KU-235-908

Napier Polytechnic Library

HARRAP'S
New Standard
FRENCH AND ENGLISH DICTIONARY

VOLUME FOUR

ENGLISH—FRENCH

L—Z

SUB-EDITORS

Hazel Curties, B.A. (née Catterall)
Flora Elphick, B.A.
H. R. Elphick
Muriel Holland Smith
Elizabeth A. H. Strick, M.A.
Helen Zarb, B.A.

PRINCIPAL COLLABORATORS AND TECHNICAL ADVISERS

Jean Bétesta, *Chevalier de la Légion d'Honneur*
Reginald Bowen, B.A., *Docteur de l'Université de Strasbourg*
Commander Ian Forbes, DSC, RN
F. G. S. Parker, M.A.

HARRAP'S New Standard
FRENCH AND ENGLISH DICTIONARY

by

J. E. MANSION, M.A.

Revised and Edited by

R. P. L. LEDÉSERT, *Licencié-ès-Lettres*, *Licencié en Droit*,

and

MARGARET LEDÉSERT, M.A.

VOLUME FOUR

ENGLISH—FRENCH

L—Z

HARRAP LONDON

1980

First published in Great Britain February 1939
by George G. Harrap & Co. Ltd
182 High Holborn, London, WC1V 7AX

Completely revised and enlarged edition
1980

ISBN 0 245 51860 6

Text set in 8/7½ pt Photon Times, printed and bound
in Great Britain at The Pitman Press, Bath

Table of Phonetic Symbols—
Tableau des Symboles Phonétiques

CONSONANTS AND SEMICONSONANTS

[p] pat [pæt]; top [tɔp]; pepper ['pepə*r*]

[b] but [bʌt]; tab [tæb]; robber ['rɔbə*r*]

[m] mat [mæt]; ram [ræm]; hammer ['hæmə*r*]; prism ['priz(ə)m]; bomb [bɔm]; calm [kɑːm]

[f] fat [fæt]; laugh [lɑːf]; ruff, rough [rʌf]; physics ['fiziks]; elephant ['elifənt]

[v] vat [væt]; avail [ə'veil]; rave [reiv]

[t] tap [tæp]; pat [pæt]; patter ['pætə*r*]; trap [træp]; tight [tait]; time, thyme [taim]; act [ækt]; pest [pest]; debt [det]

[d] dab [dæb]; mad [mæd]; madder ['mædə*r*]; build [bild]

[n] no, know [nou]; ban [bæn]; banner ['bænə*r*]; pancake ['pænkeik]; nab [næb]; gnat [næt]; pneumonia [njuː'mouniə]

[s] sat [sæt]; scene [siːn]; sent, scent [sent]; science ['saiəns]; socks [sɔks]; mouse [maus]; toss [tɔs]; kudos ['kjuːdɔs]; ceiling ['siːliŋ]; coincide [kouin'said]; ice [ais]; psychology [sai'kɔlədʒi]

[θ] thatch [θætʃ]; ether ['iːθə*r*]; faith [feiθ]; breath [breθ]

[z] zinc [ziŋk]; zone [zoun]; buzz [bʌz]; houses ['hauziz]; business ['biznis]; adze [ædz]; odds [ɔdz]

[ð] that [ðæt]; there [ðɛə*r*]; mother ['mʌðə*r*]; breathe [briːð]

[l] lad [læd], all [ɔːl]; faithful ['feiθful]; table ['teibl]; chisel ['tʃizl]

[ʃ] sham [ʃæm]; dish [diʃ]; sugar ['ʃugə*r*]; chef [ʃef]; ocean ['ouʃ(ə)n]; nation ['neiʃ(ə)n]; machine [mə'ʃiːn]; action ['ækʃ(ə)n]; conviction [kən'vikʃ(ə)n]; lunch [lʌnʃ]

[tʃ] chat [tʃæt]; search [səːtʃ]; chisel ['tʃizl]; thatch [θætʃ]; rich [ritʃ]

[ʒ] pleasure ['pleʒə*r*]; vision ['viʒ(ə)n]; beige [beiʒ]

[dʒ] jam [dʒæm]; jail, gaol [dʒeil]; gem [dʒem]; gin [dʒin]; rage [reidʒ]; edge [edʒ]; badger ['bædʒə*r*]

[k] cup [kʌp]; cat [kæt]; kitten ['kitn]; clap [klæp]; crack [kræk]; choir, quire ['kwaiə*r*]; queen [kwiːn]; kick [kik]; key, quay [kiː]; khaki ['kɑːki]; cue, queue [kjuː]; antic ['æntik]; arctic ['ɑːktik]; pique [piːk]; accept [ək'sept]; exercise ['eksəsaiz]; expect [iks'pekt]; cox [kɔks]

[g] get [get]; give [giv]; go [gou]; ghost [goust]; grain [grein]; guard [gɑːd]; guess [ges]; guilt, gilt [gilt]; again [ə'gen]; egg [eg]; exist [eg'zist]; exact [eg'zækt]; hungry ['hʌŋgri]

[h] hat [hæt]; cohere [kou'hiə*r*]

[χ] loch [lɔχ]; pibroch ['piːbrɔχ]

[ŋ] bang [bæŋ]; sing [siŋ]; singer ['siŋə*r*]; anchor ['æŋkə*r*]; anger ['æŋgə*r*]; link [liŋk]

[r] rat [ræt]; arise [ə'raiz]; barring ['bɑːriŋ]

[*r*] (*sounded only when a final* **r** *is carried on to the next word*) far [fɑː*r*]; sailor ['seilə*r*]; finger ['fiŋgə*r*]

[j] yam [jæm]; yet [jet]; youth [juːθ]; picture ['piktjə*r*]

[w] wall [wɔːl]; await [ə'weit]; choir, quire ['kwaiə*r*]; quite [kwait]

[(h)w] what [(h)wɔt]; why [(h)wai]

VOWELS and VOWEL COMBINATIONS

[iː] bee [biː]; fever ['fiːvə*r*]; see, sea [siː]; ceiling ['siːliŋ]; ski [skiː]; release [ri'liːs]; chlorine ['klɔːriːn]

[iə] beer, bier [biə*r*]; appear [ə'piə*r*]; really ['riəli]

[i] bit [bit]; added ['ædid]; drastic ['dræstik]; sieve [siv]; helplessness ['helplisnis]; begin [bi'gin]; elect [i'lekt]; manage ['mænidʒ]

[e] bet [bet]; meant [ment]; deaf [def]; leopard ['lepəd]; menace ['menəs]; said [sed]; coalesce [kouə'les]; manageress [mænidʒə'res]

[ei] date [deit]; day [dei]; railing ['reiliŋ]; feign [fein]; rain, rein, reign [rein];

[ɛə] bear, bare [bɛə*r*], there, their [ðɛə*r*]; airy ['ɛəri]

[æ] bat [bæt]; add [æd]; graph [græf]; transact [træn'zækt]

[ai] aisle, isle [ail]; height [hait]; life [laif]; fly [flai]; beside [bi'said]; aniline ['ænilain]; guide [gaid]; guy [gai]

[ɑː] art [ɑːt]; ask [ɑːsk]; car [kɑː*r*]; father ['fɑːðə*r*]; glass [glɑːs]; castle ['kɑːsl]; palm [pɑːm]

[au] fowl, foul [faul]; house [haus]; cow [kau]; renounce [ri'nauns]

[ɔ] wad [wɔd]; wash [wɔʃ]; lot [lɔt]; what [(h)wɔt]

[ɔː] all [ɔːl]; haul [hɔːl]; saw [sɔː]; caught, court [kɔːt]; coarse, course [kɔːs]; short [ʃɔːt]; wart [wɔːt]; thought [θɔːt]; thwart [θwɔːt]

[ɔi] boil [bɔil]; toy [tɔi]; oyster ['ɔistə*r*]; loyal ['lɔiəl]

[ou] low [lou]; soap [soup]; rope [roup]; road, rode, rowed [roud]; sew, so, sow (*verb*) [sou]; though [ðou]; cohere [kou'hiə*r*]; coalesce [kouə'les]

[uː] shoe [ʃuː]; clue [kluː]; prove [pruːv]; room [ruːm]; to, two [tuː]; threw, through [θruː]; true [truː]; frugal ['fruːg(ə)l]; coupon ['kuːpɔn]; wounded ['wuːndid]; (*slightly shorter*) Rumania [ru(ː)'meiniə]

[juː] few [fjuː]; hew, hue [hjuː]; huge [hjuːdʒ]; humour ['hjuːmə*r*]; nuisance ['njuːs(ə)ns]

[(j)uː] suit [s(j)uːt]; suicide ['s(j)uːisaid]

[(j)uə] lurid ['l(j)uərid]; lure [l(j)uə*r*]

[u] put [put]; wool [wul]; wood, would [wud]; full [ful]

[ju] incubate ['inkjubeit]; regulate ['regjuleit]; duplicity [dju'plisiti]

[uə] poor [puə*r*]; sure [ʃuə*r*]

[ʌ] cut [kʌt]; sun, son [sʌn]; cover ['kʌvə*r*]; rough [rʌf]

[əː] curl [kəːl]; pearl, purl [pəːl]; herb [həːb]; terse [təːs]; girl [gəːl]; learn [ləːn]; turgid ['təːdʒid]; purr [pəː*r*]; myrrh [məː*r*]; interment [in'təːmənt]

[ə] decency ['diːsənsi]; obey [ə'bei]; Atlantic [ət'læntik]; ferment (*verb*) [fə'ment]; amend [ə'mend]; upon [ə'pɔn]; delicate ['delikət]

Abbreviations Used in the Dictionary

Abréviations Utilisées dans le Dictionnaire

A:	*archaism; ancient; in former use*	désuet
a., adj.	*adjective*	adjectif
abbr.	*abbreviation*	abréviation
abs.	*absolutely; absolute use*	emploi absolu
Ac:	*acoustics*	acoustique
acc.	*accusative*	accusatif
Adm:	*administration; civil service*	administration
adv.	*adverb*	adverbe
adv.phr.	*adverbial phrase*	locution adverbiale
Aedcs:	*aerodynamics*	aérodynamique
Aer:	*aeronautics*	aéronautique
Agr:	*agriculture*	agriculture
A. Hist:	*ancient history*	histoire ancienne
Alch:	*alchemy*	alchimie
Algae:	*algae*	algues
Amph:	*Amphibia*	amphibiens
Anat:	*anatomy*	anatomie
Ann:	*Annelida, worms*	annelés
Ant:	*antiquity, antiquities*	antiquité
Anthr:	*anthropology*	anthropologie
Ap:	*apiculture*	apiculture
approx.	*approximately*	sens approché
Arach:	*Arachnida*	arachnides
Arb:	*arboriculture*	arboriculture; sylviculture
Arch:	*architecture*	architecture
Archeol:	*archaeology*	archéologie
Arm:	*armour*	armure
Arms:	*arms; armaments*	armes; armements
art.	*article*	article
Art:	*art*	beaux-arts
Artil:	*artillery*	artillerie
Astr:	*astronomy*	astronomie
Astrol:	*astrology*	astrologie
Astro-Ph:	*astrophysics*	astrophysique
Atom. Ph:	*atomic, nuclear, physics*	sciences atomiques
attrib.	*attributive*	attributif
Austr:	*Australia; Australian(ism)*	Australie; australien; expression australienne
Aut:	*motoring; automobile industry*	automobilisme; industrie automobile
aux.	*auxiliary*	auxiliaire
Av:	*aviation; aircraft*	aviation; avions
B:	*Bible; biblical*	Bible; biblique
Bac:	*bacteriology*	bactériologie
Bak:	*baking*	boulangerie
Ball:	*ballistics*	ballistique
Bank:	*banking*	opérations de banque
Belg:	*Belgium; Belgian*	Belgique; belge
B. Hist:	*Bible history*	histoire sainte
Bib:	*bibliography*	bibliographie
Bill:	*billiards*	jeu de billard
Bio-Ch:	*biochemistry*	biochimie
Biol:	*biology*	biologie
Bookb:	*bookbinding*	reliure
Book-k:	*book-keeping*	comptabilité
Bootm:	*boot and shoe industry*	cordonnerie; industrie de la chaussure

Bot:	*botany*	botanique
Box:	*boxing*	boxe
Breed:	*breeding*	élevage
Brew:	*brewing*	brasserie
Brickm:	*brickmaking*	briqueterie
Can:	*Canada, Canadian(ism)*	Canada; canadien; expression canadienne
card.a.	*cardinal adjective*	adjectif cardinal
Cards:	*card games*	jeux de cartes
Carp:	*carpentry*	charpenterie; menuiserie du bâtiment
Cer:	*ceramics*	céramique
cf.	*refer to*	conferatur
Ch:	*chemistry*	chimie
Chess:	*chess*	jeu d'échecs
Ch. of Eng:	*Church of England*	Église anglicane
Chr:	*chronology*	chronologie
Cin:	*cinema*	cinéma
Civ:	*civilization*	civilisation
Civ. E:	*civil engineering*	génie civil
Cl:	*classical; Greek or Roman antiquity*	classique; antiquité grecque ou romaine
Clockm:	*clock and watch making*	horlogerie
Cmptr:	*computers; data processing*	ordinateurs; informatique
Coel:	*Coelenterata*	cœlentérés
cogn.acc.	*cognate accusative*	accusatif de l'objet interne
Cokem:	*cokemaking*	industrie du coke
coll.	*collective*	collectif
Com:	*commerce; business term*	(terme du) commerce
comb.fm.	*combining form*	forme de combinaison
Comest:	*comestibles, food*	comestibles
comp.	*comparative*	comparatif
Conch:	*conchology*	conchyliologie
condit.	*conditional*	conditionnel
conj.	*conjunction*	conjonction
Const:	*construction, building industry*	industrie du bâtiment
Coop:	*cooperage*	tonnellerie
Corr:	*correspondence, letters*	correspondance, lettres
Cost:	*costume; clothing*	costume; habillement
cp.	*compare*	comparer
Cr:	*cricket*	cricket
Crust:	*Crustacea*	crustacés
Cryst:	*crystallography*	cristallographie
Cu:	*culinary; cooking*	culinaire; cuisine
Cust:	*customs*	douane
Cy:	*bicycles; cycling*	bicyclettes; cyclisme
Danc:	*dancing*	danse
dat.	*dative*	datif
def.	*(i) definite; (ii) defective (verb)*	(i) défini; (ii) (verbe) défectif
dem.	*demonstrative*	démonstratif
Dent:	*dentistry*	art dentaire
Dial:	*dialectal*	dialectal
dim.	*diminutive*	diminutif
Dipl:	*diplomacy; diplomatic*	diplomatie; diplomatique
Dist:	*distilling*	distillation
Dom. Ec:	*domestic economy; household equipment*	économie domestique; ménage

Abbreviations Used in the Dictionary

Draw:	*drawing*	dessin
Dressm:	*dressmaking*	couture (mode)
Dy:	*dyeing*	teinture
Dyn:	*dynamics*	dynamique
E.	*east*	est
E:	*engineering*	industries mécaniques
Ecc:	*ecclesiastical*	église et clergé
Echin:	*Echinodermata*	échinodermes
e.g.	*for example*	par exemple
El:	*electricity; electrical engineering*	électricité; électrique; électrotechnique
Elcs:	*electronics*	électronique
Eng.	*England; English*	Angleterre; anglais, britannique
Engr:	*engraving*	gravure
Ent:	*entomology*	entomologie
Equit:	*equitation*	équitation
esp.	*especially*	surtout
etc.	*et cetera*	et cætera
Eth:	*ethics*	morale
Ethn:	*ethnology*	ethnologie
Exp:	*explosives*	explosifs
f.	*feminine*	féminin
F:	*colloquial(ism)*	familier; style de la conversation
Farr:	*farriery*	maréchalerie
Fb:	*(Association) football*	football
Fenc:	*fencing*	escrime
Fig:	*figurative*	sens figuré
Fin:	*finance*	finances
Fish:	*fishing*	pêche
For:	*forestry*	forêts
Fort:	*fortification*	fortification
Fr.	*France; French*	France; français
Fr.C:	*French Canadian*	canadien français
Fung:	*fungi*	champignons
Furn:	*furniture*	mobilier
Games:	*games*	jeux
Gaming:	*gaming; gambling*	le jeu; jeux d'argent
Gasm:	*gasmaking*	industrie du gaz
Geog:	*geography*	géographie
Geol:	*geology*	géologie
ger.	*gerund*	gérondif
Glassm:	*glassmaking*	verrerie
Golf:	*golf*	golf
Gr.	*Greek*	grec
Gr.Alph:	*Greek alphabet*	alphabet grec
Gr.Ant:	*Greek antiquity*	antiquité grecque
Gr.Civ:	*Greek civilization*	civilisation grecque
Gr.Hist:	*Greek history*	histoire grecque
Gram:	*grammar*	grammaire
Gym:	*gymnastics*	gymnastique
Hairdr:	*hairdressing*	coiffure
Harn:	*harness; saddlery*	sellerie; harnais
Hatm:	*hatmaking*	chapellerie
Her:	*heraldry*	blason
Hist:	*history; historical*	histoire; historique
Hor:	*horology*	horométrie
Hort:	*horticulture*	horticulture
Hum:	*humorous*	humoristique
Husb:	*animal husbandry*	élevage
Hyd.E:	*hydraulic engineering*	hydromécanique
Hyg:	*hygiene; sanitation*	hygiène; installations sanitaires
i.	*intransitive*	intransitif
I.C.E:	*internal combustion engines*	moteurs à combustion interne
Ich:	*ichthyology; fish*	ichtyologie; poissons
Ill:	*illuminants; lighting*	illuminants; éclairage
imp.	*imperative*	impératif
impers.	*impersonal*	impersonnel
ind.	*indicative*	indicatif
Ind:	*industry; industrial*	industrie; industriel
indef.	*indefinite*	indéfini
ind.tr.	*indirectly transitive*	transitif avec régime indirect
inf.	*infinitive*	infinitif
Ins:	*insurance*	assurance
int.	*interjection*	interjection
Internat:	*international*	international
interr.	*interrogative*	interrogatif
inv.	*invariable*	invariable
Iron:	*ironic(ally)*	ironique(ment)
Jap:	*Japanese*	japonais
Jew:	*Jewish*	juif, juive
Jewel:	*jewellery*	bijouterie
Join:	*joinery*	menuiserie
Journ:	*journalism; journalistic*	journalisme; style journalistique
Jur:	*jurisprudence; legal term*	droit; terme de palais
Knit:	*knitting*	tricot
Lacem:	*lacemaking*	dentellerie
Lap:	*lapidary arts*	arts lapidaires; taillerie
Laund:	*laundering*	blanchissage
Leath:	*leatherwork*	travail du cuir
Ling:	*linguistics; language*	linguistique; langue
Lit:	*literary use; literature; literary*	forme littéraire; littérature; littéraire
Lith:	*lithography*	lithographie
Locksm:	*locksmithery*	serrurerie
Log:	*logic*	logique
Lt.	*Latin*	latin
m.	*masculine*	masculin
Magn:	*magnetism*	magnétisme
Mapm:	*mapmaking*	cartographie
Mch:	*machines; machinery*	machines; machines à vapeur
Mch.Tls:	*machine tools*	machines-outils
Meas:	*weights and measures*	poids et mesures
Mec:	*mechanics*	mécanique
Mec.E:	*mechanical engineering*	industries mécaniques
Med:	*medicine; illnesses; medical*	médecine; maladies; médical
Metall:	*metallurgy*	métallurgie
Metalw:	*metalworking*	travail des métaux
Metaph:	*metaphysics*	métaphysique
Meteor:	*meteorology*	météorologie
Mil:	*military; army*	militaire; armée de terre
Mill:	*milling*	meunerie
Min:	*mining and quarrying*	exploitation des mines et carrières
Miner:	*mineralogy*	minéralogie
M.Ins:	*marine insurance*	assurance maritime
Moll:	*molluscs*	mollusques
Moss:	*mosses and lichens*	muscinées
Mount:	*mountaineering*	alpinisme
Mth:	*mathematics*	mathématiques
Mus:	*music*	musique
Myr:	*Myriapoda*	myriapodes
Myth:	*mythology*	mythologie
N.	*north*	nord
NAm:	*North American*	de l'Amérique du Nord
N.Arch:	*naval architecture*	architecture navale
Nat.Hist:	*natural history*	histoire naturelle
Nau:	*nautical*	terme de marine
Nav:	*navigation*	navigation
Navy:	*Navy*	marine militaire
Needlew:	*needlework*	couture (travaux d'aiguille)
neg.	*negative*	négatif
nom.	*nominative*	nominatif
Num:	*numismatics*	numismatique
num.a.	*numeral adjective*	adjectif numéral
N.Z:	*New Zealand*	(de la) Nouvelle-Zélande
O:	*obsolescent*	vieilli
Obst:	*obstetrics*	obstétrique
Oc:	*oceanography*	océanographie
occ.	*occasionally*	parfois
onomat.	*onomatopoeia*	onomatopée
Opt:	*optics*	optique
Orn:	*ornithology; birds*	ornithologie; oiseaux
Ost:	*ostreiculture; oysters*	ostréiculture; huîtres
p.	*(i) past; (ii) participle*	(i) passé; (ii) participe
P:	*uneducated speech; slang*	expression populaire; argot
Paint:	*painting trade*	peinture en bâtiment
Pal:	*paleography*	paléographie
Paleont:	*paleontology*	paléontologie
Paperm:	*papermaking*	fabrication du papier
Parl:	*parliament*	parlement
Pej:	*pejorative*	péjoratif
pers.	*person(s); personal*	personne(s); personnel
Petr:	*petroleum industry*	industrie pétrolière
Ph:	*physics*	physique

Pharm:	*pharmacy*	pharmacie
Phil:	*philosophy*	philosophie
Phot:	*photography*	photographie
Phot. Engr:	*photo-engraving; process work*	procédés photomécaniques; photogravure
phr.	*phrase*	locution
Physiol:	*physiology*	physiologie
Pisc:	*pisciculture*	pisciculture
pl.	*plural*	pluriel
Plumb:	*plumbing*	plomberie
P.N:	*public notice*	affichage; avis au public
Poet:	*poetical*	poétique
Pol:	*politics; political*	politique
Pol. Ec:	*political economy, economics*	économie politique
poss.	*possessive*	possessif
Post:	*postal services*	postes et télécommunications
p.p.	*past participle*	participe passé
pr.	*present (tense)*	présent (de l'indicatif)
pref.	*prefix*	préfixe
Prehist:	*prehistory*	préhistoire
prep.	*preposition*	préposition
prep.phr.	*prepositional phrase*	locution prépositive
Pr.n.	*proper name*	nom propre
pron.	*pronoun*	pronom
Pros:	*prosody*	prosodie; métrique
Prot:	*Protozoa*	protozoaires
Prov:	*proverb*	proverbe
pr.p.	*present participle*	participe présent
Psy:	*psychology*	psychologie
Psychics:	*psychics*	métapsychisme
p.t.	*past tense*	passé défini
Publ:	*publishing*	édition
Pyr:	*pyrotechnics*	pyrotechnie
qch.	*(something)*	quelque chose
qn	*(someone)*	quelqu'un
q.v.	*which see*	se reporter à ce mot
Rac:	*racing*	courses
Rad:	*radar*	radar
Rad.-A:	*radioactivity*	radioactivité
Rail:	*railways, railroads*	chemins de fer
R.C.Ch:	*Roman Catholic Church*	Église catholique
Rec:	*tape recorders; record players*	magnétophones; tourne-disques
rel.	*relative*	relatif
Rel:	*religion(s)*	religion(s)
Rel. H:	*religious history*	histoire des religions
Rept:	*reptiles*	reptiles
Rh:	*rhetoric*	rhétorique
Rom:	*Roman*	romain
Ropem:	*ropemaking*	corderie
Row:	*rowing*	aviron
R.t.m:	*registered trademark*	marque déposée
Rubberm:	*rubber manufacture*	industrie du caoutchouc
Rugby Fb:	*Rugby (football)*	rugby
Russ:	*Russian*	russe
S.	*south*	sud
s., sb.	*substantive, noun*	substantif, nom
s.a.	*see also*	voir
Sch:	*schools and universities; students (slang, etc.)*	écoles; universités; (argot, etc.) scolaire
Scot:	*Scotland; Scottish*	Écosse; écossais
Scout:	*Scout and Guide Movements*	scoutisme
Sculp:	*sculpture*	sculpture
Ser:	*sericulture*	sériciculture
sg., sing.	*singular*	singulier
Ski:	*skiing*	ski
Sm.a:	*small arms*	armes portatives
s.o.	*someone*	(quelqu'un)
Soapm:	*soapmaking*	savonnerie
Sp:	*sport*	sport
Space:	*astronautics; space travel*	astronautique; voyages interplanétaires
Spong:	*sponges*	spongiaires
Stat:	*statistics*	statistique

St. Exch:	*Stock Exchange*	terme de Bourse
sth.	*something*	(quelque chose)
Stonew:	*stoneworking*	taille de la pierre
sub.	*subjunctive*	subjonctif
suff.	*suffix*	suffixe
Sug.-R:	*sugar refining*	raffinerie du sucre
sup.	*superlative*	superlatif
Surg:	*surgery*	chirurgie
Surv:	*surveying*	géodésie et levé de plans
Swim:	*swimming*	natation
Sw.Fr:	*Swiss French*	mot utilisé en Suisse
Switz:	*Switzerland*	Suisse
Tail:	*tailoring*	mode masculine
Tan:	*tanning*	tannage des cuirs
Tchn:	*technical*	terme technique, terme de métier
Telecom:	*telecommunications*	télécommunications
Ten:	*tennis*	tennis
Ter:	*teratology*	tératologie
Tex:	*textiles; textile industry*	industries textiles
Tg:	*telegraphy*	télégraphie
Th:	*theatre; theatrical*	théâtre
Theol:	*theology*	théologie
thg.	*thing(s)*	(chose(s))
Tls:	*tools*	outils
Toil:	*toilet; makeup*	toilette; maquillage
Town P:	*town planning*	urbanisme
Toys:	*toys*	jouets
Tp:	*telephony*	téléphonie
tr.	*transitive*	transitif
Trans:	*transport*	transports
Turf:	*turf, horse racing*	turf
T.V:	*television*	télévision
Typ:	*typography*	typographie
Typew(r):	*typing; typewriters*	dactylographie; machines à écrire
U.S:	*United States; American*	États-Unis; américain
usu.	*usually*	d'ordinaire
usu. with sg. const.	*usually with singular construction*	verbe généralement au singulier
v.	*verb*	verbe
V:	*vulgar; not in polite use*	trivial
Veh:	*vehicles*	véhicules
Ven:	*venery; hunting*	chasse
Vet:	*veterinary science*	art vétérinaire
v.i.	*intransitive verb*	verbe intransitif
v.ind.tr.	*indirectly transitive verb*	verbe transitif indirect
Vit:	*viticulture*	viticulture
v.pr.	*pronominal verb*	verbe pronominal
v.tr.	*transitive verb*	verbe transitif
W.	*west*	ouest
Wine-m:	*wine making*	industrie du vin
with sg. or pl. const.	*with singular or plural construction*	verbe au singulier ou au pluriel
Woodw:	*woodworking*	menuiserie
Wr:	*wrestling*	lutte
W.Tel:	*wireless telegraphy and telephony; radio*	téléphonie et télégraphie sans fil; radio
W.Tg:	*wireless telegraphy*	télégraphie sans fil
W.Tp:	*wireless telephony*	téléphonie sans fil
X-Rays:	*X Rays*	Rayons X
Y:	*yachting*	yachting
Z:	*zoology; mammals*	zoologie; mammifères
=	*nearest equivalent (of an institution, an office, etc., when systems vary in the different countries)*	équivalent le plus proche (d'un terme désignant une institution, une charge, etc., dans les cas où les systèmes varient dans les différents pays)

L

L, l [el], *s.* **1.** (la lettre) L, l *m or f*; **a capital L,** un L majuscule; *Tp:* **L for Lucy,** L comme Louis; *Ling:* **liquid l, palatal(ized) l,** l mouillée. **2.** *(a)* **L iron,** fer *m* cornière, fer en équerre, en L, fer d'angle; *(b) U.S:* aile *f* (d'un bâtiment) à angle droit avec le corps principal. **3.** *U.S: F:* chemin de fer aérien.

la[1] [lɑː], *s. Mus:* **1.** (*fixed*) la *m*. **2.** (*movable*) la sus-dominante.

la[2], *s.* (*in song*) **la, la, la,** tralala *m*.

la[3], *v.tr. & i. F:* **if you don't know the words just la (the tune),** si vous ne connaissez pas les paroles, chantonnez l'air.

la[4], *int. A:* mon Dieu!

laager[1] ['lɑːgər], *s.* (*in S. Africa*) laager *m*; campement *m* avec rempart de chars à bœufs.

laager[2]. **1.** *v.tr.* former (des chars à bœufs) en laager; mettre (des gens) en laager. **2.** *v.i.* se former en laager; former le camp.

lab [læb], *s. F:* (= *laboratory*) labo *m*.

Labadism ['læbədizm], *s. Rel.H:* labadisme *m*.

Labadist ['læbədist], *a. & s. Rel.H:* labadiste (*mf*).

labanotation [læbənou'teiʃ(ə)n], *s. Danc:* labanotation *f*.

labarum, *pl.* **-ra** ['læbərəm, -rə], *s. Ecc:* labarum *m*, chrisme *m*.

labdanum ['læbdənəm], *s. Ch:* labdanum *m*; **l.-bearing plant,** plante *f* labdanifère.

label[1] ['leibl], *s.* **1.** *(a)* étiquette *f*; *Rail:* cartouche *m* (sur les wagons de marchandises); **gummed l.,** étiquette gommée; **adhesive, sticky, stick-on, l.,** étiquette adhésive; **tie-on l.,** étiquette à œillet(s); **luggage l.,** étiquette à bagages; *(b) Com:* label *m*, étiquette; **guarantee, quality, l.,** label, étiquette, de garantie, de qualité; *(c) Cmptr:* label (de bande, de fichier); *(d)* désignation *f*, qualification *f* (de qn). **2.** *(a) Atom.Ph:* marque *f*; **molecular l.,** traceur *m* moléculaire; *(b) Ac: etc:* **l. of the harmonic,** rang *m* de l'harmonique. **3.** *Jur:* queue *f* (d'un document). **4.** *Arch:* capucine *f*, lamier *m*. **5.** *Astr: A:* radiomètre *m*. **6.** *Her:* lambel *m*.

label[2], *v.tr.* (**labelled**) **1.** *(a)* étiqueter; apposer, attacher, une étiquette à, coller une étiquette sur (un paquet, une bouteille, etc.); **a bottle labelled poison,** une bouteille marquée poison; **sections labelled with numbers and letters,** sections indiquées par des chiffres et des lettres; **luggage labelled for London,** bagages enregistrés pour Londres; *(b) Com:* attribuer un label (de garantie, de qualité, etc.) à (un produit); *(c) Cmptr:* inscrire un label sur, immatriculer (une bande, un fichier); *(d)* **she hesitated to l. him a liar,** elle hésitait à le qualifier de menteur. **2.** *(a) Atom.Ph:* marquer (un atome, une molécule, etc.); **labelled compound,** composé marqué; *(b) Ac: etc:* attribuer un rang à (un harmonique).

label[3], *s. Bot:* = LABELLUM.

labellate [lə'beleit], *a. Bot:* labellé.

labeller ['leib(ə)lər], *s.* étiqueteur, -euse.

labelling ['leibəliŋ], *s.* **1.** *(a)* étiquetage *m*; *(b) Com:* attribution *f* d'un label (de garantie, de qualité); *(c) Cmptr:* inscription *f* d'un label (sur une bande, un fichier); immatriculation *f* (d'une bande, d'un fichier). **2.** *(a) Atom.Ph:* marquage *m* (d'un atome, d'une molécule); *(b) Ac: etc:* attribution d'un rang (à un harmonique).

labellum, *pl.* **-bella** [lə'beləm, -ə], *s. Bot:* labelle *m* (d'une orchidée).

labenzyme ['læbenzaim], *s. Bio-Ch:* labenzyme *f*, lab(ferment) *m*.

labial ['leibiəl]. **1.** *a.* labial, -aux; *Mus:* **l. pipe,** tuyau *m* à bouche (d'un orgue); *Ling:* **l. consonant,** consonne labiale. **2.** *s. Ling:* labiale *f*.

labialization [leibiəlai'zeiʃ(ə)n], *s. Ling:* labialisation *f*.

labialize ['leibiəlaiz], *v.tr. Ling:* labialiser.

Labiatae [leibi'eitiː], *s.pl. Bot:* labiacées *f*.

labiate [leibieit]. *Bot:* **1.** *a.* labié. **2.** *s.* labiée *f*.

Labidognatha [læbi'dɔgnəθə], *s.pl. Arch:* labidognathes *m*.

labile ['læb(a)il, 'leib(a)il], *a.* labile, instable.

lability [læ'biliti], *s.* labilité *f*.

labiodental [leibiou'dent(ə)l]. *Ling:* *(a) a.* labiodental, -aux; dentolabial, -aux; *(b) s.* labiodentale *f*.

labioglossopharyngeal ['leibiouglɔsoufæ'rindʒiəl], *a. Med:* **l. paralysis,** paralysie labioglossopharyngée.

labionasal [leibiou'neizl], *a. Ling:* labionasal, -aux.

labiopalatal [leibiou'pælətl], *a. Ling:* labiopalatal, -aux.

labiovelar [leibiou'viːlər], *a. & s. Ling:* labiovélaire (*f*).

labium, *pl.* **-a** ['leibiəm, -ə], *s.* **1.** *Bot:* lèvre *f* (de corolle labiée). **2.** *Ent:* labium *m*. **3.** *pl. Anat:* labia, lèvres (de la vulve); **labia majora,** grandes lèvres; **labia minora,** petites lèvres; nymphes *f*.

laboratory [lə'bɔrətri, *esp. NAm:* 'læbrətri], *s.* laboratoire *m*; **research l.,** laboratoire de recherches; **testing l.,** laboratoire d'essais; **l. tested,** essayé, éprouvé, en laboratoire; **technical l.,** laboratoire industriel; **bacteriological l.,** laboratoire bactériologique; **nuclear research l.,** laboratoire nucléaire; **highly radioactive,** *F:* **hot, l.,** laboratoire radioactif, *F:* chaud; **non-radioactive,** *F:* **cold, l.,** laboratoire non radioactif; **pathology l.,** laboratoire d'analyses (médicales); **dental l.,** laboratoire de prothèse dentaire; *Sch:* **language l.,** laboratoire de langues; **l. assistant,** laborantin, -ine.

laborious [lə'bɔːriəs], *a.* laborieux. **1.** travailleur, -euse; qui travaille beaucoup. **2.** pénible, fatigant.

laboriously [lə'bɔːriəsli], *adv.* laborieusement, péniblement.

laboriousness [lə'bɔːriəsnis], *s.* caractère laborieux; peine *f* (d'un travail, d'une ascension, etc.); pénibilité *f*.

labour[1] ['leibər], *s.* **1.** *(a)* travail *m*, labeur *m*, peine *f*; **manual l.,** travail manuel; travail de manœuvre; **road l.,** travaux de voirie; **material and l.,** main-d'œuvre *f* et matériel *m*; matière *f* et façon *f*; **division of l.,** division *f* du travail; **l. in vain,** peine perdue; *(b) Jur: A:* **hard l.,** réclusion criminelle. **2.** *(a)* main-d'œuvre *f*; travailleurs *mpl*; **male, female, l.,** main-d'œuvre masculine, féminine; **white l.,** travailleurs blancs; **coloured l.,** travailleurs de couleur; **native l.,** main-d'œuvre indigène; **local l.,** main-d'œuvre locale; **civil l.,** main-d'œuvre civile; **skilled, semi-skilled, unskilled, l.,** main-d'œuvre qualifiée, spécialisée, non spécialisée; **cost of l.,** prix *m* de la main-d'œuvre; **mobility of l.,** mobilité *f* de la main-d'œuvre; **shortage of l.,** pénurie *f*, crise *f*, de main-d'œuvre; **employer of l.,** employeur *m*, patron *m*; *Mil:* **l. depot, l. pool,** dépôt *m* de main-d'œuvre; **l. unit,** unité *f* de travailleurs; *(b)* **capital and l.,** le capital et la main-d'œuvre; **l. agreement,** convention collective; **l. conflicts, l. disputes, l. troubles,** conflits du travail; conflits sociaux; **l. unrest,** agitation ouvrière, malaise ouvrier; **the l. question,** le problème ouvrier; *Adm: A: & F:* **l. exchange,** bureau *m* de placement, bourse *f* du travail; **l. market,** marché *m* du travail; *A:* **l. colony, l. settlement,** colonie ouvrière; **minister of l.,** ministre *m* du travail; **International L. Office,** Bureau International du Travail; **l. legislation,** législation *f* du travail, législation ouvrière; *(c) coll. Pol:* les travaillistes *m*, le travaillisme; **the demands of l.,** les revendications ouvrières; ce que réclament les travaillistes; **the L. party,** le parti travailliste; **are you L.?** êtes-vous travailliste? **L. member (of Parliament),** député *m* travailliste; **L. mayor,** maire *m* travailliste. **3.** **the twelve labours of Hercules,** les douze travaux d'Hercule; **l. of love,** (i) travail à titre gracieux; travail gratuit; (ii) travail fait avec plaisir; **it has been a l. of love to me,** c'est avec plaisir que j'y ai travaillé. **4.** *Med:* travail; couches *fpl*; **premature l.,** accouchement *m* avant terme; **missed l.,** arrêt *m* du travail; **woman in l.,** femme *f* en couches, en travail (d'enfant); **l. pains,** douleurs *f* de l'enfantement.

labour[2]. **1.** *v.i.* *(a)* travailler, peiner; **to l. for sth.,** se donner de la peine pour obtenir qch.; **to l. to do sth.,** travailler à faire qch.; s'efforcer de, s'appliquer à, faire qch.; **to l. at, over, sth.,** travailler à qch.; peiner sur qch.; *(b)* **to l. along,** marcher, avancer, péniblement; **to l. up a hill,** gravir péniblement une côte; *(c)* **to l. under a burden,** être courbé sous un fardeau; **to l. under great difficulties,** avoir à lutter contre, avoir à combattre, de grandes difficultés; être aux prises avec de grandes difficultés; **to l. under a constant anxiety,** être travaillé par une inquiétude perpétuelle; **to l. under a sense of injustice,** nourrir un sentiment d'injustice; **to l. under an illusion, a delusion, a misapprehension,** être dans l'illusion, dans l'erreur; être (la) victime d'une illusion, d'une erreur; se faire illusion; s'illusionner, s'abuser; *(d) Mch: I.C.E: etc:* (*of engine*) fatiguer, peiner, souffrir; fonctionner péniblement; (*of ship*) bourlinguer, fatiguer, se tourmenter; **the ship is labouring,** la mer fatigue le navire; (*of car*) **to l. uphill,** peiner en côte; *(e) A:* (*of woman*) **to l. with child,** être en travail d'enfant, en mal d'enfant. **2.** *v.tr.* *(a)* élaborer (un ouvrage); travailler (son style); **I won't l. the point,** je ne m'étendrai pas là-dessus; je n'insisterai pas là-dessus; *(b) Poet: A:* labourer (la terre).

laboured ['leibəd], *a.* **1.** (style, etc.) travaillé, trop élaboré, fastidieux; (poème, etc.) martelé, qui sent l'huile; **l. irony,** ironie appuyée; **l. joke,** plaisanterie laborieuse. **2.** (respiration *f*) pénible.

labourer ['leibərər], *s.* *(a)* travailleur *m*; *Prov:* **the l. is worthy of his hire,** toute peine, tout travail, mérite salaire; il faut que le prêtre vive de l'autel; *(b) Ind:* manœuvre *m*; homme *m* de peine; **(unskilled) l.,** ouvrier non spécialisé; *(c)* **agricultural l.,** ouvrier agricole.

labouring[1] ['leibəriŋ], *a. O:* **1. l. man,** ouvrier *m*; **the l. class,** la classe ouvrière. **2. l. heart,** cœur battant, palpitant (d'émotion); cœur qui peine.

labouring[2], *s.* **1.** travail (manuel); peine *f*. **2.** *O:* **the l. of his heart,** les battements *m* de son cœur.

labourite ['leibərait], *s. Pol: Pej:* membre *m* du parti travailliste; travailliste *mf*.

labour-saving ['leibəseiviŋ], *a.* allégeant le travail; **l.-s. device,** appareil (électro) ménager, etc.

Labrador [ˈlæbrədɔːr]. *Pr.n. Geog:* le Labrador; *Oc:* **L. Current,** courant *m* du Labrador; *Bot:* **L. tea,** thé *m* du Labrador; *Miner:* **L. spar, stone,** labradorite *f,* labrador *m.* **2.** *s.* chien *m* du Labrador, labrador *m.*
Labradorian, Labradorean [læbrəˈdɔːriən], *a. & s. Geog:* (originaire *mf,* habitant, -ante) du Labrador.
labradorite [ˈlæbrədɔrait], *s. Miner:* laboradorite *f,* labrador *m.*
labret [ˈleibret], *s.* labret *m.*
Labridae [ˈleibridiː], *s.pl. Ich:* labridés *m,* les labrés *m.*
labroid [ˈleibrɔid], *a. & s. Ich:* labroïde (*m*).
labrus [ˈleibrəs], *s. Ich:* labre *m.*
Labrusca [ləˈbruskə], *s. Vit:* **L. (vine), (vitis) l.,** labrusca *m.*
laburnum [ləˈbəːnəm], *s. Bot:* laburnum *m,* laburne *m;* cytise *m* (à grappes); aubour *m;* faux ébénier; **alpine l.,** cytise des Alpes.
labyrinth [ˈlæbərinθ], *s.* **1.** *Arch: etc:* labyrinthe *m,* dédale *m.* **2.** *Anat:* labyrinthe (de l'oreille). **3.** *Turb:* **l. joint,** joint *m* à labyrinthe; **l. packing,** garniture *f* à labyrinthe.
labyrinthine [læbəˈrinθain], *a.* labyrinthique.
labyrinthitis [læb(ə)rinˈθaitis], *s. Med:* labyrinthite *f.*
labyrinthodon(t) [læbəˈrinθoudɔn(t)], *s. Paleont:* labyrinthodon(te) *m.*
Labyrinthodontia [læbərinθouˈdɔnʃiə], *s.pl. Paleont:* labyrinthodontes *m.*
labyrinthula [læbəˈrinθjulə], *s. Nat.Hist:* labyrinthule *f.*
lac[1] [læk], *s.* gomme *f* laque; laque *f;* **l. varnish,** vernis-laque *m inv;* **l.-bearing, -producing,** laccifère; **l. dye,** lac-dye *m.*
lac[2], *s.* = LAKH.
Laccadive [ˈlækədiv], *a. Geog:* **the L. Islands,** les (îles) Laquedives *f.*
laccase [ˈlækeis], *s. Bio-Ch:* laccase *f.*
laccol [ˈlækɔl], *s. Ch:* laccol *m.*
laccolite, laccolith [ˈlækəlait, -liθ], *s. Geol:* laccolite, laccolithe *f.*
lace[1] [leis], *s.* **1.** lacet *m* (de corset, de soulier); cordon *m* (de soulier); *Ind:* **laces for belts,** lacets, lanières *f,* pour courroies. **2. gold, silver, l.,** galon *m,* ganse *f,* passement *m,* d'or, d'argent; **Aleçon l.,** point *m* d'Alençon; **knitted l.,** dentelle *f* au tricot; **l. collar,** col *m* de dentelle; **l. factory,** dentellerie *f;* **l. manufacture,** dentellerie; **l. glass,** verre filigrané. **3.** dentelle *f,* point *m;* **bobbin l., pillow l.,** dentelle aux fuseaux, au coussin, au coussinet; guipure *f;* **l. pillow,** coussin *m,* coussinet *m,* à dentelle; tambour *m;* **l. frame,** métier *m* à dentelle. **4.** *Ent:* **l. bug,** tingis *m;* **pear l. bug,** tigre *m* du poirier.
lace[2], *v.tr.* **1.** (*a*) **to l. (up) a corset, shoes,** lacer un corset, des chaussures *f;* **to l. oneself, one's waist, too tightly,** se serrer trop; se sangler; (*with passive force*) (*of boots, etc.*) **to l. (up),** se lacer; **l.-up boots, shoes,** bottes *f,* chaussures, à lacets; chaussures Richelieu; (*b*) *Bookb:* **to l. in the bands,** passer les nerfs en carton; (*c*) *Nau:* transfiler (des tentes); mailler (une voile à une autre). **2. to l. sth. with sth.,** entrelacer qch. de, avec, qch. **3.** garnir, border, (un ouvrage) de dentelles; galonner. **4.** barioler, bigarrer, nuancer (une surface) (**with,** de). **5.** (*a*) *O:* soulever des vergetures *f* sur (la peau); *F: A:* **to l. s.o., s.o.'s coat,** battre, sangler, rosser, qn; (*b*) *v.i. F: O:* **to l. into s.o.,** taper sur qn; faire une sortie à, contre, qn. **6.** *F:* additionner d'alcool (une boisson); **glass of milk laced with rum,** lait *m* au rhum.
laced [leist], *a.* **1.** (soulier, etc.) lacé. **2.** garni de dentelles; galonné, à galon, à ganse. **3.** (*of bird, flower, etc.*) bariolé, bigarré, nuancé.
Lacedaemon [læsiˈdiːmən]. *Pr.n. A.Geog:* Lacédémone *f.*
Lacedaemonian [læsidiˈmouniən]. *A.Geog:* (*a*) *a.* lacédémonien; (*b*) *s.* Lacédémonien, -ienne.
lacemaker [ˈleismeikər], *s.* **1.** fabricant, -ante, de dentelles. **2.** ouvrier, -ière, en dentelles; passementier, -ière; affineuse *f.*
lacemaking [ˈleismeikiŋ], *s.* dentellerie *f.*
lacerable [ˈlæsərəbl], *a.* lacérable.
lacerate[1] [ˈlæsəreit], *v.tr.* lacérer; déchirer.
lacerate[2], *a.* **1.** *Poet:* = LACERATED 1. **2.** *Bot:* lacéré.
lacerated [ˈlæsəreitid], *a.* **1.** lacéré; déchiré; *Lit:* **l. heart,** cœur déchiré; **l. feelings,** sentiments profondément blessés. **2.** *Bot:* = LACERATE[2] 2.
laceration [læsəˈreiʃ(ə)n], *s.* **1.** lacération *f,* déchirement *m.* **2.** *Med: etc:* déchirure *f.*
lacertian [ləˈsəːʃ(ə)n], *a. & s. Rept:* lacertien (*m*).
Lacertidae [ləˈsəːtidiː], *s.pl. Rept:* lacertidés *m.*
lacertiform [ləˈsəːtifɔːm], *a. Rept:* lacertiforme; qui a la forme d'un lézard.
Lacertilia [læsəˈtiliə], *s.pl. Rept:* lacertiliens *m.*
lacertine [ləˈsəːtain], *a. Rept:* lacertien.
lacewing [ˈleiswiŋ], *s. Ent:* **l. (fly),** hémérobe *m;* demoiselle *f* terrestre; **green l.,** chrysope *f.*
lacework [ˈleiswəːk], *s.* (*a*) dentelles *fpl;* dentellerie *f;* (*b*) passementerie *f.*
Lachenalia [lækəˈneiliə], *s. Bot:* lachenalia *m.*
laches [ˈlætʃiz], *s.* (*a*) *Jur:* négligence *f,* inaction *f* (dans la poursuite d'une instance, et dont résulte la péremption); (*b*) *Lit:* négligence coupable; carence *f* (du gouvernement, etc.).
Lachesis [ˈlækəsis]. **1.** *Pr.n.f. Gr.Myth:* Lachésis. **2.** *s. Rept:* lachésis *m.*
lachrymal [ˈlækrim(ə)l], *a. & s.* lacrymal, -aux; (*a*) *Anat:* **l. (bone),** os lacrymal; unguis *m;* **l. caruncle,** caroncule lacrymale; **l. duct, l. canal,** canal lacrymal; **l. gland,** glande lacrymale; **l. sac,** sac lacrymal; **s. lachrymals,** voies lacrymales; (*b*) *Archeol:* **l. (vase),** urne *f* lacrymatoire; lacrymatoire *m.*
lachrymation [lækriˈmeiʃ(ə)n], *s.* (*a*) larmes *fpl;* (*b*) larmoiement *m.*
lachrymator [ˈlækrimeitər], *s.* (*a*) *Mil: O:* gaz *m* lacrymogène; (*b*) *Archeol:* urne *f* lacrymatoire; lacrymatoire *m.*
lachrymatory [lækriˈmeit(ə)ri], *a. & s.* (*a*) *Archeol:* urne *f* lacrymatoire; lacrymatoire *m;* (*b*) *Mil: O:* (gaz *m,* obus *m,* etc.) lacrymogène.
lachrymose [ˈlækrimous], *a.* larmoyant.
lacing [ˈleisiŋ], *s.* **1.** lacement *m,* laçage *m* (d'un corset, etc.); *Nau:* transfilage *m; Mch:* **l. of belts,** attache *f* des courroies. **2.** (*a*) lacet *m;* (*b*) galon *m,* passement *m,* tresse *f; Veh:* **coach l.,** tresse pour carrosserie; (*c*) *Civ.E:* **l. bar,** barre *f* de triangulation (de poutre composée); (*d*) *Bookb:* **l. in,** passure *f* en carton. **3.** *F: A:* fouettée *f,* rossée *f.*
lacinia, *pl.* **-iae** [læˈsiniə, -iiː], *s. Nat.Hist:* lacinia *f.*
laciniate, laciniated [læˈsinieit(id)], *a. Nat.Hist:* lacinié; (feuille) déchiquetée; **laciniate-leaved,** lacinifolié.
laciniation [læsiniˈeiʃ(ə)n], *s. Bot:* lacine *f,* laciniure *f.*
lacinula, *pl.* **-ae** [læˈsinjulə, -iː], *s. Bot:* lacinule *f.*
lacinulate [læˈsinjuleit], *a. Nat.Hist:* lacinulé.
lacis [ˈleisis], *s. Lacem:* lacis *m.*
lack[1] [læk], *s.* manque *m,* absence *f,* défaut *m,* pénurie *f* (of, de); **l. of judgment,** manque de jugement; **l. of money,** pénurie d'argent; *Mec.E:* **l. of balance,** défaut d'équilibrage; **l. of power,** manque de puissance; **we have no l. of helpers at present,** il ne nous manque pas d'aide actuellement; **she was tired from l. of sleep,** ayant peu dormi elle était fatiguée; **there is no l. of water,** on ne manque pas d'eau; **for l. of . . .,** faute de . . .; (par) manque de . . ..
lack[2], *v.tr. & i.* **to l. (for) sth.,** manquer de qch.; être dénué de qch.; ne pas avoir qch.; **we l. nothing,** nous ne manquons de rien; il ne nous manque rien; **he lacks experience,** il manque d'expérience; **they l. capital,** les capitaux *m* leur font défaut; **we were unable to do it because we lacked helpers,** nous n'avons pas pu le faire parce que nous n'avions pas assez d'aide.
lackadaisical [lækəˈdeizik(ə)l], *a.* (*of pers., manner, etc.*) affecté, affété, minaudier; apathique; d'une nonchalance affectée.
lackadaisically [lækəˈdeizik(ə)li], *adv.* d'un air, d'un ton, affecté, affété.
lackaday [lækəˈdei], *int. A:* hélas!
lackey [ˈlæki], *s.* **1.** laquais *m.* **2.** *O:* sycophante *m,* flagorneur *m,* laquais. **3.** *Ent:* **l. moth,** (bombyx *m*) livrée *f.*
lacking [ˈlækiŋ], *a. F:* **l. (in the top storey),** (un peu) simplet.
Lackland [ˈlæklænd]. *Pr.n. Hist:* **John L.,** Jean sans Terre.
lacklustre [ˈlæklʌstər], *a.* (œil *m,* etc.) terne, sans brillant, sans regard, éteint.
lac(k)moid [ˈlækmɔid], *s. Ch:* lacmoïde *m.*
Laconia [ləˈkouniə]. *Pr.n. A.Geog:* Laconie *f.*
Laconian [ləˈkouniən], *a. A.Geog:* laconien, -ienne.
laconic [ləˈkɔnik], *a.* laconique; bref en paroles; (*of answer, etc.*) bref, *f.* brève.
laconically [ləˈkɔnik(ə)li], *adv.* laconiquement.
laconism [ˈlækənizm], *s.* laconisme *m.*
lacquer[1] [ˈlækər], *s.* **1.** (*a*) vernis-laque *m inv;* vernis *m* de Chine; laque *m;* **gold l.,** batture *f;* (*b*) *Bot:* **l. tree, plant,** vernis du Japon; sumac *m* vernis. **2.** émail *m;* peinture laquée; **cellulose l.,** laque *f* cellulosique. **3.** *Hairdr:* laque *f.*
lacquer[2], *v.tr.* **1.** vernir, laquer. **2.** émailler (des meubles, etc.).
lacquered [ˈlækəd], *a.* verni, laqué.
lacquering [ˈlækəriŋ], *s.* **1.** (*a*) laquage *m,* vernissage *m;* (*b*) émaillage *m.* **2.** (*a*) vernissure *f* (en laque); (*b*) émail *m.*
lacquerwork [ˈlækəwəːk], *s.* laque(s) *m(pl);* **I can show you some fine l.,** je peux vous montrer de beau laque, de beaux laques.
lacrosse [ləˈkros], *s. Sp:* crosse *f.*
lacrymal, -ation, etc. = LACHRYMAL, -ATION, ETC.
lactalbumen [lækˈtælbjumin], *s. Ch:* lactalbumine *f.*
lactam [ˈlæktæm], *s. Bio-Ch:* lactame *f.*
lactarius [lækˈtɛəriəs], *s. Fung:* lactaire *m.*
lactase [ˈlækteis], *s. Bio-Ch:* lactase *f.*
lactate [ˈlækteit], *s. Ch:* lactate *m.*
lactation [lækˈteiʃ(ə)n], *s.* **1.** *Physiol:* lactation *f; Med:* **l. tetany,** fièvre lactée. **2.** allaitement *m.*
lacteal [ˈlæktiəl], *a.* lacté; (suc) laiteux; *Anat:* **l. vessels,** *spl.* **lacteals,** vaisseaux lactés; conduits *m* chylifères; *Med:* **l. fever,** fièvre lactée; fièvre de lait.
lactenin [ˈlæktənin], *s. Bio-Ch:* lacténine *f.*
lacteous [ˈlæktiəs], *a.* **1.** *A:* laiteux. **2.** = LACTEAL.
lactescence [lækˈtes(ə)ns], *s.* lactescence *f.*
lactescent [lækˈtes(ə)nt], *a.* lactescent; *Bot:* **l. plant,** plante lactée.
lactiacidemia [læktiæsiˈdiːmiə], *s. Med:* lacticémie *f,* lactacidémie *f.*
lactic [ˈlæktik], *a. Ch:* lactique; caséique; **l. fermentation,** lactofermentation *f.*
lactide [ˈlæktaid], *s. Ch:* lactide *m.*
lactiferous [lækˈtifərəs], *a.* lactifère.
lactific [lækˈtifik], *a.* lactifique.
lactifuge [ˈlæktifjuːdʒ], *s. Med:* lactifuge *m.*
lactim [ˈlæktim], *s. Ch:* lactime *f.*
lactivorous [lækˈtivərəs], *a.* lactivore.
lactobacillus, *pl.* **-i** [læktouˈbæsiləs, -ai], *s.* lactobacille *m,* lactobacillus *m.*
lactodensimeter [ˈlæktouˈdensimiːtər], *s.* lactomètre *m,* galactomètre *m;* lacto-densimètre *m, pl.* lacto-densimètres; pèse-lait *m inv.*
lactoflavin [læktouˈfleivin], *s. Ch:* lactoflavine *f,* riboflavine *f.*
lactogenic [læktouˈdʒenik], *a. Biol:* lactigène; **l. hormone,** prolactine *f.*
lactoglobulin [læktouˈglɔbgjulin], *s.* lactoglobuline *f.*
lactometer [lækˈtɔmitər], *s.* = LACTODENSIMETER.
lactone [ˈlæktoun], *s. Ch:* lactone *f.*
lactonic [lækˈtɔnik], *a.* lactonique.
lactonitril(e) [læktouˈnaitril], *s. Ch:* lactonitrile *m.*
lactonization [læktənaiˈzeiʃ(ə)n], *s. Ch:* lactonisation *f.*
lactoscope [ˈlæktəskoup], *s.* lactoscope *m.*
lactose [ˈlæktous], *s. Ch:* lactose *f;* sucre *m* de lait.
lactosuria [læktouˈsjuːriə], *s. Med:* lactosurie *f.*
lactucarium [læktjuˈkɛəriəm], *s. Pharm:* lactucarium *m,* thridace *f.*
lacuna, *pl.* **-ae, -as** [ləˈkjuːnə, -iː, -əz], *s.* **1.** lacune *f;* hiatus *m* (dans un ouvrage). **2.** *Moll:* lacuna *f,* lacune.
lacunar [ləˈkjuːnər], *s. Arch: Const:* **1.** lacunar *m,* plafond *m* à caissons. **2.** caisson *m* (de plafond).
lacunary [ləˈkjuːnəri], *a.* lacunaire.
Lacunidae [ləˈkjuːnidiː], *s.pl. Moll:* lacunidés *m.*
lacunose [ləˈkjuːnous], *a.* (tissu, etc.) lacuneux.
lacustrian [ləˈkʌstriən]. *Prehist:* **1.** *a.* (cité, etc.) lacustre. **2.** *s.* habitant, -ante, d'une cité lacustre.
lacustrine [ləˈkʌstrin], *a.* (plante *f,* etc.) lacustre; *Prehist:* **l. dwellings,** cité *f* lacustre.
lacy [ˈleisi], *a.* de dentelle; fin, léger, comme de la dentelle.
lad [læd], *s.* **1.** (*a*) jeune homme; garçon; *A:* **a servant l.,** un jeune domestique; **come on, lads!** allons, les gars! (*b*) **he's a real l., quite a l.,** (i) c'est un gaillard; (ii) c'est un vrai garçon; **one of the lads,** un des gars; (*c*) *Turf:* **(stable) l.,** lad *m;* **she's a l. at Martin's (the trainer),** elle est employée chez (l'entraîneur) Martin comme lad. **2.** *Bot:* **lad's love,** aurone *f* (mâle); citronnelle *f.*
ladanum [ˈlædənəm], *s. Ch:* labdanum *m.*
ladder[1] [ˈlædər], *s.* **1.** échelle *f;* (*a*) **extending l., telescopic l.,** échelle à coulisse; **folding l.,** échelle pliante, brisée; **rack l., peg l.,** rancher *m,* échelier *m;* **aerial l.,** échelle de sauvetage; *Mil:* **observation l.,** échelle-observatoire *f, pl.* échelles-observatoires; *Nau:* **accommodation l., side l.,** échelle de commandement de coupée; **gangway l.,** échelle de coupée, de côté; **quarter l.,** échelle de dunette; **stern l.,** échelle de poupe; **the social l.,** l'échelle sociale; **to climb a rung of the social l.,** gravir un échelon social; **to reach, be at, the top of the l.,** atteindre le sommet de l'échelle sociale; être au bout, au haut, de l'échelle; (*b*) *attrib. Tchn:* **l. chain,** chaîne *f* de Vaucanson, chaîne à la Vaucanson; **l. tape,** ruban *m* à jalousie(s); *Rail:* **l. track,** gril *m* de triage; *Min:* **l. shaft, way,** puits *m* aux échelles; **l. sollar,** palier *m* de repos; plate-forme *f* de repos; (*c*) *Pisc:* **fish l., salmon l.,** échelle à poissons. **2.** *Hyd.E:* (*a*) élinde *f* (de drague); **l. dredger,** drague *f* à élinde, à échelle; (*b*) **l. of locks,** suite *f* de biefs. **3.** (*in stocking*) maille filée; **I've got a l. (in my stocking),** j'ai une maille qui file; j'ai filé mon bas; **to mend a l.,** rem(m)ailler un bas.
ladder[2]. **1.** *v.tr.* (*a*) munir (un échafaudage, etc.)

d'échelles; (*b*) **I've laddered my stocking,** j'ai filé mon bas. **2.** *v.i.* (*of stocking, etc.*) se démailler; filer.

ladderback ['lædəbæk], *s.* dossier *m* (de chaise) à barres horizontales.

ladderproof ['lædəpru:f], *a.* (bas) indémaillable.

laddie ['lædi], *s.m. Scot: F:* (*a*) garçon; (*b*) (*term of endearment*) mon petit gars.

lade[1] [leid], *s.* (**mill**) **l.**, courant *m* de moulin; bief *m*, biez *m*.

lade[2], *v.tr.* (**laded; laden**) **1.** *Nau:* (*a*) charger (un navire) (**with,** de); (*b*) embarquer (des marchandises). **2.** (*p.p.* **laded**) **to l. water,** (i) puiser de l'eau (**from,** à); (ii) épuiser l'eau.

laden ['leidn], *a.* chargé. **1.** *Nau:* **fully l. ship,** navire *m* en pleine charge; **l. by the head,** chargé sur l'avant, sur le nez; **l. by the stern,** chargé sur l'arrière, sur le cul; **l. in bulk,** chargé en vrac, en grenier; **l. draught,** tirant *m* d'eau en charge. **2. heavily l. tree,** arbre chargé de fruits; *Lit:* **l. with grief,** accablé de douleur.

la-di-da(h) ['lɑ:di'dɑ:]. *F:* **1.** *s. A:* petit crevé; gommeux *m.* **2.** *a.* (*a*) *A:* (airs, etc.) de petit crevé; (*b*) **l. manner,** air affecté.

Ladin [lə'di:n], *s. Ling:* ladin *m.*

lading ['leidiŋ], *s.* (*a*) chargement *m* (d'un navire); (*b*) embarquement *m*, mise *f* à bord (de marchandises).

ladle[1] ['leidl], *s.* **1.** cuiller *f* à pot; poche *f*; **soup l.,** louche *f*; **basting l.,** louche; **punch l.,** cuiller à punch. **2.** (*a*) *Ind:* puisoir *m*, casse *f*; (*b*) *Metall:* **foundry l.,** poche de fonderie, de coulée; **casting l.,** cuiller de coulée; cuiller à couler, à fondre; **slag l.,** poche à laitier; **hand l., small l.,** houlette *f*, calebasse *f*; **l. crane,** pont *m* de coulée.

ladle[2], *v.tr.* **1. to l. (out) the soup,** servir le potage (avec la louche); **to l. out information,** débiter des renseignements; *Th: P: A:* **to l. it out,** débiter son rôle avec emphase. **2.** (*a*) *Ind:* pucher (du goudron, du sirop); (*b*) *Metall:* couler (la fonte).

ladleful ['leidlful], *s.* pleine cuiller à pot, pleine louche (**of,** de).

ladler ['leidlər], *s. Metall:* pocheur *m.*

lady ['leidi], *s.f.* dame. **1.** (*a*) (*at court*) **l. in waiting,** dame d'honneur; **l. of the bedchamber,** dame des atours; (*b*) *O:* dame, femme bien élevée; **she's a real, a perfect, l.,** c'est une femme très comme il faut, très bien élevée; **she's no l.,** c'est une femme commune, mal élevée; **she was too much the l. to stoop to doing that,** elle était trop grande dame pour s'abaisser jusqu'à faire cela; (*c*) **a l. and a gentleman,** un monsieur et une dame; **an English l.,** une dame anglaise, une Anglaise; **a young l.,** une demoiselle, une jeune fille; (*married*) une jeune dame; **an old l.,** une vieille dame; *A:* **school for young ladies,** pensionnat *m* de demoiselles, de jeunes filles; (*to child*) **how are you, young l.?** comment allez-vous, ma petite demoiselle? *Com:* **the young l. will attend to you,** la vendeuse s'occupera de vous; **I'm sorry, but this l. was before you,** je m'excuse, mais cette dame était là avant vous; *Com: P:* **here you are, l.!** voilà, ma petite dame! (*at meeting, etc.*) **ladies and gentlemen!** mesdames, mesdemoiselles, messieurs! **come in, ladies!** entrez donc, mesdames! **my dear l.!** chère madame! **now then ladies, move along please!** allons, mesdames, circulez un peu! (*on public convenience*) **ladies,** dames; (*d*) **the l. of the house,** la maîtresse de maison; *P:* **my l., the l. I work for,** la patronne; (*e*) **lady's watch,** montre *f* de dame; **ladies' tailor,** tailleur pour dames; **lady's maid,** femme de chambre; **a ladies', lady's, man,** un homme galant; *O:* (*now usu.* **woman**) **l. doctor,** femme médecin, doctoresse. **2.** *Ecc:* **Our L.,** Notre-Dame, la sainte Vierge; **L. chapel,** chapelle *f* de la Vierge; **L. altar,** autel *m* de la Vierge; **L. Day,** la fête de l'Annonciation (le 25 mars). **3.** (*a*) (*title*) (i) (*no Fr. equivalent*) **Lady X,** lady X (femme de Sir David X); (ii) (*informal address*) **Lady Y,** Madame (la Comtesse, la Marquise, etc.) de Y; (iii) (*shopkeeper, etc. addressing titled woman*) **yes, my l.,** oui, madame, milady; (iv) **the L. Mayoress,** la femme du lord-maire; (*b*) **our Sovereign L.,** notre souveraine; **the l. of the manor,** la châtelaine; (*c*) *A:* maîtresse, princesse (d'un territoire). **4.** (*a*) *A:* femme, épouse; **the colonel's l.,** la femme du colonel; (*b*) *P:* **how's your good l.?** comment va votre femme? **the old l.,** (i) ma femme, la bourgeoise; (ii) ma mère; (iii) ma vieille grand-mère, ma vieille tante, etc.; **my young l.,** (i) ma bonne amie; (ii) ma fiancée, ma future. **5.** (*a*) *Crust:* moulinet *m*; (*b*) *Ent:* **painted l.,** belle-dame *f, pl.* belles-dames; (*c*) *Hort:* **l. apple,** (pomme *f* d')api *m*; *Bot:* **lady's bower,** clématite *f* des haies; herbe *f* aux gueux; **lady's comb,** aiguillette *f*; **lady's cushion,** saxifrage mousseuse; amourette moussue; **lady's eardrop,** fuchsia *m*; **lady's finger,** (i) vulnéraire *f*; trèfle *m* jaune; (ii) gombo *m*; ketmie *f* comestible; **lady's garters,** phalaris *m*; **lady's mantle,** alchémille *f* vulgaire; manteau *m* de Notre-Dame, *F:* mantelet *m* de dame; **lady's seal,** sceau *m* de la Vierge, de Notre-Dame; taminier *m*; **lady's slipper,** cypripède *m*, *F:* sabot *m* de la Vierge, de Notre-Dame, de Vénus; souliers *mpl* de Notre-Dame; marjolaine bâtarde; **lady('s) smock,** cardamine *f* des prés; cresson élégant, des prés; **lady's thistle,** chardon *m* de Notre-Dame; **lady's thumb,** persicaire *f*; **lady's tresses,** spiranthe *m*; **l. fern,** fougère *f* femelle.

ladybird, *NAm:* **ladybug** ['leidibə:d, -bʌg], *s. Ent:* coccinelle *f*; *F:* bête *f* à bon Dieu; catherinette *f.*

lady-chair ['leiditʃɛər], *s. A:* entrecroisement *m* de mains (de deux porteurs); chaise *f* (pour le transport d'un blessé); **to carry s.o. in a l.-c.,** porter qn en chaise.

ladykiller ['leidikilər], *s. F:* bourreau des cœurs; casse-cœur *inv*; don Juan; tombeur *m* de femmes, homme à femmes.

ladylike ['leidilaik], *a.* (air, etc.) distingué, de dame; (*of pers.*) comme il faut; bien élevée; à l'air distingué; de bonne société.

ladyship ['leidiʃip], *s.* **her l., your l.,** madame (la comtesse, etc.); *Iron:* **in walked her l., their ladyships,** et madame d'entrer; et ces dames d'entrer.

Laertes [lei'ə:ti:z], *Pr.n.m. Gr.Lit:* Laërte.

laevogyrate, laevogyrous [li:vou'dʒaiəreit, -'dʒaiərəs], *a. Ch:* lévogyre.

laevorotation ['li:vourou'teiʃ(ə)n], *s. Med:* lévorotation *f* (du cœur); *Ch:* rotation *f* à gauche (du plan de polarisation).

laevorotatory ['li:vourou'teitəri], **laevorotary** [li:vou'routəri], *a. Ch:* lévogyre, sénestrogyre.

laevulose ['li:vjulous], *s. Ch:* lévulose *m or f*; sucre *m* de fruit.

lag[1] [læg], *s.* **1.** *Ph:* retard *m*; *Ind: etc:* (**time**) **l.,** décalage *m* (entre deux opérations); *Nau:* **l. of the tide,** retard (diurne) de la marée; *Aedcs: Ball:* **air l.,** traînée *f* (de bombe, etc.); *Mch:* **admission l.,** retard à l'admission; **distributed lags,** retards échelonnés; *I.C.E:* etc: **ignition l.,** retard à l'allumage; *El:* **magnetic l., l. of magnetization,** retard d'aimantation, traînage *m* magnétique; hystérésis *f*; **l. of the brushes,** décalage des balais (d'une dynamo, etc.); **time l.,** retard; **time-l. cutout,** coupe-circuit *m inv* à action différée; **phase l.,** retard de phase; décalage de phase; **l. of the current,** déphasage *m* en arrière du courant; **angle of l.,** angle *m* de retard; *Mec:* **elastic l.,** retard dû à la déformation élastique; **l. screw,** tire-fond *m inv*; vis *f* à bois à tête carrée. **2.** ralentissement *m* (d'un moteur à ressort, etc.).

lag[2], *v.i.* (**lagged**). **1. to l.** (**behind**), rester en arrière; traîner; s'attarder; se laisser distancer (par les autres); **wages are lagging far behind the cost of living,** les salaires restent bien inférieurs au coût de la vie. **2.** *Tchn:* (*of tides, etc.*) retarder; *El:* (*of current*) être déphasé en arrière.

lag[3], *s. F:* **1.** condamné *m*, déporté *m*, forçat *m*; **an old l.,** un repris de justice, un récidiviste; *F:* un cheval de retour. **2.** *A:* peine *f* de transportation; transportation *f.*

lag[4], *v.tr. F:* **1.** (*a*) *A:* déporter (un forçat); (*b*) condamner (un prisonnier) aux travaux forcés. **2.** faire arrêter, faire empoigner (qn); **to get lagged,** être mis en état d'arrestation; être fourré au bloc.

lag[5], *s.* latte *f* (d'enveloppe de chaudière); **wooden lags,** lattis (protecteur).

lag[6], *v.tr.* garnir, envelopper, revêtir (une chaudière) d'un calorifuge; calorifuger, isoler (une chaudière, etc.); *Min:* garnir (les parois d'un puits); **air-lagged,** à chemise d'air.

lagan ['lægən], *s. Hist: Jur:* lagan *m.*

lagenaria [lædʒi'nɛəriə], *s. Bot:* lagenaria *m.*

lageniform [lə'dʒenifɔ:m], *a. Nat.Hist:* lagéniforme.

lagenophora [lædʒi'nɔfərə], *s. Bot:* lagenophora *m.*

lagenostoma [lædʒi'nɔstəmə], *s. Paleont:* lagénostoma *m.*

lager ['lɑ:gər], *s.* bière blonde allemande.

lagerstroemia [leigə'stri:miə], *s. Bot:* lagerstrœmia *m.*

lagetta [lə'dʒetə], *s. Bot:* lagetta *m.*

laggard ['lægəd]. **1.** *a.* lent, paresseux; en retard. **2.** *s.* (*a*) traînard, -arde; attardé, -ée; retardataire *mf*; (*b*) *For:* arbre *m* en retard, tardif.

lagging[1] ['lægiŋ], *a.* (courant) retardé, déphasé en retard.

lagging[2], *s.* **1.** retard *m*, ralentissement *m*. **2.** *El:* déphasage *m* en arrière (du courant).

lagging[3], *s.* **1.** garnissage *m*, calorifugeage *m*, enveloppement *m* (d'une chaudière, etc.); *Min:* coffrage *m*, boisage *m*, garnissage (d'une galerie). **2.** garniture *f*, enveloppe isolante, chemise *f*, revêtement *m* calorifuge (d'une chaudière, etc.). **3.** *Const:* **l. of a centering,** couchis *m* d'un cintre.

lagidium [læ'dʒidiəm], *s. Z:* lagidium *m.*

Lagomorpha [lægou'mɔ:fə], *s.pl. Z:* lagomorphes *m.*

lagoon [lə'gu:n], *s. Geog:* **1.** (*sand, shingle, etc.*) lagune *f*; **tidal l.,** lagune à marée. **2.** lagon *m* (d'atoll).

lagophthalmos, lagophthalmus [lægɔf'θælməs], *s. Med: Vet:* lagophtalmie *f.*

lagopus ['lægəpəs], *s. Orn:* lagopède *m.*

lagorchestes [lægɔ:'kesti:z], *s. Z:* lagorcheste(s) *m.*

lagostomus [læ'gɔstəməs], *s. Z:* lagostome *m*, lagostomus *m*; **the L. family,** les lagostomidés *m.*

lagothrix ['lægouθriks], *s. Z:* lagotriche *m*, lagothrix *m.*

lah [lɑ:], *s. Mus:* (*in tonic solfa*) la sus-dominante.

lahar ['lɑ:hɑ:], *s.* coulée *f* de boue, avalanche boueuse.

laic ['leiik], *a. & s.* laïque (*mf*).

laical ['leiik(ə)l], *a.* laïque.

laicism ['leiisizm], *s.* laïcisme *m.*

laicization [leiisai'zeiʃ(ə)n], *s.* laïcisation *f.*

laicize ['leiisaiz], *v.tr.* laïciser.

laid [leid], *a.* **1.** *Paperm:* vergé; **cream-laid paper,** vergé blanc. **2.** (*of moulding, etc.*) **l. on,** rapporté.

lair[1] ['lɛər], *s.* **1.** tanière *f*, repaire *m*, antre *m*, reposée *f* (de bête fauve); liteau *m* (du loup), lit *m* (du cerf); bauge *f* (du sanglier); accul *m* (du blaireau); catiche *f* (de la loutre); **brigands' l.,** repaire, caverne *f*, de brigands. **2.** hangar *m*, abri *m*, enclos *m* (pour bestiaux de passage); (*in slaughterhouse*) bouvril *m*. **3.** *Scot:* fosse *f* (de sépulture), tombe *f*; tombeau (familial).

lair[2]. **1.** *v.tr.* (*of beast*) (*a*) coucher, reposer (dans sa tanire ou dans son enclos); (*b*) se faire un repaire. **2.** *v.tr.* loger, parquer, (les bestiaux) sous les hangars ou dans les enclos.

lairage ['lɛəridʒ], *s.* logement *m* (de bestiaux).

laird ['lɛəd], *s. Scot:* propriétaire (foncier); **the l.,** le châtelain; le laird.

lairdship ['lɛədʃip], *s. Scot:* **1.** dignité *f* de laird. **2.** petite propriété foncière.

laisser-faire, laissez-faire [lesei'fɛər], *s.* laisser-faire *m*; **l.-f. policy,** politique *f* de laisser-faire.

laity ['leiiti], *s. coll.* **the l.,** les laïques *m*; le laïcat.

lake[1] [leik], *s.* (*a*) lac *m*; **crater l.,** lac de cratère; **tectonic l.,** lac tectonique; **barrier l.,** lac de barrage; **oxbow l.,** lac en forme de croissant; **salt l.,** lac salé; **ornamental l.,** bassin *m*; pièce d'eau décorative; **L. Trasimene,** le lac Trasimène; (**the**) **L.** (**of**) **Geneva,** le lac Léman, le lac de Genève; **the Great Lakes,** les Grands Lacs (d'Amérique du Nord); **the L. District,** la région des lacs (au nord-ouest de l'Angleterre); *Lit. Hist:* **the L. poets,** les (poètes *m*) lakistes *m*; *P:* **go jump in the l.,** va te faire foutre; *P:* **tell him to go (and) jump in the l.,** envoie-le paître; (*b*) *Prehist: etc:* **l. dweller,** habitant, -ante, d'une cité lacustre; **l. dwelling,** habitation *f* lacustre; **l. dwellings,** cité lacustre.

lake[2], *s. Paint:* laque *f*; **crimson l.,** laque carminée; **madder l.,** laque de garance; **yellow l.,** laque jaune; jaune indien; stil-de-grain *m.*

lake[3]. **1.** *v.tr. Med: Physiol:* (*of ammonia, etc.*) laquer (le sang). **2.** *v.i.* (*of blood*) se laquer; **laked blood,** sang laqué.

Lakeland ['leiklənd], *attrib.* de la région des lacs (du nord-ouest de l'Angleterre); **L. tour,** voyage organisé dans la région des lacs.

lakelet ['leiklit], *s.* petit lac.

laker ['leikər], *s. NAm:* navire *m* navigant sur les Grands Lacs (de l'Amérique du Nord).

lakh [læk], *s.* lack *m* (de roupies).

Lakist ['leikist], *s. Lit.Hist:* (poète *m*) lakiste *m.*

laky ['leiki], *a.* (sang) laqué.

lallation [læ'leiʃ(ə)n], *s. Ling:* lallation *f*, la(m)bdacisme *m.*

lam [læm], *v.tr. & i.* (**lammed**) *F:* **to l. (into) s.o.,** rosser, étriller, qn.

lama ['lɑ:mə], *s. Rel:* lama *m*; **the Dalai, Grand, L.,** le dalaï, grand, Lama.

lamaism ['lɑ:məizm], *s. Rel:* lamaïsme *m.*

lamaist ['lɑ:məist], *s. Rel:* lamaïste *m.*

La Mancha [lɑ:'mæntʃə], *Pr.n. Geog:* la Manche (province d'Espagne).

Lamarckism ['læmɑ:kizm], *s.* lamarckisme *m.*

lamasery ['lɑ:məs(ə)ri], *s.* couvent *m* de lamas; lamaserie *f.*

lamb[1] [læm], *s.* **1.** (*a*) agneau *m*; **ewe l.,** agnelle *f*; **wether l.,** agneau; **my one ewe l.,** mon seul trésor; **ewe with l.,** brebis pleine; *Ecc:* **L. (of God),** Agneau (de Dieu); **paschal l.,** (i) *Jew.Rel:* agneau pascal; (ii) *Her:* (*also* **l. and flag**) agneau-pascal; *F:* **he took it, went, like a l.,** il s'est laissé faire; il n'a pas protesté; il n'a pas regimbé; (*b*) *F:* **be a l.!** sois gentil! **my l.,** mon petit; (*c*) *Hort:* **lamb's lettuce,** mâche *f*; (*d*) *Bot: F:* **lambs' tails,** chatons *m* (du noisetier). **2.** *Cu:* agneau; **l. cutlet, chop,** côtelette *f* d'agneau. **3.** *Com:* (*fur*) **Persian l.,** astrak(h)an *m* persianer, caracul *m* persianer; **shorn l.,** agneau rasé. **4.** *NAm: F:* jobard *m*, gobeur *m*, pigeon *m.*

lamb². **1.** *v.i.* (*of ewe*) agneler, mettre bas. **2.** *v.tr.* (*a*) (*in p.p. only*) **sheep lambed in February,** agneau né au mois de février; (*b*) **to l. (down) the ewes,** soigner les brebis pendant l'agnelage.

lambast [læm'bæst], **lambaste** [læm'beist], *v.tr.* fustiger.

lambda ['læmdə], *s. Gr.Alph:* lambda *m.*

lambdacism ['læmdəsizm], *s. Ling:* la(m)bdacisme *m.*

lambdoid(al) ['læmdɔid, læm'dɔidl], *a. Anat:* (suture *f*) lambdoïde.

lambency ['læmbənsi], *s.* **1.** lueur blafarde (d'une étoile, d'une flamme). **2.** *Lit:* chatoiement *m* (de l'esprit).

lambent ['læmbənt], *a.* **1.** (flamboiement, etc.) blafard; (yeux, ciel) à l'éclat adouci. **2.** (esprit, style) chatoyant.

lambing ['læmiŋ], *s.* agnelage *m*, agnèlement *m.*

lambkin ['læmkin], *s.* agnelet *m*; petit agneau.

lamblike ['læmlaik], *a.* doux, *f.* douce, comme un agneau; **don't be so l.!** montre un peu de détermination!

lambrequin ['læmbrəkin], *s. Furn: etc:* lambrequin *m.*

lambskin ['læmskin], *s.* (*a*) *Leath:* peau *f* d'agneau; (*b*) (*fur*) agnelin *m.*

lambswool ['læmzwul], *s.* laine *f* d'agneau; agneline *f.*

lame¹ [leim], *a.* **1.** (*a*) boiteux; (*through accident, etc.*) estropié; **a l. man, woman,** un boiteux, une boiteuse; **l. leg,** jambe boiteuse; **l. horse,** cheval boiteux, éclopé; **to be l. in one leg,** boiter d'une jambe; **to be, walk, l.,** boiter, clocher; traîner la jambe; **I have walked myself l.,** j'ai tant marché que je traîne la patte; **to go l.,** se mettre à boiter; (*b*) *Pros:* **l. verses,** vers *m* boiteux; vers qui boitent, qui clochent. **2. l. excuse,** mauvaise, faible, piètre, pauvre, excuse; **l. story,** histoire *f* qui ne tient pas debout; histoire louche.

lame², *v.tr.* (*a*) (*of pers.*) rendre (qn) boiteux; écloper (qn, un cheval); (*of blister, etc.*) faire boiter (qn); (*b*) estropier; **lamed through an accident, in the war,** estropié par suite d'un accident, à la guerre.

lamé ['lɑːmei], *s. Tex:* **gold l., silver, l.,** lamé *m* d'or, d'argent.

lamella, *pl.* **-ae** [lə'melə, -iː], *s.* (*a*) *Nat.Hist:* lamelle *f* (de champignon, de gastéropode, etc.); **suction l.,** ventouse *f* (d'un gecko); (*b*) *Miner:* lamelle (d'ardoise, de mica, etc.); (*c*) *Tchn:* lamelle (de l'émail, etc.).

lamellar [lə'melər], *a.* **1.** (*a*) lamellaire, lamellé; (*b*) lamelliforme. **2.** *El:* **l. field,** champ vectoriel apériodique.

Lamellariidae [læmelə'raiidiː], *s.pl. Moll:* lamellaires *m.*

lamellate(d) ['læməleit(id)], *a.* (*a*) lamellaire, lamelleux, lamellé; *Miner:* **lamellated fracture,** cassure lamelleuse, lamellaire; (*b*) lamelliforme.

lamellibranch [lə'melibræŋk], *s. Moll:* lamellibranche *m.*

lamellibranchiate [ləmeli'bræŋkieit], *a. Moll:* lamellibranche.

lamellicorn [lə'melikɔːn], *a. & s. Ent:* lamellicorne (*m*).

lamelliform [lə'melifɔːm], *a.* lamelliforme.

lamellirostral [ləmeli'rɔstr(ə)l], *a. Orn:* lamellirostre.

Lamellirostres [ləmeli'rɔstriːz], *s.pl. Orn:* lamellirostres *m.*

lamelloid ['læməlɔid], *a.* lamelloïde.

lamellose [lə'melous], *a.* lamelleux.

lamely ['leimli], *adv.* (s'excuser, etc.) imparfaitement, faiblement, mal.

lameness ['leimnis], *s.* **1.** (*a*) claudication *f*; clochement *m*, boitement *m*; (*b*) boiterie *f* (d'un cheval, etc.). **2.** imperfection *f*; faiblesse *f* (d'une excuse, etc.).

lament¹ [lə'ment], *s.* **1.** lamentation *f.* **2.** *Mus: A:* complainte *f.*

lament², *v.tr. & i.* **to l. (for, over) sth., s.o.,** se lamenter sur qch.; s'affliger, gémir, de qch.; déplorer qch.; pleurer qch., qn.

lamentable ['læməntəbl], *a.* (perte *f*, insuccès *m*, etc.) lamentable, déplorable; **it's l.!** c'est lamentable! c'est à faire pitié!

lamentably ['læməntəbli], *adv.* lamentablement, déplorablement.

lamentation [læmən'teiʃ(ə)n], *s.* lamentation *f*; *B:* **the Lamentations of Jeremiah, Lamentations,** les Lamentations de Jérémie.

lamented [lə'mentid], *a.* **the late l. X,** le regretté X.

lamenting [lə'mentiŋ], *s.* lamentation *f.*

lamia ['leimiə], *s. Myth:* lamie *f.*

Lamian ['leimiən]. (*a*) *a. A.Geog:* lamiaque; *Gr.Hist:* **the L. War,** la guerre Lamiaque; (*b*) *s.* Lamiaque *mf.*

lamina, *pl.* **-ae** ['læminə, -iː], *s.* **1.** lame *f*, lamelle *f*, feuillet *m*; **spring l.,** lame, feuille *f*, de ressort. **2.** *Bot:* limbe *m* (de feuille); écaille *f* (d'une fleur). **3.** *Anat:* lame; **l. cribrosa,** lame criblée; **l. perpendicularis,** lame perpendiculaire; **l. spiralis,** lame spirale; **l. of vertebral arch,** lame vertébrale; **l. dura,** corticale *f* alvéolaire interne.

laminar ['læminər], *a.* laminaire; *Miner:* **l. fracture,** cassure *f* laminaire; *Ph: etc:* **l. flow,** écoulement *m* laminaire (d'un fluide); *Av:* **l.-flow airfoil,** profil *m* (d'aile) laminaire; **l. boundary layer,** couche *f* limite laminaire.

laminaria [læmi'nɛəriə], *s. Algae:* laminaire *f.*

Laminariaceae [læminɛəri'eisiiː], *s. pl. Algae:* laminariacées *f.*

laminarian [læmi'nɛəriən], *a. Oc:* **l. zone,** zone *f* des laminaires; zone littorale, zone herbacée.

laminate¹ ['læmineit]. **1.** *v.tr.* (*a*) *Ind: etc:* laminer, lamifier; *Metall:* écacher (au laminoir); (*b*) diviser en lamelles; (*c*) feuilleter (du verre); stratifier (de la matière plastique); plaquer, contreplaquer (du bois); (*d*) *Bookb: etc:* plastifier (du papier, du carton, etc.); **to l. cardboard with polythene,** plastifier du carton avec du polythène. **2.** *v.i.* (*a*) se laminer; (*b*) se feuilleter; se diviser en lamelles, en écailles.

laminate², *a. Nat.Hist:* lamineux; à lamelles.

laminate³, *s.* lamifié *m.*

laminated ['læmineitid], *a.* **1.** (*a*) *Geol: Ph:* lamifié; (*b*) *Ind: etc:* laminé; *Metall:* écaché (au laminoir); (*c*) à lames, à lamelles; *Mec.E:* **l. spring,** ressort *m* à lames (superposées); *El:* **l. brush,** balai *m* (de dynamo) à lames; **l. contact,** contact *m* à lamelles; (*d*) (*of mineral, glass, metal*) feuilleté; (*of plastics*) stratifié; (*of wood*) plaqué, contreplaqué; **l. clay,** argile feuilletée; **l. coal,** charbon feuilleté; **l. plate glass,** verre *m* (de sécurité) feuilleté; *El:* **l. armature,** induit feuilleté; **l. (iron) core,** noyau (de fer) feuilleté (d'une dynamo, etc.); *Ind:* **l. plastics,** matières *f* plastiques stratifiées; stratifiés *m*; **l. polythene,** polyéthylène stratifié. **2.** (*of paper, cardboard, etc.*) plastifié; *Bookb:* **l. jacket,** jaquette plastifiée, acétatée.

laminating ['læmineitiŋ], *a.* (*a*) lamifiant; (*b*) laminant; (*c*) stratifiant; (*d*) plastifiant; **l. machine,** machine *f* à plastifier (le papier, le carton, etc.).

lamination [læmi'neiʃ(ə)n], *s.* **1.** (*a*) laminage *m*; (*b*) division *f* en lamelles; (*c*) feuilletage *m* (d'un minéral, du verre, d'un métal); stratification *f* (d'une matière plastique); plaquage *m*, contreplaquage *m* (du bois); (*d*) *Bookb:* plastification *f*, pelliculage *m.* **2.** (*a*) structure lamifiée; (*b*) lamelle *f* (de l'armature d'une dynamo, etc.); lame *f.*

laminator ['læmineitər], *s. Bookb:* machine *f* à plastifier.

laminectomy [læmi'nektəmi], *s. Surg:* laminectomie *f.*

laminiform [lə'minifɔːm], *a.* laminiforme.

laminitis [læmi'naitis], *s. Vet:* fourbure *f.*

Lammas ['læməs], *s.* **L. (Day),** le premier août (en Écosse terme de loyers); *Arb:* **L. shoot,** pousse *f* de la deuxième sève; *Agr:* **L. wheat,** blé *m* d'hiver.

lammergeier ['læməgaiər], *s. Orn:* gypaète barbu.

lamp¹ [læmp], *s.* **1.** (*a*) lampe *f*; **oil l., paraffin l.,** lampe à huile, à pétrole; **hurricane l.,** lampe tempête; **miner's l.,** lampe de mineur; **Davy l.,** lampe de Davy; **safety l.,** lampe de sûreté; (*in garage, etc.*) **portable l., inspection l.,** baladeuse *f*; **stable l.,** falot *m*; **pocket l.,** lampe de poche; **l. wick,** mèche *f* de lampe; **l. oil,** huile *f* d'éclairage, à brûler; huile lampante; pétrole lampant; *A: & Lit:* (*of work, style*) **to smell of the l.,** sentir l'huile; sentir la lampe; (*b*) **projector, projection, l.,** lampe de projection; **Morse l.,** projecteur *m* de signalisation; (*c*) lampe (de bicyclette); *Aut: O:* phare *m*; *Rail:* **head, tail, l.,** fanal *m* de tête; lanterne *f*, fanal, de queue; **signal l.,** fanal (à signaux), lanterne de signalisation; (*d*) *Furn:* **table l.,** lampe de table; **standard l.,** lampadaire *m*; lampe sur pied; **l. standard,** torchère *f*; **hanging l.,** suspension *f*; **wall l., bracket l.,** (lampe d')applique *f*; **l. bracket,** applique (pour lampe); (*e*) *Tchn:* **candling l.,** lampe de mirage (pour les œufs); *Med:* **head l.,** lampe frontale; *Dent:* **mouth l.,** lampe de bouche; *Mec.E: etc:* **indicator l., warning l.,** lampe témoin; *El:* **loading l., power-control l.,** lampe de charge (d'un condensateur, etc.); *Tp:* **call l.,** lampe d'appel; **engagement l.,** *U.S:* **busy l.,** lampe d'occupation. **2.** *El:* (*bulb*) lampe, ampoule *f*; **filament l.,** lampe à filament; **two-filament l.,** lampe à filament double; **carbon(-filament) l.,** lampe à filament de carbone; **metal-filament l.,** lampe à filament métallique; **argon l.,** lampe à argon; **krypton l.,** lampe à krypton; **neon l.,** lampe au néon; **mercury-vapour l.,** lampe à vapeur de mercure; **sodium-vapour l.,** lampe à vapeur de sodium; **discharge l.,** lampe à décharge; **fluorescent l.,** lampe fluorescente; **incandescent l.,** lampe à incandescence; **ultra-violet l.,** lampe à rayons ultra-violets; **infra-red l.,** lampe infra-rouge; **l. adapter,** douille volante. **3.** *Moll:* **l. shell,** brachiopode *m*; térébratule *f.*

lamp². **1.** *v.tr.* (*a*) *A:* fournir, garnir, (qch.) de lampes; (*b*) *Poet:* éclairer, illuminer; (*c*) *U.S: P:* voir; regarder. **2.** *v.i.* luire, reluire.

lampas¹ ['læmpəs], *s. Vet:* lampas *m*, fève *f.*

lampas², *s. Tex:* lampas *m.*

lampblack¹ ['læmpblæk], *s.* noir *m* de fumée, de lampe.

lampblack², *v.tr.* passer (du cuir, etc.) au noir de fumée.

lampern ['læmpən], *s. Ich:* lamproie *f* d'alose; lamproie fluviatile.

lampholder ['læmphouldər], *s. El:* douille *f* (de lampe); porte-ampoule *m inv*; **screw l.,** douille à vis.

lampion ['læmpiən], *s.* lampion *m.*

lamplight ['læmplait], *s.* lumière *f* de la lampe; **to work by l.,** travailler à la lampe; **I saw her once in the l.,** je l'ai vue une fois, c'était à la lumière de la lampe, à la clarté d'une lampe.

lamplighter ['læmplaitər], *s. O:* (*pers.*) allumeur *m* de réverbères; lampiste *m.*

lampman, *pl.* **-men** ['læmpmæn, -men], *s.m.* lampiste.

lampoon¹ [læm'puːn], *s.* pasquinade *f*, libelle *m*, satire *f*, brocard *m.*

lampoon², *v.tr.* lancer des satires, des brocards, contre (qn); chansonner (qn); mettre (qn) en chansons; brocarder (qn).

lampooner, lampoonist [læm'puːnər, -ist], *s.* libelliste *m*, satiriste *m*; auteur *m* de pasquinades.

lampoonery [læm'puːnəri], *s.* satire *f*; esprit *m* satirique.

lamp-post ['læmppoust], *s.* **1.** (*a*) (*in street*) (montant *m*, poteau *m*, de) réverbère *m*; (*b*) *F:* **what a l.-p. (he is)!** quelle grande perche! quel grand échalas! **2.** *Ind: Civ.E:* (*high*) mât *m* d'éclairage; (*low*) poteau d'éclairage; **lattice l.-p.,** pylône *m* d'éclairage.

lamprey, *pl.* **-eys** ['læmpri, -iz], *s. Ich:* lamproie *f*; *F:* marbrée *f*; **river l.,** lamproie d'alose; lamproie fluviatile; **larval l.,** lamproyon *m*, lamprillon *m*; **sea l.,** lamproie marine.

lamprophyre ['læmproufaiər], *s. Miner:* lamprophyre *f.*

lampshade ['læmpʃeid], *s.* abat-jour *m inv.*

lampstand ['læmpstænd], *s.* pied *m* de lampe.

lampyrid ['læmpirid], *a. & s. Ent:* **1.** *a.* des lampyridés. **2.** *s.* lampyre *m.*

Lampyridae [læm'piridiː], *s.pl. Ent:* lampyridés *m.*

lanarkite ['lænɑːkait], *s. Miner:* lanarkite *f.*

Lancashire ['læŋkəʃ(i)ər]. *Pr.n. Geog:* le comté de Lancastre.

Lancaster ['læŋkəstər]. *Pr.n. Geog:* (la ville de) Lancastre; *O:* **L. cloth,** moleskin *f*, molesquine *f.*

Lancastrian [læŋ'kæstriən]. *Hist:* (*a*) *a.* lancastrien; (*b*) *s.* Lancastrien, -ienne.

lance¹ [lɑːns], *s.* **1.** lance *f*; haste *f*; **blunt l., coronal l.,** lance courtoise (de tournoi); **sharp-point l.,** lance à outrance; **l. pennon,** flamme *f* de lance; *Mil:* banderole *f*; *A: & Lit:* **to break a l. with s.o.,** rompre une lance avec qn; croiser le fer avec qn; jouter avec qn; contredire qn. **2.** (*pers.*) *Hist:* (*a*) lance; (*b*) (*man-at-arms with his attendants*) lance fournie. **3.** *Med:* = LANCET 1. **4.** *Mil:* **l. corporal,** (i) soldat *m* de première classe; (ii) sous-brigadier *m* de police; **l. sergeant,** (i) caporal-chef *m*, *pl.* caporaux-chefs; (ii) (*mounted arms*) brigadier-chef *m*, *pl.* brigadiers-chefs. **5.** (*a*) *Ich:* **l. fish** = LAUNCE; (*b*) *Rept:* **l. head, l.-headed snake,** trigonocéphale *m* jaune, vipère *f* fer de lance.

lance², *v.tr.* **1.** donner un coup de lance à (qn); percer (qn) d'un coup de lance. **2.** *Med:* donner un coup de bistouri, de lancette, à (un abcès); percer, inciser (un abcès); ouvrir (un abcès, etc.) avec une lancette.

lanced [lɑːnst], *a. Bot:* lancéiforme.

lancelet ['lɑːnslit], *s. Ich:* amphioxus *m*, lancelet *m.*

lanceolate(d) ['lɑːnsiəleit(id)], *a. Bot:* lancéolé, hastiforme; en fer de lance.

lancer ['lɑːnsər], *s.* **1.** *Mil:* lancier *m*; *A:* **l. cap,** chapska *m.* **2.** *pl.* **lancers,** (quadrille *m* des) lanciers; **to dance a set of lancers,** danser le quadrille des lanciers; danser les lanciers.

lancet ['lɑːnsit], *s.* **1.** *Med:* lancette *f*, bistouri *m*, phlébotome *m.* **2.** *Arch:* **l. (arch),** lancette.

lanceted [lɑːn'setid], *a. Arch:* (fenêtre *f*) à lancette; (église *f*) aux fenêtres à lancette.

lancewood ['lɑːnswud], *s.* (*a*) *Bot:* (i) (*Cuban*) duguétie *f*; (ii) (*Jamaican*) oxandre *m*; (*b*) *Com:* bois *m* souple pour brancards, pour cannes à pêche.

lanciform ['lɑːnsifɔːm], *a.* lancéiforme, hastiforme.

lancinating ['lɑːnsineitiŋ], *a.* (*of pain*) lancinant; **l. pains,** élancements *m.*

lancing ['lɑːnsiŋ], *s.* percement *m* (d'un abcès); coup *m* de lancette; coup de bistouri.

land¹ [lænd], *s.* **1.** (*a*) (*opposed to sea*) terre *f*; **dry l.,** terre ferme; **high, low-lying, l.,** terre(s) haute(s), basse(s); **l. reclaimed from the sea,** terres prises, gagnées, terrain pris, gagné, sur la mer; *Geog:* **Land's End,** la pointe de Cornouaille; **to travel by l.,** voyager par voie de terre; **l. route,** itinéraire *m* terrestre, voie *f* de terre; **l. breeze,** brise *f* de terre; *Nau:* **l. in sight,** terre en vue; **l. ho!** terre (en vue)! **to make, sight, l.,** reconnaître la terre; arriver en vue de la terre; atterrir; **to lose sight of the l.,** perdre la terre de vue; perdre terre; **to keep close to l.,** côtoyer la terre; **to touch l.,** toucher terre, aborder, atterrir; **to see how the l. lies,** (i) *Nau:* prendre le gisement de la terre; (ii) *Fig:* sonder, tâter, le terrain; prendre le vent; prendre l'aire du vent; *Mil:* **to attack by l., sea and air,** attaquer par terre, par mer et par air; **l. warfare,** guerre *f* sur terre; **l. operation,** opération *f* terrestre, sur terre; **l. defence,** défense *f* terrestre, du côté de la terre; **l. battle,** bataille *f* terrestre, combat *m* sur terre; **l. training installation,** centre *m* d'instruction pour les forces terrestres; **l. army,** armée *f* de terre; *Hist:* **Women's L. Army,** corps *m* de travailleuses agricoles; *Av: Ball:* **l. station,** station *f* à terre, au sol; *Av: Navy:* **l. service,** service *m* à terre; *Civ.E:* **l. arch,** arche *f* de rive (d'un pont); *Const:* **l. tie,** étai *m*, contrefort *m*; (*b*) *Agr: etc:* terre, terrain, sol *m*; terre arable, labourable; **ploughed l.,** terre labourée; **unploughed l.,** (terre en) jachère *f*; **waste l.,** terre inculte; terrain vague; **back to the l.,** retour aux champs, à la terre; **man lives off the l.,** c'est la terre qui nourrit les hommes; *Jur:* **l. act,** loi *f* agraire; **l. laws,** lois agraires; **l. bank,** crédit foncier, crédit agricole; *Hist:* **the L. League,** la Ligue agraire (formée par Parnell, 1879); **L. Leaguer,** membre de la Ligue agraire. **2.** (*country*) terre, pays *m*, contrée *f*; **distant lands,** pays lointains; **unknown lands,** pays inconnus; **the Holy L.,** la Terre Sainte; **the l. of dreams,** le pays des rêves; **theatre l.,** le quartier des spectacles. **3.** *Jur:* terre(s); fonds *m* de terre; bien-fonds *m, pl.* biens-fonds; propriété foncière; **to buy l.,** acheter des terres; **l. is expensive in London,** le terrain se vend cher à Londres; **l. and buildings,** terrains et bâtiments; *Prov:* **he that has l. has trouble at hand,** qui terre a, guerre a; *attrib.* **l. tax,** contributions foncières (sur les propriétés non bâties); **l. agent,** (i) intendant *m*, régisseur *m*, d'un domaine; administrateur foncier; (ii) agent immobilier; (iii) gérant *m*, syndic *m*, d'immeuble(s), de propriété(s); **l. agency,** (i) agence immobilière; (ii) gérance *f* d'immeubles, de propriétés; **l. registration,** inscription *f* (d'un bien-fonds) au cadastre; **l. registry (office),** bureau *m*, service *m*, du cadastre; **l. register,** registre *m* du cadastre. **4.** *Agr:* planche *f*; **ploughing in lands,** labour *m* en planches. **5.** *Scot:* maison *f* de rapport; immeuble divisé en appartements. **6.** (*a*) plat *m*, intervalle *m* (entre cannelures ou gorges); **lands of a rifle,** cloisons *f* entre les rayures d'un fusil; *I.C.E:* **piston lands,** cordons *m* de piston; **top l.** cordon supérieur; **oil l.,** quatrième cordon; (*b*) *Rec:* partie vierge, non enregistrée (d'un disque); (*c*) *N.Arch:* recouvrement *m* (dans un canot à clin). **7.** *U.S: F:* (*euphemism for* **Lord**) **good l.!** mon Dieu! **for land's sake!** pour l'amour de Dieu!

land². **1.** *v.tr.* (*a*) mettre, faire descendre, (qn) à terre; mettre (qch.) à terre; débarquer (qn, qch.); (*of vehicle*) déposer (qn à l'hôtel, etc.); décharger (des marchandises); **to l. an aircraft,** atterrir un avion; (*b*) **to l. a fish,** amener un poisson à terre; prendre un poisson; **to l. a prize, a fortune,** remporter un prix; décrocher une fortune; (*c*) amener, planter (**s.o. somewhere,** qn quelque part); **that will l. you in prison,** cela vous vaudra de la prison; **decision that may l. one in difficulties,** décision qui peut entraîner des inconvénients, des ennuis; **you've landed us in a nice fix, mess, in the soup, in it!** vous nous avez mis dans de beaux draps! **I was landed with an encyclopaedia I didn't want,** je me suis trouvé forcé d'accepter une encyclopédie dont je n'avais que faire; (*d*) *Rac:* (*of jockey*) **to l. one's horse first,** arriver premier avec son cheval; (*e*) *Nau:* placer, amener, faire reposer (un mât, une vergue); (*f*) *F:* **to l. s.o. a blow in the face,** allonger, porter, flanquer, à qn un coup au visage; **I landed him one in the face, on the nose,** je lui ai collé, fiché, une beigne à la figure. **2.** *v.i.* (*a*) (*of pers.*) descendre à terre; prendre terre; débarquer; (*of ship*) aborder, accoster la terre, atterrir; (*of aircraft, pilot*) atterrir; (*of aircraft on deck of aircraft carrier*) apponter; **to l. on the moon,** alunir; **to l. on the sea,** amérir, amerrir; **on landing,** au débarqué; (*b*) tomber (à terre); **we landed in a bog,** nous sommes tombés dans une fondrière; **he slipped and landed in a puddle,** il a glissé et est tombé dans une flaque d'eau; *F:* **he landed on us for a fortnight,** il est arrivé chez nous à l'improviste et y est resté quinze jours; (*c*) (*from a vehicle*) mettre pied à terre; (*after jumping*) tomber, retomber; **to l. on one's feet,** retomber sur ses pieds; retomber d'aplomb; *F:* **he always lands on his feet,** il retombe toujours sur ses pattes; il se débrouille toujours; (*d*) *Equit:* (*of horse, after jumping*) se recevoir; (*e*) *Rac:* (*of horse*) **to l. first,** arriver (le) premier.

landau ['lændɔ:], *s. A.Veh:* landau *m, pl.* landaus.

landaulet(te) [lændə'let], *s. Aut: A:* landaulet *m*, landaulette *f*.

landed ['lændid], *a.* **1.** (voyageur) débarqué; mis à terre; *Nau: Com:* **l. cost,** prix *m* à quai. **2. l. property,** propriété foncière, territoriale, *Jur:* prédiale; biens immobiliers; biens immeubles; bien-fonds *m, pl.* biens-fonds; **l. proprietor, l. aristocracy,** propriétaire terrien, aristocratie terrienne.

lander ['lændər], *s.* (*pers.*) *Min:* receveur *m*; ouvrier *m* de la recette.

landfall ['lændfɔ:l], *s.* **1.** *Nau:* atterrissage *m*; **to make a l.,** atterrir; **to make a bad l.,** manquer son atterrissage. **2.** *Nau: Av:* arrivée *f* en vue de terre; **to make a l.,** arriver en vue de terre.

landgirl ['lændgə:l], *s.f. O:* travailleuse agricole.

landgrave ['lændgreiv], *s. Hist:* landgrave *m*.

landgraviate [lænd'grævieit], *s. Hist:* landgraviat *m*.

landgravine ['lændgrəvi:n], *s.f. Hist:* landgravine.

landholder ['lændhouldər], *s.* **1.** propriétaire foncier. **2.** affermataire *m* (d'une terre).

landing ['lændiŋ], *s.* **1.** (*a*) *Fish:* sortie *f* de l'eau, prise *f* (d'un poisson); **l. net,** épuisette *f*; (*b*) *Nau: etc:* débarquement *m*, mise *f* à terre, atterrissage *m* (de qn, de qch.); *Com: etc:* **l. certificate,** certificat *m* de déchargement; **l. charges,** frais *m* de déchargement; **l. permit, l. order,** permis *m* de débarquement; **l. number,** numéro *m* de débarquement; **(passenger's) l. card, ticket,** ticket *m*, carte *f*, carton *m*, de débarquement; **l. place,** atterrage *m*, atterrissage; *Navy:* point *m* de débarquement; **l. steps,** échelle *f* de débarquement, d'embarquement (d'une jetée, d'un navire); **l. stage,** débarcadère *m*, embarcadère *m*; embarcadère flottant; ponton *m* de débarquement; appontement *m*; (*c*) *Mil: Navy:* débarquement; descente *f* (sur une côte ennemie); **assault l.,** débarquement de vive force; **to operate a l.,** effectuer, exécuter, un débarquement; **l. force, party,** troupes *fpl*, compagnie *f*, de débarquement; **l. operation,** opération *f* de débarquement; **l. barge,** chaland *m* d'accostage; **l. craft,** chaland, péniche *f*, engin *m*, de débarquement; **l. craft tanks,** chaland de débarquement de chars, chaland porte-chars; **l. ship,** bâtiment *m*, navire *m*, de débarquement; **l. ship assault,** transport *m* d'assaut; transport de chalands de débarquement; **l. ship tanks,** bâtiment, navire, de débarquement de chars; **l. ramp,** rampe *f* de débarquement, d'accostage; (*d*) *Av:* (*of aircraft*) (*on land*) atterrissage; (*on sea*) amerrissage *m*; (*on deck of ship*) apontage *m*; **blind l., instrument l.,** atterrissage sans visibilité, aux instruments; **visual l.,** atterrissage à vue; **radio-controlled l.,** atterrissage radio-guidé; **dead-stick l., stall l., l. with engine cut off,** atterrissage (avec) hélice calée, moteur calé; **glide l.,** atterrissage (avec) moteur réduit, atterrissage plané; **level l., wheel l.,** atterrissage sur les roues; **tail-down l.,** atterrissage sur la queue; **three-point l.,** atterrissage à trois points (avec train tricycle, à béquille arrière); **pancake l.,** atterrissage à plat, en asseyant l'avion de haut; **hot l.,** atterrissage à grande vitesse; **spot l.,** atterrissage de précision; **touch-and-go l.,** atterrissage avec décollage immédiat; **normal l.,** atterrissage normal; **smooth l.,** atterrissage en douceur; **bad l.,** mauvais atterrissage; **to make a crash l.,** faire un atterrissage, atterrir, en catastrophe; s'écraser à l'atterrissage; *F:* casser du bois; **to make a forced, an emergency, l.,** faire un atterrissage forcé; *attrib.* **l. gear,** train *m* (d'atterrissage); atterrisseur *m*; **wheel l. gear,** train, atterrisseur, à roues; **main l. gear,** train, atterrisseur, principal; **auxiliary l. gear,** train, atterrisseur, auxiliaire; **nose l. gear, l. gear nose unit,** train avant; **steerable nose l. gear,** train avant orientable; **nose-wheel l. gear, tricycle l. gear,** train tricycle; **tail l. gear, l. gear tail unit,** train arrière; **tail-wheel l. gear,** train à une roue arrière; **faired l. gear,** train caréné; **fixed l. gear,** train, atterrisseur, fixe; **retractable l. gear,** train, atterrisseur, escamotable, relevable; **to retract the l. gear,** escamoter, relever, rentrer le train; **retracted l. gear, l. gear up,** train rentré; **l. gear retraction, l. gear up cycle,** escamotage *m*, rentrée *f*, remontée *f*, du train; **to extend, lower, the l. gear,** sortir le train; **extended, lowered, l. gear, l. gear down,** train sorti; **l. gear extension, l. gear down cycle,** sortie du train; **l. gear attachments,** points *m* de fixation du train; **l. gear, leg, strut,** jambe *f* du train, de l'atterrisseur; **l. gear motor,** moteur *m* du train, de l'atterrisseur; **l. gear position indicator, l. gear warning system,** indicateur *m* de position du train, de l'atterrisseur; **ski l. gear,** train, atterrisseur, à skis; **track-tread l. gear,** train, atterrisseur, à chenilles; **l. area,** aire *f* d'atterrissage; **l. field, l. ground,** terrain *m* d'atterrissage; **l. strip,** bande *f*, piste *f*, d'atterrissage; **l. place,** lieu *m* d'atterrissage; étape *f* (aérienne); *Mil.Av:* **l. zone,** zone *f* d'atterrissage (des troupes aéroportées); *Navy:* **l. check,** pont *m* d'atterrissage (d'un porte-avions, d'un porte-hélicoptères); **l. deceleration,** ralentissement *m* à l'atterrissage; **l. distance,** distance *f* d'atterrissage, longueur *f* de roulement à l'atterrissage; **l. roll, l. run,** roulement *m* à l'atterrissage; **l. speed,** vitesse *f* d'atterrissage; **l. flap,** volet *m* d'atterrissage; **l. beacon,** radiophare *m* d'atterrissage; **l. flare,** bengale *m*, fusée *f*, d'atterrissage; **l. light,** balise *f*, phare *m*, d'atterrissage; **l. lights,** feux *mpl*, rampe *f*, d'atterrissage. **2.** (*a*) *Const:* palier *m* (de repos) (d'un escalier); repos *m*, carré *m*; **top l.,** trapan *m*; (*b*) débarcadère; (*c*) *Min:* recette *f*; **bottom l.,** recette du fond; accrochage *m* du fond; **top l.,** recette, accrochage, du jour; (*d*) *Telecom: etc:* atterrissement (de câble). **3.** *N.Arch:* recouvrement *m* des cans (dans une construction à clins).

landlady ['lændleidi], *s.f.* **1.** propriétaire *f* (d'un immeuble). **2.** (*keeping furnished apartments*) logeuse (en garni). **3.** aubergiste, hôtelière.

landlegs ['lændlegz], *s.pl. F:* (*of sailor*) **to get one's l.,** se familiariser de nouveau avec la terre.

landless ['lændlis], *a.* sans terre(s).

landline ['lændlain], *s. Tp: Tg:* (*a*) ligne *f* terrestre, circuit *m* filaire; (*b*) ligne rurale.

landlocked ['lændlɔkt], *a. Geog:* enfermé entre les terres; enserré par la terre; entouré de terre; méditerrané; **l. sea,** mer intérieure; **l. port,** port entouré de terre; **l. roadstead,** rade fermée.

landlord ['lændlɔ:d], *s.* **1.** propriétaire (foncier). **2.** propriétaire (d'un immeuble). **3.** (*keeping furnished apartments*) logeur *m* (en garni). **4.** aubergiste *m*, hôtelier *m*.

landlubber ['lændlʌbər], *s. Nau: F:* marin *m* d'eau douce; hale-bouline *m, pl.* hale-boulines; terrien *m*; éléphant *m*.

landmark¹ ['lændmɑ:k], *s.* **1.** borne *f* limite. **2.** (*a*) (point *m* de) repère *m*; point coté (sur une carte, etc.); (*b*) *Av:* repère, point de repérage (au sol); **l. beacon,** balise *f*, phare *m*, de repérage; **l. navigation,** navigation observée, à vue; (*c*) *Nau:* amer *m*, indice *m*, remarque *f* (à terre); point à terre; **l. radar,** amer radar. **3.** point décisif, événement marquant (dans l'histoire d'un pays, etc.); (*of event, writing*) **to be a l.,** faire époque; **events that stand out as landmarks in a period,** événements qui jalonnent une époque.

landmark², *v.tr.* (*of events, etc.*) jalonner (une époque, etc.).

landmine ['lændmain], *s.* mine *f* terrestre.

landocracy [læn'dɔkrəsi], *s. F:* aristocratie terrienne.

landolphia [læn'dɔlfiə], *s. Bot:* landolphie *f*.

landowner ['lændounər], *s.* propriétaire foncier.

landrail ['lændreil], *s. Orn:* râle *m* de genêt.

landscape¹ ['læn(d)skeip], *s.* (*a*) paysage *m*; *Adm:* **l. conservation,** conservation *f* des sites; **he is more interested in l. than architecture,** il s'intéresse davantage aux paysages qu'à l'architecture; **these factories are a blot on the l.,** ces usines déparent le paysage, la campagne; *F:* **she's a blot on the l.,** elle fait tache; (*b*) **l. design,** *U.S:* **architecture,** architecture *f* de paysage; **l. gardener,** jardinier *m* paysagiste; **l. garden,** jardin *m* à l'anglaise; *Art:* **to paint landscapes,** peindre des paysages; faire du paysage; **l. painter,** paysagiste *m*, peintre *m* de paysages.

landscape², *v.tr.* aménager (un terrain) en parc; **they had their garden landscaped,** ils ont employé un jardinier paysagiste pour aménager leur propriété.

landscapist ['læn(d)skeipist], *s.* paysagiste *m*, peintre *m* de paysages.

landslide ['lændslaid], *s.* **1.** éboulement *m*, affaissement *m*, glissement *m* (de terrain). **2.** *Pol:* (*a*) débâcle *f*, défaite accablante (d'un parti politique aux élections); raz de marée (électoral); (*b*) victoire écrasante.

landslip ['lændslip], *s.* = LANDSLIDE 1.

landsman, *pl.* **-men** ['lændzmən], *s.m.* homme à terre; terrien.

landward ['lændwəd]. **1.** *adv.* **(to) l.,** du côté de la terre; vers la terre. **2.** *a.* (*a*) **on the l. side,** vers l'intérieur; du côté de la terre; (*b*) *Scot:* campagnard.

landwards ['lændwədz], *adv.* du côté de la terre; vers la terre.

landworker ['lændwə:kər], *s.* ouvrier *m* agricole.

lane [lein], *s.* **1.** (*in country*) chemin vicinal, rural; *O:* (*in town*) ruelle *f*, passage *m*; **to pass through a l. of people,** passer entre une double haie de gens; **to form a l.,** faire la haie; *F: A:* **the long l., the red l.,** le gosier; *Prov:* **it's a long l. that has no turning,** tout vient à point qui sait attendre. **2.** (*a*) (*in icefield*) fissure *f*, passage; (*b*) *Nau:* route *f* de navigation; *Av:* **air l.,** couloir aérien, route de navigation aérienne; (*c*) *Aut: etc:* **(traffic) l.,** voie *f*; **four l. road, highway,** route à quatre voies (de circulation), à quadruple courant; **fast l., slow l.** = voie de gauche, de droite; **get into l.** = serrez à gauche, à droite; (*d*) *Sp:* couloir.

langaha [lɑ:ŋ'gɑ:hɑ:], *s. Rept:* langaha *m* (de Madagascar).

langbanite ['læŋbənait], *s. Miner:* langbanite *f.*

langbeinite ['læŋbainait], *s. Miner:* langbeinite *f.*

langite ['læŋait], *s. Miner:* langite *f.*

lang syne ['læŋ'sain]. *Scot:* **1.** *adv.* autrefois, jadis, au temps jadis. **2.** *s.* **(auld) l. s.,** le temps jadis; les jours *m* d'autrefois, d'antan.

language ['læŋgwidʒ], *s.* **1.** *(a)* langue *f* (d'un peuple); **the English l.,** la langue anglaise; **foreign languages,** langues étrangères; **dead languages,** langues mortes; **modern languages,** langues vivantes; **modern l. master, mistress,** professeur *m* de langues vivantes; *Ling:* **source l.,** langue de départ; **target l.,** langue d'arrivée; *(b)* langage *m*; **have animals a l.?** les animaux ont-ils un langage? **the l. of flowers,** le langage des fleurs; *(c)* **cipher l.,** langage chiffré; chiffre *m*; **code l.,** langage convenu; code *m*; **business l.,** langage, langue, des affaires, langage de gestion; *Cmptr:* **computer l., machine l.,** langage machine; **object l., target l.,** langage d'exécution; **program(me), programming, l.,** langage de programmation. **2.** langage; **strong l.,** langage violent, expressions vives; injures *fpl*; **bad l.,** langage grossier; grossièretés *fpl*; gros mots *mpl*; **to use bad l.,** parler vertement; lâcher des gros mots; **mind your l.!** surveillez votre langage!

langued [læŋd], *a. Her:* **l. or,** *(of bird)* langué d'or; *(of animal)* lampassé d'or.

langue de bœuf ['lɑ̃:ŋdəbə:f], *s. A.Arms:* langue-de-bœuf *f*, coutille *f.*

Languedocian [læŋgə'dousiən]. *Geog:* *(a) a.* languedocien; du Languedoc; *(b) s.* Languedocien, -ienne.

languet ['læŋgwit], *s.* languette *f* (de tuyau d'orgue).

languid ['læŋgwid], *a.* languissant, langoureux, faible; mou, *f.* molle; **to feel l.,** se sentir faible, sans vie, sans énergie; **l. look,** regard languissant, sans animation; **l. eye,** œil triste, mourant; **l. voice,** voix traînante; **l. movements,** mouvements lents, traînants.

languidly ['læŋgwidli], *adv.* languissamment, langoureusement, faiblement; mollement, sans animation.

languidness ['læŋgwidnis], *s.* langueur *f*, faiblesse *f*, mollesse *f.*

languish ['læŋgwiʃ], *v.i.* languir. **1.** dépérir; *(of plant)* s'étioler. **2.** *(a)* **to l. after, for, s.o., sth.,** languir après, pour, qn, qch.; **to l. in prison,** languir en prison; *(b) O:* **she smiles and languishes,** elle sourit, elle prend des airs langoureux, des airs pâmés.

languishing ['læŋgwiʃiŋ], *a.* languissant, langoureux; (regard) plein de langueur; (amant) langoureux.

languishingly ['læŋgwiʃiŋli], *adv.* langoureusement.

languishment ['læŋgwiʃmənt], *s. A:* **1.** langueur *f*, faiblesse *f*, abattement *m.* **2.** *pl.* airs langoureux.

languor ['læŋgər], *s.* langueur *f.*

languorous ['læŋgərəs], *a.* langoureux.

languorously ['læŋgərəsli], *adv.* langoureusement.

langur [lʌŋ'guər], *s. Z:* entelle *m*, langur *m*, semnopithèque *m.*

laniard ['lænjɑ:d], *s.* = LANYARD.

laniary ['læniəri], *a. & s. Z:* (dent *f*) laniaire *(f)*; **the laniaries,** les canines *f.*

laniferous [læ'nifərəs], **lanigerous** [læ'nidʒərəs], *a.* lanifère, lanigère.

laniflorous [læni'flɔ:rəs], *a. Bot:* laniflore.

Laniidae [lə'naiidi:], *s.pl. Orn:* laniidés *m*, les pies-grièches *f.*

lank [læŋk], *a.* **1.** *(of pers.)* maigre; sec, *f.* sèche; efflanqué; *(of animal)* efflanqué; **l. body,** corps décharné. **2. l. hair,** cheveux plats.

lankiness ['læŋkinis], *s.* taille grande et maigre (de qn); aspect efflanqué.

lankness ['læŋknis], *s.* maigreur *f* (sans vigueur).

lanky ['læŋki], *a.* grand et maigre; grand et sec, *f.* grande et sèche; **l. legs,** jambes longues et minces; **a great l. boy, a l.-legs,** un grand flandrin; un grand maigre; un grand efflanqué; un grand dégingandé.

lanner ['lænər], *s. Orn:* faucon *m* lanier.

lanneret ['lænərət], *s. Orn:* laneret *m.*

lanolin(e) ['lænəli(:)n], *s. Ch: Pharm:* lanoline *f*, graisse *f* de laine.

lansfordite ['lænsfə:dait], *s. Miner:* lansfordite *f.*

lansquenet ['lænskənet], *s. Hist: & Cards:* lansquenet *m.*

lantana [læn'tɑ:nə], *s. Bot:* lantanier *m.*

lantern ['læntən], *s.* **1.** *(a)* lanterne *f*, falot *m*; *Nau:* fanal, -aux, *m*; verrine *f*; *Mil:* **guard house l.,** falot de ronde; **dark l., bull's eye l.,** lanterne sourde; **Chinese l.,** lanterne vénitienne; *F: A:* **the parish l.,** la lune; *(b) A:* **magic l.,** lanterne magique; lanterne à projection(s). **2.** *Arch:* lanterne, lanterneau *m* (de dôme, de faîte). **3.** *Mec.E:* **l. (pinion, wheel),** (roue *f* à) lanterne. **4. l. jaws,** (i) joues creuses; mâchoire allongée; (ii) menton *m* en galoche; **l.-jawed,** (i) aux joues creuses, à la mâchoire allongée; (ii) au menton en galoche. **5.** *(a) Ich:* **l. fish,** scopélide *m*, myctophide *m*; *(b) Ent:* **l. fly,** fulgore *m* porte-lanterne.

lanthanide ['lænθənaid], *s. Ch:* lanthanide *m.*

lanthanite ['lænθənait], *s. Miner:* lanthanite *f.*

lanthanum ['lænθənəm], *s. Ch:* lanthane *m.*

lanthorn ['læntən], *s. A:* = LANTERN **1.**

lanuginous [lə'nju:dʒinəs], *a. Bot: etc:* lanugineux.

lanugo [læ'nju:gou], *s. Biol:* lanugo *m.*

lanyard ['lænjɑ:d, -jəd], *s.* **1.** *Nau:* aiguillette *f*; ride *f* (de hauban); *(of knife, etc.)* amarrage *m*; *(of oar)* sauvegarde *f.* **2.** *Artil:* (cordon *m*, cordeau *m*) tire-feu *m inv.*

Lao [lau]. *Geog: a. & s.* = LAOTIAN.

Laodamia [leioudə'maiə], *Pr.n.f. Myth:* Laodamie.

Laodicea [leioudi'siə], *Pr.n. A.Geog:* Laodicée *f.*

Laodicean [leioudi'siən], *a. & s.* **1.** *A.Geog:* *(a) a.* laodicéen; *(b) s.* Laodicéen, -éenne. **2.** *a. A: & Lit:* *(of pers.)* tiède, peu zélé (en ce qui concerne la religion, la politique).

Laomedon [lei'ɔmidən], *Pr.n.m. Gr.Myth:* Laomédon.

Laos ['leiɔs, laus], *Pr.n. Geog:* Laos *m.*

Laotian [lei'ouʃ(ə)n], *a. & s. Geog:* *(a) a.* laotien; *(b) s.* Laotien, -ienne.

lap[1] [læp], *s.* **1.** *(a) O:* pan *m*, basque *f* (d'un vêtement); *(b)* **ear l.,** lobe *m* de l'oreille. **2.** *(a)* genoux *mpl*; *Lit:* giron *m*; sein *m*; **Madonna holding the Child in her l.,** la Vierge tenant l'enfant dans son giron, sur ses genoux; **to sit in, on, s.o.'s l.,** s'asseoir sur les genoux de qn; **to catch sth. in one's l.,** attraper qch. dans son tablier, dans sa jupe; **whether I shall see him again is in the l. of the gods,** le reverrai-je? Dieu seul le sait, c'est sur les genoux des dieux; **he expects everything to fall into his l.,** il pense qu'il n'y a qu'à se baisser et à prendre; *(b)* **l. pack (parachute),** parachute ventral. **3.** *Lit:* creux *m*, pli *m* (d'une colline).

lap[2], *s.* **1.** *(a) Mch:* recouvrement *m* (du tiroir); **exhaust l.,** avance *f* à l'échappement; **l.-and-lead** [li:d] **lever,** levier *m* d'avance; *(b) Const:* chevauchement *m*, recouvrement (des tuiles, des ardoises, etc.); **tiles with a l. of 5 cm,** tuiles avec un recouvrement de 5cm; *(c) I.C.E:* chevauchement (des soupapes); **zero l.,** chevauchement nul; *(d) Tchn:* recouvrement (des plaques de revêtement, etc.); **butt l., end l.,** recouvrement d'abouts; **seam l.,** recouvrement des cans; *Metalw:* **l. seam, joint,** ourlet *m*; **l. rivet(t)ing,** assemblage *m* par recouvrement; **l. weld(ing),** soudure *f* à recouvrement, en écharpe, par amorces; *(e) Mapm: Phot:* recouvrement (des feuilles, des clichés); **side l.,** recouvrement latéral; *Cin:* **l. dissolve,** fondu enchaîné; enchaînement *m.* **2.** *El:* guipage *m* (de coton); couche isolante (de caoutchouc, etc.); **l. winding,** bobinage *m* à boucles; enroulage *m*, enroulement *m*, imbriqué. **3.** *(a)* tour *m* (d'une corde autour d'un cylindre, etc.); *(b) Sp:* tour (de piste, de circuit); boucle *f*, circuit *m*; **to do three laps,** faire trois tours de circuit; **to cover a l. in six minutes,** boucler le circuit en six minutes; **to be on the last l.,** en être à la dernière étape; **l. of honour,** tour d'honneur.

lap[3], *v.* **(lapped** [læpt]) **1.** *v.tr.* *(a)* **to l. sth. round sth.,** enrouler qch. autour de qch.; **to l. sth. round, up, with sth.,** envelopper, entourer, qch. de qch.; *esp. NAm:* **to l. s.o. in sth.,** envelopper qn de qch.; **to l. s.o. in luxury,** entourer qn de luxe; *(b) Const:* enchevaucher (des planches); poser (des planches) à recouvrement; donner du recouvrement à (des tuiles, etc.); **to l. a joint with sheet metal,** chaperonner un assemblage; *(c) El:* guiper (un câble, etc.); *(d) Sp:* (i) **to l. an opponent,** prendre un tour d'avance sur un concurrent; (ii) **to l. the course,** boucher le circuit. **2.** *v.i.* **to l. over sth.,** retomber, se rabattre, sur qch.; dépasser, recouvrir, qch.; *(of tiles, etc.)* chevaucher qch.; **the boards l.,** les planches sont posées à recouvrement.

lap[4], *s. Tls: Metalw: & Lap:* *(a)* rodoir *m*; *(b)* polissoir *m*, polisseuse *f*; meule *f* polissoire.

lap[5], *v.tr.* *(a) Metalw:* roder, rectifier; polir; **to l. in the gears,** roder les pignons; **to l. to size,** roder à la dimension; *(b) Metalw: & Lap:* polir (au polissoir, etc.).

lap[6], *s.* **1.** gorgée *f* (de lait, etc.); **the cat drank up his milk in two laps,** le chat a lapé son lait en deux coups de langue. **2.** clapotement *m*, clapotis *m*, batillement *m* (des vagues). **3.** *F:* **(cat's) l.,** lavasse *f*, ripopée *f.*

lap[7]. **1.** *v.tr.* *(of animal)* **to l. (up) milk,** laper du lait; *F:* **he laps up, down, everything you tell him,** il avale, gobe, tout ce qu'on lui dit; **it was sheer flattery but he lapped it all up,** c'était de la flatterie pure et simple mais il a tout gobé, avalé. **2.** *v.i.* *(of waves)* clapoter, batiller.

lapacho [lə'pætʃou], *s. Bot:* lapacho *m.*

laparocele ['læpərousi:l], *s. Med:* laparocèle *f.*

laparoscopy [læpə'rɔskəpi], *s. Med:* laparoscopie *f.*

laparotomy [læpə'rɔtəmi], *s. Surg:* laparotomie *f.*

lapdog ['læpdɔg], *s.* chien *m* d'appartement, de salon, de manchon.

lapel [lə'pel], *s. Tail:* revers *m* (d'un habit).

lapelled [lə'peld], *a. Tail:* à revers.

lapeyrousia [læpei'ru:ziə], *s. Bot:* lapeyrousia *m.*

lapful ['læpful], *s.* plein son tablier, plein sa jupe **(of,** de).

laphygma [lə'figmə], *s. Ann:* laphygma *m.*

lapicide ['læpisaid], *s.* lapicide *m*; graveur *m* sur pierre.

lapidary ['læpid(ə)ri], *a. & s.* lapidaire *(m).*

lapidate ['læpideit], *v.tr. Lit:* lapider; tuer (qn) à coups de pierres.

lapidation [læpi'deiʃ(ə)n], *s. Lit:* lapidation *f.*

lapidicolous [læpi'dikələs], *a. Nat.Hist:* lapidicole.

lapidification [læpidifi'keiʃ(ə)n], *s.* lapidification *f.*

lapidify [læ'pidifai], *v.tr.* lapidifier; donner à (qch.) la consistance de la pierre.

lapies, lapiés [lə'pi:z, 'læpieis], *s.pl. Geol:* lapiés *m*, lapiez *m*, lapiaz *m.*

lapilli [lə'pilai, 'læpili], *s.pl. Geol:* lapilli *m.*

lapis lazuli ['læpis'læzjul(a)i], *s. Miner:* lazulite *m*; lapis (-lazuli) *m inv*; ultramarine *f*, outremer *m.*

Lapithae ['læpiθi:], *Pr.n.pl. Gr.Myth:* Lapithes *m.*

lap-joint ['læpdʒɔint], *v.tr.* **1.** *(a)* assembler (des planches) à clin; *(b)* assembler (des poutres) (i) à mi-fer; (ii) à mi-bois. **2.** ourler (une tôle).

Lapland ['læplænd], *Pr.n. Geog:* Laponie *f.*

Laplander ['læplændər], *s. Geog:* Lapon, -one.

laportea [lə'pɔ:tiə], *s. Bot:* laportea *m.*

Lapp [læp]. **1.** *Geog:* *(a) a.* lapon; *(b) s.* Lapon, -one. **2.** *s. Ling:* lapon *m.*

lapped [læpt], *a.* **1.** *Carp: Mec.E: etc:* (joint *m*) à recouvrement; **l. tiles,** tuiles chevauchées; *Nau:* **l. seam,** couture *f* à clin. **2.** *El:* **single-l. wire, double-l. wire,** fil *m* à guipage simple, double.

lappet ['læpit], *s.* **1.** *(a)* pan *m*, basque *f* (de vêtement); *(b)* revers *m* (de vêtement); *(c)* barbe *f* (de coiffe, de cornette); *(d) Ecc:* rabat *m*; *(e) pl. Ecc:* **lappets,** fanons *m* (de mitre d'évêque); *(f) O:* **ear l.,** oreillette (de casquette). **2.** *(a) A: Anat:* lobe *m* (de l'oreille); *(b)* fanon (de dindon); *(c) Ent:* **l. moth,** lasiocampide *m.* **3.** cache-entrée *m inv* (de trou de serrure).

lapping[1] ['læpiŋ], *s.* **1.** recouvrement *m*, chevauchement *m.* **2.** *El:* (i) guipage *m*, (ii) guipure *f* (d'un câble, etc.).

lapping[2], *s.* *(a)* rodage *m*; rectification *f*; *(b)* polissage *m* (à la meule, au tour, etc.); **l. machine,** (i) machine *f* à roder, à rectifier; (ii) meule *f* polissoire.

lapping[3], *s.* **1.** lapement *m* (d'un animal). **2.** clapotement *m*, clapotis *m*, batillement *m* (des vagues).

Lappish ['læpiʃ]. **1.** *a. Geog:* lapon. **2.** *s. Ling:* lapon *m.*

lapsana ['læpsənə], *s. Bot:* lampsane *f.*

lapse[1] [læps], *s.* **1.** *(a) (mistake)* erreur *f*, faute *f*; **l. of memory,** défaillance *f*, absence *f*, trou *m*, de mémoire; oubli *m*; *(b) (moral fault)* chute *f*, faute, défaillance; faux pas; écart *m* de conduite; **l. from one's principles,** dérogation *f* à ses principes; **l. from one's duty,** manquement *m* à son devoir; *Theol:* **l. from faith, into heresy,** apostasie *f.* **2.** *(a) Jur:* déchéance *f* (d'un droit); *(b) Ecc:* dévolu *m*, dévolution *f* (d'un bénéfice). **3.** *A:* (i) écoulement *m*, (ii) chute (des eaux). **4.** cours *m*, marche *f* (du temps); laps *m* de temps; **after a l. of three months,** après un délai de trois mois; au bout de trois mois; **after a l. of so many years,** après tant d'années écoulées. **5.** *Meteor:* décroissement *m* (de la température, etc., avec l'élévation de l'altitude); **l. rate,** gradient vertical de température.

lapse[2], *v.i.* **1.** *(a)* déchoir; faillir; **to l. from duty,** manquer au devoir; s'écarter de son devoir; **to l. (back) into idleness,** (re)tomber dans la paresse; **to l. into silence, into obscurity,** rentrer dans le silence, dans l'ombre; *(b)* manquer à ses devoirs; être coupable d'un écart de conduite; faire un faux pas. **2.** *Jur:* *(of right, patent, etc.)* périmer, se périmer; tomber en désuétude; *(of credits, etc.)* tomber en annulation; *(of estate)* devenir disponible; *(of legacy)* devenir caduc; *(of benefice)* tomber en dévolu; *(of law)* s'abroger; cesser d'être en vigueur; *Ins:* *(of policy, etc.)* cesser d'être en vigueur; *(of right, estate, etc.)* **to l. to s.o.,** passer à qn; **to allow a right to l.,** laisser périmer, laisser tomber, un droit; **to have lapsed,** être périmé. **3.** *(a) A:* *(of stream)* s'écouler; *(b) (of time)* **to l. (away),** s'écouler, passer.

lapsed [læpst], *a.* **1.** déchu; **a l. Christian,** un chrétien déchu. **2.** *(a)* (billet, mandat-poste) périmé; *Jur:* (droit) périmé; (legs) tombé en dévolu, dévolu par péremption; (contrat, legs) caduc (*f.* caduque); *(b)* (membre) déchu.

lapsing ['læpsiŋ], *s.* **1.** déchéance *f.* **2.** caducité *f* (d'un legs); *Ecc:* dévolution *f* (d'un bénéfice).

lapstone ['læpstoun], *s. Bootm:* bouisse *f*, buisse *f.*

lapstrake, lapstreak ['læpstreik, -stri:k], *s. N.Arch:* canot (bordé) à clin.

lapsus ['læpsəs], *s.* lapsus *m*; **l. calami, linguae,** lapsus calami, linguæ.

lapweld ['læpweld], *v.tr. Metalw:* souder en écharpe, à recouvrement.

lapwing ['læpwiŋ], *s. Orn:* vanneau (huppé); **Cayenne l.,** vanneau armé de Cayenne; **spur-winged l.,** vanneau armé; **wattled l.,** vanneau caronculé.

lar[1], *pl.* **lares** [lɑːr, 'lɑːriːz], *s. Rom.Ant:* lare *m*; *esp. pl.* dieux lares; **to move with one's Lares and Penates,** transporter ailleurs ses lares et ses pénates.

lar[2], *s. Z:* **l. (gibbon),** gibbon *m* aux mains blanches.

larboard ['lɑːbəd], *s. Nau: A:* bâbord *m*.

larcener ['lɑːsənər], **larcenist** ['lɑːsənist], *s. Jur:* voleur *m*.

larcenous ['lɑːsənəs], *a.* voleur, -euse; adonné au vol; (action) que l'on peut qualifier de vol.

larceny ['lɑːsəni], *s.* (*a*) vol *m*; (*b*) *Jur:* **petty l.,** vol simple; vol minime; (*c*) *Jur:* **l. by a bailee,** carambouillage *m*.

larch [lɑːtʃ], *s.* **1.** (*a*) *Bot:* mélèze *m*; **American l., black l., red l.,** mélèze d'Amérique; (*b*) **l. (wood),** bois *m* de mélèze. **2.** *Ent:* **l.-miner (moth),** teigne *m* du mélèze.

lard[1] [lɑːd], *s.* (*a*) saindoux *m*; panne *f*; graisse *f* de porc; (*b*) *Pharm: Ind:* axonge *f*.

lard[2], *v.tr. Cu:* larder, barder, piquer (la viande); **larded joint,** larde *f*; *F:* **to l. one's writings with quotations,** larder, entrelarder, ses écrits de citations.

lardaceous [lɑː'deiʃəs], *a. Med:* (tissu) lardacé; **l. degeneration,** dégénérescence graisseuse, lardacée.

larder ['lɑːdər], *s.* garde-manger *m inv.*

larding ['lɑːdiŋ], *s.* lardage *m*, entrelardement *m*; **l. needle, pin,** lardoire *f*.

lardon ['lɑːd(ə)n], *s. Cu:* lardon *m*; barde *f* (de lard).

lardy ['lɑːdi], *a.* lardeux; *Cu:* **l. cake,** gâteau fait de farine, de saindoux et de fruits secs.

large [lɑːdʒ], *a., adv. & s.*

I. *a.* **1.** (*a*) grand; gros, vaste, fort, considérable; de grandes, de fortes, dimensions; **l.(-sized),** de grand format; **a l. woman,** (i) une grande femme; (ii) une grosse femme; **l. hands,** de grandes mains; **l. town, river,** grande ville, grand fleuve; **l. book, parcel,** gros livre; gros paquet, paquet volumineux; **the largest room,** la pièce la plus vaste; **to grow l., larger,** grossir, grandir; **as l. as life,** (i) (*of statue, etc.*) de grandeur naturelle; (ii) *F:* (*of pers.*) aucunement rabaissé dans sa propre estime; **the day after his defeat he turned up again as l. as life,** le lendemain de sa défaite il a reparu comme si de rien n'était; **there she is as l. as life,** la voilà, c'est bien elle! (*b*) **a l. sum,** une grosse, forte, somme; une somme considérable; **l. fortune,** grande, belle, fortune; **heiress to a l. fortune,** grosse héritière; **to incur l. losses,** éprouver, subir, des pertes sensibles; **l. family,** famille nombreuse; **l. meal,** repas copieux; **l. whisky,** double whisky *m*; **to a l. extent,** en grande partie; **criminal on a l. scale,** criminel *m* de grande envergure; **to see, do, things on a l. scale,** voir, faire, les choses en grand, sur une grande échelle; **to trade on a l. scale,** faire les affaires en grand. **2.** (*a*) (*liberal*) **l. views,** idées *f* larges; **l. tolerance,** large tolérance *f*; *O:* **l. hospitality,** large hospitalité *f*; (*b*) (*wide, extensive*) **l. powers,** pouvoirs larges, étendus; (*c*) *Art:* (style *m*) large.

II. *adv. Nau:* **to sail l.,** aller largue, courir largue; naviguer vent largue; avoir du largue.

III. *s.* **1.** (*a*) **to set a prisoner at l.,** élargir, relaxer, un prisonnier; **to be at l.,** être libre, en liberté; **the murderer is still at l.,** l'assassin n'est pas encore arrêté; (*b*) **society, the people, at l.,** le grand public; la grande masse du public; (*c*) **at l.,** tout au long; en détail; **to speak at l. on sth.,** parler longuement sur qch.; s'étendre sur qch.; (*d*) **to talk at l.,** parler au hasard. **2. in l.,** en grand; **details shown in l.,** détails *m* en grand.

large-handed ['lɑːdʒ'hændid], *a.* **1.** à grandes mains. **2.** généreux, libéral, -aux.

large-hearted ['lɑːdʒ'hɑːtid], *a.* **1.** magnanime. **2.** généreux.

largely ['lɑːdʒli], *adv.* **1.** en grande partie; pour une grande part; dans une large mesure; **they come very l. from Birmingham,** ils viennent pour une grande part de Birmingham. **2. that is l. sufficient,** cela suffit grandement, largement; c'est largement suffisant, amplement suffisant.

largeness ['lɑːdʒnis], *s.* **1.** (*a*) grosseur *f* (des articulations, du corps); (*b*) grandeur *f* (des profits, d'une majorité; ampleur *f* (d'un repas). **2.** (*a*) étendue *f* (d'un pouvoir); (*b*) largeur *f* (d'idées); grandeur (d'âme).

large-scale ['lɑːdʒ'skeil], *a.* grosse (entreprise); (carte *f*) à grande échelle; **l.-s. farmer,** gros agriculteur.

largess(e) [lɑː'ʒes], *s.* largesse *f*.

larghetto [lɑː'getou], *adv. & s. Mus:* larghetto (*m*).

largish ['lɑːdʒiʃ], *a.* assez grand; plutôt grand; assez gros; plutôt gros.

largo ['lɑːgou], *adv. & s. Mus:* largo (*m*).

lariat ['læriət], *s.* **1.** corde *f* à piquet. **2.** lasso *m*.

Laridae ['læridiː], *s.pl. Orn:* laridés *m*.

larigot ['lærigət], *s.* jeu *m* de larigot (de l'orgue).

Larissa [lə'risə]. *Pr.n. Geog:* Larisse *f*, Larissa *f*.

lark[1] [lɑːk], *s.* **1.** *Orn:* alouette *f*; **bar-tailed desert l.,** alouette élégante; **black l.,** alouette mègre; **calandra l.,** alouette calandrelle; **desert l.,** alouette isabelline; **lesser short-toed l.,** alouette pispolette; **shore l.,** *NAm:* **horned l.,** alouette hausse-col, alouette oreillarde; *Fr.C:* alouette cornue; **short-toed l.,** alouette calandrelle; **thick-billed l.,** alouette de Clot-bey; **white-winged l.,** alouette leucoptère; **wood l.,** alouette lulu; **crested l., tufted l.,** cochevis huppé; **short-billed crested, Thekla, l.,** cochevis de Thékla; **bifasciated l.,** sirli *m* des déserts; **Dupont's l.,** sirli de Dupont; **magpie l.,** gralline *f*; **to rise with the l.,** se lever au chant du coq; **she sings like a l.,** elle chante comme un rossignol; **lark's head (knot),** nœud *m* en tête d'alouette; *Ven:* **l.-mirror,** miroir *m* à alouettes. **2.** *Cu:* alouette, mauviette *f*. **3.** *Bot:* **lark's heel,** (i) grande capucine; cresson *m* du Pérou; (ii) = LARKSPUR.

lark[2], *s. F:* (*a*) farce *f*, rigolade *f*, blague *f*; **to do sth. for a l.,** faire qch. histoire de rire, de rigoler; **what a l.!** quelle farce! (*b*) **I'd like to know what his little l. is,** je me demande ce qu'il tripote.

lark[3], *v.i.* **to l. (about),** faire des farces; rigoler.

larkspur ['lɑːkspəːr], *s. Bot:* (*a*) pied-d'alouette *m*, *pl.* pieds-d'alouette; delphinette *f*, dauphinelle *f*, delphinium *m*; (*b*) **field l.,** consoude royale.

larky ['lɑːki], *a. F:* farceur; qui aime à jouer des tours.

larn [lɑːn], *v.tr. P:* **that'll l. him!** ça lui fera les pieds! ça lui apprendra!

larnax, *pl.* **larnakes** ['lɑːnæks, -əkiːz], *s. Gr.Ant:* larnax *m*.

larnite ['lɑːnait], *s. Miner:* larnite *f*.

larrikin ['lærikin], *s. Austr: F:* vaurien *m*; petit voyou; gamin *m* (des rues).

larrup ['lærəp], *v.tr.* (**larruped**) *F: O:* battre (qn) comme plâtre; rosser (qn); flanquer une raclée à (qn).

larruping ['lærəpiŋ], *s. F: O:* rossée *f*, raclée *f*.

larry[1] ['læri], *s. Const:* **(mortar) l.,** broyon *m* à mortier; bouloir *m*; doloire *f* (à corroyer la chaux).

Larry[2]. *Pr.n. F:* **as happy as L.,** heureux comme un poisson dans l'eau.

larsenite ['lɑːsənait], *s. Miner:* larsénite *f*.

larva, *pl.* **-vae** ['lɑːvə, -viː], *s. Rom.Ant: Ent:* larve *f*; *Biol:* **l. shaped,** larviforme.

larval ['lɑːvl], *a.* **1.** *Ent:* larvaire; de larve; en forme de larve. **2.** *Med:* (*of disease*) latent, larvé; **l. fever,** fièvre larvée.

larvated ['lɑːveitid], *a. Med:* = LARVAL 2.

larvacide, larvicide ['lɑːvəsaid], *s. Agr:* larvicide *m*.

larvicolous [lɑː'vikələs], *a. Ent:* larvicole.

larviform ['lɑːvifɔːm], *a. Biol:* larviforme.

larviparous [lɑː'vipərəs], *a. Ent:* larvipare.

larvivorous [lɑː'vivərəs], *a. Nat.Hist:* larvivore.

larvule ['lɑːvjul], *s. Ent:* larvule *f*.

laryngeal [lærin'dʒiəl, læ'rindʒiəl]. **1.** *a.* (*of artery, etc.*) laryngé; **l. cavity,** cavité laryngienne; **l. tube,** tube laryngien. **2.** *Ling:* (*also* **laryngal**) (*a*) *a.* laryngal, -aux; (*b*) *s.* laryngale *f*.

laryngectomee [lærin'dʒektəmiː], *s. Surg:* laryngectomisé, -ée.

laryngectomy [lærin'dʒektəmi], *s. Surg:* laryngectomie *f*.

laryngismus, *pl.* **-mi** [lærin'dʒizməs, -mai], *s. Med:* laryngisme *m*.

laryngitic [lærin'dʒitik], *a. Med:* laryngitique.

laryngitis [lærin'dʒaitis], *s. Med:* laryngite *f*.

laryngocatarrh [lə'riŋgoukə'tɑːr], *s. Med:* catarrhe *m* du larynx.

laryngocele [lə'riŋgousiːl], *s. Med:* laryngocèle *f*.

laryngological [læriŋgou'lɔdʒikl], *a. Med:* laryngologique.

laryngologist [læriŋ'gɔlədʒist], *s. Med:* laryngologiste *mf*, laryngologue *mf*.

laryngology [læriŋ'gɔlədʒi], *s. Med:* laryngologie *f*.

laryngoparalysis ['læriŋgoupə'ræləsis], *s. Med:* laryngoplégie *f*.

laryngopharyngeal ['læriŋgoufæ'rindʒiəl], *a.* laryngopharyngé.

laryngophone [læ'riŋgoufoun], *s. Tp:* laryngophone *m*.

laryngophony [læriŋ'gɔfəni], *s. Tp:* laryngophonie *f*.

laryngoplegia [læriŋgou'pleidʒiə], *s. Med:* laryngoplégie *f*.

laryngoscope [læ'riŋgouskoup], *s. Med:* laryngoscope *m*.

laryngoscopic [læriŋgou'skɔpik], *a.* laryngoscopique.

laryngoscopy [læriŋ'gɔskəpi], *s. Med:* laryngoscopie *f*.

laryngospasm [læriŋgou'spæzm], *s. Med:* laryngospasme *m*.

laryngotome [læ'riŋgətoum], *s. Surg:* laryngotome *m*.

laryngotomy [læriŋ'gɔtəmi], *s. Surg:* laryngotomie *f*.

laryngotracheal [læriŋgoutræ'kiːəl], *a. Anat:* laryngotrachéal, -aux.

laryngotracheitis [læriŋgoutræki'aitis], *s. Med:* laryngo-trachéite *f*.

laryngotracheotomy [læriŋgoutræki'ɔtəmi], *s. Surg:* laryngo-trachéotomie *f*.

larynx, *pl.* **larynges** ['læriŋks, læ'rindʒiːz], *s. Anat:* larynx *m*.

lascar ['læskər], *s.* lascar *m*.

lascivious [lə'siviəs], *a.* lascif; **l. smile,** sourire provocant, lascif.

lasciviously [lə'siviəsli], *adv.* lascivement.

lasciviousness [lə'siviəsnis], *s.* lasciveté *f*.

laser ['leizər], *s. Elcs:* laser *m*; *Med:* **l. therapy,** laserothérapie *f*; *Cmptr:* **l. memory,** mémoire *f* à laser.

laserpitium [læsə'piʃiəm], *s. Bot:* laserpitium *m*, sermontain *m*.

lash[1] [læʃ], *s.* **1.** (*a*) coup *m* de fouet; sanglade *f*, cinglon *m*; (*b*) (i) lanière *f* (de fouet); (ii) *occ.* mèche *f* (de fouet); (*c*) *A:* **(the penalty of) the l.,** le supplice du fouet; **prisoner sentenced to the l.,** prisonnier condamné au fouet, *A:* aux étrivières; **sentenced to six strokes of the l.,** condamné à six coups de fouet; **to be under the l. of criticism,** être exposé aux coups de la critique; être flagellé par la critique. **2.** *Mec.E:* jeu *m*; **side l.,** jeu latéral. **3.** *Anat:* cil *m*.

lash[2], *v.*

I. *v.tr. & i.* **1.** (*a*) fouailler, cingler (un cheval, etc.); (*of rain*) **to l. down, to l. (against) the windows, the face,** tomber à verse; fouetter les vitres, cingler le visage; **wind that lashes the water,** vent *m* qui tourmente l'eau; (*of waves*) **to l. (against) the shore,** battre, fouetter, le rivage; **to l. the sea into fury,** mettre la mer en fureur; **to l. oneself into a fury,** entrer dans une violente colère, *F:* dans une colère bleue; (*b*) (*of animal*) **to l. its tail,** se battre les flancs avec la queue; (*of whale, etc.*) **to l. the sea,** battre la mer de sa queue; (*c*) (*verbally*) cingler; **to l. s.o. with one's tongue,** adresser à qn des paroles cinglantes, des reproches sanglants. **2.** *v.i. Mec.E:* (*of running part*) fouetter.

II. (*compound verb*) **lash out,** *v.i.* (*a*) (*of horse*) ruer; lancer une ruade; **to l. out at s.o.,** invectiver qn; (*b*) se livrer à de folles dépenses; faire des folies; **I lashed out on a fur coat,** j'ai fait la folie de me payer un manteau de fourrure.

lash[3], *v.tr.* lier, attacher; *Nau:* amarrer; saisir (l'ancre); aiguilleter; **to l. down a load on a trailer,** lier, brider, brêler, une charge sur une remorque; **to l. down bridge planking, etc.,** guinder les planches d'un pont militaire, etc; **to l. boats side by side,** amarrer des bateaux côte à côte; **to l. two wires together,** ligaturer, ligoter, deux fils.

lashed [læʃt], *a.* (*with adj. prefixed, e.g.*) **long-l. eyes,** yeux *m* aux longs cils.

lasher ['læʃər], *s.* **1.** (*a*) *A:* fouetteur *m*; (*b*) *Ich:* **1. bullhead,** scorpion *m* de mer. **2.** *Nau:* = LASHING[3] 2. **3.** *Hyd.E:* (*a*) déversoir *m* (d'une rivière); (*b*) remous *m* au pied du déversoir.

lashing[1] ['læʃiŋ], *a.* (*of rain*) cinglant; (*of criticism*) acéré, cinglant.

lashing[2], *s.* **1.** (*a*) coups *mpl* de fouet; le fouet; (*b*) fouettée *f*; sanglade *f*; (*c*) *Mec.E:* fouettement *m*. **2.** *pl. F:* **lashings of sth.,** des tas *m*, des tapées *f*, de qch; **we had lashings of drink, to drink,** ce qu'il y avait à boire, en veux-tu!

lashing[3], *s.* **1.** *Nau:* amarrage *m*, aiguilletage *m*; *Mil.E:* brêlage *m*; **l. of cables, of wires,** ligature *f* de câbles, de fils; **l. rope,** (i) corde *f* de brêlage, de bridage; (ii) *Nau:* risse *f*; (iii) *Artil: etc:* prolonge *f*. **2.** *Nau:* amarre *f*; point *m* d'amarrage; aiguillette *f*; *Mil.E:* corde de brêlage; commande *f* (de pontons); *Const:* drisse *f*, vingtaine *f* (d'échafaudage); *Nau:* **gun lashings,** aiguillettes d'amarrage; saisines *f*; **hammock lashings,** hanets *m*, rabans *m*, de hamac; **head l. (of sheers),** portugaise *f*.

lash-out ['læʃaut], *s.* ruade *f* (d'un cheval).

lash-up ['læʃʌp], *s. F:* (*a*) expédient *m*; moyen *m* de fortune; *El:* installation *f* provisoire; (*b*) **you've got a good l.-up here,** vous êtes bien installé ici.

lasiocampid [leiziou'kæmpid], *s. Ent:* lasiocampide *m*.

Lasiocampidae [leiziou'kæmpidiː], *s.pl. Ent:* lasiocampides *m*.

lasius ['leiʃiəs], *s. Ent:* lasius *m*.

lasque [læsk], *s. Miner:* lasque *m*.

lass [læs], *s.f. esp. Scot: & N.Eng:* jeune fille; **country l.,** jeune campagnarde; **a lover and his l.,** deux jeunes amoureux *m*.

lassie ['læsi], *s.f. esp. Scot:* fillette, gamine; **a wee l.,** une (toute) petite fille.

lassitude [ˈlæsitjuːd], *s.* lassitude *f.*

lasso[1] [læˈsuː], *s.* lasso *m.*

lasso[2], *v.tr.* prendre au lasso.

last[1] [lɑːst], *s. Bootm:* forme *f* (à chaussure); *Prov:* **let the shoemaker stick to his l.,** à chacun son métier et les vaches seront bien gardées; cordonnier, mêlez-vous de votre pantoufle! cordonnier, ne regarde pas plus haut que ta chaussure! **l. maker,** formier *m.*

last[2], *v.tr. Bootm:* mettre (l'empeigne) sur la forme.

last[3], *s. A.Meas:* **1.** last(e) *m* (de laine, de malt, etc.) (poids de deux tonneaux de mer ou 2000 kilogrammes). **2.** mesure *f* de 12 barriques (de morue ou de harengs).

last[4], *a., s. & adv.*

I. *a.* dernier. **1.** (*a*) **the l. two, the two l.,** les deux derniers; **the l. ten to be rescued,** les dix derniers rescapés; **the L. Day,** le jugement dernier; **the l. guest to arrive,** le dernier des invités à arriver; **the l. but one, the second l.,** l'avant-dernier, *pl.* avant-derniers; **the l. syllable but one,** la (syllabe) pénultième; **the l. but three,** le troisième avant le dernier; **l. but not least,** le dernier (nommé), mais non le moindre; **I should be the l. to believe it,** je serais le dernier à le croire; **you are the l. one who should criticize,** vous devriez être le dernier à critiquer; **that's the l. thing to try,** ce serait la dernière ressource! drôle de remède! **that's the l. thing that's worrying me,** ça c'est le cadet de mes soucis; **in the l. resort, as a l. resort, as a l. resource,** en fin de compte; en dernière ressource; en dernier recours; en désespoir de cause; **to judge in the l. resort,** juger souverainement; **in the l. place,** en dernier lieu; pour finir; **in the l. analysis,** en dernière analyse; **to have the l. word,** (i) parler le dernier; (ii) avoir le dernier mot; **hotel that is the l. word in comfort,** hôtel qui est le dernier mot du confort; **the l. word in art,** les toutes dernières créations de l'art; **to pay one's l. respects to s.o.,** rendre les derniers devoirs à qn; **pupils in their l. term (at school),** élèves sortants; **l. date for registration,** dernier délai pour l'inscription; **l. in first out system,** système *m* dernier entré premier sorti; **Jane Austen's l. novel,** le dernier roman de Jane Austen; **is this his l. novel, or has he written another since?** est-ce son dernier roman, ou en a-t-il publié un autre depuis? **his new novel is interesting, but I like his l. one better,** son nouveau roman est intéressant, mais je préfère son dernier; **I'm down to my l. pound,** il ne me reste plus qu'une livre; *esp. NAm:* (*intensive*) **to spend every l. penny,** dépenser jusqu'au dernier sou; **every l. scrap of bread had been eaten,** on avait mangé jusqu'à la dernière miette; **at the l. moment, minute,** au dernier moment; **l.-minute decision,** décision *f* de dernière heure, de dernière minute; **l. thing at night,** tard dans la soirée; **the l. day of the month,** le dernier jour du mois; (*b*) *O: & NAm:* **a matter of the l. importance,** une affaire de la plus haute importance, de la dernière importance; (*c*) (*lowest*) **that isn't his l. price,** ce n'est pas son dernier prix; **now the l. of the nations, though once the first,** aujourd'hui la dernière des nations, bien qu'autrefois la première. **2.** (*of past time*) **l. Tuesday, Tuesday l.,** mardi dernier; **l. Christmas,** à Noël dernier; **l. January,** au mois de janvier dernier; **the l. time I saw him,** la dernière fois que je l'ai vu; **the time before l.,** l'avant-dernière fois; **l. week,** la semaine dernière; la semaine passée; **l. evening,** hier (au) soir; **l. night,** (i) la nuit dernière; (ii) hier soir; **I slept badly l. night,** j'ai mal dormi cette nuit; **the night before l.,** (i) la nuit d'avant-hier; (ii) avant-hier (au) soir; **these l. six years,** ces six dernières années; **I haven't seen him for the l. four days,** je ne l'ai pas vu depuis quatre jours; il y a quatre jours que je ne l'ai vu; **in the l. fortnight, the l. few weeks,** au cours, dans le courant, de cette dernière quinzaine, de ces dernières semaines; **the l. few weeks he was with us,** pendant les dernières semaines de son séjour chez nous; **in the l. fifty years,** dans les cinquante ans qui viennent de s'écouler; pendant les cinquante dernières années; **this day l. week,** il y a aujourd'hui huit jours; **this day l. year,** l'an dernier à pareil jour.

II. *s.* **1. this l.,** ce dernier, cette dernière; **these l. had heard nothing,** ces derniers (arrivés, nommés) n'avaient rien entendu; *B:* **the l. shall be first,** les derniers seront les premiers. **2.** (*a*) **we shall never hear the l. of it,** on ne nous le laissera pas oublier; **we haven't heard the l. of it,** tout n'est pas dit; **that's the l. I saw of him,** je ne l'ai pas revu depuis; **when shall we see the l. of him?** quand verrons-nous ses talons? **thank goodness I've seen the l. of him, her!** Dieu merci, m'en voilà débarrassé! **that's (just about) the l. of it!** et en voilà la fin! (*b*) **to, till, the l.,** jusqu'au bout, jusqu'à la fin, jusqu'au dernier moment; **faithful to the l.,** fidèle jusqu'au bout; (*c*) *adv.phr.* **at l., at long l.,** enfin; à la fin (des fins); **daylight had come at l.,** le jour avait fini par venir; enfin c'était le jour; **now at l. I understand,** du coup, finalement, je comprends; (*d*) **to look one's l. on sth.,** jeter un dernier regard sur qch.; voir qch. pour la dernière fois; (*e*) (*death*) fin *f*; **to be near one's l.,** toucher à sa fin; **towards the l.,** vers la fin.

III. *adv.* (*a*) **when I l. saw him, when I saw him l.,** la dernière fois que je l'ai vu; **he was l. seen at Cherbourg,** la dernière fois qu'on l'a vu était à Cherbourg; **when did you l. eat?** de quand date, à quand remonte, votre dernier repas? (*b*) **he spoke, came, l.,** il a parlé, est arrivé, le dernier; **he visited me l. of all,** il a passé chez moi en dernier; (*c*) **first cajolery, and l. threats,** d'abord des cajoleries, pour aboutir à des menaces; **l. but not least,** enfin et surtout.

last[5]. **1.** *v.i.* durer, se maintenir; **it's too good to l.,** c'est trop beau pour durer; **if the good weather, the frost, lasts,** si le beau temps, la gelée, tient; si le beau temps se maintient; **how long does your leave l.?** quelle est la durée de votre congé? **the supplies will not l. (out) two months,** les vivres *m* n'iront pas deux mois, ne feront pas deux mois; **this soap lasts longer,** ce savon est plus durable; **fashion that will not l.,** mode *f* qui passera, qui ne durera pas; **material that will not l. long,** tissu *m* qui n'est pas solide, qui ne tiendra pas; **their friendship won't l. long,** leur amitié ne fera pas long feu; **this dress has lasted me three years,** j'ai cette robe depuis trois ans (et je la porte toujours); **it will l. me a lifetime,** j'en ai pour la vie; **he won't l. long in that job,** il ne fera pas long feu dans cette situation. **2.** *v.tr.* **to l. s.o. out,** (i) (*of pers.*) survivre à qn; (ii) (*of thg*) durer autant que qn; **to l. the year out,** durer, aller, jusqu'au bout de l'année; **my overcoat will l. the winter out,** mon pardessus fera encore l'hiver.

last-ditcher [lɑːstˈditʃər], *s.* jusqu'au-boutiste *mf*; irréconciliable *mf.*

Lastex [ˈlæsteks], *Pr.n. R.t.m:* Lastex *m.*

lasting[1] [ˈlɑːstiŋ], *s. Bootm:* mise *f* sur la forme.

lasting[2]. **1.** *a.* (*a*) durable, permanent, de longue durée; (*of material, etc.*) résistant, de bon usage; **l. peace,** paix *f* durable; (*b*) persistant; **l. cold,** rhume persistant. **2.** *s. Tex:* **lasting(s),** lasting *m.*

lastingly [ˈlɑːstiŋli], *adv.* d'une manière durable, permanente.

lastly [ˈlɑːstli], *adv.* pour finir; en dernier lieu.

latakia [lætæˈkiːə], *s.* lattaquié *m*, latakieh *m*, tabac *m* de Lattaquié.

latania [ləˈteiniə], *s. Bot:* latanier *m.*

latch[1] [lætʃ], *s.* **1.** (*a*) loquet *m*, clenche *f*; (*for shutters, etc.*) **small l.,** loqueteau; **spring l.,** loquet à ressort; (*b*) pène *m*, gâche *f* (de portière de véhicule, etc.); **lock l.,** pène de serrure; (*c*) serrure *f* de sûreté (avec clef de maison); **to leave the door on the l.,** (i) fermer la porte au loquet, à la clenche; (ii) fermer la porte (sans la verrouiller); fermer la porte à demi-tour. **2.** *Mec.E:* (*a*) verrou *m* (de levier, d'une pièce mécanique mobile); valet *m* d'arrêt (d'une plaque tournante, etc.); chien *m* (d'arrêt); *Mec.Tls:* **disengaging l.,** verrou de débrayage; *attrib.* **l. handle, l. lever,** poignée *f*, levier *m*, de verrouillage; **l. release, handle, lever,** poignée, levier, de déverrouillage, de débloquage; **l. jaws,** mâchoires *f* de blocage, de verrouillage; **l. stop pin,** goupille *f* de verrouillage; (*b*) accrochage *m* (d'une pièce mécanique mobile); **automatic l.,** accrochage automatique; **l. hook,** crochet *m* de retenue.

latch[2], *v.tr.* **1.** (*a*) fermer (la porte) au loquet, à la clenche, à demi-tour; (*b*) fermer (la porte) sans mettre le verrou. **2.** *Mec.E:* verrouiller, bloquer (un levier, une pièce mécanique mobile). **3.** *F:* **to l. on to (s.o., sth.),** s'attacher à (qn); saisir (qch.); s'emparer de (qch.).

latchet [ˈlætʃit], *s. A:* cordon *m* (de soulier); *B:* **whose shoe's l. I am not worthy to unloose,** et je ne suis pas digne de délier la courroie de ses souliers.

latching [ˈlætʃiŋ], *s.* verrouillage *m*, blocage *m*; **l. device, l. mechanism,** dispositif *m*, mécanisme *m*, de verrouillage, de blocage.

latchkey [ˈlætʃkiː], *s.* clef *f* de maison; clef de porte d'entrée; *A:* **l. voter,** électeur *m* qui vote du fait qu'il est locataire d'une chambre.

latchstring [ˈlætʃstriŋ], *s.* cordon *m* (de loquet).

late [leit], *a. & adv.*

I. *a.* **(later; latest;** *s.a.* LATTER *and* LAST[4]**) 1.** (*a*) (*after the appointed time*) en retard; **to be l. (for sth.),** être en retard (pour qch.); se faire attendre; **am I l.?** suis-je en retard? **I shall be l. for my lesson,** je serai en retard à ma leçon; **I don't want to make you l.,** je ne veux pas vous mettre en retard; **the train is l., is ten minutes l.,** le train a du retard, a dix minutes de retard, a un retard de dix minutes; (*b*) (*delayed*) retardé; *I.C.E:* **l. cut-off of the admission,** retard à la ferme de l'admission; fermeture retardée. **2.** (*a*) (*far on in the day, etc.*) tard; **it is l.,** il est tard; **it is getting l.,** il se fait tard; **it is too l.,** il est trop tard; il n'est plus temps; **I was too l.,** je ne suis pas arrivé à temps; je suis arrivé trop tard; **am I too l. to see him?** est-il trop tard pour que je le voie? **what is the latest you can come?** à quel moment pouvez-vous venir au plus tard? **the latest I can come,** le plus tard que je puisse venir; **the latest date,** date *f* limite; *Post:* **latest time for posting,** heure *f* limite de dépôt; *W.Tel: T.V:* **is there a, any, later news?** y a-t-il encore un bulletin d'informations? y a-t-il un autre bulletin d'informations ce soir? **I did not think it was so l.,** je ne pensais pas qu'il fût si tard; **it is l. in the day to change your mind,** il est un peu tard pour changer d'avis; **I was l. going to bed,** je me suis couché tard; **l. party,** réunion *f* (i) qui commence tard, (ii) qui finit tard; **at a l. hour (in the day, in the night),** bien avant, très avant, fort avant, dans la journée, dans la nuit; à une heure avancée de la nuit; **in the l. afternoon,** tard dans l'après-midi; vers la fin de l'après-midi; **in l. summer, in l. autumn,** vers la fin de l'été, de l'automne; **Easter is l. this year,** Pâques est tard cette année; **it was getting l. in the season,** la saison s'avançait; *Prov:* **it's never too l. to mend,** il n'est jamais trop tard pour se corriger, pour s'amender, pour bien faire; **later events proved that . . .,** la suite des événements a démontré que . . .; **later generations,** les générations (i) suivantes, (ii) futures; **at a later meeting,** dans une séance ultérieure; **later will,** testament subséquent; **the latest posterity,** la postérité la plus reculée; **in later life,** plus tard dans la vie; **it is twelve o'clock at (the) latest,** c'est tout au plus s'il est midi; **on Wednesday at the latest,** mercredi au plus tard; **latest date,** (i) *Jur:* terme fatal; (ii) *Com:* terme de rigueur, délai *m* de rigueur; (*b*) (*far on in period*) **l. stained glass,** vitraux *m* de la dernière époque (du moyen âge, etc.); **the later kings of the pre-Conquest period,** les derniers en date des rois d'avant la Conquête; **the later centuries of the Middle Ages,** les siècles tardifs du moyen âge; **in the l. (eighteen) eighties,** dans les années approchant 1890. **3.** (*fruit, etc.*) tardif; **l. frosts,** gelées tardives, printanières; **wild flowers are later than garden ones,** les fleurs des champs retardent sur celles des jardins. **4.** (*a*) ancien, ex-; **the l. minister,** l'ancien ministre, l'ex-ministre; le ci-devant ministre; *Com:* **Martin, l. Thomas,** Martin, ancienne maison Thomas; Martin, ci-devant Thomas; Martin successeur de Thomas; maison Thomas, Martin successeur; (*b*) feu, défunt, décédé; **my l. father,** feu mon père; **the l. queen,** feu la reine, la feue reine. **5.** (*of recent date*) récent, dernier; **the l. rains,** les dernières pluies; **the l. war,** la guerre récente; **of l. years,** (dans) ces dernières années; depuis quelques années; **of l.,** dernièrement, récemment, depuis peu; depuis quelque temps; **this author's latest work,** le dernier ouvrage de cet auteur; **Mr X tells us that his latest book will be his last,** M. X nous annonce que son récent ouvrage sera le dernier que nous aurons de sa main, que son dernier ouvrage ne sera suivi d'aucun autre; **in this book will be found his latest views on the subject,** dans ce livre on trouvera ses vues les plus récentes sur ce sujet; *Com:* **latest novelties,** dernières nouveautés; **the very latest improvements,** les tout derniers perfectionnements; *Journ:* **latest intelligence, latest news,** informations *fpl* de la dernière heure; dernières nouvelles; **the very latest news,** les informations de toute dernière heure; **is there any later news?** a-t-on des nouvelles plus récentes? **that's the latest,** (i) c'est ce qu'il y a de plus nouveau; (ii) *F:* ça, c'est le comble! **have you heard the latest?** savez-vous la dernière nouvelle? **X's latest,** (i) la dernière plaisanterie de X; (ii) le dernier exploit de X; (iii) la dernière conquête de X.

II. *adv.* **(later; latest;** *see also* LAST[4]**) 1.** (*after the appointed time*) en retard; **to arrive too l.,** arriver trop tard; arriver après coup; *Prov:* **better l. than never,** mieux vaut tard que jamais. **2.** (*far on in day, etc.*) tard; **he came home very l.,** il est rentré fort tard; **if I come it will be fairly l.,** si je viens ce sera sur le tard; **John arrived later than the others and Charles arrived latest of all,** Jean est arrivé plus tard que les autres et Charles est arrivé le dernier; **early and l.,** à toute heure du jour; du matin au soir; **early or l., sooner or later,** tôt ou tard; **to keep s.o. l.,** attarder qn; **to sit up, stay up, l., to go to bed l.,** (se) coucher tard; veiller tard; **to sleep, stay in bed, l.,** faire la grasse matinée; **to stay up l. doing sth.,** s'attarder à faire qch.; **very l. at night,** bien avant, fort avant, dans la nuit; **l. into the night,** jusqu'à une heure avancée de la nuit; **he came l. in the afternoon,** il est venu vers la fin de l'après-midi; **very l. in the day,** à une heure avancée de la journée; très avant dans la journée; sur le tard; **l. in the year,** vers la fin de l'année; **l. in March,** dans les derniers jours de mars; **l.**

in life, à un âge avancé; sur le tard; **he married l. in life,** il se maria tard, sur le tard; **I saw him as l. as yesterday, no later than yesterday,** hier encore je l'ai vu; je l'ai vu pas plus tard qu'hier; **traces remained as l. as the seventeenth century,** des traces en restaient encore au dix-septième siècle; **a moment later,** l'instant d'après; **this happened later (on),** cela est arrivé après, plus tard, ultérieurement; **a few days later,** à quelques jours de là; **as we shall see later,** comme nous le verrons plus tard, dans la suite; **this is the latest published Agatha Christie,** c'est le roman d'Agatha Christie le plus récent; *F:* **see you later!** à bientôt! **3.** *Poet:* = LATELY. **4.** (*formerly*) **l. of London,** dernièrement domicilié à Londres; autrefois établi à Londres.

late-blooming ['leit'blu:miŋ], *a. Bot:* tardiflore.

latecomer ['leitkʌmər], *s.* retardataire *mf*; tard-venu, -venue, *pl.* tard-venus, -venues.

lateen [lə'ti:n], *a. Nau:* **l. sail,** voile latine; **storm l. sail,** tréou *m*; **l. yard,** antenne *f*; **l. mast,** mât *m* de calcet.

late-flowering ['leit'flauəriŋ], *a. Bot:* tardiflore.

lately ['leitli], *adv.* dernièrement, récemment; dans ces derniers temps; il y a peu de temps; depuis peu; **what have you been doing l.?** qu'avez-vous fait ces derniers temps? **we have not heard from him l.,** nous sommes restés sans nouvelles de lui ces temps derniers; **until l.,** jusqu'à ces derniers temps; jusqu'à une époque récente; **as l. as yesterday,** hier encore; pas plus tard qu'hier; **it is only l. that the matter has become known,** la chose n'a été sue que ces jours-ci.

laten ['leit(ə)n]. *Lit:* **1.** *v.i.* (*of hour, season*) s'avancer. **2.** *v.tr.* retarder (l'heure de qch.).

latence, latency ['leitəns(i)], *s. Biol: Ph: etc:* (*a*) latence *f*, état latent; *Tchn:* **l. time of a detector,** temps *m* de latence d'un détecteur; (*b*) temps *m* de latence.

lateness ['leitnis], *s.* **1.** arrivée tardive (de qn); tardiveté *f* (d'un fruit, etc.). **2. the l. of the hour,** l'heure avancée.

latent ['leit(ə)nt], *a. Biol: Ph: Tchn:* latent, qui dort, qui couve; **l. period, l. time,** temps *m* de latence; **l. state, fading,** disparition *f* de l'image latente; *Ph:* **l. electricity,** électricité latente; **l. heat,** chaleur latente; **l. heat of vaporization,** chaleur latente de vaporisation; *Atom.Ph:* **l. neutron,** neutron retardé; *Med:* **l. disease,** maladie latente; **l. injury,** lésion latente; (*b*) *Mil:* **l. war,** guerre larvée; (*c*) caché, invisible; *Jur:* **l. defect,** vice caché; *Bot:* **l. bud,** œil dormant, latent; (*d*) *Mth:* **l. roots,** valeurs *f* propres, valeurs spectrales (calcul matriciel).

latently ['leitəntli], *adv.* d'une manière latente, cachée.

lateral ['læt(ə)rəl], *a.* latéral, -aux; **l. road, l. route,** rocade *f*; **l. avenue,** contre-allée *f*, *pl.* contre-allées; **l. canal,** canal latéral; *Geol:* **l. cone,** cône adventif, parasitaire (d'un volcan); *Mec:* **l. motion,** mouvement latéral; **l. flexure,** flambage *m*; **l. play,** jeu latéral, vrillage *m*; *W.Tel:* **l. deviation,** diffusion *f* oblique; diffraction *f* de l'onde de sol; *Av:* **l. axis,** axes transversal; **l. attitude,** assiette latérale; **l. stability,** stabilité latérale; **l. trim,** centrage latéral; *Rec:* **l. recording,** gravure transversale (d'un disque); *Hyd.E:* **l. wall of a lock,** (mur) bajoyer *m* d'une écluse; *Bot:* **l. bud,** *s.* **lateral,** bourgeon latéral; *Ich:* **l. line,** ligne latérale; *Anat:* **l. incisor,** incisive latérale; *Ling:* **l. consonant,** consonne latérale.

laterally ['læt(ə)rəli], *adv.* latéralement.

Lateran ['lætərən], *Pr.n.m. Ecc.Hist:* Latran; **the L. Palace,** le palais de Latran; **the L. (church), Saint John L.,** la basilique de Latran; Saint-Jean de Latran; *Ecc.Hist:* **the L. Councils,** les Conciles *m* de Latran.

laterifloral [lætəri'flɔ:rəl], *a. Bot:* latériflore.

laterigrade ['lætərigreid], *a. & s. Nat.Hist:* latérigrade (*m*).

laterite ['lætərait], *s. Geol:* latérite *f*.

lateritic [lætə'ritik], *a. Geol:* latéritique.

laterization [lætərai'zeiʃ(ə)n], *s. Geol:* latérisation *f*.

laterodorsal [lætərou'dɔ:sl], *a. Anat:* latérodorsal, -aux.

lateroflexion [lætərou'flekʃ(ə)n], *s. Obst:* latéroflexion *f*.

lateroposition [lætəroupə'ziʃ(ə)n], *s. Obst:* latéroposition *f*, latéroversion *f*.

lateroventral [lætərou'ventrl], *a. Anat:* latéro-ventral, -aux.

lates ['leiti:z], *s. Ich:* latès *m*.

latewood ['leitwud], *s. Arb:* bois *m* d'automne.

latex ['leiteks], *s. Bot:* latex *m*; **l.-bearing,** laticifère; **rubber l.,** latex caoutchoutifère.

lath[1] [læθ, lɑ:θ], *s.* **1.** *Const:* (*a*) latte *f*; (*in loam work*) palançon *m*; **partition l.,** latte jointive; **l. and plaster,** enduit *m* de pan de bois; plâtrage *m*; **l.-and-plaster partition,** cloison lattée et plâtrée; **l. nail,** clou *m* à latter; **l. hammer, hatchet,** hachotte *f*; *F:* **that's all l. and plaster,** c'est du plâtrage, tout ça; (*b*) **slate l.,** (latte) volige *f*. **2.** (*of Venetian blind*) lame *f*. **3.** batte *f*, latte, sabre *m* de bois (d'Arlequin). **4.** échalas *m* (de treillis); *U.S:* **l. screen,** abri *m* pour semis.

lath[2], *v.tr.* (*a*) latter (une cloison); (*b*) voliger (un toit).

lathe[1] [leið], *s.* **1.** *Mch.Tls:* tour *m*; (*a*) **metal-working l.,** tour à métaux; **wood-turning l.,** tour à bois; **parallel l.,** tour parallèle; **precision l.,** tour de précision; *Join:* **bench l.,** tour d'établi; **made on the l.,** fait au tour, à la machine; **to put work on the l.,** monter une pièce sur le tour; **automatic, semi-automatic, l.,** tour automatique, semi-automatique; **hand l.,** tour à main; **foot l., pedal l., treadle l.,** tour (marchant) au pied, tour à pédale; **motor-driven l., power l.,** tour à moteur; **high-speed l.,** tour à grande vitesse, tour (à marche) rapide; **apron l.,** tour à tablier; **bed l.,** tour à banc; **short-bed l.,** tour à banc court; **l. bed,** banc *m*, bâti *m*, de tour; **l. centre,** pointe *f* de tour; **l. head,** poupée *f* de tour; **l. bearer,** toc *m* de tour, pour tours; doguin *m*; **break l., gap l.,** tour à banc rompu; **capstan l., turret l., revolver l.,** tour (à) révolver; **centre l.,** tour à pointes; **duplex l.,** tour à double outil; **multi-tool l.,** tour à outils multiples; **face l.,** tour en l'air, à plateau; **geared l.,** tour à engrenages; **ungeared l., plain l.,** tour sans engrenages, tour simple; *F:* bidet *m*; **spring-pole l.,** tour à perche élastique; **chasing l., spinning l.,** tour à repousser; **bulging l.,** tour à repousser les métaux; **copying l.,** tour à copier, à reproduire; *F:* tour à singer; **forming l.,** tour à profiler, à copier; **gauge l.,** tour à gabarit; **relieving l.,** tour à dégager, à dépouiller, à détalonner; **screw-cutting l., thread-cutting l., threading l.,** tour à fileter; **slicing l.,** tour à décolleter; **cutting-off l.,** tour à tronçonner; **slide l., sliding l.,** tour à charioter, tour parallèle; **second-operation l.,** tour à reprise; **universal l.,** tour universel; (*b*) touret *m*; **polishing l.,** touret à polir, de polisseur; *I.C.E:* **valve-grinding l.,** touret à rectifier les soupapes; (*c*) *Mec.E:* **gun l.,** forerie *f*. **2. potter's l.,** tour de potier.

lathe[2], *v.tr.* tourner; charioter; dresser (une pièce) au tour.

lathe[3], *s. Tex:* battant *m*, chasse *f* (d'un métier).

lathe[4], *s.* division administrative (du comté de Kent).

lather[1] ['læðər], *s.* **1.** mousse *f* de savon; **to make a l.,** faire lever la mousse. **2.** (*on horse*) écume *f*; **horse all in a l.,** cheval couvert d'écume; *F:* **to work oneself into a l.,** s'énerver; **she's in a terrible l.,** elle a les nerfs en pelote, elle est à cran.

lather[2]. **1.** *v.tr.* (*a*) savonner (**s.o.'s chin,** le menton à qn); **to l. one's face,** se savonner; **lathered chin,** menton couvert de savon; (*b*) *F: O:* (*thrash*) rosser, savonner (qn); fouailler (un cheval). **2.** *v.i.* (*a*) (*of soap*) mousser; (*b*) (*of horse*) jeter de l'écume.

lathering ['læðəriŋ], *s.* savonnage *m* (du mention de qn). **2.** *F: O:* rossée *f*, savonnage.

lathery ['læðəri], *a.* **1.** (liquide) mousseux, écumeux. **2.** (*a*) (menton) couvert de savon; (*b*) (cheval) couvert d'écume.

lathe-turned ['leiðtə:nd], *a.* fait au tour; façonné au tour; tourné.

lathework ['leiðwə:k], *s.* travail *m* au tour; tournage *m*; chariotage *m*.

lathi [lɑ:'ti:], *s.* (*in India*) bâton ferré (de policier); bambou ferré.

lathing ['læθiŋ, 'lɑ:θiŋ], *s.* **1.** (*a*) lattage *m*; (*b*) voligeage *m*. **2.** *coll.* (*also* **lathwork**) lattis *m*.

lathwood ['læθwud, 'lɑ:θ-], *s.* bois *m* de fente.

lathyrism ['læθirizm], *s. Med:* lathyrisme *m*.

lathyrus ['læθirəs], *s. Bot:* lathyrus *m*.

laticiferous [læti'sifərəs], *a. Bot:* laticifère.

laticlave ['lætikleiv], *s. Rom.Ant:* laticlave *m*.

latifoliate [læti'foulieit], *a. Bot:* latifolié.

latifundia [læti'fʌndiə], *s.pl.* latifundia *m*; grandes propriétés.

Latin ['lætin]. **1.** (*a*) *a.* latin; **the L. races,** les races latines; *Geog:* **L. America,** Amérique latine; (*b*) *s.* Latin, -ine. **2.** (*a*) *s. Ling:* latin *m*; **classical L.,** latin classique; **low, vulgar, L.,** bas latin; **late L.,** latin de la décadence; **written in L.,** écrit en latin; *F:* **dog L.,** latin de cuisine; **thieves' L.,** argot *m* des voleurs; (*b*) *a. Typ:* **L. characters,** lettres romaines; (*c*) *a.* (*in Paris*) **the L. Quarter,** le Quartier latin.

Latin-American ['lætinə'merikən], (*a*) *a.* latino-américain, *pl.* latino-américains; (*b*) *s.* Latino-américain, -aine.

Latinism ['lætinizm], *s.* **1.** latinisme *m*; tournure latine. **2.** action *f*, influence *f*, (i) des races latines, (ii) de l'Église latine.

Latinist ['lætinist], *s.* latiniste *mf*; latinisant, -ante.

Latinity [lə'tiniti], *s.* latinité *f*.

Latinization [lætinai'zeiʃ(ə)n], *s.* latinisation *f*.

latirostral [læti'rɔstrəl], **latirostrate** [læti'rɔstreit], *a. Orn:* latirostre.

Latirostres [læti'rɔstri:z], *s.pl. Orn: A:* latirostres *m*.

latish ['leitiʃ]. **1.** *a.* (*a*) un peu en retard; (*b*) un peu tard; un peu tardif; **at a l. hour,** à une heure plutôt avancée, assez avancée. **2.** *adv.* (*a*) (arriver) un peu en retard; (*b*) (se réveiller, etc.) un peu tard; **l. in the day,** à une heure assez avancée de la journée; sur le tard.

latitude ['lætitju:d], *s.* **1.** (*a*) *A:* largeur *f*, étendue *f*; (*b*) **to allow s.o. the greatest l.,** laisser à qn la plus grande latitude, la plus grande liberté d'action; accorder de la marge à qn; **to allow s.o. l. of thought,** montrer de la tolérance pour les opinions de qn; **to translate with some l.,** traduire sans serrer le texte de trop près; **he relates the facts with considerable l.,** il raconte les faits sans trop s'attacher à la vérité. **2.** *Geog: Nau:* latitude; **north, south, l.,** latitude nord, sud; **in northern, southern, latitudes,** dans les latitudes boréales, australes; **high, low, l.,** latitude haute, basse; **horse latitudes,** zone *f* des calmes tropicaux; **at 30° north,** par 30° (de) latitude nord; **l. by dead reckoning,** latitude estimée; **l. by observation,** latitude observée; **to find the l. by the pole star,** faire une latitude par la polaire; **l. scale,** échelle *f* des latitudes; **in these latitudes,** sous ces latitudes; *Lit:* **in other latitudes,** sous d'autres climats; sous d'autres ciels. **3.** *Astr:* **celestial l.,** latitude céleste.

latitudinal [læti'tju:din(ə)l], *a.* latitudinal, -aux; transversal, -aux.

latitudinarian [lætitju:di'nɛəriən], *a. & s. Rel.H:* latitudinaire *mf*; latitudinarien, -ienne; partisan, -ane, du tolérantisme (en matière de religion).

latitudinarianism [lætitjudi'nɛəriənizm], *s. Rel.H:* latitudinarisme *m*; tolérantisme *m* (en matière de religion).

Latona [lə'tounə], *Pr.n.f. Myth:* Latone.

latria [lə'traiə], *s. R.C.Ch:* latrie *f*.

latrines [lə'tri:nz], *s.pl.* latrines *f*; *Mil: F:* la casemate; *Nau: F:* la poulaine; les poulaines; *Navy:* (*for officers*) la bouteille; les bouteilles.

latrodectus [lætrou'dektəs], *s. Arach:* latrodecte *m*, latrodectus *m*.

latten ['lætən], *s. Metall:* **1.** *Archeol:* variété de laiton *m* (qui contient de l'étain); **black l.,** fer-blanc *m*. **2. l. brass,** laiton en feuilles, laiton laminé.

latter ['lætər], *a.* **1.** (*second-mentioned*) dernier (des deux); **the l.,** ce, le, dernier; cette, la, dernière; ces, les, derniers, -ières; celui-ci, celle-ci; ceux-ci, celles-ci. **2.** (*belonging to the end*) **the l. half, part, of June, of the story,** la deuxième moitié de juin, de l'histoire; **the l. half of August was fine,** pendant la seconde quinzaine d'août il a fait beau; **l. end,** (i) dernière moitié, fin *f* (d'une époque); (ii) *A:* mort *f*, fin (de qn); *Rel:* **the L. Day,** le jugement dernier. **3.** *A:* (*later*) **the l. rain,** la pluie de l'arrière-saison; **l. grass,** regain *m*.

latter-day ['lætə'dei], *a. O:* récent, moderne, d'aujourd'hui; **l.-d. opinions,** les opinions contemporaines; *Rel.H:* **the L.-d. Saints,** les Saints *m* du dernier jour; les Mormons *m*.

latterly ['lætəli], *adv.* **1.** (*a*) dans les derniers temps; vers la fin (d'une époque); (*b*) dans la suite. **2.** récemment.

lattermost ['lætəmoust], *a.* dernier.

lattice[1] ['lætis], *s.* **1.** (*a*) treillis *m*, treillage *m*; **l. window,** (i) fenêtre treillagée, treillissée; (ii) fenêtre à losanges, à vitraux sertis de plomb; *Civ.E: etc:* **l. beam, l. girder, l. truss, l. frame,** poutre *f* en treillis, à croisillons; poutre contre-fichée; **l. bridge,** pont *m* en treillis; **l. bracing,** charpente *f* à croisillons; **sliding l. door,** porte à croisillons coulissante; **l. tower,** pylône *m* en treillis; *N.Arch:* **l. boom,** mât *m* de charge en treillis; **l. mast,** (i) *N.Arch:* mât en treillis; (ii) *Civ.E:* (*supporting electric wires, etc.*) pylône métallique; (*b*) lacis *m*, entrecroisement *m*; **l. of boughs,** lacis de branchages, entrecroisement de branches; (*c*) *A:* résille *f* (de vitrail); (*d*) *Her:* treillis. **2.** (*a*) *Cryst:* **crystal l.,** réseau cristallin; **l. defects,** défauts *m*, imperfections *f*, du réseau cristallin; **l. twin,** macle *f* à charnière multiple; (*b*) *Atom.Ph:* réseau *m* (de réacteur); **dry, wet, l.,** réseau sec, humide; **paired l.,** réseaux appariés; **l. arrangement, l. array,** disposition *f* du réseau; **l. design,** géométrie *f* du réseau; **l. calculation,** calcul *m* du, des, réseau(x); **l. constant, l. parameter, l. spacing,** constante *f* du réseau; **l. pitch,** pas *m* du réseau; **l. point,** point *m* du réseau; **l. sites,** nœuds *m* du réseau; **l. vacancy,** lacune *f* du réseau; **l. structure,** (i) structure *f* réticulaire; (ii) structure du réseau; **l. reactor,** réacteur *m* à réseau. **3.** *El:* **l.(-wound) coil,** bobine *f* en nid d'abeille; **l. network,** réseau maillé. **4.** *Geol:* **l. structure,** structure fenestrée; *Bot:* **l. leaf,** feuille fenestrée.

lattice[2], *v.tr.* treillager, treillisser (un mur, etc.).

latticed ['lætist], *a.* treillissé, treillagé; **l. boughs,** rameaux entrecroisés; **window l. with iron,** fenêtre grillagée de fer; **l. window,** fenêtre treillagée, treillissée.

latticing, latticework ['lætisiŋ, -wə:k], *s.* treillage *m*, treillis *m*; (*metal*) grillage *m*.

Latvia ['lætviə], *Pr.n.* Lettonie *f*, Latvia *f*, Latvie *f*.

Latvian ['lætviən]. **1.** *Geog:* (*a*) *a.* lettonien, letton, lette, latvien; **the L. Soviet Socialist Republic,** la République socialiste soviétique de Lettonie; (*b*) *s.* Lettonien, -ienne; Letton, -one; Lette *mf.* **2.** *s. Ling:* letton *m*, lettonien *m*, lette *m*.

laubanite ['lɔːbənait], *s. Miner:* laubanite *f.*

laud[1] [lɔːd], *s.* **1.** *Lit:* louange *f.* **2.** *pl. Ecc:* **lauds,** laudes *f.*

laud[2], *v.tr. Lit:* louer, panégyriser (qn); chanter les louanges de (qn); faire l'éloge de (qn); **to l. s.o. to the skies,** faire d'excessives louanges de qn.

laudability [lɔːdə'biliti], *s.* caractère *m* louable (**of,** de).

laudable ['lɔːdəbl], *a.* **1.** louable; digne de louanges; digne d'éloges. **2.** *Med: A:* (**pus** *m*) louable.

laudably ['lɔːdəbli], *adv.* louablement, d'une manière louable.

laudanum ['lɔːd(ə)nəm], *s. Pharm:* laudanum *m*; **containing l.,** laudanisé.

laudation [lɔː'deiʃ(ə)n], *s. Lit:* louange *f.*

laudative ['lɔːdətiv], *a. Lit:* = LAUDATORY.

laudator [lɔː'deitər], *s.* louangeur, -euse; laudateur, -trice.

laudatory ['lɔːdət(ə)ri], *a.* élogieux, louangeur, -euse; laudatif.

laugh[1] [lɑːf], *s.* rire *m*; **to burst into a (loud) l.,** éclater de rire; partir d'un éclat de rire; **to give a hearty l.,** rire de bon cœur; **to force a l., to give a forced l.,** rire du bout des dents, du bout des lèvres; rire faux, rire jaune; **he gave a short l.,** il a eu un court éclat de rire; **grating l.,** ricanement *m*; **with a l.,** en riant; **to join in the l.,** rire avec les autres; **we have had many a good l. over it,** cela nous a souvent fait rire; **he loves a l.,** il aime à rire; il aime la plaisanterie; **to raise a l.,** faire rire; **to raise a l. at one's own expense,** faire rire de soi; **to draw a l. from the audience,** arracher un rire à l'auditoire; **the l. was against him,** les rieurs étaient contre lui; *F:* **to do sth. for a l.,** faire qch. histoire de rire; *F:* **that's good for a l.!** histoire de rigoler un peu! *F:* **that's a l.!** quelle blague! c'est marrant! *F:* **to have, get, the l. of s.o.,** l'emporter sur qn; faire le poil à qn; *F:* **the laugh's on us,** c'est nous qui perdons; on nous a bien refaits.

laugh[2], *v.* **1.** *v.i.* rire; (*a*) **to l. heartily,** rire de bon cœur; **l. and the world laughs with you,** qui rit s'entoure d'amis; **to l. uproariously,** rire à gorge déployée, à ventre déboutonné; *F:* se crever de rire; **he's always laughing,** (i) il est très rieur; (ii) il ne fait que rire; **to l. and cry at the same time,** pleurer d'un œil et rire de l'autre; **to l. till one cries, till the tears come,** rire (jusqu')aux larmes; **to l. till one's sides ache,** rire à s'en tenir les côtes; **we laughed loud and long,** nous avons ri comme des fous; *F:* **it's enough to make a cat l.,** c'est à dérider un mort; **to l. to oneself,** rire tout seul; rire tout bas; *F:* **to l. all the way to the bank,** rire à la caisse; **to l. in, up, one's sleeve,** *A:* **in one's beard, inwardly,** rire sous cape; rire dans sa barbe; rire en dedans; **to l. in s.o.'s face,** rire au nez, à la barbe, de qn; *F:* **I soon made him l. on the wrong side of his face, on the wrong side of his mouth,** je lui ai bientôt fait passer son envie de rire; *F:* **don't make me l.!** laissez-moi rire! *Prov:* **he laughs best who laughs last,** rira bien qui rira le dernier; **l. today and cry tomorrow; l. on Friday, cry on Sunday,** tel qui rit vendredi dimanche pleurera; (*b*) **to l. at, over, sth.,** rire de qch.; **there's nothing to l. at,** il n'y a pas de quoi rire; ce n'est pas pour rire; **to l. at s.o.,** se moquer, (se) rire, s'amuser, se jouer, de qn; railler qn; **they simply laughed at him,** on lui a ri au nez; **to l. at s.o.'s threats,** (se) rire des menaces de qn; **I'm afraid of being laughed at,** j'ai peur de prêter à rire; **I won't be laughed at,** je ne souffrirai pas qu'on se moque de moi. **2.** *v.tr.* (*a*) *with cogn. acc.* **he laughed a bitter l.,** il eut un rire amer; **he laughed his approval,** il approuva en riant; (*b*) **to l. s.o. out of his bad humour; to l. s.o. back into good humour,** chasser la mauvaise humeur de qn, rendre à qn sa bonne humeur, à force de plaisanteries, en le faisant rire; **we laughed him out of it,** nous nous sommes tellement moqués de lui qu'il y a renoncé; **to l. down a proposal,** tuer une proposition par le ridicule, à force d'en rire; **to l. s.o. out of court,** se moquer des prétentions de qn; refuser d'écouter qn; *Lit:* **to l. s.o. to scorn,** accabler qn de ridicule; **he laughed the matter off,** il tourna la chose en plaisanterie; il a pris la chose en riant; **to l. a question aside,** traiter une question en plaisanterie; écarter une question en riant; **to l. away the time,** faire passer le temps à raconter des histoires joyeuses, des plaisanteries.

laughable ['lɑːfəbl], *a.* risible, comique, plaisant, ridicule; **l. offer,** offre *f* dérisoire.

laughableness ['lɑːfəb(ə)lnis], *s.* ridicule *m*, côté *m* comique (d'une situation, etc.).

laughably ['lɑːfəbli], *adv.* risiblement; d'une manière risible, comique.

laugher ['lɑːfər], *s.* rieur, -euse.

laughing[1] ['lɑːfiŋ], *a.* riant; rieur; *Orn:* **l. thrush,** garrulax *m*, grive-geai *f*; **black-gorgeted l. thrush,** garrulax à poitrine noire; **white-crested l. thrush,** garrulax à huppe blanche; **white-throated l. thrush,** garrulax à gorge blanche.

laughing[2], *s.* rires *mpl*; (*a*) **in a l. mood,** en humeur de rire; **I'm in no l. mood,** je n'ai pas le cœur à rire; **it's no l. matter,** il n'y a pas de quoi rire; cela ne prête pas à rire; (*b*) *Anat:* **l. muscle,** risorius *m*; (*c*) **l. gas,** gaz hilarant.

laughingly ['lɑːfiŋli], *adv.* en riant.

laughingstock ['lɑːfiŋstɔk], *s.* (objet *m* de) risée *f*; objet de raillerie; **to make a l. of oneself,** se faire moquer de soi.

laughter ['lɑːftər], *s.* rire(s) *m(pl)*; **peals of l.,** éclats *m* de rire; **to cause l.,** provoquer, exciter, les rires, l'hilarité *f*; **he made us cry with l.,** il nous a fait rire aux larmes; **to be convulsed, to shake, to rock, with l.,** se tordre de rire; rire à se tordre; se tenir les côtes de rire; *F:* se désopiler; rire comme un bossu; se rouler, se gondoler; **he convulsed them with l.,** il les faisait tordre, mourir, de rire; **to roar, shout, scream, with l.,** éclater de rire; rire aux éclats; rire à gorge déployée; s'esclaffer; *F:* **to split one's sides, die, with l.,** crever de rire; mourir de rire; **to be overcome with l., to be seized with uncontrollable l.,** avoir un accès de fou rire; être pris d'un rire convulsif; **uncontrollable fit of l.,** fou rire.

laumon(t)ite [lou'mɔn(t)ait], *s. Miner:* laumonite *f*, laumontite *f.*

launce [lɑːns], *s. Ich:* lançon *m*.

launch[1] [lɔːnʃ, *occ.* lɑːnʃ], *s. Nau:* chaloupe *f*; **motor l.,** vedette *f*; **police l.,** vedette de la police.

launch[2], *s.* **1.** (*a*) lancement *m*; *Space:* **l. window,** corridor *m* de lancement; **l. pad,** base *f* de lancement; (*b*) *N.Arch:* cale *f* de lancement. **2.** essor *m* (d'un oiseau).

launch[3]. **1.** *v.tr.* (*a*) lancer (*a missile, a blow, at s.o.*, un projectile, un coup, à qn); **to l. threats, censure, against s.o.,** proférer des menaces contre qn; se répandre en critiques contre qn; **to l. a proclamation,** lancer une proclamation; (*b*) *Nau:* lancer (un navire); mettre (un navire ou une embarcation) à l'eau, à la mer; **to l. a boat (from a ship),** débarquer un canot; mettre une embarcation à la mer; **to l. a torpedo,** lancer une torpille; **to l. a mine,** mouiller une mine; (*c*) lancer (qn, une affaire); **to l. an inquiry,** lancer une enquête; *Mil:* **to l. an offensive,** déclencher une offensive. **2.** *v.i.* (*a*) **to l. out at, against, s.o.,** (i) lancer un coup à qn; (ii) faire une sortie à, contre, qn; (*b*) **to l. out,** *Lit:* **to l. forth,** mettre à la mer; *B:* **l. out into the deep,** mène en pleine mer; **the first man to l. out beyond the Hebrides, into polar seas,** le premier homme qui a osé voguer au delà des Hébrides, dans les mers polaires; *Lit:* **to l. into eternity,** partir pour l'autre monde; **to l. out into life,** se lancer dans la vie; (*c*) **to l. out on an enterprise,** se lancer dans une affaire; **to l. out into explanations,** se répandre en explications; **to l. into abuse of s.o.,** se répandre en invectives contre qn; **once he is launched on this subject,** une fois lancé sur ce sujet; **to l. out (into expense),** se lancer dans la dépense; se mettre en frais.

launcher ['lɔːn(t)ʃər], *s.* (*a*) appareil *m*, dispositif *m*, de lancement; lanceur *m* (de projectiles, de fusées); *Mil:* **grenade l.,** lance-grenades *m inv* (à fusil); *Mil: etc:* **rocket l.,** lance-fusées *m inv*; *Mil.Av:* **airborne l.,** dispositif de lancement, lanceur (d'engins), aéroporté; (*b*) *Ball:* affût *m*, rampe *f*, plateforme *f*, de lancement (de fusées, de missiles); (*c*) *Av:* catapulte *f* de lancement (d'avions).

launching ['lɔːn(t)ʃiŋ, *occ.* 'lɑː-], *s.* lancement *m*. **1.** *Nau:* (*a*) lancement, mise *f* à l'eau (d'un navire); **end l.,** lancement en long; **side l.,** lancement en travers; **double-way l., two-way l.,** lancement sur flanc, sur double coulisse; **single-way l.,** lancement sur quille, sur savate; **ship completing after l.,** navire *m* en (cours d') achèvement à flot; **l. cradle,** berceau *m* de lancement; **l. drags,** bosses cassantes, chaînes *f* de retenue; **l. ways,** voie *f* de lancement, chemin *m* de glissement; *Av:* slip *m* (pour hydravions); (*b*) mise à l'eau (d'une embarcation logée à terre ou sur un navire); (*c*) *Navy:* lancement (d'une torpille); **l. carriage,** chariot *m* (de torpille). **2.** (*a*) *Ball:* lancement (d'un projectile, d'une fusée); **l. pad, l. platform,** plateforme *f* de lancement (de fusées, de missiles); **l. ramp,** rampe *f* de lancement; **l. rail,** rail *m* de lancement; **l. site,** (i) aire *f* de lancement, (ii) *esp. U.S:* base *f*, complexe *m*, station *f*, de lancement ou de tir (de fusées, de missiles); (*b*) *Av:* **catapult l.,** lancement (d'avions) par catapulte; **l. catapult,** catapulte *f* de lancement; **l. stand,** rampe *f* de lancement. **3.** (*a*) *Com: Fin:* lancement (d'une affaire, d'un emprunt, etc.); (*b*) *Mil:* **l. of an attack, of an offensive action,** déclenchement *m*, lancement, d'une attaque, d'une offensive.

launder[1] ['lɔːndər], *s. Min:* auge *f*, caniveau *m*.

launder[2], *v.tr.* blanchir (le linge); (*with passive force*) (*of fabric*) **to l. well, badly,** se laisser blanchir, ne pas se laisser blanchir.

launderable ['lɔːndrəbl], *a.* qui peut passer au blanchissage.

launderer ['lɔːndərər], *s.* blanchisseur, -euse.

launderette [lɔːndə'ret], *s.* laverie *f*, blanchisserie *f*, automatique.

laundering ['lɔːnd(ə)riŋ], *s.* blanchissage *m*; **fine l.,** blanchissage de fin.

laundress ['lɔːndres], *s.f.* **1.** blanchisseuse; **fine l.,** blanchisseuse de fin; repasseuse de linge fin. **2.** femme de charge (des études des *Inns of Court*).

laundromat ['lɔːndroumæt], *s. U.S:* laverie *f* automatique.

laundry ['lɔːndri], *s.* **1.** blanchisserie *f*; buanderie *f.* **2.** lessive *f*; linge (i) blanchi, (ii) à blanchir; **l. list,** liste *f* de blanchissage.

laundryman, *pl.* **-men** ['lɔːndrimən], *s.m.* (*a*) propriétaire d'une blanchisserie; (*b*) blanchisseur; (*c*) livreur (de blanchisserie).

Laura ['lɔːrə], *Pr.n.f.* Laure.

Lauraceae [lɔː'reisiiː], *s.pl. Bot:* lauracées *f.*

lauraceous [lɔː'reiʃəs], *a. Bot:* lauracé.

laureate[1] ['lɔːriət]. **1.** *a.* (*a*) *Num:* (buste, etc.) lauré; (*b*) lauréat; **poet l.** (*pl.* **poets laureate),** poète lauréat (dignité conférée par la Couronne). **2.** *s.* lauréat, -ate.

laureate[2] ['lɔːrieit], *v.tr. Sch: A:* conférer un grade honorifique à (qn).

laurel ['lɔrəl], *s.* **1.** *Bot:* (*a*) laurier *m*; **noble l., bay l.,** laurier commun, vrai, d'Apollon, des poètes; laurier-sauce *m*, *pl.* lauriers-sauce; (*b*) **Alexandrian l.,** (i) laurier d'Alexandrie, danaé *f*; (ii) calophyllum *m*; **big l.,** (i) (*or* **l. magnolia),** laurier-tulipier *m*, *pl.* lauriers-tulipiers; (ii) (*or* **great l.**), laurier des marais; **cherry l.,** laurier-cerise *m*, *pl.* lauriers-cerise(s); laurier amandier; **Japan(ese) l.,** aucuba *m*; **mountain l., American l.,** kalmie *f* à larges feuilles; **sheep l.,** kalmie à feuilles étroits; **Portugal l.,** laurier du Portugal; **rose l.,** (i) laurier-rose *m*, *pl.* lauriers-rose(s); (ii) laurier des marais; **spurge l., wood l.,** daphné *m* lauréole, lauréole *f*, laurier des bois. **2. l. wreath,** couronne *f* de lauriers; **crowned with laurel(s),** couronné, ceint, de lauriers; **to reap, win, laurels,** cueillir, moissonner, des lauriers; faire une moisson de lauriers; **to rest on one's laurels,** se reposer sur ses lauriers; **he must look to his laurels,** il est en passe d'être éclipsé.

laurelled ['lɔrəld], *a.* couronné, ceint, de lauriers, lauré.

Laurence ['lɔrəns]. *Pr.n.m.* Laurent.

Laurentian [lɔ'renʃən], *a.* laurentien; **the L. Shield,** le bouclier canadien.

Laurentide ['lɔːrəntaid], *a. Can: Geog:* laurentien.

lauric ['lɔ(ː)rik], *a. Ch:* laurique.

laurinoxylon [lɔri'nɔksilɔn], *s. Paleont:* laurinoxylon *m*.

laurionite ['lɔ(ː)riənait], *s. Miner:* laurionite *f.*

laurite ['lɔ(ː)rait], *s. Miner:* laurite *f.*

laurustine ['lɔrəstain], **laurustinus** [lɔrəs'tainəs], *s. Bot:* laurier-thym *m*, *pl.* lauriers-thym; laurier-tin *m*, *pl.* lauriers-tin.

laurvikite ['lau(ə)vikait], *s. Miner:* laurvikite *f.*

lav [læv], *s. F:* petit endroit, cabinets *mpl.*

lava ['lɑːvə], *s.* lave *f*; **basic, vitreous, l.,** lave basique, vitreuse; **cellular l.,** scories *f* volcaniques; **l. stream, l. flow,** coulée *f* de lave; coulée lavique; nappe éruptive; **l. field,** champ *m* de lave.

lavabo, *pl.* **-os,** *s.* (*a*) [lə'veibou, -ouz], *Ecc:* lavabo *m*; (*b*) ['lævəbou, -ouz], *Dom.Ec: NAm:* lavabo.

lavage ['lævɑːʒ], *s. Med:* lavage *m*.

lavatera [lævə'tiərə], *s. Bot:* lavatère *f.*

lavation [lə'veiʃ(ə)n], *s.* lavage *m*; ablution *f.*

lavatory ['lævətri], *s.* **1.** *A:* & *NAm:* (*a*) cabinet *m* de toilette; (*b*) lavabo *m*. **2.** (*a*) cabinets *mpl*; **(public) l.,** toilette *f*; (*b*) ensemble W.C.; **l. pan,** cuvette *f* de W.C.

lave [leiv], *v.tr.* **1.** *Lit:* laver (les mains, etc.); (*of stream, sea*) baigner, laver (un pré, le rivage); arroser (un pré). **2.** *Med:* bassiner (une plaie).

lavement [leivmənt], *s. Med: A:* lavement *m*.

lavender ['lævindər]. **1.** *s. Bot:* lavande *f*; **true l.,** lavande vraie, lavande femelle; **French l., spike l., great l., common l.,** lavande commune, mâle, officinale; *F:* aspic *m*, spic *m*; **sea l.,** statice *m*; **oil of l.,** essence *f* de lavande; **l. cotton,** santoline *f*; aurone *f* femelle; **l. growing,** lavandiculture *f*; **l. water,** eau *f* de lavande. **2.** *a.* (*colour*) lavande *inv*; *Cin:* **l. print,** copie *f* lavande.

lavenite ['lævənait], *s. Miner:* lavenite *f.*

laver[1] ['leivər], *s. Algae:* varech *m* comestible.

laver[2], *s.* **1.** *B:* cuve *f* (du temple de Salomon). **2.** *A:* & *Lit:* aiguière *f.*

laverock ['lævərək], *s. Lit:* alouette *f.*

Lavinia [lə'viniə], *Pr.n.f.* Lavinie.

lavish[1] ['læviʃ], *a.* **1.** (*of pers.*) prodigue (**in, of,** de); **to be l. in, of, praises,** prodiguer des louanges; être prodigue de louanges; se prodiguer en éloges; **he is not l. with his praise,** il ne prodigue pas les éloges; **to be l. with one's apologies,** se confondre en excuses; **l. in spending,** prodigue de son argent. 2. (*of thg*) somptueux; abondant; **l. meal,** repas plantureux; **l. expenditure,** dépenses folles; **l. installation,** installation princière; **to live in a l. style,** mener la vie à grandes guides.

lavish[2], *v.tr.* prodiguer (son argent); répandre (son argent, l'aumône, etc.); **to l. sth. on s.o.,** prodiguer qch. à qn; **she lavishes herself on her children,** elle se prodigue pour ses enfants.

lavishly ['læviʃli], *adv.* avec prodigalité; à pleines mains; **to spend l.,** dépenser de l'argent à profusion, à poignée(s), à pleine(s) main(s); dépenser sans compter; être prodigue de son argent.

lavishness ['læviʃnis], *s.* prodigalité *f.*

law[1] [lɔː], *s.* 1. (*a*) loi *f*; **to pass a l.,** voter une loi; **to repeal a l.,** abroger une loi; **the laws in force,** la législation en vigueur; **labour laws,** législation du travail; (*b*) loi (de la nature, etc.); **organic l.,** loi organique; *Ch:* **Avogadro's l.,** loi d'Avogadro; **l. of definite, of constant, proportions,** loi des proportions constantes; **l. of multiple proportions,** loi des proportions multiples; **l. of mass action,** loi de l'action de masse; *Ph:* **distribution l.,** loi de distribution, de répartition (des vitesses, etc.); **the laws of gravity,** les lois de la pesanteur; *Atom.Ph:* **radiation l.,** loi de radiation; **radioactive decay l.,** loi de la décroissance radioactive; *El:* **Ampère's l., Faraday's l.,** loi d'Ampère, loi de Faraday; *Mth:* **l. of sines, of cosines,** loi des sinus, des cosinus; **exponential l.,** loi exponentielle; *Pol.Ec:* **l. of supply and demand,** loi de l'offre et de la demande; **l. of diminishing returns,** loi des rendements décroissants; **Gresham's l.,** loi de Gresham; *Ling:* **Grimm's l.,** loi de Grimm; (*c*) *Phil: etc:* principe *m*; **l. of causation, of causality,** principe de causalité; **l. of contradiction, of identity,** principe de contradiction, d'identité; (*d*) **laws of a game,** règles d'un jeu. 2. (*a*) **the l.,** la loi; **to put the l. into force, to carry out the l.,** appliquer la loi; **the l. forbids, allows, it,** la loi le défend, le permet; **to keep the l.,** observer la loi; **to break the l.,** enfreindre la loi; **as the l. at present stands,** en l'état actuel de la législation; **custom that has become l.,** usage *m* qui a passé en loi; **to have the force of l.,** faire loi, avoir force de loi; **to give a measure the force of l.,** consacrer une mesure en droit; **judgment possessing force of l.,** décision ayant force de chose jugée; *A:* **the King's will is l.,** si veut le roi, si veut la loi; **his word is l.,** sa parole fait loi, a force de loi; ses ordres font loi; c'est lui qui donne la loi; on ne jure que par lui; *F:* c'est la loi et les prophètes; **to lay down the l.,** (i) expliquer la loi; (ii) faire la loi (à qn); **he loves laying down the l.,** il aime pontifier, dogmatiser, sur tout; il tranche sur tout; **he thinks he's above the l.,** il se croit tout permis; **to be a l. unto oneself,** n'en faire qu'à sa tête; *Prov:* **necessity, hunger, has no l., knows no l.,** nécessité n'a point de loi; la faim chasse le loup des bois; **to have one l. for the rich and another for the poor,** avoir deux poids et deux mesures; (*b*) **Divine l.,** la loi divine; (*c*) *Rel.H:* **the L., the l. of Moses,** la loi mosaïque. 3. droit *m*; **civil l.** = droit civil; **common l.,** (i) droit coutumier; (ii) droit civil; **criminal l.,** droit pénal, criminel; législation criminelle; **commercial l., mercantile l., l. merchant,** droit commercial; code *m* de commerce; **air l.,** droit aérien; **maritime l.,** droit maritime; **naval l.,** loi navale; **international l.,** droit international; **l. of nations,** droit des gens; **l. of contract** = droit des obligations; **municipal l.,** droit national; **Roman l.,** droit romain; **statute l.,** droit écrit; **case l.,** droit jurisprudentiel; **statutory l.,** droit légal; **substantive l.,** droit positif; **judgment quashed on a point of l.,** arrêt cassé pour vice de forme; **to read, study, l.,** étudier le droit, faire son droit; **l. student,** étudiant, -ante, en droit; **Bachelor, Doctor, of Laws** = licencié(e), docteur, en droit; **to practise l.,** exercer une profession juridique; **L. Society,** organisation de *solicitors* qui cumule à l'échelle nationale les fonctions de Chambre des Notaires et Chambre des Avoués; **l. officer,** conseiller *m* juridique; **l. lord,** membre *m* juriste de la Chambre des Lords; *Scot:* **l. agent** = avoué *m*. 4. (*a*) (*justice*) **court of l.,** cour *f* de justice; tribunal *m*, -aux; **to go to l.,** avoir recours à la justice; recourir à la justice; aller en justice; **to settle a matter without going to l.,** arranger une affaire à l'amiable; **to come to an arrangement is better than going to l.,** s'arranger vaut mieux que plaider; **to go to l. with s.o.,** citer, poursuivre, qn en justice; faire, intenter, un procès à qn; *P:* **I'll have the l. on you!** je vais vous poursuivre en justice; **to have recourse to the l.,** employer les voies judiciaires; **to put the l. into motion,** mettre en jeu l'appareil de la loi; faire agir la loi; **to come under the l.,** tomber sous le coup de la loi; **to hand s.o. over to the l.,** remettre qn à la justice; **action at l.,** action *f* en justice; **to be at l.,** être en procès; **to take the l. into one's own hands,** (i) se faire justice à soi-même; (ii) passer outre à la loi; agir de soi-même sans avoir recours à la justice; **the l. had its way,** la justice suivit son cours; *Adm: Com:* **l. department,** bureau *m*, service *m*, du contentieux; le contentieux; **l. costs,** frais *mpl* de procédure; (*b*) *F:* **the l.,** (i) la police; (ii) un policier, un flic; **limb of the l.,** représentant *m* de la loi. 5. (*a*) *Sp: Ven:* **to give (fair) l. to . . .,** donner de l'avance à . . .; laisser . . . prendre du champ; (*b*) **to give s.o. three day's l.,** accorder à qn trois jours de grâce.

law[2], **laws** [lɔː(z)], *int. P:* (= *Lord*) mon Dieu! Seigneur!

law-abiding ['lɔːəbaidiŋ], *a.* respectueux des lois; soumis aux lois; qui observe la loi; **l.-a. people,** amis *m* de l'ordre.

lawbook ['lɔːbuk], *s.* livre *m* de droit.

lawbreaker ['lɔːbreikər], *s.* transgresseur *m* de la loi; violateur, -trice, infracteur, -trice, de la loi.

lawbreaking ['lɔːbreikiŋ], *s.* infraction *f* à la loi.

lawcourt ['lɔːkɔːt], *s.* cour *f* de justice; tribunal *m*.

lawful ['lɔːf(u)l], *a.* légal, -aux. 1. permis, licite; **l. trade,** trafic *m* licite. 2. (droit *m*, union *f*, enfant *m*, etc.) légitime; (contrat *m*) valide; **l. currency,** cours légal; (*of inheritance*) **l. share,** portion virile; *Jur:* **l. day,** jour *m* utile. 3. (revendication *f*, etc.) juste. 4. *occ.* = LAW-ABIDING.

lawfully ['lɔːfuli], *adv.* légalement; légitimement.

lawfulness ['lɔːf(u)lnis], *s.* légalité *f*; légitimité *f*.

lawgiver ['lɔːgivər], *s.* législateur *m*; **the lawgivers of the nation,** les sénateurs *m* de la nation.

lawk(s) [lɔːk(s)], *int. P:* = LAW[2].

lawless ['lɔːlis], *a.* 1. sans loi; **l. times,** temps *m* d'anarchie. 2. sans frein; déréglé, désordonné.

lawlessness ['lɔːlisnis], *s.* dérèglement *m*, désordre *m*, licence *f*; anarchie *f*.

lawmaker ['lɔːmeikər], *s.* législateur *m*.

lawn[1] [lɔːn], *s.* 1. *Tex:* batiste *f*; (*fine*) linon *m*; **bishop's surplice with sleeves of l.,** surplis *m* d'évêque avec manches en linon. 2. *F: A:* **the l.,** l'épiscopat *m*. 3. *Cer:* **l. sieve,** tamis fin.

lawn[2], *s.* pelouse *f*; (parterre *m* de) gazon *m*; **l. sweeper,** balayeuse mécanique (pour pelouses); **l. sprinkler,** arrosoir *m* de pelouse; tourniquet arroseur; *U.S:* **l. party,** garden-party *f*, réception *f* en plein air; *Bot:* **l. grass,** gramen *m*, *F:* herbette *f*.

lawnmower ['lɔːnmouər], *s.* tondeuse *f* (de gazon).

Lawrence ['lɔrəns], *s. Pr.n.m.* Laurent; *F:* **a (lazy) L.,** un fainéant.

lawrencite ['lɔrənsait], *s. Miner:* laurencite *f*.

lawsonite ['lɔːsənait], *s. Miner:* lawsonite *f*.

lawsuit ['lɔːsjuːt], *s.* procès *m*; poursuites *f* judiciaires; action *f* judiciaire; *F:* affaire *f*; **to engage in a l.,** engager un procès; **to bring a l. against s.o.,** intenter un procès à qn.

lawyer ['lɔːjər], *s.* 1. homme *m* de loi; juriste *m*; jurisconsulte *m*; = (i) avocat *m*, (ii) avoué *m*, (iii) notaire *m*; **common l.** = civiliste *mf*; **poor man's l.,** avocat (dédommagé par l'État) qui donne des consultations gratuites; *F:* **barrackroom l.,** chicaneur *m*, mauvais coucheur, râleur *m*; *Prov:* **a good l. makes a bad neighbour,** bon avocat, mauvais voisin. 2. *F: A:* **Penang l.,** canne *f* de palmier à fruits épines (avec laquelle on dit que l'on réglait les différends à Penang).

lax [læks], *a.* 1. (*a*) (*of conduct, principles*) relâché; (*of pers.*) négligent, inexact; (discipline *f*) lâche; (gouvernement) mou; **l. morals,** morale facile, peu sévère; mœurs débraillées; **l. conscience,** conscience *f* élastique; **to be l. in (carrying out) one's duties,** ne pas toujours observer ses devoirs; être inexact à remplir ses devoirs; **to be l. in one's conduct,** avoir une conduite peu régulière; **to become l.,** se relâcher; **l. attendance,** irrégularité *f* de présence; (*b*) (*of ideas, interpretation, etc.*) vague; peu exact; **l. use of a word,** emploi peu exact, peu précis, d'un mot; emploi abusif d'un mot. 2. (*limp*) mou, *f.* molle; flasque. 3. *Med:* (ventre) lâche, relâché. 4. *Bot:* (inflorescence *f*, etc.) lâche.

laxative ['læksətiv], *a. & s. Med:* laxatif (*m*), cathartique (*m*); *a.* solutif.

laxism ['læksizm], *s. Phil:* laxisme *m*.

laxist ['læksist], *s. Phil:* laxiste *mf*.

laxity ['læksiti], *s.* 1. (*a*) relâchement *m* (des mœurs, de la discipline); **l. in one's duties,** inexactitude *f* à remplir ses devoirs; **the l. of his predecessor,** la mollesse de son prédécesseur; (*b*) vague *m*, imprécision *f*, peu *m* d'exactitude (de langage, etc.). 2. flaccidité *f*, mollesse, laxité *f* (de tissu, etc.). 3. *Med:* relâchement (du ventre).

laxly ['læksli], *adv.* 1. (*a*) négligemment; peu rigoureusement; (*b*) vaguement, sans exactitude. 2. mollement, flasquement.

lay[1] [lei], *s.* 1. lai *m*, chanson *f*. 2. poème *m* (lyrique). 3. poème, chant, récité par un ménestrel.

lay[2], *a.* 1. laïque, lai; (*a*) *Ecc:* **l. brother,** frère lai, frère convers, frère servant; **l. sister,** sœur laie, sœur converse; **l. clerk,** chantre *m*; **l. reader, preacher,** prédicateur laïque; (*b*) **l. lord,** membre *m* de la Chambre des Lords qui n'est pas juriste; **to the l. mind it seems complicated,** aux yeux du profane cela est compliqué. 2. *Cards:* **l. suit,** couleur autre que celle d'atout. 3. *Com: Nau:* **l. days,** jours *m* de planche; jours de starie; (jours d')estarie *f*; temps *m* d'escale (accordé en vertu de la charte-partie); **extra l. days,** jours de surestarie. 4. **l. figure,** (i) *Art:* mannequin *m* (en bois, etc.); (ii) mannequin; personnage *m* (de roman, etc.) sans individualité; fantoche *m*.

lay[3], *s.* 1. *P:* genre *m* d'affaires, spécialité *f*; **that's not my l.,** ce n'est pas de ma partie; **he isn't on his old l.,** il n'est plus à son ancienne occupation. 2. tors *m*, commettage *m* (d'un cordage). 3. **l. of the land,** configuration *f*, disposition *f*, du pays, du terrain; accidents *mpl* de terrain; **to steer by the l. of the land,** gouverner d'après la configuration de la côte. 4. *Typ:* **to mark the l. on a page,** repérer une page; **good l., bad l.,** bon, mauvais, repérage; **l. mark,** repère *m*. 5. *Nau:* (*whaling*) part *f* (des bénéfices de la pêche); **to be on the hundredth l.,** avoir droit à un centième de la pêche; **by the l.,** à la part. 6. *Ost:* huîtrière *f*. 7. **hens in full l.,** poules *f* en pleine ponte. 8. (*a*) *Mus:* table *f* (de bec de clarinette); (*b*) *Mec.E: Aut:* **l. shaft,** arbre *m* intermédiaire (de changement de vitesse); arbre de couche, de renvoi. 9. *P:* (*a*) **to have a l.,** coucher avec, s'envoyer, une femme; (*b*) femelle *f*; **she's an easy l.,** c'est une môme facile, une Marie-couche-toi-là; elle a la cuisse hospitalière.

lay[4], *v.* **(laid [leid]; laid)**

I. *v.tr.* 1. coucher; (*a*) (*with complement*) **to l. s.o., sth., low, flat,** (i) coucher, étendre, qn, qch. (par terre); (ii) terrasser, abattre, qn; **a bullet laid him low,** une balle l'étendit mort; **to l. (a building, etc.) in ashes,** réduire (un bâtiment, etc.) en cendres; **to l. low an empire,** mettre à bas un empire; **laid low by sickness,** terrassé par la maladie; (*b*) (*of wind, rain*) coucher, verser, abattre (le blé); (*c*) *Needlew:* remplier (un ourlet, etc.); (*d*) *P:* **to l. a girl,** s'envoyer une fille. 2. (*cause to subside*) (*a*) abattre (la poussière, les vagues, etc.); *Prov:* **small rain lays great dust,** petite pluie abat grand vent; (*b*) exorciser, conjurer (un fantôme); *O:* **to l. s.o.'s fears,** dissiper les craintes de qn; **to l. a bogey,** écarter à tout jamais un sujet d'inquiétude, un cauchemar; (*c*) *Nau:* **to l. the land,** noyer la terre. 3. (*deposit*) mettre, placer, poser (**sth. on sth.,** qch. sur qch.); **to l. one's hand on s.o.'s shoulder,** mettre la main sur l'épaule de qn; **to l. a book on the table,** poser un livre sur la table; **to l. one's head on the pillow,** mettre, poser, sa tête sur l'oreiller; **to have nowhere to l. one's head,** ne pas avoir où reposer la tête; ne pas avoir de gîte; **to l. a child to sleep,** coucher un enfant; **to l. s.o. to rest, in the grave,** mettre, coucher, qn au tombeau; déposer qn dans le tombeau; ensevelir qn; **to l. one's homage at s.o.'s feet,** déposer ses hommages aux pieds de qn. 4. (*of hen, etc.*) pondre (un œuf); *v.i.* **hen beginning to l. again,** poule qui commence à repondre. 5. faire (un pari); parier (une somme); mettre (un enjeu, une somme); **to l. so much on a horse,** mettre, parier, miser, tant sur un cheval; **to l. ten pounds,** y aller de dix livres; **to l. 5 francs on a colour,** miser 5 francs sur une couleur. 6. (*place*) (*a*) **to l. a spark to the train,** mettre le feu aux poudres; **to l. a ship alongside (the quay),** accoster un navire le long du quai; **to l. the hounds on the scent,** mettre les chiens sur la voie; (*b*) *Artil: Ball:* pointer (une arme à feu, un missile, etc.) (**on,** sur); **to l. a gun on a target,** pointer une pièce sur un objectif; **to l. a gun by quadrant,** pointer une pièce au niveau; **to l. for elevation,** pointer en hauteur; **to l. for line,** pointer en direction. 7. soumettre (une question, une demande) (**before s.o.,** devant qn); exposer (les faits); **he laid before me all the facts of the case,** il me présenta tous les faits; **to l. complete information before the House,** donner connaissance à la Chambre de tous les faits; *Jur:* **to l. a complaint,** déposer une plainte; porter plainte; **to l. a matter before the court,** saisir le tribunal d'une affaire; **to l. an information,** présenter une information. 8. (*a*) imposer (une peine, une obligation, une charge) (**upon s.o.,** à qn); infliger (une amende, etc.); **the obligation laid on him,** l'obligation à lui imposée; (*b*) **to l. a tax on sth.,** mettre un impôt sur qch.; frapper qch. d'un impôt; (*c*) *O:* **to l. a stick on s.o.'s back, to l. (it) on s.o.,** *P:* **to l. into s.o.,** rosser qn; rouer qn de coups; taper ferme sur qn; **to l. about one,** frapper de tous côtés; frapper d'estoc et de taille; s'escrimer; frapper, taper, comme un sourd. 9. (*dispose, arrange*) (*a*) poser, jeter, asseoir (des fondements); ranger (des briques); poser (une voie ferrée); poser, immerger (un câble); verser (le béton) en place; to **l. the table, the cloth,** mettre, dresser, le couvert; mettre la nappe; mettre la table; **to l. for three,** mettre la table pour trois personnes; mettre trois couverts; **to l. a carpet,** poser, tendre, un tapis; **to l. the fire,** préparer le feu; **well laid road,** route solidement établie; *Nau:* **to l. a deck,** border un pont; *Navy:* **to l. a mine,** poser, mouiller, une mine; (*b*) dresser, tendre (un piège); disposer, dresser, placer, tendre (une embuscade); (*c*) former, faire (un projet); former, ourdir, tramer, concerter (un complot); (*d*) *Th:* **the scene is laid in Paris,** la scène se passe à Paris; (*e*) *Nau:* **to l. the course,** tracer, donner, la route; (*f*) *Agr:* **the laid places (in a field),** les endroits versés (dans un champ). **10.** *Ropem:* commettre (un cordage); **back-laid,** commis de droite à gauche.

II. *v.i. P:* (*incorrectly used for* **lie**) **to l. in bed,** rester couché.

III. (*compound verbs*) **1. lay aside,** *v.tr.* enlever, quitter (un vêtement); se dépouiller de (ses vêtements, ses préjugés, sa réserve); abandonner, mettre de côté (un travail); écarter (un papier); mettre (un papier) de côté; remiser (qch.); épargner (de l'argent); mettre (de l'argent) de côté; déposer (la couronne); **to l. one's sword aside,** pendre, mettre, son épée au croc; **to l. aside all ambition,** se désintéresser de toute ambition; **laying aside all personal feeling,** faisant abstraction de tout sentiment personnel.

2. lay away, *v.tr.* (*a*) *Tan:* mettre (les peaux) en potée; (*b*) **hen that lays away,** poule qui pond loin du nid.

3. lay back, *v.tr.* retourner, rabattre (qch.); **the horse laid back its ears,** le cheval rabattit, coucha, les oreilles.

4. lay by, *v.tr.* mettre (qch.) de côté; réserver (qch.); **to l. money by,** faire des économies; mettre de l'argent en réserve (pour l'avenir); mettre de l'argent de côté.

5. lay down. (*a*) *v.tr.* (i) déposer, poser (qch.); **to l. down one's arms,** mettre bas, rendre, les armes; *Cards:* **to l. down one's hand,** étaler, abattre, son jeu; (ii) coucher, étendre (qn); **to l. oneself down,** se coucher; (iii) quitter, se démettre de, résigner (ses fonctions); abdiquer, résigner (le pouvoir); (iv) **to l. down one's life,** donner, sacrifier, sa vie, faire le sacrifice de sa vie (**for,** pour); **we would l. down our lives for each other,** c'est entre nous à la vie, à la mort; (v) **to l. down a ship,** mettre un navire en chantier; mettre un navire sur cale; poser la quille; **to l. down a railway,** asseoir, établir, poser, une voie ferrée; (vi) poser, imposer, établir, instituer, formuler (un principe, une règle); fixer (des conditions); spécifier (des fonctions); tracer, indiquer, prescrire (une ligne de conduite); **the doctrine laid down by Monroe,** le principe posé par Monroe; **to l. down general rules,** arrêter des dispositions générales; **I l. it down as an absolute rule to . . .,** je m'impose comme règle absolue de . . .; **to l. it down (as a principle) that . . .,** poser en principe que . . .; **to l. down that . . .,** stipuler que . . .; spécifier que . . .; **to l. down conditions to s.o.,** imposer des conditions à qn; (vii) tracer, marquer (qch. sur une carte, un plan); **to l. down a map of the district,** lever le plan, dresser la carte, de la région; *Nau:* **to l. down a coast,** relever une côte; (viii) **to l. down land to, under, with, grass,** mettre du terrain en pré; (ix) mettre (du vin) en cave, sur chantier; parquer (des huîtres); (*b*) *v.i.* (i) *P:* = LIE DOWN; (ii) (*of prosecutor*) **to l. down on a charge,** retirer une plainte.

6. lay in, *v.tr.* (*a*) faire provision, s'approvisionner, de (qch.); **to l. in provisions,** faire des provisions; *Com:* **to l. in goods, stock,** emmagasiner des marchandises; (*b*) *Nau:* **to l. in the oars,** rentrer les avirons; (*c*) *Hort:* (i) mettre en jauge (les jeunes plantes); (ii) diriger, conduire (une plante).

7. lay off. (*a*) *v.tr.* (i) licencier, congédier, renvoyer temporairement (des ouvriers); mettre (une chaudière) en repos; (ii) *Nau:* **to l. off a bearing,** porter un relèvement (sur la carte); **to l. off a line of position on the chart,** tracer une droite de hauteur sur la carte; (iii) *Ins:* **to l. off a risk,** effectuer une réassurance; *Turf: etc:* **to l. off a bet,** faire la contre-partie d'un pari; (iv) *Fb:* **to l. off a ball to s.o.,** faire une passe à qn; (*b*) *v.i.* (i) *F:* se reposer; prendre, s'offrir, un congé; *P:* **l. off!** fiche-moi la paix! laisse tomber! (ii) *Nau:* rester au large.

8. lay on, *v.tr.* (*a*) étendre, coucher, appliquer (un enduit, etc.); *Art:* **to l. on the paint,** peindre dans la pâte, en pleine pâte; **to l. the colour on too thick,** ne pas ménager les couleurs; *F:* **to l. it on,** ne pas y aller de main morte; *F:* **to l. it on thick, with a trowel,** (i) flatter qn grossièrement; ne pas épargner les compliments; ne pas y aller avec le dos de la cuiller; (ii) faire (qch.) à l'excès; exagérer; en remettre; *Typ:* **to l. on colours,** toucher des couleurs; (*b*) (i) **to l. on the lash,** appliquer le fouet; (ii) *v.i. F: O:* porter des coups; frapper; (*c*) (i) installer (le gaz, l'électricité); amener (l'eau, le gaz) (dans la maison); **(bed)room with water laid on,** chambre *f* avec eau courante; (ii) *F:* arranger, préparer, organiser (qch.); **I'll l. on (a) dinner,** je vais arranger un dîner; **I'll l. on a car for you at the station,** je vais vous faire chercher en voiture à la gare; (*d*) *Typ:* marger (une feuille à tirer); (*e*) (i) **to l. on a bloodhound,** mettre un limier sur la piste; (ii) *Ven:* laisser courre (les chiens).

9. lay out, *v.tr.* **1.** arranger, disposer (des objets); étaler, déployer (des marchandises); servir (un repas); **his clothes were laid out on the bed,** ses vêtements étaient préparés sur le lit; *Nau:* **to l. out a cable, an anchor,** élonger, mouiller, un câble, une ancre. **2.** (*a*) ensuairer (un mort); faire la toilette (d'un mort); (*b*) *F:* étendre (qn) d'un coup; coucher (qn) par terre, sur le carreau; mettre (qn) hors de combat; aplatir (qn); *Box:* envoyer (l'adversaire) au tapis. **3. to l. out money,** dépenser, débourser, de l'argent; faire des débours. **4.** dresser, tracer, aligner, marquer (un camp); dessiner, disposer (un jardin); tracer, planter (une avenue); tracer (une courbe); faire le tracé (d'une route); construire (une route); aménager (un champ de mines); **to l. out a piece of (building) work,** mettre un travail en chantier. **5. to l. oneself out to make everyone feel at ease,** faire de son mieux, se mettre en frais, se dépenser, pour mettre tout le monde à l'aise; **to l. oneself out to please,** chercher à plaire.

10. lay over. *NAm:* (*a*) *v.tr.* (i) remettre, renvoyer à plus tard (un projet, etc.); (ii) *F:* surpasser (qn, qch.); (*b*) *v.i.* faire étape, passer la nuit (dans un endroit).

11. lay up, *v.tr.* (*a*) mettre (qch.) en réserve; accumuler, amasser (des provisions, etc.); **to l. up sth. for a rainy day,** garder une poire pour la soif; **you are laying up trouble for yourself,** vous vous apprêtez bien des ennuis; (*b*) désarmer, déséquiper (un navire); mettre (un navire) en rade; dérader (des bateaux de pêche); **to l. up a car,** mettre une voiture sur cales; (*c*) **to be laid up,** être alité, obligé de garder le lit; (*d*) déposer; *Mil:* **to l. up the colours,** déposer un drapeau (quand un régiment est dissous).

layabout ['leiəbaut], *s. F:* paresseux *m*; vaurien *m*.

layaway ['leiəwei], *s. Tan:* **l. pit,** fosse *f* de potée.

layby ['leibai], *s.* **1.** (*a*) (*on river*) gare *f*; (*b*) *Rail:* voie *f* de garage; (*c*) (*on road*) garage *m*; terre-plein *m*, bande *f*, de stationnement; (*on motorway*) = aire *f* (de stationnement). **2.** *A:* économies *fpl*, épargne *f*.

layer¹ ['leiər], *s.* **1.** (*pers.*) (*a*) poseur *m* (de tuyaux, de rails, de dalles, etc.); tendeur *m* (de pièges); **l. out,** (i) dessinateur *m* (de jardins, etc.); (ii) ensuaireuse *f*, ensevelisseuse *f* (d'un mort); *Typ:* **l. on,** margeur *m*, pointeur *m*; (*b*) *Artil:* pointeur; (*c*) *Rac:* **layers and backers,** parieurs *m* contre et pour. **2.** (*hen, etc.*) **good l.,** bonne pondeuse. **3.** (*a*) couche *f* (de peinture, etc.); **a l. of manure,** un lit de fumier; **a l. of natural gas,** une nappe de gaz naturel; **there was a l. of oil over the engine,** une buée d'huile couvrait le moteur; *Cu:* **alternate layers of potatoes and minced meat,** des lits alternés de pommes de terre et de hachis de viande; **l. cake,** gâteau fourré de couches de crème; *F:* **bundled up in l. upon l. of clothes,** vêtu comme un oignon; (*b*) **the upper layers of the atmosphere,** les couches supérieures, les hautes couches, de l'atmosphère; **friction l.,** couche de frottement; **Heaviside l.,** couche de Heaviside; **Appleton l.,** couche d'Appleton; *Oc:* **deep scattering, surface scattering, l.,** couche diffusante profonde, en surface; *Aedcs:* **(laminar, turbulent) boundary l.,** couche limite (laminaire, tourbillonnaire); (*c*) *El:* **barrier l., blocking l.,** couche d'arrêt; **conducting l.,** couche conductrice; **magnetic l.,** feuillet *m* magnétique; **l. winding,** bobinage *m* en couches; (*d*) *Phot: etc:* **antihalo l.,** couche anti-halo; **sensitive l.,** couche sensible; (*e*) *Anat:* **cortical l.,** couche corticale; **horny l., keratinous l.,** couche cornée; (*f*) *Const:* assise *f*, lit (de béton, de briques, etc.); *Geol:* couche, assise, strate *f* (de roches, etc.); **underlying l.,** sous-couche *f*, *pl.* sous-couches; (*g*) *Mapm:* **hypsometric l.,** teinte *f* hypsométrique; **l. colouring,** système *m* de teintes hypsométriques; **l. step,** équidistance *f* des teintes hypsométriques. **4.** *Hort:* marcotte *f*; provin *m* (de vigne); **l. stool,** pied *m* mère. **5.** *Agr:* (*a*) champ *m* de trèfle; (*b*) plage *f* de blé versé. **6.** *A:* huîtrière *f*; parc *m* à huîtres.

layer². **1.** *v.tr.* (*a*) poser, disposer, en couches; (*b*) *Hort:* marcotter (un rosier, etc.); provigner (une vigne). **2.** *v.i.* (*of wheat, etc.*) se coucher; (se) verser.

layered ['leiəd], *a.* **1.** (roche, etc.) en couches, en strates. **2.** *Mapm:* (carte *f*) avec teintes hypsométriques.

layette [lei'et], *s.* layette *f*.

laying¹ ['leiiŋ], *a.* **l. hen,** poule pondeuse.

laying², *s.* **1.** pose *f* (de rails, de tuyaux, de câbles, etc.); assise *f* (de fondements); immersion *f* (d'un câble sous-marin); commettage *m* (d'un cordage); mouillage *m* (d'une mine). **2.** ponte *f* (des œufs). **3.** *Artil: Ball:* pointage *m* (d'une arme à feu, d'un missile, etc.); **direct, indirect, l.,** pointage direct, indirect; **l. for line, for elevation,** pointage en direction, en hauteur. **4.** (*a*) *Tan:* **l. away,** mise *f* en potée; (*b*) **l. down,** (i) établissement *m* (d'un principe, etc.); (ii) pose *f* (d'une canalisation, d'un câble); assiette *f* (d'un ligne); mise en chantier, sur cale (d'un navire); (iii) dépôt *m* (des armes); (*c*) **l. in,** emmagasinage *m* (de marchandises); approvisionnement *m*; (*d*) **l. off,** (i) licenciement *m* (de la main-d'œuvre); mise en repos (d'une machine); (ii) *Ins:* réassurance *f*; (*e*) **l. on,** (i) application *f* (d'un enduit, etc.); (ii) installation *f* (de l'eau, etc.); *Ecc:* **l.-on of hands,** imposition *f* des mains; *Typ:* **l.-on table,** table *f* à marger; *Ven:* **l. on of the pack,** laisser-courre *m inv*; (*f*) **l. out,** (i) arrangement *m*, disposition *f*; étalage *m*; (ii) toilette *f* (d'un mort); (ii) tracement *m*, tracé *m* (d'une ville, etc.); dessin *m* (d'un jardin); (*g*) **l. up,** désarmement *m* (d'un navire); mise sur cales (d'une voiture).

layman, *pl.* **-men** ['leimən], *s.m.* **1.** *Ecc:* laïque *m*, séculier *m*. **2.** personne *f* qui n'est pas du métier; profane *m*, civil *m*.

layoff ['leiɔf], *s. Ind:* (période *f* de) licenciement *m* (temporaire).

layout ['leiaut], *s.* **1.** (*a*) tracé *m* (d'une construction, d'une ville, etc.); dessin *m* (d'un jardin); *Surv:* tracé, maquette *f* (d'un levé topographique); **l. sheet,** feuille *f* de tracé; (*b*) *Mec.E:* agencement *m*, disposition *f*, des pièces (dans un ensemble mécanique); *Ind: Mec.E: W.Tel:* schéma *m* de montage; vue *f* schématique montrant l'emplacement des pièces; (*c*) *Typ: Typew:* (i) disposition *f* typographique, (mode *m* de) présentation *f* (d'un texte, d'un état, d'une annonce, etc.); (ii) mise *f* en page; (*d*) tableau *m* des mises (à la roulette). **2.** étude *f* (pour la construction d'une machine, etc.); *Aut:* **chassis l.,** étude de châssis.

laystall ['leistɔl], *s. A:* dépôt *m* d'immondices.

laywoman, *pl.* **-women** ['leiwumən, -wimin], *s.f.* **1.** laïque. **2.** femme qui n'est pas du métier.

lazar ['læzər], *s.m. A:* **1.** malade indigent. **2.** lépreux; **l. house,** léproserie *f*, maladrerie *f*, hôpital *m* de lépreux.

lazaret(to) [læzə'ret(ou)], *s.* **1.** = LAZAR HOUSE. **2.** *Nau:* lazaret *m* (de quarantaine).

lazarist ['læzərist], *s. Rel.H:* lazariste *m*.

Lazarus ['læzərəs], *Pr.n.m. B:* Lazare.

laze¹ [leiz], *s. F:* **an hour's l.,** une heure de paresse, de flânerie.

laze², *v.tr. & i.* **to l. (about), to l. away one's time,** paresser, fainéanter; faire le lézard; lézarder; **to l. in bed,** traînasser au lit; faire la grasse matinée.

lazily ['leizili], *adv.* paresseusement; (passer le temps) dans la paresse, dans la fainéantise; (vivre) en paresseux.

laziness ['leizinis], *s.* paresse *f*, fainéantise *f*.

lazulite ['læzjulait], *s. Miner:* lazulite *m*; pierre *f* d'azur.

lazurite ['læzjurait], *s. Miner:* outremer *m*.

lazy ['leizi], *a.* **1.** paresseux, fainéant; **l. pupil,** élève paresseux; **a l. person,** un paresseux, une paresseuse; **he's very l. about getting up,** il est paresseux à se lever; **I feel too l. to do it,** je n'ai pas l'énergie de le faire. **2. l. moments,** moments *m* de paresse; **l. weather,** temps accablant, qui dispose à la paresse; **to have a l. fit,** se laisser aller à la paresse; *Nau:* **l. guy, sheet,** fausse écoute. **3.** (*a*) *Tls:* **l. tongs,** (i) zigzag *m*; (ii) pince *f* à zigzags; (*b*) *Mec.E:* **l. pinion,** (i) roue folle, décalée; (ii) roue de renvoi; (*c*) *Hort:* **l. bed,** planche *f* (de pommes de terre) entre tranchées.

lazybones, *A:* **lazyboots** ['leizibounz, -bu:ts], *s. F:* paresseux, -euse; fainéant, -ante.

lea¹ [li:], *s. Lit:* prairie *f*; pâturage *m*.

lea², *a. Agr:* (*of land*) en jachère.

lea³, *s. Tex:* échevette *f* (de fil).

leach¹ [li:tʃ], *s. Tan:* fosse *f* à jusée.

leach². **1.** *v.tr.* (*a*) filtrer (un liquide); (*b*) lessiver, lixivier (du minerai, de l'écorce); (*c*) **to l. away, l. out, salts,** extraire des sels par lixiviation, par lessivage. **2.** *v.i.* (*of liquid*) filtrer (**through,** à travers).

leaching ['li:tʃiŋ], *s.* **1.** filtration *f*. **2.** lessivage *m*, lixiviation *f*.

leachy ['li:tʃi], *a.* (sol *m*) perméable.

lead¹ [led], *s.* **1.** plomb *m*; (*a*) **l. ore,** minerai *m* de plomb; colombin *m*; **argentiferous l., silver l.,** plomb argentifère; **corneous l., horn l.,** plomb corné; phosgénite *f*; **green l.,** plomb vert, pyromorphite *f*; **l. carbonate,** (i) (*ore*) plomb carbonaté; (ii) *Ch:* carbonate *m* de plomb; **l. chromate,** (i) (*ore*) plomb chromaté, plomb rouge (de Sibérie), crocoïse *f*; (ii) *Ch:* chromate *m* de plomb; **l. galena, l. glance, l. sulphide,** galène *f*, sulfure *m*, de plomb; **white l.,** (i) (*ore*) plomb blanc, cérusite *f*; (ii) *Ch:* blanc *m* de plomb, céruse *f*; **yellow l.,** (i) (*ore*) plomb jaune, wulfénite *f*; (ii) *Ch:* massicot *m*; **l.**

acetate, sugar of l., acétate de plomb; **l. arseniate,** arséniate *m* de plomb; **l. bromide,** bromure *m* de plomb; **l. oxide, dioxide,** oxyde *m,* bioxyde *m,* de plomb; **l. sulphate,** sulfate *m* de plomb; **l. salt,** sel *m* de plomb; **potter's l.,** alquifoux *m*; *Cer:* **l. glaze,** glaçure *f* plombifère; vernis *m* de plomb; **l. glazed,** à glaçure plombifère; *Petr:* **tetraethyl l.,** tétraéthyle *m* de plomb; *Nau:* **black l.,** graphite *m,* plombagine *f* (pour enduire la coque); **l. content,** indice *m* de plomb (dans un carburant); (*b*) *Metall: etc:* **pig l.,** plomb en saumon; **l. pig,** saumon *m* de plomb; **sheet l.,** plomb laminé, plomb en feuille, feuille *f* de plomb; **l. foil,** mince feuille de plomb, papier *m* d'étain; **l. plate,** plomb en plaque, plaque *f* de plomb; **l. wire,** plomb filé, fil *m* de plomb; **l. dust,** plomb pulvérulent; **antimonial l., hard l.,** plomb antimonial, antimonié; plomb aigre, dur; **l. covering, encasing, sheathing,** gainage *m* en plomb; **l. covered, encased, sheathed,** sous (gaine de) plomb; **l. coating,** emplombage *m*; **l. coated,** emplombé, garni de plomb; **l. lining,** chemisage *m,* doublage *m,* de plomb; **l. lined,** chemisé, doublé, de plomb; **l. glass,** verre *m* de, au, plomb; **l. pipe,** tuyau *m* de plomb; **l. piping,** tuyauterie *f* de plomb, canalisations *fpl* en plomb; **l. accumulator, l. battery, l. (acid) cell,** accumulateur *m* en plomb; *Tls:* **l. dresser,** batte *f* de plombier, rabattoir *m*; (*c*) *Const:* **roof leads,** plombs de couverture; **window leads,** plombs de vitrail, de vitraux; *Hist:* **the Leads (of Venice),** les Plombs (de Venise); (*d*) *Sm.a:* **l. shot,** grenaille *f* de plomb, petit plomb; (*e*) *Med:* **l. colic,** coliques saturnines, de plomb; **l. palsy,** paralysie saturnine; **l. poisoning,** intoxication saturnine, par le plomb; saturnisme *m.* **2.** mine *f* (de crayon); **l. pencil,** crayon *m* à la mine de plomb. **3.** *Nau:* (plomb de) sonde *f*; **hand l.,** sonde à main, petite sonde; **deep-sea l.,** grande sonde; **l. line,** ligne *f* de sonde; **to arm the l.,** suiffer la sonde; garnir (de suif) le plomb de sonde; *F:* **to swing the l.,** tirer au flanc; **l. swinger,** tireur *m* au flanc. **4.** *Typ:* interligne *f.*

lead² [led], *v.* (**leaded** ['ledid]; **leading** ['lediŋ]) **1.** *v.tr.* (*a*) plomber (un toit); couvrir, garnir, (un objet) de plomb; (*b*) *Fish:* plomber, lester, caler (une ligne, un filet); (*c*) enchâsser (des vitraux) dans les plombs; (*d*) *Typ:* interligner (des lignes de composition); **to l. out matter,** donner de l'air à, blanchir, la composition; **to l. out the type,** espacer les lettres. **2.** *v.i.* (*of gun barrel*) s'encrasser.

lead³ [li:d], *s.* **1.** (*a*) conduite *f*; **to follow s.o.'s l.,** se laisser conduire par qn; suivre l'exemple de qn; prendre exemple sur qn; **to give the l.,** montrer la voie (à suivre); **to give s.o. a l.,** (i) amener qn sur un sujet; (ii) mettre qn sur la voie; (*b*) **to take the l.,** (i) prendre la tête; (ii) prendre la direction; (iii) *Sp: etc:* devancer ses concurrents; **to take the l. of, over, s.o.,** prendre le pas, gagner les devants, sur qn; prendre le dessus de qn; **to keep one's l. over s.o.,** garder son avance sur qn; **to have a l. over s.o.,** avoir le pas sur qn; **to have a l. of ten metres,** avoir une avance de dix mètres; **to have one minute's l. over s.o.,** avoir une minute d'avance sur qn; **to take the l. in the conversation,** mener, diriger, la conversation; (*c*) *attrib. esp. NAm:* (bœufs, chevaux, etc.) de tête; *Mus:* **l. violin,** violon principal; (*d*) **l. time,** délai *m* d'approvisionnement, d'obtention; *Cmptr:* **l. blanked,** avec espaces à gauche. **2.** *Cards:* primauté *f*; **to have the l.,** jouer le premier; avoir la main; **your l.!** à vous de jouer (le premier)! **to return a l.,** renvoyer la couleur demandée; rejouer une couleur; **to follow the l. in clubs,** fournir du trèfle. **3.** *Th:* premier rôle; (rôle de) vedette *f*; **he, she, takes the leads,** c'est lui, elle, qui joue les premiers rôles; **juvenile l.,** jeune premier, jeune première. **4.** (*a*) *Mec.E:* hauteur *f* du pas (d'une vis); **l. screw,** vis-mère *f, pl.* vis-mères (de tour); (*b*) *Mch: I.C.E:* avance *f* (du tiroir, de la manivelle, de l'allumage, etc.); (*c*) *El:* **(angle of) l. of brushes,** (angle *m* de) (dé)calage *m* en avant, (angle d')avance, des balais; **magneto l.,** avance *f* d'une magnéto; **l. of the current, (phase) l.,** déphasage *m* en avant; (*d*) *Ball: Artil:* (angle *m* de) visée *f* en avant (d'un objectif mobile); pointage *m* sur objectif futur; **to aim off a l. in front of a moving target,** viser en avant d'un objectif mobile; **to direct a gun, a missile, the required l. in front of a target,** pointer une pièce, un missile, à la distance requise en avant d'un objectif; **l. angle,** angle *m* d'avance, de correction-but; **ballastic l.,** correction-but *f* balistique; **kinetic l.,** correction-but cinétique. **5.** (*a*) (*for dog, etc.*) laisse *f*; **dogs must be kept on a l.,** les chiens doivent être tenus en laisse; (*b*) *Harn:* **l. reins,** grandes guides; **l. bars,** volée *f* de devant. **6.** *Hyd.E:* canal, -aux *m,* d'amenée; canal de prise, (canal de) dérivation *f*; **mill l.,** bief *m* de moulin. **7.** *El:* câble *m,* branchement *m,* de canalisation; amenée *f* de courant; fil électrique; **positive, negative, l. (of a dynamo),** conducteur positif, négatif (d'une dynamo); **l. and return,** conducteur d'amenée et de retour. **8.** (*a*) (*in icefield*) canal, chenal, -aux *m,* passage *m,* fissure *f*; (*b*) *Min:* filon *m.* **9.** *Artil:* raccordement *m* (de la chambre). **10.** *Nau:* (*a*) parcours *m,* retour *m* (d'une manœuvre); (*b*) **fair l.,** margouillet *m.*

lead⁴ [li:d], *v.* (**led** [led]; **led**)

I. *v.tr.* **1.** (*a*) mener, conduire, guider (**s.o. to a place,** qn à un endroit); **the guide led the party (a)round the exhibition,** le guide a conduit le groupe dans l'exposition; **to l. s.o. out of his way,** détourner qn de sa route, de son dessein; **to l. s.o. into temptation,** entraîner qn dans la tentation; induire qn en erreur, en tentation; *Ecc:* **l. us not into temptation,** ne nous soumets pas à la tentation; **to be led astray,** se laisser entraîner; *Jur:* **to l. a witness,** poser des questions tendancieuses à un témoin; (*b*) **to l. the way, to l. the van,** montrer le chemin; marcher le premier, en tête; aller devant; précéder les autres; ouvrir la marche; **to l. the conversation back to a subject,** ramener la conversation sur un sujet. **2.** conduire, guider (un aveugle, etc.) par la main; mener (un cheval) par la bride; tenir (un chien) en laisse; **led horse,** cheval mené en main; **he led the blind man down the stairs,** il a aidé l'aveugle à descendre l'escalier; **she led the horse down, up, the hill,** elle a descendu, monté, la colline en tenant le cheval par la bride; **he led the animals away from the fire,** il a emmené les animaux hors du danger de l'incendie; **he took the child by the hand and led him in, led him into the room,** il a pris la main de l'enfant et l'a fait entrer (dans la salle); *Prov:* **some can be led who won't be driven,** tout par amour et rien par force; **he is easily led,** il va comme on le mène; **to l. a woman to the altar,** conduire une femme à l'autel. **3.** induire, porter, pousser (**s.o. to do sth.,** qn à faire qch.); **this led her to reflect,** cela l'a fait réfléchir; **that leads me to believe that . . .,** cela me mène à croire que . . .; **his name would l. one to believe that. . .,** son nom ferait croire que . . .; **I was led to the conclusion that . . .,** je fus amené à conclure que . . .. **4.** amener (de l'eau à un endroit); faire passer (un cordage à travers une poulie). **5.** (*a*) mener (une vie heureuse, malheureuse); (*b*) **to l. s.o. a wretched existence, a dog's life,** faire une vie d'enfer, une vie de chien, à qn. **6.** (*a*) commander (une armée); **leading his troops,** à la tête de ses troupes; (*b*) mener (la danse, le chant); **to l. an orchestra,** jouer premier violon; **to l. a party,** être chef de parti; **to l. a movement,** être à la tête d'un mouvement; (*c*) *v.i.* (*of barrister*) être l'avocat principal (dans un procès). **7.** (*a*) (*in race, etc.*) **to l. the field,** mener le champ; tenir la tête; **to l. (s.o.) by eight points,** mener (qn) par huit points; **France is leading Belgium (by) 2 to 1.,** la France mène la Belgique par 2 à 1; **to l. s.o. by one minute,** avoir une minute d'avance sur qn; (*b*) *Ven:* **to l. a bird by three metres,** viser trois mètres en avant du gibier. **8.** *Cards:* (*a*) **to l. a card,** entamer, attaquer, d'une carte; **to l. clubs,** jouer, attaquer, trèfle; (*b*) *v.i.* ouvrir le jeu; jouer le premier, entamer; **to l. from one's long suit,** attaquer dans sa longue.

II. *v.i.* **1.** (*of road*) mener, conduire (**to,** à); **road that leads to the town,** chemin *m* qui mène, va, à la ville; **which road leads to the station?** quel est le chemin de la gare? **door that leads into the garden,** porte *f* qui communique avec le jardin, qui donne accès au jardin; **the garden leads down to the river,** le jardin descend jusqu'à la rivière; **the path leads to a lake,** le chemin aboutit à un lac; **the bells are rung by ropes which l. down from the belfry,** on sonne les cloches au moyen des cordes qui descendent du haut de la tour. **2. to l. to a good result,** aboutir à un bon résultat; produire un heureux effet; **to l. to a discovery,** conduire, aboutir, à une découverte; amener une découverte; **excessive drinking leads to other vices,** la boisson conduit à d'autres vices; **one thing leads to another,** une chose mène à une autre; **what will it l. to?** à quoi cela aboutira-t-il? **to l. to nothing,** n'aboutir, ne mener, à rien; **a simple act of carelessness may l. to a fire,** une simple négligence peut déterminer un incendie; **policy that would l. to rebellion,** politique qui amènerait un soulèvement; **action which led to criticism,** action qui a motivé des critiques.

III. (*compound verbs*) **1. lead off,** *v.i. & tr.* (*a*) commencer, débuter (**with,** par); (*b*) entamer les débats; jouer le premier; *Bill:* donner l'acquit; *Danc:* ouvrir le bal; **to l. off an attack,** lancer une attaque.

2. lead on. (*a*) *v.tr.* **to l. s.o. on to talk,** encourager qn à parler; *F:* **to l. s.o. on,** (i) entraîner qn; (ii) tromper, duper, qn; (*b*) *v.i.* **l. on!** en avant!

3. lead up, *v.i.* **to l. up to a subject,** amener un sujet; **to l. up to the climax,** amener le dénouement; **the opening chapter of this book leads up to the revolution,** le premier chapitre de ce livre nous amène à la révolution.

lead-bearing ['ledbɛəriŋ], *a.* plombifère.

leaded ['ledid], *a.* **1.** (*of window, cane, etc.*) plombé; **l. cable,** câble (armé) sous plomb. **2.** *Typ:* interligné.

leaden ['ledn], *a.* de plomb; **l. complexion,** teint couleur de plomb; teint plombé; **l. sky,** ciel *m* de plomb; **l.-eyed,** aux yeux ternes; **l.-footed,** à la démarche pesante; **l. limbs,** membres inertes, engourdis.

leader ['li:dər], *s.* **1.** (*pers.*) (*a*) conducteur, -trice; guide *m*; (*b*) *Mil: etc:* chef *m*; **file l.,** chef de file; **platoon l.,** chef de section; **company leaders,** les commandants *m* de compagnies; **he is cut out for a l. (of men),** il a l'étoffe d'un grand capitaine; il est taillé pour commander; (*c*) chef, directeur *m* (d'un parti); meneur *m* (d'une émeute); **to be the l. of a party,** être en chef dans un parti; **the l. of the Liberal party,** le leader du parti libéral; **L. of the House of Commons,** chef de la majorité ministérielle à la Chambre des Communes; **the leaders of society,** la haute société; *Sp:* **team l.,** chef d'équipe; (*d*) *Mus:* premier violon; (*of a group*) chef; (*e*) *Jur:* avocat principal (dans une cause); (*f*) chef, premier, -ière (d'une file); (*g*) *Surv:* jalonneur *m*; (*h*) *Ind: etc:* **major group, l. in its field,** important groupe, leader dans sa branche. **2.** cheval *m* de volée, de tête, d'avant; (*of unicorn team*) cheval en arbalète; **the leaders,** l'attelage *m* de devant. **3.** question, observation, faite pour orienter la conversation, pour amener un sujet. **4.** (*a*) *Agr:* conduit *m*; (*b*) *Anat:* tendon *m*; (*c*) *Rec: Cin: etc:* amorce *f* (de bande magnétique, de film); **l. connector,** raccord *m* mâle (de bande magnétique); **running, start, head, l.,** amorce initiale; **end, tail, stop, l.,** amorce de sortie; *Cmptr:* **l. card,** carte *f* d'ouverture; (*d*) *Const:* tuyau *m* de descente; descente *f* d'eau; conduit d'eau; *Civ.E:* (*of embankment, etc.*) **water l.,** dalot *m*; (*e*) *Fish:* avançon *m* (de la ligne); (*f*) *Hort:* pousse terminale; bourgeon terminal; (*g*) *Journ:* article principal, de fond, de tête; éditorial, -aux; *F:* leader; **l. writer,** éditorialiste *m*; (*h*) *Mec.E:* roue maîtresse; (*i*) *Geol: Min:* **l. (vein),** conducteur; filon *m* guide; (*j*) *Nau:* conduit, guide, chaumard *m* (pour cordages); (*k*) *Typ:* **leaders,** points conducteurs; (*l*) *Com:* **loss l.,** article sacrifié.

leaderless ['li:dəlis], *a.* sans chef, sans conducteur, sans guide.

leadership ['li:dəʃip], *s.* **1.** (*a*) conduite *f*; **to be under s.o.'s l.,** être sous la conduite de qn; (*b*) qualités requises pour conduire des hommes; qualités de chef; (*c*) sens *m* du commandement. **2.** (*a*) *Mil:* commandement *m*; (*b*) fonctions *fpl* de chef; direction *f* (d'un parti, etc.).

leadhillite ['ledhilait], *s. Miner:* leadhillite *f.*

lead-in ['li:din], *s.* **1.** (*a*) *El: Tp: etc:* entrée *f* (de câble, *W.Tel:* de poste); **rubber-sheathed l.-in,** entrée (de poste) sous (gaine de) caoutchouc; **l.-in insulator,** isolateur *m* (d'entrée en poste); (*b*) *W.Tel: etc:* descente *f* d'antenne; **l.-in pipe,** pipe *f* d'antenne; *Rec:* **l.-in groove, spiral,** sillon initial (de disque). **2.** *Av:* guidage *m* (d'un avion vers un aérodrome, une piste d'atterrissage, etc.); **l.-in lights,** feux *m* de guidage.

leading¹ ['lediŋ], *s.* **1.** (*a*) plombage *m*; (*b*) *coll.* plombs *mpl*; (*c*) *Arch:* mise *f* en plomb. **2.** *Typ:* **l. (out),** interlignage *m.* **3.** (*of gun barrel*) encrassement *m.*

leading² ['li:diŋ], *a.* **1.** (*a*) *Ch: etc:* **l. tube,** tube abducteur; (*b*) **l. question,** (i) question tendancieuse; (ii) *Jur:* question posée au témoin de manière à suggérer la réponse; **l. case,** décision *f* d'un cas d'espèce créant un précédent et fixant la jurisprudence; **l. cases,** cas d'espèce qui font autorité; (*c*) *Mus:* **l. note,** note *f* sensible; (*d*) *Nau:* **l. buoy,** bouée-balise *f, pl.* bouées-balises; **l. marks,** alignement *m*; amers *mpl.* **2.** (*chief*) premier; principal, -aux; important; **a l. man,** (i) un homme important; un des chefs; une notabilité; (ii) *Navy:* quartier-maître *m*; matelot *m* de première classe; **the l. surgeon in Manchester,** le premier chirurgien de Manchester; **the l. statesmen of Europe,** les hommes d'État dirigeants de l'Europe; **a. l. shareholder,** un des principaux actionnaires; un gros actionnaire; **available from the l. jewellers,** en vente chez les principaux bijoutiers; **one of the l. firms of the country,** une des plus puissantes maisons du pays; **l. motive of an action,** mobile principal d'une action; **l. idea,** idée dominante, directrice, maîtresse (d'une œuvre, etc.); **l. article,** (i) *Journ:* = LEADER 4 (*g*); (ii) *Com:* article *m* (de) réclame; spécialité *f* de réclame; *Th:* **l. part,** premier rôle; **l. man, lady,** premier rôle; vedette *f*; **to play a l. part in a matter,** jouer un rôle prépondérant dans une affaire. **3.** (*in front*) (*a*) **l. car,** voiture *f* de, en, tête; *Sp:* **l. ski,** ski actif (dans un virage); *Navy:* **l. column, ship,** colonne *f,* bâtiment *m,* de tête; **the l. ship,** le chef de file; *Mil:* **l. elements, l. troops, l. units,** éléments *m,* unités *f,* de tête, de premier échelon; éléments, unités, avancé(e)s; **the l. echelon,** le premier échelon, l'échelon avancé; **l. patrol,** patrouille *f* de tête; **l. scout,** éclaireur *m* de tête; (*b*) *Veh:* **l. axle, wheels,** essieu porteur d'avant; essieu avant; roues porteuses d'avant (d'une locomotive, etc.); *Av: Nau:* **l. edge (of wing, of propeller),** bord *m* d'attaque, d'entrée; arêtier *m* avant (de l'aile); (*c*) *El:* **l. current,** courant déphasé en avant; (*d*) *Cards:* **l. card,** première carte; (*e*) *Hort:* **l. shoot,** pousse principale, terminale; (*f*) **l. end,** début *m* (de bande magnétique); *Cmptr:* **l. character,** caractère *m* de gauche, de poids fort, en tête; **l. edge,** bord *m* avant (de carte, etc.). **4.** (*driving*) (*a*) *Nau:* **l. wind,** vent portant, traversier; (*b*) *Mec.E:* **l. screw,** vis-mère *f*, *pl.* vis-mères (de tour).

leading[3] ['li:diŋ], *s.* **1.** conduite *f*, menage *m* (de chevaux, etc.); *Harn:* **l. rein,** longe *f*, plate-longe *f*, *pl.* plates-longes; *Husb:* **l. staff,** bâton fixé à l'anneau nasal d'un taureau; *F:* **to be in l. strings,** être à la lisière; **to keep s.o. in l. strings,** tenir, mener, qn en laisse, en lisière. **2.** (*a*) *Mil: etc:* conduite, commandement *m* (de la troupe, d'une unité); **the l. of the higher, the lower, units,** la conduite des grandes, des petites, unités; (*b*) direction *f* (d'une entreprise, etc.); influence *f*; exemple *m*. **3.** amenée *f* (de l'eau à un moulin, etc.).

leadless ['ledlis], *a. Cer:* (glaçure *f*) sans plomb.

lead-out ['li:daut], *s.* sortie *f*; *El: Tp: etc:* **l.-o. connection,** sortie de fils; *Rec:* **l.-o. groove,** sillon final, sillon de sortie (d'un disque).

leadplant ['ledplɑ:nt], *s. Bot: U.S:* indigo bâtard.

leadsman, *pl.* **-men** ['ledzmən], *s.m. Nau:* sondeur; **leadsmen in the chains!** les sondeurs à leurs postes!

leadwork ['ledwə:k], *s.* (*a*) plomberie *f*; (*b*) *Arch:* plombs *mpl* (d'un vitrail).

leadwort ['ledwə:t], *s. Bot:* dentelaire *f* d'Europe.

leaf[1], *pl.* **leaves** [li:f, li:vz], *s.* **1.** (*a*) feuille *f* (de plante, d'arbre); *Bot:* **l. bud,** bourgeon *m* à feuille, à bois; bourgeon foliipare; **l. blade,** limbe *m* de feuille; **l. cushion,** coussinet *m* foliaire; **l. organ,** organe *m* foliaire; **l. scar,** phyllule *f*; *Hort:* **l. mould,** terreau *m* de feuilles; terre *f* d'engrais; humus *m*; **bed of l. mould,** tombe *f*; *Husb:* **l. fodder,** feuillage vert (pour fourrage); feuillard *m*; *Hort: etc:* **l. blight, l. rust,** rouille *f* des feuilles; **peach l. curl,** cloque *f* du pêcher; (*of plant, tree*) **to put out leaves, to come into l.,** (se) feuiller; **to shed its leaves,** s'effeuiller; **in l.,** couvert de feuilles, en feuille; **the trees are coming into l.,** les arbres se couvrent de feuilles; **the fall of the l.,** la chute des feuilles; effeuillaison *f*; *Art:* **l. and dart (moulding),** raide-cœur *m*, *pl.* rais-de cœur; (*b*) *F:* pétale *f* (de fleur); (*c*) **l. tobacco,** tabac *m* en feuilles; **outer l. of a cigar,** robe *f* d'un cigare; (*d*) *Ent:* **l. insect,** phyllie *f*; **l. butterfly,** kallima *m*; **l. roller (moth),** tordeuse *f*, rouleuse *f*; **the l. rollers,** les tortricidés *m*; **l. beetle,** chrysomèle *f*; galéruque *f*; **l. cutter, l.-cutting bee,** (abeille) (dé)coupeuse de feuilles; mégachile *f*; **l. miner,** adèle *f*; **l.-dwelling insects,** insectes *m* frondicoles; *Z:* **l. monkey,** entelle *m*, langur *m*; *Ich:* **l. fish,** poisson *m* feuille; (*e*) *O:* **l. lard,** saindoux *m*; **l. fat,** couche *f* de graisse (de ventre de porc); (*f*) *a. & s.* **l. green,** vert pré (*m*) *inv.* **2.** (*a*) feuillet *m* (de livre); *Bookb:* **single l.,** carton *m* de deux pages; **to turn over the leaves of a book,** feuilleter un livre; (*of pers.*) **to turn over a new l.,** (i) changer de conduite; faire peau neuve; se corriger; rentrer dans le bon chemin; revenir de ses erreurs; (ii) faire plan neuf; changer de méthode, de politique; **to take a l. out of s.o.'s book,** prendre exemple, modèle, sur qn; imiter, suivre, l'exemple de qn; prendre qn pour exemple, pour modèle; (*b*) **counterfoil and l.,** talon *m* et volant *m* (d'un carnet de chèques, etc.). **3.** feuille (d'argent, d'or, etc.); **l. brass,** laiton *m* en feuilles; **l. metal,** or faux en feuilles (pour dorure). **4.** (*a*) battant *m*, vantail, -aux *m* (de porte); battant (de contrevent); panneau, -eaux *m* (de paravent); tablier *m* (de pont-levis); *Mec.E: etc:* obturateur *m* (de vanne); aile *f* (de pignon); lame *f*, feuille, feuillet (de ressort); **l. spring,** ressort *m* à lame(s); lame-ressort *f*, *pl.* lames-ressorts; **l. of a table,** (i) (*inserted*) rallonge *f*, (ii) (*hinged, also* **drop l.,** *U.S:* **fall l.**) battant, de table; *Sm.a:* **l. sight,** hausse *f* (à charnière); **sight l., l. of back sight, of rear sight,** planche *f* de hausse; **movable (sight) l.,** planche (de hausse) mobile; (*b*) *Tex:* (*set of heddles*) lame.

leaf[2], *v.i.* **1.** (se) feuiller; pousser des feuilles; se couvrir de feuilles. **2. to l. through a book,** feuilleter un livre.

leafage ['li:fidʒ], *s.* **1.** feuillage *m*; (*for fodder*) ramée *f*. **2.** *Art:* feuillé *m*, feuillée *f*.

leafbird ['li:fbə:d], *s. Orn:* verdin *m*.

leafcup ['li:fkʌp], *s. Bot:* polymnia *m*.

leafhopper ['li:fhɔpər], *s. Ent:* cicadelle *f*, cicadellide *m*.

leafiness ['li:finis], *s.* abondance *f* de feuillage (d'un arbre).

leafing ['li:fiŋ], *s.* feuillaison *f*, foliation *f*.

leafless ['li:flis], *a.* sans feuilles, dépourvu de feuilles; (i) dénudé, effeuillé; (ii) aphylle.

leaflessness ['li:flisnis], *s.* absence *f* de feuilles; nudité *f* (d'un arbre).

leaflet ['li:flit], *s.* **1.** *Bot:* foliole *f*; petite feuille. **2.** (*a*) feuillet *m* (de papier); feuille volante, feuille mobile; imprimé *m*; (*b*) *Com: etc:* imprimé, papillon *m*, publicitaire; prospectus *m*; *Pol:* tract *m*.

leaflike ['li:flaik], *a.* foliacé; phylloïde.

leaf-nosed ['li:fnouzd], *a. Z:* **l.-n. bat,** fer-de-lance *m*, *pl.* fers-de-lance.

leafstalk ['li:fstɔ:k], *s. Bot:* pétiole *m*.

leafwork ['li:fwə:k], *s. Arch: etc:* feuilles *fpl*, feuillage *m*.

leafy ['li:fi], *a.* feuillu; couvert de feuilles; *Lit:* **l. canopy,** dais *m* de feuillage, de verdure.

league[1] [li:g], *s. A.Meas:* lieue *f*; **marine l.,** lieue marine; lieue géographique; **a hundred square leagues,** cent lieues superficielles.

league[2], *s.* (*a*) ligue *f*; **to form a l. against s.o.,** se liguer contre qn; **everyone is in l. against them,** tout le monde est ligué, s'est conjuré, contre eux; **he was in l. with them,** il était ligué, il était d'intelligence, de connivence, avec eux; *Hist:* **the L. of Nations,** la Société des Nations; *Hist:* **the Solemn L. and Covenant,** le Covenant; *Fb:* **l. matches,** matchs de championnat (professionnels); (*b*) catégorie *f*; *F:* **I'm not in your l.,** je ne suis pas de votre classe.

league[3]. **1.** *v.tr.* **to be leagued with s.o.,** être ligué avec qn; **to be leagued together,** être ligués, être d'intelligence. **2.** *v.i.* **to l. (together),** se liguer, se conjurer (**with, against,** avec, contre; **in order to,** pour).

leaguer[1] ['li:gər], *s. Hist:* ligueur, -euse.

leaguer[2], *s. A:* **1.** (*a*) camp *m* des assiégeants; (*b*) armée *f* d'investissement. **2.** investissement *m*, siège *m*.

Leah ['li:ə], *Pr.n.f. B.Hist:* Lia.

leak[1] [li:k], *s.* **1.** (*a*) fuite *f*, écoulement *m* (d'un liquide); perte *f* d'eau; (*b*) infiltration *f*, rentrée *f* (d'eau, etc.); *Nau:* voie *f* d'eau; (*of ship*) **to spring a l.,** (se) faire une voie d'eau; avoir, contracter, une voie d'eau; **to stop a l.,** (i) étancher, aveugler, boucher, maîtriser, une voie d'eau; (ii) remédier à, étancher, une fuite (d'eau, etc.); **l. detector,** indique-fuite(s) *m*, *pl.* indique-fuites; cherche-fuite(s) *m*, *pl.* cherche-fuites; *El:* indicateur *m* de pertes à la terre; déceleur *m* de fuites; (*c*) fuite (de secrets officiels, etc.). **2.** *W.Tel: etc:* **grid l.,** résistance *f* du circuit de la grille, de fuite de la grille.

leak[2]. **1.** *v.i.* (*a*) (*of tank, etc.*) avoir une fuite; fuir, couler, suinter; perdre (son eau); (*of liquid*) fuir, couler; **the boiler is leaking,** il y a une fuite à la chaudière; **our tanks were leaking,** nos citernes ne retenaient plus l'eau; **to l. away,** (*of liquid*) se perdre; *Ph:* (*of energy*) se dégrader; (*of truth, news, etc.*) **to l. (out),** s'ébruiter, se divulguer, transpirer; **how did it l. out?** comment cela s'est-il su? **it's bound to l. out,** cela se saura forcément; (*b*) (*of ship, etc.*) faire eau; avoir une voie d'eau; **roof that leaks,** toit qui laisse entrer la pluie; **my shoes l.,** mes chaussures prennent l'eau. **2.** *v.tr. F:* laisser filtrer (des informations, etc.).

leakage ['li:kidʒ], *s.* **1.** (*a*) défaut *m* d'étanchéité; fuite *f* (d'eau, de gaz, d'un tonneau); perte *f*, échappement *m*, coulage *m* (d'eau); perte, fuite, déperdition *f*, déviation *f* (d'électricité) (par dispersion); *Tg:* dérivation *f*; **l. of wine (from cask),** avalage *m* du vin (d'un tonneau); **l. loss of a canal,** perte d'infiltration d'un canal; *I.C.E:* **gasket l.,** défaut d'étanchéité des joints; fuite de joint; *El:* **l. current,** courant *m* d'excitation; **earth l.,** perte à la terre; mauvais isolement; **armature l.,** dispersion *f* d'induit; **surface l. of insulator,** décharge superficielle sur l'isolateur; *Tp: W.Tel:* **l. noises,** (bruits *m* de) friture *f*; (*b*) fuites, pertes, coulage. **2.** (*a*) coulage (dans une maison de commerce); (*b*) **l. of official secrets,** fuite de secrets officiels.

leakance ['li:kəns], *s. El:* perditance *f*.

leakiness ['li:kinis], *s.* inétanchéité *f*; manque *m* d'étanchéité; tendance *f* à couler, à faire eau.

leaking[1] ['li:kiŋ], *a.* = LEAKY 1.

leaking[2], *s.* = LEAKAGE 1 (*a*).

leakproof ['li:kpru:f], *a.* étanche; à l'épreuve des fuites.

leaky ['li:ki], *a.* **1.** (*a*) (tonneau *m*) qui coule, qui perd, qui fuit; **l. pipes,** tuyauterie disjointe; *I.C.E:* **l. induction,** fuites *fpl* à l'admission; (*b*) (bateau) qui fait eau; (bateau) gercé; **l. shoes,** chaussures *f* qui prennent l'eau; **l. roof,** toit qui laisse entrer la pluie. **2.** *F: O:* (*a*) (*of pers., tongue*) indiscret, -ète; bavard; (*b*) **l. memory,** mémoire *f* peu fidèle.

leal [li:l], *a. Scot:* loyal, -aux; fidèle; *Lit:* **the land of the l.,** le royaume des cieux, des bienheureux.

lealty ['li:əlti], *s. A:* loyauté *f*, fidélité *f*.

lean[1] [li:n]. **1.** *a.* maigre; (*a*) amaigri, décharné; (*of animal*) efflanqué, étique; **l. horse,** cheval élancé; *F:* **as l. as a shotten herring,** maigre comme un hareng, comme un clou; gras comme un cent de clous; (*b*) **l. meat,** viande *f* maigre; (*c*) **l. crops,** maigres récoltes *f*; **l. years,** années *f* maigres, déficitaires; années de disette; période *f* de vaches maigres; **l. clay,** argile *f* pauvre; **l. coal,** houille *f* maigre; **l. diet,** maigre régime; régime frugal; *I.C.E:* **l. mixture,** mélange *m* pauvre (d'air et de carburant). **2.** *s.* maigre *m* (de la viande).

lean[2], *s.* inclinaison *f*; **onward l.,** inclinaison en dehors.

lean[3] (*p.t. & p.p.* **leaned** [li:nd] *or* **leant** [lent]) **1.** *v.i.* (*a*) s'appuyer (**against, on, sth.,** contre, sur, à, qch.); **to l. on one's elbow(s),** s'accouder; **to l. (up, back) against a wall, with one's back to, against, a wall,** s'adosser à, contre, un mur; **leaning against a wall,** appuyé, adossé, accoté, à, contre, un mur; **to l. back in one's chair,** se renverser dans son fauteuil; **to l. on s.o.,** (i) s'appuyer sur qn; (ii) *F:* serrer la vis à qn; **to l. on a broken reed,** s'appuyer sur un roseau; *Mil:* **to l. on a wood,** être appuyé à un bois; s'appuyer sur un bois; (*b*) **to l. forward,** se pencher en avant; **to l. over, towards, sth.,** se pencher sur, vers, qch.; **she was leaning over his shoulder,** elle se penchait sur son épaule; **to l. out of the window,** se pencher à, par, la fenêtre; **that wall is leaning towards the right,** ce mur incline, penche, déverse, vers la droite; (*c*) **to l. towards an opinion,** incliner pour une opinion; **to l. towards socialism, towards romance,** pencher au socialisme; donner dans le romanesque; (*d*) *F:* **to l. over backwards to do sth.,** (i) se mettre en quatre, mettre tout en œuvre, pour faire qch.; (ii) aller aux concessions extrêmes pour faire qch. **2.** *v.tr.* **to l. a ladder against a wall,** appuyer une échelle contre, à, un mur; **to l. sth. against sth.,** (i) (*with its back*) adosser, (ii) (*with its side*) accoter, qch. à, contre, qch.; **to l. one's head forward, back,** pencher la tête en avant; renverser la tête.

Leander [li'ændər], *Pr.n.m. Gr.Myth:* Léandre.

leaning[1] ['li:niŋ], *a.* penché, penchant; **l. wall,** mur *m* qui penche, hors d'aplomb; **the l. tower of Pisa,** la tour penchée de Pise.

leaning[2], *s.* **1.** inclination *f*, obliquité *f*, penchement *m* (d'une tour, etc.). **2.** inclination (**towards,** pour); penchant *m* (**towards,** pour, vers); tendance *f* (**towards,** à); **to have leanings towards a party,** pencher pour un parti; **he has leanings towards communism,** il penche vers le communisme; c'est un communisant.

leanness ['li:nnis], *s.* (*a*) maigreur *f*; (*b*) *I.C.E:* pauvreté *f* (du mélange).

lean-to ['li:ntu:]. **1.** *a.* **l.-to roof,** comble *m* en appentis; toit *m* à un égout. **2.** *s.* appentis *m*; abat-vent *m inv.*

leap[1] [li:p], *s.* **1.** saut *m*, bond *m*; soubresaut *m* (d'un cheval); **to take a l.,** faire un saut; **to take a l. in the dark,** faire un saut dans l'inconnu; s'aventurer; agir en aveugle; **his heart gave a l.,** son cœur bondit; il eut un bondissement de cœur; **after business had taken a l. forward,** après le rebondissement des affaires; **to advance, progress, by leaps and bounds,** avancer par bonds et par sauts; prendre un essor prodigieux; **he is progressing by leaps and bounds,** il avance à pas de géant; **prices are rising by leaps and bounds,** les prix augmentent, montent, d'une manière folle; **the circulation went up by leaps and bounds,** le tirage (du journal) allait augmentant à une allure vertigineuse. **2.** obstacle *m* (à sauter); saut; **salmon l.,** chute *f* d'eau (que les saumons doivent sauter pour remonter). **3. l. day,** jour *m* intercalaire; le 29 février; **l. year,** année bissextile.

leap[2], *v.* (*p.t. & p.p.* **leaped** [li:pt] *or* **leapt** [lept]) **1.** *v.i.* (*a*) sauter, bondir; (*of horse, etc.*) soubresauter; **to l. to one's feet,** se lever brusquement; être sur pied d'un bond; **to l. over a ditch,** sauter un fossé; franchir un fossé (d'un bond); **to l. on to one's horse,** sauter à cheval; (*of fish*) **to l. at flies,** moucheronner; **to l. at an offer,** sauter sur une offre; **to l. at the opportunity,** saisir l'occasion au vol; **to l. for joy,** sauter de joie; **his heart leapt for joy,** son cœur bondit, tressaillit, de joie; **he nearly leapt out of his skin,** il a sauté au plafond; **to l. up in indignation,** sursauter d'indignation; (*b*) (*of flame, etc.*) **to l. (up),** jaillir. **2.** *v.tr.* (*a*) sauter (un fossé); franchir (un fossé) d'un saut; (*b*) (*cause to leap*) **to l. a horse over a ditch,** faire sauter, faire franchir, un fossé à un cheval.

leaper ['li:pər], *s.* sauteur, -euse.

leapfrog[1] ['li:pfrɔg], *s.* (*a*) **to play l.,** jouer à saute-mouton *m*; (*b*) *Cmptr:* **l. test,** test *m* saute-mouton; (*c*) *Mil:* (manœuvre *f* de) dépassement *m*.

leapfrog[2], *v.tr. & i.* (**leapfrogged**) (*a*) sauter (qch.) comme à saute-mouton; (*b*) *Mil:* opérer une manœuvre de dépassement, un dépassement; avancer, progresser, par dépassement.

leapfrogging ['li:pfrɔgiŋ], *s.* (*a*) jeu *m* de saute-mouton; (*b*) *Mil:* (manœuvre *f* de) dépassement *m*; avance *f*, progression *f*, par dépassement; **to relieve forward units by l.,** relever des unités de premier échelon par dépassement.

leaping[1] ['li:piŋ], *a.* **1.** (animal, etc.) sautillant, bondissant; (*of gait, etc.*) capricant. **2. l. flames,** flammes jaillissantes.

leaping[2], *s.* **1.** (*a*) action *f* de sauter; le saut; (*b*) sauts. **2.** franchissement *m* (d'une haie, etc.).

learn [lə:n], *v.tr. & i.* (*p.t. & p.p.* **learnt** [lə:nt], *occ.* **learned** [lə:nd]) **1.** apprendre (le français, les mathématiques, etc.); **to l. to read,** apprendre à lire; **to l. sth. by heart,** apprendre qch. par cœur; **to l. a new technique,** s'initier à une nouvelle technique; **he has learnt his lesson,** (i) il a appris sa leçon; (ii) *F:* il a eu une leçon; **to l. from one's mistakes,** mettre à profit les fautes commises; **he has everything to l. about. . .,** il ignore tout de . . .; **to like learning,** aimer à apprendre, à s'instruire; **they (just) don't want to l.,** ils n'ont aucune envie d'apprendre; **I've learnt better since then,** je sais à quoi m'en tenir maintenant; *Prov:* **it is never too late to l.,** on apprend à tout âge. **2.** apprendre (une nouvelle, etc.); **we are sorry to l. that . . .,** nous sommes désolés d'apprendre que . . .; **to l. sth. about s.o.,** apprendre qch. sur le compte de qn; **I have yet to l. why they did it,** j'ignore toujours pourquoi ils l'ont fait. **3.** *A: & P:* **(teach) to l. s.o. sth.,** apprendre qch. à qn; *P:* **I'll l.** [lə:n] **you to speak to me like that!** je vous apprendrai à me parler de la sorte! **that'll l. him!** ça lui apprendra!

learnable ['lə:nəbl], *a.* qui peut être appris; qui peut s'apprendre; **that's not l. in six easy lessons,** ça ne s'apprend pas comme ça, dans un clin d'œil.

learned ['lə:nid], *a.* savant, instruit, érudit, docte; **Alfonso the L.,** Alphonse le sage; **l. treatise,** traité savant; **l. words,** mots savants; **l. profession,** profession libérale; **to be l. in the law,** être versé dans le droit; être grand juriste.

learnedly ['lə:nidli], *adv.* savamment; doctement, avec érudition.

learnedness ['lə:nidnis], *s.* instruction *f,* érudition *f,* savoir *m,* connaissances *fpl.*

learner ['lə:nər], *s.* **1.** celui qui apprend; **to be a quick l.,** apprendre facilement. **2.** élève *mf,* commençant, -ante, débutant, -ante; apprenti *m*; *Aut:* **l. (driver),** apprenti conducteur.

learning ['lə:niŋ], *s.* **1.** action *f* d'apprendre, étude *f*; apprentissage *m.* **2.** science *f,* instruction *f,* érudition *f,* savoir *m,* connaissances *fpl*; **seat of l.,** centre intellectuel; **man of great l.,** homme de grand savoir; **advantages of l.,** avantages *m* de l'instruction; *Hist:* **the New L.,** la Renaissance.

leasable ['li:səbl], *a.* affermable.

lease[1] [li:s], *s. Tex:* envergeure *f,* encroix *m.*

lease[2], *s. Jur:* (*a*) bail *m, pl.* baux; **l. of a dwelling, house-letting l.,** bail à loyer; **l. of a farm, farming l., l. of ground, of land,** bail à ferme; **l. of livestock,** bail à cheptel; **long l.,** bail à long terme, à longue échéance; **ninety-nine year l., building l.,** bail emphytéotique; **to let out (sth.) on l., to grant (sth.) under l.,** louer, donner, (qch.) à bail; affermer (une terre); **lands out on l.,** terres louées à bail, affermées; **to take (sth.) on l.,** prendre (qch.) à bail, affermer (une terre); **to hold (sth.) on l.,** tenir (qch.) à bail; **to cancel a l.,** résilier un bail; **to take a new l., to renew the l., of a flat, of a house,** renouveler le bail d'un appartement, d'une maison; **l. to be renewed by tacit agreement, by tacit reconduction,** bail renouvelable par tacite reconduction; **expiration of a l.,** expiration *f* d'un bail; *Fig:* **to take on a new l. of life,** renaître à la vie, faire corps neuf; *F:* repartir pour un nouveau bail; **the sea air gave him a new l. of life,** l'air de la mer lui a donné un renouveau, un regain, de vie; (*b*) concession *f* (d'une source d'énergie, etc.).

lease[3], *v.tr.* **1. to l. (out),** louer; donner (une maison) à bail; affermer (une terre); amodier (une ferme, des droits de pêche, etc.). **2.** prendre (une maison) à bail; louer (une maison); affermer (une terre).

lease[4], *v.tr. Tex:* mettre (le fil, etc.) en échevettes.

leasehold ['li:should]. **1.** *s.* (*a*) tenure *f* à bail, *esp.* tenure en vertu d'un bail emphytéotique; (*b*) propriété *f,* immeuble *m,* loué(e) à bail. **2.** *a.* tenu à bail.

leaseholder ['li:shouldər], *s.* locataire *mf,* affermataire *mf,* à bail.

lease-lend ['li:s'lend], *s. Pol.Ec:* prêt-bail *m* (*no plural*).

leash[1] [li:ʃ], *s.* **1.** (*a*) laisse *f,* attache *f*; **to put a dog on the l.,** mettre un chien en laisse, à l'attache; **to hold a dog on a short l.,** tenir un chien de court; **to strain at the l.,** (i) (*of dog*) tirer sur la laisse; (ii) (*of pers.*) ruer dans les brancards; (*b*) *Her:* (*for falcon*) longe *f.* **2.** (*a*) *Ven:* harde *f* (de trois chiens, de trois faucons, etc.); (*b*) **a l. of . . .,** un trio de . . . . **3.** *Tex:* lisse *f*; cordon transversal de lame.

leash[2], *v.tr.* **1.** mettre (un chien) à l'attache; attacher la laisse à (un chien). **2.** *Ven:* harder par trois (des chiens courants, etc.).

leashed [li:ʃt], *a.* (*a*) *Ven:* **l. hounds,** chiens à l'accouple; (*b*) *Her:* (faucon) longé.

leasing[1] ['li:siŋ], *s.* location *f* à bail; affermage *m.*

leasing[2] ['li:ziŋ], *s. A: & B:* mensonge(s) *m* (*pl*).

least [li:st]. **1.** *a.* (*a*) **(the) l.,** (le, la) moindre, (le, la) plus petit(e); **he hasn't the l. chance,** il n'a pas la moindre chance; **he flares up at the l. thing,** il se fâche pour un rien, pour un oui ou pour un non; **I'm not the l. bit musical,** je ne suis pas musicien pour un sou; *Mth:* **the l. common multiple,** le plus petit commun multiple; **l. squares,** moindres carrés; (*b*) le moins important; **this was not the l. of his services,** ce n'est pas le moindre des services qu'il nous a rendus; **that's the l. of my worries,** ça c'est le dernier, le moindre, de mes soucis; (*c*) *Orn:* **l. bittern,** petit butor. **2.** (*a*) *s.* **(the) l.,** (le) moins; **to say the l. (of it),** pour ne pas dire plus, mieux; pour ne rien dire de plus; pour ne pas mieux dire; au bas mot; **it's the l. I can do,** c'est la moindre des choses; *Prov:* **(the) l. said (the) soonest mended,** moins on en parle mieux cela vaut; mieux vaut se taire que mal parler; trop gratter cuit, trop parler nuit; (*b*) *adv. phrs.* **at l.,** (tout) au moins; **I can at l. try,** je peux toujours essayer; **but at l. it must. . .,** encore faut-il que . . .; **it cost him at l. £1000,** cela lui a coûté mille livres au bas mot; **it would at l. be advisable to . . .,** il conviendrait tout le moins de . . .; **you should at l. have warned me,** au moins auriez-vous dû m'avertir; **he is back, at l. so it's said, they say,** il est de retour, du moins on l'affirme; **he is at l. as tall as you,** il est pour le moins aussi grand que vous; **not in the l.,** pas le moins du monde; pas du tout; aucunement, nullement; **it doesn't matter in the l.,** cela n'a pas la moindre importance; cela n'a aucune importance; **I don't understand in the l. what you are saying,** je n'entends rien à ce que vous dites. **3.** *adv.* **(the) l.,** (le) moins; **the l. unhappy,** le moins malheureux; **he deserves it l. of all,** il le mérite moins que tous les autres, moins que personne; **don't tell anyone, l. of all your brother,** n'en dites rien, à votre frère moins qu'à personne.

leastways ['li:stweiz], *adv. Dial:* en tout cas . . .; ou du moins . . ..

leat [li:t], *s. Hyd.E:* canal *m* d'amenée; (canal de) dérivation *f*; bief *m,* biez *m,* buse *f,* abée *f,* bée *f* (de moulin); rayère *f,* reillère *f.*

leather[1] ['leðər], *s.* **1.** cuir *m*; **undressed l.,** cuir d'œuvre; cuir inapprêté; cuir cru; **waxed l., tallowed l.,** cuir en suif; **cup l.,** cuir embouti; **white l.,** cuir mégis, cuir blanc, cuir aluné; **brown l.,** cuir havane; **Russia l.,** cuir de Russie; **l. bottle,** outre *f*; **l. shoes,** chaussures *f* en cuir; **l. apron,** tablier *m* de cuir; **fancy l. goods,** maroquinerie *f*; **l. suitcase,** valise *f* en cuir; *Mil:* **l. equipment,** buffleterie *f*; **l. paper,** papier *m* maroquin; **l. dressing,** mégisserie *f,* peausserie *f*; **l. dresser,** mégissier *m,* peaussier *m*; *Equit: F: O:* **to lose l.,** s'écorcher, s'excorier; *F:* faire du bifteck; *Lit:* **nothing like l.!** = vous êtes orfèvre, Monsieur Josse! **2.** (*a*) cuir (de pompe, de soupape, etc.); **hand l.,** manique *f* (de cordonnier, etc.); *Nau:* paumelle *f* (de voilier, etc.); (*of shoe*) **upper l.,** empeigne *f*; *Sp: F: O:* **the l.,** *Cr:* la balle; *Fb:* le ballon; (*b*) **(stirrup) l.,** étrivière *f*; **to shorten one's leathers,** raccourcir ses étrivières; (*c*) *O:* **leathers,** (i) culotte *f,* (ii) guêtres *fpl,* de cuir. **3.** *O:* **artificial l.,** similicuir *m.*

leather[2], *v.tr.* **1.** (*a*) garnir (qch.) de cuir; (*b*) **to become leathered,** durcir; prendre la consistance du cuir. **2.** *F:* tanner le cuir à (qn); étriller, rosser (qn).

leatherback ['leðəbæk], *s. Rept:* tortue *f* à cuir; tortue lyre, tortue luth.

leatherboard ['leðəbɔ:d], *s.* carton-cuir *m, pl.* cartons-cuir.

leather-bound ['leðəbaund], *a.* (livre) relié (en) cuir.

leathercloth ['leðəkləθ], *s.* toile *f* cuir.

leatherette [leðə'ret], *s. O:* similicuir *m*; (i) papier-cuir *m, pl.* papiers-cuir; (ii) tissu *m* cuir; toile *f* cuir.

leathering ['leðəriŋ], *s. F:* raclée *f,* rossée *f*; **to give s.o. a l.,** tanner le cuir à qn.

leatherjacket ['leðədʒækit], *s.* **1.** *Ich:* (*a*) baliste *m*; (*b*) monacanthe *m.* **2.** *Ent:* larve *f* de la tipule.

leathern ['leðən], *a. O: & Lit:* de cuir; en cuir.

leatherneck ['leðənek], *s.m. F:* soldat *m* de l'infanterie de marine.

leatherwood ['leðəwud], *s. Bot:* dirca *m*; bois-cuir *m.*

leatherwork ['leðəwə:k], *s.* **1.** travail *m* en cuir; travail du cuir. **2.** (*a*) cuirs (d'une carrosserie, etc.); (*b*) **fancy l.,** maroquinerie *f.*

leatherworker ['leðəwə:kər], *s.* maroquinier *m.*

leatherworking ['leðəwə:kiŋ], *s.* maroquinerie *f.*

leathery ['leðəri], *a.* qui ressemble au cuir; (*of food*) coriace; *Rept:* **l. turtle** = LEATHERBACK.

leave[1] [li:v], *s.* **1.** permission *f,* autorisation *f,* permis *m*; **l. to go out,** permission (de sortir); exeat *m*; **l. to land,** permis de débarquer; **to beg l. to do sth.,** (i) demander la permission de faire qch.; demander à faire qch.; (ii) prendre la liberté de faire qch.; **to give, grant, s.o. l. to do sth.,** donner, accorder, à qn la permission de faire qch.; permettre à qn, accorder à qn, de faire qch.; autoriser qn à faire qch.; **to take l. to do sth.,** prendre la liberté de faire qch.; se permettre de faire qch.; **by your l., with your l.,** avec votre permission; si vous le voulez bien; ne vous en déplaise; **with not even a by your l., without even saying by your l.,** sans même en demander la permission; **he didn't ask anybody's l., he just went ahead and did it,** il n'a demandé la permission de personne, il l'a simplement fait. **2.** (*a*) *Adm: Mil: etc:* congé *m*; **sick l.,** congé de maladie; **compassionate l.,** congé, permission *f,* pour affaires de famille; **to apply for l.,** demander un congé, une permission; *Nau:* **shore l.,** sortie *f* à terre; permission d'aller à terre; *Mil: etc:* **short, long, l.,** permission de courte, de longue, durée; **indefinite l.,** congé illimité; **all l. is cancelled,** toutes les permissions sont suspendues; **absence without l.,** absence illégale; **to break l.,** s'absenter sans permission; **to overstay one's l.,** dépasser son congé; **l. book,** cahier *m* des permissionnaires; (*b*) *Jur: A:* **release of prisoner on ticket of l.,** libération conditionnelle; **to be out on ticket of l.,** être libéré conditionnellement; **to break one's ticket of l.,** rompre son ban; **ticket-of-l. man,** (prisonnier) libéré *m* conditionnellement. **3.** adieux *mpl,* congé; **to take one's l.,** prendre congé; faire ses adieux; **to take l. of s.o.,** prendre congé de qn; faire ses adieux à qn; *F:* **to take l. of pleasures,** dire adieu aux plaisirs; **to take French l.,** filer à l'anglaise, sans prendre congé; s'éclipser, s'esquiver; brûler la politesse (à qn). **4.** *Bill:* jeu livré à l'adversaire; **to give one's opponent a l.,** livrer du jeu à son adversaire.

leave[2], *v.* (**left** [left]; **left**)

I. *v.tr.* **1.** laisser; (*a*) **he left his hat on the table,** il a laissé son chapeau sur la table; **he left his pen behind, at home,** il a oublié son stylo; **to l. things (lying) about,** laisser traîner des choses; *F:* **take it or l. it,** c'est à prendre ou à laisser; (*b*) **to l. a wife and three children,** laisser une femme et trois enfants; **to be left well off, badly off,** être laissé à l'aise, dans la gêne; (*c*) **to l. one's money to s.o.,** laisser, léguer, sa fortune à qn; **he was left a legacy,** il lui a échu un héritage; (*d*) (*with complement*) **to l. the door open,** laisser la porte ouverte; **the house was left empty for a few minutes,** la maison se trouvait vide pendant quelques minutes; **to l. sth. unfinished,** laisser qch. inachevé; **to l. a page blank,** laisser une page en blanc; **blue cover with title left in white,** couverture bleue avec titre en réserve blanche; **to l. s.o. free to do what he wants,** laisser qn libre de faire ce qu'il veut; **l. me alone!** laissez-moi en paix! ne me dérangez pas! **you won't l. me to have my dinner alone?** vous n'allez pas me laisser dîner tout seul? **don't l. her standing there,** ne la laissez pas plantée là; **she had been left a widow at thirty,** elle était restée veuve à trente ans; **left to oneself,** livré à soi-même; **l. him to himself,** laissez-le faire; **left to myself I should act differently,** si j'étais libre j'agirais autrement; **let us l. it at that,** *F:* **l. it,** demeurons-en là; **it's bad psychology—we'll l. it at that,** c'est de la mauvaise psychologie.—Soit, et n'en parlons plus; (*e*) **to l. hold, l. go, of sth.,** lâcher qch.; **don't l. go of the rope,** ne lâchez pas la corde; (*f*) **to l. one's bag, hat, in the cloakroom,** laisser, déposer, sa valise à la consigne; déposer son chapeau au vestiaire; **left luggage,** bagages déposés à la consigne; **left-luggage office,** consigne; **left-luggage ticket,** bulletin *m* de consigne; **left-luggage lockers,** consigne automatique; **to l. sth. with s.o.,** déposer qch. entre les mains de qn; confier qch. à qn; **to l. s.o. in charge of sth.,** laisser à qn la garde de qch.; **to go away without leaving one's address,** partir sans laisser son adresse; **to l. a message for s.o. (that . . .),** laisser un mot, un billet, pour qn; faire dire à qn que . . ., (faire) prévenir qn que . . .; **has anything been left for me?** a-t-on déposé quelque chose pour moi? (*g*) **to l. s.o. to do sth.,** laisser qn faire qch.; laisser à qn le soin de faire qch.; **then the judge leaves the jury to find their verdict,** le juge suspend l'audience pour que le jury puisse délibérer; **I l. the reader to judge,** je laisse à juger au lecteur; **I l. it to you,** je m'en remets à vous, je m'en rapporte à vous, je m'en fie à vous; **l. it to me,** remettez-vous-en à moi; laissez-moi faire; je m'en charge; j'en fais mon affaire; **l. it to time,** laissez faire le temps; laissez faire au temps; **nothing was left to accident,** on avait paré à toutes les éventualités; **I l. it to you to decide,** je vous laisse le soin de décider; **I l. it to you to judge whether I am right or wrong,** je vous laisse à juger si j'ai tort ou raison; **he left it to others to work out the details,** il laissait à d'autres le soin d'élaborer les détails; **it was left for his sons to complete the work,** ce fut à ses fils d'achever le travail; (*h*) *Bill:* **to l. the balls in a good, bad, position,** donner un bon, mauvais, acquit; **to l. nothing for one's opponent,** tirer la carotte; jouer la carotte; (*i*) **to be left,** rester; **there are three bottles left,** il reste trois bouteilles; **there are no strawberries left,** il ne reste plus de fraises; **I have none left,** il ne m'en reste plus; **to stake what money one has left,** jouer le reste de son argent; **to gather together what is left of one's fortune,** réunir les débris de sa fortune; **he had no choice left,** il ne lui restait plus de choix; **nothing was left to me but to . . .,** il ne me restait qu'à . . .; (*j*) *Mth:* **three from seven leaves four,** trois ôté de sept reste quatre. **2.** (*a*) quitter (un endroit, qn); **he has left London,** il est parti de Londres; il a quitté Londres; **I l. home at eight o'clock,** je pars de la maison à huit heures; **she never leaves the house,** elle ne sort jamais de la maison; **to l. the room,** sortir (de la pièce); *Sch:* **may I l. the room?** puis-je sortir? **to l. one's bed,** quitter le lit; sortir de son lit; **you may l. us,** vous pouvez nous laisser; vous pouvez vous retirer; **his eyes never left her,** il ne la quittait pas des yeux; **to l. the table,** se lever de table; **on leaving the theatre, the meeting,** à la sortie du théâtre; à l'issue de la réunion; **to l. one's job,** quitter son emploi; *Mil: Navy:* **to l. the service,** quitter le service; **on leaving school he went into an office,** au sortir du collège, sitôt après l'école, il entra dans un bureau; **I'm leaving at Christmas,** je quitte l'école, je quitte mon emploi, à Noël; (*of small bird, F: of child*) **to l. the nest,** prendre sa volée; **we left the church on our right,** nous avons laissé l'église à droite; **how did you l. your family?** comment se portaient vos parents quand vous les avez quittés? *Nau:* **to l. harbour,** sortir du port; *v.i.* **we l. tomorrow,** nous partons demain; **we are leaving for Paris,** nous partons pour Paris; **he left again yesterday,** il est reparti hier; **he has just left,** il sort d'ici; **(just) as he was leaving, on leaving,** au moment de son départ; en sortant, en partant; **I was just leaving when . . .,** j'étais sur mon départ lorsque . . .; (*b*) abandonner; *B:* **they left all and followed Him,** abandonnant tout ils le suivirent; **to l. one's wife,** quitter sa femme; se séparer d'avec sa femme; (*c*) **they left me behind,** ils sont partis sans moi; *Sp: etc:* **to be left behind, left standing,** être dépassé, distancé (par ses concurrents); (*d*) (*of train*) **to l. the track, the rails,** dérailler; **the car left the road,** la voiture a quitté la route; (*of gramophone needle*) **to l. the sound groove,** dérailler; (*e*) (*of valve*) **to l. its seat,** décoller.

II. (*compound verbs*) **1. leave in,** *v.tr.* inclure, retenir (un passage dans un article, etc.).

2. leave off. (*a*) *v.tr.* (i) cesser de porter, ne plus mettre (un vêtement); (ii) quitter, renoncer à (une habitude); **to l. off smoking,** renoncer au tabac; **to l. off work,** cesser le travail; (*b*) *v.i.* cesser, s'arrêter; **where did we l. off?** où en sommes-nous restés (dans notre lecture, etc.)? **if the rain doesn't l. off,** si la pluie continue, persiste; si la pluie ne cesse pas; *P:* **l. off!** ça suffit comme ça!

3. leave out, *v.tr.* (*a*) exclure (qn); (*b*) omettre (qch.); (*c*) oublier (qch.); **to l. out a line,** sauter une ligne; *Mus:* **to l. out notes,** croquer des notes.

4. leave over, *v.tr.* (*a*) remettre (qch.) à plus tard; (*b*) **to be left over,** rester; **if there are any goods left over from the sale,** s'il reste encore des articles après la vente; **you can keep what is left over,** vous pouvez garder le surplus.

leave³, *v.i.* = LEAF².

leaved [li:vd], *a.* **1.** (*a*) feuillé, feuillu; *Her:* feuillé; (*b*) (*with adj. or num. prefixed, e.g.*) **thick-l.,** aux feuilles épaisses; **three-l.,** (volet *m*, paravent *m*, etc.) à trois feuilles; **broad-l. tree,** arbre feuillu, à larges feuilles; *Bot:* **long-l.,** longifolié; **narrow-l.,** à feuilles étroites, linéaires; *Bot:* angustifolié, sténophylle; **ivy-l.,** à feuilles de lierre. **2.** (porte *f*) à deux battants; (table *f*) à rallonges.

leaven¹ ['lev(ə)n], *s.* levain *m*; *Lit:* **to purge out the old l.,** se défaire du vieux levain (du péché); **a l. of revolt, of hate,** un levain de révolte, de haine.

leaven², *v.tr.* **1.** faire lever (le pain, la pâte). **2.** modifier, transformer (le caractère d'un peuple, etc.) (**with,** par); imprégner (**with,** de); **to l. the masses,** noyauter les masses.

leavening ['lev(ə)niŋ], *a.* **l. influences,** influences transformatives.

leaver ['li:vər], *s.* **(school) leavers,** élèves sortants; **early l.,** (i) *Sch:* élève qui abandonne ses études de bonne heure; (ii) personne qui quitte une réunion, etc., de bonne heure.

leavetaking ['li:vteikiŋ], *s.* adieux *mpl.*

leaving ['li:viŋ], *s.* **1.** départ *m*; *Sch: A:* **l. examination,** examen *m* de sortie; *A:* **l. certificate,** certificat *m* d'études (secondaires). **2.** *pl.* **leavings,** (i) restes *m*; débris *m*; reliefs *m* (d'un repas); (ii) *Min:* stériles *m*. **3.** *Ind: etc:* **l.-off time,** cessation *f* du travail; heure *f* de (la) sortie (des ateliers, etc.).

lebachia [li'beikiə], *s. Paleont: Bot:* lebachia *m*.

Lebanese [lebə'ni:z]. *Geog:* (*a*) *a.* libanais; (*b*) *s.* Libanais, -aise.

Lebanon ['lebənən], *Pr.n. Geog:* le Liban; *Bot:* **cedar of L., L. cedar,** cèdre *m* du Liban.

lebbek ['lebek], *s. Bot:* **l. (tree),** albizzia *m* lebbek, bois à feu.

lebensraum ['leibənzraum], *s.* espace vital.

lebia ['li:biə], *s. Ent:* lebia *f*.

lecanium [li'keiniəm], *s. Ent:* lecanium *m*.

lecanora [lekə'nɔ:rə], *s. Moss:* lécanore *f*.

lecher ['letʃər], *s. A:* libertin *m*, débauché *m*.

lecherous ['letʃərəs], *a.* lascif, libertin, lubrique, débauché; (*of old man*) paillard.

lecherously ['letʃərəsli], *adv.* lascivement, lubriquement; en libertin.

lecherousness ['letʃərəsnis], **lechery** ['letʃəri], *s.* lasciveté *f*, lubricité *f*, libertinage *m*, luxure *f*; paillardise *f*.

Lecidea [li'sidiə], *s. Moss:* lecidea *m*.

lecithin ['lesiθin], *s. Ch:* lécithine *f*.

lecithinase [le'siθineis], *s. Bio-Ch:* lécithinase *f*.

lecontite ['lekəntait], *s. Miner:* lecontite *f*.

lectern ['lektən], *s. Ecc:* lutrin *m*, aigle *m*; **to read from the l.,** lire au lutrin.

lectionary ['lekʃənəri], *s. Ecc:* lectionnaire *m*.

lectisternium [lekti'stə:niəm], *s. Rom.Ant:* lectisterne *m*.

lector ['lektɔ:r], *s.* **1.** *Ecc: A:* lecteur *m*. **2.** *Sch:* chargé *m* de cours.

lecture¹ ['lektʃər], *s.* **1.** (*a*) conférence *f* (**on,** sur); **to give, attend, a l.,** faire, assister à, une conférence; **course, series, of lectures,** série *f* de conférences; **l. hall,** salle *f* de conférence; (*b*) *Sch:* cours *m*; **history l.,** cours d'histoire; **l. on Napoleon,** cours sur Napoléon; **to attend lectures,** suivre un cours; **he always cuts his lectures,** il n'assiste jamais aux cours. **2.** *F:* sermon *m*, semonce *f*, mercuriale *f*; **to read s.o. a l.,** faire une semonce, faire la morale, à qn; semoncer qn; sermonner qn; chapitrer qn; **to get a l.,** recevoir une semonce.

lecture². **1.** *v.i.* faire une conférence, des conférences; *Sch:* faire un cours (**on,** sur); **he lectured on Eastern affairs,** il a traité des affaires d'Orient; **after lecturing for half an hour,** après avoir discouru une demi-heure; **to l. to students,** faire une conférence, des conférences, faire un cours, à des étudiants. **2.** *v.tr. F:* sermonner, semoncer, réprimander, chapitrer (qn); faire la morale à (qn); faire la leçon à (qn).

lecturer ['lektʃərər], *s.* **1.** conférencier, -ière. **2.** *Sch:* **(junior, assistant) l.** = maître assistant; **(senior) l.** = maître de conférences.

lectureship ['lektʃəʃip], *s. Sch:* maîtrise *f* de conférences.

lecturing ['lektʃəriŋ], *s.* cours *mpl*; conférences *fpl*.

lecyth ['lesiθ], *s. Bot:* lécythis *m*.

Lecythidaceae [lesiθi'deisi:], *s.pl. Bot:* lécythidacées *f*.

lecythis [le'siθis], *s. Bot:* lécythis *m*; **l. ollaria,** jacapucayo *m*.

lecythus, *pl.* **-i** ['lesiθəs, -ai], *s. Archeol:* lécythe *m*.

led [led], *a.* **l. horse,** cheval *m* à, de, main; cheval mené en main.

Leda ['li:də]. **1.** *Pr.n.f. Gr.Myth:* Léda. **2.** *s. Moll:* léda *f*.

ledge¹ [ledʒ], *s.* **1.** rebord *m*; saillie *f*; (*on wall, building*) corniche *f*, épaulement *m*, projecture *f*. **2.** (*a*) **l. of rock,** corniche de rocher, plateforme rocheuse; (*b*) (*awash or under water*) rocher *m* à fleur d'eau, banc *m* de rochers, récif *m*, écueil *m*; (*c*) *Geol:* filon *m*, veine *f* (de minerai, etc.). **3.** *Mec.E:* épaulement *m*, rebord *m*, méplat *m* (d'une pièce mécanique). **4.** *Civ.E:* berme *f*, ressaut *m* (d'une voie).

ledge². **1.** *v.tr. O:* poser (qch.) sur un rebord, sur une saillie. **2.** *v.i.* former un rebord, une saillie.

ledger ['ledʒər], *s.* **1.** *Book-k:* grand livre (de frais, de ventes, d'achats, etc.); **payroll l.,** grand livre de paie, *Navy:* cahier *m* de solde. **2. l. (pole),** moise *f*, filière *f* (d'échafaudage). **3. l. (stone),** dalle *f* tumulaire; dalle funéraire; pierre tombale. **4.** *Min:* **l. (wall),** chevet *m* (de filon). **5.** *Tex:* **l. blade,** lame *f* femelle (de tondeuse). **6.** *Fish:* **l. bait, l. tackle,** appât *m*, appareil *m*, de fond; **l. line,** ligne dormante, de fond; bricole *f*; **l. hook,** hameçon *m* de ligne dormante. **7.** *Mus:* **l. line,** ligne postiche, supplémentaire, additionnelle, ajoutée (à la portée).

ledum ['li:dəm], *s. Bot:* ledum *m*.

lee [li:], *s.* (*a*) *Nau:* côté *m* sous le vent; **l. shore,** terre *f* sous le vent; **under the l. of the land,** sous le vent, à l'abri, de la terre; **to bring a vessel by the l.,** empanner un navire; **l. current,** courant *m* portant sous le vent; **l. helm,** barre *f* dessous; **l. sheet,** écoute *f* sous le vent; **l. tide,** marée *f* qui porte sous le vent; (*b*) abri *m* (contre le vent); **in the l. of a rock, of a hill,** abrité par un rocher, par une colline; **on the l. side of a house,** à l'abri d'une maison, abrité par une maison.

leeboard ['li:bɔ:d], *s. Nau:* aile *f*, semelle *f*, de dérive.

leech¹ [li:tʃ], *s.* **1.** *Ann:* sangsue *f*; **the leeches,** les sangsues, les bdellaires *m*; **l. breeding,** hirudi(ni)culture *f*; *Med:* **to apply leeches to s.o.,** mettre, poser, des sangsues à qn. **2.** *Med:* **artificial l.,** sangsue artificielle; ventouse scarifiée. **3.** *F:* (*pers.*) importun, -e; colleur, -euse, sangsue, crampon *m*.

leech², *s. F: A:* médecin *m*, *A:* mire *m*; **horse l.,** vétérinaire *m*.

leech³, *s. Nau:* chute *f* arrière (de voile); **l. line,** cargue-bouline *f*, *pl.* cargues-boulines; **l. rope,** ralingue *f* de chute.

leechcraft ['li:tʃkrɑ:ft], *s. F: A:* la médecine; l'art *m* de guérir.

leek [li:k], *s. Bot:* poireau *m*; **stone l.,** ciboule *f*; **sand l.,** rocambole *f*; **house l.,** joubarbe *f*; **cobweb house l.,** joubarbe aranéeuse; *F: A:* **to eat the l.,** filer doux; avaler un affront; *F:* avaler un crapaud, une couleuvre; **l. green,** vert poireau (*m*) *inv.*

leemost ['li:moust], *a.* (navire, etc.) le plus éloigné du côté sous le vent.

leer¹ ['liər], *s.* (*a*) œillade *f* en dessous; regard de côté (malicieux et mauvais); (*b*) regard paillard, polisson.

leer², *v.i.* **to l. at s.o.,** (i) lorgner, guigner, (qn) d'un air méchant; (ii) lancer des œillades à qn; fixer sur qn un regard paillard, polisson.

leer³, *s. Glassm:* four *m* à recuire; four de recuite.

leering ['liəriŋ], *a.* (regard) en dessous, paillard, polisson.

leeringly ['liəriŋli], *adv.* **1.** avec un regard narquois et méchant. **2.** avec un regard paillard, polisson.

leery ['liəri], *a. P: A:* **1.** rusé, malin. **2. to be l. of s.o.,** soupçonner qn.

lees [li:z], *s.pl.* lie *f* (de vin, etc.); **to drink, drain, the cup to the l.,** boire la coupe jusqu'à la lie; *O:* **the l. of society,** les bas-fonds *m* de la société; le rebut, la lie, de la société.

leeward ['lu:əd, 'li:wəd]. *Nau:* **1.** *a. & adv.* sous le vent; *Geog:* **the L. Islands,** les Iles *f* sous le Vent (i) de l'Océanie française, (ii) des Antilles. **2.** *s.* côté *m* sous le vent; **to drop, drift, fall, sag, to l.,** tomber sous le vent; être dépalé; **to pass to l. of a ship,** passer sous le vent d'un navire.

leewardly ['lu:ədli, 'li:wəd-], *a. Nau:* (navire) qui dérive beaucoup, qui tient mal le plus près; (navire) mauvais boulinier.

leeway ['li:wei], *s.* (*a*) *Nau:* dérive *f*; **to make l.,** dériver (à la voile); (*b*) **he has considerable l. to make up,** il a un fort retard à rattraper.

left [left]. **1.** *a.* gauche; **l. bank of a river,** rive *f* gauche d'un fleuve; **on my l. hand,** à ma gauche. **2.** *adv. Mil:* **l. turn!** à gauche, gauche! **eyes l.!** tête (à) gauche! **3.** *s.* (*a*) (i) (*left hand*) gauche *f*; **on the l., to the l.,** à gauche; *Aut: etc:* **keep (to the) l.,** tenir la gauche; (ii) (*left fist, arm*) *Box:* gauche *m*; **to feint with the l.,** feinter du gauche; (iii) *Ven:* coup *m* (de fusil) à gauche, coup du canon gauche; (*b*) (*left wing*) *Mil:* gauche *f*; l'aile *f* gauche; (*c*) *Pol:* **the L.,** les gauches *m*; la gauche.

lefthand ['lefthænd], *a.* **1.** (poche, etc.) de gauche; **l. blow,** coup *m* de la main gauche; *Box:* coup du gauche; **on the l. side,** à gauche; **the l. drawer,** le tiroir de gauche; **the l. corner of the sheet,** le coin à gauche de la feuille; *Mth:* **l. side of an equation,** premier membre d'une équation; **l. turn,** virage *m* à gauche. **2.** *Tchn:* (serrure *f*, vis *f*, foret *m*) à gauche; (filin) commis à gauche; **l. thread (of a screw),** filet *m* à gauche (d'une vis); **filet** renversé; *Av:* **l. propeller,** hélice *f* à pas à gauche.

lefthanded ['left'hændid]. **1.** *a.* (*a*) (*of pers.*) gaucher, -ère; (*b*) *F:* (*of pers.*) gauche, maladroit; (*c*) *F:* suspect, équivoque; **l. compliment,** compliment peu flatteur; compliment douteux; (*d*) **l. marriage,** mariage *m* de la main gauche; (i) mariage morganatique; (ii) concubinage *m*; (*e*) (club *m* de golf, etc.) pour gaucher; (*f*) *Tchn:* = LEFTHAND 2. **2.** *adv.* (*a*) (virer, etc.) à gauche; (*b*) **to play tennis l.,** jouer au tennis de la main gauche.

lefthandedness ['left'hændidnis], *s.* habitude *f* de se servir de la main gauche.

lefthander ['left'hændər], *s.* **1.** (*pers.*) gaucher, -ère. **2.** (*a*) *Box:* coup *m* du gauche; fausse garde, gaucher; (*b*) *F:* coup déloyal.

leftism ['leftizm], *s.* politique *f* de gauche; gauchisme *m*.

leftist ['leftist], *a. & s. Pol:* gauchiste (*mf*); (homme) de gauche.

left-off ['leftɔf], *a.* **l.-o. clothing,** *s.* **left-offs,** (i) vieilles frusques; (ii) *Com:* friperie *f*.

leftover ['leftouvər]. **1.** *a.* (provisions *f*, etc.) de surplus, en surplus; *Com:* **l. stock,** restes *m.* **2.** *s.* (*a*) survivance *f* (des temps passés); (*b*) *F: O:* (*of pers.*) vieille baderne; (*c*) *Com: Cu:* **leftovers,** restes.

leftward ['leftwəd]. **1.** *a.* de gauche, à gauche. **2.** *adv.* = LEFTWARDS.

leftwards ['leftwədz], *adv.* vers la gauche; à gauche.

left-wing ['leftwiŋ], *a.* (politique *f*) de gauche.

left-winger ['left'wiŋər], *s. Pol:* gauchiste *mf*; député *m* de la gauche; **the left-wingers,** les gauches *m,* les gauchistes, la gauche.

leg[1] [leg], *s.* **1.** (*a*) jambe *f* (d'homme, de cheval); patte *f* (de chien, d'oiseau, d'insecte, de reptile); **artificial l.,** jambe artificielle; **wooden l.,** jambe de bois; pilon *m*; **to take to one's legs,** prendre ses jambes à son cou; **I ran as fast as my legs would carry me,** j'ai couru à toutes jambes; **to have good legs, a good pair of legs,** (i) avoir de bonnes jambes; être bon marcheur; (ii) avoir des jambes bien tournées; **to put one's best l. foremost, forward,** (i) avancer vite, à toute allure; presser, allonger, le pas; partir du bon pied; (ii) pousser la besogne; faire de son mieux; faire appel de toute son énergie; (iii) se mettre à l'ouvrage; **to stand on one l.,** se tenir sur un pied; **to jump on one l.,** sauter sur un pied; sauter à cloche-pied; **to be on one's legs,** être debout; (*of public speaker*) être en train de parler; avoir la parole; **I have been on my legs all day,** j'ai été toute la journée sur les jambes; **I was never off my legs,** j'étais toujours debout; **to get on one's legs,** (i) se lever; (ii) prendre la parole; (iii) s'établir; se faire une clientèle; **to get on one's legs again,** (i) se relever; (ii) se rétablir; **to set s.o. on his legs again,** (i) relever qn; remettre qn debout; (ii) rétablir qn dans ses affaires; tirer qn d'affaire; **to set a business on its legs,** mettre une affaire sur pied, *F:* sur ses pattes; **to be on one's last legs,** tirer vers sa fin; ne plus battre que d'une aile; en être à sa dernière ressource; être à la dernière extrémité; être à bout de ressources; être aux abois; **his business is on its last legs,** son affaire ne marche plus; **to be carried off one's legs,** être emporté; perdre pied; **to feel, find, one's legs,** (i) se trouver en état de se tenir debout; (ii) prendre conscience de ses forces; (iii) se faire une clientèle; être assuré de l'avenir; **to keep one's legs,** se maintenir debout; ne pas tomber; ne pas se laisser emporter (par le courant); **to give s.o. a l. up,** (i) faire la courte échelle à qn; (ii) aider qn à monter en selle; (iii) *F:* donner à qn un coup d'épaule; *O:* **to have the legs of s.o.,** battre qn à la course; **to pull s.o.'s l.,** se payer la tête de qn; monter un bateau à qn; faire marcher qn; **somebody's been pulling your l.,** c'est un farceur, un blagueur, qui vous aura dit cela; on vous a monté un bateau; *F: O:* **to shake a l.,** danser, gambiller; *F: O:* **to show a l.,** (i) quitter son lit; se lever; (ii) y mettre du sien, de l'énergie; *F:* **l. show,** spectacle *m* de music-hall (où les girls montrent leurs jambes); *A:* **to make a l.,** (i) faire, tirer, une révérence; (ii) tendre le jarret; *Cr:* **l. before wicket,** (mis hors jeu) à pied obstructif; **l. bye,** (point obtenu par) jambe touchée; *Wr:* **l. lock,** passement *m* de pied; *Med: F:* **l. iron,** attelle *f* en fer; *Equit:* **l. strap,** trousse-pied *m inv* (pour cheval rétif); *Cost:* **l. hole,** entrée *f* (de bas, de chaussette); **l. space,** place *f* pour les jambes; *Aut:* dégagement antérieur du siège arrière; **l. rest,** appui-jambes *m inv*; bout *m* de pied (d'une chaise longue); *Med:* étrier *m*; (*b*) *Her:* **eagle's l.,** main *f* d'aigle. **2.** *Cu:* **l. of chicken,** cuisse *f* de poulet; **l. of veal,** cuisseau *m* de veau; **roast l. of pork,** cuissot *m* de porc rôti; **frogs' legs,** cuisses de grenouille; **l. of lamb, mutton,** gigot *m*; *Cost: O:* **l.-of-mutton sleeves,** manches *f* à gigot; *Nau:* **l.-of-mutton sail,** voile *f* triangulaire, à houari. **3.** (*a*) jambe (de pantalon); tige *f* (de bas, etc.); (*b*) *Mch:* **(water) l. of a boiler,** culotte *f,* cuissard *m,* d'une chaudière. **4.** (*a*) pied *m* (de table, de chaise); jambe (de trépied, de pied d'appareil photographique, de mât tripode, etc.); jambage *m,* montant *m* (de chevalet); bras *m,* anche *f,* montant (d'une bigue, d'une chèvre); *Min:* montant, pied-droit *m, pl.* pieds-droits (de châssis de mine); *Av:* jambe (d'atterrisseur); **articulated l., lever-type l.,** jambe articulée, jambe à levier; **compression l.,** jambe à amortisseur pneumatique; **oleo l.,** jambe à amortisseur oléopneumatique, jambe amortisseuse; **telescopic l.,** jambe télescopique; (*b*) *Nau:* béquille *f* (pour étayer un bateau échoué); *Tchn:* **support l.,** jambe d'appui; (*c*) branche *f* (de compas). **5.** (*a*) *Surv:* côté *m* d'un triangle (de canevas géodésique); **l. of traverse,** élément *m* d'un cheminement (compris entre deux stations de triangulation successives); (*b*) *Av:* élément, segment *m* (d'une ligne, d'une trajectoire de vol); étape *f*; **approach l.,** élément d'un circuit d'approche; **base l.,** étape de base; **cross-wind l.,** étape vent de travers; **down-wind l.,** étape vent arrière; (*c*) *Nau:* bordée (courue par un navire en louvoyant); **to make long, short, legs,** courir, faire, de grandes, de petites, bordées; (*d*) (i) *El:* élément (d'un circuit électrique); *Elcs:* **(radio-range) l.,** chenal *m* radioélectrique, faisceau *m* de radioalignement. **6.** *Cr:* le terrain à gauche et en arrière du joueur qui est au guichet; **l. drive,** coup *m* arrière à gauche. **7.** *Sp: etc:* manche *f*; **the first l.,** la première manche.

leg[2], *v.tr.* **(legged; legging) 1.** *F:* **to l. it,** (i) faire la route à pied; *F:* prendre le train onze; (ii) marcher, courir, rapidement; *F:* jouer des jambes; tricoter. **2.** *Cr:* chasser (la balle) à gauche.

legacy ['legəsi], *s.* legs *m*; **to leave a l. to s.o.,** faire un legs à qn; **he was left a l.,** il lui échut un héritage; **to come into a l.,** faire un héritage; **this desk is a l. from my predecessor,** j'ai hérité ce bureau de mon prédécesseur; **l. duty,** droits *mpl* de succession.

legal ['li:g(ə)l], *a.* **1.** légal, -aux; licite; **l. commerce,** commerce *m* licite; **the l. fare,** le prix du tarif (d'un taxi, etc.). **2.** (*a*) légal; judiciaire, juridique; selon les lois; **l. charges,** (i) (*in an action*) frais *m* judiciaires; (ii) (*in a transaction*) frais juridiques; **l. entity,** personne civile, morale; **l. crime,** crime légal; crime prévu par la loi; **by l. process,** par voies légales; par voies de droit; **forms of l. procedure,** formes processives; **to be brought to a l. trial,** être jugé selon les lois; **l. redress,** recours *m* à la justice; **l. security,** caution *f* judiciaire; **l. claim to sth.,** titre *m* juridique à qch.; **l. document,** acte *m* authentique; **l. ties,** liens *m* juridiques; (*of corporation, etc.*) **to acquire l. status,** acquérir la personnalité juridique, civile, morale; (*b*) **l. year,** année civile; **l. charges,** frais *m* judiciaires; (*of bank, etc.*) **l. department,** service *m,* bureau *m,* du contentieux; **to go into the l. profession,** se faire une carrière dans le droit; *usu. Pej:* **the l. fraternity,** les gens *m* de palais; la basoche; **l. practitioner,** homme *m* de loi; **l. expert,** jurisconsulte *m*; avocat *m* conseil; **of great l. experience,** qui a une profonde connaissance de la procédure; **l. adviser,** conseiller *m* juridique; **to take l. advice** = consulter un avocat; **l. writer,** juriste *m*; **l. language,** phraséologie *f* juridique; **l. term,** terme *m* de pratique; **the l. mind,** l'esprit *m* juridique; (*c*) **l. owner,** propriétaire *m* légitime, en titre. **3.** *Theol:* légal; se rapportant à la loi de Moïse.

legalism ['li:gəlizm], *s.* (*a*) juridisme *m*; (*b*) légalisme *m.*

legalist ['li:gəlist], *s.* légaliste *m.*

legality [li(:)'gæliti], *s.* légalité *f.*

legalization [li:gəlai'zeiʃ(ə)n], *s.* légalisation *f.*

legalize ['li:gəlaiz], *v.tr.* rendre (un acte) légal; autoriser (un acte); légaliser, certifier, authentiquer (un document).

legally ['li:gəli], *adv.* légalement ((i) licitement, (ii) judiciairement, juridiquement); **l. responsible,** responsable en droit; **l. justifiable,** légitime en droit.

legate[1] ['legət], *s. Ecc: Rom.Ant:* légat *m*; *Ecc:* **the Papal L.,** le légat du Pape; **l. a latere,** légat a latere.

legate[2] [li'geit], *v.tr.* léguer.

legatee [legə'ti:], *s.* légataire *mf*; **general, universal, l.,** légataire universel; **residuary l.,** légataire à titre universel.

legatine ['legəti:n], *s. Tex:* légatine *f.*

legation [li'geiʃ(ə)n], *s. Dipl: Ecc:* légation *f* ((i) la fonction, (ii) l'hôtel de la légation, (iii) le personnel de la légation); **secretaryship of a l.,** chancellerie *f* diplomatique; **l. fees,** droits *m* de chancellerie.

legato [li'gɑ:tou], *adv. Mus:* legato; coulé.

legator [li'geitər], *s.* testateur, -trice.

legend ['ledʒənd], *s.* **1.** légende *f*; *Lit:* **the Golden L.,** la Légende dorée. **2.** (*a*) inscription *f,* légende (sur une médaille, etc.); (*b*) explication *f,* légende (d'une carte, etc.); (*c*) *N.Arch:* **l. speed,** vitesse prévue.

legendary ['ledʒənd(ə)ri]. **1.** *a.* légendaire. **2.** *s. A:* (*writer or book*) légendaire *m.*

legerdemain ['ledʒədəmein], *s.* (tours *mpl* de) passe-passe *m*; tour d'adresse; magie blanche; prestidigitation *f*; escamotage *m.*

legged [legd], *a. Her:* **l. or,** (oiseau) membré d'or.

-legged ['legid, legd], *a.* (*with adj. or num. prefixed, e.g.*) **short-l.,** aux jambes courtes; court enjambé; **two-l.,** à deux jambes; à deux pattes.

leggings ['leginz], *s.pl. Cost:* jambières *f*; guêtres *f*; *F:* leggin(g)s *m*; **overall l.,** jambières, cuissards *m* (de cycliste).

leggy ['legi], *a.* aux longues jambes; dégingandé; (cheval) haut-monté, *pl.* haut-montés; **a l. girl,** une fille toute en jambes.

Leghorn ['leg(h)ɔ:n]. **1.** *Pr.n. Geog:* Livourne *f.* **2.** *s. Cost:* **l. (hat),** chapeau *m* de paille d'Italie. **3.** *s. Husb:* **(white) L.,** leghorn *f.*

legibility [ledʒi'biliti], *s.* lisibilité *f,* caractère *m* lisible, netteté *f* (d'une écriture).

legible ['ledʒibl], *a.* (écriture) lisible, nette, qui se lit facilement.

legibly ['ledʒibli], *adv.* (écrire) lisiblement.

legion ['li:dʒ(ə)n], *s.* légion *f*; **the Roman legions,** les légions romaines; *Mil.Hist:* **the Foreign L.,** la Légion étrangère; **the L. of honour,** la Légion d'honneur; **the British L.,** l'Association (anglaise) des anciens combattants; *Lit:* **their name is L.,** ils sont innombrables; ils s'appellent Légion.

legionary ['li:dʒənəri]. **1.** *a.* qui se rapporte à une légion, aux légions; légionnaire. **2.** *s.* légionnaire *m.*

legislate ['ledʒisleit], *v.i. & tr.* faire des, les, lois; légiférer; **to l. a people into poverty,** réduire un peuple à la misère à force de multiplier les lois; juguler un peuple sous l'étreinte des lois.

legislation [ledʒis'leiʃ(ə)n], *s.* **1.** législation *f*; **internal l.,** législation nationale; **the l. in force,** la législation en vigueur; **anti-trust l.,** législation anti-trust. **2.** *Parl:* programme législatif.

legislative ['ledʒislətiv]. **1.** *a.* (*a*) législatif; **the L. Assembly,** l'Assemblée législative; (*b*) **l. power,** la puissance législatrice. **2.** *s. U.S:* = LEGISLATURE.

legislator ['ledʒisleitər], *s.* législateur, -trice.

legislatorial [ledʒislə'tɔ:riəl], *a.* législatif.

legislature ['ledʒislətjər], *s.* législature *f*; pouvoir législatif; corps législatif.

legist ['li:dʒist], *s.* légiste *m.*

legitimacy [li'dʒitiməsi], *s.* **1.** légitimité *f* (d'un enfant, d'un successeur au trône); filiation *f* légitime; descendance *f* (d'un prince) en ligne directe. **2.** légitimité (d'une opinion).

legitimate[1] [li'dʒitimət], *a.* **1.** (*a*) (enfant *m,* héritier *m,* souverain *m,* autorité *f,* etc.) légitime; (*b*) **l. stage, the l.,** le vrai théâtre; le théâtre régulier. **2.** (raisonnement *m,* etc.) légitime; **to draw l. conclusions from the facts,** tirer des conséquences légitimes des faits.

legitimate[2] [li'dʒitimeit], *v.tr.* légitimer (un enfant, etc.).

legitimately [li'dʒitimətli], *adv.* légitimement; à bon droit.

legitimation [lidʒiti'meiʃ(ə)n], *s.* **1.** légitimation *f* (d'un enfant). **2.** légalisation *f* (de la monnaie, etc.).

legitimatize [li'dʒitimətaiz], légitimer (un enfant, etc.).

legitime ['ledʒitim], *s. Jur: Scot:* réserve (à laquelle ont droit les enfants du défunt).

legitimism [li'dʒitimizm], *s.* légitimisme *m.*

legitimist [li'dʒitimist], *a. & s.* légitimiste (*mf*).

legitimize [li'dʒitimaiz], *v.tr.* = LEGITIMATIZE.

legless ['leglis], *a.* sans jambes; **l. cripple,** cul-de-jatte *m, pl.* culs-de-jatte.

legman, *pl.* **-men** ['legmæn, -men], *s. NAm:* reporter *m* qui fait la chronique des chiens écrasés.

leg-pull ['legpul], *s. F:* blague *f,* attrape *f,* carotte *f,* mystification *f.*

leg-puller ['legpulər], *s. F:* blagueur, -euse; farceur, -euse; mystificateur, -euse.

legume ['legjum], **legumen** [le'gju:men], *s.* **1.** fruit *m* d'une légumineuse. **2.** *pl.* **legumes,** légumineuses *f.*

legumin [le'gju:min], *s. Ch:* légumine *f.*

Leguminosae [legju:mi'nousi:], *s.pl. Bot:* légumineuses *f.*

leguminous [le'gju:minəs], *a. Bot:* légumineux; **l. plant,** légumineuse *f.*

Leibni(t)zian [laib'nitsiən], *a. & s. Phil:* leibni(t)zien, -ienne.

Leibnizianism [laib'nitsiəniz(ə)m], *s. Phil:* leibnizianisme *m.*

Leicester ['lestər], *s. Husb:* (*sheep*) dishley *m.*

leiomyoma [laioumai'oumə], *s. Med:* léiomyome *m.*

leiomyosarcoma ['laioumaiousɑ:'koumə], *s. Med:* léiomyosarcome *m.*

leiothrix [laiou'θriks], *s. Orn:* leiothrix *m,* liothrix *m, F:* rossignol *m* du Japon.

leipoa [lai'pouə], *s. Orn:* lipoa *m,* leipoa *m.*

leishmania [li:ʃ'meiniə], *s. Prot:* leishmanie *f.*

leishmaniasis [li:ʃmə'naiəsis], *s.* leishmaniose *f*; *Med:* **visceral l.,** kala-azar *m*; **post-kala-azar dermal l.,** leishmanide *f.*

leishmanioid [li:ʃ'meiniɔid], *s. Med:* **(dermal) l.,** leishmanide *f.*

leishmaniosis [li:ʃmeini'ousis], *s. Med:* leishmaniose *f.*

leister[1] ['li:stər], *s. Fish:* trident *m.*

leister[2], *v.tr. Fish:* prendre (un saumon) au trident.

leisure ['leʒər], *s.* loisir(s) *m(pl)*; **to have l.,** avoir du loisir; **to have enough l. for reading,** avoir le loisir, le temps, de lire; **to enjoy some l. time,** prendre des loisirs; disposer de loisirs; avoir du temps libre; **he attends to our business when he has the l.,** il s'occupe de notre affaire selon ses disponibilités; **to do sth. at one's l.,** faire qch. à loisir, à tête reposée, dans ses moments de loisir; **do it at your l.,** faites-le à (votre) loisir; **people of l.,** les désœuvrés *m*; **l. hours,** heures *f* de loisir; **in my l. moments,** à mes moments perdus; *F:* **I'm a lady of l. at the moment,** je ne travaille pas à présent; *F:* **to be a**

gentleman of l., vivre de ses rentes; **how do you spend your l. time?** comment occupez-vous vos loisirs?

leisured ['leʒəd], *a.* **1.** (*of life, etc.*) de loisir; désœuvré. **2.** (*of pers.*) qui a des loisirs; désœuvré; **the l. classes,** les rentiers *m*.

leisureliness ['leʒəlinis], *s.* absence *f* de hâte; peu *m* de hâte, lenteur *f* (**in doing sth.,** à faire qch.).

leisurely ['leʒəli]. **1.** *a.* (*of pers.*) qui n'est jamais pressé; **l. air,** air désœuvré; **l. pace,** allure mesurée, posée, tranquille; **to ride at a l. pace,** chevaucher à l'amble, sans hâte, sans se presser; **l. journey,** voyage *m* par petites étapes; **he took a l. walk,** il s'est promené doucement; **to do sth. in a l. fashion,** faire qch. sans se presser. **2.** *adv.* (*a*) à tête reposée; (*b*) posément; sans se presser.

leitmotiv ['laitmouti:f], *s.* leitmotiv *m*.

leitneria [lait'niəriə], *s. Bot:* leitneria *m*.

lek [lek], *s. Orn:* arène *f*, lek *m*.

leman[1] ['li:mən, 'lemən], *s. A:* amant *m*, amante *f*.

Leman[2]. *Pr.n. Geog:* **Lake L.,** le lac Léman.

lemma[1], *pl.* **-as, -ata** ['lemə, -əz, -ətə], *s.* **1.** *Log: Mth:* lemme *m*. **2.** en-tête *m inv* (d'une composition littéraire).

lemma[2], *s. Bot:* glumelle *f*.

lemming ['lemiŋ], *s. Z:* lemming *m*.

lemna ['lemnə], *s. Bot:* lemna *f*; lemne *f*; lenticule *f*.

Lemnaceae [lem'neisii:], *s.pl. Bot:* lemnacées *f*.

Lemnian ['lemniən], *a. & s. Geog:* **1.** *a.* lemnien. **2.** *s.* Lemnien, -ienne. **3.** *Miner: A.Med:* **L. earth, bole,** terre lemnienne.

lemniscate [lem'niskeit], *s. Mth:* lemniscate *f*.

lemniscus, *pl.* **-nisci** [lem'niskəs, -'niski:], *s. Rom.Ant: Pal:* lemnisque *m*.

lemon[1] ['lemən]. **1.** *s.* (*a*) *Bot:* citron *m*; (*as a drink*) **fresh l.,** citron pressé; **l. squash,** (i) sirop *m* de citron; (ii) limonade non gazeuse (faite avec (i)); *Cu:* **l. cheese, curd,** confiture composée d'œufs, de beurre et de jus de citron; **l. drop,** bonbon *m* au citron; **l. kali,** tartrate de soude bicarbonatée (pour la préparation de la limonade gazeuse); **oil of lemons, l. oil,** (essence *f* de) citron; **l. squeezer,** presse-citrons *m inv*; (*b*) **l. (tree),** citronnier *m*; (*c*) *F:* **the answer's a l.,** rien à faire! des clous! bernique! **my last car was a l.,** ma dernière voiture était un loup; **I felt a real l.,** je me sentais bien bête; (*d*) personne, chose, qui ne vaut rien; **she's a l.,** c'est un remède d'amour. **2.** *s. Bot:* **l. balm,** mélisse officinale: citronnelle *f*; **l. plant, l. verbena,** verveine *f* citronnelle; verveine odorante. **3.** *a.* **l. (coloured),** (jaune) citron *inv*.

lemon[2], *s. Ich:* **l. sole,** plie *f* sole; **l. dab,** limande *f* sole.

lemonade [lemə'neid], *s.* limonade *f*; **still l.,** (i) citronnade *f*; (ii) limonade non gazeuse.

lemongrass ['lemәngrɑ:s], *s. Bot:* schénanthe *m*; jonc odorant.

Lemoniidae [lemə'naiidi:], *s.pl. Ent:* lémoniidés *m*.

lemonwood ['lemənwud], *s. Bot:* pittospore *m*.

lemur ['li:mər], *s.* **1.** *Rom.Ant:* (*pl.* **lemures** ['lemjuri:z]) lémure *m*. **2.** *Z:* lémur *m*, lemur *m*; maki *m*; **ring-tailed l.,** maki catta; lemur catta; **mouse l.,** (i) chéirogale *m*; (ii) microcèbe *m*; **dwarf l.,** microcèbe; **flying l.,** dermoptère *m*, galéopithèque *m*; **sifaka l.,** propithèque *m*; **woolly l.,** avahi *m*.

lemurian [li'mjuəriən], *a. Z:* lémurien.

Lemuridae [li'mju:ridi:], *s.pl. Z:* lémuridés *m*.

lemuroid ['lemjurɔid], *a. & s. Z:* lémurien (*m*).

Lemuroidea [lemju'rɔidiə], *s.pl. Z:* lémuriens *m*.

lend[1] [lend], *v.tr.* (**lent** [lent]; **lent**) **1.** (*a*) prêter (**sth. to s.o., s.o. sth.,** qch. à qn); **l. me a pencil,** prêtez-moi un crayon; **to l. money at interest,** prêter de l'argent à intérêt; **to l. against security,** prêter sur gages; **to l. stock,** se faire reporter; *Mil:* **to l. an officer to s.o.,** détacher un officier auprès de qn; (*b*) **to l. (out) books,** louer des livres; tenir une bibliothèque de prêt. **2.** (*a*) **to l. s.o. a (helping) hand,** donner un coup de main à qn; (*b*) **to l. an ear, one's ear(s), to . . .,** prêter l'oreille à . . .; (*c*) **to l. dignity to sth.,** donner, prêter, de la dignité à qch.; **distance lends enchantment to the view,** tout paraît beau (vu) de loin. **3.** *v.pr.* **to l. oneself, itself, to sth.,** se prêter à qch.; **I would not l. myself to such a transaction,** je ne me prêterais pas à un trafic de cette sorte.

lend[2], *s. P:* **if you've read that book can I have the l. of it?** si vous avez lu ce livre, est-ce que je peux l'emprunter?

lender ['lendər], *s.* prêteur, -euse.

lending[1] ['lendiŋ], *a.* prêteur, -euse.

lending[2], *s.* prêt *m* (d'un objet, de l'argent); *Fin:* prestation *f* (de capitaux); *St.Exch:* placement *m* (de titres en report); **l. (out) of books,** location *f* de livres; **l. library,** bibliothèque *f* de prêt; *Fin:* **l. capital,** prestation *f* de capitaux; **l. bank,** banque *f* de crédit; **l. institution,** établissement *m*, institution *f*, de crédit; **l. banker,** banquier prêteur; **l. officer,** agent prêteur (d'un établissement de crédit).

lend-lease ['lend'li:s], *s. Pol.Ec:* prêt-bail *m* (*no pl.*).

length [leŋθ], *s.* **1.** longueur *f*; **overall l.,** longueur totale, longueur hors tout, longueur d'encombrement; **to be two metres in l.,** avoir deux mètres de longueur, de long; **over the whole l. of the course,** sur toute l'étendue de la piste; **total l. of a pipeline,** parcours global d'une conduite; **the canal will take heavy barges throughout its l.,** le canal est praticable aux gros chalands dans toute sa longueur; **to cut rails, etc., to l.,** araser des rails, etc.; (*of firearm*) **l. in calibres,** longueur en calibres; (*of ship*) **l. at water line,** longueur à la flottaison; **l. of run,** longueur à la coulée; **l. of stroke,** (i) course *f* (d'un outil); (ii) *Mch: etc:* (longueur de) course (du piston); (*of ship, car, etc.*) **to turn in its own l.,** virer sur place; *Row: Turf:* **to win by a l., by half a l.,** gagner d'une longueur, d'une demi-longueur; **throughout the l. and breadth of the country,** dans toute l'étendue du pays; **that's about the l. and breadth of it,** voilà de quoi il s'agit; **to walk the whole l. of the street,** parcourir la rue d'un bout à l'autre; **I fell full l. on the ground,** je suis tombé de tout mon long; **lying full l.,** étendu de tout son long. **2.** longueur (d'un livre, d'un voyage, d'un discours, etc.); **to make a stay of some l.,** faire un séjour assez prolongé, d'une certaine durée; **l. of a lease,** durée d'un bail; **l. of service,** ancienneté *f*; **the l. of time required to do sth.,** le temps qu'il faut pour faire qch.; **he does nothing for any l. of time,** il ne fait rien d'une façon suivie; *Lit:* **our l. of days,** la durée de notre vie; *adv.phr.* **at l.,** (i) longuement; (ii) enfin; **to speak at l. on a subject,** parler longuement sur un sujet; **to explain sth. at l.,** expliquer qch. en détail; **he lectured me at great l.,** il m'a fait une longue semonce; **at l. he agreed,** enfin, à la fin, il a consenti. **3.** (*a*) *Scot:* distance *f*; **to go the l. of London,** aller jusqu'à Londres; (*b*) **to go to the l. of doing sth.,** aller jusqu'à faire qch.; **he would go to any lengths,** rien ne l'arrêterait; il ne reculerait devant rien; **I did not think you would go to such lengths,** je ne pensais pas que vous iriez aussi loin, que vous pousseriez les choses aussi loin, jusqu'à ce point; **to go to dangerous lengths,** se risquer trop loin. **4.** *Pros:* longueur (d'une voyelle, d'une syllabe). **5.** *Ten: Cr:* longueur de balle; **to keep a good l.,** conserver une bonne longueur de balle. **6.** morceau *m*, bout *m* (de ficelle, etc.); pièce *f*, coupon *m* (d'étoffe); morceau (de bois); pan *m* (de mur); tronçon *m* (de tuyau); **to cut a bar into lengths,** tronçonner une barre; *Dressm: Tail:* **dress l., trouser l.,** coupon de robe, de pantalon; **what l. do I need for . . .?** quel métrage faut-il pour . . .?

lengthen ['leŋθən]. **1.** *v.tr.* allonger, rallonger (une jupe, une chaîne, une table, etc.); prolonger (un intervalle, la vie, une voyelle, etc.); **to l. out a story,** étendre un récit. **2.** *v.i.* s'allonger, se rallonger; (*of days*) augmenter, croître, grandir; (*of time*) se prolonger; **his face lengthened,** son visage s'allongea.

lengthened ['leŋθənd], *a.* prolongé.

lengthening ['leŋθəniŋ], *s.* allongement *m*, rallongement *m*; agrandissement *m* (en long); prolongation *f* (d'un séjour, etc.); **l. piece,** allonge *f*, rallonge *f*; **l. tube,** allonge (de cornue, etc.); *Min:* **l. rod,** rallonge (de sonde).

lengthily ['leŋθili], *adv.* (parler, écrire) longuement, avec prolixité; (raconter) tout au long.

lengthiness ['leŋθinis], *s.* longueurs *fpl*; prolixité *f* (d'un discours).

lengthways ['leŋθweiz], *adv.* longitudinalement; dans le sens de la longueur; en longueur; de long; en long; **bus with seats arranged l.,** autobus *m* avec places disposées en long; **to fold cloth l.,** plier le drap en longueur; fauder le drap.

lengthwise ['leŋθwaiz]. **1.** *adv.* = LENGTHWAYS. **2.** *a.* (coupe) en long, en longueur; **l. motion,** déplacement longitudinal.

lengthy ['leŋθi], *a.* (discours, récit) (très) long, plein de longueurs, prolixe, qui n'en finit pas.

leniency ['li:njənsi], *s.* clémence *f*; douceur *f*, indulgence *f* (**to, towards,** pour).

lenient ['li:njənt], *a.* clément; doux, *f.* douce; indulgent (**to, towards,** envers, pour); **to adopt l. measures,** adopter des mesures de douceur.

leniently ['li:njəntli], *adv.* avec clémence, avec douceur, avec indulgence; indulgemment.

Lenin ['lenin, le'ni:n], *Pr.n.m.* Lénine.

Leningrad ['leningræd], *Pr.n. Geog:* Léningrad *m*.

Leningrader ['leningrɑ:dər], *s.* habitant, -ante, originaire *mf*, de Léningrad.

Leninism ['leninizm], *s. Pol:* léninisme *m*.

Leninist ['leninist], **Leninite** ['leninait], *a. & s. Pol:* léniniste (*mf*).

lenition [le'niʃ(ə)n], *s. Ling:* lénition *f*.

lenitive ['lenitiv]. **1.** *a. & s. Med:* lénitif (*m*); adoucissant (*m*). **2.** *s.* palliatif *m*, adoucissement *m*.

lenity ['leniti], *s.* = LENIENCY.

leno ['li:nou], *s. Tex:* toile *f* à patron.

lens [lenz], *s.* **1.** *Opt:* (*a*) lentille *f*; **converging, condensing, l.,** lentille convergente; **diverging, dispersing, l.,** lentille divergente; **concave l.,** lentille concave; **biconcave, double-concave, l.,** lentille biconcave, lentille concave-concave; **convex l.,** lentille convexe; **biconvex, double-convex, l.,** lentille biconvexe; **Fresnel l., step l.,** lentille de Fresnel, lentille (de phare, de projecteur) à échelons; **prismatic l.,** lentiprisme *m*; **l.-shaped,** lenticulé, lenticulaire, lentiforme; **plano-concave l.,** lentille plan-concave; **plano-convex l.,** lentille plan-convexe; **bull's eye l.,** lentille plan-convexe à court foyer; **field l. (of surveying instrument),** lentille de champ (d'instrument topographique); **eye l.,** lentille supérieure d'oculaire; verre *m* d'œil; (*b*) (*magnifying glass*) loupe *f*, verre grossissant; (*c*) verre (de lunettes); **contact l., corneal l.,** verre de contact, lentille cornéenne; (*d*) *Phot:* **(camera) l.,** objectif *m* (photographique); **simple, single, landscape, l.,** objectif simple, à paysage; **compound l.,** objectif composé; **double l.,** objectif double; **three-component, four-component, l.,** objectif à trois, à quatre, lentilles; **front, back, l.,** système antérieur, postérieur (d'un objectif); **fast l.,** objectif lumineux; **portrait l.,** objectif à portrait; **supplementary l.,** lentille additionnelle, bonnette *f*; **photomicrographic object l.,** micro-objectif *m*, *pl.* micro-objectifs; **single l. reflex (camera),** reflex mono-objectif; **twin l. reflex,** reflex à deux objectifs; **soft focus l.,** objectif anachromatique, pour le flou; **telephoto(graphic) l.,** téléobjectif *m*; **wide-angle l.,** grand angulaire; objectif grand angle; **zoom l.,** zoom *m*; objectif à focale, à foyer, variable; **l. aperture,** ouverture *f* de l'objectif; **l. cap,** couvercle *m* d'objectif; couvre-objectif *m*, *pl.* couvre-objectifs; **l. holder,** porte-objectif *m*, *pl.* porte-objectifs; **l. hood, shade,** parasoleil *m*, garde-soleil *m inv* (d'objectif); **l. mount(ing), tube,** monture *f* d'objectif; porte-objectif; **l. panel, front,** planchette *f* d'objectif; porte-objectif; **l. turret,** tourelle *f* à objectifs, d'objectifs; (*e*) **mirror l.,** objectif à lentille spéculaire; (*f*) *Elcs:* **electron l.,** lentille électronique; **electrostatic l.,** lentille électrostatique; **magnetic l.,** lentille magnétique. **2.** *Anat:* **crystalline l.,** cristallin *m* (de l'œil): *F:* lentille.

lensman ['lenzmən], *s. U.S: F:* photographe *m*.

lens(o)meter [len'zɔmitər, 'lenzmi:tər], *s. Opt:* focomètre *m*.

Lent [lent], *s. Ecc:* le carême; **to keep L.,** faire carême; **the first Sunday in L.,** le premier dimanche de carême; *Sch:* **L. term,** deuxième trimestre *m* de l'année scolaire; *Bot:* **L. lily, rose,** (i) narcisse *m* des prés; (ii) lis blanc.

lenten ['lentən], *a.* de carême; *A:* **l. face,** face *f* de carême.

Lentibulariaceae [lentibjuləri'eisii:], *s.pl. Bot:* lentibulariacées *f*.

lenticel ['lentisel], *s.* **1.** *Bot:* lenticelle *f*. **2.** *Anat:* glande *f* ciliaire.

lenticellate [lenti'seleit], *a. Bot:* lenticellé.

lenticular [len'tikjulər], **lentiform** ['lentifɔ:m], *a.* lenticulaire, lentiforme; **l. body,** lentille *f* de minerai.

lentiginous [len'tidʒinəs], *a.* lentigineux.

lentigo, *pl.* **-tigines** [len'taigou, -'tidʒini:z], *s. Med:* lentigo *m*.

lentil ['lentil], *s.* lentille *f*; *Cu:* **l. soup,** potage *m* de lentilles, purée *f* de lentilles; *Bot:* **water l.,** lentille d'eau.

lentiscus [len'tiskəs], **lentisk** ['lentisk], *s. Bot:* lentisque *m*.

lento ['lentou], *adv. & s. Mus:* lento (*m*).

lentoid ['lentɔid], *a.* lentiforme.

Leo ['li:ou], *Pr.n.* **1.** Léon *m*. **2.** *Astr:* le Lion.

Leon. **1.** *Pr.n.m.* ['li:ɔn] Léon. **2.** *Pr.n. Geog:* [lei'ɔn] Léon *m*.

Leonard ['lenəd], *Pr.n.m.* Léonard.

Leonardo da Vinci [liə'nɑ:doudɑ:'vintʃi], *Pr.n.m.* Léonard de Vinci.

Leonese [li:ə'ni:z], *a. & s. Geog:* **1.** *a.* (*a*) (*in Brittany*) léonais, léonard; (*b*) (*in Spain*) léonais. **2.** *s.* (*a*) (*in Brittany*) Léonais, -aise; Léonard, -arde; (*b*) (*in Spain*) Léonais, -aise. **3.** *s. Ling:* léonais *m*.

Leonid, *pl.* **-es** ['li:ənid, -'ɔnidi:z], *s. Astr:* Léonide *f*.

Leonidas [li(:)'ɔnidæs], *Pr.n.m. Gr.Hist:* Léonidas.

leonine[1] ['li(:)ənain], *a.* **1.** de lion(s); léonin. **2.** *Jur:* **l. convention,** contrat léonin; **l. partnership,** partage léonin.

Leonine[2], *a.* **1.** *Pros:* **L. verse,** *s.pl.* **Leonines,** vers léonins. **2. the L. city,** la cité Léonine (de Rome).

leonite ['li:ənait], *s. Miner:* léonite *f*.

Leonora [li:ə'nɔ:rə], *Pr.n.f.* Léonore.

leonotis [li:ə'noutis], *s. Bot:* léonotis *m*.

leontiasis [li:ɔn'taiəsis], *s. Med:* léontiasis *f*.

leontodon [li:'ɔntədɔn], *s. Bot:* léontodon *m*.

leontopodium [li:ɔntou'poudiəm], *s. Bot:* léontopodium *m.*

leonurus [li:ə'nju:rəs], *s. Bot:* léonure *m*, leonurus *m.*

leopard ['lepəd], *s.* **1.** *Z:* léopard *m*; *B:* **can the Ethiopian change his skin or the l. his spots?** le More changera-t-il sa peau et le léopard ses taches? *F:* **can a l. change his spots?** il mourra dans sa peau. **2.** (*a*) *Z:* **American l.,** jaguar *m*; **hunting l.,** guépard *m*; léopard à crinière; **l. cat,** ocelot *m*; **snow l.,** panthère *f*, léopard, des neiges; **sea l., l. seal,** léopard de mer; **clouded l.,** panthère longibande; (*b*) *Amph:* **l. frog,** grenouille *f* léopard; *Ent:* **l. moth,** zeuzère *f*, zeugère *f*; (*c*) *Bot:* **leopard's bane,** doronic *m*; herbe *f* aux panthères; **l. plant,** ligulaire *f.*

leopardé ['lepədei], *a. Her:* léopardé.

leopardess ['lepədis], *s. Z:* léopard *m* femelle.

leopardwood ['lepədwud], *s. Bot:* bois *m* de lettres; lettre mouchetée.

Leopold ['li:əpould], *Pr.n.m.* Léopold.

leopoldinia [li:əpoul'diniə], *s. Bot:* léopoldinia *m.*

leopoldite ['li:əpouldait], *s. Miner:* léopoldite *f.*

Leopoldville ['li:əpoul(d)vil], *Pr.n. Geog: Hist:* Léopoldville.

leotard ['li:əta:d], *s. Cost:* maillot *m* (de danseur, de danseuse); justaucorps *m.*

lepadogaster [lepədou'gæstər], *s. Ich:* lépadogastre *m*, lépadogaster *m*; porte-écuelle *m inv.*

Lepanto [li'pæntou], *Pr.n. Hist:* Lépante.

lepas ['li:pəs], *s. Crust:* lépas *m*, anatif(e).

leper ['lepər], *s.* lépreux, -euse; **l. hospital, colony,** léproserie *f*; *A:* **l. house,** (ma)ladrerie *f.*

lepidagathis [lepidə'geiθis], *s. Bot:* lépidagathis *m.*

lepidine ['lepidi:n], *s. Ch:* lépidine *m.*

lepidium [lə'pidiəm], *s. Bot:* lépidium *m.*

lepidocrocite [lepidou'krousait], *s. Miner:* lépidocrocite *f.*

Lepidodendraceae [lepidouden'dreisii:], *s.pl. Paleont:* lépidodendracées *f.*

lepidodendron [lepidou'dendrən], *s. Paleont:* lépidodendron *m.*

lepidolite [le'pidəlait], *s. Miner:* lépidolit(h)e *m.*

lepidomelane [lepidou'melein], *s. Miner:* lépidomélane *m.*

lepidophloios [lepidou'flɔiɔs], *s. Paleont:* lépidophloios *m.*

lepidophyllous [lepidou'filəs], *a. Bot:* lépidophylle.

lepidophyllum [lepidou'filəm], *s. Paleont:* lépidophyllum *m.*

lepidopter [lepi'dɔptər], *s. Ent:* lépidoptère *m.*

Lepidoptera [lepi'dɔptərə], *s.pl. Ent:* lépidoptères *m.*

lepidopteran [lepi'dɔptərən], *a. & s. Ent:* lépidoptère (*m*).

lepidopterist [lepi'dɔptərist], *s.* (*pers.*) lépidoptériste *m.*

lepidopterology [lepidɔptə'rɔlədʒi], *s.* lépidoptérologie *f.*

lepidopterous [lepi'dɔptərəs], *a. Ent:* lépidoptère.

lepidosaphes [lepi'dɔsəfi:z], *s. Ent:* lépidosaphes *m.*

Lepidosauria [lepidou'sɔ:riə], *s.pl. Rept:* lépidosauriens *m.*

lepidosiren [lepidou'sairən], *s. Ich:* lépidosirène *m.*

Lepidostei [lepi'dɔsti:ai], *s.pl. Ich:* lépidostées *m.*

lepidostrobus [lepi'dɔstrəbəs], *s. Paleont:* lépidostrobus *m.*

lepidurus [lepi'dju:rəs], *s. Crust:* lépidurus *m.*

Lepidus ['lepidəs], *Pr.n.m. Rom.Hist:* Lepidus, Lépide.

lepiota [lepi'outə], *s. Fung:* lépiote *f.*

lepisma [le'pizmə], *s. Ent:* lépisme *m.*

lepisosteus [lepi'sɔstiəs], *s. Ich:* lépidostée *m.*

Leporidae [le'pɔridi:], *s.pl. Z:* léporidés *m.*

leporide ['lepərid], *s. Z:* léporide *m.*

leporine ['lepərain], *a.* de lièvre.

Lepospondyli [lepou'spɔndilai], *s.pl. Paleont:* lépospondyles *m.*

lepothrix ['lepəθriks], *s. Med:* lépothrix *m*, trichomycose noueuse.

leprechaun ['leprəkɔ:n, -hɔ:n], *s. Myth:* farfadet *m*, lutin *m.*

leprid ['leprid], *s. Med:* lépride *f.*

leproma [le'proumə], *s. Med:* léprome *m.*

leprosy ['leprəsi], *s. Med:* lèpre *f*; **spotted l.,** lèpre maculeuse; **nodular l.,** lèpre tuberculeuse; **anaesthetic l.,** lèpre anesthésique.

leprous ['leprəs], *a.* (*a*) *Med:* lépreux; (*b*) **l. old walls,** vieux murs lépreux.

Leptidae ['leptidi:], *s.pl. Ent:* leptidés *m.*

leptite ['leptait], *s. Miner:* leptite *f.*

leptobos ['leptəbɔs], *s. Paleont:* leptobos *m.*

leptocardian [leptou'ka:diən], *s. Ich:* leptocardien *m.*

leptocephalic [leptousi'fælik], *a. Z:* leptocéphale; au crâne étroit.

leptocephalus [leptou'sefələs], *s.* **1.** *Ich:* leptocéphale *m.* **2.** *Med:* (*a*) microcéphalie *f*; (*b*) (*pers.*) microcéphale *mf.*

leptocephaly [leptou'sefəli], *s. Med:* microcéphalie *f.*

leptodactyl [leptou'dæktil], *a. & s. Orn:* leptodactyle (*m*).

Leptodactylidae ['leptoudæk'tilidi:], *s.pl. Amph:* leptodactylidés *m.*

leptodactylous [leptou'dæktiləs], *a. Orn:* leptodactyle.

leptodora [lep'tɔdərə], *s. Crust:* leptodore *f*, leptodora *f.*

leptokurtic [leptou'kə:tik], *a. Stat:* leptocurtique.

Leptolepidae [leptou'lepidi:], *s.pl. Paleont:* leptolépidés *m.*

leptolepis [lep'tɔləpis], *s. Paleont:* leptolepis *m.*

leptom(e) ['leptɔm, -oum], *s. Bot:* leptome *m.*

leptomeningitis ['leptoumenin'dʒaitis], *s. Med:* leptoméningite *f.*

leptomeryx [lep'tɔməriks], *s. Paleont:* leptoméryx *m.*

leptomonas [lep'tɔmənəs], *s. Prot:* leptomonas *m.*

lepton ['leptɔn], *s. A.Num: Moll: Atom Ph:* lepton *m.*

leptoprosopic [leptouprə'sɔpik], *a. Anthr:* leptoprosope.

leptoprosopy [leptou'prɔsəpi:], *s. Anthr:* leptoprosopie *f.*

leptor(r)hine ['leptərain], **leptorrhinian, leptorrhinic** [leptə'riniən, -'rinik], *a. Nat.Hist:* leptorhinien.

leptorrhiny ['leptəraini], *s. Nat.Hist:* leptorhinie *f.*

leptosomatic, -somic [leptousou'mætik, -'soumik], *a. Anthr:* leptosome.

leptosome ['leptousoum]. *Anthr:* **1.** *a.* leptosome. **2.** *s.* leptosome *mf.*

leptospermum [leptou'spə:məm], *s. Bot:* leptospermum *m.*

leptospira[1], *pl.* **leptospira, -as, -ae** [leptou'spairə, -əz, -i:], *s. Bac:* leptospire *m.*

Leptospira[2], *s. Bac:* leptospira *m or f.*

leptospirosis ['leptouspai'rousis], *s. Med:* leptospirose *f.*

Leptosporangiatae ['leptouspɔrændʒi'eiti:], *s.pl. Bot:* leptosporangiées *f.*

Leptostraca [lep'tɔstrəkə], *s.pl. Crust:* leptostracés *m.*

leptotene ['leptəti:n], *s. Biol:* leptotène *m.*

leptotenic [leptə'ti:nik], *a. Biol:* leptotène.

leptothrix ['leptəθriks], *s. Bac:* leptothrix *m.*

Leptotyphlopidae [leptoti'flɔpidi:], *s.pl. Rept:* leptotyphlopidés *m.*

leptura ['leptjurə], *s. Ent:* lepture *m.*

leptus ['leptəs], *s. Arach:* lepte *m.*

leptynite ['leptinait], *s. Geol:* leptynite *f.*

leptynolite [lep'tinəlait], *s. Geol:* leptynolite *f.*

Lerna ['lə:nə], *Pr.n. A.Geog:* **the L. Marsh,** le marais de Lerne.

Lernaea [lə:'ni:ə], *s. Crust:* lernée *f.*

Lernaean[1] [lə:'ni:ən], *a. Gr.Myth:* **the L. hydra,** l'hydre *f* de Lerne.

lern(a)ean[2], *s. Crust:* lernée *f.*

lerot ['lerɔt], *s. Z:* lérot *m*, loir *m.*

Lesbia ['lezbiə], *Pr.n.f.* Lesbie.

Lesbian ['lezbiən]. **1.** *a.* (*a*) *Geog:* lesbien; (*b*) (*usu. not cap.*) lesbien. **2.** *s.* (*a*) *Geog:* Lesbien, -ienne; (*b*) lesbienne *f.*

lesbianism ['lezbiənizm], *s.* lesb(ian)isme *m.*

lese-majesty ['leiz'mæʒestei], *s. Jur:* lèse-majesté *f.*

lesion ['li:ʒ(ə)n], *s.* **1.** *Jur:* lésion *f* (**to s.o.'s rights,** des droits de qn). **2.** *Med:* **functional l.,** lésion fonctionnelle; **structural l.,** lésion structurale; **tissue l.,** lésion du tissu, des tissus; lésion tissulaire.

lesleyite ['lezliait], *s. Miner:* lesleyite *f.*

lespedeza [lespə'di:zə], *s. Bot:* lespedeza *m.*

less [les]. **1.** *a.* (*comp.* **lesser**) (*a*) (*smaller*) moindre; **a question of less(er) importance, l. important question,** question *f* de moindre importance; **people of l. importance, l. important, than oneself,** les gens moindres que soi; **they are l. than slaves,** ils sont moindres qu'esclaves; **the distance between these two towns is l. than I thought,** la distance entre ces deux villes est moindre que je ne le pensais; **of l. value,** d'une moindre valeur; de moindre valeur; **in a lesser degree,** à un moindre degré; à un degré inférieur; **quantities, sums, l. than . . .,** quantités *f*, sommes *f*, au-dessous de . . .; **to grow l.,** s'amoindrir; **to grow gradually l.,** aller décroissant; (*of oscillations*) s'amortir; (*b*) (*not so much, not so many*) **eat l. meat,** mangez moins de viande; **one mouth l. to feed,** une bouche de moins à nourrir; **in l. time than it takes to tell,** en moins de temps qu'il ne faut, n'en faut, pour le dire; **he devoted l. time to his studies,** il consacrait moins de temps à ses études; **l. trouble, difficulty,** moins de peine, de difficulté; **he does (all) the l. work,** il n'en fait que moins de travail; **with a few l. windows the house would be warmer,** avec quelques fenêtres de moins la maison serait plus chaude; (*c*) (*younger*) **he is l. than thirty,** il a moins de trente ans; **men (of) l. than thirty,** les hommes de moins de trente ans, les moins de trente ans; (*d*) *A:* moins important; *Hist:* **Napoleon the L.,** Napoléon le Petit; *Ecc:* **James the L.,** Jacques le Mineur. **2.** *prep.* **four hundred francs a month, l. fines,** quatre cents francs par mois, moins les amendes; **purchase price l. 10%,** prix *m* d'achat moins 10%, sous déduction de 10%; **cost of machine l. accessories,** coût *m* de la machine sans les accessoires; **eight l. five equals three,** huit moins cinq égale trois; **a year l. two days,** une année moins deux jours. **3.** *s.* moins *m*; **in l. than an hour,** en moins d'une heure; **in l. than no time,** en moins de rien; **I'll have it done in l. than no time,** je vais vous faire ça en un rien de temps; **I shall see him in l. than a fortnight,** je le verrai avant quinze jours (d'ici); **this aircraft takes off in l. than 500 m,** cet avion décolle en moins de 500 m.; **some have more, others l.,** les uns ont plus, les autres (ont) moins; **do you earn fifty pounds a week?—sometimes more, sometimes l.,** gagnez-vous cinquante livres par semaine?—tantôt plus, tantôt moins; **so much the l. to do,** d'autant moins à faire; **I can't let you have it for l.,** je ne peux pas vous le laisser à moins (**than,** de); **I can't sell it at l. than cost price,** je ne peux pas le vendre à moins du prix de revient; **I can't sell it for l.,** je ne peux pas le vendre moins cher; et c'est mon dernier mot. **4.** *adv.* **l. (well) known,** moins (bien) connu; **if I had loved him l.,** si je l'eusse aimé moins; si je l'eusse moins aimé; si je l'avais moins aimé; **I want nothing l.,** (i) je ne veux rien de moins; (ii) cela ne m'arrange pas du tout; **one man l.,** un homme de moins; **the visitors to the motor show were 20% l. (than last year),** au salon de l'automobile il y a eu 20% de visiteurs de moins, en moins (que l'année dernière); **not a penny l.,** pas un sou de moins; **it cost him a thousand, not a penny l.,** cela lui a coûté mille livres, rien de moins; **I received ten pounds l. (than I should have done),** j'ai reçu dix livres en moins (de ce qui m'était dû); **you could have had the horse for twenty pounds l.,** vous auriez pu avoir le cheval pour vingt livres de moins; **l. than six,** moins de six; **l. and l.,** de moins en moins; **the elder boy is very clever, the younger (is) l. so,** l'aîné est très intelligent, le cadet l'est moins; **she is l. pretty than her sister,** elle est moins jolie que sa sœur; **he is l. knowledgeable than you think,** il est moins savant que vous ne croyez; **the l. you think of it the better,** moins vous y penserez mieux cela vaudra; **the l. said about it the better,** moins on en parle mieux cela vaut; **the more he is punished the l. he works,** plus on le punit moins il travaille; **he will do no more, no l.,** il n'en fera ni plus ni moins; **I was (all) the l. surprised as . . .,** j'en ai été d'autant moins étonné, surpris, que . . .; **I think all the l. of him for it,** je l'en estime d'autant moins; **still l., even l.,** moins encore; **I do not say that he is negligent, much l., still l., that he is dishonest,** je ne dis pas qu'il soit négligent, et encore moins qu'il manque de probité; **l. than ever,** moins que jamais; **he continued none the l.,** il n'en continua pas moins; **though lame he is none the l. active,** bien qu'estropié il n'en est pas moins actif; **he came in first none the l.,** néanmoins il est arrivé premier. **5.** (*a*) **nothing l. than:** (i) (*at the very least*) rien (de) moins que; pour le moins; **he will take nothing l. than £5,** il ne veut pas prendre moins de £5; il en veut £5 au bas mot; **he wants nothing l. than to step into your shoes,** il n'aspire à rien (de) moins qu'à vous supplanter; **it's nothing l. than monstrous!** c'est absolument monstrueux! **nothing l. than a public apology will make me forgive him,** je ne lui pardonnerai pas à moins d'une rétractation publique; **he is nothing l. than a hero,** il n'est rien (de) moins qu'un héros; (ii) (*anything rather than*) rien moins que; (*b*) **no l.,** (i) **with no l. skill than courage,** avec autant d'habileté que de courage; **the imports are no l. important than the exports,** les importations ne sont pas moins importantes que les exportations; **this wall is no l. than a metre thick,** ce mur n'a pas moins d'un mètre d'épaisseur; **no l. good,** également bon; (ii) **they have no l. than six cars, six cars, no l.!** ils ont six voitures, pas moins, six voitures, s'il vous plaît; (iii) **no l. than a masterpiece,** rien moins qu'un chef-d'œuvre; **it was no l. a person than the duke, the duke himself, no l.!** ce n'était rien moins que le duc; c'était le duc, s'il vous plaît! **the letter was signed by X, no l.,** la lettre était signée de X, rien de moins! **what were they hunting?—lions, no l.!** qu'est-ce qu'ils chassaient?—des lions, s'il vous plaît! (iv) **he dislikes it no l. than I (do),** il ne le déteste pas moins que moi; **he fears them no l. than me,** il a aussi peur d'eux que de moi; **I expected no l. from you,** je n'en attendais pas moins de vous.

lessee [le'si:], *s.* **1.** locataire *mf* (à bail) (d'un immeuble, etc.); tenancier, -ière (d'un casino, etc.); preneur, -euse (d'une terre); fermier *m* (d'une ferme); amodiataire *m* (d'une pêche). **2.** concessionnaire *mf.*

lessen ['les(ə)n]. **1.** *v.i.* s'amoindrir, diminuer; (*of symptoms, etc.*) s'atténuer; (*of receding object*) (se) rapetisser. **2.** *v.tr.* amoindrir, diminuer; rapetisser; atténuer (le bruit, un crime); ralentir (son activité, son ardeur); **air travel has lessened distances,** les transports aériens ont rapproché les distances; *Artil:* **to l. the range,** raccourcir le tir.

lessening ['lesəniŋ], *s.* amoindrissement *m*, diminution *f*; atténuation *f*, rapetissement *m*.

lesser ['lesər], *a.* **1.** petit; **the l. rivers of France,** les petits cours d'eau de France; **the l. talents,** les petits talents; *Astr:* **the L. Bear,** la Petite Ourse; *Ph:* **l. calory,** petite calorie. **2.** (*a*) moindre; **to choose the l. of two evils, the l. evil,** de deux maux choisir le moindre; **the l. of the two scoundrels, the l. scoundrel of the two,** le moins scélérat des deux; **his l. writings are not lacking in interest,** ses œuvres *f* secondaires ne sont pas sans intérêt; (*b*) *A:* **L. Asia,** l'Asie mineure.

lesson[1] ['les(ə)n], *s.* **1.** leçon *f*; (*a*) *Sch:* cours *m*; (*in primary school*) leçon; **French, physics, l.,** cours de français, de physique; **swimming l.,** leçon, cours, de natation; **she's taking dancing lessons,** elle suit un cours de danse; **to give private lessons,** donner des leçons particulières, des répétitions; **object l.,** (i) *A:* leçon de choses; (ii) exemple *m*; **to be an object l. to s.o.,** servir d'exemple à qn; *Sch: A:* **to hear the lessons,** faire réciter les leçons; (*b*) **the lessons of experience,** les leçons de l'expérience; **to learn a l. from sth.,** tirer enseignement, une leçon, de qch.; **let that be a l. to you!** que cela vous serve d'exemple, de leçon! *F: O:* **to read s.o. a l.,** réprimander qn; faire la leçon à qn. **2.** *Ecc:* lecture *f* de l'Ecriture sainte.

lesson[2], *v.tr. F: A:* faire la leçon à (qn); **he had been well lessoned,** on lui avait fait la leçon.

lessor [le'sɔːr], *s.* bailleur, -eresse.

lest [lest], *conj.* **1.** *esp. Lit:* de peur, de crainte, que . . . (ne) + *sub.;* **do not let him have so much power, l. he (should) misuse it,** ne lui laissez pas tant de pouvoir, de peur qu'il n'en abuse; **l. the reader be led astray . . .,** de manière (à ce) que le lecteur ne se méprenne point . . .; afin que le lecteur ne se méprenne point . . .; **l. we forget,** de peur que nous n'oubliions. **2.** *A:* (*after verbs of fearing*) **I feared l. he should fall,** je craignais qu'il (ne) tombât; **I feared l. I should fall,** j'avais peur de tomber; je craignais de tomber.

lestobiosis ['lestoubai'ousis], *s. Biol:* lestobiose *f*.

lestodon ['lestoudɔn], *s. Paleont:* lestodon *m*.

let[1] [let], *s.* **1.** *A:* empêchement *m*. **2.** *Ten:* **l. (ball),** coup *m*, balle *f*, à remettre; balle de filet.

let[2], *v.tr. A:* (*p.t. & p.p.* **letted** *or* **let**) empêcher; entraver (la justice); retarder (qn).

let[3], *s.* location *f*; *F:* **when I get a l. for the season I spend the time abroad,** quand je loue ma maison, etc., pour la saison je passe le temps à l'étranger.

let[4], *v.* (*p.t. & p.p.* **let;** *pr.p.* **letting**)

I. *v.tr.* **1.** (*a*) (*allow*) permettre; laisser; **to l. s.o. do sth.,** laisser qn faire qch.; permettre à qn de faire qch.; **he l. him go,** il l'a laissé partir; **I l. them talk,** je les ai laissés dire, *occ.* laissé dire; **to l. the wounded take a little exercise,** laisser prendre aux blessés, laisser les blessés prendre, un peu d'exercice; **to l. oneself be guided,** se laisser guider; **he l. them ruin themselves,** il les a laissés se ruiner; **they l. themselves be swindled,** ils se sont laissé filouter; **l. me tell you that . . .,** permettez-moi de vous dire que . . .; **if the weather will l. us,** si le temps (nous) le permet; **I was never l. run wild,** on ne m'a jamais laissé courir en liberté; **to l. fall, slip,** laisser échapper (qch.); **they l. the opportunity go by,** ils ont laissé échapper l'occasion; **he l. go (of) the rope,** il a lâché la corde; **when can you l. me have my coat? I'll l. you have it tomorrow,** quand pourrai-je avoir mon manteau? vous l'aurez, je vous le donnerai, demain; (*b*) (*cause*) **to l. s.o. know sth., about sth.,** faire savoir, faire connaître, qch. à qn; faire part de qch. à qn; **l. me know when . . .,** faites-moi savoir quand . . .; **I will l. him know you are here,** je vais le prévenir que vous êtes ici; **you should have l. him know,** vous auriez dû le lui faire savoir; **I thought I ought to l. you know about it,** j'ai cru devoir vous en faire part; **l. me hear the story,** racontez-moi l'histoire; (*c*) **the police would not l. anyone into the street, on the bridge,** la police ne laissait passer personne par la rue, sur le pont; **they l. him go over the factory,** on lui a permis de visiter l'usine; **the captain l. no one on board,** le capitaine n'a permis à personne de monter à bord; (*d*) *A.Med:* **to l. blood,** pratiquer une saignée; saigner qn. **2.** louer (une maison, etc.); **house to l.,** maison à louer; **to be l. with immediate possession,** à louer présentement; (*with passive force*) **house that would l. easily,** maison qui se louerait facilement.

II. *v. aux.* (*supplying 1st & 3rd pers. of imperative*) **let's hurry!** dépêchons-nous! **l. us pray,** prions; **l. you and me try now!** essayons maintenant vous et moi! **don't l. us, don't let's, start yet,** ne partons pas encore; **now, don't let's have any nonsense!** allons, pas de bêtises! *A:* **l. us to supper,** allons souper; passons à la salle à manger; **l. him do it at once!** qu'il le fasse tout de suite! **l. it be done!** que cela se fasse! **l. there be no mistake about it!** qu'on ne s'y trompe pas! *B:* **l. there be light,** que la lumière soit; **so l. it be!** (i) *Lit:* soit! (ii) *Ecc:* ainsi soit-il! *Mth:* **l. AB be equal to CD,** supposons que AB soit égal à CD; **l. me see!** voyons! attendez un peu! **l. me die if . . .,** que je meure si . . .; **l. them all come!** qu'ils viennent tous! vienne qui voudra! **don't l. me see you here again!** que je ne vous retrouve plus ici! **just l. me catch you at it again!** que je vous y reprenne! **l. them do what they will,** ils auront beau faire; **l. them look at the matter in any way they wish,** de quelque façon qu'ils envisagent la question; (*hypothetical*) **l. the machine stop and there will be an accident,** que la machine vienne à s'arrêter et il y aura un accident.

III. (*compound verbs*) **1. let down,** *v.tr.* (*a*) baisser (la glace, un store, etc.); **to l. down one's hair,** (i) défaire son chignon; laisser tomber ses cheveux; (ii) *F:* abandonner toute réserve; se laisser aller; (*b*) allonger (une robe, etc.); (*c*) **the chair was broken and l. him down,** la chaise cassée s'est affaissée sous son poids; *F:* **to l. s.o. down lightly, gently,** user de tact pour faire comprendre à qn qu'il est dans son tort, pour lui refuser qch.; traiter (un coupable) avec indulgence; **l. him down lightly!** ne soyez pas trop dur avec lui! (*d*) *F:* laisser (qn) en panne; faire faux bond à (qn); désappointer (qn); trahir (les intérêts de) qn; faire un affront à (qn); humilier (qn); **I won't l. you down,** vous pouvez compter sur moi; **one should never l. the firm down,** il faut toujours prendre le parti de la maison; **he has been badly l. down,** il a été gravement déçu; (*e*) *Mch: etc:* **to l. the fires down,** laisser tomber les feux; (*f*) détendre, débander (un ressort); dégonfler (un pneu); *Metall:* **to l. down the temper of a chisel,** faire, laisser, revenir un burin; recuire, éteindre, un burin; **to l. down a metal to quenching temperature,** adoucir un métal.

2. let in, *v.tr.* (*a*) laisser entrer, faire entrer, admettre (qn); ouvrir la porte à (qn); laisser entrer (l'air, la pluie); **he's got a key, so he can l. himself in,** comme il a une clef il peut entrer dans la maison; **my shoes l. in water,** mes chaussures prennent l'eau; (*b*) **to l. s.o. in on a secret,** initier qn à un secret; *Rac: etc: F:* **to l. s.o. in on a good thing,** tuyauter qn; (*c*) *Dressm: etc:* ajouter, introduire (une pièce); (*d*) *F:* **I've been l. in for £1000,** j'y suis de £1000; j'ai fait une perte sèche de £1000; **they l. me in for the expenses,** on m'a laissé payer la note; **I've been l. in for a speech,** on m'a forcé de faire un discours; **I didn't know what I was letting myself in for,** je ne savais pas à quoi je m'engageais.

3. let into, *v.tr.* (*a*) laisser entrer, faire entrer, (qn) dans la maison, etc.; **to l. s.o. into a secret,** dévoiler un secret à qn; mettre qn dans le secret; (*b*) *Dressm: etc:* **to l. a piece into a skirt, etc.,** mettre, ajouter, une pièce à une jupe, etc.; (*c*) *P: A:* **to l. into s.o.,** s'attaquer à qn; se jeter sur qn.

4. let off, *v.tr.* (*a*) faire partir (un fusil, un pétard); tirer, faire partir (un feu d'artifice); décocher (une flèche, une épigramme); détendre brusquement (un ressort); (*b*) lâcher, laisser échapper (de l'eau, de la vapeur); (*c*) **to l. off a house into flats,** louer un immeuble en appartements; **to l. off a flat,** louer un appartement pris sur l'immeuble; (*d*) **to l. s.o. off from sth., from doing sth.,** décharger qn d'une corvée, etc.; dispenser qn de faire qch.; **I'll l. you off,** je vous en tiens quitte, je vous en dispense; **you l. him off too easily,** vous lui faites la part trop belle; **she offered to l. him off (from his engagement),** elle lui proposa de rompre; (*e*) **to l. s.o. off,** faire grâce à qn; **I'll l. you off this time,** je vous pardonne, je vous fais grâce, (pour) cette fois-ci; **to be l. off with a fine,** en être quitte pour une amende; **to l. s.o. off the fine,** faire grâce de l'amende à qn.

5. let on, *v.tr. & i. F:* (*a*) **don't l. on that I was there,** n'allez pas dire que j'y étais; **he didn't l. on that he saw her,** (i) il n'a pas dit qu'il l'avait vue; (ii) il a fait semblant de ne pas la voir; **if you l. on to him about it!** si vous lui en parlez, lui en soufflez mot! **don't l. on!** pas un mot! ne vendez pas la mèche! (*b*) feindre; faire semblant; **he wasn't as ill as he l. on,** il faisait semblant d'être plus malade qu'il ne l'était.

6. let out, *v.tr. & i.* (*a*) *v.tr.* laisser sortir (qn); ouvrir la porte à (qn); laisser échapper (un oiseau); élargir (un prisonnier); **to be l. out on bail,** être relâché sous caution; **to l. out the air from sth.,** laisser échapper l'air de qch.; dégonfler (un ballon, etc.); **to l. out the bath water,** vider la baignoire; *F:* **to l. out a yell,** laisser échapper un cri; *Aut: etc: F:* **l. her out,** mettez les gaz; laissez-la filer; (*b*) *v.tr.* **to l. out a garment,** lâcher les coutures d'un vêtement; élargir (un vêtement); *Nau:* lâcher (un cordage); larguer (une voile); (*c*) *v.tr.* **to l. chairs out (on hire),** louer des chaises; **to l. out sth. on contract,** affermer qch.; (*d*) *v.tr.* **to l. out a secret,** laisser échapper un secret; lâcher, révéler, divulguer, un secret; (*e*) *v.i. F:* **to l. out at s.o. with one's foot, fist, etc.,** décocher un coup de pied, de poing, à qn; **to l. out at s.o.,** faire une algarade à qn; dire son fait à qn.

7. let through, *v.tr.* (*a*) laisser passer (qn); laisser passer, filtrer (la lumière); (*b*) *Sch: F:* (*of borderline candidate*) **shall we l. him through?** est-ce qu'il est admissible? est-ce qu'on le reçoit?

8. let up, *v.i.* (*of rain, pressure of business, etc.*) diminuer; (*of frost, etc.*) s'adoucir; (*of pers.*) **once he's started he never lets up,** une fois lancé il ne s'arrête plus, jamais il ne se relâche; *F:* **oh, l. up!** ça suffit! taistoi!

let-down ['letdaun], *s.* **1.** *Av:* descente *f* (en vue de l'atterrissage); **flight engineers monitor let-downs,** le mécanicien de bord contrôle les descentes; **l.-d. pattern,** circuit *m*, figures *fpl*, de descente. **2.** *Petr: etc:* **l.-d. vessel,** réservoir *m* de détente. **3.** *F:* désappointement *m*, déception *f*, déboire *m*.

lethal ['li:θ(ə)l], *a.* mortel, lét(h)al; léthifère; **l. (chemical) agent,** agent (chimique) mortel; **l. chamber,** chambre *f* à gaz (d'une fourrière, etc.); **l. dose,** dose mortelle, dose lét(h)ale; *Biol:* **l. gene,** gène lét(h)al; *Mil: etc:* **l. weapon,** arme meurtrière, léthifère; **l. wound,** blessure mortelle; **l. radius,** rayon *m* de destruction physique, d'efficacité (d'une bombe atomique, etc.).

lethality [li:'θæliti], *s.* mortalité *f*, lét(h)alité *f*.

lethargic(al) [li'θɑːdʒik(l)], *a.* **1.** *Med:* léthargique; **l. sleep,** sommeil *m* léthargique; sopor *m*. **2.** léthargique, lent, nonchalant.

lethargically [li'θɑːdʒikli], *adv.* d'une manière léthargique; lourdement, paresseusement.

lethargy ['leθədʒi], *s.* **1.** *Med:* léthargie *f*; **to sink into a state of l.,** tomber en léthargie. **2.** torpeur *f*; inertie *f*, inaction *f*.

Lethe ['li:θi], *Pr.n. Gr.Myth:* le Léthé.

Lethean [li:'θi:ən], *a. Myth:* du Léthé; **the L. waters, springs,** les eaux *f* du Léthé.

lethiferous [li'θifərəs], *a.* léthifère.

lethocerus [le'θɔsərəs], *s. Ent:* lethocerus *m*.

Lethrinidae [le'θrainidi:], *s.pl. Ich:* léthrinidés *m*.

let-out ['letaut], *s. F:* excuse *f*; *Com:* **l.-o. (clause),** clause *f* échappatoire.

Lett [let], *s.* **1.** *Ethn:* Lettonien, -ienne; Letton, -one. **2.** *Ling:* lette *m*, lettique *m*, letton *m*.

lettable ['letəbl], *a.* qui peut se louer; (immeuble) en état d'être loué.

letter[1] [letər], *s.* **1.** (*a*) lettre *f* (de l'alphabet); *Typ:* lettre, caractère *m*; **to teach a child his letters,** apprendre son alphabet à un enfant; *Typ:* **printed l.,** lettre moulée; **drop l.,** lettre deux-points; **primed l.,** lettre accentuée; **compound letters,** ligature *f*; **l. cutting,** coupe *f* de caractères; **l. cutter,** coupeur *m* de caractères; **reference l., superior l., initial l.,** lettrine *f*; *Mapm:* **grid l.,** lettre du quadrillage; (*b*) **according to the l. of the law,** selon la lettre de la loi; **to obey to the l.,** obéir à la lettre, au pied de la lettre; **to remain a dead l.,** rester lettre morte; *B:* **the l. killeth but the spirit giveth life,** la lettre tue mais l'esprit vivifie; (*c*) *Engr:* **proof before the l.,** épreuve *f* avant la lettre; **open l. proof,** estampe *f* après la lettre; (*d*) **code l.,** (i) lettre d'un code de chiffrement; lettre-code *f*, *pl.* lettres-code(s); (ii) *W.Tel:* indicatif littéral; **letters check,** vérification *f* des lettres (d'un code, etc.); **nonsignificant l.,** lettre nulle (d'un message chiffré); *W.Tel: etc:* **call letters,** indicatif *m* d'appel, d'identification (d'une station radio, etc.); *Nau:* **signal letters, call letters,** lettres signalétiques, d'identification (d'un navire); (*e*) **l. lock,** serrure *f*, cadenas *m*, à combinaisons, à chiffres; (*for steel wire*) **l. gauge,** jauge *f* alphabétique. **2.** (*a*) lettre, missive *f*; **business l.,** lettre d'affaires; **set-form l.,** lettre type, passe-partout; lettre modèle circulaire; **thank-you l.,** *F:* **bread-and-butter l.,** lettre de remerciement; **I've had a l. from him,** j'ai reçu une lettre de lui; **exchange of letters,** échange *m* de lettres; correspondance *f*; **to open one's letters,** ouvrir son courrier; **we must send off the letters before five,** il faut mettre le courrier à la poste avant cinq heures; *Post:* **sealed l.,** lettre close; **registered l.,** lettre recommandée; **express l.,** lettre exprès; **air (mail) l.,** lettre-avion *f*, *pl.* lettres-avion; **surcharged l.,** lettre taxée, avec surtaxe; **returned l.,** lettre renvoyée à l'expéditeur; **dead, unclaimed, l.,** lettre de, au, rebut; **night l. telegram,** télégramme-lettre *m*, *pl.* télégrammes-lettres; **l. rate,** tarif *m* (d'affranchissement des) lettres; **to send a l. first class, second class,** envoyer une lettre à tarif d'urgence, à tarif normal; (*to* *secretary)* **would you take a l. in French,** je vais vous dicter une lettre en français; *P:* **French l.,** capote anglaise; *attrib.* **l. paper,** papier *m* à lettres; **l. pad,** bloc *m* de papier à lettres; **l. opener,** ouvre-lettres *m inv*; **l. tray,** corbeille *f*, panier *m* (à lettres, à courrier); **l. balance, scales,** pèse-lettres *m inv*; **l. rack,** porte-lettres *m inv*; **l. file,** classeur *m* de lettres; classe-lettres *m inv*; **l. sorter,** machine *f* à trier le courrier; *(b)* **letters patent,** lettres de patentes; **letters patent of nobility,** lettres de noblesse; *Dipl:* **l. of recall (of ambassador, etc.),** lettre de rappel (d'un ambassadeur, etc.); *(c) Bank: Com: etc:* **l. of credit, of exchange,** lettre de crédit, de change; **l. of advice,** lettre d'avis; **l. of guaranty,** lettre d'aval; **follow-up l.,** lettre de relance (à un client); **l. of reminder,** lettre de rappel, de mise en demeure (à un débiteur); **accompanying l.,** lettre d'envoi; **l. of acknowledgement,** accusé *m* de réception; **l. of complaint,** lettre de réclamation; **l. of application,** (lettre de) demande *f* (d'emploi, etc.); **l. of appointment,** lettre de nomination, *Adm:* d'affectation (à un emploi); *St.Exch:* **l. of allotment,** lettre d'allocation; avis *m* d'attribution, de répartition; *Jur:* **letters of administration,** lettres d'administration (nommant un administrateur à la succession d'un défunt intestat). **3.** *pl.* **letters,** (belles-)lettres; littérature *f*; **man of letters,** homme de lettres, littérateur *m*; **the republic, the commonwealth, of letters,** la république des lettres.

letter[2], *v.tr.* **1.** marquer (un objet) avec des lettres; graver des lettres sur (un objet); estampiller. **2.** mettre le titre à (un livre ou sa couverture). **3.** *Com: Jur:* coter (des pièces).

letter[3], *s.* **1.** loueur, -euse. **2.** *A:* **l. of blood,** saigneur *m*.

letterbox ['letəbɔks], *s.* boîte *f* aux lettres; boîte à lettres.

lettercard ['letəkɑːd], *s.* carte-lettre *f*, *pl.* cartes-lettres.

lettercase ['letəkeis], *s.* porte-lettres *m inv*.

lettered ['letəd], *a.* **1.** marqué avec des lettres. **2.** (homme) lettré.

lettergram ['letəgræm], *s. esp. NAm:* télégramme-lettre *m*, *pl.* télégrammes-lettres.

letterhead ['letəhed], *s.* en-tête *m inv* de lettre (imprimé).

lettering ['let(ə)riŋ], *s.* **1.** lettrage *m*; estampillage *m*; **instant l.,** lettrage-calque *m*; *Typ:* **l. by hand,** repoussage *m*. **2.** lettres *fpl*; inscription *f*; titre *m* (d'un livre); **embossed l.,** inscription en relief; **sunken l.,** inscription en creux; **freehand l.,** dessin *m* de lettres à main levée; **marginal l.,** inscriptions marginales (sur une carte); **l. guides,** normographe *m*.

letter-perfect ['letə'pəːfikt], *a.* **to be l.-p.,** savoir (son rôle) par cœur.

letterpress ['letəpres], *s.* **1.** *Typ:* impression *f* typographique; **l. printing,** typographie *f*. **2.** texte *m* (accompagnant une illustration). **3.** presse *f* à copier.

letterweight ['letəweit], *s.* presse-papiers *m inv*, serre-papiers *m inv*.

letterwood ['letəwud], *s. Bot:* bois *m* de lettres; lettre mouchetée.

letter-writer ['letəraitər], *s.* **1.** auteur *m* de lettres; épistolier, -ière. **2.** *O:* recueil *m* de modèles de lettres.

Lettic ['letik], **Lettish** ['letiʃ]. **1.** *Geog: (a) a.* letton; *(b) s.* Letton, -one. **2.** *s. Ling:* lette *m*, lettique *m*, letton *m*.

letting ['letiŋ], *s.* **1.** louage *m*; location *f* (d'une maison); **l. value,** valeur locative. **2.** *Metall:* **l. down,** revenu *m*, recuit *m*, adoucissage *m*.

Lettonian [le'tounian], *Ethn: (a) a.* lettonien, letton; *(b) s.* Lettonien, -ienne; Letton, -one.

lettuce ['letis], *s. (a)* laitue *f*; **cabbage l.,** laitue pommée; **cos l.,** (laitue) romaine *f*; **long-leaved l.,** alfange *f*; **wall l.,** laitue des murailles; **lamb's l.,** mâche *f*; **shot, bolted l.,** laitue montée en graine; **I'll buy some l. for lunch,** je vais acheter de la salade pour le déjeuner; *(b) Algae:* **sea l.,** laitue de mer, ulve *f*.

let-up ['letʌp], *s. F:* diminution *f* **(in,** de); changement *m* (du temps); **there will be no l.-up in our efforts,** il n'y aura pas la moindre diminution, le moindre relâchement, de nos efforts; **to work fifteen hours without a l.-up,** travailler quinze heures d'affilée.

Leucadia [lju'keidiə], *Pr.n. Geog:* (l'île *f* de) Leucade, Leukas.

Leucadian [lju'keidiən], *a. Geog:* **the L. Promontory,** le cap de Leucade.

leucaena [l(j) u'kiːnə], *s. Bot:* lucæna *m*.

leucania [lju'keiniə], *s. Ent:* leucanie *f*.

leuchaemia [lju'kiːmiə], *s. Med:* leucémie *f*.

leuchaemic [lj'u'kiːmik], *a. Med:* leucémique.

leucine ['ljuːs(a)in], *s. Bio-Ch:* leucine *f*.

Leucippus [lju'sipəs], *Pr.n.m. Gr.Phil:* Leucippe.

leucite ['ljuːsait], *s.* **1.** *Miner:* leucite *m*, amphigène *m*; schorl blanc. **2.** *Bot:* leucite, leucoplaste *m*.

leucitite ['ljuːsitait], *s. Miner:* leucitite *f*.

leuco(-) ['lju(ː)kou], *pref.* leuco-; *Bio-Ch:* **l. base,** leucocobase *f*, leucodérivé *m*.

leucoblast ['ljuːkoublæst], *s. Biol:* leucoblaste *m*.

leucoblastic [ljuːkou'blæstik], *a. Biol:* leucoblastique.

leucoblastosis [ljuːkoublæs'tousis], *s. Med:* leucoblastose *f*.

leucobryum [lju'koubriəm], *s. Moss:* leucobryum *m*.

leucochalcite [ljuːkou'kælsait], *s. Miner:* leucochalcite *f*.

leucocratic [ljuːkou'krætik], *a. Geol:* leucocrate.

leucocyte ['ljuːkousait], *s. Physiol:* leucocyte *m*.

leucocythaemia [ljuːkousai'θiːmiə], *s. Med:* leucocythémie *f*, leucémie *f*.

leucocytic [ljuːkou'sitik], *a. Med:* leucocytaire.

leucocytogenesis [ljuːkousaitou'dʒenəsis], *s. Biol:* leucogénèse *f*, leucocytogénèse *f*.

leucocytopoiesis [ljuːkousaitoupɔi'iːsis], *s. Med:* leucopoïèse *f*.

leucocytosis [ljuːkousai'tousis], *s. Med:* leucocytose *f*.

leucoderm(i)a [ljuːkou'dəːm(i)ə], *s. Med:* leucodermie *f*, leucomélanodermie *f*.

leucodermic [ljuːkou'dəːmik], *a. Med:* leucoderme.

leucoencephalitis [ljuːkouensefə'laitis], *s. Med:* leucoencéphalite *f*.

leucokeratosis [ljuːkouKerə'tousis], *s. Med:* leucokératose *f*.

leucoma [lju'koumə], *s. Med:* leucome *m*.

leucomaine ['ljuːkoumein], *s. Bio-Ch:* leucomaïne *f*.

leucomyelitis [ljuːkoumaiə'laitis], *s. Med:* leucomyélite *f*.

leucon ['ljuːkɔn], *s. Spong:* leucon *m*.

leuconostoc [ljuːkou'nɔstɔk], *s. Bac:* leuconostoc *m*.

leuconychia [ljuːkou'nikiə], *s. Med:* leuconychie *f*.

leucopedesis [ljuːkou'pedisis], *s. Physiol:* leucopédèse *f*.

leucopenia [ljuːkou'piːniə], *s. Med:* leucopénie *f*.

leucopenic [ljuːkou'piːnik], *a. Med:* leucopénique.

leucophane ['ljuːkoufein], **leucophanite** [ljukou'feinait], *s. Miner:* leucophane *m*.

leucoplakia, leucoplasia [ljuːkou'pleikiə, -'pleiziə], *s. Med:* leucoplasie *f*.

leucoplast ['ljuːkouplæst], **leucoplastid** [ljuːkou'plæstid], *s. Biol:* leucoplaste *m*, leucite *m*.

leucopoiesis [ljuːkoupɔi'iːsis], *s. Med:* leucopoïèse *f*.

leucopyrite [ljuːkou'pai(ə)rait], *s. Miner:* leucopyrite *f*.

leucorrhoea [ljukə'riːə], *s. Med:* leucorrhée *f*.

leucorrhoeal [ljukə'riːəl], *a. Med:* leucorrhéique.

leucosapphire [ljuːkou'sæfaiər], *s. Miner:* rubis blanc.

leucosin ['ljuːkous(a)in], *s. Biol:* leucosine *f*.

leucosphenite [ljuːkou'sfiːnait], *s.* leucosphénite *f*.

leucothoe [ljuː'kɔθəwiː], *s. Bot:* leucothoé *f*.

leucotomy [lju'kɔtəmi], *s. Surg:* leucotomie *f*, lobotomie *f*.

leucotoxic [ljuːkou'tɔksik], *a. Med:* leucotoxique.

leucoxene [lju'kɔksiːn], *s. Miner:* leucoxène *m*.

Leuctra ['ljuːktrə], *Pr.n. A.Geog:* Leuctres.

leud [ljuːd], *s. Fr.Hist:* leude *m*; vassal *m*, -aux.

leuk(a)emia [lju'kiːmiə], *s. Med:* leucémie *f*.

leuk(a)emic [lju'kiːmik], *a. Med:* leucémique.

leuko- ['lju(ː)kou], *comb.fm.* = LEUCO-.

Levant[1] [li'vænt]. *Geog:* **1.** *Pr.n.* **the L.,** le Levant. **2.** *attrib.* du Levant; levantin; *Hist:* **the L. Company,** la Compagnie du Levant.

levant[2], *v.i. F:* partir sans payer; *(esp.* of bookmaker) décamper sans payer; lever le pied.

levanter[1] [li'væntər], *s. Meteor:* levantin *m*; vent *m* aigre de l'est (dans la Méditerranée).

levanter[2], *s. F:* bookmaker *m* qui décampe sans payer.

Levantine ['levəntain, lə'væn-]. **1.** *Geog: (a) a.* levantin; *(b) s.* Levantin, -ine. **2.** *s. Tex: (silk)* levantine *f*.

levator [li'veitər], *s. Anat:* élévateur *m*; (muscle) releveur *m*.

levee[1] ['levi], *s. (a) Hist:* lever *m* (du roi); *(b) A:* réception royale (tenue l'après-midi et pour hommes seulement); *(c)* réception mondaine (en l'honneur de qn).

levee[2], *s. Civ.E:* levée *f*, digue *f*, endiguement *m* (d'une rivière).

levee[3], *v.tr. Civ.E:* endiguer (une rivière).

level[1] ['lev(ə)l], *s., a. & adv.*

I. *s.* **1.** *Tls: etc: (a)* niveau *m* (de charpentier, etc.); **air l., bubble l.,** niveau à bulle (d'air); **l. bubble,** bulle *f* du niveau; **collimating l.,** niveau (à) collimateur; **surveyor's l.,** niveau à lunette; **spirit l.,** niveau à bulle d'air, à alcool; **hydrostatic l.,** hydrostatimètre *m*; **trueing-up l.,** niveau de réglage; **striding l.,** niveau à pattes; **l. vial,** fiole *f* du niveau; *(b)* **l. (rule),** latte *f*, règle *f*, de niveau; *(c) Mch:* **water l.,** niveau d'eau, clinomètre *m*. **2.** *(a)* niveau (de la mer, d'un cours d'eau, d'un liquide dans un récipient, etc.); *Geog: Surv:* altitude *f*, niveau; **mean sea l.,** niveau moyen de la mer; **pressure at sea l.,** pression *f* au niveau de la mer; **reduction to sea l.,** réduction *f* au niveau de la mer; *Surv:* **datum l., reference l.,** niveau de référence; **difference in l.,** différence *f* d'altitude, de niveau; dénivellation *f*, dénivellement *m*; *Civ.E: etc:* **change of l.,** ressaut *m*, dénivellation; **at a higher, lower, l.,** en contre-haut, en contre-bas **(than,** de); **at eye l.,** à la hauteur de l'œil, à hauteur des yeux; **on a l. with sth.,** au niveau, à la hauteur, de qch.; de niveau avec qch.; sur le même plan que qch.; **fanlight on a l. with the ceiling,** vasistas *m* à hauteur du plafond; **kitchen on a l. with the garden,** cuisine *f* de plain-pied avec le jardin; **split l. house,** maison à ressaut, à paliers; *Adm: Can:* maison à mi-étages; **out of l.,** (i) *(of billiard table, etc.)* dénivelé; (ii) *(of tiles, etc.)* désaffleurant; **to be out of l.,** (i) être dénivelé; (ii) désaffleurer; **to throw an instrument out of l.,** déniveler un instrument; *attrib.* **l. meter,** (appareil) mesureur *m* de niveau; limnimètre *m*, limnomètre *m*; **l. gauge, l. indicator,** indicateur *m* de niveau; **l. recorder,** enregistreur *m* de niveau; limnigraphe *m*; **l. regulator,** régulateur *m* de niveau; *(b)* niveau (des prix, des salaires, etc.); **to maintain prices at a high l.,** maintenir les prix à un niveau élevé; *Mil: etc:* **l. of supply,** niveau d'approvisionnement; *(c) Ph: etc:* **energy l.,** niveau énergétique; **intensity l.,** niveau d'intensité; **sound (intensity) l.,** niveau d'intensité sonore; **noise l.,** niveau de bruit (d'un moteur, d'un appareil); **radiation l.,** niveau de radiation; *El:* **acceptor, donor, l.,** niveau accepteur, donneur; *W.Tel:* **receiving, transmission, l.,** niveau de réception, de transmission; *(d) Mec.E:* **oil l.,** niveau d'huile (de graissage); **oil-l. indicator,** indicateur de niveau d'huile; *(e)* niveau, étage *m* (de la société, etc.); **to be on a l. with s.o.,** être au niveau de qn; être sur un pied d'égalité avec qn; être l'égal de qn; **to come down to s.o.'s l.,** se mettre au niveau, à la portée, de qn; **to find one's (own) l.,** parvenir à un niveau (social, professionnel, etc.) digne de ses mérites; **at ministerial l.,** à l'échelon ministériel; *Mil: etc:* **l. of command,** échelon de commandement, de la hiérarchie (militaire); *(f) Cmptr:* niveau; moment *m* (de code); **8-l. code,** code *m* à 8 moments; **8-l. tape,** bande *f* à 8 canaux. **3.** *(a)* surface *f*, trajectoire *f*, de niveau; terrain *m* de niveau; *Aut: Rail: Av:* palier *m*; **dead l.,** niveau parfait, palier absolu; **on the l.,** (i) sur un terrain plat; (ii) *(of pers.)* loyal, -aux; de bonne foi; (iii) *F:* en toute honnêteté; en toute sincérité; loyalement; *Aut: etc:* **speed on the l.,** vitesse *f* en palier; *Civ.E:* **formation l.,** plate-forme *f* de tassement; *(b) Min:* (i) niveau, étage; (ii) galerie *f*, voie *f* (de niveau); **blind l.,** galerie à siphon; **deep l.,** niveau profond; *(c) Geol:* étage; *(d) Geog:* plaine *f*; *(e)* bief *m*, biez *m* (d'un canal).

II. *a.* **1.** *(a) (not sloping)* horizontal, -aux; (terrain) de niveau, à niveau; (route, etc.) en palier; *Aut: Rail:* **l. run, l. stretch,** palier *m*; *Av:* **l. flight,** vol horizontal; **l.(-flight) bombing,** bombardement *m* en vol horizontal; *(b) (flat)* égal, -aux, uni; *(c)* **l. with . . .,** de niveau avec . . .; au niveau, à (la) hauteur, de . . .; affleurant avec . . .; *Rail:* **l. crossing,** passage *m* à niveau; **l. with the water,** à fleur de l'eau; à fleur d'eau; au ras de l'eau; **l. with the ground,** à fleur du sol; au ras du sol; à ras de terre; à rase terre; **to lay a building l. with the ground,** raser un édifice; **to make two walls l. (with one another),** affleurer deux murs; **the water is l. with the top of the bank,** l'eau affleure le haut de la rive; **l. spoonful,** cuillerée rase; *Sp:* **to draw l. with . . .,** arriver à (la) hauteur de . . .; *(in rowing)* venir bord à bord avec . . .. **2. l. tone,** ton soutenu, uniforme; **l. head,** tête bien équilibrée; **to keep a l. head,** garder sa tête, son sang-froid; **to do one's l. best,** faire tous ses efforts, faire tout son possible; faire de son mieux.

III. *adv. Av:* **to fly l.,** (i) voler en palier; (ii) attaquer le palier.

level[2], *v.* **(levelled)**

I. *v.tr.* **1.** *(a)* niveler; mettre (un billard, etc.) à niveau, de niveau; *(b)* niveler, aplanir, aplatir, égaliser, unir (une surface); araser (un terrain, un mur, etc.); *(c)* **to l. a town, a building (to the ground),** raser une ville, un édifice; *(d) Lit:* **to l. s.o. to the ground,** étendre qn par terre (d'un coup de poing, etc.) **2.** pointer (un fusil), braquer (un canon), diriger (une longue-vue) **(at,** sur); **to l. one's gun at, against, s.o.,** ajuster, viser, qn avec son fusil; coucher, mettre, qn en joue; **to l. sarcasms, accusations, at s.o.,** lancer, diriger, des sarcasmes, des accusations, contre qn; **to l. a blow at s.o.,** porter un coup à qn. **3.** *Surv:* effectuer des opérations de nivellement dans (une région); niveler (une région). **4.** *v.i. esp. NAm: F:* **to l. with s.o.,** parler franchement.

II. *(compound verbs)* **1. level down,** *v.tr. (a)* araser (un mur, etc.); *(b)* abaisser (qn, qch.) à son niveau; niveler par le bas, au plus bas.

2. level off, *(a) v.tr.* aplanir (qch.); *(b) v.i.* (i) s'arrêter à un certain niveau; (ii) *Av:* voler en palier.

3. level out, *(a) v.tr.* égaliser (une surface, etc.); *(b) v.i.* (i) *(of prices)* s'équilibrer; (ii) *(of aircraft)* attaquer le palier.

4. **level up,** *v.tr.* (*a*) égaliser (un terrain, etc.) (en comblant les creux); (*b*) élever (qch.) au niveau de (qch.); niveler au plus haut.

level-headed ['lev(ə)l'hedid], *a.* qui a la tête bien équilibrée; pondéré; **he's l.-h.,** c'est une tête carrée, une tête bien organisée; il a l'esprit rassis.

level-headedness ['lev(ə)l'hedidnis], *s.* esprit bien équilibré; pondération *f.*

leveller ['lev(ə)lər], *s.* **1.** (*pers.*) (*a*) niveleur, -euse; (*b*) *Pol:* égalitaire *mf.* **2.** *Civ.E:* **road l.,** (i) rouleau compresseur; (ii) niveleuse *f* de route.

levelling[1] ['lev(ə)liŋ], *a.* **1.** *Ph: Mec:* nivelant; niveleur, -euse; nivelateur, -trice; **the l. action of erosion,** l'action nivelante, nivelatrice, de l'érosion. **2.** *Pol:* égalitaire.

levelling[2], *s.* **1.** (*a*) nivellement *m*; (i) mise *f* à niveau, de niveau; (ii) aplanissement *m* (d'une surface); égalisation *f* (de la chaussée); *Civ.E:* régalement *m* (d'un terrain); **l. up, down,** nivellement par le haut, par le bas; *Surv:* **barometric l.,** nivellement barométrique; **geodetic l.,** nivellement géodésique; **precise l.,** nivellement de précision; **l. instrument,** instrument *m* de nivellement; **l. pole, rod, staff,** mire *f* (de nivellement); jalon *m* d'arpentage; balise *f*; (*b*) arasement *m*, dérasement *m* (d'un mur); (*c*) *Mec.E:* **l. jack,** vérin *m* de mise de niveau, de calage; **l. screw,** vis calante, de calage; (*d*) *Adm:* classement *m* à l'ancienneté; nivellement par le bas. **2.** pointage *m*, braquage *m*, d'une arme à feu.

levelness ['lev(ə)lnis], *s.* (*a*) nature plate, unie (d'une surface); (*b*) position *f* de niveau.

lever[1] ['li:vər], *s.* **1.** *Mec:* levier *m*; **l. of the first order,** levier du premier genre; levier intermobile; **l. of the second order,** levier du deuxième genre; levier interrésistant; **l. of the third order,** levier du troisième genre; levier interpuissant. **2.** (*a*) *Tls:* levier; *Artil:* espar(t) *m* (de manœuvre de canon); **claw l.,** levier à griffe, à pince; (*b*) *Mec.E:* levier, manette *f*; **actuating l., control l., driving l., operating l.,** levier de commande, de manœuvre; **hand l., manual l.,** levier (de commande) à main; **clutch l., coupling l., engaging l., in-gear l., meshing l.,** levier d'embrayage, d'enclenchement, d'engagement; **disconnecting l., disengaging l., releasing l., throw-out l.,** levier de débrayage, de déclenchement, de dégagement; **starting l.,** levier de démarrage, de mise en marche; *Navy:* levier de prise d'air (d'une torpille); **reverse l., reversing l.,** levier de renversement de marche; levier de marche arrière, de renvoi; levier inverseur, d'inversion, de marche; *Aut:* **change-speed l., change-gear l., gear(-shift) l.,** levier de changement de vitesse, levier des vitesses; **handbrake l.,** levier de frein à main; **l. arm,** bras *m* de levier; **l. brake,** frein *m* à levier; **l. valve,** soupape *f* à levier; **l. jack,** cric *m* à levier; *I.C.E:* **gas l., throttle l., compression l.,** manette des gaz; **sparking l., timing l.,** levier d'avance à l'allumage; *Mch.Tls:* **feed l.,** levier d'avance; **l. feed,** pression *f* à levier; **l.-feed drilling machine,** perceuse *f*, foreuse *f*, à levier; **arresting l.,** levier d'arrêt; **catch l.,** levier d'accrochage; **clamping l., locking l.,** levier de blocage, de serrage, de verrouillage, de sûreté; **unclamping, unlocking, releasing, l.,** levier de déblocage, de déverrouillage; **angle l., bent l., crank l., elbow l., knee l.,** levier coudé, brisé; levier d'équerre, levier à renvoi; **ball(-jointed) l.,** levier à rotule; **pawl l.,** levier à cliquet; **rocking l.,** levier à mouvement latéral, levier oscillant; **toggle l.,** levier à bascule, levier articulé; *Mch:* **gab l.,** bielle *f* à chapeau, à cage ouverte; (*c*) *Rail:* **point l., switch l.,** levier d'aiguille, levier de manœuvre des aiguilles; **signal l.,** levier (de manœuvre) de signal; **l. skid,** appui *m* de levier (d'aiguillage, etc.); (*d*) *Sm.a:* **arming l., cocking l.,** levier d'armement; **bolt l.,** levier de culasse (mobile), levier de manœuvre; *Exp:* **firing l.,** levier de mise de feu; *Mil.Av:* **bomb-dropping, bomb-releasing, l.,** levier de lance-bombes; (*e*) *Av:* guignol *m*; **aileron l.,** guignol d'aileron; **elevator l.,** guignol de gouverne de profondeur; **tail-skid l.,** guignol de béquille; (*f*) *Locksm:* bascule *f* (d'une serrure); *Clockm:* **regulating l.,** raquette *f* (de montre); **l. watch,** montre *f* à ancre, à échappement; **l. escapement,** échappement *m* à ancre; (*g*) **l. engine,** machine *f* à balancier; **l. balance,** peson *m* à contrepoids; **l. scales,** balance romaine; *El:* **l. switch,** commutateur *m* à manette, à bascule.

lever[2]. **1.** *v.i.* manœuvrer un levier; (*of part, etc.*) **to l. against sth.,** faire levier sur qch. **2.** *v.tr.* **to l. sth. up,** soulever qch. au moyen, à l'aide, d'un levier; exercer une pesée pour soulever qch.

leverage ['li:vəridʒ], *s.* **1.** (*a*) force *f*, puissance *f*, de levier; abattage *m* (de la manivelle d'un treuil); **l. movement,** effet *m*, mouvement *m*, de levier; *Mec:* **l. of a force,** bras *m* de levier d'une force; rapport *m* des bras de levier; *Row:* **l. of the oar,** levier *m* de l'aviron; (*b*) **to bring l. to bear on (a door, etc.),** exercer des pesées *f* sur (une porte, etc.); (*c*) **to give s.o. l.,** donner un avantage à qn (sur soi-même); **we have no l. we could bring to bear on him,** nous n'avons pas de prise sur lui. **2.** système *m* de leviers.

leveret ['levərit], *s. Z:* levraut *m.*

lever-grip ['li:vəgrip], *a. Tls: Metalw:* **l.-g. tongs,** écrevisse *f.*

Levi ['li:vai], *Pr.n.m. B.Hist:* Lévi.

leviable ['leviəbl], *a.* **1.** (impôt *m*) percevable. **2.** (personne *f*) imposable.

leviathan [li'vaiəθ(ə)n], *s.* **1.** *B:* léviathan *m.* **2.** *F:* (navire *m*) monstre *m.*

levigate ['levigeit], *v.tr.* **1.** léviger; réduire en poudre. **2.** délayer (**with,** avec).

levigation [levi'geiʃ(ə)n], *s.* lévigation *f.*

levirate ['li:vireit], *s. Jew.Hist:* lévirat *m.*

levitate ['leviteit]. *Psychics:* **1.** *v.i.* se soulever (par lévitation). **2.** *v.tr.* soulever (qch., qn) (par lévitation).

levitation [levi'teiʃ(ə)n], *s. Psychics:* lévitation *f.*

Levite ['li:vait], *s. B:* lévite *m.*

Levitical [li'vitik(ə)l], *a. B:* **1.** lévitique; des lévites. **2. L. degrees,** degrés de parenté ou d'alliance prohibitifs de mariage; **marriage within the L. degrees,** mariage *m* entre parents ou alliés au degré prohibé.

Leviticus [li'vitikəs], *s. B:* le Lévitique.

levity ['leviti], *s.* **1.** légèreté *f*; manque *m* de sérieux. **2.** *Ph: etc:* légèreté.

levoglucosan [li:vou'glu:kousæn], *s. Ch:* lévoglucosane *m.*

levogyrate, levogyrous [li:vou'dʒaiəreit, -'dʒaiərəs], **levorotatory** [li:vourou'teitəri], *a. Ch: etc:* lévogyre.

levulinic [levju'linik], *a. Ch:* (acide) lévulique.

levulose ['levjulous], *s.* lévulose *m or f.*

levulosuria [levjulou'sju:riə], *s. Med:* lévulosurie *f.*

levy[1] ['levi], *s.* **1.** (*a*) levée *f* (d'un impôt); (*b*) *Mil:* levée (des troupes); réquisition *f* (des chevaux, etc); *Mil:* **l. in mass,** levée en masse. **2.** impôt *m*, contribution *f*; **trade union that collects a political l. from its members,** syndicat *m* qui fait payer à ses membres une cotisation pour l'action politique; **capital l.,** prélèvement *m* sur le capital.

levy[2], *v.tr.* **1.** (*a*) lever, percevoir (un impôt); imposer (une amende); **to l. a duty on goods,** imposer des marchandises; frapper des marchandises d'un droit; **to l. a fine on s.o.,** frapper qn d'une amende; **to l. tithes,** prélever la dîme; (*b*) **members are levied £x a year for the pension fund,** les traitements sont sujets à un prélèvement annuel de £x comme contribution à la caisse de retraite. **2.** *Mil:* (*a*) lever (des troupes); (*b*) mettre en réquisition, réquisitionner (des denrées, etc.). **3.** (*a*) *Jur:* **to l. execution on s.o.'s goods,** faire une saisie-exécution sur les biens de qn; (*b*) *O:* **to l. war on s.o.,** faire la guerre à, contre, qn; **to l. blackmail,** faire du chantage; **to l. blackmail on s.o.,** soumettre qn à un chantage.

levying ['leviiŋ], *s.* levée *f* (d'impôts, de troupes); perception *f* (d'impôts).

lewd [lju:d], *a.* **1.** impudique, lascif, lubrique, paillard, crapuleux; **l. smile,** sourire lascif, égrillard. **2.** *A: & B:* bas, vil, ignoble.

lewdly ['lju:dli], *adv.* impudiquement, lascivement, lubriquement, crapuleusement.

lewdness ['lju:dnis], *s.* **1.** impudicité *f*, lasciveté *f*, paillardise *f*, libidinosité *f*, lubricité *f.* **2.** luxure *f*, débauche *f.*

lewis[1] ['lu:is], *s.* **1.** louve *f* (à pierres) en trois pièces. **2.** (*freemasonry*) louveteau *m.*

lewis[2], *v.tr. Stonew:* encastrer une louve dans (une pierre).

Lewis[3], *Pr.n.m.* Louis.

Lewis[4], *Pr.n. Mil: A:* **L. gun,** fusil mitrailleur.

lewisite[1] ['lu:isait], *s. Miner:* lewisite *f.*

lewisite[2], *s. Ch:* lewisite *f.*

lewisson ['lu:isən], *s.* = LEWIS[1] 1.

lexeme ['leksi:m], *s. Ling:* lexème *m.*

lexical ['leksik(ə)l], *a.* lexical, -aux.

lexicographer [leksi'kɔgrəfər], *s.* lexicographe *mf.*

lexicographical [leksikə'græfik(ə)l], *a.* lexicographique.

lexicography [leksi'kɔgrəfi], *s.* lexicographie *f.*

lexicological [leksikə'lɔdʒik(ə)l], *a.* lexicologique.

lexicologist [leksi'kɔlədʒist], *s.* lexicologue *mf.*

lexicology [leksi'kɔlədʒi], *s.* lexicologie *f.*

lexicon ['leksikən], *s.* lexique *m.*

lexiconization [leksikənai'zeiʃ(ə)n], **lexiconizing** [leksikə'naiziŋ], *s.* lexicalisation *f.*

lexiconize ['leksikənaiz], *v.tr.* lexicaliser.

lexigraphy [lek'sigrəfi], *s.* lexigraphie *f.*

ley [li:, lei], *s. Lit:* prairie *f*; *Agr:* **l. farming,** cultures *fpl* en assolement; prairies temporaires.

Leyden ['laid(ə)n], *Pr.n.* (*a*) *Geog:* Leyde *f*; (*b*) *El:* **L. jar,** bouteille *f* de Leyde.

liability [laiə'biliti], *s.* **1.** *Jur:* responsabilité *f*; **joint l.,** responsabilité conjointe; **several l.,** responsabilité séparée; **joint and several l.,** responsabilité (conjointe et) solidaire; responsabilité solidaire et indivise; solidarité *f*; coobligation *f*; **employer's l.,** responsabilité patronale, de l'employeur (pour les accidents du travail); *A:* **Employers' L. Act,** loi sur les accidents du travail; **absolute l.,** responsabilité totale, obligation inconditionnelle; **contractual l.,** responsabilité contractuelle; obligation contractée, souscrite; **civil l.,** responsabilité civile. **2.** *Com: Fin:* (*a*) **contingent l.,** (i) engagements éventuels; passif éventuel, exigible; (ii) tierce caution; *Bank:* **contingent l. in respect of acceptances,** débiteurs *mpl* par aval; (*b*) *pl.* **liabilities,** ensemble *m* des dettes; engagements, obligations *fpl*, valeurs passives, dettes passives; le passif; (*in bankruptcy*) masse passive (d'une liquidation après faillite); **assets and liabilities,** actif *m* et passif; **current liabilities,** exigibilités *f*; **to meet one's liabilities,** faire face à ses engagements, à ses échéances; **their liabilities are very large,** leur passif est considérable; (*c*) (*on bills of exchange*) encours *m*; **l. as drawer,** encours tiré; **l. as maker, as transferor,** encours cédant. **3.** (*a*) **l. to a fine,** risque *m* d'(encourir une) amende; **l. for, to, military service,** obligation *f* du service militaire; (*b*) disposition *f*, tendance *f* (**to sth., to do sth.,** à qch., à faire qch.); **to have a l. to catch cold,** avoir une disposition à s'enrhumer; être susceptible de s'enrhumer; (*c*) (*of product, etc.*) **l. to explode,** danger *m* d'explosion.

liable ['laiəbl], *a.* **1.** *Jur:* responsable (**for,** de); **you are l. for the damage,** vous êtes responsable du dommage; **I'm l. if there's an accident,** en cas d'accident je suis responsable. **2.** sujet, assujetti, tenu, astreint (**to,** à); redevable, passible (**to,** de); **l. to stamp-duty,** assujetti au timbre; **l. to a tax,** assujetti à un impôt; redevable, passible, d'un impôt; **dividends l. to income tax,** dividendes soumis à l'impôt sur le revenu; **to make sth. l. to a tax,** assujettir qch. à un impôt; **l. to a fine,** passible d'une amende; **l. to arrest,** contraignable par corps; **l. to military service,** astreint au service militaire; **they are making themselves l. to proceedings,** ils s'exposent à des poursuites. **3.** sujet, apte, exposé (**to,** à); **l. to make mistakes,** enclin à faire des fautes; **car l. to overturn,** voiture sujette à verser; **ground l. to be flooded,** terrain exposé aux inondations, en danger d'être inondé; **goods l. to go bad,** marchandises *f* susceptibles de se corrompre; **at my age one is l. to rheumatism,** à mon âge on est sujet au rhumatisme; **to be l. to catch cold,** avoir une disposition à s'enrhumer; **l. to be swayed by self-interest,** accessible à l'intérêt. **4.** (*a*) **difficulties are l. to occur,** des difficultés *f* sont susceptibles de se présenter; **rule l. to exceptions,** règle *f* qui souffre des exceptions; **plan l. to modifications,** projet *m* qui pourra subir des modifications; **when he gets angry he is l. to do anything,** quand il se met en colère il est capable de tout; (*b*) *U.S:* (= *likely*) **he is l. to go,** il est probable qu'il ira.

liaise [li:'eiz], *v.i. Mil: etc: F:* faire, effectuer, assurer, la liaison.

liaison [li'eizɔn], *s.* **1.** *Mil: etc:* **l. agent,** agent *m* de liaison; **l. officer,** officier *m* de liaison; **l. detachment,** détachement *m* de liaison; **l. set,** appareil *m* radio de liaison; **l. aircraft,** avion *m* de liaison. **2.** union *f* illicite. **3.** *Cu:* liaison *f* (d'une sauce). **4.** *Ling:* **to make a l.,** faire la liaison (entre deux mots).

liana [li'ɑ:nə], *s. Bot:* liane *f.*

liar ['laiər], *s.* menteur, -euse; **he's an out and out l.,** c'est un menteur fieffé; **you l.!** menteur que tu es! quel menteur (tu fais)! **I'm a bit of a l. myself, but there are limits!** je veux bien qu'on soit menteur, mais pas à ce point-là!

lias ['laiəs], *s. Geol:* **1.** (*rock*) liais *m.* **2.** (*stratum*) lias *m.*

lias(s)ic [lai'æsik], *a. Geol:* lias(s)ique.

libation [lai'beiʃ(ə)n], *s.* libation *f.*

libationer [lai'beiʃənər], *s. Rom. & Gr.Ant:* faiseur *m* de libations; sacrificateur *m.*

libeccio [li'betʃiou], *s. Meteor:* libeccio *m.*

libel[1] ['laibl], *s.* **1.** (*a*) diffamation *f*, calomnie *f*; (*b*) *Jur:* diffamation (par écrit); écrit *m* diffamatoire; libelle *m*; **to utter a l. against s.o.,** publier un article, un écrit, diffamant contre qn; **action for l., l. action, l. case,** procès *m*, plainte *f*, en diffamation; **to bring an action for l.,** *U.S:* **to file a l., against s.o.,** intenter un procès en diffamation à qn; **to serve s.o. with a writ for l.,** assigner qn en diffamation; **the portrait is a l. on him, this portrait is more a l. than anything else,** ce portrait ne le flatte pas, est peu flatteur, ressemble à une caricature. **2.** *Jur: Scot:* libellé *m* de la plainte.

libel[2], *v.tr.* (**libelled**) *Jur:* **1.** diffamer (qn) (par écrit); publier une calomnie contre (qn); calomnier (qn). **2.** (*a*) *Ecc: & Scot:* libeller une plainte contre (qn); (*b*) intenter un procès à (un armateur, etc.) devant la Cour de l'Amirauté.

libellant ['laibələnt], *s. Jur:* (*Ecc:* & *Nau:*) requérant, -ante.

libellee [laibə'li:], *s.* défendeur, -eresse (dans un procès en diffamation).

libeller ['laibələr], *s.* diffamateur, -trice.

libelling ['laibəliŋ], *s.* diffamation *f.*

libellous ['laibələs], *a.* (écrit) diffamatoire, diffamant, calomnieux.

libellously ['laibələsli], *adv.* calomnieusement.

libellula [li'beljulə], *s. Ent:* libellule *f.*

Libellulidae [libə'lju:lidi:], *s.pl. Ent:* libellulidés *m.*

liber ['laibər], *s. Bot:* liber *m* (de l'écorce).

liberal ['lib(ə)rəl], *a.* **1.** (*a*) libéral, -aux; **l. education,** éducation libérale; *A:* **the l. arts,** les arts libéraux; (*b*) (*of pers.*) d'esprit large; sans préjugés; **in the most l. sense of the word,** au sens le plus large du mot. **2.** (*a*) libéral, généreux, prodigue; **l. with one's money, promises,** prodigue de son argent, de promesses; **l. to, towards, s.o.,** généreux pour, envers, qn; (*b*) ample, abondant; **l. supply of food,** nourriture abondante; **l. provision of . . .,** ample provision *f* de . . . . **3.** *a.* & *s. Pol:* libéral, -ale.

liberalism ['lib(ə)rəlizm], *s.* libéralisme *m.*

liberality [libə'ræliti], *s.* libéralité *f.* **1.** largeur *f* (de vues). **2.** (*a*) générosité *f*; (*b*) **he has impoverished himself by his l.,** il s'est appauvri par ses libéralités, par ses prodigalités *f.*

liberalization [lib(ə)rəlai'zeiʃ(ə)n], *s.* libéralisation *f*; élargissement *m* (des idées).

liberalize ['lib(ə)rəlaiz], *v.tr.* libéraliser (les idées, un peuple).

liberally ['lib(ə)rəli], *adv.* libéralement. **1.** dans un esprit large; sans étroitesse. **2.** généreusement, largement; **to give l.,** donner généreusement.

liberate ['libəreit], *v.tr.* **1.** libérer; mettre en liberté; élargir (un prisonnier); affranchir (un esclave); lâcher (des pigeons). **2.** *Ch:* **to l. a gas,** libérer, dégager, un gaz. **3.** *Fin:* **to l. capital,** mobiliser des capitaux.

liberating ['libəreitiŋ], *a.* libérateur, -trice.

liberation [libə'reiʃ(ə)n], *s.* **1.** (*a*) libération *f*; mise *f* en liberté; élargissement *m* (d'un prisonnier); affranchissement *m* (d'un esclave); *Hist:* (*World War II*) **after the l.,** après la libération (de la France); (*b*) **to enjoy the sense of l.,** se réjouir d'être libéré. **2.** *Ch: Ph:* mise en liberté, dégagement *m* (d'un gaz); **l. of heat,** dégagement de chaleur. **3.** *Fin:* **l. of capital,** mobilisation *f* de capitaux.

liberationism [libə'reiʃ(ə)nizm], *s.* politique *f* de séparation de l'Église et de l'État.

liberationist [libə'reiʃ(ə)nist], *s.* partisan, -ane, de la séparation de l'Église et de l'État.

liberator ['libəreitər], *s.* libérateur, -trice.

Liberia [lai'biəriə], *Pr.n. Geog:* Libéria *m.*

Liberian [lai'biəriən], *Geog:* (*a*) *a.* libérien; (*b*) *s.* Libérien, -ienne.

libertarian [libə'tɛəriən]. **1.** *a.* & *s. Pol:* libertaire (*mf*). **2.** *s. Phil: Rel.H:* partisan, -ane, du libre arbitre.

liberticide[1] [li'bə:tisaid], *a.* & *s.* (*pers.*) liberticide (*mf*).

liberticide[2], *s.* (*crime*) liberticide *m.*

libertinage ['libətinidʒ], *s. esp. Rel: A:* libertinage *m*, libertinisme *m*; libre pensée *f.*

libertine ['libətain, -ti:n], *a.* & *s.* **1.** *a.* (*a*) *Rel: A:* libertin; (*b*) libertin, débauché. **2.** *s.* (*a*) *Rel: A:* libre penseur *m*; libertin, -ine; (*b*) libertin, -ine; débauché, -ée.

libertinism ['libərtinizm], *s.* **1.** *Rel: A:* libertinisme *m*; libre pensée *f.* **2.** libertinage *m*; mœurs dissipées; débauche *f.* **3.** *A:* libertinage, liberté *f.*

liberty ['libəti], *s.* **1.** liberté *f*; (*a*) **l. of conscience, of thought,** liberté de conscience, de pensée; **l. of the press,** liberté de la presse; **the l. of the subject,** la liberté civile; **to have full l. of action,** avoir pleine liberté d'action; **l. to do sth.,** liberté, permission *f*, de faire qch.; **at l.,** (i) en liberté; *Navy:* en permission; (ii) libre, disponible; **to give s.o. his l.,** mettre qn en liberté; **to be at l. to do sth.,** être libre de faire qch.; **you are at l. to believe me or not,** libre à vous, permis à vous, de ne pas me croire; **Statue of L.,** statue *f* de la Liberté; **this is L. Hall,** vous êtes ici comme chez vous; *Navy:* **l. boat,** vedette *f* de permissionnaires; **l. list,** cahier *m* des permissionnaires; **l. ticket,** permission de terre, d'aller à terre; (feuille, *f*, titre *m*, de) permission; *Nau:* **l. ship,** (*World War II*) liberty-ship *m*; (*b*) **to take the l. of doing, to do, sth.,** prendre la liberté, se permettre, de faire qch.; **I take the l. of drawing your attention to . . .,** je me permets d'attirer votre attention sur . . .; (*c*) **to take liberties with s.o.,** prendre des libertés, se permettre des privautés, prendre des licences, avec qn; **he takes a good many liberties,** il se permet bien des choses; **to take liberties with a text,** prendre des libertés avec un texte. **2.** *pl. Jur: A:* **liberties,** (*a*) parties d'un comté non soumises à l'autorité judiciaire du shérif; (*b*) régions hors des confins d'une cité mais y appartenantes; (*c*) alentours *m* de certaines prisons, où il était permis aux détenus de demeurer.

libertyman, *pl.* **-men** ['libətimæn, -men], *s.m. Navy:* permissionnaire.

libethenite [li'beθənait], *s. Miner:* libéthénite *f.*

libidinal [li'bidinəl], *a. Psy:* (désirs *m*, etc.) de la libido.

libidinous [li'bidinəs], *a.* libidineux, lascif, lubrique.

libidinously [li'bidinəsli], *adv.* lascivement.

libidinousness [li'bidinəsnis], *s.* libidinosité *f*, lasciveté *f.*

libido [li'bi:dou, -'bai-], *s. Psy:* libido *f.*

Libra ['laibrə, 'li:-], *Pr.n. Astr:* la Balance.

librarian [lai'brɛəriən], *s.* bibliothécaire *mf*; conservateur, -trice, de bibliothèque.

librarianship [lai'brɛəriənʃip], *s.* poste *m*, emploi *m*, de bibliothécaire.

library ['laibrəri], *s.* bibliothèque *f* (collection *f* de livres ou salle *f* de lecture); (*a*) **lending l.,** bibliothèque de prêt; **reference l.,** bibliothèque d'ouvrages de référence; salle de lecture; bibliothèque dont les livres se consultent sur place; bibliothèque qui ne consent pas le prêt; **public, municipal, l.,** bibliothèque publique, municipale; bibliothèque de la ville; **circulating l.,** bibliothèque de prêt payante; cabinet *m* de lecture; **subscription l.,** bibliothèque dont les lecteurs paient un abonnement; **mobile l.,** bibliobus *m*; **private l.,** bibliothèque privée; **newspaper l.,** hémérothèque *f*; **photographic l.,** photothèque *f*; **map l.,** cartothèque *f*; **film l.,** cinémathèque *f*, filmothèque *f*; collection de films; **sound-film l.,** phonothèque *f*, discothèque *f*; **music l.,** musicothèque *f*; **record l.,** discothèque; collection de disques; **tape l.,** magnétothèque *f*; **l. edition,** (i) édition *f* grand format; (ii) édition sur grands papiers; édition soignée; (*b*) *F:* **he's a walking l.,** c'est une bibliothèque ambulante, c'est une encyclopédie vivante.

librate ['laibreit], *v.i.* osciller (comme un balancier); balancer.

libration [lai'breiʃ(ə)n], *s.* **1.** (*a*) oscillation *f*, balancement *m*; (*b*) équilibre *m*. **2.** *Astr:* libration *f* (de la lune).

libratory ['laibrətəri], *a.* (mouvement *m*) oscillatoire.

librettist [li'bretist], *s. Th:* librettiste *m.*

libretto, *pl.* **-i, -os** [li'bretou, -i:, -ouz], *s.* libretto *m*, *pl.* libretti, librettos; livret *m* (d'opéra, etc.).

Liburnia [lai'bə:niə, li-], *Pr.n. A.Geog:* Liburnie *f.*

Liburnian [lai'bə:niən, li-], *a.* & *s. A.Geog:* (*a*) *a.* liburnien; (*b*) *s.* Liburnien, -ienne.

Libya ['libiə], *Pr.n. Geog:* Libye *f.*

Libyan ['libiən], *a.* & *s. Geog:* **1.** *a.* libyen, libyque; **the L. desert,** le désert de Libye. **2.** *s.* Libyen, -yenne. **3.** *s. A.Ling:* libyque *m.*

Libytheidae [libi'θi:idi:], *s.pl. Ent:* libythéidés *m.*

licareol [li'ka:ri:ɔl], *s. Ch:* licaréol *m*, linalol *m.*

lice [lais]. *See* LOUSE.

licence[1] ['lais(ə)ns], *s.* **1.** (*a*) permission *f*, autorisation *f*; **under l. from the author, from the inventor,** avec l'autorisation de l'auteur, de l'inventeur; *F:* **it's a l. to print money!** c'est une affaire d'or! (*b*) **release (of a prisoner) on l.,** libération conditionnelle (d'un prisonnier); (*c*) *Adm:* permis *m*, autorisation, patente *f*, licence *f*, privilège *m*; **l. to sell sth.,** licence pour vendre qch.; **l. to sell beer, wine and spirits,** *esp. NAm:* **liquor l.,** licence de débitant; **off l.,** (i) licence permettant exclusivement la vente des boissons à emporter; (ii) débit *m* où on vend les boissons à emporter; **late l., extended l.,** autorisation exceptionnelle (à un café) de rester ouvert au delà de l'heure normale; **occasional l.,** autorisation spéciale; *A:* **pedlar's l.,** autorisation de colportage; patente de colporteur; **trading l.,** carte de commerce; **printer's l.,** brevet *m* d'imprimeur; **trades subject to a l., requiring a l.,** métiers *m* patentables; **manufacturing l.,** brevet, licence, de fabrication; **made, manufactured, under l.,** construit, fabriqué, sous licence; **theatre l., tobacco l.,** autorisation d'exploiter une salle de spectacles, un débit de tabac; **television l.,** impôt (annuel) sur un appareil de télévision; **import, export, l.,** licence d'importation, d'exportation; **building l.,** permis de construire, de bâtir; **marriage l., special l.** = dispense *f* des certificats de publication de mariage; **shooting l., game l.,** permis de chasse; **gun l.,** permis de port d'arme(s); *F:* port *m* d'arme(s); **carrying a weapon without a l.,** port d'arme prohibée; **to take out a l.,** se faire inscrire à la patente; **to take out a dog l.,** acquitter la taxe pour son chien; **l. holder,** patenté, -ée; licencié, -ée; **car l.,** permis de circulation, *F:* = carte grise; **l. number,** numéro *m* d'immatriculation; **driving l.,** permis de conduire; **heavy goods (vehicle) l.,** permis poids lourds; **l. to drive a public service vehicle,** permis transports en commun; *Av:* **pilot's l.,** brevet de pilote; (*d*) *Min:* **mining l.,** acte *m* de concession de mines; **prospecting l.,** permis de recherche. **2.** (*a*) (*abuse of freedom*) licence; **poetic l.,** licence poétique; (*b*) = LICENTIOUSNESS.

licence[2], *v.tr. NAm:* = LICENSE[1].

license[1] ['lais(ə)ns], *v.tr.* accorder un permis, une patente, un brevet, un privilège, à (qn); patenter, privilégier (qn); **to l. s.o. to sell drink,** délivrer à qn une patente de débit de boissons; autoriser qn à tenir un débit de boissons; **to be licensed to sell beer, wines and spirits,** autorisé, *Fr.C:* licencié, à vendre des boissons alcooliques; **to be licensed to sell sth.,** avoir l'autorisation de vendre qch.; **to l. a play,** autoriser la représentation d'une pièce; (*of merchant, etc.*) **to be duly licensed,** payer patente; **church licensed for the celebration of marriages,** église dûment autorisée à célébrer les mariages.

license[2], *s. NAm:* = LICENCE[1].

licensed ['laisənst], *a.* **1.** *Adm:* autorisé, patenté; **l. dealer,** patenté, -ée; **l. house, premises,** débit *m* de boissons; *Av:* **l. pilot,** pilote patenté, breveté; **l. victualler,** débitant *m* de boissons, de spiritueux; cafetier *m*; **the l. victuallers,** le commerce des boissons et spiritueux. **2.** privilégié.

licensee [lais(ə)n'si:], *s.* patenté, -ée; titulaire *mf*; concessionnaire *mf*; détenteur, -trice, d'une patente, d'un permis; gérant, -ante, propriétaire *mf* (d'un restaurant, d'un café, etc.).

licenser ['lais(ə)nsər], *s.* (*a*) octroyeur *m*, concesseur *m* (d'une permission); (*b*) censeur *m* (de pièces de théâtre, etc.).

licensing ['laisənsiŋ], *s.* autorisation *f* (de qn à faire qch.); octroiement *m* d'un permis, d'une autorisation (à qn); **l. requirements,** conditions *f* d'autorisation; **l. acts, laws,** lois relatives aux débits de boissons alcooliques, lois sur les patentes de débitants.

licentiate [lai'senʃiət], *s.* **1.** *Sch:* diplômé, -ée. **2.** *Ecc:* aspirant *m* à un pastorat (de l'Église réformée); novice *m* qui a obtenu ses diplômes.

licentious [lai'senʃəs], *a.* licencieux, déréglé, dévergondé, débauché.

licentiously [lai'senʃəsli], *adv.* licencieusement.

licentiousness [lai'senʃəsnis], *s.* licence *f*, dérèglement *m*, dévergondage *m*; débauche *f*; débordement(s) *m*(*pl*).

lichen ['laikən, 'litʃən], *s.* **1.** *Moss:* lichen *m*; **(grey)beard l.,** usnée barbue; **hairy l.,** lichen filamenteux, chevelu; **manna l.,** manne-lichen *f*, *pl.* manne-lichens. **2.** *Med:* lichen; **l. planus,** lichen plan. **3.** *Ent:* **L. moths,** lithosides *mpl.*

lichened ['laikənd], *a.* couvert de lichen.

lichenification [laikenifi'keiʃ(ə)n], *s. Med:* lichénification *f.*

lichenin ['laikənin], *s. Bio-Ch:* lichénine *f.*

lichenoid ['laikənɔid], *a.* lichénoïde.

lichenology [laikən'ɔlədʒi], *s.* lichénologie *f.*

lichenous ['laikənəs], *a.* **1.** lichénique; couvert de lichen. **2.** *Med:* lichéneux.

lichgate ['litʃgeit], *s.* porche d'entrée de cimetière surmonté d'un petit toit (pour abriter le cercueil en attendant l'arrivée du prêtre).

licit ['lisit], *a.* licite.

licitly ['lisitli], *adv.* licitement.

lick[1] [lik], *s.* **1.** (*a*) coup *m* de langue; **to give sth., s.o., a l.,** lécher qch., qn; *F:* **to give oneself a l. and a promise,** se faire un bout, un brin, de toilette; se faire une toilette de chat; *F:* **to get a l. at sth.,** tenter de faire qch., tâter de qch., se faire la main à qch.; (*b*) *F:* petite quantité; petite part; **a l. of paint would make all the difference,** cela a bien besoin d'une petite couche de peinture; *U.S:* **he won't do a l.,** il ne fait rien de rien. **2.** *A:* coup (porté à qn). **3.** *F:* **at (a) great l., at full l.,** à toute allure; à toute vitesse; *F:* en quatrième vitesse; **we were going at a hell of a l.,** nous allions d'un train d'enfer. **4.** *Husb:* **salt l.,** (i) pain salé; saunière *f*; salègre *m*; (ii) terrain *m* salifère (où les bêtes viennent lécher le sol); *U.S:* **deer l.,** roches couvertes de sel (qui attirent les daims).

lick[2], *v.* **1.** *v.tr.* lécher; **the dogs would come and l. my hand,** les chiens venaient me lécher la main; **the cat was licking her kittens,** la chatte léchait ses petits; **the flames were already licking the walls,** déjà les flammes léchaient les murs; **to l. one's lips,** *F:* **one's chops,** s'en lécher les babines; se (pour)lécher les babines; *F:* **to l. s.o.'s boots,** lécher les bottes à qn; *F:* **to l. s.o. into shape,** former, dégrossir, dégourdir, qn; **to l. sth. into shape,** mettre qch. au point; finir un travail; boucler une affaire; **to l. sth. up,** (*of animal*) laper qch.; (*of flame*) dévorer qch.; **the cat licked up all the spilt milk,** le chat a léché tout le lait répandu; **he licked the cream off his fingers,** d'un coup de langue il a enlevé la crème de ses doigts; **to l. the spoon (clean),** lécher la cuiller; *F:* **to l. the platter, plate, clean,** faire les plats nets; torcher le plat. 2. *v.tr. F:* (*a*) battre, rosser (qn); donner une volée de coups, une rossée, une raclée, à qn; (*b*) battre, vaincre, écraser, griller (un adversaire); **this licks me,** ça me dépasse; je n'y comprends rien. 3. *v.i. F:* **as hard as he could l.,** à toute allure; à toute vitesse; en quatrième vitesse.

licker-in ['likə'rin], *s. Tex:* tambour *m* de réunisseuse.

lickerish ['likəriʃ], *a. A:* 1. (*a*) friand, délicat; (*b*) gourmand; avide. 2. = LECHEROUS.

licking ['likiŋ], *s.* 1. (*a*) lèchement *m*; (*b*) pourlèchement *m* (des babines). 2. *F:* (*a*) raclée *f*, roulée *f*, tripotée *f*; **to give s.o. a (good) l.,** (i) donner une volée de coups, une rossée, une raclée, à qn; (ii) vaincre, écraser, griller, qn; **to take one's l. like a man,** recevoir sa raclée sans flancher; (*b*) défaite *f*.

lickspittle ['likspitəl], *s. F: O:* parasite *m*, flagorneur *m*; lécheur, -euse.

licorice ['likəris], *s.* = LIQUORICE.

lictor ['liktər], *s. Rom.Ant:* licteur *m*.

lid [lid], *s.* 1. (*a*) couvercle *m* (de boîte, etc.); **snap l.,** couvercle à ressort; *F:* **that puts the l. on it!** il ne manquait plus que ça! ça c'est le comble! (*b*) *F:* chapeau *m*; couvre-chef *m*, *pl.* couvre-chefs; casque *m*. 2. paupière *f*. 3. *Nat.Hist:* opercule *m*.

lidded ['lidid], *a.* 1. (*a*) (boîte *f*, etc.) à couvercle; (*b*) *Nat.Hist:* (capsule *f*, coquille *f*, etc.) à opercule. 2. (*with adj. prefixed, e.g.*) **heavy-l. eyes,** yeux *m* aux paupières lourdes.

lidless ['lidlis], *a.* 1. sans couvercle. 2. (*a*) (yeux *mpl*) sans paupières; (*b*) *Poet:* (yeux) toujours éveillés, toujours vigilants.

lido ['li:dou], *s.* lido *m*.

lie[1] [lai], *s.* (*a*) mensonge *m*; **white l.,** pieux mensonge; *Theol:* mensonge officieux; **downright l.,** mensonge flagrant; gros mensonge; **it's all lies! it's a pack of lies!** c'est un tissu de mensonges! pure invention tout cela! **the papers are always inventing new lies,** les journaux ne savent quoi inventer; **to tell a l.,** faire, dire, un mensonge; **to tell lies,** mentir; **to act a l.,** agir faussement; **that's a l.!** c'est un mensonge! vous mentez! **a direct l.,** un mensonge effronté; **l. detector,** détecteur *m* de mensonges; (*b*) **to give s.o. the l. (direct), to give the l. (direct) to an assertion,** donner un démenti (formel) à qn, à une assertion; démentir qn, une assertion (formellement); opposer à qn un démenti formel.

lie[2], *v.i. & tr.* (**lied** [laid]; **lying** ['laiiŋ]) mentir (**to s.o.,** à qn); **to l. about one's age,** tricher sur sa date de naissance; cacher son âge; *F:* **to l. like the devil, like blazes, like mad,** mentir comme un arracheur de dents; *A:* **you l. in your teeth, in your throat,** vous en avez menti par la gorge; **to l. oneself into, out of, a scrape,** s'attirer une mauvaise affaire, se tirer d'affaire, par des mensonges.

lie[3], *s.* 1. disposition *f* (du terrain, etc.); *Geol:* gisement *m* (d'une couche); *Civ.E:* tracé *m* (d'une route); **l. of the land,** configuration *f*, disposition, du terrain; topographie *f*; *Nau:* **to know the l. of the coast,** connaître le gisement de la côte; *Min:* **l. of the lodes,** gisement; (*in quarrying*) **l. of the stone,** lit *m* de la pierre. 2. *Golf:* position *f*, assiette *f* (de la balle). 3. *Ven:* retraite *f*, gîte *m* (d'un animal).

lie[4], *v.* (**lay** [lei]; **lain** [lein]; **lying** ['laiiŋ])

I. *v.i.* 1. (*of pers., animal*) (*a*) être couché (à plat); **to l. on one's side, on the ground,** être couché sur le côté, sur le sol; **he lay motionless,** il restait étendu sans mouvement; *Min:* **to work lying on one's side,** travailler à col tordu; **to l. against a wall,** être couché, étendu, contre un mur; **to be lying ill in bed,** être (malade et) alité; **to l. asleep,** être endormi; **to l. at the point of death,** être à l'article de la mort; **to l. dead,** être étendu (sur son lit de) mort; être mort; **we found him lying dead,** nous l'avons trouvé mort; (*of the dead*) **to l. in state,** être exposé sur un lit de parade; **the body was lying in state,** le corps reposait sur son lit de parade; **to l. in the churchyard,** reposer au cimetière; **to l. (buried) at a place,** reposer, être enterré, à un endroit; (*of gravestones*) **here lies . . .,** ci-gît . . .; (*b*) *A:* coucher (dans un local); **that night we lay at Southwark,** nous passâmes la nuit à Southwark; **to l. with a woman,** coucher avec une femme; (*c*) être, rester, se tenir; **to l. in bed,** rester au lit; **to l. awake,** rester éveillé; **to l. in prison,** être en prison; **to l. at s.o.'s mercy,** être, se trouver, à la merci de qn; **to l. in ambush,** se tenir en embuscade; **to l. still,** rester, se tenir, tranquille; **to l. hidden,** rester, se tenir, caché; **to l. under an obligation to do sth.,** être, se trouver, dans l'obligation de faire qch.; **to l. under a charge,** être sous le coup d'une accusation; **to l. under suspicion,** être soupçonné; *Mil:* **a large force lay to the south,** une forte armée se trouvait au sud; *Rac:* **to l. on a competitor,** serrer un concurrent; **to l. low,** (i) se tapir; rester tapi; se tenir accroupi; (ii) *F:* rester coi; se tenir coi; faire le mort; **to l. in wait,** se tenir en embuscade; être à l'affût, être aux aguets; (*of animal*) être à l'affût; **to l. in wait for s.o.,** se tenir à l'affût de qn; attendre qn à l'affût; dresser une embûche à qn; tendre un guet-apens à qn; guetter le passage de qn; attendre qn au passage. 2. (*of thg*) (*a*) être, se trouver; **the papers lay on the table,** les papiers étaient (étendus) sur la table; **his clothes were lying on the ground,** ses habits étaient éparpillés par terre; **let it l. there!** laissez-le là! **the snow lies deep,** la neige est épaisse; **to l. open,** être ouvert; (*of building*) **to l. in ruins,** être en ruines; **the obstacles that l. in our way,** les obstacles *m* dont notre chemin est jonché; *Nau:* **ship lying at her berth,** navire mouillé, amarré, à son poste; (*b*) rester, séjourner; **the petition lies at our office,** la pétition se trouve actuellement dans nos bureaux, a été déposée dans nos bureaux; (*of money*) **to l. in the bank,** être déposé à la banque; **the snow did not l.,** la neige n'a pas tenu; **these books are lying on my hands,** je ne sais que faire de ces livres; (*of ground*) **to l. waste,** rester en friche; (*c*) (*of food*) **to l. (heavy) on one's stomach,** peser sur l'estomac; être un poids sur l'estomac; charger l'estomac; rester à qn sur l'estomac; **sins that l. heavy on the conscience,** péchés qui pèsent sur la conscience; **time lies heavy on my hands,** le temps me pèse; (*d*) **the onus of proof lies upon, with, them,** c'est à eux qu'incombe le soin de faire la preuve; **the responsibility lies with the author,** la responsabilité incombe à l'auteur; **it lies (entirely) with you to do it,** il dépend de vous de le faire; il ne tient qu'à vous de le faire; (*e*) être situé; **town lying in a plain,** ville située dans une plaine; **the village lies below the castle,** le village se trouve en contrebas du château; **his house lies on our way,** sa maison se trouve sur notre chemin; **the coast lies east and west,** la côte s'étend à l'est et à l'ouest; **to know how the coast lies,** connaître le gisement de la côte; **the truth lies between these extremes,** la vérité est entre ces extrêmes; **he knows where his interest lies,** il sait où se trouve son intérêt; **his fate lies in your hands,** sa destinée dépend de vous; **the difference lies in this, that . . .,** la différence consiste, réside, en ceci que . . .; **the fault lies with you, lies at your door,** la faute vous est imputable; la faute retombe sur vous; la faute en est à vous; *Lit:* **as far as in me lies,** autant qu'il est en mon pouvoir; autant qu'il m'est possible; (*f*) **a vast plain lay before us,** une vaste plaine s'étendait devant nous; **a brilliant future lies before him,** un brillant avenir s'ouvre devant lui; (*g*) **road that lies between two mountains, across a swamp,** route *f* qui passe entre deux montagnes, à travers un marais; **our road lay along the valley,** notre route longeait la vallée; **our way lies through the woods,** notre chemin passe par les bois; **my talents do not l. in that direction,** je n'ai pas de dispositions pour cela; là n'est pas mon talent. 3. *Jur:* (*of action, appeal*) être recevable; se soutenir; **it was decided that the action would not l.,** l'action fut jugée non recevable; **a criminal action lies against him,** une action criminelle a été intentée contre lui; il est sous le coup d'un procès au criminel; **no appeal lies against the decision,** la décision ne souffre pas d'appel. 4. *Nau:* (*of ship*) **to l. her course,** être en route; porter, tenir, en route.

II. (*compound verbs*) 1. **lie about,** *v.i.* (*of thg*) traîner (çà et là); **to leave one's papers lying about,** laisser traîner ses papiers.

2. **lie back,** *v.i.* (*a*) se laisser retomber; se renverser (dans son fauteuil); (*b*) **when you retire you can l. back and take things easy,** quand vous aurez pris votre retraite vous pourrez vous reposer.

3. **lie by,** *v.i.* **to have sth. lying by,** avoir qch. en réserve.

4. **lie down,** *v.i.* (*a*) se coucher, s'étendre; **to l. down on one's bed,** s'étendre sur son lit; *F:* **I'd like to l. down and die!** c'est désespérant! j'y renonce! **to l. down on the ground,** se coucher, s'allonger, par terre; **l. down for a bit,** reposez-vous un peu; (*to dog*) **l. down!** couche! (*b*) **to l. down under a defeat, under an insult; to take a defeat, an insult, lying down,** se laisser battre sans résistance; ne pas relever une insulte; **he took it lying down,** il n'a pas dit mot; *F:* il a filé doux; **he won't take it lying down,** il ne se laissera pas faire; il va se rebiffer.

5. **lie in,** *v.i.* (*a*) *O:* (*of woman*) être en couches; faire ses chouches; **lying-in hospital,** maternité *f*; (*b*) faire la grasse matinée.

6. **lie off,** *v.i.* (*of ship*) rester au large.

7. **lie over,** *v.i.* (*of thg*) être remis à plus tard; rester en suspens; se trouver ajourné; **the motion was allowed to l. over,** la motion a été ajournée; **to let a bill l. over,** différer l'échéance d'un effet.

8. **lie to,** *v.i.* (*of ship*) être à la cape; tenir la cape; capeyer; (*of sailing ship also*) rester en panne.

9. **lie up,** *v.i.* 1. *F:* (*of pers.*) garder le lit; garder la chambre. 2. (*of ship*) désarmer.

lie-abed ['laiəbed], *s. O:* paresseux, -euse (qui fait la grasse matinée); grand dormeur, grande dormeuse.

liebenerite ['li:b(ə)nərait], *s. Miner:* liebenerite *f*.

Liebig ['li:big], *Pr.n. Ch:* **L. condenser,** réfrigérant *m* de Liebig.

liebigite ['li:bigait], *s. Miner:* liebigite *f*.

lie-by ['laibai], *a. & s. Rail:* **l.-by (road),** voie *f* de dédoublement, d'évitement.

Liechtenstein ['li:ʃtənʃtain], *Pr.n. Geog:* **(the principality of) L.,** (la principauté de) Liechtenstein (*m*).

lie-down ['lai'daun], *s.* **to go for, to have, a l.-d.,** faire une sieste, un petit somme.

lief [li:f], *adv. A:* volontiers; **I would, had, as l. go to Paris as anywhere else,** j'aimerais autant aller à Paris qu'autre part; **I would as l. have died, I would liefer have died,** j'aurais préféré mourir.

liege [li:(d)ʒ], *a. & s. Hist:* 1. (vassal) lige *m*; **to our trusty lieges,** à nos féaux sujets. 2. **l. lord,** (seigneur) suzerain *m*.

liegeman, *pl.* **-men** ['li:dʒmən], *s.m. Hist:* homme lige.

lie-in ['lai'in], *s.* **to have a l.-in,** faire la grasse matinée.

lien [li:(ə)n], *s. Jur:* privilège *m* (sur un meuble, etc.); droit *m* de rétention; droit de nantissement; **general l.,** privilège général; **vendor's l.,** privilège du vendeur; **l. on goods,** droit de rétention de marchandises; **to have a l. (up)on a cargo,** avoir un recours sur un chargement; **to have a l. on the personal property of a debtor,** avoir un privilège sur les meubles d'un débiteur.

lienholder ['li:ənhouldər], *s.*, **lienor** ['li:ənər], *s. Jur:* rétentionnaire *m* (de marchandises).

lienteric [laiən'terik], *a. Med:* (flux *m*) lientérique.

lientery ['laiəntəri], *s. Med:* lientérie *f*.

lierne [li:'ə:n], *s. Arch:* lierne *f*, nervure *f* secondaire (de voûte).

lieu [lju:, lu:], *s.* **in l. of . . .,** au lieu de . . .; au lieu et place de . . .; en remplacement de . . .; **to stand in l. of . . .,** tenir lieu de . . .; **he gave him a month's wages in l. of notice,** il lui a donné un mois de salaire et l'a congédié (sur-le-champ); **I'll take something else in l.,** je prendrai quelque chose d'autre à la place.

lieutenancy [lef'tenənsi, *esp. U.S:* lu:-], *s.* 1. *Hist:* lieutenance *f*. 2. *Mil: A:* grade *m* de lieutenant.

lieutenant [lef'tenənt, *esp. U.S:* lu:-], *s.* 1. (*a*) *Hist:* lieutenant *m*, délégué *m*; (*b*) *Adm:* **lord l.,** lord-lieutenant *m* (d'un comté); **l. governor** (*pl.* **lieutenant governors**), (i) *Can:* lieutenant gouverneur (d'une province); (ii) *U.S:* gouverneur adjoint (d'un État); (*c*) aide *mf*; **my most trusted l.,** mon collaborateur le plus précieux. 2. (*a*) *Mil:* lieutenant; (*W.R.A.C.*) deuxième classe *f*; *U.S:* **first l.,** lieutenant; **second l.,** sous-lieutenant *m*, *pl.* sous-lieutenants; **l.-colonel** (*pl.* **lieutenant-colonels**), lieutenant-colonel *m*, *pl.* lieutenants-colonels; **l. general** (*pl.* **lieutenant generals**), général *m* de corps d'armée; (*b*) *Navy:* lieutenant de vaisseau; **sub l.,** *U.S:* **l. junior grade,** enseigne *m* (de vaisseau) première classe; **acting sub l.,** enseigne deuxième classe; **l. commander** (*pl.* **lieutenant commanders**), capitaine *m* de corvette; (*c*) *Mil.Av:* **flight l.,** capitaine (d'aviation); *U.S:* **first, second, l.,** lieutenant, sous-lieutenant (aviateur); *U.S:* **l.-colonel,** lieutenant-colonel; *U.S:* **l. general,** général (de corps aérien); (*d*) lieutenant (de l'Armée du Salut).

lievrite ['li:vrait], *s. Miner:* liévrite *f*.

life, *pl.* **lives** [laif, laivz], *s.* 1. (*a*) (*existence*) vie *f*; **to have l.,** être en vie; vivre; **everything that has l.,** tout ce qui a vie; **l. force,** force vitale; élan vital; **to give l. to s.o.,** donner la vie à qn; **to come to l.,** s'animer; **to come to l. again,** revenir à la vie; (i) ressusciter; (ii) se ranimer; **to bring s.o. to l. again, to recall s.o. to l.,** ramener, rappeler, qn à la vie; (i) ressusciter qn; (ii) ranimer qn; **it is a matter of l. and death,** (i) c'est une question de vie ou de mort; il y va de la vie; (ii) c'est une question d'importance capitale; **he is hovering between l. and death,** il est entre la vie et la mort; **l.-and-death struggle,** lutte désespérée; guerre *f* à mort; **to take s.o.'s l.,** tuer qn; **to take one's own l.,** se suicider; **to save s.o.'s l.,** sauver la vie à qn; *Space: etc:* **l. support equipment,** équipement *m* de survie; **l. support pack,** appareil *m* autonome de survie; **to beg for one's l,** demander la vie; **to grant s.o. his l.,** accorder la vie à qn; **to sell one's l. dearly,** vendre cher sa peau; **he was carrying his l. in his hands,** il risquait la mort; il risquait sa vie; **to risk one's l., to risk l. and limb,** risquer sa peau; risquer corps et âme; **without accident to l. or limb,** sans accident personnel; **to escape with one's l., with l. and limb,** s'en tirer la vie sauve; **to beat s.o. within an inch of his l.,** battre qn à le laisser pour mort; battre qn comme plâtre; hacher qn menu comme chair à pâté; **to lose one's l.,** perdre la vie; périr; **many lives were lost,** beaucoup (de personnes) ont péri, ont perdu la vie; il y a eu beaucoup de morts; **there were no lives lost,** personne n'a été tué; **the catastrophe resulted in great loss of l.,** la catastrophe a fait beaucoup de victimes; **the town was taken with great sacrifice of l.,** la ville fut prise au prix de beaucoup de sang répandu; **to fly, run, for one's l., for dear l.,** chercher son salut dans la fuite; s'enfuir à toutes jambes; **run for your l.!** fuyez, ou vous êtes un homme mort! **run for your lives!** sauve qui peut! **he was rowing for dear l.,** il ramait de toutes ses forces; **I cannot for the l. of me understand,** il m'est absolument impossible de comprendre; je ne comprends absolument pas; *F:* **I wouldn't do it for the l. of me,** je ne le ferais pour rien au monde; **not on your l.!** jamais de la vie! *A:* **'pon my l.!** sur ma vie! **to have as many lives as a cat,** avoir la vie dure; être dur à cuire; avoir l'âme chevillée au corps; (*b*) (*vivacity*) **to be full of l.,** être plein de vie, d'entrain; **picture full of l.,** tableau animé; **the streets were full of l.,** les rues étaient pleines de mouvement, d'animation; **to give l. to sth.,** donner de la vie à qch.; animer (la conversation, etc.); **to give new l. to s.o., sth., to put new l. into s.o., sth.,** redonner des forces à qn; rendre la vie à qn; ranimer, ressusciter, qn; ranimer, *F:* galvaniser (une entreprise, etc.); **a little drop of spirits will put new l. into him,** un petit verre va le ravigoter; **to put fresh l. into the conversation, into the meeting,** ranimer la conversation, l'assemblée; **he's the l. and soul of the party,** c'est le boute-en-train de la compagnie; c'est lui qui met tout en train; **he's the l. and soul of the undertaking,** il est l'âme *f* de l'entreprise; *F:* **put a bit of l. into it!** mets-y du nerf! grouille-toi! **there's no l. in this place,** ça manque d'entrain ici; (*c*) *Art: Lit:* **to draw from l.,** dessiner sur le vif, d'après nature; **drawing from l.,** dessin *m* d'après nature; **portrait from l.,** portrait fait sur le vivant; **l. class,** classe *f* où on dessine des académies; **to paint sth. to the l.,** peindre qch. au naturel; **it was Martin to the l.,** c'était Martin pris sur le vif; **he could imitate his master to the l.,** il imitait son maître à s'y méprendre; **characters taken from l.,** caractères pris sur le vif; **true to l.** (roman, etc.) vécu, senti; **his acting is absolutely true to l.,** son jeu est tout à fait naturel; **as large as l.,** grand comme nature; (*d*) *coll.* **animal, vegetable, l.,** la vie animale, végétale; **bird l.,** les oiseaux *m*; **the water swarms with l.,** la vie pullule dans l'eau; **there was very little l. to be seen,** on ne voyait presque personne; *Art:* **still l.,** nature morte. **2.** (*period of existence*) (*a*) vie, vivant *m* (de qn); **the seventy-two years of his l.,** les soixante-douze ans qu'il avait vécu; **to which I owe my long l.,** à quoi je dois ma longévité; **to cut short one's l.,** abréger sa vie, sa destinée; **he worked all his l.,** il a travaillé durant toute sa vie, sa vie durant; **never in (all) my l.,** jamais de la vie; **at my time of l.,** à mon âge; **early l.,** enfance *f*; **in his early l.,** quand il était (i) enfant, (ii) jeune; **single l.,** vie célibataire; **married l.,** vie conjugale; **working l.,** période *f*, années *fpl*, d'activité, de travail; **he began l. a . . .,** il commença sa vie, sa carrière, comme . . .; **tired of l.,** las de vivre; **to hold a post for l.,** occuper une situation à vie; **appointed for l.,** nommé à vie; **l. annuity, pension,** pension, rente, viagère; pension à vie; **l. interest,** usufruit *m* (d'un bien); viager *m*; rente viagère; **l. estate,** propriété viagère, en viager; **l. peer,** pair *m* à vie; **l. peerage,** pairie personnelle, à vie; **l. senator,** sénateur *m* inamovible; **l. imprisonment, imprisonment for l.,** emprisonnement perpétuel; **penal servitude for l.,** travaux forcés à perpétuité; (*of animal, bird*) **to mate for l.,** s'accoupler, s'unir, pour la vie; (*b*) *Ins:* **l. assurance, insurance,** assurance *f* sur la vie, assurance-vie *f*; **expectation of l.,** vie moyenne, probable; **expectation of l. tables,** tables *f* de mortalité, de survie; **to be a good l.,** être un bon sujet d'assurance, un bon risque; (*c*) *Lit:* biographie *f*; **to write s.o.'s l.,** écrire la vie de qn; **Plutarch's Lives,** les Vies de Plutarque; (*d*) vie, durée *f* (d'une société, d'un phénomène, etc.); durée, vie, longévité *f* (d'un appareil, d'un câble, d'une lampe, etc.); **useful l.,** vie, durée, utile (d'une machine, etc.); *Fin:* **l. of a loan,** durée d'un emprunt; *Atom.Ph:* **average l., mean l.,** vie moyenne (d'un atome, d'un isotope). **3.** (*a*) **this l.,** la vie sur terre; **to depart this l.,** mourir, quitter ce monde; (*b*) **way of l.,** manière *f* de vivre; (train *m* de) vie; **the American way of l.,** la vie américaine; **hermit's l.,** vie d'hermite; **high l.,** la vie mondaine; **to lead a gay l.,** mener joyeuse vie; **night l.,** la vie nocturne; **that sort of l. is doing your health no good,** à vivre ainsi vous vous abîmez la santé; **l. is pleasant here,** il fait bon vivre ici; *F:* **how's l.?** comment ça va? **what a l.!** quelle vie! quel métier! **such is l.!** ainsi va la vie! c'est la vie! **to see l.,** (i) se frotter au monde; (ii) s'amuser; faire la noce; **he has seen l.,** il a beaucoup vécu; **I've seen something of l.,** je connais la vie; **he makes her l. a burden, a misery,** il lui rend la vie dure.

lifebelt ['laifbelt], *s.* ceinture *f* de sauvetage; (*inflated*) nautile *m*.

lifeblood ['laifblʌd], *s.* (*a*) *Lit:* sang *m* (de qn); (*b*) âme *f* (d'une entreprise, etc.); (*c*) **oil has become the l. of their economy,** le pétrole est devenu le pivot de leur économie.

lifeboat ['laifbout], *s.* (*a*) **(coastal) l.,** canot *m* de sauvetage; **l. station,** station *f*, poste *m*, de sauvetage; **the Royal National L. Institution** = la Société de sauvetage des naufragés; (*b*) **(ship's) l.,** embarcation *f* de sauvetage.

lifeboatman, *pl.* **-men** ['laifboutmən], *s.* sauveteur *m*.

lifebuoy ['laifbɔi], *s.* bouée *f*, couronne *f*, de sauvetage; **sling l.,** bouée de sauvetage pour va-et-vient.

life-giving ['laifgiviŋ], *a.* vivifiant; (principe, pouvoir) animateur; (soleil, fleuve) fécondant; **l.-g. heat,** chaleur féconde.

lifeguard, life guard ['laifgɑːd], *s.* **1.** *Mil:* (*a*) garde *f* du corps; (*b*) (*in British Army*) **the L. Guards,** le corps de cavaliers appartenant à la maison du roi; les Gardes du corps. **2.** (*at the seaside*) gardien *m* de plage. **3.** (*device*) *Rail:* chasse-pierres *m inv*; (*trams*) ramasse-piétons *m inv*.

Life Guardsman, *pl.* **-men** ['laifgɑːdzmən], *s.m. Mil:* cavalier faisant partie des *Life Guards*; cavalier de la Garde.

lifejacket ['laifdʒækit], *s.* brassière *f*, gilet *m*, de sauvetage.

lifeless ['laiflis], *a.* sans vie; (i) mort; (ii) sans vigueur; (style, etc.) mou, inanimé, froid; (soirée *f*) sans entrain; **l. little town,** petite ville sans mouvement, *F:* bled *m*.

lifelessly ['laiflisli], *adv.* sans vie; sans vigueur; sans entrain.

lifelessness ['laiflisnis], *s.* (i) absence *f* de vie; (ii) absence de mouvement; (iii) manque *m* d'animation; mollesse *f* (de style, etc.).

lifelike ['laiflaik], *a.* (portrait, etc.) vivant, très ressemblant, qui a de la vie; **he could give a l. imitation of his master,** il imitait son maître à s'y méprendre; *Art:* **l. flesh,** chairs vraies.

lifeline ['laiflain], *s.* **1.** *Nau:* (*a*) ligne *f* de sauvetage; **l. throwing gun,** (canon *m*) lance-amarre *m*, *pl.* lance-amarres; (*b*) (*aboard ship*) garde-corps *m inv*, attrape *f*; sauvegarde *f*; (*at the seaside, etc.*) **to swim between the lifelines,** nager entre les cordages *m*; (*c*) corde *f* de communication (de scaphandrier); (*d*) ligne de pompier. **2.** (*in hand reading*) la ligne de vie.

lifelong ['laiflɔŋ], *a.* (amitié *f*, etc.) de toute la vie; **a l. friend,** un ami de toujours.

lifepreserver ['laifprizəːvər], *s.* **1.** *Nau:* appareil *m* de sauvetage. **2.** casse-tête *m inv*; canne plombée; nerf *m* de bœuf.

lifer ['laifər], *s. F: O:* (*a*) forçat *m* à perpétuité; (*b*) travaux forcés à perpétuité; **he was given a l.,** il fut condamné à perpétuité, *F:* à perpète.

liferent ['laifrent], *s. Jur: Scot:* **1.** usufruit *m* (d'un bien). **2.** rente viagère.

liferenter ['laifrentər], *s. Jur: Scot:* **1.** usufruitier, -ière. **2.** rentier, -ière, à vie.

lifesaver ['laifseivər], *s.* **1.** (*pers.*) sauveteur *m*. **2.** *F:* planche *f* de salut.

lifesaving ['laifseiviŋ], *s.* sauvetage *m*; **l. apparatus,** appareils *mpl*, engins *mpl*, de sauvetage; **l. rocket,** fusée *f*, harpon *m*, porte-amarre; **l. drill,** exercices *mpl* de sauvetage; **l. medal,** médaille *f* de sauvetage.

life-size(d) ['laifsaiz(d)], *a.* (portrait, etc.) de grandeur naturelle, grandeur nature; (statue) en grand.

lifetime ['laiftaim], *s.* (*a*) vie *f*; **in, during, his l.,** en son vivant, de son vivant; (*a*) **a l. of happiness,** toute une vie de bonheur; **it is the labour of a l.,** c'est le travail de toute une vie; **you can wear it for a l.,** c'est inusable; **it's the chance of a l.,** cette chance n'arrive qu'une fois dans la vie; *F:* **it's all in a l.,** c'est la vie! (*b*) *Ph:* durée *f*, vie (d'un phénomène); *Atom.Ph:* durée de vie, longévité *f* (d'un atome, d'un isotope); **l. of excitation energy, of excited state,** durée de l'énergie, de l'état, d'excitation; **fuel l.,** (durée de) vie du combustible.

lifework ['laifwəːk], *s.* travail *m* de toute une vie.

lift[1] [lift], *s.* **1.** (*a*) (*act of raising*) haussement *m*; élévation *f* (du bras, etc.); levée *f* (d'un fardeau, etc.); **abrupt l.,** levée brusque; **the l. of the waves,** le soulèvement des flots; **to give s.o. a l.,** (i) faire monter qn (en voiture) avec soi; (ii) *F:* remonter le moral à qn; **can I give you a l.?** est-ce que je peux vous conduire quelque part? *F:* **to get a l. up (in the world),** monter un degré, avancer d'un cran, dans l'échelle sociale; **with a l. of the head,** en levant la tête; (*b*) (*sth. raised*) palanquée (de marchandises, etc.); emport *m* (d'un avion); **l. capacity,** capacité *f* d'emport, de transport (d'un avion, etc.); **l. truck,** chariot élévateur (pour la manutention des marchandises); **fork l. truck,** chariot (élévateur) à fourche. **2.** (*a*) (*extent of rise*) hauteur *f* de levage (d'une grue, etc.); hauteur d'élévation (d'une pompe); *Mec.E:* levée *f* (d'un clapet); levée, course *f* (d'un pilon de bocard); **cam l.,** levée de la came; **l. valve,** (i) soupape *f*; (ii) clapet; **l. of a (canal) lock,** (hauteur de) chute *f* d'un bief; **l. lock,** écluse *f* double, à sas; **l. wall,** mur *m* de chute (d'une écluse); **l. pump,** pompe élévatoire; (*b*) différence *f* de niveau (entre paliers, etc.); *Min:* **l. between two levels,** hauteur verticale entre deux galeries; **quarry worked in lifts of 10 metres,** carrière exploitée en étages de 10 mètres. **3.** (*raising power*) (*a*) force ascensionnelle (d'un ballon); **l. of a gas,** force ascensionnelle d'un gaz; (*b*) *Av: etc:* portance *f*, poussée *f* (aérodynamique); sustentation *f*; **l. cœfficient,** coefficient *m* de portance, de poussée; **l. component,** composante *f* de portance; **l. drag ratio,** finesse *f* (d'un avion); **l. engine,** moteur *m* de sustentation; **l. fan,** soufflante *f*, ventilateur *m*, de sustentation; **l. strut,** mât *m* de soutien; **l. wire,** câble *m* de levée; câble, fil *m*, portant; hauban *m* de soutien; **l. angle,** angle *m* de cabrage; **l. spoiler,** volet *m* de freinage du cabrage; **jet l.,** portance par réaction; **l. jet,** réacteur *m* de sustentation. **4.** (*raising device*) (*a*) ascenseur *m*; **(goods) l.,** monte-charge *m inv*, élévateur *m*; **dinner l., service l.,** monte-plats *m inv*; **l. to all floors,** ascenseur à tous les étages; **l. cage,** cabine *f* d'ascenseur; **l. shaft,** cage *f* d'ascenseur; **l. gate,** barrière oscillante; **l. attendant,** liftier, -ière; (*boy*) garçon d'ascenseur; (*b*) (*of aircraft carrier*) monte-charge; ascenseur; **centreline l., deck-edge l.,** ascenseur axial, latéral; (*c*) **ski l.,** (re)monte-pente *m*, *pl.* remonte-pentes; **chair l.,** télésiège *m*; (*d*) *Mil: Av:* **bomb l.,** treuil *m* de chargement de bombes; (*e*) *Nau:* balancine *f* (de vergue, etc.); brécin *m*, martinet *m*; **quarter l.,** balancine de gui. **5.** (*a*) *Min:* **l. of (mine) pumps,** jeu *m* de pompes; (*b*) *Rail:* rame *f* (de wagons).

lift[2], *v.*

I. *v.tr.* **1.** (*a*) lever, soulever (un poids); lever, élever, hausser (le bras); lever, dresser (la tête); lever (les yeux); **crane to l. twenty tons,** grue *f* d'une puissance de levage de vingt tonnes; **the tide will l. the boat,** la marée soulèvera le bateau, renflouera le bateau, remettra le bateau à flot; **to l. one's hand against s.o.,** lever la main sur qn; **to l. sth. up (again),** élever, soulever, relever, qch.; **to l. s.o. up,** (i) aider qn à se relever ou à se soulever; (*in bed*) aider qn à se mettre sur son séant; (ii) prendre (un enfant) dans ses bras; **to l. up one's head,** (i) relever, redresser, la tête; (ii) reprendre courage; **to l. up one's hands to heaven,** lever les bras au ciel; **to l. up one's voice,** élever la voix; **to l. sth. down (from a shelf, etc.),** descendre qch. (d'un rayon, etc.); **he lifted her (down) from the horse,** il la prit dans ses bras et la descendit de cheval; **to l. the lid off a box,** enlever le couvercle d'une boîte; soulever le couvercle; **the wind lifted him off his feet,** il a été soulevé par le vent; **he lifted the spoon to his mouth,** il a porté la cuiller à sa bouche; **trees lifted by the frost,** arbres déchaussés par la gelée; *Av:* **to l. the nose of the aircraft,** redresser l'avion (avant l'atterrissage); *Artil:* **to l. the fire,** allonger le tir; (*b*) **the cypress lifts its dark foliage,** le cyprès élève son feuillage noir; **the church lifts its spire to the skies,** l'église *f* dresse sa flèche vers le ciel; (*c*) élever (l'âme, le cœur); **to be lifted up by a momentary success,** s'enorgueillir d'un succès momentané; (*d*) **to have one's face lifted,** se faire tirer la peau du visage; se faire remonter les bajoues; (*e*) *Nau:* soulager (une voile); **to l. the rudder,** soulager le gouvernail; (*f*) *Scot:* ramasser (qch.); *Golf:* **to l. one's ball,** ramasser la balle. **2.** (*a*) *Agr:* lever, arracher, récolter (les pommes de terre); **to l. seedlings,** dépiquer les plants (pour les repiquer); (*b*) *Min:* remonter (le minerai, le pétrole); (*c*) *Cer:* démouler (la porcelaine); (*d*) *Com:* enlever (des marchandises); (*e*) transporter (des voyageurs, etc.) en avion. **3.** *Cr: Golf:* donner de l'essor à (la balle); *Ten:* lifter (un coup). **4.** *F:* (*a*) voler, lever (qch.); **to l. cattle,** voler du bétail; **to l. s.o.'s purse,** voler le porte-monnaie de qn; **to l. a passage from an author,** plagier un auteur; démarquer un passage appartenant à un auteur; **these lines are shamelessly lifted from Donne,** ces vers sont un démarquage flagrant de Donne; (*b*) *Sp:* remporter (une coupe). **5.** lever (un embargo). **6.** *U.S:* purger (une hypothèque). **7.** *U.S:* argumenter, accroître (un impôt, les prix, etc.).

II. *v.i.* **1.** (*a*) (*of valve, etc.*) se lever, se soulever; (*b*) (*of floor*) se soulever (sous l'action de l'humidité, etc.). **2.** (*a*) (*of fog*) s'élever; se dissiper; (*b*) *U.S:* (*of rain*) cesser; **the rain is lifting,** le temps s'éclaircit. **3.** *Nau:* (*a*) (*of vessel*) s'élever à la lame; (*b*) (*of sail*) faseyer; (*c*) (*of land or constellation*) monter à l'horizon; émerger. **4.**

Av: (*of aircraft*); décoller (*of hydroplane floats*) **to l. (off the water)**, se déjauger. **5.** *Sp:* (*in walking race*) marcher sur la pointe des pieds.

lifter ['liftər], *s.* **1.** (*pers.*) (*a*) souleveur *m*; (*b*) **cattle l.,** voleur *m* de bétail. **2.** (*thg*) (*a*) *Tls:* crochet *m* (de levage) (pour couvercle de fourneau, etc.); *Metalw:* crochet de fonderie; (*moulder's tool*) crochet à ramasser; (*b*) *I.C.E:* **exhaust-valve l.,** décompresseur *m*; (*c*) **magnet l.,** électro-aimant *m* de levage, *pl.* électro-aimants de levage; (*d*) *Mec.E:* came *f*, virgule *f*, levée *f*, alluchon *m*; **valve l.,** poussoir *m* de soupape.

lifting [liftiŋ], *s.* **1.** levage *m*, relevage *m*, soulèvement *m* (d'un poids, etc.); *Artil:* allongement *m*, report *m* (du tir); **l. apparatus,** appareil *m* de levage; **l. appliances, l. tackle,** appareils, engins *mpl*, appareillage *m*, de levage; **l. gear,** appareil(s) de levage; élévateur *m*; **l. machinery,** machines *fpl* à soulever, machines élévatoires, machines acrobatiques; **l. jack,** cric *m*, vérin *m*, de levage; **l. magnet,** électro-aimant *m* de levage; **l. valve,** soupape soulevante; **l. wheel,** roue *f* élévatoire; **l. eye, l. ring,** anneau *m* de levage; **l. handle,** poignée *f* de levage, de soulèvement; **l. hook,** crochet *m* de levage, croc *m* de hissage; *Aut:* **l. ramp, platform,** pont élévateur; **l. capacity, l. power,** force *f*, puissance *f*, de levage; force élévatoire; force portante (d'un aimant); **l. height,** hauteur *f* de levage; *Av:* **l. force, l. power,** force de sustentation, puissance ascensionnelle; **l. propeller,** hélice sustentatrice, rotor sustentateur; **l. surface,** plan sustentateur; surface portante, sustentatrice, surface alaire. **2.** (*a*) *Agr:* arrachage *m*, récolte *f* (des pommes de terre); (*b*) *Min:* remontée *f* (du minerai); (*c*) *Cer:* démoulage *m* (de la porcelaine). **3.** (*a*) **l. of customs barriers,** désarmement douanier; (*b*) *F:* vol *m* (action de dérober qch.); (*c*) (*of literary work*) démarquage *m*.

liftman, *pl.* **-men** ['liftmæn, -men], *s.m.* liftier; garçon d'ascenseur.

lift-off ['liftɔf], *s. Av: Ball:* décollage *m*, soulèvement *m* (d'un hélicoptère, d'un véhicule sur coussin d'air); décollage (d'une fusée, d'un missile); **l.-o. speed,** vitesse *f* de soulèvement.

lift-up[1] ['liftʌp], *a. F:* (siège *m*, etc.) à bascule, rabattable; **l.-up seat,** strapontin *m* (de taxi, de théâtre).

lift-up[2], *s. F:* **to give s.o. a l.-up,** remonter le moral à qn.

ligament ['ligəmənt], *s. Anat:* ligament *m*.

ligamental, ligamentary, ligamentous [ligə'ment(ə)l, -'mentəri, -'mentəs], *a.* ligamenteux.

ligan ['laigən], *s. Nau: Jur:* épave marquée par une bouée.

ligate ['laigeit], *v.tr. Surg:* ligaturer, faire une ligature à.

ligation [lai'geiʃ(ə)n], *s. Surg:* ligature *f* (action de ligaturer).

ligature[1] ['ligətjər], *s.* **1.** *Surg:* ligature *f*; **retaining, stabilizing, l.,** ligature de stabilisation. **2.** *Typ:* ligature. **3.** *Mus:* liaison *f*.

ligature[2], *v.tr.* (*a*) *Surg:* ligaturer, barrer (une veine); (*b*) lier; (*c*) entrelacer (a et e); **ligatured o e,** o et e entrelacés.

light[1] [lait], *s.* **1.** lumière *f*; (*a*) **natural, artificial, electric, l.,** lumière naturelle, artificielle, électrique; **by the l. of the sun, of the moon,** à la lumière du soleil; au clair, à la clarté, de la lune; **the l. of day,** la lumière du jour; le jour; **at first l.,** à l'aube; aux premières lueurs du jour; **to bring (sth.) to l.,** (i) mettre (qch.) à jour, au jour; déterrer, exhumer (qch.); (ii) mettre (qch.) en lumière, en évidence; dévoiler, révéler (qch.); (*of crime, etc.*) **to come to l.,** se dévoiler, se découvrir; **some curious facts have come to l.,** on a découvert des choses curieuses; *Austr: N.Z: F:* **I asked him for a loan and he came to l. with $100,** je lui ai demandé de me prêter de l'argent et il m'a offert $100; **to see the l.,** (i) voir le jour, la lumière; (ii) être convaincu, converti; (iii) trouver son chemin de Damas; **his book will never see the l. of day,** son ouvrage ne sera jamais (i) terminé, (ii) publié; **secret that would never bear the l. of day,** secret qui ne supporterait pas de voir le jour, qu'on ne pourrait jamais divulguer, révéler; (*b*) *Ph: etc:* **bright l.,** lumière vive; **diffused l., scattered l.,** lumière diffuse; **incident l.,** lumière incidente; **polarized l.,** lumière polarisée; **reflected l.,** lumière réfléchie; **stray l.,** lumière parasite; **transmitted l.,** lumière transmise; **black l.,** lumière noire; **infrared l.,** lumière infrarouge; **ultraviolet l.,** lumière ultraviolette; **monochromatic l.,** lumière monochromatique; *Phot:* **safe l.,** lumière inactinique; *Atom.Ph:* **l. of recombination,** lumière de recombinaison; **scintillation l.,** lumière de scintillation; **diffusion of l.,** diffusion *f* de la lumière; **propagation of l.,** propagation *f* de la lumière; **velocity of l.,** vitesse *f* de la lumière; **energy of l.,** énergie *f* de la lumière; **intensity of l., l. output,** intensité *f* de la lumière, intensité lumineuse; **modulation of l.,** modulation *f* de la lumière; **polarization of l.,** polarisation *f* de la lumière; **source of l., l. source,** source lumineuse; **point of l.,** point lumineux; **spot of l., l. spot,** tache lumineuse; **l. beam,** faisceau lumineux; pinceau *m* de lumière; **l. flux,** flux lumineux; **l. ray,** rayon lumineux; **l. unit,** unité *f* d'intensité lumineuse; **l. wave,** onde lumineuse; *Phot:* **l. filter,** écran *m* orthochromatique; *Opt:* **l. aperture,** pinnule *f* (d'instrument d'optique); (*c*) *Astr:* **l. year,** année-lumière *f*, *pl.* années-lumière; **l. change,** variation *f* d'éclat (d'une étoile); (*d*) **good, bad, l.,** bon, mauvais, éclairage; **to give a good, bad, l.,** éclairer bien, mal; **to put, turn, on the l.,** donner de la lumière; allumer; **rent, including heat and l.,** loyer, y compris chauffage et éclairage; **oblique, slanting, l.,** lumière, éclairage, oblique; **picture hung in a good l.,** tableau accroché dans un bon jour; **against the l., with one's, its, back to the l., in one's own l.,** à contre-jour; **to stand in s.o.'s l.,** (i) cacher le jour, la lumière, à qn; (ii) mettre des bâtons dans les roues à qn; **to stand in one's own l.,** (i) tourner le dos à la lumière; (ii) être trop modeste, ne pas se faire valoir; **to see sth. in a new l.,** voir, considérer, qch. sous un jour nouveau, sous un nouvel aspect, d'un nouveau point de vue; **I don't look on it in that l.,** ce n'est pas ainsi que j'envisage, que je considère, la chose; **to present sth. in a favourable l.,** présenter qch. sous un jour favorable, sous de belles couleurs; **to see sth. in its true, proper, l.,** voir qch. sous son vrai jour; **the question should be considered in the l. of these facts,** on devrait considérer la question dans ce contexte; en considérant la question on devrait tenir compte de ces faits; (*e*) **to throw, shed, l. on (sth.),** jeter du jour sur (qch.); éclairer, éclaircir (qch.); **that throws (a) l. on many things,** cela résout beaucoup de problèmes; cela c'est toute une révélation; **the l. of reason,** les lumières de la raison; **to act according to one's lights,** agir dans la mesure de son intelligence; agir selon ses lumières; (*f*) *Rel:* **the inner l.,** la parole intérieure du Saint-Esprit. **2.** (*a*) lumière; bougie *f*; lampe *f*; **carrying a l.,** une lampe, une bougie, à la main; **you can see the lights of the motorway from here,** d'ici on voit les lumières de l'autoroute; **she put a l. in the window as a signal,** elle a mis une lumière, une lampe, à la fenêtre en guise de signal; *Adm:* **all night, half night, lights,** éclairage public intense, réduit; *Mil:* **lights out,** (sonnerie *f* de) l'extinction *f* des feux; *F:* **to go out like a l.,** s'évanouir; tomber dans les pommes; *F:* **one of the leading lights of the town,** une des personnalités de la ville; (*b*) (*for controlling traffic, etc.*) **traffic lights,** feux *m* de circulation, de signalisation routière; feux de croisement, de carrefour, *F:* feu rouge; (*at crossroads*) **winking l.,** feu clignotant; **red, amber, green, l.,** feu rouge, orange, vert; **turn right at the (traffic) lights,** tourner à droite au feu rouge; *Fig:* **to see the red l.,** se rendre compte du danger, sentir le danger; **to give s.o. the green l.,** donner le feu vert à qn; *Av:* **airfield, airport, lights,** feux d'aérodrome, d'aéroport; **boundary lights,** feux de balisage (d'aérodrome); **course light(s), runway light(s),** feu(x) de piste; **obstruction l.,** feu d'obstacle; **airway l.,** phare de jalonnement, de repérage *m*, au sol; phare de ligne; **approach l.,** feu d'approche; **landing light(s), contact light(s),** feu(x) d'atterrissage; *Nau:* **harbour lights,** feux (d'entrée) de port; **pierhead l.,** feu de musoir; **tidal l.,** feu de marée; **sectored l.,** feu à secteur; (*on lighthouse*) **fixed l.,** feu fixe; **blinker l.,** feu clignotant; **flashing l.,** feu à éclats; **intermittent l.,** feu isophase; **occulting l.,** feu à occultations, à éclipses; **revolving l.,** feu tournant; **beacon l.,** feu de balisage; **range l.,** *Av:* feu d'alignement; *Nau:* feu de direction (au milieu d'obstacles, le long d'un chenal, etc.); (*c*) (*on vehicle, etc.*) *Aut:* **rear lights,** feux rouges; **stop l.,** feu (rouge) d'arrêt; **parking lights,** feux de position, de stationnement; **reversing l.,** phare *m* de recul; *Aut: Rail:* **gauge lights,** feux d'encombrement; *Rail: etc:* **front l., tail l.,** lanterne *f*, fanal *m*, de tête, de queue (d'un train, d'un convoi de véhicules, d'une colonne de troupes à pied); **red l.,** lanterne rouge; **signal l.,** fanal; **warning l.,** fanal avertisseur; *Aut:* **dip your lights,** roulez en code; **charged with driving without lights,** inculpé d'avoir circulé avec absence totale d'éclairage; *Nau: Av:* (*on ship, aircraft*) **green l., red l., white l.,** feu vert, rouge, blanc; **navigation lights, position lights, running lights, signal lights,** feux de route, de navigation, de position; **side l.,** feu de côté, feu latéral; **port l.,** feu de bâbord; **starboard l.,** feu de tribord; **identification l., recognition l.,** feu d'identification; (*on ship*) **range l.,** feu additionnel, feu de pointe; **anchor lights, riding lights,** feux de mouillage, de position; **masthead l., steaming l.,** feu de tête de mât; **(after) range l.,** feu de mât arrière; **top l.,** feu de hune; **stern l.,** feu d'arrière, feu de poupe, ratière *f*; **not-under-command l.,** feu d'impossibilité de manœuvre; **towing l.,** feu de remorque; **working lights,** feux de pêche; **to steam without lights,** naviguer, faire route, tous feux éteints, à feux masqués; (*of ship*) **she was showing no lights,** il navigait, faisait route, tous feux éteints; ses feux n'étaient pas allumés; (*on aircraft*) **wing-tip l.,** feu de position, feu latéral; (*d*) *Tchn: etc:* **control l., warning l.,** voyant lumineux; **dial l.,** lampe de cadran (d'un appareil); *Aut: etc:* **dashboard l., panel l.,** lampe de tablier, du tableau de bord; (*in car*) **courtesy l.,** éclairage intérieur automatique; *Cin: T.V:* **cue l.,** éclairage de prise de vues; **hot l.,** éclairage principal; **operating l.,** (i) *Surg:* éclairage de salle, de table, d'opération; (ii) *Dent: etc:* éclairage de cabinet; (*of recording apparatus*) **l. spot,** spot lumineux; *Cin:* **l. valve,** valve *f* de lumière; **l.-valve recording,** enregistrement *m* (du son) par valve de lumière; **l. pen, l. gun,** crayon lumineux, électronique; stylet pointeur; (*e*) *Mil: etc:* **l. bomb, grenade, shell,** bombe, grenade, éclairante; obus éclairant; **l. tracer,** balle traceuse, obus traceur, projectile traceur; **l. flare,** fusée éclairante; (*f*) (*in Pr.n.*) phare; **the Portland L.,** le phare de Portland. **3.** (*a*) (*fire*) **to set l. to sth.,** mettre le feu à qch.; (*of smoker*) **could you give me a l., please?** pouvez-vous me donner du feu, s'il vous plaît? (*b*) feu, éclat *m* (du regard); **you should have seen the l. in his eye!** si vous aviez vu comme ses yeux brillaient! **4.** (*a*) fenêtre *f*; lucarne *f*; jour *m* (de fenêtre à meneaux); carreau *m* (de serre); vitre *f*; *Aut:* glace *f*; **rear l.,** lunette *f* arrière; **window of six lights,** fenêtre de six carreaux; **fixed l.,** verre dormant; vitrage dormant; **hidden l.,** vue dérobée; (*b*) *Jur:* **right of l.,** droit *m* de vues (et de jours); servitude *f* de jour; **ancient lights,** servitude de vue. **5.** *Art: Phot:* lumière, clair *m*; **l. effects,** effets *m* de lumière; luminosité *f*; **l. and shade,** les clairs et les ombres; le clair-obscur; *Mus: Lit:* nuances *f*; **l. and shade effects,** jeux *m* de lumière. **6. lights of an acrostic,** mots, vers, dont les lettres initiales et finales donnent la solution de l'acrostiche.

light[2], *v.tr. & i.* (*p.t. & p.p.* **lit,** *occ.* **lighted**) **1.** (*a*) allumer (une lampe, une cigarette, etc.); **to l. a fire,** allumer un feu; faire du feu; **the fire, the match, won't l.,** le feu, l'allumette, ne prend pas, ne s'allume pas; (*b*) éclairer, illuminer (une pièce, une rue); **the house was lit by oil lamps,** la maison était éclairée par des lampes à pétrole; **the bedroom is lit from the courtyard,** la chambre prend jour sur la cour; (*c*) **to l. the way for s.o.,** éclairer qn; **to l. s.o. downstairs,** éclairer qn qui descend l'escalier. **2. to l. up,** (i) allumer; mettre la lumière; (ii) *Mch: etc:* mettre les feux; (iii) *F:* allumer sa cigarette, sa pipe; **a smile lit up her face,** un sourire a éclairé, a illuminé, son visage; **her face was lit up (with joy, with a smile),** son visage rayonnait de joie, était illuminé d'un sourire; la joie, un sourire, éclairait, illuminait, son visage; **his eyes lit up,** ses yeux se sont animés; **his face was lit up with envy,** son regard témoignait la convoitise; *F:* **to be lit up,** (i) être légèrement ivre, allumé, pompette; (ii) être drogué, camé.

light[3], *a.* **1.** (*a*) **it is l., will soon be l.,** il fait, fera bientôt, jour; **the long, l. summer evenings,** les longues soirées claires de l'été; (*b*) (*of room, etc.*) clair; (bien) éclairé. **2.** (*a*) **painted in l. tones,** peint en tons clairs, lumineux; (*b*) (*of hair, complexion*) blond; (*of colour*) clair; **l. blue,** bleu clair *inv*, bleu lavé *inv*; **l. green,** vert gai *inv*; **l. brown,** clair-brun, *pl.* clair-bruns.

light[4], *a. & adv.*

I. *a.* **1.** (*a*) **l. burden,** fardeau léger; **l. as a feather,** aussi leger qu'une plume; **lighter than air,** de moindre densité que l'air; **l. soil,** terre *f* meuble; **l. pastry,** pâte légère; **l. blow, l. touch,** coup léger, touche légère; **l. stroke of the pen,** trait de plume léger; **l. chair,** chaise volante; (*b*) **with a l. step,** d'un pas léger; **l. of foot,** agile, leste; **to be l. on one's feet,** avoir le pas léger; danser légèrement; **l. movements,** mouvements souples, gracieux; (*c*) **l. wine,** vin léger; petit vin; **wine l. in alcohol,** vin léger en alcool; **l. beer,** bière légère; **l. wind,** vent léger; **l. breeze,** brise faible, molle, légère brise; *Nau:* **l. airs,** temps *m* presque calme; fraîcheurs *f*; petite brise; (*d*) (*deficient*) **l. weight,** poids *m* faible; **l. coin,** pièce faible, légère, de mauvais aloi. **2.** (*a*) *Mil:* **l. artillery,** artillerie légère, de petit calibre; **l. anti-aircraft,** artillerie anti-aérienne légère; **l. battery,** (i) (*field, AA. artillery*) groupe *m*, (ii) (*other branches*) batterie *f*, d'artillerie légère; **l. infantry,** infanterie légère; = les chasseurs (à pied); **l. infantryman,** = chasseur *m* (à pied); **l. cavalry,** cavalerie légère; **l. armour,** les (unités *f* de) blindés légers; **l. battle order,** tenue de campagne allégée; **l. duty,** service réduit; **l. weapons,** les armes légères; **l. automatic,** fusil *m* automatique; fusil-mitrailleur *m*, *pl.* fusils-mitrailleurs; **l.-automatic section,** demi-groupe *m* de fusiliers; **l. automatics,** les armes automatiques légères; **l. cannon, l. gun,** pièce légère, canon *m* de petit calibre;

Metall: **l. castings,** petites pièces (de fonderie); *Typ:* **l. face,** œil léger, caractère *m* maigre; (*b*) non chargé; *Nau:* **l. boat,** bateau *m* lège; **l. (water) line,** ligne *f* de flottaison lège; **l. sails,** voiles hautes, supplémentaires; (*of engine*) **to run l.,** (i) *Mch:* marcher à vide, à blanc; (ii) *Rail:* aller haut-le-pied; **l. running,** (i) *Mch:* marche *f* à vide, à blanc; (ii) *Rail:* marche haut-le-pied; *Rail:* **l. engine,** locomotive *f* haut-le-pied; (*c*) **l. crop,** faible récolte *f*; **to take a l. supper,** souper légèrement; (*d*) **l. sleep,** sommeil léger; **to be a l. sleeper,** avoir le sommeil léger. **3.** (*a*) **l. punishment,** peine légère; **l. taxation,** faible imposition *f*; (*b*) **l. task,** tâche *f* facile; **l. work,** petits travaux; travail peu fatigant. **4.** (*a*) **l. comedy,** comédie légère; **l. style,** style léger, badin; **l. reading,** lecture(s) amusante(s), récréative(s), délassante(s); livres *mpl* d'agrément; *Mus:* **l. piece,** divertissement *m*; (*b*) *O:* **l. woman,** femme légère, de vertu légère; **l. talk,** propos frivoles, légers; (*c*) **to make l. of sth.,** faire peu de cas de qch.; traiter qch. à la légère; traiter qch. de bagatelle; **to make l. of dangers,** mépriser les dangers; **to make l. of an accusation,** attacher peu d'importance à une accusation; se rire d'une accusation; **to make l. of doing sth.,** se faire un jeu de faire qch.

II. *adv.* légèrement; **to sleep l.,** (i) avoir le sommeil léger; (ii) dormir d'un sommeil léger; **to travel l.,** voyager avec peu de bagages; **sorrows sit l. on him,** la douleur ne l'accable pas, les soucis ne lui pèsent guère.

light[5], *v.* (*p.t. & p.p.* **lighted** *or* **lit**) **1.** *v.tr.* (*a*) *A:* alléger; (*b*) *Nau:* **to l. along the fall,** alléger le garant; **l. the sail out to windward!** portez la toile au vent! **2.** *v.i.* (*a*) (*of bird*) s'abattre, se poser; (*of thg*) s'abattre, tomber; (*b*) (*of pers.*) **to l. on one's feet,** tomber debout; retomber sur ses pieds; (*c*) **to l. on s.o., sth.,** rencontrer qn, qch.; trouver qn, qch., par hasard; **his eyes lighted on the picture,** ses yeux rencontrèrent le tableau; **to l. on an interesting fact,** tomber sur, rencontrer, un fait intéressant; (*d*) *NAm: F:* **to l. out,** décamper.

light-armed ['lait'ɑːmd], *a. Mil: etc:* légèrement armé; doté, muni, d'armes légères.

light-coloured ['laitkʌləd], *a.* clair.

light-duty ['lait'djuːti], *a.* **l.-d. machine,** machine *f* de faible puissance; machine auxiliaire; **l.-d. vehicle,** véhicule *m* de poids léger.

lighted ['laitid], *a.* **1.** allumé; **l. end of a cigarette,** bout allumé d'une cigarette. **2.** éclairé, illuminé; **l. road,** chemin éclairé, pourvu d'un éclairage public.

lighten[1] ['lait(ə)n]. **1.** *v.tr.* (*a*) éclairer (les ténèbres, le visage); désassombrir (une habitation, etc.); (*b*) éclaircir (une couleur, le ciel); dégrader (une couleur). **2.** *v.i.* (*a*) s'éclairer, s'illuminer; se désassombrir; **the sky lightened,** le ciel s'éclaira, s'éclaircit; **his eyes lightened (up),** son regard s'éclaira; (*b*) **it's lightening,** il fait des éclairs.

lighten[2]. **1.** *v.tr.* alléger; délester, alester (un navire); réduire le poids de (qch.); **to l. the taxes,** alléger les impôts; **to l. a task,** alléger une tâche; **to l. a sorrow,** alléger, soulager, une douleur; **to l. s.o.'s grief,** adoucir les peines de qn; **to l. a sentence,** mitiger, adoucir, une sentence, une peine; **to l. one's conscience,** décharger sa conscience. **2.** *v.i.* **my heart lightened,** mon cœur fut soulagé.

lightened ['laitənd], *a.* allégé; (*of girder, beam, etc.*) **l. web,** âme allégée (de poutre métallique, de barrot, etc.); *Nau:* **l. plate frame,** membrure *f* à évidement.

lightening ['laitniŋ], *s.* allégement *m* (d'un poids, d'un bateau, d'un impôt, d'une douleur); allégeage *m* (d'un bateau); *Tchn:* **l. hole,** évidement *m,* trou *m,* d'allégement; **this is a great l. of the burden of the State,** c'est une grande décharge pour l'Etat.

lighter[1] ['laitər], *s.* **1.** (*pers.*) allumeur, -euse. **2.** (*device*) allumeur, allumoir *m*; **(cigarette, cigar) l.,** briquet *m*; (*in car*) allume-cigarette(s) *m,* allume-cigare(s) *m*; **petrol l.,** briquet à essence; **l. fuel,** essence *f* pour briquet; **gas l.,** (i) briquet à gaz; (ii) allume-gaz *m* (pour cuisinière à gaz).

lighter[2], *s. Nau:* allège *f,* gabare *f*; bette *f,* chaland *m*; chatte *f*; *Navy:* **ammunition l.,** bugalet *m.*

lighter[3], *v.tr.* bateler (des marchandises); décharger (des marchandises) par allèges; transporter (des marchandises) par chalands.

lighterage ['laitəridʒ], *s. Nau:* **1.** déchargement *m* par allèges, par gabares; transport *m* par chalands; gabarage *m.* **2.** droits *mpl,* frais *mpl* de chaland(s), d'allège, de gabarage.

lighterman, *pl.* **-men** ['laitəmən], *s.m. Nau:* gabarier, batelier.

lighter-than-air ['laitəðə'nɛər], *a.* (*of aircraft*) plus léger que l'air.

lightfaced ['laitfeist], *a. Typ:* **l. type,** caractère léger, maigre.

light-fingered ['lait'fiŋgəd], *a.* **1.** à la main légère; aux doigts agiles; habile de ses dix doigts. **2. he's l.-f.,** c'est un voleur, *esp.* un voleur à la tire, un pickpocket; *A:* **the l.-f. gentry,** les pickpockets, les voleurs à la tire.

lightfooted ['lait'futid], *a.* agile, leste; au pied léger.

light-handed ['lait'hændid], *a.* **1.** à la main légère; habile de ses mains. **2.** aux mains peu encombrées.

lightheaded ['lait'hedid], *a.* **1. to be l.,** avoir le délire; être en délire; **to feel l.,** avoir, se sentir, le cerveau vide (par défaut de nourriture, etc.). **2.** à la tête légère; étourdi, écervelé.

lightheadedness ['lait'hedidnis], *s.* **1.** (*a*) délire *m*; (*b*) étourdissement *m*; transport *m* au cerveau. **2.** légèreté *f* (de caractère); manque *m* de sérieux; étourderie *f.*

lighthearted ['lait'hɑːtid], *a.* au cœur léger; gai, enjoué; allègre.

lightheartedly ['lait'hɑːtidli], *adv.* gaiement; le cœur léger; de gaieté de cœur.

lightheartedness ['lait'hɑːtidnis], *s.* gaieté *f,* gaîté *f* (de cœur), enjouement *m.*

lighthouse ['laithaus], *s.* **1.** *Nau:* phare *m*; (*on board*) tourelle *f* de fanaux; **revolving-light l., fixed-light l.,** phare à feu tournant, à feu fixe; **flashing-light l.,** phare à éclats; **l. keeper,** gardien *m* de phare; **l. tender,** baliseur *m.* **2.** *Elcs:* **l. tube,** tube-phare *m, pl.* tubes-phares; tube *m* à disques scellés; **l. transmitter-receiver,** émetteur-récepteur *m, pl.* émetteurs-récepteurs, à tubes-phares, à disques scellés.

lighting ['laitiŋ], *s.* **1.** allumage *m* (d'une lampe, etc.). **2.** éclairage *m*; illumination *f*; **fluorescent, incandescent, l.,** éclairage par fluorescence, par incandescence; **direct, indirect, l.,** éclairage direct, indirect; **emergency l.,** éclairage de secours; **street l.,** éclairage urbain, des rues; *Adm:* **l.-up time,** heure *f* d'éclairage; **l. engineer,** (ingénieur *m*) éclairagiste *m*; **l. engineering,** éclairagisme *m*; *Av:* **runway l.,** éclairage, rampe(s) *f* (*pl.*), de piste; **ground l.,** balisage (lumineux) (d'un aérodrome, d'un itinéraire); *Phot: etc:* **uniform, flat, l.,** éclairage d'ambiance; **studio l.,** jour *m,* éclairage, d'atelier; *Art: etc:* (*of parts of picture, etc.*) **half l.,** demi-jour *m*; *Th:* **stage l.,** éclairage scénique, de la scène; **l. effects,** jeux *m* de lumière. **3.** éclairage, exposition *f* (d'un tableau).

lightly ['laitli], *adv.* **1.** légèrement, à la légère; **to trace, rub, l.,** tracer, frotter, légèrement; **to stroke sth. l.,** effleurer qch.; **l. clad,** vêtu légèrement; **to walk, step, l.,** (i) marcher d'un pas léger; (ii) étouffer son pas; **to skip l. from rock to rock,** sauter agilement de rocher en rocher; **to pass l. over, touch l. on, a delicate matter,** glisser légèrement, couler, sur un point délicat; **his hand ran l. over the strings (of the harp),** sa main effleura les cordes (de la harpe); *Agr:* **to plough (land) l.,** effleurer la terre; **his responsibilities sit l. on him,** ses responsabilités ne lui pèsent pas, ne l'accablent pas; **to sleep l.,** dormir légèrement. **2. to get off l.,** s'en tirer à bon compte, à bon marché. **3. to speak l. of sth.,** parler de qch. à la légère; **to think l. of sth.,** faire peu de cas de qch.; attacher peu d'importance à qch.; **to commit oneself l.,** s'engager à la légère.

light-minded ['lait'maindid], *a.* léger, volage, étourdi, frivole.

light-negative ['lait'negətiv], *a. Ph:* photorésistant.

lightness ['laitnis], *s.* **1.** légèreté *f*; **l. of foot,** agilité *f*; **l. of heart,** gaieté *f* de cœur; **l. of touch,** légèreté de main (d'un médecin, etc.); légèreté de plume, de pinceau, de style. **2. l. of a task,** (i) facilité *f* d'une tâche; (ii) caractère peu fatigant d'une tâche.

lightning ['laitniŋ], *s.* éclairs *mpl,* foudre *f*; **a flash of l.,** un éclair; **chain(ed) l.,** éclairs sinueux; **forked l.,** éclairs arborescents, ramifiés; éclairs en zigzag; **summer l., heat l.,** éclairs de chaleur; **ribbon l., streak l.,** éclairs fulminants, en sillons; **beaded l.,** éclairs en chapelet; **ball l.,** globe *m* de feu; **sheet l.,** éclairs diffus, éclairs en nappe(s); **the l. struck the church,** la foudre est tombée sur l'église; **struck by l.,** frappé de, par, la foudre; **l. discharge, l. stroke,** coup *m* de foudre, de tonnerre; **l. arrester, l. conductor, l. discharger, l. protector,** parafoudre *m,* paratonnerre *m*; **horn-type l. arrester,** parafoudre à cornes; **plate l. discharger,** paratonnerre à lames; **vacuum l. arrester,** parafoudre à air raréfié; **l. rod,** (tige *f* de) paratonnerre; *El:* **l. switch,** commutateur *m* antenne-terre, interrupteur *m* de mise à la terre; **l. surge,** surtension due à la foudre; **as quick as l., with l. speed,** *F:* **like greased l., like (a streak of) l.,** aussi vite que l'éclair, (rapide) comme l'éclair; à toute vitesse, en un clin d'œil; **l. progress,** progrès foudroyants; **l. blow,** coup raide comme (une) balle; **l. war,** guerre *f* éclair; **l. attack,** attaque *f* éclair; **l. visit,** visite *f* éclair; *Ind:* **l. strike,** grève surprise; **l. change,** changement *m* rapide de toilette; *Th:* travestissement *m* rapide; *Med:* **l. pains,** douleurs fulgurantes.

light-o'-love ['laitəlʌv], *s. A: & Lit:* femme légère; **he is with his l.-o'-l.,** il est avec sa mie.

light-positive ['lait'pɔzitiv], *a. Ph:* photoconducteur, -trice.

lightproof ['laitpruːf], *a.* opaque.

light-resistant ['laitri'zistənt], *a.* photorésistant.

lights [laits], *s.pl. Cu:* mou *m* (de bœuf, etc.).

light-sensitive ['lait'sensitiv], *a. Ph:* photosensible.

light-sensitization ['laitsensitai'zeiʃ(ə)n], *s.* photosensibilité.

lightship ['laitʃip], *s. Nau:* bateau-feu *m, pl.* bateaux-feux; bateau-phare *m, pl.* bateaux-phares; phare flottant.

lightsome ['laitsəm], *a. A: & Lit:* **1.** léger, gracieux. **2.** au cœur léger, gai. **3.** agile, preste.

light-tight ['laittait], *a.* étanche, inaccessible, à la lumière; *Phot:* **l.-t. shutter of a dark slide,** rideau *m* hermétique d'un châssis.

lightweight ['laitweit]. **1.** *s.* (*a*) *Box:* poids léger; (*b*) *F:* personne insignifiante. **2.** *attrib:* (*of garment, etc.*) léger.

lightwood ['laitwud], *s.* **1.** *Bot:* (*a*) mélanoxylon *m*; (*b*) amyris *f.* **2.** *Com:* bois léger. **3.** *U.S: F:* bois qui brûle facilement; bois résineux.

ligia ['lidʒiə], *s. Crust:* ligie *f,* lygie *f.*

lignaloes [lain'ælouz], *s.* **1.** *Pharm:* aloès *m.* **2.** *Bot:* bois *m* d'aloès, bois d'aigle.

ligneous ['ligniəs], *a.* ligneux.

lignicolous [lig'nikələs], *a.* lignicole.

ligniferous [lig'nifərəs], *a.* lignifère.

lignification [lignifi'keiʃ(ə)n], *s.* lignification *f.*

ligniform ['lignifɔːm], *a.* ligniforme.

lignify ['lignifai]. **1.** *v.tr.* lignifier. **2.** *v.i.* se lignifier; (*of young shoot*) aoûter.

lignin ['lignin], *s. Bot: Ch:* lignine *f.*

lignite ['lignait], *s. Miner:* lignite *m.*

lignitic [lig'nitik], *a.* ligniteux.

lignitiferous [ligni'tifərəs], *a. Geol:* lignitifère.

lignivorous [lig'nivərəs], *a. Nat.Hist:* lignivore.

lignoceric [lignou'serik], *a. Ch:* (acide *m*) lignocérique.

lignum vitae ['lignəm'vaitiː], *s. Bot:* (bois *m* de) gaïac *m*; bois saint.

ligroin(e) ['ligroin], *s. Ch:* ligroïne *f.*

ligula ['ligjulə], *s.* **1.** *Bot:* ligule *f* (de graminée); languette *f* (de fleur) **2.** (*a*) *Ann:* ligule; (*b*) *Ent:* ligule (du labium).

ligularia [ligju'lɛəriə], *s. Bot:* ligulaire *f,* ligularia *m.*

ligulate ['ligjulət], *a. Bot:* ligulé; **l. floret,** demi-fleuron *m, pl.* demi-fleurons.

ligule ['ligjul], *s. Bot:* = LIGULA **1.**

Liguliflorae [ligjuli'flɔːriː], *s.pl. Bot:* liguliflores *f,* chicoracées *f.*

liguliflorous [ligjuli'flɔːrəs], *a. Bot:* liguliflore, demi-flosculeux.

Ligures [li'gjuːriːz], *s.pl. Hist:* Ligures *m.*

Liguria [li'gjuːriə], *Pr.n. Geog:* Ligurie *f.*

Ligurian [li'gjuːriən], *a. & s. Geog:* (*a*) *a.* ligurien; (*b*) *s.* Ligurien, -ienne.

ligurite ['ligjurait], *s. Miner:* ligurite *f.*

ligusticum [li'gʌstikəm], *s. Bot:* ligustique *m.*

ligustrum [li'gʌstrəm], *s. Bot:* ligustrum *m.*

liguus ['ligjuːəs], *s. Moll:* liguus *m.*

likable, likableness ['laikəbl, -nis] = LIKEABLE, LIKEABLENESS.

like[1] [laik], *a., prep., adv., & s.*

I. *a.* **1.** semblable, pareil, tel; (*a*) **two l. cases,** deux cas *m* semblables, pareils, analogues; **walking sticks and l. objects,** cannes et objets similaires; **on this and the l. subjects,** sur ce sujet et les sujets similaires; **l. causes produce l. effects,** les mêmes causes produisent les mêmes effets; **two plants of l. species,** deux plantes de même espèce; **to treat s.o. in l. manner,** traiter qn de même, pareillement; **l. father, l. son,** tel maître tel valet; tel père tel fils; *Mth:* **l. terms,** termes *m* semblables; **l. quantities,** quantités *f* semblables; *El:* **l. poles,** pôles *m* semblables, de même nom; (*b*) ressemblant; **the portrait is very l., not l.,** le portrait est très, peu, ressemblant; **they are as l. as two peas,** ils se ressemblent comme deux gouttes d'eau, à s'y méprendre. **2.** (*a*) **I want to find one l. it,** je veux trouver le pareil, la pareille; **I have one (exactly) l. it,** j'en ai un (tout) pareil; **a critic l. you,** un critique comme vous, tel que vous; **people l. you,** des gens de votre sorte; **liker to God than to man,** qui ressemble plus à Dieu qu'à l'homme; qui ressemble à Dieu plus qu'à l'homme; **to be l. s.o., sth.,** être semblable à qn, à qch., être pareil à qch.; ressembler à qn, à qch.; **to be l. one's father,** ressembler à son père; tenir de son père; **she is l. nobody else,** elle est à part; **what is that tree l.?** à quoi ressemble cet arbre? **what's the weather l.?** qu'est-ce que dit le temps? **whom is he l.?** *F:* **who is he l.?** à qui ressemble-t-il? **what is he l.?** comment est-il? **you know what he is l.,** vous savez comme il est; **he was l. a father**

to me, il m'a servi de père; il fut pour moi un père; **she wore a dress rather l. this one,** elle portait une robe dans le genre de celle-ci; **rather l., very much l., a Picasso,** un peu, tout à fait, dans le genre de Picasso; **when I hear things l. that,** quand j'entends des choses semblables; **old people are l. that,** les vieilles gens sont ainsi faits; **I know plenty of people l. that,** je connais pas mal de gens comme ça; **there are thousands of us l. that,** nous sommes ainsi des milliers; **I never saw anything l. it,** (i) je n'ai jamais rien vu de pareil, de semblable; (ii) je n'ai rien vu d'approchant; **he was magnificent; I have never seen him anything l. it,** il a été magnifique; jamais je ne l'ai vu s'acquitter si brillamment; **something very much l. it,** quelque chose qui y ressemble beaucoup, qui en approche beaucoup; quelque chose de très approchant; **he had been given something very l. judicial powers,** on lui avait donné quelque chose d'approchant à des pouvoirs judiciaires; **it costs something l. £10,** cela coûte quelque dix livres; **the total amounts to something l. £100,** la somme s'élève à environ cent livres, à quelque cent livres; **I had now been in France something l. five years,** cela faisait maintenant dans les cinq ans que j'étais en France; **it's just l. (at) home,** c'est tout comme chez nous; **that's something l. a day!** voilà une belle journée! **that's something l. rain!** voilà qui s'appelle pleuvoir! *F:* **that's something l.!** à la bonne heure! voilà qui a bon air! voilà qui est réussi! *F:* **let's get this place looking something l.!** mettons-y un peu d'ordre! **France? there's no country l. it,** la France? il n'y a pas de pays qui en approche; **it's l. sailing in a boat,** c'est comme si on était en bateau; **there's nothing l. it,** il n'y a rien de semblable, de pareil; il n'y a que cela; **there's nothing l. health,** rien de tel que la santé; **there's nothing l. speaking frankly, l. being frank,** (il n'y a) rien de tel que de parler franchement; **there's nothing l. walking,** il n'y a rien de plus agréable que la marche; **she is nothing l. so, as, pretty as you,** elle est bien loin d'être aussi jolie que vous; **he's nothing l. good enough to play your accompaniments,** il s'en faut de beaucoup qu'il soit à même de jouer vos accompagnements; (*b*) **that's just l. a woman!** voilà bien les femmes! **it's just l. him to say so,** c'est bien de lui de dire cela; **that's l. his cheek!** voilà bien son toupet! **that's just l. him!** c'est bien de lui! c'est bien digne de lui! voilà comme il est! le voilà bien! je le reconnais bien là; **just l. you!** tout comme vous! **3.** *A:* **he is l. to succeed,** il est probable qu'il réussira; il a des chances de réussir; **he is l. to die,** il est en cas de mourir; **it is l. we shall see him no more,** il est probable que nous ne le reverrons plus.

II. *prep.* comme; **I think l. you,** je pense comme vous, de même que vous; je suis du même avis que vous; **you don't hold your pencil l. me,** vous ne tenez pas votre crayon de la même façon que moi; **just l. anybody else,** tout comme un autre; **to act l. a soldier,** (i) agir comme (le ferait) un soldat; (ii) agir en soldat (maintenir sa dignité de soldat); *F:* **he ran l. anything, l. blazes, l. hell, l. the (very) devil, l. mad,** il courait comme un dératé; **don't talk l. that,** ne parlez pas comme ça; **to fit s.o. l. a glove,** aller à qn comme un gant; **to pace up and down l. a caged animal,** aller et venir comme une bête en cage; **he stood there l. a statue,** il se tenait debout comme une statue; **they live l. cavemen,** ils vivent à la façon des troglodytes; **to hate s.o. l. poison,** haïr qn comme la peste; **he cherished me l. a son,** il me chérissait à l'égal d'un fils; *P:* **that's something l.!** ça, c'est quelque chose de bien!

III. *adv.* **1.** (*a*) *A:* **l. as . . .,** comme . . ., ainsi que . . ., de même que . . .; (*b*) *F:* **l. enough, very l.; (as) l. as not,** probablement, vraisemblablement; (*c*) *P:* comme qui dirait; **he looked angry l.,** il était comme en colère; il avait l'air furieux. **2.** (*a*) (= AS) *F:* comme; **do l. I do,** faites comme moi; **I can't knit l. mother does,** je ne sais pas tricoter comme (le fait) maman; **l. I said,** comme je l'ai (si bien) dit; (*b*) (= AS IF) *F:* **he treated me l. I was dirt,** il m'a traité(e) comme si j'étais de la crotte.

IV. *s.* **1.** semblable *mf,* pareil, -eille; **a cloth the l. of which is not seen nowadays,** un drap comme on n'en voit plus; **we shall never look upon his l. again,** nous ne reverrons plus son semblable, son pareil; **he and his l.,** *P:* **he and the likes of him,** lui et ses semblables; *P:* **it's too good for the likes of me,** c'est trop bon pour des personnes comme moi; **music, painting, and the l.,** la musique, la peinture, et autres choses du même genre; *Prov:* **l. will to l.,** qui se ressemble s'assemble; *F:* **I've never seen the l. of it,** je n'ai jamais vu chose pareille; c'est le monde renversé! **to do the l.,** en faire autant, faire de même; **to give s.o. back the l.,** rendre la pareille, la réciproque, à qn; **to give, return, l. for l.,** rendre la pareille. **2.** *Golf:* **the l.,** autant; **to play the l.,** jouer le coup d'autant.

like[2], *s.* (*usu. pl.*) goût *m,* préférence *f,* inclination *f;* **likes and dislikes,** sympathies *f* et antipathies *f;* goûts *m;* **everyone has his likes and dislikes,** des goûts et des couleurs il ne faut pas discuter.

like[3], *v.tr.* **1.** aimer (qch.); aimer, avoir de la sympathie pour (qn); **I l. him,** je l'aime bien; il me plaît; **my father liked his horses and dogs equally,** mon père aimait également ses chevaux et ses chiens; **I came to l. him,** il m'est devenu sympathique; **I don't l. his looks,** son visage ne me revient pas; **how do you l. him?** comment le trouvez-vous? **she seems to l. you,** elle semble avoir un faible pour vous; **they l. each other,** ils se conviennent; **I l. the offer,** l'offre *f* me plaît, m'agrée, me convient; **he likes school,** il se plaît à l'école; **I should l. time to consider it,** j'aimerais avoir le temps d'y réfléchir; **would you l. the armchair?** voulez-vous le fauteuil? **have a glass of beer; or would you l. tea?** prenez un verre de bière; ou préféreriez-vous, voulez-vous, du thé? **I should l. some tea,** je prendrais bien une tasse de thé; **I should l. nothing better,** je ne demande pas mieux; **as much as ever you l.,** tant que vous voudrez; **do you l. tea?** aimez-vous le thé? **how do you l. your tea?** (i) comment prenez-vous votre thé? (ii) comment trouvez-vous votre thé? **your father won't l. it,** votre père ne sera pas content; **I don't l. it at all,** cela ne me plaît guère; je ne trouve pas cela bon, bien, du tout; **if he doesn't l. it he can go elsewhere,** si ça ne lui va pas qu'il aille ailleurs; **I should l. it more than anything else,** cela me ferait le plus grand plaisir; **whether he likes it or not,** qu'il le veuille ou non; bon gré, mal gré; **plant that likes a sandy soil,** plante *f* qui aime, se plaît dans, les lieux sablonneux; **these plants don't l. the damp,** ces plantes craignent l'humidité; *F:* **I l. your cheek!** j'admire votre toupet! **(well) I l. that!** en voilà une bonne! par exemple! elle est bien bonne, celle-là! **I l. oysters but they don't l. me,** j'aime les huîtres mais je ne les supporte pas, cela ne me réussit pas. **2.** (*a*) **I l. to see them now and again,** j'aime (à) les voir de temps à autre; **I l. to be obeyed,** j'aime qu'on m'obéisse; **some people l. travelling by bus, others prefer the train,** il plaît aux uns de prendre l'autobus, aux autres de prendre le train; **I hardly l. to interfere,** j'ai quelque scrupule à intervenir; **he doesn't l. people to talk about it,** il n'aime pas qu'on en parle; **I do not l. them to smoke,** je n'aime pas les voir fumer; **I l. her to be near me,** j'aime qu'elle soit près de moi; **they don't l. your going out so often,** on trouve à redire à ce que vous sortiez si souvent; **he doesn't l. our going into town,** il n'aime pas que nous allions en ville; **would you l. a cigarette?** voulez-vous, désirez-vous, une cigarette? **I should l. to go,** je voudrais bien y aller; **I should very much l. to go,** j'aimerais beaucoup y aller; je ne demande pas mieux que d'y aller; **would you l. to come with us?** vous plairait-il de nous accompagner? **would you l. me to go with you?** voulez-vous que je vous accompagne? **I should l. to be able to help you,** j'aimerais bien pouvoir vous aider; **I shouldn't l. to be in your shoes,** je ne me voudrais pas à votre place; **I should l. to know whether . . .,** je voudrais bien savoir, je me demande, si . . .; **I should l. to have been there,** j'aurais bien voulu, j'aurais aimé, m'y trouver, y être; **I should so much have liked to see him!** j'aurais tant aimé, tant voulu, le voir! (*b*) **as you l.,** comme vous voudrez; **I can do as I l. with him,** je fais de lui ce que je veux; **he is free to act as he likes,** il est libre d'agir à sa guise, comme il lui plaira; **just as you l.,** (c'est, ce sera) comme vous voudrez; comme il vous plaira; **to do just as one likes,** en faire à sa tête, à son idée; **if you l.,** si vous voulez; si cela peut vous être agréable; **she is pretty, if you l., but not a beauty,** elle est jolie, je ne dis pas, mais ce n'est pas une beauté; **when I l.,** quand je veux; **when you l.,** quand il vous plaira; **I can go there when(ever) I l.,** je peux y aller quand j'en ai envie, quand il me plaît; **he thinks he can do anything he likes,** il se croit tout permis; **people may say what they l.,** on a beau dire (mais . . .); **do what you l. with it,** faites-en ce que vous voudrez; **take as many as you l.,** prenez-en autant que vous le voudrez; **as much as you l.,** tant que vous voudrez. **3.** *impers. A:* **it likes me (well) to do sth.,** cela me plaît, me convient, de faire qch.

likeable ['laikəbl], *a.* (*of pers.*) agréable, aimable, sympathique.

likeableness ['laikəblnis], *s.* agrément *m;* charme *m* (de qn).

likelihood, likeliness ['laiklihud, -nis], *s.* vraisemblance *f,* probabilité *f,* apparence *f;* **there is little l. of his succeeding,** il y a peu de chances, il n'est guère probable, qu'il réussisse; **there is every likelihood that you will be charged,** il y a toutes les chances pour que vous soyez accusé; vous avez toutes les chances d'être accusé; **in all likelihood,** selon toute probabilité; selon toute apparence; selon toute prévision; selon toute vraisemblance; vraisemblablement.

likely ['laikli], *a. & adv.*

I. *a.* **1.** vraisemblable, probable; **l. source of infection,** source *f* probable d'infection; **a l. story,** une histoire vraisemblable; *F:* **that's a l. story!** la belle histoire! en voilà une bonne! **it's more than l.,** c'est plus que probable; **it's l. to rain,** il y a des chances pour qu'il pleuve; le temps est à la pluie; **it's not l. (that) I shall see him again,** je ne le reverrai vraisemblablement plus; il est peu probable que je le revoie; **it's not l. he'll come,** il n'est pas probable, il est peu probable, qu'il vienne; **is he l. to come?** est-il probable qu'il vienne? **he is not l. to act in this way,** ce n'est pas un homme à agir de la sorte, comme cela; **he is hardly l. to succeed,** il a peu de chances de réussir; **he is quite l. to do it,** il est probable qu'il le fasse; il est dans le cas de le faire. **2. books l. to interest young people,** ouvrages *m* susceptibles d'intéresser la jeunesse, les jeunes; **motives l. to influence judgement,** motifs *m* de nature à influer sur le jugement; **prospectus l. to interest customers,** prospectus *m* susceptible d'intéresser la clientèle; **this plan is most l. to succeed,** ce projet offre le plus de chances de succès; **they made a proposal which was l. to appeal to him,** on lui fit une proposition qui devait lui plaire; **a l. place for mushrooms,** un endroit où l'on trouvera sûrement des champignons; **the likeliest place to find him in,** l'endroit où on a le plus de chances de le trouver; **the most l. candidates,** les candidats *m* qui ont le plus de chances; les candidats de premier plan; **I asked every l. person for information,** j'ai demandé des renseignements à toute personne (que je croyais) susceptible de me les donner. **3. a l. lad,** (i) un joyeux gaillard; (ii) un gars qui promet; *esp. NAm:* **a l. child,** (i) un bel enfant; (ii) un enfant qui promet.

II. *adv.* **most l., very l.,** *esp. NAm:* **l.,** vraisemblablement; très probablement; *NAm:* **this species will l. establish itself in America,** cette espèce va probablement s'établir en Amérique; **as l. as not,** vraisemblablement; (pour) autant que je sache; **he will succeed as l. as not,** il se pourrait bien qu'il réussisse; *F:* **not l.!** plus souvent! pas de danger! jamais de la vie! *Scot:* **you'll l. be staying here?** (i) vous allez sans doute rester ici? (ii) vous êtes en séjour ici peut-être?

like-minded ['laik'maindid], *a.* dans les mêmes dispositions, du même avis; qui ont les mêmes goûts.

likemindedness ['laik'maindidnis], *s.* communauté *f* de vues.

liken ['laik(ə)n], *v.tr.* **1.** *Lit:* comparer, assimiler (**to, unto, with,** à, avec); **to what can I l. thee?** à quoi puis-je te comparer? *B:* **the kingdom of Heaven is likened unto a man who . . .,** le royaume des cieux ressemble à, est semblable à, un homme qui . . .. **2.** assimiler, faire ressembler (**sth. to sth.,** qch. à qch.); rendre semblable (**to,** à).

likeness ['laiknis], *s.* **1.** ressemblance *f* (**between,** entre; **to,** à); similitude *f* (de deux personnes, de deux objets); **a close l.,** une ressemblance étroite; **family l.,** air *m* de famille; **in the l. of s.o.,** à l'image de qn. **2.** apparence *f.* **3.** portrait *m,* image *f;* **the picture is a good, a poor, l.,** le portrait est très, peu, ressemblant.

likewise ['laikwaiz], *adv.* **1.** (*moreover*) de plus, également, de même, aussi. **2.** (*similarly*) *only in the phr.* **to do l.,** faire de même, en faire autant.

liking ['laikiŋ], *s.* goût *m,* penchant *m;* **to one's l.,** à souhait; **is it to your l.?** cela est-il à votre goût, à votre gré *m?* est-ce que cela vous plaît? **a l. for business,** le goût des affaires; **his l. for study,** son goût pour l'étude; **his l. for me,** son penchant pour moi; **natural l. for a food,** goût, attirance *f,* pour un aliment; **to have a l. for sth.,** avoir du goût, de l'attachement, pour qch.; aimer qch.; **career for which I have no l.,** carrière *f* qui n'a pas d'attrait pour moi; **to have a l. for s.o.,** trouver qn sympathique; se sentir de l'attrait pour qn; affectionner qn; **to take a l. for, to, sth.,** prendre goût à qch.; **to take a l. for, to, s.o.,** concevoir de l'amitié pour qn; prendre qn en affection, en amitié; se prendre de sympathie pour qn; **I have taken a l. to him,** il m'est devenu sympathique.

lilac ['lailək]. **1.** *s. Bot:* (*a*) lilas *m;* **Persian l.,** lilas de Perse; (*b*) **California l.,** céanothe *m,* céanothus *m;* **Indian l.,** (i) lilas des Indes, mélia *m;* (ii) langerstrœmia *m.* **2.** *a.* **l.(-coloured),** lilas *inv.*

Liliaceae [lili'eisii:], *s.pl. Bot:* liliacées *f.*

liliaceous [lili'eiʃəs], *a. Bot:* liliacé.

Liliales [lili'eili:z], *s.pl. Bot:* liliales *f.*

lilied ['lilid], *a.* **1.** *Poet:* (teint) lilial, -aux, de lis. **2.** (gazon, étang) couvert de lis. **3.** *Her:* (étendard, écu) fleurdelisé.

Lilioideae [lili'ɔidii:], *s.pl. Bot:* lilioïdées *f.*

lillianite ['liliənait], *s. Miner:* lillianite *f.*

Lilliputian [lili'pju:ʃ(ə)n], *Lit:* (*a*) *a.* lilliputien; (*b*) *s.* Lilliputien, -ienne.
lilt[1] [lilt], *s.* **1.** *A: & Scot:* chant (joyeux); air (bien cadencé). **2.** rythme *m*, cadence *f* (des vers); **the lines go with a l.,** les vers *m* ont du rythme, sont bien cadencés.
lilt[2], *v.tr. & i.* chanter mélodieusement, chanter gaiement.
lilting ['liltiŋ], *a.* **l. metre,** rythme musical; **l. air,** air cadencé, scandé; **l. stride,** pas cadencé.
lily ['lili], *s.* **1.** (*a*) *Bot:* lis *m*; **white l., madonna l., Ascension l.,** lis blanc; **belladonna l.,** amaryllis *f* belle-dame; lis de Saint-Jacques; **Mexican l.,** lis du Mexique; **Egyptian l., Ethiopian l., calla l., trumpet, l.,** richardie *f* d'Afrique; **Guernsey l.,** nérine *f*; lis du Japon; **branched l.,** asphodèle *m* rameau; **atamasco l., fairy l.,** zéphyrantes *m*; **butterfly l., ginger l.,** hedychium *m*; **day l.,** hémérocalle *f*, hémérocallis *m*; **Nile l.,** nélombo *m*, nélumbo *m*; **St. Bruno's l.,** anthericum *m*; **tiger l.,** lis tigré; (*b*) *U.S:* **l. pad,** feuille *f* de nénuphar; (*c*) *Hist:* **the lilies,** les fleurs *f* de lis (des Bourbons, de la royauté française). **2.** *Bot:* **l. of the valley,** muguet *m*; lis des vallées, de mai; convallaire *f*. **3.** *Pr.n.f.* **Lily,** Lily, Lili. **4.** *Fish:* **l. iron,** harpon *m* à tête mobile (pour la pêche de l'espadon). **5.** *U.S:* *P:* tapette *f*.
lily-like ['lililaik], *a.* blanc, *f.* blanche, comme le lis.
lily-livered ['lililivəd], *a. A:* peureux, poltron, lâche.
lily-trotter ['lilitrɔtər], *s. Orn:* jacana *m*, *F:* oiseau-chirurgien *m*, *pl.* oiseaux-chirurgiens.
lilywhite ['lili(h)wait], *a.* **1.** (*a*) blanc, *f.* blanche, comme le lis; d'une blancheur de lis; lilial, -aux; (*b*) *F:* **she's not so l.!** ce n'est pas un prix de vertu! **2.** *U.S:* *A:* opposé à la participation des nègres aux affaires politiques.
Lima[1] ['li:mə]. *Pr.n. Geog:* Lima; **L. bean,** haricot *m* de Lima; *Pharm:* **L. bark,** quinquina gris Huanaco.
lima[2] ['laimə, 'li:mə], *s. Moll:* lime *f*.
limaceous [lai'meiʃəs], **limacine** ['laiməs(a)in], *a. Moll:* limacien.
liman [li:'mæn], *s. Geog:* liman *m*, lagune *f* (à l'entrée d'un estuaire).
limanda [li'mændə], *s. Ich:* limande *f*.
limb[1] [lim], *s.* **1.** (*a*) membre *m*; **the lower limbs,** les membres inférieurs; **large of l.,** membru; aux gros os; **to tear an animal l. from l.,** mettre un animal en pièces; (*b*) *O:* (*as a genteelism*) jambe *f*. **2.** (*a*) **l. of the devil, of Satan,** tison *m* d'enfer, suppôt *m* de Satan; (*b*) *O: & NAm: F:* enfant *m* terrible; petit démon; polisson *m*. **3.** (*a*) (grosse) branche (d'un arbre); bras *m* (d'une croix); branche (d'un siphon, d'un électro-aimant, etc.); rameau *m*, contrefort *m* (d'une chaîne de montagnes); membre (d'une phrase); (*b*) *F:* **to be out on a l.,** être en plan; être sur la corde raide.
limb[2], *v.tr.* **1.** *F:* démembrer (un corps); *O:* **I'll l. him,** je lui mangerai, arracherai, le cœur. **2.** ébrancher (un arbre).
limb[3], *s. Astr: Bot: Mth:* limbe *m*.
limbate ['limbeit], *a. Bot:* limbifère.
limber[1] ['limbər], *s.* **1.** *Artil:* avant-train *m*, *pl.* avant-trains (d'affût de canon); **wagon l.,** avant-train de caisson; **l. box, l. chest,** coffre *m* d'avant-train. **2.** *Veh:* **limber (pole),** timon *m*; *O:* **l. horse,** (cheval *m*) limonier *m*.
limber[2], *v.tr. & i. Artil:* **to l. a gun,** attacher une pièce de canon à l'avant-train; **to l. up,** amener, accrocher, mettre, l'avant-train; *Mil:* **limbered wagon,** voiturette *f* (de mitrailleuse, de mortier, etc.).
limber[3], *s. Nau:* **limber (hole),** anguiller *m*; **l. boards, l. plates,** parclose *f*; **l. chain,** chaîne *f* d'anguiller; **l. passage,** canal *m* des anguillers.
limber[4], *a.* (*a*) souple, flexible; (*b*) (*of pers.*) souple, agile.
limber[5]. **1.** *v.tr.* assouplir; *Aut:* **to l. up the engine,** dégommer le moteur. **2.** *v.i. Sp: etc:* **to l. up,** se chauffer les muscles; **limbering up exercises,** exercices *m* d'assouplissement.
limbic ['limbik], *a. Anat:* (lobe *m*) limbique (du cerveau).
limbless ['limlis], *a.* (personne) (i) sans membres, (ii) à qui il manque un ou plusieurs membres; **l. ex-servicemen,** mutilés *m* de guerre (qui ont perdu un ou plusieurs membres).
limbo ['limbou], *s.* **1.** *Theol:* les limbes *m*; *F:* **to descend into l.,** tomber dans l'oubli; **to pass into the l. of things outworn,** aller où vont les vieilles lunes. **2.** *F: A:* prison *f*; **in l.,** en prison; à l'ombre.
Limburger ['limbə:gər], *s.* fromage *m* de Limbourg.
limburgite ['limbə:gait], *s. Geol:* limburgite *f*.
limbus ['limbəs], *s. Bot:* limbe *m* (de feuille).
lime[1] [laim], *s.* **1.** *A:* (= BIRDLIME) glu *f*; **l. twig,** gluau *m*, pipeau *m*. **2.** chaux *f*; **caustic l.,** chaux vive; **fat l.,** chaux grasse; **quiet l.,** chaux maigre; **slaked, slack(ed), l.,** chaux éteinte; **air-slaked l.,** chaux éteinte à sec; chaux fusée; **hydraulic l.,** chaux hydraulique; **l. sulphur,** bouillie soufrée, bouillie sulfocalcique; **l. pit,** carrière *f* de pierre à chaux; **l. burning,** chaufournerie *f*; cuisson *f* de la chaux; *Agr:* **l. spreader,** chauleuse *f*, distributeur *m* de chaux. **3.** *Tan:* **l. (pit),** plain *m*, pelain *m*.
lime[2], *v.tr.* **1.** gluer (des ramilles); enduire (des ramilles) de glu; **to l. birds,** prendre des oiseaux à la glu, au gluau. **2.** *Agr:* chauler (un terrain). **3.** *Tan:* plainer, plamer, pelainer (les peaux).
lime[3], *s. Bot:* **1.** lime *f*; **sweet l.,** limette *f*, lime douce, citron doux; **acid l.,** lime acide; **l. juice,** jus *m* de lime douce, de citron doux. **2. l.(-tree),** limettier *m*.
lime[4], *s. Bot:* **l. (tree),** tilleul *m*; **European l., broad-leaved l.,** tilleul à grandes feuilles; tilleul de Hollande; **American l.,** tilleul d'Amérique; **white l.,** tilleul argenté.
limeburner ['laimbə:nər], *s.* chaufournier *m*, chaulier *m*.
limecast ['laimkɑ:st], *s. Const:* crépi *m*.
lime-juicer ['laimdʒu:sər], *s. U.S: P: A:* (*a*) navire anglais; (*b*) matelot anglais; (*c*) Anglais *m*.
limekiln ['laimkiln], *s.* four *m* à chaux, chaufour *m*; *F:* **to have a throat like a l.,** avoir une soif de tous les diables.
limelight[1] ['laimlait], *s.* (*a*) lumière *f* oxhydrique; (*b*) **in the l.,** sous les feux de la rampe; très en vue; en vedette.
limelight[2], *v.tr.* (*p.t. & p.p.* **limelighted** *or* **limelit**). *Th:* diriger les projecteurs sur (la vedette).
limen ['laimen], *s. Psy: Physiol:* seuil *m* (de la conscience, etc.).
limenitis [laimə'naitis], *s. Ent:* sylvain *m*; liménitide *m*.
limerick ['limərik], *s.* poème *m* en cinq vers, toujours comique et absurde, aux rimes a a b b a; exemple en français: il y avait un gars de Madère, qui venait de tuer son père; on demanda pourquoi, il répondit: ma foi, vous n'avez pas connu mon père! (l'origine s'en rattache vaguement à la ville de Limerick, en Irlande).
limestone ['laimstoun], *s.* (*a*) *Geol:* calcaire *m*; **organic l.,** calcaire organogène; **coral l.,** calcaire coralligène; **dolomitic l.,** calcaire dolomitique; **magnesian l.,** dolomie *f*, dolomite *f*; **siliceous l.,** calcaire siliceux; **freshwater l.,** travertin *m*; **carboniferous l.,** calcaire carbonifère; **Jurassic l.,** calcaire jurassique; (*b*) *Ind: etc:* pierre *f* à chaux; *Metall:* **l. flux,** castine *f*; *Const:* **shell, shelly, l.,** coquillart *m*, calcaire coquillier.
limewash[1] ['laimwɔʃ], *s.* **1.** lait *m* de chaux; blanc *m* de chaux; badigeon (blanc). **2.** *Tan:* enchaux *m*.
limewash[2], *v.tr.* blanchir (un mur) à la chaux; chauler (un mur).
limewashing ['laimwɔʃiŋ], *s.* blanchiment *m*, blanchissage *m*, à la chaux; chaulage *m*.
limewater ['laimwɔ:tər], *s. Pharm: etc:* eau *f* de chaux.
limewort ['laimwə:t], *s. Bot:* véronique cressonnée, *F:* cresson *m* de cheval, de chien.
limey ['laimi], *s. P: esp. U.S: Austr:* (*a*) Anglais *m*; (*b*) matelot anglais.
Limicolae [lai'mikɔli:], *s.pl. Orn:* limicoles *m*, charadriidés *m*.
limicolous [lai'mikələs], *a.* limicole.
liminal ['liminəl], *a. Psy:* liminal.
liming ['laimiŋ], *s.* **1.** *Agr:* chaulage *m*. **2.** *Tan:* plainage *m*, plamage *m*, pelainage *m*.
limit[1] ['limit], *s.* **1.** limite *f*; borne *f*; (*a*) **within the limits of the city,** dans les limites, le périmètre, de la ville; **within a ten kilometre l.,** dans un rayon de dix kilomètres; **the southern l. of the desert,** la limite sud du désert; **the limits of decency,** les frontières de la bienséance; **within the limits of my power, of my authority,** pour autant qu'il est en mon pouvoir; **it is true within (certain) limits,** c'est vrai dans de certaines limites, dans une certaine limite; **to fix, set, a l., limits (to sth.),** fixer, mettre, une limite, des limites, des bornes (à qch.); borner (son ambition, ses désirs); **without l.,** sans limites, sans bornes; **age l.,** limite d'âge; **time l.,** (i) limite de temps (imposée à un orateur, etc.); (ii) délai *m* (de paiement, etc.); (iii) durée *f* (d'un privilège, etc.); **size l., weight l.,** limite de dimension, de poids; **speed l.,** vitesse *f* limite, maximum, maximale; *Av:* **l. of endurance,** autonomie *f* pratique; *Veh: etc:* **load l.,** charge *f* maximum, limite; *Com:* **l. of free delivery area,** rayon, périmètre, de livraison gratuite, de livraison franco domicile; *Fin: etc:* **credit l., l. of credit,** limite, plafond *m*, du crédit; **to fix a l. for a budget,** fixer un plafond à un budget; *Mth:* **method of limits,** méthode *f* des limites; (*b*) *Mec: etc:* **elastic (stretch) l.,** limite d'élasticité; **strength, yield, l.,** limite de résistance; **stress l.,** limite de fatigue; **fatigue l.,** limite d'endurance; **l. angle,** angle *m* de déplacement, etc.; *Elcs:* **pitch l.,** limite des fréquences audibles; (*c*) *Ins:* plein *m*; **to fix a l.,** fixer les pleins; **table of limits,** tableau *m* des pleins; (*d*) **there's a l. to everything!** il y a limite à tout! *F:* **the sky's the l.,** il n'y a pas de limite; **that the l.!** ça c'est le comble! ça c'est par trop fort! il ne manquerait plus que ça! **he's the l.!** il est impayable! il est impossible! **you're the l.!** vous êtes unique! vous exagérez! **2.** *Mec.E:* tolérance *f*; **plus and minus limits,** tolérances maxima et minima; *Tls:* **l. gauge,** calibre *m* de tolérance; (*external*) bague *f* à tolérance; (*internal*) tampon *m*, bouchon *m*, à tolérance.
limit[2], *v.tr.* limiter, borner, restreindre (qn, qch.); **their sphere of activity is limited to . . .,** leurs opérations se bornent à . . .; **to l. oneself to . . .,** se borner à . . .; **to l. oneself to strict necessities, to essentials,** se restreindre au strict nécessaire, à faire l'essentiel; **rain that limits the view,** pluie *f* qui bouche la vue.
limitary ['limitəri], *a.* **1.** limité, restreint. **2.** qui est situé à la frontière. **3.** qui sert de limite, de borne.
limitation [limi'teiʃ(ə)n], *s.* **1.** limitation *f*, restriction *f*; **l. of a promise,** restriction apportée à une promesse. **2. there are many limitations on my liberty (of action),** de nombreuses servitudes entravent ma liberté d'action; **limitations of an administration,** limitations imposées à l'action d'une administration; **he has his limitations,** ses connaissances, ses capacités, sont bornées; **I know his limitations,** je sais ce dont il est capable et ce qu'il ne faut pas lui demander de faire. **3.** *Jur:* prescription (extinctive); **term of l.,** délai *m* de prescription; (*in a suit*) **time l.,** péremption *f*.
limitative ['limitətiv], *a.* limitatif; **l. clause,** article restrictif.
limited ['limitid], *a.* limité, borné, restreint; **l. capacity,** capacité limitée, restreinte; **l. intelligence,** intelligence bornée; **to be of l. understanding,** avoir l'esprit court; *Com:* **l. market,** marché étroit, restreint; *Geol:* **l. deposit,** gisement cantonné; **l. number,** nombre limité, restreint; **only a l. number of passengers was allowed to land,** seuls quelques passagers furent autorisés à débarquer; **l. supply,** *U.S:* **l. procurement,** approvisionnement limité; **l. storage,** emmagasinage *m*, entreposage *m*, de durée limitée; **the expenditure, however l. . . .,** les dépenses *fpl*, si réduites soient-elles . . .; *St.Exch:* **l. prices,** cours limités; *Publ:* **l. edition,** (édition *f* à) tirage restreint; *Mil:* **l. attack,** attaque *f* à objectif(s) limité(s); **l. war,** (i) guerre limitée quant au nombre et aux objectifs des belligérants; (ii) guerre limitée dans l'espace, guerre localisée; *Jur:* **l. owner,** propriétaire *m* sous conditions; usufruitier, -ière; *U.S: F:* **l. divorce,** séparation *f* de corps; *Mil:* **l. mobilization,** mobilisation partielle; **l. service,** service *m* auxiliaire; *Rail:* **l. train,** train *m* accessible aux voyageurs ayant acquitté un supplément spécial; *U.S:* train de luxe.
limiter ['limitər], *s.* **1.** *Mec.E:* limiteur *m*, régulateur *m* (de puissance, de vitesse, etc.); **oil-pressure l.,** limiteur de pression d'huile. **2.** *El: Ph:* **l. (of half-wave or full wave),** limiteur (d'une ou deux alternances). **3.** *Cmptr:* borne *f*, drapeau *m*, séparateur *m* (de zones, etc.).
limiting[1] ['limitiŋ], *a.* limiteur, -euse; limitatif, -ive; **l. angle,** angle *m* limite; **l. case,** cas *m* limite; **l. speed, l. velocity,** vitesse *f* limite; *Jur:* **l. clause,** clause limitative, article limitatif (d'un contrat, etc.); *El:* **l. circuit,** circuit *m* de limitation; **l. coil,** bobine limiteuse; **(charge-)l. device,** limiteur *m* (de tension, de charge); **l. frequency,** fréquence *f* limite, fréquence de coupure; **l. resistor,** résistance *f* de protection.
limiting[2], *s. El: Ph:* **l. (of half-wave or full wave),** écrêtage *m* (d'une ou deux alternances).
limitless ['limitlis], *a.* sans bornes, illimité.
limitrophe ['limitrouf], *a.* limitrophe (**to,** de).
limivorous [lai'miv(ə)rəs], *a.* limivore, limnivore, pélophage.
limn [lim], *v.tr. A:* **1.** enluminer (un missel, etc.) **2.** (*a*) faire le portrait de (qn); dessiner (qch.); (*b*) peindre (un portrait).
limnanthes [lim'nænθi:z], *s. Bot:* limnanthe *m*.
limner ['lim(n)ər], *s. A:* (*a*) enlumineur *m*; (*b*) peintre *m*.
limnetic [lim'netik], *a. Biol:* limnétique.
limnimeter [lim'nimitər], *s.* limnimètre *m*.
limning ['lim(n)iŋ], *s. A:* (*a*) enluminement *m*; (*b*) enluminure *f*, peinture *f*.
limnite ['limnait], *s. Miner:* limnite *f*.
limnograph ['limnougræf], *s.* limnigraphe *m*.
limnology [lim'nɔlədʒi], *s.* limnologie *f*.
limnometer [lim'nɔmitər], *s.* limnimètre *m*.
limnopithecus [limnou'piθikəs], *s. Paleont:* limnopithèque *m*.
Limnophilidae [limnou'filidi:], *s.pl. Ent:* limnophilides *m*.
limnoplankton [limnou'plæŋktən], *s. Biol:* limnoplancton *m*.
limnoscelis [lim'nɔsilis], *s. Rept;* limnoscelis *m*.
limon[1] ['li:mən], *s. Geol:* limon *m*.
limon[2] ['laimən], *s. Bot:* lémonime *m*.
limonene ['liməni:n], *s. Ch:* limonène *m*.
limonite ['laimənait], *s. Miner:* limonite *f*; **nodular l.,** œtite *f*.
limonium [li'mouniəm], *s. Bot:* limonium *m*.
limosella [laimə'selə], *s. Bot:* limoselle *f*.

limousine [limu'zi:n], *s. Aut:* limousine *f*; *A:* **l.-brougham,** coupé *m* limousine.

limp[1] [limp], *s.* boitement *m*, clochement *m*, claudication *f*; **to walk with a l., to have a l.,** boiter.

limp[2], *v.i.* boiter, clopiner, claudiquer; tirer, traîner, la jambe; **to l. along, past, away,** aller, passer, s'en aller, en boitant, *F:* clopin-clopant; **to l. up, down,** monter, descendre, en boitant.

limp[3], *a.* mou, *f.* molle; flasque; sans consistance; *Bookb:* **l. binding,** cartonnage *m* souple, cartonnage à l'anglaise; (*of linen*) **to become l.,** devenir mou; (*of starched linen*) se désempeser; (*of pers.*) **to feel l.,** se sentir mou, sans énergie; se sentir fatigué; **to feel as l. as a rag,** se sentir mou, flasque, comme une chiffe; être comme une loque; **he was l. with fear,** la peur lui cassait bras et jambes; **l. with the heat,** abattu par la chaleur; **heat that leaves one l.,** chaleur accablante, déprimante.

limpet ['limpit], *s.* **1.** *Moll:* lepas *m*, patelle *f*, arapède *m*; lampotte *f*; **cup-and-saucer l.,** calyptrée *f*; **blue-rayed l.,** helcion *m*. **2.** *F:* (*pers.*) crampon *m*.

limpid ['limpid], *a.* limpide, pellucide, clair, transparent.

limpidity [lim'piditi], **limpidness** ['limpidnis], *s.* limpidité *f*, clarté *f*.

limpidly ['limpidli], *adv.* clairement; avec limpidité.

limping[1] ['limpiŋ], *a.* boiteux; **l. verse,** (i) vers *mpl* boiteux; (ii) vers qui traînent.

limping[2], *s.* = LIMP[1].

limpingly ['limpiŋli], *adv.* en boitant; *F:* clopin-clopant.

limpkin ['limpkin], *s. Orn:* courlan *m*, *F:* oiseau *m* des lamentations.

limply ['limpli], *adv.* **1.** mollement, flasquement. **2.** sans énergie.

limpness ['limpnis], *s.* mollesse *f*; manque *m* de fermeté (d'un tissu); manque d'énergie (de qn).

limpwort ['limpwə:t], *s. Bot:* véronique cressonnée, *F:* cresson *m* de cheval, de chien.

limy ['laimi], *a.* **1.** (sol *m*) calcique, calcaire. **2.** enduit de glu; gluant.

linage ['lainidʒ], *s.* **1.** nombre *m* de lignes (d'un article de journal, etc.). **2.** paiement *m* à la ligne.

linaloe [li:'næloua], *s. Bot:* linaloé *m*; **l. oil,** essence *f* de linaloé.

linalol ['linəlɔl], **linalool** [li'næluəl], *s. Ch:* linalol *m*.

linaria [lai'nɛəriə], *s. Bot:* linaire *f*; muflier bâtard.

linarite ['linərait], *s. Miner:* linarite *f*.

linchcap ['lin(t)ʃkæp], *s. Veh:* coiffe *f* d'esse (de l'essieu).

linchpin ['lin(t)ʃpin], *s. Veh:* esse *f*; clavette *f* de bout d'essieu; cheville *f* d'essieu.

linctus ['liŋktəs], *s. Pharm:* sirop *m*.

lindackerite [lin'dækərait], *s. Miner:* lindackérite *f*.

lindane ['lindein], *s.* lindane *m*.

linden ['lindən], *s. Bot: Lit:* **l. (tree),** tilleul *m*; **l. lea,** prairie entourée de tilleuls.

lindera ['lindərə], *s. Bot:* lindera *m*.

line[1] [lain], *s. Tex:* lin sérancé.

line[2], *s.* **1.** (*cord, wire, etc.*) (*a*) *Nau: etc:* ligne *f*, corde *f*, cordage *m*; amarre *f*; **heaving l.,** ligne d'attrape; lance *f* amarre; **reeving l.,** passeresse *f*; **log l.,** ligne de loch; **lead l., sounding l.,** ligne de sonde; **tripping l.,** calebas *m*; hale-bas *m inv*; **tricing l.,** lève-nez *m inv*; suspensoir *m*; **grab l. (becket),** filière *f* en guirlande; *Dom.Ec:* **clothes l.,** corde à (étendre le) linge; étendoir *m*; *Civ.E: etc:* **snubbing l.,** élingue *f* de retenue; (*b*) *Fish:* ligne (de pêche); **ground l.,** ligne de fond; **trawl l.,** palangre *f*, corde; ligne flottante, dormante; **level l.,** soie *f* parallèle; **l. fishing,** pêche à la ligne; **l. fisherman,** pêcheur *m* à la ligne; **to give a fish plenty of l.,** donner du mou à un poisson; (*c*) *Tp:* **single-wire l., two-wire l.,** ligne unifilaire, bifilaire; **direct l.,** ligne directe; **branch l.,** ligne de branchement; **extension l.,** ligne supplémentaire; **shared l., party l.,** ligne partagée; *Pol:* **the hot l.,** (i) (*Élysée to Kremlin*) la ligne verte; (ii) (*U.S.A. to Kremlin*) la ligne rouge; **the line's very bad, we've got a very bad l.,** la communication est mauvaise; j'ai du mal à vous entendre; **I've just been on the l. to him,** je viens de l'avoir au bout du fil; *attrib.* **l. constant,** constante *f* linéique; **l. noise,** bruit *m* de ligne; **l. scratches,** (bruits de) friture *f*; **l. test equipment,** appareillage *m* pour essai de ligne; (*d*) *El:* **high-tension l.,** ligne à haute tension; **leak l.,** ligne de fuite; *El: Tp:* **overhead l., overhanging l.,** ligne aérienne; **l. carried on brackets,** ligne sur consoles; **pole l.,** ligne sur poteaux; **underground l., buried l.,** ligne souterraine, ligne enterrée; *attrib.* **l. breaker,** conjoncteur-disjoncteur *m, pl.* conjoncteurs-disjoncteurs; **l. drop,** perte *f* en ligne; (*e*) *Surv: Const:* cordeau *m*; **laid out by the l., by rule and l.,** tiré au cordeau; (*f*) *B:* **the lines are fallen unto me in pleasant places,** les cordeaux me sont échus en des lieux agréables; *F:* **it's hard lines,** c'est dur, c'est bien rude; c'est de la malchance; **it's hard lines on you!** c'est bien malheureux pour vous! vous n'avez pas de chance! **hard lines!** pas de chance! (*g*) *esp. U.S: Equit:* **the lines,** les rênes; les guides; (*h*) *Her:* (*for falcon*) longe *f*. **2.** *Nau:* collecteur *m*; **main bilge l.,** collecteur d'assèchement; **main suction l.,** collecteur d'aspiration; **main discharge l.,** collecteur de refoulement. **3.** (*a*) ligne; trait *m*; raie *f*; *Mth: etc:* **straight l.,** (ligne) droite *f*; **parallel straight lines,** droites parallèles; **perpendicular l.,** (ligne, droite) perpendiculaire *f*; **secant l.,** ligne sécante; **secant straight l.,** (droite) sécante *f*; **tangent l.,** ligne tangente, ligne tangentielle; **tangent straight l.,** (droite) tangente *f*, droite tangentielle; **l. of tangency,** ligne de tangence; *Ball:* **l. of elevation,** tangente à la trajectoire à l'origine; **l. of fall,** tangente à la trajectoire à son point de rencontre avec le plan horizontal; **l. of impact,** tangente à la trajectoire à l'arrivée; *Art: etc:* **l. drawing,** dessin *m* au trait; **l. of colour,** trait de couleur; **broken l.,** (i) ligne brisée; (ii) trait discontinu; **continuous l., dash l., full l., solid l.,** ligne pleine, trait plein; **heavy l.,** gros trait; **jagged l.,** ligne brisée; **wavy l.,** trait ondulé; *Typ:* **pecked l.,** ligne en tirets, trait tireté; **to draw a l.,** tirer, tracer, une ligne, un trait; **to copy sth. l. by l.,** copier qch. trait pour trait; **l. engraving,** gravure *f* au trait; **l. engraver,** graveur *m* au trait; **l. process,** photogravure *f* au trait; **l. work,** travail *m* de trait; **colour l. work,** travail de trait en couleur; **fine l. work,** travail de trait fin; **l. block,** cliché *m* trait; **l. copy,** original *m* de trait; **l. subject,** modèle *m* de trait; **border l.,** filet *m* d'encadrement (d'une gravure, etc.); **gold lines (on binding, etc.),** filets dorés (sur une reliure, etc.); *Nau:* **water l.,** ligne de flottaison; **load l.,** ligne de charge; **load water l.,** ligne de flottaison en charge; **base l.,** ligne d'eau zéro; **l. of soundings,** ligne des fonds; *Mec.E: etc:* **reference l., check l., adjusting l.,** (ligne, trait) repère *m*; **datum l.,** ligne de référence; **dimension l.,** ligne de cote; (*supplied with writing pad*) **guide lines,** transparent *m*; guide-âne(s) *m*; *Ten:* **service l.,** ligne de service; **on the l.,** sur la raie; *T.V:* **l. system lines,** linéature *f*; **definition of 625 lines,** définition *f* de 625 lignes (d'exploration); *Aut:* **white l.,** *U.S:* **yellow l.** = ligne blanche, bande médiane; **stop l.,** bande d'arrêt; **single dotted l.,** bande simple pointillée; **double yellow lines** = ligne rouge (d'interdiction de stationnement); **(single) yellow l.** = stationnement limité; *P.N:* **no white lines,** signalisation horizontale provisoirement supprimée; marquages routiers interrompus; pas de signalisation au sol; (*b*) *Geol: Geog:* **ridge l.,** ligne de crête, de faîte; **snow l.,** ligne, limite *f*, des neiges; **fault l.,** ligne de faille; **l. of weakness,** ligne faible; **fall l.,** ligne de changement de pente; ligne, zone *f*, de chutes, de rapides; (*of glacier*) **flow l.,** ligne de flux; **isoseismal l.,** ligne isos(é)iste; **geodetic l.,** ligne géodétique; (*c*) **l. of light,** filet de lumière; **l. of colour,** trait de couleur; *Ph:* **lines of the spectrum,** raies noires du spectre; **absorption lines,** raies d'absorption; **cadmium red l.,** raie rouge d'émission du cadmium; **the lines of the hand,** les lignes de la main; **the l. of life, the life l.,** la ligne de vie; **the lines on his forehead,** les rides *f*, les sillons *m*, de son front; **there was a hard l. across his forehead,** un pli dur barrait son front; (*d*) *Geog:* **the l.,** la Ligne (équatoriale); l'équateur *m*; (*e*) *Opt:* **l. of collimation,** ligne de collimation (d'une lunette d'approche, d'un sextant); **l. of sight, l. of sighting,** ligne de visée, de tir, champ *m* de vision; *Artil: Sm.a:* ligne de mire; **l.-of-sight coverage,** couverture *f* optique; **l.-of-sight range,** portée *f* optique; **l. of vision,** ligne de visée, rayon visuel; *Artil: Sm.a:* **aiming l.,** ligne de mire, ligne de visée; *Ball:* **l. of fire,** ligne de tir; **l. of departure,** ligne de tir au départ, ligne de départ; **l. of site,** ligne de site; *Ph:* **l. of force,** ligne de force, ligne de champ; **neutral l.,** ligne neutre; (*f*) *Art:* **picture hung on the l.,** tableau pendu sur la cimaise; (*g*) *F:* **to get a l. on sth.,** (i) obtenir des tuyaux, se tuyauter, sur qch.; (ii) se rendre compte de qch., arriver à comprendre qch.; **to give s.o. a l. on sth.,** tuyauter qn sur qch.; **to get a l. on s.o.,** se renseigner, se rencarder, sur qn; (*h*) (*contour*) ligne (de l'horizon); contours *mpl* (d'un rivage, d'un visage); lignes (d'une voiture, d'un navire, etc.); mouvement *m* (d'une robe, etc.); **the l. of the nose,** la ligne du nez; **the lines of the mouth,** les lignes de la bouche; **the hard lines of his face,** ses traits durs; **dress, car, etc., that has good lines,** robe, voiture, etc., qui a de la ligne; (*of car, etc.*) **good, clean, lines,** lignes élégantes, élancées; formes fines; *N.Arch:* **body lines,** lignes de carène; **keel l.,** ligne de quille; *Art:* **boldness, purity, of l.,** fermeté *f*, pureté *f*, des lignes; **the broad lines of a work,** les grandes lignes d'un ouvrage; **the main lines of a party's policy,** les directives *f* politiques d'un parti; **to govern on Conservative lines,** gouverner d'après les principes conservateurs; **to work on the same lines as s.o., on the lines laid down by s.o.,** travailler d'après le modèle tracé par qn; **to be working on the right lines,** être en bonne voie; **committee constituted on the following lines,** comité constitué, établi, de la manière suivante; **established on completely new lines,** établi sur un pied tout nouveau; **lines on which an understanding can be reached,** modalités *f* d'une entente; (*i*) (*limit*) **demarcation l.,** ligne de démarcation; *Hist:* **the Mason-Dixon L.,** la frontière sud de la Pennsylvanie (qui séparait les États libres des États esclavagistes); **the Oder-Neisse L.,** la ligne, la frontière, Oder-Neisse (entre l'Allemagne Fédérale et la Pologne); **one must draw the l. somewhere,** il y a une limite à tout; il faut savoir s'arrêter; **I draw the l. at that,** je ne vais pas jusqu'à ce point-là; **to overstep the l.,** dépasser la mesure. **4.** (*row of pers. or thgs*) (*a*) (*side by side*) ligne, rangée *f* (de personnes, d'objets); **to put (out) things in a l.,** aligner des objets; **building l. (of a street),** alignement *m* (plastique) (d'une rue); **to project beyond the building l.,** déborder, dépasser, l'alignement; **street l.,** alignement de voirie; (*of pers.*) **to fall, get, into l., to form a l.,** se mettre en ligne, en rangs; former les rangs; s'aligner; **out of l.,** désaligné; **to fall out of l.,** se désaligner; (*of individual*) quitter les rangs, sortir des rangs; **to fall into l. with s.o.'s ideas,** se conformer aux idées de qn; **his decision is not in l., out of l., with government policy,** sa décision ne se conforme pas, n'est pas d'accord, avec la politique du gouvernement; **we must try to bring him into l. with the others,** il faut essayer de le mettre d'accord avec les autres; *Nau:* **to come into l. with two landmarks,** fermer deux amers; **to come into l. with the majority,** se ranger, se mettre d'accord, avec la majorité; **that's not in l. with his character,** cela ne s'accorde pas, n'est pas en harmonie, avec son caractère; (*b*) (*one behind the other*) file *f*; *esp. NAm:* queue *f*; **l. of locks and canals,** chapelet *m* de biefs et de canaux; **twenty cars in a l.,** vingt voitures à la file; **l. of traffic,** colonne *f* de véhicules en marche; (*of vehicle*) **to get into the l. of traffic,** prendre la file; *Ind:* **assembly l.,** chaîne *f* de montage; (*in abattoir*) **killing l.,** abattage *m* à la chaîne; (*of pipeline, etc.*) **to bring a section into l. with the others,** mettre un tronçon dans le prolongement exact du premier; (*of pers.*) **to stand in a l.,** (i) se tenir à la file; (ii) faire la queue; *P.N: NAm:* **l. entrance,** faites la queue ici; tête de queue; *F:* **l. jumper,** resquilleur, -euse; carotteur, -euse; (*c*) *Mil: etc:* **fighting l., l. of battle,** ligne de combat, de bataille; **l. of attack,** ligne d'attaque; **division drawn up in three lines,** division formée, articulée, en trois lignes; **the front lines, rear lines,** le front, l'arrière; **l. of assaulting troops,** vague *f* d'assaut; *O:* **infantry of the l.,** infanterie *f* de ligne; **soldier of the l.,** fantassin *m*; **the 20th regiment of the l.,** le 20e régiment de ligne; *Navy: A:* **ship of the l.,** vaisseau *m* de ligne; **twenty sails of the l.,** vingt vaisseaux de ligne; **to win all along the l.,** gagner sur toute la ligne; (*d*) *pl. Mil:* lignes (de fortification, etc.); **to retire within one's lines,** rentrer dans ses lignes; (*e*) *Petr:* **l. and tack,** alignement et pointage; (*f*) ligne (de mots écrits, imprimés); vers *m* (de poésie); **first l. of a paragraph,** alinéa *m*; (*in dictating*) **next l., new l.,** à la ligne; *F:* **I'll drop you a l.,** je vous enverrai un petit mot; **I had a l., a few lines, from him,** j'ai reçu un mot de lui; **just a l. to tell you . . .,** deux mots, un petit mot, pour vous dire . . .; *Typ: Typew:* **l. space,** entre-ligne *m*, interligne *m*; **adjustable l. space,** interligne réglable; **l.-space lever, l. spacer,** levier *m* d'interligne; **l. spacing,** interlignage *m*; *Typ: etc:* **l. printing,** impression *f* ligne par ligne; **l. printer,** imprimante *f* ligne par ligne; *M.Ins:* (*of underwriter*) **to write a l.,** prendre une part d'un risque; *Th:* (*of actor*) **he doesn't know his lines,** il ne sait pas son rôle; *F:* **marriage lines,** acte *m* de mariage. **5.** ligne, compagnie *f* (de paquebots, etc.); **shipping l.,** compagnie de navigation; messageries *fpl* maritimes. **6.** ligne de descendants, d'ascendants; ligne (généalogique); **male, female, l.,** ligne masculine, féminine; **long l. of ancestors,** longue suite d'ancêtres; **in direct l.,** en ligne directe. **7.** (*a*) ligne (de marche, d'intercommunication); voie *f* (de communication); *Mil: etc:* **l. of advance,** ligne de progression, direction *f* de marche; **l. of withdrawal,** ligne, direction, de repliement; ligne de repli; (*b*) *Rail:* voie; ligne; **main l.,** voie principale; grande ligne; **local l., branch l.,** ligne, chemin *m* de fer, d'intérêt local; **collecting l.,** voie de formation; **deviation l.,** voie de déviation; **single-track, double-track, l.,** ligne à voie unique, à double voie; **up l., down l.,** voie montante, descendante; **l. blocked,** voie, section, bloquée; **l. clear,** voie libre; section débloquée; **l. in operation,** ligne en exploitation; voie exploitée; (*c*) **l. of conduct,** ligne de conduite; **l. of thought,** suite *f* d'idées; **l. of argument,** raisonnement *m*; **in the l. of French tradition,** dans l'axe de la tradition française; **what l. are you going to take?** quel parti allez-vous prendre? **to take a l. of one's own,** aller de son côté; **he insisted on taking a very tough l. with the rebels,** il a insisté pour qu'on prenne des mesures très sévères à l'égard des rebelles, pour que les rebelles soient traités avec la plus grande rigueur; (*d*) *F:* genre *m* d'affaires; métier *m*; **what's his l.?** quel est son métier? quelle est sa spécialité? qu'est-ce qu'il fait? **he's in the building l.,** il est dans le bâtiment; **that's not my l.,** ce n'est pas mon rayon; **tennis isn't my l.,** le tennis n'est pas mon fait; je ne joue pas au tennis; **that's more (in) my l.,** cela est plus dans mon genre; ça me connaît; **here's something in your l.,** voici quelque chose qui va vous intéresser; (*e*) *Com:* série *f* (d'articles); article *m*; **leading lines,** articles, spécialités *f,* de réclame; **it's not one of our lines,** nous ne vendons pas cet article; *F:* **something in the fish l.,** un plat de poisson quelconque; **a rice pudding or something in that l.,** un gâteau de riz ou quelque chose dans ce genre(-là); **she's got a fine l. in slang,** elle a un choix d'argot. **8.** *Atom.Ph:* filière *f* (de réacteurs).

line[3], *v.*

I. *v.tr.* **1.** ligner, régler, rayer (un morceau de papier); **pain had lined her face,** son visage était ridé par la douleur; (*of forehead, face*) **to become lined,** se rider. **2.** border; **to l. a walk with poplars,** border une allée de peupliers; **to l. the roads with troops,** aligner des troupes sur les routes; **the banks were lined with soldiers,** les rives étaient bordées de soldats; **the crowd lined the street,** la foule s'alignait le long du trottoir; **the troops lined the streets,** les troupes faisaient, formaient, la haie; les rues étaient garnies de troupes. **3.** érafler, rayer; strier de lignes.

II. (*compound verbs*) **1. line in,** *v.tr. Art:* **to l. in a figure in a picture,** esquisser une figure dans un tableau; **to l. in a contour,** réchampir un contour.

2. line off, *v.tr. Tchn:* **to l. off a piece of wood, a stone,** cingler, tringler, dresser, ligner, une pièce de bois; tracer la coupe d'une pierre.

3. line out, *v.i. Rugby: Fb:* se mettre en deux lignes parallèles pour la touche.

4. line up, (*a*) *v.tr.* (i) aligner, mettre en ligne (des personnes, des objets); (ii) dresser (une machine); (*b*) *v.i.* (i) (*of pers.*) s'aligner; se mettre en ligne; se ranger; faire la queue; prendre la file; prendre sa file; **to l. up for the theatre,** faire queue devant le guichet (du théâtre); (ii) *Mec.E:* (*of parts*) se repérer.

line[4], *v.tr.* (*a*) *Tail: Dressm: etc:* doubler (un vêtement) (**with,** de); **fur-lined gloves,** gants fourrés; (*b*) **to l. a box with paper, with zinc,** tapisser une boîte de papier; doubler une boîte de zinc; **box lined with silk,** coffret avec intérieur en soie; *Cu:* **to l. a tin with pastry,** foncer un moule de pâte; **a membrane lines the stomach,** une membrane tapisse l'estomac; *F:* **to have nothing to l. one's stomach with,** n'avoir rien à se mettre dans le buffet; **nest lined with moss,** nid garni de mousse; (*c*) *Tchn:* **to l. a bearing block,** garnir, recouvrir, un palier; **to l. a gun, a cylinder,** chemiser un fusil, un cylindre; **to l. a wall, a furnace,** revêtir, incruster, un mur, un fourneau (**with,** de); **to l. the foot of a wall,** rechausser un mur; **walls lined with panelling,** murs revêtus de boiseries; **to l. a well, a mine shaft,** tuber, cuveler, un puits; **to l. a flue with cement,** enduire un carneau de ciment; **to l. a shaft with metal,** blinder un puits; *Nau:* **to l. a sail,** renforcer une voile.

line[5], *v.tr.* (*of dog, wolf*) couvrir, lacer, monter, aligner (la chienne, la louve).

lineage ['liniidʒ], *s.* lignée *f,* lignage *m*; race *f,* famille *f*; **to boast an ancient l.,** se vanter d'une longue généalogie.

lineal ['liniəl], *a.* (*a*) linéal, -aux; **l. succession,** succession linéale, en ligne directe; **l. (descendant),** descendant, -ante, en ligne directe; *Jur:* **l. relative,** lignager *m*; **in l. descent from . . .,** en descendance directe de . . .; (*b*) *Mil:* **l. promotion,** avancement *m* à l'ancienneté; **l. rank,** ancienneté *f* dans le grade.

lineally ['liniəli], *adv.* en ligne directe; **to be l. descended from . . .,** descendre en ligne directe de . . ..

lineament ['liniəmənt], *s. usu. pl.* trait *m*, linéament *m*.

linear ['liniər], *a.* **1.** linéaire; (*a*) **l. measure,** mesure *f* linéaire, mesure de longueur; **l. foot,** pied *m* linéaire; **l. metre,** mètre courant; *Mth:* **l. equation,** équation *f* linéaire, équation du premier degré; **l. space,** espace vectoriel; (*b*) *Ph:* **l. expansion,** dilatation *f* linéaire; (*c*) *Atom.Ph:* **l. acceleration,** accélération *f* linéaire; **l. (particle) accelerator,** accélérateur *m* linéaire (de particules); **l. electron accelerator,** accélérateur linéaire d'électrons; **l. resonance accelerator,** accélérateur linéaire de résonance; **l. range,** parcours *m* linéaire; (*d*) *El:* **l. network,** réseau *m* linéaire; *W.Tel: etc:* **l. amplification,** amplification *f* linéaire; **l. amplifier,** amplificateur *m* linéaire; **l. distortion,** distorsion *f* linéaire; **l. array,** réseau (d'antennes) linéaire; (*e*) *Mec:* **l. energy transfer,** transfert *m* linéaire d'énergie; **l. speed,** vitesse *f* linéaire; (*f*) *Cmptr:* **l. programming,** programmation *f* linéaire. **2.** *Bot:* **l. leaf,** feuille *f* linéaire.

linearity [lini'æriti], *s.* linéarité *f*; *T.V:* **l. control,** réglage *m* du nombre de lignes.

linearization [liniərai'zeiʃ(ə)n], *s. Ph: etc:* linéarisation *f.*

linearize ['liniəraiz], *v.tr.* linéariser; *Mth:* ramener (une équation) au premier degré; *Ch:* **catalyst that linearizes polyethylene,** catalyseur *m* qui linéarise le polyéthylène.

linearly ['liniəli], *adv.* linéairement.

lineate ['linieit], *a. Bot:* ligné, rayé.

lineation [lini'eiʃ(ə)n], *s.* **1.** lignage *m*, lignes *fpl.* **2.** tracé *m* (de lignes).

lined[1] [laind], *a.* **1.** (*a*) ligné; **l. leaf,** feuille lignée; **l. paper,** papier réglé, rayé; *Phot: Engr:* **cross-l. screen,** trame quadrillée; **deeply l. forehead,** front creusé de rides; (*b*) strié; ripé. **2. straight-l.,** à lignes droites. **3.** *Her:* (faucon) longé.

lined[2], *a.* (manteau) doublé; (gant) fourré; (frein) garni; *Min:* **l. gallery,** galerie coffrée; **leather-l. throughout,** doublé entièrement en peau; **felt-l.,** garni de feutre; **steel-l. cylinder,** cylindre chemisé d'acier; **well l. purse,** bourse ronde, bien garnie.

lineman, *pl.* **-men** ['lainmən], *s.m.* **1.** *Rail:* cantonnier. **2.** *Tg: Tp:* (i) poseur de lignes; (ii) surveillant de ligne.

line-out ['lainaut], *s. Rugby: Fb:* alignement *m* des deux équipes pour la touche.

linen ['linin], *s.* **1.** (*a*) *Tex:* toile *f* (de lin); **l. towel,** serviette *f* de, en, toile; **l. thread,** fil *m* de lin; **l. sheets,** draps *m* fil; **l. trade,** commerce *m* des toiles; **l. industry,** industrie linière, toilière; **l. warehouse,** magasin *m* de blanc; **l. manufacturer,** toilier *m*; **l. prover,** compte-fils *m inv*; quart-de-pouce *m, pl.* quarts-de-pouce; (*b*) **l.(-finish(ed)) paper, l.-faced paper,** papier toilé. **2.** linge *m*; lingerie *f*; **table l.,** linge de table; **a piece of l., a l. rag,** un linge; **dirty l.,** linge sale; *F:* **one shouldn't wash one's dirty l. in public,** il faut laver son linge sale en famille; **l. press, cupboard,** armoire *f* à, au, linge; **l. room,** lingerie; (*in hotel, etc.*) **l. maid,** lingère *f.*

linenfold ['lininfould], *attrib. Arch: Furn:* **l. panel,** panneau *m* à étoffe(s) pliée(s), à pli(s) de serviette.

liner[1] ['lainər], *s.* **1.** (*pers.*) traceur *m* de filets; fileteur *m*. **2.** (paquebot *m*) transatlantique *m*; **cargo l.,** navire de charge régulier; **l. freighting,** affrètement *m* à la cueillette; **l. rate,** frêt *m* à la cueillette.

liner[2], *s.* **1.** (*pers.*) doubleur, -euse (de manteaux, etc.). **2.** (*a*) cale *f* d'épaisseur (en fer, en bois); (*b*) *Mch: I.C.E:* fourreau *m*, chemise (intérieure), manchon (intérieur) (de cylindre); **wet l.,** chemise humide; (*c*) *Mch:* contre-porte *f* (de chaudière); (*d*) *Mec.E:* **footstep l.,** plaque *f* de butée.

linesman, *pl.* **-men** ['lainzmən], *s.m.* **1.** *Mil: O:* soldat de la ligne; *F:* lignard. **2.** = LINEMAN. **3.** *Fb: Ten:* arbitre de lignes; *Fb:* arbitre, juge, de touche.

line-up ['lainʌp], *s.* **1.** (*a*) mise *f* en rang, en ligne; alignement *m*; (*b*) (i) *esp. NAm:* queue *f* (de personnes); (ii) rangée *f* de personnes (assemblées par la police pour l'identification d'un suspect); (*c*) *Sp:* formation *f* (d'une équipe sur le terrain) **2.** *Mec.E: etc:* **l.-up mark,** marque-repère *f, pl.* marques-repères.

linework ['lainwəːk], *s. Art:* dessin *m* au trait; gravure *f* en relief.

ling[1] [liŋ], *s. Ich:* lingue *f*; morue longue; julienne *f.*

ling[2], *s. Bot:* bruyère commune; callune *f* vulgaire.

linga(m) ['liŋgə(m)], *s. Hindu Rel:* linga(m) *m*.

linger ['liŋgər], *v.i.* (*a*) tarder, s'attarder, traîner; **to l. behind the others,** traîner derrière les autres; **to l. about, (a)round, a place; to l. over a subject,** s'attarder dans un endroit; s'attarder sur, à, un sujet; **he had lingered to say goodnight to her,** il s'était attardé à lui dire bonsoir; **to l. over a meal,** s'attarder sur, prolonger, un repas; **to l. over a pipe, over one's port,** savourer une pipe, son porto; **a doubt still lingered in his mind,** un doute subsistait encore dans son esprit; *v.tr.* **to l. away one's time,** perdre son temps en flâneries; **to l. out one's days, one's life,** traîner une vie pénible jusqu'à la tombe; (*b*) (*of invalid*) **to l. (on),** languir, traîner.

lingerer ['liŋgərər], *s.* traînard *m*; retardataire *mf.*

lingerie ['lɛ̃ːʒəri(ː)], *s.* lingerie *f* (pour femmes); *Com:* **l. department,** rayon *m* de blanc.

lingering[1] ['liŋg(ə)riŋ], *a.* **1. l. look,** regard prolongé; **l. doubt,** doute *m* qui subsiste encore; **there was a l. hope that . . .,** on conservait un vague espoir que . . .. **2. l. disease,** maladie *f* qui traîne, maladie chronique; **l. death,** mort lente.

lingering[2], *s.* lenteurs *fpl*; retard *m*, attardement *m*.

lingo ['liŋgou], *s.* (*pl.* **lingoes** ['liŋgouz]) *F:* **1. the l. of the country,** (i) la langue du pays; (ii) le jargon, le patois, du pays. **2.** argot *m* (du théâtre, etc.).

lingua franca ['liŋgwə'fræŋkə], *s. Ling:* sabir *m*.

lingual ['liŋgwəl]. **1.** *a. Anat: Ling:* lingual, -aux. **2.** *s. Ling:* linguale *f.*

linguatula [liŋ'gwætjulə], *s. Arach:* linguatule *f.*

linguatulosis [liŋgwætju'lousis], *s. Vet:* linguatulose *f.*

linguiform ['liŋgwifɔːm], *a.* linguiforme.

linguist ['liŋgwist], *s.* linguiste *mf*; **to be a good l., no l.,** être, ne pas être, doué pour les langues.

linguistic [liŋ'gwistik], *a.* linguistique; **l. minorities,** minorités *f* linguistiques.

linguistically [liŋ'gwistik(ə)li], *adv.* linguistiquement.

linguistics [liŋ'gwistiks], *s.pl.* (*usu. with sg. const.*) linguistique *f*; **structural l.,** linguistique structurale.

lingula ['liŋgjulə], *s. Moll:* lingule *f*; (*genus*) lingula *f.*

lingulate ['liŋgjuleit], *a. Nat.Hist:* lingulaire, lingulé.

linguodental ['liŋgwou'dent(ə)l]. *Ling:* **1.** *a.* linguodental, -aux. **2.** *s.* linguodentale *f.*

linhay ['lini], *s. Dial:* appentis *m*, hangar *m*.

liniment ['linimənt], *s.* liniment *m*.

linin ['linin], *s. Biol:* linine *f* (du noyau de la cellule).

lining[1] ['lainiŋ], *s.* **1.** doublage *m*, garnissage *m*; revêtement intérieur; *I.C.E:* **l. of cylinders,** garnissage des cylindres. **2.** (*a*) *Dressm: etc:* doublure *f* (de robe); coiffe *f* (de chapeau); **tobacco pouch with rubber l.,** blague *f* à tabac avec intérieur caoutchouc; (*b*) *Tchn:* garniture *f*, fourrure *f* (de frein, de coussinet, d'embrayage); chemise *f* (de fourneau, de pompe); revêtement *m*, cuvelage *m* (de puits); parois *fpl* (de cheminée); paroi (d'un tunnel); *Mch:* grain *m* (d'un palier à poussée); **antifriction l.,** fourrure d'antifriction; *Nau:* **l. of a sail,** doublage, renfort *m*, d'une voile; **top l.,** tablier *m*; *Const:* **l. of a wall,** incrustation *f* d'un mur; *I.C.E:* **steel l. of a cylinder,** chemise d'acier d'un cylindre; *Com: etc:* **zinc l. of a case,** paroi de zinc d'une caisse; *Min: etc:* **plank l.,** planches *fpl* de coffrage (de puits); (*of scabbard*) **wooden l.,** alèze *f.*

lining[2], *s.* saillie *f* (de la chienne).

linitis [lai'naitis], *s. Med:* linite *f.*

link[1] [liŋk], *s.* **1.** (*a*) chaînon *m*, maillon *m*, maille *f*, anneau *m* (d'une chaîne); *Nau:* paillon *m* (de câble-chaîne); **l. and stud,** maille à talon; (*b*) maille (de tricot); (*c*) **cuff links,** boutons de manchette (jumelés), à chaînettes; jumelles *f* de manchettes; (*d*) *Meas: A:* centième partie *f* de la chaîne (d'arpenteur) = 7.92 pouces = 20 cm. **2.** *Mec.E: etc:* (*a*) pièce *f* de liaison, tige *f* d'assemblage; bielle *f*, biellette *f*; *Aut:* bielle d'accouplement (des roues avant); **breaking l.,** bielletts de sécurité; **coupling l.,** bielle d'accouplement, de couplage; **l. connection,** transmission *f* par biellettes; **l. mechanism,** embiellage *m*; (*b*) **(fork) l,** étrier *m*; **l. mounting,** monture *f* d'étrier; (*c*) menotte *f* (de ressort); (*d*) *Mch:* coulisse *f* (de machine à vapeur); **l. lever,** levier *m* de changement de marche, de renversement; **l. motion,** distribution *f* par, à, coulisse; **l. plate,** flasque *m* de coulisse. **3.** lien *m*, liaison *f*, trait *m* d'union (**between,** entre); *Ch:* **co-ordinate l.,** coordinence *f*, covalence *f*; *Av:* **air l.,** liaison aérienne; *Elcs:* **radio l.,** câble hertzien, faisceau hertzien; liaison radiophonique; **l. relay,** relais hertzien; *Cmptr:* **data l.,** liaison pour l'acheminement des données; **he is a l. between the old world and the new,** il sert de trait d'union entre le vieux monde et le nouveau; **missing l.,** (i) vide *m*, lacune *f* (dans une théorie); (ii) *Biol:* forme intermédiaire disparue; *F:* (l')anneau manquant, (le) pithécanthrope; *F:* **he's the missing l.!** quel chimpanzé!

link[2]. **1.** *v.tr.* enchaîner, (re)lier, (re)joindre, attacher (**with, to,** à); **line that links (up) two towns,** ligne *f* (de chemin de fer) qui relie deux villes; **to l. up one's lands at A with those at B,** réunir sa terre de A à sa terre de B; **to l. up records,** relier entre eux des documents; **one can see how things are linked (up) with one another,** on voit comme les choses s'enchaînent; **to l. one question with another,** rattacher une question à une autre; **our business is linked (up) with Australian trade,** notre maison est en rapport intime avec le commerce australien; **wages linked to the cost of living,** salaires indexés sur le coût de la vie; *F:* **to be linked for life to s.o.,** être uni à qn pour la vie; **facts closely linked together,** faits étroitement unis; **to l. hands, arms,** se donner la main, le bras; **she linked her arm in mine,** elle me prit le bras; *Ling:* **to l. two words,** lier deux mots. **2.** *v.i.* **to l. on to sth., to l. in, up, with sth.,** s'attacher, se joindre, s'unir, à qch.

link[3], *s. A:* **1.** torche *f*, flambeau *m* (dont se faisaient précéder ceux qui circulaient à la nuit tombée). **2. l.(-boy),** porte-flambeau *m inv*; porteur *m* de torche.

Link[4], *Pr.n. Av:* **L. trainer,** appareil *m* d'entraînement au pilotage sans visibilité.

linkage ['liŋkidʒ], *s.* **1.** système *m* de chaînons. **2.** *Mec.E:* (*a*) liaison *f*, raccord *m*, accouplement *m*, couplage *m*, attache *f*; (*b*) embiellage *m*; transmission *f* par tringles, tringlerie *f*; *Aut:* timonerie *f* (de la direction, de commande de carburateur, etc.). **3.** *Ph: Ch: etc:* enchaînement *m*, concomitance *f* (de faits, de phénomènes).

linked [liŋkt], *a.* lié, joint, associé, uni; *Mch: Mec.E:* articulé; *Mil:* **l. battalions,** bataillons formant brigade; **l. traffic signals, lights,** feux synchronisés.

linking ['liŋkiŋ], *s.* **l. (up),** enchaînement *m*, liaison *f*, union *f* (d'intérêts, etc.); *Space:* **l. up of two spacecraft,** jonction *f* de deux engins spatiaux.

linkman, *pl.* **-men** ['liŋkmən], *s.m.* **1.** *A:* = LINK³ 2. **2.** *U.S: Th: Cin:* commissionnaire.

linkpin ['liŋkpin], *s. Mec.E: etc:* (*a*) axe *m* d'articulation; tourillon *m*; (*b*) goujon *m* de chaîne (de bicyclette, etc.); fuseau *m* (de chaîne à rouleaux).

links [liŋks], *s.pl.* (*a*) *Scot:* dunes *f*; (*b*) (*usu. with sg. const.*) (**golf**) **l.,** terrain *m*, parcours, *m*, de golf.

link(-)up ['liŋkʌp], *s.* lien *m*, liaison *f* (**between,** entre).

linkword ['liŋkwəːd], *s. Ling:* mot-outil *m*, *pl.* mots-outils.

linnaea [li'ni(ː)ə], *s. Bot:* linnée *f*.

Linn(a)ean [li'niːən], *a. Bot:* linnéen, -éenne.

linnaeite ['liniait], *s. Miner:* linnéite *f*.

Linnaeus [li'niːəs]. *Pr.n.m.* Linné.

linneite ['liniait], *s. Miner:* linnéite *f*.

linneon ['liniɔn], *s. Nat.Hist:* linnéon *m*.

linnet ['linit], *s. Orn:* linotte (mélodieuse); **green l.,** verdier *m*.

lino¹ ['lainou], *s. F:* linoléum *m*.

lino², *s. Typ: F:* linotype *f*.

linocut ['lainoukʌt], *s. F:* lino *m*.

linoleic [linou'liːik], *a. Ch:* (acide *m*) linoléique.

linoleum [li'nouliəm], *s.* linoléum *m*.

Linotype¹ ['lainoutaip], *s. R.t.m: Typ:* Linotype *f*; **setting by l.,** linotypie *f*; **l. operator,** linotypiste *m*.

linotype², *v.tr.* linotyper.

linotyper ['lainoutaipər], **linotypist** ['lainoutaipist], *s. Typ:* linotypiste *m*.

linsang ['linsæŋ], *s. Z:* linsang *m*; **banded l.,** linsang à bandes; **spotted l.,** linsang tacheté.

linseed ['linsiːd], *s.* graine *f* de lin; linette *f*; **l. meal,** farine *f* de lin; **l. cake,** tourteau *m* de lin; **l. poultice,** cataplasme *m* de farine de lin.

linsey-woolsey ['linzi'wulzi], *s. Tex: A:* tiretaine *f*; *A:* breluche *f*, breluchet *m*.

linstock ['linstɔk], *s. A.Arms:* boutefeu *m*.

lint [lint], *s.* **1.** *Med:* (*a*) *A:* charpie *f*; (*b*) pansement ouatiné. **2.** peluche *f* (de laine, de coton, de chiffon, etc.); *Paperm:* poussière (de papier).

lintel ['lint(ə)l], *s.* **1.** linteau *m*, sommier *m* (de porte, de fenêtre); *Arch:* **l. course,** plate-bande *f*, *pl.* plates-bandes. **2.** travers *m* (de manteau de cheminée).

lintelled ['lint(ə)ld], *a.* (porte) à linteau.

linters ['lintəz], *s.pl. Paperm: etc:* bourres *f* de coton.

lion ['laiən], *s.* **1.** *Z:* (*a*) lion *m*; **lion('s) cub, whelp,** lionceau *m*; **l. hunter,** tueur *m* de lions; **l. house,** fauverie *f*; **lion's den,** antre *m* du lion; **the lion's share,** la part du lion; la part léonine; **to take the l.'s share,** se faire la part du lion; *F:* tirer la couverture à soi; **to put one's head into the lion's mouth,** se fourrer dans la gueule du loup, dans la gueule du lion; **a l. in the way, in the path,** un danger, un obstacle (surtout imaginaire); **a l. at home, a mouse abroad,** rogue chez lui, timide dans le monde; **it's the ass in the lion's skin,** c'est l'âne couvert de la peau du lion; **the British L.,** le Lion britannique; **to twist the lion's tail,** mettre à l'épreuve la patience de la nation anglaise; faire bisquer les Anglais; (*b*) **American, mountain, l.,** lion d'Amérique, du Pérou; couguar *m*; **l. monkey,** marikina *m*, petit-lion *m*, *pl.* petits-lions; (*c*) *Bot:* **lion's ear,** leonotis *m*; **lion's foot,** *F:* (i) pied-de-lion *m*; (ii) manteau *m* de Notre-Dame; **lion's leaf,** léontice *f*. **2.** (*a*) *A:* **to see, show, the lions of a place,** visiter, montrer, les curiosités, les beautés naturelles, d'un endroit; (*b*) célébrité *f*; personnage marquant; lion; **the l. of the day,** la célébrité du jour; **to make a l. of s.o.,** faire une célébrité de qn; mettre qn en vedette. **3.** *Geog:* **the Gulf of Lions,** le golfe du Lion. **4.** *Astr:* **the L.,** le Lion. **5. the (British) Lions,** équipe britannique internationale de rugby.

lioncel ['laiənsel], *s. Her:* lionceau *m*.

lioness ['laiənes], *s.f. Z:* lionne.

lionheart ['laiənhɑːt], *s.* homme courageux; *Hist:* **(Richard) the L.,** Richard Cœur de Lion.

lionhearted ['laiənhɑːtid], *a.* au cœur de lion.

lionism ['laiənizm], *s. A: Lit:* lionnerie *f*.

lionize ['laiənaiz], *v.tr.* faire une célébrité de (qn); mettre (qn) en vedette.

lion-tailed ['laiənteild], *a. Z:* **l.-t. macaque,** macaque *m* silène.

lip¹ [lip], *s.* **1.** (*a*) lèvre *f* (de qn); babine *f* (d'un animal); **lower, bottom, under, l.,** lèvre inférieure; **thick (lower) l., blubber l.,** lippe *f*; **upper, top, l.,** lèvre supérieure; **to keep a stiff upper l.,** ne pas broncher; garder son courage et faire contre mauvaise fortune bon cœur; serrer les dents; **to do, pay, show, l. service to s.o., to sth.,** rendre à qn, à qch., des hommages peu sincères; payer de paroles; **he pays l. service,** il le dit des lèvres, mais le cœur n'y est pas; **to hang one's l.,** faire la moue; **a cigar between his lips,** un cigare aux lèvres; **with tight, set, lips,** les lèvres serrées; **with parted lips,** la bouche entrouverte; les lèvres entrouvertes; **to bite one's lip(s),** se mordre les lèvres; **to purse, screw up, one's lips,** pincer les lèvres; faire la moue; **to smack, lick, one's lips over sth.,** se lécher les babines; se pourlécher; **to open one's lips,** (i) écarter les lèvres; ouvrir la bouche; (ii) desserrer les dents, les lèvres; parler; **he didn't open his lips, not a word passed his lips,** il n'a pas desserré les dents; il ne lui est pas échappé une parole; il n'a pas dit mot; **this sounds strange from your lips,** ceci semble étrange sur vos lèvres; **no food has passed his lips today,** il n'a pris aujourd'hui aucune nourriture; **no complaint ever passes his lips,** jamais il ne se plaint; *Harn:* **l. strap,** fausse gourmette; **l. microphone,** *F:* **l. mike,** microphone *m* moustache; microphone de bouche; *Ling:* **l. consonant,** consonne labiale; labiale *f*; **l.-teeth consonant,** consonne labio-dentale; dentilabiale *f*; (*b*) *P:* effronterie *f*, insolence *f*; **don't give me, I don't want, any of your l.!** ne te fiche pas de moi! ne te paie pas ma tête! ne la ramène pas! **none of your l.!** on ne me répond pas sur ce ton-là! en voilà assez! (*c*) lèvre (d'une plaie); *Bot:* lèvre (de corolle labiée); labelle *m* (d'orchidée). **2.** (*a*) (*rim*) bord *m*, rebord *m* (d'une tasse, d'une cavité); margelle *f* (de puits); orle *m*, lèvre (de cratère); labelle (d'une coquille); **l. of a furnace,** rive *f* d'un four; (*b*) **pouring l.,** bec *m* (de vase, d'éprouvette); coulée *f* (de creuset); **I've broken the l. off the jug,** j'ai égueulé le pot; (*projection*) rebord, saillie *f*; balèvre *f* (d'assise de maçonnerie); couronne *f* (de came); *O:* visière *f* (de cheminée de locomotive); (*d*) *Tls:* lèvre, tranchant *m* (de mèche anglaise); (*e*) **l. curb,** contrebord *m* à pente douce; *Mec.E:* languette *f*, ergot *m*; **l. bolt,** boulon *m* à ergot.

lip², *v.tr.* (**lipped** [lipt]) **1.** *O:* (*a*) mettre les lèvres à (une tasse, etc.); emboucher (un instrument à vent); (*b*) baiser (la main de qn). **2.** (*of water*) toucher, lécher (les rochers). **3.** *Golf:* **to l. the hole,** envoyer la balle juste au bord du trou.

lip(a)emia [li'piːmiə], *s. Med:* excès de lipides dans le sang.

Lipari ['lipɑːri], *Pr.n. Geog:* **the L. Islands,** les îles *f* Lipari.

Liparian [li'pεəriən], *a. & s. Geog:* (*a*) *a.* liparéen; (*b*) *s.* Liparéen, -éenne.

Liparidae [li'pæridiː], *s.pl. Ent:* liparidés *m*.

liparis ['lipəris], *s. Bot:* liparis *m*.

liparite ['lipərait], *s. Miner:* liparite *f*, rhyolit(h)e *f*.

lipase ['lipeis], *s. Ch:* lipase *f*.

lipeurus [li'pjuːrəs], *s. Ent:* lipeure *m*.

lipid(e) ['lip(a)id], *s. Bio-Ch:* lipide *m*.

lipidic [li'pidik], *a. Bio-Ch:* lipidique.

lipochrome ['lipoukroum], *s. Bio-Ch:* lipochrome *m*.

lipodystrophy [lipou'distrəfi], *s. Med:* lipodystrophie *f*; **progressive l.,** lipodystrophie progressive.

lipogenesis [lipou'dʒenisis], *s. Biol:* lipogénèse *f*.

lipogram ['lipougræm], *s. Lit:* lipogramme *m*.

lipography [li'pɔgrəfi], *s.* haplographie *f*.

lipoid ['lipɔid], *a. & s. Bio-Ch:* lipoïde (*m*); *s.pl.* **lipoids,** lipides *m*.

lipoidic [li'pɔidik], *a. Bio-Ch:* lipoïdique.

lipolysis [li'pɔlisis], *s. Biol:* lipolyse *f*.

lipolytic [lipə'litik], *a. Biol:* lipolytique.

lipoma [li'poumə], *s. Med:* lipome *m*.

lipomatosis [lipoumə'tousis], *s. Med:* lipomatose *f*.

lipomatous [li'pɔmətəs], *a. Med:* lipomateux.

lipophilia [lipou'filiə], *s. Ch:* lipophilie *f*.

lipophile, lipophilic ['lipoufail, lipou'filik], *a. Ch:* lipophile.

lipoprotein [lipou'proutiːn], *s. Bio-Ch:* lipoprotéine *f*.

liposoluble [lipou'sɔljubl], *a. Ch:* liposoluble.

lipothymic [lipou'θimik], *a. Med:* lipothymique.

lipothymy [li'pɔθimi], *s. Med:* lipothymie *f*; défaillance *f*, évanouissement *m*.

lipotrop(h)ic [lipou'trɔpik, -'trɔfik], *a. Bio-Ch:* lipotrope.

lipovaccine ['lipouvæksiːn], *s. Med: etc:* lipovaccin *m*.

lipoxydase [li'pɔksideis], *s. Ch:* lipoxydase *f*.

lipped [lipt], *a.* **1.** (*with adj. prefixed, e.g.*) **thin-l.,** aux lèvres minces; **thick-l., blubber-l.,** lippu; **red-l.,** aux lèvres rouges. **2.** *Bot:* labié. **3.** (tuyau *m*, etc.) à rebord; (cruche *f*) à bec.

lipper ['lipər], *s. Nau:* rides *fpl* (à la surface de l'eau); remous *m*, clapotis *m*; **wind l.,** revolin *m*.

lipping ['lipiŋ], *s. Mus:* embouchure *f*, manière *f* d'emboucher (une flûte, etc.).

lip-read ['lipriːd], *v.i.* (*of the deaf*) lire sur les lèvres; interpréter les mots parlés d'après le mouvement des lèvres.

lipreading ['lipriːdiŋ], *s.* lecture *f* sur les lèvres; lecture labiale.

lipsalve ['lipsælv, -sɑːv], *s.* **1.** pommade *f* pour les lèvres. **2.** *F: A:* flagornerie *f*; pommade.

lipstick ['lipstik], *s.* rouge *m*, crayon *m*, à lèvres; crayon-lèvres *m*, *pl.* crayons-lèvres; **pink l.,** rouge à lèvres rose; **I'll just put on a bit of l.,** je vais mettre un peu de rouge aux lèvres.

lipuria [li'pjuːriə], *s. Med:* lipurie *f*.

liquate ['laikweit], *v. Metall:* **1.** *v.tr.* liquater (le cuivre et le plomb, etc.). **2.** *v.i. & tr.* **to l. out,** séparer (le plomb, etc.) par liquation; (*of tin, etc.*) se séparer par liquation.

liquation [li'kweiʃ(ə)n], *s. Metall:* liquation *f*.

liquefacient [likwi'feiʃənt], *s.* liquéfiant *m*.

liquefaction [likwi'fækʃ(ə)n], *s.* liquéfaction *f*.

liquefactive [likwi'fæktiv], *a.* liquéfiant.

liquefiable [likwi'faiəbl], *a.* liquéfiable.

liquefy ['likwifai]. **1.** *v.tr.* (*a*) liquéfier (un gaz, etc.); (*b*) *Ling:* mouiller (une consonne). **2.** *v.i.* (*a*) (*of gas, etc.*) se liquéfier; se fluidifier; (*b*) (*of oil, etc.*) se défiger.

liquescence [li'kwes(ə)ns], *s. Ch:* liquescence *f*.

liquescent [li'kwes(ə)nt], *a.* liquescent.

liqueur¹ [liː'kəːr, li'kjuər], *s.* (*a*) liqueur *f* (de dessert); **l. glass,** verre *m* à liqueur; **l. wine,** vin *m* de liqueur; **l. brandy** = fine champagne; *F:* fine *f*; **l. chocolates,** bonbons *mpl* à la liqueur; (*b*) *Wine-m:* liqueur (pour doser le champagne); liqueur d'expédition.

liqueur², *v.tr. Wine-m:* doser (le champagne).

liquid ['likwid], *a. & s.* **1.** *a.* (*a*) liquide, liquidien; **to reduce sth. to a l. state,** liquéfier qch.; *Ph:* **l. air,** air *m* liquide; **l. fire,** (i) *Mil: O:* pétrole enflammé; (ii) (*raw spirit*) tord-boyaux *m inv*; **l. pitch,** poix *f* liquide; **l. fuel,** combustible *m* liquide; (*b*) (air, œil, etc.) limpide, clair, transparent; (*c*) (son) doux, harmonieux, clair; (*d*) *O:* élastique, changeant, inconsistant; (*e*) *Fin:* (argent *m*) liquide, disponible; **l. assets,** valeurs *f* disponibles; actif *m* liquide; disponible *m*; disponibilités *fpl*; **l. debt,** dette liquide, dette claire; (*f*) *Ling:* (consonne *f*) liquide. **2.** *s.* (*a*) liquide *m*; **l. measure,** mesure *f* de capacité pour les liquides; (*b*) **l.-cooling,** refroidissement *m* par liquide; **l.-cooled engine,** moteur *m* à refroidissement par liquide; **freezing, refrigerating, l.,** liquide réfrigérant; (*c*) *Ch:* **mother l.,** liqueur-mère *f*, *pl.* liqueurs-mères; (*d*) *Ling:* (consonne) liquide *f*.

liquidambar [likwid'æmbər], *s. Bot:* liquidambar *m*; copalme *m*.

liquidate ['likwideit], *v.* **1.** *v.tr.* (*a*) liquider (une société, une dette); amortir (une dette); mobiliser (des capitaux); (*b*) *F:* **to l. s.o.,** liquider qn. **2.** *v.i.* entrer en liquidation; liquider.

liquidation [likwi'deiʃ(ə)n], *s.* liquidation *f* (d'une société, d'une dette); amortissement *m* (d'une dette); mobilisation *f* (de capitaux); (*of company*) **to go into l.,** entrer en liquidation; **compulsory, voluntary, l.,** liquidation forcée, volontaire; **l. subject to supervision of court,** liquidation judiciaire.

liquidator ['likwideitər], *s.* liquidateur, -trice (d'une société en liquidation).

liquidity [li'kwiditi], *s.* **1.** liquidité *f*. **2.** *Fin:* liquidité (d'une dette); **l. ratio,** coefficient *m*, taux *m*, de liquidité; **l. preference,** préférence *f* pour la liquidité.

liquidize ['likwidaiz], *v.tr.* liquéfier.

liquidizer ['likwidaizər], *s. Dom.Ec:* mixe(u)r *m*.

liquidometer [likwi'dɔmitər], *s.* liquidomètre *m*; jauge *f* à liquide.

liquor¹ ['likər], *s.* **1.** (*a*) boisson *f* alcoolique; **fermented liquors,** boissons fermentées; **to be the worse for l.,** être ivre; être pris de boisson; (*b*) *esp. NAm:* (*gin, whisky, etc.*) alcool *m*; *Can:* **the L. Commission** = la Régie des Alcools. **2.** *Tchn:* (*a*) *Leath:* **tan(ning) l.,** jusée *f*; **dyeing l.,** jusée colorante; (*b*) *Tex:* liqueur *f*; (*c*) *Brew:* eau *f*; (*d*) *Gasm:* **gas l.,** eau ammoniacale. **3.** *Cu:* (i) *O:* jus *m* (d'un rôti); bouillon *m*; graisse *f* de friture; (ii) eau (des huîtres) **4.** (*a*) *Ch: Pharm:* solution *f*, liqueur; **mother l.,** liqueur-mère *f*, *pl.* liqueurs-mères; (*b*) *Physiol:* liqueur; **l. amnii** ['laikwɔːr'æmniai] liqueur amniotique.

liquor², *v.tr.* (*a*) *A:* graisser (le cuir, les bottes); (*b*) *Brew:* mélanger (le malt) avec l'eau; (*c*) *F:* **to l. s.o. (up),** enivrer qn.

liquorice ['likəris], *s.* **1.** *Bot:* réglisse *f*; **Indian l.,** abrus *m* à chapelet; liane *f* réglisse. **2.** *Comest:* (bâton *m*, bonbon *m* de) réglisse; *Pharm:* **(extract of) l.,** pâte *f* de réglisse.

lira, *pl.* **lire, liras** ['liərə, 'liəri, 'liərəz], *s. Num:* lire *f.*

liriodendron [liriou'dendrən], *s. Bot:* liriodendron *m*; tulipier *m.*

Lisbon ['lizbən], *Pr.n. Geog:* Lisbonne *f.*

liskeardite [li'skɑːdait], *s. Miner:* liskéardite *f.*

lisle [lail], *a. & s. Tex:* **l. (thread),** fil *m* d'Écosse; **l. stockings,** bas *m* de fil.

lisp¹ [lisp], *s.* **1.** zézaiement *m*, susseyement *m*, blèsement *m*, chuintement *m*; (*of baby*) bégaiement *m*; **to have a l., to speak with a l.,** zézayer, susseyer, bléser, chuinter; parler d'une voix zézayante; (*of baby*) bégayer. **2.** *Lit:* bruissement *m*, murmure *m* (des feuilles, d'un ruisseau).

lisp², *v.i. & tr.* zézayer, susseyer, bléser; être blèse; chuinter; (*of baby*) bégayer; **to l. sth. (out),** dire qch. en zézayant.

lisper ['lispər], *s.* personne *f* blèse, qui zézaie.

lisping¹ ['lispiŋ], *a.* blèse, zézayant; (*of baby*) bégayant.

lisping², *s.* zézaiement *m*, blésité *f*, susseyement *m*, chuintement *m*; (*of baby*) bégaiement *m.*

lispingly ['lispiŋli], *adv.* en zézayant; comme un petit enfant.

lissom ['lisəm], *a.* souple, agile, leste.

lissomness ['lisəmnis], *s.* souplesse *f* (de taille).

lissotrichous [li'sɔtrikəs], *a. Anthr:* lissotriche, lissotrique.

list¹ [list], *s.* **1.** *Tex:* (*a*) lisière *f*; **coloured end l.,** entre-bande *f*, *pl.* entre-bandes; (*b*) *A:* **to line the edges of a door with l.,** calfeutrer une porte avec des lisières; mettre des bourrelets à une porte; **l. slippers,** chaussons *m* de lisière. **2.** *pl. A:* **lists,** lice *f*; champ clos; **to enter the lists (against s.o.),** entrer en lice (contre qn); se mettre sur les rangs; descendre dans l'arène *f.*

list², *v.tr. A:* calfeutrer (une porte); garnir (une porte) de lisières, de bourrelets.

list³, *s.* (*a*) liste *f*; *Adm: etc:* bordereau *m*; **alphabetical l.,** liste par ordre alphabétique; répertoire *m* alphabétique; **l. of names,** liste nominative; état, contrôle, nominatif; **his name is on the l.,** son nom se trouve, est (porté), sur la liste; **shopping l.,** liste des achats; **wedding l.,** liste de mariage; **check l., control l.,** liste de contrôle, de vérification; (*in restaurant*) **wine l.,** carte *f* des vins; **l. of applicants, of applications,** (i) liste des candidats, des postulants; (ii) *Fin:* liste des souscripteurs (à un emprunt, etc.); *St.Exch:* **l. of quotations,** bulletin *m* de cours; **official l.,** bulletin de la cote, cote officielle; **attendance l.,** liste, feuille *f*, de présence; **callover, absence, l.,** *Nau:* **muster l.,** liste d'appel; **the Army, Navy, Air Force, L.,** l'annuaire de l'armée de terre, de la Marine, de l'Aéronautique; **to remove s.o. from the Army L.,** rayer qn de la liste de l'armée (de terre); **on the detached l.,** hors cadres; *Mil: etc:* **casualty l.,** état *m* des pertes; *Nau:* **crew l.,** rôle *m* d'équipage; *Nau:* **l. of sailings,** tableau *m* des départs (des navires); tableau de marche; *Adm:* **civil l.,** liste civile; **free l.,** (i) *Cust:* liste des marchandises importées en franchise; (ii) *Th:* liste des personnes à qui l'entrée est gratuite; (*in hospital*) **danger l.,** liste des grands malades; **to be on the danger l.,** être gravement malade, dans un état grave; *Turf: F:* (*of geldings in training*) **horse added to the l.,** cheval *m* hongre; *Cmptr:* **assembly l.,** liste d'assemblage; **pop-up, push-up, l.,** liste directe; **push-down l.,** liste refoulée; *Bank: etc:* **l. of investments,** (bordereau *m* de) portefeuille *m*; **l. of bills for collection, for discount,** bordereau d'effets à l'encaissement, à l'escompte; bordereau d'encaissement, d'escompte; **to make out, draw up, a l.,** établir, dresser, une liste; **to make out a l. of one's assets, of one's liabilities, of one's investments,** faire l'inventaire *m* de son actif, de son passif, de son portefeuille; **to enter (sth.) on a l.,** porter (qch.) sur une liste; **to strike (a name) off a l.,** rayer (un nom) d'une liste; (*b*) *Com:* catalogue *m*; **mailing l.,** liste d'envoi; liste des abonnés; **l. on application,** catalogue sur demande; **price l.,** prix-courant *m*, *pl.* prix-courants; tarif *m*; **publisher's monthly l.,** bulletin mensuel d'une maison d'édition; **market price l.,** mercuriale *f.*

list⁴. **1.** *v.tr.* (*a*) inscrire, mettre, porter, (des noms, etc.) sur une liste; enregistrer (qch.); inventorier (des marchandises, etc.); *Fin:* **listed securities, stock,** valeurs admises, inscrites, à la cote (officielle); **these articles are listed in the catalogue,** ces articles figurent dans le catalogue; (*b*) *Cmptr:* lister (sur imprimante, etc.). **2.** *v.i. Mil: F: A:* (*of soldier*) s'engager, s'enrôler.

list⁵, *s. Nau:* faux bord; bande *f*, gîte *f*; **to have, take, a l.,** donner de la bande; avoir un faux bord; prendre de la gîte; pencher sur le côté; **l. to starboard,** gîte à tribord.

list⁶, *v.i. Nau:* donner de la bande (**to starboard,** à tribord); avoir un faux bord; prendre de la gîte; incliner; gîter; **the ship is listing,** le navire penche sur le côté; **to l. heavily,** donner fortement de la bande.

list⁷, *v.tr. A:* (*3rd pers. sg., pr.t.* **l.** *or* **listeth;** *p.t.* **l.** *or* **listed**) (*a*) *impers.* plaire; sembler bon; **he shall do what him listeth,** il fera comme bon lui semblera; **he did as him l.,** il a fait comme il lui a plu; (*b*) **ye who l. to hear,** vous qui voulez entendre; **the wind bloweth where it listeth,** le vent souffle où cela lui plaît.

list⁸, *v. A:* écouter.

listel ['list(ə)l], *s. Arch:* listel *m*, *pl.* -eaux.

listen¹ ['lisn], *s.* **to be on the l.,** être aux écoutes; tendre l'oreille; être tout oreilles.

listen², *v.ind.tr.* **1.** écouter; **to l. to s.o., to sth.,** écouter qn, qch.; **to l. attentively to s.o.,** prêter une oreille attentive à qn; **to l. with both ears,** écouter de toutes ses oreilles; **to l. with half an ear,** n'écouter que d'une oreille; **to l. to s.o. singing,** écouter chanter qn; **to l. for a footstep,** écouter, tendre l'oreille, pour entendre un pas; **l.! here's an idea,** écoutez donc, j'ai une idée. **2.** faire attention; écouter; **if people listened to me,** si on m'écoutait; **he wouldn't l. (to us),** il n'a rien voulu savoir; il a refusé de nous entendre; **you've been listening to tales,** vous vous êtes laissé raconter des histoires; **to l. to a few home truths,** empocher quelques bonnes vérités. **3.** *W.Tel:* **to l. in,** écouter la radio; **to l. (in) to the news,** écouter les informations; *Tp:* **to l. in to other people's conversations,** écouter les conversations d'autrui.

listener ['lisnər], *s.* (*a*) (i) auditeur, -trice; (ii) (*usu. Pej:*) écouteur, -euse; **he's a good l.,** il sait écouter; **he is more of a l. than a reader,** il écoute plus volontiers qu'il ne lit; *Prov:* **listeners never hear good of themselves,** qui écoute aux portes entend plus qu'il ne désire; (*b*) *Mil: Tp: etc:* écouteur; (*c*) *W.Tel:* **listener(-in),** auditeur.

listening ['lis(ə)niŋ], *s.* écoute *f*; *Mil: etc:* **l. apparatus,** appareil *m* d'écoute; écouteur *m*; *Mil: Tp: W.Tel:* **l. post, station,** poste *m*, station *f*, d'écoute; écoute *f*; (*in record shop*) **l. booth,** cabine *f* d'audition; *Mil:* **l. gallery,** galerie *f* d'écoute.

lister¹ ['listər], *s. Cmptr:* (imprimante *f*) listeuse *f.*

lister², *s. Agr:* buttoir *m.*

listing¹ ['listiŋ], *s.* **1.** *A:* calfeutrage *m*, calfeutrement *m* (d'une porte, etc.). **2.** *coll. Tex:* lisière *f.*

listing², *s.* (*a*) inscription *f*, mise *f*, sur une liste; (*b*) inscription, mise, au catalogue; catalogement *m*; (*c*) (*act of listing*) inventaire *m.*

listing³, *s. Nau:* bande *f*, gîte *f.*

listless ['listlis], *a.* **1.** nonchalant, indifférent, distrait; apathique, sans énergie. **2.** *A: & Lit:* **l. of sth.,** inattentif, indifférent, à qch.; **l. of the future, of praise,** indifférent à l'avenir, aux louanges.

listlessly ['listlisli], *adv.* nonchalamment; apathiquement; sans énergie.

listlessness ['listlisnis], *s.* nonchalance *f*, apathie *f*; indifférence *f.*

litany ['litəni], *s. Ecc:* litanies *fpl*; **l. of the Blessed Virgin,** litanies de la Sainte Vierge.

litchi ['liːtʃiː, 'lai-], *s. Bot:* litchi *m*, letchi *m.*

literacy ['litərəsi], *s.* fait *m* de savoir lire et écrire; (degré *m* d') aptitude *f* à lire et écrire; degré d'instruction; **l. campaign,** campagne *f* contre l'analphabétisme; **percentage of l.,** pourcentage *m* de gens qui savent lire et écrire.

literal ['litərəl], *a.* **1.** (*a*) littéral, -aux; **l. translation,** traduction littérale, mot à mot; (*b*) **in the l. sense of the word,** au sens propre du mot; **to take sth. in a l. sense,** prendre qch. à la lettre, au pied de la lettre; **to use a word in its l. sense,** employer un mot au propre; (*c*) (*of pers.*) terre à terre; prosaïque; positif; sans imagination. **2.** (*a*) *Mth:* (coefficient) littéral; **l. notation,** notation littérale; (*b*) *Typ:* **l. error,** *s.* **literal,** coquille *f.*

literalism ['litərəlizm], *s.* littéralisme *m.*

literalist ['litərəlist], *s.* **to be a l.,** prendre les choses à la lettre.

literalistic [litərə'listik], *a.* littéraliste.

literally ['litərəli], *adv.* littéralement; **to translate l.,** traduire littéralement, mot à mot; **to take an article l.,** interpréter un article à la lettre; **it is l. true,** cela est littéralement vrai; **he was l. blown to pieces by a shell,** il fut littéralement déchiqueté par un obus; **l. speaking,** à proprement parler; *Sp:* **in the hundred metres he l. flew down the track,** dans le cent mètres il a pour ainsi dire volé sur le terrain.

literal-minded ['litərəlmaindid], *a.* prosaïque; sans imagination.

literalness ['litərəlnis], *s.* littéralité *f.*

literary ['litərəri], *a.* littéraire; **l. work,** (i) travaux *mpl* littéraires; (ii) œuvre *f* littéraire; **l. agent,** agent *m* littéraire; **l. agency,** agence *f* littéraire; **l. property,** propriété *f* littéraire; **l. Greek,** le grec littéral, littéraire; **l. man,** homme *m* de lettres; littérateur *m*; **l. society,** société *f* littéraire.

literate ['litərət]. **1.** *a.* (*a*) qui sait lire et écrire; (*b*) lettré; *Sch: A:* **Lady L. in Arts,** diplôme octroyé aux femmes (après examen) par l'Université de St Andrews; (sorte de) Brevet supérieur (aboli vers 1930). **2.** *s. Ecc: A:* prêtre qui a été admis aux ordres sans grade universitaire.

literati [litə'rɑːtiː], *s.pl.* littérateurs *m*; hommes *m* de lettres.

literature ['litərətjər], *s.* **1.** littérature *f*; (*a*) la carrière des lettres; (*b*) œuvres *f* littéraires; **light l.,** lectures amusantes; livres amusants; (*c*) **the l. of a country,** la littérature d'un pays; **French l.,** la littérature française. **2.** (*a*) **the l. of a subject,** les écrits traitant d'un sujet; la bibliographie d'un sujet; (*b*) *Com: etc:* prospectus *mpl*, brochures *fpl*; **to distribute Communist l.,** distribuer des tracts *m* communistes; **l. sent free on request,** documentation envoyée gratuitement sur demande.

lith [liθ], *s.* loge *f* (d'orange).

litham [liː'θæm], *s. Cost:* litham *m.*

litharge [li'θɑːdʒ], *s. Ch: Ind:* litharge *f.*

lithe [laið], *a.* (*a*) (*of pers. or animal*) souple, agile; (*b*) **to make one's muscles l.,** s'assouplir les muscles.

litheness ['laiðnis], *s.* souplesse *f*; agilité *f* (de corps).

lithesome ['laiðsəm], *a.* souple, agile, leste.

lithia ['liθiə], *s.* **1.** *Ch:* lithine *f.* **2. l. (water),** eau lithinée.

lithiasis [li'θaiəsis], *s. Med:* lithiase *f*, lithiasie *f.*

lithium ['liθiəm], *s. Ch:* lithium *m*; **l. carbonate,** carbonate *m* de lithium; **l. hydride,** hydrure *m* de lithium.

litho- ['liθou, li'θɔ], *pref.* litho-.

litho¹ ['laiθou], *s. F:* (= LITHOGRAPHY) litho *f.*

litho², *attrib.* (= LITHOGRAPHIC) **l. chalk, l. crayon,** crayon *m* lithographique; **l. stone,** pierre *f* lithographique; **l. writing ink,** encre *f* d'écrivain litho; **flatbed l. machine,** machine *f* litho plate.

lithobius [li'θoubiəs], *s. Myr;* lithobie *f.*

lithochromatic [liθoukrou'mætik]. **1.** *a.* lithochromique. **2.** *s.pl.* (*usu. with sg. const.*) **lithochromatics,** la lithochromie.

lithodomus [li'θɔdəməs], *s. Moll:* lithodome *m.*

lithogenesis [liθou'dʒenisis], *s.* **1.** *Geol:* lithogénèse *f.* **2.** *Med:* lithogénie *f.*

lithogenous [li'θɔdʒənəs], *a. Geol: Med: Nat.Hist:* lithogène.

lithoglyptics [liθou'gliptiks], *s.pl.* (*usu. with sg. const.*) lithoglyphie *f.*

lithograph¹ ['liθəgræf], *s. Engr:* lithographie *f*; image lithographiée.

lithograph², *v.tr.* lithographier.

lithographer [li'θɔgrəfər], *s.* lithographe *m*; **l. draughtsman,** dessinateur *m* litho(graphe).

lithographic [liθə'græfik], *a.* lithographique; **l. printer,** imprimeur *m* lithographe, offsetiste *m.*

lithography [li'θɔgrəfi], *s.* lithographie *f*; procédés *m* lithographiques.

lithoid(al) [li'θɔid(l)], *a. Nat.Hist:* lithoïde.

lithological [liθə'lɔdʒikl], *a. Geol:* lithologique.

lithology [li'θɔlədʒi], *s. Geol: Med:* lithologie *f.*

lithop(a)edion [liθou'piːdiən], *s. Obst:* lithopédion *m.*

lithophaga [li'θɔfəgə], *s. Moll:* lithophage *m*, lithodome *m.*

lithophagous [li'θɔfəgəs], *a.* (mollusque) lithophage.

lithophane ['liθoufein], *s. Cer:* lithophanie *f.*

lithophilous [li'θɔfiləs], *a. Bot:* lithophile.

lithophysa [liθou'faizə], *s. Geol:* lithophyse *f.*

lithophyte ['liθoufait], *s. Coel:* lithophyte *m.*

lithopone ['liθoupoun], *s. Ind:* lithopone *m.*

lithosia [li'θousiə], *s. Ent:* lithosie *f.*

Lithosiidae [liθou'siːidiː], *s.pl. Ent:* lithosides *m.*

lithosis [li'θousis], *s. Med:* phtisie *f* des tailleurs de pierre; chalicose *f*, *F:* cailloute *f.*

lithosol ['liθousɔl], *s. Geol:* lithosol *m.*

lithospermum [liθou'spəːməm], *s. Bot:* lithospermum *m.*

lithosphere ['liθə'sfiər], *s. Geol:* lithosphère *f.*

lithothamnion [liθou'θæmniən], *s. Algae:* lithothamnion *m.*

lithotome ['liθoutoum], *s. Surg:* lithotome *m.*

lithotomy [li'θɔtəmi], *s. Surg:* lithotomie *f.*

lithotriptic [liθou'triptik], *a. & s.* lithotriptique (*m*).

lithotriptor [liθou'triptər], **lithotrite** ['liθoutrait], **lithotritor** ['liθoutraitər], *s. Surg:* lithotriteur *m.*

lithotrity [li'θɔtriti], *s. Surg:* lithotritie *f.*

lithotypy [li'θɔtipi], *s. Typ:* lithotypographie *f.*

Lithuania [liθju'einiə]. *Pr.n. Geog: Hist:* Lit(h)uanie *f.*

Lithuanian [liθju'einiən]. *Geog: Hist:* (*a*) *a.* lit(h)uanien; **the L. Soviet Socialist Republic,** la République socialiste soviétique de Lit(h)uanie; (*b*) *s.* Lit(h)uanien, -ienne.

litigant ['litigənt]. *Jur:* **1.** *a.* **l. parties,** parties plaidantes, en litige. **2.** *s.* plaideur, -euse.

litigate ['litigeit]. **1.** *v.i.* plaider; être en procès. **2.** *v.tr.* contester (une question); mettre (une question, une propriété) en litige.

litigation [liti'geiʃ(ə)n], *s. Jur:* litige *m*; procès *mpl*; **in l.,** en litige.

litigious [li'tidʒəs], *a.* **1.** (point, cas) litigieux, contentieux. **2.** (homme) litigieux, processif, procédurier; (homme) à procès.

litigiously [li'tidʒəsli], *adv.* (*a*) contentieusement; (*b*) par pure chicane.

litigiousness [li'tidʒəsnis], *s.* esprit litigieux; esprit de chicane; humeur processive.

litmus ['litməs], *s. Dy: Ch:* tournesol *m*; **l. paper,** papier *m* (de) tournesol; **l. solution,** teinture *f* de tournesol.

litotes ['laitouti:z], *s. Rh:* litote *f.*

litre[1] ['li:tər], *s. Meas:* litre *m.*

litre[2] ['laitər], *s. Her:* litre *f*; ceinture *f* de deuil.

litter[1] ['litər], *s.* **1.** (*a*) *Veh:* litière *f*; **to be carried in a l.,** être porté en litière; (*b*) civière *f* (pour le transport des blessés). **2.** (*a*) *Agr: Hort: Husb:* litière (de paille, etc.); **to change the horses' l.,** renouveler la litière des chevaux; **peat l.,** poussier *m* de mottes; (*b*) fumier *m* (d'écurie, etc.). **3.** (*a*) immondices *fpl,* détritus *m*; papiers *m* et objets *m* malpropres (qui jonchent les rues, etc.); papiers gras; (*in street, etc.*) **l. bin,** boîte *f* à ordures; (*b*) fouillis *m,* désordre *m*; **to make a l.,** mettre tout en désordre, mettre tout sens dessus dessous; **l. of useless knowledge,** fatras *m* de connaissances. **4.** portée *f,* ventrée *f,* mise *f* bas (d'un animal); (*of pigs*) cochonnée *f*; (*of pups*) chiennée *f*; (*of kittens*) chattée *f*; **five young at a l., in one l.,** cinq petits d'une portée.

litter[2], *v.tr. & i.* **1.** *v.tr.* (*a*) **to l. (down) a horse,** faire la litière à un cheval; (*b*) **to l. (down) a stable,** étendre de la paille dans une écurie; (*c*) *Hort:* empailler (des plantes). **2.** (*a*) *v.tr.* mettre en désordre (une chambre, etc.); **to l. papers about, over, the floor,** éparpiller des papiers sur le plancher; joncher le plancher de papiers; **room littered with books,** pièce *f* où des livres traînent partout; **table littered with papers,** table encombrée, jonchée, de papiers; (*b*) *v.i. esp. NAm: P.N:* **please do not l.,** défense de jeter des ordures. **3.** *v.i.* (*of animal*) mettre bas, avoir une portée.

litterbug ['litəbʌg], **litterlout** ['litəlaut], *s. F:* personne qui laisse traîner des ordures.

littermates ['litəmeits], *s.pl.* petits *m* d'une même portée.

little ['litl], *a., s. & adv.*

I. *a.* (*for comp. and sup.* **less, least, smaller, smallest,** *q.v., are used; there is also a F: form* **littler, littlest.**) **1.** petit; **l. boy,** petit garçon; garçonnet *m*; **l. girl,** petite fille; fillette *f*; **l. ones,** (i) enfants *m, F:* mioches *m*; (ii) petits *m* (d'un animal); **l. David,** le petit David; **poor l. girl!** pauvre petite! *F:* **the littlest one,** le bébé de la famille; **the l. people,** les fées *f*; *F:* **a tiny l. house,** une toute petite maison; **wait a l. while!** attendez un petit moment! **for so l. a matter,** pour une chose si insignifiante; **the littlest things of daily life,** les choses les plus insignifiantes de la vie quotidienne; *Prov:* **l. and good,** dans les petits pots les bons onguents; **the l. finger,** le petit doigt; *Astr:* **the L. Bear,** la petite Ourse; *Orn:* **the l. grebe,** le petit grèbe. **2.** peu (de); **l. money,** peu d'argent; **a l. money,** un peu d'argent; **she knows a l. music,** elle sait quelque peu de musique; **to gain l. advantage from sth.,** ne tirer que peu d'avantage de qch.; **they get l. if any, l. or no, salary,** ils ne reçoivent que peu ou point de traitement; *F:* **ever so l.,** un tout petit peu (de), un tantinet (de); **be it ever so l.,** si peu que ce soit. **3.** mesquin; **a l. mind,** un petit esprit.

II. *s.* (*comp. and sup.* **less, least**) **1.** peu *m*; **to eat l. or nothing,** manger peu ou point; **he eats very l.,** il ne mange pas grand-chose; **he knows very l.,** il sait peu de chose; il ne sait pas grand-chose; **he has done l. for us,** il a peu fait pour nous; **I had l. to do with it,** j'y ai été pour peu de chose; **I got very l. out of it,** je n'en ai tiré que très peu, que peu de chose; **I see very l., of him,** je ne le vois guère; (*of scheme, etc.*) **to come to l.,** aboutir à pas grand-chose; **the l. I know,** le peu que je sais; **he did what l. he could,** il a fait le peu qu'il pouvait; **you are welcome to what l. there is,** le peu qu'il y a est à votre disposition; **to think l. of s.o.,** tenir qn en médiocre estime; **to make, think, l. of sth.,** faire peu de cas de qch.; **he makes l. of physical pain,** il fait bon marché de la douleur physique; **he thinks very l. of a ten kilometre walk,** pour lui ce n'est pas une grande affaire de faire dix kilomètres à pied; *adv.phr.* **l. by l.,** petit à petit; peu à peu; **l. by l. she told me everything,** brin à brin, de fil en aiguille, elle m'a tout raconté; *Prov:* **every l. helps,** (i) tout fait nombre; un peu d'aide fait grand bien; les petits ruisseaux font les grandes rivières; (ii) il n'y a pas de petites économies; (iii) on fait feu de tout bois. **2.** (*a*) **he knows a l. of everything,** il sait un peu de tout; **a l. more,** encore un peu; **a l. more and he would have been killed,** peu s'en fallut qu'il ne fût tué; *F:* un peu plus il était tué; **a l. makes us laugh,** un rien nous fait rire; **for a l.,** pendant un certain temps; pendant quelques instants; **after, in, a l.,** au bout de quelque temps; après un certain temps; dans un instant; (*b*) (*used adverbially*) **he helped him a l., not a l.,** il l'a aidé un peu, il l'a beaucoup aidé; **I was a l. afraid,** j'avais un peu peur; **as soon as one is a l. known,** dès qu'on est tant soit peu connu; **wait a l.!** attendez un peu! attendez un petit moment! *Nau:* **starboard a l.!** à droite doucement!

III. *adv.* (*comp. and sup.* **less, least**) peu; **l. known,** peu connu; **he is l. richer than he was,** il n'est guère plus riche qu'il n'était; **l. more than an hour ago,** il n'y a guère qu'une heure; **do you see him?—very l.,** le voyez-vous?—guère; très peu; **he l. knows . . ., thinks . . ., suspects . . .,** il ne sait guère . . ., il ne pense guère . . ., il ne se doute guère . . ..

little-go ['litlgou], *s. Sch: F: A:* premier examen d'admissibilité au grade de B.A. (à l'Université de Cambridge).

littleness ['litlnis], *s.* **1.** petitesse *f*; petite taille (de qn, etc.). **2.** mesquinerie *f,* petitesse.

littoral ['litərəl]. **1.** *a.* littoral, -aux; du littoral. **2.** *s.* littoral *m.*

littorina [litə'rainə], *s. Moll:* littorine *f.*

liturgic(al) [li'tə:dʒik(l)], *a.* liturgique.

liturgist ['litədʒist], *a.* liturgiste *m.*

liturgy ['litədʒi], *s.* liturgie *f.*

livable ['livəbl], *a.* = LIVEABLE.

live[1] [laiv], *a.* **1.** (*a*) vivant; en vie; **l. weight,** poids vif, vivant (d'un animal de boucherie); *F:* **a real l. burglar,** un cambrioleur en chair et en os; *Fish:* **l. bait,** amorce vive; **to fish with l. bait,** pêcher au vif; **l. box,** boutique *f*; **l. birth,** naissance *f,* mise *f* au monde, accouchement *m,* d'un enfant vivant; *Vet:* naissance, mise bas, parturition *f,* d'un petit vivant; **l. born,** né vivant; *Ich: Rept:* **l.-bearing,** vivipare; *Bot: U.S:* **l. oak,** chêne vert; (*b*) *T.V: W.Tel:* **l. broadcast,** émission *f* en direct; **l. pickup,** prise *f* de vues en direct; (*as distinct from film, etc.*) **l. show,** spectacle *m* sur une scène de théâtre; (*c*) (récit) vivant; (homme) plein de vie; **a thoroughly l. play,** une pièce pleine de vie; (*d*) **l. question,** question *f* d'actualité; (*e*) **l. coals,** charbons ardents; **l. rock,** roc vif; (*f*) *Fin:* **l. claims,** créances *f* valables, qui subsistent (à l'égard d'un établissement de crédit). **2.** (*a*) *Mil:* **l. ammunition,** (i) munitions actives; (ii) munitions de guerre; **l. bomb,** bombe active, amorcée, armée; **l. cartridge,** cartouche *f* à balle, cartouche réelle; (*b*) *El:* (*of cable, line, etc.*) sous tension, chargé, en charge; **l. circuit,** circuit *m* sous tension; **l. conductor,** conducteur *m* en charge; **l. resistance, l. resistor,** résistance *f* sous tension; **l. wire,** câble *m,* fil *m,* sous tension, en charge, chargé, électrisé; *F:* **he's a (real) l. wire,** il est énergique; il a de l'allant; il va toujours de l'avant; il est très entreprenant; c'est un brasseur d'affaires; **the l. wire of the business,** l'âme, l'animateur, la cheville ouvrière, de l'affaire; (*c*) *Mch:* **l. steam,** vapeur vive, fraîche, vierge. **3.** (*a*) *Tchn:* **l. load,** charge roulante, charge mobile, poids roulant; **l. weight,** charge utile; (*b*) *Mec.E:* **l. axle,** essieu moteur; *Mch.Tls:* **l. head (of lathe),** poupée *f* fixe.

live[2] [liv], *v.*

I. *v.tr. & i.* **1.** *v.i.* vivre; (*a*) (*be alive*) **is he still living?** vit-il encore? **while my father lives, lived,** du vivant de mon père; **long l. the king!** vive le roi! **he hasn't long to l.,** il n'en a plus pour longtemps à vivre; **he hasn't a year to l.,** il n'en a pas pour un an; **he will l. to be a hundred,** il atteindra la centaine; **I shall never l. to see it,** je ne vivrai pas assez longtemps pour voir cela; **as long, so long, as I l.,** tant que je vivrai; **he'll be a fool as long as he lives,** il mourra dans la peau d'un imbécile; **he won't l. through the winter,** il ne passera pas l'hiver; (*of ship, etc.*) **to l. through a storm,** survivre à une tempête; **he lived through all these events,** il a été spectateur de tous ces événements; *O:* **as I l.!** sur ma vie! *Prov:* **l. and learn,** (i) on apprend à tout âge; (ii) qui vivra verra; **l. and let l.,** il faut que tout le monde vive; il faut laisser chacun manger avec sa cuiller; (*b*) durer; **his name will l.,** son nom vivra, durera, sera immortalisé; (*c*) (*subsist*) **to l. on vegetables,** vivre de légumes, se nourrir de légumes; **to l. on hope,** vivre d'espérance; **to l. on charity,** vivre d'aumônes; **he earns enough to l. on,** il gagne de quoi vivre; **to l. on £200 a month,** vivre avec £200 par mois; **this will be enough for us to l. on,** cela nous suffira pour vivre; **to l. on one's relations,** (i) vivre aux crochets de ses parents; (ii) se débrouiller grâce à des amis bien placés; **to l. on one's capital,** vivre sur son capital; **to l. on one's reputation,** vivre sur, de, sa réputation; **to l. by one's work,** vivre de son travail; gagner sa vie à travailler; **he lives by his pen,** il vit de sa plume; sa plume est son gagne-pain; **a man must l.!** il faut bien que je gagne ma vie! il faut bien vivre! *Prov:* **man lives by hope,** l'espérance fait vivre (l'homme); (*d*) (*pass life*) **to l. honestly, like a saint,** vivre honnêtement; vivre en saint; **to l. in style,** mener grand train; **to l. riotously,** faire la vie, faire la noce; mener une vie de bâton de chaise; **at the rate at which they l. they will soon be ruined,** au train dont ils vivent ils seront bientôt ruinés; **to l. well,** faire bonne chère; ne rien se refuser; **to l. up to one's principles,** vivre conformément à ses principes, selon ses principes; conformer sa vie à ses principes; **to l. up to one's income,** (i) mener un train de vie en rapport avec sa fortune; (ii) dépenser tout son revenu, tout ce qu'on gagne; **to l. up to one's reputation,** faire honneur à sa réputation; **to l. up to one's promise,** remplir sa promesse; *Prov:* **as we l., so shall we end,** telle vie telle fin; (*e*) (*reside*) **to l. in Paris,** habiter, demeurer à, Paris; **to l. in the country,** demeurer, habiter, à la campagne; **where do you l.?** où est-ce que vous habitez? **I live at 10 St Martin's Square,** j'habite au 10 place Saint-Martin; **to l. on the fifth floor,** habiter, demeurer, loger, au cinquième, *NAm:* au sixième; **did you l. there long?** y êtes-vous resté longtemps? est-ce que vous y avez habité longtemps? **the house we used to l. in,** notre ancienne maison; la maison où nous avons habité, demeuré, vécu, autrefois; **this house isn't fit to l. in,** cette maison est inhabitable, n'est pas habitable; **the house doesn't seem to be lived in,** la maison ne paraît pas habitée; (*f*) **to l. with s.o.,** vivre, habiter, avec qn; **he is living with his grandparents,** il habite chez ses grands-parents; **to l. happily with s.o.,** mener une vie heureuse, faire bon ménage, avec qn; (*g*) (*cohabit*) **she is living with him, they l. together,** ils vivent ensemble; font ménage à deux; *F:* elle s'est collée avec lui. **2.** *v.tr.* (*a*) (*with cogn. acc.*) **to l. a happy life,** mener, passer, une vie heureuse; **is life worth living?** cela vaut-il la peine de vivre? **once more life seemed worth living,** de nouveau la vie lui semblait bonne; (*b*) **to l. a lie,** vivre dans un perpétuel mensonge; **the author seemed (to me) to have lived his story,** il me semblait que l'auteur avait vécu ce qu'il a raconté; *Th:* **to l. a part,** entrer dans la peau d'un personnage; (*c*) *F:* **to l. it up,** faire la noce; mener une vie de bâton de chaise.

II. (*compound verbs*) **1. live down,** *v.tr.* **to l. down a scandal, one's past,** faire oublier un scandale à la longue; faire oublier son passé; **it took him a long time to l. it down,** on ne l'a pas oublié si tôt.

2. live in, *v.i.* (*of servants*) coucher à la maison; *O:* (*of shop assistants*) loger dans l'établissement même, dans les locaux affectés au commerce; **the employees l. in,** les employés sont logés et nourris.

3. live out, *v.i.* (*of servant*) coucher à son domicile; venir en journée; *O:* (*of shop assistants*) loger hors de l'établissement.

liveable ['livəbl], *a.* **1.** (*of house, room*) habitable, logeable. **2.** (*of life*) tenable, supportable. **3.** (*of pers.*) **l. (with),** accommodant, sociable; avec qui on peut vivre.

live-forever ['livfə'revər], *s. NAm: Bot:* grand orpin, orpin reprise.

livelihood ['laivlihud], *s.* vie *f*; moyens *mpl* d'existence; gagne-pain *m inv*; **to earn, gain, get, make, a l.,** gagner sa vie, son pain; gagner de quoi vivre; **to deprive s.o. of his l.,** enlever à qn son gagne-pain, *F:* lui ôter le pain de la main, de la bouche.

liveliness ['laivlinis], *s.* vivacité *f,* animation *f,* entrain *m,* vie *f*; *Fin:* animation (du marché).

livelong[1] ['livlɔŋ], *a. Lit:* **the l. day, night,** toute la (sainte) journée; toute le long du jour; toute la nuit.

livelong[2], *s. Bot:* grand orpin, orpin reprise; *F:* herbe *f* aux charpentiers, herbe à la coupure.

lively ['laivli], *a.* **1.** *A:* (portrait) vivant. **2.** (*a*) vif, animé; plein d'entrain; **l. imagination,** imagination vive; **l. description, conversation,** description, conversation, animée, pleine de vie; **l. scene,** scène animée, pleine de vie; **l. music,** musique allante, égayante, entraînante, pleine d'entrain; *Nau:* **l. breeze,** jolie brise; (*b*) *F:* **to make it, things, l. for s.o.,** rendre la vie dure à qn; embêter qn; **things are getting l.,** ça chauffe; **to have a lively time of it,** (i) avoir fort à faire; (ii) en voir de toutes les couleurs; (*c*) **l. satisfaction,** vive satisfaction; **to feel a l. pleasure,** éprouver un vif plaisir; **to take a l. interest in sth.,** s'intéresser vivement à qch.; (*d*) *Ch:* **l. reaction,** réaction active, énergique; **a more l. combustion,** une combustion plus active. **3.** (*of colour*) vif. **4.** (*of pers.*) gai, joyeux, enjoué; guilleret, -ette; **as l. as a cricket,** gai comme un pinson; *F:* **she's a l. one,** c'est une dégourdie. **5.** *Nau:* (canot) léger sur l'eau, vif. **6.** *Sp:* (*of cricket pitch, tennis court, etc.*) vite à rebondir.

liven ['laiv(ə)n]. **1.** *v.tr.* **to l. (up),** animer, égayer (qn, une réunion, etc.); activer, *F:* chauffer (une affaire); *Th:* mouvementer (l'action); **to l. up the conversation,** ranimer la conversation; donner plus d'entrain à la conversation; **in order to l. up the company,** pour mettre tout le monde en train. **2.** *v.i.* **to l. up,** s'animer, s'activer; *F:* s'échauffer.

liveness ['laivnis], *s.* animation *f.*

liver[1] ['livər], *s.* **1.** *(a) Anat:* foie *m*; **l. disease, complaint,** maladie *f* de foie; **l. fluke,** douve *f* du foie; *Vet:* **l. rot,** pourriture *f* du foie; *Cu:* **calf's l.,** foie de veau; **l. pâté,** pâté *m* de foie; *(b) a.* **l. and white spaniel,** épagneul *m* foie et blanc *inv.* **2.** *Ch:* **l. of antimony, of sulphur,** foie d'antimoine, de soufre.

liver[2], *s.* *(of pers.)* **good l.,** (i) homme rangé; (ii) amateur *m* de bonne chère; **fast l.,** viveur, -euse, noceur, -euse; **loose liver,** libertin *m*, dissolu *m*, débauché *m*.

liverberry ['livəberi], *s. Bot:* streptopus *m.*

liveried ['livərid], *a.* en livrée; **to be a l. servant,** porter la livrée.

liverish ['livəriʃ], *a. F:* qui a le foie dérangé; **to feel l.,** avoir une crise de foie; se sentir mal en train.

liverleaf ['livəli:f], *s. U.S: Bot:* hépatique trilobée; trinitaire *f*; herbe *f* à la Trinité.

Liverpudlian [livə'pʌdliən]. *Geog:* *(a) a.* de Liverpool; *(b) s.* Liverpoolien, -ienne.

liverwort ['livəwə:t], *s. Bot:* **1.** hépatique trilobée; trinitaire *f*; herbe *f* à la Trinité. **2. stone l.,** hépatique terrestre, des fontaines.

livery[1] ['livəri], *s.* **1.** *(a)* livrée *f*; **full l.,** grande livrée; **in l.,** en livrée; **out of l.,** sans livrée; **l. servant,** domestique *m* en livrée; *Lit:* **the l. of spring,** la livrée du printemps; *(b) coll. A:* **the l.,** la livrée; les domestiques; *(c)* **l. company,** corporation *f* d'un corps de métier (de la cité de Londres) (chaque corporation portait autrefois un uniforme distinctif); **to take up one's l.,** entrer dans une des *livery companies.* **2.** *(a) A:* pension *f* (pour chevaux); **to take, keep, horses at l.,** prendre, avoir, des chevaux en pension, à l'attache; *(b)* **l. horse,** cheval *m* de louage; **l. stables,** écuries *fpl* de chevaux de louage. **3.** *Jur:* *(a)* mise *f* en possession; *(of minor)* **to sue (for) one's l.,** réclamer ses biens à ses tuteurs; *(b)* émancipation *f* (d'un mineur); *(c)* **l. of seisin,** envoi *m* en possession; saisine *f.* **4.** *Furn: A:* **l. cupboard,** (i) armoire *f* à provisions; (ii) panetière *f.*

livery[2], *a.* **1.** (couleur de) foie *inv.* **2.** *(of soil)* gras. **3.** *F:* = LIVERISH.

liveryman, *pl.* **-men** ['livərimən], *s.m.* **1.** loueur de chevaux; remiseur. **2.** membre d'une des corporations de la cité de Londres.

livestock ['laivstɔk], *s. Husb:* bétail *m*, bestiaux *mpl*; animaux *mpl* sur pied; *Jur:* cheptel *m.*

liveware ['laivwɛər], *s. Cmptr:* personnel informaticien.

livid ['livid], *a.* (teint *m*) livide, blême; (ciel) plombé; **the l. tinge of death,** le bleu de la mort; **to be l. with anger,** *F:* **absolutely l.,** être blême de colère, dans une colère blanche; *F:* **it makes me l.!** ça me met en boule!

lividity [li'viditi], **lividness** ['lividnis], *s.* lividité *f.*

living[1] ['liviŋ], *a.* **1.** *(a)* vivant, vif; en vie; **a l. man,** un homme vivant; **while he was l.,** de son vivant; **l. or dead,** mort ou vif; **l. creatures,** êtres vivants; êtres animés; créatures vivantes; **there is not a l. soul to be seen,** on ne rencontre pas âme qui vive, *F:* pas un chat; **no l. man could do better,** personne au monde ne pourrait mieux faire; **he has done more for them than any man l.,** il a fait plus pour eux que n'importe qui; **the first among l. artists,** le premier des artistes contemporains; *s.* **the l.,** les vivants; **he's still in the land of the l.,** il est encore vivant, toujours vivant, encore en vie, encore de ce monde; **l. language,** langue vivante; **l. pictures,** tableaux vivants; *F:* **he's a l. skeleton,** c'est un squelette; **a l. death,** une vie pire que la mort; *(b)* **l. rock,** roc vif; **l. water,** eau vive; **l. force,** force vive; *(c) B:* **I am the l. bread,** je suis le pain vivant. **2.** *(with adj. prefixed, e.g.)* **clean-l.,** de vie réglée; de bonnes mœurs; **evil-l.,** de mœurs dissolues.

living[2], *s.* **1.** *(a)* vie *f*; **l. in the country,** la vie à la campagne; **style of l., rate of l.,** train *m* de vie; *Pol.Ec:* **standard of l.,** niveau *m* de vie; **cheap l.,** la vie à bon marché; **l. is dear here,** la vie est chère ici; il fait cher vivre ici; **to be fond of good l.,** aimer la bonne chère; aimer la table; **riotous l.,** la noce; **plain l. and high thinking,** une vie sobre et de hautes pensées; **l. space,** espace vital; *(b)* **l. in,** logement *m* (d'une bonne, etc.) chez l'employeur; **l. out,** logement hors de chez l'employeur; **l.-out allowance,** indemnité *f* de logement. **2.** *(livelihood)* **to earn one's l.,** gagner sa vie; **to work for one's l., for a l.,** travailler pour vivre, pour gagner sa vie; **to work hard for one's l.,** gagner laborieusement sa vie; **to beg for a l.,** mendier sa vie; **to write for a l.,** vivre de sa plume; **he gets a good l.—I won't say he earns it,** je ne dis pas qu'il mérite son salaire, mais il est très bien payé; **what does he do for a l.?** qu'est-ce qu'il fait? quel est son métier? **to make a l.,** gagner de quoi vivre; gagner sa vie; **he has always made his own l.,** il s'est toujours suffi; **he makes a l. out of it,** il en vit; **there's no l. to be had from poetry,** la poésie ne nourrit pas son homme; **l. wage,** minimum vital. **3.** *Ecc:* bénéfice *m*, cure *f*; **crown l.,** bénéfice à la nomination de la Couronne.

livingroom ['liviŋru:m], *s.* salle *f* de séjour; living-room *m*; *Fr.C:* vivoir *m.*

livingstonite ['liviŋstənait], *s. Miner:* livingstonite *f.*

Livonia [li'vouniə]. *Pr.n. Hist:* Livonie *f.*

Livonian [li'vouniən]. *Hist:* *(a) a.* livonien; *(b) s.* Livonien, -ienne.

Livy ['livi]. *Pr.n.m. Lt.Lit:* Tite-Live.

lixiviate [lik'sivieit], *v.tr.* lixivier, lessiver (la cendre de bois).

lixiviation [liksivi'eiʃ(ə)n], *s.* lixiviation *f*, lessivage *m* (des cendres de bois).

lixivium [lik'siviəm], *s.* lessive *f*; dissolution alcaline.

lizard ['lizəd], *s.* **1.** *Rept:* lézard *m*; **common l.,** lézard vivipare; **sand l.,** lézard des souches; **mangrove l.,** lézard de mangrove; **desert night l.,** lézard nocturne; **leaf-green spiny-tailed l.,** lézard épineux vert végétal; **(Australian) frilled l.,** lézard à collier (australien); **(Australian) bearded l., Jew l.,** lézard à barbe, lézard barbu (australien); **eyed l.,** lézard ocellé; **(Australian) pine-cone l.,** lézard pomme-de-pin; **fence l., pine l.,** lézard des palissades; scélopore *m*; **(North American) fence l.,** iguane *m* des haies; **lace l.,** faux iguane australien; **water l.,** agame *m* aquatique; **North American horned l.,** phrynosome *m*; **(oriental) flying l.,** dragon volant (oriental); **alligator l.,** lézard-caïman *m*, *pl.* lézards-caïmans; **grey l.,** margouillat *m*; **the Old World lizards,** les lacertidés *m.* **2.** *(a) Orn:* **l. cuckoo,** saurothère *m*; *(b) Moll:* **sea l.,** glaucus *m.* **3.** *Nau:* margouillet *m*, manchette *f.*

Lizzie, Lizzy ['lizi]. **1.** *Pr.n.f.* *(dim. of Elizabeth)* Lisette. **2.** *s. F: A:* **Tin Lizzie,** (i) auto *f* Ford; (ii) voiture *f* à bon marché; voiture de type économique; (iii) vieille Ford. **3.** *s. Bot: F:* **busy L.,** balsamine *f.*

llama ['lɑ:mə], *s. Z:* lama *m.*

llanero [l(j)æ'nɛərou], *s.* llanero *m.*

llano ['l(j)ɑ:nou], *s.* llano *m*, grande plaine (de l'Amérique du Sud).

lo [lou]. **1.** *int. A: & Lit:* voici, voilà, voyez, voilà que . . .; *Hum:* **lo and behold there he was,** et voilà qu'il était là. **2.** *s. U.S: F:* indien, -ienne; **Mr Lo,** monsieur le Peau-Rouge (facétie sur un vers de Pope: *Lo, the poor Indian . . .*).

loach [loutʃ], *s. Ich:* loche *f*; **common stone l.,** loche franche; *F:* petit barbot; barbotte *f*; **spined l.,** loche épineuse; loche.

load[1] [loud], *s.* **1.** *(a)* fardeau *m*; **to carry a l. on one's shoulders, on one's back,** porter un fardeau sur ses épaules, sur son dos; **to have a l. on one's mind,** être accablé de soucis; **you've taken a l. off my mind,** vous m'avez soulagé (l'esprit); **that's a l. off my mind!** quel soulagement! *(b)* charge *f*, chargement *m* (d'un camion, d'un navire, d'un avion, etc.); **full l.,** chargement complet; **prescribed l.,** chargement réglementaire; **l. (carrying) capacity,** charge utile; charge limite; **useful l.,** charge utile; **additional l.,** surcharge *f*; **commercial l., pay l.,** charge marchande, payante; **disposable l.,** charge disponible; **working l.,** charge de travail, charge pratique; **dead l.,** charge constante; **l. curve,** courbe *f* de charge; *Av: etc:* **balancing l.,** poids compensateur; **fuel l.,** poids du carburant, du combustible; **gross l.,** poids brut; *Av:* **l. factor,** coefficient *m* de charge; **flight l.,** charge en vol; **touchdown l.,** charge imposée à l'impact; *Nau:* **deck l.,** chargement sur le pont; (chargement en) pontée *f*; **l. displacement,** déplacement *m* en charge; **l. (water) line,** ligne *f* de charge, de flottaison en charge; *(c) (contents of vehicle)* camion *m*, tombereau *m* (de gravier, etc.); **I bought five loads of wood,** j'ai acheté cinq charges de bois; *F:* **it's a l. of rubbish, of nonsense,** c'est du bidon; *P:* **get a l. of that!** (i) écoute un peu ça! (ii) regarde ça! *(d) F:* **he's got loads of them,** il en a des quantités, des tas; **we've done it loads of times,** nous l'avons fait je ne sais combien de fois; **we've got loads of time,** nous en avons largement le temps. **2.** *(a) Mec: etc:* charge; **distribution of l.,** répartition *f* de la charge; **distributed l.,** charge répartie; **l. per unit,** taux *m* de charge; **maximum permissible l.,** charge maximum admissible; **safe l.,** charge de sécurité; **breaking l.,** charge de rupture; **torque l.,** couple *m* de serrage, de torsion; **torsional l.,** effort *m* de torsion; *Av:* **basic l.,** charge unitaire; **transverse l., wing l.,** charge alaire; *Av: etc:* **dynamic l.,** charge dynamique; *(b) Mch:* **operating l.,** charge de fonctionnement; **full l.,** pleine charge, pleine puissance; **machine working (at) full l.,** machine *f* qui fonctionne, qui travaille, à pleine charge; **under l.,** en charge; **to put the motor under l.,** mettre le moteur en charge; **starting under l.,** démarrage *m* en charge; **starting l.,** charge de démarrage; **charging l.,** régime *m* de charge; **machine at constant l.,** machine en régime permanent; **without l., zero l., no l.,** à vide, charge nulle; **machine running with, on, no l.,** machine qui marche à vide; *(c) El:* *(of circuit, line)* charge; **base l.,** charge minimum (d'un générateur); **normal, operating, l.,** charge normale; **ultimate l.,** charge limite; **peak l.,** charge maximum, de pointe; **balanced l.,** charge équilibrée; **rated l.,** charge de régime; **resistive l.,** charge résistante; **condenser l.,** charge capacitive; **anode l.,** charge d'anode; **inductive, inductance, l.,** charge inductive; **l. circuit,** circuit *m* de charge, d'utilisation; **l. current,** courant *m* de charge; **l. impedance,** impédance *f* de charge, d'utilisation; **l. resistor,** résistance *f* de charge; **l. curve,** courbe *f* de charge; **l. diagram, l. graph,** diagramme *m* de charge; **l. distribution, l. sharing,** répartition *f* de la charge; **l. dispatcher,** répartiteur *m* de charge; **l. regulator,** régulateur *m* de charge; **to shed the l.,** délester; **l. shedding,** délestage *m*; *(d) Atom.Ph:* charge (d'un réacteur); *(e) Cmptr:* charge, chargement (d'un ordinateur); **l. card,** carte *f* de chargement; **l. time,** moment *m* du chargement; **l. factor,** densité *f* d'occupation.

load[2]. **1.** *v.tr.* *(a)* charger (un camion, un navire, etc.); **to l. a cargo on to a ship,** charger une cargaison sur un navire; **to l. s.o. with sth., to l. sth. on to s.o.,** charger qn de qch.; *(of bus)* **to l. passengers,** prendre des voyageurs; **stomach loaded with food,** estomac chargé de nourriture; **to l. oneself up with luggage,** se charger de bagages; **to be loaded up with . . .,** être encombré de . . .; *St.Exch:* **to be loaded up with stock,** avoir en portefeuille plus de valeurs qu'on n'en peut écouler; *(b)* **to l. s.o. with favours, with praise,** combler qn de faveurs, de louanges; **to l. s.o. with abuse,** accabler qn d'injures; **loaded with cares,** accablé de soucis; *(c)* **to l. a gun,** charger un fusil (à balle); **my gun wasn't loaded,** mon fusil, mon revolver, n'était pas chargé; *Aut:* **to l. the grease gun,** armer le graisseur; *Phot:* **to l. a slide,** charger un châssis; *(d)* **to l. a spring,** serrer, bander, un ressort; *(e)* alcooliser (un vin); charger (le papier); *(f)* plomber (une canne); piper (des dés); *(g) Tp:* **to l. a line (with inductances),** pupiniser une ligne; *(h) Ins:* majorer (une prime). **2.** *v.i.* *(a) (of ship, etc.)* **to l. (up),** prendre charge; faire la cargaison; **loading for Bombay,** en charge pour Bombay; **ship loading,** navire *m* en chargement, en charge; *(in street)* **one can stop for a few minutes to l. and unload,** des arrêts brefs sont autorisés pour charger et décharger; *(b) Aut: F:* *(of engine)* **to l. up,** s'engorger d'essence; se noyer; *(c) P:* *(of pers.)* **to l. up,** se bourrer (de nourriture); boire jusqu'à plus soif.

loaded ['loudid], *a.* **1.** *(a)* (camion, navire, etc.) chargé; *(b) Mec.E:* (ressort) bandé. **2.** *(a)* **l. cane,** canne plombée; **l. dice,** dés pipés, chargés; *I.C.E:* **spring-l. valve,** soupape rappelée sur son siège par un ressort; *(b) Paperm:* **l. paper,** papier chargé; *(c) Med:* **l. urine,** urine chargée (de sels); *(d) (of pers.) P:* (i) soûl; (ii) richissime; (iii) drogué, camé. **3.** *Ins:* **l. premium,** prime majorée; surprime *f.*

loader ['loudər], *s.* **1.** *(pers.)* *(a)* chargeur *m*, manœuvre *m*; *(b) (with shooting party)* chargeur des fusils. **2.** *(device)* chargeuse *f*; *Civ.E:* chargeur; **bucket l.,** chargeuse à godets; **back l.,** rétrochargeuse *f*; **front(-end), fore(-end), l.,** chouleur *m*, chargeur frontal. **3. single l.,** fusil *m* à un coup; **breech l.,** fusil, pièce *f*, se chargeant par la culasse; **muzzle l.,** pièce se chargeant par la bouche.

loading ['loudiŋ], *s.* **1.** *(a)* chargement *m* (d'un camion, d'un wagon, d'un navire, d'un avion); **end-on l.,** chargement en bout, en enfilade; **side l.,** chargement par le côté, par le travers; **bulk l.,** chargement en vrac; **l. gear,** appareil *m* de chargement; **l. point,** point *m*, endroit *m*, de chargement; *Mil:* chantier *m* de chargement, d'embarquement (du matériel); **l. ramp, rack,** rampe *f* de chargement; **l. chute,** couloir *m* de chargement; **l. board,** pont volant; **l. bay, platform,** quai *m* de chargement; **l. gauge,** gabarit *m* de chargement; *Nau:* **l. port, berth,** port *m*, poste *m*, de chargement; **l. on the berth,** affrètement *m* à la cueillette; **l. net,** élingue *f* en filet; *Av:* **l. apron, area,** aire *f* de chargement; *Mil:* **l. centre,** centre *m* de ravitaillement; *(b) Artil: Sm.a:* chargement (d'un canon, d'un fusil, d'un pistolet); **breech l.,** chargement par la culasse; **muzzle l.,** chargement par la bouche; **single l.,** chargement coup par coup; **self l. (system),** chargement automatique; **l. clip,** lame-chargeur *f*, *pl.* lames-chargeurs; *(of machine gun)* **l. belt,** bande-chargeur *f* (*pl.* bandes-chargeurs) souple; **l. strip,** bande-chargeur rigide; *Artil:* **l. tray,** plateau *m*, planchette *f*, de chargement; *(c) Phot:* chargement (de l'appareil, des châssis); **l. magazine,** chargeur *m* de caméra; (*d*) *Atom.Ph:* chargement (du réacteur en combustible); chargement, enfournement *m* (du combustible); (*e*) *Cmptr:* chargement (de programme); mise *f* en place (d'une bande magnétique); garnissage *m* (d'un registre); **l. tray,** rampe de chargement; (*f*) *U.S: F:* **free l.,** (grands) repas pris aux frais d'autrui. **2.** (*a*) *Av:* **wing l.,** charge *f* alaire; (*b*) *Paperm:* **(clay) l.,** charge; (*c*) *Tp:* **coil l.,** pupinisation *f*; **l. coil,** bobine *f* Pupin *m*, de charge; (*d*) *Aut: F:* engorgement *m*, noyade *f* (du moteur).

loadstone ['loudstoun], *s.* = LODESTONE.

loaf[1], *pl.* **loaves** [louf, louvz], *s.* **1.** pain *m*; **round l.,** pain rond, boulot; **tin(ned) l.,** pain moulé; **French l.,** baguette *f*; flûte *f*; (*very thin*) ficelle *f*; **sandwich l.,** pain de mie; **farmhouse l.,** pain de campagne, pain paysan; **large (home-made) l.,** pain de ménage; **cottage l.** = double miche *f*; = calotte bretonne; *O:* **quartern l.,** pain de quatre livres; *U.S:* **l. cake,** gâteau carré cuit au moule; *Prov:* **half a l. is better than no bread,** faute de grives on mange des merles. **2. sugar l.,** pain de sucre; **l. sugar,** sucre *m* en pains. **3.** (*a*) tête *f*, cœur *m* (de chou, de laitue); (*b*) *F:* tête, caboche *f*; **use your l.,** fais un peu travailler tes méninges.

loaf[2], *v.i.* (*of cabbage, etc.*) pommer.

loaf[3], *pl.* **loafs,** *s.* flânerie *f*.

loaf[4]. **1.** *v.i.* **to l. (about, around),** flâner; fainéanter; traîner. **2.** *v.tr.* **to l. away the time,** passer son temps à flâner, à fainéanter.

loafer ['loufər], *s.* **1.** (*pers.*) flâneur, -euse; fainéant, -ante; **young l.,** voyou *m*. **2.** *NAm: Cost:* **loafers** = mocassins *m*.

loafing[1] ['loufiŋ], *a.* fainéant; flâneur.

loafing[2], *s.* flânerie *f*; fainéantise *f*.

loam[1] [loum], *s.* **1.** *Agr: Geol:* terreau *m*; terre grasse, forte, franche, végétale, naturelle; terre de gazon; *Vit:* herbue *f*. **2.** *Metall: etc:* terre glaise; glaise *f*; terre (de coulage); potée *f*; **l. cake,** motte *f* de recouvrement; **l. board,** échantillon *m*; planche *f* à trousser. **3.** (*a*) torchis *m*, pisé *m*; **l. hut,** cabane *f* de bousillage, de torchis, en torchis; cabane en pisé; (*b*) *Arb:* engluement *m*, torchis.

loam[2], *v.tr.* recouvrir (une paroi, etc.) de torchis; torcher; glaiser.

loamy ['loumi], *a.* (*of soil*) (i) gras, fort; (ii) argileux, glaiseux; **l. sand,** sable gras.

loan[1] [loun], *s.* **1.** (*a*) prêt *m*; avance *f* (de fonds); **l. of money,** prêt, avance, d'argent; **to oblige s.o. with a l.,** rendre à qn un service d'argent; avancer de l'argent à qn; **to offer s.o. sth. on l.,** offrir qch. à qn à titre de prêt; **on l. from the Louvre,** prêt du Louvre; *Mil: etc:* (*of officer, etc.*) **on l.,** détaché (to, auprès de); **may I have the l. of . . .?** puis-je vous emprunter . . .? puis-je vous demander de me prêter . . .? (*b*) (*money advanced*) prêt, emprunt *m*; **l. at interest,** prêt à intérêt; **l. at call, l. repayable on demand,** prêt, emprunt, remboursable sur demande; **l. at notice,** prêt, emprunt, à terme; **long-dated l., long-term l.,** prêt, emprunt, à long terme; **short(-term) l.,** prêt, emprunt, à court terme; **time l.,** prêt, emprunt, à terme fixe; **l. by the week, l. with payment of weekly interest,** prêt, emprunt, à la petite semaine; **secured l.,** prêt, emprunt, gagé, garanti; **l. on collateral,** prêt sur gage, sur nantissement; **l. on mortgage, mortgage l.,** prêt, emprunt, hypothécaire, sur hypothèque; **l. on securities, on stock,** prêt, emprunt, sur titres; **l. on trust,** prêt d'honneur; **unsecured l., l. without security, l. on overdraft,** prêt, emprunt, à découvert; **tied l.,** prêt conditionnel, emprunt à emploi spécifié; *Nau:* **l. on respondentia,** prêt, emprunt, à la grosse sur facultés; **l. office,** caisse *f* d'emprunts; établissement *m* de prêt; **l. society, company,** société *f*, établissement, de crédit; **l. bank,** caisse de prêt; *F:* **l. shark,** usurier *m*; **l. certificate,** titre *m* de prêt; **to apply for a l.,** demander, solliciter, un prêt; **application for a l.,** demande *f* de prêt; **to allow, grant, a l.,** accorder, consentir, un prêt, un emprunt; **to contract, raise, take up, a l.,** contracter un prêt, un emprunt; faire un emprunt; **to raise a l. on an estate,** emprunter de l'argent sur une terre; **to redeem, refund, repay, a l.,** rembourser, amortir, un prêt, un emprunt; **redemption, refunding, repayment, of a l.,** remboursement *m*, amortissement *m*, d'un prêt, d'un emprunt; (*c*) **it's a l., you can have it as a l.,** je vous le prête; c'est à titre de prêt. **2.** *Fin: etc:* emprunt; **government l.,** emprunt d'État; **public l.,** emprunt public; **internal l.,** emprunt interne; **municipal l.,** emprunt communal, emprunt de ville(s); **utility l.,** emprunt des services publics; **foreign l., external l.,** emprunt extérieur; **perpetual l.,** emprunt perpétuel; **consolidation l., funding l.,** emprunt de consolidation; **consolidated l.,** emprunt consolidé; **conversion l.,** emprunt de conversion; **debenture l.,** emprunt obligataire; **gold l.,** emprunt or; **indexed l.,** emprunt indexé; **to issue a l.,** émettre un emprunt; **issue of a l.,** émission *f* d'un emprunt; **to float a l.,** lancer un emprunt; **to place a l.,** placer un emprunt; **the l. was undersubscribed, oversubscribed,** l'emprunt n'a pas été couvert, a été très largement couvert. **3.** *Ling:* mot *m* d'emprunt; **l. translation,** calque *m*.

loan[2]. **1.** *v.tr. & i.* prêter (**sth. to s.o.,** qch. à qn); **loaned by the Louvre,** prêt *m* du Louvre. **2.** *v.tr. F:* emprunter (qch.).

loanable ['lounəbl], *a.* **1.** prêtable; (capital *m*) disponible pour investissement, pour placement; fonds *m* à prêter. **2.** que l'on peut emprunter.

loanee [lou'ni:], *s.* emprunteur, -euse.

loaner ['lounər], *s.* prêteur, -euse.

loaning ['louniŋ], *s.* **1.** action *f* de prêter; prêt *m*. **2.** action d'emprunter; emprunt *m*.

loanword ['lounwə:d], *s. Ling:* mot *m* d'emprunt; mot emprunté (à une autre langue).

Loasaceae [louə'seisii:], *s.pl. Bot:* loasacées *f*.

loath [louθ], *a.* **to be l. to do sth.,** avoir de la répugnance à faire qch., répugner à faire qch.; être peu disposé, peu enclin, à faire qch.; faire qch. à contrecœur; ne pas vouloir faire qch.; **I am l. to punish you,** (i) j'hésite à vous punir; (ii) c'est à regret que je vous punis; *esp. Lit:* **nothing l.,** très volontiers, sans hésiter, sans se faire prier.

loathe [louð], *v.tr.* détester, exécrer, *F:* abominer (qn, qch.); avoir, éprouver, de l'aversion, du dégoût, pour (qn, qch.); avoir (qn, qch.) en horreur; **I l. wine,** le vin me répugne; je ne peux pas souffrir le vin; **that made me l. wine,** cela m'a fait prendre le vin en dégoût; **to l. doing sth.,** détester faire qch.; **I l. doing it,** il me répugne de le faire; **he loathes being praised,** il déteste qu'on lui fasse des éloges.

loathing ['louðiŋ], *s.* dégoût *m*, aversion *f*, répugnance *f* (**for,** pour); **to take, conceive, a l. for s.o.,** prendre qn en dégoût; **to have a l. for milk,** avoir, éprouver, du dégoût pour le lait.

loathliness ['louðlinis], *s. A: & Lit:* = LOATHSOMENESS.

loathly ['louðli], *a. A: & Lit:* = LOATHSOME.

loathness ['louθnis], *s.* répugnance *f*, aversion *f* (**to do sth.,** à faire qch.).

loathsome ['louðsəm], *a.* repoussant, écœurant, dégoûtant, répugnant; (*of smell*) nauséabond.

loathsomely ['louðsəmli], *adv.* d'une manière repoussante, répugnante; dégoûtamment; **l. ugly,** (homme) dégoûtant par sa laideur.

loathsomeness ['louðsəmnis], *s.* nature repoussante, dégoûtante (de qch.).

lob[1] [lɔb], *s. Dial: A:* rustre *m*, lourdaud *m*.

lob[2], *s. Sp:* lob *m*; (balle envoyée en) chandelle *f*; *Ten:* **to play a l. against s.o.,** lober qn; **l. volley,** lob-volée *m*, *pl.* lobs-volées.

lob[3]. **1.** *v.i.* (*a*) *O:* **to l. (along),** se traîner lourdement; (*of shell, etc.*) voler lourdement; **to. l. up, down,** monter, descendre, en chandelle; (*b*) *Sp:* lober; *Ten:* renvoyer des chandelles. **2.** *v.tr. Sp:* envoyer (la balle, etc.) en chandelle; lober (la balle, etc.); **to l. one's opponent,** lober son adversaire.

lobar ['loubər], *a. Nat.Hist:* lobaire; *Med:* **l. pneumonia,** pneumonie *f* lobaire.

lobate ['loubeit], *a.* lobé, lobaire.

lobby[1] ['lɔbi], *s.* **1.** (*a*) couloir *m*, antichambre *f*, vestibule *m*; promenoir *m* (d'un tribunal, etc.); entrée *f* (d'un théâtre); (*b*) (*in Parliament*) **the l. of the House,** la salle des pas perdus; les couloirs de la Chambre; **the division lobbies,** les vestibules où passent les députés lorsqu'ils se divisent pour voter. **2.** *Pol: etc:* lobby *m*, groupe *m* de pression; **they constitute a powerful l.,** ils représentent un lobby puissant.

lobby[2], *v.tr. & i.* **to l. (members),** fréquenter la salle des pas perdus de la Chambre (en quête de nouvelles, pour influencer des membres du Parlement); faire les couloirs; *U.S:* **to l. a bill through,** faire passer une mesure à force d'intrigues.

lobbying ['lɔbiiŋ], *s.* intrigues *fpl* de couloirs.

lobbyist ['lɔbiist], *s.* intrigant *m* (qui fréquente les couloirs de la Chambre).

lobe [loub], *s.* **1.** (*a*) *Arch: Bot:* lobe *m* (d'une rosace, d'une feuille); (*b*) *Anat:* lobe (de l'oreille); **lower l. of the ear,** auricule *f* de l'oreille. **2.** (*a*) *Metall: F:* oreille *f* (d'une pièce coulée, etc.); (*b*) *Mec.E:* bossage *m*, renflement *m* (d'une pièce mécanique, etc.); **cam l.,** bossage, nez *m*, de came. **3.** *Elcs:* pétale *m* (de diagramme de rayonnement); lobe (d'une antenne directrice, d'une antenne de radar); *W.Tel:* **l. switching,** commutation *f*, déplacement *m*, de lobe.

lobectomy [lou'bektəmi], *s. Surg:* lobectomie *f*.

lobed [loubd], *a. Nat.Hist:* lobé.

lobefoot ['loubfut], *s. Orn:* lobipède *m*.

lobelet ['loublit], *s. Bot:* lobule *m*.

lobelia [lə'bi:liə], *s. Bot:* lobélie *f*.

Lobeliaceae [loubili'eisii:], *s.pl. Bot:* lobéliacées *f*.

lobeline ['loubəli:n], *s. Pharm:* lobéline *f*.

lobiole ['loubioul], *s. Bot:* lobiole *f*.

lobitis [lou'baitis], *s. Med:* lobite *f*.

loblolly ['lɔb'lɔli], *s.* **1.** *A:* gruau *m*, bouillie *f* (pour malades, etc.); *Navy: A:* **l. boy, l. man,** infirmier *m*. **2.** *Bot: U.S:* **l. bay,** gordonie *f* à feuilles glabres.

lobo ['loubou], *s. Z: U.S:* **l. (wolf),** loup *m* d'Amérique du Nord.

lobopod ['louboupɔd], **lobopodium** [loubou'poudiəm], *s.* lobopode *m*.

lobosa [lou'bousə], *s.pl. Prot:* lobosa *m*.

lobotomy [lou'bɔtəmi], *s. Surg:* lobotomie *f*, leucotomie *f*.

lobscouse ['lɔbskaus], *s. Cu:* ratatouille *f*, ragoût *m*.

lobster ['lɔbstər], *s.* **1.** *Crust:* homard *m*; **hen l.,** homard femelle; **squat l.,** galathée *f*; **American l.,** homard d'Amérique; **spiny l., rock l.,** langouste *f*; **Norway l.,** langoustine *f*; **l. crab,** porcellane *f*; **l. boat,** (i) homardier *m*; (ii) langoustier *m*; **l. pot,** casier *m* (i) à homards, (ii) à langoustes; **l. net,** (i) caudrette *f*; (ii) langoustier, langoustière *f*. **2.** *Ent:* **l. moth,** staurope *m*; **l. caterpillar,** chenille *f* du staurope; **oak l. moth,** écureuil *m*, harpye *f*, du hêtre.

lobsterman, *pl.* **-men** ['lɔbstəmæn, -men], *s.* (*a*) homardier *m*; (*b*) langoustier *m*.

lobular ['lɔbjulər], *a.* lobulaire.

lobulate ['lɔbjuleit], *a. Nat.Hist:* lobulé, lobuleux.

lobule ['lɔbjul], *s. Nat.Hist:* lobule *m*.

lobulose ['lɔbjulous], **lobulous** ['lɔbjuləs], *a.* lobulé, lobuleux.

lobworm ['lɔbwə:m], *s.* arénicole *f* des pêcheurs; *F:* ver *m* des pêcheurs; ver rouge.

local[1] ['loukl]. **1.** *a.* (*a*) local, -aux; régional, -aux; du pays, de la localité, de la région; **l. authorities,** autorités locales, régionales; **l. government** = l'administration (i) départementale, (ii) communale; **l. bank,** banque locale, régionale; **l. name,** nom régional, de terroir; **l. news,** informations locales, de la région; **l. information,** information recueillie sur les lieux; **l. wine,** vin *m* du pays; **l. colour,** couleur locale; **l. time,** heure légale (selon le fuseau horaire); **l. horizon,** horizon apparent, visible; **the l. doctor,** le médecin du quartier, de l'endroit; **the l. grocer,** l'épicier *m* (i) du pays, (ii) du coin; **l. interests, quarrels,** intérêts *m*, disputes *f*, de clocher; **it's just a matter of l. politics,** c'est une question de politique de clocher; **this project has roused a great deal of l. feeling,** ce projet a causé beaucoup de controverses dans le pays, parmi les gens du pays; **l. train,** omnibus *m*; **l. bus,** (i) = autobus municipal; (ii) car *m* qui dessert les villages des environs; **l. road,** route locale; chemin vicinal; *Ecc:* **l. preacher,** laïque autorisé à célébrer l'office (chez les méthodistes); **l. thunder,** orages locaux; **l. showers,** averses éparses; *Meteor:* **l. attraction,** déviation locale (du compas) (due au voisinage de terres magnétiques); (*b*) *Post:* **local,** en ville; *Bank: Com:* **l. business,** les affaires *f* de la place; **l. bill,** effet *m* sur place; **l. agent,** agent *m* fixe; **l. trade,** commerce local, de la place, de la localité; **l. purchases,** achats *m* sur place; (*c*) **l. disease, pain,** maladie, douleur, localisée, locale, topique; **l. remedy,** remède topique, local; topique *m*; **l. anaesthetic,** anesthésique local. **2.** *s.* (*a*) **the locals,** (i) les gens *m*, les habitants *m*, du pays; (ii) *Sp:* l'équipe locale, du pays; (*b*) *F:* anesthésique local; (*c*) *esp. NAm:* = **local train, local bus, etc.;** (*d*) *F:* **the l.,** le bistro du village, du coin; (*e*) *Sch: O:* **Oxford, etc. L.,** examen tenu sous les auspices de l'université d'Oxford, etc.

locale [lou'kɑ:l], *s.* localité *f*; scène *f*, théâtre *m* (des événements).

localism ['loukəlizm], *s.* **1.** amour (excessif) de sa ville, de sa région; esprit *m* de clocher. **2.** (*a*) locution régionale; (*b*) accent régional, du pays; (*c*) coutume *f*, habitude *f*, du pays.

localite ['loukəlait], *s. esp. U.S: F:* habitant, -ante, d'une localité.

locality [lou'kæliti], *s.* **1.** (*a*) caractère local (d'un usage, etc.); (*b*) *Psy:* **(sense of) l.,** localisation *f* (d'un stimulus); (*c*) **to have a good sense of l., the bump of l.,** savoir s'orienter; avoir la bosse de l'orientation. **2.** (*a*) localité *f*; habitat *m* (d'une faune, d'une flore, etc.); emplacement *m* (d'un gisement, etc.); (*b*) localité; endroit *m*; voisinage *m*; **in our l.,** chez nous; dans notre pays, notre région; (*c*) *Mil:* point *m* (sur le terrain); **strategic l.,** point stratégique; **tactical l.,** point d'importance tactique; **battalion l.,** quartier *m*; **company l.,** sous-quartier *m*; **defended l.,** point d'appui, centre *m* de résistance.

localizable [loukə'laizəbl], *a.* localisable.

localization [loukəlai'zeiʃ(ə)n], *s.* localisation *f* (d'une épidémie, etc.).

localize ['loukəlaiz], *v.tr.* **1.** *(a)* localiser (une épidémie, une conflagration, etc.); *(of disease)* **to become localized,** se localiser (dans un organe); *X Rays:* **localizing apparatus,** localisateur *m*; *(b)* localiser (un mythe, une légende). **2.** = LOCATE 1 *(a)*.

localizer ['loukəlaizər], *s. Av:* **(runway) l.,** radiophare *m* d'alignement (de piste), appareil *m* de radioguidage à l'atterrissage; **glide path l.,** indicateur *m* de pente.

locally ['loukəli], *adv.* localement; **staff engaged l.,** personnel engagé sur place; **he is well known l.,** il est bien connu dans son pays, dans la région; **l. produced wine,** vin *m* du pays.

Locarno [lə'kɑ:nou]. *Pr.n. Geog:* Locarno; *Hist:* **the L. Pact, the Treaty of L.,** les Accords *m* de Locarno.

locate [lə'keit]. **1.** *v.tr.* *(a)* localiser (qch.); situer (qch.); établir, déterminer, reconnaître, la situation de (qch.); **to l. the root of the trouble,** découvrir, repérer, le siège du mal; **to l. an event in history,** fixer la date d'un événement dans l'histoire; **the police have located the headquarters of the gang,** la police a repéré le quartier général de la bande; *El:* **to l. a fault,** repérer, localiser, déterminer, un dérangement; *Mil:* **to l. a machine-gun position,** repérer un emplacement de mitrailleuse; *Nau:* **to l. a ship at sea,** déterminer la position d'un navire (en mer); *(b) esp. U.S:* fixer, décider, l'emplacement de (qch.); *(c) Mec.E:* maintenir (une pièce) en place. **2.** *v.i. U.S:* s'établir (dans un endroit); habiter (quelque part).

locater [lə'keitər], *s.* = LOCATOR.

locating [lə'keitiŋ], *s.* *(a)* détermination *f* (d'une fuite de gaz, etc.); relève *f* (d'un défaut dans un appareil); *Artil: etc:* repérage *m* (d'une batterie, etc.); *El:* **l. of faults,** recherche *f*, détermination *f*, de dérangements; *(b) Mec.E:* **l. dowel pin,** goujon *m* d'assemblage; **l. peg, l. pin,** ergot *m* de centrage; goupille *f* de montage, de repérage; **l. slot,** encoche *f* de mise en place.

location [lə'keiʃ(ə)n], *s.* **1.** = LOCATING. **2.** situation *f*, emplacement *m*. **3.** *(a) (in S. Africa)* réserve *f* indigène; *(b) Austr:* élevage *m* (de moutons, etc.); *(c) esp. U.S:* concession minière. **4.** *Jur: Scot: (letting for hire)* location *f*. **5.** *Cin:* **to be on l.,** tourner en extérieur; **l. shot,** extérieur *m*.

locative ['lɔkətiv], *a. & s. Gram:* locatif *(m)*; **in the l.,** au locatif.

locator [lə'keitər], *s.* **1.** *(pers.)* trouveur, -euse. **2.** *(a) Mec.E:* pièce *f* de repérage; repère *m*; ergot *m*, goupille *f*, de position, d'assemblage; gabarit *m* de montage; *(b) Elcs:* phare *m* (pour radiocompas); *Petr:* **electronic pipe l.,** localisateur *m* de canalisation en place.

loch [lɔχ], *s. Scot:* **1.** lac *m*. **2. sea l.,** bras *m* de mer; loch *m* maritime; fjord *m*.

lochia ['lɔkiə], *s.pl. Obst:* lochies *f*; suites *f* de couches.

lochial ['lɔkiəl], *a. Obst:* lochial, -aux.

lock[1] [lɔk], *s.* **1.** *(a)* mèche *f*, boucle *f* (de cheveux); *(b) pl. A: & Lit:* **locks,** cheveux *m*, chevelure *f*; **scanty locks,** rares cheveux. **2.** flocon *m* (de laine); **l. wool, locks,** écouailles *fpl*.

lock[2], *s.* **1.** serrure *f*; fermeture *f*; **double l.,** serrure à double tour; **spring l.,** serrure à ressort; serrure bec-de-cane; **mortise l.,** serrure à larder, à mortaiser; **flush l.,** serrure encastrée, à encastrer, à entailler; **dead l.,** serrure à pêne dormant; **two-bolt l.,** serrure à deux pênes; **drawback l.,** serrure camarde; **double-sided l.,** serrure bénarde; **cylinder l.,** serrure à cylindre; **box l.,** serrure auberonnière; *(for door)* serrure palastre; **safety l.,** serrure de sûreté; **Bramah l.,** serrure Bramah, serrure à pompe; **Yale l.,** serrure Yale; **combination l.,** serrure à combinaisons; **piped-key l.,** serrure à broche; **letter-keyed l.,** cadenas *m* à chiffres, à combinaisons; **to put a l. on a door,** poser une serrure à une porte; **l. plate,** palastre *m* de serrure; **under l. and key,** sous clef; *(of pers.)* sous les verrous, **to pick a l.,** crocheter une serrure. **2.** *Mec.E: etc:* *(a)* verrou *m*, *pl.* verrous; verrouillage *m*, blocage *m*; *Veh:* enrayage *m*, enraiement *m*, blocage (des roues); **automatic l.,** verrouillage automatique; **coupling l.,** verrou d'accouplement; **hydraulic l.,** verrouillage, blocage, hydraulique; **l. lug, l. pin,** axe *m*, goupille *f*, de verrouillage, d'arrêt; **l. ring,** bague *f* de blocage; *Av:* **pitch l.,** (i) verrou de pas d'hélice; (ii) verrouillage du pas d'hélice; **up and down l.,** verrou de train (d'atterrissage); *Artil: Sm.a:* **breech l.,** verrou de culasse; **l. mechanism,** mécanisme *m* de verrouillage; **travelling l.,** verrou de route (de canon, de char, etc.); *Rail:* **switch l., control l.,** verrou de blocage des aiguilles; **l. and block system,** système *m* de bloc enclenché; *(b)* crabotage *m*; *Aut:* **direct-drive l.,** crabotage de prise directe. **3.** *(a)* platine *f* (de fusil); *(b)* **l., stock and barrel,** tout sans exception; tout le fourbi. **4.** *Wr:* étreinte *f*, clef *f*; **arm l.,** clef de bras; **leg l.,** passement *m* de pied; **waist l.,** ceinture *f*. **5.** *Aut: etc:* angle *m* de braquage; **car with a good l.,** voiture *f* qui braque bien; **to have a l. of 30°,** braquer à 30°; **on full l.,** braqué au maximum. **6.** *(a) Hyd.E:* écluse *f*; **flash l.,** écluse simple; **pound l.,** écluse à sas; **l. chamber,** sas *m*; chambre *f* (d'écluse); **l. gate,** porte *f* d'écluse; **ship-canal l.,** ascenseur-écluse *m*, *pl.* ascenseurs-écluses; **to pass a boat through a l.,** écluser, sasser, un bateau; *(of boat)* **to pass through a l.,** passer par une écluse; *(b) (of boiler room, etc.)* **air l.,** sas à air, sas pneumatique *(cf.* **airlock**); poche d'air (dans un tuyau, etc.); *(c) T.V: W.Tel:* **sound l.,** sas. **7.** *Med: A:* **l. (hospital),** hôpital *m* pour les maladies vénériennes. **l. chain,** chaîne *f* à enrayer (les roues); **l. lever,** levier *m* de blocage, de verrouillage; **l. nut,** écrou *m* de calage, de freinage; **l. pawl,** cliquet *m* de fermeture, de verrouillage; **l. pin,** goupille *f* de verrouillage, de fixation; **l. ring,** bague *f* d'arrêt, de blocage, de verrouillage; collier *m* de serrage; **l. screw,** vis *f* de blocage, de serrage, d'arrêt; **l. sleeve,** manchon *m* de serrage, de sécurité; **l. wire** = LOCKWIRE. **3.** *Elcs: (of radar, sensor, etc.)* **l. on,** accrochage *m* (d'un objectif); *Space:* **the l. on the sun by one of the sensors,** l'accrochage du soleil par l'un des capteurs. **4.** *Hyd.E:* éclusage *m*, sassement *m* (d'un bateau).

lock[3], *v.*

I. *v.tr.* **1.** *(a)* fermer à clef; donner un tour de clef à (une porte); *(with passive force)* **trunk that won't l.,** malle *f* dont la serrure est abîmée, qu'on ne peut pas fermer à clef; **the door locks on the inside,** la serrure (de la porte) joue à l'intérieur; **all these boxes l.,** tous ces coffrets se ferment à clef; *(b)* **to l. s.o. in a room,** enfermer qn dans une chambre; **to l. sth. (away) in a drawer,** enfermer qch. dans un tiroir. **2.** *(a)* enrayer, bloquer, caler (les roues); enclencher (les pièces d'un mécanisme); *Sm.a:* verrouiller (la culasse); *Dent:* **locked tooth,** dent barrée; **to l. the turret of a lathe,** bloquer, verrouiller, la tourelle d'un tour; **to l. a screw,** arrêter une vis; **the lever has become locked,** le levier se trouve verrouillé; *Rail:* **to l. a switch,** verrouiller une aiguille; **ship locked in ice,** navire pris dans les glaces; *(b) (of pers.)* **to be locked (together) in a struggle,** être engagés corps à corps dans une lutte; **to be locked in each other's arms,** se tenir étroitement embrassés, être enlacés; *(d)* **to l. one's teeth,** serrer les dents; **his jaws were tightly locked,** ses dents étaient serrées. **3.** *Hyd.E:* *(a)* écluser (un canal); pourvoir (un canal) d'écluses; *(b)* **to l. a boat,** écluser, sasser, un bateau. **4.** *v.ind.tr. Elcs: etc: (of radar, sensor, etc.)* **to l. on to (sth.),** accrocher (un objectif); **one sensor had locked on to the sun,** l'un des capteurs avait accroché le soleil.

II. *v.i.* **1.** *(a) (of wheels, etc.)* s'enrayer, se bloquer; *(b)* **the parts l. into each other,** (i) les parties s'enclavent; (ii) les parties s'enclenchent. **2.** *Mil: (of ranks)* emboîter le pas. **3.** *Hyd.E: (of boat)* passer par une écluse. **4.** *Aut:* **l. left, right,** braquer à gauche, à droite.

III. *(compound verbs)* **1. lock in,** *v.tr.* enfermer (qn) à clef; mettre (qn) sous clef.

2. lock out, *v.tr.* *(a)* **to l. s.o. out,** fermer la porte à clef (quand il y a qn qui n'est pas rentré); **I found myself locked out,** en rentrant j'ai trouvé la porte fermée (à clef); *(b) Ind:* lock(-)outer (le personnel); *(c) Cmptr: etc)* verrouiller, interdire l'utilisation (d'un appareil).

3. lock up, *v.tr.* *(a)* mettre, serrer, (qch.) sous clef; enfermer (qch.); **to l. s.o. up,** enfermer qn; mettre qn sous les verrous, en lieu sûr; écrouer qn au dépôt; **to l. up a house,** fermer une maison à clef; **it's time to l. up,** c'est l'heure de fermer la maison; *(b) Typ:* **to l. up the forms,** serrer les formes; *(c) Fin:* **to l. up capital,** immobiliser, bloquer, engager, des capitaux; **to l. up a stock,** boucler une valeur.

lockable ['lɔkəbl], *a.* verrouillable; qu'on peut fermer à clef.

lockage ['lɔkidʒ], *s. Hyd.E:* **1.** différence *f* de niveau (entre biefs). **2.** éclusage *m*, sassement *m* (d'un bateau). **3.** péage *m* d'écluse; droit *m* d'écluse. **4.** construction *f* d'écluses. **5.** *coll.* écluses *fpl*.

locker ['lɔkər], *s.* **1.** armoire *f*, coffre *m* (fermant à clef); **l. room,** vestiaire *m* (d'une école, d'une usine, d'un pavillon de sports, etc.); **every member of the club has his l.,** chaque membre du club a son armoire, sa case. **2.** *Nau:* *(a)* caisson *m*, coffre; **signal, flag, l.,** coffre aux pavillons; coffre, caisson, à signaux; *(b)* soute *f*; **sail l.,** soute à voiles; **rope l.,** soute à filin; **cable l.,** (i) soute aux câbles; (ii) puits *m* aux chaînes; **ready-use l.,** parc *m*; **lamp l.,** lampisterie *f*.

locket ['lɔkit], *s.* **1.** médaillon *m* (porté en parure). **2.** *Sm.a:* bracelet *m*, agrafe *f*, de fourreau.

lockful ['lɔkful], *s. Hyd.E:* éclusée *f* (d'eau).

locking[1] ['lɔkiŋ], *a.* **1.** qui se ferme à clef. **2.** à verrouillage, à enclenchement.

locking[2], *s.* **1.** fermeture *f* à clef; **l. up,** mise *f* sous clef; fermeture (d'une maison, etc.); *Typ:* serrage *m* (des formes); **l. up of capital,** immobilisation *f* de capitaux. **2.** *Mec.E: etc:* blocage *m*, verrouillage *m*, enclenchement *m*, immobilisation *f*; *Veh:* enrayage *m*, enrayement *m*, blocage (des roues); **l. of a nut,** blocage d'un écrou; *Rail:* **l. of points,** verrouillage des aiguilles; **l. device, l. mechanism,** dispositif *m*, mécanisme *m*, de blocage, de verrouillage; *Aut: etc:* **handle with interior l. device,** poignée *f* (de portière) à condamnation; **seat with a l. device,** siège *m* à dispositif de blocage; **l. bar,** (i) barre-verrou *f*, *pl.* barrettes-verrous; (ii) *Rail:* pédale *f* de calage; **l. bolt,** verrou de blocage; **l. cam,** came *f* de verrouillage; **l. catch,** encliquetage *m* d'arrêt;

lockjaw ['lɔkdʒɔ:], *s. Med:* (i) trisme *m*; trismus *m*; (ii) *F:* tétanos *m*; *Vet: F:* mal *m* de cerf.

lock-keeper ['lɔkki:pər], *s.* gardien *m* d'écluse; éclusier *m*.

locknut ['lɔknʌt], *s.* **1.** contre-écrou *m*, *pl.* contre-écrous; écrou *m* de blocage; **adjustment l.,** contre-écrou de réglage. **2.** écrou indesserrable.

lock-on ['lɔkɔn], *s. Elcs:* accrochage *m*, capture *f* (d'un objectif par un radar ou un détecteur).

lockout ['lɔkaut], *s. Ind:* lock-out *m inv*.

locksman, *pl.* **-men** ['lɔksmən], *s.* = LOCK-KEEPER.

locksmith ['lɔksmiθ], *s.* serrurier *m*.

locksmithery ['lɔksmiθəri], *s.* serrurerie *f*.

lockstep ['lɔkstep], *s.* **to march in l.,** emboîter le pas.

lockstitch ['lɔkstitʃ], *s.* point *m* de navette (d'une machine à coudre); point indécousable; point noué; point de piqûre; **double l.,** point redoublé.

lockup ['lɔkʌp], *s.* **1.** *Sch: etc:* fermeture *f* des portes (pour la nuit). **2.** *Fin:* *(a)* immobilisation *f*, blocage *m*, engagement *m* (de capital); *(b)* capital immobilisé, engagé; **l. holding,** placement *m* à long terme. **3.** hangar *m*, etc., fermant à clef; **l. shop,** (petit) magasin (construit sans habitation attenante); **l. garage,** (i) box *m* (dans un garage); (ii) garage (construit à côté d'un immeuble, etc.); **l. desk,** bureau *m* fermant à clef. **4.** *F:* poste *m* de police, le violon, le bloc; **he's in the l.,** il est au poste, au violon.

lockwire ['lɔkwaiər], *s. Mec.E:* fil *m* à freiner; frein *m*; jonc *m* d'arrêt.

loco[1] ['loukou], *s. Rail: F:* loco *f*.

loco[2], *s. F:* **1.** = LOCOWEED. **2.** *Vet:* **l. (disease),** vertigo *m*. **3.** *(a) a. & s. NAm:* (animal) atteint de vertigo; *(b) a. F: (pers.)* fou, *f.* folle; maboul, toqué.

loco[3], *adv. Com:* loco; **l. price,** prix *m* loco.

locoed ['loukoud], *a. NAm: Vet:* (animal) atteint de vertigo.

locoism ['loukouizm], *s. Vet:* vertigo (dû à l'astragale).

locomote ['loukəmout], *v.i. esp. U.S: F:* se déplacer.

locomotion [loukə'mouʃ(ə)n], *s.* locomotion *f*.

locomotive [loukə'moutiv]. **1.** *a.* locomotif, -ive; locomobile; **l. faculty,** faculté locomotive, locomotrice; locomotilité *f*, locomotivité *f*. **2.** *s. Rail:* locomotive *f*; **diesel (powered) l.,** locomotive (à moteur) diesel; **diesel-electric l.,** locomotive (à moteur) diesel-électrique; **electric l.,** locomotive électrique; **gas turbine l.,** locomotive à turbine à gaz; **steam l.,** locomotive à vapeur; **rack l.,** locomotive à crémaillère; **l. shed,** dépôt *m* de(s) locomotives, de(s) machines; **l. works,** atelier *m* de construction de locomotives; **l. engineer,** conducteur *m*, mécanicien *m*, de locomotive.

locomotivity [loukəmou'tiviti], *s.* locomotivité *f*.

locomotor ['loukəmoutər]. **1.** *a.* locomoteur, -trice; *Med:* **l. disorder,** troubles locomotifs; **l. ataxia,** ataxie locomotrice. **2.** *s.* locomoteur *m*.

locomotory [loukə'moutəri], *a.* locomotif; locomoteur, -trice; *Med:* **disorder of the l. organs,** troubles locomotifs.

locoweed ['loukouwi:d], *s. Bot:* (variété *f* toxique d'astragale *m*.

Locrian ['lɔkriən], *a. & s. A.Geog:* *(a) a.* locrien; *(b) s.* Locrien, -ienne.

Locris ['lɔkris]. *Pr.n. A.Geog:* la Locride.

locular ['lɔkjulər], *a. Nat.Hist:* loculaire.

loculate(d) ['lɔkjuleit(id)], *a. Nat.Hist:* loculé, loculeux.

locule ['lɔkjul], *s. Bot:* loge *f*.

loculicidal [lɔkjuli'said(ə)l], *a. Bot:* (déhiscence *f*, etc.) loculicide.

loculose ['lɔkjulous], *a. Bot:* loculé, loculeux.

loculus, *pl.* **-li** ['lɔkjuləs, -lai], *s.* *(a) Nat.Hist: A:* locule *f*; *(b) Bot:* loge *f*.

locum ['loukəm], *s.* **1. l. (tenens),** remplaçant, -ante; suppléant, -ante (d'un médecin, d'un ecclésiastique); **to act as l. (tenens) for a doctor,** faire l'intérim *m* d'un médecin; faire un remplacement. **2. l. (tenency),** poste *m* de remplaçant.

locus, *pl.* **loci** ['loukəs, 'lousai, 'lousi:], *s.* **1.** *Scot: Jur:* situation *f* (d'une concession, d'un bâtiment, etc.); scène *f* (d'un crime, etc.); *Jur:* **l. standi,** (i) statut personnel; (ii) droit *m* de comparaître devant la cour. **2.**

Mth: lieu *m* géométrique; **loci curve,** courbe *f* de lieux géométriques. **3.** *Biol:* locus *m* (d'un chromosome).

locust ['loukəst], *s.* **1.** *Ent:* acridien *m*, criquet *m*; grande sauterelle d'Orient; **migratory l.,** criquet pèlerin, migrateur; locuste *f*; **grouse l.,** tétrix *m*. **2.** *Bot:* (*a*) **l. (bean),** caroube *f*; (*b*) **l. (tree),** (i) caroubier *m*; (ii) robinier *m*; faux acacia; acacia vulgaire; (iii) courbaril *m*; (*c*) *Com:* **l. (wood),** (i) caroubier; (ii) robinier; (iii) courbaril.

locution [lou'kju:ʃ(ə)n], *s.* locution *f*.

locutory ['lɔkjutəri], *s. Ecc:* (*a*) parloir *m* (de couvent); (*b*) grille *f* (du parloir).

loddigesia [lɔdi'dʒi:ziə], *s. Orn:* loddigésie *m*.

lode [loud], *s. Geol: Min:* filon *m*, veine *f*; **blind l.,** filon aveugle, sans affleurement; **branched l.,** filon ramifié; **champion l., main l., master l., mother l.,** filon principal, filon mère; **barren l.,** filon stérile; **rotten l.,** filon pourri; **worked-out l., dead l.,** filon épuisé, veine épuisée; **copper(-bearing) l.,** filon de cuivre, filon cuprifère; **tin l.,** filon d'étain, filon stanifère; **l. mining,** exploitation filonienne; **l. deposits,** gisement en filons; **l. formation,** formation filonienne; **l. gold,** or filonien; **l. tin,** étain *m* de roche.

loden ['loudən], *s. Tex:* **l. (cloth),** loden *m*.

lodestar ['loudsta:r], *s.* **1.** étoile directrice; *esp.* **the l.,** l'étoile polaire. **2.** point *m* d'attraction, point de mire (de l'attention, etc.).

lodestone ['loudstoun], *s. Miner:* aimant naturel; pierre *f* d'aimant; magnétite *f*.

lodge[1] [lɔdʒ], *s.* **1.** (*a*) loge *f* (de concierge, etc.); (*b*) **keeper's l.,** maison *f* de garde-chasse; **(gate) l.,** pavillon *m* d'entrée (d'une propriété); pavillon du garde; **forester's l.,** maison forestière; **l. keeper,** portier *m*. **2.** **shooting l.,** pavillon de chasse. **3.** (*a*) loge, atelier *m* (des francs-maçons); **the Grand L. of France,** le Grand Orient (de France); (*b*) **l. (meeting),** tenue *f*. **4.** *Sch:* (*at Cambridge*) **master's l.,** résidence *f* du principal. **5.** terrier *m* (de loutre); hutte *f* (de castor). **6.** hutte (des Indiens de l'Amérique), wigwam *m*. **7.** *Min:* recette *f*, accrochage *m*.

lodge[2], *v.*

I. *v.tr.* **1.** (*a*) loger (qn); héberger (qn); avoir (qn) comme locataire (en garni); **we were well lodged,** nous étions très bien logés; (*b*) **the two divisions lodged themselves on the enemy's flank,** les deux divisions s'établirent, prirent position, sur le flanc de l'ennemi. **2.** *Ven:* (r)embûcher (le cerf). **3.** (*a*) déposer, remettre; **to l. money with s.o.,** consigner, déposer, de l'argent chez qn; confier, remettre, de l'argent à qn; **to l. securities with a bank,** déposer des titres dans une banque, confier des titres à une banque; **securities lodged as collateral,** titres déposés, remis, en nantissement; (*b*) **to l. a bullet on the target,** loger une balle dans la cible; (*c*) recevoir; *Navy:* **to l. a projectile,** encaisser un coup; (*d*) *Jur:* **to l. an appeal,** interjeter appel, faire appel; **to l. a claim against s.o. for damages,** réclamer des dommages-intérêts à qn; **to l. a complaint against s.o.,** porter plainte contre qn; *A:* **to l. power in the hands of s.o.,** donner pouvoir à qn. **4.** (*of wind, rain*) verser, coucher, abattre (le blé).

II. *v.i.* **1.** (*a*) (*of pers.*) (se) loger (quelque part); **to l. with s.o.,** (i) louer une chambre, des chambres, chez qn; (ii) être en pension chez qn; (*b*) *Ven:* (*of stag*) s'embûcher. **2.** (*of thg*) rester, se loger; **his ball lodged on the roof,** son ballon est resté, s'est logé, sur le toit; **a fishbone lodged in his throat,** il a eu une arête coincée dans son gosier. **3.** (*of wheat, etc.*) verser; se coucher.

lodged [lɔdʒd], *a.* (*of stag*) (*a*) *Ven:* embûché; (*b*) *Her:* couché.

lodg(e)ment ['lɔdʒmənt], *s.* **1.** (*a*) *Mil:* installation *f* (dans un ouvrage pris à l'ennemi); **l. area,** ensemble *m* de têtes de pont constituant une base d'opérations; (*b*) prise *f*; point *m* d'appui; assiette *f* (de pied). **2.** *Jur:* dépôt *m*, remise *f* (d'argent, de valeurs) **(with,** chez). **3.** (*a*) accumulation *f*, dépôt (de sable, de boue, etc.) (dans une canalisation, etc.); (*b*) *Min:* recette *f* à eau; **l. level,** galerie *f* de drainage.

lodger ['lɔdʒər], *s.* locataire *mf* (en meublé); sous-locataire *mf*, *pl.* sous-locataires; pensionnaire *mf*; **to take (in) lodgers,** louer des appartements, des chambres; prendre des pensionnaires.

lodging ['lɔdʒiŋ], *s.* **1.** (*a*) hébergement *m* (de qn); **l. house,** hôtel garni; maison meublée; *A:* **common l. house,** dépôt *m* de mendicité; *Rail:* **l. turn,** système qui consiste à faire passer la nuit à un terminus au personnel d'un train qui retourne à son point d'attache par un train en sens inverse le lendemain matin; (*b*) dépôt *m*, consignation *f*, remise *f* (d'argent, de valeurs, etc.); (*c*) *Jur:* déposition *f* (d'une plainte), interjection *f* (d'appel); (*d*) verse *f* (du blé). **2.** logement *m*; **to find a night's l.,** trouver où se coucher pour la nuit; **board and l.,** le vivre et le couvert; chambre(s) *f* avec pension; *Mil: etc:* **l. allowance,** indemnité *f* de logement. **3.** (*usu. in pl.*) logement, logis *m*, appartement meublé; **to let lodgings,** louer des chambres; louer en garni; **to live, be, in lodgings,** loger, habiter, en garni, en (hôtel) meublé.

lodicule ['lɔdikju:l], *s. Bot:* lodicule *f*.

loellingite ['leliŋait], *s. Miner:* lœllingite *f*.

loess [lə:s], *s. Geol:* lœss *m*.

loeweite, loewigite ['lə:vait, -vigait], *s. Miner:* lovéite *f*, lœwéite *f*.

loft[1] [lɔft], *s.* **1.** grenier *m*, soupente *f*. **2.** (*a*) pigeonnier *m*, colombier *m*; (*b*) **a l. of pigeons,** un vol de pigeons. **3.** galerie *f*, tribune *f* (dans une église, une salle, etc.); **organ l.,** tribune de l'orgue. **4.** *Ind:* atelier *m*; *N.Arch:* **drawing l., mould(ing) l.,** salle *f* de gabarits; *Ind:* **l. department,** service *m* de traçage; **l. floor,** aire *f*, table *f*, de traçage. **5.** *Golf:* angle *m* de la face (d'une crosse).

loft[2], *v.tr.* **1.** *Golf:* **to l. the ball,** donner de la hauteur à la balle. **2.** garder (des pigeons) dans un pigeonnier. **3.** *Ind:* tracer; faire le gabarit de (qch.); gabarier.

lofted ['lɔftid], *a. Golf:* (crosse) à face renversée.

loftily ['lɔftili], *adv.* **1.** (situé) en haut. **2.** (répondre) avec hauteur; fièrement, altièrement.

loftiness ['lɔftinis], *s.* **1.** hauteur *f*, élévation *f* (d'un édifice, d'une salle, du plafond). **2.** hauteur (dans les manières); ton hautain. **3.** *A: & Lit:* (*a*) élévation (des sentiments); (*b*) sublimité *f*, élévation (du style).

lofting ['lɔftiŋ], *s. Ind:* traçage *m*; gabariage *m*; exécution *f* de tracés en vraie grandeur.

lofty ['lɔfti], *a.* **1.** (*of mountain, tree, building, etc.*) haut, élevé; **l. stature,** haute taille; taille élevée; *F:* (*as form of address*) **hi, l.!** bonjour, mon grand! **2.** (*of pers., manner*) hautain, orgueilleux, altier; (*b*) (air) condescendant, protecteur. **3.** (*a*) (*of aim, desire, etc.*) élevé; **l. soul,** âme élevée, grande âme; (*b*) (*of style, etc.*) élevé, relevé, sublime, soutenu.

log[1] [lɔg], *s.* **1.** bloc *m* de sciage; grosse bûche; tronçon *m* de bois; rondin *m*; **chopping l.,** billot *m*; **timber in the l.,** bois *m* de brin; bois en grume; **l. basket,** panier *m* à bois; **l. cabin, hut,** hutte *f* de troncs d'arbre, cabane *f* de bois; cabane en rondins; **l. running,** flottage *m* du bois; *Carp:* **l. screw,** tire-fond *m inv*; *Veh:* **l. transporter,** fardier *m*; **don't stand there like a l.!** ne reste pas là comme une souche! **to sleep like a l.,** dormir comme une souche, comme un loir; **to fall like a l.,** tomber comme une masse; **a King L.,** un roi soliveau, un roi solive. **2.** *Nau:* (*a*) loch *m*; **patent l.,** loch enregistreur, à hélice; sillomètre *m*; **hand l.,** loch à main; **l. glass,** sablier *m*; **l. line,** ligne *f* de loch; **l. reel,** touret *m* de loch; tambour *m* de loch; **l. ship, chip,** bateau *m* de loch; **to heave, throw, stream, the l.,** jeter, filer, le loch; **to haul in the l.,** rentrer le loch; **to sail by the l.,** naviguer au loch; (*b*) (*in engine room*) indicateur *m* de vitesse. **3.** carnet *m* de route, de bord; *Nau:* journal *m*, -aux; *Petr: etc:* carnet de sondage; **ship's l.,** journal (i) de navigation, (ii) de bord; **mate's l.,** journal de bord; **to write up the l.,** noter les détails du voyage; **the entries in the l.,** les éléments du carnet, du journal.

log[2], *v.tr.* **1.** (*a*) tronçonner (le bois); débiter (le bois) en bûches; (*b*) **to l. a piece of forest,** abattre (et débiter) les arbres d'une coupe. **2.** (*of ship*) filer (tant de nœuds). **3.** (*a*) *Nau: etc:* porter (un fait) au journal; (*b*) *Ind:* noter (des résultats, etc.) sur le registre. **4.** *W.Tel:* repérer, étalonner (une station).

log[3], *s. Mth: F:* log *m*.

loganberry ['lougənberi], *s. Hort:* ronce-framboise *f*, *pl.* ronces-framboises.

Loganiaceae [lougeini'eisii:], *s.pl. Bot:* loganiacées *f*.

loganstone ['lougənstoun], *s. Geol:* rocher branlant; pierre branlante.

logaoedic [lɔgə'i:dik], *a. & s. Pros:* (vers) logaédique (*m*).

logarithm ['lɔgəriθm], *s.* logarithme *m*; **Napierian l., natural l., hyperbolic l.,** logarithme népérien, naturel; **Briggs's l., decimal l., common l.,** logarithme ordinaire, à base 10; **law of iterated logarithms,** loi *f* des logarithmes itérés.

logarithmic [lɔgə'riθmik], *a.* **1.** (courbe *f*, papier *m*) logarithmique; (papier) à divisions logarithmiques; **l. computation,** calcul *m* logarithmique; **l. chart, l. diagram,** diagramme *m* logarithmique; **double-l. chart,** diagramme bilogarithmique; **l. decrement,** décrément *m* logarithmique; **l. energy decrement,** décrément logarithmique d'énergie. **2. l. table,** table *f* des logarithmes.

logarithmically [lɔgə'riθmik(ə)li], *adv.* au moyen de(s) logarithmes.

logbook ['lɔgbuk], *s.* **1.** *Nau:* livre *m* de loch. **2.** (*a*) *Nau:* **ship's l.,** (i) journal *m* de navigation, (ii) journal de bord; (*b*) *Aut:* carnet *m* de route; (*c*) *Av:* livre, carnet, de vol; (*d*) *Ind: etc:* journal de travail (d'une machine); registre *m*; *W.Tel:* carnet d'écoute; *Min:* **driller's l.,** carnet de sondage. **3.** *Aut:* *F:* = carte grise.

logger ['lɔgər], *s.* bûcheron *m*; forestier *m*.

loggerhead ['lɔgəhed], *s.* **1.** *A:* sot *m*, lourdaud *m*. **2.** *Nau:* boulet *m* à brai. **3.** (*a*) *Rept:* caouan(n)e *f*; (*b*) *Orn:* canard *m* vapeur. **4. to be at loggerheads with s.o.,** être en conflit (d'intérêts, d'opinions), en désaccord, en querelle, avec qn; *F:* être à couteaux tirés avec qn; **he's at loggerheads with the mayor,** il fait mauvais ménage avec le maire.

loggia, *pl.* **-ias, -ie** ['lɔdʒiə, -iəz, -iei], *s. Arch:* loge *f*, loggia *f*.

logging ['lɔgiŋ], *s.* (*a*) exploitation *f* des bois et forêts; abattage *m* et façonnage *m*; **l. wheels,** triqueballe *m or f*; (*b*) inscription *f* (d'un fait) dans le journal, le carnet de route, etc.; *W.Tel:* étalonnage *m*.

logic ['lɔdʒik], *s.* logique *f*; **combinatory l.,** logique combinatoire; **formal l.,** logique formelle; **modal l.,** logique modale; **predicate l.,** logique fonctionnelle, logique des termes; **prepositional l.,** logique prépositionnelle; **scientific l.,** logique scientifique; **the l. of events,** la contrainte des événements; **l. chopping,** byzantinisme *m*; *F:* **feminine l.,** logique féminine.

logical ['lɔdʒik(ə)l], *a.* (*of thg, pers.*) logique; **it's only l.!** ce n'est (quand même) que logique! **do be l.!** sois quand même logique!

logically ['lɔdʒik(ə)li], *adv.* logiquement.

logician [lə'dʒiʃ(ə)n], *s.* logicien, -ienne.

logicism ['lɔdʒisizm], *s. Phil:* logicisme *m*.

logicist ['lɔdʒisist], *s.* logiciste *mf*.

logistic[1] [lə'dʒistik], *a. Phil: Mil:* logistique; *Mil:* **l. resources,** moyens *m* logistiques; **l. support,** soutien *m* logistique; **air l. support,** soutien logistique aérien; **naval mobile l. support,** soutien (logistique) mobile de la flotte; **underway l. support,** soutien logistique en mer, ravitaillement *m* à la mer.

logistic[2], *s.* (*a*) *Phil:* logistique *f*; (*b*) *Mil:* **logistics,** logistique.

logistician [lɔdʒis'tiʃ(ə)n], *s. Phil: Mil:* logisticien, -ienne.

logjam ['lɔgdʒæm], *s.* (*a*) embâcle *m* de bûches; (*b*) *NAm:* impasse *f*; situation *f* inextricable.

logoclonia [lɔgou'klouniə], *s. Med: Psy:* logoclonie *f*.

logographer [lɔ'gɔgrəfər], *s. Gr.Ant:* logographe *m*.

logogriph ['lɔgəgrif], *s.* logogriphe *m*, énigme *f*, anagramme *f*.

logomachic(al) [lɔgou'mækik(l)], *a.* logomachique.

logomachy [lɔ'gɔməki], *s.* logomachie *f*; dispute *f* de mots.

logomania [lɔgou'meiniə], *s. Med:* logorrhée *f*.

logopedics [lɔgou'pi:diks], *s.pl.* (*usu. with sg. const.*) logopédie *f*.

logorrhea [lɔgou'riə], *s. Med:* logorrhée *f*.

logos ['lɔgɔs], *s.* (*a*) *A.Phil:* logos *m*; (*b*) *Theol:* **Logos,** Logos, le Verbe.

logotype ['lɔgətaip], *s. Typ:* logotype *m*.

logroll ['lɔgroul], *v.i.* **1.** *For:* rouler les billes jusqu'à la rivière. **2.** se prêter les uns aux autres une entr'aide intéressée; faire du battage.

logroller ['lɔgroulər], *s.* **1.** manœuvre *m* qui roule les billes jusqu'à la rivière. **2.** personne qui prête à une autre une aide intéressée.

logrolling ['lɔgrouliŋ], *s.* **1.** transport *m* des billes à la rivière. **2.** (*a*) alliance *f* politique dans un but intéressé; (*b*) battage *m* littéraire, camaraderie *f* littéraire; **l. criticism,** critique *f* d'admiration mutuelle.

logrunner ['lɔgrʌnər], *s. Orn: Austr:* orthonyx *m*.

logwood ['lɔgwud], *s. Bot:* (*a*) (*wood*) (bois *m* de) campêche *m*; (*b*) (*tree*) campêcher *m*; (*c*) *Dy:* extrait *m* de campêche.

loin [lɔin], *s.* **1.** *pl.* **loins,** reins *m*; *Anat:* lombes *m*; *Lit:* **to gird up one's loins,** ceindre ses reins; se ceindre les reins; **sprung from the loins of . . .,** sorti des reins de . . .. **2.** (*a*) esquine *f* (d'un cheval); (*b*) *Cu:* filet *m* (de mouton, de veau); longe *f* (de veau); carré *m* (de mouton); aloyau *m* et faux-filet (de bœuf); échine *f*, filet *m* (de porc); **l. chop,** côtelette *f* de filet; côte première.

loincloth ['lɔinkləθ], *s.* pagne *m*, bande-culotte *f*, *pl.* bandes-culottes.

loir ['lɔiər], *s. Z:* loir *m*.

loiter ['lɔitər], *v.i.* (*a*) flâner, traîner; s'attarder (en route); (*b*) *Jur:* rôder (d'une manière suspecte dans un endroit fréquenté); (*said by police*) **now then, no loitering!** circulez!

loiterer ['lɔitərər], *s.* (*a*) flâneur, -euse; musard, -arde; (*b*) rôdeur, -euse.

loitering ['lɔitəriŋ], *s.* flânerie *f*.

loligo [lou'laigou], *s. Moll:* loligo *m*; *F:* calmar *m*, encornet *m*.

loll [lɔl]. **1.** *v.i.* (*a*) (*of tongue*) **to l. out,** pendre; (*b*) (*of* *pers.*) être étendu (paresseusement); **lolling back in an armchair,** étendu, renversé, nonchalamment, paresseusement, dans un fauteuil; **to l. against a wall,** s'appuyer mollement contre un mur; (*c*) **to l. about,** flâner, fainéanter. **2.** *v.tr.* (*of dog, etc.*) **to l. out its tongue,** laisser pendre la langue.

Lollard ['lɔləd], *s. Rel.H:* lollard *m.*

Lollardism ['lɔlədizm], *s. Rel.H:* lollardisme *m.*

löllingite ['leliŋait], *s. Miner:* lœllingite *f.*

lollie ['lɔli], *s. F:* sucette *f.*

lollipop ['lɔlipɔp], *s.* (*a*) sucrerie *f*; sucre *m* d'orge; sucette *f*; **lollipops,** bonbons *m*; (*b*) *F:* **l. man, woman,** gardien, -ienne, de passage clouté (pour les écoliers).

lollop ['lɔləp], *v.i. F:* **to l. along,** marcher lourdement; se traîner; **the rabbit was lolloping across the field,** le lapin traversait le champ par bonds.

lolly ['lɔli], *s. F:* **1.** (*a*) sucette *f*; **ice(d) l.,** sucette glacée; (*b*) *Austr:* bonbon *m.* **2.** fric *m*, galette *f.*

Lombard ['lɔmbəd], *a. & s.* **1.** *a. Geog:* lombard; *Arch:* **L. bands,** bandes lombardes; *Hist:* **the L. bankers,** les Lombards *m.* **2.** *s. Geog:* Lombard, -arde.

Lombardic [lɔm'bɑ:dik], *a.* lombard, lombardique; de Lombardie.

Lombardy ['lɔmbədi]. *Pr.n. Geog:* Lombardie *f.*

lomentaceous [lɔmen'teiʃəs], *a. Bot:* lomentacé.

London ['lʌndən]. *Pr.n.* **1.** (*a*) *Geog:* Londres *f, occ. m*; **Greater L.,** le grand Londres; (*b*) *attrib.* londonien, de Londres; **L. fogs,** les brouillards londoniens; **a typical L. street,** une rue typique de Londres; **this town is basically a L. dormitory,** cette ville sert essentiellement de dortoir pour Londres; **a firm with a L. office,** une maison qui a un bureau à Londres; *Geol:* **L. clay,** argile *f* du Bassin de Londres. **2.** *Bot:* **L. pride,** saxifrage ombreuse; désespoir *m* des peintres; amourette *f*, mignonnette *f*, mignonnet *m.*

Londoner ['lʌndənər], *s.* Londonien, -ienne; habitant, -ante, de Londres; **L. born and bred,** un vrai Londonien de Londres.

lone [loun], *a.* **1.** *esp. Lit:* (*of pers., thg*) solitaire, seul; (*of place*) isolé, désert; **a l. pine,** un pin solitaire. **2. to play a l. hand,** (i) (*at cards*) faire la chouette; (ii) agir tout seul; être seul contre tous; *s. O:* **to be on one's lone(s), by one's lone(s),** être seul avec soi-même. **3.** *A:* **l. woman,** femme seule, non mariée; veuve; **I'm a poor l. woman,** je suis une pauvre femme livrée à ses propres ressources.

loneliness ['lounlinis], *s.* **1.** solitude *f*, isolement *m.* **2.** sentiment *m* d'abandon.

lonely ['lounli], *a.* solitaire, isolé; **to feel very l.,** se sentir bien seul; **l. spot,** endroit désert; solitude *f.*

lonesome ['lounsəm]. **1.** *a.* solitaire, seul; seulet, -ette; **to feel l.,** se sentir seul. **2.** *s. F:* **to be on one's l.,** être seul avec soi-même.

lonesomeness ['lounsəmnis], *s. esp. Lit:* solitude *f*; sentiment *m* d'abandon.

long[1] [lɔŋ], *a., s. & adv.*

I. *a.* (**longer** ['lɔŋgər], **longest** ['lɔŋgist]) long, *f.* longue. **1.** (*a*) **l. measure,** mesure *f* de longueur; **how l. is the table?** quelle est la longueur de la table? de quelle longueur est la table? **to make sth. longer,** allonger, rallonger, qch.; **a garden longer than it is wide,** un jardin plus long que large; **to be six metres l.,** avoir une longueur de six mètres; être long de six mètres; **to go the longest way round,** prendre par le plus long; **it's not as l. as (all) that,** ce n'est pas aussi long que ça; **the best by a l. way,** de beaucoup le meilleur; **we went on (in the rain) for ten l. kilometres,** nous avons avancé (sous la pluie) pendant dix bons kilomètres; *F:* **words as l. as your arm,** mots longs d'une toise; (*b*) **l. dress,** robe longue; **should I wear a l. dress?** devrais-je mettre une robe de soirée? *A.Cost:* **l. clothes,** *A:* **l. coats,** maillot anglais (de nouveau-né); cache-maillot *m*; (*c*) **a l. face,** (i) une figure allongée; (ii) une triste figure; **to pull a l. face,** avoir la mine longue; faire longue figure; faire une tête; **face as l. as a fiddle,** figure d'enterrement, longue d'une aune; **to have a l. tongue,** avoir la langue trop longue, bien pendue; **l. in the leg,** haut jambé; **to be l. in the arm, to have l. arms, to be l.-armed,** avoir les bras longs; (*d*) *Typ:* **l. S,** S allongé; (*e*) *Cr:* **l. stop,** chasseur posté en arrière du garde-guichet; **l. off, l. on,** chasseur éloigné à la droite, à la gauche, du batteur. **2.** (*in time*) **a l. life,** une longue vie; **how l. are the holidays?** quelle est la durée des vacances? **the l. vacation,** les grandes vacances; **the days are getting longer,** les jours rallongent; **it will take a l. time,** cela prendra longtemps; ce sera long; **a l. time has elapsed,** beaucoup de temps s'est écoulé; **they're a l. time, a l. while, coming,** ils mettent du temps, ils tardent, à venir; ils se font attendre; **she was a l. time getting over it,** elle a mis longtemps à s'en remettre; **it's a l. time since I saw him, I haven't seen him for a l. time,** il y a longtemps que je ne l'ai vu; **he has been gone a l. time,** il y a longtemps qu'il est parti; **a l. time ago,** il y a (bien) longtemps; **it was a l. time before these facts were acknowledged,** on a été longtemps à reconnaître ces faits; **it will be a l. time before the agitation dies down,** l'agitation n'est pas près de se calmer; **to wait for a l. time,** attendre longtemps; **to have been waiting for a l. time,** attendre depuis longtemps; **for a l. time he was thought to be dead,** pendant longtemps on l'a cru mort; **he had been contemplating this step for a l. time,** depuis longtemps, de longue date, il méditait cette démarche; **it won't happen for a l. time,** cela ne se fera pas de longtemps; **it will be a l. job,** cela va prendre longtemps; ce sera un travail de longue haleine; **three days at the longest,** trois jours (tout) au plus; **a l. memory,** une mémoire tenace; **to have a l. story to tell,** en avoir long à conter; **to have a l. talk with s.o.,** parler longuement avec qn; avoir un long entretien avec qn; *Pros: etc:* **l. syllable,** syllabe longue; *Mil: etc:* **l. service,** engagement *m* à long terme; **l. servicemen,** engagés *m* à long terme. **3.** *Com:* **l. hundred,** grand cent, cent vingt; **l. dozen,** treize; *O:* **l. family,** grande famille; **l. price,** grand prix, prix élevé; *F: O:* **l. firm,** bande noire; (groupe de) carambouilleurs *mpl.*

II. *s.* **1.** (*a*) **the l. and short of it, of the matter, is that . . .,** le fin mot de l'affaire c'est que . . .; en somme . . .; **that's the l. and short of it,** voilà ni plus ni moins l'affaire; et voilà tout! (*b*) **longs and shorts,** (i) *Pros:* longues *f* et brèves *f*; (ii) *Const:* chaîne *f* d'encoignure, de liaison; (*c*) *Mus: A:* longue; (*d*) *Sch: O:* **the l.,** les grandes vacances. **2.** (*shortened form of* **a long time**) **before l.,** *Lit:* **ere l.,** avant peu; dans peu; sous peu; dans un avenir prochain; **for l.,** pendant longtemps; **I haven't l. to live,** je n'ai pas longtemps à vivre; je n'en ai pas pour longtemps; **it won't take l.,** cela ne prendra pas longtemps; ce sera tôt fait, ce ne sera pas long; **it won't take me l.,** je n'en ai pas pour longtemps; **I had only l. enough to . . .,** je n'ai eu que le temps de . . ..

III. *adv.* **1.** (*a*) longtemps; **I didn't wait l.,** je n'ai pas attendu longtemps; **have you been here l.?** y a-t-il longtemps que vous êtes ici, que vous attendez? **he has been gone so l.,** il y a beau temps qu'il est parti; **he's not l. for this world,** il ne vivra plus longtemps; il ne fera pas de vieux os; **l. live the King, the Queen!** vive le roi, la reine! **so l. as, as l. as,** (i) aussi longtemps que; (ii) tant que; (iii) pourvu que; **as l., so l., as I live,** tant que je vivrai; **do as you like so, as, l. as you leave me alone,** faites tout ce que vous voudrez pourvu que vous me laissiez tranquille; **stay as l. as you like,** restez aussi longtemps que vous voudrez; **he was not l. coming,** il n'a pas tardé à venir; **he wasn't l. putting things straight,** il eut bientôt fait de mettre tout en ordre; **don't be too l. packing,** ne soyez pas trop longtemps, ne mettez pas trop de temps, à faire vos valises; **you weren't l. about it, over it, doing it,** vous l'avez vite fait; vous n'avez pas pris longtemps (à le faire); **he won't be l.,** (i) il ne tardera pas; (ii) il l'aura vite fait; **it won't be l. now,** ça ne va plus durer longtemps; **now we shan't be l.!** nous n'en avons plus pour longtemps; **it won't be l. before you see him again,** vous le reverrez avant longtemps; **it's not l. since I saw him,** il n'y a pas longtemps que je l'ai vu; **we shan't have to wait long before seeing him, before he comes,** nous ne tarderons pas à le voir venir; *F:* **so l.!** au revoir! à bientôt! à tantôt! à toute à l'heure! *Fin:* **to lend, to borrow, l.,** prêter, emprunter, à longue échéance; (*b*) depuis longtemps; **I have l. been convinced of it,** j'en suis convaincu depuis longtemps; **l. felt want,** besoin senti depuis longtemps; (*c*) **how l.?** combien de temps? **how l. have you been here?** il y a combien de temps que vous êtes ici? vous êtes ici depuis combien de temps? **how l. will it be until, before . . .?** combien de temps faudra-t-il pour que . . .? **how much longer shall we be?** pour combien de temps avons-nous encore? **how l. does your leave last?** quelle est la durée de votre congé? **how l. will you need (to do it)?** combien de temps vous faudra-t-il (pour le faire)? **how l. is it since then?** combien de temps y a-t-il de cela? **2. l. before, l. after,** longtemps avant, après; **not l. before, after,** peu de temps avant, après; **l. ago,** il y a longtemps; **he died l. ago,** *Lit:* **l. since,** il est mort depuis longtemps; il y a longtemps qu'il est mort; **he died not very l. ago,** il n'y a pas longtemps qu'il est mort; il est mort depuis peu; **in the days of l. ago,** autrefois, anciennement; *Lit:* au temps jadis; **tales of l. ago,** contes *m* du temps jadis, d'autrefois; **the l.-ago days of my youth,** les jours lointains de ma jeunesse; **I knew it l. before,** je le savais de longue date. **3. all day, all night, l.,** tout le long du jour, de la nuit; pendant toute la journée, la nuit. **4. I could no longer see him,** je ne pouvais plus le voir; **they were no longer very young,** ils n'étaient plus très jeunes; **I couldn't wait any longer,** je ne pouvais pas attendre plus longtemps; **five minutes longer,** cinq minutes de plus; encore cinq minutes; **it will be longer than that,** ce sera plus long, plus longtemps, que ça; **the longer you stay the better,** plus vous resterez, mieux cela vaudra.

long[2], *v.i.* **to l. for sth.,** désirer qch. fortement, ardemment; avoir grande envie de qch.; soupirer pour, après, qch.; **to l. for home,** avoir la nostalgie du foyer; **to l. for s.o.'s return,** attendre impatiemment le retour de qn; **to l. to do sth.,** avoir bien envie, avoir une furieuse envie, de faire qch.; être impatient de faire qch.; brûler, rêver, de faire qch.; **I'm longing to see him again,** j'attends de le revoir avec impatience.

longan ['lɔŋgən], *s. Bot:* longanier *m.*

longanimity [lɔŋgə'nimiti], *s. Lit:* longanimité *f.*

longbeard ['lɔŋbi:əd], *s. Moss:* mousse *f* d'Espagne; barbe *f* de vieillard.

longbill ['lɔŋbil], *s. Orn:* (*a*) bécassine *f*; (*b*) oiseau *m* longirostre.

longboat ['lɔŋbout], *s. Nau:* grand canot; chaloupe *f.*

long-boled ['lɔŋ'bould], *a.* (arbre) à fût long.

longbow ['lɔŋbou], *s. Mil.Hist:* arc *m* d'homme d'armes; *F:* **to draw the l.,** exagérer, hâbler; conter des couleurs; dire des gasconnades; faire le Gascon; outrer les choses; en conter d'incroyables; dire, raconter, des craques.

longcase ['lɔŋkeis], *a.* **l. clock,** horloge *f* de parquet.

longclaw ['lɔŋklɔ:], *s. Orn:* alouette *f* sentinelle.

longcloth ['lɔŋklɔθ], *s. Tex:* (sorte de) calicot *m.*

long-dated ['lɔŋ'deitid], *a. Fin:* à longue échéance; **l.-d. bills,** billets *m*, papiers *m*, à longue échéance; *F:* papiers longs.

long-distance ['lɔŋ'distəns], *a. Tp: etc:* à longue distance; *Rail: etc:* de grand parcours; **l.-d. aircraft,** (avion) long courrier; *Sp:* **l.-d. runner,** coureur, -euse, de fond; fondeur *m.*

long-drawn-out ['lɔŋ'drɔ:'naut], *a.* (*of sigh, etc.*) prolongé; (*of story, explanation, etc.*) interminable.

longe [lʌndʒ], *s.* = LUNGE[1].

long-eared ['lɔŋ'iə:d], *a.* aux longues oreilles; **l.-e. bat,** oreillard *m*; **l.-e. fox,** otocyon *m.*

longeron ['lɔndʒərən], *s. Av:* longeron *m.*

long-established ['lɔŋis'tæbliʃt], *a.* établi depuis longtemps.

longevity [lɔn'dʒeviti], *s.* longévité *f.*

longevous [lɔn'dʒi:vəs], **longeval** [lɔn'dʒi:v(ə)l], *a.* longévital, -aux; de longue durée; qui vit longtemps.

long-forgotten ['lɔŋfə'gɔt(ə)n], *a.* oublié depuis longtemps.

long-grained ['lɔŋ'greind], *a.* à fibres longues.

longhair ['lɔŋhɛər], *s.* **1.** chat *m* à poils longs. **2.** *F:* (*pers.*) intellectuel *m.*

longhaired ['lɔŋhɛəd], *a.* (homme) à cheveux longs; (chat) à poils longs.

longhand ['lɔŋhænd], *s.* écriture ordinaire, courante, non-abrégée; **to take (down) a letter in l.,** prendre une lettre en clair.

long-headed ['lɔŋ'hedid], *a.* **1.** à (la) tête allongée; *Anthr:* dolichocéphale. **2.** *O:* sagace, perspicace, avisé; fin matois; calculateur, -trice.

long-headedness ['lɔŋ'hedidnis], *s.* **1.** *Anthr:* dolichocéphalie *f.* **2.** *O:* sagacité *f*, perspicacité *f.*

longhorn ['lɔŋhɔ:n], *a. & s.* **1.** *Z:* (bœuf *m*) à longues cornes. **2.** *Ent:* **l. (beetle),** longicorne *m*, capricorne *m*; **Alpine l.,** rosalie *f.*

longhouse ['lɔŋhaus], *s.* maison commune (des Iroquois, etc.).

longicaudate [lɔndʒi'kɔ:deit], *a. Nat.Hist:* longicaude; à longue queue.

longicauline [lɔndʒi'kɔ:lain], *a. Bot:* longicaule; à longue tige.

longicorn ['lɔndʒikɔ:n]. *Ent:* **1.** *a.* (coléoptère *m*) longicorne. **2.** *s.* céréambyx *m*; capricorne *m*, longicorne *m.*

longimanous [lɔn'dʒimənəs], *a. Z:* longimane; à longues mains.

longing[1] ['lɔŋiŋ], *a.* qui désire ardemment, qui attend impatiemment; **to look at sth. with l. eyes,** couver qch. des yeux; regarder qch. avec convoitise.

longing[2], *s.* (*a*) désir ardent, grande envie (**for, after,** de); aspiration *f* (**for, after,** à); (*b*) *Med:* **longings,** envies (de femme enceinte).

longingly ['lɔŋiŋli], *adv.* avec envie, avec ardeur, avec un vif désir; **to look l. at sth.,** couver qch. des yeux.

Longinus [lɔn'dʒainəs]. *Pr.n.m. Gr.Lit:* Longin.

longipedate [lɔn'dʒipədeit], *a. Z:* longipède.

longipennate [lɔndʒi'peneit], *a. Orn:* longipenne.

longish ['lɔŋiʃ], *a.* assez long, plutôt long; *F:* longuet, -ette.

longitude ['lɔndʒitju:d], *s.* **1.** *A:* longueur *f.* **2.** *Astr: Geog:* longitude *f*; **east l.,** longitude est, orientale; **west**

l., longitude ouest, occidentale; **in l. 20°**, par 20° de longitude; **in the l. of . . .**, sous, par, la longitude de . . .; **l. of fix**, longitude du point estimé; **l. scale**, échelle *f* des longitudes; **difference of l.**, différence *f* en longitude; **corrected l.**, longitude corrigée; **celestial l.**, longitude céleste; **l. by chronometer**, longitude par différence d'heure; **l. by dead reckoning**, longitude par l'estime, longitude estimée; **l. by observation**, longitude par l'observation, longitude observée.

longitudinal [lɔndʒi'tju:din(ə)l]. **1.** *a.* longitudinal, -aux; en long; **l. beam, l. girder, l. member, l. runner**, longeron *m*, longrine *f*; *Av:* **l. stringer**, raidisseur longitudinal; **l. trim**, centrage longitudinal; *Ph:* **l. vibration**, vibration longitudinale; **l. wave**, onde longitudinale; *Opt:* **l. aberration**, aberration longitudinale; *Mec:* **l. stress**, effort longitudinal, fatigue longitudinale; *Mch.Tls:* (*of lathe*), **l. traverse**, chariotage longitudinal; *Draw:* **l. section**, coupe longitudinale, coupe en long; profil longitudinal, profil en long. **2.** *s.* (*a*) *Av:* longeron *m*; (*b*) *N.Arch:* **l. frame**, longitudinale *f*; **l. bulkhead**, cloison longitudinale.

longitudinally [lɔndʒi'tju:dinəli], *adv.* longitudinalement; en long.

long-jointed ['lɔŋ'dʒɔintid], *a.* (cheval) long-jointé, *pl.* long-jointés.

longleaf ['lɔŋli:f], *s. Bot:* **l. (pine)**, pin *m* à longues feuilles.

long-leaved ['lɔŋ'li:vd], *a.* à longues feuilles; longifolié; **l.-l. lettuce**, alfange *f*; **l.-l. pine**, pin *m* à longues feuilles.

long-legged ['lɔŋ'legid], *a.* à longues jambes; haut enjambé, *pl.* haut enjambés; (*of horse*) haut-perché, haut-jointé, *pl.* haut-perchés, -jointés, aux jambes allongées; (*of bird*) à longues pattes; **a l.-l., gawky, young woman**, une grande gigue.

long-limbed ['lɔŋ'limd], *a.* longiligne.

long-line[1] ['lɔŋ'lain], *a.* **l.-l. brassière**, soutien-gorge *m* à basque; (*strapless*) bustier *m*.

longline[2], *s. Fish:* ap(pe)let *m*.

long-lived ['lɔŋ'livd], *a.* (*a*) qui a la vie longue; qui vit longtemps; *Nat.Hist:* longévital, -aux; vivace; (*b*) **l.-l. error**, erreur persistante, vivace; **l.-l. fame**, célébrité *f* de longue durée.

long-lost ['lɔŋ'lɔst], *a.* perdu depuis longtemps.

long-playing ['lɔŋ'pleiiŋ], *a. Rec:* **l.-p. record, disc**, disque *m* de longue durée, (disque) microsillon *m*.

long-range ['lɔŋ'reindʒ], *a.* (avion) long courrier; (canon, radar) à longue portée; *Meteor:* **l.-r. forecast**, prévision *f* à longue échéance.

Longshanks ['lɔŋʃæŋks]. **1.** *Pr.n. Hist: F:* **Edward L.**, Édouard Longues-Jambes. **2.** *s. Orn:* échassier *m*.

longshore ['lɔŋʃɔ:ər], *a.* qui vit sur la côte; qui rôde sur la plage.

longshoreman, *pl.* **-men** ['lɔŋʃɔ:mən], *s.m. Nau:* (*a*) homme qui travaille dans le port; débardeur; (*b*) pêcheur de moules, ramasseur de varech, etc.

longsighted ['lɔŋ'saitid], *a.* **1.** (*a*) presbyte; (*b*) hypermétrope. **2.** prévoyant.

longsightedness ['lɔŋ'saitidnis], *s.* **1.** (*a*) presbytie *f*; (*b*) hypermétropie *f*. **2.** prévoyance *f*.

longspur ['lɔŋspə:r], *s. Orn:* bruant *m*; **chestnut-collared l.**, bruant à ventre noir; **Lapland l.**, bruant lapon; **McCown's l.**, bruant à collier gris; **Smith's l.**, bruant de Smith.

longstanding ['lɔŋ'stændiŋ], *a.* ancien; de longue date; de vieille date; **l. accounts**, notes dues depuis longtemps; vieux comptes.

long-styled ['lɔŋ'staild], *a. Bot:* (fleur) longistyle.

longsuffering ['lɔŋ'sʌf(ə)riŋ]. **1.** *s.* (*a*) patience *f*, endurance *f*; (*b*) longanimité *f*, indulgence *f*. **2.** *a.* (*a*) patient, endurant; (*b*) longanime, indulgent.

longtail ['lɔŋteil], *s.* **1.** *Z:* lévrier *m*. **2.** *Orn:* (*a*) phaéton *m*; (*b*) harelde *f* de Miquelon.

long-tailed ['lɔŋ'teild], *a.* à longue queue; longicaude; (crustacé *m*) macroure; *Orn:* **l.-t. tit (mouse)**, mésange *f* à longue queue; **l.-t. duck**, harelde *f* de Miquelon.

long(-)term ['lɔŋtə:m], *a.* à long terme; **l. credit, loan**, crédit *m*, emprunt *m* à long terme; **l. policy**, politique *f* à long terme, à longue échéance.

long-waisted ['lɔŋ'weistid], *a.* (*of pers., dress*) long de taille.

longways ['lɔŋweiz], **longwise** ['lɔŋwaiz], *adv.* en long, en longueur; dans le sens de la longueur.

longwinded ['lɔŋ'windid], *a.* **1.** (histoire *f*) de longue haleine, interminable. **2.** (*of speaker*) verbeux, prolixe, diffus; intarissable. **3.** *Sp:* (*of pers., horse*) qui ne s'essouffle pas; qui a du fond.

long-winged ['lɔŋ'wiŋd], *a. Orn:* longipenne.

loo[1] [lu:], *s.* **1.** *Cards:* la mouche. **2.** *Furn:* **l. table** = guéridon *m*.

loo[2], *s. F:* **the l.**, les cabinets, la toilette; **to go to the l.**, aller aux cabinets; **l. paper**, papier *m* hygiénique; **l. cover, l. mat**, dessus *m* d'abattant, tapis *m* d'entourage, de W.C.

looby ['lu:bi], *s. esp. U.S: F:* nigaud *m*, lourdaud *m*.

loofah ['lu:fə], *s. Bot: Toil:* loofa(h) *m*, luffa, louffa *m or f*; éponge végétale.

look[1] [luk], *s.* **1.** regard *m*; **to have a l. at sth.**, regarder qch.; jeter un coup d'œil sur qch.; **may I have a l.?** puis-je regarder? **he had a good, a hard, l. at it**, il l'a examiné attentivement, longuement; **to take a good l. at s.o.**, (i) scruter qn du regard; (ii) dévisager qn; **he gave a l. at his brother**, il a jeté, lancé, un coup d'œil vers son frère; **he gave me a severe l.**, il m'a regardé d'un œil sévère; **to have a l. round the town**, faire un tour de ville; **would you like to have a l. round the house?** est-ce que vous voudriez voir la maison? **have a l. round and see if you can find my keys**, cherche un peu si tu peux trouver mes clefs; **I'll have a l. upstairs**, je vais regarder en haut; **to have a l. round the room**, (i) promener son regard autour de la pièce; (ii) chercher dans la pièce (pour trouver qch.). **2.** (*a*) aspect *m*, air *m*, apparence *f* (de qn, de qch.); mine *f* (de qn); **his face took on a vacant l.**, il a pris un air hébété; **there was an ugly l. on his face**, il faisait mauvaise mine; **the business has a suspicious l. about it**, l'affaire paraît suspecte, louche, ne dit rien de bon; **by her l. one can see that . . .**, à sa mine on voit que . . .; **to judge by looks**, juger d'après les apparences; **to judge by his looks**, à le voir; **I like the l. of him**, il me plaît, je le trouve sympathique; **I don't like the l. of him**, (i) il ne me plaît pas, ne m'est pas sympathique; (ii) il a l'air louche; (iii) il a l'air (bien) malade; **by, from, the l. of him I think it probable**, à le voir cela me paraît très probable; **she has a l. of her mother**, elle ressemble à sa mère; **this town has a European l. (about it)**, cette ville a un aspect, un air, européen; *Com:* **new l.**, nouvelle apparence, nouvelle mode; (*b*) **good looks**, belle mine, bonne mine, beauté *f*; **she has looks but no money**, elle a la beauté mais pas la fortune.

look[2], *v.*

I. *v.i. & tr.* **1.** *v.i.* regarder; (*a*) **to l. through, out of, the window**, regarder par la fenêtre; **to l. in at the window**, regarder à la fenêtre; **to l. through a telescope**, regarder au télescope, dans le télescope; **to l. over a wall**, regarder par-dessus un mur; **to l. down a list**, parcourir une liste; **to l. down, up, the street**, jeter un coup d'œil le long de la rue; **we looked down on the crowd from the top of the tower**, nous avons regardé la foule du haut de la tour; **to l. about one**, regarder autour de soi; s'orienter; **to l. away from s.o., from sth.**, détourner les yeux, le regard, de qn, de qch.; **to l. the other way**, (i) regarder de l'autre côté; (ii) détourner les yeux; **to l. in s.o.'s direction, towards s.o.**, tourner les yeux, la tête, vers qn; *F: A:* **I l. towards you!** à votre santé! **to l. into s.o.'s eyes**, regarder dans les yeux de qn; regarder qn dans les yeux; *Prov:* **l. before you leap**, regardez à deux fois avant de sauter; il faut réfléchir avant d'agir; (*b*) **l. (and see) what time it is**, regardez quelle heure il est; **l. where you're going!** regardez où vous allez; prenez garde où vous marchez; attention! (*c*) **I l. to you to help me, for protection**, je compte sur votre aide, votre protection; *Lit:* **I had looked to find a stern master**, je m'attendais à trouver un maître sévère; *A:* **to l. to sth.**, s'occuper de qch.; veiller à qch.; **it is time to l. to it**, il est temps d'aviser; (*d*) (i) **which way does the house l.?** quelle est l'exposition de la maison? **it looks south, to, towards, the south, towards the sea**, elle est exposée orientée, vers le sud, au midi, vers la mer; **the drawing room looks on to the garden**, le salon donne sur le jardin; (ii) **to l. to, towards, the future**, envisager l'avenir. **2.** *v.tr.* (*a*) **to l. s.o. (full, straight) in the face**, regarder qn (bien) en face, dans les yeux, dans le blanc des yeux, entre les deux yeux; dévisager qn; **I can never l. him in the face again**, je me sentirai toujours honteux devant lui; **to l. s.o. up and down**, regarder qn de haut en bas; mesurer qn des yeux; toiser qn; (*b*) **to l. one's last on sth.**, voir qch. pour la dernière fois; jeter un dernier regard sur qch. **3.** *v.i.* avoir l'air, paraître, sembler; **to l. happy**, avoir l'air heureux, avoir la mine heureuse; **she looks tired**, elle a l'air bien fatigué(e); **to l. old**, paraître, faire, vieux; **he is only thirty, but he looks fifty**, il n'a que trente ans, mais il en paraît cinquante; **to l. older, younger, than one really is**, porter, marquer, plus que son âge, moins que son âge; **he's not as stupid as he looks**, il est moins bête qu'il n'en a l'air; **she is not so thin as she looks**, c'est une fausse maigre; **he looks young for his age**, il porte bien son âge; **she looks her age**, elle paraît son âge; **she doesn't l. her age**, elle ne porte pas son âge; on ne lui donnerait pas son âge; **he was frightened, and (he) looked it**, il avait peur, et cela se voyait; **you still l. the same**, vous avez toujours même visage; **to l. ill**, avoir l'air malade; avoir mauvaise mine; **to l. well**, (i) (*of pers.*) avoir l'air bien portant; avoir bonne mine, bon visage; (ii) (*of thg*) faire bien; faire bon effet; avoir de l'apparence; **he looks well in uniform**, l'uniforme lui va; **vases that l. well on the mantelpiece**, vases *m* qui font bien sur la cheminée; **it doesn't l. well**, (i) cela manque de cachet; (ii) (*of conduct, etc.*) cela fait mauvais effet; **that dress looks well on you**, cette robe vous va bien; **business is looking promising**, les affaires vont bien, prennent une bonne allure; **the crops l. promising**, la récolte s'annonce bien; **things are looking bad, black**, les choses prennent une mauvaise, une vilaine, tournure, une mauvaise allure; **this chicken looks good**, ce poulet a l'air appétissant; **how does my hat l.?** comment trouvez-vous mon chapeau? **he looks as though, as if, he wanted to . . .**, il a l'air de vouloir . . .; **you l. as if you'd slept badly**, vous avez l'air d'avoir mal dormi; **it looks as if he didn't want to go**, il semble qu'il ne veuille pas y aller; **it looks as if, as though, it were going to be fine, to rain, it looks like fine weather, like rain**, le temps a l'air de se mettre au beau, à la pluie; on dirait qu'il va faire beau, va pleuvoir; **it doesn't l. to me as if. . .**, il ne me semble pas que + *sub.*; **what does he l. like?** comment est-il? à quoi ressemble-t-il? **he looks like a soldier**, il a l'air d'un militaire; on dirait un soldat; **he looked so like a Frenchman that . . .**, il avait si bien l'air d'un Français que . . .; **it looks like an elephant**, on dirait un éléphant; **this rock looks like granite**, cette roche ressemble à du granit; **step back a bit to see what it looks like**, reculez un peu pour juger du coup d'œil; **this looks to me like the way in**, je crois que c'est là l'entrée; *esp. U.S: P:* **looks like to me that. . .**, il me semble que . . .; **he looks a rogue**, il a l'air d'un coquin; **he looks the part**, il est fait pour ce rôle; il a le physique de l'emploi; **to l. like doing sth.**, avoir l'air de vouloir faire qch.; **he looks like winning**, on dirait qu'il va gagner. **4. l. here!** écoutez donc! dites donc! regardez! tenez! voyons! *F:* **l. alive! l. sharp! l. slippy!** dépêchez-vous! grouillez-vous!

II. (*compound verbs*) **1. look after**, *v.ind.tr.* soigner (qn, qch.); s'occuper de, avoir soin de (qn, qch.); veiller sur (qn, qch.); **she doesn't l. after her husband properly**, elle néglige son mari; **my husband will l. after the children**, mon mari va s'occuper des enfants, surveiller les enfants; **I don't know what I'd do without you to l. after me**, je me passerais mal de tous tes soins; **you're well looked after**, vous êtes bien soigné, bien servi; **he can l. after himself, is quite capable of looking after himself**, il sait se débrouiller; il sait bien s'occuper de son propre ménage; **to l. after one's (own) interests**, veiller à, ménager, ses intérêts; **I l. after my own car, I l. after my car myself**, j'entretiens ma voiture moi-même; **the car has been well looked after**, la voiture a été bien entretenue; **I also l. after the garden**, je m'occupe aussi du jardin.

2. look at, *v.ind.tr.* (*a*) regarder (qn, qch.); **what are you looking at?** qu'est-ce que vous regardez? **let me l. at your work**, faites voir un peu votre travail; **just l. at that!** regardez-moi ça! **it doesn't cost anything to l. at it**, la vue n'en coûte rien; **what time is it? l. at your watch!** quelle heure est-il? regardez (à), consultez, votre montre! *F:* **she won't l. at a man**, elle dédaigne les hommes; les hommes lui sont indifférents; **what's he like to l. at?** quel air a-t-il? **it's not much to l. at**, cela ne paie pas de mine; (*b*) **if you l. at the result**, si vous considérez le résultat; **I don't like his way of looking at things**, je n'aime pas la manière dont il voit les choses; **however, whichever way, you l. at it, it's strange**, de n'importe quel point de vue, de quelque façon que vous l'envisagiez, c'est curieux.

3. look back, *v.i.* (*a*) regarder en arrière; **to l. back on the past**, faire un retour sur le passé; se reporter au passé; **to l. back with regret**, se souvenir (de qch.) avec tristesse; (*b*) *F:* **he has never looked back since that day**, depuis ce jour il a fait des progrès ininterrompus.

4. look down, *v.i.* **to l. down on s.o.**, mépriser, dédaigner, qn.

5. look for, *v.ind.tr.* (*a*) chercher (qn, qch.); **go and l. for him**, allez le chercher; **I've been looking for my book everywhere**, j'ai cherché mon livre partout; **he's looking for a job**, il cherche une situation; **a journalist looking for copy**, un journaliste en quête de copie; (*b*) s'attendre à (qch.); **I had never looked for such a result as this**, je n'avais pas envisagé, prévu, un tel résultat.

6. look forward, *v.i.* **to l. forward to sth.**, (i) s'attendre à qch.; (ii) attendre qch. avec plaisir; jouir d'avance de qch.; se faire une fête de qch.; **I'm looking forward to seeing her again**, ce sera un grand plaisir de la revoir; **we are looking forward to our holiday in France**, nous attendons avec impatience nos vacances en France; *Corr:* **I shall l. forward to hearing from you again soon,**

j'attends avec impatience votre prochaine lettre.

7. **look in,** *v.i.* (*a*) entrer en passant; **I've just looked in for a moment,** je ne fais qu'entrer et sortir; **he looked in at his office to sign his letters,** il a passé à son bureau pour signer ses lettres; **I'll look in again tomorrow,** je repasserai demain; (*b*) *O:* regarder la télévision.

8. **look into,** *v.ind.tr* examiner, étudier (une question); prendre (une question) en considération; **I'll l. into it thoroughly,** je vais l'examiner à fond.

9. **look on.** (*a*) *v.i.* être spectateur; **I'm only looking on,** je ne fais que regarder; **suppose you help me instead of looking on,** donne-moi un coup de main au lieu de me regarder faire; (*b*) *v.ind.tr.* considérer, envisager (qn, qch.); **I l. on him as a friend,** je le considère comme un ami; **to l. on sth. as a crime,** regarder qch. comme un crime; **to l. on s.o. as a child,** traiter qn en enfant; **I don't l. on it in that light,** ce n'est pas ainsi que j'envisage la chose; **l. on it as done,** tenez cela pour fait.

10. **look out.** (*a*) *v.i.* (i) **to l. out for s.o.,** guetter (l'arrivée de) qn; *Nau:* **l. out forward!** veillez bien devant! ouvrez l'œil devant! (ii) prendre garde; être sur ses gardes; **l. out!** attention! prenez garde! (*b*) *v.tr.* chercher (qch.); **I'll l. you out some interesting books, some good pears,** je vais vous choisir des livres intéressants, de belles poires.

11. **look over,** *v.tr.* jeter un coup d'œil sur (qch.); examiner (qch.); parcourir (des papiers, etc.); visiter (une maison à vendre, etc.); **to l. over one's accounts,** examiner, vérifier, ses comptes; **to l. over one's neighbour's paper,** lire le journal par-dessus l'épaule de son voisin; **may I l. over your book?** puis-je partager votre livre?

12. **look round,** *v.i.* (*a*) regarder autour de soi; faire un tour d'horizon; **I haven't time to l. round!** je n'ai pas le temps de me retourner! (*b*) tourner la tête; se retourner (pour voir); **don't l. round!** ne regardez pas en arrière, derrière vous!

13. **look through,** *v.tr.* (*a*) parcourir, examiner rapidement (des papiers, etc.); (*b*) **to l. s.o. through and through,** transpercer qn du regard; regarder qn d'un œil perçant.

14. **look up.** (*a*) *v.i.* (i) lever les yeux; relever la tête; (ii) **to l. up to s.o.,** respecter, estimer, qn; (iii) **business is looking up,** les affaires *f* reprennent, prennent une meilleure tournure; la situation s'améliore; **shares are looking up,** les actions *f* remontent, tendent à la hausse; (*b*) *v.tr.* (i) **to l. up a train in the timetable,** chercher un train dans l'indicateur; **to l. up a word in a dictionary,** chercher un mot dans un dictionnaire; consulter un dictionnaire; (ii) **to l. s.o. up,** aller voir qn; passer chez qn; **(come and) l. me up,** venez me voir.

15. **look upon,** *v.ind.tr. O:* = LOOK ON (*b*).

lookdown ['lukdaun], *s. Ich;* **l. (fish),** poisson *m* dollar.

looker ['lukər], *s.* **1. l.-on,** *pl.* **lookers-on,** spectateur, -trice **(at,** de); assistant, -ante **(at,** à). **2.** *F:* **(good) l.,** bel homme, belle femme.

look-in ['lukin], *s.* **1.** courte visite; courte apparition; visite éclair. **2.** *Sp: etc:* **he won't have, get, a l.-in,** il n'a pas la moindre chance.

looker-out [lukə'raut], *s.* pointeur, -euse.

looking-glass ['lukiŋglɑːs], *s.* (*a*) miroir *m*, glace *f*; (*b*) *Bot:* **Venus's l.-g.,** (spéculaire *f*) miroir de Vénus; mirette *f*; campanule *f* doucette.

lookout ['lukaut], *s.* **1.** guet *m*, surveillance *f*, garde *f*, observation *f*; *Nau:* veille *f*; **to keep a l.,** avoir l'œil au guet, être aux aguets; *Nau:* veiller; être en vigie, de vigie; **I shall keep a l.,** j'y aurai l'œil; **to be on the l.,** (i) être en observation; *Nau:* être de veille; (ii) être sur ses gardes; être sur le qui-vive; **to be on the l. for s.o.,** être à l'affût de qn; guetter qn; **shoppers on the l. for bargains,** acheteurs *m* à la recherche de soldes. **2.** (*a*) *Mil: Nau:* **l. (post, station),** poste *m* d'observation, de guetteur, de guet, de vigie; guérite *f*; *Rail:* **l. seat,** guérite (d'un wagon de train de marchandises); (*b*) (*pers.*) **l. (man),** (i) *Mil:* guetteur *m*; (ii) *Nau:* homme *m* de veille, de bossoir, de vigie; veilleur *m*. **3.** vue *f*, perspective *f*; *F:* **that's a poor l. for him,** c'est de mauvais augure pour lui; c'est une triste perspective; **that's his l.!** c'est affaire à lui! ça c'est son affaire! ça le regarde! qu'il s'arrange! qu'il se débrouille!

lookover ['lukouvər], *s. F:* **to give sth. a l.,** examiner qch. rapidement.

look-see ['luksiː], *s. F:* visite *f*, coup *m* d'œil, d'inspection; **I'll go and have a l.-s.,** je vais y aller voir.

look-through ['lukθruː], *s. Paperm:* **wild l.-t.,** épair nuageux, irrégulier.

loom[1] [luːm], *s. Tex:* métier *m* à tisser.

loom[2], *s.* silhouette estompée, agrandie (par la brume, etc.); **l. (of a lighthouse),** lueur (d'un phare) (reflétée sur la mer).

loom[3], *v.i.* apparaître indistinctement; s'élever, se dessiner, s'estomper, dans le lointain, dans le brouillard; **the island loomed out of the fog,** (la silhouette de) l'île apparut à travers le brouillard, se dégagea du brouillard, naissait du brouillard; **a ship loomed up out of the fog,** un navire surgit, sortit, du brouillard; **a form loomed up in the darkness,** une forme surgit, se dessina, dans l'obscurité; **dangers looming ahead,** dangers qui menacent, qui paraissent imminents; (*of event*) **to l. large,** paraître imminent; **his own interests l. large in his mind,** ses propres intérêts occupent le premier plan dans son esprit.

loom[4], *s. Row:* **1.** manche *m* (d'un aviron). **2.** genou *m*, giron *m*, collet *m* (de l'aviron).

loom[5], *s. Orn:* (plongeon *m*) catmarin *m*.

looming[1] ['luːmiŋ], *s. Tex:* remettage *m*, rentrage *m*.

looming[2], *a.* (silhouette, etc.) vague, estompée.

loon[1] [luːn], *s. A: & Scot:* **1.** garçon *m*, jeune homme *m*. **2.** (*a*) vaurien *m*, chenapan *m*, drôle *m*; (*b*) rustre *m*, lourdaud *m*.

loon[2], *s. Orn:* **1.** plongeon *m*, *Fr.C:* huart *m*; **Arctic, Pacific, black-throated, l.,** plongeon arctique, lumme, à gorge noire, *Fr.C:* huart arctique; **common l.,** plongeon imbrin, *Fr.C:* huart à collier; **red-throated l.,** plongeon catmarin, à gorge rousse, *Fr.C:* huart à gorge rousse; **yellow-billed l.,** plongeon à bec blanc; *Fr.C:* huart à bec jaune. **2. greater l.,** grèbe huppé; **smaller l.,** petit grèbe.

loony ['luːni], *a. & s. F:* fou, *f.* folle; louftingue, loufoque, timbré, -ée; **l. bin,** maison *f* de fous.

loop[1] [luːp], *s.* **1.** (*a*) boucle *f* (de ruban, de ficelle, etc.); boucle, œil *m*, anse *f*, ganse *f* (d'un cordage); coque *f* (de cravate); boucle, poche *f* (de lettre écrite); **running l.,** boucle à nœud coulant; *Furn:* **curtain-l.,** embrasse *f* de rideau; *Harn:* **strap l.,** passant *m*; **fixed l.,** passant fixe; *Cost:* **epaulette l.,** bride *f*, attente *f*, d'épaulette; **scabbard l.,** tirant *m* de fourreau; *Needlew:* **l. stitch,** picot *m*; (*b*) *Anat:* anse *f*; **capillary l.,** anse capillaire; **intestine l.,** anse intestinale; **nerve l.,** anse nerveuse; (*c*) méandre *m*, sinuosité *f*, boucle (de rivière); (*d*) *Rail:* **l. (line),** voie *f* d'évitement; voie de raccordement; ligne *f* de contournement; (*at terminus*) boucle d'évitement; (*e*) *Sp:* (*skating*) croisé *m*; (*f*) *Av:* **(inside) l.,** boucle, looping *m*; **normal l.,** looping normal; **inverted normal l.,** looping normal après vol renversé; **outside l.,** looping inversé; **ground l.,** chevaux *mpl* de bois; (*g*) tour *m*, spire *f* (de spirale, de bobine); (*h*) *Cin:* boucle (de film). **2.** (*a*) *Ph:* ventre *m*, antinœud *m* (d'une onde); **oscillation l.,** ventre de vibration; *El:* **current l.,** ventre d'intensité; **potential l., voltage l.,** ventre de tension; (*b*) *El:* boucle, bouclage *m*; **l. connection,** montage *m* en boucle; **battery l.,** bouclage par batterie; **l. resistance,** bouclage de circuit par résistance; **l. circuit,** circuit bouclé; **l. current,** courant *m* circulant dans un circuit bouclé; **l. line,** ligne bouclée; (*c*) *Atom.Ph:* boucle, circuit (de réacteur); **control l.,** boucle, circuit, de contrôle, de réglage; **coolant, cooling, l.,** boucle, circuit, de refroidissement; (*d*) *Cmptr:* boucle (i) d'itération, (ii) de bande pilote; circuit (de graphe); **to go into a l.,** tourner sur une boucle; **closed, open, l.,** boucle bloquée, ouverte; **nesting loops,** boucles emboîtées; **(magnetic) hysteresis l.,** boucle hystérésis; **l. controlled,** commandé par bande pilote; **l. stop,** arrêt bouclé; **l. memory,** boucle-mémoire *f*, *pl.* boucles-mémoires; **l. storage bin,** puits *m* à dépression (de dérouleur); (*e*) *Tp:* circuit (branché); ligne dérivée; **l. circuit,** circuit bifilaire; **l. dialling,** appel *m* sur circuit; (*f*) *Elcs: etc:* **(direction-finding) l.,** cadre *m* (radiogoniométrique); **l. antenna, aerial,** cadre d'antenne, antenne-cadre *f*, *pl.* antennes-cadres; **l. receiving,** réception *f* sur cadre; **l. galvanometer,** galvanomètre *m* sur cadre.

loop[2]. **1.** *v.tr.* (*a*) faire une boucle, des boucles, à (une ficelle, etc.); boucler (un ruban, etc.); (*b*) enrouler **(sth. with sth.,** qch. de qch.); (*c*) **to l. back a curtain,** retenir un rideau avec une embrasse; (*d*) *Av: etc:* **to l. the loop,** faire un looping; boucler la boucle; (*e*) *El:* boucler; **to l. in,** dériver sans épissure. **2.** *v.i.* (*a*) faire une boucle; former des boucles; boucler; (*b*) *Cmptr:* tourner sur une boucle; se bloquer; **to l. through a sequence (of operations),** itérer sur une suite d'opérations.

loop[3], *s. Metall:* loupe *f*, balle *f*, renard *m*.

looper ['luːpər], *s. Ent:* arpenteuse *f*.

loophole[1] ['luːphoul], *s.* **1.** (*a*) *Fort:* meurtrière *f*, créneau *m*, taillade *f*; *Arch:* rayère *f*; (*for gun*) canonnière *f*; (*for crossbows*) arbalétrière *f*; (*for arrows*) arch(i)ère *f*; (*b*) trou *m*, ouverture *f*. **2.** échappatoire *f*; **to find a l. of escape,** trouver une échappatoire; se ménager une issue; **it affords a l. for recriminations,** c'est la porte ouverte aux récriminations.

loophole[2], *v.tr. Fort:* créneler (un mur); percer (un mur) de meurtrières.

looping ['luːpiŋ], *s.* **1.** *Av:* **l. (the loop),** looping *m*. **2.** (*a*) *Cmptr:* itération *f*; (*b*) *El:* **l. in,** dérivation *f* sans épissure.

loopway ['luːpwei], *s.* route déviée; route d'évitement.

loopy ['luːpi], *a. F:* toqué, timbré, dingo, loufoque, louftingue.

loose[1] [luːs], *a.* **1.** (*a*) (*of fixed part*) dégagé, mal assujetti; branlant; (*of page*) détaché; (*of knot*) défait, délié; **l. plank,** planche désajustée; **l. stone (in wall),** pierre branlante; **l. horseshoe,** fer *m* qui lâche; **l. tooth,** dent mobile, qui branle, qui remue; *El:* **l. connection,** raccord déconnecté, desserré; **to come l., to get l.,** se dégager, se détacher; (*of knot*) se défaire, se délier; (*of screw*) se desserrer; (*of iron bar from stonework, etc.*) se desceller; **some of the pages have come l.,** quelques-unes des pages se sont détachées; **he tried to get his hand l.,** il a cherché à dégager sa main; **to work l.,** (*of machine parts*) se desserrer, se désunir; prendre du jeu; (*of handle*) se démancher; (*of spokes*) dérayer; (*of chisel, etc.*) **to be l. in the handle,** branler dans le manche; (*b*) (*of animal*) déchaîné, échappé, lâché; **to let a dog l.,** lâcher, détacher, un chien; **to let l. one's anger,** donner libre cours à sa colère; lâcher la bonde à sa colère; **to let l. one's passions,** lâcher la bride à ses passions; **to let l. a torrent of abuse,** lâcher, déchaîner, un torrent d'injures; **the boat let l. a swarm of tourists,** le bateau a débarqué une foule de touristes; *Rac:* **l. horse,** cheval *m* sauvage; (*c*) non assujetti; mobile; (câble) volant; **l. sheets,** feuilles volantes; **l. cards,** fiches *f* mobiles; **l. floorboards,** plancher *m* mobile; *Ind:* **l. plant,** matériel *m* mobile; *Mec.E:* **l. wheel, pulley,** roue folle, décalée; poulie folle; **l. pinion,** satellite *m*; **l. headstock,** poupée *f* mobile (de tour); *Metall:* **l. piece,** pièce rapportée, pièce de rapport; *Carp:* **l. tongue,** languette rapportée; **beam with ends l.,** poutre posée; **l. end (of rope),** bout pendant (d'une corde); **to be at a l. end,** se trouver désœuvré, sans rien à faire, sans occupation; avoir une heure à perdre; (*of rope, etc.*) **to hang l.,** pendre, flotter; **her hair fell l. over her shoulders,** ses cheveux (i) se répandaient, étaient répandus, sur ses épaules, (ii) tombaient sur ses épaules; (*d*) **the money was l. in his pocket,** l'argent *m* était à même sa poche; **l. cash, change,** menue monnaie; *Com:* **l. goods,** marchandises *f* en vrac; *Civ.E:* **bank of l. stones,** remblai *m* de pierres sèches; (*e*) *Ch:* (à l'état) libre, non-combiné; (*f*) *Dy:* **l. colour,** couleur fugitive. **2.** (*slack*) (*a*) détendu; **l. rope,** câble mou, détendu; **l. knot,** nœud *m* lâche; (*of shoelace*) **to come l.,** se relâcher; **l. skin,** peau *f* flasque; **l. garment,** vêtement *m* (trop) large, ample; **l. draperies, l. coat,** draperies flottantes, manteau flottant; **he has a l. tongue,** il ne sait pas retenir sa langue; (*b*) *Med:* **l. cough,** toux grasse; (*of cough*) **to get looser,** se dégager; **l. bowels,** ventre *m* lâche; corps dérangé; (*c*) *Bookb:* **binding with a l. back,** reliure *f* à dos brisé. **3. l. earth, soil,** terre *f* meuble; terrain inconsistant, sans consistance; terrain ébouleux, coulant, mouvant; **l. fabric,** tissu *m* lâche, à claire-voie; **l. handwriting,** écriture informe; *Nau:* **l. bottom,** fond *m* de mauvaise tenue (pour l'ancre); *Mil:* **l. order,** ordre dispersé. **4.** vague, peu exact; (style) lâche, décousu; **l. ideas,** idées vagues, décousues, sans liaison; **l. thinker,** esprit décousu; **l. translation,** traduction approximative, qui ne serre pas le texte d'assez près; **to do sth. in a l. manner,** faire qch. sans méthode; *Sp:* **l. ball,** (i) *Cr:* balle mal lancée; (ii) *Ten:* coup *m* faible. **5.** dissolu, relâché, débauché, libertin, licencieux; **l. living,** mauvaise vie; inconduite *f*; excès *mpl* de conduite; **to lead a l. life,** avoir une mauvaise conduite; **l. morals,** mœurs relâchées; **l. woman,** femme *f* de mauvaise vie; *s.* **to be on the l.,** être en bordée, en vadrouille, en rupture de ban; courir la prétantaine; mener une vie de polichinelle.

loose[2], *v.tr.* **1.** délier, détacher; **to l. s.o. from his bonds,** délivrer qn de ses liens; libérer qn; **to l. s.o.'s tongue,** délier, dénouer, la langue à qn; **to l. one's hold,** lâcher prise; **to l. hold of sth.,** lâcher qch. **2.** délier, dénouer, défaire (un nœud, etc.); dénouer, détacher (ses cheveux); *Nau:* larguer (une amarre); déferler (une voile); **to l. out a sail,** larguer une voile. **3.** (*a*) décocher (une flèche); (*b*) *v.i. Mil: F:* **to l. off,** tirer (avec une mitrailleuse); lâcher, envoyer, une giclée.

loose-fitting ['luːs'fitiŋ], *a.* non ajusté; (vêtement *m*) ample, large; (col) dégagé.

loose-jointed, -limbed ['luːs'dʒɔintid, -'limd], *a.* (*of pers.*) démanché; dégingandé; **l.-l. horse,** cheval décousu.

loose-leaf ['luːsliːf], *a.* (album *m*, etc.) à feuilles mobiles; **l.-l. ledger,** grand livre biblorhapte; **l.-l. binder,** grebiche *f*.

loosely ['luːsli], *adv.* **1.** (tenir qch.) sans serrer; **to be**

(too) **l. fixed,** être mal serré, mal ajusté; avoir du jeu; **his hands were hanging l. (by his sides),** ses bras lui pendaient mollement; **l. packed,** emballé peu soigneusement; **her dress hung l. on her body,** elle flottait dans sa robe. **2.** vaguement, inexactement; (parler) inexactement, sans précision; **word l. employed,** mot employé inexactement, d'une manière abusive; **laws l. administered,** lois mollement appliquées. **3.** (vivre) d'une manière dissolue.

loosen ['lu:s(ə)n]. **1.** *v.tr.* (*a*) (i) défaire, délier (un nœud); (ii) relâcher (un nœud); desserrer, dégager, décoller (un écrou, etc.); faire décoller (une soupape, etc.); donner du jeu à (un ressort); relâcher, détendre (une corde); **to l. the saddle girths,** desserrer, relâcher, les sangles; **to l. s.o.'s bonds,** dénouer les liens de qn; **to l. one's grip,** relâcher son étreinte; **to l. s.o.'s tongue,** délier, dénouer, la langue à qn; faire parler qn; *Mec.E:* **to l. a bearing,** dégripper un palier; *O:* **to l. one's purse strings,** délier les cordons de sa bourse; *Agr:* **to l. the soil,** ameublir, mouver, serfouir, la terre; *Med:* **to l. the bowels,** relâcher le ventre; dégager les intestins; **to l. a cough,** dégager une toux; (*b*) détacher (**sth. from sth.,** qch. de qch.); (*c*) relâcher (la discipline). **2.** *v.i.* (*a*) (*of knot, etc.*) se délier, se défaire; (*of screw, etc.*) se desserrer; (*of guy rope, etc.*) se relâcher; (*of machinery, etc.*) prendre du jeu; *Med:* (*of cough*) se dégager; (*b*) (*of pers.*) **to l. up,** (i) se dégourdir; (ii) se mettre à l'aise; ne plus se gêner; (iii) *F: O:* se montrer généreux.

looseness ['lu:snis], *s.* **1.** (*a*) état branlant (d'une dent, d'une pierre); desserrage *m* (d'un écrou); jeu *m* (d'une cheville, etc.); (*b*) flaccidité *f* (de la peau). **2.** (*a*) peu *m* de tension, relâchement *m* (d'une corde); ampleur *f* (d'un vêtement); (*b*) *Med:* **l. of the bowels,** relâchement du ventre; dévoiement *m* du corps. **3.** inconsistance *f* (du terrain). **4.** (*a*) vague *m* (d'une pensée); imprécision *f* (de terminologie); décousu *m* (du style); (*b*) relâchement (de la discipline, de ses principes); (*c*) licence *f*; vie dissolue.

loosening ['lu:sniŋ], *s.* **1.** dégagement *m*, détachement *m*; desserrage *m* (d'un écrou); relâchement *m* (d'un cordage); dégrippage *m* (d'un palier, etc.); dénouement *m* (d'un lien); *Agr:* ameublissement *m*, assouplissement *m* (du sol). **2.** *Med:* dégagement (d'une toux).

loosestrife ['lu:sstraif], *s. Bot:* **1. (yellow) l.,** lysimachie *f*, lysimaque *f*. **2. (purple) l.,** salicaire commune.

loot[1] [lu:t], *s.* **1.** pillage *m*; **soldiers on the l.,** soldats *m* en maraude *f*. **2.** butin *m*.

loot[2], *v.tr.* **1.** piller, saccager, mettre à sac (une ville, etc.); *v.i.* se livrer au pillage. **2.** (*of soldiers, etc.*) voler (du bétail, etc.).

looter ['lu:tər], *s.* pilleur, -euse; pillard, -arde.

looting ['lu:tiŋ], *s.* pillage *m*; sac *m* (d'une ville, etc.).

lop[1] [lɔp], *s. For:* **l. and top, l. and crop,** élagage *m*, émondes *fpl*.

lop[2], *v.tr.* (**lopped** [lɔpt]) (*a*) élaguer, ébrancher, tailler, émonder, égayer (un arbre); **to l. away, l. off, a branch,** couper, élaguer, ravaler, une branche; (*b*) *A:* **to l. off a head, a limb,** abattre une tête, un membre; (*c*) **to l. off (a credit, workers, etc.),** réduire (un crédit, la main-d'œuvre, etc.).

lop[3], *v.i.* **1. to l. (over),** retomber; pendre flasque. **2.** *O:* & *NAm:* **to l. about,** flâner; se trimbaler çà et là. **3.** *NAm:* **to l. down in an armchair,** se laisser tomber dans un fauteuil. **4.** (*of animals*) bondir; **to l. along,** avancer par bonds.

lop[4], *s. Nau:* clapotis *m*.

lop[5], *v.i.* (*of sea*) clapoter; déferler en vagues courtes.

lope[1] [loup], *s.* pas de course allongé; **the buck was coming on at an easy l.,** le daim approchait à petits bonds.

lope[2], *v.i.* (*a*) *A:* bondir; (*b*) **to l. along,** courir à petits bonds; avancer à un demi-trot aisé.

lop(-ear) ['lɔpi:ər], *s.* lapin *m* aux oreilles pendantes.

lop-eared ['lɔpi:əd], *a.* (lapin *m*, etc.) aux oreilles pendantes, à oreilles avalées; (cheval) oreillard.

lophiid [lou'faiid], *s. Ich:* lophiidé *m*.

Lophiidae [lou'faiidi:], *s.pl. Ich:* lophiidés *m*.

lophiodon [lou'faiədɔn], *s. Paleont:* lophiodon *m*.

lophiomys [lou'faiəmis], *s. Z:* lophiomys *m*.

lophobranch ['loufoubræŋk], **lophobranchiate** [loufou'bræŋkieit], *a.* & *s. Ich:* lophobranche (*m*).

Lophobranchii [loufou'bræŋkii:], *s.pl. Ich:* lophobranches *m*, phtinobranches *m*.

lophodont ['loufoudɔnt], *a.* & *s. Z:* lophodonte (*m*).

lophophora [lou'fɔfərə], *s. Bot:* lophophora *m*.

lophophore ['loufoufɔ:r], *s. Nat.Hist:* lophophore *m*.

lophophorus [lou'fɔfərəs], *s. Orn:* lophophore *m*.

lopped [lɔpt], *a.* (arbre) élagué, émondé, coupé; *Bot: Z:* tronqué; **l. tree, branch,** écot *m*.

lopper ['lɔpər], *s. Tls:* élagueur *m*, échenilloir *m*.

lopping ['lɔpiŋ], *s.* **1.** élagage *m*, ébranchement *m* (d'un arbre); **l. shears,** élagueur *m*, échenilloir *m*. **2.** *pl.* **loppings,** élagage, émondes *fpl*; rameaux coupés.

lopsided [lɔp'saidid], *a.* qui penche trop d'un côté; qui manque de symétrie; déjeté, déversé; de guingois; *F:* (*of pers.*) bancal; **l. chair,** chaise bancale; **to make sth. l.,** déjeter qch.; **l. ship,** navire *m* qui a un faux bord, un faux côté; (navire) bordier (*m*).

lopsidedness [lɔp'saididnis], *s.* (*a*) manque *m* de symétrie; déjettement *m*; (*b*) (*of ship*) faux bord.

loquacious [lə'kweiʃəs], *a.* loquace.

loquaciously [lə'kweiʃəsli], *adv.* avec loquacité.

loquaciousness [lə'kweiʃəsnis], **loquacity** [lə'kwæsiti], *s.* loquacité *f*.

loquat ['loukwɔt], *s. Bot:* nèfle *f* du Japon; bibasse *f*, bibace *f*; **l.-tree,** néflier *m* du Japon; bibassier *m*, bibacier *m*.

lor' [lɔ:r], *int. P:* mon Dieu! Seigneur!

Loran ['lɔræn], *s. Av: Nau:* Loran *m*; **L. chain,** chaîne Loran; **L. fix,** position obtenue par Loran; **L. set,** appareil récepteur Loran; **L. station,** station émettrice Loran.

lorandite ['lɔrəndait], *s. Miner:* lorandite *f*.

loranskite [lə'rænskait], *s. Miner:* loranskite *f*.

Loranthaceae [louræn'θeisii:], *s.pl. Bot:* loranthacées *f*.

lord[1] [lɔ:d], *s.m.* **1.** seigneur, maître; **our sovereign l. the king,** notre seigneur souverain, le roi; *Hist:* **l. of the manor,** seigneur (censier, foncier); châtelain; *F:* **her l. and master,** son seigneur et maître; son mari; **the cotton lords,** les rois du coton, les magnats *m* du coton. **2.** *Ecc:* **L. God Almighty,** Seigneur Dieu Tout-puissant; **the L.,** le Seigneur; Dieu; **Our L.,** Notre-Seigneur; **in the year of our L. . . .,** en l'an de grâce . . .; **the Lord's Day,** le jour du Seigneur; le dimanche; **the Lord's Prayer,** l'oraison *f*, la prière, dominicale; *F:* **(good) L.! O L.! bless my soul!** mon Dieu! Seigneur (Dieu)! **L. knows if. . .,** Dieu sait si. . .. **3.** (*a*) lord *m* (titre des barons, vicomtes, comtes, et marquis); **Lord X,** lord X; *F:* milord X; *Pol:* **the House of Lords,** *F:* **the Lords,** la Chambre des Lords; **to live like a l.,** mener une vie de grand seigneur; **my l.,** (i) monsieur le baron, le comte, le marquis, etc.; (ii) (*to bishop*) monseigneur; (*to judge*) monsieur le juge; (*b*) **L. High Constable,** grand connétable; **L. High Admiral,** grand amiral; **the L. Mayor,** le lord maire (de Londres et de plusieurs autres grandes villes). **4.** *Bot:* **lords and ladies,** (i) arum maculé; gouet *m*; pied-de-veau *m*, *pl.* pieds-de-veau; (ii) arisæma *m*.

lord[2]. **1.** *v.i.* *F:* **to l. it,** prendre le haut du pavé; faire l'important; poser au grand seigneur; trancher du grand seigneur; **to l. it over s.o.,** vouloir dominer qn; vouloir en imposer à qn; le prendre de haut avec qn; **to l. it over everyone,** vivre comme en pays conquis. **2.** *v.tr. A:* anoblir (qn).

lordliness ['lɔ:dlinis], *s.* **1.** (*a*) dignité *f*; (*b*) magnificence *f* (d'un château, etc.). **2.** hauteur *f*, orgueil *m*, morgue *f*.

lordling ['lɔ:dliŋ], *s.* petit seigneur.

lordly ['lɔ:dli], *a.* **1.** de grand seigneur; noble, majestueux; magnifique. **2.** hautain, altier; **to put on a l. air,** prendre des airs, des manières, de grand seigneur; **in a l. manner,** avec hauteur; avec importance.

lordosis [lɔ:dousis], *s. Med:* lordose *f*.

lordotic [lɔ:'dɔtik], *a. Med:* lordosique.

lordship ['lɔ:dʃip], *s.* **1.** suzeraineté *f*; seigneurie *f* **(over,** de); **l. of a demesne,** possession *f* d'un domaine. **2.** domaine *m*, seigneurie. **3. your l.,** votre Seigneurie; (*to nobleman*) monsieur le comte, etc.; (*to bishop*) monseigneur.

lore[1] [lɔ:r], *s.* science *f*, savoir *m*; **country l.,** connaissance *f* intime de la campagne; *O:* **bird l.,** ornithologie *f*; **fairy l.,** la tradition et la littérature concernant les fées.

lore[2], *s. Nat.Hist:* lore *m* (d'une araignée, d'un oiseau).

Lorenzo [lɔ'renzou]. *Pr.n.m. Hist:* **L. the Magnificent,** Laurent le Magnifique.

lorgnette [lɔ:'njet], **lorgnon** ['lɔ:njɔn], *s.* **1.** face-à-main *m*, *pl.* faces-à-main. **2.** jumelle *f* (de théâtre) à manche.

lorica [lə'raikə], *s. Nat.Hist:* lorique *f*.

loricarian [lɔri'kɛəriən], *a.* & *s. Ich:* loricaire (*f*).

Loricariidae [lɔrikə'raiidi:], *s.pl. Ich:* loricariidés *m*.

Loricata [lɔri'keitə], *s.pl. Z: Rept:* loricates *m*.

loricate ['lɔrikeit], **loricated** ['lɔrikeitid], *a. Nat.Hist:* loriqué.

lorikeet [lɔri'ki:t], *s. Orn:* loriquet *m*; **musk l.,** loriquet musqué; **Swainson's l.,** loriquet de Swainson; **varied l.,** loriquet varié.

loris ['lɔris], *s. Z:* loris *m*; **slender l.,** loris grêle, loris de l'Inde; **Asiatic slow l.,** nycticèbe *m*.

Lorisidae [lɔ'risidi:], *s.pl. Z:* lorisidés *m*.

lorn [lɔ:n], *a. Lit:* délaissé, solitaire; **lone l. creature,** pauvre femme abandonnée à elle-même.

Lorrainer [lɔ'reinər], *s. Geog:* Lorrain, -aine.

lorry ['lɔri], *s.* **1.** camion *m*; **five-ton l.,** camion de cinq tonnes; **heavy l.,** camion lourd, de fort tonnage; poids lourd; **articulated l.,** véhicule articulé; semi-remorque *f* *or m*, *pl.* semi-remorques; **breakdown l.,** camion de dépannage; **crane l., derrick l.,** camion-grue *m*, *pl.* camions-grues; **tank l.,** camion-citerne *m*, *pl.* camions-citernes; **winch l.,** camion à treuil; **workshop l.,** camion-atelier *m*, *pl.* camions-ateliers; **l. driver,** conducteur *m*, chauffeur *m*, (i) de camion, (ii) de poids lourd, *F:* routier *m*. **2.** (*a*) fardier *m*, diable *m*; (*b*) *Rail:* lorry *m*.

lory ['lɔ:ri:], *s. Orn:* lori *m*; **chattering l.,** lori noir.

Los Angeleno [lɔsændʒə'li:nou], *s.* habitant, -ante, originaire *m f* de Los Angeles.

lose [lu:z], *v.tr.* (*p.t.* **lost** [lɔst]; *p.p.* **lost;** *pr.p.* **losing** [lu:ziŋ]) **1.** (*a*) perdre, égarer (son parapluie, etc.); **your cheque has been lost,** votre chèque a été égaré; **it is easily lost,** cela se perd facilement; **lost, a diamond ring,** il a été perdu une bague de diamants; (*b*) perdre (un droit, son argent, etc.); **I lost a thousand francs,** j'ai perdu mille francs; *F:* j'en ai été de mille francs; (*at cards, etc.*) **to l. heavily,** perdre une forte somme; *F:* boire un bouillon; **it is so much money lost,** c'est de l'argent perdu, flambé; **to l. a thousand francs to s.o.,** se faire gagner mille francs par qn; **to stand to l. nothing,** (i) n'avoir rien à perdre; (ii) être en position de gagner de toutes les façons; **you will l. nothing by waiting,** vous ne perdrez rien pour attendre; **I haven't lost by it,** je n'y ai rien perdu; **the incident did not l. in the telling,** cet incident ne perdit rien à la narration; **to l. in value, in interest,** perdre de sa valeur, de son intérêt; **to l. in public esteem,** baisser dans l'estime publique; *Rac: etc:* **to l. (ground) to a competitor,** perdre sur un concurrent; lui laisser prendre de l'avance; (*c*) **he has lost an arm,** il lui manque un bras; **he has lost his left arm,** il est manchot du bras gauche; **he lost one eye at . . .,** il eut un œil crevé à . . .; **to l. one's voice,** avoir, attraper, une extinction de voix; **to l. one's reason,** perdre la raison; **to l. one's reputation,** se perdre de réputation; **he had lost interest in his work, his work had lost interest for him,** son travail ne l'intéressait plus; **to l. strength,** s'affaiblir; **the patient is losing strength,** le malade baisse; **to l. weight,** perdre de son poids; **I've lost 10 kilos,** j'ai maigri de 10 kilos; (*d*) perdre (son père, etc.); **she has just lost her old aunt,** elle vient de perdre sa vieille tante; (*of doctor*) **to l. a patient,** (i) ne pas réussir à sauver un malade; (ii) perdre un client; *Com:* **to l. a customer,** perdre un client; **to be lost at sea,** périr, être perdu, en mer; périr dans un naufrage; **the ship was lost,** le navire a péri; *v.i.* **both armies lost heavily,** les deux armées subirent de fortes pertes. **2. to l. one's way, to l. oneself, to get lost,** perdre son chemin; se perdre, s'égarer; **to l. oneself, to be lost, in the crowd,** se perdre, se dissimuler, dans la foule; se mêler à, dans, la foule; *F:* **I'm lost! you've lost me!** je n'y suis plus! *P:* **(go and) get lost! l. yourself!** fiche-moi le camp! **his voice was lost in the laughter,** sa voix se perdit parmi les rires; **to l. oneself in a book,** s'absorber dans la lecture d'un livre; **to be lost in conjecture, in apologies,** se perdre en conjectures; se confondre en excuses; **lost in amazement,** perdu d'étonnement; **to l. sight of s.o.,** perdre qn de vue; **mountain lost in the clouds,** montagne perdue dans les nuages; **lost in the haze,** (horizon) embrumé. **3.** gaspiller, perdre (son temps); perdre (sa peine); **lost labour,** peine perdue; *Mec.E:* **lost motion,** (i) perte *f* de mouvement; déplacement *m* à vide; (ii) jeu *m*; **the joke was lost on him,** il n'a pas saisi la plaisanterie; **he spoke for half an hour, but it was all lost on me,** il a parlé pendant une demi-heure, mais ce fut en pure perte en ce qui me concernait, mais je n'y ai pas compris un mot. **4. clock that loses five minutes a day,** pendule *f* qui retarde de cinq minutes par jour; *v.i.* **my watch is losing,** ma montre retarde. **5.** (*a*) manquer (le train, etc.); (*b*) **I lost several words of his reply,** plusieurs mots *m* de sa réponse m'ont échappé. **6.** perdre (une partie, une bataille, un procès); **to l. a race,** être battu dans une course; (*in debate*) **the motion was lost,** la motion a été rejetée. **7.** faire perdre (qch. à qn); **that mistake lost him the match, his job,** cette faute lui fit perdre, lui coûta, la partie, son poste. **8.** *v.i.* **to l. out,** ne pas réussir; échouer.

loser ['lu:zər], *s.* **1. he'll be the l.,** c'est lui qui perdra; **he's a born l.,** il ne réussit jamais; il met toujours les pieds dans le plat. **2.** (*a*) **to be the l. of a battle,** perdre une bataille; être battu dans une bataille; (*b*) *Sp: etc:* perdant, -ante; **the winners and the losers,** les gagnants et les perdants, les vainqueurs et les vaincus; **to be a good l.,** être bon, beau, joueur; **to be a bad l.,** être mauvais joueur. **3.** *Sp:* coup perdant.

losh [lɔʃ], *int. Scot:* Seigneur! mon Dieu!

losing[1] ['lu:ziŋ], *a.* perdant; **l. bargain,** mauvais marché; **l. battle,** bataille *f* de vaincu; **l. game,** partie perdue d'avance; **to play a l. game,** (i) jouer un jeu à perdre; (ii) jouer à qui perd gagne; (iii) défendre une cause perdue; **the l. side,** les vaincus; *Sp:* l'équipe perdante.

losing[2], *s.* **1.** perte *f.* **2.** *pl.* **his losings at cards,** ses pertes de jeu.

loss [lɔs], *s.* **1.** (*a*) perte *f* (d'un parapluie, etc.); égarement *m* (d'un document, etc.); (*b*) **l. of sight,** perte, privation *f,* de la vue; **l. of voice,** extinction *f* de voix; **total l. of reason,** éclipse totale de la raison; **l. of time,** perte de temps; **without l. of time,** sans perte de temps, sans perdre de temps, sans tarder; **with l. of honour,** aux dépens de l'honneur; **l. of morale,** démoralisation *f*; *Com:* **l. of custom,** perte de clientèle, désachalandage *m*; **l. of market,** perte de marché, de débouché; *Jur:* **l. of a right,** perte, déchéance *f,* d'un droit; **l. of civil rights,** perte des droits civiques, dégradation *f* civique; *Ind:* **l. of service,** rupture *f* de contrat de travail, de contrat entre employeur et employé (portant préjudice à l'employeur); *Theol:* **l. of grace,** amission *f* de la grâce. **2.** (*a*) **to meet with a l.,** subir une perte, un préjudice; **he had a heavy l.,** il a beaucoup perdu; **to sustain, suffer, heavy losses,** subir de grosses pertes; **dead l.,** perte sèche; **to make up the losses,** réparer les dommages; compenser ses pertes; *Com:* **to sell at a l.,** vendre à perte; mévendre; **sale of goods at a l.,** mévente *f* de marchandises; **to cut one's losses,** faire la part du feu; **it is her l., the l. is hers,** c'est elle qui y perd; **he, it, is no l.,** la perte n'est pas grande; (*b*) *Ins:* sinistre *m*; **to estimate the l.,** évaluer le sinistre; *M.Ins:* **(actual) total l.,** perte totale; **constructive total l.,** perte censée totale; (*c*) **the l. of her husband,** la perte, la disparition, de son mari; **she cannot get over her l.,** elle est inconsolable de sa perte; *Mil: etc:* **to suffer heavy losses,** éprouver, subir, de grosses, de lourdes, pertes. **3.** (*a*) déperdition *f*; *Ph: etc:* **diminution of weight by l. of water,** perte de poids par départ d'eau; **l. of heat,** perte de chaleur; **heat transfer losses,** pertes de chaleur par conductivité; *Mec:* **l. of pressure,** *Hyd: Mch:* **l. of head,** perte de charge; *Mec.E:* **l. of power, of energy,** perte de puissance, d'énergie; travail *m* nuisible; déperdition; *Metall:* **l. of temper,** perte de trempe; **l. factor,** coefficient *m,* facteur *m,* de perte; *Atom.Ph:* **l. on ignition,** perte par grillage; **l. of neutrons by escape,** perte de neutrons par fuite; *El:* **copper, iron, losses,** pertes dans le cuivre, dans le fer; **charge l.,** perte de charge; **eddy (current) losses,** pertes par courants parasites, par courants de Foucault; **impedance losses,** pertes en charge; **line losses, power losses,** pertes en ligne; **ohmic losses, resistance losses,** pertes ohmiques, pertes par effet Joule; **watt l.,** perte en watt; **commutator l.,** perte au collecteur, au commutateur; **l. due to arcing,** perte par crachement aux balais; *Magn:* **hysteresis losses,** pertes par hystérésis; (*b*) *Ind: Trans:* freinte *f,* frainte *f,* déperdition (d'un produit en cours de fabrication ou de transport); **l. in transit,** freinte, déchet *m,* de route; **l. in weight,** freinte de poids; (*c*) *Med:* écoulement *m,* perte. **4. to be at a l.,** être embarrassé, dans l'embarras; être désorienté; être à quia; **I am quite at a l.,** je ne sais que faire; je m'y perds; **he seemed at a l.,** il avait l'air dépaysé, désorienté; **he is never at a l.,** il ne s'embarrasse de rien, rien ne l'embarrasse; il sait se retourner; **to be at a l. to . . .,** avoir de la peine à . . .; être en peine de . . .; **I should be at a l. to answer,** je serais bien embarrassé s'il me fallait répondre; **never to be at a l. to find an excuse, at a l. for an excuse,** ne jamais être en peine de trouver une excuse; **one would be very much at a l. if one had to . . .,** on serait bien empêché s'il fallait . . .; **a foreigner is at a l. when he tries to understand us,** l'étranger se trouve désemparé quand il veut nous comprendre; **to be at a l. what to do, what to say,** ne savoir que faire, que dire; **he was at a l. how to apologize,** il ne savait que faire pour s'excuser; **never to be at a l. for an answer,** avoir, trouver, réponse à tout; **he is never at a l. for a word,** il n'est jamais embarrassé pour trouver le mot; **I am at a l. for words to express . . .,** les mots me manquent pour exprimer . . .; **he is never at a l. for words, for sth. to say,** il n'est jamais à court (de mots); **I'm at a bit of a l. for money,** je suis à court d'argent.

lost [lɔst], *a.* perdu; (*a*) **l. property office,** service *m* des objets trouvés; *U.S:* **l. river,** rivière souterraine; **to give s.o. up for, as, l.,** abandonner tout espoir de retrouver, de sauver, qn; **to give sth. up for l.,** abandonner tout espoir de retrouver qch.; *F:* faire son deuil de qch.; **they were already given up for l.,** on les considérait déjà comme perdus; (*b*) **l. soul,** âme perdue, âme damnée; un damné; **he is like a l. soul,** il est comme un corps sans âme; **to wander like a l. soul,** errer comme une âme en peine; (*c*) **he seems l., looks l.,** il a l'air dépaysé; il a l'air de ne savoir que devenir; (*d*) **when he is listening to music he is l. to the world,** quand il écoute la musique le monde n'existe plus pour lui; **to be l. to all sense of duty, of shame,** avoir perdu tout sentiment de devoir, de honte; avoir perdu toute honte.

lot[1] [lɔt], *s.* **1.** (*a*) **to draw, cast, lots for sth.,** tirer au sort pour qch.; tirer qch. au sort; **to throw in, cast, one's l. with s.o.,** partager le sort, la fortune, de qn; unir sa destinée à celle de qn; s'attacher à la fortune de qn; (*b*) sort *m*; tirage *m* au sort; **drawn by l. from . . .,** tiré au sort parmi . . .; **Lombardy fell to him by l.,** la Lombardie lui échut au sort; *Fin:* **the debentures are redeemed by l.,** les obligations sont rachetées par voie de tirage. **2.** (*a*) sort, part *f,* partage *m*; *Lit:* **the l. fell upon him,** le sort tomba sur lui; **to fall to s.o.'s l.,** échoir, tomber, en partage à qn; **it fell to my l. to decide,** c'était à moi de décider; **all the dirty work seems to fall to my l.,** c'est à moi qu'arrivent toutes les sales besognes; (*b*) destin *m,* destinée *f*; **the poor man's l.,** la condition, la destinée, du pauvre; **it's the l. of everyone,** tout le monde y passe; **to envy s.o.'s l.,** envier la destinée de qn; **to submit to one's l.,** se soumettre à sa destinée. **3.** (*a*) (lot *m* de) terrain *m*; *Cin:* **(studio) l.,** terrain (de studio); **parking l.,** parcage *m, F:* parking *m*; (*b*) (*at auction*) lot; (*c*) *Com: etc:* lot, paquet *m*; **l. of goods,** lot de marchandises; **in lots,** par parties; **to buy, sell, in one l.,** acheter, vendre, en bloc; *Fin:* **l. of shares,** paquet de titres, d'actions; **to sell shares in small lots,** vendre des actions par petits paquets; (*d*) **a bad l.,** un mauvais sujet; un vaurien; un mauvais garnement; une crapule; un dévoyé; une canaille; **he's, she's, a bad l.,** il, elle, ne vaut pas cher; *Iron:* **you're a nice l.!** vous êtes admirables, vous! (*e*) **the l.,** le tout; **that's the l.,** c'est tout; **the whole l. of you,** vous tous (sans exception); **the whole l. of them,** toute la bande; *F:* **and the whole damn l.,** et tout le bazar; et tout le bataclan. **4.** (*a*) **a l. of . . .,** beaucoup de . . .; **a l. of butter,** beaucoup de beurre; **a l. of sheep,** beaucoup de moutons, un grand nombre de moutons; **what a l.!** en voilà-t-il! **what a l. of people!** que de monde! que de gens! **what a l. of time you waste!** ce que vous en perdez du temps! **such a l.,** tellement; **I've had such a l. of people today!** j'ai eu tant de monde aujourd'hui! **quite a l.,** une quantité considérable; **he knows quite a l. about you,** il en sait long sur votre compte; **I saw quite a l. of him in Paris,** je l'ai vu assez souvent pendant mon séjour à Paris; **we are rather a l. for dinner this evening,** nous sommes nombreux à dîner ce soir; **he must have a l. to say,** il doit en avoir à dire; **he would have given a l. to . . .,** il aurait donné gros pour . . .; **I haven't a l. of money,** je n'ai pas beaucoup d'argent; **they're just a l. of good-for-nothings,** c'est une bande de vauriens; **well they are a l.!** quelle engeance! *F:* **it's a (whole) l. of nonsense, of rubbish,** c'est du bidon; *adv.* **times have changed a l.,** les temps *m* ont bien changé; (*b*) *F:* **we've (got) lots of time,** nous avons tout le temps; **lots of people,** beaucoup de gens; **lots of money,** un argent fou, énormément d'argent; **I've lots of things to do,** j'ai un tas de choses à faire; *adv.* **I feel lots better,** je me sens infiniment mieux.

lot[2], *v.tr.* **(lotted) to l. out a piece of ground,** lotir un terrain.

Lot[3]. *Pr.n.m. B.Hist:* Loth.

loth [louθ] = LOATH.

Lothair [ˈlouθɛər]. *Pr.n.m. Hist:* Lothaire.

Lotharingia [lɔθəˈrindʒiə]. *Pr.n. Hist:* Lotharingie *f.*

Lothario [lɔˈθɛəriou]. *Pr.n.m. Lit:* **a gay L.,** un joyeux viveur, un Don Juan.

lotion [ˈlouʃ(ə)n], *s. Pharm: Toil:* lotion *f*; *Hairdr:* **setting l.,** lotion pour mise en plis; *Toil:* **sun l.,** lotion antisolaire.

lotophagi [louˈtɔfədʒai], *s.pl. Gr.Myth:* lotophages *m,* mangeurs *m* de lotus.

lottery [ˈlɔtəri], *s.* loterie *f*; **to draw a l.,** tirer une tombola; **life, marriage, is a l.,** la vie, le mariage, est une loterie, est une affaire de chance; *Fin:* **l. loan,** emprunt *m* à lots.

lotto [ˈlɔtou], *s. Games:* loto *m.*

lotus, *pl.* **-uses** [ˈloutəs, -əsiz], *s.* **1.** (*a*) *Gr.Myth:* lotus *m*; **l. eater,** (i) mangeur *m* de lotus; lotophage *m*; (*b*) *Fig:* rêveur, -euse; indolent, -ente. **2.** *Bot:* (*a*) lotus *m,* lotier *m*; *esp.* lotier corniculé, trèfle cornu; (*b*) **Egyptian l.,** nélombo *m,* nélumbo *m*; lotus égyptien; lis *m* du Nil; (*c*) **l. (tree),** micocoulier *m*; (*d*) **l.-shaped,** lotiforme. **3.** *Orn:* **l. bird,** jacana *m.*

loud [laud]. **1.** *a.* (*a*) bruyant, retentissant; **l. noise, l. cry,** grand bruit, grand cri; **l. report,** détonation violente, retentissante; **l. laugh,** rire sonore; gros rire; **l. voice,** voix forte, voix haute; **l. and metallic voice,** voix claironnante; **in a l. voice,** à haute voix; **in a very l. voice,** en criant très fort; **one could hear snatches of l. conversation,** on entendait des éclats de voix; **l. cheers, l. applause,** vifs applaudissements, applaudissements tumultueux; **to be l. in one's admiration, in one's praise, of sth.,** louer qch. chaudement; *Lit:* **the woods are l. with the song of birds,** les bois *m* retentissent du chant des oiseaux; (*b*) (*of pers., behaviour*) bruyant, tapageur; vulgaire, commun; (*c*) (*of colour, etc.*) criard, voyant; (*of costume*) tapageur, affichant. **2.** *adv.* (crier, parler) haut, à haute voix; **to shout, bark, louder,** crier, aboyer, plus fort; **louder!** parlez plus haut! **it was a case of who could shout the loudest,** ils criaient à qui mieux mieux; **we laughed l. and long,** nous avons ri comme des fous; **a l.-ticking clock,** une pendule à tic-tac sonore.

louden [ˈlaud(ə)n]. **1.** *v.tr.* rendre (un son) plus fort. **2.** *v.i.* devenir plus bruyant; (*of sound, noise*) devenir plus fort; augmenter.

loudhailer [ˈlaudˈheilər], *s.* porte-voix *m inv.*

loudly [ˈlaudli], *adv.* **1.** (crier) haut, fort, à voix haute; (rire) bruyamment, avec grand bruit; **to call l. for sth.,** réclamer qch. à grands cris; **they were shouting l.,** ils criaient à qui mieux mieux; **to knock l. at the door,** frapper rudement à la porte; **to proclaim l. that . . .,** annoncer hautement que . . .. **2. she dresses very l.,** elle affecte des toilettes extravagantes, criardes; **l. dressed,** à toilette tapageuse.

loudmouth [ˈlaudmauθ], *s. F:* gueulard, -arde.

loudmouthed [ˈlaudmauðd], *a. F:* fort en gueule.

loudness [ˈlaudnis], *s.* **1.** force *f,* sonorité *f* (d'un bruit, etc.); grand bruit (d'une cataracte, etc.); caractère bruyant (d'une démonstration). **2.** conduite vulgaire, tapageuse; **the l. of her dress,** sa toilette tapageuse, criarde.

loudspeaker [laudˈspiːkər], *s.* haut-parleur *m, pl.* haut-parleurs; **(electro)dynamic l., moving-coil l.,** haut-parleur électrodynamique; **(electro)magnetic l., moving-armature l.,** haut-parleur électromagnétique; **ionic l.,** haut-parleur ionique; **pneumatic l.,** haut-parleur pneumatique; **cone(-shaped) l.,** haut-parleur à cône; diffuseur *m*; **duo-cone l.,** haut-parleur à deux cônes, haut-parleur mixte; **horn l.,** haut-parleur à pavillon; **dual loudspeakers,** haut-parleurs accouplés; **outdoor l.,** haut-parleur d'extérieur; **l. diaphragm,** membrane *f* de haut-parleur; **l. moving coil,** bobine *f* mobile de haut-parleur; **l. rectifier,** redresseur *m* d'excitation de haut-parleur.

lough [lɔχ], *s.* (*in Ireland*) **1.** lac *m.* **2.** bras *m* de mer.

Louis [ˈluːi]. *Pr.n.m.* Louis; **L. the Fourteenth,** Louis Quatorze; **L. Quinze, L. Seize, furniture, etc.,** meubles *m* Louis Quinze, Louis Seize; *Bootm:* **L. heel,** talon *m* Louis XV.

Louisa [lu(ː)ˈiːzə]. *Pr.n.f.* Louise.

Louisiana [lu(ː)iːziˈænə]. *Pr.n. Geog:* Louisiane *f*; *Bot:* **L. cypress,** cyprès *m* de la Louisiane, cyprès chauve; *Orn:* **L. heron,** héron *m* à ventre blanc; **L. tanager,** tangara *m* à tête rouge; **L. water thrush,** fauvette *f* hochequeue.

Louisianian [lu(ː)iːziˈæniən]. *Geog:* (*a*) *a.* louisianais; (*b*) *s.* Louisianais, -aise.

lounge[1] [laundʒ], *s.* **1.** (*a*) *O:* flânerie *f*; *F: O:* **l. lizard,** gigolo *m*; (*b*) *A:* allure nonchalante; (*c*) **l. suit,** complet veston *m.* **2.** (*a*) promenoir *m*; (*in hotel*) hall *m*; **cocktail l., l. bar,** bar *m* (où l'on sert des cocktails, etc.); **coffee is served in the l.,** on sert le café (i) au salon, (ii) au bar; (*b*) (*in house*) salon; **sun l.,** véranda *m*; (*c*) *Th: Av: etc:* foyer *m* (du public). **3.** *NAm:* (*a*) *Furn:* canapé *m*; **l. chair,** fauteuil *m*; (*b*) *Rail:* **l. car,** voiture-salon *f, pl.* voitures-salons.

lounge[2], *v.i.* **1. to l. (about),** flâner; **to l. along,** avancer en traînant le pas; *v.tr.* **to l. away the time,** passer le temps en flânant, à flâner. **2.** s'étaler, s'étendre, paresseusement (sur un canapé, etc.); **to l. against the wall,** s'appuyer mollement au mur.

lounger [ˈlaundʒər], *s.* **1.** flâneur, -euse; oisif, -ive; désœuvré, -ée. **2.** *Furn:* (*a*) *NAm:* canapé *m*; (*b*) **(sun) l.,** fauteuil *m* de relaxation. **3.** *U.S: Cost:* tenue *f* de loisirs.

lounging[1] [ˈlaundʒiŋ], *a.* (*a*) flânant; de flâneur; de flânerie; (*b*) *U.S: Cost:* de loisirs.

lounging[2], *s.* flânerie *f.*

lour [ˈlauər], *s. & v.i.,* **louring** [ˈlauəriŋ], *a.,* **louringly** [ˈlauəriŋli], *adv.* = LOWER[2,3], LOWERING[3,4], LOWERINGLY.

lourie [ˈluːriː], *s. Orn:* (*S. Africa*) touraco *m.*

louse[1], *pl.* **lice** [laus, lais], *s.* (*a*) *Ent:* pou *m, pl.* poux; **bee l.,** braule *f*; **plant l.,** aphis *m,* puceron *m*; **infested with lice,** pouilleux; (*b*) *Crust:* **carp l.,** argule foliacé; pou des poissons; **sea l.,** (i) cymothoé *m,* caligе *m*; *F:* pou de mer; (ii) limule *m* polyphème; crabe *m* des Moluques; **whale l.,** cyame *m,* cyamus *m*; (*c*) *P:* fripouille *f*; salaud *m.*

louse[2], *v. P:* (*a*) *v.i.* **to l. around,** traîner, traînasser; (*b*) *v.tr.* **to l. (sth.) up,** gâcher, bousiller (qch.).

lousewort ['lauswəːt], *s. Bot:* pédiculaire *f*; herbe *f* aux poux.

lousiness ['lauzinis], *s.* état pouilleux.

lousy ['lauzi], *a.* **1.** pouilleux; pédiculaire; plein de poux. **2.** *F:* (*a*) sale, ignoble; miteux, moche; **a l. trick,** un sale coup; un sale tour; **a l. hole,** (i) une vraie pouillerie; (ii) un vrai bled; **he's a l. type,** c'est un petit pouilleux; **l. weather,** sale temps *m*, temps de chien; **a l. meal,** un repas bien moche; **a l. crossing,** une traversée affreuse (de la Manche, etc.); (*b*) **this place is l. with . . .,** ça grouille de . . .; **he's l. with money,** c'est un gros richard.

lout [laut], *s.* (*a*) lourdaud *m*; rustre *m*; maladroit *m*; **you clumsy l.!** espèce de lourdaud! (*b*) **he was attacked by a bunch of louts,** il a été attaqué par une bande de voyous.

loutish ['lautiʃ], *a.* rustre, rustaud, lourdaud.

loutishness ['lautiʃnis], *s.* grossièreté *f*; **there's too much l. at football matches these days,** de nos jours il y a trop de voyous aux matchs de football.

louver, louvre ['luːvər], *s.* **1.** *Arch: A:* lucarne *f.* **2.** (*a*) *Arch:* **l. (board),** abat-vent *m inv*, abat-son *m*, *pl.* abat-sons (de clocher); (*b*) *Nau:* louvre *m*; jalousie *f* (de sabord, etc.); *Aut: Av:* persienne *f*, volet *m* (d'aérage, de capot); *Mec.E:* ouïe *f* (de prise d'air).

louvered ['luːvəd], *a.* **1.** *Arch:* (clocher *m*) à abat-sons. **2.** (*a*) *Nau:* muni d'un louvre, de louvres; (sabord *m*, etc.) à jalousies; (*b*) *Aut: Av:* (capot *m*) à persiennes, à volet; *Mec.E:* **l. opening,** orifice muni d'ouïes.

lovable ['lʌvəbl], *a.* aimable; chérissable; qu'on peut aimer; **he's got a l. nature,** il a un caractère aimable, sympathique; **cats are very l. creatures,** les chats sont bien sympathiques.

lovableness ['lʌvəbəlnis], *s.* caractère *m* aimable, sympathique (de qn).

lovage ['lʌvidʒ], *s. Bot:* **(Italian, common) l.,** livèche *f*; ache *f* de(s) montagne(s).

love[1] [lʌv], *s.* **1.** (*a*) amour *m*; affection *f*, tendresse *f*, attachement *m*; *Lit:* **courtly l.,** amour courtois; **l. of, for, s.o.,** amour de, pour, envers, qn; affection pour qn; **l. of, for, sth.,** amour de qch.; **full of l.,** plein de tendresse; **there's no l. lost between them,** ils ne s'aiment pas outre mesure; ils ne peuvent pas se sentir; *Lit:* **the l. you bear me,** l'amour que vous me portez; **for the l. of God,** pour l'amour de Dieu; **he learnt French for the l. of it,** il a appris le français par attrait pour cette langue; **to play for l.,** jouer pour l'honneur, pour le plaisir; **I don't want to work for l.,** je ne veux pas travailler pour rien, pour le roi de Prusse; **give my l. to your parents,** faites mes amitiés à vos parents; **my l. to all,** mes amitiés à tous; **mother sends her l.,** ma mère vous envoie son affectueux souvenir; *Corr:* **with much l.,** je vous embrasse de tout mon cœur; **with l. from all,** avec mille amitiés de notre part à tous; **it can't be had for l. or money,** on ne peut se le procurer à aucun prix; il est absolument impossible de s'en, se le, procurer; **I wouldn't do it for l. or money,** je ne le ferais pour rien au monde; **l. of one's neighbour,** l'amour *m* du prochain; **l. feast,** (i) *Ecc.Hist:* agape *f*; (ii) *U.S: Pol: etc:* banquet *m* de réconciliation; (*b*) (*between lovers*) amour (*the pl. is fem. in Lit: use*); **first l.,** les premières amours; **it's l. at first sight,** c'est le coup de foudre; **l. life,** vie amoureuse; **l. match,** mariage *m* d'amour, d'inclination; **to marry for l.,** épouser qn par amour; faire un mariage d'inclination; **l. letter,** billet doux; **l. story,** histoire *f*, roman *m*, d'amour; **l. song,** (i) chant *m* d'amour; (ii) chanson *f* d'amour; romance *f*; *Th: etc:* **l. scene,** scène *f* d'amour; **l. knot,** lacs *m* d'amour; *Lit:* **l. philtre, potion,** philtre *m*; **l. child,** enfant naturel, illégitime; enfant d'amour, de l'amour; *Furn: U.S:* **l. seat,** causeuse *f*; *A:* **l. apple,** pomme *f* d'amour; tomate *f*; *Lit:* **l. laughs at locksmiths,** l'amour force toutes les serrures; **to be in l. with s.o.,** être amoureux, épris, de qn; **to win s.o.'s l.,** se faire aimer de qn; **head over heels, over ears, in l.,** amoureux fou, éperdument amoureux; **to fall in l. with s.o.,** tomber amoureux de qn; **to make l. to s.o.,** (i) faire la cour à qn; (ii) faire l'amour avec qn; **l. in a cottage,** une chaumière et un cœur; **love's young dream,** le parfait amour; **he learnt French for (the) l. of her,** il a appris le français par amour pour elle. **2.** (*pers.*) (*a*) **(my) l.,** mon amour; mon ami, mon amie; (mon) chéri, (ma) chérie; **an old l. of mine,** une de mes anciennes amours; (*b*) *F:* (*between women; usu. not translated*) **more coffee, l.?** tu prends encore du café? *Com: etc: P:* **there you are, l.!** voilà, ma petite dame! **3.** (*a*) **Love,** l'Amour, Cupidon; (*b*) **what a l. of a child,** *A:* **of a hat!** quel amour d'enfant, de chapeau! **4.** *Ten: etc:* zéro *m*, rien *m*; **three l.,** trois à zéro; **l. all,** zéro partout; **l. fifteen, fifteen l.,** rien à quinze, quinze à rien; **l. game,** jeu blanc.

love[2], *v.tr.* **1.** (*a*) aimer, affectionner (qn); **to l. one another,** s'aimer, s'entr'aimer; **the disciple whom Jesus loved,** le disciple bien-aimé (de Jésus); *F:* **Lord l. you!** Seigneur Dieu! *Prov:* **l. me l. my dog,** qui m'aime aime mon chien; (*b*) aimer (d'amour); **I l. you!** je t'aime! *Prov:* **l. me little l. me long,** qui aime peu aime longtemps; les passions ardentes sont passagères. **2.** aimer (passionnément) (son chez-soi, etc.); *B:* **he that loveth his life shall lose it,** qui aime sa vie la perdra; **as you l. your life,** si vous tenez à la vie; **I l. horse racing,** les courses de chevaux me passionnent; **I l. music,** j'adore la musique; **to l. to do sth., to l. doing sth.,** aimer (à) faire qch.; adorer faire qch.; **he loves to be praised,** il aime qu'on le loue; **will you come with me?—I should l. to,** voulez-vous m'accompagner?—je ne demande pas mieux; avec le plus grand plaisir; très volontiers; **she'll l. me to go with you,** elle sera enchantée que je vous accompagne.

lovebird ['lʌvbəːd], *s.* (*a*) *Orn:* perruche *f* inséparable; **black-cheeked l.,** inséparable *mf* à joues noires; **Fischer's l.,** inséparable de Fischer; **masked l.,** inséparable masquée; **Nyasa l.,** inséparable de Liliane; **peach-faced l.,** inséparable à face rose; (*b*) *pl. F:* (*of pers.*) **lovebirds,** tourtereaux *m.*

love-in-a-mist ['lʌvinə'mist], *s. Bot:* nigelle *f* (de Damas); cheveux *mpl* de Vénus, patte-d'araignée *f.*

love-in-idleness ['lʌvin'aidəlnis], *s. Bot:* pensée *f*; herbe *f* de la Trinité.

love-in-winter ['lʌvin'wintər], *s. Bot:* chimaphile *f.*

Lovelace ['lʌvleis], *s.m. A:* séducteur; libertin.

loveless ['lʌvlis], *a.* sans amour. **1.** insensible à l'amour. **2.** pour qui personne ne ressent d'amour; délaissé, privé d'amour.

lovelessness ['lʌvlisnis], *s.* **1.** insensibilité *f* à l'amour. **2.** privation *f* d'amour.

love-lies-bleeding ['lʌvlaiz'bliːdiŋ], *s. Bot:* amarante *f* à fleurs en queue; queue-de-renard *f*, *pl.* queues-de renard.

loveliness ['lʌvlinis], *s.* beauté *f*, charme *m* (d'une femme, d'un paysage, etc.).

lovelock ['lʌvlɔk], *s.* accroche-cœur *m*, *pl.* accroche-cœur(s).

lovelorn ['lʌvlɔːn], *a. O:* délaissé, abandonné; éperdu d'amour.

lovely ['lʌvli], *a.* **1.** (*a*) beau, *f.* belle, charmant, ravissant, séduisant, gracieux; **wouldn't it be l. to win the first prize!** ce serait merveilleux de gagner le premier prix! **what a l. woman!** la belle femme! quelle femme ravissante! **what a l. jewel!** quel amour de bijou! **my l.!** ma belle! (*b*) **it's been just l. being with you!** ça a été charmant de me trouver avec vous! **that l. scene in which the bishop is caught with the girls,** cette scène délicieuse où l'évêque est surpris au milieu des jeunes filles. **2.** *F:* (personne *f*) très aimable.

lovemaking ['lʌvmeikiŋ], *s.* (*a*) cour (amoureuse); (*b*) rapports sexuels.

lover ['lʌvər], *s.* **1.** (*a*) (i) amoureux *m*, prétendant *m*; (ii) fiancé *m*; **Lovers' Lane,** Sentier *m* des amoureux; (*b*) **her l.,** son amant; son ami intime; **they were lovers,** ils étaient amants, amant-amante. **2.** amateur *m*, ami(e) (des livres, de la nature, etc.); **music l.,** amateur de musique; musicien, -ienne; **l. of the past,** ami(e) du passé.

lovesick ['lʌvsik], *a.* défaillant d'amour; qui languit d'amour.

lovesickness ['lʌvsiknis], *s.* mal *m* d'amour.

lovey(-)dovey ['lʌvidʌvi], *P:* **1.** *s.* mon petit chou; ma mie. **2.** *a.* (parler) sentimental, mignard.

loving ['lʌviŋ], *a.* **1.** affectueux, affectionné, tendre; *Corr:* **your l. mother,** ta mère affectueuse, qui t'aime. **2.** (*with noun prefixed*) **money l., home l.,** qui aime l'argent, son chez-soi. **3. l. cup,** coupe *f* de l'amitié.

lovingkindness [lʌviŋ'kaindnis], *s.* bonté *f* (d'âme, de cœur).

lovingly ['lʌviŋli], *adv.* affectueusement, tendrement.

low[1] [lou], *a., adv., & s.*

I. *a.* **1.** bas, *f.* basse; **l. wall,** mur bas, peu élevé; **l. forehead,** front bas; **l. relief,** bas-relief *m*; **dress with a l. neckline,** robe décolletée; **l. collar,** (i) col bas; (ii) col rabattu; **the fire is burning l.,** le feu baisse; **light turned l.,** lumière *f* en veilleuse; **l. tide, l. water,** marée basse; basse mer, mer basse; **the river is l.,** la rivière est basse; **l. water mark,** (*of river*) étiage *m*; (*of sea*) (i) niveau *m* des basses eaux; (ii) laisse *f* de basse mer, de basse marée; (*of pers.*) **to be in l. water,** (i) être dans la gêne, dans des difficultés; (ii) être déprimé, malade; **my purse was getting l.,** mes ressources baissaient; ma bourse se dégarnissait; **my stocks are rather l.,** mes stocks sont un peu dégarnis; *Typ:* **letter l. to paper,** caractère *m* qui n'affleure pas. **2.** (*a*) **l. ceiling,** plafond bas, peu élevé; **l. bow,** profonde révérence; **to make s.o. a l. bow,** saluer qn profondément; *Geog:* **the L. Countries,** les Pays-Bas; *Aut:* **l. chassis,** châssis surbaissé; (*b*) **to bring s.o. l.,** humilier, abaisser, abattre, ravaler, qn; *B:* **he brought Babylon l.,** il abaissa Babylone; **to lie l.,** (i) se tapir; rester tapi; se tenir accroupi; (ii) rester coi; se tenir coi; faire le mort; (*c*) **lower part,** bas *m* (d'une échelle, etc.); **the lower part of the town,** la basse ville; **the lower Alps,** les basses Alpes; **lower Normandy,** la basse Normandie; **the lower Thames, the lower Seine (valley),** la vallée inférieure de la Tamise, de la Seine; **the lower regions,** les régions infernales; **the lower jaw,** la mâchoire inférieure; **lower tooth,** dent *f* du bas; (*d*) *Ling:* **l. German,** le bas allemand; **l. Latin,** le bas latin. **3.** (*a*) **l. birth,** basse naissance; **all the people, high and l.,** tous, du haut en bas de l'échelle sociale; **there was something low about her,** elle avait un je ne sais quoi de peuple, de canaille; **the lower classes,** *A:* **orders,** les basses classes; le bas peuple; **lower ranks,** rangs inférieurs (de l'armée, etc.); **lower court,** tribunal inférieur; *Pol:* **the lower house,** la Chambre basse; **lower end of the table,** bas bout de la table; *Sch:* **the lower school, the lower forms,** les petites classes; (*b*) bas, peu élevé; **of a l. type of intelligence,** d'une intelligence peu développée; **the lower animals,** les animaux inférieurs; **l. comedy,** la comédie à gros effets; le bas comique; **l. comedian,** comédien *m* à emplois bouffons, à rôles chargés; (*c*) bas, vil, trivial, canaille; **l. company,** mauvaise compagnie; basses fréquentations; **a l. woman,** (i) une femme vulgaire, grossière; (ii) une femme de mauvaise vie; **the lowest of the l.,** le dernier des derniers; **l. expression,** expression *f* canaille; **a l. type of face,** une vraie tête de brute; **to get into l. habits,** s'encanailler; **l. district,** quartier mal famé; **l. cunning,** fourberie *f*; **that's a l. trick!** ça c'est un sale coup! **4. l. diet,** régime sévère, peu substantiel; régime débilitant; diète *f*; (*of invalid*) **to be very l., in a very l. state,** être bien bas; aller très mal; **to feel l., to be in l. spirits,** se sentir déprimé; être abattu; *F:* avoir le cafard; *Med:* **l. physical condition,** atonie *f.* **5. l. price,** bas prix; prix faible; **at a l. figure, at a l. price,** à bas prix; à bon compte; à bon marché; **the lowest price,** le dernier prix; **the lowest freight,** le minimum de fret; **it will cost a hundred pounds at the very lowest,** cela coûtera cent livres au bas mot, pour le moins; **l. wages,** salaires peu élevés; **l. temperature,** basse température; **to cook sth. over a l. heat, a l. fire,** faire cuire qch. à feu doux; **water with l. radioactive content,** eau légèrement radioactive; **l. speed,** petite vitesse, faible vitesse; **l.-consumption lamp,** lampe *f* à faible consommation; **l. gradient,** pente *f* faible; **l. fever,** fièvre lente; **l. latitudes,** basses latitudes; *Cards:* **the l. cards,** les basses cartes; *Metall:* **l. steel,** acier *m* à faible teneur en carbone. **6. l. note,** note basse; **l. sound,** (i) son bas, grave; (ii) faible son; **l. murmur,** faible murmure *m*; **l. cry,** cri sourd; **in a l. voice,** à voix basse, à mi-voix; **she has a l. voice,** elle a une voix basse, au timbre grave; **to speak to s.o. in a l. whisper,** parler tout bas à qn. **7.** *A:* **l. date,** date récente. **8.** *Ecc:* **l. mass,** la messe basse; **L. Sunday,** Pâques closes, (dimanche *m* de) la Quasimodo; **L. Week,** la semaine de la Quasimodo.

II. *adv.* **1.** (*a*) (pendre, viser) bas; **the village stands lower than the castle,** le village se trouve en contrebas du château, au-dessous du château; **to bow l.,** s'incliner profondément; saluer très bas; **I never fell so l. as that,** je ne suis jamais tombé si bas; **dress cut l. in the back,** robe décolletée dans le dos; **she wears her hair l. on the forehead,** ses cheveux *m* mordent sur le front; *F: O:* **that's playing it l.,** c'est agir d'une façon peu loyale, peu digne; *F:* c'est un coup rosse; *Box:* **to hit l.,** toucher bas; (*b*) (*of bird, aircraft*) **to fly l.,** voler bas; (*bird*) *a.* **l. flyer,** bas voleur. **2. to play l.,** jouer petit jeu; **the lowest paid employees,** les employés les moins payés. **3.** (*a*) (parler) à voix basse; (*b*) *Mus:* **I cannot get as l. as that,** je ne peux pas descendre si bas (dans la gamme); **to set (a song, etc.) lower,** baisser (une chanson, etc.); **music transposed two tones lower,** musique transposée (de) deux tons au-dessous. **4.** *A:* (*of dates*) **as l. as . . .,** aussi récemment que . . ..

III. *s.* **all-time l.,** record le plus bas, record de médiocrité; **to reach a new l.,** descendre encore plus bas.

low[2], *s.* meuglement *m* (d'une vache, du troupeau).

low[3], *v.i.* (*of cattle*) meugler; (*occ. of bull, etc.*) beugler.

low-angle ['lou'æŋgl], *a. Artil: etc:* **l.-a. fire,** tir *m* de plein fouet.

lowborn ['loubɔːn], *a.* **1.** de basse naissance. **2.** d'humble naissance.

lowboy ['loubɔi], *s. Furn: U.S:* commode basse (sur pieds).

lowbred ['loubred], *a.* mal élevé; grossier.

lowbrow ['loubrau], *F:* **1.** *a.* terre à terre *inv*; peu intellectuel. 2. *s.* personne *f* terre à terre, dépourvue de sens artistique; bourgeois, -oise; philistin, -ine.

low-browed ['loubraud], *a.* **1.** au front bas. **2.** (*a*) (*of building*) à entrée basse; (*b*) (*of rock*) surplombant.

low-budget ['lou'bʌdʒit], *a.* bon marché; économique.

low-built ['loubilt], *a.* bas, peu élevé; *Nau:* de bas bord; ras (sur l'eau); **l.-b. fortification,** fortification rasante; *Aut:* **l.-b. chassis,** châssis surbaissé.

low-capacitance ['loukə'pæsitəns], *a. El:* à faible capacité; **l.-c. conductor,** conducteur *m* à faible capacité.

low-capacity ['loukə'pæsiti], *a. Ph: etc:* à faible capacité; *Cmptr:* **l.-c. memory,** mémoire *f* à faible capacité; *Tp:* **l.-c. line,** ligne *f* à faible capacité (de trafic).

low-class ['loukla:s], *a.* de bas étage; vulgaire, inférieur; sans distinction.

low-cut ['loukʌt], *a.* (*of dress*) décolleté.

lowdown[1] ['loudaun], *a.* **1.** bas, *f.* basse; près du sol; *Cr:* **he made a fine l. catch,** il a happé la balle presque à ras de terre avec une adresse remarquable. **2.** bas, vil, ignoble, canaille; (*of attempt at fraud, etc.*) inavouable; **a l. business,** une affaire honteuse; **l. methods,** procédés déloyaux; **that's a l. trick,** ça c'est un coup rosse.

lowdown[2], *s. F:* **to give s.o. the l.,** renseigner qn; porter les faits véritables à la connaissance de qn; tuyauter qn (**on,** sur).

low-drag ['loudræg], *a. Aedcs:* profilé; aérodynamique; *Av:* **l.-d. strut,** hauban profilé.

low-energy ['lou'enədʒi], *a. Atom.Ph:* **l.-e. particle,** particule *f* à faible énergie; **l.-e. reactor,** réacteur *m* de faible puissance.

lower[1] ['louər]. **1.** *v.tr.* (*a*) baisser (la tête, les yeux); abaisser (les paupières); abaisser, rabattre (son voile, son chapeau); *Mil:* **to l. the colour (in salute),** saluer du drapeau; *Th:* **to l. the curtain,** faire baisser le rideau; (*b*) **to l. s.o. on a rope,** affaler, (faire) descendre, qn au bout d'une corde; **to l. a barrel into the cellar,** descendre un tonneau dans la cave; **to l. a ladder,** descendre une échelle; *Nau:* **to l. a mast,** amener, caler (un mât); **l. away!** laissez aller! **to l. a boat,** amener une embarcation; mettre une embarcation à la mer; **to l. the boats to the water's edge,** amener les embarcations à fleur d'eau; (*c*) abaisser (qch.); diminuer la hauteur de (qch.); *Aut:* **to l. the chassis,** surbaisser le châssis; (*d*) baisser, rabaisser (un prix); réduire, abaisser (la pression); baisser (la lumière); amoindrir (un contraste); **to l. rents,** diminuer, baisser, les loyers; **to l. the bank rate,** abaisser le taux de l'escompte; **to l. the temperature,** abaisser la température; (*e*) baisser (la voix, le ton); **to l. s.o.'s spirits,** déprimer, démoraliser, qn; **to l. the enemy's morale,** déprimer le moral de l'ennemi; (*f*) (r)abaisser, faire baisser, (r)abattre, aplatir (l'orgueil de qn); abaisser, avilir (qn); **to l. one's pride,** rabattre de sa fierté; **to l. oneself,** s'abaisser, se rabaisser, se ravaler (**to,** à); s'avilir; **he would think he was lowering himself if he accepted,** il croirait déroger en acceptant; **that would l. you in the eyes of the public,** cela vous diminuerait aux yeux du public. **2.** *v.i.* (*a*) (*of ground, etc.*) s'abaisser, descendre; (*b*) (*of prices, rents, bank rate, etc.*) diminuer, baisser.

lower[2] ['lauər], *s.* **1.** air renfrogné, menaçant. **2.** assombrissement *m* (du ciel); menace *f* (de la tempête).

lower[3] ['lauər], *v.i.* **1.** (*of pers.*) se renfrogner; froncer les sourcils; **to l. upon, at, s.o.,** regarder qn d'un mauvais œil; menacer qn du regard. **2.** (*of sky*) s'assombrir, s'obscurcir, se couvrir; (*of clouds*) s'amonceler; (*of storm*) menacer.

lowering[1] ['louəriŋ], *a.* **1.** (*of action, conduct*) abaissant. **2.** *Med:* (régime) débilitant.

lowering[2] ['louəriŋ], *s.* **1.** (*a*) abaissement *m*; baissement *m* (de la tête, etc.); (*b*) descente *f* (d'une échelle dans un puits, etc.); *Nau:* calage *m* (d'un mât); mise *f* à la mer (d'une embarcation); **l. mast,** mât *m* rabattable; (*c*) abaissement, diminution *f* de la hauteur (de qch.). **2.** rabattage *m*, rabais *m*, diminution (des prix); réduction *f* (de la pression); **l. of taxation,** diminution des impôts; *Phot:* **l. of sensitiveness,** dépression *f* de la sensibilité.

lowering[3] ['lauəriŋ], *a.* **1.** (air) renfrogné, menaçant; (front) sombre. **2.** (ciel) sombre, menaçant, orageux.

lowering[4] [lauəriŋ], *s.* = LOWER[2].

loweringly ['lauəriŋli], *adv.* **1.** (regarder) d'un air renfrogné, menaçant. **2.** *Lit:* **l. the clouds gathered,** les nuages menaçants s'amoncelaient.

lowermost ['louəmoust], *a.* le plus bas.

low-flying ['lou'flaiiŋ], *a.* (*a*) *Orn:* (faucon) bas voleur; (*b*) *Av:* **l.-f. aircraft,** avion *m* volant bas, volant à basse altitude; **l.-f. attack,** attaque *f* (par des avions volant) à basse altitude; **l.-f. patrol,** patrouille *f* (d'avions volant) à basse altitude.

low-frequency ['lou'fri:kwənsi], *a. El:* (courant) de basse fréquence.

low-grade ['lou'greid], *a.* de qualité inférieure; pauvre.

lowing[1] ['louiŋ], *a.* (troupeau) meuglant; beuglant.

lowing[2], *s.* meuglement *m*; beuglement *m*.

lowland ['loulənd], *s.* plaine (basse); terre *f* en contrebas; *Geog:* **the Lowlands,** la Basse-Écosse; *attrib.* **the L. counties,** les comtés de la Basse-Écosse.

lowlander ['louləndər], *s.* habitant, -ante (i) de la plaine, (ii) de la Basse-Écosse.

low-level ['lou'levl], *a.* **1.** bas, *f.* basse. **2.** en contrebas; *Rail:* **l.-l. station,** gare (i) en contrebas, (ii) souterraine. **3.** *Cmptr:* **l.-l. flowchart,** organigramme détaillé; **l.-l. language,** langage peu évolué.

lowliness ['loulinis], *s.* humilité *f.*

low-living ['lou'liviŋ], *a.* de mauvaise vie; aux mœurs grossières.

lowly[1] ['louli], *adv.* **1.** *O:* **l. born,** (i) de basse naissance; (ii) de naissance modeste. **2.** humblement.

lowly[2], *a. A: & Lit:* humble, modeste, sans prétention; *s.pl.* **the l.,** les humbles *m*, les petites gens *m*; **l. rank,** rang *m* infime.

low-lying ['lou'laiiŋ], *a.* situé en bas, dans la plaine; (terrain) bas, enfoncé.

low-masted ['lou'ma:stid], *a. Nau:* peu mâté.

low-necked ['lou'nekt], *a.* **l.-n. dress,** robe décolletée, à encolure dégagée.

lowness ['lounis], *s.* **1.** manque *m* de hauteur (d'un mur, etc.); petitesse *f* (d'un arbre, etc.); situation basse (d'une île); faible altitude *f* (d'une île, des collines). **2.** humilité *f* (de situation). **3.** (*a*) gravité *f* (d'un son); (*b*) faiblesse *f* (d'un bruit); peu *m* d'élévation (de la température); modicité *f* (de prix). **4.** bassesse *f* (de conduite). **5. l. (of spirits),** abattement *m*, découragement *m*, dépression *f.*

low-pass ['loupa:s], *a. W.Tel:* **l.-p. filter,** filtre *m* passe-bas.

low-pitched ['lou'pitʃt], *a.* **1.** (*a*) (son *m*) grave; (*b*) (piano) accordé à un diapason bas. **2.** *Const:* (comble *m*) à faible inclinaison, à faible pente; (chambre *f*) au plafond bas, à plafond bas.

low-powered ['lou'pauəd], *a.* de faible puissance.

low-pressure ['lou'preʃər], *a.* (*a*) *Meteor:* (zone *f*) de basse pression; (*b*) (cylindre *m*, machine *f*) à basse pression, à basse tension.

low-slung ['lou'slʌŋ], *a.* (meuble, etc.) bas; *Aut:* (châssis) surbaissé.

low-speed ['lou'spi:d], *a.* (machine *f*) à petite vitesse, à vitesse réduite.

low-spirited ['lou'spiritid], *a.* abattu, triste, déprimé, découragé; **to be l.-s.,** broyer du noir.

low-voiced ['lou'vɔist], *a.* **1.** à la voix grave, profonde. **2.** à la voix basse.

low-wing(ed) ['lou'wiŋ(d)], *a. Av:* (*of monoplane*) à aile(s) basse(s), à aile(s) surbaissée(s), à voilure basse.

loxoclase ['lɔksəkleis], *s. Miner:* loxoclase *f.*

loxodont ['lɔksədɔnt], *a. Z:* loxodonte.

loxodrome ['lɔksədroum], *s. Nau: Av:* loxodromie *f.*

loxodromic [lɔksə'droumik], *a. Nau: Av:* (navigation *f*, etc.) loxodromique; (ligne) loxodromique *f*; **l. tables,** tables *f* loxodromiques.

loxodromics [lɔksə'droumiks], *s.pl.* (*usu. with sg. const.*) navigation *f* loxodromique.

loxodromy [lɔk'sɔdrəmi], *s.* loxodromie *f.*

loxolophodont [lɔksə'lɔfədɔnt], *s. Paleont:* loxolophodonte *m.*

loxomma [lɔk'sɔmə], *s. Paleont:* loxomma *m.*

loxygen ['lɔksidʒən], *s. Pyr:* oxygène *m* liquide.

loyal ['lɔiəl], *a.* (*a*) (ami, etc.) fidèle, dévoué (**to,** à); loyal, -aux (**to,** envers); (*b*) fidèle au roi, à la famille royale; **to drink the l. toast,** boire le toast au roi, au souverain; *s.pl. A:* **the loyals,** les partisans assurés du roi, de la famille royale.

loyalism ['lɔiəlizm], *s. Pol:* loyalisme *m.*

loyalist ['lɔiəlist], *s.* loyaliste *mf.*

loyally ['lɔiəli], *adv.* fidèlement.

loyalty ['lɔiəlti], *s.* (*a*) *A:* fidélité *f* à sa promesse, à son serment, etc.; (*b*) fidélité à la Couronne; loyalisme *m*; **l. to one's party, to one's friends,** fidélité à son parti; loyauté *f* envers ses amis; *Geog:* **L. Island,** l'île Loyauté.

lozenge ['lɔzindʒ], *s.* **1.** *Mth: Her:* losange *m.* **2.** *Pharm:* pastille *f*, tablette *f.*

lozenged ['lɔzindʒd], *a.* **1.** losangique; en losange, en losanges. **2.** *Her:* = LOZENGY.

lozengy ['lɔzindʒi], *a. Her:* losangé; **l. barry,** losangé en barre.

lubber ['lʌbər], *s.* **1.** (*a*) lourdaud *m*, balourd *m*; (*b*) *Nau:* terrien *m*, maladroit *m*, empoté *m.* **2.** *Nau:* **lubber's hole,** trou *m* du chat (entre mât et hune); *Av: Nau:* **lubber('s) line (of compass, of cathode-ray indicator),** ligne *f* de foi (d'un compas de navigation, d'un radiogoniomètre à oscilloscope).

lubberliness ['lʌbəlinis], *s.* **1.** balourdise *f*, gaucherie *f*; rusticité *f.* **2.** lourdeur *f* de corps.

lubberly ['lʌbəli]. **1.** *a.* lourdaud, balourd; empoté, gauche; rustre. **2.** *adv.* lourdement, gauchement; d'un air empoté.

lubra ['lu:brə], *s. Austr:* femme aborigène.

lubricant ['lu:brikənt], *a. & s.* (*a*) lubrifiant (*m*), lubrificateur, -trice; graisse *f*, huile *f* (pour machines, etc.); **gear l.,** graisse pour engrenages; **extreme-pressure l.,** lubrifiant pour haute pression; (*b*) *Tex:* lubrificatum *m.*

lubricate ['lu:brikeit], *v.tr.* **1.** lubrifier; graisser, huiler; **synovia lubricates the joints,** la synovie lubrifie les articulations; **to l. the wheels,** graisser les roues. **2.** *F:* (*a*) graisser la patte à (qn); (*b*) **to be well lubricated,** être soûl.

lubricating[1] ['lu:brikeitiŋ], *a.* lubrifiant; lubrificateur, -trice.

lubricating[2], *s.* lubrification *f*, graissage *m*; **l. oil,** huile *f* de graissage; **light l. oil,** huile de graissage fluide; *Mec.E:* **l. cap,** chapeau graisseur; **l. cup,** godet *m* de graissage; **l. rack,** rampe *f* de graissage; **l. ring,** anneau *m* de graissage; **l. wick,** mèche *f* de graissage; **l. system,** système *m* de graissage.

lubrication [lu:bri'keiʃ(ə)n], *s.* lubrification *f*, lubrifaction *f*; graissage *m*; **dry-sump l.,** graissage à carter sec; **drip l., drop-feed l.,** graissage à (compte-)gouttes; **gravity-feed l.,** graissage par gravité; **splash l.,** graissage par barbotage, par projection; **spray l.,** graissage par brouillard d'huile; **l. system,** circuit *m* de graissage; **l. diagram,** schéma *m* (du circuit) de graissage.

lubricator ['lu:brikeitər], *s.* graisseur *m*; appareil *m* de graissage; **cap l.,** graisseur à chapeau; **drop l.,** graisseur compte-gouttes; **hand-pump l.,** (graisseur à) coup-de-poing *m*, *pl.* coups-de-poing; **telescope l.,** graisseur à trombonne; **gravity-feed l.,** graisseur par gravité; **forced-feed l.,** graisseur à, sous, pression; **l. cap,** chapeau graisseur.

lubricity [lu'brisiti], *s.* **1.** (*a*) onctuosité *f* (d'un lubrifiant); (*b*) *A:* nature glissante; caractère fuyant (de qn); caractère rusé; matoiserie *f*, fourberie *f.* **2.** lubricité *f*, lasciveté *f.*

lubrify ['lu:brifai], *v.tr. A:* lubrifier.

Lucan[1] ['lu:kən], *a. B.Hist:* de (saint) Luc.

Lucan[2]. *Pr.n.m. Lt.Lit:* Lucain.

Lucania [lu(:)'keiniə]. *Pr.n. A.Geog:* la Lucanie.

Lucanian [lu(:)'keiniən]. *A.Geog:* (*a*) *a.* lucanien; (*b*) *s.* Lucanien, -ienne.

Lucanidae [lu:'kænidi:], *s.pl. Ent:* lucanidés *m.*

lucanus [lu(:)'keinəs], *s. Ent:* lucane *m*, cerf-volant *m*, *pl.* cerfs-volants.

Lucca ['lʌkə]. *Pr.n. Geog:* Lucques *f.*

luce [lju:s], *s. Ich:* brochet *m* (adulte).

lucency ['lu:sənsi], *s.* brillance *f*, luminosité *f.*

lucent ['lu:sənt], *a.* **1.** brillant, lumineux. **2.** clair, transparent.

lucernal [lu:'sə:n(ə)l], *a.* **l. microscope,** microscope lucernal.

lucernaria [lu:sə'na:riə], *s. Cœl:* lucernaire *f.*

lucern(e)[1] [lu:'sə:n], *s. Bot: Agr:* luzerne *f.*

Lucerne[2]. *Pr.n. Geog:* Lucerne *f*; **the Lake of L.,** le lac des Quatre-Cantons.

Lucian ['lu:siən, -ʃiən]. *Pr.n.m. Gr.Lit:* Lucien.

Lucianic [lu:si'ænik], *a.* lucianesque; satirique (à la manière de Lucien).

lucid ['lu:sid], *a.* **1.** (*a*) *Lit:* brillant, lumineux; (*b*) *Ent: Bot:* luisant; (*c*) *Astr:* (étoile *f*) visible à l'œil nu. **2.** (*a*) (esprit *m*, style *m*) lucide; **l. explanation,** explication claire; (*b*) *Med:* **l. interval,** intervalle *m* lucide, de lucidité; (*c*) *Lit:* (*of water, etc.*) clair, transparent.

lucidity [lu:'siditi], *s.* **1.** (*a*) luminosité *f*; (*b*) transparence *f.* **2.** (*a*) lucidité *f* (d'esprit, de style); (*b*) lucidité (d'un malade entre périodes de démence); (*c*) *Psy:* lucidité, cryptesthésie *f.*

lucidly ['lu:sidli], *adv.* lucidement; avec lucidité.

lucidness ['lu:sidnis], *s.* = LUCIDITY, 1, 2, (*a*).

Lucifer[1] ['lu:sifər]. *Pr.n.m.* **1.** *Astr:* Lucifer; Vénus *f.* **2.** *B:* Lucifer.

lucifer[2], *s. A:* **l. (match),** allumette *f* (chimique).

lucifer[3], *s. Crust:* lucifer *m.*

luciferase [lu:'sifəreis], *s. Bio-Ch:* luciférase *f.*

luciferin [lu:'sifərin], *s. Bio-Ch:* luciférine *f.*

lucifugous [lu:'sifjugəs], *a.* (insecte *m*, etc.) lucifuge.

lucilia [lu:'siliə], *s. Ent:* lucilie *f*; mouche dorée de la viande.

lucimeter [lu:'simitər], *s. Opt:* lucimètre *m.*

Lucina [lu:'sainə]. **1.** *Pr.n.f. Rom.Myth:* Lucine. **2.** *s. Moll:* lucine *f.*

luciola [lu:'si:oulə]. *s. Ent:* luciole *f.*

luck [lʌk], *s.* **1.** hasard *m*, chance *f*, fortune *f*; **good l.,** bonne chance, heureuse fortune, bonheur *m*; **good l. (to you)!** bonne chance! *Iron:* **good l. to him! and the best of (British) l. to him!** qu'il le fasse si ça lui chante! **ill l., bad l.,** mal(e)chance *f*, mauvaise fortune, fortune adverse; malheur *m*; déveine *f*, guigne *f*, guignon *m*; **good l., bad l., cannot last for ever,** il n'y a chance qui ne rechange; **he's had terribly bad l.,** il a eu une déveine extraordinaire; **I always had the best of l.,** la chance m'a toujours été favorable; **to be down on one's l.,** avoir de la déveine, la guigne; être dans la déveine, dans l'adversité; **he's having a run of bad l.,** il est en pleine déveine; **to bring s.o. bad, good, l.,** porter malheur, bonheur, à qn; **it'll be hard, bad, l. if . . .,** ce sera bien malheureux, bien le diable, si . . .; **to try one's l.,** tenter la fortune, la chance; **to push one's l.,** pousser sa chance; **better l. next time!** ça ira mieux une autre fois; **just my l.!** c'est bien de ma chance! pas de veine! **worse l.!** tant pis! **hard l.!** pas de chance! **to tell a hard l. story,** raconter ses malheurs (pour inspirer la pitié); **it's bad l. to walk under a ladder,** passer sous une échelle porte malheur; **by good l.,** heureusement, par bonheur; **by, through, bad l.,** par malheur; **he avoided an accident more by l. than (by) judgement,** il a évité un accident par chance plutôt que par adresse; **as l. would have it I was there,** le hasard a voulu que je m'y trouvasse. **2.** bonheur *m*, bonne fortune, (bonne) chance; **to have the l. to . . .,** avoir la chance de . . ., être assez heureux pour . . .; **to keep sth. for l.,** garder qch. comme porte-bonheur; **bit, piece, stroke, of l.,** coup *m* de fortune, coup de veine; aubaine *f*; **to be in l., in luck's way,** être en veine, en bonheur; jouer de bonheur; avoir de la chance, de la veine; avoir le vent en poupe; **you're in l. and no mistake,** pour de la chance, c'est de la chance! **to be out of l.,** être en guigne, jouer de malheur, être en malheur; **my luck's in!** quelle veine! **my luck's out,** c'est la guigne! **he's having a run of l.,** il est en veine; **he has all the l.,** c'est un veinard; **to have the devil's own l., the l. of the devil,** avoir un bonheur insolent, une chance de tous les diables; avoir de la corde de pendu dans sa poche; **as l. would have it,** par bonheur.

luckily ['lʌkili], *adv.* heureusement, par bonheur; **l. for me nobody saw me,** j'ai eu la chance de ne pas être remarqué.

luckiness ['lʌkinis], *s.* bonheur *m*; bonne fortune; chance *f*.

luckless ['lʌklis], *a.* *O:* **1.** (*of pers.*) malheureux, malchanceux, infortuné. **2. l. day,** jour malencontreux; **l. hour,** heure fatale.

lucklessness ['lʌklisnis], *s.* *O:* malchance *f*, malheur *m*.

lucky ['lʌki], *a.* (*a*) heureux, fortuné; chanceux, veinard; qui a de la chance, de la veine; *F:* **the l. man,** le marié; *F:* **(you) l. devil! l. beggar!** *O:* **l. dog!** veinard! **to be l.,** avoir de la chance, jouer de bonheur; *Iron:* **you'll be l.!** tu peux toujours courir! **he was born l.,** il est né coiffé; **l. in love, at cards,** heureux en amour, au jeu; (*b*) **l. hit, l. shot,** coup heureux; coup de bonheur, de veine; trouvaille *f*; **to make a l. hit, guess,** tomber juste; **l. hour, moment,** heure *f*, moment *m*, propice; **l. day,** jour *m* faste, de veine; **it's not my l. day,** je n'ai pas de chance aujourd'hui; **now isn't that l.? how l.!** quelle chance! **how l. you came!** quelle chance que vous soyez venu! **it was l. for him that he did (it),** il a été bien inspiré de le faire; **to strike (it) l.,** jouer de chance; gagner le gros lot; (*c*) **l. charm,** porte-bonheur *m inv*; **l. pig, etc.,** petit cochon, etc., porte-bonheur; (*of thg*) **to be l.,** porter bonheur; (*d*) **l. dip,** baquet rempli de son où l'on plonge la main pour en retirer une surprise (à une vente de charité, etc.).

lucrative ['lu:krətiv], *a.* lucratif.

lucratively ['lu:krətivli], *adv.* d'une manière lucrative; lucrativement.

lucrativeness ['lu:krətivnis], *s.* bon rapport; **l. of a trade,** gros bénéfices que rapporte un métier.

lucre ['lu:kər], *s.* **1.** lucre *m*; **to do sth. for (filthy) l.,** agir par amour de gain, de lucre. **2.** *A:* **l. of gain,** l'amour du lucre.

Lucretia [lu:'kri:ʃ(i)ə], *Pr.n.f. Rom.Hist:* Lucrèce.

Lucretian [lu:'kriʃ(i)ən], *a.* de Lucrèce; qui se rapporte à la philosophie de Lucrèce.

Lucretius [lu:'kri:ʃ(i)əs], *Pr.n.m. Rom.Lit:* Lucrèce.

lucubrate ['lu:kjubreit], *v.i.* *Lit:* écrire des élucubrations; travailler tard dans la nuit.

lucubration [lu:kju'breiʃ(ə)n], *s.* *Lit:* **1.** élucubration *f*, veilles *fpl*. **2.** (*often pl.*) élucubration(s).

lucubrator ['lu:kjubreitər], *s.* *Lit:* élucubrateur, -trice.

lucule, *pl.* **-ae** ['lu:kjul, -i:], *s.* *Astr:* lucule *f*.

Lucy ['lu:si], *Pr.n.f.* Lucie.

lud [lʌd], *s.* (*in addressing judge in law courts*) **my l.** [mlʌd] (= *my lord*), monsieur le président; monsieur le juge.

Luddism ['lʌdizm], *s.* *Hist:* luddisme *m*.

Luddite ['lʌdait], *s.* *Hist:* luddite *m*.

Ludian ['lu:diən], *a.* & *s.* *Geol:* ludien (*m*).

ludicrous ['lu:dikrəs], *a.* risible, comique, ridicule, grotesque, plaisant.

ludicrously ['lu:dikrəsli], *adv.* risiblement, comiquement, ridiculement, grotesquement, plaisamment.

ludicrousness ['lu:dikrəsnis], *s.* côté plaisant, aspect *m* comique, côté risible (d'un incident); absurdité *f* (d'une réclamation, etc.).

Ludlovian [lʌd'louviən], *a.* & *s.* *Geol:* ludlovien (*m*), ludlowien (*m*).

ludwigite ['lʌdwigait], *s.* *Miner:* ludwigite *f*.

lues ['lu:i:z], *s.* *Med:* (*a*) *F:* peste *f*; (*b*) syphilis *f*.

luetic [lu:'etik], *a.* *Med:* syphilitique.

luff[1] [lʌf], *s.* *Nau:* **1.** lof *m*, ralingue *f* du vent, chute *f* avant (d'une voile); (*of sail*) **to tear from l. to leech,** se déchirer dans toute sa longueur, dans toute sa largeur. **2.** *N.Arch:* épaule *f* (de l'avant). **3. l. (tackle),** palan *m* à croc; dispositif *m* de relevage (d'une grue). **4. to spring the l.,** faire une aulof(f)ée; **to keep the l.,** tenir le vent; tenir le plus près.

luff[2], *v.tr.* & *i.* **1.** *Nau:* (*a*) *v.i.* lof(f)er; oloffer; faire une aulof(f)ée; **luff!** loffe! **l. round!** loffe tout! (*b*) *v.tr.* **to l. the boat (up),** faire loffer la barque; (*c*) *v.tr.* (*in yachting*) **to l. an antagonist away,** passer au vent d'un concurrent. **2.** *v.tr.* (*of crane*) transborder (la charge) par la volée.

luffa ['lʌfə], *s.* *Bot:* *Toil:* luffa *m*.

lufferboard ['lʌfəbɔ:d], *s.* = LOUVER 2.

luffing ['lʌfiŋ], *s.* **1.** aulof(f)ée *f*, oloffée *f*; *Y:* **to have a l. match with s.o.,** disputer le vent à qn. **2.** (*of crane*) **l. gear,** dispositif *m* de relevage.

lug[1] [lʌg], *s.* = LUGWORM.

lug[2], *s.* *Nau:* = LUGSAIL.

lug[3], *s.* **1.** *F:* (*a*) (*ear*) oreille *f*; (*b*) oreillette *f* (de casquette). **2.** *Tchn:* (*a*) oreille; **l. of a foundry flask,** oreille d'un châssis de fonderie; **lugs of a shackle,** oreille d'une manille; **l. union,** raccord *m* à oreilles; (*b*) patte *f*, bride *f*; **attaching l., attachment l., fastening l., fixing l.,** patte, étrier *m* d'attache, de fixation; *El:* **accumulator-plate l.,** patte, queue *f*, de plaque d'accu(mulateur); **earthing l.,** patte de mise à la terre; *Tp:* **l. of insulator,** patte de console (d'isolateur); (*c*) *Metall:* **l. of a casting, of a mould,** tasseau *m* d'une pièce venue de fonderie, d'un moule (de fonderie); (*d*) saillie *f*, bossage *m*, bouton *m*, taquet *m*, tenon *m*, ressaut *m*; mentonnet *m* (d'un obus, d'une bombe); (*on gearing, etc.*) ergot *m*; *I.C.E:* **lugs of the piston,** bossages du piston; *Mec.E:* **retaining l.,** tenon de fixation; **stop l.,** taquet arrêtoir, tenon arrêtoir.

lug[4], *s.* traction violente, subite.

lug[5], *v.tr.* **(lugged) 1.** traîner, tirer (qch. de pesant); **to l. sth. along, away,** entraîner qch.; **to l. sth. about with one,** promener, trimbaler, qch. avec soi. **2.** *P:* *esp. Austr:* **to l. s.o.,** emprunter de l'argent à qn.

luge[1] [lu:ʒ], *s.* *Sp:* luge *f*.

luge[2], *v.i.* *Sp:* luger; faire de la luge.

luger ['lu:dʒər], *s.* *Sp:* lugeur, -euse.

luggage ['lʌgidʒ], *s.* **1.** bagage(s) *m* (*pl*); **hand l.,** bagages à main; **heavy l.,** gros bagages; **excess l.,** excédent *m* de bagages; **20 kilos of l. are allowed free (of charge),** on a droit à 20 kilos de bagages en franchise; **l. in advance,** bagages non accompagnés; *Rail:* **l. van,** fourgon *m* (aux bagages); *Nau:* **l. room, hold,** soute *f* aux bagages; **cabin l.,** bagages de cabine; **hold l., l. not wanted on the voyage,** bagages de cale; *Av:* **l. bay, compartment,** compartiment *m*, soute, à bagages; **l. rack,** (i) *Rail:* filet *m*, porte-bagages *m inv*; (ii) *Aut:* galerie *f*, porte-bagages; **l. label,** étiquette *f* à bagages; **his only l. was a briefcase and an umbrella,** il avait pour tout bagage une serviette et un parapluie. **2.** *esp.* *NAm:* *Com:* articles *mpl* de voyage.

lugger ['lʌgər], *s.* *Nau:* lougre *m*; **coasting l.,** hovari *m*; chasse-marée *m inv*.

lughole ['lʌghoul], *s.* *P:* oreille *f*; **pin back your lugholes!** écarquillez vos esgourdes!

lugsail ['lʌgseil, 'lʌgsl], *s.* *Nau:* voile *f* à bourcet, au tiers; tréou *m*; taille-vent *m inv*.

lugubrious [lə'gu:briəs], *a.* lugubre.

lugubriously [lə'gu:briəsli], *adv.* lugubrement.

lugubriousness [lə'gu:briəsnis], *s.* caractère *m* lugubre; aspect *m* lugubre (d'un endroit, etc.).

lugworm ['lʌgwɔ:m], *s.* arénicole des pêcheurs, *F:* ver *m* des pêcheurs, ver rouge.

luidia [lə'widiə], *s.* *Echin:* luidia *m*.

Luke [lu:k]. *Pr.n.m.* Luc; **Saint L.,** saint Luc.

lukewarm ['lu:kwɔ:m], *a.* (*of water, friendship, etc.*) tiède; (*of water*) dégourdi; **to become l.,** s'attiédir; **to make l.,** (at)tiédir (l'eau, etc.).

lukewarmness [lu:k'wɔ:mnis], *s.* tiédeur *f* (de l'eau, d'un accueil, etc.).

lull[1] [lʌl], *s.* moment *m* de calme; (*before storm*) bonace *f*; *Nau:* accalmie *f*, embellie *f*; **there was a l. in the storm,** il y a eu une accalmie; **there was a l. in the wind, in the conversation,** le vent, la conversation, tomba.

lull[2]. **1.** *v.tr.* (*a*) bercer, endormir (qn); **to l. a child to sleep,** endormir un enfant; (*b*) endormir (les soupçons de qn); assoupir (une douleur); **to l. s.o. with false hopes,** bercer qn d'espérances trompeuses; (*c*) calmer, apaiser (la tempête); **the winds were lulled,** les vents *m* se calmèrent. **2.** *v.i.* (*of storm, sea*) se calmer, s'apaiser, tomber; *Nau:* calmir.

lullaby ['lʌləbai], *s.* *Mus:* berceuse *f*.

lulu ['lu:lu:], *s.* *F:* (*a*) *as m*; chic type; jolie fille; (*b*) **it's a l.!** c'est hors concours!

lumachel ['lu:məkel], **lumachelle** [lumə'ʃel], *s.* *Miner:* lumachelle *f*.

lumbago [lʌm'beigou], *s.* *Med:* lumbago *m*.

lumbar ['lʌmbər], *a.* & *s.* *Anat:* lombaire (*f*).

lumber[1] ['lʌmbər], *s.* **1.** (*a*) vieux meubles; objets encombrants; fatras *m*; **l. room,** (pièce *f* de) débarras *m*; (*b*) *Sp:* *Turf:* excès *m* de chair. **2.** *NAm:* (*a*) bois *m* de charpente, de construction; bois en grume; (*b*) *Cost:* **l. jacket,** blouson *m*; canadienne *f*.

lumber[2]. **1.** *v.tr.* (*a*) encombrer, embarrasser (un lieu); remplir (un lieu) de fatras; **to l. (up) a room with furniture,** encombrer une pièce de meubles; (*b*) entasser (des objets) pêle-mêle; (*c*) *F:* **to be lumbered with a mistress,** avoir un fil à la patte; **I don't want to be lumbered with him for the whole evening,** je ne veux pas le traîner à mes trousses pendant toute la soirée. **2.** *v.tr.* & *i.* *NAm:* débiter (le bois).

lumber[3], *v.i.* (*a*) **to l. along, in, out, up,** avancer, entrer, sortir, monter, à pas lourd, d'un pas lourd, lourdement; (*b*) **to l. about,** se trimbaler çà et là.

lumbered ['lʌmbəd], *a.* encombré (**with,** de); rempli de fatras.

lumberer ['lʌmbərər], *s.* *NAm:* bûcheron *m*.

lumbering[1] ['lʌmbriŋ], *s.* **1.** encombrement *m* (d'un lieu). **2.** *NAm:* (i) débit *m* des bois; (ii) exploitation forestière.

lumbering[2], *a.* lourd, pesant.

lumberjack ['lʌmbədʒæk], *s.* *NAm:* bûcheron *m*.

lumberman, *pl.* **-men** ['lʌmbəmən], *s.m.* *NAm:* (*a*) exploitant de forêts; (*b*) marchand de bois; (*c*) bûcheron *m*.

lumbersome ['lʌmbəs(ə)m], *a.* lourd, pesant.

lumberyard ['lʌmbəja:d], *s.* *NAm:* chantier *m* de bois.

lumbosacral [lʌmbou'sækrəl], *a.* *Anat:* lombo-sacré.

lumbrical ['lʌmbrik(ə)l], *a.* & *s.* *Anat:* (muscle) lombrical, -aux (*m*).

lumbricoid ['lʌmbrikɔid], *a.* & *s.* lombricoïde (*m*).

lumbricus ['lʌmbrikəs], *s.* *Ann:* lombric *m*.

lumen, *pl.* **-mina** ['lu:men, -minə], *s.* **1.** *Anat:* *Surg:* ouverture *f*, passage *m*. **2.** *Ph.Meas:* (*pl.* **lumens**) lumen *m* (unité de flux lumineux); **l. output,** intensité (lumineuse) en lumens; **l. hour,** lumenheure *m*; **l. meter,** lumenmètre *m*.

luminance ['lu:minəns], *s.* *Ph:* luminance *f*.

luminant ['lu:minənt]. **1.** *a.* lumineux, luminogène. **2.** *s.* source lumineuse.

luminarism ['lu:minərizm], *s.* *Art:* luminisme *m*.

luminarist ['lu:minərist], *s.* *Art:* luminariste *m*, luministe *m*.

luminary ['lu:minəri], *s.* **1.** corps lumineux; luminaire *m*, astre *m*. **2.** (*of pers.*) lumière *f*; flambeau *m* (de la science, etc.); **discovery vouched for by several luminaries of physics,** découverte attestée par plusieurs physiciens éminents.

luminesce [lu:mi'nes], *v.i.* devenir luminescent.

luminescence [lu:mi'nesəns], *s.* luminescence *f*; **l. microscope,** microscope *m* à luminescence; **threshold of l.,** seuil *m* de luminescence.

luminescent [lu:mi'nesənt], *a.* luminescent, luminogène; **l. material,** substance luminescente, luminogène; **l. centre,** centre luminescent, luminogène; *Elcs:* **l. screen tube,** tube *m* à écran luminescent.

luminiferous [lu:mi'nifərəs], *a.* luminifère; qui répand, qui transmet, la lumière.

luminism ['lu:minizm], *s.* *Art:* luminisme *m*.

luminist ['lu:minist], *s.* *Art:* luministe *m*, luminariste *m*.

luminophor(e) ['lu:minoufɔ:ər], *s.* **1.** luminophore *m*, substance luminescente. **2.** phosphore *m*.

luminosity [lu:mi'nɔsiti], *s.* luminosité *f*; **l. curve,** courbe *f* de luminosité; **l. factor,** facteur *m*, coefficient *m*, de luminosité.

luminous ['lu:minəs], *a.* **1.** lumineux; (*a*) *Ph:* **l. density,** densité lumineuse; luminance *f*; **l. efficiency,** efficacité lumineuse, rendement lumineux, coefficient *m* d'efficacité lumineuse; **l. flux,** flux lumineux; **l. intensity,** intensité lumineuse; **l. sensitivity,** sensibilité lumineuse, photosensibilité *f*; **l. standard,** étalon *m* photométrique; (*b*) **l. dial,** cadran lumineux; **l. pointer,** indicateur lumineux; **l. screen,** écran lumineux; **l. paint,** peinture lumineuse, peinture au radium; *Elcs:* **l.(-discharge) tube,** tube luminescent haute tension, tube à décharge à cathode froide. **2.** (génie, etc.) illuminant; (explication) lumineuse; **the examples that make his lectures so l.,** les exemples *m* dont il illumine ses conférences.

lumme ['lʌmi], *int. F:* mon Dieu!

lump[1] [lʌmp], *s.* **1.** (*a*) gros morceau, bloc *m* (de pierre); motte *f* (de terre, d'argile); morceau (de sucre); masse *f* (de plomb, etc.); grugeon *m* (de cassonade); (*in porridge, etc.*) boule *f*, grumeau *m*; *Paperm:* pâton *m* (dans le papier); *B: Lit:* **to leaven the whole l.,** faire lever toute la pâte; **to sell sth. in the l.,** vendre qch. en bloc, en gros, globalement; **l. sum,** (i) somme grosse, globale; prix global; (ii) prix à forfait; paiement *m* forfaitaire; **to have a l. in one's throat,** avoir la gorge serrée; avoir un serrement de gorge, une boule dans la gorge; se sentir le cœur gros; (*b*) (*caused by bruise*) bosse *f* (au front, etc.); (*c*) *Med: etc:* excroissance *f*; grosseur *f*. **2.** *F:* (*of pers.*) empoté *m*, pataud *m*, lourdaud *m*; **great lump of a girl,** grosse dondon; **great l. of a man,** gros plein de soupe; grand mollasse; **fat l. of a man,** gros patapouf. **3.** *Civ.E: etc: F:* **the l.,** ouvriers indépendants (qui évitent le fisc).

lump[2]. **1.** *v.tr.* (*a*) mettre en bloc, en masse, en tas; (*b*) **to l. things together,** réunir des choses ensemble; **to l. persons together,** considérer des personnes en bloc; **items lumped under the heading . . .,** articles qui sont bloqués, réunis, sous la rubrique . . .. **2.** *v.i.* (*a*) (*of earth*) former des mottes; (*b*) **to l. along,** marcher lourdement, à pas pesants; **to l. down,** tomber lourdement.

lump[3], *v.tr. F:* s'arranger à contrecœur de (qch.); **if he doesn't like it, he can l. it, he can like it or l. it,** si cela ne lui plaît pas, qu'il s'arrange; s'il n'est pas content, qu'il aille le dire à Rome.

lumped [lʌmpt], *a.* **1.** concentré, massé. **2.** *Elcs: El:* (*a*) localisé; **l. capacity,** capacité localisée; **l. constants,** constantes localisées; **l.-constants filter,** filtre *m* à constantes localisées; **l. load,** charge localisée; (*b*) composé; **l. circuit,** circuit composé; **l. voltage,** tension composée; *W.Tel:* **l. characteristic,** caractéristique composée.

lumper ['lʌmpər], *s. Nau:* déchargeur *m*, débardeur *m*.

lumpfish ['lʌmpfiʃ], *s. Ich: F:* lompe *m*, lump *m*; gros-mollet *m*, (gras) mollet *m*, seigneur *m*.

lumpiness ['lʌmpinis], *s.* **1.** tendance *f* (de la terre, etc.) à se mettre en mottes. **2.** profusion *f* de mottes, de bosses; **the l. of the paper,** les nombreux pâtons dans le papier.

lumping[1] ['lʌmpiŋ], *a. F:* gros, énorme.

lumping[2], *s.* réunion *f* (de plusieurs choses dans la même catégorie, sous la même rubrique).

lumpish ['lʌmpiʃ], *a.* **1.** gros, lourd, balourd, pesant, pataud, godiche, godichon; **great, l. man,** lourdaud *m*, pataud *m*, mastoc *m*. **2.** *F:* à l'esprit lent; à l'intelligence peu ouverte.

lumpishness ['lʌmpiʃnis], *s.* **1.** lourdeur *f*, balourdise *f*. **2.** *F:* stupidité *f*.

lumpkin ['lʌm(p)kin], *s. A: & Dial:* lourdaud *m*, butor *m*; **a Tony L.,** un grand dadais, un godelureau.

lumpsucker ['lʌmpsʌkər], *s. Ich:* = LUMPFISH.

lumpy ['lʌmpi], *a.* (*a*) (*of earth*) rempli de mottes; (*of sauce, etc.*) grumeleux; (*of paper*) chantonné; (*b*) **l. sea,** mer courte, houleuse, clapoteuse; (*c*) couvert de protubérances; (front, etc.) couvert de bosses; *Vet: F:* **l. jaw,** actinomycose *f*.

lunacy ['lu:nəsi], *s.* **1.** aliénation mentale; folie *f*; *Jur:* démence *f*; **commission of l.,** commission chargée de prononcer sur un cas présumé d'aliénation mentale; **the Commissioners in l.,** les inspecteurs *m* des asiles d'aliénés; **master in l.,** magistrat chargé d'examiner les cas présumés d'aliénation mentale et le cas échéant d'aviser à la tutelle du dément. **2.** *F:* action, idée, folle; folie; **it's sheer l.,** c'est de la folie (pure et simple).

lunar ['lu:nər], *a.* **1.** lunaire; de (la) lune; *Astr:* **l. cycle,** cycle *m* lunaire; **l. month,** mois *m* lunaire; mois de consécution. **2.** en forme de croissant; *Anat:* **l. bone,** os *m* semi-lunaire.

lunaria [lu:'nɛəriə], *s. Bot:* lunaire *f*.

lunarian [lu:'nɛəriən]. **1.** (*a*) *a.* lunarien, -ienne; (*b*) *s.* habitant *m* de la lune; lunicole *m*. **2.** *s.* observateur *m* de la lune.

lunate ['lu:neit], *a. Nat.Hist:* luné, luniforme; en forme de croissant; **bearing l. markings,** lunifère.

lunatic ['lu:nətik]. **1.** *a.* (*a*) de fou(s), d'aliéné(s); *F:* **l. behaviour,** conduite folle, extravagante; **the l. fringe,** les originaux *m*, les extrémistes *m*, les cinglés *m*; (*b*) *B:* lunatique. **2.** *s.* fou, *f.* folle; aliéné, -ée; *Jur:* dément, -ente.

lunation [lu:'neiʃ(ə)n], *s.* lunaison *f*.

lunch[1] [lʌnʃ], *s.* (*a*) déjeuner *m*; *Fr.C: Belg:* dîner *m*; **the children have school l.,** les enfants déjeunent à la cantine; **they have l. at one o'clock,** ils déjeunent à une heure; **I only have a snack l.,** je ne prends qu'un tout petit repas, un casse-croûte, à midi; **we had a picnic l.,** nous avons pique-niqué à midi; (*b*) *NAm:* petit repas, casse-croûte (pris à n'importe quelle heure); (*c*) *A:* café, casse-croûte (pris au milieu de la matinée).

lunch[2]. **1.** *v.i.* (*a*) déjeuner; (*b*) *NAm:* prendre un petit repas; manger un morceau sur le pouce. **2.** *v.tr.* donner à déjeuner à (qn); faire déjeuner (qn); **I lunched him well at the Hilton,** je lui ai offert un bon déjeuner au Hilton.

luncheon ['lʌnʃ(ə)n], *s.* (*a*) *A:* collation *f* (de midi); (*b*) (*usu. formal meal*) déjeuner *m*; **there were about thirty guests at the l.,** il y avait une trentaine d'invités au déjeuner; (*c*) *Rail: etc:* **first, second, l.,** premier, deuxième, service; **l. basket,** (i) panier *m* à provisions; (ii) panier-repas *m*, *pl.* paniers-repas; *Com: etc:* **l. voucher,** chèque-repas *m*, *pl.* chèques-repas.

luncher ['lʌnʃər], *s.* déjeuneur, -euse.

lune [lu:n], *s. Mth:* lunule *f*, croissant *m*; **spherical l.,** trochoïde *m*.

lunette [lu(:)'net], *s. Arch: Fort:* lunette *f*.

lung [lʌŋ], *s.* **1.** poumon *m*; **to shout at the top of one's lungs,** crier à tue-tête; **to have good lungs,** avoir de bons poumons; avoir la voix forte; **inflammation of the lungs,** congestion *f* pulmonaire; **cancer of the l., l. cancer,** cancer *m* du poumon; *Med:* **iron l.,** poumon d'acier. **2.** *Bot:* **lungs of oak** = LUNGWORT.

lunge[1] [lʌndʒ], *s. Equit:* **1.** longe *f*, allonge *f*; plate-longe *f*, *pl.* plates-longes. **2.** piste *f* (circulaire).

lunge[2], *v.tr. Equit:* faire trotter (un cheval) à la longe; dresser (le cheval) à la longe.

lunge[3], *s.* **1.** *Fenc:* botte *f*; développement *m*; coup droit; coup de pointe; **to make a full l.,** se fendre à fond. **2.** (*a*) mouvement (précipité) en avant; (*b*) **with each l. of the ship,** chaque fois que le navire tanguait; à chaque coup de roulis.

lunge[4], *v.i.* **1.** (*a*) *Fenc:* se fendre; **to l. at the adversary,** porter, pousser, allonger, une botte à l'adversaire; (*b*) **to l. at s.o. with one's stick,** lancer un coup de pointe à qn avec sa canne; **to l. out at s.o.,** (i) (*of pers.*) allonger un coup de poing à qn; (ii) (*of horse*) lancer une ruade à qn; *v.tr.* (*of insect*) **to l. out its sting,** darder son aiguillon. **2. to l. forward,** se précipiter en avant; se jeter en avant.

lunge[5], *s. NAm: Ich: F:* maskinongé *m* (*Fr.C.*).

lunged [lʌŋd], *a.* **1.** *Ich:* muni de poumons. **2.** (*with adj. prefixed, e.g.*) **strong-l., weak-l.,** aux poumons forts, faibles.

lunger ['lʌŋər], *s. U.S: F:* poitrinaire *mf*, tuberculeux, -euse, *F:* tubard *m*.

lungfish ['lʌŋfiʃ], *s. Ich:* dipnoïque *m*, dipneuste *m*, poisson *m* à poumons; **African l.,** protoptère *m*.

lunging ['lundʒiŋ], *s. Equit:* exercice *m* à la longe; **l. rein,** (al)longe *f*.

lungoor ['lʌŋguər], *s. Z:* entelle *f*, langur *m*.

lungwort ['lʌŋwə:t], *s. Bot:* pulmonaire *f*; herbe *f* au cœur; herbe aux poumons.

luniform ['lu:nifɔ:m], *a.* luniforme, luné; en forme de croissant.

lunisolar [lu:ni'soulər], *a.* (année *f*, etc.) luni-solaire.

lunistice ['lu:nistis], *s. Astr:* lunistice *m*.

lunitidal [lu:ni'taid(ə)l], *a. Oc:* **l. interval,** intervalle *m* entre le passage de la lune au méridien et la haute marée.

lunker ['lʌŋkər], *s. NAm: F:* gros poisson.

lunkhead ['lʌŋkhed], *s. F:* idiot, -ote; andouille *f*, nouille *f*.

lunula, *pl.* **-ae** ['lu:njulə, -i:], *s. Anat: Mth:* lunule *f*.

lunular ['lu:njulər], *a.* lunulaire.

lunulate(d) ['lu:njuleit(id)], *a. Nat.Hist:* lunulé, lunulaire.

lunule ['lu:nju:l], *s. Anat: Mth: etc:* lunule *f*.

lupa ['lu:pə], *s. Crust:* lupa *f*.

Lupercalia [lu:pə'keiliə], *s.pl. Rom.Ant:* lupercales *f*.

lupin ['lu:pin], *s. Bot:* lupin *m*.

lupine ['lu:pain], *a.* lupin; de loup.

lupinosis [lu:pi'nousis], *s. Vet:* lupinose *f*.

lupulin ['lu:pjulin], *s.* **1.** *Bot: Brew:* lupulin *m*, lupuline *f*. **2.** *Ch:* lupuline.

lupus ['lu:pəs], *s. Med:* lupus *m*.

lurch[1] [lə:tʃ], *s.* déconfiture *f*; *used in the phr.* **to leave s.o. in the l.,** laisser qn dans l'embarras, en panne, en plan, dans le pétrin; planter là qn; laisser là qn; laisser qn le bec dans l'eau.

lurch[2], *s.* **1.** embardée *f*, coup *m* de roulis (d'un navire); **l. to starboard,** embardée à tribord; **lee l.,** arrivée *f*. **2.** cahot *m*, embardée (d'une voiture). **3.** pas titubant, embardée (d'un ivrogne); titubation *f*.

lurch[3], *v.i.* **1.** (*a*) (*of ship, etc.*) faire une embardée; embarder; (*b*) *Veh:* embarder; avoir un fort cahot. **2.** (*of pers.*) **to l. along,** marcher en titubant; **to l. in, out,** entrer, sortir, en vacillant, en titubant.

lurcher ['lə:tʃər], *s.* **1.** (*a*) filou *m*, *pl.* filous; (*b*) chipeur, -euse; chapardeur, -euse. **2.** *Z:* lévrier bâtard.

lurching ['lə:tʃiŋ], *s.* **1.** (*a*) *Nau:* coups *mpl* de roulis; embardage *m*; (*b*) embardage, cahots *mpl* (d'une voiture). **2.** titubation *f*; marche *f* en zigzag.

lure[1] ['l(j)uər], *s.* **1.** (*a*) *Ven:* leurre *m* (de fauconnier); (*b*) *Fish:* leurre; appât *m* factice. **2.** (*a*) piège *m*; **he fell a victim to her lures,** il est tombé dans le piège; il s'est laissé séduire; (*b*) attrait *m*; **the l. of the sea,** l'attrait de la mer.

lure[2], *v.tr.* **1.** (*a*) *Ven:* leurrer (un faucon); (*b*) leurrer (un poisson, etc.). **2.** attirer, séduire, allécher; **to be lured into the trap,** être attiré, entraîné, dans le piège; **to l. s.o. away from duty,** détourner qn d'un devoir; débaucher qn; **to l. s.o. with dazzling prospects,** faire miroiter l'avenir aux yeux de qn; **to be lured on to destruction,** être entraîné à sa perte.

lurid ['l(j)uərid], *a.* **1.** (*a*) (ciel) blafard, fauve; (teint) livide, blafard, *Med:* luride; **l. light,** lueur blafarde, sinistre; **this casts a l. light on the facts,** cela jette une lumière sinistre, tragique, sur les faits; (*b*) *Nat.Hist:* luride. **2.** (*a*) cuivré; **l. flames,** flammes rougeoyantes; (*b*) corsé; (récit) fortement coloré; (langage) haut en couleur; (film, etc.) à effets corsés.

luridly ['l(j)uəridli], *adv.* **1.** (*a*) avec une lueur blafarde; (*b*) sinistrement, tragiquement. **2.** (*a*) en rougeoyant; (*b*) en corsant les effets.

luridness ['l(j)uəridnis], *s.* **1.** lueur blafarde, aspect *m* sinistre (du ciel, etc.). **2.** ton cuivré, rougeoiement *m* (de l'horizon, etc.).

luring ['l(j)uəriŋ], *a.* séduisant, attrayant.

Luristan [luri'stɑ:n]. *Pr.n. Geog: Archeol:* Louristan *m*; *attrib.* (céramique) de Louristan.

lurk [lə:k], *v.i.* se cacher; se tenir caché; rester tapi (dans un endroit); **the thieves were lurking in an alley way,** les voleurs se cachaient dans une venelle.

lurker ['lə:kər], *s.* **1.** personne cachée. **2.** personne aux aguets; espion *m*.

lurking[1] ['lə:kiŋ], *a.* caché; secret, -ète; **a l. suspicion,** un vague soupçon; **a l. thought of revenge,** une arrière-pensée de vengeance, de revanche.

lurking[2], *s.* **l. place,** (i) cachette *f*, retraite *f*; repaire *m* (de voleurs); (ii) *Ven:* affût *m*.

Lusatia [lu:'seiʃə]. *Pr.n. A.Geog:* Lusace *f*.

Lusatian [lu:'seiʃ(ə)n]. *A. Geog:* (*a*) *a.* lusacien; (*b*) *s.* Lusacien, -ienne.

luscious ['lʌʃəs], *a.* **1.** succulent, savoureux, délicieux; (fruit) fondant. **2.** *Pej:* (*a*) (vin) liquoreux, trop sucré; un peu écœurant; (*b*) (style) trop riche, trop fleuri; (*c*) (littérature, musique) d'un charme trop voluptueux; (*d*) *F:* **a l. piece,** une femme bien en chair.

lusciousness ['lʌʃəsnis], *s.* **1.** succulence *f* (d'un fruit); goût délicieux. **2.** *Pej:* douceur extrême, affadissante.

lush[1] [lʌʃ], *a.* **1.** (*of grass, plant*) plein de sève; luxuriant. **2.** (*a*) *Pej: F:* extravagant, trop orné; trop riche; écœurant; (*b*) *P:* **she's a l. piece!** ce qu'elle est bath, juteuse!

lush[2], *s. P:* **1.** *A:* boisson *f* (alcoolique). **2.** ivrogne *mf*; soûlard *m*.

lush[3]. *P:* **1.** *v.tr.* payer à boire à (qn); rincer la dalle à (qn); arroser (les copains). **2.** *v.i.* (*a*) boire (au bistro, etc.); (*b*) s'enivrer, se soûler.

lushness ['lʌʃnis], *s.* surabondance *f*, luxuriance *f* (de l'herbe, etc.).

Lusiad (the) [ðə'lu:siæd], *s. Lit:* les Lusiades *f*.

Lusitania [lu:si'teiniə]. *Pr.n. A.Geog:* Lusitanie *f*.

Lusitanian [lu:si'teiniən]. *A.Geog:* (*a*) *a.* lusitanien, lusitain; (*b*) *s.* Lusitanien, -ienne; Lusitain, -aine.

lust[1] [lʌst], *s.* **1.** (*a*) *Theol:* appétit *m* (coupable); convoitise *f*; **lusts of the flesh, fleshly lusts,** concupiscence *f*; **to mortify carnal lusts, the lusts of the flesh,** mortifier les appétits; **to arouse unholy lusts in s.o.,** allumer des convoitises, des désirs malsains, chez qn; (*b*) luxure *f*; désir (charnel, libidineux). **2.** *Lit:* **l. of honours, riches, of power,** soif *f* des honneurs, des richesses, du pouvoir; **l. of battle, of conquest,** désir effréné de se battre, de faire des conquêtes.

lust[2], *v.ind.tr. Lit:* **1.** (*a*) **to l. for, after, sth.,** convoiter qch.; (*b*) **to l. after a woman,** désirer une femme. **2. to l. for riches, for power, for revenge,** avoir soif des richesses, du pouvoir; avoir soif de vengeance.

lusterer ['lʌstərər], *s. Tex:* lustreur *m*.

lustful ['lʌstful], *a. Lit:* lascif, sensuel, libidineux, luxurieux, lubrique; **to cast l. eyes on s.o.,** regarder qn avec désir, d'un œil de convoitise.

lustfully ['lʌstfuli], *adv.* lascivement, libidineusement.
lustfulness ['lʌstfulnis], *s.* appétits charnels, sensuels; luxure *f*; libidinosité *f.*
lustily ['lʌstili], *adv.* (travailler, etc.) vigoureusement, de toutes ses forces; (chanter, crier) à pleine poitrine, à pleine gorge; (se battre) vaillamment; **they were shouting l.,** ils criaient à qui mieux mieux.
lustiness ['lʌstinis], *s.* vigueur *f*; santé exubérante.
lusting[1] ['lʌstiŋ], *a.* **1.** (œil) de convoitise. **2.** = LUSTFUL.
lusting[2], *s.* **1.** convoitise *f.* **2.** désir (charnel).
lustral ['lʌstrəl], *a.* **1.** lustral, -aux; *Rom.Ant:* **l. games,** jeux lustraux; *Ecc:* **l. water,** eau lustrale. **2.** quinquennal, -aux.
lustrate ['lʌstreit], *v.tr. Rom.Ant: etc:* purifier (qn, une ville).
lustration [lʌs'treiʃ(ə)n], *s.* lustration *f.*
lustre[1] ['lʌstər], *s.* **1.** éclat *m*, brillant *m*, lustre *m*; nitescence *f*; *Tex:* cati *m*, lustre (du drap); *Cer:* burgos *m*; *Min:* **soapy l.,** éclat gras; *Lit:* **to shed l. on a name, to add fresh l. to a name,** donner du lustre à un nom; ajouter un nouveau lustre à un nom; **action that added fresh l. to his fame,** action *f* qui a relevé sa gloire; **work that has conferred l. on his name,** ouvrage *m* qui a rendu son nom illustre. **2.** (*a*) pendeloque *f* (de lustre); (*b*) lustre (de plafond). **3.** *Tex:* **(cotton) l.,** lustrine *f.*
lustre[2], *v.tr.* **1.** *Tex:* lustrer, catir (un tissu). **2.** *Cer:* lustrer (la poterie).
lustre[3], *s. Rom.Ant:* lustre *m* (espace de cinq ans).
lustreless ['lʌstəlis], *a.* mat, terne; (bijoux, yeux) sans éclat.
lustreware ['lʌstəwɛər], *s. Cer:* poterie *f* à reflets métalliques; poterie lustrée.
lustrine ['lʌstrin], *A:* **lustring**[1] ['lʌstriŋ], *s. Tex: A:* lustrine *f.*
lustring[2], *s. Tex:* lustrage *m*; catissage *m.*
lustrous ['lʌstrəs], *a.* brillant, éclatant; (*of material*) lustré, satiné.
lustrousness ['lʌstrəsnis], *s.* éclat *m*, lustre *m.*
lustrum, *pl.* **-a, -ums** ['lʌstrəm, -ə, -əmz], *s. Rom.Ant: etc:* = LUSTRE[3].
lusty ['lʌsti], *a.* vigoureux, fort, robuste; puissant (de corps); (garçon) solidement découplé, bien bâti.
lute[1] [lu:t], *s. Mus:* luth *m*; **l. player** = LUTENIST; **l. maker,** luthier *m.*
lute[2], *s.* **1.** lut *m*, mastic *m* (pour cornues, etc.); *Metall:* brasque *f.* **2.** *Arb:* mastic *m* à greffer, engluement *m.*
lute[3], *v.tr.* **1.** luter, boucher, mastiquer (une cornue, etc.); *Metall:* brasquer (un creuset, etc.); **to l. a flue with cement,** enduire un carneau de ciment. **2.** *Arb:* enduire (une greffe) de mastic.
lutecium [lu:'ti:ʃiəm], *s. Ch:* lutécium *m.*
lutein ['lu:tiin], *s. Biol: Ch:* lutéine *f.*
lutenist ['lu:tənist], *s. Mus:* joueur, -euse, de luth; luthiste *mf.*
luteous ['lu:tiəs], *a. Nat.Hist:* orangé.
lutestring ['lu:tstriŋ], *s. Tex:* = LUSTRINE.
Lutetia [lu:'ti:ʃ(i)ə]. *Pr.n. A.Geog:* Lutèce *f.*
Lutetian [lu:'ti:ʃ(i)ən], *a. & s. Geol:* lutétien (*m*).
Lutheran ['lu:θərən], *a. & s. Rel.H:* luthérien, -ienne.
Lutheranism ['lu:θərənizm], *s. Rel.H:* luthéranisme *m.*
lutianid, lutjanid [lu:'tʃænid], *s. Ich:* lutjanide *m.*
Lutianidae, Lutjanidae [lu:'tʃænidi:], *s.pl. Ich:* lutjanidés *m*, lutjanides *m.*
luting ['lu:tiŋ], *s.* **1.** lutation *f*, lutage *m*; masticage *m.* **2.** = LUTE[2].
lutjanus [lu:'tʃeinəs], *s. Ich:* lutjan *m.*
lux, *pl.* **luces** [lʌks, 'lju:si:z], *s. Ph.Meas:* lux *m* (unité de lumière).
luxate ['lʌkseit], *v.tr.* luxer; déboîter (l'épaule, etc.).
luxation [lʌk'seiʃ(ə)n], *s.* luxation *f*; déboîtement *m* (de l'épaule, etc.).
Luxembourg ['lʌksəmbə:g]. *Pr.n. Geog:* le Luxembourg (province de Belgique).
Luxemb(o)urg ['lʌksəmbə:g]. *Pr.n. Geog:* **the Grand Duchy of L.,** le grand-duché de Luxembourg.
Luxemb(o)urger ['lʌksəmbə:gər], *s. Geog:* Luxembourgeois, -eoise.
luxmeter ['lʌksmi:tər], *s.* luxmètre *m.*
Luxor ['lʌksɔ:r]. *Pr.n. Geog:* Louxor *m*, Louqsor *m.*
luxuriance [lʌg'zju:riəns, lʌk's-], *s.* exubérance *f*, luxuriance *f* (de la végétation, de style, etc.).
luxuriant [lʌg'zju:riənt, lʌk's-], *a.* exubérant, luxuriant; plantureux; **l. growth of hair,** chevelure abondante; **l. foliage,** feuillage abondant, luxuriant.
luxuriantly [lʌg'zju:riəntli, lʌk's-], *adv.* avec exubérance; en abondance.
luxuriate [lʌg'zju:rieit, lʌk's-], *v.i.* **1.** (*of vegetation*) croître avec exubérance; pousser dru. **2.** (*of pers.*) (*a*) **to l. in an armchair,** prendre ses aises dans un fauteuil; (*b*) **to l. in dreams,** se griser de rêves; **he luxuriated in this new life,** il jouissait avec délices de cette vie nouvelle; il se livrait avec délices à cette vie nouvelle.
luxurious [lʌg'zju:riəs, lʌk's-], *a.* **1.** (appartement) luxueux, somptueux; **l. life,** vie *f* de luxe; vie luxueuse. **2.** (*of pers.*) (*a*) adonné au luxe; (*b*) sensuel; voluptueux. **3.** *A:* adonné à la luxure; luxurieux.
luxuriously [lʌg'zjuriəsli, lʌk's-], *adv.* **1.** luxueusement; avec luxe; dans le luxe. **2.** avec volupté.
luxuriousness [lʌg'zju:riəsnis, lʌk's-], *s.* luxe *m*; somptuosité *f.*
luxury ['lʌkʃəri], *s.* **1.** luxe *m*; **to live in (the lap of) l.,** vivre dans le luxe, au sein de l'abondance; **bred in (the lap of) l.,** élevé au sein du luxe; **I have never known either want or l.,** je n'ai jamais connu ni le besoin ni le luxe. **2.** objet *m* de luxe; **l. article,** objet de luxe; **to let, l. flat,** appartement *m* de luxe à louer; **strawberries at Christmas are a l.,** les fraises à Noël sont un luxe; **the luxuries of life,** les superfluités *f* agréables de la vie; **I can't afford luxuries,** je n'ai pas les moyens de me payer des douceurs, de faire du luxe; **to indulge in the l. of a cigar,** se payer le luxe d'un cigare; **it is quite a l. for us,** c'est du luxe pour nous; c'est un régal pour nous; **what a l. to be free at this time!** quel délice d'être libre à cette heure! **l. tax,** taxe *f* de luxe; **the l. trades,** le commerce des articles de luxe; **l. car,** voiture *f* de (grand) luxe. **3.** luxe (d'un appartement, etc.). **4.** *A:* luxure *f.*
Luzon [lu:'zɔn]. *Pr.n. Geog:* Luçon *m.*
lycaena [lai'si:nə], *s. Ent:* lycène *f.*
lycaenid [lai'si:nid], *s. Ent:* lycénide *m.*
Lycaenidae [lai'si:nidi:], *s.pl. Ent:* lycénidés *m.*
lycanthrope ['laikænθroup], *s.* **1.** lycanthrope *m.* **2.** loup-garou *m*, *pl.* loups-garous.
lycanthropy [lai'kænθrəpi], *s.* lycanthropie *f.*
lycaon [lai'keiən], *s. Z:* lycaon *m*; loup peint.
Lycaonia [laikei'ouniə]. *Pr.n. A.Geog:* Lycaonie *f.*
Lycaonian [laikei'ouniən]. *A.Geog:* (*a*) *a.* lycaonien; (*b*) *s.* Lycaonien, -ienne.
Lyceum [lai'siəm], *s.* **1.** *Gr.Ant:* **the Lyceum,** le Lycée (où enseignait Aristote). **2.** (*literary institution, etc.*) Lycée, Lycéum *m.*
lychee ['laitʃi:], *s. Bot:* litchi *m.*
lychgate ['litʃgeit], *s.* = LICHGATE.
lychnis ['liknis], *s. Bot:* lychnide *f*, lychnis *m*; **rock l.,** viscaire *f*, viscaria *m.*
Lycia ['lisiə]. *Pr.n. A.Geog:* Lycie *f.*
Lycian ['lisiən]. *A.Geog:* (*a*) *a.* lycien; (*b*) *s.* Lycien, -ienne.
lycoperdon [laikou'pə:dɔn], *s. Fung:* lycoperdon *m.*
lycopod ['laikoupɔd], *s. Bot:* lycopode *m.*
Lycopodiaceae [laikoupɔdi'eisii:], *s.pl. Bot:* lycopodiacées *f.*
Lycopodineae [laikoupou'dinii:], *s.pl. Bot:* lycopodinées *f.*
lycopodium [laikou'poudiəm], *s.* **1.** *Bot:* = LYCOPOD. **2.** *Pharm: etc:* poudre *f* de lycopode; soufre végétal.
Lycopsida [lai'kɔpsidə], *s.pl. Bot:* lycopsides *f.*
lycopsis [lai'kɔpsis], *s. Bot:* lycopside *f.*
lycopus [lai'koupəs], *s. Bot:* lycope *m*; chanvre *m* d'eau.
lycosid [lai'kousid], *s. Arach:* lycose *f.*
lyctid ['liktid], *s. Ent:* lycte *m.*
Lycurgus [lai'kə:gəs]. *Pr.n.m. Gr.Hist:* Lycurgue.
lyddite ['lidait], *s. Exp:* lyddite *f.*
Lydia ['lidiə]. **1.** *Pr.n. A.Geog:* Lydie *f.* **2.** *Pr.n.f.* Lydie.
Lydian ['lidiən]. **1.** *a. A.Geog:* lydien; *A.Mus:* **L. mode,** mode lydien. **2.** *s. A.Geog:* Lydien, -ienne.
lye [lai], *s.* lessive *f* (de soude, de potasse); **caustic soda l.,** lessive de soude caustique; *A:* **l. water,** eau seconde, des savonniers; lessive faible; *Agr: Glassm:* **l. ashes,** charrée *f.*
lygeum [lai'dʒi:əm], *s. Bot:* lygée *f.*
lying[1] ['laiiŋ], *a.* (*of pers., appearance*) menteur, -euse; faux, *f.* fausse; (récit, etc.) mensonger; **l. tongue,** langue trompeuse.
lying[2], *s.* le mensonge.
lying[3], *a.* couché, étendu.
lying[4], *s.* **1. l.(-down) position,** position couchée; *Med: etc:* décubitus *m.* **2.** *A:* **l. in,** couches *fpl*; accouchement *m*; **l.-in hospital,** maternité *f.*
lymantriid [lai'mæntriid], *s. Ent:* lymantriidé *m.*
Lymantriidae [laimæn'traiidi:], *s.pl. Ent:* lymantriidés *m.*
lyme-grass ['laimgrɑ:s], *s. Bot:* élyme *m* (des sables).
lymnaea [lim'ni:ə], *s. Moll:* limnée *f.*
Lymnaeidae [lim'ni:idi:], *s.pl. Moll:* limnéidés *m.*
lymph [limf], *s.* **1.** *Physiol:* lymphe *f*; **l. cell, l. corpuscle,** cellule *f*, corpuscule *m*, lymphatique; lymphocyte *m.* **2.** *Med:* vaccin *m*; **calf l.,** vaccin de génisse; **seed l.,** lymphe d'ensemencement.
lymphad ['limfæd], *s. Her:* galère *f.*
lymphadenectomy [limfæde'nektəmi], *s. Surg:* lymphadénectomie *f.*
lymphadenia [limfæ'di:niə], *s. Med:* lymphadénie *f.*
lymphadenitis [limfæde'naitis], *s. Med:* lymphadénite *f*; *Vet:* **caseous l.,** pseudo-tuberculose *f.*
lymphadenoma [limfæde'noumə], *s. Med:* lymphadénome *m.*
lymphangiectasia, lymphangiectasis [limfændʒ-ek'teiziə, -ektəsis], *s. Med:* lymphangiectasie *f.*
lymphangioma [limfændʒi'oumə], *s. Med:* lymphangiome *m.*
lymphangitis [limfæn'dʒaitis], *s. Med:* lymphangite *f*; *Vet:* **ulcerative l.,** lymphangite ulcéreuse.
lymphatic [lim'fætik]. *Physiol:* **1.** *a.* lymphatique; **l. gland,** glande *f*, ganglion *m*, lymphatique; **l. node, l. nodule,** ganglion lymphatique; **deep, superficial, l. gland,** glande lymphatique profonde, ganglion lymphatique profond, superficiel; **l. temperament,** tempérament *m* lymphatique. **2.** *s. Physiol:* (vaisseau) lymphatique *m.*
lymphatism ['limfətizm], *s. Med:* lymphatisme *m.*
lymphatitis [limfə'taitis], *s. Med:* lymphatite *f.*
lymphoblast ['limfoublæst], *s. Biol:* lymphoblaste *m.*
lymphocyte ['limfəsait], *s. Physiol:* lymphocyte *m.*
lymphocythaemia [limfousai'θi:miə], *s. Med:* lymphocytémie *f.*
lymphocytogenesis, lymphocytopoiesis [limfousaitou'dʒenisis, -pɔi'i:sis], *s. Physiol:* lymphocytogénèse *f.*
lymphocytosis [limfousai'tousis], *s. Med:* lymphocytose *f.*
lymphogenesis [limfou'dʒenisis], *s. Physiol:* lymphogénèse *f.*
lymphogenic [limfou'dʒenik], **lymphogenous** [lim'fɔdʒənəs], *a. Physiol:* lymphogène.
lymphogranulomatosis ['limfou'grænjuloumə'tousis], *s. Med:* lymphogranulomatose *f*; **benign l.,** lymphogranulomatose bénigne.
lymphography [lim'fɔgrəfi], *s. Med:* lymphographie *f.*
lymphoid ['limfɔid], *a.* (cellule *f*) lymphoïde.
lymphoma [lim'foumə], *s. Med:* lymphome *m*, lymphadénome *m.*
lymphopoiesis [limfoupɔi'i:sis], *s. Physiol:* lymphopoièse *f.*
lymphoreticulosis [limfouretikju'lousis], *s. Med:* lymphoréticulose *f.*
lymphosarcoma [limfousɑ:'koumə], *s. Med:* lymphosarcome *m.*
lymph-producing ['limfprədju:siŋ], *a.* **1.** lymphogène. **2.** vaccinogène.
lyncean [lin'siən], *a.* (perspicacité, œil) de lynx; (personne) aux yeux de lynx.
Lynceus [lin'si:əs]. *Pr.n.m. Gr.Myth:* Lyncée.
lynch [linʃ], *v.tr.* lyncher.
lyncher ['linʃər], *s.* lyncheur *m.*
lynchet ['linʃet], *s. Geog:* terrasse *f.*
lynching ['linʃiŋ], *s.* lynchage *m.*
lynx [liŋks], *s. Z:* lynx *m*; loup-cervier *m*, *pl.* loups-cerviers; **she-l.,** loup-cerve *f*, *pl.* loups-cerves; **Persian l.,** carcal, -als *m*, lynx du désert; **spotted l.,** lynx pard d'Espagne, lynx pardelle; **Canada l.,** chat *m* du Canada, lynx canadien; **bay l.,** lynx roux.
lynx-eyed ['liŋksaid], *a.* aux yeux de lynx.
Lyon ['laiən], *s. Her:* **L. King of Arms, L. Herald,** le roi d'armes d'Écosse.
Lyon(s) ['li:ɔn, 'laiənz]. *Pr.n. Geog:* Lyon *m.*
lyophilic [laiou'filik], *a.* lyophile.
lyophilization [laiɔfilai'zeiʃ(ə)n], *s.* lyophilisation *f.*
lyophilize [lai'ɔfilaiz], *v.tr.* lyophiliser.
lypemania [laipi'meiniə], *s.* lypémanie *f.*
Lyra ['laiərə]. *Pr.n. Astr:* la Lyre.
lyrate ['laiəreit], *a. Nat.Hist:* lyré; en forme de lyre.
lyre ['laiər], *s.* **1.** *Mus:* lyre *f.* **2.** *Mec.E:* tête *f* de cheval de tour; cœur *m* de renversement.
lyrebird ['laiəbə:d], *s. Orn:* oiseau-lyre *m*, *pl.* oiseaux-lyres; ménure *m.*
lyreflower ['laiəflauər], *s. Bot:* cœur-de-Marie *m*, cœur-de-Jeannette *m*, *pl.* cœurs-de-Marie, -de-Jeannette.
lyric ['lirik]. **1.** *a.* (poète *m*, drame *m*) lyrique. **2.** *s.* poème *m* lyrique; **Wordsworth's lyrics,** la poésie lyrique de Wordsworth; *Th:* **lyrics by . . .,** les chansons du livret sont de . . .; **l. writer,** parolier *m.*
lyrical ['lirik(ə)l], *a.* (*a*) lyrique; (*b*) dit, écrit, sur un ton lyrique, sur un ton de faux lyrisme; *F:* **she got positively l. about it,** elle y a montré un enthousiasme fou.
lyricism ['lirisizm], *s.* (*a*) lyrisme *m*; **the l. of the Bible,** le lyrisme de la Bible; (*b*) (faux) lyrisme.
lyricist ['lirisist], *s.* poète *m* lyrique.
lyriform ['lirifɔ:m], *a.* lyriforme.
lyrism ['lirizm], *s.* = LYRICISM.
lyrist ['lirist], *s.* **1.** *Mus:* joueur *m* de lyre. **2.** = LYRICIST.
Lysander [lai'sændər]. *Pr.n.m. Gr.Hist:* Lysandre.
lyse [laiz], *v.tr. Biol:* (*of lysin*) lyser, dissoudre (une cellule).

lysergic [lai'sə:dʒik], *a.* lysergique; **l. acid diethylamide,** acide *m* lysergique (synthétique) diéthylamine (LSD).
lysidine ['lisidain], *s. Ch:* lysidine *f.*
lysigenic [lisi'dʒenik], **lysigenous** [li'sidʒinəs], *a. Biol:* lysigène.
Lysimachus [lai'simakəs]. *Pr.n.m. A.Hist:* Lysimaque.
lysimeter [li'simitər], *s.* lysimètre *m.*
lysin [laisin], *s. Biol: Ch:* lysine *f.*
Lysippus [lai'sipəs]. *Pr.n.m. Gr.Art:* Lysippe.
lysis ['laisis], *s. Biol: Med:* lyse *f*; lysis *m.*
Lysistratus [lai'sistrətəs]. *Pr.n.m.* Lysistrate.
lysol ['laisɔl], *s. Pharm:* lysol *m.*
lysosoma [laisou'soumə], *s. Biol:* lysosome *m.*
lysozyme ['laisouzaim], *s. Biol:* lysozyme *m.*
lyssa ['lisə], *s. Med:* rage *f.*
lyssophobia [lisou'foubiə], *s.* lyssophobie *f.*
Lythraceae [li'θreisii:], *s.pl. Bot:* lythracées *f,* lythrariées *f.*
lythrum ['liθrəm], *s. Bot:* lythrum *m.*
lytic ['litik], *a. Biol:* (action *f,* sérum *m*) lytique.
lytta ['litə], *s. Ent:* lytta *m.*
lyxose ['liksous], *s. Ch:* lyxose *m.*

M

M, m [em], *s.* (la lettre) M, m *f*; *Tp:* **M for Mary,** M comme Marcel.

ma [mɑː], *s.f.* maman.

ma'am [mɑːm; *at Court in addressing members of the royal family:* mæm; *from servant to mistress:* mʌm], *s.* **1.** madame. **2.** *F:* **school-m.** [mɑːm], maîtresse *f* d'école.

mac[1] [mæk], *s. F:* imper *m.*

mac[2], *s. U.S: P:* mec *m.*

macabre [mə'kɑːbr], *a.* macabre.

macaco[1], [mə'keikou], *s. Z:* maki *m*, mococo *m*, lémur *m.*

macaco[2], *s.* **1.** *Z:* = MACAQUE. **2. m. worm,** ver *m* macaque.

macadam [mə'kædəm], *s. Civ.E:* macadam *m*; **tar m.,** macadam au goudron; **m. road,** route macadamisée; **cement-bound m.,** macadam-ciment *m*; **waterbound m.,** macadam à l'eau; **m. plant,** installation *f* pour macadamisation.

macadamization [məkædəmai'zeiʃ(ə)n], *s. Civ.E:* macadamisage *m*, macadamisation *f.*

macadamize [mə'kædəmaiz], *v.tr. Civ.E:* empierrer, macadamiser (une route); **macadamized road,** macadam *m.*

macadamizing [mə'kædəmaiziŋ], *s. Civ.E:* macadamisage *m.*

macaque [mə'kæk], *s. Z:* macaque *m*, magot *m*; **bonnet(ed) m.,** bonnet chinois; **pig-tailed m.,** macaque à queue de cochon.

Macarius [mə'kɛəriəs]. *Pr.n.m. Ecc.Hist:* Macaire.

macaroni [mækə'rouni], *s.* **1.** *Cu:* macaroni *m*; **m. cheese,** macaroni au gratin. **2.** (*pl.* **macaronies**) *Hist:* (i) élégant *m*; (ii) fat *m*; petit-maître, *pl.* petits-maîtres.

macaronic [mækə'rɔnik]. **1.** *a.* macaronique. **2.** *s.pl.* **macaronics,** vers *m* macaroniques.

macaronicism [mækə'rounisizm], *s. Lit:* macaronisme *m.*

macaronism [mækə'rounizm], *s. Hist:* dandysme *m.*

macaroon [mækə'ruːn], *s. Cu:* macaron *m.*

Macassar [mə'kæsər]. **1.** *Pr.n. Geog:* Macassar. **2.** *s.* **m. (oil),** huile *f* de Macassar. **3.** *s.* **m. (ebony),** macassar *m.*

macaw[1] [mə'kɔː], *s. Orn:* ara *m*; **blue and yellow m.,** ara ararauna; **hyacinthine m.,** ara hyacinthe; **red and blue m.,** ara macao; **red and green m.,** ara militaire; **red and yellow m.,** ara chloroptère.

macaw[2], *s. Bot:* **m. tree, palm,** (palmier) acrocomia *m.*

maccabaw ['mækəbɔː], *s.* = MACCABOY.

Maccabean [mækə'biːən], *a. B.Hist:* Macchabéen; des Macchabées.

Maccabees ['mækəbiːz]. *Pr.n.m.pl. Hist:* (les) Macchabées.

Maccabeus [mækə'biːəs]. *Pr.n.m. Hist:* Macchabée.

maccaboy ['mækəbɔi], *s.* (tabac *m*) macouba *m.*

mace[1] [meis], *s.* **1.** *A.Arms:* masse *f* d'armes; massue *f* (de guerre). **2.** (*a*) masse (portée par le massier devant un fonctionnaire); (*b*) = MACEBEARER. **3.** *A. Bill:* masse (avec laquelle on queutait la bille). **4.** *Bot:* **reed m.,** massette *f*; roseau *m* des étangs; quenouille *f.*

mace[2], *s. Bot: Cu:* macis *m*; fleur *f* de muscade.

macebearer ['meisbɛərər], *s.* massier *m*, porte-masse *m inv*; appariteur *m* (d'une Université, d'une corporation).

macédoine [mæsei'dwɑːn], *s. Cu:* macédoine *f.*

Macedonia [mæsi'douniə], *A:* **Macedon** ['mæsidən]. *Pr.n. Geog:* Macédoine *f.*

Macedonian [mæsi'douniən]. *Geog: Hist:* (*a*) *a.* macédonien; (*b*) *s.* Macédonien, -ienne.

macer ['meisər], *s.* **1.** massier *m.* **2.** *Jur: Scot:* huissier audiencier.

macerate ['mæsəreit]. **1.** *v.tr.* macérer; faire macérer; infuser (des herbes, etc.) à froid. **2.** *v.i.* macérer.

macerating ['mæsəreitiŋ], **maceration** [mæsə'reiʃ(ə)n], *s.* macération *f.*

macerator ['mæsəreitər], *s. Ind:* cuve *f* de macération; macérateur *m.*

Mach [mæk], *s. Aedcs: Meas:* **M. (number),** (nombre *m* de) Mach; **M. angle, cone, effect, front, wave,** angle *m*, cône *m*, effet *m*, front *m*, onde *f*, de Mach.

machaerodus [mə'kiərədəs], *s. Paleont:* machérode *m.*

machete [mə'tʃeiti, -'tʃeti], *s.* machette *f.*

Machiavelli [mækiə'veli]. *Pr.n.m. Hist:* Machiavel.

Machiavellian [mækiə'veliən], *a.* Machiavélique.

Machiavellism [mækiə'velizm], *s.* Machiavélisme *m.*

Machiavellist [mækiə'velist], *s.* Machiavéliste *m.*

machicolated [mə'tʃikəleitid], *a. A.Fort:* (porte *f*, etc.) à mâchicoulis.

machicolation [mætʃikə'leiʃ(ə)n], **machicoulis** [mæʃi'kuːli], *s.* mâchicoulis *m.*

Machilidae [mə'kilidiː], *s.pl. Ent:* machilidés *m.*

machilis [mə'kilis, 'mækəlis], *s. Ent:* machilis *m.*

machinability [məʃiːnə'biliti], *s. Metalw:* usinabilité *f* (d'un métal).

machinable [mə'ʃiːnəbl], *a. Metalw:* usinable.

machinate ['mækineit, 'mæʃ-], *v.i.* comploter; tramer des complots.

machination [mæki'neiʃ(ə)n, mæʃ-], *s.* machination *f*, complot *m*, intrigue *f*; **the machinations of our opponents,** les agissements *m* de nos adversaires.

machinator ['mækineitər, 'mæʃ-], *s.* machinateur, -trice; intrigant, -ante.

machine[1] [mə'ʃiːn], *s.* machine *f*; **compound, simple, m.,** machine composée, simple; **the m. age,** l'âge *m* des machines; (*a*) (*for office use, etc.*) **business m.,** machine de bureau; **adding, subtracting, multiplying, m.,** machine à additionner, à soustraire, à multiplier; **copying m.,** machine à (poly)copier; **dictating m.,** machine à dicter; **teaching m.,** machine à enseigner, à apprendre; (*b*) *Ind: etc:* **grinding m.,** rodeuse *f*; **rivet(t)ing m.,** riveuse *f*; **boring m.,** (i) *Mec.E:* foreuse *f*, perceuse *f*; (*for cylinders*) alésoir *m*, aléseuse *f*; (ii) *Min: etc:* sondeuse *f*, sonde *f*, foreuse; (iii) perforatrice *f*; **milling m.,** fraiseuse *f*, machine à fraiser; **screw-cutting m.,** machine à fileter, à décolleter; décolleteuse *f*; *Typ:* **type-setting m.,** compositeur *m*; **m. compositor,** claviste *m*; **to run sheets through the m.,** passer les feuilles à la machine; *E:* **balancing m.,** indicateur *m* de position; (*c*) *attrib.* (i) **m. production,** production *f* en série, à la machine; **m. work,** travail *m* à la machine; usinage *m*; **m. bending,** cintrage *m* à la machine; **m. made,** fait à la machine; **m.-made lace,** dentelle *f* mécanique; **m. winding,** bobinage *m* mécanique; **m.-wound,** bobiné à la machine; **m. cut,** taillé à la machine; **m. stitched,** cousu à la machine; **m. turned,** fait au tour; (ii) **m. oil,** huile *f* à machine; (iii) **m. bolt,** boulon *m* mécanique; **m. screw,** vis *m* mécanique; **m. saw,** scie *f* mécanique; (*d*) *El:* générateur *m*, génératrice *f*; **acyclic m.,** machine acyclique, générateur unipolaire; **induction m.,** machine à induction, générateur asynchrone; **influence m.,** machine à influence, générateur électrostatique; **synchronous m.,** générateur synchrone; (*e*) *Med:* **heart-lung m.,** cœur artificiel; **kidney m.,** rein artificiel; (*f*) *Com: etc:* **slot m.,** distributeur *m* automatique, *F:* machine à sous; **cigarette m.,** distributeur de cigarettes; **ticket m.,** distributeur de billets; **fruit m.,** (i) distributeur automatique (qui vend des fruits); (ii) *F:* tire-pognon *m*; (*g*) *Dom.Ec:* **sewing m.,** machine à coudre; **washing m.,** machine à laver; **washing-up m.,** lave-vaisselle *m inv.* (automatique); (*h*) *F:* (i) voiture *f*; (ii) bicyclette *f*; (iii) avion *m*, appareil *m*; (iv) *U.S:* pompe *f* à incendie; (v) machine à coudre; (vi) machine à écrire; (vii) machine à laver; lave-vaisselle; (*i*) (*pers.*) automate *m*, robot *m*, machine; **he's just a money-making m.,** c'est une machine à faire de l'argent; (*j*) **the industrial m.,** les rouages *m*, l'organisation *f*, de l'industrie; *Pol:* **the party m.,** les rouages, l'appareil *m*, les leviers *m* de commande, du parti; **to get caught up in the m.,** être pris dans l'engrenage.

machine[2], *v.tr.* **1.** *Ind:* (*a*) façonner (une pièce); travailler (qch.) à la machine; (*b*) usiner, ajuster; **to m. a casting,** ajuster une pièce fondue; **to m. down the metal,** amincir le métal. **2.** *Dressm:* coudre, piquer, à la machine.

machine-cut [mə'ʃiːnkʌt], *v.tr.* tailler à la machine.

machined [mə'ʃiːnd], *a.* **1.** (*a*) façonné; (*b*) travaillé à la machine; usiné; **as m.,** brut d'usinage; **rough-m.,** ébauché; **finish-m.,** complètement usiné. **2.** cousu, piqué, à la machine.

machine-finish [mə'ʃiːn'finiʃ], *v.tr.* (*a*) *Metalw: etc:* finir, polir, à la machine; usiner; (*b*) *Paperm:* apprêter (le papier) à la machine.

machine-gun[1] [mə'ʃiːngʌn], *s.* mitrailleuse *f*; (*a*) **heavy m.-g.,** mitrailleuse lourde; **light m.-g.,** mitrailleuse légère; fusil-mitrailleur *m*; **anti-aircraft m.-g.,** mitrailleuse antiaérienne; **twin m.-guns.,** mitrailleuses jumelées; **m.-g. carrier,** voiturette *f*, chenillette *f*, porte-mitrailleuse; (*b*) *Mil.Av: Phot:* **m.-g. camera,** mitrailleuse photo(graphique).

machine-gun[2], *v.tr.* mitrailler.

machine-gunner [mə'ʃiːngʌnər], *s.* mitrailleur *m.*

machine-gunning [mə'ʃiːngʌniŋ], *s.* mitraillade *f*, mitraillage *m.*

machine pistol [mə'ʃiːnpist(ə)l], *s.* (*a*) pistolet-mitrailleur *m*, *pl.* pistolets-mitrailleurs; (*b*) mitraillette *f.*

machinery [mə'ʃiːn(ə)ri], *s.* **1.** mécanisme *m*; machines *fpl*, machinerie *f*; appareil(s) *m(pl)*, outillage *m*; **auxiliary m.,** machines auxiliaires; *Ind:* **driving m.,** *Nau:* **propelling m.,** appareil moteur; *N.Arch:* **m. casing,** encaissement *m* des machines; **m. space,** tranche *f* des machines. **2. the m. of government,** les rouages *m* du gouvernement, de la machine gouvernementale; **administrative m.,** l'appareil administratif, la machine administrative; *Fin:* **compensation m.,** mécanisme de compensation; **I shall put in motion the m. at my disposal,** je mettrai en œuvre les organes *m* dont je dispose; **no m. exists for putting this law into effect,** les moyens *m* manquent pour mettre cette loi en vigueur. **3.** *Lit: Th:* le merveilleux.

machining [mə'ʃi:niŋ], *s.* **1.** usinage *m*; ajustage *m* mécanique; **m. down,** amincissement *m*; **m. allowance,** surépaisseur *f* pour ajustage; **m. operations,** travaux *m* d'usinage, d'ajustage. **2.** *Typ:* tirage *m* à la machine. **3.** *Dressm:* couture *f*, piquage *m*, à la machine.

machinism ['mæʃinizm], *s. Pol.Ec:* machinisme *m*.

machinist [mə'ʃi:nist], *s.* **1.** *Ind:* (*a*) machiniste *m*; mécanicien *m*; (*b*) ajusteur *m* de machines-outils. **2.** *Ind:* (*at sewing machine*) mécanicienne *f*.

machmeter ['mækmi:tər], *s. Aedcs: Av:* machmètre *m*.

mack [mæk], *s. F:* imper *m*.

mackerel ['mæk(ə)rəl], *s.* (*a*) *Ich:* maquereau *m*, scombre *m*; merlan bleu; **m. shark,** requin *m* marsouin; *Fish:* **m. boat, smack,** maquilleur *m*, maquereautier *m*; (*b*) **m. breeze,** bonne brise; **m. sky,** ciel pommelé, moutonné.

mackinac ['mækinæk], **mackinaw** ['mækinɔ:], *s. U.S:* **1.** (i) manteau court, (ii) couverture *f*, en laine épaisse. **2.** bateau plat des Grands Lacs.

mackintosh ['mækintɔʃ], *s.* **1.** (manteau *m* en) caoutchouc *m*; mackintosh *m*; imperméable *m*; waterproof *m*. **2.** tissu caoutchouté; tissu imperméable.

mackintoshite ['mækintɔʃait], *s. Miner:* mackintoshite *f*.

mackle[1], **macle**[1] ['mækl], *s. Typ:* bavochure *f*, maculature *f*, frison *m*.

mackle[2], **macle**[2]. *Typ:* **1.** *v.tr.* maculer, bavocher, mâchurer (une feuille). **2.** *v.i.* (*of paper*) (se) maculer; (*of type*) bavocher; (*of proof*) friser, papilloter.

mackled ['mækld], *a. Typ:* bavocheux.

mackling ['mækliŋ], *s. Typ:* papillotage *m*.

macle[3], *s. Cryst: Miner:* macle *f*.

macled [mækld], *a. Cryst:* maclé.

maconite ['mækənait], *s. Miner:* maconite *f*.

macramé [mə'krɑ:mi], *s.* macramé *m*.

macrergate ['mækrəgeit], *s. Ent:* ouvrière *f* macroergate.

macro- ['mækrou], *comb.fm.* macro-.

macrobian [mə'kroubiən], *a. Biol:* macrobien.

macrobiosis [mækroubai'ousis], *s. Biol:* macrobie *f*, longévité *f*.

macrobiote [mækrou'baiout], *s.m. Biol:* macrobite *m*.

macrobiotic [mækroubai'ɔtik], *a.* macrobiotique.

macrobiotics [mækroubai'ɔtiks], *s.* macrobiotique *f*.

macrobiotus [mækroubai'outəs], *s. Biol:* macrobiotus *m*.

Macrobius [mə'kroubiəs]. *Pr.n.m. Lt.Lit:* Macrobe.

macrocephalic [mækrouse'fælik], **macrocephalous** [mækrou'sefələs], *a. Z: Bot:* macrocéphale.

macrocephaly [mækrou'sefəli], *s.* macrocéphalie *f*.

macrochaeta, *pl.* **-ae** [mækrou'ki:tə, -i:], *s. Ent:* macrochète *m*.

macroch(e)ilia [mækrou'kailiə], *s. Anthr:* macrocheilie *f*.

macrocheira [mækrou'kairə], *s. Crust:* macrocheire *m*.

macroch(e)iria [mækrou'kairiə], *s. Med:* macrochirie *f*.

macrochemical [mækrou'kemik(ə)l], *a.* macrochimique.

macrochemistry [mækrou'kemistri], *s.* macrochimie *f*.

macroclimate [mækrou'klaimət], *s.* macroclimat *m*.

macroclimatic [mækrouklai'mætik], *a.* macroclimatique.

macrocosm ['mækroukɔzm], *s.* macrocosme *m*.

macrocosmic [mækrou'kɔzmik], *a. Phil:* macrocosmique.

macrocyst ['mækrousist], *s. Bot:* macrocyste *m*.

macrocystis [mækrou'sistis], *s. Algae:* macrocystis *m*.

macrocyte ['mækrousait], *s. Med:* macrocyte *m*.

macrocytic [mækrou'sitik], *a. Med:* macrocytaire.

macrocytosis [mækrousai'tousis], *s. Med:* macrocytose *f*.

macrodactyl [mækrou'dæktil], **macrodactylous** [mækrou'dæktiləs], *a. Z:* macrodactyle.

macrodactyly [mækrou'dæktili], *s.* macrodactylie *f*.

macrodont ['mækroudɔnt], *a. Med:* macrodonte.

macrodontia [mækrou'dɔntiə], *s. Med:* macrodontie *f*.

macroeconomic [mækrouekə'nɔmik], *a.* macroéconomique.

macroeconomics [mækrouekə'nɔmiks], *s.* macroéconomie *f*.

macroergate [mækrou'ə:geit], *s. Ent:* ouvrière *f* macroergate.

macroevolution [mækroui:və'luʃ(ə)n], *s.* macroévolution *f*.

macrogamete [mækrou'gæmi:t], *s. Biol:* macrogamète *m*.

macrogametocyte [mækrougæ'mi:tousait], *s. Prot:* macrogamétocyte *m*, macrogamonte *m*.

macrogenitosomia [mækroudʒenitou'soumiə], *s. Med:* macrogénitosomie *f*.

macroglobulin [mækrou'glɔbjulin], *s. Bio-Ch:* macroglobuline *f*.

macroglobulin(a)emia [mækrouglɔbjuli'ni:miə], *s. Med:* macroglobulinémie *f*.

macroglossa [mækrou'glɔsə], *s. Ent:* (*genus*) macroglosse *m*.

macroglossal [mækrou'glɔs(ə)l], *a. Med:* macroglosse.

macroglossia [mækrou'glɔsiə], *s. Med:* macroglossie *f*.

macrognathia [mækrou'gneiθiə], *s. Med:* macrognathie *f*, hypergnathie *f*.

macrognathic [mækrou'næθik], *a. Med:* macrognathe, hypergnathe.

macrograph ['mækrougræf], *s.* épreuve *f* macrographique, macrographie *f*.

macrographic [mækrou'græfik], *a.* macrographique.

macrography [mæ'krɔgrəfi], *s.* macrographie *f*.

Macrolepidoptera [mækroulepi'dɔptərə], *s.pl. Ent:* macrolépidoptères *m*.

macrolymphocyte [mækrou'limfousait], *s.* macrolymphocyte *m*.

macrolymphocytosis [mækroulimfousai'tousis], *s. Med:* macrolymphocytose *f*.

macromelia [mækrou'mi:liə], *s. Med:* macromélie *f*.

macromere ['mækroumi:ər], *s. Z:* macromère *m*.

macromolecular [mækroumə'lekjulər], *a. Ch:* macromoléculaire.

macromolecule [mækrou'mɔlikju:l], *s. Ch:* macromolécule *f*.

macron ['mækrɔn], *s. Pros: Gram:* marque *f* de longueur (d'une voyelle).

macronuclear [mækrou'nju:kliər], *a. Z:* macronucléaire.

macronucleate(d) [mækrou'nju:klieit, -'nju:klieitid], *a.* macronucléé.

macronucleus [mækrou'nju:kliəs], *s. Prot:* macronucléus *m*.

macroparticle [mækrou'pɑ:tikl], *s. Atom.Ph:* macroparticule *f*.

macrophage ['mækroufeidʒ], *s. Biol: Physiol:* macrophage *m*.

macrophagic [mækrou'feidʒik], *a. Biol: Physiol:* macrophage.

macrophotograph [mækrou'foutəgræf], *s. Phot:* épreuve *f* macrophotographique, photomacrographique; macrophotographie *f*, photomacrographie *f*.

macrophotographic [mækroufoutə'græfik], *a.* macrophotographique, photomacrographique.

macrophotography [mækroufə'tɔgrəfi], *s.* macrophotographie *f*, photomacrographie *f*.

macrophyllous [mæ'krɔfiləs], *a. Bot:* macrophylle.

macrophysics [mækrou'fiziks], *s.* macrophysique *f*.

macropod ['mækroupɔd], *a.* & *s. Z:* macropode (*m*).

macropodia [mækrou'poudiə], *s. Med:* macropodie *f*.

macropodid [mækrou'pɔdid], *a.* & *s. Z:* macropode (*m*).

Macropodidae [mækrou'pɔdidi:], *s.pl. Z:* macropodidés *m*.

macropodous [mæ'krɔpədəs], *a. Z: Bot:* macropode.

macroporosity [mækroupɔ:'rɔsiti], *s.* macroporosité *f*.

macropterous [mæ'krɔptərəs], *a. Ich: Orn:* macroptère.

macrorhinus [mækrou'rainəs], *s. Z:* macrorhine *m*.

macroscelia [mækrou'si:liə], *s. Med:* macroscélie *f*, macroskélie *f*.

macroscelid [mækrou'selid], *s. Z:* macroscélide *m*.

Macroscelidae [mækrou'selidi:], *s.pl. Z:* macroscélidés *m*.

macroscelidous [mækrou'selidəs], *a. Z:* macroscélide.

Macroscelidoidea [mækrouseli'dɔidiə], *s. pl. Z:* macroscélidoïes *m*.

macroscopic [mækrə'skɔpik], *a.* macroscopique.

macroscopy [mæ'krɔskəpi], *s. Ph:* macroscopie *f*.

macroseism ['mækrousiazm], *s. Geol:* macroséisme *m*.

macroseismic [mækrou'saizmik], *a. Geol:* macrosismique.

macrosomatic [mækrousou'mætik], *a. Med: Z:* macrosomatique.

macrosomia [mækrou'soumiə], *s. Med:* macrosomie *f*.

macrosporangium [mækrouspə'rændʒiəm], *s. Bot:* macrosporange *m*.

macrospore ['mækrouspɔ:r], *s. Bot:* macrospore *f*.

macrosporophyll [mækrou'spɔroufil], *s. Bot:* macrosporophylle *m*.

macrostomia [mækrou'stoumiə], *s. Med:* macrostomie *f*.

macrostomus [mæ'krɔstəməs], *s. Med:* macrostoma *m*; bec-de-lièvre *m*, *pl.* becs-de-lièvre.

macrostructural [mækrou'strʌktjur(ə)l], *a. Ch:* macrostructural.

macrostructure [mækrou'strʌktjuər], *s.* macrostructure *f*.

macrotherium [mækrou'θiəriəm], *s. Paleont:* macrothérium *m*.

macrozamia [mækrou'zeimiə], *s. Bot:* macrozamia *m*.

macruran [mæ'kruərən], *s. Crust:* macroure *m*.

Macruridae [mæ'kru:ridi:], *s.pl. Ich:* macruridés *m*.

macrurous [mæ'kru:rəs], *a.* macroure.

macrurus [mæ'krurəs], *s. Crust:* macroure *m*.

macula, *pl.* **-ae** ['mækjulə, -i:], *s.* **1.** *Astr: Med: Miner: etc:* macule *f*. **2.** *Ant:* tache *f* jaune (de la rétine); **m. lutea,** macula *f* (lutea); **m. acustica,** tache auditive.

macular ['mækjulər], *a. Med:* pigmentaire; maculeux.

maculate ['mækjuleit], *v.tr.* maculer, souiller.

maculation [mækju'leiʃ(ə)n], *s.* **1.** maculation *f*, maculage *m*. **2.** *Astr: Med:* disposition *f* des macules.

maculature [mæ'kju:lətjər], *s. Phot.Engr:* maculature *f*.

macule ['mækjul], *s.* **1.** (*a*) *Med:* macule *f*; (*b*) *Anat:* macula *f* (lutea). **2.** *Typ:* = MACKLE[1].

maculicole [mæ'kju:likoul], *a. Fung:* maculicole.

maculose ['mækjulous], *a.* maculeux.

mad [mæd], *a.* (**madder, maddest**) **1.** fou, *f.* folle; aliéné; dément; *A: F:* **m. doctor,** médecin *m* des fous; médecin aliéniste; **a m. doctor, who makes terrible experiments,** un médecin dément, pris de folie, qui fait des expériences épouvantables; **raving m.,** fou furieux; atteint de folie furieuse; *F:* **(stark) m. raving m., as m. as a hatter, as m. as a March hare,** tout à fait fou; complètement fou; fou à lier; archifou, -folle; bon à enfermer; *F:* **to be a bit m.,** être maboul, marteau; avoir un grain; **to drive s.o. m.** rendre qn fou; affoler qn; faire perdre la tête à qn; **it is enough to drive you m.,** il y a de quoi devenir fou; c'est à vous rendre fou; **to go m.,** *A:* & *Lit:* **to run m.,** devenir fou; perdre la tête; tomber en démence; être pris de folie; **nationalism gone m.,** nationalisme forcené; *F:* **you've gone m. with the salt,** tu y a mis trop de sel; **m. with pain,** fou de douleur; **m. with joy,** ivre de joie; **m. with fear,** affolé (de peur); **he was m. to try,** c'était une folie de sa part que d'essayer; **a m. hope,** un fol espoir; **a m. plan,** un projet insensé; **a m. gallop,** un galop furieux, effréné; *F:* **like m.,** comme un enragé, comme un perdu; follement; **to run like m.,** courir comme un dératé; *Nau:* **the compass is m.,** le compas est fou, affolé. **2. m. for revenge,** assoiffé de revanche; **to be m. about, on,** *occ.* **after sth.,** être fou de qch.; aimer qch. à la folie; avoir la folie, la rage, la manie, de qch.; être entiché de qch.; raffoler de qch.; **to be m. on sport,** avoir la passion des sports; **she is m. on dancing, dancing m.,** elle ne pense qu'à danser; **he's m. on fishing, on pictures,** c'est un pêcheur enragé; il a la passion des tableaux; *Dial:* **he was m. to try,** il brûlait d'essayer. **3.** *F:* furieux, furibond; **to be m. with,** *U.S:* **at, s.o.,** être furieux contre qn; **it made me m. just to see him,** rien que de le voir me rendait furieux; **hopping m.,** fou furieux, hors de soi. **4.** (*a*) **m. bull,** taureau furieux, enragé; (*b*) *Vet:* **m. dog,** chien enragé. **5.** *adv. F:* **m. keen (on sth.),** fou de, emballé de (qch.).

Madagascan [mædə'gæskən], *a. Ethn: Geog:* malgache.

Madagascar [mædə'gæskər]. *Pr.n. Geog:* Madagascar *m*; *Z:* **M. cat,** maki *m*, maque *m*.

madam ['mædəm], *s.f.* **1.** (*title of address in business and commerce and from servant to mistress*) madame, mademoiselle; **M. Chairman,** Madame la Présidente; (*in letters*) **Dear M.,** Madame, Mademoiselle. **2.** (*pl.* **madams**) tenancière de bordel, maquerelle. **3.** *F:* (*pl.* **madams**) **she's a bit of a m.,** elle aime à le prendre de haut; elle a sa petite tête à elle.

Madame [mæ'dæm, 'mædəm], *s.f. O:* (*professional title*) **Madame X,** Madame X.

madapol(l)am [mædə'pɔləm, mə'dæpələm], *s. Tex:* madapol(l)am *m*.

madarosis [mædə'rousis], *s. Med:* madarosis *f*, madarose *f*.

madcap ['mædkæp], *a.* & *s.* écervelé, -ée; étourdi, -ie; **m. scheme,** projet insensé.

madden [mædn]. **1.** *v.tr.* (*a*) rendre (qn) fou; exaspérer (qn); (*b*) **fear-maddened,** affolé de peur. **2.** *v.i.* devenir fou; se mettre en rage.

maddening ['mæd(ə)niŋ], *a.* à rendre fou; exaspérant.

madder[1] ['mædər], *s.* **1.** (*a*) *Bot:* garance *f*; **m. root,** alizari *m*; (*b*) *Dy:* teinture *f* de garance; **dyeing with m.,** garançage *m*. **2.** *Ind:* **m. dye,** alizarine *f*.

madder[2], *v.tr.* garancer.

madding ['mædiŋ], *a. Poet:* fou, *f.* folle; furieux; **far from the m. crowd,** loin de la foule insensée, loin de la foule et du bruit.

made [meid], *a.* **1.** fait, fabriqué, confectionné. **2.** *Civ.E: etc:* **m. ground,** terre rapportée; terre de rapport; *Nau:* **m. mast,** mât *m* d'assemblage; mât en plusieurs pièces. **3.** *Equit:* **m. horse,** cheval fait. **4.** *F:* **he's a m. man,** le voilà arrivé; son avenir, son sort, est assuré; sa fortune est faite.

Madeira [mə'di:ərə]. **1.** *Pr.n. Geog:* Madère *f.* **2.** *attrib.* (*a*) **M. wine,** *s.* **madeira,** vin *m* de Madère; madère *m*; (*b*) **M. cake,** gâteau *m* de Savoie; (*c*) *Bot:* **M. vine,** boussingaultiat *f*; *U.S: O:* **M. wood,** acajou *m.*

Madeiran [mə'diərən]. *Geog:* (*a*) *a.* madérien; madérois; (*b*) *s.* Madérien, -ienne; Madérois, -oise.

madeleine ['mæd(ə)lein], *s. Cu:* madeleine *f.*

Madel(e)ine ['mæd(ə)lin]. *Pr.n.f.* Madeleine.

made-up ['meid'ʌp], *a.* **1. m.-up box,** caisse assemblée; *Rail:* **m.-up train,** rame *f* de wagons. **2.** artificiel, factice; faux, *f.* fausse; **m.-up story,** histoire inventée. **3.** (vêtement) tout fait. **4.** *Adm:* **non m.-up road,** route non aménagée.

Madge [mædʒ]. *Pr.n.f.* (*dim. of* **Margaret**) Margot.

madhouse ['mædhaus], *s.* (*a*) *A:* maison *f* de fous; asile *m* d'aliénés; (*b*) *F:* **the place is a m.!** on se croirait à Charenton!

madia ['meidiə], *s. Bot:* madi *m*, madia *m*, madie *f*; *Husb:* **madia oil,** huile *f* de madi.

madly ['mædli], *adv.* **1.** follement; en fou; comme un fou. **2.** (aimer) à la folie, éperdument. **3.** furieusement. **4.** *F:* très, drôlement; **it's m. expensive,** c'est fou ce que c'est cher.

madman, *pl.* **-men** ['mædmən, -men], *s.m.* fou, insensé, aliéné; **to fight like a m.,** se battre en désespéré, comme un forcené; **to scream like a m.,** crier comme un perdu.

madness ['mædnis], *s.* **1.** folie *f,* fureur *f*; démence *f*; **fit of m.,** accès *m* de folie; *Med:* accès démentiel; **in a fit of m.,** dans un accès de folie; dans un moment de folie; *F:* **it is sheer m. for him to go out in this weather,** c'est insensé qu'il sorte, c'est folie de sa part de sortir, par le temps qu'il fait; **midsummer m.,** (i) le comble de la folie; (ii) une aberration qui passera. **2.** *A: & Dial:* (*rage*) rage *f,* fureur, furie *f.* **3.** (*of animals*) rage; hydrophobie *f.*

madonna [mə'dɔnə], *s.f.* madone; *A:* **to wear one's hair m.-braided,** se coiffer à la Vierge.

Madras [mə'dræs]. **1.** *Pr.n. Geog:* Madras *m.* **2.** *Tex:* madras *m*; **M. (handkerchief),** (foulard *m* de) madras.

Madrasi [mə'dræsi], *a. & s. Geog:* (habitant, -ante, originaire *mf*) de Madras.

madreporaria [mædripə'rɛəriə], *s.pl. Coel: Biol: Z:* madréporaires *m.*

madrepore ['mædripɔ:r], *s. Coel:* madrépore *m.*

madreporic [mædri'pɔrik], **madreporiform** [mædri'pɔ:rifɔ:m], *a.* madréporique, madréporien.

madreporite [mædri'pɔ:rait], *s. Echin:* madréporite *f*; plaque *f* madréporique.

madrier ['mædriər], *s. A.Mil:* madrier *m.*

madrigal ['mædrig(ə)l], *s. Lit: Mus:* madrigal, -aux *m.*

madrigalian [mædri'geiliən], *a.* madrigalique.

madrigalist ['mædrigəlist], *s.* madrigaliste *m.*

Madrilenian [mædri'li:niən], *a. & s. Geog:* Madrilène (*mf*); de Madrid.

madwort ['mædwə:t], *s. Bot:* alysse *f,* alysson *m*, corbeille *f* d'or, râpette *f.*

maeandra [mi'ændrə], *s. Coel:* méandrine *f.*

Maecenas [mi(:)'si:næs]. **1.** *Pr.n.m. Lt.Lit:* Mécène. **2.** *s.* mécène *m*, protecteur *m* (d'un artiste).

Maelstrom ['meilstroum], *s.* **1.** *Geog:* **the M.,** le Maelström. **2. a m.,** un tourbillon, un gouffre; **the m. of modern life,** le tourbillon de la vie moderne.

maenad ['mi:næd], *s.f. Gr.Myth:* ménade.

ma(e)rl [mɑ:l], *s. Algae: Agr:* maërl *m*, merl *m.*

maestoso [mai'stousou], *adv. Mus:* maestoso.

maestro, *pl.* **-tri** ['maistrou, -tri:], *s.m. Mus:* maestro, *pl.* maestros.

Mae West ['mei'west], *s. O:* Mae West *m*, gilet *m* de sauvetage.

mafeesh [mɑ:'fi:ʃ], *a. & adv. P: A:* **1.** fini; plus rien! **2.** mort.

maf(f)ia ['mɑ:fiə, mæfiə], *s.* maf(f)ia *f.*

maffick ['mæfik], *v.i. F: O:* se livrer dans la rue à des réjouissances bruyantes, extravagantes, (comme celles qui accueillirent la délivrance de Mafeking en 1900).

mafficker ['mæfikər], *s. F: O:* chahuteur *m.*

mafficking ['mæfikiŋ], *s. F: O:* réjouissances bruyantes; manifestation extravagante de la joie publique; chahut *m.*

mag[1] [mæg], *s. P: A:* sou *m.*

mag[2], *s. F:* **1.** = MAGAZINE 3. **2.** = MAGNETO.

magazine [mægə'zi:n], *s.* **1.** (*a*) *A:* dépôt *m* de marchandises; (*b*) (i) *Mil:* magasin *m*; dépôt (d'armes, de vivres, d'équipement, de matériel); (ii) *Navy:* soute *f* à munitions; **powder m.,** (i) *Mil:* poudrière *f,* dépôt d'explosifs; (ii) *Navy:* soute aux poudres, à poudre; soute aux explosifs. **2.** (*a*) *Sm.a:* chargeur *m*, magasin; **(box-type) m.,** boîte-chargeur *f, pl.* boîtes-chargeurs; **drum m.,** tambour chargeur *m*; **m. platform,** planche-élévateur *f* (*pl.* planches-élévateurs), élévateur *m*, de la boîte-chargeur; **m. spring,** ressort élévateur; **m. rifle,** fusil *m* à répétition, à magasin, à chargeur; (*b*) *Phot:* magasin; **m. camera,** (i) appareil *m* à magasin; (ii) *Cin:* camera *f* à chargeur; *Cin:* **take-up m.,** magasin récepteur; **supply m.,** magasin débiteur; (*c*) *Cmptr:* magasin (de mémoire, d'alimentation en cartes); **input, output, m.,** magasin d'alimentation, de réception. **3.** revue *f* ou recueil *m* périodique; périodique *m*; **illustrated m.,** revue illustrée, magazine *m*; *Publ:* **m. rights,** droits *m* de reproduction dans les périodiques; *W.Tel: T.V:* **m. (programme),** magazine.

magazinist [mægə'zi:nist], *s.* collaborateur, -trice, d'un périodique.

Magdalen(e) ['mægdələn, 'mægdəli(:)n, -'lini]. **1.** (*a*) *Pr.n.f.* Madeleine; (*b*) *A:* **Magdalen asylum, hospital,** maison *f* de filles repenties des Madelonnettes. **2. Magdalen College (Oxford)** et **Magdalene College (Cambridge)** se prononcent ['mɔ:dlin'kɔlidʒ].

Magdalenian [mægdə'li:niən], *a. & s. Geol: Prehist:* magdalénien, -ienne.

Magdeburg ['mægdəbə:g]. *Pr.n. Geog:* Magdebourg *m.*

Magellanic [mæge'læ:nik], *a.* magellanique; *Astr:* **M. clouds,** nuées *f* magellaniques.

magenta [mə'dʒentə], *s. & a.* (*colour*) magenta (*m*) *inv.*

Maggie ['mægi]. *Pr.n.f.* (*dim. of* **Margaret**) Margot.

Maggiore [mæ'dʒɔ:ri]. *Pr.n. Geog:* **Lake M.,** le lac Majeur.

maggot ['mægət], *s.* **1.** larve *f* apode; *F:* ver *m*, asticot *m*; ver de viande. **2.** *F: A:* caprice *m*, lubie *f.*

maggoty ['mægəti], *a.* véreux, plein de vers.

Maghreb (the) [ðəmə'greb]. *Pr.n. Geog:* le Maghreb.

magi ['meidʒai], *s.pl. see* MAGUS.

magian ['meidʒiən]. **1.** *a.* des mages. **2.** *s. Rel.H:* magiste *mf.*

magianism ['meidʒiənizm], *s. Rel.H:* magisme *m.*

magic ['mædʒik]. **1.** *s.* magie *f,* enchantement *m*; **black m., white m.,** magie noire, blanche; **as if by m., like m.,** comme par enchantement; **the m. of his eloquence,** la magie de son éloquence. **2.** *a.* (*a*) magique, enchanté; **m. wand,** baguette *f* magique; **his m. skill with the brush,** son pinceau magique; (*b*) *Elcs:* **m. eye,** œil *m* magique; (*c*) *Mth:* **m. numbers,** nombres *m* magiques; **m. square,** carré *m* magique.

magical ['mædʒik(ə)l], *a.* magique.

magically ['mædʒik(ə)li], *adv.* magiquement; (comme) par enchantement.

magician [mə'dʒiʃ(ə)n], *s.* magicien, -ienne.

magicianly [mə'dʒiʃənli], *a.* (adresse *f*) de magicien.

magism ['meidʒizm], *s. Rel.H:* magisme *m.*

magisterial [mædʒis'tiəriəl], *a.* **1.** (air, ton) magistral, -aux; (air) de maître. **2.** de magistrat.

magisterially [mædʒis'tiəriəli], *adv.* **1.** (*a*) magistralement, d'une façon magistrale; (*b*) en maître. **2.** (*a*) en qualité de magistrat, de juge; (*b*) (interrogé, jugé, etc.) par des magistrats, par des juges.

magisterium [mædʒi'stiəriəm], *s.* **1.** *Alch:* magistère *m.* **2.** *R.C.Ch:* magistère.

magistery ['mædʒist(ə)ri], *s. Alch:* magistère *m.*

magistracy ['mædʒistrəsi], *s.* **1.** magistrature *f.* **2.** *coll.* **the magistracy,** la magistrature; les magistrats *m.*

magistral [mə'dʒistrəl], *a.* **1.** *Pharm:* (remède) magistral, -aux. **2.** *Fort:* (*of line, gallery*) magistral.

magistrate ['mædʒistreit], *s.* magistrat *m*, juge *m*; **police-court m.,** juge d'instance; **magistrate's court** = tribunal *m* d'instance.

magistrateship ['mædʒistrətʃip], **magistrature** ['mædʒistrətjər], *s.* magistrature *f.*

Maglemosian [mæglə'mouziən], *a. Prehist:* maglemosien.

magma, *pl.* **-mata, -mas** ['mægmə, -mətə, -məz], *s. Ch: Geol:* magma *m*; pâte *f*; **parental m.,** magma primaire.

magmatic [mæg'mætik], *a. Geol:* magmatique; **m. water,** eau *f* magmatique, juvénile.

Magna Carta ['mægnə'kɑ:tə], *s. Engl.Hist:* la Grande Charte (de l'année 1215).

magnaflux[1] ['mægnəflʌks], *s. Elcs:* **m. test,** essai *m* magnétique à la limaille.

magnaflux[2], *v.tr. Elcs:* faire un essai magnétique à la limaille.

Magna Graecia ['mægnə'gri:ʃiə]. *Pr.n. A.Geog:* la Grande-Grèce.

magnalium [mæg'neiliəm], *s. Metall:* magnalium *m.*

magnanimity [mægnə'nimiti], *s.* (*a*) grandeur *f* d'âme; (*b*) magnanimité *f,* générosité *f.*

magnanimous [mæg'næniməs], *a.* (*a*) **to be m.,** faire preuve de grandeur d'âme; (*b*) magnanime.

magnanimously [mæg'næniməsli], *adv.* (*a*) noblement; (*b*) magnanimement, avec magnanimité.

magnate ['mægneit], *s.* **1.** *Hist:* magnat *m* (de la Pologne ou de la Hongrie). **2.** magnat (de l'industrie, de la finance).

magnesia [mæg'ni:ʃə, -ʒə], *s.* **1.** *Ch:* magnésie *f*; oxyde *m* de magnésium. **2.** *Pharm:* magnésie blanche; **milk of m.,** magnésie hydratée.

magnesian [mæg'ni:ʃ(ə)n, -ʒ(ə)n], *a. Ch:* magnésien.

magnesic [mægni:zik], *a. Ch:* magnésique.

magnesiferous [mægni'zifərəs], *a.* magnésifère.

magnesiocopiapite [mægni:ziou'koupiəpait], *s. Miner:* knoxvillite *f.*

magnesioferrite [mægni:ziou'ferait], *s. Miner:* magné(sio)ferrite *f.*

magnesite ['mægnisait], *s. Miner:* giobertite *f*; magnésite *f.*

magnesium [mæg'ni:ziəm], *s. Ch:* magnésium *m*; **m. oxide,** magnésie *f,* oxyde *m* de magnésium; **m. ribbon,** ruban *m* de magnésium; *Phot:* **m. light, flash,** éclair *m* au magnésium; *Ill:* **m. flare,** fusée éclairante au magnésium; **m. powder,** poudre *f* de magnésium; *Mil:* **m. bomb,** bombe *f* au magnésium.

magnet ['mægnit], *s.* **1.** aimant *m*; **artificial m.,** aimant artificiel; **natural m.,** aimant naturel; **permanent m.,** aimant permanent; **temporary m.,** aimant temporaire, aimant induit; **bar m.,** aimant en barreau, barreau aimanté; **horseshoe m., U-shaped m.,** aimant en fer à cheval; **straight m.,** aimant droit; **compound m., bunch of magnets,** faisceau aimanté; aimant à lames; **m. steel,** acier *m* à aimant; *Nau: Av:* **compensating m.,** aimant compensateur, aimant correcteur; **m. core,** âme *f* de l'aimant, noyau aimanté, noyau magnétique; **m. gap,** entrefer *m*; *Nau:* **m. bar,** aimant de la rose du compas; **m. chamber, m. space,** chambre *f* à aimant (du compas); *Fig:* **it's a m. for tourists,** cela attire beaucoup de touristes. **2.** électro-aimant *m, pl.* électro-aimants; (*of crane*) **lifting m.,** électro-aimant de levage; **snap m.,** électro-aimant à rupture brusque.

magnetic [mæg'netik], *a.* **1.** (*a*) (barreau, etc.) aimanté; **m. needle,** aiguille aimantée; **m. iron ore,** aimant naturel, pierre *f* d'aimant; **m. pyrites,** magnétopyrite *f,* pyrrhotite *f*; (*b*) (attraction, champ, circuit, perturbation, etc.) magnétique; **m. deflection,** déviation *f* magnétique, du compas; **m. force, intensity,** force *f* magnétique, intensité *f* de champ magnétique; **m. interference,** champs *m* magnétiques parasites; **m. layer, shell,** feuillet *m* magnétique; *Atom.Ph:* **m. focusing,** focalisation *f,* concentration *f,* magnétique; **m. lens,** lentille *f* magnétique; *Nau:* **m. bearing, pole, heading,** relèvement *m*, pôle *m*, cap *m*, magnétique; *El:* **m. amplifier, recording,** amplificateur *m*, enregistrement *m*, magnétique; *Cmptr:* **m. card,** carte *f* magnétique; **m.-card file,** fichier *m* magnétique; **m. reader,** lecteur *m* magnétique; magnéto-lecteur *m, pl.* magnéto-lecteurs; *Mec.E:* **m. brake,** frein *m* magnétique; *Navy:* **m. mine, detector,** mine *f,* détecteur *m*, magnétique. **2.** (*of pers., power*) magnétique, hypnotique; **his eyes are m.,** il a le regard magnétique.

magnetically [mæg'netik(ə)li], *adv.* magnétiquement; par magnétisme.

magnetics [mæg'netiks], *s.pl.* (*usu. with sg.const.*) magnétisme *m.*

magnetimeter [mægni'timitər], *s. Ph:* magnétimètre *m*, magnétomètre *m.*

magnetism ['mægnitizm], *s.* **1.** *Ph:* magnétisme *m*; aimantation *f*; **induced m.,** magnétisme induit; **nuclear m.,** magnétisme nucléaire; **permanent, residual, temporary, m.,** magnétisme permanent, rémanent, temporaire. **2. animal m.,** magnétisme animal; **(personal) m.,** magnétisme (personnel); fascination *f.*

magnetite ['mægnitait], *s. Miner:* magnétite *f*; aimant naturel; pierre *f* d'aimant.

magnetite-olivinite ['mægnitaitɔ'livinait], *s. Miner:* magnétite-olivinite *f.*

magnetizability [mægnitaizə'biliti], *s. Ph:* susceptibilité *f* magnétique.

magnetizable ['mægnitaizəbl], *a.* aimantable, magnétisable.

magnetization [mægnitai'zeiʃ(ə)n], *s.* **1.** *Ph:* aimantation *f,* magnétisation *f*; **m. by electricity, by influence,** aimantation par l'électricité, par influence; **m. coefficient,** coefficient *m* d'aimantation; **m. curve,** courbe *f* de magnétisation. **2.** *A:* magnétisation (par hypnotisme).

magnetize ['mægnitaiz], *v.tr.* **1.** (*a*) aimanter (une aiguille, etc.); (*b*) (*with passive force*) (*of iron, etc.*) s'aimanter. **2.** (*a*) *A:* magnétiser, hypnotiser (qn); (*b*) magnétiser, attirer (qn, par magnétisme personnel).

magnetizer ['mægnitaizər], *s.* **1.** dispositif *m* d'aimantation. **2.** *A:* (*pers.*) magnétiseur, -euse.

magnetizing[1] ['mægnitaiziŋ], *a.* magnétisant, d'aimantation; **m. coil,** bobine *f* d'aimantation, d'excitation; **m. current,** courant magnétisant, de magnétisation; **m. field,** champ magnétisant; **m. force, m. power,** force magnétisante.

magnetizing[2], *s.* **1.** aimantation *f,* magnétisation;

permeability under low m., perméabilité *f* (magnétique) à faible aimantation. **2.** magnétisation *f* (de qn, des esprits).

magneto [mæg'ni:tou], *s. El:* magnéto *f*; **adjustable-lead m.**, magnéto à avance réglable, variable; **automatic-lead m.**, magnéto à avance automatique; **revolving (-armature) m., shuttle-type m.**, magnéto à induit tournant; **anti-clockwise m.**, magnéto pour rotation à gauche; **stationary(-armature) m.**, magnéto à induit fixe; **booster m.**, magnéto à survolteur; **make-and-break m.**, magnéto à rupture; **starting m.**, magnéto de démarrage, de départ; *I.C.E:* **the m. won't fire,** la magnéto n'allume pas; **m. booster,** magnéto de départ; **m. bell,** sonnerie *f* magnétique, sonnette *f* à magnéto; **m. (telephone) system,** système *m* téléphonique à magnéto.

magnetocaloric [mægni:toukæ'lɔ:rik], *a.* magnétocalorique.

magnetochemical [mægni:tou'kemik(ə)l], *a.* magnétochimique.

magnetochemistry [mægni:tou'kemistri], *s.* magnétochimie *f.*

magnetodynamic [mægni:toudai'næmik], *a.* magnétodynamique.

magnetodynamics [mægni:toudai'næmiks], *s.pl.* (*usu. with sg.const.*) magnétodynamique *f.*

magneto-electric [mægni:toui'lektrik], *a. Ph:* magnéto-électrique.

magnetogram [mæg'ni:tougræm], *s.* magnétogramme *m.*

magnetograph [mæg'ni:tougræf], *s.* magnétographe *m.*

magnetohydrodynamic [mæg'ni:touhaidroudai'næmik], *a.* magnétohydrodynamique.

magnetohydrodynamics [mæg'ni:touhaidroudai'næmiks], *s.pl.* (*usu. with sg. const.*) magnétohydrodynamique *f.*

magnetometer [mægni'tɔmitər], *s. Ph:* magnétomètre *m.*

magnetometric [mægni:tou'metrik], *a.* magnétométrique.

magnetometry [mægni'tɔmitri], *s.* magnétométrie *f.*

magnetomotive [mægni:tou'moutiv], *a. Ph:* magnétomoteur, -trice; **m. force,** force magnétomotrice.

magneton [mæg'ni:tɔn], *s. Ph:* magnéton *m*; **Bohr m.,** magnéton de Bohr; **nuclear m.,** magnéton nucléaire.

magneto-optical [mægni:tou'ɔptik(ə)l], *a.* magnéto-optique.

magneto-optics [mægni:tou'ɔptiks], *s.pl.* (*usu. with sg. const.*) magnéto-optique *f.*

magnetoplumbite [mægni:tou'plʌmbait], *s. Miner:* magnétoplumbite *f.*

magnetoresistance [mægni:touri'zist(ə)ns], *s. El:* magnétorésistance *f.*

magnetoscope [mæg'ni:touskoup], *s. T.V:* magnétoscope *m.*

magnetosphere [mæg'ni:tousfi:ər], *s.* magnétosphère *f.*

magnetostatic [mægni:tou'stætik], *a. Ph:* magnétostatique.

magnetostatics [mægni:tou'stætiks], *s.pl.* (*usu. with sg.const.*) *Ph:* magnétostatique *f.*

magnetostriction [mægni:tou'strikʃ(ə)n], *s. Ph:* magnétostriction *f.*

magnetostrictive [mægni:tou'striktiv], *a. Ph:* à magnétostriction.

magnetotherapy [mægni:tou'θerəpi], *s. Med:* magnétothérapie *f.*

magnetron ['mægnitrɔn], *s. Elcs:* magnétron *m*; **cavity m.,** magnétron à cavités; **multi-segment m.,** magnétron à secteurs multiples; **slotted-anode m., split-anode m.,** magnétron à anode fendue; **fixed-tune m.,** magnétron à accord fixe; **m. oscillator,** oscillateur *m* à magnétron.

magnific [mæg'nifik], *a. A: & Lit:* magnifique.

magnificat [mæg'nifikæt], *s. Ecc:* magnificat *m.*

magnification [mægnifikeiʃ(ə)n], *s.* **1.** *Opt: etc:* grossissement *m*, grandissement *m*, amplification *f*; **tenfold m.,** grossissement: dix; **high m.,** fort grossissement; **optimum m.,** grossissement optimal; **m. factor,** coefficient *m* de grossissement; **m. ratio,** rapport *m* de grossissement, d'amplification; *El:* **voltage m.,** gain *m* en tension. **2.** *A:* exaltation *f*, glorification *f* (de qn, de qch.).

magnificence [mæg'nifis(ə)ns], *s.* magnificence *f.*

magnificent [mæg'nifis(ə)nt], *a.* **1.** magnifique; (repas) somptueux; **m. jewels,** bijoux *m* de toute beauté. **2.** *A:* magnifique; d'une libéralité princière.

magnificently [mæg'nifis(ə)ntli], *adv.* magnifiquement.

magnifico [mæg'nifikou], *s.* (*a*) *Hist:* magnifique *m*, grand *m* (de Venise); (*b*) grand seigneur.

magnified ['mægnifaid], *a.* grossi, agrandi; (son) amplifié, renforcé.

magnifier ['mægnifaiər], *s.* verre grossissant; loupe *f*; *Phot:* bonnette *f* d'approche; **focussing m.,** loupe de mise au point.

magnify ['mægnifai], *v.tr.* **1.** (*a*) grossir, agrandir (une image); amplifier, renforcer (un son); (*b*) **to m. an incident,** grossir, exagérer, un incident; donner à un incident une importance exagérée. **2.** *Ecc:* magnifier (le Seigneur); *A:* exalter, glorifier (qn, qch.).

magnifying ['mægnifaiiŋ], *s. Opt: etc:* grossissement *m*, amplification *f*; **m. power,** pouvoir grossissant, grossissement (d'une lentille, d'un objectif); **m. glass,** verre grossissant, loupe *f*; **m. lens,** lentille *f* dioptrique; **m. prism,** prisme grossissant.

magniloquence [mæg'niləkwəns], *s.* grandiloquence *f.*

magniloquent [mæg'niləkwənt], *a.* grandiloquent.

magnitude ['mægnitjud], *s.* (*a*) grandeur *f*, importance *f*; ampleur *f*; **the m. of the interests at stake,** l'importance *f* des intérêts en jeu; (*b*) *Astr:* magnitude *f*; **star of the first m.,** étoile *f* de première magnitude; **star of m. 3·0,** étoile de magnitude 3·0; (*c*) *Mth:* grandeur, valeur *f*; **m. range, order of m.,** ordre *m* de grandeur; **m. at an instant,** valeur instantanée.

magnochromite [mægnou'kroumait], *s. Miner:* magnochromite *f.*

magnoferrite [mægnou'ferait], *s. Miner:* magnéferrite *f*, magnoferrite *f*, magnésioferrite *f.*

magnolia [mæg'nouliə], *s.* **1.** *Bot:* (*a*) magnolia *m*; (*b*) **m. (tree),** magnolia, magnolier *m*; **m. grandiflora, evergreen m., laurel m.,** magnolier à grandes fleurs, laurier-tulipier *m*, *pl.* lauriers-tulipiers; **m. virginiana,** arbre *m* de castor. **2.** *Metall:* **m. (metal),** magnolia.

Magnoliaceae [mægnouli'eisii:], *s.pl. Bot:* magnoliacées *f.*

magnum, *pl.* **-ums** ['mægnəm(z)], *s.* magnum *m* (de champagne, etc.).

magnum opus ['mægnəm'oupəs, -'ɔpəs]. *Lt.s.phr.* grand ouvrage; chef-d'œuvre *m*; **how's the m. o. getting on?** et votre grand ouvrage, ça avance?

magot ['mægət, 'mægou], *s.* **1.** *Z:* magot *m*; singe *m* sans queue (de Gibraltar, etc.). **2.** magot (de porcelaine, d'ivoire); magot de Chine.

magpie ['mægpai], *s.* **1.** (*a*) *Orn:* pie *f*; jacasse *f*; *NAm:* **American m.,** pie bavarde; **Spanish blue m.,** pie bleue; **azure-winged m.,** pie bleue à calotte noire; (*b*) *Austr:* flûteur *m*, gymnorhine *m*; **paradise m.,** astrapie *f*; **green m.,** pirolle *f*; **m. lark,** grallinе *f*; **m. robin,** dyal *m*; (*c*) *F:* (*pers.*) bavard(e), pie. **2.** *Mil: F:* coup *m* (de fusil) qui atteint l'avant-dernier cercle extérieur de la cible; (il est signalisé par un fanion blanc et noir).

magus, *pl.* **-gi** ['meigəs, -dʒai], *s. Rel.H:* mage *m*; *B.Hist:* **the Three Magi,** les trois (rois) mages.

Magyar ['mægjɑ:r]. **1.** *Ethn:* (*a*) *a.* magyar; (*b*) *s.* Magyar, -are. **2.** *Cost:* **M. sleeves,** manches *f* kimono.

Magyarization [mægjuɑrai'zeiʃ(ə)n], *s.* magyarisation *f.*

Magyarize ['mægjɑraiz], *v.tr.* magyariser.

mahaleb ['mɑ:həleb], *s.* mahaleb *m*; (i) cerisier *m*, (ii) bois *m*, de Sainte-Lucie.

maharajah [mɑ:hə'rɑ:dʒə], *s.m.* maharajah.

maharani, *A:* **maharanee** [mɑ:hə'rɑ:ni:], *s.f.* maharani; la femme du maharajah.

mahatma [mə'hɑ:tmə, -'hæt-], *s.* mahatma *m.*

Mahdi ['mɑ:di], *s.* mahdi *m.*

Mahdism ['mɑ:dizm], *s.* mahdisme *m.*

Mahdist ['mɑ:dist], *a. & s.* mahdiste (*mf*).

mahem [mə'hem], *s. Orn:* (*S. Africa*) grue couronnée.

mah-jong(g) ['mɑ:'(d)ʒɔŋ], *s. Games:* ma(h)-jong *m.*

mahlstick ['mɔ:lstik], *s.* = MAULSTICK.

mahoe [mə'hou], *s. Bot:* **seaside m.,** thespesia *m.*

mahogany [mə'hɔgəni], *s.* **1.** (*a*) *Bot:* acajou *m*; (*b*) (bois *m* d')acajou; **m. table,** table *f* en acajou; **m. complexion,** teint *m* acajou *inv.* **2. bastard m.,** (bois) caïlcédra *m*; **white m.,** primavera *m*; **Indian m.,** (espèce de) cedrela *m.*

Mahomet [mə'hɔmet]. *Pr.n.m. Rel.H:* Mahomet.

Mahometan [mə'hɔmətən], *a. & s.* musulman, -ane.

Mahometanism [mə'hɔmətənizm], *s.* islamisme *m.*

mahonia [mə'houniə], *s. Bot:* mahonia *m.*

Mahound [mə'hu:nd]. *Pr.n.m. A:* **1.** *Rel.H:* Mahomet. **2.** *Scot:* Satan.

mahout [mə'haut], *s.* cornac *m.*

Mahratta [mə'rætə]. **1.** *Ethn:* (*a*) *a.* mahratte; (*b*) *s.* Mahratte (*mf*). **2.** *s. Ling:* mahratte *m.*

Mahratti [mə'ræti:], *s. Ling:* mahratte *m.*

mahseer ['mɑ:siər], *s. Ich:* mahaseer *m.*

mahua ['mɑ:wə], *s.* **m. butter,** beurre *m* d'illipé.

maia ['maiə], *s. Crust:* maïa *m.*

maianthemum [mai'ænθəməm], *s. Bot:* maïanthème *m.*

maid [meid], *s.f.* **1.** *Lit:* jeune fille. **2.** *A: & Lit:* vierge; **the M. (of Orleans),** la Pucelle (d'Orléans). **3. old m.,** (i) vieille fille; (ii) *Moll:* mye *f*; **to remain an old m.,** rester fille; coiffer sainte Catherine. **4.** bonne, domestique, servante; **lady's m.,** femme de chambre; **(general) m., m. of all work,** bonne à tout faire. **5. m. of honour,** (i) fille d'honneur (de la reine, d'une princesse); (ii) *NAm:* (*at wedding*) première demoiselle d'honneur; (iii) *Cu:* tartelette feuilletée au lait caillé ou aux amandes.

maidan [mai'dɑ:n], *s.* (*in India*) esplanade *f*, promenade *f.*

maiden [meidn], *s.* **1.** (*a*) jeune fille *f*; (*b*) vierge *f*; (*c*) *Hist:* **the (Scottish) m.,** la "guillotine" (érigée à Édimbourg dès le XVIe siècle). **2.** *attrib.* (*a*) **m. aunt,** tante non mariée, restée fille; **m. lady,** demoiselle *f*; (*b*) **m. modesty,** modestie *f* de jeune fille; **m. name,** nom *m* de jeune fille; (*c*) *Jur:* **m. assize,** assises *fpl* où il n'y a pas de causes à juger; session blanche; *Cr:* **m. over,** série *f* de balles où aucun point n'a été marqué; *Rac:* **m. horse,** cheval *m* qui n'a jamais gagné de prix; (*d*) *Arb:* **m. tree,** arbre franc de pied; (*e*) **m. voyage, m. flight,** premier voyage, premier vol; **m. speech,** premier discours (en public); discours de début (d'un député).

maidenhair ['meidnhɛər], *s. Bot:* **m. (fern),** adiante *m*, capillaire *m*; cheveu *m* de Vénus; **m. tree,** ginkgo *m.*

maidenhead ['meidnhed], *s. A:* **1.** virginité *f*, pucelage *m.* **2.** étrenne *f* (de qch.). **3.** *Anat:* hymen *m.*

maidenhood ['meidnhud], *s.* célibat *m* (de fille); condition *f* de fille.

maidenliness ['meidnlinis], *s. Lit:* qualités *fpl*, tenue *f*, de jeune fille.

maidenly ['meidnli]. **1.** *a.* de jeune fille, virginal, -aux; modeste. **2.** *adv.* en jeune fille; avec modestie, avec pudeur.

maidservant ['meidsə:v(ə)nt], *s.f.* domestique; bonne.

maieutics [mai'ju:tiks], *s.pl. Phil:* maïeutique *f.*

mail[1] [meil], *s.* **1.** (*a*) *Arm:* mailles *fpl*; **clad in m.,** vêtu d'une cotte de mailles; (*b*) *Moll:* **m. shell,** chiton *m*, oscabrion *m.* **2.** *Tex:* maille, maillon *m.*

mail[2], *v.tr. Arm:* revêtir (qn) de mailles, d'une cotte de mailles.

mail[3], *s.* **1.** courrier *m*; lettres *fpl*; **early m.,** courrier du matin; **incoming m.,** courrier (à l') arrivée; **outgoing m.,** courrier (au) départ; **inward m.,** courrier en provenance de l'étranger, de la province; **outward m.,** courrier (en partance) pour l'étranger, pour la province; **to open, deal with, one's m.,** dépouiller, faire, son courrier; **when does the next m. leave?** à quand le prochain départ du courrier? *Mil:* **m. clerk,** vaguemestre *m*; **m. orderly,** planton *m* du vaguemestre. **2.** (*a*) *A.Veh:* malle *f*; malle-poste *f*, *pl.* malles-poste(s); (*b*) *Rail: A:* **limited m.,** train-poste *m*, *pl.* trains-poste(s); (*c*) la poste; **the Royal M.** = le Service des postes; *Nau: A:* **the Indian m.,** la malle des Indes; *Nau:* **m. flag,** pavillon postal; **m. boat, steamer,** navire postal, paquebot-poste *m*, *pl.* paquebots-poste; **m. van,** fourgon *m* des postes; *Rail:* **m. van, car,** wagon-poste *m*, *pl.* wagons-poste; **m. coach,** (i) *A:* malle-poste *f*, *pl.* malles-poste(s); (ii) *Rail:* wagon-poste; **m. plane,** avion postal; **m. train,** train-poste *m*; *Nau:* **m. room,** soute *f* aux dépêches; *Com:* **m. order,** commande *f* par correspondance; **m. order business,** (achat *m* et) vente *f* par correspondance, sur catalogue; **m. order catalogue,** tarif-album *m*, *pl.* tarifs-albums.

mail[4], *v.tr.* envoyer par la poste, expédier (des lettres, des paquets); mettre (une lettre) à la poste.

mail[5], *s. Scot:* impôt *m*, tribut *m*, loyer *m.*

mailable ['meiləbl], *a. U.S:* transmissible par la poste.

mailbag ['meilbæg], *s.* sac postal, sac de dépêches.

mailbox ['meilbɔks], *s. NAm:* boîte *f* à lettres.

mailed [meild], *a.* **1.** (*a*) *Arm:* (guerrier) revêtu de mailles, maillé; *O:* (navire) cuirassé; (*b*) **the m. fist,** la main gantelée; la force armée; **to show the m. fist,** recourir à la manière forte. **2.** *Z:* cuirassé.

mailing ['meiliŋ], *s.* envoi *m* par la poste; mise *f* à la poste; **m. list,** liste *f* de diffusion; liste d'adresses (de clients éventuels, etc.); **please add our name to your m. list,** veuillez nous faire régulièrement le service de votre documentation, de vos catalogues, de vos prix courants, etc.

maim [meim], *v.tr.* estropier, mutiler (qn); *Fig:* mutiler (un texte).

maimed [meimd], *a.* estropié, mutilé.

main[1] [mein], *s.* **1.** *A:* vigueur *f*, force *f*; *still used in the phr.;* **with might and m.,** de toutes mes, ses, forces; **to hit out with might and m.,** frapper à coups redoublés, à bras raccourcis, à tour de bras. **2.** *Poet:* océan *m*, haute mer. **3. in the m.,** en général, en gros, en somme, généralement (parlant), pour la plupart, à tout prendre. **4.** (*a*) *Civ.E:* canalisation maîtresse, principale; *El:* conducteur principal; câble *m* de distribution; **m. water,** eau de la ville; **the mains,** les communications *f*; **town mains,** canalisation de la ville, réseau *m* de distribution de la ville; **electric mains,** canalisations électriques; **gas mains,** conduites *fpl* de gaz; **water mains,** canalisations, conduites, d'eau; *Nau:* **the fire mains,** les collecteurs *m* d'incendie; *El:* **to take one's power from the mains,** brancher sur le secteur; *W.Tel:* **mains set,** poste *m* secteur; **all-mains set,** poste secteur tous-courants; (*b*) *Nau:* grand-mât.

main[2], *a.* **1. by m. force,** de vive force; de haute lutte; à main armée. **2.** principal, -aux, premier, essentiel; (*a*) **m. body,** gros *m* (de l'armée, de la flotte, etc.); plus grande partie; *Agr:* **m. crop,** culture principale; (*b*) **m. point, m. thing,** l'essentiel, le principal; **the m. thing is to understand one another,** il s'agit surtout, le tout est, de bien se comprendre; **the m. thing is that no one shall know anything about it,** le principal est que personne n'en sache rien; **m. idea,** idée *f* mère (d'une œuvre, etc.); **m. features of a speech,** linéaments *m*, grands traits, points saillants, d'un discours; **one of his m. objects in life,** un des maîtres buts de sa vie; *Com: Ind:* **m. office,** direction générale; siège social; **factory contained in three m. buildings,** usine *f* en trois corps de bâtiment; *Gram:* **m. clause,** proposition principale; *Cu:* **m. course, dish,** plat *m* de résistance; (*c*) **m. air current,** courant d'air principal; **m. road,** grande route; route à grande circulation; **m. street,** rue principale; **m. sewer,** égout collecteur; grand collecteur; **m. drain,** maître drain; drain collecteur; **to be on m. drainage,** avoir le tout à l'égout; **m. leaf,** lame maîtresse (d'un ressort); *El:* **m. cable,** câble principal; *Min:* **m. lode,** filon principal, filon mère; *Av:* **m. wing,** aile sustentatrice; **m. rib (of wing),** nervure principale; *Rail: etc:* **m. line,** voie principale, grande ligne; (*d*) *Nau:* **m. masts,** les mâts majeurs; **m. hatch,** grand panneau; **m. pump,** pompe royale; **m. yard,** grand-vergue *f*; **m. deck,** pont principal; premier pont; franc tillac; **m. boiler,** chaudière principale; **m. breadth,** fort *m* (d'un navire).

Main[3] **(the)** [ðə'mein]. *Pr.n. Geog:* le Main.

mainbrace ['meinbreis], *s. Nau:* grand bras de vergue; *F:* **to splice the m.,** boire un coup.

Maine [mein]. *Pr.n. Geog:* le Maine ((i) ancienne province de France; (ii) État des États-Unis).

mainland ['meinlænd], *s.* continent *m*; terre *f* ferme; grande terre.

mainly ['meinli], *adv.* **1.** principalement, surtout. **2.** dans une large mesure, en grande partie.

mainmast ['meinmɑːst, -məst], *s. Nau:* grand mât; (*of lateen-rigged ship*) (arbre *m* de) mestre *m*.

mainsail ['meinseil, 'meinsl], *s. Nau:* grand-voile *f*, *pl.* grand(s)-voiles; (*of lateen-rigged ship*) voile *f* de mestre; (*of boat*) taille-vent *m inv*; **the mainsails,** le fard de grand mât.

mainsheet ['meinʃiːt], *s. Nau:* grand-écoute *f*, *pl.* grand-écoutes.

mainspring ['meinspriŋ], *s.* **1.** grand ressort; ressort moteur (d'une pendule, etc.). **2.** mobile essentiel, cause principale, cheville ouvrière; **m. of our actions,** principe *m* de nos actions.

mainstay ['meinstei], *s.* **1.** *Nau:* étai *m* de grand mât. **2.** soutien principal; point *m* d'appui (d'une cause, etc.); **he was the m. of his family,** c'était le principal soutien de sa famille.

maintain [mein'tein], *v.tr.* **1.** maintenir (l'ordre, la discipline); soutenir (une guerre, un siège, une lutte, un procès, la conversation, sa dignité, sa réputation); entretenir (des relations, une correspondance); conserver (la santé); garder, observer (une attitude, le silence); garder (son sang-froid); **to m. the speed, the pace,** conserver l'allure; **to m. s.o., sth., in a position,** maintenir qn, qch., dans une position; **the improvement is maintained,** l'amélioration se maintient. **2.** entretenir, soutenir, nourrir, faire vivre, faire subsister (une famille, etc.); **to have to m. s.o.,** avoir qn à sa charge; **he undertook to m. me,** il prit à sa charge les frais de mon entretien; **maintained school,** école subventionnée; *Jur:* **to neglect to m. one's family,** négliger de subvenir aux besoins de sa famille. **3.** entretenir (une armée, une route, un feu); *El:* **to m. a battery,** entretenir un accu; **well-maintained road,** route bien entretenue. **4.** soutenir, défendre (une cause); **to m. one's rights,** défendre ses droits. **5.** garder (un avantage); se maintenir dans (un poste); **they maintained their ground for three hours,** ils ont tenu pendant trois heures; **at the end of the day we had maintained our ground,** à la fin de la journée nous restions sur nos positions. **6.** (s'obstiner à) soutenir (une opinion, un fait); **to m. (that) . . .,** maintenir, soutenir, prétendre, que . . .; **he maintains that he is innocent,** il affirme qu'il est innocent; il affirme son innocence.

maintainable [men'teinəbl], *a.* **1.** (position *f*) tenable. **2.** (opinion *f*) soutenable.

maintainer [men'teinər], *s.* **1.** (*a*) celui qui maintient, soutient (l'ordre, etc.); protecteur *m*, souteneur *m* (d'un système); (*b*) *Sch:* soutenant, -ante (d'une thèse). **2.** soutien *m* de famille; personne *f* qui pourvoit aux besoins de sa, d'une famille.

maintenance ['meintənəns], *s.* **1.** maintien *m* (de l'ordre, de qn dans un emploi); *Com:* **resale price m.,** prix imposés. **2.** (*a*) entretien *m* (d'une famille, des troupes, etc.); *Sch:* **m. grant,** bourse *f* d'entretien; (*b*) *Jur:* pension *f* alimentaire; **m. order,** obligation *f* alimentaire; **separate m.,** (i) pension alimentaire servie par le mari à se femme séparée de corps; (ii) séparation *f* de biens (judiciaire); (*c*) *Adm: Fin:* alimentation *f*, financement *m* (d'un fonds, d'une caisse). **3.** (*a*) *Tchn:* entretien, conservation *f* (du matériel, des bâtiments, des routes, etc.); **corrective m.,** dépannage *m*; **preventive m.,** entretien préventif; **routine m., scheduled m.,** entretien courant, périodique; entretien de routine; *Av: etc:* **line m.,** petit entretien, entretien d'escale; **m. allowance,** allocation *f* d'entretien; **m. charges, m. expenses,** frais *mpl* d'entretien; **m. equipment,** matériel *m* d'entretien; **m. handbook,** manuel *m* d'entretien; **m. kit,** trousse *f* d'entretien; **m. personnel, m. staff,** personnel *m* d'entretien, équipe(s) *f(pl)* d'entretien; **m. engineer,** ingénieur *m*, technicien *m*, d'entretien; **m. shop,** atelier *m* d'entretien; **m. vehicle,** camion-atelier *m*, *pl.* camions-ateliers; *Mil:* **organization(al) m.,** entretien courant d'unité; (*b*) (*management upkeep*) maintenance *f*; *Ind: Mil:* **m. programme, m. project,** programme *m* de maintenance; **m. requirements,** moyens *m* de maintenance exigés, indispensables; **m. resources,** moyens de maintenance (dont on dispose); *Mil:* **base m.,** maintenance de base (d'opérations); **depot m.,** maintenance de dépôt; **combat m.,** maintenance de combat; (*c*) *Rail: Tp: etc:* surveillance *f* (des voies, des lignes); *Tp:* **m. department,** service *m* de surveillance des lignes. **4. m. of one's rights,** défense *f* de ses droits. **5.** *Jur:* aide pécuniaire apportée à une des parties, intervention officieuse et vexatoire (dans un procès où l'on n'est pas intéressé).

main-top ['meintɔp], *s. Nau:* grand-hune *f*, *pl.* grand-hunes.

Mainz [maints]. *Pr.n. Geog:* Mayence *f*.

Maioidea [mai'ɔidiə], *s.pl. Crust:* majidés *m*.

maison(n)ette [meizə'net], *s.* **1.** appartement *m* prélevé sur un immeuble, *esp.* (appartement) duplex *m*. **2.** *A:* maisonnette *f*.

maitlandite ['meitləndait], *s. Miner:* maitlandite *f*.

maize [meiz]. **1.** *s.* maïs *m*; blé *m* de Turquie, d'Inde, d'Espagne; turquet *m*; **water m.,** maïs d'eau. **2.** *a. & s.* (*colour*) jaune maïs *inv*; maïs *inv*.

majestic(al) [mə'dʒestik(əl)], *a.* majestueux, auguste; **majestic bearing,** maintien plein de majesté.

majestically [mə'dʒestik(ə)li], *adv.* majestueusement.

majesty ['mædʒəsti], *s.* majesté *f*; (*a*) **the m. of the Roman people,** la majesté du peuple romain; **God in all His m.,** Dieu dans toute sa majesté; (*b*) **His M., Her M.,** Sa Majesté le Roi, Sa Majesté la Reine; *Hist:* **his Most Christian M.,** sa Majesté Très Chrétienne (le roi de France); **his Catholic M.,** sa Majesté catholique (le roi d'Espagne); **Your M. has deigned to visit your humble servant,** Votre Majesté a daigné visiter son humble serviteur; **on His, Her, M.'s Service,** (pour le) service de Sa Majesté (= service de l'État); *Post:* en franchise.

Majidae ['mædʒidiː], *s.pl. Crust:* majidés *m*.

majolica [mə'dʒɔlikə], *s. Cer:* majolique *f*, maïolique *f*.

major[1] ['meidʒər], *s. Mil:* (*a*) commandant *m*, chef *m* de bataillon (d'infanterie); *Fr.C:* major *m*; (*in W.R.A.C.*) hors classe *f*; **m. general,** général *m* de division; (*b*) chef d'escadron (de cavalerie, des blindés); chef d'escadron (d'artillerie, du train).

major[2]. **1.** *a.* (*a*) **the m. portion,** la majeure partie, la plus grande partie; **the m. poets, prophets,** les grands poètes, prophètes; *Ecc:* **the m. orders,** les ordres majeurs; **m. decision,** décision très importante, capitale; **m. illness,** maladie *f* grave; *Mil:* **a m. command,** un haut commandement; **m. units,** les grandes unités; **m. offensive,** vaste offensive; *Log:* **m. premiss,** prémisse majeure; *Mth:* **m. axis,** axe *m* transverse, grand axe (d'une ellipse); *Mus:* **m. key,** ton majeur; mode majeur; **m. third,** tierce majeure; *Aut:* **m. road,** route *f* à grand circulation; route à priorité; *Cards:* (*at bridge*) **the m. suits,** les couleurs principales (pique et cœur); (*b*) **tierce m.,** tierce majeure; *Sch:* **Martin m.,** Martin aîné, l'aîné des deux Martin. **2.** *s.* (*a*) *Jur:* (*pers.*) majeur, -eure; personne majeure; (*b*) *Log:* majeure *f*; (*c*) *Sch: U.S:* (i) sujet (d'études) principal, spécial (d'un étudiant); (ii) **philology m.,** étudiant, -ante, qui se spécialise dans la philologie.

major[3], *v.i. Sch: U.S:* **to m. in a subject,** se spécialiser dans un sujet; **to m. in English** = faire sa licence d'anglais.

Majorca [mə'dʒɔːkə, mai'ɔːkə]. *Pr.n. Geog:* Majorque *f*.

Majorcan [mə'dʒɔːkən, mai'ɔːkən]. **1.** *a. Geog:* majorquin, mayorquin. **2.** *s.* Majorquin, -ine, Mayorquin, -ine.

major-domo, *pl.* **-os** ['meidʒə'doumou, -ouz], *s.* major-dome *m*.

majorette [meidʒə'ret], *s.f. NAm:* majorette.

majority [mə'dʒɔriti], *s.* **1.** majorité *f* (des voix, des suffrages); (*a*) **absolute m.,** majorité absolue; **simple, relative, m.,** majorité relative; **a two-thirds m.,** une majorité de deux tiers, de deux contre un; **to be in a m., in the m.,** être en majorité, avoir la majorité; **to be in a m. over . . .,** avoir la majorité sur . . .; **to secure a m.,** remporter la majorité; **m. decision, decision taken by a m.,** décision prise à la majorité (des voix); **elected by a m.,** élu à la pluralité des voix; **elected by a m. of ten,** élu à dix voix de majorité, à la majorité de dix voix; **election by an absolute m.,** scrutin *m* majoritaire; **narrow m.,** faible majorité; **by an overwhelming m.,** en nombre écrasant; **m. vote,** vote *m* majoritaire; **m. party,** parti *m* majoritaire; *Jur:* **m. verdict,** verdict *m* de la majorité (du jury); verdict non-unanime; (*b*) la plus grande partie, le plus grand nombre (des hommes, etc.); **to join the (great) m.,** mourir; s'en aller ad patres; (*c*) *U.S:* majorité absolue. **2.** *Jur:* majorité; **to attain one's m.,** atteindre sa majorité; devenir majeur. **3.** *Mil:* = MAJORSHIP; **he has just obtained his m.,** il vient de passer commandant.

majorship ['meidʒəʃip], *s. Mil:* grade *m* de commandant.

majuscule ['mædʒəskjul], *a. & s.* majuscule (*f*).

make[1] [meik], *s.* **1.** (*a*) façon *f*, forme *f*, fabrication *f*, construction *f*; coupe *f* (d'une robe, etc.); (*b*) *Com: Ind:* marque *f* (d'un produit); **of French m.,** de fabrication française, de construction française; **our own m.,** de notre marque; **cars of all makes,** voitures *f* de toutes marques; **a good m. of car, etc.,** voiture, etc., d'excellente fabrication, de première marque; **standard m.,** marque courante. **2.** caractère *m*, aspect *m* (de qn); **men of his m. are rare,** des hommes comme lui sont rares. **3.** *F:* **to be on the m.,** être âpre au gain, chercher à faire fortune par tous les moyens. **4.** *El:* fermeture *f* (du circuit); **at m.,** en circuit; **m. position,** position *f* de fermeture du circuit; *Tp:* **m. contact,** contact *m* de travail. **5.** *P:* **easy m.,** femme *f* facile.

make[2], *v.* **(made** [meid]; **made)**

I. *v.tr.* **1.** (*a*) faire, construire (une machine, une boîte, etc.); faire, façonner (un vase, etc.); faire, fabriquer (du papier, etc.); faire, confectionner (des vêtements, etc.); **God made man,** Dieu a fait, a créé, l'homme; **to m. an opening for the wires,** ménager une ouverture pour les fils; **you are made for this work,** vous êtes fait pour ce travail; **they seem made for each other,** ils semblent créés l'un pour l'autre; *Knitting:* **to m. one,** faire un jeté simple; **to m. two,** faire un jeté double, faire deux augmentations; *F:* **he's as sharp as they m. them** ['meikm], c'est un malin s'il en est; **life is what you m. it,** la vie est faite de ce que nous y mettons; (*b*) **bread is made of wheat,** le pain est fait de blé, le pain se fait avec du blé; **there would be no wheat to m. bread (with),** il n'y aurait pas de blé pour faire le pain; **what is it made of?** en quoi est-ce? c'est en quoi? **what is brass made of?** de quoi le laiton se compose-t-il? **to m. a box out of a piece of mahogany,** faire une boîte d'un morceau d'acajou; **to m. a friend of s.o.,** faire de qn son ami; s'attirer l'amitié de qn; **he made a business of politics,** il faisait de la politique son occupation; **I don't know what to m. of it, I can m. nothing of it,** je n'y comprends rien; **what do** ***you*** **m. of it?** et vous, qu'en pensez-vous? **you'd m. more of it than I would,** (i) vous en profiteriez mieux que moi; vous en tireriez meilleur parti que moi; (ii) vous le comprendriez mieux que moi; **to show what one is made of,** donner sa mesure; (*c*) **to m. milk into butter,** transformer le lait en beurre; (*d*) **to m. one's will,** faire son testament; *Fin:* **to m. a promissory note, a bill of exchange,** souscrire un billet à ordre; libeller une lettre de change; (*e*) **to m. the bed, the tea,** faire le lit, le thé; **to m. a fire,** faire du feu; *Cards:* **to m. the cards,** battre les cartes; (*f*) **to m. trouble,** causer, occasionner, des désagréments; causer des ennuis (à qn); provoquer le désordre; **to m. objections,** soulever des objections; **d'you want to m. an issue of it,** *P:* **something of it?** veux-tu en faire toute une histoire, du grabuge? **to m. a noise,** faire du bruit; **to m. peace,** faire, conclure, la paix; **to m. an opportunity, to m. it possible, for s.o. to do sth.,** ménager à qn l'occasion de faire qch.; (*g*) **to m. a law,** faire une loi; **to m. a rule,** établir une règle; **to m. a distinction,** faire une distinction; (*h*) **to m. a payment, a deal,** effectuer, faire, un versement, une transaction; **to m. a change,** opérer un changement; (*i*) **to m. a speech,** faire un discours; **to m. an attempt to do sth.,** essayer de faire qch.; **to m. a mis-**

take, faire, commettre, une erreur; se tromper; **you have made me m. a mistake,** c'est à cause de vous que je me suis trompé; **to m. war,** faire la guerre; **to m. a good dinner,** faire un bon dîner; bien dîner; **to m. one's escape,** s'échapper, se sauver; **to m. excuses,** faire des excuses; s'excuser; **this recommendation was made by . . .,** cette recommandation émane de . . .; **he made a sudden gesture,** il a fait un mouvement brusque; (*j*) **we made the whole journey in two days,** nous avons fait tout le trajet en deux jours; **we just made it,** nous sommes arrivés juste à temps. **2.** (*a*) établir, assurer (**a connection between . . .,** le raccordement de . . .); *El: (of contact points)* **to m. the circuit,** fermer le circuit; (*b*) (*constitute*) **two and two m. four,** deux et deux font, égalent, quatre; **this book makes pleasant reading,** ce livre est d'une lecture agréable; **they m. a handsome couple,** ils font un beau couple; **to m. a good husband, a good wife,** se montrer bon époux, bonne épouse; **she made him a good wife,** elle a été pour lui une excellente épouse; **will you m. one of the party?** voulez-vous être des nôtres? *Prov:* **the cowl does not m. the monk,** l'habit ne fait pas le moine. **3.** (*acquire*) faire (de l'argent); **to m. £100 a week,** gagner, se faire, £100 par semaine; **to m. a, one's, fortune,** faire fortune; gagner une fortune; *F:* **to m. a bit (on the side),** se faire de la gratte; **to m. a name, friends,** se faire un nom, des amis; **to m. profits,** réaliser des bénéfices; **to m. a good deal by . . .,** tirer beaucoup de profit de . . .; **what will you m. by it?** qu'est-ce que vous en tirerez? *Com: (of goods)* **to m. a price,** rapporter un prix; **the prices made yesterday,** les cours pratiqués hier; *Cards:* **to m. a trick,** faire une levée; **to m. one's contract,** réussir son contrat; **little slam bid and made,** petit chelem demandé et réussi; *v.i. (of card)* **to m.,** faire la levée; *P:* **to m. sth.,** voler, faucher, faire, qch.; *P:* **I made (it with) her,** je l'ai tombée; j'ai couché avec elle; *F:* **to m. it,** réussir, y arriver; **he's got it made,** le voilà arrivé; son avenir est assuré; **can you m. it on Friday?** pouvez-vous venir, y aller, vendredi? *F:* **I just made my train,** j'ai eu mon train tout juste; **do you think he'll m. university?** pensez-vous qu'il sera admis à l'université? **4.** (*a*) faire la fortune de (qn); **the cotton trade made Manchester,** l'industrie cotonnière a fait la prospérité de Manchester; **this book made him, made his name,** ce livre lui a assuré la célébrité, la renommée; ce livre l'a rendu célèbre; **this will m. him or break him,** cela sera ou son succès ou sa ruine; ou il réussira ou il sombrera; (*b*) **that made my day,** ça m'a rendu heureux pour toute la journée; **that makes my day!** (i) je n'attendais que ça! (ii) *Iron:* ça c'est le comble! **that little touch makes the picture, the dress, the room,** c'est ce petit détail qui fait le tableau, la robe, la pièce; **it makes all the difference,** ça change tout; (*c*) *Equit:* **to m. a horse,** refaire un cheval. **5. to m. s.o. happy,** rendre qn heureux; **to m. s.o. hungry, thirsty, sleepy, hot,** donner faim, soif, sommeil, chaud, à qn; **to m. a box too heavy,** rendre une boîte trop lourde; **to m. s.o. angry,** fâcher qn; **to m. a dish hot,** (faire) chauffer un plat; **to m. s.o. an earl,** faire qn comte; **they made him their leader,** on le prit pour chef; **to m. s.o. one's heir,** constituer qn son héritier; **to m. s.o. a judge,** nommer qn juge; **he wants to m. his son a barrister,** il veut que son fils devienne avocat; **this made him a hero,** cela fit de lui un héros; **to m. s.o. rich,** rendre qn riche; enrichir qn; **to m. sth. known, felt, understood,** faire connaître, sentir, comprendre, qch.; **to m. oneself heard,** se faire entendre; **to m. oneself comfortable,** se mettre à l'aise; **to m. oneself ill,** se rendre malade; **to m. oneself tired,** se fatiguer; **to m. it a rule, one's aim, to . . .,** se faire une règle, un but, de . . .; **what makes you so late?** qu'est-ce qui vous met si en retard? **can you come at six?—m. it half past,** pouvez-vous venir à six heures?—plutôt la demie. **6.** (*represent as*) **Irving made Shylock a tragic figure,** Irving faisait de Shylock, représentait Shylock comme, une figure de tragédie; **what do you m. the time? what time do you m. it?** quelle heure est-il à votre montre? *F:* quelle heure avez-vous? **I m. it five kilometres,** j'évalue la distance à cinq kilomètres. **7.** (*cause, compel*) **to m. s.o. speak, sleep,** faire parler, dormir, qn; **to m. s.o. behave stupidly,** faire faire des bêtises à qn; **you should m. him do it,** vous devriez le lui faire faire; vous devriez le forcer à le faire; **I made him stop,** je l'ai fait arrêter; **what made you go?** (i) qu'est-ce qui vous a déterminé à partir? (ii) pourquoi y êtes-vous allé? **what made you say that?** pourquoi avez-vous dit cela? **his answer made her wonder whether he was sincere,** sa réponse l'a fait douter de sa sincérité; **the events that m. things what they are,** les événements *m* qui font que les choses sont ce qu'elles sont. **8.** *Nau:* (*a*) **we hope to m. Falmouth tomorrow night,** nous espérons arriver à Falmouth demain soir; **to m. a headland,** (i) arriver en vue d'un cap; reconnaître un cap; (ii) doubler, franchir, une pointe; **to m. a light,** reconnaître un feu; **to m. the island,** atterrir sur l'île; (*b*) (*of ship*) **to m. twenty knots,** faire vingt nœuds; filer à vingt nœuds; **we made bad weather all the way,** nous avons essuyé du mauvais temps pendant toute la traversée.

II. *v.i.* **1. to m. for, towards, a place,** se diriger vers un endroit; se rendre dans un lieu; filer sur un endroit; **to m. for the door,** gagner la porte; se diriger vers la porte; **I was making for home,** je me rendais chez moi; **to m. for Paris,** se diriger vers, se rendre à, Paris, prendre le chemin de Paris; **he was making for Greece,** il était en route pour la Grèce; **the crowd made for the square,** la foule s'est portée vers la place; **he made for, after, at, me like a madman,** il s'est élancé, s'est précipité, sur moi comme un fou; **to m. for the sound of guns,** marcher au canon; *F:* **she made at me with her umbrella,** elle m'a menacé de son parapluie; *Nau:* **to m. for . . .,** faire route sur . . ., mettre le cap sur . . .; **ship making for Hull,** navire *m* à destination de Hull; **to m. for the open sea,** prendre le large; **to m. for the anchorage,** se rendre au mouillage. **2. this cannot m. for happiness,** cela ne peut pas contribuer au bonheur; **these agreements m. for peace,** ces accords tendent à maintenir la paix; **this fine weather makes for optimism,** ce beau temps porte à l'optimisme; **to m. against sth.,** nuire à, être contraire à, qch. **3. to m. as if, as though, to do sth.,** faire mine, faire semblant, de faire qch.; **he made as if to speak,** il a eu l'air de vouloir parler; **he made as if to strike me,** (i) il a fait un geste comme pour me frapper; (ii) il a fait semblant de vouloir me frapper. **4.** (*of tide*) se faire; (*of floodtide*) monter; (*of ebb*) baisser. **5.** *El:* (*of current*) **to m. and break,** s'interrompre et se rétablir.

III. (*compound verbs*) **1. make away,** *v.i. F:* **to m. away with sth.,** détruire, faire disparaître, enlever, qch.; dérober (de l'argent, etc.); **to m. away with s.o.,** tuer, descendre, supprimer, qn; **to m. away with oneself,** se suicider; se donner la mort.

2. make believe, *v.i.* (*esp. of children and politicians*) (jouer à) faire semblant.

3. make do, *v.* (*a*) *v.i.* **I need a hundred pounds but I could m. do with fifty,** j'ai besoin de cent livres mais cinquante feraient mon affaire; **with prices rising I can't m. do any longer,** maintenant que les prix montent je ne peux plus m'arranger avec ce que j'ai; **to m. do and mend,** rafistoler; (*b*) *v.tr.* **we'll have to m. the milk do,** il faut nous contenter du peu de lait que nous avons.

4. make off, *v.i. F:* se sauver; décamper, tourner court; s'éclipser, filer, déguerpir; gagner la porte; **to m. off with the cash,** filer avec l'argent; **he made off to America with the money,** il a filé sur l'Amérique avec l'argent; **somebody's made off with my overcoat,** on m'a volé, chipé, subtilisé, mon pardessus.

5. make out, (*a*) *v.tr.* faire, établir, dresser (une liste, etc.); dresser, rédiger (un mémoire); établir, dresser, relever (un compte); faire, tirer, créer (un chèque); **to m. out a cheque to s.o.,** établir un chèque au nom de qn; **to m. out a document in duplicate,** établir un document en double (exemplaire); (*b*) *v.tr.* établir, prouver (qch.); **how do you m. that out?** comment arrivez-vous à ce résultat, à cette conclusion? (ii) **to m. s.o. out to be richer than he is,** faire qn plus riche qu'il ne l'est; **they made out that they were friends of ours,** ils prétendaient être de nos amis; ils se disaient de nos amis; **he's not such a fool as people m. out,** il n'est pas aussi bête qu'on le dépeint, qu'on le croit, qu'on le fait; **the climate's not so bad as you m. out,** le climat n'est pas si mauvais que vous le dites; (*c*) *v.tr.* (i) comprendre (une énigme, un problème, un caractère); démêler (les raisons de qn, la signification de qch.); déchiffrer (une écriture); débrouiller (une affaire); **I can't m. the boy out,** ce garçon est une énigme pour moi; **I can't m. it out,** je ne puis m'y retrouver; je n'y comprends rien; c'est incompréhensible; (ii) distinguer, discerner (qch.); **to m. out a light,** reconnaître un feu; (*d*) *v.i. F:* (i) réussir, faire son chemin, prospérer, faire des progrès; aller, marcher, bien, mal; **he's making out very well,** il fait de bonnes affaires; **how do your children m. out at school?** comment vos enfants se débrouillent-ils au collège? **how did you m. out in the exam?** ça a marché, ton examen? (ii) subsister; **I can m. out on bread and water,** je peux vivre de pain et d'eau.

6. make over, *v.tr.* (i) céder, transférer, transmettre (**sth. to s.o.,** qch. à qn); **to m. over the whole of one's property to s.o.,** disposer de tous ses biens en faveur de qn; faire donation entière de ses biens à qn; faire l'abandon de tous ses biens à qn; (ii) refaçonner, arranger (un vêtement, une maison).

7. make up, (*a*) *v.tr.* (i) compléter, parfaire (une somme); parfournir (des commandes); combler, suppléer à (un déficit); **to m. up the difference,** parfaire la différence; **to m. up the even money,** faire l'appoint; **to m. up the missing numbers of a publication,** compléter sa collection d'une publication; (ii) **to m. up lost ground,** regagner le terrain perdu; **to m. up back payments,** solder l'arriéré; **to m. it up to s.o. for sth.,** dédommager qn de qch.; indemniser qn; **the lost day will be made up,** la journée chômée sera récupérée; (iii) faire (un paquet); *Pharm:* préparer, exécuter (une ordonnance); **to m. up goods into a parcel,** faire un paquet des marchandises; (iv) (α) faire, confectionner, façonner, monter (des vêtements); arranger (du tissu); **customers' own material made up,** on travaille à façon; tailleur à façon; (β) dresser (une liste); (γ) régler, établir, arrêter (un compte); régler, balancer (les livres); **to m. up one's accounts,** vider ses comptes; **to m. up a balance sheet,** confectionner un bilan; (δ) inventer, forger (une histoire, des excuses); **made-up story,** histoire inventée de toutes pièces; histoire faite à plaisir; **the whole thing is made up!** pure invention tout cela! (v) rassembler, réunir (une compagnie); rassembler (une somme d'argent); renformir (un mur); **to m. up the fire,** ajouter du combustible au feu; (re)charger le poêle; arranger le feu; *v.i. Typ:* **to m. up,** mettre en pages; (vi) former, composer (un ensemble); **all animals are made up of cells,** tous les animaux sont composés de cellules; **the bones and muscles that m. up the body,** les os et les muscles qui forment le corps; **this lens is made up of four elements,** cet objectif comporte quatre éléments; **the payments m. up a considerable total,** ces versements atteignent une somme considérable; **the train is made up at Crewe,** le train se forme à Crewe; (vii) **to m. (oneself) up,** se maquiller; *Th:* faire sa figure; (*of man*) se grimer; **to m. up for a part,** se faire la tête d'un rôle; **to m. s.o. up,** maquiller qn; (viii) **to m. up one's mind,** se décider, prendre son parti; (ix) arranger, accommoder (un différend); **to m. it up (again),** se réconcilier, se remettre bien ensemble; se raccommoder; (*b*) *v.i.* (i) **to m. up for lost time,** rattraper, réparer, le temps perdu; **to m. up for one's losses,** compenser ses pertes; se rattraper de ses pertes; **that will m. up for your losses,** cela vous dédommagera de vos pertes; **to m. up for one's faults,** racheter, réparer, ses erreurs; **that makes up for it,** c'est une compensation; **you've no garden but the terrace makes up for it,** vous n'avez pas de jardin, mais en revanche vous avez la terrasse; **to m. up for the lack of sth.,** suppléer au manque de qch.; **as there wasn't much meat I had to m. up with vegetables,** faute de viande il a fallu me rattraper sur les légumes; (ii) **to m. up on a ship, on a competitor,** gagner sur un navire, sur un concurrent; (iii) **to m. up to s.o.,** faire des avances, faire la cour, à qn; courtiser qn.

make-and-break ['meikənd'breik], *s.* (*a*) *El:* conjoncteur-disjoncteur *m*, *pl.* conjoncteurs-disjoncteurs; interrupteur-distributeur *m*, *pl.* interrupteurs-distributeurs; trembleur *m*, vibreur *m*, coupleur *m*; *I.C.E:* dispositif *m*, levier *m*, de rupture; autorupteur *m*; rupteur-distributeur; **m.-a.-b. cam,** came *f* de distribution d'allumage; **m.-a.-b. coil,** bobine *f* à rupteur, à trembleur; **m.-a.-b. current,** courant intermittent; **m.-a.-b. key,** brise-circuit *m inv*; *Tp:* **m.-a.-b. contact,** contact *m* repos-travail; (*b*) *Cmptr:* branchement *m*, débranchement *m*.

make-believe ['meikbili:v]. **1.** *s.* semblant *m*, feinte *f*, trompe-l'œil *m inv*; **that's all m.-b.,** tout cela est feint; tout ça c'est du chiqué; **all this cordiality is only m.-b.,** toute cette cordialité n'est qu'une comédie; **the land of m.-b.,** le pays des chimères. **2.** *a.* **m.-b. soldiers, etc.,** soldats, etc., pour rire; **he lives in a m.-b. world,** il vit dans un monde imaginaire.

make-do ['meikdu:], *s. F:* moyen *m* de fortune; **m.-do airfield,** terrain *m* d'atterrissement (i) de fortune, (ii) de secours.

makefast ['meikfa:st], *s. Nau:* amarre *f*.

maker ['meikər], *s.* **1.** faiseur, -euse; *Com: Ind:* fabricant *m* (de drap, etc.); constructeur *m* (de machines); **biscuit m.,** fabricant de biscuits. **2.** *Rel:* **our M., the M. of all,** le Créateur. **3.** *A: Lit:* auteur *m* (d'un livre, etc.). **4. m. up,** (i) *Typ:* metteur *m* en pages; (ii) *Th:* maquilleur, -euse; (iii) mesureur-emballeur-expéditeur *m*.

makeready ['meikredi], *s. Typ:* mise *f* en train.

makeshift ['meikʃift], *s.* pis aller *m*, expédient *m*; moyen *m* de fortune; dispositif *m* de circonstance, de fortune; **m. equipment,** installation *f* de fortune; **a m. peace,** une paix d'expédient; une paix telle quelle; **a m. government,** un gouvernement, des gouvernants, de rencontre; **a m. dinner,** un dîner de fortune.

makeup ['meikʌp], *s.* **1.** (*a*) composition *f*, arrangement *m* (de qch.); confection *f* (des vêtements); contexture *f*; (*b*) (*of pers.*) caractère *m*. **2.** (*a*) maquillage *m*; fard *m*; **eye, leg, body, m.,** maquillage pour les yeux, les jambes, le corps; **evening m.,** maquillage du soir; **m. bag,** *Th: etc:* **m. box,** trousse *f*, boîte *f*, à maquillage; **where's my m.?** où est mon rouge, ma poudre, etc.? **m. remover,** démaquillant *m*; **to remove one's m.,** enlever son maquillage; *Th: etc:* **m. man, girl,** maquilleur, -euse; (*b*) **Irving's m. in Hamlet,** la présentation physique de Hamlet, comme la comprenait Irving. **3.** *Typ:* mise *f* en pages; imposition *f*. **4.** invention *f*; histoire inventée (de toutes pièces). **5.** appoint *m*; (*of pipe, etc.*) **m. length,** pièce jointive; pièce de raccordement.

makeweight ['meikweit], *s.* complément *m* de poids; supplément *m*; **as a m.,** (i) pour parfaire le poids; (ii) pour faire nombre.

making ['meikiŋ], *s.* **1.** (*a*) fabrication *f* (de la toile, du papier); confection *f*, façon *f* (de vêtements); construction *f* (d'un pont, d'une machine); composition *f* (d'un poème); création *f* (du monde, d'un poste); **ingredients that go (in)to the m. of . . .,** ingrédients qui entrent dans la composition de. . .; **the marriage was none of her m.,** ce n'était pas elle qui avait arrangé le mariage; **the war was not of England's m.,** ce n'est pas l'Angleterre qui a déclenché la guerre, qui a voulu la guerre; **this incident was the m. of him,** c'est à cet incident qu'il devait sa fortune, tout son succès; **this failure was the m. of him,** cet échec a réformé son caractère; **that will be the m. of him,** cela fera sa fortune; cela le posera; **history in the m.,** l'histoire en train de se faire; la genèse de l'histoire; **mankind in the m.,** l'humanité en voie de progrès; (*b*) *El:* **m. and breaking,** fermeture *f* et ouverture *f* (du circuit). **2.** (*a*) **to have the makings of . . .,** avoir tout ce qu'il faut pour devenir. . .; **I have not the makings of a hero (in me),** je n'ai rien du héros; **he has the makings of a statesman,** il y a en lui l'étoffe d'un homme d'État; (*b*) **we've got the makings of a good cocktail here,** nous avons de quoi faire un bon cocktail; (*c*) *NAm:* **makings,** de quoi rouler une cigarette. **3. m. up,** (*a*) compensation *f* (**for losses, errors,** de pertes, d'erreurs); (*of pipe*) **m. up length,** pièce *f* de raccordement; **m. up strip,** cale *f* d'ajustage; (*b*) *Pharm:* préparation *f* (d'un médicament); (*c*) (i) confection *f*, façon *f* (de vêtements); (ii) *Com: Fin:* confection (d'un bilan); arrêté *m* (des comptes); clôture *f* (des livres); *St.Exch:* **m. up price,** cours *m* de compensation; (iii) invention *f* (d'une histoire, d'excuses); (*d*) *Typ:* **m. up and imposing,** mise *f* en pages; (*e*) composition, formation *f* (d'un ensemble); renformis *m* (d'un mur); (*f*) *Th: etc:* maquillage *m*; (*g*) arrangement *m*, raccommodement *m* (d'un differend).

mal- [mæl], *pref.* mal-; mé-.

Malabar ['mæləbɑːr]. **1.** *Pr.n. Geog:* Malabar *m*. **2.** (*a*) *a.* malabare; **the M. Coast,** la côte de Malabar; (*b*) *s.* Malabare *mf*. **3.** *s. Ling:* malabare *m*.

Malacca [mə'lækə]. **1.** *Pr.n. Geog:* Malacca; **M. Straits,** détroit *m* de Malacca. **2.** *s.* **M. (cane),** (canne *f* de) jonc *m*.

malaceous [mə'leiʃəs], *a. Bot:* pomacé.

Malachi ['mæləkai]. *Pr.n.m. B.Hist:* Malachie.

malachite ['mæləkait], *s. Miner:* malachite *f*; vert *m* de cuivre, de montagne; cendre verte; **m. green,** vert *m* malachite de cuivre, de montagne.

malacia [mə'leiʃiə], *s. Med:* malacie *f*, malacia *f*.

malacobdella [mæləkɔb'delə], *s. Ann:* malacobdelle *f*.

malacoderm ['mæləkoudəːm], *a. & s. Z: Ent:* malacoderme (*m*).

malacodermatous [mæləkou'dəːmətəs], *a. Z:* malacoderme.

Malacodermidae [mæləkou'dəːmidiː], *s.pl. Ent:* malacodermes *m*.

malacologist [mælə'kɔlədʒist], *s.* malacologiste *m*.

malacology [mælə'kɔlədʒi], *s.* malacologie *f*.

malacon ['mælәkɔn], *s. Miner:* malacon *m*, malakon *m*.

malacophilous [mælə'kɔfiləs], *a. Bot:* malacophile.

Malacopoda [mælə'kɔpədə], *s.pl. Z:* malacopodes *m*.

malacopterygian [mæləkɔptə'ridʒiən], *a. & s. Ich:* malacoptérygien (*m*).

Malacostraca [mælə'kɔstrəkə], *s.pl. Crust:* malacostracés *m*.

malacostracan [mælə'kɔstrəkən], *a. & s. Crust:* malacostracé (*m*).

malacotic [mælə'kɔtik], *a. Med:* hypocalcifié.

maladaptation [mælædæp'teiʃ(ə)n], *s. Biol: etc:* défaut *m* d'adaptation.

maladjusted [mælə'dʒʌstid], *a. & s.* inadapté, -ée.

maladjustment [mælə'dʒʌstmənt], *s.* (*a*) *Mec.E:* (i) défaut *m* d'ajustage; (ii) mauvais réglage; (*b*) *El: Elcs:* déréglage *m* (d'un appareil); désaccord *m*; (*c*) inadaptation *f*; **emotional m.,** déséquilibre émotif; *PolEc:* **m. in the balance of trade,** déséquilibre dans la balance commerciale.

maladministration [mælədminis'treiʃ(ə)n], *s.* mauvaise administration; mauvaise gestion (des affaires publiques, etc.); *Jur:* forfaiture *f*; **m. of justice,** prévarication *f*.

maladministrator [mæləd'ministreitər], *s. Jur:* forfaiteur *m*.

maladroit [mælæ'drɔit], *a.* maladroit.

maladroitly [mælæ'drɔitli], *adv.* maladroitement.

maladroitness [mælæ'drɔitnis], *s.* maladresse *f*.

malady ['mælədi], *s.* maladie *f*; mal *m*.

mala fide [mælə'faidiː], *a. & adv. Jur:* de mauvaise foi.

Malaga ['mæləgə]. **1.** *Pr.n. Geog:* Malaga *m*. **2.** *s.* vin *m* de Malaga; malaga *m*.

Malagasy [mælə'gæsi]. **1.** *Pr.n. Geog:* **(the) M. (Republic),** la République malgache. **2.** *Ethn:* (*a*) *a.* malgache, madécasse; (*b*) *s.* Malgache *mf*, Madécasse *mf*. **3.** *s. Ling:* malgache *m*.

malaguetta [mælə'getə], *s.* **m. (pepper),** graines *fpl* de Guinée, de paradis; poivre *m* de Guinée; malaguette *f*.

malaise [mæ'leiz], *s.* malaise *m*.

malakon ['mæləkɔn], *s. Miner:* malakon *m*, malacon *m*.

malalignment [mælə'lainmənt], *s.* alignement défectueux (des dents, etc.).

malanders ['mæləndəz], *s.pl. Vet:* malandre *f*, malandres *fpl*.

malapert ['mæləpəːt], *a. & s. A:* **1.** *a.* insolent, impertinent, malappris. **2.** *s.* insolent, -ente; péronnelle *f*.

malapropism ['mæləprɔpizm], *s.* **1.** emploi *m* de mots savants déformés, hors de propos; incongruité *f*. **2.** mot employé hors de propos.

malapropos [mælæprə'pou], *adv. & a.* mal à propos; inopportun; inopportunément.

malapterurus [mælæptə'ruːrəs], *s. Ich:* malapterurus *m*, malaptérure *m*.

malar ['meilər], *a. & s. Anat:* (os *m*) malaire (*m*).

malaria [mə'lɛəriə], *s. Med:* malaria *f*; fièvre paludéenne; paludisme *m*.

malarial [mə'lɛəriəl], *a. & s.* (*a*) *a.* malarique; malarien; **m. fever,** fièvre paludéenne; **m. infection,** infection paludéenne; **m. germ,** germe *m* du paludisme; (*b*) *s.* malarique *mf*.

malariotherapy [məlɛəriou'θerəpi], *s. Med:* malariathérapie *f*; impaludation *f*; paludothérapie *f*.

malarious [mə'lɛəriəs], *a.* **m. swamps,** marécages impaludés.

malate ['mæleit, 'mei-], *s. Ch:* malate *m*.

Malawi [mə'lɑːwi]. **1.** *Pr.n. Geog:* Malawi *m*. **2.** *s.* (*pers.*) Malawi *mf inv*.

malaxate ['mæləkseit], *v.tr.* malaxer.

malaxation [mælək'seiʃ(ə)n], *s.* malaxage *m*.

malaxator ['mæləkseitər], *s.* malaxeur *m* (à argile, à beurre, etc.).

Malay [mə'lei]. **1.** *Geog:* (*a*) *a.* malais; **the M. Peninsula,** la presqu'île Malaise; Malacca *m*; **the M. Archipelago,** la Malaisie; *Bot:* **M. apple,** janolac *m*; (*b*) *s.* Malais, -aise. **2.** *s. Ling:* malais *m*.

Malaya [mə'leiə], *Pr.n. Geog:* Malaisie *f*.

Malayan [mə'leiən]. *Geog:* (*a*) *a.* malais; (*b*) *s.* Malais, -aise.

Malayo-Polynesian [mə'leioupɔli'niːziən], (*a*) *a. Ethn:* malayo-polynésien; (*b*) *s. Ling:* malayo-polynésien *m*.

Malaysia [mə'leiʒə, -'leiziə]. *Pr.n. Geog:* Malaysia *f*; la Fédération de Grande Malaisie; Malaisie *f*.

Malaysian [mə'leiʒən, -'leiziən]. *Geog:* (*a*) *a.* malais; (*b*) *s.* Malais, -aise.

malbrouck ['mælbruk], *s. Z:* malbrouck *m*; (espèce de) cercopithèque *m*.

malconformation [mælkɔnfɔː'meiʃ(ə)n], *s. Med: etc:* mauvaise conformation.

malcontent ['mælkəntent], *a. & s.* mécontent, -ente.

maldevelopment [mældi'veləpmənt], *s. Med:* développement anormal; dysplasie *f*.

Maldive ['mɔːldiv]. *Pr.n. Geog:* **the M. Islands,** les Iles Maldives.

maldonite ['mɔːldənait], *s. Miner:* maldonite *f*.

male [meil]. **1.** *a.* (*a*) mâle; **m. sex,** sexe masculin; **m. child,** enfant *m* mâle; enfant du sexe masculin; **m. heir,** héritier *m* mâle; **a m. cousin,** un cousin; **a m. friend,** un ami; **m. line (of descent),** ligne masculine; **on the m. side,** du côté de la barbe; (*b*) **m. hormone,** hormone *f* mâle; **m. flower, fern,** fleur *f*, fougère *m*, mâle; (*c*) *Tchn:* mâle; **m. screw,** vis *f* mâle. **2.** *s.m.* mâle.

malediction [mæli'dikʃ(ə)n], *s.* malédiction *f*.

maledictory [mæli'dikt(ə)ri], *a.* de malédiction.

malefaction [mæli'fækʃ(ə)n], *s.* méfait *m*.

malefactor ['mælifæktər], *s.* malfaiteur, -trice.

malefic [mə'lefik], *a.* maléfique.

maleficence [mə'lefisəns], *s.* malfaisance *f*.

maleficent [mə'lefisənt], *a.* **1.** malfaisant (**to,** envers). **2.** (*of pers.*) criminel.

maleic [mə'liːik, -'leiik], *a. Ch:* (acide) maléique.

malesherbia [mæli'zəːbiə], *s. Bot:* malesherbia *f*.

Malesherbiaceae [mælizəːbi'eisiiː], *s.pl. Bot:* malesherbiacées *f*.

malevolence [mə'levələns], *s.* malveillance *f* (**towards,** envers).

malevolent [mə'levələnt], *a.* malveillant.

malevolently [mə'levələntli], *adv.* avec malveillance; (regarder) d'un œil malveillant.

malfeasance [mæl'fiːz(ə)ns], *s.* **1.** *Jur:* agissements *m* coupables; malversation *f*. **2.** méfait *m*.

malfeasant [mæl'fiːz(ə)nt], *a. Jur:* contrevenant; criminel.

malformation [mælfɔː'meiʃ(ə)n], *s. Med: etc:* malformation *f*, difformité *f*; défaut *m*, vice *m*, de conformation.

malformed [mæl'fɔːmd], *a.* mal conformé; difforme.

malfunction[1] [mæl'fʌŋkʃən], *s.* fonctionnement défectueux, irrégulier (d'un mécanisme, d'un organe); dérèglement *m*.

malfunction[2], *v.i.* fonctionner mal.

Mali[1] ['mɑːliː]. *Pr.n. Geog:* (*country*) le Mali.

Mali[2]. *Geog:* (*a*) *a.* malien; (*b*) *s.* (*pers.*) Malien, -ienne.

malic ['meilik, 'mæ-], *a. Ch:* malique.

malice ['mælis], *s.* **1.** (*a*) malice *f*, malveillance *f*, méchanceté *f*; rancune *f*; **out of m.,** par malice, par méchanceté; **he is without m.,** il est sans malice; **to bear m. to, towards, s.o., to bear s.o. m.,** vouloir du mal à qn, en vouloir à qn; garder rancune à qn; avoir de la rancune contre qn; **I bear him no m.,** je ne lui garde pas de rancune; **no m., I hope,** sans rancune, j'espère; (*b*) *A:* désir *m* de taquiner; malice, espièglerie *f*. **2.** *Jur:* intention criminelle, délictueuse; **with, of, through, m. prepense, with m. aforethought,** avec intention criminelle; avec préméditation; de propos délibéré.

malicious [mə'liʃəs], *a.* **1.** (*a*) méchant, malveillant; **m. rumours, gossip,** racontars malveillants; (*b*) rancunier; (*c*) *A:* taquin, espiègle, malicieux; malin, -igne. **2.** *Jur:* fait avec intention criminelle, délictueuse; criminel; **m. intent,** intention délictueuse; **m. destruction of property,** sabotage *m*; **m. prosecution,** poursuites intentées par malveillance.

maliciously [mə'liʃəsli], *adv.* **1.** (*a*) avec méchanceté, avec malveillance; (*b*) par rancune; (*c*) *A:* malicieusement; avec une intention taquine. **2.** *Jur:* avec intention criminelle; dans l'intention de nuire; avec préméditation.

maliciousness [mə'liʃəsnis], *s.* (*a*) méchanceté *f*, malveillance *f*; (*b*) malice *f*.

malign[1] [mə'lain], *a.* **1.** (*of thg*) pernicieux, nuisible. **2.** *Astrol:* (astre) malin; (planète) maligne. **3.** *Med:* malin, *f.* maligne. **4.** *A:* (*of pers.*) malveillant.

malign[2], *v.tr.* calomnier, diffamer, noircir (qn); dire du mal de (qn); **I've heard you maligned in every way,** on m'en a dit de toutes les couleurs sur votre compte; **much maligned man,** homme dont on dit beaucoup de mal (souvent sans raison).

malignancy [mə'lignənsi], *s.* **1.** malignité *f*, méchanceté *f*, malveillance *f*. **2.** *Med:* malignité, virulence *f* (d'une maladie).

malignant [mə'lignənt], *a.* **1.** (*a*) malin, *f.* maligne; méchant; (*b*) *Astrol:* = MALIGN[1] 2. **2.** *Med:* malin; **m. fever,** fièvre maligne; **m. tumour,** tumeur maligne. **3.** *s.pl. Hist:* **the malignants,** les dissidents (opposés au parti de Cromwell); les malcontents; les partisans de Charles Ier.

malignantly [mə'lignəntli], *adv.* avec malignité; méchamment.

maligner [mə'lainər], *s.* calomniateur, -trice; diffamateur, -trice.

malignity [mə'ligniti], *s.* = MALIGNANCY.

Malines [mæ'liːn]. *Pr.n. Geog:* Malines; **M. lace,** point *m*, dentelle *f*, de Malines; *Husb:* **M. fowl,** coucou *m* de Malines.

malinger [mə'liŋgər], *v.i.* faire le malade; simuler une maladie, *F:* tirer au flanc.

malingerer [mə'liŋgərər], *s.* faux malade, simulateur *m*, *F:* tireur *m* au flanc.

malingering [mə'liŋgəriŋ], *s.* simulation *f* (de maladie); *F:* tirage *m* au flanc.

malinowskite [mæli'nɔfskait], *s. Miner:* malinofskite *f*, malinowskite *f*.

mall [mɔːl], *s.* **1.** *Games: A:* (*a*) mail *m*, maillet *m* (pour le jeu de mail); (*b*) le (jeu de) mail; (*c*) l'allée *f* (du jeu de mail). **2.** (*a*) mail; promenade publique; (*b*) [mæl] **the M.,** le Mall (avenue qui longe St James's Park, à Londres); (*c*) *NAm:* centre commercial (fermé à la circulation automobile).

mallard ['mælɑːd], *s. Orn:* canard *m* col-vert, canard sauvage, *Fr.C:* canard malard; *NAm:* **m. shooting,** chasse au canard.

mallardite ['mælədait], *s. Miner:* mallardite *f.*

malleability [mæliə'biliti], *s.* malléabilité *f.*

malleabilization [mæliəbilai'zeiʃ(ə)n], *s. Metall:* malléabilisation *f.*

malleable ['mæliəbl], *a.* malléable; forgeable; (fer) doux; (*of pers.*) **m. nature,** caractère *m* malléable.

malleabl(e)ize ['mæliəb(ə)laiz], *v.tr. Metall:* malléabiliser.

malleal, mallear ['mæliəl, -iər], *a. Anat:* malléal, malléaire.

mallee ['mæli:], *s. Bot:* (espèce d')eucalyptus *m* d'Australie.

mallein ['mæli:in], *s. Vet:* malléine *f.*

malleinization [mæli:inai'zeiʃ(ə)n], *s. Vet:* malléin(is)ation *f.*

malleinize ['mæli:inaiz], *v.tr. Vet:* malléin(is)er.

mallenders ['mæləndəz], *s.pl. Vet:* malandre(s) *f(pl).*

malleolar [mæ'li:oulər], *a. Anat:* malléolaire.

malleolus, *pl.* **-li** [mə'li:ələs, -lai], *s. Anat:* malléole *f.*

mallet ['mælit], *s.* **1.** (*a*) maillet *m,* mailloche *f;* (*b*) tapette *f* (pour enfoncer les bouchons). **2.** *Games:* maillet (de croquet, de polo).

malleus, *pl.* **-ei** ['mæliəs, -iai], *s. Anat:* marteau *m* (de l'oreille).

Mallophaga [mæ'lɔfəgə], *s.pl. Ent:* mallophages *m.*

mallow ['mælou], *s. Bot:* (*a*) (*often pl. with sg. const.*) mauve *f;* **Jews' m.,** guimauve potagère; **rose m.,** rose trémière; passe-rose *f, pl.* passe-rose(s); **tree m.,** lavatère *f* (en arbre); **Indian m.,** (i) abutilon *m;* (ii) sida *m;* (*b*) guimauve, althée *f.*

malm [mɑ:m], *s.* **1.** *Geol:* malm *m.* **2.** *Agr: etc:* marne *f.*

malmignatte [mælmi'njæt], *s. Arach:* malmignat(t)e *f.*

malmsey ['mɑ:mzi], *s.* vin *m* de Malvoisie; malvoisie *m or f.*

malnutrition [mælnju'triʃ(ə)n], *s.* malnutrition *f;* sous-alimentation *f;* alimentation défectueuse.

malocclusion [mælə'klu:ʒ(ə)n], *s. Dent:* inocclusion *f.*

malodorous [mæ'loudərəs], *a.* malodorant; vireux, nauséabond.

malonate ['mæləneit], *s. Ch:* malonate *m.*

malonic [mə'lounik], *a. Ch:* malonique.

malonylurea [mælənilju'riə], *s. Bio-Ch:* malonylurée *f.*

malpighia [mæl'pigiə], *s. Bot:* malpighia *f,* malpighie *f.*

Malpighiaceae [mælpigi'eisii:], *s.pl. Bot:* malpighiacées *f.*

Malpighian [mæl'pigiən], *a. Anat:* (corpuscules, etc.) de Malpighi.

malposition [mælpə'ziʃ(ə)n], *s.* (*a*) *Obst:* malposition *f,* position anormale; (*b*) *Dent:* malposition.

malpractice [mæl'præktis], *s.* **1.** méfait *m.* **2.** *Jur:* (*a*) négligence *f,* incurie *f* (d'un médecin); (*b*) malversation *f.*

malt[1] [mɔ:lt], *s. Brew: etc:* malt *m;* **m. liquor,** bière *f;* **m. kiln,** touraille *f;* **m. loft,** germoir *m;* **m. floor,** côtière *f;* *Pharm: etc:* **m. extract, extract of m.,** extrait *m* de malt.

malt[2]. **1.** *v.tr. Brew:* malter (l'orge); convertir (l'orge) en malt. **2.** *v.i.* (*of grain*) se convertir en malt.

Malta ['mɔ:ltə]. *Pr.n. Geog:* Malte *f;* *Med:* **M. fever,** fièvre *f* de Malte; *Hist:* **the Knights of M.,** les Chevaliers *m* (de l'ordre) de Malte.

maltase ['mɔ:lteis], *s. Ch:* maltase *f.*

malted ['mɔ:ltid], *a.* (lait) malté.

Maltese [mɔ:l'ti:z]. **1.** *a.* (*a*) *Geog:* maltais; (*b*) *Hist:* de l'ordre de Malte; (*c*) *Her: Mec.E: etc:* **M. cross,** croix *f* de Malte. **2.** *s. Geog:* Maltais, -aise. **3.** *s. Ling:* maltais *m.* **4.** *a. & s.* **M. (dog),** (chien) maltais.

maltha ['mælθə], *s. Miner:* malthe *f;* bitume glutineux; pissasphalte *m.*

malthenes ['mælθi:nz], *s.pl. Ch:* malthènes *m.*

malithite ['mælθait], *s. Miner:* malthe *f.*

malthouse ['mɔ:lthaus], *s. Brew:* malterie *f.*

Malthusian [mæl'θ(j)u:ziən], *a.* malthusien.

Malthusianism [mæl'θ(j)u:ziənizm], *s.* malthusianisme *m.*

malting ['mɔ:ltiŋ], *s. Brew:* **1.** maltage *m;* **m. water,** trempe *f.* **2.** malterie *f.*

maltman, *pl.* **-men** ['mɔ:ltmən], *s.m.* malteur.

maltose ['mɔ:ltous], *s. Ch:* maltose *m.*

maltreat [mæl'tri:t], *v.tr.* maltraiter, malmener, brutaliser (qn); maltraiter, déshonorer (un tableau, un arbre, etc.).

maltreating, maltreatment [mæl'tri:tiŋ, -mənt], *s.* mauvais traitement.

maltster ['mɔ:ltstər], *s.m.* malteur.

malurine ['mæljur(a)in], *s. Orn:* malure *m.*

Malvaceae [mæl'veisii:], *s.pl. Bot:* malvacées *f.*

malvaceous [mæl'veiʃəs], *a. Bot:* malvacé; de la famille des malvacées.

Malvasia [mælvæ'si:ə, -'zi:ə]. *Pr.n. Geog:* Malvoisie *f,* Malvasia *f.*

malversation [mælvə:'seiʃ(ə)n], *s.* **1.** malversation *f.* **2.** mauvaise administration, gestion *f* coupable (**of public money,** de fonds publics).

mam [mæm], *s.f. F:* maman.

mamba ['mæmbə], *s. Rept:* mamba *m.*

mamelon ['mæmilən], *s.* mamelon *m.*

mameluke ['mæmilu:k], *s. Hist:* mamel(o)uk *m.*

mamill- ['mæmil], *see* **mam(m)ill-.**

mam(m)a ['mæmɑ:, mə'mɑ:], *s.f. F:* maman.

mamma, *pl.* **-ae** ['mæmə, -i:], *s. Anat:* mamelle *f.*

mammal ['mæməl], *s.* mammifère *m.*

Mammalia [mæ'meiliə], *s.pl.* mammifères *m.*

mammalian [mæ'meiliən], *a. & s.* mammifère (*m*).

mammalogical [mæmə'lɔdʒikl], *a.* mammalogique.

mammalogist [mæ'mælədʒist], *s.* mammalogiste *mf.*

mammalogy [mæ'mælədʒi], *s.* mammalogie *f.*

mammary ['mæməri], *a. Anat:* mammaire; **the m. glands,** *s.* **the mammaries,** les glandes *f* mammaires; les mammaires *f;* **m. tissue,** tissu *m* mamellaire.

mammate ['mæmeit], *a.* mammifère.

mammectomy [mæ'mektəmi], *s. Surg:* mastectomie *f, F:* mammectomie *f.*

mammee [mæ'mi:], *s. Bot:* mammea *m,* mammée *f;* arbre *m* aux mamelles; abricotier *m* de Saint-Domingue.

mammiferous [mæ'mifərəs], *a. Z:* mammifère.

mammiform ['mæmifɔ:m], *a.* mammiforme.

mam(m)illa, *pl.* **-ae** [mæ'milə, -i:], *s. Anat:* mamelon *m.*

mam(m)illaplasty [mæmilə'plæsti], *s. Surg:* mamilloplastie *f.*

mam(m)illary ['mæmiləri], *a.* (*a*) *Anat:* mamillaire; (*b*) mammiforme; (*c*) *Anat: Geog:* mamelonné.

mam(m)illate(d) ['mæmileit(id)], *a. Anat: Geog:* mamelonné.

mam(m)illiform [mæ'milifɔ:m], *a.* mamelliforme.

mammitis [mæ'maitis], *s.* (*a*) *Med:* mastite, *F:* mammite *f;* (*b*) *Vet:* mammite.

Mammon ['mæmən]. *Pr.n. B:* Mammon *m;* **you cannot serve God and M.,** vous ne pouvez servir Dieu et l'Argent.

mammoth ['mæməθ]. **1.** *s. Paleont:* mammouth *m.* **2.** *a.* géant, monstre; énorme, gigantesque, colossal; *Com:* **m. reduction,** rabais géant.

mammy ['mæmi], *s.f.* **1.** *F:* maman. **2.** *U.S:* (*a*) bonne d'enfants noire; (*b*) *Pej:* noire. **3.** (*in W. Africa*) **m. bus,** vieux car (qui transporte les gens au marché, etc.).

mampalon ['mæmpələn], *s. Z:* cynogale *f.*

man[1], *pl.* **men** [mæn, men], *s.m.* **1.** (*a*) (*human being*) homme; **the rights of m.,** les droits de l'homme; **God was made m.,** Dieu se fit homme; **one can see, recognize, the hand of m. in it,** on y reconnaît la main de l'homme; *A:* **accommodation for m. and beast,** ici on loge à pied et à cheval; **this food's not fit for m. nor beast,** un chien ne mangerait pas cela; **every m.,** tout le monde; tous; **any man,** n'importe qui; **I don't think any m. could do it,** je ne vois personne capable de le faire; **any m., every m. alive, on earth, knows that . . .,** tout le monde sait que . . .; **ask any m.,** demandez à n'importe qui; **some men think that . . .,** certains pensent que . . .; il y a des gens qui pensent que . . .; **few men,** peu de gens; **no m. living could . . .,** personne n'est capable de . . .; **no man's land,** (i) terrains *m* vagues; (ii) *Mil:* zone *f* neutre, terrain inoccupé entre les lignes adverses; **a m. has a right to speak,** on a bien le droit de parler; **a m. must live,** il faut bien vivre; **what could a m. do in such a case?** qu'est-ce qu'on pouvait faire, que faire, en pareil cas? **with initiative a m. can achieve anything,** on peut faire n'importe quoi si on a de l'initiative; (*b*) (*mankind*) l'homme; **the brain of m.,** le cerveau de l'homme; **m. proposes, God disposes,** l'homme propose et Dieu dispose; **m. does not live by bread alone,** on ne se nourrit pas que de pain; (*c*) *Theol:* **the inner m.,** l'homme intérieur; **the old, the new, m.,** le vieil homme, le nouvel homme; *F:* **the inner m.,** l'estomac *m;* **to satisfy the inner m.,** se restaurer; bien manger; (*d*) *Ind: etc:* **m. hour,** heure *f* de travail, de main-d'œuvre; heure-homme *f, pl.* heures-homme; **m. day,** journée *f* de travail. **2.** (*adult male*) homme; (*a*) **men and women,** les hommes et les femmes; *P.N:* (*on public convenience*) **men,** messieurs; **I've lived here m. and boy for forty years,** j'habite ici depuis mon plus jeune âge, ce qui fait quarante ans; **a helpful m. showed us the way,** un homme bien disposé nous a montré le chemin; **she's a m. hater,** elle déteste tous les hommes; *Com:* **men's department,** rayon *m* hommes; **m. for m.,** homme pour homme; **between m. and m.,** d'homme à homme; **may I speak to you as m. to m.?** puis-je parler d'homme à homme? **to fight m. against m.,** se battre homme à homme; **they were killed to a m.,** ils furent tués jusqu'au dernier; **they replied as one m.,** ils répondirent d'une seule voix, comme un seul homme; **I like him as a m.,** je l'aime comme homme; **to show oneself a m.,** se montrer homme; **to make a m. of s.o.,** faire un homme de qn; rendre qn viril; **to bear sth. like a m.,** supporter qch. avec courage; **to be m. enough to refuse,** avoir assez de courage pour refuser; **he is not the m. to (refuse, etc.),** il n'est pas homme à (refuser, etc.); **he seems to be the very m. for the job,** il paraît tout indiqué pour ce travail; **I'm your m.,** (i) je suis votre homme; je vous suis tout acquis; (ii) cela ma va! **he's just the m. for me,** c'est mon homme; **to be one's own m.,** (i) être maître de soi; (ii) ne dépendre que de soi; s'appartenir; être à soi; **I'm my own m. again,** je suis de nouveau indépendant, libre de mes activités; **he's not the m. for that,** il n'est pas fait pour cela; **a man's m.,** un vrai homme, un homme que les autres hommes admirent; **a lady's m.,** un galant; *Pej:* **what are you doing here, my m.?** qu'est-ce que vous faites là, dites donc! *F:* **look at that, m.!** regarde un peu mon vieux! *F:* **m., you're crazy!** mais mon pauvre vieux, tu es fou! *F: esp. U.S:* **(m. oh) m.!** dis donc! ben alors! **come here, young m.!** venez ici (i) jeune homme, (ii) mon petit! *O:* **goodbye old m.!** au revoir, mon vieux! (*b*) **an old m.,** un vieillard; **a dirty old m.,** un vieux paillard; **a dangerous m.,** un esprit dangereux; **an ambitious m.,** un ambitieux; **the head m.,** le chef; **a dead m.,** (i) un mort; (ii) *F:* (*empty bottle*) un cadavre; *Rail: etc:* **dead man's handle,** l'homme-mort; **he's an important, *F:* a big m.,** c'est une personnalité; *F:* c'est quelqu'un; **a small m.,** (i) un petit commerçant; (ii) un rien du tout; *Pej:* **the m. Thomas,** le nommé, le dit Thomas; **this m. Thomas,** (i) Thomas que voilà; ce vaurien de Thomas; (*c*) **the men of Somerset,** les originaires, les habitants, du Somerset; **an Oxford m.,** (i) un originaire, un habitant, d'Oxford; (ii) un étudiant de l'Université d'Oxford; (iii) un homme qui a fait ses études à l'Université d'Oxford; (*d*) **odd-job m.,** homme à tout faire; *F:* **the weather m.,** Monsieur Météo. **3.** (*husband, lover*) **m. and wife,** mari et femme; **to live as m. and wife,** vivre maritalement; faire ménage ensemble; **he made them m. and wife,** il les a mariés; *F:* **her m.,** son mari, son homme; *F:* **my old m.,** (i) mon mari, mon homme; (ii) mon père, le vieux; *F:* **my young m.,** (i) mon bon ami; (ii) mon fiancé. **4.** (*a*) *Hist:* (*vassal*) homme; (*b*) (*manservant*) domestique, valet; (*c*) *Ind: etc:* **employers and men,** les patrons et les ouvriers; (*d*) *Mil:* **officers, N.C.O.'s and men,** officiers, sous-officiers, et hommes de troupe; (*e*) *Sp:* joueur; *Cr:* **twelfth m.,** le joueur de réserve; (*lacrosse*) **third m.,** demi. **5.** *Games:* (*chess*) pièce *f;* (*draughts*) pion *m.*

man[2], *v.tr.* **(manned) 1.** (*a*) fournir du personnel à (une organisation, etc.); être affecté à (une organisation, etc.); assurer le service d'(une machine), la manœuvre d'(un appareil); être membre de l'équipe d'(un avion, etc.); **to m. the assembly line,** travailler à la chaîne de montage; **to m. a crane,** assurer la manœuvre d'une grue; **to m. a night shift,** composer une équipe de nuit; (*b*) *Mil:* **to m. a fort,** mettre une garnison dans un fort; occuper, garnir, un fort; **to m. a trench,** occuper, garnir, une tranchée; **to m. a gun,** (i) mettre les servants d'une pièce à leur poste; (ii) servir, manœuvrer, une pièce; **each gun was manned,** (i) les servants *m* de chaque pièce étaient à leur poste; (ii) toutes les pièces étaient servies; (*c*) *Nau:* armer, équiper (un canot); **boat manned by . . .,** embarcation montée par . . .; **fully manned boat,** canot *m* à armement complet; **to m. a prize,** amariner, armer, une prise; **to m. a rope,** se mettre à, sur, une manœuvre; **to m. the pumps,** armer les pompes; *Navy:* (*in salute, etc.*) **to m. ship,** faire passer l'équipage à la bande; **to m. the yards,** monter les vergues; **man the side!** du monde sur le bord! **2. to m. oneself,** se fortifier; se donner du cœur; s'armer de courage. **3.** *Ven:* (*falconry*) apprivoiser, affaiter.

Man[3]. *Pr.n. Geog:* **the Isle of M.,** l'île *f* de Man.

manacle[1] ['mænəkl], *s. usu. pl.* **manacles,** (i) menottes *f;* (ii) chaînes *f;* entraves *f.*

manacle[2], *v.tr.* mettre les menottes à (qn); emmenotter (qn).

manage ['mænidʒ], *v.tr.* **1.** (*a*) manier (un outil, un instrument); (*b*) **to m. the stage effects with great skill,** diriger, ménager, avec beaucoup d'habileté les effets de scène. **2.** conduire (une entreprise, etc.); administrer, diriger, gérer (une affaire, une société, une banque, etc.); gouverner (une banque); régir (une propriété); mener (une affaire); **to m. s.o.'s affairs,** gérer les affaires de qn; **to m. the household,** diriger l'intérieur; **to m. a quarry,** diriger l'exploitation d'une carrière; **to have a fortune to m.,** être à la tête d'une fortune; **he knows how to m. his (own) business,** il sait bien mener sa barque. **3.** gouverner, mater (qn); venir à bout de (qn); tenir (des enfants, etc.); maîtriser, dompter (un animal); **to know how to m. s.o.,** savoir prendre qn; **he**

is a difficult person to m., il faut savoir le prendre. 4. arranger, conduire (une affaire); **to m. to do sth.,** s'arranger pour faire qch.; arriver, parvenir, à faire qch.; faire en sorte, venir à bout, de faire qch.; trouver moyen de faire qch.; **I shall m. it,** j'en viendrai à bout; ça ira; **I think I can m. it,** je crois que je pourrai le faire; **I must m. it,** il faut que j'y arrive; **I know how to m. it,** je sais comment m'y prendre; je m'y connais; **he managed it very cleverly,** il en est venu à bout très adroitement; il ne s'y est pas mal pris; **if I can see how to m. it,** si je vois moyen de le faire; **at last he managed to get rid of it,** il a réussi enfin à s'en débarrasser; **I shall never m. to learn it,** jamais je n'arriverai, je ne réussirai, à l'apprendre; **I managed to have him put in my battalion,** j'ai réussi à, j'ai trouvé moyen de, le faire placer dans mon bataillon; **to m. matters so well that . . .,** faire tant et si bien que . . .; **I don't know how they managed it,** (i) je ne sais pas comment ils en sont venus à bout; (ii) je ne sais pas comment ils firent leur compte, (mais . . .); **he managed to fail at the oral,** il a trouvé moyen de se faire recaler à l'oral; **how do you m. not to dirty your hands?** comment faites-vous pour ne pas vous salir les mains? **he managed to profit by it,** il a su en profiter; **I managed to master my anger,** j'ai su maîtriser ma colère; **a hundred pounds is the most that I can m.,** cent livres, c'est tout ce que je peux faire (pour vous); **he managed to see the minister,** il est arrivé jusqu'au ministre; **if you can m. to see him,** si vous pouvez vous arranger pour le voir; **I managed to see him again,** j'ai pu le revoir; **try to m. to have everything done methodically,** tâchez d'arriver à ce que tout se fasse avec ordre; **can you m. a few more cherries?** pouvez-vous manger encore quelques cerises? 5. *v.i.* **she manages well,** (i) elle sait s'y prendre; (ii) elle est bonne maîtresse de maison, bonne ménagère; **m. as best you can,** arrangez-vous comme vous pourrez; débrouillez-vous; **we shall m. better next time,** nous ferons mieux la prochaine fois; **with your help I shall m. all right,** avec votre aide je m'arrangerai très bien, je me tirerai d'affaire, je m'en tirerai; **he'll m. all right,** il saura bien se retourner; il se débrouillera; **with ten pounds I could m.,** avec dix livres je pourrais arriver; **we could just m.,** on vivait bien juste; on arrivait juste à se tirer d'embarras; **perhaps we can m. with that,** peut-être cela suffira-t-il; **how will you m. about the children?** et pour les enfants, comment ferez-vous? **how did you m. since you didn't speak Spanish?—Oh, we managed!** comment faisiez-vous, puisque vous ne parliez pas l'espagnol?—on s'est débrouillé! on s'est tiré d'affaire (tout de même)!

manageable ['mænidʒəbl], *a.* 1. (*of thg*) maniable; (canot *m*) manœuvrable. 2. (*of pers.*) maniable, traitable, docile, facile à diriger, gouvernable. 3. (*of undertaking*) praticable, faisable; **business grown too big to be m.,** entreprise devenue si grosse qu'on ne peut plus la diriger.

management ['mænidʒmənt], *s.* 1. (*a*) maniement *m* (d'un outil, des hommes, des affaires); (*b*) direction *f*, conduite *f* (d'une affaire); gérance *f*, gestion *f* (d'une usine, d'une propriété); exploitation *f* (d'une carrière, etc.); **state m.,** exploitation *f* en régie; **m. science,** recherche opérationnelle; science *f* de la gestion; **business m.,** gestion des affaires; **personnel m.,** direction *f*, administration *f*, du personnel; **m. consultant,** ingénieur-conseil *m*, *pl.* ingénieurs-conseils; conseil *m* en gestion; conseiller *m* de direction; **m. committee,** comité *m* de direction; **bad m.,** mauvaise organisation; **owing to bad m.,** faute d'organisation; **under new m.,** (i) changement *m* de propriétaire; (ii) nouvelle direction. 2. adresse *f*; savoir-faire *m*. 3. *coll.* les administrateurs *m*; les directeurs *m*; l'administration *f*, la direction; **the m. regrets any inconvenience caused by the rebuilding,** la direction prie les clients de l'excuser de tout dérangement causé par la reconstruction.

manager ['mænidʒər], *s.* 1. (*a*) directeur *m*, gérant *m* (d'une société, etc.); administrateur *m*, gestionnaire *m* (de biens); régisseur *m* (d'une propriété); *Cin: Sp: F:* manager *m*; **joint m.,** cogérant *m*; **general m.,** directeur général; **acting m.,** directeur, gérant, intérimaire; **business m.,** (i) gérant d'affaires; (ii) directeur commercial; (iii) *Journ:* administrateur; (iv) *Th:* impresario *m* (d'une actrice, etc.); **branch m.,** directeur de succursale; **departmental m.,** chef *m* de service; **district m.,** directeur régional; **engineering m.,** directeur technique; **production m.,** directeur de la production, chef de l'ordonnancement; **sales m.,** directeur commercial; **office m.,** chef de bureau; **personnel, staff, m.,** chef, directeur, du personnel; *Rail:* **traffic m.,** chef de l'exploitation; *Ind:* **works m.,** chef du service (des) ateliers; directeur d'usine; (*b*) *U.S:* chef (d'un parti politique); **city m.,** chef des services municipaux. 2. ménager, -ère; **she's a good m.,** elle est bonne ménagère, bonne maîtresse de maison; **he's no m.,** il n'a aucune entente des affaires, aucun sens pratique; **what a capital m. you are!** comme vous vous entendez bien à arranger les choses! 3. *Jur:* **receiver and m.,** administrateur (d'une faillite, d'une succession grevée); syndic *m* de faillite.

manageress ['mænidʒəres], *s.f.* directrice, gérante; **joint m.,** cogérante.

managerial [mænə'dʒiəriəl], *a.* directorial, -aux; **the m. staff,** les cadres *m*; **m. position,** poste *m* de commande.

managership ['mænidʒəʃip], *s.* direction *f*, gérance *f*; intendance *f*; gouvernement *m* (d'une entreprise, etc.).

managing[1] ['mænidʒiŋ], *a.* 1. directeur, -trice; gérant; **m. director,** (i) administrateur directeur; (ii) administrateur délégué; (iii) administrateur gérant; **m. clerk,** *Adm: Com:* chef *m* de bureau; commis *m* chef; commis principal. 2. *usu. Pej:* autoritaire; **a m. woman,** une maîtresse femme.

managing[2], *s.* = MANAGEMENT 1.

manakin ['mænəkin], *s. Orn:* manakin *m*.

Manasseh [mə'næsi]. *Pr.n.m. B.Hist:* Manassé.

man-at-arms, *pl.* **men-at-arms** [mænət'ɑ:mz, men-], *s.m. A:* homme d'armes.

manatee [mænə'ti:], *s. Z:* lamantin *m*; **m. butter,** graisse *f* de lamantin.

manbarklak ['mænbɑ:klæk], *s.* (*a*) (*tree*) eschweilera *m*; (*b*) (*timber*) manbarklak *m*.

Manchester ['mæn(t)ʃistər]. *Pr.n. Geog:* Manchester; *O:* **M. goods, wares,** produits cotonniers; tissus *m* de coton; *Pol.Ec:* **the M. School,** l'école *f* de Manchester; les libre-échangistes *m*.

manchineel [mæntʃi'ni:l], *s. Bot:* 1. mancenille *f*. 2. **m. (tree),** mancenillier *m*.

Manchu [mæn'tʃu:]. 1. *Ethn:* (*a*) *a.* mandchou; *Hist:* **the M. dynasty,** la dynastie mandchoue; (*b*) *s.* Mandchou, -oue. 2. *s. Ling:* mandchou *m*.

Manchukuo [mæntʃu'kwou]. *Pr.n. Hist:* Mandchoukouo *m*.

Manchuria [mæn'tʃu:riə]. *Pr.n. Geog:* Mandchourie *f*.

Manchurian [mæn'tʃu:riən]. 1. *Geog:* (*a*) *a.* mandchou; (*b*) *s.* Mandchou, -oue. 2. *Orn: a.* **M. crane,** grue blanche de Mandchourie.

manciple ['mænsipl], *s. Hist:* intendant *m*, économe *m*, dépensier *m* (d'un collège, d'une communauté, etc.).

Mancunian [mæŋ'kju:niən], *a. & s. Geog:* (originaire, habitant, -ante) de Manchester.

mandamus [mæn'deiməs], *s. Jur:* mandement *m* (de la *Court of Queen's, King's, Bench* à une cour inférieure, à un fonctionnaire, etc.).

mandarin[1] ['mændərin], *s.* 1. *Chinese Hist:* mandarin *m*; *Toys:* **nodding m.,** branle-tête *m inv.*; *Orn:* **m. duck,** canard *m* mandarin. 2. *F:* haut fonctionnaire; mandarin.

mandarin[2], **mandarine** ['mændəri:n], *s.* 1. *Bot:* mandarine *f*; **m. orange tree,** mandarinier *m*. 2. *Dist:* mandarine. 3. *a. & s.* (*colour*) **m. (orange, yellow),** mandarine *inv.*

mandatary ['mændət(ə)ri], *s. Jur:* mandataire *mf*.

mandate[1] ['mændeit], *s.* 1. *Lit:* commandement *m*, ordre *m*. 2. (*a*) *Hist: Jur:* mandement *m*; *Ecc.Jur: Scot.Jur:* mandat *m*; (*b*) *Bank:* **m. form,** lettre *f* de signatures autorisées. 3. *Pol:* (*a*) *Hist:* mandat; **international m.,** mandat international (donné par la Société des Nations); **the m. for Palestine,** le mandat sur la Palestine; **to confer a m. on a power,** attribuer un mandat à une puissance; (*b*) **electoral m.,** mandat de député; **the government has no m. to ruin the country,** personne n'a autorisé le gouvernement à, n'a attribué un mandat au gouvernement de, ruiner le pays.

mandate[2], *v.tr. Hist:* **to m. a country to one of the powers,** attribuer sous mandat un pays à une des puissances; mettre un pays sous le mandat d'une des Puissances; **the mandated territories,** les territoires *m* sous mandat.

mandatory ['mændət(ə)ri]. 1. *a.* (*a*) qui prescrit, qui enjoint; **m. writ,** mandement *m* impératif; (*b*) obligatoire; **m. instructions,** mandat impératif; (*c*) *Hist:* **m. states,** états *m* mandataires. 2. *s.* = MANDATARY.

mandatum [mæn'deitəm], *s. Ecc:* mandatum *m*; mandé *m*.

mandible ['mændibl], *s.* 1. *Z:* mandibule *f*. 2. *Anat:* mâchoire inférieure.

mandibular [mæn'dibjulər], *a. Z:* mandibulaire.

mandibulate [mæn'dibjuleit], *a.* (insecte) mandibulé; (organe *m*) mandibulaire.

mandola [mæn'doulə], *s. Mus:* mandore *f*.

mandolin(e) ['mændəlin], *s. Mus:* mandoline *f*.

mandolinist ['mændəlinist], *s. Mus:* mandoliniste *mf*.

mandora [mæn'dɔ:rə], *s. Mus:* mandore *f*.

mandorla [mæn'dɔ:lə], *s. Art:* mandorle *f*.

mandragora [mæn'drægərə], *s.* = MANDRAKE.

mandrague ['mændræg], *s. Fish:* madrague *f*.

mandrake ['mændreik], *s. Bot:* 1. mandragore *f*; anthropomorphe *m*. 2. *NAm:* podophylle *m* en bouclier.

mandrel[1], **mandril** ['mændril], *Mec.E:* 1. mandrin *m*, arbre *m* (de tour); douille filetée; **chucking m.,** mandrin pour tour en l'air; **hollow m.,** mandrin à manchon. 2. (*a*) *Metalw:* mandrin (pour évaser les tubes); (*b*) (*for rings*) triboulet *m*. 3. *Dial:* pic *m* (de mineur) à deux pointes.

mandrel[2], *v.tr.* mandriner, évaser (un tube).

mandrill ['mændril], *s. Z:* mandrill *m*.

manducable ['mændjukəbl], *a.* manducable.

manducate ['mændjukeit], *v.tr.* mâcher; mastiquer (chaque bouchée).

manducation [mændju'keiʃ(ə)n], *s.* (*a*) mastication *f* (des aliments); (*b*) *Ecc:* manducation *f*; participation actuelle à l'eucharistie.

manducatory [mændju'keitəri], *a.* masticatoire.

mane [mein], *s.* crinière *f* (du cheval, du lion, etc.); **the m. and tail,** les crins *m* (d'un cheval); **horse with flowing m. and tail,** cheval à tous crins; **hog m.,** crinière coupée en brosse.

maneater ['mæni:tər], *s.* (*pl.* **maneaters**) 1. (*of pers.*) anthropophage *m*, cannibale *m*. 2. (*of animal*) (*a*) mangeur *m* d'hommes; (*b*) cheval *m* qui mord.

maneating ['mæni:tiŋ], *a.* 1. (tribu etc.) anthropophage, cannibale. 2. (tigre, etc.) mangeur d'hommes; (cheval) qui mord; **m. shark,** requin blanc, carcharodon, mangeur *m* d'hommes.

maned [meind], *a.* (*a*) à crinière; **black-m.,** à la crinière noire; (*b*) *Her:* criné; **a lion gules m. or,** à un lion de gueules criné d'or.

manege [mæ'neiʒ], *s. Equit:* 1. manège *m* (du cheval). 2. (salle *f* de) manège.

manes ['meini:z, 'mɑ:ni:z], *s.pl. Rom.Ant:* mânes *m*.

maneuver [mə'nu:vər], *s. & v. NAm:* = MANOEUVRE.

manful ['mænful], *a.* vaillant, courageux, hardi, intrépide, viril.

manfully ['mænfuli], *adv.* vaillamment, courageusement, hardiment, intrépidement; avec virilité.

manfulness ['mænfulnis], *s.* vaillance *f*; hardiesse *f*, virilité *f*.

mangabey ['mæŋgəbi], *s. Z:* (singe) cercocèbe *m*; mangabey *m*; **the mangabeys, the m. monkeys,** les cercocèbes; **white-collared m.,** cercocèbe à collier blanc; **grey-cheeked m.,** cercocèbe à gorge blanche.

manganapatite [mæŋgə'næpətait], *s. Miner:* manganapatite *f*.

manganate ['mæŋgəneit], *s. Ch:* manganate *m*.

manganese [mæŋgə'ni:z], *s.* 1. *Miner:* (oxyde noir de) manganèse *m*; péroxyde *m* de manganèse; **red m.,** rhodonite *f*; **dioxide of m., grey oxide of m.,** bioxyde *m*, ferroxyde *m*, de manganèse; **grey m. ore,** manganite *f*; **bog m.,** bog-manganèse *m*, écume *f* de manganèse; **m. epidote,** manganépidote *f*; **m. spar,** manganspath *m*, rhodochrosite *f*. 2. *Ch:* manganèse; **m. oxide,** (i) *or* **m. dioxide,** bioxyde *m* de manganèse, *F:* magnésie *f* des peintres; (ii) oxyde manganeux; (iii) *or* **m. sesquioxide,** oxyde manganique; *Metall:* **m. pig,** fonte manganésée; **m. bronze,** bronze *m* au manganèse, bronze manganésé; **m. steel,** acier *m* au manganèse.

manganesian [mæŋgə'ni:ziən], *a. Ch:* manganésien.

manganic [mæŋ'gænik], *a. Ch:* manganique; **m. oxide,** oxyde *m* manganique.

manganiferous [mæŋgə'nifərəs], *a.* manganésifère, manganésien.

manganin ['mæŋgənin], *s. Metall:* manganine *f*.

manganite ['mæŋgənait], *s.* 1. *Miner:* manganite *f*, acerdèse *f*. 2. *Ch:* manganite.

manganocalcite [mæŋgənou'kælsait], *s. Miner:* manganocalcite *f*.

manganophyllite [mæŋgənou'filait], *s. Miner:* manganophyllite *f*.

manganosite ['mæŋgənousait, mæŋ'gænousait], *s. Miner:* manganosite *f*.

manganostibiite [mæŋgənou'stibiait], *s. Miner:* manganostibite *f*.

manganotantalite [mæŋgənou'tæntəlait], *s. Miner:* manganotantalite *f*.

manganous ['mæŋgənəs], *a. Ch:* manganeux; **m. oxide,** oxyde manganeux.

mange [mein(d)ʒ], *s. Vet:* gale *f*, *F:* rogne *f* (du chien, du chat, etc.).

mangel-wurzel ['mæŋgl'wə:zl], *s.* betterave *f* champêtre; betterave fourragère.

manger ['meindʒər], *s.* 1. mangeoire *f*, crèche *f*; auge *f* d'écurie; *F:* **he's a dog in the m.,** il fait comme le chien du jardinier (qui ne mange pas de choux et ne laisse pas les autres en manger). 2. *N.Arch:* gatte *f*.

mangerful ['meindʒəful], *s.* augée*f.*
manginess ['meindʒinis], *s.* état galeux (d'un chien, etc.).
mangle[1] ['mæŋgl], *s. Laund:* essoreuse *f* (à rouleaux).
mangle[2], *v.tr.* essorer (le linge) (dans une essoreuse à rouleaux).
mangle[3], *v.tr.* **1.** déchirer, lacérer, écraser, mutiler (qn, les membres de qn); charcuter, massacrer (une volaille, un morceau de viande); **the body was found frightfully mangled,** on a retrouvé le corps affreusement mutilé. **2.** mutiler, déformer (un mot); estropier (une citation); mutiler, dénaturer (un texte).
mangling[1] ['mæŋgliŋ], *s.* essorage *m* (dans une essoreuse à rouleaux).
mangling[2], *s.* lacération *f*; mutilation *f.*
mango, *pl.* **-oes** ['mæŋgou, -ouz], *s. Bot:* **1.** mangue *f.* **2. m. (tree),** manguier *m*; (*in India*) **the m. trick,** le tour du manguier qui pousse à vue d'œil. **3.** *Ich:* **m. fish,** polynème *m* mangue.
mangold ['mæŋgould], *s.* = MANGEL-WURZEL.
mangonel ['mæŋgənel], *s. A.Arms:* mangonneau *m.*
mangosteen ['mæŋgəsti:n], *s. Bot:* **1.** mangouste *f.* **2. m. (tree),** mangoustan *m.*
mangrove ['mæŋgrouv], *s. Bot:* **1.** mangle *f.* **2. m. (tree),** manglier *m*, palétuvier *m*; **m. bark,** écorce *f* de manglier; **m. swamp,** mangrove *f.*
mangy ['meindʒi], *a.* **1.** galeux. **2.** (*a*) *F:* (*of furniture, etc.*) minable, miteux; (*b*) *P:* sale, moche.
manhandle ['mænhændl], *v.tr.* **1.** manutentionner (des marchandises, etc.); transporter, déplacer, (un canon, etc.) à force de bras; *Nau:* haler, enlever, (qch.) à la main. **2.** brutaliser, maltraiter, malmener, bousculer (qn).
Manhattanese [mænhætə'ni:z], *a. & s.* (originaire, habitant, -ante) de Manhattan.
manhole ['mænhoul], *s.* **1.** trou *m* d'homme (de chaudière); trou de visite, regard *m* (d'aqueduc, d'égout); bouche *f* d'accès (d'égout); **m. cover, lid,** (i) plaque *f* d'égout; (ii) *Mch:* autoclave *m* d'un trou d'homme; **m. door,** porte *f* autoclave. **2.** *Rail:* refuge *m*, abri *m*, retraite *f*, niche *f* (de tunnel, etc.). **3.** *Min:* passage *m* pour les hommes.
manhood ['mænhud], *s.* **1.** humanité *f*; nature humaine. **2.** âge *m* d'homme; âge viril; virilité *f*; *Pol: A:* **m. suffrage,** suffrage universel. **3.** *A:* = MANLINESS.
manhunt ['mænhʌnt], *s.* chasse *f* à l'homme.
mania ['meiniə], *s.* **1.** *Med:* (i) manie *f*; folie *f*; délire *m*; (ii) folie furieuse; **suicidal m.,** folie du suicide. **2.** manie, passion *f* (de qch.); **speed m.,** la passion de la vitesse; **she's got a real m. for gardening,** elle a la folie du jardinage.
maniac ['meiniæk]. **1.** *a. & s. Med:* fou furieux, folle furieuse; *Psy:* maniaque (*mf*); **sex m., sexual m.,** obsédé sexuel. **2.** *s.* maniaque, enragé, -ée (de qch.); **he's a real m. about it,** il en a la manie, la folie; il ne peut pas penser à autre chose.
maniacal [mə'naiək(ə)l], *a. Med:* **1.** fou, folle. **2.** de fou; de fou furieux, maniacal.
manic ['mænik], *a. Psy:* (désir, etc.) qui tient de la folie; **m. depressive,** maniaco-dépressif, -ive; **m.-depressive psychosis,** psychose maniaco-dépressive, maniaque dépressive.
Manichean [mæni'ki:ən]. *Rel.H:* **1.** *a.* manichéen; des Manichéens. **2.** *s.* (*also* **Manichee**) manichéen, -éenne.
Manicheism ['mæniki:izm], *s. Rel.H:* manichéisme *m.*
manichord(on) [mæni'kɔ:d(ən)], *s. A.Mus:* manic(h)ordion *m*, manicorde *m.*
manicure[1] ['mænikjuər], *s.* **1.** soin *m* des mains; toilette *f* des ongles; **m. set,** trousse *f* de manucure; onglier *m*; **to have a m.,** se faire faire les ongles, les mains, se faire soigner les mains; **to give oneself a m.,** se faire les ongles. **2.** (*pers.*) manucure *mf.*
manicure[2], *v.tr.* **1.** soigner les mains de (qn); faire les mains, les ongles, à (qn). **2. to m. one's nails,** se faire les ongles.
manicurist ['mænikjuərist], *s.* manucure *mf.*
Manidae ['mænidi:], *s.pl. Z:* manidés *m.*
manifest[1] ['mænifest], *a.* manifeste, évident, clair; **to make sth. m.,** manifester qch.; rendre qch. manifeste.
manifest[2], *s.* (*a*) *Nau:* **(inward, outward) m.,** manifeste *m* (d'entrée, de sortie); (*b*) *Av:* état *m* de chargement.
manifest[3]. **1.** *v.tr.* (*a*) manifester, témoigner, montrer (qch.); **they manifested great activity,** ils faisaient preuve d'une grande activité; (*b*) **no disease has manifested itself,** il ne s'est manifesté, ne s'est révélé, aucune maladie; (*c*) *Nau:* (i) déclarer (une cargaison) en douane; (ii) faire figurer (une marchandise) sur le manifeste. **2.** *v.i.* (*a*) *Pol: etc: O:* manifester; prendre part à une manifestation; (*b*) *Psychics:* (*of ghost, spirit*) se manifester.
manifestation [mænifes'teiʃ(ə)n], *s.* manifestation *f*; *Pol:* **mass m.,** manifestation de masse, collective; *Med:* **clinical m.,** manifestation clinique.
manifestly ['mænifestli], *adv.* manifestement; **she is m. wrong,** il est clair qu'elle a tort.
manifesto [mæni'festou], *s. Pol: etc:* manifeste *m*, proclamation *f*; déclaration publique (d'un parti, etc.).
manifold[1] ['mænifould]. **1.** *a.* (*a*) divers, varié; de diverses sortes; dans diverses directions, dans divers secteurs; **the m. wisdom of God,** la sagesse infiniment variée de Dieu; (*b*) multiple, nombreux; **m. temptations,** de nombreuses tentations; *B:* **how m. are thy works!** que tes œuvres sont en grand nombre! (*c*) **m. increase,** (i) dépassement *m* du taux normal; (ii) *Pharm:* surdosage *m.* **2.** *s.* (*a*) *Phil:* diversité *f*; (*b*) *Com: etc: A:* polycopie *f*; document polycopié; copie (tirée sur un polygraphe); **m. writer,** appareil *m* à polycopier; appareil de reproduction graphique; polygraphe *m*; *Typew:* **m. paper,** papier *m* à copies multiples; (*c*) *I.C.E: etc:* tubulure *f*, tuyauterie *f*; collecteur *m*, culotte *f*; *Mch:* collecteur (du surchauffeur); **exhaust m.,** tubulure d'échappement; tuyautage *m* d'échappement; collecteur d'échappement; culotte d'échappement; **inlet m., admission m.,** tuyauterie d'aspiration, d'admission; **oil m.,** collecteur d'huile; (*d*) *Mth:* **vector m.,** multiplicité vectorielle.
manifold[2], *v.tr. A:* polycopier, autocopier.
manifoldly ['mænifouldli], *adv.* **1.** diversement; de diverses manières. **2.** en nombre multiple.
manifoldness ['mænifouldnis], *s.* multiplicité *f*, diversité *f*; aspects variés (de qch.).
manikin ['mænikin], *s.* **1.** petit homme; petit bout d'homme; homoncule *m*, nabot *m.* **2.** *Art: Med: Surg:* mannequin *m.* **3.** *Orn:* = MANAKIN.
Manil(l)a [mə'nilə]. *Pr.n. Geog:* Manille *f*; *Com:* **m. hemp,** abaca *m*; (i) chanvre *m* de Manille; (ii) (*tree*) bananier *m* textile; **m. rope,** cordage *m* en manille; manille *f*; **m. cheroot,** cigare *m* de Manille; manille *m*; *Paperm:* **m. paper,** papier *m* bulle.
manille [mæ'nil], *s. Cards:* manille *f.*
manioc ['mæniɔk], *s.* **1.** *Bot:* manioc *m.* **2.** *Cu:* cassave *f.*
maniple ['mænipl], *s.* **1.** *Rom.Ant:* manipule *m*; compagnie *f* d'infanterie. **2.** *Ecc:* manipule, fanon *m.*
manipulable [mə'nipjuləbl], *a.* maniable.
manipular [mə'nipjulər]. **1.** *a. & s. Rom.Ant:* manipulaire (*m*). **2.** *a.* = MANIPULATIVE.
manipulatable [mənipju'leitəbl], *a.* maniable.
manipulate [mə'nipjuleit], *v.tr.* **1.** manipuler (un objet); manœuvrer, actionner (un dispositif mécanique); agir sur (un levier, une pédale). **2.** *Pej:* **to m. accounts,** tripoter, cuisiner, arranger, des comptes; *St.Exch:* **to m. the market,** agir sur le marché; travailler le marché; provoquer des mouvements de Bourse.
manipulation [mənipju'leiʃ(ə)n], *s.* manipulation *f.* **1.** *Med:* exploration *f* (des organes). **2.** manœuvre *f*; **wrong m.,** fausse manœuvre. **3.** *Pej:* tripotage *m*; **m. of the market,** tripotages en Bourse; agiotage *m.*
manipulative [mə'nipjulətiv], *a.* de manipulation; accompli au moyen de manipulations; **m. surgery,** thérapeutique manuelle.
manipulator [mə'nipjuleitər], *s.* **1.** manipulateur. **2.** *Pej:* tripoteur *m*; *St.Exch:* agioteur *m.* **3.** *Atom.Ph:* **remote m.,** télémanipulateur *m.*
Manitoban [mæni'toubən], *a. & s.* (originaire, habitant, -ante) du Manitoba.
manjack ['mændʒæk], *s.* **1.** *Bot:* cordia *m.* **2.** *Miner:* manjac *m*, majak *m.*
mankind, *s. coll.* **1.** [mæn'kaind], le genre humain; l'homme *m*; l'humanité *f*; l'espèce humaine. **2.** ['mænkaind] (*opp. to womankind*) les hommes.
manlike ['mænlaik], *a.* **1.** (*a*) d'homme; mâle; digne d'un homme; *Lit:* **m. he stood his ground,** en homme qu'il était, il tint bon; (*b*) (*of woman*) hommasse. **2.** semblable à un homme; **the m. apes,** les anthropoïdes *m.*
manliness ['mænlinis], *s.* caractère mâle, viril; virilité *f.*
manly ['mænli], *a.* d'homme; mâle, viril; **m. voice,** voix *f* mâle; **m. qualities,** les qualités qui conviennent à l'homme.
man(-)made ['mænmeid], *a.* fait par la main de l'homme; artificiel, synthétique; **m.-m. laws,** les lois faites par l'homme; **m.-m. fibres,** fibres *f* synthétiques.
manna ['mænə], *s.* **1.** *B: etc:* manne *f*; *Fig:* **it was m. from heaven,** cela tombait des mains des dieux. **2.** *Bot: Pharm: etc:* manne du frêne; **m. lichen,** lichen *m* à la manne; **Turkish, Syrian, m.,** tréhala *m*; **m. grass,** manne de Pologne; **m. in tears,** manne en larmes; **m. in sorts,** manne en sortes; **m. sugar,** mannitol *m.*
manned [mænd], *a.* (*a*) (*of administrative, technical, agency*) doté, pourvu, de personnel; (*b*) (*of machine, apparatus*) (i) doté d'un homme, de personnel, chargé du service, de la manœuvre; (ii) servi, manœuvré; (*c*) (*of vehicle, aircraft*) (i) doté d'un pilote, d'un équipage; (ii) à conduite humaine, piloté; (*of spacecraft*) habité.
mannequin ['mænikin], *s.* (*pers.*) mannequin *m*; **permanent m.,** mannequin de cabine; **freelance m.,** mannequin volant.
manner ['mænər], *s.* **1.** (*a*) manière *f*, façon *f* (de faire qch.); **in this m.,** de cette manière, de cette façon; ainsi; **no one would use it in that m.,** personne n'en userait de la sorte; **the m. in which . . .,** la manière dont . . .; **he is religious after his own m.,** il est religieux à sa façon; **in the same,** *Lit:* **like, m.,** de la même manière; de même; **in such a m. that . . .,** de manière que, de sorte que + *ind. or sub.* **in the same m. as . . .,** de la même manière que . . ., de même que . . .; **in a m. (of speaking),** en quelque sorte, en quelque manière; dans un certain sens; d'un certain point de vue; pour ainsi dire; **it's a m. of speaking,** c'est une façon de parler; *Gram:* **adverb of m.,** adverbe *m* de manière; (*b*) *Lit:* manière; **the m. and the matter,** la forme et le fond; **novel in the m. of Dickens,** roman *m* à la (manière de) Dickens; **painted in the Watteau m.,** peint dans le goût, dans le style, de Watteau; **it sounds rather like Verdi in his early m.,** cela ressemble à du Verdi de la première manière. **2.** *A: & Lit:* manière, coutume *f*, habitude *f*; **Paul, as his m. was, . . .,** Paul, comme c'était son habitude, . . .; **after the m. of the kings of old,** à la manière, selon l'habitude, des rois d'autrefois; à l'instar des anciens rois; **he does it as (if) to the m. born,** il le fait comme s'il était né pour cela, comme si de sa vie il n'avait fait que cela. **3.** *pl.* mœurs *f*, usages *m* (d'un peuple); **such were the manners of the time,** telles étaient les mœurs de l'époque; **manners change with the times,** autres temps, autres mœurs. **4.** maintien *m*, tenue *f*, air *m*, abord *m*; **his easy m.,** son air dégagé; **I do not like his m.,** je n'aime pas son attitude; **he has a bad m.,** il ne sait pas se présenter. **5.** *pl.* (*a*) manières; **bad manners,** mauvaises manières; manque *m* de savoir-vivre; manque de tenue; **it is bad manners to stare,** il est mal élevé de dévisager les gens; **he needs to be, should be, taught better manners,** il a besoin qu'on lui apprenne à vivre; (*b*) **(good) manners,** bonnes manières, savoir-vivre *m*, politesse *f*, bienséance *f*; **to teach s.o. manners,** donner à qn une leçon de politesse, de bienséance; **I'll teach him manners!** je lui apprendrai à vivre! *F:* **to forget one's manners,** oublier les convenances; s'oublier; (*to child*) **don't forget your manners! where are your manners?** c'est comme ça qu'on se tient? en voilà une tenue! *F:* d'où sors-tu? **he has no manners,** c'est un malappris; il ne sait pas vivre; il manque d'éducation, de savoir-vivre, d'usage; **lack of manners,** manque de procédés; *A:* (*at table*) **to leave a piece for manners,** laisser un morceau par bienséance. **6.** espèce *f*, sorte *f*; **what m. of man is he?** quelle espèce d'homme est-il? quel genre d'homme est-ce? **all m. of people, of things,** toutes sortes de gens, de choses; **no m. of doubt,** aucune espèce de doute; **you have no m. of right to interfere,** vous n'avez aucunement le droit de vous en mêler.
mannered ['mænəd], *a.* **1.** (*with a. or adv. prefixed, e.g.*) **rough-m.,** aux manières rudes; (homme *m*) brusque; **well-m.,** bien élevé. **2.** *Art: Lit:* maniéré; affecté; (style) recherché, précieux; **I find the style slightly m.,** je trouve un peu de maniérisme, un peu de recherche, dans l'expression.
mannerism ['mænərizm], *s.* **1.** maniérisme *m*, affectation *f.* **2.** particularité *f* (d'un écrivain, etc.); **he has his mannerisms,** il a sa manière.
mannerist ['mænərist], *s. & a. Art: Lit:* maniériste (*mf*).
mannerless ['mænəlis], *a.* aux mauvaises manières; sans tenue; qui manque de savoir-vivre.
mannerliness ['mænəlinis], *s.* bonnes manières; courtoisie *f*; politesse *f.*
mannerly ['mænəli], *a.* poli; courtois; qui a de bonnes manières; bien élevé.
mannide ['mænaid], *s. Ch:* mannide *m.*
manniferous [mæ'nifərəs], *a. Ent:* mannipare.
mannikin ['mænikin], *s. Orn:* spermète *m*, capucin *m*; **black-headed m.,** capucin à tête noire; **bronze m.,** spermète à capuchon; **rufous-backed m.,** spermète à dos brun; **white-headed m.,** capucin à tête blanche; **Bengalese m.,** moineau *m* du Japon.
manning ['mæniŋ], *s.* **1.** (*a*) affectation *f* de personnel (à une organisation, au service d'une machine, à la manœuvre d'un appareil, etc.); *Artil:* armement *m* (d'une pièce); *Nau:* armement (d'un canot, du cabestan); amarinage *m* (d'une prise); (*b*) personnel affecté (à une organisation, au service d'une machine, à la manœuvre d'un appareil); effectifs *mpl*; **m. table,** tableau *m* d'effectifs; *Mil:* **m. depot,** dépôt *m* d'effectifs. **2.** *Ven:* (*falconry*) apprivoisement *m*, affaitage *m.*
mannish ['mæniʃ], *a.* **1.** d'homme; qui caractérise l'homme. **2.** (*of woman*) hommasse; **m. ways,** façons

garçonnières; **to be m. in one's dress,** s'habiller d'une manière masculine.

mannishness ['mæniʃnis], *s.* **1.** caractère masculin. **2.** caractère hommasse (d'une femme).

mannitan ['mænitæn], *s. Ch:* mannitane *m.*

mannitol ['mænitɔl], *s. Ch:* mannitol *m.*

mannonic [mæ'nounik], *a. Ch:* (acide) mannonique.

mannose ['mænous], *Bio-Ch:* mannose *m.*

Manoeline ['mænjuəlain], *a. Arch:* manuélin.

manœuvre[1] [mə'nu:vər], *s.* manœuvre *f.* **1.** *Mil: etc:* (*a*) (*action*) *Mil:* **encircling m.,** manœuvre d'encerclement; **enveloping, surrounding, m.,** manœuvre d'enveloppement, enveloppante; **outflanking m.,** manœuvre de débordement; **freedom of m.,** liberté *f* de manœuvre; **pivot of m.,** pivot *m* de manœuvre; **the whole m. hinged on the deployment of the left flank,** toute la manœuvre reposait sur l'articulation du flanc gauche; **to upset, ward off, a m.,** déjouer, parer, une manœuvre; **evasive m.,** manœuvre de dérobement; (*b*) (*exercise*) *chiefly pl.* **air manœuvres,** manœuvres aériennes; **army manœuvres,** manœuvres de l'armée de terre; grandes manœuvres; **fleet manœuvres,** manœuvres d'escadre, de la flotte; **troops on manœuvres,** troupes *f* en manœuvre; **firing manœuvres,** manœuvres avec tirs réels; **one-sided, two-sided, m.,** manœuvre à simple, à double, action; **map manœuvres,** manœuvres à double action sur la carte; **m. scheme,** thème *m* de manœuvre. **2.** (*a*) *F:* **a clever, a false, m.,** une manœuvre habile, une fausse manœuvre; **vote-catching m.,** manœuvre électorale; (*b*) *pl. Pej:* **(underhand) manœuvres,** menées *f,* intrigues *f* (contre le gouvernement, etc.).

manœuvre[2]. **1.** *v.tr.* manœuvrer, faire manœuvrer (une armée, une flotte); **to m. the enemy out of a position,** user de moyens adroits pour déloger l'ennemi; **to m. s.o. into a corner,** (i) acculer qn dans un coin; (ii) amener adroitement qn dans une impasse. **2.** *v.i.* (*of troops, etc.*) manœuvrer; *Nau:* (*of ship*) évoluer; **to m. for position,** s'efforcer d'obtenir une bonne position initiale, de se mettre en bonne posture.

manœuvrability [mənu:vrə'biliti], *s.* maniabilité *f,* manœuvrabilité *f.*

manœuvrable [mə'nu:vrəbl], *a.* (avion *m,* etc.) manœuvrable, maniable.

manœuvrer [mə'nu:vrər], *s.* **1.** manœuvrier *m* (d'une armée, etc.). **2.** *Pej:* intrigant, -ante.

manœuvring [mə'nu:vriŋ], *s.* **1.** manœuvres *fpl*; *Tchn:* **m. gear,** appareil *m* de manœuvre; *Mec.E:* **m. lever,** levier *m* de manœuvre; **m. valve,** soupape *f* de manœuvre, robinet *m* à main; *Mil:* **m. area,** zone *f* de manœuvre; **m. element, force,** élément *m* de manœuvre; **m. troops,** troupes *f* de, en, manœuvre. **2.** *Pej:* intrigues *fpl,* menées *fpl.*

man-of-war, *pl.* **men-of-war** ['mænəv'wɔ:r, 'men-], *s.* **1.** *Nau: A:* vaisseau *m,* bâtiment *m,* de guerre; vaisseau de ligne. **2.** *Coel:* **Portuguese m.-of-w.,** physalie *f,* galère *f.* **3.** *Orn:* **(magnificent) m.-of-w. bird,** frégate *f* superbe.

manograph ['mænəgræf], *s. Tchn:* manographe *m.*

manometer [mæ'nɔmitər], *s. Ph: etc:* manomètre *m.*

manometric(al) [mænou'metrik(l)], *a.* manométrique.

manometry [mæ'nɔmitri], *s. Ph:* manométrie *f.*

manor ['mænər], *s.* (*a*) *Hist:* seigneurie *f*; **capital m.,** domaine *m* d'un seigneur suzerain; (*b*) **m. (house),** manoir *m, Hist:* demeure seigneuriale; (*c*) (*esp. of police*) **it's not in my m.,** ce n'est pas sur mon territoire.

manorial [mə'nɔ:riəl], *a.* seigneurial, -aux.

manostat ['mænoustæt], *s. Tchn:* manostat *m.*

manpower ['mænpauər], *s.* **1.** *Mec.E:* la force des bras. **2.** *coll. Ind: etc:* main-d'œuvre *f*; *Mil:* effectifs *mpl*; **shortage of m.,** crise *f* de main-d'œuvre, d'effectifs.

mansard ['mænsa:d], *s.* **m. (roof),** toit *m,* comble *m,* en mansarde; comble à la mansarde; comble brisé; **m.-roofed,** mansardé.

manse [mæns], *s. Ecc:* maison *f* du pasteur.

manservant, *pl.* **menservants** ['mænsə:vənt, 'mensə:vənts], *s.m.* domestique; valet (de chambre).

mansion ['mænʃ(ə)n], *s.* **1.** (*in country*) château *m*; (*in town*) hôtel (particulier); **m. (house),** manoir *m,* château seigneurial; **a 16th century m.,** une demeure du 16e siècle; *B:* **in my Father's house there are many mansions,** il y a beaucoup de demeures dans la maison du Père. **2.** *Astrol:* mansion *f,* maison. **3.** *A.Th:* mansion.

mansized ['mænsaiz(d)], *a.* (*a*) (*of shadow on wall, etc.*) de la grandeur d'un homme; (*b*) (*of handkerchief, helping of food, etc.*) qui convient à un homme; de taille; (*c*) (travail) d'homme; **she's done a m. job,** elle a abattu un travail d'homme.

manslaughter ['mænslɔ:tər], *s. Jur:* (*a*) homicide *m* involontaire, par imprudence; (*b*) homicide sans préméditation; **voluntary m.,** meurtre *m.*

mansuetude ['mænswitju:d], *s. A:* mansuétude *f.*

manta ['mæntə], *s.* **1.** *U.S: Dial:* couverture *f.* **2.** *Ich:* **m. (ray),** mante *f,* diable *m* de mer.

mantel ['mæntl], *s.* = MANTELPIECE.

mantelet ['mæntlit], *s.* = MANTLET.

mantelpiece ['mæntlpi:s], *s.* **1.** manteau *m,* linteau *m,* chambranle *m,* de cheminée. **2.** (*also* **mantleshelf**) dessus *m,* tablette *f,* de cheminée; cheminée *f.*

mantilla [mæn'tilə], *s. Cost:* mantille *f.*

Mantinea [mænti'niə]. *Pr.n. A.Geog:* Mantinée *f.*

mantis ['mæntis], *s.* **1.** *Ent:* mante *f*; **praying m.,** mante religieuse; prie-Dieu *f inv.* **2.** *Crust:* **m. shrimp, prawn,** squille *f*; mante de mer.

mantispid ['mæntispid], *s. Ent:* mantispe *m.*

Mantispidae [mæn'tispidi:], *s.pl. Ent:* mantispidés *m.*

mantissa [mæn'tisə], *s. Mth:* mantisse *f* (d'un logarithme).

mantle[1] ['mæntl], *s.* **1.** *A: Cost:* (*a*) manteau *m* (sans manches); cape *f*; (*b*) mante *f,* pèlerine *f* (de femme). **2.** (*a*) manteau (de lave, de neige, de lierre); *Geol:* **inner, outer, m.,** enveloppe pierreuse interne, externe; (*b*) voile *m* (d'obscurité, de brume). **3.** *Moll:* manteau. **4.** (*a*) manchon *m* (de bec de gaz à incandescence); (*b*) *Metall:* (i) chemise extérieure, enveloppe extérieure (de haut-fourneau); (ii) manteau, surtout *m* (de moule); (*c*) *Const:* parement *m* (d'un mur).

mantle[2]. **1.** *v.tr.* (*a*) *A:* couvrir, vêtir, envelopper (qn) d'un manteau, d'une mante, d'une cape; (*b*) jeter un manteau sur (qch.); cacher, voiler (qch.); (*c*) couvrir, envelopper **(with,** de); **wall mantled with ivy,** mur tapissé de lierre. **2.** *v.i.* (*a*) (*of liquid*) écumer, mousser; se couvrir d'une couche d'écume; (*b*) *Lit:* (*of blood, blush*) se répandre **(over the cheeks,** sur les joues); (*of face, cheeks*) rougir, s'empourprer; **the dawn mantles in the sky,** l'aurore *f* envahit le ciel.

mantlet ['mæntlit], *s.* **1.** *A.Cost:* mantelet *m.* **2.** *Mil:* (*a*) *A:* mantelet (de siège); (*b*) pare-balles *m inv* (d'une pièce).

mantling ['mæntliŋ], *s. Her:* courtine *f*; lambrequin *m* (de casque, etc.).

mantrap ['mæntræp], *s.* piège *m* à hommes, à loups; chausse-trape *f, pl.* chausse-trapes.

mantua[1] ['mæntjuə], *s. A.Cost:* (*a*) mante *f*; (*b*) robe flottante.

Mantua[2]. *Pr.n. Geog:* Mantoue *f.*

Mantuan ['mæntjuən]. *Geog:* (*a*) *a.* mantouan; (*b*) *s.* Mantouan, -ane.

manual ['mænjuəl]. **1.** *a.* manuel; **m. work,** travail manuel, travail de manœuvre; **m. control,** commande manuelle; **m. remote control,** commande manuelle à distance; **m. operation,** fonctionnement *m* à la main; commande manuelle; **m. haulage,** traction *f* à bras d'homme; *Tp:* **m. telephone (system),** téléphone manuel, téléphonie manuelle; **m. exchange,** bureau téléphonique manuel; **m. switchboard,** tableau manuel; **m. operating,** exploitation manuelle; **the m. alphabet,** l'alphabet manuel, l'alphabet des sourds-muets; **m. method of communication,** méthode *f* dactylologique, dactylologie *f.* **2.** *s.* (*a*) (*handbook*) manuel *m*; (*b*) *Mus:* clavier *m* (d'un orgue); **grand m.,** clavier du grand orgue.

manually ['mænjuəli], *adv.* manuellement; à la main.

manucode ['mænjukoud], *s. Orn:* manucode *m.*

manufactory [mænju'fækt(ə)ri], *s. A:* fabrique *f,* usine *f,* manufacture *f.*

manufacture[1] [mænju'fæktʃər], *s.* **1.** fabrication *f,* élaboration *f* (d'un produit industriel); confection *f* (de vêtements, etc.); **article of foreign m.,** article fabriqué à l'étranger; article de fabrication étrangère. **2.** produit fabriqué; produit manufacturé.

manufacture[2], *v.tr.* fabriquer, manufacturer (un produit industriel); confectionner (des vêtements, etc.).

manufacturer [manju'fæktʃərər], *s.* fabricant *m,* industriel *m*; **cloth m.,** fabricant de draps; **boiler m.,** constructeur *m* de chaudières.

manufacturing[1] [mænju'fæktjəriŋ], *a.* industriel; **m. town,** ville industrielle.

manufacturing[2], *s.* fabrication *f*; confection *f* (de vêtements).

manul ['mæn(ə)l], *s. Z:* manoul *m,* manul *m*; chat *m* de Pallas, du désert.

manumission [mænju'miʃ(ə)n], *s. Hist:* manumission *f,* affranchissement *m,* émancipation *f* (d'un esclave); mainmise *f* (d'un serf).

manumit [mænju'mit], *v.tr.* **(manumitted)** *Hist:* affranchir, émanciper (un esclave); mainmettre (un serf).

manumitter [mænju'mitər], *s. Hist:* affranchisseur *m,* émancipateur *m* (d'un esclave).

manure[1] [mə'njuər], *s.* engrais *m*; **farmyard m.,** fumier *m* (d'étable); **fish m.,** engrais de poisson; **chemical m.,** engrais chimique; **liquid m.,** engrais flamand; eaux-vannes *fpl,* purin *m*; **m. heap,** tas *m* de fumier; *Hort:* meule *f*; **m. pit,** trou *m* au fumier; **liquid m. pit, sump,** fosse *f* à purin; **m. crop,** culture sidérale; **green m.,** engrais vert; verdage *m.*

manure[2], *v.tr.* fumer, engraisser (la terre).

manuring [mə'nju:riŋ], *s.* fumage *m,* fumure *f,* engraissement *m.*

manuscript ['mænjuskript]. **1.** *s.* manuscrit *m*; **m. library, room,** bibliothèque *f* protypographique. **2.** *a.* manuscrit; écrit à la main.

manuterge ['mænjutə:dʒ], **manutergium** [mænju'tə:dʒiəm], *s. R.C.Ch:* manuterge *m.*

Manutius [mə'nju:ʃiəs]. *Pr.n. Hist:* Manuce.

Manx [mæŋks]. **1.** *a. Geog:* mannois; manxois; manx; de l'île de Man; **old M. customs,** les vieilles mœurs manxes; **M. cat,** chat *m* sans queue de l'île de Man; *Orn:* **M. shearwater,** puffin *m* des Anglais. **2.** *s.* (*a*) *Ling:* le mannois, le manx, le manxois; (*b*) *pl.* **the M.,** les Mannois; les habitants de l'île de Man.

Manxman, *pl.* **-men,** *f.* **-woman,** *pl.* **-women** ['mæŋksmən, -mən, -wumən, -wimin], *s. Geog:* Mannois, -oise.

many ['meni]. **1.** *a. & s.* **(more, most,** q.v.) un grand nombre (de); beaucoup (de); bien des; plusieurs; *Lit:* maint, force; **m. times,** beaucoup de fois, bien des fois; **m. a time,** *Lit:* **m. a time and oft,** mainte(s) fois; mainte et mainte fois; de multiples fois; **m. a man, m. a one,** bien des gens; plus d'un; **many's the time I've heard that song,** j'ai entendu cette chanson bien des fois, plus d'une fois; **m. people,** beaucoup de gens, bien des gens; **m. customers write to us,** de nombreux clients, nombre de clients, nous écrivent; **we shall see him before m. days, before m. weeks, have passed,** nous le verrons avant qu'il soit longtemps; **of m. kinds,** de toutes sortes; **in m. instances,** dans bien des cas; **it can be done in m. ways,** on peut le faire de plusieurs manières; **for m. years,** pendant de longues années; **I have known him for (so) m. years,** je le connais depuis des années, tant d'années; **so m. times,** je ne sais combien de fois; **he made m. mistakes, his mistakes were m.,** il faisait de nombreuses erreurs, beaucoup d'erreurs; *Prov:* **m. hands make light work,** à plusieurs la besogne va vite; à plusieurs mains l'ouvrage avance; **m. of us, of them,** beaucoup, un grand nombre, d'entre nous, d'entre eux; **m. of his observations have proved correct,** beaucoup de ses observations se sont vérifiées; **m. have seen it,** beaucoup de personnes l'ont vu; il y en a beaucoup qui l'ont vu; **there were so m.,** ils étaient si nombreux; il y en avait tant; **like so m. others,** comme tant d'autres; comme il y en a tant; **the boys climb like so m. monkeys,** les garçons grimpent comme autant de singes, comme de vrais singes; **he told me in so m. words that . . .,** il m'a dit en propres termes que . . .; **too m. people,** trop de monde; **they are too m.,** ils sont trop; **three of you are none too m. for the job,** vous n'êtes pas trop de trois pour ce travail; **a card too m.,** une carte de trop; **how m. horses have you?** combien de chevaux avez-vous? **how m. of you are there?** vous êtes combien? **I have as m. books as you,** j'ai autant de livres que vous; **how m. (of them) can I have?** combien puis-je en avoir? **as m. as you like, as you need,** autant que vous voulez, qu'il vous en faut; **as m. again, as m. more, twice as m.,** deux fois autant, encore autant; **three times as m.,** trois fois autant; **as m. as ten people saw it,** il y a bien dix personnes qui l'ont vu; **as m. words as make up a line,** le nombre de mots nécessaire pour faire une ligne; **admit as m. as come,** laissez entrer tous ceux qui viendront; **four accidents in as m. days,** quatre accidents en autant de jours; **a great m. people,** un grand nombre de personnes; **a good m. things,** un assez grand nombre de choses; pas mal de choses; **a good m. people saw him,** bon nombre, pas mal, de gens l'ont vu; **there are a good m.,** il y en a pas mal; **those, not very m., who . . .,** ceux, en petit nombre, qui . . .. **2.** *s.* **the m.,** la multitude; la foule.

many-coloured ['meni'kʌləd], *a.* multicolore.

many-fingered ['meni'fiŋgəd], *a. Nat.Hist:* multidigité.

many-headed ['meni'hedid], *a.* (monstre) aux têtes nombreuses; à plusieurs têtes.

manyplies ['meniplaiz], *s.pl. Dial:* feuillet *m*; troisième poche *f* de l'estomac (des ruminants).

many-sided ['meni'saidid], *a.* **1.** (figure *f*) à plusieurs côtés. **2.** (problème) complexe, compliqué. **3.** (personne) aux talents variés.

many-sidedness ['meni'saididnis], *s.* **1.** complexité *f* (d'une question). **2.** diversité *f,* variété *f,* de talents; **his m.-s.,** la diversité de ses talents.

Maoism ['mauizm], *s. Pol:* maoïsme *m.*

Maoist ['mauist], *a. & s. Pol:* maoïste (*mf*).

Maori ['ma:əri]. **1.** *Ethn:* (*a*) maori; **M. civilization,** la civilisation maorie; (*b*) *s.* Maori, -ie. **2.** *s. Ling:* maori *m.*

map[1] [mæp], *s.* (*a*) carte *f* (géographique); **m. of the world,** mappemonde *f*; **physical m.,** carte physique; **relief m.,** carte topographique, en relief; **contour m.,** carte hypsométrique; **geological m.,** carte géologique; **photo m.,** carte photographique; **ordnance survey m.** = carte d'état-major; **political m.,** carte politique; **sketch m.,** croquis *m*; **squared m., grid(ded) m.,** carte quadrillée, carroyée; **outline, skeleton, m.,** carte muette; **large-scale, small-scale, m.,** carte à grande, à petite, échelle; **1:500,000 m.,** carte au 500.000ème; **one in a million, one in two million, m.,** carte au millionième, au deux-millionième; **air, aeronautical, m.,** carte aéronautique; **air navigation m.,** carte de navigation aérienne; *Av:* **moving m.,** routier *m* automatique; **astronomical m.,** carte astronomique, céleste; *Mil:* **battle m., m. of positions,** plan directeur; **intelligence m.,** carte renseignée, de renseignements; **strategic m.,** carte stratégique; **target m.,** carte d'objectifs; **to lay down a bearing on a m.,** porter un relèvement sur une carte; **to orient(ate) a m.,** orienter une carte; **is it shown on the m.?** est-ce que c'est marqué sur la carte? **what is the distance on the m.?** quelle est la distance sur la carte? **to read a m.,** lire une carte; **m. reading,** lecture *f* des cartes; **m. reference,** référence *f* cartographique, topographique; coordonnées *fpl*; **m. library,** cartothèque *f*; *Av:* **m. display,** indicateur *m* cartographique; *Mil: etc:* **m. reconnaissance,** reconnaissance *f* sur la carte; **m. fire, m. firing,** tir *m* d'après la carte; (*b*) **our village is really off the m.,** notre village est vraiment au bout du monde; **the building of the atomic pile will put our village on the m.,** la construction de la pile atomique va mettre notre village en vedette.

map[2], *v.tr.* **(mapped) 1.** dresser une carte, un plan, de (la région, etc.). **2. to m. out a route,** tracer un itinéraire; **to m. out a course of action,** se tracer un plan d'action; **to m. out a programme,** dresser, tracer, un programme; **to m. out one's time,** dresser, arranger, son emploi du temps.

mapholder ['mæphouldər], (*also* **map case** ['mæpkeis]) *s.* porte-cartes *m inv*; poche *f* à cartes.

maple ['meipl], *s. Bot:* **1. m. (tree),** (*a*) érable *m*; **English m., common m., field m.,** érable champêtre; **silver m.,** érable du Canada; **sugar m., rock m.,** érable à sucre; **m. sugar,** sucre *m* d'érable; **m. syrup,** sirop *m* de sucre d'érable; **ash-leaved m.,** négundo *m* à feuilles de frêne, érable négundo; **flowering m.,** abutilon *m*; **Norway m.,** érable plane; **m. grove,** érablière *f*; (*b*) **great m.,** sycomore *m* maple, (érable) faux platane, *F:* (érable) sycomore. **2.** (bois *m* d')érable.

mapping ['mæpiŋ], *s.* **1.** (*a*) cartographie *f*; levé *m* (de carte, de plan, etc.); **photographic m.,** cartographie photographique; (*b*) repérage *m* (d'un point du terrain, etc., sur la carte). **2.** *Rad:* cadrage *m*. **3.** *Mth:* application *f*; **canonical, natural, m.,** application canonique; **linear m.,** application linéaire; **one-to-one m.,** application biunivoque.

maquis ['mæki:], *s. Geog:* maquis *m*; *Pol: etc:* **to take to the m.,** prendre le maquis; **he's in the m.,** c'est un maquisard.

mar [ma:r], *v.tr.* **(marred)** gâter, gâcher (le plaisir de qn); troubler (la joie de qn); défigurer (un paysage, etc.); déparer (la beauté de qn); **to make or m. s.o.,** faire la fortune ou la ruine de qn; **such ordeals either make or m. a man,** ce sont de ces épreuves qui trempent le caractère ou qui l'énervent à tout jamais; **that will either mend or m. matters,** cela va tout arranger ou tout gâcher; **serious defects m. his work,** de graves imperfections déparent son œuvre; **detail that mars a picture,** détail qui fait tache dans un tableau, qui gâte un tableau.

mara ['ma:rə], *s. Z:* mara *m*, lièvre patagon; lièvre des pampas.

marabou ['mærəbu:], *s.* **1.** *Orn:* marabout *m*; cigogne *f* à sac; **m. feather, plume,** plume *f* de marabout. **2.** *coll.* duvet *m* de marabout.

marabout ['mærəbu:t], *s. Rel:* marabout (musulman).

maram ['mærəm], *s.* = MARRAM.

Marantaceae [mæræn'teisii:], *s.pl. Bot:* marantacées *f*.

maraschino [mærəs'ki:nou], *s. Dist:* marasquin *m*; **m. cherries,** cerises *f* au marasquin.

marasmius [mə'ræzmiəs], *s. Fung:* marasmius *m*, marasme *m*.

marasmus [mə'ræzməs], *s. Med:* marasme *m*.

Marathon ['mærəθ(ə)n]. *Pr.n.* (*a*) *Geog:* Marathon; (*b*) *Sp: etc:* **m. (race),** marathon *m*; **m. runner,** marathonien *m*; **diplomatic m.,** marathon diplomatique; *F:* **dancing m.,** concours *m* d'endurance de danseurs; marathon de danse; **m. speech,** marathon oratoire.

Marattiaceae [mæræti'eisii:], *s.pl. Bot:* marattiacées *f*.

Marattiales [mæræti'eili:z], *s.pl. Bot:* marattiales *f*.

maraud [mə'rɔ:d]. **1.** *v.i.* **to go marauding,** marauder; aller en maraude, aller à la maraude. **2.** *v.tr. O:* piller (un village, etc.).

marauder [mə'rɔ:dər], *s.* maraudeur, -euse.

marauding[1] [mə'rɔ:diŋ], *a.* maraudeur, -euse; de maraudeurs.

marauding[2], *s.* maraude *f*; *Jur:* maraudage *m*.

marble[1] ['ma:bl], *s.* **1.** marbre *m*; (*a*) **Brabançon m.,** petit antique; **clouded m.,** marbre tacheté; brocatelle *f*; **landscape m.,** marbre fleuri; **onyx m., branded m.,** marbre onyx; **imitation m.,** similimarbre *m*; **m. statue,** statue *f* de marbre; **m. pavement,** dallage *m* en marbre; dalles *fpl* de marbre; **the m. industry,** l'industrie marbrière; (*pers.*) **m. cutter,** marbrier *m*; **m. cutting,** marbrerie *f*; **m. quarry,** carrière *f* de marbre; marbrière *f*; (*b*) *Art:* **(collection of) marbles,** (collection *f* de) marbres; **the Elgin marbles,** les marbres d'Elgin. **2.** *Games:* bille *f*; **to play marbles,** jouer aux billes; **glass m.,** agate *f*.

marble[2], *v.tr.* marbrer (une boiserie, etc.); *Bookb:* marbrer, raciner (les plats); jasper, marbrer (les tranches).

marbled ['ma:bld], *a.* **1.** marbré; *Bookb:* (*of cover*) raciné, marbré; (*of edge*) jaspé, marbré; **m. calf,** veau marbré, raciné. **2.** (salle, etc.) à revêtement de marbre. **3. m. meat, beef, etc.,** viande persillée, bœuf persillé.

marble-edged ['ma:bl'edʒd], *a. Bookb:* marbré sur tranche; à tranches marbrées.

marbleize ['ma:bəlaiz], *v.tr. U.S:* = MARBLE[2].

marbler ['ma:blər], *s. Bookb:* (*pers.*) marbreur, -euse; racineur *m* (des plats); jaspeur *m* sur tranches.

marbling ['ma:bliŋ], *s.* marbrure *f*; *Bookb:* racinage *m* (des plats); jaspage *m*, jaspure *f* (des tranches).

marc [ma:(k)], *s.* marc *m* (de raisin, etc.); *Agr:* tourte *f* (de lin, pour engrais).

marcasite ['ma:kəsait], *s. Miner:* marcas(s)ite *f*.

marcel[1] [ma:'sel], *s. Hairdr: A:* **m. (wave),** ondulation *f*.

marcel[2], *v.tr. A:* faire une ondulation à (une chevelure); **to have one's hair marcelled,** se faire faire une ondulation.

marcescence [ma:'sesəns], *s. Bot:* marcescence *f*, flétrissure *f*.

marcescent [ma:'sesənt], *a. Bot:* marcescent.

March[1] [ma:tʃ], *s.* (*a*) mars *m*; **in M.,** en mars, au mois de mars; **(on) the first, the seventh, of M.,** le premier, le sept, mars; **M. winds,** vents *m* de mars; (*b*) *Ent:* **M. fly,** bibion *m*.

march[2], *s. Hist:* (*often in pl.*) marche *f*; frontière *f* (militaire).

march[3], *v.i.* (*of country, domain*) **to m. (up)on, with . . .,** confiner à, être adjacent à, être limitrophe de, aboutir à . . .; **lands marching on an estate,** tenants *m* d'une propriété.

march[4], *s.* **1.** *Mil: etc:* (*a*) marche *f*; **m. in column, in line,** marche en colonne, en ligne; **m. in step,** marche au pas; **m. at attention,** marche au pas cadencé; **m. at ease,** marche sans cadence; **m. at route step,** marche au pas de route; **m. past,** défilé *m* (de prise d'armes, etc.); **route m.,** marche militaire; **movement by m. route,** déplacement *m* à pied; **cross-country m.,** marche à travers champs; **diurnal m.,** marche de jour; **night m.,** marche de nuit; **practice m.,** marche d'entraînement, d'exercice; **order of m.,** ordre *m* de marche; **rate of m.,** vitesse *f* de marche; **day's m.,** étape *f*, journée *f* de marche; **to do a day's m.,** faire, couvrir, fournir, une étape; **approach m.,** marche d'approche; **enveloping m.,** marche d'enveloppement; **flank m.,** marche de flanc; **retreat m.,** marche en retraite; **stolen m.,** marche dérobée; **on the m.,** en marche, en mouvement; **protection on the m.,** sûreté *f* en marche; **to lead the m.,** ouvrir la marche; **m. column,** colonne *f* de route; **m. discipline,** discipline *f* de marche; **m. formation,** formation *f* de marche; **m. schedule,** horaire *m* de marche; **m. unit,** (*of troops*) unité *f* de marche; (*of column of vehicles*) rame *f*; **m. unit commander,** (i) commandant *m* d'une unité de marche; (ii) chef *m* de rame; (*b*) pas *m*, allure *f*; **double m.,** pas gymnastique; **quick m.,** pas cadencé; **parade m., slow m.,** pas de parade; marche, pas, redoublé. **2.** marche, progrès *m* (des événements, du temps, de l'esprit humain); **the m. of thought,** le cheminement de la pensée. **3.** *Mus:* marche; **dead m.,** marche funèbre; **wedding m.,** marche nuptiale.

march[5]. **1.** *v.i.* (*a*) *Mil: etc:* marcher; avancer; **to m. in, out, away,** entrer, sortir, partir, au pas; **to m. off,** (i) se mettre en marche; (ii) *F:* décamper, plier bagage; **the column marched off,** la colonne s'ébranla; **to m. by, past (s.o.),** défiler (devant qn); **to m. at attention,** marcher au pas cadencé; **quick . . . m.!** (*when stationary*) en avant . . . marche! (*at the double*) pas cadencé . . . marche! **march at . . . ease!** sans cadence . . . marche! **to m. at route step,** marcher au pas de route; **to m. in close order,** marcher, avancer, en ordre serré; **to m. in column, in line,** marcher en colonne, en ligne; **to m. in front,** ouvrir la marche; **to m. in the rear,** fermer la marche; **to m. without halting,** brûler les étapes; (*b*) (*of enterprise, events*) marcher, avancer, faire des progrès; **time marches on,** l'heure s'avance; le temps s'écoule. **2.** *v.tr.* (*a*) faire marcher, mettre en marche (des troupes); (*b*) **he was marched off, away, to gaol,** il a été emmené en prison.

marchantia [ma:'ʃæntiə], *s. Bot:* marchantie *f*; (*genus*) marchantia *f*.

Marchantiales [ma:ʃænti'eili:z], *s.pl. Bot:* marchantiales *f*.

marching[1] ['ma:tʃiŋ], *a. Mil:* (régiment *m*) de ligne.

marching[2], *s. Mil: etc:* marche *f*; **in (heavy, light) m. order,** en tenue de campagne (complète, allégée); **m. orders,** ordre *m* de mise en route, feuille *f* de route; *F:* **to give s.o. his m. orders,** signifier, donner, son congé à qn; mettre qn à la porte; **m. song,** chanson *f* de route.

marchioness ['ma:ʃənes], *s.f.* marquise.

marchite ['ma:kait], *s. Miner:* marchite *f*.

marchland ['ma:tʃlænd], *s.* marches *fpl*; pays *m* frontière.

marchpane ['ma:tʃpein], *s. Cu: A:* massepain *m*.

Marcianus [ma:si'einəs]. *Pr.n.m. Hist:* Marcien.

Marcomanni [ma:kou'mæni], *s.pl. Hist:* Marcomans *m*.

marconi [ma:'kouni], *v.tr. W.Tel: A:* transmettre (un message) par sans-fil.

marconigram [ma:'kounigræm], *s. W.Tel: A:* marconigramme *m*, radiotélégramme *m*; dépêche *f* par sans-fil; *F:* sans-fil *m inv*.

Marcus ['ma:kəs]. *Pr.n.m.* Marcus; Marc.

mare ['mɛər], *s.* (*a*) jument *f*; **the grey m. is the better horse,** c'est la femme qui porte la culotte; **the discovery turned out to be a mare's nest,** la découverte s'est avérée illusoire; (*b*) **mare's tail,** (i) *Bot:* pesse *f* d'eau; (ii) *Bot:* prêle *f*; (iii) *Meteor:* queue-de-chat *f, pl.* queues-de-chat.

mareca [mə'ri:kə], *s. Orn:* maréca *m*; canard siffleur.

maregraph ['mærigræf], *s. Oc:* marémètre *m*; maréomètre *m*; maréographe *m*.

marekanite [mæ'rekənait], *s. Miner:* marécanite *f*, marékanite *f*.

maremma [mə'remə], *s. Geog:* maremme *f*; **the M.,** la Maremme.

marennin [mæ'renin], *s.* marennine *f*.

margarate ['ma:gəreit], *s. Ch:* margarate *m*.

Margaret ['ma:g(ə)rit]. *Pr.n.f.* Marguerite.

margaric [ma:'gærik], *a. Ch:* (acide *m*) margarique.

margarin ['ma:gərin], *s. Ch:* margarine *f*.

margarine [ma:dʒə'ri:n], *s. Com:* margarine *f*; **m. manufacturer,** margarinier *m*.

margarite ['ma:gə'rait], *s. Miner:* margarite *f*.

Margarodes [ma:gæ'roudi:z], *s. Ent:* margarodes *m*.

margarodite ['ma:gəroudait], *s. Miner:* margarodite *f*.

margarosanite [ma:gə'rɔsənait], *s. Miner:* margarosanite *f*.

margay ['ma:gei], *s. Z:* margay *m*; chat-tigre *m, pl.* chats-tigres.

marge[1] [ma:dʒ], *s. Poet:* = MARGIN[1] 1.

marge[2], *s. F:* margarine *f*.

Margery ['ma:dʒəri]. *Pr.n.f.* Marguerite.

margin[1] ['ma:dʒin], *s.* **1.** (*a*) marge *f*; bord *m*; lisière *f* (d'un bois); bord, rive *f* (d'un lac, d'une rivière, etc.); *Nat.Hist:* marge (d'une feuille, de l'aile d'un insecte, etc.); *Anat:* bord, rebord *m* (d'une cavité, d'un orifice); **alveolar m.,** bord alvéolaire; **cervical m.,** rebord cervical; **gingival m.,** (re)bord gingival, bord de la gencive; *N.Arch:* **m. plank,** pièce *f* de bordure (de pont); **m. plate,** tôle *f* de côté, de flanc (de ballast, etc.); (*b*) marge, écart *m*; **the m. between the rates of interest in the two countries,** l'écart entre les taux d'intérêt dans les deux pays; **m. of profit, profit m.,** marge bénéficiaire; **to allow s.o. some m.,** accorder quelque marge, quelque liberté, à qn; **m. of error,** marge d'erreur; **to allow a m. for error,** faire la part des erreurs possibles; calculer large; **m. of £100 for unforeseen expenses,** disponibilité *f* d'imprévus de £100; **to have plenty of m.,** avoir de la marge; (*c*) *Com: Fin:* marge, couverture *f*; provision *f*; *St.Exch:* acompte (versé à un courtier); couverture; (*d*) *Mec.E: etc:* **tolerance m.,** marge de tolérance; **m. of power,** marge de puissance; **safety m.,** marge de sécurité; **thickness m., length m.,** tolérance sur l'épaisseur, sur la longueur. **2.** marge, blanc *m* (d'une page, etc.); rive *f* (de papier d'imprimante); *Phot:* liseré *m* (d'une épreuve); **to write sth. in the m.,** écrire qch. en marge; faire une note marginale; *Typ:* **head m., top m.,** marge supérieure; **tail m., bottom m.,** marge inférieure; **back m., inner m.,**

marge intérieure, de fond; **outer m.,** marge extérieure; grand fond; **faulty m.,** petit fond; *Typew: etc:* **m. stop,** margeur *m*; curseur *m*, régulateur *m*, de marges; **m. release,** déclenche-marge *m inv*; *Cmptr:* **m.-punched card,** carte *f* à perforations marginales; **m. remover,** appareil *m* à couper les rives; **m. scale,** réglette graduée.

margin². **1.** *v.tr.* mettre une marge à (une page). **2.** *v.i. esp. NAm: St.Exch:* **to m. (up),** verser les couvertures requises.

marginal ['mɑːdʒin(ə)l], *a.* **1.** (*a*) marginal, -aux; *Nat.Hist:* **m. hair,** filament marginal; *Bot:* **m. placentation,** placentation marginale; *Anat:* **m. convolution,** convolution marginale (du cerveau); *Geog:* **m. sea,** mer bordière; **m. crevasse,** crevasse marginale; **m. moraine,** moraine marginale; *Opt: Phot:* **m. sharpness,** définition, netteté *f*, aux bords (de l'image); **m. rays,** rayons *m* périphériques; (*b*) **m. case,** cas *m* limite; **m. preoccupations,** préoccupations marginales; *Pol:* **m. seat,** point chaud, siège chaudement disputé; (*c*) *Com: etc:* **m. profit,** bénéfice marginal; **firm with only a m. profit,** entreprise marginale; **m. productivity, utility,** productivité, utilité, marginale; *Agr:* **m. land,** terres *fpl* d'un maigre rendement; **to lead a m. existence,** avoir à peine de quoi vivre; tirer le diable par la queue; (*d*) *Aedcs:* **m. layer,** couche limite; *Cmptr:* **m. check(ing), test(ing),** contrôle *m* des tolérances. **2.** marginal, en marge; **m. note,** note, glose, marginale; **to make m. notes in a book,** annoter un livre en marge; *Typew:* **m. stop,** margeur *m*; curseur *m*, régulateur *m*, de marge; *Cmptr:* **m. punching,** perforations marginales; **m.-punched card,** carte *f* à perforations marginales.

marginalia [mɑːdʒi'neiliə], *s.pl. Lit:* notes marginales.

marginalism ['mɑːdʒinəlizm], *s. Pol.Ec:* marginalisme *m.*

marginalist ['mɑːdʒinəlist], *s. Pol.Ec:* partisan, -ane, du marginalisme; marginaliste *mf.*

marginality [mɑːdʒi'næliti], *s.* caractère, état, marginal; nature marginale.

marginally ['mɑːdʒinəli], *adv.* d'une manière marginale; en marge; **to live m.,** avoir à peine de quoi vivre; **the shares were m. lower,** les actions avaient légèrement baissé.

marginate ['mɑːdʒineit], *a. Nat.Hist:* marginé.

margrave ['mɑːgreiv], *s. Hist:* margrave *m.*

margravial [mɑː'greiviəl], *a. Hist:* margravial, -aux.

margraviate [mɑː'greivieit], *s. Hist:* margraviat *m.*

margravine ['mɑːgrəviːn], *s. Hist:* margrave *f*, margravine *f.*

marguerite [mɑːgə'riːt], *s. Bot:* (*a*) (*oxeye daisy*) leucanthème *m* vulgaire; grande marguerite, marguerite de la Saint-Jean; marguerite des champs; (*b*) (*Paris daisy*) marguerite en arbre; chrysanthème frutescent; anthémis *f*; (*c*) **blue m.,** agathée *f* amelloïde; agathée céleste.

Maria [mə'raiə]. *Pr.n.f.* Maria; *F:* **black M.,** la voiture cellulaire; le panier à salade.

marialite [mə'riːəlait], *s. Miner:* marialite *f.*

Marian¹ ['mæriən]. *Pr.n.f.* Marianne.

Marian² ['mɛəriən, 'mæriən], *a.* **1.** de (la Vierge) Marie; *Theol:* marial, -aux. **2.** *Hist:* (*a*) de Marie (reine d'Angleterre, ou de Marie Stuart, reine d'Écosse); (*b*) *s.* partisan, -ane, de Marie Stuart. **3.** *Rom.Hist:* de Marius.

Marianas [mæri'ɑːnəz], *a. Geog:* **the M. Islands,** les îles Mariannes; les îles des Larrons.

marianism ['mɛəriənizm], *s. Rel.H:* marianisme *m.*

maricolous [mə'rikələs], *a. Nat.Hist:* marin.

Marignano [mærig'nɑːnou]. *Pr.n. Geog:* Marignan.

marigold ['mærigould], *s. Bot:* **1.** souci *m.* **2. African m.,** rose *f* d'Inde; **French m.,** œillet *m* d'Inde. **3. corn m., field m., yellow m.,** marguerite dorée; **bur(r) m.,** bidens *m*, bident *m.*

marigot ['mærigɔt], *s.* (*in W. Africa*) marigot *m*; bras *m* de fleuve.

marigram ['mærigræm], *s. Oc:* marégramme *m.*

marigraph ['mærigræf], *s. Oc:* maré(o)graphe *m.*

marihuana, marijuana [mæri'(h)wɑːnə], *s.* marihuana *f*, marijuana *f.*

marikina [mæri'kiːnə], *s. Z:* marikina *m*, rosalie *f*, tamarin *m* rosalie.

marina [mə'riːnə], *s.* port *m* de plaisance, marina *f.*

marinade¹ [mæri'neid], *s. Cu:* marinade *f.*

marinade², marinate ['mærineid, -eit], *v.tr. Cu:* (faire) mariner.

marine [mə'riːn]. **1.** *a.* (*a*) marin; **m. fauna, flora,** faune, flore, marine; **m. crab,** crabe marin; **m. life,** la vie dans les mers, dans les océans; *Geol:* **m. deposits,** gisements, dépôts, marins; **m. alluvium,** alluvions marines; *esp. NAm:* **m. belt,** eaux territoriales; *Art:* **m. painter,** peintre *m* de marines; mariniste *mf*; *Rail:* **m. station,** gare *f* maritime; (*b*) **m. barometer,** baromètre marin; **m. clock,** montre *f* de bord; **m. boiler,** chaudière *f* de marine; **m. engine,** moteur marin; **m. nuclear reactor,** réacteur marin; **m. railway,** slip *m* de carénage; **m. architecture,** génie *f* maritime, architecture navale; **m. architect,** ingénieur *m* des constructions navales; **m. engineer,** (i) mécanicien *m* de marine; (ii) ingénieur mécanicien de marine; **m. engineering,** ingénierie *f* de marine; mécanique navale; (*in port*) **m. superintendent,** capitaine *m* d'armement; (*c*) **m. forces,** troupes *f* de marine; **m. infantry,** infanterie *f* de marine; **m. artillery,** artillerie *f* de marine; (*d*) **m. insurance,** assurance *f* maritime; **m. policy, risk,** police *f* (d'assurance), risque *m*, maritime; **m. surveyor,** expert *m* maritime; (*e*) *Ch: etc:* **m. acid,** acide *m* chlorhydrique; **m. glue,** colle marine; **m. oil,** huile marine; **m. soap,** savon *m* pour lavage à l'eau de la mer. **2.** *s.* (*a*) marine *f*; **merchant, mercantile, m.,** marine marchande, de commerce; (*b*) soldat *m* de marine; = fusilier marin; **the Royal Marines, the U.S. Marine Corps** *approx.* = les fusiliers marins; *F:* **tell that to the (horse) marines!** allez conter ça ailleurs! à d'autres! *F:* **he's in the horse marines,** c'est un amiral suisse, un plongeur à cheval; (*c*) *Art:* marine; (*d*) *F:* **dead m.,** bouteille *f* vide, cadavre *m.*

marined [mə'riːnd], *a. Her:* mariné.

mariner ['mærinər], *s. Nau:* marin *m* (officier ou matelot).

Marinism [mə'riːnizm], *s. Lit.Hist:* Marinisme *m.*

Marinist [mə'riːnist], *s. Lit.Hist:* Mariniste *m.*

Mariolater [mɛəri'ɔlətər], *s. Theol:* Mariolâtre *mf.*

Mariolatry [mɛəri'ɔlətri], *s. Theol:* Mariolâtrie *f.*

Marialogy [mæriɔlədʒi], *s. Theol:* mariologie *f.*

marionette [mæriə'net], *s.* marionnette *f.*

mariposite [mæri'pousait], *s. Miner:* mariposite *f.*

marisca [mə'riskə], *s. Med:* marisque *f*, hémorroïde *f.*

Marist ['mɛərist], *s. R.C.Ch:* Mariste *m.*

marital ['mærit(ə)l], *a.* **1.** marital, -aux. **2.** matrimonial, -aux.

maritally ['mæritəli], *adv.* maritalement.

maritime ['mæritaim], *a.* maritime; **m. climate,** climat *m* maritime; **the great m. powers,** les grandes puissances maritimes; *NAm:* **m. city,** ville *f* maritime; **the M. Provinces,** *s.* **the Maritimes,** les Provinces *f* Maritimes (du Canada); **m. law,** droit *m*, législation *f*, maritime; **m. lien,** privilège *m*, droit *m* de rétention, maritime; **m. loan,** prêt *m*, emprunt *m*, à la grosse; *Ins:* **m. peril,** péril *m*, fortune *f*, de mer; **m. risk,** risque *m* maritime, risque de mer.

Maritimer ['mæritaimər], *s.* originaire *mf*, habitant, -ante, des Provinces Maritimes.

marjoram ['mɑːdʒərəm], *s. Bot:* origan *m*, marjolaine *f*; **wild m.,** origan commun; **sweet m.,** marjolaine; *Pharm:* **m.-tops,** sommités *f* d'origan.

mark¹ [mɑːk], *s.* **1.** (*a*) (*target*) but *m*, cible *f*; **to hit the m.,** (i) atteindre le but, frapper juste; (ii) (*of pers.*) réussir; tomber, deviner, juste; **to miss the m.,** (i) manquer le but; passer à côté; (ii) ne pas réussir; se tromper; **wide of the m.,** (i) loin du but; (ii) loin de la réalité, de la vérité; **I think that's near the m., I don't think I'm far from the m.,** je ne crois pas me tromper beaucoup, être loin de la vérité; **close to the thousand m.,** tout près du millier; **that's beside the m.,** cela est hors de propos, à côté de la question; (*b*) *F:* **he's an easy m.,** c'est un crédule, une dupe, une andouille; (*c*) *Box:* **blow on the m.,** coup *m* au creux de l'estomac, à la pointe du sternum, à l'épigastre. **2.** (*sign, proof*) (*a*) marque *f*, preuve *f*, signe *m*, témoignage *m*; **m. of resentment,** marque, signe, de dépit; **as a m. of (my) respect,** en signe de respect; comme marque de mon respect; **it bears the m. of strong convictions,** cela porte l'empreinte d'une forte conviction; **it bears every m. of poverty,** cela porte tous les stigmates de la misère; (*b*) (*of horse*) **m. of mouth,** marque d'âge (aux dents); germe *m* de fève; cornet *m*; **to have m. of mouth,** marquer; avoir de la dent; **to lose m. of mouth,** démarquer; **horse that has lost m. of mouth,** cheval rasé. **3.** (*visible trace*) (*a*) marque, tache *f*, signe, empreinte; **m. on the skin,** marque sur la peau; **marks of a blow,** marques d'un coup; (*of scar, etc.*) **it won't leave any permanent m.,** cela ne laissera aucune trace; **to bear the marks of suffering on one's face,** porter sur son visage la trace de la souffrance; **his fingers had left their m.,** ses doigts avaient laissé leur marque, leurs traces; (*b*) **man of m.,** homme marquant, de marque; **to make one's m.,** se faire un nom, une réputation; arriver; exercer une influence; *Lit:* **by his m. you shall know him,** à la griffe, à l'ongle, on connaît le lion; *Rugby Fb:* **to make a m.,** faire une marque; signifier un arrêt de volée; *Lit:* **God save the m.!** Dieu me pardonne! **4.** (*distinguishing sign; indication of quality, value*) (*a*) **distinguishing m.,** marque distinctive; **identification m.,** marque d'identification; **registration m.,** marque d'immatriculation; *Av:* **nationality m.,** marque de nationalité; *Com:* **certification m.,** marque de garantie; (*on gold and silver*) (**assay**) **m.,** poinçon *m* de garantie; *F:* **he's not up to the m.,** (i) il ne va pas bien, il n'est pas dans son assiette; (ii) il n'est pas à la hauteur; **you don't look up to the m.,** vous avez mauvaise mine; **that's hardly up to the m., doesn't come up to the m.,** cela laisse à désirer, ne répond pas aux exigences; (*b*) *Ind: Mil:* **m. II, III,** série II, III; (*c*) *For:* (*blaze*) blanchi(s) *m*; (*d*) *Typ: etc:* **punctuation marks,** signes de ponctuation; **interrogation m., question m.,** point *m* d'interrogation; **as he couldn't write he made his m.,** ne sachant pas écrire il a fait une croix; (*e*) *Sch:* point, note *f*; (*of teacher*) **he never gives high marks for essays,** il ne donne jamais de bonnes notes pour une dissertation; **examination marks,** notes d'examen; **good m.,** bon point; **bad m., black m.,** mauvais point; (*f*) **you've left the price m. on your new dress,** tu as laissé l'étiquette avec le prix sur ta nouvelle robe; (*g*) *St.Exch:* cote *f* (d'une valeur); **to lodge an objection to (the) m.,** mettre des oppositions à la cote. **5.** (*indication of position; limit; reference* (*on instrument, etc.*) (*a*) marque, repère *m*; **chalk m.,** marque, repère, à la craie; **reference m., guide m., lay m.,** point de repère; **gauge m.,** trait *m* de repère (pour mesurer); **scriber m.,** trait de point à tracer, trace de style; **boundary m.,** borne *f* de limitation; *Mec.E:* **assembly m.,** repère de montage, d'ajustage; **dead-centre m.,** repère de point mort; **index m.,** marque de repérage, repère (sur une pièce); **setting m.,** repère de calage; **to adjust, set, an instrument, etc., by reference marks, guide marks,** repérer un instrument, etc.; (*b*) *Nau:* amer *m*, point de reconnaissance; (*on a buoy*) voyant *m*; (*on ship*) **freeboard marks,** marques de franc-bord; **freshwater m.,** marque de franc-bord en eau douce; **Plimsoll m.,** ligne *f* Plimsoll; *Oc:* **high-water m.,** niveau *m*, laisse *f*, des hautes eaux, de la haute mer; **low-water m.,** niveau, laisse, des basses eaux, de la basse mer; (*c*) *Cmptr:* **end m.,** drapeau indicateur; **file m.,** drapeau de fichier; **group m., record m., tape m.,** drapeau de groupe, d'article, de bande; **m. reading, scanning, sensing,** lecture *f* (optique) de marques; **m. reader,** lecteur *m* de marques; (*d*) *Opt:* **fiducial m.,** marque-repère *f*, *pl.* marques-repères; fente *f* de repère; (*e*) *Rad:* **distance m., range m.,** marque de repère, de distance; (*f*) *Sp:* ligne de départ; **on your marks! get set! go!** à vos marques! prêts! partez! **to get off the m. quickly, to be quick off the m.,** démarrer vite.

mark², *v.*

I. *v.tr.* **1.** (*a*) marquer, chiffrer (du linge, de l'argenterie, des arbres, des marchandises); estampiller (des marchandises); *For:* griffer (des baliveaux); *Tchn:* signer (de la bijouterie, etc.); **to m. timber (for sawing), stones (for cutting),** établir du bois, des pierres; **to m. the cards,** biseauter, piper, piquer, maquiller, les cartes; **marked** *breakable*, revêtu de la mention *fragile*; (*b*) (*usu. passive*) **face marked with smallpox,** visage marqué de, par, la petite vérole; **my trousers were scarcely marked,** mon pantalon était à peine taché (de vin, etc.); *Nat.Hist:* **to be marked with spots, stripes,** être marqué de taches, de lignes. **2.** (*a*) **to m. (the price of) an article,** mettre le prix à un article; *St.Exch:* **to m. stock,** coter des valeurs; (*b*) *Sch:* **to m. an exercise,** corriger, noter, un devoir; **marked out of 10, 20,** noté sur 10, sur 20. **3. to m. s.o., sth., as . . .,** désigner, choisir, qn, qch., pour . . .; **I marked him as an easy prey,** je l'ai jugé une proie facile; **cattle marked for slaughter,** bestiaux désignés pour être tués. **4.** (*a*) marquer, repérer, indiquer; **to m. the points in a game, to m. the game,** marquer les points du jeu; **to m. the degrees on a thermometer,** repérer les degrés sur un thermomètre; **to m. a place on the map,** indiquer un lieu sur la carte; **to m. the wrecks in a channel,** baliser les épaves d'un chenal; (*b*) **stream that marks the boundary of the estate,** ruisseau *m* qui marque la limite de la propriété; **post marking the course,** poteau indicateur de piste; (*c*) indiquer; **this marks a change in public opinion,** cela indique un changement d'orientation de l'opinion publique; **X marks the spot,** la croix, X, indique l'endroit. **5.** (*a*) **to m. one's approval, displeasure,** témoigner, montrer, son approbation, son mécontentement; **to m. the rhythm,** accentuer le rythme; *Danc:* **to m. (out) (a step, a movement),** marquer (un pas, un mouvement); **to m. time,** (i) *Mil:* marquer le pas; (ii) *F:* piétiner sur place; attendre; (iii) *F:* vivre sur son acquis; **we're marking time,** on n'avance pas; (*b*) **the cordiality which has marked our dealings,** la cordialité qui a été (la) caractéristique de nos rapports; **his reign was marked by great victories,** de grandes victoires signalèrent son règne; son règne fut marqué, signalé, par de grandes victoires; **to m. an era,** faire époque. **6.** (*a*) *Lit:* observer, regarder, guetter (qn, qch.); **he marked him closely,** il l'observait attentivement; (*b*) *Ven:* **to m. where the birds fall,** distinguer, repérer, le point de chute des oiseaux; (*c*) observer, remarquer, noter (qch.); **m. my words!** écoutez-moi bien! notez bien ce que je vous dis! prenez-y garde! **m. you, you mustn't tell him anything he doesn't like,** par exemple, notez bien, il ne faut rien dire qui lui déplaise; *Lit:* **m. well what I say!** faites bien attention à ce que je dis! **7.** *Sp:* marquer (un adversaire).

II. (*compound verbs*) **1. mark down,** *v.tr.* (*a*) **to m. down (the price of) an article,** baisser un article de prix; **to m. down goods,** démarquer des marchandises; *Sch:* **to m. down (a paper),** baisser la note (d'une copie); (*b*) *Ven:* repérer (le gibier); rembûcher (un cerf).

2. mark off, *v.tr.* (*a*) *Surv:* **to m. off a line, a road,** bornoyer, jalonner, une ligne, une route; **to m. off a distance on the map,** (i) prendre, mesurer, (ii) rapporter, une distance sur la carte; (*b*) **to m. s.o., sth., off from . . .,** distinguer, séparer, qn, qch., de . . .; **qualities which m. him off from his colleagues,** qualités *f* qui le distinguent de ses confrères; (*c*) cocher (une liste).

3. mark out, *v.tr.* (*a*) **to m. out boundaries,** délimiter, aborner, tracer, des frontières; **to m. out a course,** tracer un itinéraire; **to m. out a field,** borner, bornoyer, un champ; **to m. out a claim,** jalonner une concession; **to m. out a tennis court,** marquer un tennis; (*b*) **to m. s.o., sth., out for . . .,** destiner qn, qch., à . . .; désigner qn, qch., pour . . ..

4. mark up, *v.tr. Com:* élever le prix de (qch.); *Sch:* hausser la note (d'une copie).

mark[3], *s. Num:* mark *m*; **gold marks,** marks or.

Mark[4]. *Pr.n.m.* Marc; **the Gospel according to Saint M.,** l'évangile *m* selon saint Marc; *Rom.Hist:* **M. Antony,** Marc-Antoine.

marked [mɑ:kt], *a.* **1.** (*a*) (*after accident*) **badly m. face,** visage balafré; (*b*) **m. card,** carte marquée, biseautée, piquée, maquillée. **2. m. man,** homme marqué (par ses ennemis); homme repéré, qui va tomber d'un jour à l'autre; **he's a m. man,** son sort est réglé, *F:* il est fichu. **3.** marqué, prononcé, accusé; **m. difference,** différence marquée, prononcée; **m. improvement,** amélioration marquée, sensible; **strongly m. features,** traits fortement accentués, fortement accusés; **strongly m. tendency,** tendance fortement marquée; **to have a very m. German accent,** avoir un accent allemand très prononcé, très accusé; **the change is becoming more m.,** le changement s'accentue; **to treat s.o. with m. discourtesy,** traiter qn avec une impolitesse marquée; **there was a m. absence of applause,** les applaudissements ne se faisaient guère entendre.

markedly ['mɑ:kidli], *adv.* d'une façon marquée; **four m. different kinds,** quatre espèces d'une différence marquée, d'une différence très prononcée; **this method is m. better,** cette méthode est nettement meilleure; **m. polite,** d'une politesse marquée.

marker ['mɑ:kər], *s.* **1.** (*pers.*) (*a*) marqueur, -euse (de linge, de bétail, etc.); (*b*) (*at games*) marqueur, pointeur *m*; (*c*) *Mil: etc:* (i) jalonneur *m*; (ii) (*at butts*) marqueur; (*d*) *Sch:* **generous m.,** professeur *m* qui donne des notes élevées. **2.** (*a*) *Ind: Mec.E:* marqueuse *f*; machine *f* à marquer, à estampiller; *Needlew:* arrondisseur *m* (de jupe); (*b*) *Ten: etc:* **(court) m.,** marqueur à chaux; *Bill:* **automatic m.,** marqueur automatique. **3.** (*a*) jalon *m*; repère *m*; fanion *m*, piquet *m*, d'alignement, de jalonnement, de repérage; *Av: etc:* (radio)phare *m*, (radio)balise *f*; *Cmptr:* marque *f*, drapeau *m*; **air m.,** repère aéronautique; **sea m.,** repère (aéronautique) en mer; (*b*) *Surg:* **pocket m., instrument m.,** pince *f* à repérer les culs-de-sac; **(radio-)beacon m.,** radiophare indicateur, feu avertisseur; **boundary m.,** borne *f*, feu, de balisage; balise de délimitation, d'extrémité (d'aérodrome); **I.L.S. (Instrument Landing System) m.,** balise radio d'atterrissage; **holding m.,** radiobalise d'attente; **outer m.,** balise d'approche; **middle m.,** balise (d'approche) intermédiaire; **m. beacon,** (radio)phare de balisage, de repérage; phare secondaire d'approche; **m. cone,** borne de balisage; **m. light,** balise lumineuse; **flush m. light,** plot lumineux d'atterrissage; **m. bomb,** marqueur; (*c*) *Geol: Min:* **m. (bed),** guidon *m*; (*d*) liseuse *f*, signet *m*.

market[1] ['mɑ:kit], *s.* **1.** (*a*) marché *m*; **open-air m.,** marché en plein air, en plein vent; **covered m.,** halle(s) *f(pl)*, marché couvert; **to go to m.,** aller au marché; **cattle m., fish m.,** marché aux bestiaux, aux poissons; **m. day,** jour *m* de marché; **m. square, m. place,** place *f* du marché; **m. town,** ville où se tient un marché; **m. gardening,** culture maraîchère; maraîchage *m*; **m. garden,** jardin maraîcher; **m.-garden produce,** produits maraîchers; **m. gardener,** maraîcher, -ère; (*b*) *Com:* **commodity m.,** marché des matières premières; **capital goods m.,** marché d'équipement; **cotton, tin, m.,** marché du coton, de l'étain; **real estate m.,** marché (de l')immobilier; (*c*) *Com: Pol.Ec:* marché; débouchés *mpl* (d'un produit); **the home m.,** le marché intérieur, national; **foreign, overseas, markets,** marchés extérieurs, étrangers, d'outre-mer; **free, open, m.,** marché libre; *Jur:* **m. overt,** marché public; **regulated m.,** marché réglementé; **the Common M.,** le Marché Commun; **black m.,** marché noir, parallèle; **grey m., semi-black m.,** marché gris; **m. research, analysis,** étude *f*, analyse *f*, de marché; **m. forecast,** prévision *f* du marché; **buyers', sellers', m.,** marché à la baisse, à la hausse; **to buy at the top of the m.,** acheter au cours, au prix, le plus élevé; **to put an article on the m.,** mettre un article sur le marché; **to be on the m., come into the m.,** être à vendre, en vente; (*of pers.*) **to be in the m. for sth.,** être acheteur, se porter acquéreur, de qch.; **to find a m. for sth.,** trouver un débouché, des acheteurs, pour qch.; **to find a ready m.,** être facile à vendre, d'un débit facile; se placer facilement; **to open up new markets,** créer, ouvrir, de nouveaux débouchés; **to glut, flood, the m.,** encombrer, saturer, le marché; **m. price,** prix marchand, courant; **to price oneself out of the m.,** perdre sa clientèle en demandant des prix excessifs; (*d*) *Fin: St.Exch:* **foreign exchange m.,** marché des changes, des devises; **forward exchange m.,** marché des changes à terme, marché à terme des devises; **credit m.,** marché du crédit; **stock m.,** marché des titres, des valeurs; bourse *f* des valeurs; **settlement m.,** marché à terme (des valeurs); **shares on the m.,** titres flottants; **official m.,** marché officiel, en bourse; parquet *m*; **unofficial m., m. in unlisted shares,** *U.S:* **over-the-counter m.,** marché hors cote; **outside, curbstone, m.,** marché en coulisse; **to make a m., to rig the m.,** se porter contre-partiste (occulte); **m. rigger,** contrepartiste *m* occulte; **m. rigging,** contrepartie *f* occulte; **to play the m.,** spéculer. **2.** *A:* achat *m* et vente *f*; trafic *m*; affaire *f*; **to make a m. of one's honour,** faire trafic de son honneur; trafiquer de son honneur.

market[2], *v.* **(marketed) 1.** *v.i. U.S:* **to m., to go marketing,** faire son marché, (aller) faire ses courses, aller aux provisions. **2.** *v.tr.* vendre; trouver des débouchés pour (ses marchandises); lancer (un article) sur le marché.

marketability [mɑ:kitə'biliti], *s.* valeur marchande, commerciale (d'un produit).

marketable ['mɑ:kitəbl], *a.* (*a*) (*of goods*) vendable; d'un débit facile; (*b*) **m. value,** valeur marchande, vénale.

marketeer [mɑ:ki'tiər], *s.* **black m.,** trafiquant *m* du marché noir; **Common M.,** partisan, -ane; du Marché Commun.

marketing ['mɑ:kitiŋ], *s.* **1.** (*a*) achat *m*, vente *f* (de qch.) au marché; **to do one's m.,** aller faire son marché, ses courses; aller aux provisions; (*b*) commercialisation *f*; service commercial (d'un produit); *Adm:* **the Milk M. Board,** le Comité de contrôle de la vente du lait; (*c*) (i) étude *f* des marchés; marketing *m*; (ii) prospection *f* du client. **2.** *U.S:* denrées (apportées au marché).

markhor ['mɑ:kɔ:r], *s. Z:* markhor *m*.

marking ['mɑ:kiŋ], *s.* **1.** (*a*) marquage *m* (du linge, du bétail, etc.); *For:* établissement *m*, marquage (du bois à couper); **m. ink,** encre *f* à marquer; (*b*) estampillage *m*; poinçonnage (de l'or, de l'argent, etc.); **m. awl, m. tool,** pointe *f* à tracer; **m. wheel,** molette imprimante; *Carp:* **m. gauge,** trusquin *m* (à pointe); **m. off,** séparation *f* (de qch. d'avec qch.); **m.-off tool,** outil *m* de traçage; (*c*) *Mec.E: etc:* repérage *m* (du point mort, etc.); *Surg:* **m. of pocket depth,** repérage de la profondeur des culs-de-sac; (*d*) **m. (out),** tracement *m*, tracé *m*, jalonnage *m*, (*with beacons*) balisage *m* (d'un itinéraire, etc.); traçage *m*, tracé (d'un tennis); bornage *m*, abornement *m* (d'un champ); *Mil: etc:* **m. pennant,** fanion *m* (de jalonnement, d'alignement); *Nau:* **m. buoy,** bouée *f* de balisage; *Tp:* **m. post,** borne *f* de repérage; (*e*) *St.Exch:* cotation *f* (des valeurs). **2.** (*a*) **markings,** marques *f*; (*on animal*) taches *f*, rayures *f*; **distinctive marking(s),** marques distinctives; *Av:* **(wing, fuselage) m.,** cocarde *f*; (*b*) estampille *f*. **3.** *Sch:* (*a*) correction *f*, notation *f* (d'un devoir); (*b*) copies *f* à corriger; **I've a lot of m. this evening,** j'ai beaucoup de devoirs à corriger ce soir.

marksman, *pl.* **-men** ['mɑ:ksmən], *s.* bon tireur; tireur d'élite, de première classe.

marksmanship ['mɑ:ksmənʃip], *s.* adresse *f*, habileté *f*, au tir.

marl[1] [mɑ:l], *s. Agr:* marne *f*; *Geol:* caillasse *f*; **m. pit,** marnière *f*.

marl[2], *v.tr. Agr:* marner (le sol).

marl[3], *v.tr. Nau:* merliner (une ralingue, une voile); **to m. down a rope,** guirlander un cordage.

marl[4], *s. Austr: Z:* (espèce de) péramèle *m*.

marlberry ['mɑ:lberi], *s. Bot:* ardisia *f*.

Marlburian [mɔ:l'bju:riən], *s.* (i) élève, (ii) ancien élève, de Marlborough College.

marled [mɑ:ld], *a. Scot:* bigarré.

marlin ['mɑ:lin], *s. Ich:* poisson *m* épieu.

marline ['mɑ:lin], *s. Nau:* (*two yarns*) lusin *m*; (*three yarns*) merlin *m*; **m. spike,** (*also* **marlingspike**), épissoir *m*; épinglette *f*; burin *m*; **m. spike, hitch,** nœud *m*, de tressillon, de griffe.

marling[1] ['mɑ:liŋ], *s. Agr:* marnage *m*.

marling[2], *s. Nau:* guirlande *f*; **m. hitch,** nœud *m* de croc double.

marly ['mɑ:li], *a.* (sol) marneux.

marmalade ['mɑ:məleid], *s. Cu:* confiture *f* d'oranges; **grapefruit m.,** confiture de pamplemousses.

marmalite ['mɑ:məlait], *s. Miner:* marmolite *f*.

marmarization [mɑ:mərai'zeiʃ(ə)n], *s. Geol:* marmorisation *f*.

marmarize ['mɑ:məraiz], *v.tr. Geol:* marmoriser.

marmatite ['mɑ:mətait], *s. Miner:* marmatite *f*.

marmolite ['mɑ:məlait], *s. Miner:* marmolite *f*.

Marmora ['mɑ:mərə]. *Pr.n. Geog:* **the Sea of M.,** la mer de Marmara.

marmoreal, marmorean [mɑ:'mɔ:riəl, -riən], *a. Poet:* marmoréen; de marbre.

marmorization [mɑ:mərai'zeiʃ(ə)n], *s. Geol:* marmorisation *f*.

marmorize ['mɑ:məraiz], *v.tr. Geol:* marmoriser.

marmoset [mɑ:mə'zet], *s. Z:* ouistiti *m*, marmouset *m*; **silky m.,** tamarin *m*.

marmot ['mɑ:mət], *s. Z:* marmotte *f*; **Canadian m.,** siffleur *m*; **bobak m.,** marmotte bobak.

marocain ['mærəkein], *s. Tex:* crêpe marocain.

Maronite ['mærənait], *s. Rel.H:* maronite *m*.

maroon[1] [mə'ru:n]. **1.** *a. & s.* (*colour*) marron pourpré *inv*; rouge foncé *inv*. **2.** *s. Pyr:* marron *m*; fusée *f* à pétard.

maroon[2], *s.* **1.** *Hist:* nègre marron, négresse marronne. **2.** personne abandonnée dans une île déserte, sur une côte sans habitants.

maroon[3]. **1.** *v.tr.* (*a*) abandonner (qn) dans une île déserte; (*b*) **riverside dwellers marooned by the floods,** riverains isolés par les inondations. **2.** *v.i.* (*a*) (*of negro slave*) s'enfuir dans les bois; (*b*) *U.S: O:* flâner; mener une vie oisive.

marooner [mə'ru:nər], *s. A:* boucanier *m*.

marplot ['mɑ:plɔt], *s. O:* brouillon *m*; brouille-tout *m inv*; gaffeur *m*.

marque [mɑ:k], *s. Hist:* **1. letters of m. (and reprisal),** lettres *f* de marque; lettres de représailles. **2. letter of m.,** corsaire (muni de lettres de marque); vaisseau armé en course.

marquee [mɑ:'ki:], *s.* grande tente.

Marquesan [mɑ:'keizən], *Geog:* (*a*) *a.* marquésan, marquisien; (*b*) *s.* Marquésan, -anne; Marquisien, -ienne.

Marquesas (the) [ðəmɑ:'keisəs]. *Pr.n. Geog:* les Iles *f* Marquises.

marquess, marquis ['mɑ:kwis], *s.* marquis *m*.

marquetry ['mɑ:kitri], *s.* marqueterie *f*.

marquisate ['mɑ:kwizeit], *s.* marquisat *m*.

marquise [mɑ:'ki:z], *s.* **1.** (*of foreign nobility*) marquise *f*. **2.** (*a*) **m. ring,** marquise; (*b*) *O:* **m. sunshade,** marquise; (*c*) *Hort:* **m. pear,** marquise.

mar(r)am ['mærəm], *s. Bot:* **m. (grass),** gourbet *m*; (*in N. of Fr.*) oyat *m*.

marriage ['mæridʒ], *s.* **1.** mariage *m*; union (conjugale); **to give s.o. in m.,** donner qn en mariage; **to take s.o. in m.,** épouser qn; **to seek s.o.'s hand, in m.,** rechercher qn en mariage; **proposal of m.,** demande *f* en mariage; **uncle by m.,** oncle *m* par alliance; **a m. has been arranged between . . . and . . .,** on annonce le prochain mariage de . . . avec . . .; **the m. will take place at . . .,** le mariage aura lieu à . . .; **theirs was a happy m.,** leur mariage a été heureux; **their m. is on the rocks,** leur mariage est en ruines; **civil m.,** mariage civil; **m. settlement,** contrat *m* de mariage; **m. certificate,** *F:* **m. lines,** acte *m* de mariage; **m. service,** célébration *f* du mariage; **the m. tie,** le lien conjugal; *Adm:* **m. rate,** nuptialité *f*. **2.** mariage, union (entre les choses); **the m. of line and colour,** l'union de la ligne et de la couleur. **3.** *Cards:* (*bezique*) mariage.

marriageable ['mæridʒəbl], *a.* (*a*) (fille *f*, âge *m*) nubile; **she is of m. age,** elle est d'âge à se marier, en âge de se marier; (*b*) **to have three m. daughters,** avoir trois filles mariables, à marier.

married ['mærid], *a.* (*a*) **m. man,** homme marié; **a (happily) m. couple,** un ménage (heureux); **the young, newly, m. couple,** les jeunes, nouveaux, mariés; (*b*) **the m. state,** l'état *m* de mariage; **m. life,** la vie conjugale; le mariage; **the first year of their m. life,** leur première année de mariage; **m. name,** nom *m* de femme mariée, de mariage.

marrow ['mærou], *s.* **1.** (*a*) moelle *f*; **spinal m.,** moelle épinière; *Cu:* amourettes *fpl* (de mouton, etc.); **to be frozen to the m.,** être transi de froid; être glacé jusqu'à la moelle; (*b*) moelle, essence *f* (de qch.). **2.** *Hort:* **vegetable m.,** courge *f*; courgette *f*.

marrowbone ['mærouboun], *s.* os *m* à moelle.

marrowfat ['mæroufæt], *s.* **1.** graisse *f* de moelle. **2.** *Hort:* **m. (pea),** pois carré.

marrowless ['mæroulis], *a.* (*a*) (os *m*) sans moelle; (*b*) *F: A:* (*of pers.*) sans énergie; veule.

marrowy ['mæroui], *a.* **1.** (os) plein de moelle. **2.** qui ressemble à de la moelle; onctueux.

marrubium [mə'ru:biəm], *s. Bot:* marrube *m*.

marry[1] ['mæri], *v.tr.* **1.** (*of priest, parent*) marier; unir (en mariage); **he married his daughter to my eldest son,** il a marié sa fille à mon fils aîné; **she has three daughters to m. off,** elle a trois filles à marier, à caser; **they were married by the bishop, by the mayor,** l'évêque, le maire, les a mariés. **2.** (*a*) se marier avec (qn); épouser (qn); **he married his cook,** il a épousé sa cuisinière; (*b*) *v.tr. & i.* **to m., to get married,** se marier; **to m. (for) money,** faire un mariage d'argent, *F:* épouser le sac; **of an age to be married,** (i) en âge de, d'âge à, se marier; (ii) *Physiol:* (*of girl*) nubile; **why have you never married?** pourquoi ne vous êtes-vous jamais marié? **to m. again, a second time,** se remarier; **to m. into a family,** s'allier, s'apparenter, à une famille; entrer par alliance dans une famille; **to m. beneath one,** se marier au-dessous de son rang; se mésallier; faire une mésalliance; **he has married well,** il a fait un beau mariage; *Prov:* **m. in haste and repent at leisure,** tel se marie à la hâte qui s'en repent à loisir. **3.** *Nau:* marier (deux cordages).

marry[2], *int. A:* par la sainte Vierge! pardi! ma foi! **m. come up!** ta, ta, ta! turlututu!

marrying[1] ['mæriiŋ], *a. F:* **he's not the m. sort,** il n'est pas enclin au mariage; il n'est pas porté à se marier.

marrying[2], *s.* union *f* en mariage; **of a m. age,** en âge de se marier; d'âge à se marier.

Mars [mɑ:z]. *Pr.n.m. Rom.Myth: Astr:* Mars; **the planet M.,** la planète Mars.

Marsala [mɑ:'sɑ:lə]. **1.** *Pr.n. Geog:* Marsala. **2.** *s.* vin *m* de Marsala; marsala *m*.

Marseille(s) [mɑ:'sei(lz)]. *Pr.n. Geog:* Marseille.

marsh [mɑ:ʃ], *s.* (*a*) marais *m*, marécage *m*; **salt m.,** marais salant; (*b*) *Bot:* **m. marigold,** souci *m* d'eau; populage *m*; **m. samphire,** salicorne *f*; (*c*) *Orn:* **m. hen,** poule *f* d'eau; **m. harrier,** busard *m* des roseaux, busard harpaye; **m. hawk,** busard Saint-Martin; **m. sandpiper,** chevalier *m* stagnatile; (*d*) **m. gas,** gaz *m* des marais, *Ch:* formène *m*, méthane *m*.

marshal[1] ['mɑ:ʃ(ə)l], *s.* **1.** *Hist:* maréchal, -aux *m*; **knight-m.,** maréchal de la Maison du Roi (et chef de la sûreté dans la zone où réside le roi). **2.** (*a*) *Mil:* **field m.** = maréchal (de France); (*b*) *Mil: Av:* **M. of the R.A.F.** = Commandant en Chef des Forces aériennes; **Air Chief M.** = général d'armée aérienne; **Air M.** = général de corps d'armée aérienne; **Air Vice M.** = général de division d'armée aérienne; (*c*) **M. of the Diplomatic Corps,** Chef *m* du Protocole. **3.** (*a*) maître *m* des cérémonies; **city m.,** fonctionnaire chargé de l'application des lois de la Cité de Londres (et qui précède le lord-maire dans les processions); (*b*) *U.S:* (i) fonctionnaire ayant les attributions d'un shérif; (ii) *occ.* = commissaire *m* de police; (*c*) **fire m.,** chef du service d'incendie (dans une région, une usine). **4. judge's m.,** secrétaire *m* d'un juge en tournée.

marshal[2], *v.* **(marshalled) 1.** *v.tr.* (*a*) placer (des personnes) en ordre, en rang; (*b*) *Mil:* ranger (des troupes); (*c*) **to m. facts,** rassembler des faits et les mettre en ordre; *Jur:* **to m. the assets,** établir l'ordre entre les éléments d'actif (d'une succession); (*d*) *Her:* **to m. two coats of arms in one shield,** disposer deux blasons sur un écu; (*e*) *Rail:* classer, trier, manœuvrer (des wagons); (*f*) (*of usher, footman, etc.*) introduire **(s.o. into a room,** qn dans une salle); **to m. s.o. out,** reconduire qn (cérémonieusement). **2.** *v.i.* se ranger, se placer en ordre; **we marshalled in the yard,** nous nous sommes mis en rang, nous avons pris nos rangs, dans la cour.

marshaller ['mɑ:ʃələr], *s.* (*a*) *Rail:* chef *m* de manœuvre; (*b*) *Av:* placeur *m*.

marshalling ['mɑ:ʃəliŋ], *s.* **1.** disposition *f* en ordre (de personnes, de choses); *Jur:* **m. the assets,** ordre établi par l'exécuteur testamentaire entre les éléments d'actif (d'une succession). **2.** *Rail:* classement *m*, triage *m*, manœuvre *f* (des wagons); **m. yard,** gare *f* de triage.

marshalship ['mɑ:ʃəlʃip], *s.* maréchalat *m*; dignité *f* de maréchal.

marshiness ['mɑ:ʃinis], *s.* état marécageux (du terrain).

marshite ['mɑ:ʃait], *s. Miner:* marshite *f*.

marshland ['mɑ:ʃlænd], *s.* terrain marécageux, terrain uliginaire, marécages *mpl*.

marshmallow [mɑ:ʃ'mælou], *s.* (*a*) *Bot:* guimauve *f*, althée *f*; (*b*) *Comest:* (pâte de) guimauve.

marshy ['mɑ:ʃi], *a.* (sol, air) marécageux.

marsupial [mɑ:'s(j)u:piəl]. **1.** *a.* marsupial, -iaux; *Amph:* **m. frog,** nototrème *m*; *Z:* **m. anteater,** myrmécobie *m*; **m. mole,** notorycte *m*; **m. mouse, (brush-tailed) m. rat,** phasco(lo)gale *m*; **m. wolf,** thylacine *m*. **2.** *s. Z:* marsupial *m*; **the marsupials,** les marsupiaux; les didelphes *m*, les métathériens *m*.

Marsupiala [mɑ:s(j)u:pi'eilə], *s.pl. Z:* marsupiaux *m*.

marsupialization [mɑ:s(j)u:piəlai'zeiʃ(ə)n], *s. Surg:* marsupialisation *f*.

marsupialize [mɑ:'s(j)u:piəlaiz], *v.tr. Surg:* marsupialiser.

marsupium, *pl.* **-ia** [mɑ:'s(j)u:piəm, -iə], *s.* (*a*) *Z: etc:* marsupium *m*; poche ventrale; (*b*) *Anat:* marsupium (de l'œil).

mart [mɑ:t], *s.* **1.** *A:* (*a*) place *f* du marché; (*b*) centre *m* de commerce; marché. **2. (auction) m.,** salle *f* de vente; **car m.,** auto-marché *m*, *pl.* auto-marchés.

martagon ['mɑ:təgɔn], *s. Bot:* **m. (lily),** martagon *m*, *F:* turban *m*.

martel-de-fer ['mɑ:teldə'fɛər], *s. A.Arms:* marteau *m* d'armes.

martello [mɑ:'telou], *s. Fort:* **m. tower,** martello *m*, tour *f* à la Martello; fort *m* circulaire (défendant les côtes).

marten[1] ['mɑ:tin], *s. Z:* mart(r)e *f*; **beech m., stone m.,** fouine *f*; **pine m.,** martre des pins; martre commune; **Asiatic yellow-throated m.,** martre asiatique à gorge jaune.

marten[2], *s. Orn:* = MARTIN[2].

martensite ['mɑ:tenzait], *s. Metall:* martensite *f*.

Martha ['mɑ:θə]. *Pr.n.f.* Marthe.

martial[1] ['mɑ:ʃ(ə)l], *a.* **1.** martial, -aux, guerrier; **m. bearing,** air martial; **m. spirit,** esprit martial, guerrier; **m. exercises,** exercices *m* de guerre; *A:* **m. array,** ordre *m* de bataille; **m. law,** loi martiale; (*in a town*) **to declare m. law,** proclamer l'état *m* de siège. **2.** *Pharm: etc: A:* ferrugineux, martial.

Martial[2]. *Pr.n.m. Lt.Lit:* Martial.

martially ['mɑ:ʃəli], *adv.* martialement; d'une manière martiale; en guerrier.

Martian ['mɑ:ʃiən]. **1.** *a.* martien, de la planète Mars. **2.** *s.* Martien, -ienne; habitant, -ante, de Mars.

Martin[1] ['mɑ:tin]. *Pr.n.m.* Martin; **St Martin's day,** la Saint-Martin; **St Martin's summer,** été *m* de la Saint-Martin.

martin[2], *s. Orn:* **(house) m.,** hirondelle *f* de fenêtre; **purple m.,** hirondelle pourprée; **sand m., bank m.,** hirondelle de rivage, *Fr.C:* hirondelle des sables; **black m., screech m.,** martinet noir; arbalétrier; **crag m.,** hirondelle des rochers.

martinet[1] [mɑ:ti'net], *s. Orn: A:* hirondelle *f* de fenêtre.

martinet[2], *s. Mil: etc:* officier *m* à cheval sur la discipline, *F:* qui fait pivoter ses hommes; *F:* pètesec *m*; **he's a regular m.,** c'est un vrai garde-chiourme; il fait marcher ses employés militairement; **she's a m.,** c'est un vrai gendarme.

martingale[1] ['mɑ:tiŋgeil], *s.* **1.** *Harn:* martingale *f*. **2.** *Nau:* (*a*) **m. (guy, stay),** martingale du beaupré; (*b*) (*dolphin striker*) arc-boutant *m* de martingale. **3.** *Gaming:* martingale.

martingale[2], *v.i. Gaming:* martingaler.

Martinican [mɑ:ti'ni:kən]. *Geog:* (*a*) *a.* martiniquais; (*b*) *s.* Martinquais, -aise.

Martinique [mɑ:ti'ni:k]. *Pr.n. Geog:* la Martinique.

Martinmas ['mɑ:tinmæs], *s.* la Saint-Martin.

martite ['mɑ:tait], *s. Miner:* martite *f*.

martlet ['mɑ:tlet], *s.* **1.** *Orn: A:* hirondelle *f* de fenêtre. **2.** *Her:* merlette *f*.

martyr[1] ['mɑ:tər], *s.* martyr, *f.* martyre; **to be a m. to gout, to rheumatism,** être sujet à la goutte, aux rhumatismes; être torturé par la goutte; être travaillé de, par, la goutte; être perclus de rhumatismes; souffrir (beaucoup) des rhumatismes; **he makes a perfect m. of himself,** il se torture le cœur à plaisir; il se donne gratuitement de la peine; **to die a m. in, to, a cause,** mourir martyr d'une cause; mourir pour une cause; **the martyrs (in the cause) of science,** les martyrs de la science.

martyr[2], *v.tr.* martyriser (qn); **a martyred people,** un peuple martyr.

martyrdom ['mɑ:tədəm], *s.* martyre *m*; **these cruel trials had made his life one long m.,** ces cruelles épreuves avaient fait de sa vie un long supplice, un long calvaire.

martyrization [mɑ:tərai'zeiʃ(ə)n], *s.* martyre *m* **(of s.o.,** de qn).

martyrize ['mɑ:təraiz], *v.tr.* **1.** faire subir le martyre à (qn). **2.** martyriser (ses domestiques, etc.).

martyrizing ['mɑ:təraiziŋ], *s.* **1.** martyre *m*. **2.** persécution *f*.

martyrological [mɑ:tərə'lɔdʒik(ə)l], *a.* martyrologique.

martyrologist [mɑ:tə'rɔlədʒist], *s.* martyrologiste *m*.

martyrology [mɑ:tə'rɔlədʒi], *s.* **1.** (*list of martyrs*) martyrologe *m*; (*in the Gr. Church*) ménologe *m*. **2.** (*history of martyrs*) martyrologie *f*.

martyry ['mɑ:təri], *s.* martyrium *m*; chapelle commémorative d'un martyr.

marvel[1] ['mɑ:v(ə)l], *s.* **1.** (*a*) merveille *f*; **the marvels of science,** les merveilles de la science; (*b*) **it's a m. to me that . . .,** cela m'étonne beaucoup que . . .; **it was a m. that he wasn't killed,** merveille qu'il ne se soit pas tué; *A:* **no m. then if . . .,** il n'est donc pas étonnant si . . .; **the house was a m. of neatness,** la maison était une merveille de propreté; **to work marvels,** faire des merveilles; **these injections work marvels,** ces piqûres *f* font merveille; (*c*) *P:* **you're a bloody m.!** (i) espèce d'andouille! (ii) tu te crois, mon vieux! **2.** *A:* étonnement *m*, émerveillement *m*. **3.** *Bot:* **m. of Peru,** belle *f* de nuit.

marvel[2], *v.i.* **(marvelled)** *O:* s'émerveiller, s'étonner **(at,** de); **I m. that he should remain so calm,** je m'étonne (de ce) qu'il reste si calme.

marvellous ['mɑ:v(ə)ləs]. **1.** *a.* merveilleux, étonnant, miraculeux; **it would be m. if . . .,** ce serait merveilleux si . . .; *F:* **I feel m.,** je me sens rudement bien; *Iron:* **isn't it m.!** ça c'est le bouquet, le comble! **2.** *s.* **it savours of the m.,** cela tient du prodige; **I don't believe in the m.,** je ne crois pas au merveilleux.

marvellously ['mɑ:v(ə)ləsli], *adv.* à merveille; merveilleusement; miraculeusement; **m. well done,** fait à merveille, à miracle.

Marxian ['mɑ:ksiən], *a. & s. Pol.Ec:* marxiste (*mf*).

Marx(ian)ism ['mɑ:ks(iən)izm], *s. Pol.Ec:* marxisme *m*.

Marxianize ['mɑ:ksiənaiz], *v.tr. Pol:* marxistiser (un pays, etc.).

Marxist ['mɑ:ksist], *a. & s. Pol.Ec:* marxiste (*mf*).

Mary ['mɛəri]. *Pr.n.f.* **1.** Marie; **M. Stuart, M. Queen of Scots,** Marie Stuart; **Bloody M.,** (i) *Hist: F:* Marie Tudor; (ii) *F:* cocktail composé de vodka et de jus de tomate. **2.** *F:* **little M.,** l'estomac *m*.

Maryland ['mɛərilænd]. *Pr.n. Geog:* le Maryland; **M. tobacco,** maryland *m*; *Orn:* **M. yellowthroat,** fauvette masquée; *Cu:* **M. chicken,** poulet sauté Maryland.

Marylander ['mɛərilændər], *a. & s.* (habitant, -ante; originaire) du Maryland.

marzipan [mɑ:zi'pæn], *s. Cu:* massepain *m*; **m. dates,** dattes farcies.

mascagnine, mascagnite [mæ'skænji:n, -njait], *s. Miner:* mascagnine *f*.

mascara [mæs'kɑ:rə], *s. Toil:* mascara *m*.

Mascarene [mæskə'ri:n]. *Pr.n. Geog:* **the M. Islands,** les (îles) Mascareignes.

mascaron ['mæskərən], *s. Art:* mascaron *m*.

mascle [mæskl], *s. A.Arm: Her:* macle *f*.

mascled ['mæ'skəld], *a. Her:* maclé.

mascon ['mæskɔn], *s.* (*on moon*) mascon *m*.

mascot ['mæskət], *s.* mascotte *f*; porte-bonheur *m inv*; *Aut:* **radiator m.,** fétiche *m*, mascotte, de bouchon de radiateur.

masculine ['mæskjulin], *a.* **1.** masculin, mâle; **m. descent,** descendance *f* mâle; **m. style,** style mâle, viril; **m. woman,** femme masculine, hommasse. **2.** *Gram:* **m. noun,** substantif masculin; **this word is m.,** ce mot est du masculin; **in the m. gender,** *s.* **in the m.,** au masculin; *Pros:* **m. rhyme,** rime masculine.

masculineness ['mæskjulinnis], **masculinity** [mæskju'liniti], *s.* masculinité *f*.

masculinize ['mæskjulinaiz], *v.tr.* masculiniser (la femme, etc.).

masculy ['mæskjuli], *a. Her:* maclé.

maser ['meizər], *s. Atom.Ph:* maser *m*; **ammonia m.,** maser à ammoniac; **gas m.,** maser à gaz; **infra-red m.,** maser infrarouge; **optical m.,** maser optique; **ruby m.,** maser à rubis; **solid-state m.,** maser solide.

mash[1] [mæʃ], *s.* **1.** *Brew:* fardeau *m* (de malt et d'eau chaude); **m. tub, m. tun,** cuve *f* matière; brassin *m*. **2.** *Husb:* mash *m* (pour chevaux); pâtée *f* (pour cochons et volaille); **bran m.,** barbotage *m*, pâtée de son (pour chevaux et bestiaux); son mouillé. **3.** *F:* purée *f* de pommes de terre; **sausages and m.,** purée avec saucisses. **4.** mélange *m*; pâte *f*; bouillie *f*; **to reduce sth. to m.,** réduire (du papier, etc.) en pâte, en bouillie.

mash[2], *v.tr.* **1.** (*a*) *Brew:* brasser, mélanger, démêler (le moût); (*b*) *Dial:* **to m. the tea,** faire infuser le thé; *v.i.* (*of tea*) **to m.,** infuser. **2. to m. sth. (up),** broyer, écraser, qch.; *Cu:* **to m. potatoes, turnips,** faire une purée de pommes de terre, de navets.

mash[3], *s. F: A:* béguin *m*; (*a*) **to have a m. on s.o.,** avoir un béguin pour qn; (*b*) **to be out with one's m.,** se promener avec son béguin.

mash[4], *v.tr. F: A:* **1.** (*a*) faire la conquête de (qn); (*b*) faire des avances à (qn); faire de l'œil à (qn). **2. to be mashed on s.o.,** avoir un béguin pour qn; être emballé pour qn.

mashed [mæʃt], *a.* **1.** écrasé. **2.** *Cu:* en purée; **m. potatoes,** purée *f* de pommes de terre; pommes *f* mousseline.

masher[1] ['mæʃər], *s. Tchn:* (*device*) broyeur *m*, écraseur *m*, mélangeur *m*.

masher[2], *s. A: F:* gommeux *m*, bellâtre *m*, dandy *m*.

mashie, mashy ['mæʃi], *s. Golf:* mashie *m*.

mashing ['mæʃiŋ], *s. Brew:* brassage *m*, mélange *m*, démêlage *m* (du moût).

mask[1] [mɑːsk], *s.* **1.** (*a*) masque *m*; (*silk or velvet*) loup *m*; **to put a m. on s.o.,** masquer qn; **to put on a m.,** se masquer; **carnival m.,** masque de carnaval; **under the m. of friendship,** sous le masque, sous le voile, sous le semblant, de l'amitié; sous de faux semblants d'amitié; **to throw off, drop, the m.,** lever le masque; jeter, mettre bas, le masque; se démasquer; **with the m. off,** à visage découvert; (*b*) **protective m.,** masque de protection; **(fencing) m.,** masque protecteur, masque d'escrime; *Ind:* **welder's m.,** capot protecteur; (*c*) *Gr.Th:* **the tragic m.,** le masque tragique. **2.** *Ven:* face *f* (de renard, etc.); **mounted m.,** face naturalisée sur écusson. **3.** moulage *m*, masque (d'un visage). **4.** *Art:* mascaron *m*. **5.** *Phot:* **(printing) m.,** cache *m*; **soft m.,** cache flou; **sharp m.,** cache net.

mask[2], *v.tr.* **1.** masquer; **to m. one's face,** se masquer. **2.** (*a*) *Mil:* masquer (une batterie, une place forte); **to m. one's own batteries,** masquer ses propres batteries; gêner le tir de ses propres batteries; (*b*) **to m. a light beam,** masquer un faisceau lumineux. **3.** (*a*) *Phot:* poser un cache à (un cliché); (*b*) *Paint:* poser un papier-cache à (une surface à protéger). **4.** (*a*) cacher; déguiser (ses sentiments, ses pensées); voiler (ses défauts, etc.); (*b*) *Med:* masquer, déguiser, blanchir (une maladie).

Maskat [mæs'kæt]. *Pr.n. Geog:* Mascate.

masked [mɑːskt], *a.* **1.** masqué; **m. man,** homme masqué; **m. ball,** bal masqué; *Bot:* **m. flower,** fleur personnée. **2.** *Mil:* **m. battery,** batterie masquée. **3.** (*a*) **m. smile,** sourire caché; **m. dictatorship,** dictature larvée; (*b*) *Med:* **m. fever,** fièvre larvée.

maskelynite ['mæskilinait], *s. Miner:* maskelynite *f*.

masker ['mɑːskər], *s.* (*pers.*) **1.** masque *m*. **2.** *Th: A:* acteur *m* (d'un masque).

masking ['mɑːskiŋ], *s.* **1.** (*a*) pose *f* d'un masque ou d'un cache; couverture *f*; *Paint:* **m. paper,** papier-cache *m*, *pl.* papiers-caches; **m. tape,** bande *f* de papier-cache; (*b*) *Cin:* **m. blade,** secteur *m* d'obscuration (de l'obturateur). **2.** déguisement *m* (de sa pensée, etc.).

maslin ['mæzlin], *s. Agr:* méteil *m*, dragée *f*; (blé *m*) mouture *f*.

masochism ['mæsoukizm], *s. Psy:* masochisme *m*.

masochist ['mæsoukist], *s. & a. Psy:* masochiste (*mf*).

masochistic [mæsou'kistik], *a.* masochiste.

mason[1] ['meis(ə)n], *s.* **1.** maçon *m*; **foreman m.,** appareilleur *m*. **2.** franc-maçon *m*, *pl.* francs-maçons. **3.** *Ent:* **m. bee,** abeille maçonne; **m. wasp,** guêpe maçonne; eumène *m*; **m. ant,** fourmi maçonne; *Ann:* **sand m. worm,** maçon des sables.

mason[2], *v.tr.* **(masoned)** maçonner (un mur, etc.); construire (qch.) en maçonnerie.

masoned ['meis(ə)nd], *a. Her:* maçonné.

masonic [mə'sɔnik], *a.* (franc-)maçonnique; des francs-maçons, de la franc-maçonnerie.

masonite ['meisənait], *s. Miner:* masonite *f*.

masonry ['meisənri], *s.* **1.** (*a*) maçonnerie *f*, maçonnage *m*; (*b*) **piece of m.,** ouvrage *m* en pierre. **3.** franc-maçonnerie *f*.

Masora(h) [mə'sɔːrə], *s. Rel.Lit:* massore *f*, massora(h) *f*.

Masorete, Masorite ['mæsəriːt, -ait], *s. Rel.H:* massorète *m*.

Masoretic [mæsə'retik], *a. Rel.H:* massorétique.

masque [mɑːsk], *s. Lit: Th:* masque *m* (pantomime ou féerie).

masquerade[1] [mæskə'reid], *s.* mascarade *f*; (i) bal masqué; troupe masquée; (ii) déguisement *m*.

masquerade[2], *v.i.* se masquer, aller en masque, faire une mascarade; **to m. as . . .,** se déguiser en . . .; **soldier masquerading as a general,** soldat *m* qui se fait passer pour un général.

masquerader [mæskə'reidər], *s.* **1.** masque *m* (qui prend part à une mascarade). **2.** (*a*) personne déguisée, masquée; déguisé, -ée; (*b*) imposteur *m*.

masquerading [mæskə'reidiŋ], *s.* mascarade *f*, déguisement *m*.

mass[1] [mæs, mɑːs], *s.* (*a*) *Ecc:* messe *f*; **high m., sung m.,** grand-messe *f*, (*since 1958*) messe chantée; **low m.,** messe basse, (*since 1958*) messe lue; **requiem m., m. for the dead,** messe de requiem, messe des morts; **to hear m.,** assister à la messe; **to celebrate, say, m.,** célébrer, dire, la messe; **we had masses said for him,** nous avons fait dire des messes pour le repos de son âme; **m. book,** livre *m* de messe, missel *m*; *A:* **dry m.,** messe sèche, missa sicca; *Mus:* **to compose a m.,** composer une messe; (*b*) **black m.,** messe noire.

mass[2] [mæs], *s.* **1.** (*a*) masse *f*, amas *m*; **air m.,** masse d'air; **rock m.,** masse rocheuse; **m. of metal,** masse de métal; **m. of ore, of sand,** amas de minerai, de sable; **a m. of snow broke away from the mountain side,** une masse de neige s'est détachée de la montagne; (*b*) *Ch:* **molecular m.,** masse moléculaire; *Atom.Ph:* **atomic m.,** masse atomique, masse de l'atome, poids *m* atomique isotopique; **law of m. action,** loi *f* d'action de masse; *Atom.Ph:* **critical, subcritical, m.,** masse critique, subcritique; **electron m.,** masse électronique, masse de l'électron; **neutron m.,** masse neutronique, masse du neutron; **nuclear m.,** masse nucléaire, masse du noyau; **proton m.,** masse protonique, masse du proton; **relativistic m.,** masse relativiste; **rest m.,** masse au repos (de l'électron); **m. analyser,** analyseur *m* de masse; **m. balance,** bilan *m* matière; **m. decrement,** décrément *m* de masse; **m. formula,** formule *f* massique, formule de masse; **empirical, semi-empirical, m. formula,** formule empirique, semi-empirique, de masse; **m. number,** nombre *m* de masse (d'un noyau nucléaire); **m. spectrum,** spectre *m* de masse; (*c*) *Mec:* **unit of m.,** unité *f* de masse; **power per unit of m.,** puissance *f* unitaire massique; *attrib.* **m. balance,** équilibrage *m* statique; **m. impact,** impulsion *f* mécanique. **2.** (*a*) (*large quantity*) **a m. of people,** une foule, une multitude, des masses, de gens; **to gather in masses,** se masser; **a solid m. of traffic,** une masse compacte, serrée, de voitures; **m. meeting,** réunion *f*, assemblée *f*, en masse; grand rassemblement, grand concours, de gens; **a m. of letters,** des quantités *f*, une collection, de lettres; un courrier abondant, volumineux; *F:* **I've masses (of things) to do,** j'ai un tas de choses à faire; **a m. of evidence,** des témoignages en abondance; **a m. of sound,** un grand volume de son; **the exercise was nothing but a m. of mistakes,** le devoir était rempli, cousu, de fautes; **he was a m. of bruises,** il était tout couvert de meurtrissures; il n'était que meurtrissures; **he's a m. of complexes,** il est bourré de complexes; **m. grave,** tombe collective; *Ind:* **m. production,** fabrication *f*, production *f*, en série; *Cmptr:* **m. memory, m. storage,** mémoire *f* de grande capacité; *Mil:* **m. of manœuvre,** masse de manœuvre; **covering m.,** masse courante; **m. formation,** formation massive, compacte; **m. attack,** action massive (contre l'ennemi); (*b*) (*the majority, the bulk*) **the great m. of the people,** la plupart des gens; la plus grande partie, la majorité, de la population; **the masses,** les masses; le grand public; la foule; **m. psychology,** psychologie *f* des foules; **the power of m. suggestion,** la puissance de la suggestion sur les masses; **m. communication,** communication *f* avec les masses, avec le grand public; **m. media,** moyens de communication avec, d'action sur, les masses, le grand public; **in the m.,** en masse, en bloc; **m. protest,** protestation *f* en masse; **m. observation,** études et enquêtes sociales; **the great m. of the exports consists of raw materials,** la majeure partie des exportations est constituée par des matières premières.

mass[3] [mæs]. **1.** *v.tr.* masser (des troupes, etc.); **arms were being massed on the frontier,** on concentrait des armements sur la frontière. **2.** *v.i.* (*of troops*) se masser; (*of clouds*) s'amonceler.

massacre[1] ['mæsəkər], *s.* **1.** massacre *m*, tuerie *f*, hécatombe *f* (d'hommes, de gibier). **2.** *Her:* massacre.

massacre[2], *v.tr.* massacrer (des hommes, une symphonie, une langue); faire un massacre de (gibier).

massacrer ['mæsəkrər], *s.* massacreur, -euse.

massacring ['mæsəkriŋ], *s.* massacre(s) *m*(*pl*).

massage[1] ['mæsɑːʒ], *s.* (*a*) *Med:* massage *m*; **hand m.,** massage manuel; (*b*) *Hairdr:* **(scalp) m.,** friction *f*.

massage[2], *v.tr. Med:* masser (le corps); malaxer (les muscles).

Massalian [mæ'seiliən]. *A.Geog:* (*a*) *a.* massaliote; (*b*) *s.* Massaliote *mf* (de l'ancienne Marseille).

massasauga [mæsə'sɔːgə], *s. Rept:* **m. (rattler),** sistrure *m*.

Massawa [mə'sɑːwə]. *Pr.n. Geog:* Massaoua, Massouah.

massé ['mæsi], *s. Bill:* massé *m*; **to take a m. (shot),** masser la bille; faire un massé.

massecuite [mæs'kwiːt], *s. Sug-R:* masse-cuite *f*, *pl.* masses-cuites.

masseter [mæ'siːtər], *a. & s. Anat:* (muscle) masséter *m*.

masseteric [mæsi'terik], *a. Anat:* massétérin.

masseur, *f.* **masseuse** [mæ'səːr, mæ'səːz], *s. Med:* masseur, -euse.

massicot ['mæsikɔt], *s. Ch: Ind:* massicot *m*.

massif ['mæsif], *s. Geog:* massif *m*.

massing ['mæsiŋ], *s.* amoncellement *m* (de nuages); réunion *f*, rassemblement *m*, (de troupes) par masses; agglomération *f* (d'individus, des neiges, etc.).

massive ['mæsiv], *a.* **1.** (*a*) (monument, etc.) massif; *Mil:* **m. work,** ouvrage *m* à fort profil; **cup in m. gold,** coupe *f* en or massif; (*b*) **m. undertaking,** entreprise *f* à grande échelle; *Pharm: etc:* **m. dose,** dose massive. **2.** *Geol:* aggloméré; sans structure cristalline.

massively ['mæsivli], *adv.* massivement.

massiveness ['mæsivnis], *s.* caractère, aspect, massif (d'un monument, etc.).

Massorah [mə'sɔːrə], **Massorete** ['mæsəriːt], **Massoretic** [mæsə'retik] = MASORA(H), etc.

massotherapy [mæsou'θerəpi], *s.* massothérapie *f*.

Massowah [mə'sɑːwə]. *Pr.n. Geog:* Massaoua, Massouah.

mass-produce ['mæsprə'djuːs], *v.tr. Ind:* fabriquer en série.

mast[1] [mɑːst], *s.* **1.** (*a*) *Nau:* mât *m*; (*of lateen rig*) arbre *m*; **the masts,** les mâts, la mâture; **small m.,** mâtereau *m*; **lower m.,** bas mât; **upper m.,** mât supérieur; **lattice m.,** mât en treillis; **bipod m., sheer m.,** mât bipode; **tripod m.,** mât tripode; **twin masts,** mâts jumelés; **hinged m.,** mât basculant, à bascule; mât de pont; **telescopic m.,** mât télescopique; **pole m.,** mât à pible; **m. cap,** chouque(t) *m* de mât; **m. collar,** bourrelet *m* d'étambrai; **m. funnel,** manchon *m* de capelage; **m. hole,** (trou *m* d')étambrai *m*; **m. heel,** pied *m* de mât; **m. rope,** guinderesse *f*; **m. step,** emplanture *f* de mât; **to strike the masts of a ship,** démâter un navire; **before the m.,** en avant du grand mât; **to sail before the m.,** servir comme simple matelot; (*b*) **Venetian m.,** mât de pavoisement. **2.** *W.Tel:* pylône *m*; **aerial m.,** mât d'antenne; **lattice m.,** mât croisillonné; **stayed m.,** mât haubanné; **m. anchor,** ancrage *m* de pylône.

mast[2], *v.tr. Nau:* **1.** mâter (un bâtiment). **2.** hisser haut (une vergue).

mast[3], *s.* **(ground) m.,** faînes *fpl* (de hêtre); faînée *f*; glands *mpl* (de chêne); glandée *f*; châtaignes (données en nourriture aux porcs); **m.-fed,** (porc) élevé au pâturage.

mastaba ['mæstəbə], *s.* mastaba; *m*.

Mastacembelidae [mæstəsem'belidiː], *s.pl. Ich:* mastacembelidés *m*.

mastectomy [mæs'tektəmi], *s. Surg:* mastectomie *f*.

masted ['mɑːstid], *a. Nau:* (*a*) mâté; **heavily m.,** fortement mâté; (*b*) **three-m., four-m., ship,** navire à trois, à quatre, mâts.

-master ['mɑːstər], *s. Nau:* **three-m., four-m.,** trois-mâts *m inv*, quatre-mâts *m inv*; navire *m* à trois, à quatre, mâts.

master[1] ['mɑːstər], *s.* **1.** (*man in control*) (*a*) maître *m*; **the m. of the house,** le maître de la maison; **to be m. in one's own house,** être maître chez soi; **if I were m.,** si j'étais le maître; **to be m. of oneself,** être maître de soi; **to be one's own m.,** s'appartenir; ne dépendre que de soi; n'avoir de comptes à rendre à personne; **I am not my own m.,** je n'ai pas la liberté d'agir; **a dog learns to obey his m.,** le chien apprend à obéir à son maître; **to be m. of a large fortune,** disposer d'une grosse fortune; **to be m. of the situation,** être maître de la situation, dominer la situation; **to remain m. of the field,** rester maître du champ de bataille; **to meet one's m.,** trouver son maître; **to be m. of a subject,** posséder un sujet à fond; **to make oneself m. of sth.,** (i) se rendre maître de qch.; (ii) apprendre qch. à fond; (*b*) (*employer*) maître, patron *m*, chef *m*; **like m. like man,** tel maître tel valet; *O:* (*said by servant*) **the m. is not at home,** monsieur n'y est pas; *A:* **job m.,** loueur *m* de chevaux et de voitures; remiseur *m* (de voitures); (*c*) (*director*) (*esp. at Oxford, Cambridge*) directeur *m*, principal, -aux *m* (de certains collèges universitaires); (*d*) *Nau:* patron (d'un bateau de pêche); capitaine *m*, commandant *m* (d'un navire marchand); **m. of a coasting vessel,** patron au cabotage; (*e*) *Ven:* **M. of foxhounds,** maître d'équipage; grand veneur; *Adm:*

M. of the Mint, directeur de la Monnaie; **m. of ceremonies,** maître des cérémonies; (*at Court*) introducteur *m* des ambassadeurs, etc.; *Jur:* **M. in Chancery,** conseiller *m* à la cour de la Chancellerie; **M. of the Rolls** = vice-président *m* de la Cour de Cassation; **M. of the King's, Queen's, Music** = Maître de chapelle du Roi; *Th:* **chorus m.,** répétiteur *m*; *Mil:* **billet m.,** répartiteur *m* (des billets de logement); *Hist:* **the M. of the Horse,** le Grand Écuyer; (*Fr.Hist.*) Monsieur le Grand; (*f*) (*freemasonry*) vénérable *m*. **2.** *Sch:* (*a*) (*primary*) maître; instituteur *m*; (*secondary*) professeur *m*; **form m.,** professeur principal (d'une classe); **French m.,** professeur de français; (*at certain large public schools*) **high, chief, m.,** directeur; (*b*) **fencing m.,** maître d'escrime; **dancing m.,** maître de danse; **riding m.,** professeur d'équitation; (*c*) **M. of Arts, of Science** = (i) maître ès lettres, ès sciences; (ii) (*at certain universities*) licencié, -ée, ès lettres, ès sciences. **3.** (*a*) *A:* artisan établi à son compte, travaillant en chambre; (*b*) **m. of an art,** maître d'un art; **to make oneself m. of a language,** se rendre maître d'une langue; apprendre à fond une langue; **to be a m. of one's art,** posséder son art en maître; **painter, sculptor, who is a m. of his craft,** peintre *m*, sculpteur *m*, qui a du métier; **already his writing was that of a m.,** déjà il écrivait en maître; *Art:* **old m.,** (i) maître, (ii) tableau *m* de maître. **4.** (*as title*) (*a*) *A:* Messire *m*, Maître; **good M. Francis,** maître François; **my masters,** messieurs; (*b*) *O:* (*form of address to small boys*) (i) **M. David Thomas,** Monsieur David Thomas; (ii) (*said by servant*) **M. David,** Monsieur David; (*c*) *Scot:* titre *m* de l'héritier d'une pairie au-dessous du rang de *earl*. **5.** *attrib.* (*a*) **m. carpenter, m. mason,** maître charpentier, maître maçon; *Const:* **m. builder,** (i) entrepreneur *m* de bâtiments; constructeur *m* (de maisons); (ii) passé maître en architecture; **m. mariner,** capitaine au long cours; capitaine marchand; *Mil: U.S:* **m. sergeant,** sergent-chef *m*, *pl.* sergents-chefs; (*b*) **m. hand,** main *f* de maître; **it is the work of a m. hand,** c'est fait de main de maître; **he's a m. hand at (doing sth.),** il est passé maître dans l'art de (faire qch.); **m. stroke,** coup *m* de maître; (*c*) **m. passion,** passion dominante; *Cards:* **m. card,** carte maîtresse; (*d*) principal, -aux; **m. plan,** plan d'ensemble détaillé; **m. key,** passe-partout *m inv*; **m. word,** maître-mot *m*; **m. race,** race supérieure; **m. map,** carte *f* mère; **m. compass,** compas principal; *Metalw: etc:* **m. form,** matrice *f*; (*plastics, etc.*) **m. batch,** mélange maître *m*; *Mec.E: etc:* **m. rod,** bielle maîtresse; **m.-rod assembly,** embiellage *m*; **m. tap,** taraud *m* mère; (taraud) matrice; **m. wheel,** roue maîtresse; **m. gauge,** (i) *Mec.E:* calibre *m* mère, d'ensemble; (ii) *Rail:* gabarit *m* passe-partout; **m. cylinder,** maître-cylindre *m*, *pl.* maîtres-cylindres (de frein hydraulique); *El:* **m. relay,** relais principal; **m. switch,** commutateur, disjoncteur, principal; **m. oscillator,** (i) *Elcs:* maître-oscillateur *m*, *pl.* maîtres-oscillateurs; oscillateur *m* pilote; (ii) *Rad:* pilote *m*; *Cmptr:* **m. computer unit,** ordinateur *m*, unité *f*, pilote; **m. file,** fichier permanent, maître; **m. data,** données permanentes; **m. program(me), m. routine,** programme principal; *Rec:* **m. record,** (disque) original *m*; **m. tape,** bande *f* mère; *Cin: etc:* **m. print,** copie originale.

master², *v.tr.* **1.** dompter, maîtriser (qn); se rendre maître, maîtresse, de (qn); vaincre (un cheval). **2.** maîtriser, dompter (ses passions); surmonter (sa colère); apprendre (un sujet) à fond; **to m. a difficulty,** surmonter une difficulté; triompher d'une difficulté; venir à bout d'une difficulté; **to have mastered a subject,** posséder un sujet à fond; **to m. the meaning of sth.,** saisir la signification de qch.; **to m. the use of a tool, to m. the saxophone,** se familiariser avec le maniement d'un outil, avec le saxophone. **3.** régir (la maison, etc.).

masterful ['mɑːstəf(u)l], *a.* (*of pers., manner, etc.*) impérieux, dominateur, -trice, autoritaire.

masterly ['mɑːstəli], *a.* de maître; magistral, -aux; **m. stroke,** coup *m* de maître; **m. work,** œuvre magistrale; **m. work on . . .,** savant ouvrage sur . . .; **in a m. manner,** de main de maître; magistralement, supérieurement.

mastermind¹ ['mɑːstəmaind], *s.* (*a*) esprit supérieur, magistral; (*b*) cerveau *m* (d'une entreprise, d'un complot).

mastermind², *v.tr.* diriger (un projet, etc.); tramer (un complot, etc.).

masterpiece ['mɑːstəpiːs], *s.* chef-d'œuvre *m*, *pl.* chefs-d'œuvre; **it's a m.,** c'est fait de main de maître; c'est un chef-d'œuvre; **a minor m.,** un petit chef-d'œuvre.

mastership ['mɑːstəʃip], *s.* **1.** autorité *f* **(over,** sur); maîtrise *f* **(over,** de). **2. M. of the Rolls,** dignité *f* de *Master of the Rolls*. **3.** *Sch:* (*a*) poste *m* de principal (de certains collèges universitaires ou d'une école secondaire); (*b*) **(assistant) m.,** poste de professeur. **4.** connaissance approfondie (d'un sujet).

mastersinger ['mɑːstəsiŋər], *s. Mus.Hist:* maître chanteur.

masterstroke ['mɑːstəstrouk], *s.* coup *m* de maître.

masterwort ['mɑːstəwəːt], *s. Bot:* impératoire *f*; **black m.,** astrance *f*.

mastery ['mɑːst(ə)ri], *s.* **1.** maîtrise *f* **(of,** de); autorité *f*, domination *f* **(over,** sur); **to gain the m.,** l'emporter **(over,** sur); avoir le dessus. **2.** connaissance approfondie (d'un sujet); **his m. of the violin,** sa maîtrise du violon.

masthead¹ ['mɑːsthed], *s. Nau:* tête *f*, ton *m*, de mât; haut *m* du mât; **m. light,** feu *m* de tête de mât; (*of pers.*) **to be at the m.,** être en vigie.

masthead², *v.tr. Nau:* envoyer (qn) en haut du mât.

mastic ['mæstik], *s.* **1.** (*resin*) mastic *m*. **2.** (*cement*) mastic; *Carp:* **glue and sawdust m.,** futée *f*. **3.** *Bot:* **m. (tree),** lentisque *m*.

masticate ['mæstikeit], *v.tr.* **1.** mâcher, mastiquer (un aliment). **2.** *Ind:* triturer (le caoutchouc, etc.); malaxer.

mastication [mæsti'keiʃ(ə)n], *s.* **1.** mastication *f*, mâchement *m*. **2.** *Ind:* trituration *f*.

masticator ['mæstikeitər], *s.* **1.** (*a*) *Anat:* **m. muscles,** muscles masticateurs; (*b*) *pl. F: O:* **masticators,** mâchoires *f*; (*c*) (*animal*) masticateur *m*. **2.** *Ind:* (*apparatus*) masticateur; triturateur *m* (de caoutchouc, etc.); malaxeur *m*.

masticatory [mæsti'keitəri]. **1.** *a.* masticateur, -trice; **m. teeth,** dents mâchelières (des ruminants). **2.** *s. Pharm:* masticatoire *m*.

mastiff ['mæstif], *s.* mâtin *m*; dogue anglais; **m. pup,** mâtineau *m*; **m. bat,** molosse *m*.

mastigure ['mæstigjuər], *s. Rept:* uromastix *m*, *F:* fouette-queue *m*, *pl.* fouette-queues.

masting ['mɑːstiŋ], *s. Nau:* (*a*) mâture *f*, mâts *mpl*, (d'un navire); (*b*) mâtage *m*.

mastitis [mæs'taitis], *s. Med:* mastite *f*; *Vet:* **streptococcal m.,** mammite *f* à streptocoques.

mastless ['mɑːstlis], *a.* **1.** sans mât(s). **2.** dématé.

mastocyte ['mæstousait], *s. Biol:* mastocyte *m*.

mastodon ['mæstoudɔn], *s. Paleont:* mastodonte *m*.

mastodonsaurus [mæstoudɔn'sɔːrəs], *s. Paleont:* mastodonsaurus *m*.

mastodynia [mæstou'diniə], *s. Med:* mastodynie *f*.

mastoid ['mæstɔid], *a.* & *s. Anat:* mastoïde; **m. process,** *s.* **mastoid,** apophyse *f* mastoïde; *Med:* **inflammation of the m.,** *F:* **mastoids,** mastoïdite *f*.

mastoidean [mæs'tɔidiən], *a. Anat:* mastoïdien.

mastoidectomy [mæstɔi'dektəmi], *s. Surg:* mastoïdectomie *f*.

mastoiditis [mæstɔi'daitis], *s. Med:* mastoïdite *f*.

mastoido-humeral [mæstɔidou'hjuːmərəl], *a. Z:* mastoïdo-huméral, -aux.

mastopexy [mæstou'peksi], *s. Surg:* mastopexie *f*.

mastoplasty [mæstou'plæsti], *s. Surg:* mammoplastie *f*.

masturbate ['mæstəbeit], *v.i.* & *tr.* (se) masturber.

masturbation [mæstə'beiʃ(ə)n], *s.* masturbation *f*.

mastwood ['mɑːstwud], *s. Bot:* calophyllum *m*.

mat¹ [mæt], *s.* **1.** (*a*) natte *f* (de paille, de jonc); (*b*) (petit) tapis, carpette *f* (de laine, etc.); **prayer m.,** tapis à prière; **chair m.,** dessous *m* de siège; (*c*) (*at entrance door*) paillasson *m*; essuie-pieds *m inv*; **coir m., (coconut-)fibre m.,** tapis-brosse *m*, *pl.* tapis-brosses; **wire m.,** essuie-pieds métallique; tapis décrottoir; **steel scraper m.,** grille *f* décrottoir; **rubber m.,** tapis en caoutchouc; *F:* **to be on the m.,** être sur la sellette; **he's been on the m.,** on lui a passé un savon; (*d*) **table m.,** (i) dessous *m* de plat; (ii) (*also* **place m.**), rond *m* de table, porte-assiette *m*, *pl.* porte-assiettes; (*e*) *Wr:* tapis; (*f*) *Hort:* abrivent *m*; **grass m.,** rabane *f* de raphia; (*g*) *Typ:* empreinte *f* (de clichage). **2.** *Nau:* paillet *m*, sangle *f*, baderne *f*; **chafing m.,** paillet de portage; **collision m.,** paillet d'abordage; bonnette lardée; **cargo m.,** natte, toile *f*, de fardage. **3.** *Hyd.E:* clayonnage *m*.

mat², *v.tr.* **(matted) 1.** *A:* natter (une chambre), couvrir (une chambre) de nattes. **2.** *Hort:* **to m. (up),** paillassonner, empailler (des semis, des espaliers, etc.). **3.** *Hyd.E:* **to m. the bank of a canal,** clayonner le talus d'un canal. **4.** (*a*) natter, tresser (le jonc); (*b*) emmêler (les cheveux, etc.); (*c*) *v.i.* (*of hair, fibres, etc.*) s'emmêler, se coller ensemble.

mat³. 1. *a.* (*of colour, surface*) mat; **m. complexion,** teint mat; *Phot:* **m. paper,** papier mat; **semi-m. paper,** papier demi-brillant; **m. varnish,** (vernis *m*) mattolin *m*. **2.** *s.* (*a*) (*for gilding*) mat *m*, dorure mate; (*b*) monture dorée, filet *m* d'or mat, *U.S:* filet (doré ou non) (d'une gravure, etc.); (*c*) *Metalw:* surface matie (granitée ou dépolie).

mat⁴, *v.tr.* **(matted)** *Tchn:* matir (la dorure); mater (le cuivre, etc.); dépolir (le verre).

Matabele [mætə'biːli], *s. Ethn:* Matabélé, -ée.

matador ['mætədɔːr], *s.* **1.** matador *m*. **2.** *Cards: etc:* matador.

matamata [mætæmə'tɑː], *s. Rept:* matamata *f*, tortue *f* à gueule.

match¹ [mætʃ], *s.* **1.** (*a*) (*of pers.*) égal, -ale; pareil, -eille; **to find, meet, one's m.,** trouver à qui parler; trouver son homme, avoir affaire à forte partie, *F:* trouver chaussure à son pied; **to meet more than one's m.,** trouver, s'attaquer à, plus fort que soi; trouver son maître; **to be a m. for s.o.,** être de force à lutter avec qn; pouvoir le disputer à qn; **you're no m. for him,** vous n'êtes pas de force, de taille, à lutter, à vous mesurer, avec lui; il vous mettrait dans sa poche; **to be more than a m. for s.o.,** (i) être trop fort pour qn; rendre des points à qn; (ii) circonvenir qn; **he has not his m.,** il n'a pas son pareil; (*b*) (*of thgs*) **to be a bad m.,** aller mal ensemble; **to be a (good) m.,** aller bien ensemble; être bien assortis; **perfect m. of colours,** assortiment parfait de couleurs. **2.** *Sp:* lutte *f*, partie *f*, match *m*; **tennis m.,** partie de tennis; **football m.,** match de football; *Box:* **m. of twenty rounds,** match en vingt reprises; **to win the m.,** gagner la partie; **m. ball, m. point,** balle *f* de match; point *m* dont dépend l'issue du match; **m. play,** (i) *Ten:* jeu *m* de match; (ii) *Golf:* partie *f* par trous; *Golf:* **m. play competition,** concours *m* par trous. **3.** (*a*) mariage *m*; alliance *f*; **to make a good m.,** faire un beau mariage; *F:* **they made a m. of it,** ils se sont mariés; (*b*) **he's a good m.,** c'est un bon, un excellent, parti.

match². 1. *v.tr.* (*a*) *A:* **to m. s.o. with s.o.,** faire épouser qn à qn; donner qn en mariage à qn; unir qn à qn; (*b*) égaler (qn); être l'égal de (qn); rivaliser avec (qn); **evenly matched,** de force égale; **no country can m. France for wine,** en fait de vins aucun pays ne saurait rivaliser avec la France; **there's nobody to m. him,** il n'a pas son pareil; **I can m. your story,** j'en sais une qui vaut bien la vôtre; (*c*) **to m. s.o. against s.o.,** opposer qn à qn; mettre qn aux prises avec qn; *Sp:* **to m. opponents,** matcher des adversaires; (*d*) apparier, rapparier (des gants, des bas); rappareiller (un service à thé, etc.); appareiller (des chevaux); assortir, allier (des couleurs); (*of husband and wife*) **a well matched couple,** un couple bien assorti; **cushions to m. the colour of her dress,** coussins assortis à la couleur de sa robe; **I need a new hat to m. my suit,** j'ai besoin d'un nouveau chapeau qui aille avec mon tailleur; **have you any material to m. this?** avez-vous du tissu comme, pareil à, celui-ci? *Com:* **articles difficult to m.,** rassortiments *m* difficiles à obtenir; **this picture wants another to m. it,** il faut un pendant à ce tableau; *St.Exch: U.S:* **matched orders,** ordres couplés d'achat et de vente (pour stimuler le marché); (*e*) *Carp:* **to m. boards,** bouveter, embrever, des planches. **2.** *v.i.* s'assortir; s'harmoniser; **ornaments that m.,** ornements *m* qui se font pendant, qui se correspondent; **colours to m.,** couleurs assorties; **dress with hat to m.,** robe avec chapeau assorti; **paper and envelopes to m.,** papier *m* et enveloppes *fpl* assortis; **to m. well,** aller bien ensemble, être bien assortis, faire la paire.

match³, *s.* **1.** allumette *f*; **safety m.,** allumette de sûreté; **book matches,** allumettes plates; **book of matches,** pochette *f* d'allumettes; **to strike a m.,** frotter une allumette; **m. manufacturer,** allumettier, -ière; *F:* **to put a m. to an explosive situation,** mettre le feu aux poudres. **2.** *A. Artil:* mèche *f*; *Min:* canette *f*, raquette *f*; **slow m.,** corde *f* à feu; *F:* **to set a m. to the train,** mettre le feu aux étoupes.

match⁴, *v.tr.* mécher (un fût, une barrique).

matchable ['mætʃəbl], *a.* assortissable; que l'on peut rassortir; auquel on peut trouver un pendant.

matchboard ['mætʃbɔːd], *s. Carp:* planche bouvetée.

matchboarding ['mætʃbɔːdiŋ], *s. Carp:* planches bouvetées; assemblage *m* à rainure; jointes *fpl*; planches de recouvrement.

matchbook ['mætʃbuk], *s. NAm:* pochette *f* d'allumettes.

matchbox ['mætʃbɔks], *s.* boîte *f* à allumettes; boîte d'allumettes; *F:* **a little m. house,** une maison de rien du tout.

matcher ['mætʃər], *s.* **1.** *Com:* (*pers.*) assortisseuse *f*. **2.** *Carp:* machine *f* à bouveter.

matchet ['mætʃit], *s.* machette *f*; grand coutelas; coupe-coupe *m inv*.

matching[1] ['mætʃiŋ], *a.* **m. colours,** couleurs assorties; **these pictures are a m. pair,** ces deux tableaux forment pendant.

matching[2], *s.* **1.** (*a*) assortiment *m*, appareillement *m* (de couleurs); appariement *m*, appariation *f* (d'objets); (*b*) *Tchn:* liaison *f*, synchronisation *f*; (*c*) *El: Elcs:* adaptation *f* (d'impédance); **m. device,** système *m* d'adaptation; **m. impedance,** impédance *f* caractéristique; **m. transformer,** transformateur *m* d'adaptation. **2.** *Carp:* **m. machine,** machine *f* à bouveter. **3.** *St.Exch: U.S:* application *f*.

matchless ['mætʃlis], *a.* incomparable, inimitable; sans égal, sans pareil, sans second.

matchlessly ['mætʃlisli], *adv.* incomparablement.

matchlessness ['mætʃlisnis], *s.* incomparabilité *f*.

matchlock ['mætʃlɔk], *s. Hist:* fusil *m* à mèche.

matchmaker[1] ['mætʃmeikər], *s.* faiseur, -euse, de mariages; *F:* agenceuse *f* de mariages; courtière *f* en mariages; marieur, -euse; **she's a regular m.,** c'est une marieuse acharnée; elle ne pense qu'à marier les gens.

matchmaker[2], *s.* fabricant *m* d'allumettes; allumettier, -ière.

matchmaking ['mætʃmeikiŋ], *s.* manie *f* d'arranger des mariages.

matchmark ['mætʃmɑ:k], *s. Mec.E:* (trait *m* de) repère *m*.

matchstick ['mætʃstik], *s.* allumette *f*; *F:* **to have legs like matchsticks,** avoir des jambes comme des allumettes; avoir des mollets de coq.

matchwood ['mætʃwud], *s.* bois *m* d'allumettes; **smashed, reduced, to m.,** mis en miettes; mis en capilotade.

mate[1] [meit], *s. Chess:* échec *m* et mat *m*; **fool's m.,** coup *m* du berger.

mate[2], *v.tr. Chess:* faire (le roi) échec et mat; mater (le roi); **to m. in three,** faire (échec et) mat en trois coups.

mate[3], *s.* **1.** camarade *mf*, compagnon, *f.* compagne; *F:* copain, *f.* copine; *Ind:* **(workman's) m.,** compagnon; **plumbers never work without a m.,** le plombier ne travaille jamais seul; *F:* **hi, m.!** dis donc, mon vieux! **2.** (*a*) (*one of a united pair*) (*of pers., birds*) compagnon, compagne; (*of birds*) mâle *m* ou femelle *f*; *O:* (*of pers.*) mari *m* ou femme *f*; (*b*) **litter mates,** animaux *m* d'une même portée. **3.** *Nau:* (*a*) (*on merchant vessel*) officier *m*; **first m., chief m.,** second *m*; **second m.,** lieutenant *m*; **third m.,** second lieutenant; **the master and the mates,** le capitaine et les officiers; (*b*) *Navy:* second maître; **carpenter's m.,** second maître charpentier; contre-maître charpentier. **4.** *esp. U.S: Mec.E:* pièce *f* qui s'accouple (avec une autre), qui s'emboîte (dans une autre); pièce correspondante.

mate[4]. **1.** *v.tr.* (*a*) *O:* marier, unir (**s.o. with s.o.,** qn à qn); (*b*) accoupler (des oiseaux), apparier (des animaux); (*c*) *Tchn: Mec.E:* assembler, réunir (des éléments); **to m. rocket stages,** adapter, assembler, les étages d'une fusée; **the axle is mated to the wheel,** l'essieu *m* s'emboîte dans, est réuni à, la roue. **2.** *v.i.* (*a*) *O:* (*of pers.*) **to m. with s.o.,** s'unir à qn; se marier avec qn; épouser qn; (*b*) (*of birds*) s'accoupler, s'apparier; (*c*) *A:* (*of pers.*) tenir compagnie (**with,** à); frayer (**with,** avec); vivre en compagnie (**with,** de); (*d*) *Mec.E: etc:* (*of parts*) s'adapter, correspondre (**to,** à); aller (**to,** sur); s'accoupler (**to,** à); s'emboîter (**to,** dans).

maté ['mɑ:tei], *s.* maté *m*; thé *m* du Paraguay, des Jésuites.

mateless ['meitlis], *a.* sans compagnon, sans compagne.

matelote ['mætlɔt], *s. Cu:* matelote *f*.

mater ['meitər], *s.* **1.** *Anat:* **dura m.,** dure-mère *f*; **pia m.,** pie-mère *f*. **2.** *F: O:* **the m.,** ma mère; maman.

material [mə'tiəriəl].

I. *a.* **1.** (*a*) *Phil: Ph: Theol:* matériel; (*b*) (*of conduct, point of view*) matériel, grossier, terre-à-terre, matérialiste; **to be engrossed in m. things,** être enfoncé dans la matière; (*c*) (*of comfort, interests*) matériel; **to have enough for one's m. comfort, for one's m. needs,** avoir de quoi vivre matériellement; *F:* avoir sa matérielle. **2.** (*a*) important, essentiel (**to,** pour); **it has been of m. use to me,** cela m'a rendu un service sensible, considérable, appréciable; **m. witnesses,** témoins essentiels; (*b*) (fait) pertinent; *Jur:* **m. evidence,** témoignages pertinents.

II. *s.* **1.** (*a*) matière *f*; matériau, -aux *m*; **raw material(s),** matière(s) première(s); **unprocessed, unrefined, m.,** matière brute, non travaillée; **filling m.,** matière de remplissage; **sealing m.,** matière obturatrice; **absorbent m.,** matière absorbante; **filter m.,** matière filtrante; **foam m.,** matière spongieuse; **synthetic m.,** matière synthétique; **refractory m.,** matériau réfractaire; *El:* **insulating m.,** matière isolante; isolant *m*; **building materials,** matériaux de construction; **roofing materials,** matériaux de couverture; *Atom.Ph:* **reactor materials,** matériaux de réacteurs, de piles atomiques; **core materials,** matériaux de cœur; *Dent:* **impression m.,** matériau pour empreinte; (*b*) *Atom.Ph:* **active m.,** matière active; **fertile m.,** matière fertile; **fissionable m.,** matière fissile; **impoverished m.,** matière appauvrie; (*c*) *Geol:* **parent materials,** matériaux d'origine; (*d*) **the m. for a play,** le matériau d'une pièce; **he was collecting m. for a book on China,** il se documentait pour écrire un livre sur la Chine; **to provide m. for conversation,** fournir des sujets de conversation; alimenter la conversation. **2.** (*a*) **railway m.,** matériel *m* de chemin de fer, de voie; **war m.,** matériel de guerre; **replacement m.,** matériel de remplacement; (*b*) **photographic materials,** fournitures *f*, accessoires *m*, pour la photographie; **writing materials,** de quoi écrire; tout ce qu'il faut pour écrire; **artists' materials,** matériel de l'artiste. **3.** (*a*) *Tex:* tissu *m*; étoffe *f*; **cotton m.,** tissu de coton; **waterproof m.,** tissu imperméable; **dress m.,** tissu pour robes; **customers' own m. made up,** on travaille à façon; (*b*) **glass is a brittle m.,** le verre est un matériau cassant; **protective m.,** matériel de protection; (*c*) *Agr:* **liming materials,** amendements *m* calcaires.

materialism [mə'tiəriəlizm], *s. Phil:* matérialisme *m*.

materialist [mə'tiəriəlist]. **1.** *s.* matérialiste *mf*. **2.** *a.* (*a*) matérialiste; (*b*) matériel.

materialistic [mətiəriə'listik], *a.* **1.** matérialiste. **2.** (*of pleasures, mind, etc.*) matériel.

materialistically [mətiəriə'listikli], *adv.* matériellement.

materiality [mətiəri'æliti], *s.* **1.** matérialité *f*. **2.** *Jur:* importance *f* (d'un fait, etc.).

materialization [mətiəriəlai'zeiʃ(ə)n], *s.* **1.** matérialisation *f*. **2.** aboutissement *m* (d'un projet, etc.).

materialize [mə'tiəriəlaiz]. **1.** *v.tr.* (*a*) matérialiser (l'âme, qn); (*b*) *Psychics:* donner une forme matérielle à (un esprit); faire apparaître (un esprit). **2.** *v.i.* (*a*) (*of psychic ectoplasm*) se matérialiser; (*b*) (*of occurrence*) se réaliser, s'actualiser, se concrétiser; (*of policy*) prendre forme, prendre corps; (*of plans*) aboutir; se réaliser; **sneezes that don't m.,** éternuements qui ne viennent pas.

materializing [mə'tiəriəlaiziŋ], *s.* **1.** matérialisation *f*. **2.** réalisation *f*.

materially [mə'tiəriəli], *adv.* **1.** matériellement, essentiellement; *Log:* **formally correct but m. false,** exact quant à la forme, mais faux quant au fond. **2.** sensiblement; d'une manière appréciable; **this route will shorten our journey m.,** cette route raccourcira sensiblement notre trajet.

materia medica [mə'tiəriə'medikə], *s. Med:* matière médicale.

materiel, matériel [mə'tiəriəl], *s. Mil: etc:* matériel *m*.

maternal [mə'tə:n(ə)l], *a.* maternel; **m. grandfather,** aïeul maternel.

maternally [mə'tə:nəli], *adv.* maternellement.

maternity [mə'tə:niti], *s.* maternité *f*; **m. hospital,** maternité; **m. ward,** salle *f* des accouchées; service *m* de la maternité; **m. centre,** centre *m* d'accouchement; **m. dress,** robe *f* de maternité; **m. grant, benefit,** allocation *f* de maternité.

matey ['meiti], *a. F:* **to be m.,** être à tu et à toi; être copains.

matgrass ['mætgrɑ:s], *s. Bot:* nard *m* raide.

mathematical [mæθə'mætik(ə)l], *a.* **1.** (science *f*, calcul *m*) mathématique; **m. accuracy,** précision *f* mathématique; **m. analysis,** analyse *f* mathématique; **m. expression,** expression *f* mathématique; *Cmptr:* **m. programming,** programmation *f* linéaire; *Ins:* **m. premium,** prime nette. **2.** (étudiant, -ante) en mathématiques; (professeur *m*, livre *m*) de mathématiques; (connaissance *f*) des mathématiques; (connaissances) en mathématiques; (disposition *f*) pour les mathématiques; (carrière *f*) de mathématicien; **to be m., to have a m. turn of mind,** être doué pour les mathématiques; **he's a m. genius,** c'est un mathématicien de génie.

mathematically [mæθə'mætik(ə)li], *adv.* mathématiquement.

mathematician [mæθəmə'tiʃ(ə)n], *s.* mathématicien, -ienne.

mathematics [mæθə'mætiks], *s.pl.* (*usu. with sg. const.*) mathématiques *fpl*; **pure m.,** mathématiques pures; **applied m.,** mathématiques appliquées; **modern m.,** mathématiques modernes; **to study m.,** étudier les mathématiques.

mathiola [mə'θaiələ], *s. Bot:* = MATTHIOLA.

maths [mæθs], *s.pl. F:* math(s) *f*.

Mathurin ['mæθjurin]. *Rel.H:* **1.** *Pr.n.m.* Mathurin; *A:* **malady of St M.,** colique *f* de Saint-Mathurin. **2.** (*a*) *a.* de l'ordre des mathurins; **M. friar,** mathurin *m*; (*b*) *s.m.* mathurin.

Matilda [mə'tildə]. *Pr.n.f.* Mathilde.

matildite [mə'tildait], *s. Miner:* matildite *f*.

matinée ['mætinei], *s.* (*a*) *Th:* (représentation *f* en) matinée *f*; (*b*) *Cost:* **m. coat,** matinée.

matiness ['meitinis], *s. F:* camaraderie *f*.

mating ['meitiŋ], *s.* **1.** union *f* (de personnes); accouplement *m* (d'oiseaux); appareillement *m*, appariation *f*, appariment *m*, appariement *m* (d'animaux); **the m. season,** la saison des amours; (*of domestic animals*) la monte. **2.** *Tchn:* accouplement *m*, raccordement *m*; (*of gears*) conjugaison *f*; **m. flange,** collerette *f* de raccordement; **m. parts,** pièces *f* qui s'accouplent, qui s'emboîtent, qui se raccordent; pièces correspondantes.

matins ['mætinz], *s.pl.* (*a*) *R.C.Ch:* matines *f*; **the bell was ringing for m.,** la cloche sonnait matines; (*b*) *Ch. of Eng:* office *m* du matin.

matlockite ['mætlɔkait], *s. Miner:* matlockite *f*.

matrass ['mætræs], *s. Ch:* matras *m*; ballon *m* (à long col).

matriarch ['meitriɑ:k], *s.f.* femme qui exerce une autorité matriarcale.

matriarchal ['meitriɑ:k(ə)l], *a.* matriarcal, -aux.

matriarchy ['meitriɑ:ki], *s.* matriarcat *m*.

matric[1] ['meitrik, 'mæ-], *a. Mth:* matriciel; **m. equation,** équation matricielle.

matric[2] [mə'trik], *s. F: A:* = MATRICULATION 2.

matricidal ['meitrisaidl], *a.* matricide.

matricide[1] ['meitrisaid], *s.* (*pers.*) matricide *mf*.

matricide[2], *s.* (*crime*) matricide *m*.

matriclan ['meitriklæn], *s. Anthr:* matriclan *m*.

matriculant [mə'trikjulənt], *s. Sch:* étudiant, -ante, qui s'inscrit (à l'université).

matriculate [mə'trikjuleit]. **1.** *v.tr.* immatriculer (un étudiant). **2.** *v.i. A:* passer l'examen d'entrée à l'université (et prendre ses inscriptions).

matriculation [mətrikju'leiʃ(ə)n], *s. A: Sch:* **1.** immatriculation *f*, inscription *f* (comme étudiant). **2.** *A:* examen *m* de fin d'études secondaires (qui admet à l'université).

matrilineal, matrilinear [mætri'liniəl, -'liniər; meit-], *a.* (descendance) par ligne maternelle; *Anthr:* matrilinéaire.

matrilocal [mætri'louk(ə)l, mei-], *a. Anthr:* matrilocal, -aux.

matrimonial [matri'mounjəl], *a.* matrimonial, -aux; conjugal, -aux.

matrimony ['mætriməni], *s.* **1.** le mariage; la vie conjugale; **to join in m.,** conjoindre matrimonialement; *Ecc:* **joined in holy m.,** unis par les saints nœuds du mariage. **2.** *Cards:* mariage. **3.** *Bot:* **m. vine,** jasmin bâtard.

matrix, *pl.* **-ixes, -ices** ['meitriks, 'meitriksiz, 'meitrisi:z; 'mæt-], *s.* **1.** *Anat:* matrice *f*, utérus *m*; **cervical m.,** matrice cervicale. **2.** *Geol: Miner:* matrice, gangue *f*, gaine *f*; roche *f* mère; **emerald m.,** roche d'émeraude; **m. gem,** pierre précieuse engagée dans sa gangue. **3.** *Metall: Typ: etc:* matrice, moule *m*; *Art: Cer:* mère *f* (de moulages en plâtre, etc.); *Rec:* matrice de disques; matrice de réserve. **4.** *Mth: etc:* matrice; **basis m.,** matrice de base; **correlation m.,** matrice de corrélation; **covariance m.,** matrice de covariance; **diagonal, quasi-scaler, m.,** matrice diagonale; **inverse m.,** matrice inverse; **negative, positive, m.,** matrice négative, positive; **rectangular m.,** matrice rectangulaire; **singular m.,** matrice non inversible; **non-singular m.,** matrice régulière; **square m.,** matrice carrée; **stochastic m.,** matrice stochastique; **transition m.,** matrice de passage, de transition; **m. inversion,** inversion *f* de matrice; **m. mechanics,** mécanique *f* matrice; **m. representation,** représentation matricielle; *Cmptr:* **m. storage, m. store,** mémoire (à sélection) matricielle; **m. analysis,** analyse matricielle; **m. coefficient,** coefficient matriciel.

matroclinic, matroclinous [mætrou'klinik, -'klainəs], *a. Biol:* matrocline.

matrocliny [mætrou'klaini], *s. Biol:* matroclinie *f*.

matron ['meitrən], *s.f.* **1.** matrone; mère de famille; femme d'un certain âge; **m. of honour,** dame d'honneur; *A.Jur:* **jury of matrons,** jury de matrones (appelé à décider de la grossesse d'une femme condamnée à mort). **2.** (*a*) intendante (d'une institution); (*b*) infirmière en chef (d'un hôpital); (*c*) intendante, infirmière (d'un pensionnat).

matronal ['meitrənəl], *a.* matronal, -aux; de matrone; **matronal duties,** devoirs *m* domestiques.

matronly ['meitrənli], *a.* matronal, -aux; de matrone; **a m. woman,** une femme qui s'impose; **at thirty she looked quite m.,** à trente ans elle en portait au moins quarante; *Cost:* **m. styles,** modes *f* pour dames d'un certain âge.

matronymic [mætrə'nimik], *s.* matronyme *m.*
matt [mæt], *a.* & *s.* = MAT[3].
matte [mæt], *s. Metall:* matte *f.*
matted ['mætid], *a.* **1.** (*a*) (plancher, etc.) natté, couvert de nattes; (*b*) (chaise, etc.) de jonc, de paille. **2. m. hair,** cheveux emmêlés, entremêlés; (*of cloth, etc.*) feutré.
matter[1] ['mætər], *s.* **1.** matière *f*; substance *f*; (*a*) *Phil: etc:* **form and m.,** la forme et la matière; la forme et le fond; (*b*) **inanimate m.,** matière inanimée; **organic, inorganic, m.,** matière organique, inorganique; **vegetable m.,** matières végétales; **colouring m.,** matière colorante; **m. in suspension in a liquid,** matières en suspension dans un liquide; **the indestructibility of m.,** l'indestructibilité *f* de la matière; *Bio-Ch:* **dry m.,** extrait sec; *Atom.Ph:* **nuclear m.,** matière nucléaire; *Anat:* **grey m.,** matière grise; *F:* **to have plenty of grey m.,** être très intelligent. **2.** *Med:* matière (purulente); pus *m*, sanie *f*; **to squeeze m. out of a wound,** faire sortir du pus d'une plaie. **3.** (*a*) **(subject) m.,** matière, sujet *m* (d'un discours, d'un livre, etc.); **reading m.,** livres *mpl*, choses *fpl* à lire; **I haven't any reading m.,** je n'ai rien à lire; **m. of, for, astonishment,** sujet d'étonnement; **it is a m. of astonishment to me that . . .,** je ne cesserai jamais de m'étonner que . . .; **m. of dispute,** sujet de controverse; **one could have an interesting discussion on this m.,** voilà un beau sujet de discussion; **it is a m. for regret,** c'est à regretter; **it's no laughing m.,** il n'y a pas matière à rire; (*b*) *Typ:* matière, copie *f*; **plain m.,** composition *f* en plein; **mixed m.,** composition lardée; (*c*) *Adm:* **postal m.,** lettres et paquets postaux; *NAm:* **first-class m.,** lettre close, paquet clos; **second-class m.,** imprimé *m* périodique; **third-class m.,** imprimé non périodique; **fourth-class m.,** échantillons *mpl.* **4. no m.!** n'importe! cela ne fait rien! tant pis! **no m. what you do, he is never satisfied,** quoi qu'on fasse il n'est jamais content; **no m. how you do it,** de n'importe quelle manière que vous le fassiez; **no m. when you do it,** à n'importe quel moment que vous le fassiez; **no m. how fast you run you won't catch him,** vous avez beau courir, vous ne le rattraperez pas; **any service, no m. what it was, was rewarded,** jamais un service, tel qu'il fût, n'a été sans récompense. **5.** affaire *f*; chose *f*; cas *m*; **we'll deal with this m. tomorrow,** nous nous occuperons de ce problème demain; nous traiterons demain ce chapitre; **let's come back to the m. in hand,** revenons à nos moutons; **it's an easy, no easy, m.,** c'est, ce n'est pas, facile; **it's no easy m. to . . .,** il n'est pas facile de . . .; **it's no great m., it's a m. of little importance,** ce n'est pas grand-chose; c'est peu de chose; ce n'est pas là une affaire; **for so small a m.,** pour si peu de chose; **that's quite another m.,** cela c'est tout autre chose; ça c'est une autre paire de manches; **as matters stand,** au point où en sont les choses; **money matters,** affaires d'intérêt, d'argent; **business matters,** affaires; **in all matters of . . .,** en tout ce qui concerne, qui a rapport à . . .; **in matters of religion,** en ce qui concerne la religion; **in the m. of . . .,** quant à . . ., en ce qui concerne . . .; **in this m.,** à cet égard; *Jur:* **in the m. of the Companies Act of 1929,** vu la loi de 1929 sur les sociétés; **a m. of business,** une question d'affaires; **a m. of taste, of opinion,** une affaire, une question, de goût, d'opinion; **m. of conscience,** cas de conscience; **it's a m. of historical fact,** c'est un fait historique; **a m. of habit,** une question d'habitude; **it's simply a m. of time,** c'est une simple question de temps; **it's just a m. of £100,** c'est l'affaire, une affaire, de £100; il y va de £100; **that will cost you a m. of £50,** cela vous coûtera dans les £50, une cinquantaine de livres; **it will be a m. of ten days,** cela prendra dans les dix jours; ce sera l'affaire de dix jours; **within a m. of hours,** en, au bout de, quelques heures; **it was only a m. of minutes before he came back,** deux ou trois minutes s'étaient à peine écoulées que déjà il était de retour; **for that m., for the m. of that,** pour ce qui est de cela; quant à cela; si ce n'est que cela; d'ailleurs; aussi bien; **as a m. of fact,** (i) à la vérité, en réalité, à vrai dire; (ii) aussi bien; **nor, for that m., do I regret it,** et à vrai dire je ne le regrette pas; **what's the m.?** qu'est-ce qu'il y a? qu'y a-t-il? de quoi s'agit-il? qu'est-ce qui se passe? **what's the m. with you?** qu'est-ce que vous avez? qu'avez-vous? qu'est-ce qui vous prend? **is there anything the m. (with you)?** y a-t-il quelque chose qui ne va pas? **there's something the m.,** il y a quelque chose; **there's something the m. with him,** il a quelque chose; **there's nothing the m. with you,** vous n'avez rien du tout; **I don't know what's the m. with me,** je ne sais pas ce que j'ai; je me sens je ne sais comment; **as if nothing was the m.,** comme si de rien n'était; **there's something the m. with his throat,** il a quelque chose à la gorge; **is there anything the m. with the engine?** est-ce qu'il y a quelque chose qui ne marche pas au moteur? **don't you like the book? what's the m. with it?** vous n'aimez pas ce livre? qu'est-ce que vous y trouvez à redire?
matter[2], *v.i.* **1.** importer (**to s.o.,** à qn); avoir de l'importance; **what really matters is that . . .,** ce qui est vraiment important, c'est que . . .; **it doesn't m.,** ce n'est pas important; cela ne fait rien; peu importe; **it doesn't m. whether . . .,** peu importe que + *sub.*; **it doesn't m. a bit, in the least,** cela n'a pas la moindre importance; **it doesn't m. much,** cela n'a pas grande importance; **what does it m. to you?** qu'est-ce que cela vous fait? **it matters a great deal to me,** cela a beaucoup d'importance pour moi; cela me préoccupe beaucoup; **a day or two more or less doesn't m.,** nous n'en sommes pas à un ou deux jours près; **nothing else matters,** tout le reste n'est rien. **2.** (*of wound*) suppurer.
Matterhorn (the) [ðə'mætəhɔ:n]. *Pr.n. Geog:* le (Mont) Cervin.
matter-of-course ['mætərəv'kɔ:s], *a.* naturel; qui va de soi.
matter-of-fact ['mætərəv'fækt], *a.* (*of pers., manner, statement, etc.*) pratique, positif; terre-à-terre; prosaïque.
matter-of-factly ['mætərəv'fæktli], *adv.* prosaïquement; d'une manière pratique, terre-à-terre.
matter-of-factness ['mætərəv'fæktnis], *s.* prosaïsme *m*; esprit *m* pratique.
Matthew ['mæθju:]. *Pr.n.m.* Mat(t)hieu.
Matthias [mə'θaiəs]. *Pr.n.m.* Mat(t)hias.
matthiola [mə'θaələ], *s. Bot:* matthiole *f*; matthiola *f.*
matting[1] ['mætiŋ], *s.* **1.** (*a*) enchevêtrement *m*, emmêlement *m* (de fils, etc.); (*b*) paillassonnage *m* (des plantes); (*c*) tressage *m* (de la paille). **2.** (*a*) natte(s) *f(pl)*, paillassons *mpl*; **Indian m.,** natte de Chine; (*b*) *Hort:* rabane *f*, auvent *m*, abrivent *m.*
matting[2], *s.* matage *m* (de la dorure, du cuivre); dépolissage *m* (du verre); *Metalw:* **m. tool,** matoir *m.*
mattins ['mætinz], *s.pl.* = MATINS.
mattock[1] ['mætək], *s. Tls: Agr:* hoyau *m*; pioche *f*; pioche-hache *f*, *pl.* pioches-haches; bigot *m.*
mattock[2], *v.tr.* piocher (la terre).
mattress ['mætris], *s.* **1.** (*a*) matelas *m*; **hair m., wool m.,** matelas de crin, de laine; **foam-rubber m.,** matelas de mousse; **inflatable m.,** matelas pneumatique, de camping; **m. carder,** matelassier, -ière; **to turn the mattress,** retourner le matelas; (*b*) sommier *m*; **spring (interior) m., box m.,** sommier à ressorts; **wire m.,** sommier métallique. **2.** *Hyd.E:* clayonnage *m*, claie *f.*
maturant ['mætjurənt], *s. Med:* maturatif *m.*
maturate ['mætjureit]. **1.** *v.tr. Med:* mûrir, faire mûrir (un abcès). **2.** *v.i.* (*of abscess, etc.*) (*a*) mûrir; (*b*) suppurer.
maturation [mætju'reiʃ(ə)n], *s.* maturation *f* (d'un fruit, d'un abcès, etc.); développement *m* (de l'intelligence, etc.).
maturative [mə'tjuə:rətiv], *a.* & *s. Med:* maturatif (*m*).
mature[1] [mə'tjuər], *a.* **1.** (*of fruit, intelligence, person, etc.*) mûr; **person of m. years,** personne *f* d'âge mûr; **after m. consideration,** après mûre réflexion; **he's not very m. for his age,** (i) pour son âge il n'a pas l'esprit assez mûr; (ii) (*of child*) il n'est pas particulièrement avancé pour son âge. **2.** *Fin:* (papier) échu.
mature[2]. **1.** *v.tr.* (*a*) mûrir (une plante, qn); vieillir, affiner (le vin, le fromage); *Cer:* vieillir (la pâte); (*b*) **his plans were not yet matured,** ses projets n'étaient pas encore mûris, pas encore mûrs. **2.** *v.i.* (*a*) (*of plant, wine, etc.*) mûrir; (*b*) **to let a plan m.,** laisser mûrir un projet; (*c*) *Fin:* (*of bill*) échoir; arriver à échéance; **bills to m.,** papier *m* à échéance.
matured [mə'tjuəd], *a.* **1.** mûr, mûri; (vin) mûri, fait, en boite, de bonne boite; (cigare) sec. **2.** *Fin:* échu; **m. capital,** capitaux *mpl* dont la date de paiement est échue.
maturely [mə'tjuəli], *adv.* mûrement; d'une manière réfléchie.
matureness [mə'tjuənis], *s.* maturité *f* (du jugement, du style, etc.).
maturing [mə'tjuəriŋ], *s.* maturation *f* (du tabac, etc.); affinage *m* (du vin, du fromage).
maturity [mə'tjuəriti], *s.* **1.** maturité *f* (d'un fruit, etc.); maturité, boite *f* (du vin); **to come to m.,** arriver à maturité, à plein développement; **the years of m.,** l'âge mûr, l'âge moyen (de qn); **work of his m.,** œuvre *f* de sa maturité; *For:* **age of m.,** âge d'exploitabilité (d'une forêt). **2.** *Fin: Com:* **(date of) m.,** échéance *f* (d'une traite, d'un billet); **payable at m.,** payable à l'échéance.
matutinal [mæ'tju:tinəl], *a. Lit:* matutinal, -aux, matinal, -aux; du matin.
Maud[1] [mɔ:d]. *Pr.n.f.* Mathilde; *Hist:* **the Empress M.,** Mathilde, Mahaut, d'Angleterre.
maud[2], *s. A:* **1.** châle *m*, plaid *m*, à rayures grises (de berger écossais). **2.** couverture *f* de voyage en étoffe rayée.
maudlin ['mɔ:dlin], *a.* **1.** larmoyant, pleurard, pleurnicheur; d'une tendresse exagérée; **m. voice,** voix pleurarde; **m. sentimentality,** sentimentalité larmoyante; **to be m. in one's cups,** avoir le vin triste, tendre. **2.** dans un état d'ivresse larmoyante.
maul[1] [mɔ:l], *s.* **1.** *Tls:* maillet *m*, mailloche *f*, mail *m*, masse *f*; batterand *m* (de carrier); *N.Arch:* **pin m.,** moine *m.* **2.** *A.Arms:* massue *f.*
maul[2], *v.tr.* **1.** (*a*) meurtrir, malmener (qn); (*of crowd*) houspiller (qn); **to be mauled by a tiger,** être écharpé, mutilé, lacéré, par un tigre; **to m. s.o. about,** tirer qn de ci de là; tripatouiller (une femme); (*b*) éreinter (un auteur, une œuvre). **2.** *U.S:* fendre (une bûche) au coin.
mauling ['mɔ:liŋ], *s.* (*a*) (*by tiger, etc.*) lacération *f*; (*b*) tripotée *f*; mauvais quart d'heure.
maulstick ['mɔ:lstik], *s. Art:* appui-main *m*, *pl.* appuis-main.
maunder ['mɔ:ndər], *v.i.* **1. to m. (along),** flâner, baguenauder; se trimbaler. **2. to m. (on),** divaguer, radoter.
maundy ['mɔ:ndi], *s.* **1.** *Hist:* cérémonie *f* du lavement des pieds des pauvres par le monarque, le jeudi saint; *Ecc:* **M. Thursday,** le jeudi saint. **2.** largesse *f* du jeudi saint; **m. money,** pièces frappées pour les largesses du jeudi saint.
maurandia [mɔ:'rændiə], *s. Bot:* maurandie *f.*
Mauresque [mɔ:'resk], *a.* & *s. Art: etc:* mauresque (*f*), moresque (*f*).
Mauritania [mɔri'teiniə]. *Pr.n. Geog:* Mauritanie *f*; **the Islamic Republic of M.,** la République islamique de Mauritanie.
Mauritanian [mɔri'teiniən]. *Geog:* (*a*) *a.* mauritanien; (*b*) *s.* Mauritanien, -ienne.
Mauritian [mə'riʃ(ə)n]. *Geog:* (*a*) *a.* mauricien; (*b*) *s.* Mauricien, -ienne.
Mauritius [mə'riʃəs]. *Pr.n. Geog:* l'île *f* Maurice.
Mauser ['mauzər], *s. Sm.a:* **M. (rifle),** Mauser *m.*
mausoleum, *pl.* **-lea, -leums** [mɔ:sə'li:əm, -'li:ə, -'li:əmz], *s.* mausolée *m.*
mauve [mouv], *a.* & *s.* (*colour*) mauve (*m*).
mauveine ['mouvi:n], *s. Ch: Dy:* mauvéine *f.*
maverick ['mævərik], *s.* **1.** *NAm:* bouvillon *m* errant sans marque de propriétaire. **2.** *esp. U.S:* non-conformiste *mf*; politicien réfractaire, indépendant.
mavis ['meivis], *s. Orn: Poet:* grive (chanteuse); calandrette *f.*
maw [mɔ:], *s.* **1.** (*a*) *Z:* quatrième poche *f* de l'estomac (d'un ruminant); caillette *f*; (*b*) jabot *m* (d'oiseau); (*c*) *F:* estomac *m*, panse *f*; **to fill one's m.,** se remplir le jabot, la panse. **2.** gueule *f* (du lion, du brochet).
mawkish ['mɔ:kiʃ], *a.* (*a*) fade, insipide; (*b*) d'une sensiblerie outrée.
mawkishly ['mɔ:kiʃli], *adv.* (*a*) fadement; avec fadeur; (*b*) sentimentalement.
mawkishness ['mɔ:kiʃnis], *s.* (*a*) fadeur *f*, insipidité *f*; (*b*) sensiblerie *f*; fausse sentimentalité.
mawseed ['mɔ:si:d], *s.* graine *f* de pavot.
mawworm ['mɔ:wə:m], *s.* **1.** ver intestinal; ascaride *m*, ascaris *m*, oxyure *f.* **2.** *Lit: A:* hypocrite *m.*
Maxentius [mæk'senʃəs]. *Pr.n.m.* Maxence.
maxi ['mæksi], *a.* & *s. Cost: F:* (jupe, manteau) maxi (*m or f*).
maxilla, *pl.* **-ae** [mæk'silə, -i:], *s.* **1.** *Anat:* (os *m*) maxillaire *m*; maxillaire supérieur. **2.** *Ent: Crust:* maxille *m.*
maxillary [mæk'siləri], *a. Anat:* maxillaire.
maxillipede [mæk'silipi:d], *s. Arach: Crust:* maxillipède *m*, patte-mâchoire *f*, *pl.* pattes-mâchoires.
maxillodental [mæksilou'dent(ə)l], *a. Anat:* maxillodentaire.
maxillula [mæk'siljulə], *s. Ent: Crust:* maxillule *f.*
maxim[1] ['mæksim], *s.* **1.** maxime *f*, dicton *m*; **it was a m. of his that one should . . .,** il tenait pour maxime que l'on devrait . . .. **2.** *Jur:* brocard *m*; maxime du droit.
Maxim[2], *s. Artil:* **M. (machine gun),** mitrailleuse *f* Maxim.
maximal ['mæksiməl], *a.* maximal, -aux.
maximalism ['mæksiməlizm], *s. Pol.Hist:* maximalisme *m.*
maximalist ['mæksiməlist], *a.* & *s. Pol.Hist:* maximaliste (*mf*).
Maximian [mæk'simiən]. *Pr.n.m. Rom.Hist:* Maximien.
Maximilian [mæksi'miliən]. *Pr.n.m.* Maximilien.
maximize ['mæksimaiz], *v.tr.* maximaliser, maximiser; porter (qch.) au maximum.
maximum, *pl.* **-a** ['mæksiməm, -ə]. **1.** *s.* maximum *m*, *pl.* -ums, -a; **to the m.,** au maximum; **up to a m. of . . .,** jusqu'à concurrence de . . .; **to raise production to a m.,** porter la production au maximum; **to run the m. of**

risks, courir le maximum de risques; **to reach one's m.,** plafonner; **m. thermometer,** thermomètre *m* à maxima. **2.** *a.* maximum; *occ.* maximal, -aux; **m. efficiency,** maximum de rendement; **m. load,** charge *f* limite; **m. price,** prix maximum; **m. output,** rendement maximum; **m. pressure,** pression maximum; **to be condemned to the m. sentence,** être condamné au maximum de la peine; **m. speeds,** vitesses maxima; **m. temperatures,** températures maximales; **the average m. diurnal temperature,** la moyenne des maxima diurnes.

Maximus ['mæksiməs]. *Pr.n.m. Rom.Hist:* Maxime.

may[1] [mei], *v.aux.* (*2nd pers. sing. A:* **thou mayest, mayst;** *3rd pers. sing.* **he may;** *p.t.* **might** [mait]; *no pres. or past participle*) **1.** (*expressing possibility*) (*a*) **he m. return at any moment,** il peut revenir d'un moment à l'autre; **with luck I m. succeed,** avec de la chance je peux réussir; **he m. not be hungry,** il n'a peut-être pas faim; il se peut qu'il n'ait pas faim; **that m. or m. not be true,** (i) cela est peut-être vrai ou peut-être pas; (ii) je me demande si cela est vrai; c'est une affirmation dont il est permis de douter; **the air m., might, revive her,** l'air peut, pourrait, la ranimer, la remettre; **it is still possible that one of the bills m. be passed,** il est encore possible que l'une des lois soit votée; **he m., might, miss the train,** il se peut, se pourrait, qu'il manque le train; **I m. (possibly) have done it, have said so,** j'ai pu le faire, le dire; **he might have dropped it in the street,** (i) il aurait pu, (ii) il a pu, le laisser tomber dans la rue; **he m. have lost it,** il a pu le perdre; peut-être qu'il l'a perdu; il se peut qu'il l'ait perdu; **any sum which m. be allocated,** toute somme qui viendrait à être allouée; **such documents as m. be of interest to you,** les documents susceptibles de vous intéresser; **he recognized the place, as well he might, seeing that. . .,** il a reconnu l'endroit, et rien d'étonnant, vu que . . .; (*b*) **how old might she be?** quel âge peut-elle bien avoir? **she might be thirty,** elle aurait peut-être trente ans; **and how old might you be?** quel âge avez-vous, sans indiscrétion? **and who might** *you* **be?** (i) qui êtes-vous, sans indiscrétion? (ii) pour qui vous prenez-vous? **and what might** *you* **be doing here?** peut-on savoir ce que vous faites là? **mightn't it be just as well to warn him?** est-ce qu'on ne ferait pas bien de l'avertir? **I wonder what I m. have done to offend him,** je me demande ce que j'ai bien pu faire pour le fâcher; (*c*) **it m., might, be that. . .,** il se peut, se pourrait, bien que + *sub.*; il peut, pourrait, se faire que + *sub.*; **be that as it m.,** quoi qu'il en soit; **be that as it m., I heard you,** toujours est-il que je vous ai entendu; **that's as m. be,** c'est selon; **as you m. suppose,** comme vous (le) pensez bien; **he might be impatient, he might be restless, but he remained faithful to his wife,** s'il lui arrivait de se montrer impatient, agité, il est resté pourtant fidèle à sa femme; **whatever faults he m. have he is never dull,** quels que soient ses défauts, il n'est jamais ennuyeux; **run as he might he could not overtake me,** il a eu beau courir, il n'a pas pu me rattraper; *Lit:* **he mounted his horse with what speed he might,** il monta à cheval en toute hâte; (*d*) **you might have won the prize if you had worked harder,** vous auriez pu gagner le prix si vous aviez travaillé davantage; **he might have arrived in time if he had run more quickly,** il aurait pu arriver à temps s'il avait couru plus vite; **you m. see him if you stay another hour,** vous le verrez peut-être si vous y restez encore une heure; **we m., might, as well stay where we are,** autant vaut, vaudrait, rester où nous sommes; (*e*) **you might shut the door!** vous pourriez bien fermer la porte! si vous vouliez bien fermer la porte! **he might have offered to help,** il aurait bien pu offrir son aide; **all the same, you might have made less noise,** tout de même vous auriez (bien) pu faire moins de bruit. **2.** (*asking or giving permission*) **m. I?** vous permettez? **m. I come in?** puis-je entrer? **m. I leave the table, m. I get down?** puis-je sortir de table, m'en aller? **you m. go out when you have finished,** vous pourrez sortir quand vous aurez fini; **you m. go,** (i) vous pouvez partir; (ii) (*at end of interview*) vous pouvez disposer; **you m. go if you want to,** vous pouvez y aller si vous en avez envie; *Sch:* **m. I leave the room?** puis-je sortir? **m. I give you some wine?** puis-je vous offrir du vin? **if I m. be allowed to express an opinion,** si vous me permettez d'exprimer mon avis; **if I m. say so,** si j'ose (le) dire; se je l'ose dire; si l'on peut dire; si je puis dire; s'il est permis de s'exprimer ainsi; **the council m. decide . . .,** il appartient, au besoin, au conseil de décider . . .; **any friend of the family m. send flowers or a wreath,** tout ami de la famille est autorisé à envoyer des fleurs ou une couronne. **3.** (*in clauses expressing purpose, fear, etc.*) **I only hope it m. last!** pourvu que cela, ça, dure! **I was afraid it might be true,** j'avais peur que ce ne fût vrai; **I hoped it might come true,** j'espérais que cela se réaliserait; **I was afraid he might have done it,** j'avais peur qu'il ne l'eût fait; **the catastrophe which he had hoped might have been averted,** la catastrophe qu'il avait espéré voir conjurer. **4.** (*expressing a wish*) **m. I rather die!** puissé-je plutôt mourir! que je meure plutôt! **m. God bless you!** (que) Dieu vous bénisse! **m. he rest in peace!** qu'il repose en paix! **much good m. it do you!** grand bien vous fasse! **long m. you live to enjoy it!** puissiez-vous vivre longtemps pour en jouir! **m. he, she, defend our laws,** puisse-t-il, -elle, défendre nos lois.

May[2], *s.* **1.** (*a*) mai *m*; **in (the month of) M.,** en mai; au mois de mai; **(on) the first, the seventh, of M.,** le premier, le sept, mai; *Ecc: etc:* **the M. meetings,** les assemblées *f* (de l'Église libre, etc.) du mois de mai; **Queen of the M., M. queen,** reine *f* du premier mai; *Lit:* **M. and December,** une jeune fille qui épouse un vieillard, qui est unie à un vieillard; *Prov:* **a hot M. makes a fat churchyard,** chaleur en mai engraisse le cimetière; (*b*) *Lit:* **in the M. of life,** au printemps de la vie. **2.** (*a*) *Bot:* **m. (tree),** aubépine *f*; **m. (blossom),** fleurs *fpl* d'aubépine; (*b*) *Ent:* **M. bug, M. beetle,** (i) hanneton *m*; (ii) *U.S:* (*in southern states*) phyllophage *m.* **3.** *Sch:* (*Cambridge*) **M. week,** la semaine des courses à aviron (fin mai).

May[3]. *Pr.n.f.* (*dim. of Mary*) May, Marie.

Maya ['maiə], *s.* **1.** *Hindu Rel:* maya *f*, mâyâ *f.* **2.** *Phil:* maya, illusion *f.*

Maya(n) ['maiə(n)]. **1.** *Ethn:* (*a*) *a.* maya; (*b*) *s.* Maya *mf.* **2.** *s. Ling:* maya *m.*

mayapple ['meiæpl], *s. Bot: NAm:* podophylle *m* en bouclier.

maybe ['meibi:], *adv.* peut-être; **m. yes, m. no,** peut-être bien que oui, et peut-être bien que non; **I don't mean m.,** et pas d'erreur; *F:* et c'est pas peut-être.

maybush ['meibuʃ], *s.* aubépine *f.*

Mayday ['meidei]. **1.** *s.* (*also* **May Day**) le premier mai. **2.** *int.* (*signal of distress*) mayday!

mayflower ['meiflauər], *s.* **1.** *Bot:* (*a*) primevère *f*, coucou *m*; (*b*) cardamine *f* des prés; cresson *m* des prés; cresson élégant; (*c*) *NAm:* épigée rampante. **2.** (*in U.S:*) **an old M. family,** une vieille famille de souche anglaise (dont les ancêtres ont fait la traversée de l'Atlantique dans le *Mayflower*).

mayfly ['meiflai], *s. Ent:* éphémère *m* vulgaire; **the mayflies,** les éphéméridés *m.*

mayhap ['meihæp], *adv. A: & Lit:* peut-être.

mayhem[1] ['meihem], *s. Jur: A: & NAm:* (*a*) mutilation *f*; action *f* d'estropier qn; (*b*) *NAm:* **to commit m. on s.o.,** se livrer à des voies de fait contre qn.

mayhem[2], *v.tr. Jur: A: & NAm:* mutiler, estropier (qn).

maying ['meiiŋ], *s.* **1. to go m.,** (i) fêter le premier mai; (ii) *A:* se promener en douce compagnie au mois de mai. **2.** *U.S:* cueillette *f* des fleurs d'aubépine.

mayonnaise [meiə'naiz, maiə'nez], *s. Cu:* mayonnaise *f.*

mayor ['mɛər], *s.m.* maire; **deputy m.,** adjoint (au maire); maire adjoint; *Belg:* échevin.

mayoralty ['mɛərəlti], *s.* mairie *f* (i) exercice *m* des fonctions de maire; (ii) mandat *m* de maire.

mayoress ['mɛəres], *s.f.* femme du maire.

maypole ['meipoul], *s.* **1.** mai *m*; **to set up a m.,** planter un mai. **2.** *F:* (*tall man*) échalas *m*; (*tall woman*) grande perche.

mayweed ['meiwi:d], *s. Bot:* camomille puante; maroute *f.*

mazapilite [mæ'zæpilait], *s. Miner:* mazapilite *f.*

maz(z)ard ['mæzəd], *s. Bot:* cerise noire; guigne *f.*

mazarine [mæzə'ri:n, 'mæzəri:n]. **1.** *a. & s.* bleu foncé *inv.* **2.** *s. Ent:* **m. (blue),** (papillon *m*) adonis *m*; argus bleu.

maze[1] [meiz], *s.* labyrinthe *m*, dédale *m*; **to be lost in a m.,** se perdre dans un dédale (de complications, etc.); **m. of streets,** enchevêtrement *m* de rues; **to be in a m.,** être désorienté; ne pas savoir où donner de la tête.

maze[2], *v.tr. O:* égarer, troubler, embrouiller, désorienter, *F:* méduser (qn).

mazurka [mə'zə:kə], *s. Mus: Danc:* mazurka *f.*

me [*unstressed* mi, *stressed* mi:], *pers. pron., objective case.* **1.** (*unstressed*) (*a*) me, (*before vowel sound*) m'; **they can't see me,** ils ne peuvent pas me voir; **they were looking at me,** ils me regardaient; **he told me so,** il me l'a dit; **he saw you and me,** il nous a vus, vous et moi; **listen to me,** écoutez-moi; **give me some,** donnez-m'en; **lend it (to) me,** prêtez-le-moi; **would you lend it to me?** voudriez-vous me le prêter? **he wrote me a letter,** il m'a écrit une lettre; (*b*) (*refl.*) moi; **I'll take it with me,** je le prendrai avec moi; **I closed the door behind me,** j'ai refermé la porte derrière moi; (*c*) (*refl.*) *A: & Lit:* **I laid me down,** je me suis couché. **2.** (*stressed*) moi; **big enough to hold you and me,** assez grand pour que nous y tenions, vous et moi; **he loves me (and me alone),** il n'aime que moi; **he was thinking of me,** il pensait à moi; **nobody ever thought of me,** personne ne pensait à ma pauvre petite personne; **that's for me,** ça c'est pour moi; **he gave it to me, not to you,** c'est à moi qu'il l'a donné, pas à vous; **do you suspect me?** vous me soupçonnez, moi? **3.** (*complement of verb* **to be**) **it's me!** c'est moi! **it's not me,** (i) ce n'est pas moi; (ii) *F:* ce n'est pas mon genre; **he's younger than me,** il est plus jeune que moi. **4.** (*in int.*) **dear me!** mon Dieu! vraiment! par exemple! *A:* **ah me!** pauvre de moi! que je suis malheureux! *O: & Lit:* **ah me, what a beautiful night!** mon Dieu, quelle belle soirée!

mead[1] [mi:d], *s.* hydromel *m.*

mead[2], *s. Lit:* = MEADOW.

meadow ['medou], *s.* (*a*) pré *m*; prairie *f*; **water m.,** noue *f*, prairie susceptible d'être inondée; **m. grass,** pâturin *m*, herbe *f* des prés; **rough m. grass,** pâturin commun; **English m. grass,** ray-grass anglais; (*b*) *Bot:* **m. saffron,** colchique *m* d'automne; safran *m* des prés; *F:* mort *f* aux chiens; veillotte *f*, veilleuse *f*; **m. sage,** sauge *f* sauvage, des prés; **white m. saxifrage,** saxifrage granulée; casse-pierre(s) *m inv*; perce-pierre *f*, *pl.* perce-pierres; christemarine *f*; **m. rhubarb, m. rue,** pigamon *m*, rue *f*, des prés; fausse rhubarbe; rhubarbe des paysans, des pauvres; (*c*) *Orn:* **m. pipit,** pipit *m* des prés, farlouse *f.*

meadowland ['medoulænd], *s.* prairie(s) *f*(*pl*); pâturages *mpl*; herbage *m.*

meadowlark ['medoulɑ:k], *s. Orn:* (*a*) pipit *m* (des prés); farlouse *f*; (*b*) *NAm:* grande sturnelle, sturnelle à collier, *Fr.C:* sturnelle des prés; **western m.,** sturnelle de l'ouest.

meadowsweet ['medouswi:t], *s. Bot:* (spirée *f*) ulmaire *f*; reine *f* des prés; vignette *f*; herbe *f* aux abeilles.

meagre[1] ['mi:gər], *a.* (*a*) *A:* (*of pers.*) maigre, décharné; (*b*) maigre, peu copieux, rudimentaire; **m. soil,** sol ingrat, terre maigre; *F:* **it was a bit m.,** ça ne valait pas grand-chose.

meagre[2], *s. Ich:* maigre *m* (d'Europe).

meagrely ['mi:gəli], *adv.* maigrement, pauvrement; **m. furnished room,** pièce pauvrement meublée.

meagreness ['mi:gənis], *s.* maigreur *f*; pauvreté *f* (d'un repas, d'un sujet à traiter).

meal[1] [mi:l], *s.* (*a*) farine *f* (d'avoine, de seigle, d'orge, de maïs); (*b*) farine, poudre *f* (de diverses substances); (*c*) *Ent:* **m. beetle,** ténébrion *m* de la farine; cafard *m*, escarbot *m*, meunier *m*; **m. mite,** acaride *m* de la farine; **m. moth,** pyrale *f.*

meal[2], *v.tr. Pyr:* égruger (la poudre).

meal[3], *s.* **1.** repas *m*; **large, square, m.,** repas copieux, solide; ample repas; **light m.,** repas léger; petit repas; *F:* **a proper, sit-down, m.,** un vrai repas; **I've had a huge m.,** j'ai mangé comme quatre; **to make a m. of it,** en faire son repas; *F:* **don't make a m. of it!** n'exagère pas! *Pharm:* **to be taken before, after, meals,** à prendre avant, après, le repas, avant, après, manger. **2.** *Husb:* (lait fourni par une vache à chaque) traite *f.*

mealie ['mi:li], *s. usu.pl. Dial:* **mealies,** maïs *m.*

mealiness ['mi:linis], *s.* (*a*) nature farineuse (d'un produit); (*b*) *O:* onctuosité *f* (de paroles).

mealing ['mi:liŋ], *s. Pyr:* égrugeage *m.*

mealtime ['mi:ltaim], *s.* heure *f* du repas; **at mealtimes,** aux heures de repas.

mealworm ['mi:lwə:m], *s. Ent:* ver *m* de farine.

mealy ['mi:li], *a.* **1.** farineux; (fruit) cotonneux; **m. potatoes,** pommes de terre farineuses. **2.** (*a*) saupoudré de blanc; poudreux; (fruit) cotonné, duveteux; (*b*) *F: O:* (visage *m*) de papier mâché; (visage) terreux. **3.** (cheval) moucheté.

mealybug, mealywing ['mi:libʌg, -wiŋ], *s. Ent: F: esp. U.S:* aleurode *m*; cochenille *f* des serres.

mealymouthed [mi:li'mauðd], *a. F:* doucereux, mielleux, patelin; au parler onctueux.

mean[1] [mi:n], *s.* **1.** (*a*) milieu *m*; moyen terme; **the golden m., the happy m.,** le juste milieu; la juste mesure; (*b*) *Mth:* moyenne *f*; **arithmetical m.,** moyenne arithmétique; **geometrical m.,** moyenne géométrique; moyenne proportionnelle; **weighted m.,** moyenne pondérée. **2.** *pl.* (*often with sg. const.*) **means,** moyen(s) *m*(*pl*), voie(s) *f*(*pl*); **to find (a) means to do sth.,** trouver moyen de faire qch.; **to use every possible means to do sth.,** employer tous les moyens pour accomplir qch.; **the best means of doing sth.,** le meilleur moyen de faire qch.; **there is no means of escape,** il n'y a aucun moyen de fuite; **by any means it must be done,** il faut le faire à n'importe quel prix; **there is no means of doing it,** il n'y a pas moyen; *F:* il n'y a pas mèche; **it has been the means of extending our trade,** c'est par ce moyen, c'est grâce à cela, que nous avons élargi nos affaires; **he has been the means of . . .,** c'est par lui que . . .; **by all (manner of) means,** (i) par tous les moyens (possibles); (ii) mais certainement! mais oui! je vous en prie! mais faites donc! **do it by all means,** que rien ne vous en empêche! **may I come in?—by all means!** puis-je entrer?—je vous en prie; **by no (manner of) means,** en aucune façon; aucunement; nullement; pas du tout; pas le moins du monde; **by no means is it possible to . . .,** par aucun moyen l'on ne peut . . .; **he is not by any means a hero,** il n'est rien moins qu'un héros; **by this, that, means,** par ce moyen; **by some means or other,** de manière ou d'autre; **by means of s.o.,** par l'entremise de qn; **by means of sth.,** au moyen, par le moyen, de qch.; à la faveur de qch.; en se servant de qch.; **not by any means,** jamais de la vie; **a means to an end,** un moyen d'arriver au but. **3.** *pl.* moyens (de vivre); ressources *fpl*; fortune *f*; **according to our means,** selon nos moyens; **it isn't within my means,** je n'en ai pas les moyens; **to live beyond one's means,** vivre au delà de ses moyens; dépenser plus que son revenu; **this car is beyond my means,** cette voiture est hors de ma portée, n'est pas dans mes prix; **private means,** ressources personnelles; fortune personnelle; **he's a man of means,** c'est un homme qui a des ressources; il a une belle fortune; **the man who has the means,** l'homme qui a de la fortune; **to be without means,** (i) être sans ressources; (ii) être sans fortune; *Adm:* **means test** = enquête *f* sur la situation (de fortune).

mean[2], *a.* moyen; **m. quantity, pressure,** quantité, pression, moyenne; **m. time,** temps moyen; **m. reaction time,** temps moyen de réaction; *Mth:* **m. proportional,** moyenne proportionnelle; *Com:* **m. tare,** tare commune; *Nau:* **m. draft,** tirant d'eau moyen.

mean[3], *a.* **1.** (*a*) misérable, pauvre; humble; minable; **a m. little room,** une petite pièce d'aspect minable; *O:* **of m. birth,** de basse extraction; d'humble naissance; **the meanest flowers,** les plus humbles des fleurs; **that ought to be clear to the meanest intelligence,** cela devrait être compris par l'esprit le plus borné; **they had the meanest opinion of him,** ils le tenaient en très médiocre estime; (*b*) (i) **no m.,** excellent; **he's no m. scholar,** c'est un grand érudit; **he's no m. violinist,** il joue admirablement du violon; c'est un violoniste de premier ordre; *Lit:* **no m. city,** une ville importante, florissante; (ii) *esp. NAm: F:* superbe, formidable; **he plays a m. guitar,** c'est un guitariste formidable; (*c*) *NAm:* **to feel m.,** se sentir mal en train; ne pas être dans son assiette. **2.** (*a*) (*of pers., character, action*) bas, méprisable, vil, mesquin; **a m. trick,** un vilain tour; un tour déloyal; *F:* un sale coup; **that's m. of him,** ce n'est pas chic de sa part; **don't be so m.!** soyez plus gentil! **to take a m. advantage of s.o.,** exploiter indignement qn; **I feel very m. about not going,** j'ai honte de ne pas y aller; (*b*) *esp. NAm:* difficile; de mauvaise humeur; vicieux; **m. horse,** cheval rétif. **3.** avare, chiche, regardant; **he's very m. about tipping,** il n'aime pas donner de pourboires; pour les pourboires il est très chiche; **don't be so m. with the food,** ne lésinez pas sur la nourriture; **he's m. beyond words,** il n'y a pas plus avare.

mean[4], *v.tr.* (**meant** [ment]; **meant**) **1.** (*purpose*) (*a*) avoir l'intention (**to do sth.,** de faire qch.); se proposer (de faire qch.); **do you m. to stay long?** avez-vous l'intention de rester longtemps? comptez-vous rester longtemps? **what do you m. to do?** que comptez-vous faire? **he meant to do me a service,** il voulait me rendre service; **I meant to write, to have written,** je voulais vous écrire; j'avais l'intention de vous écrire; **I never meant to go,** je n'ai jamais eu l'intention d'y aller; **he didn't m. them to think that he meant them to hear,** il ne voulait pas leur donner à penser que ceci était dit à leur intention; **I certainly m. them to give it back to me,** je prétends bien qu'ils me le rendent; **he means no harm,** il n'y entend pas malice; il ne pense pas à mal; **I m. him no harm,** je ne lui veux pas de mal; **he meant no offence,** il n'avait nullement l'intention de vous offenser; **he didn't m. (to do) it,** il ne l'a pas fait exprès, à dessein; il n'en avait pas l'intention; **I never meant it,** ce n'a jamais été mon intention; **without meaning it,** sans le vouloir; sans intention; sans y prendre garde; **the letter was meant to irritate him,** la lettre avait été écrite dans l'intention de l'irriter; (*b*) **to m. well by s.o.,** avoir de bonnes intentions à l'égard de qn; vouloir le bien de qn; vouloir du bien à qn; **he means well,** il a de bonnes intentions; il est bien intentionné; il agit dans les meilleures intentions; ses intentions sont bonnes; (*c*) **I m. to be obeyed,** j'entends qu'on m'obéisse; je veux absolument être obéi; **I m. to succeed,** je veux réussir; **I m. to have it,** je suis résolu à l'avoir; **I don't m. to put up with that insult,** je n'entends pas avaler cette insulte; **I m. him to do it,** il le fera, je le veux. **2.** (*destine*) (*a*) **I meant this purse for you,** je vous destinais cette bourse; *A:* **he was meant for a soldier,** on le destinait à la carrière militaire; (*b*) **the remark was meant for you,** la remarque s'adressait à vous; c'est à vous que s'adresse cette observation; **he meant that for you,** c'est pour vous qu'il a dit cela; **he meant the blow for you,** c'est à vous qu'il destinait le coup; (*c*) **do you m. me?** est-ce de moi que vous parlez? est-ce moi à qui vous faites allusion? **I don't m. you, I m. David,** il ne s'agit pas de vous mais de David; **this portrait is meant to be the duke,** ce portrait est censé représenter le duc. **3.** (*signify*) (*a*) (*of word, phrase*) vouloir dire; signifier; **what does that word m.?** que signifie ce mot? **the word means nothing to me,** ce mot n'a pas de sens pour moi; **the name means nothing to me,** ce nom ne me dit rien; **what is meant by . . .?** que veut dire . . .? **all this means nothing,** tout cela ne rime à rien; (*b*) (*of pers.*) vouloir dire; **what do you m.?** que voulez-vous dire? **what do you m. by that?** qu'entendez-vous par là? **what do you m. by such behaviour?** que signifie une pareille conduite? qu'est-ce que cela signifie? **what do you m. by coming late?** qu'est-ce que c'est que ces façons d'arriver en retard? **what do you m. by doing such a thing?** a-t-on jamais vu faire chose pareille? **what exactly do you m.?** expliquez-vous; **this is what I m.,** je m'explique . . .; **does he m. what he says?** dit-il réellement sa pensée? **do you think he meant what he said?** pensez-vous qu'il l'ait dit sérieusement? **they don't m. anything by it,** cela ne signifie rien; **you mustn't think he meant anything by it,** il ne faut pas y voir malice; **I didn't m. that,** ce n'est pas cela que je voulais dire; je me suis mal exprimé; **these figures are not meant to be accurate,** je ne veux pas dire que ce soient là des chiffres précis; **I meant the remark for a joke,** j'ai dit cela par plaisanterie; **he meant it as a kindness,** il l'a fait par bonté; **I never say what I don't m.,** je ne dis jamais ce que je ne pense pas; **do you m. that . . .?** ai-je bien compris que . . .? est-ce à dire que . . .? **you don't m. it!** vous voulez rire! vous plaisantez! vous n'y pensez pas! pas possible! vous ne parlez pas sérieusement! **I m. it,** je parle sérieusement; c'est sérieux; **when I say** *no,* **I m.** *no,* quand je dis non, c'est non, c'est pour tout de bon, je sais ce que je veux dire; **I say what I m. and I m. what I say,** (i) je parle tout carrément et ce que je dis c'est ce que je pense; (ii) ce que je dis j'ai l'intention de le faire; et si je le dis je le ferai; (*c*) **his refusal means ruin for me,** s'il refuse c'est la ruine pour moi; **liberty need not m. anarchy,** liberté ne signifie pas nécessairement anarchie; **£100 means a lot to him,** £100, c'est une somme pour lui; **the price means nothing to him,** le prix n'est rien pour lui; **all that means nothing,** tout cela est sans importance; **if you knew what it means to live alone!** si vous saviez ce que c'est que de vivre seul! **I cannot tell you what he has meant to me,** je ne saurais vous dire tout ce qu'il a été pour moi.

Meander[1] [mi'ændər]. **1.** *Pr.n. Geog: A:* **the (river) M.,** le Méandre. **2.** *s.* (*a*) *Geog:* méandre *m* (d'un cours d'eau); **incised m.,** méandre encaissé; **cut-off m.,** méandre recoupé; **flood-plain m.,** méandre divagant; **rock-defended m.,** méandre à armature rocheuse; (*b*) *Art:* méandre, frettes *fpl.*

meander[2], *v.i.* **1.** (*of river*) serpenter, se replier; faire des méandres; **the river meanders through the plain,** la rivière fait des méandres à travers la plaine. **2.** (*of pers.*) errer çà et là; errer à l'aventure.

meandering[1] [mi:'ændəriŋ], *a.* **1.** (rivière) qui fait des méandres; (sentier, etc.) sinueux, tortueux, serpentant. **2.** (discours, etc.) sans plan, qui passe d'un sujet à l'autre, sans suite.

meandering[2], *s.* méandres *mpl* (d'un cours d'eau); sinuosités *fpl,* détours *mpl,* replis *mpl,* serpentement *m.*

meandrine [mi'ændrin], *a. Coel:* **m. coral,** méandrine *f.*

meanie ['mi:ni], *s. F:* (*a*) rapiat, -ate; pingre *mf*; (*b*) **what a m.!** quelle vache! qu'il est vache!

meaning[1] ['mi:niŋ], *a.* **1.** (*with adv. prefixed*) **well m.,** bien intentionné. **2.** (regard) significatif; (sourire) d'intelligence.

meaning[2], *s.* (*a*) signification *f,* sens *m,* acception *f* (d'un mot, etc.); **what is the m. of this word?** que signifie, que veut dire, ce mot? **figurative m. of a word,** acception figurée d'un mot; **in the fullest m. of the word,** dans toute l'acception du mot; *Ling:* **area of m.,** champ sémantique, linguistique, notionnel; **this translation does not bring out the full m. of the passage,** cette traduction ne rend pas, ne fait pas valoir, la vraie signification du passage; (*expressing indignation*) **what's the m. of this?** qu'est-ce que cela signifie? (*b*) **to understand s.o.'s m.,** comprendre ce que qn veut dire; **that's not my m.,** ce n'est pas là ce que je veux dire; ce n'est pas là ma pensée; **you've mistaken my m.,** vous ne m'avez pas compris; (*c*) **look full of m.,** regard significatif.

meaningful ['mi:niŋful], *a.* (*a*) plein de sens; (*b*) significatif; qui en dit long; *esp. Pol:* **m. talks,** conversations constructives.

meaningfully ['mi:niŋfuli], *adv.* = MEANINGLY.

meaningless ['mi:niŋlis], *a.* dénué, vide, de sens; qui n'a pas de sens; qui ne signifie rien; **a m. act, remark,** un non-sens.

meaningly ['mi:niŋli], *adv.* d'un air, d'un ton, significatif; avec une intention marquée.

meanly ['mi:nli], *adv.* **1.** misérablement, pauvrement, humblement; **m. furnished,** pauvrement meublé; **to live m.,** vivre petitement; *O:* **m. born,** de basse, d'humble, naissance; **to think m. of sth.,** avoir une piètre, une médiocre, opinion de qch.; faire peu de cas de qch. **2.** (agir, se conduire) peu loyalement, mesquinement, indignement. **3.** chichement, en lésinant.

meanness ['mi:nnis], *s.* **1.** médiocrité *f,* pauvreté *f,* petitesse *f* (de qch.); bassesse *f,* petitesse, platitude *f* (d'esprit); *O:* bassesse (de naissance). **2.** (*a*) mesquinerie *f,* avarice *f,* ladrerie *f*; (*b*) vilenie *f.*

meanspirited [mi:n'spiritid], *a.* à l'âme basse; vil, abject.

meantime, meanwhile ['mi:ntaim, -(h)wail], *s. & adv.* **in the meantime, (in the) meanwhile,** dans l'intervalle, dans l'entre-temps; pendant ce temps-là; en attendant; d'ici là; sur ces entrefaites; **meanwhile for the meantime, pay up, we'll arrange things later,** payez toujours, on verra après.

meany ['mi:ni], *s. F:* = MEANIE.

measled ['mi:zld], *a.* (*a*) (*of pers.*) atteint de rougeole; qui a la rougeole; (*b*) *Vet:* (porc *m*, etc.) ladre, atteint de ladrerie.

measles ['mi:zlz], *s.pl.* (*usu. with sg. const.*) (*a*) *Med:* rougeole *f*; (*b*) *Med:* **German m.,** rubéole *f*; (*c*) *Vet:* ladrerie *f* (des porcs, etc.).

measly ['mi:zli], *a.* **1.** (*a*) (éruption *f,* etc.) qui ressemble à la rougeole; (*b*) *Vet:* (porc) ladre, atteint de ladrerie. **2.** *F:* insignifiant, misérable; de peu de valeur; minable; **a m. present,** un petit cadeau de rien du tout; **a m. lot,** un tas de minables.

measurability [meʒ(ə)rə'biliti], *s.* mensurabilité *f.*

measurable ['meʒ(ə)rəbl], *a.* mesurable, mensurable; *Ch: etc:* (constituent) dosable; **within m. distance of success,** à peu de distance du succès; en bonne voie de réussite; à deux doigts de la réussite.

measurably ['meʒərəbli], *adv.* **1.** *esp. U.S:* dans une certaine mesure; jusqu'à un certain point. **2.** à un degré appréciable; sensiblement.

measure[1] ['meʒər], *s.* **1.** (*a*) mesure *f*; **linear m., m. of length,** mesure linéaire, de longueur; **square m.,** mesure de superficie, de surface; **cubic m.,** mesure de volume; **liquid m.,** mesure de capacité pour les liquides; **dry m.,** mesure (de capacité) pour les matières sèches; **pression m.,** mesure de pression; **weights and measures,** poids *m* et mesures; **heaped-up m.,** mesure comble; **strike m., bare m.,** mesure rase; **give me good m.,** faites-moi bonne mesure; **to pour s.o. out a m. of rum,** verser une mesure de rhum à qn; (*b*) *Tail: etc:* **made to m.,** fait sur mesure(s); **to have a suit made to m.,** se faire faire un complet sur mesure(s); *Fig:* **to take s.o.'s m.,** prendre la mesure d'un homme; jauger un homme; (*c*) *Nau:* cubage *m,* jaugeage *m*; **m. goods,** marchandises *f* de cubage, d'encombrement; (*d*) *Typ:* **narrow m.,** petite justification; (*e*) *Fenc:* mesure; **to be out of m.,** être hors de mesure; (*f*) *Metalw:* **stop m.,** calé-étalon *f.* **2.** (*instrument for measuring*) (*a*) mesure (à grains, à lait, etc.); *Ch: etc:* **graduated m.,** mesure graduée, éprouvette graduée, verre gradué, gobelet gradué; (*b*) **(tape) m.,** mesure, mètre *m* (à ruban). **3.** (*limit*) (*a*) mesure, limite *f*; **to know no measures,** ignorer toute mesure; **he annoys me beyond m.,** il m'irrite outre mesure, sans mesure; (*b*) **in some m.,** dans une certaine mesure; jusqu'à un certain point; **he enjoys a large m. of liberty,** il jouit d'une très grande liberté; **a m. of independence,** une certaine indépendance. **4.** (*a*) mesure, démarche *f,* manœuvre *f*; **preventive, protective, measures,** mesures préventives, de protection; **security, safety, measures,** mesures de sécurité; **forcible m.,** mesure contraignante; **disciplinary m.,** mesure disciplinaire; **defence measures,** mesures de défense; **measures of conciliation,** voies *f* d'accommodement; **the success of this m.,** le résultat de cette manœuvre; **he took all necessary measures,** il a pris tous les arrangements nécessaires; **to take extreme measures,** employer les grands moyens; **to drive s.o. to extreme measures,** pousser qn à des extrémités; **to take legal measures,** avoir recours aux voies légales, de droit; **as a m. of economy,** par mesure d'économie; (*b*) projet *m* de loi. **5.** *Mth: O:* facteur *m,* diviseur *m* (d'un nombre); **greatest common m.,** plus grand commun diviseur. **6.** *Min:* **coal measures,** gisements houillers; série *f* carbonifère; **barren measures,** morts-terrains *m.* **7.** *Pros:*

etc: mesure.

measure², *v.*

I. *v.tr. & i.* 1. *v.tr.* (*a*) mensurer; mesurer (le débit d'un cours d'eau, l'intensité d'un courant électrique, une distance, le temps, etc.); métrer (un mur, etc.); cuber (le bois, des pierres); stérer (du bois de chauffage); **to m. a piece of ground,** mesurer, arpenter, toiser, un terrain; faire l'arpentage d'un terrain; **to m. sth. with compasses,** mesurer qch. au compas; compasser (des dimensions); (*of pers.*) (*for height*) **to be measured,** passer à la toise; **to m. the tonnage of a ship,** jauger un navire; **to m. one's length (on the ground),** s'étaler par terre; tomber tout de son long, de tout son long; **to m. s.o. (with one's eye),** mesurer, toiser, qn (du regard); prendre la mesure de qn; **the gravity of the situation could be measured by their anxiety,** on pouvait mesurer à leur anxiété la gravité de la situation; (*b*) *Dressm: Tail:* mesurer (qn); prendre la mesure de (qn); prendre mesure à (qn); **I am going to be measured for an overcoat,** je vais me faire prendre mesure, je vais faire prendre mes mesures, pour un pardessus; (*c*) **to m. one's strength, oneself, with s.o.,** mesurer ses forces avec qn; se mesurer avec, contre, qn; (*d*) **to m. one's words,** mesurer, peser, ses paroles. 2. *v.i.* (*a*) **A4 paper measures 210 mm by 297,** le papier A4 a 297 mm de long sur 210 mm de large; **column that measures 10 metres,** colonne *f* qui mesure 10 mètres; (*b*) **the paper would m. more easily on the table,** il serait plus simple d'étaler le papier sur la table pour le mesurer.

II. (*compound verbs*) 1. **measure off,** *v.tr.* mesurer (du tissu, etc.); **m. off 10 cm from the end of the line,** mesurez 10 cm à partir du bout de la ligne.

2. **measure out,** *v.tr.* (*a*) mesurer (un terrain de tennis, etc.); (*b*) distribuer (les parts qui reviennent à chacun); répartir (qch.); mesurer (du blé, etc.); verser (qch.) dans une mesure; **he measured out a tot of rum to each of us,** il nous a servi à chacun un petit verre de rhum, mesuré de justesse.

3. **measure up.** (*a*) *v.tr.* mesurer (du bois); (*b*) *v.i.* **to m. up to one's job,** se montrer à la hauteur de sa tâche; **to m. up to s.o., to sth.,** être à la mesure de qn, de qch.; égaler, être l'égal de, qn.

measured ['meʒəd], *a.* 1. (*of time, distance, etc.*) mesuré, déterminé; *Nau:* **m. ton,** tonneau *m* d'encombrement. 2. (*a*) (mouvement, pas) cadencé; **m. tread,** marche scandée; *Equit:* **m. movements,** mouvements écoutés; (*b*) **with m. steps,** à pas mesurés, à pas comptés. 3. **m. language,** langage modéré; paroles mesurées, pondérées; **to speak in m. tones,** parler sur un ton modéré, parler avec mesure; **with m. insolence,** avec une insolence calculée. 4. *Pros:* (vers, etc.) mesuré.

measureless ['meʒəlis], *a. esp. Lit:* infini, illimité, sans bornes; **a m. expanse,** un paysage fuyant à perte de vue; **m. insolence,** une insolence sans bornes.

measurement ['meʒəmənt], *s.* 1. mesure *f*; mesurage *m*; **range m.,** mesure des distances; **m. of time, of heat,** mesure du temps, de la chaleur; **radiation m.,** mesure du rayonnement, des radiations; *Mec.E:* **m. between centres,** mesure entre axes, entre pointes; *Const: etc:* **inside, outside, m.,** mesure dans œuvre, hors œuvre; **m. reading,** relevé *m* de mesure. 2. *Nau:* (*a*) jaugeage *m* (d'un bâtiment); **certificate of m.,** certificat *m* de jaugeage; (*b*) cubage *m*, encombrement *m* (du fret); **m. converted into weight,** cubage converti en poids; **to pay for cargo by m.,** payer le fret au cubage, au volume; **m. freight,** fret selon encombrement, selon volume; **m. goods,** marchandises *f* de cubage, d'encombrement; **m. ton,** tonneau *m* d'encombrement, de mer. 3. (*of pers.*) **head, bust, waist, hip, measurements,** tour *m* de tête, de poitrine, de taille, de hanches; *Anthr:* **face, skull, measurements,** mensuration *f* de la face, du crâne; **to take s.o.'s measurements,** prendre (i) les mesures, (ii) *Anthr:* les mensurations, de qn; *Tail:* **to take a customer's measurements,** mesurer un client.

measurer ['meʒərər], *s.* 1. (*pers.*) mesureur, -euse; arpenteur *m*; toiseur *m*; métreur *m*. 2. (*device*) mesureur; mesureuse.

measuring ['meʒəriŋ], *s.* (*a*) mesurage *m* (du drap, etc.); mensuration *f*; métrage *m*; mesure *f* (du temps); arpentage *m* (d'un terrain); cubage *m* (de pierres, etc.); stérage *m* (de bois de chauffage); (*with compasses*) compassement *m*; *Nau:* jaugeage *m* (d'un bâtiment); *Ch: etc:* dosage *m*; **m. tube,** tube *m* pour dosage; **m. cylinder,** (tube) mesureur *m*; **m. glass,** verre gradué; **m. tape,** mètre *m* (à) ruban; **m. rod,** (i) pige *f*, réglette-jauge *f*, *pl.* réglettes-jauges; (ii) mètre *m* (de drapier, etc.); *Surv:* **m. staff,** règle divisée; **m. chain,** chaîne d'arpenteur, d'arpentage; *El:* **m. bridge,** pont *m* de mesure; **m. circuit,** circuit *m* de mesure; **m. instrument,** appareil *m*, instrument *m*, de mesure; **m. accuracy,** précision *f* de mesure; **m. range,** champ *m*, plage *f*, de mesure; **m. sensitivity,** sensibilité *f* de mesure; (*b*) *Ent:* **m. worm,** (chenille *f*) arpenteuse *f*.

meat [mi:t], *s.* 1. (*a*) viande *f*; **fresh m.,** viande fraîche; **frozen, chilled, m.,** viande congelée, frigorifiée; **butcher's m.,** viande de boucherie; **red m.,** viande rouge; **white m.,** viande blanche; blanc *m* (de poulet); *esp. Can:* **fancy meats, variety meats,** abats *m* comestibles; **processing m.,** viande de fabrication; *Cu:* **cold m.,** viande froide; *P:* **to make cold m. of s.o.,** tuer, refroidir, qn; **luncheon m.** = pâté *m* de viande; **pressed m.,** viande pressée; **minced m.,** *U.S:* **ground m.,** hachis *m* (de viande); **dog's m., cat's m.,** viande pour chiens, pour chats; *F:* **to make cat's m. of s.o.,** abîmer le portrait à, de, qn; **abstention from m.,** abstinence *f* des viandes; *Ecc:* **to abstain from m.,** faire maigre; **m. diet,** régime carné, gras; **he has been forbidden to eat m.,** l'alimentation carnée lui est interdite; **m. eater,** mangeur, -euse, de viande; (animal) carnivore *m*; **m. broth,** bouillon gras; *Bac:* **(gelatine) m. broth,** bouillon de culture; **m. hook,** croc *m* de boucherie; allonge *f* de boucher; **m. saw,** scie *f* de boucher; **m. chopper,** feuille *f* de boucher; hache-viande *m inv*; **m. tea,** thé-collation *m*, goûter *m*, auquel on sert un plat de viande; (*b*) *A: & U.S:* chair *f* (d'huître, de fruit, de noix); (*c*) *Med: F:* préparations *f* microscopiques. 2. (*a*) (i) *A:* aliment *m*, nourriture *f*; (ii) **m. and drink,** le manger et le boire; **it was m. and drink to them,** c'était ce qui les faisait vivre; c'était leur passion, leur plus grand plaisir; **to get the m. out of a book,** extraire la moelle d'un livre; **there's no m. in this,** cela n'a rien de substantiel; cela est dépourvu de toute solidité; *Prov:* **one man's m. is another man's poison,** ce qui guérit l'un tue l'autre; ce qui nuit à l'un nuit à l'autre; (*b*) (i) *A:* repas *m*; (ii) **grace before m.,** bénédicité *m*; prière *f* avant le repas. 3. *P:* **a (nice) bit of m.,** une putain, une poule.

meatball ['mi:tbɔ:l], *s. Cu:* boulette *f* (de viande).

meathead ['mi:thed], *s. P: esp. U.S:* idiot, -ote; andouille *f*, gourde *f*.

meatless ['mi:tlis], *a.* 1. (ville assiégée) à court de viande. 2. (repas *m*) maigre.

meatotome [mi'eitoutoum], *s. Surg:* méatotome *m*.

meatotomy [miə'tɔtəmi], *s. Surg:* méatotomie *f*.

meatus, *pl.* **-us, -uses** [mi'eitəs, -əsiz], *s. Anat:* méat *m*.

meaty ['mi:ti], *a.* 1. charnu. 2. (odeur *f*, etc.) de viande. 3. (livre, etc.) plein de substance.

mebbe ['mebi], *adv. P:* (= *may be*) peut-être; ça se peut.

mebos ['mi:bəs], *s. Cu:* (*in S. Africa*) (espèce de) pâte *f* d'abricots.

Mecca ['mekə]. *Pr.n. Geog:* la Mecque; *F:* **Stratford-on-Avon, the tourists' M.,** Stratford-on-Avon, la Mecque des touristes.

Meccan ['mekən]. *Geog:* (*a*) *a.* mecquois, de la Mecque; (*b*) *s.* Mecquois, -oise.

mechanic [mi'kænik], *s.* 1. *A:* artisan *m*; ouvrier *m*. 2. mécanicien *m*; **garage, motor, m.,** mécanicien de garage, mécanicien auto; **air(craft) m.,** mécanicien d'avion, d'aviation; **radio m.,** mécanicien radio; **radar m.,** mécanicien (de) radar; **dental m.,** mécanicien dentiste, prothésiste *mf* dentaire.

mechanical [mi'kænik(ə)l], *a.* 1. *Mec:* mécanique; **m. advantage,** effet *m* mécanique (d'un levier, d'une presse hydraulique, etc.); **m. efficiency,** rendement *m* mécanique; **m. energy,** (i) énergie *f* mécanique; (ii) travail moteur, travail mécanique; **m. equivalent of heat,** équivalent *m* mécanique de la chaleur; **m. force, power,** force *f*, puissance *f*, mécanique. 2. (*a*) **m. engineering,** constructions *f* mécaniques; **m. calculator,** machine *f* à calculer mécanique; *Mec.E:* **m. drive,** entraînement *m* mécanique; **m. joint,** accouplement *m*, connexion *f*, mécanique; **m. linkage,** liaison *f* mécanique; **m. failure,** panne *f* mécanique; (*b*) *El:* **m. impedance, reactance,** impédance *f*, réactance *f*, mécanique; (*c*) **m. drawing,** dessin industriel, géométrique; **he has no m. skill,** il ne peut pas manier un outil; *O:* **m. arts,** les arts *m* mécaniques; (*d*) (contraceptif) local. 3. (*a*) (*of reply, smile, etc.*) machinal, -aux; automatique; (*b*) (*of pianist, etc.*) **his playing is very m.,** il joue d'une façon très mécanique.

mechanicalism [mi'kænikəlizm], *s.* 1. *Phil:* mécanisme *m*. 2. *A:* mécanicité *f* (d'une profession, etc.).

mechanically [mi'kænik(ə)li], *adv.* 1. mécaniquement; **m. driven, operated,** actionné, entraîné, mécaniquement; **m. propelled vehicle,** véhicule *m* à propulsion, à traction, mécanique; *Cmptr:* **m. produced report,** état établi mécanographiquement. 2. machinalement; par habitude.

mechanician [mekə'niʃ(ə)n], *s. esp. NAm:* mécanicien *m* constructeur.

mechanics [mi'kæniks], *s.pl.* 1. (*usu. with sg. const.*) la mécanique; **analytical, pure, theoretical, m.,** mécanique analytique, rationnelle; **applied m.,** mécanique appliquée; **celestial m.,** mécanique céleste; **matrix m.,** mécanique matricielle; **quantum m.,** mécanique quantitique; **Newtonian m.,** mécanique newtionienne, de Newton; **fluid m.,** mécanique des fluides, mécanique hydraulique; **wave m.,** mécanique ondulatoire. 2. mécanisme *m* (du corps humain, etc.).

mechanism ['mekənizm], *s.* 1. *Phil: Psy: etc:* mécanisme *m*; **defence m.,** (i) *Psy:* mécanisme de défense; (ii) *Z: etc:* système *m* de défense. 2. appareil *m*; dispositif *m*; mécanisme; mécanique *f*; **a delicate piece of m.,** un mécanisme délicat; **safety m.,** mécanisme de sécurité; *Mec.E:* **drive m.,** mécanisme de commande, d'entraînement; mécanisme moteur; **operation m.,** mécanisme de manœuvre, de fonctionnement; **feed m.,** (i) *Mch.Tls:* mécanisme d'avance; (ii) *Artil:* mécanisme d'alimentation; *Artil:* **firing m.,** mécanisme de détente, de mise à feu; **traversing m.,** mécanisme de pointage en direction; **elevating m.,** mécanisme de pointage en hauteur; **automatic prediction m.,** mécanisme d'extrapolation automatique; *Av:* **integrator m.,** mécanisme d'intégration.

mechanist ['mekənist], *s.* 1. *Phil:* mécaniste *mf*. 2. *A:* mécanicien *m* (constructeur).

mechanistic [mekə'nistik], *a. Phil:* mécanistique.

mechanization [mekənai'zeiʃ(ə)n], *s.* mécanisation *f*.

mechanize ['mekənaiz], *v.tr.* mécaniser (une industrie, etc.); **mechanized army,** armée mécanisée.

mechanotherapy [mekənou'θerəpi], *s.* mécanothérapie *f*.

Mechlin ['meklin]. 1. *Pr.n. Geog:* Malines *f*. 2. *s.* **M. (lace),** dentelle *f* de Malines; malines *f*.

Mecklenburg ['meklənbə:g]. *Pr.n. Geog:* Mecklembourg *m*.

meconate ['mekəneit], *s. Ch:* méconate *m*.

meconic [mi'kɔnik], *a. Ch:* (acide) méconique.

meconin ['mekənin], *s. Ch:* méconine *f*.

meconium [mi'kouniəm], *s. Physiol:* méconium *m* (du nouveau-né).

meconoid ['mekənɔid], *a. Physiol:* méconial, -aux.

Mecoptera [me'kɔptərə], *s.pl. Ent:* mécoptères *m*.

Mecopteroidea [mekɔptə'rɔidiə], *s.pl. Ent:* mécoptéroïdes *m*.

Med (the) [ðə'med]. *Pr.n. F:* la Méditerranée.

médaillon [me'daijɔn], *s. Cu:* médaillon *m*.

medal ['med(ə)l], *s.* médaille *f*; **campaign m.,** médaille commémorative; **to award a m. to s.o.,** médailler qn; décerner une médaille à qn; **to wear,** *F:* **sport, all one's medals,** porter, mettre, toutes ses décorations; *F:* sortir sa batterie de cuisine; *F:* **a putty m.,** une médaille en carton; **the reverse of the m.,** le revers de la médaille; *F:* **you're showing your medals,** votre braguette est déboutonnée.

medallion [me'dæliən], *s.* médaillon *m*.

medallist ['medəlist], *s.* 1. médailliste *m*; amateur *m* de médailles. 2. médailleur *m*; graveur *m* en médailles. 3. médaillé, -ée; **gold m.,** titulaire *mf* d'une médaille d'or.

meddle ['medl], *v.i.* **to m. with sth.,** se mêler de qch.; **to m. in sth.,** s'immiscer dans qch.; s'ingérer dans qch.; intervenir dans qch.; **to m. in, with, other people's affairs,** se mêler des affaires d'autrui; **don't m. with my tools!** ne touchez pas à mes outils! ne dérangez pas mes outils! **it's dangerous to m. with him,** il ne fait pas bon (de) se frotter à lui; **I don't want the women meddling,** je ne veux pas que les femmes s'en mêlent; *Prov:* **m. and smart for it,** qui s'y frotte s'y pique.

meddler ['medlər], *s.* officieux, -euse; intrigant, -ante; touche-à-tout *m inv*; *F:* **he's a (terrible) m.,** il se mêle de tout, met son grain de sel dans tout.

meddlesome ['med(ə)lsəm], **meddling**¹ [medliŋ], *a.* officieux, intrigant; qui se mêle de tout; qui touche à tout.

meddlesomeness ['med(ə)lsəmnis], *s.* manie *f* de se mêler des affaires d'autrui.

meddling², *s.* 1. intervention *f*, ingérence *f*, immixtion *f* **(in, with, sth.,** dans une affaire). 2. manigances *fpl*, menées *fpl*.

Mede [mi:d], *s.* (*a*) *Hist:* Mède *m*; (*b*) **it is like the laws of the Medes and Persians,** c'est réglé comme du papier à musique, comme une pendule, comme une horloge.

Medea [mi'diə]. *Pr.n.f. Gr.Myth:* Médée.

media¹, *pl.* **-iae** ['mi:diə, -ii:], *s.* 1. *Ling:* consonne moyenne. 2. *Anat:* unique moyenne (des artères).

Media². *Pr.n. A.Geog:* la Médie.

media³. *See* MEDIUM.

mediaeval [medi'i:vəl], *a.* 1. du moyen âge; médiéval, -aux; **m. architecture, literature,** architecture *f*, littérature *f*, médiévale, du moyen âge. 2. *F:* **you're positively m.!** tu es moyenâgeux! tu vis dans le passé!

mediaevalism [medi'i:vəlizm], *s.* 1. culture médiévale. 2. médiévisme *m*.

mediaevalist [medi'i:vəlist], *s.* médiéviste *mf*.

medial ['mi:diəl]. **1.** *a.* (*a*) intermédiaire (**to**, entre); *Nat.Hist:* (*of line, etc.*) médian; *Ling:* (*of letter*) médial, -als, -aux; **m. letter,** médiale *f*; (*b*) de grandeur moyenne, de dimensions moyennes. **2.** *s. Ling:* médiale *f*.

medialize ['mi:diəlaiz], *v.tr. Ling:* sonoriser (une consonne occlusive).

medially ['mi:diəli], *adv.* médialement.

median[1] ['mi:diən], (*a*) *a.* médian; (*b*) *a.* & *s. Anat:* (nerf) médian; (veine) médiane; (*c*) *a.* & *s. Mth:* (ligne) médiane; *Stat:* **m. of a distribution,** médiane d'une distribution; (*d*) *a. NAm: Aut:* **m. strip,** terre-plein central; berme centrale; *Fr.C:* médiane.

Median[2]. **1.** *A.Geog:* (*a*) *a.* médique, mède; (*b*) *s.* Mède *mf.* **2.** *s. Ling:* mède *m*.

mediant ['mi:diənt], *s. Mus:* médiante *f*.

mediastinitis [mi:diæsti'naitis], *s. Med:* médiastinite *f*.

mediastinotomy [mi:diæsti'nɔtəmi], *s. Surg:* médiastinotomie *f*.

mediastinum, *pl.* **-a** [mi:diəs'tainəm, -ə], *s. Anat:* médiastin *m*.

mediate[1] ['mi:dieit], *a.* **1.** médiat, intermédiaire, interposé (**between,** entre). **2.** *Hist:* **m. lord,** prince médiat. **3.** *Log:* **m. inference,** déduction médiate; *Jur:* **m. testimony,** témoignage *m* de seconde main.

mediate[2]. **1.** *v.i.* (*a*) (*of pers.*) s'entremettre, s'interposer; agir en médiateur, servir de médiateur (**between . . . and . . .**, entre. . . et. . .); (*b*) (*of thg*) former un lien, un trait d'union (entre deux choses). **2.** *v.tr.* **to m. a peace,** intervenir en qualité de médiateur pour amener la paix.

mediating ['mi:dieitiŋ], *a.* **1.** (*of opinion, etc.*) modéré. **2.** (*of party, etc.*) médiateur, -trice.

mediation [mi:di'eiʃ(ə)n], *s.* médiation *f*; intervention (amicale); **offer of m.,** offre *f* d'intervention; **through the m. of. . .**, par l'entremise *f* de . . ..

mediative ['mi:diətiv], *a.* médiateur, -trice.

mediatization [mi:diətai'zeiʃ(ə)n], *s. Hist:* médiatisation *f* (d'un état).

mediatize ['mi:diətaiz], *v.tr. Hist:* médiatiser (un état).

mediator ['mi:dieitər], *s.* (*f. occ.* **mediatress** ['mi:dieitris], **mediatrix** ['mi:diətriks]) médiateur, -trice; intermédiaire *mf*; entremetteur, -euse.

mediatory ['mi:diətəri], *a.* médiateur, -trice.

medic ['medik], *s. F:* (*a*) étudiant, -ante, en médecine, carabin *m*; (*b*) médecin *m*, toubib *m*.

medicable ['medikəbl], *a.* guérissable.

medical ['medik(ə)l]. **1.** *a.* médical, -aux; de médecine; **the m. profession,** (i) le corps médical; (ii) la profession de médecin; **m practitioner,** *F:* **m. man,** médecin *m*; **m. adviser,** médecin (traitant); **you need m. attention, advice,** il faut vous faire soigner par un médecin; il faut voir un médecin, un docteur; **m. attention,** soins médicaux; **m. school,** école *f* de médecine; **m. student,** étudiant, -ante, en médecine; **m. books,** livres *m* de médecine; **m. officer,** (i) (*in hospital*) chef *m* de service; (ii) *Ind:* médecin du travail; (iii) *Mil:* médecin militaire; *Mil:* **regimental m. officer,** médecin(-chef) du corps, du régiment, du bataillon; **m. assistant,** médecin auxiliaire; **to come before the m. officer,** passer (à) la visite; *Adm:* **m. officer of health** = médecin départemental; (*esp. in hospital*) **ancillary m. personnel,** auxiliaires médicaux; **m. examination,** examen médical; **m. control,** contrôle médical, sanitaire; **m. inspection,** visite médicale, inspection *f* sanitaire; **m. record,** dossier médical, fiche médicale; **m. equipment, supplies,** matériel médical, sanitaire; *Mil:* approvisionnements médicaux, sanitaires, du service de santé; *Mil:* **m. supply officer,** officier *m* d'approvisionnement du service de santé; **m. service, department,** *U.S:* **m. corps,** service *m* de santé militaire; **m. collecting unit,** unité médicale de ramassage (des blessés); **m. reception station,** centre médical de répartition (des blessés). **2.** *s. F:* (*a*) étudiant, -ante, en médecine; carabin *m*; (*b*) examen médical.

medically ['medik(ə)li], *adv.* **m. speaking,** médicalement parlant; **viewed m.,** considéré au point de vue médical; **m. trained,** qui a reçu un enseignement médical; **to be m. examined,** subir un examen médical.

medicament [me'dikəmənt], *s.* médicament *m*.

medicate ['medikeit], *v.tr.* **1.** donner un traitement médical à, traiter (un malade). **2.** rendre (du vin) médicamenteux; rendre (du coton) hydrophile.

medicated ['medikeitid], *a.* (papier) médicamenté; (vin) médicamenteux; (savon) hygiénique; (coton) hydrophile.

medication [medi'keiʃ(ə)n], *s.* **1.** médication *f*; emploi *m* de médicaments; *U.S:* **it's time for the patient to have his m.,** il faut donner ses médicaments, son traitement, au malade. **2.** imprégnation *f* (du papier, etc.) avec des médicaments.

medicative ['medikətiv], *a.* curatif; médicateur, -trice.

Medici ['meditʃi(:)]. *Pr.n.pl. Hist:* **the M.,** les Médicis; **Lorenzo de' M.,** Laurent de Médicis.

medicinal [me'disin(ə)l], *a.* médicinal, -aux; médicamenteux; **m. baths,** bains médicinaux; **m. rash,** éruption médicamenteuse; **m. plants,** plantes médicamenteuses.

medicinally [me'disinəli], *adv.* médicalement, comme médicament; **I take a little whisky m.,** je prends un peu de whisky comme, à titre de, médicament.

medicine[1] ['med(i)sin], *s.* **1.** la médecine; **allopathic, hom(o)eopathic, m.,** médecine allopathique, homéopathique; **clinical m.,** médecine clinique; **social m.,** médecine sociale; **industrial m.,** médecine du travail; **aviation m.,** médecine aéronautique, médecine de l'air; **space m.,** médecine spatiale, médecine de l'espace; **nuclear m.,** médecine nucléaire, atomique; **radiological m.,** médecine radiologique; **to study m.,** étudier la médecine; **to practise m.,** exercer la médecine. **2.** (*a*) médicament *m*, remède *m*; drogue *f*; **to give s.o. a taste, a dose, of his own m.,** rendre la pareille à qn; **to take one's m.,** avaler la pilule; supporter les conséquences (de son action); **m. chest, cupboard,** (coffre *m* à) pharmacie *f*; armoire *f* à pharmacie; (*b*) *F: O:* purgatif *m*, médecine; **to take m.,** se purger; (*c*) *Sp:* **m. ball,** medicine-ball *m*; (*d*) (*among NAm. Indians, etc.*) (i) sorcellerie *f*, magie *f*; (ii) charme *m*; **m. man, woman,** (sorcier *m*) guérisseur *m*; (sorcière *f*) guérisseuse *f*.

medicine[2], *v.tr. A:* traiter (qn) par des médicaments; médicamenter (qn).

medick ['medik], *s. Bot:* **(purple) m.,** luzerne *f*; **black m., hop m.,** luzerne houblon; triolet *m*, lupuline *f*; petit trèfle jaune; minette (dorée); **yellow m., sickle m.,** luzerne en faux.

medico ['medikou], *s. F:* (*a*) médecin *m*, toubib *m*; (*b*) étudiant, -ante, en médecine; carabin *m*.

medico-legal ['medikou'li:g(ə)l], *a.* médico-légal, -aux.

medico-surgical ['medikou'sə:dʒik(ə)l], *a.* médico-chirurgical, -aux.

medieval, medievalism [medi'i:v(ə)l, -'i:vəlizm] = MEDIAEVAL, MEDIAEVALISM.

medifixed ['mi:difikst], *a. Bot:* médifixe.

Medina[1] [me'di:nə]. *Pr.n. Geog:* Médine *f*.

medina[2], *s.* (*in N. Africa*) médina *f*.

medinal ['medin(ə)l], *s. Pharm:* véronal *m* sodique.

mediocarpal [mi:diou'ka:p(ə)l], *a. Anat:* médiocarpien.

mediocre [mi:di'oukər], *a.* (*a*) médiocre; *s.* **to rise above the m.,** s'élever au-dessus du médiocre; (*b*) *s.pl.* **the m.,** les médiocrités *f*.

mediocrity [mi:di'ɔkriti], *s.* **1.** médiocrité *f* (de qn, de qch.). **2.** (*pers.*) **a m.,** une médiocrité.

medio-dorsal [mi:diou'dɔ:s(ə)l], *a. Anat:* médio-dorsal, -aux.

mediopalatal [mi:diou'pælət(ə)l]. *Ling:* (*a*) *a.* médiopalatal, -aux; (*b*) *s.* médiopalatale *f*.

mediopassive [mi:diou'pæsiv], *a.* & *s. Ling:* médiopassif (*m*).

mediotarsal [mi:diou'tɑ:s(ə)l], *a. Anat:* (articulation) médiotarsienne.

meditate ['mediteit]. **1.** *v.tr.* méditer (un projet, une entreprise); projeter (un ouvrage); **to m. mischief,** méditer un mauvais coup; **to m. doing sth.,** méditer de faire qch.; se proposer de faire qch.; avoir l'intention de faire qch.; penser à faire qch. **2.** *v.i.* (*a*) méditer (**on, upon,** sur); réfléchir (**on, upon,** sur, à); (*b*) se livrer à la méditation; méditer; se recueillir.

meditation [medi'teiʃ(ə)n], *s.* **1.** méditation *f* (**upon,** sur); recueillement *m*; **to be plunged in m.,** être plongé dans la méditation. **2.** *Lit:* **the Meditations of Marcus Aurelius,** les Pensées *f* de Marc-Aurèle.

meditative ['meditətiv], *a.* méditatif, recueilli; **m. walks,** promenades consacrées à la méditation.

meditatively ['meditətivli], *adv.* d'un air méditatif; avec recueillement.

meditativeness ['meditətivnis], *s.* nature méditative; recueillement *m*.

meditator ['mediteitər], *s.* penseur, -euse; rêveur, -euse; méditatif, -ive.

Mediterranean [meditə'reiniən]. **1.** *a. Geog:* méditerrané; (*a*) qui est au milieu des terres; (*b*) qui est entouré par des terres; **the M. Sea,** *s.* **the M.,** la (mer) Méditerranée; **m. climate,** climat méditerranéen. **2.** *s. pl.* **the Mediterraneans,** les races *f* du littoral méditerranéen.

medium[1], *pl.* **-a, -ums** ['mi:diəm, -ə, -əmz], *s.* **1.** milieu *m*; moyen terme (**between,** entre); **happy m.,** juste milieu. **2.** (*a*) *Ph:* milieu, véhicule *m*; **air is the m. of sound,** l'air *m* est le véhicule du son; **the air is the m. in which we live,** l'air est le milieu dans lequel nous vivons; (*b*) **(social) m.,** milieu, atmosphère *f*, ambiance *f*; (*c*) *Biol:* **culture m.,** bouillon *m* de culture; (*d*) *Pharm: Paint:* véhicule; (*e*) *Typ:* **carrying m.,** véhicule (de l'encre); **opaquing m.,** opacifiant *m*; **shading m.,** relief *m* de gélatine; **tinting m.,** blanc *m* de mélange. **3.** (*a*) intermédiaire *m*, entremise *f*; **to impose peace through the m. of war,** imposer la paix par la voie des armes; **through the m. of the press,** par l'intermédiaire de la presse, par voie de presse, par la voie des journaux; (*b*) moyen *m* (d'expression, de communication); agent *m*, organe *m*; **advertising m.,** organe *m* de publicité; **the newspaper, the television, as a m. for advertising,** le journal, la télévision, comme moyen de publicité, de réclame; **mass media, the media,** moyens de communication(s) et d'information(s) de (la) masse; *attrib.* **it's just a media sales gimmick,** ce n'est qu'un truc, une réclame, pour attirer le (grand) public; *Pol.Ec:* **circulating m., m. of circulation, of exchange,** agent de circulation, agent monétaire; (*c*) agent (chimique); (*d*) moyen d'expression; **sculptor whose favourite m. is marble,** sculpteur *m* qui préfère travailler le marbre. **4.** *Psychics:* médium *m*.

medium[2], *a.* moyen; **of m. height,** de taille moyenne; **of m. length,** demi-long; **m. sized,** de grandeur moyenne, de taille moyenne; **m. dry wine,** vin demi-sec; *W.Tel:* **m. wave,** onde moyenne.

mediumism ['mi:diəmizm], *s. Psychics:* médiumnité *f*.

mediumistic [mi:diə'mistik], *a. Psychics:* médiumnique, médianique, médianimique.

mediumship ['mi:diəmʃip], *s. Psychics:* médiumnité *f*; profession *f* de médium.

medlar ['medlər], *s. Bot:* **1.** (*a*) nèfle *f*; (*b*) **m.(-tree),** néflier *m*. **2. Japan m.,** (i) nèfle du Japon; (ii) (*tree*) néflier du Japon; bibassier *m*, bibacier *m*; **Neapolitan m.,** (i) azerole *f*; (ii) (*tree*) azerolier *m*.

medley[1] ['medli]. **1.** *s.* (*a*) mélange *m*, confusion *f*, méli-mélo *m*, *pl.* mélis-mélos, pêle-mêle *m inv*, olla-podrida *f*, ambigu *m* (de personnes, d'objets); bigarrure *f* (de couleurs, etc.); bariolage *m* (d'idées, d'expressions); *Lit:* macédoine *f*; *Mus:* pot pourri; **m. of all kinds of people,** mélange hétéroclite de toutes sortes de gens; *Swim:* **400 metres m. race,** 4 × 100 mètres quatre nages; (*b*) *A:* bagarre *f*, rixe *f*. **2.** *a.* (*a*) *A:* (*of colour, cloth*) bariolé, bigarré; (*b*) mêlé, mélangé, hétéroclite.

medley[2], *v.tr. A:* entremêler (des choses mal assorties).

medulla [me'dʌlə], *s.* **1.** *Bot:* médulle *f*, moelle *f*. **2.** *Anat:* moelle (d'un os, d'un poil); **the m. oblongata,** le bulbe rachidien, la moelle allongée.

medullary [me'dʌləri], *a. Anat:* médullaire; *Bot:* médullaire, médulleux; **m. sheath,** (i) *Bot:* étui *m* médullaire; vaisseaux *m* primaires; (ii) *Anat:* myéline *f*; *Bot:* **m. ray,** rayon *m*, prolongement *m*, médullaire; *Anat:* **m. canal, cavity,** canal *m*, cavité *f*, médullaire.

medullated ['medjuleitid], *a. Anat:* médullaire; *Bot:* médullaire, médulleux; à moelle.

medullitis [medju'laitis], *s. Med:* médullite *f*.

Medusa [mi'dju:sə, -zə]. **1.** *Pr.n.f. Gr.Myth:* Méduse; *Bot: Echin:* **Medusa's head,** tête *f* de Méduse. **2.** *s. Coel:* méduse *f*.

medusan [mi'dju:sən, -zən], **medusoid** [mi'dju:sɔid, -zɔid]. *Coel:* **1.** *a.* médusaire. **2.** *s.* médusaire *m*, acalèphe *m*, discophore *m*.

meed [mi:d], *s. Lit:* récompense *f*; **to offer one's m. of praise,** apporter sa part, son tribut, d'éloges, de louanges.

meek [mi:k], *a.* doux, *f.* douce; humble, soumis, résigné; **m. creatures,** douces et humbles créatures; *F:* **m. as a lamb, m. as Moses,** doux comme un agneau, comme un mouton; *s. B:* **blessed are the m.,** bienheureux les débonnaires.

meekly ['mi:kli], *adv.* avec douceur; avec soumission; humblement.

meekness ['mi:knis], *s.* douceur *f* de caractère; soumission *f*, humilité *f*, mansuétude *f*; **m. of spirit,** résignation *f*.

meerschaum ['miəʃəm], *s.* **1.** *Miner:* magnésite *f*, écume *f* (de mer). **2. m. (pipe),** pipe *f* d'écume (de mer), en écume (de mer).

meet[1] [mi:t], *a. A:* & *Lit:* convenable; séant; **diamonds m. for a queen,** diamants *m* qui conviendraient à une reine, dignes d'une reine, propres à une reine; **it is m. that we should do so,** il convient que nous le fassions; **as was m.,** comme il convenait.

meet[2], *s.* **1.** (*a*) *Ven:* rendez-vous *m* de chasse; assemblée *f* de chasseurs; rassemblement *m* de la meute; (*b*) *O:* réunion *f* (de cyclistes, etc.). **2.** *Mth:* point *m* de section (de deux lignes); point de tangence, de rencontre (de deux courbes).

meet[3], *v.* (**met** [met]; **met**)

I. *v.tr.* **1.** rencontrer (qn); faire la rencontre de (qn); se rencontrer avec (qn); **I hope to m. you soon,** j'espère avoir sous peu l'occasion, le plaisir, de vous rencontrer; **to m. s.o. on the stairs,** croiser qn, se croiser avec qn, faire une rencontre, dans l'escalier; **to m. a ship,** rencontrer un navire; **to m. another car,** croiser une autre voiture; **he met his death, his fate, at . . .,** il trouva la mort, sa perte, à . . .; **it's not something you m. every day,** c'est le trèfle à quatre feuilles. **2.** (*a*) rencontrer (l'ennemi, qn en duel); (*b*) affronter (la mort, une épreuve, un danger); parer à (un danger); faire face à (une difficulté). **3.** *Nau:* **to m. her with the helm, to m. the helm,** rencontrer (l'embardée) avec la barre; **m. her!** rencontrez! **4.** rejoindre, (re)trouver (qn); se rencontrer avec (qn); **to come forward to m. s.o.,** s'avancer à la rencontre de qn; **to go to m. s.o.,** aller au-devant de qn; aller à la rencontre de qn; **when there is danger ahead I go to m. it,** quand il y a du danger je vais au-devant; **to m. s.o. at the station,** aller chercher, aller recevoir, aller attendre, qn à la gare; **to send s.o. to m. s.o.,** envoyer qn au-devant de qn; envoyer qn chercher qn; **the bus meets the train,** il y a une correspondance entre le train et l'autobus; **to arrange to m. s.o.,** donner (un) rendez-vous à qn; fixer un rendez-vous avec qn; **I arranged to m. him at three o'clock,** j'ai pris rendez-vous avec lui pour trois heures; **we'll m. again at the station,** nous nous retrouverons à la gare. **5.** faire la connaissance de (qn); **we must give a party for people to m. our new neighbours,** il nous faut donner une réception en l'honneur de nos nouveaux voisins; **I met her at the Martins',** je l'ai rencontrée chez les Martin; **he met his wife in Paris,** il a rencontré sa femme pour la première fois à Paris; **m. Mr Thomas,** je vous présente M. Thomas; **it was a great pleasure to m., meeting, you,** j'ai été enchanté de faire votre connaissance. **6. he met my request by saying that . . .,** en réponse à ma demande il a dit que . . .; **as we went in we were met by the smell of cabbage,** dès l'entrée une odeur de choux saisit notre odorat; **the scene that met my eyes,** le spectacle qui s'offrait à mes yeux; **there's more in this than meets the eye,** on ne voit pas le dessous des cartes; **my eye met his,** nos regards se sont croisés; **I dared not m. his eye,** je n'osais pas le regarder en face; **a strange sound met our ears,** un bruit étrange nous a frappé l'oreille. **7. here the road meets the railway,** c'est ici que la route rencontre, rejoint, croise, le chemin de fer; **the point where the Saône meets the Rhône,** l'endroit où la Saône et le Rhône confluent, où la Saône se jette dans le Rhône. **8.** (*a*) **to m. s.o.,** faire des concessions à qn; s'efforcer d'être agréable à qn; **I'll do my best to m. you,** (i) je vais faire mon possible pour vous donner satisfaction, pour me conformer à vos désirs; (ii) *Com:* on va s'arranger, quant au prix; (*b*) satisfaire à, parer à, remplir (un besoin); faire face à (une demande, un besoin); satisfaire à, prévoir, prévenir (une objection); **that meets a long-felt want,** cela répond à un besoin qui s'est fait longtemps ressentir; **that does not m. the difficulty,** cela ne remédie pas à l'inconvénient; **to m. s.o.'s wishes,** satisfaire, remplir, les désirs de qn; **your wishes have been met,** vos désirs *m* ont reçu satisfaction; **it doesn't m. my requirements,** cela ne répond pas à mes besoins; (*c*) *Com:* faire honneur à, faire bon accueil à, accueillir (un effet, une lettre de change); honorer (un chèque); **to m. one's commitments,** faire honneur à ses engagements; remplir ses engagements; (*d*) **to m. expenses,** faire face aux dépenses, à ses dépenses; supporter les dépenses; subvenir aux frais; **he met all expenses,** il a subvenu à tout; **I myself can m. all expenses,** moi seul je suffis à toutes les dépenses.

II. *v.i.* (*a*) (*of pers.*) se rencontrer, se voir; **they met in 1960,** ils se sont connus en 1960; **we met in Paris,** nous nous sommes rencontrés à Paris; **we have met before,** nous nous sommes déjà vus; **when shall we m. again?** quand nous reverrons-nous? (*b*) (*of society, assembly*) se réunir (en session); s'assembler; **the society meets at . . .,** la société tient ses réunions à . . .; **Parliament meets tomorrow,** les Chambres *f* se réunissent demain; (*c*) (*of thgs*) se rencontrer, se réunir, se joindre; **two lines that m.,** deux lignes *f* qui se rencontrent; **two rivers that m.,** deux rivières *f* qui confluent, qui se (re)joignent; *Prov:* **extremes m.,** les extrêmes *m* se touchent; **our eyes met,** nos regards se sont croisés; **these boards do not m.,** ces planches *f* ne joignent pas; **to make (both) ends m.,** joindre les deux bouts; attraper le bout de l'année; arriver à boucler son budget; **we make both ends m. and nothing more,** on s'en tire, voilà tout; (*d*) **to m. with sth.,** rencontrer, trouver, découvrir, qch.; **to m. with a warm reception,** être accueilli avec bonté; recevoir un accueil plein de bonté; **to m. with difficulties,** éprouver des difficultés; rencontrer des obstacles; **to m. with a check, a loss,** éprouver, essuyer, subir, un échec, une perte; **to m. with losses,** faire des pertes; **to m. with a refusal,** essuyer un refus; être éconduit; **to m. with an accident,** être victime d'un accident; **he has met with an accident,** il lui est arrivé un accident; **to m. with a fall,** faire une chute; **to m. with death,** trouver la mort; *Nau:* **to m. with a gale,** essuyer un coup de vent; **we met up with him in Paris,** nous l'avons rencontré (par hasard) à Paris.

meeting ['mi:tiŋ], *s.* **1.** rencontre *f* (de personnes, de routes, etc.); **he's very shy at a first m.,** il a l'abord timide; il est timide quand il rencontre quelqu'un pour la première fois; **right of public m.,** droit *m* de réunion; **m. place, point,** lieu *m* de réunion; rendez-vous *m*; **m. point,** point *m* de jonction; *Mth:* point de rencontre (de deux courbes). **2.** (*a*) assemblée *f*, réunion *f*, séance *f*; **to hold a m.,** tenir une réunion; **the m. will be held at . . .,** la réunion aura lieu à . . .; **the association holds its meetings at . . .,** l'association se réunit à . . .; **the m. will be held tomorrow,** la réunion est prévue pour demain; **to hold a public m.,** se réunir en séance publique; **m. of shareholders,** assemblée d'actionnaires; **to call a m. of the shareholders,** convoquer les actionnaires; **notice of m.,** convocation *f*; *Jur:* **m. of creditors,** assemblée de créanciers; **at the m. in London,** à la séance tenue à Londres; dans une réunion tenue à Londres; **to open the m.,** déclarer la séance ouverte; **to dissolve the m.,** lever la séance; **to address the m.,** prendre la parole; **to put a resolution to the m.,** mettre une résolution aux voix; (*b*) *Sp:* réunion, meeting *m*; *Turf:* (réunion de) courses *fpl*; **mixed m.,** réunion mixte; **jumping m.,** journée *f* de l'obstacle; (*c*) *Rel:* (*of Quakers*) **to go to m.,** aller au temple; **m. house,** temple; (*of Methodists*) **class m.,** réunion en semaine (d'un groupe de fidèles); *O:* **(Sunday) go-to-m. clothes,** habits *m* du dimanche.

meetness ['mi:tnis], *s. A:* convenance *f*; à-propos *m inv*.

Meg [meg]. *Pr.n.f.* (*dim. of Margaret*) Margot.

mega- [(')megə], *comb.fm.* méga-.

megabarye ['megəbæri], *s. Ph.Meas:* mégabarye *f*.

megacaryocyte [megə'kæriousait], *s. Physiol:* mégacaryocyte *m*.

megacephalic [megəse'fælik], **megacephalous** [megə'sefələs], *a. Anthr:* mégacéphale, mégalocéphale.

megaceros [me'gæsərəs], *s. Paleont:* mégacéros *m*.

megachile [megə'kaili], *s. Ent:* mégachile *f*.

Megachiroptera [megəkai'rɔptərə], *s.pl. Z:* mégachiroptères *m*.

megacolon [megə'koulən], *s. Med:* mégacôlon *m*.

megacycle ['megəsaikl], *s. El.Meas:* mégacycle *m*.

Megaderm(at)idae [megədə:'mætidi:, -'də:midi:], *s.pl. Z:* mégadermidés *m*.

megadont ['megədɔnt], *a. Anat:* mégadonte.

megadontism, megadonty [megə'dɔntizm, -'dɔnti], *s. Anat:* macrodontie *f*, gigantisme *m* dentaire.

megadyne ['megədain], *s. Mec.Meas:* mégadyne *f*.

mega-electron-volt ['megəi'lektrɔn'voult], *s. Ph:* méga(-)électron(-)volt *m*.

Megaera [me'giərə]. *Pr.n.f. Gr.Myth:* Mégère.

megahertz ['megəhə:ts], *s. El.Meas:* mégahertz *m*.

megajoule ['megədʒu:l], *s. El.Meas:* mégajoule *m*.

megakaryocyte [megə'kæriousait], *s. Physiol:* mégacaryocyte *m*.

megalith ['megəliθ], *s. Prehist:* mégalithe *m*.

megalithic [megə'liθik], *a.* mégalithique.

megalo- ['megəlou], *comb.fm.* mégalo-.

megaloblast ['megəloublæst], *s. Physiol:* mégaloblaste *m*.

megaloblastic ['megəlou'blæstik], *a. Physiol:* mégaloblastique.

megalocephalic ['megəlouse'fælik], **megalocephalous** [megəlou'sefələs], *a. Anthr:* mégalocéphale.

megalocephaly [megəlou'sefəli], *s. Anthr:* mégalocéphalie *f*.

megaloceros [megə'lɔsərəs], *s. Paleont:* mégacéros *m*.

megalocornea [megəlou'kɔ:niə], *s. Med:* mégalocornée *f*.

megalocyte ['megələusait], *s. Physiol:* mégalocyte *m*.

megalocytosis [megəlousai'tousis], *s. Med:* mégalocytose *f*.

megalodon ['megəloudən], *s. Paleont:* mégalodon *m*.

megalodont ['megəloudɔnt], *a.* mégadonte.

megalomania [megəlou'meiniə], *s.* mégalomanie *f*; folie *f* des grandeurs.

megalomaniac [megəlou'meiniæk], *a. & s.* (de) mégalomane (*mf*).

megalonyx [megə'lɔniks], *s. Paleont:* mégalonyx *m*.

megalophthalmus [megəlɔf'θælməs], *s. Med:* mégalophtalmie *f*.

megalopolis [megə'lɔpəlis], *s.* mégalopolis *f*.

megalopolitan [megəlou'pɔlit(ə)n], *a. & s.* mégalopolitain, -aine.

megalops ['megəlɔps], *s. Crust:* mégalops *m*.

megalopsia [megə'lɔpsiə], *s. Med:* mégalopsie *f*.

Megaloptera [megə'lɔptərə], *s.pl. Ent:* mégaloptères *m*.

Megalopygidae [megəlou'pi:dʒidi:], *s.pl. Ent:* mégalopygides *m*.

megalosaurus [megəlou'sɔ:rəs], *s. Paleont:* mégalosaure *m*.

megalosplenia [megəlou'spli:niə], *s. Med:* mégalosplénie *f*.

megaloureter ['megəlouju'ri:tər], *s. Med:* méga-uretère *m*.

Meganisoptera [megæni'sɔptərə], *s.pl. Ent: Paleont:* méganisoptères *m*.

megaphone ['megəfoun], *s.* mégaphone *m*.

megaphyll ['megəfil], *s. Bot:* mégaphylle *f*.

megaphyton [me'gæfitən], *s. Paleont:* mégaphyton *m*.

megapod(e) ['megəpɔd, -poud], *s. Orn:* mégapode *m*.

Megapodiidae [megəpɔ'daiidi:], *s.pl. Orn:* mégapodidés *m*.

Megara ['megərə]. *Pr.n. A.Geog:* Mégare *f*.

megarhinus [megə'rainəs], *s. Ent:* mégarhine *m*.

Megarian [me'gɛəriən]. **1.** *a.* (*also* **Megaric**) *A.Geog:* mégarien; *Phil:* **the M. school,** l'École de Mégare; **M. philosophy,** philosophie mégarique. **2.** *s. A.Geog:* Mégarien, -ienne; Mégaréen, -éenne.

Megaris ['megəris]. *Pr.n. A.Geog:* la Mégaride.

megascope ['megəskoup], *s. A.Opt:* mégascope *m*.

Megasecoptera [megəsi'kɔptərə], *s.pl. Ent: Paleont:* mégasécoptères *m*.

megaseism ['megəsaizm], *s. Geol:* tremblement de terre violent.

megaseme ['megəsi:m], *a. Anthr:* mégasème.

megasoma ['megəsoumə], *s. Ent:* mégasome *m*.

megasporangium [megəspɔ'rændʒiəm], *s. Bot:* macrosporange *m*, mégasporange *m*.

megaspore ['megəspɔ:r], *s. Bot:* macrospore *m*, mégaspore *m*.

megasporophyll [megə'spɔroufil], *s. Bot:* macrosporophylle *m*.

megass [me'gæs], *s. Sug.-R:* bagasse *f*.

megatherium, *pl.* **-ia** [megə'θiəriəm, -iə], *s. Paleont:* mégathérium *m*.

megatherm ['megəθə:m], *s. Biol:* mégatherme *f*.

Megathymidae [megə'θaimidi:], *s.pl. Ent:* mégathymides *m*.

megaton ['megətʌn], *s. Exp:* mégatonne *f*.

megavolt ['megəvoult], *s. El.Meas:* mégavolt *m*.

megawatt ['megəwɔt], *s. El.Meas:* mégawatt *m*.

megerg ['megə:g], *s. Mec.Meas:* mégerg *m*.

megilp [me'gilp], *s. Art:* véhicule (de couleur) composé d'huile et de vernis.

megohm ['megoum], *s. El.Meas:* mégohm *m*.

megohmmeter ['megoumi:tər], *s.* mégohmmètre *m*.

megrim[1] ['mi:grim], *s. A:* **1.** *Med:* (*a*) migraine *f*; (*b*) **to have the megrims,** avoir (i) le spleen, les vapeurs; (ii) *Vet:* le vertigo. **2.** fantaisie *f*, lubie *f*.

megrim[2], *s. Ich:* géline *f*; fausse limande, limande salope.

mehari [me'hɑ:ri], *s. Z:* méhari *m*.

meharist [me'hɑ:rist], *a. & s.* mehariste (*m*).

meiocene ['maiousi:n], *a. & s.* = MIOCENE.

meionite ['maiənait], *s. Miner:* méionite *f*.

meiosis [mai'ousis], *s.* **1.** *Rh:* litote *f*. **2.** *Biol:* méiose *f*.

Mekong ['mi:kɔŋ]. *Pr.n. Geog:* Mékong *m*.

melaconite [me'lækənait], *s. Miner:* mélaconite *f*.

melaena [me'li:nə], *s. Med:* melæna *m*, méléna *m*.

melamine ['meləmain], *s. Ch:* mélamine *f*.

Melampsoraceae [melæm(p)spɔ:'reisii:], *s.pl. Fung:* mélampsoracées *f*.

melampyrum [meləm'pairəm], *s. Bot:* mélampyre *m*.

melancholia [melən'kouliə], *s. Med:* mélancolie *f*.

melancholic [melən'kɔlik], *a.* mélancolique.

melancholically [melən'kɔlik(ə)li], *adv.* mélancoliquement.

melancholy ['melənkəli]. **1.** *s.* mélancolie *f*; vague tristesse *f*. **2.** *a.* (*a*) (*of pers.*) atrabilaire; (*b*) (*of pers.*) mélancolique; triste; (*c*) **m. news,** triste nouvelle; nouvelle attristante.

Melanellidae [melə'nelidi:], *s.pl. Moll:* mélanellidés *m*.

Melanesia [melə'ni:ziə]. *Pr.n. Geog:* la Mélanésie.

Melanesian [melə'ni:ziən]. *Geog:* (*a*) *a.* mélanésien; (*b*) *s.* Mélanésien, -ienne.

melanic [me'lænik], *a. Med:* mélanique; atteint de mélanose.

Melaniidae [melə'naiidi:], *s.pl. Moll:* mélaniidés *m*.

melanin ['melənin], *s. Ch: etc:* mélanine *f*.

melanism ['melənizm], *s. Physiol: etc:* mélanisme *m*.

melanistic [melə'nistik], *a. Biol:* mélanique.

melanite ['melənait], *s. Miner:* mélanite *f*.

melanization [melənai'zeiʃ(ə)n], *s. Geol:* mélanisation *f*.

melanoblast ['melənoublæst], *s. Biol:* mélanoblaste *m*.

melanocarcinoma ['melənoukɑ:si'noumə], *s. Med:*

mélanocarcinome *m.*

melanocerite [melənou'si:rait], *s. Miner:* mélanocérite *f.*

melanochroite [melənou'krouait], *s. Miner:* mélanochroïte *f.*

melanocrate ['melənoukreit], *s. Geol:* roche *f* mélanocrate.

melanocratic [melənou'krætik], *a. Geol:* mélanocrate.

melanocyte ['melənousait], *s. Biol:* mélanocyte *m.*

melanoderm(i)a [melənou'də:m(i)ə], *s. Med:* mélanodermie *f.*

melanodermic [melənou'də:mik], *a. Anthr:* mélanoderme.

melanoid ['melənɔid], *a. Med:* (tumeur) mélanoïde.

melanoma [melə'noumə], *s. Med:* mélanome *m.*

melanophore ['melənoufɔ:r], *s. Biol:* mélanophore *f.*

melanorrhoea [melənə'ri:ə], *s. Bot:* mélanorrhœa *m.*

melanosarcoma ['melənousɑ:'koumə], *s. Med:* mélanosarcome *m.*

melanose ['melənous], *a. Med:* (tumeur *f*, etc.) mélanique.

melanosis [melə'nousis], *s. Med:* mélanose *f.*

melanostibian [melənou'stibiən], *s. Miner:* mélanostibiane *f.*

melanotekite [melənou'ti:kait], *s. Miner:* mélanotékite *f.*

melanotic [melə'nɔtik], *a. Med:* mélanique.

melanotus [melə'noutəs], *s. Ent:* mélanote *m.*

melanterite [me'læntərait], *s. Miner:* mélantérie *f*, mélantérite *f.*

melanuria [melə'njuəriə], *s. Med:* mélanurie *f*, mélanurèse *f.*

melaphyre ['meləfaiər], *s. Miner:* mélaphyre *m.*

melassigenic [melæsi'dʒenik], *a.* mélassigène.

Melastomaceae [melæstou'meisii:], *s.pl. Bot:* mélastomacées *f.*

Melchisedec, Melchizedek [mel'kizidek]. *Pr.n.m. B.Lit:* Melchisédech.

Melchite ['melkait], *s. Rel.H:* Melchite *m.*

meld[1] [meld], *s. Cards:* combinaison *f.*

meld[2]. *Cards:* **1.** *v.tr.* étaler (des cartes) pour former une combinaison. **2.** *v.i.* étaler une combinaison.

Meleager [meli'eidʒər]. *Pr.n.m. Gr.Myth:* Méléagre.

melee, mêlée ['melei], *s.* mêlée *f.*

melezitose [me'lezitous], *s. Ch:* mélézitose *m.*

Meliaceae [meli'eisii:], *s.pl. Bot:* méliacées *f.*

Melianthaceae [mi:liæn'θeisii:], *s.pl. Bot:* mélianthacées *f.*

melianthus [meli'ænθəs], *s. Bot:* mélianthe *m.*

melibiose [meli'baious], *s. Ch:* mélibiose *m.*

Meliboeus [meli'bi:əs]. *Pr.n.m. Lt.Lit:* Mélibée.

melic[1] ['melik], *a. Gr.Lit:* (poésie *f*) mélique.

melic[2], *a. & s. Bot:* **m. (grass),** mélique *f.*

melica ['melikə], *s. Bot:* mélique *f.*

meliceric, melicerous [meli'siərik, -'siərəs], *a.* mélicérique.

melicocca [meli'kɔkə], *s. Bot:* mélicoque *m*, mélicocca *m.*

melilite ['melilait], *s. Miner:* mélil(l)ite *f.*

melilot ['melilɔt], *s. Bot:* mélilot *m.*

melinite ['melinait], *s. Exp:* mélinite *f.*

meliorate ['mi:liəreit], *v.tr. & i.* améliorer.

melioration [mi:liə'reiʃ(ə)n], *s.* **1.** amélioration *f.* **2.** *Ling:* mélioration *f.*

meliorism ['mi:liərizm], *s. Phil:* méliorisme *m.*

meliorist ['mi:liərist], *a. & s. Phil:* mélioriste (*mf*).

Meliphagidae [meli'fædʒidi:], *s.pl. Orn:* méliphagidés *m*, méliphages *m.*

melipona [me'lipənə], *s. Ent:* mélipone *f.*

melissa [me'lisə], *s. Bot:* mélisse *f*; *F:* citronnelle *f*; *Pharm: O:* **m. cordial,** eau *f* de mélisse.

melitaea [meli'ti:ə], *s. Ent:* mélitée *f*, damier *m.*

melittis [me'litis], *s. Bot:* mélitte *f*; mélisse *f* sauvage.

melituria [meli'tju:riə], *s. Med:* méliturie *f*, glycosurie *f.*

Mellifera [me'lifərə], *s.pl. Ent:* mellifères *m.*

melliferous [me'lifərəs], *a.* mellifère.

mellific [me'lifik], *a.* mellifique.

mellification [melifi'keiʃ(ə)n], *s. Ent:* mellification *f.*

mellifluence [me'lifluəns], *s.* mellifluité *f* (d'un discours, etc.).

mellifluous [me'lifluəs], *a.* (*of eloquence, words, etc.*) mielleux, doucereux; melliflu (*usu. f.*); **m. eloquence,** éloquence melliflue.

mellite ['melait], *s. Miner:* mellite *f.*

mellivorous [me'livərəs], *a. Z:* mellivore.

mellow[1] ['melou], *a.* **1.** (fruit) fondant, mûr; vermeil; (vin) moelleux, velouté; **m. old town,** vieille ville qui a la patine de l'âge. **2.** (terrain *m*) meuble. **3.** (*of voice, light, sound*) moelleux; doux, *f.* douce; (*of colour*) doux, tendre, voilé; **m. whites,** blancs onctueux; **life there is pleasantly m.,** il y règne une agréable douceur de vivre. **4.** (esprit, caractère) mûr; **to grow m.,** mûrir; s'adoucir. **5.** (*of pers.*) (*a*) jovial, -aux, enjoué, débonnaire; (*b*) *F:* un peu gris; entre deux vins.

mellow[2]. **1.** *v.tr.* (*a*) (faire) mûrir (des fruits); donner du moelleux à (un vin, une couleur, un son); **old church mellowed by age,** vieille église patinée par le temps; (*b*) ameublir (le sol); (*c*) mûrir, adoucir (le caractère de qn). **2.** *v.i.* (*a*) (*of fruit, wine*) mûrir; prendre du velouté; (*of sound, light*) prendre du moelleux; (*of colour*) prendre de la patine; s'atténuer; (*b*) (*of character*) s'adoucir.

mellowing ['melouiŋ], *s.* **1.** maturation *f* (des fruits, du vin); adoucissement *m* (de la voix, des couleurs, du caractère). **2.** *Agr:* ameublissement *m* (du sol).

mellowly ['melouli], *adv.* moelleusement; d'un ton doux.

mellowness ['melounis], *s.* **1.** maturité *f* (des fruits); moelleux *m* (du vin, d'un tableau); velouté *m* (du vin); velouté, moelleux (de la voix); douceur *f* (du caractère); **the m. of these pastels,** le fondu de ces pastels. **2.** maturité, richesse *f* (du sol).

melocactus, *pl.* **-ti** [melou'kæktəs, -tai], *s. Bot:* mélocacte *m*, mélocactus *m.*

melodeon, melodion [me'loudiən], *s. Mus:* **1.** *A:* mélodion *m*, mélodium *m*; orgue expressif. **2.** accordéon *m.*

melodic [me'lɔdik], *a. Mus:* (progression, etc.) mélodique.

melodious [me'loudiəs], *a.* mélodieux, harmonieux.

melodiously [me'loudiəsli], *adv.* mélodieusement; avec harmonie.

melodiousness [me'loudiəsnis], *s.* caractère mélodieux; mélodie *f* (du style, d'un poème).

melodist ['melədist], *s.* mélodiste *m.*

melodize ['melədaiz]. **1.** *v.i.* faire des mélodies; chanter des mélodies. **2.** *v.tr.* (*a*) rendre (qch.) mélodieux; (*b*) mettre (un chant) en musique.

melodrama ['melədrɑ:mə], *s.* mélodrame *m.*

melodramatic [melədrə'mætik], *a.* mélodramatique.

melodramatically [melədrə'mætik(ə)li], *adv.* d'un air, d'un ton, mélodramatique; d'un air de mélodrame.

melodramatist [melou'dræmətist], *s.* auteur *m* de mélodrames; mélodramatiste *m.*

melodramatize [melou'dræmətaiz], *v.tr.* mélodramatiser (un sujet).

melody ['melədi], *s.* **1.** mélodie *f*, air *m*, chant *m*; **old Irish melodies,** vieux airs irlandais, vieilles mélodies irlandaises; **m. writer,** mélodiste *m.* **2.** *Mus:* (*a*) chant *m*, thème *m*; **m. taken up by the clarinets,** chant repris par les clarinettes; **to emphasize the m.,** mettre le thème bien en dehors; (*b*) (*as opposed to harmony*) mélodie.

meloe ['meləwi], *s. Ent:* méloé *m.*

melograph ['melougræf], *s. Mus:* mélographe *m.*

Meloidae [me'lɔidi:], *s.pl. Ent:* méloïdés *m.*

melolonthid [melou'lɔnθid], *s. Ent:* mélolonthe *m.*

melolonthoid [melou'lɔnθɔid], *a. Ent:* mélolonthoïde.

melomania [melou'meiniə], *s.* mélomanie *f.*

melomaniac [melou'meiniæk], *s.* mélomane *mf.*

melon ['melən], *s.* **1.** melon *m*; **musk m.,** (melon) cantaloup *m*; **sugary m.,** (melon) sucrin *m*; **water m.,** pastèque *f*; **m. bed,** melonnière *f.* **2.** *F:* melon (sur la tête du cachalot); **the m. is the spermaceti organ,** le melon est l'organe du spermaceti. **3.** *NAm: F:* gros bénéfices (à distribuer); **to carve, cut up, the m.,** distribuer les bénéfices.

melonite ['melənait], *s. Miner:* mélonite *f.*

Melonites [melə'naiti:z], *s. Paleont:* melonites *m.*

melon-shaped ['melənʃeipt], *a.* en forme de melon, melonné.

meloplasty [melou'plæsti], *s. Surg:* méloplastie *f.*

Melpomene [mel'pɔmini]. *Pr.n.f. Gr.Myth:* Melpomène.

melt[1] [melt], *s. Metall: etc:* **1.** fusion *f*, fonte *f*; **on the m.,** en fusion. **2.** coulée *f* (de métal); **five melts a week,** cinq coulées, cinq fontes, par semaine.

melt[2], *v.*

I. *v.i.* **1.** fondre; se fondre; (*of jelly*) se déprendre; **butter melts in the sun,** le beurre fond au soleil; **to begin to m.,** commencer à fondre; (*of glass, metals*) entrer en fusion; *F:* **money melts in his hands,** l'argent lui fond entre les mains, entre les doigts; **the fog was beginning to m. into a drizzle,** le brouillard commençait à se résoudre en bruine; **we were all melting,** nous étions tous en eau, en nage. **2.** (*of pers.*) s'attendrir; fléchir; **his heart melted with pity,** son cœur (se) fondait de pitié; la pitié lui attendrissait le cœur; **to m. into tears,** fondre en larmes. **3.** (*a*) (*of solid in liquid*) fondre, se dissoudre; **pear that melts in the mouth,** poire fondante; (*b*) (*of colour, etc.*) **to m. into . . .,** se fondre dans . . ., se perdre dans . . .; **to m. into thin air,** disparaître.

II. *v.tr.* **1.** (faire) fondre (la glace, les métaux); **melted snow,** neige fondue. **2.** attendrir, émouvoir (qn). **3.** (faire) fondre, (faire) dissoudre (un sel, etc.).

III. (*compound verbs*) **1. melt away,** *v.i.* (*a*) (*of snow, etc.*) fondre complètement; (*b*) (*of clouds, vapour*) se dissiper; (*of crowd*) se disperser; disparaître; **his money is gradually melting away,** son argent fond, s'écoule, peu à peu; **his anger was melting away,** sa colère s'évaporait.

2. melt down, *v.tr.* fondre (de la ferraille, des bijoux, de l'argenterie).

melt[3], *s.* rate *f* (des mammifères).

melter ['meltər], *s.* **1.** (*pers.*) fondeur *m.* **2.** creuset *m.*

melting[1] ['meltiŋ], *a.* **1.** (*a*) (neige *f*, cire *f*) qui (se) fond; (neige) fondante; (*b*) (*of voice, etc.*) attendri; **m. mood,** attendrissement *m*; (*c*) (fruit) fondant. **2.** (*of words, scene, etc.*) attendrissant, émouvant.

melting[2], *s.* **1.** fonte *f*, fusion *f* (de la neige, des métaux); *Metall:* **fractional m.,** fusion fractionnée; **m. point, temperature,** point *m*, température *f*, de fusion; **m. pot,** creuset *m*; pot *m*, chaudière *f*, à fusion; *F:* **everything's in the m. pot,** on est en train de tout refondre; tout est à refaire. **2.** attendrissement *m* (des cœurs).

meltingly ['meltiŋli], *adv.* d'une manière attendrissante.

meltwater ['meltwɔ:tər], *s. esp. NAm:* eaux *fpl* de fonte.

Melursus [me'lə:səs], *s. Z:* mélurse *m.*

Melusina [melju(:)'si:nə]. *Pr.n.f. Myth:* Mélusine.

member ['membər], *s.* **1.** (*a*) *A:* membre *m* (du corps); (*b*) **m. of Christ,** membre de Jésus-Christ; (*c*) *Nat.Hist:* organe *m.* **2.** (*a*) *Arch:* membre (d'une façade, etc.); *Carp:* pièce *f* (d'une charpente); *Civ.E:* barre *f* (de membrure); longeron *m* (d'un pont, etc.); *Mec.E:* organe (d'une machine); **auxiliary members of a framework,** éléments *m* auxiliaires d'un système articulé; *Const:* **diagonal members,** jambes *f* de force en croix; (*b*) *Gram: Mth:* membre (de la phrase, d'une équation); *Mth:* **left-hand m. of the equation,** premier membre de l'équation; **right-hand m.,** deuxième membre. **3.** (*a*) membre (d'une famille, d'une société, d'un corps politique); adhérent, -ente (d'un parti); **he's a m. of the family,** il fait partie de la famille; **m. of the audience,** assistant, -ante; **m. of a learned, etc., society,** sociétaire *mf*; **to become a m. of an association,** devenir membre d'une société; **to elect s.o. as a m. (of a learned body, etc.),** élire qn membre (d'une société); s'associer qn; associer qn à ses travaux; **the new m. delivered his speech,** le récipiendaire prononça son discours; **ordinary members, paying members, of an association,** cotisants *m*; (*b*) **m. of Parliament,** membre de la Chambre des Communes; député *m*; **our m.,** notre représentant (à la Chambre).

membered ['membəd], *a.* **1.** qui a des membres; à membres. **2.** *Her:* membré.

membership ['membəʃip], *s.* **1.** qualité *f* de membre; sociétariat *m*; adhésion *f* (à un parti); **qualifications for m.,** titres *m* d'éligibilité; **conditions of m.,** conditions *f* d'adhésion; **m. card,** carte *f* de membre, de sociétaire; **to pay one's m. (fee),** payer sa cotisation, son abonnement; **to renew one's m.,** renouveler sa carte (de membre); **to accept m. on a commission,** accepter de faire partie d'une commission; *Pol:* **m. drive,** campagne *f* de recrutement. **2.** (*a*) nombre *m* des membres, effectif *m* (d'une société, etc.); **club with a m. of a thousand,** club *m* de mille membres; (*b*) **the opinion of the majority of our m.,** l'avis *m* de la majorité de nos membres.

membracid ['membrəsid], *s. Ent:* membracide *m.*

Membracidae [mem'bræsidi:], *s.pl. Ent:* membracides *m.*

membranaceous [membrə'neiʃəs], *a. Biol:* membraneux.

membrane ['membrein], *s.* (*a*) *Nat.Hist:* membrane *f*; **mucous m.,** (membrane) muqueuse *f*; **investing m.,** enveloppe *f*; tunique *f* (d'un organe); **nictitating m.,** membrane nictitante, clignotante; paupière *f* interne; **semi-permeable m.,** membrane semi-perméable; (*b*) *Med:* **false, diphtheritic, m.,** fausse membrane; **basement m.,** (membrane) basale *f*; couche *f* sous-épidermique, sous-épithéliale; **basilar m.,** membrane basilaire; (*c*) *Ph: Ind: etc:* **porous m.,** membrane poreuse.

membraned ['membreind], *a.* (doigt, orteil) membrané.

membraniform [mem'breinifɔ:m], *a.* membraniforme.

membranipora [membrei'nipərə], *s. Prot:* membranipore *m.*

membranous ['membrənəs], *a.* membraneux, membrané.

membranula [mem'breinjulə], *s. Anat:* membranule *f.*

membrum virile ['membrəmvi'raili], *s. Anat:* membre viril.

memento, *pl.* **-oes, -os** [me'mentou, -ouz], *s.* **1.** mémento *m*, souvenir *m*; **m. mori** ['mɔ:rai], memento mori *m*; tête *f* de mort. **2.** *Ecc:* (*R.C. Liturgy*) mémento.

memo ['memou], *s. F:* mémo *m*; **m. pad,** bloc-notes *m*, *pl.* blocs-notes.

memoir ['memwɑ:r], *s.* (*a*) mémoire *m*, dissertation *f*, étude *f* (scientifique, etc.); (*b*) (i) notice *f* biographique;

(ii) *Journ:* article *m*, notice, nécrologique; (*c*) *pl.* **memoirs,** mémoires; mémorial *m.*

memoirist ['memwɑːrist], *s.* auteur *m* de mémoires, d'un mémoire.

memorabilia [mem(ə)rə'biliə], *s.pl.* événements *m* mémorables.

memorable ['mem(ə)rəbl], *a.* mémorable; **a sail round this island is m.,** faire le tour de l'île en bateau laisse un souvenir impérissable.

memorably ['memərəbli], *adv.* mémorablement.

memorandum, *pl.* **-da, -dums** [memə'rændəm, -də, -dəmz], *s.* **1.** mémorandum *m*; note *f*; **to make a m. of sth.,** prendre note de qch.; noter qch. **2.** (*a*) mémoire *m* (d'un contrat, d'une vente, etc.); sommaire *m* des articles (d'un contrat); (*b*) *Jur:* **m. of association,** charte constitutive d'une société à responsabilité limitée; acte *m* de société; **m. and articles of association,** statuts *mpl.* **3.** (*a*) *Adm:* circulaire *f*; (*b*) note diplomatique; mémorandum. **4.** *Com:* bordereau *m*; **m. book,** carnet *m*, calepin *m*, agenda *m.*

memorial [mi'mɔːriəl]. **1.** *a.* (*of statue, festival, etc.*) commémoratif; *U.S:* **M. Day,** fête *f* en mémoire des morts de la guerre. **2.** *s.* (*a*) monument (commémoratif); **as a m. of sth.,** en commémoration, en souvenir, de qch.; **war m.,** monument aux morts (de la guerre); (*b*) *pl.* **memorials,** mémoires *mpl*, mémorial *m*; (*c*) mémorial (diplomatique); (*d*) pétition, demande, requête (adressée à un gouvernement); (*e*) *Jur:* **m. of a deed,** extrait *m* pour enregistrement.

memorialist [mi'mɔːriəlist], *s.* **1.** pétitionnaire *mf.* **2.** mémorialiste *m*; auteur *m* de mémoires, d'un mémoire.

memorialize [mi'mɔːriəlaiz], *v.tr.* **1.** commémorer (qn, qch.). **2.** pétitionner (qn); présenter une requête à (qn).

memorization [memərai'zeiʃ(ə)n], *s.* mémorisation *f.*

memorize ['meməraiz], *v.tr.* **1.** rappeler (qn, qch.) au souvenir. **2.** apprendre (qch.) par cœur.

memory ['meməri], *s.* **1.** (*a*) mémoire *f*; **to have a good, bad, m.,** avoir (une) bonne mémoire, (une) mauvaise mémoire; *F:* **m. like a sieve,** mémoire de lièvre; **I have a bad m. for names,** je n'ai pas la mémoire des noms; **my lack of m.,** mon peu de mémoire; **to lose one's m.,** perdre la mémoire; **loss of m.,** perte *f* de mémoire; amnésie *f*; **the incident has stuck in my m.,** l'incident s'est gravé dans ma mémoire; **it escaped, slipped, my m., it went out of my m.,** cela m'est sorti de la mémoire, de l'esprit; **if my m. serves me (well), to the best of my m.,** si mes souvenirs sont exacts; si j'ai bonne mémoire; autant que je m'en souvienne; **it didn't happen within my m.,** mes souvenirs ne remontent pas si loin que cela; **within living m., within the m. of man,** de mémoire d'homme; **beyond the m. of man, from time beyond all m.,** de temps immémorial; *Jur:* **time of legal m.,** période *f* qui remonte au commencement du règne de Richard Ier (1189); **to play, recite, sth. from m.,** jouer, réciter, qch. de mémoire; **to paint from m.,** peindre de mémoire, de pratique; *U.S:* **m. book,** album *m* (de découpures, etc.); (*b*) *Cmptr:* mémoire; **core m.,** mémoire à tores magnétiques; **dynamic m.,** mémoire dynamique; **external, internal, m.,** mémoire externe, interne; **high-speed m.,** mémoire rapide; **random-access m.,** mémoire à accès sélectif; **m. capacity, size,** capacité *f* de la mémoire; **m. diagram, layout, map,** topogramme *m* (de la) mémoire; **m. fill,** remplissage *m*, garnissage *m*, de la mémoire; **m. dump,** vidage *m* de la mémoire. **2.** mémoire, souvenir *m* (de qn, de qch.); **to retain a clear m. of sth.,** conserver un souvenir net de qch.; **childhood memories,** souvenirs d'enfance; **that dates from my earliest memories,** cela remonte à mes souvenirs les plus lointains; **I have wonderful memories of our holiday in Greece,** je garde des souvenirs magnifiques de nos vacances en Grèce; **I have very pleasant memories of your friend,** je garde, je conserve, un excellent souvenir de votre ami; **to keep s.o.'s m. alive, green,** garder le souvenir de qn; **in m. of . . .,** en mémoire de . . .; à la mémoire de . . .; en souvenir de . . .; *Lit:* **of glorious, of happy, m.,** de glorieuse, d'heureuse, mémoire; **the late king, of blessed m.,** le feu roi, d'heureuse mémoire.

Memphian ['memfiən]. **1.** *A.Geog:* (*a*) *a.* (*also* **Memphite** ['memfait], **Memphitic** [mem'fitik]) memphite, memphitique; (*b*) *s.* (*also* **Memphite**) Memphite *mf.* **2.** *a.* & *s.* *Geog:* (habitant, -ante, originaire *mf*) de Memphis (Tennessee).

memsahib ['memsɑːib], *s.f.* *O:* (*in India, etc.*) (*a*) (i) **a m.,** une dame européenne; **my m.,** ma maîtresse; (ii) (*as title*) madame; (*b*) *F: Pej:* femme huppée.

menaccanite [me'nækənait], *s.* *Miner:* ménaccanite *f.*

menace[1] ['menəs], *s.* menace *f*; **it is a m. to our safety,** c'est une menace pour notre sûreté; **in dry weather forest fires are a m.,** par temps sec les forêts sont menacées d'incendie; **there was m. in his voice,** il parlait d'un ton menaçant; *F:* **he's an awful m.,** c'est une vraie plaie.

menace[2], *v.tr.* **1.** menacer (qn); **my plan is menaced with ruin,** mon projet est menacé de ruine. **2. those who m. war,** ceux qui nous menacent de la guerre.

menacer ['menəsər], *s.* menaceur, -euse.

menacing[1] ['menəsiŋ], *a.* menaçant; **in a m. voice,** d'une voi menaçante.

menacing[2], *s.* menaces *fpl.*

menacingly ['menəsiŋli], *adv.* d'un air, d'un ton, menaçant; d'une voix menaçante.

ménage [mei'nɑːʒ], *s.* ménage *m.*

menagerie [mi'nædʒəri], *s.* ménagerie *f.*

Menander [mi'nændər]. *Pr.n.m.* *Gr.Lit:* Ménandre.

menarche [me'nɑːki], *s.* *Physiol:* ménarche *m.*

mend[1] [mend], *s.* **1.** (*in fabric, etc.*) reprise *f*, raccommodage *m.* **2.** amélioration *f*; (*of pers.*) **to be on the m.,** être en train de se remettre, être en voie de guérison; **trade is on the m.,** les affaires *f* reprennent.

mend[2], *v.*

I. *v.tr.* **1.** raccommoder (un vêtement, des souliers); repriser, ravauder (des bas); rem(m)ailler (un filet); réparer (un outil, une route, etc.); *Civ.E:* repiquer (une route); **to m. one's clothes,** raccommoder ses vêtements; **to m. invisibly,** stopper (un vêtement); **that broken-legged table could be mended,** on pourrait réparer cette table aux pieds cassés; **to m. the fire,** arranger le feu; remettre du combustible sur le feu; *A:* **to m. a pen,** tailler une plume. **2.** rectifier, corriger; **to m. one's manners,** changer de manières, changer de ton; **to m. one's ways,** changer de conduite, de vie; s'amender, se corriger; rentrer dans le bon chemin. **3.** (*a*) réparer (une faute, un mal); *Prov:* **least said soonest mended,** trop gratter cuit, trop parler nuit; moins on parle, mieux cela vaut; (*b*) **to m. matters,** améliorer la situation, arranger les choses; **it does not m. matters to . . .,** cela n'arrange pas les choses de . . .; **crying will not m. matters,** pleurer n'arrangera pas les choses; (*c*) *O:* **to m. one's pace,** hâter, presser, le pas.

II. *v.i.* **1.** (*of invalid, etc.*) se remettre; **my health is mending,** ma santé se rétablit, s'améliore; **the weather is mending,** le temps se remet au beau. **2.** (*of pers.*) s'amender, se corriger. **3.** (*a*) (*of fault*) se corriger; (*b*) (*of condition*) s'améliorer; (*of broken bones*) se ressouder.

mendable ['mendəbl], *a.* **1.** (vêtement) raccommodable; (outil, etc.) réparable. **2.** (faute) corrigible; (condition) améliorable.

mendacious [men'deiʃəs], *a.* menteur, -euse; mensonger.

mendaciously [men'deiʃəsli], *adv.* mensongèrement.

mendaciousness [men'deiʃəsnis], **mendacity** [men'dæsiti], *s.* **1.** penchant *m* au mensonge; habitude *f* du mensonge. **2.** fausseté *f.* **3. barefaced mendacities,** mensonges éhontés.

mendelevium [mendə'liːviəm], *s.* *Ch:* mendélévium *m.*

Mendelian [men'diːliən], *a.* *Biol:* mendélien.

Mendelism ['mendəlizm], *s.* *Biol:* mendélisme *m.*

mender ['mendər], *s.* raccommodeur, -euse; ravaudeur, -euse (de vêtements); repriseuse *f* (de dentelles, etc.); réparateur *m* (de bicyclettes, etc.); **invisible m.,** stoppeur, -euse.

mendicancy ['mendikənsi], *s.* mendicité *f.*

mendicant ['mendikənt]. **1.** *a.* mendiant, de mendiant; *Ecc:* **m. orders,** ordres mendiants. **2.** *s.* mendiant, -ante.

mendicity [men'disiti], *s.* mendicité *f.*

mending, *s.* **1.** raccommodage *m* (de vêtements, etc.); ravaudage *m*, reprisage *m* (de bas); réparation (d'un mur, etc.); *Civ.E:* repiquage *m* (d'une route); *Dom.Ec:* **m. kit,** trousse *f* de raccommodage; **m. cotton,** coton *m* à repriser; **invisible m.,** (i) stoppage *m*; (ii) rem(m)aillage *m* (de bas); **to repair sth. by invisible m.,** stopper (un vêtement, un trou); rem(m)ailler (des bas). **2. pile of m.,** tas *m* de vêtements à raccommoder.

mendipite ['mendipait], *s.* *Miner:* mendipite *f.*

mendozite [men'douzait], *s.* *Miner:* mendozite *f.*

mene, tekel, upharsin ['menei'tek(ə)l, ju'fɑːsin], *B:* mané, thécel, pharès.

meneghinite [mene'giːnait], *s.* *Miner:* ménéghinite *f.*

Menelaus [meni'leiəs]. *Pr.n.m.* *Gr.Lit:* Ménélas.

menfolk ['menfouk], *s.m.pl.* les hommes (de la famille); **their m. were all away fishing,** leurs hommes étaient tous partis à la pêche.

menhaden [men'heidn], *s.* *Ich:* menhaden *m*; **m. oil,** huile *f* de menhaden.

menhir ['menhiər], *s.* *Prehist:* menhir *m*; pierre levée; (*in Brittany*) peulven *m*; **inscribed m.,** statue-menhir *f*, *pl.* statues-menhirs.

menial ['miːniəl]. **1.** *a.* (*of duties, offices*) de domestique; servile; bas, *f.* basse. **2.** *s.* *usu. Pej:* domestique *mf*; valet *m*, laquais *m.*

menially ['miːniəli], *adv.* servilement.

Ménière ['menjeːr]. *Pr.n.* *Med:* **Ménière's disease, syndrome,** maladie *f*, syndrome *m*, de Ménière.

menilite ['menilait], *s.* *Miner:* ménilite *f.*

meningeal [me'nindʒiəl], **meningic** [me'nindʒik], *a.* *Anat:* méningé; **m. artery,** artère méningée; *Med:* **m. involvement,** complication méningée.

meninges, *s.pl.* See MENINX.

meningioma, *pl.* **-omas, -omata** [menindʒi'oumə, -'oumәz, -'oumətə], *s.* *Med:* méningiome *m.*

meningism ['menindʒizm], **meningismus** [menin'dʒizməs], *s.* *Med:* méningisme *m*, pseudo-méningite *f.*

meningitis [menin'dʒaitis], *s.* *Med:* méningite *f*; **spinal m.,** méningo-myélite *f*; **cerebrospinal m.,** méningite cérébro-spinale.

meningocele [me'niŋgousiːl], *s.* *Med:* méningocèle *f.*

meningococc(a)emia [meniŋgoukɔk'siːmiə], *s.* *Med:* méningococcémie *f.*

meningococcus, *pl.* **-cocci** [meniŋgou'kɔkəs, 'kɔksai], *s.* *Bac:* méningocoque *m.*

meningoencephalitis [meniŋgouensefə'laitis], *s.* *Med:* méningo-encéphalite *f.*

meningomyelitis [meniŋgoumaii'laitis], *s.* *Med:* méningo-myélite *f.*

meningorrhagia [meniŋgou'reidʒiə], *s.* *Med:* méningorragie *f.*

meninx, *pl.* **meninges** ['miːniŋks, me'nindʒiːz], *s.* *Anat:* méninge *f.*

Menippus [me'nipəs]. *Pr.n.m.* *Gr.Lit:* Ménippe.

meniscitis [meni'saitis], *s.* *Med:* méniscite *f.*

meniscus [me'niskəs], *s.* *Mth:* *Ph:* *etc:* ménisque *m*; *Opt:* **converging m.,** ménisque convergent; lentille *f* convexo-concave; **diverging m.,** ménisque divergent; lentille concavo-convexe.

menisperm ['menispəːm], *s.* *Bot:* ménisperme *m.*

Menispermaceae [menispəː'meisiiː], *s.pl.* *Bot:* ménispermacées *f.*

menispermaceous [menispəː'meiʃəs], *a.* *Bot:* ménispermacé.

Mennonite ['menənait], *s.* *Rel.H:* Mennonite *m*, Mennoniste *m.*

menology [me'nɔlədʒi], *s.* *Gr.Church:* ménologe *m.*

Menominee [me'nɔminiː], *s.* **1.** *Ethn:* (indien) Ménomène *m.* **2.** *Can:* riz *m* sauvage.

menopause ['menəpɔːz], *s.* *Physiol:* ménopause *f.*

menorrhagia [menə'reidʒiə], *s.* *Med:* ménorragie *f.*

menorrhagic [menə'reidʒik], *a.* *Med:* ménorragique.

menorrhoea [menə'riə], *s.* *Med:* ménorrhée *f.*

menostasis [me'nɔstəsis], *s.* *Med:* ménostase *f.*

menses ['mensiːz], *s.pl.* *Physiol:* menstrues, *f*, règles *f* (d'une femme).

Menshevik ['menʃəvik], **Menshevist** ['menʃəvist], *a.* & *s.* *Pol:* menchevik (*m*).

menstrual ['menstruəl], *a.* *Physiol:* menstruel; **m. flow,** écoulement menstruel, menstrues *fpl*; **m. cycle,** cycle menstruel.

menstruate ['menstrueit], *v.i.* *Physiol:* avoir ses menstrues, ses règles.

menstruation [menstru'eiʃ(ə)n], *s.* *Physiol:* menstruation *f.*

menstruum, *pl.* **-a** ['menstruəm, -ə], *s.* *Ch:* dissolvant *m.*

mensurability [mensjərə'biliti], *s.* mensurabilité *f.*

mensurable ['mensjərəbl], *a.* **1.** mensurable, mesurable. **2.** *A.Mus:* mesuré, rythmé.

mensuration [mensjə'reiʃ(ə)n], *s.* **1.** mesurage *m*, mesure *f.* **2.** *Mth:* mensuration *f.*

menswear ['menzwɛər], *s.* *Com:* vêtements *mpl* d'hommes; habillement *m* pour hommes.

mental[1] ['ment(ə)l], *a.* mental, -aux; de l'esprit; **his m. outlook,** sa mentalité; **m. age,** âge mental; **m. reservation,** restriction mentale; arrière-pensée *f*, *pl.* arrière-pensées; **m. arithmetic,** calcul mental, de tête; **m. disease,** maladie mentale; **m. deficiency,** déficience mentale; petite mentalité, débilité mentale; **m. defective,** déficient, -ente; petit mental, débile intellectuel(le); *Jur:* irresponsable *mf* (pénalement); *Med:* **a m. case,** un aliéné, une aliénée; **m. hospital, m. home,** hôpital *m*, clinique *f*, psychiatrique; maison *f* de santé; **m. specialist,** médecin *m* aliéniste; *F:* **he's m.,** il est fou; il déménage.

mental[2], *a.* *Anat:* *etc:* mentonnier; du menton; **m. foramen,** trou mentonnier.

mentality [men'tæliti], *s.* (*a*) mentalité *f*, état mental (de qn); (*b*) **the oriental m.,** la mentalité orientale; **it is difficult to understand their m.,** on comprend difficilement leur mentalité, leur esprit.

mentally ['mentəli], *adv.* mentalement; du point de vue mental; **m. deficient, defective,** débile; **m. retarded child,** enfant attardé, arriéré.

menthadiene [menθə'daiiːn], *s.* *Ch:* menthadiène *m.*

menthane ['menθein], *s. Ch:* menthane *m.*
menthanol ['menθənɔl], *s. Ch:* menthanol *m.*
menthanone ['menθənoun], *s. Ch:* menthanone *f.*
menthene ['menθi:n], *s. Ch:* menthène *m.*
menthenol ['menθənɔl], *s. Ch:* menthénol *m.*
menthenone ['menθənoun], *s. Ch:* menthénone *f.*
menthol ['menθɔl], *s. Ch:* menthol *m*; *Med:* **m. pencil,** crayon mentholé; **m. cigarettes,** cigarettes *f* menthol.
mentholated ['menθəleitid], *a. Pharm:* (*of vaseline, etc.*) mentholé, mentholique.
menthone ['menθoun], *s. Ch:* menthone *f.*
menthyl ['menθil], *s. Ch:* menthyle *m.*
mention[1] ['menʃ(ə)n], *s.* **1.** mention *f* (de qn, de qch.); **to make m. of sth.,** faire mention de qch., parler de qch.; **m. was made of . . .,** on a parlé de . . .; **to make no m. of sth.,** passer qch. sous silence; **there was never any m. of that,** il n'a jamais été question de cela. **2.** *Sch: etc:* **honourable m.,** mention (honorable); accessit *m.*
mention[2], *v.tr.* mentionner, citer, faire mention de, parler de (qn, qch.); relever (un fait); **the firm mentioned on the accompanying slip,** la maison indiquée sur le bordereau ci-joint; **I may m. as an example . . .,** je citerai en exemple, comme exemple . . .; **I will m. that I have seen you,** je dirai que je vous ai vu; **we need hardly m. that . . .,** il est bien entendu que . . .; **I had forgotten to m. that . . .,** j'avais oublié de vous dire que . . .; **you have never mentioned it,** vous ne m'en avez jamais rien dit; **I shall m. it to him,** je lui en toucherai un mot; **it must never be mentioned again,** il ne faut plus jamais en reparler; **the custom is mentioned in . . .,** il est fait mention de cette coutume dans . . .; **nothing of the kind is mentioned in the report,** le rapport ne porte rien de tout cela; **too numerous to m.,** trop nombreux pour les citer; **it isn't worth mentioning,** cela est sans importance; **I have no money worth mentioning,** je n'ai presque, pour ainsi dire, pas d'argent; **as mentioned above, below,** comme mentionné ci-dessus, ci-dessous; **not to m . . .,** pour ne rien dire de . . .; sans parler de . . .; sans compter . . .; **not to m. the fact that . . .,** outre que . . .; **I could m. a house where . . .,** je sais une maison où . . .; je sais telle maison où . . .; **the price mentioned gave us a start,** l'énoncé *m* du prix nous a fait sauter; **I heard my name mentioned,** j'ai entendu prononcer mon nom; **you must never m. his name,** il ne faut jamais prononcer son nom; **we never m. her,** jamais nous ne parlons d'elle; **he is always mentioned with respect,** son nom est toujours prononcé avec respect; **to write mentioning s.o.'s name,** écrire en se recommandant de qn; **I have promised not to m. his name,** j'ai promis de taire son nom; **he mentioned no names,** il n'a nommé personne; **to m. s.o. in one's will,** coucher qn sur son testament; **don't m. it!** (i) ne m'en parlez pas! n'en parlez pas! cela ne vaut pas la peine d'en parler! (ii) *P:* il n'y a pas de quoi!
Mentor ['mentɔ:r]. **1.** *Pr.n.m. Gr.Lit:* Mentor. **2.** *s.* mentor *m*, guide *m.*
menu ['menju], *s.* menu *m*; **m. card,** menu; **m. holder,** porte-menu *m inv*; **today's m.,** carte *f* du jour.
menura [me'nju:rə], *s. Orn:* ménure *m*; oiseau-lyre *m, pl.* oiseaux-lyres.
Menuridae [me'nju:ridi:], *s.pl. Orn:* ménuridés *m.*
menyanthes [meni'ænθi:z], *s. Bot:* ményanthe *m* (à trois feuilles); trèfle *m* d'eau.
meow[1] [mjau], *int. & s.* miaou(!).
meow[2], *v.i.* (*of cat*) miauler.
Mephistophelean [mefistə'fi:liən], *a.* méphistophélique.
Mephistopheles [mefis'tɔfili:z]. *Pr.n.m.* Méphistophélès.
Mephistophelian [mefistə'fi:liən], *a.* méphistophélique.
mephitic [me'fitik], *a.* méphitique; **m. air,** air *m* méphitique, mofette *f.*
mephitis [me'faitis], **mephitism** ['mefitizm], *s.* méphitisme *m.*
meralgia [me'rældʒiə], *s. Med:* méralgie *f.*
mercantile ['mə:k(ə)ntail], *a.* (*a*) mercantile, marchand, commercial, -aux, commerçant, de commerce; **m. operations,** opérations *f* mercantiles; **m. nation,** nation commerçante; **m. broker,** agent *m* de change; **m. agency,** agence commerciale; **m. agent,** agent commercial; **m. marine,** marine marchande; **m. law,** droit commercial; code *m* de commerce; (*b*) *Pol.Ec:* **the m. system, the m. theory,** la théorie de l'argent source de richesse; le système mercantile; (*c*) *Pej:* mercantile, intéressé.
mercantilism ['mə:kəntilizm], *s.* mercantilisme *m.*
mercantilist ['mə:kəntilist], *a. & s.* mercantiliste (*m*).
mercaptal [mə:'kæptæl], *s. Ch:* mercaptal *m.*
mercaptan [mə:'kæptæn], *s. Ch:* mercaptan *m.*
mercaptide [mə:'kæptaid], *s. Ch:* mercaptide *m.*
mercaptomerin [mə:kæp'tɔmərin], *s. Ch:* mercaptomérine *f.*
Mercator [mə:'keitɔ:r]. *Pr.n.* Mercator; **Mercator's sailing,** navigation *f* loxodromique; navigation plane; **Mercator's projection,** projection *f* de Mercator.
Mercatorial [mə:kə'tɔ:riəl], *a.* (méridien *m*) de la projection de Mercator.
Mercedarian [mə:si'dɛəriən], *s. Ecc:* mercédaire *m.*
mercenarily ['mə:sinərili], *adv.* mercenairement, d'une manière mercenaire.
mercenariness ['mə:sin(ə)rinis], *s.* mercenarisme *m.*
mercenary ['mə:sin(ə)ri]. **1.** *a.* (âme *f*, esprit *m*) mercenaire, intéressé. **2.** *s.* (*soldier*) mercenaire *m.*
mercer ['mə:sər], *s. A:* **1. (silk) m.,** marchand, -ande, de soieries. **2.** mercier, -ière.
mercerization [mə:sərai'zeiʃ(ə)n], *s. Tex:* mercerisage *m.*
mercerize ['mə:səraiz], *v.tr. Tex:* merceriser.
mercerized ['mə:səraizd], *a.* (coton) mercerisé.
mercerizing ['mə:səraiziŋ], *s. Tex:* mercerisage *m.*
mercery ['mə:səri], *s. O:* **1.** commerce *m* des soieries. **2.** *coll:* soieries *fpl.*
merchandise[1] ['mə:tʃəndaiz], *s.* marchandise(s) *f*(*pl*).
merchandise[2], *v.i.* faire du commerce, du négoce.
merchandising ['mə:tʃəndaiziŋ], *s.* techniques marchandes.
merchant ['mətʃ(ə)nt]. **1.** *s.* (*a*) négociant, -ante; commerçant, -ante; marchand, -ande, en gros; **m. prince,** grand négociant, prince *m* du commerce; *O:* **m. tailor,** marchand-tailleur *m, pl.* marchands-tailleurs; **wine m.,** négociant en vins; (*b*) *Scot: & NAm:* marchand, -ande, boutiquier, -ière; (*c*) *F: O:* type *m*, individu *m*; *Aut:* **speed m.,** chauffard *m.* **2.** *a.* (*a*) marchand; de, du, commerce; **m. bank,** banque *f* d'affaires; **m. marine, m. navy, m. service, m. shipping,** marine marchande; **m. seaman,** matelot marchand; **m. ship, vessel,** navire marchand; navire de commerce; *Metall:* **m. bar, m. iron,** fer marchand; **m. steel,** acier marchand; (*b*) **the law m.,** le droit commercial; **m. shipping law,** droit maritime.
merchantable ['mə:tʃ(ə)ntəbl], *a.* **1.** en état d'être livré au commerce; vendable. **2.** de débit facile, de bonne vente.
merchantman, *pl.* **-men** ['mə:tʃ(ə)ntmən], *s.* navire marchand, navire de commerce.
merchantry ['mə:tʃəntri], *s. A:* commerce *m.*
Mercia ['mə:ʃiə, -siə]. *Pr.n. Hist:* Mercie *f.*
Mercian ['mə:ʃiən, -siən]. *Hist:* (*a*) *a.* mercien; (*b*) *s.* Mercien, -ienne.
merciful ['mə:sif(u)l], *a.* miséricordieux (**to,** pour); clément (**to,** envers); pitoyable; *Lit:* **be m. to me,** faites-moi miséricorde; *B:* **blessed are the m.,** bienheureux sont les miséricordieux.
mercifully ['mə:sif(u)li], *adv.* miséricordieusement; avec clémence; avec pitié.
mercifulness ['mə:sif(u)lnis], *s.* miséricorde *f*, clémence *f*, pitié *f.*
merciless ['mə:silis], *a.* impitoyable; sans pitié, sans merci, sans indulgence.
mercilessly ['mə:silisli], *adv.* impitoyablement; sans pitié, sans indulgence, sans merci.
mercilessness ['mə:silisnis], *s.* caractère *m* impitoyable; manque *m* de pitié.
mercuration [mə:kju'reiʃ(ə)n], *s. Ch:* mercuration *f.*
mercurial [mə:'kju:riəl]. **1.** *a.* (*a*) *Astr: Rom.Myth:* de Mercure; (*b*) (*of pers.*) vif, éveillé; à l'esprit prompt; ingénieux; (*c*) (*of pers.*) inconstant; d'humeur changeante; (*d*) *Med: Pharm:* mercuriel. **2.** *Med: Pharm:* (*a*) *a.* (produit) mercuriel, hydrargyrique; **m. poisoning,** mercurialisme *m*, hydrargyrisme *m*; **m. ointment,** onguent mercuriel double; (*b*) *s. Pharm:* produit mercuriel; préparation mercurielle.
mercurialism [mə:'kju:riəlizm], *s. Med:* mercurialisme *m*, hydrargyrisme *m*; intoxication *f* par le mercure.
mercuriality [mə:kjuri'æliti], *s.* **1.** vivacité *f*; ingéniosité *f*; promptitude *f* d'esprit. **2.** inconstance *f*; esprit changeant.
mercurialize [mə:'kju:riəlaiz], *v.tr. Med: Pharm:* mercurialiser.
mercuric [mə:'kju:rik], *a. Ch:* (sel, etc.) mercurique; **red m. sulphide,** cinabre *m*; **m. chloride,** chlorure *m* de mercure.
mercurification [mə:kjurifi'keiʃ(ə)n], *s.* mercurification *f*; extraction *f* du mercure (d'un minerai).
mercurify [mə:'kju:rifai], *v.tr.* extraire le mercure (d'un minerai).
mercurophylline [mə:kjurou'fili:n], *s. Pharm:* mercurophylline *f.*
mercurous ['mə:kjurəs], *a. Ch:* (sel) mercureux.
Mercury ['mə:kjuri]. **1.** *Pr.n.m. Myth: Astr:* Mercure. **2.** *s. Ch:* mercure *m*; (*a*) **m. ore,** minerai *m* de mercure; cinabre *m*; **m. bichloride,** bichlorure *m* de mercure; **m. chloride,** chlorure *m* de mercure; **m. cyanide,** cyanure *m* de mercure; **m. fulminate,** fulminate *m* de mercure; **m. oxide,** oxyde *m* de mercure; **m. sulphide,** sulfure *m* de mercure; *Pharm:* **ammoniated m.,** mercure précipité blanc; (*b*) *Tchn:* **m. barometer, thermometer,** baromètre *m*, thermomètre *m*, à mercure; **m. column,** colonne *f* de mercure; *Mch:* **m. gauge,** manomètre *m* à mercure; *El:* **m. switch,** interrupteur *m* à mercure; **m. (vapour) lighting,** éclairage *m* à vapeur de mercure; *Cmptr:* **m. delay line,** ligne *f* à retard à mercure; **m. storage,** mémoire *f* à ligne à retard à mercure. **3.** *s. Bot:* (*a*) mercuriale *f*, *F:* vignette *f*; **dog's m., wild m.,** mercuriale vivace; chou *m* de chien; **annual m., French m., garden m.,** mercuriale annuelle; foirolle *f*, foirande *f*; (*b*) **English m., false m.,** épinard *m* sauvage, bon-henri *m, pl.* bons-henris.
mercury-bearing ['mə:kjuribɛəriŋ], *a. Miner:* mercurifère.
mercy ['mə:si], *s.* miséricorde *f*; grâce *f*; merci *f*; pitié *f*; (*a*) **the infinite m. of God,** la miséricorde infinie de Dieu; **divine m.,** la miséricorde divine; **he was left to the m. of God,** il fut abandonné à la grâce de Dieu; **no sin but should find m.,** à tout péché miséricorde; *Ecc:* **Lord have m.! Christ have m.!** Seigneur prends pitié! (ô) Christ prends pitié! **m. seat,** (i) *B:* propitiatoire *m*; (ii) le trône de Dieu; (*b*) **to show m. to s.o.,** faire miséricorde à qn; **to have m. on s.o.,** avoir pitié de qn; **to be without m., to have no m.,** être impitoyable, sans pitié; **I have no m. for stupidity of that kind,** je ne puis pardonner une pareille stupidité; **to call, beg, for m.,** demander grâce; crier merci; **to throw oneself on s.o.'s m.,** s'abandonner à la merci de qn; **for mercy's sake,** de grâce; par pitié; **m.!** grâce! *O:* **m. on us!** grand Dieu! miséricorde! *O:* **m. me!** merci de ma vie! merci de moi! *Jur:* **with a recommendation to m.,** en demandant au chef d'État d'user de son droit de grâce; **the jury recommended the murderer to m.,** les jurés ont signé le recours en grâce; **m. killing,** euthanasie *f*; (*c*) **at the m. of s.o., of sth.,** à la discrétion, à la merci, de qn, de qch.; **I have him at my m.,** il est à ma merci; je le tiens à la gorge; **at the m. of the waves,** au gré des flots, à la dérive; **we are all at the m. of fortune,** nous dépendons tous de la fortune; *Iron:* **I leave him to your tender mercies,** je le livre, je l'abandonne, à votre merci, à vos soins; (*d*) **to be thankful for small mercies,** être reconnaissant des moindres bienfaits; **it's a m. you were able to come,** c'est un vrai bonheur que vous ayez pu venir; **what a m.!** quel bonheur! quelle chance! (*e*) **works of m.,** œuvres *f* de charité; *Can: Austr: etc: Av:* **m. flight,** vol *m* pour transporter un malade à l'hôpital (d'un endroit isolé).
mere[1] [miər], *s. Lit: & Dial:* lac *m*, étang *m.*
mere[2], *s. A:* limite *f*, borne *f.*
mere[3], *a.* (*a*) simple, pur, seul; rien que . . .; **m. justice demands that . . .,** la simple justice exige que . . .; **a m. glance will show that . . .,** il suffit d'un coup d'œil pour se rendre compte que . . .; **a m. coincidence,** une pure et simple coïncidence; **as a m. spectator,** en simple observateur; **out of m. spite,** par pure méchanceté; **it's m. chance,** c'est un pur hasard; **it was only by the merest chance that . . .,** ce n'est que par le plus grand des hasards que . . .; **by the merest accident I heard that . . .,** par pur accident j'ai appris que . . .; **the m. sight of her,** sa seule vue; **I shudder at the m. thought of it, the m. thought of it makes me shudder,** je frissonne rien que d'y penser; cette seule pensée me fait frissonner; **to condemn s.o. on a m. suspicion,** condamner qn sur un simple soupçon; **he's a m. boy,** ce n'est qu'un enfant; *F:* ce n'est qu'un gosse; **for a m. halfpenny,** pour un misérable sou; (*b*) minime; **the neutron occupies a m. fraction of the effective space inhabited by the electrons,** le neutron occupe simplement une fraction minime de l'espace réellement habité par les électrons.
merely ['miəli], *adv.* simplement, seulement; purement (et simplement); tout bonnement; **the invitation is m. formal,** l'invitation est de pure forme; **m. a word,** rien qu'un mot; **not m. . . .,** non pas seulement . . .; **not m. . . ., but also . . .,** non seulement . . ., mais encore . . .; **he m. smiled,** il se contenta de sourire; **I m. observed that . . .,** je me suis borné à faire remarquer que . . .; **I said it m. as a joke,** j'ai dit cela histoire de rire; **m. to tell of it made him tremble,** il tremblait rien qu'en le racontant, rien que de le raconter; **he came m. to see me,** il est venu uniquement pour me voir.
merenchyma [me'renkimə], *s. Bot:* mérenchyme *m.*
merestone ['miəstoun], *s. A:* borne *f* (de bornage).
meretricious [meri'triʃəs], *a.* **1.** *A:* de courtisane. **2.** (style, etc.) factice, d'un éclat criard, truqué.
meretriciously [meri'triʃəsli], *adv.* avec un faux brillant.
meretriciousness [meri'triʃəsnis], *s.* clinquant *m*, faux

brillant (du style, etc.).

meretrix, *pl.* **meretrices** ['meritriks, meri'traisi:z], *s.* **1.** *A: & Lit:* courtisane *f*, prostituée *f*. **2.** *Moll:* mérétrice *f*, mérétrix *f*.

merganser [mə:'gænsər], *s. Orn:* harle *m*, *Fr.C:* bec-scie *m*; **hooded m.,** harle couronné, bec-scie couronné; **red-breasted m.,** harle huppé, bec-scie à poitrine rousse; **American m.,** harle bièvre, grand harle.

merge[1] [mə:dʒ]. **1.** *v.tr.* fondre, fusionner (deux systèmes, deux classes); *Cmptr:* interclasser; **to m. sth. in, into, sth.,** fondre qch. dans qch.; amalgamer qch. avec qch.; **these states were, became, merged in the Empire,** ces États furent englobés dans l'Empire; *Jur:* **rights that are merged in one person,** droits confus en une personne. **2.** *v.i.* se fondre, se perdre (**in, into,** dans); se confondre (**in, into,** avec); (*of banks, etc.*) s'amalgamer, fusionner.

merge[2] *s. Cmptr:* fusion *f*; **m. routine,** programme *m* de fusion; **m. generator,** générateur *m* (de programme) d'interclassement; **m. key,** indicatif *m* de classement.

merger ['mə:dʒər], *s.* **1.** *Fin:* fusion *f*, amalgamation *f* (de plusieurs sociétés en une seule); **industrial m.,** unification industrielle; **m. company,** sociétés réunies. **2.** *Jur:* extinction *f* par consolidation, confusion, ou fusion; consolidation *f* (de l'usufruit avec la nue propriété).

merging ['mə:dʒiŋ], *esp. NAm:* **mergence** ['mə:dʒ(ə)ns], *s.* (*a*) fusion *f* (de deux choses) (**into,** en); fusionnement *m*; (*b*) *Cmptr:* **merging,** fusion, interclassement *m*; **m. sort,** rangement *m* par interclassement.

mericarp ['merika:p], *s. Bot:* méricarpe *m*.

meridian [mə'ridiən]. **1.** *s.* (*a*) méridien *m*; **terrestrial, geographical, m.,** méridien géographique; **arc of m.,** arc *m* de méridien; **first, prime, zero, m.,** premier méridien, méridien d'origine; méridien-origine *m*, *pl.* méridiens-origines; **Greenwich, Paris, m.,** méridien de Greenwich, de Paris; **magnetic m.,** méridien magnétique; (*b*) *Astr:* méridien, point culminant (d'un astre); **celestial m.,** méridien céleste, *Nau:* cercle *m* de déclinaison; **m. passage,** passage *m* (d'un astre) au méridien; *Fig:* **at the m. of his glory,** au zénith, à l'apogée, de sa gloire; *Lit:* **the m. of life,** le midi de la vie, la force de l'âge. **2.** *a.* (*a*) *Astr:* méridien, -enne; **m. altitude,** altitude, hauteur, méridienne; **m. angle,** angle méridien; **m. latitude,** latitude méridienne; **m. line,** (ligne) méridienne *f*; **m. zenith distance,** distance zénithale méridienne; (*b*) *Lit:* culminant; **he was at his m. splendour,** il était dans toute sa splendeur; il était au zénith, à l'apogée, de sa gloire; sa gloire était à son zénith, à son apogée.

meridional [mə'ridiənl]. **1.** *a. & s.* (*a*) méridional, -ale, -aux; du sud; (*b*) du midi de la France; méridional. **2.** *a.* (*of line, altitude, etc.*) méridien; *Astr:* **m. zenith distance,** distance zénithale méridienne.

meringue [mə'ræŋ], *s. Cu:* meringue *f*.

meringued [mə'ræŋd], *a. Cu:* meringué.

merino [mə'ri:nou], *s. Husb: Tex:* mérinos *m*; **m. ewe,** brebis *f* mérinos.

merismatic [meriz'mætik], *a.* (*a*) *Biol:* (reproduction *f*, etc.) mérismatique; (*b*) *Bot:* **m. tissue,** méristème *m*.

meristele ['meristi:l], *s. Bot:* méristèle *f*.

meristem ['meristem], *s. Bot:* méristème *m*.

merit[1] ['merit], *s.* **1.** mérite *m*; (*a*) *Rel:* **to acquire m.,** gagner du mérite; (*b*) **to be rewarded according to one's merits,** être récompensé selon ses mérites; (*c*) *Jur:* **the merits of a case,** le bien-fondé d'une cause; le fond (par opposition à la forme); **the case is at issue upon its merits,** le fond de la cause est en état; **to judge (a proposal) on its merits,** juger (une proposition) au fond, en considérant ses qualités intrinsèques; **to discuss, go into, the merits of sth.,** discuter qch.; discuter le pour et le contre de qch. **2.** valeur *f*, mérite; **book of considerable m.,** livre de véritable valeur; **of little m.,** de peu de mérite, sans grande valeur; **man of m.,** homme de valeur; **in order of m.,** par ordre de mérite; *Sch: etc:* **certificate of m.,** accessit *m*; *Ind: etc:* **m. bonus,** prime *f* au rendement.

merit[2], *v.tr.* mériter (une récompense, une punition); **he does not m. our trust,** il ne mérite pas notre confiance; **the plan scarcely merits consideration,** ce projet ne mérite guère, n'est guère digne de, notre considération.

merithal ['meriθæl], **merithallus,** *pl.* **-i** [meri'θæləs, -ai], *s. Bot:* mérithalle *m*; entre(-)nœud *m*, *pl.* entre(-)nœuds.

meritocracy [meri'tɔkrəsi], *s.* aristocratie *f* du mérite.

meritorious [meri'tɔ:riəs], *a.* (*of pers.*) méritant; (*of deed*) méritoire; (*of conduct*) digne, méritoire.

meritoriously [meri'tɔriəsli], *adv.* méritoirement; d'une façon méritoire.

meritoriousness [meri'tɔ:riəsnis], *s.* mérite *m*.

merlin[1] ['mə:lin], *s.* (faucon *m*) émerillon *m*.

Merlin[2]. *Pr.n.m. Lit:* Merlin.

merlon ['mə:lən], *s. Fort:* merlon *m*.

mermaid ['mə:meid], *s.* **1.** (*a*) *Myth:* (*Poet: occ.* **mermaiden**) sirène *f*; (*b*) *F: A:* sirène, enchanteresse *f*. **2.** (*a*) *Ich:* **m. fish,** ange *m* de mer, angelot *m*; **mermaid's purse,** oreiller *m* de mer; (*b*) *Bot:* **m. weed,** proserpinaca *m*.

merman, *pl.* **-men** ['mə:mæn, -men], *s.m. Myth:* triton.

mero-[1] ['merou, me'rɔ], *comb.fm. Biol: etc:* méro-.

mero-[2] ['miərou], *comb.fm. Med: etc:* méro-.

meroblastic [merou'blæstik], *a. Biol:* méroblastique.

merocele ['miərousi:l], *s. Med:* mérocèle *f*.

merocrine ['meroukrain], *a.* (glande) mérocrine.

merocyte ['merousait], *s. Biol:* mérocyte *m*.

merogony [me'rɔgəni], *s. Biol:* mérogonie *f*.

merohedral, merohedric [merou'hi:dr(ə)l, -'hi:drik], *a. Cryst:* mériédre.

merohedrism [merou'hi:drizm], *s. Cryst:* mériédrie *f*.

meromorphic [merou'mɔ:fik], *a. Med:* méromorphe.

Meropidae [me'rɔpidi:], *s.pl. Orn:* méropidés *m*, les guêpiers *m*.

Merostomata [merou'stoumətə], *s.pl. Paleont:* mérostomes *m*.

merotomy [me'rɔtəmi], *s. Biol:* mérotomie *f*.

Merovingian [merou'vin(d)ʒiən]. *Hist:* (*a*) *a.* mérovingien; (*b*) *s.* Mérovingien, -ienne.

Merovius [me'rouviəs]. *Pr.n.m. Hist:* Mérovée.

merozoite [merou'zouait], *s. Prot:* mérozoïte *m*.

merrily ['merili], *adv.* gaiement, joyeusement; avec entrain; **the sails of the windmill are turning m.,** les ailes du moulin tournent à toute volée.

merriment ['merimənt], *s.* gaieté *f*, hilarité *f*, réjouissance *f*, divertissement(s) *m*(*pl*), amusement(s) *m*(*pl*).

merry[1] ['meri], *s. Bot: Hort:* **1.** merise *f*. **2. m. (tree),** merisier *m*.

merry[2], *a.* (**merrier, merriest**) **1.** (*a*) joyeux, gai; jovial, -aux; **m. as a lark, as a cricket, as a grig, as m. as the day is long,** gai comme un pinson; **to lead a m. life,** mener joyeuse vie; **to be always m. and bright,** être toujours plein d'entrain; avoir toujours l'air heureux et content; **to make m.,** se divertir, s'amuser, s'égayer, se réjouir; *O:* **to make m. over sth.,** se divertir, se moquer, de qch.; (**a**) **m. Christmas!** joyeux Noël! **the m. monarch,** le gai monarque (Charles II d'Angleterre); *Prov:* **the more the merrier,** plus on est de fous, plus on rit; (*b*) *F:* éméché; un peu parti, un peu gris; *O:* **to be m. in one's cups,** avoir le vin gai. **2.** *A: & Lit:* (*a*) agréable, aimable; **m. England,** l'aimable Angleterre; **the m. month of May,** le gentil mois de mai; (*b*) **Robin Hood and his m. men,** Robin des Bois et sa troupe de gaillards.

merry-andrew ['meri'ændru:], *s.m. O:* paillasse, bouffon, pitre, baladin.

merry-go-round ['merigouraund], *s.* (manège *m* de) chevaux *mpl* de bois; carrousel *m*.

merrymaker ['merimeikər], *s.* (*a*) celui qui se divertit, qui se réjouit, qui s'amuse; **the merrymakers,** la bande joyeuse; (*b*) noceur, -euse; fêtard, -arde.

merrymaking ['merimeikiŋ], *s.* (*a*) réjouissances *fpl*, divertissement *m*; (*b*) réunion joyeuse, partie *f* de plaisir.

merrythought ['meriθɔ:t], *s.* lunette *f*, fourchette *f* (d'une volaille).

Merseburg ['mə:səbə:g]. *Pr.n. Geog:* Mersebourg.

merulius [mə'ru:liəs], *s. Fung:* mérule *f*.

Mervig ['mə:vig]. *Pr.n.m. Hist:* Mérovée.

Merychippus [meri'kipəs], *s. Paleont:* merychippus *m*.

merycism ['merisizm], *s. Med:* mérycisme *m*.

Merycopotamus [merikou'pɔtəməs], *s. Paleont:* merycopotamus *m*.

mesa ['mi:sə], *s.* **1.** *Geog:* mesa *f*. **2.** *Elcs:* **m. transistor,** transistor *m* mesa.

mesaconic [mezə'kɔnik], *a. Ch:* mésaconique.

mesail ['meseil], *s. A.Arm:* mézail *m* (de casque).

mesarteritis [meza:tə'raitis], *s. Med:* mésartérite *f*.

mesaticephalic, mesaticephalous [mezætise'fælik, -'sefələs], *a. Anthr:* mésaticéphale.

mesaticephalism, mesaticephaly [mezæti'sefəlizm, -'sefəli], *s. Anthr:* mésaticéphalie *f*.

mescal [mes'kæl], *s.* **1.** *Bot:* **m. (buttons),** mescal *m*. **2.** *Dist:* mescal.

mescalin(e) ['meskəl(a)in], *s. Pharm:* mescaline *f*.

Mesdames [mei'dæm], *s.f.pl.* (*used for pl. of Mrs*) Mesdames.

meseems [mi'si:mz], *v.impers. A: & Lit:* il me semble; m'est avis (**that,** que).

Mesembryanthemaceae ['mezembriænθi'meisii:], *s.pl. Bot:* mésembryanthémées *f*, mésembryanthémacées *f*.

mesembryanthemum [mezembri'ænθiməm], *s. Bot:* mésembryanthème *m*, ficoïde *f*.

mesencephalic [mezense'fælik], *a. Anat:* mésencéphalique.

mesencephalon [mezen'sefələn], *s. Anat:* mésencéphale *m*, mésocéphale *m*.

mesenchyma [me'seŋkimə], *s. Biol:* mésenchyme *m*.

mesenteric [mesen'terik], *a. Anat:* mésentérique.

mesenteritis [mesentə'raitis], *s. Med:* mésentérite *f*.

mesentery ['mesənt(ə)ri], *s. Anat:* mésentère *m*; *Z:* fraise *f*.

meseta [me'si:tə], *s. Geog:* meseta *f*.

mesh[1] [meʃ], *s.* **1.** (*a*) maille *f* (d'un filet, d'un tamis); **double m.,** contre-maille *f*, *pl.* contre-mailles; **fine-m. screen,** crible *m* à mailles fines; **m. 60, 60 gauge m.,** (tamis de) maille 60; **100 m. ore,** minerai broyé passant à la maille 100; **wire m.,** toile *f* métallique; **to mend the meshes of a net,** re(m)mailler un filet; *Com:* **m. bag,** (sac *m*) filet; *Geol: etc:* **m. structure,** structure maillée; *Cmptr:* **m. sort,** rangement *m* par interclassement; (*b*) *Nat.Hist:* **meshes,** réseau *m* (vasculaire, etc.). **2.** *Mec.E:* prise *f*, engrènement *m*, engrenage *m*; **constant m.,** prise continue; **constant m. gear,** pignons *mpl* constamment en prise; pignons de prise constante; **in m. with (a pinion, etc.),** en prise avec (un pignon, etc.); *Fig:* **to be caught in the meshes,** être pris dans l'engrenage. **3.** *El:* **m. circuit,** montage polygonal; **m. connection,** connexion polygonale; **three-phase m. connection,** connexion en triangle; **four-phase m. connection,** connexion en carré.

mesh[2]. **1.** *v.tr.* (*a*) prendre (des poissons) au filet; (*b*) *occ.* mailler (un filet); (*c*) *Mec.E:* endenter, engrener (des roues dentées); coordonner (qch. à qch.). **2.** *v.i.* (*a*) (*of fish*) se laisser prendre au filet; (*b*) se coordonner, s'agencer; (*of teeth of wheel*) engrener, s'engrener; être, se mettre, en prise (**with,** avec).

meshed [meʃt], *a.* **1.** à mailles; **fine-m., wide-m.,** à mailles fines, à larges mailles; *El:* **wide-m. grid,** grillage *m* (d'accumulateur) à larges alvéoles. **2.** *Mec.E:* engrené.

meshing ['meʃiŋ], *s.* **1.** *Mec.E: etc:* (*a*) prise *f*, venue *f* en prise; engrènement *m*, endentement; (*b*) mise *f* en prise; (*c*) *attrib.* **m. jaw,** mâchoire (d'étau, etc.) dentelée, striée; *El:* **m. solenoid,** enclencheur *m* magnétique. **2.** (*a*) mailles *fpl* (d'un filet); (*b*) **wire m.,** treillis *m* métallique, en fil de fer.

mesial ['mi:ziəl], *a. Anat:* (*a*) (*as opposed to* **distal**) mésial; (*b*) médian; médial, -als, -aux.

mesially ['mi:ziəli], *adv.* médialement.

mesic ['mezik], *a. Atom.Ph:* mésique, mésonique.

mesidine ['mezidi:n], *s. Ch:* mésidine *f*.

mesitine, mesitite ['mezitain, -tait], *s. Miner:* mésitine *f*.

mesityl ['mezitil], *s. Ch:* mésityle *m*.

mesitylene [me'zitili:n], *s. Ch:* mésitylène *m*.

meslin ['mezlin], *s.* = MASLIN.

mesmerian, mesmeric [mez'miəriən, -'merik], *a.* mesmérien, mesmérique, magnétique, hypnotique.

mesmerism ['mezmərizm], *s.* mesmérisme *m*, magnétisme *m* (animal); hypnotisme *m*.

mesmerist ['mezmərist], *s.* **1.** hypnotiseur *m*. **2.** *occ.* = MESMERITE.

mesmerite ['mezmərait], *s.* mesmérien, -ienne; partisan, -ane, du mesmérisme; *Hist:* partisan de Mesmer.

mesmerize ['mezməraiz], *v.tr.* hypnotiser.

mesmerizer ['mezməraizər], *s.* hypnotiseur *m*.

mesne [mi:n], *a. Jur:* intermédiaire; **m. process,** cours *m* de l'instance (entre les actes introductifs et le jugement); **m. profits,** bénéfices retirés d'un bien pendant un intervalle de détention illégitime; *Hist:* **m. lord,** vassal d'arrière-fief; vavasseur *m*.

meso- ['mezou, 'mi:zou, 'mesou], *pref.* méso-.

mesoblast ['mezoublæst], *s. Biol:* mésoblaste *m*, mésoderme *m*.

mesocarp ['mezouka:p], *s. Bot:* mésocarpe *m*.

mesocarpus [mezou'ka:pəs], *s. Algae:* mésocarpe *f*.

mesocephal ['mezousef(ə)l], *s. Anthr:* mésocéphale *mf*.

mesocephalic ['mezouse'fælik], *a. Anthr:* mésocéphale; *Anat:* mésocéphalique.

mesocephaly [mezou'sefəli], *s. Anthr:* mésocéphalie *f*.

mesocoelic [mezou'si:lik], *a. Anat:* mésocœliaque.

mesocolon [mezou'koulən], *s. Anat:* mésocôlon *m*.

mesocotyl ['mezoukɔtil], *s. Bot:* mésocotyle *m*.

mesocratic [mezou'krætik], *a. Geol:* mésocrate.

mesoderm ['mezoudə:m], *s. Biol:* mésoderme *m*, mésoblaste *m*.

mesodermal, mesodermic [mezou'də:m(ə)l, -'də:mik], *a. Biol:* mésodermique.

Mesodevonian [mezoudi'vouniən], *a. & s. Geol:* mésodévonien (*m*).

mesodont(ic) ['mezoudɔnt, mezou'dɔntik], *a. Anat:* mésodonte.

mesodonty ['mezoudɔnti], *s. Anat:* mésodontie *f*.

Mesoenatidae [meze'nætidi:], *s.pl. Orn:* mésœnatidés *m.*
mesogaster [mezou'gæstər], *s. Anat:* mésogastre *m.*
mesogastric [mezou'gæstrik], *a. Anat:* mésogastrique.
Mesogastropoda [mezougæ'strɔpədə], *s.pl. Moll:* mésogastropodes *m.*
mesogl(o)ea [mezou'gli:ə], *s. Coel: Spong:* mésogléе *f.*
mesohippus [mezou'hipəs], *s. Paleont;* mésohippus *m.*
mesokurtic [mezou'kə:tik], *a. Stat:* mésocurtique.
mesolabe ['mezouleib], *s. A.Mth:* mésolabe *m.*
mesole ['mezoul], *s. Miner:* mésole *m.*
mesolite ['mezoulait], *s. Miner:* mésolite *f.*
Mesolithic [mezou'liθik], *a. & s. Prehist:* (ère *f*) mésolithique (*m*).
mesologic(al) [mezou'lɔdʒik(l)], *a. Biol:* mésologique.
mesology [me'zɔlədʒi], *s. Biol:* mésologie *f.*
mesomere ['mezoumiər], *s. Biol:* mésomère *f.*
mesomeric [mezou'merik], *a. Ch:* mésomère, mésomérique.
mesomerism [me'zɔmərizm], *s. Ch:* mésomérie *f.*
mesomorph ['mezoumɔ:f], *s. Cryst:* mésomorphe *m.*
mesomorphic, mesomorphous [mezou'mɔ:fik, -'mɔ:fəs], *a. Cryst:* mésomorphe.
mesomorphism, mesomorphy [mezou'mɔ:fizm, -'mɔ:fi], *s. Cryst:* mésomorphisme *m.*
Mesomyodi [mezoumai'oudai], *s.pl. Orn:* mésomyodés *m.*
meson ['mezɔn], *s. Atom.Ph:* méson *m*; électron lourd; **light, heavy, m.,** méson léger, lourd; **positive, negative, neutral, m.,** méson positif, négatif, neutre; **scalar m.,** méson scalaire; **pseudo-scalar m.,** méson pseudoscalaire; **virtual m.,** méson virtuel; **mu m.,** méson mu; **pi m.,** méson pi; **K m.,** méson K; **m. physics,** physique *f* des mésons; **m. beam,** faisceau *m* de mésons; **m. field,** champ *m* mésonique; **m. scattering,** diffusion *f* des mésons; **m. threshold,** seuil *m* mésonique; **m. theory of nuclear forces,** théorie *f* mésonique des forces nucléaires.
mesonephros [mezou'nefrɔs], *s. Biol:* mésonéphros *m.*
mesonic [me'zɔnik], *a. Atom.Ph:* mésonique, mésique; **m. atom,** atome *m* mésonique, mésique; **m. charge,** charge *f* mésonique, mésique.
mesonotum [mezou'noutəm], *s. Ent:* mésonotum *m.*
mesonyx ['mezouniks], *s. Paleont:* mésonyx *m.*
mesopause ['mezoupɔ:z], *s. Meteor:* mésopause *f.*
mesophile ['mezoufail], *a. Bac:* mésophile.
mesophragm(a) ['mezoufræm, mezou'frægmə], *s. Z:* mésophragme *m.*
mesophragmal [mezou'frægm(ə)l], *a. Z:* mésophragmatique.
mesophyll(um) ['mezoufil, mezou'filəm], *s. Bot:* mésophylle *m.*
mesophyllic, mesophyllous [mezou'filik, -'filəs], *a. Bot:* mésophyllien.
mesophyte ['mezoufait], *s. Bot:* mésophyte *f.*
mesophytic [mezou'fitik], *a. Bot:* mésophyte.
mesoplodon [me'zɔplədɔn], *s. Z:* mésoplodon *m.*
Mesopotamia [mesəpə'teimiə]. *Pr.n. Geog: Hist:* Mésopotamie *f.*
Mesopotamian [mesəpə'teimiən], (*a*) *a.* mésopotamien; (*b*) *s.* Mésopotamien, -ienne.
mesopotamic [mesəpə'tæmik], *a.* mésopotamien, situé entre deux fleuves.
mesor(r)hinian [mezou'riniən], *a. & s. Anthr:* mésorhinien, -ienne.
mesosaur ['mezousɔər], *s. Paleont:* mésosaure *m.*
mesoseme ['mezousi:m], *a. Anthr:* mésosème.
mesosoma [mezou'soumə], *s. Z:* mésosoma *m.*
mesosphere ['mezousfiər], *s. Meteor:* mésosphère *f.*
mesosternal [mezou'stə:n(ə)l], *a. Anat: Ent:* mésosternal, -aux.
mesosternum [mezou'stə:nəm], *s. Anat: Ent:* mésosternum *m.*
Mesostomatidae [mezoustou'mætidi:], *s.pl. Ann:* mésostomatidés *m.*
mesostomid [mezou'stoumid], *s. Ann:* mésostome *m.*
mesotartaric [mezoutɑ:'tærik], *a. Ch:* (acide) mésotartrique.
Mesot(a)eniales [mezouti:ni'eili:z], *s.pl. Algae:* mésoténiales *f.*
mesothelioma [mezouθi:li'oumə], *s. Med:* mésothéliome *m.*
mesothelium [mezou'θi:liəm], *s. Anat:* mésothélium *m.*
mesotherium, *pl.* **-ia** [mesou'θiəriəm, -iə], *s. Paleont:* mésothérium *m.*
mesotherm ['mezouθə:m], *s. Bot:* mésotherme *f.*
mesothermal [mezou'θəm(ə)l], *a.* (*a*) *Ph: Geol:* mésothermal, -aux; (*b*) *Bot:* mésotherme.
mesothoracic [mezouθɔ'ræsik], *a. Anat: Ent:* mésothoracique.
mesothorax [mezou'θɔ:ræks], *s. Anat: Ent:* mésothorax *m.*
mesothorium [mezou'θɔ:riəm], *s. Ch:* mésothorium *m.*
mesot(r)on ['mezout(r)ɔn], *s. Atom.Ph:* mésot(r)on *m.*
mesotype ['mezoutaip], *s. Miner:* mésotype *f.*
mesoxalic [mezɔk'sælik], *a. Ch:* mésoxalique.
mesozoic [mezou'zouik], *a. Geol:* mésozoïque.
mesozone ['mezouzoun], *s. Geol:* mésozone *f.*
mesozoon, *pl.* **-zoa** [mezou'zouən, -'zouə], *s. Prot:* mésozoaire *m.*
Mespot ['mespɔt]. *Mil: P: A:* = MESOPOTAMIA.
mesquit(e) ['meski:t, me'ski:t], *s. Bot:* **1.** prosopis *m.* **2. m. grass,** bouteloue *m.*
mess[1] [mes], *s.* **1.** (*food*) (*a*) *A:* plat *m*; mets *m*; *B:* **m. of pottage** = plat de lentilles; (*b*) *Husb: O:* ration *f*, pâtée *f* (pour les animaux). **2.** saleté *f*; **to make a m. of the tablecloth,** salir la nappe; **to clear up the m. made by the cat,** enlever les saletés du chat. **3.** fouillis *m*, désordre *m*; gâchis *m*; **everything's in a m.,** tout est en désordre; **what a m.!** quel désordre! quel gâchis! quelle pagaille! **he's left me to clear up the m.,** il m'a laissé le soin de tout remettre en ordre, de tout débrouiller; (*of pers.*) **to be in a m.,** être dans le pétrin, dans de beaux draps; **to get, help, s.o. out of a m.,** sortir qn d'un mauvais pas, du pétrin; repêcher qn; **to make a m. of a job,** gâcher, bousiller, un travail; **to make a m. of things,** tout gâcher; **you've made a nice, a fine, m. of it!** voilà un joli gâchis, du beau travail! *F:* **he always makes a m. of things!** il n'en rate pas un! **you've made a fine m. of my watch!** vous avez bien arrangé ma montre! (*after air raid, etc.*) **the town's in a frightful m.,** la ville est en marmelade; (*after accident, etc.*) **my car's a m.,** ma voiture ne vaut plus rien, est bien amochée; *P:* **to make a m. of s.o.,** tabasser, amocher, qn; *F:* **after the fight his face was a terrible m.,** après la bagarre il avait le visage tout amoché; *P:* **she's an awful m.!** ce qu'elle est moche! **4.** *Mil: etc:* (i) mess *m*, table *f*, *F:* popote *f* (des officiers, des sous-officiers); ordinaire *m* (des hommes); *Navy:* plat *m*; (ii) (*room*) (salle *f* de) mess; réfectoire *m* (des hommes); *Navy:* carré *m* (des officiers); *Navy:* **m. deck,** poste *m* des matelots, d'équipage; *Mil:* **m. tent,** (i) tente *f* mess, *F:* tente popote (des officiers); (ii) tente réfectoire (des hommes); **m. kit,** (i) ustensiles *mpl*, matériel *m*, d'ordinaire, de campement; (ii) couvert individuel; **m. kettle,** (i) *Mil:* marmite *f*, plat *m*, de campement; bouteillon *m*; (ii) *Navy:* gamelle *f*; **m. tin,** gamelle (individuelle); **m. dress,** *F:* **kit,** tenue *f* de mess, de soirée; **m. jacket,** spencer *m*; **m. president,** président (i) *Mil:* de table, (ii) *Navy:* de carré; **officers', etc., m.,** mess des officiers, etc.; **m. officer, sergeant, corporal,** officier *m*, sergent *m*, caporal *m*, d'ordinaire; **m. attendant, orderly, servant,** serveur *m*; *Navy:* matelot d'office; serveur *m*; **m. commission, committee,** commission *f* du mess; **m. accounts,** comptabilité *f* de l'ordinaire; **m. bill,** note *f* (de mess).
mess[2], *v.*
I. *v.tr. & i.* **1.** *v.tr.* salir, souiller (qch.). **2.** *Mil: etc:* (*a*) *v.i.* (*of officers*) faire table, (*of men*) faire plat; manger en commun, faire gamelle (**with,** avec); **to m. together,** manger à la même table; *F:* faire popote ensemble; **privates must m. together,** la troupe doit manger à l'ordinaire; (*b*) *v.tr.* **to m. a regiment, a crew,** approvisionner la table d'un régiment; aplater un équipage.
II. (*compound verbs*) **1. mess about,** (*a*) *v.tr.* (i) houspiller (qn); abîmer, tripoter (qch.); (ii) (*also* **mess around**) déranger qn; mettre la confusion dans les projets de (qn); **I don't like being messed about (around),** je n'aime pas qu'on me dérange, qu'on me prenne pour une girouette; (*b*) *v.i.* (*also* **mess around**) (i) bricoler; gaspiller son temps; traîner; *F:* **to m. about (around) with a girl,** caresser, peloter, *P:* tripoter, une fille.
2. mess up, *v.tr.* **to m. up a piece of work,** gâcher, bousiller, un travail; **don't m. up my watch,** n'abîmez pas ma montre; **you've really messed it up this time!** en voilà un beau gâchis!
message[1] ['mesidʒ], *s.* **1.** (*a*) message *m*; communication *f* (téléphonique, etc.); **radio m.,** message radio (télégraphique); **telephone(d) m.,** message téléphoné, téléphonique; *Nau: etc:* **distress m.,** message de détresse; **weather m.,** message météo(rologique); *Av:* **dropped, weighted, m.,** message lesté, lancé d'avion; *Tp: Tg:* **service m.,** message de service; **through m.,** message en transit; **code m., cipher m., m. in code,** message chiffré, en code; **message in clear,** message en clair; **routine m.,** message ordinaire; **priority m., urgent m.,** message prioritaire, urgent; **emergency m.,** message extrême urgent; **flash m.,** message instantané, immédiat, flash; message en priorité absolue; **deferred m.,** message différé; **misrouted m.,** message mal acheminé; **m. book,** carnet *m* de messages; *Mil: etc:* **m. centre,** centre *m* de régulation des messages; **m. shell,** projectile *m* porte-message; *Cmptr:* **m. handling, switching,** traitement *m*, commutation *f*, de messages; **to send a m. to s.o.,** envoyer, transmettre, un message à qn; **I'll give him the m.,** je lui transmettrai le message; je lui ferai la commission; **to leave a m. for s.o.,** laisser un message, un mot, pour qn; (*b*) **the King's, the Queen's, m.,** discours télévisé et radiodiffusé du roi, de la reine, le jour de Noël; *U.S:* **President's m.,** discours du Président au Congrès; (*c*) *F:* **have you got the m.?** as-tu bien compris? tu as pigé? **2.** (*errand*) commission, course *f*; **to send s.o. on a m.,** envoyer qn faire une commission, une course. **3.** (*a*) prédiction *f*, révélation *f*, évangile *m*, prédiction *f* (d'un prophète); (*b*) message, leçon (spirituelle), enseignement *m* (d'un écrivain, d'un livre, etc.).
message[2], *v.tr. esp. U.S:* **1.** envoyer, transmettre, (une communication) par messager. **2.** transmettre (un ordre, etc.) par signaux, par télégramme, par radio; signaler (un message).
Messalian [me'seiliən], *s. Rel.Hist:* Messalien, -ienne.
Messalina [mesə'li:nə]. *Pr.n.f. Rom.Hist:* Messaline.
messelite ['mesəlait], *s. Miner:* messelite *f.*
Messene [me'si:ni]. *Pr.n. Geog:* Messène *f.*
messenger ['mesindʒər], *s.* **1.** (*a*) messager, -ère; courrier *m*; (*b*) *Mil:* agent *m* de transmission, coureur *m*, estafette *f*; *Navy:* timonier coureur; **motorcycle m.,** estafette motocycliste; **m. service,** service *m* d'estafettes; **m. dog,** chien *m* de transmission; chien-estafette *m*, *pl.* chiens-estafettes; **m. pigeon,** pigeon voyageur; **m. plane,** avion *m* de liaison; (*c*) *Adm:* courrier (diplomatique, etc.); **King's, Queen's, m.** = courrier d'État; (*d*) commissionnaire *m*; **by m.,** par porteur; **m. boy,** garçon *m* de courses; **hotel m.,** chasseur *m*; **office m.,** garçon de bureau; coursier, -ière; **telegraph m.,** préposé *m* télégraphiste, facteur *m* télégraphiste; **auctioneer's m.,** garçon de salle; (*e*) *A:* porteur *m*, annonciateur *m* (**of good tidings,** de bonnes nouvelles); (*f*) *Civ.E: El: etc:* **m. cable,** câble *m* porteur. **2.** *Nau:* tournevire *m* (du cabestan); marguerite *f* (de l'ancre, etc.). **3.** (*on kite string*) postillon *m.*
Messenia [me'si:niə]. *Pr.n. Geog:* la Messénie.
Messenian [me'si:niən]. *Geog:* **1.** *a.* messénien. **2.** *s.* Messénien, -ienne.
Messiah [me'saiə]. *Pr.n.* Messie *m.*
messianic [mesi'ænik], *a.* messianique.
messianism [me'saiənizm], *s.* messianisme *m.*
Messina [me'si:nə]. *Pr.n. Geog:* Messine *f*; **the Strait of M.,** le détroit de Messine.
Messinese [mesi'ni:z]. *Geog:* **1.** *a.* messinois. **2.** *s.* Messinois, -oise.
messing ['mesiŋ], *s.* **1.** habitude *f* de manger en commun; *F:* popote *f* en commun; **m. allowance,** indemnité *f* de table. **2.** *Mil: etc:* approvisionnement *m* de la table (d'un régiment, etc.).
messmate ['mesmeit], *s.* (*a*) commensal, -ale, -aux; camarade *m* de table; *Navy:* camarade de plat; convive *m*; (*b*) *Z:* commensal.
Messrs ['mesəz], *s.m.pl. Com: etc:* Messieurs, *abbr.* MM; **Messrs J. Martin & Co.,** Messieurs J. Martin et Cie.
messuage ['meswidʒ], *s. Jur:* maison, dépendances et terres *fpl*; *A:* manse *m*; **ancient m.,** maison bâtie avant le règne de Richard Ier, et qui de ce fait jouit de droits de prescription; **capital m.,** manse seigneurial.
mess-up ['mesʌp], *s. F:* **1.** gâchis *m.* **2.** embrouillement *m*, embrouillamini *m*; contretemps *m*; cafouillage *m*; **there's been a bit of a mess-up over booking the seats,** il y a eu je ne sais quel malentendu pour la location, *Rail:* la réservation, des places.
messy ['mesi], *a. F:* **1.** (*a*) sale, malpropre; (*b*) en désordre. **2.** qui salit; salissant; **cleaning the car oneself is a m. business,** à entretenir soi-même la voiture on salit tout; **oranges are a m. fruit,** les oranges vous poissent les doigts.
mestiza [mes'ti:zə], *s.f.* métisse.
mestizo, *pl.* **-os** [mes'ti:zou, -ouz], *s.m.* métis.
mestome ['mestoum], *s. Bot:* mestome *m.*
met [met], *a. F:* météo; **the m. office,** la météo; **the m. officer,** le météo.
Meta ['mi:tə], *s. Ch: R.t.m.* Méta *m.*
meta- ['metə, metə, me'tæ], *pref.* méta-.
metabasis [me'tæbəsis], *s.* métabase *f.*
metabiosis [metə'baiousis], *s. Biol:* métabiose *f.*
metabisulphite [metəbai'sʌlfait], *s. Ch:* métabisulfite *m.*
Metabola [me'tæbələ], *s.pl. Ent:* métaboles *m.*
metabolic [me'tæbɔlik], *a. Biol:* métabolique.
metabolism [me'tæbəlizm], *s. Biol:* métabolisme *m*; **constructive m.,** anabolisme *m*; **destructive m.,** catabolisme *m*; **fat, protein, m.,** métabolisme lipidique, protidique; **basal m.,** métabolisme basal.

metabolite [me'tæbəlait], *s. Biol:* métabolite *m.*

metabolize [me'tæbəlaiz], *v.tr.* transformer (un tissu, etc.) par métabolisme.

metabolous [me'tæbələs], *a. Biol:* métabole.

metaborate [metə'bɔ:reit], *s. Ch:* métaborate *m.*

metaboric [metə'bɔ:rik], *a. Ch:* métaborique.

metabrushite [metə'brʌʃait], *s. Miner:* métabrushite *f.*

metacarpal [metə'kɑ:p(ə)l], *a. & s. Anat:* (os) métacarpien (*m*).

metacarpophalangeal [metəkɑ:poufæ'lændʒiəl], *a. Anat:* métacarpo-phalangien.

metacarpus [metə'kɑ:pəs], *s. Anat:* métacarpe *m.*

metacentre ['metəsentər], *s. Hyd:* métacentre *m*; **height of the m.,** hauteur *f* métacentrique.

metacentric [metə'sentrik], *a.* (courbe, etc.) métacentrique.

metacercaria [metəsə:keəriə], *s. Ann:* métacercaire *f.*

Metachlamydeae [metəklæ'mi:dii:], *s.pl. Bot:* métachlamydées *f.*

metachromasia [metəkrou'meiziə], **metachromasy** [metə'krouməsi], *s. Biol:* métachromasie *f.*

metachromatic [metəkrou'mætik], *a. Biol:* métachromatique.

metachromatin [metə'kroumətin], *s. Biol:* métachromatine *f,* volutine *f.*

metachromatism [metə'kroumətizm], *s. Biol:* métachromatisme *m.*

metacinnabar [metə'sinibɑ:r], *s. Miner:* métacinnabre *m.*

metacinnabarite [metə'sinibərait], *s. Miner:* métacinnabarite *f.*

metadyne ['metədain], *s. El:* métadyne *f.*

metagalaxy [metə'gæləksi], *s.* métagalaxie *f.*

metage ['mi:tidʒ], *s.* **1.** mesurage *m,* pesage *m.* **2.** taxe *f* de pesage, etc.

metagenesis [metə'dʒenisis], *s. Biol:* métagénèse *f.*

metagenetic [metədʒe'netik], *a. Biol:* métagénésique.

metageometry [metədʒi:'ɔmitri], *s.* métagéométrie *f.*

metagnomy [me'tænəmi], *s.* métagnomie *f.*

metal[1] ['met(ə)l], *s.* **1.** (*a*) métal, -aux; **base m., non-precious m.,** métal commun, non précieux; métal vil; **precious m., noble m.,** métal précieux, noble; **ferrous, non-ferrous, metals,** métaux ferreux, non ferreux; **tipped with m., m. tipped,** ferré; **m. engraver,** graveur *m* sur métaux; **m. polish,** nettoie-métaux *m inv*; *Fin:* **standard m.,** métal-étalon *m, pl.* métaux-étalons; (*b*) *Metall:* métal, fonte *f*; **crude, raw, m.,** métal cru, brut; **coarse m.,** matte *f*; **high-melting, low-melting, m.,** métal à basse, à haute, température de fusion; **liquid m.,** métal fondu; **molten m.,** métal en fusion; **sheet m.,** métal en feuilles; (de la) tôle; **sheet m. work,** chaudronnerie *f*; (*in factory*) **sheet m. shop,** (atelier *m* de) chaudronnerie; **m. foil,** métal en feuilles très minces; **to convert ore into m.,** métalliser le minerai; **conversion (of ore) into m.,** métallisation *f* (du minerai); **to coat, cover, a surface with m.,** métalliser une surface; **to spray with m.,** métalliser au pistolet, par projection; **m. founding,** moulage *m* des métaux; **m. refining,** affinage *m* des métaux; corroyage *m*; **m. refinery,** usine *f* d'affinage des métaux, usine métallique d'affinage; (*c*) **bearing m., bush m., white m.,** métal à coussinets, métal rose; **filler m.,** métal d'apport (pour soudure autogène); **joining m.,** métal de liaison; **structural metals,** métaux de construction; (*d*) **m. casing,** enveloppe *f* métallique; **m. covering,** revêtement *m* métallique; **m. framework,** bâti *m,* structure *f,* métallique; (*e*) *Ph:* **m. fog, m. mist,** métal en suspension (dans un électrolyte). **2.** *Glassm:* verre *m* en fusion. **3.** (*a*) *Min:* pierre *f* de mine; minerai; (*b*) *Min:* roc *m*; (*c*) *Civ.E:* (matériau *m* d') empierrement *m*; ballast *m* (de voie ferrée); **road m.,** cailloutis *m,* pierraille *f*; caillasse *f,* chaille *f.* **4.** *Typ:* caractères *mpl,* métal, plomb *m*; **old m.,** vieille matière; **to print down on m.,** copier sur métal, sur plomb; **to read in the m.,** lire sur le métal, sur le plomb; **to coat upon the m.,** coucher le métal, le plomb; **m. printing room,** salle *f* de copie sur métal. **5.** *Rail: etc:* **the metals,** les rails *m*; (*of engine, etc.*) **to leave, jump, the metals,** quitter les rails; dérailler. **6.** *Her:* métal; **the metals,** les métaux (or et argent).

metal[2], *v.tr.* **(metalled) 1.** empierrer, ferrer, macadamiser, caillouter (une route). **2.** (*a*) métalliser (le bois, etc.); (*b*) doubler de métal (une carène de navire, etc.).

metalanguage ['metəlæŋgwidʒ], *s. Ling:* métalangage *m.*

metal-bearing ['metlbeəriŋ], *a.* métallifère.

metal carbonyl [metl'kɑ:bənil], *s. Ch:* métal-carbonyle *m.*

metaldehyde [me'tældihaid], *s. Ch:* métaldéhyde *f.*

metalepsis [metə'lepsis], *s. Rh:* métalepse *f.*

metalimnion [metə'limniɔn], *s. Oc: etc:* métalimnion *m.*

metalinguistic [metəliŋ'gwistik], *a. Ling:* métalinguistique.

metallation [metə'leiʃ(ə)n], *s. Ch:* métallation *f.*

metalled ['metld], *a.* **m. road,** route empierrée, ferrée, en cailloutis; **m. road surface,** revêtement *m* en empierrement.

metallescent [metə'les(ə)nt], *a.* métallescent.

metallic [mi'tælik], *a.* métallique, métallin; (*a*) *Ch:* **m. bond,** liaison *f* métallique; **m. element,** corps *m* simple métallique, élément *m* métallique; **m. oxide,** oxyde *m* métallique; **m. antimony, m. sodium,** antimoine *m,* sodium *m,* métallique; **m. paint,** peinture *f* métallique; (*b*) *El:* **m. arc,** arc *m* métallique; **m. circuit,** circuit *m* sans retour à la terre, circuit magnétique; *Rail:* **m. return circuit,** circuit de retour par conducteur séparé; (*c*) **m. shield,** écran *m* métallique; *Mch:* **m. packing,** garniture *f* métallique (d'un piston); (*d*) *Fin:* **m. currency,** monnaie *f* de métal, monnaie métallique; **m. standard,** étalon *m* métallique; **m. reserve,** réserve *f* métallique; (*e*) *Fig:* (*brilliant, iridescent*) **m. aspect,** aspect *m* métallique, métallin; **m. lustre,** éclat *m* métallique; **m. colour,** couleur *f* métallique; **a m. blue, green,** un bleu, un vert, métallique; (*f*) (*harsh, sharp*) **m. sound,** son *m* métallique; **m. voice, laughter,** voix *f,* rire *m,* métallique; **the m. note of the bellbird,** la note métallique de l'oiseau-cloche; (*g*) **m. taste,** goût *m* de métal.

metalliferous [metə'lifərəs], *a.* métallifère.

metalliform [me'tælifɔ:m], *a.* métalliforme.

metalline ['metəlain], *a.* métallin.

metalling ['metəliŋ], *s.* **1.** *Civ.E:* (*a*) empierrement *m* (des routes); macadam *m*; (*b*) couche *f* d'empierrement. **2.** métallisation *f,* métallisage *m* (d'une surface).

metallization [metəlai'zeiʃ(ə)n], *s.* **1.** métallisation *f,* métallisage *m.* **2.** vulcanisation *f* (du caoutchouc).

metallize ['metəlaiz], *v.tr.* **1.** métalliser (une surface). **2.** vulcaniser (le caoutchouc).

metallochromy [metælou'kroumi], *s.* métallochromie *f.*

metallogeny [metə'lɔdʒəni], *s. Geol:* métallogénie *f.*

metallographer, metallographist [metə'lɔgrəfər, -'lɔgrəfist], *s.* métallographe *mf.*

metallographic [metəlou'græfik], *a.* métallographique.

metallography [metə'lɔgrəfi], *s.* métallographie *f.*

metalloid ['metəlɔid], *a. & s.* métalloïde (*m*).

metalloidal [metə'lɔidəl], *a. Ch:* métalloïdique.

metalloscope [me'tælouskoup], *s.* métalloscope *m.*

metallurgic(al) [metə'lə:dʒik(l)], *a.* métallurgique.

metallurgically [metə'lə:dʒikəli], *adv.* métallurgiquement.

metallurgist [me'tælədʒist], *s.* métallurgiste *m.*

metallurgy [me'tælədʒi, metə'lə:dʒi], *s.* métallurgie *f*; **the m. of iron,** la sidérotechnie; la sidérurgie; **powder m.,** métallurgie des poudres.

metalmark ['met(ə)lmɑ:k], *s. Ent:* **the metalmarks,** les riodinides *m,* les érycinides *m.*

metalogical [metə'lɔdʒik(ə)l], *a. Phil:* métalogique.

metalwork ['met(ə)lwə:k], *s.* **1.** (*a*) travail *m* des métaux; serrurerie *f*; **art m.,** ferronnerie *f,* serrurerie d'art; (*b*) métal ouvré; **open m.,** grillage *m.* **2.** *pl.* (*usu. with sg. const.*) **metalworks,** (i) usine *f* métallurgique; (ii) tôlerie *f.*

metalworker ['met(ə)lwə:kər], *s.* ouvrier *m* en métaux; serrurier *m*; **art m.,** ferronnier *m,* serrurier, d'art; **metalworkers,** (ouvriers) métallurgistes *m*; *F:* métallos *m.*

metalworking ['met(ə)lwə:kiŋ], *s.* travail *m* sur métaux.

metamathematical [metəmæθə'mætik(ə)l], *a.* métamathématique.

metamathematics [metəmæθə'mætiks], *s.pl.* (*usu. with sg. const.*) métamathématiques *f.*

metamer ['metəmə:r], *s. Ch:* composé *m* métamère.

metamere ['metəmiər], *s. Nat.Hist:* métamère *m.*

metameric [metə'merik], *a. Ch:* métamère.

metamerism, metamery [me'tæmərizm, -əri], *s. Nat.Hist: Ch:* métamérie *f.*

metamerization [metæmərai'zeiʃ(ə)n], *s. Biol:* métamérisation *f.*

metamerized [me'tæməraizd], *a. Biol:* métamérisé; (*of embryo*) métamérique.

metamict ['metəmikt], *a. Atom.Ph:* métamicte.

metamorphic [metə'mɔ:fik], *a.* **1.** *Geol:* métamorphique. **2.** *Nat.Hist:* métamorphosique.

metamorphism [metə'mɔ:fizm], *s.* métamorphisme *m*; **contact m., local m.,** métamorphisme de contact; **general m.,** métamorphisme général; **endomorphic, exomorphic, m.,** métamorphisme endomorphe, exomorphe.

metamorphopsia, metamorphopsy [metəmɔ:'fɔpsiə, -'mɔ:fəpsi], *s. Med:* métamorphopsie *f.*

metamorphosable [metəmɔ:'fouzəbl], *a.* métamorphosable.

metamorphose [metə'mɔ:fouz]. **1.** *v.tr.* métamorphoser, transformer (**to, into,** en). **2.** *v.i.* se transformer (**into,** en).

metamorphosis, *pl.* **-oses** [metə'mɔ:fəsis, -əsi:z], *s.* métamorphose *f.*

metamorphotic [metəmɔ:'foutik], *a. Nat.Hist:* métamorphosique.

metamyelocyte [metə'maiəlousait], *s. Med:* métamyélocyte *m.*

Metamynodon [metə'minoudɔn], *s. Paleont:* métamynodon *m.*

metanauplius [metə'nɔ:pliəs], *s. Crust:* métanauplius *m.*

metanephros [metə'nefrɔs], *s. Biol:* métanéphros *m.*

métaphase ['metəfeiz], *s. Biol:* métaphase *f.*

metaphenylenediamene [metə'fenili:n'daiəmi:n], *s. Ch:* métaphénylènediamine *f.*

metaphony [me'tæfəni], *s. Ling:* métaphonie *f*; modification *f* vocalique.

metaphor ['metəfər], *s.* métaphore *f*; image *f*; **mixed m.,** métaphore disparate, incohérente; **Homer is full of metaphors,** presque tout est image dans Homère; **to speak in metaphors,** parler par métaphores; métaphoriser.

metaphoric(al) [metə'fɔrik(l)], *a.* métaphorique.

metaphorically [metə'fɔrik(ə)li], *adv.* métaphoriquement.

metaphosphate [metə'fɔsfeit], *s. Ch:* métaphosphate *m.*

metaphosphoric [metəfɔs'fɔrik], *a. Ch:* métaphosphorique.

metaphrase ['metəfreiz], *s.* métaphrase *f*; traduction *f* mot à mot; traduction littérale.

metaphrast ['metəfræst], *s.* métaphraste *m.*

metaphrastic [metə'fræstik], *a.* métaphrastique; (traduction *f*) mot à mot.

metaphysical [metə'fizik(ə)l], *a.* métaphysique.

metaphysically [metə'fizik(ə)li], *adv.* métaphysiquement.

metaphysician [metəfi'ziʃ(ə)n], *s.* métaphysicien, -ienne.

metaphysicize [metə'fizisaiz], *v.i.* métaphysiquer.

metaphysics [metə'fiziks], *s.pl.* (*usu. with sg. const.*) métaphysique *f.*

metaphysis [me'tæfisis], *s. Anat:* métaphyse *f.*

metaphyte ['metəfait], *s. Bot:* métaphyte *m.*

metaplasia [metə'pleiziə], *s. Physiol:* métaplasie *f.*

metaplasm[1] ['metəplæzm], *s. Gram: Rh:* métaplasme *m.*

metaplasm[2], *s. Biol:* deutoplasma *m,* deutoplasme *m,* métaplasme *m.*

metapsychic(al) [metə'saikik(l)], *a.* métapsychique.

metapsychics [metə'saikiks], *s.pl.* (*usu. with sg. const.*) métapsychique *f.*

metapsychist [metə'saikist], *s.* métapsychiste *mf.*

metapsychology [metəsai'kɔlədʒi], *s.* métapsychologie *f.*

metargon [me'tɑ:gɔn], *s. Ch:* métargon *m.*

metarsenious [metɑ:'si:niəs], *a. Ch:* (acide) métaarsénieux.

metarsenite [me'tɑ:sənait], *s. Ch:* métaarsénite *m.*

metasequoia [metəsi'kwɔijə], *s. Bot:* métaséquoia *m.*

metasilicate [metə'silikeit], *s. Ch:* métasilicate *m.*

metasilicic [metəsi'lisik], *a. Ch:* métasilicique.

metasoma [metə'soumə], *s. Z:* métasoma *m.*

metasomatic [metəsou'mætik], *a. Z: Geol:* métasomatique.

metasomatism [metə'soumətizm], **metasomatosis** [metəsoumə'tousis], *s. Geol:* métasomatose *f.*

metastable [metə'steibl], *a. Ph:* (état *m*) métastable.

metastannic [metə'stænik], *a. Ch:* (acide) métastannique.

metastasis [me'tæstəsis], *s.* **1.** *Med:* métastase *f.* **2.** *Biol:* métabolisme *m.*

metastatic [metə'stætik], *a.* (abcès, etc.) métastatique.

metasternal [metə'stə:n(ə)l], *a. Ent:* métasternal, -aux.

metasternum [metə'stə:nəm], *s. Ent:* métasternum *m.*

metastibnite [metə'stibnait], *s. Miner:* métastibnite *f.*

metatarsal [metə'tɑ:s(ə)l], *a. Anat: Nat.Hist:* métatarsien.

metatarsalgia [metətɑ:'sældʒiə], *s. Med:* métatarsalgie *f.*

metatarsus, *pl.* **-i** [metə'tɑ:səs, -ai], *s. Anat: Nat.Hist:* métatarse *m.*

metatheory [metə'θi:əri], *s.* métathéorie *f.*

Metatheria [metə'θiəriə], *s.pl. Z:* méthathériens *m.*

metatherian [metə'θiəriən], *a. & s. Z:* métathérien (*m*).

metathesis, *pl.* **-eses** [me'tæθəsis, -əsi:z], *s.* **1.** *Ling: Surg: Phil:* métathèse *f.* **2.** *Ch:* décomposition *f* double; substitution *f.*

metathoracic [metəθɔ:'ræsik], *a. Ent:* métathoracique.

metathorax [metə'θɔ:ræks], *s. Ent:* métathorax *m.*

metatype ['metətaip], *s. Biol:* métatype *m.*

metatypic [metə'tipik], *a. Biol:* métatypique.

metatypism [metə'taipizm], *s. Biol:* métatypie *f.*

Metaurus [me'tɔ:rəs]. *Pr.n. Geog:* **the (river) M.,** le Métaure.

metavoltine [metə'vɔltain], *s. Miner:* métavoltine *f.*

metaxite [me'tæksait], *s. Miner:* métaxite *f.*

metazo(a)ea [metəzou'i:ə], *s. Crust:* métazoé *m.*

metazoan [metə'zouən], *Nat.Hist:* **1.** *a.* métazoaire; des métazoaires. **2.** *s.* métazoaire *m.*

metazoic [metə'zouik], *a. Nat.Hist:* métazoaire.

metazoon, *pl.* **-zoa** [metə'zouɔn, -'zouə], *s. Nat.Hist:* métazoaire *m.*

mete[1] [mi:t], *s. Jur:* **metes and bounds,** bornes *f.*

mete[2], *v.tr. Lit:* **1.** mesurer. **2. to m. (out) punishments, rewards,** assigner des punitions; distribuer, décerner, des récompenses.

metel ['mi:təl], *s. Bot:* métel *m.*

metempiric(al) [metem'pirik(l)], *a.* métempirique.

metempsychosis, *pl.* **-oses** [metem(p)s(a)i'kousis, -ousi:z], *s.* métempsyc(h)ose *f*; **believer in m.,** métempsyc(h)osiste *mf.*

metencephalon [meten'sefəlɔn], *s. Anat:* métencéphale *m.*

metensomatosis [metensoumə'tousis], *s.* métensomatose *f.*

meteor ['mi:tiər], *s.* météore *m*; **aerial, aqueous, igneous, meteors,** météores aériens, aqueux, ignés.

meteoric [mi:ti'ɔrik], *a.* **1.** météorique; **m. stones,** pierres *f* météoriques; **m. iron,** sidérolithe *f*; **m. rise in the social scale,** montée *f* rapide de l'échelle sociale. **2.** atmosphérique; **m. agents,** agents *m* d'intempérisme.

meteorically [mi:ti'ɔrik(ə)li], *adv.* (briller, surgir, etc.) comme un météore.

meteorism ['mi:tiərizm], *s. Med: Vet:* météorisation *f*, météorisme *m.*

meteorite ['mi:tiərait], *s.* météorite *m or f*; aérolithe *m.*

meteoritic [mi:tiə'ritik], *a. Meteor:* météoritique.

meteorograph ['mi:tiərougræf], *s. Meteor:* météorographe *m*; **radio m.,** radio-sonde *f*, *pl.* radio-sondes.

meteoroid ['mi:tiərɔid], *s.* météore *m*, météorite *m or f*; **m. detector plate,** plaquette *f* de détection de météorites.

meteorolite ['mi:tiəroulait], *s.* météorite *m or f.*

meteorological [mi:tiərə'lɔdʒik(ə)l], *a.* météorologique; aérologique; **m. coverage,** couverture *f* météorologique; **m. office,** bureau *m* météorologique; **m. report,** bulletin *m* météorologique; **m. radio broadcast,** bulletin météorologique (radiodiffusé); **m. reporting station,** station *f* de renseignements météorologiques; *Mil.Av:* **m. briefing office,** bureau d'exposé météorologique; **m. unit,** unité *f* météo(rologique); **m. observing unit,** unité d'observation météorologique.

meteorologist [mi:tiə'rɔlədʒist], *s.* météorologiste *mf*, météorologue *mf.*

meteorology [mi:tiə'rɔlədʒi], *s.* météorologie *f.*

meter[1] ['mi:tər], *s.* **1.** *A:* (*pers.*) (*a*) mesureur *m*, peseur *m*; (*b*) arpenteur *m.* **2.** (*device*) appareil *m* de mesure, compteur *m*, jaugeur *m*; **certified m.,** compteur agréé; **direct-reading m.,** appareil de mesure, compteur, à lecture directe; **electric m.,** compteur électrique; **flow m.,** compteur de fluide, débitmètre *m*; **gas m.,** compteur à gaz; **water m.,** compteur à eau; **excess m.,** compteur à dépassement; **hour m., time m.,** compteur horaire; **slot m.,** compteur à paiement préalable; *Aut:* **parking m.,** parcomètre *m*, *Fr.C:* compteur de stationnement; **exposure m.,** (i) *Ph:* photomètre *m*, actinomètre *m*; (ii) *Phot:* posemètre *m*; *Opt:* **light m.,** luxmètre *m*; *Av:* **airflow m.,** appareil à mesurer le débit d'air; *El:* **integrating m.,** compteur intégrateur; *Tp:* **position m.,** compteur d'appels; **m. error,** tolérance *f* de mesure (d'un compteur, etc.); **m. multiplier,** multiplicateur *m* d'échelle; **m. reading,** lecture *f* d'un appareil de mesure; relevé *m* de(s) compteur(s); (*pers.*) **m. reader,** releveur, -euse, de(s) compteur(s).

meter[2], *v.tr.* (*a*) (*of gas company, etc.*) mesurer (le gaz, etc.) au compteur; (*b*) (*of apparatus*) mesurer (le débit de gaz, etc.); (*c*) **do they make a fixed charge for water or is it metered?** est-ce qu'on paie l'eau à forfait ou bien à la consommation?

meterage ['mi:təridʒ], *s.* mesurage *m*; pesage *m*; mesurage au compteur.

metered ['mi:təd], *a.* mesuré, calibré, jaugé; *I.C.E:* **m. distribution,** distribution calibrée.

metering ['mi:t(ə)riŋ], *s.* mesurage *m*, mesure *f*, comptage *m*, calibrage *m*, jaugeage *m*; *Mec.E: Tchn:* **m. device,** dispositif *m*, système *m*, de mesure; dispositif calibreur; **m. dial,** cadran *m* de mesures; **m. head,** sonde *f* de mesure; **m. pin,** pointeau calibreur; **m. port,** orifice *m* de dosage; **m. screw,** vis *f* de réglage; *El:* **m. relay,** relais *m* de comptage (d'impulsions).

methacrylic [meθæ'krilik], *a. Ch:* mét(h)acrylique.

methaemoglobin [meθi:mou'gloubin], *s. Bio-Ch:* méthémoglobine *f.*

methaemoglobin(a)emia [meθi:mougloubi'ni:miə], *s. Med:* méthémoglobinémie *f.*

methane ['meθein], *s. Ch:* méthane *m*; formène *m*; *F:* gaz *m* des marais; **phenyl m.,** toluène *m*; **m. series,** carbures saturés; **m. pipeline,** méthanoduc *m*; *Nau:* **m. tanker,** méthanier *m.*

methanization [meθənai'zeiʃ(ə)n], *s.* méthanisation *f.*

methanol ['meθənɔl], *s. Ch:* méthanol *m*; alcool *m* méthylique.

methemalbumin [meθe'mælbjumin], *s. Bio-Ch:* méthémalbumine *f.*

methinks [mi'θiŋks], *v.impers.* (*p.t.* **methought** [mi:θɔ:t]) *A: Lit:* il me semble.

methionic [meθi'ɔnik], *a. Ch:* méthionique.

methionine [me'θaiənain], *s. Bio-Ch:* méthionine *f.*

method ['meθəd], *s.* (*a*) (*research, science*) méthode *f*; **backward m.,** méthode indirecte, rétrograde; **forward m.,** méthode directe, progressive; **case m.,** méthode des cas concrets; **deductive, inductive, m.,** méthode déductive, inductive; **experimental m.,** méthode expérimentale; **exponential m.,** méthode exponentielle; **interpolation m.,** méthode d'interpolation; **iteration m.,** méthode d'itération; **m. of concomitant variations,** méthode des variations concomitantes; **m. of least, of minimum, squares,** méthode des moindres carrés; **m. of residues,** méthode des résidus; **m. of substitution,** méthode de substitution; **product m.,** méthode des nombres; **successive approximations m., trial-and-error m.,** méthode des approximations successives; **zero m., null m., balanced m.,** méthode du zéro, méthode de compensation; (*b*) méthode, manière *f* (**of doing sth.,** de faire qch.); procédé *m* (pour faire qch.); modalités *fpl*; **m. of application of a treaty,** modalités d'application d'un traité; *Adm:* **m. of payment,** modalités de paiement; *Mil:* **tactical methods,** procédés de combat; *Ind:* **production m.,** procédé(s) de fabrication, de production; **m. of working, m. of operation,** méthode de travail, d'exploitation; *Surg:* **operative m.,** méthode opératoire; (*c*) *Ind:* **methods engineer,** ingénieur *m* des méthodes; **methods engineering,** étude *f* des méthodes; **methods office,** bureau *m* des méthodes; (*d*) **man of m.,** homme *m* d'ordre; homme méthodique; **to work without m.,** travailler sans méthode, à bâtons rompus; **lack of m.,** absence *f* de méthode; manque *m* de suite *f*, d'esprit de suite; **there's m. in his madness,** il n'est pas si fou qu'il en a l'air.

methodical [mi'θɔdik(ə)l], *a.* méthodique; **m. life,** vie réglée, ordonnée; **m. man,** homme *m* d'ordre; homme méthodique; **to be m.,** avoir l'esprit méthodique, avoir de l'ordre; **he is very m.,** il a beaucoup de méthode.

methodically [mi'θɔdik(ə)li], *adv.* méthodiquement, avec méthode.

methodism ['meθədizm], *s.* **1.** souci exagéré de la méthode. **2.** *Med.Hist: Rel.H:* méthodisme *m.*

methodist ['meθədist], *a.* & *s. Med.Hist: Rel: H:* méthodiste *mf.*

Methodius [me'θoudiəs]. *Pr.n.m. Ecc.Hist:* Méthode.

methodization [meθədai'zeiʃ(ə)n], *s.* méthodisation *f.*

methodize ['meθədaiz], *v.tr.* ordonner, régler; mettre de la méthode dans (une nomenclature, etc.).

methodological [meθədə'lɔdʒikl], *a.* méthodologique.

methodology [meθə'dɔlədʒi], *s.* méthodologie *f.*

methol ['meθɔl], *s. Ch:* méthol *m.*

methoxyl [me'θɔksil], *s. Ch:* méthoxyle *m.*

meths [meθs], *s. F:* alcool *m* à brûler.

Methuselah [me'θju:zələ]. *Pr.n.m. B:* Mathusalem; **as old as M.,** vieux comme Hérode.

methyl ['meθil], *s. Ch:* méthyle *m*; (*a*) **m. alcohol,** alcool *m* méthylique; **m. acetate,** acétate *m* de méthyle; **m. bromide,** bromure *m* de méthyle; **m. chloride,** chlorure *m* de méthyle; **m. iodide,** iodure *m* de méthyle; **m. sulphide,** sulfure *m* de méthyle; **m. cellulose,** méthylcellulose *f*; **m. ethyl ketone,** méthyléthylcétone *f*; **m. isobutyl ketone,** méthylisobutylcétone *f*; (*b*) *Dy:* **m. orange,** méthylorange *m*; **m. violet,** méthylviolet *m*; **m. yellow,** méthyljaune *m*; **m. red,** méthylrouge *m.*

methylal ['meθilæl], *s. Ch:* méthylal *m.*

methylamine ['meθil'æmain], *s. Ch:* méthylamine *f.*

methylaniline ['meθil'ænilain], *s. Ch:* méthylaniline *f.*

methylate[1] ['meθileit], *s. Ch:* méthylate *m.*

methylate[2], *v.tr. Ch:* méthyler.

methylated ['meθileitid], *a.* **m. spirit,** alcool dénaturé; alcool à brûler.

methylation [meθi'leiʃ(ə)n], *s. Ch:* méthylation *f.*

methylbenzene ['meθil'benzi:n], *s. Ch:* méthylbenzène *m.*

methylene ['meθili:n], *s. Ch:* méthylène *m*; (*a*) **m. chloride,** chlorure *m* de méthylène; **m. iodide,** iodure *m* de méthylène; (*b*) *Dy:* **m. blue, m. green,** bleu *m*, vert *m*, de méthylène.

methylic [me'θilik], *a. Ch:* méthylique.

methylpentose ['meθil'pentous], *s. Ch:* méthylpentose *m.*

methylpropane ['meθil'proupein], *s. Ch:* méthylpropane *m.*

metic ['metik], *s. Gr.Ant:* métèque *m.*

meticulosity [metikju'lɔsiti], *s.* méticulosité *f.*

meticulous [me'tikjuləs], *a.* méticuleux; minutieux; **to be m. in the choice of words,** avoir des scrupules dans le choix des mots; **to be m. in little things,** observer les points et les virgules.

meticulously [me'tikjuləsli], *adv.* méticuleusement; **to be always m. accurate,** avoir le souci de l'exactitude; **m. dressed,** habillé avec un soin méticuleux.

meticulousness [me'tikjuləsnis], *s.* méticulosité *f*; minutie *f.*

métier ['meitjei], *s.* avocation *f*; **he has found his m.,** il a trouvé sa voie.

meting ['mi:tiŋ], *s.* **1.** mesurage *m.* **2. m. out,** allocation *f*, distribution *f*, décernement *m.*

metis ['meitis], *s. esp. Can:* métis, -isse.

metol ['metɔl], *s. Phot:* métol *m.*

Metonic [me'tɔnik], *a. Astr:* **the M. cycle,** le cycle métonien.

metonymical [metə'nimik(ə)l], *a. Rh:* métonymique.

metonymy [me'tɔnimi], *s. Rh:* métonymie *f.*

metope ['metəpi], *s. Gr.Arch:* métope *f.*

metopic [me'tɔpik], *a. Anat:* métopique; **m. suture,** suture *f* métopique.

metoposcopy [metou'pɔskəpi], *s.* métoposcopie *f.*

metralgia [me'træl(d)ʒiə], *s. Med:* métralgie *f*; douleur utérine.

metre[1] ['mi:tər], *s. Pros:* mètre *m*, mesure *f*; **in m.,** en vers.

metre[2], *s. Meas:* mètre *m*; **linear m., running m.,** mètre courant; **square m.,** mètre carré; **cubic m.,** mètre cube; *Com:* **stacked cubic m.,** stère *m* (de bois).

metric[1] ['metrik], *a. Meas:* métrique; **the m. system,** le système métrique; **m. area, volume,** métrage *m*; **m. ton,** tonne *f* (métrique); *F:* (*of country*) **to go m.,** adopter le système métrique.

metric[2]**(al)** ['metrik(l)], *a.* (poésie *f*, etc.) métrique.

metrically[1] ['metrikəli], *adv.* **to express oneself m.,** écrire en vers.

metrically[2], *adv.* **everything is labelled m.,** on utilise le système métrique partout.

metricate ['metrikeit]. **1.** *v.i.* introduire le système métrique. **2.** *v.tr.* **to m. one's system (of measures),** remplacer son système (de poids et mesures) par le système métrique.

metrication [metri'keiʃən], *s.* adoption *f*, introduction *f*, utilisation *f*, du système métrique; établissement *m* du système métrique (dans un pays).

metrician [me'triʃ(ə)n], *s. Pros:* métricien *m.*

metrics ['metriks], *s.pl. Pros:* (*usu. with sg. const.*) métrique *f.*

metrist ['metrist], *s. Pros:* versificateur *m*, métricien *m.*

metritis [me'traitis], *s. Med:* métrite *f*; inflammation *f* de la matrice.

metrological [metrə'lɔdʒik(ə)l], *a.* métrologique.

metrologist [me'trɔlədʒist], *s.* métrologiste *mf*, métrologue *mf.*

metrology [me'trɔlədʒi], *s.* métrologie *f.*

metromania [metrou'meiniə], *s.* métromanie *f.*

metromaniac [metrou'meiniæk], *s.* métromane *mf.*

metronome ['metrənoum], *s. Mus:* métronome *m.*

metronomic [metrə'nɔmik], *a.* métronomique.

metropolis [mi'trɔpəlis], *s.* **1.** métropole *f*, capitale *f*; ville métropolitaine. **2.** *Ecc:* siège métropolitain; métropole.

metropolitan [metrə'pɔlit(ə)n]. **1.** *a.* métropolitain; **m. police, railway,** police métropolitaine, chemin de fer métropolitain; **the m. area,** l'ensemble *m* des *boroughs* de la ville de Londres. **2.** *s.* (*a*) habitant, -ante, de la métropole, de la capitale; (*b*) *Ecc:* (i) métropolitain *m*, archevêque *m*; (ii) = METROPOLITE.

metropolite [me'trɔpəlait], *s. Ecc:* métropolite *m* (de l'Église russe).

metrorrhagia [mi:trou'reidʒiə], *s. Med:* métrorragie *f*; hémorragie utérine.

metrorrhagic [mi:trou'reidʒik], *a. Med:* métrorragique.

Metroxylon [me'trɔksilɔn], *s. Bot:* metroxylon *m.*

metsat ['metsæt], *s.* satellite *m* météorologique.

mettle ['metl], *s.* **1.** (*of pers.*) ardeur *f*, courage *m*, feu *m*; (*of horse*) fougue *f*; **full of m.,** (*of pers.*) courageux, plein de courage, plein d'ardeur; (*of horse*) fougueux, plein de fougue; **to try a horse's m.,** pousser un cheval;

to try s.o.'s m., tâter le courage de qn; **to put s.o. on his m.,** piquer qn d'honneur; exciter l'émulation de qn; stimuler l'amour-propre, le zèle, de qn; pousser qn à faire de son mieux; **to be on one's m.,** se sentir poussée à faire de son mieux; se piquer d'honneur; **I was on my m.,** je m'étais piqué au jeu. **2.** caractère *m*, disposition *f*, tempérament *m*; **to show one's m.,** donner sa mesure, faire ses preuves; **he showed the m. he was made of,** il a montré de quel bois il se chauffait.

mettlesome ['metlsəm], *a.* (*of pers.*) ardent, vif, plein de courage; (*of horse*) fougueux.

meum ['mi:əm], *s. Bot:* méum *m.*

mew[1] [mju:], *s. Orn:* (**sea**)**m.,** mouette *f*, goéland *m*; *F:* mauve *f.*

mew[2], *s.* mue *f*, cage *f* (pour les faucons); **pheasant m.,** volière *f* à faisans.

mew[3], *v.tr.* **1.** (r)enfermer (un faucon) dans une mue; mettre (des faisans) en cage. **2. to m. s.o. (up),** cloîtrer, claquemurer, renfermer, qn.

mew[4], *v.tr. & i. Orn: O:* **to m. (its feathers),** muer.

mew[5], *s.* (*of cat, seagull*) miaulement *m.*

mew[6], *v.i.* (*of cat, seagull*) miauler.

mewing[1] ['mju:iŋ], *s. Orn: O:* mue *f.*

mewing[2], *s.* (*of cat, etc.*) miaulement *m.*

mewl [mju:l], *v.i. O:* (*of infant*) vagir, piailler; (*of cat*) miauler.

mewling[1] ['mju:liŋ], *a. O:* (enfant) piaillard.

mewling[2], *s. O:* vagissement *m*, piaillerie *f*, miaulement *m.*

mews [mju:z], *s.* (*originally pl., now used as sg.*) **1.** écuries *fpl.* **2.** impasse *f*, ruelle *f* (sur laquelle donnaient des écuries); **m. house, flat,** maison *f*, appartement *m*, aménagé(e) dans une ancienne écurie.

Mexican ['meksikən]. **1.** *a. Geog:* mexicain; *Z:* **M. hog,** pécari *m.* **2.** *s. Geog:* Mexicain, -aine.

Mexico ['meksikou]. *Pr.n. Geog:* **1.** Mexique *m.* **2. M. (City),** Mexico *f.*

meyerhofferite [maiə'hɔfərait], *s. Miner:* meyerhofférite *f.*

mezcal ['mezkæl], *s. Bot:* mescal *m*, mezcal *m.*

mezereon [mi'ziəriən], *s. Bot:* mézéréon *m*, lauréole *f*; *F:* bois gentil, garou *m* des bois.

mezzanine ['me(t)zəni:n], *s.* **1.** *Arch:* **m. (floor),** mezzanine *f*, entresol *m*; **m. window,** fenêtre *f* d'entresol; mezzanine. **2.** *Th:* premier dessous (de la scène).

mezza voce ['metzə 'voutʃi], *adv. Mus:* à demi-voix; mezza voce.

mezzo ['metsou]. *Mus:* **1.** *adv.* mezzo; **m. forte,** mezzo forte. **2.** *s.* **m. soprano,** *F:* **m.,** mezzo-soprano *m, pl.* mezzo-sopranos, -ni.

mezzo-relievo ['metzouri'li:vou], *s.* demi-relief *m, pl.* demi-reliefs.

mezzotint[1] ['metzoutint], *s. Engr:* **1.** mezzo-tinto *m inv*; gravure *f* à la manière noire. **2.** estampe *f* à la manière noire.

mezzotint[2], *v.tr.* graver (qch.) à la manière noire.

mezzotinter [metzou'tintər], *s.* graveur *m* à la manière noire.

mi [mi:], *s. Mus:* **1.** (*fixed mi*) mi *m.* **2.** (*movable mi, in tonic solfa also* **me**) la médiante.

Miacidae [mai'æsidi:], *s.pl. Paleont:* miacidés *m.*

miacis ['maiəsis], *s. Paleont:* miacis *m.*

miaow[1] [mi(:)'au]. **1.** *s.* miaulement *m*, miaou *m* (du chat). **2.** *int. F:* **m.!** que tu es rosse!

miaow[2], *v.i.* (*of cat*) miauler.

miargyrite [mai'ɑ:dʒirait], *s. Miner:* miargyrite *f.*

miasm ['maiæzm], **miasma,** *pl.* **-ata, -as** [mi'æzmə, -ətə, -əz], *s.* miasme *m.*

miasmal [mi'æzm(ə)l], **miasmatic** [miæz'mætik], **miasmic** [mi'æzmik], *a.* miasmatique.

miastor [mai'æstər], *s. Ent:* miastor *m.*

miaul [mi(:)'aul], *v.i.* (*a*) miauler; (*b*) *F:* chanter comme un chat.

miauling [mi:'auliŋ], *s.* miaulement *m.*

mica ['maikə], *s. Miner:* mica *m*; **rhombic m.,** phlogopite *f*; **pearl m.,** margarite *f*; **m. flakes,** écailles *f* de mica; **m. schist, m. slate,** schiste micacé; micaschiste *m*; mica schistoïde; **m.-schistose, -schistous,** micaschisteux; *El: etc:* **m. sheet,** feuille *f*, lamelle *f*, de mica; **m. plate,** plaque *f* en mica; **m. capacitor,** condensateur *m* au mica.

micaceous [mai'keiʃəs], *a.* micacé; **m. chalk,** tuf(f)eau *m.*

Micah ['maikə]. *Pr.n.m. B.Hist:* Michée.

micanite ['maikənait], *s. El:* micanite *f.*

micarta [mai'kɑ:tə], *s. R.t.m:* micarta *m.*

mice [mais]. *See* MOUSE[1].

micella, *pl.* **-ae** [mai'selə, -i:], **micelle** [mai'sel], *s. Ch: Biol:* micelle *f.*

micellar [mai'selər], *a. Ch: Biol:* micellaire.

Michael ['maikl]. *Pr.n.m.* Michel.

Michaelmas ['mikəlməs], *s.* **1.** la Saint-Michel; **M. term,** *Sch:* premier trimestre (de l'année scolaire); *Jur:* session *f* de la Saint-Michel. **2.** *Bot:* **M. daisy,** marguerite *f* de la Saint-Michel, marguerite d'automne; aster *m* œil-du-Christ.

Michelangelesque [maikəl'æn(d)ʒəlesk], *a. Art:* Michelangélesque.

Michelangelo [maikəl'æn(d)ʒəlou], *Pr.n.m. Art:* Michel-Ange; (*of museum*) **we have two Michelangelos,** nous avons deux œuvres de Michel-Ange.

Michigander [miʃi'gændər], *s. Geog:* habitant, -ante, du Michigan.

Michler ['miklər]. *Pr.n. Ch:* **Michler's ketone,** cétone *f* de Michler.

Mick, Mickey ['miki]. **1.** *Pr.n.m.* (*dim. of Michael*) Michel. **2.** *s. m. F: Pej:* Irlandais. **3.** *s. F:* **to take the m. out of s.o.,** se payer la tête de qn, faire marcher qn, mettre qn en boîte. **4.** *s.pl. F:* **mickies,** pommes de terres cuites aux braises. **5.** *s. F:* **Mickey Finn,** boisson droguée. **6.** *s. P:* **to do a mickey,** s'enfuir, déguerpir.

mickle ['mikl]. *A: & Scot:* **1.** *a.* (*a*) moult; beaucoup de; (*b*) grand. **2.** *s. Prov:* **many a little, many a pickle, makes a m.,** *F:* **many a m. makes a muckle,** les petits ruisseaux font les grandes rivières.

miconia [mai'kouniə], *s. Bot:* miconia *m*, miconie *f.*

micraster [mai'kræstər], *s. Paleont:* micraster *m.*

micro- [(')maikrou], *pref.* micro-.

microammeter [maikrou'æmitər], *s. El:* microampèremètre *m.*

microampère [maikrou'æmpɛər], *s. El:* microampère *m.*

microanalysis [maikrouə'nælisis], *s. Ch: Biol:* microanalyse *f.*

microanalyst [maikrou'ænəlist], *s. Ch: Biol:* microanalyste *mf.*

microanalytic(al) [maikrouænə'litik(l)], *a. Ch: Biol:* microanalytique.

microbalance [maikrou'bæləns], *s. Ph:* microbalance *f.*

microbar ['maikroubɑ:r], *s. Ph.Meas:* microbar *m.*

microbarograph [maikrou'bærəgræf], *s. Ph:* microbarographe *m.*

microbe ['maikroub], *s.* microbe *m.*

microbeam ['maikroubi:m], *s. Atom.Ph:* microfaisceau, -eaux *m.*

microbial, microbian [mai'kroubiəl, -iən], *a.* microbien; **m. disease,** maladie microbienne; **m. infection,** infection microbienne, microbisme *m* pathogène; **m. fermentation,** fermentation microbienne.

microbic [mai'kroubik], *a.* microbique, microbien.

microbicidal [mai'kroubisaidl], *a.* microbicide.

microbicide [mai'kroubisaid], *s.* microbicide *m.*

microbiologic(al) [maikroubaiə'lɔdʒik(l)], *a.* microbiologique.

microbiologist [maikroubai'ɔlədʒist], *s.* microbiologiste *mf.*

microbiology [maikroubai'ɔlədʒi], *s.* microbiologie *f.*

microbism ['maikroubizm], *s. Med:* microbisme *m*; **latent m.,** microbisme latent.

microblast ['maikroublæst], *s. Biol:* microblaste *m.*

microbus ['maikroubʌs], *s. Veh:* microbus *m.*

microcalorimeter [maikroukælɔ'rimitər], *s. Ph:* microcalorimètre *m.*

microcalorimetric [maikroukælɔri'metrik], *a. Ph:* microcalorimétrique.

microcalorimetry [maikroukælɔ'rimitri], *s. Ph:* microcalorimétrie *f.*

microcamera [maikrou'kæmərə], *s.* appareil *m* de microphotographie.

microcapsule [maikrou'kæpsjul], *s.* microcapsule *f.*

microcard ['maikroukɑ:d], *s.* microfiche *f.*

microcebus [maikrou'si:bəs], *s. Z:* microcèbe *m.*

microcephalic [maikrouse'fælik], *a. & s. Nat.Hist:* microcéphale (*mf*).

microcephalous [maikrou'sefələs], *a.* microcéphale.

microcephaly [maikrou'sefəli], *s.* microcéphalie *f.*

microchemical [maikrou'kemikl], *a.* microchimique; **m. analysis,** analyse *f* microchimique.

microchemically [maikrou'kemik(ə)li], *adv.* microchimiquement.

microchemistry [maikrou'kemistri], *s.* microchimie *f.*

Microchiroptera [maikroukai'rɔptərə], *s.pl. Z:* microchiroptères *m.*

microchiropteran [maikroukai'rɔptərən], *s. Z:* microchiroptère *m.*

microcinematographic [maikrousinimætə'græfik], *a.* microcinématographique.

microcinematography [mikrousinimə'tɔgrəfi], *s.* microcinématographie *f.*

microcircuit [maikrou'sə:kit], *s. Elcs:* microcircuit *m.*

microclimate [maikrou'klaimət], *s.* microclimat *m.*

microclimatic [maikrouklai'mætik], *a.* microclimatique.

microclimatologic(al) [maikrouklaimətə'lɔdʒik(l)], *a.* microclimatologique.

microclimatology [maikrouklaimə'tɔlədʒi], *s.* microclimatologie *f.*

microcline ['maikrouklain], *s. Miner:* microcline *f.*

micrococcus, *pl.* **-cocci** [maikrou'kɔkəs, -'kɔksai], *s. Biol:* micrococcus *m.*

microcode ['maikroukoud], *s. Cmptr:* micro-code *m, pl.* micro-codes.

micrococing ['maikroukoudiŋ], *s. Cmptr:* microprogrammation *f.*

microcopy[1] ['maikroukɔpi], *s.* cliché *m* de microfilm, reproduction *f* sur microfilm; photomicrographie *f.*

microcopy[2], *v.tr.* microfilmer, reproduire sur microfilm.

micro-corneal [maikrou'kɔ:niəl], *a. Opt:* micro-cornéen.

microcosm ['maikroukɔzm], *s.* microcosme *m.*

microcosmic [maikrou'kɔzmik], *a.* **1.** microcosmique. **2.** *Ch:* **m. salt,** phosphate *m* acide double d'ammoniaque et de soude.

microcosmus [maikrou'kɔzməs], *s. Moll:* microcosmus *m*, *F:* violet *m*, figue *f* de mer.

microcrystal [maikrou'kristəl], *s.* microcristal *m.*

microcrystalline [maikrou'kristəl(a)in], *a.* microcristallin.

microcurie [maikrou'kju:ri], *s. Ph.Meas:* microcurie *m.*

Microcyprini [maikrousi'pri:nai], *s.pl. Ich:* cyprinodontidés *m.*

microcyte ['maikrousait], *s. Physiol:* microcyte *m.*

microcythemia [maikrousai'θi:miə], *s. Med:* microcyt(h)émie *f.*

microcytic [maikrou'saitik], *a. Med:* microcytique; **m. anaemia,** anémie *f* microcytique.

microcytosis [maikrousai'tousis], *s. Med:* microcytose *f.*

microdactylia [maikroudæk'tiliə], *s.* microdactylie *f.*

microdactylous [maikrou'dæktiləs], *a.* microdactyle.

microdetector [maikroudi'tektər], *s. Elcs: Atom.Ph:* microdétecteur *m.*

microdissection [maikroudi'sekʃ(ə)n], *s. Biol:* microdissection *f.*

microdistillation [maikroudisti'leiʃ(ə)n], *s. Ch:* microdistillation *f.*

microdont ['maikroudɔnt], **microdontous** [maikrou'dɔntəs], *a.* microdonte, qui a de petites dents.

microdontia, microdontism, microdonty [maikrou'dɔntiə, -'dɔntizm, -'dɔnti], *s. Anat:* microdontisme *m*, nanisme *m* dentaire.

microdot ['maikroudɔt], *s.* micropoint *m.*

microeconomics [maikroui:kə'nɔmiks], *s.* micro-économie *f.*

micro-electronics [maikrouelek'trɔniks], *s.* micro-électronique *f.*

microelectrophoresis [maikrouilektroufɔ'ri:sis], *s.* micro-électrophorèse *f.*

microelement [maikrou'eləmənt], *s. Ch:* microélément *m.*

micro-encapsulation [maikrouenkæpsju'leiʃ(ə)n], *s.* microencapsulation *f.*

microengine ['maikrouendʒin], *s.* micro-moteur *m, pl.* micro-moteurs.

microevolution [maikroui:və'l(j)u:ʃ(ə)n], *s.* microévolution *f.*

microevolutionary [maikroui:və'l(j)u:ʃən(ə)ri], *a.* microévolutif.

microfacies [maikrou'feiʃii:z], *s. Geol:* microfaciès *m.*

microfarad [maikrou'færæd], *s. El.Meas:* microfarad *m.*

microfauna [maikrou'fɔ:nə], *s.* faune microbienne.

microfelsite [maikrou'felsait], *s. Miner:* microfelsite *f.*

microfibril(la) [maikrou'faibril, -fai'brilə], *s. Ch: Biol:* microfibrille *f.*

microfiche ['maikroufi:ʃ], *s. Cmptr: etc:* microfiche *f*; **to publish out-of-print volumes in m.,** publier les numéros épuisés (d'un périodique) en microfiches.

microfilaria [maikroufi'lɛəriə], *s.* microfilaire *f.*

microfilm[1] ['maikroufilm], *s.* microfilm *m*; **m. records,** archives *f*, documents *m*, sur microfilm; **m. file,** fichier *m* sur microfilm; **m. viewer,** lecteur *m*, visionneuse *f*, de microfilm.

microfilm[2], *v.tr.* microfilmer.

microfilmer ['maikroufilmər], *s.* **1.** (*pers.*) photographe *m* sur microfilm. **2.** (*device*) appareil *m* à microfilm.

microfilming ['maikroufilmiŋ], *s.* microfilmage *m.*

microflora [maikrou'flɔ:rə], *s.* flore microbienne.

microfossil ['maikroufɔsil], *s.* microfossile *m.*

microgamete [maikrou'gæmi:t], *s. Biol:* microgamète *m.*

microgametocyte [maikrougæ'mi:tousait], *s. Biol:* microgamétocyte *m.*
microgaster [maikrou'gæstər], *s. Ent:* microgastre *m.*
microglossia [maikrou'glɔsiə], *s. Med:* microglossie *f.*
micrognathia, micrognathism [maikro'neiθiə, -'neiθizm], *s. Med:* micrognathie *f.*
microgram ['maikrougræm], *s. Phot:* = MICROGRAPH[1].
microgram(me) ['maikrougræm], *s. Meas:* microgramme *m.*
microgranite ['maikrougrænit], *s. Miner:* microgranit(e) *m.*
microgranular [maikrou'grænjulər], *a. Miner:* microgrenu.
micrograph[1] ['maikrougræf], *s.* **1.** appareil *m* photographique pour préparation microscopique. **2.** micrographie *f*; **electron m.,** micrographie électronique.
micrograph[2], *v.tr.* micrographier.
micrographer [mai'krɔgrəfər], *s.* (*pers.*) micrographe *mf.*
micrographic [maikrou'græfik], *a.* micrographique.
micrography [mai'krɔgrəfi], *s.* micrographie *f.*
microgroove ['maikrougru:v], *s.* microsillon *m.*
microgyria [maikrou'dʒairiə], *s.* microgyrie *f.*
microhenry ['maikrouhenri], *s. El.Meas:* microhenry *m.*
microhm ['maikroum], *s. El.Meas:* microhm *m.*
microhmmeter ['maikroum(m)i:tər], *s. El.Meas:* microhmmètre *m*; micro-ohmmètre *m, pl.* micro-ohmmètres.
Microhylidae [maikrou'hailidi:], *s.pl. Amph:* microhylidés *m.*
micro-irradiation [maikrouireidi'eiʃ(ə)n], *s. Atom.Ph:* micro-irradiation *f.*
Microlepidoptera [maikroulepi'dɔptərə], *s.pl. Ent:* microlépidoptères *m.*
microlite ['maikroulait], *s.* **1.** *Miner:* microlite *f.* **2.** *Cryst:* microlite *m.*
microlith ['maikrouliθ], *s. Prehist:* microlit(h)e *m.*
microlithic [maikrou'liθik], *a. Prehist:* microlit(h)ique.
microlitic [maikrou'litik], *a. Geol:* microlitique.
micrological [maikrou'lɔdʒikl], *a.* micrologique.
micrology [mai'krɔlədʒi], *s.* micrologie *f.*
micromanipulation [maikroumænipju'leiʃ(ə)n], *s.* micromanipulation *f.*
micromanipulator [maikroumæ''nipjuleitər], *s.* micromanipulateur *m.*
micromanometer [maikroumæ'nɔmitər], *s. Ph:* micromanomètre *m.*
micromastia [maikrou'mæstiə], *s. Med:* micromastie *f.*
micromelia [maikrou'mi:liə], *s. Med:* micromélie *f.*
micromelic [maikrou'mi:lik], *a. Med:* micromélien.
micromere ['maikroumiər], *s. Biol:* micromère *m.*
micromerism [maikrou'miərizm], *s. Biol:* micromérisme *m.*
micromesh ['maikroumeʃ], *a. Com:* (bas) à mailles très fines.
micrometallography [maikroumetə'lɔgrəfi], *s.* micrométallographie *f.*
micrometeorite [maikrou'mi:tiərait], *s.* micrométéorite *m*; **m. detector plate,** plaquette *f* de détection des micrométéorites.
micrometer [mai'krɔmitər], *s.* micromètre *m*, palmer *m*; **depth m.,** palmer de profondeur; **external m., outside m.,** palmer extérieur; **internal m., inside m.,** palmer intérieur; **pneumatic m.,** micromètre pneumatique; **m. with clamp-screw,** micromètre avec vis d'arrêt; **m. with ratchet-stop,** micromètre avec bouton à friction, avec tête à friction; **m. balance,** microbalance *f*; **m. caliper(s), m. gauge,** calibre *m* à vis micrométrique; palmer; **sliding m. gauge,** compas *m* à coulisse; **m. dial,** cadran *m* micrométrique; **m. screw,** vis *f* micrométrique; **m. thimble,** poignée *f* de palmer; *Opt:* **m. eyepiece,** oculaire *m* à micromètre.
micromethod ['maikroumeθəd], *s.* microméthode *f.*
micrometric(al) [maikrou'metrik(l)], *a.* micrométrique.
micrometry [mai'krɔmitri], *s.* micrométrie *f.*
micromillimetre [maikrou'milimi:tər], *s. Meas:* **1.** micromillimètre *m*, millionième *m* de millimètre. **2.** = MICRON.
micromodule [maikrou'mɔdjul], *s. Elcs:* micro-module *m, pl.* micro-modules.
micromutation [maikroumju'teiʃ(ə)n], *s. Biol:* micromutation *f.*
micromycete [maikrou'maisi:t], *s. Fung:* micromycète *m.*
micron ['maikrɔn], *s. Meas:* micron *m*, millième *m* de millimètre.
Micronesia [maikrə'ni:ziə]. *Pr.n. Geog:* Micronésie *f.*
Micronesian [maikrə'ni:ziən]. *Geog:* (*a*) *a.* micronésien; (*b*) *s.* Micronésien, -ienne.
micronize ['maikrənaiz], *v.tr. Ch:* microniser.
micronuclear [maikrou'nju:kliər], *a. Prot:* micronucléaire.
micronucleate [maikrou'nju:klieit], *a. Prot:* micronucléé.
micronucleus [maikrou'nju:kliəs], *s. Prot:* micronucléus *m.*
micro-organic [maikrouɔ:'gænik], *a.* micro-organique, *pl.* micro-organiques.
micro-organism [maikrou'ɔ:gənizm], *s.* micro-organisme *m, pl.* micro-organismes.
micropal(a)eontologist [maikroupæliɔn'tɔlədʒist], *s.* micropaléontologiste *mf.*
micropal(a)eontology [maikroupæliɔn'tɔlədʒi], *s.* micropaléontologie *f.*
micropantograph [maikrou'pæntougræf], *s.* micrographe *m.*
microparticle [maikrou'pɑ:tikl], *s. Atom.Ph:* microparticule *f.*
microphage [maikrou'feidʒ], *s. Biol:* microphage *m.*
microphagous [mai'krɔfəgəs], *a. Biol:* microphage.
microphagy [mai'krɔfədʒi], *s. Biol:* microphagie *f.*
microphone ['maikrəfoun], *s.* microphone *m*; (*a*) *Tp: etc:* **carbon m.,** microphone à charbon; **carbon-dust, carbon-powder, m.,** microphone à poudre (de charbon); **carbon-granule m.,** microphone à grenaille (de charbon); **carbon-stick m.,** microphone à crayon; (*b*) *Elcs: etc:* **anti-noise m.,** microphone antivibrateur; **capacitor m., condenser m.,** microphone à condensateur, microphone électrostatique; **crystal m., piezo-electric m.,** microphone piézo-électrique; **diaphragmless m.,** microphone sans diaphragme, microphone statique; **(electro)dynamic m., moving-coil m.,** microphone électrodynamique; **electromagnetic m.,** microphone électromagnétique; **inset m.,** microphone à capsule; **magnetostrictive, magnetostriction, m.,** microphone à magnétostriction; **parabolic-horn m.,** microphone à concentrateur parabolique; **pressure m.,** microphone à pression; **pressure-gradient m.,** microphone à gradient de pression; **directional m.,** microphone directionnel; **semi-directional m.,** microphone semi-directionnel; **unidirectional m.,** microphone unidirectionnel; **bidirectional m.,** microphone bidirectionnel; **concealed m.,** microphone caché; espion *m*; (*worn under tie, etc.*) **miniature m.,** micro-cravate *m*; **neck, lapel, m.,** petit micro(phone) porté au cou, au revers d'un vêtement; **lip m.,** microphone de bouche, *F:* microphone moustache; *Av:* **throat m.,** laryngophone *m*; *Cin:* **following m.,** microphone mobile; (*c*) *attrib.* **m. adapter,** prise *f* pour microphone; **m. amplifier,** amplificateur *m* microphonique; **m. capsule, m. inset,** capsule *f*, pastille *f*, microphonique; **m. circuit,** circuit *m* microphonique; **m. hiss,** souffle *m* microphonique; **m. transformer,** transformateur *m* microphonique.
microphonic [maikrə'fɔnik], *a.* microphonique.
microphonicity [maikroufou'nisiti], *s. Ph: Elcs:* microphonicité *f*, sensibilité *f* à l'effet microphonique.
microphonics [maikrə'fɔniks], *s.pl.* (*usu. with sg. const.*) *Ph: Elcs:* **1.** microphonie *f.* **2.** effet *m* microphonique.
microphonous [mai'krɔfənəs], *a.* microphone.
microphony [mai'krɔfəni], *s.* = MICROPHONICITY.
microphotograph [maikrou'foutəgræf], *s.* microphotographie *f.*
microphotography [maikroufə'tɔgrəfi], *s.* microphotographie *f.*
microphotometer [maikroufə'tɔmitər], *s. Opt:* microphotomètre *m.*
microphotometric [maikroufoutou'metrik], *a. Opt:* microphotométrique.
microphthalmia [maikrɔf'θælmiə], *s.* microphtalmie *f.*
microphthalmic [maikrɔf'θælmik], *a.* microphtalme, microphtalmique.
microphyll ['maikroufil], *s. Bot:* microphylle *f.*
microphyllous [mai'krɔfiləs], *a. Bot:* microphylle.
microphysics [maikrou'fiziks], *s.pl.* (*usu. with sg. const.*) microphysique *f.*
microphysical [maikrou'fizikl], *a.* microphysique.
microphyte ['maikroufait], *s. Bot:* microphyte *m*; microbe végétal.
Micropodidae [maikrou'pɔdidi:], *s.pl. Orn:* micropodidés *m.*
Micropodiformes [maikroupɔdi'fɔ:mi:z], *s.pl. Orn:* micropodiformes *m.*
microporosity [maikroupɔ:'rɔsiti], *s.* microporosité *f.*
microprobe ['maikrouproub], *s.* micro-sonde *f, pl.* micro-sondes.
microprogram(me)[1] [maikrou'prougræm], *s. Cmptr:* microprogramme *m.*
microprogram(me)[2], *v.tr. Cmptr:* microprogrammer.
microprogramming [maikrou'prougræmiŋ], *s. Cmptr:* microprogrammation *f.*
micropsia, micropsy [mai'krɔpsiə, -'krɔpsi], *s. Med:* micropsie *f.*
micropterous [mai'krɔptərəs], *a. Orn: Ent:* microptère.
micropterygid [maikrɔp'teridʒid], *s. Ent:* microptérygide *m.*
Micropterygidae [maikrɔptə'ridʒidi:], *s.pl. Ent:* microptérygides *m.*
micropyle ['maikroupail], *s. Biol:* micropyle *m.*
microradiograph [maikrou'reidiougræf], *s.* microradiographie *f*, épreuve *f* microradiographique.
microradiographer [maikroureidi'ɔgrəfər], *s.* microradiographe *mf.*
microradiography [maikroureidi'ɔgrəfi], *s.* microradiographie *f.*
microradiometer [maikroureidi'ɔmitər], *s. Ph:* microradiomètre *m.*
microreader ['maikrouri:dər], *s.* microlecteur *m*, microliseuse *f*; lecteur *m*, visionneuse *f*, de microphotographie, de microfilm.
microray [maikrou'rei], *s.* = MICROWAVE.
microreproduction [maikrouri:prə'dʌkʃ(ə)n], *s.* (*a*) microreproduction *f* photographique; (*b*) reproduction *f* sur microfilm.
microscope ['maikrəskoup], *s.* microscope *m*; **binocular, monocular, m.,** microscope binoculaire, monoculaire; **compound, simple, m.,** microscope composé, simple; **light m.,** microscope optique; **phase m., phase-contrast m., phase-difference m.,** microscope à contraste de phase; **polarizing m.,** microscope polarisant; **ultraviolet m.,** microscope à ultra-violets; **X-ray m.,** microscope à rayons X; **dark field m.,** microscope en lumière noire; **field emission m.,** microscope à champ émissif; **two-stage m.,** microscope à deux longueurs d'onde; **electron m.,** microscope électronique; **proton m.,** microscope protonique; **to examine an object under the m.,** examiner un objet au microscope; **visible under the m.,** visible au microscope.
microscopic [maikrə'skɔpik], *a.* **1.** (animalcule, etc.) microscopique. **2. m. examination,** examen *m*, essai *m*, au microscope; essai microscopique; **m. anatomy,** anatomie *f* microscopique.
microscopically [maikrə'skɔpikəli], *adv.* **1.** (examiner qch.) au microscope. **2.** microscopiquement.
microscopist [mai'krɔskəpist], *s.* microscopiste *mf.*
microscopy [mai'krɔskəpi], *s.* microscopie *f.*
microsecond [maikrou'sekənd], *s.* microseconde *f.*
microseism ['maikrousaizm], *s. Geol:* micros(é)isme *m.*
microseismic [maikrou'saizmik], *a. Geol:* micros(é)ismique.
microseismograph [maikrou'saizmougræf], *s. Geol:* micros(é)ismographe *m.*
microseismometer [maikrousaiz'mɔmitər], *s. Geol:* micros(é)ismomètre *m.*
microseismometry [maikrousaiz'mɔmitri], *s. Geol:* micros(é)ismométrie *f.*
microsociology [maikrousousi'ɔlədʒi], *s.* microsociologie *f.*
microsoma, *pl.* **-somata, microsome** [maikrə'souma, -'soumətə, 'maikrəsoum], *s. Biol:* microsome *m.*
microsomia [maikrə'soumiə], *s.* microsomie *f*, microsomatie *f.*
microsommite [maikrou'sɔmait], *s. Miner:* microsommite *f.*
microspectroscope [maikrou'spektrəskoup], *s. Opt:* microspectroscope *m.*
microspectroscopy [maikrouspek'trɔskəpi], *s. Opt:* microspectroscopie *f.*
microsporange, microsporangium [maikrouspɔ'rændʒ, -'rændʒiəm], *s. Bot:* microsporange *m.*
microspore ['maikrouspɔər], *s.* **1.** *Med:* microsporon *m.* **2.** *Bot:* microspore *f.*
microsporiasis [maikrouspɔ'raiəsis], *s. Med:* microsporie *f.*
microsporon [mai'krɔspərən], *s. Med:* microsporon *m.*
microsporophyll [maikrou'spɔ:roufil], *s. Bot:* microsporophylle *m.*
microstome ['maikroustoum], *s. Ich:* microstome *m.*
microstomia [maikrou'stoumiə], **microstomus** [mai'krɔstəməs], *s. Med:* microstomie *f.*
microstomous [mai'krɔstəməs], *a. Med:* microstome.
microstructural [maikrou'strʌktjərəl], *a.* microstructural, -aux.
microstructure [maikrou'strʌktjər], *s.* microstructure *f*, structure *f* microscopique.
microswitch ['maikrouswitʃ], *s. El:* micro-contact *m*, *pl.* micro-contacts; micro-rupteur *m*, *pl.* micro-rupteurs.

microtasimeter [maikroutæ'simitər], *s. Ph:* microtasimètre *m.*

microtelephone [maikrou'telifoun], *s.* microtéléphone *m.*

microtext ['maikroutekst], *s.* texte microfilmé, sur microfilm.

microtherm ['maikrouθə:m], *s.* **1.** *Bot:* microtherme *f.* **2.** *Ph.Meas:* microthermie *f.*

microthermal [maikrou'θə:məl], *a. Ph:* microthermal, -aux.

microthermic [maikrou'θə:mik], *a. Ph:* microthermique.

microthoracic [maikrouθɔ:'ræsik], *a. Z:* microthoracique.

microthorax [maikrou'θɔ:ræks], *s. Z:* microthorax *m.*

Microtinae [mai'krɔtini:], *s.pl. Z:* microtinés *m.*

microtome ['maikroutoum], *s.* microtome *m*; **m. section,** tranche coupée au microtome, microtomique.

microtomy [mai'krɔtəmi], *s. Biol:* microtomie *f.*

microtron ['maikrətrɔn], *s. Atom.Ph:* microtron *m.*

microvolt ['maikrəvoult], *s. El.Meas:* microvolt *m.*

microvoltmeter [maikrə'voultmi:tər], *s. El:* microvoltmètre *m.*

microwatt ['maikrəwɔt], *s. El.Meas:* microwatt *m.*

microwave[1] ['maikrouweiv], *s. Elcs: W.Tel:* (*a*) micro-onde *f, pl.* micro-ondes; onde ultra-courte; onde centimétrique; **m. spectrum,** spectre *m* de micro-ondes, d'ondes ultra-courtes; *Mil:* **m. early warning,** radar *m* d'alerte sur dix centimètres; (*b*) hyperfréquence *f*; **m. receiver,** récepteur *m* d'hyperfréquences; **m. tube,** tube *m* hyperfréquences; (*c*) *attrib.* hertzien; **m. beam, m. link,** câble hertzien, faisceau hertzien; **m. relay,** relais hertzien.

microwave[2], *v.i.* transmettre sur hyperfréquences, sur micro-ondes.

microwear ['maikrouwɛər], *s. Prehist:* (*on flint instruments, etc.*) usure *f* microscopique, visible au microscope.

microzoan, microzoic [maikrou'zouən, -'zouik], *a.* microzoaire.

microzoon, *pl.* **-zoa** [maikrou'zouɔn, -'zouə], *s.* microzoaire *m.*

microzyma [maikrou'zaimə], **microzyme** ['maikrouzaim], *s. Biol:* microzyma *m.*

micrurgy ['maikrə:dʒi], *s.* micrurgie *f,* microchirurgie *f.*

micturate ['miktjureit], *v.i. Med:* uriner.

micturition [miktju'riʃ(ə)n], *s. Med:* **1.** micturition *f.* **2.** *F:* urination *f,* miction *f.*

mid [mid], *a.* (*a*) mi-, du milieu; **in m. afternoon,** au milieu de l'après-midi; **m. ocean sea,** haute mer, pleine mer; **in m. ocean,** au milieu de l'océan; **in m. channel,** au milieu du chenal; **in m. Channel,** au milieu de la Manche; à moitié chemin de la traversée; **in m. air,** entre ciel et terre; au milieu des airs; **from m. June to m. August,** de la mi-juin à la mi-août; **m. season,** demi-saison *f, pl.* demi-saisons; **m. Lent,** la mi-carême; *Mch:* **m. stroke,** mi-course *f* (du piston); *Hist:* **m.-Renaissance, m.-Victorian, style,** le style du milieu de la Renaissance, du milieu de l'époque victorienne; *St.Exch:* **m. month, m. (month) account, settlement,** le 15 du mois, la liquidation de quinzaine; *For:* **m. diameter,** diamètre *m* (d'un arbre) à mi-hauteur; *Cr:* **m. off,** (i) chasseur *m* en avant et à droite (du batteur); (ii) l'endroit où ce chasseur se tient; **m. on,** (i) chasseur en avant et à gauche (du batteur); (ii) l'endroit où ce chasseur se tient; **to stop in m. career,** rester, demeurer, en (beau) chemin; **to stop s.o. in m. career,** arrêter qn au milieu de sa course, en pleine course; **in m. course,** au milieu de sa carrière; en pleine carrière; (*b*) médian, moyen, central; *Mth: etc:* **m. line,** ligne médiane; **m. plane,** plan médian; **m. point,** point médian, moyen, central; **m. position,** position médiane, moyenne; **m. section,** section médiane; *Mec.E:* **m. bearing,** palier *m* intermédiaire; *Ling:* **m. vowel,** médiane *f*; *Elcs:* **m. value,** valeur centrale (d'une fréquence, etc.).

mid[2], *prep. Poet:* = AMID.

midbrain ['midbrein], *s. Anat:* = cerveau *m* moyen.

midday ['middei, 'mid'dei], *s.* midi *m*; **m. heat,** chaleur *f* de midi; chaleur méridienne; **m. meal,** repas *m* de midi.

midden ['midn], *s.* **1.** (tas *m* de) fumier *m*; **m. pit,** fosse *f* à fumier et à purin. **2.** *Prehist:* **kitchen m.,** kjœkkenmœdding *m.*

middle[1] ['midl]. **1.** *a.* du milieu; central, -aux; moyen, intermédiaire; **seated at the m. table,** assis à la table du milieu; **the m. house,** la maison du milieu; **m. position,** position médiale, centrale, intermédiaire; **m. wall,** mur *m* de refend; *Const:* **m. post,** poinçon *m* (de comble); **put this book on the m. shelf,** mettez ce livre sur le rayon du milieu; **the m. region of the air,** la moyenne région de l'air; **m. point of a straight line,** milieu d'une droite; **the m. points,** les points milieux; **to take a m. course,** prendre un parti moyen, un entre-deux; **there is no m. course,** il n'y a pas de milieu; *Lit:* il faut qu'une porte soit ouverte ou fermée; **m. age,** âge mûr; **man of m. age,** homme d'âge mûr; **to be past m. age,** être sur le retour; être sur le déclin (de la vie); *Hist:* **the M. Ages,** le moyen âge; **the m. class(es),** la classe moyenne; la bourgeoisie; **the upper, higher, m. class,** la haute bourgeoisie; **the lower m. class,** la petite bourgeoisie; **m.-class prejudices,** préjugés bourgeois; *Pej:* **it's terribly m. class!** c'est du dernier bourgeois! **m. name,** second prénom; *F:* **self-denial is my m. name,** je suis l'abnégation personnifiée; **m. size,** grandeur moyenne; *St.Exch:* **m. price,** cours moyen; *Log:* **m. (term),** moyen terme; *Gr.Gram:* **m. voice,** voix moyenne; *Ling:* **M. English,** moyen anglais; *Geog:* **(the) M. East,** le Moyen-Orient; **M. Eastern,** du Moyen-Orient; **(the) M. West,** les États de la Prairie; *Anat:* **m. ear,** l'oreille moyenne; barillet *m*; **m. finger,** médius *m,* doigt *m* du milieu; doigt majeur; *Nau:* **m. watch,** quart de minuit à quatre heures; *Typ:* **m. space,** espace moyen; *Husb:* **M. White,** porc blanc intermédiaire (de la race de Yorkshire). **2.** *s.* (*a*) milieu, centre *m*; **the m. of the century,** le milieu du siècle; **in the m. of. . .,** au milieu de . . .; **the ball hit him in the m. of the back,** la balle l'atteignit en plein dos; **to accost s.o. in the m. of the street,** aborder qn en pleine rue; **in the m. of the summer,** au cœur de l'été; en plein été; **about the m. of August,** à la mi-août; **in the very m. of. . ., right in the m. of . . .,** au beau milieu de . . .; **in the m. of the night,** en pleine nuit; **I was in the m. of reading,** j'étais en train de lire; j'étais en pleine lecture; (*b*) *F:* taille *f,* ceinture *f*; **round his m.,** autour de sa taille; **to seize s.o. round the m.,** prendre qn à bras-le-corps; **he was up to his m. in water,** il était dans l'eau jusqu'à la ceinture; **the water came up to his m.,** l'eau venait à mi-corps; **I've a pain in my m.,** j'ai mal au ventre.

middle[2], *v.tr.* **1.** *Tchn:* centrer (un poinçon, etc.); placer (qch.) au centre. **2.** *Nau:* plier (une voile) en deux.

middle-aged [midl'eidʒd], *a.* (*of pers.*) entre deux âges; d'un certain âge, d'âge mûr.

middleman, *pl.* **-men** ['midlmæn, -men], *s.m.* **1.** *Com:* intermédiaire, revendeur. **2.** *Pej:* entremetteur.

middlemost ['midlmoust], *a.* le plus au milieu; le plus au centre; central, -aux.

middle-of-the-road ['midləvðə'roud], *a.* (politique) modéré, du juste milieu.

middleweight ['midlweit], *a.* & *s. Box:* (poids *m*) moyen *m.*

middling ['midliŋ]. **1.** *a.* (*a*) (i) médiocre; (ii) passable, assez bon; *F:* **how are you?—m.,** comment allez-vous?—assez bien; pas mal; comme ci comme ça; (*b*) *Com:* entre-fin; bon ordinaire; de qualité moyenne. **2.** *adv. F:* assez bien; passablement; ni bien ni mal. **3.** *s.pl.* **middlings,** (*a*) *Com:* marchandises entre-fines; (*b*) *Mill:* issues *f* de blé; remoulage mêlé; recoupe *f*; (*c*) *Min:* mixtes *m.*

middy ['midi], *s. F:* **1.** *Nau:* aspirant *m* (de marine), *F:* midship. **2.** *Cost:* **m. (blouse),** marinière *f.*

Mideastern [mid'i:stən], *a.* du Moyen-Orient.

midge [midʒ], *s.* **1.** *Ent:* moucheron *m*; cousin *m.* **2.** = MIDGET 1.

midget ['midʒit], *s.* **1.** nain, *f.* naine; nabot, -ote; *F:* **she's a m.,** elle est minuscule; c'est une miniature. **2.** *attrib.* minuscule, miniature; **m. submarine,** sous-marin *m* de poche; **m. camera,** appareil *m* miniature; *Mec.E:* **m. chuck,** mandrin *m* miniature.

midi ['midi], *a.* & *s. Cost: F:* (jupe) de longueur moyenne; midi (*m*).

Midianite ['midiənait], *s. B.Hist:* Madianite *mf.*

midiron ['midaiən], *s. Golf:* fer moyen; crosse moyenne en fer.

midland ['midlənd]. **1.** *a.* (*a*) du centre (d'un pays); **the m. plains,** les plaines *f* du centre; (*b*) *A:* **the M. Sea,** la (mer) Méditerranée. **2.** *s.pl.* **the Midlands,** (i) les comtés *m* du centre (de l'Angleterre); (ii) les États *m* du centre (des États-Unis).

midleg ['midleg], *adv.* **m. (high, deep),** jusqu'à mi-jambe; jusqu'aux genoux; **to walk m. (deep) through the mud,** marcher enfoncé jusqu'à mi-jambe dans la boue; **to stand m. deep in water,** avoir de l'eau jusqu'à mi-jambe.

midmorning [mid'mɔ:niŋ], *a.* & *adv.* **m. coffee break,** pause-café *f* (au milieu de la matinée); **she always comes about m.,** elle arrive toujours au milieu de la matinée.

midmost ['midmoust]. **1.** *a.* (le) plus près du milieu; central, -aux. **2.** *adv. Lit:* tout au centre de . . ..

midnight ['midnait], *s.* minuit *m*; *Astr:* **Greenwich, local, apparent m.,** minuit apparent de Greenwich, local; **towards m.,** vers minuit; **on the stroke of m.,** sur le coup de minuit; **m. mass,** messe *f* de minuit; **m. sun,** soleil *m* de minuit; **the land of the m. sun,** l'Arctique *f*; **to take the m. train,** prendre le train de minuit; **to burn the m. oil,** travailler, veiller, fort avant dans la nuit.

midnoon ['mid'nu:n], *s. A:* = MIDDAY.

midrib ['midrib], *s. Bot:* nervure médiane, côte *f* (d'une feuille).

midriff ['midrif], *s. Anat:* diaphragme *m*; **to get a blow in the m.,** recevoir un coup au creux de l'estomac; *F:* **I've got sunburnt in the m. because of my two-piece swimsuit,** j'ai un coup de soleil au milieu (du corps) à cause de mon (maillot) deux-pièces.

midsection [mid'sekʃən], *s.* section médiane; partie médiane, centrale.

midship[1] ['midʃip], *s. N.Arch:* milieu *m* du navire; **m. frame,** maître couple *m*; **half m. section,** demi-coupe *f* au maître.

midship[2], *v.tr. Nau:* **to m. the helm,** mettre la barre à zéro.

midshipman, *pl.* **-men** ['midʃipmən], *s.m. Nau:* aspirant (de marine); *F:* midship.

midships ['midʃips], *adv. Nau:* au milieu du navire; par le travers.

midst [midst], *s.* (*a*) **in the m. of sth.,** au milieu de, parmi, qch.; **in the m. of his work,** au milieu de son travail; **in the m. of pleasure,** au milieu des plaisirs; **in the m. of the storm,** au milieu, au fort, de l'orage; **in the m. of winter,** en plein hiver; au cœur de l'hiver; **in the m. of all this,** sur ces entrefaites; **I was in the m. of reading,** j'étais en train de lire; (*b*) **in our, your, their, m.,** au milieu de nous, de vous, d'eux; parmi nous, vous, eux.

midstream [mid'stri:m], *s.* **in m.,** au milieu du courant.

midsummer ['midsʌmər], *s.* (*a*) milieu *m* de l'été; plein *m* de l'été; cœur *m* de l'été; (*b*) le solstice d'été; **m. day,** la Saint-Jean.

midway [mid'wei]. **1.** *adv.* à mi-chemin, à moitié chemin; **m. up the hill,** à mi-côte; **m. between . . . and . . .,** à mi-distance, à mi-chemin, entre . . . et . . .; **a style m. between X's and Y's,** un style intermédiaire entre celui de X et celui de Y. **2.** *s. U.S:* allée centrale (d'une exposition).

midweek [mid'wi:k], (*a*) *s.* milieu *m* de la semaine; *attrib.* **m. party,** réunion *f* au milieu de la semaine; (*b*) *adv.* **I don't go out much m.,** je ne sors pas beaucoup au milieu de la semaine.

midwife, *pl.* **-wives** ['midwaif, -waivz], *s.f.* sage-femme, *pl.* sages-femmes; accoucheuse.

midwifery ['midwif(ə)ri], *s.* **1.** profession *f* de sage-femme. **2.** obstétrique *f*; tocotechnie *f.*

midwinter ['mid'wintər], *s.* (*a*) milieu *m* de l'hiver, fort *m* de l'hiver, cœur *m* de l'hiver; *attrib.* **m. frosts,** gelées *f* du fort de l'hiver; **m. weather on midsummer day,** un temps d'hiver à la Saint-Jean; **a real m. day,** une vraie journée d'hiver; (*b*) le solstice d'hiver.

mien [mi:n], *s. Lit:* mine *f,* air *m,* contenance *f,* aspect *m* (de qn); **lofty m.,** port hautain.

miersite ['mi:əsait], *s. Miner:* miersite *f.*

miff[1] [mif], *s. F: O:* **1.** boutade *f*; accès *m* d'humeur; fâcherie *f*; **to be in a m.,** être de mauvaise humeur. **2.** pique *f,* brouille *f* (entre deux personnes).

miff[2]. *F: O:* **1.** *v.i.* se brouiller, se fâcher (**with s.o.,** avec qn); **to m. at sth.,** prendre la mouche au sujet de qch. **2.** *v.tr.* **to be miffed,** être froissé, piqué, fâché.

might[1] [mait], *s.* **1.** puissance *f,* force(s) *f*(*pl*); **the m. of God,** la puissance de Dieu; *O:* **man of m.,** homme fort et vaillant; **to work with all one's m.,** travailler de toute sa force, de toutes ses forces; **m. against right,** la force contre le droit; le droit du plus fort; *Prov:* **m. is right,** force passe droit; la force prime le droit; la raison du plus fort est toujours la meilleure; les gros poissons mangent les petits. **2.** *A: Dial:* grande quantité, tas *m* (de difficultés, etc.).

might[2], *v. see* MAY[1].

might-have-been ['maitəvbi:n], *s. F:* **he's a m.-h.-b.,** c'est un raté.

mightily ['maitili], *adv.* **1.** puissamment, fortement, vigoureusement. **2.** *F:* extrêmement, fameusement; **we enjoyed ourselves m.,** on s'est fameusement, rudement, amusé(s).

mightiness ['maitinis], *s.* **1.** puissance *f,* force *f*; grandeur *f.* **2.** *Iron:* **His High and Mightiness,** sa Toute-Puissance (un tel).

mighty ['maiti]. **1.** *a.* (*a*) puissant, fort; **a m. nation,** une grande nation; *B:* **m. works,** miracles *m,* prodiges *m*; *s. B:* **he hath put down the m. from their seats,** il a renversé de dessus leurs trônes les puissants; (*b*) grand, vaste, grandiose; (*c*) *F:* grand, considérable; **there was a m. bustle,** il ya eu un grand remue-ménage; **you're in a m. hurry,** vous êtes diablement pressé. **2.** *adv. F:* fort, extrêmement, rudement; **that's m. good,** c'est rudement bon; **you're making a m. big mistake,** vous commettez là une fameuse erreur.

migmatite ['migmətait], *s. Geol:* migmatite *f.*

mignonette [minjə'net], *s.* **1.** *Bot:* réséda odorant; *F:* herbe *f* d'amour. **2. m. (lace),** mignonnette *f.*

migraine ['mi:grein], *s. Med:* migraine *f.*

migrainous [mi'greinəs], *a. Med:* migraineux.

migrant ['maigrənt]. **1.** *a.* (*a*) = MIGRATORY 1; (*b*) *Med:* (érysipèle, etc.) ambulant. **2.** *s.* (*pers., bird, etc.*) migrateur, -trice; (*pers.*) émigrant, -ante; nomade *mf*; **migrants like the swallow,** les oiseaux émigrants comme l'hirondelle.

migrate [mai'greit], *v.i.* (*of pers.*) émigrer, passer (**from one country to another,** d'un pays dans un autre); (*of birds*) émigrer, voyager; *Geol:* migrer.

migration [mai'greiʃ(ə)n], *s.* **1.** (*a*) migration *f* (des oiseaux, etc.); foule *f* (du caribou); **the mass m. of holidaymakers to southern countries,** la migration massive des vacanciers vers les pays méridionaux; (*b*) émigration *f.* **2.** (*a*) *Ch: Ph:* migration (des éléments, de l'énergie, etc.); **ion m.,** migration d'ions; **surface m.,** migration superficielle; **m. area,** aire *f* de migration; **m. length,** longueur *f* de migration; (*b*) *Geol:* migration (du pétrole brut, du gaz, à travers les roches); (*c*) *Biol:* migration (de cellules, de tissus, etc.); **epithelial m.,** migration épithéliale; **distal m.,** migration distale, distogression *f*; **mesial m.,** migration mésiale, mésiogression *f.*

migrator [mai'greitər], *s.* = MIGRANT 2.

migratory ['maigrət(ə)ri, mai'greitəri], *a.* **1.** (peuple) migrateur, nomade; (travailleur) saisonnier; (tribu) migratrice; (oiseau) migrateur, émigrant, voyageur, de passage; (gibier) nomade. **2.** (mouvement) migratoire.

mihrab ['miəræb], *s.* (*of mosque*) mihrâb *m.*

mike[1] [maik], *s. F:* **1.** microphone *m, F:* micro *m.* **2.** *esp. Med:* microscope *m.* **3.** *Mec.E:* micromètre *m.*

mike[2], *v.i. P:* paresser; tirer au flanc.

Mike[3]. *Pr.n.m.* (*dim. of Michael*) Michel; *F:* **for the love of M.,** pour l'amour de Dieu.

mil [mil], *s.* **1.** *Meas:* (*a*) *Pharm:* millilitre *m*; (*b*) *Ind:* millième *m* de pouce (unité de mesure des fils métalliques); (*c*) *Artil:* millième (unité d'angle). **2.** *Com:* **so much per m.,** tant par mille.

milage ['mailidʒ], *s.* = MILEAGE.

Milanese [milə'ni:z]. **1.** *Geog:* (*a*) *a.* milanais; de Milan; (*b*) *s.* Milanais, -aise; (*c*) *Hist:* **the M.,** le Milanais. **2.** *s. Tex:* milanaise *f,* milanèse *f.*

milarite ['milərait], *s. Miner:* milarite *f.*

milch [miltʃ], *a. Husb:* à lait, laitière; **m. cow,** (i) (vache) laitière *f*; (ii) *F:* (*pers.*) vache à lait; **m. ewe,** brebis allaitante.

milcher ['miltʃər], *s.* (vache, etc.) laitière *f.*

mild [maild], *a.* **1.** (*of pers., remark*) doux *f.* douce; **m. look,** air doux; **to be m. tempered,** être d'une disposition douce; **m. reply,** réponse conciliatrice; **m. criticism,** critique anodine; **the mildest man alive,** le plus doux des hommes; *Lit:* **as m. as a dove, as milk,** doux comme un mouton, douce comme une colombe. **2.** (*of regulation, punishment*) doux, peu sévère, peu rigoureux; **milder measures,** des mesures moins rigoureuses; **m. punishment,** punition légère. **3.** (climat) doux, tempéré; (air) tiède; (ciel) clément; (hiver) doux, bénin; **the weather is getting milder,** le temps s'adoucit, devient plus doux; **it has turned milder with the south wind,** le vent du sud a radouci le temps. **4.** (*a*) (plat) doux, peu relevé; (médicament) doux, bénin; (tabac) doux; **m. cigar,** cigare doux, suave; **m. laxative,** purgatif bénin, qui agit doucement; *O:* **m. beer,** *s.* **mild,** bière brune (sous pression); *F: O:* **draw it m.!** tout doux! n'exagérez pas! ne vous emballez pas! (*b*) *Med:* bénin, *f.* bénigne; clément; **a m. form of measles,** une forme bénigne de la rougeole. **5.** (exercice) modéré; (amusement) innocent, anodin; **m. applause,** applaudissements *m* peu enthousiastes; **the play was a m. success,** la pièce a obtenu un succès d'estime, un succès modéré; **to make only the mildest of efforts,** ne faire qu'un faible effort. **6. m. steel,** acier doux.

milden ['maild(ə)n]. *O:* **1.** *v.tr.* adoucir; rendre plus doux. **2.** *v.i.* s'adoucir; devenir plus doux.

mildew[1] ['mildju:], *s.* **1.** (*a*) *Agr:* rouille *f* (sur le froment, etc.); (*b*) mildiou *m,* mildew *m* (sur les vignes, les arbres, etc.); *Vit:* rosée *f* de farine; oïdium *m* (des vignes); **apple m.,** (i) oïdium du pommier; (ii) podosphaera *m*; **rose m.,** blanc *m* du rosier; *Winem:* **m. specks,** fleurs *f* de vin; (*c*) chancissure *f* (sur le pain, etc.). **2.** moisissure *f,* taches *fpl* d'humidité, piqûres *fpl* (sur le papier, le cuir).

mildew[2]. **1.** *v.tr.* (*a*) *Agr:* rouiller, moisir (une plante); frapper (une plante) de rouille, de mildiou; (*b*) (*of damp, etc.*) piquer (le papier, etc.); chancir (le pain, les confitures). **2.** *v.i.* (*a*) (*of plant*) se rouiller, se moisir; (*b*) (*of paper, etc.*) se piquer.

mildewed ['mildjud], *a.* **1.** (*a*) (blé) rouillé; (*b*) **m. vine,** vigne mildiousée, atteinte de mildiou, de mildew; (*c*) (pain, etc.) chanci. **2.** (papier, etc.) piqué, taché d'humidité.

mildewy ['mildjui], *a.* **1.** (blé) moisi, rouillé; atteint de mildiou; mildiousé. **2.** (odeur *f*) de moisi.

mildly ['maildli], *adv.* **1.** doucement; avec douceur. **2.** modérément; **to put it m.,** pour ne pas en dire plus.

mildness ['maildnis], *s.* **1.** douceur *f,* clémence *f* (de qn, du temps); caractère anodin (d'une critique); légèreté *f* (d'une punition). **2.** *Med:* bénignité *f* (d'une maladie).

mile [mail], *s. Meas:* mille *m*; **five miles,** cinq milles, = huit kilomètres; **statute m.,** mille anglais (1609 m 31); **nautical m., geographical m.,** mille marin (= 1853 m 25); **international nautical m.,** mille marin international (= 1852 m); **measured m.,** base *f* (pour essais de vitesse); *Sp:* **four minute m.,** mille couru en quatre minutes; **square m.,** mille carré; **speed limit of 50 miles an hour,** vitesse limitée à 50 milles à l'heure, = à 80 kilomètres à l'heure; **my car does 25 miles to the gallon,** ma voiture fait 25 milles au gallon, = *approx.* fait onze litres au 100 kilomètres; **a thirty m. journey,** un voyage de trente milles, = d'une cinquantaine de kilomètres; *Mil:* **they attacked on a m. front,** ils ont attaqué sur un front de bataille d'un mille; **for miles and miles you can see nothing but trees,** on parcourt des kilomètres sans voir autre chose que des arbres; **he lives miles away,** il habite loin d'ici; il habite au diable; *F:* **to be miles away,** être dans la lune; *F:* **he's miles better,** (i) il va beaucoup mieux; (ii) il vaut infiniment mieux; **nobody comes, is, within a m. of him,** personne ne lui monte à la cheville; *F:* **you can see it a m. off,** ça se voit à une lieue, d'une lieue; *F:* **it sticks out, stands out, a m.,** ça vous crève les yeux, ça vous saute aux yeux.

mileage ['mailidʒ], *s.* (*a*) distance *f* en milles; *Fr.C:* millage *m*; = kilométrage *m*; **m. of a rail(road) system,** longeur *f* des lignes d'un réseau; **daily m.,** parcours kilométrique journalier; parcours journalier (d'une locomotive); *Aut:* **the m. on our speedometer is 10,000,** notre compteur marque 10.000 milles; **m. minder,** compteur totalisateur; **car with a very small m.,** voiture qui a très peu roulé; **what m. do your tyres do?** quelle est la durée kilométrique de vos pneus? (*for train, taxi, etc.*) **m. rate,** tarif *m* par mille; *Adm: Com: etc:* **m. (allowance),** indemnité *f* de déplacement.

mileometer [mai'lɔmitər], *s. Aut: etc:* compteur *m* kilométrique.

milepost ['mailpoust], *s.* borne routière.

Milesian[1] [m(a)i'li:ziən]. *A.Geog:* (*a*) *a.* milésien, milésiaque; (*b*) *s.* Milésien, -ienne; Milésiaque *mf.*

Milesian[2]. (*a*) *s. Myth:* descendant, -ante, de Milésius (dont les fils conquirent l'Irlande); (*b*) *A:* (i) *a.* irlandais; (ii) *s.* Irlandais, -aise.

milestone ['mailstoun], *s.* (*a*) borne routière, = borne kilométrique; (*b*) événement important; **this discovery is a m. in cancer research,** cette découverte marque une étape importante dans les recherches sur le cancer; **these events stand out as milestones in his career,** ces événements jalonnent sa carrière.

Miletus [mi'li:təs]. *Pr.n. A.Geog:* Milet *m.*

milfoil ['milfɔil], *s. Bot:* millefeuille *f*; **musk m.,** génépi (musqué); **water m.,** (i) volant *m* d'eau; (ii) millefeuille aquatique.

Milian ['mi:liən], (*a*) *a.* mélien, de Milo; (*b*) *s.* Mélien, -ienne.

miliaria [mili'ɛəriə], *s. Med:* fièvre *f* miliaire; suette *f* miliaire; miliaire *f.*

miliary ['miliəri], *a. Physiol: Med:* miliaire; **m. fever,** fièvre *f* miliaire *f,* suette *f* miliaire; **m. eruption,** millet *m.*

milieu ['mi:ljə:], *s.* milieu (social, géographique); **guests drawn from every m.,** des invités de tous les milieux.

miliola [mi'laioulə], *s. Prot:* miliole *f.*

militancy ['militənsi], *s.* esprit militant; militantisme *m.*

militant ['militənt]. **1.** *a.* militant; **the Church m.,** l'Église militante; *Hist:* **m. suffragette,** *s.* **m.,** suffragette *f* activiste. **2.** *s. Pol: etc:* **the militants,** les activistes *mf*; les partisans, -anes, de l'action directe.

militarily ['militərili], *adv.* militairement; **to occupy a town m.,** occuper une ville militairement.

militarism ['militərizm], *s.* militarisme *m.*

militarist ['militərist], *s.* militariste *mf.*

militarization [milit(ə)rai'zeiʃ(ə)n], *s.* militarisation *f.*

militarize ['militəraiz], *v.tr.* militariser.

military ['milit(ə)ri]. **1.** *a.* militaire; (*a*) **m. authorities,** autorités *f* militaires; **under m. control,** sous l'autorité, sous contrôle, militaire; **m. government,** gouvernement *m* militaire, dans les mains des militaires; stratocratie *f*; **m. man,** militaire *m*; **m. age,** âge *m* de servir, de la conscription; **m. service,** service *m* militaire; **available, fit, for m. service,** bon pour le service (militaire); **m. status,** statut *m* militaire; **m. records,** état(s) *m*(*pl*) de service; **m. area,** (i) zone *f* militaire; (ii) région *f,* subdivision *f,* militaire; **m. reservation,** domaine *m,* terrain *m,* militaire; *Can:* **m. district,** région militaire; **m. subdistrict,** subdivision militaire; **m. aviation,** aviation *f* militaire; **m. airfield,** champ *m* d'aviation militaire; (*b*) *Jur:* **m. court, m. tribunal,** tribunal *m* militaire; **m. jurisdiction,** juridiction *f* militaire; **m. justice,** justice *f* militaire; **m. law,** code *m* (de justice) militaire; **subject to m. law,** justiciable des tribunaux militaires; **m. offence,** délit *m* ressortissant aux tribunaux militaires; **m. police,** police *f* militaire, police aux armées, prévôté *f*; **m. policeman,** membre *m* de la police militaire, de la prévôté; *F:* prévôt *m*; (*c*) *Med: A:* **m. fever,** fièvre *f* des armées; peste *f* de guerre; le typhus; la fièvre typhoïde. **2.** *s.pl. coll.* **the m.,** les militaires *m,* les soldats *m*; la force armée; l'armée *f*; **the m. were called in,** on fit venir la force armée.

militate ['militeit], *v.i.* **1.** militer (**in favour of, against,** en faveur de, contre); **facts that m. against the prisoner,** faits *m* qui militent contre l'accusé. **2.** *A:* servir (dans l'armée); se battre, combattre.

militia [mi'liʃə], *s.* (*a*) milice *f*; = garde nationale; **m. troops,** milices; (*b*) *U.S: F:* hommes d'âge militaire.

militiaman, *pl.* **-men** [mi'liʃəmən], *s.m.* milicien, soldat de la milice; = garde national.

milk[1] [milk], *s.* **1.** (*a*) lait *m*; **new m.,** lait (encore) chaud; lait du jour; **m. fresh from the cow,** lait fraîchement trait; **raw m.,** lait cru; **chilled m.,** lait frappé; **whole m.,** lait entier; **homogenized m.,** lait homogénéisé; **tuberculin tested,** *F:* **TT, m.,** lait cru certifié; **curdled m.,** lait caillé; **cow in m.,** vache *f* en train de donner du lait; **m. diet,** régime lacté, diète lactée; **to go on (to) a m. diet,** se mettre au lait; **m. and vegetable diet,** régime lacto-végétarien; **m. foods,** laitage *m*; **m. jelly, jellied m.,** lait gélifié; **m. loaf,** pain *m* de fantaisie; **m. powder, powdered m.,** lait en poudre; *Cu:* **m. pudding,** riz *m,* sagou *m,* tapioca *m,* etc., au lait; entremets sucré au lait; crème *f* (à la vanille, etc.); **m. punch,** lait au rhum; **m. shake,** lait battu, fouetté; **chocolate m. shake,** frappé *m* au chocolat; **m. chocolate,** chocolat *m* au lait; **m. toast,** pain perdu; **with m.,** au lait; **m. jug,** pot *m* à, au, lait; **m. bottle,** bouteille *f* à lait; **m. pail,** seau *m* à lait; **m. pan,** jatte *f,* terrine *f* (à lait); (**domestic**) **m. can,** boîte *f* à lait; (**dairyman's**) **m. can,** berthe *f*; **m. gauge, tester,** lacto-densimètre *m, pl.* lacto-densimètres; lactomètre *m,* pèse-lait *m inv*; **m. round,** tournée *f* de laitier; **m. float,** *A:* **m. cart,** voiture *f* de laitier; **m. train,** train *m* qui s'arrête à toutes les gares; **m. bar,** milk-bar *m, pl.* milk-bars; *F:* **to come home with the m.,** rentrer au petit jour; *Lit:* **land of m. and honey,** pays *m* de cocagne; **the m. of human kindness,** le lait de la tendresse humaine, de l'humaine tendresse; **m. and water,** lait coupé (d'eau); **m.-and-water (literature, discipline),** (littérature *f,* discipline *f*) fade, insipide, sans sel, à l'eau de rose; **m. white,** blanc comme du lait, d'une blancheur de lait; (liquide) lactescent; **m. white stone, gem,** pierre laiteuse; *Prov:* **it's no use crying over spilt m.,** ce qui est fait est fait; inutile de pleurer, ça ne changera rien; à chose faite point de remède; (*b*) *Med: F:* **m. crust,** croûtes *fpl* de lait; **m. fever,** fièvre laiteuse, fièvre lactée, fièvre de lait; *F:* **m. leg,** leucophlegmasie *f*; œdème blanc douloureux; *Anat:* **m.-bearing (gland, etc.),** (glande, etc.) galactogène; **m. duct,** vaisseau *m* galactophore; **m. tooth,** dent *f* de lait; **m. teeth,** dentition *f* de lait; dents de lait; *Toil:* **cleansing m.,** lait démaquillant, de démaquillage; (*c*) *Bot:* **m. thistle,** chardon argenté; chardon Marie; lait Sainte-Marie; **m. vetch,** tragacanthe *f,* astragale *m*; **m. tree,** galactodendron *m*; arbre *m* à lait; **m. willowherb,** salicaire *f*; (*d*) *Fung:* **m. cap,** lactaire *m*; **saffron m. cap,** lactaire délicieux; *Orn:* **pigeon('s) m.,** lait de pigeon; (*e*) *Glassm:* **m. glass,** opaline *f.* **2.** lait, eau *f* (de noix de coco); **m. of almonds, of lime,** lait d'amandes, de chaux; **m. of sulphur,** lait de soufre.

milk[2], *v.tr.* **1.** traire (une vache, etc.); *F: O:* **to m. the ram, the bull,** vouloir accomplir des impossibilités; entreprendre l'impossible. **2.** *F:* dépouiller, écorcher (qn); exploiter (qn); **to m. the till,** barboter la caisse. **3.** (*a*) **to m. sap from a tree,** saigner un arbre; **to m. the venom from a snake,** capter le venin d'un serpent; (*b*) *Tg: Tp: F: O:* **to m. a message, to m. the wire,** capter une communication (à l'écoute).

milker ['milkər], *s.* **1.** (*a*) (*pers.*) trayeur, -euse; (*b*) **mechanical m.,** trayeuse mécanique. **2.** (*cow, etc.*) **good, bad m.,** bonne, mauvaise laitière.

milkiness ['milkinis], *s.* couleur laiteuse, trouble laiteux, aspect laiteux, lactescence *f* (d'un liquide, etc.).

milking ['milkiŋ], *s.* **1.** traite *f,* mulsion *f* (d'une vache, etc.); **m. machine,** trayeuse *f* mécanique. **2.** *Tg: Tp: F: O:* captation *f* (d'une communication). **3.** *El:* **m. cell,** élément *m* supplémentaire d'une batterie.

milkmaid ['milkmeid], *s.f.* trayeuse; fille de laiterie.

milkman, *pl.* **-men** ['milkmən], *s.m.* (*a*) laitier, crémier; (*b*) livreur de lait.

milksop ['milksɔp], *s. F:* poule mouillée; poule laitée; poltron *m*; **you little m.!** petit peureux!

milkweed ['milkwi:d], *s. Bot:* plante *f* à suc laiteux; *esp.* (*a*) laiteron *m*, lait *m* d'âne; (*b*) fenouil *m* de porc; (*c*) réveille-matin *m inv*; (*d*) *U.S:* asclépiade *f* de Syrie; plante *f* à soie; apocyn *m* à ouate soyeuse; soyeuse *f*; coton *m* sauvage.

milkwort ['milkwɔ:t], *s. Bot:* **1.** polygale commun; laitier *m*; herbe *f* au lait. **2. sea m.,** glaux *m*; glauque *f*.

milky ['milki], *a.* laiteux; lactescent; blanchâtre; (*of gem*) pâteux; *Astr:* **the M. Way,** la Voie lactée; la Galaxie; *El:* **m. accumulator,** accumulateur perlé, laiteux.

mill[1] [mil], *s.* **1.** (*a*) **(flour) m.,** moulin *m* (à farine); (*large*) minoterie *f*; **m. hopper,** trémie *f*; **m. leat, run, race,** bief *m* de moulin; chenal, -aux *m*; coursier *m*; **m. wheel,** roue *f* de moulin; **m. cake,** (i) *Husb:* tourteau *m*; (ii) *Exp:* bloc *m* de poudre; *F:* **to put s.o. through the m.,** passer qn au laminoir, en faire voir de dures à qn; faire passer qn par la filière; **he's been through the m.,** il a passé par de rudes épreuves; il a mangé de la vache enragée; il en a vu de dures, de toutes les couleurs; (*of artist, etc.*) il a de l'acquis, il est passé par l'école; **m. hand,** ouvrier de minoterie; garçon meunier; *F:* **run of the m.,** banal; quelconque; **it was very much a run of the m. play,** c'était chose quotidienne, normale; *F:* cela faisait partie du programme; (*b*) **coffee m., pepper m.,** moulin à café, à poivre; **vegetable m.,** moulin à légumes; (*c*) **(crushing) m.,** broyeur *m*, concasseur *m*; **roller m.,** broyeur à meules horizontales; **cutter-type m.,** broyeur à couteaux; **ink m.,** broyeur d'encre; **paint m.,** broyeur malaxeur; **kneading m.,** malaxeur *m*; (*d*) **cider m.,** pressoir *m* (à pommes); **cane m.,** moulin à canne (à sucre). **2.** (*a*) **lapidary's m.,** meule *f* lapidaire; lapidaire *m*; (*b*) *Metalw:* **(rolling) m.,** laminoir *m*, train *m* (de laminage); **blooming, cogging, m.,** laminoir, train, ébaucheur; **roughing m.,** laminoir, train, dégrossisseur; **finishing m.,** laminoir, train, finisseur; **reversing m.,** train réversible; **two-high, three-high, m.,** laminoir duo, trio; **universal m.,** laminoir universel; **bar m.,** laminoir, train, à barres; **continuous bar m.,** train continu à barres; **merchant m.,** laminoir, train, marchand, à fers marchands; **rail m.,** laminoir à rails; **(heavy) plate, medium plate, m.,** laminoir, train, à grosses tôles, à tôles moyennes; **sheet m.,** laminoir, train, à tôles minces; **strip m.,** laminoir à bandes, à feuillards; **wide-strip m.,** laminoir, train, à larges bandes; **section m., shape rolling m.,** laminoir à, pour, profilés; (*c*) *Num:* **m. (and screw),** presse *f* monétaire. **3.** *Tls:* fraise *f*, fraiseuse *f*; **side m.,** fraise de côté, fraise latérale; **face m.,** fraise de face, fraise plane, fraise à surfacer; **end m.,** fraise en bout; **two-lipped end m.,** fraise en bout à deux arêtes de coupe; **spiral-fluted m.,** fraise hélicoïdale; **roughing, finishing, slot m.,** fraise à dégrossir, à finir les rainures; **slot m.,** fraise à rainurer. **4.** (*a*) usine *f*, *esp.* usine textile; **spinning m.,** filature *f*; **weaving m.,** usine de tissage; **cotton m.,** filature de coton; **cloth m.,** fabrique *f* de drap; **m. hand,** ouvrier, -ière, textile, de filature; **m. girl,** ouvrière de filature; (*b*) **sugar m.,** raffinerie *f* de sucre; **(olive, vegetable) oil m.,** huilerie *f*; moulin à huile; **paper m.,** papeterie *f*, fabrique *f* de papier; **m. finish(ing),** apprêt *m*, apprêtage *m* (du papier). **5.** *F:* bagarre *f*; combat *m* à coups de poing; assaut *m* de boxe. **6.** *Crust:* **gastric m.,** moulinet *m* gastrique. **7.** *Min:* cheminée *f* à minerai.

mill[2]. **1.** *v.tr.* (*a*) moudre (le blé, la farine); (*b*) broyer; bocarder (du minerai); (*c*) *Tex:* fouler (le drap); (*d*) *Mec.E:* fraiser, tailler (des engrenages, etc.); **to m. between centres,** fraiser entre pointes; **to m. off,** enlever à la fraise; **to m. out a part,** travailler une pièce à la fraise; (*e*) molet(t)er, godronner (la tête d'une vis); *Num:* créneler (une pièce de monnaie); (*f*) faire mousser (du chocolat, de la crème); (*g*) *F:* moudre, rouer, (qn) de coups. **2.** *v.i.* (*a*) **to m. (about, around),** (i) (*of cattle, etc.*) tourner en masse; (ii) (*of crowd*) fourmiller; tourner en rond; (iii) (*of whale*) revenir sur son sillon; **in the milling crowd,** dans les remous de la foule; (*b*) *F:* boxer, cogner.

mill[3], *s. U.S:* millième *m* (de dollar).

millboard ['milbɔ:d], *s.* carton-pâte *m inv*; fort carton, gros carton, carton épais (pour reliure, pour dessin).

millcourse ['milkɔ:s], *s.* canal, -aux *m*, courant *m*, bief *m*, de moulin.

milled [mild], *a.* **1.** (*a*) *Mec.E:* (écrou) moleté, godronné; (*b*) *Num:* crénelé; (*on coin*) **m. edge,** crénelage *m*, grènetis *m*, cordon *m*. **2.** *Tex:* foulé.

millefeuille [mi:l'fœ:j], *s. Comest:* millefeuille *m*.

millefiori [milǝfi'ɔ:ri], *s. Glassm:* sulfure *m*, millefiori *m*.

millefleurs [mi:l'flœ:r], *s. Toil:* mille-fleurs *f inv*.

millenarian [mili'nɛǝriǝn]. *Rel.H:* **1.** *s.* millénaire *m*, millénariste *m*. **2.** *a.* qui se rapporte au millénium.

millenarianism [mili'nɛǝriǝnizm], *s. Rel.H:* millénarisme *m*.

millenary [mi'lenǝri, 'milinǝri]. **1.** *a.* (*a*) millénaire (de mille ans); (*b*) *Rel.H:* du millénium. **2.** *s.* millénaire *m* (période de mille ans).

millennial [mi'leniǝl]. **1.** *a.* millénaire; du millénaire; qui dure depuis mille ans. **2.** *s.* millième anniversaire *m*.

millennialism, millenniarism [mi'leniǝlizm, -rizm], *s. Rel.H:* millénarisme *m*.

millennium [mi'leniǝm], *s.* **1.** *Rel.H:* millénium *m*; règne *m* millénaire (du Messie). **2.** millénaire *m*; mille ans *m*; *Archeol:* **it dates from the 3rd m. B.C.,** il date du troisième millénaire avant J.-C.

millepede ['milipi:d], *s.* **1.** *Myr:* mille-pattes *m inv*, millepieds *m inv*. **2.** *Crust:* armadille *m or f*.

millepore ['milipɔ:r], *s. Coel:* millépore *m*.

miller ['milǝr], *s.* **1.** meunier *m*; (*of mill*) minotier *m*; **the miller's wife,** la meunière. **2.** *Mec.E:* (*a*) (*pers.*) fraiseur *m*; (*b*) (*machine*) fraiseuse *f*; machine *f* à fraiser. **3.** *Ent:* *F:* (*a*) hanneton *m*; (*b*) (variétés de) chenille *f* (saupoudrées de blanc). **4.** *Ich:* *F:* **miller's dog,** cagnot *m*; **miller's thumb,** chabot *m* de rivière; meunier, cabot *m*.

millerite ['milǝrait], *s. Miner:* millérite *f*.

millesimal [mi'lesimǝl], *a. & s.* millième (*m*).

millet ['milit], *s. Bot:* (*a*) millet *m*, mil *m*; **African, Indian, black, m.,** sorgho *m*; millet d'Afrique, d'Inde; doura *m*; **Italian m.,** panic *m* d'Italie; **m. seed,** graine *f* de millet; (*b*) **(wood) m. grass,** millet.

milli- ['mili], *comb.fm.* milli-.

milliammeter [mili'æmitǝr], *s. El:* milliampèremètre *m*.

milliamp ['miliæmp], *s. El: F:* = MILLIAMPERE.

milliampere [mili'æmpɛǝr], *s. El.Meas:* milliampère *m*.

milliamperemeter [mili'æmpɛǝmi:tǝr], *s.* = MILLIAMMETER.

milliard ['miljɑ:d], *s.* milliard *m* (10^9).

milliary ['miliǝri], *a. & s. Rom.Ant:* **m. (column),** borne *f* milliaire; colonne *f* milliaire.

millibar ['milibɑ:r], *s. Meteor.Meas:* millibar *m*.

millicurie [mili'kjuǝri], *s. Ph.Meas:* millicurie *m*.

millieme ['milieim], *s. Artil:* millième *m* (d'artilleur).

milliequivalent [milii'kwivǝlǝnt], *s.* milliéquivalent *m*.

milligrade ['miligreid], *s. Meas:* milligrade *m*.

milligram(me) ['miligræm], *s. Meas:* milligramme *m*.

millihenry ['milihenri], *s. El.Meas:* millihenry *m*.

millilitre ['milili:tǝr], *s. Meas:* millilitre *m*.

millimetre ['milimi:tǝr], *s. Meas:* millimètre *m*; **m. scale,** échelle *f* millimétrique.

millimicron ['milimaikrɔn], *s. Ph.Meas:* millimicron *m*.

millimole ['milimoul], *s. Meas:* millimole *f*.

milliner ['milinǝr], *s.* marchand, -ande, de modes; **milliner's shop,** magasin *m* de modes.

millinery ['milinǝri], *s.* (articles *mpl* de) modes *fpl*.

milling ['miliŋ], *s.* **1.** métier *m* de meunier, de minotier; meunerie *f*, minoterie *f*. **2.** (*a*) mouture *f*, moulage *m* (du grain); **wheat of high m. value,** blé *m* de grande valeur boulangère; (*b*) broyage *m*; bocardage *m* (du minerai); (*c*) foulage *m* (du drap). **3.** *Metalw:* (*a*) fraisage *m*, fraisement *m*; dressage *m* à la fraise; **angle m., angular m.,** fraisage d'angle; **end m.,** fraisage en bout; **side m.,** fraisage de côté; **jig m.,** fraisage au calibre; **face m.,** surfaçage *m* à la fraise; **m. machine,** fraiseuse *f*, machine *f* à fraiser; **automatic m. machine,** fraiseuse automatique; **hand m. machine,** fraiseuse à main; **horizontal, vertical, m. machine,** machine à fraiser horizontale, verticale; **knee-and-column m. machine,** fraiseuse à console; **single-spindle, double-spindle, m. machine,** fraiseuse à broche unique, à deux broches; **m. cutter,** fraise *f*, fraiseuse; **m. tool,** (i) fraise, fraiseuse; (ii) godronnoir *m*; porte-molette *m*, *pl.* porte-molettes; **m. spindle,** porte-fraise *m*, *pl.* porte-fraises; **m. head,** tête *f* porte-fraise; **m. jig,** calibre *m* de fraisage; (*b*) moletage *m*, godronnage *m* (d'une vis, d'un bouton de réglage, etc.); (*c*) *Num:* cordonnage *m* (d'une médaille, d'une pièce de monnaie). **4.** cordon *m*, grènetis *m*, tranche cannelée (d'une médaille, d'une pièce de monnaie). **5.** *F:* coups *mpl* de poing; raclée *f*, rossée *f*.

million ['miliǝn], *s.* (*a*) million *m*; **a m. men, one m. men,** un million d'hommes; **two m. men,** deux millions d'hommes; **four m. four thousand men,** quatre millions quatre mille hommes; **one thousand million(s),** un milliard, un billion; **a quarter of a m. men,** deux cent cinquante mille hommes; **half a m. men,** un demi-million d'hommes; (*of pers.*) **worth millions, worth ten millions,** riche à millions; dix fois millionnaire; *F:* **they have millions and millions,** ils sont archimillionnaires; **to talk in millions,** ne parler que mille et cents; **a two-million pound machine,** une machine coûtant deux millions de livres; (*b*) **a one in a m. map,** une carte au millionième; **a two in a m. map,** une carte au deux millionième; (*c*) *O:* **the millions,** la foule, les masses *f*.

millionaire [miliǝ'nɛǝr], *a. & s.* millionnaire (*mf*).

millionth ['miliǝnθ], *a. & s.* millionième (*m*).

millirœntgen, -röntgen [mili'rø:ntgen], *s.* milliröntgen *m*.

millisecond ['milisekǝnd], *s. Meas:* milliseconde *f*.

millivolt ['milivoult], *s. El.Meas:* millivolt *m*.

millivoltmeter [mili'voultmi:tǝr], *s.* millivoltmètre *m*.

millowner ['milounǝr], *s.* (*a*) propriétaire *m* de moulin; minotier *m*; (*b*) (*of oil mill*) moulinier *m*; (*c*) filateur *m*.

millpond ['milpɔnd], *s.* (*a*) réservoir *m* de moulin; retenue *f*; **as calm, as smooth, as a m.,** (mer) calme comme un lac; (mer) d'huile; (*b*) *F:* *O:* **the M.,** l'Atlantique *m*.

millrace ['milreis], *s.* bief *m* de moulin; chenal, -aux *m*; coursier *m*.

millrind ['milraind], *s. Mill: Her:* anille *f*.

millstone ['milstoun], *s.* **1.** *Geol:* **m. (grit),** meulière *f*, grès meulier; **formation of m.,** meuliérisation *f*; **m. quarry,** meulière. **2.** meule *f* (de moulin); **upper m.,** meule courante, meule tournante; surmeule *f*; **lower m.,** *A:* **nether m.,** meule gisante, de dessous; gite *m*; **heart as hard as the nether m.,** cœur aussi dur que la pierre, que le roc; cœur de pierre; **to be between the upper and the nether m.,** être entre l'enclume et le marteau; **to see far into a m.,** être très perspicace; **it will be a m. round his neck all his life,** c'est un boulet qu'il trainera toute sa vie; **m. manufacturer,** meulier *m*.

millstream ['milstri:m], *s.* **1.** courant *m* d'eau qui actionne la roue d'un moulin. **2.** = MILLRACE.

milltail ['milteil], *s.* bief *m* d'aval, biez *m* de fuite (d'un moulin).

millwright ['milrait], *s.* constructeur *m* de moulins; *Ind:* **m. work,** petit outillage.

Milo[1] ['mailou]. *Pr.n.m. A.Hist:* Milon.

Milo[2] ['mi:lou]. *Pr.n. Geog:* Milo; *Art:* **the Venus of M.,** la Vénus de Milo.

milreis [mil'reis], *s. Num:* milreis *m*.

milt[1] [milt], *s.* **1.** rate *f* (des mammifères). **2.** laitance *f*, laite *f* (des poissons).

milt[2], *v.tr. Ich:* féconder.

milter ['miltǝr], *s. Ich:* poisson laité; poisson mâle.

Miltiades [mil'taiǝdi:z]. *Pr.n.m. Gr.Hist:* Miltiade.

Miltonian, Miltonic [mil'touniǝn, -'tɔnik], *a. Lit:* miltonien.

miltwaste, miltwort ['miltweist, -wɔ:t], *s. Bot:* cétérac officinal.

Mimallonidae [mimǝ'lɔnidi:], *s.pl. Ent:* mimallonides *m*.

mimbar ['mimbɑ:r], *s.* minbar *m* (d'une mosquée).

mime[1] [maim], *s. Th:* mime *m* (comédie ou acteur); **m. writer,** mimographe *m*.

mime[2]. **1.** *v.tr.* mimer (une scène). **2.** *v.i.* jouer par gestes.

mimeograph[1] ['mimiougræf], *s.* **1.** autocopiste *m* (au stencil). **2.** polycopie *f*.

mimeograph[2], *v.tr.* polycopier.

mimesis [mai'mi:sis], *s.* **1.** *Rh:* mimèse *f*. **2.** *Nat.Hist:* mimétisme *m*.

mimetene ['mimiti:n], **mimetesite** [mi'metisait], *s. Miner:* mimétèse *f*, mimétite *f*.

mimetic [mai'metik], *a.* **1.** d'imitation; imitatif. **2.** = MIMIC[1] 1. **3.** *Nat.Hist:* (papillon *m*, etc.) mimétique.

mimetically [mai'metik(ǝ)li], *adv.* par mimique; par mimétisme.

mimetism ['maimitizm], *s. Nat.Hist:* mimétisme *m*.

mimetite ['mimitait], *s. Miner:* mimétèse *f*, mimétite *f*.

mimiambics [maimai'æmbiks], *s.pl. A.Pros:* mimiambes *m*.

mimic[1] ['mimik]. **1.** *a.* (*a*) (*of gesture, etc.*) mimique; imitateur, -trice; **the m. art,** la mimique; (*b*) (*of warfare, etc.*) factice. **2.** *s.* (*a*) mime *m*; (*b*) imitateur, -trice; contrefaiseur, -euse; **he's a great m.,** c'est un grand imitateur, *F:* c'est un vrai singe; (*c*) *Nat.Hist:* être mimant.

mimic[2], *v.tr.* (**mimicked**) **1.** imiter, mimer, contrefaire; *F:* singer (qn). **2.** imiter, contrefaire (la nature, etc.); **some insects m. leaves,** certains insectes imitent les feuilles.

mimicker ['mimikǝr], *s.* contrefaiseur, -euse; imitateur, -trice; *F:* singe *m*.

mimicry ['mimikri], *s.* **1.** mimique *f*, imitation *f*. **2.** *Nat.Hist:* mimétisme *m*.

Mimidae ['mimidi:], *s.pl. Orn:* mimidés *m*.

miminy-piminy ['mimini'pimini], *a. F:* *O:* affété, précieux, prétentieux.

mimmation [mi'meiʃ(ǝ)n], *s. Ling:* mimmation *f*.

mimographer [mai'mɔgrǝfǝr], *s. A:* mimographe *m*; auteur *m* de mimes.

mimosa [mi'mouzǝ], *s. Bot:* mimosa *m*.

Mimosaceae [mimou'zeisii:], *s.pl. Bot:* mimosacées *f*.

Mimoseae [mi'mouzii:], *s.pl. Bot:* mimosées *f.*
mimulus ['mimjuləs], *s. Bot:* mimule *m*, mimulus *m.*
Mimusops [mi'mju:sɔps], *s. Bot:* mimusops *m.*
mina[1], *pl.* **-ae, -as** ['mainə, -i:, -əz], *s. A.Meas: & Num:* mine *f.*
mina[2], *s. Orn:* mainate religieux.
minacious [mi'neiʃəs], *a. Lit:* menaçant; *Jur:* comminatoire.
minaciously [mi'neiʃəsli], *adv. Lit:* d'un ton, d'un air, menaçant.
minar [mi'nɑ:r], *s.* (*in India*) **1.** phare *m.* **2.** tourelle *f.*
minaret [minə'ret], *s.* minaret *m.*
minasragrite [minæs'rægrait], *s. Miner:* minasragrite *f.*
minatory ['minətəri], *a.* menaçant; *Jur:* comminatoire.
mince[1] [mins], *s. Cu:* (*a*) hachis *m* (de viande); (*b*) **m. pie,** tarte *f* contenant du *mincemeat.*
mince[2], *v.tr.* **1.** hacher, hacher menu, mincer (de la viande, etc.). **2.** (*always in the neg.*) **not to m. one's words,** avoir son franc parler; ne pas mâcher ses mots; parler carrément (**with s.o.,** à qn); **he didn't m. his words,** il n'a pas ménagé ses termes; **not to m. matters,** pour parler net, carrément; **I did not m. matters (with him),** je n'ai pas pris de mitaines, je n'ai pas usé de ménagements, pour le lui dire; je lui ai dit tout net ce que je pensais; **he doesn't m. matters,** il n'y va pas par quatre chemins. **3. to m. one's words,** *v.i.* **to m.,** parler avec une élégance affectée, parler du bout des lèvres; (*of woman*) minauder; (*of man*) mignarder; faire des grimaces, des simagrées, des manières. **4.** *v.i.* marcher d'un air affecté.
minced [minst], *a. Cu:* haché; **m. veal,** hachis *m* de veau; **m. meat,** hachis.
mincemeat ['minsmi:t], *s. Cu:* compote de raisins secs, de pommes, d'amandes, d'écorce d'orange, etc., liée avec de la graisse et conservée avec du cognac; *F:* **to make m. of sth.,** hacher menu qch.; *F:* **to make m. of s.o.,** réduire qn en chair à pâté; hacher qn menu comme chair à pâté; réduire qn en bouille.
mincer ['minsər], *s. Dom.Ec:* hachoir *m.*
mincing[1] ['minsiŋ], *a.* (*a*) (*of manner, tone*) affecté, minaudier, affété; (*of man*) mignard; (*of woman*) minaudière; (*b*) **to take m. steps,** marcher à petits pas.
mincing[2], *s.* **1.** mise *f* en hachis (de la viande, etc.); **m. machine,** hachoir *m.* **2.** airs affectés; afféteries *fpl.*
mincingly ['minsiŋli], *adv.* d'un ton, d'un air, affecté; avec une élégance affectée; mignardement.
mind[1] [maind], *s.* **1.** (*remembrance*) (*a*) souvenir *m*, mémoire *f*; **to bear, keep, sth. in m.,** (i) se souvenir de qch.; garder la mémoire de qch.; songer à qch.; avoir soin de faire qch.; ne pas oublier qch.; (ii) tenir compte de qch.; **keep, bear, him in m.,** songez à lui; **I shall keep your advice in m.,** je tiendrai compte de vos conseils; je n'oublierai pas vos conseils; **this is the goal we should keep in m.,** voilà le but qu'il ne faut pas perdre de vue; **we must bear in m. that she is only a child,** il nous faut nous rappeler, il ne faut pas oublier, que ce n'est qu'une enfant; **I shall try to keep it in m.,** je tâcherai de m'en souvenir; **to call sth. to m.,** se rappeler, se souvenir, de qch.; évoquer le souvenir de qch.; **to put s.o. in m. of s.o., of sth.,** rappeler qn à qn; faire penser qn à qn, à qch.; **he puts me in m. of his father,** il me rappelle son père; **she puts me in m. of a sparrow,** elle me rappelle, me fait penser à, un moineau; **a curious story came into my m.,** je me suis souvenu d'une histoire curieuse; *O:* **to go, pass, out of m.,** tomber dans l'oubli; **it went (completely, clean) out of my m.,** cela m'est (entièrement) sorti de l'esprit; je l'ai (complètement) oublié; (*b*) *Ecc: O:* **year's m.,** (messe *f*, office *m*, du) bout de l'an; **month's m.,** messe du bout de mois (messe célébrée un mois après la mort de quelqu'un). **2.** (*a*) (*opinion*) pensée *f*, avis *m*, idée *f*; *O:* **to tell s.o. one's m., to let s.o. know one's m.,** dire sa façon de penser à qn; *F:* **I gave him a piece, a bit, of my m.,** je lui ai dit son fait, ses vérités; je lui ai parlé carrément; je lui ai dit carrément ce que j'en pensais; je lui ai flanqué un savon; **to be of the same m. as s.o.,** *O:* **to be of s.o.'s m., of a m. with s.o.,** être du même avis que qn; être d'accord avec qn; (*of several pers.*) **to be of one m., of the same m.,** *O:* **of a m.,** être du même avis, être d'accord; avoir les mêmes vues; **to my m.,** à, selon, mon avis; selon moi; à ce que je pense; (*b*) (*purpose, desire*) **to know one's own m.,** savoir ce qu'on veut; **he doesn't know his own m.,** (i) il ne sait pas ce qu'il veut; (ii) il est indécis; **to make up one's m.,** prendre son parti; se décider; prendre une décision; **come on, make up your m.!** allons, décidez-vous! **a man who cannot make up his m.,** un indécis; **to make up one's m. to do sth.,** se décider, se résoudre, à faire qch.; **to make up one's m. about sth.,** prendre une décision au sujet de qch.; *O:* **to make up one's m. to, for, sth.,** (i) se résigner à qch.; (ii) décider en faveur de qch.; **my m. is made up,** ma résolution est prise; mon parti est pris; c'est tout réfléchi; **she couldn't make up her m. what to do,** elle ne pouvait pas décider quoi faire; **to be in two minds about (doing) sth., to be in two minds what to do,** être indécis sur qch., pour faire qch., quant au parti à prendre; balancer si l'on fera qch.; ne pas trop savoir si l'on fera qch.; **to change, alter, one's m.,** changer d'avis, de pensée, d'idée; se raviser; **I've a good m. to do it,** j'ai bien l'intention de le faire; **I've half a m. to go out this evening,** je vais peut-être sortir ce soir; *O:* **do as you have a m.!** faites à votre idée, à votre guise! *O:* **if you have a m. for it,** si le cœur vous en dit; *O:* **to have no m. to do sth.,** n'avoir aucun désir, aucune intention, de faire qch.; (*c*) **to set one's m. on sth.,** vouloir absolument avoir qch.; désirer qch. ardemment; être déterminé, s'être promis, de faire qch.; **he has set his m. on writing a novel,** il s'est mis dans la tête d'écrire un roman; **once he sets his m. on doing sth. nothing will stop him,** quand il s'est mis dans la tête, en tête, de faire qch. rien ne l'arrêtera; **his m. turned to . . .,** sa pensée s'est tournée vers . . .; **to give one's m. to sth.,** s'adonner, s'appliquer, à qch.; s'occuper de qch.; **to give one's whole m. to sth.,** appliquer toute son attention à qch.; **to bring one's m. to bear on sth.,** porter son attention vers qch.; **to keep one's m. on sth.,** se concentrer sur qch.; **to have sth. in m.,** avoir qch. en vue; **the person I have in m.,** la personne à qui je pense; *O:* **to find sth. to one's m.,** trouver qch. à son goût, à son gré. **3.** esprit *m*, âme *f*; **state of m.,** état *m* d'esprit; **turn of m.,** mentalité *f* (de qn.); **he has a mechanical turn of m.,** il est bon mécanicien; **attitude of m.,** manière *f* de penser; **he wasn't in a state of m. to . . .,** (i) il n'était pas disposé à . . .; (ii) il n'était pas en état de . . .; **to be in a bad state, frame, of m.,** être mal disposé, de mauvaise humeur; **peace of m.,** tranquillité *f* d'esprit; **peace of m. is essential to . . .,** la paix de l'âme, la tranquillité, est essentielle à . . .; **to enjoy peace of m.,** avoir l'esprit en repos; **to disturb s.o.'s peace of m.,** troubler l'esprit de qn, la tranquillité de qn; **he has no strength of m.,** c'est un homme sans caractère. **4.** (*a*) *Phil: Psy:* (*opposed to body*) âme; (*opposed to matter*) esprit; (*opposed to emotions*) intelligence *f*; (*b*) esprit; idée; **such a thought had never entered his m.,** une telle pensée ne lui était jamais venue à l'esprit; **it never entered my m. that I already had an appointment,** j'avais complètement oublié que j'étais déjà pris; **to have sth. on one's m.,** (i) avoir qch. qui vous préoccupe; (ii) avoir qch. sur la conscience; **in the mind's eye,** dans l'imagination; **to take s.o.'s m. off his sorrows,** distraire qn de son chagrin; **a walk will take my m. off it,** une promenade me changera d'idées; **to be easy, uneasy, in one's m.,** avoir, ne pas avoir, l'esprit tranquille; **he wants to be clear about it in his own m.,** il veut y voir clair; **that's a weight off my m.,** voilà qui me soulage l'esprit; **put it out of your m.,** n'y pensez plus; (*c*) **a noble m.,** une belle âme; *Prov:* **great minds think alike,** les beaux esprits, les grands esprits, se rencontrent; (*d*) **the m. of man,** l'esprit de l'homme; l'esprit humain; **the religious m.,** l'esprit religieux; *O:* **to rouse the public m.,** agiter les esprits; (*e*) *attrib.* **m. reader,** liseur, -euse, de pensées; **m. reading,** lecture *f* de la pensée; **m. picture,** représentation mentale; *Lit:* **m. child,** enfant imaginaire; camarade imaginaire (d'un enfant solitaire). **5.** raison *f*; **to be out of one's m.,** avoir perdu la raison, la tête; n'avoir plus sa raison; être fou; **to go out of one's m.,** perdre la raison, la tête, l'esprit; tomber en démence; **you'll send, drive, me out of my m.!** vous me rendrez fou! **are you out of your m.? you must be out of your m.!** vous êtes fou! **his m. has given way,** il a perdu la raison; **his misfortunes have unsettled his m.,** ses malheurs ont troublé sa raison; **to be in one's right m.,** avoir toute sa raison; **of sound m., sound in m.,** sain d'esprit; en possession de toutes ses facultés.
mind[2], *v.tr.* **1.** (*a*) (*attend to, pay attention to*) faire attention à, prêter (son) attention à (qn, qch.); **never m. him, never m. what he says,** ne faites pas attention à lui, à ce qu'il dit; ne vous préoccupez pas de ce qu'il dit; *O:* **you should m. your elders,** vous devriez écouter vos aînés; **never m. the money,** ne faites pas attention à l'argent; ne regardez pas à l'argent; **never m. the rest,** je vous tiens quitte du reste; **nobody seems to m.,** personne ne paraît y prêter attention; *F:* **never you m.!** ça c'est mon affaire! **m. you, I've always thought that . . .,** notez bien, et pourtant, j'ai toujours pensé que . . .; (*b*) (*apply oneself to*) s'occuper de, se mêler de (qch.); **m. your own business!** occupez-vous, mêlez-vous, de ce qui vous regarde! occupez-vous de vos affaires, de vos oignons! on ne vous demande pas l'heure (qu'il est)! (*c*) (*take care, pay attention*) **m. that she is kept quiet,** veillez à ce qu'elle reste tranquille; **m. you're not late!** prenez soin de ne pas être en retard! et surtout ne soyez pas en retard! **m. you wake me up early!** n'oubliez pas de me réveiller de bonne heure! **m. you write to him!** écrivez-lui sans faute! ne manquez pas, n'oubliez pas, de lui écrire! **m. what you're doing!** prenez garde, faites attention, à ce que vous faites! **m. you don't stay too long!** gardez-vous de rester trop longtemps! **m. what you say!** prenez garde à vos paroles! **m. your language!** ne jurez pas comme ça! **m. you don't fall!** prenez garde de tomber! **m. the step!** attention à la marche! **m. the paint!** attention à la peinture! **m. your backs (please)!** dégagez (s'il vous plaît)! **m. the doors!** = attention au départ! (*d*) *F:* **m. you, . . .,** tu sais . . .; **don't be late, m.!** surtout, ne sois pas en retard! **2.** (*a*) (*object to*) **would you m. if . . .?** cela vous gênerait-il que . . .? **if you don't m.,** si cela ne vous dérange pas, ne vous fait rien; si vous le voulez bien; **I shouldn't m. that,** cela ne me déplairait pas; **I don't m.,** (i) cela m'est égal; (ii) je le veux bien; **I hope you don't m.,** j'espère que vous n'y voyez pas d'inconvénient, que cela ne vous dérange pas; **if nobody minds,** si personne n'y voit d'inconvénient; **I don't m. trying,** je veux bien essayer; **he didn't m. admitting that . . .,** il ne se refusait pas de reconnaître que . . .; **he won't m. doing it,** il le fera volontiers; **if you don't m. my saying so,** cela ne vous froisse pas que je vous le dise? **I don't m. saying that . . .,** je n'hésite pas à dire que . . .; **I wonder if you'd very much m. waiting a few more minutes,** ne serait-ce trop vous demander d'attendre encore quelques minutes? **do you m. my asking . . .?** puis-je vous demander sans indiscrétion . . .? **if you don't m.,** si vous n'y voyez pas d'inconvénient; **would you m. repeating that?** répétez, s'il vous plaît; **would you m. shutting the door,** voudriez-vous bien fermer la porte; **do you m. if I open the window, my opening the window?** cela ne vous dérange pas si j'ouvre la fenêtre? **do you m. if I smoke?** cela ne vous dérange pas, ne vous gêne pas, ne vous incommode pas, que je fume? **I wouldn't m. a cup of tea,** je prendrais volontiers une tasse de thé; *P:* **another drop of wine?—I don't m. if I do,** encore un peu de vin?—ce n'est pas de refus; (*b*) (*trouble oneself about*) **don't m. them,** ne vous inquiétez pas d'eux; **never m. the consequences,** ne vous souciez pas des conséquences; **don't you m. being thought a fool?** cela ne vous fait rien qu'on ne vous prenne pour un imbécile? **never m.!** (i) n'importe! peu importe! ça ne fait rien! rien! tant pis! (ii) ne vous inquiétez pas! **I don't m. what people say,** je ne m'inquiète guère, je me moque, de ce qu'on dit; **who minds what he says?** qui s'occupe de ce qu'il dit? **I don't m. the cold,** le froid ne me gêne pas; **he doesn't m. hard work,** le travail ne lui fait pas peur; **never m. the expense,** ne regardez pas à la dépense; **I don't m.,** cela m'est égal; cela n'a pas d'importance, ne me dérange pas. **3.** (*look after*) soigner (qn); surveiller, avoir l'œil sur (des enfants); garder (des animaux, etc.); **to m. the house,** garder, veiller sur, la maison; **to m. the shop,** s'occuper du magasin, garder le magasin. **4.** *A: & Dial:* (*remember*) se souvenir de, se rappeler (qn, qch.).
mind-bender ['maindbendər], *s. P:* drogue *f*, etc., qui affine l'intelligence; euphorisant *m.*
mind-bending ['maindbendiŋ], *a. P:* qui affine l'intelligence; euphorique.
mind-blower ['maindblouər], *s. P:* (*a*) expérience inaccoutumée; (*b*) choc soudain, coup *m* de massue; (*c*) drogue *f* hallucinogène extatique, bonbon *m* à kick.
mind-blowing ['maindblouiŋ], *a. P:* qui donne (i) des expériences inaccoutumées, (ii) un coup de massue, (iii) des hallucinations extatiques.
minded ['maindid], *a.* (*a*) disposé, enclin (à faire qch.); *O:* **if you are so m.,** si le cœur vous en dit; si vous y êtes disposé; (*b*) (*with adv.*) **commercially m.,** commerçant; **architecturally m.,** qui s'intéresse à l'architecture; (*c*) (*with s. or a. prefixed*) **feeble m.,** à l'esprit faible; **healthy m.,** à l'esprit sain; **acute m.,** sagace; **money m.,** obsédé, hanté, par l'argent; **air m.,** qui aime voyager en avion; **the right m.,** les bien-pensants *m.*
Mindel ['mindəl], *s. Geol:* mindel *m.*
minder ['maindər], *s.* **1.** (*a*) gardeur, -euse (de bestiaux); surveillant, -ante (d'enfants); *esp. NAm:* **baby m.,** garde-bébé *mf, pl.* garde-bébés; (*b*) *Ind:* **(machine) m.,** surveillant, *Typ:* conducteur *m*, de machines. **2.** *A:* enfant commis à la garde d'une crèche, etc.
mindful ['maindful], *a.* **1.** attentif (à sa santé, etc.); soigneux (de); **he is always m. of others,** il pense toujours aux autres. **2. to be m. of sth.,** se souvenir de qch.; ne pas oublier qch.
mindless ['maindlis], *a.* **1.** (*a*) sans esprit, sans intelligence; (*b*) **m. destruction,** destruction irresponsable. **2.** (*a*) insouciant (**of,** de); indifférent (à); (*b*) oublieux (de).

mine[1] [main], *s.* **1.** (*a*) mine *f*; **coal m.,** mine de houille, de charbon; **gold m., lead m., salt m.,** mine d'or, de plomb, de sel; **iron ore m.,** mine de fer; **opencast, surface, m.,** mine à ciel ouvert; **deep-level m.,** mine à grande profondeur; **undersea, underwater, m.,** mine sous-marine; **to work a m.,** exploiter une mine; **m. inspector, surveyor, viewer,** inspecteur *m* des mines; (*b*) **a m. of knowledge,** un puits de science; **a m. of information,** (i) (*pers.*) un véritable bureau de renseignements; (ii) (*book, etc.*) une mine, un trésor, de renseignements, d'information. **2.** *A:* (*ore*) mine, minerai *m*, de fer. **3.** *Mil: Navy: etc:* mine; **atomic demolition m.,** mine atomique; **delayed-action m.,** mine à retardement; **land m.,** mine terrestre; **bounding m.,** mine bondissante; **anti-personnel m.,** mine antipersonnel; **anti-tank m.,** mine antichar; **sea m.,** mine marine; **submarine m.,** mine sous-marine; **floating m.,** mine flottante; **drifting m.,** mine dérivante; **moored m.,** mine à orin; **ground m.,** mine de fond, mine dormante; **acoustic m.,** mine acoustique; **contact m.,** mine de contact, à antennes; **influence m.,** mine à influence; **magnetic m.,** mine magnétique; **pressure m.,** mine à dépression; **radio-controlled m.,** mine télécommandée; **coast-controlled m.,** mine télécommandée de la côte; **tube-type m.,** mine à mouillage par tube; **aerial m.,** mine aérienne, à mouillage par avion; **activated, deactivated, m.,** mine amorcée, désamorcée; **m. belt,** ceinture *f* de mines; **m. thrower,** lance-mines *m inv*, mortier *m* de tranchée; *Navy:* **m. watching,** guet *m* au mouillage de mines; **m.-watching radar,** radar *m* de guet au mouillage de mines; **m. watcher,** guetteur *m* contre les mines; **m. dredger,** drague *f* pour mines; **m. anchorage,** crapaud *m* (de mine flottante); **m. clearance,** déminage *m*; enlèvement *m* des mines; **m. clearance diver,** plongeur démineur; **m. detector,** détecteur *m* de mines; **m. firing pin, m. horn,** antenne *f* de mine; **m. sterilizer,** neutralisateur *m* de mine(s); **to arm a m., to make a m. live,** armer une mine; **to disarm a m.,** désarmer, neutraliser, une mine; **to lay a m.,** poser, mouiller, une mine; **to lift, pick up, a m.,** relever une mine; **to spring, touch off, fire, a m.,** faire jouer, sauter, une mine; **to blow up, explode, a m.,** faire sauter une mine; **to be blown up by a m.,** sauter sur une mine; **the m. went up,** la mine a sauté.

mine[2], *v.tr. & i.* **1.** (*a*) **to m. (under) the earth,** fouiller (sous) la terre, creuser la terre; **to m. a hole,** creuser un trou; faire un sondage; (*b*) *Mil:* miner, saper (une muraille); **river that mines the foundations of a house,** rivière qui creuse, fouille, mine, sape, les fondements d'une maison; **to m. the foundations of a doctrine,** saper les fondements d'une doctrine; (*c*) *Navy:* **to m. the sea,** poser, semer, des mines en mer; **to m. a harbour,** miner un port; **mined area,** zone semée de mines. **2.** *Min:* **to m. (for) coal, gold,** exploiter le charbon, l'or; **to m. a coal seam,** exploiter une couche de houille; **to m. coal by undercutting,** abattre le charbon par havage.

mine[3]. **1.** *poss.pron.* le mien, la mienne, les miens, les miennes; (*a*) **your country and m.,** votre patrie et la mienne; **this letter is m.,** (i) cette lettre est à moi, m'appartient; c'est ma lettre; (ii) cette lettre est de moi; **this signature, criticism, is not m.,** cette signature, cette critique, n'est pas de moi; **your interests are m.,** vos intérêts sont les miens; **lend me your gloves, m. are too dirty,** prêtez-moi vos gants, les miens sont trop sales; **he gave presents to his brothers and m.,** il a donné des cadeaux à ses frères et aux miens; **I took her hands in both of m.,** je pris ses mains dans les deux miennes; **a friend of m.,** un(e) de mes ami(e)s; un(e) ami(e) à moi; **a friend of yours and m.,** un de vos amis et des miens; **that house of m. in the country,** ma maison à la campagne; **it is no business of m.,** ce n'est pas mon affaire; **no effort of m.,** aucun effort de ma part; (*b*) (*my family*) **be good to me and m.,** soyez gentil pour moi et les miens; (*c*) (*my property*) **m. and thine,** le mien et le tien; *F:* **what's yours is mine, what's mine's my own,** ce qui est à toi est à moi; ce qui est à moi c'est le mien. **2.** *poss.a. A: & Poet:* mon, *f.* ma, *pl.* mes; (*a*) (*before a noun or adj. beginning with a vowel or h*) **m. ears, m. heart,** mes oreilles, mon cœur; **m. only son,** mon fils unique; *Hum:* **m. host,** l'aubergiste; (*b*) (*after voc.*) **mistress m.!** ma (belle) maîtresse!

mineable ['mainəbl], *a.* **1.** *Mil:* minable, qui peut être miné. **2.** *Min:* (charbon, etc.) exploitable.

minefield ['mainfi:ld], *s. Mil: Navy:* champ *m* de mines; **to clear a m.,** déblayer un champ de mines.

minehead ['mainhed], *s. Min:* front *m* de taille.

minelayer ['mainleiər], *s. Navy:* (bâtiment) mouilleur *m* de mines; **coastal m.,** mouilleur de mines côtier; **fleet m.,** mouilleur de mines d'escadre; **submarine m.,** sous-marin mouilleur de mines.

minelaying ['mainleiiŋ], *s. Mil: Navy:* pose *f*, mouillage *m*, de mines; **aerial m.,** mouillage de mines par avion; **m. aircraft,** avion mouilleur de mines; **m. vessel** = MINELAYER.

mineowner ['mainounər], *s.* propriétaire *mf* de mine(s), de houillères.

miner ['mainər], *s.* **1.** (*a*) *Min:* (ouvrier *m*) mineur *m*; ouvrier du fond; **miner's lamp,** lampe *f* de mineur; **miner's compass,** boussole *f* de mine; *O:* **miners' disease,** maladie *f*, anémie *f*, des mineurs; (*b*) *Mil:* mineur, sapeur *m*. **2.** *Ent:* larve mineuse.

mineral ['minərəl]. **1.** *a.* minéral, -aux; **the m. kingdom,** le règne minéral; **m. spring,** source (d'eau) minérale; **m. waters,** (i) eaux minérales; (ii) *Com:* boissons gazeuses; **m. coal,** charbon *m* de pierre, de terre; houille *f*; **m. charcoal,** charbon fossile; **m. oil,** huile minérale; **m. naphtha,** naphte minéral, huile de roche; **m. tar,** goudron minéral; **m. wax,** cire minérale, cérésine *f*; **m. acid,** acide minéral; **m. jelly,** vaseline *f*. **2.** *s.* (*a*) minéral *m*; **original m.,** minéral originel; **contact m.,** minéral de contact; **related minerals,** minéraux apparentés; **m. cleavage,** clivage *m* des minéraux; *Min:* **m. deposits,** gisements miniers, minéraux; **m. rights,** droits miniers; **m. concession, claim,** concession minière; **the m. resources of a country,** les ressources minières d'un pays; (*b*) *Atom.Ph:* **secondary m.,** minerai *m* secondaire; (*c*) *Com: F:* **minerals,** boissons gazeuses.

mineral-bearing ['minərəlbɛəriŋ], *a.* (*of rock*) minéralisé.

mineralizable [minərə'laizəbl], *a.* minéralisable.

mineralization [minərəlai'zeiʃ(ə)n], *s.* (*a*) minéralisation *f* (de l'eau, des métaux, etc.); (*b*) calcification *f*, minéralisation (des os); **m. of teeth,** calcification des dents.

mineralize ['minərəlaiz], *v.tr.* minéraliser.

mineralized ['minərəlaizd], *a.* **1.** minéralisé. **2.** *Adm: Com:* **m. methylated spirits,** alcool dénaturé additionné de naphte.

mineralizer ['minərəlaizər], *s.* minéralisateur *m*.

mineralizing ['minərəlaiziŋ], *a.* minéralisateur, -trice.

mineralocorticoid [minərəlou'kɔ:tikɔid], *s. Bio-Ch:* minéralocorticoïde *m*.

mineralogical [minərə'lɔdʒik(ə)l], *a.* minéralogique.

mineralogist [minə'rælədʒist], *s.* minéralogiste *mf*.

mineralogy [minə'rælədʒi], *s.* minéralogie *f*; **descriptive, economic, physical, m.,** minéralogie descriptive, économique, physique.

Minerva [mi'nə:və]. **1.** *Pr.n.f. Rom.Myth:* Minerve. **2.** *s. Typ:* **M. (jobbing machine),** minerve *f*.

mineshaft ['mainʃɑ:ft], *s.* puits *m* de mine.

minestrone [minis'trouni], *s. Cu:* minestrone *m*.

minesweeper ['mainswi:pər], *s. Navy:* dragueur *m* de mines; **coastal m.,** dragueur (de mines) côtier; **fleet m.,** dragueur (de mines) d'escadre; **inshore m.,** dragueur (de mines) de petits fonds.

minesweeping ['mainswi:piŋ], *s. Navy:* draguage *m* des mines.

minette [mi'net], *s. Miner:* minette *f*.

minever ['minivər], *s.* = MINIVER.

mingle ['miŋgl]. **1.** *v.tr.* mêler, mélanger (**sth. with sth.,** qch. avec qch.; **two things together,** deux choses ensemble); **the Seine and the Marne m. their waters,** la Seine et la Marne confondent leurs eaux; **respect mingled with admiration,** respect mêlé d'admiration; *Lit:* **to m. one's tears with s.o.'s,** mêler ses larmes à celles de qn; confondre ses larmes avec celles de qn. **2.** *v.i.* (*a*) (*of thg*) se mêler, se mélanger, se confondre (**with,** avec); (*b*) (*of pers.*) se mêler (**in, with, a company,** à une compagnie); **to m. with the crowd,** se mêler à, dans, la foule.

mingle-mangle ['miŋgl'mæŋgl], *s. F: O:* mélange *m*, confusion *f* (de personnes, d'objets).

mingling ['miŋgliŋ], *s.* mélange *m*, mêlement *m*.

mingy ['mindʒi], *a. F:* **1.** mesquin, chiche, pingre, grigou; **don't be so m.!** ne sois pas si chiche! **2.** misérable, insignifiant; **a m. helping,** une portion minuscule.

mini ['mini], *s.* **1.** *Cost: F:* mini *m* or *f*. **2.** *Aut: R.t.m:* mini *f*.

mini- ['mini], *comb.fm.* mini-.

miniature ['mini(ə)tjər]. **1.** *s.* miniature *f*; (*a*) **temple which is a m. of the Parthenon,** temple qui est un Parthénon en miniature, qui est un modèle réduit du Parthénon; **to paint in m.,** peindre en miniature; **a Niagara in m.,** un Niagara en miniature, en petit; **the family is society in m.,** la famille est la société en raccourci; (*b*) (portrait *m* en) miniature; **m. painter,** peintre *m* de miniatures; miniaturiste *mf*; **m. painting,** miniature; (*c*) **Japanese gardeners can produce from a tree normally 30 metres high a m. of barely 15 centimetres,** les jardiniers japonais savent, d'un arbre qui normalement aurait 30 mètres de haut, faire une miniature d'à peine 15 centimètres; (*d*) *Com:* bouteille miniature (de cognac, de whisky, etc.). **2.** *a.* en miniature, en raccourci; **a m. edition of a book,** une édition minuscule d'un livre; **m. mountain,** montagne *f* minuscule; **our pond was a m. lake,** notre étang *m* était un lac en miniature, en petit; **he's a m. Napoleon,** c'est un Napoléon au petit pied; **m. camera,** appareil *m* de petit format; **m. model,** miniature, maquette *f*; **m. garden,** jardin miniature; **m. golf,** golf miniature; **m. car,** motocar *m*; *Elcs:* **m. resistor,** résistance *f* miniature; **m. tube,** tube *m* miniature; *Mil: etc:* **m. range,** stand *m*, galerie *f*, de tir réduit.

miniaturist ['mini(ə)tjərist], *s.* miniaturiste *mf*; peintre *m* en miniature.

miniaturization [mini(ə)tjərai'zeiʃ(ə)n], *s.* miniaturisation *f*.

miniaturize ['mini(ə)tjəraiz], *v.tr.* miniaturiser.

minibudget ['minibʌdʒet], *s.* budget *m* intermédiaire.

minibus ['minibʌs], *s.* minibus *m*, microbus *m*.

minicab ['minikæb], *s.* radio-taxi *m*, *pl.* radio-taxis.

minification [minifi'keiʃ(ə)n], *s.* amoindrissement *m*, réduction *f*.

minify ['minifai], *v.tr.* amoindrir, réduire, diminuer; **to m. an accident,** réduire l'importance d'un accident.

minikin ['minikin]. **1.** *s.* (*a*) homuncule *m*, nabot *m*; petite poupée (de femme); (*b*) **m. (pin),** camion *m*; (*c*) *Typ:* diamant *m* (corps 3½). **2.** *a.* (*a*) tout petit, mignon; (*b*) affecté, précieux, minaudier.

minim ['minim], *s.* **1.** *Mus:* blanche *f*; (*in plain song*) minime *f*. **2.** *A: Meas:* goutte *f*. **3.** *F: A:* Homoncule *m*, homuncule *m*, bout *m* d'homme, bout de femme. **4.** *Ecc.Hist:* **(mendicant order of) minims,** (ordre mendiant des) minimes *m*. **5.** (*handwriting*) jambage *m*.

minimal ['miniməl], *a.* **1.** minime. **2.** minimal, -aux; minimum; *Ph:* **m. temperature,** température minimale; **m. volume,** volume minimal; *Mth:* **m. function,** fonction minimale; **m. value,** valeur minimale, minimum.

minimalist ['miniməlist], *s. Hist:* minimaliste *mf*; menchevik *m*.

minimax ['minimæks], *s. Mth:* minimax *m*; minimum *m* des maximums; **m. criterion, m. rule,** critère *m*, règle *f*, du minimax; **m. estimate,** estimation *f* minimax.

minimism ['minimizm], *s. Theol:* minimisme *m*.

minimization [minimai'zeiʃ(ə)n], *s.* minimisation *f*; réduction *f* au minimum.

minimize ['minimaiz], *v.tr.* minimiser, réduire au minimum; restreindre (le bruit, le frottement, etc.) au minimum; **to m. an accident,** mettre au minimum l'importance d'un accident.

minimum, *pl.* **-a** ['miniməm, -ə], *s.* minimum *m*, *pl.* minimums, minima; **to reduce sth. to a m.,** réduire qch. au minimum; minimiser qch.; **m. price,** prix *m* minimum; **m. width,** largeur *f* minimum, largeur minima; **m. altitudes,** altitudes *f* minima, minimums; **m. speed,** minimum de vitesse; **the m. densities,** les minimums de densité; *Mth:* **m. value,** valeur minima; **m. thermometer,** thermomètre *m* à minima.

minimus, *pl.* **-mi** ['miniməs, -mai]. **1.** *s.* (*a*) *A:* homoncule *m*, homuncule *m*; nabot, -ote; (*b*) *A:* petit doigt (de la main, du pied). **2.** *a. Sch:* **Thomas m.,** le plus jeune des Thomas (qui sont au moins trois).

mining ['mainiŋ], *s.* **1.** exploitation minière, des mines; **diamond, gold, tin, iron ore, m.,** exploitation des mines de diamant, d'or, d'étain, de minerai de fer; **opencast, surface, m.,** abattage *m*, exploitation, extraction *f*, à ciel ouvert, au jour; **deep m.,** abattage en profondeur, exploitation profonde; **lode, vein, m.,** exploitation filonienne, des filons; **placer m.,** exploitation placérienne, des placers; **the m. industry,** l'industrie minière; **m. area,** domaine minier; région minière; **m. town,** ville minière; **m. engineer,** ingénieur *m* des mines; **m. engineering,** ingéniérie, technique, minière; **m. equipment,** matériel *m*, outillage *m*, de mines; **m. timber,** bois *m* de mines; **m. explosives,** explosifs *m* de mines; *St.Exch:* **m. shares,** valeurs minières. **2.** (*a*) *Mil:* sape *f*; (*b*) *Navy:* pose *f* de mines, minage *m*. **3.** *Ent:* **m. bee,** abeille fouisseuse, terrassière.

minion ['minjən], *s.* **1.** *Pej:* (*a*) *A:* favori, -ite; mignon, -onne; (*b*) *A:* amante *f*, maîtresse *f*; (*c*) **the minions of the law,** les recors *m* de la justice; (*d*) *F: Iron:* subordonné, -ée; domestique *mf*; **one of my minions will do it,** un de mes gens, un des sous-fifres, le fera. **2.** *Typ:* mignonne *f*, corps 7.

minish ['miniʃ], *v.tr. & i. A:* diminuer.

miniskirt ['miniskə:t], *s. Cost:* minijupe *f*.

minister[1] ['ministər], *s.* **1.** (*a*) *Pol:* ministre *m* (d'État); (*b*) *Dipl:* **British m. in Paris,** ministre britannique à Paris. **2.** *Ecc:* (*a*) ministre, pasteur *m* (d'un culte réformé); **M. of the Gospel,** ministre de l'Évangile; (*in Scot.*) **minister's man,** bedeau *m*; *Adm:* **m. of religion,** prêtre *m*, pasteur; (*b*) *R.C.Ch:* ministre (des

Jésuites); **m. general,** ministre général.

minister². **1.** *v.i.* (*a*) **to m. to s.o., to s.o.'s needs,** soigner qn; pourvoir, subvenir, aux besoins de qn; donner ses soins à qn; (*b*) *Ecc:* **to m. to a parish,** desservir une paroisse. **2.** *v.tr. A:* fournir, procurer (de la consolation); fournir (du secours).

ministerial [minis'tiəriəl], *a.* **1.** exécutif; **m. functions,** fonctions exécutives; *Jur: Adm:* **m. act,** acte accompli par un fonctionnaire dans l'exercice de ses fonctions. **2.** accessoire, subsidiaire; **to be m. to . . .,** contribuer à . . .; aider à . . .. **3.** *Ecc:* (*of duties, life, etc.*) de ministre; sacerdotal, -aux. **4.** *Pol:* ministériel, gouvernemental, -aux; du gouvernement; **the m. benches,** les bancs ministériels (des Chambres); **m. team,** équipe gouvernementale; **m. reverse,** échec *m* du gouvernement. **5.** *s.* homme *m* lige, vassal *m*.

ministerialism [minis'tiəriəlizm], *s.* **1.** *Pol:* appui prêté au ministère. **2.** *Ecc:* caractère *m* de ministre, caractère sacerdotal.

ministerialist [minis'tiəriəlist], *s. Pol:* ministériel *m*; partisan *m* du gouvernement.

ministerially [minis'tiəriəli], *adv.* **1.** ministériellement; en ministre. **2.** en ministre, en prêtre.

ministering¹ ['minist(ə)riŋ], *a.* (ange, etc.) secourable.

ministering², *s.* soins *mpl*, service *m* (**to**, de).

ministrant ['ministrənt]. **1.** *a.* **m. to s.o., sth.,** (i) qui sert qn, qui subvient à qch.; (ii) *Ecc:* qui dessert la paroisse; qui officie à l'église, au temple. **2.** *s.* (*a*) ministre *m*; dispensateur, -trice (**of,** de); (*b*) *Ecc:* desservant *m*, officiant *m*.

ministration [minis'treiʃ(ə)n], *s.* **1.** service *m*; ministère *m*, soins *mpl*; **thanks to the ministrations of two devoted nurses,** grâce aux soins dévoués de deux gardes-malades. **2.** *Ecc:* (*a*) saint ministère; sacerdoce *m*; (*b*) **to go about one's ministrations,** vaquer à ses devoirs sacerdotaux; **to receive the ministrations of a priest,** être administré par un prêtre.

ministry ['ministri], *s.* **1.** (*a*) *Pol:* ministère *m*, gouvernement *m*; **to form a m.,** former un ministère; (*b*) *Adm:* ministère, département *m*; **the M. of Defence,** le Ministère de la Défense. **2.** *Ecc:* **the m.,** le saint ministère; *R.C.Ch:* le ministère des autels, le sacerdoce; **he was intended for the m.,** il fut destiné à l'Église. **3.** ministère, entremise *f* (**of,** de).

minium ['miniəm], *s.* minium *m*; plomb *m* rouge.

miniver ['minivər], *s.* **1.** *Z: A:* petit-gris *m*, *pl.* petits-gris. **2.** (*fur*) petit-gris.

minivet ['minivet], *s. Orn:* minivet *m*.

mink [miŋk], *s.* **1.** *Z:* (**American**) **m.,** vison *m*; martre *f* du Canada; **m. farm,** visonnière *f*. **2.** (*fur*) vison; **simulated m.,** visonnette *f*; **a m. coat,** *F:* **a m.,** un manteau de vison, *F:* un vison.

minkery ['miŋkəri], *s. Breed:* visonnière *f*.

Minkies (the) [ðə'miŋkiz]. *Pr.n. Geog:* le plateau des Minquiers.

minnow ['minou], *s.* **1.** *Ich:* vairon *m*; (*also loosely*) épinoche *f*. **2.** *Fish:* devon *m*.

Minoan [mi'nouən], *a. A.Hist:* minoen.

minor ['mainər]. **1.** *a.* (*a*) (*lesser*) petit, mineur; **m. planets,** petites planètes; *Ecc:* **m. orders,** ordres mineurs; *Rel.H:* **m. (friar),** frère mineur; (*b*) (*comparatively unimportant*) petit, menu, peu important; **m. poet,** petit poète, poète de second ordre; **m. accidents,** accidents *m* minimes, peu graves; **m. expenses,** menus frais; **m. repairs,** petites réparations; menues réparations; réparations peu importantes; **question of m. interest,** question *f* d'intérêt secondaire; *Parl:* **m. amendment,** amendement *m* subsidiaire, de portée restreinte; **this drawback is of m. importance,** cet inconvénient est secondaire, de moindre importance; **to play a m. part,** jouer un rôle subalterne, accessoire; **m. roads,** routes secondaires; *Mth:* **m. axis,** petit axe (d'une ellipse); *Cards:* **m. suit,** petite couleur (trèfle ou carreau); *Med:* **m. surgery,** petite chirurgie; chirurgie ministrante; **m. operation,** opération *f* d'importance secondaire; (*c*) *Log:* **m. term,** *s.* **m.,** petit terme; mineure *f*; (*d*) *Mus:* **m. scale,** gamme mineure; **m. third,** tierce mineure; **in the m. (key),** en mineur; **in a m.,** en la mineur; *F:* **his conversation was pitched in a m. key,** sa conversation était plutôt triste; (*e*) *Sch:* **Jones m.,** le plus jeune des Jones (qui sont deux). **2.** *s.* (*a*) *Jur:* mineur, -eure; (*b*) *Ecc:* **the Minors,** les frères mineurs; l'ordre *m* de saint François d'Assise.

Minorca [mi'nɔːkə]. **1.** *Pr.n. Geog:* Minorque *f*. **2.** *s. Husb:* coq *m*, poule *f*, de Minorque; minorque *f*.

Minorcan [mi'nɔːkən]. *Geog:* (*a*) *a.* minorquin; (*b*) *s.* Minorquin, -ine.

Minorite ['mainərait], *s. Ecc:* frère mineur; franciscain *m*; **the M. order,** l'ordre *m* des frères mineurs; l'ordre de saint François d'Assise.

minority [mi'nɔriti, mai-], *s.* **1.** (*a*) minorité *f*; **to be in a, the, m.,** être en minorité; **to be in a m. of one,** être seul de son opinion; (*b*) **minorities have their rights,** les minorités ont leurs droits; **m. member,** membre *m* (d'un comité) qui représente une minorité; **m. report,** rapport (d'une commission d'enquête) rédigé par la minorité; **m. party,** parti minoritaire. **2.** *Jur:* minorité; **during the m. of Louis XV,** pendant la minorité de Louis XV.

Minotaur ['m(a)inətɔːr]. *Pr.n. Gr.Myth:* **the M.,** le Minotaure.

minster ['minstər], *s.* (*a*) église abbatiale; (*b*) grande église; cathédrale *f*; **York M.,** la cathédrale d'York.

minstrel ['minstrəl], *s.* **1.** (*a*) *Hist:* ménestrel *m*; (*b*) *Lit:* poète *m*, musicien *m*, chanteur *m*; *Lit:* chantre *m* (de hauts faits). **2.** *A:* **negro minstrels, nigger minstrels, Christy minstrels,** troupe *f* de chanteurs et de comiques déguisés en nègres (dont le répertoire est censé être d'origine nègre).

minstrelsy ['minstrəlsi], *s. Lit:* **1.** art *m* du ménestrel; chant *m* des ménestrels. **2.** *coll.* chants (d'une nation, d'une région). **3.** *coll.* ménestrandise *f*.

mint¹ [mint], *s.* **1. the M.,** l'Hôtel *m* de la Monnaie; l'Hôtel des Monnaies; la Monnaie; (*of coin*) **fresh from the m.,** à fleur de coin; (*of medal, stamp, print, book, etc.*) **in m. state, in m. condition,** à l'état (de) neuf; *Fin:* **m. par,** pair *m* intrinsèque, pair théorique; *F:* **to be worth a m. (of money),** (i) (*of pers.*) rouler sur l'or; (ii) (*of thg*) valoir une somme fabuleuse, une fortune; **to spend a m. (of money),** dépenser des sommes folles; **it costs a m. (of money),** cela coûte les yeux de la tête. **2.** *Lit:* source *f*, origine *f*; **the m. of our noblest speech,** la source de ce qu'il y a de plus noble dans notre langue.

mint², *v.tr.* **1.** (*a*) **to m. money,** (i) frapper de la monnaie, battre monnaie; (ii) *F:* amasser de l'argent à la pelle; (*b*) monnayer (de l'or, etc.). **2.** *Lit:* inventer, forger, fabriquer, créer (un mot, une expression).

mint³, *s.* (*a*) *Bot:* menthe *f*; **garden m.,** baume vert, menthe verte; **wild m.,** menthe sauvage, baume des champs; **horse m.,** menthe aquatique, sauvage; **m. geranium,** balsamite *f*, baume des jardins, menthe-coq *f*, menthe de Notre-Dame; (*b*) *Pharm:* **m. camphor,** menthol *m*; (*c*) *Comest:* bonbon *m* à la menthe; pastille *f* de menthe; **m. chocolate, after-dinner m.,** chocolat fourré de crème à la menthe; **m. sauce,** vinaigrette *f* à la menthe; **m. tea,** (i) thé *m* à la menthe; (ii) infusion *f* à la menthe; *esp. U.S:* **m. julep, m. sling,** boisson alcoolique parfumée à la menthe.

mintage ['mintidʒ], *s.* **1.** (*a*) monnayage *m*; frappe *f* de la monnaie; (*b*) *Lit:* invention *f* (d'un mot); fabrication *f* (d'une théorie). **2.** espèces monnayées (de telle date, de telle Monnaie). **3.** droit *m* de monnayage; droit de frappe. **4.** *Num:* empreinte *f*.

minter ['mintər], *s.* monnayeur *m*.

minting ['mintiŋ], *s.* monnayage *m*; **m. press,** presse *f* monétaire.

mintmark ['mintmɑːk], *s. Num:* déférent *m*, différent *m*; nom *m*, marque *f*, de l'atelier monétaire.

mintmaster ['mintmɑːstər], *s.m.* directeur de la Monnaie.

Minturnae [min'təːniː]. *Pr.n. A.Geog:* Minturnes *fpl*.

minuend ['minjuend], *s. Mth:* nombre duquel on soustrait.

minuet [minju'et], *s. Mus: Danc:* menuet *m*.

minus ['mainəs]. **1.** *prep.* moins; **ten m. eight leaves two,** dix moins huit égale deux; **he managed to escape, but m. his luggage,** il a réussi à s'enfuir, mais sans (ses) bagages, mais privé de ses bagages; **I got out of it m. one eye,** je m'en suis tiré avec un œil en moins; **a pedestal m. its statue,** un piédestal veuf de sa statue; **bond m. its coupons,** titre démuni de coupons. **2.** *a. Mth:* **m. sign,** *s.* **m.,** moins *m*; **m. quantity,** quantité négative; *F:* **it's a m. quantity,** cela n'existe pas; *F:* **he's a m. quantity,** il est nul.

minuscule ['minəskjuːl]. **1.** *a.* minuscule. **2.** *s. Pal:* minuscule *f*.

minute¹ ['minit], *s.* **1.** (*a*) minute *f* (de temps); **to wait ten minutes,** attendre dix minutes; **it's ten minutes to three, ten minutes past three,** il est trois heures moins dix, trois heures dix; **to live ten minutes from the station,** habiter à dix minutes de la gare; **m. hand,** aiguille *f* des minutes, grande aiguille (d'une montre, etc.); **m. gun,** coup *m* de canon de minute en minute (en signe de deuil, *Nau:* comme signal de détresse); (*b*) **a minute's rest,** un moment de repos; **wait a m.!** attendez un instant! **he's come in this (very) m.,** il rentre à l'instant (même); il vient juste de rentrer; **he was here a m. ago,** il était là il y a un instant; il vient de sortir; **I'll come, be with you, in a m.,** j'arrive(rai), je suis à vous, dans un instant; **he'll be here any m.,** je l'attends d'un moment à l'autre; **in a few minutes,** dans quelques minutes; **I shan't be a m., many minutes,** j'en ai pour une seconde; je ne serai pas longtemps; je ne fais qu'aller et (re)venir; **it won't take a m.,** ce n'est que l'affaire d'un instant; **I've just looked, slipped, popped, in for a m.,** je ne fais qu'entrer et sortir; **just give me a m. to sign my letters,** le temps de signer mes lettres et je suis à vous; **I haven't a free m.,** je n'ai pas une minute pour moi; **to arrive on the m.,** être ponctuel, exact; arriver à l'heure précise; **he arrived at nine on the m.,** il est arrivé à neuf heures tapant; **two hours to the m.,** deux heures montre en main; **to be punctual to the m.,** être à la minute; **I'll send him to you the m. he arrives,** je vous l'enverrai dès qu'il arrivera, dès son arrivée; **the m. I heard the news,** dès que j'ai su la nouvelle. **2.** *Mth: Astr:* minute (de degré); **centesimal m.,** minute centésimale. **3.** minute, brouillon *m*, projet *m* (d'un contrat, etc.). **4.** (*a*) note *f* (de service); **ephemeral m.,** note volante; **to make a m. of sth.,** prendre note de qch.; faire la minute (d'une transaction, etc.); **to take minutes of a conversation,** noter une conversation; **m. of dissent,** insertion *f* au procès-verbal de l'avis contraire d'un membre (de la commission); (*b*) **minutes of a meeting,** procès-verbal *m* d'une séance; **to confirm the minutes of the last meeting,** approuver le procès-verbal de la dernière séance; **to keep the minutes of the meetings,** tenir le procès-verbal des réunions; *Dipl:* **minutes of a convention,** recez *m* d'une convention; **m. book,** (i) registre *m* des procès-verbaux, des délibérations; (ii) *Adm:* journal *m* de correspondances et d'actes; (iii) *Jur:* minutier *m*; (*c*) **treasury m.,** approbation *f* de la Trésorerie; communiqué *m* de la Trésorerie.

minute² ['minit], *v.tr.* **1.** compter (une entrevue, etc.) à la minute; *Sp:* chronométrer (une course). **2.** (*a*) faire la minute de, minuter (un contrat, etc.); (*b*) **to m. sth. down,** prendre note de qch.; noter qch.; prendre acte de qch.; (*c*) **to m. (the proceedings of) a meeting,** dresser le procès-verbal, le compte rendu, d'une séance; verbaliser une séance.

minute³ [mai'njuːt], *a.* **1.** (*a*) tout petit; menu, minuscule, minime; **m. particle,** parcelle *f* minuscule; **m. graduations,** graduations *f* minimes; (*b*) **the minutest particulars,** les moindres détails, les détails les plus infimes, les derniers détails. **2.** minutieux; **m. examination,** inspection minutieuse; **m. account,** compte rendu très détaillé.

minutely [mai'njuːtli], *adv.* minutieusement; en détail; dans les moindres détails.

minuteness [mai'njuːtnis], *s.* **1.** petitesse *f*, exiguïté *f*. **2.** minutie *f*; exactitude minutieuse; détails minutieux.

minutia, *pl.* **-iae** [mai'njuːʃiə, -iiː], *s.* (*usu.pl.*) **minutiae,** minuties *f*; petits détails; détails infimes.

minx [miŋks], *s.f. F:* friponne, coquine; **you little m.!** petite espiègle! petite polissonne! **she's a sly little m.,** c'est une fine mouche.

Minyan ['miniən]. *A.Hist:* (*a*) *a.* minyen; (*b*) *s.* Minyen, -enne.

Miocene ['maiousiːn], *a.* & *s. Geol:* miocène (*m*).

miohippus [maiou'hipəs], *s. Paleont:* miohippus *m*.

miosis [mai'ousis], *s. Med:* myosis *m*.

mirabelle ['mirəbel], *s. Hort:* **m. (plum),** mirabelle *f*.

mirabilite [mi'ræbilait], *s. Miner:* mirabilite *f*.

miracle ['mirəkl], *s.* **1.** (*a*) miracle *m*; **to work, accomplish, do, a m.,** faire, opérer, un miracle; **by a m.,** par miracle; (*b*) miracle, prodige *m*; **it sounds like a m.,** cela tient du miracle, du prodige; **it's a m. that . . .,** c'est (un) miracle que + *sub.*; **m. of ingenuity,** merveille *f* d'ingéniosité. **2.** *Lit:* **m. (play),** miracle.

miraculous [mi'rækjuləs], *a.* (*a*) miraculeux; (*b*) miraculeux, extraordinaire, merveilleux; **there's something m. about that,** cela tient du miracle, du prodige; **to have a m. escape,** échapper comme par miracle.

miraculously [mi'rækjuləsli], *adv.* (*a*) miraculeusement; (*b*) par miracle.

miraculousness [mi'rækjuləsnis], *s.* caractère miraculeux; le miraculeux (d'un événement, d'une guérison, etc.).

mirador ['mirədɔːr], *s.* mirador(e) *m*; belvédère *m*.

mirage ['mirɑːʒ], *s.* mirage *m*.

mirbane ['məːbein], *s. Ch:* mirbane *f*; **essence, oil, of m.,** essence *f* de mirbane.

mire¹ ['maiər], *s.* (*a*) bourbier *m*; fondrière *f*; (*b*) boue *f*, bourbe *f*, fange *f*; **to sink into the m.,** (i) s'enfoncer dans la boue, dans un bourbier; s'embourber; (ii) s'embourber, s'avilir; (iii) s'embourber, s'embarrasser; se mettre dans le pétrin; **to drag s.o., s.o.'s name, through the m.,** traîner qn dans la boue, dans la fange; (*c*) *Orn: A:* **m. crow,** mouette rieuse.

mire². *A:* **1.** *v.tr.* (*a*) embourber (qn, une charrette, etc.); enfoncer (qn) dans un bourbier; (*b*) salir (qn) de boue; crotter (qn). **2.** *v.i.* s'embourber; s'enfoncer dans un bourbier; tomber dans la fange.

mire-drum ['maiərdrʌm], *s. Orn: F:* butor *m.*
mirific [mi'rifik], *a.* mirifique.
miriness ['maiərinis], *s.* état boueux, état fangeux (des routes, etc.).
mirliton ['miəlitən], *s. Mus:* mirliton *m.*
mirror[1] ['mirər], *s.* **1.** miroir *m*; (*a*) *Opt: Ph:* **burning m.,** miroir ardent; **concave, convex, m.,** miroir concave, convexe; **hyperbolic, parabolic, m.,** miroir hyperbolique, parabolique; **plane m.,** miroir plan; **Fresnel mirrors,** miroirs de Fresnel; *Atom.Ph:* **magnetic m.,** miroir magnétique; **m. nuclei,** noyaux *m* miroirs; **m. nucleides,** nucléides *m* miroirs; (*b*) miroir, glace *f*; **hand m.,** miroir, glace, à main; **shaving m.,** miroir à raser, à barbe; **facet m., segmented m.,** miroir à facettes; **triple m.,** miroir (pliant) à trois faces; **magnifying m.,** miroir grossissant; **distorting m.,** miroir déformant; **m. wardrobe,** armoire *f* à glace; *Com: Ind:* **m. manufacture, m. trade,** la miroiterie; **m. factory,** miroiterie; **m. maker,** miroitier *m*; **m. writing,** écriture *f* en miroir, écriture spéculaire; (*c*) *Tchn:* **illuminating m.,** miroir d'éclairage; *Aut:* **driving m., rear view m.,** (miroir) rétroviseur *m*; *Dent:* **dental m., mouth m.,** miroir dentaire, buccal; *Med:* **head m.,** miroir frontal; *Mil:* **laying m.,** miroir de pointage; (*on aircraft carrier*) **landing m., m. side deck landing aid,** miroir d'apontage; **m. finish, m. polish,** fini *m*, polissage *m*, spéculaire; *El:* **m. galvanometer,** galvanomètre *m* à miroir; **m. oscilloscope,** oscilloscope *m* à miroir; *Phot:* **m. lens,** objectif *m* à lentille spéculaire; (*d*) **the press is the m. of public opinion,** la presse est le miroir de l'opinion publique; *Lit:* **the eyes are the mirrors of the soul,** les yeux sont les miroirs de l'âme. **2.** *Elcs:* réflecteur *m* parabolique pour micro-ondes.
mirror[2], *v.tr.* refléter; **the steeple is mirrored in the lake,** le clocher se reflète, se mire, dans le lac.
mirth [mə:θ], *s.* gaieté *f*, allégresse *f*; réjouissance *f*; rire *m*, hilarité *f*.
mirthful ['mə:θful], *a.* **1.** gai, joyeux. **2.** amusant, désopilant.
mirthfully ['mə:θfuli], *adv.* gaiement, joyeusement.
mirthfulness ['mə:θfulnis], *s.* allégresse *f*; gaieté *f*.
mirthless ['mə:θlis], *a.* sans gaieté; triste; **m. laughter,** rire forcé, amer.
mirthlessness ['mə:θlisnis], *s.* manque *m* de gaieté; tristesse *f*.
miry [m'aiəri], *a.* **1.** fangeux, bourbeux, boueux; vaseux. **2.** fangeux, ignoble.
mis- [mis], *pref.* **1.** mé-, més-. **2.** mal (+ *vb*); mauvais (+ *s*); peu (+ *adj.*).
misaddress [misə'dres], *v.tr.* mal adresser (une lettre, etc.).
misadventure [misəd'ventjər], *s.* mésaventure *f*, contretemps *m*; avatar *m*.
misadvise [misəd'vaiz], *v.tr.* mal conseiller (qn).
misaligned [misə'laind], *a.* mal aligné; *Mec.E:* (*of wheel, etc.*) excentré.
misalignment [misə'lainmənt], *s.* mauvais alignement; défaut *m* d'alignement.
misalliance [misə'laiəns], *s.* mésalliance *f*.
misanthrope ['misənθroup], *s.* misanthrope *mf*.
misanthropic(al) [misən'θrɔpik(l)], *a.* (personne *f*, caractère *m*) misanthrope; (humeur *f*, réflexion *f*) misanthropique.
misanthropist [mi'sænθrəpist], *s.* = MISANTHROPE.
misanthropy [mis'ænθrəpi], *s.* misanthropie *f*, misanthropisme *m*.
misapplication [misæpli'keiʃ(ə)n], *s.* **1.** mauvaise application, emploi abusif (d'un mot, etc.); mauvais usage (d'un remède). **2.** emploi injustifié (d'une somme d'argent); détournement *m* (de fonds).
misapply [misə'plai], *v.tr.* **1.** mal appliquer (qch.); appliquer (qch.) mal à propos; faire un mauvais usage (d'un remède). **2.** faire un emploi injustifié (d'une somme d'argent); détourner (des fonds).
misapprehend [misæpri'hend], *v.tr.* mal comprendre (qn, qch.); se méprendre sur (les paroles de qn); mal saisir (un mot).
misapprehension [misæpri'henʃ(ə)n], *s.* malentendu *m*, méprise *f*; **m. of the facts,** fausse interprétation, idée fausse, des faits; **to do sth. under a m.,** faire qch. par méprise, pour s'être mal rendu compte des faits.
misapprehensive [misæpri'hensiv], *a.* qui se méprend (**of,** sur); qui comprend mal, qui a mal saisi.
misappropriate [misə'prouprieit], *v.tr.* détourner, distraire, dilapider (des fonds).
misappropriation ['misəproupri'eiʃ(ə)n], *s.* détournement *m*, distraction *f*, dilapidation *f*, divertissement *m*, déprédation *f* (de fonds); *Jur:* abus *m* de confiance; **m. of public funds,** détournement des deniers de l'État, des deniers publics; concussion *f*.
misbegotten [misbi'gɔt(ə)n], *a.* **1.** (*a*) (enfant) illégitime, bâtard; (*b*) **m. plant, animal,** avorton *m*. **2.** vil, misérable; qui ne ressemble à rien; **another of his m. plans!** encore un de ses projets biscornus, qui ne riment à rien, qui n'aboutissent à rien.
misbehave [misbi'heiv], *v.i.* se mal conduire; avoir une mauvaise conduite; **I hope the children haven't misbehaved,** j'espère que les enfants n'ont pas été méchants.
misbehaviour [misbi'heivjər], *s.* (*a*) mauvaise conduite; inconduite *f*; (*b*) faute *f*; écart *m* de conduite.
misbelief [misbi'li:f], *s.* **1.** (*a*) *Theol:* fausse croyance; (*b*) opinion erronée. **2.** *A:* incrédulité *f*.
miscalculate [mis'kælkjuleit]. **1.** *v.tr.* mal calculer (une somme, un effort, une distance, etc.). **2.** *v.i.* **to m. about sth.,** se tromper sur qch.
miscalculation [misk:ækju'leiʃ(ə)n], *s.* faux calcul; calcul erroné; mécompte *m*; erreur *f* de calcul, erreur de compte; **a m. of the distance,** une fausse appréciation de la distance.
miscall [mis'kɔ:l], *v.tr.* **1.** mal nommer; nommer improprement; attribuer un faux nom à (qn); **he was miscalled *the Good*,** on l'a appelé à tort *le Bon*. **2.** *Dial:* injurier, invectiver (qn).
miscarriage [mis'kæridʒ], *s.* **1.** égarement *m*, perte *f* (d'une lettre, d'un colis, confiés à la poste ou au chemin de fer). **2.** (*a*) avortement *m*, insuccès *m*, échec *m*, échouement *m* (d'un projet); (*b*) *Jur:* **m. of justice,** erreur *f* judiciaire; mal-jugé *m*; déni *m* de justice. **3.** *Med:* fausse couche; avortement (spontané); **to have a m.,** faire une fausse couche.
miscarry [mis'kæri], *v.i.* **1.** (*of letter*) (i) s'égarer, se perdre; (ii) parvenir à une fausse adresse. **2.** (*of scheme, enterprise*) avorter, échouer; ne pas réussir; manquer, rater, mal tourner; **plan that looks like miscarrying,** projet *m* qui fait long feu. **3.** *Med:* faire une fausse couche; avorter.
miscegenation [misidʒi'neiʃ(ə)n], *s.* métissage *m*; croisement *m* (de races).
miscellanea [misə'leiniə], *s.pl. Lit:* miscellanées *f*; mélanges *m*.
miscellaneous [misə'leiniəs], *a.* **1.** varié, mêlé, mélangé, divers; **m. remarks,** remarques diverses; **m. news,** nouvelles variées; **m. prose works,** mélanges *m* en prose; *Journ:* **m. column,** avis *mpl* divers; (*in catalogue*) **m. (items),** mélanges. **2.** (*of pers.*) à l'esprit souple; qui a écrit en plusieurs genres.
miscellaneously [misə'leiniəsli], *adv.* avec variété; diversement; de diverses façons; **to write m.,** écrire sur des sujets variés.
miscellaneousness [misə'leiniəsnis], *s.* variété *f*, diversité *f*.
miscellanist [mi'selənist], *s. Lit:* anthologiste *mf*.
miscellany [mi'seləni], *s.* **1.** mélange *m*; collection *f* d'objets variés. **2.** *Lit:* (*a*) **miscellanies,** miscellanées *f*, mélanges *m*; (*b*) mélange, recueil *m*; anthologie *f*; **prose m.,** mélanges en prose.
mischance[1] [mis'tʃɑ:ns], *s.* **1.** mauvaise chance. **2.** malheur *m*, mésaventure *f*, accident *m*, infortune *f*; **by m.,** par mal(e)chance.
mischance[2], *v.i. A:* méchoir.
mischief ['mistʃif], *s.* **1.** mal *m*, tort *m*, dommage *m*, dégât(s) *m(pl)*; mauvais coup; **to do m.,** faire du mal; **to do s.o. a m.,** faire du mal, du tort, à qn; porter un mauvais coup à qn; faire un malheur; **to mean m.,** chercher à nuire; méditer un mauvais coup; avoir de mauvais desseins, des intentions malveillantes; **to make m.,** apporter le trouble, semer la zizanie (dans un ménage, dans une famille); semer la discorde; **to make m. between two people,** créer de la discorde entre deux personnes; brouiller deux personnes. **2.** malice *f*; **out of pure m.,** par pure malice; (i) par pure espièglerie; (ii) par pure méchanceté; **he's full of m.,** il est malin comme un singe; il est très espiègle; c'est un petit diable; **ready for m.,** (i) prêt à jouer des tours; (ii) prêt à toutes les méchancetés; (*of child*) **to be always getting into m.,** être toujours à faire des siennes; **don't get into m.! keep out of m.!** (i) ne faites pas de bêtises! (ii) faites attention à ne pas vous attirer d'ennuis! **to keep s.o. out of m.,** empêcher qn de faire des sottises, des bêtises; **that'll keep him out of m.,** ça l'occupera, le tiendra occupé; **he's up to (some) m.,** (i) il médite une malice, une espièglerie; (ii) il médite quelque mauvais tour, quelque vilenie, un mauvais coup; **I wonder what m. he's up to,** je me demande ce qu'il fricote; *Prov:* **Satan finds some m. still for idle hands to do,** l'oisiveté est la mère de tous les vices. **3.** (*pers.*) fripon, -onne; malin, -igne; **little m.,** petit(e) espiègle, petit(e) coquin(e); petit(e) d'enfant; *O:* **she looks a little m.,** elle a l'œil fripon.
mischiefmaker ['mistʃifmeikər], *s.* brandon *m* de discorde; tison *m* de discorde; mauvaise langue.
mischiefmaking[1] ['mistʃifmeikiŋ], *a.* malfaisant, tracassier; qui sème la discorde.
mischiefmaking[2], *s.* tracasserie *f*; méchanceté *f*; **to like m.,** aimer à tracasser les gens, à semer la discorde.
mischievous ['mistʃivəs], *a.* **1.** (*a*) (*of pers.*) méchant, malfaisant; *Tp:* **m. call,** appel malveillant; (*b*) (*of thg*) mauvais, malfaisant, nuisible, pernicieux. **2.** (enfant) espiègle, malicieux, gamin; **m. eye,** œil fripon; **m. trick, prank,** espièglerie *f*, farce *f*; **as m. as a monkey,** malin, malicieux, comme un singe.
mischievously ['mistʃivəsli], *adv.* **1.** (*a*) méchamment; par malveillance; (*b*) nuisiblement. **2.** malicieusement; par espièglerie.
mischievousness ['mistʃivəsnis], *s.* **1.** nature malfaisante; (*a*) méchanceté *f*; (*b*) nature nuisible (de qch.). **2.** malice *f*, espièglerie *f*, gaminerie *f* (d'un enfant).
mischmetal ['miʃmetl], *s.* mischmétal *m*.
miscibility [misi'biliti], *s.* miscibilité *f*.
miscible ['misibl], *a.* miscible (**with,** avec).
miscolour [mis'kʌlər], *v.tr.* représenter (qch.) sous un faux jour; dénaturer (un fait).
miscomputation [miskɔmpju'teiʃ(ə)n], *s.* faux calcul; erreur *f* de calcul; mécompte *m*.
miscompute [miskəm'pju:t], *v.tr.* & *i.* mal compter, mécompter; faire une erreur de calcul.
misconceive [miskən'si:v]. **1.** *v.ind.tr.* **to m. of one's duty,** mal concevoir son devoir. **2.** *v.tr.* mal comprendre (un mot); prendre (un passage) de travers.
misconceived [miskən'si:vd], *a.* **1.** mal conçu. **2. to have a m. idea of sth.,** avoir une fausse idée de qch.
misconception [miskən'sepʃ(ə)n], *s.* **1.** conception erronée; idée fausse. **2.** malentendu *m*.
misconduct[1] [mis'kɔndʌkt], *s.* **1.** mauvaise administration, mauvaise gestion (d'une affaire). **2.** (*of pers.*) (*a*) mauvaise conduite; inconduite *f*; déportements *mpl*; (*b*) *Jur:* adultère *m*; **m. took place,** il y a eu faute, inconduite.
misconduct[2] [miskən'dʌkt], *v.tr.* **1.** mal diriger, mal gérer (une affaire). **2. to m. oneself,** se mal conduire.
misconjecture [miskən'dʒektjər], *s.* fausse conjecture.
misconstruction [miskən'strʌkʃ(ə)n], *s.* fausse interprétation; mésinterprétation *f*; contre-sens *m*.
misconstrue [miskən'stru:], *v.tr.* mal interpréter, mésinterpréter (qch.); interpréter (qch.) à contresens; prendre (qch.) à rebours, à contre-pied; tourner (une action) en mal; **you have misconstrued my words,** vous avez mal pris mes paroles; vous avez pris le contre-sens de mes paroles.
miscopy [mis'kɔpi], *v.tr.* copier de travers; mal copier.
miscount[1] ['miskaunt], *s.* (*a*) erreur *f* de calcul; faux calcul; (*b*) erreur d'addition; *Pol:* erreur dans le dépouillement du scrutin.
miscount[2] [mis'kaunt], *v.tr.* & *i.* mal compter; faire une erreur de calcul.
miscreant ['miskriənt]. **1.** *a.* (*a*) scélérat, misérable; (*b*) *A:* infidèle; sans croyance. **2.** *s.* (*a*) scélérat *m*, misérable *m*, vaurien *m*, gredin *m*; (*b*) *A:* mécréant *m*, infidèle *m*.
miscue[1] [mis'kju:], *s. Bill:* fausse queue; faux coup de queue.
miscue[2], *v.i. Bill:* faire fausse queue.
misdate [mis'deit], *v.tr.* mal dater (une lettre, un chèque, un événement historique).
misdating [mis'deitiŋ], *s.* erreur *f* de date.
misdeal[1] [mis'di:l], *s. Cards:* maldonne *f*, fausse donne, mauvaise donne; **it's a m.,** il y a maldonne.
misdeal[2], *v.tr.* & *i.* (**misdealt** [mis'delt]) *Cards:* **to m. (the cards),** faire maldonne; maldonner.
misdeed [mis'di:d], *s.* méfait *m*; (*a*) mauvaise action; (*b*) crime *m*, délit *m*.
misdelivery [misdi'livəri], *s.* erreur *f* de livraison.
misdemean [misdi'mi:n], *v.pr. A:* & *Lit:* **to m. oneself,** se mal comporter, se mal conduire.
misdemeanant [misdi'mi:nənt], *s. Jur:* délinquant, -ante; coupable *mf*.
misdemeanour [misdi'mi:nər], *s.* **1.** *Jur:* délit contraventionnel (coups et blessures, fraude, faux témoignage, diffamation); acte délictueux (de moindre gravité que la *felony*); **high m.,** grave délit. **2.** *A:* & *Lit:* écart *m* de conduite; méfait *m* (d'un enfant, etc.).
misdescription [misdi'skripʃ(ə)n], *s. Jur:* fausse désignation (d'un article de commerce).
misdirect [misdi'rekt], *v.tr.* **1.** mal adresser, mal acheminer (une lettre). **2.** mal diriger (un coup); mal viser avec (un revolver, etc.). **3.** mal diriger (une entreprise, etc.). **4.** mal renseigner, mal diriger (qn); mettre (qn) sur la mauvaise voie. **5.** *Jur:* (*of judge*) **to m. the jury,** mal instruire le jury (sur un point de droit, de fait).
misdirected [misdi'rektid], *a.* **1.** (*of letter, parcel, etc.*) mal adressé; mal acheminé. **2.** (coup) frappé à faux; (feu) mal ajusté, mal visé. **3.** (zèle) mal employé.

misdirection [misdi'rekʃ(ə)n], *s.* **1.** (*a*) (*on letter*) erreur *f* d'adresse; fausse adresse; (*b*) indication erronée, renseignement erroné; *Jur:* **m. of the jury,** indications inexactes de la part du juge sur des points de droit, de fait, dans le résumé qu'il adresse au jury. **2.** *A:* mauvaise direction.
misdoing [mis'du:iŋ], *s.* méfait *m*, faute *f*.
misdoubt [mis'daut], *v.tr. A: & Dial:* **1.** douter de (qch., qn); **there was no misdoubting it,** il n'y avait pas de doute là-dessus. **2.** se douter de (qch.); soupçonner (qch.).
mise [mi:z], *s. Hist:* **1.** don *m* de joyeux avènement. **2.** accord *m*; **the M. of Amiens, the M. of Lewes,** l'Accord d'Amiens, de Lewes.
misemploy [misim'plɔi], *v.tr.* mal employer; faire un mauvais emploi de (son temps, son argent, ses talents, etc.).
misemployment [misim'plɔimənt], *s.* mauvais emploi, mauvais usage (de son temps, etc.).
misenite [mi'zenait], *s. Metall:* misénite *f*.
misenter [mis'entər], *v.tr. Book-k:* contre-poser.
misentry [mis'entri], *s.* inscription erronée, inexacte; *Book-k:* contre-position *f*, *pl.* contre-positions.
Misenum [mai'si:nəm]. *Pr.n. Geog:* le cap Misène.
miser[1] ['maizər], *s.* avare *mf*, amasseur, -euse; grigou *m*; ladre *m*.
miser[2], *s. Min:* tarière *f* à gravier.
miserabilism ['mizərəbəlizm], *s. Phil:* misérabilisme *m*.
miserable ['miz(ə)rəbl], *a.* **1.** (*of pers.*) malheureux, triste; **utterly m.,** malheureux comme les pierres; **to make s.o.'s life m.,** rendre la vie dure à qn. **2.** (*of event, condition*) misérable, déplorable; **what m. weather!** quel chien de temps! **m. journey,** voyage *m* pénible, désagréable. **3.** (*a*) misérable, pauvre, piteux, pitoyable; **m. dwelling,** logement *m* misérable, sordide; **her m. dress,** sa méchante robe; **m. sum,** somme insignifiante; **m. speech,** pauvre, piteux, discours; **it was a m. performance,** la représentation a été lamentable; **m. wage,** salaire *m* dérisoire; (*b*) **I want only a m. seven hundred pounds to get straight,** il ne me faudrait que sept cents misérables livres pour me remettre d'aplomb; **at the end of thirty years' work he had saved a m. five or six hundred pounds,** au bout de trente ans de travail, il avait amassé cinq ou six pauvres cents livres.
miserableness ['miz(ə)rəb(ə)lnis], *s.* état malheureux, état misérable.
miserably ['miz(ə)rəbli], *adv.* misérablement; (*a*) malheureusement, lamentablement; **to die m.,** mourir misérablement; (*b*) pauvrement, piètrement; **m. dressed,** vêtu piètrement; **to be m. paid,** avoir un salaire dérisoire, de misère.
misère [mi'zɛər], *s. Cards:* misère *f*; **to go m.,** jouer la misère.
miserere [mizə'riəri], *s. Ecc:* **1.** miséréré *m*, miserere *m*. **2. m. (seat)** = MISERICORD 1 (*b*).
misericord [mi'zerikɔ:d], *s.* **1.** *Ecc:* (*a*) miséricorde *f* (de monastère); (*b*) miséricorde, patience *f* (de stalle). **2.** *A:* **m. (dagger),** miséricorde.
miserliness ['maizəlinis], *s.* avarice *f*, ladrerie *f*.
miserly ['maizəli], *a.* **1.** (*of pers.*) avare, pingre, ladre. **2.** (*of habits, etc.*) d'avare; sordide.
misery ['mizəri], *s.* **1.** souffrance(s) *f*(*pl*), supplice *m*; **to put s.o. out of his m.,** mettre fin aux souffrances de qn; **to put an animal out of its m.,** achever un animal; donner le coup de grâce à un animal; **his life was sheer m.,** sa vie était un martyre. **2.** détresse *f*; **to make s.o.'s life a m.,** rendre la vie malheureuse à qn; **what a m.!** quel malheur! **3.** (*pers.*) *F:* geigneur, -euse; geignard, -arde.
misestimate[1] [mis'estimət], *s.* mésestimation *f*.
misestimate[2] [mis'estimeit], *v.tr.* mésestimer (qch.); estimer (qch.) à tort.
misexplain [misiks'plein], *v.tr.* donner une fausse explication de (qch.); expliquer mal (qch.).
misfeasance [mis'fi:z(ə)ns], *s. Jur:* infraction *f* à la loi; *esp.* abus *m* de pouvoir; abus d'autorité.
misfeasor [mis'fi:zər], *s. Jur:* contrevenant *m*; personne *f* commettant un abus de pouvoir, d'autorité.
misfeed[1] [mis'fi:d], *s.* défaut *m* d'alimentation (d'une arme automatique, d'une machine, d'un ordinateur); passage défectueux (d'une carte dans un ordinateur).
misfeed[2], *v.i.* (*of automatic weapon, machine, computer*) mal s'alimenter.
misfeeding [mis'fi:diŋ] = MISFEED[1].
misfile [mis'fail], *v.tr.* mal classer (des documents, etc.).
misfire[1] [mis'faiər], *s.* **1.** (*a*) *Sm.a: Artil:* (*of round of ammunition*) raté *m* (de percussion); (*b*) *Exp:* raté d'allumage (d'un fourneau de mine); raté d'explosion; (*c*) *Ball:* raté d'allumage, de mise à feu (de la charge propulsive d'une fusée, d'un missile); (*d*) *I.C.E:* raté d'allumage. **2.** *Brickm:* brique mal cuite.
misfire[2], *v.i.* **1.** (*a*) *Sm.a: Artil:* (*of round of ammunition*) rater, faire long feu; (*b*) *exp.* (*of mine*) ne pas exploser, rater, faire long feu; (*c*) *Ball:* (*of propulsive charge of rocket*) ne pas s'allumer, avoir un raté d'allumage; (*d*) *I.C.E:* (*of engine*) avoir des ratés; rater; ne pas donner; *F:* bafouiller, cafouiller. **2.** (*of joke, etc.*) manquer son effet; tomber à plat.
misfiring [mis'faiəriŋ], *s.* **1.** = MISFIRE[1]. **2.** *Elcs:* **m. of fluorescent tube,** désamorçage *m* d'un tube fluorescent.
misfit ['misfit], *s.* (*a*) vêtement, etc., manqué, mal réussi; *Com:* laissé-pour-compte *m*, *pl.* laissés-pour-compte; (*b*) (*pers.*) inadapté, -ée; **he's a m.,** c'est un inadapté.
misfortune [mis'fɔ:tjən], *s.* infortune *f*, malheur *m*, calamité *f*; **that has been his m.,** c'est cela qui a fait son malheur; **to fall into m.,** tomber dans le malheur; **it is more his m. than his fault,** il est plus à plaindre qu'à blâmer; *Prov:* **misfortunes never come singly,** un malheur ne vient jamais seul; un malheur en appelle un autre; *F: A:* **her husband's had a m.,** son mari est sous les verrous.
misframe ['misfreim], *s. Cin: T.V:* décadrage *m*.
misgive [mis'giv], *v.tr.* (**misgave** [mis'geiv]; **misgiven** [mis'givn]) *A: & Lit:* **my heart, mind, misgives me,** j'ai de mauvais pressentiments, des doutes, des inquiétudes; **my heart misgives me that . . .,** j'ai le pressentiment que . . ..
misgiving [mis'giviŋ], *s.* doute *m*, crainte *f*, méfiance *f*, soupçon *m*, pressentiment *m*, inquiétude *f* (**about sth.,** sur qch.); **not without misgivings,** non sans hésitation; **I am not without misgivings,** je suis assez peu rassuré; **his own prospects caused him no misgivings,** son propre avenir ne l'inquiétait point; **I had a m. that I was going to have a bad time,** j'avais le pressentiment que je passerais par de rudes épreuves.
misgovern [mis'gʌvən], *v.tr.* mal gouverner.
misgovernment [mis'gʌvənmənt], *s.* mauvais gouvernement; mauvaise administration.
misguidance [mis'gaid(ə)ns], *s.* **1.** renseignements erronés. **2.** mauvais conseils *mpl*.
misguide [mis'gaid], *v.tr.* **1.** mal guider (qn); égarer (qn). **2.** mal conseiller (qn).
misguided [mis'gaidid], *a.* **1.** (*of pers.*) qui manque de jugement; dont l'enthousiasme porte à faux; qui se fourvoie; **these m. people,** ces malheureux. **2.** (*of conduct*) peu judicieux; (*of zeal*) hors de propos; (*of attempt*) malencontreux.
misguidedly [mis'gaididli], *adv.* sans jugement.
misguidedness [mis'gaididnis], *s.* manque *m* de jugement.
mishandle [mis'hændl], *v.tr.* **1.** (*a*) malmener, maltraiter, rudoyer, bousculer, (qn); (*b*) mal traiter (un sujet). **2.** mal manier, mal manœuvrer, mal utiliser (un outil, un appareil, etc.); *F:* malmener (une machine, un appareil).
mishandling [mis'hændliŋ], *s.* **1.** (*a*) mauvais traitements, brimades *fpl*, vexations *fpl* (à l'égard de qn.); (*b*) traitement défectueux, imparfait, erroné (d'un sujet). **2.** maniement défectueux (d'un outil, etc.); fausse manœuvre (dans l'utilisation d'un appareil, etc.).
mishap ['mishæp], *s.* mésaventure *f*, contretemps *m*; désagrément *m*; accident *m*; avatar *m*; **after many mishaps,** après bien des péripéties; **the horse and the jockey met with a slight m.,** le cheval et le jockey ont eu un léger accroc.
mishear [mis'hiər], *v.tr.* (**misheard** [mis'hə:d]) mal entendre.
mish-mash ['miʃmæʃ], *s. F: O:* fatras *m*, mélange *m*, méli-mélo *m*; salade *f*.
mishna(h) ['miʃnə], *s. Rel.H:* mis(c)hna *f*.
Mishnaic [miʃ'neiik], *a. Rel.H:* mishnaïque, mischnique.
misinform [misin'fɔ:m], *v.tr.* mal renseigner.
misinformation [misinfə'meiʃ(ə)n], *s.* fausse information, faux renseignement(s); renseignements erronés.
misinformed [misin'fɔ:md], *a.* mal informé; mal renseigné.
misinterpret [misin'tə:prit], *v.tr.* mal interpréter, mésinterpréter (qn, les paroles de qn); mal traduire la pensée de (qn).
misinterpretation [misintə:pri'teiʃ(ə)n], *s.* **1.** fausse interprétation. **2.** (*in translating*) contre-sens *m inv*.
misjoin [mis'dʒɔin], *v.tr. Jur:* constituer faussement (les parties).
misjoinder [mis'dʒɔindər], *s. Jur:* **m. of parties,** fausse constitution de parties.
misjudge [mis'dʒʌdʒ], *v.tr.* mal juger (qn, qch.); se tromper sur le compte de (qn); ne pas se rendre compte de (qch.); mal juger de (qch.); méconnaître (qn); **to m. a motive,** se méprendre sur un motif; **to m. the distance,** se tromper dans l'estimation de la distance.
misjudg(e)ment [mis'dʒʌdʒmənt], *s.* jugement erroné; fausse estimation (d'une distance); méprise *f*.
mislay [mis'lei], *v.tr.* (**mislaid** [mis'leid]; **mislaid**) égarer, perdre (son parapluie, etc.); *Jur:* adirer (un document, etc.).
mislead [mis'li:d], *v.tr.* (**misled** [mis'led]; **misled**) **1.** (*a*) induire (qn) en erreur; tromper (qn); **to m. s.o. about one's intentions,** tromper, abuser, qn sur ses intentions; (*b*) égarer, fourvoyer (qn). **2.** corrompre, dévoyer (qn).
misleading [mis'li:diŋ], *a.* trompeur, -euse; fallacieux.
mislike[1] [mis'laik], *s.* = MISLIKING.
mislike[2], *v.tr. A: & Dial:* ne pas aimer; détester; **to m. s.o.,** trouver qn peu sympathique.
misliking [mis'laikiŋ], *s. A: & Dial:* répugnance *f*, aversion *f*.
mislocate [mislou'keit], *v.tr.* mal placer, mal situer (qch.).
mismanage [mis'mænidʒ], *v.tr.* mal conduire, mal diriger, mal administrer, mal gérer (une affaire, une entreprise).
mismanagement [mis'mænidʒmənt], *s.* (*a*) mauvaise administration, mauvaise gestion; (*b*) **there has been some m.,** l'affaire a été mal menée.
mismatch[1] [mis'mætʃ], *s.* **1.** *O:* (*a*) erreur *f* d'assortiment; (*b*) lutte inégale (entre combattants, entre concurrents dans une épreuve sportive ou technique); **the contest between the two men was an obvious m.,** la lutte entre les deux hommes était incontestablement inégale. **2.** *Tchn:* défaut *m* d'adaptation.
mismatch[2], *v.tr.* **1.** *O:* mal assortir; commettre, faire, une erreur d'assortiment. **2.** *Tchn:* mal adapter, désadapter.
mismatched [mis'mætʃt], *a.* **1.** *O:* mal assorti; **m. couple,** couple mal assorti. **2.** *Tchn:* mal adapté, non adapté, désadapté.
mismatching [mis'mætʃiŋ], *s.* **1.** erreur *f* d'assortiment. **2.** *Tchn:* non adaptation *f*, désadaptation *f*; *Elcs: El:* **impedance m.,** désadaptation d'impédance; **m. factor,** coefficient *m* de réflexion, de transition.
misname [mis'neim], *v.tr.* mal nommer (qn, qch.); nommer (qn, qch.) improprement.
misnomer [mis'noumər], *s.* **1.** *Jur:* erreur *f* de nom. **2.** (*a*) nom mal approprié; (*b*) **changes which, by a great m., are called progress,** changements auxquels on donne fort mal à propos le nom de progrès.
misnumber [mis'nʌmbər], *v.tr.* mal numéroter; commettre, faire, une erreur de numérotage, de numérotation.
misnumbering [mis'nʌmb(ə)riŋ], *s.* erreur *f* de numérotage, de numérotation.
misogamist [m(a)isɔgəmist], *s.* misogame *mf*.
misogamy [m(a)i'sɔgəmi], *s.* misogamie *f*.
misogynist [m(a)i'sɔdʒinist], *s.* misogyne *mf*.
misogynous [m(a)i'sɔdʒinəs], *a.* misogyne.
misogyny [m(a)i'sɔdʒini], *s.* misogynie *f*.
misologist [m(a)i'sɔlədʒist], *s.* misologue *m*.
misology [m(a)i'sɔlədʒi], *s.* misologie *f*.
misoneism [m(a)isou'ni:izm], *s.* misonéisme *m*.
misoneist [m(a)isou'ni:ist], *s.* misonéiste *mf*.
misoneistic [m(a)isouni'istik], *a.* misonéiste.
mispickel ['mispikəl], *s. Miner:* mispickel *m*; fer arsenical; pyrite arsenicale; arsénopyrite *f*.
misplace [mis'pleis], *v.tr.* **1.** placer à faux (l'accent tonique, etc.). **2.** mal placer (ses affections, sa confiance). **3.** se tromper en remettant en place (un livre, etc.); déplacer (un livre, etc.).
misplaced [mis'pleist], *a.* **1.** (*of confidence, etc.*) mal placé. **2.** (mot) déplacé; (observation *f*) hors de propos.
misplacement [mis'pleismənt], *s.* erreur *f* de mise en place; déplacement *m*.
misplead [mis'pli:d], *v.i. Jur:* faire erreur dans la production des moyens de droit.
mispocket ['mispɔkit], *s. Cmptr:* erreur *f* de case.
misprint[1] ['misprint], *s. Typ:* faute *f* d'impression; erreur *f* typographique; *F:* coquille *f*.
misprint[2] [mis'print], *v.tr.* imprimer (un mot) incorrectement.
misprision[1] [mis'priʒ(ə)n], *s.* **1.** *Jur:* **m. of treason, of felony,** non-révélation *f* de haute trahison, d'un crime. **2.** *A:* méprise *f*; erreur *f* d'interprétation.
misprision[2], *s. A:* **1.** mépris *m*. **2.** méconnaissance *f* (de la valeur de qch., etc.); sous-estimation *f*.
misprize [mis'praiz], *v.tr. A:* **1.** mépriser. **2.** méconnaître (qn); sous-estimer (qn, qch.).
mispronounce [misprə'nauns], *v.tr.* mal prononcer (un mot).
mispronunciation [misprənʌnsi'eiʃ(ə)n], *s.* mauvaise prononciation; prononciation incorrecte; faute *f* de prononciation.
misquotation [miskwou'teiʃ(ə)n], *s.* citation inexacte.

misquote [mis'kwout], *v.tr.* citer (qch.) à faux, inexactement; **to m. a writer,** citer un auteur incorrectement.

misread[1] [mis'ri:d], *v.tr.* (**misread** [mis'red]; **misread**) mal lire, mal interpréter (un texte, etc.).

misread[2] ['misri:d], *s. Cmptr:* erreur *f* de lecture.

misreading [mis'ri:diŋ], *s.* lecture erronée; interprétation erronée (des faits, de la loi).

misreasoning [mis'ri:zniŋ], *s.* raisonnement erroné, erreur *f* de jugement.

misreckon [mis'rek(ə)n]. **1.** *v.tr.* mal calculer; mal compter. **2.** *v.i.* calculer à faux; manquer de perspicacité.

misreckoning [mis'rekəniŋ], *s.* **1.** calcul erroné. **2.** manque *m* de perspicacité.

misrelate [misri'leit], *v.tr.* raconter, rapporter, (qch.) inexactement.

misrelated [misri'leitid], *a.* **1.** rapporté inexactement. **2. m. facts,** faits qui n'ont rien en commun, qui ne vont pas ensemble. **3.** *Gram:* (participe) isolé, indépendant, sans soutien.

misrelation [misri'leiʃ(ə)n], *s.* **1.** rapport inexact; récit inexact. **2. the m. of the facts,** le mauvais groupement des faits.

misreport[1] [misri'pɔ:t], *s.* rapport inexact, narration inexacte.

misreport[2], *v.tr.* rapporter (les faits) inexactement.

misrepresent [misrepri'zent], *v.tr.* mal représenter; dénaturer, travestir (les faits); présenter (les faits) sous un faux jour.

misrepresentation [misreprizen'teiʃ(ə)n], *s.* faux rapport, faux exposé; présentation erronée des faits, d'un bilan, etc.; *Jur:* (i) fausse déclaration; (ii) réticence *f*; **wilful m.,** dol *m*; fraude civile.

misroute [mis'ru:t], *v.tr.* mal acheminer, mal diriger (un message, un appel téléphonique, etc.); acheminer (qch.) par la mauvaise voie, route.

misrouting [mis'ru:tiŋ], *s.* erreur *f* d'acheminement (d'un message, d'un paquet, d'un appel téléphonique, etc.); fausse direction.

misrule[1] [mis'ru:l], *s.* mauvaise administration, mauvais gouvernement, désordre *m*, confusion *f*; *Hist:* **Lord, Abbot, Master, of M.,** évêque *m* de la déraison, pape *m* des fous (dans les réjouissances de Noël).

misrule[2], *v.tr.* mal gouverner.

miss[1] [mis], *s.* **1.** coup manqué (pour n'avoir pas atteint le but); coup perdu; *Bill:* manque *m* de touche; manque à toucher; *Bill:* **to give a m.,** éviter de toucher; **to score a m.,** marquer un point du fait que l'adversaire a manqué à toucher; *F:* **it was a near m.,** (i) je l'ai, il l'a, raté à un cheveu près; (ii) les deux avions, les deux voitures, etc., ont failli se heurter; **to give (s.o., sth.) a m.,** passer le tour de (qn); ne pas aller voir, visiter (un monument), sécher un cours; **we'll give the museum a m.,** quant au musée, on n'y va pas! (*at dinner*) **I'll give the fish course a m.,** je ne prendrai pas de poisson; *Prov:* **a m. is as good as a mile,** manquer de près ou de loin, c'est toujours manquer. **2.** *F:* (*miscarriage*) fausse couche. **3.** *A:* manque, absence *f*, défaut *m* (**of,** de).

miss[2], *v.tr.* **1.** (*fail to hit or to find*) (*a*) manquer; *F:* rater (le but); **to m. one's mark, one's aim,** manquer son coup, son but; tirer à côté; frapper à faux, à vide; **his blow missed the mark,** le coup a donné à côté, il a manqué son coup, tapé dans le vide; **the bullet missed me by a hair's breadth,** la balle m'a manqué à un cheveu près; *v.i.* **he never misses,** il ne manque jamais son coup; **missed!** à côté! manqué! **to m. the point (in one's answer),** répondre à côté; **this criticism misses the point,** cette critique porte à faux; *Bill:* **to m.,** manquer à toucher; manquer de touche; *Th:* (*of actor*) **to m. one's entrance,** louper son entrée; **to m. one's cue,** manquer la réplique; *Nau:* **to m. stays,** manquer à virer; (*of ship*) refuser de virer; *I.C.E:* (*of engine*) **to m. fire,** *v.i.* **to m.,** = **misfire**[2] (*b*); (*b*) **to m. one's way,** se tromper de route; s'égarer; **he missed his footing,** le pied lui manqua; (*c*) ne pas trouver, ne pas rencontrer (qn); **I called at his house yesterday, but missed him (by two minutes),** je suis passé chez lui hier, mais je l'ai manqué, mais je ne l'ai pas rencontré, *F:* mais je l'ai raté (de deux minutes, à deux minutes près); (*d*) manquer, *F:* rater (un train, le bateau); (*e*) manquer, laisser échapper, laisser passer, *F:* rater (une occasion); **an opportunity not to be missed,** une occasion à saisir; une occasion qu'il ne faut pas manquer; **I have missed my turn,** j'ai perdu mon tour; **do come back, you're missing all the fun!** revenez donc! vous ne savez pas comme on s'amuse! **if you don't see it you'll be missing sth.,** si vous n'allez pas voir ça vous allez rater quelque chose de bien; *F:* **you haven't missed much!** vous n'avez pas raté grand-chose! **to m. the market,** laisser échapper le moment favorable pour la vente; *F:* **to m. the boat, the bus,** laisser échapper l'occasion; *Sch:* **he just missed a first** = il a juste manqué d'avoir une mention très bien; (*f*) ne pas se voir décerner (une récompense, un honneur); **I missed my holiday this year,** je n'ai pas eu de vacances cette année; (*g*) manquer (une conférence, un rendez-vous, un repas); *F:* sécher (un cours); **I would not have missed his speech for anything,** pour rien au monde je n'aurais voulu manquer son discours; **I never m. going there,** je ne manque jamais d'y aller; **how many lessons have you missed?** combien de leçons avez-vous manquées? (*h*) **he narrowly missed, just missed, being killed,** il a failli se faire tuer; (*i*) **to m. a remark, a joke,** ne pas saisir une observation, une plaisanterie ((i) ne pas l'entendre; (ii) ne pas la comprendre); **you have missed the real meaning of the text,** le sens véritable du texte vous a échappé; **to m. the obvious,** chercher midi à quatorze heures; **I missed the church you told me about,** je n'ai pas vu l'église dont vous m'aviez parlé; **I missed the house,** j'ai passé la maison sans m'en apercevoir; **you can't m. the house,** la maison s'impose à la vue; vous ne pouvez pas manquer de reconnaître la maison. **2.** (*a*) (*omit*) **to m. (out) a word, a line,** omettre, passer, sauter, un mot, une ligne; **to m. (out) a stop,** brûler un arrêt; **his heart missed a beat,** il a eu un pincement au cœur; (*at dinner*) **to m. out the fish course,** ne pas prendre de poisson; (*b*) *v.i. F:* **to m. out on sth.,** rater qch. **3.** (*a*) (*notice absence of*) remarquer l'absence de (qn, qch.); s'apercevoir de la disparition de (qch.); remarquer qu'il manque (qn, qch.); **he missed some money from his cashbox,** il s'aperçut qu'il manquait de l'argent dans sa caisse; **I m. the tree that used to be near the window,** je regrette cet l'arbre qui était près de la fenêtre; **I missed my spectacles,** je ne trouvais plus mes lunettes; **it will never be missed,** on ne s'apercevra pas que cela n'y est plus; **we are sure to be missed,** on s'apercevra sûrement de notre absence; **all at once I missed him,** (i) tout à coup je le perdis de vue, il disparut à mes yeux; (ii) tout à coup je m'aperçus qu'il n'était plus là; (*b*) (*feel lack of*) regretter (qn); regretter l'absence de (qn); **I m. you,** vous me manquez; **to m. an absent friend,** regretter un ami absent; **they will miss one another,** ils se manqueront; **I am not allowed cigarettes, but I do not m. them,** on me défend les cigarettes, mais je n'en sens pas le besoin, mais ce n'est pas une privation; **the late Mr Martin is sadly missed,** M. Martin a laissé, emporté, des regrets.

miss[3], *s.f.* **1. Miss Martin,** *pl.* **the Miss Martins, the Misses Martin,** mademoiselle, Mlle Martin; les demoiselles Martin; (*as address*) mademoiselle Martin, Mesdemoiselles; **thank you, Miss Martin,** merci mademoiselle; **I knew her when she was Miss X,** je l'avais connue demoiselle; **Miss World,** Miss Monde. **2.** *P:* (*with omission of proper name*) **Yes, M.; good morning, M.; three whiskeys, M.,** oui, mam'selle; bonjour mam'selle; trois whiskys, mam'selle. **3.** (*a*) *F: often Pej:* demoiselle; **a modern m.,** une jeune fille moderne; **is that little m. a friend of yours?** elle est de vos amies, cette jeune demoiselle? (*b*) *Com: O:* fillette; **shoes for misses,** chaussures *f* pour fillettes.

missal ['mis(ə)l], *s. Ecc:* missel *m*.

missel (thrush) ['mis(ə)l(θrʌʃ)], *s. Orn:* draine *f*; grive *f* draine, de gui.

mis-shapen [mis'ʃeip(ə)n], *a.* (*of pers., limb, etc.*) difforme, contrefait; (*of hat, figure, etc.*) déformé; (*of building, mind*) biscornu.

missile ['misail, -(ə)l]. **1.** *a.* (arme *f*) de jet, de trait. **2.** *s.* (*a*) projectile *m*; (*b*) *Mil:* missile *m*, engin *m*; **air-to-air m.,** missile, engin, air-air; **air-to-surface m.,** missile, engin, air-sol; *Navy:* **missile air-surface,** air-mer; **surface-to-surface m.,** missile, engin, sol-sol; *Navy:* **surface-surface,** missile, engin, mer-mer; *Navy:* **underwater-to-surface m.,** (missile) mer-sol *m inv.*; *Av:* **air-launched m.,** engin lancé en vol; **air-breathing m., cruise-type m., flying m., non-ballistic m.,** missile, engin, atmosphérique; **ballistic m.,** missile, engin, balistique; **(radio-)guided, radio-controlled, m.,** missile, engin, (télé)guidé; **homing m.,** missile, engin, autoguidé, à tête chercheuse; **intercontinental ballistic m.,** missile balistique intercontinental; **intermediate-range, medium-range, ballistic m.,** missile balistique à portée intermédiaire, à portée moyenne; **antiballistic m.,** missile antifusée(s); **anti-missile m.,** engin antimissile(s); **multiple-warhead m.,** missile à têtes, à ogives, multiples; **radar-homing m.,** engin antiradar; **tactical m.,** missile tactique; **m. base,** base *f* de lancement de missiles; **m. gap,** retard(s) *m(pl)* dans le domaine des missiles; **m. guidance,** guidage *m* de missiles; **m. launcher,** (appareil) lanceur *m* de missiles; affût *m*, rampe *f*, de lancement de missiles; **m. launching,** lancement *m*, tir *m*, de missiles; **m. range,** champ *m* de tir de missiles, d'engins.

missileer [misə'li:ər], **missileman** ['misəlmən], *s. U.S:* (*a*) *Mil:* servant *m* de lanceur de missiles, missilier *m*; (*b*) (i) projeteur *m*, (ii) constructeur *m*, de missiles.

missil(e)ry ['misəlri], *s.* technique *f* de la construction des missiles; missilerie *f*.

missing[1] ['misiŋ], *a.* absent; égaré, perdu; disparu, manquant; **the m. umbrella was found at the Martins',** le parapluie égaré a été retrouvé chez les Martin; **some books are m.,** il manque quelques livres; **one man is m.,** un homme manque; **there is only one m.,** il n'en manque qu'un(e); **he has been m. for two days,** voilà deux jours qu'on ne l'a vu; on est sans nouvelles de lui depuis deux jours; *Mil: etc:* **to report s.o. m.,** porter qn disparu; **killed, wounded, or m.,** tués, blessés, ou disparus; *s.pl.* **the m.,** les disparus.

missing[2], *s.* **1. m. of a chance,** perte *f* d'une occasion. **2.** *I.C.E:* ratés *mpl*, *F:* bafouillage *m*, cafouillage *m*.

missiology [misi'ɔlədʒi], *s. Ecc:* missiologie *f*.

mission ['miʃ(ə)n], *s.* mission *f*. **1.** (*task*) **to charge, entrust, s.o. with a m.,** charger qn d'une mission, confier une mission à qn; **to carry out, execute, fulfil, a m.,** effectuer, exécuter, remplir, une mission; s'acquitter d'une mission; **m. accomplished,** mission accomplie; **to be sent on a m. to s.o.,** être envoyé en mission auprès de qn; **minister on a special m. to Paris,** ministre *m* en mission spéciale à Paris; **she thinks her m. in life is to help lame dogs,** elle croit avoir mission de secourir les malheureux; **he failed in his m.,** il a failli dans sa mission; *Mil:* **day, night, m.,** mission de jour, de nuit; **general, special, m.,** mission générale, particulière; **primary, secondary, m.,** mission principale, secondaire; **air m.,** mission aérienne; **air force m.,** mission assignée aux forces aériennes, à l'aviation; mission de l'aviation; **fire m.,** mission de tir; **reconnaissance m.,** mission de reconnaissance; **scouting m.,** mission d'exploration; **support m.,** mission de soutien. **2.** (*body of persons entrusted with a mission*) (*a*) *U.S:* ambassade *f*; représentation *f* diplomatique; (*b*) **economic, scientific, military, trade, m.,** mission économique, scientifique, militaire, commerciale; **to exchange cultural missions,** échanger des missions culturelles; *Ecc:* **foreign, home, missions,** missions étrangères, métropolitaines; **the m. field,** les missions (étrangères); (*c*) *attrib. U.S:* **m. architecture, m. furniture,** architecture *f*, mobilier *m*, de l'époque des missions espagnoles (en Californie, etc.). **3.** (*place*) *Ecc:* **mission (station),** mission *f*.

missionary ['miʃən(ə)ri]. **1.** *a.* (prêtre *m*, œuvre *f*, esprit *m*) missionnaire; (société *f*) de missionnaires; (vocation *f*) de missionnaire; (tronc *m*) des missions. **2.** *s.* (*a*) missionnaire *mf*; (*b*) *A:* **police-court m.,** délégué(e) d'une œuvre de miséricorde auprès des tribunaux de simple police; (*c*) *U.S: Com:* prospecteur *m*.

missioner [miʃ(ə)nər], *s.* missionnaire (préposé aux œuvres d'une paroisse).

missis ['misiz], *s.f. P:* = MISSUS.

missish ['misiʃ], *a. F: O:* (manières *f*, etc.) de petite pensionnaire.

Mississippi (the) [ðəmisi'sipi]. *Pr.n. Geog:* le Mississipi.

Mississippian [misi'sipiən]. **1.** *a.* mississipien. **2.** *s.* Mississipien, -ienne.

missive ['misiv]. **1.** *a. Hist: & Jur:* **letter m.,** lettre missive. **2.** *s.* lettre *f*, missive *f*.

missort ['mis'sɔ:t], *s. Cmptr:* erreur *f* de tri.

Missourian [mi'zu:riən], *a. & s.* **1.** *a.* missourien. **2.** *s.* Missourien, -ienne.

mis-spell ['mis'spel], *v.tr.* (*p.t.* **mis-spelt** ['mis'pelt]; *p.p.* **mis-spelt**) mal épeler, mal orthographier; écrire (un mot) incorrectement.

mis-spelling ['mis'speliŋ], *s.* faute *f* d'orthographe.

mis-spend ['mis'spend], *v.tr.* (*p.t.* **mis-spent** ['mis'spent]; *p.p.* **mis-spent**) dépenser (de l'argent) mal à propos; mal employer (son argent, son temps); gâcher (son argent); faire un mauvais emploi de (son temps); **a mis-spent youth,** (i) une jeunesse mal employée; (ii) une jeunesse passée dans la dissipation.

mis-state ['mis'steit], *v.tr.* exposer, rapporter, (qch.) incorrectement; rendre un compte inexact de (qch.); altérer (des faits).

mis-statement ['mis'steitmənt], *s.* exposé inexact, rapport inexact, compte rendu erroné; **chapter full of mis-statements,** chapitre rempli d'erreurs de fait.

misstep ['mis'step], *s.* faux pas; faute *f*.

mis-suit ['mis'sju:t], *v.tr. Lit:* convenir mal à (qn), messeoir à (qn).

missus ['misəs, 'misəz], *s.f. P:* (*corruption of mistress*) (*a*) madame; **I say, M.!** eh dites donc, la petite mère! (*b*) (*wife*) femme; **the m., my m.,** ma femme, ma légitime, la patronne; **your m.,** votre dame; (*c*) *O:* (*used by ser-*

vants) **(the) m. is in the drawing room,** madame est au salon; (*d*) (*owner of pet*) maîtresse.

mist [mist], *s.* **1.** (*a*) *Meteor:* brume *f*, *Nau:* brumaille *f*; **heavy m.,** embrun *m*; **morning m.,** brume matinale; **Scotch m.,** bruine *f*, crachin *m*; *Fig:* **lost in the mists of time,** perdu dans la nuit des temps; (*b*) *Ch:* **hydrocarbon m.,** brouillard *m* d'hydrocarbure; *Mec.E:* **oil m.,** brouillard d'huile. **2.** buée *f* (sur une glace, etc.); **to have a m. before one's eyes,** avoir un voile devant les yeux; **to see things through a m.,** voir trouble.

mist². **1.** *v.tr.* couvrir (une glace, etc.) de buée. **2.** *v.i.* **to m. over,** (i) (*of landscape, etc.*) disparaître sous la brume; (ii) (*of mirror, etc.*) se couvrir de buée; (iii) (*of eyes*) se voiler; **misted-up windscreen,** pare-brise embué.

mistakable [mis'teikəbl], *a.* **1.** sujet à méprise. **2. easily m. for sth.,** facile à confondre avec qch.

mistake¹ [mis'teik], *s.* erreur *f*, inadvertance *f*; méprise *f*, faute *f*; **m. in calculation,** faux calcul; erreur de calcul; **m. in labelling,** erreur d'étiquetage; **m. in the date,** erreur de date; **exercise full of mistakes,** exercice plein de fautes; **grammatical, spelling, mistakes,** fautes de grammaire, d'orthographe; **m. in gender,** erreur sur le genre; **to make a m.,** faire une faute; commettre une faute, une erreur, une confusion; se méprendre, se tromper (**about, over,** sur, au sujet de, quant à); **you made me make a m.,** vous m'avez fait tromper; **to make a bad m.,** commettre une grave erreur; **to make the m. of doing sth.,** avoir le tort de faire qch.; **he made the m. of speaking too soon,** il a eu le tort de parler trop tôt; **to do sth. by m.,** faire qch. par erreur, par inadvertance, par mégarde, par méprise; **to acknowledge one's m.,** avouer (être dans) son tort; **it is a m. to believe that . . .,** c'est se tromper que de croire que . . ., c'est un abus (que) de croire que . . .; **it was a great m. to ask him for advice,** nous avons fait une grave erreur en lui demandant conseil; **there is some m.!** il y a erreur! **there must be some m.,** il doit y avoir confusion; **there is, can be, no m. about that,** il n'y a pas à s'y tromper, à s'y méprendre; *F:* c'est bien le cas de le dire; **let there be no m. about it: make no m.,** que l'on ne s'y trompe pas; **I'm unlucky and no m.!** décidément je n'ai pas de chance! **he was angry and no m.!** il était absolument furieux; **it's warm and no m.!** il fait chaud, pas d'erreur! **to take s.o.'s umbrella in m. for one's own, to take s.o. else's umbrella by m.,** se tromper de parapluie.

mistake², *v.tr.* (**mistook** [mis'tuk]; **mistaken** [mis'teik(ə)n]) **1.** comprendre mal (les paroles de qn); se méprendre sur (les paroles, les intentions, de qn); **to m. the time, one's way,** se tromper d'heure, de route; **I have mistaken the house,** je me suis trompé de maison; **if I'm not mistaken,** *A:* **if I m. not,** si je ne me trompe; **if I'm not mistaken about him,** si je ne me trompe pas sur son compte; **there is no mistaking the facts,** on ne peut pas se tromper à cet égard; **there's no mistaking it,** il n'y a pas à s'y méprendre; **there can be no mistaking his words,** on ne peut pas se méprendre sur le sens de ses paroles; **you have mistaken your man,** vous vous adressez mal. **2. to m. s.o., sth., for s.o., sth.,** confondre qn, qch., avec qn, qch.; prendre qn, qch., pour qn, qch.; **to m. s.o. for somebody else,** prendre qn pour quelqu'un d'autre.

mistaken [mis'teik(ə)n], *a.* **1. m. opinion,** opinion erronée; **m. zeal,** zèle mal entendu, hors de propos; **m. ideas,** idées fausses; **m. kindness,** bonté mal placée. **2. m. identity,** erreur *f* sur la personne; **m. statement,** (i) déclaration mal comprise; (ii) déclaration erronée.

mistakenly [mis'teik(ə)nli], *adv.* **1.** par erreur, par méprise. **2.** sans réflexion, peu judicieusement.

mistakenness [mis'teik(ə)nnis], *s.* erreur *f*, fausseté *f* (de vues, d'opinions).

mister ['mistər], *s.* **1.** (*always abbreviated to* **Mr**) **Mr Thomas,** Monsieur Thomas; M. Thomas; (*on address*) monsieur Thomas, **Mr Chairman,** Monsieur le président; *Com:* **our Mr A,** notre représentant M. A.; **2.** *F: O:* **a mere m.,** un simple particulier, un bourgeois. **3.** (*with omission of proper name*) m'sieur; **what's the time, m.?** quelle heure est-il, m'sieur?

misterm ['mis'tə:m], *v.tr.* (dé)nommer (qch.) improprement, abusivement.

mistily ['mistili], *adv.* (voir qch.) dans la brume, obscurément.

mistime ['mis'taim], *v.tr.* faire (qch.) mal à propos, à contretemps; mal calculer (un coup).

mistimed ['mis'taimd], *a.* inopportun, mal à propos; (coup) mal calculé.

mistiness ['mistinəs], *s.* **1.** (*a*) état brumeux, obscurité *f*; (*b*) **owing to the m. of the windscreen . . .,** à cause de la buée qui obscurcissait le pare-brise . . .. **2.** brouillard *m*, brume *f*; vapeurs *fpl.*

mistle-thrush ['mislθrʌʃ], *s. Orn:* grive *f* draine.

mistletoe ['misltou, 'miz], *s. Bot:* gui *m*; **red-berried m.,** gui d'Espagne; *Orn:* **m. thrush,** grive *f* draine, de gui; **m. bird,** dicée *m.*

mistral ['mistrəl, mis'tra:l], *s. Meteor:* mistral *m.*

mistranslate [mistræns'leit, -tra:-], *v.tr.* mal traduire; interpréter (une phrase) à contresens.

mistranslation ['mistræns'leiʃ(ə)n, -tra:-], *s.* mauvaise traduction; traduction inexacte; erreur *f* de traduction; contresens *m.*

mistress ['mistris], *s.f.* **1.** (*a*) maîtresse (qui exerce l'autorité); **to be one's own m.,** être indépendante; être sa propre maîtresse; **to be m. of oneself, of one's emotions,** être maîtresse de soi(-même); avoir de l'empire sur soi-même; **she is m. of her subject,** elle possède son sujet à fond; (*b*) **m. of a family, of a household,** maîtresse de maison; *A:* (*to servant*) **is your m. at home?** madame y est-elle? **my m., (the) m., is not at home,** madame n'y est pas; (*c*) (*owner of pet*) maitresse; (*d*) *Com: A:* patronne; **speak to the m.,** adressez-vous à la patronne; (*e*) maîtresse (d'école), institutrice; professeur *m* (de lycée); **kindergarten m.,** jardinière d'enfants; **the French m.,** le professeur de français; **she is a music m.,** elle est professeur de musique; elle enseigne la musique. **2.** (*a*) *A:* amante, maîtresse (recherchée en mariage); bien-aimée, *pl.* bien-aimées; (*b*) maîtresse, concumbine; *F:* bonne amie; amie; **kept m.,** femme entretenue. **3.** (*in titles*) (*a*) *A:* Madame; **Mistress Quickly,** Madame Quickly; (*b*) (*now always abbreviated to* **Mrs** ['misiz]) **Mrs Martin,** Madame Martin.

mistrial [mis'traiəl], *s.* (*a*) erreur *f* judiciaire; (*b*) jugement entaché d'un vice de procédure.

mistrust¹ [mis'trʌst], *s.* méfiance *f*, défiance *f* (**of,** de); soupçons *mpl* (**of,** à l'endroit de, à l'égard de); manque *m* de confiance (**of,** en).

mistrust², *v.tr.* se méfier de, se défier de, soupçonner (qn, qch.); ne pas avoir confiance en (qn).

mistrustful [mis'trʌstful], *a.* méfiant; défiant; soupçonneux (**of,** à l'égard de).

mistrustfully [mis'trʌstfuli], *adv.* avec méfiance, avec défiance.

mistrustfulness [mis'trʌstfulnis], *s.* méfiance *f*, défiance *f*.

mistune [mis'tju:n], *v.tr.* mal accorder, désaccorder (un piano, etc.).

misty ['misti], *a.* (temps, lieu, etc.) brumeux, brumailleux, embrumé; **m. light,** lumière vaporeuse; **it's m.,** le temps est brumeux; il brumasse; **m. outlines,** contours vagues, flous; formes estompées; **the mountain tops were a m. purple,** les cimes des montagnes étaient d'un violet brumeux; **m. eyes,** yeux embués, troublés; regard ému; **the windscreen is all m.,** le pare-brise est tout couvert de buée; **m. recollection,** souvenir vague, confus.

misunderstand [misʌndə'stænd], *v.tr.* (**misunderstood** [misʌndə'stud]; **misunderstood**) **1.** mal comprendre (qch., qn); mal entendre, se méprendre sur (qch.); mal interpréter (une action); **if I have not misunderstood,** si j'ai bien compris; **you have misunderstood this passage,** vous avez mal compris ce passage; vous avez pris ce passage à contresens; **we misunderstood each other,** il y a eu un malentendu. **2.** méconnaître (qn); se méprendre sur le compte de (qn).

misunderstanding [misʌndə'stændiŋ], *s.* **1.** (*a*) conception erronée; (*b*) malentendu *m*; quiproquo *m*; **through a m.,** faute de s'entendre; par malentendu. **2.** mésintelligence *f*, malentente *f*, mésentente *f*, brouille *f*.

misusage [mis'ju:zidʒ], *s.* **1.** mauvais traitements *mpl.* **2.** *A:* = MISUSE¹.

misuse¹ [mis'ju:s], *s.* abus *m*, mauvais usage, emploi abusif, mauvais emploi, mésusage *m* (de qch.); malmenage *m* (d'un instrument de précision, etc.); **m. of authority,** abus d'autorité; **m. of words,** confusion *f* de mots; emploi abusif des mots, *Jur:* **fraudulent m. of funds,** détournement *m* de fonds; abus de confiance.

misuse² [mis'ju:z], *v.tr.* **1.** faire (un) mauvais usage, (un) mauvais emploi, de (qch.); mésuser de (qch.); abuser de (qch.); **to m. a word,** employer un mot à tort, mal à propos, abusivement. **2.** maltraiter, malmener (qn).

misused [mis'ju:zd], *a.* **1.** (chien) maltraité. **2.** (sens) abusif (d'un mot).

misuser [mis'ju:zər], *s. Jur:* abus *m* (d'un droit); abus de jouissance.

miswrite [mis'rait], *v.tr.* (**miswrote** [mis'rout]; **miswritten** [mis'rit(ə)n]) mal écrire (un mot); écrire (un mot) incorrectement.

mite [mait], *s.* **1.** *A:* & *Lit:* (*a*) **the widow's m.,** le denier de la veuve; **to offer one's m.,** donner son obole; (*b*) **m. of consolation,** brin *m* de consolation; **there's not a m. left,** il n'en reste plus une miette. **2.** petit gosse, petite gosse; mioche *mf*, bambin, -ine; moutard *m*; **he was a little m., a m. of a child,** il était haut comme ma botte; **poor little m.!** pauvre petit marmot! pauvre petit! pauvre petite! **3.** *Arach:* acarien *m*; mite *f*; **cheese m.,** mite du fromage; **cheese alive with mites,** fromage plein de mites.

mitella [mi'telə], *s.* **1.** *Bot:* mitelle *f*. **2.** *Surg:* mitelle, écharpe *f*.

Mithra ['miθrə]. *Pr.n.m.* Mithra(s).

Mithradates [miθri'deiti:z]. *Pr.n.m.* = MITHRIDATES.

Mithraic [mi'θreiik], *a. Rel.H:* mithriaque.

Mithraism ['miθreiizm], *s. Rel.H:* mithracisme *m*, mithraïsme *m.*

Mithras ['miθræs]. *Pr.n.m. Rel.H:* Mithra(s).

mithridate ['miθrideit], *s. A: Pharm:* mithridate *m.*

Mithridates [miθri'deiti:z]. *Pr.n.m. Hist:* Mithridate.

Mithridatic [miθri'deitik], *a. Hist:* mithridatique.

mithridatism ['miθrideitizm], *s. Med:* mithridatisation *f*; mithridatisme *m.*

mithridatize [mi'θridətaiz], *v.tr. Med:* mithridatiser, immuniser (qn) contre un poison.

mitigate ['mitigeit], *v.tr.* **1.** adoucir (la colère de qn). **2.** adoucir, atténuer (la souffrance, le chagrin, un mal); apaiser (la douleur); alléger (un fardeau); amoindrir (un mal); mitiger, modérer, atténuer (une peine, la sévérité d'une peine); adoucir (une critique). **3.** tempérer (la chaleur, un climat); adoucir (le froid). **4.** atténuer (un crime, une faute).

mitigating ['mitigeitiŋ], *a.* **1.** adoucissant, atténuant, mitigeant. **2. m. circumstances,** circonstances atténuantes.

mitigation [miti'geiʃ(ə)n], *s.* **1.** adoucissement *m* (d'une douleur); amoindrissement *m* (d'un mal); mitigation *f*, réduction *f*, atténuation *f*, modération *f* (d'une peine); allègement *m* (d'un fardeau); *Jur:* **plea in m. of damages,** demande *f* en réduction de dommages-intérêts. **2.** atténuation (d'une faute).

mitochondrion, *pl.* **-dria** [maitou'kɔndriən, -driə], *s. Biol:* mitochondrie *f*.

mitosis, *pl.* **-toses** [mai'tousis, -'tousi:z], *s. Biol:* mitose *f*, karyokinèse *f*, caryocinèse *f*.

mitotic [mai'tɔtik], *a.* mitotique.

mitral ['maitrəl], *a. Anat: Med:* mitral, -aux; **m. valve,** valvule mitrale; **m. regurgitation,** insuffisance *f* mitrale.

mitre¹ ['maitər], *s.* (*a*) *Ecc.Cost:* mitre *f*; (*b*) *Moll:* **m. (shell),** mitre, mitra *m*; **bishop's m.,** mitre épiscopale.

mitre², *s.* **1.** (*a*) *Carp:* **m. (joint),** (assemblage *m* à) onglet *m*; **m. box,** boîte *f* à onglet(s); (*b*) *Tls:* **m. (square),** équerre *f* (à) onglet; onglet; angle *m* oblique; **m. plane,** guillaume *m* à onglets; **m. rule,** biveau *m* (de tailleur de pierres). **2.** (*a*) *Mec.E:* **m. gear,** engrenage *m* à onglet, à 45°; engrenage d'équerre; **m. (wheel),** roue *f* d'angle, roue (dentée) conique; engrenage conique; roue, pignon *m*, d'échange; (*b*) *Hyd.E:* **m. gates,** portes busquées; **m. post,** poteau busqué; poteau battant; montant *m* de busc; **m. sill,** busc *m*; seuil *m* d'écluse; (*c*) *I.C.E: etc:* **m. valve,** soupape *f* conique.

mitre³, *v.tr.* **1.** (*a*) *Carp: Metalw: etc:* tailler (une pièce) à onglet; (*b*) *Bookb:* **to m. the fillets,** biseauter les filets. **2.** assembler (deux pièces) à onglet.

mitred¹ ['maitəd], *a. Ecc:* mitré; coiffé d'une mitre; **m. abbot,** abbé mitré.

mitred², *a. Carp:* en onglet, à onglet.

mitrewort ['maitəwə:t], *s. Bot:* mitelle *f*; **false m.,** tiarella *m.*

Mitridae ['mitridi:], *s.pl. Moll:* mitridés *m.*

mitriform ['maitrifɔ:m], *a. Nat.Hist:* mitriforme.

mitring ['mait(ə)riŋ], *s.* **1.** *Carp:* assemblage *m* à onglet; **m. machine,** machine *f* à couper les onglets. **2.** *Bookb:* biseautage *m.*

mitt [mit], *s.* **1.** = MITTEN 1. **2.** *F:* main *f*, patte *f*; **to give s.o. the frozen m.,** tourner le dos à qn.

mitten ['mit(ə)n], *s.* **1.** mitaine *f*; *F: A:* **to give a suitor the m.,** éconduire un soupirant; **to get the m.,** (i) être éconduit; (ii) (*of official, employee, etc.*) être congédié; recevoir son congé; *F:* être sa(c)qué. **2.** moufle *f*. **2.** *pl. Box: F:* **mittens,** gants *mpl*, les mitaines.

mittimus ['mitiməs], *s.* **1.** *Jur:* mandat *m* de dépôt (d'un prévenu). **2.** *A:* renvoi *m*; **to get one's m.,** (i) être mis à la porte; (ii) avoir son affaire; recevoir son compte.

Mitylene [miti'li:ni]. *Pr.n. Geog:* Mytilène.

mix¹ [miks], *s.* **1.** (*a*) mélange *m* (de mortier, de plâtre, etc.); *Com: etc:* assortiment *m*, éventail *m* (de produits); *Mil:* **weapon m.,** combinaison *f* d'armes; (*b*) *Com:* **cake, etc., m.,** préparation *f* pour gâteaux, etc. **2.** *F:* **to be in a m.,** avoir les idées brouillées. **3.** *Cin:* fondu, enchaîné; enchaînement *m* (des images).

mix², *v.*

I. *v.tr.* **1.** *v.tr.* & *i.* (*a*) mêler, mélanger (**several things together, sth. with sth.,** plusieurs choses ensemble, qch. à, avec, qch.); allier (des métaux); **to m. wine with water,** mêler, mélanger, diluer, du vin avec de l'eau; allonger, couper, du vin; **to m. two races,** mêler deux

races; (*b*) préparer, faire (un gâteau, etc.); préparer (une boisson); *Pharm:* mixtionner (des drogues); (*c*) brasser (des billets de loterie, etc.); malaxer (le mortier, etc.); gâcher (du mortier, du plâtre); *Glassm:* macler (le verre); *Cu:* retourner, fatiguer (la salade); *U.S: Cards:* battre, mélanger (les cartes); (*d*) confondre (des faits); (*e*) *esp. U.S: P:* **to m. it (up),** en venir aux coups. **2.** *v.i.* se mêler, se mélanger (**with,** avec, à); (*of fluids*) s'allier; (*of colours, etc.*) **to m. well,** aller bien ensemble; s'accorder; (*of pers.*) **to m. with people,** s'associer à, avec, des gens; fréquenter les gens; **to m. with the crowd,** se mêler à la foule.
II. (*compound verb*) **mix up,** *v.tr.* (*a*) mêler, mélanger (plusieurs substances, qch. à, avec, qch.); embrouiller (ses papiers, etc.); (*b*) confondre (**with,** avec); **I was mixing you up with your brother,** je faisais confusion avec vous et votre frère; (*c*) **to be mixed up in a complicated business,** être mêlé à une affaire compliquée; se trouver engagé, être compromis, être impliqué, dans une affaire compliquée; **mixed up with a gang,** accointé avec une bande; (*d*) embrouiller (qn); **I was getting all mixed up,** je ne savais plus où j'étais; **everything had got mixed up,** tout était en désordre, en pagaille.

mixed [mikst], *a.* **1.** mêlé, mélangé, mixte; (*a*) **m. forest,** (forêt *f* de) peuplement mélangé; **m. metal,** alliage *m*; **m. race,** race *f* de sang mêlé; **person of m. blood,** sang-mêlé *mf inv*; *Cu: etc:* **m. grill,** mixed-grill *m, pl.* mixed-grills; **m. ice, m. salad,** glace, salade, panachée; **m. sweets,** *NAm:* **m. candies,** bonbons assortis; **m. vegetables,** jardinière *f,* macédoine *f,* de légumes; **m. wines,** vins mélangés; **m. feelings,** sentiments mêlés; **to act from m. motives,** agir pour des motifs divers, complexes; **the speaker had a m. reception,** l'orateur a été accueilli par un concert d'acclamations et de huées, a reçu un accueil mitigé; *Ling:* **m. vowel,** voyelle métisse; **m. sound,** son mixte, métis; (*b*) **m. company,** compagnie mêlée, monde mêlé, milieu *m* hétéroclite; **m. society,** société hétérogène; *Rail:* **m. train,** train *m* mixte; *Ins:* **m. policy,** police *f* au temps et au voyage; **m. sea and land risks,** risques *m* mixtes maritimes et terrestres; *Jur:* **m. action,** action *f* mixte; *Nau:* **m. cargo,** cargaison *f* mixte, chargement *m* de divers; *Ven:* **m. bag,** carnassière *f,* tableau *m* (de chasse), où il y a un peu de tout; *F:* (*of pers.*) **they were a m. bag,** il y en avait de tous les milieux; *F:* **these novels are a m. bag,** certains de ces romans sont bons, mais quant aux autres . . .! *Mth:* **m. number,** nombre *m* fractionnaire; **m. integer problem,** problème *m* partiellement en nombres entiers; **m. base,** base *f* mixte (de numération); **m.-base, m.-radix, notation,** numération *f* à base multiple; (*c*) *Mec.E:* **m. turbine,** turbine *f* mixte; **m.-flow compressor,** compresseur *m* à écoulement mixte; **m.-matrix radiator,** radiateur *m* mixte; *El:* **m. semi-conductor,** semi-conducteur *m* mixte. **2. m. school,** école *f* mixte; école pour garçons et filles; *Ten:* **m. doubles,** double *m* mixte; **to play in the m. doubles,** jouer en double mixte; *A:* **m. bathing,** bains *m* mixtes.

mixed-up ['mikst'ʌp], *a. F:* (*of pers.*) complexé.

mixen ['miks(ə)n], *s. Dial:* tas *m* de fumier.

mixer ['miksər], *s.* **1.** (*pers.*) (*a*) *Metall: Ind:* brasseur *m*; (*b*) *Cin:* opérateur *m* des sons. **2.** (*machine*) (*a*) *Ind: etc:* mélangeur *m*; mélangeuse *f*; barboteur *m*; malaxeur *m*, agitateur *m*; **counter-flow m.,** malaxeur à contre-courant; **m. preheater,** mélangeur-réchauffeur *m, pl.* mélangeurs-réchauffeurs; **mortar m.,** tonneau *m* à mortier; (*b*) *Cin:* mélangeur de sons; (*c*) *I.C.E:* diffuseur *m*; (*d*) *Elcs:* changeur *m* de fréquence, mélangeur; **m. circuit,** montage *m* de conversion; **m. stage,** étage *m* de conversion, de changement de fréquence; **m. crystal,** cristal mélangeur, quartz mélangeur; (*e*) *Dom.Ec:* **(electric) m.,** batteur *m* (électrique); **m. (tap),** mitigeur *m*; **shower m.,** mitigeur de douche. **3.** (*pers.*) **to be a good m.,** être très sociable; être liant avec tout le monde; savoir se rendre sympathique (dans tous les milieux); **he's a bad m.,** il est sauvage; c'est un ours; il ne sait pas s'adapter à son entourage.

mixing ['miksiŋ], *s.* **1.** mélange *m* (de qch. avec qch.); **the m. of social classes,** le mélange, *F:* le brassage, des classes sociales; *Tchn:* **vacuum m.,** mélange sous vide. **2.** (*a*) brassage *m* (des billets de loterie, etc.); (*b*) barbotage *m* (des liquides); **m. bowl,** terrine *f,* bol *m* à mélanger; **m. glass,** verre mélangeur; **m. tap,** *NAm:* **faucet,** robinet mélangeur; **m. knife,** couteau *m* à broyer l'encre; (*c*) gâchage *m*, malaxage *m* (du mortier, du plâtre); *Glassm:* maclage *m* (du verre); *Pharm:* mixtion *f* (d'une préparation, d'un onguent); **m. machine,** malaxeur *m*; mélangeoir *m*; mélangeur *m*, mélangeuse *f*; **m. mill,** broyeur malaxeur, broyeur mélangeur; **m. cylinder,** cylindre malaxeur; **m. drum,** mélangeur (à tambour); **m. tank,** réservoir *m* de mélange; **m. trough,** baç *m*, cuve *f,* de mélange; **m. valve,** (i) *Mec.E:* vanne *f* de mélange; (ii) *Elcs:* tube mélangeur; tube changeur de fréquence, lampe changeuse de fréquence; *I.C.E:* **m. chamber,** chambre *f* de mélange, de carburation, de pulvérisation; **m. cone,** diffuseur *m*; (*d*) *Cin: etc:* mixage *m*, mélange des sons; **m. apparatus,** appareil *m* de mélange; **m. panel,** mélangeur de sons; tableau *m* de mélange, de mixage; **m. table,** table *f* de mixage.

mixite ['miksait], *s. Miner:* mixite *f.*

mixoploid ['miksouplɔid], *s.* mixoploïde *f.*

Mixosaurus [miksou'sɔ:rəs], *s. Paleont:* mixosaurus *m.*

mixtilineal [miksti'liniəl], **mixtilinear** [miksti'liniər], *a.* mixtiligne.

mixtion ['mikstʃ(ə)n], *s. Art: etc:* mixtion *f,* mordant *m* (pour la dorure).

mixture ['mikstjər], *s.* **1.** (*a*) mélange *m* (de choses, de personnes); amalgame *m*; **a m. of every nation under the sun,** un amalgame de toutes les nations; **a m. of brutality and sentimentality,** un mélange de brutalité et de sentimentalité; **pipe m.,** mélange (de tabac) pour la pipe; **cake, etc., m.,** préparation *f* pour gâteaux, etc.; (*b*) *Ch:* **intimate m.,** mélange intime; **homogeneous, heterogeneous, m.,** mélange homogène, hétérogène; **gaseous m.,** mélange gazeux; *Exp:* **explosive, detonating, m.,** mélange explosif, détonant; *Atom.Ph: Ch:* **m. of isotopes, isotopic m.,** mélange d'isotopes; **reactive m.,** mélange réactif; (*c*) *I.C.E:* **fuel-air m.,** mélange air-carburant; **explosive m.,** mélange (dé)tonant; **lean, weak, m.,** mélange pauvre; **rich m.,** mélange riche; **priming m.,** mélange d'amorçage; *Av:* **altitude m.,** mélange pour vol en altitude; **(automatic) m. control,** commande *f,* correcteur *m*, (automatique) de mélange; **m. control valve,** soupape *f* d'étranglement; **m. ratio,** dosage *m*, taux *m*, du mélange. **2.** *Pharm:* mixtion *f,* mixture *f.* **3.** *Tex:* tissu mélange. **2.** *Pharm:* mixtion *f,* mixture *f.* **3.** *Tex:* tissu *m* de) fourniture *f,* jeu de mixture (d'un orgue). **6.** *Mth:* **rule of mixtures,** règle *f* d'alliage.

mix-up ['miksʌp], *s.* **1.** confusion *f,* embrouillement *m*; embouteillage *m* (de voitures, etc.); *F:* pagaïe *f,* pagaille *f*; **what a m.-up!** (i) quelle cohue! (ii) quel embrouillamini! **there's been a bit of a m.-up over the booking of the seats,** il y a eu je ne sais quel malentendu pour la réservation des places. **2.** *F:* bagarre *f.*

Mizpah ['mizpə]. *Pr.n. B:* Mitspa; **M. ring,** anneau donné en gage d'amour.

mizzen ['miz(ə)n], *s. Nau:* **m. (sail),** artimon *m*; **m. topsail,** perroquet *m* de fougue; **m. topmast,** mât *m* de perroquet de fougue; mât de hune d'artimon, mât de flèche d'artimon; **m. topgallant sail,** perruche *f*; **m. topgallant mast, yard,** mât, vergue *f,* de perruche; **m. royal,** cacatois *m* de perruche.

mizzenmast ['miz(ə)nmɑ:st], *s. Nau:* mât *m* d'artimon.

mizzentop ['miz(ə)ntɔp], *s. Nau:* hune *f* d'artimon.

mizzenyard ['miz(ə)njɑ:d], *s. Nau:* vergue *f* de perroquet.

mizzle[1] ['mizl], *s. Dial:* bruine *f,* crachin *m.*

mizzle[2], *v.i. Dial:* bruiner, brouillasser, crachiner.

mizzle[3], *v.i. P:* (*a*) déguerpir, filer; (*b*) rouspéter, râler.

mizzly ['mizli], *a. Dial:* bruineux; **m. rain,** petite pluie fine; **m. morning,** matin *m* de pluie fine.

mnemonic [ni'mɔnik]. **1.** *a.* mnémonique; **m. code,** code *m* mnémonique; **m. symbol,** symbole *m* mnémonique. **2.** *s.* (*a*) aide-mémoire *m inv*; moyen *m* mnémotechnique; (*b*) *pl.* (*usu. with sg. const.*) **mnemonics,** mnémonique *f,* mnémotechnie *f.*

mnemonist ['ni:mənist], *s.* mnémotechnicien, -ienne.

mnemonize ['ni:mənaiz], *v.tr.* mnémoniser.

mnemotechnic [ni:mou'teknik], *a.* mnémotechnique.

mnemotechny [ni:mou'tekni], *s.* mnémotechnie *f,* mnémonique *f.*

mo [mou], *s. F:* une seconde; **half a mo!** une petite minute!

moa ['mouə], *s. Orn:* dinornis *m*, moa *m.*

Moabite ['mouəbait]. *B.Hist:* (*a*) *a.* moabite; (*b*) *s.* Moabite *mf.*

moan[1] [moun], *s.* (*a*) gémissement *m*, plainte *f*; *F:* **to have a (good) m.,** grogner, ronchonner; (*b*) **the m. of the wind,** le gémissement du vent.

moan[2]. **1.** *v.i.* gémir; pousser des gémissements; se lamenter; (*of wind*) gémir; **he's always moaning (and groaning),** ce sont des lamentations à n'en plus finir; **he's always moaning about his health,** il se plaint toujours de sa santé; **she's always moaning about being short of money,** elle se plaint toujours d'être à court d'argent. **2.** *v.tr.* (*a*) *A: & Lit:* gémir de, sur (qch.); se lamenter sur (qch.); pleurer (qn); (*b*) dire (qch.) en gémissant; **to m. out a prayer,** gémir une prière.

moaner ['mounər], *s. F:* ronchonneur, -euse; râleur, -euse.

moaning[1] ['mouniŋ], *a.* (enfant, vent) gémissant; *F:* **she's a real m. Minnie,** c'est une vraie geignarde, rouspéteuse.

moaning[2], *s.* gémissement *m*; *F:* **his constant m. gets me down,** ses plaintes continuelles m'énervent.

moat[1] [mout], *s.* fossé *m*, douve *f* (d'un château, de fortifications).

moat[2], *v.tr.* entourer (un château) d'un fossé.

moated ['moutid], *a.* (château) entouré d'un fossé, de fossés.

mob[1] [mɔb], *s.* **1.** *Pej:* **the m.,** la populace; *F:* le populo; **m. law,** la loi de la populace; **m. rule,** voyoucratie *f*; **m. oratory,** éloquence tribunitienne; **to join the m.,** descendre dans la rue. **2.** (*a*) foule (agitée), cohue *f,* rassemblement *m*; attroupement *m*, ameutement *m*; bande *f* d'émeutiers; (*of people in pursuit*) meute *f*; **to form a m., to gather into a m.,** s'attrouper, s'ameuter; **the army had degenerated into a m.,** l'armée *f* n'était plus qu'une cohue; **m. psychology,** psychologie *f* des foules; (*b*) *esp. Austr:* troupeau *m* (de moutons, etc.). **3.** *P: A:* **the swell m.,** la haute pègre; pickpockets bien fringués.

mob[2], *v.* **(mobbed) 1.** *v.tr.* (*a*) (*of angry crowd*) houspiller, attaquer, malmener (qn); **to be mobbed by the crowd,** être attaqué, molesté, malmené, par la foule; *Orn:* **passerines that gather round an owl and m. it,** passereaux qui se rassemblent autour d'un hibou pour le harceler; (*b*) (*of admiring crowd*) assiéger (qn); faire foule autour de (qn). **2.** *v.i.* s'attrouper; former un rassemblement.

mob-cap ['mɔbkæp], *s. A.Cost:* bonnet *m* (de femme) (s'attachant sous le menton); charlotte *f.*

mobile[1] ['moubail], *a.* **1.** (*a*) (*of limb, component part, etc.*) mobile; **m. features,** physionomie changeante, mobile; *W.Tel:* **m. aerial, m. antenna,** antenne *f* orientable; (*b*) *Ph:* **m. equilibrium,** équilibre indifférent. **2.** (*a*) itinérant, mobile; **m. laboratory,** laboratoire itinérant, mobile; **m. library,** bibliothèque itinérante, bibliobus *m*; **m. unit,** élément itinérant, mobile (d'une bibliothèque, d'un hôpital, etc.); groupe *m* (électrogène, etc.) mobile; *W.Tel:* **m. transmitter, m. radio unit,** émetteur *m* mobile; *F:* **are you m.?** vous êtes motorisé? vous avez votre voiture? (*b*) *Mil:* **m. defence,** défense *f* mobile; **m. medical, surgical, unit,** unité médicale, chirurgicale, mobile; **m. radar control post,** poste *m* mobile de contrôle radar; **m. reserve,** réserve *f* mobile; **m. warfare,** guerre *f* de mouvement. **3.** (*of pers., character*) changeant, versatile.

mobile[2] ['moubail], *s. Art:* mobile *m.*

mobile[3] ['moubili], *s. A.Astr: A.Phil:* **the primum m.,** le premier mobile.

mobiliary [mou'biljəri], *a.* **1.** *Jur:* mobilier. **2.** *Mil:* (facilités *fpl*) de mobilisation.

mobility [mou'biliti], *s.* **1.** mobilité *f*; **m. of features,** mobilité de physionomie; **social m.,** mobilité sociale. **2.** *Ph:* **ion m.,** mobilité d'un ion.

mobilizable [moubi'laizəbl], *a.* mobilisable.

mobilization [moubilai'zeiʃ(ə)n], *s.* mobilisation *f* (des troupes, de capitaux, etc.); **m. order,** (i) (*public*) appel *m*, (ii) (*personal*) ordre *m*, de mobilisation.

mobilize ['moubilaiz]. **1.** *v.tr.* mobiliser (des troupes, des capitaux); effectuer la mobilisation (d'une flotte, etc.). **2.** *v.i.* (*of army*) entrer en mobilisation.

Möbius ['mɔ:biəs]. *Pr.n.* **1.** *Mth:* **M. band, strip,** ruban *m* de Möbius. **2.** *Med:* **Möbius's disease,** maladie *f* de Möbius.

mobocracy [mɔ'bɔkrəsi], *s. F: Pej:* voyoucratie *f,* démagogie *f.*

mobsman, *pl.* **-men** ['mɔbzmən], *s.m. P: O:* filou chic; **the mobsmen,** la haute pègre; *A:* **swell m.,** pègre *m* de la haute; escroc de haut vol; pickpocket bien fringué.

moccasin ['mɔkəsin, mə'kæsin], *s.* **1.** *Cost:* mocassin *m.* **2.** *Rept:* **water m., cottonmouth m.,** mocassin d'eau, aquatique. **3.** *Can: F:* **m. telegraph,** téléphone *m* arabe.

Mocha ['moukə]. **1.** *Pr.n. Geog:* Moka. **2.** *s.* (*a*) *Miner:* **m. (stone),** pierre *f* de Moka; agate mousseuse; *Ent:* **m. (moth),** éphyre *f*; (*b*) **m. (coffee),** (café *m*) moka *m*; *Cu:* **m. cake,** moka.

mock[1] [mɔk], *s.* **1.** *A:* moquerie *f,* dérision *f.* **2.** *O:* sujet *m* de moquerie; (*still so used in*) **to make a m. of s.o., of sth.,** se moquer de qn, de qch.; tourner qn, qch., en ridicule. **3.** *A:* semblant *m*, simulacre *m.* **4.** *Sch: F:* examen blanc.

mock[2], *a.* d'imitation; feint, contrefait; faux, *f.* fausse; pour rire; burlesque; **m. tortoiseshell,** écaille *f* imitation; *Cu:* **m. turtle soup,** consommé *m* à la tête de veau (imitation d'un consommé à la tortue); *Meteor:* **m. moon,** parasélène *f*; **m. sun,** parhélie *m*; soleil apparent; faux soleil; **m. prophet,** faux prophète; **m. king,** roi *m* pour rire; **m. tragedy,** tragédie *f* burlesque; **m.-heroic poem,** poème *m* héroï-comique; **to indulge in m.**

heroics, jouer au, se prendre pour un, héros; **m. modesty,** fausse modestie; **m. trial,** simulacre *m* de procès; procès dérisoire; **m. fight,** simulacre de combat; petite guerre; *Sch:* **m. examination,** examen blanc.

mock[3]. **1.** *v.tr. & i.* **to m. (at) s.o., sth.,** se moquer de qn, de qch.; railler qn, qch.; bafouer qn. **2.** *v.tr.* (*a*) narguer (qn); (*b*) se jouer de, tromper (qn); (*c*) imiter, contrefaire, singer (qn, qch.).

mocker [ˈmɔkər], *s.* **1.** (*a*) moqueur, -euse; railleur, -euse; (*b*) trompeur, -euse; (*c*) *P:* **to put the mockers on s.o., sth.,** jeter un sort sur qn, qch. **2.** *esp. U.S:* = MOCKINGBIRD.

mockery [ˈmɔkəri], *s.* **1.** moquerie *f*, raillerie *f*, dérision *f*. **2.** sujet *m* de moquerie, de raillerie; objet *m* de risée, de dérision; **this makes a m. of the whole thing,** cela tourne tout en dérision. **3.** semblant *m*, simulacre *m* (**of,** de); **his trial was a mere m.,** son procès n'a été qu'un simulacre; son procès a été une pure moquerie.

mocking[1] [ˈmɔkiŋ], *a.* moqueur, -euse, railleur, -euse; **m. irony,** ironie gouailleuse.

mocking[2], *s.* moquerie *f*, raillerie *f*.

mockingbird [ˈmɔkiŋbəːd], *s. Orn:* (*a*) moqueur *m* (polyglotte); (*b*) *Austr: F:* atrichornis *m*.

mockingly [ˈmɔkiŋli], *adv.* en se moquant; d'un ton moqueur, railleur; par moquerie, par dérision.

mock-up [ˈmɔkʌp], *s.* maquette *f*.

Mod[1] [moud], *s. Scot:* = jeux floraux.

mod[2] [mɔd]. *F:* modification *f*.

modal [ˈmoud(ə)l], *a.* modal, -aux; *Gram:* de mode; **m. auxiliary,** auxiliaire *m* de mode; *Log:* **m. proposition,** modale *f*; *Jur:* **m. legacy,** legs conditionnel; *Mus:* **m. note,** modale *f*.

modality [mouˈdæliti], *s.* modalité *f*.

mode [moud], *s.* **1.** (*manner*) (*a*) mode *m*, méthode *f*, manière *f* (**of,** de); **m. of life,** façon *f*, manière, de vivre; train *m*, mode, de vie; **m. of operation,** mode de fonctionnement; **m. of application,** (i) *Jur:* modalités *fpl*, (ii) *Pharm: etc:* mode, d'application; (*b*) *Cmptr:* **access, control, m.,** mode d'accès, de contrôle; **hold, freeze, m.,** état *m* d'interruption; **operate, compute, m.,** état de fonctionnement; **reset m.,** condition initiale. **2.** (*fashion*) mode *f*; **it's the m. of the day,** c'est à la mode. **3.** *Mus:* (*a*) mode *m*; **major, minor, m.,** mode majeur, mineur; **ecclesiastical, Gregorian, m.,** mode ecclésiastique; (*b*) mode *m* (de plain-chant). **4.** *Phil:* mode *m*.

model[1] [ˈmɔd(ə)l], *s.* **1.** (*a*) modèle *m*; maquette *f*; **(small)-scale m.,** modèle réduit, à petite échelle; **full-scale m.,** maquette, modèle, en vraie grandeur, (en) grandeur naturelle; **demonstration m.,** (i) modèle, appareil *m*, de démonstration; (ii) maquette d'enseignement; **study m.,** maquette, modèle, d'étude; **working m.,** modèle pouvant fonctionner; **m. aircraft, yacht,** maquette, modèle (réduit) d'avion, de yacht; avion *m*, yacht *m*, miniature; **m. maker,** maquettiste *mf*; modéliste *m*; **m. making,** modélisme *m*; construction *f* de maquettes, de modèles réduits; **to make a m. of a statue,** (i) modeler une statue; (ii) faire la maquette d'une statue; **constructed after m.,** construit sur maquette, sur modèle; *Cin:* **m. work,** prise *f* de vues avec maquette; (*b*) *N.Arch: etc:* gabarit *m*; (*c*) *Surv:* plan *m* en relief. **2.** (*a*) *Art:* **figure drawn from the m.,** figure dessinée d'après le modèle; **to draw, paint, without a m.,** dessiner, peindre, de chic; **anatomical m.,** écorché *m*; (*b*) **on the m. of sth., of s.o.,** à l'imitation de qch., de qn; **to take s.o. as one's m.,** prendre modèle sur qn; prendre qn pour modèle; **to be a m. of virtue,** être un modèle, un exemple, de vertu; *attrib.* **m. pupil,** écolier, -ière, modèle; **m. husband, m. wife,** mari *m*, épouse *f*, modèle; le modèle des maris, des épouses; **m. farm,** ferme modèle; (*c*) *Dressm: etc:* modèle; patron *m*; **m. gown, hat,** modèle (de robe, de chapeau); **Paris models,** modèles de la haute couture parisienne; (*d*) *Pol.Ec:* **decision m., praxeological m.,** modèle de décision, de praxéologie; **feasibility m.,** modèle probatoire; **predictive m.,** modèle de prévision; **prescriptive m.,** modèle normatif; **m. construction,** élaboration *f* des modèles; **integrity of a m.,** validité *f* d'un modèle. **3.** (*pers.*) (*a*) *Art:* modèle; (*b*) **(fashion) m.,** mannequin *m*; (*c*) *F:* prostituée *f*.

model[2], *v.tr.* (**modelled**) **1.** modeler (une figure, un groupe); **she has a beautifully modelled figure,** elle a une belle plastique. **2. to m. sth. after, on, upon, sth.,** modeler qch. sur qch.; former, faire, qch. d'après le modèle de qch.; **to m. oneself on s.o.,** se modeler sur qn, se faire la copie de qn; prendre exemple sur qn. **3.** (*a*) (*of mannequin*) présenter (une robe, etc.); (*b*) *v.i.* **she models,** elle travaille comme mannequin, comme modèle.

modeller [ˈmɔdələr], *s.* modeleur, -euse (**of,** de).

modelling [ˈmɔd(ə)liŋ], *s.* **1.** (*a*) modelage *m*; **m. board,** (i) table *f* de modeleur; (ii) *Metall:* échantillon *m*; **m. clay,** argile *f* à modeler; (*b*) facture *f* sur modèle, sur gabarit. **2.** création *f* de modèles. **3.** présentation *f* (d'une robe, etc.) par un mannequin.

modem [ˈmɔdem], *s. Elcs:* modem *m*; modulateur-démodulateur *m*.

Modena [ˈmɔdənə]. **1.** *Pr.n. Geog:* Modène *f*. **2.** *s.* **M. (red),** pourpre foncé.

Modenese [mɔdəˈniːz]. *Geog:* (*a*) *a.* modénais; (*b*) *s.* Modénais, -aise.

moder [ˈmoudər], *s. Geol:* moder *m*.

moderantism [ˈmɔdərəntizm], *s.* modérantisme *m*.

moderantist [ˈmɔdərəntist], *s.* modérantiste *mf*.

moderate[1] [ˈmɔdərət]. **1.** *a.* (*a*) modéré; moyen, ordinaire, raisonnable; **m. in one's demands on s.o.,** modéré envers qn; **m. man,** (i) (*in opinions*) homme modéré; (ii) (*in conduct*) homme réglé; **m. drinker,** buveur tempéré; buveur plutôt sobre; **m. language,** langage mesuré; **m. price,** prix modéré, doux, modique, moyen; **m. income,** revenus *mpl* modiques; **m. capacities,** talents *m* ordinaires, moyens; **m. pace,** allure modérée; **m. size,** grandeur moyenne; **of m. size, m. sized,** de grandeur moyenne; **m. wind,** vent modéré; **m. sea,** mer *f* maniable; (*b*) *Ecc: Pol:* **m. party, opinions,** parti modéré, opinions modérées; (*c*) **m. meal,** repas *m* sobre. **2.** *s.* (*pers.*) *Ecc: Pol:* modéré, -ée.

moderate[2] [ˈmɔdəreit]. **1.** (*a*) *v.tr.* modérer (ses exigences, ses désirs); ralentir (son zèle); modérer, tempérer (l'ardeur du soleil); **to m. one's pretensions,** rabattre de ses prétentions; (*b*) *Atom.Ph:* modérer, ralentir (un réacteur). **2.** *v.i.* (*of storm*) diminuer d'intensité, faiblir; se modérer. **3.** *Ecc: esp. Scot:* (*a*) *v.i.* présider (une assemblée); (*b*) *v.i. & v.tr.* **to m. (in) a call,** entériner l'invitation à remplir un pastorat.

moderated [ˈmɔdəreitid], *a.* modéré, ralenti; *Atom.Ph:* **m. reactor,** pile *f*, réacteur *m*, à modérateur, à ralentisseur; **graphite-m. reactor,** réacteur modéré au graphite; **heavy-water-m., light-water-m., reactor,** réacteur modéré à l'eau lourde, à l'eau légère; **organic-m. reactor,** réacteur à modérateur organique, modéré par fluide organique.

moderately [ˈmɔd(ə)rətli], *adv.* modérément; avec modération; mesurément, sobrement; modiquement, médiocrement, moyennement, passablement; **m. priced,** de prix moyen.

moderateness [ˈmɔd(ə)rətnis], *s.* **1.** modération *f* (dans les opinions); modicité *f* (de prix). **2.** médiocrité *f* (du travail, etc.).

moderating [ˈmɔdəreitiŋ], *a.* (*a*) **m. influence,** influence modérante, modératrice, apaisante; (*b*) *Atom.Ph:* **m. medium,** milieu modérateur; **m. power,** pouvoir *m* de ralentissement; **m. process,** processus *m* de modération, de ralentissement; **m. ratio,** rapport *m* de modération.

moderation [mɔdəˈreiʃ(ə)n], *s.* **1.** modération *f*, mesure *f*, retenue *f*; sobriété *f* (de langage); **with m.,** avec modération, mesurément; **in m.,** avec modération, avec mesure, modérément; **to eat and drink in m.,** manger et boire avec sobriété, avec frugalité, frugalement. **2.** *Atom.Ph:* modération, ralentissement *m* (d'un réacteur, etc.); **m. of neutrons,** modération des neutrons; thermalisation *f*; **m. length,** longueur *f* de modération, de ralentissement. **3.** *pl. Sch:* (*at Oxford*) **moderations,** premier examen pour le grade de *Bachelor of Arts*.

moderato [mɔdəˈrɑːtou], *adv. Mus:* moderato.

moderator [ˈmɔdəreitər], *s.* **1.** (*a*) président *m* (d'une assemblée); *Ecc:* (dans l'Église réformée) président de l'assemblée paroissiale, de l'assemblée régionale des ministres; *Scot:* **M. of the General Assembly,** modérateur *m*, président, de l'Assemblée générale (de l'Église d'Écosse); (*b*) *Sch:* (i) *A:* cathédrant *m* (président à une soutenance de thèse); (ii) (*at Cambridge*) président du jury pour le *tripos* en mathématiques; (iii) (*at Oxford*) examinateur *m* pour les *moderations*. **2.** (*a*) *Atom.Ph:* modérateur *m*, ralentisseur *m* (de réacteur, etc.); **neutron m.,** modérateur, ralentisseur, des neutrons; **graphite m.,** modérateur en graphite; **heavy water, light water, m.,** eau lourde, légère, servant de ralentisseur; **hydrogenous m.,** modérateur hydrogénique; **m. coolant,** modérateur-refroidisseur *m*, *pl.* modérateurs-refroidisseurs; **m. lattice,** réseau *m* du modérateur; **m. level,** niveau *m* du modérateur; **m. material,** substance modératrice, substance de ralentissement; (*b*) *A:* **m. (lamp),** lampe *f* à modérateur.

moderatorship [ˈmɔdəreitəʃip], *s. esp. Ecc:* fonctions *fpl* de modérateur; présidence *f*.

modern [ˈmɔd(ə)n]. **1.** *a.* moderne; **m. house,** maison *f* moderne; **to build in the m. style,** bâtir à la moderne; **m. times,** le temps présent, les temps modernes; **m. languages,** langues vivantes; **m. mathematics,** mathématiques *f* modernes; *Sch:* **m. side,** enseignement *m* moderne. **2.** *s.* **the ancients and the moderns,** les anciens *m* et les modernes *m*.

modernism [ˈmɔdə(ː)nizm], *s.* **1.** (*a*) modernité *f*; caractère *m* moderne; (*b*) modernisme *m*; goût *m* du moderne; (*c*) *Theol:* modernisme. **2.** (*a*) nouveauté *f*; usage nouveau, moderne; (*b*) *Ling:* néologisme *m*.

modernist [ˈmɔdə(ː)nist], *s. Theol: etc:* moderniste *mf*.

modernistic [mɔdə(ː)ˈnistik], *a.* (doctrine, etc.) moderniste.

modernity [mɔˈdəːniti], *s.* modernité *f*.

modernization [mɔdə(ː)naiˈzeiʃ(ə)n], *s.* modernisation *f*.

modernize [ˈmɔdə(ː)naiz], *v.tr.* moderniser; rénover; mettre (ses idées, etc.) à jour.

modernizing [ˈmɔdə(ː)naiziŋ], *s.* modernisation *f*.

modernness [ˈmɔdə(ː)nnis], *s.* modernité *f*.

modest [ˈmɔdist], *a.* (*a*) modeste; **m. hero,** héros *m* modeste; **to be m. about one's achievements,** avoir le succès modeste; (*b*) *O:* (*of woman*) pudique, modeste, chaste; (*c*) modéré; **to be m. in one's requirements,** être peu exigeant; **m. fortune,** fortune *f* modeste; (*d*) (*of style, etc.*) sans prétentions.

modestly [ˈmɔdistli], *adv.* **1.** modestement; avec modestie. **2.** pudiquement, chastement. **3.** modérément. **4.** sans prétentions; sans faste.

modesty [ˈmɔdisti], *s.* **1.** modestie *f*; **let it be said with all due m.,** soit dit sans vanité, avec toute la modestie du monde. **2.** (*a*) *O:* pudeur *f*, pudicité *f*; **to offend m.,** commettre un outrage à la pudeur; *A.Cost:* **m. (front),** modestie; (*b*) *Furn:* **m. panel,** cache-jambes *m inv.* **3.** modération *f* (d'une demande, etc.); modicité *f* (d'une dépense). **4.** absence *f* de prétention; simplicité *f* (de décor, etc.).

modicum [ˈmɔdikəm], *s.* **a m. of . . .,** une petite portion, une faible quantité, de . . .; **a m. of truth,** une petite part de vérité; **good intentions are of no use without a m. of intelligence,** les bonnes intentions ne valent rien si on est dépourvu de bon sens; *A:* **to live on a small m.,** vivre de peu.

modifiable [ˈmɔdifaiəbl], *a.* **1.** modifiable. **2.** susceptible d'atténuation.

modification [mɔdifiˈkeiʃ(ə)n], *s.* **1.** modification *f* (d'un plan, *Ling:* d'une voyelle); **to make modifications in sth.,** apporter des modifications à qch. **2.** atténuation *f*.

modificative [mɔdifiˈkeitiv], *a. & s. Gram:* modificatif (*m*).

modificatory [mɔdifiˈkeitəri], *a.* modificateur, -trice.

modified [ˈmɔdifaid], *a.* modifié; *Jur:* **m. penalty,** peine mitigée.

modifier [ˈmɔdifaiər], *s.* modificateur, -trice; *Cmptr:* **m. register, m. store,** registre *m*, mémoire *f*, d'index.

modify [ˈmɔdifai], *v.tr.* **1.** (*a*) modifier; apporter des modifications à (qch.); (*b*) mitiger, atténuer (une peine); **to m. one's demands,** rabattre de ses prétentions. **2.** *Gram: Ling:* modifier (le verbe, une voyelle, etc.).

modifying [ˈmɔdifaiiŋ], *a.* mitigeant.

modillion [məˈdiljən], *s. Arch:* modillon *m*.

Modiolus [mɔˈdaiələs], *s. Moll:* modiole *f*.

modish [ˈmoudiʃ], *a. O:* **1.** *usu. Pej:* qui se pique d'être à la mode; (*of pers.*) faraud, *f.* faraude; **a m. hat,** un chapeau à la dernière mode. **2.** à la mode.

modishly [ˈmoudiʃli], *adv. O:* (habillé(e)) très à la mode.

modishness [ˈmoudiʃnis], *s. O:* conformité *f* à la mode; asservissement *m* à la mode; élégance affectée (d'une toilette, etc.).

modiste [mɔˈdiːst], *s.f.* modiste et marchande de modes.

mods [mɔdz], *s.pl. Sch: F:* (*at Oxford*) premier examen pour le grade de *Bachelor of Arts*.

modular [ˈmɔdjulər], *a.* (*a*) *Arch: Mth:* modulaire; (*b*) *Const: etc:* modulaire; fait d'éléments normalisés (préfabriqués); **m. construction, m. design,** construction *f* modulaire, construction au moyen d'éléments normalisés; **m. furniture,** mobilier composé d'éléments normalisés (pouvant se juxtaposer ou se superposer de façon à constituer un même meuble plus ou moins grand); (*c*) (*of spacecraft*) modulaire; composé d'éléments s'arrimant les uns aux autres.

modulate [ˈmɔdjuleit]. **1.** *v.tr.* (*a*) moduler (sa voix, des sons, *Ph:* l'amplitude, etc.); (*b*) ajuster, approprier (**sth. to sth.,** qch. à qch.). **2.** *v.i. Mus:* **to m. from one key (in)to another,** passer d'un ton à, dans, un autre; moduler.

modulated [ˈmɔdjuleitid], *a.* modulé; *El: Elcs:* **amplitude m., frequency m.,** modulé en amplitude, en fréquence; **m. amplifier,** étage modulateur; **m. current,** courant modulé; **m. wave,** onde modulée; **m. continuous wave,** onde entretenue modulée; **pulse-m. wave,** onde modulée par impulsions; **m. output power,** puissance modulée, watts modulés; *Cin:* **m. parts of**

the sound track, parties modulées de la bande photophonique.

modulating ['mɔdjuleitiŋ], *a.* modulateur, -trice; *El: Elcs:* **m. choke,** self modulatrice; self de modulation, de parole; **m. electrode,** électrode modulatrice, de modulation; **m. frequency,** fréquence *f* de modulation; **m. voltage,** tension *f* de modulation; *W.Tel: etc:* **m. valve, m. tube,** lampe (à vide) modulatrice, tube (à vide) modulateur.

modulation [mɔdju'leiʃ(ə)n], *s.* **1.** modulation *f,* inflexion *f* (de la voix). **2.** *Mus:* modulation. **3.** *El: Elcs:* modulation; **anode, cathode, m.,** modulation dans l'anode, dans la cathode; **direct m.,** modulation dans l'étage final; **grid m.,** modulation dans la grille; **absorption m.,** modulation par absorption; **grid bias m.,** modulation par variation de polarisation de grille; **pulse m.,** modulation par impulsions; **pulse code m.,** modulation par impulsions codées; **phase shift m.,** modulation par déphasage; **light m.,** modulation de lumière; **phase m.,** modulation de phase; **power m.,** modulation de puissance; **A-class, B-class, m.,** modulation classe A, classe B; **constant current m.,** modulation à courant constant; **remote m.,** modulation à distance; **series m.,** modulation à tension constante; **spurious m.,** modulation parasite; *T.V:* **brilliance m.,** modulation d'intensité; **negative-light, positive-light, m.,** modulation négative, positive; **m. amplifier,** amplificateur *m* de modulation; **m. capability,** taux *m* maximum de modulation sans distorsion; **m. distortion,** distorsion *f* de modulation; **m. factor, m. index,** facteur *m,* indice *m,* de modulation; **m. level, m. percentage,** taux de modulation; **m. wave,** onde *f* de modulation; **m. meter, monitor,** vumètre *m*; **m. tube,** tube *m,* lampe *f,* de modulation.

modulator ['mɔdjuleitər], *s.* **1.** *Mus:* (*pers.*) modulateur, -trice. **2.** *Mus:* tableau *m* pour solfège (donnant toutes les notes de la gamme, d'après le système *sol-fa*). **3.** *El: Elcs:* modulateur *m*; **balanced m.,** modulateur équilibré; **pulse m.,** modulateur d'impulsions; **reactance m.,** modulateur (de tube) à réactance; **ring m.,** modulateur en anneau; **vacuum tube m.,** modulateur à lampe; **modulator-demodulator,** modulateur-démodulateur *m, pl.* modulateurs-démodulateurs; modem *m*; **m. electrode,** électrode modulatrice, de modulation; **m. stage,** étage modulateur; **m. valve, m. tube,** lampe (à vide) modulatrice, tube (à vide) modulateur.

module ['mɔdju:l], *s.* **1.** (*a*) *Arch: Hyd: etc:* module *m*; (*b*) *Mec.E:* module, pas diamétral (d'un engrenage). **2.** (*a*) *Civ.E: etc:* module, élément normalisé (préfabriqué) (d'une construction, d'un ensemble); (*b*) *Space:* module, cabine *f,* compartiment *m,* élément (d'un véhicule spatial composé de parties indépendantes s'arrimant les unes aux autres); **service m.,** module de service; compartiment des servitudes; **lunar m.,** module lunaire; **command m.,** module de commande.

modulus, *pl.* **-i** ['mɔdjuləs, -ai], *s. Mth: Mec:* module *m,* coefficient *m*; *Mth:* **m. of common logarithms,** module de logarithmes communs; *Mec:* **m. of compression,** coefficient d'écrasement; **m. of elasticity,** module, coefficient, d'élasticité; **m. of rupture, of resistance,** module, coefficient, de rupture, de résistance; **shearing m.,** module, coefficient, de cisaillement; **Young's m.,** module de Young.

modus operandi ['moudəsɔpə'rændai, -di:], *s.* modus *m* operandi; façon *f,* manière *f,* d'opérer.

modus vivendi ['moudəsvi'vendai, -di:], *s.* **1.** modus *m* vivendi; manière *f* de vivre. **2.** *Jur:* modus vivendi; accord *m.*

Moesia ['mi:siə]. *Pr.n. A.Geog:* Mésie *f.*

Moesogoth ['misougɔθ], *s. Hist:* Goth *m* de Mésie.

Moesogothic [mi:sou'gɔθik], (*a*) *a. Hist:* mésogothique; (*b*) *s. Ling:* mésogothique *m.*

mofette [mɔ'fet], *s. Geol:* mo(u)fette *f.*

moggy ['mɔgi], *s. F:* chat *m*; **come on, m.!** viens, minou!

mogiphonia [mɔgi'founiə], *s. Med:* mogiphonie *f.*

Mograbin ['mɔ:grəbin]. *Geog:* (*a*) *a.* mograbin; (*b*) *s.* Mograbin, -ine.

Mogul ['mougəl], *s.* **1.** *Hist:* mogol *m*; **the Great, Grand, M.,** le Grand Mogol. **2.** *F:* gros bonnet; huile *f*; **movie m.,** magnat *m* du cinéma.

mohair ['mouhɛər], *s.* mohair *m*; poil *m* de chèvre angora; turcoin *m.*

Mohammed [mə'hæmid]. *Pr.n.m.* **1.** Mohammed. **2.** *Rel.H:* Mahomet.

Mohammedan [mə'hæmidən], *a.* & *s. O: Rel:* musulman, -ane; mahométan, -ane.

Mohammedanism [mə'hæmidənizm], *s. Rel: O:* islam(isme) *m*; mahométisme *m.*

mohatra [mou'hætrə], *s. Jur: A:* contrat *m* mohatra.

mohawkite ['mouhɔ:kait], *s. Miner:* mohawkite *f.*

Mohican ['mouikən]. *Ethn:* (*a*) *a.* des Mohicans; (*b*) *s.* Mohican, -ane.

Mohr [mɔ:r]. *Pr.n. Ch:* **Mohr's salt,** sel *m* de Mohr.

Mohs [mouz]. *Pr.n. Miner:* **Mohs' scale,** échelle *f* de Mohs.

moider ['mɔidər]. *Dial:* **1.** *v.tr.* embrouiller, troubler, ahurir (qn). **2.** *v.i.* divaguer.

moidore ['mɔidɔ:r], *s. Num: A:* moïdore *f* (du Portugal).

moiety ['mɔiəti], *s. A:* & *Jur:* **1.** moitié *f*; *Jur:* **cheptel by m.,** cheptel *m* à moitié. **2.** part *f,* demi-portion *f,* une des deux fractions (d'un tout).

moil [mɔil], *v.i.* **to toil and m.,** peiner, travailler dur; suer sang et eau; s'acharner; gagner son pain à la sueur de son front.

moire [mwɑ:r], *s. Tex:* moire *f*; **m. crêpe,** crêpe ondé.

moiré[1] ['mwɑ:rei]. **1.** *a.* & *s. Tex:* moiré (*m*). **2.** *s. Metalw:* moiré *m,* moirure *f*; **m. effect, pattern,** moirage *m.*

moiré[2], *v.tr.* **1.** *Tex:* moirer (des rubans, etc.). **2.** *Metalw:* moirer (le métal).

moissanite ['mɔisənait], *s. Miner:* moissanite *f.*

moist [mɔist], *a.* **1.** (climat, région, chaleur, etc.) humide; (peau, main, chaleur) moite; **eyes m. with tears,** yeux mouillés, humectés, de larmes; **to grow m.,** se mouiller, s'humecter; devenir humide; (*of horse*) **m. mouth,** bouche fraîche; *Paint:* **m. colours,** couleurs *f* moites. **2.** *Med:* purulent; qui coule; qui jette du pus.

moisten ['mɔis(ə)n]. **1.** *v.tr.* (*a*) mouiller, humecter; moitir, amoitir (la peau); arroser (la pâte, etc.); bassiner (la pâte); *Tchn:* humidifier, madéfier; (*b*) **to m. a cloth, a sponge, with . . .,** imbiber un chiffon, une éponge, de . . . . **2.** *v.i.* se mouiller, s'humecter.

moistener ['mɔis(ə)nər], *s.* (*device*) mouilleur *m.*

moistening ['mɔis(ə)niŋ], *s.* mouillage *m,* mouillement *m*; humidification *f,* humectage *m,* humectation *f*; arrosage *m,* arrosement *m* (de la pâte).

moistness ['mɔistnis], *s.* humidité *f*; moiteur *f* (de la peau).

moisture ['mɔistjər], *s.* **1.** humidité *f*; buée *f* (sur une glace, etc.); **inherent m.,** humidité interne; **m.-laden air,** air chargé d'humidité; **m. proof, m. repellent,** protégé contre, à l'épreuve de, l'humidité; étanche; hydrofuge; **m. content,** teneur *f* en humidité, en eau; degré hygrométrique (de l'air); **m. diverter,** gouttière *f*; **m. extractor, m. separator,** séparateur *m* d'humidité, d'eau. **2.** *Physiol:* moiteur *f* (de la peau).

moither ['mɔiðər], *v.tr.* & *i. Dial:* = MOIDER.

moke [mouk], *s.* **1.** *F:* bourricot *m,* bourrique *f*; âne *m.* **2.** *U.S: P: Pej:* nègre *m.*

mol [moul], *s. Ch.Meas:* mole *f.*

mola ['moulə], *s. Ich:* môle *f.*

molar[1] ['moulər]. **1.** *a.* (dent) molaire. **2.** *s.* molaire *f,* grosse dent, dent du fond; **milk m.,** molaire de lait. **3.** *a. Obst:* **m. pregnancy,** grossesse *f* môlaire.

molar[2], *a. Ph:* **1.** qui se rapporte à la masse, à la molécule-gramme; (concrétion, etc.) molaire; **m. physics,** physique *f* molaire; **m. ratio,** rapport *m* molaire. **2.** moléculaire; **m. conductivity, m. resistivity,** conductibilité *f,* résistivité *f,* moléculaire.

molarity [mou'læriti], *s. Ch:* molarité *f.*

molasse [mou'læs], *s. Geol:* mol(l)asse *f.*

molasses [mə'læsiz], *s.pl.* (*with sg. const.*) mélasse *f.*

mold (*etc.*) [mould]. *NAm:* = MOULD (*etc.*).

Moldavia [mɔl'deiviə]. *Pr.n. Hist:* Moldavie *f.*

Moldavian [mɔl'deiviən]. *Hist:* (*a*) *a.* moldave; (*b*) *s.* Moldave *mf.*

moldavite ['mɔldəvait], *s. Miner:* moldavite *f.*

mole[1] [moul], *s.* **1.** grain *m* de beauté (au visage). **2.** nævus *m.*

mole[2], *s.* (*a*) *Z:* taupe *f*; **African, golden, m.,** taupe dorée, chrysochlore *m*; **marsupial m.,** taupe marsupiale; **star-nosed m.,** taupe étoilée; **m. rat,** rat-taupe *m, pl.* rats-taupes; spalax *m*; **Cape m. rat,** bathyergue *m* (de mer), blesmol *m*; **European lesser m. rat,** spalax européen; **(East African) naked m. rat,** hétérocéphale *m*; **m. trap,** taupière *f*; **m.-shaped,** talpiforme; (*b*) *Ent:* **m. cricket,** taupe-grillon *f, pl.* taupes-grillons; courtilière *f*; tridactyle *m.*

mole[3], *s.* môle *m*; brise-lames *m inv*; digue *f*; jetée *f.*

mole[4], *s. Obst:* **hydatidiform m.,** môle *f* hydatiforme.

mole[5], *s. Meas:* **1.** *Ch:* mole *f.* **2.** *Ph:* molécule-gramme *f, pl.* molécules-grammes; **m. fraction,** fraction *f* molaire.

molecast ['moulkɑ:st], *s.* taupinière *f.*

molecular [mə'lekjulər], *a. Ph:* moléculaire; **m. attraction,** attraction *f* moléculaire; **m. bond,** liaison *f* moléculaire; **m. diffusion, m. scattering,** diffusion *f* moléculaire; **m. heat,** chaleur *f* moléculaire; **m. mass, m. weight,** masse *f,* poids *m,* moléculaire; **m. structure,** structure *f* moléculaire; **m. velocity,** vitesse *f* moléculaire; **m. volume,** volume *m* moléculaire; *Atom.Ph:* **m. label,** traceur *m* moléculaire.

molecularity [məlekju'læriti], *s.* **1.** qualité *f* moléculaire. **2.** force *f* moléculaire.

molecule ['mɔlikju:l], *s. Ch: Ph:* molécule *f*; **atomic, diatomic, m.,** molécule atomique, diatomique; **monoatomic m.,** molécule monoatomique; **gas m.,** molécule gazeuse; **homonuclear m.,** molécule homonucléaire; **ionized m.,** molécule ionisée; **labelled, tagged, m.,** molécule marquée; **neutral m.,** molécule neutre.

molehill ['moulhil], *s.* taupinière *f.*

moleskin ['moulskin], *s.* **1.** (peau *f* de) taupe *f*; **m. coat,** manteau *m* en taupe. **2.** (*a*) *Tex:* velours *m* de coton; (*b*) *A.Cost:* **moleskins,** pantalon *m* en velours de coton (de garde-chasse, etc.).

molest [mə'lest], *v.tr.* (*usu. in neg. implications*) **1.** *A:* & *Jur:* molester, importuner, inquiéter (qn). **2.** rudoyer (qn); se livrer à des voies de fait contre (qn).

molestation [moules'teiʃ(ə)n], *s.* **1.** molestation *f.* **2.** voies *fpl* de fait.

Molgula ['mɔlgjulə], *s. Nat.Hist:* molgule *f.*

Molidae ['mɔlidi:], *s.pl. Ich:* molidés *m.*

molimen [mɔ'laimən], *s. Med:* molimen *m.*

moline [mou'lain]. **1.** *s. Mill: Her:* anille *f.* **2.** *a. Her:* **cross m.,** croix anillée.

Molinism[1] ['mɔlinizm], *s. Theol:* molinisme *m*; la doctrine de Molina.

Molinism[2], *s. Ecc. Hist:* molinosisme *m*; la doctrine de Molinos; quiétisme *m.*

Molinist[1] ['mɔlinist], *s. Theol:* moliniste *mf.*

Molinist[2], *s. Ecc.Hist:* molinosiste *mf.*

Moll [mɔl]. **1.** *Pr.n.f.* = MOLLY[1]. **2.** *s.f. P:* (*a*) **(gangster's) m.,** poule, môme, d'un gangster; (*b*) *A:* catin, goton.

mollie ['mɔli], *s. Ich:* mollienisia *m,* molly *m.*

mollienisia [mɔlie'nisiə], *s. Ich:* mollienisia *m,* molly *m.*

mollifiable [mɔli'faiəbl], *a.* (colère) qu'on peut adoucir, apaiser; (personne) dont on peut apaiser la colère.

mollification [mɔlifi'keiʃ(ə)n], *s.* apaisement *m,* adoucissement *m* (de qn, de la colère de qn).

mollifier ['mɔlifaiər], *s.* **1.** (*pers.*) apaiseur *m.* **2.** (*thg*) adoucissant *m.*

mollify ['mɔlifai], *v.tr.* **to m. s.o.,** adoucir, apaiser, qn, la colère de qn; émousser la colère de qn; **he refused to be mollified (by them),** il leur tenait rigueur.

mollifying ['mɔlifaiiŋ], *a.* **in a m. tone,** d'un ton doux.

mollusc ['mɔləsk], *s.* mollusque *m.*

Mollusca [mɔ'lʌskə], *s.pl.* mollusques *m.*

Molluscoid(e)a [mɔlə'skɔid(i)ə], *s.pl. Z: O:* molluscoïdes *m.*

molluscum [mɔ'lʌskəm], *s. Med:* molluscum *m*; verrue sébacée.

Molly[1] ['mɔli]. *Pr.n.f.* (*dim. of Mary*) Mariette, Manon.

Molly[2], *s. Ich:* mollienisia *m,* molly *m.*

mollycoddle[1] ['mɔlikɔd(ə)l], *s. F:* (*a*) petit(e) chéri(e) à sa maman; (*b*) (homme) douillet *m*; (*c*) poule mouillée.

mollycoddle[2], *v.tr. F:* dorloter, câliner, ouater (un enfant); élever (un enfant) dans du coton.

mollymawk ['mɔlimɔ:k], *s. Orn: F:* albatros *m,* pétrel géant.

Moloch ['moulɔk]. **2.** *Pr.n.m. B:* Moloch. **2.** *s. Rept:* moloch (épineux).

Molossian [mə'lɔsiən]. *A.Geog:* (*a*) *a.* molosse; *A:* **M. (dog, hound),** molosse *m*; (*b*) *s.* Molosse *mf.*

molossic [mə'lɔsik], *a. A.Pros:* molossique, molosse.

Molossidae [mə'lɔsidi:], *s.pl. Z:* molossidés *m.*

molossus, *pl.* **-i** [mə'lɔsəs, -ai], *s.* **1.** *A.Pros:* molosse *m.* **2.** *Z:* (*mastiff bat*) (chauve-souris *f*) molosse *m.*

molten ['moult(ə)n], *a.* **1.** *Metall: Glassm:* fondu, en fusion; **m. lead,** plomb fondu; **m. gold,** or *m* en fusion, en bain. **2.** *A:* (*of statue, etc.*) venu de fonte; coulé.

Molucca [mɔ'lʌkə]. *Pr.n. Geog:* **1. the Moluccas, the M. Islands,** les Moluques *f.* **2.** *Bot:* (*a*) **M. balm,** molucelle *f* lisse; mélisse *f* des Moluques; moluque odorante; (*b*) **M. bean,** bonduc *m* jaune; œil-de-chat *m, pl.* œils-de-chat; guénic *m.*

moly ['mouli], *s.* **1.** *Myth:* Moly *m.* **2.** *Bot:* ail doré; moly.

molybdate [mɔ'libdeit], *s. Ch:* molybdate *m.*

molybdenite [mɔ'libdənait], *s. Miner:* molybdénite *f.*

molybdenum [mɔ'libdinəm], *s. Miner:* molybdène *m*; **m. oxide,** oxyde *m* de molybdène.

molybdic [mɔ'libdik], *a. Miner:* molybdique; **m. ochre,** molybdénocre *f.*

molybdite [mɔ'libdait], *s. Miner:* molybdine *f.*

molybdomancy [mɔ'libdoumænsi], *s. Gr.Ant:* molybdomancie *f.*

molybdomenite [mɔlibdou'mi:nait], *s. Miner:* molybdoménite *f.*

molybdophyllite [mɔlibdou'filait], *s. Miner:* molybdophyllite *f.*

molysite ['mɔlisait], *s. Miner:* molysite *f.*

mombin [moum'bin], *s. Bot:* mombin *m,* monbin *m.*

moment ['moumənt], *s.* **1.** moment *m*, instant *m*; **I haven't a m. to spare,** je n'ai pas un instant de libre; *F:* **I've had my moments,** j'ai eu mes bons moments; j'ai fait mes entourloupettes *f*; **wait a m.! just a m.! one m.!** *F:* **half a m.!** une petite minute! une seconde! un moment! un instant! attendez une seconde! **to flare up one m. and calm down the next,** s'emporter et se calmer, tour à tour; **every m.,** à chaque instant; **to expect s.o. (at) any m.,** attendre qn d'un moment, d'un instant, à l'autre; **he may return at any m.,** il peut revenir d'un instant à l'autre; **you may expect me at any m.,** j'arriverai incessamment; **he'll be here any m. now,** il peut arriver d'un instant à l'autre; **one hour to a m.,** une heure à une minute près; **his entry was timed to the m.,** son entrée était calculée à la minute; **I have just, only, this m. heard about it,** je viens de l'apprendre à l'instant; je l'apprends à l'instant; **I saw him a m. ago,** je l'ai vu il y a un instant; **I came the (very) m. I heard about it,** je suis venu aussitôt que, dès que, je l'ai appris; **the m. I saw him I recognized him,** je ne l'ai pas plus tôt vu que je l'ai reconnu; **the m. he arrives,** dès son arrivée; **the m. I came in,** au moment où je suis entré; **from the m. when . . .,** dès l'instant où . . .; du moment que . . .; **at this m., at the present m.,** en ce moment; actuellement; **I'm busy at the m.,** je suis occupé pour le moment, en ce moment; **I was busy at the m.,** j'étais occupé à ce moment; **I don't need anything at the m.,** il ne me faut rien pour le moment; **he's there at the m., this m.,** il est là en, à, ce moment; **at the m. I thought . . .,** sur le moment j'ai pensé . . .; **at that m. I could have killed him,** à ce moment(-là) je l'aurais tué; **at the (very) m.,** au même instant; **at the last m.,** à la dernière minute; **the book appeared just at the right m.,** le livre a paru à point nommé; **to arrive at an awkward m.,** arriver dans un mauvais moment; **to study at odd moments,** étudier à ses moments perdus; **I'll come in a m.,** je viendrai dans un instant; **I'll be with you in a m.,** je suis à vous dans un moment, une minute; **it's done in a m.,** c'est l'affaire d'un instant; **it was all over, it all happened, in a m.,** cela s'est fait en un clin d'œil; **I want nothing for the m.,** je n'ai besoin de rien pour le moment; **nothing more for the m.,** rien de plus pour le moment; **I forget for the m.,** j'oublie pour le moment, pour l'instant; **I stood listening for a m.,** je suis resté à écouter pendant un moment; **he disappeared for a m.,** il a disparu momentanément; **may I disappear for a m.?** excusez-moi un instant; **for a m. I was at a loss,** sur le moment je n'ai su que faire; **not for a m.!** (i) pas encore! (ii) jamais de la vie! pour rien au monde! **not a moment's hesitation,** pas un moment d'hésitation; **the man of the m.,** l'homme du jour, du moment; *F:* **who's the man of the m.?** qui est le grand préféré? **writer of the m.,** écrivain *m* du moment; **the m. of truth,** la minute de vérité; **psychological m.,** moment psychologique; **on the spur of the m.,** sur le moment. **2.** *(a)* *Mth: Mec:* moment (d'une force); **m. of (a) force about a point,** moment de force par rapport à un point; **m. of a couple,** moment d'un couple; **m. of inertia,** moment d'inertie; **m. of momentum,** moment des quantités de mouvement; **bending m., m. of flexure,** moment fléchissant, moment de flexion; (*of piece*) **to carry the bending m.,** travailler à la flexion; **friction m.,** moment de frottement; **torsional, twisting, m., m. of torsion,** moment de torsion; *Magn:* **magnetic m.,** moment magnétique; *Av:* **diving, stalling, m.,** moment piqueur, cabreur; **hinge m.,** moment de charnière (d'une gouverne); **pitching m.,** moment de tangage; **rolling m.,** moment de roulis; **restoring, righting, m.,** moment de retour; **yawing m.,** moment de lacet, d'embardée, de giration; *(b)* *Nau:* **m. of a sail,** moment de voilure; **m. of stability,** moment de stabilité; **heeling m.,** moment d'inclinaison; **righting m.,** moment de redressement; **rudder m.,** moment d'évolution; *Veh:* **m. of braking couple,** moment de freinage. **3.** (*of fact, event*) **to be of m.,** être important; être de conséquence; **of great, little, no, m.,** de grande, de petite, d'aucune, importance; **it is of no m. whether . . .,** peu importe que + *sub.*; **of the first m.,** de première importance.

momentarily [moumən'terili], *adv.* **1.** momentanément, passagèrement. **2.** d'un moment à l'autre; à tout moment.

momentary ['moumənt(ə)ri], *a.* **1.** momentané, passager. **2.** de tous les moments; **in m. fear of falling,** craignant à chaque instant de tomber.

momently ['mouməntli], *adv. esp. U.S:* **1.** *A:* à tout moment. **2.** d'un moment à l'autre; d'un instant à l'autre. **3.** momentanément.

momentous [mou'mentəs], *a.* important; **m. decision,** décision capitale; **on this m. occasion,** en cette occasion mémorable; **the risks of war are too m. to be faced lightly,** la guerre offre des risques trop graves pour qu'on les traite à la légère.

momentousness [mou'mentəsnis], *s.* importance capitale.

momentum, *pl.* **-ta** [mou'mentəm, -tə], *s.* *(a)* *Mec: Ph:* force vive, force d'impulsion; quantité *f* de mouvement; *Atom.Ph:* impulsion *f* (d'une particule); **angular m.,** moment *m* angulaire, cinétique; **m. distribution,** répartition *f* de la force vive, *Atom.Ph:* distribution *f* d'impulsions; **m. transfer,** transfert *m* de la force vive, *Atom.Ph:* transfert d'impulsions; *(b)* (*impetus*) vitesse acquise; élan *m*; **carried away by my own m.,** emporté par mon (propre) élan; (*of movement*) **to gather m.,** acquérir de la force (vive), de la vitesse; *Mil:* **the m. of the assault, of the attack,** la force vive de l'assaut, de l'attaque.

momot ['moumɔt], *s. Orn:* momot *m.*

Momotidae [mou'mɔtidi:], *s.pl. Orn:* momotidés *m.*

Momotus [mou'moutəs], *s. Orn:* momot *m.*

Momus ['mouməs]. *Pr.n.m. Gr.Myth:* Momus, Momos.

monacanthid [mɔnə'kænθid], *a. & s. Ich:* monacanthe (*m*).

Monacanthidae [mɔnə'kænθidi:], *s.pl. Ich:* monacanthidés *m*, monocanthes *m.*

monacanthous [mɔnə'kænθəs], *a. Z:* monacanthe.

monac(h)al ['mɔnək(ə)l], *a.* monacal, -aux.

monachism ['mɔnəkizm], *s.* monachisme *m.*

Monaco [mɔ'nɑ:kou]. *Pr.n. Geog:* **Principality of M.,** Principauté *f* de Monaco.

monad ['mɔnæd], *s. Phil: Biol: Ch:* monade *f.*

monadelph ['mɔnədelf], *s. Bot:* plante *f* monadelphe.

monadelphia [mɔnə'delfiə], *s. A.Bot:* monadelphie *f.*

monadelphous [mɔnə'delfəs], *a. Bot:* monadelphe.

monadic [mɔ'nædik], *a.* **1.** *Ch:* univalent, monoatomique. **2.** *Phil:* monadiste; monadaire.

monadism ['mɔnædizm], *s. Phil:* monadisme *m.*

monadology [mɔnæ'dɔlədʒi], *s. Phil:* monadologie *f.*

monal [mɔ'nɔ:l], *s. Orn:* lophophore *m.*

Mona Lisa ['mounə'li:zə]. *Pr.n.f. Art:* la Joconde.

monander [mɔ'nændər], *s. Bot:* plante *f* monandre.

monandria [mɔ'nændriə], *s. A.Bot:* monandrie *f.*

monandrous [mɔ'nændrəs], *a. Bot:* monandre.

monandry [mɔ'nændri], *s. Anthr:* monandrie *f.*

monanthous [mɔ'nænθəs], *a. Bot:* monanthe.

monarch ['mɔnək], *s.* **1.** monarque *m.* **2.** *Ent:* danaïde *f.*

monarchic(al) [mɔ'nɑ:kik(l)], *a.* monarchique; de monarque.

monarchically [mɔ'nɑ:kik(ə)li], *adv.* monarchiquement; (i) en monarque; (ii) en monarchie.

monarchism ['mɔnəkizm], *s. Pol:* monarchisme *m.*

monarchist ['mɔnəkist], *s. Pol:* monarchiste *mf.*

monarchize ['mɔnəkaiz]. **1.** *v.tr.* monarchiser (une nation). **2.** *v.i.* faire le monarque; se conduire en monarque.

monarchy ['mɔnəki], *s.* monarchie *f*; **limited m.,** monarchie tempérée.

monarda [mɔ'nɑ:də], *s. Bot:* monarde *f.*

monarticular [mɔnɑ:'tikjulər], *a. Med:* monoarticulaire.

monastery ['mɔnəstri], *s.* monastère *m.*

monastic [mə'næstik], *a.* **1.** monastique; monacal, -aux; claustral, -aux. **2.** *Bookb:* **m. binding,** reliure dorée à froid.

monastically [mə'næstik(ə)li], *adv.* monastiquement; en moine.

monasticism [mə'næstisizm], *s.* **1.** vie *f* monastique. **2.** système *m* monastique; monachisme *m.*

monatomic [mɔnə'tɔmik], *a. Ch:* monoatomique.

monaural [mɔ'nɔ:rəl], *a. Ac:* monaural, -aux.

monaxial [mɔ'næksiəl], *a.* **1.** *Biol:* monoaxe. **2.** *Bot:* monoaxifère.

monaxon(ic) [mɔ'nækson, mɔnæk'sɔnik], *a. Spong:* monoaxe.

monazite ['mɔnəzait], *s. Miner:* monazite *f.*

mond [mɔnd], *s. Her:* monde *m.*

Monday ['mʌndi], *s.* lundi *m*; **he comes on Mondays,** il vient le lundi; *occ.* il vient les lundis; **he comes every M.,** il vient tous les lundis; **to take M. off,** *A:* **to keep Saint M.,** fêter la Saint-Lundi; chômer, faire, le lundi; *F:* **that M. morning feeling,** l'humeur *f*, le cafard, du lundi; l'après-weekend *m.*

Mondayish ['mʌndiiʃ], *a. F:* qui a la maladie du lundi; **that M. feeling,** l'humeur *f*, le cafard, du lundi.

Monegasque ['mɔnigæsk]. *Geog:* *(a)* *a.* monégasque; *(b)* *s.* Monégasque *mf.*

Monel ['mounel], *s. Metall: R.t.m:* **M. metal,** monel *m.*

moneme ['mouni:m], *s. Ling:* monème *m.*

monergol ['mɔnəgɔl], *s. Av:* monopropellant *m.*

moneron, *pl.* **-a** ['mɔnərɔn, -ə], *s. Prot:* monère *f.*

monetary ['mʌnit(ə)ri], *a.* monétaire; **m. area,** zone *f* monétaire; **m. authority,** autorité *f* monétaire; **m. circulation,** circulation *f* monétaire; **m. convention,** convention *f* monétaire; **m. policy, m. management,** politique *f* monétaire; **m. reform,** réforme *f*, assainissement *m*, monétaire; **m. standard,** étalon *m* monétaire; **m. unit,** unité *f* monétaire; **to have a m. interest,** avoir un intérêt pécuniaire.

monetite ['mɔnitait], *s. Miner:* monétite *f.*

monetization [mʌnitai'zeiʃ(ə)n], *s.* monétisation *f.*

monetize ['mʌnitaiz], *v.tr.* monétiser (de l'argent, etc.).

money ['mʌni], *s.* **1.** monnaie *f*, argent *m*; espèces (monnayées, numéraires); numéraire *m*; *(a)* (*coins*) **gold, silver, m.,** monnaie d'or, d'argent; **nickel m.,** monnaie de nickel; **copper m.,** monnaie de bronze, de cuivre, de billon; **piece of m.,** pièce *f* de monnaie; **to coin, mint, m.,** frapper de la monnaie, battre monnaie; *F:* **he's (just) coining m.,** il gagne un argent fou; il fait fortune; *F:* **that's giving him a licence to print m.,** comme ça il va amasser l'argent à la pelle; *Pol.Ec:* **bank m., deposit m., representative m.,** monnaie de banque, monnaie scripturale; **commodity m.,** monnaie marchandise; **common m., token m.,** monnaie fiduciaire, fictive; **counterfeit, base, bad, m.,** fausse monnaie; **current m.,** monnaie qui a cours; **divisional, fractional, subsidiary, m.,** monnaie divisionnaire, monnaie d'appoint; **effective, real, m.,** monnaie effective, réelle; **foreign m.,** monnaie étrangère; **lawful m.,** monnaie légale; **paper m., soft m.,** billets *mpl* (de banque), papier *m* monnaie; **standard m.,** monnaie intrinsèque, droite; **hard m.,** espèces (monnayées); *Fin: Bank:* **cheap, easy, m.,** argent à bon marché; **m. at, on, call; call m.,** argent remboursable sur demande; argent, dépôt *m*, à vue; **blocked call m.,** dépôt(s) à vue bloqué(s); **m. that bears, yields, interest,** argent qui rapporte (un intérêt); **m. interest,** intérêt de l'argent, intérêt pécuniaire; **price of m.,** loyer *m* de l'argent; **m. rate,** taux *m* de l'argent; **m. market,** marché *m* de l'argent; marché monétaire, financier; place *f* de change; bourse *f*; **m. changing,** change *f*; **m. changer,** (i) (*pers.*) agent *m* de change; changeur *m*; (ii) (*machine*) distributeur *m* de monnaie; *Com:* **ready m.,** argent comptant, argent liquide; **to pay in ready m.,** payer (au) comptant; **m. allowance,** allocation *f* en deniers, en espèces; **m. payment,** paiement *m* en argent, en espèces, en numéraire; **m. supply,** masse *f* monétaire; **to throw good m. after bad,** s'enfoncer davantage dans une mauvaise affaire; **m. lying idle, dead m.,** argent improductif, qui dort; argent mort; **m. matters,** affaires *f* d'argent, questions financières; **it's like m. in the bank,** c'est un placement, c'est du blé au grenier; **m. means nothing to him,** il ne regarde pas à l'argent; l'argent n'est rien pour lui; l'argent ne lui coûte guère; *Post:* **m. order,** mandat-poste *m*, *pl.* mandats-poste; **international, foreign, m. order,** mandat international, sur l'étranger; *(b)* **my own m.,** mon argent personnel; **I bought it with my own m.,** je l'ai acheté avec mon argent personnel; je l'ai payé de mes propres deniers; **spending m.,** argent de poche; argent pour dépenses courantes; **to be worth a lot of m.,** (i) (*of thg*) valoir de l'argent; avoir du prix, de la valeur; (ii) (*of pers.*) être riche, avoir de la fortune; *F:* **he's made of m., rolling in m., in the m., he's got pots of m.,** il est immensément riche; il roule sur l'or; *F:* **I'm not made of m.,** je ne suis pas cousu d'or; **to be well provided with m.,** être bien pourvu d'argent; **to be short of m.,** être démuni, à court, d'argent; **I want to get my m. back,** je voudrais récupérer mon argent, rentrer dans mes fonds; **your m. or your life!** la bourse ou la vie! **to earn, make, m.,** gagner, faire, de l'argent; **he made his m. by selling . . .,** il s'est enrichi, il a fait fortune, en vendant . . .; **to do sth. for m.,** faire qch. pour l'argent, à prix d'argent; **there should be some m. in it,** c'est une bonne affaire; on devrait en tirer de l'argent; **there's plenty of m., big m., in it,** c'est une mine d'or; cela rapportera gros; **it's a job that brings in the m.,** c'est un travail qui rapporte, qui nourrit son homme; **m. makes m.,** l'argent va à l'argent; un sou amène l'autre; un bien acquiert un autre; **to spend, part with, one's m.,** débourser; **it's not everybody's m.,** ce n'est pas au goût de tout le monde; **you've had your money's worth,** vous en avez eu pour votre argent; **you can live there for next to no m.,** on peut y vivre pour pas cher; **it's m. thrown away, down the drain,** c'est de l'argent gaspillé, jeté par la fenêtre; **he's the man for my m.,** c'est mon homme; *F:* **to put your m. where your mouth is,** soutenir une cause par son argent, par ses efforts personnels, et non seulement par de belles paroles; *attrib.* **m. belt,** ceinture *f* à porte-monnaie; *F:* **m. spinner,** (i) (*pers.*) amasseur *m* d'argent; (ii) (*business, product, etc.*) mine *f* d'argent; *Arach:* **m. spider, m. spinner,** petite araignée rouge (qui annonce la richesse à ceux sur qui elle tombe). **2.** *(a)* (*pl.* **moneys,** *occ.* **monies**) pièce *f* de monnaie; monnaie (particulière); **m. of ac-**

count, monnaie de compte; (b) A: & Jur: **moneys, monies,** argent, fonds *mpl*; **moneys paid out,** versements (opérés); **moneys paid in,** recettes (effectuées); **public moneys,** deniers publics; le trésor public; **sundry monies owing to him,** diverses sommes à lui dues.

moneybag ['mʌnibæg], s. 1. (a) sac *m* à argent; sacoche *f* (d'une receveur d'autobus, etc.); (b) *pl. F:* sacs d'argent, d'or; sacs; **to marry s.o. for her moneybags,** épouser qn pour son sac d'écus, pour son magot. 2. *F: O: (pers.)* **moneybags,** richard, -arde; rupin, -ine.

moneybox ['mʌnibɔks], s. 1. tirelire *f*. 2. caisse *f*, cassette *f*.

moneyed ['mʌnid], a. 1. riche; qui a de l'argent; **m. man,** homme riche; *Pej: F:* capitaliste *m*, richard *m*; **the m. classes,** les classes possédantes, les gens fortunés. 2. **the m. interest,** les rentiers *m*, les capitalistes; **m. resources,** ressources *f* pécuniaires, en argent.

moneygrubber ['mʌnigrʌbər], s. grippe-sou *m, pl.* grippe-sous; pingre *m*, thésauriseur *m*, homme *m* d'argent.

moneygrubbing[1] ['mʌnigrʌbiŋ], a. cupide, avare.

moneygrubbing[2], s. thésaurisation *f*.

moneylender ['mʌnilendər], s. 1. prêteur *m* d'argent; banquier usurier; maison *f* de prêt. 2. *Com:* bailleur *m* de fonds.

moneyless ['mʌnilis], a. sans argent; *F:* sans le sou.

moneymaker ['mʌnimeikər], s. (a) (*pers.*) amasseur *m* d'argent; (b) (*thg*) (bonne) source d'argent; métier *m*, etc., qui rapporte.

moneymaking[1] ['mʌnimeikiŋ], a. (commerce, etc.) qui rapporte.

moneymaking[2], s. acquisition *f* de l'argent.

moneywort ['mʌniwə:t], s. *Bot:* (lysimaque *f*, lysimachie *f*) nummulaire *f*; monnayère *f*; herbe *f* aux écus.

Mongol ['mɔŋgəl]. 1. a. (a) *Geog:* mongol; mongolien; **the M. invasions,** les invasions mongoles; (b) *Med:* mongolien; **M. spot,** tache bleue mongolique. 2. s. (a) *Geog:* Mongol, -ole; (b) *Med:* mongolien, -ienne; (c) *Ling:* mongol *m*.

Mongolia [mɔŋ'gouliə]. *Pr.n. Geog:* Mongolie *f*; **Inner M.,** Mongolie intérieure; *A:* **Outer M.,** Mongolie extérieure.

Mongolian [mɔŋ'gouliən]. 1. a. (a) *Geog:* mongol; mongolien; **M. People's Republic,** République *f* populaire de Mongolie; (b) *Med:* mongolien; **M. spot,** tache bleue mongolique. 2. s. (a) *Geog:* Mongol, -ole; (b) *Med:* mongolien, -ienne; (c) *Ling:* mongol *m*.

mongol(ian)ism ['mɔŋgəlizm, mɔŋ'gouliənizm], s. *Med:* mongolisme *m*.

Mongolic [mɔŋ'gɔlik]. 1. a. *Ethn:* mongol. 2. s. *Ling:* mongol *m*.

Mongoloid ['mɔŋgəlɔid], a. & s. (a) *Ethn:* mongol, -ole; (b) *Med:* mongoloïde (*mf*); mongolien, -ienne.

mongoose, *pl.* **-ses** [mɔn'gu:s, -siz], s. *Z:* mangouste *f*; **striped m.,** mangouste zébrée; **marsh m.,** mangouste des marais; **crab-eating m.,** mangouste crabière; **the Malagasy mongooses,** les galidiinés *m*.

mongrel ['mʌŋgrəl]. 1. s. (*of dog, animal, pers.*) métis, -isse; (*of dog*) bâtard, -arde. 2. a. (a) (animal) métis; (plante) métisse; **m. cur,** roquet *m*; (b) *F:* (peuple) mélangé, métis.

mongrelize ['mʌŋgrəlaiz], *v.tr.* métisser.

monheimite [mɔn'haimait], s. *Miner:* monheimite *f*.

monial ['mouniəl], s. *Arch:* meneau *m*.

Monica ['mɔnikə]. *Pr.n.f.* Monique.

monilia [mɔ'niliə], s. *Fung:* monilia *f*; **m. disease,** moniliose *f*.

moniliform [mɔ'nilifɔ:m], a. moniliforme.

Monimiaceae [mɔnimi'eisii:], *s.pl. Bot:* monimiacées *f*.

monimolite [mɔ'nimoulait], s. *Miner:* monimolite *f*.

monism ['mɔnizm], s. *Phil:* monisme *m*.

monist ['mɔnist], s. *Phil:* moniste *mf*.

monistic [mɔ'nistik], a. *Phil:* monistique, moniste.

monition [mə'niʃ(ə)n], s. 1. (a) *A:* avertissement *m* (**of a danger,** d'un danger); (b) *Ecc:* monition *f*. 2. *Jur:* citation *f* (à comparaître).

monitor[1] ['mɔnitər], s. 1. (*pers.*) (a) moniteur, -trice; (b) *Sch:* élève choisi (i) pour maintenir la discipline, (ii) pour aider le professeur dans les travaux pratiques, etc.; (c) *Tp:* (i) opérateur *m* d'interception; (ii) opératrice chargée des réclamations; (d) *Cin: T.V:* **m. (man),** ingénieur *m* du son. 2. *Rept:* varan *m*; **Komodo m.,** varan de Komodo; **desert m.,** varan des déserts. 3. appareil *m* de contrôle, de surveillance; moniteur *m*; (a) *Elcs: W.Tel: etc:* **m. receiver,** récepteur *m* de contrôle; **m. loudspeaker,** moniteur, haut-parleur *m* de contrôle; *Cin:* **m. room,** cabine *f* d'enregistrement sonore; cabine, box *m*, d'écoute (pour le contrôle acoustique); **projection room m.,** haut-parleur de cabine, de contrôle; *T.V:* **m. (screen),** écran *m* de contrôle; (b) *Cmptr:* **m. program(me), m. routine,** (programme) moniteur; **m. printer, m. typewriter,** imprimante *f*, machine *f* à écrire, de contrôle; (c) *Atom.Ph:* **m. chamber,** chambre *f* de contrôle; **m. ionization chamber,** chambre d'ionisation de contrôle; **m. fan,** soufflante *f* de contrôle; **area m.,** détecteur local; **air m.,** détecteur de la radioactivité de l'air; moniteur atmosphérique; **alpha, beta, gamma, (contamination) m.,** détecteur (de contamination) alpha, bêta, gamma; **burst can m.,** *U.S:* **failed element m.,** détecteur, moniteur, de rupture de gaine; **health m.,** détecteur, moniteur, de radioprotection; **radioactive, radiation, m.,** détecteur de radioactivité, de rayonnement; (d) *Civ.E:* **m. (nozzle),** monitor *m*; (e) *U.S:* **m. roof, top,** lanterneau *m* (d'atelier, de wagon).

monitor[2], *v.tr.* (a) *W.Tel: etc:* surveiller (des émissions); *Tp:* brancher un appareil d'écoute, entrer en écoute, (sur une conversation); se mettre en surveillance (sur un circuit de transmissions); (b) *Cin:* contrôler (l'enregistrement sonore); (c) *Cmptr:* (i) surveiller, suivre (le déroulement d'une opération); (ii) examiner, tester (l'état d'un mot qualitatif, etc.); (d) *Atom.Ph:* contrôler, surveiller (le degré de radioactivité d'un corps, etc.); **detector designed to m. atomic explosions,** détecteur destiné à déceler les explosions atomiques.

monitorial [mɔni'tɔ:riəl], a. 1. = MONITORY 2. *Sch:* **m. system,** système *m* d'éducation où la discipline est en partie assurée par des moniteurs.

monitoring ['mɔnit(ə)riŋ], s. (a) *W.Tel:* monitoring *m*, interception *f* (des émissions); **m. station,** station *f*, centre *m*, d'écoute; **news m.,** service *m* des écoutes *f* radiotéléphoniques; **m. technique,** méthode *f* de contrôle; (b) *Tp:* (i) écoute (d'une conversation); (ii) *Mil:* écoute (des transmissions ennemies); écoute de contrôle (des transmissions amies); (iii) surveillance *f* (d'un circuit de transmissions); (c) *Cin:* contrôle *m* (de l'enregistrement sonore); (d) *Cmptr:* analyse *f*, contrôle, surveillance (du déroulement d'une opération); (e) *Atom.Ph:* contrôle (du degré de radioactivité d'un corps, etc.); (*f*) *Med:* **(patient) m.,** surveillance continue (de malades).

monitory ['mɔnit(ə)ri]. 1. a. (a) (mot *m*) d'admonition, d'avertissement; (b) *Ecc:* monitoire; monitorial, -aux; **m. letter,** monitoire *m*. 2. s. *Ecc:* monitoire.

monitress ['mɔnitris], *s.f.* 1. monitrice. 2. *Sch:* élève choisie (i) pour maintenir la discipline, (ii) pour aider le professeur dans les travaux pratiques, etc.

monitron ['mɔnitrɔn], s. *Atom.Ph:* appareil avertisseur; détecteur *m*.

monk [mʌnk], *s.m.* 1. moine, religieux; **to be a m.,** porter le froc; **black m.,** bénédictin; **white m.,** (moine) cistercien. 2. *Z:* **m. seal,** moine; phoque *m* à ventre blanc.

monkbird ['mʌŋkbə:d], s. *Orn:* gymnocéphale *m*, *F:* oiseau *m* mon-père.

monkery ['mʌŋkəri], s. *F: & Pej:* 1. moinerie *f*; esprit *m* monastique. 2. *coll.* moines *mpl*, moinaille *f*. 3. monastère *m*.

monkey[1] ['mʌŋki], s. 1. (a) *Z:* singe *m*; **female m., she-m.,** guenon *f*, guenuche *f*, singesse *f*; **patas, red, m.,** singe pleureur, rouge; **pigtailed m.,** singe cochon; **woolly m.,** singe laineux; **long-tailed m.,** guenon; **proboscis m.,** nasique *m*; guenon à long nez; **green m.,** callitriche *m*; **spider m.,** atèle *m*; singe-araignée *m*, *pl.* singes-araignées; **squirrel m.,** sagouin *m*; **snub-nosed m.,** rhinopithèque *m*; **white-nosed m.,** blanc-nez *m*, *pl.* blancs-nez; **m. gland,** testicule *m* de chimpanzé; *Surg:* **m. gland operation,** greffe *f* de testicules de chimpanzé; **m. house,** singerie *f*; pavillon *m* des singes; **m.-like,** simiesque; (b) *F:* **you little, young, m.!** petit polisson! mauvais garnement! petit(e) espiègle! **little m. face,** petite frimousse espiègle; **to get, put, s.o.'s m. up,** mettre qn en colère, en rogne; **to get one's m. up,** se mettre en colère; se fâcher; prendre la mouche; **his monkey's up,** il est d'humeur massacrante; il est en rogne; **to make a m. (out) of s.o.,** se payer la tête de qn; **m. business,** (i) affaire peu sérieuse, peu loyale; fricotage *m*; (ii) conduite *f* malhonnête; procédé irrégulier; (iii) coup fourré; (iv) fumisterie *f*; **I won't stand any m. business,** vous n'allez pas me la faire! **m. tricks,** singeries *fpl*; tours *mpl* de singe; chinoiseries *fpl*; espiègleries *fpl*; (c) *Nau:* **m. boat,** plate *f*; **m. forecastle,** teugue *f*; **m. block,** poulie *f* à émerillon, retour *m* de palan; **monkey's fist,** nœud *m* de ligne d'attrape; **m.-rigged,** à gréement léger; (d) *Bot:* **m. bread,** pain *m* de singe; calebasse *f*; **m. bread (tree),** baobab *m*; arbre *m* à pain; **m. flower,** mimule *m*; **m. nut,** (i) *Bot:* pistache *f* de terre; arachide *f*; (ii) *Com:* caca(h)ouette *f*, cacahuète *f*; **m. pot,** marmite *f* de singe; **m. pot (tree),** lécythis *m*; eschweilera *m*; **m. puzzle(r),** araucaria *m*, araucarie *f*; pin *m* du Chili; (e) *Cost: O:* **m. jacket,** veste courte (de garçon de café, etc.); spencer *m* (militaire); *Wr:* **m. climb,** planchette japonaise. 2. *Glassm: etc:* **m. (pot),** alcarazas *m*. 3. *Civ.E: etc:* mouton *m*, singe (de sonnette); **m. carriage,** chariot *m* de roulement (d'un pont roulant); *Min:* **m. drift,** galerie *f* de recherches, de prospection; *Tls: NAm:* **m. wrench,** clef anglaise; clef à molette; clef réglable. 4. *Metall:* trou *m* à laitier, trou de la scorie. 5. *P:* billet *m*, faf(f)iot *m*, de cinq cents livres, *U.S:* de cinq cents dollars; gros talbin.

monkey[2]. 1. *v.tr. F: O:* imiter, singer (qn). 2. *v.i.* (a) faire des tours de singe; (b) *F:* **to m. (about, around) with sth.,** tripoter qch.; toucher à qch. (qu'il faut laisser tranquille); **don't m. around with me!** (i) c'en est assez! (ii) (à) bas les mains!

monkeypod ['mʌŋkipɔd], s. *Bot:* pithecolobium *m*.

monkeyshines ['mʌŋkiʃainz], *s.pl. NAm: F:* tours *m* de singe; singeries *f*.

monkfish ['mʌŋkfiʃ], s. *Ich:* (i) ange *m* de mer, angelot *m*; (ii) baudroie *f*; lotte *f*.

monkhood ['mʌŋkhud], s. 1. monachisme *m*. 2. *coll.* moinerie *f*, *F:* moinaille *f*.

monkish ['mʌŋkiʃ], a. *Pej:* de moine; monacal, -aux.

monkshood ['mʌŋkshud], s. *Bot:* (aconit *m*) napel *m*; char *m* de Vénus; casque *m* de Jupiter; coqueluchon *m*; madriette *f*; capuce *m* de moine.

mono- ['mɔnou, 'mɔnə, mə'nɔ], *comb.fm.* mono-.

mono ['mɔnou], a. *Rec: F:* monaural, mono.

monoacid [mɔnou'æsid], s. *Ch:* monoacide *m*.

monoacidic [mɔnouæ'sidik], a. *Ch:* monoacide.

monoamid(e) [mɔnou'æm(a)id], s. *Ch:* monoamide *m*.

monoatomic [mɔnouæ'tɔmik], a. *Ch:* monoatomique.

monobasal [mɔnou'beisl], a. *Cryst:* monobase.

monobase ['mɔnoubeis], s. *Ch:* monobase *f*.

monobasic [mɔnou'beisik], a. 1. *Ch:* (acide) monobasique. 2. *Bot:* (phanérogame) monobase.

monobloc ['mɔnoublɔk], a. & s. monobloc *m* (*adj. inv.*).

monocalcium [mɔnou'kælsiəm], a. *Ch:* monocalcique.

monocarpellary [mɔnouka:'peləri], a. *Bot:* monocarpellaire.

monocarpian, monocarpic [mɔnou'ka:piən, -'ka:pik], a. *Bot:* monocarpien, monocarpique.

monocarpous [mɔnou'ka:pəs], a. *Bot:* 1. monocarpellaire; monocarpe. 2. monocarpien, monocarpique.

monocellular [mɔnou'seljulər], a. *Biol:* unicellulaire.

monocephalous [mɔnou'sefələs], a. *Bot:* monocéphale.

Monoceros [mɔ'nɔsərəs], s. *Astr: A:* la Licorne.

Monochlamydeae [mɔnouklæ'midii:], *s.pl. Bot:* monochlamydées *f*.

monochloride [mɔnou'klɔ:raid], s. *Ch:* monochlorure *m*.

monochlorinated [mɔnou'klɔ:rineitid], a. *Ch:* monochloré.

monochord ['mɔnoukɔ:d], s. 1. *A.Mus:* monocorde *m*. 2. *Ph:* monocorde, sonomètre *m*.

monochromatic [mɔnoukrou'mætik], a. monochromatique.

monochromator [mɔnou'kroumətər], s. *Opt:* monochromateur *m*.

monochrome ['mɔnəkroum]. 1. a. monochrome. 2. s. (peinture *f*) monochrome *m*.

monochromic, monochromous [mɔnə'kroumik, -'krouməs], a. monochrome.

monochromy ['mɔnəkroumi], s. monochromie *f*.

monocle ['mɔnəkl], s. monocle *m*.

monoclinal [mɔnou'klainl], a. *Geol:* monoclinal, -aux.

monocline ['mɔnəklain], s. *Geol:* pli monoclinal.

monoclinic [mɔnou'klinik], a. *Cryst:* monoclinique.

monoclinous [mɔnou'klainəs], a. *Geol:* monoclinal, -aux.

monocoque ['mɔnəkɔk], s. avion *m* monocoque.

monocotyledon [mɔnoukɔti'li:d(ə)n], s. *Bot:* monocotylédone *f*.

monocotyledonous [mɔnoukɔti'li:dənəs], a. *Bot:* monocotylédone, monocotylé.

monocracy [mɔ'nɔkrəsi], s. monocratie *f*.

monocrystal [mɔnou'kristəl], s. monocristal *m*.

monocrystalline [mɔnou'kristəlain], a. monocristallin.

monocular [mɔ'noukjulər], a. monoculaire.

monoculture ['mɔnəkʌltjər], s. *Agr:* monoculture *f*.

monocyclic [mɔnou'saiklik], a. monocyclique.

monocyte ['mɔnousait], s. *Biol:* monocyte *m*.

monocytosis [mɔnousai'tousis], s. *Med:* monocytose *f*.

monodactylous [mɔnou'dæktiləs], a. *Z:* monodactyle.

monodelph ['mɔnoudelf], s. *Z:* monodelphe *m*.

Monodelphia [mɔnou'delfiə], *s.pl. Z:* monodelphes *m*, euthériens *m*.

monodelphian, monodelphic [mɔnou'delfiən, -'delfik], a. *Z:* monodelphe.

monodermic [mɔnou'də:mik], a. monodermique.

monodic [mɔ'nɔdik], a. *Mus:* monodique.

monodromic [mɔnou'droumik], *a. Mth:* monodrome.
monody ['mɔnədi], *s. Gr.Lit: etc:* monodie *f.*
Monoecia [mɔ'ni:ʃiə], *s.pl. A: Bot:* monœcies *f.*
monoecian [mɔ'ni:ʃiən], *s. Bot:* monœcie *f.*
monoecious [mɔ'ni:ʃiəs], *a.* **1.** *Bot:* monœcique, monoïque. **2.** *Z:* hermaphrodite.
monoecism [mɔ'ni:sizm], *s.* **1.** *Bot:* monœcie *f.* **2.** *Z:* hermaphrodisme *m.*
monoenergetic [mɔnouenə'dʒetik], **monoenergic** [mɔnoue'nə:dʒik], *a. Atom.Ph:* monoénergétique.
monoethylenic [mɔnoueθi'li:nik], *a. Ch:* (acide) monoéthylénique.
monogamic [mɔnou'gæmik], *a.* **1.** (*of rule, custom*) monogamique. **2.** (*of pers.*) monogame.
monogamist [mə'nɔgəmist], *s.* **1.** monogamiste *mf.* **2.** monogame *mf.*
monogamous [mə'nɔgəməs], *a.* monogame.
monogamy [mə'nɔgəmi], *s.* monogamie *f.*
monogenesis [mɔnou'dʒenisis], *s.* monogénèse *f.*
monogenetic [mɔnoudʒə'netik], *a.* **1.** *Geol:* (roche) monogénique. **2.** *Biol:* (*a*) (reproduction) monogène, monogénésique; (*b*) (espèce, trématode, etc.) monogénèse.
monogenic [mɔnou'dʒenik], *a.* **1.** *Geol:* monogénique. **2.** *Mth:* (fonction) monogène. **3.** *Biol:* monogène, monogénésique.
monogenism [mɔ'nɔdʒənizm], *s. Biol:* monogénisme *m.*
monogenist [mɔ'nɔdʒənist], *s.* monogéniste *mf.*
monoglot ['mɔnouglɔt], *a. Ling:* monoglotte.
monogony [mɔ'nɔgəni], *s. Biol:* monogonie *f.*
monogram[1] ['mɔnəgræm], *s.* monogramme *m*, chiffre *m.*
monogram[2], *v.tr.* (**monogrammed**) broder, décorer, d'un monogramme; **monogrammed handkerchief,** mouchoir brodé d'initiales.
monogrammatic [mɔnəgrə'mætik], *a.* monogrammatique.
monograph ['mɔnəgræf], *s.* monographie *f.*
monographer, monographist [mə'nɔgrəfər, -grəfist], *s.* monographe *m*, monographiste *m.*
monographical [mɔnou'græfikl], *a.* monographique.
Monograptidae [mɔnou'græptidi:], *s.pl. Paleont:* monograptidés *m.*
monogynous [mɔ'nɔdʒinəs], *a.* **1.** *A: Bot:* monogyne. **2.** (homme) monogame.
monogyny [mɔ'nɔdʒini], *s.* **1.** *A: Bot:* monogynie *f.* **2.** *Anthr:* monogamie *f.*
monohybrid [mɔnou'haibrid], *s. Biol:* monohybride *m.*
monohydrate [mɔnou'haidreit], *s. Ch:* monohydrate *m.*
monohydrated [mɔnouhai'dreitid], *a. Ch:* monohydraté.
monohydric [mɔnou'haidrik], *a. Ch:* (composé) monohydrique.
monoid ['mɔnɔid], *a. & s. Mth:* monoïde (*m*).
monoideic [mɔnouai'di:ik], *a. Phil:* monoïdéiste.
monoideism [mɔnou'aidiizm], *s. Phil:* monoïdéisme *m.*
monoideistic [mɔnouaidi'istik], *a. Phil:* monoïdéiste *m*
monokinetic [mɔnouk(a)i'netik], *a. Ph:* monocinétique.
monolingual [mɔnou'liŋgwəl], *a. & s.* monolingue (*mf*).
monolith [mɔnəliθ], *s.* monolithe *m.*
monolithic [mɔnə'liθik], *a.* **1.** (monument) monolithe, *F:* monolithique; (époque, âge) des monolithes. **2.** *Pol: etc:* monolithique.
monolithism ['mɔnəliθizm], *s.* monolithisme *m.*
monologist [mɔ'nɔlədʒist], *s.* monologueur, -euse.
monologize [mɔ'nɔlədʒaiz], *v.i.* monologuer.
monologue[1] ['mɔnəlɔg], *s.* monologue *m.*
monologue[2], *v.i.* monologuer.
monologuist [mɔ'nɔlɔgist], *s.* monologueur, -euse.
monomania [mɔnou'meiniə], *s.* monomanie *f.*
monomaniac [mɔnou'meiniæk], *s.* monomane *mf*, monomaniaque *mf.*
monomaniacal [mɔnoumə'naiəkl], *a.* monomane, monomaniaque.
monomer ['mɔnoumər], *s. Ch:* monomère *m.*
monomeric [mɔnou'merik], *a. Ch:* monomère.
monomerous [mɔ'nɔmərəs], *a. Bot:* monomère.
monometallic [mɔnoumə'tælik], *a. Pol.Ec: etc:* (pays, système) monométalliste.
monometallism [mɔnou'metəlizm], *s. Pol.Ec: etc:* monométallisme *m.*
monometallist [mɔnou'metəlist], *s. Pol.Ec: etc:* monométalliste *m.*
monometer [mɔ'nɔmitər], *s. Pros:* monomètre *m.*
monometric [mɔnou'metrik], *a.* **1.** *Pros:* (*also* **monometrical**) monométrique. **2.** *Cryst:* isométrique; tesséral.
monomial [mɔ'noumiəl], *a. & s. Mth:* monôme (*m*).
monomolecular [mɔnoumo'lekjulər], *a. Ch: etc:* monomoléculaire.
monomorphic, monomorphous [mɔnou'mɔ:fik, -'mɔ:fəs], *a.* (insecte) monomorphe, qui ne subit pas de métamorphose.
monomorphism [mɔnou'mɔ:fizm], *s. Ent:* monomorphisme *m.*
Monomyaria [mɔnoumai'εəriə], *s.pl. Moll:* monomyaires *m.*
mononuclear, mononucleated [mɔnou'nju:kliər, -'nju:klieitid], *a.* mononucléaire.
mononucleosis [mɔnoun:jukli'ousis], *s. Med:* mononucléose *f.*
monopetalous [mɔnou'petələs], *a. Bot:* monopétale.
monophagous [mɔ'nɔfəgəs], *a. Z:* monophage.
monophasic [mɔnou'feizik], *a.* **1.** *El:* (*also* **monophase**) monophasé. **2.** *Biol: Psy:* monophasique.
monophonic [mɔnou'fɔnik], *a. Ac:* monophonique.
monophonous [mɔ'nɔfənəs], *a. Ac:* monophonique.
monophony [mɔ'nɔfəni], *s. Ac:* monophonie *f.*
monophthalmic [mɔnɔf'θælmik], *a.* monophtalme.
monophthong ['mɔnɔfθɔŋ], *s.* monophtongue *f*, voyelle *f* simple.
monophthongal [mɔnɔf'θɔŋg(ə)l], *a.* monophtongue.
monophthongization [mɔnɔfθɔŋgai'zeiʃ(ə)n], *s.* monophtongaison *f.*
monophydont [mɔnou'faidɔnt], *a. Z:* monophydonte.
monophyletic [mɔnoufai'letik], *a. Biol:* monophylétique; (espèces) à souche commune.
monophylet(ic)ism [mɔnou'failetizm, -fail'letisizm], *s. Biol:* monophylétisme *m.*
monophyllous [mɔnou'filəs], *a. Bot:* monophylle.
monophysism [mɔ'nɔfisizm], *s. Rel.H:* monophysisme *m.*
monophysite [mɔ'nɔfisait], *a. & s. Rel.H:* monophysite (*m*).
monophysitism [mɔ'nɔfisaitizm], *s. Rel.H:* monophysisme *m.*
monophytic [mɔnou'fitik], *a. Bot:* monophyte.
monopiece ['mɔnəpi:s], *a. Aut:* **m. body,** carrosserie *f* monocoque, coque auto-porteuse.
monoplane ['mɔnəplein]. *Av:* **1.** *s.* monoplan *m.* **2.** *a.* **m. empennage,** empennage monoplan.
monoplast(id) ['mɔnouplæst, mɔnou'plæstid], *s. Biol:* monoplastide *m.*
monoplegia [mɔnou'pli:dʒiə], *s. Med:* monoplégie *f.*
monopode [mɔnou'poud]. **1.** *a.* monopode. **2.** *s. Ter:* monopode *m.*
monopodial [mɔnou'poudiəl], *a. Bot:* monopode.
monopodium [mɔnou'poudiəm], *s. Bot:* monopode *m.*
monopodous [mɔ'nɔpədəs], *a. Bot:* monopode.
monopolist [mə'nɔpəlist], *s.* **1.** monopolisateur, -trice; accapareur, -euse. **2.** *Pol:* partisan, -ane, du monopole.
monopolistic [mənɔpə'listik], *a.* monopolistique; monopolisant; monopolisateur, -trice.
monopolization [mənɔpəlai'zeiʃ(ə)n], *s.* monopolisation *f.*
monopolize [mə'nɔpəlaiz], *v.tr.* **1.** *Com:* monopoliser, accaparer (une denrée, etc.). **2.** accaparer (qn, qch.); **to m. the conversation,** s'emparer de la conversation.
monopolizer [mə'nɔpəlaizər], *s.* monopolisateur, -trice; accapareur, -euse.
monopolizing [mə'nɔpəlaiziŋ], *s.* monopolisation *f.*
monopoly [mə'nɔpəli], *s.* monopole *m*; **to have a m. of sth.,** *U.S:* **on sth.,** avoir, faire, le monopole de qch.; avoir l'exclusivité de qch.; monopoliser qch.; **state m.,** monopole d'État; **m. control,** contrôle *m* monopolistique.
monopropellant [mɔnouprə'pelənt]. **1.** *s.* (*rocket fuel*) monergol *m*, monopropulsant *m.* **2.** *a.* (*of fuel*) à un seul constituant.
monopteral [mɔ'nɔptərəl], *a.* **1.** *Arch:* monoptère. **2.** *Ich: Z:* monoptère.
monopteros [mɔ'nɔptərəs], *s. Arch:* temple *m* monoptère.
monorail ['mɔnoureil], *a. & s. Rail: etc:* monorail (*m*); **m. transporter,** chariot transbordeur sur monorail.
monorchid [mɔ'nɔ:kid], *a. & s. Physiol:* monorchide (*m*).
monorchis, *pl.* **-ides** [mɔ'nɔ:kis, -idi:z], *s. Physiol:* monorchide *m.*
monorchism [mɔ'nɔ:kizm], *s. Physiol:* monochidie *f.*
monorefringent [mɔnouri'frindʒənt], *a. Ph:* monoréfringent, uniréfringent.
monorhyme, monorime ['mɔnouraim], *a. & s. Pros:* monorime (*f*).
monosaccharide [mɔnou'sækəraid], *s. Ch:* monosaccharide *m.*
monoscope ['mɔnəskoup], *s. T.V:* monoscope *m.*
monosepalous [mɔnou'sepələs], *a. Bot:* monosépale.
monoshell ['mɔnouʃel], *a. Aut:* monocoque.
monosome ['mɔnousoum], *s.* **monosomic** [mɔnou'soumik], *a. & s. Biol:* monosomique (*m*).
monospar ['mɔnouspɑ:r]. *Civ.E: Mec.E:* **1.** *a.* à longeron unique. **2.** *s.* monolongeron *m.*
monospermous [mɔnou'spə:məs], *a. Bot:* monosperme.
monosporous [mɔnou'spɔ:rəs], *a. Bot:* monosporé.
monostable ['mɔnousteibl], *a. Elcs:* monostable.
monostely ['mɔnɔstiæli], *s. Bot:* monostélie *f.*
monostich ['mɔnoustik]. *Pros:* **1.** *a.* monostique. **2.** *s.* monostique *m*, monostiche *m.*
monostichous [mɔ'nɔstikəs], *a. Cryst:* monostique.
monostomatous [mɔnou'stoumətəs], *a. Ann:* monostome.
monostome ['mɔnoustoum], *a. & s. Ann:* monostome (*m*).
monostrut ['mɔnoustrʌt]. *Civ.E: Mec.E:* **1.** *s.* monomât *m*, jambe *f* de force unique. **2.** *attrib.* à jambe de force, à mât, unique.
monosubstituted [mɔnou'sʌbstitjutid], *a. Ch:* monosubstitué.
monosyllabic [mɔnousi'læbik], *a.* monosyllable, monosyllabique.
monosyllabism [mɔnousilə'bizm], *s.* monosyllabisme *m.*
monosyllable [mɔnou'siləbl], *s.* monosyllabe *m.*
monothalamous [mɔnou'θæləməs], *a.* monothalame.
monotheism [mɔnou'θi:izm], *s.* monothéisme *m.*
monotheist [mɔnou'θi:ist], *s.* monothéiste (*mf*).
Monothelite [mɔ'nɔθəlait], *s. Rel.H:* monothélite *mf.*
Monothelitic [mɔnouθi'litik], *a. Rel.H:* monothélite.
Monothelitism [mɔ'nɔθəlaitizm], *s. Rel.H:* monothélisme *m.*
monotint ['mɔnətint], *s. Art:* monochrome *m*; **in m.,** en monochrome, en camaïeu.
monotone ['mɔnətoun]. **1.** *a.* monotone; qui ne change pas de ton. **2.** *s.* débit *m* monotone, uniforme, sans modulation; **to speak in a m.,** parler d'une voix uniforme, monotone.
monotonic [mɔnə'tɔnik], *a. Ph:* monotone; *Mth:* **m. function,** fonction *f* monotone; *Ph: Mth:* **m. quantity,** invariant *m.*
monotonous [mə'nɔtənəs], *a.* **1.** (*a*) monotone, dont le ton ne varie pas; (*b*) (instrument) qui ne donne qu'une note. **2.** monotone, sans variété; (travail) ennuyeux, fastidieux.
monotonously [mə'nɔtənəsli], *adv.* monotonement.
monotony [mə'nɔtəni], *s.* monotonie *f.*
Monotremata [mɔnou'tri:mətə], *s.pl. Z:* monotrèmes *m*, protothériens *m.*
monotreme ['mɔnoutri:m], *a. & s. Z:* monotrème (*m*).
monotriglyph [mɔnou'traiglif], *s. Arch:* monotriglyphe *m.*
monotriglyphic [mɔnoutrai'glifik], *a. Arch:* monotriglyphe.
monotropa [mɔ'nɔtrəpə], *s. Bot:* monotrope *m.*
Monotropaceae [mɔnoutrou'peisii:], *s.pl. Bot:* monotropacées *f.*
monotype ['mɔnətaip], *s.* **1.** *Nat.Hist:* espèce *f* unique. **2.** *Typ: R.t.m.* Monotype *f.*
monotypic(al) [mɔnou'tipik(l)], **monotypous** [mɔ'nɔtipəs], *a. Nat.Hist:* monotype.
monovalence, monovalency [mɔnou'veiləns, -'veilənsi], *s. Ch:* monovalence *f*, univalence *f.*
monovalent [mɔnou'veilənt], *a. Ch:* monovalent, univalent.
monovular [mɔ'nɔvjulər], *a. Biol:* univitellin, monozygote.
monoxenous [mɔ'nɔksənəs], *a. Biol:* monoxène.
monoxide [mɔ'nɔksaid], *s. Ch:* **carbon m.,** oxyde *m* de carbone; **lead m.,** oxyde de plomb.
monozygotic [mɔnouzai'gɔtik], **monozygous** [mɔnou'zaigəs], *a. Biol:* monozygote, univitellin.
Monroe [mən'rou]. *Pr.n.m. U.S:* **the M. doctrine,** la doctrine de Monroe.
Monroeism [mən'rouizm], *s. U.S: Hist:* la doctrine de Monroe.
Monroeist [mən'rouist], *s. U.S: Hist:* partisan, -ane, de la doctrine de Monroe.
mons, *pl.* **montes** [mɔnz, 'mɔnti:z], *s. Anat:* **m. pubis,** pénil *m*; **m. veneris,** (i) *Anat:* mont *m* de Vénus; (ii) (*palmistry*) monticule *m*, mont, de Vénus.
monsignor, *pl.* **-ori** [mɔnsi:'njɔ:r, -ɔ:ri], *s.m. Ecc:* monseigneur, *pl.* messeigneurs, nosseigneurs; (*of papal prelates*) monsignore, *pl.* monsignori.
monsoon [mɔn'su:n], *s. Meteor:* mousson *f*; **wet m., summer m.,** mousson d'été; **dry m., winter m.,** mousson d'automne.
monsoonal [mɔn'su:nəl], *a.* de la mousson.
monster ['mɔnstər]. **1.** *s.* (*a*) *Ter:* monstre *m*; monstruosité *f*; *Jur:* monstre; avorton *m*; enfant viable mais qui n'a pas forme humaine; (*b*) *Myth: etc:* monstre; **the monsters of the deep,** les monstres marins; (*c*) colosse *m*; géant, -ante. **2.** *a. F:* monstre, monstrueux; colossal, -aux; énorme; immense.

monstrance ['mɔnstrəns], *s. Ecc:* ostensoir *m.*

monstrosity [mɔn'strɔsiti], *s.* monstruosité *f*; (i) monstre *m*; (ii) énormité *f* (d'un crime, etc.).

monstrous ['mɔnstrəs]. **1.** *a.* (*a*) (*of offspring*) monstrueux; contre nature; (*b*) odieux, monstrueux; *F:* **it is perfectly m. that such a thing should be allowed,** c'est monstrueux que cela soit permis; (*c*) monstrueux, énorme; colossal, -aux; immense. **2.** *adv. A:* énormément; **m. wise,** d'une sagacité prodigieuse.

monstrously ['mɔnstrəsli], *adv.* monstrueusement, énormément, prodigieusement.

monstrousness ['mɔnstrəsnis], *s.* monstruosité *f*, énormité *f* (d'un crime, etc.).

montage ['mɔntɑ:ʒ], *s. Cin:* montage *m.*

Montanian [mɔn'teinjən], *a. & s. Geog:* (habitant, -ante, originaire *mf*) du Montana.

Montanism ['mɔntənizm], *s. Rel.H:* montanisme *m.*

Montanist ['mɔntənist], *a. & s. Rel.H:* montaniste *mf.*

montbretia [mɔnt'bri:ʃiə], *s. Bot:* montbrétie *f*, montbrétia *f*, tritonie *f.*

montebrasite [mɔnti'breizait], *s. Miner:* montebrasite *f.*

Monte Carlo [mɔnti'kɑ:lou]. *Pr.n. Geog:* Monte-Carlo; *Pol.Ec: etc:* **M. C. method, model,** méthode *f*, modèle *m*, de Monte-Carlo.

Monte Cassino [mɔntikə'si:nou]. *Pr.n. Geog:* le Mont Cassin.

Montenegrin [mɔnti'ni:grin]. *Hist:* (*a*) *a.* monténégrin; (*b*) *s.* Monténégrin, -ine.

Montenegro [mɔnti'ni:grou]. *Pr.n. Hist:* Monténégro *m.*

Monte Rosa [mɔnti'rouzə]. *Pr.n. Geog:* le Mont Rose.

Montgolfier [mɔnt'gɔlfiər]. *Pr.n. Aer:* **M. (balloon),** montgolfière *f.*

month [mʌnθ], *s.* mois *m*; **lunar m.,** mois lunaire; mois de consécution; **calendar m.,** mois du calendrier; mois civil, commun; **in the m. of August,** au mois d'août; en août; **current m.,** mois en cours; **at the end of the current m., of the present m.,** fin courant; **what day of the m. is this?** le combien sommes-nous? c'est le combien (du mois) aujourd'hui? **this day m., a m. (from) today,** dans un mois, jour pour jour; **a m. ago today,** il y a un mois aujourd'hui; il y a aujourd'hui un mois; **a thirteen months' old baby,** un(e) enfant de treize mois; **to hire sth. by the m.,** louer qch. au mois; **from m. to m.,** de mois en mois; **once a m.,** une fois par mois; mensuellement; **twice a m.,** bimensuellement; **to receive one's month's pay,** toucher son mois; **a month's credit,** un mois de crédit; *Fin:* **bill at three months,** papier *m* à trois mois (d'échéance); *Ecc:* (*R.C.Ch.*) **the M. of Mary,** le mois de Marie; *F:* **a m. of Sundays,** une éternité; **never in a m. of Sundays,** jamais de la vie.

monthly[1] ['mʌnθli]. **1.** *a.* (*a*) mensuel; **m. occurrence,** événement *m* qui se produit tous les mois; *Physiol:* **m. periods,** règles *f*; *Com:* **m. payment, m. instalment,** mensualité *f*; **m. statement (of account),** relevé *m*, situation *f*, de fin de mois; (*b*) *Rail: etc:* **m. season ticket,** (billet d')abonnement *m* valable pour un mois. **2.** *s.* revue mensuelle; publication mensuelle.

monthly[2], *adv.* mensuellement; une fois par mois; chaque mois; tous les mois.

Montian ['mɔnʃiən], *a. & s. Geol:* montien (*m*).

monticellite [mɔnti'selait], *s. Miner:* monticellite *f.*

monticule ['mɔntikju(:)l], *s.* **1.** monticule *m.* **2.** *Anat: Z:* petite éminence.

montmartrite [mɔnt'mɑ:trait], *s. Miner:* montmartrite *f.*

montmorillonite [mɔntmɔ'rilənait], *s. Geol:* montmorillonite *f.*

Montreal [mɔntri'ɔ:l]. *Pr.n. Geog:* Montréal; **Greater M.,** le Grand Montréal; l'agglomération montréalaise; *Can:* **M. canoe,** canot *m* du maître.

montroydite [mɔn'trɔidait], *s. Miner:* montroydite *f.*

monument ['mɔnjumənt], *s.* **1.** monument *m*; **the M.,** la colonne commémorative de l'incendie de 1666 (Cité de Londres); **ancient monuments,** monuments historiques. **2.** monument funéraire; pierre tombale. **3.** document *m*; *pl.* archives *f.*

monumental [mɔnju'mentəl], *a.* **1.** (*a*) (*of statue, etc.*) monumental, -aux; (*b*) (*of literary work, etc.*) monumental; de longue haleine, de grande envergure; **m. ignorance,** ignorance monumentale, prodigieuse. **2. m. mason,** marbrier *m*; entrepreneur *m* de monuments funéraires.

monzonite ['mɔnzənait], *s. Miner:* monzonite *f.*

moo[1] [mu:], (*of cow, etc.*) (*a*) *s.* meuglement *m*, beuglement *m*; (*b*) *int.* **m.!** meuh!

moo[2], *v.i.* **(mooed)** (*of cow, etc.*) meugler, beugler.

mooch[1] [mu:tʃ], *s. P: O:* flânerie *f*; **to be on the m.,** (i) passer son temps à flâner; (ii) rôder (en quête d'un coup à faire).

mooch[2]. *P:* **1.** *v.i.* **to m. about,** flâner, traîner; se balader; baguenauder; **to m. about the streets,** battre le pavé. **2.** *v.tr.* chiper, chaparder (qch.). **3.** *v.i. & tr.* emprunter (qch. à qn); taper (qn); **to m. on s.o.,** vivre aux dépens de qn.

moocha ['mu:tʃə], *s. Cost:* pagne *m* (de Cafre).

moocher ['mu:tʃər], *s. P:* **1.** flâneur, -euse; traîneur, -euse. **2.** (*a*) chipeur, -euse; chapardeur, -euse; (*b*) mendiant, -ante.

moocow ['mu:kau], *s. F:* (*child's language*) vache *f*, meu-meu *f.*

mood[1] [mu:d], *s.* (*a*) *Log:* mode *m*; (*b*) *Gram:* mode; **the indicative m.,** l'indicatif *m*; (*c*) *esp. U.S: Mus:* mode.

mood[2], *s.* **1.** (*a*) humeur *f*, disposition *f*; état *m* d'âme; **to be in a good, bad, m.,** être bien, mal, disposé; être de bonne, de mauvaise, humeur; **he is in one of his good, bad, moods,** il est bien, mal, luné, disposé; **try to catch him in one of his good moods,** tâchez de le prendre dans un de ses bons moments; **to be in a generous m.,** être en veine de générosité; **to be in the m. to write,** être en disposition d'écrire; **to be in the m. for reading,** être en humeur de lire; **to feel, be, in no m. for laughing, in no laughing m.,** ne pas avoir le cœur à rire; n'avoir aucune envie de rire; ne pas être d'humeur à rire; ne pas être en humeur de rire; **to fall in with the prevailing m.,** se mettre au diapason général; **to put s.o. in the right m. for sth.,** mettre qn en haleine pour qch.; **to be in the m. to refuse point blank,** être d'humeur à refuser net; (*b*) *Med:* **m. elevating,** psychotonique; **m. elevator,** psychotonique *m.* **2.** *pl.* **to have moods,** être caractériel; avoir ses mauvaises heures.

moodily ['mu:dili], *adv.* d'un air chagrin, d'un air morose; maussadement.

moodiness ['mu:dinis], *s.* **1.** humeur chagrine; morosité *f*, maussaderie *f.* **2.** humeur changeante.

moody ['mu:di], *a.* **1.** chagrin, morose, maussade, atrabilaire. **2. to be m.,** (i) être d'humeur changeante; (ii) être maussade; être mal luné.

moon[1] [mu:n], *s.* **1.** (*a*) lune *f*; **new m.,** nouvelle lune; **the m. is new,** c'est la nouvelle lune; **full m.,** pleine lune; **she's got a face like a full m.,** elle a un visage de pleine lune; **April m.,** lune rousse; **there's a m. tonight,** il fait clair de lune ce soir; **there was no m.,** c'était une nuit sans lune; **to land on the m.,** atterrir, se poser, sur la lune; *F:* alunir; **m. walker,** piéton *m* lunaire; *Fig:* **to cry for the m., to ask for the m. and stars,** faire des demandes par-dessus les maisons; demander la lune; **to promise s.o. the m. and stars,** promettre la lune à qn; promettre monts et merveilles à qn; **once in a blue m.,** tous les trente-six du mois; en de rares occasions; une fois par extraordinaire; une fois en passant; **the man in the m.,** l'homme *m* de la lune; **m. blind,** (i) (*of horse*) lunatique, fluxionnaire, sujet à l'ophtalmie périodique; (ii) (*of pers.*) frappé de cécité passagère (pour avoir dormi sous les rayons de la lune); (*of horse*) **m. blindness,** œil *m* lunatique; fluxion *f* périodique des yeux; **m. blink,** moment *m* de cécité (de ceux qui, sous les tropiques, ont dormi sous les rayons de la lune); (*b*) **the moons of Saturn,** les lunes de Saturne. **2.** (*month*) *Astr:* lunaison *f*; *Poet:* lune, mois *m.* **3.** lunule *f* (des ongles).

moon[2]. *F:* **1.** *v.i.* **to m. about, along,** muser, musarder, flâner. **2.** *v.tr.* **to m. away two hours,** passer deux heures à musarder, à flâner.

moonbeam ['mu:nbi:m], *s.* rayon *m* de lune; *F:* **to chase moonbeams,** courir après des chimères.

mooncalf ['mu:nkɑ:f], *s.* **1.** *A:* monstre *m*, avorton *m*, non viable. **2.** *F:* idiot, -ote; crétin, -ine.

mooneye ['mu:nai], *s. Vet:* œil *m* lunatique (de cheval).

mooneyed ['mu:naid], *a.* **1.** (*of horse*) lunatique, fluxionnaire, sujet à l'ophtalmie périodique. **2.** (plume, etc.) à lunule(s).

moonface ['mu:nfeis], *s.* visage *m* lunaire.

moonfaced ['mu:nfeist], *a.* à visage lunaire.

moonfish ['mu:nfiʃ], *s. Ich:* vomer *m*; poisson-lune *m*, *pl.* poissons-lunes.

moonflower ['mu:nflauər], *s. Bot:* **1.** (*a*) marguerite dorée; (*b*) marguerite des champs; œil-de-bœuf *m*, *pl.* œils-de-bœuf. **2.** ipomée *f* bonne-nuit.

moonless ['mu:nlis], *a.* (nuit, etc.) sans lune.

moonlight[1] ['mu:nlait] *s.* clair *m* de lune; **in the m., by m.,** au clair de lune; à la clarté, la lumière, de la lune; **it was m.,** il y avait, il faisait, clair de lune; **it was a glorious m. night,** il faisait un clair de lune merveilleux; **m. walk,** promenade *f* au clair de lune; *F:* **m. flit,** déménagement *m* à la cloche de bois.

moonlight[2], *v.i. F:* cumuler deux emplois, deux fonctions.

moonlighter ['mu:nlaitər], *s.* **1.** *Irish Hist:* assassin, -ine, nocturne (qui agissait contre ceux qui étaient désignés par la Ligue agraire); terroriste *mf.* **2.** *U.S:* distillateur *m* illicite. **3.** *F:* cumulard *m.*

moonlighting ['mu:nlaitiŋ], *s.* **1.** (*a*) méfaits *mpl* nocturnes; (*b*) *Irish Hist:* terrorisme nocturne (auquel se livraient les membres de la Ligue agraire). **2.** travail noir.

moonlit ['mu:nlit], *a.* éclairé par la lune.

moonquake ['mu:nkweik], *s.* tremblement *m* de lune.

moonraker ['mu:nreikər], *s. Nau:* (*sail*) papillon *m*; contre-cacatois *m inv.*

moonrise ['mu:nraiz], *s.* lever *m* de la lune.

moonrock ['mu:nrɔk], *s.* = MOONSTONE 2.

moonscape ['mu:nskeip], *s.* paysage *m* lunaire.

moonseed ['mu:nsi:d], *s. Bot:* ménisperme *m.*

moon-shaped ['mu:nʃeipt], *a.* en forme de lune, lunaire; lunulé, lunulaire.

moonshine ['mu:nʃain], *s.* **1.** clair *m* de lune. **2.** *F:* balivernes *fpl*, calembredaines *fpl*, fariboles *fpl*, sornettes *fpl*; contes *mpl* en l'air; **that's all m.,** tout ça c'est de la blague. **3.** *NAm: F:* alcool (i) illicitement distillé, (ii) de contrebande.

moonshiner ['mu:nʃainər], *s. NAm: F:* (i) contrebandier *m* de boissons alcooliques; (ii) bouilleur non patenté; bouilleur de contrebande.

moonstone ['mu:nstoun], *s.* **1.** *Lap:* adulaire *f*; feldspath nacré; pierre *f* de lune. **2. a sample of m.,** du rocher de la lune.

moonstruck ['mu:nstrʌk], *a.* **1.** (*a*) à l'esprit dérangé; toqué; (*b*) halluciné. **2.** *F:* abasourdi, médusé, hébété; sidéré.

moonstuff ['mu:nstʌf], *s.* lunite *f.*

moonwort ['mu:nwə:t], *s. Bot:* botrychium *m* lunaire.

moony ['mu:ni], *a.* **1.** (lueur, etc.) de lune. **2.** en forme de lune, de croissant; ressemblant à la lune. **3.** (*of pers.*) (i) rêveur, -euse, musard; (ii) perdu dans de vagues rêveries; dans les nuages, dans la lune.

moor[1] [muər], *s.* **1.** *A:* terrain marécageux; **high m.,** plateau marécageux. **2.** (*a*) lande *f*, brande *f*, bruyère *f*; *Orn:* **m. buzzard,** busard *m* des marais; harpaye *f*; (*b*) *Scot:* chasse réservée.

moor[2] [mɔ:r], *s. Nau:* amarrage *m*, affourchage *m*; **to make a running m.,** mouiller avec de l'erre.

moor[3] [mɔ:r], *v. Nau:* **1.** *v.tr.* amarrer, (*with 2 anchors*) affourcher (un navire); mouiller (une bouée, une mine); **to m. alongside,** s'amarrer à quai; **to m. a ship stern and bow,** *U.S:* **head and stern,** embosser un navire. **2.** *v.i.* s'amarrer, s'affourcher; prendre le corps mort; **to m. with a spring, kedge,** s'embosser en faisant croupiat.

Moor[4] [muər], *s.* Maure *m*, More *m*; Mauresque *f*; *Her:* **Moor's head,** tête *f* de Maure.

moorage ['mɔ:ridʒ], *s. Nau:* **1.** amarrage *m*, affourchage *m*, mouillage *m.* **2.** droits *mpl* d'ancrage, de corps mort; (*in river*) droits de rivage.

moorcock ['muəkɔk], *s. Orn:* lagopède *m* d'Écosse mâle.

moorfowl ['muəfaul], *s. Orn:* lagopède *m* rouge d'Écosse.

moorgrass ['muəgrɑ:s], *s. Bot:* **1.** drosère *f* à feuilles rondes; sesleria *m*, seslérie *f.* **2.** *Scot:* potentille ansérine; argentine *f.* **3.** linaigrette commune; lin *m* des marais.

moorhen ['muəhen], *s. Orn:* **1.** poule *f* d'eau; (*also*) gallinule commune, *Fr.C:* **2.** lagopède *m* rouge d'Écosse (femelle).

mooring ['mɔ:riŋ], *s. Nau:* **1.** (*a*) amarrage *m*, affourchage *m* (d'un navire); **m. on, to, a buoy,** amarrage mouillage *m*, sur corps mort; **m. bridle,** patte *f* d'oie de corps mort; **m. block, m. clump,** crapaud *m* (de corps mort); **m. pendant,** itague *f* de corps mort; **m. dues** = MOORAGE 2; **m. pile, m. post, bollard,** pieu *m* d'amarrage; borne *f* d'amarrage; **m. ring,** organeau *m*; **m. swivel, m. shackle,** émerillon *m*, maillon *m* d'affourche; *Aer: Av:* amarrage, ancrage *m*; **m. band,** sangle *f* d'ancrage (d'un ballon captif); **m. cone,** cône *m* d'ancrage (d'un dirigeable); **m. gear,** appareil *m*, dispositif *m*, d'amarrage, d'ancrage; **m. line,** câble *m* d'amarrage; **m. mast, m. tower,** mât *m*, pylône *m*, d'amarrage (pour dirigeable); (*b*) poste *m* d'amarrage; **ship at her moorings,** navire sur ses amarres; **to pick up one's moorings,** prendre son coffre.

Moorish ['muəriʃ], *a.* **1.** mauresque, moresque, maure, more; **a Moorish woman,** une Mauresque. **2.** *Ich:* **M. idol,** tranchoir *m*, zancle cornu.

moorland ['muələnd], *s.* (*a*) *A:* terrain marécageux; (*b*) lande *f*, brande *f*, bruyère *f.*

moorstone ['muəstoun], *s. Miner:* granit *m* de Cornouailles.

moorva ['muəvə], *s. Bot:* sansevière *f.*

moose [mu:s], *s.* (*pl.* **moose**) *Z:* (*a*) **American m.,** orignal *m*, élan *m* du Canada; *Can:* **m. yard,** pâturage *m* d'hiver de l'orignal; (*b*) **Eurasiatic m.,** élan *m.*

moosebird ['mu:sbə:d], *s. Orn: Can:* mésangeai *m* du Canada, *Fr.C:* geai gris.

moosecaller ['mu:skɔ:lər], *s.* bourgot *m* (*Fr.C.*).

moot[1] [mu:t], *s.* **1.** *Hist:* assemblée *f* (du peuple). **2.** (*at Gray's Inn*) parlotte *f*; procès fictif (exercice d'étudiants); conférence *f* de stage; **m. court,** salle *f* où se tiennent les procès fictifs.

moot[2], *a.* (*of question, etc.*) sujet à controverse; discutable, disputable; pendant, indécis; **that's a m. point,** c'est un point que l'on peut discuter; *Jur:* **m. case, m. point,** point de droit.

moot[3], *v.tr.* soulever (une question); **this question has been mooted again,** cette question a été remise sur le tapis.

mop[1] [mɔp], *s.* **1.** (*a*) balai *m* à laver, balai-éponge *m, pl.* balais-éponges; balai à franges; lavette *f* (à vaisselle); **baker's oven m.,** écouvillon *m*; (*b*) *Nau:* faubert *m*, vadrouille *f*, guipon *m*. **2. m. of hair,** tignasse *f*; vadrouille; toison *f*.

mop[2], *v.* (**mopped**)

I. *v.tr.* éponger, essuyer, (le parquet) avec un balai; *Nau:* fauberder, fauberter (le pont); **to m. one's brow (with one's handkerchief),** s'éponger, se tamponner, le front avec son mouchoir; *Bak:* **to m. the oven,** écouvillonner le four.

II. (*compound verb*) **mop up,** *v.tr.* (*a*) éponger (de l'eau); **to take a piece of bread to m. up one's sauce, gravy,** prendre un morceau de pain pour finir sa sauce; (*b*) *Mil: etc:* liquider, exterminer (les derniers résistants); **to m. up (a position, a trench),** nettoyer (une position, une tranchée); (*c*) *P:* aplatir, rouler (un rival, un concurrent).

mop[3], *s. A:* **mops and mows,** grimaces *f*, grimaceries *f*.

mop[4], *v.i. A:* **to m. and mow,** grimacer.

mop[5], *s. A:* **m. (fair),** foire *f* de louage.

mope[1] [moup], *v.i.* être triste, mélancolique; s'ennuyer; broyer du noir; **to m. in solitude,** languir dans la solitude.

mope[2], *s.* **1.** personne *f* triste, mélancolique. **2.** *F: O:* **to have the mopes,** avoir des idées noires; broyer du noir; avoir le cafard.

moped ['mouped], *s. F:* cyclomoteur *m*; mobylette *f* (*R.t.m.*)

mopey ['moupi], **mopish** ['moupiʃ], *a.* triste, mélancolique, morose.

mophead ['mɔphed], *s.* **1.** tête *f* de balai (à laver). **2.** *F:* tignasse *f*, toison *f*.

mopishness ['moupiʃnis], *s.* tristesse *f*, mélancolie *f*, morosité *f*.

mopoke ['moupouk], *s. Orn:* (*a*) *Austr:* podarge *m* de Cuvier; (*b*) *N.Z:* hibou *m*; (*c*) (*Tasmania*) engoulevent *m*.

mopper-up ['mɔpərʌp]. *s. Mil:* nettoyeur *m* (de position, de tranchée, après une attaque).

moppet ['mɔpit], *s. F:* gamin, -ine, gosse *mf*.

mopping[1] ['mɔpiŋ], *s.* (*a*) **m. (up),** épongeage *m*, essuyage *m* (du parquet, etc.); (*b*) *Mil:* **m. up,** nettoyage *m* (d'une position, d'une tranchée); **m. up operations,** opérations *f* de nettoyage; (*c*) *Bak:* écouvillonnage *m* (du four).

mopping[2], *s. A:* **m. and mowing,** grimacerie *f*.

mopy ['moupi], *a.* = MOPEY.

moquette [mɔ'ket], *s. Tex:* moquette *f*.

mor [mɔ:r], *s. Geol:* mor *m*.

mora ['mɔrə], *s. Games:* la mourre.

Moraceae [mɔ'reisii:], *s.pl. Bot:* moracées *f*, morées *f*.

morainal, morainic [mɔ'rein(ə)l, -'reinik], *a. Geol:* morainique.

moraine [mɔ'rein], *s. Geol:* moraine *f*; **terminal m., lateral m., medial m.,** moraine frontale, latérale, médiane.

moral ['mɔr(ə)l], *a. & s.*

I. *a.* **1.** moral, -aux; **the m. sciences,** les sciences morales; **the m. faculties,** les facultés morales; **m. precepts,** préceptes moraux; **m. sense,** sentiment *m* du bien et du mal; sens moral; **to raise the m. standard of the community,** moraliser la société; relever les mœurs de la société. **2. to live a m. life,** se conduire moralement; avoir de bonnes mœurs; **m. books,** livres moraux. **3. the m. nature of man,** la nature morale, le côté moral, de l'homme; **m. virtues,** vertus morales; **m. courage,** courage moral; **m. victory,** victoire morale. **4. m. certainty,** certitude morale.

II. *s.* **1.** morale *f*, moralité *f* (d'un conte); **story with a m.,** conte moral. **2.** *pl.* **morals,** moralité, mœurs *f*; **man without morals,** homme sans mœurs; **man of loose morals,** homme de moralité douteuse, de mœurs douteuses; **of good morals,** de bonnes mœurs; **to reform, improve, the morals of a country,** moraliser un pays. **3.** = MORALE. **4.** *Lit:* **morals,** morale(s) (de Sénèque, etc.); **the Morals of Epictetus,** la Morale d'Épictète.

morale [mɔ'rɑ:l], *s.* (*no pl.*) moral *m* (d'une armée, etc.); **the high m. of the troops,** l'excellent moral des troupes; **to undermine the m. of the army,** démoraliser les troupes; **loss of m.,** démoralisation *f*.

moralism ['mɔrəlizm], *s.* moralisme *m*.

moralist ['mɔrəlist], *s.* moraliste *mf*.

moralistic [mɔrə'listik], *a.* moraliste; didactique.

morality [mə'ræliti], *s.* **1.** *A:* (*ethics*) morale *f*. **2.** (*a*) moralité *f*; principes moraux; sens moral; **commercial m.,** probité commerciale; (*b*) bonnes mœurs; conduite *f*; (*c*) *pl.* **moralities,** principes moraux. **3.** réflexion morale; moralité; **I am tired of your moralities,** j'en ai assez de vos sermons. **4.** *Th:* **m. (play),** moralité.

moralization [mɔrəlai'zeiʃ(ə)n], *s.* **1.** *Lit:* interprétation morale. **2.** (*a*) prédication morale; (*b*) réflexions morales. **3.** moralisation *f* (de qn, d'une race).

moralize ['mɔrəlaiz]. **1.** *v.i.* moraliser, faire de la morale (**on, upon, sth.,** sur qch.). **2.** *v.tr.* (*a*) donner une interprétation morale à (qch.); (*b*) élever le niveau moral de (qch.).

moralizing[1] ['mɔrəlaiziŋ], *a.* moralisant; moralisateur, -trice.

moralizing[2], *s.* = MORALIZATION 2, 3.

morally ['mɔrəli], *adv.* moralement; **m. bound to do sth.,** moralement obligé de faire qch.; **to live m.,** vivre moralement; avoir des mœurs; **m. certain,** moralement certain; **m. speaking,** moralement parlant; du point de vue moral.

morass [mə'ræs], *s.* marais *m*, marécage *m*, fondrière *f*; **m. of vice,** bourbier *m* de vice.

morassic [mə'ræsik], *a.* marécageux.

moratorial [mɔrə'tɔ:riəl], *a.* (*of interest, etc.*) moratoire.

moratorium [mɔrə'tɔ:riəm], *s. Fin:* moratorium *m, pl.* moratoria, moratoires *m*; **to announce a m.,** décréter un moratoire; **debt for which a m. has been granted,** dette moratoriée.

moratory ['mɔrətəri], *a.* moratoire.

Moravia [mə'reiviə]. *Pr.n. Geog:* Moravie *f*.

Moravian[1] [mə'reiviən]. **1.** *Geog:* (*a*) *a.* morave; (*b*) *s.* Morave *mf*. **2.** *Rel.H:* **M. brethren,** frères *m* moraves; hern(h)utes *m*.

Moravian[2], *a. & s. Geog:* (habitant, -ante, originaire *mf*) de Moray (en Écosse).

moray [mə'rei], *s. Ich:* murène *f*.

morbid ['mɔ:bid], *a.* **1.** (symptôme *m*, idée *f*) morbide; **m. curiosity,** curiosité *f* morbide, malsaine, maladive; **to have a m. outlook on life,** voir les choses en noir. **2.** *Med:* **m. anatomy,** anatomie *f* pathologique.

morbidezza [mɔ:bi'detsə], *s. Art:* morbidesse *f*.

morbidity [mɔ:'biditi], *s.* **1.** (*a*) morbidité *f*; état maladif; (*b*) tristesse maladive (des pensées de qn). **2.** morbidité (d'un pays, etc.).

morbidly ['mɔ:bidli], *adv.* morbidement, maladivement.

morbidness ['mɔ:bidnis], *s.* = MORBIDITY 1.

morbiferous, morbific [mɔ:'bifərəs, -'bifik], *a. Med:* morbifique.

morbilliform [mɔ:'bilifɔ:m], *a. Med:* morbilliforme.

morcellation [mɔ:sə'leiʃ(ə)n], *s. Surg:* morcellement *m* (d'une tumeur).

mordacity [mɔ:'dæsiti], **mordancy** ['mɔ:d(ə)nsi], *s.* mordacité *f*, causticité *f* (d'une critique, etc.).

mordant[1] ['mɔ:d(ə)nt]. **1.** *a.* (*a*) (acide) mordant, caustique; (*b*) (sarcasme) mordant, caustique, incisif; (*c*) *O:* **m. pain,** douleur aiguë. **2.** *s.* (*a*) (acide) mordant *m*; (*b*) *Dy: etc:* mordant; *Phot:* **m. toning,** (virage *m* par) mordançage *m*.

mordant[2], *v.tr. Dy: etc:* mordancer.

mordanting ['mɔ:d(ə)ntiŋ], *s. Dy: etc:* mordançage *m*.

Mordecai [mɔ:di'keiai]. *Pr.n.m. B.Hist:* Mardochée.

mordellid [mɔ:'delid], *s. Ent:* mordelle *f*.

Mordellidae [mɔ:'delidi:], *s.pl. Ent:* mordellidés *m*.

mordenite ['mɔ:dənait], *s. Miner:* mordénite *f*.

mordent ['mɔ:d(ə)nt], *s. Mus:* mordant *m*.

more [mɔ:r]. **1.** *a. & indef. pron.* plus (de); **he has m. patience than I (have),** il a plus de patience que moi; **there is m. truth in it than you imagine,** il y a plus de vérité là-dedans que vous ne (le) croyez; **we need m. men,** il nous faut un plus grand nombre d'hommes; il nous faut un surcroît de main-d'œuvre; **he is afraid it means m. work,** il craint un surcroît de besogne; **there were m. (people) than we had expected,** ils étaient plus nombreux, en plus grand nombre, que nous ne l'avions prévu; **he has m. money than he knows what to do with,** il a de l'argent à n'en savoir que faire; **m. than ten men,** plus de dix hommes; **I don't want to pay m. than £5,** je ne veux pas payer plus de £5; **one m.,** un de plus, encore un; **one or m.,** un ou plusieurs; **if I'd had one m. hour I would have finished,** si j'avais eu une heure de plus, j'aurais terminé; **there's only one m. problem to solve,** il n'y a plus qu'un problème à résoudre; **£10 m.,** £10 de plus; encore £10; **I'll give you £10, not a penny m.,** je vous donnerai £10 sans plus; **(some) m. bread, please!** encore du pain, s'il vous plaît! **to have some m. wine,** reprendre du vin; **I've had some m.,** j'en ai repris; **is there any m.?** y en a-t-il encore? en reste-t-il? **there is hardly, scarcely, any m.,** il en reste à peine; **there's plenty m.,** il en reste des quantités; il y en a encore à foison, en abondance; **do you want (any, some) m.?** en voulez-vous encore? **what m. do you want?** que vous faut-il de plus? **what m. could you ask?** que pourrait-on demander de plus? **what m. can I say?** que puis-je dire de plus? **I need a little m.,** il m'en faut encore un peu; **nothing m.,** plus rien; **there is nothing m. to be said,** il n'y a plus rien à dire; **have you any m. books?** avez-vous d'autres livres? **a few m.,** encore quelques-uns; **with a few m. days I could manage it,** avec quelques jours de plus j'en viendrais à bout; **I need a good deal m., a good many m.,** il m'en faut encore pas mal; **I need still m.,** il m'en faut encore davantage; **I need much m., a lot m.,** il m'en faut encore beaucoup, des quantités; **many m. were killed,** beaucoup d'autres encore furent tués; **give me as many m.,** donnez-m'en encore autant. **2.** *s. or indef. pron.* **I cannot give m.,** je ne peux donner davantage; **he gave what he promised and m.,** il a donné ce qu'il avait promis et même plus, et même davantage; **Oliver Twist has asked for m.!** Oliver Twist en a redemandé! **I needn't say m.,** pas besoin d'en dire davantage; c'est tout dire; **it is m. than I asked for,** c'est aller au delà de mes désirs; **that's m. than enough,** c'est plus qu'il n'en faut (to, pour); **that hat costs m. than this one,** ce chapeau-là coûte plus cher que celui-ci; **I earn m. than you,** je gagne plus que vous; **he knows m. about it than you,** il en sait plus que vous, plus long que vous, là-dessus; **I hope to see m. of him,** j'espère faire plus ample connaissance avec lui; j'espère le voir plus souvent à l'avenir; **I hope to hear m. of him,** j'espère bien avoir encore de ses nouvelles; **that is m. than I can tell, than I can say,** cela, je n'en sais rien; **how he manages to live is m. than I can tell,** comment il fait pour vivre, ça me dépasse; **one or m., two or m.,** un ou plusieurs, deux ou plusieurs; **he's m. than 30,** il a plus de 30 ans; il a dépassé la trentaine; **he is 30 and m.,** il a 30 ans et même davantage; **children of 12 years old and m.,** les enfants de 12 ans et au-dessus; **this incident, of which m. anon,** cet incident, sur lequel nous reviendrons; **what is m.,** (et) qui plus est; bien plus; de plus; **he is lazy and, what is m., he is a liar,** il est paresseux et, de plus, il est menteur; **kind hearts are m. than coronets,** un cœur chaud vaut mieux que des lettres de noblesse; **it is little m. than petty pilfering,** ce n'est guère que du chapardage; **she was m. of a tie than a companion,** elle était une attache plutôt qu'une compagne; **she's m. of an artist than her sister,** elle est plus artiste que sa sœur; **it costs £5, neither m. nor less,** cela coûte £5, ni plus ni moins. **3.** *adv.* (*a*) plus, davantage; **m. easily,** plus facilement; **this is far m. serious,** c'est bien autrement sérieux; c'est bien, beaucoup, plus sérieux; **to make sth. m. difficult,** augmenter la difficulté de qch.; **m. and m.,** de plus en plus; **I feel it m. and m. every day,** je le ressens chaque jour davantage; **they are far m. numerous,** ils sont beaucoup plus nombreux; **it couldn't have been m. pathetic,** la chose était on ne peut plus pathétique; **he was m. surprised than annoyed,** il était plutôt surpris que fâché; **m. than half dead,** plus qu'à demi mort; plus d'à demi mort; **m. than satisfied,** plus que satisfait; satisfait au delà de ses souhaits; **his total debts are m. than covered by his assets,** le chiffre de ses dettes est couvert et au delà par son actif; **she is m. attentive than you,** elle est plus attentive que vous; **nobody is m. expert at it than he,** il s'y connaît comme personne; **m. than usually brilliant,** plus brillant encore que d'ordinaire; **do it m. like this,** faites-le plutôt comme ça; **there were m. like a hundred than two hundred,** il y en avait plutôt cent que deux cents; **one should pay m. attention to details,** il faut faire plus d'attention aux détails; **I didn't do it any m. than you did,** je ne l'ai pas fait plus que vous; *F:* **that's m. like it!** voilà ce qu'il me, nous, faut! ça, c'est mieux! c'est comme ça qu'il faut faire! **m. or less,** plus ou moins; sensiblement; **silence was m. or less restored,** le silence fut rétabli plus ou moins; **they are m. or less cousins,** ils sont tant soit peu cousins; **neither m. nor less than ridiculous,** ni plus ni moins que ridicule; (*b*) **once m.,** encore une fois, une fois de plus; **if I see him any m.,** si jamais je le revois. **4. (the) more;** (*a*) *a.* **he only does (all) the m. harm,** il n'en fait que plus (de) mal; **(the) m. fool you (to have done it),** vous êtes d'autant plus sot (de l'avoir fait); **(the) more's the pity,** c'est d'autant plus malheureux, plus regrettable; tant pis! (*b*) *s.* **the m. one has the m. one wants,** plus on a, plus on désire avoir; *Prov:* l'appétit vient en mangeant; **the m.**

books I read, the m. I learn, plus je lis de livres, plus j'apprends; **the m. I read, the less I remember,** plus je lis, moins je retiens; (*c*) *adv.* **all the m. (reason),** à plus forte raison; d'autant plus; raison de plus; **I am all the m. surprised as. . .,** j'en suis d'autant plus surpris que . . .; **it makes me all the m. proud,** je n'en suis que plus fier; **the worse his arguments are, the m. he believes in them,** plus ses arguments sont mauvais, plus il y croit; **the m. famous the novel to be filmed, the greater the difficulties of adaptation,** plus célèbre est le roman qu'il s'agit de porter à l'écran, plus l'adaptation s'en avère difficile; **the fewer the joys of life, the m. we value them,** on attache d'autant plus de prix aux joies de la vie qu'elles sont moins nombreuses; **the m. he drinks the thirstier he gets,** (tant) plus (qu')il boit, (tant) plus il a soif. **5. no m., not any m.,** plus (*with ne expressed or understood*); (*a*) *a.* **I have no m. money,** je n'ai plus d'argent; **no m. soup, thank you,** plus de potage, merci; **I don't want to hear any m. talking; no m. talking!** je n'en veux plus entendre parler; silence! **(there is) no m. doubt,** (il n'y a) plus de doute; **I won't give any m. examples,** je ne donnerai pas davantage d'exemples; (*b*) *s.* **I have no m.,** je n'en ai plus; **I can do no m.,** je ne peux pas en faire davantage; **to say no m.,** ne pas en dire davantage; **I need say no m.,** inutile d'en dire plus long; c'est tout dire; **let us say no m. about it,** qu'il n'en soit plus question; n'en parlons plus; brisons là; tranchons là; **say no m.!** cela suffit! je comprends; **there remains no m. but to thank you,** il ne reste plus qu'à vous remercier; **I had no m. than half of my men left,** il ne me restait plus que la moitié de mes hommes; **he's just a good friend, nothing m.,** c'est un bon ami, rien de plus; **nothing m. is needed to finish it,** il ne faut pas davantage pour le finir; (*c*) *adv.* (i) **I can't see her any m.,** je ne peux plus la voir; **he is not in England any m.,** il n'est plus en Angleterre; **we won't go there any m.,** nous n'y irons plus; **do you go there?—not any m.,** y allez-vous quelquefois?—plus maintenant; **I don't want to go there any m.,** je ne veux jamais plus y aller; **he doesn't drink any m.,** il ne boit plus; **he doesn't know any m. about it,** il n'en sait pas davantage; **when I am no m.,** quand je ne serai plus; **the house is no m.,** la maison n'existe plus; **to return no m.,** ne plus jamais revenir; **I shall see her no m.,** je ne la verrai jamais plus; (ii) (*just as little*) **he is no longer young, no m. am I,** il n'est plus jeune, ni moi non plus; **he is no m. a lord than I am,** il n'est pas plus, pas davantage, (un) lord que moi; **she is no m. like you than her brother is,** non plus que son frère elle ne vous ressemble; **he thought you didn't want to see him—no m.** *do* **I!** il a pensé que vous ne vouliez pas le voir—ce qui est parfaitement juste; **I can't make out how it happened—no m. can I,** je ne m'explique pas comment c'est arrivé—ni moi non plus.

Morea [mə'riə]. *Pr.n. Geog:* la Morée.

moreen [mə'ri:n], *s. Tex:* moreen *f.*

more(-)ish ['mɔ:riʃ], *s. F:* appétissant; **this cake is very m.,** ce gâteau a un goût de revenez-y.

morel [mə'rel], *s. Bot:* morelle *f*; **great m.,** morelle furieuse; belladone *f*; **petty m.,** morelle noire; crève-chien *m inv*; herbe *f* à la gale.

morel(le) [mə'rel], *s. Fung:* morille *f.*

morello [mə'relou], *s. Hort:* **m. (cherry),** griotte *f*; **m. (cherry) tree,** griottier *m.*

morendo [mə'rendou], *adv. Mus:* morendo; en mourant.

morenosite [mə'renousait], *s. Miner:* morénosite *f.*

Moreote ['mɔriɔt]. *Geog:* (*a*) *a.* moréote; (*b*) *s.* Moréote *mf.*

moreover [mɔ:'rouvər], *adv.* d'ailleurs; du reste; au reste; de plus; au surplus; en outre; et qui plus est; **m. circumstances are favourable,** aussi bien les circonstances sont-elles favorables; **and m.,** bien plus.

morepork ['mɔ:pɔ:k], *s. Orn:* = MOPOKE.

Moresque [mɔ:'resk], *a. & s.* mauresque (*f*).

Morgagni [mɔ:'gæɲi:]. *Pr.n. Anat:* (*in male*) **sessile, stalked, hydatid of M.,** hydatide *f* sessile, pédiculée, de Morgagni.

Morgan ['mɔ:gən]. *Pr.n.f. Lit:* **M. le Fay,** la Fée Morgane; Morgane la Fée.

morganatic [mɔ:gə'nætik], *a.* morganatique.

morganatically [mɔ:gə'nætikli], *adv.* morganatiquement.

morgue[1] [mɔ:g], *s. Lit:* morgue *f*, orgueil *m.*

morgue[2], morgue *f*; dépôt *m* mortuaire; **this place is like a m.,** c'est lugubre comme un dépôt mortuaire.

moribund ['moribʌnd], *a. & s.* moribond, -onde.

morillon [mɔ'rilən], *s. Vit:* morillon *m.*

morin ['morin], *s. Ch:* morin *m.*

morindin [mə'rindin], *s. Ch:* morindine *f.*

Moringuidae [moriŋ'g(j)u:idi:], *s.pl. Ich:* moringuidés *m.*

morion[1] ['mɔriən], *s. A: Arm:* morion *m.*

morion[2], *Miner:* **m. (quartz),** morion *m.*

Morisco [mə'riskou]. (*a*) *a.* mauresque, moresque; (*b*) *s.* Maure *m*, More *m.*

morish ['mɔ:riʃ], *a. F:* = MORE(I)SH.

Mormon ['mɔ:mən], *a. & s. Rel:* mormon, -one.

Mormonism ['mɔ:mənizm], *s. Rel:* mormonisme *m.*

mormyrid [mɔ:'mairid], *s. Ich:* mormyre *m.*

Mormyridae [mɔ:'miridi:], *s.pl. Ich:* mormyridés *m.*

Mormyrus [mɔ:'mairəs], *s. Ich:* mormyre *m.*

morn [mɔ:n], *s. Poet:* matin *m.*

morne [mɔ:n], *s. A.Arms:* morne *f* (de lance courtoise).

morning ['mɔ:niŋ], *s.* **1.** (*a*) matin *m*; **to work from m. till night; to work m., noon and night,** travailler du matin au soir; **I saw him this m.,** je l'ai vu ce matin; **tomorrow m.,** demain matin; **the next m., the m. after,** le lendemain matin; **the morning before, the previous m.,** la veille au matin; *F:* **the m. after the night before,** le lendemain de la bombe, de la cuite; **I'm feeling like the m. after the night before,** j'ai la gueule de bois; **every Monday m.,** tous les lundis matin; **on the m. of Thursday the second,** le jeudi deux au matin; **four o'clock in the m.,** quatre heures du matin; **(the) first thing in the m.,** dès le matin; à la première heure; en vous levant; au saut du lit; au sortir du lit; **early in the m.,** matinalement, de grand matin; **I work best in the m.,** c'est le matin que je travaille mieux; **what do you do in the m.?** que faites-vous le matin? **good m.,** bonjour; (*b*) matinée *f*; **all the m.,** toute la matinée; **in the course of the m.,** dans la matinée; **the m. was wet,** il a plu dans la matinée; **m. off,** matinée de congé; **a morning's work,** une matinée de travail; **that's my morning's work,** (i) voilà ce que je fais le matin; (ii) voilà ce que j'ai fait ce matin; **on a cold winter('s) m.,** par une froide matinée d'hiver; (*c*) *Lit:* **in the m. of life,** à l'aube *f* de la vie. **2.** *attrib.* (*of breeze, etc.*) matinal, -aux; du matin; *A:* **m. girl,** bonne *f* qui vient faire le ménage le matin; **m. tea,** tasse de thé prise au lit avant de se lever; **m. room,** petit salon; *Bot:* **m. glory,** volubilis *m* des jardins; liseron *m* pourpre; **m. star,** (i) étoile *f* du matin; (ii) *A.Arms:* fléau *m* d'armes; *Nau:* **m. watch,** quart *m* du jour.

Moroccan [mə'rɔkən]. *Geog:* (*a*) *a.* marocain; (*b*) *s.* Marocain, -aine.

Morocco [mə'rɔkou]. **1.** *Pr.n. Geog:* le Maroc; *Hist:* **the Empire of M.,** l'empire du Maroc; l'empire chérifien. **2.** *s.* (*a*) **M. (leather),** maroquin *m*; **French m.,** maroquin français; **Levant m.,** maroquin du Levant; **M. (leather) tanning,** maroquinage *m*, maroquinerie *f*; **M. (leather) tannery,** maroquinerie; **M. (leather) goods,** maroquinerie; **M. (leather) tanner, dresser,** maroquinier *m*; **lined m., squared m.,** maroquin quadrillé; *Bookb:* **in m., m. bound,** (relié) en maroquin; (*b*) **M. paper,** maroquin.

moron ['mɔ:rɔn], *s.* **1.** (homme, femme) faible d'esprit, anormal(e). **2.** *F:* idiot, -ote, crétin *m.*

morose[1] [mə'rous], *a.* (*of pers., of disposition*) chagrin, morose; **to be m.,** voir tout en noir.

morose[2], *a. Theol:* qui s'attarde (sur une pensée); *esp.* **m. delectation,** délectation *f* morose.

morosely [mə'rousli], *adv.* chagrinement; d'un air chagrin, morose.

moroseness [mə'rousnis], *s.* morosité *f*; humeur chagrine, morose.

moroxite [mə'rɔksait], *s. Miner:* moroxite *f.*

morph [mɔ:f], *s. Nat.Hist:* **the various morphs of a polymorphic species,** les formes diverses d'une espèce polymorphe.

morphea [mɔ:'fi:ə], *s. Med:* morphée *f.*

morpheme ['mɔ:fi:m], *s. Ling:* morphème *m.*

morphemic [mɔ:'fi:mik], *a. Ling:* morphématique.

Morpheus ['mɔ:fiəs]. *Pr.n.m. Myth:* Morphée; *Lit:* **in the arms of M.,** dans les bras de Morphée.

morphia ['mɔ:fiə], **morphine** ['mɔ:fi:n], *s.* morphine *f*; **m. addict,** morphinomane *mf*; **the m. habit,** la morphinomanie.

morphinism ['mɔ:finizm], *s.* morphinisme *m.*

morphi(n)omania [mɔ:fi(n)ou'meiniə], *s.* morphinomanie *f.*

morphi(n)omaniac [mɔ:fi(n)ou'meiniæk], *a. & s.* morphinomane (*mf*).

Morpho ['mɔ:fou], *s. Ent:* morpho *m.*

morphogenesis [mɔ:fou'dʒenisis], *s. Biol:* morphogenèse *f.*

morphogenetic [mɔ:foudʒə'netik], *a. Biol:* (hormone, etc.) morphogénétique, morphogène.

morphogenic [mɔ:fə'dʒenik], *a. Physiol:* morphogène, morphogénétique.

morphogeny [mɔ:'fɔdʒəni], *s. Physiol:* morphogenèse *f.*

Morphoidae [mɔ:'fouidi:], *s.pl. Ent:* morphides *m.*

morphological [mɔ:fə'lɔdʒik(ə)l], *a.* morphologique.

morphologically [mɔ:fə'lɔdʒikli], *adv.* morphologiquement.

morphologist [mɔ:'fɔlədʒist], *s.* morphologue *mf.*

morphology [mɔ:'fɔlədʒi], *s.* morphologie *f.*

morphometry [mɔ:'fɔmitri], *s.* morphométrie *f.*

morphophonemics [mɔ:foufou'ni:miks], *s.* morphophonologie *f.*

morphosis, *pl.* **-oses** [mɔ:'fousis, -ousi:z], *s. Biol:* morphose *f.*

morphotropic [mɔ:fou'trɔpik], *a.* morphotropique.

morphotropism, morphotropy [mɔ:fou'troupizm, -'troupi], *s.* morphotropie *f.*

morra ['mɔrə], *s. Games:* la mourre.

Morris ['mɔris]. **1.** *Pr.n.m.* Maurice. **2.** *attrib.* **M. chair,** fauteuil *m* à dossier réglable; *Sm.a:* **M. tube,** tube réducteur (de calibre). **3.** *attrib.* **M. dance,** (sorte de) danse *f* folklorique; **M. dancer,** danseur, -euse, de cette danse folklorique.

morrow ['mɔrou], *s. A: & Lit:* lendemain *m*; **on the m.,** le lendemain; **what has the m in store for us?** qu'est-ce que demain nous réserve? **good m.,** bonjour.

morse[1] [mɔ:s], *s. Z:* morse *m.*

Morse[2]. *Pr.n.* **1.** *Tg:* **M. alphabet, code,** (alphabet *m* code *m*) Morse *m*; **M. inkwriter,** scripteur *m* Morse; **M. (sending) key,** manipulateur *m* (Morse); **M. receiver,** récepteur *m* Morse. **2.** *Mch.Tls:* **M. taper shank,** cône *m* Morse.

morse[3], *v.i. Tg: O:* télégraphier en morse.

morse[4], *s. Ecc.Cost:* mors *m*, fermail *m* (de chape).

morsel[1] ['mɔ:s(ə)l], *s.* (petit) morceau; **choice m., dainty m.,** morceau friand, de choix; **not a m. of bread,** pas une bouchée de pain.

morsel[2], *v.tr.* **(morselled)** morceler (une terre, etc.).

mort[1] [mɔ:t], *s. Ven:* hallali *m*; **to blow the m.,** sonner l'hallali.

mort[2], *s. Fish:* saumon *m* de trois ans.

mort[3], *s. A: & Dial:* **I've a m. of things to do,** j'ai un tas, des tas, de choses à faire; **she's had a m. of trouble,** elle a eu toutes sortes de malheurs.

mortadella [mɔ:tə'delə], *s.* **m. (sausage),** mortadelle *f.*

mortal ['mɔ:t(ə)l], *a.* **1.** (*a*) mortel, sujet à la mort; **all men are m.,** tous les hommes sont mortels; **m. remains,** dépouille mortelle; **unknown to m. man,** inconnu de tous; (*b*) *s.* **the mortals,** les mortels; *F: A:* **she's a queer m.,** c'est une drôle de femme; (*c*) humain; **the biggest head I ever saw on m. shoulders,** la plus grosse tête que j'aie jamais vue sur des épaules humaines. **2.** (*a*) mortel, qui cause la mort; funeste; fatal, -als **(to,** à); **m. blow, disease,** coup mortel, maladie mortelle; **m. poison,** poison mortel; (*b*) **m. sin,** péché mortel. **3. m. enemy,** ennemi mortel; ennemi à mort; **m. hatred, affront,** haine mortelle; affront mortel; **m. combat,** combat *m* à outrance, à mort. **4. m. struggles,** affres *f* de la mort. **5.** (*a*) **m. anxiety,** inquiétude mortelle; **to be in m. anxiety,** avoir la mort dans l'âme; **to be in m. fear of. . .,** avoir une peur mortelle, *F:* une peur bleue, de . . .; (*b*) *F:* **I waited two m. hours for him,** je l'ai attendu deux mortelles heures, deux heures interminables; **you're in a m. hurry,** vous êtes bien pressé; (*c*) *F:* **any m. thing,** n'importe quoi; **it's no m. use,** ça ne sert absolument à rien. **6.** *adv. P: A:* très; **she was m. angry,** elle était dans une colère bleue.

mortality [mɔ:'tæliti], *s.* **1.** mortalité *f* (de l'homme, d'un péché). **2.** *coll.* les mortels *m*, les humains *m*. **3.** mortalité; nombre *m* des décès; **infant m.,** mortalité infantile; **epidemic with a heavy m.,** épidémie *f* qui a entraîné une forte mortalité; *Ins:* **m. tables,** tables *f* de mortalité.

mortally ['mɔ:təli], *adv.* **1.** mortellement; **m. wounded,** blessé à mort. **2. m. offended,** mortellement offensé; **he was m. afraid of women,** il avait une peur bleue des femmes.

mortar[1] ['mɔ:tər], *s.* **1.** (*a*) *Pharm: etc:* mortier *m* (pour piler); *Dom.Ec:* égrugeoir *m*; **pestle and m.,** pilon *m* et mortier; (*b*) *Artil:* mortier; lance-bombes *m inv*; **m. carrier,** véhicule *m*, voiturette *f*, porte-mortier; **m. shell,** obus *m*, projectile *m*, de mortier; **m. squad,** équipe *f* de mortiers; **m. platoon,** section *f* de mortiers; **rifled, smoothbore, m.,** mortier rayé, à âme lisse. **2.** *Const:* (*a*) mortier, enduit *m*; **lime m.,** mortier ordinaire; **cement m.,** mortier ou enduit de ciment; **slow-setting m., slow-hardening m.,** mortier à prise lente; **strong m.,** mortier résistant; **hydraulic m.,** mortier hydraulique; **rich, lean, m.,** mortier gras, maigre; **m. trough,** auge *f* à mortier; (*b*) **clay and straw m.,** bauge *f.*

mortar[2], *v.tr. Const:* lier (les pierres) avec du mortier.

mortarboard ['mɔ:təbɔ:d], *s.* **1.** *Const:* planche *f* à mortier; taloche *f*. **2.** toque universitaire anglaise.

mortgage[1] ['mɔ:gidʒ], *s.* hypothèque *f*; **blanket m., general m.,** hypothèque générale; **chattel m.,** hypothèque mobilière, hypothèque sur biens meubles; **first, prior, m.,** hypothèque de premier rang; **second**

m., seconde hypothèque; **burdened, encumbered, with m.**, grevé d'hypothèque; **by, on, m.**, hypothécairement; **to borrow, lend, on m.**, emprunter, prêter, sur hypothèque; **to create a m.**, constituer une hypothèque; **to raise a m.**, prendre une hypothèque; **to buy a house on a m.**, prendre une hypothèque pour acheter une maison; **to secure a debt by m.**, hypothéquer une créance; **to register a m. on a property**, inscrire une hypothèque sur un bien; **to pay off, redeem, a m.**, purger une hypothèque; **m. bond, m. debenture**, obligation *f* hypothécaire; **first m. bonds**, obligations de première hypothèque; **m. charge**, affectation *f* hypothécaire; **m. creditor, creditor on m.**, créancier *m* hypothécaire; **m. debt, debt on m.**, dette *f* hypothécaire; **m. debtor**, débiteur *m* hypothécaire; **m. deed**, contrat *m* hypothécaire; **m. loan, loan on m.**, prêt *m* hypothécaire; **m. registrar; registrar, recorder, of mortgages**, conservateur *m* des hypothèques; **m. registration**, inscription *f* hypothécaire; **m. registry**, conservation *f* des hypothèques.

mortgage[2], *v.tr.* (*a*) hypothéquer, grever (une terre, un immeuble, des titres); engager, mettre en gage (des marchandises, des titres); déposer (des titres) en nantissement; **mortgaged estate**, domaine affecté d'hypothèques; (*b*) **I've already mortgaged my month's salary**, j'ai déjà disposé de tout mon mois; **to m. one's happiness**, engager son bonheur; **to m. one's reputation**, risquer sa réputation.

mortgageable ['mɔːgidʒəbl], *a.* hypothécable.

mortgagee [mɔːgi'dʒiː], *s.* (créancier *m*) hypothécaire (*m*).

mortgager, mortgagor ['mɔːgidʒər], *s.* débiteur *m* hypothécaire; débiteur sur hypothèque.

mortice ['mɔːtis], *s.* & *v.tr.* = MORTISE[1,2].

mortician [mɔː'tiʃ(ə)n], *s.* *U.S:* entrepreneur *m* de pompes funèbres.

mortiferous [mɔː'tifərəs], *a.* mortifère.

mortification [mɔːtifi'keiʃ(ə)n], *s.* **1.** mortification *f*; **m. of the body, of the passions**, mortification corporelle; mortification des passions. **2.** mortification, déconvenue *f*, humiliation *f*. **3.** *Med:* mortification, sphacèle *m*, sphacélisme *m*, gangrène *f*; **m. is setting in**, la plaie, le membre, se gangrène.

mortified ['mɔːtifaid], *a.* **1.** mortifié, humilié. **2.** *Med:* gangrené, mortifié, sphacélé.

mortify ['mɔːtifai]. **1.** *v.tr.* (*a*) mortifier, châtier (son corps, ses passions); (*b*) mortifier, humilier (qn); (*c*) *Med:* mortifier, gangrener, sphacéler. **2.** *v.i.* *Med:* se gangrener, se mortifier.

mortifying[1] ['mɔːtifaiiŋ], *a.* **1.** mortifiant, humiliant. **2.** mortifère.

mortifying[2], *s.* mortification *f*; **m. of the flesh (by fasting, etc.)**, macération *f* (par le jeûne, etc.).

mortise[1] ['mɔːtis], *s.* *Carp:* mortaise *f*; **to join two pieces by open m.**, affourcher deux pièces; **m. lock**, serrure *f* à mortaiser; serrure encastelée, encastrée, encloisonnée; **m. gauge**, trusquin *m* (de menuisier).

mortise[2], *v.tr.* mortaiser; **to m. two beams together**, emmortaiser, emboîter, deux poutres.

mortised ['mɔːtist], *a.* assemblé à mortaise; emmortaisé, emboîté.

mortising ['mɔːtisiŋ], *s.* mortaisage *m*; **m. machine**, machine *f* à mortaiser; mortaiseuse *f*; **m. tool**, outil mortaiseur; **m. axe**, besaiguë *f*.

mortmain ['mɔːtmein], *s.* *Jur:* mainmorte *f*; **goods in m.**, biens *m* de mainmorte; **to hold sth. in m.**, conserver qch. posthumement sous son empire.

mortuary ['mɔːtj(u)əri]. **1.** *a.* mortuaire. **2.** *s.* (*a*) dépôt *m* mortuaire; salle *f* mortuaire (d'hôpital, etc.); (*b*) morgue *f*; (*c*) *Jur:* *A:* droit mortuaire (prélevé sur la succession du défunt au profit du prêtre de la paroisse).

morula, *pl.* **-ae** ['mɔːrjulə, -iː], *s.* *Biol:* morula *f*.

mosaic[1] [mou'zeiik], *s.* (*a*) *Art:* *etc:* mosaïque *f*; **worker in m.**, mosaïste *mf*; *attrib.* **m. floor**, dallage *m* en mosaïque; (*b*) *Phot:* **(aerial) m.**, assemblage *m*, montage *m*, mosaïque, photographique; **m. (map)**, relevé *m* topographique; *attrib.* **m. screen film**, film *m* en trichromie à réseau mosaïque; (*c*) *T.V:* mosaïque; **photoelectric m.**, mosaïque photoélectrique; (*d*) *attrib.* *Ch:* **m. gold**, or mussif; (*e*) *Hort:* **m. disease, (leaf) m.**, mosaïque *f*; **severe m.**, frisolée *f* (mosaïque); **tobacco m. virus**, mosaïque du tabac; **tomato m. virus**, mosaïque des tomates; (*f*) *Biol:* **m. (hybrid)**, hybride *m* mosaïque; *Z:* **m. tailed rat**, uromys *m*.

Mosaic[2], *a.* *B.Hist:* (loi *f*, etc.) mosaïque, de Moïse.

mosaicist [mou'zeiisist], *s.* *Art:* *etc:* mosaïste *mf*.

Mosaism ['mouzeiizm], *s.* *Rel.Hist:* Mosaïsme *m*.

mosandrite ['mɔsændrait], *s.* *Miner:* mosandrite *f*.

mosasaur ['mousəsɔːr], *s.* *Paleont:* mosasaure *m*.

Mosasauri(a) [mousə'sɔːri(ə)], *s.pl.* *Paleont:* mosasauriens *m*.

mosasaurid [mousə'sɔːrid], *s.* *Paleont:* mosasaure *m*.

mosasaurus [mousə'sɔːrəs], *s.* *Paleont:* mosasaure *m*.

moschatel [mɔskə'tel], *s.* *Bot:* **(tuberous) m.**, moscatelle *f*; *F:* herbe *f* du musc; petite musquée.

moschiferous [mɔs'kifərəs], *a.* moschifère.

Moscow ['mɔskou]. *Pr.n.* *Geog:* Moscou; *Hist:* **the retreat from M.**, la retraite de Russie.

moselle [mou'zel], *s.* vin *m* de Moselle; moselle *m*.

Moses ['mouziz]. *Pr.n.m.* **1.** (*a*) *B.Hist:* Moïse; *int.* *P:* *O:* **Holy M.!** grand Dieu! par exemple! (*b*) *F:* *A:* **to be taken in like Moses at the fair**, faire l'échange de l'Indien. **2.** *P:* *Pej:* *O:* (désigne un) juif, usurier.

mosey ['mouzi], *v.i.* *U.S:* *P:* **1.** filer, décamper. **2.** se grouiller. **3. to m. along**, aller son petit bonhomme de chemin.

Moskva (the) [ðə'mɔskvɑː]. *Pr.n.* *Geog:* la Moscova.

Moslem ['mɔzlem]. (*a*) *a.* musulman; (*b*) *s.* musulman, -ane; moslem *m*.

Moslemism ['mɔzlemizm], *s.* islam(isme) *m*.

mosque [mɔsk], *s.* mosquée *f*.

mosquito, *pl.* **-oes** [məs'kiːtou, -ouz], *s.* (*a*) *Ent:* moustique *m*; **yellow-fever m.**, stégomyie *f*; **m. bite**, piqûre *f* de moustique; **m. net, curtain**, moustiquaire *f*; (*b*) *Ich:* **m. fish**, poisson-moustique *m*.

moss [mɔs], *s.* **1.** (*a*) *A:* marais *m*, marécage *m*; (*b*) **(peat) m.**, tourbière *f*; *Scot:* **m. hag**, tourbière (épuisée); fondrière *f*. **2.** *Bot:* (*a*) mousse *f*; **tree m.**, usnée *f*; **beard m.**, usnée barbue; **cord m.**, funaria *m*, funaire *m*; **dyer's m.**, orseille *f*; **Florida, Spanish, m.**, mousse d'Espagne; barbe *f* de vieillard; **(hair) cap m.**, polytric *m*; **lattice m.**, criblette *f*; **reindeer m.**, cladonie *f* (des rennes); **scale m.**, jungermannie *f*; **the mosses**, les muscinées *f*; (*b*) *Algae:* *etc:* **Irish m., pearl m.**, carragheen *m*; mousse perlée; mousse d'Irlande; chondrus *m*; **Ceylon m.**, agar-agar *m*; **sea m.**, (i) coralline *f*; (ii) bryozoaire *m*; (*c*) **Japanese m.**, helxine *f*; **m. rose**, rose moussue; *F:* rose mousseuse; **m. pink**, phlox subulé; (*d*) *U.S:* **house m.**, moutons *mpl*. **3.** *Miner:* **m. agate**, agate mousseuse. **4.** *Knit:* **(double) m. stitch**, point *m* de riz (double).

mossback ['mɔsbæk], *s.* *NAm:* **1.** *Hist:* embusqué *m*. **2.** *Pol:* *A:* *F:* vieille baderne; retardataire *m*; conservateur *m* à outrance; réactionnaire *m*.

mossbunker ['mɔsbʌŋkər], *s.* *Ich:* *U.S:* menhaden *m*.

moss-clad, moss-grown ['mɔsklæd, -groun], *a.* couvert de mousse; moussu.

moss-trooper ['mɔstruːpər], *s.* *Hist:* maraudeur *m* des frontières d'Écosse (au XVIIe siècle).

mossy ['mɔsi], *a.* moussu; **m. stone**, pierre moussue.

most[1] [moust]. **1.** *a.* (*a*) le plus (de); **you have made (the) m. mistakes**, c'est vous qui avez fait le plus de fautes; **he has the m. power**, c'est lui qui a le plus de pouvoir; (*b*) **m. men**, la plupart des hommes; **m. people have forgotten him**, la plupart des gens l'ont oublié; **in m. cases**, dans la généralité des cas; dans la majorité des cas; **for the m. part**, (i) pour la plupart, pour la plus grande partie, en majeure partie; (ii) le plus souvent; presque toujours; pour la plupart du temps. **2.** *s.* & *indef. pron.* (*a*) le plus; **do the m. you can**, faites le plus que vous pourrez; **at (the) (very) m.**, au maximum; (tout) au plus; **at the m. there are only about twenty women in the hall**, c'est tout au plus si l'on peut compter jusqu'à vingt femmes dans la salle; **to make the m. of sth.**, (i) tirer le meilleur parti possible, le plus grand parti possible, de qch.; faire valoir (son argent); bien employer (son temps); exploiter (son talent); ménager le plus possible (ses provisions, etc.); bien gouverner (ses ressources); (ii) représenter qch. sous son plus beau jour ou sous son plus vilain jour; accentuer (ses souffrances, etc.); **to make the m. of one's hair**, se coiffer à son plus grand avantage; **to make the m. of one's wares**, faire valoir sa marchandise; **he doesn't know how to make the m. of himself**, il ne sait pas se faire valoir; **to know how to make the m. of one's time**, savoir tirer le meilleur parti possible de son temps; (*b*) la plupart; **m. of the work**, la plupart, la plus grande partie, du travail; **he had eaten m. of the cake**, il avait mangé les trois quarts du gâteau; **m. of the time**, la plupart du temps; la majeure partie du temps; **he spends m. of his time (in) gambling**, il passe le plus clair de son temps à jouer; **m. of his friends, m. of them, have forgotten him**, la plupart de ses amis, la plupart d'entre eux, l'ont oublié; (*c*) **he is more reliable than m.**, on peut compter sur lui plus que sur la plupart des hommes. **3.** *adv.* *as superlative of comparison* (*a*) (*with vb*) le plus; **what I want m.**, ce que je désire le plus, surtout, par-dessus tout; (*b*) (*with adj.*) **the m.**, le plus, la plus, les plus; **the m. intelligent child, children**, l'enfant le plus intelligent; les enfants les plus intelligents; **the m. beautiful woman**, la plus belle femme; (*c*) (*with adv.*) le plus; **those who have answered m. accurately**, ceux qui ont répondu le plus exactement. **4.** *adv.* (*intensive*) très, fort, bien; **m. displeased**, fort mécontent; **m. unhappy**, bien malheureux; **that's m. strange**, c'est bien étrange; voilà qui est très curieux, fort curieux; **m. likely, m. probably**, très probablement; **a m. expensive car**, une voiture des plus coûteuses; **he has been m. rude**, il a été on ne peut plus impoli; **he is m. strict with his pupils**, il est extrêmement sévère avec ses élèves; **it is m. remarkable**, c'est tout ce qu'il y a de plus remarquable; **a m. dangerous man**, un homme dangereux entre tous; un homme des plus dangereux; **the M. Honourable . . .**, le Très Honorable . . .; *Hist:* **His m. Christian Majesty**, sa Majesté très chrétienne. **5.** *adv.* *Dial:* *F:* (= ALMOST) **m. everybody's here**, presque tout le monde est là; **m. all we have done**, à peu près tout ce que nous avons fait.

most[2], *s.* *Elcs:* mos(t) *m*.

mostly ['moustli], *adv.* **1.** pour la plupart; principalement; **they come m. from Scotland**, ils viennent surtout, pour la plupart, de l'Écosse; **the town is m. built of brick**, la ville est pour la plus grande partie bâtie en briques. **2.** le plus souvent, (pour) la plupart du temps; **she is m. out on Sundays**, elle sort presque toujours le dimanche.

Mosul ['mous(ə)l]. *Pr.n.* *Geog:* Mossoul *m*.

mot [mou], *s.* *Lit:* bon mot; mot piquant; trait *m* d'esprit.

Motacillidae [moutə'silidiː], *s.pl.* *Orn:* motacillidés *m*, les bergeronnettes *f*, les pipits *m*.

mote[1] [mout], *s.* *Lit:* atome *m* de poussière; *B:* **the m. in thy brother's eye**, la paille dans l'œil de ton frère.

mote[2], *s.* *A:* (*a*) monticule *m*, butte *f*; (*b*) motte *f* (place du château).

motel [mou'tel], *s.* motel *m*.

motet [mou'tet], *s.* *Mus:* motet *m*.

moth [mɔθ], *s.* **1.** *Ent:* (*a*) **(clothes) m.**, mite *f*; teigne *f* des draps, ver *m* des étoffes, artison *m*, gerce *f*; **wood m.**, artison; **black-cloaked clothes m.**, teigne des tapisseries; **single-spotted clothes m.**, teigne des pelleteries; **casemaking clothes m.**, pelletière *f*; **honeycomb m.**, fausse teigne; teigne de la cire; **m. worm**, chenille *f* de la teigne; mite; *F:* **the moths have been at my fur coat**, mon manteau de fourrure est tout mangé, rongé, de mites; (*b*) papillon *m* nocturne, de nuit; phalène *f*; **cabbage m.**, plutelle *f*, teigne des crucifères; **corn m.**, (fausse) teigne des blés, des grains; alucite *f* (des céréales); **plume m.**, alucite; **dart m.**, agrotide *f*; agrotis *f* des moissons; **turnip m.**, agrotide des moissons; **emperor m.**, paon *m* de nuit; **atlas m.**, saturnie *f* atlas; **ghost m., hepialid m.**, hépiale *m* du houblon; **goat m.**, (cossus *m*) gâte-bois *m inv*; **gypsy m.**, zigzag *m*; **hawk m.**, sphinx *m*; crépusculaire *m*, smérinthe *m*; **hummingbird hawk m.**, moro-sphinx *m inv*; sphinx moineau; macroglosse *m*, sphinx, du caille-lait; **death's head m.**, sphinx tête de mort; **luna m.**, lunaire *m*; **silk(worm) m.**, bombyx *m* du ver à soie, du mûrier; **silver silk m., tailed comet m.**, papillon comète (de Madagascar); **tiger m.**, arctie *f*; *F:* **he's like a m. round a candle flame**, il va se brûler à la chandelle comme un papillon. **2.** *Bot:* **m. mullein**, molène *f* blattaire; herbe *f* aux mites.

mothball[1] ['mɔθbɔːl], *s.* boule *f* de naphtaline.

mothball[2], *v.tr.* *Mil:* *Navy:* (*of equipment, ship, weapon*) mettre en cocon, encoconer; conditionner (un matériel) en vue de sa conservation.

motheaten ['mɔθiːtn], *a.* **1.** rongé, mangé, des mites, des vers; mangé aux mites; mité; piqué (des vers); criblé de mangeures; **to get m.**, se miter. **2.** *F:* *O:* (*of idea, scheme, etc.*) suranné. **3.** *F:* misérable; sans valeur; miteux; **m. hotel**, hôtel miteux.

mother[1] ['mʌðər], *s.f.* **1.** (*a*) mère; **yes, m.!** oui, maman! **please remember me to your m.**, rappelez-moi au bon souvenir de (madame) votre mère; *Cu:* **like m. makes it**, appétissant, succulent; **m. to be**, future maman; **m. of six**, mère de six enfants; **mother's day**, fête *f* des mères; **every mother's son**, tous, sans exception; *F:* **mother's ruin**, le gin; *Fig:* **Greece, m. of the arts**, la Grèce, mère des arts; (*b*) *attrib.* **m. hen**, mère poule; **m. earth**, la terre notre mère, la terre nourricière; **m. country**, (i) mère-patrie *f*, *pl.* mères-patries; (ii) métropole *f* (d'une colonie); **m. tongue**, (i) langue maternelle; (ii) (*also* **m. language**) langue mère, langue matrice (d'une autre langue); **m. wit**, le bon sens, le sens commun; **m. church**, (i) église mère, église matrice; (ii) notre sainte mère l'Église; *Biol:* **m. cell**, cellule *f* mère; *For:* **m. tree**, (arbre) porte-graine *m inv*; *Nau:* **m. ship**, ravitailleur *m*; navire-gigogne *m*, *pl.* navires-gigognes; **m. aircraft**, (i) avion porteur (d'un plus petit appareil); (ii) avion guide (d'un appareil aérien téléguidé); (iii) avion ravitailleur (en vol). **2.** *A:* *F:* (*elderly woman*) **(old) M. Martin**, la mère Martin; **M. Goose stories**, contes *m* de ma mère l'Oie. **3.** *Ecc:* **reverend m.**, (i) (sœur) supérieure; (ii) *Corr:* Madame la Supérieure; (iii) (*form of address*) ma mère; **the M. Superior,** la Mère supérieure. **4.** (*a*) *Geol: etc:* **m. rock,** roche *f* mère; **m. of coal,** charbon fossile; **m. emerald,** mère *f* d'émeraude; **m. crystal, m. quartz,** quartz naturel; **m. of pearl,** nacre *f*; **m.-of-pearl button,** bouton *m* de, en, nacre; *Min:* **m. lode,** filon *m* mère; *Metall:* **m. metal,** métal *m* mère; (*b*) *Ch:* **m. liquid, liquor, lye, water,** eau *f*, solution *f*, mère; **m. of vinegar,** mère de vinaigre; (*c*) *Bot:* **m. of millions, of thousands,** (linaire *f*) cymbalaire *f*.

mother², *v.tr.* **1.** *F:* donner naissance à (qch.); enfanter (qch.). **2.** (*a*) donner des soins maternels à (qn); servir de mère à (qn); (*b*) dorloter (qn). **3.** (*a*) se faire passer pour la mère de (qn); (*b*) s'avouer l'auteur de (qch.); (*c*) adopter (un enfant). **4.** (*a*) *O:* **to m. a child (up)on s.o.,** attribuer la maternité d'un enfant à qn; (*b*) **to mother a wolf cub on a bitch,** faire élever un louveteau par une chienne.

mothercraft ['mʌðəkrɑːft], *s.* puériculture *f*.

motherhood ['mʌðəhud], *s.* maternité *f*.

mothering ['mʌðəriŋ], *s.* **1.** soins maternels. **2. M. Sunday,** la fête des mères (en Angleterre le dimanche de la mi-carême).

mother-in-law ['mʌðərinlɔː], *s.f.* **1.** belle-mère, *pl.* belles-mères (mère du mari ou de la femme de qn). **2.** *A:* belle-mère (deuxième femme du père de qn).

motherland ['mʌðəlænd], *s.* patrie *f*; pays natal.

motherless ['mʌðəlis], *a.* sans mère; orphelin (de mère).

motherliness ['mʌðəlinis], *s.* **1.** affection maternelle. **2.** bonté *f*, affection *f*, digne d'une mère.

motherly ['mʌðəli], *a.* **1.** maternel, de mère. **2.** digne d'une mère.

motherwort ['mʌðəwəːt], *s. Bot:* cardiaire *f*, cardiaque *f*; léonure *m*; agripaume *f*; queue-de-lion *f*, *pl.* queues-de-lion.

mothery ['mʌðəri], *a.* (vin) couvert de moisissures.

moth-hole ['mɔθhoul], *s.* piqûre *f*, trou *m*, de mite.

mothkiller ['mɔθkilər], *s.* anti-mites *m*.

mothproof¹ ['mɔθpruːf], *a.* anti-mites, à l'épreuve des mites.

mothproof², *v.tr.* antimiter.

motif [mou'tiːf], *s.* **1.** *Dressm:* motif *m* (de broderie). **2.** *Art: Mus:* motif.

motile ['moutail], *a. Nat.Hist:* (spore, cellule) mobile.

motility [mou'tiliti], *s. Biol:* mobilité *f*, motilité *f*.

motion¹ ['mouʃ(ə)n], *s.* **1.** mouvement *m*, déplacement *m*; (*a*) *Mec: Ph:* **in m.,** en mouvement, en marche; **body in m.,** corps *m* en mouvement; **accelerated m.,** mouvement accéléré; **uniformly accelerated m.,** mouvement uniformément accéléré; **atomic m.,** mouvement des atomes; **collective mode of m.,** mouvement collectif; **compound m.,** mouvement composé; **curvilinear m., m. in a curve,** mouvement curviligne; **equable, uniform, m.,** mouvement uniforme; **impressed m.,** mouvement acquis; **pendular, pendulous, swinging, m.,** mouvement pendulaire; **perpetual, continuous, m.,** mouvement perpétuel, continu; **rectilinear, straight-line, m.,** mouvement rectiligne; **simple m.,** mouvement simple; **thermal m.,** mouvement thermique; **variable m.,** mouvement varié; **uniformly variable m.,** mouvement uniformément varié; (*b*) *Mec.E: Mch:* **back m.,** mouvement de rappel, jeu *m* arrière; **back-and-forth, to-and-fro, m.,** mouvement d'avance et de recul, de va-et-vient; **up-and-down m.,** mouvement ascendant et descendant; **coiling, winding, m.,** mouvement d'enroulement; **hoisting m.,** mouvement de levage; **lateral m., side m.,** mouvement latéral; **reverse m.,** mouvement inversé, marche *f* arrière; (*of machine part*) **travelling m.,** mouvement de translation (d'un organe de machine); (*of derrick boom*) **lifting, derricking, m.,** mouvement de relevage (de la flèche); **traversing m.,** mouvement de direction (de la flèche); **m. bar,** règle *f*, guide *m* (de la tête du piston); **m. rod,** tringle *f* de transmission du mouvement; **m. study,** analyse *f* du mouvement; chronophotographie *f*; (*c*) (*of vehicle, apparatus*) marche *f*, mouvement; **car in m.,** voiture *f* en mouvement, en marche; **smooth m.,** allure régulière, roulement silencieux (d'une voiture); marche régulière, silencieuse (d'un appareil); **to put, set, (sth.) in m.,** mettre (qch.) en mouvement, en marche, en jeu; imprimer un mouvement à (qch.); faire mouvoir, faire aller, faire jouer (qch.); faire agir (la loi); **to set a machine in m.,** mettre une machine en marche, en route, en train; embrayer une machine; **to set the apparatus in m.,** mettre l'appareil en marche; faire fonctionner, déclencher, l'appareil; (*d*) *esp. NAm: Cin:* **m. picture,** film *m*; (*e*) *Astr:* **m. of stars,** mouvement des étoiles; **apparent, proper, m.,** mouvement apparent, propre (des astres). **2.** (*a*) mouvement (du bras, etc.); **to go through the motions (of doing sth.),** exécuter les mouvements; *F:* **to go through the motions,** faire semblant d'agir selon les règles; (*b*) signe *m*, geste *m*; *Ind: etc:* **m. efficiency,** rendement *m* du geste; **m. analysis,** analyse des mouvements; **time and motion consultant,** organisateur-conseil *m*, *pl.* organisateurs-conseils. **3.** (*a*) *A:* **to do sth. of one's own m.,** faire qch. de sa propre initiative; **on whose m.?** sous l'impulsion de qui? (*b*) motion *f*, proposition *f*; **to propose, move, bring forward, a m.,** faire une proposition; présenter une motion; **to put the m.,** mettre la proposition aux voix; **to carry a m.,** faire adopter une motion; **the m. was carried,** la motion fut adoptée; **to speak for the m., to support the m.,** soutenir la motion; **to speak against the m.,** soutenir la contre-partie; (*c*) *Jur:* demande *f*, requête *f*. **4.** (*a*) mécanisme *m*; **reversing m.,** mécanisme de renversement de marche; **planetary m.,** engrenage *m* planétaire; (*b*) *Clockm: etc:* mouvement (d'une montre). **5.** *Mus:* **similar m., contrary m., oblique m.,** mouvement semblable, contraire, oblique. **6.** *Med:* évacuation *f*, selle *f*; **to have a m.,** aller à la selle; **two motions daily,** deux selles par jour.

motion², *v.tr.* & *i.* *A:* **to m. (to) s.o. to do sth.,** faire signe à qn de faire qch.; **to m. s.o. away, in,** faire signe à qn de s'éloigner, d'entrer.

motional ['mouʃən(ə)l], *a.* (*a*) de mouvement; motionnel; *El:* **m. impedance,** impédance motionnelle; (*b*) cinétique.

motionless ['mouʃ(ə)nlis], *a.* immobile; immobilisé; sans mouvement; **to remain m.,** (i) ne pas bouger, rester immobile; (ii) ne pas broncher.

motivate ['moutiveit], *v.tr.* motiver (une action, etc.).

motivation [mouti'veiʃ(ə)n], *s.* motifs *mpl*; *esp. Psy:* motivation *f*.

motivational [mouti'veiʃən(ə)l], *a.* (études) de motivation.

motive¹ ['moutiv]. **1.** *a.* (*a*) moteur, -trice; **m. power,** force motrice; source *f* d'énergie; moyen *m* de propulsion; (*b*) *Mec:* **m. energy,** énergie *f* cinétique. **2.** *s.* (*a*) motif *m* (**for acting,** d'action); **to act for, from, a given m.,** agir poussé par un motif déterminé; **to have a m. in doing sth.,** avoir un motif à, pour, faire qch.; **from a religious m.,** poussé par un sentiment religieux; (*b*) mobile *m* (d'une action); **the crime was committed from a political m.,** le mobile du crime était politique; **interest is a powerful m.,** l'intérêt est un puissant ressort; **I wonder what his m. is,** je me demande pourquoi, pour quelle raison, il fait cela. **3.** *s. Art:* motif (d'un tableau, etc.).

motive², *v.tr.* motiver (une action).

motivity [mou'tiviti], *s.* **1.** motilité *f*; *Biol:* motricité *f* (des neurones). **2.** *Mec:* énergie *f* cinétique.

motley ['mɔtli]. **1.** *a.* (*a*) bariolé, bigarré; *A:* **m. fool,** bouffon *m* (de cour) en livrée; (*b*) divers, mêlé, bigarré; **m. crowd,** foule bigarrée, panachée, mélangée. **2.** *s.* (*a*) couleurs bigarrées; (*b*) mélange *m* (de choses disparates); (*c*) *A:* livrée *f* de fou de cour, de bouffon de cour; **to don the m.,** revêtir la livrée de bouffon; faire le bouffon.

motmot ['mɔt'mɔt], *s. Orn:* momot *m*.

motocross ['moutoukrɔs], *s. Sp:* moto-cross *m*.

motometer [mou'tɔmitər], *s. Mec.E:* compteur *m* de tours; compte-tours *m inv.*

motor¹ ['moutər]. **1.** *a.* moteur, -trice; (*a*) *Anat:* **m. muscle, nerve,** muscle, nerf, moteur; **m. area, centre,** centre moteur, praxique (du cerveau); **m. response,** réponse motrice; *Med:* **m. paralysis,** paralysie *f* des centres moteurs; (*b*) *Mec:* **m. torque,** couple moteur. **2.** *s.* moteur *m*; (*a*) **clockwork m.,** mouvement *m* d'horlogerie; **spring m.,** moteur à ressort; **pneumatic m.,** moteur à air comprimé; **water, hydraulic, m.,** moteur à eau, moteur hydraulique; **driving m.,** moteur d'entraînement, de commande; **starting m.,** moteur de démarrage; **auxiliary m.,** moteur auxiliaire; servo-moteur, *pl.* servo-moteurs; *Mch.Tls: etc:* **travelling m.,** moteur de translation; (*of crane, derrick boom*) **hoist(ing) m.,** moteur de levage; **slewing m.,** moteur d'orientation; **traverse m.,** moteur de direction; *I.C.E:* **four-stroke, two-stroke, m.,** moteur à quatre, à deux, temps; **bicycle with m. attachment,** bicyclette *f* avec moteur auxiliaire; *F:* **clap-on m.,** moteur amovible, auxiliaire, pour bicycle; *attrib.* **m. vehicle,** voiture *f* automobile; véhicule *m* à traction automotrice; **m. saw,** motoscie *f*; **m.(-driven) pump,** motopompe *f*; **m. scythe,** motofaucheuse *f*; **m. convoy,** convoi *m* automobile, de véhicules automobiles; **m. show,** salon *m* de l'automobile; **m. tour,** randonnée *f*, voyage *m*, en voiture; *NAm:* **m. court,** motel *m*; *Rail:* **m. coach,** *NAm:* **m. car,** motrice *f*; *O:* **m. bus, m. coach,** autobus *m*; autocar *m*; (*b*) *El:* **(electric) m.,** moteur électrique; **alternating-current m.,** moteur à courant alternatif, alternomoteur *m*; **continuous-current, direct-current, m.,** moteur à courant continu, électromoteur *m*; **asynchronous, synchronous, m.,** moteur asynchrone, synchrone; **commutator m.,** moteur à collecteur; **compound(-wound) m.,** moteur à excitation composée, moteur compound; **monophase m.,** moteur monophasé; **multiphase, polyphase, m.,** moteur polyphasé; **pole-changing m.,** moteur à plusieurs polarités; **shunt(-wound) m.,** moteur excité en dérivation, moteur shunt; **series(-wound) m.,** moteur (excité) en série; **slip-ring, wound-rotor, m.,** moteur à rotor bobiné; **m. generator,** groupe convertisseur, moteur-générateur, *pl.* moteurs-générateurs; **m. brush,** balai *m* de moteur; **m. rheostat,** rhéostat *m* de démarrage; *Rail:* **(electric) m. carriage,** (voiture) motrice *f*.

motor². **1.** *v.i.* voyager, circuler, en automobile, en voiture. **2.** *v.tr.* *O:* conduire, transporter, (qn) en voiture.

motorail ['moutəreil], *s. Rail:* **m. (service),** train(s) *m* (à) auto-couchettes.

motor-assisted ['moutərə'sistid], *a.* (bicyclette) à moteur.

motorboat ['moutəbout], *s.* vedette *f* automobile; canot *m* automobile, à moteur; **harbour m.,** vedette de port; **coastal m.,** vedette de défense côtière.

motorboating ['moutəboutiŋ], *s.* motonautisme *m*; promenades *fpl* en canot automobile; sport *m* motonautique.

motorcade ['moutəkeid], *s.* défilé *m* de voitures.

motorcar ['moutəkɑːr], *s.* automobile *f*, voiture *f*.

motorcycle ['moutəsaikl], *F:* **motorbike** ['moutəbaik], *s.* motocyclette *f*, *F:* moto *f*; **(lightweight) m.,** vélomoteur *m*, cyclomoteur *m*; *Mil:* **m. scout,** éclaireur *m* motocycliste; **m. troop,** peloton *m* motocycliste; **I came on my m., by m.,** je suis venu à motocyclette, *F:* en moto.

motorcycling ['moutəsaikliŋ], *s.* motocyclisme *m*.

motorcyclist ['moutəsaiklist], *s.* motocycliste *mf*; *Mil:* **m. orderly,** estafette *f* motocycliste.

motor-driven ['moutədriv(ə)n], *a.* actionné, commandé, par moteur; à (électro)moteur.

motordrome ['moutədroum], *s.* autodrome *m*; circuit *m* de vitesse.

motorial [mou'tɔːriəl], *a. Physiol:* moteur, -trice; **m. excitement,** excitation motrice.

motoring ['moutəriŋ], *s.* automobilisme *m*; tourisme *m* automobile; **school of m.,** auto-école *f*, *pl.* auto-écoles; **two summonses for m. offences,** deux contraventions *f* pour infractions au code de la route.

motorist ['moutərist], *s.* automobiliste *mf*; **a veteran m.,** un vétéran du volant.

motorization [moutərai'zeiʃ(ə)n], *s.* motorisation *f*.

motorize ['moutəraiz], *v.tr.* motoriser.

motorized ['moutəraizd], *a.* motorisé; à moteur; **m. bicycle,** bicyclette *f* à moteur; cyclomoteur *m*, vélomoteur *m*; **m. agriculture,** motoculture *f*.

motorless ['moutəlis], *a.* sans moteur.

motorman, *pl.* **-men** ['moutəmæn, -men], *s.m.* wattman (de tramway); conducteur (de tramway, de train de métro).

motorway ['moutəwei], *s.* autoroute *f*.

motory ['moutəri], *a. Anat:* (*of nerve, etc.*) moteur, -trice.

motte [mɔt], *s. Archeol:* motte *f*.

mottle¹ ['mɔtl], *s.* **1.** tache *f*, tacheture *f*, moucheture *f*. **2.** (*a*) marbrure *f*, diaprure *f*; (*b*) *Tex:* laine chinée.

mottle², *v.tr.* tacheter, diaprer, marbrer, moucheter; **to m. metal,** moirer le métal; **to m. (-finish),** jasper (des outils, etc.); **cold mottles the skin,** le froid marbre la peau; **the clouds that m. the sky,** les nuages *m* qui marbrent le ciel.

mottled ['mɔtld], *a.* truité, tiqueté, tacheté, moucheté, diapré, marbré, pommelé; **m. soap,** savon marbré, madré; **m. wood,** bois madré; **m. bakelite,** bakélite marbrée; *Leath:* **m. chamois,** chamois moucheté; *Bookb:* **m. skin,** peau marbrée; *Metall:* **m. pig (iron),** fonte truitée; *Tex:* **m. fabric,** tissu chiné.

mottling ['mɔtliŋ], *s.* marbrure *f*, diaprure *f*, tiqueture *f*; *Tex:* chinage *m*, chiné *m*; *Phot:* **m. of the gelatine,** réticulation *f* de la gélatine.

motto, *pl.* **-oes** ['mɔtou, -ouz], *s.* **1.** devise *f*; **cracker m.,** devise de diablotin. **2.** *Her:* mot *m*, âme *f* (d'une devise). **3.** *Typ:* épigraphe *f* (en tête de chapitre). **4.** *Mus:* motif *m*.

mottramite ['mɔtrəmait], *s. Miner:* mottramite *f*.

moucharaby [mu'ʃærəbi], *s.* moucharabieh *m*.

moufflon ['muːflɔn], *s. Z:* mouflon *m*; **maned m., ruffled m.,** mouflon à manchettes.

moujik ['muːʒik], *s.* moujik *m*.

mould¹ [mould], *s.* terre végétale, franche, meuble, naturelle; **vegetable m.,** terreau *m*, humus *m*; *Agr:* **m. board,** orillon *m*, oreille *f*, versoir *m* (de charrue); *A: Lit:* **man of m.,** (i) homme mortel; (ii) homme bien doué.

mould[2], *v.tr. Hort:* butter (des pommes de terre, etc.).

mould[3], *s.* **1.** *Const: etc:* (*template*) calibre *m*, profil *m*; *N.Arch: Av:* gabarit *m*; **frame m.**, gabarit de membrure; **m. loft**, salle *f* des gabarits, des modèles; salle à tracer; **to lay off the m. loft**, porter sur le plancher de la salle des gabarits, de la salle à tracer. **2.** (*a*) *Art: Cer: etc:* moule *m*; mère *f*; **bullet m.**, moule à balles; **button m.**, moule de bouton (de vêtement); *Glassm:* **parison m.**, moule mesureur; **m. blowing**, pressé-soufflé *m*; *Dom.Ec:* **jelly m.**, moule à gelée; *Lit:* **to be cast in an heroic m.**, être de la pâte, du bois, dont on fait les héros; **characters cast in the same m.**, caractères jetés dans le même moule; **man cast in a simple m.**, homme tout d'une pièce; (*b*) *Metall:* **casting m.**, moule à fonte; **built-up m.**, moule monté; **box m.**, châssis *m* (de moule); **half m.**, coquille *f* (de moule); **outer m.**, surtout *m*; **dry sand m.**, moule en sable sec, en sable gras; **green sand m.**, moule en sable vert, en sable maigre; moule à vert; **open sand m.**, moule à découvert; **loam m.**, moule en terre; **m. press**, serre *f*; machine *f* à mouler sous pression; **to cast the piece in the m.**, couler la pièce au moule; **to withdraw a pattern from the m.**, démouler un modèle; (*c*) *Typ:* **(type) m.**, matrice *f* (de caractère); *Rec:* **(record) m.**, matrice (de disque). **3.** (*a*) *Geol:* **(outer, inner) m.**, moule (externe, interne) (de coquillage fossile); (*b*) *Typ:* empreinte (prise sur la forme); flan *m*. **4.** *Cu:* **rice m.**, gâteau *m* de riz. **5.** *Arch:* moulure *f*.

mould[4], *v.tr.* **1.** mouler, façonner; **to m. in wax**, mouler en cire; **to m. s.o.'s character**, pétrir, former, façonner, le caractère de qn; **easily moulded character**, caractère docile, malléable; caractère de cire. **2.** *Bak:* (*a*) pétrir (la pâte); (*b*) mettre (le pain) en forme. **3.** *N.Arch:* gabarier (la quille, etc.). **4.** (*a*) *Typ:* **to m. a page**, prendre l'empreinte d'une page; (*b*) **to m. a (gramophone) record**, presser un disque.

mould[5], *s.* moisi *m*, moisissure *f*, chancissure *f*.

mould[6], *v.i.* (se) moisir; **blue-moulded cheese**, fromage à pâte persillée.

mould[7], *s. Anat: Dial:* fontanelle *f*.

moulded ['mouldid], *a.* **1.** moulé, façonné; **m. glass**, verre moulé; **m. plastic**, plastique moulé, matière plastique moulée; **m. steel**, acier moulé; **m. piece, m. casting**, pièce moulée; *El:* **m. resistor**, résistance moulée. **2.** *N.Arch:* **m. breadth**, largeur *f* hors membrures; **m. displacement**, déplacement *m* hors membres; **m. depth**, creux *m* sur quille; **m. draught**, profondeur *f* de carène; **m. form.** forme *f* sur gabarit.

moulder[1] ['mouldər], *v.i.* tomber en poussière; s'effriter; (*of empire, etc.*) tomber en ruine; (*of institution, etc.*) dépérir; **to m. in one's grave**, subir la corruption du temps.

moulder[2], *s.* (*pers.*) *Cer: Metall: etc:* mouleur *m*, façonneur *m*.

mouldering[1] ['mouldəriŋ], *a.* qui tombe en poussière.

mouldering[2], *s.* effritement *m*.

mouldiness ['mouldinis], *s.* **1.** état moisi. **2.** moisissure *f*, moisi *m*.

moulding[1] ['mouldiŋ], *s. Hort:* buttage *m*.

moulding[2], *s.* **1.** (*a*) *Metall: etc:* moulage *m*; **compression m., pressure m.**, moulage sous pression; **extrusion m.**, moulage par extrusion; **injection m.**, moulage par injection; **chill m.**, moulage en coquille; **dry sand m.**, moulage en sable sec, en sable gras; **green sand m.**, moulage à vert, en sable vert, en sable maigre; **open sand m.**, moulage à découvert; **loam m.**, moulage en terre; **shell m.**, moulage en carapace; **m. box, m. flask**, châssis *m* (à mouler); **m. floor**, chantier *m* de moulage; moulerie *f*; **m. hole**, fosse *f* de moulage; **m. machine**, machine *f* à mouler; **m. press**, serre *f*; machine à mouler sous pression; **m. shop**, atelier *m* de moulage; moulerie; (*b*) *N.Arch:* gabariage *m*; **m. loft**, salle *f* des gabarits; salle à tracer; (*c*) *Bak:* (i) pétrissage *m*; (ii) mise *f* en forme (du pain); **m. board**, planche *f* à pâtisserie; (*d*) *Rec:* pressage *m* (d'un disque); (*e*) formation *f* (du caractère, etc.); manipulation *f*, mise *f* en condition (de l'opinion publique). **2.** moulure *f*, moulage; profil mouluré; profilé *m*; (*a*) *Const: etc:* **frame m.**, chambranle *m* (de porte, etc.); **cover-joint m.**, baguette *f* couvre-joint; (*b*) **(drip, weather (tight)) m.**, rejéteau *m*, jet *m* d'eau (de fenêtre, de porte); larmier *m*; (*c*) *Arch:* baguette; **arch m.**, voussure *f*; **plain m.**, listeau *m*, listel *m*; **grooved m.**, moulure à gorge; **m. machine**, machine à faire les moulures, à moulurer; **spindle m. machine**, toupie *f*; **m. plane**, rabot *m* à moulures; mouchette *f*; (*for grooves*) bouvet *m*, gorget *m*, tarabiscot *m*; (*for doucines*) doucine *f*; **neck m. plane**, congé *m*; (*d*) *N.Arch:* liston *m*; (*e*) (*goldsmith's work*) **pellet m.**, greneté *m*.

mouldwarp ['mouldwɔ:p], *s. Dial:* taupe *f*.

mouldy ['mouldi], *a.* (*a*) moisi; **m. bread, jam**, pain moisi, chanci, confiture chancie; **to go m.**, (se) moisir; **to smell m.**, sentir le moisi; (*b*) *F: O:* lamentable, moche; **to feel m.**, (i) se sentir patraque; ne pas être dans son assiette; (ii) avoir le cafard.

moulinet [mu:li'net], *s. Fenc: Danc:* moulinet *m*.

moult[1] [moult], *s.* mue *f*; **bird in the m.**, oiseau *m* en mue.

moult[2]. **1.** *v.i.* (*of bird, reptile, etc.*) muer; perdre ses plumes, sa peau, sa carapace. **2.** *v.tr.* perdre (ses plumes, sa peau, sa carapace).

moulting[1] ['moultiŋ], *a.* en mue.

moulting[2], *s.* (*of bird, reptile*) **m. (season)**, mue *f*.

mound[1] [maund], *s.* **1.** (*a*) (*artificial*) tertre *m*, monticule *m*, butte *f*; *Civ.E: etc:* remblai *m*; **low m.**, champignon *m*; **burial mound**, tumulus *m*; (*b*) monceau *m*, tas *m* (de pierres, etc.); (*c*) (*natural*) monticule; (*d*) *Orn:* **m. bird, m. builder**, mégapode *m*. **2.** *Anat: etc:* mont *m*.

mound[2], *v.* **1.** *v.tr.* (*a*) recouvrir de terre; *Petr: etc:* **mounded tank**, réservoir recouvert de terre; (*b*) *A:* entourer d'une clôture, d'un remblai de terre; fortifier (une position de batterie, etc.) au moyen d'un épaulement, d'un parapet, de terre. **2.** *v.i.* se former, s'amonceler, en monticule(s).

mound[3], *s. Her:* monde *m*; globe *m*.

mount[1] [maunt], *s.* **1.** mont *m*, montagne *f*; **M. Sinai**, le mont Sinaï. **2.** *Palmistry:* mont *m*.

mount[2], *s.* **1.** montage *m*; support *m*; (*a*) armement *m*, piètement *m* (d'une machine); bâti *m*, socle *m* (d'une machine, d'un moteur); *Artil: etc:* affût *m*; trépied *m*; affût, pied *m*, monture *f* (de télescope); pied (d'un appareil photographique, etc.); **brass mounts**, ferrures *f* en cuivre; (*b*) monture (d'une lentille, d'un prisme); **lens m.**, porte-objectif *m inv* (d'un microscope); *Phot: etc:* **flange m.**, monture normale (de l'objectif); (*c*) monture (d'un éventail); (*d*) monture (d'une pierre précieuse); (*e*) *Art: etc:* carton *m* de montage, pourtour *m* (d'un tableau, etc.); **white open m., cut m.**, passe-partout anglais; *Phot:* **sunk m.**, monture rentrante; (*f*) **stamp m.**, charnière *f* (de philatéliste). **2.** (*a*) saut *m*; **he leapt on his horse with a flying m.**, il a sauté sur son cheval d'un mouvement rapide; (*b*) *Gym:* rétablissement *m* (à la barre fixe, etc.); (*c*) *Breed:* monte *f*. **3.** (*a*) monture (d'un cavalier); cheval *m*, etc.; **my m. was a camel**, j'étais monté sur un chameau. **4.** *Turf:* monte; **jockey who has had three mounts during the day**, jockey *m* qui a eu trois montes dans la journée.

mount[3], *v.*

I. *v.i.* **1.** monter; **the blood mounted to his head**, le sang lui est monté à la tête. **2.** *Equit:* se mettre en selle; monter, sauter, à cheval. **3.** (*of total, bill, etc.*) se monter, s'élever (**to so much**, à tant).

II. *v.tr. & i.* **1. to m. (on) a chair**, monter sur une chaise; **to m. (on) the scaffold**, monter sur l'échafaud; **to m. the throne**, monter sur le trône; **to m. the pulpit**, monter en chaire; **to m. the breach**, monter sur la brèche; (*of car, etc.*) **to m. the pavement**, monter sur le trottoir; *Gym:* **to m. (on a horizontal bar, etc.)**, faire un rétablissement (à la barre fixe, etc.); **by mounting on one another's shoulders**, en faisant la courte échelle. **2. to m. (on) a horse, a bicycle**, monter sur, enfourcher, un cheval, une bicyclette; sauter à cheval; **horse hard to m.**, cheval *m* difficile au montoir. **3.** *Breed:* (*of male*) couvrir (une femelle).

III. *v.tr.* **1.** monter, gravir (l'escalier, une colline); **to m. a ladder**, monter à une échelle; **to m. a stepladder**, monter sur un escabeau. **2. to m. s.o. (on a horse)**, (i) hisser qn sur un cheval; (ii) pourvoir (qn) d'un cheval; **to m. a squadron of cavalry**, monter un escadron de cavalerie. **3.** (*a*) fixer (qch.) sur la monture; mettre (qch.) sur (son) pied, sur (son) socle; mettre (une machine, un moteur) sur (son) bâti; (*b*) *Artil: etc:* **to m. a gun**, mettre un canon, une pièce, sur (son) affût; **to m. the gun**, mettre la mitailleuse, la pièce, sur le trépied, sur l'affût; (ii) déployer le bipied du fusil mitrailleur); **to m. guns in a battery, in a fort**, armer une batterie, un fort; **fort, ship, mounting eighty guns**, fort, vaisseau, armé de quatre-vingts canons; **to m. the guns in their emplacements**, mettre les pièces en batterie; (*c*) **to m. guard**, monter la garde. **4.** (*a*) monter, installer (une machine, un moteur, etc.); monter, armer (un métier à tisser, etc.); monter (une scie, un outil); monter, sertir (une pierre précieuse); sertir (une lentille, un objectif photographique, etc.) dans une monture; *Fish:* monter, empiler (un hameçon); entoiler, monter (un tableau, une photographie, une carte (géographique)); monter, naturaliser (une fourrure, etc.); **diamonds mounted in platinum**, diamants montés sur platine, sertis de platine; (*b*) *Th:* mettre (une pièce) à la scène; (*c*) *Mil: etc:* **to m. an offensive (action), a landing operation**, monter une offensive, une opération de débarquement.

IV. (*compound verb*) **mount up**, *v.i.* croître, monter, augmenter; **the bill was mounting up**, la facture augmentait; **it all mounts up**, les petits ruisseaux font les grandes rivières; tout fait nombre.

mountain ['mauntin], *s.* **1.** (*a*) montagne *f*; **range, chain, of mountains, m. range, chain**, chaîne *f* de montagnes; **the Italian mountains**, les montagnes de l'Italie; **the Rocky Mountains**, les montagnes Rocheuses; **to spend one's holidays in the mountains**, passer ses vacances à la montagne; **the seaside is pleasant enough, but I prefer mountains**, la plage n'est pas désagréable, mais je préfère la montagne; **to make a m. out of a molehill**, (se) faire une montagne d'un obstacle insignifiant; se faire d'une mouche un éléphant; se faire d'un œuf un bœuf; se faire des monstres de tout; **he makes a m. out of every molehill**, il se noierait dans une goutte d'eau, dans un crachat; **the waves rose m. high**, les vagues étaient hautes, se dressaient, comme des montagnes; **if the m. won't go to Mohammed, Mohammed must go to the m.**, si la montagne ne vient pas à nous il faut aller à elle; **m. scenery**, paysage *m* de montagne; **m. pass**, col *m*; défilé *m* (de montagne); **m. stream**, ruisseau *m* de montagne; **m. flowers**, fleurs *f* des montagnes; **m. pasture**, pâturage *m* de montagne; montagne à vaches; **m. retreat**, retraite montagnarde; **m. tribe**, tribu montagnarde; **m. rescue**, secours *m* en montagne; **m. sickness**, mal *m* de montagne; (*b*) *Z:* **m. sheep**, mouton *m* des montagnes Rocheuses; **m. panther**, once *f*; léopard *m* des neiges; (*c*) *Bot:* **m. pine**, pin *m* de montagne; **m. ash**, sorbier *m* des oiseaux, des oiseleurs; sorbier commun, sauvage; arbre *m* à grives; cochène *m*; **m. rice**, orysopsis *m*; (*d*) *Miner:* **m. cork**, liège *m* fossile, de montagne; **m. leather**, cuir *m* fossile, de montagne; **m. paper**, carton fossile, minéral, de montagne; **m. soap**, savon blanc, minéral, de montagne; (*e*) *Mil:* **m. troops**, troupes alpines, de montagne; **m. infantry**, infanterie alpine, de montagne; **m. rifle battalion**, bataillon *m* de chasseurs alpins; **m. artillery**, artillerie *f* de montagne; **m. battery**, batterie *f* de montagne; **m. gun**, canon *m*, pièce *f*, de montagne; **m. warfare**, guerre *f* en montagne; (*f*) **a (whole) m.**, (**of cabbages, of papers, etc.**), une montagne, un tas énorme (de choux, de documents, etc.); *F:* **a great m. of a man**, un colosse, une armoire à glace. **2.** *Hist:* **the M.**, la Montagne (parti de Robespierre et de Danton).

mountaineer[1] [maunti'niər], *s.* **1.** *A:* montagnard; -arde. **2.** alpiniste *mf*.

mountaineer[2], *v.i.* faire de l'alpinisme.

mountaineering [maunti'niəriŋ], *s.* alpinisme *m*.

mountainous ['mauntinəs], *a.* **1.** (pays, etc.) montagneux. **2. m. seas**, vagues hautes comme des montagnes.

mountant ['mauntənt], *s. Phot:* colle *f* pour épreuves.

mountebank ['mauntibæŋk], *s.* (*a*) saltimbanque *m*, bateleur *m*, faiseur *m* de tours, baladin *m*; (*b*) charlatan *m*; **political m.**, paillasse *m*, cabotin *m*, polichinelle *m*, de la politique.

mounted ['mauntid], *a.* **1.** monté; (*of precious stone*) monté, serti; *Artil: etc:* (canon) (mis) sur affût; (mitrailleuse) (mise) sur trépied, sur affût. **2.** monté (à cheval); **the m. police**, la police montée; **the Royal Canadian M. Police**, la Gendarmerie royale du Canada; **well m., badly m., troops**, troupes bien, mal, montées.

mounter ['mauntər], *s.* monteur, -euse (de photographies, de diamants, de machines, etc.); metteur *m* en œuvre (de diamants, etc.).

Mountie ['maunti], *s. F:* membre *m* de la Gendarmerie royale du Canada.

mounting ['mauntiŋ], *s.* **1.** (*a*) mise *f* (de qch.) sur (son) pied, sur (son) socle; fixation *f*, installation *f* (d'un télescope, etc.) sur sa monture; (*b*) *Artil: etc:* mise (d'un canon) sur (son) affût; mise (d'une mitrailleuse) sur (son) trépied, sur (son) affût; dépliement *m* du bipied (du fusil mitrailleur); (*c*) *Mec.E:* montage *m*, assemblage *m*, installation (d'une machine, d'un moteur, etc.); **antivibration m.**, montage antivibrations; **floor m.**, montage sur le sol; **frame m.**, montage sur cadre; **panel m.**, montage sur panneau; **pillar m.**, montage sur colonnette(s), sur pilotis; **rack m.**, montage sur châssis; **wall m.**, montage mural; **m. bracket**, support *m*, patte *f*, de montage; **m. flange, m. lug, m. pad**, bride *f*, patte, de montage, d'assemblage, de fixation; **m. pin**, goupille *f* d'assemblage, axe *m* de fixation; **m. screw**, vis *f* d'assemblage, de fixation; (*d*) collage *m*, entoilage *m*, montage (d'une photographie, d'un tableau); entoilage, montage (d'une carte (géographique)); *Phot:* **dry m.**, collage à sec; **dry m. tissue**, adhésif *m*; **m. paper**, papier *m* d'emmargement; (*e*) *Fish:* montage, empilage *m* (d'un hameçon); (*f*) *Th:* mise à la scène (d'une pièce); (*g*) *Equit:* **m. block**, montoir *m*. **2.** (*a*) support *m*; armement *m*, pietement *m* (d'une machine); bâti *m*, socle *m* (d'une machine, d'un moteur); monture *f*, garniture *f* (de fusil, etc.); monture (d'hameçon, d'éventail, etc.); **engine mountings,** pièces *f* d'assemblage d'un moteur; **iron mountings,** ferrures *f*; garniture de fer; **door mountings,** ferrures de porte; (*b*) *Artil:* affût *m*; (*of machine-gun*) affût, trépied *m*; affût-trépied *m, pl.* affûts-trépieds; **bipod m.,** support-bipied *m, pl.* supports-bipieds (de fusil-mitrailleur, etc.); **tripod m.,** affût-trépied; **cradle m.,** affût-berceau *m, pl.* affûts-berceaux; **fixed m.,** affût à poste fixe; **pedestal m.,** affût à piédestal, à pivot central; **railway m.,** affût-truc *m, pl.* affûts-trucs; **to fire with clamped m.,** (i) *Artil:* tirer avec l'affût bloqué; (ii) (*machine-gun*) tirer avec le support bloqué; (*c*) *Tex:* harnais *m* (de métier à tisser).

mourn ['mɔːn], *v.i. & tr.* pleurer, (se) lamenter, s'affliger; **to m. (for, over) sth.,** pleurer, déplorer, qch.; **to m. for s.o.,** pleurer (la mort de) qn; **to m. for one's lost youth,** pleurer sa jeunesse perdue; **you find us mourning the death of a friend,** vous nous trouvez tout tristes de la mort d'un ami; *B:* **blessed are they that m.,** heureux les affligés.

mourner ['mɔːnər], *s.* **1.** affligé, -ée; personne *f* qui porte le deuil. **2.** personne qui suit le cortège funèbre; **the mourners,** le convoi; le cortège funèbre; le deuil; **to be chief m.,** mener, conduire, le deuil. **3.** (*a*) *A:* (*professional*) pleureur, -euse; (*b*) *Art:* pleurant *m*, deuillant *m*. **4.** *NAm: Ecc:* pénitent, -ente; **mourner's bench,** le banc des pénitents.

mournful ['mɔːnful], *a.* triste, lugubre, mélancolique; *F:* (air *m*, figure *f*) d'enterrement; (voix *f*) funèbre.

mournfully ['mɔːnfuli], *adv.* tristement, lugubrement, funèbrement, mélancoliquement.

mournfulness ['mɔːnfulnis], *s.* tristesse *f* (d'un chant, etc.); aspect *m* lugubre (d'un lieu); air funèbre; air désolé (d'une campagne).

mourning[1] ['mɔːniŋ], *a.* **1.** qui pleure, s'afflige, se lamente. **2.** en deuil. **3.** *Bot:* **m. bride,** (fleur *f* de) veuve *f*.

mourning[2], *s.* **1.** tristesse *f*, affliction *f*, deuil *m*, désolation *f*; **the whole country was plunged in m.,** tout le pays était plongé dans le deuil. **2.** (*a*) deuil; **house of m.,** maison endeuillée; **m. coach,** voiture *f* d'enterrement, de deuil; (*b*) habits *m* de deuil; **in deep m.,** en grand deuil; **to go into m.,** se mettre en deuil; prendre le deuil; **m. band,** (i) crêpe *m*; brassard *m* de deuil; (ii) *Her:* litre *f*; **to wear m., be in m. (for s.o.),** porter le deuil (de qn); être en deuil (de qn); être vêtu (tout) de noir; être en noir; **to go out of m.,** quitter le deuil; *F:* **fingernails in m.,** ongles *m* en deuil; **eye in m.,** œil *m* au beurre noir.

mouse[1], *pl.* **mice** [maus, mais], *s.* **1.** *Z:* (*a*) souris *f*; **young m.,** souriceau *m*; **wood m.,** mulot *m*; souris de terre; **meadow m.,** campagnol *m*; **jumping m.,** (i) souris sauteuse de montagne; (ii) zapode *m*; **(American) white-footed m., deer m.,** péromysque *m*, souris à pattes blanches; **Papuan arboreal m.,** souris arboricole papoue; **Australian marsupial m., pouched m.,** souris marsupiale australienne; **striped grass m.,** rat rayé; **pocket m.,** pérognathe *m*; (*b*) **m. deer,** chevrotain *m*; **m. lemur,** (i) microcèbe *m*, lémur-souris *m*; (ii) ch(é)irogale *m*, lémurien inférieur. **2.** *a. & s.* **m. grey, m. colour(ed),** gris (*m*) (de) souris. **3.** *F:* (*a*) fille, femme, timide; souris; (*b*) **are you a man or a m.?** tu es un homme ou une bûche? **4.** *Bot:* **m. ear (hawkweed),** oreille *f* de souris; piloselle *f*; **m. ear (scorpion grass),** myosotis *m* (des marais), oreille de souris; **m. ear (chickweed),** céraiste (cotonneux); argentine *f*; oreille de souris; **m. ear (cress),** arabidopsis *m*; oreille de souris. **5.** *Nau:* (*a*) aiguilletage *m* (de croc); (*b*) *A:* guirlande *f*, bouton *m* (d'un cordage). **6.** contre-poids *m inv* (de fenêtre à guillotine). **7.** *P: A:* (*a*) meurtrissure *f*, bleu *m*; (*b*) œil *m* au beurre noir.

mouse[2]. **1.** *v.i.* (*a*) (*of cat, etc.*) chasser aux souris; chasser les souris; (*b*) *F:* **to m. (about),** fouiner, fureter. **2.** *v.tr. U.S:* **to m. sth. out,** dénicher qch. **3.** *v.tr. Nau:* (*a*) faire une guirlande à (un cordage); (*b*) moucheter, aiguilleter, guirlander (un croc).

mousebird ['mausbəːd], *s. Orn:* (*a*) coliou *m*, oiseau-souris *m, pl.* oiseaux-souris; (*b*) *Austr: F:* atrichornis *m*.

mousehole ['maushoul], *s.* trou *m* de souris.

mouser ['mausər], chasseur *m* de souris; (*cat, etc.*) souricier *m*; **good m.,** chat bon souricier.

mousetail ['mausteil], *s. Bot:* queue-de-rat *f, pl.* queues-de-rat; ratoncule *f*, myosure *m*.

mousetrap ['maustræp], *s.* souricière *f*; tapette *f*; **(round wire) m.,** calotte *f* à souris; **m. (cheese),** fromage (genre Cheddar), sec, de mauvaise qualité (dont on se sert pour armer une souricière); *Fr.C:* fromage à souris.

mousing ['mausiŋ], *s.* **1.** chasse *f* aux souris. **2.** *Nau:* aiguilletage *m*.

mousse [muːs], *s. Cu:* mousse *f* (au chocolat, etc.).

moustache [məs'tɑːʃ], *s.* **1.** moustache(s) *f*(*pl*); **to wear, have, a m.,** porter la moustache; **short m., clipped m.,** moustache courte, en brosse; **m. trainer,** fixe-moustaches *m inv.* **2.** *Z:* **m. monkey,** moustac *m*.

moustached [məs'tɑːʃt], *a.* moustachu.

Mousterian [mus'tiəriən], *a. & s. Prehist:* moustérien (*m*).

mousy ['mausi], *a.* **1.** (*a*) gris sale; gris pisseux; (*b*) *F:* (cheveux) queue-de-vache *inv.* **2.** (odeur, etc.) de souris. **3.** infesté de souris. **4.** (*of pers.*) qui aime à s'effacer; timide; **m. little woman,** petite souris.

mouth[1] [mauθ], *s.* (*pl.* **mouths** [mauðz]). **1.** (*of pers.*) bouche *f*; *Med:* **m. to m. artificial respiration,** bouche-à-bouche *m*; **with a pipe in his m.,** une pipe à la bouche; **to have one's m. full,** avoir la bouche pleine; **it makes one's m. water,** cela fait venir l'eau à la bouche; *O:* **to make a wry m.,** faire la moue, une grimace; *F:* **big m.,** gueulard *m*, grande gueule; **you open your m. too wide!** (i) tu ne sais pas te taire! (ii) tu demandes trop! *P:* **to shoot one's m. off,** (i) être atteint de diarrhée verbale; (ii) vendre la mèche; *A:* **to make a poor m.,** crier famine; crier, pleurer, misère; *A:* **to make mouths at s.o.,** faire des grimaces à qn; **to have a pleasant, a nasty, taste in one's m.,** avoir bonne, mauvaise, bouche; **the whole business left a nasty taste in my m.,** l'affaire m'a laissé un arrière-goût désagréable; (tout) cela m'a dégoûté; **to condemn oneself out of one's own m.,** se condamner par ses propres paroles; **she didn't dare open her m. (to speak),** elle n'osait pas ouvrir la bouche; **to put words into s.o.'s m.,** attribuer des paroles à qn; **the news spread from m. to m.,** la nouvelle s'est communiquée, a volé, de bouche en bouche; **by word of m.,** de bouche à oreille; *F:* **to be down in the m.,** avoir le cafard; *P:* **I'll stop your m. for you!** je vais te faire taire! **to stop s.o.'s m. with a bribe,** acheter le silence de qn; **to have seven mouths to feed,** avoir sept bouches à nourrir. **2.** bouche (de cheval, d'âne, de bœuf, de mouton, d'éléphant, de baleine, de poisson); gueule *f* (de chien, d'animaux carnassiers, de requin, de brochet, et autres gros poissons); *Equit:* **horse with a hard m.,** cheval fort en bouche, sans bouche, pesant à la main; cheval à l'appui lourd; **soft m.,** bouche tendre, sensible; **horse with a delicate m.,** cheval délicat d'embouchure; **to spoil a horse's m.,** égarer un cheval; *F:* **it's straight from the horse's m.,** (i) ça vient de la source; je l'ai de première main; (ii) c'est un tuyau increvable; *Ven: A:* (*of hounds*) **to give m.,** donner de la voix. **3.** (*a*) bouche (de puits, de volcan); orifice *m*, halde *f* (de puits de mine); amorce *f* (de galerie de mine); goulot *m* (de bouteille); pavillon *m* (d'entonnoir); guichet *m* (de boîte à lettres); gueule (de sac, de canon, de four); ouverture *f*, entrée *f* (de tunnel, de caverne); gueulard *m* (de haut fourneau); dégorgement *m* (d'égout); bée *f*, abée *f* (de bief); entrée *f* (de port, de rade, d'un détroit); *Tls:* lumière *f* (d'un rabot); **m. of a hole,** entrée d'un trou; (*b*) embouchure *f* (de rivière); **the mouths of the Ganges, of the Rhône,** les embouchures, les bouches, du Gange; les bouches du Rhône.

mouth[2] [mauð]. **1.** *v.tr.* (*a*) **to m. one's words,** déclamer ses phrases; (*b*) former (des mots) avec les lèvres (sans faire entendre de son); (*c*) prendre (qch.) dans la bouche; (*d*) *Equit:* assurer la bouche (d'un cheval). **2.** *v.i.* (*a*) *esp. NAm:* grimacer; faire des grimaces; (*b*) déclamer.

mouthful ['mauθful], *s.* **1.** bouchée *f*; **to swallow sth. in, at, one m.; to make one m. of sth.,** ne faire qu'une bouchée, qu'un morceau, de qch.; **not to miss a m.,** ne pas perdre un coup de dent, une bouchée; **m. of soup,** gorgée *f*, cuillerée *f*, de potage; *F:* **won't you have just a m. of soup?** tu prendras bien une petite goutte de soupe? **m. of wine,** gorgée, lampée *f*, de vin; *Swim:* **I've swallowed, got, a m. (of water),** j'ai bu une tasse, un bouillon. **2.** *F:* (*a*) mot, nom, long d'une aune, qui vous remplit la bouche; (*b*) **you've said a m.!** vous avez parlé d'or!

mouthing ['mauðiŋ], *s.* **1.** emphase *f*, enflure *f* (dans le discours). **2.** grimaces *fpl.*

mouthorgan ['mauθɔːg(ə)n], *s.* harmonica *m*.

mouthpiece ['mauθpiːs], *s.* **1.** (*a*) embouchure *f* (de chalumeau, etc.); embout *m* (de porte-voix); tuyau *m*, bout *m*, bouquin *m* (de pipe à tabac); (*b*) *Mus:* bec *m* (de clarinette, etc.); (embouchure en) bocal *m* (de cornet, etc.); (*c*) *Tp:* cornet *m*, microphone *m*; (*d*) cuvette *f* (d'un fourreau d'arme blanche). **2.** (*a*) **the m. of a party,** le porte-parole *inv* d'un parti; (*b*) *P:* avocat *m*.

mouthwash ['mauθwɔːʃ], *s. Pharm:* collutoire *m*; eau *f* dentifrice; bain *m* de bouche.

mouth-watering ['mauθwɔːt(ə)riŋ], *a.* qui fait venir l'eau à la bouche.

mouthy ['mauði], *a. F:* (*a*) fort en gueule; braillard; (*b*) emphatique, ampoulé.

mov(e)ability [muːvə'biliti], *s.* mobilité *f*.

mov(e)able ['muːvəbl]. **1.** *a.* (*a*) mobile; **m. feast,** (i) fête *f* mobile; (ii) *F:* repas pris à n'importe quelle heure; *Typ:* **m. type,** caractère(s) *m* mobile(s); mobile(s) *m*(*pl*); **m. flange,** bride *f* mobile (de tuyau); *Mec.E:* **m. gear,** baladeur *m*; *Av:* **m. surfaces,** gouvernes *f*; (*b*) *Jur:* mobilier, meuble; **m. effects,** effets mobiliers; **m. property,** biens *m* meubles. **2.** *s.pl.* **movables,** (*a*) mobilier *m*; agencements *m* amovibles; (*b*) *Jur:* biens mobiliers, biens meubles; meubles (meublants).

mov(e)ableness ['muːvəb(ə)lnis], *s.* mobilité *f*.

move[1] [muːv], *s.* **1.** (*a*) *Chess: etc:* coup *m*; **mate in four moves,** (échec et) mat en quatre coups; **knight's m.,** marche *f* du cavalier; (*at the start*) **to allow s.o. two moves,** donner deux traits à qn; **to have first m.,** avoir le trait; **to make a m.,** jouer; **to take back a m.,** déjouer; **whose m. is it?** c'est à qui de jouer? **your m.,** à vous de jouer; (*b*) coup, démarche *f*; **smart m.,** coup habile; **what's the next m.?** qu'est-ce qu'il faut faire maintenant? **the next m. is with you,** c'est (à) votre tour d'agir; **to make the first m.,** faire le premier pas; **he must make the first m.,** c'est à lui d'agir le premier; **a new m. on the part of France,** (i) une nouvelle mesure, une nouvelle démarche, une nouvelle action, (ii) un nouveau coup, une nouvelle manœuvre, de la part de la France; *F:* **he's up to every m., he knows every m. (in the game),** on ne la lui fait pas; **he's up to a m. or two,** il a plus d'un tour dans son sac; **he has made a good m.,** (i) (*at chess, draughts*) il a bien joué; (ii) *F:* il a fait acte de bonne politique. **2.** mouvement *m*; **to make a m. towards sth.,** faire un mouvement vers qch.; **we must make a m., we must be, get, on the m.,** il faut partir; en route! **time to make a m.!** il est temps de songer à partir, à nous retirer, à prendre congé; **to be always on the m.,** être toujours en mouvement; s'agiter toujours; ne jamais rester en place; ne faire qu'aller et venir; être toujours par monts et par vaux; **on the m.,** en marche; *F:* **to get a m. on,** se dépêcher; se presser; lever l'ancre; se grouiller; **get a m. on!** activez! remuez-vous un peu! secouez-vous! grouillez-vous! **3.** déménagement *m*.

move[2], *v.*

I. *v.tr.* **1.** (*a*) déplacer (un meuble, etc.); **he's always moving the furniture (about),** il aime déplacer les meubles, changer les meubles de place; **to m. sth. from its place,** changer qch. de place; déranger qch.; **to m. one's position,** changer de place; **to m. one's chair,** changer sa chaise de place; **to m. one's chair near the fire,** approcher son fauteuil du feu; **he was moved to London,** on l'a envoyé (travailler) à Londres; **we moved the bookcase into the dining room,** nous avons transporté la bibliothèque dans la salle à manger; *Sch:* **to be moved up,** passer dans la classe supérieure; **to m. troops,** déplacer des troupes; **the faith that moves mountains,** la foi qui transporte les montagnes; *Chess:* **to m. a piece,** jouer une pièce; **you m. first,** à vous le trait; (*b*) **to m. (house),** déménager; **to m. to the country,** aller s'installer à la campagne; (*c*) *Cmptr:* transférer (des informations). **2.** (*a*) remuer, bouger (la tête, etc.); **not to m. hand or foot,** ne remuer ni pied ni patte; **not to m. a muscle,** ne pas sourciller; ne pas cligner (des yeux); **stone that cannot be moved,** pierre qu'on ne peut pas bouger; **the wind was moving the branches,** le vent agitait, remuait, les branches; (*b*) mouvoir, animer (qch.); mettre (qch.) en mouvement; mettre en marche (une machine); **water moves the mill wheel,** l'eau meut, fait mouvoir, fait marcher, la roue du moulin; **moved by a spring,** mû par un ressort; (*c*) **to m. the bowels,** provoquer une selle; relâcher le ventre. **3.** (*a*) faire changer d'avis à (qn); ébranler la résolution de (qn); **he is not to be moved, nothing will m. him,** il est inébranlable, inflexible; (*b*) **to m. s.o. to do sth.,** pousser, inciter, qn à faire qch.; *Lit:* **the spirit moved him to speak,** il se sentit poussé à prendre la parole; **I'll do it when the spirit moves me,** je le ferai quand j'y serai disposé, quand cela me plaira, quand le cœur m'en dira; (*c*) émouvoir, toucher, affecter (qn); **these demonstrations don't really m. me,** ces démonstrations me touchent très peu; **moved by the news,** affecté par, de, la nouvelle; **easily moved,** émotionnable; **moved with anger,** mû par la colère; sous le coup de la colère; **to m. s.o. to anger,** provoquer la colère de qn; **to m. s.o. to laughter,** faire rire qn; **to m. s.o. to tears,** émouvoir qn (jusqu') aux larmes; toucher qn à le faire pleurer; attendrir qn; **to be easily moved to tears,** avoir la larme facile; avoir toujours la larme à l'œil; **to m. s.o. to pity,** exciter la pitié de qn; **tears will not m. him,** les larmes ne le fléchiront pas. **4.** *A:* **to m. anger, pity, laughter,** exciter la colère, la pitié, les rires. **5.** **to m. a resolution,** proposer une motion; mettre aux voix une résolution; déposer une résolution; **to m. that . . .,** faire la proposition que . . .; proposer que + *sub.*; **his counsel moved that the case be adjourned for a week,** son avocat a conclu à ce que la cause soit remise à huitaine; *v.i. Pol:* **to m. for papers,** demander que les pièces soient soumises à la Chambre; demander la publication des pièces.

II. *v.i.* **1.** (*a*) se mouvoir, se déplacer; **the crowd moving in the street,** la foule qui circule dans les rues; **the traffic was heavy but kept moving,** la circulation était intense mais fluide; **keep moving! m. along (please)!** circulez! **to m. one step,** faire un pas, se déplacer d'un pas; **to m. sideways,** se déplacer latéralement; **to m. to another seat,** changer de place; aller s'asseoir autre part; **body moving at a speed of . . .,** mobile animé d'une vitesse de . . .; **moving train,** train *m* en marche; **his hand moved over the strings,** sa main effleura les cordes (de la harpe); (*of pers.*) **to m. in high society,** fréquenter la haute société; pratiquer le grand monde; **real life does not m. on the political plane,** la vie réelle n'évolue pas sur le plan politique; (*b*) *Nau:* (*of ship*) déhaler (avec la machine, des remorqueurs, des amarres); (*c*) **to m. (about),** faire un mouvement; bouger, (se) remuer; aller et venir; **don't m.!** ne bougez pas! **lights were moving in the darkness,** des lumières *f* s'agitaient dans l'obscurité; *Mec.E:* (*of part*) **to m. freely,** jouer librement; (*d*) marcher, aller; s'avancer, défiler; **the earth moves round the sun,** la terre se meut autour du soleil; **the procession moved through the streets,** le cortège défilait par les rues; **to m. towards a place,** aller, se diriger, s'avancer, vers un endroit; **he moved with dignity,** il avait une démarche digne; **things are moving slowly,** les choses marchent, avancent, lentement; **the old man's life was moving towards its end,** la vie du vieillard s'acheminait vers sa fin; **it's time we were moving, we must be moving,** il est temps de partir; *Chess:* **the bishop moves diagonally,** le fou marche diagonalement. **2.** agir; **it is for him to m. first in the matter,** c'est à lui d'agir le premier dans l'affaire. **3.** *A:* **to m. to s.o.,** saluer qn (d'une inclination de tête).

III. (*compound verbs*) **1. move away.** (*a*) *v.tr.* écarter, éloigner (qch.); (*b*) *v.i.* s'éloigner, s'écarter, s'en aller, se retirer; **they've moved away from here,** ils ont déménagé, ils n'habitent plus ici.

2. move back. (*a*) *v.tr.* (faire) reculer; **the police moved us back on to the pavement,** la police nous fit reculer jusqu'au trottoir; (*b*) *v.i.* (i) (se) reculer; (ii) **they have moved back to London,** ils sont revenus habiter à Londres.

3. move forward. (*a*) *v.tr.* avancer (la main, etc.); faire avancer, porter en avant (des troupes); (*b*) *v.i.* (s')avancer; (*of troops*) se porter en avant.

4. move in. (*a*) *v.tr.* (i) emménager (son mobilier); (ii) *Cmptr:* introduire (une information) en mémoire; (*b*) *v.i.* (i) (*of crowd*) entrer, pénétrer, dans la salle de spectacle, etc.; (ii) emménager; s'installer (quelque part).

5. move off. (*a*) *v.i.* (i) s'éloigner, s'en aller; (*of army, train, etc.*) se mettre en marche, se mettre en branle, s'ébranler; (*of motor, etc.*) démarrer; **the train, etc., is moving off,** nous voilà partis; le train, etc., part; (ii) déboîter (d'une file d'hommes ou de véhicules); **to m. off to the right,** déboîter vers la droite; (*b*) *v.tr.* **the police moved them off,** la police les a chassés, les a fait circuler.

6. move on. (*a*) *v.tr.* faire circuler (la foule, etc.); (*b*) *v.i.* (i) avancer; continuer son chemin, passer son chemin; **m. on, please!** circulez, s'il vous plaît! **to get the crowd to m. on,** faire écouler la foule; (ii) (*of car, etc.*) se remettre en route.

7. move out. (*a*) *v.tr.* (i) sortir (qch.); faire sortir (qn); *Cmptr:* sortir (une information) de la mémoire; (ii) déménager (ses meubles); (*b*) *v.i.* déménager.

8. move over, *v.i.* se déplacer (vers le côté); se ranger; **m. over!** pousse-toi!

9. move round. (*a*) *v.tr.* tourner (la table, sa chaise, etc.); (*b*) *v.i.* tourner en rond; faire le tour (pour se rendre de l'autre côté).

10. move up, *v.i.* se déplacer, se pousser (pour faire place à qn); *Sch:* être transféré à une classe supérieure; *St.Exch:* (*of shares*) se relever; reprendre (de la valeur).

movement ['mu:vmənt], *s.* **1.** mouvement *m*; déplacement *m*; (*a*) **there was a general m. towards the door,** tout le monde s'est dirigé vers la porte; **to follow s.o.'s movements,** suivre, surveiller, les mouvements, les allées et venues, de qn; **to watch the movements of the crowd,** regarder les mouvements de la foule, regarder la foule qui circule; (*b*) mouvement, marche *f* (d'un glacier); **to study the m. of the stars,** étudier le mouvement des astres; *Ph: etc:* **Brownian m.,** mouvement brownien; **m. of ions,** mouvement des ions, mouvement ionique; **nuclear m.,** mouvement du noyau (d'un atome); mouvement nucléaire; **m. blur,** flou *m* cinématique; *T.V:* **m. of lines,** défilement *m* des lignes; (*c*) mouvement, circulation *f* (des véhicules); mouvement, déplacement, transport *m* (des marchandises); **m. control,** régulation *f* de la circulation; *Mil: etc:* **m. control officer,** officier régulateur de la circulation; **m. order,** feuille *f* de route; (*d*) *Mil: etc:* mouvement, manœuvre *f*; **parallel-to-the-front m.,** mouvement parallèle au front, mouvement de rocade; **retrograde m.,** mouvement rétrograde, de repli; **wrong m.,** fausse manœuvre; **m. area,** aire *f*, zone *f*, de manœuvre; (*e*) *Pol.Ec: etc:* circulation (des capitaux, etc.); mouvement (de baisse, de hausse) (des prix, des valeurs en bourse); **free m. of workers, of labour,** libre circulation des travailleurs, de la main-d'œuvre; **cyclical movements,** mouvements cycliques, conjoncturels. **2.** (*a*) mouvement (du bras, etc.); **m. of impatience,** geste *m* d'impatience; (*in massage*) **passive movements,** gymnastique passive; (*b*) *Physiol:* selle *f*. **3.** mouvement (politique, littéraire, religieux, etc.); **the Romantic M.,** le mouvement romantique; **the Labour M.,** le mouvement travailliste; **period marked by a strong m. towards individualism,** période marquée par un fort courant, une forte tendance, individualiste. **4.** mouvement, mécanisme (d'horlogerie). **5.** *Mus:* mouvement; **symphony in three movements,** symphonie *f* en trois mouvements.

mover ['mu:vər], *s.* **1.** moteur *m*; **God, the sovereign M. of nature,** Dieu, souverain moteur de la nature; **prime m.,** (i) *Mec:* moteur primaire; (ii) *Phil:* (*pers.*) premier moteur; premier mobile; animateur *m*, -trice, inspirateur *m*, -trice (d'un projet, etc.); **the prime m. of the enterprise,** l'âme *f* de l'entreprise. **2.** auteur *m*, proposeur *m* (d'une motion, d'une proposition); motionnaire *m*. **3.** *Chess:* **three m.,** problème *m* en trois coups.

movie ['mu:vi], *s. esp. NAm: Cin: F:* film *m*; **the movies,** le cinéma; **m. star,** vedette *f* de cinéma, de l'écran; **m. house,** cinéma.

moving[1] ['mu:viŋ], *a.* **1.** en mouvement, mobile, mouvant; (*a*) *Ph: Mec:* **m. body,** corps *m* en mouvement; mobile *m*; **m. part,** pièce *f*, organe *m*, élément *m*, mobile, en mouvement; **m. masses, m. parts,** masses *f*, parties, mobiles, en mouvement; *Atom.Ph:* **m. particle,** particule mouvante; (*b*) **m. platform,** *U.S:* **m. sidewalk,** trottoir roulant; **m. staircase, m. stairway,** escalier roulant, mobile, mécanique; (*c*) *Mil:* **m. target,** but *m*, cible *f*, mobile; objectif *m* mobile, en mouvement; **m.-target course,** exercice *m* de tir sur cible mobile; *Rad:* **m. target indicator,** éliminateur *m*, suppresseur *m*, d'échos fixes; (*d*) *El:* **m. armature,** induit *m* mobile; **m.-armature loudspeaker,** haut-parleur *m* magnétique; **m. coil,** bobine *f* mobile; **m.-coil instrument,** appareil *m* à cadre mobile; **m.-coil loudspeaker,** haut-parleur électromagnétique; **m.-coil microphone,** microphone *m* électrodynamique; (*e*) *Surv:* **m. coordinate system,** système *m* de coordonnées mobiles; (*f*) *Cin:* **m. picture,** film *m*. **2.** (*of force, etc.*) moteur, -trice; **m. power,** (i) force motrice; (ii) impulsion *f* mécanique; **the m. spirit,** l'âme *f* (d'une entreprise); le meneur du jeu. **3.** (ton, etc.) émouvant, touchant, attendrissant, pathétique; **m. story,** histoire émouvante, touchante.

moving[2], *s.* **1.** mouvement *m*, déplacement *m* (de qch.). **2.** **m. (out),** déménagement *m*; **m. (in),** emménagement *m*; **m. day,** jour *m* du déménagement; *F:* **m. man,** déménageur *m*.

movingly ['mu:viŋli], *adv.* d'une manière émouvante, touchante.

moviola [mouvi'oulə], *s. Cin:* moviola *f*.

mow[1] [mou], *s. Dial: & NAm:* **1.** (*a*) meule *f*, moie *f* (de foin); (*b*) tas *m* (de blé en grange). **2.** las *m* (de grange).

mow[2] [mau], *s. A: & Lit:* moue *f*, grimace *f*.

mow[3] [mau], *v.i. A: & Lit:* faire la moue; grimacer.

mow[4] [mou], *v.tr.* **(mowed; mown) 1.** faucher, moissonner (le blé, un champ); **to m. down the enemy,** faucher l'ennemi. **2.** tondre (le gazon).

mower ['mouər], *s.* **1.** (*pers.*) faucheur, -euse. **2.** (*machine*) faucheuse *f*; **(lawn) m.,** tondeuse *f* (de gazon); **motor m.,** (i) faucheuse, (ii) tondeuse, mécanique, à moteur.

mowing ['mouiŋ], *s.* **1.** (*a*) fauchage *m*, moissonnage *m* (du foin, etc.); (*b*) tonte *f*, tondaison *f* (du gazon); (*c*) **m. machine,** (i) faucheuse *f*; (ii) tondeuse *f* (de gazon). **2.** fauchée *f*.

moxa ['mɔksə], *s. Med:* moxa *m*.

moxie ['mɔksi], *s. NAm: P:* **1.** courage *m*, cran *m*. **2.** savoir-faire *m*, habileté *f*.

Mozabite ['mɔzəbait]. *Geog:* (*a*) *a.* mozabite; (*b*) *s.* Mozabite *mf*.

Mozambican, Mozambiquan [mouzæm'bi:kən], *a. & s.* (habitant, -ante, originaire *mf*) du Mozambique.

Mozambique [mouzæm'bi:k]. *Pr.n.* Mozambique *m*.

Mozarab [mɔ'zærəb], *s. Rel.H:* Mozarabe *mf*.

Mozarabic [mɔ'zærəbik], *a. Rel.H: Arch:* mozarabique, mozarabe.

mozetta [mɔ'zetə], *s. Ecc.Cost:* mosette *f*.

Mr ['mistər], (*form of address; not used without name*) **Mr Thomas,** Monsieur Thomas.

Mrs ['misiz], (*form of address; not used without name*) **Mrs Long,** Madame Long.

M/s [miz], (*form of address; not used without name*) **M/s Martin,** (i) Mademoiselle, (ii) Madame, Martin.

mu[1] [mju:], *s.* **1.** *Gr.Alph:* mu *m*. **2.** *Ph.Meas:* millimicron *m*; nanomètre *m*. **3.** *W.Tel:* **mu (factor),** coefficient *m* d'amplification.

mu[2], *s.* (*abbrev. of* '*mutual conductance*') *W.Tel:* pente *f*; **variable mu valve,** lampe *f* à pente variable.

much [mʌtʃ]. **1.** *a.* (*a*) beaucoup (de); bien (du, de la, des); **m. care,** beaucoup de soin; bien des soins; **I had m. difficulty in convincing her,** j'ai eu beaucoup de mal à la convaincre; **we haven't had m. rain,** nous n'avons pas eu beaucoup de pluie; il n'a pas plu beaucoup; *Iron:* **m. good may it do you!** grand bien vous fasse! **we haven't m. garden,** notre jardin est bien petit; (*b*) **how m.?** combien? **how m. bread?** combien de pain? **how m. time do you need?** combien de temps vous faut-il? **how m. is it?** c'est combien? combien cela coûte-t-il? **how m. a kilo is it?** c'est combien, cela coûte combien, le kilo? **2.** *adv.* beaucoup, bien; **(very) m. better,** beaucoup mieux; **m. worse,** bien pis; **it doesn't matter m.,** cela ne fait pas grand-chose; ce n'est pas très important; **he's m. richer than I am,** il est beaucoup plus riche que moi; **m. less pleasant,** beaucoup moins agréable; **I don't like it very m.,** cela ne me plaît guère; **m. to be desired,** fort à désirer; **m. the largest,** de beaucoup le plus grand; le plus grand de beaucoup; **thank you very m. (for . . .),** merci beaucoup, je vous remercie infiniment (de . . .); **I enjoyed it very m.,** cela m'a fait bien du plaisir; **m. the same age, m. of an age,** à peu près du même âge; **it's (pretty, very) m. the same thing,** c'est à peu près la même chose; **he's m. (about) the same,** il est toujours pareil; **m. to my astonishment, m. to my regret,** à mon grand étonnement, à mon grand regret; **I don't want two, m. less three,** il ne m'en faut pas deux, encore moins trois; *P:* **not m. (he doesn't, etc.)!** et comment! **3.** *s.* (*a*) **m. still remains to be done,** il reste encore beaucoup à faire; **m. has happened while you have been away,** il s'est passé bien des choses pendant votre absence; **I'm not paid m.,** je ne suis pas payé lourd; **m. of the paper is damaged,** une bonne partie du papier est avariée; **the total does not amount to m.,** le total ne s'élève pas à une très forte somme; **there is not m. of it,** il n'y en a pas beaucoup; **do you see m. of one another?** vous voyez-vous souvent? **there is not m. to see,** il n'y a pas grand-chose à voir; **to have m. to be thankful for,** avoir tout lieu d'être reconnaissant; **it's not worth m.,** *F:* **it's not up to m.,** cela ne vaut pas grand-chose; cela ne vaut pas cher; ce n'est pas fameux; **he's not up to m.,** (i) il ne vaut pas grand-chose; (ii) il n'est pas dans son assiette; **his work isn't up to m.,** son travail est quelconque; **there's not m. in it, nothing m. in it,** (i) *Turf: Sp:* les chances sont à peu près égales; (ii) *F:* ça se vaut; **there's not m. in him,** il manque d'étoffe; il n'a rien de remarquable; **no matter how m. of a quack he is, I believe in him,** quelque charlatan qu'il puisse être, j'ai confiance en ses soins; **he's not m. of a scholar,** ce n'est pas ce qu'on appelle un savant; **he wasn't m. of a teacher,** il ne valait pas grand-chose comme professeur; **I'm not m. of a theatre goer,** je ne vais guère au théâtre; **he's not m. of a father,** ce n'est pas le modèle des pères; **he's, she's, not m. to look at,** ce n'est pas une beauté; **not m. of a dinner,** un dîner médiocre; un pauvre dîner; *Iron:* **m. he knows about it!** il n'en sait absolument rien! comme s'il y connaissait quelque chose! *Prov:* **m. will have more,** l'appétit vient en mangeant; (*b*) **this m.,** autant que ceci; **that m.,** autant que cela; **this m., that m., too big,** trop grand de ceci, de cela; **the sleeves are too long by that m.,** les manches sont trop longues de tout cela; **cut that m. off,** coupez-en long comme ça; **give me that m.,** donnez-m'en cette quantité-là; **can you spare this m.?** pouvez-vous me donner un bout comme ça? **I'll say this m. for him,** je dirai ceci en sa faveur; **he did tell me that m.,** voilà ce qu'il m'a dit; **he admitted that m.,** il est allé jusque-là dans ses aveux; **there's not (all) that m.,** il n'y en a pas tellement; **this m. is certain, that . . .,** il y a ceci de certain que . . .; **you haven't grown up without knowing that m.,** vous n'avez pas grandi sans savoir au moins cela; (*c*) **to make m. of sth.,** (i) attacher beaucoup d'importance à qch.; faire beaucoup de cas, grand cas, de qch.; (ii) vanter qch.; **m. has been made of the incident,** on a beaucoup parlé de cet incident; **to make m. of s.o.,** (i) faire fête à qn; être aux petits soins pour qn, auprès de qn; (ii) câliner, choyer, dorloter, mignoter (un enfant, etc.); (iii) flatter qn; **to make m. of a horse,** caresser un cheval; faire des caresses à un cheval; **I didn't make m. of that book,** je n'ai pas compris grand-chose à ce livre; **I don't think m. of it,** j'en fais peu de cas; je n'en fais pas grand cas; ça ne me dit pas grand-chose; **I don't think m. of his work,** je n'ai pas une bien haute idée de son travail; **I don't think m. of him,** (i) je ne l'estime pas beaucoup; (ii) il ne m'est guère sympathique. **4.** *adv.phrs.* (*a*) **m. as,** pour autant; **m. as I like him,** quelle que soit mon affection pour lui; **m. as we should like to help you,** pour autant que nous voudrions vous aider; **m. as I dislike it,** pour autant que cela me déplaise; j'ai beau ne pas l'aimer; **m. as I tried I could never find it again,** j'ai eu beau chercher, je ne l'ai pas retrouvé; (*b*) **as m.,** autant (de); **as m. again,** encore autant; **one and a half times as m., half as m. again,** moitié plus; la moitié en plus; **quite as m.,** tout autant; **twice as m. water,** deux fois autant d'eau; **three times as m.,** trois fois autant, *occ.* deux fois autant; **I expected as m., I thought as m., I guessed as m.,** je m'y attendais; c'est (bien) ce que je pensais; je m'en doutais bien; **can you do as m.?** êtes-vous capable d'en faire autant? **I'll help you, but you must do as m. for me,** je vais vous obliger, mais c'est à titre de revanche, c'est à charge d'autant; **there is as m. to be said about him,** il y en a autant à dire de lui; (*c*) **as m. as,** autant que; **as m. as possible,** autant que possible; **do as m. as you can,** faites(-en) autant que vous pourrez; **I have three times as m. as I want,** j'en ai trois fois plus qu'il ne m'en faut; j'en ai trois fois autant qu'il m'en faut; **quite as m. as . . .,** tout autant que . . .; non moins que . . .; **it is as m. your fault as mine,** c'est autant votre faute que la mienne; **he hates you as m. as you like him,** autant vous l'aimez, autant il vous déteste; **it is as m. as he can do to keep out of debt,** il a toutes les peines du monde à ne pas contracter des dettes; **it is as m. as he can do to read,** c'est tout juste s'il sait lire; **it was as m. as I could do not to cry,** je me tenais à quatre pour retenir mes larmes; **it is as m. as saying that I am a liar,** autant dire que je mens; **he looked at me as m. as to say . . .,** il me regarda avec l'air de (vouloir) dire . . .; **I would give as m. as fifty pounds,** j'irais jusqu'à cinquante livres; **the wall must be as m. as 20 metres high,** le mur ne doit pas avoir moins de 20 mètres de haut; (*d*) **as m. (as), so m. (as),** tant (que), autant (que); **to like nothing as m. as fighting,** n'aimer rien (au)tant que de se battre; **one cannot say so m. for everybody,** on ne peut pas en dire autant de tout le monde; **he does not like me as m. as her,** il ne m'aime pas autant qu'il l'aime; **do you owe him as m. as that?** est-ce que vous lui devez autant que cela? **do you love her as m. as that?** vous l'aimez donc tant, à ce point-là? **he is not so m. a scholar as a writer,** il est plutôt un écrivain qu'un érudit; **oceans do not so m. divide the world as unite it,** les océans ne divisent pas tant le monde qu'ils l'unissent; **I would not even have done so m.,** je n'en aurais pas même fait autant; **I haven't so m. as my fare,** je n'ai pas même, seulement, le prix de mon voyage; **he went away without so m. as saying goodbye,** il s'en est allé sans même dire au revoir; **he would not so m. as look at it,** il n'a pas même voulu le regarder; **I would not so m. as raise a finger to help him,** je ne lèverais pas même, pas seulement, le petit doigt pour l'aider; (*e*) **so m.,** tant (de), autant (de); **so m. money,** tant d'argent; **I did not know he was so m. respected,** je ne le savais pas autant respecté; **so m. of his time is spent on trifles,** il perd une si grande partie de son temps à des vétilles; **he has drunk so m. that . . .,** il a tant, tellement, bu que . . .; **that's so m. to the good,** c'est autant de gagné; **so m. the better,** tant mieux; **so m. the more, the less, as . . .,** d'autant plus, moins, que . . .; **it will be so m. the less to pay,** ce sera autant de moins à payer; **so m. so that . . .,** à ce point que . . .; au point que . . .; à tel point que . . .; *F:* à telle(s) enseigne(s) que . . .; **so m. for our journey; and now . . .,** voilà pour notre voyage; maintenant . . .; **so m. for his friendship!** et voilà ce qu'il appelle l'amitié! **so m. for that !** voilà tout ce qu'il y a à dire là-dessus; voilà une affaire finie; *F:* et d'une; **so m. for him!** voilà son compte réglé! *F:* **not so m. of it, of that!** ça suffit! (*f*) **so m. per cent,** tant pour cent; **so m. a kilo,** tant le kilo; (*g*) **too m.,** trop (de); **too m. bread,** trop de pain; **m. too m.,** beaucoup trop (de); **£10 too m.,** 10 livres de trop; **they were too m. for him,** il n'était pas de taille à leur résister; **it is too m. by half,** c'est trop de moitié; **to cost too m.,** coûter trop cher; **he was going to say too m.,** il allait trop en dire, en dire trop; **to think too m. of oneself,** s'en faire accroire; **to make too m. of sth.,** attacher trop d'importance à qch.; s'exagérer la portée de qch.; **to make too m. of trifles,** (i) s'attacher superstitieusement aux choses sans intérêt; (ii) attacher trop d'importance à des vétilles; **don't make too m. of it,** ne vous impressionnez pas; ne vous frappez pas; **this author has been made too m. of,** on a surfait cet auteur; **this is (really) too m.!** *F:* **that's a bit m.!** c'est vraiment trop fort! **that's too m. of a good thing,** cela passe la mesure; cela passe les bornes; **one can have too m. of a good thing,** tout lasse à la fin; **you can't have too m. of a good thing,** abondance de bien ne nuit pas; **too m. is as bad as none at all,** trop et trop peu n'est pas mesure.

muchly ['mʌtʃli], *adv. F:* beaucoup.

muchness ['mʌtʃnis], *s.* **1.** *A:* (*a*) quantité *f*; (*b*) grandeur *f.* **2.** *F:* **it's much of a m.,** c'est bonnet blanc et blanc bonnet; c'est chou vert et vert chou; c'est kif-kif.

muciform ['mju:sifɔ:m], *a.* muciforme.

mucigen ['mju:sidʒen], *s. Bio-Ch:* mucigène *m.*

mucilage ['mju:silidʒ], *s.* **1.** mucilage (végétal, animal). **2.** *esp. NAm:* colle *f* (de bureau); colle de poisson, gomme *f* arabique.

mucilaginous [mjusi'lædʒinəs], *a.* mucilagineux.

mucin ['mju:sin], *s. Ch:* mucine *f.*

muck[1] [mʌk], *s.* **1.** (*a*) fumier *m*; **horse m.,** crottin *m* de cheval; *Agr:* **m. spreader,** épandeur *m*; (*b*) fange *f*; (*from the streets*) crotte *f,* ordures *fpl*; (*from drain, etc.*) curures *fpl*; (*from machinery*) cambouis *m*; **to be all covered in m.,** être crotté de la tête aux pieds; *F:* **to be in a m. sweat,** être tout en nage; suer à grosses gouttes; *F:* **where there's m. there's money,** on trouve de l'argent dans les ordures. **2.** *F:* (i) saletés *fpl,* choses dégoûtantes; (ii) camelote *f*; **I must clear up all this m.,** il me faut me débarrasser de toutes ces saletés; **this book's awful m.,** ce livre ne vaut absolument rien, n'est qu'une suite de bêtises; **they serve nothing but m. in this restaurant,** dans ce restaurant il n'y a rien de mangeable, on ne sert que des saletés; **I shan't buy anything here—there's nothing but m.,** je ne vais rien acheter ici; il n'y a que de la camelote. **3.** *F:* (*a*) confusion *f,* désordre *m,* pagaille *f*; **I must clear up the m. before getting down to work,** il me faut tout remettre en ordre avant de me mettre au travail; (*b*) **to make a m. (up) of sth.,** faire un véritable gâchis de qch. **4.** *Metall:* **m. bar,** barre *f* de fer brut; ébauché *m*; **m. iron,** fer ébauché; **m. roll,** dégrossisseur *m.*

muck[2], *v.*

I. *v.tr.* (*a*) **to m. (out) a stable,** nettoyer une écurie; (*b*) salir, souiller, crotter (qch.); (*c*) *F:* **to m. (up) a job,** bousiller un travail; **you've mucked it (up) completely,** tu as fait un beau gâchis.

II. (*compound verbs*) **1. muck about, around,** *v.i. F:* (*a*)traîner, flâner; bricoler; (*b*) **don't m. me about,** (i) ne dérange pas, ne salis pas, ma robe, etc.; (ii) *P:* laissez-moi tranquille! à bas les pattes!

2. muck in, *v.i. F:* **to m. in with s.o.,** chambrer avec qn; faire gourbi ensemble; *F:* **he mucks in well with us,** nous nous entendons bien tous ensemble.

mucker ['mʌkər], *s. P:* **1.** (*pers.*) *esp. NAm:* homme grossier, rustre *m.* **2.** chute *f,* culbute *f,* bûche *f*; **to come a m.,** tomber, ramasser un billet de parterre.

muckheap ['mʌkhi:p], *s.* tas *m* de fumier, d'ordures; *F:* **that's only fit for the m.,** ça, c'est à jeter, à mettre à la poubelle.

muckiness ['mʌkinis], *s.* saleté *f,* malpropreté *f.*

muckite ['mʌkait], *s. Miner:* muckite *f.*

muckle ['mʌkl], *s. Scot: See* MICKLE.

muckrake[1] ['mʌkreik], *s.* racloir *m* à boue; râteau *m* à fumier.

muckrake[2], *v.i. F:* déterrer, publier, des scandales, des cas de corruption.

muckraker ['mʌkreikər], *s. F:* déterreur *m* de scandales, *P:* fouille-merde *m inv.*

muckworm ['mʌkwə:m], *s.* **1.** (*a*) *Ent:* larve *f* du bousier; (*b*) *F:* ver *m* de fumier. **2.** *P: A:* grippe-sou *m, pl.* grippe-sous; avare *mf*; ladre, *f.* ladresse; pingre *m.*

mucky ['mʌki], *a.* sale, crotté, souillé, malpropre; *F:* (*to child*) **you're a m. pup!** que tu es sale!

mucocele ['mju:kousi:l], *s. Med:* mucocèle *f.*

mucoid ['mju:kɔid], *s. Bio-Ch:* mucoïde *m.*

mucoitin-sulphuric [mju'kɔitinsʌl'fju:rik], *a.* (acide) mucoïtine-sulfurique.

muconic [mju'kɔnik], *a.* (acide) muconique.

mucopurulent [mjukou'pju:rjulənt], *a. Med:* muco-purulent, *pl.* muco-purulent(e)s.

mucopus ['mju:koupʌs], *s. Med:* muco-pus *m.*

mucor ['mju:kɔ:r], *s. Fung:* mucor *m.*

Mucoraceae [mjukɔ:'reisii:], *s.pl. Fung:* mucoracées *f.*

Mucorales [mjukɔ:'reili:z], *s.pl. Fung:* mucorales *f.*

mucosa [mju'kousə], *s.* muqueuse *f*; **lining m.,** muqueuse de revêtement.

mucosity [mju'kɔsiti], *s. Physiol:* mucosité *f.*

mucous ['mju:kəs], *a.* muqueux; **m. membrane,** muqueuse *f.*

mucro, *pl.* **-os, -ones** ['mju:krou, -ouz, mju'krouni:z], *s. Bot:* mucron *m,* pointe *f.*

mucronate(d) ['mju:krouneit(id)], *a. Bot:* mucroné.

mucus ['mju:kəs], *s.* **1.** *Physiol:* mucus *m,* mucosité *f,* glaire *f.* **2.** *Bot:* mucosité.

mud[1] [mʌd], *s.* (*a*) boue *f*; bourbe *f*; *Lit:* fange *f*; **(river) m.,** vase *f*; (*used as fertilizer*) wagage *m*; (*of river, etc.*) **m. bottom,** vasard *m*; **caked m.,** boue agglomérée; **to be covered in m., to be all over m.,** être crotté de la tête aux pieds, jusqu'à l'échine; **to get stuck, to sink, in the m.,** s'embourber; (*of ship*) s'envaser; **vessel stuck in the m.,** navire supé; *Nau:* **m. berth,** souille *f*; **m. barge, m. lighter, m. dredger,** marie-salope *f, pl.* maries-salopes; **m. hut,** hutte *f* de terre; adobe *m*; **m. wall,** mur bousillé en torchis, en pisé; *Av:* **m. strip,** piste *f* en terre; **to drag s.o.'s name in the m.,** lancer des calomnies contre qn; traîner qn dans la boue; **to fling, throw, m. at s.o.,** couvrir qn de boue, de fange; déblatérer contre qn; **if you throw m. enough some of it will stick,** calomniez, il en reste toujours quelque chose; *F:* **his name is m.,** (i) sa réputation ne vaut pas cher, est moins que rien; (ii) c'est un homme fini; *F:* **if I'm late my name will be m.,** si j'arrive en retard je vais me faire appeler Arthur; *P:* **here's m. in your eye!** à votre santé! à la (bonne) vôtre! *F:* **as clear as m.,** clair comme de l'eau de boudin, du jus de chique; (*b*) *Med:* **m. bath,** bain *m* de boue; illutation *f*; **m. cure,** illutation; **to give a patient a m. bath,** donner un bain de boue à un malade; illuter un malade; **m. poultice,** cataplasme *m* de boue; *Toil:* **m. pack, m. mask,** emplâtre *m* de boues; (*c*) *attrib. Geog: etc:* **m. avalanche,** avalanche boueuse; **m. geyser,** source jaillissante boueuse; **m. spring,** fontaine *f* de boue; **m. flat,** plaine boueuse; plage *f* de vase; *Oc:* banc *m* de boue; (*consolidated by vegetation*) tanguaie *f*; *F:* **m. pie,** pâté de sable, de boue (fait par un enfant); (*d*) *Mch:* boue; tartres boueux; **red m.,** les boues rouges; **m. hole,** trou *m* de sel (d'une chaudière); trou de vidange; vasière *f*; **m. cock,** purgeur *m*; robinet *m* d'ébouage; **m. plug,** bouchon *m* de nettoyage; **m. scraper,** décrottoir *m* (de cylindre compresseur); **m. shovel,** bogue *f*; (*e*) *Petr:* **(drilling) m.,** boue (de forage); **m. pit,** bassin *m* à boue; **m. mixer,** mélangeur *m* de boue; **m. socket,** cuiller *f* à clapet (pour l'extraction des boues); **m. chemicals,** produits *m* pour boue; (*f*) *Ich:* **m. minnow,** umbre *m*; **m. pusser,** molliensie *f*; *Amph:* **m. puppy,** salamandre géante américaine ((i) cryptobranche *m*; (ii) axolotl *m*; (iii) necture *m*); *Echin:* **m. star,** luidia *m*; *Rept:* **m. turtle, m. terrapin, m. tortoise,** tortue bourbeuse; *Ent:* **m. dauber,** (i) pélopée *m,* scéliphron *m*; (ii) guêpe maçonne.

mud[2], *v.* **(mudded) 1.** *v.tr.* (*a*) recouvrir de boue; (*b*) enterrer, enfouir, dans la boue; (*c*) rendre bourbeux, troubler (un liquide); (*d*) *Petr:* **to m. (off),** obturer avec de la boue, embouer (une venue de liquide). **2.** *v.i.* (*of fish, etc.*) se dissimuler, s'enfouir, s'enfoncer, dans la boue.

mudar [mʌ'dɑ:r], *s. Bot: Pharm:* calotropis *m*; mudar *m.*

mudbank ['mʌdbæŋk], *s.* (*in river, etc.*) banc vaseux.

mudded ['mʌdid], *a.* crotté; couvert de boue; (*of pers.*) **m. all over,** crotté jusqu'à l'échine, jusqu'aux oreilles; crotté comme un barbet.

muddied ['mʌdid], *a.* **1.** = MUDDED. **2.** (cours d'eau) bourbeux.

muddiness ['mʌdinis], *s.* **1.** état crotté; saleté *f.* **2.** turbidité *f,* état *m* trouble (d'un liquide).

mudding ['mʌdiŋ], *s. Petr: etc:* **m. (off),** embouage *m.*

muddle[1] ['mʌdl], *s.* confusion *f,* emmêlement *m,* embrouillement *m,* (em)brouillamini *m,* fouillis *m*; **to be in a m.,** (i) (*of thgs*) être en confusion, en désordre, en pagaille; (ii) (*of pers.*) avoir les idées brouillées; **to get into a m. (about sth.),** s'embrouiller (au sujet de qch.); **his business was in a complete m.,** ses affaires étaient complètement embrouillées, en désordre, en pagaille.

muddle[2], *v.*

I. *v.tr.* (*a*) embrouiller, brouiller (qch.); emmêler (une histoire); brouiller, gâcher (une affaire); **to m. things (up),** embrouiller les choses; *F:* brouiller les fils; **to m. (up) a drawer,** déranger un tiroir; tripoter, *F:* farfouiller, dans un tiroir; **business muddled from the start,** affaire mal emmanchée; (*b*) brouiller l'esprit à (qn); embrouiller (qn).

II. (*compound verbs*) **muddle along, on, through,** *v.i.* vivre au jour le jour; se débrouiller, s'en tirer, tant bien que mal.

muddled ['mʌd(ə)ld], *a.* **1.** (*of thgs*) brouillé; en désordre. **2.** (*of pers.*) (*a*) confus, brouillé, embrouillé; (*b*) **m. with drink,** un peu gris; éméché; hébété par la boisson.

muddlehead ['mʌdlhed], *s.* brouillon, -onne.

muddleheaded [mʌdl'hedid], *a.* à l'esprit confus; brouillon, -onne; **m. ideas,** idées confuses, embrouillées.
muddleheadedness [mʌdl'hedidnis], *s.* confusion *f* d'esprit.
muddler ['mʌdlər], *s.* brouillon, -onne; esprit brouillon.
muddling ['mʌdliŋ], *a.* **1.** (*of pers.*) qui embrouille tout; brouillon, -onne. **2.** (*of thg*) qui embrouille l'esprit.
muddy[1] ['mʌdi], *a.* **1.** (*a*) (chemin) boueux, fangeux, bourbeux, détrempé; (cours d'eau) bourbeux, vaseux, limoneux; *Nau:* **m. bottom,** fond *m* de vase; (*b*) (vêtement, etc.) crotté, couvert de boue. **2.** (*a*) (liquide *m*, vin *m*, etc.) trouble; **m. ink,** encre pâteuse, épaisse; (*b*) (couleur) sale, enfumée; (lumière *f*) terne (dans le brouillard, etc.); **m. complexion,** teint brouillé, terreux. **3. to taste m.,** avoir un goût de vase.
muddy[2], *v.tr.* **1.** encrotter, crotter (ses habits, etc.). **2.** (*a*) troubler (l'eau); (*b*) brouiller (le teint).
mud-eating ['mʌdi:tiŋ], *a. Z:* limivore, pélophage.
Mudejar ['mu:deiha:r]. *Hist: Arch:* (*a*) *a.* mudéjar; (*b*) *s.* Mudéjar, -are.
mudfish ['mʌdfiʃ], *s. Ich:* amie *f.*
mudguard ['mʌdga:d], *s.* garde-boue *m inv*, pare-boue *m inv* (de véhicule); *A:* aile *f* (d'automobile).
mudlark[1] ['mʌdla:k], *s.* **1.** *Orn: Austr:* grailline *f.* **2.** *F:* gamin *m* des rues; loupiot *m.*
mudlark[2], *v.i. F:* (*of street urchins*) jouer dans le ruisseau.
mudskipper ['mʌdskipər], *s. Ich: F:* gobie marcheur, des marais.
mudslinger ['mʌdsliŋər], *s. F:* calomniateur, -trice; médisant, -ante.
mudslinging ['mʌdsliŋiŋ], *s. F:* calomnies *fpl*; médisance *f.*
mud-stained ['mʌdsteind], *a.* (vêtement) souillé de boue.
mudworm ['mʌdwə:m], *s.* appât *m* de vase.
mudwort ['mʌdwə:t], *s. Bot:* limoselle *f.*
muezzin [mu'ezin], *s.* muezzin *m.*
muff[1] [mʌf], *s.* **1.** *Cost:* manchon *m.* **2.** *Mec.E:* manchon d'accouplement (de tuyaux); **m. coupling,** (i) accouplement *m* à manchon; (ii) manchon d'accouplement.
muff[2], *s. F:* **1.** (*pers.*) empoté *m*; andouille *f*, tourte *f*, cornichon *m*, nouille *f.* **2.** *Sp:* coup raté; **to make a m. of a catch, etc.,** rater la balle, etc.; rater, louper, son coup.
muff[3], *v.tr. F:* rater, bousiller, louper; *Golf: etc:* **to m. a shot, a stroke,** manquer, rater, un coup; *Cr: etc:* **to m. a catch,** rater, manquer, une balle (en essayant de l'attraper).
muffetee [mʌfi'ti:], *s. A:* manchette *f* de tricot; miton *m.*
muffin ['mʌfin], *s. Cu:* (*NAm:* **English m.**) muffin *m*; *A:* **m. man,** marchand de muffins ambulant; **m. bell,** sonnette *f* de marchand de muffins; *F:* **m. face,** visage rond sans expression.
muffle[1] ['mʌf(ə)l], *s.* mufle *m* (de bœuf, de vache).
muffle[2], *s.* **1.** *Cost:* moufle *f*, mitaine *f.* **2.** *Metall: Cer:* moufle *m*; **m. furnace,** (four *m* à) moufle.
muffle[3], *v.tr.* **1.** emmitoufler; **to m. oneself up,** s'emmitoufler; **to m. up one's throat,** s'emmitoufler la gorge. **2.** (*a*) envelopper (qch., pour amortir, assourdir, voiler, le son); assourdir (les avirons, une cloche); *Mus:* voiler, assourdir (un tambour); (*b*) **the carpet muffles every footstep,** le tapis éteint, étouffe, tout bruit de pas; **the snow muffled the approaches to the camp,** la neige ouatait les abords du camp; (*c*) envelopper la tête, la bouche, de (qn, pour l'empêcher de crier); bâillonner (qn).
muffled ['mʌf(ə)ld], *a.* **1.** emmitouflé. **2.** (son) sourd; (aviron) assourdi; **m. drums,** tambours voilés; **m. voice,** voix étouffée.
muffler ['mʌflər], *s.* **1.** cache-nez *m inv*; cache-col *m, pl.* cache-col(s). **2.** *A:* (*a*) *Box:* gant *m*; (*b*) *F:* moufle *f*, mitaine *f.* **3.** (*a*) *Mus:* étouffoir *m* (de piano); (*b*) *Mch:* **(exhaust) m.,** (i) gueule-de-loup *f, pl.* gueules-de-loup; (ii) *I.C.E:* pot *m* d'échappement; silencieux *m.*
muffling ['mʌfliŋ], *s.* assourdissement *m* (d'un tambour, d'une cloche).
mufti ['mʌfti], *s.* **1.** *Moslem Rel:* mufti *m*, muphti *m.* **2.** *Mil: etc:* tenue civile; **in m.,** en civil.
mug[1] [mʌg], *s.* **1.** (*for beer*) chope *f*, pot *m*; (*for tea, etc.*) (grosse) tasse (à parois verticales); gobelet *m*; (*made of metal*) timbale *f.* **2.** *F:* (*a*) visage *m*, fiole *f*, binette *f*; **nice little m.,** jolie petite frimousse; *P:* **ugly m.,** vilain museau, gueule *f* d'empeigne; (*b*) *esp. NAm:* photo *f* (*esp.* d'un criminel); **mugs and dabs,** photo et empreintes digitales; (*c*) bouche *f*, bec *m*; *P:* **shut your (ugly) m.!** ta gueule! la ferme! **3.** *F:* (*pers.*) (*a*) dupe *f*, poire *f*; **it's a mug's game,** c'est bon pour les poires; **to be had for a m.,** être trompé, dupé; (*b*) idiot, -ote; andouille *f*; nouille *f*; (*c*) *Sch: O:* bûcheur, -euse; potasseur *m.*
mug[2], *v.* **(mugged)** *esp. NAm: F:* **1.** *v.tr.* photographier (un criminel). **2.** *v.i.* faire des grimaces (soi-disant amusantes).
mug[3], *v.tr. Sch: F:* **to m. up a subject,** bûcher, potasser, un sujet.
mug[4], *v.tr. F:* attaquer (qn) à main armée; tabasser (qn).
mugful ['mʌgful], *s.* chope *f*, pot *m* (de bière); timbale *f* (d'eau, etc.).
mugger[1] ['mʌgər], *s. Z:* crocodile *m* des marais, de l'Inde.
mugger[2], *s. F:* voleur *m* à main armée; cogneur *m.*
mugginess ['mʌginis], *s.* **1.** chaleur *f* humide, lourdeur *f* (du temps). **2.** manque *m* d'air, odeur *f* de renfermé (d'une salle).
mugging ['mʌgiŋ], *s. F:* vol *m* avec agression; attaque *f* à main armée.
muggins ['mʌginʒ], *s.* **1.** *F:* idiot, -ote, nouille *f*, cruche *f*; **I suppose m. will have to do it!** tant pis! ce sera à moi de le faire! **2.** (*dominoes*) variété *f* de) matador *m.*
muggy ['mʌgi], *a.* **1.** (temps) mou, lourd; (temps) chaud et humide. **2.** (salle, etc.) qui manque d'air, qui sent le renfermé.
Mugilidae [mju:'dʒilidi:], *s.pl. Ich:* mugilidés *m.*
mug-up ['mʌgʌp], *s. NAm: F:* casse-croûte *f.*
mugwort ['mʌgwə:t], *s. Bot:* armoise commune; barbotine *f*; herbe *f* à cent goûts.
mugwump ['mʌgwʌmp], *s. F:* **1.** personnage important; gros bonnet; grosse légume. **2.** *Pol:* (*a*) dissident, -ente; (*b*) neutre *m.* **3.** idiot, -ote; andouille *f.*
mujik ['mu:ʒik], *s.* moujik *m.*
Mukden ['mukdən]. *Pr.n. Hist: Geog:* Moukden *m.*
mulatto [mju(:)'lætou]. **1.** *a.* (*a*) mulâtre; (*b*) (teint) basané. **2.** *s.* mulâtre *mf*; mulâtresse *f.*
mulberry ['mʌlb(ə)ri]. **1.** *s. Bot:* (*a*) mûre *f*; (*b*) **m. (bush, tree),** mûrier *m.* **2.** *Pr.n. Hist:* **M. (Harbour),** Port de la libération, port flottant.
mulch[1] [mʌltʃ], *s. Hort:* paillis *m*; litière *f* en décomposition; **surface m.,** couverture *f* d'humus.
mulch[2], *v.tr. Hort:* pailler; fumer (avec des feuilles mortes).
mulching ['mʌltʃiŋ], *s.* paillage *m*, paillement *m.*
mulct[1] [mʌlkt], *s.* amende *f.*
mulct[2], *v.tr.* **1.** *Jur:* mettre (qn) à l'amende; frapper (qn) d'une amende; *A:* mulcter (qn); **to m. s.o. (of, in) a certain sum,** infliger à qn une amende d'une certaine somme; **he was mulcted (of, in) five pounds,** on lui a imposé une amende de cinq livres; *A:* on l'a mulcté de cinq livres. **2.** priver **(s.o. of sth.,** qn de qch.); **to m. a man of a week's pay,** suspendre la solde d'un homme pour huit jours.
mule[1] [mju:l], *s.* **1. (he) m.,** mulet *m*; **(she) m., m. mare,** mule *f*; **m. foal, young m.,** muleton, -onne; jeune mulet; mulasse *f*; **m. breeder,** mulassier *m*; **m. breeding,** l'industrie mulassière; **m. path,** sentier muletier; **m. train,** équipage muletier; **m. driver,** muletier *m*; **on a m., on m. back,** à dos de mulet; **as stubborn as a m.,** têtu comme un mulet. **2. m. deer,** cerf *m* à queue noire. **3.** métis, -isse; hybride *m*; **m. canary,** arlequin *m.* **4.** *Tex:* **m. (jenny),** mule-jenny *f, pl.* mule-jennys; renvideur *m.* **5.** *U.S:* tracteur *m* électrique (pour le halage des bateaux, etc.).
mule[2], *s.* (*slipper*) mule *f.*
muleheaded [mju:l'hedid], *a. F:* têtu comme une mule.
muleteer [mju:lə'tiər], *s.* muletier *m.*
muley ['mju:li], *a. & s. U.S:* (vache) sans cornes.
mulish ['mju:liʃ], *a.* **1.** de mulet. **2.** entêté, têtu, comme un mulet; rétif; opiniâtre.
mulishly ['mju:liʃli], *adv.* avec entêtement; par pure obstination.
mulishness ['mju:liʃnis], *s.* entêtement *m*, obstination *f*; caractère têtu.
mull[1] [mʌl], *s. Tex:* **1.** mousseline *f*; **silk m.,** mousseline de soie. **2.** *Bookb:* mousseline (de relieur), singalette *f.*
mull[2], *s. F: O:* gâchis *m*; **to make a m. of sth.,** gâcher, *F:* bousiller (une affaire); rater (un coup).
mull[3], *v.tr.* **1.** *Sp:* rater, manquer (la balle); bousiller (une affaire). **2.** *F:* **to m. over an idea,** ruminer une idée; tourner une idée dans son esprit.
mull[4], *v.tr.* chauffer (du vin, de la bière) avec des épices; **mulled wine,** vin chaud épicé.
mull[5], *s. Scot:* cap *m*, promontoire *m.*
mull[6], *s. Scot:* tabatière *f.*
mull[7], *s. Geol:* mull *m.*
mulla(h) ['mʌlə], *s. Moslem Rel:* mollah *m.*
mullein ['mʌlin], *s. Bot:* molène *f*, cierge *m*; **great m.,** molène commune; bouillon-blanc *m, pl.* bouillons-blancs; cierge de Notre-Dame; **m. pink,** coquelourde *f*; passe-fleur *f, pl.* passe-fleurs.
mullen ['mʌlin], *s. Paperm:* résistance *f* à l'éclatement.
mullentypery [mʌlen'tipəri], *s. Rept:* **(South Australian) m.,** chélodine *f.*
muller ['mʌlər], *s.* molette *f*, porphyre *m* (de broyeur de couleurs, de pharmacien).
mullet[1] ['mʌlit], *s. Ich:* **1.** muge *m*, mulet *m*; **common grey m.,** muge capiton, mulet; **striped m.,** muge à grosse tête; mulet de mer. **2.** mulle *m*; **red m.,** rouget *m*; rouget-barbet *m*; surmulet *m*; mulle barbu. **3.** *Fish:* **m. net,** mulier *m*, muletières *fpl.*
mullet[2], *s. Her:* molette *f* (d'éperon).
Mullidae ['mʌlidi:], *s.pl. Ich:* mullidés *m.*
mulligan ['mʌligən], *s. NAm: Cu: F:* ragoût *m*; matelote *f.*
mulligatawny [mʌligə'tɔ:ni], *s.* potage *m* au cari, au curry.
mullion ['mʌliən], *s. Arch:* meneau (vertical).
mullioned ['mʌliənd], *a. Arch:* (fenêtre *f*) à meneau(x).
mullite ['mʌlait], *s. Miner:* mullite *f.*
mullock ['mʌlək], *s. Austr:* (*a*) roche *f* non aurifère; (*b*) déchets *mpl* de roche aurifère.
multangular [mʌl'tæŋgjulər], *a. Mth:* multangulaire.
multeity [mʌl'ti:iti], *s.* **1.** pluralité *f.* **2.** nombre *m* considérable.
multi- ['mʌlti], *comb.fm.* multi-.
multi-address ['mʌltiə'dres], *a.* à plusieurs adresseses, à plusieurs destinations; multiadresse, multidestinataire; collectif; **m.-a. instruction,** instruction multidestinataire, collective.
multi-articulate [mʌltia:'tikjuleit], *a. Z:* multiarticulé.
multibarrelled [mʌlti'bærəld], *a.* (*of gun*) multitube.
multibranched, multibranchiate [mʌlti'bra:nʃt, -'bræŋkieit], *a.* multibranche.
multicapsular, multicapsulate [mʌlti'kæpsjulər, -'kæpsjuleit], *a. Bot:* multicapsulaire.
multicauline [mʌlti'kɔ:lain], *a. Bot:* multicaule.
multicellular [mʌlti'seljulər], *a.* multicellulaire, pluricellulaire; *Atom.Ph:* **m. counter tube,** compteur *m* multicellulaire.
multichannel [mʌlti'tʃænəl], *a. Elcs: T.V:* à plusieurs canaux, à plusieurs voies; à canaux, à voies, multiples; multicanal, -aux; multivoie; multipiste; **m. amplifier,** amplificateur *m* multivoie, à plusieurs voies; **m. detector, oscillator,** détecteur, oscillateur, multicanal, à canaux multiples; **m. recorder,** enregistreur *m* multipiste.
multicoloured [mʌlti'kʌləd], *a.* multicolore.
multicomponent [mʌltikəm'pounənt], *a.* à composantes multiples; complexe; *Elcs:* **m. signal,** signal *m* complexe.
multicomputer [mʌltikəm'pju:tər], *s.* multicalculateur *m.*
multicomputing [mʌltikəm'pju:tiŋ], *s.* multicalcul *m.*
multicuspidate [mʌlti'kʌspideit], *a. Bot:* multicuspidé.
multicylinder [mʌlti'silindər], *a.* (moteur) à plusieurs cylindres, polycylindrique.
multidentate [mʌlti'denteit], *a. Bot: etc:* multidenté, pluridenté.
multidigitate [mʌlti'didʒiteit], *a. Z:* multidigité.
multidimensional [mʌltid(a)i'menʃənəl], *a.* multidimensionnel.
multi-element [mʌlti'elimənt], *a.* à plusieurs éléments, à éléments multiples; complexe; *Mch:* **m.-e. oil cooler,** radiateur *m* à éléments multiples; *Elcs:* **m.-e. tube,** tube *m* complexe, polyode, à plusieurs électrodes.
multi-engined ['mʌlti'endʒind], *a.* à plusieurs moteurs; multimoteur, -trice.
multi-exchange [mʌltieks'tʃeindʒ], *a. Tp:* à plusieurs (postes) centraux; **m.-e. area,** circonscription *f*, secteur *m*; réseau *m* à plusieurs centraux.
multifarious [mʌlti'fɛəriəs], *a.* varié, divers; multiple; **my m. duties,** le nombre et la variété de mes occupations.
multifariousness [mʌlti'fɛəriəsnis], *s.* variété *f*, diversité *f*; multiplicité *f.*
multifid ['mʌltifid], **multifidous** [mʌl'tifidəs], *a. Nat.Hist:* multifide.
multifield [mʌlti'fi:ld], *a.* **m. research,** recherche *f* pluridisciplinaire.
multifile ['mʌltifail], *a. Cmptr:* **m. reel, tape,** bobine *f*, bande *f*, multifichier.
multifloral, multiflorous [mʌlti'flɔ:rəl, -'flɔ:rəs], *a. Bot:* multiflore, pluriflore.
multifoil ['mʌltifɔil], *s. Arch:* (arc) polylobé.
multiform ['mʌltifɔ:m], *a.* multiforme.
multiformity [mʌlti'fɔ:miti], *s.* caractère *m* multiforme; diversité *f.*
multigrade ['mʌltigreid], *a. Aut: etc.* (*of oil, etc.*) multigrade.
multigrid ['mʌltigrid], *a. Elcs: W.Tel:* **m. tube, valve,** tube *m* (électronique) multigrille.
multigroup ['mʌltigru:p], *a. Atom.Ph:* multigroupe; **m. model,** modèle *m* multigroupe, à plusieurs groupes; **m. theory,** théorie *f* multigroupe.
multihull ['mʌltihʌl], *a. & s. N.Arch:* multicoque (*m*).
multilane ['mʌltilein], *a.* (route) à plusieurs voies, à voies

multiples.
multilateral [mʌlti'lætərəl], *a.* multilatéral; **m. disarmament,** désarmement multilatéral; **m. agreement,** accord multilatéral, plurilatéral; **m. guarantees,** garanties plurilatérales; *Mil:* **m. force,** force multilatérale; **m. school** = groupe *m* scolaire.
multilayer [mʌlti'leiər], *a.* à plusieurs couches; *Paint:* multicouche; *El:* **m. winding,** enroulement *m* à plusieurs couches; *Phot:* **m. film,** film *m* à émulsions superposées, à plusieurs couches sensibles.
multilevel [mʌlti'lev(ə)l], *a.* à plusieurs niveaux; à plusieurs étages.
multilinear [mʌlti'liniər], *a.* multilinéaire.
multilingual [mʌlti'liŋgwəl], *a.* (*pers.*) polyglotte; (*country*) plurilingue.
multilobate, multilobated, multilobular [mʌlti'loubeit, -lou'beitid, -'lɔbjulər], *a. Nat.Hist:* multilobé.
multilocular, multiloculate(d) [mʌlti'lɔkjulər, -'lɔkjuleit(id)], *a. Bot:* (ovaire) multiloculaire, pluriloculaire.
multimeter ['mʌltimi:tər], *s. Ph.Meas:* multimètre *m*, polymètre *m*, appareil *m* de mesure universel.
multimillionaire [mʌltimiliə'nɛər], *a. & s.* multimillionnaire (*mf*), milliardaire (*mf*).
multimission ['mʌltimiʃ(ə)n], *a.* (*of aircraft, weapon, etc.*) polyvalent, (à) toutes fins.
multimodal [mʌlti'moudəl], *a. Pol.Ec:* (distribution) plurimodale.
multimode ['mʌltomoud], *a. Elcs:* (oscillateur) à plusieurs modes de fonctionnement.
multinegative [mʌlti'negətiv], *s. Phot:* négatif *m* à plusieurs poses.
multinervate, multinervous [mʌlti'nə:veit, -'nə:vəs], *a. Nat.Hist:* multinervé.
multinomial [mʌlti'noumiəl], *a. & s. Mth:* polynôme (*m*).
multioffice [mʌlti'ɔfis], *a. U.S: Tp:* à plusieurs (postes) centraux.
multiparity [mʌlti'pæriti], *s. Biol:* multiparité *f.*
multiparous [mʌl'tipərəs], *a. Biol:* multipare.
multipartite [mʌlti'pɑ:tait], *a.* à divisions multiples; multiparti(te).
multipath ['mʌltipɑ:θ], *a. Elcs: W.Tel:* (onde *f*, signal *m*) suivant différents trajets, émis sous plusieurs angles; **m. effect,** effet *m* d'échos dus à un signal ayant suivi différents trajets; **m. transmission,** transmission *f* sous plusieurs angles.
multiped ['mʌltiped], *a.* (tracteur *m*) multipédale.
multiperforate [mʌlti'pə:fəreit], *a.* multiperforé.
multipetalous [mʌlti'petələs], *a.* multipétalé.
multiphase ['mʌltifeiz], *a. El:* (courant, alternateur) polyphasé, multiphasé; *Atom.Ph:* **m. structure,** structure multiphasée.
multipin ['mʌltipin], *a. Mec.E:* multibroche.
multiple ['mʌltipl]. **1.** *a.* (*a*) multiple; **m. stores,** magasin *m* à succursales (multiples); **m. ownership,** multipropriété *f* (d'un immeuble, etc.); **m. plough,** multisoc *m*; **m. boiler,** chaudière *f* multitubulaire; *Mec.E: etc:* **m. machining, milling,** usinage *m*, fraisage *m*, en série; **m. spindle drill,** perceuse *f* multiple, à broches multiples; **m. punching machine,** poinçonneuse *f* multiple; **m.-operator welding set,** groupe *m* de soudage à postes multiples; *Pol.Ec:* **m.-use principle,** principe *m* de polyvalence; *Psy:* **m. personality,** personnalité multiple, alternante, à dédoublement; (*b*) *Atom.Ph:* **m. bond,** liaison *f* multiple; **m. collision,** collision *f* multiple; **m. decay, m. disintegration,** désintégration *f* multiple; **m. formation, m. production,** formation *f*, production *f*, multiple; **m. fractionation,** fractionnement *m* multiple; **m. ionization,** ionisation *f* multiple; **m. relay,** relais multiple; **m. scattering,** diffusion *f* multiple; (*c*) *El:* **batteries in m.,** accus *m* en parallèle; **m. connection,** couplage *m* en batterie, en dérivation, en parallèle; **m.-series connection,** couplage en séries parallèles, couplage mixte; **m.-current generator,** génératrice *f* polymorphe; **m. system,** montage *m* en parallèle; **m. winding,** enroulement *m* multiple; **m. plug,** fiche *f* multiple; (*d*) *Elcs: W.Tel: etc:* **m. reception,** réception *f* multiple; **m. tube, m. valve,** tube *m* (électronique) multiple, mixte; **m. switch,** combinateur *m*; **m.(-unit) antenna,** antenne *f* multiple, complexe; **m. courses (of radio guidance),** axes *m* multiples (de radioguidage); *Cmptr:* **m. address code,** instruction *f* multiadresse; **m. tape lister,** imprimante *f* multibande; **m. reel file,** fichier *m* multibobine; **m. use card,** carte *f* à usages multiples; (*e*) *Tp:* **m. circuit,** circuit *m* multiple; **m. conductor,** câble *m*, fil *m*, multiple; **m. jack,** jack général; **m. joint,** branchement *m*; **m. switchboard,** multiple *m* (téléphonique); **m. twin,** quarte *f* (Dieselhorst-Martin); **m.-twin cable,** câble multipaire; **m.-twin quad,** quarte à deux paires torsadées. **2.** *s.* (*a*) *Mth:* multiple; **lowest, least, common m.,** plus petit commun multiple; **twelve is a m. of two,** douze est un multiple de deux; (*b*) *Tp:* multiplage *m*; **m. field,** champ *m* de multiplage.
multiple-line [mʌltipl'lain], *a.* multiligne.
multiplet ['mʌltiplet], *s. Opt:* multiplet *m* (d'un spectre).
multiplex[1] ['mʌltipleks], *s. W.Tel:* multiplex *m*; **m. operation,** fonctionnement *m* en multiplex; **m. printer,** transcripteur *m* en multiplex.
multiplex[2], *v.tr. W.Tel:* multiplexer (un message, un signal).
multiplexer ['mʌltipleksər], *s. W.Tel:* multiplexeur *m*; **m. channel,** canal multiplexeur.
multiplexing ['mʌltipleksiŋ], *s. W.Tel:* multiplexage *m*; **m. rack,** châssis *m* multiplexeur.
multipliable [mʌlti'plaiəbl], **multiplicable** [mʌlti'plikəbl], *a.* multipliable.
multiplicand [mʌltipli'kænd], *s. Mth:* multiplicande *m.*
multiplication [mʌltipli'keiʃ(ə)n], *s.* multiplication *f*; (*a*) **m. of the human species,** multiplication du genre humain; (*b*) *Mth:* **rules of m.,** règles *f* de la multiplication; **m. table,** table *f* de multiplication; **it's simply a matter of m.,** vous n'avez qu'à multiplier les deux (etc.) nombres; (*c*) *Mec.E:* **speed m.,** amplification *f* de vitesse; multiplication de vitesse.
multiplicative [mʌlti'plikətiv], *a.* multiplicatif.
multiplicity [mʌlti'plisiti], *s.* multiplicité *f*; **a m. of interests,** une multiplicité, une multitude, d'intérêts.
multiplied ['mʌltiplaid], *a.* multiplié; multiple.
multiplier ['mʌltiplaiər], *s.* **1.** *Mth:* multiplicateur *m*; *Cmptr:* **analog(ue), digital, m.,** multiplicateur analogique, numérique. **2.** *El:* résistance additionnelle en série; multiplicateur.
multiply ['mʌltiplai]. **1.** *v.tr.* multiplier; (*a*) **to m. one's examples,** multiplier ses exemples; (*b*) *Mth:* **to m. two numbers together,** multiplier deux nombres l'un par l'autre. **2.** *v.i.* (*a*) (*of species, etc.*) se multiplier; (*b*) *Mth:* multiplier, faire une multiplication.
multiplying[1] ['mʌltiplaiiŋ], *a.* multipliant; multiplicateur, -trice; multiplicatif; *Opt:* **m. glass,** (verre) multipliant *m.*
multiplying[2], *s.* multiplication *f*; *Cmptr:* **m. punch,** calculatrice *f* perforatrice.
multipolar [mʌlti'poulər], **multipole** ['mʌltipoul], *a. El: etc:* multipolaire; **m. moment,** moment *m* multipolaire.
multiprocessing [mʌlti'prousesiŋ], *s. Cmptr:* multitraitement *m* (des données).
multiprocessor [mʌlti'prousesər], *s. Cmptr:* multicalculateur *m.*
multiprogramming [mʌlti'prougræmiŋ], *s. Cmptr:* multiprogrammation *f.*
multipropellant [mʌltiprə'pelənt], *s.* combustible *m* (pour fusée) à plusieurs constituants; polergol *m.*
multipurpose [mʌlti'pə:pəs], *a.* polyvalent, plurivalent; à usages multiples; (à) tous usages, (à) toutes fins; universel; **m. aircraft,** avion polyvalent; **m. vehicle,** véhicule *m* tous usages, toutes fins; *Elcs:* **m. tube,** tube (électronique) universel.
multiracial [mʌ'lti'reiʃəl], *a.* multiracial, -aux.
multirate ['mʌltireit], *a.* à plusieurs tarifs, à tarifs multiples; à plusieurs taux; *El: etc:* **m. meter,** compteur *m* change-tarif, compteur différentiel; **m. tariff,** tarif *m* à tranches.
multirôle ['mʌltiroul], *a.* (*of aircraft, etc.*) polyvalent; (à) toutes fins.
multiseat ['mʌltisi:t], *a. Av:* **m. fighter,** multiplace *m* de combat.
multiseater [mʌlti'si:tər], *s. Av:* multiplace *m*, avion *m* à plusieurs places.
multislot ['mʌltislɔt], *a. Av:* (volet d'aile, de gouverne) multifente.
multispindle ['mʌlti'spindl], *a.* multibroche; **m. drill, lathe,** perceuse *f*, tour *m*, multibroche, à broches multiples.
multistage ['mʌltisteidʒ], *a.* **1.** *Elcs: Mec.E:* à plusieurs étages, à étages multiples; **m. amplifier, transformer,** amplificateur *m*, transformateur *m*, à plusieurs étages; **m. compressor, turbine,** compresseur *m*, turbine *f*, à plusieurs étages; **m. rocket,** fusée composite, gigogne, fusée à plusieurs étages. **2.** *Ind: etc:* **m. process,** processus échelonné.
multistorey ['mʌlti'stɔ:ri], *a.* (*N.Am: usu.* **multistory**) (immeuble) à plusieurs étages; **m. car park,** *U.S:* **m. parking garage,** garage *m* à étages.
multisyllabic [mʌltisi'læbik], *a.* polysyllabique.
multitape ['mʌltiteip], *a. Cmptr: etc:* multibande; **m. memory,** mémoire *f* à bandes multiples.
multi-tenancy [mʌlti'tenənsi], *s.* appartement *m* qui a plusieurs locataires; **girls living in multi-tenancies,** jeunes filles qui partagent la location d'un appartement, d'une maison.
multiterminal [mʌlti'tə:min(ə)l], *s. Elcs: Tp:* multiterminal *m.*
multitone ['mʌltitoun], *a. Aut:* **m. horn,** avertisseur *m* à sons multiples.
multitool ['mʌltitu:l], *a.* (*of lathe, etc.*) à outils multiples.
multitransferring [mʌltitræns'fə:riŋ], *a. Typ:* à reports; **m. machine,** machine *f* à reports.
Multituberculata [mʌltitjubə:kju'leitə], *s.pl. Paleont:* multituberculés *m.*
multitude ['mʌltitju:d], *s.* **1.** multitude *f*, multiplicité *f* (de raisons, etc.). **2.** multitude, foule *f*, affluence *f*; **play that will appeal to the m.,** pièce qui plaira à la multitude, au peuple, à la foule.
multitudinous [mʌlti'tju:dinəs], *a.* **1.** nombreux, innombrable. **2.** de toutes sortes; multiple. **3.** immense, vaste; **m. sound,** flot *m* de sons.
multivalence [mʌlti'veiləns], *s. Ch:* polyvalence *f.*
multivalent [mʌlti'veilənt], *a. Ch:* polyvalent.
multivalve ['mʌltivælv], *a. & s. Moll:* multivalve (*m* or *f*).
multivalvular [mʌlti'vælvjulər], *a.* multivalve.
multivariate [mʌlti'vɛərieit], *a.* (*a*) *Mth: etc:* à plusieurs variables; **m. analysis,** analyse *f* à plusieurs variables; **m. process,** processus vectoriel; (*b*) *Psy:* (analyse) multivariée.
multivarious [mʌlti'vɛəriəs], *a.* multivarié; extrêmement divers.
multivibrator [mʌltivai'breitər], *s. W.Tel:* multivibrateur *m.*
multivitamin [mʌlti'v(a)itəmin], *s.* multivitamine *f.*
multiway ['mʌltiwei], *a.* multivoie, à plusieurs voies; *Cmptr:* **m. conversion,** multiconversion *f.*
multiwire ['mʌltiwaiər], *a.* multifiliaire; *W.Tel:* **m. antenna,** antenne *f* multifiliaire; antenne en cage, en nappe.
multure ['mʌltjər], *s.* mouture *f* (salaire *m* du meunier).
mum[1] [mʌm], *int. & a.* **mum's the word!** motus (et bouche cousue)! chut! bouche close! avale ta langue! **to keep m. (about sth.),** ne pas souffler mot, ne pas sonner mot (de qch.).
mum[2] [mʌm], *s. F:* maman *f.*
mum[3] ['m], *s. F: O:* (*form of address, Com: and from servant to mistress*) madame, mademoiselle; *Com:* ma petite dame.
mum[4] [mʌm], *v.i.* (**mummed**) mimer.
mumble[1] ['mʌmbl], *s.* marmottage *m*; paroles marmottées.
mumble[2], *v.tr. & i.* (*a*) marmotter, marmonner; barboter (ses mots); parler entre ses dents; manger ses mots; **to m. a prayer,** marmotter, mâchonner, une prière; **he mumbled a few words,** il a prononcé quelques mots entre ses dents; **to m. through a sermon,** ânonner un sermon; (*b*) *A:* mâchonner (de la nourriture).
mumbler ['mʌmblər], *s.* **1.** marmotteur, -euse. **2.** *A:* mâchonneur, -euse.
mumbling[1] ['mʌmbliŋ], *a.* **1.** qui marmotte, marmonne; marmottant. **2.** *A:* qui mâchonne.
mumbling[2], *s.* **1.** marmottage *m.* **2.** *A:* mâchonnement *m.*
mumblingly ['mʌmbliŋli], *adv.* indistinctement, en marmottant.
mumbo-jumbo ['mʌmbou 'dʒʌmbou], *s.* **1.** (*a*) idole *f* (de certaines tribus africaines); (*b*) objet auquel on rend un culte ridicule. **2.** (*a*) culte superstitieux; (*b*) baragouin *m*, charabia *m*; galimatias *m.*
mumchance ['mʌmtʃɑ:ns], *a. A:* **to sit, keep, m.,** rester coi, *f.* coite.
mummer ['mʌmər], *s.* **1.** acteur *m* de pantomimes; mime *m.* **2.** *Pej: F: O:* acteur, -trice; cabotin, -ine.
mummery ['mʌməri], *s.* **1.** *Th: A:* pantomime *f.* **2.** *Pej:* momerie *f.*
mummification [mʌmifi'keiʃ(ə)n], *s.* momification *f.*
mummiform ['mʌmifɔ:m], *a.* (sarcophage *m*, etc.) en forme de momie.
mummify ['mʌmifai]. **1.** *v.tr.* momifier. **2.** *v.i.* se momifier.
mumming ['mʌmiŋ], *s.* momerie *f*; momeries *fpl.*
mummy[1] ['mʌmi], *s.* **1.** (*a*) *Med: A:* poudre *f* de momie; *F:* **to beat sth. to a m.,** réduire qch. en poussière, en miettes, en bouillie; (*b*) *Art:* momie *f* (couleur brune). **2.** (*a*) momie (égyptienne); **m. cloth,** bandelette *f* (de momie); (*b*) momie, codaure desséché.
mummy[2], *v.tr.* (**mummied**) momifier.
mummy[3], *s. F:* maman *f.*
mump[1] [mʌmp], *v.i. & tr. A:* mendier, coquiner.
mump[2], *v.i. A:* **1.** bouder. **2.** prendre une mine confite; faire la sainte nitouche.
mumps [mʌmps], *s.pl.* (*usu. with sg. const.*) **1.** *Med:* parotidite ourlienne; oreillons *mpl.* **2.** *A:* bouderie *f*, maussaderie *f*; **to have the m.,** broyer du noir; avoir le

cafard.

munch [mʌn(t)ʃ], *v.tr.* mâcher, mâchonner; *v.i.* **to m. away,** jouer des mâchoires.

mundane ['mʌndein], *a.* mondain. **1.** terrestre; *Lit:* sublunaire. **2. m. pleasures,** plaisirs mondains. **3.** cosmique.

mundaneness ['mʌndeinnis], **mundanity** [mʌn'dæniti], *s.* mondanité *f.*

mungo ['mʌŋgou], *s. Tex:* (drap *m* de) laine *f* (de) renaissance.

mungoose, *pl.* **mongooses** ['mʌŋgu:s], *s. Z:* mangouste *f.*

munia ['mju:niə], *s. Orn:* munie *f,* damier *m;* (*Austr: species*) donacole *m;* **chestnut-bellied m.,** capucin *m* à tête noire.

municipal [mju:'nisipl], *a.* **1.** municipal, -aux; **m. loans,** emprunts *m* de ville; **m. buildings** = mairie *f;* hôtel *m* de ville; *Can: Austr:* **m. district** = municipalité *f.* **2.** *Jur:* **m. law,** droit national, interne; législation *f* d'Etat, intérieure.

municipalism [mju'nisipəlizm], *s.* **1.** municipalisme *m.* **2.** esprit *m* de clocher.

municipality [mjunisi'pæliti], *s.* municipalité *f.*

municipalization [mjunisipəlai'zeiʃ(ə)n], *s.* municipalisation *f.*

municipalize [mju'nisipəlaiz], *v.tr.* municipaliser.

municipally [mju'nisip(ə)li], *adv.* municipalement.

municipium, *pl.* **-ia** [mju(:)ni'sipiəm, -iə], *s. Rom.Ant:* municipe *m.*

munificence [mju'nifisəns], *s.* munificence *f;* grande libéralité; **through the m. of an anonymous donor,** grâce à la générosité d'un donateur anonyme.

munificent [mju'nifisənt], *a.* munificent, généreux, libéral, -aux.

munificently [mju'nifisəntli], *adv.* avec munificence; libéralement, généreusement.

muniment ['mju:nimənt], *s.* **1.** *pl.* **muniments,** titres *m,* chartes *f,* archives *f,* documents *m;* **m. of title,** acte *m* de propriété. **2.** *attrib.* **m. room,** archives.

munition[1] [mju'niʃ(ə)n], *s.* **munition(s) of war,** munitions *f* de guerre; **m. factory,** fabrique *f,* usine *f,* de munitions; **m. worker,** ouvrier, -ière, d'une fabrique de munitions; *A:* **the Ministry of Munitions,** le Ministère de l'Armement.

munition[2], *v.tr. O:* approvisionner; ravitailler en munitions (une armée); armer (un vaisseau).

muntjac, muntjak ['mʌntdʒæk], *s. Z:* muntjac *m,* muntjak *m;* cerf aboyeur.

muon ['mju:ɔn], *s. Atom.Ph:* muon *m.*

muraena [mju'ri:nə], *s. Ich:* murène *f.*

Muraenidae [mju'ri:nidi:], *s.pl. Ich:* murénidés *m.*

mural ['mju:rəl]. **1.** *a.* mural, -aux; **m. paintings,** peintures murales; *Rom.Ant:* **m. crown,** couronne murale; *Astr:* **m. circle,** cercle mural. **2.** *s.* peinture murale.

murchisonite ['mə:tʃisənait], *s. Miner:* murchisonite *f.*

Murcia ['mə:siə]. *Pr.n. Geog:* Murcie *f.*

murder[1] ['mə:dər], *s.* meurtre *m; Jur:* homicide *m* volontaire; **premeditated m.,** *U.S:* **m. in the first degree,** assassinat *m; U.S:* **m. in the second degree,** meurtre *m;* **to commit (a) m., to do m.,** commettre un meurtre, un assassinat; *B:* **thou shalt do no m.,** tu ne tueras point; *F:* **it's downright m. to . . .,** c'est un meurtre de . . .; *F:* **it's (sheer, downright) m. in the rush hours,** c'est (absolument) épouvantable, impossible, aux heures de pointe, d'affluence; **m.!** au meurtre! à l'assassin! **to cry m.,** crier à l'assassin; *F:* **to scream blue m.,** crier, gueuler, à tue-tête, comme un perdu; *F:* **like blue m.,** à une vitesse vertigineuse; *F:* **he'd get away with m.,** il s'en tire toujours à bon compte; **m. will out,** tôt ou tard la vérité se fait jour.

murder[2], *v.tr.* **1.** (*a*) assassiner; *Jur:* **person murdered,** personne homicidée; (*b*) *P:* **I'll m. you (for that)!** je vais te tabasser, te battre comme plâtre! **2.** *F:* estropier (un mot, un vers, une citation); massacrer, saboter, assassiner (une valse, une chanson); écorcher (le français, l'anglais).

murderer ['mə:d(ə)rər], *s.m.* meurtrier, assassin.

murderess ['mə:d(ə)res], *s.f.* meurtrière.

murdering[1] ['mə:d(ə)riŋ], *a.* qui assassine; meurtrier, assassin.

murdering[2], *s.* **1.** assassinat *m,* meurtre *m.* **2.** *F:* massacre *m.*

murderous ['mə:d(ə)rəs], *a.* meurtrier, assassin; **m. weapons,** armes meurtrières; **m. war,** guerre *f* homicide; **with m. intent,** dans une intention homicide.

murderously ['mə:d(ə)rəsli], *adv.* d'une manière meurtrière, sanguinaire; **to attack s.o. m.,** se livrer à une attaque sanguinaire contre qn.

mure [mjuər], *v. ind.tr. A: & Lit:* **1. to m. in a town,** murer une ville. **2. to m. up a window,** murer, condamner, une fenêtre. **3. to be mured up in a small room all day,** être cloîtré, claquemuré, dans une petite chambre pendant toute la journée.

murex, *pl.* **-exes, -ices** ['mju:reks, -eksiz, isi:z], *s. Moll:* murex *m;* rocher épineux.

murexide [mju'reksaid], *s. Ch:* murexide *f.*

muriate ['mju:rieit], *s. A.Ch: Com:* (*also* **muriatic acid**) muriate *m,* chlorure *m.*

muricate ['mju:rikeit], *a. Nat.Hist:* muriqué.

Muricidae [mju'risidi:], *s.pl. Moll:* muricidés *m.*

muriculate [mju'rikjuleit], *a. Bot:* muriculé.

Muridae ['mju:ridi:], *s.pl. Z:* muridés *m.*

muriform ['mju:rifɔ:m], *a. Med:* mûriforme.

Murinae ['mju:rini:], *s.pl. Z:* murinés *m.*

murine ['mju:r(a)in], *a. Z:* murin.

murk [mə:k], *s.* (*a*) obscurité *f,* ténèbres *fpl;* (*b*) fumée *f;* brume *f.*

murkiness ['mə:kinis], *s.* obscurité *f.*

murky ['mə:ki], *a.* obscur, ténébreux; **m. darkness,** ténèbres épaisses; **m. sky,** ciel brouillé; **m. past,** passé obscur, ténébreux.

Murmansk [mə:'mænsk]. *Pr.n. Geog:* Mourmansk; **M. coast,** côte mourmane.

murmur[1] ['mə:mər], *s.* **1.** (*a*) murmure *m* (des vagues, d'un ruisseau, de la foule); bruissement *m;* (*b*) *Med:* **cardiac m.,** murmure cardiaque; bruit *m* cardiaque. **2.** (*a*) murmure (d'approbation, d'improbation); **he swallowed it without a m.,** il l'a avalé sans murmurer, sans broncher; (*b*) **in murmurs,** à voix basse.

murmur[2], *v.i. & tr.* **1.** murmurer, susurrer; (*of brook*) bruire. **2.** *O:* **to m. at sth., against s.o.,** murmurer contre qch., contre qn. **3.** murmurer, dire (qch.) à voix basse.

murmuring[1] ['mə:məriŋ], *a.* (*of stream, etc.*) murmurant, susurrant.

murmuring[2], *s.* **1.** murmure *m.* **2.** murmures (**against,** contre).

muromontite [mjurou'mɔntait], *s. Miner:* muromontite *f.*

murphy ['mə:fi], *s. F: O:* pomme *f* de terre.

murra ['mʌrə], *s. Rom.Ant:* murrhe *f.*

murrain ['mʌrin], *s.* **1.** *A:* peste *f;* **a m. on him!** (la) peste soit de lui! **2.** *Vet:* épizootie *f.*

murrained ['mʌrind], *a. Vet:* (troupeau) atteint d'une épizootie.

murre [mə:r], *s. Orn: NAm:* **Brünnich's m.,** guillemot de Brünnich, *Fr.C:* marmette *f* de Brünnich; **common m., Atlantic m.,** guillemot de Troïl, guillemot à capuchon, *Fr.C:* marmette commune.

murrelet ['mə:lət], *s. Orn:* **ancient m.,** alque *f* à cou blanc; **marbled m.,** alque marbrée.

murrhine ['mʌr(a)in], *a. & s. Cer: Glassm:* murrhin (*m*).

Musaceae [mju'zeisii:], *s.pl. Bot:* musacées *f.*

muscardine [mʌs'kɑ:din], *s. Ser:* muscardine *f.*

muscarine ['mʌskərain], *s. Ch:* muscarine *f.*

muscat[1] ['mʌskæt], *a. & s.* = MUSCATEL.

Muscat[2]. *Pr.n. Geog:* Mascate.

muscatel [mʌskə'tel], *a. & s.* (vin, raisin) muscat (*m*); **m. raisins,** *s.* **muscatels,** raisins secs de Malaga.

muschetours ['mu:ʃtu:ər], *s.pl. Her:* mouchetures *fpl.*

Muscicapidae [mʌsi'kæpidi:], *s.pl. Orn:* muscicapidés *m.*

muscicole ['mʌsikoul], **muscicolous** [mʌ'sikələs], *a. Nat.Hist:* muscicole.

Muscidae ['mʌsidi:], *s.pl. Ent:* muscidés *m.*

muscle[1] ['mʌsl], *s.* muscle *m;* **smooth m., striated m.,** muscle lisse, strié; **to have m.,** avoir du muscle; **he has plenty of m.,** il est bien musclé; **man of m.,** homme musculeux, musclé; *F:* **m. man,** costaud *m,* homme à poigne, gorille *m.*

muscle[2], *v.i. F:* **to m. in,** s'immiscer (**on sth.,** dans une affaire); se pousser, jouer des coudes; **he muscled his way in,** il s'est introduit de force; il a forcé la porte; **to m. in on a conversation,** s'injecter dans une conversation.

muscoid ['mʌskɔid], *a.* muscoïde.

muscology [mʌs'kɔlədʒi], *s. Bot:* muscologie *f,* bryologie *f.*

muscovado [mʌskə'vɑ:dou], *s. Sug.-R:* cassonade *f;* sucre brut.

Muscovite ['mʌskəvait], *s.* **1.** (*a*) *a.* moscovite; (*b*) *s.* Moscovite *mf.* **2.** *s. Miner:* muscovite *f.*

Muscovy ['mʌskəvi]. *Pr.n. A.Geog:* Moscovie *f; Orn:* **M. duck,** canard musqué, *F:* de Barbarie; *Miner: O:* **M. glass,** muscovite *f.*

muscular ['mʌskjulər], *a.* **1.** (*of system, tissue, action*) musculaire. **2. m. man,** homme musculeux, musclé, bien découplé; **to be m.,** avoir du biceps.

muscularity [mʌskju'læriti], *s.* **1.** muscularité *f* (d'un tissu). **2.** musculosité *f* (d'un membre); vigueur *f* musculaire.

musculation [mʌskju'leiʃ(ə)n], *s. Anat: Art:* musculature *f.*

musculature ['mʌskjulətjər], *s. Anat: Art:* musculature *f.*

musculocutaneous ['mʌskjuloukju'teiniəs], *a. & s. Anat:* (nerf) musculo-cutané *m.*

muse[1] [mju:z], *s.* (*a*) *Myth:* muse *f;* **the (nine) muses,** les muses, les neuf sœurs; (*b*) *Lit:* **to call on one's m.,** invoquer sa muse.

muse[2], *s. Lit:* rêverie *f,* méditation *f;* **to fall into a m. over sth.,** se mettre à méditer sur qch.

muse[3], *v.i.* méditer, rêver, rêvasser; **to m. on, upon, about, sth.,** méditer sur qch.; réfléchir à qch.; **to m. on an idea,** ruminer une idée; **to m. on the future,** rêvasser à l'avenir; **"that's queer," he mused,** "voilà qui est bien étrange," murmura-t-il d'un ton rêveur.

museography [mjuzi'ɔgrəfi], *s.* muséographie *f.*

museologist [mjuzi'ɔlədʒist], *s.* muséologue *mf.*

museology [mjuzi'ɔlədʒi], *s.* muséologie *f.*

muser ['mju:zər], *s.* rêveur, -euse; rêvasseur, -euse; contemplateur, -trice.

musette [mju'zet], *s. Mus:* musette *f.*

museum [mju(:)'ziəm], *s.* (*a*) musée *m* (d'antiquités, d'arts et métiers); **natural history m.,** muséum *m* d'histoire naturelle; **m. piece,** pièce *f* de musée; (*b*) **m. beetle,** anthrène *m* des musées, *F:* amourette *f.*

mush[1] [mʌʃ], *s.* **1.** *Cu: esp. U.S:* bouillie *f* de farine de maïs. **2.** *F:* (*a*) bouillie, panade *f;* (*b*) *W.Tel: etc:* cafouillage *m;* (bruits *mpl* de) friture *f;* brouillage *m; T.V:* **background m.,** brouillard *m* de fond. **3.** *F:* sentimentalité *f* (à l'eau de rose). **4.** [muʃ], *P:* (*a*) visage *m,* museau *m;* gueule *f;* (*b*) individu *m,* type *m,* mec *m.*

mush[2], *s. NAm:* voyage *m* en traîneau (tiré par des chiens).

mush[3], *v.i. NAm:* voyager sur la neige (avec traîneaux et chiens); (*to dogs*) **m.!** en avant! tirez!

mushiness ['mʌʃinis], *s.* **1.** état détrempé, spongieux; manque *m* de consistance (d'un aliment, du terrain, etc.); état bourbeux (des rues, etc.). **2.** fadeur *f* (de sentiments); sensiblerie *f.*

mushroom[1] ['mʌʃru:m], *s.* **1.** *Fung:* (*a*) champignon (blanc); **cultivated mushrooms,** champignons de couche, de Paris; **button m.,** champignon encore en bouton; **m. bed,** couche *f* de champignons; meule *f* à champignons; champignonnière *f;* **m. grower,** champignonnier *m,* champignonniste *m; Cu:* **m. sauce, m. soup,** sauce *f,* potage *m,* aux champignons; (*b*) *F:* **penny-bun m.,** cèpe *m;* **club-top m.,** clavaire *f;* **Caesar's m.,** oronge *f;* **fool's m.,** amanite vireuse. **2.** *F:* (*a*) *A:* (*pers.*) parvenu, -ue; (*b*) **m. town,** ville *f* champignon. **3.** (*a*) **m. cloud,** (i) nuage *m* en forme de champignon; (ii) champignon (atomique); (*b*) *Needlew:* œuf *m,* boule *f,* à repriser; (*c*) **m. anchor,** champignon; (*d*) *Mec.E: etc:* **m. valve,** (soupape *f* à) champignon; soupape circulaire; clapet *m;* (*e*) *Coel:* **m. coral,** fongia *f,* fongie *f,* fungia *f,* fungie *f.*

mushroom[2], *v.i.* **1.** ramasser, faire la cueillette, des champignons. **2.** (*a*) (*of bullet, etc.*) faire champignon; s'aplatir; (*b*) (*of fire, etc.*) **to m. out,** se répandre; (*c*) *F:* pousser comme un champignon, champignonner.

mushrooming ['mʌʃru:miŋ], *s.* **1.** cueillette *f* des champignons; **to go m.,** aller aux champignons. **2.** aplatissement *m* (d'une balle de fusil, etc.).

mushy ['mʌʃi], *a.* **1.** (*of food, etc.*) détrempé; spongieux; sans consistance; baveux; (*of ground, etc.*) détrempé, bourbeux; (*of pear, etc.*) blet, *f.* blette. **2.** *F:* **m. sentimentality,** sensiblerie *f,* sentimentalité *f* (à l'eau de rose).

music[1] ['mju:zik], *s.* musique *f;* **to set words to m.,** mettre des paroles en musique; **instrumental m.,** musique instrumentale; **orchestral m.,** musique d'orchestre; **chamber m.,** musique de chambre; **sacred m.,** musique religieuse, sacrée; **background m.,** musique d'ambiance de fond; **m. while you work,** travail *m* en musique; **programme m.,** musique de genre; **incidental m. for a play,** musique pour une pièce; **to be fond of, to appreciate, m.,** aimer la musique; être musicien, -ienne; **to have an ear for m.,** avoir l'oreille musicale; **m. lover,** amateur, -trice, de musique; musicien, -ienne; **m. hater,** mélophobe *mf;* **m. book,** cahier *m* de musique; **m. cabinet,** casier *m* de musique; **m. case,** porte-musique *m inv;* **m. stand,** pupitre *m* à musique; **m. paper,** papier *m* à, de, musique; **m. rest,** tablette *f* de piano; **m. stool,** tabouret *m* de piano; **m. roll,** rouleau perforé, bande perforée (pour piano mécanique); *A.Phil:* **the m. of the spheres,** l'harmonie *f* céleste.

music[2]. *O:* (**musicked; musicking**) **1.** *v.tr.* mettre (des paroles) en musique; *A:* musiquer (des vers, etc.). **2.** *v.i.* musiquer; faire de la musique.

musical ['mju:zik(ə)l]. **1.** *a.* (*a*) musical, -aux; **m. evening,** soirée musicale; **to have a m. ear,** avoir l'oreille musicale; **m. instrument,** instrument *m* de musique; **m. box,** boîte *f* à musique; **toy m. box,** moulinet *m* à musique; **m. watch,** montre *f* à carillon; *W.Tel: T.V:* **m. frequency,** fréquence musicale; **m. cushion,** remplissage musical; (*b*) (*pers.*) **to be m.,** aimer la musique; être (bon) musicien, (bonne) musicienne; (*c*) (*of sound*) harmonieux, mélodieux, chantant; **m. voice,** voix harmonieuse, mélodieuse; *Aut:* **m. horn,** avertisseur *m* à tonalité musicale. **2.** *s.* = opérette *f.*

musicale [mju:zi'kɑ:l], *s. U.S:* soirée, matinée, musicale.

musicality [mju:zi'kæliti], *s.* musicalité *f.*

musically ['mju:zikli], *adv.* **1.** musicalement. **2.** mélodieusement, harmonieusement.

musicalness ['mju:zik(ə)lnis], *s.* mélodie *f,* harmonie *f,* qualité chantante (des vers, de la voix).

music hall ['mju:zikhɔ:l], *s.* music-hall *m, pl.* music-halls.

musician [mju'ziʃ(ə)n], *s.* musicien, -ienne.

musicographer [mju:zi'kɔgrəfər], *s.* musicographe *mf.*

musicographic [mju:zikou'græfik], *a.* musicographe.

musicography [mju:zi'kɔgrəfi], *s.* musicographie *f.*

musicologist [mju:zi'kɔlədʒist], *s.* musicologue *mf.*

musicology [mju:zi'kɔlədʒi], *s.* musicologie *f.*

musicomania [mju:zikou'meiniə], *s.* musicomanie *f,* mélomanie *f.*

musicotherapy [mju:zikou'θerəpi], *s.* musicothérapie *f.*

musing[1] ['mju:ziŋ], *a.* pensif, contemplatif, méditatif; rêveur, -euse.

musing[2], *s.* rêverie *f* (**on,** à); méditation *f* (**on,** sur); contemplation *f* (**on,** de); **idle musings,** rêvasseries *f.*

musingly ['mju:ziŋli], *adv.* d'un air songeur, rêveur, méditatif; pensivement.

musk [mʌsk], *s.* (*a*) musc *m*; *Z:* **m. deer,** porte-musc *m inv*; musc; **m. ox,** bœuf musqué; ovibos *m*; **m. cat,** civet *m*; **m. cavy,** hutia *m*; *Rept:* **m. turtle, m. terrapin, m. tortoise,** tortue musquée; *Ent:* **m. beetle,** capricorne musqué; (*b*) odeur *f* fauve (du corps); (*c*) *Bot:* **m. (plant),** musc; **m. rose,** rose musquée; (*bush*) rosier musqué; **m. mallow,** mauve musquée; **m. mallow of India,** ambrette *f*; *Toil:* **m. seed,** ambrette; *Hort:* **m. pear,** poire musquée, muscat *m,* muscadelle *f.*

muskeg ['mʌskeg], *s. Can:* fondrière *f,* marécage *m.*

muskelunge ['mʌskəlʌndʒ], *s. Ich:* maskinongé *m* (*Fr.C*).

musket ['mʌskit], *s. Sm.a: A:* mousquet *m*; **m. shot,** coup *m* de mousquet, *A:* mousquetade *f*; **within m. shot,** à portée de fusil.

musketeer [mʌski'tiər], *s. A:* mousquetaire *m.*

musketoon [mʌski'tu:n], *s. A:* mousqueton *m.*

musketry ['mʌskitri], *s. Mil:* **1.** *A:* mousqueterie *f.* **2.** tir *m*; **m. instruction,** exercices *mpl* de tir; école *f* de tir; **instructor in m.,** instructeur *m* de tir.

muskiness ['mʌskinis], *s.* odeur *f,* goût *m,* de musc.

muskrat ['mʌskræt], *s. Z:* **1.** rat musqué; ondatra *m.* **2.** desman musqué.

musky ['mʌski], *a.* musqué; qui sent le musc; **m. smell,** (i) odeur *f* de musc; (ii) odeur fauve.

Muslim ['mʌzlim], *a. & s.* = MOSLEM.

muslin ['mʌzlin], *s.* **1.** *Tex:* (*a*) mousseline *f*; **foundation m.,** mousseline forte; *F: A:* **a bit of m.,** une fille; une jeune femme; **his bit of m.,** sa petite amie; (*b*) *NAm:* calicot *m.* **2. m. glass,** (verre *m*) mousseline.

Musophagidae [mju:sou'feidʒidi:], *s.pl. Orn:* musophagidés *m.*

musquash ['mʌskwɔʃ], *s.* **1.** *Z:* rat musqué; ondatra *m.* **2.** *Com:* castor *m* du Canada.

muss[1] [mʌs], *s. NAm: F:* désordre *m,* fouillis *m.*

muss[2], *v.tr. NAm: F:* **to m. up s.o.'s hair,** déranger la coiffure de qn; **hair all mussed up,** cheveux ébouriffés; **to m. up a dress,** froisser, chiffonner, une robe; **to m. up one's hands,** se salir les mains; **I'm all mussed up,** je ne sais plus où j'en suis.

mussel ['mʌsl], *s. Moll:* moule *f*; **freshwater m.,** mulette *f*; **the m. industry,** l'industrie moulière; **m. bank, bed, farm,** banc *m* de moules; moulière *f*; parc *m* mytilicole; bouchot *m*; **m. breeder,** bouchot(t)eur *m,* mytiliculteur *m*; **m. breeding,** mytiliculture *f.*

mussitation [mʌsi'teiʃ(ə)n], *s. Med:* mussitation *f.*

Mussulman, *pl.* **-mans** ['mʌslmən, -mənz], *s. O:* musulman, -ane.

mussy ['mʌsi], *a. NAm: F:* en désordre; dérangé, froissé; sale.

must[1] [mʌst], *s. Vit:* moût *m*; vin doux; **new m.,** surmoût *m.*

must[2], *s.* moisi *m*; moisissure *f.*

must[3], *a. & s.* **m. elephant, elephant in m.,** éléphant *m* en rage; éléphant furieux; **to go m.,** se mettre en rage.

must[4], *modal aux. v. inv.* (**must not** *is often contracted into* **mustn't**) (*finite tenses of*) falloir, devoir. **1.** (*a*) (*expressing obligation*) **you m. be ready at four o'clock,** vous devrez être prêt, il faut, faudra, que vous soyez prêt, à quatre heures; **I m. go and see him,** il faut que j'aille le voir; **you m. hurry up,** il faut vous dépêcher; **you mustn't tell anyone,** il ne faut le dire à personne; **it m. be done,** il faut que cela se fasse; **the subject m. be dealt with in a different manner,** le sujet demande à être traité autrement; **plant that m. have continual attention,** plante qui demande, qui réclame, des soins continuels; **all drivers m. pass an examination,** pour tous les chauffeurs un examen est obligatoire; tous les chauffeurs sont astreints à passer un examen; **cars m. not be parked in front of this gate,** défense de stationner devant cette grille; **it mustn't go on like that,** cela ne peut pas continuer, durer, ainsi, comme ça; **I m. sell something in order to pay my bills,** il me faut, je suis obligé de, vendre quelque chose pour régler mes comptes; **you (simply)** *must* **meet him,** il faut absolument que vous fassiez sa connaissance; **I** *must* **have a new dress,** il faut absolument que j'achète une nouvelle robe; **he (simply)** *must* **come,** il faut absolument, il est de toute nécessité, qu'il vienne; **you** *must* **visit the Louvre,** une visite au Louvre s'impose; **you m. stay until tomorrow, you just** *must,* il faut absolument que vous restiez jusqu'à demain; **well, if you m.!** si vous l'exigez; **why m. you always be interfering?** pourquoi vous mêlez-vous toujours de ce qui ne vous concerne pas? **he's stupid, I m. say,** il est stupide, il faut l'avouer; **the reader m. understand that . . .,** le lecteur comprendra que . . .; **the room, you m. understand, was panelled,** je dois vous dire que la pièce était lambrissée; (*b*) (*expressing probability*) **there's a ring; it m. be the doctor,** on sonne, ce doit être le médecin; **you m. be hungry after your walk,** vous devez avoir faim après votre promenade; **it m. be getting on for two (o'clock),** il ne doit pas être loin de deux heures; **he m. have missed the train,** il aura manqué le train; **I m. have made a mistake,** j'ai dû me tromper; **if he says so it m. be true,** s'il le dit c'est que c'est vrai; **he** *must* **be in,** il est sûrement chez lui; **if you do as I say you m. win,** si vous faites comme je vous dis vous êtes sûr de gagner; **you m. know that it isn't true,** vous savez pourtant bien, vous n'êtes pas sans savoir, que cela n'est pas vrai; **you** *must* **know him,** vous n'êtes pas sans le connaître; vous ne pouvez pas ne pas le connaître. **2.** (*past tense*) (*a*) **he agreed that he m. take the consequences,** il a convenu qu'il lui fallait en subir les conséquences; **if he had looked he m. have seen it,** s'il avait regardé, il l'aurait sûrement vu, il n'a pas pu manquer de le voir; **I saw that he m. have suspected something,** j'ai bien vu qu'il avait dû se douter de quelque chose; (*b*) **as we were about to start what m. the child do but sit down in a puddle,** au moment du départ voilà l'enfant qui s'assied dans une flaque d'eau; **the idiot m. needs come while we were having dinner,** et cet imbécile qui est arrivé pendant que nous étions à table! **just as I was at my busiest he m. come worrying me,** au moment où j'étais le plus occupé il a fallu qu'il vienne me tracasser.

must[5], *s. F:* chose *f* à ne pas manquer, à faire à tout prix; **it's a m.,** c'est une nécessité; **of course the Louvre's a m.,** une visite au Louvre s'impose, naturellement; **this film's a m.,** ça, c'est un film à ne pas manquer.

mustache [mə'stæʃ], *s. NAm:* moustache *f.*

mustachio, *pl.* **-os** [mʌs'tɑ:ʃiou, mu-, -ouz], *s. A:* = MOUSTACHE.

mustang ['mʌstæŋ], *s. Z:* mustang *m.*

mustard ['mʌstəd], *s.* **1.** (*a*) *Comest:* moutarde *f*; **French m.** = moutarde de Dijon; **m. pot,** moutardier *m*; pot *m* à moutarde; (*b*) *Med:* **m. bath,** bain sinapisé; **m. poultice,** cataplasme sinapisé; **m. plaster,** emplâtre *m* à la moutarde; *O:* **m. leaf, paper,** sinapisme *m*; papier rigollot; (*c*) *Mil:* (*1914–18 war*) **m. gas,** ypérite *f*; gaz *m* moutarde. **2.** *Bot:* (*a*) moutarde; **black m.,** moutarde noire; sénevé *m*; **white m.,** moutarde blanche; **m. seed,** (i) graine *f* de moutarde; (ii) *U.S:* cendrée *f,* menu plomb (de chasse); *B:* **grain of m. seed,** grain *m* de sénevé; (*b*) **wild m.,** moutarde des champs; moutardin *m,* moutardon *m*; sanve *f*; (*c*) **hedge m.,** sisymbre officinal; *F:* herbe *f* aux chantres; tortelle *f,* vélar *m*; **treacle m.,** (i) tabouret *m* des champs; *F:* monnayère *f,* herbe aux écus; (ii) vélar fausse-giroflée; **poor man's m.,** alliaire officinale; *Hort:* **m. and cress,** moutarde blanche et cresson alénois.

Mustelidae [mʌs'telidi:], *s.pl. Z:* mustélidés *m.*

muster[1] ['mʌstər], *s.* **1.** (*a*) rassemblement *m* (d'une tribu, etc.); (*b*) *Mil:* revue *f*; **to make, take, a m. of troops,** faire la revue des troupes; passer des troupes en revue; **m. parade,** inspection *f*; **to pass m.,** passer, être passable; être à la hauteur; **work that will pass m.,** travail *m* acceptable; (*c*) *Nau:* appel *m*; (*d*) **m. roll,** feuille *f* d'appel; *Mil:* contrôles *mpl*; *Nau:* rôle *m* de l'équipage; *Navy:* casernet *m* d'appel; **to be on the m. roll,** figurer sur les cadres; (*e*) *esp. Austr:* rassemblement (des troupeaux). **2.** (*a*) assemblée *f,* réunion *f*; **to turn out in full m.,** se présenter au grand complet; (*b*) **m. of peacocks,** troupe *f* de paons.

muster[2]. **1.** *v.tr.* (*a*) rassembler (ses partisans, etc.); **society that musters a hundred (members),** association qui compte cent membres, qui s'élève à cent membres; **we mustered ten,** nous étions dix; (*b*) *Mil:* passer (des troupes) en revue; faire, passer, la revue (des troupes); (*c*) *Nau:* faire l'appel (des hommes); assembler (l'équipage); (*d*) rassembler (ses troupeaux, etc.); **to m. (up) one's courage,** rassembler toutes ses forces; prendre son courage à deux mains. **2.** *v.i.* s'assembler, se réunir, se rassembler.

mustiness ['mʌstinis], *s.* moisi *m*; moisissure *f*; goût *m,* odeur *f,* de moisi; relent *m*; remugle *m.*

musty ['mʌsti], *a.* **1.** (*a*) (goût *m,* odeur *f*) de moisi; **to smell m.,** sentir le moisi; (*of room, etc.*) sentir le renfermé; (*of food*) sentir l'évent; **m. smell, taste,** relent *m*; (*b*) (pain, etc.) moisi; **to grow m.,** moisir. **2.** *F: O:* suranné; vieux jeu *inv*; **m. old laws,** vieilles lois désuètes.

mutability [mju:tə'biliti], *s.* **1.** mutabilité *f,* variabilité *f.* **2.** *A:* inconstance *f*; humeur changeante.

mutable ['mju:təbl], *a.* **1.** (*a*) muable, changeant, variable; (*b*) *A:* inconstant; d'humeur changeante. **2.** *Ling:* (*of consonant or vowel*) sujet à la mutation.

mutage ['mju:tidʒ], *s.* mutage *m* (du vin).

mutagen ['mju:tədʒen], *s.* agent *m* mutagène.

mutant ['mju:tənt], *a. & s. Biol:* mutant, -ante.

mutarotation ['mju:tərou'teiʃ(ə)n], *s. Ch:* mutarotation *f* (des sucres).

mutation [mju:'teiʃ(ə)n], *s.* **1.** *Biol:* mutation *f,* altération *f,* changement *m*; *Biol:* **m. of type,** métatypie *f*; **controlled m.,** mutation dirigée. **2.** *Mus:* (*a*) *A:* muance *f*; (*b*) **m. stop,** jeu *m* de mutation. **3.** *Ling:* mutation (d'une consonne initiale, etc.); **vowel m.,** mutation vocalique; métaphonie *f.*

mutationism [mju:'teiʃ(ə)nizm], *s. Biol:* mutationnisme *m.*

mutationist [mju:'teiʃənist], *a. & s. Biol:* mutationniste (*mf*).

mutch [mʌtʃ], *s. Scot:* bonnet (blanc), coiffe *f* (de femme).

mute[1] [mju:t], *a. & s.*

I. *a.* **1.** (*of pers., appeal, etc.*) muet; *F:* **m. as a fish,** muet comme un poisson, comme une carpe; **she stood m. with wonder,** elle restait immobile, dans un étonnement muet, muette d'étonnement; *Jur:* **to stand m. (of malice),** refuser de plaider, de répondre; *Ven:* **m. hound,** chien secret. **2.** *Ling:* (*a*) **m. letter,** lettre muette; **h m.,** h muet; (*of sound*) **to become m.,** s'amuïr; (*b*) **m. consonant,** consonne sourde.

II. *s.* **1.** (*pers.*) (*a*) muet, -ette; (*b*) employé *m* des pompes funèbres; (i) croque-mort *m, pl.* croque-morts; (ii) *A:* pleureur *m*; (*c*) *Th:* personnage muet; (*d*) (*in the Orient*) muet (du sérail). **2.** *Ling:* consonne sourde. **3.** *Mus:* sourdine *f*; **with the m. on,** en sourdine.

mute[2], *v.tr.* **1.** amortir, étouffer, assourdir (un son). **2.** *Mus:* mettre une sourdine à, assourdir (un violon, etc.). **3.** *Vit:* muter (le vin).

mute[3], *v.i. A: & Dial:* (*of birds*) fienter.

muted ['mju:tid], *a. Mus:* (violon *m*) en sourdine; (corde) sourde.

mutely ['mju:tli], *adv.* muettement; en silence.

muteness ['mju:tnis], *s.* **1.** mutisme *m.* **2.** mutisme, silence *m.*

mutilate ['mju:tileit], *v.tr.* mutiler, estropier (qn); mutiler (une statue, une pièce de théâtre); tronquer (un passage, une citation).

mutilating ['mju:tileitiŋ], **mutilation** [mju:ti'leiʃ(ə)n], *s.* mutilation *f.*

mutilator ['mju:tileitər], *s.* mutilateur, -trice.

mutillid ['mju:tilid], *s. Ent:* mutille *f.*

mutineer [mju:ti'niər], *s. Mil: Nau:* révolté *m,* mutiné *m,* mutin *m.*

muting ['mju:tiŋ], *s.* **1.** amortissement *m,* assourdissement *m,* atténuation *f* (d'un son). **2.** mise *f* d'une sourdine à (un violon, etc.). **3.** *Vit:* mutage *m.*

mutinous ['mju:tinəs], *a.* rebelle, mutiné, mutin; (équipage *m*) en révolte.

mutinously ['mju:tinəsli], *adv.* d'un air, d'un ton, de révolte.

mutinousness ['mju:tinəsnis], *s.* tendance *f* à la révolte; insoumission *f.*

mutiny[1] ['mju:tini], *s.* révolte *f,* mutinerie *f*; *Hist:* **the Indian M.,** la Révolte des cipayes.

mutiny[2], *v.i.* se révolter, se mutiner (**against,** contre).

mutism ['mju:tizm], *s.* mutisme *m*; mutité *f.*

mutoscope ['mju:təskoup], *s. A:* mutoscope *m.*

mutt [mʌt], *s. F:* **1.** idiot, -ote; andouille *f*; **poor m.!** pauvre mec! **2.** *NAm:* chien *m* (sans race).

mutter[1] ['mʌtər], *s.* murmure *m* (entre les dents).
mutter[2], *v.tr. & i.* marmonner, marmotter, murmurer, grommeler; *F:* maronner; (*of thunder*) gronder; **to m. an oath,** grommeler, maronner, un juron; **to m. at, against, s.o.,** murmurer contre qn.
mutterer ['mʌtərər], *s.* marmotteur, -euse.
muttering[1] ['mʌt(ə)riŋ], *a.* qui marmotte, qui marmonne; murmurant, grondant.
muttering[2], *s.* marmottage *m*, grommellement *m*, murmures *mpl*; rumeurs sourdes; grondement *m* (du tonnerre); **hostile mutterings,** hostilité sourde; **mutterings of revolt,** grondements de l'émeute.
mutton ['mʌt(ə)n], *s. Cu:* mouton *m*; **leg of m.,** gigot *m*; **shoulder of m.,** épaule *f* de mouton; **m. chop, cutlet,** côtelette *f* de mouton; *F:* **m.-chop whiskers,** favoris *m* en côtelette; *F:* (*of woman*) **m. dressed (up) as lamb,** vieux tableau; *F: O:* **to eat s.o.'s m.,** manger la soupe avec qn; **m. fat,** graisse *f* de mouton; suif *m* de mouton.
mutton-bird ['mʌtənbə:d], *s. Orn:* puffin *m*, pétrel *m*; **Australian m.-b.,** puffin à bec grêle; **New Zealand m.-b.,** puffin fuligineux.
muttonhead ['mʌt(ə)nhed], *s. F:* idiot, -ote; andouille *f*.
muttonheaded [mʌt(ə)n'hedid], *a. F:* bête comme ses pieds.
mutual ['mju:tjuəl], *a.* **1.** (*a*) (*of feelings, etc.*) mutuel, réciproque; **m. improvement,** enseignement mutuel; **to arrange a transaction on m. principles, on m. terms,** conclure un marché stipulant un échange de services, avec stipulation de réciprocité; **m. benefit society,** société *f* de secours mutuels; **member of a m. benefit society,** mutualiste *mf*; **m. assurance,** coassurance *f*; **m. assurance company,** compagnie *f* d'assurances mutuelles; mutuelle *f*; *Jur:* **m. testament,** donation *f* au dernier survivant; (*b*) *El: Elcs:* **m. attraction, m. repulsion,** attraction, répulsion, mutuelle; **m. capacitance, m. impedance, m. inductance,** capacitance, impédance, inductance, mutuelle; **m. conductance,** pente *f* (d'un tube électronique); **m. interaction,** action(s) *f* réciproque(s), réactions mutuelles. **2.** commun; (*a*) *Tchn:* **m. branch,** branche commune (d'un réseau téléphonique, etc.); **m. point,** point commun; *Cmptr:* **m. key,** critère commun (de classement); (*b*) **our m. friends,** nos amis communs.
mutualism ['mju:tjuəlizm], *s. Nat.Hist: Pol.Ec:* mutualisme *m*.
mutualist ['mju:tjuəlist], *s. Nat.Hist: Pol.Ec:* mutualiste *mf*.
mutuality [mju:tju'æliti], *s.* mutualité *f*, réciprocité *f*.
mutualization ['mju:tjuəlai'zeiʃ(ə)n], *s.* mutualisation *f*.
mutually ['mju:tjwəli], *adv.* mutuellement, réciproquement; d'un commun accord.
mutulary ['mju:tjuləri], *a. Arch:* mutulaire.
mutule ['mju:tju:l], *s. Arch:* mutule *f*.
muzzle[1] ['mʌzl], *s.* **1.** museau *m* (d'un animal). **2.** bouche *f*, gueule *f* (d'une arme à feu); *Artil:* **m. loader,** pièce *f* se chargeant par la bouche; **m. brake,** frein *m* de bouche; **m. ring,** ceinture *f* de bouche (de canon); **m. cover,** couvre-bouche *m, pl.* couvre-bouches (de pièce d'artillerie); capuchon *m* (de canon de fusil); **m. flash,** lueur *f* de départ; **m. velocity,** vitesse initiale, à la bouche. **3.** muselière *f* (pour chiens, etc.); bâillon *m* (pour chevaux).
muzzle[2], *v.tr.* **1.** museler (un chien, *F:* la presse, etc.); *F:* bâillonner (la presse, etc.). **2.** *Nau:* haler bas (une voile); diminuer (de voiles).
muzzler ['mʌzlər], *s. Nau:* coup *m* de vent contraire.
muzzling ['mʌzliŋ], *s.* musellement *m*, bâillonnement *m*.
muzzy ['mʌzi], *a.* **1.** (*a*) (*of pers.*) brouillé dans ses idées; hébété; au cerveau fumeux; (*b*) (*of ideas*) confus, vague; (*of outline*) flou, estompé; **m. painting,** peinture floue; (*c*) (*of weather, place*) brumeux, embrumé, sombre. **2.** un peu gris; éméché; enfumé par la boisson.
my [mai], *poss.a.* **1.** mon, *f.* ma, *pl.* mes; (*in the fem. before a vowel sound*) mon; **my book and my pen,** mon livre et ma plume; **my shoes and socks,** mes souliers et mes chaussettes; **my opinion and yours,** mon opinion et la vôtre; **one of my friends,** un de mes amis; un ami à moi; **my father and mother,** mon père et ma mère; *Jur:* mes père et mère; **my king and master,** mon roi et maître; **my own son,** mon propre fils; **my two,** les deux miens; **I fell on my back,** je suis tombé sur le dos; **I have broken my arm,** je me suis cassé le bras; **my hair is grey,** j'ai les cheveux gris; (*emphatic*) *my* **idea would be to . . .,** mon idée à moi serait de . . .; *Games: etc:* **my turn! my ball!** à moi! *int. F: O:* **my!** sapristi! rien que ça! par exemple! **2.** (*ethical*) **I know my Homer from beginning to end,** je connais mon Homère d'un bout à l'autre.
Mya ['maiə], *s. Moll:* mya *f*.
myalgia [mai'ældʒiə], *s. Med:* myalgie *f*, myodynie *f*.
myall ['maiəl], *s.* **1.** *Bot:* acacia *m* d'Australie. **2.** *Austr:* aborigène *mf* (sauvage).
myasis [mai'eisis], *s. Med:* my(i)ase *f*.
myasthenia [maiæs'θi:niə], *s. Med:* myasthénie *f*.
myatony [mai'ætəni], *s. Med:* myatonie *f*.
myatrophy [mai'ætrəfi], *s. Med:* myatrophie *f*, amyotrophie *f*.
mycelial [mai'si:liəl], *a. Fung:* mycélien.
mycelium [mai'si:liəm], *s. Fung:* mycélium *m*, mycélion *m*, *F:* blanc *m* de champignon.
Mycenae [mai'si:ni:]. *Pr.n. Geog: Archeol:* Mycènes.
Mycenaen [mai'si:niən], *a. Geog: Archeol:* mycénien.
Mycetes [mai'si:ti:z], *s. Z:* mycètes *m*.
mycetology [maisi'tələdʒi], *s.* mycétologie *f*.
mycetoma [maisi'toumə], *s. Med:* mycétome *m*.
mycetophagous [maisi'təfəgəs], *a. Ent:* mycétophage.
mycetophilid [maisi'təfilid], *a. & s. Ent:* mycétophile (*f*).
Mycetozoa [maisitòu'zouə], *s.pl. Bot: Fung:* mycétozoaires *m*.
Mycobacteriaceae [maikoubæktiəri'eisii:], *s.pl. Fung:* mycobactériées *f*.
mycocecidium [maikousi'sidiəm], *s. Bot:* mycocécidie *f*.
mycoderm ['maikoudə:m], **mycoderma** [maikrou'də:mə], *s. Fung:* mycoderme *m*.
mycodermic, mycodermatoid [maikou'də:mik, -'də:mətɔid], *a. Fung:* mycodermique.
mycologic(al) [maikou'lɔdʒik(l)], *a. Bot:* mycologique.
mycologist [mai'kɔlədʒist], *s. Bot:* mycologue *mf*.
mycology [mai'kɔlədʒi], *s. Bot:* mycologie *f*.
mycophagist [mai'kɔfədʒist], *s.* mycophage *mf*.
mycophagous [mai'kɔfəgəs], *a.* mycophage.
mycor(r)hiza [maikou'raizə], *s. Fung:* mycor(r)hize *f*.
mycosis [mai'kousis], *s. Med:* mycose *f*; **m. fungoides,** mycosis *m* fongoïde.
mycostatic [maikou'stætik], *a.* fongostatique.
myctophid ['miktoufid], *s. Ich:* myctophide *m*.
Myctophidae [mik'tɔfidi:], *s.pl. Ich:* myctophidés *m*.
mydriasis [mi'draiəsis], *s. Med:* mydriase *f*.
mydriatic [midri'ætik]. **1.** *a. Med:* mydriatique, mydriadique. **2.** *s. Pharm:* mydriatique *m*.
myel(a)emia [maiə'li:miə], *s. Med:* myélémie *f*, myélocytémie *f*.
myelencephalon [maiəlen'sefələn], *s. Anat:* myélencéphale *m*.
myelin(e) ['maiəl(a)in], *s. Anat:* myéline *f*.
myelinic [maiə'li:nik], *a. Anat:* myélinique.
myelitis [maiə'laitis], *s. Med:* myélite *f*.
myeloblast ['maiəloublæst], *s. Physiol:* myéloblaste *m*.
myelocele ['maiəlousi:l], *s. Anat:* myélocèle *f*.
myelocystocele [maiəlou'sistousi:l], *s. Med:* myélocystocèle *f*.
myelocyte ['maiəlousait], *s. Physiol:* myélocyte *m*.
myelogenous [maiə'lɔdʒinəs], *a. Anat:* myélogène; *Med:* **m. leuk(a)emia,** leucémie *f* myélogène.
myelogram [mai'elougræm], *s. Med:* myélogramme *m*.
myelographic [maiəlou'græfik], *a. Med:* myélographique.
myelography [maiə'lɔgrəfi], *s. Med:* myélographie *f*.
myeloid ['maiəlɔid], *a. Med:* myéloïde; **m. tumour,** tumeur *f* myéloïde.
myeloma [maiə'loumə], *s. Med:* myélome *m*; **multiple m.,** myélome multiple.
myelomatosis [maiəloumə'tousis], *s. Med:* myélomatose *f*.
myelomatous [maiə'lɔmətəs], *a. Med:* myélomateux.
myelomeningitis [maiəloumenin'dʒaitis], *s. Med:* myélo-méningite *f*.
myelopathy [maiə'lɔpəθi], *s. Med:* myélopathie *f*.
myelophthisis [maiəlɔf'θaisis], *s. Med:* myélophtisie *f*.
myeloplax ['maiəlouplæks], *s. Anat:* myéloplaxe *m*.
myelosarcoma [maiəlousɑ:'koumə], *s. Med:* myélosarcome *m*.
mygale ['migəli], *s. Arach:* mygale *f*.
myiasis [maii'eisis], *s. Med:* my(i)ase *f*.
Myliobatidae [miliou'bætidi:], *s.pl. Ich:* myliobatidés *m*.
mylohoyid [milou'hɔid], *a. & s. Anat:* (muscle) mylo-hoïdien *m*.
mylonite ['mailənait], *s. Miner:* mylonite *f*.
Mymaridae [mai'mæridi:], *s.pl. Ent:* mymarides *m*.
myna(h) ['mainə], *s. Orn:* martin *m*; **common m.,** martin triste; **grey-headed m.,** martin à tête grise; **Brahminy m.,** martin des pagodes; **pied m.,** martin-pie *m*; **hill m.,** mainate (religieux); **crested m.,** étourneau huppé (*Fr.C.*).
myoblast ['maioublæst], *s. Physiol:* myoblaste *m*.
myocarditis [maioukɑ:'daitis], *s. Med:* myocardite *f*.
myocardium [maiou'kɑ:diəm], *s. Anat:* myocarde *m*.
myocyte ['maiousait], *s.* myocyte *m*.
myodynamia [maioudai'neimiə], *s.* myodynamie *f*.
myoedema [maiou'i:dimə], *s. Med:* myœdème *m*.
myoelectric [maioui'lektrik], *a.* myoélectrique.
myoepithelioma [maiouepiθi:li'oumə], *s. Med:* myoépithéliome *m*.
myofunctional [maiou'fʌŋkʃən(ə)l], *a. Med:* **m. therapy,** myothérapie *f*.
myogenesis [maiou'dʒenisis], *s.* myogénie *f*.
myogenetic [maioudʒe'netik], *a.* myogène.
myoglobin [maiou'gloubin], *s. Physiol:* myoglobine *f*.
myoglobinurea [maiougləbi'nju:riə], *s. Med:* myoglobinurie *f*.
myogram ['maiougræm], *s. Med:* myogramme *m*.
myograph ['maiougræf], *s. Med:* myographe *m*.
myographic [maiou'græfik], *a. Med:* myographique.
myographist [mai'ɔgrəfist], *s. Med:* myographe *m*.
myography [mai'ɔgrəfi], *s. Med:* myographie *f*.
myoh(a)emoglobin [maiouhi:mou'gloubin], *s. Physiol:* myoglobine *f*.
myokinetic [maioukai'netik], *a.* myokinétique.
myolemma [maiou'lemə], *s. Med:* myolemme *m*.
myologic(al) [maiou'lɔdʒik(l)], *a. Anat:* myologique.
myologist [mai'ɔlədʒist], *s. Anat:* myologiste *mf*.
myology [mai'ɔlədʒi], *s. Anat:* myologie *f*.
myoma [mai'oumə], *s. Med:* myome *m*.
myomere ['maioumiər], *s. Anat:* myomère *m*.
myometrium [maiou'mi:triəm], *s. Anat:* myomètre *m*.
Myomorpha [maiou'mɔ:fə], *s.pl. Z:* myomorphes *m*.
myopathic [maiou'pæθik], *a.* myopathique.
myopathy [mai'ɔpəθi], *s. Med:* myopathie *f*.
myope ['maioup], *s.* myope *mf*.
myopia [mai'oupiə], *s.* myopie *f*.
myopic [mai'ɔpik], *a.* **1.** (*suffering from myopia*) myope. **2.** (*relating to myopia*) myopique.
myoplastic [maiou'plæstik], *a. Surg:* myoplastique.
myoplasty ['maiouplæsti], *s. Surg:* myoplastie *f*.
myopotamus [maiou'pɔtəməs], *s. Z:* myopotame *m*.
myorrhaphy [maiou'ræfi], *s. Surg:* myorraphie *f*.
myosclerosis [maiouskle'rousis], *s. Med:* myosclérose *f*.
myosin ['maiousin], *s. Physiol:* myosine *f*.
myosis [mai'ousis], *s. Med:* myosis *m*.
myositis [maiou'saitis], *s. Med:* myosite *f*.
myosotis [maiou'soutis], *s. Bot:* myosotis *m*.
myotic [mai'ɔtik], *a. Med:* myotique.
myotome ['maioutoum], *s. Anat:* myotome *m*.
myotomy [mai'ɔtəmi], *s. Surg:* myotomie *f*.
myotonia [maiou'touniə], *s. Med:* myotonie *f*.
myotonic [maiou'tɔnik], *a.* myotonique.
Myoxidae [mai'ɔksidi:], *s.pl. Z:* myoxidés *m*.
myrcene ['mə:si:n], *s. Ch:* myrcène *m*.
myria- ['miriə], *pref.* myria-.
myriad ['miriəd]. **1.** *s.* myriade *f*. **2.** *a. Lit:* innombrable.
myriagramme ['miriəgræm], *s. Meas:* myriagramme *m*.
myriameter ['miriəmi:tər], *s. Meas:* myriamètre *m*.
myriametric [miriə'metrik], *a. Meas:* myriamétrique; *Ph:* **m. wave,** onde *f* myriamétrique.
myriapod ['miriəpɔd], *s. Nat.Hist:* myriapode (*m*); *F:* mille-pattes *m inv.*
Myriapoda [miriə'poudə], *s.pl. Nat.Hist:* myriapodes *m*.
myriapodous [miri'æpədəs], *a. Nat.Hist:* myriapode.
myrica ['mirikə], *s. Bot:* myrica *m*.
Myricaceae [miri'keisii:], *s.pl. Bot:* myricacées *f*.
myringa [mi'riŋgə], *s. Anat:* myringe *f*, membrane *f* du tympan.
myringitis [mirin'dʒaitis], *s. Med:* myringite *f*.
myringotomy [miriŋ'gɔtəmi], *s. Surg:* myringotomie *f*.
myriophyllum [miriou'filəm], *s. Bot:* myriophylle *m*.
myristic [mi'ristik], *a. Ch:* (acide) myristique.
Myristicaceae [miristi'keisii:], *s.pl. Bot:* myristicacées *f*.
myristin ['miristin], *s. Ch:* myristine *f*.
Myrmecobiidae [mə:mi:kou'baiidi:], *s.pl. Z:* myrmécobiidés *m*.
myrmecological [mə:mikə'lɔdʒik(ə)l], *a. Ent:* myrmécologique.
myrmecologist [mə:mi'kɔlədʒist], *s. Ent:* myrmécologiste *m*.
myrmecology [mə:mi'kɔlədʒi], *s. Ent:* myrmécologie *f*.
Myrmecophagidae [mə:mikou'fædʒidi:], *s.pl. Z:* myrmécophagidés *m*.
myrmecophagous [mə:mi'kɔfəgəs], *a. Nat.Hist:* myrmécophage.
myrmecophilous [mə:mi'kɔfiləs], *a. Nat.Hist:* myrmécophile.
myrmecophily [mə:mi'kɔfili], *s. Nat.Hist:* myrmécophilie *f*.
myrmecophyte [mə:'mi:koufait], *s. Bot:* myrmécophyte *m*.
myrmeleon [mə:'mi:liən], *s. Ent:* formica-leo *m*; fourmilion *m*.

Myrmidon ['mə:mid(ə)n]. **1.** *Pr.n. Gr.Myth:* Myrmidon *m*. **2.** *s. F:* (*a*) assassin *m* à gages; spadassin *m*; (*b*) *A:* **the myrmidons of the law,** les officiers publics; les policiers *m*; les stipendiaires *m*, les sbires *m*, de la police; les suppôts *m* de la loi.
myrmillo [mə:'milou], *s. Ant:* mirmillon *m*.
myrobalan [mai'rɔbələn], *s.* **1.** *Bot:* myrobalan *m*, myrobolan *m*. **2. m. plum,** prunier myrobolan.
myronic [mai'rɔnik], *a.* myronique.
myrosin ['mirəsin], *s. Bio-Ch:* myrosine *f*.
myroxylon [mai'rɔksilɔn], *s. Bot:* myroxylon *m*; toluifera *m*.
myrrh[1] [mə:r], *s.* myrrhe *f*.
myrrh[2], *s. Bot:* myrrhide odorante; cerfeuil odorant, musqué, d'Espagne.
Myrsinaceae [mə:si'neisii:], *s.pl. Bot:* myrsinacées *f*.
Myrtaceae [mə:'teisii:], *s.pl. Bot:* myrtacées *f*.
myrtaceous [mə:'teiʃəs], *a.* myrtacé.
myrtiform ['mə:tifɔ:m], *a.* myrtiforme.
myrtle ['mə:tl], *s. Bot:* **1.** myrte *m*. **2. bog m., Dutch m.,** myrte bâtard, des marais; trèfle *m* d'eau; galé (odorant); piment royal; poivre *m* de Brabant; bois-sent-bon *m*; **blue m.,** céanothe *m*, céanothus *m*. **3.** *NAm:* pervenche grimpante. **4. m. wax,** cire *f* de myrica.
myrtleberry ['mə:tlberi], *s.* **1.** baie *f* de myrte. **2.** airelle *f* myrtille.
myself [mai'self], *pers. pron.* (*a*) (*emphatic*) moi (-même); **I did it m.,** je l'ai fait moi-même; **I saw it m.,** je l'ai vu moi-même, de mes propres yeux; *F:* **I'm not quite m.,** je ne suis pas dans mon assiette; **I m. believe, speaking for m. I believe, that. . .,** (quant à) moi, pour ma part, je crois que . . .; (*b*) (*reflexive*) me; **I've hurt m.,** je me suis fait mal; **I was enjoying m. very much,** je m'amusais beaucoup; **I did it, I couldn't help m.,** je l'ai fait, je n'ai pu m'empêcher de le faire; (*at meal*) **I can help m.,** je peux me servir, moi-même; (*c*) (*after preposition*) **I live by m.,** je vis tout seul; **I was laughing to m.,** je riais tout seul; **I'm not speaking for m.,** je ne parle pas en mon nom; **I'll keep it for m.,** je le garderai pour moi(-même).
Mysia ['maisiə]. *Pr.n. A.Hist:* Mysie *f*.
mysid ['maisid], *s. Crust:* myside *m*.
Mysidacea [maisi'deisiə], *s.pl. Crust:* mysidacés *m*.
Mysidae ['maisidi:], *s.pl. Crust:* mysides *m*, mysidés *m*.
mysis ['maisis], *s. Crust:* mysis *m*.
mystagogue ['mistəgɔg], *s. Gr.Ant:* mystagogue *m*.
mystagogy ['mistəgɔdʒi], *s. Gr.Ant:* mystagogie *f*.
mysterious [mis'tiəriəs], *a.* **1.** mystérieux; **a m. business,** une affaire mystérieuse, une ténébreuse affaire; *s.* **men are always attracted by the m.,** le mystérieux séduit toujours les hommes. **2.** (*of pers.*) mystérieux; qui aime le mystère.
mysteriously [mis'tiəriəsli], *adv.* mystérieusement; **he's behaving very m.,** il agit d'une façon très étrange, très mystérieuse.
mysteriousness [mis'tiəriəsnis], *s.* caractère mystérieux (**of,** de); mystère *m*.
mystery[1] ['mist(ə)ri], *s.* **1.** mystère *m*; **to make a m. of sth.,** faire mystère de qch.; **I see no m. about it,** je n'y vois rien de mystérieux; **it's a m. to me,** pour moi c'est un mystère; c'est lettre close pour moi; **there was some m. about it that I didn't understand,** il y avait là un mystère que je ne comprenais pas; **wrapped in m.,** enveloppé de mystère; **the key to the m.,** la clef du mystère. **2.** *A.Th:* **m. (play),** mystère. **3.** *Theol:* **the Holy Mysteries,** les saints mystères; l'eucharistie *f*.
mystery[2], *s. A:* **arts and mysteries,** arts et métiers *m*.
mystic ['mistik]. **1.** *a.* (*a*) (*of rites, arts*) ésotérique, cabalistique, mystique; (*b*) (*of power*) occulte; (*of formula*) magique; (*c*) surnaturel; **the m. hour of midnight,** minuit, l'heure des mystères; (*d*) *Theol:* mystique; (*e*) **the m. dove,** la colombe mystique; *Jur:* **m. will,** testament *m* mystique. **2.** *s.* (*a*) magicien *m*, initié *m*; (*b*) *Theol:* mystique *mf*.
mystical ['mistik(ə)l], *a.* mystique; **m. theology,** mystique *f*.
mystically ['mistik(ə)li], *adv.* mystiquement; avec mysticisme.
Mysticeti [misti'si:ti], *s.pl. Z:* mysticètes *m*.
mysticism ['mistisizm], *s.* mysticisme *m*.
mystification [mistifi'keiʃ(ə)n], *s.* **1.** mystification *f*; farce jouée à qn. **2.** embrouillement *m*, désorientation *f* (de l'esprit de qn); obscurcissement *m*, complication *f* (d'une question).
mystifier ['mistifaiər], *s.* **1.** mystificateur, -trice. **2.** embrouilleur, -euse; personne qui désoriente l'esprit de qn, qui obscurcit, complique, une question.
mystify ['mistifai], *v.tr.* **1.** mystifier (qn); **mystified by . . .,** intrigué par . . .. **2.** désorienter, dérouter. **3.** envelopper, parer, (qch.) de mystère; faire un mystère de (qch.); embrouiller, obscurcir, compliquer (une question).
mystique [mis'ti:k], *s.* mystique *f*.
myth [miθ], *s.* (*a*) mythe *m*; (*b*) **is justice a m.?** la justice est-elle un mythe?
mythical ['miθik(ə)l], *a.* mythique.
mythicize ['miθisaiz], *v.tr.* **1.** donner un caractère mythique à (un phénomène naturel, etc.). **2.** interpréter (les saintes Écritures, etc.) mythologiquement.
mythographer [mi'θɔgrəfər], *s.* mythographe *m*.
mythography [mi'θɔgrəfi], *s.* mythographie *f*.
mythological [miθə'lɔdʒik(ə)l], *a.* mythologique.
mythologically [miθə'lɔdʒik(ə)li], *adv.* mythologiquement.
mythologist [mi'θɔlədʒist], *s.* mythologue *mf*, mythologiste *mf*.
mythology [mi'θɔlədʒi], *s.* mythologie *f*.
mythomania [miθou'meiniə], *s.* mythomanie *f*.
mythomaniac [miθou'meiniæk]. **1.** *a.* mythomaniaque. **2.** *s.* mythomane *mf*.
mythopoeic [miθou'pi:ik], **mythopoetic** [miθoupou'etik], *a.* qui crée des mythes.
Mytilacea [miti'leiʃiə], *s.pl. Moll:* mytilacés *m*.
Mytilene [miti'li:ni]. *Pr.n. Geog:* Mytilène.
Mytilidae [mi'tilidi:], *s.pl. Moll:* mytilidés *m*.
mytilotoxine [mitilou'tɔksin], *s. Ch:* mytilotoxine *f*.
myurous [mai'ju:rəs], *a. Med:* myure; **m. pulse,** pouls *m* myure.
myxa ['miksə], *s. Orn:* myxa *f*.
myxamoeba [miksæ'mi:bə], *s. Prot:* myxamibe *f*.
myxine ['miksain], *s. Ich:* myxine *f*.
myxobacterium, *pl.* **-ia** [miksoubæk'tiəriəm, -iə], *s.* myxobactérie *f*.
myxochondroma [miksoukɔn'droumə], *s. Med:* myxochondrome *m*.
myx(o)edema [miksi'di:mə], *s. Med:* myxœdème *m*.
myx(o)edematous [miksi'demətəs], *a. Med:* myxœdémateux.
myxofibroma [miksoufai'broumə], *s. Med:* myxofibrome *m*.
myxoid ['miksɔid], *a.* myxoïde.
myxoma, *pl.* **-ata** [mik'soumə, -ətə], *s. Med:* myxome *m*.
myxomatosis [miksoumə'tousis], *s.* myxomatose *f*.
myxomatous [mik'sɔmətəs], *a.* myxomateux.
Myxomycetes [miksoumai'si:ti:z], *s.pl. Fung:* myxomycètes *m*.
myxomyoma [miksoumai'oumə], *s. Med:* myxomyome *m*.
Myxophyceae [miksou'f(a)isii:], *s.pl. Algae:* cyanophycées *f*.
myxorrhea [miksə'ri:ə], *s. Med:* myxorrhée *f*.
myxosarcoma [miksousɑ:'koumə], *s. Med:* myxosarcome *m*.
Myxosporidia [miksouspɔ'ridiə], *s.pl. Prot:* myxosporidies *f*.
Myzostomata [maizoustou'meitə], *s.pl. Ann:* myzostomes *m*.
myzostome ['maizoustoum], *s. Ann:* myzostome *m*.

N

N, n [en], *s.* (*a*) (la lettre) N, n *f*; *Tp:* **N for Nellie,** N comme Nicolas; *Ecc:* **what is your name—N or M?** comment vous appelez-vous?—N ou M? *Ph:* **n. rays,** rayons *m* n; *Aut:* (*in Fr.*) **the N seven,** la N sept; (la Route nationale sept); (*b*) *Mth:* **to the** n^{th} **(power),** à la $n^{ième}$ puissance; **the** n^{th} **power of x is written** x^n, la $n^{ième}$ puissance de x s'écrit x^n; *F:* **to the** n^{th}, au suprême degré; **I'm telling you for the** n^{th} **time,** je te le dis pour l'énième, la nième, fois; (*c*) *Typ:* **N (quadrat),** demi-cadratin *m*; **line of 50 n's,** ligne *f* de 50 n; **indent 2 n's,** à rentrer d'un cadratin.

naartje ['nɑːtʃə], *s. Hort:* (*in S. Africa*) mandarine *f*.

nab [næb], *v.tr.* (**nabbed**) *P:* **1.** (*a*) saisir, arrêter; *P:* pincer, choper, poisser, épingler (qn); **the police nabbed him,** il s'est fait pincer par la police; **the police nabbed the lot,** la police les a tous cueillis, embarqués, ratissés; **to get nabbed,** se faire pincer; se faire poisser; se faire piger; se faire cueillir; se faire choper; (*b*) prendre (qn) sur le fait; prendre (qn) la main dans le sac. **2.** escamoter, chiper, chaparder, barboter (qch.); **he's nabbed my watch,** il m'a chipé, il m'a fauché, ma montre.

Nabataean [næbə'tiːən]. **1.** *Hist:* (*a*) *a.* nabatéen; (*b*) *s.* Nabatéen, -éenne. **2.** *s. A.Ling:* nabatéen *m*.

nabla ['næblə], *s.* **1.** *Mus:* nabla *m*. **2.** *Mth:* (opérateur) nabla (*m*).

nabob ['neibɔb], *s.* (*a*) nabab *m*, nabob *m*; (*b*) homme *m* très riche; (*c*) Européen *m* qui a fait une grosse fortune dans l'Inde.

Naboth ['neibɔθ]. *Pr.n.m. B.Hist:* Naboth; **Naboth's vineyard,** la vigne de Naboth.

Nabothian [nə'bouθiən], *a. Med:* **N. cyst, follicle,** œuf *m* de Naboth.

nacarat ['nækəræt], *a. & s.* **1.** *Dy:* nacarat (*m*); **n. ribbons,** rubans *m* nacarat. **2.** *Tex:* **n. (crape),** nacarat (du Portugal).

nacelle [næ'sel], *s.* **1.** *Aer:* nacelle *f* (de ballon, de dirigeable); **streamlined n.,** nacelle profilée. **2.** *Av:* carlingue *f*, habitacle *m*; **(engine) n.,** fuseau-moteur *m*, *pl.* fuseaux-moteur; **gun n.,** (i) fuseau-canon *m*, *pl.* fuseaux-canon; (ii) fuseau-mitrailleuse(s) *m*, *pl.* fuseaux-mitrailleuse(s); **inboard, outboard, n.,** fuseau (-moteur) intérieur, extérieur; **wing n.,** fuseau(-moteur) dans l'aile.

nacre ['neikər], *s.* **1.** *Moll: A:* pinne marine. **2.** nacre *f*.

nacreous ['neikriəs], **nacrous** ['neikrəs], *a.* (coquillage, etc.) nacré; (nuage, etc.) nacré, perlaire.

nacrite ['neikrait], *s. Miner:* nacrite *f*.

nadir ['neidiːər], *s. Astr:* nadir *m*; **a people at the n. of degradation,** un peuple tombé au plus bas de la dégradation.

nadiral ['neidərəl], *a. Astr:* nadiral.

nadorite ['nædərait], *s. Miner:* nadorite *f*.

N(a)emorh(a)edus [nemə'riːdəs], *s. Z:* nemorhædus *m*.

n(a)eniae ['neniiː], *s.pl. Gr. & Rom.Ant:* nénies *f*.

naevus, *pl.* **-i** ['niːvəs, -ai], *s. Med:* (*a*) nævus *m*, *pl.* nævi; **pigmented, vascular, n.,** nævus pigmentaire, vasculaire; (*b*) tumeur *f* érectile.

nag[1] [næg], *s. F:* (*a*) *A:* petit cheval (de selle); bidet *m*; (*b*) bidet, canard *m*, canasson *m*, bique *f*, bourrin *m*.

nag[2], *s.* chamaillerie *f*; **n., n., all day long,** rien que des criailleries, que des querelles, pendant toute la journée.

nag[3], *v.tr. & i.* (**nagged**) quereller (qn); gronder (qn) sans cesse; criailler (**at s.o.,** contre qn); **to be always nagging (at) s.o.,** être toujours après qn; être toujours sur le dos de qn; être toujours à critiquer qn; harceler qn de querelles, de plaintes; **she nagged him into going with her,** à force de le harceler elle a obtenu qu'il l'accompagne.

naga ['nɑːgə], *s.* (*a*) *Myth:* naga *m inv*; (*b*) *Ling:* naga *m*.

nagaika [nə'gaikə], *s.* nagaïka *f*, nahaïka *f*.

nagana [nə'gɑːnə], *s. Vet:* nagana *m*; trypanosomiase communiquée par la mouche tsétsé.

Nagari ['nægəri], *s.* (*often attrib.*) *Ling:* nagari *f*.

nagger ['nægər], *s.* querelleur, -euse; grondeur, -euse; chamailleur, -euse; *F:* chipie *f*.

nagging[1] ['nægiŋ], *a.* **1.** (*of pers.*) querelleur, -euse, grondeur, -euse, chamaillard, hargneux, -euse. **2.** (*of pain, etc.*) agaçant, énervant.

nagging[2], *s.* chamaillerie *f*.

nagyagite ['nægjægait], *s. Miner:* nagyagite *f*, élasmose *f*.

nahoor [nə'huər], *s. Z:* nahor *m*.

naiad, *pl.* **-ads, -ades** ['naiæd, -ædz, -ədiːz]. **1.** *Myth:* naïade *f*; nymphe *f* des eaux. **2.** *Bot: Moll:* naïade. **3.** *Ent:* nymphe.

Naiadaceae [naiæ'deisiiː], *s.pl. Bot:* naïadacées *f*.

naiant ['neiənt], *a. Her:* nageant.

naif [nai'iːf], *a. Jewel:* naïf.

nail[1] [neil], *s.* **1.** (*a*) (*of pers., occ. of animal, bird*) ongle *m* (de doigt, d'orteil); *Toil:* **n. brush,** brosse *f* à ongles; **n. cleaner,** cure-ongle(s) *m inv*; **n. file,** lime *f* à ongles; **n. scissors,** ciseaux *m* à ongles; ongliers *m*; **n. varnish, polish, enamel,** vernis *m* à ongles; **n. varnish remover,** dissolvant *m* (pour ongles); **to bite one's (finger)nails,** se ronger les ongles; **to bite one's nails with impatience,** mordre ses doigts; se ronger les ongles; *Med:* **n. biting,** onychophagie *f*; *Anat:* **n. bed,** lit *m* de l'ongle; **n. groove,** gouttière, rainure, unguéale; **n. plate,** manteau *m* de l'ongle; **n. shaped,** onglé; (*b*) lamelle *f* (du bec du canard, etc.). **2.** clou *m*, *pl.* clous; **brass-headed n.,** clou à tête de laiton, clou doré; **cast n.,** clou fondu; **diamond n.,** clou à tête de diamant; **dog n.,** clou à grosse tête, (clou) caboche *f*; **flat(headed) n.,** clou à tête plate; **forged n., wrought n.,** clou forgé; **French n., wire n.,** clou, pointe *f*, de Paris; **wing n.,** aile *f* de mouche; **n. box,** cloutière *f*; **n. hole,** (i) clouure *f*; trou fait par un clou; (ii) (*in hinge, horseshoe, etc.*) étampure *f*, estampure *f*; (iii) (*on blade of penknife*) onglet *m*; **n. factory, works,** clouterie *f*; **wire n. works,** pointerie *f*; **n. dealer, maker, manufacturer,** cloutier *m*; **n. making,** clouterie *f*; **n. making machine,** machine cloutière; **wire n. cutting machine, n. cutter,** bistoquet *m*; *Tls:* **n. claw, drawer, extractor, wrench,** arrache-clou *m*, *pl.* arrache-clous; arrache-pointe(s) *m inv*; tire-clou(s) *m inv*; pied-de-biche *m*, *pl.* pieds-de-biche; **n. set, punch,** chasse-clou *m*, chasse-pointe *m*, chasse-goupille *m*, *pl.* chasse-clous, -pointes, -goupilles; **to drive in a n.,** enfoncer un clou; **to drive a n. into a wall,** planter un clou dans un mur; **to drive the n. home,** mener une affaire à bonne fin; **to draw, take out, a n.,** arracher un clou; *F:* **to hit the n. (right) on the head,** frapper, tomber, juste; mettre le doigt dessus; *Prov:* **one n. drives out another,** un clou chasse l'autre. **3.** *F:* **to pay on the n.,** payer argent comptant; payer recta; payer rubis sur l'ongle. **4.** *A.Meas:* nail *m*.

nail[2], *v.*

I. *v.tr.* **1.** clouer; **to n. (up) a notice on, to, a wall,** clouer une affiche au mur; fixer, attacher, une pancarte au mur avec un clou, avec des clous; **he stood nailed to the spot,** il est resté cloué au sol. **2.** clouter (des chaussures, une porte, etc.); **if you are going to do any climbing you should have your boots nailed,** si vous avez l'intention de faire de l'alpinisme, vous devriez faire mettre des clous à vos bottes. **3.** (*a*) *P:* attraper, saisir, tenir, coincer (qn); mettre la main sur (qn); (*b*) *F:* **to n. a lie,** exposer un mensonge.

II. (*compound verbs*) **1. nail down,** *v.tr.* (*a*) clouer (le couvercle d'une boîte); (*b*) *F:* **to n. s.o. down (to his promise),** obliger qn à tenir sa promesse; **he tried to wriggle out of the argument but we nailed him down,** il cherchait une échappatoire, mais nous l'avons acculé, nous l'avons mis au pied du mur.

2. nail up, *v.tr.* (*a*) clouer (une caisse); condamner (une porte); (*b*) *Hort:* palisser (un arbre fruitier).

nailed [neild], *a.* **1.** (*a*) cloué; (*b*) clouté; garni de clous; **n. shoes,** souliers cloutés; **heavily n. door,** porte garnie, ornementée, de gros clous. **2.** pourvu d'ongles; **long-n.,** aux ongles longs.

nailer ['neilər], *s.* **1.** (*a*) cloutier *m*; (*b*) cloueur *m* (de caisses, de peaux, etc.). **2.** *F: A:* (*of pers.*) bon type; type épatant; (*of thg*) chose épatante; **to be a n. at sth.,** être de première force à qch.; **he's a n. at it,** c'est un artiste dans la matière; c'est un as.

nailery ['neiləri], *s.* clouterie *f*.

nailhead ['neilhed], *s.* **1.** tête *f* de clou. **2.** *Arch:* pointe *f* de diamant.

nailheaded ['neilhedid], *a.* **1.** à tête de clou. **2.** *Arch:* (moulure, etc.) à pointes de diamant.

nailing[1] ['neiliŋ], *a. F: A:* excellent, épatant; **a n. good day with the hounds,** une épatante journée de chasse.

nailing[2], *s.* **1.** (*a*) clouage *m*, clouement *m*; **n. up,** (i) condamnation *f* (d'une porte); (ii) *Hort:* palissage *m* (d'un pêcher, etc.); (*b*) cloutage *m*; (*c*) *Med:* **intramedullary n.,** enclouage *m* médullaire. **2.** (*a*) les clous *m*; **the n. gave way,** les clous ont lâché; (*b*) clouterie *f*.

nailless ['neillis], *a.* **1.** sans ongles. **2.** sans clous.

nailsmith ['neilsmiθ], *s.* cloutier *m*.

nainsook ['neinsuk], *s. Tex:* nansouk *m*.

nais ['neiis], *s. Ann:* naïs *f*.

naissant ['neisənt], *a. Her:* naissant.

naïve, naive [nai'iːv], *a.* (*of pers., manner, etc.*) naïf, *f.* naïve; ingénu; **n. girl,** fille naïve, oie blanche; **to make n. remarks,** dire des simplicités, des naïvetés; *Art:* **n. art,** l'art naïf; **the naïves,** les naïfs.

naïvely [nai'iːvli], *adv.* naïvement, ingénument.

naïveté, naïvety [nai'iːvtei, -ti], *s.* naïveté *f*.

naja ['neidʒə], *s. Rept:* naja *m*.

naked ['neikid], *a.* **1.** (*a*) (*of pers.*) nu, sans vêtements; *F:* à poil; **stark n.,** tout nu; entièrement, complètement, nu; *F:* nu comme un ver, comme la main; **to strip (oneself) n.,** se mettre à nu, *F:* à poil; *s. B:* **to cover the n.,** couvrir celui qui est nu, ceux qui sont nus; (*b*) (bras, dos, etc.) découvert, nu; **the toga left the right arm n.,** la toge laissait à découvert, à nu, le bras droit; (*c*) (mur, etc.) nu, dégarni, sans ornement; (pays) dénudé, pelé;

(paysage) sans verdure, sans arbres; (arbre) dénudé, dépouillé de ses feuilles, sans feuillage; *Nat.Hist:* (*of stalk, tail, etc.*) nu; *Bot: F:* **n. lady, n. boys,** colchique *m* d'automne; safran *m* des prés; *F:* tue-chiens *m inv*; veillotte *f*. **2.** (*a*) sans protection; à découvert; **n. sword,** sabre nu; épée nue; **n. light,** feu nu, flamme nue; lumière *f* sans fanal; *Min:* lampe *f* à feu libre; (*b*) sans aide; **visible to the n. eye,** visible à l'œil nu; **to look at stars with the n. eye,** observer des étoiles à l'œil nu; (*c*) **the n. truth,** la vérité toute nue, sans fard; la pure vérité; **n. facts,** faits bruts; (*d*) *O:* **to believe sth. upon s.o.'s n. assertion,** croire à qch. sur le simple dire de qn; *Jur: Com:* nu, sans garantie; **n. bond,** contrat *m* sans garantie; **n. contract,** contrat sans contrepartie; contrat non exécutable; **n. debenture,** obligation *f* non valable.

nakedly ['neikidli], *adv.* (s'exposer) sans voiles, à nu; (conter des faits) nûment, simplement, sans déguisement.

nakedness ['neikidnis], *s.* nudité *f* (de qn, des murs, des rochers, etc.); pauvreté *f*, indigence *f* (d'esprit, etc.); **to reveal the crime in all its n.,** faire voir le crime dans toute sa nudité; *B:* **to see the n. of the land ye are come,** vous êtes venus pour remarquer les lieux faibles du pays.

namby-pamby ['næmbi'pæmbi]. **1.** *a.* (*of style, etc.*) fade; (*of pers.*) maniéré, affecté; sentimental, -aux; minaudier; gnangnan *inv*; **to behave in a n.-p. fashion,** faire la petite bouche; minauder. **2.** *s.* (i) personne maniérée, affectée, sentimentale, minaudière; (ii) *F:* mollasson *m*, poule mouillée.

namby-pambyism ['næmbi'pæmbiizm], *s.* afféterie *f*, fadeur *f*, sentimentalisme *m*, mignardise *f* (de qn, du style).

name[1] [neim], *s.* **1.** (*a*) nom *m*; **full n.,** nom et prénoms *mpl*; **Christian n., first n.,** *esp. NAm:* **given n.,** prénom; **baptismal n.,** nom de baptême; **family n., second n., last n.,** nom de famille; **boy's n., girl's n.,** prénom masculin, féminin; **maiden n.,** *Adm:* **n. at birth,** nom de jeune fille; **married n.,** nom de femme mariée, de mariage; **n. day,** (i) fête *f* (de qn); (ii) *St.Exch:* deuxième jour *m* de liquidation; **n. tape, tab,** marque *f* à linge; **to give a child the n. (of) George,** appeler un enfant Georges; **what's your n.?** quel est votre nom? comment vous appelez-vous? comment vous nommez-vous? **my n. is . . .,** je m'appelle . . .; je me nomme . . .; **what's his Christian n.?** quel est son prénom? **his Christian n. is John,** il se prénomme Jean, il a le prénom de Jean; **his real n. is Thomas,** de son vrai nom il s'appelle Thomas; **n. assumed when travelling,** nom de voyage; **n. of a ship,** devise *f*, nom, d'un navire; **to change the n. of a ship,** débaptiser un navire; **he knows the names of all the engines,** il connaît toutes les locomotives par leur nom; **n. of a firm, corporate n.,** raison sociale, nom social (d'une maison de commerce); **n. of a company,** raison sociale d'une société; **the n. of the company is . . .,** la société a pour dénomination . . ., la société prend la dénomination de . . .; **n. of an account,** intitulé *m* d'un compte; **n. of the payee,** nom du bénéficiaire; *Com:* **registered n., trade n.,** nom déposé; **brand n.,** marque de fabrique; **a man, X by n., by n. X, of the n. of X,** un homme du nom de X; *Jur:* le (dé)nommé X; *F:* **pleasant by n., pleasant by nature,** un joli nom, une jolie nature; **to have, bear, a n.,** porter un nom; **to go by, under, the n. of . . .,** être connu sous le nom de . . .; **he was known, went, by the n. of Martin,** on le connaissait sous le nom de Martin; (*of dog, etc.*) **he answers to his n.,** il répond à son nom; **to know s.o. (only) by n.,** (ne) connaître qn (que) de nom; **to refer to s.o. by n.,** désigner qn nominalement; **he was called upon by n. to answer,** il a été sommé nominativement de répondre; **to mention s.o. by n.,** nommer qn; mentionner qn nommément; **to mention sth. by n.,** nommer qch.; **he mentioned no names,** il n'a nommé personne; **certain members, I mention no names . . .,** certains membres, je ne précise pas . . .; **her n. is never mentioned in our house,** on ne la nomme jamais chez nous; **to give one's (full) n.,** décliner son nom et ses prénoms; (*to caller*) **what n. shall I say?** qui dois-je annoncer? **the caller went away without giving his n.,** le visiteur s'en est allé sans avoir donné son nom, sans s'être nommé; *F:* **give it a n.!** qu'est-ce que vous prenez? **to send in one's n.,** (i) se faire inscrire (dans un concours, etc.); (ii) se faire annoncer; **to set, put, one's n. to a document,** signer un document; mettre sa signature au bas d'un document; **to put one's n. down (for sth.),** (i) poser sa candidature; (ii) s'inscrire (pour qch.); **before he was thirty he had his n. up in Harley St.,** avant trente ans il avait sa plaque dans Harley Street; (*at Oxford or Cambridge*) **to have one's n. on the books,** être inscrit sur les registres; **to take one's n. off the books,** se faire rayer du registre; **list of names,** liste nominative; *F:* (*of police*) **to take s.o.'s n. and address,** dresser une contravention à qn; **in the n. of. . .,** au nom de . . ., de la part de . . .; **in the n. of the law,** au nom de la loi; **in the n. of the Father, the Son,** au nom du Père, du Fils; **I am speaking in the n. of Mr . . .,** je parle au nom de M. . . .; **speaking for myself and in the n. of Mr X,** parlant en mon nom et au nom de M. X; **the shares are in my n.,** les actions sont à mon nom; **in the n. of the king,** de par le roi; (*of official*) **to act in one's own n.,** agir en son nom personnel; *F:* **what in the n. of goodness are you doing?** que diable faites-vous là? **what in the n. of goodness is that?** pour l'amour de Dieu qu'est-ce que c'est que ça? **a king in n. only,** un roi de nom seulement; **to be master in n. only,** n'être maître que de nom; **it exists only in n.,** cela n'existe que nominalement; *F:* **I'll do it, or my n. isn't (Martin, etc.),** je le ferai ou j'y perdrai mon nom; (*b*) terme *m*; **endearing names,** termes d'amitié; **insulting n.,** appellation injurieuse; (*c*) **names of things,** noms de choses; **names of the different parts of sth.,** noms, dénomination *f*, des différentes parties de qch.; *Gram:* **proper n.,** nom propre; **another n. for . . .,** autre nom pour . . .; **by whatever n. you call it,** de quelque nom qu'on le nomme; **to give a new plant a n.,** dénommer une nouvelle plante; (*d*) titre *m* (d'une pièce de théâtre, d'un roman, etc.); **n. part,** rôle *m* qui donne le titre à une pièce, à un film, etc.; **n. story,** conte *m* qui donne le titre à un recueil. **2.** réputation *f*, renommée *f*; **he has a good, a bad, n.,** il a (une) bonne, (une) mauvaise, réputation; **to get a bad n.,** se faire un mauvais renom; **trademark with a good n.,** marque réputée; **to defend one's good n.,** défendre sa réputation; **to forfeit one's good n.,** se perdre de réputation, perdre sa réputation; **man who has lost his good n.,** homme décrié; homme perdu de réputation; **he already has several successful plays to his n.,** il a déjà fait jouer plusieurs pièces à succès; **a big n. in the theatre, the business, world,** un nom bien connu dans le monde du théâtre, des affaires; *F:* **his n. is mud for doing it,** on trouve mauvais qu'il le fasse; **if I'm late my n. will be mud,** si j'arrive en retard je vais me faire appeler Arthur; *Prov:* **a good, a fair, n. is better than riches,** bonne renommée vaut mieux que ceinture dorée; **he has a n. for honesty; he has the n. of being honest,** il est connu, réputé, pour son honnêteté; **he had made a n. as a weather prophet,** il s'était fait une réputation d'oracle du temps; **to make, achieve, a n. for oneself, to make one's n.,** se faire un grand nom; se faire une réputation (**as,** de); sortir du rang; **author who is beginning to make a n.,** auteur *m* qui commence à percer; **it made his n.,** cela a fait sa réputation; **to have nothing but one's n. and sword,** n'avoir que la cape et l'épée; **to lend one's n. to an undertaking,** prêter son nom pour une entreprise.

name[2], *v.tr.* **1.** (*a*) nommer; donner un nom à (qn, qch.); **to n. s.o. sth.,** nommer qn qch.; **he was named Peter,** (i) on lui a donné le nom de Pierre; on l'a appelé, on l'a nommé, Pierre; (ii) il s'appelait, se nommait, Pierre; **a person named Thomas,** un nommé Thomas; **to n. a new mineral,** dénommer un nouveau minéral; **way of naming plants,** appellation *f* des plantes; **to n. s.o. after s.o.,** *U.S:* **for s.o.,** donner à qn le nom de qn; **he is named after his father,** il porte le prénom de son père; (*b*) **I know his face, but I can't n. him,** je le connais de vue mais je ne me rappelle pas son nom, mais son nom m'échappe. **2. to n. s.o. to an office,** nommer qn à un poste; **to n. s.o. mayor,** nommer qn maire. **3.** (*a*) désigner (qn, qch.) par son nom; mentionner, dénommer (qn); **n. the kings of England,** donnez les noms des rois d'Angleterre; *Parl:* (*to member making insinuation*) **n.! n.!** nommez-le! son nom? (*b*) (*of the Speaker, in House of Commons*) **to n. a member,** signaler à la Chambre l'indiscipline d'un membre. **4.** (*a*) citer (un exemple, un fait); *F:* **you n. it, (he's done it, got it, etc.),** tout ce qu'on peut imaginer, (il l'a fait, le possède, etc.); (*b*) fixer (le jour, l'heure, une somme); **n. any price you like,** fixe tel prix que vous voudrez; **to n. a day for . . .,** indiquer, arrêter, un jour pour . . ..

nam(e)able ['neiməbl], *a.* que l'on peut nommer.

nameboard ['neimbɔ:d], *s. Nau:* tableau *m* (d'un navire).

named [neimd], *a.* (*a*) nommé; **on the n. day,** à jour nommé; *Ins:* **party n., person n.,** accrédité, -ée; **policy to a n. person,** police nominative; (*b*) (bien) connu; (*c*) *a. & s. Jur:* **afore n.,** précité, -ée; **the first n.,** celui-là, celle-là; **the last n.,** celui-ci, celle-ci.

name-dropper ['neimdrɔpər], *s. F:* celui, celle, qui se dit ami(e) de chacun dont on parle dans les journaux.

name-dropping ['neimdrɔpiŋ], *s. F:* habitude *f* de se dire ami(e) des gens connus.

nameless ['neimlis], *a.* **1.** (*of pers., etc.*) sans nom, inconnu, obscur. **2.** (écrivain, etc.) anonyme; **s.o. who shall be, remain, n.,** qn dont je tairai le nom, que je ne nommerai pas; **n. grave,** tombe *f* sans nom, sans inscription. **3.** (*a*) (*of dread, grief, etc.*) indéfinissable, indicible, inexprimable, ineffable; (*b*) (vice, etc.) abominable, inouï, innommable.

namely ['neimli], *adv.* c'est-à-dire; (à) savoir; nommément; **n. X,** je nomme X.

nameplate ['neimpleit], *s.* plaque *f* (de porte, etc.); écusson *m*, médaillon *m* (avec le nom); (*of street*) plaque indicatrice de rue; (*on machine, apparatus, etc.*) **manufacturer's n.,** plaque de constructeur.

namesake ['neimseik], *s.* **he's my n.,** il a le même nom que moi; il s'appelle comme moi; il porte mon nom.

naming ['neimiŋ], *s.* **1.** attribution *f* d'un nom; **there was a great deal of discussion over the n. of the child,** on a beaucoup discuté sur le choix du prénom, des prénoms, à donner à l'enfant; **n. of a ship,** baptême *m* d'un navire. **2.** nomination *f* (d'un fonctionnaire). **3.** désignation *f*, dénommement *m* (de qn, qch.).

Namurian [næ'mju:riən], *a. & s. Geol:* namurien (*m*).

Nan [næn]. *Pr.n.f.* (*dim. of Anne*) Nanette, Annette.

nana ['nænə], *s.f. F:* grand-maman, mémé, mamé.

Nancy ['nænsi]. **1.** *Pr.n.f.* (*dim. of Anne*) Nanette, Annette. **2.** *s. P:* **n. (boy),** (i) mignon *m*, giton *m*, tapette *f*; (ii) femmelette *f*. **3.** *F:* **n. (story, tale),** (i) conte *m* légendaire des Noirs; (ii) conte en l'air; tissu *m* d'absurdités.

nandine ['nændin], *s. Z:* nandinie *f*.

nandu ['nændu:], *s. Orn:* nandou *m*, rhée *f*.

nanism ['nænizm], *s. Nat.Hist:* nanisme *m*.

nankeen [næŋ'ki:n], *s.* **1.** *Tex:* nankin *m*. **2.** *A: pl.* **nankeens,** pantalon *m* de nankin. **3. n. (yellow),** chamois *inv*, nankin *inv*, jaune pâle *inv*. **4.** *Cer:* porcelaine *f* de Nankin; *Com:* porcelaine de Chine.

Nanking [næn'kiŋ]. *Pr.n. Geog:* Nankin.

nannoplankton [nænou'plæŋktən], *s. Nat.Hist:* nanoplankton *m*, plankton nain.

Nanny ['næni]. **1.** *Pr.n.f. A:* = NANCY 1. **2.** *s.f.* bonne d'enfant, nurse; (*child's speech*) nounou. **3.** *s.f.* **n. (goat),** chèvre; *F:* bique, biquette.

nano- ['nænou, 'nænə, næ'nɔ], *comb.fm.* nano-.

nanocephalic, nanocephalous [nænouse'fælik, nænou'sefələs], *a. Med:* nanocéphale.

nanocephalus [nænou'sefələs], *s. Med:* nanocéphale *mf*.

nanocephaly [nænou'sefəli], *s. Med:* nanocéphalie *f*.

nanocormia [nænou'kɔ:miə], *s. Med:* nanocormie *f*.

nanocormus [nænou'kɔ:məs], *s. Med:* nanocorme *mf*.

nanomelia [nænou'mi:liə], *s. Med:* nanomélie *f*.

nanomelous [næ'nɔmələs], *a. Med:* nanomèle.

nanomelus [næ'nɔmələs], *s. Med:* nanomèle *mf*.

nanoplankton [nænou'plæŋktən], *s. Nat.Hist:* nanoplankton *m*.

nanosecond [nænou'sekənd], *s.* nanoseconde *f*.

nanosomia [nænou'soumiə], *s. Med:* nanosomie *f*.

nanosomus [nænou'souməs], *s. Med:* nanosome *mf*.

nantokite ['næntəkait], *s. Miner:* nantokite *f*.

Naomi ['neiəmi]. *Pr.n.f. B.Hist:* Noémi.

naos ['neiɔs], *s. Gr.Ant:* naos *m*.

nap[1] [næp], *s.* petit somme, petit assoupissement; **afternoon n.,** sieste *f*, méridienne *f*; **to take a n., have a n.,** faire un petit somme; *F:* piquer un roupillon; piquer un chien; (*after lunch*) faire la sieste.

nap[2], *v.i.* (**napped**) faire un petit somme; sommeiller; **to catch s.o. napping,** (i) surprendre qn en train de dormir; (ii) *F:* surprendre la vigilance de qn; prendre qn à l'improviste, au dépourvu; prendre qn sans vert; prendre le lièvre au gîte; (iii) *F:* surprendre qn en défaut, en faute; trouver qn en faute; *F:* **to be caught napping,** (i) être pris au dépourvu; (ii) être pris en faute.

nap[3], *s.* **1.** *Tex:* (*a*) (*of velvet, cloth, felt*) poil *m*; (*of cloth*) duvet *m*, lainer *m*; **cloth with raised n.,** étoffe nolletonnée, tirée à poil, garnie; **short n. velvet,** velours ras, à fils courts; **against the n.,** à contre-poil, à rebrousse-poil, à rebours; **to wear off the n. of a garment,** élimer un vêtement; **his overcoat had lost its n.,** son pardessus était élimé; **cloth that is beginning to show a n.,** drap *m* qui commence à (se) cotonner, à pelucher; (*b*) *pl. Tex: A:* **naps,** draps à poil. **2.** *F:* duvet (d'un fruit).

nap[4], *v.tr. Tex:* garnir, gratter, lainer, rebrousser, rebourser, tirer à poil (le drap, etc.); molletonner (la laine, le coton); faire la peluche (d'un tissu).

nap[5], *s.* **1.** *Cards:* napoléon *m*; nap *m*; **to go n.,** demander les cinq levées; *F:* **to go n. on sth.,** être sûr et certain de qch., en mettre sa main au feu; **to deal oneself a n. hand,** se donner un beau jeu; **to hold a n. hand,** avoir en main toutes les cartes pour réussir. **2.** *Turf:* tuyau sûr.

nap[6], *v.tr. Turf: F:* **to n. a winner,** donner un tuyau assuré; recommander une certitude.

Napa ['næpə]. **1.** *Pr.n. Geog:* Napa. **2.** *s. U.S:* **N. (leather),** cuir mégissé.

napalm ['neipɑ:m], *s.* napalm *m*; **n. bomb,** bombe *f* au napalm.

nape [neip], *s.* **n. (of the neck),** nuque *f.*

napery ['neipəri], *s. A: & Scot:* linge *m* de table; nappage *m.*

naphtha ['næfθə], *s.* (*a*) *Ind:* (huile *f* de) naphte *m*; bitume *m* liquide; essence lourde; solvant *m*; **petroleum n.,** naphte de pétrole; **virgin n., straight run n.,** naphte de première distillation; **crude n.,** naphte brut; **coal tar n.,** naphte de goudron; huile de houille; **laboratory n.,** solvant de laboratoire; **light n.,** essence solvante légère; **shale n.,** naphte de schiste; (*b*) *Ch:* naphta *m.*

naphthacene ['næfθəsi:n], *s. Ch:* naphtacène *m.*

naphthalene, -ine ['næfθəli:n], *s. Ch: Com:* naphtaline *f*, naphtalène *m.*

naphthalenesulphonic ['næfθəli:nsʌl'fɔnik], *a. Ch:* naphtalène-sulfonique.

naphthalenic [næfθə'lenik], *a. Ch:* naphtalénique.

naphthein, naphthine ['næfθi:n], *s. Miner:* naphtéine *f.*

naphthenate ['næfθəneit], *s. Ch:* naphténate *m.*

naphthene ['næfθi:n], *s. Ch:* naphtène *m*; **n.-base crude petroleum,** pétrole brut à base naphténique.

naphthenic [næf'θi:nik], *a. Ch:* naphténique.

naphthoic [næf'θouik], *a. Ch:* naphtoïque.

naphthol ['næfθɔl], *s. Ch: Pharm:* naphtol *m.*

naphtholsulphonic ['næfθoulsʌl'fɔnik], *a. Ch:* naphthol-sulfonique.

naphthoquinone, naphthaquinone ['næfθoukwi'noun, -næfθə-], *s. Ch:* naphtoquinone *f.*

naphthoyl ['næfθɔil], *s. Ch:* naphtoyle *m.*

naphthyl ['næfθil], *s. Ch:* naphtyle *m.*

naphthylamine ['næfθil'æmain], *s. Ch:* naphtylamine *f.*

naphthylene ['næfθili:n], *s. Ch:* naphtylène *m.*

naphthylic [næf'θilik], *a. Ch:* naphtylique.

napierian [nei'piəriən], *a. Mth:* (logarithme) népérien.

napiform ['neipifɔ:m], *a. Bot:* (racine *f*, etc.) napiforme.

napkin ['næpkin], *s.* **1.** (*a*) **(table) n.,** serviette *f* (de table); **paper n.,** serviette en papier; **n. ring,** rond *m* de serviette; (*b*) *Ecc:* (*for consecrated bread, etc.*) tavaïole *f.* **2. (baby's) n.,** couche *f* (de bébé), pointe *f*; *U.S:* **(sanitary) n.,** serviette hygiénique. **3.** *A:* petite serviette, torchon *m.*

napless ['næplis], *a.* **1.** (drap *m*) sans poil. **2.** (drap, etc.) râpé, usé, élimé.

Napoleon [nə'pouliən]. **1.** *Pr.n.m. Hist:* Napoléon. **2.** *s.* (*a*) *Num: A:* napoléon *m*; pièce *f* d'or de vingt francs; (*b*) *Cost: A:* **n. boots, napoleons,** bottes *f* de chasse; bottes à revers; (*c*) *Cards: A:* napoléon; nap *m.*

Napoleonic [nəpouli'ɔnik], *a.* napoléonien; **the N. Wars,** les guerres napoléoniennes.

Napoleonism [nə'pouliənizm], *s. Hist:* napoléonisme *m.*

Napoleonist [nə'pouliənist], *s. Hist:* napoléonien, -ienne.

napoleonite [nə'pouliənait], *s. Geol:* napoléonite *f.*

napoo[1] [nɑ:'pu:]. *P: O:* **1.** *int.* rien à faire! ça ne prend pas! tu peux te gratter, te taper! on ne me la fait pas! macache! des nèfles! **2.** *a.* (*a*) fini, épuisé; (*b*) bon à rien; (*c*) mort; fichu, capout.

napoo[2], *v.tr. P: A:* tuer (qn); faire son affaire à (qn); faire capout (à) (qn).

nappe [næp], *s.* **1.** *Hyd.E:* nappe *f* d'eau. **2.** *Mth:* nappe (d'hyperboloïde). **3.** *Geol:* nappe; **overthrust n.,** nappe de charriage, de chevauchement.

napper[1] ['næpər], *s. Tex:* **1.** (*pers.*) garnisseur, -euse; gratteur, -euse; laineur, -euse. **2.** (*machine*) laineuse *f.*

napper[2], *s. P: A:* **1.** tête *f*, caboche *f.* **2.** bouche *f*, gueule *f*; **you keep your n. shut!** ferme ça! la ferme! ta gueule!

napping ['næpiŋ], *s.* garnissage *m*, grattage *m*, lainage *m*, rebroussement *m*, rebroussement *m*, tirage *m* à poil; **n. machine,** laineuse *f*; **n. comb,** rebroussoir *m*, rebroussette *f*, reboursoir *m.*

nappy[1] ['næpi], *a.* **1.** (drap, etc.) poilu, pelucheux. **2.** *A:* (*of ale, etc.*) (*a*) écumeux, mousseux; (*b*) capiteux, fort.

nappy[2], *s.* couche *f* (de bébé), pointe *f*; **cotton n.,** lange *m*; **disposable n.,** couche à jeter.

napu ['nɑ:pu:], *s. Z:* napu *m.*

narceine ['nɑ:sii:n], *s. Ch:* narcéine *f.*

narcissism ['nɑ:sisizm], *s. Psy:* narcissisme *m.*

narcissistic [nɑ:si'sistik], *a. Psy:* (*of instinct, etc.*) narcissique.

Narcissus [nɑ:'sisəs]. **1.** *Pr.n.m.* Narcisse. **2.** *s.* (*pl.* **narcissi, narcissuses** [nɑ:'sisai, -'sisəsiz]) *Bot:* narcisse *m*, genette *f*; **poet's n.,** narcisse des poètes; œillet *m* de Pâques; œil-de-faisan *m, pl.* œils-de-faisan; jeannette blanche.

narcoanalysis [nɑ:kouə'næləsis], *s. Med:* narco-analyse *f, pl.* narco-analyses.

narcodiagnosis [nɑ:koudaiə'gnousis], *s. Med:* narco-diagnostic *m, pl.* narco-diagnostics.

narcolepsy ['nɑ:koulepsi], *s. Med:* narcolepsie *f.*

narcoleptic [nɑ:kou'leptik], *a. & s. Med:* narcoleptique (*mf*).

narcolysis [nɑ:'kɔlisis], *s. Med:* narco-analyse *f, pl.* narco-analyses.

narcomania [nɑ:kou'meiniə], *s. Med:* narcomanie *f.*

Narcomedusae [nɑ:koumi'dju:si:], *s.pl. Z:* narcoméduses *f.*

narcosis [nɑ:'kousis], *s. Med:* narcose *f*; (*diving*) **nitrogen n.,** narcose; ivresse *f* des profondeurs.

narcosynthesis [nɑ:kou'sinθəsis], *s. Psy:* narcosynthèse *f.*

narcotherapy [nɑ:kou'θerəpi], *s. Med:* narcothérapie *f.*

narcotic [nɑ:'kɔtik], *a. & s.* narcotique (*m*), stupéfiant (*m*); somnifère (*m*).

narcotine ['nɑ:kəti:n], *s. Ch: Med:* narcotine *f.*

narcotism ['nɑ:kətizm], *s.* **1.** *Med:* narcotisme *m.* **2.** influence *f* narcotique (du tabac, etc.).

narcotization [nɑ:kətai'zeiʃ(ə)n], *s.* action *f* narcotique **(of, sur).**

narcotize ['nɑ:kətaiz], *v.tr. Med:* narcotiser (qch.); donner un narcotique à (qn).

nard [nɑ:d], *s.* **1.** *Bot:* nard *m.* **2.** *A.Pharm:* **Indian n.,** nard indien.

nares ['næri:z], *s.pl. Anat:* narines *f.*

nargileh, narghile ['nɑ:gili:], *s.* narghilé *m*, narguilé *m*, narghileh *m.*

naringenin [nærin'dʒenin], *s. Ch:* naringénine *f.*

naringin [nə'rindʒin], *s. Ch:* naringine *f.*

nark[1] [nɑ:k], *s. P:* **(copper's) n.,** espion *m* de police; mouchard *m*; mouton *m*; bourrique *f*, casserole *f.*

nark[2]. *P:* **1.** *v.tr.* (*a*) prendre (qn) à rebrousse-poil; mettre (qn) en colère, en rogne; fâcher, irriter (qn); **to get narked,** être en colère; se mettre en rogne; **I was narked,** j'étais embêté; (*b*) **n. it!** écrase! la ferme! fous-moi la paix! **2.** *v.i.* faire l'espion; en croquer, en manger.

narky ['nɑ:ki], *a. P:* en colère; fâché; en rogne; de mauvais poil; **don't get n.!** ne te fâche pas! ne te mets pas en rogne!

narrate [nə'reit], *v.tr.* narrer, raconter, relater (qch.).

narration [nə'reiʃ(ə)n], *s.* **1.** (*also* **narrating**) narration *f* (d'une histoire, etc.). **2.** (*a*) récit *m*, narration, relation *f*; histoire *f*, conte *m*; (*b*) *Rh:* narration; (*c*) *Book-k:* libellé *m* (d'un article de journal).

narrative[1] ['nærətiv], *s.* **1.** récit *m*, narration *f*, relation *f*; histoire *f*, conte *m.* **2.** (l'art *m* de) la narration.

narrative[2], *a.* (style, poème) narratif; **n. writer,** narrateur, -trice.

narrator [nə'reitər], *s.* (*a*) narrateur, -trice; (*b*) (*in oratorio*) récitant, -ante.

narrow[1] ['nærou]. **1.** *a.* (*a*) (chemin, etc.) étroit; (vallon, etc.) serré, resserré, encaissé; (passage, chenal) étranglé; (juper, cour, etc.) étriquée; **the strait and n. way,** la voie étroite; **shoes n. at the toe(s),** chaussures étroites du bout; **n.(-)chested,** (i) (*of pers.*) à poitrine étroite; (ii) (*of article of clothing*) étriqué de poitrine; **n. across the shoulders,** (i) (*of pers.*) étroit de carrure; (ii) (*of article of clothing*) étriqué aux épaules; **n. (-)shouldered,** aux épaules étroites; **to grow n.,** se rétrécir; **the road becomes narrower as one goes on,** la route va en se rétrécissant; *Com:* **n. goods,** rubans *mpl.*; *Rail:* **n. gauge (railway),** (chemin *m* de fer à) voie étroite; *Min:* **n. work,** travail *m* à l'étroit; travaux étriqués; *A:* **the n. seas,** la Manche et la mer d'Irlande; (*on canal*) **n. boat,** berge *f*; (*of vase, etc.*) **n.(-)mouthed,** à embouchure étroite; (*of bottle, etc.*) **n.(-)necked,** à goulot étroit, étranglé; **n.-ringed, n.-zoned, tree,** arbre *m* à couches minces; (*b*) restreint, étroit; de faibles dimensions, de peu d'étendue; (esprit) étroit, borné, rétréci; (existence) limitée, bornée, circonscrite; **n. limits,** limites restreintes; **within n. bounds,** dans des limites étroites; **within a n. compass,** sur une petite échelle; **in the narrowest sense,** dans le sens le plus étroit, le plus strict, le plus exact; (*c*) (examen, etc.) minutieux, soigneux, appliqué, méticuleux; (*d*) **a n. majority,** une faible majorité; une majorité bien juste; **to have a n. escape,** *F:* **a n. squeak,** l'échapper belle; *Sp:* **n. victory,** victoire *f* de justesse; (*e*) *Ling:* **n. vowel,** voyelle tendue. **2.** *s.pl.* **narrows,** passe étroite (entre deux terres); goulet *m* (d'un port); étranglement *m* (de rivière, de détroit, de vallée); pertuis *m* (de fleuve).

narrow[2], *v.*

I. *v.tr. & i.* **1.** *v.tr.* (*a*) resserrer, rétrécir (une rue, l'esprit, etc.); **narrowed eyelids,** paupières mi-closes; (*b*) restreindre, limiter, borner; rétrécir (un espace, les idées, etc.); *Phot:* **to n. the field,** restreindre le champ; (*c*) *A: & Lit:* mettre (qn) à l'étroit; gêner les mouvements de (qn); acculer (qn). **2.** *v.i.* (*a*) devenir plus étroit; se resserrer, se rétrécir; (*of channel*) s'étrangler; (*of cat, etc.*) **his eyes narrowed to slits,** ses yeux se réduisirent à deux petites fentes; (*b*) *Equit:* (*of horse*) s'étrécir.

II. (*compound verb*) **narrow down.** (*a*) *v.tr.* **further inquiries have narrowed the search down to two men,** de plus amples renseignements ont limité l'enquête à la recherche de deux hommes; (*b*) *v.i.* **here the stream narrows down to a few feet,** ici le cours d'eau se rétrécit jusqu'à n'avoir plus que quelques pieds; **the struggle has narrowed down to a fight between socialism and radicalism,** la lutte s'est rétrécie entre le socialisme et le radicalisme.

narrowing[1] ['nærouiŋ], *a.* **1.** (*a*) qui resserre, qui rétrécit; (*b*) (*of influence, etc.*) qui restreint, qui limite, qui borne. **2.** qui se resserre, qui se rétrécit.

narrowing[2], *s.* **1.** resserrement *m*, rétrécissement *m* (d'une rue, etc.); contraction *f* (d'une route); *Knit:* diminution *f*, rétrécie *f.* **2.** restriction *f*, limitation *f.*

narrowish ['nærouiʃ], *a.* assez étroit, plutôt étroit.

narrowly ['nærouli], *adv.* **1.** (*a*) (interpréter qch.) strictement, étroitement, rigoureusement; (*b*) (examiner qch.) minutieusement, soigneusement, attentivement, méticuleusement, de près. **2.** (enfermer qch.) étroitement, à l'étroit. **3.** tout juste; **the match was n. won by . . .,** le match a été gagné de bien peu par . . .; **he n. missed being run over,** il a failli être écrasé; **in crossing the road he n. avoided a taxi,** en traversant la rue, il a esquivé de justesse un taxi; **he n. escaped falling,** il a failli tomber; peu s'en faut, il s'en faut de peu, qu'il ne soit tombé.

narrow-minded [nærou'maindid], *a.* (d'un esprit) borné; à l'esprit étroit, à l'esprit rétréci; illibéral, -aux; *F:* qui porte des œillères; **n.-m. ideas,** idées étroites, mesquines; **n.-m. person,** personne *f* aux idées étroites.

narrow-mindedly [nærou'maindidli], *adv.* sans largeur de vues.

narrow-mindedness [nærou'maindidnis], *s.* étroitesse *f*, petitesse *f*, d'esprit; esprit borné, rétréci, mesquin.

narrowness ['nærounis], *s.* **1.** (*a*) étroitesse *f* (d'un sentier, des épaules, etc.); rétrécissement *m*, manque *m* de largeur (d'un passage, etc.); *Med:* angustie *f* (du bassin); (*b*) petitesse *f*, exiguïté *f*, manque d'étendue (d'un espace, etc.); limitation *f*, circonscription *f* (de la vie, de l'intelligence, etc.); insuffisance *f*, étroitesse (des moyens de qn); **n. of mind,** étroitesse d'esprit. **2.** minutie *f*; caractère soigneux, appliqué, méticuleux (d'un examen, des recherches).

narsarsukite [nɑ:sə'sʌkait], *s. Miner:* narsarsukite *f.*

narthecium [nɑ:'θi:siəm], *s. Bot:* narthecium *m.*

narthex ['nɑ:θeks], *s. Arch:* narthex *m.*

narwhal ['nɑ:wəl], *s. Z:* narval *m, pl.* narvals; licorne *f* de mer.

nasal ['neiz(ə)l]. **1.** *a.* (*a*) *Anat:* nasal, -aux; **the n. fossae,** les fosses nasales; *Anthr:* **n. index,** indice nasal; *Hum:* **n. organ,** nez *m*; (*b*) (*of sound, letter, etc.*) nasal; **n. accent,** accent nasillard; **to have a n. voice,** parler du nez; *Ling:* (*of vowel, etc.*) **to lose its n. sound,** se dénasaliser. **2.** *s.* (*a*) *Arm:* nasal *m* (de casque); (*b*) *Anat:* épine nasale; (*c*) *Ling:* nasale *f.*

nasality [nei'zæliti], *s.* nasalité *f* (d'articulation, etc.).

nasalization [neizəlai'zeiʃ(ə)n], *s.* nasalisation *f* (d'une voyelle, etc.).

nasalize ['neizəlaiz]. **1.** *v.tr.* nasaliser (une syllabe, etc.). **2.** *v.i.* nasiller; parler du nez.

nasally ['neizəli], *adv.* nasalement; **to speak n.,** parler du nez, d'un ton nasillard; nasiller; **to pronounce a vowel n.,** nasaliser une voyelle.

nasard [nə'zɑ:d], *s. Mus:* nasard *m.*

nascent ['neis(ə)nt, 'næs-], *a.* (*of plant, society, etc.*) naissant; *Ch:* (corps, élément) à l'état naissant.

nase [neiz], *s. Geog:* promontoire *m*, cap *m*, pointe *f.*

naseberry ['neizbəri], *s. Bot:* **1.** sapotille *f.* **2. n. (tree),** sapotillier *m.*

nasicorn ['neizikɔ:n], *a. Z:* nasicorne.

nasion ['neiziɔn], *s. Anthr:* nasion *m*; point nasal.

nasolabial [neizou'leibiəl], *a. Anat:* naso-labial, *pl.* naso-labiaux.

nasolachrymal [neizou'lækriməl], *a. Anat:* nasolacrymal, -aux.

nasonite ['neisənait], *s. Miner:* nasonite *f.*

nasopalatine [neizou'pælətain], *a. Anat:* naso-palatin, *pl.* naso-palatins.

nasopharyngeal [neizoufə'rindʒiəl], *a. Anat:* nasopharyngien; naso-pharyngé, *pl.* naso-pharyngés; rhynopharyngien; rhynopharingien.

nasopharyngitis [neizoufærin'dʒaitis], *s. Med:* rhynopharyngite *f.*

nasopharynx [neizou'færinks], *s. Anat:* nasopharynx *m.*

nassa ['næsə], **Nassarius** [nə'sɛəriəs], *s. Moll:* nasse *f.*

nastic ['næstik], *a. Bot:* (*of plants*) **n. movement,** nastie *f.*

nastily ['nɑ:stili], *adv.* **1.** désagréablement, d'une façon dégoûtante; **to behave n.,** se conduire méchamment, d'une manière déplaisante. 2. (*a*) malproprement, salement; (*b*) indécemment, d'une façon obscène.

nastiness ['nɑːstinis], *s.* 1. mauvais goût, odeur *f* désagréable. 2. (*of pers.*) méchanceté *f*, rosserie *f*. 3. (*a*) saleté *f*, malpropreté *f*; (*b*) indécence *f*, obscénité *f*.

nasturtium [nə'stəːʃəm], *s. Bot:* 1. nasturce *m*; cresson *m* de fontaine. 2. capucine *f*; cresson d'Inde; **dwarf n., Tom Thumb n.,** capucine naine; **n. seeds,** (i) graines *f* de capucines; (ii) câpres *f* capucines.

nasty ['nɑːsti], *a.* 1. (*a*) désagréable, dégoûtant; nauséabond; **to smell n.,** sentir mauvais; **his behaviour left me (with) a n. taste in my, the, mouth,** sa conduite m'a laissé un mauvais souvenir; (*b*) **n. weather,** sale, mauvais, vilain, temps; **a n. job,** une besogne difficile, dangereuse, désagréable; une sale besogne; **n. corner,** tournant dangereux; **n. illness, accident,** maladie grave, accident sérieux; **n. wound,** vilaine blessure; **he's had a n. attack of bronchitis,** il a fait une mauvaise bronchite; **to get a n. blow,** (i) recevoir un mauvais coup; (ii) (*of fortune*) *F:* recevoir une tuile; **that's a n. one!** (i) quelle tuile! (ii) *Games:* quelle balle impossible! **to have a n. look in one's eye,** avoir l'air mauvais, menaçant; **a n. little vase,** un vilain petit vase. 2. (*of pers.*) méchant, déplaisant, hargneux, *F:* rosse; **to turn n.,** prendre un air méchant; **to be n. to s.o.,** être vilain avec qn; faire des méchancetés à qn; être désobligeant envers qn; **don't be n.!** ne fais donc pas le méchant! **n. trick,** vilain tour; *F:* sale tour, rosserie *f*. 3. (*a*) sale, malpropre, immonde; *F:* **he's a n. piece of work,** c'est un sale individu, un sale type, un vilain coco, une rosse; (*b*) (*of language, book, etc.*) indécent, obscène, ordurier, malpropre; **n. word,** vilain mot; **to have a n. mind,** avoir l'esprit mal tourné; voir des obscénités où il n'y en a pas; **n.-minded,** à l'esprit graveleux, malsain.

nasua ['neisjuːə], *s. Z:* nasua *m*.

natal[1] ['neit(ə)l], *a.* natal, -als (*very rarely used in pl.*); de naissance.

Natal[2] [nə'tæl]. *Pr.n. Geog:* Natal *m*.

natalis [nə'teilis], *s. A.Rel:* natalice *f*.

natality [nə'tæliti], *s.* natalité *f*; **n. statistics,** la statistique des naissances.

natant ['neitənt], *a. Bot:* (*of leaf, plant*) nageant, natant.

natation [nə'teiʃ(ə)n], *s. Nat.Hist:* natation *f*.

Natatores [neitə'tɔːriːz], *s.pl. Orn:* les nageurs *m*.

natatorial [neitə'tɔːriəl], **natatory** ['neitət(ə)ri], *a. Nat.Hist:* (organe *m*, membrane *f*) natatoire.

natatorium [neitə'tɔːriəm], *s. NAm:* piscine *f*.

nates ['neitiːz], *s.pl. Anat:* 1. fesses *f*. 2. nates *m*, tubercules quadrijumeaux antérieurs (du cerveau).

Nathan ['neiθ(ə)n]. *Pr.n.m.* Nathan.

Nathaniel [nə'θæniəl]. *Pr.n.m.* Nathanael.

nath(e)less ['neiθlis], *adv. A:* = NEVERTHELESS.

Natica ['nætikə], *s. Moll:* natice *f*.

Naticidae [nə'tisidiː], *s.pl. Moll:* naticidés *m*.

nation ['neiʃ(ə)n], *s.* 1. (*a*) nation *f*; **the nations of Europe,** les nations de l'Europe; les peuples européens; **people of all nations,** des gens de toutes les nationalités; *A.Sch:* **the four nations of the university,** les quatre nations de l'université; *Pol:* **United Nations (Organization),** (Organisation *f* des) Nations Unies; *Hist:* **the Battle of the Nations,** la bataille des Nations; la bataille de Leipzig; (*b*) *B.Hist:* **the Nations,** les nations, les gentils *m*. 2. **the whole n. rose in arms,** tout le pays se souleva; **the voice of the n.,** la voix du peuple; **to serve the n.,** servir l'État *m*.

national ['næʃ(ə)n(ə)l]. 1. *a.* (*a*) national, -aux; de l'État; *Adm:* **n. status,** nationalité *f*; *Nau:* **n. flag,** pavillon *m* de nation; **n. forces,** armée nationale; **n. service,** service *m* militaire; **N. Guard,** (i) *U.S:* = compagnie nationale de sécurité; (ii) *Fr.Hist:* garde nationale; les sectionnaires *m*; *Fr.Hist:* **n. guard(sman),** sectionnaire; *Eng.Hist:* **N. (Coalition) Government,** gouvernement *m* de coalition nationale; *Pol.Hist:* **n. socialism,** national-socialisme *m*; **n. socialist,** national(e)-socialiste (*mf*), *pl.* nationaux-socialistes, *f.* nationales-socialistes; *Turf:* **n. hunt (races, racing),** courses *fpl* d'obstacles; **n. hunt jockey,** jockey *m* d'obstacles; *A:* **n. school,** (i) école communale; (ii) école établie par la *National Society;* (*b*) **n. poet,** poète national; **n. dress,** costume *m* du pays; costume national; **n. custom,** coutume *f* du pays; **he's intensely n.,** il est d'un nationalisme extrême. 2. *s.* ressortissant *m* (d'un pays); **a French n.,** un(e) Français(e); **this law militates against our own nationals,** cette loi défavorise nos compatriotes. 3. *s. Turf: F:* **the Grand N.,** la course classique de steeple (qui se court à Aintree, Liverpool).

nationalism ['næʃ(ə)nəlizm], *s.* nationalisme *m*.

nationalist ['næʃ(ə)nəlist]. 1. *s.* nationaliste *mf*. 2. *a.* nationaliste; **N. China,** la Chine nationaliste.

nationalistic ['næʃ(ə)nəlistik], *a.* nationaliste.

nationality [næʃ(ə)'næliti], *s.* 1. nationalité *f*; **twenty nationalities were represented,** vingt nationalités étaient représentées; **he is of Italian n.,** il est de nationalité italienne; **to take British n.,** prendre la nationalité britannique; **dual n.,** double nationalité. 2. nationalisme *m*, patriotisme *m*, esprit national.

nationalization [næʃənəlai'zeiʃ(ə)n], *s.* 1. nationalisation *f* (d'un peuple, etc.). 2. naturalisation *f* (d'un étranger). 3. nationalisation, étatisation *f* (d'une industrie).

nationalize ['næʃənəlaiz], *v.tr.* 1. nationaliser (un peuple, etc.). 2. naturaliser (un étranger, etc.); **to become nationalized,** se naturaliser; obtenir des lettres de naturalisation. 3. nationaliser, étatiser (une industrie, etc.).

nationally ['næʃənəli], *adv.* nationalement; du point de vue national.

nationwide ['neiʃənwaid], *a.* **n. movement,** mouvement répandu par tout le pays.

native ['neitiv], *s. & a.*

I. *s.* 1. (*a*) originaire *mf*, (d'un pays, d'une ville); *Adm: Jur:* régnicole *mf*; **n. of Australia,** Australien, -ienne, de naissance; **he speaks English like a n.,** il parle anglais comme un Anglais, comme un habitant du pays, comme si c'était sa langue maternelle, comme vous et moi; (*b*) (*esp. of foreign country, of colony*) indigène *mf*; aborigène *m*; *F:* (*of white man*) **to go n.,** adopter la vie des indigènes; s'encanaquer; s'assimiler aux indigènes; (*c*) *F: Hum:* **let's ask the natives,** il faut demander ça aux habitants. 2. (*a*) (*of plant, animal*) indigène; **the elephant is a n. of Asia,** l'éléphant *m* est originaire de l'Asie; (*b*) *pl.* **natives,** huîtres anglaises (de Colchester). 3. *Hist:* esclave natif; serf *m* de naissance.

II. *a.* 1. (*a*) (*of qualities, etc.*) natif; naturel, inhérent, inné; **n. wit,** esprit naturel; **n. to s.o., to sth.,** inhérent à qn, à qch.; (*b*) *A:* (*of state, colours, feelings, etc.*) simple, naturel, natif; **to behave with n. ease,** se conduire avec naturel. 2. (*a*) (*of country, place*) natal, -als de naissance; **n. land,** terre natale; patrie *f*, pays; **my n. place,** le lieu où je suis né; mon pays natal, ma ville natale, ma maison natale; **n. inhabitant of . . .,** habitant, -ante, originaire de . . .; **n. language,** langue maternelle; **to breathe one's n. air,** respirer l'air natal; **he returned to his n. London,** il est revenu à Londres, sa ville natale; (*b*) (costume, huîtres) du pays; **they were guaranteed the use of their n. customs and religion,** on leur a garanti l'usage de leurs coutumes et de leur religion propres, particulières; (*c*) *Adm: Jur:* (*of pers.*) régnicole. 3. (*a*) (*of metals, minerals*) (à l'état) natif; **n. silver,** argent natif; *Miner:* **n. soda,** natrite *f*, natron *m*, natrum *m*; (*b*) *Ch:* **n. substance,** principe immédiat; (*c*) **n. albumin,** albumine naturelle. 4. (*of plants, inhabitants, etc.*) indigène (**to,** de, à); originaire, aborigène (**to,** de); *Ling:* **n. word,** mot *m* indigène; **a n. rising,** une insurrection des indigènes; *Hist:* **N. States,** États indigènes (de l'Inde anglaise); **n. labour,** main-d'œuvre *f* indigène; *Orn:* **n. companion,** grue *f* d'Australie.

native-born ['neitivbɔːn], *a.* 1. indigène, natif; **a n.-b. German,** un Allemand, une Allemande, de naissance. 2. *A:* (enfant d'Européens) né(e) aux colonies, dans l'Inde, etc.

natively ['neitivli], *adv.* nativement; de sa nature; par nature.

nativism ['neitivizm], *s.* 1. *Pol: esp. U.S: Hist:* exclusivisme *m* en faveur des natifs. 2. *Phil:* innéisme *m*. 3. *Psy:* nativisme *m*.

nativist ['neitivist], *s.* 1. *Pol: esp. U.S: Hist:* partisan, -ane, de l'exclusivisme en faveur des natifs. 2. *Phil:* nativiste *mf*.

nativistic [neiti'vistik], *a. Psy:* nativiste.

nativity [nə'tiviti], *s.* 1. (*a*) *A:* naissance *f*; **land of one's n.,** pays *m* de naissance; (*b*) nativité *f*, naissance (du Christ, de la Vierge, de saint Jean-Baptiste); (*c*) *Ecc:* **the (festival of the) N.,** la Nativité; la fête de Noël; **n. scene,** crèche *f*; *Th:* **n. play,** mystère *m* de la Nativité. 2. *Astrol:* nativité, horoscope *m*; **to cast s.o.'s n.,** faire, dresser, tirer, l'horoscope de qn.

Nato ['neitou], *s.* l'Otan *m*; **N. member states,** pays *mpl* membres de l'Otan.

natraemia [næ'triːmiə], *s.* natrémie *f*.

natrium ['neitriəm], *s. A:* natrium *m*, sodium *m*.

natrochalcite [neitrou'kælsait], *s. Miner:* natrocalcite *f*.

natrolite ['nætroulait, 'nei-], *s. Miner:* natrolite *f*.

natron ['neitrɔn], *s.* (*a*) *Miner:* natron *m*, natrum *m*; (*b*) *Ch:* soude carbonatée.

natter[1] ['nætər], *s. F:* **to have a n.,** bavarder, jacter.

natter[2], *v.i. F:* bavarder, jacter.

natterjack ['nætədʒæk], *s. Amph:* **n. (toad),** crapaud *m* des roseaux; calamite *f*.

Nattier ['nætiei]. *Pr.n.* **N. blue,** bleu *m* Nattier.

nattily ['nætili], *adv.* 1. coquettement; d'une façon pimpante; avec soin. 2. adroitement, habilement; avec adresse.

nattiness ['nætinis], *s.* 1. coquetterie *f*, élégance *f* (de qn, de la mise de qn). 2. adresse (manuelle); dextérité *f* (de qn).

natty ['næti], *a.* 1. (*of pers., dress, etc.*) pimpant; coquet, -ette; soigné. 2. (*a*) (*of pers.*) adroit (de ses mains); (*b*) (*of gadget, etc.*) habilement exécuté; bien ménagé; commode; **a n. little gadget,** un petit dispositif bien trouvé, bien imaginé.

natural ['nætjərəl], *a. & s.*

I. *a.* 1. (*a*) naturel; qui est conforme à la nature; **n. law,** loi naturelle; loi de la nature; **n. right,** droit naturel; **n. size,** grandeur *f* nature; de grandeur normale; **n. day,** jour vrai; **n. magic,** magie blanche; **n. life,** vie mortelle, vie sur terre; *s. P:* **for the rest of my n.,** pour le reste de ma vie; **death from n. causes,** mort naturelle; **n. tone of voice,** ton naturel; **n. modesty,** modestie *f* simple, sans affectation; **be n.!** soyez naturel! **his acting is absolutely n.,** son jeu est tout à fait nature; **that'll look more n.,** ça fera plus nature; (*b*) **in the n. state,** à l'état naturel, primitif; à, dans, l'état de nature; *Civ.E:* **n. drainage,** écoulement naturel; *Ph: Ch:* **n. gas,** gaz naturel; **n. magnet,** aimant naturel; *Atom.Ph:* **n. radioactivity,** radioactivité naturelle; **n. uranium,** uranium naturel; *Tex:* **n. wool,** laine *f* beige; **cloth in n. colour,** tissu *m* beige; (*c*) *Mth:* **n. logarithms,** logarithmes naturels, hyperboliques, népériens; **n. sines, n. cosines, n. tangents,** sinus *m*, cosinus *m*, tangentes *f*, ordinaires, hyperboliques; (*d*) *Mus:* **n. note,** (note) naturelle *f*; **n. keys,** tons naturels. 2. (*a*) naturel, natif, inherent, inné; **n. goodness,** bonté foncière; **n. gift,** don naturel; **n. inclination,** penchant naturel; **to have a n. tendency to do sth.,** avoir une tendance naturelle à faire qch.; **it comes n. to him,** c'est un don chez lui; c'est un de ses talents naturels; *F:* **it comes n. to him to . . .,** il a une facilité innée pour . . .; *F:* **it comes n. to him to write in verse,** il lui est naturel d'écrire en vers; **laughter is n. to man,** le rire est le propre de l'homme; **it comes, is, n. for a man to . . .,** il est dans, de, la nature de l'homme de . . .; **the cat is the n. enemy of the dog,** le chat est l'ennemi naturel du chien; **n.-born subject,** Anglais, Français, etc., de naissance; **she's a n.-born nurse,** c'est une infirmière née; (*b*) *Ph:* **n. frequency,** fréquence *f* propre; **n. oscillation,** oscillation propre, fondamentale; **n. period,** période *f* propre; **n. wave,** onde fondamentale; **n. wavelength,** longueur *f* d'onde propre; *Ac:* **n. resonance,** résonance *f* propre; (*c*) **it's n. (that) . . .,** il est (bien) naturel que + *sub.*; rien de surprenant à ce que + *sub.*; **it's n. he should go away,** il est (bien) naturel qu'il s'en aille; **it's only n. that. . .,** il est, c'est, tout à fait normal que + *sub.*; **as is n.,** comme de raison. 3. **n. child,** enfant naturel, illégitime. 4. **the n. world,** le monde physique; **n. history,** histoire naturelle; *O:* **n. historian,** naturaliste *mf*.

II. *s.* 1. *A:* idiot, -ote (de naissance); **the village n.,** l'innocent *m* du village. 2. **as an actor, he's a n.,** c'est un acteur né. 3. *Mus:* (*a*) (note) naturelle *f*; (*b*) (*sign*) bécarre *m*. 4. *Cards:* **to have a n.,** avoir vingt et un d'entrée.

naturalism ['nætjərəlizm], *s.* naturalisme *m*.

naturalist ['nætjərəlist], *a. & s.* naturaliste (*mf*).

naturalistic [nætjərə'listik], *a.* 1. *Art: Lit: etc:* naturaliste. 2. *Phil: Lit:* naturiste.

naturalistically [nætjərə'listikli], *adv.* **to paint n.,** être de l'école des naturalistes; *F:* peindre nature.

naturalization [nætjərəlai'zeiʃ(ə)n], *s.* 1. naturalisation *f* (d'un étranger, d'un mot étranger); **letters of n.,** déclaration *f* de naturalisation; **to take out (French) n. papers,** se faire naturaliser (français). 2. acclimatation *f* (d'une plante, d'un animal).

naturalize ['nætjərəlaiz]. 1. *v.tr.* (*a*) naturaliser (un étranger, un mot); (*b*) acclimater (une plante, un animal); (*c*) rendre (l'art, etc.) conforme à la nature; donner du naturel à (son style, etc.); (*d*) *A:* expliquer (le surnaturel, etc.) selon les lois naturelles. 2. *v.i.* (*a*) (*of plant, etc.*) s'acclimater; (*b*) *O:* faire de l'histoire naturelle (en plein air); herboriser.

naturalized ['nætjərəlaizd], *a.* naturalisé; **to become a n. Frenchman,** se faire naturaliser français.

naturalizing ['nætjərəlaiziŋ], *s.* 1. naturalisation *f*; acclimatation *f* (d'une plante, d'un animal). 2. *O:* histoire naturelle en plein air; herborisation *f*.

naturally ['nætjərəli], *adv.* 1. (*a*) naturellement; de sa nature, par nature, nativement; **n. lazy,** paresseux de sa nature, par tempérament; **n. curly hair,** cheveux *m* qui frisent naturellement; **he was n. of a kind disposition,** il était foncièrement bon; **he's n. shy,** il est timide de nature; il est d'une nature timide; **he's n. cheerful,** il est gai de sa nature; **it comes n. to him to . . .,** il est dans sa nature, il lui est naturel, de . . .; **it comes n. to him,** il tient ça de sa nature; **dancing comes n. to her,** elle est douée pour la danse; (*b*) **to speak n.,** parler naturellement, sans affectation, sans art, simplement; **to behave n.,** se conduire avec naturel; (*c*) **to die n.,** mourir de sa belle mort. **2.** (= *of course*) naturellement; **he n. does not wish . . .,** comme il est naturel, naturellement, comme de raison, il ne veut pas . . .; **you answered him?—n.,** vous lui avez répondu?—naturellement; cela va sans dire; **these questions were n. somewhat embarrassing,** ces questions, comme vous le pensez bien, n'étaient pas sans m'embarrasser; **he was attacked, and n. hit back,** on l'attaqua et naturellement il riposta.

naturalness ['nætjərəlnis], *s.* **1.** (*a*) caractère naturel (d'une action, etc.); (*b*) **the portrait lacks n.,** le portrait manque de naturel. **2.** naturel *m*; absence *f* d'affectation; **to behave with n.,** se conduire avec naturel.

nature ['neitjər], *s.* **1.** (*a*) (*of thg*) nature *f*, essence *f*, caractère *m*; **n. of the climate, of the soil,** nature du climat, du sol; **the n. of fish is to swim,** le propre des poissons est de nager; **love is jealous by n.,** il est de l'essence de l'amour d'être jaloux; l'amour est jaloux par nature; **it is in the n. of things that . . .,** il est dans l'ordre des choses que . . .; **in, by, from, the n. of things, of the case, we cannot hope for more,** vu la nature de l'affaire nous ne pouvons espérer mieux; *Phil:* **the true n. of things,** l'être *m* véritable des choses; (*b*) (*of pers.*) nature; naturel *m*, caractère, tempérament *m*; **a jealous n.,** un caractère jaloux; une nature jalouse; **to have, to be of, a happy n.,** être d'un heureux naturel; **he has an envious n.,** il est envieux par nature; **it's not in his n.,** ce n'est pas dans sa nature; **it's not in his n. to . . .,** il n'est pas dans, de, sa nature de . . .; **by n.,** par nature, par tempérament, de (sa) nature, naturellement; **he's shy by n.,** il est timide de nature; il est d'une nature timide; il est naturellement timide; **monkeys are mischievous by n.,** le singe est malicieux de nature; **he is envious by n.,** il est envieux par nature; **it comes to him by n., it's in his n.,** cela lui vient tout naturellement; il tient cela de nature; **habit is a second n.,** l'habitude *f* est une seconde nature; **it has become second n. to him,** il le fait par instinct; il est fait à cela comme un chien à aller à pied; **there are some natures that cannot stand the cold,** il y a des natures qui ne supportent pas le froid; (*c*) **human n., divine n.,** nature humaine, nature divine; *Theol:* **the union of two natures in Christ,** l'union *f* des deux natures en Jésus-Christ. **2.** espèce *f*, sorte *f*, genre *m*; **things of this n.,** les choses *f* de ce genre; **something in the n. of a . . .,** une espèce, une sorte, de . . .; **invitation in the n. of a command,** invitation *f* en forme d'ordre; **his words were in the n. of a threat,** ses paroles *f* tenaient de la menace; **this news was of a n. to alarm her,** ces nouvelles étaient faites pour l'alarmer; **n. of contents,** nature, désignation *f*, du contenu. **3.** (*a*) nature; **Mother N.,** la Nature; **the laws of n.,** les lois *f* de la nature; les lois naturelles; **n. study,** histoire naturelle; **n. gods,** dieux naturels; **n. worship,** adoration *f* des phénomènes naturels; **n. lover, lover of n.,** ami, -e, amant, -ante, amoureux, -euse, de la nature; **n. myth,** mythe naturel; **to draw, paint, from n.,** dessiner, peindre, d'après nature; *Phot.Engr:* **n. print(ing),** impression naturelle directe; **against n.,** (i) contre nature; (ii) miraculeux; **crime against n.,** crime *m* contre nature; **in n.,** dans la nature; **in a state of n.,** (i) en l'état de pure nature; à, dans, l'état de nature; à l'état naturel; (ii) *F:* dans le costume d'Adam, d'Ève; **return to n.,** retour *m* à l'état de nature; *U.S: F:* **that beats all n.,** ça dépasse tout (au monde); ça c'est le comble! (*b*) force vitale, fonctions vitales, naturelles (de l'homme); **diet insufficient to support n.,** régime insuffisant pour entretenir la vie, pour se sustenter.

naturism ['neitjərizm], *s.* naturisme *m*.

naturist ['neitjərist], *s.* naturiste *mf*.

naturistic [neitjə'ristik], *a.* naturiste.

naucorid ['nɔ:kərid], *s. Ent:* naucore *f*.

naught [nɔ:t], *s.* **1.** *A: & Lit:* rien *m*, néant *m*; **to come to n.,** échouer; n'aboutir à rien; **the attempt came to n.,** la tentative n'a pas abouti; **to bring an attempt to n.,** faire échouer, faire avorter, une tentative; **to bring s.o.'s plans to n.,** confondre les projets de qn; **to set the law at n.,** ne tenir aucun compte, aller à l'encontre, de la loi; passer outre, faire échec, à la loi; braver la loi; **to set advice at n.,** ne tenir aucun compte, faire peu de cas, d'un conseil; *B:* **set at n.,** chargé de mépris; méprisé; **all for n.,** en vain, inutilement; **his efforts were all for n.,** ce furent des efforts perdus; **a man of n.,** un homme de néant, de rien. **2.** *Mth:* zéro *m*.

naughtily ['nɔ:tili], *adv.* **to behave n.,** se mal conduire; ne pas être sage; être méchant.

naughtiness ['nɔ:tinis], *s.* **1.** mauvaise conduite, désobéissance *f* (de qn). **2.** *F:* caractère risqué, grivois (d'un conte, d'un mot).

naughty ['nɔ:ti], *a.* **1.** vilain, méchant; pas sage; désobéissant; **you n. child!** petit méchant! oh, le laid! oh, la laide! petit polisson! **he's been a n. boy,** il a été méchant; il n'a pas été sage. **2.** *F:* (*of tale*) risqué, grivois, leste; **n. song,** chanson gaillarde, polissonne; **to tell n. stories,** conter des gaillardises *f*; en raconter de corsées, de salées, d'égrillardes; **to make rather n. jokes,** plaisanter un peu lestement; **n. word,** vilain mot; **the n. nineties,** les années 1890–1900 (qui ont été un peu polissonnes).

naumachia, *pl.* **-iae, -ias** [nɔ:'meikiə, -ii:, -iəz], *s. Rom.Ant:* naumachie *f*.

naumannite ['nɔ:mənait], *s. Miner:* naumannite *f*.

Nauplia ['nɔ:pliə]. *Pr.n. Geog:* Nauplie.

nauplius, *pl.* **-plii** ['nɔ:pliəs, -pliai], *s. Crust:* nauplius *m*.

nausea ['nɔ:siə], *s.* **1.** (*a*) nausée *f*, envie *f* de vomir, soulèvement *m* de cœur; **to be overcome with n.,** avoir mal au cœur; avoir des nausées; (*b*) mal *m* de mer. **2.** dégoût *m*, nausée, écœurement *m*.

nauseate ['nɔ:sieit]. **1.** *v.tr.* (*a*) *A:* refuser (la nourriture, etc.) avec dégoût; avoir du dégoût pour (qch.); prendre (qch.) en dégoût; (*b*) écœurer, dégoûter (qn); donner des nausées, donner mal au cœur, à (qn). **2.** *v.i. A:* avoir mal au cœur; éprouver des nausées.

nauseating ['nɔ:sieitiŋ], *a.* **1.** *Med:* nauséeux. **2.** nauséabond, dégoûtant, écœurant; **it's n.,** cela soulève le cœur; cela donne mal au cœur; cela donne des nausées; cela vous donne la nausée; *F:* **I find him n.,** il m'écœure.

nauseatingly ['nɔ:sieitiŋli], *adv.* d'une façon dégoûtante, écœurante; *F:* **he's n. hypocritical,** il est d'une hypocrisie répugnante.

nauseous ['nɔ:siəs], *a.* = NAUSEATING.

nauseousness ['nɔ:siəsnis], *s.* caractère nauséabond, dégoûtant, écœurant (de qch.).

nautch [nɔ:tʃ], *s.* (*India*) natche *f*; ballet *m*; **n. girl,** danseuse *f* de natche; bayadère *f*.

nautical ['nɔ:tik(ə)l], *a.* nautique, marin; naval, -als; **n. chart,** carte marine; **n. term,** terme *m* de navigation, de marine; **n. terms,** termes navals; **n. star,** étoile *f* servant aux observations; **n. almanac,** connaissance *f* des temps; éphémérides *fpl* nautiques; **n. day,** jour *m* astronomique; **n. twilight,** crépuscule *m* nautique; *Sch:* **n. school,** école *f* de navigation (de la marine marchande); **n. club,** club *m* nautique; *F:* **n. yarn,** histoire *f* de marin; conte bleu; **n. matters,** questions navales; **article on n. matters,** article *m* sur la marine.

nautically ['nɔ:tik(ə)li], *adv.* d'une façon nautique; **n. speaking . . .,** nautiquement parlant . . .; pour parler en marin . . ..

nautilus, *pl.* **-uses, -i** ['nɔ:tiləs, -əsiz, -ai], *s. Moll:* nautile *m*; **paper n.,** argonaute *m*, voilier *m*; chaloupe cannelée; **pearly n.,** nautile flambé.

Navaho ['nævəhou], *s. Ethn:* Navaho *mf*.

Navajo ['nævəhou], *s. Ethn:* Navajo *mf*.

naval ['neiv(ə)l], *a.* naval, -als; de marine (de guerre); marinier; **n. power,** puissance *f* maritime; **n. forces of a State,** marine *f* (de guerre, militaire), armée navale, de mer, d'un État; flotte *f* de guerre d'un État; **n. war(fare),** guerre navale; **n. engagement,** combat naval, bataille navale; combat sur mer; **n. rating,** marin *m* de l'État, de la Marine nationale; **n. officer,** (i) officier *m* de marine; (ii) *U.S:* douanier chargé de recevoir les déclarations d'entrée; **n. attaché,** attaché naval; **the N. College,** l'École navale; **to enter the N. College,** entrer à Navale; **to be at the N. College,** faire (l'École) Navale; **n. station,** station navale; **n. base,** base navale; **n. repair base,** base navale de réparations; **n. dockyard,** arsenal *m* maritime; **n. constructor,** ingénieur *m* du génie maritime; **N. Control Service,** Direction *f* des Routes; **n. stores,** (i) approvisionnements *mpl*, matériel *m*; fournitures *fpl* de navires; (ii) produits résineux retirés des conifères; *Rom.Ant:* **n. crown,** couronne navale, rostrale.

navally ['neivəli], *adv.* au point de vue naval.

navarch ['neivɑ:k], *s. Gr.Ant:* navarque *m*.

Navarino [nævə'ri:nou]. *Pr.n. Geog:* Navarin.

Navarra [næ'vɑ:rə]. *Pr.n. Geog:* (*in Spain*) Navarre *f*.

Navarre [næ'vɑ:r]. *Pr.n. Hist:* (*in Fr.*) **(the kingdom of) N.,** (le royaume de) Navarre *f*.

Navarrese [nævə'ri:z]. **1.** *Hist: & Geog:* (*a*) *a.* navarrais; (*b*) *s.* Navarrais, -aise. **3.** *s. Ling:* navarrais *m*.

nave[1] [neiv], *s.* moyeu *m* (de roue); **n. box,** boîte *f* de roue; douille *f* de roulement; **n. hole,** emboîture *f* de moyeu.

nave[2], *s.* nef *f*, vaisseau *m* (d'église); vaisseau de la nef.

navel ['neiv(ə)l], *s.* (*a*) *Anat:* nombril *m*, ombilic *m*; **n. string,** cordon ombilical; (*b*) *Fig:* milieu *m*, centre *m*, cœur *m* (d'un pays, d'une forêt, etc.); **n. hole,** trou *m* de meule de moulin; *Hort:* **n. orange,** orange *f* navel *inv* (avec une petite orange incluse dans le fruit); (*c*) *Her:* **n. (point),** nombril (de l'écu); (*d*) *Nau:* **n. pipe,** écubier *m* de pont.

navelwort ['neiv(ə)lwə:t], *s. Bot:* ombilic *m*, *F:* nombril *m* de Vénus.

navicert ['nævisə:t], *s. Nau: O:* navicert *m*.

navicular [næ'vikjulər]. **1.** *a. & s. Anat:* **n. (bone),** os *m* naviculaire; *Vet:* **n. (disease),** maladie *f* naviculaire; encastelure *f*. **2.** *a. Anat:* naviculaire; **n. fossa,** (i) (*in ear*) fossette *f* de l'anthélix; (ii) (*in urethra*) fosse *f* naviculaire; *Bot:* naviculaire.

navicularthritis [nævikjulɑ:θ'raitis], *s. Vet:* maladie *f* naviculaire.

navigability [nævigə'biliti], **navigableness** ['nævigəblnis], *s.* navigabilité *f* (d'un fleuve, d'un vaisseau); dirigeabilité *f* (d'un aérostat).

navigable ['nævigəbl], *a.* (fleuve *m*, canal *m*) navigable; (aérostat *m*) dirigeable; **n. river,** rivière navigable, marchande; **n. airspace,** espace (aérien) navigable; **n. waters,** eaux *f* navigables; **waters n. by seagoing vessels,** eaux accessibles aux bâtiments de mer; **ship in n. condition,** vaisseau *m* en bon état de navigabilité, en état de prendre la mer.

navigate ['nævigeit]. **1.** *v.i.* naviguer. **2.** *v.tr.* (*a*) parcourir (les mers); naviguer dans, sur (les mers, etc.) naviguer les mers; voyager (dans l'air); bourlinguer; (*b*) naviguer (un navire, un avion); gouverner, diriger (un navire); piloter (un aérostat); **navigating officer,** officier *m* de navigation; officier navigateur; officier des montres.

navigating ['nævigeitiŋ], *s.* navigation *f*; *Aer:* **n. room,** cabine *f* de navigation.

navigation [nævi'geiʃ(ə)n], *s.* navigation *f*; conduite *f* (d'un navire, d'un aérostat); **the art of n.,** la marine; **deep-sea n., high-seas n., ocean n., foreign n.,** navigation au long cours, hauturière, au large; **radio n.,** radionavigation *f*; **radar-monitored n.,** navigation au radar; **loxodromic n.,** navigation loxodromique; **orthodromic n., great-circle n.,** navigation orthodromique, navigation sur arc de grand cercle; **celestial, astronomical, n.,** navigation astronomique; **the n. laws,** le code maritime; *Hist:* **N. Act,** Acte *m* de navigation; **n. officer,** (i) *Nau: Av:* officier *m* de navigation; officier navigateur; officier des montres; (ii) *A: Aer:* officier du corps des aérostiers; *A:* **n. school,** école *f* d'hydrographie; *Av:* **air, aerial, n.,** navigation aérienne; *Ball: Space:* **space n.,** navigation spatiale, interplanétaire; **improper n.,** navigation fautive; **n. aids,** aides *f* à la navigation; **automatic n. system,** système *m* automatique de navigation.

navigational [nævi'geiʃən(ə)l], *a.* (instrument *m*, etc.) de navigation; **n. equipment,** appareils *mpl* de navigation; **n. aids,** aides *f* à la navigation.

navigator ['nævigeitər], *s.* **1.** (*a*) navigateur *m* (d'un navire, d'un avion, d'un engin spatial, etc.); *Nau: Av:* officier navigateur; (*b*) navigateur, marin *m*; *Hist:* **Henry the N.,** Henri le Navigateur. **2.** *A:* ouvrier occupé à construire un canal; terrassier *m*.

navvy[1] ['nævi], *s.* **1.** (*pers.*) terrassier *m*. **2.** *Civ.E: etc:* **(mechanical) n.,** excavateur, -trice; pelle *f* à vapeur; piocheuse *f*; *A:* **steam n.,** terrassier à vapeur.

navvy[2], *v.i.* (**navvied**) travailler comme terrassier.

navvying ['nævi:iŋ], *s.* travaux *mpl* de terrassier, de terrassement.

navy ['neivi], *s.* **1.** marine *f* de guerre, marine militaire; forces navales, armée *f* de mer; **to serve in the n.,** servir sur mer; **his son is in the n.,** son fils est dans la marine de guerre, dans la flotte; **n. agent,** agent *m* maritime; **the Royal N.,** la Marine nationale britannique; **seaman in the N.,** matelot *m* de l'État; *F:* **Wavy N.,** la marine de réserve (RNVR); **the merchant n.,** la marine marchande; **the NATO navies,** les forces navales de l'Otan; **minister,** *U.S:* **secretary, for the N.** = ministre *m* de la Marine; *U.S:* **the N. Department,** le ministère de la Marine; *A:* **the N. Board** = division navale du ministère de la Défense; *Com:* **n. cut,** carotte de tabac hachée. **2.** *A:* **the navies of Solomon,** les flottes de Salomon. **3. n. (blue),** bleu *m* marine *inv*; bleu foncé *inv*; **n. uniforms,** uniformes *m* bleu marine.

nawab [nə'wɑ:b], *s.* **1.** *Hist:* (*a*) vice-roi *m* sous l'Empire mogol; (*b*) prince musulman. **2.** = NABOB.

nay [nei]. **1.** *adv.* (*a*) *A:, Lit: & Dial:* non; (*b*) *Lit:* (*introducing a more emphatic statement*) (et) même, ou plutôt, pour mieux dire, bien plus, qui plus est, voire; **I am astounded, n., disgusted,** j'en suis ahuri, voire révolté; **a friend, n., a brother!** un ami, que dis-je! un frère! **2.** *s. A: & Lit:* non *m*; **he will not take n.,** il n'accepte pas de refus; **I cannot say him n.,** je ne peux pas le lui refuser; **no one dared to say him n.,** personne

n'osait l'empêcher; **yea and n.,** barguignage *m*; (*in voting*) **ayes and nays,** voix *f* pour et contre.
nazard [nə'zɑːd], *s. Mus:* nasard *m.*
Nazarene ['næzəriːn], *a. & s.* (*a*) *B.Hist:* nazaréen, -éenne; (*b*) *Art:* **the N. School, the Nazarenes,** l'école nazaréenne.
Nazarite ['næzərait], *s.* **1.** *Rel.H:* naziréen, -éenne; nazaréen, -éenne; nazir *m.* **2.** *B.Hist:* (*rare*) = NAZARENE.
nazaritism ['næzəraitizm], *s. Rel.H:* naziréisme *m*; naziréat *m*, nazaréat *m.*
naze [neiz], *s. Geog:* promontoire *m*, cap *m*, pointe *f.*
Nazi ['nɑːtsi], *a. & s. Hist: Pol:* nazi, -ie.
nazify ['nɑːtsifai], *v.tr.* nazifier.
Naziism ['nɑːtsiːizm], *s. Hist: Pol:* nazisme *m.*
Nazirite ['næzərait], *s.* **1.** *Rel.H:* = NAZARITE. **2.** *B.Hist:* (*rare*) = NAZARENE.
Nazism ['nɑːtsizm], *s. Hist: Pol:* nazisme *m.*
Neandert(h)al [niː'ændətɑːl]. **1.** *Pr.n. Geog:* Néandert(h)al; *Anthr:* **N. man,** l'homme de Néanderthal. **2.** *s. Anthr:* néandert(h)alien, -ienne.
Neandert(h)alian [niːændə'tɑːliən], *a. & s. Anthr:* néandert(h)alien, -ienne.
Neandert(h)aloid [niːændə'tɑːlɔid], *a. Anthr:* néandert(h)aloïde.
neap[1] [niːp], *a. & s.* **n. tide,** marée *f* de morte-eau; **n. tides, neaps,** (marées de) mortes-eaux *f*; marées de quadrature; marées bâtardes; **n. season,** époque *f* des mortes-eaux; **at dead neaps,** à la plus basse marée des mortes-eaux.
neap[2]. **1.** *v.i.* (*a*) (*of tides*) aller en décroissant vers les mortes-eaux; décroître; (*b*) (**of n. tide**), être aux mortes-eaux. **2.** *v.tr.* (*of ship*) **to be neaped,** être retenu par manque d'eau; être échoué jusqu'aux vives-eaux; être amorti; être au plein; **to get neaped,** amortir.
Neapolitan [niːə'pɔlit(ə)n]. *Geog:* (*a*) *a.* napolitain; de Naples; **N. ice cream,** tranche napolitaine; (*b*) *s.* Napolitain, -aine; habitant, -ante, originaire *mf*, de Naples.
near[1] [niər], *adv., prep. & a.*
I. *adv.* **1.** (*a*) (*denoting proximity in space and time*) près, proche; **to stand quite n.,** se tenir tout près; se tenir à proximité; **he lives quite n.,** il habite tout près; **to come n., draw n.,** s'approcher; **to come, draw, n. to s.o., sth.,** (s')approcher de qn, qch.; **come nearer,** venez plus près; approchez-vous; **as the mountains came nearer,** à l'approche *f* des montagnes; **he drew nearer,** il s'est approché davantage; il s'est rapproché; **the time is drawing n.,** l'heure *f* approche; **when they drew n. the group dispersed,** à leur approche le groupe s'est dispersé; **to bring sth. nearer,** rapprocher qch. **(to,** de); **nearer and nearer,** de plus en plus proche; **n. at hand,** (*of thg*) tout près, à portée de la main, à proximité; (*of event*) tout proche; **he lives quite n. (at hand),** il habite tout près; **it was very n. (to) Christmas,** on touchait à Noël; c'était aux approches de Noël; **keep n. to me,** restez près de moi; **he was standing n. the table,** il se tenait auprès de la table; **n. to where I was sitting,** près de l'endroit où j'étais assis; **we live n. (to) them,** nous habitons près de chez eux; **he has been very n. to death's door,** il a vu la mort de près; **with Chateaubriand we are very n. to the Romantic period,** avec Chateaubriand nous touchons à l'époque romantique; (*b*) (*of ship*) près du vent; (*to man at the helm*) **no nearer!** pas plus au vent! **as n. as she can!** au plus près! (*c*) (*closely connected by kinship or intimacy*) proche; **those n. and dear to him,** ceux qui lui touchent de près. **2.** (*a*) **he was as n. as could be to getting drowned,** il n'a tenu à rien qu'il ne se noyât; **as n. as I can remember,** autant que je puisse m'en souvenir; autant qu'il m'en souvient, qu'il m'en souvienne; **there are a thousand of them, as n. as makes no difference, no matter,** il y en a mille à peu de choses près; **that's as n. as you can get,** vous ne trouverez pas mieux; **keep as n. as possible to the prices quoted,** ne vous écartez pas trop des prix indiqués; **I came n. to crying,** j'ai été sur le point de pleurer; *A:* **n. upon thirty men,** près de trente hommes; (*b*) *A: & Lit:* (= NEARLY) presque, à peu près; **he was very n. asleep,** il était presque endormi; **these conditions lasted n. a century,** ces conditions durèrent à peu près, environ, un siècle; (*c*) **he's nowhere n. so, as, strong as you,** il n'est pas à beaucoup près aussi fort que vous; il s'en faut de beaucoup qu'il (ne) soit aussi fort que vous; **is he anywhere n. finished?** est-il près d'avoir fini? **he's nowhere n. finished,** il est loin d'avoir fini; **is the bus anywhere n. full?** s'en faut-il de beaucoup que l'autobus (ne) soit plein? **3. horse that goes, stands, n. behind,** cheval serré de derrière. **4.** *A:* **to live n.,** vivre parcimonieusement.
II. *prep.* **1.** près de, auprès de (qn, qch.); **n. the village,** près, auprès, du village; *Adm: Jur:* proche le village, proche du village; **situated n. the church,** situé près (de) l'église; **the houses n. the mountains,** les maisons *f* dans le voisinage des montagnes; **as we drew n. the mountains,** à l'approche des montagnes; **bring your chair near(er) the fire,** (r)approchez votre chaise du feu; **stand n. him,** mettez-vous, tenez-vous, auprès de lui; **to come, draw, n. (to) s.o., sth.,** (s')approcher de qn, qch.; **don't come n. me,** ne m'approchez pas; **we are getting n. London,** nous approchons de Londres; **we live n. them,** nous habitons près de chez eux; **being n. the station is an advantage,** le voisinage de la gare est un avantage. **2.** près de, sur le point de; **n. twelve o'clock,** près de midi; **n. death,** près de mourir; sur le point de mourir; **to be n. the end, the goal,** toucher à la fin, au but; **his hopes were n. fulfilment,** ses espoirs *m* étaient près de se réaliser; **he came n. (to) being run over,** il a failli être écrasé; **the plan came n. (to) being realized,** ce projet a été sur le point de se réaliser. **3. to be, to come, n. s.o., sth.,** se rapprocher de qn, de qch., (par la ressemblance); ressembler à qn, à qch.; **language that is nearer (the) Latin than (the) Italian,** langue *f* qui est plus près du latin que de l'italien, qui ressemble plus au latin qu'à l'italien; **it's the same (thing) or n. it,** c'est la même chose ou peu s'en faut; **nobody can come anywhere n. her,** il n'y a personne à son niveau; **he's nowhere n. it!** il n'y est pas du tout! **4.** *Com:* **n. beer,** imitation *f* de bière; **n. seal,** fourrure *f* genre loutre; **n. silk,** soie artificielle; **she gave a n. smile,** elle a esquissé un sourire.
III. *a.* **1.** (*of relative*) proche; (*of friend*) intime, cher; **our n. relations,** nos proches (parents); **they are n. relatives (of each other),** ils se touchent de près; **the nearest heir to the throne,** le plus proche héritier du trône. **2. the n. horse,** le cheval de gauche; (*of team*) le porteur; **n. foreleg,** pied *m* du montoir; **n. rein,** rêne *f* du dedans. **3.** (*of place, time, event*) proche; **the nearest inn,** l'auberge la plus voisine, la plus proche, (la plus) prochaine; **go to the nearest chemist's,** allez à la prochaine pharmacie; **glasses that make objects look nearer,** lunettes *f* qui rapprochent les objets; **to get a nearer view of sth.,** examiner qch. de plus près; **n. work,** travail fin, délicat; **the hour is n.,** l'heure *f* est proche; **n. prospect of happiness,** attente *f* d'un bonheur proche; **give the measurements to the nearest metre,** donnez les mesures à un mètre près; **he would guess your weight to the nearest kilo,** il devinerait votre poids à un kilo près. **4.** (*of road*) court, direct; **to go by the nearest road,** prendre par le plus court. **5.** qui touche, serre, de près; **it is a very n. concern of mine,** c'est une affaire qui me touche de très près; **n. translation,** traduction serrée, qui serre le texte de près; **n. resemblance,** grande ressemblance; **n. portrait,** portrait très ressemblant; **n. guess,** conjecture *f* à peu près juste; **n. race,** course très disputée; **n. offer,** offre approchante; **it was a n. thing, a n. escape,** *F:* **a n. go,** nous l'avons échappé belle; il s'en est fallu de peu; il était moins cinq. **6.** (*of pers.*) *O:* regardant, chiche, parcimonieux, ladre.
near[2], *v.tr. & i.* (s')approcher (de qn, de qch.); **as we were nearing Oxford,** comme nous approchions d'Oxford; **he is nearing his end,** il est près de sa fin; il s'éteint; **the road is nearing completion,** la route est près d'être achevée; **we are nearing the goal,** nous touchons au but; nous approchons du but.
nearby [niə:'bai]. **1.** *adv.* tout près, tout proche; **n. stood a windmill,** près de là se trouvait un moulin à vent; **he lives n.,** il habite tout près. **2.** *prep. O:* tout près de, tout proche de; **n. the church,** tout près de l'église; *Adm: Jur:* proche (de) l'église. **3.** *a.* ['niəːbai], **he came out of a n. house,** il est sorti d'une maison avoisinante.
Nearchus [ni'ɑːkəs]. *Pr.n.m. A.Hist:* Néarque.
nearctic [ni'ɑːktik], *a. Z: etc:* néarctique.
nearly ['niəːli], *adv.* **1.** (*a*) presque, à peu près, près de; **it's n. midnight,** il est bientôt minuit; **it's n. six (o'clock),** il est près de six heures; il n'est pas loin de six heures; **they were n. home,** ils étaient presque arrivés chez eux; **we're n. there now,** nous voilà bientôt arrivés; **n. all of the electors,** la presque totalité des électeurs; **I've got n. all of them,** je les ai presque tous; **the two results are pretty n. equal,** les deux résultats se valent à peu (de chose) près; **it's the same thing or n. so,** c'est la même chose ou peu s'en faut; **it's done or n. so,** c'est achevé ou peu s'en faut; **is he dead?—pretty n.,** est-il mort?—il ne s'en faut guère; **very n.,** peu s'en faut; **she's very n. twenty,** elle a tout près de vingt ans; elle va sur ses vingt ans; **he was n. appointed,** il a été près d'être nommé; **I n. caught them,** j'ai été près de les attraper; **I n. fell,** j'ai failli tomber; j'ai manqué de tomber; **it n. broke his heart,** cela lui a presque brisé le cœur; **the doctors n. killed me,** les médecins ont failli me tuer; **he very n. died,** il a frôlé la mort; **I very n. threw him out,** pour un peu je l'aurais jeté dehors; **we very n. shouted,** pour un peu on eût crié; **he was very n. run over,** il s'en est fallu de peu qu'il n'ait été écrasé; (*b*) **she's not n. so, as, old as me,** elle est loin d'être aussi âgée que moi; **it's not n. as, so, good,** il s'en faut qu'il (ne) soit aussi bon. **2.** (de) près; **do not approach too n.,** ne vous approchez pas trop (près); **we are n. related,** nous sommes proches parents; **to be n. acquainted with the people of a country,** connaître intimement le peuple d'un pays; *Nat.Hist:* **n. allied species,** espèces voisines; **they resemble each other very n.,** ils se ressemblent beaucoup; **news that concerns you very n.,** nouvelles *f* qui vous touchent de très près.
nearness ['niənis], *s.* **1.** (*a*) (*of time, place*) proximité *f*; (*of place*) voisinage *m*; (*b*) (*of translation*) fidélité *f*, exactitude *f*; (*c*) (*of friends*) intimité *f*; **n. of relationship,** proche parenté *f.* **2.** *A:* parcimonie *f*, économie *f*, ladrerie *f.*
nearside ['niəːsaid], *s.* (*a*) côté *m* gauche (d'un cheval); côté (du) montoir; (*b*) (*esp. in U.K.*) *Aut:* gauche *f* (de la route); côté gauche (d'une voiture); **n. door,** portière *f* gauche; **Dover, keep to the n. lane,** serrez à gauche pour Douvres.
nearsighted [niəː'saitid], *a.* myope; **she's n.,** elle a la vue basse.
nearsightedness [niəː'saitidnis], *s.* myopie *f.*
nearthrosis [niːɑː'θrousis], *s. Med:* néarthrose *f.*
neat[1] [niːt], *s.* (*a*) *A:* bœuf *m*, bétail *m*; **n. house,** vacherie *f*; étable *f* à vaches; **neat's leather,** cuir *m* de vache; *Cu:* **neat's tongue,** langue *f* de bœuf; (*b*) *Leath:* **neat's-foot (oil),** huile *f* de pied de bœuf.
neat[2], *a.* **1.** (*of spirits*) pur, sans eau; **to take, drink, one's whisky n.,** boire son whisky sec; **to drink the juice n.,** boire le jus nature. **2.** (*a*) (*of clothes, etc.*) simple et de bon goût; (*of room, drawer, etc.*) bien rangé, en ordre; (*of exercise book, etc.*) bien tenu, propre; (*of garden, etc.*) bien tenu, coquet, *F:* propret; **n. handwriting,** écriture nette; **n. ankles,** fines chevilles, fines attaches; **n. leg,** jambe bien tournée, bien faite; **she has a n. figure,** elle est bien faite; elle a une gentille tournure; **his n. attire,** sa mise soignée; **as n. as a new pin,** tiré à quatre épingles; propre comme un sou neuf; (*b*) (*of style*) élégant, choisi; (*of phrase, answer, etc.*) bien trouvé, bien tourné, adroit; **n. little speech,** petit discours bien tourné, bien troussé; **n. piece of work,** ouvrage bien exécuté; **to make a n. job of sth.,** faire du bon travail. **3.** (*of pers.*) ordonné, qui a de l'ordre; propre; **to be n. with one's hands,** être adroit de ses mains.
neaten ['niːtn], *v.tr.* ajuster (qch.); donner meilleure tournure à (qch.).
neath [niːθ], *prep. Poet:* sous; au-dessous de.
neat-handed ['niːt'hændid], *a. Lit:* aux mains adroites; adroit de ses mains.
neatherd ['niːthəːd], *s. A:* bouvier *m*, vacher *m.*
neatly ['niːtli], *adv.* **1.** (ranger, etc.) d'une manière soignée, ordonnée, avec ordre; **n. written,** écrit avec netteté; **n. dressed,** habillé avec goût; **she was poorly but n. dressed,** elle était vêtue pauvrement, mais avec soin; **quietly and n. dressed,** vêtue avec une simplicité de bon goût. **2.** adroitement, dextrement; **n. turned compliment,** compliment bien tourné, *F:* bien troussé; **that is n. put,** c'est joliment dit.
neatness ['niːtnis], *s.* **1.** simplicité *f*, bon goût (dans la mise); apparence soignée (d'un jardin); netteté *f* (d'écriture, de style); bon ordre (d'une chambre, d'un tiroir, etc.); propreté *f* (d'un cahier, etc.); jolie ligne (de jambe); finesse *f* (de la cheville, des attaches); tournure adroite (d'une phrase). **2.** (*of pers.*) (*a*) ordre *m*, propreté; (*b*) adresse *f*, habileté *f*, dextérité *f.*
neb [neb], *s. esp. Scot:* **1.** (*a*) bec *m* (d'oiseau, de tortue); (*b*) (i) bouche *f*, (ii) nez *m* (de qn); museau *m* (d'animal). **2.** bout *m*, pointe *f*, extrémité *f* (de qch.).
Nebalia [ne'beiliə], *s. Crust:* nébalie *f.*
Nebria ['nebriə], *s. Ent:* nébrie *f.*
nebris ['nebris], *s. Gr.Ant:* nébride *f.*
Nebuchadnezzar [nebjukəd'nezər], **Nebuchadrezzar** [nebjukə'drezər]. **1.** *Pr.n.m. B.Hist:* Nabuchodonosor. **2.** *s.* nabuchodonosor *m* (bouteille de 8 litres).
nebula, *pl.* **-ae** ['nebjulə, -iː], *s.* **1.** *Astr:* nébuleuse *f.* **2.** *Med:* (*a*) (*on eye*) taie *f*; néphélion *m*; (*b*) liquide *m* pour vaporisation. **3.** brume *f.*
nebular ['nebjulər], *a. Astr:* nébulaire.
nebule ['nebjuːl], *s.* **1.** *Astr:* nébuleuse *f.* **2.** brume *f*, buée *f.* **3.** *Arch:* nébule *f.*
nebulé ['nebjulei], **nebuly** ['nebjuli], *a.* **1.** *Her:* nébulé, nuagé. **2.** *Arch:* **n. moulding,** nébules *fpl.*
nebulium [ne'bjuːliəm], *s. Ch:* nébulium *m.*
nebulosity [nebju'lɔsiti], **nebulousness** ['nebjuləsnis], *s.* nébulosité *f.*

nebulous ['nebjuləs], *a. Astr: etc:* nébuleux; **n. thoughts,** pensées nébuleuses, fumeuses, brumeuses, vagues; **n. character, n. part,** personnage flou.

nebulously ['nebjuləsli], *adv.* nébuleusement.

necessarian [nesi'sɛəriən], *a. & s.* nécessarien, -ienne; déterministe (*mf*).

necessarianism [nesi'sɛəriənizm], *s.* doctrine *f* des nécessariens; déterminisme *m.*

necessarily [nesi'serəli], *adv.* nécessairement, de (toute) nécessité; inévitablement, infailliblement, forcément, inéluctablement; **what he says is not n. what he thinks,** ce qu'il dit n'est pas forcément ce qu'il pense; **it does not n. follow that the ring is lost,** il ne s'ensuit pas que la bague soit perdue; **this will n. remind him of his promise,** cela ne pourra manquer de lui rappeler sa promesse; **you don't n. have to read the whole book,** vous n'êtes pas obligé de lire le livre entier; **I don't n. have to go with them,** rien ne m'oblige à les accompagner.

necessary ['nesis(ə)ri]. **1.** *a.* (*a*) nécessaire, indispensable (**to, for, s.o., sth.,** à qn, qch.); **n. for doing sth.,** nécessaire, indispensable, pour faire qch.; **it is n. to (do sth.),** il est nécessaire, il est besoin, de (faire qch.); il faut (faire qch.); **it is n. for him to return,** il faut qu'il revienne; **matters n. to be known,** choses *f* qu'il est nécessaire de savoir; **I find it n. to . . .,** je juge nécessaire de . . .; **it is n. that. . .,** il est nécessaire, il faut, que + *sub.*; **is it n. for me to . . .? is it n. that I should . . .?** est-il nécessaire que je + *sub.*; **I shall do everything n. to . . .,** je ferai tout ce qu'il faudra pour . . .; **to make all n. arrangements,** prendre toutes dispositions utiles; **rendered n. by circumstances,** commandé par les circonstances; **to make it n. for s.o. to do sth.,** mettre qn dans la nécessité de faire qch.; **this clause makes it n. for us to . . .,** cette clause entraîne pour nous l'obligation de . . .; **if n.,** si cela est nécessaire; s'il le faut; s'il y a lieu; le cas échéant; au besoin; en cas de besoin; **if a meeting is n.,** s'il y a lieu de se réunir; **to do what is n.,** faire le nécessaire; **not to do more than is absolutely n.,** ne faire que le strict nécessaire, que l'essentiel; **you have more knowledge than is n.,** vous avez plus de connaissances qu'il n'en faut; **is all that n.?** faut-il de tout cela? **is all that fuss n.?** faut-il faire tant de façons? **to stay no longer than is strictly n.,** réduire la durée de son séjour à l'indispensable; **I did not go beyond what was strictly n.,** je me suis borné au strict nécessaire, à l'indispensable; **don't take more than is strictly n.,** ne prenez que l'indispensable; **we shall do what is n. to . . .,** nous ferons le nécessaire pour . . .; (*b*) (résultat *m*, conclusion *f*, loi *f*, etc.) nécessaire, inévitable, inéluctable; (*c*) *Phil:* **n. agent,** agent *m* nécessaire. **2.** *s.* (*a*) *usu. pl.* = NECESSITY 2; (*b*) *F:* **the n.,** de l'argent *m*; **his father will provide the n.,** son père fournira les frais de l'entreprise; **to do the n.,** faire le nécessaire; *esp.* payer la note.

necessitarian [nisesi'tɛəriən], *a. & s.* nécessarien, -ienne; déterministe (*mf*).

necessitarianism [nisesi'tɛəriənizm], *s.* doctrine *f* des nécessariens; déterminisme *m.*

necessitate [ni'sesiteit], *v.tr.* nécessiter (qch.), rendre (qch.) nécessaire; **process that necessitates very high pressures,** procédé *m* qui impose, comporte, des pressions très élevées.

necessitating [ni'sesiteitiŋ], *a. Theol:* (*of grace, action*) nécessitant.

necessitous [ni'sesitəs], *a.* nécessiteux, pauvre, besogneux; **to be in n. circumstances,** être dans le besoin, dans la nécessité.

necessitousness [ni'sesitəsnis], *s.* nécessité *f*, indigence *f*, dénuement *m.*

necessity [ni'sesiti], *s.* **1.** (*a*) nécessité *f*; obligation *f*, contrainte *f*, force *f*; **dire n. compels me to . . .,** la dure nécessité me force à . . .; **by, from, out of, n.,** par nécessité, par force, par la force des choses; **to do sth. out of n.,** être réduit à la nécessité de faire qch.; **of n.,** de (toute) nécessité; nécessairement, inévitablement; **of absolute n.,** de nécessité absolue; **this journey is a matter of n.,** ce voyage est une nécessité; **to be under the n. of doing sth., to be compelled by n. to do sth.,** être dans la nécessité, être contraint, se trouver dans l'obligation, de faire qch.; **to throw upon s.o. the n. of doing sth.,** mettre qn dans l'obligation de faire qch.; **to lay, put, s.o. under the n. of doing sth.,** mettre qn dans la nécessité de faire qch.; **the thing has become a n.,** la chose est devenue nécessaire; **case of absolute n.,** cas *m* de force majeure; *Phil:* **doctrine of n.,** doctrine *f* des nécessariens; déterminisme *m*; *Prov:* **n. is the mother of invention,** de tout s'avise à qui pain faut; nécessité est mère d'industrie, d'invention; *Num:* **n. money,** monnaies *fpl* de nécessité; (*b*) nécessité, besoin *m*; **the n. for sth.,** le besoin de qch.; **you understand the n. for your return,** vous comprenez la nécessité de votre retour; **if the n. arose, should arise,** si le besoin s'en faisait sentir; **in case of n.,** au besoin, en cas de besoin; **is there any n.?** est-il besoin? **there is no n. for you to come,** vous n'avez pas besoin de venir; il n'y a pas urgence à ce que vous veniez; **the n. of doing sth.,** le besoin, la nécessité, de faire qch.; (*c*) **a logical n.,** une nécessité logique; **heat follows friction as a n.,** le frottement entraîne nécessairement la chaleur. **2.** *usu. pl.* **necessities,** ce qui est nécessaire à l'existence; le nécessaire; **the bare necessities,** le strict nécessaire; **the necessities of life,** les nécessités de la vie; l'indispensable *m*; *Jur:* les aliments *m*; **to deny oneself the necessities of life,** se refuser les nécessaires; **travel necessities,** articles *m* indispensables au voyageur; **a car is a n. of life nowadays,** aujourd'hui une voiture est un objet de nécessité, est indispensable. **3.** *A:* nécessité, indigence *f*, dénuement *m*, besoin; **to be in n.,** être dans la nécessité, dans le besoin.

neck[1] [nek], *s.* **1.** (*a*) cou *m* (d'une personne, d'un animal); **n. feathers (of a bird),** plumes *f* collaires, camail *m* (d'un oiseau); **stiff n.,** (i) torticolis (passager); (ii) *A: & Lit:* opiniâtreté *f*; **to have a stiff n.,** avoir un, le, torticolis; **to be up to one's n. in sth.,** être dans qch. jusqu'au cou; *F:* **to be up to one's n. in work,** avoir du travail par-dessus la tête; être débordé de travail; en avoir jusque là; **he's in it up to his n.,** il y est (mouillé) jusqu'au cou; il trempe dans le bain; **to throw, fling, one's arms round s.o.'s n.,** sauter, se jeter, au cou de qn; **he held me round the n.,** il me tenait par le cou; **to break one's n.,** se casser le cou; **to save one's n.,** sauver sa peau; échapper à la potence; *F:* **you've got a n.,** quel toupet! quel culot! *F:* **to get it in the n.,** écoper; en avoir pour son compte, pour son grade; **the n. and withers (of a horse),** l'encolure *f* (d'un cheval); *Rac:* **to win by a n.,** gagner par une encolure; **to finish n. and n.,** arriver à égalité; finir dead-heat; **they ran a kilometre n. and n.,** ils se sont disputé la première place pendant un kilomètre; **we're n. and n.,** nous sommes manche à manche; *F:* **n. and crop,** tout entier; à corps perdu; **to be thrown out on one's n.,** être flanqué dehors avec perte(s) et fracas; **it's n. or nothing,** il faut tout hasarder; il faut risquer, jouer, le tout pour le tout; **he rode at the fence n. or nothing,** il a lancé son cheval à corps perdu contre la barrière; (*b*) *Cu:* collet *m* (d'agneau, etc.); **n. (of) beef,** collier *m* de bœuf; **best end of (the) n.,** côtelettes premières (d'agneau); (*c*) *Cost:* encolure (de robe, de chemise); **square n., round n.,** encolure carrée, ronde; **V n.,** encolure en pointe, en V; **high n.,** col haut, montant; **low n.,** décolleté *m*; **n. flap,** couvre-nuque *m, pl.* couvre-nuques (de képi, etc.). **2.** (*a*) orifice *m*, tubulure *f*; goulot *m*, col *m* (de bouteille); col (d'un vase); goulet *m* (d'un port); rétrécissement *m*, étranglement *m* (de tuyau); col (de cornue); appendice *m*, raccordement *m*, manchon *m* (de ballon); *Anat:* col (de l'utérus); *Ch:* **three-n. bottle,** flacon *m* à trois tubulures; **to knock the n. off a bottle,** faire sauter le goulot d'une bouteille; (*b*) langue *f* (de terre); collet (de ciseau, de dent, de vis, etc.); manche *m*, collet (d'un instrument à cordes); coude *m* (de baïonnette); gorge, raccordement (de cartouche); gorge (d'arme à feu); *Arch:* gorge, gorgerin *m*, colarin *m* (de chapiteau dorique); **n. mould(ing),** annelets *mpl* (de chapiteau); *Bot:* collet (de racine, de champignon, etc.); *Mec.E:* fusée *f*, tourillon *m*, gorge (d'essieu); **n. of a jack,** col d'un vérin; **swivel n.,** collet tournant; *Geol:* **(volcanic) n.,** neck *m.*

neck[2]. **1.** *F: v.tr.* pinter, lamper (de la bière, etc.). **2.** *v.i. P:* (*of couple*) se bécoter, se peloter; se faire des papouilles, des mamours.

neck[3], *s. Dial:* dernière gerbe de la moisson.

neckband ['nekbænd], *s.* tour-du-cou *m, pl.* tours-du-cou (de chemise); col *m.*

neckcloth ['neklɔθ], *s. A:* foulard *m*, cravate *f*, tour *m* de cou; cache-col *m, pl.* cache-col(s).

neckerchief ['nekətʃif], *s. A:* foulard *m*; mouchoir *m*, tour *m* de cou; cache-col *m, pl.* cache-col(s).

necking ['nekiŋ], *s.* **1.** *Arch:* gorge *f* (de colonne). **2.** *Mch:* anneau *m* de serrage; grain *m* (d'une boîte à étoupe); *Metalw:* **n. down,** (con)struction *f.* **3.** *F:* caresses *fpl*, câlinerie *f*; papouilles *fpl.*

necklace ['neklis], *s.* **1.** collier *m* (de diamants, etc.). **2.** *Nau:* collier (de mât).

necklet ['neklit], *s.* collier *m* (de perles, de fourrure, etc.).

neckline ['neklain], *s. Cost:* encolure *f*, échancrure *f* (d'une robe de jour); (*low*) décolletage *m*, décolleté *m* (d'une robe de soir).

neckpiece ['nekpi:s], *s. A:* (*a*) collet *m* (d'un vêtement); (*b*) *Arm:* colletin *m*, collerette *f* (d'une armure).

necktie ['nektai], *s. Cost:* cravate *f*; **made-up n.,** nœud tout fait; *U.S: P:* **n. party,** lynchage *m.*

neck-verse ['nekvə:s], *s. Hist:* verset *m* de psaume latin que l'on donnait à lire à ceux qui revendiquaient le bénéfice de clergie (pour échapper à la potence); **the n.-v.,** le premier verset du psaume LI: "Miserere mei."

neckwear ['nekwɛər], *s. Com:* cols *mpl*, cravates *fpl*, foulards *mpl*, etc.

necro- ['nekrou, ne'krɔ, nekrə], *comb.fm.* nécro-.

necrobacillosis [nekroubæsi'lousis], *s. Vet:* nécrobacillose *f.*

necrobia [ne'kroubiə], *s. Ent:* nécrobie *f.*

necrobiosis [nekroubai'ousis], *s. Med:* nécrobiose *f.*

necrobiotic [nekroubai'ɔtik], *a. Med:* nécrobiotique.

necrodes ['nekrədi:z], *s. Ent:* nécrode *m.*

necrogenic [nekrou'dʒenik], **necrogenous** [ne'krɔdʒənəs], *a. Bot:* nécrogène.

necrographer [ne'krɔgrəfər], *s.* nécrologue *m.*

necrolatry [ne'krɔlətri], *s.* nécrolâtrie *f.*

necrological [nekrə'lɔdʒik(ə)l], *a.* nécrologique.

necrologist [ne'krɔlədʒist], *s.* nécrologue *m.*

necrology [ne'krɔlədʒi], *s.* **1.** nécrologe *m* (d'une église, d'une année, etc.). **2.** nécrologie *f.*

necromancer ['nekrəmænsər], *s.* nécromancien, -ienne.

necromancy ['nekrəmænsi], *s.* nécromancie *f.*

necromantic [nekrə'mæntik], *a.* nécromantique.

necrophagous [ne'krɔfəgəs], *a. Z:* nécrophage.

necrophile ['nekroufail], *s. Med:* nécrophile *mf.*

necrophilia [nekrou'filiə], *s. Med:* nécrophilie *f.*

necrophiliac [nekrou'filiæk], *a. & s. Med:* nécrophile (*mf*).

necrophilic [nekrou'filik], *a. & s. Med:* nécrophile (*mf*).

necrophily [ne'krɔfili], *s. Med:* nécrophilie *f.*

necrophobia [nekrou'foubiə], *s. Med:* nécrophobie *f.*

necrophobic [nekrou'foubik], *a. Med:* nécrophobe, nécrophobique.

necrophore ['nekroufɔ:r], *s. Ent:* nécrophore *m.*

necropolis [ne'krɔpəlis], *s.* nécropole *f.*

necropsy [ne'krɔpsi], *s. Med:* **1.** autopsie *f*, *occ.* nécropsie *f.* **2.** dissection *f.*

necroscopy [ne'krɔskəpi], *s.* autopsie *f.*

necrose [ne'krous], *v.i.* se nécroser.

necrosis [ne'krousis], *s.* **1.** *Med:* nécrose *f*; gangrène *f* des os; mortification *f*; **n. of the jaw,** nécrose phosphorée; **to cause n. in a bone,** nécroser un os. **2.** *Bot:* nécrose.

necrospermia [nekrou'spə:miə], *s. Med:* nécrospermie *f.*

necrotic [ne'krɔtik], *a. Med:* nécrosique, nécrotique.

necrotize ['nekrətaiz], *v.i. Med:* se nécroser.

Nectandra [nek'tændrə], *s. Bot:* nectandra *m.*

nectar ['nektər], *s. Myth: Bot:* nectar *m.*

nectared ['nektəd], **nectareous, nectarious** [nek'tɛəriəs], **nectarous** ['nektərəs], *a. A: & Lit:* nectaréen.

nectariferous [nektə'rif(ə)rəs], *a. Bot:* nectarifère.

nectarine[1] ['nektəri(:)n], *s. Hort:* (*a*) brugnon *m*; **n. tree,** brugnonier *m*; (*b*) nectarine *f.*

nectarine[2] ['nektərin], *a. A: & Lit:* nectaréen.

Nectariniidae [nektəri'naiidi:], *s.pl. Orn:* nectarini(i)dés *m.*

nectarivorous [nektə'riv(ə)rəs], *a. Orn: etc:* nectarivore.

nectary ['nektəri], *s.* **1.** *Bot:* nectaire *m.* **2.** *Ent:* cornicule *f* (de puceron).

necton ['nektɔn], *s. Biol:* necton *m.*

nectria ['nektriə], *s. Fung:* nectria *m.*

necturus [nek'tjuərəs], *s. Amph:* necture *m.*

Ned [ned]. *Pr.n.m.* (*dim. of Edward*) Édouard.

Neddy ['nedi]. **1.** *Pr.n.m.* = NED. **2.** *s. F:* bourricot *m*, âne *m.*

née [nei], *Fr. p.p.* née; **Mrs Thomas, née Long,** Mme Thomas, née Long.

need[1] [ni:d], *s.* **1.** (*a*) besoin *m*; **to feel, satisfy, a n.,** éprouver, satisfaire, un besoin; **if need(s) be, in case of n.,** en cas de besoin, au besoin; si cela est nécessaire, s'il le faut; s'il (en) est besoin, si besoin (en) est; s'il y a lieu; le cas échéant; en cas d'urgence; **I shall come if n. be,** je viendrai si besoin est; **the n. for teachers,** les besoins en professeurs; **there is no n. for violence,** la violence n'est pas de mise; point n'est besoin de violence; **there is no n. to . . .,** il n'est pas nécessaire de . . ., il n'est pas besoin de . . .; **there is no n. for him to come on Monday,** il n'a pas de besoin de venir lundi; **there's no n. for you to do it,** vous pouvez vous dispenser de le faire; rien ne vous oblige à le faire; **what n. is there to send for him?** à quoi bon le faire venir? **what n. is there to go?** qu'est-il besoin d'y aller? **what n. was there for doing that?** quelle nécessité y avait-il de faire cela? **no n. to say that . . .,** inutile de dire, point n'est besoin de dire, que . . .; **no n. to insist,** pas besoin d'insister; **to have n. to do sth.,** avoir besoin de, avoir à, devoir, être dans la nécessité de, faire qch.; **he had n. to remember that**

. . ., il devait, devrait, se rappeler que . . .; **you had no n. to speak,** vous n'aviez que faire de parler; (*b*) **to be in n., have n., stand in n., of sth.,** avoir besoin de qch.; manquer de qch.; **should you be in n. of . . .,** si vous avez besoin de . . .; **premises in great n., badly in n., of repair,** local *m* qui a grand besoin de réparations; **I am in great n. of his assistance,** j'ai grand besoin de son aide; **I have no n. for his help,** je n'ai que faire de son aide; je n'ai aucun besoin de son aide; **you will have n. of me some day,** un jour viendra où vous aurez besoin de moi; **she is in n. of a rest,** elle a besoin de se reposer, de repos. **2.** (*a*) adversité *f*, difficulté *f*, embarras *m*; **in times of n., in the hour of n.,** aux moments difficiles; **to fail s.o. in his n.,** abandonner qn dans l'adversité; (*b*) besoin, indigence *f*, dénuement *m*, misère *f*; **to be in n.,** être dans la nécessité, dans le besoin; **to be in great n.,** être dans le plus grand besoin, dans la misère noire; **their n. is greater than mine,** ils en ont plus besoin que moi; ils sont plus malheureux que moi. **3. present needs,** besoins actuels; **my needs are few,** il me faut peu de chose; peu me suffit; **to attend, minister, to s.o.'s needs, to supply the needs of s.o.,** pourvoir aux besoins de qn; **that will meet my needs,** cela fera mon compte, mon affaire.

need[2], *v.* **1.** *v.tr.* (*3rd pers. sg. pr. ind.* **needs;** *p.t. & p.p.* **needed**) (*a*) (*of pers.*) avoir besoin de (qn, qch.); (*of thg*) réclamer, exiger, demander (qch.); **to n. rest,** avoir besoin de repos; **I work because I n. the money,** je travaille par besoin d'argent; **I n. you,** j'ai besoin de vous; **after all, they n. one another,** tout compte fait, ils ont besoin l'un de l'autre; **take what you n.,** prenez ce qui vous est nécessaire; **work that needs much care,** travail *m* qui exige, réclame, nécessite, beaucoup de soin; **the soil needs rain,** la terre demande de la pluie; **this plant needs water,** cette plante a besoin d'eau; **this will n. explaining, some explanation,** ceci demande à être expliqué; **there's still a lot that needs explaining,** il reste encore beaucoup de faits qui demandent une explication; **these facts n. no comment,** ces faits *m* se passent de commentaire; **situation that needs tactful handling,** situation qui demande à être maniée avec tact; **this chapter needs to be rewritten,** ce chapitre a besoin d'être remanié, demande à être remanié; **what he needs is a thrashing,** ce qu'il mérite, ce qu'il lui faudrait, c'est une bonne raclée; **to n. a lot of asking,** se faire prier; se faire tirailler; **I shall n. you to take down some letters,** j'aurai quelques lettres à vous dicter; (*b*) **to n. to do sth.,** être obligé, avoir besoin, de faire qch.; **I n. to clean the room,** il faut que je nettoie la chambre; **I n. to go to London,** j'ai besoin de me rendre à Londres; **they n. to be told everything,** il faut qu'on leur dise tout; **business that needs to be dealt with carefully,** affaire qui veut être conduite avec soin; **do you n. to work?** avez-vous besoin, êtes-vous obligé, de travailler? **I didn't n. to be reminded of it,** je n'avais pas besoin qu'on me le rappelât; **he didn't n. to be told twice,** il ne se l'est pas fait dire deux fois; **you only needed to ask,** vous n'aviez qu'à demander; **we shall not n. to reflect whether . . .,** nous n'aurons pas à nous demander si . . .; **some people use ten times more words than they n. (to use),** il y a des gens qui emploient dix fois plus de mots qu'il ne faut. **2.** *modal aux.* (*3rd pers. sg. pr. ind.* **n.;** *p.t.* **n.;** *no pr.p.; no p.p.*) **n. he go?** a-t-il besoin, est-il obligé, d'y aller? **n. he go so soon?** y a-t-il urgence à ce qu'il parte? est-il besoin qu'il parte si tôt? **adults only n. apply,** les adultes seuls peuvent postuler; **he needn't go, n. he?** il n'est pas tenu d'y aller, n'est-ce pas? **he needn't go if he doesn't want to,** s'il ne veut pas y aller, il n'y est pas tenu; **you needn't trouble yourself,** (vous n'avez) pas besoin de vous déranger; **you needn't wait,** inutile (pour vous) d'attendre; ne m'attendez pas, je vous en prie; **he needn't write to me,** il est inutile qu'il m'écrive; **you needn't do, say, any more,** inutile de dire, de faire, davantage; je vous fais grâce du reste; **I n. hardly tell you . . .,** point n'est besoin de vous dire . . .; point n'est besoin que je vous dise . . .; **I n. hardly tell you how grateful I am,** il n'est pas, il n'y a pas, besoin de vous dire combien je vous suis reconnaissant; **why n. he bother us?** qu'a-t-il besoin de nous déranger? **you needn't be in such a hurry,** ce n'est pas la peine de tant vous presser; **he n. not have been in such a hurry,** il n'avait pas besoin de tant se presser; **you needn't have knocked,** c'était inutile de frapper; **don't be longer than you n. (be),** faites aussi vite que possible; **there n. be no questions asked,** point besoin de questions; **why n. there be . . .?** qu'est-il besoin de . . .? **3.** *impers.* **it needs a great deal of skill for this work,** il faut beaucoup d'habileté pour ce travail; **it needed the horrors of war to open our eyes,** il a fallu les horreurs de la guerre pour nous ouvrir les yeux; *A:* **there needs a new spirit of brotherhood,** besoin est d'un nouvel esprit de fraternité. **4.** *v.i. A: & Lit:* être dans le besoin, dans la gêne; **to give to those that n.,** donner à ceux qui sont dans le besoin.

needed ['ni:did], *a.* nécessaire, dont on a besoin; **a much n. lesson,** une leçon dont on avait grand besoin.

needful ['ni:dful], *a.* nécessaire (**to, for,** à, pour); *O:* **the one thing n.,** la chose indispensable; **as much as is n.,** autant qu'il est besoin, autant qu'il en faut; *s. F:* **the n.,** l'argent *m* (nécessaire); *F:* **to do the n.,** (i) faire ce qui est nécessaire; (ii) payer, casquer.

needfulness ['ni:dfulnis], *s.* nécessité *f*, besoin *m* (**of,** de).

neediness ['ni:dinis], *s.* indigence *f*, nécessité *f*, dénuement *m*.

needle[1] ['ni:dl], *s.* **1.** (*a*) aiguille *f* (à coudre, à tricoter, etc.); **wool n., tapestry n.,** aiguille pour tapisserie; **bearded, spring n.,** aiguille à bec, à barbe, aiguille faisant ressort; **two-piece, compound, n.,** aiguille composée, à deux éléments; **latch n.,** aiguille à charnière, à loquet, à palette, aiguille articulée; **n. case,** étui *m* à aiguilles; porte-aiguilles *m inv*, cousette *f*; **n. book,** jeu *m* d'aiguilles; sachet *m* d'aiguilles; **n. threader,** filifère *m*; enfile-aiguilles *m inv*; **n. holder,** porte-aiguille *m, pl.* porte-aiguille(s); **n. paper,** papier *m* antirouille; **n. lace,** dentelle *f* à l'aiguille; *Surg:* **suture n.,** aiguille à suture; *Med:* **vaccinator n.,** aiguille à vaccin; **hypodermic n.,** aiguille pour injections hypodermiques; *F:* **he's a n. fiend,** il se pique; *Med:* **n. bath,** douche *f* en pluie fine sous pression; *Nau:* **roping n.,** aiguille à ralinguer; **n. trade, n. making, n. factory,** aiguillerie *f*; **n.(-)shaped,** en forme d'aiguille; (stylet, etc.) aiguillé; (cristal *m*) aciculaire; **to look for a n. in a haystack,** chercher une aiguille, une épingle, dans une botte de foin; (*b*) *Bot:* **(pine) n.,** aiguille (de pin); **Adam's n., beggar's n., shepherd's n.,** scandix *m*; peigne *m* de Vénus; aiguille de berger; aiguillette *f* de berger; **n. furze, gorse,** genêt épineux; *Ent: NAm:* **n. bug,** ranatra *f*, ranatre *f*; (*c*) *P:* **to get the n.,** se froisser; se fâcher; piquer une crise; **to give s.o. the n.,** taper sur les nerfs à qn; agacer qn. **2.** *Tchn:* (*a*) *O:* aiguille (de tourne-disque, etc.); *A:* **n. cup,** godet *m* à aiguilles (de phonographe); **n. box,** sébile *f* à aiguilles (de phonographe); (*on record player*) **n. noise, scratch,** bruit *m* d'aiguille; *El:* **n. gap,** éclateur *m* à pointes; *I.C.E:* pointeau *m* (de carburateur); *Mec.E:* **valve n.,** pointeau de soupape, de robinet; **n. valve,** soupape *f* à pointeau, à aiguille; robinet *m* à pointeau; **n. seat,** siège *m* de pointeau; **n. bearing,** roulement *m* à aiguilles; **self-aligning n. bearing,** roulement à aiguilles à autocentrage; **n. roller,** aiguille de roulement; **n. lubricator,** graisseur *m* à bouteille; *Exp:* **blasting n., priming n.,** aiguille, épinglette *f*; *Sm.a:* **firing n.,** aiguille de percussion; percuteur *m*; *A:* **n. gun,** fusil *m* à aiguille; *Metalw:* **assayer's n., touch n., test n.,** aiguille d'essai; touch(e)au *m*; *Art:* **engraving n.,** pointe *f* pour taille-douce; pointe sèche; (*b*) *Cmptr:* aiguille (de tri, etc.); **n. sorting,** tri *m* à l'aiguille; **n. sort card,** carte *f* à perforations marginales (pour le tri à l'aiguille); **n.-sorted cards,** cartes triées à l'aiguille; (*c*) aiguille (de boussole, d'indicateur de vitesse, etc.); aiguille, langue *f*, languette *f* (de balance); **compass, magnetic, mariner's, n.,** aiguille aimantée; **telegraph n.,** aiguille, index *m*; **n. telegraph,** télégraphe *m* à cadran; **n. dial,** cadran *m* à aiguille. **3.** (*a*) *Arch:* obélisque *m*; **Cleopatra's N.,** l'Obélisque, l'aiguille, de Cléopâtre; (*b*) *Geol: Geog:* aiguille (rocheuse); (*c*) *Ch: Miner:* **crystalline needles,** aiguilles cristallines. **4.** *Civ.E:* cale *f* d'étayage; **n. beam,** aiguille (de pont); *Hyd.E:* **n. dam, gate, weir,** barrage *m* à aiguilles, à fermettes.

needle[2]. **1.** *v.tr.* (*a*) *A:* coudre (un vêtement, etc.); (*b*) *Surg:* opérer (une cataracte) avec l'aiguille; (*c*) *F:* **to n. s.o.,** irriter, exciter, agacer, qn; chiner, empoisonner, qn; (*d*) *Cmptr:* trier (des cartes) à l'aiguille; (*e*) *Const:* caler en sous-œuvre (un mur); encastrer une cale d'étayage dans (un mur); (*f*) *U.S: F:* ajouter de l'alcool à (une consommation); renforcer (une consommation). **2.** *v.i.* (*a*) *A:* coudre; (*b*) *Miner: etc:* se cristalliser en aiguilles.

needlecord ['ni:dlkɔ:d], *s. Tex:* velours *m* mille-raies.

needlecraft ['ni:dlkra:ft], *s.* travaux *mpl* à l'aiguille; la couture.

needlefish ['ni:dlfiʃ], *s. Ich:* aiguille *f* de mer.

needleful ['ni:dlful], *s.* aiguillée *f* (de fil).

needlelike ['ni:dllaik], *a. Cryst: etc:* apiciforme, aciculaire.

needlepoint ['ni:dlpoint], *s.* **1.** (*a*) pointe *f* d'aiguille; (*b*) pointe sèche (de compas). **2. n. (lace),** dentelle *f* à l'aiguille.

needle-pointed ['ni:dlpointid], *a.* (rocher, flèche, etc.) en pointe d'aiguille.

needless ['ni:dlis], *a.* inutile, peu nécessaire, superflu; **n. remark,** remarque déplacée, peu nécessaire; **(it is) n. to say that . . .,** (il est) inutile de dire que . . ., point n'est besoin de dire que . . .; **n. to say we shall refund the money,** il va de soi que nous rembourserons l'argent; **she is, n. to say, very pleased about it,** il va sans dire qu'elle en est très contente; **comment is n.,** voilà qui se passe de commentaire; pas besoin de commentaire; **all this discussion is n.,** toute cette discussion ne sert à rien.

needlessly ['ni:dlisli], *adv.* inutilement, sans nécessité.

needlessness ['ni:dlisnis], *s.* inutilité *f* (de qch.); caractère déplacé (d'une remarque, etc.).

needlewoman, *pl.* **-women** ['ni:dlwumən, -wimin], *s.f.* **1. she's a good n.,** elle coud bien; elle sait coudre; elle travaille adroitement à l'aiguille; **I'm no n.,** je ne sais pas coudre; je ne suis pas une femme d'aiguille. **2.** *O:* couturière à la journée; (*in boarding school, etc.*) lingère.

needlework ['ni:dlwə:k], *s.* travail *m* à l'aiguille; travaux à l'aiguille, ouvrages *mpl* de dames; (*school subject*) couture *f*; **she's never without her n.,** elle a toujours son ouvrage à la main; **n. case,** mallette *f* de couture.

needs [ni:dz], *adv. O:* (*used only before or after* **must**) (*a*) nécessairement, de toute nécessité, par un besoin absolu; **he must n. obey, he n. must obey,** (i) force lui est d'obéir; (ii) force lui fut d'obéir; **there's no train, so we must n. walk,** il n'y a pas de train, il (nous) faudra donc faire le trajet à pied; **if n. must . . .,** s'il le faut . . .; *Prov:* **n. must when the devil drives,** nécessité n'a pas de loi; (*b*) *Pej:* **he n. must interfere!** il a fallu qu'il vienne s'en mêler! **he had no money, but she must n. go and marry him,** il était sans le sou, mais la voilà qui commet la sottise de l'épouser, mais il a fallu qu'elle aille l'épouser.

needy ['ni:di], *a.* (*of pers.*) nécessiteux, besogneux, indigent; **to be in n. circumstances,** être dans l'indigence; **n. old people,** vieillards *mpl* dans le besoin; *s.* **the n.,** les nécessiteux.

neem [ni:m], *s. Bot:* margousier *m*.

neep [ni:p], *s. Scot:* navet *m*.

ne'er [nɛər], *adv. Poet:* (ne . . .) jamais; **ne'er the less,** néanmoins.

ne'er-do-well ['nɛə:du:wel]. **1.** *a.* propre à rien. **2.** *s.* vaurien, -ienne; **he's, she's, a n.-do-w.,** c'est un, une, propre à rien.

nefarious [ni'fɛəriəs], *a.* (*of pers., purpose, etc.*) infâme, scélérat, vilain.

nefariously [ni'fɛəriəsli], *adv.* d'une manière infâme, scélérate.

nefariousness [ni'fɛəriəsnis], *s.* scélératesse *f*.

negate [ni'geit], *v.tr.* **1.** *Lit:* nier; **if you n. the soul,** si vous niez l'existence de l'âme. **2.** nullifier (la loi, etc.). **3.** *Gram:* mettre au négatif.

negation [ni'geiʃ(ə)n], *s.* négation *f* (d'un fait, etc.).

negative[1] ['negətiv], *a., s. & adv.*

I. *a.* (*a*) négatif; **to have a n. voice,** avoir voix négative; *Nau:* **n. signal,** triangle *m* non; (*b*) **n. virtues,** vertus négatives; **n. evidence,** preuve négative; **to maintain a n. attitude,** se tenir sur la négative; (*c*) *Mth:* **n. quantity,** quantité négative; **n. sign,** (signe *m*) moins *m*; *El:* **n. electrode,** cathode *f*; *Med:* **n. result, test,** examen négatif; *Opt:* **n. optical system,** système optique divergent, négatif.

II. *s.* **1.** (*a*) négative *f*; *Gram:* négation *f*; **to answer in the n.,** répondre négativement; répondre par la négative; **the answer is in the n.,** la réponse est négative, est non; **to argue in the n.,** soutenir la négative; **two negatives make an affirmative,** deux négations valent une affirmation; (*b*) *Mth:* valeur, quantité, négative. **2.** (*a*) *Phot:* négatif *m*; épreuve négative; cliché (négatif); **brownprint n.,** brun négatif; *Phot.Engr:* **contact n.,** négatif par contact; **continuous tone n.,** négatif à tons continus; **direct n.,** phototype négatif; **halftone n., screened n.,** négatif tramé; **line n.,** négatif de trait; **mirror n., reversed n.,** négatif inversé; **stripping n.,** négatif pelliculaire; **tint n.,** négatif de teinte (plate); **flat n.,** cliché, négatif, sans contrastes; (*b*) *Rec:* **n. (record),** poinçon *m*; **master n.,** poinçon de réserve; **metal n.,** original *m*, père *m*; (*c*) *El:* plaque négative (de pile).

III. *adv. Av: Space:* (*in answer to a question*) non.

negative[2], *v.tr.* **1.** (*a*) s'opposer à, rejeter (un projet, etc.); **to n. an amendment,** repousser un amendement; (*b*) *U.S:* refuser (un candidat). **2.** réfuter (une hypothèse); contredire, nier (un rapport); *Nau: etc:* **to n. a signal,** annuler un signal. **3.** neutraliser (un effet, etc.).

negatively ['negətivli], *adv.* négativement.

negativism ['negətivizm], *s. Psy:* négativisme *m*.

negativity [negə'tiviti], *s. Phil:* négativité *f*.

negatory ['negətəri], *a.* négatoire.

negatoscope ['negətəskoup], *s. Med:* négatoscope *m*.

negat(r)on ['negət(r)ɔn], *s. Atom.Ph:* négaton *m*.

neglect[1] [ni'glekt], *s.* **1.** (*a*) manque *m* d'égards (**of,** envers, pour); (*b*) manque de soin(s); **to leave one's children in utter n.,** laisser ses enfants à l'abandon; **to die in total n.,** mourir complètement abandonné; (*c*) mauvais entretien (d'une machine, etc.). **2.** négligence *f*, inattention *f*; **out of n., from n., through n.,** par négligence; **n. of proper precautions,** négligence, manque, de précautions convenables; **n. of one's duties,** oubli *m* de ses devoirs; inattention à ses devoirs.

neglect[2], *v.tr.* **1.** (*a*) manquer d'égards envers (qn); négliger (qn); laisser (qn) de côté; (*b*) manquer de soins pour (qn); ne prendre aucun soin de, négliger (ses enfants, etc.); **he utterly neglected his family,** il laissait sa famille à l'abandon; **to n. one's health,** négliger sa santé; **to n. oneself,** négliger sa personne, sa mise, sa tenue; se négliger; prendre peu de soin de sa personne; **everything's being neglected,** tout va à vau-l'eau. **2.** négliger, oublier (ses devoirs, un avis, etc.); **to n. an opportunity,** laisser échapper une occasion; **to n. to do sth.,** négliger, omettre, de faire qch.

neglectable [ni'glektəbl], *a. A:* négligeable.

neglected [ni'glektid], *a.* (*a*) **n. wife,** femme délaissée; épouse négligée; **a n. cold may develop into bronchitis,** un rhume négligé peut dégénérer en bronchite; (*b*) (*of appearance, etc.*) **n. beard,** barbe mal soignée; **n. garden,** jardin à l'abandon; jardin mal tenu; **n. house,** intérieur négligé.

neglectful [ni'glektful], *a.* négligent; **to be n. of sth., of s.o.,** négliger qch., qn; être négligent, oublieux, de qch., de qn; **n. of his interests,** insoucieux de ses intérêts; *Lit:* **to be n. to do sth.,** omettre de faire qch.

neglectfully [ni'glektfuli], *adv.* négligemment; avec négligence.

neglectfulness [ni'glektfulnis], *s.* négligence *f*.

négligé(e) ['neglizei], *s. Cost:* négligé *m*.

negligence ['neglidʒəns], *s.* **1.** (*a*) négligence *f*, incurie *f*; manque *m* de soins; inobservation *f* des règlements; **through n.,** par négligence; (*b*) nonchalance *f*, insouciance *f*, indifférence *f*; (*c*) *Jur:* négligence; **criminal n.,** négligence coupable, criminelle; **gross n.,** négligence grave, grosse; *Ins:* **n. clause,** clause *f* (de) négligence. **2. negligences,** négligences, fautes *f* d'omission.

negligent ['neglidʒənt], *a.* **1.** négligent; **to be n. of sth.,** négliger qch.; être oublieux de (ses devoirs, etc.). **2.** (air, ton) nonchalant, insouciant.

negligently ['neglidʒəntli], *adv.* **1.** négligemment; avec négligence. **2.** nonchalamment; avec insouciance.

negligible ['neglidʒibl], *a.* négligeable; *Mth:* **n. quantity,** quantité *f* négligeable; **she considered him a n. quantity,** elle le jugeait négligeable.

negotiability [nigouʃiə'biliti], *s.* négociabilité *f*, commercialité *f* (d'un effet, etc.).

negotiable [ni'gouʃiəbl], *a.* **1.** *Fin: etc:* (effet *m*, titre *m*, etc.) négociable; bancable; **stocks n. on the Stock Exchange,** titres négociables en Bourse; **not n.,** non-négociable; (*of military pension, etc.*) incessible. **2.** (barrière, etc.) franchissable; (chemin, etc.) praticable.

negotiate [ni'gouʃieit]. **1.** *v.tr.* (*a*) négocier, traiter (une affaire, un mariage); négocier (un emprunt); (*b*) **to n. a bill,** négocier, trafiquer, un effet; **bills difficult to n.,** valeurs *f* difficiles à placer; **to n. a treaty,** (i) négocier un traité; (ii) conclure un traité; (*c*) franchir (une haie, une côte); surmonter (une difficulté); **to n. a difficult road,** venir à bout d'un chemin difficile; *Aut:* **to n. a bend,** négocier un virage; prendre un virage; **he can't n. the hills,** (i) il ne sait pas prendre les côtes; (ii) sa voiture n'est pas capable de monter les côtes. **2.** *v.i.* (*a*) **to be negotiating with s.o. for . . .,** être en traité, en marché, avec qn pour . . .; **to n. for peace,** entreprendre des pourparlers de paix; traiter de la paix; **to n. for new premises,** traiter pour un nouveau local; (*b*) **they refuse to n.,** ils refusent de négocier.

negotiation [nigouʃi'eiʃ(ə)n], *s.* **1.** négociation *f* (d'un traité, d'un emprunt, etc.); **under n.,** en négociation; **by n.,** par voie de négociations; de gré à gré; **price a matter for n.,** prix *m* à débattre; **to be in n. with s.o.,** être en pourparler(s) avec qn; **to enter into, upon, negotiations with s.o.,** engager, entamer, des négociations avec qn; entrer en pourparler, entamer des pourparlers, avec qn; **to start negotiations with s.o.,** engager des négociations avec qn; **who will conduct the negotiations?** qui va conduire, mener, les négociations? **negotiations are proceeding,** des négociations sont en cours; **to break off negotiations,** rompre les négociations; **to resume negotiations,** reprendre les négociations. **2.** franchissement *m* (d'un obstacle); prise *f* (d'un virage).

negotiator [ni'gouʃieitər], *s.* négociateur, -trice.

negotiatress [ni'gouʃieitris], **negotiatrix** [ni'gouʃieitriks], *s.f. Jur:* négociatrice.

negress ['ni:gris], *s.f.* noire; *Anthr: & Pej:* négresse.

negrillo [ni'grilou], *s.* **1.** négrillon, -onne. **2.** *Anthr:* négrille *m*.

Negritic [ni'gritik], *a. Anthr:* négroïde.

Negrito [ni'gri:tou], *a. & s. Anthr:* (*a*) *a.* négrito; **the N. race,** la race négrito; (*b*) *s.* Négrito *m*.

Negritoid [ni'gri:tɔid], *a. Anthr:* négritoïde.

negro, *pl.* **-oes** ['ni:grou, -z], *a. & s.* (*a*) *a.* noir, nègre; **the n. race,** la race noire, nègre; *U.S: Hist:* **the N. States,** les États *m* esclavagistes; (*b*) *s.* noir *m*; *Pej:* nègre *m*; *Anthr:* **the negroes,** les nègres; la race noire, nègre.

Negro-African ['ni:grou'æfrikən], *s. Ling:* les langues négro-africaines.

negrohead ['ni:grouhed], *s.* **1.** tabac noir en carotte. **2.** caoutchouc *m* de qualité inférieure.

negroid ['ni:grɔid], *a. & s. Anthr:* négroïde (*mf*).

negrophile ['ni:grəfail], **negrophilist** [ni:'grɔfilist], *s.* négrophile *mf*.

Negropont ['ni:grəpɔnt]. *Pr.n. Geog:* Nègrepont *m*, Eubée *f*.

negus[1] ['ni:gəs], *s.* nég(o)us *m* (d'Éthiopie).

negus[2], *s.* vin épicé et aromatisé; nég(o)us *m*.

Nehemiah [ni:i'maiə]. *Pr.n.m. B.Hist:* Néhémie.

neigh[1] [nei], *s.* hennissement *m*.

neigh[2], *v.i.* hennir.

neighbour[1] ['neibər], *s.* **1.** voisin, -ine; **to have good, bad, neighbours,** avoir des voisins agréables, désagréables; **all the neighbours are talking about it,** tout le voisinage en parle; **my right-hand, left-hand, n.,** mon voisin de droite, de gauche. **2.** *B: etc:* prochain *m*; **love thy n. as thyself,** aime ton prochain comme toi-même; **one's duty towards one's n.,** le devoir envers son prochain; **it isn't easy to love one's n. as oneself,** il n'est pas facile d'aimer autrui comme soi-même; **to covet one's neighbour's property,** convoiter le bien d'autrui.

neighbour[2], *v.tr. & ind.tr. esp. NAm:* (*of pers.*) **to n. (with) s.o.,** être le voisin de qn; (*of lands*) **to n. (with, on) an estate,** avoisiner (avec) une terre.

neighbourhood ['neibəhud], *s.* **1.** *A:* voisinage *m*; rapports *mpl* entre voisins; **good n.,** bons rapports entre voisins; relations *fpl* de bon voisinage. **2.** voisinage, proximité *f* (**of,** de); **to live in the (immediate) n. of . . .,** demeurer à proximité de . . .; *F:* **something in the n. of ten pounds, of fifteen kilometres,** environ dix livres, quinze kilomètres; une somme dans les dix livres. **3.** (*a*) alentours *mpl*, environs *mpl*, approches *fpl* (d'un lieu); **in the n. of the town,** aux alentours, aux approches, de la ville; (*b*) voisinage, quartier *m*; parages *mpl*; **there's no park in this n.,** il n'y a pas de parc dans ce quartier; **the fruit grown in that n.,** les fruits cultivés dans cette localité; **all the young people of the n.,** tous les jeunes du voisinage; **the whole n. is talking about it,** tout le voisinage en parle.

neighbouring ['neibəriŋ], *a.* avoisinant, voisin; proche.

neighbourliness ['neibəlinis], *s.* (*of pers.*) (relations *fpl* de) bon voisinage; bons rapports entre voisins.

neighbourly ['neibəli], *a.* (*of pers.*) obligeant, amical, -aux; bon voisin; (*of action, etc.*) de bon voisin; de bon voisinage; **to act in a n. way,** agir en bon voisin; **to be n. with s.o.,** voisiner avec qn; **n. visits,** visites *f* de bon voisinage.

neighbourship ['neibəʃip], *s. A:* **1.** = NEIGHBOURHOOD 1. **2.** proximité *f*.

neighing[1] ['neiiŋ], *a.* (cheval) hennissant.

neighing[2], *s.* hennissement *m*.

neither ['naiðər, *esp. NAm:* 'ni:ðər]. **1.** *adv. & conj.* (*a*) **n. . . . nor . . .,** ni . . . ni . . .; **he will n. eat nor drink,** il ne veut ni manger ni boire; **he n. eats nor drinks,** il ne mange ni ne boit; **I n. like nor dislike her,** je ne l'aime ni ne l'aime pas; **n. my mother nor I know where they are,** ni ma mère ni moi ne savons où ils sont; je ne sais pas où ils sont, ni ma mère non plus; **n. Peter nor Henry is there,** ni Pierre ni Henri ne sont (*occ.* n'est) là; **I have n. wife nor child nor friends,** je n'ai ni femme ni enfants ni amis; **it is n. more nor less than a crime,** ce n'est ni plus ni moins qu'un crime; **n. here nor anywhere else,** ni ici ni ailleurs; **is she happy or merely resigned?—n. (the) one nor the other,** est-elle heureuse ou seulement résignée?—ni l'un ni l'autre; (*b*) non plus; **as he does not work, n. will I,** puisqu'il ne travaille pas, (moi) je ne travaillerai pas non plus; **if you do not go n. shall I,** si vous n'y allez pas, je n'irai pas non plus; (*c*) **I don't know, n. can I guess,** je n'en sais rien et je ne peux pas davantage le deviner; **I haven't read it, n. do I intend to,** je ne l'ai pas lu et d'ailleurs je n'en ai pas l'intention. **2.** *a. & pron.* ni l'un(e) ni l'autre; aucun(e); **n. tale, n. of the tales, is true,** aucune, ni l'une ni l'autre, des deux histoires n'est vraie; **n. car was seriously damaged,** ni l'une ni l'autre des voitures n'a subi de dégâts importants; **n. driver was killed,** ni l'un ni l'autre des conducteurs n'a été tué; **n. (of them) knows,** ils ne le savent ni l'un ni l'autre; ni l'un ni l'autre ne le savent; **n. (of them) saw it,** ni l'un ni l'autre ne l'a vu; **n. of them ever speaks about it,** ils n'en parlent jamais ni l'un ni l'autre; **on n. side,** ni d'un côté ni de l'autre.

nekton ['nektɔn], *s. Biol:* necton *m*.

Nell, Nellie, Nelly[1] [nel, 'neli]. *Pr.n.f.* (*dim. of Ellen*) Éléonore, Hélène; *P:* **not on your nellie!** jamais de la vie! rien à faire!

nelly[2], *s. Orn:* pétrel géant.

nelson ['nelsən], *s. Wr:* nelson *m*; **double, full, n.,** double nelson.

nelumbium [ni'lʌmbiəm], **nelumbo** [ne'lʌmbou], *s. Bot:* nélombo *m*, nélumbo *m*.

Nemalion [ni'meiliən], *s. Algae:* némalion *m*.

Nemalionales [nimeiliə'neili:z], *s.pl. Algae:* némalionales *f*.

nemalite ['neməlait], *s. Miner:* némalite *f*.

nemathelminth [nemə'θelminθ], *s. Ann:* némathelminthe *m*.

nematic [ni'mætik], *a. Ph: Ch:* nématique.

nemato- ['nemətə-, nemə'tɔ-, nemə'tou-], *comb.fm.* némato-.

nematoblast ['nemətəblɑ:st], *s. Biol:* nématoblaste *m*.

Nematocera [nemə'tɔsərə], *s.pl. Ent:* nématocères *m*.

nematoceran, nematocerous [nemə'tɔsərən, -rəs], *a. Ent:* nématocère, némacère.

nematocyst ['nemətəsist], *s. Biol:* nématocyste *m*, cnidoblaste *m*.

Nematoda [nemə'toudə], *s.pl. Ann:* nématodes *m*.

nematode ['nemətoud], *s. Ann:* nématode *m*.

nematoid ['nemətɔid], **nematoidean** [nemə'tɔidiən], *a. & s. Ann:* nématoïde (*m*).

Nematophora [nemə'tɔfərə], *s.pl. Coel:* nématophores *m*.

nematus ['nemətəs], *s. Ent:* némate *m*.

nem. con. ['nem'kɔn], **nem. diss.** ['nem'dis]. *Lt.adv.phr.* (*nemine contradicente, nemine dissidente*) unanimement; à l'unanimité; sans opposition; **to vote a law n. c.,** voter une loi sans opposition.

Nemea [ni'mi:ə]. *Pr.n. Hist:* Némée.

Nemean [ni'mi:ən], *a. & s. Hist:* (*a*) *a.* néméen; **the N. games,** les jeux néméens; *Myth:* **the N. lion,** le lion de Némée; (*b*) *s.* Néméen, -éenne.

Nemertea [ni'mə:tiə], *s.pl. Ann:* némertiens *m*, némertes *f*.

nemertean [ni'mə:tiən], **nemertine** ['neməti:n], *a. & s. Ann:* (*a*) *a.* némertien; (*b*) *s.* némerte *f*, nemertes *m*; némertien *m*.

nemesia [ni'mi:siə], *s. Bot:* nemesia *m*.

Nemesis ['nemisis]. *Pr.n.f. Myth:* Némésis.

nemobius [ni'moubiəs], *s. Ent:* némobie *m*.

Nemocera [ni'mɔsərə], *s.pl. Ent:* nématocères *m*.

nemophila [ni'mɔfilə], *s. Bot:* némophila *m*, némophile *f*.

nemopterid [ni'mɔptərid], *a. & s. Ent:* némoptère (*m*).

Nemopteridae [ni:mɔp'teridi:], *s.pl. Ent:* némoptères *m*.

nemoral ['nemərəl], *a.* (*a*) *Lit:* némoral, -aux; (*b*) *Rom.Ant:* némoréen, -éenne.

nemoricole [ni'mɔrikoul], **nemoricoline, nemoricolous** [nemə'rikəlain, -'rikələs], *a. Orn:* némoricole.

nemourid [ni'murid], *s. Ent:* némoure *f*, nemura *m*.

nenuphar ['nenjufɑ:r], *s. Bot:* nénuphar *m*, nénufar *m*.

neo- ['ni:ou], *pref.* néo-.

neoabietic [ni:ouæbi'etik], *a. Ch:* (acide) néoabiétique.

neoarsphenamine [ni:ouɑ:'sfenəmain], *s. Pharm:* néoarsphénamine *f*.

neo-Babylonian [ni:oubæbi'louniən]. (*a*) *a. Hist:* néo-babylonien; (*b*) *s. Ling:* chaldéen *m*.

neobalaena [ni:oubæ'li:nə], *s. Z:* néobaleine *f*.

neobisium [ni:ou'baisiəm], *s. Arach:* neobisium *m*.

neoblast ['ni:oublæst], *s. Biol:* néoblaste *m*.

neoblastic [ni:ou'blæstik], *a. Biol:* néoblastique.

neocapitalism [ni:ou'kæpit(ə)lizm], *s.* néocapitalisme *m*.

neo-Catholic [ni:ou'kæθ(ə)lik], *a.* néo-catholique.

neo-Catholicism [ni:oukə'θɔlisizm], *s.* néo-catholicisme *m*.

neo-Celtic [ni:ou'keltik], *a.* néo-celtique.

Neocene ['ni:ousi:n], *a. & s. Geol:* néogène (*m*).

neoceratodus [ni:ousə'rætədəs], *s. Ich:* neoceratodus *m*.

neo-Christian [ni:ou'kristjən], *a. & s.* néo-chrétien, -ienne.

neo-Christianity [ni:oukristi'æniti], *s.* néo-christianisme *m*.

neo-classic(al) [ni:ou'klæsik(l)], *a.* néo-classique.

neo-classicism [ni:ou'klæsisizm], *s.* néoclassicisme *m*.

neocolonialism [ni:oukə'louniəlizm], *s. Pol:* néo-colonialisme *m*.

neocolonialist [ni:oukə'louniəlist], *a. & s.* néo-colonialiste (*mf*).
Neocomian [ni:ou'koumiən], *a. & s. Geol:* néocomien (*m*).
neo-Confucianism [ni:oukən'fju:ʃənizm], *s.* néo-confucianisme *m.*
neo-Confucianist [ni:oukən'fju:ʃənist], *s.* néo-confucianiste *mf.*
neo-criticism [ni:ou'kritisizm], *s. Phil:* néo-criticisme *m.*
neocyte ['ni:ousait], *s. Biol:* néocyte *m.*
neo-Darwinian [ni:oudɑ:'winiən], *a.* néo-darwinien.
neo-Darwinism [ni:ou'dɑ:winizm], *s. Biol:* néo-darwinisme *m.*
neo-Darwinist [ni:ou'dɑ:winist], *s.* néo-darwiniste *mf.*
neodymium [ni:ou'dimiəm], *s. Ch:* néodyme *m.*
neofascism [ni:ou'fæʃizm], *s. Pol:* néo-fascisme *m.*
neofascist [ni:ou'fæʃist], *a. & s.* néo-fasciste (*mf*).
neoformation [ni:ouʃɔ:'meiʃ(ə)n], *s. Biol:* néo-formation *f.*
Neogene ['ni:oudʒi:n], *a. & s. Geol:* néogène (*m*).
neogenesis [ni:ou'dʒenəsis], *s. Biol:* néogenèse *f.*
neogenetic [ni:oudʒə'netik], *a.* néogénétique.
neo-gothic [ni:ou'gɔθik], *a. & s. arch:* Néo-gothique (*m*).
neography [ni:'ɔgrəfi], *s.* néographie *f.*
neo-Greek [ni:ou'gri:k], *a.* néo-grec, *f* -grecque.
neo-Hebraic [ni:ouhe'breiik], *a.* néo-hébraïque.
neo-Hebrew [ni:ou'hi:bru:], *s. Ling:* neo-hébreu *m.*
neo-Hegelian [ni:ouhe'geiliən], *a. Phil:* néo-hégélien, -ienne.
neo-Hegelianism [ni:ouhe'geiliənizm], *s. Phil:* néo-hégélianisme *m.*
neo-Hellenism [ni:ou'helinizm], *s.* néo-hellénisme *m.*
neo-impressionism [ni:ouim'preʃənizm], *s. Art:* néo-impressionnisme *m.*
neo-impressionist [ni:ouim'preʃənist], *a. & s.* néo-impressionniste (*mf*).
neo-Kantian [ni:ou'kæntiən], *a. & s. Phil:* néo-kantien, -ienne.
neo-Kantianism [ni:ou'kæntiənizm], *s.* néo-kantisme *m.*
neo-Lamarckian [ni:oulæ'mɑ:kiən], *a. & s. Biol:* néo-lamarckien, -ienne.
neo-Lamarckism [ni:ou'læmɑ:kizm], *s. Biol:* néo-lamarckisme *m.*
neo-Latin [ni:ou'lætin], *a.* néo-latin.
neo-liberalism [ni:ou'lib(ə)rəlizm], *s. Pol:* néo-libéralisme *m.*
neolith ['ni:ouliθ], *s. Prehist:* outil *m*, arme *f*, néolithique.
neolithic [ni:ou'liθik]. **1.** *a.* néolithique. **2.** *s.* **the N.,** l'âge *m* de la pierre polie, le néolithique.
neolocal [ni:ou'loukl], *a. Ethn:* néolocal, -aux.
neologian [ni:ou'loudʒiən], *s.* néologiste *m.*
neological [ni:ou'lɔdʒikl], *a.* néologique.
neologism [ni'ɔlədʒizm], *s.* néologisme *m.*
neologist [ni'ɔlədʒist], *s.* néologiste *m*, néologue *m.*
neology [ni'ɔlədʒi], *s.* **1.** néologisme *m.* **2.** néologie *f.*
neo-Malthusian [ni:oumæl'θu:ziən], *a. & s.* néo-malthusien, -ienne.
neo-Malthusianism [ni:oumæl'θu:ziənizm], *s.* néo-malthusianisme *m.*
neomenia [ni:ou'mi:niə], *s. Ant:* néoménie *f.*
neomycin [ni:ou'maisin], *s. Pharm:* néomycine *f.*
neon ['ni:ɔn], *s. Ch:* néon *El:* **n. lighting,** éclairage luminescent, au néon; **n. tube,** tube fluorescent, *F:* au néon; **n. sign,** enseigne au néon.
neonatal [ni:ou'neitl], *a. Med:* néo-natal.
neo-naturalism [ni:ou'nætjərəlizm], *s. Art:* néo-naturalisme *m.*
neophobia [ni:ou'foubiə], *s.* néophobie *f.*
neophron ['ni:oufrɔn], *s. Orn:* néophron *m.*
neophyte ['nioufait], *s.* (*a*) *Rel:* néophyte *mf*; (*b*) débutant, -ante, néophyte.
neoplasia [ni:ou'pleiziə], *s. Med:* néoplasie *f.*
neoplasm ['ni:ouplæzm], *s. Med:* néoplasme *m*; **infiltrating n.,** infiltration *f* néoplasique.
neoplastic [ni:ou'plæstik], *a.* **1.** (*a*) *Med:* néoplasique; (*b*) *Surg:* néoplastique. **2.** *Art:* relatif au néo-plasticisme.
neoplasticism [ni:ou'plæstisizm], *s. Art:* néo-plasticisme *m.*
neoplasticist [ni:ou'plæstisist], *s.* néo-plasticiste *mf.*
neoplasty ['ni:ouplæsti], *s. Surg:* néoplastie *f.*
Neoplatonic [ni:ouplə'tɔnik], *a. Phil:* néoplatoncien, -ienne.
Neoplatonism [ni:ou'pleitənizm], *s.* néoplatonisme *m.*
Neoplatonist [ni:ou'pleitənist], *s.* néoplatonicien, -ienne.
neo-positivism [ni:ou'pɔzitvizm], *s. Phil:* néo-positivisme *m.*
neo-positivist [ni:ou'pɔzitivist], *a. & s.* néo-positiviste (*mf*).
neo-positivistic [ni:oupɔziti'vistik], *a.* néo-positiviste.
Neoprene ['ni:oupri(:)n], *s. R.t.m:* néoprène *m.*
Neoptera [ni:'ɔptərə], *s.pl. Ent:* néoptères *m.*
Neoptolemus [niɔp'tɔliməs]. *Pr.n.m. Gr.Lit: Hist:* Néoptolème.
neo-Pythagorean [ni:oupaiθægə'ri:ən], *a. & s. Phil:* néo-pythagorien, -ienne.
neo-Pythagoreanism ['ni:oupaiθægə'ri:ənizm], *s.* néo-pythagorisme *m.*
neo-realism [ni:ou'ri:əlizm], *s.* néo-réalisme *m.*
neo-realist [ni:ou'ri:əlist], *a. & s.* néo-réaliste (*mf*).
neo-realistic [ni:ouri:ə'listik], *a.* néo-réaliste.
neo-romantic [ni:ourou'mæntik], *a. & s.* néo-romantique.
neo-romanticism [ni:ourou'mæntisizm], *s.* néo-romantisme *m.*
neo-scholastic [ni:ouskə'læstik], *a. & s.* néo-scolastique (*mf*).
neo-scholasticism [ni:ouskə'læstisizm], *s.* néo-scolastique *f.*
neostigmine [ni:ou'stigmain], *s. Pharm:* néostigmine *f.*
neostomy [ni:'ɔstəmi], *s. Surg:* néostomie *f.*
Neo-Syriac [ni:ou'siriæk], *s. Ling:* néo-syriaque *m.*
neotantalite [ni:ou'tæntəlait], *s. Miner:* néotantalite *f.*
neoteinia [ni:ou'ti:niə], *s. Biol:* néoténie *f.*
neote(i)nic [ni:ou'ti:nik], **neotenous** [ni:'ɔtənəs], *a. Biol:* néoténique.
neoteny [ni:'ɔtəni], *s. Biol:* néoténie *f.*
neoteric [ni:ou'terik], *a.* récent, moderne.
neo-Thomism [ni:ou'toumizm], *s. Rel:* néo-thomisme *m.*
neo-Thomist [ni:ou'toumist], *a. & s. Rel:* néo-thomiste (*mf*).
neo-Thomistic [ni:outou'mistik], *a.* néo-thomiste.
neotoma [ni:'ɔtəmə], *s. Z:* néotome *m.*
Neotraginae [ni:ou'trædʒini:], *s.pl. Z:* néotraginés *m.*
neotragus [ni:ɔtrəgəs], *s. Z:* néotrague *m.*
Neotremata [ni:ou'tri:mətə], *s.pl. Z:* néotremata *m.*
neottia [ni'ɔtiə], *s. Bot:* neottia *m*, néottie *f.*
neo-vitalism [ni:ou'vaitəlizm], *s.* néo-vitalisme *m.*
neo-vitalist [ni:ou'vaitəlist], *a. & s.* néo-vitaliste (*mf*).
neovolcanic [ni:ouvɔl'kænik], *a. Geol: A:* néovolcanique.
neoytterbium [ni:oui'tə:biəm], *s. Ch:* néoytterbium *m.*
Neozoic [ni:ou'zouik], *a. & s. Geol:* néozoïque (*m*).
nepa ['ni:pə], *s. Ent:* nèpe *f*; scorpion *m* d'eau.
Nepal [ne'pɔ:l]. *Pr.n. Geog:* Népal *m.*
Nepalese [nepə'li:z], **Nepali** [ne'pɔ:li]. **1.** *a.* népalais. **2.** *s.* Népalais, -aise.
nepenthe, nepenthes [ne'penθi:(z)], *s.* **1.** *Gr.Lit:* népenthès *m.* **2.** *Bot:* népenthès; plante *f* distillatoire.
neper ['ni:pər], *s. Ph:* néper *m.*
nepeta ['nepətə], *s. Bot:* népète *f.*
nephalism ['nefəlizm], *s.* néphalisme *m.*
nephalist ['nefəlist], *s.* néphaliste *mf.*
nepheline ['nefilain], *s. Miner:* néphéline *f.*
nephelinic [nefi'linik], *a.* néphélinique.
nephelinite [ne'felinait], *s. Geol:* néphélinite *f.*
nephelite ['nefilait], *s. Miner:* néphéline *f.*
nephelometer [nefi'lɔmitər], *s. Ph:* néphélomètre *m.*
nephelometry [nefi'lɔmitri], *s.* néphélométrie *f.*
nephelosphere ['nefilousfiər], *s. Astr:* zone *f* de nuages (autour d'une planète).
nephew ['nefju], *s.m.* neveu.
nephila ['nefilə], *s. Arach:* néphile *f.*
nephology [ne'fɔlədʒi], *s.* science *f* des nuages.
nephoscope ['nefəskoup], *s. Meteor:* néphoscope *m.*
nephralagia [ne'frældʒiə], *s. Med:* néphralgie *f.*
nephralgic [ne'frældʒik], *a. Med:* néphralgique.
nephrectomy [ne'frektəmi], *s. Surg:* néphrectomie *f*; **to perform a n. on s.o.,** néphrectomiser qn.
nephridium, *pl.* **-a** [ne'fridiəm, -ə], *s. Ent: Ann:* néphridie *f.*
nephrite ['nefrait], *s. Miner:* néphrite *f*; jade *m*; néphrétique *f.*
nephritic [ne'fritik], *a. Med:* néphrétique.
nephritis [ne'fraitis], *s. Med:* néphrite *f*; douleur rénale.
nephro- ['nefrou], *pref.* néphro-.
nephrocyte ['nefrousait], *s. Biol:* néphrocyte *m.*
nephrolepis [nefrou'lepis], *s. Bot:* néphrolépis *m.*
nephrolith ['nefrouliθ], *s. Med:* (*rare*) néphrolithe *m.*
nephrolithiasis [nefrouli'θaiəsis], *s. Med:* néphrolithiase *f.*
nephrolithic [nefrou'liθik], *a.* néphrolithique.
nephrolithotomy [nefrouliθ'ɔtəmi], *s. Surg:* néphrolithotomie *f.*
nephrologist [ne'frɔlədʒist], *s. Med:* néphrologue *m.*
nephrology [ne'frɔlədʒi], *s. Med:* néphrologie *f.*
nephrolysis [ne'frɔlisis], *s. Surg:* néphrolyse *f.*
nephron ['nefrɔn], *s. Anat:* néphron *m.*
nephropathy [ne'frɔpəθi], *s. Med:* néphropathie *f.*
nephropexy [nefrou'peksi], *s. Surg:* néphropexie *f.*
nephrops ['nefrɔps], *s. Crust:* néphrops *m.*
nephroptosis [nefrɔp'tousis], *s. Med:* néphroptose *f*; rein flottant, mobile.
nephrorrhagia [nefrou'reidʒiə], *s. Med:* néphrorragie *f.*
nephrorrhaphy [nefrou'ræfi], *s. Med:* néphrorraphie *f*
nephrosclerosis [nefrousklɛə'rousis], *s. Med:* néphrosclérose *f.*
nephrosis, *pl.* **-es** [ne'frousis, -i:z], *s. Med:* néphrose *f.*
nephrostomy [ne'frɔstəmi], *s. Surg:* néphrostomie *f*; **to perform a n. on s.o.,** néphrostomiser qn.
nephrotic [ne'frɔtik], *a. Med:* néphrotique.
nephrotome ['nefroutoum], *s. Anat:* néphrotome *m.*
nephrotomy [ne'frɔtəmi], *s. Surg:* néphrotomie *f.*
nephrotoxin [nefrou'tɔksin], *s.* néphrotoxine *f.*
nephro-ureterectomy [nefroujuri:tə'rektəmi], *s. Surg:* néphro-urétérectomie *f.*
Nepidae ['nepidi:], *s.pl. Ent:* népidés *m.*
nepotism ['nepətizm, 'ni:-], *s.* népotisme *m.*
nepouite [ne'pu:ait], *s. Miner:* népouite *f.*
nepticulid [nep'tikjulid], *a. & s. Ent:* nepticulide (*m*).
Nepticulidae [nepti'kju:lidi:], *s.pl. Ent:* nepticulides *m.*
Neptune ['neptju:n]. *Pr.n.m. Myth: Astr:* Neptune.
neptunian [nep'tju:niən], *a. & s. Geol:* neptunien (*m*).
neptunism ['neptjunizm], *s.* neptunisme *m.*
neptunist ['neptjunist], *s.* neptunien, -ienne.
neptunite ['neptjunait], *s. Miner:* neptunite *f.*
neptunium [nep'tju:niəm], *s. Ch:* neptunium *m.*
nereid ['neriəd], *s. Myth: Ann:* néréide *f.*
nereis, *pl.* **-ides** ['neriəs, ne'ri:idi:z], *s. Ann:* néréidien *m.*
Nereus ['neriəs]. *Pr.n.m. Myth:* Nérée.
nerine [ne'raini], *s. Bot:* nérine *f.*
nerita [ne'raitə], *s. Moll:* nérite *f.*
neritic [ne'ritik], *a. Oc:* (zone *f*, faune *f*) néritique.
Neritidae [ne'ritidi:], *s.pl. Moll:* néritidés *m.*
neritina [neri'tainə], *s. Moll:* néritine *f.*
nerium ['niəriəm], *s. Bot:* nerium *m.*
Nero ['niərou]. *Pr.n.m. Rom.Hist:* Néron.
neroli ['nerəli], *s.* néroli *m.*
Neronian [niə'rouniən], **Neronic** [niə'rɔnik], *a.* néronien.
nerval ['nə:v(ə)l], *a. Anat: etc:* nerval, -aux; neural, -aux.
nervate ['nə:veit], *a. Bot:* nervé.
nervation [nə'veiʃ(ə)n], *s. Bot: etc:* nervation *f.*
nerve [nə:v], *s.* **1.** (*a*) *Anat:* nerf *m*; **optic n.,** nerf optique; **abducens n.,** nerf moteur oculaire externe; **accessory n.,** nerf accessoire; **acoustic, auditory, n.,** nerf acoustique, auditif; **afferent n.,** nerf afférent; **cranial n.,** nerf crânien; **dental n.,** nerf dentaire; **facial n.,** nerf facial; **motor n.,** nerf moteur; **sensory n.,** nerf sensitif, sensoriel; **spinal n.,** nerf spinal; **n. cell,** cellule nerveuse, neurone *m*; **n. centre,** centre nerveux; **n. fibre,** fibre nerveuse; **n. knot,** ganglion nerveux; **n. impulse,** influx nerveux; *Mil: etc:* **n. gas,** gaz *m* neurotoxique; *Med:* **n. case, n. patient,** névropathe *mf*; **n. specialist,** neurologue *mf*; **to have cast-iron nerves,** avoir les nerfs à toute épreuve; *F:* **fit of nerves,** attaque *f*, crise *f*, de nerfs; **to be in a state of nerves,** être énervé; avoir ses nerfs; **(s)he's a bundle of, (s)he's all, nerves,** c'est un paquet de nerfs; **he doesn't know what nerves are,** rien ne le démonte; il reste toujours calme; **to get on s.o.'s nerves,** porter, donner, taper, sur les nerfs à qn; énerver, crisper, qn; **that child gets on my nerves,** cet enfant m'agace, m'horripile, me porte, me tape, sur les nerfs, **to live on one's nerves,** vivre sur les nerfs; **my nerves are on edge,** j'ai les nerfs à vif, en boule, en pelote; **it gets on my nerves to see him always there,** cela m'agace qu'il soit toujours là; (*b*) courage *m*, assurance *f*, fermeté *f*, sang-froid *m*; **to lose one's n.,** perdre son sang-froid, avoir le trac; **his n. failed (him), went, he lost his n.,** le courage lui a manqué, ses nerfs ont lâché; (*c*) *F:* audace *f*, aplomb *m*; **to have the n. to . . .,** avoir l'aplomb de . . .; *F:* **you *have* got a n.! *you've* got a n.!** tu en as un toupet! quel culot! tu n'as pas la trouille! **he's got a n. (doing that)!** il en a de (bien) bonnes (de faire cela)! **2.** *Bot: Ent: Arch:* nervure *f.* **3.** (*a*) *Lit:* tendon *m*, nerf; **to strain every n. to do sth.,** mettre toute sa force à faire qch.; faire des pieds et des mains pour faire qch.; se mettre en quatre pour faire qch.; **good communications are the very nerves of the country,** de bonnes voies de communication sont l'armature, les nerfs mêmes, du pays; (*b*) *A:* force *f* (musculaire); vigueur *f.*
nerve², *v.tr.* (*a*) fortifier; donner du nerf, de la force, à (son bras, etc.); encourager (qn); donner du courage à (qn); (*b*) **to n. oneself to do sth., to doing sth.,** s'armer

de courage, de sang-froid, pour faire qch.; rassembler, faire appel à, tout son courage pour faire qch.; **to n. oneself to make a speech,** s'enhardir à parler; **she cannot n. herself to going,** elle ne se sent pas le courage d'y aller.
nerved [nɔ:vd], *a. Bot:* nervé.
nerveless ['nɔ:vlis], *a.* **1.** (*of pers., limb, etc.*) inerte, faible, sans force; (style, etc.) sans vigueur, mou, languissant; **n. hand,** main (i) défaillante, (ii) inerte. **2.** (*a*) *Anat: Z:* sans nerfs; (*b*) *Bot:* (*of leaf*) sans nervures; énervé.
nervelessly ['nɔ:'vlisli], *adv.* d'une manière inerte, faible; mollement; sans force.
nervelessness ['n:vlisnis], *s.* inertie *f*; manque *m* de force, d'énergie.
nerveracking ['nɔ:vrækiŋ], *a.* énervant, horripilant; qui martyrise les nerfs.
Nervii ['nɔ:viai], *s.pl. Hist:* Nerviens *m.*
nervine ['nɔ:vi:n], *a. & s. Pharm:* nervin (*m*).
nerviness ['nɔ:vinis], *s. F:* nervosité *f*; énervement *m.*
nervose ['nɔ:rvous], *a.* **1.** *Anat: A:* nerveux; nerval, -aux; des nerfs. **2.** *Bot:* nervé; à nervures.
nervosism ['nɔ:vəsizm], *s. Med:* nervisme *m.*
nervosity [nɔ:'vɔsiti], *s.* nervosité *f.*
nervotabes [nɔ:vou'teibi:z], *s. Med:* nervo-tabès *m.*
nervous ['nɔ:vəs], *a.* **1.** (*of pers.*) (*a*) excitable; irritable; (*b*) inquiet, -ète; ému; intimidé; (*c*) timide, peureux, craintif; **to feel n.,** se sentir ému; (*of singer, etc.*) avoir le trac; **any sound of a shot made her feel n.,** la moindre détonation l'effrayait; elle s'effrayait de, à, la moindre détonation; **to feel n. in s.o.'s presence,** se sentir intimidé en présence de qn; **to get n.,** s'intimider; **n. state of mind,** état *m* d'agitation; émoi *m*; nervosité *f*; **I was n. on his account,** j'avais peur pour lui; **to be n. of (doing) sth.,** avoir peur de (faire) qch.; **it makes me n.,** cela m'intimide; **to be n. that sth. might happen,** craindre, avoir peur, que qch. se fasse. **2.** *A: & Lit:* (style, etc.) nerveux, énergique. **3.** (*a*) *Anat:* nerveux; des nerfs; **n. system,** système nerveux; **central n. system,** névraxe *m*; (*b*) *Med:* **n. diathesis,** nervosisme *m*; **n. involvement,** complication nerveuse; **n. complaint,** maladie *f* de nerfs.
nervously ['nɔ:vəsli], *adv.* **1.** (*a*) timidement; d'un air ou d'un ton ému ou intimidé; (*b*) craintivement. **2.** *A: & Lit:* avec vigueur; énergiquement.
nervousness ['nɔ:vəsnis], *s.* **1.** (*a*) nervosité *f*, état nerveux, état d'agitation; (*b*) timidité *f*; *F:* trac *m.* **2.** *A: & Lit:* vigueur *f*, force *f*, puissance *f.*
nervure ['nɔ:vjər], *s. Bot: Ent:* nervure *f.*
nervy ['nɔ:vi], *a.* **1.** *F:* (*a*) énervé, irritable; à cran; **to feel n., to be in a n. state,** être dans un état d'agacement, d'énervement; avoir les nerfs agacés; avoir les nerfs en pelote; être à cran; **she's n.,** elle est très nerveuse; c'est un paquet de nerfs; **to soothe s.o. when he is n.,** calmer les nervosités de qn; (*b*) **n. movement,** mouvement nerveux, sec, saccadé. **2.** *A: & Poet:* vigoureux, fort, puissant.
nescience ['nesiəns], *s.* nescience *f*; ignorance *f* (**of,** de).
nescient ['nesiənt]. **1.** *a.* nescient; ignorant (**of,** de). **2.** *a. & s.* agnostique (*mf*).
nesodon ['nesoudɔn], *s. Paleont:* nesodon *m.*
nesokia [ne'soukiə], *s. Z:* nésocie *m*, nesokia *m*, (rat) perchal *m.*
Nesomyinae [nesou'maiini:], *s.pl. Z:* nésomyinés *m.*
Nesotragus [ne'sɔtrəgəs], *s. Z:* nésotrague *m.*
nesquehonite [neskwi'hounait], *s. Miner:* nesquehonite *f.*
ness [nes], *s.* promontoire *m*, cap *m.*
nest[1] [nest], *s.* **1.** (*a*) nid *m* (d'oiseaux, de guêpes, de souris, etc.); **the bird is building its n.,** l'oiseau fait, façonne, son nid; **n. box,** pondoir *m*; **squirrel's n.,** bauge *f*; **caterpillar's n.,** chenillère *f*; *F:* **love n.,** nid d'amoureux; **n. egg,** (i) *Husb:* nichet *m*; œuf *m* en faïence; (ii) *F:* argent mis de côté, pécule *m*, boursicot *m*; **a nice little n. egg,** un bas de laine bien garni (d'écus); un bon petit magot; une gentille petite somme en banque; (*b*) repaire *m*, nid (de brigands, etc.). **2.** nichée *f* (d'oiseaux, etc.). **3.** série *f*, jeu *m* (d'objets); **n. of boxes,** jeu de boîtes; **n. of tables,** table *f* gigogne; **n. of drawers,** (i) chiffonnier *m*; (ii) classeur *m* (à tiroirs); *Mch: etc:* **n. of boiler tubes,** faisceau *m* tubulaire; **n. of springs,** faisceau de ressorts; **n. of gear-wheels,** équipage *m* d'engrenage; *Mil:* **machine-gun n.,** nid de mitrailleuses; *Rail:* **n. of short tracks** (*leading from main line*), épi *m* de voies.
nest[2]. **1.** *v.i.* (*of birds, etc.*) se nicher; nicher; faire son nid. **2.** *v.tr.* emboîter (des tubes, etc.) les uns dans les autres; (*with passive force*) **boxes that nest in each other,** boîtes qui s'emboîtent l'une dans l'autre; **nested boxes,** caisses emboîtées; *Geol:* **nested cone,** cône emboîté.
nestful ['nestful], *s.* nichée *f.*
nesticus ['nestikəs], *s. Arach:* nesticus *m.*
nesting[1] ['nestiŋ], *a.* (oiseau) nicheur.
nesting[2], *s.* **1. n. time,** époque *f* des nids; **n. box,** pondoir *m.* **2.** (*a*) emboîtage *m*; (*b*) emboîture *f*, emboîtement *m.*
nestle [nesl], *v.i. & tr.* **1.** *occ.* = NEST[2] 1. **2.** se nicher, se pelotonner; **to n. (down) in an armchair,** se blottir, se pelotonner, dans un fauteuil; **to n. close (up) to s.o.,** se serrer contre qn; **to n. (one's face) against s.o.'s shoulder,** se blottir sur l'épaule de qn; **village nestling in a valley, in a wood, among the trees,** village blotti, tapi, dans une vallée; village niché dans un bois, parmi les arbres.
nestling ['nestliŋ], *s.* oisillon *m*; petit oiseau (encore au nid).
Nestor ['nestɔ:r]. *Pr.n.m. Gr.Lit: & F:* Nestor.
Nestorian [nes'tɔriən], *a. & s. Rel.H:* Nestorien, -ienne.
Nestorianism [nes'tɔ:riənizm], *s. Rel.H:* Nestorianisme *m.*
Nestorius [nes'tɔ:riəs]. *Pr.n.m. Rel.H:* Nestorius.
net[1] [net], *s.* **1.** filet *m*; (*a*) **fishing n.,** filet de pêche; **butterfly n.,** filet à papillons; *Fish:* **bag n., poke n.,** bâche volante, traînante; **cast(ing) n.,** épervier *m*; **crayfish n.,** balance *f* à écrevisses; **gill n., entangling n., tangle n.,** filet maillant, manet *m*; **hand n.,** salabre *m*; **prawn n.,** treille *f*; **set n.,** filet fixe, dormant; **shrimp(ing) n.,** filet à crevettes, crevettière *f*, haveneau *m*, treille; **square n.,** carrelet *m*; **tunny n.,** combrière *f*; **to cast, lay, spread, a n.,** jeter, tendre, un filet; **to haul in a n.,** relever un filet; (*b*) *Ven:* **(game) n.,** pan *m*, panneau *m*; filet; **to make a n.,** lacer un filet; **to spread a n.,** tendre un filet; **to be caught in the n.,** être pris au filet, au piège; (*c*) **hair n.,** filet, résille *f* (pour cheveux); (*for horse*) **fly n.,** émouchette *f*, émouchette *f*; **n. bag,** *U.S:* **marketing n.,** filet à provisions; *Nau:* **cargo n., loading n.,** filet de chargement, d'élingue; (*d*) *Ten: etc:* filet; **to go, come, up to the n.,** monter au filet; **n. play,** jeu *m* au filet; (*e*) *Ind:* **guard n.,** filet de protection; *Mil:* **(camouflage) n.,** filet (de camouflage); **gun n.,** filet de pièce d'artillerie, de mitrailleuse; **garnished n.,** filet garni (de plumetis, etc.); **pre-garnished n.,** filet fourni garni; **ungarnished, empty, n.,** filet nu; *Navy:* **submarine n.,** filet anti-sous-marins; **scramble n.,** filet de débarquement; **n. laying,** mouillage *m*, pose *f*, de filets; **n.-laying ship, n. layer,** (bâtiment *m*) mouilleur *m* de filets; (*f*) (*at circus, etc.*) **safety n.,** filet; (*g*) *Aer:* filet (de ballon). **2.** *Tex:* tulle *m*; **Brussels n.,** tulle bruxelles; **spotted n.,** tulle à pois; tulle point d'esprit; **figured n.,** tulle façonné, brodé; **foundation n.,** mousseline forte; **n. curtain,** rideau *m* de tulle. **3.** = NETWORK.
net[2], *v.* **(netted) 1.** *v.tr.* (*a*) prendre (des poissons, des lièvres, etc.) au filet; (*b*) pêcher dans (une rivière, etc.) au moyen de filets; tendre des filets dans (une rivière); (*c*) *Sp:* envoyer (le ballon, la balle) dans le filet; (*d*) *Mil:* camoufler (un emplacement, etc.) avec un filet; recouvrir d'un filet de camouflage; (*e*) *Hort:* protéger (des petits pois, etc.) avec un filet; (*f*) faire (un hamac, etc.) au filet. **2.** *v.i.* faire du filet.
net[3]. **1.** *a.* (*of weight, price, etc.*) net, *f.* nette; **n. yield,** revenu, rendement, net; **n. proceeds of a sale,** (produit) net *m* d'une vente; **terms strictly n.,** sans déduction; payable au comptant. **2.** *s.* prix, poids, bénéfice, etc., net.
net[4], *v.tr.* **(netted) 1.** (*of pers.*) toucher net, gagner net (tant de bénéfices, etc.); **I netted (a full profit of) £2000,** cela m'a donné, rapporté, un bénéfice net de £2000. **2.** (*of enterprise, etc.*) rapporter net, produire net (une certaine somme).
netball ['netbɔ:l], *s. Sp:* netball *m.*
netful ['netful], *s.* (plein) filet (**of,** de).
nether ['neðər], *a.* inférieur, bas; **the n. lip,** la lèvre inférieure; *Hum:* **n. garments,** pantalon *m*; **the n. regions, the n. world,** l'enfer *m*; les régions infernales.
Netherlander ['neðəlændər], *s.* Néerlandais, -aise; Hollandais, -aise.
Netherlandish ['neðəlændiʃ]. **1.** *a.* néerlandais, hollandais. **2.** *s. Ling:* le hollandais.
Netherlands (the) [ðə'neðələndz]. *Pr.n.pl. Geog:* les Pays-Bas *m*; la Hollande; **in the N.,** dans les, aux, Pays-Bas.
nethermost ['neðəmoust], *a.* le plus bas; le plus profond.
netlike ['netlaik], *a.* rétiforme.
netsuke ['netsu:kei], *s. Cost:* netsuké *m.*
nett [net], *a.* = NET[3].
nettapus ['netəpus], *s. Orn:* nettapus *m.*
netted ['netid], *a.* **1.** couvert d'un filet, d'un réseau. **2.** (*a*) *Tex:* (tissu *m*) en filet; (*b*) (*of veins, paths, etc.*) en lacis, en réseau; (*c*) *Nat.Hist: etc:* réticulé.
netter ['netər], *s.* filetier *m*; fabricant, -ante, de filets; laceur, -euse.
netting ['netiŋ], *s.* **1.** fabrication *f* du filet; **n. needle,** navette *f*; **n. pin,** moule *m* (pour filets). **2.** (*a*) pêche *f*, capture *f*, du gibier, au(x) filet(s); filetage *m*; (*b*) pose *f* de filets. **3.** (*a*) filet(s) (de protection); *Nau:* filet (de pavois, de hune, etc.); **nettings,** bastingages *mpl*; **camouflage n.,** filet(s) de camouflage; (*b*) grillage *m*, treillage *m*, treillis *m*; **wire n.,** treillis métallique, grillage en fil de fer; (*c*) *Tex:* tulle *m.*
nettle[1] ['netl], *s. Bot:* (*a*) ortie *f*; **stinging n.,** ortie brûlante; **annual n., great n.,** ortie dioïque; grande ortie; **perennial n., small n.,** ortie grièche; petite ortie; **dead n.,** ortie blanche; lamier (blanc); **red dead n.,** ortie rouge, lamier pourpre; **n. sting,** piqûre *f* de l'ortie; urtication *f*; *Med:* **n. rash,** urticaire *f*; fièvre ortiée; cnidose *f*; (*b*) **n. tree,** micocoulier *m*, perpignan *m.*
nettle[2]. *v.tr.* **1.** (*a*) ortier; fustiger (qn) avec des orties; (*b*) **to n. oneself,** se piquer à des orties. **2.** *F:* (*a*) piquer, irriter (qn); faire monter la moutarde au nez de (qn); (*b*) piquer (qn) d'honneur; stimuler (qn).
nettled ['netld], *a. F:* piqué, irrité, vexé.
net-veined ['netveind], *a. Bot:* rétinerve, rétinervé.
network[1] ['netwɔ:k], *s.* **1.** (*a*) travail *m* au filet; (*b*) ouvrage *m* en filet; (*c*) **wire n.,** treillis *m* (métallique); lacis *m* de fils de fer. **2.** réseau *m*; (*a*) réseau, lacis (de canaux, de rues, de tranchées, de voies ferrées, de nerfs, de veines dans le corps humain ou la roche, etc.); enchevêtrement *m* (de ronces, etc.); **road n., highway n.,** réseau routier; (*b*) *El:* **balancing n.,** réseau d'équilibrage; **distribution n.,** réseau de distribution électrique; **electric n.,** réseau électrique; **high-tension n.,** réseau haute tension; **lattice n.,** réseau maillé; **lighting n.,** réseau d'éclairage; **phase-shift n.,** réseau déphaseur; **primary, secondary, n.,** réseau primaire, secondaire; **quarter-phase, two-phase, n.,** réseau diphasé; **three-phase n.,** réseau triphasé; **tree n.,** réseau non maillé; **two-terminal, four-terminal, n.,** réseau dipôle, quadripôle; *Tp:* **local n.,** réseau urbain; *El: Tp:* **overhead n.,** réseau aérien; **underground n.,** réseau souterrain; **n. constants, n. parameters,** constantes *f* de réseau; **n. diagram,** plan *m* de, du, réseau; **n. protector,** protecteur *m* de réseau; poste *m*, station *f*, de disjonction; **n. relay,** disjoncteur *m* de réseau; (*c*) *T.V: W.Tel:* chaîne *f* (de télévision, de radiodiffusion); *U.S:* **n. show,** programme *m* de chaîne; (*d*) *W.Tel:* **aerial n.,** réseau d'antennes; (*e*) *Av: etc:* **ground n.,** infrastructure *f* (d'aides à la navigation, etc.); **meteorological n., n. of meteorological stations,** réseau de stations météo(rologiques); (*f*) *Cmptr:* réseau, graphe *m*; **analog(ue) n.,** réseau analogique; **switched n.,** réseau commuté; **n. analog(ue) (device),** réseau d'étude analogique; **n. analyser, n. calculator,** analyseur *m* de réseau, simulateur *m* d'étude de réseau. **3.** réseau (d'alliances, d'espionnage, etc.); **spy n.,** réseau d'espionnage; **resistance n.,** réseau de résistance; *F:* **the old-boy n.** = la franc-maçonnerie des grandes écoles.
network[2], *v.tr. T.V: U.S:* transmettre (un programme).
neum(e) [nju:m], *s. A.Mus:* neume *m.*
neumatic [nju:'mætik], *a. A.Mus:* neumatique.
neuragmia [nju:'rægmiə], *s. Physiol:* névragmie *f.*
neural ['nju:r(ə)l], *a.* **1.** *Anat:* (*of cavity, etc.*) neural, -aux. **2.** (*of remedy*) nerval, -aux.
neuralgia [nju:'rældʒiə], *s. Med:* névralgie *f.*
neuralgic [nju:'rældʒik], *a. Med:* névralgique.
neurapophysis [nju:rəpou'faisis], *s. Anat:* neurapophyse *f.*
neurasthenia [nju:rəs'θi:niə], *s. Med:* neurasthénie *f.*
neurasthenic [nju:rəs'θi:nik], *a. & s. Med:* neurasthénique (*mf*).
neuration [nju:'reiʃ(ə)n], *s.* nervation *f.*
neuraxis [nju:'ræksis], *s. Anat: A:* névraxe *m.*
neuraxitis [nju:ræk'saitis], *s. Med:* névraxite *f.*
neurectomy [nju:'rektəmi], *s. Surg:* névrectomie *f.*
neurilemma [nju:ri'lemə], *s. Anat:* névrilème *m.*
neurilemmal [nju:ri'leməl], **neurilemmatic** [nju:rile'mætik], **neurilemmatous** [nju:ri'lemətəs], *a.* névrilématique.
neurine ['nju:rain], *s.* **1.** *Anat:* tissu nerveux. **2.** *Ch:* névrine *f*, neurine *f.*
neurinoma [nju:ri'noumə], *s. Med:* neurinome *m.*
neuritic [nju:'ritik], *a. Med:* névritique.
neuritis [nju:'raitis], *s. Med:* névrite *f.*
neuro- ['nju:rou], *pref.* neuro-, névro-.
neuroanatomy [nju:rouə'nætəmi], *s.* neuroanatomie *f.*
neuroarthritism [nju:rou'ɑ:θritizm], *s. Med:* neuro-arthritisme *m.*
neuroblast ['nju:roublæst], *s. Anat:* neuroblaste *m.*
neuroblastoma [nju:roublæs'toumə], *s. Med:* neuroblastome *m.*
neurocirculatory ['nju:rousə:kju'leitəri], *a. Anat: Med:* neurocirculatoire.
neurocrinism [nju:'rɔkrinizm], *s. Med:* neurocrinisme *m.*

neurocriny [nju:'rɔkrini], *s. Physiol:* neurocrinie *f.*
neurodermatitis ['nju:roudə:mə'taitis], *s. Med:* névrodermite *f*, neurodermatose *f.*
neuro-epithelium ['nju:rouepi'θi:liəm], *s. Anat:* neuro-épithélium *m.*
neurofibril [nju:rou'faibril], *s. Anat:* neurofibrille *f.*
neurofibroma [nju:roufai'broumə], *s. Med:* neurofibrome *m.*
neurofibromatosis ['nju:roufaibroumə'tousis], *s. Med:* neurofibromatose *f.*
neurogenesis [nju:rou'dʒenəsis], *s. Biol:* neurogénèse *f*, névrogénèse *f.*
neurogenic [nju:rou'dʒenik], *a. Med:* neurogène, névrogène.
neuroglia [nju:'rɔgliə], *s. Anat:* névroglie *f.*
neurogliac [nju:'rɔgliæk], **neuroglial** [nju:'rɔgliəl], **neurogliar** [nju:'rɔgliər], *a. Med:* névroglique.
neuroglioma [nju:rouglai'oumə], *s. Med:* neurogliome *m.*
neurogliosis [nju:rouglai'ousis], *s. Med:* neurogliomatose *f.*
neurogram ['nju:rougræm], *s. Med:* neurogramme *m.*
neurographic [nju:rou'græfik], *a. Med:* neurographique.
neurography [nju:'rɔgrəfi], *s.* neurographie *f.*
neurokeratin [nju:rou'kerətin], *s. Bio-Ch:* névrokératine *f*, neurokératine *f.*
neuroleptic [nju:rou'leptik], *s. Med:* neuroleptique *m.*
neurological [nju:rə'lɔdʒik(ə)l], *a.* névrologique, neurologique.
neurologist [nju:'rɔlədʒist], *s.* neurologue *mf*, neurologiste *mf.*
neurology [nju:'rɔlədʒi], *s.* névrologie *f*, neurologie *f.*
neurolymphomatosis ['nju:roulimfoumə'tousis], *s. Vet:* neurolymphomatose *f.*
neurolysis [nju:'rɔlisis], *s. Med:* neurolyse *f.*
neurolytic [nju:rou'litik], *a.* neurolytique.
neuroma, *pl.* **-mata** [nju:'roumə, -mətə], *s. Med:* névrome *m*, neurome *m.*
neuromuscular [nju:rou'mʌskjulər], *a.* neuro-musculaire.
neuromyelitis [nju:roumaii'laitis], *s. Med:* **n. optica,** neuromyélite *f* optique.
neuron ['nju:rɔn], *s. Physiol:* neurone *m.*
neuronal [nju:'rounəl], *a.* neuronal, -aux.
neuronic [nju:'rɔnik], *a.* neuronique.
neuropath ['nju:roupæθ], *s. Med:* névropathe *mf.*
neuropathic [nju:rou'pæθik], *a.* névropathique.
neuropathology [nju:roupə'θɔlədʒi], *s.* névropathologie *f*, neuropathologie *f.*
neuropathy [nju:'rɔpəθi], *s.* névropathie *f.*
neurophile ['nju:roufail], **neurophilic** [nju:'rɔfilik], *a. Med:* neurophile.
neurophysiology [nju:roufizi'ɔlədʒi], *s.* neurophysiologie *f.*
neuroplegic [nju:rou'pli:dʒik], *a. Med:* neuroplégique; **n. substance,** neuroplégique *m.*
neuropsychiatric [nju:rousə'kaiætrik], *a.* neuropsychiatrique.
neuropsychiatrist [nju:rousə'kaiətrist], *s.* neuro-psychiatre *mf.*
neuropsychiatry [nju:rousə'kaiətri], *s.* neuro-psychiatrie *f.*
neuropsychic [nju:rou'saikik], *a.* neuropsychique.
neuropsychological [nju:rousaikə'lɔdʒikl], *a.* neuropsychologique.
neuropsychologist [nju:rousai'kɔlədʒist], *s.* neuro-psychologue *mf.*
neuropsychology [nju:rousai'kɔledʒi], *s.* neuro-psychologie *f.*
Neuroptera [nju:'rɔptərə], *s.pl. Ent:* névroptères *m.*
neuropteran [nju:'rɔptərən], *a. & s. Ent:* névroptère (*m*).
Neuropterideae [nju:rɔptə'ridii:], *s.pl. Paleont:* neuroptéridés *m*, névroptéridés *m.*
neuropteris [nju:'rɔptəris], *s. Paleont:* neuroptéris *m*, névroptéris *m.*
Neuropteroidea [nju:rɔptə'rɔidiə], *s.pl.* névroptéroïdes *m.*
neuropterous [nju:'rɔptərəs], *a.* névroptère.
neuroretinitis [nju:roureti'naitis], *s. Med:* neurorétinite *f.*
neurorrhaphy [nju:rou'ræfi], *s. Med:* neurorrhaphie *f.*
neurosecretion [nju:rousi'kri:ʃ(ə)n], *s.* neurosécrétion *f.*
neurosis [nju:'rousis], *s. Med:* névrose *f.*
neurosome ['nju:rousoum], *s. Anat:* neurosome *m.*
neurosurgeon [nju:rou'sə:dʒən], *s.* neurochirurgien, -ienne.
neurosurgery [nju:rou'sə:dʒəri], *s.* neurochirurgie *f.*
neurotic [nju:'rɔtik]. **1.** *a. Med:* (*a*) (*of pers.*) névrosé; *F:* **he's positively n. about it,** c'est une obsession chez lui; (*b*) (*of drug*) névrotique; nerval, -aux; (*c*) (*relating to a neurosis*) névrosique. **2.** *s.* névrosé, -ée.
neuroticism [nju:'rɔtisizm], *s.* caractère névrosé.
neurotization [nju:rɔtai'zeiʃ(ə)n], *s. Physiol:* neurotisation *f.*
neurotomy [nju:'rɔtəmi], *s.* névrotomie *f.*
neurotoxic [nju:'rou'tɔksik], *a.* neurotoxique.
neurotoxin [nju:rou'tɔksin], *s.* neurotoxine *f.*
neurotropic [nju:rou'trɔpik], *a. Med:* neurotrop(iqu)e.
neurotropism [nju:rou'trɔpizm], **neurotropy** [nju:'rɔtrəpi], *s. Med:* neurotropisme *m.*
neurovegetative [nju:rou'vedʒitətiv], *a. Med:* neurovégétatif.
neurovisceral [njurou'visərəl], *a.* neuroviscéral, -aux.
neurula ['nju:rələ], *s. Biol:* neurula *f.*
neuston ['nju:stɔn], *s. Biol:* neuston *m.*
Neustria ['nju:striə]. *Pr.n. A.Geog:* Neustrie *f.*
Neustrian ['nju:striən]. *A.Geog:* **1.** *a.* neustrien. **2.** *s.* Neustrien, -ienne.
neuter[1] ['nju:tər]. **1.** *a.* (*a*) *Gram:* (genre *m*, verbe *m*, etc.) neutre; **this word is n.,** ce mot est du neutre; (*b*) *Biol:* neutre, asexué; **n. bee,** abeille *f* neutre; **n. flower,** fleur neutre, asexuée; (*c*) = NEUTRAL 1 (*a*). **to stand n.,** garder la neutralité. **2.** *s.* (*a*) *Gram:* (genre) neutre *m*; **in the n.,** au neutre; (*b*) abeille, fourmi, asexuée, ouvrière; (*c*) animal châtré.
neuter[2], *v.tr. Vet:* châtrer (un chat, etc.).
neutral ['nju:tr(ə)l]. **1.** *a.* (*a*) *Pol: etc:* neutre; **n. country, n. power,** pays *m*, puissance *f*, neutre; **to remain n.,** rester neutre, garder la neutralité; (*b*) neutre, indéterminé, intermédiaire, moyen; *Ch:* (sel, etc.) neutre; *Ph:* **n. equilibrium,** équilibre indifférent; *Opt:* **n. filter,** filtre *m* neutre; **n. oil,** huile *f* neutre; *Ch:* **n. state,** neutralité *f* (d'une substance); *Art: Dy:* **n. tint,** teinte *f* neutre; (*c*) *El:* (câble, etc.) neutre, non chargé; **n. conductor, n. wire,** conducteur *m*, fil *m*, neutre; **n. grid,** neutre *m* (d'un réseau); **n. line,** (i) *El:* fil neutre; (ii) *Magn:* ligne *f* neutre (d'un barreau aimanté); **n. terminal,** borne *f* neutre (d'un appareil électrique polyphasé); (*d*) *Atom.Ph:* **n. molecule, n. particle,** molécule *f*, particule *f*, neutre. **2.** *s.* (*a*) (État *m*, pays) neutre *m*; **rights of neutrals,** droits *m* des neutres; (*b*) ressortissant, -ante, d'un État neutre; (*c*) *El:* **grounded n.,** neutre *m* à la terre; **insulated n.,** neutre isolé; **n. earthing,** mise *f* à la terre du neutre; (*d*) *Mec.E:* **in n.,** au point mort.
neutralism ['nju:trəlizm], *s.* neutralisme *m.*
neutralist ['nju:trəlist], *s.* neutraliste *mf.*
neutrality [nju(:)'træliti], *s.* (*a*) *Pol: etc:* neutralité *f*; **armed n.,** neutralité armée; **breach of n.,** violation *f* de la neutralité; (*b*) *Ch:* neutralité, indifférence *f* (d'un sel).
neutralization [nju:trəlai'zeiʃ(ə)n], *s.* neutralisation *f.*
neutralize ['nju:trəlaiz], *v.tr.* neutraliser; **to n. one another,** (i) (*of chemical agents*) se neutraliser; (ii) (*of forces*) se détruire, s'annuler.
neutralizer ['nju:trəlaizər], *s.* neutralisant *m.*
neutralizing ['nju:trəlaiziŋ]. **1.** *a.* (*a*) *Ch: Ph: etc:* neutralisant, de neutralisation; *Ch:* **a n. agent,** un neutralisant; (*b*) *El:* isolant, de neutralisation, de neutrodynage; **n. condenser,** condensateur *m* de neutralisation, condensateur neutrodyne; **n. tool,** outil isolant; (*c*) *Mil:* **n. fire,** tir *m* de neutralisation. **2.** *s.* neutralisation *f.*
neutrally ['nju:trəli], *adv.* neutralement.
neutretto [nju:'tretou], *s. Atom.Ph:* méson *m* neutre; neutretto *m.*
neutrino [nju:tri:nou], *s. Atom.Ph:* neutrino *m*; **pertaining to the n.,** neutrinien, -ienne; neutrinique.
neutrodyne[1] ['nju:troudain], *a. & s. W.Tel:* neutrodyne (*m*); **n. receiver,** récepteur *m* neutrodyne.
neutrodyne[2], *v.tr. W.Tel:* neutrodyner.
neutrodyning ['njutroudainiŋ], *s. W.Tel:* neutrodynation *f.*
neutron ['nju:trɔn], *s. Atom.Ph: El:* neutron *m*; **cold n.,** neutron froid; **delayed n.,** neutron différé, retardé; **delayed-n. fraction,** fraction *f*, taux *m*, de neutrons différés; **fast, slow, n.,** neutron rapide, lent; **fission n.,** neutron de fission; **high-energy n.,** neutron de grande énergie; **low-energy n.,** neutron à basse, de faible, énergie; **prompt n.,** neutron immédiat, instantané, prompt; **prompt-n., fraction,** fraction, taux, de neutrons prompts; **stray n.,** neutron erratique, vagabond; **thermal n.,** neutron thermique; **virgin, non-virgin, n.,** neutron vierge, non vierge; **relating to neutrons,** neutronique; **the study of neutrons,** la neutronique; **n. beam,** faisceau *m*, pinceau *m*, de neutrons; **n. beam, photograph,** neutrographie *f*; **n. density,** densité *f*, nombre *m* volumique, des neutrons; **n. distribution,** distribution *f* neutronique, répartition *f* des neutrons; **n. escape, n. leakage,** fuite *f* de(s) neutrons; **n. monitoring,** contrôle *m* neutronique; **n. physics,** physique *f* neutronique; **n. radiation,** rayonnement *m* neutronique; **n. scattering,** diffusion *f* des neutrons; **n. thermopile,** thermopile *f* à neutrons.
neutropenia [nju:trou'pi:niə], *s. Med:* neutropénie *f.*
neutrophil(e) ['nju:trouf(a)il], **neutrophilic** [nju:'trɔfilik], *a. Med:* neutrophile.
neutrophilia [nju:trou'filiə], *s. Med:* neutrophilie *f.*
névé ['neve], *s. Geol:* névé *m.*
never ['nevər], *adv.* (*a*) (ne . . .) jamais; **I n. go there,** je n'y vais jamais; **I n. drink anything but water,** je ne bois jamais que de l'eau; **there is n. any mustard in the pot,** il n'y a jamais de moutarde dans le moutardier; **n. again, n. more,** jamais plus; plus jamais (. . . ne); **he was n. heard of again,** on n'a jamais plus eu de ses nouvelles; on n'a jamais plus entendu parler de lui; **he n. came back,** il n'est jamais revenu; **the thing had n. before been seen,** jusqu'alors la chose ne s'était jamais vue; **it had n. been heard of before,** on n'en avait encore jamais entendu parler; **I have n. yet seen . . .,** jusqu'ici je n'ai jamais vu . . .; je n'ai encore jamais vu . . .; **I have n. found a fault in him yet,** j'en suis encore à lui trouver un défaut; **n. was a woman more unhappy,** jamais femme ne fut plus malheureuse; **I shall n. forget it, n.!** jamais, au grand jamais, je ne l'oublierai; **n. in (all) my life, n. in all my born days,** jamais de la vie; **I n. heard such a speech!** de la vie je n'ai entendu pareil discours! *A: F:* **tomorrow come n.,** à la Saint-Glinglin; **that n. to be forgotten day,** ce jour inoubliable; **the N. N. Land,** (i) le nord du Queensland; (ii) *F:* le pays de cocagne; (*b*) (*emphatic neg.*) **I n. expected him to come,** je ne m'attendais aucunement à ce qu'il vînt; **it n. seemed to have occurred to him,** ça n'avait pas l'air de lui être (jamais) venu à l'esprit; **he n. said a word to him about it,** il ne lui en a pas dit le moindre mot; **he n. paused in his speech,** pas un instant il ne s'est arrêté de parler; *O:* **n. a one,** pas un seul; *Lit:* **he answered n. a word,** il ne répondit pas un (seul) mot; **you (surely) n. left him all alone!** ne me dites pas que vous l'avez laissé tout seul! **you have n. forgotten to post that letter, have you?** ne me dites pas que vous avez oublié de mettre cette lettre à la poste! **he has eaten it all—n.!** il a tout mangé—pas possible! jamais de la vie! **well I n. (did)!** par exemple! c'est formidable! *P:* **no, I n.!** non, c'était pas moi! (*c*) *A: Lit:* **be he n. so brave,** quelque courageux qu'il soit; si courageux soit-il; **tread he n. so lightly,** si léger que soit son pas.
never-ending ['nevər'endiŋ], *a.* perpétuel, éternel; sans fin; incessant; qui n'en finit plus; **it's a n.-e. job,** c'est une tâche interminable; c'est le rocher de Sisyphe; c'est la toile de Pénélope.
nevermore [nevə'mɔ:ər], *adv.* (ne . . .) plus jamais, (ne . . .) jamais plus; **n. shall we hear his voice,** plus jamais nous n'entendrons sa voix; **n.!** jamais plus! plus jamais!
never-never ['nevə'nevər], *s. F:* **to buy sth. on the n.-n.,** acheter qch. à crédit, à tempérament.
nevertheless [nevəðə'les], *adv.* néanmoins, quand même, tout de même, cependant, toutefois, pourtant; **I shall do it n.,** je le ferai quand même; **I dislike it, n. I am eating it,** je ne l'aime pas, néanmoins je le mange; **it n. makes me anxious,** cela ne laisse pas (que) de m'inquiéter; cela n'empêche pas que je sois inquiet; toujours est-il que cela m'inquiète.
new [nju:], *a. & adv.*
I. *a.* **1.** (*a*) nouveau, -elle; **n. fashion, newest fashion,** nouvelle mode; mode nouvelle; **n. theory,** nouvelle théorie; théorie nouvelle; **ever n. topic,** sujet toujours nouveau; **Mr X's n. novel,** le nouveau roman de M. X; **I am reading a new novel,** je lis un roman nouveau: **what's n.?** qu'est-ce qu'il y a de neuf? **here's something n,** (i) voici quelque chose de nouveau; (ii) *F:* voici du nouveau! en voici bien d'une autre! **to find something n.,** trouver du neuf, du nouveau; **it was something n. for a woman to be called to the bar,** il était nouveau qu'une femme se fît avocat; *F:* **that's nothing n.! tell us something n.!** rien de nouveau à cela! **n. ideas,** idées nouvelles, idées neuves; **n. country,** pays neuf; **n. ground,** terre *f* vierge; **a district quite n. to me,** une région qui est toute nouvelle pour moi, qui m'est toute nouvelle; **to add three n. rooms to one's house,** ajouter trois nouvelles chambres à sa maison; **this beauty preparation will give you a completely n. skin,** ce produit de beauté vous rénovera la peau; **it has made a n. man of him,** cela a fait de lui un autre homme; **to become a n. man,** faire peau neuve; **he wears a new suit every day,** il porte tous les jours un nouveau complet; **I need a n. battery for my transistor,** j'ai besoin d'une pile pour mon transistor; **n. batteries cost 20p.,** les piles de rechange coûtent vingt pence; *Mil:* **the n. guard,** la garde montante; *Sch:* **the n. boys,** les nouveaux; les élèves entrants; *Games:* **n. player,** rentrant, -ante; (*b*) (*of pers.*) **to be n. to business,** être nouveau, neuf, aux affaires; **n. to his trade,** neuf dans son métier; **I was n.**

to that kind of work, je n'étais pas fait, habitué, à ce genre de travail; **I'm n. to this town,** je suis nouveau venu dans cette ville. 2. (*a*) neuf, *f.* neuve; non usagé; **n. garment,** vêtement neuf; **to be dressed in n. clothes,** être habillé de neuf; **he wore n. gloves,** il était ganté de frais; **this dress is far from (being) n.,** cette robe ne date pas d'hier; *Com:* **in n. condition, as n.,** à l'état (de) neuf; **absolutely as n.,** état neuf absolu; **to make, do up, sth. like n.,** remettre qch. à neuf; (*b*) **n. ideas,** idées neuves; **the subject is quite n.,** ce sujet est neuf, n'a pas encore été traité. 3. **n. bread,** pain frais, tendre; **n. potatoes,** pommes de terre nouvelles; **n. wine,** vin nouveau, jeune; **wines that are palatable when n.,** vins bons dans la primeur; **n. leaves,** jeunes feuilles *f*; **n. grass,** herbe *f* tendre; *Geol:* **n. red sandstone,** grès bigarré.

II. *adv.* (*used to form compound adjs.*) nouvellement; **n.-set-up business,** commerce nouvellement établi; **n. blown,** (fleur) fraîche épanouie; **n. mown hay,** foin fraîchement coupé.

III. (*in geographical names*) **N. Amsterdam,** Nouvelle-Amsterdam; **N. Britain,** Nouvelle-Bretagne; **N. Brunswick,** Nouveau-Brunswick; **N. Caledonia,** Nouvelle-Calédonie; **N. Caledonian,** (i) *a.* néo-calédonien; (ii) *s.* Neo-Calédonien, -ienne; **N. Castile,** Nouvelle-Castille; **N. Delhi,** Nouvelle-Delhi; **N. England,** Nouvelle-Angleterre; **N. Englander,** habitant, -ante, de la Nouvelle-Angleterre; **N. Guinea,** Nouvelle-Guinée; Papouaisie *f*; **N. Guinean,** (i) *a.* néo-guinéen; (ii) *s.* Néo-Guinéen, -éenne; **the N. Hebrides,** les Nouvelles-Hébrides; **N. Jersey,** New Jersey *m*; **N. Mexico,** Nouveau-Mexique; **N. Orleans,** Nouvelle-Orléans; **N. South Wales,** Nouvelle-Galles-du-Sud; **N. South Welshman, Welshwoman,** Néo-Gallois, -oise; **N. York,** New York; *attrib.* newyorkais; **N. Yorker,** New yorkais, -aise; **N. Zealand,** Nouvelle-Zélande; **N. Zealander,** Néo-Zélandais, -aise.

newberyite ['nju:beriait], *s. Miner:* newberyite *f.*

newborn ['nju:bɔ:n], *a.* 1. nouveau-né; **n. children,** enfants nouveau-nés; **n. daughter,** fille nouveau-née; **a. n. passion,** une passion de fraîche date. 2. *Theol:* régénéré.

Newcastle ['nju:kɑ:sl]. *Pr.n. Geog:* Newcastle; *Vet:* **N. disease (of fowl),** maladie *f* de Newcastle; pseudopeste *f.*

newel ['nju:əl], *s. Const: etc:* 1. noyau *m* (d'escalier tournant, de vis d'Archimède); **open, hollow, n. stair,** vis *f* à jour. 2. **n. post,** pilastre *m* (de rampe d'escalier).

newfangled ['nju:fæŋg(ə)ld], *a. Pej:* (*of word, notion, etc.*) d'une modernité outrée; *F:* du dernier bateau; **determined opponent of n. ideas,** misonéiste endurci(e).

Newfie ['n(j)u:fi], *s. F:* Terre-Neuvien, -ienne.

newfound ['nju:faund], *a.* récemment découvert.

Newfoundland ['nju:fəndlænd, -lənd, -'faundlənd]. 1. *Pr.n. Geog:* Terre-Neuve; **the N. fishermen, fishing boats,** les terre-neuviers *m*, les terre-neuviens *m.* 2. *s.* [nju:'faundlənd], **N. (dog),** chien *m* de Terre-Neuve; terre-neuve *m inv.*

Newfoundlander ['nju:fəndlændər, nju:'faundləndər], *s.* 1. *Geog:* Terre-neuvien, -ienne. 2. *Fish:* (*pers. or ship*) terre-neuvien, terre-neuvier *m.*

Newgate ['nju:geit], *s.* (du nom de l'ancienne prison à Londres) *F: A:* **N. bird,** gibier *m* de potence; **N. knocker,** accroche-cœur *m, pl.* accroche-cœurs; rouflaquette *f.*

newly ['nju:li], *adv.* (*usu. hyphenated when in conjunction with a.*) récemment, nouvellement, fraîchement; **he is n. arrived,** il est tout fraîchement arrivé; il est arrivé tout dernièrement; **he was n. shaven,** il était rasé de frais; **the n.-elected members,** les députés nouveaux élus; **the n.-born child,** le nouveau-né, la nouveau-née; **n.-painted wall,** mur fraîchement peint; **a child's n.-awakened curiosity,** la curiosité neuve d'un enfant; **n.-formed bud,** bourgeon naissant; **n.-formed friendship,** amitié *f* de fraîche date, de date récente.

newlyweds ['nju:liwedz], *s.pl.* nouveaux mariés.

Newmanism ['nju:mənizm], *s. Rel.H:* la doctrine de Newman (avant sa conversion au catholicisme).

Newmanite ['nju:mənait], *s. Rel.H:* adhérent, -ente, à la doctrine de Newman, du mouvement d'Oxford.

newness ['nju:nis], *s.* 1. (*a*) nouveauté *f* (d'une idée, etc.); (*b*) inexpérience *f* (d'un employé, etc.). 2. état neuf (d'un vêtement, etc.). 3. (*a*) fraîcheur *f* (du pain, etc.); (*b*) jeunesse *f* (du vin); manque *m* de maturité (d'un fromage, etc.).

news [nju:z], *s.pl.* (*usu. with sg. const.*) 1. nouvelle *f*; nouvelles; **what's the n.?** quelles nouvelles? qu'est-ce qu'il y a de nouveau, de neuf? quoi de nouveau, de neuf? **I've some n. for you,** j'ai une nouvelle à vous annoncer; **that's n. to me,** ça, c'est du nouveau; **that's no n.!** ça, ce n'est pas une nouvelle! ça, c'est vieux! **it will be n. to you that . . .,** vous apprendrez avec surprise que . . .; **a sad piece of n., sad n.,** une triste nouvelle; **to break the n. to s.o.,** faire part d'une mauvaise nouvelle à qn; préparer qn à entendre la nouvelle; **n. has reached us from America that . . .,** d'Amérique nous vient la nouvelle que . . .; **we've had no n. of him for a long time,** il n'a pas donné signe de vie depuis longtemps; voilà longtemps qu'on n'a pas eu de ses nouvelles; **bad n. travels fast,** les mauvaises nouvelles ont des ailes; les malheurs s'apprennent bien vite; **no n. is good n.,** point de nouvelles, bonnes nouvelles. 2. (*a*) *Journ: etc:* **official n.,** communiqué officiel; **financial n.,** chronique financière; **n. from America,** reportage *m* d'Amérique; **n. in brief** = faits divers; **to be in the n.,** faire vedette; avoir les honneurs de la presse, défrayer la chronique; **X was in the n.,** on parlait beaucoup d'X dans les journaux; **the cold war was very much in the n.,** la guerre froide était à l'ordre du jour; **n. writer,** journaliste *mf*; **n. agency,** agence *f* d'informations; **n. stand,** kiosque *m* (où l'on vend des journaux); (*b*) *W.Tel: T.V: etc:* **the n.,** le radiojournal; le téléjournal; *Cin:* les actualités *f*; **n. theatre, cinema,** cinéma *m* où on montre des films d'actualités; (*c*) sujet *m* propre au reportage; **to make n.,** faire sensation; **a pub brawl isn't n.,** une rixe dans un bistro ne fait pas sensation, est sans intérêt pour le public.

newsagent ['nju:zeidʒənt], *s.* marchand, -ande, dépositaire *mf*, de journaux.

newsboy ['nju:zbɔi], *s.m.* vendeur de journaux.

newscast ['nju:zkɑ:st], *s. W.Tel: T.V:* bulletin *m* d'informations, les informations.

newscaster ['nju:zkɑ:stər], *s. W.Tel: T.V:* speaker, speakerine.

newscasting ['nju:zkɑ:stiŋ], *s.* radioreportage *m*; téléreportage *m.*

newsdealer ['nju:zdi:lər], *s.* marchand, -ande, de journaux.

newshawk, newshound ['njuzhɔ:k, -haund], *s. F:* reporter *m*, chasseur *m* de copie.

newsletter ['nju:zletər], *s.* bulletin *m* (d'informations); circulaire *f.*

newsman, *pl.* **-men** ['nju:zmæn, -men], *s.m.* 1. reporter. 2. vendeur de journaux.

newsmonger ['nju:zmʌŋgər], *s.* colporteur, -euse, de nouvelles, de cancans.

newspaper ['nju:zpeipər], *s.* journal, -aux *m*; **daily n.,** (journal) quotidien *m*; **weekly n.,** (journal) hebdomadaire *m*; **electric n.,** journal lumineux; **to be on a n.,** être attaché à la rédaction d'un journal; **n. report,** reportage *m*; **n. cuttings,** coupures *f* de journaux; **n. rack,** porte-journaux *m inv*; **n. man,** (i) journaliste *m*; (ii) marchand *m* de journaux; **I'll wrap it up for you in n.,** je vais vous l'envelopper dans du papier journal.

newsprint ['nju:zprint], *s.* papier *m* (de) journal.

newsreel ['nju:zri:l], *s. Cin:* actualités *fpl.*

newsroom ['nju:zru:m], *s.* 1. *Journ:* salle *f* de rédaction des informations. 2. (*in library*) salle des journaux.

newsvendor ['nju:zvendər], *s.* marchand, -ande, de journaux.

newsy ['nju:zi], *a. F:* (*a*) (*of letter, etc.*) plein de nouvelles; (*b*) *Journ:* propre au reportage; qui fera parler, qui fera sensation.

newt [nju:t], *s. Amph:* triton *m*; salamandre *f* aquatique; **crested n., greater water n.,** triton crêté, à crête; **smooth n.,** triton ponctué; **Californian n.,** salamandre aquatique de Californie; **marbled n.,** triton marbré.

Newton ['nju:tən]. 1. *Pr.n.* Newton; *Opt:* **Newton's disc, rings,** disque *m*, anneaux *m*, de Newton. 2. *s. Ph:* newton *m.*

Newtonian [nju:'touniən], *a.* newtonien, de Newton; **N. physics, mechanics,** physique, mécanique, newtonienne; **N. fluid,** fluide *m* à viscosité constante; *Opt:* **N. aberration,** cercle *m* de réfrangibilité.

Newtonianism [nju:touniənizm], *s.* newton(ian)isme *m.*

next [nekst], *a., adv. & prep.*

I. *a.* 1. (*of place*) prochain, le plus proche, (le plus) voisin; **the n. town,** la ville prochaine, la ville la plus proche; **let's stop at the n. hotel we see,** arrêtons-nous au prochain hôtel que nous apercevrons; **the n. room,** la chambre voisine; la chambre prochaine; **her room is n. to mine,** sa chambre est à côté de, est contiguë à, avec, la mienne; sa chambre touche à la mienne; **the garden n. to mine,** le jardin attenant au mien; **the chair n. to the piano,** la chaise à côté, tout près, du piano; **seated n. to me,** assis à côté de moi; **I was sitting n. to a barrister at table,** je voisinais à table avec un avocat; **they sat down right n. to one another,** elles se sont assises tout près l'une de l'autre; **they were standing n. to one another,** ils étaient debout, l'un près de l'autre; **the n. house,** la maison d'à côté; **the n. house but one,** la deuxième maison à partir d'ici; deux portes plus loin; **two houses n. to each other,** deux maisons voisines; **n. door,** la maison d'à côté; **the girl (from) n. door,** la jeune fille (de la maison) d'à côté; **to live n. door to s.o.,** demeurer porte à porte avec qn; **he lives n. door (to us),** il habite dans la maison voisine; il habite à côté (de chez nous); nous habitons porte à porte; **he lives n. door to the school,** il demeure à côté de l'école; **n.-door neighbours,** voisins *m* d'à côté, de porte à porte; voisins immédiats; **to be n.-door neighbours,** demeurer porte à porte. 2. (*a*) (*of time*) prochain, suivant; **the n. year, week,** l'année suivante, la semaine suivante; **the n. day,** le lendemain, le jour (d')après; **the n. day but one,** le surlendemain; **the n. Sunday after Easter,** le dimanche qui suit Pâques; *Ecc:* **the Sunday n. before Easter,** le dimanche avant Pâques; **on the n. Wednesday but one after my birthday,** le deuxième mercredi après mon anniversaire; **(the) n. morning,** le lendemain matin; **the n. instant,** l'instant d'après; **from one moment to the n.,** d'un instant à l'autre; **one minute she's smiling (and) the n. (minute) she's sulking,** tantôt elle sourit et tantôt elle boude; **the n. three days,** les trois jours suivants; (*future time*) **n. year, n. week,** l'année prochaine, la semaine prochaine; **for the n. fortnight,** pour les quinze prochains jours; **in the n. few days,** dans les prochains jours; **by this time n. year,** dans un an d'ici; **the year after n.,** dans deux ans; **n. Friday, (on) Friday n.,** vendredi prochain; **not this Sunday but Sunday n., but n. Sunday,** pas dimanche prochain, mais le dimanche suivant; **n. April, in April n.,** en avril prochain; **on the third of n. month,** le trois du mois prochain; (*b*) (*of order*) **the n. chapter,** le chapitre suivant; *Journ:* **continued in the n. column,** la suite à la colonne suivante; **the n. number, copy (of a periodical),** le prochain numéro (d'un périodique); **I'll tell you in my n. letter,** je vous le dirai dans ma prochaine lettre; **her n. (child) was a girl,** l'enfant qui a suivi a été une fille; **the n. time I see him,** la prochaine fois que je le verrai; la première fois que je le reverrai; **the n. time I saw him,** la première fois que je l'ai revu; **ask the n. person you meet,** demandez à la première personne que vous rencontrerez; **the n. thing is to . . .,** maintenant il s'agit de . . .; **in the n. place . . .,** ensuite . . .; *F:* **what(ever) n.!** par exemple! et quoi encore! **n. (person), please!** au suivant! **who's n., who comes n.? whose turn (is it) n.?** à qui le tour? **you're n., your turn n.,** c'est votre tour; à vous maintenant; **n. came the band,** ensuite venait la musique; **I come n. to him,** je viens (immédiatement) après lui; **he is n. before me, n. after me,** il me précède, me suit, immédiatement; (*c*) (*in shoes, etc.*) **the n. size (larger),** la pointure au-dessus; **the n. size (smaller),** la pointure au-dessous; **the n. town to London in size,** la première ville, pour l'étendue, après Londres; **the n. best thing would be to . . .,** à défaut de cela, le mieux serait de . . .; à défaut de cela, ce qu'il y aurait de mieux à faire ce serait de . . .; *F:* **I got it for n. to nothing,** je l'ai eu pour presque rien, pour un rien, pour une bouchée de pain; **to eat n. to nothing,** se nourrir de rien; **n. door to nothing,** autant dire rien; **there is n. to no evidence,** il n'y a pour ainsi dire pas de preuves; **there was n. to nobody at the meeting,** il n'y avait presque personne à la réunion; **that's n. to impossible,** cela est pour ainsi dire impossible; **n. door to sth.,** approchant de qch.; qui avoisine qch.; **flattery is n. door to lying,** de la flatterie au mensonge il n'y a qu'un pas; la flatterie frise le mensonge; **ideas n. door to madness,** idées *f* qui avoisinent, qui frisent, la folie, idées qui touchent à, qui confinent à, la folie; **if he isn't a quack, he's n. door to it,** si ce n'est pas un charlatan, il ne s'en faut de guère. 3. *Jur:* **n. friend,** ami le plus proche; représentant *m* ad litem. 4. *esp. U.S: F:* **to get n. to s.o.,** faire la connaissance de qn; se mettre bien avec qn; **to get n. to an idea,** saisir une idée.

II. *adv.* 1. ensuite, après; **n. we went to the Martin's,** ensuite nous sommes allés chez les Martin; **what shall we do n.?** qu'est-ce que nous allons faire maintenant, après cela? **he is an Irishman first, critic n.,** il est tout d'abord Irlandais et critique en second lieu, et puis critique. 2. la prochaine fois; **when you're there n.,** la prochaine fois que vous passerez par là; **when I n. saw him,** quand je l'ai revu; **when shall we meet n.?** quand nous reverrons-nous?

III. *prep. A: & Lit:* auprès de, à côté de; **I was sitting n. to him,** j'étais assis auprès de lui, à côté de lui; **he placed his chair n. to hers,** il mit sa chaise auprès de la sienne; **the carriage n. to the engine,** la première voiture près de la locomotive; **I can't bear wool n. to my skin,** je ne peux pas supporter la laine à même la peau.

nexus ['neksəs], *s.* connexion *f*, liaison *f*, lien *m*; **causal n.,** connexion causale.

niacin ['naiəsin], *s. Pharm:* niacine *f.*

Niagara [nai'æg(ə)rə]. *Pr.n. Geog:* Niagara *m*; **the N. Falls,** les chutes *f* du Niagara.
niaouli [ni:'auli:], *s. Bot:* niaouli *m*.
nib[1] [nib], *s.* **1.** (*a*) *A:* taillon *m* (de plume d'oie); (*b*) (bec *m* de) plume *f*; **broad n.,** grosse plume; plume à gros bec; **fine n.,** plume fine; plume à bec fin; fausset *m*. **2.** (*a*) pointe *f* (d'outil, etc.); (*b*) talon *m*, crochet *m* (de tuile). **3.** graine *f*, fève *f*, de cacao décortiquée.
nib[2], *v.tr.* (**nibbed**) (*a*) *A:* tailler (une plume); (*b*) mettre une plume à (un porte-plume).
nibbed [nibd], *a.* **1.** (plume) à bec; **hard-n. pen,** plume *f* à bec dur; plume dure. **2.** (*a*) (outil) à pointe; (*b*) (tuile) à talon, à crochet.
nibble[1] ['nibl], *s.* **1.** (*a*) grignotage *m*, grignotement *m*, mordillure *f*; **to have a n. at the cake,** grignoter le gâteau; (*b*) *Fish:* touche *f*; **I didn't get, have, a n. all day,** le poisson n'a pas mordu de toute la journée. **2.** juste de quoi grignoter, de quoi brouter; petit morceau (de biscuit); petite touffe (d'herbe). **3.** *F:* **nibbles,** amuse-gueules *m*.
nibble[2]. **1.** *v.tr. & i.* grignoter, mordiller (qch.); (*of sheep*) brouter (l'herbe); **to n. (at) a biscuit,** grignoter, mangeot(t)er, un biscuit; **he nibbles at his food,** il mange du bout des dents, des lèvres; (*of fish, F: of pers.*) **to n. (at the bait),** toucher; piquer; mordre à l'hameçon; (*of fish*) **to n. off the bait,** manger l'appât (sans s'enferrer); **to n. at an offer,** être attiré par une offre (sans pouvoir se décider); être tenté; *F:* **to n. at sth.,** critiquer qch.; chicaner, ergoter, sur qch. **2.** *v.tr.* (*a*) *Metalw:* découper (une tôle) à vive arête; grignoter (une tôle); (*b*) gruger (le verre); arrondir (une lentille).
nibbler ['niblər], *s.* grignoteur, -euse.
nibbling ['nibliŋ], *s.* grignotement *m*, grignotage *m*, mordillage *m*; arrondissage *m* (d'une lentille); *Tchn:* **n. machine,** machine *f* à découper, à grignoter, à gruger; grignoteuse *f*.
niblick ['niblik], *s. Golf:* niblick *m*.
nibs [nibz], *s. F:* **his n.,** sa majesté; le gros bonnet, *P:* la grosse légume; **who should walk in but his n.!** à la porte apparaît sa seigneurie elle-même!
Nicaea [nai'si:ə]. *Pr.n. Hist:* Nicée.
Nicaean [nai'si:ən], *a.* = NICENE.
Nicandra [nai'kændrə], *s. Bot:* nicandre *f*, nicandra *m*.
Nicaragua [nikə'rægjuə]. *Pr.n. Geog:* Nicaragua *m*.
Nicaraguan [nikə'rægjuən]. *Geog:* (*a*) *a.* nicaraguayen; (*b*) *s.* Nicaraguayen, -enne.
niccolite ['nikəlait], *s. Miner:* nickéline *f*, niccolite *f*.
nic(c)olo ['nikəlou], *s. Miner:* niccolo *m*.
nice [nais], *a.* **1.** *Lit:* (*a*) (*of pers.*) (i) difficile, délicat, exigeant; (ii) *O:* scrupuleux, méticuleux; **to be n. about, in, the choice of words,** avoir des scrupules dans le choix des mots; **to be n. about one's food,** être difficile pour sa nourriture; **he is not too n. about the means,** il n'est pas trop scrupuleux quant aux moyens; (*b*) (*of experiment, question, etc.*) délicat; (*of distinction, taste, etc.*) subtil, fin, recherché; (*of inquiry, etc.*) minutieux; (*of ear, eye, etc.*) sensible, juste; **that's a very n. point,** voilà une question délicate. **2.** *F:* (*a*) (*of pers.*) gentil, *f* gentille; sympathique, agréable, aimable; **child of a n. disposition,** enfant d'un bon naturel; **to be n. to s.o.,** se montrer gentil, aimable, avec qn, pour qn, envers qn; **that's very n. of you,** vous êtes bien aimable, très gentil; **he was as n. as could be,** il s'est montré aimable au possible; **it is n. of you to . . .,** vous êtes bien aimable de . . .; **how n. of you to come!** comme c'est gentil, bien, à vous d'être venu! **it's not n. of you to make fun of him,** ce n'est pas bien de vous moquer de lui; **it's not n. (of you) to be jealous,** c'est vilain (de votre part) d'être jaloux, **he's a n. chap,** c'est un gentil garçon; *Iron:* **you're a n. one to talk like that!** c'est du joli de parler comme ça! **and a n. sort of chap you are!** eh, bien, tu es gentil, toi! **you look very n. in that dress,** tu es très bien dans cette robe-là; **she's a n.-looking woman,** c'est une jolie, belle, femme; elle est bien de sa personne; (*b*) (*of thg*) joli, bon; **n. dinner,** bon dîner; **n. evening,** soirée *f* agréable; **n. car,** jolie voiture; **the garden is beginning to look n.,** le jardin s'embellit; **what a n.-looking vase,** quel joli, beau, vase; **n. plump chicken,** bon poulet bien en chair; **to have a n. long chat,** faire une bonne petite causette; **a n. little sum,** une somme grassouillette, rondelette; **it's not n. to be poor,** il ne fait pas bon être pauvre; **it's n. here,** il fait bon ici; **how n.!** ça c'est chic! (*c*) (*intensive*) *F:* **n. and handy,** bien commode; **n. and cosy,** bien à l'aise, tout bien; **it's n. and cool,** le temps est agréablement frais, d'une fraicheur agréable; **they're n. and warm in their cots,** ils sont bien au chaud dans leurs petits lits; **it's n. and easy,** c'est très facile; **I like my tea n. and sweet,** j'aime le thé bien sucré; **how n. and early you are,** c'est bien gentil à vous de venir de si bonne heure; **thank you for doing it so n. and quickly,** merci de l'avoir fait si rapidement; **you'll be n. and ill in the morning!** ce que tu vas être malade demain matin! **everything's as n. as n. can be,** tout est agréable au possible; (*d*) **n. people,** des gens bien; **not n.,** désagréable; pas tout à fait convenable; peu convenable; **it's not a n. story,** c'est une histoire peu savoureuse; (*e*) *Iron:* **we are in a n. mess!** nous voilà dans de beaux draps! **that's a n. way to behave!** voilà une jolie conduite! **that's a n. way to talk!** c'est du joli ce que vous dites là! **that's a n. state of affairs!** ça c'est du propre!
nicely ['naisli], *adv.* **1.** *Lit:* (*a*) minutieusement, scrupuleusement, méticuleusement, soigneusement; **n. turned epigram,** épigramme joliment tournée; (*b*) exactement; avec justesse. **2.** joliment, gentiment, bien, agréablement; de la bonne façon; **n. situated house,** maison agréablement située; **everything was n. done,** tout était bien fait; **those will do (very) n.,** ceux-là feront très bien l'affaire; **he spoke to me very n.,** il m'a parlé très aimablement, très gentiment; **he spoke very n. about you,** il m'a parlé de vous en très bons termes; **he's getting on n.,** (i) (*of invalid*) il fait du progrès; (ii) ses affaires ne marchent pas mal; **that's n. done, said!** voilà qui est bien! *Sp:* **n.!** bien! bravo!
Nicene [nai'si:n], *a.* nicéen; de Nicée; **the N. councils,** les conciles *m* de Nicée; *Theol:* **the N. creed,** le symbole de Nicée.
niceness ['naisnis], *s.* **1.** *Lit:* (*a*) (*of pers.*) (i) goût *m* difficile, délicatesse exagérée; (ii) scrupulosité *f*, méticulosité *f*; (*b*) (*of experiment, etc.*) délicatesse *f*; (*of distinction, taste*) subtilité *f*, finesse *f*; (*of inquiry, etc.*) minutie *f*; (*of ear, eye*) sensibilité *f*, justesse *f*. **2.** gentillesse *f*, amabilité *f* (de qn); agrément *m*, caractère *m* agréable (de qch.).
nicety ['naisiti], *s.* **1.** = NICENESS 1 (*a*). **2.** (*a*) exactitude *f*, justesse *f*, précision *f* (d'un calcul, etc.); **to a n.,** exactement, à la perfection; **her dress fits her to a n.,** sa robe lui va à merveille, comme un gant; **roast done to a n.,** rôti cuit juste à point; (*b*) subtilité *f*, délicatesse *f* (d'une question, etc.); **a point of great n.,** une question très délicate, très subtile. **3.** *pl.* **niceties** (*a*) *A:* bonnes choses (à manger, etc.); (*b*) minuties *f*; **niceties of a craft,** finesses *f* d'un métier.
niche[1] [nitʃ], *s.* (*a*) niche *f* (pour une statue, etc.); **secret n.,** resserre *f*; *Nat.Hist:* **ecological n.,** niche écologique; **to make a n. for oneself,** (trouver à) se caser; (*b*) *Mil:* niche (d'une tranchée).
niche[2]. **1.** *v.tr.* placer (une statue, etc.) dans une niche. **2.** *v.pr.* se nicher, se caser (dans un coin, etc.).
Nicholas ['nikələs]. *Pr.n.m.* Nicolas.
nichrome ['naikroum], *s. Metall:* nichrome *m*.
Nick[1] [nik]. *Pr.n.m.* (*dim. of Nicholas*) Nicolas; *F:* **Old N.,** le diable.
nick[2], *s.* **1.** (*a*) (*in plank, etc.*) entaille *f*, encoche *f*, cran *m*; (*in tally stick, etc.*) coche *f*, encoche, hoche *f*; (*in screwhead*) fente *f*; *Typ:* (*in shank of type*) cran; (*b*) saignée *f* (de graissage, etc.); onglet *m* (de lame de couteau); gorge *f*; (*c*) brèche *f* (au tranchant d'une lame). **2.** (*in dice games*) coup gagnant. **3.** point nommé, moment *m* critique; **(just) in the n. of time,** à point nommé; fort à propos; au bon moment; juste à temps, juste à point; **you've come just in the n. of time,** vous tombez bien; vous tombez à pic. **4.** *P:* **in good n.,** en bon état. **5.** *P:* prison *f*, taule *f*.
nick[3]. **1.** *v.tr.* (*a*) entailler, encocher, cocher (un bâton, etc.); fendre (la tête d'une vis); biseauter (les cartes); *Typ:* créner (la tige d'une lettre); dumdum(is)er (une balle); **to n. a tally,** faire une coche à une taille; hocher une taille; (*b*) anglaiser, niqueter (la queue d'un cheval, un cheval); (*c*) pratiquer une saignée dans (une surface de glissement, etc.); (*d*) ébrécher (une lame, etc.); (*e*) **to n. oneself,** se couper. **2.** *v.tr. F:* (*a*) deviner (la vérité, etc.); **to n. it,** deviner juste; **he's nicked it!** il y est! (*b*) **to n. the time,** arriver à point nommé, juste à temps; **I just nicked the boat,** je suis parvenu tout juste à attraper le bateau; (*c*) (*in dice games*) gagner (un coup); (*d*) *P:* (*esp. of police*) pincer, choper qn; **to get nicked,** se faire pincer, épingler; (*e*) *P:* chiper, faucher, barboter (qch.). **3.** *v.i.* (*a*) *Rac:* **to n. in,** couper son concurrent; s'insinuer; (*b*) *Breed:* (*of stock*) se croiser heureusement.
nicked [nikt], *a.* **1.** (*a*) (*of stick, etc.*) entaillé, encoché, coché; (*of bullet*) dumdum(is)é, mâché; **n.-tooth milling cutter,** fraise *f* à denture interrompue; (*b*) (*of horse's tail*) niqueté, anglaisé. **2.** ébréché.
nickel[1] ['nikl], *s.* **1.** (*a*) *Metall:* nickel *m*; **n. iron,** fer *m* au nickel, fer-nickel *m*; *Metall:* **n. chrome, n. chromium,** nickel-chrome *m*, chrome-nickel *m*; nichrome *m*; **n. chrome steel,** acier *m* au chrome-nickel; **n. plating,** nickelage *m*, nickelure *f*; **n.-plated,** nickelé; **n. plater,** nickeleur *m*; (*b*) *Miner:* **n. ochre, n. bloom,** nickélocre *m*; annabergite *f*; **n. glance,** nickelglanz *m*, gersdorffite *f*; **n. gymnite,** nickelgymnite *f*; **n.-bearing,** nickélifère; (*c*) *Ch: Miner:* **n. arsenide,** arséniure *m* de nickel; **n. sulphide,** sulfure *m* de nickel; *Ch:* **n. carbonyl,** nickel-carbonyle *m*, nickel-tétracarbonyle *m*. **2.** (*a*) pièce *f* de monnaie en nickel; (*b*) *NAm:* pièce de cinq *cents*.
nickel[2], *v.tr.* (**nickelled**) (*also* **nickel-plate**) nickeler (des objets en métal oxydable); nickéliser.
nickelage ['nikəlidʒ], *s.* = NICKELLING.
nickelic ['nikəlik], *a.* nickélique.
nickeliferous [nifə'lifərəs], *a. Miner:* nickélifère.
nickeline ['nikəli:n], *s. Metall:* maillechort *m*.
nickelite ['nikəlait], *s. Miner:* = NICCOLITE.
nickelization [nikəlai'zeiʃ(ə)n], *s.* = NICKELLING.
nickelize ['nikəlaiz], *v.tr.* = NICKEL[2].
nickelled ['nikəld], *a.* (*of spoon, etc.*) nickelé.
nickelling ['nikəliŋ], *s.* **1.** (*action*) nickelage *m*, nickélisage *m*. **2.** nickelure *f*.
nickernut ['nikənʌt], *s. Bot:* œil-de-chat *m*, *pl.* œils-de-chat.
nicking ['nikiŋ], *s.* **1.** (*a*) entaillage *m*; (*b*) *Typ:* crénage *m* (de la tige d'une lettre); (*c*) anglaisage *m* (de la queue d'un cheval), **2.** ébrèchement *m* (d'un ciseau, etc.).
nick-nack ['niknæk], *s.* colifichet *m*, babiole *f*, bibelot *m*.
nick-nackery ['niknækəri], *s.* bibelots *mpl*, bimbeloterie *f*.
nickname[1] ['nikneim], *s.* **1.** surnom *m*. **2.** (*a*) (*in derision*) sobriquet *m*; (*b*) (*shortened name*) diminutif *m*.
nickname[2], *v.tr.* **1.** surnommer (qn). **2.** (*a*) donner un sobriquet à (qn); **nicknamed the Hunchback,** connu sous le sobriquet de Bossu; (*b*) appeler (qn) par, de, son diminutif.
Nicobar ['nikəba:r]. *Pr.n. Orn:* **N. pigeon,** nicobar *m*.
Nicobarese [nikə'ba:ri:z], *a. & s.* **1.** *Geog:* (*a*) *a.* nicobarais; (*b*) *s.* Nicobarais, -aise. **2.** *s. Ling:* nicobarais *m*.
Nicodemus [nikə'di:məs]. *Pr.n.m. B.Hist:* Nicodème.
Nicol ['nik(ə)l]. *Pr.n. Opt:* **Nicol('s) prism,** prisme *m* de Nicol; nicol *m*.
Nicolaitan [nikə'leiitən], *s. Rel.H:* nicolaïte *m*.
Nicolette [nikə'let]. *Pr.n.f.* Nicolette, Colinette.
Nicomachean [naikəmə'ki:ən], *a. Gr.Lit:* **the N. Ethics,** l'Éthique *f* à Nicomaque (d'Aristote).
Nicomachus [nai'kəməkəs]. *Pr.n.m. Gr.Ant:* Nicomaque.
Nicomedes [nikə'mi:di:z]. *Pr.n.m. A.Hist:* Nicomède.
Nicosia [nikə'si:ə]. *Pr.n. Geog:* Nicosie, Nicosia.
nicotein(e) ['nikəti:n], *s. Ch:* nicotéine *f*.
nicotian [ni'kouʃ(i)ən], *s. A:* **1.** tabac *m*. **2.** fumeur, -euse (de tabac).
nicotiana [nikouʃi'a:nə], *s. Bot:* nicotiane *f*.
nicotinamid(e) [nikə'ti:nəmid, -maid], *s. Ch:* nicotinamide *f*.
nicotine ['nikəti:n], *s. Ch:* nicotine *f*; **n. poisoning,** nicotinisme *m*, tabagisme *m*.
nicotinic [nikə'ti:nik], *a. Ch:* (acide, etc.) nicotinique, nicotique; tabagique.
nicotinism ['nikəti:nizm], *s. Med:* nicotinisme *m*, tabagisme *m*.
nicotinize ['nikəti:naiz], *v.tr.* nicotiniser, nicotiser.
nict(it)ate ['nikt(it)eit], *v.i.* cligner les yeux; ciller; (*of horses*) nicter.
nict(it)ating ['nikt(it)eitiŋ], *a.* nictitant; *Z:* **n. membrane,** membrane nictitante, clignotante; paupière *f* interne, onglet *m* (d'oiseau, etc.).
nict(it)ation [nik(ti)'teiʃ(ə)n], *s.* nict(it)ation *f*, clignotement *m*, cillement *m*.
nidation [nai'deiʃ(ə)n], *s. Physiol:* nidation *f*.
niddering ['nidəriŋ], *a. & s. A:* poltron, -onne; scélérat, -ate; misérable (*mf*).
nide [naid], *s. A:* couvée *f*, nichée *f* (de faisans).
nidicolous [nai'dikələs], *a. Orn:* nidicole.
nidification [nidifi'keiʃ(ə)n], *s.* nidification *f*.
nidifugous [nai'difjugəs], *a. Orn:* nidifuge.
nidify ['nidifai], *v.i.* (*of birds*) nidifier.
nidus, *pl.* **-uses, -i** ['naidəs, -əsiz, -ai], *s.* **1.** (*a*) nid *m* (d'insectes, etc.); (*b*) dépôt *m* d'œufs (d'insectes, etc.). **2.** *Bot:* endroit *m* favorable (pour la croissance des spores, des graines). **3.** endroit d'origine, foyer *m*, source *f* (d'une maladie, d'une doctrine, etc.).
niece [ni:s], *s.f.* nièce.
niellist [ni'elist], *s.* nielleur, -euse.
niello [ni'elou], *s. Metalw:* **1.** nielle *m*; **to inlay with n.,** nieller; **inlaying with n.,** niellage *m*. **2. n. (work),** niellure *f*, niellage; **n. worker,** nielleur, -euse; **n. enamels,** émaux *m* de niellure.
nielloed [ni'eloud], *a.* (argent, or, sabre, etc.) niellé.
Nietzschean ['ni:tʃiən], *a. & s. Phil:* nietzschéen, -éenne.
nietzsch(ean)ism ['ni:tʃ(iən)izm], *s. Phil:* nietzschéisme *m*.
nife [naifi], *s. Geol:* nifé *m*.

niff[1] [nif], *s. P:* puanteur *f*, mauvaise odeur.

niff[2], *v.i. P:* puer; cocoter, (s)chlinguer; **to n. of garlic,** puer l'ail.

niffy ['nifi], *a. P:* puant.

nifty ['nifti], *a. O:* **1.** *F:* (*a*) (*of pers.*) adroit, débrouillard; (*b*) (*of thg*) commode; bien imaginé. **2.** *P:* puant. **3.** *NAm: F:* coquet, pimpant.

nigella [nai'dʒelə], *s. Bot:* nigelle *f*.

Niger ['naidʒər]. *Pr.n. Geog:* (*a*) (*river*) Niger *m*; (*b*) (République du) Niger.

Nigeria [nai'dʒiəriə]. *Pr.n. Geog:* Nigeria *m*.

Nigerian [nai'dʒiəriən]. *Geog:* **1.** (*in Niger*) (*a*) *a.* nigérien; (*b*) *s.* Nigérien, -ienne. **2.** (*in Nigeria*) (*a*) *a.* nigérian; (*b*) *s.* Nigérian, -ane.

niggard ['nigəd]. **1.** *s.* grippe-sou *m*, *pl.* grippe-sou(s); ladre,*f.* ladresse; pingre *m*, avare *mf.* **2.** *a. Poet:* avare, parcimonieux, ladre.

niggardliness ['nigədlinis], *s.* ladrerie *f*, pingrerie *f*, parcimonie *f*, avarice *f*, mesquinerie *f*.

niggardly[1] ['nigədli], *a.* (*of pers.*) chiche, ladre, pingre, parcimonieux, mesquin; (*of sum, portion*) mesquin.

niggardly[2], *adv.* chichement, parcimonieusement, mesquinement.

nigger ['nigər], *s.* **1.** (*a*) *P: Pej:* nègre *m*, *f.* négresse; bougnoul(e) *m*, bamboula *m*; **a little n. boy,** un négrillon; (*b*) *F:* **there's a n. in the woodpile,** il y a (quelque) anguille sous roche; **that's the n. in the woodpile!** voilà le fin mot de l'histoire! **he's the n. in the woodpile,** c'est un empêcheur de tourner rond; (*c*) *a.* & *s.* (*colour*) (*not used in U.S.*) **n. brown,** (tête-de-) nègre *inv.* **2.** *Ent:* larve *f* de la tenthrède. **3.** *Tchn:* (*for loading logs*) nègre.

niggle ['nigl], *v.i.* vétiller; tatillonner; *Art:* fignoler, pignocher, blaireauter; **to n. over trifles,** s'attarder à des vétilles, à des riens.

niggler ['niglər], *s.* tatillon, -onne; *Art:* pignocheur, -euse.

niggling[1] ['nigliŋ], *a.* (*a*) (*of details, etc.*) insignifiant; de rien du tout; (*of work*) fignolé; léché; (*of pers.*) tatillon, -onne; (*b*) **n. handwriting,** pattes *fpl* de mouche.

niggling[2], *s.* vétillerie *f*, chicanerie *f*.

niggly ['nigli], *a.* (*a*) = NIGGLING[1]; (*b*) *F:* de mauvaise humeur; ronchonnard.

nigh [nai]. *Poet: Dial:* **1.** *adv.* près, proche; **n. unto death,** à l'article de la mort; près de mourir; presque, à peu près. **2.** *prep.* près de, auprès de (qn, qch.). **3.** *a.* proche.

night [nait], *s.* **1.** (*a*) nuit *f*, soir *m*; **last n.,** la nuit dernière; cette nuit; hier (au) soir; **I dreamt a great deal last n.,** j'ai beaucoup rêvé cette nuit; **the n. before,** la veille (au soir); **the n. before last,** la nuit d'avant-hier; avant-hier au soir; **tomorrow n.,** demain soir; **I saw him on Thursday n.,** je l'ai vu jeudi soir; **the n. from Monday to Tuesday,** la nuit de lundi à mardi, du lundi au mardi; **ten o'clock at n.,** dix heures du soir; **far into the n.,** jusqu'à une heure avancée de la nuit; **all n. long, the whole n., (all) the livelong n.,** toute la nuit; **to sit up all n., spend the n., doing sth.,** passer la nuit à faire qch.; **to be accustomed to late nights,** avoir l'habitude de veiller, de se coucher tard; être accoutumé aux veilles; **to have a good, a bad, night('s sleep),** bien, mal, dormir; passer une bonne, une mauvaise, nuit; **I didn't close my eyes, sleep a wink, all n.,** je n'ai pas dormi de la nuit; j'ai passé une nuit blanche; **good n.!** bonsoir! (*when going to bed*) bonne nuit! **(I wish you) good n.,** (je vous souhaite une) bonne nuit; **he was saying good n. to her,** il lui disait bonsoir; il lui souhaitait le bonsoir; **he will not live through the n.,** il ne passera pas la nuit; **to make a n. of it,** faire la noce toute la nuit; tirer une bordée; **we made a n. of it,** nous avons passé la nuit à faire la fête; **the maid's n. out,** le soir de sortie de la bonne; **Saturday is our theatre n.,** c'est samedi soir que nous allons au théâtre; **to work day and n.,** travailler nuit et jour; **to turn day into n. and n. into day,** faire de la nuit le jour et du jour la nuit; **to say one's prayers n. and morning,** dire ses prières matin et soir; **at n.,** (à la) nuit; **to set off at n.,** partir de nuit; **in the n.,** (pendant) la nuit; **to get up in the n.,** se (re)lever la nuit; **by n.,** de nuit; nuitamment; **to travel by n., at n.,** voyager de nuit, la nuit; **we stayed (there) the n.,** nous y avons passé la nuit; **night's lodging,** logement *m* pour la nuit; **to pay for one's night's lodging,** payer pour sa nuit; **n. clothes, n. attire,** vêtements *mpl*, toilette *f*, de nuit; **n. boat, n. train, n. service,** bateau *m*, train *m*, service *m*, de nuit; **n. traffic,** (i) circulation *f* de nuit; (ii) *Tp:* trafic *m* de nuit; *Aut:* **n. driving can be dangerous,** conduire la nuit peut être dangereux; **n. work,** travail *m* de nuit; **to do n. work, to be on n. duty,** *F:* **to work nights, to be on nights,** travailler la nuit; **n. shift,** équipe *f* de nuit; **he's on (the) n. shift,** il est de nuit; **n. watch,** (i) garde *f*, veille *f* (de nuit); (ii) *Nau:* quart *m* de nuit; **n. watchman,** veilleur *m* de nuit; garde *m*, gardien *m*, de nuit; *Av:* **n. bomber, n. fighter,** bombardier *m*, chasseur *m*, de nuit; **n. flight, n. flying,** vol *m* de nuit; **n. stop,** escale *f* de nuit; *Mil:* **n. attack, n. engagement,** attaque *f*, combat *m*, de nuit, nocturne; **n. firing,** tir *m* de nuit; *Opt:* **n. glass,** lunette *f* de nuit; **n. glasses,** jumelles *f* (d'observation) de nuit; **n. blind,** héméralope, héméralopique; **n. blindness,** héméralopie *f*; **my n. vision isn't good,** je vois mal la nuit; **n. prowler,** rôdeur *m* de nuit; *U.S:* **n. rider,** bandit masqué (qui terrorise les gens pendant la nuit); *A:* **n. chair,** chaise percée; chaise garde-robe; **n. lamp, light,** veilleuse *f*; *Nau:* **n. lights,** feux *m* de position; *Nau:* **n. finder,** noctoviseur *m*; **n. shelter,** asile *m* de nuit; *Hyg:* **n. soil,** matières *fpl* de vidange; vidanges *fpl*; gadoue *f*; poudrette *f*; *A:* **n. cart,** voiture *f* de vidange; *Orn:* **n. bird,** oiseau *m* de nuit; **n. birds,** nocturnes *mpl*; *Can:* **black-crowned n. heron,** bihoreau *m* à couronne noire; **yellow-crowned n. heron,** bihoreau violacé; *Z:* **n. ape,** singe *m* nocturne, nyctipithèque *m*, douroucouli *m*; *Rept:* **(African) n. adder,** vipère-flèche *f*; *Bot:* **n. flower,** fleur *f* nocturne; **n.-flowering,** noctiflore; (*b*) *Th: etc:* représentation *f*; **first n.,** première *f*; **the last nights,** les dernières représentations (d'une pièce, etc.); **Wagner n.,** soirée musicale consacrée à Wagner; festival *m* Wagner; **n. scene,** scène *f* nocturne. **2.** obscurité *f*, nuit, ténèbres *fpl*; **n. is falling, coming on,** la nuit vient, tombe; il commence à faire nuit; il se fait nuit; **n. had come, had fallen, had closed in,** la nuit était venue; **n. was falling on the plain,** la plaine s'enténébrait; *Lit:* **to go forth into the n.,** s'en aller dans les ténèbres, dans l'obscurité; *Paint:* **n. effect, n. scene,** effet *m* de nuit; **n. piece,** (i) *Mus:* nocturne *m*; (ii) *Art: Lit:* effet de nuit; *Lit:* **the n. of ignorance,** les ténèbres de l'ignorance; **the n. of time,** la nuit des temps.

nightcap ['naitkæp], *s.* **1.** *A.Cost:* (i) bonnet *m* de nuit (de femme); (ii) bonnet de coton, de nuit (d'homme); **wearing a cotton n.,** coiffé d'un bonnet de coton. **2.** *F:* boisson (prise avant de se coucher).

nightclub ['naitklʌb], *s.* boîte *f* de nuit; cabaret *m*.

nightdress ['naitdres], *s.* chemise *f* de nuit (de femme, d'enfant); *Fr.C:* jaquette *f*.

nighterie, *also* **nightery** ['naitəri], *s. esp. U.S: F:* boîte *f* de nuit.

nightfall ['naitfɔ:l], *s.* tombée *f* du jour, de la nuit; la brune; **at n.,** à la nuit tombante; à la tombée de la nuit, au tomber du jour; à la brune.

nightgown ['naitgaun], *s.* = NIGHTDRESS.

nighthawk ['naithɔ:k], *s.* **1.** *Orn:* engoulevent *m*; **American n., common n., booming n.,** engoulevent d'Amérique, *Fr.C:* engoulevent commun. **2.** *F:* rôdeur *m* de nuit. **3.** *esp. U.S: F:* taxi *m* noctambule.

nightie, *also* **nighty** ['naiti], *s. F:* NIGHTDRESS.

nightingale ['naitiŋgeil], *s. Orn:* rossignol *m* (philomèle); **thrush n.,** rossignol progné; **Japanese n.,** rossignol du Japon, leiothrix *m*; **to sing like a n.,** chanter comme un rossignol; **to have a nightingale's throat,** avoir un gosier de rossignol.

nightjar ['naitdʒɑ:r], *s. Orn:* engoulevent *m* (d'Europe); **Egyptian n.,** engoulevent d'Égypte; **pennant-winged n.,** engoulevent à balanciers; **standard-winged n.,** engoulevent porte-étendards; **red-necked n.,** engoulevent à collier roux, tête-chèvre *m*, *pl.* tête-chèvres.

nightlock ['naitlɔk], *v.tr. U.S:* fermer (une porte) pour la nuit.

nightlong ['naitlɔŋ], *s.* (veille, fête, etc.) qui dure toute la nuit.

nightly ['naitli]. **1.** *a.* (*a*) (*happening at night*) de nuit, de soir, nocturne; (*b*) de tous les soirs, de toutes les nuits; **n. performance,** représentation *f* (de) tous les soirs; soirée quotidienne; **it's a n. occurrence,** cela arrive tous les soirs, chaque nuit. **2.** *adv.* tous les soirs, toutes les nuits; **performances n.,** représentations tous les soirs.

nightman, *pl.* **-men** ['naitmən], *s.m. A:* vidangeur.

nightmare ['naitmeər], *s.* cauchemar *m*; **to have a n., to have nightmares,** avoir le cauchemar; **the prospect was a n. to me,** cette perspective me donnait le cauchemar; ça me cauchemardait, cette perspective.

nightmarish ['naitmeəriʃ], *a.* qui ressemble à un cauchemar, aux cauchemars; qui donne des cauchemars; cauchemardesque, cauchemardeux.

nightshade ['naitʃeid], *s. Bot:* **(black) n.,** morelle noire; crève-chien *m inv*; raisin *m* de loup; **woody n.,** douce-amère *f*, *pl.* douces-amères; vigne *f* de Judée, de Judas; **enchanter's n.,** circée *f*; sorcier *m*; herbe *f* à la magicienne; **deadly n.,** (atrope *f*) belladone *f*; morelle furieuse; herbe empoisonnée; belle-dame *f*, *pl.* belles-dames; **Malabar n.,** baselle *f*.

nightshirt ['naitʃɔ:t], *s. Cost:* chemise *f* de nuit (d'homme).

nightstick ['naitstik], *s. U.S:* casse-tête *m inv*; matraque *f* (d'agent de police).

nightstool ['naitstu:l], *s. A:* chaise percée; chaise garde-robe.

night(-)time ['naittaim], *s.* la nuit; **at n.,** la nuit; **in the n.,** de nuit; pendant la nuit.

nightwalker ['naitwɔ:kər], *s.* **1.** *A:* (*a*) rôdeur *m* de nuit; (*b*) prostituée *f*, pierreuse *f*. **2.** animal *m* noctambule.

nightwalking ['naitwɔ:kiŋ], *s.* noctambulisme *m*.

nightwear ['naitweər], *s.* vêtements *mpl* de nuit.

nignog ['nignɔg], *s. P:* **1.** nigaud, -aude. **2.** *Pej:* nègre *m*, *f.* négresse.

nigre ['naigər], *s. Soapm:* nègre *m*.

nigrescence [nai'gres(ə)ns], *s. Nat.Hist:* teinte *f* noirâtre; noirceur *f* (de peau, etc.).

nigrescent [nai'gres(ə)nt], *a. Nat.Hist:* nigrescent, noirâtre; qui tire sur le noir.

nigrine ['naigrin], *s. Miner:* nigrine *f*.

nigrite ['naigrait], *s. El:* nigrite *f*.

Nigritia [nai'gri:ʃə]. *Pr.n. Hist:* Nigritie *f*.

Nigritian [nai'gri:ʃ(ə)n], *a. Hist:* nigritique.

nigritude ['nigritju:d], *s.* noirceur *f*.

nigrosine ['naigrəsi:n], *s. Ch:* nigrosine *f*.

nihilism ['nai(h)ilizm], *s. Phil: Pol:* nihilisme *m*.

nihilist ['nai(h)ilist], *s.* nihiliste *mf*.

nihilistic [nai(h)i'listik], *a.* nihiliste.

nihility [nai'(h)iliti], *s.* **1.** néant *m*. **2.** rien *m*, bagatelle *f*.

Nijmegen ['naimeigən]. *Pr.n. Geog:* Nimègue.

nil [nil], *s.* rien *m*; (*on report sheet, etc.*) néant *m*; *Sp:* zéro *m*; **they won three n.,** ils ont gagné par trois (buts) à zéro; **the balance is n.,** le solde est nul.

Nile [nail]. *Pr.n. Geog:* Nil *m*; *Hist:* **the Battle of the N.,** la bataille d'Aboukir; *Ch:* **N. blue,** bleu *m* de Nil.

nilg(h)ai ['nilgai], *s. Z:* nylgaut *m*, nilgau *m*.

nilometer [nai'lɔmitər], *s.* nilomètre *m*, niloscope *m*.

nilometric [nailou'metrik], *a.* nilométrique.

nilometry [nai'lɔmitri], *s.* nilométrie *f*.

nilotic [nai'lɔtik], *a. Geog: Ethn:* nilotique.

nilpotent ['nilpoutənt], *a. Mth:* nilpotent.

nimbed [nimd], *a. Lit:* nimbé.

nimble ['nimbl], *a.* (*of pers., etc.*) agile, leste, preste, alerte; (*of mind, etc.*) délié subtil, agile, prompt; (*of old pers.*) **still n.,** encore ingambe; **n. fingers,** doigts *mpl* de fée; **n. at, in, doing sth.,** agile à faire qch.; **n.(-)fingered,** aux doigts agiles, souples, de fée; agile de ses doigts; **n.(-)footed,** aux pieds agiles, lestes, légers; **n.(-)minded, n.(-)witted,** (i) à l'esprit délié, subtil; (ii) à l'esprit prompt; **he's n. minded,** il saisit vite.

nimbleness ['nimbəlnis], *s.* agilité *f*, souplesse *f* (de membres, etc.); subtilité *f*, vivacité *f* (d'esprit, etc.).

nimbly ['nimbli], *adv.* agilement; avec agilité; lestement, prestement, souplement, légèrement; **to run n. up the stairs,** gravir d'un pas alerte, gravir allègrement, les degrés de l'escalier.

nimbostratus [nimbou'strɑ:təs, -'streitəs], *s. Meteor:* nimbostratus *m inv*.

nimbus, *pl.* **-i, -uses** ['nimbəs, -ai, -əsiz], *s.* **1.** nuage lumineux; gloire *f* (environnant une divinité, etc.). **2.** (*a*) *Art:* nimbe *m*, auréole *f*, gloire; (*b*) *Meteor:* aréole *f* (autour de la lune). **3.** *Meteor:* nimbus *m*; **insulated n.,** haut-pendu *m*, *pl.* hauts-pendus.

nimbused ['nimbəst], *a.* nimbé.

niminy-piminy ['nimini'pimini], *a.* = NAMBY-PAMBY 1.

Nimrod ['nimrɔd]. *Pr.n.m.* (*a*) *B.Hist:* Nemrod; (*b*) *s.* Nemrod; chasseur habile et infatigable.

nincompoop ['niŋkəmpu:p], *s. F:* nigaud, -aude, niais, -aise, niguedouille *mf*, serin, -ine; nicodème *m*.

nine [nain], *num.a.* & *s.* neuf (*m*); *Sp: NAm:* équipe *f* de baseball; **n. times out of ten,** neuf fois sur dix; en général, d'ordinaire; (*of cat, pers., etc.*) **to have n. lives,** avoir l'âme chevillée au corps; *Mth: A:* **to cast out the nines,** faire la preuve par neuf; **two nines, n. twos, are eighteen, n. times two is eighteen,** deux fois neuf, neuf fois deux, font dix-huit; **number n.,** le numéro neuf; *Cards:* **the n. of diamonds,** le neuf de carreau; **(in) chapter n.,** (dans le) chapitre neuf; **in (the year) n. B.C., A.D.,** en l'an *m* neuf av. J.-C., A.D.; *Myth:* **the N. (Muses),** les neuf sœurs *f*; les Muses *f*; *Mus:* **n.-eight (time),** (mesure *f* à) neuf-huit *m*; *Pros:* **n. line stanza,** neuvain *m*; *Golf:* **n. hole course,** parcours *m* de neuf trous; neuf-trous *m inv*; *adv.phr. F: O:* **dressed up to the nines,** habillé(e) à la perfection.

ninefold ['nainfould]. **1.** *a.* (*a*) divisé en neuf parties; (*b*) neuf fois aussi grand. **2.** *adv.* neuf fois autant; **to increase n.,** (se) multiplier par neuf; faire, devenir, neuf fois aussi grand.

nineholes ['nainhoulz], *s. Games: A:* trou-madame *m*, *pl.* trous-madame.

ninepence ['nainpəns], *s.* (somme *f*, *A:* pièce *f*, de) neuf pence *m*.

ninepin ['nainpin], *s.* **1.** *pl.* **ninepins,** (jeu *m* de) quilles *fpl.* **2.** quille; *F:* **to go down like ninepins,** tomber comme autant de quilles, comme des capucins de cartes; *Nau:* **n. block,** marionnette *f.*

nineteen [nain'ti:n], *num.a.* & *s.* dix-neuf (*m*); **she is n.,** elle a dix-neuf ans; **n.** ['nainti:n] **houses,** dix-neuf maisons; *F:* **to talk n. to the dozen,** bavarder comme une pie.

nineteenth [nain'ti:nθ]. **2.** *num.a.* & *s.* dix-neuvième (*mf*); *Golf: F:* **the n. (hole),** le bar (d'un club de golf). **2.** *s.* (*fraction*) dix-neuvième *m.*

nineteenthly [nain'ti:nθli], *adv.* dix-neuvièmement.

ninetieth ['naintiəθ], *num.a.* & *s.* quatre-vingt-dixième.

ninety ['nainti], *num.a.* & *s.* (*a*) quatre-vingt-dix (*m*); **n.-one, n.-nine,** quatre-vingt-onze, quatre-vingt-dix-neuf; **the nineties,** les années entre 1890 et 1900; = la belle époque; **in the nineties,** dans les années quatre-vingt-dix; **he's in his nineties,** il est nonagénaire; *Jur:* **n.-nine years' lease,** bail *m* emphytéotique; (*b*) *Med:* **say n.-nine!** = dites trente-trois!

Nineveh ['ninivə]. *Pr.n. A.Geog:* Ninive *f.*

Ninevite ['ninivait]. *A.Geog:* (*a*) *a.* ninivite; (*b*) *s.* Ninivite *mf.*

ninny ['nini], *s. F: O:* niais, -aise; serin, -ine; nigaud, -aude; niguedouille *mf*; andouille *f.*

ninon ['ni:nɔn], *s. Tex:* crêpe *m* Ninon.

ninth [nainθ]. **1.** *num.a.* & *s.* neuvième (*mf*); **the n. (boy) in the class,** le neuvième (élève) de la classe. **2.** *s.* (*fraction*) neuvième *m.* **3.** *s. Mus:* neuvième *f.*

ninthly ['nainθli], *adv.* neuvièmement, en neuvième lieu.

Niobe ['naiəbi]. *Pr.n.f. Myth:* Niobé.

niobic [nai'oubik], *a. Ch:* (acide, etc.) niobique.

niobite ['naiəbait], *s. Miner:* niobite *f*, colombite *f.*

niobium [nai'oubiəm], *s. Ch:* niobium *m*, colombium *m.*

nip[1] [nip], *s.* **1.** (*a*) pincement *m*, pinçade *f*, pince *f*; **to give s.o. a n.,** pincer qn; faire un pinçon à qn; **tool that has no n.,** outil *m* qui manque de pince; (*b*) étranglement *m*, resserrement *m* (d'une chaîne, etc.); (*c*) prise *f*, enclavement *m* (d'un navire dans les glaces); (*d*) *Min:* étreinte *f*, serrement *m* (d'un filon). **2.** (*a*) *Nau:* portage *m*, étrive *f* (d'une manœuvre); **to freshen the n.,** changer le portage; (*b*) *Mec.E:* **spring n.,** sabot *m* de ressort. **3.** (*a*) morsure *f* (de la gelée, du froid); *Hort:* coup *m* de gelée; (*b*) **the n. of the early morning air,** le froid, le piquant, du petit jour; *F:* **there's a n. in the air,** ça pince; ça pique; le fond de l'air est froid. **4.** *esp. U.S: Geog:* échancrure *f* (du littoral). **5.** *NAm: F:* **to race along n. and tuck with s.o.,** courir manche à manche avec qn.

nip[2] *v.* **(nipped)**

I. *v.tr.* **1.** pincer; **he nipped his finger,** il s'est pincé le doigt; **her arm was nipped black and blue,** elle avait le bras couvert de pinçons; *F:* **he nipped her bottom,** il lui a pincé les fesses; **pincers that n. the iron,** tenaille *f* qui mord le fer; **ship nipped in the ice,** navire pris dans les glaces, enclavé; *Nau:* **to n. a cable,** étriver, étrangler, un cordage. **2.** *Hort:* pincer, éborgner (des bourgeons, etc.); *F:* **to n. (sth.) in the bud,** écraser, tuer, détruire, étouffer, (qch.) dans l'œuf; étouffer, (une rébellion) dans le germe, au berceau; écraser (une révolte) au nid. **3.** (*of cold, frost*) (*a*) pincer, piquer, mordre (la figure, les doigts, etc.); (*b*) brûler (les bourgeons, etc.); (*of sun*) brouir (les bourgeons, etc.); **nipped by the frost,** (*of plant*) brûlé par la gelée; gelé; (*of fruit tree, etc.*) champlé; **the vines will be nipped,** les vignes *f* vont geler.

II. *v.i.* **1.** *Nau:* **the footrope nips round the stay,** la ralingue est étrivée par l'étai, étrive l'étai. **2.** *F:* **just n. across, along, down, over, round, up, to the baker's and get a loaf,** cours vite chez le boulanger, fais donc un saut, file donc, chez le boulanger, prendre un pain; **n. upstairs and fetch me a handkerchief,** monte vite me chercher un mouchoir; **he nipped on to a bus,** il a sauté sur un bus qui passait; **to n. in and out of the traffic,** se faufiler adroitement parmi les voitures.

III. (*compound verbs*) **1. nip in,** (*a*) *v.i. F:* entrer lestement; **to n. in for a moment,** ne faire qu'entrer et sortir; (*b*) *v.tr.* **nipped-in waist,** taille cintrée.

2. nip off. (*a*) *v.i. F:* filer, s'esquiver; (*b*) *v.tr.* enlever, couper (qch.) en le pinçant.

3. nip out. *F:* (*a*) *v.i.* sortir lestement; s'esquiver; (*b*) *v.tr.* sortir prestement (un revolver, etc.).

4. nip up. *F:* (*a*) *v.i.* monter lestement; (*b*) *v.tr.* ramasser vivement (qch.).

nip[3], *s. F:* goutte *f*, petit verre, doigt *m* (de cognac, etc.); (*after coffee*) rincette *f*; **to have, take, a n.,** boire, prendre, une goutte.

nip[4], *v.i.* **(nipped)** *F:* boire la goutte; siroter.

Nip[5], *s. P: Pej:* Jap(onais, -aise) *mf.*

nipper ['nipər], *s.* **1.** *usu.pl.* **(pair of) nippers,** (*a*) pince(s) *f(pl)* (de serrage); pincette(s) *f(pl)*, tenaille(s) *f(pl)*; **spring nippers,** brucelles *f*; (*b*) cisaille(s) *f(pl)*; bec-de-corbeau *m*, *pl.* becs-de-corbeau; **ticket n.,** pince à contrôle; (*c*) *Civ.E:* déclic *m* (de sonnette); (*d*) pince-nez *m inv.* **2.** (*a*) dent incisive, pince (d'un herbivore); (*b*) pince (d'un homard, etc.). **3.** *Nau:* **(rope) n.,** garcette *f* de tournevire. **4.** *F:* gamin, -ine, gosse *mf*; **my little n.,** mon petit bonhomme; mon, ma, mioche.

nippiness ['nipinis], *s.* agilité *f* (d'une personne).

nipping[1] ['nipiŋ], *a.* **1.** (*of tool, etc.*) qui pince; *Bookb:* **n. press,** presse *f* à percussion. **2.** (*of language, tone, etc.*) mordant, caustique; (*of frost, wind, etc.*) coupant, âpre, cuisant.

nipping[2], *s.* **1.** pincement *m* (d'un objet). **2.** *Nau:* (*a*) étrive *f*, étranglement *m* (d'un cordage, etc.); (*b*) enclavement *m* (d'un navire dans les glaces). **3.** *Hort:* pincement, pinçage *m*, éborgnage *m.*

nipple ['nipl], *s.* **1.** (*a*) *Anat:* mamelon *m*; bout *m* de mamelle; bout de sein; (*b*) **n. (shield),** bout de sein (en caoutchouc, etc.); (*c*) tétine *f* (de biberon). **2.** (*a*) (*in glass, metal, on mountain summit, etc.*) mamelon; (*b*) *Sm.a: A:* cheminée *f* (d'un fusil à percussion); (*c*) *Tchn:* raccord *m*, jonction *f* (d'un bec, d'une conduite de vapeur, etc.); jet raccordé (de chalumeau); nipple *m*; *Cy: etc:* douille *f*, écrou *m* (d'un rayon de roue, etc.); **n. key,** clé *f* pour écrou de rayon; *Mec.E:* **grease n.,** graisseur *m*; **hook n.,** raccord à crochet; *Plumb:* **barrel n.,** mamelon double; (*d*) *Bot:* **n. cactus,** mamillaire *f.*

nipplewort ['niplwə:t], *s. Bot:* lampsane *f*; herbe *f* aux mamelles.

Nippon [ni'pɔn]. *Pr.n. Geog:* Nippon *m.*

Nipponese [nipə'ni:z]. *Geog:* (*a*) *a.* nippon; japonais; (*b*) *s.* Nippon, -one; Japonais, -aise.

nippy ['nipi], *a. F:* **1.** (*a*) alerte, dispos, vif; rapide; **tell him to be n. about it,** dis-lui de se grouiller; (*b*) *s.f. A:* **Nippy,** serveuse (dans certains restaurants). **2.** (*a*) (vent, etc.) froid, coupant, âpre; (*b*) (condiment) piquant.

nirvana [niə:'vɑ:nə, niə-], *s. Rel:* nirvâna *m*; **cult of n.,** nirvanisme *m*; *Psy:* **n. principle,** principe *m* de nirvâna.

Nisei [ni'sei], *s. U.S:* Américain, -aine, né(e) d'immigrés japonais.

nisetru [ni:'zetru:], *s. Ich:* (esturgeon *m*) nisetru *m.*

Nish [niʃ]. *Pr.n. Geog:* Nich, Nis.

nisi ['naisai]. *Lt.conj. Jur:* (*of decree, order, etc.*) provisoire; (*of decision*) rendu sous condition; **n. prius court,** tribunal civil.

nit [nit], *s.* **1.** lente *f*; œuf *m* de pou. **2.** *F:* (*pers.*) nigaud, -aude; niguedouille *mf*; andouille *f*; **you silly n.!** espèce d'œuf!

nite [nait], *s. U.S: F:* nuit *f.*

nitery ['naitəri], *s. U.S: F:* boîte *f* de nuit.

nitramine ['naitrəmi:n], *s. Ch:* nitramine *f.*

nitraniline [nai'trænilin], *s. Ch:* nitraniline *f.*

nitrate[1] ['naitreit], *s. Ch:* nitrate *m* (d'argent, d'ammonium, de calcium, etc.); **(sodium) n.,** nitrate de sodium (du Chili); **(potassium) n.,** *O:* **n. of potash,** nitrate de potassium; salpêtre *m*, nitre *m*; **basic n.,** sous-nitrate *m*, *pl.* sous-nitrates; *Agr:* **n. fertilizers,** *F:* **nitrates,** engrais azotés; **exploitation of n. fields,** exploitation *f* des nitrières; *St.Exch:* **n. shares,** *F:* **nitrates,** (valeurs) nitratières.

nitrate[2], *v.tr. Ch:* (*a*) traiter (une matière) avec, de, l'acide nitrique; nitrer; (*b*) traiter (une matière) avec un nitrate; nitrater.

nitrated [nai'treitid], *a.* (*a*) nitré; (*b*) nitraté.

nitratine ['naitrəti:n], *s. Miner:* nitratine *f*, matronite *f.*

nitration [nai'treiʃ(ə)n], *s. Ch:* nitration *f*, nitratage *m.*

nitre ['naitər], *s.* nitre *m*, salpêtre *m*; nitrate *m* de potassium; **cubic n.,** nitre cubique; salpêtre du Chili; nitrate de sodium; **to turn into n.,** (se) nitrifier; **n. works,** nitrière *f.*

nitrebed ['naitəbed], *s.* nitrière *f.*

nitric ['naitrik], *a. Ch:* nitrique; **n. acid,** acide *m* (trioxo)nitrique; *Com:* eau-forte *f*; **n. dioxide,** bioxyde *m*, dioxyde *m*, d'azote; **n. oxide,** oxyde *m* nitrique.

nitridation [naitri'deiʃ(ə)n], *s. Ch:* nitruration *f.*

nitride[1] ['naitraid], *s. Ch:* nitrure *m*, nitruré *m.*

nitride[2], *v.tr.* nitrurer.

nitrided ['naitraidid], *a. Ch: Ind:* nitruré.

nitriding ['naitraidiŋ]. (*a*) *a.* nitrant; (*b*) *s.* nitruration *f.*

nitrification [naitrifi'keiʃ(ə)n], *s.* nitrification *f.*

nitrify ['naitrifai]. (*a*) *v.tr.* nitrifier; (*b*) *v.i.* se nitrifier.

nitril(e) ['naitril], *s. Ch:* nitrile *m.*

nitrite ['naitrait], *s. Ch:* nitrite *m.*

nitroamine [naitrou'æmi:n], *s. Ch:* nitramine *f.*

nitroaniline [naitrou'ænilin], *s. Ch:* nitraniline *f.*

nitrobacter, bacterium, *pl.* **-teria** ['naitroubæktər, -bæk'tiəriəm, -'tiəriə], *s. Biol:* nitrobacter *m*, nitrobactérie *f.*

nitrobarite, *also* **nitrobaryte** [naitrou'bærait], *s. Miner:* nitrobaryte *f.*

nitrobenzene [naitrou'benzi:n], *s. Ch:* nitrobenzène *m*, nitrobenzine *f*; nitrobenzol *m*; (essence *f* de) mirbane *f.*

nitrocalcite [naitrou'kælsait], *s. Miner:* nitrocalcite *f.*

nitrocellulose [naitrou'seljulous], *s. Ch:* nitrocellulose *f*; **n. product,** produit *m* cellulosique; *Aut: etc:* **n. finish,** enduit *m* cellulosique.

nitrocellulosic [naitrouselju'lousik], *a. Ch:* nitrocellulosique.

nitrochloroform [naitrou'klɔrəfɔ:m], *s. Ch:* nitrochloroforme *m.*

nitrocompound ['naitroukɔmpaund], *s. Ch:* dérivé, composé, nitré.

nitroethane [naitrou'i:θein], *s. Ch:* nitro-éthane *m*, *pl.* nitro-éthanes; nitréthane *m.*

nitro-explosive [naitrouiks'plousiv], *s. Exp:* explosif nitraté; poudre nitratée.

nitrogelatin(e) [naitrou'dʒelətin, -ti:n], *s. Exp:* nitrogélatine *f*; gélatine détonante, explosive.

nitrogen ['naitrədʒən], *s. Ch:* azote *m*; **aerial n.,** azote de l'air; **ammonia n.,** azote ammoniacal; **n. cycle,** cycle *m* de l'azote; **n. fixation,** fixation *f* de l'azote; **n. gas,** gaz *m* azote; **n. monoxide,** (i) protoxyde *m* d'azote; oxyde nitreux, azoteux; (ii) oxyde nitrique; **n. peroxide,** bioxyde *m*, dioxyde *m*, d'azote; *Exp:* **n. powder,** poudre azotée; **n. trioxide,** anhydride nitreux, azoteux; **n.-hardened,** nitruré.

nitrogenize [nai'trɔdʒənaiz], *v.tr.* azoter.

nitrogenous [nai'trɔdʒənəs], *a. Ch:* azoté.

nitroglycerin(e) [naitrou'glisəri:n], *s. Exp:* nitroglycérine *f.*

nitrometer [nai'trɔmitər], *s. Ch:* nitromètre *m.*

nitromethane [naitrou'mi:θein], *s. Ch:* nitrométhane *m.*

nitronaphthalene [naitrou'nafθəli:n], *s. Ch:* nitronaphtalène *m.*

nitronium [nai'trouniəm], *s. Ch:* nitronium *m.*

nitroparaffin [naitrou'pærəfin], *s. Ch:* nitroparaffine *f.*

nitrophenol [naitrou'fi:nɔl], *s. Ch:* nitrophénol *m.*

nitrophilous [nai'trɔfiləs], *a. Bot:* nitrophile.

nitrophyte ['naitroufait], *s. Bot:* plante *f* nitrophile.

nitrophytic [naitrou'fitik], *a. Bot:* nitrophile.

nitrosate ['naitrouseit], *s. Ch:* nitrosate *m.*

nitrosation [naitrou'seiʃ(ə)n], *s. Ch:* nitrosation *f.*

nitrosite ['naitrousait], *s. Ch:* nitrosite *f.*

Nitrosomonas [naitrou'sɔmənəs], *s. Bac:* nitrosomonas *m.*

nitrosulphuric [naitrousʌl'fjuərik], *a. Ch:* (acide, etc.) nitrosulfurique.

nitrosyl ['naitrousil], *s. Ch:* nitrosyle *m.*

nitrotoluene [naitrou'tɔljui:n], *s. Ch: Exp:* nitrotoluène *m.*

nitrous ['naitrəs], *a.* nitreux; **n. acid,** acide nitreux; **n. anhydride,** anhydride nitreux, azoteux; **n. oxide,** oxyde nitreux, azoteux; protoxyde *m* d'azote; **to become n.,** se nitrifier.

nitr(ox)yl [nai'trɔksil, 'naitril], *s. Ch:* nitryle *m.*

nitty ['niti], *a.* (*of hair, etc.*) plein de lentes.

nitty-gritty ['niti'griti], *s. F:* (fin) fond, tréfonds *m* (d'une affaire); substratum *m.*

nitwit ['nitwit], *s. F:* idiot, -ote; imbécile *mf*; crétin, -ine.

nitwitted ['nitwitid], *a. F:* idiot; faible d'esprit.

nival ['naiv(ə)l], *a. Geog:* nival, -aux.

nivation [nai'veiʃ(ə)n], *s. Geol:* nivation *f*; **n. cirque,** niche *f* de nivation.

niveous ['ni:viəs], *a.* neigeux; niviforme, nivéen.

nix [niks]. *F:* **1.** *s.* rien *m* (du tout); peau *f* de balle; **to work for n.,** travailler pour des prunes, pour le roi de Prusse. **2.** *int.* pas mèche! rien à faire! vingt-deux! **to keep n.,** faire le pet.

nix(ie) ['niks(i)], *s. Myth:* nixe *f*; nymphe *f* des eaux; ondine *f.*

Nizam [nai'zæm]. *Pr.n.m. Hist:* Nizam (d'Haïderabad).

no[1] [nou], *a., adv.* & *s.*

I. *a.* **1.** nul, pas de, point de, aucun (*with* ne *expressed or understood*); **no hope,** nul espoir; **he has no bread,** il n'a pas de pain; **this fact is of no importance whatever,** ce fait n'a aucune importance; **he made no reply,** il ne fit aucune réponse; il ne répondit pas; **he has no cause for complaint,** il n'a nulle raison de se plaindre; **to have no intention of doing sth.,** n'avoir nulle intention, aucune intention, de faire qch.; **no father was ever more indulgent,** jamais père ne fut plus indulgent; **no words can describe what I felt,** il n'y a pas de mots, les mots me manquent, pour décrire ce que j'ai éprouvé; **he has no talent whatsoever for music,** il n'a absolument aucun talent pour la musique; **he had no business at all to be there,** ce n'était nullement sa place; **he spared no pains to get it,** il n'a rien épargné, il ne s'est pas épargné, pour l'obtenir; il n'y avait pas de soins qu'il n'eût pris pour l'obtenir; **I have no room to write any more,** la place me manque pour vous en écrire davantage; **it's no distance,** ce n'est pas loin; c'est tout près; **no one man could have done it,** aucun homme n'aurait pu le faire à lui seul; **no one example will do,** il ne suffit pas d'un seul exemple; **no two men are alike,** il n'y a pas deux hommes qui se ressemblent; **I am in no way surprised,** je n'en suis aucunement étonné; **details of no interest,** détails *m* de peu d'intérêt, sans intérêt; *Corr:* **letter of no date,** lettre *f* sans date; **there must be no talking about it,** il ne faudra en parler à personne; **no surrender!** on ne se rend pas! **no nonsense!** pas de bêtises! *P.N:* **no admittance (except on business),** (i) entrée interdite, (ii) défense d'entrer dans les chantiers, (iii) *Nau:* défense de monter à bord (sauf pour affaires); **no smoking,** défense de fumer; *Com:* **no sale,** non-vente *f*; **no man's land,** (i) terrains *mpl* vagues; no man's land *m*; (ii) *Mil:* no man's land, zone *f* neutre, terrain contesté; (iii) *Nau:* trou *m* de la drome, parc *m*. **2.** (*a*) peu; ne . . . pas (du tout); **with no pleased air,** d'un air peu content; **it's no easy job,** ce n'est pas une tâche facile; **he was no great walker,** il n'était pas grand marcheur; **it's no small matter,** ce n'est pas une petite affaire; **no such thing,** pas du tout; nullement; (*b*) ne . . . pas; **he's no artist,** il n'est pas artiste; **she's no beauty,** ce n'est pas une beauté; elle n'est pas belle du tout; **he was no general,** il n'avait aucune des qualités d'un général; **he's no friend of mine,** il n'est pas de mes amis, tant s'en faut; **brother or no brother, he has no right to interfere,** qu'il soit mon frère ou non, il n'a pas le droit d'intervenir; **it's no place for me,** ce n'est pas un endroit pour (une personne comme) moi; *Cr: etc:* **no ball,** balle nulle; **to no-ball the bowler,** déclarer nulle la balle servie par le bôleur; (*c*) (*with gerund*) ne . . . pas; **there's no agreeing with him, no pleasing him,** il n'y a pas moyen de s'accorder avec lui, de le satisfaire; **there's no getting out of it,** impossible de s'en tirer; impossible de sortir de là. **3. no one:** (*a*) *see* **1.** (*above*); (*b*) = NOBODY 1; **no one knew anyone else there,** personne ne se connaissait.

II. *adv.* **1.** *A: Lit: & Scot:* **or no,** ou non; **pleasant or no, it's true,** agréable ou non, c'est vrai; **do you want it or no?** le voulez-vous, ou non? **whether or no,** que cela soit ou non; **I may see him tomorrow, but I'll write to you whether or no,** il se peut que je le voie demain, mais je vous écrirai dans tous les cas. **2.** (*with comparatives*) ne . . . plus, ne . . . pas; **I'm no taller, no richer, than him, than he is,** je ne suis pas plus grand, plus riche, que lui; **the patient is no better,** le malade ne va pas mieux; **he's no longer here,** il n'est plus ici; **no sooner had she opened it than . . .,** elle ne l'avait pas plus tôt ouvert que. . . . **3.** non; **have you seen him?—no,** l'avez-vous vu?—non; **no, no, you're wrong!** mais non, mais non, vous vous trompez! (*expressing incredulity, etc.*) **oh, no!** ça alors! **to say no,** (i) dire non; (ii) (*deny*) dire que non; **my answer is no,** je réponds par la négative.

III. *s.* (*pl.* **noes**) non *m inv*; **he won't take no for an answer,** il n'acceptera pas, il n'admettra pas, de refus; (*in voting*) **ayes and noes,** votes *m*, voix *f*, pour et contre; **the noes have it,** les voix contre, les non, l'emportent; le vote est contre, la majorité est défavorable.

no[2] [nou], *s. Japanese Th:* nô *m*.

Noachian [nou'eikiən], *a.* de Noé; du temps de Noé.

Noah ['nouə]. *Pr.n.m. B.Hist:* Noé; **Noah's ark,** l'arche *f* de Noé.

nob[1] [nɔb], *s. P:* tête *f*, coco *m*, caboche *f*; *Cards:* (*at cribbage*) **one for his n.,** point marqué par le joueur qui a le valet de la couleur retournée.

nob[2], *s. P:* aristo *m*; gommeux *m*; **the nobs,** les rupins *m*.

nobble ['nɔbl], *v.tr. P:* **1.** *Turf:* (i) doper, donner un narcotique à (un cheval), (ii) écloper (un cheval) (avant la course). **2.** soudoyer, acheter (qn, un journal, etc.); **to n. the votes of . . .,** capter les suffrages de . . . . **3.** faucher, filouter, voler, qch. **4.** (*a*) pincer, choper, piger (un voleur); (*b*) attraper (qn) (au passage).

nobby ['nɔbi], *a. P: O:* chic, élégant.

nobelium [nou'bi:liəm], *s. Ch:* nobélium *m*.

nobiliary [nou'biliəri], *a.* (rang, etc.) nobiliaire; **the n. particle,** la particule nobiliaire.

nobility [nou'biliti], *s.* **1.** noblesse *f* (de rang, de cœur, etc.); *Hist:* **patent of n.,** lettres *fpl* d'anoblissement. **2.** *coll.* noblesse; (la classe des) nobles *m*; *A:* **the n. and gentry,** la haute et la petite noblesse; **the old n.,** la noblesse d'épée; **she wanted to marry into the n.,** elle voulait se marier dans la noblesse.

noble ['noubl]. **1.** *a.* (*a*) (naissance, personne, etc.) noble; **his n. birth on his mother's side,** sa (haute) noblesse par sa mère; **n. family,** famille *f* noble; **to be of n. descent, of n. birth,** être de grande naissance, de naissance noble; être noble de race; (*b*) (sentiment, etc.) noble, sublime, relevé, généreux, grand; **n. soul,** grande âme; (*c*) (*of monument, proportions, etc.*) empreint de grandeur; superbe, admirable, grandiose; **to do things on a n. scale,** faire les choses en grand, en prince; faire grandement les choses; **a n. mountain,** une montagne altière, magnifique, imposante; **n. building,** édifice aux dimensions impressionnantes, empreint de grandeur; **n. wine,** grand vin; (*d*) (*of metals, stones*) noble, précieux; (*e*) *Ch:* **n. gas,** gaz *m* rare; (*f*) *Ven:* (*of hawk*) de haute volerie; (faucon) haut voleur. **2.** *s.* noble *m*, aristocrate *mf*; gentilhomme *m*, *pl.* gentilshommes; **a newly created n.,** un anobli (de date récente).

nobleman, *pl.* **-men** ['noub(ə)lmən], *s.m.* noble, aristocrate; gentilhomme, *pl.* gentilshommes.

nobleminded ['noub(ə)l'maindid], *a.* (*of pers.*) magnanime, généreux; aux nobles sentiments; à l'âme noble, haute.

noblemindedness ['noub(ə)l'maindidnis], *s.* magnanimité *f*, générosité *f*; noblesse *f* d'âme; noblesse de sentiments.

nobleness ['noub(ə)lnis], *s.* **1.** noblesse *f* (de naissance, etc.). **2.** (*a*) noblesse, magnanimité *f*, générosité *f* (d'esprit, d'une action, etc.); **n. of mind,** grandeur *f* d'âme; (*b*) proportions *f* superbes, admirables (d'une statue, d'un cheval, etc.); dimensions impressionnantes (d'un édifice, etc.).

noblewoman, *pl.* **-women** ['noub(ə)lwumən, -wimin], *s.f.* (femme) noble; aristocrate.

nobly ['noubli], *adv.* **1.** noblement, d'une manière noble; **n. born,** noble de naissance. **2.** magnifiquement, superbement (proportionné, etc.); généreusement; **you did n.!** vous avez été magnifique!

nobody ['noubədi]. **1.** *pron.* (*a*) personne *m*, nul *m*, aucun *m* (*with* ne *expressed or understood*); **I spoke to n.,** je n'ai parlé à personne; **n. spoke to me,** personne ne m'a parlé; **n. has come,** personne n'est venu; **who's there?—n.,** qui est là?—personne; **n. knows it,** personne, nul, ne le sait; **n. knows it better (than him, than he does),** il le sait aussi bien, mieux, que personne; **n. is more aware than he is that . . .,** il sait mieux que personne que . . .; **n. is better placed than we are to . . .,** nul n'est mieux placé que nous pour . . .; **n. is perfect,** nul n'est parfait; **n. is more expert at it than him, than he is,** il s'y connaît comme personne, comme pas un; **n. is to leave,** que personne ne sorte; **there's n. killed,** il n'y a personne de mort; **n. has been injured,** il n'y a personne de blessé; **there is n. better informed,** il n'y a personne de mieux renseigné; **n. was more surprised than me, than I was,** cela m'a étonné plus que personne; **did n. among you notice anything?** personne de vous, d'entre vous, n'a rien remarqué? **n. is happier than me, than I am,** il n'y a personne de plus heureux que moi; **n. is in his, their, place,** personne n'est à sa place; **n. could find his, their, place,** personne n'arrivait à trouver sa place; **I shall marry my cousin or n.,** j'épouserai ma cousine ou personne; **there was n. else on board,** personne (d')autre n'était à bord; **n. who was there heard anything,** aucun de ceux qui étaient là, personne parmi tous ceux qui étaient là, n'a rien entendu; **there was n. there, n. about,** il n'y avait personne (là); l'endroit était désert; *F:* **who's broken it?—Mr N.,** qui est-ce qui l'a cassé?—Monsieur Personne; (*b*) **I knew him when he was n.,** j'ai été en relations avec lui alors qu'il était encore inconnu; **before that success he was n.,** avant ce succès c'était un inconnu. **2.** *s.* (*pers.*) nullité *f*, zéro *m*; personne *f* de rien (du tout); homme *m* d'hier; **he's a little, a mere, n.,** c'est un petit rien-du-tout; c'est un homme de rien; **they're (mere) nobodies,** ce sont des gens *m* de rien; **to treat s.o. as a mere n.,** traiter qn comme le dernier venu; *F:* **there was only a handful of nobodies,** il n'y avait que trois pelés et un tondu, que trois teigneux et un pelé.

nock[1] [nɔk], *s.* encoche *f*, coche *f* (d'une flèche, de l'arc).

nock[2], *v.tr.* **1.** encocher (une flèche); tailler les coches de (l'arc). **2.** ajuster (la flèche).

nock[3], *s. Nau:* empointure *f* (d'une voile carrée).

noctambulant [nɔk'tæmbjulənt], *a.* **1.** somnambule. **2.** noctambule.

noctambulism [nɔk'tæmbjulizm], *s.* **1.** somnambulisme *m*. **2.** noctambulisme *m*.

noctambulist [nɔk'tæmbjulist], *s.* **1.** somnambule *mf*. **2.** noctambule *mf*.

noctambulous [nɔk'tæmbjuləs], *a.* = NOCTAMBULANT.

noctiflorous [nɔkti'flɔ:rəs], *a. Bot:* noctiflore.

Noctilionidae [nɔktili:'ɔnidi:], *s.pl. Z:* noctilionidés *m*.

noctiluca, *pl.* **-cas, -cae** [nɔkti'lju:kə, -kəz, -si:], *s. Prot:* noctiluque *f*.

noctua ['nɔktjuə], **noctuid** ['nɔktjuid], *s. Ent:* noctuelle *f*.

Noctuidae [nɔk'tju:idi:], *s.pl. Ent:* noctuidés *m*.

noctule ['nɔktju:l], *s. Z:* **n. (bat),** noctule *f*.

nocturn ['nɔktə:n], *s. R.C.Ch:* nocturne *m*.

nocturnal [nɔk'tə:n(ə)l]. **1.** *a.* nocturne. **2.** *s.pl. Orn:* **nocturnals,** nocturnes *m*.

nocturne ['nɔktə:n], *s.* **1.** *Mus:* nocturne *m*. **2.** *Art:* effet *m* de nuit.

nocuous ['nɔkjuəs], *a.* nocif, nuisible.

nod[1] [nɔd], *s.* **1.** (*a*) inclination *f* de la tête; signe *m* d'assentiment, signe de tête affirmatif; **to give a n. of assent,** donner, faire, un signe de consentement; **to answer with a n.,** répondre d'une inclination, d'un mouvement, de tête; *F:* **on the n.,** (i) *Com:* à crédit; (ii) *Parl: etc:* sans débats; (*b*) signe de tête (impératif); **to be at s.o.'s n.,** être assujetti aux moindres caprices de qn. **2.** (*a*) (*greeting*) signe de la tête; **he gave me a n.,** il m'a fait un petit signe de la tête; (*b*) **after a n. in the direction of France,** après un coup de chapeau vers la France, après quelques remarques aimables envers la France. **3.** penchement *m* de tête (dû au sommeil); **the land of N.,** le pays des songes; **to go to the land of N.,** s'endormir; partir pour le pays des songes.

nod[2], *v.tr.* & *i.* (**nodded**) **1. to n. (one's head),** faire un signe de tête (de haut en bas); incliner la tête; **to n. to s.o.,** faire un signe, une inclination, de tête à qn; **to n. assent, approval, to n. yes,** faire signe que oui; faire un signe de consentement; consentir d'un signe de tête; **I nodded to him and he opened another bottle,** sur mon signe (affirmatif) il a débouché encore une bouteille. **2.** dodeliner (de) la tête; somnoler, sommeiller; **the old man's head was nodding,** le vieillard dodelinait de la tête; *F:* **to n. off,** s'endormir; piquer un roupillon; **(even) Homer sometimes nods,** Homère lui-même se trompe quelquefois; **there's hardly an author who isn't caught nodding sometimes,** il n'y a guère d'auteur qui ne sommeille, qui ne se trompe, quelquefois, qui ne soit quelquefois sujet à des inadvertances. **3.** (*a*) (*of plumes, etc.*) ballotter, danser; **plumes nodding in the wind,** panaches agités par le vent; (*b*) (*of tree, etc.*) pencher; **trees with heads nodding in different directions,** arbres à têtes inclinées chacune de son côté; *A:* (*of building, empire, etc.*) **to n. to its fall,** pencher vers sa ruine; menacer ruine.

nodal ['noud(ə)l], *a. Opt: Ph:* nodal, -aux; **n. points,** points nodaux.

nodding[1] ['nɔdiŋ], *a.* **1.** (vieillard, etc.) à la tête dodelinante, branlante; somnolent; (fleur, panache) qui se balance (au vent, etc.). **2.** *O:* (édifice, etc.) chancelant, qui menace ruine. **3.** *Nat.Hist:* (*of leaf, horn, etc.*) penché, incliné.

nodding[2], *s.* **1.** inclination *f* de tête; **to have a n. acquaintance with s.o.,** connaître qn vaguement; **I have a n. acquaintance with him,** nous nous saluons; **to have a n. acquaintance with Greek,** avoir une légère teinture de grec. **2.** (*from drowsiness, old age, etc.*) dodelinement *m* (de la tête). **3.** balancement *m* (d'un panache, des fleurs, etc.).

noddle ['nɔdl], *s. F:* tête *f*, boule *f*, caboche *f*, ciboulot *m*, citron *m*; **to get sth. into one's n.,** (i) se mettre qch. dans la tête, dans la caboche; (ii) s'enticher (d'une idée).

noddy ['nɔdi], *s.* **1.** *F: O:* niais, -aise; nigaud, -aude; niguedouille *mf*. **2.** *Orn:* noddi (niais).

node [noud], *s.* **1.** *Astr: Mth: Ph:* nœud *m*, point nodal (d'une orbite d'astre, d'une courbe, d'une onde, etc.); **moon's n.,** point nodal de la lune; *El: W.Tel:* (*in circuit, aerial*) **potential n.,** nœud de potentiel, de tension. **2.** (*a*) *Bot:* nœud, nodosité *f* (d'un tronc d'arbre, etc.); nœud, articulation *f*, bracelet *m* (des graminées); (*b*) *Med:* nœud, nodosité, nodus *m*, nodule *m*; **lymph n.,** ganglion *m* lymphatique.

nodose [nou'dous], *a.* noueux.

nodosity [nou'dɔsiti], *s.* **1.** nodosité *f*; état noueux. **2.** nodosité, nœud *m*.

nodular ['nɔdjulər], *a. Geol: Med: etc:* (concrétion, etc.) nodulaire.

nodule ['nɔdju:l], *s.* **1.** (*a*) *Geol:* nodule *m*, rognon *m*; **flint n.,** rognon de silex; *Miner:* (*in greensand*) **n. of phosphate of lime,** coquin *m*; (*b*) *Cer:* géode *f*, druse *f* (dans la porcelaine). **2.** *Med: Bot:* nodule, petite nodosité.

noduled ['nɔdju:ld], *a.* nodulaire, noduleux; couvert de nœuds.

nodulose ['nɔdjulous], **nodulous** ['nɔdjuləs], *a.* noduleux.

nodus, *pl.* **-i** ['noudəs, -ai], *s. Lit:* nœud *m* (de la question); point *m* difficile.

noegenesis [noui'dʒenisis], *s. Psy:* noégénèse, noogénèse, nougénèse *f*.

Noël. 1. *s.* [nou'el], Noël *m*. **2.** *Pr.n.m.* ['nouəl], Noël.

noesis [nou'i:sis], *s. Phil:* noèse *f*.

noetic [nou'etik]. **1.** *a.* (*of truth, activity, etc.*) intellectuel. **2.** *s.* (*also* **noetics,** *s.pl.*) science *f* de l'intellect, de l'intelligence.

nog[1] [nɔg], *s.* **1.** *Const:* cheville *f* de bois. **2.** (*on tree*) chicot *m*. **3.** *pl. Min:* **nogs,** soliveaux de soutènement (empilés à plat).

nog[2], *v.tr.* **1.** *Const:* cheviller (un joint, etc.). **2.** *Const: Min:* hourder (une cloison, un mur).

nog[3], *s.* (*a*) *A:* bière forte; (*b*) = lait *m* de poule.

nogaku ['nougɑ:ku:], *s. Japanese Th:* nô *m*.

nogged [nɔgd], *a.* (*of wall, etc.*) hourdé.

noggin ['nɔgin], *s.* **1.** (*a*) (petit) pot; (*b*) son contenu. **2.** *A.Meas:* quart *m* de pinte; deux canons *m*. **3.** *F:* tête *f*, caboche *f*.

nogging ['nɔgiŋ], *s. Const:* hourdage *m*, hourdis *m*; remplissage *m* (en briques); **n. piece,** moise *f* (d'une cloison).

no-go ['nou'gou], *attrib.a. esp. Town P:* **no-go areas,** régions où l'autorité du gouvernement est impuissante, n'est pas reconnue.

no-good ['nougud]. *F:* (*a*) *a.* bon à rien; (*b*) *s.* vaurien, -ienne.

noh [nou], *s. Japanese Th:* nô *m*.

nohow ['nouhau], *adv. P:* **1.** aucunement, nullement, en aucune façon. **2.** (être, se sentir, avoir l'air) mal à l'aise, mal en train; **I feel all n.,** je ne me sens pas dans mon assiette, je suis tout patraque; (*of thg*) **all n.,** dérangé, mal fait, mal entretenu.

noil(s) [nɔil(z)], *s.* (*pl.*) *Tex:* blousse *f*.

noise[1] [nɔiz], *s.* **1.** bruit *m*, tapage *m*, vacarme *m*, fracas *m*; **the n. of cars hooting,** le tintamarre des avertisseurs; **n. of cracking branches,** bruit de branches qui se cassent; **n. of tramping,** bruit de pas marqués, lourds; **n. fit to wake the dead,** bruit à tout casser, à tout rompre; **n. abatement campaign,** campagne *f*, lutte *f*, contre le bruit; **to make a n.,** (i) faire du bruit, du vacarme, du tapage; (ii) (*of horse*) corner; *F:* **to make a n. in the world,** faire du bruit dans le monde; faire parler de soi; **to make a lot of n. about a novel,** faire du tintamarre autour d'un roman; **don't make a n.!** ne faites pas de bruit! (*to child*) **there's nothing to make a n. about,** il n'y a pas de quoi pleurer; *F:* **hold your n.!** taisez-vous! tais-toi! *F:* **the big n.,** le grand manitou (de l'entreprise); **a big n.,** un gros bonnet; une grosse légume. **2.** (*a*) bruit; son *m*; **clicking n.,** cliquetis *m*; **hammering n.,** bruit de marteau, martèlement *m*, martellement *m*; **tinkling n.,** tintement *m*; **the n. of the bells, of a detonation,** le son des cloches, le bruit d'une détonation; **to have noises in one's ears,** avoir des bourdonnements dans les oreilles; (*b*) *W.Tel: Elcs: etc:* bruit; parasite(s) *m*(*pl*); **background n.,** bruit de fond; **buzzing n.,** bourdonnement *m*, ronflement *m* (d'un appareil, d'une machine, etc.); **cavitation n.,** bruit de cavitation; **circuit n., line n.,** bruit de circuit, de ligne; (**crackling, sizzling**) **n.,** (bruit de) friture *f*; (*of record player*) **needle n., record n., surface n.,** bruit de surface; bruissement *m* d'aiguille; **parasitic, spurious, n.,** bruit(s) parasite(s); **random n.,** bruit complexe, aléatoire; **room n.,** bruit ambiant, bruit de salle; **white n.,** bruit blanc; **n. analyser,** analyseur *m* de bruit; **n. cone,** cône *m* de bruit; **n. eliminator, n. suppressor,** (i) *Elcs: W.Tel:* (dispositif *m*) antiparasite *m*; (ii) *Mec.E:* silencieux *m inv*; **n. factor,** facteur *m* de bruit; **n. filter,** filtre *m* antiparasite; **n. generator,** générateur *m* de bruit; **n. level,** niveau *m* de bruit; **n. contour,** courbe *f* de niveau de bruit; **n. limiter,** (i) *Ac:* (appareil, dispositif) atténuateur *m*, limiteur *m*, de bruit; (ii) *Elcs: W.Tel:* écrêteur *m* de bruit; **n. maker,** (i) *Ac:* (appareil, dispositif) émetteur *m* de bruit; bruiteur *m*; (ii) *Th: etc:* instrument *m*, dispositif, de bruitage; **n. silencer,** étouffeur *m* de bruit; silencieux; **n. reduction,** réduction *f* des bruits; **flicker n.,** bruit de scintillation; **n.-free,** (i) *Elcs: W.Tel:* déparasité; (ii) *Mec.E:* silencieux; **n.-proof,** insonorisé; **n.-reducing,** atténuateur, -trice, réducteur, -trice, de bruit, de parasites; (*c*) *Ph:* **n. fatigue,** fatigue des matériaux due aux vibrations acoustiques; (*d*) *Th: Cin: T.V:* (*pers.*) **noises off,** bruiteur *m*, bruitiste *m*.

noise[2], *v.tr. A:* **to n. sth. abroad,** ébruiter, divulguer, publier (un scandale, une nouvelle, etc.); **it was noised abroad that . . .,** le bruit s'est répandu que . . .

noiseless ['nɔizlis], *a.* sans bruit; (appareil, mouvement) silencieux; **with n. tread,** à pas feutrés.

noiselessly ['nɔizlisli], *adv.* silencieusement, en silence; sans bruit.

noiselessness ['nɔizlisnis], *s.* silence *m*; absence *f* de bruit; **n. of a machine,** marche silencieuse, silence de fonctionnement, d'une machine.

noisily ['nɔizili], *adv.* bruyamment, tapageusement; avec grand bruit.

noisiness ['nɔizinis], *s.* caractère bruyant, caractère tapageur (de qn, qch.); turbulence *f* (des enfants, etc.); **the n. of the streets,** le tintamarre des rues.

noisome ['nɔisəm], *a.* **1.** (*of plant, germ, etc.*) nocif, nuisible. **2.** (*of smell, water, etc.*) puant, fétide, infect, méphitique. **3. n. task,** tâche *f* désagréable, repoussante, répugnante.

noisomeness ['nɔisəmnis], *s.* **1.** nocivité *f* (d'une plante, etc.). **2.** puanteur *f*, fétidité *f*, infection *f*. **3.** caractère désagréable, répugnant (d'un travail).

noisy ['nɔizi], *a.* **1.** bruyant, tapageur; tintamarresque; (enfant) turbulent; (*of crowd, street*) tumultueux; (*of pers.*) **to be n.,** faire du bruit, du tapage, du vacarme; **the street was very n.,** il y avait beaucoup de bruit dans la rue; *Jur:* **premises for carrying on n. or noxious trades,** établissements *m* incommodes. **2.** (*of colours, etc.*) voyant, criard.

nolens volens ['noulenz'voulenz]. *Lt.phr.* bon gré, mal gré; de gré ou de force.

nolle prosequi ['nɔliprɔ'sekwai]. *Lt.phr. Jur:* minute *f* de désistement (des poursuites); abandon *m* de poursuites.

no-load ['nou'loud], *attrib.a. Ind: Mec.E:* (marche *f*) à vide; *El:* **no-l. current,** courant *m* à vide; **no-l. release,** (i) déclenchement *m* à vide; (ii) disjoncteur *m*, interrupteur *m*, à vide, à zéro.

noma ['noumə], *s. Med:* noma *f*.

nomad ['noumæd], *a. & s.* nomade (*mf*).

nomadic [nou'mædik], *a.* nomade.

nomadism ['noumædizm], *s.* nomadisme *m*.

nomadization [noumædai'zeiʃ(ə)n], *s.* nomadisation *f*.

nomadize ['noumædaiz]. (*a*) *v.tr.* nomadiser; (*b*) *v.i.* nomadiser; vivre en nomade(s).

nomarch ['nɔmɑːk], *s.* (*a*) *A.Hist:* (*in Egypt*) nomarque *m*; (*b*) *Adm:* (*in Greece*) nomarque *m*.

nomarchy ['nɔmɑki], *s. Adm:* (*in Greece*) nomarchie *f*, nome *m*.

nombril ['nɔmbril], *s. Her:* nombril *m* (de l'écu).

nom de plume ['nɔmdə'pluːm], (*pl.* **noms de plume**), *s.* pseudonyme *m* (d'un auteur).

nome [noum], *s.* (*a*) *A.Hist:* (*in Egypt*) nome *m*; (*b*) *Adm:* (*in Greece*) nome, nomarchie *f*.

nomenclature [nə'meŋklətjər], *s.* nomenclature *f*.

nominal ['nɔmin(ə)l], *a.* **1.** (*a*) nominal, -aux; **n. authority,** autorité nominale; **to be the n. head,** n'être chef que de nom; **n. rent,** loyer insignifiant, payable pour la forme; (*b*) *Book-k:* **n. accounts,** comptes *m* de choses; **n. ledger,** grand livre général; *Fin:* **n. capital,** capital nominal; *St.Exch:* **n. market,** marché insignifiant, presque nul; **n. price,** prix fictif; **n. value,** valeur nominale; (*c*) *Elcs:* **n. frequency,** fréquence nominale; **n. line width,** inverse *m* du nombre de lignes par unité de longueur; **n. voltage,** tension nominale; *El: Mec:* **n. load,** charge nominale; **n. output, n. power, n. rating,** puissance nominale; **n. size,** cote nominale; (*d*) *Psy:* **n. scale,** échelle nominale. **2.** nominatif; **n. list,** liste nominative, état nominatif; *Mil: etc:* **n. roll,** contrôle, état, nominatif.

nominalism ['nɔminəlizm], *s. Phil:* nominalisme *m*.

nominalist ['nɔminəlist], *s. Phil:* nominaliste *m*.

nominalistic [nɔminə'listik], *a. Phil:* nominaliste.

nominalization [nɔminəlai'zeiʃ(ə)n], *s. Ling:* nominalisation *f*.

nominalize ['nɔminəlaiz], *v.tr. Ling:* nominaliser.

nominally ['nɔmin(ə)li], *adv.* **1.** nominalement; de nom; **he's only n. head,** il n'est chef que de nom. **2.** nommément, nominativement.

nominate ['nɔmineit], *v.tr.* **1.** *occ.* (*a*) nommer (qn, qch.); désigner (qn, qch.) par son nom; (*b*) fixer (un lieu de rendez-vous, une date, etc.). **2.** (*a*) nommer, choisir, désigner (qn); **to n. s.o. to, for, a post,** nommer qn à un emploi; (*b*) proposer, présenter (un candidat); (*c*) présenter la candidature de qn.

nomination [nɔmi'neiʃ(ə)n], *s.* **1.** (*a*) nomination *f* (de qn à un emploi, etc.); (*b*) droit *m* de nommer qn à un poste, de désigner qn pour un poste; (*c*) *Pol:* investiture *f* (d'un candidat). **2.** présentation *f* (d'un candidat).

nominatival [nɔminə'taiv(ə)l], *a. Gram:* nominatif.

nominative ['nɔminətiv]. **1.** *Gram:* (*a*) *a. & s.* nominatif (*m*); **noun in the n. (case),** substantif *m* au nominatif, au cas sujet; **n. of address,** vocatif *m*; **n. absolute,** nominatif absolu; (*b*) *s.* sujet *m* (de la phrase). **2.** *a.* (fonctionnaire, candidat, membre) désigné, nommé; **the n. and elective members,** les membres désignés et les membres élus.

nominator ['nɔmineitər], *s.* présentateur, -trice (d'un candidat).

nominee [nɔmi'niː], *s.* **1.** (*for an annuity, etc.*) personne dénommée; *Ecc: A:* (*for a living*) nominataire *m*. **2.** (*for a post*) personne nommée, désignée; candidat, -ate, désigné, -e, choisi, -e.

nomogram, -graph ['nɔməgræm, -græf], *s. Mth:* nomogramme *m*, nomographie *f*.

nomographer [nɔ'mɔgrəfər], *s.* nomographe *m*.

nomographical [nɔmə'græfik(ə)l], *a. Mth:* (table) nomographique.

nomography [nɔ'mɔgrəfi], *s.* nomographie *f*.

nomos ['nɔmɔs], *s.* = NOME.

nomothete ['nɔmouθiːt], *s. Gr.Hist:* nomothète *m*.

non- [nɔn], *pref.* non-; in-; sans; peu.

non(-)ability ['nɔnə'biliti], *s.* incapacité *f*.

non(-)absorbent ['nɔnəb'sɔːbənt], *a.* (matériel, etc.) non perméable.

non(-)acceptance ['nɔnək'septəns], *s. Com: etc:* non-acceptation *f*, inacceptation *f*, refus *m* d'acceptation (d'un effet, d'une traite); **draft returned under protest for n.,** traite protestée faute d'acceptation.

non(-)access [nɔn'ækses], *s. Jur:* **to plead n.,** plaider l'impossibilité légale de cohabitation (dans un déni de paternité).

non(-)accomplishment [nɔnə'kɔmpliʃmənt, -'kʌm-], *s.* inaccomplissement *m*.

non(-)actinic [nɔnæk'tinik], *a. Ph: Ch:* inactinique.

non(-)activity [nɔnæk'tiviti], *s.* non-activité *f*.

non(-)adjustable [nɔnə'dʒʌstəbl], **non(-)adjusting** [nɔnə'dʒʌstiŋ], *a.* non réglable.

nonage ['noundiʒ], *s.* **1.** minorité *f*; **to be still in one's n.,** être encore mineur; n'avoir pas encore atteint sa majorité. **2.** immaturité *f*, enfance *f* (d'une nation, etc.).

nonagenarian [nounədʒi'nɛəriən], *a. & s.* nonagénaire (*mf*).

nonagesimal [nounə'dʒesim(ə)l], *a. & s. Astr:* **the n. (degree, point),** le nonagésime (degré).

non(-)aggression [nɔnə'greʃ(ə)n], *s.* non-agression *f*; **n.(-)a. pact,** pacte *m* de non-agression.

nonagon ['nɔnəgɔn], *s. Mth:* nonagone *m*.

non(-)alcoholic [nɔnælkə'hɔlik], *a.* (*of drinks*) non alcoolisé.

non(-)aligned [nɔnə'laind], *a. Pol:* non aligné; non engagé; **the n.(-)a. countries,** les (pays) non alignés.

non(-)alignment [nɔnə'lainmənt], *s. Pol:* non-alignement *m*; non-engagement *m*; neutralisme *m*.

nonane ['nounein], *s. Ch:* nonan(e) *m*.

non(-)appearance [nɔnə'piərəns], *s. Jur: etc:* défaut *m* (de comparution).

non(-)arcing [nɔn'ɑːkiŋ], *a. El:* (fusible) antiarc(s), brise-arcs *inv*; **n.(-)a. gear,** antiarcs *mpl*.

non(-)arrival [nɔnə'raiv(ə)l], *s.* non-arrivée *f*.

nonary ['nounəri], *s. Mth:* **1.** *a.* (système de numération) ayant neuf comme base. **2.** *s.* groupe *m* de neuf.

non(-)assessable [nɔnə'sesəbl], *a. Adm:* (revenu, etc.) non imposable.

non(-)assessment [nɔnə'sesmənt], *s. Adm:* non-imposition *f* (d'un revenu, etc.).

non(-)assistance [nɔnə'sistəns], *s. Jur:* non-assistance *f*.

non(-)attendance [nɔnə'tendəns], *s.* absence *f*.

non(-)availability [nɔnəveilə'biliti], *s.* non-disponibilité *f*.

non(-)available [nɔnə'veiləbl], *a.* non-disponible.

non(-)axial [nɔn'æksiəl], *a. Mec.E: etc:* décalé, désaxé.

non(-)believer [nɔnbi'liːvər], *s.* incroyant, -ante.

non(-)belligerency [nɔnbi'lidʒər(ə)nsi], *s.* non-belligérence *f*.

non(-)belligerent [nɔnbi'lidʒər(ə)nt], *a. & s.* non-belligérant, -ante.

non(-)beneficed [nɔn'benifist], *a.* (prêtre) habitué.

non(-)breeding [nɔn'briːdiŋ], *a.* **1.** *Physiol:* stérile. **2.** *Atom.Ph:* non régénérateur, -trice; **n.(-)b. material,** matière non régénératrice.

nonce [nɔns], *s.* **for the n.,** pour la circonstance; pour l'occasion, pour le coup; **n. word,** mot créé, forgé, pour l'occasion; mot de circonstance.

nonchalance ['nɔnʃələns], *s.* nonchalance *f*, indifférence *f*; **out of n.,** par nonchalance.

nonchalant ['nɔnʃələnt], *a.* nonchalant; indifférent.

nonchalantly ['nɔnʃələntli], *adv.* nonchalamment; avec nonchalance; d'un air négligent, indifférent.

non(-)claim ['nɔn'kleim], *s. Jur:* défaut *m* de porter plainte dans les délais.

non(-)clogging [nɔn'klɔgiŋ], *a.* **1.** (ajutage, etc.) imbouchable. **2.** (huile) qui n'encrasse pas.

non(-)collegiate [nɔnkə'liːdʒiit]. **1.** *a. & s.* (étudiant, -ante, d'université) n'appartenant à aucun collège. **2.** *a.* (université) qui n'est pas divisée en collèges.

non-com ['nɔn'kɔm], *s. Mil: F: A:* sous-officier *m*; gradé *m*; sous-off *m*, *pl.* sous-offs.

non(-)combattant [nɔn'kɔmbətənt], *a. & s. Mil:* non-combattant (*m*).

non(-)commissioned ['nɔnkə'miʃ(ə)nd], *a. Mil:* sans brevet; **n.(-)c. officer,** sous-officier *m*; gradé *m*.

noncommittal [nɔnkə'mit(ə)l], *a.* (*of answer, etc.*) qui n'engage à rien; diplomatique; (*in answering*) **to be n.,** observer une sage, une prudente, réserve; être très réservé; **I'll be quite n.,** je ne m'engagerai à rien.

non(-)communicant [nɔnkə'mjuːnikənt], *s. Ecc:* non-communicant, -ante.

non(-)completion [nɔnkəm'pliːʃ(ə)n], *s.* non-achèvement *m* (d'un travail); non-exécution *f* (d'un contrat).

non(-)compliance [nɔnkəm'plaiəns], *s.* refus *m* (de consentement); insoumission *f*; inobservation *f* (d'un contrat souscrit); **n.(-)c. with an order,** résistance *f*, refus d'obéissance, à un ordre.

non(-)compressible [nɔnkəm'presibl], *a.* incompressible.

non(-)condensing [nɔnkən'densiŋ], *a.* (machine) sans condensation, à échappement libre.

non(-)conductibility [nɔnkəndʌkti'biliti], *s. Ph:* défaut *m* de conductibilité; mauvaise conductibilité.

non(-)conducting [nɔnkən'dʌktiŋ], **non(-)conductive** ['nɔnkən'dʌktiv], *a. Ph:* non-conducteur, -trice; mauvais conducteur; *El:* inconducteur, -trice; (*with heat*) calorifuge.

non(-)conductor [nɔnkən'dʌktər], *s. Ph:* non-conducteur *m*, mauvais conducteur; *El:* inconducteur; (*of heat*) calorifuge *m*.

nonconformist [nɔnkən'fɔːmist], *a. & s.* non-conformiste (*mf*); dissident, -ente.

nonconformity [nɔnkən'fɔːmiti], *s.* non-conformité *f.*

non(-)content [nɔnkən'tent], *s. Parl:* voix *f* contre (à la Chambre des Lords).

non(-)contradiction [nɔnkɔntrə'dikʃ(ə)n], *s. Phil:* non-contradiction *f.*

non(-)contributory [nɔnkən'tribjut(ə)ri], *a.* (caisse de retraite, etc.) sans versements de la part des bénéficiaires.

non(-)corrosive [nɔnkə'rousiv], *a.* **1.** non corrosif. **2.** inaltérable, inoxydable, inattaquable.

non(-)cumulative [nɔn'kjuːmjulətiv], *a. Fin:* non cumulatif; **n.(-)c. shares,** actions non cumulatives.

non(-)dazzle ['nɔn'dæzl], *a.* anti-éblouissant; *Aut:* **n.-d. headlight,** (i) phare anti-éblouissant; (ii) phare-code *m*, *pl.* phares-codes.

non(-)delivery [nɔndi'livəri], *s.* non-livraison *f*; défaut *m* de livraison; non-réception *f* (de marchandises, etc.); non-remise *f* (d'une lettre).

nondescript ['nɔndiskript], *a. & s.* (personne, chose) indéfinissable, inclassable; difficile à décrire, à classer; quelconque; **n. costume,** costume *m* hétéroclite.

non(-)detachable [nɔndi'tætʃəbl], *a.* non démontable; (pièce) inamovible.

non(-)directional [nɔndə'rekʃən(ə)l, -di-], *a. Elcs: W.Tel:* non directionnel; **n.(-)d. aerial, antenna,** antenne non directionnelle; **n.(-)d. radio beacon,** radiophare non directionnel.

non(-)directive [nɔndə'rektiv, -di-], *a. Psy:* **n.(-)d. therapy,** non-directivisme *m*.

non(-)disclosure [nɔndis'klouʒər], *s. Jur:* réticence *f.*

non(-)dissemination [nɔndisemi'neiʃ(ə)n], *s.* non-dissémination *f* (des armes nucléaires, etc.).

none [nʌn]. **1.** *pron.* (*with* (i) *pl.* (ii) *O: sg., verb*) (*a*) aucun; **n. of them is, are, known to me, I know n. of them,** je n'en connais aucun; **I trust n. of them,** je ne me fie à aucun d'entre eux; **I waited for two hours but n. of them came,** j'ai attendu deux heures, sans qu'aucun d'entre eux arrivât; **n. of you can tell me,** personne d'entre vous, aucun d'entre vous, ne peut me dire; **those weaknesses from which n. of us are free,** ces faiblesses dont aucun de nous n'est exempt; **we n. of us have one,** aucun de nous, personne d'entre nous, n'en possède; **n. of the boys has, have, gone out,** aucun des garçons n'est sorti; **n. of this concerns me,** rien de ceci ne me regarde; **I want n. of these things,** je ne veux aucune de ces choses; **n. news today?—n.,** pas de nouvelles aujourd'hui?—aucune(s); **do you know any of her relations?—n.,** connaissez-vous quelqu'un de ses parents?—aucun; **strawberries! there are n.,** des fraises! il n'y en a pas; **we have masses of fruit but n. ripe,** nous avons des quantités de fruits, mais aucun (de) mûr; **n. at all,** pas un(e) seul(e); **any occupations is better than n. at all,** une occupation quelle qu'elle soit est préférable à pas d'occupation du tout; **half a loaf is better than n. (at all),** il vaut mieux avoir la moitié d'un pain que rien du tout; **for this reason if for n. other, I wish to . . .,** pour cette raison, à défaut d'une autre, je voudrais . . .; **I'll have n. of it!** je ne veux pas en entendre parler! **n. of your impudence!** pas d'insolences de votre part! *F:* **n. of that!** pas de ça! **his nature is n. of the calmest,** sa nature n'est pas des plus calmes; **I looked for peace and found n.,** j'ai cherché la paix et ne l'ai pas trouvée; (*b*) personne, nul; **n. can tell,** personne ne le sait; nul ne le sait; **n. had ever asked her that before,** personne ne lui avait encore jamais posé cette question; **he is aware, n. better, that . . .,** il sait mieux que personne que . . .; **n. but he knew of it,** lui seul le savait, nul que lui ne le savait; **I have told n. but you,** je n'en ai parlé à personne d'autre que vous; **n. but a fool would do such a thing,** il n'y a qu'un imbécile pour faire une chose pareille; **the visitor was n. other than the king,** le visiteur n'était autre que le roi; (*c*) *Adm:* (*in schedules, etc.*) **n.,** néant. **2.** *a. A:* **money I had n.,** de l'argent, d'argent, je n'en avais pas, point; **sounds there were n., save the barking of a dog,** de sons aucun, sauf les aboiements d'un chien; **village there was n.,** de village point. **3.** *adv.* (*a*) **he is n. the happier for his wealth,** ce n'est pas sa richesse qui le rend plus heureux; pour être riche, il n'en est pas plus heureux; **I like him n. the better, n. the worse, for that,** je ne l'en aime pas mieux, pas moins; (*b*) **he was n. too soon,** il est arrivé juste à temps; il était temps qu'il arrive; **he was n. too happy about it,** il n'en était pas trop content; **the wages are n. too high,** le salaire n'est pas énorme; **it was n. too warm,** il ne faisait pas chaud; **his position is n. too secure,** sa position n'est rien moins qu'assurée; **he was n. too amiable,** il ne s'est pas montré trop aimable; il a manqué d'amabilité; **it's n. too easy,** ça n'est pas si facile que ça.

non(-)effective [nɔni'fektiv]. **1.** *a.* ineffectif. **2.** *a. & s. Mil: Navy:* (officier, etc.) en non-activité; (homme) non-valide.

non(-)ego [nɔn'egou, -'iːgou], *s. Phil:* non-moi *m*.

non(-)elective [nɔni'lektiv], *a. Pol:* (chambre) non-élective.

non-engaged [nɔnin'geidʒd], *a. Lit:* (écrivain) non-engagé.

non-engagement [nɔnin'geidʒmənt], *s. Lit: etc:* non-engagement *m*.

nonentity [nɔn'entiti], *s.* **1.** non-être *m*, non-existence *f*, néant *m*. **2.** (*a*) personne insignifiante, de peu d'importance; mince personnage *m*; non-valeur *f*; nullité *f*; (*b*) *Th: F:* panne *f.*

nones [nouz], *s.pl.* **1.** *Rom.Ant:* nonnes *f.* **2.** *Ecc:* none.

non(-)essential [nɔni'senʃ(ə)l], *a.* non essentiel.

non(e)such ['nʌnsʌtʃ]. **1.** (*a*) *a.* non pareil; sans égal; incomparable; (*b*) *s.* personne, chose, sans pareille. **2.** *s.* (*a*) *Bot:* (**black**) **n.,** lupuline *f*; petit trèfle jaune; triolet *m*; minette (dorée); (*b*) **n. apple,** nonpareille *f.*

nonet [nou'net], *s. Mus:* nonetto *m*.

non-Euclidean [nɔnjuː'klidiən], *a. Mth:* **n.-E. geometry,** géométrie non-euclidienne.

non-event [nɔni'vent], *s. F:* événement manqué; **it was the n.-e. of the year,** c'était tout ce qu'on peut imaginer de plus ennuyeux.

non(-)existence [nɔnig'zist(ə)ns], *s.* non-existence *f*, non-être *m*; néant *m*.

non(-)existent [nɔnig'zist(ə)nt], *a.* non-existant; inexistant; **almost n.(-)e. capital,** capitaux presque nuls.

non(-)expendable [nɔniks'pendəbl], *a. Mil: etc:* (approvisionnements, fournitures) non consommables, récupérables.

non-explosive [nɔniks'plousiv], *a.* inexplosif, non détonant.

non(-)extensile [nɔniks'tensail], *a.* inextensible.

non(-)feasance [nɔn'fiːz(ə)ns], *s. Jur:* délit *m* par abstention.

non(-)ferrous [nɔn'ferəs], *a.* non-ferreux.

non-fiction [nɔn'fikʃ(ə)n], *s.* **n.-f. (books),** ouvrages généraux.

non(-)figurative [nɔn'figjərətiv], *a.* (art) non-figuratif.

non(-)fissile, non(-)fissionable [nɔn'fisail, -'fiʃ(ə)nəbl], *a. Atom.Ph:* non fissile, non fissible, non scissile.

non(-)forfeiture [nɔn'fɔːfitjər], *s. Jur:* non-déchéance *f*, non-résiliation *f*, prolongation *f*, reconduction *f*; *Ins:* **n.(-)f. clause,** clause *f* de reconduction automatique.

non-freezing [nɔn'friːziŋ], *a.* incongelable.

non(-)fulfilment [nɔnful'filmənt], *s.* non-exécution *f*, inexécution *f* (d'un contrat, etc.).

non-greasy [nɔn'griːsi], *a.* (onguent, etc.) qui ne laisse pas de traces grasses, qui ne graisse pas.

non-icing [nɔn'aisiŋ], *a.* antigivrant; *Av:* **n.-i. equipment,** équipement, dispositif, antigivrant; antigivreur *m*.

nonillion [nou'niliən], *s. Mth:* nonillion *m*.

non(-)inductive [nɔnin'dʌktiv], *a. El:* (circuit, condensateur) non inductif.

non(-)inflammable [nɔnin'flæməbl], *a.* ininflammable, ignifuge.

non(-)interference [nɔnintə'fiərəns], *s. Pol:* non-ingérence *f*, non-intervention *f.*

non(-)intervention [nɔnintə'venʃ(ə)n], *s. Pol:* non-intervention *f.*

non(-)interventionist [nɔnintə'venʃənist], *a. & s. Pol:* non-interventionniste (*mf*); de non-intervention.

non(-)ionizing [nɔn'aiənaiziŋ], *a. Atom.Ph:* non ionisant.

non-iron ['nɔn'aiən], *a.* (*of clothes, material*) ne nécessitant, n'exigeant, aucun repassage; lavé-repassé *inv.*

non(-)joinder [nɔn'dʒɔindər], *s. Jur:* fait de ne pas mettre en cause une personne qui aurait dû être partie à une instance.

non(-)juring [nɔn'dʒuəriŋ], *a. Hist:* (prêtre) non-jureur, insermenté, inassermenté, non assermenté.

non(-)juror [nɔn'dʒuːrər], *s. Hist:* non-jureur *m*; (prêtre) insermenté, inassermenté.

non(-)jury [nɔn'dʒuːri], *a. & s. Jur:* **n.(-)j. (case, action),** procès dans lequel la présence du jury n'est pas requise.

non(-)ladder [nɔn'lædər], *a.* (bas) indémaillable.

non-liability [nɔnlaiə'biliti], *s. Jur:* non-responsabilité *f*; **n.-l. clause,** clause *f* de non-responsabilité.

non-lifting [nɔn'liftiŋ], *a. Av:* non-porteur, non portant; non sustentateur, -trice; **n.-l. surface,** surface non sustentatrice.

non(-)linear [nɔn'liniər], *a.* non linéaire.

non(-)linearity [nɔnlini'æriti], *s.* non-linéarité *f.*

non(-)malignant [nɔnmə'lignənt], *a. Med:* **n.(-)m. tumour,** tumeur bénigne.

non(-)member [nɔn'membər], *s.* (*at club, etc.*) invité, -ée; **open to n.-members,** ouvert au public.

non(-)metal [nɔn'metəl], *s. Ch:* non-métal *m*, métalloïde *m*.

non(-)metallic [nɔnmi'tælik], *a.* non-métallique; *Ch:* métalloïdique.

non(-)migrant, non(-)migratory [nɔn'maigrənt, -'maigrət(ə)ri], *a.* (oiseau) sédentaire.

non(-)mobile [nɔn'moubail], *a. Mil:* **n.(-)m. troops,** troupes *f* sédentaires.

non(-)negotiable [nɔnni'gouʃiəbl], *a.* (billet, etc.) non-négociable.

non(-)observance [nɔnəb'zəːv(ə)ns], *s.* inobservance *f* (des lois, du carême, etc.); inobservation *f.*

non(-)operable [nɔn'ɔp(ə)rəbl], *a.* hors d'état de fonctionner.

non(-)oxidizing [nɔn'ɔksidaiziŋ], *a.* inoxydable.

nonpareil [nɔnpə'rel]. **1.** (*a*) *a.* nonpareil; sans égal; incomparable; (*b*) *s.* personne, chose, sans pareille. **2.** *s.* (*a*) *Typ:* nonpareille *f*; corps *m* six; (*b*) (*apple, sweet*) nonpareille; (*c*) *Orn:* nonpareil *m*; **pin-tailed n.,** (diamant *m*) quadricolore *m*; pape *m* des prairies.

non(-)participating [nɔnpɑː'tisipeitiŋ], *a. Ins:* (police) sans participation aux bénéfices.

non(-)payment [nɔn'peimənt], *s.* non-paiement *m*; défaut *m*, faute *f*, de paiement (d'un effet de commerce, etc.).

non(-)performance [nɔnpə'fɔːməns], *s.* non-exécution *f*, inexécution *f* (d'un contrat, d'une obligation, etc.).

nonplus[1] [nɔn'plʌs], *s.* embarras *m*, perplexité *f*; **to be at a n.,** être réduit à quia; ne savoir que faire; **to bring, reduce, s.o. to a n.,** réduire, mettre, qn à quia.

nonplus[2], *v.tr.* (**nonplussed**) embarrasser, confondre, interdire, interloquer (qn); mettre, réduire, (qn) à quia; **this question nonplussed the candidates,** cette question a dérouté les candidats; **to be nonplussed,** être désemparé; **I was absolutely nonplussed,** je ne savais plus que penser.

non(-)poisonous [nɔn'pɔizənəs], *a.* atoxique.

non(-)printing [nɔn'printiŋ], *a.* (i) (*of machine*) non imprimant; (ii) (*of character*) qui ne s'imprime pas.

non(-)profit [nɔn'prɔfit], *attrib.a.* (association) sans but lucratif; **n.(-)p.-making company,** association à but non lucratif.

non-proliferation [nɔnprəlifə'reiʃ(ə)n], *s.* non-prolifération *f*; **n.-p. treaty,** traité *m* de non-prolifération (des armes nucléaires).

non(-)reactive [nɔnriː'æktiv], *a.* **1.** *Ch: Physiol:* sans réaction, non réactif. **2.** *El:* sans self, non selfique, passif.

non-recoil(ing) [nɔnri'kɔiliŋ], *a.* (canon, etc.) sans recul.

non(-)recurring [nɔnri'kəːriŋ], *a.* exceptionnel, extraordinaire; **n.(-)r. expenditure,** frais *mpl*, dépenses *fpl*, extraordinaires.

non(-)residence [nɔn'rezid(ə)ns], *s.* **1.** non-résidence *f* (d'un prêtre, d'un propriétaire). **2.** *Sch: etc:* externat *m* (d'un étudiant, etc.).

non(-)resident [nɔn'rezid(ə)nt], *a. & s.* **1.** (*a*) (*of priest, etc.*) non-résident (*m*); **the canons were n.(-)r.,** les chanoines ne résidaient pas; (*b*) **n.(-)r. landowner,** propriétaire forain. **2.** *Sch: etc:* externe (*mf*); **n.(-)r. medical officer,** externe (des hôpitaux); (*in hotel*) hôte *m* de passage; **open to n.(-)residents,** repas servis aux voyageurs de passage.

non(-)resistance [nɔnri'zist(ə)ns], *s.* non-résistance *f.*

non(-)return [nɔnri'təːn], *s.* (*a*) non-retour *m*; **n.(-)r. to reference, to zero,** non-retour à zéro (dans un appareil de mesure, etc.); *Av: Space: etc:* **point of n.(-)r.,** point *m* de non-retour; (*b*) *Aut: etc:* **n.(-)r. handle,** manivelle *f* à retour empêché; *Hyd.E: Mec.E:* **n.(-)r. valve,** clapet *m*, soupape *f*, de non-retour, de retenue.

non(-)returnable [nɔnri'təːnəbl], *a.* perdu; **n.(-)r. packing,** emballage perdu, non repris, non consigné, logé.

non(-)reversible [nɔnri'vəːsibl], *a.* irréversible.

non(-)rigid [nɔn'ridʒid], *a. Aer:* (aérostat) souple, non rigide.

non(-)run ['nɔn'rʌn], *a.* (bas, collant, etc.) indémaillable.

non-rust ['nɔn'rʌst], *a.* **1.** (peinture, produit) antirouille. **2.** (métal) inoxydable.

non-scheduled [nɔn'ʃedju:ld], *a. Trans:* (service) spécial, extraordinaire, irrégulier.

nonsense ['nɔns(ə)ns], *s.* **1.** non-sens *m.* **2.** (*a*) absurdité *f*, déraison *f*; **a piece of n.,** une bêtise, une absurdité, une extravagance, une ânerie, une ineptie; **to talk (a lot of) n.,** déraisonner; dire des bêtises, des sottises, des absurdités, des imbécillités, des inepties, des âneries; débiter des balivernes, divaguer, radoter; **why do you talk such n.?** pourquoi dire des bêtises comme ça? **he talked a lot of (wild) n.,** il a dit un tas d'extravagances; **this passage is n.,** ce passage est inintelligible; **to make sense out of n.,** attacher un sens à l'inintelligible; **whoever heard (of) such n.!** a-t-on jamais entendu la pareille! **that's all n.!** imbécillités que tout cela! **(what) n.!** quelle bêtise! pas possible! allons donc! (dites cela) à d'autres! quelle blague! vous me faites rire! avec ça! **it's n. to think that . . .,** il est absurde de penser que . . .; **he'll stand no n., he won't stand (for) any n.,** il n'est pas d'humeur facile; il ne permet pas qu'on prenne des libertés avec lui; il ne permet pas de bêtises; il ne plaisante pas là-dessus; **that'll take, knock, the n. out of him!** voilà qui l'assagira! cela lui fera passer ses lubies! cela le ramènera à la raison! **now, no n.!** allons, pas de bêtises! pas d'enfantillage! (*b*) *Lit:* **n. verse,** vers *m* amphigouriques; **n. rhyme,** cliquette *f*; (*c*) *attrib.* (*of pers.*) no-n., (i) (trop) sérieux; (ii) sévère.

nonsensical [nɔn'sensik(ə)l], *a.* **1.** (*of speech, reason, etc.*) absurde; qui n'a pas de sens, qui n'a pas le sens commun. **2. don't be n.!** ne soyez pas si bête! ne dites pas de bêtises, d'absurdités!

nonsensically [nɔn'sensik(ə)li], *adv.* absurdement; contre le bon sens; contre le sens commun.

non sequitur [nɔn'sekwitər], *s.* fausse conclusion, absurdité *f*, illogicité *f*.

non(-)skid(ding) [nɔn'skid(iŋ)], **non(-)slip(ping)** [nɔn'slip(iŋ)], *a. Aut: etc:* antidérapant; **n.(-)skid tyre,** (pneu) antidérapant *m.*

non(-)smoker [nɔn'smoukər], *s.* **1.** (*pers.*) **I'm a n.(-)s.,** je ne suis pas fumeur; je ne fume pas. **2.** *Rail: Av:* compartiment de non fumeurs.

non(-)smoking [nɔn'smoukiŋ], *a. Rail: Av:* **n.(-)s. compartment,** compartiment de non fumeurs.

non(-)spherical [nɔn'sferik(ə)l], *a. Opt: etc:* asphérique.

non(-)spill ['nɔn'spil], *a.* anti-gouttes *inv.*

non(-)standard [nɔn'stændəd], *a.* non normalisé, non standard(isé); spécial; personnalisé.

non(-)starter [nɔn'stɑ:tər], *s.* (*a*) *Sp: etc:* non-partant *m*; (*b*) *F:* (projet, etc.) fichu d'avance; **this makes the proposition a n.(-)s.,** cela fait que la proposition tombe à l'eau, n'a pas de raison d'être.

non-stick ['nɔn'stik], *a.* **n.-s. (saucepan),** (casserole) avec revêtement anti-adhésif, qui n'attache pas; **n.-s. rice,** riz *m* décollable.

nonstop ['nɔnstɔp]. **1.** *a.* **n. train,** train direct; train faisant le trajet sans arrêt; **n. journey,** trajet sans arrêt; *Av:* **n. flight,** vol *m* sans escale; *Cin:* **n. performance,** spectacle permanent. **2.** *adv.* sans arrêt; **we flew n.,** nous y avons volé sans escale; **she talked for two hours n.,** elle a parlé sans arrêt, sans cesse, pendant deux heures; **to argue n.,** discuter à perdre haleine.

non(-)stretching [nɔn'stretʃiŋ], *a.* (courroie, etc.) inextensible.

nonsuit[1] ['nɔn's(j)u:t], *s. Jur:* **1.** *A:* désistement *m* d'instance. **2.** débouté *m*, déboutement *m*; ordonnance *f* de non-lieu; **to direct a n.,** rendre une ordonnance de non-lieu.

nonsuit[2], *v.tr.* débouter (un plaideur) (de son appel); renvoyer (qn) de sa demande, des fins de sa plainte; mettre (qn) hors de cour; rendre une ordonnance de non-lieu à (qn); **to be nonsuited,** être débouté de sa demande; être déclaré irrecevable en son action.

non(-)symmetrical [nɔnsi'metrik(ə)l], *a.* dissymétrique.

non-taxable [nɔn'tæksəbl], *a. Adm:* (revenu, etc.) non imposable.

non(-)transferable [nɔn'trænsfərəbl], *a.* non transmissible, incessible; nominatif; **n.(-)t. shares,** actions nominatives.

non(-)transportable [nɔntræns'pɔ:təbl], *a.* (blessé, produit) intransportable.

nontronite ['nɔntrənait], *s. Miner:* nontronite *f.*

non(-)uniform [nɔn'ju:nifɔ:m], *a.* inégal, irrégulier, variable; *Elcs:* **n.(-)u. field,** champ irrégulier, variable.

non(-)union [nɔn'ju:niən], *a.* (ouvrier) non-syndiqué.

non(-)unionist [nɔn'ju:niənist], *s.* non-syndiqué, -ée.

non(-)usage [nɔn'ju:zidʒ], **non(-)user** [nɔn'ju:zər], *s. Jur:* non-usage *m.*

non-utilization [nɔnju:tilai'zeiʃ(ə)n], *s.* non-utilisation *f.*

non(-)viability [nɔnvaiə'biliti], *s. Med:* non-viabilité *f* (d'un enfant nouveau-né).

non(-)viable [nɔn'vaiəbl], *a. Med:* (enfant) non-viable.

non-vintage [nɔn'vintidʒ], *a. Vit:* (vin) sans appellation.

non(-)violence [nɔn'vaiələns], *s.* non-violence *f*; **advocate of n.(-)v.,** partisan, -ane, de la non-violence; non-violent, -ente.

non(-)violent [nɔn'vaiələnt], *a.* (mouvement, etc.) non-violent.

non-warranty [nɔn'wɔr(ə)nti], *s.* non-garantie *f*; **n.-w. clause,** clause *f* de non-garantie.

non-woven [nɔn'wouv(ə)n], *a. Tex:* (tissu) non-tissé.

nonyl ['nɔnil], *s. Ch:* nonyle *m.*

noodle ['nu:dl], *s.* **1.** *Cu:* (*usu.pl.*) **(ribbon) noodles,** nouilles *f*; (*small*) nouillettes *f.* **2.** *F:* bêta, -asse; niais, -aise, nigaud, -aude; cornichon *m*, nouille *f.*

noogenesis [nouo'dʒenəsis], *s. Psy:* noogénèse *f.*

nook [nuk], *s.* (*a*) coin *m*, recoin *m*; **nooks and crannies,** coins et recoins; (*b*) renfoncement *m* (dans une pièce).

noon [nu:n], *s.* midi *m*; **Greenwich apparent n., mean n.,** midi apparent, midi moyen, de Greenwich; **local apparent n., mean n.,** midi apparent, midi moyen, local; **local true n.,** midi vrai local; **local mean n.,** midi moyen local; **it is twelve n.,** il est midi; **to arrive about n.,** arriver sur le midi, *F:* sur les midi; **the sun at n.,** le soleil de midi; **shadow at n.,** ombre méridienne; **at the height of n., at high n.,** au milieu du jour.

noonday ['nu:ndei], *O:* **noontide** ['nu:ntaid], *s.* midi *m*; plein jour; **the n. sun,** le soleil de midi; *Lit:* **he was at the n. of his prosperity,** il était à l'apogée *m* de sa prospérité.

noose[1] [nu:s], *s.* (*a*) nœud coulant; (*for trapping animals*) lacet *m*, lacs *m*, collet *m*; **running n.,** nœud coulant; (*b*) **hangman's n.,** corde *f* (de potence); *F:* **to put one's head in the (marriage) n.,** se mettre la corde au cou; (*c*) lasso *m.*

noose[2], *v.tr.* **1.** faire un nœud coulant à (une corde); **to n. a rope round s.o.'s neck,** mettre la corde au cou de qn. **2.** (*a*) prendre (un lièvre, etc.) au lacet, au collet, dans un lacs; (*b*) attraper (une bête) au lasso.

nopal ['noup(ə)l], *s. Bot:* nopal *m*, *pl.* -als; cochenillier *m*; *F:* raquette *f*, semelle *f* du pape.

nopalry ['noupəlri], *s. Hort:* nopalerie *f*; nopalière *f* (pour l'éducation de la cochenille).

nope [noup], *adv. esp. U.S: P:* (= *no*) non.

nor[1] [nɔ:r], *conj.* **1.** (*continuing the force of a neg.*) (ne, ni . . .) ni; **he has neither father n. mother, he has no mother n. father,** il n'a père ni mère, il n'a pas de père ni de mère; **he hasn't any, n. have I,** il n'en a pas, ni moi non plus; **neither you n. I know,** ni vous ni moi ne le savons; je n'en sais rien, ni vous non plus; **not a man, woman n. child could be seen,** on ne voyait ni homme ni femme ni enfant; **he's not going, n. you either,** il n'ira pas, ni vous non plus; **I have never known him n. seen him,** je ne l'ai jamais connu ni vu. **2.** (*and not*) (*a*) **I do not know, n. can I guess,** je n'en sais rien et je ne peux pas le deviner; **I will not apologize, n. will I admit that I'm wrong,** je ne ferai pas d'excuses, et je n'admets pas non plus que j'aie tort; **he had promised not to interfere, n. did he,** il avait promis de ne pas intervenir et il a tenu sa promesse; **n. does it seem that . . .,** il ne semble pas non plus que . . .; il ne semble pas davantage que . . .; d'ailleurs il ne semble pas que . . .; **n. was this all,** et ce n'était pas tout; **n. had I forgotten the wine,** je n'avais pas non plus oublié le vin; **n. had I ever thought of . . .,** jamais non plus je n'avais songé à . . .; (*b*) *A: & Lit:* (*with no other neg. expressed*) **n. thou n. I have made the world,** ni toi ni moi n'avons créé la terre.

nor[2], *conj. Dial: P:* (= THAN) **he works better n. you,** il travaille mieux que vous.

Nora(h) ['nɔ:rə]. *Pr.n.f.* Éléonore.

noradrenalin [nɔ:rə'drenəlin], *s. Ch:* noradrénaline *f.*

Nordic ['nɔ:dik]. (*a*) *a.* nordique, scandinave; (*b*) *s.* Nordique *mf*, Scandinave *mf.*

nor'east, *etc. See* NORTHEAST, *etc.*

Norfolk ['nɔ:fək]. *Pr.n. Geog:* (le comté de) Norfolk *m*; **N. jacket,** (sorte de) veston *m* (de chasse); *F:* **N. dumpling,** habitant, -ante, du Norfolk; **N. capon,** hareng saur.

noria ['nɔ:riə], *s. Hyd.E:* noria *f.*

norite ['nɔ:rait], *s. Geol:* norite *f.*

norland ['nɔ:lənd], *s. Dial:* les régions *f* du nord.

norlander ['nɔ:ləndər], *s. Dial:* = NORTHERNER 1.

norm [nɔ:m], *s.* (*a*) norme *f*; **according to the n.,** selon la norme; normal, -aux; (*b*) règle *f.*

normal ['nɔ:m(ə)l]. **1.** *a.* (*a*) *Mth:* (*of line, etc.*) normal, -aux, perpendiculaire **(to,** à); (*b*) normal, de régime, régulier, ordinaire; **n. person,** personne normale, ordinaire, saine de corps et d'esprit; **outside n. experience,** qui échappe à la norme; **n. working, n. running (of engine, etc.),** régime *m*; **n. speed,** vitesse *f* de régime; **n. bed of a river,** lit mineur d'une rivière; *El:* **n. current,** courant *m* de régime; **n. power,** puissance-régime *f*, *pl.* puissances-régimes; *Med:* **n. temperature,** température moyenne, normale; (*c*) *Ch:* (*of solution, etc.*) normal, titré; **n. salt,** sel *m* neutre; (*d*) *Sch: NAm:* **n. school,** école normale. **2.** *s.* (*a*) *Mth:* normale *f*, perpendiculaire *f*; (*b*) condition normale; **the office was not at (its) n.,** le bureau n'était pas dans son état normal; *Med:* **temperature above the n.,** température au-dessus de la normale.

normalcy ['nɔ:m(ə)lsi], *s.* normalité *f*, normativité *f*; vie normale.

normality [nɔ:'mæliti], *s.* normalité *f.*

normalization [nɔ:məlai'zeiʃ(ə)n], *s.* normalisation *f.*

normalize ['nɔ:məlaiz]. **1.** *v.tr.* (*a*) ramener (qch.) à l'état normal, à la normale; rendre (qch.) normal; normaliser, régulariser; **to n. sth. to unity,** ramener qch. à l'unité; (*b*) *Metall:* normaliser (un métal); **to n. steel,** recuire l'acier et le laisser refroidir à l'air. **2.** *v.i.* se normaliser, redevenir normal.

normalizing ['nɔ:məlaiziŋ]. **1.** *a.* normalisant, qui normalise; de normalisation. **2.** *s.* normalisation *f*; *Metall:* **n. furnace,** four *m* de normalisation.

normally ['nɔ:məli], *adv.* **1.** normalement. **2.** *Mth:* normalement (to, à).

Norman ['nɔ:mən]. (*a*) *a.* normand; **N. architecture,** (i) l'architecture normande; (ii) l'architecture romane (anglaise); *Hist:* **the N. Conquest,** la conquête normande; *Ling: Hist:* **N. French,** normand *m*; (*b*) *s.* Normand, -ande.

Normandy ['nɔ:məndi]. *Pr.n. Geog:* Normandie *f.*

normative ['nɔ:mətiv], *a.* normatif.

normed [nɔ:md], *a.* normé.

normoblast ['nɔ:moublæst], *s. Med:* normoblaste *m.*

normocyte ['nɔ:mousait], *s. Physiol:* normocyte *m.*

Norn [nɔ:n]. *Pr.n.f. Myth:* Norne.

Norroy ['nɔrɔi], *s. Her:* **N. and Ulster King of Arms,** norroy *m*, roi *m* d'armes (ayant juridiction au nord de la rivière Trent et dans l'Irlande du Nord).

Norse [nɔ:s]. **1.** *a.* (*a*) norvégien; **N. mythology,** mythologie *f* scandinave; (*b*) *Hist:* nor(r)ois, normannique. **2.** *s.* (*a*) *pl.* Nordiques *mf*, Scandinaves *mf*, *esp.* Norvégiens, -iennes; (*b*) *Ling:* (i) les langues *f* nordiques, scandinaves, *esp.* norvégien *m*; (ii) (*in Orkneys, Shetlands, etc.*) norse *m*; *Hist:* **Old N.,** langue nordique; (vieux) nor(r)ois; normannique *m.*

Norseland ['nɔ:slənd]. *Pr.n. Hist:* Scandinavie *f*; Norvège *f.*

Norseman, *pl.* **-men** ['nɔ:smən], *s.m. Hist:* Scandinave; Norvégien; Viking.

north[1] [nɔ:θ]. **1.** *s.* (*a*) nord *m*; **true n.,** nord vrai, géographique; **magnetic n.,** nord magnétique; pôle *m* magnétique; *Mapm:* **grid n.,** nord du quadrillage; **house facing (the) n.,** maison exposée au nord; **to look (to the) n.,** regarder vers le nord; **on the n. of, to the n. of,** au nord de; **bounded on the n. by . . .,** borné au nord par . . .; **to the n. the hotel overlooks the lake,** du côté du nord l'hôtel a vue sur le lac; (*of wind*) **to veer (round to the) n.,** (*a*) nordir; tourner au nord; **the wind is in the n.,** le vent est au nord; **of the n., from the n.,** du nord; **in the n.,** au nord, dans le nord; (*b*) **to live in the n. of England,** habiter dans le nord de l'Angleterre; **he lives somewhere in the n.,** il habite quelque part dans le nord (de Londres, de l'Angleterre, de l'Europe, etc.); (*c*) *U.S: Hist:* **the N.,** les États *m* du nord (des États-Unis); les États anti-esclavagistes; (*d*) **the Canadian Far N.,** le Grand Nord Canadien. **2.** *adv.* au nord; **to travel n.,** voyager vers le nord; *F:* **he's from up n.,** il vient du nord (de l'Angleterre); *F:* **I'm going up n.,** je vais dans le nord (de l'Angleterre); **Canterbury is n. of Dover,** Cantorbéry est (situé) au nord de Douvres; **the wind is blowing n.,** le vent vient, souffle, du nord; le vent est (du) nord; **to sail due n.,** aller droit vers le nord; avoir le cap au nord; faire du nord; **n. by east,** nord-quart-nord-est; **n. by west,** nord-quart-nord-ouest. **3.** *a.* nord *inv*; septentrional, -aux; (pays) du nord; (mur, etc.) exposé au nord; **n. aspect,** exposition *f* au nord; **studio with a n. light,** atelier *m* qui reçoit la lumière du nord; **on the n. side,** du côté nord; **the n. wind,** (i) le vent du nord; (ii) *Nau:* le nord; (iii) *Lit: & Poet:* la bise; **n. coast,** côte *f* nord; **the N. Country,** le Nord (de l'Angleterre); **a N.-country girl,** une jeune fille du Nord (de l'Angleterre); **N. countryman,** homme du Nord (de l'Angleterre); **N. Africa,** Afrique *f* du Nord; **N. African,** (i) *a.* nord-africain; (ii) *s.* Nord-africain, -aine, *pl.* Nord-africains; **the N. Sea,** la mer du Nord; **N. Sea oil, gas,** pétrole *m*, gaz *m*, de la mer du Nord; *F:* **we've just been converted to N. Sea gas,** on vient d'installer le gaz de la mer du Nord chez nous; **the N. Pole,** le Pôle Nord; **the N. Channel,** le Canal du Nord; *Arch:* (*in church*) **n. transept,** transept septentrional.

north², *v.i.* **1.** (*of star in S. hemisphere*) passer le méridien. **2.** (*of ship*) courir vers le nord; faire route au nord.

northbound ['nɔːθbaund], *a.* (train, etc.) allant vers le nord; (*on underground*) en direction de la banlieue nord; *Aut:* **the n. carriageway (of the motorway),** la voie nord de l'autoroute.

northcaper [nɔːθ'keipər], *s. Z:* baleine *f* de Biscaye.

northeast [nɔːθ'iːst], *Nau:* **nor'east** [nɔː'riːst]. **1.** *s.* nord-est *m*; *Nau:* nordé *m*; (*of wind*) **to veer to the n.,** tourner au nord-est; *Nau:* nordester. **2.** *a.* (du) nord-est *inv*; **n. wind,** nord-est. **3.** *adv.* vers le nord-est; **we live n. of the town,** nous habitons au nord-est de la ville; **n. by east,** nord-est-quart-est; **n. by north,** nord-est-quart-nord.

northeaster [nɔːθ'iːstər], *Nau:* **nor'easter** [nɔː'riːstər], *s.* vent *m* du nord-est.

northeasterly [nɔːθ'iːstəli], *Nau:* **nor'easterly** [nɔː'riːstəli]. **1.** *a.* (*of wind, etc.*) (du) nord-est *inv*; (*of district, etc.*) (au, du) nord-est; (*of direction*) vers le nord-est. **2.** *adv.* vers le nord-est. **3.** *s.* (*wind*) nord-est.

northeastern [nɔːθ'iːstən], *Nau:* **nor'eastern** [nɔː'riːstən], *a.* (du) nord-est *inv*.

northeastward [nɔːθ'iːstwəd]. **1.** *s.* nord-est *m*. **2.** *a.* (au, du) nord-est *inv*. **3.** *adv.* vers le nord-est.

northeastwards [nɔːθ'iːstwədz], *adv.* vers le nord-est.

norther ['nɔːðər], *s. U.S:* vent *m* du nord; tempête venue du nord.

northerly ['nɔːðəli]. **1.** *a.* (*of wind, etc.*) du nord; (*of district, etc.*) (du, au) nord *inv*; (*of direction*) vers le nord; **n. latitude,** latitude *f* nord, boréale; **n. aspect,** exposition *f* au nord. **2.** *adv.* vers le nord.

northern ['nɔːðən], *a.* (du) nord *inv*; septentrional, -aux; **the n. counties,** les comtés *m* du nord; **N. Ireland,** l'Irlande *f* du Nord; **n. hemisphere,** hémisphère nord; **n. lights,** aurore boréale; **cold n. slope of a valley,** envers *m* d'une vallée.

northerner ['nɔːðənər], *s.* **1.** habitant, -ante, du Nord (de l'Angleterre, etc.); personne *f* du nord; **the Northerners,** les septentrionaux *m*. **2.** *U.S: Hist:* nordiste *m*.

northernmost ['nɔːðənmoust], *a.* (point, etc.) le plus au nord.

northing ['nɔːθiŋ], *s.* **1.** *Nau:* chemin *m* nord; marche *f*, route *f*, vers le nord. **2.** (*of star in S. hemisphere*) passage *m* au méridien; médiation *f*. **3.** *Mapm:* ordonnée *f* (d'un quadrillage cartographique).

northland ['nɔːθlənd], *s.* **the n.,** le nord du pays; **the northlands,** les pays du nord.

Northman, *pl.* **-men** ['nɔːθmən], *s.m.* **1.** *Hist:* Scandinave, Norvégien. **2.** habitant d'un pays du nord.

northmost ['nɔːθmoust], *a.* (point, etc.) le plus au nord.

north-northeast [nɔːθnɔːθ'iːst], *Nau:* **nor'nor'east** [nɔːnɔː'riːst]. **1.** *a. & s.* nord-nord-est (*m*) *inv.* **2.** *adv.* vers le nord-nord-est.

north-northwest [nɔːθnɔːθ'west], *Nau:* **nor'nor'west** [nɔːnɔː'west]. **1.** *a. & s.* nord-nord-ouest (*m*) *inv.* **2.** *adv.* vers le nord-nord-ouest.

Northumbrian [nɔː'θʌmbriən], *a. & s. Geog:* northumbrien, -ienne; du Northumberland; *s. Ling:* northumbrien *m*.

northupite ['nɔːθəpait], *s. Miner:* northupite *f*.

northward ['nɔːθwəd]. **1.** *s.* nord *m*; direction *f* du nord; **to the n.,** au nord. **2.** *a.* au, du, nord; du côté du nord. **3.** *adv.* vers le nord.

northwards ['nɔːθwədz], *adv.* vers le nord.

northwest [nɔːθ'west], *Nau:* **nor'west** [nɔː'west]. **1.** *s.* nord-ouest *m*; (*of wind*) **to veer to the n.,** tourner au nord-ouest; *Nau:* nordouester; **Alaska is to the n. of the United States,** l'Alaska est au nord-ouest des États-Unis. **2.** *a.* (du) nord-ouest *inv*; **n. wind,** (vent *m* du) nord-ouest; *Nau:* norois *m*, noroît *m*. **3.** *adv.* vers le nord-ouest; **n. by west,** nord-ouest-quart-ouest; **n. by north,** nord-ouest-quart-nord.

northwester [nɔːθ'westər], *Nau:* **nor'wester** [nɔː'westər], *s.* (vent *m* du) nord-ouest; *Nau:* norois *m*, noroît *m*.

northwesterly [nɔːθ'westəli], *Nau:* **nor'westerly** [nɔː'westəli]. **1.** (*of wind, etc.*) du nord-ouest; (*of district, etc.*) (au, du) nord-ouest *inv*; (*of direction*) vers le nord-ouest. **2.** *adv.* vers le nord-ouest. **3.** *s.* (*wind*) (vent du) nord-ouest; *Nau:* norois *m*, noroît *m*.

northwestern [nɔːθ'westən], *Nau:* **nor'western** [nɔː'westən], *a.* (du) nord-ouest *inv*.

northwestward [nɔːθ'westwəd]. **1.** *s.* nord-ouest *m*. **2.** *a.* (au, du) nord-ouest *inv*. **3.** *adv.* vers le nord-ouest.

northwestwards [nɔːθ'westwədz], *adv.* vers le nord-ouest.

Norway ['nɔːwei]. *Pr.n. Geog:* Norvège *f*.

Norwegian [nɔː'wiːdʒən]. **1.** *a.* norvégien. **2.** *s.* (*a*) Norvégien, -ienne; (*b*) *Ling:* norvégien *m*.

nor'west, *etc. See* NORTHWEST, *etc.*

nor'wester [nɔː'westər], *s.* **1.** *Nau:* NORTHWESTER. **2.** *F: A:* grand verre d'eau-de-vie, de whisky, etc. **3.** *Cost: Nau: A:* suroît *m*.

nose¹ [nouz], *s.* **1.** (*a*) (*of pers.*) nez *m*; (*of many animals*) museau *m*; (*of horse*) museau, chanfrein *m*; (*of dog, etc.*) nez; **n. bag,** musette *f* (mangeoire); moreau *m*, pochet *m* (de cheval); sac *m* à fourrages; **n. ring,** (i) anneau nasal, nasière *f*, mouchette *f* (de taureau, de porc); (ii) (*of pers.*) anneau porté au nez; **snub n.,** nez court, camus; **turn(ed)-up n.,** nez retroussé; **flat n.,** nez épaté, camus; **his n. is bleeding,** il saigne du nez; *Med:* **n. spray(er),** insufflateur *m*; **to blow one's n.,** se moucher; *P:* **n. rag, wiper,** mouchoir *m*; tire-jus *m inv*; **to hold one's n.,** se boucher le nez; *P:* **he gets up my n.,** il me fait monter la moutarde au nez; **to speak through one's n.,** parler du nez; nasiller; parler d'une voix nasillarde; *F:* **at three o'clock on the n.,** à trois heures précises, pile; *Turf: U.S: F:* **to back a horse on the n.,** parier un cheval gagnant; (*of fowl*) **the parson's, pope's, n.,** le croupion; l'as *m* de pique; le bonnet d'évêque; *F:* **it's under your n.,** vous l'avez sous le nez; ça vous crève les yeux; **he took it from under my very n.,** il l'a enlevé à mon nez (et à ma barbe); **I did it under his very n.,** je l'ai fait sous son nez; **they burgled the house under the very noses of the police,** ils ont cambriolé la maison au nez et à la barbe de la police; **he can't see any further than the end of his n.,** il ne voit pas plus loin que le bout de son nez; **to have one's n. in a book,** avoir le nez dans son livre; **to poke one's n. into sth.,** frotter son nez à, dans, qch.; **to poke one's n. into everything, into other people's business,** fourrer, mettre, son nez partout, dans les affaires des autres; intervenir dans les affaires des autres; **to look down one's n.,** faire un nez; **to look down one's n. at s.o.,** regarder qn de haut en bas; *O:* **to make a long n. at s.o.,** faire un pied de nez à qn; **to cut off one's n. to spite one's face,** s'arracher, se couper, le nez pour faire dépit à son visage; bouder contre son ventre; **to lead s.o. by the n.,** mener, conduire, qn par le bout du nez; *F:* **to count, tell, noses,** (i) faire le compte (de ses adhérents, etc.); (ii) compter les voix; *F: A:* **n. warmer,** brûle-gueule *m inv*; pipe courte; (*b*) *Z:* **n. ape, monkey,** nasique *m*. **2.** *F:* **to have a n. round,** faire le tour de la maison, du village, etc., en furetant dans tous les recoins. **3.** (*a*) odorat *m*; **to have a good n.,** avoir bon nez, le nez fin, creux; avoir un odorat exquis, avoir l'odorat fin; **dog with a good n.,** chien qui a du flair, du nez; *F:* (*of pers.*) **to have a n. for sth.,** avoir un flair, du flair, pour qch.; (*b*) bouquet *m* (d'un vin, du thé, etc.); parfum *m* (du foin, etc.). **4.** *Tchn:* (*a*) nez, avant *m* (d'un véhicule, d'un navire, d'un avion); nez (du moteur, d'un dirigeable); *Aut: etc:* **n. to tail,** pare-choc(s) à, contre, pare-choc(s); à la queue leu leu; **n. cone,** (i) *Av:* cône *m* de nez (d'un avion); (ii) *Ball:* ogive *f* (d'une fusée); *Av:* **n. (landing) gear, n. undercarriage,** train *m* (d'atterrissage) avant; atterrisseur *m* avant; **steerable n. gear,** train avant orientable; **n. spar,** arêtier *m* (de plan); **n. dip, dive,** vol piqué; piquage *m* (de nez); piqué *m*; **spiral n. dive,** descente *f* en spirale; **n. lift,** cabrage *m*; **n. over,** capotage *m*, culbutage *m*; (*of aircraft*) **n. heavy,** lourd du nez, de l'avant; **n. heaviness,** lourdeur *f* dans le nez; tendance *f* à piquer (du nez); (*b*) *Tls:* bec *m*, nez (d'un outil); bec (d'un burin, d'une pince); pilote *m* (de fraise); tête *f* (d'un poinçon); *Mch.Tls:* nez (d'un mandrin, d'un arbre porte-foret); (*c*) *Mec.E:* ajutage *m* (d'un tuyau); bec (d'un loquet); buse *f* (du porte-vent d'une tuyère); mentonnet *m* (d'une clavette); **n. pipe,** bec, buse, tuyère (de soufflet, de haut fourneau); ajutage; **n. key, wedge,** contre-clavette *f*, *pl.* contre-clavettes; *Metall:* bec de coulée, calotte *f* (d'un convertisseur Bessemer); (*d*) *Ball:* pointe *f*, ogive (d'une balle, d'un obus, d'un missile); *Navy:* cône de choc (d'une torpille); **n. cap,** (i) *Sm.a:* embouchoir *m* à quillon (du fusil); (ii) (α) *Aer:* coiffe *f* (de dirigeable); (β) *Av:* cône avant (de l'hélice); (γ) *Artil:* coiffe (d'obus); **n. adapter,** fausse ogive (d'obus); **n. fuse,** fusée *f* d'ogive, de tête.

nose², *v.*

I. *v.tr. & i.* **1.** (*a*) *v.tr.* (i) *O:* flairer, sentir, mettre le nez dans (qch.); (ii) pousser du nez; **the dog nosed the door open,** le chien a ouvert la porte en la poussant du nez; le chien a poussé la porte du nez pour l'ouvrir; (*b*) *v.i. F:* **to n. about, (a)round,** fouiller, fureter, fouiner; fourrer le nez partout; **to n. about the village,** se promener dans le village en fouinant dans tous les coins; **to n. into the crowd,** s'insinuer dans la foule; **to n. into s.o.'s business,** mettre le nez dans les affaires de qn; **to n. after, for, sth.,** chercher qch. (en furetant); (*c*) *v.i. & tr.* **the ship nosed (her way) through the fog,** le navire s'avançait à l'aveuglette à travers le brouillard; (*of ship*) **to n. (her way) along the coast,** longer la côte. **2.** *v.tr. Const:* garnir d'un nez (la marche d'un escalier).

II. (*compound verbs*) **1. nose dive,** *v.i. Av:* piquer du nez; descendre en piqué.

2. nose down, *v.i. Av:* faire piquer l'appareil.

3. nose lift, *v.i.* (*of aircraft*) se cabrer, lever le nez.

4. nose out, *v.tr.* (i) (*of dog*) **to n. out the game,** flairer le gibier; (ii) *F:* **to n. out a secret,** découvrir, éventer, un secret; **to have a gift for nosing things out,** avoir du flair; **to n. s.o. out,** dépister, dénicher, qn.

5. nose over, *v.i.* (*of aircraft*) capoter, culbuter.

6. nose up, *v.i.* (*of aircraft*) se cabrer, monter.

nosean ['nouziːən], *s. Miner:* = NOSELITE.

noseband ['nouzbænd], *s. Harn:* muserol(l)e *f*; dessus *m* de nez; cache-nez *m inv*.

nosebleed ['nouzbliːd], *s.* saignement *m* de nez; **to have a n.,** saigner du nez.

nosed [nouzd], *a.* (*with adj. prefixed, e.g.*) **red-n.,** au nez rouge; **brass-n.,** à nez de laiton.

nosegay ['nouzgei], *s.* bouquet *m* (de fleurs).

noselite ['nouzəlait], *s. Miner:* nos(él)ite *f*, noséane *f*, nosiane *f*.

nosema [nou'siːmə], *s. Ap:* nosema *m*; **n. disease,** nosémose *f*.

nosepiece ['nouzpiːs], *s.* **1.** (*a*) *Arm:* nasal *m* (du heaume); (*b*) *Harn:* = NOSEBAND. **2.** ajutage *m*, bec *m* (de tuyau d'arrosage, etc.); buse *f*, tuyère *f* (de soufflet); *Opt:* porte-objectifs *m inv* (de microscope); **revolving n.,** revolver *m* (porte-objectifs) (de microscope).

noser ['nouzər], *s. Nau: F: A:* **dead n.,** fort vent debout.

nosewheel ['nouz(h)wiːl], *s. Av:* roue *f* avant, roulette *f* avant, train *m* avant (d'atterrissage); roulette de nez; **steerable n.,** roue avant orientable.

nosewipe ['nouzwaip], *s. P:* tire-jus *m inv*.

nosey ['nouzi], *a.* = NOSY.

nosh¹ [nɔʃ], *s. F:* nourriture *f*; mangeaille *f*, repas *m*.

nosh², *v.i. F:* manger; bouffer.

nosh-up ['nɔʃʌp], *s. P:* **a good n.-up,** une bonne boustifaille.

nosing ['nouziŋ], *s.* **1.** *Const:* (*of stair tread*) nez *m*, profil *m*, astragale *m*; *Arch:* arête *f* (de moulure). **2.** (*of door bolt*) gâche *f*.

nosogeny [nɔ'sɔdʒəni], *s. Med:* nosogénie *f*.

nosographic [nɔsou'græfik], *a. Med:* nosographique.

nosographist [nɔ'sɔgrəfist], *s. Med:* nosographe *mf*.

nosography [nɔ'sɔgrəfi], *s. Med:* nosographie *f*.

nosological [nɔsou'lɔdʒik(ə)l], *a. Med:* nosologique.

nosologist [nɔ'sɔlədʒist], *s. Med:* nosologiste *mf*; nosographe *mf*.

nosology [nɔ'sɔlədʒi], *s. Med:* nosologie *f*.

nostalgia [nɔs'tældʒiə], *s.* nostalgie *f*; mal *m*, maladie *f*, du pays.

nostalgic [nɔs'tældʒik], *a.* nostalgique.

nostalgically [nɔs'tældʒikli], *adv.* nostalgiquement.

nostoc ['nɔstɔk], *s. Algae:* nostoc *m*, nodulaire *f*; *F:* crachat *m* de lune.

nostomania [nɔstou'meiniə], *s. Psy:* nostomanie *f*.

nostril ['nɔstril], *s.* (*of pers.*) narine *f*; aile *f* du nez; (*of horse, ox, etc.*) naseau *m*.

nostrum ['nɔstrəm], *s.* panacée *f*, drogue *f*, orviétan *m*, remède *m* empirique, universel, de charlatan.

nosy ['nouzi], *a. F:* **1.** fouinard, fouineur, fureteur; indiscret; **don't be so n.!** ne soyez pas si curieux! mêlez-vous de vos (propres) affaires! **n. parker,** fouinard *m*, fouine *f*, furet *m*, fureteur, -euse; indiscret, -ète. **2.** au nez fort. **3.** *A:* d'odeur désagréable; qui sent.

not [nɔt], *adv.* (ne) . . . pas, (ne) . . . point. **1.** *A: & Lit:* (*following the verb*) **I know n.,** je ne sais pas; **fear n.,** n'ayez pas peur; n'ayez point de crainte. **2.** (*a*) (*following the aux. verb, usually affixed as* **n't**) **I don't, do n., know,** je ne sais pas; **he won't, will n., come,** il ne viendra pas; **he won't come until after dinner,** il ne viendra qu'après le dîner; **he won't come at all,** il ne viendra pas du tout; **is he coming?—no, he isn't, he's n.,** vient-il?—non; **will he come?—I say he won't,** viendra-t-il?—je dis que non; **she isn't there,** elle n'est pas là; **don't move,** ne bougez pas; **I'm n. in the least surprised,** je ne suis nullement étonné; **I haven't seen him yet,** je ne l'ai pas encore vu; **you understand, don't you?** vous comprenez; n'est-ce pas? **you'll be home early, won't you?** tu rentreras de bonne heure, n'est-ce pas? **isn't it disgusting?** c'est dégoûtant, non? **I bet it isn't,** je parie que non; **please don't!** je vous en prie! **we can't n. do it,** impossible de s'en abstenir; **we can't do it but we can't n. try,** nous ne pouvons pas le faire mais il faut essayer; (*b*) (*stressed*) **I am ready—you're *n*.,** je suis prêt—(non), vous ne l'êtes pas; **no, she would *n*. wear an apron!** non! un tablier, elle n'en porterait pas; (*c*) (*elliptically, in answers, etc.*) **what's she like?—n. pretty,** comment est-elle?—pas jolie; **n. at all, n. a bit of it,** pas du tout; **you're angry, aren't you?—n. at all!** vous êtes fâché, n'est-ce pas?—mais pas du tout! en aucune façon! que non pas! **thank you so much!—n. at all!** merci beaucoup!—je vous en prie (monsieur, madame, mademoiselle)! **are you going there?—certainly n.,** y allez-vous?—ah ça, non! **if it's fine we'll go out, if n., we won't,** s'il fait beau nous sortirons, sinon, pas; *F:* **n. if I know it, n. if I've (got) anything to do with it, n. likely,** jamais de la vie! **why n.?** pourquoi pas? **I wish it weren't (so),** je voudrais (bien) que non, que cela ne soit pas; **I don't care whether he comes or n.,** qu'il vienne ou non, cela m'est égal; **you are free to believe it or n.,** libre à vous de ne pas le croire; **whether he likes it or n.,** que cela lui plaise ou non; **we walk little or n. at all,** nous marchons peu ou pas, peu ou point; **I think n.,** je crois que non, il me semble que non; **I'm afraid n.,** j'ai peur que non; **I hope n.,** j'espère que non; **wasn't he invited?—he says n.,** est-ce qu'on ne l'a pas invité?—il dit que non; **n. always,** pas toujours; **n. yet,** pas encore; **mine n. yet worked,** mine non encore exploitée; **lilac n. yet in bloom,** des lilas pas encore fleuris; **n. even in France,** (non) pas même en France; **n. negotiable,** non négociable; **n. guilty,** non coupable. **3.** (*with the verb infinite*) **n. wishing to be seen, I drew the curtain,** ne désirant pas être vu, comme je ne désirais pas être vu, j'ai tiré le rideau; **n. including . . ., n. to mention . . .,** sans compter . . .; *F:* **n. to worry!** ne vous en faites pas! ne nous en faisons pas! **he asked me n. to do it,** il m'a demandé de ne pas le faire; **he did wrong in n. speaking,** il a eu tort de ne pas parler; **I didn't know what to do, or what n. to do,** je ne savais ni que faire, ni de quoi m'abstenir. **4. n. that . . .,** ce n'est pas que . . ., ce n'est point à dire que . . ., non (pas) que . . .; **n. that I fear him,** non (pas) que je le craigne; **(it's) n. that I don't pity you,** non que je ne vous plaigne; **what's he doing now? n. that I care,** qu'est-ce qu'il fait maintenant? d'ailleurs je m'en soucie peu! **n. that he is handsome,** non pas qu'il soit beau; **n. that I can remember,** pas autant qu'il m'en souvienne. **5.** (*in contrasts*) **she's n. my mother but yours,** elle n'est pas ma mère à moi, mais la vôtre; **she's n. my mother but my aunt,** ce n'est pas ma mère, c'est ma tante; **she's your aunt, (and) n. mine,** elle est votre tante à vous et non la mienne; **he is respected but n. loved,** il est respecté mais non pas aimé; **n. only . . . but also . . .,** non seulement . . . mais encore . . .. **6.** (*with pronoun*) **n. I,** pas moi; **n. one replied,** pas un(e) n'a répondu; **are you going to tell him?—n. I!** allez-vous le lui dire?—moi? bien sûr que non! **he'll never pay, n. he!** il ne paiera jamais, cela c'est sûr! **she wouldn't agree—n. she!** elle n'y consentirait pas, vous la connaissez bien! **7.** (*understatement*) **I wasn't sorry to go,** j'étais très content de partir; **there were n. a few women amongst them,** il y avait pas mal de femmes parmi eux; **the news caused n. a little surprise,** la surprise a été grande à cette nouvelle; **he is n. a little ashamed of himself,** il est rempli de honte; **n. a beautiful town,** une ville pas belle; **n. far from the town,** non loin de la ville; **n. once (n)or twice,** plusieurs fois; bien des fois; **n. without reason,** non sans raison; *F:* **n. half!** et comment! tu peux y aller! tu parles! **8. n. a word was spoken,** pas un mot n'a été dit; **n. a murmur was heard,** pas un murmure ne se fit entendre; **five wounded and n. a man killed,** cinq blessés et pas un (seul) homme tué; **who will believe it?—n. a soul,** qui le croira?—pas un. **9.** *Cmptr:* **n. element,** élément *m* non; inverseur *m*; **n. operation,** opération *f* non; **n.-and element,** élément non et.

nota bene [noutə'benei, -'bi:ni]. *Lt. phr:* nota bene.

notability [noutə'biliti], *s.* **1.** (*pers.*) notabilité *f*, notable *mf*, célébrité *f*, personne, *f* considérable. **2.** notabilité, caractère *m* notable, prééminence *f* (d'un fait, etc.).

notable ['noutəbl], *a.* **1.** (*a*) (*of pers., thg*) notable, considérable, insigne, remarquable; (*of pers.*) éminent; (*b*) *s.* notable *m*; *esp. Fr.Hist:* **Assembly of Notables,** Assemblée *f* des notables. **2.** *Ch:* (*of quantity, etc.*) perceptible, sensible. **3.** *a. A:* (femme) économe; bonne ménagère.

notably ['noutəbli], *adv.* **1.** notablement, remarquablement. **2.** notamment, particulièrement, spécialement.

notarial [nou'teəriəl], *a. Jur:* **1.** (*of functions, seal, etc.*) notarial, -aux; (*of style, etc.*) de notaire. **2.** (*of deed, etc.*) notarié.

notary ['noutəri], *s.* **1.** *Jur: Scot:* **n. (public),** notaire *m*; **before a n.,** par-devant notaire. **2.** *Ecc:* **apostolical n.,** notaire apostolique.

notate [nou'teit], *v.tr. Mus: Danc:* noter.

notated [nou'teitid], *a. Mus: Danc:* noté.

notation [nou'teiʃ(ə)n], *s.* notation *f*; **algebraic, musical, n.,** notation algébrique, musicale; **dance n.,** notation chorégraphique; **n. of a sound by a symbol,** figuration *f* d'un son par un symbole; *Mth:* **decimal n.,** numération, notation, décimale; **binary n.,** numération binaire; *Cmptr:* **prefix n., parentheses-free n., Polish n., Lukasiewicz n.,** notation préfixée; **base n., radix n.,** indication *f* de la base.

notator [nou'teitər], *s. Mus: Danc:* noteur *m.*

notch[1] [nɔtʃ], *s.* **1.** (*a*) entaille *f*, encoche *f*, cran *m*; hoche (faite sur une taille); enfourchement *m* (de tenon); trait *m* (de scie); cran, dent *f* (d'une roue); barbe *f* (de pêne); *U.S: Artil: etc:* cran de mire de la hausse; *Dressm:* cran; *For:* (*in tree to be cut*) blanchi(s) *m*, miroir *m*; *Mec.E:* **lock n., stop n.,** cran d'arrêt; **expansion n.,** cran de détente; **neutral n.,** cran de point mort, cran neutre; *Aut: etc:* **to adjust (the brakes, etc.) a n.,** faire un cran (aux freins, etc.); (*in jumping*) **to raise the bar one n.,** hausser la barre d'un cran; *Artil: Sm.a:* **first n. of the cocking piece,** cran de l'abattu; **sight(ing) n.,** cran de mire; **full cock n.,** cran de l'armé, cran de départ; *Carp:* **skew n.,** embrèvement *m*; *Cmptr:* encoche (de carte magnétique, etc.); **n. coding,** encochage *m* (de cartes à encoches marginales); (*b*) brèche *f* (dans une lame, etc.); (*c*) échancrure *f*; *Anat:* **sciatic n.,** échancrure sciatique; **mandibular n., sigmoid n.,** échancrure sigmoïde. **2.** *NAm:* défilé *m*, gorge *f* (de montagne); (*in Newfoundland*) entrée *f* d'un port.

notch[2], *v.tr.* **1.** (*a*) entailler, encocher, cocher, hocher (un bâton, etc.); denteler, créneler (une roue, etc.); *For:* griffer (de jeunes baliveaux); **to n. a tally,** faire une hoche, une coche, à une taille; *Dressm:* **to n. a seam, an armhole,** faire des crans à, échancrer, cranter, une couture, une emmanchure; *Carp:* **to n. two planks together,** assembler deux planches à entailles; **to n. a post, a beam (where it is to bed),** ruiner un poteau, une poutre; (*b*) ébrécher (une lame, etc.). **2.** *Const:* **to n. steps in a staircase,** poser les marches d'un escalier. **3. to n. up, down, a sum, items,** cocher une somme, des détails. **4.** ajuster (une flèche).

notchboard ['nɔtʃbɔ:d], *s. Const:* limon *m* d'escalier.

notched [nɔtʃt], *a.* (*a*) (*of plank, stick, etc.*) entaillé, à entailles, à coches, à crans, à encoches; (*of wheel, chisel, etc.*) à dents; **n. quadrant,** secteur denté; *Carp:* **n. joint,** trave *f*, assemblage *m* à entailles; (*b*) (*of blade, etc.*) ébréché; *Cin:* **n. blade,** pale échancrée (de l'obturateur de l'appareil de projection); (*c*) *Nat.Hist:* dentelé.

notcher ['nɔtʃər], *s. Metalw: Tls:* grugeoir *m.*

notching ['nɔtʃiŋ], *s.* entaillage *m*, encochement *m* (d'un bâton, etc.); bretture *f* (de la pierre avec une gradine); *For:* griffage *m*; *Carp:* ruinure *f* (d'un poteau, d'une poutre); *Metalw: etc:* grugeage *m*; **n. machine,** machine *f* à encocher, grugeoir *m.*

note[1] [nout], *s.* **1.** *Mus: etc:* (*a*) note *f*; caractère *m* de musique; (*b*) touche *f* (d'un piano, etc.); (*c*) note, son *m*; **the seven notes of the scale,** les sept notes de la gamme; **the leading n.,** la (note) sensible; (*as cue for singer, dancer, etc.*) **to give a n., to strike the n.,** donner la note; **to sing, play, a false n.,** faire une fausse note; (*d*) chant *m*, ramage *m* (d'oiseau); (*of bird*) **to give n.,** chanter; **a n. of originality,** une note d'originalité; **there was a n. of impatience in his voice,** son ton indiquait une certaine impatience; *Lit:* **to sound the n. of war,** parler de guerre; **speech that strikes the right n.,** discours *m* dans la note voulue. **2.** (*a*) marque *f*, signe *m*, indice *m* (d'un fait, d'une qualité, etc.); (*b*) *A:* **n. of infamy,** stigmate *m*; marque déshonorante; **to set a n. of infamy on sth.,** marquer qch. d'un stigmate, d'une note d'infamie; (*c*) *Typ: etc:* **n. of exclamation, of interrogation,** point *m* d'exclamation, d'interrogation. **3.** (*a*) note, mémorandum *m*, mémento *m*; **n. on an agreement,** note ayant trait à un contrat; **let me have a n. on the matter,** remettez-moi une note de l'affaire; *Sch:* **lecture notes,** notes de cours; **to make, take (down), notes,** prendre des notes; **to take, make, a n. of sth.,** prendre note de qch., prendre qch. en note, noter qch.; **to take n. of a declaration,** prendre acte d'une déclaration; **to take n. of events,** tenir registre des événements; **to take due n. of sth.,** prendre bonne note de qch.; **to keep a n. of sth.,** garder note de qch.; **to speak from, with, notes,** prononcer un discours en s'aidant de notes; **to preach without notes,** prêcher sans notes; (*b*) note, commentaire *m*, annotation *f*, remarque *f* (sur un texte); **critical notes on a work,** remarques critiques sur un ouvrage; **notes on Tacitus,** commentaire sur Tacite; **to write, make, notes on a text,** annoter un texte, accompagner un texte de notes, de remarques; (*at end of book*) **bibliographical n.,** souscription *f*; (*c*) billet *m*; petite lettre; mot *m*; **I wrote a n. to her at once,** je lui ai tout de suite écrit un mot; (*d*) **diplomatic n.,** note diplomatique, mémorandum. **4.** *Fin: Com:* (*a*) billet, bordereau *m*; **n. of hand,** reconnaissance *f* (de dette); billet simple; **promissory n.,** billet (simple); bon *m*; **commission n.,** bon de commission; **discount n.,** bordereau d'escompte; **credit n.,** note, facture *f*, bordereau, de crédit, d'avoir; **debit n.,** note, bordereau, de débit; **advice n.,** note, lettre, d'avis; **dispatch n.,** bordereau d'expédition; *St.Exch:* **contract n.,** bordereau d'achat, de vente; **customhouse n.,** bordereau de douane; (*b*) billet (de banque); **hundred-franc notes,** coupures *f* de cent francs; **country notes,** billets de banque de province; *U.S:* **n. broker,** courtier *m* de change. **5.** (*a*) distinction *f*, marque *f*, renom *m*; **a man of n.,** un homme marquant, de renom, de marque, de note; un homme bien connu; une notoriété; **all the people of n. in the town had received invitations,** on avait convié toutes les notabilités de la ville; (*b*) attention *f*, remarque *f*; **it is worthy of n. that. . .,** il sied de noter que . . .; **nothing of n.,** rien d'important; **to take n. of sth.,** retenir qch. dans sa mémoire; remarquer qch.; faire la remarque de qch.

note[2], *v.tr.* **1.** noter, constater, remarquer, prendre note de (qch.); **to n. a misprint, a mistake,** relever une faute d'impression, une erreur; **to n. a resemblance between . . .,** constater une ressemblance entre . . .; **the improvement noted is being maintained,** l'amélioration enregistrée se maintient; **to n. sth. as a fact, to n. a fact,** constater, noter, un fait; prendre acte d'un fait; **which fact is hereby duly noted,** dont acte; **I n. that you do not deny it,** je constate que vous ne vous en défendez pas; **it should be noted that. . .,** il est à noter que . . .; **may I ask you to n. that,** puis-je vous prier d'observer que . . .; **we duly n. that . . .,** nous prenons bonne note (de ce) que . . .; **you will n. that there is an error in the account,** vous remarquerez qu'il y a erreur dans le compte; *Com:* **we have noted your order,** nous avons pris bonne note de votre commande. **2. to n. sth. (down),** écrire, inscrire, prendre note de, qch.; **to n. events in one's books,** tenir registre des événements. **3.** *A:* annoter (un texte).

notebook ['noutbuk], *s.* carnet *m*, calepin *m*, mémorandum *m*, agenda *m*; (*for shorthand, etc.*) bloc-notes *m*, *pl.* blocs-notes: (*larger*) cahier *m*; **pocket n.,** carnet de poche.

notecase ['noutkeis], *s.* portefeuille *m*; porte-coupures *m inv*; porte-billets *m inv.*

noted ['noutid], *a.* (*of pers.*) distingué, célèbre, éminent, illustre; (*of thg*) fameux, célèbre, remarquable (**for sth.,** par qch.).

notehead ['nouthed], *s. esp. U.S:* en-tête *m inv*; **n. paper,** papier *m* à en-tête.

notepad ['noutpæd], *s.* bloc-notes *m*, *pl.* blocs-notes; bloc *m* (de correspondance).

notepaper ['noutpeipər], *s.* papier *m* à lettres, à écrire.

noter ['noutər], *s.* remarqueur, -euse; **great n. of events,** grand enregistreur des événements.

noteworthiness ['noutwə:ðinis], *s.* importance *f*, qualité *f* remarquable (d'un fait, etc.).

noteworthy ['noutwə:ði], *a.* (*of fact, etc.*) remarquable, mémorable, digne d'attention, de remarque; **it is n. that . . .,** il convient de noter que . . ..

nothing ['nʌθiŋ], *pron.. s. & adv.*

I. *pron.* rien (*with* ne *expressed or understood*) (*a*) **he does n.,** il ne fait rien; **to spend the day doing n.,** passer la journée à (ne) rien faire; **I ate n. for three days,** je n'ai rien mangé pendant trois jours; **I saw n.,** je n'ai rien vu; **what are you doing?—n.,** que faites-vous?—rien; **n. interests him,** rien ne l'intéresse; **it's all or n.,** c'est tout ou rien; **it's better than n.,** cela vaut mieux que rien; **n. could be simpler,** rien de plus simple; c'est tout ce qu'il y a de plus simple; **n. could be finer than . . .,** rien de plus beau que . . .; **I see n. that I like,** je ne vois rien qui me plaise; **n. that I saw pleased me,** rien de ce que j'ai vu ne m'a plu; **you can't live on n.,** on ne peut pas vivre de rien; **to live on (next to) n.,** vivre de l'air du temps; **for next to n.,** pour trois fois rien; **one can live here for next to n.,** la vie est pour rien ici; **to get sth. for (next to) n.,** avoir, obtenir, qch. pour rien; *F:* **I feel like n. on earth,** je ne sais pas ce que je ressens; **it looks like n. (else) on earth,** cela ne ressemble à rien; **you look like n. on earth in, with, that hat!** de quoi avez-vous l'air avec ce chapeau! **as if n. had happened,** comme si de rien n'était; **fit for n.,** propre, bon, à rien; **I can do n. in the matter,** je n'y peux rien; **say n. about it,** n'en dites rien; **to say n. of . . .,** sans parler de . . .; **they quarrel about n., for n.,** ils se querellent à propos de rien; **he gets angry about n.,** il se fâche de rien, pour des riens; un rien le fâche; **they know n. about it,** ils n'en savent rien; **n. at all,** rien du tout; **he knows n. (whatever), absolutely n., n. at all, about anything,** il ne sait rien de rien, il sait deux fois rien; **the purse had n. in it,** il n'y avait rien dans la bourse; la bourse était vide; **there's n. in these rumours,** ces bruits sont sans fondement; **there's n. in it,** (i) cela n'a pas d'importance; c'est sans intérêt; ce n'est pas une affaire; (ii) (*in choice*) l'un vaut l'autre; ça se vaut; *F:* **there's n. to it, in it,** c'est simple comme bonjour; **the house is n. without the garden,** la maison n'est rien sans le jardin; **he was n. if not discreet,** il était surtout discret; il était discret avant tout; **to rise from n.,** partir de rien, de zéro; **to create an army out of n.,** créer une armée de toutes pièces; **my father's conservative, my brother's liberal, but I'm n.,** mon père est conservateur, mon frère libéral, mais moi je ne suis rien, je n'appartiens à aucun parti; **catholics, protestants, and people who are n.,** catholiques, protestants, et ceux qui n'appartiennent à aucune religion; *F:* **no tea, no coffee, no milk, no n.,** pas de thé, pas de café, pas de lait, rien de rien; *Prov:* **n. ventured, n. gained,** qui ne risque rien n'a rien; (*b*) (*followed by adj.*) rien de . . .; **n. new,** rien de nouveau, rien de neuf; **that's n. unusual,** cela n'a rien d'anormal; **there is n. heroic about him,** il n'a rien d'un héros; **n. much,** pas grand-chose; **n. good will come out of it,** cela n'annonce rien de bon; **I had n. much to complain of except my poverty,** je n'avais guère à me plaindre d'autre chose que de ma pauvreté; **he's a good N.C.O., n. more,** c'est un bon gradé, sans plus; **there is n. more to be said,** il n'y a rien de plus à dire; il n'y a plus rien à dire; **we had n. more to say to each other,** nous n'avions plus rien, rien de plus, à nous dire; (*c*) **I have n. to do,** je n'ai rien à faire; **there is n. to be done,** il n'y a rien à faire; **to have n. to do with sth.,** n'avoir rien à faire, n'avoir aucun rapport, avec qch.; **he had n. to do with the matter, with it,** il n'était pour rien dans l'affaire; il n'entrait pas dans l'affaire; **I'll have n. to do with it,** je ne veux rien avoir à faire avec; **that's n. to do with it,** cela ne fait rien à l'affaire; cela n'entre pas en ligne de compte; **that's n. to do with you,** ce n'est pas votre affaire; vous n'avez rien à y voir; cela ne vous regarde pas; **there is n. to cry about,** il n'y a pas de quoi pleurer; **there's n. to laugh at,** il n'y a pas de quoi rire; **that's n. to be proud of,** il n'y a pas de quoi être fier; **he has n. to say for himself,** (i) il ne parle guère; (ii) il ne sait pas se faire valoir; (iii) il ne peut rien dire pour se défendre; il est sans excuse; **I had n. to say against the proposal,** je n'avais rien à objecter à la proposition; (*d*) **he has n. of his father in him,** il n'a rien de son père; **he's n. of a scholar,** ce n'est pas du tout un savant; il n'est rien moins qu'un savant; (*e*) **n. else,** rien d'autre; **n. but . . .,** rien que . . .; **n. else but . . ., n. else than . . .,** rien d'autre que . . .; **I have n. (else) to do but . . .,** je n'ai rien (d'autre) à faire que de . . .; **n. else could be done,** (i) on ne pouvait rien faire de plus; (ii) on ne pouvait faire autrement; **n. else matters,** tout le reste n'est rien; **it is n. else but, than, pure laziness,** c'est de la paresse pure et simple; **n. but the truth,** rien que la vérité; **there was n. of the bear left but the skin,** il ne restait (rien) de l'ours que la peau; **he does n. but go in and out,** il ne fait qu'entrer et sortir; **there is n. for it but to submit,** il n'y a qu'à se soumettre; il n'y a pas d'autre alternative, il ne reste rien à faire, que de se soumettre; il n'y a pas d'alternative, il faut céder; **there is n. for it but to go yourself,** vous ne pouvez pas faire autrement, il n'y a rien (d'autre) à faire, que d'y aller vous-même; **there was n. for it but to wait,** force nous était d'attendre; **there's n. else for it,** c'est inévitable; **you walked back?—there was n. else for it,** vous êtes revenu à pied?—il a bien fallu; **there's n. like knowing how to listen,** rien de tel que de savoir écouter; (*f*) **to do sth. for n.,** (i) faire qch. en vain, inutilement; (ii) faire qch. sans raison, à propos de rien; (iii) faire qch. gratuitement; **it's not for n. that . . .,** (i) ce n'est pas sans raison que . . .; (ii) ce n'est pas sans motif que . . .; **he let me have it for (almost) n.,** il me l'a cédé pour (presque) rien, pour une bouchée de pain; **all my work went for n., I got n. out of it,** j'ai travaillé pour le roi de Prusse; j'en suis pour mes frais; **all my efforts went for n.,** c'étaient des efforts perdus; **all that goes for n.,** tout cela ne compte pas; **to count for n.,** ne compter pour rien; *Prov:* **n. for n.,** point d'argent, point de Suisse; (*g*) **n. for s.o., sth.,** (i) indifférent à qn; (ii) pas comparable à qn, à qch.; **she is n. to him,** elle lui est indifférente; **is he a relative?—no, he's n. to me,** est-il un parent?—non, il ne m'est rien; **£1000 is n. to him,** mille livres ne sont rien pour lui; **it's n. to me whether he comes or not,** qu'il vienne ou non, cela m'est égal; **it's n. to me either way,** cela m'est égal; **that's n. to you,** (i) pour vous ce n'est rien; (ii) cela ne vous intéresse pas; (iii) cela ne vous regarde pas; **at tennis she's n. to her sister,** au tennis elle n'est rien à côté de sa sœur; (*h*) **to make, think, n. of sth.,** (i) ne pas se soucier de qch.; n'attacher aucune importance à qch.; ne faire aucun cas de qch.; (ii) ne pas se faire scrupule de faire qch.; **he makes n. of walking 10 km,** il se fait un jeu de faire 10 km à pied; **he thinks n. of borrowing from the till,** il ne se fait pas scrupule d'emprunter à la caisse; **he thinks n. of a lie,** un mensonge ne lui coûte rien; (*i*) **I can make n., n. at all, of it,** je n'y comprends rien, rien du tout, absolument rien.

II. *s.* **1.** *Mth:* zéro *m.* **2.** néant *m*; rien; **to come to n.,** ne pas aboutir; se réduire, tomber, à rien; (*of hopes, etc.*) s'anéantir; **the negotiations came to n.,** les négociations n'ont pas abouti; **the scheme has come to n.,** le projet s'est effondré; **the colours have faded away to n.,** les couleurs sont complètement passées; **to reduce an army to n.,** anéantir une armée. **3.** bagatelle *f*; vétille *f*; rien *m*; **airy nothings,** des bagatelles; **a mere n.,** si peu que rien; **a hundred francs? a mere n.!** cent francs? une misère! une bêtise! **to punish a child for a mere n.,** punir un enfant pour une vétille; **it's n. to him,** cela ne le touche pas; **have you hurt yourself?—oh, it's n.,** vous vous êtes fait mal?—oh, ce n'est rien; **in those days it was n. to see . . .,** en ce temps-là on voyait facilement . . .

III. *adv.* aucunement, nullement; pas du tout; *O:* **this helps us n.,** ceci ne nous avance pas du tout; *O:* **that is n. to the purpose,** cela ne fait rien à l'affaire; *A:* & *Lit:* **n. loath,** volontiers, sans hésiter; **it was n. like as, so, wonderful as we'd imagined,** ce n'était nullement aussi merveilleux qu'on se l'était figuré; **n. like, near, so big, as big,** loin d'être aussi grand; **it is n. less than madness,** c'est de la folie ni plus ni moins.

nothingness ['nʌθiŋnis], *s.* néant *m*; **to pass into n.,** s'anéantir; rentrer dans le néant; **to return to everlasting n.,** rentrer dans un éternel néant; **God created the world out of n.,** Dieu a tiré l'univers du néant; **the n. of human greatness,** le vide des grandeurs humaines.

notice[1] ['noutis], *s.* **1.** (*a*) avis *m*, notification *f*, intimation *f*; **n. of receipt,** avis de réception; **n. of delivery,** avis, accusé *m*, de réception; (*b*) préavis *m*, avertissement *m*; **n. in writing,** avis par écrit; **to give s.o. n. of sth.,** prévenir qn de qch.; **to give s.o. n. of one's intentions,** avertir qn de ses intentions; **I must have n.,** il faudra m'en avertir, m'en donner avis préalable; **to give official n. of . . ., that . . .,** donner acte de . . ., que . . .; **to give s.o. formal n. of sth.,** intimer qch. à qn; **to give n. of . . ., that . . .,** donner avis de . . ., que . . .; **without (prior) n.,** sans préavis; **without n. he sold the house,** sans avis préliminaire, sans avis préalable, sans en aviser personne, il a vendu la maison; **to give n. to the authorities,** informer, prévenir, l'autorité (**of, de**); *Pol:* **to give n. of a question, of an amendment,** donner avis préalable d'une interpellation, d'un amendement; **I must have n. of that question,** je demande que cette interpellation soit inscrite à l'ordre du jour; **to give out a n.,** lire une communication; faire l'annonce de qch.; **take n. that after the twelfth of July . . .,** vous êtes prévenu, avisé, qu'à partir du douze juillet . . .; **n. is hereby given that . . .,** le public est avisé que . . .; on fait savoir que . . .; **public n.,** avis au public; **important n.,** avis important; **n. of a meeting,** convocation *f* d'assemblée; *Ecc:* **the weekly notices,** les annonces de la semaine; **until further n.,** jusqu'à nouvel ordre; jusqu'à nouvel avis; jusqu'à avis contraire; **n. of termination of a treaty,** dénonciation *f* d'un traité; *Jur:* **n. of measures about to be taken,** dénonciation des mesures que l'on va prendre; (*c*) avis formel, instructions formelles; (*served by bailiff, etc.*) exploit *m*; **to give s.o. n. to do sth.,** aviser qn de faire qch.; **to send s.o. a second n.,** réavertir qn; *Jur:* **peremptory n. to do sth.,** mise en demeure formelle de faire qch.; **n. of appeal,** intimation *f*; **to receive n. to do sth.,** être mis en demeure de faire qch.; **n. to pay,** avertissement; **n. to perform a contract,** sommation *f*; mise *f* en demeure; **to give n. of distraint,** dénoncer une saisie; **to serve a n. on s.o.,** signifier un arrêt à qn; (*d*) **at short n.,** à court délai; à bref délai; **I can't do it at such short n.,** je ne peux pas le faire dans un aussi court délai; **always ready to start at short n., at a day's n.,** toujours prêt à partir à l'instant, du jour au lendemain; **to give s.o. short n.,** prendre qn de court; **I had to leave at half an hour's n.,** j'ai dû partir une demi-heure après avoir reçu avis; **at a moment's, a minute's, n.,** à la minute, à l'instant, sur-le-champ; **without a moment's n.,** sans crier gare; **to replace s.o. at a moment's n., without a moment's n.,** *F:* remplacer qn au pied levé; **to dismiss s.o. at a moment's n.,** renvoyer qn sans avertissement préalable, sur-le-champ, du jour au lendemain; **weapons ready for use at a moment's n.,** armes prêtes à servir au premier signal; **term of n.,** délai de préavis; **to give previous n. to s.o.,** préaviser qn; **to give six months' n. of sth.,** donner avis de qch. six mois d'avance; **to require three months' n.,** exiger un préavis de trois mois; *Com:* **can be delivered at three days' n.,** livrable dans un délai de trois jours; *Fin:* **realizable at short n.,** réalisable à court terme; *Bank:* **deposit at seven days' n.,** dépôt à sept jours de préavis; **n. of withdrawal,** mandat *m*; *Nau:* **n. for steam** = les délais d'appareillage; position *f* d'attente; **to remain at six hours' n.,** tenir les chaudières, les feux, à six heures d'appareillage; **what n. are you at?** quel est l'état de vos feux? (*e*) **n. (to quit),** (avis de) congé *m*; *Jur:* intimation de vider les lieux; **to give a tenant n. to quit, to serve n. upon a tenant,** donner congé, signifier son congé, à un locataire; **to be under n. to quit,** avoir reçu son congé; **he received n. to quit within twenty-four hours,** on lui a notifié qu'il eût à déménager dans les vingt-quatre heures; **what n. do you require?** quel est le terme du congé? **to give n.,** (i) (*of landlord, employer*) donner, signifier, son congé (à qn); (ii) (*of tenant, employee*) donner, demander, (son) congé; signifier, donner, sa démission; **you have to give a month's n.,** il faut donner congé un mois d'avance; **a week's n.,** un congé, un préavis, de huit jours; **to give s.o. a week's n.,** donner ses huit jours à qn. **2.** (*a*) affiche *f*; indication *f*; **n. (to the public),** avis (au public); placard *m*; (*on a card*) écriteau *m*; **I saw a n.** *for sale* **in front of the house,** j'ai vu un écriteau annonçant *à vendre* devant la maison; **n. of sale by auction,** publication *f* de vente aux enchères; **to stick up a n.,** placarder une affiche; **n. board,** (i) (*on house for sale, etc.*) écriteau; (*in schools, clubs, etc.*) tableau *m* d'affichage, d'annonces, de publicité; porte-affiches *m inv*; (ii) panneau indicateur (de route); panneau de signalisation routière; plaque indicatrice; (*b*) (*in newspaper, etc.*) annonce *f*, note *f*, notice *f*, entrefilet *m*; **notices of new publications,** bulletin *m* littéraire; **to put a n. in the papers,** mettre une annonce, faire passer une note, dans les journaux; (*c*) revue *f* (d'un ouvrage). **3.** (*a*) attention *f*, connaissance *f*, observation *f*; **to take n. of s.o., sth.,** faire attention, prêter (son) attention, à qn, à qch.; observer qn, qch.; tenir compte, prendre connaissance, de qn, de qch.; **take n.!** avis au public; **to take no, not the least, n. of sth.,** ne faire aucune attention, ne pas prêter la moindre attention, à qch.; **to take no n. of an objection,** passer outre à une objection; **without seeming to take any n.,** sans faire semblant de rien; **I was there but nobody took any n. of me,** j'étais présent mais personne n'a pris garde à moi, personne ne s'est intéressé à moi; **I should take no n., I shouldn't take any n., of it,** je n'y prendrais pas garde; **I didn't take any particular n.,** je n'y ai pas fait particulièrement attention; **the news received no particular n.,** les nouvelles n'ont excité que peu d'intérêt; **the fact came to his n. that . . .,** son attention a été attirée par le fait que . . .; **to attract n.,** se faire remarquer, s'afficher; commencer à être connu; **author who is beginning to attract n.,** auteur qui commence à percer; **to avoid n.,** se dérober aux regards; **to bring, call, sth., s.o., to s.o.'s n.,** appeler, porter, attirer, l'attention de qn sur qch., qn; signaler, désigner, recommander, qch., qn, l'attention de qn; faire observer qch., qn, à qn; **it's not worth n., it's beneath n.,** cela ne vaut pas la peine qu'on y fasse attention; cela est indigne de notre attention; (*b*) **the baby is beginning to take n.,** le bébé commence à avoir conscience des choses; *F:* **to sit up and take n.,** se réveiller; dresser l'oreille.

notice[2], *v.tr.* **1.** observer, remarquer, s'apercevoir de, tenir compte de, prendre garde à (qn, qch.); faire la remarque de (qch.); relever (des fautes); **to n. s.o. in a crowd,** remarquer qn dans la foule; **let us now n. the effect of . . .,** considérons maintenant l'effet de . . .; **I've never noticed it,** je n'y ai jamais pris garde; je ne l'ai jamais remarqué; **without his noticing it,** sans qu'il y prît garde; **he didn't seem to n.,** il n'a pas tiqué; **I hadn't noticed that the bus was running past the stop,** je n'avais pas pris garde que le car dépassait l'arrêt; **I noticed from the appearance of the room that . . .,** j'ai reconnu à l'aspect de la pièce que . . .; **he noticed she was less attentive,** il la voyait moins attentive; **I noticed her wipe away a tear,** j'ai vu qu'elle essuyait une larme; **to be noticed, to get oneself noticed, by s.o.,** attirer l'attention de qn (sur soi); **mistake that is noticed at once,** faute qui attire l'attention, qui saute aux yeux; *F:* (*with passive force*) **does it n.?** est-ce que ça se voit? **the darn doesn't n.,** la reprise ne se voit pas. **2.** donner congé, signifier son congé, à (un locataire, etc.). **3.** *A:* **to n. sth. to s.o.,** mentionner, faire remarquer (qch. à qn); faire la remarque de qch. à qn. **4.** *O:* donner la revue, le compte rendu, d'une pièce, etc.; **the play was noticed in the Sunday papers,** les journaux de dimanche ont publié un compte rendu de la pièce.

noticeable ['noutisəbl], *a.* **1.** (*of fact, etc.*) digne d'attention, de remarque; **to be n. because of sth.,** se faire remarquer par qch. **2.** perceptible, sensible; apparent; **it isn't n., it's not n.,** cela ne se voit pas, ne s'aperçoit pas; **the difference is very n.,** la différence est très sensible.

noticeably ['noutisəbli], *adv.* perceptiblement, sensiblement, visiblement.

notifiable ['noutifaiəbl], *a.* (maladie) dont la déclaration aux autorités est obligatoire.

notification [noutifi'keiʃ(ə)n], *s.* avis *m*, notification *f*, annonce *f* (d'un fait, etc.); déclaration *f* (de naissance); *Jur:* cédule *f* (de citation); **letter of n.,** lettre notificative.

notify ['noutifai], *v.tr.* annoncer, notifier (qch.); déclarer (une naissance, etc.); **to n. s.o. of sth.,** avertir, aviser, qn de qch.; notifier qch. à qn; faire connaître qch. à qn; **to n. s.o. of the day of one's visit,** aviser qn du jour de sa visite; **to n. the authorities of a fact,** saisir l'administration d'un fait; **to n. the police of sth.,** signaler qch. à la police; **to be notified of sth.,** recevoir notification de qch.; être avisé, averti, de qch.; **he was notified that he must leave at once,** on lui a signifié de partir sur-le-champ; *Jur:* **to n. the parties,** faire des intimations aux parties; **to n. s.o. of a decision,** signifier un arrêt à qn.

notion ['nouʃ(ə)n], *s.* **1.** *Phil:* notion *f*, concept *m*. **2.** (*a*) notion, idée *f*; **the n. of good and evil,** la notion du bien et du mal; **to form a true, false, n. of sth.,** se former une idée exacte, fausse, de qch.; **to have no n. of sth.,** n'avoir pas la moindre notion, n'avoir guère conscience, ne pas se douter, de qch.; **to have no n. of time,** n'avoir pas le sens, la notion, de l'heure; **I haven't the first n. about it,** je n'en ai pas la moindre idée; je n'en sais pas le premier mot; **I haven't the faintest n. of what he means,** je n'ai aucune idée, notion, de ce qu'il veut dire; (*b*) opinion *f*, pensée *f*, idée, sentiment *m*; **I have a n. that . . .,** j'ai dans l'idée que . . .; je me suis mis en tête que . . .; il me vient à la pensée que . . .; **such is the common n.,** telle est l'opinion commune; (*c*) caprice *m*; **as the n. takes him,** selon son caprice; **to have a n. to do sth.,** s'aviser, se mettre en tête, de faire qch.; **I have no n. of letting myself be . . .,** je n'ai pas l'intention de me laisser . . .. **3.** (*a*) *A:* invention *f*; (*b*) *pl.* **notions,** petites inventions; petits articles ingénieux; (*c*) *pl. NAm:* **notions,** mercerie *f*.

notional ['nouʃ(ə)nəl], *a.* **1.** (*of knowledge, etc.*) spéculatif. **2.** (*of thgs, relations, etc.*) imaginaire. **3.** *esp. U.S:* (*of pers.*) capricieux, fantasque, visionnaire. **4.** *Ling:* notionnel.

notobranchiate [noutou'bræŋkiət], *a. Ann:* dorsibranche.

notochord ['noutoukɔ:d], *s. Biol:* notoc(h)orde *f*.

notodontid [noutou'dɔntid], *s. Ent:* notodontide *m*.

Notodontidae [noutou'dɔntidi:], *s.pl. Ent:* notodontides *m*.

Notog(a)ean [noutou'dʒi:ən], *a.* de la région australienne; **the N. Islands,** les îles *f* de la région australienne.

notonecta [noutou'nektə], *s. Ent:* notonecte *m*.

Notoptera [nou'tɔptərə], *s.pl. Ent:* notoptères *m*.

notopterid [nou'tɔptərid], *a. & s. Ich:* notoptère (*m*).

notoriety [noutə'raiəti], *s.* **1.** notoriété *f*; *Pej:* **to bring s.o., sth., into n.,** faire connaître qn, qch.; **to seek n.,** chercher à se faire remarquer; rechercher la gloriole; s'afficher. **2.** (*pers.*) notabilité *f*, notable *m*.

notorious [nou'tɔ:riəs], *a.* **1.** *A:* (fait) notoire, bien connu, reconnu; **it is n. that . . .,** il est de notoriété publique que . . .; il est reconnu que . . .. **2.** d'une triste notoriété; (menteur, etc.) insigne; (malfaiteur) reconnu, notoire; (endroit) mal famé; (voleur) fieffé; **a n. woman,** une femme perdue de réputation; **the n. case of . . .,** le cas si tristement célèbre de . . ..

notoriously [nou'tɔ:riəsli], *adv.* notoirement; **n. cruel,** connu pour sa cruauté.

notoriousness [nou'tɔ:riəsnis], *s.* notoriété *f*.

notornis [nou'tɔ:nis], *s. Orn:* notornis *m*.

notoryctid [noutou'riktid], *s. Z:* notorycte *m*.

Notoryctidae [noutou'riktidi:], *s.pl. Z:* notoryctidés *m*, les taupes marsupiales.

nototheniid [noutou'θeniid], *s. Ich:* notothénide *m*.

Nototheniidae [noutouθen'i:idi:], *s.pl. Ich:* notothénidés *m*, notothénides *m*.

no-trumper [nou'trʌmpər], *s. Cards:* jeu *m* de sans-atout.

notwithstanding [nɔtwiθ'stændiŋ]. **1.** *prep.* malgré, en dépit de, nonobstant; **n. all I could say,** malgre tout ce que j'ai pu dire; **he went n. our remonstrances,** il est parti malgré, en dépit de, nos remontrances; *Lit:* **this n., his accent betrayed him,** ce nonobstant, son accent le trahissait; *Jur:* **n. the provisions of . . .,** par dérogation aux dispositions de . . .; **this rule n. . . .,** par, en, dérogation à cette règle . . .. **2.** *adv.* quand même, tout de même; néanmoins, nonobstant; pourtant; **he knows the road is dangerous but takes it n.,** il sait que le chemin est dangereux, mais il le suit tout de même, quand même. **3.** *conj. A:* quoique, en dépit de ce que, bien que + *sub.*; **n. (that) I enjoyed myself, I am glad to be back,** quoique je me sois bien amusé, je suis content d'être de retour.

nougat ['nu:gɑ:, 'nʌgit], *s.* nougat *m*.

nought [nɔ:t], *s.* **1.** = NAUGHT 1. **2.** *Mth:* zéro *m*; **to get a n. (in an exam),** avoir, attraper, un zéro (dans un examen); *Cmptr:* **n. state,** état *m* zéro; *Games:* **noughts and crosses** = morpion *m*.

noumenon, *pl.* **-na** ['nu:minɔn, 'nau-; -nə], *s. Phil:* noumène *m*.

noun [naun], *s. Gram:* substantif *m*, nom *m*; **common n.,** nom commun; **proper n.,** nom propre; **n. clause,** proposition substantive.

nourish ['nʌriʃ], *v.tr.* **1.** (*a*) nourrir (qn, une plante, etc.); alimenter (qn); sustenter (le corps, etc.); **to n. s.o. on, with, sth.,** nourrir qn de qch.; **to be well nourished,** être bien nourri; (*b*) *Ind:* **to n. the wood,** nourrir le bois; **to n. leather,** entretenir le cuir. **2.** *O:* nourrir, entretenir (un sentiment, un espoir, etc.).

nourishing ['nʌriʃiŋ], *a.* nourrissant, nutritif; **milk is n.,** le lait nourrit; **it is too n.,** cela nourrit trop.

nourishment ['nʌriʃmənt], *s.* **1.** (*a*) alimentation *f*, nourriture *f* (de qn, qch.); (*b*) *Leath:* entretien *m* (du cuir). **2.** nourriture, aliments *mpl*; **to take (some) n.,** prendre de la nourriture; *F:* **he's sitting up and taking n.,** il est en bonne voie de s'en remettre.

nous [naus], *s.* **1.** *Gr.Phil:* **the n.,** l'esprit *m*. **2.** *F:* intelligence *f*, sagacité *f*; savoir-faire *m*.

nouveau riche, *pl.* **nouveaux riches** ['nu:vou'ri:ʃ], *s.* nouveau riche.

nova, *pl.* **-ae** ['nouvə, -i:], *s. Astr:* nova *f*, *pl.* novæ.

novaculite [nou'vækjulait], *s. Geol:* novaculite *f*.

Novara [nə'vɑ:rə]. *Pr.n. Geog:* Novare.

Nova Scotia ['nouvə'skouʃə]. *Pr.n. Geog:* Nouvelle-Écosse *f*.

novation [nou'veiʃ(ə)n], *s. Jur:* novation *f* (de débiteur, de contrat, etc.).

Novaya Zemlya ['nɔvəjɑ:'zemljɑ:]. *Pr.n. Geog:* Nouvelle-Zemble *f*.

novel[1] ['nɔv(ə)l], *s.* **1.** *Lit:A:* nouvelle *f*. **2.** *Lit:* roman *m*; **detective n.,** roman policier; **social n.,** roman de mœurs; **autobiographical n.,** roman personnel, autobiographique; **tendenz n.,** roman à thèse; **n. writer,** romancier, -ière; **his adventures read like a n.,** ses aventures ont tout l'intérêt d'un roman. **3.** *Rom: Jur:* novelle *f*.

novel[2], *a.* nouveau, -elle; original, -aux; singulier; **that's a n. idea!** voilà qui est original!

novelette [nɔvə'let], *s.* **1.** *Lit:* (*a*) nouvelle *f*; (*b*) petit roman (à) bon marché; **she was a great reader of cheap novelettes,** elle était grande liseuse de romans d'amour de troisième ordre, de romans à l'eau de rose. **2.** *Mus:* novelette *f*.

novelist ['nɔvəlist], *s. Lit:* romancier, -ière.

novelistic [nɔvə'listik], *a.* du, de, roman.

novelize ['nɔvəlaiz]. *F: v.tr.* mettre (une pièce, l'histoire) en roman; **to n. a film,** écrire la version romancée d'un film; **novelized biography,** biographie romancée.

novella [nou'velə], *s. Lit:* nouvelle *f*.

novelty ['nɔvəlti], *s.* **1.** (*a*) chose nouvelle; innovation *f*; *Com:* (article *m* de) nouveauté *f*; **the latest novelties,** les articles de haute nouveauté, les dernières nouveautés; (*b*) **novelties** = farces *f* et attrapes *f*. **2.** nouveauté, étrangeté *f* (de qch.); **the charm of n.,** le charme de la nouveauté.

November [nə'vembər], *s.* novembre *m*; **in N.,** au mois de novembre; en novembre; **(on) the first, the fifth, of N., (on) N. the first, the fifth,** le premier, le cinq, novembre.

novena [nou'vi:nə], *s. R.C.Ch:* neuvaine *f*.

novercal [nə'vɔ:k(ə)l], *a.* de belle-mère; de marâtre.

novice ['nɔvis], *s.* **1.** *Ecc:* novice *mf*. **2.** (*a*) novice, apprenti, -ie, débutant, -ante; **to be a n. in, at, sth.,** être novice dans, à, qch.; **he's no n.,** il n'en est pas à son coup d'essai; il n'est pas novice; (*b*) (*at horse show, dance competition, etc.*) cheval, personne, qui n'a jamais gagné un prix.

noviciate, novitiate [nou'viʃiət], *s.* **1.** *Ecc:* (temps *m* du) noviciat *m*; **to go through one's n.,** faire son noviciat. **2.** *A:* = NOVICE. **3.** *Ecc:* noviciat; maison *f* des novices.

novocaine ['nouvəkein], *s. Pharm:* novocaïne *f*.

now [nau], *adv., conj. & s.*

I. *adv.* **1.** (*a*) maintenant, en ce moment, à présent, actuellement, à l'heure actuelle; *F:* à l'heure qu'il est; **he is n. in London,** il est actuellement à Londres; **what shall we do n.?** qu'est-ce que nous allons faire maintenant? **the rain is falling n.,** la pluie tombe maintenant; **the methods n. in force,** les méthodes appliquées actuellement; **n. or never, n. if ever, is the time to . . .,** c'est le cas ou jamais de . . .; *F:* **(it's a case of) n. or never,** c'est le cas, le moment, ou jamais; **n. or never!** allons-y! risquons le coup! *F:* **goodbye n.!** au revoir! **goodbye for n.!** à bientôt! **that'll do for n.,** ça suffit pour le moment; (*b*) maintenant; dans ces circonstances; **he won't be long n.,** il ne tardera plus guère; **even n., I don't understand,** même maintenant je ne comprends pas; **I cannot n. very well refuse,** dans ces circonstances je ne peux guère refuser; (*c*) maintenant; tout de suite; immédiatement; **it's going to begin n.,** cela va commencer tout de suite, dans un instant; **and n. I must go,** sur ce je vous quitte; **n. I'm ready,** me voilà prêt; **n. is the time to . . .,** c'est le bon moment pour . . .; **right n.,** tout de suite; **I'm going (right) n.,** j'y vais de ce pas; (*d*) (*in narrative*) alors, à ce moment-là; **all was n. ready,** dès lors tout était prêt; **he was even n. on his way,** il était déjà en route; (*e*) **just n.,** (i) (*past, also A:* **even n., but n.**) tout à l'heure, il y a un instant, il y a peu de temps; (ii) (*present*) en ce moment; **I saw him just n.,** je l'ai vu il y a un instant, tout à l'heure; *O:* **I have just n., only n., arrived,** je ne fais que d'arriver; **I can't do it just n.,** je ne puis pas le faire tout de suite, en ce moment; (*f*) **(every) n. and then, (every) n. and again,** de temps en temps, de temps à autre; de loin en loin; parfois, par intervalles, par moments, par occasion, par-ci par-là; **n. . . . n. . . ., n. . . . then . . ., n. . . . and again . . .,** tantôt . . . tantôt . . .; **n. here n. there,** tantôt ici tantôt là, par-ci par-là; **up to n.,** jusqu'ici; **even n.,** même à cette heure tardive; **from n. on,** dès maintenant; **a good harvest is n. assured,** une belle récolte est désormais assurée; **it's two years (ago) n.,** ça fait déjà deux ans. **2.** (*without temporal significance*) (*a*) (*explanatory, or in development of an argument*) or; **n. to come back to what we were saying,** or, pour revenir à ce que nous disions; **n. that dog of mine . . .,** tenez, mon chien à moi . . .; (*in story*) **n. it happened that . . .,** or il advint que . . .; **n. . . ., therefore . . .,** or . . ., donc . . .; (*b*) (*interjectional expletive*) **n. what's the matter with you? n. what's all this about?** qu'avez-vous donc? voyons, qu'est-ce que vous avez? **n. what do you mean?** que voulez-vous donc dire? **come n.!** voyons! **n., n.! stop quarrelling!** voyons, voyons! assez de querelles! **n. don't nag!** allons, ne faites pas de sermons! **well n.!** eh bien! **n. then!** (i) attention! (ii) voyons! allons! **n. then, look out!** allons, faites attention! **n. then, where have you been?** or çà, d'où venez-vous?

II. *conj.* maintenant que, à présent que; **n. I'm older I think differently,** maintenant que je suis plus âgé je pense autrement; **n. that the cost of living is so high,** maintenant que la vie est si chère; **it's not worth it n. we've waited so long,** ce n'est plus la peine, depuis le temps que nous attendons.

III. *s.* le présent, le temps actuel; **I shall see you between n. and then,** je vous verrai d'ici là; **in three or four days from n.,** d'ici trois ou quatre jours; **he ought to be here by n., he ought to have been here before n.,** il devrait déjà être arrivé; **you ought to be ready by n.,** vous devriez être prêt maintenant; **until n.,** jusqu'ici, jusqu'à présent; **from n. (on),** dès maintenant, dès à présent, à partir de maintenant; **from n. on he'll stop doing it,** (à partir de) maintenant il cessera de le faire.

nowaday ['nauədei], *a. & adv. A:* (*a*) *a.* d'aujourd'hui; (*b*) *adv.* aujourd'hui.

nowadays ['nauədeiz], *adv.* aujourd'hui; de nos jours; à l'heure actuelle; *F:* à l'heure qu'il est; au jour d'aujourd'hui; **that isn't done n.,** cela ne se pratique plus aujourd'hui.

noway(s) ['nouwei(z)], *adv.* = NOWISE.

nowel[1] [nou'el], *int. & s. A:* Noël (*m*)!

nowel[2] ['nouəl], *s. Metall:* grand noyau (de moule).

nowhere ['nou(h)wɛər]. **1.** *adv.* nulle part, en aucun lieu; **he was n. to be found,** on ne le trouvait nulle part; il restait introuvable; **he's n. near as tall as you,** il n'est pas à beaucoup près aussi grand que vous; il s'en faut de beaucoup qu'il soit aussi grand que vous; **it's n. near big enough,** ce n'est pas à beaucoup près assez grand; *F:* (*in race, examination, etc.*) **to be n.,** être distancé; être battu à plate(s) couture(s); **my horse was n.,** mon cheval est arrivé dans les choux; **flattery will get you n.,** la flatterie ne vous mènera à rien. **2.** *s.* le néant; **he seemed to come from n.,** il semblait apparaître tout d'un coup.

nowise ['nouwaiz], *adv. O:* en aucune façon; aucunement, nullement.

nowt [naut], *pron. & s. Dial: & P:* (ne . . .) rien (*m*); **I've got n.,** je n'ai rien; **I don't do owt for n.,** je ne fais rien pour rien.

noxious ['nɔkʃəs], *a.* nuisible, nocif; malfaisant, malsain; pernicieux; *Med:* nociceptif; (plante) délétère, vireuse; (gaz) méphitique, délétère; (exhalation) miasmatique; (air) contagieux; **n. plants, animals,** plantes, animaux, nuisibles; **they are n. even to man,** ils nuisent, sont nuisibles, même aux hommes.

noxiously ['nɔkʃəsli], *adv.* nuisiblement; d'une manière malsaine, pernicieuse.

noxiousness ['nɔkʃəsnis], *s.* nuisibilité *f*, nocivité *f*; nature malfaisante, pernicieuse (de qch.).

nozzle ['nɔzl], *s.* (*a*) ajutage *m*; jet *m* (de tuyau); lance *f* (de tuyau de pompe à incendie, d'un lance-flammes); canule *f* (de seringue); **water hose n.,** (i) ajutage (de tuyau d'arrosage), lance à eau, lance d'arrosage; bec *m* de lance; (ii) robinet *m* du flexible; **petrol pump delivery n.,** pistolet *m* de distribution d'essence; (*b*) bec, tuyau *m*, buse *f* (de soufflet); injecteur *m*; ventouse *f*, suceur *m*, buse aspiratrice (de nettoyeuse par le vide); tuyère *f*, ajutage (d'injecteur, de turbine, etc.); **spray n.,** (i) ajutage d'arrosage; (ii) *I.C.E:* gicleur *m*, diviseur *m* d'essence; **drip n.,** ajutage à gouttes réglables; (*in jet engine*) **(thrust) n.,** tuyère (d'éjection); **deflected thrust n.,** tuyère orientable; **variable area n.,** tuyère à section variable; *Gasm:* (*of coke oven*) **gas n.,** busette *f*.

nozzleman, *pl.* **-men** ['nɔzlmən], *s.m.* porte-lance *inv* (de lance-flammes).

nu [nju:], *s. Gr.Alph:* nu *m inv*.

nuance ['nju:ɑ̃(n)s], *s.* nuance *f*.

nub [nʌb], *s.* **1.** petit morceau (de charbon, etc.); **n. sugar,** sucre concassé. **2.** bosse *f*, protubérance *f*. **3. the n. of the matter,** l'essentiel *m* de l'affaire; *U.S: F:* **worn (down) to the n., to a n.,** usé jusqu'au trognon, au bout; vanné.

nubbin ['nʌbin], *s. NAm: F:* épi de maïs petit et mal formé.

nubble ['nʌbl], *s.* = NUB 1, 2.

nubbly ['nʌbli], *a.* **1.** (*of coal, etc.*) en petits morceaux. **2.** couvert de bosses, de protubérances.

nubecula, *pl.* **-ae** [nju:'bekjulə, -i:], *s.* **1.** nubécule *f*, taie *f* (sur l'œil); *Med:* néphélion *m*. **2.** *Astr:* nuée *f* magellanique.

Nubia ['nju:biə]. *Pr.n. Geog:* Nubie *f*.

Nubian ['nju:biən], *a. & s.* **1.** *Geog:* (*a*) *a.* nubien; (*b*) *s.* Nubien, -ienne. **2.** *s. Ling:* nubien *m*.

nubile ['nju:bail], *a.* nubile.

nubility [nju:'biliti], *s.* nubilité *f*.

nucellus [nju:'seləs], *s. Bot:* nucelle *f* (d'ovule).

nucha ['nju:kə], *s. Anat:* nuque *f*.

nuchal ['nju:k(ə)l], *a. Anat:* de la nuque; nuc(h)al, -aux.

nuciferous [nju:'sifərəs], *a. Bot:* nucifère.

nuciform ['nju:sifɔ:m], *a. Bot: Anat: etc:* nuciforme.

nucivorous [nju:'sivərəs], *a. Z:* nucivore.

nuclear ['nju:kliər], *a.* (*a*) *Atom.Ph:* nucléaire, atomique; **n. physics,** physique *f* nucléaire, atomique; **n. physicist,** physicien, -ienne, nucléaire, atomique; **n. chemistry,** chimie *f* nucléaire; **n. engineering,** génie *m* atomique; atomistique *f*; **n. scientist,** atomiste *m*, nucléiste *m*; **n. energy,** énergie *f* nucléaire, atomique; **n. power,** (i) force motrice nucléaire; énergie nucléaire, atomique; (ii) électricité *f* d'origine nucléaire; **n. power station, plant,** centrale *f* atomique; centrale (d'énergie) nucléaire; centrale électro-nucléaire; **n. mass, matter,** masse *f*, matière *f*, nucléaire; **n. (chain) reaction,** réaction *f* nucléaire (en chaîne); **n. bombardment,** bombardement *m* nucléaire (de l'atome); **n. charge, collision, disintegration,** charge *f*, collision *f*, désintégration *f*, nucléaire; **n. weapon,** arme *f* nucléaire; **n. ship,** navire *m* à propulseur atomique; **n. (-powered, -propelled) submarine,** sous-marin *m* à (pro)pulsion atomique, nucléaire, sous-marin atomique; **n. war(fare),** guerre *f* nucléaire, atomique; **n. explosion,** explosion *f* nucléaire, atomique; **n. radiation,** rayonnement *m* nucléaire, atomique; (*b*) *Pol:* **the N. Powers,** les puissances *f* nucléaires; (*c*) *Biol:* **n. sex,** sexe chromatinien; *Bio-Ch:* **n. hybridization,** hybridation *f* cellulaire.

nuclease ['nju:klieis], *s. Ch:* nucléase *f*.

nucleate[1] ['nju:klieit]. **1.** *v.tr.* former (qch.) en noyau; assembler (plusieurs choses) en noyau. **2.** *v.i.* se former, s'assembler, en noyau.

nucleate[2] ['nju:kliət], **nucleated** ['nju:kli:eitid], *a. Biol: etc:* nucléé.

nucleic [nju:'kli:ik], *a. Ch:* (acide) nucléique.

nuclein ['nju:kli:in], *s. Ch:* nucléine *f*.

nucleobranch ['nju:klioubræŋk], *s. Moll:* nucléobranche *m*.

Nucleobranchiata [nju:klioubræŋki'eitə], *s.pl. Moll:* nucléobranches *m*.

nucleolar [nju:kli:ələr], *a.* nucléolaire.

nucleolate(d) [nju:'kli:əleit(id)], *a. Biol:* nucléolé.

nucleole ['nju:klioul], **nucleolus,** *pl.* **-i** [nju:kli'ouləs, -ai], *s. Biol:* nucléole *m*.

nucleon ['nju:kliɔn], *s. Atom.Ph:* nucléon *m*.

nucleonic [nju:kli'ɔnik], *a. Atom.Ph:* nucléonique.

nucleonics [nju:kli'ɔniks], *s.pl. Atom.Ph:* nucléonique *f*.

nucleophilic [nju:kliou'filik], *a. Ch:* nucléophile.

nucleophilicity [nju:kliouf i'lisiti], *s. Ch:* nucléophilie *f*.

nucleoplasm ['nju:klioupl æzm], *s. Biol:* nucléoplasme *m*.

nucleoproteid, nucleoprotein [nju:kliou'prouti:d, -'prouti:n], *s. Bio-Ch:* nucléoprotéide *f*.

nucleoside ['nju:kliousaid], *s. Bio-Ch:* nucléoside *m*.

nucleothermic [nju:kliou'θə:mik], *a. Atom.Ph:* nucléothermique.

nucleus, *pl.* **-ei** ['nju:kliəs, -iai], *s.* (*a*) *Ph: Biol: Astr:* noyau *m* (d'atome, de cellule, de comète); *Ph:* **atomic n.,** noyau atomique; **naturally radioactive n.,** noyau naturellement radioactif; **artificially radioactive n.,** noyau artificiellement radioactif; **daughter n.,** noyau enfanté, engendré; **parent n.,** noyau original, noyau père; **even-even, even-odd, n.,** noyau pair-pair, pair-impair; **odd-odd, odd-even, n.,** noyau impair-impair, impair-pair; **compound n.,** noyau composé; **crystal n.,** germe *m* de cristallisation; *Ch:* **benzene n.,** noyau benzénique; *Biol:* **n. of crystallization,** noyau de cristallisation; (*b*) noyau, embryon *m* (d'une organisation, d'un établissement, etc.;) **the n. of a library,** un embryon, un commencement, de bibliothèque; **the n. of the affair,** le fond, l'essentiel *m*, de l'affaire; *Mil: etc:* **n. of resistance,** noyau de résistance.

nuclide ['nju:klaid], *s. Atom.Ph:* nucléide *m*.

nucula ['nju:kjulə], *s. Moll:* nucule *f*.

nude [nju:d]. **1.** *a.* (*a*) (*of pers., limbs, etc.*) nu; *Art:* **to paint n. figures,** peindre des nus *m*, des nudités *f*, des académies *f*; peindre des figures nues, académiques; *Com: A:* **n. stockings,** bas *m* couleur chair; (*b*) *Jur:* (*of contract*) unilatéral, -aux. **2.** *s.* (*a*) *Art:* **(the) n.,** (le) nu, (la) nudité, (la) figure nue; **studies from the n.,** des nus, des académies; **to draw, paint, from the n.,** dessiner, peindre, d'après le nu; dessiner, peindre, des académies; **to sit in the n.,** poser pour le nu; (*b*) **to bathe in the n.,** se baigner tout nu.

nudge[1] [nʌdʒ], *s.* coup *m* de coude.

nudge[2], *v.tr.* pousser (qn) du coude; donner un coup de coude à (qn); **I nudged him to stand up,** je l'ai poussé du coude pour le faire lever.

nudibranch ['nju:dibræŋk], *s. Moll:* nudibranche *m*.

Nudibranchi(at)a [nju:di'bræŋkiə, -bræŋki'eitə], *s.pl. Moll:* nudibranches *m*.

nudism ['nju:dizm], *s.* nudisme *m*, naturisme *m*.

nudist ['nju:dist], *s.* nudiste *mf*, naturiste *mf*; **n. camp, colony,** camp de vacances réservé aux naturistes.

nudity ['nju:diti], *s.* **1.** nudité *f* (de qn, etc.). **2.** *Art:* nudité; figure nue; nu *m*.

'nuff [nʌf], *adv. P:* (*enough*) **'n. said,** pas besoin d'en dire plus long, d'en dire davantage.

nugatory ['nju:gət(ə)ri], *a.* frivole, futile, sans valeur; (*of law, attempt, etc.*) nul, inefficace.

nugget ['nʌgit], *s.* pépite *f* (d'or); nugget *m*; **gold in nuggets,** or brut.

nuggety ['nʌgiti], *a. Miner:* en pépites; **n. gold,** or *m* en pépites.

nuisance ['nju:s(ə)ns], *s.* **1.** *Jur:* dommage *m*; atteinte portée (i) aux droits du public, (ii) à la moralité publique, (iii) aux droits privés des voisins; *P.N: A:* **commit no n.,** (i) défense *f* d'uriner; (ii) défense de déposer des immondices. **2.** *F:* (*a*) (*pers.*) casse-pieds *m inv*, peste *f*, fléau *m*; gêneur, -euse; **he's a perfect n.,** il est assommant, sciant; **what a n. that child is!** quel tourment que cet enfant-là! **go away, you('re a) n.!** va-t'en, tu m'embêtes! **to make oneself a n. to one's neighbours,** incommoder, embêter, ses voisins; **one of those public nuisances who . . .,** un de ces individus, véritables fléaux sociaux, qui . . .; (*b*) (*thg*) ennui *m*, incommodité *f*; chose fâcheuse; embêtement *m*; désagrément *m*; **long skirts are a n.,** les jupes longues sont gênantes; **it has a certain n. value,** cela sert au moins, sinon à autre chose, à embêter les gens; **it's a n. for, to, me to . . .,** cela me gêne de . . .; **that's a n.!** voilà qui est bien ennuyeux! **what a n.!** quel ennui! quelle contrariété! comme c'est ennuyeux! que c'est embêtant, agaçant! quelle tuile! *P:* **what a bloody n.!** que c'est emmerdant! **he's a bloody n.!** c'est un emmerdeur!

null [nʌl]. **1.** *a.* (*a*) *Jur: etc:* (*of decree, act, etc.*) nul, *f.* nulle; (*of legacy*) caduc, *f.* caduque; **n. and void,** nul et de nul effet, nul et sans effet, nul et non avenu, radicalement nul; **to declare a contract n. and void,** déclarer un contrat nul et non avenu; **to render n.,** annuler, infirmer (un décret, un testament); (*b*) (*of thg*) inefficace, sans valeur; (*of pers.*) nul, insignifiant; (*c*) *El:* **n. indicator,** indicateur *m* de zéro; **n. method,** méthode *f* de zéro; **n. point,** point *m* d'équilibre; **n. position,** zéro *m*; *Cmptr:* **n. representation,** caractère nul; **n. string,** chaîne *f* vide. **2.** *s.* (*dummy letter in cipher*) nulle *f*.

nullah ['nʌlə], *s.* (*Anglo-Indian*) ravine *f*, ravin *m*; cours *m* d'eau; lit *m* de rivière, de torrent.

nullification [nʌlifi'keiʃ(ə)n], *s.* annulation *f*, infirmation *f*.

nullify ['nʌlifai], *v.tr.* annuler, nullifier; infirmer (un acte); dirimer (un contrat, etc.); **his marriage was nullified,** son mariage a été déclaré nul.

nulliparous [nʌ'lipərəs], *a. Jur: etc:* (femme) nullipare.

nullity ['nʌliti], *s.* **1.** *Jur:* (*a*) nullité *f*, invalidité *f* (d'un mariage, etc.); caducité *f* (d'un legs, etc.); *Jur:* **n. suit,** demande *f* en nullité d'un mariage; (*b*) **to declare an act a n.,** déclarer un acte nul. **2.** (*a*) nullité (de qn, etc.); (*b*) (*pers.*) **a n.,** une non-valeur; un zéro; un homme nul; (*c*) (*of an army, etc.*) **to shrink to a n.,** se réduire à zéro, à rien.

Numantia [nju:'mænʃiə]. *Pr.n. A.Geog:* Numance *f*.

numb[1] [nʌm], *a.* (*of limb, mind, etc.*) engourdi; (*of limb*) privé de sentiment; gourd; **hands n. with cold,** mains engourdies par le froid; mains gourdes; **my foot's gone n.,** mon pied s'est engourdi.

numb[2], *v.tr.* engourdir (les membres, l'esprit, etc.).

numbed [nʌmd], *a.* engourdi **(with,** par); transi; gourd.

number[1] ['nʌmbər], *s.* **1.** (*a*) *Mth:* nombre *m*; **three-figure n.,** nombre de trois chiffres; **even, odd, prime, n.,** nombre pair, impair, premier; **whole, integral, n.,** nombre entier; **binary n.,** nombre binaire; **amicable n.,** nombre amiable; **complex n.,** quantité *f* complexe; **imaginary n.,** nombre imaginaire; **random n.,** nombre aléatoire, fortuit; **pseudo-random n.,** nombre pseudo-aléatoire; **the law of numbers,** la loi des grands nombres; **the n. theory,** la théorie des nombres; *Ph:* **atomic n.,** nombre atomique; **mass n.,** nombre de masse, nombre massique; **wave n.,** nombre d'onde; **quantum n.,** nombre quantique; **magic numbers,** nombres magiques; *Cmptr:* **base n.,** base *f* de numération; **n. base,** base de numérotation; *Pol.Ec:* **index n.,** nombre index; *Ecc:* **golden n.,** nombre d'or; (*b*) **the n. of people present,** le nombre des assistants; **the greater n. are of this opinion,** le plus grand nombre est de cet avis; **the greatest n. on record is 50 persons,** le plus grand nombre enregistré est de 50 personnes; **we were in equal numbers,** nous étions en nombre égal; **given equal numbers we would be the stronger,** à nombre égal nous serions les plus forts; **to swell the number(s),** faire nombre; **to swell the n. of subscribers,** grossir la liste des souscripteurs; **come and help make up the number(s),** venez pour faire nombre; **they volunteered to the n. of 10,000,** ils se sont engagés au nombre de 10.000; **they were six in n.,** ils étaient au nombre de six; **an army small in n.,** une armée numériquement faible; **they are few in n.,** ils sont en petit nombre; **they are more in n. than . . .,** ils sont plus nombreux que . . .; **they exceed us in n.,** ils nous dépassent en nombre, par le nombre; **without n.,** sans nombre; **books without n.,** des livres innombrables; (*c*) **a (certain) n. of . . .,** (bon) nombre de . . ., un certain nombre de . . ., un assez grand nombre de . . .; plusieurs . . .; **we have a great n. of apples,** nous avons une quantité de pommes; **a large n. of men were killed,** nombre d'hommes, de nombreux hommes, ont été tués; **a small n. were saved,** un petit nombre de gens ont été sauvés; **such a n. of . . .,** un si grand nombre de . . .; **any n. of . . .,** un grand nombre de . . ., bon nombre de . . .; une quantité de . . .; (*d*) *pl.* **numbers of people died of it,** nombre de personnes, de nombreuses personnes, en moururent; **to be present in small numbers, in (great) numbers,** être présents en petit nombre, en grand nombre; **they were in such numbers that . . .,** ils étaient si nombreux que . . .; **they are coming in ever increasing numbers,** ils viennent de plus en plus nombreux; **the power of numbers,** le pouvoir du nombre; **they conquered by force of numbers,** ils ont vaincu par le nombre, par la force du nombre; **to be overpowered by numbers, to succumb to numbers,** succomber sous le nombre; céder au nombre; **victory does not depend on numbers,** la victoire ne dépend pas du nombre; (*e*) compagnie *f*, groupe *m* (de personnes); **one of their n.,** (l')un d'entre eux; **he is not of our n.,** il n'est pas des nôtres; il n'est pas de notre compagnie; **he was now added to the n. of my enemies,** il a fait dès lors partie de mes ennemis; (*f*) *B:* **(the Book of) Numbers,** le Livre des Nombres; les Nombres. **2.** chiffre *m*; **to write the n. on a page,** mettre le chiffre à une page; numéroter une page. **3.** (*a*) numéro *m* (d'une maison, d'un commissionnaire, etc.); (numéro) matricule *m* (d'un soldat, d'un fusil, d'un prisonnier, etc.); **I live at n. 40,** j'habite, je demeure, au numéro 40; **the chemist at n. 2, rue Lepic,** le pharmacien du numéro 2, rue Lepic; **my room is n. 20,** j'ai la chambre numéro 20; *Mil: Navy:* **n. one uniform,** *F:* **n. ones,** tenue *f* numéro un; *Navy:* **n. eight uniform,** *F:* **n. eights** = tenue de travail; bleu *m* de chauffe; *F:* (*child's language*) **to do n. one,** faire pipi, faire sa petite commission; **to do number two,** faire sa grosse commission; *F:* **to look after n. one,** penser à mézigue, tirer la couverture à soi; **running n.,** numéro de série, d'ordre; **to give a running n. to each record**

file, donner un numéro d'ordre à chaque dossier d'archives; **registered, registration, n.,** numéro matricule; *Aut:* **registration n.,** (i) numéro d'immatriculation, numéro de police; (ii) *Adm:* numéro minéralogique; **car (with registration) n. DHK 295P,** voiture immatriculée DHK 295P; **n. plate,** (i) plaque *f* d'immatriculation; (ii) *Adm:* plaque minéralogique; **to take a car's n.,** relever le numéro d'une voiture; *F:* **to take, get, s.o.'s n.,** savoir ce que vaut qn; **to have s.o.'s n.,** en savoir long sur qn; **I've got his n.,** je connais le numéro; **chassis n.,** numéro d'ordre, numéro de fabrication, du châssis; **to stamp the n. on an engine,** matriculer un moteur; **road n.,** numéro (administratif) d'une route; *Nau:* **ship's, boat's, n.,** numéro (officiel), lettres *f* signalétiques, d'un navire, d'un bateau; **equipment n.,** nombre d'armement; **n. signal,** signal *m* numérique; numéraire *m*; *Com:* **reference n.,** numéro de commande; **marks and numbers of cases,** marques *f* et numéros de colis; *Com: Ind:* **lot n.,** numéro de lot; **designation, specification, n.,** numéro de classification, numéro distinctif; *Tp:* **telephone n.,** numéro d'appel; **subscriber's n.,** numéro d'abonné; *Mapm: etc:* **sheet n.,** numéro d'une feuille (de carte); *Bank:* **cheque n.,** numéro du chèque; *Th: Trans: Sp: etc:* **ticket n.,** numéro du billet, du ticket; *Sp:* **n. board,** tableau *m* d'affichage; (*at lottery, conscription, etc.*) **to draw a lucky, a wrong, n.,** tirer un bon, un mauvais, numéro; *F:* **his number's up,** il a son affaire, son affaire est faite; il va mourir; il est fichu, flambé; son compte est bon; (*b*) *Ch: etc:* (*in analysis*) **acetyl n., iodine n.,** indice *m* d'acétyle, d'iode; (*c*) *Tex:* numéro, titre *m* (des fils du coton, etc.). **4.** *Gram:* nombre. **5.** (*a*) *Th:* numéro; **the last n. on the programme,** le dernier numéro du programme; **vocal n.,** tour *m* de chant; (*b*) *Journ:* numéro (d'un journal, etc.); *Publ:* livraison *f*, fascicule *m* (d'un ouvrage qui paraît par fascicules); **current n.,** numéro du jour, de la semaine, du mois; dernier numéro; **the Christmas n.,** le numéro de Noël; **back n.,** vieux numéro; *F:* (*of pers.*) **to be a back n.,** être vieux jeu; ne plus être à la page; *F:* **she's a cute little n.,** ce qu'elle est appétissante! **6.** *pl. A:* (*a*) *Mus:* mesures *f*; **soft numbers,** doux accords; (*b*) vers *mpl*, poésie *f*.

number[2], *v.tr.* **1.** (*a*) compter; **to n. the stars,** compter, dénombrer, les étoiles; **his days are numbered,** il n'a plus longtemps à vivre, ses jours sont comptés; (*b*) **to n. s.o. among one's friends,** mettre, compter, qn au nombre de, parmi, ses amis; **the society numbers some poets among its members,** la société compte quelques poètes parmi ses membres; **this painting is numbered among the treasures of the gallery,** ce tableau compte parmi les trésors du musée; (*c*) **the town, the army, numbers thirty thousand,** la ville, l'armée, compte trente mille habitants, trente mille hommes; **to n. about a thousand,** s'élever environ à mille; **they n. several thousand,** ils sont au nombre de plusieurs mille; leur nombre se chiffre par milliers; **our company numbered forty,** nous étions quarante; *A:* **he numbers fourscore years,** il a quatre-vingts ans. **2.** (*a*) numéroter (les maisons d'une rue, etc.); **to n. serially,** numéroter en série; **10 cases numbered 1 to 10,** 10 caisses numérotées de 1 à 10; (*b*) *v.i. Mil:* **to n. (off),** se numéroter; **(from the right) n.!** numérotez-vous (à partir de la droite)!

numberer ['nʌmbərər], *s.* (*pers.*) compteur, -euse.

numbering ['nʌmbəriŋ], *s.* **1.** comptage *m*, compte *m*, dénombrement *m* (d'objets, de personnes). **2.** numérotage *m*, numérotation *f* (de maisons, de routes, etc.); **n. machine, stamp,** numéroteur *m*; (*for pages of ledgers, etc.*) folioteur *m*, folioteuse *f*; **automatic (dating and) n. machine,** composteur *m*; *Cmptr:* **n. machine,** numérateur automatique.

numberless ['nʌmbəlis], *a.* **1.** innombrable; **n. cars,** des voitures sans nombre. **2. a n. car,** une voiture sans plaque d'immatriculation, non immatriculée.

numbfish ['nʌmfiʃ], *s. Ich:* torpille *f*, crampe *f*.

numbles ['nʌmblz], *s.pl. A:* entrailles *f* (de cerf, etc.).

numbly ['nʌmli], *adv.* d'une manière engourdie.

numbness ['nʌmnis], *s.* engourdissement *m* (des doigts, etc.); torpeur *f* (de l'esprit).

numbskull ['nʌmskʌl], *s.* = NUMSKULL.

numdah ['nʌmdə], *s. Equit:* tapis *m* de selle (aux Indes).

numerable ['nju:mərəbl], *a.* nombrable; que l'on peut compter, dénombrer.

numeracy ['nju:mərəsi], *s.* degré *m* d'aptitude (i) en mathématiques, (ii) en calcul.

numeral ['nju:mərəl]. **1.** *a.* (*of word, letter, etc.*) numéral, -aux; *Nau:* **n. signal,** signal *m* numérique; numéraire *m*. **2.** *s.* (*a*) chiffre *m*, nombre *m*; *Cmptr:* **n. system,** système *m* de numération; (*b*) **the cardinal numerals,** les numéraux cardinaux; (*c*) nom *m* de nombre.

numerally ['nju:mərəli], *adv.* numéralement.

numerary ['nju:mərəri], *a.* (valeur, etc.) numéraire; *Nau:* **n. signal,** signal *m* numérique; numéraire *m*.

numerate[1] ['nju:məreit], *v.tr.* énumérer, dénombrer.

numerate[2] ['nju:mərət], *a.* ayant un degré d'aptitude en mathématiques.

numeration [nju:mə'reiʃ(ə)n], *s. Mth:* numération *f*; **binary n.,** numération binaire.

numerator ['nju:məreitər], *s.* **1.** *Mth:* numérateur *m* (d'une fraction). **2.** (*pers.*) compteur, -euse.

numeric [nju:'merik]. *Cmptr:* (*a*) *a.* numérique; **n. coding,** codage *m* numérique; (*b*) *s.pl.* **numerics,** chiffres *m*, caractères *m*, numériques.

numerical [nju:'merik(ə)l], *a.* (valeur, supériorité, etc.) numérique; **ascending n. order,** ordre *m* numérique (normal); **descending n. order,** ordre numérique inverse; **n. analysis,** analyse *f* numérique; **n. data,** données *f* numériques; *Cmptr:* **n. (control) tape,** bande-pilote *f*, *pl.* bandes-pilotes, de commande de machine-outil.

numerically [nju:'merik(ə)li], *adv.* numériquement; *Cmptr:* **n. controlled machine tool,** machine-outil *f*, *pl.* machines-outils, à commande numérique.

numerous ['nju:mərəs], *a.* **1.** (*a*) nombreux; **the competitors are not n.,** les concurrents sont peu nombreux, il n'y a pas beaucoup de concurrents; (*b*) *A:* **the n. voice of the people,** la voix du peuple en foule; **a n. dinner,** un dîner de nombreux convives. **2.** *A:* (*esp. of verse*) cadencé, harmonieux; nombreux.

numerously ['nju:mərəsli], *adv.* **1.** en grand nombre; abondamment. **2.** *A:* harmonieusement; en vers cadencés; avec nombre.

Numidia [nju:'midiə]. *Pr.n. Geog:* la Numidie.

Numidian [nju:'midiən]. **1.** *a.* numide. **2.** *s.* Numide *mf*.

numinous ['nju:minəs], *a.* (*a*) surnaturel; mystérieux; (*b*) sacré.

numismatic [nju:miz'mætik], *a.* numismatique.

numismatics [nju:miz'mætiks], *s.pl.* (*usu. with sg. const.*) la numismatique.

numismatist [nju:'mizmətist], **numismatologist** [nju:mizmə'tɔlədʒist], *s.* numismate *mf*, numismatiste *mf*.

numismatology [nju:mizmə'tɔlədʒi], *s.* la numismatique.

nummary ['nʌməri], *a.* (*of weight, language, etc.*) monétaire; **n. pound,** livre *f* numéraire.

nummular ['nʌmjulər], *a.* rond; ovale.

nummulary ['nʌmjuləri], *a.* = NUMMARY.

nummulite ['nʌmjulait], *s. Paleont:* nummulite *f*; *Geol:* **n. limestone,** calcaire *m* à nummulites; pierre *f* à liards.

nummulitic [nʌmju'litik], *a. Geol:* (calcaire *m*) nummulitique.

numnah ['nʌmnə], *s. Equit:* tapis *m* de selle (aux Indes).

numskull ['nʌmskʌl], *s. F:* nigaud, -aude; bêta, -asse; idiot, -ote.

nun [nʌn]. **1.** *s.f. Ecc:* religieuse; **to become a n.,** entrer en religion; se faire religieuse; **he was nursed by the nuns,** il a été soigné par les religieuses, par les sœurs. **2.** *s. Orn:* (*a*) mésange bleue; (*b*) harle *m* piette; (*c*) pigeon *m* nonnain, à capuchon. **3.** *Ent:* **n. (moth),** psilure *m* moine.

nunatak ['nʌnətæk], *s. Geol:* nunatak *m*.

Nunc dimittis ['nʌŋkdi'mitis], *s. Ecc:* Nunc dimittis *m inv*.

nunciature ['nʌnʃiətjər], *s. Ecc:* nonciature *f*.

nuncio ['nʌnʃiou], *s. Ecc:* nonce *m*; **papal n.,** nonce du Pape.

nuncupate ['nʌnkjupeit], *v.tr. Jur: A:* **to n. a will,** faire un testament nuncupatif.

nuncupation [nʌnkju'peiʃ(ə)n], *s. Jur: A:* nuncupation *f*.

nuncupative ['nʌnkjupeitiv], *a. Jur: A:* (testament) nuncupatif.

nunhood ['nʌnhud], *s.* état *m* de religieuse.

nunnation [nʌ'neiʃ(ə)n], *s. Ling:* nunnation *f*.

nunnery ['nʌnəri], *s.* couvent *m* (de religieuses).

nuphar ['nju:fər], *s. Bot:* nuphar *m*; nénuphar *m* jaune; lis *m* des étangs; jaunet *m* d'eau.

nuptial ['nʌpʃəl]. *Lit:* **1.** *a.* nuptial, -iaux; *Ent: etc:* **n. flight,** vol nuptial. **2.** *s.pl.* **nuptials,** noces *f*; *A: & Dial:* épousailles *f*.

nuptiality [nʌpʃi'æliti], *s.* nuptialité *f*.

Nuremberg ['nju:rəmbə:g]. *Pr.n. Geog:* Nuremberg.

Nuremberger ['nju:rəmbə:gər]. *Geog:* (*a*) *a.* nurembergeois, de Nuremberg; (*b*) *s.* Nurembergeois, -oise.

nurse[1] [nə:s], *s.* **1.** (*a*) **(wet) n.,** nourrice *f*; **to put a baby out to n.,** mettre un bébé en nourrice; **a child at n.,** un enfant en nourrice; (*b*) (*A:* **dry**) **n.,** nourrice (*A:* sèche); (*c*) nurse *f*, bonne *f* (d'enfants); (*d*) *Amph:* **n. frog,** alyte *m*, crapaud accoucheur. **2. (sick) n.,** infirmier, -ière; garde-malade *mf*, *pl.* gardes-malades; **night n.,** (i) (*in hospital*) infirmière de nuit, (ii) (*privately employed*) garde *f* de nuit; *O:* **district n.,** infirmière visiteuse; **nursery n.,** puéricultrice *f*; *Surg:* **theatre n.,** instrumentiste *f*; **army n.,** infirmier, -ière, militaire; **air n.,** hôtesse médicale de l'air. **3.** (*a*) *Ent:* (*of bees, ants*) ouvrière *f*; (*b*) *Z:* nourrice. **4.** *For:* **n. (tree),** arbre *m* d'abri; **n. crop,** peuplement *m* d'abri.

nurse[2], *v.tr.* **1.** nourrir (de son lait), allaiter (un enfant); **nursed in luxury,** élevé dans le luxe. **2.** (*a*) soigner (un malade); **she nursed him back to health,** elle lui a fait recouvrer la santé grâce à ses soins; (*b*) **to n. a cold,** soigner un rhume. **3.** (*a*) soigner, abriter (des plantes, etc.); ménager (un cheval, une équipe, etc.) en vue du dernier effort à donner; **this is a connection that should be nursed,** c'est une relation à cultiver; **to n. one's public,** soigner sa popularité; *Pol:* **to n. a, one's, constituency,** chauffer ses électeurs; **I managed to n. the car as far as the garage,** je suis arrivé (en y allant doucement) à conduire la voiture jusqu'au garage; (*b*) *Bill:* **to n. the balls,** rassembler les billes; conserver, garder, les billes groupées; jouer un jeu très groupé; (*c*) nourrir, entretenir (un sentiment, un espoir, un chagrin, etc.); mitonner, mijoter (un projet); (*d*) *F: O:* **to n. the fire,** couver le feu; rester au coin du feu. **4.** bercer (un enfant); tenir (qn, qch.) dans ses bras; caresser (qch.) dans ses mains; **I nursed him when he was a baby,** je l'ai dorloté tout petit enfant; **to n. one's knee,** tenir son genou dans ses mains. **5.** *Turf:* **to n. a horse,** serrer un cheval contre la corde (ou entre deux autres) pour le gêner.

nurse[3], *s. Ich:* (nom donné à diverses familles de) squale *m*.

nurseling ['nə:sliŋ], *s.* nourrisson *m*.

nursemaid ['nə:smeid], *s.f.* bonne d'enfants, nurse.

nursery ['nə:s(ə)ri], *s.* **1.** (*a*) chambre *f* des enfants; nursery *f*; *O:* **day n., night n.,** salle *f*, dortoir *m*, des enfants; **n. governess,** gouvernante *f* pour (les) jeunes enfants; **n. tale,** conte *m* de nourrice; conte pour (les) enfants; *A:* conte de ma mère l'Oie; **n. rhyme,** poésie enfantine; chanson *f* de nourrice; cliquette *f*; (*b*) **(day) n.,** crèche *f*; garderie *f*; **resident n.,** pouponnière *f*; **n. school,** maternelle *f*. **2.** (*a*) *For: Hort:* **n. (garden),** pépinière *f*; **n. gardener,** pépiniériste *mf*; **permanent n.,** pépinière fixe; **shifting n.,** pépinière volante; *Fig:* **n. of, for, soldiers, artists,** pépinière de soldats, d'artistes; (*b*) *Pisc:* alevinier *m*, vivier *m*. **3.** *Bill:* **n. (canons),** série *f* de carambolages sur billes groupées ou collées.

nurseryman, *pl.* **-men** ['nə:srimən], *s.m.* pépiniériste.

nursey ['nə:si], *s.f.* (*child's speech*) nounou, bobonne.

nursing[1] ['nə:siŋ], *a.* **1.** qui nourrit; **n. mother,** mère allaitante. **2.** qui soigne; (*in hospital*) **the n. staff,** les infirmiers, -ières.

nursing[2], *s.* **1.** allaitement *m* (d'un enfant); **during the n. period,** pendant l'allaitement. **2.** culture assidue (des plantes, d'une terre, etc.); ménagement *m*, soin *m* (d'une affaire); entretien *m* (d'un sentiment, etc.). **3.** (*a*) soins (d'une garde-malade); **good n. will soon put him right,** bien soigné, il se remettra vite; **n. home,** clinique *f*; (*b*) profession *f* de garde-malade, d'infirmière; **to take up n.,** se faire infirmier, infirmière; **she does night n.,** elle fait des gardes. **4.** bercement *m*, dorlotement *m* (d'un enfant) (dans les bras, sur les genoux).

nursling ['nə:sliŋ], *s.* nourrisson *m*.

nurture[1] ['nə:tjər], *s.* **1.** éducation *f*; soins *mpl*; **n. of the mind,** nourriture *f* de l'esprit; *Prov:* **n. is stronger than nature,** nourriture passe nature. **2.** aliments *mpl*, nourriture.

nurture[2], *v.tr.* **1.** nourrir (les enfants, etc.); nourrir, entretenir (des sentiments, etc.); **children must be nurtured on truth,** il faut nourrir les enfants de (la) vérité. **2.** élever, faire l'éducation de (qn); instruire (qn).

nurturer ['nə:tjərər], *s.* nourricier, -ière; protecteur, -trice.

nut[1] [nʌt], *s.* **1.** (*a*) (i) noix *f*; (ii) **(hazel) n.,** noisette *f*, aveline *f*; *Bot:* **African bladder n.,** royena *m*; **rush n., tiger n.,** souchet *m* comestible; **Queensland n.,** (i) (*also* **macadamia n.**), noisette de Queensland; (ii) noyer de Queensland, macadamia *m*; **n. tree,** noisetier *m*; coudrier *m*; **n.-bearing,** nucifère; *Bot: Dy:* **n. gall,** noix de galle; **n. butter,** beurre *m* de noix; *F:* **tough, hard, n. to crack,** (i) problème *m* difficile à résoudre; (ii) personne *f* difficile, peu commode; *F:* dur *m* à cuire; (iii) personne difficile à tromper; **it's a hard n. to crack,** cela n'ira pas sans peine; *F:* c'est un os bien dur à ronger; *F:* **he can't sing for nuts,** il ne sait pas chanter du tout; il n'a aucun talent; **to be nuts on s.o., on sth.,** raffoler de qn, de qch.; être entiché de qn; être mordu de qch.; **he's nuts,** il est cinglé, il travaille du chapeau; **nuts!** à d'autres! *O:* (*of thg*) **to be nuts to s.o.,** être un plaisir pour qn; (*b*) *F:* tête *f*; ciboulot *m*, caboche *f*; **to be off one's n.,** être timbré, toqué, loufoque; avoir un coup de marteau; avoir perdu la boule; **he's off his n., he's a n.**

case, il, sa tête, déménage; (*c*) *pl. V:* testicules *m*, couilles *f*. **2.** *Mec.E:* écrou *m*; **acorn n., blind n.,** écrou borgne; **adjusting n.,** écrou de réglage; **anchor n., plate n.,** écrou prisonnier, écrou à plaque; **butterfly n., fly n., thumb n., wing n., finger n.,** écrou ailé, à ailettes, à oreilles; écrou (à) papillon; **cap(ped) n.,** écrou à chape; **castellated n., castle n.,** écrou crénelé, à crénaux, à encoches; **clamping n., compression n., hold-down n.,** écrou de serrage, de fixation; **collar n.,** écrou à collet; **coupling n., fitting n., union n.,** écrou d'assemblage, écrou raccord; **elastic-stop n., self-locking n.,** écrou indesserrable; **flush n., internal-wrenching n.,** écrou noyé, encastré; **gland n.,** écrou (de) presse-étoupe; **hexagon(al) n.,** écrou hexagonal, écrou (à) six pans; **knurled n., milled n.,** écrou moleté, à molette; **ring n., round n.,** écrou cylindrique; **n. blank,** écrou brut; **n. lock,** frein *m* d'écrou; **n.-making, n.-tapping, machine,** machine *f* à fabriquer, à tarauder, les écrous; **n. wrench,** clé *f* à écrous. **3.** *Clockm:* roue droite, à denture droite (de petites dimensions). **4.** (*a*) *Mus:* sillet *m* (de violon); **tail-piece n.,** grand sillet; **n. at the neck,** petit sillet; (*b*) *Mus:* hausse *f* (d'archet); **at, with, the n.,** du talon; (*c*) *Nau:* tenon *m* (d'une ancre). **5.** *Com: Min:* **n. coal, nuts,** gailletin *m*; têtes *f* de moineau.

nut[2], *v.tr. F:* frapper (qn) à la tête.

nutant ['nju:tənt], *a. Bot:* nutant.

nutation [nju'teiʃ(ə)n], *s. Astr: Bot: Med:* nutation *f*.

nut-brown ['nʌtbraun], *a.* (couleur) noisette *inv*; **n.-b. hair,** cheveux châtains; *Poet:* **n.-b. maid,** jeune fille au teint brun (noisette).

nutcracker ['nʌtkrækər], *s.* **1. (pair of) nutcrackers,** casse-noisette(s) *m inv*, casse-noix *m inv*; *F:* **n. (nose and) chin,** (nez *m* et) menton *m* en casse-noisette, en patte de homard. **2.** *Orn:* casse-noix; **slender-billed n.,** casse-noix de Sibérie; **thick-billed n.,** casse-noix moucheté; **Clark's n.,** casse-noix américain.

nuthatch ['nʌthætʃ], *s. Orn:* sittelle *f* (torche-pot); **Corsican,** *NAm:* **red-breasted n.,** sittelle corse, *Fr.C:* sittelle à poitrine rousse; **white-breasted n.,** sittelle à poitrine blanche; **rock n.,** sittelle des rochers; **pigmy n.,** petite sittelle.

nuthouse ['nʌthaus], *s. F:* asile *m* de fous, cabanon *m*.

nutlet ['nʌtlit], *s. Bot:* nucule *f*.

nutmeg ['nʌtmeg], *s.* (noix *f*) muscade *f*, noix de Banda; **Californian n.,** noix de Californie; **calabash n.,** monodore *m* aromatique; **plume n.,** athérosperme *m*; **n. tree,** muscadier *m*; **n. grater,** râpe *f* à muscade; *Orn:* **n. bird,** damier commun.

nutria ['nju:triə], *s.* **1.** *Z:* coypou *m*, ragondin *m*. **2.** *Com:* fourrure *f* de coypou; castor *m* du Chili, loutre *f* d'Amérique, ragondin, nutria *m*.

nutrient ['nju:triənt]. **1.** *a.* nutritif, nourrissant. **2.** *s.* substance nutritive; aliment *m*; **total digestible nutrients,** matières digestibles totales.

nutriment ['nju:trimənt], *s.* nourriture *f*; aliments nourrissants; nutriment *m*.

nutrition [nju'triʃ(ə)n], *s.* nutrition *f*; alimentation *f*.

nutritional [nju'triʃənəl], *a.* alimentaire; nutritionnel.

nutritionist [nju'triʃənist], *s.* diététicien, -ienne, nutritionniste *mf*.

nutritious [njutriʃəs], *a.* nutritif, nourrissant.

nutritiousness [nju:'triʃəsnis], *s.* nutritivité *f*.

nutritive ['nju:tritiv], *a.* **1.** nutritif, nourrissant. **2.** relatif à la nutrition; nutritif.

nutritiveness ['nju:tritivnis], *s.* nutritivité *f*.

nutshell ['nʌtʃel], *s.* coquille *f* de noix; **that's the whole thing in a n.,** voilà toute l'affaire (résumée) en un mot, en deux mots; **there you have your man in a n.,** voilà votre homme campé en peu de mots; **the whole thing lies in a n.,** c'est simple comme bonjour; **to put it in a n. . . .,** pour me résumer . . ..

nutter ['nʌtər], *s. P:* toqué, -ée.

nuttiness ['nʌtinis], *s.* **1.** goût *m* de noisette. **2.** *F:* loufoquerie *f*, maboulisme *m*.

nutting ['nʌtiŋ], *s.* cueillette *f* des noisettes; **to go n.,** aller à la cueillette, faire la cueillette, des noisettes; aller aux noisettes.

nutty ['nʌti], *a.* **1.** (pays, arbre) abondant en noisettes, en noix. **2.** (vin, etc.) ayant un goût de noisette, de noix. **3.** *F:* **to be n. about s.o., sth.,** raffoler de qn, de qch.; être entiché de qn; être mordu de qch. **4.** *F:* fou, timbré, loufoque, dingue.

nux vomica ['nʌks'vɔmikə], *s. Bot: Pharm:* noix *f* vomique; **n. v. tree,** vomiquier *m*.

nuzzle ['nʌzl], *v.i. & tr.* **1.** (*of pig, etc.*) fouiller avec le groin; **to n. into the mud,** fouiller dans la boue. **2. to n. (against) s.o.'s shoulder,** (*of dog, horse*) fourrer son nez sur l'épaule de qn; faire des caresses à qn; (*of pers.*) se blottir sur l'épaule de qn; **to n. close to s.o., up to s.o.,** se serrer contre qn; **the dog came nuzzling (about) my calves,** le chien me reniflait les mollets.

nyala [nai'ɑ:lə], *s. Z:* nyala *m*.

Nyasaland [nai'æsəlænd]. *Pr.n. Hist:* Nyas(s)aland *m*; **in N.,** au Nyas(s)aland.

nychthemeral [nik'θemərəl], *a. Nat.Hist:* nycthéméral, -aux.

nychthemeron, *pl.* **-ons, -a** [nik'θemərɔn, -ɔnz, -ə], *s. Nat.Hist:* nycthémère *m*.

Nyctaginaceae [niktædʒineisii:], *s.pl. Bot:* nyctaginacées *f*.

nyctalope ['niktəloup], *s.* héméralope *mf*.

nyctalopia [niktə'loupiə], *s.* **1.** *Med:* héméralopie *f*. **2.** (*incorrectly*) nyctalopie *f*.

nyctalopic [niktə'lɔpik], *a. Med:* héméralop(iqu)e.

nyctalops ['niktəlɔps], *s. Med:* héméralope *mf*.

nyctea ['niktiə], *s. Orn:* nyctéa *m*, harfang *m*.

nycteribid [nik'teribid], *s. Ent:* nyctéribide *m*.

Nycteribiidae [nikteri'bi:idi:], *s.pl. Ent:* nyctéribides *f*.

nycterohemeral [niktərou'hemərəl], **nyctohemeral** [niktou'hemərəl], *a. Nat.Hist:* nycthémère.

nycthemeral [nik'θemərəl], *a.* nycthéméral, -aux.

nycthemeron, *pl.* **-ons, -a,** [nik'θemərɔn, -ɔnz, -ə], *s.* nycthémère *m*.

nyctinastic [nikti'næstik], *a. Bot:* nyctinastique.

nyctinasty ['niktinæsti], *s. Bot:* nyctinastie *f*.

nyctophonia [niktə'founiə], *s. Psy:* nyctophonie *f*.

nyctotemperature [niktou'tempritjər], *s. Bot:* nyctotempérature *f*.

nylghau ['nilgɔ:], *s. Z:* nylgaut *m*.

nylon ['nailɔn], *s. R.t.m: Tex:* nylon *m*; **n. stockings, nylons,** bas *m* nylon; **crêpe n. socks,** chaussettes *f* crêpe *m* mousse.

nymph [nimf], *s.f.* **1.** *Myth:* nymphe; **tree n., wood n.,** hamadryade; **ocean n.,** océanide; **grotto, mountain, n.,** oréade; **sea n.,** néréide; **water n.,** (i) *Myth:* naïade; (ii) *Bot:* nymphée *f*. **2.** *s. Ent:* nymphe *f*.

nymphae ['nimfi:], *s.pl. Anat:* nymphes *f*; petites lèvres.

nymphaea [nim'fiə], *s. Bot:* nymphée *f*, nymphéa *m*, nénuphar blanc.

nymphaeaceae [nimfi'eisii:], *s.pl. Bot:* nymphéacées *f*.

nymphaeum [nim'fi:əm], *s. Archeol:* nymphée *m or f*.

nymphal ['nimfəl], *a. Ent:* nymphal, -aux.

nymphalid ['nimfəlid]. *Ent:* **1.** *a.* concernant les nymphalidés. **2.** *s.* nymphale *m*.

Nymphalidae [nim'fælidi:], *s.pl. Ent:* nymphalidés *m*.

nymphea ['nimfiə], *s. Bot:* nymphéa *m*.

nymphean [nim'fi:ən], *a.* de nymphe; des nymphes.

nymphet ['nimfit], *s.f.* nymphette.

nympholepsy ['nimfoulepsi], *s.* nympholepsie *f*.

nympholept ['nimfoulept], *a. & s.* nympholepte *mf*.

nymphomania [nimfou'meiniə], *s. Med:* nymphomanie *f*.

nymphomaniac [nimfou'meiniæk], *a. & s.f.* nymphomane.

nyssa ['nisə], *s. Bot:* nyssa *m*.

nystagmic [ni'stægmik], *a. Med:* nystagmique.

nystagmoid [ni'stægmɔid], *a. Med:* nystagmoïde.

nystagmus [nis'tægməs], *s. Med:* nystagmus *m*, nystagme *m*.

O

O[1], **o**, *pl.* **o's, oes, os** [ou, ouz], *s.* **1.** (la lettre) O, o *m*; *Tp:* **O for Oliver,** *esp. Mil:* **O for Oscar,** O comme Oscar; *Sch:* **to take one's O-levels,** se présenter au premier examen du *General Certificate of Education.* **2.** *Tp: etc:* (*nought*) zéro *m*; **for London numbers dial 01** ['ou'wʌn], pour Londres composez zéro un; **I said 506** ['faivousiks], **not 906** ['nainousiks], j'ai dit cinq cent six pas neuf cent six. **3.** cercle *m*, rond *m*.

O[2], *int.* **1.** (*vocative*) O, ô; *Ecc:* **the O's of Advent,** les sept O de Noël. **2.** = OH.

o' [ə], *prep.* **1.** (= OF) **man-o'-war,** bâtiment *m* de guerre; **six o'clock,** six heures. **2.** *A: Dial:* (= OF *or* ON) **I dream of it o'nights,** j'en rêve la nuit.

oaf, *pl.* **-s,** *A:* **oaves** [ouf, -s, ouvz], *s.* **1.** *A:* enfant *m* de fée. **2.** (*a*) *A:* idiot *m* (de naissance); innocent *m*; (*b*) lourdaud *m*, balourd *m*, godiche *m*.

oafish ['oufiʃ], *a.* lourdaud, stupide, rustre.

oafishly ['oufiʃli], *adv.* d'un air lourdaud; stupidement.

oafishness ['oufiʃnis], *s.* balourdise *f*, stupidité *f*.

oak [ouk], *s.* **1.** (*a*) *Bot:* **o. (tree),** chêne *m*; **common, pedunculate, o.,** chêne rouvre, pédonculé; **sessile o.,** chêne à fleurs sessiles, à glands sessiles; **Turkey o.,** chêne chevelu; **holm o.,** yeuse *f*; **o. leaf,** feuille *f* de chêne; *U.S: Mil: F:* **o. leaves,** feuilles de chêne (insignes de commandant et de lieutenant-colonel); **o. gall, o. nut,** noix *f* de galle; pomme *f* de chêne; cinelle *f*; **o. mast,** glands *mpl* de chêne; glandée *f*; **o. wilt,** fanage *m* de chêne; **o. bark,** écorce *f* de chêne; **o.-bark tanned,** tanné à l'écorce de chêne; *U.S:* **dyer's o.,** chêne tinctorial, des teinturiers; *Hist:* **the Royal O.,** le chêne qui servit de cachette à Charles II; *A:* **to wear o.,** porter des feuilles de chêne à la boutonnière (le 29 mai, en souvenir de Charles II); **o. sapling,** chêne de brin; chêneau *m*; **o. plantation, grove, wood,** chênaie *f*; bois *m* de chênes; (*b*) **o. (wood),** (bois de) chêne; **bog o.,** chêne de tourbière; **o. furniture,** meubles *mpl* de, en, chêne; **dark o. (colour),** couleur *f* vieux chêne; (*c*) *Ent:* **o. moth,** tordeuse *f* des chênes; **o. beauty,** amphidasys *m* prodromaire; **great o. beauty,** boarmie *f* de chêne; **o. pest,** phylloxéra *m* du chêne; *U.S:* **o. pruner,** capricorne *m* du chêne; (*d*) porte extérieure (d'un appartement dans les universités, etc.); **to sport one's o.,** s'enfermer à double porte; défendre, condamner, sa porte. **2.** *Bot:* **o. of Cappadocia,** ambrosie *f* maritime. **3.** *Turf:* **the Oaks,** course pour pouliches de trois ans courue à Epsom; = Prix de Diane.

oakapple ['oukæpl], *s.* noix *f* de galle; pomme *f* de chêne; cinelle *f*; **O. Day,** le 29 mai, anniversaire de la Restauration de Charles II.

oaken ['ouk(ə)n], *a. O:* de, en, chêne.

oakling ['oukliŋ], *s.* chêneau *m*; baliveau *m* de chêne.

oakum ['oukəm], *s.* étoupe (noire), filasse *f*; *Nau:* **to drive o. into the seams, to pack the seams with o.,** faire entrer l'étoupe dans, étouper, les coutures; **to pick o.,** (i) démêler, tirer l'étoupe; faire de la filasse; (ii) *F:* (*as prison task*) = casser des cailloux; tresser des chaussons de lisière.

oar[1] [ɔːr], *s.* **1.** (*a*) aviron *m*, rame *f*; *Row:* (*opposed to scull*) aviron de nage; **single-banked oars,** avirons de, en, pointe; **double-banked oars,** avirons de couple, accouplés; **to pull at the oars,** tirer à la rame; *Nau:* souquer ferme; **to pull an o.,** tirer en pointe; *F:* tirer sur le bois mort; **to pull a good o.,** être bon tireur d'aviron, bon rameur; *Nau:* **oars!** lève rames! **to rest, lie, on one's oars,** (i) lever les rames, les avirons; (ii) *F:* s'accorder un moment de répit; (iii) *F:* s'endormir sur ses lauriers; *Nau:* **rest on your oars!** avirons en galère! *F:* **to put, stick, one's o. in,** intervenir (mal à propos); s'en mêler; **he has an o. in everything,** *A:* **in every man's boat,** il est mêlé à tout; (*b*) (*oarsman*) **good o.,** bon tireur d'aviron; bon rameur. **2.** *A: Lit: Poet:* (*wing, fin*) rame. **3.** *Brew:* (*for stirring mash*) vague *f*.

oar[2], *v.tr. & i. Lit:* ramer.

-oared [ɔːd], *a.* (*with num. prefixed*) **four-o., eight-o.,** à quatre, huit, rames, avirons; **eight-o. boat,** huit *m* de pointe.

oarfish ['ɔːfiʃ], *s. Ich:* (*a*) régalec *m*; (*b*) lophote *m*, poisson-licorne *m*, *pl.* poissons-licornes.

oarlocks ['ɔːlɔks], *s.pl. U.S:* dames *f* de nage; tolets *m*.

oarsman, *pl.* **-men** ['ɔːzmən], *s.m.* rameur; tireur d'aviron; *Nau:* nageur.

oarsmanship ['ɔːzmənʃip], *s.* l'art *m* de ramer; l'aviron *m*.

oarswoman, *pl.* **-women** ['ɔːzwumən, -wimin], *s.f.* rameuse; tireuse d'aviron.

oarweed ['ɔːwiːd], *s. Algae:* laminaire *f*; **flexible-stemmed o.,** laminaire à tige souple; **ribbon o.,** laminaire en ruban, laminaire rubannée.

oasal [ou'eisl], **oasitic** [ouei'sitik], *a.* oasien.

oasis, *pl.* **oases** [ou'eisis, -iːz], *s. Geog:* oasis *f*; **the o. dwellers of the Sahara,** les oasiens du Sahara; *Fig:* **an o. of calm in the middle of a built-up area,** une oasis de calme au milieu d'une agglomération urbaine.

oast [oust], *s.* séchoir *m* (à houblon); four *m* à houblon.

oasthouse ['ousthaus], *s.* sécherie *f* (pour le houblon).

oat [out], *s.* **1.** (*a*) *Bot:* avoine (commune); **naked o., Chinese o.,** avoine nue; **false o., tall meadow o.,** fromental, -aux *m*; faux froment; fenasse *f*; avoine élevée; **Tartarian o.,** avoine de Tartarie; **o. grass,** (i) folle avoine; (ii) avoine élevée; **wild oat(s),** folle avoine; haveron *m*; avoine stérile; *F:* **to sow one's wild oats,** faire des fredaines; jeter sa gourme; *Agr:* **field of oats, o. field,** champ *m* d'avione; avénière *f*, aveinière *f*; (*b*) *Husb:* **oats,** avoine; **bruised oats,** avoine égrugée; (*of horse*) **to feel its oats,** être vif; être en l'air; *F: O:* (*of pers.*) **to feel one's oats,** (i) se sentir gaillard; avoir de l'entrain; (ii) se rengorger; faire l'important; (*of horse*) **to be off its oats,** refuser de manger; être malade; (*of pers.*) **to be off one's oats,** être indispose, mal en train; (*c*) *Dom.Ec:* **(porridge) oats,** flocons *mpl* d'avoine. **2.** *A:* tige *f* d'avoine (employée comme chalumeau); chalumeau *m*.

oatcake ['outkeik], *s. Cu:* galette *f* d'avoine.

oaten ['outn], *a.* **1.** *O:* (de farine) d'avoine. **2.** *A:* (chalumeau) fait d'une tige d'avoine.

oatmeal ['outmiːl], *s.* (i) farine *f*, (ii) flocons *mpl*, d'avoine; *Cu:* **o. porridge,** *NAm:* **o.,** bouillie *f* d'avoine, porridge *m*.

oath, *pl.* **oaths** [ouθ, ouðz], *s.* **1.** serment *m*; **o. of allegiance,** serment de fidélité; *U.S:* **o. of office,** serment politique; **to swear, make, an o.,** faire un serment; jurer; **to take an o.,** *Jur:* **to take the o.,** prêter serment; **taking of an o., of the o.,** prestation *f* de serment; **I'll take my o. on it, to it,** j'en jurerais; *F:* j'en lève la main, j'en mettrais la main au feu; **to put s.o. on his o., to administer, tender, the o. to s.o.,** faire prêter serment à qn; déférer le serment à qn; assermenter qn; **on, upon, under, o.,** sous (la foi du) serment; **witness on o.,** témoin assermenté; **to declare, state, sth. on o.,** déclarer, certifier, qch. sous serment; **guarantee given on o.,** caution *f* juratoire; *O:* **on my (Bible) o. it happened as I'm telling you,** je vous jure que c'est arrivé comme je vous le dis; **to break one's o.,** fausser, rompre, son serment; manquer à son serment; se parjurer; **to release, relieve, s.o. from his o.,** délier, relever, qn de son serment; rendre son serment à qn. **2.** juron *m*; gros mot; **to let out, rap out, an o.,** laisser échapper un juron; lâcher un juron.

oba ['oubə], *s. Bot:* oba *m*; manguier *m* du Gabon.

Obadiah [oubə'daiə], *Pr.n.m.* Abdias.

obbligato [ɔbli'gɑːtou], *Mus:* **1.** *a. & s. A:* (partie) obligée. **2.** *adv.* obbligato. **3.** *s.* **violin o., flute o.,** accompagnement de violon, de flûte (ajouté à une romance, etc.).

obconic(al) [ɔb'kɔnik(l)], *a. Nat.Hist:* obconique.

obcordate [ɔb'kɔːdeit], *a. Bot:* (feuillet) obcordiforme, obcordé.

obdiplostemonous ['ɔbdiplou'stiːmənəs], *a. Bot:* obdiplostémone.

obduracy ['ɔbdjurəsi], *s.* **1.** (*a*) endurcissement *m* (de cœur); opiniâtreté *f*, entêtement *m*; (*b*) inexorabilité *f*, inflexibilité *f*. **2.** *Theol:* impénitence *f*.

obdurate ['ɔbdjurət], *a.* **1.** (*a*) endurci, obstiné, têtu, opiniâtre; (*b*) inexorable; inflexible. **2.** *Theol:* impénitent.

obdurately ['ɔbdjurətli], *adv.* (*a*) avec entêtement; opiniâtrement; (*b*) inexorablement, inflexiblement.

obdurateness ['ɔbdjurətnis], *s.* = OBDURACY.

obeah ['oubiə], *s.* **1.** fétiche *m*. **2.** sorcellerie *f* des obis; **o. man, o. doctor,** obi *m*.

obeche [ou'biːtʃiː], *s. Com:* (*wood*) samba *m*.

obedience [ə'biːdjəns], *s.* **1.** (*a*) obéissance *f*; **o. to the will of s.o.,** soumission *f* aux volontés de qn; **he expected implicit o. to his will,** il demandait une parfaite obéissance à ses volontés; **passive o.,** obéissance passive; **to enforce o. to the law,** faire obéir la loi; **to compel, secure, o. from s.o.,** se faire obéir par qn; **to reduce s.o. to o.,** mettre qn au pas; *Com: O:* **in o. to your orders,** conformément à vos ordres; en exécution de vos ordres; **to show prompt o.,** obéir au doigt et à l'œil; (*b*) **to owe o. to the king,** devoir obéissance au roi; **to return to one's o.,** rentrer dans l'obéissance. **2.** *Ecc:* (*a*) **o. of a monk to his superior,** obédience d'un religieux à son supérieur; (*b*) **the Roman o.,** l'obédience de Rome; (*c*) *Pol:* **countries of the Communist o.,** pays d'obédience communiste.

obediencer [ə'biːdjənsər], *s. Ecc:* obédiencier *m*.

obedient [ə'biːdjənt], *a.* obéissant, soumis; docile; **to be o. to s.o.,** être obéissant envers, vis-à-vis de, qn; obéir à qn; *Corr: Adm:* **your (most) o. servant,** votre très obéissant serviteur.

obediential [əbiædi'enʃl], *a. Ecc:* obédientiel.

obedientiary [əbiːdi'enʃəri], *s. Ecc:* obédiencier *m*.

obediently [ə'biːdjəntli], *adv.* avec obéissance, avec soumission; *Corr: A:* **Yours o.,** agréez, Monsieur, Madame, mes salutations empressées; votre très obéissant serviteur; *Com:* toujours à vos ordres.

obeisance [ə'beis(ə)ns], *s.* **1.** *A: & Lit:* salut *m*, révérence *f*; **to make (an) o. to s.o., to do, pay, o. to s.o.,** faire un salut à qn, s'incliner devant qn; **with many obeisances,** avec force prosternations *f*, avec force révérences. **2.** obéissance *f*, hommage *m*; **to do, make, pay, o. to s.o.,** prêter obéissance à (un prince); rendre, faire, hommage à qn.

obelia [ou'bi:liə], *s. Coel:* obélie *f*.

obelion [ou'bi:liən], *s. Anat:* obélion *m*.

obeliscal [ɔb'ːliskl], **obeliscoid** [ɔbi'liskɔid], *a.* obéliscal, -aux.

obelisk ['ɔbəlisk], *s.* **1.** obélisque *m*. **2.** *(a) Pal:* obèle *m*; *(b) Typ:* croix *f*; obèle; **double o.,** diésis *m*.

obelize ['ɔbilaiz], *v.tr. Pal:* marquer (un passage, etc.) d'un obèle.

obelus, *pl.* **-i** ['ɔbələs, -lai], *s. Pal:* obèle *m*.

obese [ou'bi:s], *a.* obèse.

obesity [ou'bi:siti], **obeseness** [ou'bi:snis], *s.* obésité *f*.

obey [ə'bei], *v.tr.* obéir à (qn, un ordre); obéir, être obéissant; **to o. s.o. implicitly,** obéir à qn au doigt et à l'œil; **he can make himself obeyed,** il sait se faire obéir; **he is obeyed,** il est obéi; **orders must be obeyed,** il faut obéir aux ordres; **the order was obeyed,** l'ordre fut obéi; **I must o. instructions,** je ne connais que la consigne; **to o. the law,** obéir, se plier, aux lois; **to o. a summons, the magistrates,** *Adm:* **an order,** obtempérer à une sommation, aux magistrats, à un ordre; **to o. the dictates of one's conscience,** écouter sa conscience; **his legs refused to o., would not o., him,** ses jambes refusaient d'obéir; *(of ship)* **to o. the helm,** obéir à la barre.

obeyer [ə'beiər], *s.* **the obeyers of the law,** ceux qui obéissent aux lois.

obfuscate ['ɔbfʌskeit], *v.tr.* **1.** *A:* obscurcir, assombrir (le ciel, etc.); éclipser (un astre). **2.** *(a)* obscurcir, offusquer (la vue, le jugement, etc.); *(b) F: A:* **to be obfuscated,** être hébété, stupéfié, par la boisson.

obfuscation [ɔbfʌs'keiʃ(ə)n], *s. A:* obscurcissement *m*; offuscation *f*.

obi[1] ['oubi], *s. Cost:* obi *m*.

obi[2], *s.* = OBEAH.

obit[1] ['ɔbit], *s. Ecc:* **1.** *A:* obit *m*. **2. o. book,** (registre *m*) obituaire (*m*).

obit[2] ['oubit, ə'bit], *s. Journ: F:* notice *f* nécrologique.

obiter ['ɔbitər]. *Lt.adv.* en passant; *Jur:* **o. dictum,** opinion judiciaire incidente; *Lit:* **o. dicta,** opinions *f* et propos *m* (d'un écrivain).

obituarist [ə'bitjurist], *s.* nécrologue *m*.

obituary [ə'bitjuri], *a. & s.* **o. (list),** registre *m* des morts; obituaire *m*, nécrologe *m*; **o. notice,** notice nécrologique; *Journ:* **the o. column, the obituaries,** la nécrologie.

object[1] ['ɔbdʒikt], *s.* **1.** objet *m*; *(a)* objet, chose *f*; **a distant o.,** un objet éloigné; **o. lesson,** (i) *A:* leçon *f* de choses; (ii) exemple *m*; **to be an o. lesson to s.o.,** servir d'exemple à qn; **the o. looked at under the microscope,** l'objet observé au microscope; *Opt:* **o. glass, o. lens,** objectif *m*; **photomicrographic o. glass,** micro-objectif *m*, *pl.* micro-objectifs; **o. plate, o. slide,** porte-objet *m* (de microscope); *(of microscope)* **o. finder,** chercheur *m* d'objet; chariot *m* (à vernier, de centrage); *(b) Surv:* objet, point *m*; **reference o.,** point de référence; **setting by o.,** orientation *f* sur un point, par rapport à un point; **o. staff,** jalon *m*; *(c) Bill:* **o. ball,** (la) bille que l'on vise; *(d) Phil:* **formal o., material o.,** objet formel, matériel. **2.** objet, sujet *m*; **o. of, for, pity,** objet, sujet, de pitié; **to be an o. for ridicule,** être en butte au ridicule; **they had become objects of universal hatred,** ils étaient devenus les objets d'une haine universelle; **the o. of one's love,** l'objet aimé; **the Flood had been the o. of his studies,** le Déluge avait été le sujet de ses études; *F:* **did you ever see such an o.?** (i) a-t-on jamais rien vu de si bizarre? (ii) a-t-on jamais vu une telle horreur? **he's a funny-looking o.,** il a l'air drôle; il a une drôle de touche. **3.** *(a)* but *m* objectif, fin *f*; **to have sth. for, as, an o.,** avoir qch. pour objectif, pour objet; avoir qch. pour but; **the o. of this letter is to inform you that . . .,** nous vous écrivons pour vous informer que . . .; **with this o.,** dans cette intention; à cette fin; **with the same o. in view,** dans le même but; avec la même intention; **to wander about without any o.,** flâner sans objet, sans but; **this law has two objects,** cette loi vise un double but, comporte un double objectif; **with the sole o. of doing sth.,** à seule fin de faire qch.; **what is the o. of all this?** à quoi vise tout cela? **what o. is there in running these risks?** à quoi bon courir ces risques? **there's no o. in doing that,** cela ne sert à rien de faire cela; **I see no o. in relating the story,** je juge inutile de raconter cette histoire; **I should be defeating my o. if I let him into the secret,** je manquerais mon but si je le mettais dans le secret; **to attain one's o., to succeed in one's o.,** atteindre son objet; **wealth is his sole o.,** il n'a pour objet que la richesse; *(b) (in applying for a post, etc.)* **salary no o.,** les appointements importent peu; *F: (through a misuse)* **expense, distance, is no o.,** on ne regarde pas à la dépense; la longueur du trajet, la distance, importe peu. **4.** *Gram:* complément *m* (d'objet); **cognate o.,** objet interne; **direct o., indirect o.,** complément direct, indirect; **o. clause,** proposition complétive. **5.** *Cmptr:* objet; **o. language,** langage objet, généré; langage d'exécution; **o. computer, machine,** machine *f* d'exécution; **o. program(me), o. routine,** programme *m* d'objet, exécutable.

object[2] [əb'dʒekt]. **1.** *v.tr.* objecter; *(a) O:* **to o. sth. to s.o., to a proposal,** objecter qch. à qn, à une proposition; **I objected that there was no time,** j'ai objecté le manque de temps; *(b) A:* **to o. sth. against s.o.,** objecter, alléguer, qch. contre qn; **what have you got to o. against him?** qu'avez-vous à alléguer contre lui? que lui reprochez-vous? **2.** *v.i.* **to o. to sth.,** faire objection, élever une objection, s'opposer, trouver à redire, à qch.; désapprouver qch.; protester, réclamer, contre qch.; **to o. to s.o.,** avoir des objections à faire contre qn; *Jur:* **to o. to a witness,** récuser un témoin; **he objects to my dress,** il désapprouve ma robe; **to o. to doing sth.,** se refuser à faire qch.; **I o. to his doing it,** je m'oppose à ce qu'il le fasse; **I strongly o. to it,** cela me répugne absolument; **I strongly o. to waiting another year,** je ne tiens pas du tout à attendre, il me déplairait fort d'attendre, encore une année; **I don't o. to waiting,** cela ne me fait rien d'attendre; **he objects to my singing,** (i) il n'aime pas ma façon de chanter; (ii) il lui déplaît que je chante; **do you o. to my smoking?** la fumée vous gêne-t-elle? cela ne vous ennuie pas que je fume? **you don't o. to my correcting your mistakes?** vous ne trouvez pas mal que je corrige vos fautes? **he objects,** il s'y oppose.

objectification [ɔbdʒektifi'keiʃ(ə)n], *s. Phil:* objectivation *f*.

objectify [ɔb'dʒektifai], *v.tr. Phil:* objectiver.

objection [əb'dʒekʃ(ə)n], *s.* **1.** objection *f*; **to raise an o.,** dresser, soulever, élever, formuler, une objection; **to raise objections to sth.,** opposer des objections à qch., soulever des objections contre qch.; faire, élever, des difficultés *f*; **the o. has been raised that the candidate is too young,** on a objecté que le candidat est trop jeune; **to find, make, an o. to sth.,** objecter à qch.; trouver un empêchement à qch.; **there is one o. to be made,** il y a un mais; **to take o. to sth.,** (i) faire des objections à qch.; (ii) se fâcher de qch.; **the only o. that can be taken to your plan is that it's too complicated,** le seul grief, la seule objection, qu'on puisse faire à votre projet est que c'est trop compliqué; *Jur:* **o. to a witness, to an arbitrator,** récusation *f* de témoin, d'arbitre; *St.Exch:* **o. to mark,** opposition *f* à la cote; **to lodge an o. to sth.,** mettre opposition à qch.; **to make no o. to, against, sth.,** ne rien objecter contre qch.; **I have no o. to that proposal,** je n'ai rien à objecter, à opposer, à cette proposition; **I have no o. to his doing so,** je ne m'oppose pas à ce qu'il le fasse; **have you any o. to my approaching him on the subject?** vous déplairait-il que je lui en touche un mot? **I have no o. to it,** (i) je ne m'y oppose pas, je n'ai rien à dire là-contre, à l'encontre; (ii) je le veux bien, je ne demande pas mieux; **I have no o. to him,** je n'ai rien à dire contre lui; **I have a decided o. to him,** il me déplaît fortement; **his youth is the chief o.,** ce qu'on lui objecte surtout, ce qu'on allègue surtout contre lui, c'est sa jeunesse; **I have a strong o. to doing that,** il me répugne (fortement) de faire cela; **if you have no o.,** si cela ne vous fait rien; si vous le voulez bien; ne vous déplaise. **2.** obstacle *m*, inconvénient *m*; **there is no o. to your leaving at once,** il n'y a pas d'obstacle à ce que vous partiez immédiatement; **the chief o. to your plan is its cost,** l'inconvénient principal, le plus grand désavantage, de votre projet, c'est le coût; **this presents objections,** cela offre des inconvénients; **there are objections to doing that,** il y a des inconvénients à faire cela; **I see no o. (to it),** je n'y vois pas d'inconvénient, pas d'obstacle; **I see no o. to doing so,** je ne vois aucun inconvénient, aucun empêchement, à ce que cela se fasse.

objectionable [əb'dʒekʃnəbl], *a.* **1.** à qui, à quoi, on peut trouver à redire; répréhensible; inadmissible; inacceptable; **most o. conduct,** conduite que l'on ne saurait qualifier, inqualifiable. **2.** désagréable, répugnant; **idea that is most o. to me,** idée qui me répugne; **to use o. language,** dire des grossièretés; tenir des propos choquants, lâcher des gros mots; **he's a most o. person,** personne ne peut le souffrir.

objectionableness [əb'dʒekʃnəb(ə)lnis], *s.* caractère répugnant, désagréable (de qn, d'une action); grossièreté *f* (de langage).

objectionably [əb'dʒekʃnəbli], *adv.* désagréablement; d'une manière répugnante.

objectivate [ɔb'dʒektiveit], *v.tr. Phil:* objectiver.

objectivation [ɔb'dʒekti'veiʃ(ə)n], *s.* objectivation *f*.

objective [ɔb'dʒektiv]. **1.** *a.* *(a) Phil: Med: etc: (of reality, symptom, etc.)* objectif; **let's be o.,** voyons les choses objectivement; *Psy:* **o. choice,** choix objectal; *Sch:* **o. test,** test objectif; *(b) Gram:* **o. (case),** cas *m* régime; cas objectif; **o. genitive,** génitif objectif; *(c) Mil:* **o. point,** objectif *m*. **2.** *s.* *(a)* but *m*, objectif; *Mil:* **primary o.,** objectif principal; **long-term o.,** objectif lointain; **to reach the o.,** atteindre l'objectif; *(b) Opt:* objectif; **coated o.,** objectif traité, bleuté; **reflecting o.,** objectif à miroir; **immersion o.,** objectif à immersion (d'un microscope).

objectively [ɔb'dʒektivli], *adv.* **1.** (contempler qch.) objectivement, d'une manière objective. **2.** *Gram:* en fonction de régime.

objectiveness [ɔb'dʒektivnis], *s. Phil:* objectivité *f*.

objectivism [ɔb'dʒektivizm], *s. Phil:* objectivisme *m*.

objectivist [ɔb'dʒektivist], *a. & s. Phil:* objectiviste (*mf*).

objectivistic [ɔbdʒekti'vistik], *a. Phil:* objectiviste.

objectivity [ɔbdʒek'tiviti], *s. Phil:* objectivité *f*.

objectless ['ɔbdʒiktlis], *a.* sans but, sans objet.

objector [əb'dʒektər], *s.* **1.** protestataire *mf*, réclameur, -euse. **2.** personne *f* qui soulève des objections; contradicteur, -trice.

objet d'art ['ɔbʒei'dɑ:], *s.* objet *m* d'art; *Pej:* sujet *m* de pendule.

objet trouvé ['ɔbʒei'tru:vei], *s. Art:* ready-made *m inv.*

objurgate ['ɔbdʒəgeit], *v.tr.* accabler (qn) de reproches.

objurgation [ɔbdʒə'geiʃ(ə)n], *s.* objurgation *f*, réprimande *f*.

objurgatory [ɔb'dʒə:gət(ə)ri], *a.* objurgatoire.

oblanceolate [ɔb'lɑ:nsiəleit], *a. Bot:* oblancéolé.

oblast ['ɔblɑ:st], *s. Russian Adm:* oblast *m*, province *f* autonome.

oblate[1] ['ɔbleit], *s. Ecc:* oblat, -ate.

oblate[2] ['ɔbleit, ə'bleit], *a. Mth: etc:* (ellipsoïde) aplati (aux pôles), raccourci.

oblateness [ɔ'bleitnis], *s. Geom: etc:* aplatissement *m* (d'un ellipsoïde, etc.).

oblation [ɔ'bleiʃ(ə)n], *s. Ecc:* oblation *f*; **the great o.,** le sacrement de l'Eucharistie; **to make an o. of sth. to God,** faire l'oblation de qch. à Dieu.

obley ['ɔbli], *s. Ecc: A:* pain *m* à chanter, pain d'autel.

obligant ['ɔbligənt], *s. Jur: Scot:* obligé, -ée; débiteur, -trice.

obligate[1] ['ɔbligeit], *v.tr.* **1.** *Jur:* **to o. s.o. to do sth.,** imposer à qn l'obligation de faire qch.; **to be obligated to do sth.,** avoir l'obligation de faire qch. **2.** *NAm: Fin:* *(a)* obliger (un bien); *(b)* donner à (des fonds) une affectation spéciale.

obligate[2], *a.* essentiel, nécessaire; *Biol:* **o. parasite,** parasite essentiel.

obligation [ɔbli'geiʃ(ə)n], *s.* *(a)* obligation *f*; **o. of humanity,** devoir *m* d'humanité; **moral obligations,** obligations morales; **greatness has its obligations,** la grandeur a ses assujettissements *m*; **to put, lay, s.o. under an o. to do sth.,** imposer à qn l'obligation de faire qch.; **to be under an o. to do sth.,** être dans l'obligation de, être astreint à, être tenu de, faire qch.; **I am under no o. to go with them,** rien ne m'oblige à les accompagner; *Com:* **without o.,** sans engagement; **no o. to buy,** entrée libre; *Ecc:* **day, holiday, of o.,** fête *f* d'obligation, de commande; *Jur:* **perfect o.,** obligation parfaite; obligation légale; **imperfect o.,** obligation imparfaite; obligation morale, naturelle; **joint and several o.,** solidarité *f*; *(b)* dette *f* de reconnaissance; **to be under obligations, under an o., to s.o.,** avoir des obligations envers qn; devoir de la reconnaissance à qn; avoir envers qn une dette de reconnaissance; **to remain under an o. to s.o.,** demeurer en reste avec qn; **I am under a great o. to him,** je lui suis redevable de beaucoup; **to lay, put, s.o. under an o.,** obliger qn; créer une obligation à qn; **I don't want him to put me under an o.,** je ne voudrais pas être son obligé; **you are laying me under an o.,** c'est à charge de revanche; *(c) Com:* **to meet, fulfil, one's obligations,** tenir ses engagements; faire face, faire honneur, à ses engagements, ses obligations; **to fail to meet one's obligations,** manquer à ses obligations.

obligato [ɔbli'gɑ:tou], *a., adv. & s.* = OBBLIGATO.

obligatorily [ə'bligət(ə)rili], *adv.* obligatoirement.

obligatory [ə'bligət(ə)ri], *a.* **1.** obligatoire; **to make it o. on, upon, s.o. to do sth.,** obliger qn à faire qch.; imposer à qn l'obligation de faire qch.; **the wearing of a jacket is o.,** le port d'un veston est de rigueur. **2.** *Jur:* **writing o.,** obligation *f* (par écrit, par acte notarié).

oblige [ə'blaidʒ], *v.tr.* **1.** *(compel)* *(a)* *usu. Jur:* obliger, astreindre, assujettir (**s.o. to do sth.,** qn à faire qch.); **to o. oneself to s.o.,** s'obliger envers qn (par engagement authentique, par devant notaire); (*b*) **to be obliged to do sth.,** être obligé, tenu, de faire qch.; *Adm:* être astreint à faire qch.; **he was obliged to go,** il a dû s'en aller; **I was obliged to obey,** j'ai été contraint d'obéir; force me fut d'obéir. **2.** (*do s.o. a favour*) obliger; (*a*) **to o. a friend,** rendre service à un ami; **o. me by thinking no more about it,** faites-moi le plaisir de l'oublier; **you would greatly o. (me) by lending me ten pounds,** vous m'obligeriez beaucoup en me prêtant, si vous me prêtiez, dix livres; **will you o. me with a cheque?** auriez-vous l'obligeance de me donner un chèque? **can you o. me with a light?** auriez-vous l'amabilité de me donner du feu? **he did it to o. (us),** il l'a fait par pure complaisance; **in order to o. you,** pour vous être agréable; **to be always willing to o.,** être toujours prêt à rendre service; être très obligeant, très complaisant; **an answer by return of post will o.,** prière de vouloir bien répondre par retour du courrier; *P:* **anything to o.,** tout ce que vous voudrez pour vous faire plaisir; **he obliged with a song,** il a eu l'obligeance, l'amabilité, de chanter; **a lady I used to o.,** une dame chez laquelle je faisais le ménage; (*b*) **to be obliged to s.o.,** être obligé à qn; **I am much obliged to you for your kindness,** je vous suis bien reconnaissant, je vous sais infiniment gré, de votre bonté; **I am obliged to you for supporting me,** je vous ai de l'obligation de m'avoir soutenu; **we should be greatly obliged if you would cease this practice,** nous vous saurions gré de vouloir bien mettre fin à cet usage.

obligee [ɔbli'dʒi:], *s.* **1.** *Jur:* créancier *m* (en vertu d'une obligation); obligataire *m.* **2.** *F:* obligé, -ée.

obliging [ə'blaidʒiŋ], *a.* obligeant, complaisant, serviable, prévenant; arrangeant; **very o. man,** homme d'une grande obligeance; **it's very o. of you,** c'est très obligeant de votre part.

obligingly [ə'blaidʒiŋli], *adv.* obligeamment, complaisamment; **the facilities you o. granted to us,** les facilités que vous avez bien voulu nous accorder.

obligingness [ə'blaidʒiŋnis], *s.* obligeance *f.*

obligor [ɔbli'gɔ:r], *s. Jur:* obligé, -ée; débiteur, -trice.

oblique[1] [ə'bli:k]. **1.** *a.* (*a*) (ligne, angle, cône, etc.) oblique (**to,** à); **o. angled,** obliquangle; **o. glance,** regard *m* de biais; *Arch:* **o. arch,** voûte biaise; **o. photograph,** photographie (aérienne) prise sous un angle oblique; *Astr:* **o. sphere,** sphère *f* oblique; *Bot:* **o. leaf,** feuille *f* oblique, asymétrique; *Anat:* **o. muscle,** oblique *m*; **superior o. muscle,** grand oblique; muscle *m* pathétique (de l'œil); *Mus:* **o. motion,** mouvement *m* oblique; *Nau:* **o. sailing,** route *f* oblique; *Mil:* **o. fire,** tir *m* oblique; tir d'écharpe; (*b*) **o. ways,** moyens indirects; **to achieve sth. by o. means,** accomplir qch. par des moyens indirects, détournés; (*c*) *Gram:* **o. case,** cas indirect, oblique; **o. oration,** discours indirect. **2.** *s.* (*a*) (i) (ligne) oblique (*f*); (ii) *Geom:* figure *f* oblique; (*b*) *Anat:* (muscle) oblique (*m*); (*c*) *Typ:* barre transversale, barre de fraction; (*d*) *Mil: etc:* (mouvement) oblique (*m*); **to make a left o.,** exécuter un oblique à gauche; obliquer à gauche.

oblique[2], *v.i. Mil: etc:* obliquer (**to the right, left,** à droite, à gauche).

obliquely [ə'bli:kli], *adv.* (*a*) obliquement, de biais, en biais; *Mil:* (tiré) en écharpe; (*b*) d'une façon indirecte, par des moyens détournés, de biais.

obliqueness [ə'bli:knis], *s.* = OBLIQUITY 1.

obliquity [ə'blikwiti], *s.* **1.** obliquité *f,* biais *m*; **o. of the eye,** l'obliquité de l'œil; *Astr:* **o. of the ecliptic,** obliquité de l'écliptique. **2.** obliquité (de conduite); manque *m* de franchise; duplicité *f.*

obliterate [ə'blitəreit], *v.tr.* **1.** (*a*) faire disparaître, effacer, gratter (des chiffres, etc.); *Journ:* **to o. a passage,** caviarder un passage; **carvings obliterated by time and weather,** sculptures effacées par le temps; **to o. the past,** faire oublier le passé; oblitérer le passé; passer l'éponge sur le passé; (*b*) oblitérer, composter (un timbre). **2.** *Anat: Med: etc:* oblitérer (un conduit, etc.).

obliterating [ə'blitəreitiŋ], *a.* (*of stamp, etc.*) oblitérateur, -trice.

obliteration [əblitə'reiʃ(ə)n], *s.* **1.** effaçage *m*; (*by scratching out*) grattage *m*; (*by crossing out*) rature *f.* **2.** oblitération *f* (d'un timbre). **3.** *Anat: Med:* oblitération (d'un conduit, etc.).

obliterative [ə'blit(ə)rətiv], *a. Nat.Hist:* **o. coloration,** homochromie *f.*

obliterator [ə'blitəreitər], *s.* effaceur, -euse.

oblivion [ə'bliviən], *s.* (*a*) (état *m* d')oubli *m*; **poem doomed to o.,** poème voué à l'oubli; **to fall into o.,** tomber dans l'oubli; **it has sunk into o.,** le souvenir en est perdu; **to rescue s.o., sth., from o.,** sauver qn, qch., de l'oubli; (*b*) oubli; **in a moment of o.,** dans un moment d'oubli; *Pol:* **Act, Bill, of O.,** (loi *f* d')amnistie *f.*

oblivious [ə'bliviəs], *a.* oublieux (**of,** de); **to be totally o. of the difficulties,** ne tenir aucun compte des difficultés; **o. of what was going on,** inconscient de ce qui se passait.

obliviously [ə'bliviəsli], *adv.* oublieusement; sans se rendre compte de ce qui se passe.

obliviousness [ə'bliviəsnis], *s.* oubli *m*; inconscience *f.*

oblong ['ɔblɔŋ]. **1.** *a.* oblong, -ongue; (sphéroïde) allongé; (rectangle) plus long que large; *Bot:* **o. leaf,** feuille allongée; *Typ: etc:* **o. format,** format oblong, à l'italienne. **2.** *s.* rectangle *m.*

obloquy ['ɔbləkwi], *s.* (*a*) calomnie *f*; blâme (malveillant); **to cover s.o. with o., to heap o. upon s.o.,** cribler qn d'attaques malveillantes; **held up to public o.,** poursuivi par, exposé à, la vindicte publique; **to come under public o.,** encourir le blâme public; (*b*) honte *f,* déshonneur *m,* opprobre *m.*

obnoxious [əb'nɔkʃəs], *a.* **1.** (*a*) (*of pers., action, etc.*) haïssable, odieux; (*of pers.*) antipathique (**to s.o.,** à qn); détesté (**to,** par); mal vu (**to,** de); **o. conduct,** conduite odieuse, détestable, exécrable; (*b*) **o. smell,** odeur repoussante, désagréable, malsaine. **2.** *A:* exposé (**to a danger,** à un danger).

obnoxiously [əb'nɔkʃəsli], *adv.* d'une façon détestable, exécrable, insupportable.

obnoxiousness [əb'nɔkʃəsnis], *s.* caractère odieux, exécrable, insupportable (de qch.).

obnubilate [ɔb'nju:bileit], *v.tr.* obnubiler, obscurcir (la vue, l'intelligence, etc.).

obnubilation [ɔbnju:bi'leiʃ(ə)n], *s. Lit: Med:* obnubilation *f* (de l'esprit, des facultés).

oboe ['oubou], *s.* **1.** *Mus:* (*a*) hautbois *m*; (*b*) (*organ stop*) (jeu *m* de) hautbois; (*c*) **o. (player),** hautboïste *mf,* oboïste *mf.* **2.** *Rad: Av:* radar *m* de navigation et de bombardement.

oboist ['oubouist], *s. Mus:* hautboïste *mf,* oboïste *mf.*

obol ['ɔbɔl], *s. Gr.Ant:* obole *f.*

obole ['ɔboul], *s. A.Num:* obole *f.*

obolus, *pl.* **-li** ['ɔbələs, -lai], *s. Gr.Ant:* obole *f.*

obovate [ɔb'ouveit], *a. Bot:* (feuille, etc.) obovale.

obovoid [ɔb'ouvɔid], *a. Bot:* (fruit, etc.) obové, obovoïde.

obpyramidal [ɔbpi'ræmidl], *a. Bot:* (fruit, etc.) obpyramidal, -aux.

obreption [ɔb'repʃ(ə)n], *s. Jur: Ecc: & Scot:* obreption *f.*

obreptitious [ɔbrep'tiʃəs], *a.* obreptice.

obscene [əb'si:n], *a.* (*a*) (chanson, mot) obscène; **to circulate o. books,** faire circuler des obscénités; **o. author,** auteur *m* obscène; (*b*) repoussant, hideux, révoltant.

obscenely [əb'si:nli], *adv.* d'une manière obscène; **to talk o.,** dire des obscénités.

obscenity [əb'seniti, -'si:n-], *s.* obscénité *f.*

obscurant [əb'skju:rənt], *s.* obscurantiste *mf.*

obscurantic [ɔbskju'ræntik], *a.* obscurantiste.

obscurantism [ɔbskju'ræntizm], *s.* obscurantisme *m.*

obscurantist [ɔbskju'ræntist]. **1.** *s.* obscurantiste *mf.* **2.** *a.* obscurantiste.

obscuration [ɔbskju'reiʃ(ə)n], *s.* **1.** obscurcissement *m.* **2.** *Astr:* obscuration *f,* éclipse *f,* occultation *f* (d'un astre).

obscure[1] [əb'skjuər], *a.* **1.** (*a*) obscur, ténébreux, sombre; **to grow, become, o.,** s'obscurcir; (*b*) (sentiment) vague; (*c*) **o. village, retreat,** village inconnu, ignoré, caché; retraite obscure; (*d*) **o. outline,** profil indistinct. **2.** (discours, livre) obscur; **o. argument,** argument obscur, peu clair; **o. illness,** maladie obscure; **o. style,** style obscur, confus, ténébreux, hermétique; **the part he played in the rebellion remains o.,** le rôle qu'il joua dans la rébellion n'a jamais été éclairci, *F:* tiré au clair. **3.** (*undistinguished*) **o. birth,** naissance obscure; **o. author,** auteur inconnu, peu connu, obscur.

obscure[2], *v.tr.* **1.** (*a*) assombrir; (*b*) obscurcir, cacher; **to o. sth. from s.o.'s view,** cacher qch. à qn; **clouds obscured the sun,** des nuages voilaient le soleil; *Nau:* **to o. the (sailing) lights,** masquer les feux; **light obscured by the land,** feu masqué par la terre; *Const:* **obscured glass,** verre non-transparent; (*c*) obscurcir (un argument, les faits); aveugler (l'entendement). **2.** (*overshadow*) éclipser, surpasser; **his fame was obscured by that of his father,** sa gloire était éclipsée, surpassée, par celle de son père.

obscurely [əb'skjuəli], *adv.* **1.** (*a*) (voir qch.) obscurément; (apparaître) indistinctement; (*b*) (sentir) vaguement; (*c*) (vivre) obscurément, dans l'obscurité. **2.** (parler) obscurément.

obscureness [əb'skjuənis], *s.* = OBSCURITY 2.

obscuring [əb'skju:riŋ], *s.* obscurcissement *m,* obscuration *f*; *Cin:* **o. period,** phase *f* d'obscuration; **o. blade,** secteur *m* d'obscuration.

obscurity [əb'skju:riti], *s.* **1.** obscurité *f* (de la nuit, d'un bois, etc.). **2.** obscurité, hermétisme *m* (du style, etc.); **to lapse into o.,** tomber dans l'obscurité; devenir obscur. **3.** obscurité (de naissance, de famille, etc.); **to live in o.,** vivre dans l'obscurité; **to spring, rise, emerge, from o.,** sortir de l'obscurité, du néant; sortir de sa chrysalide; **to sink into o.,** tomber dans l'obscurité.

obsecration [ɔbsi'kreiʃ(ə)n], *s. Ecc:* obsécration *f.*

obsequent ['ɔbsikwənt], *a. Geog:* (cours d'eau) obséquent.

obsequies ['ɔbsikwiz], *s.pl.* obsèques *f,* funérailles *f*; **to attend the o.,** suivre le convoi (de qn).

obsequious [əb'si:kwiəs], *a.* obséquieux; **o. bow,** révérence obséquieuse; **o. person,** personne obséquieuse; complimenteur, -euse.

obsequiously [əb'si:kwiəsli], *adv.* obséquieusement.

obsequiousness [əb'si:kwiəsnis], *s.* obséquiosité *f.*

observable [əb'zə:vəbl], *a.* **1.** (cérémonie, formule, etc.) à observer, à laquelle on doit se conformer. **2.** (*discernible*) observable, visible; **an o. change took place,** il y eut un changement perceptible, sensible, appréciable. **3.** (*worthy of note*) remarquable; digne de remarque, d'attention; à noter.

observably [əb'zə:vəbli], *adv.* sensiblement, visiblement, perceptiblement.

observance [əb'zə:v(ə)ns], *s.* **1.** (*a*) observation *f,* observance *f,* respect *m* (d'une loi, d'un usage, des clauses d'un contrat, etc.); **o. of the Sabbath,** observance, sanctification *f,* du dimanche; (*b*) *Ecc:* règle *f,* observance (d'un ordre religieux); **friars of the Strict O.,** frères de l'étroite observance. **2. religious observances,** pratiques religieuses; **to maintain the customary observances,** pratiquer les rites habituels.

observant [əb'zə:v(ə)nt], *a.* **1.** (*a*) observateur, -trice (**of,** de); attentif (**of,** à); (*b*) attentif; **o. (turn of) mind,** esprit observateur, d'observation; **he is very o.,** rien ne lui échappe; *F:* il a l'œil. **2.** *Ecc: A:* **O. Friar, (Friar) O.,** religieux observantin; observantin *m.*

observantly [əb'zə:v(ə)ntli], *adv.* attentivement; d'un œil pénétrant, éveillé.

observation [ɔbzə(:)'veiʃ(ə)n], *s.* observation *f.* **1.** (*a*) **to put, keep, s.o., a patient, sth., under o.,** mettre, tenir, qn, un malade, qch., en observation; **to come under s.o.'s o.,** entrer dans le champ d'observation de qn; tomber sous les yeux, le regard, de qn; **your behaviour is under constant o.,** on vous observe, surveille, continuellement; on observe, surveille, tous vos faits et gestes; **experiment carried out under the o. of the principal,** expérience effectuée, accomplie, sous le contrôle, la surveillance, du directeur; **to escape o.,** se dérober aux regards; **hidden from o.,** caché aux regards; *Mil:* **o. of the ground, the enemy,** surveillance du terrain, de l'ennemi; **aerial, air, o.,** observation aérienne; **land, ground, o.,** observation terrestre; **combined, cross, o.,** observation conjuguée; (*b*) **he has no (power of) o.,** il est peu observateur; (*c*) *Astr: Surv:* coup *m* de lunette; **observations in the dark,** visées *f* dans l'obscurité; **wind o.,** sondage *m*; **astronomical o.,** observation astronomique; **to take an o.,** prendre, faire, une observation; *Nau:* faire le point; **to enter observations,** inscrire des observations, des coups de lunette; **reading of each o.,** cote *f* de chaque observation; *Nau:* **sailing by observation(s),** navigation observée; **position by o.,** point observé; (*d*) *attrib.* **o. aircraft,** avion *m* d'observation; *Rail:* **o. coach, railcar,** voiture *f,* autorail *m,* d'observation, panoramique; *Cin:* **o. port,** fenêtre *f,* trou *m,* d'observation; *Mil:* **o. post, station,** poste *m* d'observation; observatoire *m*; poste de guet (à vue); (*in tree, etc.*), mirador *m*; **o. unit,** unité *f* d'observation, de surveillance; *Opt: etc:* **o. slit, aperture,** regard *m* (d'un appareil scientifique, etc.); *Tp:* **o. circuit,** circuit *m* d'écoute; **o. desk,** table *f* de contrôle; *Med:* **o. ward,** salle *f* des malades en observation. **2.** (*a*) remarque *f*; **he didn't make a single o. during dinner,** il n'a pas fait une seule observation, n'a pas ouvert la bouche, n'a pas soufflé mot, pendant le dîner; (*b*) **to publish one's observations on sth.,** publier ses observations sur qch.; **to make observations on the habits of ants,** faire des observations sur les habitudes des fourmis; **please let us have your observations on this matter,** veuillez nous communiquer vos observations sur cette question.

observational [ɔbzə'veiʃ(ə)nəl], *a.* (*of research, etc.*) fait par l'observation; (*of conclusion, etc.*) qui provient de l'observation.

observatory [əb'zə:vət(ə)ri], *s.* **1.** *Astr:* observatoire *m*; *Orn:* **bird o.,** station *f* d'observation des mœurs des oiseaux; *Mil:* **field o.,** échelle-observatoire *f, pl.* échelles-observatoires. **2.** belvédère *m.*

observe [əb'zə:v], *v.tr.* **1.** observer (la loi, un jeûne, etc.); se conformer à (un ordre); **to o. the conventions,** observer les convenances; **to o. silence,** garder un silence absolu; observer le silence; **to o. care in doing sth.,** apporter des précautions à faire qch.; **he observed moderation in what he said,** il a mis de la modération dans ses paroles; **to o. the Sabbath,** observer, respecter, (i) le sabbat, (ii) le dimanche; **failure to o. the law,** inobservation *f* de la loi; *F:* entorse *f* à la loi. **2.** (*a*) observer, regarder (les étoiles, etc.); (*b*) *Mil:* **to o. the enemy's movements,** surveiller l'ennemi. **3.** apercevoir, remarquer, noter (un fait, etc.); **I observed him spying on them,** je l'ai surpris à les guetter; **at last I observed a policeman,** enfin j'ai aperçu un agent de police; **I didn't o. the colour of her eyes,** je n'ai pas remarqué la couleur de ses yeux; **you will o. there is a mistake in the account,** vous remarquerez qu'il y a erreur dans le compte; **it should be observed that this is an exception,** il est à noter que cela fait exception; *v.i.* **a man who observes keenly but says little,** un homme qui observe attentivement, à qui rien n'échappe, mais qui parle peu. **4.** (*a*) dire; **'you are wrong', he observed,** 'vous avez tort', dit-il, fit-il; **I observed (to him) that somebody was following us,** je lui fis remarquer, je lui fis l'observation, que quelqu'un nous suivait; **you were going to o.?** vous alliez dire, remarquer? (*b*) *v.i.* **no one has observed on this fact,** personne n'a commenté ce fait; ce fait a été passé sous silence.

observer [əb'zəːvər], *s.* **1.** observateur, -trice (des lois, des règles, etc.); **a strict o. of etiquette,** un scrupuleux observateur de l'étiquette. **2.** (*a*) observateur, -trice (des mouvements des astres, *Mil:* des mouvements de l'ennemi); **Royal O. Corps,** corps des observateurs de la défense contre avions (1939–45); (*b*) observateur, -trice (des événements); **to send observers to a conference,** envoyer des observateurs à un congrès; **United Nations o.,** observateur des Nations Unies; **he had come as an o.,** il était venu en curieux.

observing[1] [əb'zəːviŋ], *a.* observateur, -trice; attentif; **o. mind,** esprit observateur, d'observation.

observing[2], *s.* observation *f*; surveillance *f* (de l'ennemi, etc.); **o. unit,** unité *f* d'observation; **o. angle,** angle *m* d'observation; **o. station,** poste *m* d'observation; observatoire *m.*

obsess [əb'ses], *v.tr.* (*a*) (*of evil spirit*) obséder (qn); (*b*) **to be obsessed with, by, an idea,** être obsédé d'une idée, par une idée; être travaillé, hanté, par une idée; être en proie à une idée.

obsessing [əb'sesiŋ], *a.* (*of thought*) obsédant.

obsession [əb'seʃ(ə)n], *s.* **1.** obsession *f* ((i) par un démon, (ii) par une idée). **2.** obsession; hantise *f*, monomanie *f*, idée *f* fixe; **his o. with violence,** son obsession de la violence; **he suffers from an o.,** c'est un obsédé.

obsessional [əb'seʃ(ə)nl], *a.* *Psy:* obsessionel; **o. neurosis,** névrose obsessionnelle.

obsessionist [əb'seʃənist], *s.* obsédé, -ée.

obsessive [əb'sesiv], *a.* (*of idea, image, etc.*) obsédant.

obsidian [əb'sidiən]. *Miner:* obsidienne *f*, obsidiane *f*, pierre *f*, verre *m*, des volcans; verre, silex *m*, volcanique; agate noire, d'Islande.

obsidianite [əb'sidiənait], *s. Miner:* obsidianite *f.*

obsidional [əb'sidiən(ə)l], *a.* (*of money, etc.*) obsidional, -aux; *Rom.Ant:* **o. crown,** couronne obsidionale.

obsolescence [ɔbsə'lesns], *s.* **1.** tendance *f* à tomber en désuétude, à devenir désuet; vieillissement *m*; *Ind: etc:* obsolescence *f* (d'un outillage); *Ind:* **planned o.,** obsolescence prévue; *Ind: Com:* **built-in o.,** obsolescence prévue systématiquement; *Ins:* **o. clause,** clause *f* de vétusté *f.* **2.** *Biol:* atrophie *f*, contabescence *f* (d'un organe, etc.).

obsolescent [ɔbsə'lesnt], *a.* **1.** qui tombe en désuétude; vieillissant; **o. word,** mot *m* qui a vieilli. **2.** *Biol:* (organe, etc.) atrophié, qui tend à disparaître.

obsolete[1] ['ɔbsəliːt], *a.* **1.** (*of word, etc.*) désuet, -ète; inusité; obsolète; hors d'usage; tombé en désuétude; (*of fashion*) suranné; (*of tool, etc.*) abandonné; hors d'usage; (*of engine, design, etc.*) démodé, dépassé; (*of ship*) déclassé, démodé; (*of institution*) aboli; **to grow o.,** s'abroger, passer de mode, tomber en désuétude; **the word is o.,** ce mot n'est plus usité. **2.** *Biol: etc:* obsolète; **o. groove, tooth,** sillon *m*, dent *f*, à peine visible, dont il reste à peine une trace.

obsolete[2], *v.tr. U.S:* périmer, démoder.

obsoleteness ['ɔbsəliːtnis], *s.* vétusté *f*, désuétude *f.*

obstacle ['ɔbstəkl], *s.* obstacle *m*; **to be an o. to sth., s.o.,** faire obstacle à qch.; se trouver sur le chemin de qn; **path strewn with obstacles,** voie semée d'achoppements *m*; **to pass round an o.,** doubler un obstacle; **to put obstacles in s.o.'s way,** dresser, susciter, des obstacles à qn; **to put an o. in the way of the marriage,** mettre obstacle au mariage; **the only o. to their reconciliation,** le seul obstacle, empêchement, à leur réconciliation; **fact that might have proved an o. to his promotion,** fait qui aurait pu nuire à son avancement; *Mil:* **tactical o.,** obstacle actif; **protective o.,** obstacle passif; **to set up, construct, obstacles,** établir des obstacles; **o. course,** parcours *m*, piste *f*, d'obstacles; *Av:* **o. clearance line,** ligne *f* de dégagement des obstacles; **o. light,** feu *m* d'obstacle; *Sp:* **o. race,** course *f* d'obstacles; **o. riding,** monte *f* à l'obstacle.

obstetric(al) [əb'stetrik(l)], *a.* obstétrical, -aux; *Amph:* **obstetrical toad,** crapaud accoucheur.

obstetrician [ɔbste'triʃ(ə)n], *s.* docteur *m* en obstétrique; médecin accoucheur; obstétricien, -ienne.

obstetrics [əb'stetriks], *s.pl.* (*usu. with sg. const.*) obstétrique *f.*

obstinacy ['ɔbstinəsi], *s.* **1.** obstination *f*, entêtement *m*, opiniâtreté *f*, ténacité *f*; **o. in denying sth.,** acharnement *m* à nier qch.; **to show o.,** s'obstiner; **it's sheer o.,** c'est un parti pris (chez lui). **2.** *Med:* persistance *f* (d'une maladie).

obstinate ['ɔbstinət], *a.* **1.** obstiné (**in doing sth.,** à faire qch.); opiniâtre, volontaire, tenace; **to be o.,** s'entêter; **o. nature,** caractère buté; **o. as a mule,** entêté, têtu, comme un mulet, comme une mule, comme un âne; **o. resistance to an attack,** résistance déterminée à une attaque; **o. contest,** combat acharné. **2.** *Med:* **o. fever,** fièvre *f* rebelle; **an o. cold,** un rhume obstiné.

obstinately ['ɔbstinətli], *adv.* obstinément, opiniâtrement, volontairement; **he o. refused,** il s'obstina à refuser; **he o. refuses to eat,** il s'entête à ne pas vouloir manger; **to fight o.,** se battre avec acharnement.

obstreperous [əb'strep(ə)rəs], *a.* (*a*) bruyant, tapageur; (*b*) rebelle, turbulent; **to be o.,** *F:* faire de la rouspétance; rouspéter.

obstreperously [əb'strep(ə)rəsli], *adv.* (*a*) bruyamment, tapageusement; (*b*) *F:* en rouspétant.

obstreperousness [əb'strep(ə)rəsnis], *s.* (*a*) tapage *m*; (*b*) turbulence *f*; *F:* rouspétance *f.*

obstruct [əb'strʌkt], *v.tr.* (*a*) obstruer, embarrasser, encombrer (la rue, etc.); colmater (un filtre); engorger, boucher (un tuyau, etc.); (*of ice, etc.*) embâcler (un cours d'eau); *Med:* oblitérer, obstruer (l'intestin); **to o. s.o.'s path,** barrer le chemin à qn; **do not o. the exit,** n'encombrez pas la sortie; **to o. the view,** incommoder, gêner, la vue; **building that obstructs the light,** bâtiment qui intercepte la lumière, le jour; (*b*) **to o. s.o.'s movements,** gêner, entraver, empêcher, les mouvements de qn; embarrasser qn; **to o. s.o. in the execution of his duty,** gêner qn dans l'exercice de ses fonctions; *Sp:* **to o. another player, competitor,** *v.i.* **to o.,** faire de l'obstruction; *Jur:* **to o. process,** empêcher un huissier dans l'exercice de ses devoirs; *Parl:* **to o. a bill,** faire de l'obstruction; (*c*) **to o. the traffic,** embarrasser, entraver, gêner, la circulation; **to o. navigation,** gêner la navigation.

obstruction [əb'strʌkʃ(ə)n], *s.* **1.** (*a*) engorgement *m* (d'un tuyau, etc.) colmatage *m*, encrassement *m* (d'un filtre, etc.); *Med:* encombrement *m*; **o. of the bowels, of a duct,** occlusion, obstruction, oblitération, intestinale; oblitération d'un conduit; (*b*) empêchement *m* (de qn dans ses affaires, de la circulation, etc.); **o. (of the police),** empêchement de l'action de la police; *Sp:* **o. (of a player, a competitor),** obstruction; (*c*) *Pol:* obstruction; **to practise o.,** faire de l'obstruction. **2.** encombrement, embarras *m* (dans la rue); gêne *f* (dans la circulation); entrave *f* (à la navigation); engorgement, stoppage *m* (dans un tuyau); *Rail:* **an o. on the line,** un obstacle sur la voie; **o. guard,** chasse-corps *m inv*; chasse-pierres *m inv*; *Av:* **o. light, o. marker,** feu *m*, balise *f*, d'obstacle; **o. clearance line,** ligne *f* de dégagement des obstacles.

obstructionism [əb'strʌkʃənizm], *s. Pol:* obstructionnisme *m.*

obstructionist [əb'strʌkʃənist], *s. Pol:* obstructionniste *mf.*

obstructive [əb'strʌktiv], *a.* **1.** *Med:* obstructif, obstruant. **2. o. member of the House,** membre de la Chambre qui fait de l'obstruction; obstructionniste *mf*; **o. tactics, o. measures,** tactique *f* d'obstruction; tactique obstructionniste.

obstructively [əb'strʌktivli], *adv.* (agir) d'une manière gênante; dans un but d'obstruction.

obstructiveness [əb'strʌktivnis], *s.* tactique *f* d'obstruction, de susciter des obstacles, des empêchements.

obstructor [əb'strʌktər], *s.* empêcheur, -euse.

obstruent ['ɔbstruənt]. **1.** *a. & s. Med:* obstruant (*m*). **2.** *a. Ling:* (*of vowel*) (i) fricatif; (ii) occlusif.

obtain [əb'tein]. **1.** *v.tr.* (*a*) obtenir, se procurer, avoir (qch.); **to o. information,** recueillir des renseignements; **goods that can only be obtained from an accredited agent,** marchandises qu'on ne peut se procurer que chez les agents accrédités; **difficulty in obtaining provisions,** difficulté à se procurer des provisions; **to o. sugar from beet,** retirer du sucre de la betterave; **the pleasure obtained from music,** le plaisir que l'on retire de la musique; le plaisir que donne la musique; **to o. s.o.'s appointment to a post,** obtenir la nomination de qn; faire nommer qn à un poste; **he obtained the appointment on merit,** son mérite lui a valu sa nomination; **he has just obtained his captaincy,** il vient de passer capitaine; **to o. first place,** remporter la première place (dans un concours); **I obtained permission to see him,** j'ai obtenu la permission de le voir; **to o. a week's leave,** se faire accorder huit jours de congé; *Com:* **the rates obtained at today's market,** les cours réalisés au marché d'aujourd'hui; *Fb:* **to o. the ball,** capturer le ballon; (*b*) *A:* (*attain*) **to o. one's object,** atteindre son but. **2.** *v.i. A:* avoir cours; prévaloir; **pronunciation that still obtains,** prononciation encore courante, qui prévaut encore; **practice that obtains among civil servants,** pratique, établie, qui règne, chez les fonctionnaires; **system now obtaining,** régime *m* en activité, actuellement en vigueur.

obtainable [əb'teinəbl], *a.* procurable; **where is that o.?** où cela s'obtient-il? où peut-on se procurer cela? où est-ce que ça se trouve? **these shares are not o. on our market,** il est impossible d'acquérir ces actions sur notre place.

obtainer [əb'teinər], *s.* personne *f* qui obtient, se procure, quelque chose; *F:* obtenteur, -trice.

obtaining [əb'teiniŋ], **obtainment** [əb'teinmənt], **obtention** [əb'tenʃ(ə)n], *s.* obtention *f* (**of,** de).

obtect [əb'tekt], **obtected** [əb'tektid], *a. Ent:* (*of chrysalis*) obtecté.

obtrude [əb'truːd]. **1.** *v.tr.* mettre (qch.) en avant; **to o. sth. on, upon, s.o.,** importuner qn pour lui faire acheter, accepter, qch.; **to o. one's opinions on others,** imposer ses opinions à autrui; **to o. oneself,** s'imposer à l'attention, importuner (qn). **2.** *v.i.* (*a*) (*of pers.*) s'imposer à l'attention (de qn); se montrer importun; (*b*) (*of thg*) être trop en évidence; choquer la vue.

obtruncate [əb'trʌŋkeit], *v.tr.* décapiter.

obtrusion [əb'truːʒ(ə)n], *s.* intrusion *f*; importunité *f.*

obtrusive [əb'truːsiv], *a.* **1.** (*of pers.*) importun, intrus; indiscret, -ète; qui se met en avance; (*of behaviour*) indiscret. **2. the background of the picture is too o.,** l'arrière-plan de ce tableau est trop en évidence, s'impose trop; **o. smell,** odeur pénétrante.

obtrusively [əb'truːsivli], *adv.* inopportunément; en intrus; importunément, indiscrètement.

obtrusiveness [əb'truːsivnis], *s.* importunité *f.*

obtund [əb'tʌnd], *v.tr. Med:* émousser (les facultés, etc.).

obturate ['ɔbtjureit], *v.tr.* boucher, obturer (une ouverture, un tuyau, *Artil:* la culasse, etc.).

obturating ['ɔbtjureitiŋ], *a.* obturateur, -trice; obturant.

obturation [ɔbtju'reiʃ(ə)n], *s.* obturation *f* (d'un tuyau, d'une ouverture, etc.).

obturator ['ɔbtjureitər], *s. Mec.E: Artil: Surg: Bot: etc:* obturateur *m*; *Artil:* **ring o.,** obturateur à anneau; *Sm.a:* **o. spindle,** tige *f* de tête mobile; *Dent:* **cleft-palate o.,** obturateur vélo-palatin, *pl.* vélo-palatins; *Anat:* **o. canal, foramen, muscle, nerve,** canal, trou, muscle, nerf, obturateur; **o. artery, vein, membrane,** artère, veine, membrane, obturatrice; *Mec.E:* **o. plate,** plaque obturatrice, obturante; **o. ring,** segment *m* d'étanchéité.

obtuse [əb'tjuːs], *a.* **1.** (*a*) obtus, émoussé; **o. point,** pointe obtuse; *Mth:* **o. angle,** angle obtus; **o. angled,** obtusangle; *Arch:* **o. arch,** arc surbaissé; *Bot:* **o. leaf,** feuille obtuse; (*b*) (sentiment) émoussé; **o. pain,** douleur sourde. **2.** (esprit) obtus, inintelligent, peu intelligent.

obtusely [əb'tjuːsli], *adv.* d'une manière obtuse; obtusement. **2.** stupidement, bêtement, inintelligemment.

obtuseness [əb'tjuːsnis], *s.* **1.** manque *m* de (i) tranchant, (ii) pointe. **2.** inintelligence *f*, stupidité *f.*

obtusifolious [ɔbtjuːsi'fouliəs], *a. Bot:* obtusifolié.

obverse ['ɔbvəːs]. **1.** *a. Nat.Hist:* (organe) plus large au sommet qu'à la base; renversé. **2.** *a. & s.* (*a*) *Num:* **o. (side) of a medal,** avers *m*, obvers *m*, obverse *m or f*, tête *f*, face *f*, d'une médaille; (*b*) **o. of a truth,** opposé *m* d'une vérité.

obversion [ɔb'vəːʃ(ə)n], *s.* obversion *f.*

obvert [əb'vəːt], *v.tr. Log:* retourner (une proposition).

obviate ['ɔbvieit], *v.tr.* prévenir, éviter, parer à, obvier à (une difficulté, etc.); prévenir (des scrupules, etc.); aller au-devant d'(une objection).

obvious ['ɔbviəs], *a.* (*a*) évident, clair, manifeste; de toute évidence; indiscutable; qui tombe sous les sens; **it's o. that the project will fail,** il est de toute évidence, est évident, tombe sous les sens, que le projet échouera; **it's quite o. that he is lying,** il ment, cela saute aux yeux; **it soon became o. that we were not wanted,** il apparut bientôt que nous étions de trop; **that's o.,** cela se devine, ne se demande pas; c'est clair comme bonjour; **the o. importance of this discovery,** l'importance *f* manifeste de cette découverte; **o. fact,** fait patent, évident, qui crève les yeux; **how can we deny o. facts?** comment nier l'évidence même? **o. truth,** vérité patente, évidente; **it was the o. thing to do,** c'était évidemment la chose à faire, c'est ce qu'il fallait faire; c'était tout indiqué; cela s'imposait; **an o. remark,** une vérité de (monsieur de) La Palisse; une lapalissade; **o. tricks,** finesses cousues de fil blanc; **to miss the o.,** ne pas voir l'essentiel; (*b*) **the tower is more o. than elegant,** la tour est plus voyante qu'élégante; **her rather o. clothes,** ses vêtements un peu voyants; **his patriotism is a little (too) o.,** son patriotisme sonne faux; *Nat.Hist:* **o. stripe,** raie distincte.

obviously ['ɔbviəsli], *adv.* clairement, évidemment, manifestement; **she is o. wrong,** il est clair qu'elle a tort; elle a manifestement tort; **he was o. busy,** visiblement il était très occupé; il était de toute évidence qu'il était très occupé; **accidents o. connected with poor visibility,** accidents d'évidence liés à la mauvaise visibilité.

obviousness ['ɔbviəsnis], *s.* évidence *f*, clarté *f*, caractère *m* manifeste (d'un fait, etc.); **this remark, for all its o., caused a sensation,** cette remarque, toute évidente qu'elle était, a fait sensation.

obvolute ['ɔbvəlju:t], *a. Bot:* obvoluté.

oca ['oukə], *s. Bot:* oca *m.*

ocarina [ɔkə'ri:nə], *s. Mus:* ocarina *m.*

occasion[1] [ə'keiʒ(ə)n], *s.* **1.** (*a*) sujet *m*, cause *f*, occasion *f*; **there's, you have, no o. to be alarmed,** il n'y a pas lieu de vous inquiéter; vous n'avez pas à vous inquiéter; **I have no o. for complaint,** je n'ai aucun sujet de plainte, de me plaindre; **I have no o. for his help,** je n'ai aucun besoin, je n'ai que faire, de son aide; **to give s.o. o. to do sth.,** donner à qn une occasion de faire qch.; **to give o. to an outburst of popular indignation,** donner lieu à un mouvement d'indignation populaire; **to give o. for scandal,** donner occasion à la médisance; **his return was the o. for a family gathering,** son retour a donné lieu à une réunion de famille; **what o. is there for all this unpleasantness?** pourquoi tant de désagréments? **there's no o. to crow,** il n'y a pas de quoi chanter victoire; **if there is o., should the o. arise,** s'il y a lieu; le cas échéant; (*b*) (*in contrast to cause*) cause occasionnelle; cause immédiate. **2.** *pl.* occupations *f*; **to go about one's lawful occasions,** vaquer à ses affaires (dans le cadre de la loi). **3.** occasion, occurrence *f*; **he was absent on this o.,** il fut absent en cette occasion; **on the o. of his daughter's marraige,** à l'occasion du mariage de sa fille; **on this particular o.,** (i) actuellement; cette fois; (ii) à cette occasion; cette fois; **on one o.,** une fois; **on another o.,** une autre fois; dans une autre circonstance; **on several occasions,** à plusieurs reprises; **on various occasions,** à diverses reprises; **on rare occasions,** dans de rares circonstances; rarement; **on such an o.,** en pareille occasion; **on great occasions, on state occasions,** dans les grandes, les graves, occasions; **on all occasions,** en toute occasion; **on o.,** de temps à autre, de temps en temps; **there is no country where one may feel more alone on o.,** il n'y a pas de pays où l'on se sente éventuellement plus seul; **on o. only,** occasionnellement; **on such an o.,** en pareille occasion; **as o. requires, may require, as o. arises,** suivant l'occasion; au besoin; quand les circonstances le demandent; *Jur:* à telle fin que de raison; **words appropriate to the o.,** paroles de circonstance; **to be equal to the o.,** être à la hauteur des circonstances, de la situation; **to dress to fit the o.,** faire une toilette de circonstance; **your hat doesn't exactly suit the o.,** votre chapeau n'est pas tout à fait dans la note; **law made, play written, for the o.,** loi, pièce, de circonstance; **this is not an o. for trifling,** ce n'est pas le moment de badiner; **we'll make this an o.,** ce n'est pas tous les jours fête. **4.** (*opportunity*) **I'll speak to him on the first o.,** je lui parlerai à la prochaine occasion; **if you have o. to speak to him,** si vous avez l'occasion de lui parler.

occasion[2], *v.tr.* **1.** occasionner, entraîner, déterminer (la mort, un incendie, etc.); donner lieu à (la peur, etc.); **absence occasioned by illness,** absence occasionnée par, à cause de, maladie; **incident that occasioned a rising,** incident qui provoqua une révolte; **to o. emotion,** susciter, faire naître, l'émotion. **2.** *A:* **to o. s.o. to do sth.,** porter, déterminer, qn à faire qch.

occasional [ə'keiʒ(ə)nl], *a.* **1.** (*a*) **o. play, poem, verse,** pièce *f*, poème *m*, vers *mpl*, de circonstance, de situation; (*b*) **o. table,** table de fantaisie, volante; guéridon *m*; **o. chair,** chaise volante; (*c*) *Ind:* **o. hands,** extras *m*, (employés *m*) surnuméraires (*m*). **2. an o. visitor,** un visiteur qui vient de temps en temps; **to make an, the, o. remark,** faire une remarque de temps en temps; **to have o. bouts of pain,** avoir de vives douleurs de temps à autre; **o. showers,** averses éparses; **to meet an o. tramp on the road,** rencontrer des chemineaux çà et là sur le chemin. **3.** *Phil:* **o. cause,** cause occasionnelle.

occasionalism [ə'keiʒnəlizm], *s. Phil:* occasionnalisme *m,*

occasionalist [ə'keiʒnəlist], *s. Phil:* occasionnaliste *mf.*

occasionalistic [ə'keiʒnəlistik], *a. Phil:* occasionnaliste.

occasionally [ə'keiʒnəli], *adv.* de temps en temps; par occasion; occasionnellement, parfois; par intervalles.

occident ['ɔksidənt], *s.* occident *m*, ouest *m*, couchant *m*; *Pol: etc:* **the O.,** l'Occident.

occidental [ɔksi'dentl]. **1.** *a.* (*a*) occidental, -aux; de l'ouest; *Astr:* **o. plane,** planète occidentale; (*b*) **o. turquoise,** turquoise occidentale. **2.** *s.* **Occidental,** Occidental, -e.

occidentalism [ɔksi'dentəlizm], *s.* occidentalisme *m.*

occidentalist [ɔksi'dentəlist], *s.* Occidental, -e, qui épouse l'occidentalisme; étudiant, -e, des langues occidentales.

occidentalize [ɔksi'dentəlaiz], *v.tr.* occidenntaliser.

occiduous [ɔk'sidjuəs], *a. Astr:* **o. amplitude,** amplitude *f* occase.

occipital [ɔk'sipitl], *a. & s. Anat:* (*of artery, foramen, etc.*) occipital, -aux; **o. (bone),** (os) occipital (*m*); **o. point,** point occipital maximum.

occipito-atlantal, occipito-atloid [ɔksipitouət'læntl, -'ætlɔid], *a. Anat:* occipito-atloïdien, *pl.* occipito-atloïdiens; atloïdo-occipital, *pl.* atloïdo-occipitaux.

occipito-bregmatic [ɔksipitoubreg'mætik], *a. Anat:* occipito-bregmatique, *pl.* occipito-bregmatiques.

occipito-frontal [ɔksipitou'frʌntl], *a. Anat:* occipito-frontal, *pl.* occipito-frontaux.

occipito-mental [ɔksipitou'mentl], *a. Anat:* occipito-mentonnier, *pl.* occipito-mentonniers.

occipito-parietal [ɔk'sipitoupə'raiitl], *a. Anat:* occipito-pariétal, *pl.* occipito-pariétaux.

occiput ['ɔksipʌt], *s. Anat:* occiput *m.*

occlude [ɔ'klu:d]. **1.** *v.tr.* (*a*) fermer, boucher, obstruer (un orifice, un conduit, etc.); **to o. rays of light,** occlure les rayons de lumière; *Surg:* **to o. the eyelids,** occlure les paupières; (*b*) *Ch:* (*of a metal*) absorber, condenser (et retenir) (un gaz); occlure (un gaz). **2.** *v.i.* (*of molars*) s'emboîter les unes dans les autres (quand la bouche est fermée).

occluded [ɔ'klu:did], *a.* (gaz, etc.) occlus; *Med:* **o. eyelids,** paupières occluses; *Meteor:* **o. front,** front occlus.

occlusal [ɔ'klu:sl], *a. Anat:* occlusal, -aux; **o. surface of a tooth,** surface occlusale, triturante, d'une dent.

occlusion [ɔ'klu:ʒ(ə)n], *s.* **1.** (*a*) occlusion *f*, bouchage *m*, fermeture *f* (d'un conduit, etc.); recouvrement *m* (d'une plaie, etc.); *Surg:* **o. of the eyelids,** occlusion des paupières; (*b*) *Ch:* occlusion (d'un gaz). **2.** *Dent:* occlusion (molaire, etc.); **acquired, habitual, convenience, o.,** occlusion acquise, habituelle; **balanced o.,** occlusion équilibrée. **3.** *Meteor:* **cold, hot, front o.,** occlusion à caractère de front froid, chaud.

occlusive [ɔ'klu:siv]. **1.** *a.* occlusif; *Med:* **o. dressing,** pansement occlusif. **2.** *a. & s. Ling:* **o. (consonant),** (consonne) occlusive (*f*).

occult[1] [ɔ'kʌlt]. **1.** *a.* occulte, secret, -ète; **the o. sciences,** les sciences *f* occultes. **2.** *s.* **the o.,** l'occulte *m*; les sciences occultes.

occult[2]. **1.** *v.tr.* (*a*) *Astr:* occulter, immerger (une planète, étoile, etc.); (*b*) *Nau: etc:* occulter (une lumière, un signal). **2.** *v.i. Nau: etc:* (*of light*) s'éclipser.

occultation [ɔkʌl'teiʃ(ə)n], *s. Astr:* occultation *f*, obscuration *f*, immersion *f* (d'un astre).

occulter [ɔ'kʌltər], *s.* occul(ta)teur *m.*

occulting[1] [ɔ'kʌltiŋ], *a.* (feu) occultant, clignotant, à occultations.

occulting[2], *s. Astr: Nau: etc:* occultation *f.*

occultism ['ɔkəltizm], *s.* occultisme *m.*

occultist ['ɔkəltist, ɔ'kʌl-], *a. & s.* occultiste (*mf*).

occultly [ɔ'kʌltli], *adv.* occultement.

occultness [ɔ'kʌltnis], *s.* caractère *m* occulte.

occupancy ['ɔkjupənsi], *s.* **1.** *Jur:* possession *f* à titre de premier occupant. **2.** (*a*) occupation *f*, habitation *f* (d'un immeuble); *U.S:* **industrial o.,** location *f* par une entreprise industrielle; **during his o. of the house,** pendant la période où il a occupé la maison; pendant la période de sa location; *U.S:* **store for rent, immediate o.,** magasin à louer, possession immédiate; (*b*) *U.S:* immeuble occupé; appartement occupé; (*c*) *U.S:* (*in restaurant, store*) **o. by more than 160 persons is dangerous,** il est dangereux d'admettre plus de 160 personnes. **3.** possession *f* (d'un emploi).

occupant ['ɔkjupənt], *s.* **1.** (*a*) occupeur *m*, occupant, -ante (de terres); locataire *mf* (d'une maison); *F:* **at present rats are the sole occupants,** à présent les seuls occupants, locataires, sont des rats; (*b*) *Jur:* premier occupant. **2. the occupants of the car,** les voyageurs *m*, les passagers *m*. **3.** titulaire *mf* (d'un emploi).

occupation [ɔkju'peiʃ(ə)n], *s.* occupation *f.* **1.** (*a*) *Jur:* prise *f* de possession (d'un bien, à titre de premier occupant); (*b*) **to be in o. of a house,** occuper une maison; **house fit for o.,** maison habitable; **during his o. of the house,** pendant la période où il a occupé la maison; pendant la période de sa location; **o. road,** chemin privé; chemin de passage (vers une enclave); *Adm:* **o. franchise,** droit *m* de vote à titre de locataire; (*c*) **army of o., o. troops,** armée *f*, troupes *f*, d'occupation; *Archeol:* **o. level,** niveau *m* d'occupation; **military o. authority,** autorité militaire occupante; *Hist:* **the Roman o. of Great Britain,** l'occupation romaine de la Grande-Bretagne. **2.** (*a*) **to find s.o. (some) o.,** donner de l'occupation à qn; occuper qn; **to do sth. for want of o.,** faire qch. par désœuvrement; (*b*) métier *m*, emploi *m*, profession *f*; **what is his o.?** qu'est-ce qu'il est de son métier? quel est son emploi?; **without o.,** sans travail, désœuvré, en chômage; *Adm:* (*1939–45*) **to be in a reserved o.,** être affecté spécial, avoir une affectation spéciale.

occupational [ɔkju'peiʃ(ə)nl], *a.* ayant trait à une profession, aux professions; **o. hazards,** risques *m* du métier; **o. medicine,** médecine *f* du travail; **o. disease,** maladie professionnelle; **o. therapy,** thérapeutique occupationnelle.

occupied ['ɔkjupaid], *a.* occupé. **1.** *Mil:* **o. territory,** territoire occupé. **2. I am o. at present,** je suis occupé pour l'instant; j'ai à faire en ce moment; **to be o. in doing sth.,** être occupé, s'occuper, à faire qch.; **to be o. with sth.,** être occupé à qch.; tenir la main à qch.; **o. population,** population active; **the children must be kept usefully o.,** il faut occuper les enfants à des choses utiles; **gainfully o.,** salarié; **to keep one's mind o.,** s'occuper l'esprit; **pleasantly o. with his thoughts,** agréablement absorbé par ses pensées.

occupier ['ɔkjupaiər], *s.* occupant, -ante; locataire *mf*; habitant, -ante (d'une maison).

occupy ['ɔkjupai], *v.tr.* **1.** (*a*) occuper, habiter (une maison, une chambre, etc.); **my friends o. the ground floor,** mes amis occupent le rez-de-chaussée; **this room has never been occupied,** cette pièce n'a jamais été habitée; (*b*) occuper, remplir (une fonction, un emploi); **to o. an important post,** occuper un poste important; **he occupies a high position in society,** il occupe un rang distingué dans la société, dans le monde; (*c*) occuper (un pays ennemi, etc.); garnir (une place de guerre); s'emparer d'(un point stratégique). **2.** (*a*) remplir (un espace, etc.); occuper (une place, le temps, l'attention); **the table occupies half the floor space,** la table tient la moitié de la pièce; **this seat is occupied,** cette place est occupée; **to o. an armchair,** être assis, installé, dans un fauteuil; (*b*) **to o. one's time in, with, doing sth.,** remplir, occuper, son temps à faire qch.; **the work occupied much time,** le travail a pris beaucoup de temps; **his work occupies all his time,** son travail l'absorbe; **it occupied all my time,** cela a rempli mon temps; **cooking occupies her whole morning,** la cuisine est l'unique occupation *f* de sa matinée. **3.** occuper (qn); donner du travail à (qn); donner à travailler à (qn); **to o. one's mind,** s'occuper l'esprit.

occur [ə'kə:r], *v.i.* **(occurred) 1.** (*happen*) (*of event, etc.*) avoir lieu; survenir, arriver; se présenter; se produire; (*of fire, etc.*) se déclarer; **the collision occurred at midnight,** l'abordage s'est produit à minuit; **festival that occurs every ten years,** fête qui revient tous les dix ans; **an outbreak of disease occurred in the town,** une épidémie se déclara dans la ville; **should the case o.,** le cas échéant; **a complete change has occurred,** un changement complet s'est opéré, s'est produit; **if another opportunity occurs,** si une autre occasion se présente, s'offre; **if the slightest hitch occurs,** survienne le moindre accroc; **this seldom occurs,** ce fait est assez rare; (*of difficulty, etc.*) **to o. again,** se représenter; **such a chance will not o. again,** une occasion pareille ne se retrouvera pas; **I hope it will not o. again,** j'espère que cela ne se répétera pas; **don't let it o. again!** que cela n'arrive plus! que cela ne se reproduise plus! pas de récidive! **2.** (*to be met with*) (*of objects, minerals, types, etc.*) se rencontrer, se trouver, se présenter; **mineral that occurs in nature in a native state,** minéral qui se présente dans la nature à l'état natif; **ore occurring in beds,** minerai disposé en couches; **this word occurs twice in the letter,** ce mot se rencontre deux fois dans la lettre. **3.** se présenter à l'esprit; **it occurs to me that perhaps I should act first,** il me vient à l'idée, l'idée me vient, je m'avise, que c'est à moi peut-être d'agir le premier; **the thought occurred to me that he might be ill,** il m'est venu à la pensée qu'il pouvait être malade; **I say things as they o. to me,** je dis les choses comme elles me viennent; **such an idea would never have occurred to me,** une pareille idée ne me serait jamais venue à l'esprit.

occurrence [ə'kʌrəns], *s.* **1.** (*a*) **two hours before its o.,** deux heures avant que cela eût lieu; **to be of frequent, rare, o.,** arriver souvent, peu souvent; se produire, se renouveler, fréquemment, rarement; (*b*) venue *f*, rencontre *f* (de minéraux, etc.); **o. of gold in a region,** venues aurifères dans une région. **2.** événement *m*, fait *m*, occurrence *f*; **an everyday o.,** un fait journalier; **a singular o.,** une occurrence singulière; **at the time of these occurrences,** lors de ces faits; **these occurrences are rare,** ces faits sont assez rares. **3.** *Ecc:* occurrence (de deux fêtes).

occurrent [ə'kʌrənt], *a.* **1. rarely o.,** qui ne se rencontre pas souvent; rare. **2.** *Ecc:* **o. festivals,** fêtes occurrentes.

ocean ['ouʃ(ə)n], *s.* océan *m*. **1. the Atlantic O.,** l'(océan) Atlantique (*m*); *A:* **the German O.,** la mer du Nord; **the o. waves,** les flots *m* de l'océan; **o. floor, bottom,** fond sous-marin; **o. current,** courant *m* océanique; **o. lane,** route *f* de navigation; *Av:* **o. station (vessel),** (navire) station de radioguidage transocéanique; *Nau:* **o. chart,** carte *f* à petit point; **o. navigation,** navigation au long cours, hauturière; **o. voyage,** voyage *m* au long cours; **o. carrying trade,** transports *mpl* océaniques, grande navigation; *A: & Lit:* **the o. sea,** la mer océane; l'Atlantique. **2.** *Fig:* **an o. of sand,** une mer de sable; *F:* **there's oceans of it,** il y en a des tas; **there's oceans of room,** ce n'est pas la place qui manque. **3.** *Bot: U.S:* **o. spray,** holodiscus *m*.

oceanarium, *pl.* **-iums, -ia** [ouʃə'nɛəriəm, -iəmz, -iə], *s.* aquarium *m* d'eau de mer (naturelle).

oceanaut ['ouʃənɔ:t], *s.* océanaute *mf*.

ocean-going ['ouʃ(ə)n'gouiŋ], *a.* **o.-g. ship,** navire *m* au long cours, de haute mer, hauturier; long-courrier *m*, *pl.* long-courriers; **o.-g. tug,** remorqueur *m* de haute mer.

Oceania [ouʃi'einiə], *Pr.n. Geog:* l'Océanie *f*.

Oceanian [ouʃi'einiən]. *Geog:* **1.** *a.* océanien, de l'Océanie. **2.** *s.* Océanien, -ienne.

oceanic [ouʃi'ænik]. **1.** *a.* (*a*) (voyage, climat, courant) océanique; (*b*) (faune, etc.) pélagique; (*c*) = OCEANIAN 1. **2.** *s.pl.* **oceanics,** étude *f* de la structure des fonds océaniques.

Oceanid, *pl.* **-ids, -ides** [ou'si(:)ənid, -idz, ousi'ænidi:z], *s.f. Gr.Myth:* Océanide.

oceanographer [ouʃə'nɔgrəfər], *s.* océanographe *mf*.

oceanographic(al) [ouʃənou'græfik(l)], *a.* océanographique.

oceanography [ouʃə'nɔgrəfi], *s.* océanographie *f*.

oceanology [ouʃə'nɔlədʒi], *s.* océanologie *f*.

Oceanus [ou'siənəs], *Pr.n.m. Gr.Myth:* Océan.

oceanward(s) ['ouʃ(ə)nwəd(z)], *adv.* vers l'océan.

ocellar [ə'selər], *a. Ent:* ocellaire.

ocellate ['ɔsileit], *a. Nat.Hist:* ocellé, oculé.

ocellated ['ɔsileitid], *a. Nat.Hist:* ocellé (**with,** de).

ocellation [ɔsi'leiʃ(ə)n], *s. Nat.Hist:* ocellation *f*.

ocelliform [ə'selifɔ:m], *a.* ocelliforme.

ocellus, *pl.* **-i** [ə'seləs, -ai], *s. Nat.Hist:* **1.** ocelle *m*, œil *m* simple. **2.** ocelle (d'aile de papillon); miroir *m* (de plume de paon).

ocelot ['ɔsəlɔt], *s. Z:* ocelot *m*.

ochlocracy [ɔk'lɔkrəsi], *s. Pol:* ochlocratie *f*; *F:* voyoucratie *f*.

ochlocrat [ɔklə'kræt], *s. Pol:* ochlocrate *mf*.

ochlocratic [ɔklə'krætik], *a. Pol:* ochlocratique.

ochlophobia [ɔklə'foubiə], *s. Med:* phobie *f* des foules.

ochna ['ɔknə], *s. Bot:* ochna *m*.

Ochnaceae [ɔk'neisii:], *s.pl. Bot:* ochnacées *f*.

Ochoan [ou'kouən], *a. & s. Geol:* (du) permien supérieur de l'Amérique du Nord.

ochotona [ɔkə'tounə], *s. Z:* ochotone *m*.

Ochotonidae [ɔkə'tɔnidi:], *s.pl. Z:* ochotonidés *m*.

ochraceous [ou'kreiʃəs], *a.* ocreux; *Nat.Hist:* ochracé.

ochre[1] ['oukər]. **1.** *s.* (*a*) *Miner:* ocre *f*; **red o.,** ocre rouge; arcanne *f*; **yellow o.,** jaune *m* d'ocre; ocre jaune; terre *f* de montagne; (*b*) *P:* (i) *A:* pièces *fpl* d'or; (ii) *NAm:* argent *m*; *P:* po(i)gnon *m*, blanc *m*. **2.** *a.* **o.(-coloured),** ocre *inv*; ocreux.

ochre[2], *v.tr.* ocrer.

ochrea, *pl.* **-eae** ['ɔkriə, -ii:], *s. Bot:* ocréa *f*, gaine *f*.

ochreous ['oukriəs, 'oukərəs], **ochrous** ['oukrəs], *a.* ocreux; *Nat.Hist:* ochacé.

ochring ['ouk(ə)riŋ], *s.* ocrage *m*.

ochrolite ['oukrəlait], *s. Miner:* ochrolite *f*.

ochronosis [oukrə'nousis], *s. Med:* ochronose *f*.

ochrosporous [oukrə'spɔ:rəs], *a. Fung:* ochrosporé.

o'clock [ə'klɔk], *adv.phr.* **one, two, o'c.,** une heure, deux heures; **the seven o'c. train,** le train de sept heures; *F:* *O:* **they get on like one o'c.,** ils s'entendent à merveille.

ocrea, *pl.* **-eae** ['ɔkriə, -ii:], *s. Bot:* ocréa *f*, gaine *f*.

oct(a)-, oct(o)- ['ɔkt(ə)], *comb.fm.* oct(a)-, oct(o)-.

octachord ['ɔktəkɔ:d], *Mus:* **1.** *a. & s.* octac(h)orde (*m*). **2.** *s.* série *f* de huit notes; gamme *f*.

octacosane [ɔktə'kousein], *s. Ch:* octacosane *m*.

octad ['ɔktæd], *s.* **1.** huitaine *f*; groupe *m* de huit. **2.** *Ch:* (i) corps octovalent; (ii) radical octovalent.

octadecane [ɔktə'dekein], *s. Ch:* octadécane *m*.

octadecyl [ɔktə'desil], *s. Ch:* octadécylène *m*, octodécylène *m*.

octaechos [ɔktə'i:kɔs], *s. Ecc:* octoèque *m*.

octagon ['ɔktəgən], *s. Geom:* octogone *m*; *Mec.E:* **o. nut,** écrou *m* à huit pans.

octagonal [ɔk'tægənl], *a.* octogonal, -aux; (écrou, etc.) à huit pans.

octahedral [ɔktə'hi:dr(ə)l, -'hed-], *a.* octaèdre; octaédrique.

octahedrite [ɔktə'hi:drait], *s. Miner:* octaédrite *f*.

octahedron, *pl.* **-ons, -a** ['ɔktə'hi:drən, -'hed-, -ənz, -ə], *s. Geom:* octaèdre *m*.

octal ['ɔktl], *a.* **1.** *Mth:* octal, -aux; **o. digit,** chiffre octal; **o. notation, number system,** numération octale, de base huit. **2.** *Elcs:* **o. base,** culot *m* (de tube électronique) à huit broches; **o. valve,** *NAm:* **o. tube,** tube électronique octal, avec culot à huit broches.

octally ['ɔktəli], *adv. Cmptr:* en octal.

octameter [ɔk'tæmitər], *a. & s. Pros:* (vers *m*) de huit pieds.

octan ['ɔktən], *a. Med:* **o. fever,** fièvre octane.

Octandria [ɔk'tændriə], *s.pl. Bot:* octandries *f*.

octandrian, octandrious [ɔk'tændriən, -driəs], *a. Bot:* octandre.

octane ['ɔktein], *s. Ch:* octane *m*; **high-o. petrol,** essence *f* à haut indice d'octane; **o. number,** indice *m* d'octane; **o. rating,** degré *m* en octane.

Octans ['ɔktænz], *Pr.n. Astr:* (constellation *f* de) l'Octant *m*.

octant ['ɔktənt], *s. Geom: Astr:* octant *m*.

octastich ['ɔktəstik], *s. Pros:* strophe *f* de huit vers; huitain *m*.

octastyle ['ɔktəstail], *a. Arch:* octastyle, octostyle.

Octateuch ['ɔktətju:k], *s. B:* octateuque *m*.

octavalent [ɔktə'veilənt], *a. Ch:* octovalent.

octavarium [ɔktə'vɛəriəm], **octavary** ['ɔktəvəri], *s. Ecc:* octavaire *m*.

octave[1] ['ɔktiv, 'ɔkteiv], *s.* **1.** *Ecc: usu.* ['ɔkteiv], octave *f*. **2.** *Mus: usu.* ['ɔktiv], octave; **double o.,** intervalle triplé; **o. flute,** octavin *m*, petite flûte; **o. coupler,** double-main *f* (d'orgue), *pl.* doubles-mains; **o. stop,** jeu *m* d'octave (d'orgue). **3.** *Pros:* octave; huitain *m*; **the o. of a sonnet,** les deux quatrains d'un sonnet. **4.** *Fenc:* octave. **5. o. cask,** quartaut *m*; caque *f* (de vin de champagne).

octave[2] ['ɔktiv], *v.i. Mus:* octavier.

Octavia [ɔk'teiviə], *Pr.n.f. Rom.Hist:* Octavie.

Octavius [ɔk'teivjəs], *Pr.n.m. Rom.Hist:* Octave.

octavo [ɔk'teivou], *a. & s. Typ:* in-octavo (*m*) *inv*.

octene ['ɔkti:n], *s. Ch:* octène *m*.

octennial [ɔk'tenjəl], *a.* **1.** qui dure huit ans. **2.** qui a lieu tous les huit ans.

octet [ɔk'tet], *s.* **1.** *Ch:* octet *m*. **2.** *Cmptr:* octet. **3.** *Mus:* octuor *m*. **4.** *Pros:* huitain *m*; **the o. of a sonnet,** les deux quatrains *m* d'un sonnet.

octette [ɔk'tet], *s. Mus:* octuor *m*.

octillion [ɔk'tiljən], *s.* **1.** octillion *m* (10^{48}). **2.** *NAm:* mille quatrillions *m* (10^{27}).

octine ['ɔkti:n], *s. Ch:* octyne *m*.

octobass ['ɔktəbeis], *s. Mus:* octobasse *m*.

October [ɔk'toubər], *s.* octobre *m*; **in O.,** au mois d'octobre; en octobre; (**on**) **the first, seventh, of O.,** le premier, le sept, octobre.

Octobrist [ɔk'toubrist], *s. Russian Hist:* octobriste *m*.

Octocorallia [ɔktoukə'ræliə], *s.pl. Coel:* octocoralliaires *m*.

octode ['ɔktoud], *s. Elcs:* octode *m*.

octodecimo [ɔktə'desimou], *a. & s. Typ:* in-dix-huit (*m*) *inv*.

octodon ['ɔktədɔn], *s. Z:* octodon *m*, octodonte *m*.

Octodontidae [ɔktə'dɔntidi:], *s.pl. Z:* octodontidés *m*.

octoechos [ɔktou'i:kɔs], *s. Ecc:* octoèque *m*.

octogenarian ['ɔktədʒin'ɛəriən], *a. & s.* octogénaire (*mf*).

octogynous [ɔk'tɔdʒinəs], *a. Bot:* octogyne.

octopetalous [ɔktə'petələs], *a. Bot:* octopétale.

octoploid ['ɔktəplɔid], *a. & s. Biol:* octoploïde (*m*).

octopod ['ɔktəpɔd], *a. & s. Moll:* octopode (*m*).

Octopoda [ɔk'tɔpədə], *s.pl. Moll:* octopodes *m*, poulpes *m*.

Octopodidae [ɔktə'pɔdidi:], *s.pl. Moll:* octopodidés *m*.

octopolar ['ɔktə'poulər], *a. El:* octopolaire.

octopus ['ɔktəpəs], *s. Moll:* poulpe *m*, pieuvre *f*; **Mediterranean o.,** élédone *f*.

octoroon [ɔktə'ru:n], *s. Ethn:* octavon, -onne.

octostyle ['ɔktəstail], *a. Arch:* octastyle, octostyle.

octosyllabic [ɔktəsi'læbik]. **1.** *a.* (vers, mot) octosyllabe, octosyllabique. **2.** *s. Pros:* vers *m* octosyllabe, octosyllabique.

octosyllable [ɔktə'siləbl], *s.* **1.** vers *m* octosyllabe, octosyllabique. **2.** (mot) octosyllabe (*m*).

octovalent [ɔktə'veilənt], *a. Ch:* octovalent.

octuple[1] [ɔk'tju:pl], *a. & s.* octuple (*m*).

octuple[2], *v.tr.* octupler.

octyl ['ɔktil], *s. Ch:* octyle *m*.

octylene ['ɔktili:n], *s. Ch:* octylène *m*.

octyne ['ɔktain], *s. Ch:* octyne *m*.

ocular ['ɔkjulər]. **1.** *a.* (nerf, témoin, etc.) oculaire; **o. estimate,** estimation *f* à vue d'œil. **2.** *s. Opt:* oculaire *m* (de microscope, etc.).

ocularist ['ɔkjulərist], *s.* oculariste *m*; fabricant *m* d'yeux artificiels, d'yeux de verre.

ocularly ['ɔkjuləli], *adv.* oculairement.

oculate ['ɔkjuleit], *a. Nat.Hist:* oculé, ocellé.

oculiferous [ɔkju'lifərəs], *a. Nat.Hist:* oculifère.

oculiform ['ɔkjulifɔ:m], *a. Biol:* oculiforme.

Oculinidae [ɔkju'linidi:], *s.pl. Coel:* oculinidés *m*.

oculist ['ɔkjulist], *s.* oculiste *mf*.

Oculi Sunday ['ɔkjulai'sʌndi], *s. Ecc:* Oculi *m*.

oculocardiac ['ɔkjulou'kɑ:diæk], *a. Med:* (réflexe) oculo-cardiaque, *pl.* oculo-cardiaques.

oculogyric ['ɔkjulou'dʒirik], *a. Med: Anat:* (nerf, crise) oculogyre.

oculomotor ['ɔkjul'oumoutər], *a. Anat:* (nerf) oculogyre.

oculopalpebral ['ɔkjulou'pælpibrəl], *a. Anat:* oculo-palpébral, *pl.* oculo-palpébraux.

oculoreaction ['ɔkjulouri'ækʃ(ə)n], *s. Med:* oculo-réaction *f*, *pl.* oculo-réactions.

oculus, *pl.* **-i** ['ɔkjuləs, -ai], *s. Arch:* oculus *m*, *pl.* -i.

ocypode ['ousipɔd], *s. Crust:* ocypode *m*.

Ocypodidae [ousi'pɔdidi:], *s.pl. Crust:* ocypodidés *m*.

od [ɔd], *s. F: A:* (= GOD) **od's bodikins!** cordieu!

odalisk, odalisque ['oudəlisk], *s.f.* odalisque.

odd [ɔd], *a.* **1.** (*a*) (nombre) impair; **to play at o. or even,** jouer à pair ou impair; *Cmptr:* **o.-even check,** contrôle *m* de parité; **o.-parity check,** contrôle d'imparité, de parité impair; (*b*) (i) (*usu.* = *a slightly higher amount*) **a hundred o. sheep,** cent et quelques moutons; une centaine de moutons; **fifty o. thousand,** entre cinquante et soixante mille; **fifty thousand o.,** un peu plus de cinquante mille; une cinquantaine de mille; **twenty pounds o., twenty o. pounds,** une vingtaine de livres; un peu plus de vingt livres; (ii) **a few o. grammes over,** quelques grammes de plus; **what shall we do with the o. six?** que ferons-nous avec les six qui restent? **keep the o. change, the o. money,** gardez la monnaie; (*c*) **to be the o. man (out),** rester en surnombre; **the o. day of the leap year,** le bissexte; **at o. moments,** dans mes, ses, moments perdus; **to pick up an o. bargain,** trouver une occasion; (*at tennis, cards, etc.*) **the o. game,** la belle; *Cards:* **the o. trick,** le trick, le tri; **to take, lose, the o. trick,** faire, perdre, la carte; **to play for the o. trick,** jouer la belle; *Com:* **o. money,** passe *f*; **to make up the o. money,** faire l'appoint *m*; (*d*) *s. Golf:* **the o.,** coup *m* (de crosse) de plus que l'adversaire; le plus; **to play the o.,** jouer un de plus; (*in handicapping*) **two odds,** deux de plus. **2.** (*a*) (*of one of a set*) dépareillé; (*of one of a pair*) déparié, disparate; **o. one (of pair),** demi-paire *f*; **o. glove,** gant déparié, dépareillé; **o. stockings,** bas *m* qui ne vont pas ensemble; **a few o. volumes,** quelques tomes dépareillés; **table service made up of o. pieces,** service de table désassorti; (*b*) quelconque; **any o. piece of cloth,** un bout d'étoffe quelconque; **o. moments,** moments de loisir, moments perdus; **at o. times,** par-ci par-là; **in an o. corner,** (i) dans un coin quelconque; (ii) dans un coin écarté; **o. man, o. hand,** homme à tout faire; *Com:* **o. lot,** (i) solde *m*; (ii) *occ.* lot *m* d'appoint. **3.** non usuel; (*a*) *Com: Ind:* **o. size,** dimension spéciale, non courante; *Mec.E:* **o. pitch,** pas bâtard (d'un écrou); (*b*) singulier, drôle; (*of pers.*) (i) excentrique, original; singulier; (ii) *P:* homosexuel *m*; **he knew all those o. people,** il connaissait tout ce monde curieux; **the o. thing about it is that nobody had the slightest suspicion of it,** le curieux de l'affaire, ce qui est bizarre, c'est que personne n'en avait le moindre soupçon; **it's o. your not knowing about it,** il est curieux, singulier, que vous n'en sachiez rien; **how o. that he should have forgotten it!** comme c'est drôle qu'il l'ait oublié; (**well**), **that's o.!** voilà qui est singulier! c'est curieux! c'est extraordinaire! c'est bizarre!

oddball ['ɔdbɔ:l]. *NAm: P:* **1.** *a.* excentrique, loufoque, farfelu. **2.** *s.* (*a*) drôle *m* de zigoto; farfelu *m*; (*b*) pédéraste *m*, pédé *m*.

odd-come-short ['ɔdkʌm'ʃɔ:t], *s. F:* **1.** bribe *f* d'étoffe; petit bout; coupon *m*; tombée *f* (de tissu). **2.** (*pers.*) gringalet *m*.

odd-come-shortly ['ɔdkʌm'ʃɔ:tli]. *F: O:* **1.** *adv.* un jour ou l'autre, dans quelques jours. **2.** *s.* **one of these odd-come-shortlies,** un de ces jours; un de ces quatre matins.

Oddfellow ['ɔdefelou], *s.* oddfellow *m* (membre d'une société de secours mutuels organisée en société secrète).

oddish ['ɔdiʃ], *a.* un peu bizarre.

oddity ['ɔditi], *s.* **1.** (*a*) singularité *f*, bizarrerie *f*, excentricité *f*; (*b*) **he has some little oddities,** il a quelques petits travers. **2.** (*a*) personne excentrique; original, -ale; (*b*) chose *f* bizarre; curiosité *f*.

odd-looking ['ɔdlukiŋ], *a.* bizarre, baroque.

oddly ['ɔdli], *adv.* bizarrement, singulièrement; **he behaves rather o. at times,** de temps en temps il fait quelque chose de bizarre; **o. enough nobody knew anything about it,** chose curieuse, personne n'en savait rien; **o. enough I came across him in London,** par un hasard singulier je l'ai rencontré à Londres.

odd-man-out ['ɔdmæn'aut], *s.* **1.** (*a*) homme éliminé (après avoir joué, à pile ou face, etc.); (*b*) **to be (the) o.-m.-o.,** (i) être en surnombre; (ii) ne pas être du métier, de la partie. **2. to play o.-m.-o.,** jouer à qui sera éliminé.

oddment ['ɔdmənt], *s.* bribe *f*; article dépareillé; article en solde; coupon *m* d'étoffe; **oddments,** fins *f* de série, *Publ:* défets *m*; **remnants and oddments,** soldes *m* et occasions *f*.

oddness ['ɔdnis], *s.* **1.** imparité *f* (d'un nombre). **2.** singularité *f*, bizarrerie *f*, étrangeté *f*.

odd-numbered ['ɔd'nʌmbəd], *a.* impair; portant un nombre impair.

odd-pinnate ['ɔd'pineit], *a. Bot:* imparipenné.

odds [ɔdz], *s.pl.* (*occ. with sg. const.*) **1.** inégalité *f*; **to make o. evens,** égaliser les conditions, les avantages, etc.; répartir les choses également. **2.** (*a*) avantage *m*; chances *fpl*; **the o. are against him, in his favour,** les chances sont contre lui, pour lui; **he has heavy o. against him,** toutes les chances sont contre lui; **to fight against (great, long) o,** (i) lutter, combattre, contre des forces supérieures, plus nombreuses; combattre à armes inégales; (ii) avoir affaire à forte partie, à plus fort que soi; **to fight against crushing o.,** lutter contre une supériorité écrasante; **to succumb to o.,** succomber sous le nombre; céder à la force; (*b*) différence *f*; **what's the o.?** qu'est-ce que ça fait? **it makes no o., it's no o.,** ça ne fait rien; cela n'a pas d'importance; tant pis! **it makes no o. to me whether I go or not,** ça ne me fait rien que j'y aille ou non; (*c*) *Turf:* **o. on, o. against, a horse,** cote *f* d'un cheval; **short o.,** faible cote; **long o.,** forte cote; **he may attract punters looking for long o.,** il pourra tenter les amateurs de grosses cotes; **what are the o. on his horse?** quelle cote fait son cheval? **the o. are (at) ten to one,** la cote est à dix contre un; **to give, take, o.,** faire un pari inégal; **the art of laying and taking o.,** la technique de la mise; **to play the o.,** jouer à coup presque sûr; *P:* **to shout the o.,** se vanter, faire de la gloriole; **the o. are, it's long o., that he'll succeed,** il y a gros à parier qu'il réussira; **it's within the o.,** c'est possible; **the o. are even which is the worse,** impossible à dire lequel est le pire; **by all o., a silly thing to do,** de toute façon une bêtise; (*d*) *Sp:* **to give s.o. o.,** donner (de) l'avantage, donner de l'avance, à un concurrent; concéder des points à qn; **player who has been given o.,** joueur avantagé; *U.S:* **I ask no o. from anybody,** je ne demande de faveurs à personne. **3. to be at o. with s.o.,** (i) ne pas être d'accord avec qn; (ii) être brouillé avec qn; **they are always at o.,** (i) ils sont toujours en désaccord; (ii) ils sont toujours en bisbille. **4.** (*a*) **o. and ends,** petits bouts; bribes *f* et morceaux *m*; chiffonneries *f*; (*of food*) restes *m*, reliefs *m*; **I have some o. and ends left,** j'en ai quelques restes dépareillés; (*b*) *P:* **there were just a few o. and sods,** il n'y avait que trois pelés et un tondu.

odd-shaped ['ɔdʃeipt], *a.* d'une forme bizarre.

odds-on ['ɔdz'ɔn], *a.* **o.-on bet,** pari inégal; (*with bookmaker*) pari où le client gagnera moins que son enjeu; **o.-on favourite,** grand favori; **it's an o.-on chance that he will be chosen,** il y a gros à parier qu'il sera choisi.

odd-toed ['ɔd'toud], *a. Z:* imparidigité.

ode [oud], *s.* ode *f*; **short o.,** odelette *f*; *Mus:* **the O. to Joy,** l'Hymne *m* à la joie (de Beethoven).

odeon ['oudiən], **odeum,** *pl.* **-ea** [ou'di(:)əm, -i(:)ə], *s. Gr.Ant:* odéon *m*.

Odilia [ou'diliə], *Pr.n.f.* Odile.

Odin ['oudin], *Pr.n.m. Myth.* Odin.

odious ['oudiəs], *s.* odieux (**to,** à); **to me he's o., I find him o.,** il m'est odieux; **the o. part of the business,** l'odieux *m* de l'affaire.

odiously ['oudiəsli], *adv.* odieusement, détestablement.

odiousness ['oudjəsnis], *s.* caractère odieux, (l')odieux *m* (d'une action).

odium ['oudiəm], *s.* **1.** réprobation *f*; détestation *f*; **to bring, cast, o. upon s.o.,** rendre qn odieux; **he incurred all the o. of the transaction,** il supporta toute la réprobation attachée à cette transaction; **exposed to widespread o.,** exposé à toutes les haines; **o. theologicum,** haine entre gens d'église. **2.** caractère odieux; **he realized the o. of the transaction,** il se rendait compte de l'odieux *m* de cette transaction.

Odo ['oudou], *Pr.n.m.* Odon, Eudes.

Odoacer [ɔdou'eisər], *Pr.n.m. Hist:* Odoacre.

Odobenidae [oudou'benidi:], *s.pl. Z:* odobénidés *m*.

odograph ['oudəgræf], *s. Mec:* odographe *m* (d'un mouvement).

odographic [oudə'græfik], *a. Mec:* odographique.

odography [ou'dɔgrəfi], *s. Mec:* odographie *f*.

odometer [ou'dɔmitər], *s. Surv: etc:* odomètre *m*.

odometry [ou'dɔmitri], *s. Surv: etc:* odométrie *f*.

Odonata [oudə'nɑ:tə], *s.pl. Ent:* odonates *m*, libellulidés *m*.

odonate ['oudəneit], *a. & s. Ent:* odonate (*m*).

Odonatoptera [oudənə'tɔptərə], *s.pl. Ent:* odonatoptères *m*.

odontalgia [oudɔn'tældʒiə], *s. Med:* odontalgie *f*; mal *m* de dents.

odontalgic [oudɔn'tældʒik], *a. & s. Med: Pharm:* odontalgique (*m*).

odontaspis [oudɔn'tæspis], *s. Ich:* odontaspis *m*; requin *m* de sable.

odontoblast [ou'dɔntəblæst], *s. Anat:* odontoblaste *m*.

odontocete [ou'dɔntəsi:t], *a. & s. Z:* odontocète *m*.

Odontoceti [oudɔntə'si:ti:], *s.pl. Z:* odontocètes *m*.

odontocetous [oudɔntə'si:təs], *a. Z:* odontocète.

odontogenesis [oudɔntə'dʒenisis], **odontogeny** [oudɔn'tɔdʒini], *s. Biol:* odontogénèse *f*, odontogénie. *f*; *Med:* **odontogenesis imperfecta,** disphasie *f* dentaire.

odontogenic [oudɔntə'dʒenik], **odontogenous** [oudɔn'tɔdʒinəs], *a. Biol:* odontogénique, odontogène.

odontoglossum [oudɔntə'glɔsəm], *s. Bot:* odontoglossum *m*, odontoglosse *m*.

odontogram [ou'dɔntəgræm], *s.* **1.** *Dent:* odontogramme *m*; schéma *m* dentaire. **2.** *Mec.E:* odontogramme (d'un engrenage).

odontograph [ou'dɔntəgræf], *s. Dent: Mec.E:* odontographe *m*.

odontographic [oudɔntə'græfik], *a.* odontographique.

odontography [oudɔn'tɔgrəfi], *s. Dent: Mec.E:* odontographie *f* (d'une dentition, d'un engrenage).

odontoid [ou'dɔntɔid], *a. Anat:* (*a*) (apophyse *f*) odontoïde; (*b*) (ligament) odontoïdien.

odontolite [ou'dɔntəlait], *s.* **1.** *Miner:* odontolit(h)e *f*; turquoise osseuse; turquoise occidentale. **2.** *Dent:* odontolit(h)e; tartre *m* dentaire.

odontolithiasis [oudɔntəliθi'eisis], *s. Dent:* odontolithiase *f*; formation *f* du tartre dentaire.

odontologic(al) [oudɔntə'lɔdʒik(l)], *a.* odontologique.

odontologist [oudɔn'tɔlədʒist], *s. Med:* odontologiste *mf*.

odontology [oudɔn'tɔlədʒi], *s.* odontologie *f*.

odontoma, *pl.* **-mas, -mata** [oudɔn'toumə, -məz, -mətə], **odontome** [ou'dɔntoum], *s. Med:* odontome *m*; **complex, composite, compound, o.,** odontome complexe, composé.

odontometer [oudɔn'tɔmitər], *s. Mec: Philately:* odontomètre *m*.

odontophoral [oudɔn'tɔfərəl], **odontophoran** [oudɔn'tɔfərən], *a. Moll:* odontophorin.

odontophore [ou'dɔntəfɔ:r], *s. Moll:* odontophore *m*.

odontophorine [oudɔn'tɔfəri:n]. **1.** *a. Moll:* odontophorin. **2.** *s. Orn:* odontophore *m*.

odontophorus [oudɔn'tɔfərəs], *s. Orn:* odontophore *m*.

Odontornithes [oudɔn'tɔ:niθi:z], *s.pl. Paleont:* odontornithes *m*.

odontorrhagia [oudɔntə'reidʒiə], *s. Dent:* odontorragie *f*.

odontorrhagic [oudɔntə'reidʒik], *a. Dent:* odontorragique.

odontotherapy [oudɔntə'θerəpi], *s. Med:* thérapeutique *f*, traitement *m*, dentaire.

odontotomy [oudɔn'tɔtəmi], *s. Dent:* tomodontie *f*.

odorant ['oudərənt], *s.* substance odorante.

odoriferous [oudə'rifərəs], *a.* **1.** odoriférant, odorifique; parfumé. **2.** *F:* malodorant.

odorimeter [oudə'rimitər], *s.* odorimètre *m*.

odoriphore [ou'dɔrifɔ:r], *s. Ch:* matière odorante (d'une molécule).

odorometer [oudə'rɔmitər], *s.* odorimètre *m*.

odorous ['oudərəs], *a.* (*a*) odorant; qui exhale une odeur; (*b*) qui exhale une odeur agréable; (*c*) *F:* malodorant.

odour ['oudər], *s.* **1.** (*a*) odeur *f*; **gas that has no o. at all,** gaz qui n'a aucune odeur; *Fig:* **a faint o. of his early beliefs can still be detected in his works,** on remarque encore dans son œuvre littéraire l'écho lointain, un arrière-goût, de ses croyances de jeunesse; (*b*) odeur (agréable); parfum *m*; (*c*) *F:* mauvaise odeur. **2. to be in good, bad, o. with s.o.,** être bien, mal, vu de qn; être, ne pas être, en faveur auprès de qn; **to die in (the) o. of sanctity,** mourir en odeur de sainteté; *F:* **I can't stand his o. of sanctity,** son air confit en dévotion me répugne.

odourless ['oudəlis], *a.* inodore; sans odeur.

odynerus [ou'dinərəs], *s. Ent:* odynère *m*.

Odyssean [ɔdi'siən], *a.* digne d'Ulysse; (voyage) qui ressemble à l'Odyssée.

Odyssey ['ɔdisi], *s. Gr.Lit:* **the O.,** l'Odyssée *f*; *Fig:* **his journey was a real o.,** son voyage fut une véritable odyssée.

oecanthus [i:'kænθəs], *s. Ent:* œcanthe *m*.

oecological [i:kə'lɔdʒikl], *a.* œcologique, bionomique.

oecology [i:'kɔlədʒi], *s.* œcologie *f*, bionomie *f*.

oecumenical [i:kju(:)'menikl], *a.* **1.** *Ecc:* (conseil, etc.) œcuménique. **2.** universel.

oecumenicalism [i:kju(:)menikəlizm], *s. Ecc:* œcuménisme *m*.

oecumenicity [i:kju(:)me'nisiti], *s.* œcuménicité *f*.

oedema [i(:)'di:mə], *s. Med:* œdème *m*.

oedematic [i(:)di'mætik], **oedematose** [i(:)'demətous], **oedematous** [i(:)'demətəs], *a. Med:* œdémateux.

Oedipean [i:di'pi:ən], *a. Gr.Lit: Psy:* œdipien.

Oedipus ['i:dipəs], *Pr.n.m. Gr.Lit:* Œdipe; **O. Rex, O. Tyrannus,** Œdipe roi; **O. Coloneus,** Œdipe à Colone; *Psy:* **O. complex,** complexe *m* d'Œdipe.

oenanthal [i(:)'nænθəl], *s. Ch:* œnanthal *m*.

oenanthe [i(:)'nænθi:], *s. Bot:* œnanthe *m*.

oenanthic [i(:)'nænθik], *a. Ch:* (acide, éther) œnanthique.

oenanthylate [i(:)'nænθileit], *s. Ch:* œnanthylate *m*.

oenanthylic [i(:)'nænθilik], *a. Ch:* œnanthylique.

oenochoë [i(:)'nɔkoui:], *s. Gr.Ant:* œnochoé *f*.

oenocyte ['i:nəsait], *s. Ent:* œnocyte *m*.

oenological [i:nə'lɔdʒikl], *a.* œnologique.

oenologist [i(:)'nɔlədʒist], *s.* œnologiste *mf*, œnologue *mf*.

oenology [i(:)'nɔlədʒi], *s.* œnologie *f*.

oenomel ['i:nəmel], *s. Gr.Ant:* œnomel *m*, hydromel *m*.

oenometer [i(:)'nɔmitər], *s.* œnomètre *m*, vinomètre *m*; pèse-vin *m inv*.

oenophile ['i:nəfail], *a.* œnophile.

oenophilist [i(:)'nɔfilist], *s.* œnophile *mf*.

oenophobe ['i:nəfoub], *a. & s.* œnophobe (*m*).

oenophobia [i:nə'foubiə], *s.* œnophobie *f*.

oenothera [i:nə'θiərə], *s. Bot:* œnothère *m*.

Oenotheraceae [i:nəθi'reisii:], *s.pl. Bot:* œnothéracées *f*.

o'er [ɔ:r, 'ouər], *prep.* = OVER 1.

Oerlikon ['ɔ:likən], *s. Mil:* canon anti-aérien automatique de 20 mm.

oersted ['ɔ:sted], *s. El:* œrsted *m*.

oesophageal [i:səfə'dʒiəl, i:sə'fædʒiəl], *a. Anat: Med:* (*of membrane, tube, probe, etc.*) œsophagien.

oesophagectomy [i:səfə'dʒektəmi], *s. Surg:* œsophagectomie *f*.

oesophagism [i:'sɔfədʒizm], *s. Med:* œsophagisme *m*.

oesophagitis [i:səfə'dʒaitis], *s. Med:* œsophagite *f*.

oesophagogastrostomy [i:'sɔfəgougæ'strɔstəmi], *s. Surg:* œsophago-gastrostomie *f*.

oesophagomalacia [i:'sɔfəgoumæ'leiʃə], *s. Med:* œsophagomalacie *f*.

oesophagoplasty [i:'sɔfəgou'plæsti], *s. Surg:* œsophagoplastie *f*.

oesophagoscope [i:'sɔfəgəskoup], *s. Med:* œsophagoscope *m*.

oesophagoscopic [i:sɔfəgə'skɔpik], *a. Med:* œsophagoscopique.

oesophagoscopy [i:sɔfə'gɔskəpi], *s. Med:* œsophagoscopie *f*.

oesophagostomy [i:sɔfə'gɔstəmi], *s. Surg:* œsophagostomie *f*.

oesophagotomy [i:sɔfə'gɔtəmi], *s. Surg:* œsophagotomie *f*.

oesophagus, *pl.* **-gi, -guses** [i:'sɔfəgəs, -gai, -gəsiz], *s. Anat:* œsophage *m*.

oestradiol [i:strə'daioul], *s. Bio-Ch:* œstradiol *m*.

oestral ['i:strəl], *s. Physiol:* œstral, -aux; œstrien.

Oestridae ['i:stridi:], *s.pl. Ent:* œstridés *m*.

oestriol ['i:straiəl], *s. Bio-Ch:* œstriol *m.*
oestrogen ['i:strədʒen], *s. Bio-Ch:* œstrogène *m.*
oestrogenic [i:strə'dʒenik], *a. Physiol:* œstrogénique.
oestromania [i:strə'meiniə], *s. Psy: Vet:* œstromanie *f.*
oestrone ['i:stroun], *s. Bio-Ch:* œstrone *f.*
oestrous ['i:strəs], *a. Physiol:* (*of cycle, etc.*) œstral, -aux; œstrien.
oestrum ['i:strəm], *s.* = OESTRUS 2.
oestrus ['i:strəs], *s.* **1.** *Ent:* œstre *m.* **2.** (*a*) stimulant *m*, aiguillon *m* (des sens); (*b*) *Physiol:* œstrus *m*, œstre *m*; (*of animals*) chaleur *f*, rut *m*; **o. cycle,** cycle œstral, œstrien.

of [ɔv; *weak forms* əv, v, f], *prep.* de. **1.** (*a*) (*indicating separation*) **south of,** au sud de; **within a mile of,** à moins d'une mille de; **free of,** libre de; **cured of,** guéri de; **destitute of,** dépourvu de; *NAm:* **five (minutes) of, a quarter of, one,** une heure moins cinq, moins le quart; (*b*) (i) (*origin*) **of noble birth,** de naissance noble; **works of Shakespeare,** œuvres de Shakespeare; **to buy sth. of s.o.,** acheter qch. de, à, chez, qn; **of all booksellers,** chez tous les libraires; **to expect sth. of s.o.,** attendre, s'attendre à, qch. de qn; **to ask a favour of s.o.,** demander une faveur à qn; (ii) (*cause*) **of necessity,** par nécessité; **of one's own accord,** de soi-même; **of my own choice,** de mon propre choix; **nothing can move of itself,** rien ne peut se mouvoir de soi-même; **to pray God of His mercy to forgive,** prier Dieu que dans sa miséricorde il pardonnera; **to die of a wound,** mourir (des suites) d'une blessure; **she died of grief,** elle mourut de douleur; **sick, proud, of sth.,** las, fier, de qch. **2.** (*agency*) (*a*) *A:* (= BY) **forsaken of God and man,** abandonné de Dieu et des hommes; **beloved of all,** aimé de tout le monde; (*b*) **it is very good, very kind, of you to invite me,** c'est bien aimable de votre part, c'est très aimable, très gentil, à vous, de m'inviter. **3.** (*a*) (*material*) **made of wood,** fait de, en, bois; **wall of stone,** mur en pierre; **a house of cards,** une maison de cartes; **the floor was of tiles,** le sol était carrelé; (*b*) **full of water,** plein d'eau. **4.** (*concerning, in respect of*) (*a*) (*introducing ind. obj. of verb*) **to think of s.o.,** penser à qn; **it admits of no doubt,** cela ne souffre pas de doute; **to warn s.o. of sth.,** avertir qn de qch.; **what do you think of him?** que pensez-vous de lui? **what has become of him?** qu'est-il devenu? (*b*) (*after adjs*) **guilty of,** coupable de; **capable of,** capable de; **enamoured of,** amoureux de; (*c*) **doctor of medicine,** docteur en médecine; **master of arts,** *A:* maître ès arts; (*d*) *F:* **well, what of** [ɔv] **it?** et bien, et après? **5.** (*descriptive genitive*) (*a*) (i) **name of Jones,** nom de Jones; **the city of Rome,** la cité de Rome; **state of rest,** état de repos; **man of genius,** homme de génie; **tales of children,** contes évoquant des enfants; **boots of our own manufacture,** bottes de notre fabrication; **trees of my planting,** arbres que j'ai plantés moi-même; **flag of three colours,** drapeau de trois couleurs; **people of foreign appearance, of dark complexion,** gens à l'air étranger, au teint foncé; **the isle of green meadows,** l'île aux vertes prairies; **child of ten,** enfant (âgé) de dix ans; *NAm:* **his wife of twenty years,** la femme qu'il a épousée il y a vingt ans; **the fact of your speaking to him,** le fait que vous lui avez parlé; le fait du lui avoir parlé; (ii) **to be of good cheer,** être vaillant, courageux; **to be of no account,** ne pas compter; **swift of foot,** aux pieds légers; **hard of heart,** au cœur dur; **hard of hearing,** dur d'oreille; (*b*) **a fine figure of a woman,** une belle femme, un beau corps de femme; **they possess a palace of a house,** ils possèdent une maison qui est un vrai palais; **that fool of a sergeant,** cet imbécile de sergent; (*c*) **all of a tremble,** tout tremblant; **all of a sudden,** tout d'un coup. **6.** (*a*) (*subjective genitive*) **the temptations of the devil,** les tentations du diable; **the love of a mother,** l'amour d'une mère; (*b*) (*objective genitive*) **the temptation of Eve,** la tentation d'Ève; **the fear of God,** la crainte de Dieu; **hope of relief,** espoir de secours; **great drinker of whisky,** grand buveur de whisky; **writer of theosophical treatises,** auteur de traités théosophiques; **explanation of a fact,** explication d'un fait; *P:* **to be (a-)doing of sth.,** être en train de faire qch.; **what are you a-doing of?** que faites-vous là? **7.** (*partitive*) (*a*) **three parts of the whole,** trois quarts du tout; **the whole of the apple,** toute la pomme; *F:* **no more of that!** plus de cela! **how much of it do you want?** combien en voulez-vous? **two of them died,** deux d'entre eux moururent; **many of us, several of us,** beaucoup, plusieurs, d'entre nous; **there were two, several, of us,** nous étions deux, plusieurs; **the car carried the four of us,** l'auto, la voiture, nous a transportés tous les quatre; **he is one of us,** il est des nôtres; **one of the best,** un des meilleurs; **of the twenty only one was bad,** sur les vingt un seul était mauvais; **a man of a thousand,** un homme entre mille; **there's something of good in every man,** il y a quelque chose de bon en tout homme; **to give of one's best,** faire de son mieux; (*b*) (*after superlative*) **the best of men,** le meilleur des hommes; **she had the best of teachers,** (i) elle a eu la meilleure des institutrices, (ii) elle a eu les meilleures institutrices qu'il fût possible de se procurer; **the bravest of the brave,** le brave des braves; **the one he loved most of all,** celui qu'il aimait entre tous; **first of all,** avant tout; (*c*) (*out of*) **he, of all men, of all people, should have been grateful,** lui entre tous aurait dû se montrer reconnaissant; **of all things she dreaded Tom's anger,** elle craignait au-dessus de toutes choses la colère de Tom; **it is a time of all others for rejoicing,** c'est, plus que tout autre, le moment de se réjouir; **the one thing of all others that I want,** ce que je désire surtout, par-dessus tout, avant tout; **this day of all days,** ce jour entre tous; (*d*) (*intensive*) **the Holy of Holies,** le saint des saints; **a fool of fools,** un triple sot; **he is an aristocrat of aristocrats,** c'est un aristocrate entre tous; **the virtue of all virtues is success,** la vertu qui prime toutes les autres, c'est de réussir; **at that time castor oil was the remedy of remedies,** à cette époque, le remède par excellence c'était l'huile de ricin; (*e*) *Poet:* **to drink of hemlock,** boire de la ciguë; *B:* **hast thou not eaten of the tree . . .,** n'as-tu pas mangé du fruit de l'arbre . . .. **8.** (*possession or dependence*) (*a*) **the widow of a barrister,** la veuve d'un avocat; **leg of the table,** pied de la table; **citizen of London,** citoyen de Londres; **topic of conversation,** sujet de conversation; **the first of the month,** le premier du mois; **the first of June,** le premier juin; (*b*) (+ *possessive*) **he is a friend of mine, of my father's,** c'est un de mes amis, un des amis de mon père; c'est un ami de mon père; **is he a friend of yours?** il est de vos amis? **it's no business of yours,** cela ne vous regarde pas; ce n'est pas votre affaire; **that hat of his,** ce chapeau qu'il porte; **that frail little husband of hers,** ce frêle petit homme qu'elle a pour mari; **I was reading something of Carlyle's,** je lisais quelque chose de, par, Carlyle; **that's not a bad paper of Smith's,** cette composition de Smith n'est pas mauvaise. **9.** (*in temporal phrases*) (*a*) **of late years,** (pendant) ces dernières années; **of late,** dernièrement, récemment; depuis peu; depuis quelque temps; *A:* **of a child, he was sickly,** il a été maladif dès son enfance; (*b*) *F: O:* **what do you do of a Sunday?** que faites-vous le dimanche? **he looks in of an evening,** il nous fait de temps en temps une petite visite le soir; *Dial:* **to sit up late of nights,** veiller tard la nuit.

off[1] [ɔf], *adv., prep. & a.*
I. *adv.* **1.** (*away*) (*a*) **house a mile o.,** maison à un mille de distance; **I'd know him a mile o.,** je le reconnaîtrais à des kilomètres; **some way o.,** à quelque distance; **about a year o.,** à à peu près une année de distance; **far o.,** au loin; dans le lointain; **further o.,** plus loin; **to keep s.o. o.,** empêcher qn d'approcher, de se rapprocher; tenir qn à distance; (*b*) (*departure*) **to go o.,** *F:* **be o.,** s'en aller, partir; *F:* décamper, filer; **I'm o. to church, to London,** je pars à la messe, pour Londres; **I'm o. to Paris again,** je repars pour Paris; **it's getting late, I'm off,** il se fait tard, je me sauve, je pars, je file; **it's time I was o.,** il est temps que je plie bagage; **I must be o.,** *F:* il faut que je me trotte, que je me sauve; **be o.!** allez-vous-en! partez! filez! *F:* déguerpissez! **they're o.! o. they go!** (i) les voilà partis! (ii) *F:* les voilà lancés! **she's o.!** la voilà partie (sur son sujet préféré); **o. we go!** (i) en route! *F:* fouette, cocher! (ii) nous voilà partis! **o. with him!** emmenez-le! **to go o. (to sleep),** s'endormir; **I was nearly o. myself,** moi-même j'étais presque endormi; (*for* **drive o., give o., etc.** *see verbs*) (*c*) *Nau:* au large; **to sail o. and on,** louvoyer tantôt vers le large, tantôt vers la terre; *s.a.* **4.** *infra.*; (*d*) *Th:* à la cantonade; derrière la toile. **2.** (*a*) (*removal*) **to take o. one's coat,** ôter son habit; **with one's coat o.,** en bras de chemise; **I have never seen her with her hat o.,** je ne l'ai jamais vue sans chapeau; **hat's o.!** chapeaux bas! **o. with your shoes!** ôtez vos chaussures! **a button has come o., is o.,** un bouton a sauté; **you'd better have it o.,** vous ferez bien (i) de l'enlever, (ii) de vous le faire enlever, (iii) (*of beard, etc.*) de vous la faire couper, (*of leg*) de vous la faire amputer; **to cut s.o.'s head o.,** couper la tête à qn; décapiter qn; **o. with his head!** allez! qu'on (me) le décapite! (*for* **bite o., tear o., etc.** *see verbs*); **to turn o. the gas,** fermer le gaz; (*at the main*) couper le gaz; **the water is o.,** on a coupé l'eau; **o. position,** fermé; **the brakes are o.,** les freins sont desserrés; *I.C.E:* **the ignition is o.,** l'allumage est coupé; (*in restaurant*) **dish that is o.,** plat qui est épuisé; **chicken is o.,** il n'y a plus, il ne reste plus, de poulet; **the deal, the concert, is o.,** le marché est rompu, ne se fera pas; le concert est abandonné, n'aura pas lieu; **it's all o., the whole thing is o.,** tout est rompu; *F:* l'affaire est tombée dans l'eau; **holidays are o. for us,** nous n'avons plus la possibilité de prendre des vacances; **football is o. and tennis is not yet on,** le football est fini et le tennis n'a pas encore commencé; **the play is o.,** la pièce a quitté l'affiche; (*b*) qui n'est plus frais; **meat that is slightly o.,** viande un peu avancée; *F:* **this beer's o.,** cette bière est éventée; *P:* **that's a bit o.!** ça c'est pas chic! ce n'est pas loyal! (*c*) (*completion*) **to finish o. a piece of work,** parachever un travail; *Sp:* **to run o. a heat,** courir une éliminatoire; (*for* **drink o., pay o., etc.,** *see verbs*). **3.** **to be well o.,** être à l'aise; avoir de la fortune; **to be badly, poorly, o.,** être dans la gêne, dans la misère, mal en point, à l'étroit, mal loti; **to be badly o. for sth.,** avoir grand(ement) besoin de qch.; **I am badly o. for tools,** je suis dépourvu d'outils; **we are badly o. for provisions,** nous sommes à court de vivres; **to be better o.,** (i) être plus à son aise matériellement; (ii) se trouver dans de meilleures conditions; **he is better o. where he is,** il est bien mieux, dans une meilleure situation, où il est; **he is worse o.,** sa situation a empiré. **4.** *adv.phr.* **o. and on; on and o.,** par intervalles; à différentes reprises; par instants; de temps en temps; **to be on and o. with sth.,** travailler à qch. par à-coups; **I work at it o. and on,** j'y travaille avec des interruptions; **right o., straight o.,** immédiatement, sur-le-champ, tout de suite, sans hésitation.

II. *prep.* **1.** (*a*) *usu.* de; **to fall o. sth.,** tomber de qch.; **to fall o. one's horse,** tomber à bas de son cheval; **to get o. the table,** descendre de la table; **to drive a cat o. the flowerbed,** chasser un chat du parterre; **to take a ring o. one's finger,** ôter une bague de son doigt; **to take sth. (from) o. a table,** prendre qch. sur une table; **door that is o. its hinges,** porte *f* qui est hors de ses gonds; **to eat o. silver plate,** manger dans des assiettes d'argent; **to cut a slice o. sth.,** couper une tranche de qch.; **I dined o. a leg of mutton,** j'ai dîné d'une tranche de gigot; (*of accessory, etc.*) **to work o. the engine,** marcher, fonctionner, sur le moteur; *El:* **to work o. the mains,** être branché sur le secteur; **to take sth. o. the price,** rabaisser qch. du prix; **a third o. everything,** rabais *m* d'un tiers sur tout; *adv.* **to allow 2½% o. for ready money,** faire une réduction, une remise, de 2½% pour paiement comptant; **to borrow money o. s.o.,** emprunter de l'argent à qn; **that is a great weight o. my mind,** cela me soulage l'esprit d'un grand poids; (*b*) écarté de, éloigné de; **village o. the beaten track,** village éloigné, hors, du chemin battu; **a yard o. me,** à un mètre de moi; **the car was standing o. the road,** la voiture stationnait aux abords de la route; **street o. the main road,** (i) rue qui donne sur la grande route, aboutissant à la grande route; (ii) rue éloignée de la grande route; **hair, hat, worn o. the face,** cheveux tirés, chapeau porté, en arrière; **to sing, play, o. key,** chanter, jouer, faux; *NAm: F:* **to be o. key,** manquer d'à-propos; clocher; *U.S: Mil:* **to put a public house o. limits,** consigner un café; **o. limits,** consigné à la troupe; **all that's o. the point,** tout cela est étranger à la question; *F:* **you're right o. it,** tu te trompes de tout au tout, tu déraillles; *Games:* **o. ground,** (jeu *m* du) chat perché; *Fb:* **player o. side,** joueur *m* hors jeu; **the o.-side rule,** la règle du hors jeu; *F:* **to get o. side with s.o.,** se faire mal voir de qn; (*c*) **to be o. one's food,** être dégoûté de sa nourriture; n'avoir pas d'appétit; **to be o. meat,** (i) être dégoûté de la viande, (ii) suivre un régime qui ne comporte pas de viande; **I am o. that work now,** je ne fais plus ce travail; **to have time o. (work),** avoir du temps de libre; **have you any time o. during the week?** avez-vous des heures libres, des loisirs, pendant la semaine? **to take some time o.,** prendre des loisirs; **to take a week o. housework, gardening,** se libérer des travaux ménagers, du jardinage, pendant huit jours; **an afternoon o.,** un après-midi libre; un après-midi de congé, de liberté; **day o.,** jour *m* de congé, de liberté; **to give the staff a day o.,** donner congé à son personnel pour la journée; **to arrange to take two days o.,** se libérer pour deux jours. **2.** *Nau:* (*a*) **o. the Cape,** à la hauteur du Cap; au large du Cap; **o. Calais,** devant Calais; **o. the entrance to the bay,** à l'ouvert de la baie; (*b*) **to sail o. the wind,** naviguer vent largue. **3.** (*in compounds*) **o.-white,** blanc légèrement teinté; **o.-black,** presque noir.

III. *a.* **1.** (*a*) **the o. side,** (i) *Equit:* le côté hors montoir; (ii) *Aut: etc:* le côté droit; (iii) *Turf:* l'extérieur *m* de la piste; *Equit:* **o. rein, leg,** rêne *f*, jambe, *f*, de dehors; **to mount a horse on the o. side,** monter à cheval en fauconnier; fauconner; **o. horse,** (cheval de) sous-verge *m inv*; bricolier *m*; **o. leader,** sous-verge de devant; **o. wheeler,** cheval de brancard; sous-verge de derrière; (*b*) *Cr:* **drive to the o. (side), o. drive,** coup *m* en avant à droite; **o. break,** (balle *f* qui fait une) déviation vers la droite; (*c*) *Bookb:* **o. side, o. board,** verso *m*; plat inférieur. **2.** subsidiaire; **o. street,** rue secondaire, latérale; **o. issue,** question *f* d'importance subsidiaire.

3. (*a*) **o. position,** position *f* de desserrage (des freins); *El:* position de rupture de circuit; position d'extinction (des lampes); position de repos; position "zéro", "fermé", "coupé"; (*b*) **o. day,** (i) jour *m* où l'on ne travaille pas; jour de chômage; jour férié; jour de liberté; (ii) jour où l'on n'est pas en train, où l'on ne brille pas; **it was one of his o. days,** il n'était pas dans un de ses meilleurs jours; *NAm:* **o. year,** (i) *Pol:* année sans élections d'importance; (ii) *Com: Agr:* mauvaise année. 4. *Adm:* **o. consumption,** consommation *f* (des boissons alcooliques) à domicile; **beer for o. consumption,** bière *f* à emporter; **o. licence,** licence *f* permettant exclusivement la vente des boissons à emporter; bar où l'on peut acheter des boissons à emporter. 5. *Mus:* **o. beat,** temps *m* faible; *s.a.* OFFBEAT 2.

off[2], *v.i.* 1. *Nau:* prendre le large. 2. *F: O:* (*a*) **to o. with one's coat,** mettre bas, ôter, son habit; tomber la veste; (*b*) **to o. it,** partir, s'en aller.

off[3], *s. F:* **the o.,** le départ.

offal ['ɔfəl], *s.* 1. (*a*) rebut *m*, restes *mpl*, débris *mpl*, déchets *mpl*, détritus *m*; *NAm:* **o. timber,** bois *m* de rebut; *Husb:* **o. (wheat),** blé avarié (donné aux poules, etc.); (*b*) ordures *fpl*, immondices *fpl*; (*c*) charogne *f*; (*d*) *Fish:* poissons *mpl* de qualité inférieure. 2. déchets d'abattage (de boucherie); *F:* tripaille *f*; (*edible*) abats *mpl*; (*inedible*) issues *fpl*. 3. *Mill:* issues.

offbeat ['ɔfbi:t], *a.* 1. *F:* (*of pers., conduct, etc.*) original; qui sort de l'ordinaire. 2. (*jazz*) qui accentue les deuxième et quatrième temps.

offcast ['ɔfkɑ:st]. *NAm:* 1. *a.* (chose, personne) de rebut. 2. *s.* (*a*) (*thg*) rebut *m*; (*b*) (*pers.*) rebut; déchet *m*.

off-centre, off-centred ['ɔfsentər, -təd], décentré, décalé, désaxé; qui n'est pas au centre; en porte-à-faux; *I.C.E:* **o.-c. engine,** moteur décalé; *Rad:* **o.-c. display radar,** radar *m* à information décentrée.

off-centring ['ɔfsentriŋ], *s. Tchn:* décentrage *m*, excentrage *m*, décalage *m*.

off-circuit ['ɔf'sə:kit], *a. Elcs: Tp:* hors circuit; *Tp:* **o.-c. test,** essai *m* à vide.

offcome ['ɔfkʌm], *s. Scot:* issue *f*; (i) succès *m*; (ii) moyen *m* de sortir.

off-course ['ɔf'kɔ:s], *a.* (pari) effectué hors des champs de course.

offcut ['ɔfkʌt], *s.* 1. découpure *f*; (*from wooden plank, length of cloth*) chute *f*. 2. *Bookb:* bande *f*, carton *m*; *Typ:* **imposition with o.,** imposition *f* avec coupure.

off-drive ['ɔfdraiv], *v.i.* (**off-drove, -driven**), *Cr:* faire un coup en avant à droite.

offence [ə'fens], *s.* 1. *A: & Lit:* scandale *m*; *B:* **woe unto that man by whom the o. cometh,** malheur à l'homme par qui le scandale arrive; **rock of o.,** pierre *f* de scandale; *B:* pierre d'achoppement. 2. (*a*) attaque *f*, agression *f*; **war of o.,** guerre offensive; (*b*) *NAm: Sp:* (i) attaque (d'une équipe); (ii) équipe attaquante; (l')attaque. 3. blessure faite à la susceptibilité de qn; sujet *m* de mécontentement, de déplaisir; **this music is an o. to the ear,** cette musique offense l'oreille; **to cause o. to s.o.,** formaliser, froisser, qn; **to cause o.,** déplaire; **to take o. (at sth.),** se formaliser, se froisser, se choquer (de qch.); *F:* prendre la mouche; **to take o. at the slightest thing,** s'offenser, se piquer, se blesser, d'un rien; se fâcher pour rien, pour un rien; **he took o. at not being invited,** il a mal pris qu'on ne l'ait invité; il s'est formalisé de ce qu'on ne l'avait pas invité; **to give o. to s.o.,** offenser, blesser, froisser, qn; **if I may say so without (giving) o.,** soit dit sans vous blesser; **I meant no o.,** je ne voulais offenser personne; **no o. meant—none taken;** soit dit sans offense—il n'y a pas d'offense. 4. (*a*) offense *f*, faute *f*; **minor o., trifling o.,** faute légère; **serious o.,** faute grave; *Ecc:* **pardon our offences,** pardonnez-nous nos offenses; **to commit an o. against the law,** commettre une infraction à la loi; commettre (i) un délit, (ii) un crime, puni par la loi; **to commit an o. against s.o.'s rights,** porter atteinte aux droits de qn; outrager les droits de qn; **to commit an o. against good taste, against common decency,** commettre une infraction au bon goût; faire outrage aux convenances; **o. against God,** offense faite à Dieu; (*b*) *Jur:* **indictable o.,** violation *f* de loi; crime ou délit; acte délictueux; **petty o., minor o.,** contravention *f* (de simple police); **capital o.,** crime capital; **second o.,** récidive *f*; **unnatural o.,** crime contre nature; **indecent o.,** outrage *m* aux mœurs; attentat *m* aux mœurs.

offenceless [ə'fenslis], *a. A:* 1. sans faute, innocent. 2. inoffensif.

offend [ə'fend]. 1. *v.i.* (*a*) pécher, faillir; (*b*) **to o. against the law,** violer, enfreindre, la loi; faire un délit à la loi; **to o. against the laws of courtesy,** pécher contre la politesse; **to o. against (the laws of) grammar,** offenser la grammaire. 2. *v.tr.* (*a*) *A: & B:* scandaliser; *B:* **but whoso shall o. one of these little ones,** mais quiconque scandalise un de ces petits; **if thy right hand o. thee, cut it off,** si votre main droite vous est un sujet de scandale, vous fait tomber dans le péché, coupez-la; (*b*) offenser, blesser, froisser, choquer (qn); faire une offense à (qn); *F:* marcher sur le pied à (qn); **if I have offended you by word or deed,** si je vous ai offensé par parole ou par action; *abs.* **I have no wish to o.,** je ne veux offenser personne; **to be offended at, with, by, sth.,** se piquer, se fâcher, de qch.; **to be offended with s.o.,** être fâché contre qn; **I accepted his invitation so as not to o. him,** j'ai accepté son invitation pour ne pas le désobliger; **to be easily offended,** être très susceptible; se froisser facilement; (*c*) (*of thg*) **to o. the eye,** choquer les regards, la vue; offusquer l'œil; **harsh sound that offends the ear,** son aigre qui offense l'oreille; **people whose ears are easily offended,** gens aux oreilles chatouilleuses; **it offends our sense of justice,** cela outrage notre sentiment de la justice; **idea that offends common sense,** idée qui choque le bon sens; **book that offends morals,** livre outrageant pour les bonnes mœurs.

offended [ə'fendid], *a.* 1. fâché, froissé; **in an o. tone of voice,** d'un ton bourru, d'un ton de dépit, d'une voix offensée. 2. *Jur:* **the o. party,** l'offensé, -ée.

offendedly [ə'fendidli], *adv.* d'un ton froissé.

offender [ə'fendər], *s.* 1. (*a*) pécheur, -eresse; (*b*) *Jur:* délinquant, -ante, contrevenant, -ante, malfaiteur, -trice; criminel, -elle; **a first o.,** un délinquant primaire; **the First Offenders Act,** la loi de sursis; (*in Fr.*) la loi Bérenger; **to be an old, a hardened, o.,** (i) être un récidiviste, un repris de justice, *F:* un cheval de retour; (ii) *F:* être coutumier du fait; **the chief o.,** le grand coupable. 2. offenseur *m*; **she is the o.,** c'est elle qui est l'offenseur.

offending [ə'fendiŋ], *a.* offensant, fautif.

offensive [ə'fensiv]. 1. *a.* (*a*) *Mil: etc:* offensif; **o. and defensive arms,** armes offensives et défensives; (*b*) (*of word, action*) offensant, blessant, choquant, sale; (spectacle) désagréable, repoussant; (odeur) nauséabonde, délétère, déplaisante; *Jur:* **o. trades,** métiers incommodes ou insalubres; **word o. to the ear,** mot qui choque l'oreille; mot malsonnant; **book that is morally o.,** livre outrageant pour les bonnes mœurs; (*c*) (*of pers.*) **to be o. to s.o.,** insulter qn; injurier qn; dire des grossièretés à qn; **o. answer,** réponse blessante, injurieuse; **to give an o. answer,** répondre grossièrement; **in an o. tone,** d'un ton rogue, injurieux. 2. *s. Mil: Sp: etc:* offensive *f*; **to take, assume, the o.,** prendre l'offensive; **to carry out an o.,** mener une offensive; *Mil:* exécuter une action offensive; **to resume the o.,** reprendre l'offensive; *Mil:* effectuer un retour offensif; **peace o.,** offensive de paix.

offensively [ə'fensivli], *adv.* 1. *Mil: Sp:* offensivement. 2. (*a*) désagréablement, d'une manière offensante, choquante; (*b*) d'un ton injurieux, blessant.

offensiveness [ə'fensivnis], *s.* 1. nature offensante, désagréable (d'un spectacle, d'un son, d'une odeur). 2. nature injurieuse, blessante (d'une réponse, etc.).

offer[1] ['ɔfər], *s.* 1. offre *f*, proposition *f*; (*a*) **verbal o.,** offre verbale; **to make an o. of sth. to s.o.,** faire offre de qch. à qn; offrir qch. à qn; *Com: etc:* **to make an o. for sth.,** faire une offre pour qch.; **that's the best o. I can make,** c'est le plus que je puis offrir; c'est mon dernier mot; **it's a fair o.,** (i) c'est une bonne proposition; (ii) *F:* libre à vous d'accepter; **better o.,** suroffre *f*; **to close with an o.,** accepter une offre; **on o.,** en vente; *Com:* **special o.,** article *m* (en) réclame; *NAm:* **job offers,** offres d'emploi; (*b*) **o. of marriage,** demande *f* en mariage; **Jane had had several offers,** Jane avait eu plusieurs demandes en mariage, avait plus d'une fois été demandée en mariage; **to decline an o.,** rejeter, décliner, refuser, repousser, une offre, une demande en mariage. 2. *O:* tentative *f* (**at,** de); mouvement spontané (pour faire qch.).

offer[2]. 1. *v.tr.* (*a*) offrir; **to o. s.o. sth.,** offrir qch. à qn; **to o. an apology,** présenter des excuses; **to o. (up) prayers to God,** adresser des prières à Dieu; **to o. (up) a sacrifice,** offrir un sacrifice; **to o. s.o. money,** proposer de l'argent à qn; **to o. one's services,** offrir ses services; **he was offered a post,** un emploi lui a été offert; **to o. oneself for a post,** s'offrir, se proposer, se présenter, à un emploi; poser sa candidature à un emploi; *Com:* **to o. goods (for sale),** offrir des marchandises en vente; **house offered for sale,** maison mise en vente; **this is what we have to o.,** voici ce que nous proposons; *St.Exch: etc:* **prices offered,** cours offerts, cours vendeurs; **the conditions that we are able to o. you,** les conditions que nous sommes à même de vous faire; **what will you o. me for it?** combien m'en offrez-vous? **to o. one's arm to an old lady,** offrir le bras à une vieille dame; **to o. one's lips (for a kiss),** tendre les lèvres; **to o. one's flank to the enemy,** prêter le flanc à l'ennemi; **to o. battle,** inviter le combat; **to o. to do sth.,** faire l'offre, offrir, de faire qch.; s'offrir à faire qch.; **to o. to fight s.o.,** défier qn; (*b*) **to o. a remark, an opinion,** faire une remarque; avancer une opinion; **to o. a definition,** proposer une définition; *Jur:* **to o. a plea,** exciper d'une excuse; (*c*) **the fireworks offered a fine spectacle,** le feu d'artifice a présenté, a offert, un beau spectacle; **the scheme offered considerable difficulties,** le projet présentait des difficultés considérables; *Sch:* **to o. French at an examination,** présenter le français à un examen; (*d*) essayer, tenter; **to o. resistance,** faire (de la) résistance; **to o. violence to s.o.,** faire violence à qn; *O:* **to o. to strike s.o.,** lever la main sur qn; *Th:* **offers to go,** fausse sortie; **he offers to go,** il va pour sortir; il dessine une sortie. 2. *v.i.* (*of occasion, etc.*) s'offrir, se présenter; **if a good occasion offers,** s'il s'offre une belle occasion; **if more passengers offered,** s'il se présentait plus de voyageurs.

offerer ['ɔfərər], *s.* offreur *m*; (*at sale*) **no offerers,** pas d'amateurs, d'offrants; **to the highest o.,** au plus offrant.

offering ['ɔf(ə)riŋ], *s.* 1. (*action*) offre *f*. 2. (*thg offered*) offre; *Ecc:* offrande *f*; **sin o., trespass o.,** offrande expiatoire, sacrifice *m* expiatoire; **burnt o.,** (i) holocauste *m*; (ii) *F:* viande brûlée, calcinée; plat brûlé; **to put one's o. in the alms box,** déposer son offrande dans le tronc; *F:* **the latest offerings of the publishing world,** les dernières publications, œuvres, offertes au public.

offertory ['ɔfət(ə)ri], *s. Ecc:* 1. (*a*) offertoire *m* (de la messe); (*b*) *Mus:* offertoire. 2. (*a*) quête *f* (de l'offrande); (*b*) montant *m* de la quête.

off-gauge ['ɔfgeidʒ], *a. Cmptr:* décadré.

offhand. 1. *adv.* ['ɔf'hænd]. 1. (*a*) sans préparation; sur-le-champ; au pied levé; au premier abord; à première vue; en un tour de main; **to play an accompaniment o.,** jouer un accompagnement à vue; **to speak o.,** parler impromptu; parler d'abondance; improviser un discours; (*b*) sans cérémonie, sans façon; brusquement, cavalièrement; d'un air dégagé. 2. *a. before noun* ['ɔfhænd]; *following verb* [ɔf'hænd]; (*a*) spontané, improvisé, impromptu; **o. speech,** discours impromptu, improvisé; (*b*) brusque, cavalier, dégagé, désinvolte; sans cérémonie, sans façon(s), sans-gêne *inv*; **to be o. with s.o.,** se montrer désinvolte à l'égard de qn; **to treat s.o. in an o. manner,** traiter qn d'une façon très dégagée; traiter qn sans façon, à la cavalière, cavalièrement, avec désinvolture.

offhanded [ɔf'hændid], *a.* = OFFHAND 2 (*b*).

offhandedly [ɔf'hændidli], *adv.* = OFFHAND 1 (*b*).

offhandedness [ɔf'hændidnis], *s.* brusquerie *f*; sans-façon *m*; désinvolture *f*; sans-gêne *m*.

office ['ɔfis], *s.* 1. (*a*) office *m*, service *m*; **to do s.o. a good, a bad, o.,** rendre un bon, un mauvais, service à qn; **through, owing to, the good offices of a friend,** grâce aux bons offices, par les bons soins, d'un ami; **good offices to one another,** échange *m* de services; (*b*) **last offices (to the dead),** (i) derniers devoirs (rendus à un mort); (ii) obsèques *f*; **to perform the last offices,** rendre au mort les derniers devoirs. 2. (*a*) fonctions *fpl*, devoir; **to perform the o. of secretary,** faire l'office de secrétaire; **it is my o. to pass the accounts,** il est de mon devoir, il rentre dans mes fonctions, d'approuver les comptes; (*b*) charge *f*, emploi *m*, place *f*, fonctions; **high o., important o.,** fonctions élevées; haute charge; **public o.,** fonctions publiques, emploi public; **the o. of bishop,** la dignité d'évêque; *Pol:* **the o. of Chancellor of the Exchequer,** le portefeuille des Finances; **to be in o., to hold o.,** (i) remplir un emploi; être en charge, en fonctions; (ii) (*of government*) être au pouvoir; (iii) (*of minister of State*) avoir un portefeuille; *F:* **people in o.,** les gens en place; les bureaucrates; **the noble lords in o.,** les nobles lords à la tête des affaires; **to be called to o.,** être appelé à un ministère; **to take o., to come into o.,** (i) entrer en fonctions; (ii) (*of government*) arriver au pouvoir; prendre le pouvoir; (iii) (*of minister*) entrer au ministère; accepter un portefeuille; **to continue, remain, in o.,** demeurer en fonctions; **to leave o.,** se démettre de ses fonctions; quitter ses fonctions; *abs.* se démettre; **to aim at o., to be ambitious of o.,** ambitionner un portefeuille; *F:* ambitionner le maroquin; **to act in virtue of one's o.,** agir d'office. 3. *Ecc:* **o. of the day,** office du jour; **o. for the dead,** office de morts; vigiles *fpl* des morts. 4. (*a*) bureau *m*; (*lawyer's*) étude *f*; **business o.,** bureau commercial; **head o., registered offices (of company),** bureau principal, bureau central, siège (principal, social); **complaints o.,** bureau, service *m*, des réclamations; *Post:* **telegraph o.,** bureau télégraphique; (bureau du) télégraphe; *NAm: Tp:* **the central o.,** le central; **public offices,** administrations (publiques); **o. building, block,** bâtiment administratif; **o. equipment,** matériel *m* de bureau; **o. expenses,** frais *m* de bureau; **o. hours,** heures *f* de bureau; **o. premises, o. space,** locaux *mpl* pour bureaux; **this will make very good o. space,** ceci fera, ces locaux feront, d'excellents bureaux; **o. requisites, o. supplies,** articles *m*, fournitures *f*, de bureau; **o. staff,** personnel *m* de bureau; **for o. use only,** (cadre) réservé à l'administration; **o. work,** travail *m* de bureau; **o. worker,** employé, -ée, de bureau; (*b*) **private o.,** cabinet particulier; **the manager's o.,** le bureau du directeur; **the secretary's o.,** le secrétariat; **cash o.,** caisse *f*; **porter's o.,** loge *f* du concierge; (*c*) **government o.,** ministère *m* (d'État); **the Home O.** = le ministère de l'Intérieur; **the Foreign and Commonwealth O.** = le ministère des Affaires étrangères; **the War O.** = le ministère de la Guerre; *F:* la Guerre; **War O. staff,** personnel *m* des bureaux de la Guerre; (*d*) **insurance o.,** compagnie *f* d'assurances; (*e*) *NAm:* cabinet *m* de consultation (d'un médecin, d'un dentiste); bureau *m* (d'un professeur, etc.); (*f*) *Ecc: Hist:* **the Holy O.,** le Saint-Office (de l'Inquisition); (*g*) **offices (of a house),** communs *m* et dépendances *f*; **the usual offices,** les lieux *m* d'aisances. **5.** *P: A:* **to give s.o. the o.,** avertir, prévenir, qn; *P:* passer la consigne à qn.

office-bearer ['ɔfis'bɛərər], *s.* (*a*) personne *f* qui remplit un emploi public; *Pol:* personne qui a un portefeuille; (*b*) officier *m*; fonctionnaire *m*; (*c*) membre *m* du bureau (d'une société, etc.).

office-holder ['ɔfis'houldər], *s.* **1.** = OFFICE-BEARER. **2.** *NAm:* employé *m* de l'État; fonctionnaire *m*.

officehunter ['ɔfis'hʌntər], *s. Pej:* politicien qui ambitionne un portefeuille.

officer[1] ['ɔfisər], *s.* **1.** (*a*) fonctionnaire *m*; officier *m*; **municipal o.,** officier municipal; *Adm:* **clerical o.,** secrétaire *m* d'administration; **administrative o.** = administrateur civil; **executive o.,** rédacteur *m* (de ministère); **customs o.,** douanier *m*; **police o.,** *U.S:* **o.,** agent *m* de police, de la sûreté; officier de police; *Adm:* gardien *m* de la paix; *F:* sergent *m* de ville; (*when addressing a policeman*) **excuse me, o.!** pardon monsieur! **sheriff's o.,** huissier *m*; (*b*) **the officers of a society,** les membres *m* du bureau d'une société. **2.** *Mil: etc:* officier; (*a*) **(commissioned) army o.,** officier de l'armée de terre; **assistant o.,** *U.S:* **executive o.,** officier adjoint; **field o.,** officier supérieur; **general o. commanding first army,** général commandant la première armée; **regimental o.,** officier de (corps de) troupe; **staff o.,** officier d'état-major; *F:* topo *m*; *U.S:* officier breveté de l'état-major, de l'École de Guerre; **subordinate officers,** *U.S:* **company officers,** officiers subalternes; *Sch: A:* **Officers' Training Corps,** bataillon *m* scolaire; = préparation militaire supérieure; **reserve o.,** officier de réserve; (*b*) *Mil.Av:* **flying o.,** (i) lieutenant aviateur, d'aviation; (ii) (*W.R.A.F.*) deuxième classe *f*; **pilot o.,** (i) sous-lieutenant, *pl.* sous-lieutenants, aviateur, d'aviation; (ii) (*W.R.A.F.*) troisième classe; **acting pilot o.,** aspirant *m* (d'aviation); (*c*) *Navy:* **naval o.,** officier de marine; **deck o., executive o.,** officier de pont, de manœuvre; **the executive o.,** le commandant en second; l'officier en second; *F:* le second; **non-executive o.,** officier des équipages de la flotte; **engineer o.,** officier mécanicien; **gunnery o.,** officier de tir; (*d*) *Nau:* **merchant navy o.,** officier de la marine marchande; **first o.,** (commandant en) second; second capitaine; **radio o.,** radionavigant *m*; (*e*) *Civil Av: NAm:* **first o.,** copilote *m*; (*f*) **o. in the Salvation Army,** officier, *f.* officière, de l'Armée du Salut. **3. high o. (of an order),** grand dignitaire (d'un ordre).

officer[2], *v.tr. Mil:* **1.** fournir des officiers à (un corps); encadrer (un bataillon). **2.** (*esp. in passive*) commander; **a well-officered battalion,** un bataillon bien commandé.

officering ['ɔfisəriŋ], *s.* **1.** encadrement *m* (d'un corps de troupes). **2.** commandement *m*.

office-seeker ['ɔfissi:kər], *s.* **1.** personne *f* qui ambitionne une charge, une haute fonction, *Pol:* un portefeuille. **2.** *NAm:* quémandeur *m* d'une place, d'un emploi, dans l'administration.

official [ə'fiʃ(ə)l]. **1.** *a.* (*a*) officiel; **o. letter,** pli officiel, de service; *Post:* **o. paid,** en franchise postale; **o. seal,** cachet *m* réglementaire, de service; **o. language,** langage officiel, administratif; **o. style,** style bureaucratique; *Pej:* jargon administratif; **to act in one's o. capacity,** agir dans l'exercice de ses fonctions; **the o. cars,** les voitures des officiels; **the o. party,** les Officiels; *U.S:* **the o. family,** l'entourage *m* (d'un ministre, etc.); (*b*) (*of statement, source, journal, etc.*) officiel; **o. news,** nouvelles authentiques, officielles; *Fin:* **o. quotation,** cours *m* authentique; cote officielle; **o. market,** marché officiel; parquet *m*; *Adm: U.S:* (*on document*) **o.,** pour ampliation; *Sp:* **o. record,** record homologué; (*c*) titulaire; **the o. organist,** le titulaire de l'orgue; le préposé officiel à l'orgue; (*d*) *Med:* officinal, -aux; autorisé par la pharmacopée; conforme au codex. **2.** *s.* (*a*) fonctionnaire *m*; *Pej:* bureaucrate *m*; **minor officials,** petits fonctionnaires; **senior officials,** fonctionnaires moyens; **higher officials,** hauts fonctionnaires; **the o. at the entrance,** le préposé à l'entrée; **railway o.,** employé *m* des chemins de fer; **post-office officials,** employés des Postes; (*b*) (i) (*at sports meeting, fête, etc.*) commissaire *m*; (ii) *Sp: U.S:* arbitre *m*; (*c*) *Ecc:* **o. (principal),** official *m*, -aux.

officialdom [ə'fiʃ(ə)ldəm], *s.* **1.** l'administration *f*; les milieux officiels. **2.** bureaucratie *f*, fonctionnarisme *m*.

officialese [əfiʃə'li:z], *s. F:* jargon administratif.

officialism [ə'fiʃəlizm], *s.* **1.** bureaucratie *f*, fonctionnarisme *m*, chinoiseries *fpl* (de l'administration). **2.** suffisance *f*, fatuité *f* (d'un bureaucrate).

officiality [əfiʃi'æliti], *s.* officialité *f*.

officialization [ə'fiʃəlai'zeiʃ(ə)n], *s.* officialisation *f*.

officialize [ə'fiʃəlaiz], *v.tr.* officialiser.

officially [ə'fiʃəli], *adv.* officiellement.

officiant [ə'fiʃiənt], *s. Ecc:* (*at service*) officiant *m*; (*in parish*) desservant *m*.

officiate [ə'fiʃieit], *v.i.* **1.** *Ecc:* **to o. at a service,** officier à un office; **to o. at a church, in a parish,** desservir une église, une paroisse; **officiating minister,** (ministre) officiant *m*. **2.** *O:* **to o. as host, as hostess,** remplir, exercer, les fonctions d'hôte, de maîtresse de maison; **I officiated for him during his illness,** je l'ai remplacé pendant sa maladie.

officinal [ə'fisinəl], *a. Pharm:* officinal, -aux.

officious [ə'fiʃəs], *a.* **1.** empressé; trop zélé; officieux. **2.** (*unofficial*) officieux.

officiously [ə'fiʃəsli], *adv.* **1.** avec trop de zèle; **to behave o.,** faire l'empressé. **2.** (*unofficially*) officieusement; à titre officieux.

officiousness [ə'fiʃəsnis], *s.* officiosité *f*; excès *m* de zèle, d'empressement; **letter that smacks of o.,** lettre d'un ton officieux.

offing ['ɔfiŋ], *s. Nau:* **1. the o.,** le large; la pleine mer; **in the o.,** au large; dehors. **2. to make, get, an o.,** prendre le large, gagner au large; **to keep an o.,** tenir le large. **3.** *F:* **I have a job in the o.,** j'ai une place en perspective; **a general election is in the o.,** une élection générale approche, est en vue.

offish ['ɔfiʃ], *a. O:* **1.** *F:* (*of pers.*) distant, raide, réservé; (*of manner*) raide, hautain. **2.** *P:* (*of pers.*) mal en train.

offishness ['ɔfiʃnis], *s. F: O:* raideur *f*, réserve *f*, morgue *f*.

off-line ['ɔf'lain], *a.* **1.** *Tp: Tg:* (matériel, etc.) hors circuit. **2.** *Cmptr:* **o.-l. equipment,** matériel périphérique, autonome, non connecté; **o.-l. processing,** exploitation *f* (en mode) autonome; traitement *m* en différé; **o.-l. working, operation,** (i) exploitation (en) autonome; (ii) fonctionnement *m* (en) autonome.

offload ['ɔf'loud], *v.tr.* débarquer (un excédent de marchandises, de voyageurs, etc.); *F:* **he offloads most of his work on his colleagues,** il se décharge de la plupart de son travail sur ses collègues.

off-lying ['ɔflaiiŋ], *a.* (*of island, etc.*) lointain, éloigné.

off-net ['ɔf'net], *a. W.Tel:* (station) hors réseau.

offpeak ['ɔf'pi:k], *a.* **o. hours,** heures creuses, hors pointe; **o. output,** rendement *m* en période de creux; *El:* **o. tariff,** tarif *m* de nuit; *Rail: etc:* **o. fare,** billet *m* à prix réduit.

offprint[1] ['ɔfprint], *s. Typ:* tirage *m* à part; tiré *m* à part.

offprint[2], *v.tr. Typ:* tirer à part.

off-putting ['ɔf'putiŋ], *a.* **1.** (événement) déconcertant, déroutant. **2.** (caractère) rébarbatif, répugnant.

offsaddle ['ɔfsædl]. **1.** *v.tr.* desseller (un cheval); ôter la selle à (un cheval). **2.** *v.i.* (*a*) ôter la selle; desseller; (*b*) descendre de selle; s'arrêter (pour faire étape).

offscourings ['ɔfskauriŋz], *s.pl.* rebut *m*; **the o. of humanity,** la lie du peuple.

offscreen ['ɔfskri:n], *adv. & a. Cin:* **1.** à la cantonade. **2. o., he's a modest man,** dans le privé c'est un type modeste.

offseason ['ɔfsi:zn]. **1.** *s.* morte-saison *f*, *pl.* mortes-saisons. **2.** *adv.* pendant la morte-saison. **3.** *a.* hors-saison; **o. tariff,** tarif *m* hors-saison.

offset[1] ['ɔfset], *s.* **1.** *occ.* (= OUTSET) commencement *m*; **at the o.,** au commencement, au début; **from the o.,** dès le début. **2.** (*a*) *Hort:* rejeton *m*, œilleton *m*, stolon *m*, stolone *f*; *Fig: O:* **o. of a noble house,** rejeton d'une famille noble; (*b*) *Geol:* contrefort *m* (de montagne). **3.** repoussoir *m*; **to serve as an o. to s.o.'s beauty,** faire ressortir la beauté de qn. **4.** (*a*) compensation *f*, dédommagement *m*; **as an o. to my losses,** en compensation de, pour faire contrepoids à, mes pertes; **to be an o. to a fault,** compenser une faute; (*b*) *Book-k:* compensation (d'une écriture). **5.** (*a*) *Arch:* ressaut *m*, saillie *f*, portée *f*; retrait *m* (d'un mur); (*b*) *Mec.E: etc:* désaxage *m*, décalage *m*, déport *m*, déportage *m*, décentrement *m*; **angular o.,** inclinaison *f*; (*c*) rebord *m* (de piston, etc.); bord biseauté (d'une roue, etc.); (*d*) double coude *m*, siphon *m* (d'un tuyau, pour contourner un obstacle). **6.** *Surv:* perpendiculaire *f*; ordonnée *f*. **7.** (*a*) *Typ:* maculage *m*; **o. blanket,** décharge *f*; (*b*) *Phot.Engr:* offset *m*; **deep etched o., intaglio o., o. deep,** offset en creux; **o. deep plate,** plaque *f* d'offset en creux; **printed in o.,** tiré en offset; **flat-bed o. (printing) machine,** machine offset plate; **rotary o. machine,** rotative *f* offset; **o. printing,** tirage *m* par offset; **o. process,** tirage en offset, par report; impression *f* rotocalcographique; offset. **8.** *Nau:* courant *m* en direction du large.

offset[2], *v.* (**offset; -setting**) **1.** *v.tr.* (*a*) compenser, contrebalancer (ses pertes, etc.); (*b*) *Mec.E:* désaxer, décentrer (une roue, etc.); déporter, décaler (un organe); (*c*) faire déborder (une pièce); (*d*) prévoir un dégagement, une courbure, à (un outil, etc.); faire un double coude à (un tuyau); (*e*) *Typ:* imprimer (un document) en offset. **2.** *v.i.* (*a*) *Hort:* (*of plant*) pousser des rejetons; (*b*) *Typ:* faire du maculage; maculer.

offset[3], *a. Mec.E: etc:* **1.** désaxé, déporté; en porte-à-faux; **drive o. to the left,** transmission décalée, déportée, vers la gauche; *I.C.E:* **o. connecting-rod,** bielle déportée. **2.** (coussinet, etc.) désaffleurant.

offshoot ['ɔfʃu:t], *s.* **1.** (*a*) rejeton *m* (d'un arbre, d'une famille); (*b*) *Fig:* **all the offshoots of this policy,** toutes les ramifications de cette politique. **2.** *Geol:* caprice *m* (d'un filon).

offshore ['ɔfʃɔ:r]. **1.** *adv.* vers le large, au large. **2.** *a.* (*a*) du côté de la terre; **o. wind,** vent *m* de terre, d'aval; (*b*) (i) côtier, littoral; **o. bar,** cordon littoral; **o. fishing,** pêche côtière; (ii) éloigné de la côte; en mer; **o. islands,** îles éloignées de la côte; *Petr:* **o. prospecting, drilling,** prospection pétrolière, forage pétrolier, en mer; **o. installations,** installations pétrolières marines; (*c*) **o. purchases,** achats *m* à l'étranger; *U.S:* achats américains d'armement en Europe. **3.** *s. Geol:* avant-plage *f*, *pl.* avant-plages.

offside ['ɔf'said], *adv. & a.* = OFF(-)SIDE *q.v. under* OFF[1] II. 1., III. 1.

offsider [ɔf'saidər], *s. Austr:* **1.** (cheval *m* de) sous-verge *m inv.* **2.** aide *m*, compagnon *m* (d'un ouvrier).

offspring ['ɔfspriŋ], *s.* **1.** *coll.* (*a*) *Nat.Hist:* progéniture *f*, descendance *f*, descendants *mpl*; (*b*) enfants *mpl*; **parents surrounded by their o.,** parents entourés de leurs enfants, *Hum:* par leur progéniture. **2.** (*a*) descendant, rejeton *m*; **the o. of a long line of merchants,** le rejeton d'une longue lignée de négociants; (*b*) **knowledge which is the o. of much research,** science qui est le fruit, le produit, de beaucoup de recherches.

offstage ['ɔf'steidʒ], *adv. & a.* **1.** (parler, fracas, etc.) à la cantonade, derrière la toile. **2. o. he's quite different,** dans sa vie privée il est tout autre; **his life o., his o. life,** sa vie privée. **3.** (*of work, scheming, etc.*) en secret; *Pol:* dans la coulisse.

offstreet ['ɔfstri:t], *a.* **o. parking,** parcage *m*.

offtake ['ɔfteik], *s.* **1.** écoulement *m* (de marchandises, etc.). **2.** *Min:* (i) galerie *f*, (ii) voie *f*, d'écoulement. **3.** *Hyd.E:* prise *f* d'eau (d'un canal dérivé d'une rivière, etc.); dérivation *f*.

off-type ['ɔf'taip], *a. Biol: etc:* aberrant.

offward ['ɔfwəd]. *Nau:* **1.** *adv. also* **offwards** ['ɔfwədz], vers le large; au large. **2.** *s.* côté *m* du large; **to the o.,** au large. **3.** *a.* du (côté du) large.

oflag ['ɔflæg], *s. Mil.Hist:* oflag *m*.

oft [ɔft], *adv. Poet:* souvent; **many a time and o.,** mainte(s) et mainte(s) fois; *A:* souventefois, souventes fois; **o.-told,** raconté maintes fois; **o.-recurring,** revenant fréquemment.

often ['ɔf(t)n], *adv.* souvent, fréquemment, mainte(s) fois; **o. and o.,** maintes et maintes fois; **I see him o., I o. see him,** je le vois souvent; **I don't see him very o. now,** je ne le vois plus guère; **I o. forget,** il m'arrive souvent d'oublier; **how o.?** (i) combien de fois? (ii) tous les combien? **how o. do you see him?** tous les combien le voyez-vous? **how o. do the buses run?** il y a un autobus tous les combien? *F:* **how o. have I told you!** que de fois, combien de fois, ne vous l'ai-je pas dit! **as o. as I saw him,** toutes les fois, chaque fois, que je l'ai vu; **as o. as not, more o. than not,** assez souvent, le plus souvent; **every so o.,** de temps en temps; de temps à autre; parfois; **you cannot do it too o.,** on ne peut trop le faire; **it cannot be too o. repeated,** on ne saurait trop le répéter; **once too o.,** une fois de trop.

oftentimes ['ɔf(ə)ntaimz], **oft-times** ['ɔft(t)aimz], *adv. A: & Poet:* souvent; *A:* souventefois.

ogam ['ɔgəm], *s. Pal:* = OGHAM.

Ogcocephalidae [ɔgkouse'fælidi:], *s.pl. Ich:* ogcocéphalidés *m*.

ogee ['oudʒi:], *s. Arch:* **o. (moulding),** cimaise *f*, talon *m*; **o. arch,** arc *m* en accolade; *Tls:* **o. plane,** bouvement *m*, doucine *f*.

ogham ['ɔgəm], *s. Pal:* **o. (alphabet),** og(h)am *m*.

ogival [ou'dʒaiv(ə)l], *a. Arch:* ogival, -aux; **o. bridge,** pont *m* en dos d'âne.

ogive ['oudʒaiv], *s. Arch:* ogive *f*.

ogle[1] ['ougl], *s.* œillade (amoureuse); lorgnade *f*.

ogle[2]. **1.** *v.tr.* lorgner, guigner (qn); lancer des œillades à (qn); faire les yeux doux à (qn); reluquer (qn); faire des yeux en coulisse à (qn); jeter à (qn) un regard en coulisse; *P:* faire de l'œil à (qn). **2.** *v.i.* jouer de la prunelle; lancer des œillades.

ogler ['ouglər], *s.* lorgneur, -euse; reluqueur, -euse.

ogling[1] ['oupliŋ], *a.* qui lorgne; lorgnant.

ogling[2], *s.* lorgnerie *f*; yeux doux; regards *mpl* en coulisse.

Ogpu ['ɔgpu:], *s. Russian Hist:* (le) Guépéou.

ogre, *f.* **ogress** ['ougər, -gris], *s.* **1.** ogre, *f.* ogresse; *Fig:* **the concierge was an old ogress,** la concierge était une vieille ogresse, mégère. **2.** *Her:* **ogress,** tourteau *m* de sable.

ogr(e)ish ['oug(ə)riʃ], *a.* **1.** qui ressemble à un ogre, une ogresse. **2. o. mouth,** bouche d'ogre.

Ogygia [ou'dʒidʒiə], *Pr.n. Gr.Myth:* (l'île *f* d')Ogygie *f*.

Ogygian [ou'dʒidʒiən]. *Gr.Myth:* **1.** *a.* ogygien. **2.** *s.* Ogygien, -ienne.

oh [ou], *int.* (*expressing surprise, pain, etc.*) ô, oh; **oh how tired I am!** ah! que je suis fatigué! **oh for a glass of water!** que ne donnerais-je pas pour un verre d'eau! **oh to be in England!** que ne suis-je en Angleterre! si seulement j'étais en Angleterre!

oh-be-joyful ['oubi'dʒɔif(u)l], *s. P:* bouteille *f* de rhum.

Ohm [oum]. **1.** *Pr.n.* Ohm; *Ph:* **O.'s law,** la loi d'Ohm. **2.** *s. El:* **ohm,** ohm *m*; **legal, Congress, o.,** ohm légal; **British Association o.,** ohm pratique; **acoustic o.,** ohm acoustique.

ohmic ['oumik], *a. El:* (mesure, chute, etc.) ohmique.

ohmmeter ['oummi:tər], *s. El:* ohmmètre *m*.

oho [ou'hou], *int.* oh! ah! ho, ho!

oh yes ['ou'jes], *int.* = OYEZ.

oidiomycosis [ouidioumai'kousis], *s. Med: Vet:* oïdiomycose *f*.

oidium, *pl.* **-ia** [ou'idiəm, -iə], *s. Fung: Vit:* oïdium *m*.

oil[1] [ɔil], *s.* huile *f*. **1.** (*a*) **vegetable o.,** huile végétale; **olive o.,** huile d'olive; **walnut o.,** huile de noix; **groundnut o.,** huile d'arachide; **linseed o.,** huile (de graine) de lin; **edible o., cooking o.,** huile comestible, de cuisine; **to cook in, with, o.,** faire la cuisine à l'huile; **frying o.,** huile à friture; **fried in o.,** frit à l'huile; (*b*) *Paint: Art:* **o. paint,** peinture *f* à l'huile; **boiled, raw, (linseed) o.,** huile (de lin) cuite, crue; **blown o., condensed o.,** huile soufflée; **drying o.,** huile siccative; siccatif *m*; **tung o., China wood o.,** huile de Canton; **to paint in oils,** peindre à l'huile; **o. painting,** peinture *f* à l'huile; *F:* **she's no o. painting,** ce n'est pas une Vénus; (*c*) *Ecc:* **holy o.,** les saintes huiles (pour l'extrême onction, etc.); (*d*) *Fig:* **to burn the midnight o.,** travailler, veiller, fort avant dans la nuit; **it smells of the midnight o.,** cela sent l'huile, l'étude, l'effort; **to add o. to the flames,** jeter de l'huile sur le feu; **to pour o. on troubled waters,** calmer la tempête; apaiser les esprits; apaiser le tollé général par des paroles de conciliation; (*e*) *Bot:* **o. palm, o. tree,** éléis *m* de Guinée, palmier *m* à l'huile; **o. tree,** (i) ricin commun; (ii) ricin d'Amérique; (iii) bassie *f* à longues feuilles; **o. nut,** (i) graine *f* de ricin; (ii) graine de l'éléis de Guinée; (iii) noix *f* du noyer cendré; **o. poppy,** œillette *f*. **2.** (*a*) **animal o.,** huile animale; **whale o.,** huile de baleine; **sperm o.,** huile de blanc de baleine; **cod-liver o.,** huile de foie de morue; (*b*) *Orn:* **o. gland,** glande uropygienne; (*c*) *Ent:* **o. beetle,** méloé *m*. **3.** (*a*) **mineral o.,** huile minérale; pétrole *m*; **o. prospecting,** prospection *f* pétrolifère; **o. concession,** concession *f* pétrolifère; **crude o.,** pétrole brut; **heavy o.,** (i) huile épaisse, lourde; (ii) (*distilled from tar*) oléonaphte *m*; **fuel o.,** (i) pétrole; (ii) mazout *m*; **o. heating,** chauffage *m* au mazout; **o. refinery,** raffinerie *f* à pétrole; **o. rig,** appareil *m* de sondage; installation *f* de forage; (*offshore*) île *f* de forage; barge *f*; **o. ring,** cartel *m* du pétrole, d'exploitants de gisements pétrolifères; **o. well,** puits *m* pétrolifère; puits à, de, pétrole; *Geol:* **o. sand,** sable *m*, grès *m*, pétrolifère; **o. shale,** schiste bitumineux; **o. lens,** lentille *f* de sable pétrolifère; **o. line,** canalisation *f* de pétrole; oléoduc *m*; **o. gas,** gaz *m* de pétrole; **o. tanker,** pétrolier *m*; (*b*) *St.Exch:* **o. shares, oils,** valeurs *f* pétrolières; pétroles; (*c*) *Tchn:* **lubricating o., machine o.,** huile à graisser, de graissage; **lamp o.,** (i) huile d'éclairage, lampante; (ii) pétrole lampant; **stock o.,** huile de base; *Mec.E: Mch: etc:* **cutting o.,** huile de coupe; **machine o., motor o.,** huile à machine, à moteur; **white o.,** huile blanche; **o. box,** (i) boîte *f*, (ii) godet *m*, à huile, à graisse; **o. brush,** balai graisseur; **o. buffer,** amortisseur *m* hydraulique; **o. catcher,** puisoir *m* à huile, cuiller *f* de graissage (de la bielle); arrêt *m* d'huile; **o. cleaner,** épurateur *m* d'huile; **o. cock,** robinet *m* de graissage; robinet graisseur; **o. cooling,** refroidissement *m* par huile; **o. cup,** (i) godet graisseur, à huile; (ii) collecteur *m* d'huile; **o. duct,** tube *m* de graissage; conduite *f* d'huile; **o. engine,** moteur *m* à pétrole; **heavy o. engine,** moteur à huile lourde; **o. feeder,** burette *f* à huile; alimenteur *m* à huile; **force-feed o. feeder,** burette *f* à piston; **o. filter, strainer,** filtre *m* à huile; **o. firing,** chauffe *f* au mazout; **o. gauge,** jauge *f*, manomètre *m*, d'huile; (jauge de) niveau *m* d'huile; **o. governor,** régulateur *m* d'huile; **o. groove, o. way,** rainure *f*, saignée *f*, de graissage; **o. grooves of a bearing,** pattes *f* d'araignée d'un palier graisseur; **o. guard,** pare-gouttes *m inv*, garde-gouttes *m inv*; **o. hardening,** trempe *f* à l'huile; huilage *m*; **o. hole,** trou *m* de graissage; lumière *f* (de graissage); **o. immersion,** immersion *f* dans l'huile; **o.-immersion lens, objective,** objectif *m* (de microscope) à immersion; **o. inlet,** arrivée *f*, entrée *f*, d'huile; **o. line,** canalisation *f*, conduite *f*, d'huile; **o. mist,** brouillard *m* d'huile; **o. pan,** poche *f* d'huile, à huile; carter *m* à huile; fond *m*, cuvette *f*, de carter; auge *f* de graissage; **o. pump,** pompe *f* à huile; **o. ring,** anneau graisseur; **o. screen,** filtre *m* à huile; **o. seal,** (i) disque *m* de retenue d'huile; (ii) joint *m* d'huile; **o. separator,** (i) *Aut: etc:* déshuileur *m*; épurateur *m*, séparateur *m*, d'huile; (ii) *Mch:* dégraisseur *m*, déshuileur *m*, de vapeur; **o. spray,** brouillard *m* d'huile; **o. sump,** carter *m* à huile; puisard *m* (d'huile); **o. tank,** (i) réservoir *m* d'huile; (ii) caisse *f*, soute *f*, à pétrole; **o. tanning,** tannage *m* à huile; chamoisage *m*; **o. tempering,** trempe à huile; huilage; **o. tracks,** araignée *f* (d'un palier); **o. well,** carter *m* à huile; puisard *m* (d'huile); *El:* **o. insulation,** isolation *f* à l'huile; **o. switch,** commutateur *m* à l'huile; disjoncteur *m* à bain d'huile. **4. essential o.,** huile essentielle; essence *f*; **o. of cloves,** essence de girofle; **o. of lavender,** essence de lavande; **o. of lemons,** (essence de) citron *m*. **5.** *A:* **o. of vitriol,** (huile de) vitriol *m*.

oil[2]. **1.** *v.tr.* (*a*) huiler, graisser, lubrifier (une machine, etc.); **to o. the wheels,** graisser les roues, *F:* faciliter les choses; **to o. one's tongue,** user de flatteries, parler d'un ton mielleux; **to o. s.o.'s hand, s.o.'s palm,** *NAm:* **to o. s.o.,** graisser la patte à qn; (*b*) **to o. a pool (against mosquitoes),** pétroler une mare; (*c*) huiler (la toile, etc.); (*d*) *Tex:* ensimer (la laine); (*e*) fondre (le beurre, etc.). **2.** *v.i.* (*a*) (*of butter, etc.*) devenir huileux; (*b*) *Nau:* faire le plein de mazout. **3. to o. up,** (i) *v.tr.* encrasser (d'huile); (ii) *v.i.* (*of sparking plug, etc.*) s'encrasser (d'huile).

oil-arresting ['ɔilərestiŋ], *a.* qui arrête l'huile; étanche à l'huile; *I.C.E:* **o.-a. ring,** bague *f* gratte-huile *inv* (d'un moteur diesel, etc.).

oil-bearing ['ɔilbɛəriŋ], *a.* **1.** *Bot:* (*of plant*) oléagineux, oléifère. **2.** *Geol:* (*of shade, etc.*) pétrolifère.

oilbird ['ɔilbə:d], *s. Orn:* guacharo *m*.

oilcake ['ɔilkeik], *s.* (*a*) tourteau *m* de lin; nougat *m* (pour bestiaux); (*b*) tourte *f* pour engrais.

oilcan ['ɔilkæn], *s.* **1.** (*a*) (i) bidon *m*, (ii) broc *m*, à huile; (*b*) estagnon *m* à huile. **2.** *Tls:* burette *f* à huile; **o. with a spring bottom,** burette à fond cloquant; **force-feed o.,** burette à pompe, à piston.

oilcloth ['ɔilklɔθ], *s.* **1.** (*for waterproofs, etc.*) tissu huilé. **2.** (*for covering tables, etc.*) toile cirée. **3.** (*floor-covering*) linoléum imprimé.

oil-cooled ['ɔil'ku:ld], *a.* refroidi par l'huile.

oiled [ɔild], *a.* huilé; (*a*) graissé; **to keep one's tools slightly o.,** tenir ses outils un peu gras; *F:* **well-o. tongue,** langue bien pendue; *P:* **to be well o.,** être un peu parti, (un peu) éméché; (*b*) **o. silk,** taffetas *m* imperméable; **o. paper,** papier imprégné d'huile; papier huilé.

oiler ['ɔilər], *s.* **1.** (*pers.*) (*a*) graisseur *m*; (*b*) *P: O:* individu mielleux. **2.** (*a*) burette *f* à huile; burette de graissage; graisseur *m*; **o. with a spring bottom,** burette à fond cloquant; **force-feed o.,** burette à pompe, à piston; (*b*) (*part of machine*) (i) graisseur; **plunger o.,** graisseur à plongeur; **ring o.,** graisseur à bague; **wick o.,** graisseur à mèche, (ii) godet graisseur, de graissage. **3.** *Nau:* (*a*) (navire) pétrolier (*m*); (*b*) navire chauffant (i) au mazout, (ii) au pétrole. **4.** *F:* **oilers,** blouse *f* et pantalon *m* en toile huilée; cirage *m*.

Oïleus [ou'i:ljəs], *Pr.n.m. Gr.Lit:* Oïlée.

oilfield ['ɔilfi:ld], *s.* grisement *m*, champ *m*, pétrolifère.

oil-filled ['ɔil'fild], *a. El:* **o.-f. cable,** câble *m* à huile fluide.

oil-fired ['ɔilfaiəd], *a.* (*of boiler, etc.*) chauffé (i) au pétrole, (ii) au mazout; **o.-f. central heating,** chauffage (central) au mazout.

oil-fuelled ['ɔilfjuəld], *a.* (*of ship*) chauffant, qui chauffe, (i) au pétrole, (ii) au mazout.

oil-immersed ['ɔili'mə:st], *a.* à bain d'huile.

oiliness ['ɔilinis], *s.* **1.** état graisseux; aspect graisseux; onctuosité *f* (de qch.). **2.** *Pej:* onctuosité (de qn).

oiling ['ɔiliŋ], *s.* **1.** (*a*) graissage *m*, huilement *m*, huilage *m*, lubrification *f* (d'un mécanisme, etc.); **o. ring, sleeve,** bague *f*, douille *f*, de graissage; (*b*) enduisage *m* (d'un nageur, etc.) de graisse; *A:* onction *f* (d'un athlète grec). **2.** *Hyg:* pétrolage *m* (d'une mare, etc.). **3.** *Tex:* ensimage *m* (de la laine). **4. oiling up,** encrassement *m* (d'une bougie d'allumage, etc.).

oil-insulated ['ɔil'insjuleitid], *a. El:* isolé à l'huile.

oilless ['ɔillis], *a.* sans huile; (coussinet) autolubrifiant.

oilman, *pl.* **-men** ['ɔilmən], *s.m.* **1.** (*a*) huilier, marchand d'huile; (*b*) marchand de couleurs; droguiste. **2.** graisseur (de machines, etc.). **3.** (expert) pétrolier; **one of the big oilmen,** un des rois du pétrole.

oilmeal ['ɔilmi:l], *s. Husb:* tourteau moulu.

oilpaper ['ɔilpeipər], *s.* papier à calquer; papier huilé.

oil-producing ['ɔilprədju:siŋ], *a.* **1.** (*of plant*) oléifère; (*of substance, etc.*) oléifiant. **2.** (*of shale, etc.*) pétrolifère; **o.-p. countries,** pays producteurs de pétrole.

oilseed ['ɔilsi:d], *s.* **1.** (*a*) graine *f* de lin; (*b*) semence *f* de ricin. **2.** graine oléagineuse; oléagineux *m*.

oilskin ['ɔilskin], *s.* **1.** toile cirée, vernie, huilée. **2.** (*garment*) ciré *m*, caban *m* (de matelot); **(suit of) oilskins,** cirage *m*.

oil-soluble ['ɔil'sɔljubl], *a.* soluble dans l'huile, dans la graisse; oléosoluble, liposoluble.

oilstone[1] ['ɔilstoun], *s. Tls:* pierre *f*, queue *f*, à huile (pour affûter); pierre à morfiler, à repasser; affiloir *m*, affiloire *f*.

oilstone[2], *v.tr.* passer (un outil) à la pierre à huile.

oil-tempered ['ɔiltempəd], *a. Metall:* trempé à huile.

oiltight ['ɔiltait], *a.* (*a*) étanche à l'huile, à la graisse; (ii) étanche au pétrole.

oily ['ɔili], *a.* **1.** huileux; gras, *f.* grasse; graisseux; (papier) imprégné d'huile. **2.** *F:* (*of manner, etc.*) onctueux; **o. voice,** voix grasse; **o.(-tongued) hypocrite,** hypocrite mielleux, patelin.

oil-yielding ['ɔilji:ldiŋ], *a.* = OIL-BEARING.

oink[1] [ɔiŋk], *s.* grognement *m* (d'un cochon).

oink[2], *v.i.* (*of pig*) grogner.

ointment ['ɔintmənt], *s.* onguent *m*, pommade *f*; *Pharm:* **blue, mercurial, o.,** onguent mercuriel double; onguent gris, napolitain; **diachylon o.,** onguent diachylon; **iodine o.,** pommade d'iode; **zinc o.,** pommade à l'oxyde de zinc; **sulphur o.,** pommade soufrée; *Fig:* **a fly in the o.,** une ombre au tableau; un cheveu (sur la soupe).

O.K.[1], **okay**[1] ['ou'kei]. *F:* **1.** *a.* correct, exact: **the totals are O.K.,** les sommes sont exactes; **everything is O.K.,** tout est en règle; **that's O.K. by me,** je n'y vois pas d'inconvénient; d'accord! **are you O.K.?** ça va? **O.K.!** très bien! parfait! ça va! bon! d'accord! ça colle! (*marked on document, etc.*) O.K., vu et approuvé; *Typ:* (*of proof*) bon à tirer. **2.** *s.* **to give one's O.K. to sth.,** passer, approuver (une commande, etc.); contresigner, parafer (un ordre, etc.); *Typ:* donner le bon à tirer à (une épreuve); **to give the O.K.,** donner le feu vert; **we can do nothing without the O.K.,** nous ne pouvons rien faire sans le oui, sans le feu vert.

O.K.[2] **(O.K.'d), okay**[2], *v.tr. F:* passer, approuver (une commande); contresigner, parafer (un ordre); *Typ:* donner le bon à tirer à (une épreuve).

okapi [ə'kɑ:pi], *s. Z:* okapi *m*.

oke [ouk], *int. P:* d'accord!

okenite ['oukənait], *s. Miner:* okénite *f*.

okey-doke, okey-dokey, okie-doke, okie-dokey [ouki'douk(i)], *int. P:* ça va! d'accord!

okonite ['oukənait], *s. El:* okonite *f*.

okra ['ɔkrə], *s. Bot:* (*a*) okra *m*; (*b*) gombo *m*, ketmie *f* comestible.

Olacaceae [oulə'keisii:], *s.pl. Bot:* olacacées *f*.

old [ould], *a.* **1.** (*a*) (*aged*) vieux; (*in sing. before a qualified noun beginning with a vowel or h "mute"*) vieil *or* vieux: *f.* vieille; *pl.* vieux, *f.* vieilles; âgé; **my o. father, my o. friend,** mon vieux père; mon vieil, vieux, ami; **o. in body, young in mind,** vieux de corps, jeune d'esprit; **a man is as o. as he feels,** on a l'âge de ses artères; **to be growing, getting, o.,** prendre de l'âge; avancer en âge; tirer sur l'âge; se faire vieux, vieille; vieillir; **to grow older,** vieillir; devenir vieux, vieille; **the way she dresses makes her look o.,** sa façon de s'habiller la vieillit; **she dresses too o. for her age,** elle s'habille trop vieux pour son âge; *F:* **he's as o. as Methuselah,** il est vieux comme Mathusalem, comme Hérode; **an o. man,** un homme âgé, un vieillard; **he's an o. man,** il est vieux; **the O. Man of the Mountains,** le Vieux de la Montagne; **he's like the o. man of the sea,** c'est un crampon (allusion à l'histoire de Sindbad le

Marin); *Th:* **to play o. men,** jouer les vieillards, les grimes *m*; *s.a.* 5(*b*); **an o. woman,** une vieille femme; *F:* une vieille; **o. John,** le père Jean; **o. Mrs. Brown,** (i) la vieille Madame Brown; *F:* la mère Brown; (ii) Madame Brown mère; **o. people, old folk(s),** les vieux; *F:* **us o. 'uns,** nous autres anciens; *Prov:* **there's nothing like, it takes, the o. horse for the hard road,** il n'est chasse que de vieux chiens; *s.pl.* **o. and young,** grands et petits; **o. age,** la vieillesse; **to die at a good o. age,** mourir à un grand âge, à un âge avancé, à un bel âge; **to live to (an) o. age, to live to be o.,** vivre vieux, vieille; **he's saving for his o. age,** il économise pour ses vieux jours; **in his older days,** (i) à un âge plus mûr; (ii) au déclin de sa vie; (*b*) (*of thg.*) **o. clothes,** vieux habits; **o. clothes man, woman,** marchand, -ande, d'habits d'occasion; fripier, -ière; **o. clothes shop,** boutique *f* d'habits d'occasion; friperie *f*; **o. bread,** pain rassis; **o. wine,** vin vieux. **2. how o. are you?** quel âge avez-vous? **how o. would you take him to be?** quel âge lui donnez-vous? **the oldest of the tribe,** l'aîné, -ée, de la tribu; **to be five years o.,** avoir cinq ans; être âgé de cinq ans; **he is older than I am,** il est plus âgé que moi; il est mon aîné; **he looks five years older,** il a, est, vieilli de cinq ans; **to be ten years older than one's wife,** avoir dix ans de plus que, être plus âgé de dix ans que, sa femme; **at six years o. he was playing the organ in public,** à l'âge de six ans il tenait l'orgue en public; **he left Paris at ten years o.,** il a quitté Paris à dix ans; **a two-year-o. child,** *s. F:* **a two-year-o.,** un enfant (âgé) de deux ans; *Turf:* **two-year-o., three-year-o.,** cheval, poulain *m*, pouliche *f*, de deux ans, de trois ans; **to be o. enough to do sth.,** être d'âge à faire qch.; être en âge de faire qch.; être assez grand pour faire qch.; **when you are o. enough,** quand tu seras grand; **he is o. enough to behave better,** il est en âge de, il est assez âgé pour, se conduire mieux; **he has an o. head on young shoulders,** il est sérieux pour son âge; **news a week o.,** nouvelles vieilles d'une semaine. **3.** (*a*) (*long-established*) vieux, ancien; **an o. family,** une famille de vieille souche; **an o. Norfolk family,** une vieille famille du Norfolk; **a very o. family,** une famille très ancienne; **o. debt,** dette *f* d'ancienne date; **this theory agrees with the older one,** cette théorie est d'accord avec son aînée; **he's an o. friend of mine,** c'est un de mes vieux amis; **an o. story,** une vieille histoire; **that's o. stuff,** c'est vieux; **that's an o. dodge,** c'est un coup classique; **that's as o. as the hills,** c'est vieux comme le monde, comme le Pont-Neuf, comme Hérode, comme les rues; **it's as o. as Adam,** cela remonte au déluge; (*b*) (*experienced*) vieux; **o. campaigner,** vieux soldat, vieux brisquard; **o. hand,** ouvrier expérimenté; *Nau: etc:* vétéran *m*; **to be an o. hand at sth.,** avoir le coup pour faire qch.; **he's an o. hand (at it),** il est vieux dans ce métier; il n'est pas novice; il en a l'expérience; il n'en est pas à son coup d'essai; il connaît le métier, *F:* le fourbi; **he's too o. a bird to be caught like that,** il est trop malin pour s'y laisser prendre; *A:* **he was o. in crime, in sin,** c'était un criminel de longue date, un pécheur endurci; (*c*) **to travel over o. ground,** revenir sur un terrain déjà parcouru. **4.** (*former*) ancien; (*a*) **o. boy, girl, pupil, scholar,** ancien élève, ancienne élève; **the o.-boy net(work)** = la franc-maçonnerie des grandes écoles; **o. customs,** anciennes coutumes; **we did so in the o. days,** nous l'avons fait dans notre temps; **o. memories,** (i) souvenirs *m* du temps passé; (ii) souvenirs de jeunesse; *Fin:* **one new share for two o. ones,** une nouvelle action pour deux anciennes; (*b*) **the O. World,** l'ancien monde; **o. English, French,** l'ancien anglais, français; **the O. Country,** la mère-patrie; **the O. Testament,** l'Ancien Testament; *B:* **to put off the o. man,** dépouiller le vieil homme. **5.** *F:* (*a*) (*with* **any**) **you can dress any o. how,** vous pouvez vous mettre n'importe comment; **take any o. hat,** prenez un chapeau quelconque; **any o. thing,** la première chose venue; n'importe quoi; **come any o. time,** venez quand vous voudrez; (*b*) **o. man, chap, fellow, boy, etc.,** mon vieux, mon pote; **dear, good, o. Martin,** ce bon vieux Martin; *NAm:* **o. man Martin,** le père Martin; *F:* **the o. man,** (i) papa; (ii) le patron; (iii) *Nau:* le capitaine; *P:* le capiston, le pacha; (iv) *Mil:* le colonel; *P:* le colon, le colo; *P:* **my o. man,** mon homme; **the o. woman, lady,** ma femme; *P:* la bourgeoise; ma moitié; **the o. 'un,** l'ancien; (*c*) *F:* **your o. book,** ton bouquin; **your o. pipe,** ta bouffarde; **your o. bike,** ton clou; **the o. school,** le bahut. **6. of o.:** (*a*) *adj.phr.* ancien, d'autrefois; *Lit:* **in the days of o.,** autrefois, au temps jadis; du temps que Berthe filait; **the knights of o.,** les chevaliers de jadis; (*b*) *adv.phr.* (i) jadis, autrefois; (ii) **I know him of o.,** je le connais depuis longtemps; il y a belle lurette que je le connais.

olden[1] ['ouldən], *a. Lit: & Poet:* **in o. time(s),** au temps jadis; autrefois; du temps que Berthe filait; **cities of o. time,** villes antiques; **men of o. times,** hommes d'autrefois.

olden[2], *v.i.* vieillir.

Oldenburg ['ould(ə)nbə:g]. *Pr.n. Geog:* Oldenbourg.

Oldenburger ['ould(ə)nbə:gər]. *Geog:* (*a*) *a.* oldenbourgeois; (*b*) *s.* Oldenbourgeois, -oise.

old-established ['ouldis'tæbliʃt], *a.* ancien; établi depuis longtemps.

olde-worlde ['ouldi'wə:ldi], *a.* (maison, village, etc.) qui a un aspect factice d'antan.

oldfashioned [ould'fæʃ(ə)nd]. **1.** *a.* (*a*) (*of dress, hat, etc.*) (i) à la vieille mode; à l'ancienne mode; (ii) démodé; passé de mode; suranné, antique; **o.-f. rifle,** fusil vieux modèle; **o.-f. Christmas,** Noël à l'ancienne mode; **a sweet o.-f. atmosphere,** une atmosphère doucement surannée; (*b*) (i) (*of pers.*) partisan, -ane, des anciens usages; de la vieille roche; (*of manner, etc.*) de l'ancien temps; (ii) (*of ideas, etc.*) arriéré, vieillot, vieux jeu; **I am very o.-f.,** je suis très vieux jeu; (*c*) *Dial: & F:* **o.-f. child,** enfant précoce; **o.-f. look,** regard *m* de travers. **2.** *s.* cocktail composé de whisky, d'amers, de sucre et d'eau de seltz.

oldfashionedness ['ould'fæʃ(ə)ndnis], *s.* **1.** caractère démodé, suranné (d'une installation, etc.). **2.** caractère arriéré, vieux jeu (de qn, des idées).

old-gentlemanly ['ould'dʒentlmənli], *a.* (politesse, conduite, etc.) d'un gentleman de la vieille roche.

oldhamite ['ouldəmait], *s. Miner:* oldhamite *f*.

oldie ['ouldi], *s. F:* **1.** vieillard, -arde. **2.** vieillerie *f*, antiquaille *f*; *NAm:* ancienne chanson populaire.

oldish ['ouldiʃ], *a.* vieillot, -otte; assez vieux, assez vieille; assez ancien.

old-maidish ['ould'meidiʃ], *a.* (*a*) (façons, etc.) de vieille fille; (*b*) qui a des pruderies, des manies de vieille fille; **he, she, is rather o.-m.,** il, elle, est un peu collet monté.

old man ['ould'mæn], *s.* **1.** (*pers.*) *see* **old. 2.** *Bot:* (*a*) aurone *f*, citronelle *f*; (*b*) **o. m.'s beard,** (clématite *f*) vigne blanche; vigne de Salomon; viorne *f* des pauvres; herbe *f* aux gueux; berceau *m* de la Vierge. **3.** *Const:* (*in excavating*) témoin *m*, dame *f*. **4.** *Z: Austr:* kangourou *m*.

old-standing ['ould'stændiŋ], *a.* ancien; (dette, etc.) d'ancienne date.

oldster ['ouldstər], *s. F:* **1.** vieillard *m*; vieux, *f.* vieille; **to be an o.,** n'être plus jeune. **2.** *Navy:* aspirant *m* qui a quatre ans de service.

old-style ['ould'stail], *a.* à l'ancienne mode; *Hist:* **the o.-s. calendar,** le calendrier vieux style, ancien style; le vieux calendrier.

old-time ['ould'taim], *a.* du temps jadis; **o.-t. songs,** chants *m* d'autrefois; **o.-t. ceremonial,** antique cérémonial *m*; **o.-t. dances,** danses *f* du bon vieux temps.

old-timer ['ould'taimər], *s.* vieux *m* (de la vieille); ancien *m*; vieux copain; (un) qui a passé par là.

oldwife, *pl.* **-wives** [ould'waif, -waivz], *s. Ich:* (*a*) brême *f* de mer, des rochers; (*b*) baliste *f*; arbalétrier *m*.

old-womanish ['ould'wumәniʃ], *a.* (opinions, etc.) de vieille femme; **he's very o.-w.,** il ressemble à une vieille femme.

old-world ['ould'wə:ld], *a.* **1.** (*a*) des temps anciens, antiques; de l'ancien temps; (*b*) de l'ancien monde opposé (i) au monde moderne, (ii) à l'Amérique; *Z:* **the O.-W. monkeys,** les singes de l'ancien monde. **2.** = OLD-TIME; **o.-w. appearance,** aspect *m* d'antan; **o.-w. village,** village qui n'a pas changé au cours des siècles.

oldy ['ouldi], *s.* = OLDIE.

Oleaceae [ouli'eisii:], *s.pl. Bot:* oléacées *f*.

oleaceous [ouli'eiʃəs], *a. Bot:* oléacé.

oleaginous [ouli'ædʒinəs], *a.* **1.** (*of liquid, plant, etc.*) oléagineux, huileux. **2.** *F:* (*of manner, etc.*) onctueux.

oleander [ouli'ændər], *s. Bot:* oléandre *m*; laurier-rose *m*, *pl.* lauriers-rose(s).

oleandomycin [ouliændou'maisin], *s. Med:* oléandomycine *f*.

oleandrin [ouli'ændrin], *s. Ch:* oléandrine *f*.

oleaster [ouli'æstər], *s. Bot:* oléastre *m*; olivier *m* sauvage.

oleate ['oulieit], *s. Ch: Pharm:* oléate *m*.

olecranal [ouli'kreinl], **olecranian** [ouli'kreiniən], *a. Anat:* olécrânien.

olecranon [ouli'kreinən], *s. Anat:* olécrâne *m*.

olefiant [ouli'faiənt], *a. Ch: A:* (gaz) oléfiant.

olefin ['oulifin], **olefine** ['oulifi:n], *s. Ch:* oléfine *m*.

olefinic [ouli'finik], *a. Ch:* oléfinique; **o. content,** teneur *f* en oléfines.

oleic [ou'li:ik], *a. Ch:* (acide, éther) oléique.

oleiculture ['ouliikʌltʃər], *s.* oléiculture *f*.

oleiferous [ouli'ifərəs], *a.* oléifère, oléagineux.

olein ['ouliin], *s. Ch:* oléine *f*; huile *f* de suif; huile absolue (de Braconnot).

olenellus [ouli'neləs], *s. Paleont:* olénellus *m*.

olenid ['oulinid], *s. Paleont:* olenus *m*.

Olenidae ['oulinidi:], *s.pl. Paleont:* olénidés *m*.

olenus [ou'li:nəs], *s. Paleont:* olenus *m*.

oleo- ['ouliou, ouli'ɔ], *comb.fm.* oléo-.

oleo ['ouliou], *s. F:* **1.** *Lith:* oléographie *f*. **2.** *NAm:* oléomargarine *f*.

oleobrom process ['ouliou'brɔm'prousez], *s. Phot:* oléobromie *f*; (procédé *m*) bromoïl (*m*).

oleocalcareous [oulioukæl'kɛəriəs], *a.* oléocalcaire.

oleo gear ['ouliou'giər], *s.* **1.** *Av:* = OLEO STRUT. **2.** *Mec.E:* amortisseur *m* hydraulique.

oleograph ['ouliougræf], *s. Lith:* oléographie *f*.

oleographer [ouli'ɔgrəfər], *s. Lith:* oléographe *mf*.

oleographic [ouliou'græfik], *a. Lith:* oléographique.

oleography [ouli'ɔgrəfi], *s. Lith:* oléographie *f*.

oleo leg ['ouliou'leg], *s.* = OLEO STRUT.

oleomargaric [oulioumɑ:'gærik], *a. Ch:* oléomargarique.

oleomargarine ['oulioumɑ:dʒə'ri:n, -'gəri:n], *s.* oléomargarine *f*.

oleometer [ouli'ɔmitər], *s. Ph: Ind:* oléomètre *m*.

oleophosphoric ['ouliоufɔs'fɔrik], *a. Ch:* oléophosphorique.

oleorefractometer ['ouliourifræk'tɔmitər], *s. Ph:* oléoréfractomètre *m*.

oleoresin [ouliou'rezin], *s. Ch: Ind:* oléorésine *f*.

oleoresinous [ouliou'rezinəs], *a. Ch:* oléorésineux.

oleosaccharum [ouliou'sækərəm], *s. Pharm:* oléosaccharure *m*.

oleo strut ['ouliou'strʌt], *s. Av: etc:* jambe *f* à amortisseur hydraulique, jambe oléopneumatique (de roue d'atterrissage, etc.).

oleothorax ['ouliou'θɔ:ræks], *s. Med:* oléothorax *m*.

oleraceous [ɔlə'reiʃəs], *a. Bot:* oléracé.

olericulture [ɔ'lerikʌltʃər], *s.* culture *f* des plantes potagères.

oleum ['ouliəm], *s. Ch:* oléum *m*.

olfaction [ɔl'fækʃ(ə)n], *s. Physiol:* olfaction *f*.

olfactive [ɔl'fæktiv], *a.* olfactif.

olfactometer [ɔlfæk'tɔmitər], *s.* olfactomètre *m*.

olfactometric [ɔlfæktə'metrik], *a.* olfactométrique.

olfactometry [ɔlfæk'tɔmitri], *s.* olfactométrie *f*.

olfactory [ɔl'fæktəri]. **1.** *a.* (bulbe, nerf, etc.) olfactif. **2.** *s.* organe olfactif.

olibanum [ɔ'libənəm], *s.* oliban *m*; encens *m* mâle.

olig(a)emia [ɔli'gi:miə], *s. Med:* oligohémie *f*.

oligarch ['ɔligɑ:k], *s.* oligarque *m*.

oligarchic(al) [ɔli'gɑ:kik(l)], *a.* oligarchique.

oligarchy ['ɔligɑ:ki], *s.* oligarchie *f*.

oligist ['ɔlidʒist], *s. Miner:* **o. (iron),** (fer *m*) oligiste (*m*); écume *f* de fer.

olig(o)- ['ɔlig(ou), -gɔ], *comb.fm.* olig(o)-.

oligocarpous [ɔligou'kɑ:pəs], *a. Bot:* oligocarpe.

Oligocene ['ɔligousi:n], *a. & s. Geol:* oligocène (*m*).

Oligochaeta [ɔligou'ki:tə], *s.pl. Ann:* oligochètes *m*.

oligoclase ['ɔligoukleis], *s. Miner:* oligoclase *f*.

oligodendroglia [ɔligouden'drɔgliə], *s. Anat:* oligodendroglie *f*.

oligodipsia [ɔligou'dipsiə], *s. Med:* oligodipsie *f*.

oligodynamic [ɔligoudai'næmik], *a. Bio-Ch:* oligodynamique.

oligohaemia [ɔligou'hi:miə], *s. Med:* oligohémie *f*.

oligomenorrhea [ɔligoumenə'ri:ə], *s. Med:* oligoménorrhée *f*.

oligomer ['ɔligoumər], *s. Ch:* oligomère *m*.

oligomeric [ɔligou'merik], *a. Ch:* oligomère.

oligomerization [ɔligoumərai'zeiʃ(ə)n], *s. Ch:* oligomérisation *f*.

oligomycin [ɔligou'maisin], *s. Ch:* oligomycine *f*.

Oligomyodae [ɔligou'maiədi:], *s.pl. Orn:* oligomyodés *m*.

oligonite ['ɔligənait], *s. Miner:* oligonite *f*.

oligophagous [ɔli'gɔfəgəs], *a. Nat.Hist:* oligophage.

oligophagy [ɔli'gɔfədʒi], *s. Nat.Hist:* oligophagie *f*.

oligophrenia [ɔligou'fri:niə], *s. Med:* oligophrénie *f*.

oligophrenic [ɔligou'frenik], *a. & s. Med:* oligophrène (*mf*).

oligophyllous [ɔli'gɔfiləs], *a. Bot:* oligophylle.

oligopolist [ɔli'gɔpəlist], *s. Pol.Ec:* oligopoliste *mf*.

oligopolistic [ɔligɔpə'listik], *a. Pol.Ec:* oligopoliste.

oligopoly [ɔli'gɔpəli], *s. Pol.Ec:* oligopole *m*.

oligopsony [ɔli'gɔpsəni], *s. Pol.Ec:* marché *m* où le manque d'acheteurs leur permet d'exercer une influence sur la vente.

oligosaccharide [ɔligou'sækəraid], *s. Bio-Ch:* oligosaccharide *m*.

oligosialia [ɔligousi'æliə], *s. Med:* oligosialie *f*.

oligosideric [ɔligou'sidərik], *a. Miner:* oligosidère.

oligosiderite [ɔligou'sidərait], *s. Miner:* oligosidérite *f*.

oligospermatic [ɔligouspə:'mætik], *a. Med:*

oligosperme.
oligospermia [ɔligou'spɜ:miə], *s. Med:* oligospermie *f.*
Oligotricha [ɔli'gɔtrikə], *s.pl. Prot:* oligotriches *m.*
oligotrophia [ɔligou'troufiə], *s. Med:* oligotrophie *f.*
oligotrophic [ɔligə'trɔfik], *a. Med:* oligotrophique, oligotrophe.
oliguria [ɔli'gjuriə], *s. Med:* oligurie *f.*
olio ['ouliou], *s. A:* **1.** *Cu:* oille *f,* olla-podrida *f.* **2.** *F:* pot pourri, mélange *m* (de mélodies, d'extraits littéraires, etc.).
oliphant ['ɔlifənt], *s. Lit:* olifant *m.*
oliva ['ɔlivə], *s. Moll:* olive *f.*
olivaceous [ɔli'veiʃəs], *a.* olivacé, olivâtre; vert olive *inv.*
olivary ['ɔlivəri], *a.* olivaire; *Anat:* **o. body,** olive *f* (de la moelle); **inferior o. body, o. nucleus,** olive bulbaire; **superior o. nucleus,** olive protubérentielle.
olive ['ɔliv], *s.* **1.** *Bot:* (*a*) **o. (tree),** olivier *m;* **the o. family,** les oléacées *f; B.Hist:* **the Mount of Olives,** le Mont, le Jardin, des Oliviers; **o. garden, o. yard,** oliv(er)aie *f;* jardin d'oliviers; **o. grove, o. plantation, o. wood,** olivette *f,* oliv(er)aie; **o. grower,** oléiculteur *m;* **o. branch,** rameau *m* d'olivier; **to hold out the o. branch (to s.o.),** se présenter à qn l'olivier à la main; présenter l'olivier; faire les premiers pas (pour une réconciliation); proposer la paix (à qn); (*b*) **Russian o.,** datte *f* de Trébizonde. **2.** *Bot: Cu:* olive *f;* **pickled o.,** picholine *f;* **to gather, harvest, (the) olives,** oliver; **to gather, harvest, the olives in a plantation,** oliver un champ; **o. crop, o. harvest,** olivaison *f;* récolte *f* des olives; **o. oil,** huile *f* d'olive; **o.-oil factory, mill,** oliverie *f,* moulin *m* à huile; **o.-oil manufacturer,** oléiculteur *m;* **o. season,** olivaison. **3.** *Com: Join:* **o. (wood),** (bois *m* d')olivier. **4.** *Cost: etc:* olive; *Arch:* **o. moulding,** olive. **5.** *Moll:* **o. (shell),** olive. **6.** *Cu:* **meat o.,** paupiette *f.* **7.** *a.* (*a*) **o. (green),** vert olive *inv;* (couleur d')olive; **o. ribbons,** rubans olive; (*b*) (teint, etc.) olivâtre; (*c*) *U.S:* **o. drab,** gris olivâtre (des militaires).
olivenite ['oulivənait, 'ɔl-], *s. Miner:* olivénite *f.*
Oliver[1] ['ɔlivər], *Pr.n.m.* Olivier.
oliver[2], *s. Metalw:* marteau *m* à pédale.
olive-shaped ['ɔlivʃeipt], *a.* olivaire, oliviforme.
olivet ['ɔlivet], **olivette** [ɔli'vet], *s.* **1.** *Cost:* olive *f.* **2.** (*imitation pearl*) olivette *f.*
Olivetan [ɔli'vi:t(ə)n], *s. Ecc.Hist:* olivétain *m.*
Oliveto [ɔli'vi:tou], *Pr.n. Geog:* **Monte** ['mɔnti], **O.,** le Mont-Olivet.
Olivia [ə'liviə], *Pr.n.f.* Olivie, Olivia.
Olividae [ɔ'lividi:], *s.pl. Moll:* olividés *m.*
oliviform [ɔ'livifɔ:m], *a.* oliviforme.
olivin ['ɔlivin], **olivine** [ɔli'vi:n], *s. Miner:* olivine *f;* péridot *m* (granulaire); chrysolit(h)e *f.*
olivinite ['ɔlivinait], *s. Miner:* olivinite *f.*
olla podrida ['ɔləpɔ'dri:də], *s.* = OLIO.
olm [oulm], *s. Amph:* protée *m;* anguillard *m.*
Olmec ['ɔlmek]. *Ethn:* **1.** *a.* olmèque. **2.** *s.* Olmèque *mf.*
'ologies ['ɔlədʒiz], *s.pl. F:* sciences *f; O:* **doctor in the 'o.,** savant *m* en us.
Olympia[1] [ə'limpiə], *Pr.n. A.Geog:* Olympie *f.*
Olympia[2], *Pr.n.f.* Olympe.
olympiad [ə'limpiæd], *s. Gr.Ant: Sp:* olympiade *f.*
Olympian [ə'limpiən]. **1.** *a.* (air, calme, etc.) olympien; **the O. gods,** les dieux *m* de l'Olympe. **2.** *s.* Olympien, -ienne.
Olympic [ə'limpik]. **1.** *a. Gr.Ant: Sp:* olympique; **the O. Games,** les jeux *m* olympiques; **O. stadium, champion,** stade *m,* champion *m,* olympique. **2.** *s.pl. Sp: F:* **the Olympics,** les Jeux.
Olympus [ə'limpəs], *Pr.n. Geog: Gr.Myth:* l'Olympe *m.*
Olynthiac [ə'linθiæk]. **1.** *a. A.Geog:* olynthien. **2.** *s.pl. Gr.Lit:* **the Olynthiacs,** les Olynthiennes *f* (de Démosthène).
Olynthian [ə'linθiən]. *A.Geog:* **1.** *a.* olynthien. **2.** *s.* Olynthien, -ienne.
Olynthus [ə'linθəs], *Pr.n. A.Geog:* Olynthe *m.*
omasitis [ɔmə'saitis], *s. Vet:* inflammation *f* du feuillet.
omasum, *pl.* **-a** ['ɔməsəm, -ə], *s. Z:* omasum *m,* feuillet *m.*
ombre ['ɔmbər], *s. Cards: A:* (h)ombre *m.*
ombrology [ɔm'brɔlədʒi], *s. Meteor:* ombrologie *f.*
ombrometer [ɔm'brɔmitər], *s. Meteor:* ombromètre *m,* pluviomètre *m.*
ombrometric [ɔmbrə'metrik], *a. Meteor:* ombrométrique, pluviométrique.
ombrophile ['ɔmbrəfail], *s. Bot:* ombrophile *m.*
ombrophilous [ɔm'brɔfiləs], *a. Bot:* ombrophile.
ombrophobe ['ɔmbrəfoub], *s. Bot:* ombrophobe *m.*
ombrophobous [ɔm'brɔfəbəs], *a. Bot:* ombrophobe.
ombudsman, *pl.* **-men** ['ɔmbudzmən], *s.* **1.** ombudsman *m;* médiateur *m;* protecteur *m* du citoyen; *Belg:* commissaire *m* du Parlement. **2.** *U.S:* médiateur *m* (entre acheteurs et vendeurs, etc.).

omega ['oumigə], *s. Gr.Alph:* oméga *m; Atom.Ph:* **o. (particle),** particule *f* oméga; **o. minus,** oméga moins.
omegatron ['oumigətrɔn], *s. Atom.Ph:* omégatron *m.*
omelet(te) ['ɔmlit], *s. Cu:* omelette *f;* **savoury o.,** omelette aux fines herbes; **ham o.,** omelette au jambon; **jam o.,** omelette aux confitures; *Prov:* **you cannot make an o. without breaking eggs,** on ne saurait faire une omelette sans casser des œufs.
omen[1] ['oumen], *s.* présage *m,* augure *m,* pronostic *m,* auspice *m;* **it's of good o. that the sky is clear,** il est de bon augure que le ciel est clair; **to look on sth. as a good o.,** regarder qch. comme un bon présage, comme de bon augure; **to take sth. as a good o.,** prendre qch. à bon augure; **bird of ill o.,** oiseau *m* de sinistre présage, de mauvais augure; messager *m* de malheur; portemalheur *m inv.*
omen[2], *v.tr.* augurer, présager.
-omened ['oumənd], *a.* (*with adj. or adv. prefixed*) **well-o., ill-o.,** de bon, mauvais, augure; de bon, mauvais, présage.
omental [ə'mentl], *a. Anat:* épiploïque; omental, -aux; **o. bursa,** arrière-cavité *f* des épiploons.
omentopexy [əmentou'peksi], *s. Med:* omentopexie *f.*
omentum, *pl.* **-a** [ə'mentəm, -ə], *s. Anat:* épiploon *m.*
omicron [ou'maikrən], *s. Gr.Alph:* omicron *m.*
ominous ['ɔminəs], *a.* **1. o. of good, evil,** qui présage, augure, qch. de bon, de mauvais. **2.** de mauvais augure; sinistre; inquiétant; **o.-looking sky,** ciel menaçant; **o. symptoms,** symptômes inquiétants; **an o. silence,** un silence lourd de menaces; **I heard an o. crack,** j'entendis un craquement qui ne présageait rien de bon; **o. for the future,** de mauvais augure pour l'avenir.
ominously ['ɔminəsli], *adv.* sinistrement; d'une façon menaçante, inquiétante.
ominousness ['ɔminəsnis], *s.* caractère sinistre, inquiétant (de qch.).
omissible [ə'misibl], *a.* négligeable; qui peut s'omettre.
omission [ə'miʃ(ə)n], *s.* **1.** omission *f* (d'un mot, etc.); *Com:* **errors and omissions excepted,** sauf erreur ou omission. **2.** négligence *f,* oubli *m; Theol:* omission; **to rectify, make good, an o.,** réparer un oubli; *Theol:* **sin of o.,** péché *m,* faute *f,* d'omission; **sins of commission and o.,** péchés par action ou par omission; péchés d'omission et de commission. **3.** *Typ:* bourdon *m.*
omissive [ə'misiv], *a.* (faute, etc.) d'omission.
omit [ə'mit, ou'mit], *v.tr.* **(omitted) 1.** (*a*) omettre, passer sous silence (des détails, etc.); (*b*) *Typ:* bourdonner (un mot). **2. to o. to do sth.,** oublier, omettre, de faire qch.; manquer à faire qch.; **not to o. to do sth.,** ne pas manquer de faire qch.; **to o. an opportunity of doing sth.,** manquer, laisser passer, une occasion de faire qch.
ommateum, *pl.* **-tea** [ɔmə'ti:əm, -ti:ə], *s. Ent: etc:* œil composé.
ommatidium, *pl.* **-ia** [ɔmə'tidiəm, -iə], *s. Z: Ent:* ommatidie *f.*
ommatophore [ə'mætəfɔ:r], *s. Crust:* pédoncule *m* de l'œil.
Ommiad [ɔ'maiæd]. *Pr.n. Hist:* **the O. dynasty, the Ommiads,** les Omm(é)iades *m,* les Ommeyades *m.*
omni- ['ɔmni], *comb.fm.* omni-.
omnibus, *pl.* **-uses** ['ɔmnibəs, -bəsiz]. **1.** *s. A:* (*a*) **(horse) o.,** omnibus *m;* **o. conductor,** receveur *m* d'omnibus; **o. driver,** cocher *m* d'omnibus; (*b*) **motor o.,** (*now usu.* **bus**), autobus *m; F:* **the man, woman, on the Clapham o.,** le banlieusard, la banlieusarde, typique. **2.** *a.* omnibus *inv; El: A:* **o. bar** (*now usu.* **busbar**) barre *f* omnibus; *Publ:* **o. volume, edition,** gros recueil (de contes, de poèmes, etc.); publication *f* en un volume de plusieurs ouvrages d'un auteur; *s.* **our new detective o.,** notre nouveau recueil de romans policiers; *Parl:* **o. bill,** projet *m* de loi embrassant des mesures diverses; *Th: A:* **o. box,** grande loge (louée à plusieurs abonnés).
omnicompetence ['ɔmni'kɔmpitəns], *s. Jur:* compétence *f* en toute matière; compétence générale.
omnicompetent ['ɔmni'kɔmpitənt], *a. Jur:* (juge) compétent en toute matière; (juge) de droit commun.
omnidirectional ['ɔmni'direkʃənl], *a. Rad: W.Tel:* (*of aerial*) omnidirectionnel; **o. beacon,** radiophare omnidirectionnel, d'alignement.
omnifarious [ɔmni'fɛəriəs], *a.* de toutes sortes, de toute espèce; de toute nature.
omnifariously [ɔmni'fɛəriəsli], *adv.* en grande variété.
omnificient [ɔmni'fiʃənt], *a.* qui crée, a créé, tout.
omnifont [ə'mnifɔnt], *a. Cmptr:* (lecteur) qui peut lire toutes les polices de caractères.
omniform ['ɔmnifɔ:m], *a.* omniforme.
omnigenous [ɔm'nidʒinəs], *a.* de toutes sortes.
omniparity [ɔmni'pæriti], *s.* égalité universelle.
omnipotence [ɔm'nipətəns], *s.* omnipotence *f;* toute-puissance *f.*
omnipotent [ɔm'nipətənt]. **1.** *a.* omnipotent; tout-puissant, *pl.* tout-puissants, *f.* toute-puissante, *pl.* toutes-puissantes. **2.** *s.* **the O.,** le Tout-Puissant.
omnipresence ['ɔmni'prez(ə)ns], *s.* omniprésence *f;* ubiquité *f.*
omnipresent ['ɔmni'prez(ə)nt], *a.* omniprésent.
omnirange ['ɔmni'reindʒ]. *Rad: W.Tel:* **1.** *a.* omnidirectionnel. **2.** *s.* omnirange *m;* radio-alignement omnidirectionnel.
omniscience [ɔm'nisiəns], *s.* omniscience *f; Theol:* toute-science *f.*
omniscient [ɔm'nisiənt], *a.* omniscient.
omnium ['ɔmniəm], *s. St.Exch:* omnium *m.*
omnium gatherum ['ɔmniəm'gæð(ə)rəm], *s. F:* **1.** ramassis *m,* méli-mélo *m* (de choses, de personnes). **2.** réception (mondaine) mêlée, où il y a des gens de tous les mondes.
Omnivora [ɔm'nivərə], *s.pl. Nat.Hist:* (les) omnivores *m.*
omnivorous [ɔm'nivərəs], *a.* omnivore; *Fig:* **o. reader,** lecteur *m* insatiable, qui lit tout, qui lit de tout.
omnivorously [ɔm'nivərəsli], *adv.* (se nourrir) de tout; *Fig:* **to read o.,** lire de tout.
omnivorousness [ɔm'niv(ə)rəsnis], *s.* omnivorité *f.*
omohyoid [oumə'haiɔid]. *Anat:* **1.** *a.* omo-hyoïdien, -ienne; *pl.* omo-hyoïdiens, -iennes. **2.** *s.* (muscle) omo-hyoïdien (*m*).
omoideum [ə'mɔidiəm], *s. Orn:* omoïde *m.*
omphacite ['ɔmfəsait], *s. Miner:* omphacite *f,* omphazite *f.*
omophagia [oumə'feidʒiə], **omophagy** [ə'mɔfədʒi], *s. Anthr:* omophagie *f.*
omophagic [oumə'feidʒik], **omophagous** [ə'mɔfəgəs], *a. Anthr:* omophage.
omophagist [ə'mɔfədʒist], *s. Anthr:* omophage *mf.*
omoplate ['oumәpleit], *s. Anat: A:* omoplate *f.*
Omphale ['ɔmfəli:], *Pr.n.f. Gr.Myth:* Omphale.
omphalectomy [ɔmfə'lektəmi], *s. Surg:* omphalectomie *f.*
omphalic [ɔm'fælik], *a. Anat:* ombilical, -aux.
omphalitis [ɔmfə'laitis], *s. Med:* omphalite *f.*
omphalocele ['ɔmfələsi:l], *s. Med:* omphalocèle *f;* hernie ombilicale.
omphalomesenteric ['ɔmfəloumezen'terik], *a. Anat:* omphalomésentérique.
omphalophlebitis ['ɔmfəloufli'baitis], *s. Med:* omphalophlébite *f.*
omphalorrhagia [ɔmfələ'reidʒiə], *s. Obst:* omphalorragie *f.*
omphalos, *pl.* **-li** ['ɔmfələs, -lai], *s.* **1.** *Gr.Ant:* omphalos *m* ((i) à Delphes, (ii) d'un bouclier). **2.** *Fig:* centre *m,* pivot *m* (d'un empire, etc.). **3.** *Anat:* ombilic *m.*
omphalosite ['ɔmfələsait], *s. Ter:* omphalosite *f.*
omphalotomy [ɔmfə'lɔtəmi], *s. Obst:* omphalotomie *f.*
omphalotripsy [ɔmfələ'tripsi], *s. Obst:* omphalotripsie *f.*
omphalus, *pl.* **-i** ['ɔmfələs, -ai], *s.* = OMPHALOS 2, 3.
on[1] [ɔn], *prep., adv. & a.*
I. *prep.* **1.** (*a*) *usu.* sur; **put it on the table,** mettez-le sur la table; **floating on the water,** flottant sur l'eau; **to tread on sth.,** marcher sur qch.; **do not tread on it,** ne marchez pas dessus; **on the high seas,** en haute mer; **room on the second floor,** chambre du second; **hotel on the left bank,** hôtel de la rive gauche; **scene on a Dutch river,** scène de rivière hollandaise; **can we have dinner on the train?** peut-on dîner dans le train? (*b*) **on shore,** à terre; **on foot,** à pied; **on horseback,** à cheval; **on a bicycle,** à bicyclette; **he had his rucksack on his back,** il portait le sac au dos; (*c*) (*member of*) **to be on the committee,** être membre du comité; faire partie du bureau; **to be on the staff,** faire partie du personnel; **to be on a newspaper,** être attaché à la rédaction d'un journal; **he's on the "Daily Mail",** il est au "Daily Mail"; (*d*) **to swear sth. on the Bible,** jurer qch. sur la Bible. **2.** (*a*) **hanging on the wall,** pendu au mur, contre le mur; **on the ceiling,** au plafond; **stuck on (to) the wall,** collé au mur; **he has a ring on his finger,** il a une bague au doigt; **shoes on his feet,** des souliers aux pieds; **his hat on his head,** son chapeau sur la tête; **his coat on (= over) his arm,** son manteau sur son bras; **have you any money on you?** avez-vous de l'argent (sur vous)? **dog on the lead, on the chain,** chien en laisse, à la chaîne; **to be on the phone,** (i) parler, être, au téléphone; (ii) avoir le téléphone; **he played it on his violin,** il l'a joué sur son violon; **I read it in the paper, on page four,** je l'ai lu dans le journal, à, sur, la quatrième page, à la page quatre; *Journ:* **continued on page four,** la suite en quatrième page; (*b*) (*proximity*) (i) **fort on the frontier,** forteresse sur la frontière; **house on the main road,** maison sur la grande route; *NAm:* **he lives on Sixth**

Avenue, il habite dans l'avenue VI; (ii) **just on a year ago,** il y a près d'un an; il y aura bientôt un an; **just on £5,** tout près de cinq livres. **3.** (*direction*) (*a*) **on (to),** sur, à; **to jump on (to) the table,** sauter sur la table; **to drift on to the shore,** dériver sur la terre, vers la terre, à terre; **room that looks on (to) the street,** pièce *f* qui donne sur la rue; (*b*) **on the right, left,** à droite, à gauche; **on this side,** de ce côté; **on the north,** du côté du nord; (*c*) (*towards*) **to march on London,** avancer vers, sur, Londres; **to smile on s.o.,** sourire à qn; **to turn one's back on s.o.,** tourner le dos à qn; (*d*) **to hit s.o. on the head,** frapper qn sur la tête; **to serve a writ on s.o.,** signifier un arrêt à qn; **shame on you!** honte à vous! **4.** (*basis, ground*) **based on a fact,** fondé sur un fait; **to have sth. on good authority,** savoir qch. de source certaine, de bonne part; **to act on the advice of one's lawyer,** agir d'après les conseils de son avoué; **arrested on a charge of murder,** arrêté sous l'inculpation de meurtre; **put to death on a false accusation,** mis à mort sur une fausse accusation; **on pain, penalty, of death,** sous peine de mort; **on a commercial basis,** sur une base industrielle; **on an average,** en moyenne; **tax on tobacco,** impôt sur le tabac; **interest on capital,** intérêt du capital; **to borrow money on security,** emprunter de l'argent sur nantissement; **to retire on a pension of £x a year,** prendre sa retraite avec une pension de £x par an; **to be on half-pay,** être en demi-solde; **dependent on circumstances,** qui dépend des circonstances; **on condition that nobody says anything about it,** à condition que personne n'en dise mot; **to buy sth. on good terms,** acheter qch. à d'excellentes conditions. **5.** (*in expressions of time*) (*a*) (*preposition omitted in French*) **on Sunday,** dimanche (prochain ou dernier); **on Sundays,** le(s) dimanche(s); **on the day of my arrival,** le jour de mon arrivée; **on the following day,** le lendemain; **on April 3rd,** le trois avril; **I was born on (the morning of) the fifth of May,** je suis né le (matin du) cinq mai; **on the evening of the first of June,** le premier juin au soir; (*b*) **on a fine day in June,** par une belle journée de juin; **on a warm day like this,** par une chaleur comme celle-ci, comme aujourd'hui; **light visible on a dark night,** feu visible par une nuit noire; **on certain days,** à (de) certains jours; **on and after the fifteenth,** à partir du quinze; à dater du quinze; **on or about the twelfth,** vers le douze; **on the occasion of his wedding,** à l'occasion de son mariage; **on that occasion,** à, dans, cette occasion; **on the death of his mother,** à la mort de sa mère; **on his majority,** à, lors de, sa majorité; **on my arrival,** à mon arrivée; **on application,** sur demande; **on examination,** après examen; **payable on sight,** payable à vue; **on delivery of the letter,** lors de la remise de la lettre; (*c*) **on (my) entering the room,** quand j'entrai, en entrant, dans la salle; à, dès, mon entrée dans la salle; **on our knocking the door was instantly opened,** nous avons frappé, et la porte s'est ouverte aussitôt; **on my telling him the news,** lorsque je lui ai annoncé la nouvelle; **on coming nearer to them one realizes what they are,** à les approcher on se rend compte de ce qu'ils sont; (*d*) **on time, on the minute,** ponctuel, à l'heure, à la minute; (*e*) *A:* (*sometimes abbreviated to o'*) **on nights, o'nights,** la nuit, de nuit. **6.** (*manner*) (*a*) *A:* **on this wise,** de cette manière; ainsi; (*b*) (*with adj.*) **on the cheap,** à bon marché; **on the sly,** en sourdine, en catimini. **7.** (*state*) en; **on sale,** en vente; **on tap,** en perce; *Fb:* **to keep just on side,** rester juste en deçà de la limite du hors jeu; *Fig:* **to be on side with s.o.,** être en faveur auprès de qn; être dans les petits papiers de qn, bien vu de qn. **8.** (*about, concerning*) **lecture, book, on the United Nations,** conférence, livre, sur les Nations Unies; **a lecture on history,** une conférence d'histoire; **inquiry on sth.,** enquête sur qch.; **congress on international law,** congrès de droit international; **you must read Hume Brown on John Knox,** il faut lire l'appréciation *f* de John Knox par Hume Brown; **note on an agreement,** note ayant trait à un contrat; **to congratulate s.o. on his success,** féliciter qn de son succès; **keen on sth.,** porté sur qch.; amateur de qch.; **mad on s.o.,** fou, entiché, de qn. **9.** (*engaged upon*) **I am here on business,** je suis ici pour affaires; **on tour,** en tournée; **on holiday,** en congé, en vacances; **to be (working) on sth.,** travailler à qch.; **on the way,** en chemin, chemin faisant. **10.** (*a*) **to have pity on s.o.,** avoir pitié de qn; **effect of sth. on s.o.,** effet de qch. sur qn; **attack on s.o.,** attaque contre qn; **to confer a reward on s.o.,** décerner une récompense à qn; **decision binding on s.o.,** décision obligatoire pour qn, qui lie qn; *F:* **this round (of drinks) is on me,** c'est moi qui paie cette tournée; c'est moi qui régale; **to have one on the house,** prendre une consommation aux frais du cafetier; **the police have nothing on him,** la police n'a rien contre lui; **to have something on a competitor,** avoir l'avantage sur un concurrent; (*b*) *Fin: Com:* **cheque on a bank, on Paris,** chèque sur une banque, sur Paris. **11.** (*a*) **to live on one's private income,** vivre de ses rentes; **many live on less than that,** beaucoup vivent avec moins que ça; (*b*) **he's on insulin,** il a un traitement à l'insuline; *F:* **she's on the pill,** elle prend la pilule; **he's on drugs,** il se drogue. **12.** (*added to*) **disaster on disaster,** désastre sur désastre. **13.** *Turf: Games:* **to put money on a horse, on a colour,** parier sur un cheval; miser sur une couleur.

II. *adv.* **1.** (*a*) **to put on the cloth,** mettre la nappe; **to put the kettle on,** mettre la bouilloire à chauffer; **the stew's on,** le ragoût est en cuisson; *Th:* (*of actor*) **to be on,** être en scène; (*b*) **to put on one's clothes,** mettre ses habits; **to put on one's gloves,** se ganter; **to have one's boots on,** avoir ses bottes aux pieds; être chaussé; **to have one's hat on,** avoir son chapeau sur la tête; **with his spectacles on,** avec ses lunettes; **what had he got on?** comment était-il vêtu? qu'est-ce qu'il portait? **to have nothing on,** être tout nu; **on with your coat!** mettez votre veston! **2.** (*expressing continuation*) **to fly on, go on, journey on, march on, ride on, run on, stroll on, walk on, work on,** continuer son vol, son chemin, son voyage, sa marche, sa chevauchée, sa course, sa flânerie, sa route, son travail; **to burn on, climb on, crawl on, drive on, hold on, sail on, shout on, swim on, talk on, wander on,** continuer à brûler, à grimper, à ramper, à rouler, à tenir, à naviguer, à crier, à nager, à parler, à errer; **to soldier on,** rester au service, au même emploi; **sing on!** continuez à chanter! **sleep on!** continuez à dormir! **the train didn't stop at Rugby, and I was carried on to Crewe,** le train a brûlé Rugby et j'ai été emmené jusqu'à Crewe; **go on!** allez toujours! **move on!** circulez! **on, Stanley, on!** en avant, Stanley, en avant! **to toil on and on,** peiner sans fin; **and so on,** et ainsi de suite. **3.** (*towards*) **to be broadside on to the shore,** présenter le côté à la terre; avoir la terre par le travers; **to be sideways on to sth.,** présenter le côté à qch.; **to keep an aircraft head on to the wind,** tenir un avion le nez au vent. **4.** (*in expressions of time*) **later on,** plus tard; **from that day on,** à dater de ce jour; **well on in April,** fort avant dans le mois d'avril; **well on in the evening, in the night,** à une heure avancée de la soirée, de la nuit; **to talk away well on into the small hours,** rester à causer bien avant dans la nuit; **well on in years,** d'un âge avancé. **5. to turn on the tap,** ouvrir le robinet; **on (position),** (i) (*of gas, etc.*) ouvert; (ii) *I.C.E:* marche, contact; (iii) (*of electric circuit*) fermé; **the engine was on,** la machine était en marche; **the brakes are on,** les freins sont appliqués, serrés; **the rain is on again!** voilà qu'il repleut! **a terrible row was on,** on entendait un vacarme terrible; **the performance is now on,** la représentation est commencée, a déjà commencé; **on with the show!** (i) que le spectacle commence! (ii) que le spectacle continue! **what plays are on, what is on (at the theatre), just now?** qu'est-ce qu'on joue, donne, qu'est-ce qui se joue, actuellement? qu'y a-t-il (à l'affiche) au théâtre? **the play was on for weeks,** la pièce a tenu l'affiche pendant des semaines; **I see** ***Hamlet*** **is on again,** je vois qu'on redonne *Hamlet*; **this film was on last week,** ce film a passé la semaine dernière; **what's on tonight?** (i) qu'est-ce qui se passe ce soir? (ii) *W.Tel:* qu'est-ce qu'ils donnent, *T.V:* qu'est-ce qui passe, ce soir? (iii) que fait-on ce soir? **have you anything on this evening?** avez-vous quelque chose à faire, en vue pour, ce soir? êtes-vous occupé, invité, ce soir? **there's nothing on at present,** c'est la morte-saison. **6.** *F:* (*a*) **I'm on!** je suis de la partie! j'en suis! je vous accompagne! ça me va! **I'm not on!** je ne marche pas! **he's neither on nor off,** c'est tantôt oui, tantôt non; il ne dit ni oui ni non; **it's not on,** il n'y a pas moyen; rien à faire! pas mèche! (*b*) **to be on to sth.,** comprendre, saisir, qch.; **he was on to it at once,** il a compris au premier mot; *P:* il a pigé tout de suite; **they were on to him at once,** ils ont tout de suite vu clair dans son jeu; (*c*) **to be on to a good thing,** (i) avoir un bon tuyau; (ii) être sur une bonne affaire; **the police are on to him,** la police est sur sa piste; (*d*) **I was on to him on the phone this morning,** je lui ai parlé au téléphone ce matin; **I'll put you on to him,** je vais vous donner la communication; (*e*) **he's always on at, to, me,** il s'en prend toujours à moi; il m'est toujours sur le dos; (*f*) **to have s.o. on,** monter le bateau à qn; faire marcher qn; (*g*) *Turf:* **to have a bit on,** (i) faire, (ii) avoir fait, un pari. **7. on and off** *see* OFF[1] 1, 4.

III. *a.* **1. on position,** position *f* de serrage (des freins); position de mise en marche (d'un moteur); *El:* position de fermeture (du circuit). **2.** *Cr:* **drive to the on side,** *s.* **drive to the on, on drive,** coup *m* avant à gauche. **3.** *F:* (*of athlete, etc.*) **it was not one of his on days,** il n'était pas dans un de ses meilleurs jours. **4.** *Adm:* **on consumption of intoxicants,** consommation *f* des boissons alcooliques sur les lieux; *on* **licence,** licence *f* permettant la consommation des boissons sur les lieux.

on[2], *v.i. P: A:* **to on with one's coat,** mettre sa veste.

onager, *pl.* **-gers, -gri** ['ɔnədʒər, -dʒəz, -grai], *s.* **1.** *Z:* onagre *m.* **2.** *A.Arms:* **(siege) o.,** onagre.

Onagraceae [ɔnə'greisii:], *s.pl. Bot:* œnothéracées *f*; onagra(ria)cées *f.*

onanism ['ounənizm], *s.* (i) onanisme *m*, masturbation *f*; (ii) rapport interrompu.

onanist ['ounənist], *s.* onaniste *m.*

onanistic [ounə'nistik], *a.* onaniste.

on-board ['ɔn'bɔ:d], *a. Av: etc:* (appareil, etc.) de bord.

on-call ['ɔn'kɔ:l], *a. Com:* (entretien, etc.) sur appel.

once [wʌns], *adv.* **1.** (*a*) une fois; **o. only,** une seule fois; **more than o.,** plus d'une fois; **o. a week, a fortnight,** tous les huit jours, tous les quinze jours; **o. or twice,** une ou deux fois, une fois ou deux; **o. more, o. again,** une fois de plus, encore une fois; **o. and again, o. in a way, o. in a while,** une fois par-ci par-là; une fois de temps en temps; une fois en passant, par hasard; par extraordinaire; **o. (and) for all,** une fois pour toutes, une bonne fois; **to settle a question o. and for all,** en finir avec une question; **you may do so this o., just for (this) o.,** je vous le permets pour une fois, pour cette fois(-ci); **for o. you are right,** pour une fois tu as raison; **he never o. asked himself what the outcome might be,** il ne se demanda pas un instant ce qui pourrait en résulter; **he didn't o. look our way,** pas un instant il n'a regardé de notre côté; **o. is enough,** une fois est assez; c'est assez d'une fois; **o. a thief always a thief,** qui a volé volera; (*b*) **(if) o. you hesitate it's all up with you,** dès que, une fois que, vous hésitez, pour peu que vous hésitiez, vous êtes fichu; **(when) o. you've had something to eat you'll feel better,** dès que vous aurez mangé quelque chose vous vous trouverez mieux; **o. grasp this fact and everything becomes plain,** comprenez bien cela et tout s'éclaircit. **2.** autrefois; **o. (upon a time) there was a princess,** il était une fois; il y avait jadis, une princesse; **I knew him o.,** je l'ai connu autrefois, dans le temps; **o. famous painter,** peintre célèbre autrefois, dans le temps; *A:* **his o. friend,** son ami d'autrefois; **book o. so popular,** livre autrefois si populaire; **a collar that had o. been white,** un faux col jadis blanc; **o. when I was young, I had a bad fright,** il arriva un jour, quand j'étais petit que, j'ai eu une belle peur. **3. at o.;** (*a*) (*without delay*) tout de suite; à l'instant; sur-le-champ; sur l'heure; aussitôt; immédiatement; instantanément; **come at o.!** venez tout de suite! **I'll do it at o.,** je vais le faire dès maintenant; **I'm going at o.,** (i) j'y vais de ce pas, tout de suite; (ii) je pars à l'instant; tout de suite; (*b*) (*at the same time*) **don't all speak at o.,** ne parlez pas tous à la fois, en même temps; **to do several things at o., to have several things on at o.,** faire plusieurs choses à la fois; mener plusieurs choses de front; **at o. a food and a tonic,** à la fois un aliment et un fortifiant; **to do a great deal at o.,** faire beaucoup (i) en une fois, (ii) à la fois; **to drink the whole bottle at o.,** boire toute la bouteille d'un coup.

once-over ['wʌns'ouvər], *s. F:* **to give s.o., sth., the o.-o.,** jeter un coup d'œil (scrutateur) sur qn, qch.; **to give a room a o.-o.,** (i) donner un coup de torchon à une chambre; (ii) mettre un peu d'ordre dans une chambre.

oncer ['wʌnsər], *s. F: O:* personne *f* qui ne va qu'une fois à l'église dimanche, qui n'assiste qu'à un seul office.

onchidium [ɔŋ'kidiəm], *s. Moll:* onchidie *f.*

onchocerca [ɔŋkə'sə:kə], *s. Z:* onchocerque *f.*

onchocerciasis [ɔŋkəsə'kaiəsis], **onchocercosis** [ɔŋkəsə'kousis], *s. Med:* onchocercose *f*, volvulose *f.*

onchogenic [ɔŋkə'dʒenik], **oncogenous** [ɔŋ'kɔdʒinəs], *a. Med:* (goudron, etc.) qui provoque le développement des tumeurs.

oncology [ɔŋ'kɔlədʒi], *s. Med:* étude *f* des tumeurs.

on-coming ['ɔnkʌmiŋ], *a.* **1.** (*a*) approchant, qui approche; (danger) imminent; **the o.-c. traffic,** (i) (*for vehicle*) les véhicules venant en sens inverse; la colonne montante; (*for pedestrian*) les véhicules qui approchent, approchaient; (*b*) *Ind:* **o.-c. shift,** poste entrant. **2.** *F:* (*a*) hardi, déluré, qui n'a pas froid aux yeux; peu timide; (*b*) spontané, ouvert, peu réticent.

oncorhyncus [ɔŋkəriŋkəs], *s. Ich:* oncorhyncus *m.*

oncosphere ['ɔŋkəsfiər], *s. Z:* oncosphère *f.*

oncost ['ɔnkɔst], *s. Scot:* frais généraux.

oncostman, *pl.* **-men** [ɔn'kɔstmən], *s. Scot: Min:* mineur payé à la journée.

oncotic [ɔŋ'kɔtik], *a. Biol:* (pression, etc.) oncotique.

oncotomy [ɔŋ'kɔtəmi], *s. Surg:* oncotomie *f.*

ondatra [ɔn'dætrə], *s. Z:* ondatra *m*; rat musqué.

ondograph ['ɔndəgræf], *s. El:* ondographe *m.*

ondometer [ɔn'dɔmitər], *s. El:* ondemètre *m.*

ondoscope ['ɔndəskoup], *s. El:* ondoscope *m.*

one [wʌn], *a., s. & pron.*
I. *num.a.* 1. (*a*) un; **twenty-o. apples,** *A:* **o. and twenty apples,** vingt et une pommes; **fifty-o.,** cinquante et un; **seventy-o.,** soixante et onze; **eighty-o.,** quatre-vingt-un; **a hundred and o.,** cent un; **a thousand and o.,** mille un; **the Thousand and o. Nights,** les Mille et une Nuits; **o. or two people saw it,** quelques personnes, une ou deux personnes, l'ont vu; (*b*) **he comes o. day out of two,** il vient un jour sur deux; **o. man in a hundred,** un homme entre, sur, cent; **that's o. way of doing it,** c'est une manière comme une autre de le faire; **that's o. comfort,** c'est déjà une consolation; **I can't go; for o. thing I'm short of cash,** je ne pourrai pas y aller; entre autres raisons je suis à court d'argent; **it's no use asking whether o. book fulfils its aim better than another,** inutile de demander si tel ouvrage remplit son but mieux que tel autre; **the speech of the Prime Minister in the o. House and of Lord X in the other,** le discours du Premier Ministre dans l'une des Chambres et de Lord X dans l'autre. 2. (*a*) seul, unique; **my o. and only suit,** mon seul et unique complet; **my o. and only son,** mon fils unique; *s. P:* **my o. and only,** mon cher et tendre, ma chère et tendre; **families with o. child,** familles avec un seul enfant; **the o. way to do it,** le seul moyen de le faire; **his o. care,** son seul souci; son unique souci; **the o. real danger is he might die first,** le seul véritable danger c'est qu'il pourrait mourir avant cela; **this o. thing,** cette seule et unique chose; **no o. man can do it,** il n'y a pas d'homme qui puisse le faire à lui seul, tout seul; **no o. of you could accomplish it,** pas un de vous ne pourrait l'accomplir à lui seul; **I do not limit myself to the books of any o. publishing house,** je ne me restreins pas aux publications d'une seule maison, quelle soit-elle; (*b*) **they cried out with o. voice, as o. man,** ils s'écrièrent d'une seule voix, d'une commune voix; **to advance like o. man,** avancer comme un seul homme; (*c*) même; **all in o. direction,** tous dans la même direction; **all gathered in o. spot,** tous rassemblés en un même lieu; **o. and the same thought came into our minds,** une seule et même pensée nous est venue à l'esprit; **I am sure the two visitors are o.,** je suis sûr que les deux visiteurs ne font qu'un; **to remain for ever o.,** être toujours le même; ne jamais changer; *F:* **it's all o.,** cela revient au même, c'est tout un; *P:* c'est kif-kif; **it's all o. to me whether he comes or not,** qu'il vienne ou non, ce m'est égal, cela m'est parfaitement indifférent; peu m'importe, cela ne me fait ni chaud ni froid, qu'il vienne ou non; (*d*) **God is o.,** Dieu est un; *A:* **to become o., to be made o.,** s'unir, se marier; **to be o. with sth.,** ne faire qu'une pièce avec qch.; faire corps avec qch.; **I'm o. with you,** je suis de votre avis.
II. *s.* 1. (*a*) **eleven is written with two ones,** onze s'écrit avec deux un; **chapter o.,** chapitre un, chapitre premier; **number o.,** (i) numéro un; (ii) *F:* soi-même; (iii) *P:* petit besoin; pipi; (iv) *Mil:* (*of gun crew, etc.*) chef *m* (de pièce); (*in restaurant, etc.*) **table number o.,** *F:* l'as *m*; *P:* **to look after, take care of, number o.,** avoir soin de son individu, de sa personne; soigner sa petite personne; mettre ses intérêts en premier lieu; *F:* tirer la couverture à soi; **he knows how to look after number o.,** il n'oublie jamais ses intérêts; il ne s'oublie pas; **that's for number o.,** *P:* ça c'est pour bibi; *F:* **since the year o.,** depuis un temps immémorial; *Gym: Sp:* **o., two! o. two! one deux! one deux! o., two, three, go!** un-(e), deux, trois, partez! (*b*) (*dominoes*) as; **o. blank,** l'as blanc; **double o.,** double-un *m, pl.* doubles-uns; (*c*) *Cmptr:* **o. condition, o. state,** état *m* "un"; **ones complement,** complément *m* à un. 2. (*a*) **there's only o. left,** il n'en reste qu'un; **you have fifty readers for every o. he has,** pour un qui lit ses livres ils sont cinquante qui lisent les vôtres; *F:* **there's o. born every minute,** on pend les andouilles sans les compter; **the top, bottom, stair but o.,** l'avant-dernière marche; **to arrive in ones and twos,** arriver par un et par deux, un ou deux à la fois; **to issue shares in ones,** émettre des actions en unités; **goods that are sold in ones,** marchandises qui se vendent à la pièce; **two for the price of o.,** deux pour le prix d'un; **cylinders cast in o.,** cylindres venus de fonte d'une seule pièce; **all in o. garment,** vêtement en une pièce; **two volumes in o.,** deux volumes en un; **to be at o. with s.o.,** être d'accord avec qn; **we are at o. in thinking that he's talented,** nous sommes, demeurons, tombons, d'accord pour reconnaître, nous sommes unanimes à reconnaître, qu'il a du talent; **o. of two things,** de deux choses l'une; (*b*) **o. fifty,** (i) cent cinquante; (ii) une livre cinquante (pence); (iii) un dollar cinquante (cents); (iv) deux heures moins dix; une heure cinquante; **o. (o'clock),** une heure; **I'll come between o. and two,** je viendrai entre une et deux (heures); **children (aged) from o. to ten,** des enfants de un à dix ans; *F:* **to give s.o. o. on the nose, in the eye,** donner à qn un coup de poing sur le nez, sur l'œil; **that's o. in the eye for him,** ça lui fait les pieds; **I fetched, landed, him o.,** je lui ai flanqué un marron; **to call at the pub for a quick o.,** entrer au café pour s'en enfiler une; **o. for the road,** le coup de l'étrier; **to have o. too many,** boire un verre de trop; *Sp: Games:* **to be o. up on an opponent,** être en avance d'un point, d'un jeu, d'une partie, d'un but, etc., sur un concurrent; *F:* **to be o. up,** avoir l'avantage (**on s.o.,** sur qn); avoir le dessus; **that's o. (up) for us,** et d'un dans nos filets! (*c*) *Knit:* **to make o.,** faire une augmentation; (*d*) *St.Exch:* unité *f*; unité de mille livres (au prix nominal des actions); *Turf:* **the odds are (at) ten to o.,** la cote est à dix contre un; *F:* **it's ten to o.,** *NAm:* **o. will get you ten, that he's at the office,** je parie (à) dix contre un qu'il est au bureau.
III. *dem.pron.* (*a*) **this o.,** celui-ci, *f,* celle-ci; **that o.,** celui-là, *f.* celle-là; **which o. do you prefer?** lequel, laquelle, préférez-vous? **the o. on the table,** celui, celle, qui est sur la table; **the o. who spoke,** celui qui a parlé; **the o. I spoke of,** celui, celle, dont j'ai parlé; **she is the o. who helped Louise,** c'est elle qui a aidé Louise; **that's the Mayor, the o. with glasses,** voilà monsieur le maire, celui qui porte des lunettes; (*b*) **to pick the ripe plums and leave the green ones,** cueillir les prunes mûres et laisser les vertes; **he has chosen good ones,** il en a choisi de bons; **she put her feet (she has very small ones) on a chair,** elle posa ses pieds (elle les a très petits) sur une chaise; **the portraits on the walls, especially the full-length ones,** les portraits pendus aux murs, surtout les portraits en pied; **his father was a sailor and he wants to be o. too,** son père était marin et il veut l'être aussi; **she became a Catholic and a very devout o.,** elle est devenue catholique et même catholique très dévote; **the scheme was a good one on paper,** le plan était excellent en théorie; **that's a good o.!** celle-là est bonne! **have you heard the o. about . . .?** est-ce tu as déjà entendu la blague, celle, du . . .? **it is a mere farce and not a good o.,** c'est une simple farce et qui est médiocre; **the best o.,** le meilleur, la meilleure; **he's a knowing o.,** c'est un malin; **my sweet o.,** ma chérie; **the absent o.,** l'absent; **our loved, dear, ones,** (i) ceux qui nous sont chers; (ii) nos chers disparus; **the great ones of the earth,** les grands de la terre; **the little ones,** les petits enfants; (*of animals*) les petits; **the young ones are at school,** les gamins sont à l'école; **a nest with five young ones,** un nid avec cinq petits; **the Evil O.,** le Malin, l'Esprit malin; **the Holy O.,** l'Éternel.
IV. *indef.a.* **o. day,** un jour; **o. stormy evening in January,** par une soirée orageuse de janvier; **on o. occasion I travelled in the guard's van,** il est arrivé une fois que j'ai fait le voyage dans le fourgon.
V. *indef.pron.* 1. (*pl.* **some, any**) **I haven't a pencil, have you got o.?** je n'ai pas de crayon, en avez-vous un? **I noticed two men; o. walked with a limp,** j'ai remarqué deux hommes; l'un d'eux boitait; **the word has two pronunciations, o. English and o. French,** ce mot se prononce de deux façons, à l'anglaise ou à la française; **this question is o. of extreme delicacy,** ce problème est délicat entre tous; **the idea is o. which occurs in primitive societies,** cette idée est de celles que l'on rencontre dans les sociétés primitives; **o. of them,** un d'entre eux; l'un d'eux; *F:* **he's o. of them,** il en est, c'est une tantouse; **this plan is not o. of those which appeal to everybody,** ce projet n'est pas de ceux qui ont de l'attrait pour tout le monde; **he is o. of the family,** il fait partie de la famille; il est de la famille; **to treat s.o. as o. of the family,** traiter qn comme s'il était de la famille; **I was o. of the party,** j'étais du groupe; **he is o. of us,** il est des nôtres; **will you make o. of us?** voulez-vous vous mettre de la partie? voulez-vous être des nôtres? **o. of my friends,** un de mes amis; un ami à moi; **o. of the ladies will see to it,** l'une, quelqu'une, de ces dames va s'en occuper; **you are sure to find it in o. of the other shops in the town,** vous le trouverez sûrement dans un des autres magasins de la ville; **any o. of us,** l'un quelconque d'entre nous; n'importe lequel d'entre nous; **o. and all,** tous sans exception; **they o. and all declined,** tous sans exception ont refusé; **the woman, the children, the old people, o. and all had got out,** femmes, enfants, vieillards, tout était descendu; **the anxieties he had caused o. and all,** les alarmes qu'il avait causées à tous et à chacun; **o. for all and all for o.,** un pour tous et tous pour un; (the) **o. . . . the other,** l'un . . . l'autre; **you can't have o. without the other,** l'un ne va pas sans l'autre; **when you contrast the one's stupidity with the intelligence of the other,** lorsqu'on met en contraste la stupidité de l'un et l'intelligence de l'autre; **o. after the other,** l'un après l'autre; **he drank three glasses of beer, o. after the other,** il a bu trois bières à la file; **to enter by o. or other of the doors,** entrer par l'une ou l'autre des portes; **o. by o.,** un à un, une à une; **door that lets visitors through o. by o.,** porte qui admet les visiteurs un à un; **the chestnut trees shed their leaves o. by o.,** les marronniers égrènent leurs feuilles. 2. **I want the opinion of o. better able to judge,** je voudrais avoir l'opinion de quelqu'un qui soit plus capable de juger; **he set about it with the manner of o. accustomed to the task,** il s'y mit à la manière de quelqu'un à qui la tâche était familière; **this ingratitude on the part of o. he knew so well,** cette ingratitude de la part d'un homme qu'il connaissait si bien; **o. whom I do pity is his father,** un que je plains c'est son père; **he looked like o. dead,** il avait l'air d'un mort; **o. possessed,** un (homme) possédé; **she said it in the voice of o. who repeats a lesson,** elle le dit du ton de quelqu'un qui récite, réciterait, une leçon; **to o. who can read between the lines it is evident he's dishonest,** à qui sait lire entre les lignes il est évident qu'il est malhonnête; **o. Martin,** un certain M. Martin; un homme nommé, du nom de, Martin; **I, for o., will come,** moi, entre autres, je viendrai; quant à moi je viendrai; **I, for o., do not believe it,** pour ma part je n'en crois rien; **I'm not o. to complain,** je ne suis point homme à me plaindre; **she was not o. to bear a grudge,** elle n'était pas de celles qui restent fâchées; elle n'était pas rancunière; **I'm not the o. to scoff at it,** ce n'est pas moi qui en rirais; **he's (the) o. to talk,** (i) ce n'est pas à lui de parler ainsi; (ii) il a la langue bien pendue; il a du bagout; *F:* **she was quite a o. for football,** c'était une emballée, une passionnée, du football; **I'm not much of a o. for sweets,** je ne suis pas grand amateur de bonbons; **I'm not much of a o. for making pretty speeches,** je ne suis pas expert à dire des gentillesses; *P:* **you *are* a o.!** vous êtes fameux, impayable, vous! 3. (*a*) (*nom.*) on; **o. cannot always be right,** on ne peut pas toujours avoir raison; **o. can do that easily,** cela se fait facilement; **the book is so pleasant that o. is sorry it is so short,** le livre est si agréable que l'on regrette qu'il soit si court; **were o. to judge humanity from novels, o. would have a poor opinion of it,** si l'on jugeait l'humanité d'après les romans, on n'en fera pas grand cas; (*b*) vous; **it is enough to kill o.,** il y a de quoi vous faire mourir; **this synopsis puts o. in a position to answer any argument,** ce résumé vous met à même de répondre à n'importe quel argument. 4. **one's,** son, *f.* sa, *pl.* ses; votre, *pl.* vos; **to give one's opinion,** donner son avis; **when o. is allowed to see one's friends,** quand il nous est permis de voir nos amis; **o. never knows one's own happiness,** on ne connaît jamais son bonheur; **to cut one's finger,** se couper le doigt; **o. may surely do what o. likes with (what is) one's own,** on a bien le droit de faire ce qu'on veut avec ce qui vous appartient.

one-ahead ['wʌnə'hed], *a. Cmptr:* (adressage) à progression automatique.

one-armed ['wʌn'ɑːmd], *a.* à un seul bras; (*of pers.*) manchot, -ote.

one-class ['wʌnklɑːs], *a.* (avion, paquebot, train) à classe unique.

one-design ['wʌndi'zain], *a. Sp:* **o.-d. sailing boats,** (voiliers *m*) monotypes (*m*).

one-dimensional [wʌnd(a)i'menʃnəl], *a.* (esprit, etc.) superficiel.

one-er ['wʌnər], *s. F:* = ONER.

one-eyed ['wʌnaid], *a.* 1. (*a*) *Z: etc:* unioculé; (*b*) (*of pers.*) borgne; **to be o.-e.,** n'avoir qu'un œil; être borgne; **o.-e. man, woman,** borgne *mf*; (*c*) *F:* (*of pers. outlook, etc.*) borné, étroit; **o.-e. bargain,** marché inéquitable. 2. *F:* **o.-e. town,** petite ville de rien de tout; trou perdu.

onefold ['wʌnfould], *a.* simple, clair.

one-footed ['wʌn'futid], *a. Z:* monopode.

one-handed ['wʌn'hændid], *a.* 1. (*of pers.*) manchot, -ote. 2. (*a*) (travail, etc.) fait d'une seule main; *adv.* **to do sth. o.-h.,** faire qch. d'une main; (*b*) (outil) à une main.

one-horse ['wʌn'hɔːs], *a.* 1. (*of vehicle*) à un cheval. 2. *F:* **o.-h. show,** (i) spectacle *m* de deux sous; (ii) affaire *f* de quatre sous; **o.-h. town,** petite ville de rien du tout; trou perdu.

oneiric [ou'nairik], *a.* onirique.

oneirocritic [ounairə'kritik], *a. & s.* oniro-critique (*m*), *pl.* oniro-critiques; interprète *m* des songes, onirocrite *m.*

oneirocritical [ou'nairə'kritik(ə)l], *a.* oniro-critique, *pl.* oniro-critiques.

oneirocriticism [ou'nairə'kritisizm], *s.*, **oneirocritics** [ou'nairə'kritiks], *s.pl.* (*usu. with sg. const.*) oniro-critique *f,* onirocritie *f,* interprétation *f* des songes.

oneirologist [ounai'rɔlədʒist], *s.* onirologue *mf.*

oneirology [ounai'rɔlədʒi], *s.* onirologie *f.*

oneiromancer [ou'nairəmænsər], *s.* oniromancien, -ienne.

oneiromancy [ou'nairəmænsi], *s.* oniromancie *f.*
oneirotherapy [ounairou'θerəpi], *s. Med:* onirothérapie *f.*
one-leaved ['wʌn'li:vd], *a. Bot:* unifeuillé, unifolié.
one-legged ['wʌn'legd, -'legid], *a.* **1.** (*a*) qui n'a qu'une jambe; amputé de la jambe; **o.-l. man, woman,** unijambiste *mf*; (*b*) *Z:* monopode. **2.** *F:* (contrat, etc.) inégal, -aux.
one-level ['wʌn'lev(ə)l], *a. Cmptr:* **o.-l. address,** adresse absolue, directe, réelle; **o.-l. code,** code réel; langage *m* machine; **o.-l. subroutine,** sous-programme, *pl.* sous-programmes, fermé.
one-man ['wʌn'mæn], *a.* (tâche, astronef, etc.) pour un seul homme; **o.-m. show,** (i) *Art:* exposition particulière, individuelle; (ii) *Th:* (spectacle *m*) solo (*m*); *Mus:* récital *m, pl.* récitals; (iii) entreprise individuelle; **o.-m. dog,** chien *m* qui ne s'attache qu'à une seule personne; *Com:* **o.-m. company,** société *f* à une seule personne, à personne unique; **o.-m. market,** marché fermé, contrôlé.
oneness ['wʌnnis], *s.* **1.** unité *f*; accord *m* (d'opinions). **2.** identité *f* dans le temps. **3.** unicité *f*; caractère *m* unique.
one-nighter ['wʌn'naitər], *s. Th:* soirée *f* unique.
one-off ['wʌn'ɔf], *a. Ind: Com:* (article) spécial, hors série; *T.V:* (film) en exclusivité; *Publ:* (livre) à tirage limité; **the Minister said the measures were a o.-o. operation,** le Ministre a dit que les mesures ne seraient pas répétées.
one-piece ['wʌn'pi:s], *s.* monobloc *inv*; d'une seule pièce; **o.-p. swimsuit,** maillot *m* une pièce.
one-price ['wʌn'prais], *a. Com:* **o.-p. counter,** rayon *m* à prix unique; **o.-p. store,** (magasin *m* à) prix (*m*) unique.
oner ['wʌnər], *s.* **1.** *P: O:* (*a*) personne *f* unique; type épatant; (*b*) expert *m*; as *m*. **2.** *A:* (*a*) (coup *m* d')assommoir *m*, maître coup (de poing, etc.); (*b*) mensonge *m* de taille. **3.** *Games:* coup qui compte un point.
onerous ['ɔnərəs], *a.* **1.** (devoir, impôt, etc.) onéreux; **o. responsibility,** lourde responsabilité; **o. task,** tâche pénible. **2.** *Jur:* (*Scot:*) **o. title,** titre onéreux; **o. contract,** contrat *m* à titre onéreux.
onerously ['ɔnərəsli], *adv.* onéreusement; à titre onéreux.
onerousness ['ɔnərəsnis], *s.* onérosité *f.*
oneself [wʌn'self], *pron.* (*a*) (*emphatic*) soi-même; **one must do it o.,** il faut le faire soi-même; **to do sth. all by o.,** faire qch. tout seul; (*b*) (*reflexive*) se, soi(-même); **to flatter o.,** se flatter; **to look after o.,** se soigner; avoir soin de son individu; **to come to o.,** revenir à soi(-même); **to say sth. to o.,** se dire qch. à part soi, à soi-même; **to speak of o.,** parler de soi; **to keep o. to o.,** être très casanier, peu accueillant; **to feel o. again,** se sentir rétabli.
one-shot ['wʌn'ʃɔt], *a.* **1.** *Aut:* **o.-s. lubrication,** graissage central; graissage monocoup. **2.** *NAm:* **there's no o.-s. solution to the problem,** on ne peut pas résoudre le problème une fois pour toutes; **a o.-s. effort to achieve sth.,** un seul et unique effort pour accomplir qch. **3.** *Cmptr:* **o.-s. problem,** problème non répétitif, isolé, unique. **4.** *Elcs:* **o.-s. circuit,** circuit *m* monostable.
one-sided ['wʌn'saidid], *a.* **1.** (*a*) (*of contract, etc.*) unilatéral, -aux; (*b*) **o.-s. street,** rue bâtie d'un seul côté. **2.** (*of shape, etc.*) asymétrique. **3.** (*a*) (*of contract, etc.*) inégal, -aux; injuste; inéquitable; (*b*) (*of judgment, etc.*) partial, -aux; injuste; **o.-s. information,** renseignements entachés de partialité.
one-sidedly [wʌn'saididli], *adv.* **1.** unilatéralement. **2.** inéquitablement, partialement.
one-sidedness [wʌn'saididnis], *s.* **1.** asymétrie *f.* **2.** partialité *f* (d'une opinion, etc.); manque *m* d'équité (d'un marché, etc.).
Onesimus [ou'nesiməs]. *Pr.n.m. Rel.H:* Onésime.
onestep ['wʌnstep], *s. Danc:* one-step *m.*
one-time ['wʌn'taim], *a.* **1.** (*also* **onetime**) **James Martin, o.-t. mayor,** M. Jacques Martin, ancien, autrefois, jadis, maire. **2.** ne servant qu'une fois; *Typew:* **o.-t. carbon,** carbone *m* à frappe unique; *Mil: etc:* **o.-t. (ciphering) pad,** carnet *m* de clés-blocs; *Cmptr:* **o.-t. job,** travail *m* unique.
one-to-one ['wʌntə'wʌn], *a.* **o.-to-o. relationship,** tête-à-tête *m inv*; *Mth:* **o.-to-o. correspondence,** correspondance bijective, bi-univoque; *Cmptr:* **o.-to-o. translator,** traducteur *m* ligne à ligne, un(e) pour un(e).
one-track ['wʌn'træk], *a.* **1.** *Rail:* (ligne) à voie unique. **2. o.-t. mind,** esprit obsédé par une seule idée; **to have a o.-t. mind,** être incapable d'envisager deux idées à la fois.
one-two ['wʌn'tu:], *s. Box: F:* coup sec de gauche suivi d'un direct de droite.
one-upmanship [wʌn'ʌpmənʃip], *s. F:* l'art *m* de se faire passer pour supérieur aux autres.
one-way ['wʌn'wei], *a.* **1.** (*a*) **o.-w. ticket,** billet *m* simple; billet d'aller; (*b*) *Com:* **o.-w. packing,** emballage perdu. **2.** unidirectionnel; **o.-w. street,** rue *f* à sens unique (de circulation); **o.-w. traffic,** circulation *f* en sens unique; *Mec.E:* **o.-w. seal,** segment *m* anti-retour; *El:* **o.-w. switch,** commutateur *m* à une direction, à une voie; *Tp:* **o.-w. circuit,** circuit spécialisé. **3.** *NAm: P:* **o.-w. guy,** type franc, loyal.
onfall ['ɔnfɔ:l], *s. Scot:* **1.** attaque *f.* **2.** début *m* (d'une maladie).
ongoing ['ɔngouiŋ], *a. F:* progressif; continu.
ongoings ['ɔngouiŋz], *s.pl. F:* manège *m*; agissements *mpl*; manœuvres *fpl.*
onion ['ʌniən], *s.* **1.** oignon *m*; **spring o.,** ciboule *f*; petit oignon; **Welsh o.,** ciboule; **Spanish o.,** oignon d'Espagne; **pickling o.,** petit oignon; **string of onions,** chapelet *m*, corde *f*, d'oignons; **that's the way the o. peels,** c'est ainsi que tombent les dés, que la roue tourne; *Cu:* **o. sauce,** sauce blanche à l'oignon; **stewed with spring onions,** aux petits oignons; *Hort:* **o. bed, plot,** plant *m* d'oignons; oignonière *f*; **o. seed,** graine *f* d'oignon; **o. set,** oignonet *m*. **2.** *P:* (*a*) tête *f*, *P:* ciboulot *m*, citrouille *f*; **he's off his o.,** il est maboule; (*b*) **she knows her onions,** elle connaît son affaire, s'y connaît; elle est à la hauteur, *P:* à la coule. **3.** *Bot:* **sea o.,** oignon de mer; scille *f* maritime; **o. couch, o. grass,** avoine élevée; fromental *m*. **4.** *Arch:* **o. dome,** dôme bulbeux; bulbe *m*. **5.** *Miner:* **o. marble,** cipolin *m.*
onionskin ['ʌniənskin], *s.* **1.** (*usu. 2 words*) pelure *f* d'oignon. **2.** *Com:* (papier *m*) pelure (d'oignon).
oniony ['ʌniəni], *a.* qui sent l'oignon, qui a un goût d'oignon.
Oniscidae [ou'nisidi:], *s.pl. Crust:* oniscidés *m.*
onisciform [ou'nisifɔ:m], *a. Z:* onisciforme.
oniscus [ou'niskəs], *s. Crust:* oniscus *m.*
on-line ['ɔn'lain], *a.* **1.** *Tg:* en circuit; *Mil: etc:* **on-l. (ciphering) equipment,** matériel *m* de chiffrement en circuit; téléimprimeur chiffrant. **2.** *Cmptr:* (traitement, etc.) en direct, en liaison directe, avec l'ordinateur; **on-l. operation, working,** exploitation *f* en connexion, en (mode) connecté.
onlooker ['ɔnlukər], *s.* spectateur, -trice; *F:* badaud, -e; **the onlookers,** l'assistance *f*; les assistants *m*; (*at indoor sports, etc.*) la galerie; **to be an o. at a football match,** assister à un match de football.
only ['ounli], *a., adv. & conj.*
I. *a.* seul, unique; **o. son, o. child,** fils unique, enfant unique; **o. copy extant,** exemplaire unique; **his one and o. hope,** son seul et unique espoir; **his o. answer was to burst out laughing,** pour toute réponse il a éclaté de rire; **his o. relaxation was walking,** pour toute distraction il faisait des promenades à pied; **hunting is their o. source of food,** seule la chasse leur fournit des vivres; **his o. weapon was a walking stick,** pour toute arme il avait une canne; **we are the o. people who know it,** nous sommes seuls à le savoir; **he was the o. one who noticed it,** il a été le seul à s'en apercevoir, il n'y a eu que lui pour s'en apercevoir; **they were the o. ones killed,** il n'y a eu qu'eux de tués; **you are not the o. one,** vous n'êtes pas le seul; il n'y a pas que vous; **country life is the o. life,** il n'y a rien de tel que de vivre à la campagne; **tights are the o. thing nowadays,** il n'y a que le collant aujourd'hui; **the o. thing is that it's rather expensive,** seulement ça coûte cher.
II. *adv.* seulement, ne . . . que, rien que, simplement; **he has o. one brother,** il n'a qu'un seul frère; **I have o. three—o. three?** je n'en ai que trois—que trois? **it is true, isn't it?—o. too true,** c'est bien vrai, n'est-ce pas?—que trop vrai; **o. half an hour more,** plus qu'une demi-heure; **one man o.,** un seul homme; *Rail: etc:* **ladies o.,** réservé aux dames; **(entrance for) season ticket holders o.,** entrée réservée aux abonnés; **o. an expert could advise us,** seul un expert pourrait nous conseiller; il n'y a qu'un expert qui puisse nous conseiller; **o. he can say,** lui seul saurait le dire; **o. the binding is damaged,** il n'y a que la reliure d'abîmée; **o. five men remained alive,** il ne restait de vivants que cinq hommes; **it is o. in Paris that one really lives,** on ne vit qu'à Paris; **a little chap o.** *so* **high,** un petit bonhomme pas plus haut que ça; **he can o. refuse,** il ne peut que refuser; **I o. touched it,** je n'ai fait que le toucher; **he has o. to ask for it,** il n'a qu'à le demander; **it is o. a matter of having good taste,** il suffit d'avoir du goût; **we are born o. to die,** nous ne naissons que pour mourir; **he got home o. to find his wife had gone out,** il est rentré chez lui pour trouver que sa femme était sortie; **I will o. say that I disagree,** je me bornerai à dire que je ne suis pas de cet avis; **he's going o. to please you,** il y va seulement pour vous faire plaisir; **I shall be o. too pleased to come,** je ne serai que trop heureux de venir; **o. to think of it,** rien que d'y penser; **o. to think of what might have happened!** quand je pense à ce qui aurait pu arriver! **o. think what pleasure it gave me,** imaginez un peu le plaisir que cela m'a fait; **if o. I knew where he is!** si seulement je savais où il est! **we must respect him if o. for his honesty,** il faut le respecter rien que, ne fût-ce que, ne serait-ce que, pour sa probité; **I o. wish that I had his luck,** je ne souhaite qu'une chose, c'est d'avoir sa bonne fortune; **not o. useful but also decorative,** non seulement utile, mais aussi, mais encore, décoratif; **o. yesterday,** hier encore; pas plus tard qu'hier; **o. just,** à peine.
III. *conj.* mais; **the book is interesting, o. rather too long,** le livre est intéressant, mais un peu trop long, seulement un peu long; *conj.phr.* **I would do it o. (that) I can't spare the time,** je le ferais n'était que, si ce n'était que, le temps me fait défaut; **the house looked like a castle, o. that the windows were modern,** la maison avait tout d'un ancien château, si ce n'est que les fenêtres étaient de notre époque.
only-begotten [ounlibi'gɔt(ə)n], *a. & s.* **the o.-b. (Son) of the Father,** le Fils unique du Père.
onocentaur [ɔnou'sentɔ:r], *s. Myth:* onocentaure *m.*
onoclea [ɔnə'kli:ə], *s. Bot:* onocléе *f.*
on-off ['ɔn'ɔf], *a. Tchn:* (contrôle, etc.) (par) tout ou (par) rien.
onomancy ['ɔnəmənsi], *s.* onomancie *f.*
onomastic [ɔnə'mæstik], *a.* onomastique.
onomasticon [ɔnə'mæstikən], *s.* onomasticon *m.*
onomastics [ɔnə'mæstiks], *s.pl.* (*usu. with sg. const.*) onomastique *f.*
onomatologist [ɔnəmə'tɔlədʒist], *s.* onomatologue *mf.*
onomatology [ɔnəmə'tɔlədʒi], *s.* onomatologie *f.*
onomatomania [ɔnəmætə'meinjə], *s. Psy:* onomatomanie *f.*
onomatop(e) ['ɔnəmətɔp, -toup], *s.* mot *m* onomatopéique.
onomatopoeia [ɔnəmətæ'pi(:)ə], *s. Ling: Rh:* onomatopée *f.*
onomatopoeic(al) [ɔnəmætə'pi:ik(l)], **onomatopoetic** [ɔnəmætəpou'etik], *a.* onomatopéique.
onrush ['ɔnrʌʃ], *s.* ruée *f*, attaque *f*; **swept away by the o. of the water,** enlevé par des torrents d'eau.
onset ['ɔnset], *s.* **1.** assaut *m*, attaque *f*; **to withstand the o. of the enemy,** soutenir le choc de l'ennemi. **2.** (*a*) **at the (first) o.,** d'emblée, de prime abord, à l'abord, au premier abord; **from the o.,** dès l'abord; **the o. of a disease,** la première attaque d'une maladie; (*b*) *Ch:* départ *m* (d'une réaction).
onsetter ['ɔnsetər], *s. Min:* clicheur *m.*
onsetting ['ɔnsetiŋ], *s. Min:* accrochage *m*; **o. station,** recette *f.*
onshore ['ɔnʃɔ:r], *a.* **1.** (vent, etc.) du large. **2.** (installation pétrolière, etc.) à terre.
onslaught ['ɔnslɔ:t], *s.* assaut *m*, attaque *f*; **to withstand the o. of the enemy,** soutenir le choc de l'ennemi; *Hist:* **the o. on Verdun,** la ruée vers Verdun; **to make a savage o. on the Prime Minister,** attaquer férocement, faire une charge à fond contre, le Premier Ministre.
onstage ['ɔn'steidʒ]. **1.** *adv.* (entrer, etc.) en scène. **2.** *a.* (manière de parler, style, etc.) sur la scène.
ontal ['ɔntəl], *a. Phil:* ontique.
Ontarian [ɔn'tεəriən]. *Geog:* **1.** *a.* ontarien. **2.** *s.* Ontarien, -ienne.
on-the-fly ['ɔnðə'flai], *a. Cmptr: etc:* (*of printing, printer*) à la volée.
on-the-job ['ɔnðə'dʒɔb], *a.* **on-t.-j. training,** formation *f* sur le tas, par la pratique.
ontic ['ɔntik], *a. Phil:* ontique.
onto ['ɔntu(:), 'ɔntə], *prep.* = on to *q.v. under* ON[1] I.3.
onto- ['ɔntou, ɔn'tɔ], *pref.* onto-.
ontogenesis [ɔntou'dʒenisis], **ontogeny** [ɔn'tɔdʒini], *s. Biol:* ontogénèse *f*, ontogénie *f.*
ontogenetic [ɔntoudʒi'netik], **ontogenic** [ɔntə'dʒenik], *a. Biol:* ontogénétique, ontogénique.
ontological [ɔntou'lɔdʒik(ə)l], *a. Phil:* ontologique; **o. argument,** preuve *f* ontologique.
ontologically [ɔntou'lɔdʒikəli], *adv.* ontologiquement.
ontologism [ɔn'tɔlədʒizm], *s. Phil:* ontologisme *m.*
ontologist [ɔn'tɔlədʒist], *s.* ontologiste *m.*
ontologize [ɔn'tɔlədʒaiz], *v.tr. & i.* ontologiser.
ontology [ɔn'tɔlədʒi], *s. Phil:* ontologie *f.*
onus ['ounəs], *s.* responsabilité *f*, charge *f*, obligation onéreuse; soin laissé à qn (de faire qch.); **to have the o. of proving the validity of a claim,** avoir la charge de prouver le bien-fondé d'une réclamation; **the o. lies on the government to compensate the victims,** il incombe au gouvernement d'indemniser les sinistrés; *Jur:* **o. probandi** [prə'bændai], charge, fardeau *m*, de la preuve.
onward ['ɔnwəd]. **1.** *adv.* = ONWARDS. **2.** *a.* (*of motion,*

etc.) en avant; **the o. march of ideas,** la marche en avant, la marche progressive, des idées.

onwards ['ɔnwədz], *adv.* (*a*) en avant, plus loin; **to move o.,** s'avancer; (*b*) **from tomorrow o.,** à partir de demain; **from this time o.,** désormais, dorénavant.

onychia [ɔ'nikiə], *s. Med:* onychie *f.*

onychogenic [ɔnikou'dʒenik], *a. Physiol:* onychogène.

onychogryp(h)osis [ɔnikougri'fousis, -'pousis], *s. Med:* onychogryphose *f.*

onychomycosis [ɔnikoumai'kousis], *s. Med:* onychomycose *f.*

onychophagia [ɔnikou'feidʒiə], **onychophagy** [ɔni'kɔfədʒi], *s. Med:* onychophagie *f.*

Onychophora [ɔni'kɔfərə], *s.pl. Bot:* onychophores *m.*

onychoptosis [ɔnikɔp'tousis], *s. Med:* onychoptôse *f.*

onychosis [ɔni'kousis], *s. Med:* onychose *f.*

onymous ['ɔniməs], *a.* qui porte le nom de l'auteur; signé.

onyx ['ɔniks], *s.* **1.** *Miner:* onyx *m*; **black o.,** jais artificiel. **2.** *Med:* ongle *m* (à l'œil).

oynx-bearing ['ɔniksbɛəriŋ], *a. Miner:* onychite.

onyxis [ɔ'niksis], *s. Med:* onyxis *m*; ongle incarné.

o(o)- ['ou(ə)], *pref.* o(o)-.

oocyst ['ouəsist], *s. Biol:* oocyte *m.*

oocyte ['ouəsait], *s. Biol:* ovocyste *m.*

oodles ['u:dlz], *s.pl. P:* **there's o. of it, of them,** il y en a un tas, des tas, une tapée.

ooecium [ou'i:ʃiəm], *s. Z:* oécie *f.*

oof [u:f], *s. F: O:* argent *m*, braise *f*, pognon *m.*

oofy ['u:fi], *a. P: O:* **1.** (*of pers.*) galetteux, rupin. **2.** (*of thg.*) coûteux, magnifique.

oogamy ['ouɔgəmi], *s. Biol:* oogamie *f.*

oogenesis [ouə'dʒenisis], *s. Biol:* oogénèse *f.*

oogonium, *pl.* **-ia** [ouə'gouniəm, -iə], *s. Bot:* oogone *f.*

ooja(h) ['u:dʒɑ:], **ooji** ['u:dʒi:], **oojimaflip** ['u:dʒiməflip], *s. F: O:* chose *f*, machin *m*, truc *m.*

oolite ['u:(ə)lait], *s. Geol:* **1.** jurassique supérieur; **Inferior O.,** bajocien *m.* **2.** oolithe *m.*

oolith ['ou:(ə)liθ], *s. Geol:* oolithe *m.*

oolitic [ou:(ə)'litik], *a. Geol:* oolithique.

oologic(al) [ou(ə)'lɔdʒik(l)], *a.* oologique.

oologist [ou'ɔlədʒist], *s.* **1.** ornithologiste *mf* qui se spécialise dans l'oologie. **2.** collectionneur *m* d'œufs d'oiseaux.

oology [ou'ɔlədʒi], *s. Orn:* oologie *f.*

oolong ['u:lɔŋ], *s.* variété *f* de thé entre le noir et le vert.

oom [u:m], *s.* (*in S. Africa*) oncle *m*; *Hist: F:* **O. Paul,** le Président Kruger.

oomiak ['u:miæk], *s.* canot *m* esquimau.

oomph [umf], *s. P:* (*a*) allant *m*; **to have plenty of o.,** avoir de l'allant; être énergique, dynamique; **to have no o.,** être sans entrain; (*b*) (*of girl*) sex-appeal *m*; chien *m.*

Oomycetes [ouəmai'si:ti:z], *s.pl. Fung:* oomycètes *m.*

oont [u:nt], *s.* (*in India*) chameau *m.*

oophore ['ouəfɔ:r], *s. Bot:* oophore *m.*

oophorectomy [ouəfə'rektəmi], *s. Surg:* oophorectomie *f*, ovariotomie *f.*

oophoritis [ouəfə'raitis], *s. Med:* oophorite *f*, ovarite *f.*

ooplasm ['ouəplazm], *s. Bot:* ooplasme *m.*

oops [u:ps], *int.* **1.** (*to child who has fallen down*) (*also* **oops-a-daisy** ['u:psə'deizi]) houp-là! **2.** oh là là! hélas! mon Dieu!

ooscope ['ouəskoup], *s.* ooscope *m.*

ooscopy [ou'ɔskəpi], *s.* ooscopie *f.*

oosphere ['ouəsfiər], *s. Bot:* oosphère *f.*

oospore ['ouəspɔ:r], *s. Bot:* oospore *f.*

oosporic, oosporous [ouə'spɔ:rik, -'spɔ:rəs], *a. Bot:* oospore.

oostegite [ou'ɔstidʒait], *s. Crust:* oostégite *f.*

oostegitic [ouɔsti'dʒitik], *a. Crust:* oostégitique.

ootheca, *pl.* **-ae** [ouə'θi:kə, -'θi:si:], *s. Ent: Moll:* oothèque *f.*

ootid ['ouətid], *s. Biol:* ootide *f.*

ooze[1] [u:z], *s.* **1.** (*a*) vase *f*, limon *m*; bourbe *f*, boue *f*; *Geol:* dépôt abyssal, boue; **diatom o.,** vase diatoméenne; (*b*) marais *m*, fond bourbeux. **2.** suintement *m*, infiltration *f*, dégouttement *m* (d'un liquide). **3.** *Tan:* jusée *f*, jus *m*; **o. calf, o. leather,** cuir *m* de jusée.

ooze[2]. **1.** *v.i.* (*a*) suinter; s'infiltrer; dégoutter; **to o. through the ground,** filtrer à travers le terrain; s'infiltrer dans la terre; **oil was oozing through the walls,** l'huile suintait à travers les murs; **water that oozes out from the rock,** eau qui sourd de la roche; **sap that oozes (from the tree),** sève qui s'écoule; **his courage is oozing away,** son courage l'abandonne; son ardeur se refroidit; *F:* il commence à avoir le trac; (*b*) **the walls were oozing with water,** les murs suintaient l'eau; l'eau suintait des murs; (*c*) *NAm: F:* **to o. out,** s'éclipser, se défiler, filer. **2.** *v.tr.* suer, suinter, laisser dégoutter (l'eau, etc.); *F:* **to o. hatred,** suinter la haine; **he oozes conceit,** il sue l'orgueil par tous les pores; **to o. charm,** faire du charme.

ooze[3], *s. Scot: Tex:* poil *m*, duvet *m* (des tissus non flambés).

oozing[1] ['u:ziŋ], *a.* (*a*) (*of water*) stillant; (*b*) (*of wall*) dégoulinant, suintant.

oozing[2], *s.* suintement *m*, fuite *f* (de l'eau, etc.); (déperdition *f* par) infiltration *f*; (*from rock, etc.*) stillation *f.*

oozy ['u:zi], *a.* **1.** vaseux, bourbeux, limoneux; **o. bank,** banc *m* de vase. **2.** suintant, humide.

op[1] [ɔp], *s. F:* (= OPERATION) **1.** *Med:* opération (chirurgicale). **2.** *Mil:* **combined o.,** opération combinée.

op[2], *a. Art:* (= OPTICAL) **o. art,** l'op art *m.*

opacify [ou'pæsifai]. **1.** *v.tr.* opacifier. **2.** *v.i.* s'opacifier.

opacifying[1] [ou'pæsifaiiŋ], *a.* opacifiant.

opacifying[2], *s.* opacification *f.*

opacimeter [oupə'simitər], *s. Phot:* opacimètre *m.*

opacimetry [oupə'simitri], *s. Opt:* opacimétrie *f.*

opacity [ou'pæsiti], *s.* opacité *f* (d'un corps, d'un liquide, de l'esprit); obscurité *f* (d'un texte, etc.).

opah ['oupə], *s. Ich:* opah *m.*

opal ['oup(ə)l], *s.* **1.** (*a*) opale *f*; **pitch o.,** péchopal *m*; **wood o.,** opale xyloïde; **water o.,** hyalite *f*; (*b*) *a. & s.* (*colour*) opale (*m*) *inv*; **the sea was a milky o.,** la mer était d'un opale laiteux. **2.** *Glassm:* **o. (glass),** verre opale; opaline *f*; *El:* **o. lamp,** ampoule *f* opale.

opalescence [oupə'lesəns], *s.* opalescence *f.*

opalescent [oupə'lesənt], *a.* opalescent; (*of hue*) opale *inv*; (*of haze, etc.*) opalisé.

opalesque [oupə'lesk], *a.* opalescent, opalin.

opaline ['oupəlain]. **1.** *a.* opalin. **2.** *s.* ['oupəli:n, -lain], *Glassm:* verre opalin; verre opale; opaline *f.*

opalinid [oupə'linid], *s. Prot:* opaline *f.*

Opalinidae [oupə'linidi:], *s.pl. Prot:* opalines *f.*

opalization [oupəlai'zeiʃ(ə)n], *s. Glassm:* opalisation *f.*

opalize ['oupəlaiz], *v.tr. Glassm:* opaliser (le verre).

opalized ['oupəlaizd], *a.* opalisé.

opalizing ['oupəlaiziŋ], *s. Glassm:* opalisation *f.*

opaque[1] [ou'peik]. **1.** *a.* (*a*) opaque; **to make o.,** rendre opaque, opacifier (qch.); **to become o.,** s'opacifier; *Opt:* **o. projector, projection,** projecteur *m*, projection *f*, épiscopique; (*b*) (*of pers.*) peu intelligent; à l'esprit épais, obtus; (*of mind*) lourd, épais, obtus; (*c*) (texte, etc.) difficile à comprendre; obscur. **2.** *s. Phot:* (*a*) opacifiant *m*; (*b*) cliché *m* opaque.

opaque[2]. **1.** *v.tr.* opacifier. **2.** *v.i.* s'opacifier.

opaqueness [ou'peiknis], *s.* opacité *f* (d'un liquide, de l'esprit, etc.); obscurité *f* (d'un texte, etc.).

opaquing[1] [ou'peikiŋ], *a.* opacifiant; **o. medium,** opacifiant *m.*

opaquing[2], *s.* opacification *f*; *Phot:* bouchage *m* (d'un cliché).

ope [oup], *v.tr. & i. Poet:* = OPEN[2].

open[1] ['oup(ə)n], *a.* **1.** (*a*) ouvert; **o. door, window,** porte, fenêtre, ouverte; **to fling, throw, the door wide o.,** ouvrir la porte toute grande; *Pol.Ec:* **the policy of the o. door,** la politique de la porte ouverte; **the door flew o.,** la porte s'ouvrit brusquement, en coup de vent; **to pull, push, the door o.,** ouvrir la porte (en tirant dessus; d'une poussée); **to burst the door o.,** (i) ouvrir brusquement la porte; (ii) enfoncer la porte; **half o.,** entrouvert, entrebâillé; **to keep o. house,** tenir table ouverte; *F:* tenir auberge; *NAm: Com:* **o. house,** *Sch:* **o. day,** journée *f* d'accueil; *Hyd.E:* **o. sluice,** gueule bée; (*of mill*) **to work with all sluice gates o.,** marcher à gueule bée; (*b*) (*of box, etc.*) ouvert; (*of bottle*) débouché; (*of parcel*) défait; (*of envelope*) (i) non cacheté; (ii) décacheté; **o. grave,** tombe qui attend son cercueil; *Mus:* (*of organ*) **o. pipe,** tuyau ouvert; *Ch:* **o. chain,** chaîne ouverte; *Cmptr:* **o. subroutine,** sous-programme ouvert, relogeable; **to break o., burst o., smash o., a box,** éventrer une boîte; **to slit o., rip o., an envelope,** couper, éventrer, une enveloppe; **to cut o.,** couper, ouvrir; **to bite o.,** ouvrir (qch.) avec les dents; **to lay s.o.'s skull o.,** ouvrir, fendre, le crâne à qn; **to read s.o. like an o. book,** lire à livre ouvert dans la pensée de qn; (*c*) **the offices are o. from ten to five,** les bureaux sont ouverts de dix heures à cinq heures; (*of museum, etc.*) **o. to the public,** ouvert, accessible, au public; visible; **o. all night,** ouvert la nuit; **police station o. day and night,** permanence *f* de police; *Ven:* **the season is o.,** la chasse est ouverte; (*d*) **in (the) o. court,** en plein tribunal; **to pronounce judgment in the o. court,** rendre un jugement à huis ouvert; **o. trial,** jugement public; **o. market,** marché public; (*e*) **posts o. to all,** charges accessibles à tout le monde; **career o. to very few,** carrière très fermée; *Sp:* **o. competition,** tournement, tournoi ouvert; **o. race,** *Turf:* **o. handicap,** omnium *m*; *Golf:* **o. championship,** championnat open, ouvert; omnium; **the French o.,** l'open français; *Ind:* **o. shop,** atelier *m*, chantier *m*, qui admet les ouvriers non-syndiqués. **2.** (*a*) sans limites, sans bornes; **in the o. air,** au grand air; à ciel ouvert; **this experiment must be carried out in the o. air,** il faut faire cette expérience à l'air libre, en plein air; **to sleep in the o. air,** coucher à la belle étoile, dehors; **in the o. street, fields,** en pleine rue, en pleins champs; **to sow seed in the o. ground,** semer des graines en pleine terre; **o. country,** pays découvert; **in the o. country,** en pleine, rase, campagne; (*in a forest*) **o. patch,** terrain découvert; clairière *f*; **the o. sea,** la haute mer, le large; **in the o. sea,** en pleine mer; *Mil:* **o. warfare,** guerre *f* en rase campagne; guerre de mouvement; (*b*) *s.* **in the o.,** au grand air; à ciel ouvert; **to sleep in the o.,** coucher à la belle étoile, dehors; **the house stands in the o.,** la maison est située en pleine campagne; **to come out into the o.,** venir au grand jour; se dévoiler; **trees that grow in the o.,** arbres qui croissent à l'état isolé; *Hort:* **to sow seed in the o.,** semer en pleine terre; *Nau:* **to pilot a ship into the o.,** piloter un navire vers le large. **3.** (*a*) découvert, non couvert; **o. carriage, car,** voiture découverte; **o. boat,** bateau ouvert, découvert, non-ponté; **o. mine,** mine *f* à ciel ouvert; **o. light,** feu nu; **o. wire,** *El:* fil nu; *Cmptr: etc:* fil (nu) aérien; **o.-wire line,** ligne aérienne; (*b*) **o. field,** champ ouvert, sans enclos; *Nau:* **o. roadstead,** rade foraine; (*c*) (*of coast, position, etc.*) exposé (to, à); **o. to all the winds,** ouvert à tous les vents; **fortress o. to attack from the south,** forteresse attaquable au sud; *Fb:* **to leave the goal o.,** dégarnir ses buts; (*d*) **to lay oneself o. to a charge, to criticism,** prêter le flanc, donner prise, à une accusation, à la critique; **to lay oneself o. to calumny,** s'exposer à, se mettre en butte à, la calomnie; **idea that is o. to objections,** idée qui appelle des objections, qui prête à des objections; **procedure o. to criticism,** procédure qui pourrait donner lieu à des critiques; procédure critiquable; **an author is o. to criticism,** un auteur est justiciable de la critique; **o. to doubt,** exposé au doute; douteux; **o. to ridicule,** qui prête au ridicule; (*e*) **to be o. to prejudices, to conviction,** être accessible aux préjugés, à la conviction; **to be o. to advice,** être tout prêt à accueillir des conseils; **o. to pity,** accessible à la pitié; **o. to any reasonable offer,** disposé à considérer toute offre raisonnable; **invention o. to improvement,** invention susceptible d'amélioration. **4.** (*a*) manifeste, public, -ique; **o. scandal,** scandale public; **o. secret,** secret *m* de Polichinelle; **o. letter,** lettre ouverte (communiquée à la presse); **to lay o. a plan,** mettre un projet à découvert, à nu; exposer un projet au grand jour; **o. hostilities,** guerre ouverte; *Tel: P:* **o. mike,** tribune *f* libre; (*b*) ouvert; franc, *f.* franche; déclaré; **o. admiration,** franche admiration; **o. enemy of the Government,** ennemi déclaré du Gouvernement; **he is an o. atheist,** il est franchement athée; **to be o. with s.o.,** parler franchement à qn; ne rien cacher à qn; **he is as o. as a child,** il est franc comme l'or. **5.** (*a*) (*of flower, the lips, the hand, etc.*) ouvert; **eyes wide o. with surprise,** yeux écarquillés de surprise; **to stand with o. mouth before sth.,** rester bouche bée devant qch.; **o. wound,** plaie (i) béante, (ii) non cicatrisée; (*to the feelings, etc.*), **ever-o. wound,** plaie incicatrisable; blessure toujours saignante; *Cost:* **o. at the neck,** (i) *O:* (*of dress*) échancré au col; (ii) (*of shirt*) à col ouvert; *Physiol:* **o. pores,** pores dilatés; (*b*) *Ling:* **o. vowel,** voyelle ouverte. **6.** (*a*) non serré; *For:* **o. felling,** coupe claire; *Agr:* **o. soil,** terre meuble; (*b*) *Mil:* **to attack in o. order,** attaquer en ordre dispersé; *Navy:* (*of ships*) **in o. order,** à distance normale; (*c*) (clôture) à claire-voie; (tissu) à jour; (*d*) *Fb:* **o. game, play,** jeu ouvert, dégagé. **7.** (*a*) libre, non obstrué; **o. road,** chemin *m* libre; **road o. to traffic,** route ouverte à la circulation (publique); *Rail:* **o. signal,** signal effacé; *T.V: etc:* **the line will be o. at 8 o'clock,** vous pourrez nous téléphoner (pour poser vos questions) à partir de 8 heures; **o. water,** eau *f* libre (de glace, etc.); *Can:* (i) débâcle *f* (de la glace qui couvre une rivière, etc.); (ii) période *f* entre la débâcle et l'embâcle; **to have an o. field,** avoir le champ libre devant soi; **o. view,** vue dégagée; **o. forest,** forêt *f* de haute futaie; *Aut:* **o. corner,** virage découvert; **to keep the bowels o.,** tenir le ventre libre; **o. town, city,** (i) *Mil:* ville ouverte; (ii) *U.S:* ville où la police se montre indulgente en matière de vice; *Mus:* **o. string,** corde *f* à vide; (*of wind instrument*) **o. sounds,** sons ordinaires (non bouchés); (*b*) **to keep a day o. for s.o.,** réserver un jour pour qn; *NAm:* **to have an o. hour, an hour o.,** avoir une heure de libre; **to keep a job o.,** ne pas pourvoir à un emploi; **the job is still o.,** la place est toujours vacante; **there was no course o. to me but flight,** je n'avais d'autre ressource que la fuite; **two courses are o. to us,** deux moyens s'offrent à nous; **it is o. to you to object,** il vous est permis, loisible, de faire des objections, d'y trouver à redire; **it is o. to me to do so,** j'ai toute latitude pour le faire; je peux le faire si je veux. **8.** (*a*) non résolu; **o. question,** question discutable, discutée, pendante, indécise, en suspens; **to keep an o. mind on sth.,** rester sans parti pris; ne pas avoir d'idée préconçue sur qch.; se réserver; réserver son opinion, sa liberté de jugement, sur qch.; **to leave the matter o.,** réserver la question; *Jur:* **o. contract,** contrat dont toutes les stipulations ne sont pas encore arrêtées; (*b*) *M.Ins:* **o. policy,** police flottante, d'abonnement. **9. o. weather,** temps doux; **o. winter,** hiver clément. **10.** *Fin: Com:* **o. account,** compte ouvert; compte courant; **o. credit,** crédit à découvert; crédit en blanc; **o. cheque,** chèque ouvert, non barré.

open², *v.tr. & i.* **I.** *v.tr.* **1.** (*a*) ouvrir (une porte, etc.); baisser (une glace); **to o. the door wide,** ouvrir la porte toute grande; **to half o. the door,** entrebâiller, entrouvrir, la porte; **to o. again,** rouvrir; **to o. the door to abuses,** ouvrir la porte aux abus; prêter aux abus; **to o. the door to a settlement,** rendre possible un arrangement; (*b*) déboucher, entamer (une bouteille); écailler (une huître); décacheter (une lettre); ouvrir (un livre); défaire (un paquet); déplier (un journal, etc.); déluter (une cornue à gaz); lâcher (une écluse); **to o. the mail,** dépouiller le courrier; **opened bottle,** bouteille en vidange; *El:* **to o. the circuit,** (inter)rompre, couper, le courant; *Mil:* **to o. a battery,** démasquer une batterie; *Med:* **to o. the bowels,** relâcher les intestins; (*c*) **to o. one's shop,** ouvrir son magasin; **to o. a new shop, a new branch,** ouvrir, fonder, monter, un nouveau magasin; fonder une succursale; **to o. a park to the public,** ouvrir un parc au public; **to o. a road (to traffic),** livrer une route à la circulation; (*d*) présider à l'inauguration de, inaugurer (une institution, un établissement); **to o. Parliament,** ouvrir la session du Parlement. **2.** (*a*) écarter (les jambes, etc.); ouvrir (la main, les yeux, etc.); **to o. one's shoulders,** écarter les épaules; se carrer; **he didn't o. his mouth,** il n'a pas ouvert la bouche; **I have not opened my mouth all day,** je n'ai pas desserré les dents de la journée; **not to dare to o. one's lips,** ne pas oser ouvrir la bouche; **to half o. one's eyes,** entrouvrir les yeux; *Mil:* **to o. the ranks,** ouvrir les rangs; (*b*) *Nau:* **to o. two sea marks, a bay,** ouvrir deux amers, une baie. **3. to o. a hole in a wall, etc.,** pratiquer, percer, un trou dans un mur, etc.; **to o. a vein,** ouvrir une veine; **to o. a way, path, through sth.,** ouvrir, frayer, un chemin à travers qch.; **to o. a quarry,** éventer une carrière. **4.** découvrir, exposer, révéler; **to o. one's heart, to o. oneself,** (i) épancher son cœur; (ii) ouvrir son cœur, s'ouvrir (**to s.o.,** à qn); **to o. one's mind to s.o.,** s'ouvrir à qn; *Arch:* **to o. vistas,** dégager les vues; **that opens new prospects for me,** cela m'ouvre de nouveaux horizons; cela me donne de nouvelles espérances. **5.** commencer; **to o. negotiations, a conversation, a debate,** entamer, engager, des négociations, une conversation, un débat; **his name opens the list,** son nom ouvre la liste; **to o. fire,** ouvrir le feu; commencer le tir; **to o. hostilities,** ouvrir les hostilités; **to o. ground,** défricher, défoncer, un terrain (vierge); **to o. the budget,** présenter le budget; *Com:* **to o. an account in s.o.'s name,** ouvrir un compte à qn, en faveur de qn; **to o. a loan,** ouvrir un emprunt; *Jur:* **to o. the case,** ouvrir l'affaire; exposer les faits; *Cards:* **to o. the play,** attaquer, entamer (d'une carte); **to o. clubs,** attaquer trèfle; entamer trèfle; **to o. the bidding,** ouvrir les enchères; **to o. (the bidding) with two hearts,** annoncer deux cœurs d'entrée; *v.i.* (*poker*) **to o.,** ouvrir le pot.

II. *v.i.* s'ouvrir. **1.** (*a*) (*of door, etc.*) **to half o., to o. a little,** s'entrebâiller, s'entrouvrir; **the door won't o.,** la porte tient; **door, room, that opens into, on to, the garden,** porte, salle, qui donne sur, dans, le jardin, qui ouvre sur, qui communique avec, le jardin; **rooms that o. out of one another,** pièces qui se commandent; **the exits o. directly on to the street,** les sorties donnent accès directement à la rue; **lane that opens into the main road,** chemin qui aboutit à la grande route; **stairway opening on the pavement,** escalier débouchant sur le trottoir; (*b*) *El:* (*of cutout*) décoller; (*c*) *Mch:* (*of inlet port, etc.*) se découvrir; s'ouvrir; (*d*) (*of shop, etc.*) ouvrir; **the bank opens at ten,** la banque ouvre (ses portes) à dix heures; **as soon as the season opens,** dès l'ouverture *f* de la saison. **2.** (*a*) (*of view, prospects, etc.*) s'étendre; (*b*) (*of flower*) s'épanouir, s'ouvrir; **half-opened bud,** bouton entr'éclos; (*c*) (*of bay, etc.*) s'ouvrir. **3.** commencer; **play that opens with a brawl,** pièce qui s'ouvre, commence, débute, par une rixe; **he opened with a remark about the weather,** il a entamé la conversation par une remarque à propos du temps; *St.Exch:* **coppers opened firm,** les valeurs cuprifères ont ouvert fermes. **4.** *Ven:* (*of hounds*) donner de la voix.

III. (*compound verbs*) **1. open out.** (*a*) *v.tr.* (i) ouvrir, étendre, déplier (une feuille de papier, etc.); (ii) développer (une entreprise, etc.); (iii) élargir, aléser, agrandir (un trou); évaser, mandriner (la bouche d'un tuyau); (*b*) *v.i.* (*of view, prospects, etc.*) s'ouvrir, s'étendre; (ii) **to o. out to s.o.,** s'ouvrir à qn; s'épancher; (iii) *Aut:* mettre, ouvrir, les gaz.

2. open up. (*a*) *v.tr.* ouvrir; éventer (une carrière); exposer, révéler (une perspective, etc.); frayer, pratiquer (un chemin); **to o. up a thoroughfare between two districts,** faire une percée entre deux quartiers; **to o. up a country to trade,** ouvrir un pays au commerce; *Surg:* **to o. up an abscess,** débrider un abcès; *Metall:* **to o. up a mould,** dévêtir un moule; (*b*) *v.i.* (i) (*of view, prospects, etc.*) s'ouvrir, s'étendre; (ii) *F:* ouvrir le feu; (iii) (*of pers.*) s'ouvrir (**to s.o.,** à qn); s'épancher; *F:* vider son sac; **to make a suspect o. up,** faire avouer un suspect; délier la langue à un suspect; (iv) (*of athlete, etc.*) y aller de tout son cœur, de toutes ses forces; (v) *Aut:* mettre, ouvrir, les gaz; (vi) *Com:* ouvrir une boutique, une maison, une succursale (**in, at, a place,** dans un endroit); **to o. up in a new country,** entamer des affaires dans un nouveau pays.

openable ['oup(ə)nəbl], *a.* que l'on peut ouvrir; *Th:* (porte, fenêtre) praticable.

openair ['oupənɛər], *a.* (*a*) au grand air, en plein air; **o. restaurant,** restaurant *m* en plein air; **o. life,** la vie des champs; **o. plants,** végétaux *m* de pleine terre; **o. meeting, market,** assemblée *f*, marché *m*, en plein vent; *Art:* **an o. portrait,** un plein air; *Med:* **o. treatment,** cure *f* d'air; (*b*) **she's an o. girl,** elle aime la vie, les occupations, en plein air.

open-armed ['oup(ə)n'ɑ:md], *a.* (accueil *m*) à bras ouverts; **to receive s.o. o.-a.,** accueillir qn les bras ouverts, à bras ouverts.

openbill ['oupənbil], *s. Orn:* (cigogne *f*) bec-ouvert (*m*), *pl.* becs-ouverts; anastome *m*.

opencast ['oup(ə)nkɑ:st]. **1.** *a.* (chantier *m*, exploitation *f*) à ciel ouvert. **2.** *s.* carrière *f* à ciel ouvert.

open-circuit ['oup(ə)n'sə:kit], *a. El:* (impédance *f*, etc.) en circuit ouvert; **o.-c. voltage,** tension *f* à vide; *Tg:* **o.-c. system,** système *m* à circuit ouvert.

open-eared ['oup(ə)n'i:əd], *a.* **to listen o.-e. to s.o.,** écouter qn de toutes ses oreilles.

open-end ['oupən'end], *a.* **o.-e. mortgage,** hypothèque qui peut être changée, modifiée; *Fin:* **o.-e. trust,** société *f* de gestion de portefeuille à capital variable et dont les actions sont remboursables sur demande.

open-ended ['oupən'endid], *a.* **1.** (caisse) à bout(s) ouvert(s). **2.** sans limites fixes; non déterminé; (système, procédé) extensible, qui peut être évolué; **o.-e. commitment,** engagement illimité; **o.-e. discussion,** libre discussion *f*; **o.-e. question,** question *f* qui manque de précision.

opener ['oup(ə)nər], *s.* **1.** (*pers.*) ouvreur, -euse. **2.** (*thg*) (*a*) **case o.,** ciseau *m* à déballer; arrache-clou(s) *m inv*; ouvre-caisse(s) *m inv*; **bottle o., crown cork o.,** décapsulateur *m*; **letter o.,** ouvre-lettres *m inv*; **oyster o.,** ouvre-huîtres *m inv*; **can, tin, o.,** ouvre-boîtes *m inv*; *Aut:* **leaf-spring o.,** écarte-lames *m inv*; (*b*) *Tex:* ouvreuse *f* (de la laine, du coton). **3.** (*a*) *Th: etc:* premier numéro; (*b*) *Cards:* **openers,** cartes *f* avec lesquelles on peut ouvrir (au poker).

open-eyed ['oupən'aid], *a.* **1.** (*a*) qui a les yeux ouverts; qui voit clair; qui ne se laisse pas duper; (*b*) **he acted o.-e.,** il se rendait parfaitement compte de ce qu'il faisait. **2. to look at s.o., in o.-e. astonishment, to gaze o.-e. at s.o.,** regarder qn les yeux écarquillés de surprise, en écarquillant les yeux; ouvrir de grands yeux.

open-faced ['oupənfeist], *a.* au visage franc.

open-field ['oupən'fi:ld], *a. Eng.Hist:* **o.-f. system,** système de l'openfield, des champs ouverts.

open-handed ['oupən'hændid], *a.* libéral, -aux; **to be o.-h.,** avoir la main ouverte.

open-handedly ['oupən'hændidli], *adv.* libéralement, généreusement; **to give o.-h.,** donner à pleines mains.

open-handedness ['oupən'hændidnis], *s.* libéralité *f*, générosité *f*.

open-heart ['oupən'hɑ:t], *a. Surg:* (chirurgie) à cœur ouvert.

openhearted [oupən'hɑ:tid], *a.* **1.** ouvert; franc, *f.* franche; sincère; expansif; au cœur ouvert; **to be very o.,** avoir le cœur sur la main, sur les lèvres; **in an o. moment,** dans un moment d'expansion; **o. welcome,** accueil cordial. **2.** au cœur tendre, compatissant.

openheartedly [oupən'hɑ:tidli], *adv.* franchement; à cœur ouvert; cordialement.

openheartedness [oupən'hɑ:tidnis], *s.* franchise *f*, ouverture *f* de cœur, expansion *f*; cordialité *f* (d'un accueil).

opening¹ ['oup(ə)niŋ], *a.* **1.** (*a*) (porte, etc.) qui s'ouvre; praticable; (*b*) **the o. season,** la saison qui commence; (*c*) (*of bud, etc.*) en train d'éclore. **2.** *O:* **o. medicine,** laxatif *m*.

opening², *s.* **1.** (*a*) ouverture *f* (de la porte, d'un musée, magasin, bureau, parachute, etc., de son cœur; *Com:* d'un compte); débouchage *m* (d'une bouteille); décachetage *m* (d'une lettre); dépouillement *m* (de son courrier); *Mch:* découvrement *m* (d'une lumière); *Com:* **late o. Friday** = nocturne *m* le vendredi; **o. of a new street in a congested area,** percement *m* d'une nouvelle rue dans un quartier surchargé de circulation; **o. of a street to traffic,** ouverture d'une rue à la circulation; *Ind:* **o. of an additional workshop,** mise *f* en service d'un nouvel atelier; (*b*) **formal o.,** inauguration *f*; **the o. of Parliament,** l'ouverture du Parlement; **the o. of the courts,** la rentrée des tribunaux; (*c*) commencement *m* (d'une conversation, etc.); ouverture (de négociations); *Jur:* exposition *f* des faits; *Artil: etc:* déclenchement *m* (du tir); (*d*) *Cards:* attaque *f*, ouverture; *Chess:* **the openings,** les débuts *m* de partie. **2.** (*a*) **the sudden o. of a chasm at their feet,** l'ouverture soudaine d'un gouffre à leurs pieds; (*b*) épanouissement *m*, éclosion *f* (d'une fleur, etc.); **o. (out),** développement *m* (des ailes d'un oiseau); (*c*) *El:* décollement *m* (d'un interrupteur); (*d*) commencement, début (d'une pièce de théâtre, d'une ère nouvelle, etc.). **3.** (*a*) trou *m*, jour *m*, percée *f* (à travers un mur, etc.); percée (dans une forêt); *Hyd.E:* gueule bée; **to make, cut, an o. in a wall,** faire un trou dans, pratiquer une ouverture dans, percer, un mur; **the estate has several openings on to the river,** le domaine a plusieurs percées qui mènent à la rivière; *Nau:* **gangway o.,** coupée *f*; (*b*) embrasure *f*, baie *f* (dans un mur); (*c*) échappée *f* (entre les arbres); clairière *f* (dans un bois); éclaircie *f* (dans les nuages); (*d*) orifice *m*; embouchure *f* (d'un sac, etc.); *Min:* cloche *f* (d'une carrière); amorce *f* (d'un galerie); *Mch:* **exhaust o.,** lumière *f* d'échappement; *Atom.Ph:* **experimental o.,** orifice d'expérimentation. **4.** occasion *f* favorable; *Com:* débouché *m* (pour une marchandise); **to wait for an o.,** attendre une occasion; **fine o. for a young man,** beau débouché pour un jeune homme; **to give an adversary an o.,** donner une bonne chance, prêter le flanc, à un adversaire. **5.** *attrib.* inaugural, -aux; de, du, début; **o. ceremony,** cérémonie *f* d'inauguration; **the o. day of the session,** le jour d'ouverture de la session; **o. address, speech,** discours *m* d'ouverture; **o. sentence,** phrase *f* de début; *Com:* **o. hours,** heures *f* d'ouverture; *Book-k:* **o. entry,** écriture *f* d'ouverture; *St.Exch:* **o. price,** (i) cours *m* d'ouverture, de début, premier cours (d'une séance boursière); (ii) cours d'introduction (d'une nouvelle valeur en bourse); *Cards:* **o. bid,** annonce *f* d'entrée, d'indication.

openly ['oupənli], *adv.* ouvertement, franchement, en toute franchise; publiquement, au vu (et au su) de tous, en pleine rue, à visage découvert; **to act o.,** agir à découvert, cartes sur table; jouer franc jeu; **to speak o.,** parler sans déguisement, sans réticence, sans feinte, sans rien déguiser.

openminded [oupən'maindid], *a.* qui a l'esprit ouvert, large; impartial, -aux; **to be o. on, about, sth.,** n'avoir pas de parti pris, d'idée préconçue, être libre de préjugés, avoir l'esprit libre, sur qch.

openmindedly [oupən'maindidli], *adv.* sans partialité; sans préjugés.

openmindedness [oupən'maindidnis], *s.* largeur *f* (d'esprit); absence *f* de parti pris.

openmouthed [oupən'mauðd], *a.* **1. to stand in o. astonishment,** rester bouche bée; *P:* en rester baba. **2.** bruyant.

open-necked [oupən'nekt], *a.* (chemise, robe) à col ouvert; (chemise) à col Danton.

openness ['oupənnis], *s.* **1.** situation exposée (d'une côte, etc.); aspect découvert (du terrain). **2.** contexture non serrée (d'un tissu); pénétrabilité *f* (d'un radiateur, etc.). **3.** (*a*) franchise *f*, candeur *f*, ouverture *f* de cœur; (*b*) largeur *f*, libéralité *f* (d'esprit); (*c*) douceur *f*, clémence *f* (du temps).

open-pit ['oup(ə)npit], *a. Min: NAm:* (exploitation) à ciel ouvert.

openwork ['oupənwə:k], *s.* (*a*) ouvrage ajouré, à jour; (*b*) ajours *mpl*, jours *mpl*; *Needlew:* **row of o.,** rivière *f* à jour; **faggot o.,** jours à faisceau; **o. stockings,** bas ajourés, à jour.

opera ['ɔp(ə)rə], *s.* **1.** opéra *m*; **grand o.,** (grand) opéra; (*with spoken dialogue*) opéra-comique *m*, *pl.* opéras-comiques; **comic o., o. bouffe,** opéra bouffe; **light o.,** opérette *f*; *W.Tel: T.V: F:* **soap o.,** feuilleton *m* à l'eau de rose. **2. o. (house),** (théâtre *m* de l')opéra; théâtre lyrique. **3. o. (company),** (compagnie *f* d')opéra. **4.** *attrib.* **o. cloak,** sortie *f* de bal, de théâtre; **o. dancer,**

danseur, -euse, d'opéra; **o. glasses,** jumelles *f* de théâtre; **o. goer,** amateur, -trice, de l'opéra; **o. hat,** (chapeau *m*) claque (*m*); gibus *m*; **o. singer,** chanteur *m*, cantatrice *f*, d'opéra; *Cost:* **vest with an o. top,** chemise américaine forme opéra.

operable ['ɔp(ə)rəbl], *a.* **1.** *Surg:* (malade, tumeur, etc.) opérable. **2.** (système, etc.) utilisable, praticable.

operand ['ɔpərænd], *s. Mth:* opérande *m.*

operant ['ɔpərənt], *a. & s.* opérateur, -trice.

operate ['ɔpəreit], *v.i. & tr.* **I.** *v.i.* **1.** (*a*) (*of medicine, etc.*) opérer; agir; produire son effet; avoir de l'effet; (*b*) (*of machine, etc.*) fonctionner; **motor that operates on direct current,** moteur qui fonctionne sur courant continu; (*c*) **army units that operated in Burma,** unités militaires qui ont été engagées en Birmanie; **burglar who operates in wealthy districts,** cambrioleur qui opère dans les quartiers riches; (*d*) jouer; **the rise in wages will o. from the first of January,** l'augmentation des salaires jouera à partir du premier janvier. **2.** *St.Exch:* faire des opérations; **to o. for a rise, a fall,** jouer, spéculer, à la hausse, à la baisse; **to o. against one's client,** faire de la contrepartie. **3.** *Surg:* opérer (qn, un appendice, un abcès, etc.) **to o. (on s.o.) for appendicitis,** opérer (qn) de l'appendicite; faire une appendicectomie; **to o. in the acute stage,** opérer à chaud; **to o. between attacks,** opérer à froid; **to be operated on,** subir une opération.
II. *v.tr.* **1.** opérer, effectuer, accomplir (une guérison, un changement, etc.). **2.** (*a*) (*of pers.*) **to o. a machine,** manœuvrer une machine; **to o. the breech of a rifle,** manœuvrer, faire jouer, la culasse d'un fusil; **to o. the brakes,** actionner les freins; (*b*) (*of part of machine*) **to o. another part,** commander, actionner, attaquer, un autre organe; **operated by electricity,** commandé électriquement; actionné par l'électricité; **mechanically operated valve,** soupape commandée. **3.** gérer, diriger (une maison de commerce, etc.); exploiter (un chemin de fer, une ligne d'autobus, etc.).

operatic [ɔpə'rætik]. **1.** *a.* d'opéra; **o. singer,** chanteur, -euse, dramatique, d'opéra; **o. society,** cercle *m* d'opéra d'amateurs. **2.** *s.pl. F:* **operatics,** opéra *m* d'amateurs; **at Christmas we had some operatics in the school hall,** à Noël nous avons représenté un opéra dans la grande salle du lycée.

operating[1] ['ɔpəreitiŋ], *a.* **1.** qui opère; **o. surgeon,** (chirurgien) opérateur (*m*); *Ind:* **o. staff,** personnel exploitant, d'exploitation; **o. mechanism,** mécanisme actif; *El:* **o. coil,** bobine excitatrice. **2.** *Theol:* **o. grace,** grâce opérante.

operating[2], *s.* **1.** (*a*) fonctionnement *m*; *El:* **o. angle,** angle *m* de fonctionnement (d'un tube électronique); *El:* **o. capacity,** capacité *f* utile; *Elcs: W.Tel:* **o. frequency,** fréquence de fonctionnement, de travail; fréquence utilisée; *Elcs:* **o. point,** point *m* de fonctionnement (sur la caractéristique d'un tube électronique); *Cmptr:* **o. ratio,** taux *m* d'activité; *Tp:* **o. signal,** signal *m* de service; *Cmptr:* **o. tape,** bande *f* d'exploitation; **o. time,** *Mec.E:* délai *m* de fonctionnement (d'un mécanisme); *Tp:* délai d'établissement (d'une communication); *Cmptr:* durée *f*, temps *m*, d'exécution (d'une instruction). **2.** manœuvre *f*, commande *f* (d'une machine, etc.); **o. instructions,** instructions *f*, règlements *m*, de service; *Cmptr: etc:* consignes *f* d'exploitation; **o. lever,** levier *m* de manœuvre, de commande; *Rail: NAm:* **o. rod,** bielle *f* de commande; *Tp: NAm:* **o. room,** salle *f* des opératrices. **3.** exploitation *f* (d'une compagnie de chemins de fer, etc.); **o. costs,** frais *m* d'exploitation; **o. instructions,** consignes *f*, règles *f*, d'exploitation; règles de procédure; **o. profit,** bénéfices *m* d'exploitation. **4.** *Mil:* **o. base,** base opérationnelle, d'opérations. **5.** *Pol.Ec:* **o. level of supply,** niveau fonctionnel d'approvisionnements; **o. stocks,** stocks fonctionnels. **6.** *Surg:* **o. mask,** masque *m* de chirurgien; **o. table,** table *f* d'opération; *F:* (le) billard; **o. theatre,** *occ.* **room,** salle *f* d'opération; amphithéâtre *m*; **mobile o. theatre,** ambulance chirurgicale automobile.

operation [ɔpə'reiʃ(ə)n], *s.* opération *f.* **1.** fonctionnement *m*; marche *f* (d'un appareil, d'une machine); jeu *m* (d'un mécanisme); **in o.,** (i) (machine, etc.) en marche, en fonctionnement; (ii) (loi, etc.) en application, en vigueur; **restrictions at present in o.,** restrictions actuellement en vigueur; **to be in o.,** (i) (*of machine*) fonctionner; (*of mechanism*) jouer; (ii) (*of law, etc.*) être en application, en vigueur; **to come into o.,** (i) (*of machine, etc.*) commencer à fonctionner, à jouer; (ii) (*of law, etc.*) entrer en application, en vigueur; **to bring a decree into o.,** rendre un décret opérant; appliquer un décret; mettre un décret en application, en vigueur; **to interfere with the o. of a regulation,** entraver l'action, l'application, d'un règlement; **to suspend the o. of a law,** suspendre l'action d'une loi. **2.** (*a*) commande *f* (d'une machine, etc.); **manual, mechanical, o.,** commande manuelle, mécanique; **the method of o. is always the same,** le processus est toujours le même; (*b*) exploitation *f* (d'un haut fourneau, d'un réacteur, d'un navire, d'un établissement industriel, d'un réseau de transport, etc.); **the mine is still in o.,** la mine est toujours en exploitation, en activité; **business in full o.,** affaire en pleine activité, en pleine exploitation, en plein rapport. **3.** (*a*) **mathematical o.,** opération mathématique; (*b*) *Cmptr:* **computer o.,** opération machine; **unary o.,** opération unaire; **o. code,** code *m* opération; **o. register,** registre *m* d'opération; **o. time,** temps *m* d'exécution; (*c*) travail *m*, -aux; unité *f* (de fabrication, etc.); **machining operations,** travaux d'usinage; **the process involves three operations,** le procédé comporte trois opérations; **operations research, analysis,** recherche opérationnelle; (*d*) **a firm's operations,** les activités d'une entreprise; *St.Exch:* **stock o.,** opération sur les valeurs; **credit o.,** opération à terme. **4.** *Mil:* **airborne o.,** opération aéroportée; **theatre of operations,** théâtre *m* des opérations, d'opérations; **operations room,** salle *f* d'opérations (d'un état-major). **5.** **(surgical) o.,** opération (chirurgicale); **to perform an o. for appendicitis,** faire l'opération de l'appendicite; faire une appendicectomie; **to perform an o. on s.o.,** opérer qn (**for,** de); **to undergo an o.,** se faire opérer, subir une opération (**for,** de); (*for appendicitis, etc.*) **emergency o., interval o.,** opération à chaud, à froid.

operational [ɔpə'reiʃənl], *a.* (*a*) opérationnel; relatif aux opérations; *Mil:* **o. duties,** service *m* en campagne; **o. training,** instruction *f* tactique; entraînement *m* de guerre, au combat; **o. station,** centre *m* d'opérations; *Ind: etc:* **o. costs,** coûts opérationnels; **o. environment,** (i) ambiance opérationnelle; (ii) *Cmptr:* cadre *m* d'utilisation, d'exploitation; **o. flexibility,** souplesse *f* d'utilisation (d'un appareil, etc.); **o. planning,** planification *f* des opérations; **o. research,** recherche opérationnelle; *Av:* **o. ceiling,** plafond opérationnel; *Cmptr:* **o. instruction,** instruction *f* opératoire; *Mth:* **o. calculus,** calcul opérationnel; (*b*) en état de marche, de fonctionnement, de service; **the new power station should be o. next year,** la nouvelle centrale électrique devrait (être prêt à) entrer en service l'an prochain; **in a few hours the carrier was again fully o.,** au bout de quelques heures le porte-avions était en parfait état de marche.

operative ['ɔp(ə)rətiv]. **1.** *a.* (*a*) opératif, actif; (*of law, etc.*) **to become o.,** entrer en vigueur; prendre effet; **to make a decree o.,** rendre un décret opérant; **an o. obligation,** une obligation exécutoire; **the rise in wages has been o. since May 1st,** l'augmentation des salaires joue depuis le 1er mai; *Jur:* **o. part of an act,** clause essentielle d'un acte; *F:* **the o. word,** le mot qui compte, le mot pivot; (*b*) pratique; **the o. side of an industry,** les ateliers *m*; (*c*) *Surg:* **o. field,** champ *m* opératoire. **2.** *s.* (*a*) ouvrier, -ière; artisan, -ane; (*b*) *NAm:* détective *m.*

operator ['ɔpəreitər], *s.* **1.** (*pers.*) opérateur, -trice; (*a*) *Cin: T.V:* opérateur (de caméra); *Tg:* télégraphiste *mf*; *Tp:* opérateur, téléphoniste *mf*; *Nau: etc:* **radio, wireless, o.,** (opérateur de) radio *m*; *Tp:* **switchboard o.,** standardiste *mf*; **to call the o.,** appeler le, la, standardiste, le, la, téléphoniste; (*b*) opérateur (d'une machine); **operator's handbook,** manuel *m* de l'utilisateur; (*c*) *Surg:* opérateur; (*d*) *Com: Ind:* exploitant *m* (d'une entreprise); (*e*) *St.Exch:* **o. for a fall, a rise,** opérateur, joueur *m*, à la baisse, à la hausse; (*f*) *F:* (i) brasseur *m* d'affaires (souvent douteuses); **a slick o.,** un escroc habile; (ii) pourvoyeur *m* de drogues. **2.** (*a*) *Mth:* opérateur (de logarithme, etc.); **differential, integral, o.,** opérateur différentiel, intégral; (*b*) *Mec.E: etc:* appareil *m*, mécanisme *m*, de commande; opérateur (d'une machine-outil); (*c*) *Biol:* **o. (gene),** gène opérateur.

opercle [ə'pə:kl], *s. Ich:* operculaire *m.*

opercular [ə'pə:kjulər]. **1.** *a. Nat.Hist:* operculaire. **2.** *s. Ich:* operculaire *m.*

Operculata [ə'pə:kjuleitə], *s.pl. Moll:* operculés *m.*

operculate [ə'pə:kjulət], **operculated** [ə'pə:kjuleitid], *a. Nat.Hist:* operculé.

operculiform [ə'pə:kjulifɔ:m], *a.* operculiforme.

operculum, *pl.* **-la** [ə'pə:kjuləm, -lə], *s. Nat.Hist:* opercule *m.*

operetta [ɔpə'retə], *s. Mus:* opérette *f.*

operettist [ɔpə'retist], *s.* auteur *m*, compositeur *m*, d'opérettes.

operon ['ɔpərɔn], *s. Biol:* opéron *m.*

operose ['ɔpərous], *a. A:* laborieux.

Ophelia[1] [ə'fi:ljə]. *Pr.n.f.* Ophélie.

ophelia[2], *s. Ann:* ophélie *f.*

Ophian ['oufiən], *s. Rel.H:* ophite *m.*

ophic ['ɔfik], *a.* ophique.

ophicalcite [ɔfi'kælsait], *s. Miner:* ophicalcite *f.*

Ophicephalidae [ɔfisi'fælidi:], *s.pl. Ich:* ophiocéphalidés *m.*

ophicleide ['ɔfiklaid], *s. Mus:* **1.** *A:* ophicléide *m.* **2.** (*in organ*) tuba *m.*

ophicleidist ['ɔfiklaidist], *s. A:* (joueur *m* d')ophicléide *m.*

Ophidia [ɔ'fidiə], *s.pl. Rept:* ophidiens *m*; serpents *m.*

ophidian [ɔ'fidiən], *a. & s. Rept:* ophidien (*m*); serpent *m.*

ophidiasis [ɔfi'daiəsis], **ophidism** ['ɔfidizm], *s. Med:* ophidisme *m.*

ophidium [ɔ'fidiəm], *s. Ich:* ophidie *f*; donzelle *f.*

Ophiocephalidae [ɔfiousi'fælidi:], *s.pl. Ich:* ophiocéphalidés *m.*

Ophioglossales [ɔfiouglɔ'seiliz], *s.pl. Bot:* ophioglossales *f.*

ophioglossum [ɔfiou'glɔsəm], *s. Bot:* ophioglosse *m*; langue-de-serpent, *pl.* langues-de-serpent; herbe *f* sans couture.

ophiography [ɔfi'ɔgrəfi], *s.* ophiographie *f.*

ophiolatry [ɔfi'ɔlətri], *s.* ophiolâtrie *f.*

ophiolite ['ɔfioulait], *s. Miner:* **1.** *A:* ophiolithe *m*, serpentine *f.* **2.** vert *m* antique.

ophiolitic [ɔfiou'litik], *a. Miner:* ophiolithique.

ophiologic(al) [ɔfiou'lɔdʒik(l)], *a. Nat.Hist:* ophiologique.

ophiologist [ɔfi'ɔlədʒist], *s. Nat.Hist:* ophiologiste *m.*

ophiology [ɔfi'ɔlədʒi], *s. Nat.Hist:* ophiologie *f.*

ophiomorph ['ɔfioumɔ:f], *s. Amph:* gymnophione *m*; amphibien *m* apode.

ophiomorphic, ophiomorphous [ɔfiou'mɔ:fik, -fəs], *a. Amph:* ophiomorphique.

ophion ['ɔfiɔn], *s. Ent:* ophion *m.*

ophiophagous [ɔfi'ɔfəgəs], *a. Nat.Hist:* ophiophage.

ophiopluteus, *pl.* **-tei** [ɔfiou'plu:tiəs, -tii:], *s. Echin:* ophioplutéus *m.*

ophi(o)saurus [ɔfi(ou)'sɔ:rəs], *s. Rept:* ophisaure *m.*

ophism ['ɔfizm], *s.* ophiolâtrie *f.*

ophite[1] ['ɔfait], *s. Miner:* ophite *m*; marbre serpentin; serpentine *f.*

Ophite[2], *s. Rel.H:* ophite *m.*

ophitic[1] [ɔ'fitik], *a. Miner:* ophitique.

Ophitic[2], *a. Rel.H:* ophitique.

Ophiuchus [ɔfi'ju:kəs], *Pr.n. Astr:* le Serpentaire.

ophiura [ɔfi'juərə], *s. Echin:* ophiure *f.*

Ophiurae [ɔfi'juəri:], *s.pl. Echin:* ophiurides *m.*

ophiuran [ɔfi'jurən], *s. Echin:* ophiure *f.*

ophiurid, ophiuroid [ɔfi'ju:rid, -rɔid], *a. & s. Echin:* ophiuride (*m*).

Ophiuroidea [ɔfiju'rɔidiə], *s.pl. Echin:* ophiurides *m.*

ophrys ['ɔfris], *s. Bot:* ophrys *f.*

ophthalmalgia [ɔfθæl'mældʒiə], *s. Med:* ophtalmalgie *f.*

ophthalmia [ɔf'θælmiə], *s. Med:* ophtalmie *f*; **sewerman's o.,** mitte *f*; *Vet:* **periodic o.,** ophtalmie périodique; fluxion *f* périodique des yeux.

ophthalmic [ɔf'θælmik], *a.* **1.** ophtalmique; **o. remedy,** ophtalmique *m*, collyre *m.* **2.** **o. hospital,** hôpital *m* pour les maladies des yeux; hôpital ophtalmologique.

ophthalmo-blennorrhea [ɔf'θælmoublenə'riə], *s. Med:* ophtalmoblennorr(h)ée *f.*

ophthalmocele [ɔf'θælməsi:l], *s. Med:* ophtalmocèle *f*; exophtalmie *f.*

ophthalmodynamometer [ɔf'θælmoudainə'mɔmitər], *s. Med:* ophtalmodynamomètre *m.*

ophthalmodynia [ɔfθælmou'diniə], *s. Med:* ophtalmodynie *f.*

ophthalmograph [ɔf'θælmougræf], *s. Med:* ophtalmographe *m.*

ophthalmographer [ɔfθæl'mɔgrəfər], *s. Med:* ophtalmographe *m.*

ophthalmographic [ɔfθælmou'græfik], *a. Med:* ophtalmographique.

ophthalmography [ɔfθæl'mɔgrəfi], *s. Med:* ophtalmographie *f.*

ophthalmologic(al) [ɔfθælmə'lɔdʒik(l)], *a. Med:* ophtalmologique.

ophthalmologist [ɔfθæl'mɔlədʒist], *s. Med:* ophtalmologiste *mf*, ophtalmologue *mf.*

ophthalmology [ɔfθæl'mɔlədʒi], *s. Med:* ophtalmologie *f.*

ophthalmomalacia [ɔfθælmoumə'leisiə], *s. Med:* ophtalmomalacie *f.*

ophthalmometer [ɔfθæl'mɔmitər], *s. Med:* ophtalmomètre *m.*

ophthalmometric(al) [ɔfθælmou'metrik(l)], *a. Med:* ophtalmométrique.

ophthalmometry [ɔfθæl'mɔmitri], *s. Med:* ophtalmométrie *f.*

ophthalmoplasty [ɔfθælmou'plæsti], *s. Med:* ophtalmoplastie *f.*
ophthalmoplegia [ɔfθælmou'pli:dʒiə], *s. Med:* ophtalmoplégie *f.*
ophthalmoptosis [ɔfθælmou'ptousis], *s. Med:* ophtalmoptose *f.*
ophthalmoreaction [ɔf'θælmouri'ækʃ(ə)n], *s. Med:* ophtalmo(-)réaction *f*; oculoréaction *f.*
ophthalmorrhagia [ɔfθælmə'reidʒiə], *s. Med:* ophtalmorragie *f.*
ophthalmosaurus [ɔfθælmou'sɔ:rəs], *s. Paleont:* ophtalmosaurus *m.*
ophthalmoscope [ɔf'θælməskoup], *s. Med:* ophtalmoscope *m.*
ophthalmoscopic(al) [ɔfθælmə'skɔpik(l)], *a. Med:* ophtalmoscopique.
ophthalmoscopy [ɔfθæl'mɔskəpi], *s. Med:* ophtalmoscopie *f.*
ophthalmostat [ɔf'θælmoustæt], *s. Med:* ophtalmostat *m.*
ophthalmotomic [ɔfθælmou'tɔmik], *a. Surg:* ophtalmotomique.
ophthalmotomy [ɔfθæl'mɔtəmi], *s. Surg:* ophtalmotomie *f.*
opianic [oupi'ænik], *a. Ch:* opianique.
opiate[1] ['oupiət]. **1.** *a. A:* opiacé. **2.** *s. Pharm:* opiacé *m*, opiat *m*, narcotique *m*; *Fig:* **religion, an o. for the masses,** la religion, l'opium du peuple.
opiate[2] ['oupieit], *v.tr.* opiacer (un médicament).
opiated ['oupieitid], *a. Pharm:* opiacé.
opiatic [oupi'ætik], *a. Pharm:* opiatique.
Opiliaceae [oupili'eisii:], *s.pl. Bot:* opiliacées *f.*
Opiliones [oupili'ouniz], *s.pl. Arach:* opilions *m*, opilionidés *m.*
opine [ə'pain], *v. O: & U.S:* **1.** *v.tr.* (*a*) être d'avis (**that,** que); (*b*) émettre l'avis (**that,** que). **2.** *v.i.* opiner; **they opined for peace,** ils opinèrent pour la paix.
opinion [ə'piniən], *s.* **1.** opinion *f*; (*a*) avis *m*; **in my o.,** selon mon avis, à mon sens; **in the o. of experts,** de l'avis, au dire, au jugement, des experts; suivant, selon, l'opinion des experts; **in my o. it's a liver attack,** pour moi c'est une crise de foie; **in my o. he ought to come,** je suis d'avis qu'il vienne; **in his o. there was no danger,** dans sa pensée, suivant lui, il n'y avait aucun danger; **is that really his o.?** a-t-il dit réellement sa pensée? **his o. is the result of a close examination of the problem,** son appréciation *f* résulte d'un mûr examen du problème; **cut and dried o.,** opinion toute faite; **to be of the o. that the crisis is not over,** être d'avis, estimer, que la crise n'est pas finie; **I am of (the) o. that he will never come back, in my o. he will never come back,** à mon avis il ne reviendra jamais; **to be entirely of s.o.'s o.,** abonder dans le sens de qn; **to be of the same o. as s.o.,** être du même avis que qn; **matter of o.,** affaire *f* d'opinion, d'appréciation; **to express, put forward, an o.,** émettre un avis, une opinion; **to express an o. for, against, in favour of, a proposition,** opiner pour, contre, une proposition, en faveur d'une proposition; **to give one's o.,** dire, émettre, son opinion; **to change one's o.,** changer d'avis; **to share s.o.'s o.,** partager l'opinion de qn; **to ask s.o.'s o.,** se référer à qn; demander l'avis de qn; consulter qn; **to take s.o.'s o.,** prendre l'avis, de qn; **to form an o. on s.o., sth.,** se faire une opinion sur, de, qn, qch.; **to have an o. about sth.,** avoir une opinion sur qch.; **what is your o. of him?** que pensez-vous de lui? (*b*) estime *f*; **to have, hold, a high, a low, o. of s.o.,** avoir une bonne, une mauvaise, opinion de qn; tenir qn en haute, en basse, estime; **to have a high o. of oneself,** avoir bonne opinion de soi-même; **to have no o. of sth.,** ne pas estimer qch.; ne pas faire grand cas de qch.; **to fall in s.o.'s (good) o.,** baisser dans l'estime de qn; encourir la mésestime de qn; (*c*) **public o.,** l'opinion (publique); la voix populaire; **to excite, rouse, public o.,** créer un mouvement d'opinion; *F:* battre l'appel (dans les journaux); **local financial o. inclines to the belief that bankruptcy is inevitable,** les milieux financiers de notre place inclinent à croire que la faillite est inévitable; **o. poll, survey,** sondage *m* d'opinion publique. **2.** consultation *f* (de médecin, etc.); **you ought to have another o.,** vous devriez consulter un autre médecin; *Jur:* **counsel's o.,** consultation écrite délivrée par un "barrister"; avis motivé; **to take counsel's o.,** consulter un avocat, un conseiller juridique; **after taking counsel's o.,** après consultation; *Jur:* **o. of the Court,** jugement rendu par le tribunal sur un point de droit soulevé au cours d'un arbitrage.
opinionated [ə'piniəneitid], *a.* opiniâtre; entier (dans ses opinions); imbu de ses opinions; exclusif (de caractère).
opinionatedly [ə'piniəneitidli], *adv.* opiniâtrement.
opinion(n)aire [ə'piniənɛər], *s. NAm:* questionnaire *m* pour sondage d'opinion.
opiomania [oupiou'meiniə], *s. Med:* opiomanie *f.*
opiomaniac [oupiou'meiniæk], *s. Med:* opiomane *mf.*
opisometer [ɔpi'sɔmitər], *s. Surv:* cartomètre *m.*
opisthobranch [ə'pisθoubræŋk], *a. & s. Moll:* opist(h)obranche (*m*).
Opisthobranchia [əpisθou'bræŋkiə], *s.pl. Moll:* opist(h)obranches *m.*
opisthobranchiate [əpisθou'bræŋkieit], *a. Moll:* opist(h)obranche.
Opisthocoela [əpisθou'si:lə], *s.pl. Z:* opistoocèles *m*, opisthocœles *m.*
opisthocoelan [əpisθou'si:lən], *s. Z:* opisthocèle *m*, opisthocœle *m.*
opisthocoelid [əpisθou'si:lid], *a. & s. Z:* opisthocélide (*m*), opisthocœlide (*m*).
opisthocoelian [əpisθou'si:liən], **opisthocoelous** [əpisθou'si:ləs], *a. Z:* opisthocèle, opisthocœle; opisthocœlique.
opisthodome [ɔ'pisθoudoum], **opisthodomos** [ɔpis'θɔdəməs], *s. Gr.Ant:* opisthodome *m.*
opisthoglyph [ə'pisθouglif], *a. & s. Rept:* opisthoglyphe (*m*).
Opisthoglypha [ɔpis'θɔglifə], *s.pl. Rept:* opisthoglyphes *m.*
opisthoglyphic, opisthoglyphous [ɔpis'θouglifik, -əs], *a. Rept:* opisthoglyphe.
opisthognathism [ɔpis'θɔgnəθizm], *s. Anat:* opisthognathisme *m.*
opisthognathous [ɔpis'θɔgnəθəs], *a. Anat:* opisthognathe.
opisthograph [ə'pisθəgræf], *s. Pal:* manuscrit *m* opisthographe.
opisthographic(al) [əpisθə'græfik(l)], *a. Pal:* opisthographe.
opisthography [ɔpis'θɔgrəfi], *s. Pal:* opisthographie *f.*
opisthotic [ɔpis'θɔtik], *a. & s. Anat:* opisthotique (*m*).
opisthotonos, opisthotonus [əpis'θɔtənəs], *s. Med:* opisthotonos *m.*
opium ['oupjəm], *s.* opium *m*; **o. addict, fiend,** opiomane *mf*; **o. den,** fumerie *f* d'opium; **o. eater,** mangeur, -euse, d'opium; opiophage *mf*; **o. eating,** opiophage; (*to excess*) opiomane; **o. extract,** extrait *m* thébaïque; **o. poisoning,** intoxication *f* par l'opium; thébaïsme *m*; **o. smoker,** fumeur *m* d'opium.
opiumism ['oupjəmizm], *s.* **1.** opiomanie *f.* **2.** intoxication *f* par l'opium, thébaïsme *m.*
opobalsam [ɔpou'bɔ:lsəm], *s. Pharm: etc:* opobalsamum *m*; baume *m* de la Mecque; térébenthine *f* de Judée.
opodeldoc [ɔpə'deldɔk], *s. Pharm:* opodeldoch *m.*
opodidymus [ɔpə'didiməs], *s. Ter:* opodidyme *m.*
opopanax [ə'pɔpənæks], *s. Bot: Pharm:* opopanax *m.*
Oporto [ə'pɔ:tou]. *Pr.n. Geog:* Porto *m.*
opossum, *pl.* **-um(s)** [ə'pɔsəm, -əmz], *s.* (*a*) *Z:* opossum *m*; sarigue *mf*; **South American woolly o.,** opossum laineux sud-américan; **water o.,** yapo(c)k *m*, chironecte *m*; crabier *m*; **the o. family,** les didelphidés *m*; (*b*) *Austr:* phalanger *m*, trichosure *m*; (*c*) *Bot:* **o. wood,** halesia *m*, halésie *f*; (*d*) *Crust:* **o. shrimp,** mysidacé *m.*
opotherapeutic ['ɔpouθerə'pju:tik], *a. Med:* opothérapique, organothérapique.
opotherapy [ɔpou'θerəpi], *s.* opothérapie *f*; organothérapie *f.*
Oppian[1] ['ɔpiən]. *Pr.n.m. Gr.Lit:* Oppien.
Oppian[2], *a. Rom.Hist:* oppien.
oppidan ['ɔpidən], *s.* **1.** *A:* citoyen *m.* **2.** *Sch:* élève *m* (au collège d'Eton qui n'a pas gagné de bourse).
oppidum, *pl.* **-da** ['ɔpidəm, -də], *s. Archeol:* oppidum *m.*
oppilate ['ɔpileit], *v.tr. Med:* opiler, obstruer.
oppilation [ɔpi'leiʃ(ə)n], *s. Med:* opilation *f*, obstruction *f.*
oppilative ['ɔpileitiv], *a. Med:* opilatif, obstruant.
opponens [ə'pounənz], *a. & s. Anat:* **o. (muscle),** opposant *m*; **o. pollicis, minimi digiti,** opposant du pouce, du petit doigt.
opponent [ə'pounənt]. **1.** *a.* opposé; *Anat:* **o. muscle,** opposant *m.* **2.** *s.* adversaire *mf*, antagoniste *mf* (**of,** de), opposant, -ante (**of,** à); **a formidable o.,** un adversaire redoutable; un rude jouteur.
opportune ['ɔpətju:n], *a.* (*of time*) opportun, convenable, commode; (*of action*) à propos; **you have come at an o. moment,** vous arrivez à propos; vous tombez bien; **this cheque is most o.,** ce chèque tombe à merveille.
opportunely ['ɔpətju:nli], *adv.* opportunément; en temps opportun; à propos; **it comes, happens, very o., most o.,** cela arrive à point (nommé), tombe à merveille.
opportuneness ['ɔpətju:nnis], *s.* opportunité *f*; à-propos *m.*
opportunism ['ɔpətju:nizm], *s.* opportunisme *m.*
opportunist ['ɔpətju:nist], *s.* opportuniste *mf.*
opportunity [ɔpə'tju:niti], *s.* **1.** occasion *f* (favorable); **golden o.,** affaire *f* d'or; **to throw away a golden o.,** laisser échapper une occasion magnifique; **at the first, earliest, o.,** à la première occasion; au premier jour; **when the o. occurs,** à l'occasion; **to have, get, many opportunities for doing sth.,** avoir de nombreuses occasions de faire qch.; **I have had (the) o. to come into contact with all sorts of people,** j'ai eu l'occasion de fréquenter toutes sortes de gens; **if I get an o.,** si l'occasion se présente; **if the o. comes your way,** si l'occasion se rencontre; si vous en trouvez l'occasion; **to take an o.,** saisir, prendre, une occasion; **to avail oneself of, take, the o. to do sth., of doing sth.,** profiter de l'occasion pour faire qch.; saisir, prendre, l'occasion de faire qch.; prendre occasion pour faire qch.; **to have the o. of doing sth.,** avoir (l')occasion de faire qch.; **to miss an o.,** laisser passer, perdre, manquer, une occasion; **the o. is too good to be missed,** l'occasion s'offre trop belle pour ne pas la saisir; *Com:* **unique sales opportunities,** soldes et occasions exceptionnels; **to throw away a wonderful o. of doing sth.,** laisser échapper, perdre, une belle occasion de faire qch.; **to make an o. for doing sth.,** se ménager une occasion de faire qch.; **it affords an o. for recrimination,** c'est l'entrée aux récriminations; **to provide educational opportunities,** assurer des facilités d'accès à l'éducation; *Prov:* **o. makes the thief,** l'occasion fait le larron. **2.** *Ind: etc:* **productive o.,** possibilité *f* de production; **the industry is rising to the height of its o.,** l'industrie atteint peu à peu son développement maximum. **3.** opportunité *f*, à-propos *m* (d'une démarche, etc.).
opposability [əpouzə'biliti], *s.* opposabilité *f.*
opposable [ə'pouzəbl], *a.* opposable (**to,** à).
oppose [ə'pouz], *v.tr.* **1.** opposer; (*a*) *A:* **to o. a dike to the fury of the waves,** opposer une digue à la fureur des flots; (*b*) mettre (deux couleurs, etc.) en opposition, en contraste. **2.** s'opposer à (qn, qch.); aller au contraire de (qch.); mettre obstacle, mettre opposition, à (qch.); résister à (qn, qch.); combattre (qn, qch.); contrarier, contrecarrer (qn, qch.); se bander contre (qn, qch.); **to o. s.o.'s plans,** se mettre, se jeter, à la traverse des projets de qn; **to o. the motion,** soutenir la contrepartie; parler contre; **to be opposed to sth.,** être opposé à qch.; **country life as opposed to town life,** la vie à la campagne par contraste avec la vie des grandes villes; **I do not o. it,** je ne vais pas là-contre; **I opposed it tooth and nail,** je m'y suis opposé de toutes mes forces; *v.i.* **the opposition must always o.,** l'opposition doit toujours soutenir la contrepartie; *Jur:* **to o. an action, a marriage,** se rendre opposant à un acte, un mariage.
opposed [ə'pouzd], *a.* **1.** opposé, hostile; **directly o. evidence,** témoignages *m* en contradiction directe. **2.** (*a*) *Mec:* **o. forces,** forces opposées; *I.C.E:* **horizontally o. cylinders,** cylindres opposés; **o.-cylinder engine,** moteur *m* à cylindres opposés; moteur à plat; **o.-piston engine,** moteur à pistons opposés; *Av:* **o. propeller,** hélice bi-rotative; (*b*) *Mus:* (*in counterpart*) **o. part,** contrepartie *f.*
opposer [ə'pouzər], *s.* opposant, -ante; adversaire *mf.*
opposing [ə'pouziŋ], *a.* (*of armies, characters, etc.*) opposé; (*of party, etc.*) opposant; *Sp:* **o. team,** équipe *f* adverse; *Jur:* **o. counsel,** contradicteur *m*; *Mec:* **o. couple,** couple *m* antagoniste.
opposite ['ɔpəzit]. **1.** *a.* (*a*) opposé (**to,** à); vis-à-vis (**to,** de); en face (**to,** de); **o. sides of a square,** côtés opposés d'un carré; **vertically o. angles,** angles opposés par le sommet; *Bot:* **o. leaves,** feuilles opposées; **see the diagram on the o. page,** voir la figure ci-contre; **text with illustration on the o. page,** texte avec illustration en regard; **house o. the church,** maison en face de l'église, qui fait face à l'église; **the house o.,** la maison qui est, qui fait, vis-à-vis; la maison (d')en face; **he was passing on the o. pavement,** il passait sur le trottoir d'en face; **o. number,** confrère *m*; *Mil: etc:* correspondant en grade; **we are to meet our o. numbers from abroad,** nous devons nous rencontrer avec nos confrères, homologues *mf*, d'outre-mer; (*b*) contraire (**to, from,** à); **the o. sex,** l'autre sexe *m*; *Magn:* **o. poles,** pôles *m* contraires, de nom contraire; **the o. result from what was expected,** un résultat tout le contraire de celui qu'on espérait; **to take the o. course, view,** prendre le contre-pied; **in the o. direction,** en sens inverse, en sens contraire, dans le sens opposé; **they went in o. directions,** ils prirent des directions opposées; *Nau:* **to run in o. directions, to o. points,** courir à contre; **ships going in o. directions,** navires allant à contre-bord; (*of ships*) **to steer on an o. course,** faire route inverse. **2.** *s.* opposé *m*; contre-pied; *Lit:* opposite *m*; **picture that**

does not go with its o., tableau qui ne va pas avec son pendant; **just the o. of what he says,** tout le contraire de ce qu'il dit; **he's the exact o. of his brother,** il est exactement le contraire de son frère. **3.** *adv.* vis-à-vis; en face; **we had two ladies sitting o.,** deux dames nous faisaient vis-à-vis. **4.** *prep.* en face de, vis-à-vis (de); **to stand, sit, o. s.o.,** faire vis-à-vis à qn; **o. one another,** en face l'un de l'autre; l'un en face de l'autre; vis-à-vis l'un de l'autre; l'un vis-à-vis de l'autre; **we live o. them,** nous habitons en face de chez eux; **stop o. number 128,** arrêtez-vous à la hauteur du numéro 128; **to set a mirror o. a window,** opposer une glace à une fenêtre; *Th: Cin:* **he played o. many of the stars of the day,** il a joué avec beaucoup des vedettes du jour pour partenaire; **she played o. Irving,** elle a donné la réplique à Irving.

opposition [ɔpə'ziʃ(ə)n], *s.* (*a*) opposition *f*; *Astr:* **superior, inferior, o.,** opposition supérieure, inférieure (de deux astres); **in o.,** en opposition; (*b*) **to set two things in o. (to each other),** opposer deux objets l'un à l'autre; **to place oneself in o. to the general opinion,** prendre le contre-pied de l'opinion publique; **to act in o. to public opinion,** agir contrairement à l'opinion publique; **groups in o.,** groupes qui se combattent; (*c*) résistance *f*; **to offer a determined o. to a measure,** faire une opposition résolue à une mesure; **to break down all o.,** vaincre toutes les résistances; *F:* forcer toutes les barricades; **to insist on doing sth. in spite of all o.,** faire qch. à toute force; (*d*) **the o.,** le camp adverse; *Pol:* (le parti de) l'opposition, le parti oppositionnel; **member of the o.,** membre *m* de l'opposition; oppositionnel, -elle; **o. league,** contre-coalition *f, pl.* contre-coalitions; **o. meeting,** contre-assemblée *f, pl.* contre-assemblées; (*e*) *Com:* **to start up (a shop) in o. to s.o.,** ouvrir un magasin en concurrence avec qn.

oppress [ə'pres], *v.tr.* (*a*) opprimer (un peuple vaincu, etc.); (*b*) oppresser, opprimer, accabler (l'esprit, etc.); **oppressed by asthma,** oppressé par l'asthme.

oppressed [ə'prest], *a.* (peuple) opprimé; *s.* **the o.,** les opprimés *m*.

oppression [ə'preʃ(ə)n], *s.* **1.** oppression *f* (d'un peuple, etc.); *Jur:* abus *m* d'autorité. **2.** (*a*) accablement *m* (de l'esprit); resserrement *m* de cœur; (*b*) oppression de la poitrine; **to have fits of o.,** avoir des étouffements *m*.

oppressive [ə'presiv], *a.* **1.** (*of law, etc.*) oppressif, opprimant, tyrannique; **o. regime,** régime oppressif, oppresseur, opprimant. **2.** (*a*) (*of atmosphere, etc.*) lourd, entêtant, étouffant, alourdissant; (*b*) (*of mental burden*) accablant.

oppressively [ə'presivli], *adv.* **1.** tyranniquement; d'une manière accablante, étouffante.

oppressiveness [ə'presivnis], *s.* **1.** caractère oppressif, tyrannique (d'un gouvernement, etc.). **2.** lourdeur *f* (du temps).

oppressor [ə'presər], *s.* oppresseur *m*; **the oppressors and the oppressed,** les opprimants *m* et les opprimés *m*.

opprobrious [ə'proubriəs], *a.* injurieux, outrageant, infamant.

opprobriously [ə'proubriəsli], *adv.* injurieusement.

opprobriousness [ə'proubriəsnis], *s.* caractère injurieux (d'une insinuation, etc.).

opprobrium [ə'proubriəm], *s.* opprobre *m*.

oppugn [ə'pju:n], *v.tr.* attaquer, assaillir (un principe, etc.); s'attaquer à (une opinion, un principe, etc.).

oppugner [ə'pju:nər], *s.* attaqueur *m*; antagoniste *mf*; adversaire *m*.

opsonic [ɔp'sɔnik], *a. Bac: Med:* opsonique; **o. index,** indice *m*, index *m*, opsonique.

opsonin ['ɔpsənin], *s. Bio-Ch:* opsonine *f*.

opt [ɔpt], *v.i.* **1.** opter (**for,** pour; **between,** entre). **2. to o. out of an association,** quitter une association; se retirer d'une association; **to o. out of a competition,** abandonner un concours; **to o. out of sport,** décider de ne plus faire du sport; **I'm opting out,** je ne veux pas participer; je renonce.

optant ['ɔptənt], *s.* optant, -ante.

optative ['ɔptətiv], *a. & s. Gram:* optatif (*m*); **verb in the o.,** verbe à l'optatif.

optic ['ɔptik]. **1.** *a.* optique; *Anat:* **o. nerve,** nerf *m* optique; *Physiol:* **o. angle,** angle *m* de vision, optique; *Cryst:* **o. axis,** axe *m* optique. **2.** *s.* (*a*) *F: & Hum: O:* **the optics,** les yeux *m*, les mirettes *f*, les calots *m*; **he got one on the left o.,** il a reçu un pain sur l'œil gauche; (*b*) *Opt:* (i) lentille *f*, (ii) miroir *m*, (iii) prisme *m* (d'un instrument d'optique). **3. o. measure,** mesure transparente utilisée dans les bars.

optical ['ɔptikl], *a.* **1.** (*a*) optique; **o. spectrum,** spectre *m* optique; **o. activity, rotation,** activité *f* optique; **o. axis, centre,** axe *m*, centre *m*, optique (d'une lentille); *Med:* **o. neuritis,** œdème *m* de la papille optique; (*b*) *Phot: Cin:* tireuse *f* optique; *Tchn:* **o. pyrometer,** pyromètre *m* optique; (*c*) d'optique; **o. instrument,** instrument *m* d'optique; **o. glass,** verre *m* d'optique; **o. engineer,** ingénieur opticien, en optique; **o. illusion,** illusion *f* (d')optique. **2.** *Surv:* **o. square,** équerre *f* d'arpenteur à réflexion.

optically ['ɔptik(ə)li], *adv.* optiquement.

optician [ɔp'tiʃ(ə)n], *s.* opticien, -ienne.

optics ['ɔptiks], *s.pl.* (*usu. with sg. const.*) l'optique *f*; **electron o.,** optique électronique; **geometrical, mathematical, o.,** optique géométrique; **high-precision o.,** optique de haute précision.

optimal ['ɔptim(ə)l], *a.* optimal, -aux; optimum, -ima.

optimality [ɔpti'mæliti], *s.* optimalité *f*; **principle of o.,** principe *m* d'optimalité.

optimalization [ɔptiməlai'zeiʃ(ə)n], *s.* optim(al)isation *f*.

optimalize ['ɔptiməlaiz], *v.tr.* optim(al)iser.

optimism ['ɔptimizm], *s.* optimisme *m*.

optimist ['ɔptimist], *s.* optimiste *mf*.

optimistic [ɔpti'mistik], *a.* optimiste; **to feel o. about a matter, about the future,** augurer bien d'une affaire, de l'avenir.

optimistically [ɔpti'mistik(ə)li], *adv.* d'une manière optimiste; avec optimisme.

optimization [ɔptimai'zeiʃ(ə)n], *s.* optim(al)isation *f*.

optimize ['ɔptimaiz], *v.tr.* optim(al)iser.

optimum, *pl.* **-ima** ['ɔptiməm, -imə]. **1.** *s.* optimum *m* (des conditions de croissance et de reproduction). **2.** *a.* **o. conditions,** conditions les meilleures; conditions optimum; conditions optima; **o. equilibrium,** équilibre optimal; **o. population density,** optimum de population; *Cmptr:* **o. programming,** programmation optimisée.

option ['ɔpʃ(ə)n], *s.* **1.** option *f*, choix *m*; (*a*) **to make one's o.,** faire son option, son choix; opter (**between,** entre); **it is left to the o. of the student to study German or French,** le choix de l'étude de l'allemand ou du français est laissé aux étudiants; **lease renewable at the o. of the tenant,** bail renouvelable au gré du locataire; **bonds redeemable at the o. of the government,** obligations amorties à la suite d'une décision de l'État; **local o.,** droit *m* des habitants d'une localité d'interdire ou d'autoriser le débit des boissons alcooliques; (*b*) faculté *f*; **to have the o. of doing sth.,** avoir la faculté, le choix, de faire qch.; **this leaves us no o.,** cela nous ôte toute alternative; **we have no o. but to agree,** nous ne pouvons faire autrement, nous n'avons pas d'autre choix, que de consentir; **he had no o. but to obey,** force lui fut d'obéir; **to rent a building with o. of purchase,** louer un immeuble avec faculté d'achat; *Jur:* **imprisonment without the o. of a fine,** emprisonnement *m* sans substitution d'amende; *F:* **to get six months without the o.,** être condamné à six mois d'emprisonnement sans substitution d'amende; (*c*) **which of them is the best o.,** lequel est le meilleur choix; **there were few options open to him,** il n'avait pas grand choix; **there was no soft o.,** il n'y avait pas de solution facile; *Aut:* **options,** modifications *f*, accessoires *m*, au choix de l'acheteur. **2.** (*a*) **to take an o. on all the future works of an author,** prendre une option sur tous les ouvrages à paraître d'un auteur; **to ask for an o. on the film rights of a book,** demander une option pour un sujet de film; (*b*) *St.Exch: etc:* option; (marché *m* à) prime *f*; **buyer's, seller's, o.,** prime acheteur, vendeur; **double o.,** double option, doubles primes, stellage *m*; **to buy an o. on stock,** souscrire des valeurs à option; **put o.,** prime comportant le droit de livrer; **to take up an o.,** lever une prime; consolider un marché à prime; **to declare an o.,** donner la réponse, répondre, à une prime; **taker of an o.,** optant *m*; **giver of an o.,** optionnaire *m*; **taker of o. money,** vendeur *m* de primes; **giver of o. money,** acheteur *m* de primes; **exercise of an o.,** levée *f* d'une prime; **o. dealing(s),** opérations *fpl* à prime; négociations *fpl* à prime, à option; **o. deal,** opération à prime; **to deal in options,** faire des marchés à prime; **o. day, declaration of options,** (jour *m* de la) réponse des primes; jour d'option; **to declare options,** donner la réponse; **o. rate,** dont *m*.

optional ['ɔpʃənl], *a.* facultatif; **evening dress is o.,** l'habit *m* n'est pas de rigueur; *Aut: etc:* **o. extras,** accessoires *m* au choix (de l'acheteur); **o. retirement at sixty,** retraite *f* à soixante ans sur demande; *Sch:* **o. subjects,** matières *f* à option.

opto-electronics [ɔptouilek'trɔniks], *s.pl.* (*usu. with sg. const.*) opto-électronique *f*.

optogram ['ɔptougræm], *s. Physiol:* image rétinienne.

optokinetic [ɔptouki'netik, -kai-], *a.* qui concerne, entraîne, les mouvements des yeux.

optometer [ɔp'tɔmitər], *s. Opt:* optomètre *m*.

optometric(al) [ɔptə'metrik(l)], *a.* optométrique.

optometrist [ɔp'tɔmitrist], *s.* optométriste *mf*; *NAm:* réfractionniste *mf*.

optometry [ɔp'tɔmitri], *s.* optométrie *f*.

optophone ['ɔptəfoun], *s.* optophone *m*.

opulence ['ɔpjuləns], *s.* opulence *f*, richesse *f*; **to live in o.,** vivre dans l'opulence.

opulent ['ɔpjulənt], *a.* (*a*) opulent, riche; **to marry an o. widow,** épouser une veuve opulente; (*b*) *F: A:* **her o. hair,** sa chevelure abondante: **her o. charms,** ses appas plantureux.

opulently ['ɔpjuləntli], *adv.* opulemment; avec opulence.

opuntia [ou'pʌntiə], *s. Bot:* opuntia *m*, opuntiée *f*, oponce *m*.

Opuntiales [oupʌnti'eili:z], *s. Bot:* opuntiales *f*.

opus ['oupəs, 'ɔp-], *s.* opus *m*. **1.** *Arch:* **o. incertum,** opus incertum. **2.** *Mus: etc:* **magnum o.,** chef-d'œuvre *m*, *pl.* chefs-d'œuvre; **Beethoven o. 40,** Beethoven opus, op., 40.

opuscule [ɔ'pʌskju:l, 'ɔpəs-], **opusculum,** *pl.* **-a** [ɔ'pʌskjuləm, -ə], *s.* opuscule *m*.

or[1] [ɔ:r; *unstressed* ər]. **1.** *conj.* (*a*) ou; (*with neg.*) ni; **will you have beef or ham?** voulez-vous du bœuf ou du jambon? **Mohammed or Mahomet,** Mohammed ou (bien) Mahomet; **to state the object or objects of the operation,** indiquer le ou les buts de l'opération; **the search for the motive or motives for a crime,** la recherche du ou des motifs d'un crime; **the production was 7000 tons, or no more than a third of the target,** la production a été 7000 tonnes, soit pas plus que le tiers de l'objectif; **either one or the other,** soit l'un soit l'autre; l'un ou l'autre; **either come in or (else) go out,** entrez ou (bien) sortez; **either you or he has done it; he or you have done it,** c'est vous ou (c'est) lui, c'est l'un de vous deux, qui l'a fait; **I cannot either read or write, I cannot read or write,** je ne sais ni lire ni écrire; **without money or luggage,** sans argent ni bagages; **he has not left it here or at home,** il ne l'a pas laissé ici ni chez lui; **there was no perceptible light, sound or movement,** on ne percevait ni lumière, ni son, ni mouvement; **in a day or two,** dans un ou deux jours; **a mile or so,** environ un mille; **it will cost you ten or twelve pounds,** cela vous coûtera de dix à douze livres; *F:* **he's sick or something,** il est malade, ou bien il y a quelque chose qui ne va pas; (*b*) **don't move, or I'll shoot,** ne bougez pas, sinon je tire. **2.** *s. Cmptr:* OR, réunion *f* logique; **OR element,** élément *m* OU; mélangeur *m*; **OR circuit, gate,** circuit *m* OU.

or[2], *prep and conj. A: & Poet:* avant (que); *esp.* **or e'er you leave,** avant que vous (ne) partiez.

or[3], *s. Her:* or *m*.

orach(e) ['ɔritʃ], *s. Bot:* arroche *f*; **garden o.,** arroche des jardins; bonne-dame *f*, *pl.* bonnes-dames; belle-dame *f*, *pl.* belles-dames.

oracle ['ɔrəkl], *s.* oracle *m*; (*a*) **the Delphic o.,** l'oracle de Delphes; *Lit:* le trépied de Delphes; (*b*) **to pronounce, utter, an o.,** rendre un oracle; (*c*) (prêtre, -esse, d')oracle; *F:* **to talk like an o.,** parler comme un oracle; (*d*) *F:* **to work the o.,** (i) faire agir certaines influences; (ii) arriver à ses fins; (iii) se procurer de l'argent; *F:* battre monnaie; **it's he who works the o.,** c'est lui qui tient les fils.

oracular [ɔ'rækjulər], *a.* (*a*) (style, etc.) d'oracle, oraculaire; **our o. press,** nos journaux qui tranchent sur tout; (*b*) (réponse, etc.) en style d'oracle; équivoque, obscur.

oracularly [ɔ'rækjuləli], *adv.* en (style d')oracle.

oral ['ɔ:rəl], *a.* oral, -aux; (*a*) *Sch:* **o. examination,** *s. F:* **oral,** (examen) oral (*m*); *Jur:* **o. evidence,** preuve testimoniale; *NAm:* **o. history,** histoire fondée sur interviews enregistrées; (*b*) *Anat: etc:* **o. cavity,** cavité orale, buccale; **o. administration of a drug,** administration *f* d'une drogue par la bouche; **o. vaccine,** vaccin buccal; **o. contraception,** contraception par voie orale.

orality [ɔ'ræliti], *s.* oralité *f*.

orally ['ɔ:rəli], *adv.* **1.** oralement; de vive voix. **2.** *Med:* par la bouche; par voie buccale.

orange[1] ['ɔrin(d)ʒ], *s.* **1.** orange *f*; **o. section, segment,** quartier *m*, côte *f*, tranche *f*, loge *f* (d'une orange); **bitter, Seville, o.,** orange amère; bigarade *f*; **Valencia o.,** valence *f*; **sweet o., China o.,** orange douce; **blood o.,** (orange) sanguine (*f*); **o. peel,** peau *f*, écorce *f*, *Cu:* zeste *m*, d'orange; *Cu:* **candied o. peel,** zeste d'orange confit; orangeat *m*; *F:* **to squeeze the o. dry,** sucer qn jusqu'au dernier sou, jusqu'à la moelle; **a squeezed, sucked, o.,** (i) un homme fini, vidé; (ii) une chose dont on ne peut plus rien tirer; **o. girl, man, seller,** marchand, -ande, d'oranges; oranger, -ère; **o. marmalade,** marmelade *f* d'orange(s). **2.** (*a*) **o. (tree),** oranger *m*; **o. blossom,** fleurs *fpl* d'oranger; **o. flower,** fleur d'oranger; *Dist:* **o. flower water,** eau *f* de fleur(s) d'oranger; **o. flower oil,** (essence *f* de) néroli *m*; **o. grove,** orangeraie *f*; **o. grower,** orangiste *mf*; **o. house,** orangerie *f*; **o. wood,** bois *m* d'oranger; *Toil:* **o. stick,** bâtonnet *m*; bâton *m* d'oranger; (*b*) **mock o.,** (i) seringa odorant; (ii) laurier-cerise *m*, *pl.* lauriers-cerises; (iii) (*also* **osage o.**), toxylon *m*; oranger des Osages. **3.** *a.* & *s.* orangé (*m*), orange (*m*) *inv*; **o. red,** rouge orange (*m*) *inv*; nacarat (*m*) *inv*; **o. ribbons,** rubans orangés, orange; **to dye sth. o.,** oranger qch.; *Bot:* **o. lily,** lis orangé; *Ent:* **o. tip (butterfly),** aurore *f.* **4.** *Hort:* **Blenheim, Cox's, o. (pippin),** variétés de (pommes) reinettes d'Angleterre.

Orange[2], *Pr.n. Geog:* **1. the O. (River),** le fleuve Orange; l'Orange *m*; *Hist:* **the O. River Colony, the O. Free State,** la Colonie du fleuve Orange; l'État *m* libre d'Orange. **2.** (*in S. Fr.*) Orange; *Hist:* **the Prince of O.,** le prince d'Orange.

orangeade [ɔrin'dʒeid], *s.* orangeade *f.*

orange-coloured ['ɔrin(d)ʒkʌləd], *a.* (couleur d')orange *inv*; orangé.

Orang(e)ism ['ɔrin(d)ʒizm], *s. Hist:* orangisme *m.*

Orang(e)ist ['ɔrin(d)ʒist], *a. Hist:* (*in the Netherlands*) **the O. Party,** le parti orangiste.

Orangeman, *pl.* **-men** ['ɔrin(d)ʒmən], *s.m. Hist: Pol:* orangiste (du parti protestant de l'Irlande du Nord).

orangeroot ['ɔrin(d)ʒru:t], *s. U.S: Bot:* hydrastis *m.*

orangery ['ɔrin(d)ʒ(ə)ri], *s.* orangerie *f.*

orang-outang, -utan [ɔ:ræŋ'u:tæŋ, -tæn], *s. Z:* orang-outan(g) *m*, *pl.* orangs-outan(g)s.

orant ['ɔ:rənt], *s. Art:* orant, -ante.

orate [ɔ:'reit], *v.i. Pej:* pérorer; faire un, des, laïus; piquer un laïus, laïusser.

oration [ɔ:'reiʃ(ə)n], *s.* **1.** allocution *f*, discours *m*; morceau *m* oratoire; *Pej:* harangue *f*; *Sch: F:* laïus *m*; **funeral o.,** oraison *f* funèbre. **2.** *Gram: O:* **direct, oblique, o.,** discours direct, indirect.

orator ['ɔrətər], *s.* orateur *m*; **woman o.,** femme orateur; *occ.* oratrice; **mob o.,** harangueur *m* de foules; **soap-box o.,** orateur de carrefour, de borne.

oratorial [ɔrə'tɔ:riəl], *a.* = ORATORICAL.

Oratorian [ɔrə'tɔ:riən], *a.* & *s.m. Ecc:* oratorien; **the O. fathers,** les pères de l'Oratoire.

oratorical [ɔrə'tɔrikl], *a.* **1.** (*a*) (style, talent) oratoire; **o. delivery,** débit *m* oratoire; (*b*) (discours) verbeux, ampoulé. **2. an o. speaker,** (i) un orateur disert; (ii) *Pej:* un phraseur.

oratorically [ɔrə'tɔrik(ə)li], *adv.* oratoirement; dans un style d'oration; sur un ton oratoire.

oratorio [ɔrə'tɔ:riou], *s. Mus:* oratorio *m.*

oratory[1] ['ɔrət(ə)ri], *s.* art *m* oratoire; éloquence *f*; **pulpit o.,** éloquence de la chaire; **a brilliant piece of o.,** un brillant spécimen d'art oratoire; **flight of o.,** envolée éloquente.

oratory[2], *s.* **1.** *Ecc:* oratoire *m*; chapelle privée. **2.** *Ecc.Hist:* **the O. (of St Philip Neri),** l'Oratoire (de Jésus); les pères de l'Oratoire.

orb [ɔ:b], *s.* **1.** orbe *m*; (*a*) globe *m*, sphère *f*; **the o. of the sun,** le globe du soleil; (*b*) *Poet:* corps *m* céleste; astre *m*; (*c*) (*of regalia*) globe; **the o. and the sceptre,** l'orbe et le sceptre; (*d*) *Her:* monde *m*. **2.** *Poet:* (globe de l')œil *m*. **3.** *A:* orbite *f* (d'une planète).

orbed [ɔ:bd], *a. Lit:* rond, sphérique; **full-o. moon,** lune *f* dans son plein.

orbicular [ɔ:'bikjulər], *a.* **1.** orbiculaire, sphérique. **2.** *Anat:* (muscle) orbiculaire. **3.** *Min:* **o. rock,** roche *f* orbiculaire.

orbicularis, *pl.* **-res** [ɔ:bikju'la:ris, -ri:z], *s. Anat:* (muscle) orbiculaire (*m*).

orbicularly [ɔ:'bikjuləli], *adv.* orbiculairement.

orbiculate [ɔ:'bikjuleit], *a.* orbiculaire, sphérique; *Bot:* **o. leaf,** feuille orbiculaire, orbiculée.

orbit[1] ['ɔ:bit], *s.* **1.** (*a*) *Astr: Space:* orbite *f* (d'une planète, d'un véhicule spatial); **in o.,** en, sur, orbite; **to enter, go into, o.,** se mettre, se placer, en orbite; **to put a satellite in o.,** mettre, placer, un satellite en orbite, sur (son) orbite; **parking o.,** orbite d'attente; **to make six orbits of the moon,** effectuer six révolutions sur orbite lunaire; **small states are drawn into the o. of greater ones,** les petits États sont attirés dans l'orbite, dans la sphère d'influence, d'un plus grand; **this isn't within my o.,** cela n'appartient pas à mon milieu, ne rentre pas dans ma compétence; (*b*) *Av:* circuit *m* d'attente (avant l'autorisation d'atterrir); (*c*) *Atom.Ph:* orbite (d'un électron, etc.). **2.** *Anat:* orbite (de l'œil); fosse *f* orbitaire.

orbit[2]. **1.** *v.tr.* (*a*) mettre, placer, (un satellite) en orbite, sur une orbite; (*b*) (*of satellite, etc.*) **to o. the sun,** décrire une orbite, orbiter, autour du soleil; **to o. the moon ten times,** effectuer une dizaine de révolutions sur orbite lunaire. **2.** *v.i.* (*a*) (*of satellite, etc.*) orbiter, décrire une orbite; (*b*) *Av:* (*of aircraft*) orbiter (sur un circuit d'attente).

orbital[1] ['ɔ:bitl], *a.* **1.** (*a*) *Astr: etc:* orbital, -aux; **o. moment,** moment orbital; **o. velocity,** vitesse orbitale; (*b*) *Ph:* **o. electron,** électron orbital, planétaire, satellite; (*c*) *Av:* **o. bomber,** bombardier *m* capable d'effectuer le tour de la terre; (*d*) *Civ.E:* **o. road,** route *f* de ceinture; boulevard *m* périphérique. **2.** *Anat:* (*of nerve, cavity, arch, etc.*) orbitaire; *Orn:* **o. feathers,** plumes *f* orbitaires.

orbital[2], *s. Atom.Ph:* **atomic, molecular, o.,** orbitale *f* atomique, moléculaire.

Orbitelariae [ɔ:biti'lɛərii:], *s.pl. Arach:* orbitèles *m.*

orbitelarian [ɔ:biti'lɛəriən], *Arach:* **1.** *a.* orbitèle, orbitélaire. **2.** *s.* orbitèle *m.*

orbitele [ɔ:bi'ti:l], *s. Arach:* orbitèle *m.*

orbitelous [ɔ:bi'ti:ləs], *a. Arach:* orbitèle, orbitélaire; **o. spider,** orbitèle *m.*

orbiter ['ɔ:bitər], *s. Space:* satellite artificiel en orbite (qui ne doit pas atterrir).

orbiting[1] ['ɔ:bitiŋ], *a.* (*a*) (*of satellite, spacecraft*) en, sur, orbite; **earth-o., moon-o.,** en orbite autour de la terre, de la lune; sur orbite terrestre, lunaire; (*b*) *Av:* (avion) qui orbite, en orbite (sur un circuit d'attente).

orbiting[2], *s.* orbitage *m* (d'un satellite, etc.).

orbitoid ['ɔ:bitɔid], *a.* & *s. Paleont:* orbitoïde (*m*).

orbitolina [ɔ:bitou'lainə], *s. Paleont:* orbitoline *f.*

orbitolite [ɔ:'bitəlait], *s. Paleont:* orbitolite *f.*

orbitosphenoid [ɔ:bitou'sfenɔid], *s. Anat:* petite aile du sphénoïde.

orbitostat ['ɔ:bitoustæt], *s. Anthr:* orbitostat *m.*

orc [ɔ:k], *s. Z:* orque *f*, épaulard *m.*

Orcadian [ɔ:'keidiən]. **1.** *a.* & *s. Geog:* (originaire, natif) des Orcades. **2.** *a. Geol:* **O. series,** vieux grès rouges d'Écosse.

orcanet(te), orchanet ['ɔ:kənet], *s. Bot:* orcanète *f*, orcanette *f.*

orcein ['ɔ:sii:n], *s. Ch:* orcéine *f.*

orchard ['ɔ:tʃəd], *s.* verger *m*; *Bot:* **o. grass,** dactyle pelotonné.

orcharding ['ɔ:tʃədiŋ], *s.* **1.** fructiculture *f*; arboriculture fruitière. **2.** *coll. NAm:* terrains aménagés en vergers.

orchardist ['ɔ:tʃədist], **orchardman,** *pl.* **-men** ['ɔ:tʃədmən], *s.* fructiculteur *m*, pomiculteur *m.*

orchesis [ɔ:'ki:sis], *s. Gr.Ant:* orchestique *f.*

orchesography [ɔ:ki'sɔgrəfi], *s. Danc: Mus:* orchésographie *f.*

orchestia [ɔ:kestiə], *s. Crust:* orchestie *f.*

orchestic [ɔ:'kestik], *a. Danc: Mus:* orchestique.

orchestics [ɔ:'kestiks], *s.pl.* (*usu. with sg. const.*) orchestique *f*; art *m* de la danse.

orchestra ['ɔ:kistrə], *s.* **1.** *Gr.Ant: Th:* orchestre *m*; *Th:* **the o. stalls,** *NAm:* **the o.,** les fauteuils *m* d'orchestre. **2.** *Mus:* orchestre; **string o.,** orchestre d'archets, à cordes; **with full o.,** à grand orchestre; **the members of the o.,** les musiciens *m.*

orchestral [ɔ:'kestrəl], *a.* orchestral, -aux.

orchestrate ['ɔ:kistreit], *v.tr. Mus:* orchestrer, instrumenter (une symphonie, etc.); *Fig:* **to o. a press campaign,** orchestrer une campagne de presse.

orchestrater, orchestrator ['ɔ:kistreitər], *s. Mus:* orchestrateur *m.*

orchestration [ɔ:kis'treiʃ(ə)n], *s.* orchestration *f*, instrumentation *f.*

orchestric [ɔ:'kestrik], *a.* orchestral, -aux.

orchestrina [ɔ:ki'stri:nə], *s. Mus:* orchestrino *m.*

orchestrion [ɔ:'kestriən], *s. Mus:* orchestrion *m.*

orchid ['ɔ:kid], *s.* **1.** *Bot: Hort:* orchidée *f*; (*wild*) orchis *m*; **cradle o.,** anguloa *f*; **frog o.,** (espèce *f* de) cœloglossum *m*; **(green) man o.,** acéras *m*; *F:* homme pendu; **spider o.,** ophrys *f* araignée; **spotted o.,** orchis taché; **o. grower,** cultivateur, -trice, d'orchidées; *F:* **orchids for the author,** (mes) compliments à l'auteur. **2. o. (pink),** (couleur *f*) rose (*m*) violet.

Orchidaceae [ɔ:ki'deisii:], **Orchideae** [ɔ:'kidii:], *s.pl. Bot:* orchid(ac)ées *f.*

orchidaceous [ɔ:ki'deiʃəs], *a.* **1.** *Bot:* relatif, ressemblant, aux orchidées. **2.** *F: O:* (i) (style) fleuri; (ii) (femme) d'une grande beauté.

orchidalgia [ɔ:ki'dældʒiə], *s. Med:* orchialgie *f.*

orchi(d)ectomy [ɔ:ki'(d)ektəmi], *s. Surg:* orchidectomie *f.*

orchidist ['ɔ:kidist], *s.* cultivateur, -trice, d'orchidées.

orchidologist [ɔ:ki'dɔlədʒist], *s.* orchidologiste *m.*

orchidology [ɔ:ki'dɔlədʒi], *s.* orchidologie *f.*

orchidopexy [ɔ:kidou'peksi], *s. Surg:* orchidopexie *f.*

orchidotherapy [ɔ:kidou'θerəpi], *s. Med:* orchidothérapie *f.*

orchidotomy [ɔ:ki'dɔtəmi], *s. Surg:* orchidotomie *f.*

orchil ['ɔ:tʃil], **orchilla (weed)** [ɔ:'tʃilə(wi:d)], *s. Bot: Dy:* orseille *f.*

orchis ['ɔ:kis], *s. Bot:* orchis *m*; **purple o.,** orchis pourpre.

orchitis [ɔ:'kaitis], *s. Med:* orchite *f.*

Orchomenus [ɔ:'kɔminəs], *Pr.n. A.Geog:* Orchomène.

orcin ['ɔ:sin], **orcinol** ['ɔ:sinɔl], *s. Ch:* orcine *f.*

ordain [ɔ:'dein], *v.tr.* ordonner. **1.** *Ecc:* conférer les ordres à (un prêtre); **to o. s.o. deacon,** ordonner qn diacre; **to be ordained,** recevoir les ordres; **ordained priest,** prêtre ordonné. **2.** (*of the Deity, of fate*) (*a*) destiner; *B:* **as many as were ordained to eternal life,** tous ceux qui étaient destinés à la vie éternelle; **ordained of God to be judge,** destiné de Dieu pour être juge; (*b*) ordonner, fixer; **fate ordained, it was ordained, that we should meet,** le sort a voulu que nous nous rencontrions; **the hour ordained for his death,** l'heure que Dieu avait fixée, avait décrétée, pour sa mort; (*c*) (*of pers.*) prescrire, décréter (une mesure); **the court ordained that the President should be suspended from his duties,** la cour ordonna que le Président serait interdit de ses fonctions; **to o. an inquiry,** statuer une enquête; **it was ordained by law,** c'était prescrit, commandé, par la loi.

ordainer [ɔ:'deinər], *s.* **1.** *Ecc:* ordinant *m*. **2.** ordonnateur, -trice.

ordaining [ɔ:'deiniŋ], *s. Ecc:* ordination *f* (d'un prêtre).

ordeal [ɔ:'di:l], *s.* **1.** *Hist:* épreuve *f* judiciaire; *A:* ordalie *f*; jugement *m* de Dieu; **to decide a case by o.,** trancher une cause par ordalie; **o. by fire,** épreuve du feu. **2.** épreuve; danger *m* (qui éprouve la force et le courage); **to go through a terrible o.,** passer par une rude épreuve; **it is an o. for me to make a speech,** je suis au supplice quand je dois prononcer un discours. **3.** *Bot:* **o. bean,** (i) (*plant*) physostigma *m*; (ii) fève *f* de Calabar; **o. tree,** (i) tanghin *m*, tanghen *m*; (ii) (*also* **o. bark**) mancône *f.*

order[1] ['ɔ:dər], *s.* ordre *m*. **1.** (*a*) **all orders of men,** toutes les classes sociales; **the higher, lower, orders (of society),** les classes supérieures; les classes inférieures, les basses classes, le menu peuple; **talents of the first o., of a high o.,** talents de premier ordre, d'un ordre élevé; **workmanship of the highest o.,** travail de premier ordre; **population of, in, the o. of 100,000,** population de l'ordre de 100.000 habitants; **difficulties of,** *NAm:* **on, the same o. as those previously encountered,** difficultés du même ordre que celles rencontrées auparavant; *NAm:* **something on the o. of a museum,** quelque chose dans le genre d'un musée; (*b*) *Ecc:* **holy orders,** ordres sacrés; ordres majeurs; **minor orders,** ordres mineurs; **to take (holy) orders,** prendre les ordres; recevoir les ordres; entrer dans les ordres (sacrés), dans la cléricature; recevoir la prêtrise; *R.C.Ch:* prendre la soutane; **to be in holy orders,** être prêtre; **to confer holy orders on s.o.,** ordonner qn prêtre; (*c*) **monastic o.,** ordre religieux; communauté *f*; **the Franciscan o.,** l'ordre des Franciscains; *A.Theol:* **o. of angels,** ordre d'anges; **the o. of seraphim,** l'ordre des séraphins; **o. of knighthood,** ordre de chevalerie; **the O. of the Garter,** l'Ordre de la Jarretière; (*d*) **to be wearing all one's orders,** porter tous ses ordres, toutes ses décorations; (*e*) *Arch:* **Ionic o., Doric o.,** ordre ionique, dorique; (*f*) *Mth:* **curve of the second o.,** courbe *f* du second ordre; **matrix of o. 2,** matrice *f* d'ordre 2; (*g*) *Nat.Hist:* ordre (d'un règne); *Cryst:* **first o. pyramid,** pyramide *f* de première espèce. **2.** succession *f*, suite *f*; **in alphabetical o.,** en, par, ordre alphabétique; **in chronological o.,** en, par, ordre chronologique; **in o. of date,** par ordre de dates; **in o. of age,** par rang d'âge; **in ascending, descending, o.,** en, par, ordre croissant, décroissant; **in the o. stated,** dans l'ordre indiqué; *For:* **o. of felling,** ordre d'abattage; succession des coupes; **o. of precedence,** (i) ordre de priorité; (ii) ordre de préséance; *Mil:* ordre de bataille (dans un défilé); **card out of (its) o.,** fiche *f* hors de son rang; *Mth:* **to arrange terms in ascending, descending, o.,** ordonner des termes. **3.** *Mil:* (*a*) **close o.,** ordre serré; **in close o.,** en ordre serré; en formation dense; *Navy:* à distance serrée; **o. of battle,** ordre de bataille; répartition générale des forces; *Navy:* ordre tactique; *Navy:* **scouting o.,** dispositif *m* d'éclairage; *NAm: F:* **in quick, short, o.,** (i) au plus vite; (ii) immédiatement, sur-le-champ; (*b*) tenue *f*; **drill o.,** tenue d'exercice; **fatigue o.,** tenue de corvée; **review o.,** tenue de défilé, de parade, de revue; **in gala o.,** en grande tenue; en tenue de soirée. **4.** régime *m*; **the established o.,** l'ordre établi; **the old o. of things,** l'ancien ordre des choses; l'ancien régime; **to set up a new o.,** établir un nouveau régime; **it's not in the natural o. of events,** ce n'est pas dans l'ordre des choses. **5.** (*a*) **to put things in o.,** mettre des choses en ordre; **the matter is now in o.,** l'affaire est maintenant en règle; **to put, set, one's affairs in o.,** mettre ses affaires en état, en ordre; mettre ordre à ses affaires; mettre de l'ordre dans ses affaires; régler ses affaires; **to set one's house in o.,** (i) remettre de l'ordre dans son ménage; (ii) remettre de l'ordre dans ses affaires; **the country must set its house in o.,** il faut que le pays assainisse les finances, l'administration; *Com:*

so that our accounts, books, may be kept in o., pour la bonne tenue de notre comptabilité, de nos livres (comptables); (*b*) *Adm: etc:* **in o.,** en règle; conforme aux dispositions, prescriptions, réglementaires; conforme à la règle; réglementaire; **document that is not in (legal) o.,** document *m* informe; **receipt that is not in o.,** quittance qui n'est pas en règle, pas en bonne forme; **is your passport in o.?** est-ce que votre passeport est en règle? (*c*) **cargo received in good o.,** chargement reçu en bon état; **machine in good (working) o.,** machine en bon état de fonctionnement, de marche; **out of o.,** (mécanisme) détraqué, dérangé, en mauvais état de fonctionnement; (compas, etc.) déréglé; (téléphone) en dérangement; **to get out of o.,** se détraquer, se dérégler, se déranger; **to put a machine out of o.,** détraquer, dérégler, une machine; **the machine is out of o.,** la machine ne marche, fonctionne, pas; **the lift is out of o.,** l'ascenseur est en panne; **my stomach's out of o.,** j'ai l'estomac dérangé, *F:* détraqué; (*d*) (*in meeting, etc.*) **o. of the day,** ordre du jour; *Parl:* **o. paper,** copie *f* de l'ordre du jour; **in o.,** dans le cadre de l'ordre du jour; **to rule a question out of o.,** statuer qu'une interpellation n'est pas dans les règles, n'est pas pertinente; **to rise to a point of o.,** se lever pour demander le rappel à l'ordre; **to call s.o. to o.,** rappeler qn à l'ordre, à la question; **o.! o.!** à l'ordre! **such levity is quite out of o.,** un tel manque de sérieux n'est pas de mise, est intempestif; **before leaving this subject a short résumé would not be out of o.,** avant de quitter ce sujet un petit résumé ne serait pas hors de propos, inopportun, il conviendrait peut-être de faire un petit résumé; *F:* **tape-recorders are the o. of the day,** les magnétophones sont à l'ordre du jour, en vogue; (*e*) *Ecc:* **o. of service,** office *m*. **6. law and o.,** l'ordre public; **to support law and o.,** (i) prêter main-forte à la justice; (ii) aider au maintien de l'ordre public; **to keep o. in a town,** assurer, maintenir, l'ordre dans une ville; faire la police d'une ville; *Sch:* **to keep o. in class,** maintenir, faire régner, la discipline dans une classe; tenir ses élèves (en main); **to keep the children in o.,** (i) faire régner l'ordre parmi les enfants; (ii) soumettre les enfants à la discipline; **to restore o.,** rétablir l'ordre. **7.** *Mil:* **arms at the o.,** l'arme au pied; **to return to the o. (from the slope),** revenir l'arme au pied; reposer l'arme. **8.** *conj.phr.* **in o. to do sth.,** afin de, pour, à dessein de, en vue de, faire qch.; **in o. to put you on your guard,** pour que vous soyez sur vos gardes; **in o. for them to understand,** afin qu'ils puissent le comprendre. **9.** (*a*) commandement *m*, instruction *f*; *Mil: etc:* consigne *f*; *Nau:* **engine room orders,** commandements à la machine; **verbal, written, o.,** ordre verbal, écrit; **standing orders,** ordres permanents; règlement(s) *m* (d'une assemblée, etc.); *Mil:* consigne permanente; *Mil:* **duty covered by orders,** service commandé; **to give orders for sth. to be done, that sth. should be done,** ordonner qu'on fasse qch., que qch. se fasse; **I gave orders for the goods to be packed,** j'ai donné l'ordre d'emballer la marchandise; **he gave me orders to do it,** il m'a donné (l')ordre de le faire; **I have orders to remain here,** j'ai ordre de rester ici; **he has orders to let nobody pass,** il a pour consigne de ne laisser passer personne; **orders are orders,** je ne connais que la consigne; **to obey orders,** se conformer aux ordres, à ses instructions; suivre la consigne; **to take orders only from s.o.,** n'obéir qu'aux ordres de qn; *F:* **I don't take (my) orders from him,** je ne dépends pas de lui; **until further orders,** jusqu'à nouvel ordre, nouvel avis; sauf avis contraire; **by o. of the town council,** par l'ordre du conseil municipal; **by o. of the King,** de par le roi; **it was done by o. of the board,** cela s'est fait sur les ordres du conseil d'administration; *Jur:* **forced sale by o. of the court,** vente forcée par autorité de justice; (*b*) *Fin: Com:* **pay to the o. of J. Martin,** payez à l'ordre de J. Martin; **pay J. Martin or o.,** payez à J. Martin ou à son ordre; **to our own o.,** à l'ordre de moi-même, de nous-mêmes; **bill to o.,** billet *m* à ordre; **cheque to o., o. cheque,** chèque *m* à ordre; (*c*) *Cmptr:* **initial orders,** ordres initiaux; (*d*) *Com:* commande *f*, demande *f*; **to solicit orders from s.o.,** faire à qn ses offres de service; (*of representative*) **to call for orders,** passer prendre les commandes; **to place an o. with s.o., to give s.o. an o.,** (i) confier, passer, une commande à qn; donner à (un agent) une commission pour acheter qch.; (ii) commander qch. à qn; **he gave us an o. for five tons of fertilizer,** il nous a fait une commande de, nous a commandé, cinq tonnes d'engrais; (*in restaurant*) **have you given your o.?** avez-vous commandé? **he has sent us a good o.,** il nous a fait une commande importante; **cash with o.,** payable à la commande; **o. form,** bon *m*, bulletin *m*, de commande; **o. book,** carnet *m* de commandes; **to put goods on o.,** commander des marchandises; mettre des marchandises en commande; **it's on o.,** c'est commandé; **by o. and for account of J. Martin,** d'ordre et pour compte de J. Martin; **made to o.,** (*of furniture, etc.*) fabriqué sur commande, à la demande; (*of suit*) fait sur mesure; **clothes to o.,** vêtements *m* sur commande; **books written to o.,** ouvrages écrits sur commande; *F:* **that's a tall o.,** ce que vous demandez là n'est pas une mince affaire, n'est pas facile, est un peu gros! vous en demandez un peu trop! (*e*) (i) (*goods ordered*) **to deliver an o.,** livrer une commande; (ii) *NAm:* (*in restaurant*) portion *f*. **10.** (*a*) **written o.,** ordre par écrit; *Adm:* **departmental o.,** arrêté ministériel; **general o.,** arrêt *m*; **o. in council** = décret présidentiel; arrêté ministériel; décret-loi, *pl.* décrets-lois; **o. to pay, for payment,** ordonnance *f* de paiement; ordonnancement *m*; *Com:* **o. to view,** permis *m* de visiter (une maison à vendre, etc.); *Adm:* **to issue an o.,** prendre un arrêté; *Jur:* **judge's o.,** ordonnance; **o. of the court,** injonction *f* de la cour; **deportation o.,** arrêté d'expulsion; (*of judge*) **to make an administration o.,** ordonner une gestion, une administration judiciaire; (*b*) *Mil:* **daily orders,** décision journalière; **regimental orders,** décisions du régiment; **orders in brief,** mémorandum *m*; **battle orders,** mémorandum de combat; *Navy:* **sailing orders,** ordre d'appareiller, instructions pour l'appareillage; **to be under sailing orders,** avoir reçu l'ordre d'appareiller; **sealed orders,** ordres cachetés, pli cacheté, pli secret; **orders for the night,** service *m* de nuit; (*c*) *Com: Adm:* bon *m*; **delivery o.,** bon de livraison; **issue o.,** bon de sortie (de magasin, etc.); **purchase o.,** bon d'achat, de commande; *Mil: etc:* **travel o.,** feuille *f* de déplacement; (*d*) mandat *m*; **o. on a bank,** mandat sur une banque; **to pay by banker's o.,** payer par virement bancaire; **postal o., money o.,** mandat de poste; mandat postal; mandat-poste *m*, *pl.* mandats-poste; (*e*) *Th: etc:* billet *m* de faveur.

order², *v.* **I.** *v.tr.* **1.** (*a*) arranger, ranger, ordonner (des meubles, des objets, etc.); classer, ranger (des papiers, etc.); régler (sa vie, etc.); **to o. one's affairs,** mettre ordre à, de l'ordre dans, ses affaires; mettre ses affaires en ordre; (*b*) *Mil:* **to o. arms,** (i) mettre l'arme au pied; (ii) (*from the slope*) reposer l'arme, les armes; **o. arms!** reposez armes! **2.** (*of fate, Deity*) destiner (qn à qch.); **fate ordered otherwise,** le sort a voulu autrement. **3.** (*a*) **to o. s.o. to do sth.,** ordonner, commander, à qn de faire qch.; **he's been ordered to report tomorrow,** il a reçu l'ordre de se présenter demain; *Jur:* **to be ordered to pay costs,** être condamné aux dépens; **to o. an inquiry,** ordonner une enquête; **to o. s.o. home,** ordonner à qn de rentrer (chez lui); **I was ordered abroad,** j'ai reçu l'ordre de partir pour l'étranger; **to o. an officer to Plymouth,** désigner un officier pour Plymouth; **ship ordered to the Mediterranean,** navire désigné pour la Méditerranée; (*b*) *Med:* prescrire, ordonner (un traitement, un médicament, à qn); **I have been ordered a little wine,** sur l'avis du médecin je bois un peu de vin; **the doctor ordered him a change of air, to go to the south of France,** le médecin lui a ordonné de changer d'air, un séjour dans le Midi; *F:* **that's just what the doctor ordered,** c'est tout à fait ce qu'il faut pour l'occasion; (*c*) *Com: etc:* commander, demander, commissionner (qch.); mettre qch. en commande; **to o. goods from Paris,** commander des articles, faire des commandes, à Paris; **you must o. a barrel of beer,** vous ferez venir un tonneau de bière; **to o. a taxi,** (faire) demander un taxi; **what have you ordered for dinner?** qu'avez-vous commandé pour le dîner? **4.** *Ecc: A:* conférer les ordres à, ordonner (un prêtre).

II. (*compound verbs*) **1. order about,** *v.tr. F:* faire marcher, faire aller (qn); faire pivoter (qn); **he likes ordering people about,** il aime (à) commander les autres; c'est un autoritaire.

2. order off, *v.tr.* ordonner à (qn) de s'éloigner, s'en aller; *Fb:* **to o. off a player, to o. a player off (the field),** ordonner à un joueur de quitter la partie, faire sortir un joueur du terrain.

3. order out, *v.tr.* ordonner à (qn) de sortir; **to o. s.o. out (of the room, house),** mettre (qn) à la porte; **to o. out the troops,** faire sortir des troupes; appeler la troupe.

ordered ['ɔːdəd], *a.* ordonné; en (bon) ordre; **to lead an o. life,** mener une vie régulière, réglée; *Cmptr:* **o. sequence, set, of data,** suite ordonnée d'informations; *Cryst:* **o. lattice,** réseau cristallin régulier.

orderer ['ɔːdərər], *s.* ordonnateur, -trice.

ordering ['ɔːdəriŋ], *s.* **1.** mise *f* en ordre (des affaires, de ses pensées); disposition *f* (de troupes, de sa maison, etc.); ordonnance *f* (d'un campement, etc.); arrangement *m* (des mots dans la phrase); classement *m*, rangement *m* (de documents, etc.); *Cmptr:* **o. by merging,** rangement par interclassement. **2.** *Com:* lancement *m*, passation *f*, des commandes; **cost of o.,** coût *m* de lancement des commandes. **3.** *Ecc: A:* ordination *f* (d'un prêtre).

orderless ['ɔːdəlis], *a.* sans ordre, en désordre, désordonné; *Cmptr: etc:* **o. sequence of data,** suite non ordonnée d'informations.

orderliness ['ɔːdəlinis], *s.* **1.** bonne conduite; méthode *f*. **2.** habitudes *fpl* d'ordre. **3.** discipline *f*; calme *m*, bonne conduite (d'une foule, etc.).

orderly ['ɔːdəli]. **1.** *a.* (*a*) (*of arrangement, etc.*) ordonné, méthodique; (*of life, etc.*) réglé, rangé, régulier; **books arranged in an o. fashion,** livres rangés méthodiquement, avec ordre, en bon ordre; (*of pers.*) **to be very o.,** avoir beaucoup de méthode, beaucoup de soin; (*b*) (*of crowd, etc.*) tranquille, discipliné; **quiet and o. person,** personne sage et posée; (*c*) *Mil:* **o. room,** salle *f* des rapports; **o. officer,** officier *m* de service. **2.** *s.* (*a*) *Mil:* planton *m*; **to be on o. duty,** être de planton; (*b*) **hospital o., medical o.,** aide-infirmier, -ière; *Mil:* infirmier *m*, ambulancier *m*; (*c*) *A:* **street o.,** balayeur *m*, arroseur *m* (de rues); boueur *m*.

ordinal ['ɔːdinl]. **1.** *a.* (*a*) (nombre) ordinal, -aux; (*b*) *Nat.Hist:* **o. classification,** classification ordinale. **2.** *s.* (*a*) adjectif ordinal; (*b*) *Ecc:* ordinal *m*.

ordinance ['ɔːdinəns], *s.* **1.** ordonnance *f*, décret *m*, règlement *m*; **police o.,** ordonnance de police; arrêté *m* de police; (*in Fr.*) arrêté préfectoral; **traffic o.,** ordonnance sur la circulation; **amnesty o.,** ordonnance d'amnistie. **2.** *Ecc:* (*a*) rite *m*, cérémonie *f* (du culte); (*b*) **the (sacred) O.,** l'Eucharistie *f*.

ordinand [ɔːdi'nænd], *s. Ecc:* ordinand *m*.

ordinant ['ɔːdinənt], *s. Ecc:* ordinant *m*.

ordinarily ['ɔːdin(ə)rili, *NAm:* ɔːdi'nɛərili], *adv.* ordinairement, communément, normalement; d'ordinaire, d'habitude; à l'ordinaire.

ordinariness ['ɔːdin(ə)rinis], *s.* caractère *m* peu remarquable, banalité *f* (d'un spectacle, etc.).

ordinary ['ɔːdin(ə)ri], *a.* & *s.* **I.** *a.* **1.** (*a*) ordinaire; (*of routine, etc.*) coutumier; normal, -aux; courant; **o. scale of remuneration,** barème courant de rémunération; **tools in o. use,** outils couramment employés, d'emploi courant; **o. language,** langage *m* ordinaire, accessible, de tous les jours; **the o. course of things,** le cours ordinaire des choses; **in o. times, in the o. way, it isn't done,** en temps ordinaire cela ne se fait pas; **o.-sized man,** homme de taille ordinaire; *Dipl:* **ambassador o.,** ambassadeur ordinaire; *Fin:* **o. share, shareholder,** action, actionnaire, ordinaire; **o. agent,** agent attitré; *Opt:* **o. ray,** rayon ordinaire; (*b*) **o. Englishman,** Anglais moyen, typique; **the o. reader,** le commun des lecteurs; **he was just an o. tourist,** c'était un touriste comme un autre; **he's just an o. person,** il appartient au commun des mortels. **2.** *Pej:* **a very o. kind of man,** un homme tout à fait quelconque, un homme à la douzaine; **a small and very o. room,** une petite chambre banale, très quelconque; **we can't give him an o. job,** on ne peut pas lui donner un emploi quelconque; **the two girls were anything rather than o.,** ces deux jeunes filles étaient loin d'être quelconques, n'étaient nullement banales.

II. *s.* **1.** ordinaire *m*; **out of the o.,** exceptionnel; peu ordinaire; qui sort de l'ordinaire; anormal, -aux; **that's out of the o.,** cela sort des proportions ordinaires; *F:* ça c'est pas banal; **man above the o.,** homme à part, distingué, au-dessus du commun; **physician in o. to the Queen,** médecin ordinaire de la Reine; **purveyors in o. to Her Majesty,** fournisseurs attitrés de sa Majesté. **2.** *A:* (*a*) (*in restaurant*) table *f* d'hôte; ordinaire *m*; (*b*) *NAm:* auberge *f*. **3.** *Her:* pièce *f* honorable. **4.** (*pers.*) (*a*) *Jur: Scot:* juge *m*; (*b*) *Ecc.Jur:* ordinaire (archevêque ou évêque). **5.** *Ecc:* **the O. (of the Mass),** l'Ordinaire (de la messe). **6.** *Navy:* **ship in o.,** navire en réserve, désarmé. **7.** *A:* vélocipède *m*.

ordinate ['ɔːdinət], *s. Mth:* ordonnée *f*; **o. axis,** axe *m* d'ordonnée.

ordination [ɔːdi'neiʃ(ə)n], *s.* **1.** arrangement *m*; classification *f* (des plantes, etc.). **2.** ordonnance *f* (de Dieu, etc.). **3.** *Ecc:* ordination *f*.

ordnance ['ɔːdnəns], *s.* **1.** artillerie *f*; **piece of o.,** bouche *f* à feu; pièce *f* d'artillerie; **ship with heavy o.,** navire fort en artillerie; **o. factory,** manufacture *f* d'artillerie; **naval o. officer,** ingénieur *m* de l'artillerie navale. **2.** (*a*) *Mil:* (service *m* du) matériel; **Royal Army O. Corps,** *U.S:* **O. Service,** Service du Matériel; **o. and supplies,** les ravitaillements *m*; **o. field park,** parc *m* du Matériel; **o. officer,** officier *m* du Matériel; **o. stores,** (i) magasin *m* du Matériel; (ii) matériel militaire; **o. supplies,** fournitures *f*, ravitaillements, du Service du Matériel; **o. unit,** unité *f* du Matériel; **o. workshop,** atelier *m* du (Service du) Matériel; (*b*) *Adm: Mil:* **O. Survey,** (i) = Institut Géographique National; (ii) corps *m* des ingénieurs géographes; **o.(-survey) map,** (i) = carte *f* de l'Institut Géographique National; (ii) carte d'état-major; **o. surveyor,** ingénieur *m* géographe.

ordo, *pl.* **-os, -dines** ['ɔ:dou, -ouz, -dini:z], *s. Ecc:* ordo *m*; bref *m.*

ordonnance ['ɔ:dənəns], *s.* agencement *m*, arrangement *m* (des figures d'un tableau, etc.).

Ordovician [ɔ:də'viʃiən], *a. & s. Geol:* ordovicien (*m*); silurien inférieur.

ordure ['ɔ:djuər], *s.* ordure *f*; (*a*) excrément *m*; (*b*) immondice *f*, saleté *f*; (*c*) langage ordurier; ordures.

ore [ɔ:r], *s.* minerai *m*; pierre *f* de mine; **o. minerals,** minerais; **copper, iron, o.,** minerai de cuivre, de fer; **base, low-grade, o.,** minerai de, à, basse teneur, de basse, faible, teneur; minerai pauvre; **rich, high-grade, o.,** minerai à, de, haute teneur; minerai riche; **crude o., raw o., o. as mined,** minerai brut; **crushed o.,** minerai bocardé, broyé; schlich *m*; *Miner:* **needle o.,** aciculite *f*; **o. body,** masse minérale; corps minéralisé; masse, massif *m*, corps, de minerai; **o. chute, o. shoot,** (i) (*also* **o. chimney**) colonne *f* de richesse; coulée *f* de minerai; *Min:* cheminée *f* à minerai; (ii) *Min:* couloir *m* à minerai; **o. deposit,** gisement *m* de minerai; gîte minéral; *Min:* **o. level, road, way,** voie *f* d'extraction du minerai; *Metall:* **o. dressing,** préparation *f*, traitement *m*, mécanique du minerai.

oread ['ɔ:riæd], *s.f. Gr.Myth:* oréade.

ore-bearing ['ɔ:beəriŋ], *a.* **1.** *Geol: Min:* (roche, etc.) métallifère. **2.** *Ch:* (*of solution*) minéralisant.

ore-forming ['ɔ:fɔ:miŋ], *a.* minéralisateur, -trice; *Metall:* **o.-f. flux,** fondant minéralisateur.

oregano [ɔ'regənou], *s. Bot:* origan *m*; marjolaine bâtarde.

Oregon ['ɔrigən], *Pr.n. Geog:* **1. the O.,** le fleuve Orégon, l'Orégon *m.* **2.** l'État *m* d'Orégon, l'Orégon.

Oregonian [ɔri'gouniən], *a. & s. Geog:* (originaire, natif) de l'Orégon.

Orenbourg ['ɔrənbə:g], *Pr.n. Geog:* Orenbourg *m.*

Orenburgian [ɔrən'bə:giən], *a. & s. Geol:* (étage) supérieur russe du stéphanien.

oreodon ['ouriədɔn], *s. Paleont:* oreodon *m.*

oreodont ['ouriədɔnt], *s. Paleont:* oréodonte *m.*

oreodoxa [ouriou'dɔksə], *s. Bot:* oreodoxa *m.*

oreophasis [ouriou'feisis], *s. Orn:* oréophase *m.*

oreopithecus [ouriou'piθikəs], *s. Paleont:* oréopithèque *m*, oreopithecus *m.*

oreotrochilus [ouriou'trɔkiləs], *s. Orn:* oiseau-mouche andin, *pl.* oiseaux-mouches.

Oresteia (the) [ðiɔres'taiə], *s. Gr.Lit:* l'Orestie *f.*

Orestes [ɔ'resti:z], *Pr.n.m. Gr.Myth:* Oreste.

orfe [ɔ:f], *s. Ich:* ide *m.*

orfray ['ɔ:frei], *s. Ecc.Cost:* orfroi *m*, parement *m* (de chasuble).

organ ['ɔ:gən], *s.* **1.** *Mus:* (*a*) orgue *m*; *Ecc:* orgues *fpl*; **a fine o.,** un bel orgue; de belles orgues; **the finest organs made,** les meilleurs orgues fabriqués; **grand o.,** grand orgue, grandes orgues; **choir o.,** orgue du chœur, de la maîtrise, d'accompagnement; **echo o.,** écho *m*; **full o.,** (i) orgue à plein jeu; orgue plein; (ii) (*direction to organist*) grand orgue; **to play the o.,**jouer, toucher, de l'orgue; **to be, preside, at the o.,** tenir l'orgue, les orgues; **o. blower,** (i) souffleur *m* (d'orgue); (ii) soufflerie *f* (électrique, etc.); **o. builder,** facteur *m* d'orgues; **o. building,** facture *f* d'orgues; **o. case, chest,** buffet *m*, fût *m*, d'orgue; **o. loft, gallery,** tribune *f* d'orgues; **o. pipe,** (i) tuyau *m* d'orgue; (ii) *Coel:* orgue de mer; tubipore *m*; **o. point,** point *m* d'orgue; **o. stop,** jeu *m* d'orgue; **o. screen,** jubé *m* (formant tribune d'orgue); *Dressm:* **o. folds,** plis *m* en tuyau d'orgue; (*b*) **American o.,** orgue de salon; (*c*) **street o.,** orgue de Barbarie; **o. grinder,** joueur, -euse, d'orgue de Barbarie; **bird o.,** serinette *f*; **whistle o.,** sifflet à vache; (*d*) **cinema o.,** orgue de cinéma. **2.** organe *m* (du corps humain, d'une plante, machine, etc.); **o. of hearing, hearing o.,** organe de l'ouïe; **the vocal organs,** l'appareil vocal; la voix; l'organe; *Anat:* **o. of Corti,** organe de Corti; *NAm: Cu:* **o. meat,** abats *mpl.* **3.** (*a*) organe (de gouvernement, etc.); **an efficient o. of propaganda,** un organe de propagande efficace; (*b*) journal *m*, -aux, bulletin *m*, organe, porte-parole *m inv* (du gouvernement, d'un parti, etc.); **the official o.,** l'organe officiel; le porte-parole du Gouvernement; **journal considered as a semi-official o.,** journal considéré comme un organe officieux du gouvernement.

organbird ['ɔ:gənbə:d], *s. Orn: Austr:* cassican *m* à gorge noire.

organdi(e) ['ɔ:gəndi], *s. Tex:* organdi *m.*

organelle ['ɔ:gənel], *s. Biol:* organite *m.*

organic [ɔ:'gænik], *a.* **1.** (maladie, fonction, etc.) organique. **2. o. beings,** êtres organisés; **the law of o. growth,** la loi de croissance organisée. **3.** (*a*) (dépôt, engrais, etc.) organique; (*b*) **o. chemistry,** chimie *f* organique; **o. chemist,** organicien, -ienne; **o. acid, base, compound,** acide *m*, base *f*, composé *m*, organique; *Atom.Ph:* (*of reactor*) **o.-moderated,** à modérateur, ralentisseur, organique. **4.** systématisé; **an o. whole,** un ensemble systématique. **5.** organique, fondamental, -aux; **o. part of the whole,** partie essentielle de la totalité; *Jur:* **o. law,** loi *f* organique; *Ling:* **o. consonant, vowel,** consonne *f*, voyelle *f*, organique; *Mil:* **o. unit,** unité *f* organique.

organically [ɔ:'gænik(ə)li], *adv.* organiquement; (*of pers.*) **to have something o. wrong,** souffrir d'une maladie organique; **there's nothing o. wrong with the system,** le système n'est pas foncièrement mauvais.

organicism [ɔ:'gænisizm], *s.* organicisme *m.*

organicist [ɔ:'gænisist], *s.* **1.** *Biol:* organiciste *mf.* **2.** *Med:* organicien, -ienne.

organicistic [ɔ:gæni'sistik], *a.* **1.** *Biol:* organicistique. **2.** *Med:* organicien, -ienne.

organism ['ɔ:gənizm], *s.* **1.** *Biol:* organisme *m*; **living o.,** organisme vivant. **2.** économie *f* (d'un corps, d'un système).

organist ['ɔ:gənist], *s.* organiste *mf.*

organizability [ɔ:gənaizə'biliti], *s.* organisabilité *f.*

organizable [ɔ:gə'naizəbl], *a.* organisable.

organization [ɔ:gənai'zeiʃ(ə)n], *s.* organisation *f.* **1.** aménagement *m* (d'une forêt, etc.); **inadequacy of o.,** défaut *m* d'organisation; *Ind: etc:* **o. of work,** organisation du travail; **o. of labour,** (i) régime *m* du travail; (ii) syndicalisme *m*; **o. and methods,** organisation scientifique du travail; **functional o.,** *NAm:* **staff o.,** organisation fonctionnelle, horizontale; **line o.,** organisation hiérarchique, verticale; **o. chart,** schéma *m* d'organisation, de structure; organigramme *m*; *Mil:* **o. of the forces into divisions, corps, units, etc.,** répartition *f* organique des forces. **2.** organisation, organisme *m* (politique, international, etc.); **charity o.,** organisation charitable; œuvre *f* de charité; **youth o.,** mouvement *m* de jeunesse; **travel o.,** organisation de voyage, de tourisme; **national organizations,** collectivités nationales; **International Labour O.,** Organisation internationale du travail; **United Nations O.,** Organisation des Nations Unies; **North Atlantic Treaty O.,** Organisation du traité de l'Atlantique nord; *Mil:* **the higher o.,** les grandes unités; *Av:* **ground o.,** infrastructure aérienne.

organizational [ɔ:gənai'zeiʃən(ə)l], *a.* (*a*) (défaut, etc.) d'organisation, de structure; **o. chart,** schéma *m* d'organisation, de structure; organigramme *m*; (*b*) *Mil:* (matériel, etc.) d'unité; **o. maintenance,** entretien courant d'unité; **o. unit,** unité administrative.

organizationally [ɔ:gənai'zeiʃən(ə)li], *adv.* (*a*) d'une manière organisée, structurale; (*b*) relativement à l'organisation; **the firm is o. weak,** la maison manque, a des défauts, d'organisation.

organize ['ɔ:gənaiz], *v.tr.* **1.** organiser; policer (un pays); **workmen organized into trade unions,** ouvriers organisés en syndicats; **well-organized body of adherents,** partisans bien embrigadés. **2.** (*a*) organiser, arranger (un concert, etc.); **badly organized fête,** fête mal organisée; (*b*) aménager (ses loisirs, etc.); (*c*) *F:* **to o. a week's leave,** se faire accorder un congé de huit jours; **to o. a bottle of rum,** s'emparer d'une bouteille de rhum; dénicher, *esp.* voler, une bouteille de rhum.

organized ['ɔ:gənaizd], *a.* **1.** *Biol:* organisé, pourvu d'organes. **2.** (*of society, religion, etc.*) organisé; (état) policé; **the o. bodies of the country,** les corps constitués, les organisations, du pays; **o. labour,** les organisations ouvrières; *Sch:* **o. games,** jeux dirigés.

organizer ['ɔ:gənaizər], *s.* **1.** organisateur, -trice; **the o. of the festivities,** l'organisateur, -trice, l'ordonnateur, -trice, de la fête. **2.** *Biol:* organisateur.

organizing ['ɔ:gənaiziŋ], *s.* **1.** organisation *f*; **o. ability,** qualités *fpl* d'organisation. **2.** aménagement *m* (de ses loisirs).

organogel [ɔ:'gænoudʒel], *s. Ch:* organogel *m.*

organogenesis [ɔ:gənou'dʒenisis], **organogeny** [ɔ:gə'nɔdʒəni], *s. Biol:* organogénèse *f*, organogénie *f.*

organogenetic [ɔ:gənoudʒi'netik], **organogenic** [ɔ:gənə'dʒenik], *a. Biol:* organogénique.

organogenist [ɔ:gə'nɔdʒinist], *s. Biol:* organogéniste *mf.*

organographic [ɔ:gə'nou'græfik], *a. Biol:* organographique.

organographist [ɔ:gə'nɔgrəfist], *s. Biol:* organographe *mf.*

organography [ɔ:gə'nɔgrəfi], *s. Biol:* organographie *f.*

organoid ['ɔ:gənɔid]. *Biol:* **1.** *a.* organoïde; *Med:* **o. tumour,** tumeur *f* organoïde. **2.** *s.* organite *m.*

organoleptic [ɔ:gənou'leptik], *a. Physiol:* organoleptique.

organologic [ɔ:gənou'lɔdʒik], *a. Biol:* organologique.

organology [ɔ:gə'nɔlədʒi], *s. Biol:* organologie *f.*

organomagnesium ['ɔ:gənoumæg'ni:ziəm], *a. & s. Ch:* organo-magnésien (*m*), *pl.* organo-magnésiens.

organometallic ['ɔ:gənoumi'tælik], *a. Ch:* organométallique.

organon, *pl.* **-ana** ['ɔ:gənən, -ənə], *s. Phil:* organum *m.*

organopathic [ɔ:gənou'pæθik], *a. Med:* organopathique.

organopathy [ɔ:gə'nɔpəθi], *s. Med:* organopathie *f.*

organoplastic [ɔ:gənou'plæstik], *a. Biol:* organoplastique.

organoplasty [ɔ:gənou'plæsti], *s. Biol:* organoplastie *f.*

organoscopic [ɔ:gənou'skɔpik], *a. Med:* organoscopique.

organoscopy [ɔ:gə'nɔskəpi], *s. Med:* organoscopie *f.*

organosol [ɔ:'gænəsɔl], *s. Ch:* organosol *m.*

organotherapy ['ɔ:gənou'θerəpi], *s. Med:* organothérapie *f*, opothérapie *f.*

organotropic [ɔ:gənou'trɔpik], *a. Med:* organotrope.

organum, *pl.* **-a** ['ɔ:gənəm, -ə], *s.* **1.** *Phil:* organum *m.* **2.** *A.Mus:* organum.

organzine[1] ['ɔ:gənzi:n], *s. Tex:* organsin *m*; floche *f.*

organzine[2], *v.tr. Tex:* organsiner.

orgasm ['ɔ:gæzm], *s.* **1.** paroxysme *m* (de rage, etc.); excitation *f.* **2.** *Physiol:* orgasme *m.*

orgastic [ɔ:'gæstik], *a. Physiol:* orgastique.

orgeat ['ɔ:ʒɑ:, 'ɔ:dʒiət], *s.* orgeat *m.*

orgiac ['ɔ:dʒiæk], *a.* orgiaque.

orgiast ['ɔ:dʒiæst], *s. Gr.Ant:* orgiaste *m.*

orgiastic [ɔ:dʒi'æstik], *a.* orgiastique.

orgy ['ɔ:dʒi], *s.* (*a*) *Gr. & Rom.Ant:* **orgies,** orgies *f*, bacchanales *f*; (*b*) *Fig:* orgie; débauche *f*; **drunken o.,** beuverie *f*; (*c*) **o. of colour,** orgie, profusion *f*, de couleurs.

Oribatidae [ɔri'bætidi:], *s.pl. Arach:* oribatidés *m.*

oribi ['ɔribi], *s. Z:* oribi *m*, ourébi *m.*

orichalc(h) ['ɔrikælk], **orichalcum** [ɔri'kælkəm], *s. Ant:* orichalque *m.*

oriel ['ɔ:riəl], *s. Arch:* **o. (window),** oriel *m*; fenêtre *f* (i) en saillie, (ii) en encorbellement.

orielled ['ɔ:riəld], *a. Arch:* à fenêtres (i) en saillie, (ii) en encorbellement.

orient[1] ['ɔ:riənt]. **1.** *s.* (*a*) *Astr: Geog:* orient *m*; **the O.,** l'Orient; (*b*) **(pearl of) o.,** perle orientale; (*c*) **pearl of a fine o.,** perle d'un bel orient. **2.** *a.* (*a*) *O:* oriental, -aux, de l'Orient; (*b*) **o. pearl,** (i) perle orientale; (ii) perle d'un bel orient; **o. ruby, sapphire,** rubis, saphir, oriental; (*c*) *A: & Lit:* étincelant; brillant; (*d*) *Lit:* (soleil, etc.) levant.

orient[2] ['ɔ:rient], *v.tr. & i.* = ORIENTATE.

oriental [ɔ:ri'entl]. **1.** *a.* oriental, -aux; **o. languages,** langues orientales; **o. rug,** tapis *m* d'Orient; **o. bookseller,** libraire *m* spécialiste des ouvrages sur l'Orient; **o. splendour,** luxe oriental, *F:* asiatique; **o. amethyst, pearl, topaz,** améthyste, perle, topaze, orientale; *Med:* **o. sore,** bouton *m* d'Orient, d'Alep; clou *m* de Biskra. **2.** *s.* Oriental, -ale.

orientalism [ɔ:ri'entəlizm], *s.* orientalisme *m.*

orientalist [ɔ:ri'entəlist], *s.* orientaliste *mf.*

orientalize [ɔ:ri'entəlaiz]. **1.** *v.tr.* orientaliser. **2.** *v.i.* s'orientaliser.

orientate ['ɔ:rienteit]. **1.** *v.tr.* orienter (une carte, une église, etc.); **to o. the map on the village church,** orienter la carte sur le clocher du village; **to o. oneself (physically, psychologically),** s'orienter; *Fig:* **events enabled them to o. themselves better,** les événements leur ont permis de prendre une meilleure orientation; **to o. s.o. towards a commercial career,** orienter qn vers une carrière dans le commerce. **2.** *v.i.* s'orienter **(on a star, etc.,** sur une étoile, etc.).

orientating [ɔ:riən'teitiŋ], *s.* orientation *f.*

orientation [ɔ:riən'teiʃ(ə)n], *s.* orientation *f*; (*a*) *Surv:* **o. line, point,** ligne *f*, point *m*, d'orientation; **o. table,** table *f* d'orientation; *Fig:* **the political o. of the middle classes,** l'orientation politique des classes moyennes; (*b*) *Atom.Ph:* **nuclear o.,** orientation nucléaire; **spin o.,** orientation du spin, des spins; **with preferred, random, o.,** à orientation préférentielle, non préférentielle.

orientator ['ɔ:rienteitər], *s. Surv:* (instrument) orienteur *m.*

oriented ['ɔ:rientid], *a.* **1.** orienté; *Surv:* **o. map method,** méthode *f* de la carte orientée; *Cmptr:* **o., non-o., graph,** graphe orienté, non orienté; *Tchn:* **o. cellulose, steel,** cellulose *f*, acier *m*, à grain orienté. **2. profit-o. undertaking,** entreprise *f* qui vise aux profits; *Cmptr:* **card-o., disc-o., tape-o., computer,** ordinateur *m* à cartes, disques, bandes; **computer-o. language,** langage adapté au calculateur.

orienting ['ɔ:rientiŋ], *s.* orientation *f*; *Surv:* **o. line, point,** ligne *f*, point *m*, d'orientation; **o. compass,** déclinatoire *m.*

orientite ['ɔ:riəntait], *s. Miner:* orientite *f.*

orifice ['ɔrifis], *s.* orifice *m*, ouverture *f*, trou *m*; *Petr:* **o. meter,** indicateur *m* de débit (à l'orifice d'une canalisation, etc.).
oriflamme ['ɔriflæm], *s. Hist: & Fig:* oriflamme *f.*
origan ['ɔrigən], **origanum** [ɔ'rigənəm], *s. Bot:* origan *m.*
Origen ['ɔridʒen], *Pr.n.m. Rel.Hist:* Origène.
origin ['ɔridʒin], *s.* origine *f.* **1. the o. of the universe,** la genèse des mondes; **to trace an event back to its o.,** remonter à l'origine d'un événement; *Arch: etc:* **point of o.,** point *m* d'origine, de naissance (d'une courbe, etc.); *Artil: Sm.a:* **o. of the rifling,** naissance des rayures; *Ph:* **o. distortion,** distorsion *f* d'origine. **2. word of Greek o.,** mot *m* d'origine grecque; (*of pers.*) **to be of noble o.,** être d'origine illustre; **a man of humble o.,** un homme d'humble extraction *f*; **this family had its o. in Spain,** cette famille tire son origine de l'Espagne; *Com:* **country of o.,** pays *m* de provenance; **goods of foreign o.,** marchandises *f* de provenance étrangère; *Cust:* **certificate of o.,** certificat *m* d'origine. **3.** *Anat:* (point d') attache *f* (d'un muscle). **4.** *Cryst:* centre *m* (de symétrie) (d'un cristal).
original [ɔ'ridʒinl]. **1.** *a.* (*a*) original, -aux; premier, primitif; primordial, -iaux; originaire; d'origine; **the o. aims of an association,** les fins primordiales d'une société; **o. colour of a dress,** couleur première, primitive, d'une robe; **o. idea of a work,** idée *f* mère d'une œuvre; **o. material of an experiment,** produit *m* de départ d'une expérience; **o. meaning of a word,** sens premier, originel, d'un mot; **o. member of a club,** membre originaire d'un cercle; *Com: etc:* **o. value,** valeur initiale; **o. packing,** emballage d'origine; **o. tyres of a car,** pneus d'origine d'une automobile; *Cmptr:* **o. address,** adresse *f* d'origine; *Fin:* **o. capital,** capital d'origine, primitif; **o. subscriber,** souscripteur primitif; (*b*) originel, originaire; **o. defect,** vice *m* originaire; *Theol:* **o. sin,** péché originel; (*c*) (manuscrit, texte) original; **the o. picture is in the National Gallery,** le tableau original se trouve à la *National Gallery*; *Publ:* **o. edition,** édition princeps, originale; *Engr:* **o. print,** gravure originale; *Fin: Com: etc:* **o. bill, cheque, receipt,** primata *m* de traite, de chèque, de quittance; **o. document,** (i) *Book-k:* pièce *f* comptable; (ii) *Jur:* primordial *m*, -aux; **o. invoice,** facture originale; (*d*) (écrivain, ouvrage, style, etc.) original; (spectacle, etc.) inédit; **the scheme is not o.,** ce projet n'est pas original, n'est pas inédit; **to give an o. turn to one's writing,** donner un tour original à, originaliser, ses écrits. **2.** *s.* (*a*) original *m* (d'un tableau, d'une facture, etc.); *Fin:* primata *m* (d'une traite); **to copy sth. from the o.,** copier qch. sur l'original; **to read the classics in the o.,** lire les classiques dans l'original; (*b*) **the likeness of a portrait to the o.,** la ressemblance d'un portrait à l'original; (*c*) *Lith:* matrice *f.* **3.** *s.* personne originale; original, -ale; *F:* type *m* (à part).
originality [əridʒin'æliti], *s.* originalité *f.*
originally [ə'ridʒinəli], *adv.* **1.** (*a*) originairement; à l'origine, dans l'origine; **he was o. English,** il est d'origine anglaise; il est Anglais d'origine; (*b*) originellement; dès l'origine. **2.** originalement; d'une façon originale, singulière.
originate [ə'ridʒineit]. **1.** *v.tr.* faire naître, donner naissance à, être l'auteur de (qch.); amorcer (une réforme, etc.); **he originated this industry,** ce fut lui le promoteur de cette industrie; c'est lui qui a créé cette industrie. **2.** *v.i.* tirer son origine, dériver, provenir (**from, in,** de); avoir son origine, prendre sa source (**from, in,** dans); **to o. from a common ancestor,** tirer ses origines d'un ancêtre commun; **the fire originated under the floor,** le feu a pris naissance sous le plancher; **the strike originated in demands of the lowest paid workers,** la grève a eu pour origine les revendications des ouvriers les moins payés; **the scheme originated with me,** je suis l'auteur de ce projet; *Tp:* **the call originated at a call box,** l'appel a émané, est venu, d'une cabine publique.
originating [ə'ridʒineitiŋ], *a.* d'origine; émetteur, -trice; *Cmptr:* **o. department,** service émetteur; **o. tape,** bande émettrice; *Tp:* **o. exchange,** *NAm:* **o. office,** bureau *m* d'origine, de départ.
origination [əridʒin'eiʃ(ə)n], *s.* (*a*) source *f*, origine *f*; (*b*) création *f*, invention *f* (d'une machine, etc.); ébauche *f* (d'un projet, etc.); *Cmptr:* création, émission *f* (d'une information); (*c*) naissance *f* (d'une rumeur, etc.).
originative [ə'ridʒinətiv], *a.* (*of mind, etc.*) inventif, créateur, -trice.
originator [ə'ridʒineitər], *s.* créateur, -trice; auteur *m*; initiateur, -trice; promoteur *m* (d'une industrie); premier mobile (d'un complot); *Cmptr:* émetteur *m*, créateur (d'une information); *Tp: Tg:* (i) expéditeur, -trice, (ii) origine *f* (d'un message).
orill(i)on [ɔ'ril(i)ən], *s. Fort: A:* orillon *m* (d'un bastion).
orinasal [ɔ:ri'neiz(ə)l], *a. Ling:* **o. vowel,** voyelle nasale.
Orinoco (the) [ðiɔri'noukou], *Pr.n. Geog:* l'Orénoque *m.*
oriole ['ɔ:rioul], *s. Orn:* **1.** loriot *m*, oriol(l)e *m*; **golden o.,** loriot (jaune d'Europe); merle *m* d'or; grive dorée; oiseau *m* aux cerises; compère-loriot *m*, *pl.* compères-loriots. **2.** *NAm:* troupiale *m*; *Fr.C:* oriole; **Baltimore o.,** troupiale baltimore; *Fr.C:* oriole de Baltimore; **orchard o.,** oriole des vergers (*Fr.C.*) **Bullock's o.,** oriole à ailes blanches (*Fr.C.*).
Oriolidae [ɔ:ri'oulidi:], *s.pl. Orn:* oriolidés *m.*
Orion [ɔ'raiən], *Pr.n.m. Gr.Myth: Astr:* Orion; **Orion's belt,** le baudrier d'Orion; le bâton de Jacob; les trois Rois; les trois Mages; **Orion's hound,** Sirius *m.*
orioscope ['ɔriəskoup], *s. Ph:* orioscope *m*, polariscope *m.*
orismology [ɔris'mɔlədʒi], *s.* étude *f* des terminologies.
orison ['ɔrizən], *s. A:* oraison *f*, prière *f*; **to be at one's orisons,** être en prière.
Orkneys (the) [ði'ɔ:kniz], *Pr.n.pl. Geog:* les Orcades *f.*
Orlando [ɔ:'lændou], *Pr.n.m.* **1.** *Hist:* Roland; *Lit:* **O. Furioso,** Roland Furieux. **2.** (*in Shakespeare*) Orlando.
Orleanian [ɔ:'li:niən], *a. & s.* (habitant, originaire) de la Nouvelle-Orléans.
Orleanism [ɔ:'li:ənizm], *s. Fr.Hist:* orléanisme *m.*
Orleanist [ɔ:'liənist], *a. & s. Fr.Hist:* orléaniste (*mf*).
Orleanistic [ɔ:liə'nistik], *a. Fr.Hist:* orléaniste.
Orleans [ɔ:'liənz]. **1.** *Pr.n. Geog:* Orléans. **2.** *s.* ['ɔ:liənz], (*a*) *Tex:* **O. (cloth),** orléans *f*; (*b*) pruneau *m* d'Orléans.
orlée ['ɔ:lei], *a. Her:* orlé.
orlewise ['ɔ:lwaiz], *adv. Her:* en orlé.
Orlon ['ɔ:lɔn], *s. R.t.m:* Orlon *m.*
orlop ['ɔ:lɔp], *s. Nau:* **o. (deck),** faux-pont *m*, *pl.* faux-ponts.
ormer ['ɔ:mər], *s. Moll:* ormeau *m*, ormier *m*, ormet *m*; oreille *f* de mer.
ormolu ['ɔ:məlu:], *s.* **1.** or moulu; **o. clock,** pendule *f* en or moulu. **2.** chrysocale *m.*
ornament¹ ['ɔ:nəmənt], *s.* **1.** (*a*) ornement *m* (du style, d'architecture, etc.); agrément *m*, garniture *f* (sur une robe, etc.); **by way of o.,** pour ornement; en fait d'ornements; **rich in o.,** d'une ornementation riche; (*b*) ornement; **vases and other ornaments,** vases et autres ornements; **to strip sth. of (its) ornaments,** déparer qch.; *Ecc:* **the altar ornaments,** le parement d'autel; *Fig:* **he would be an o. to any circle,** il serait un ornement pour n'importe quelle société. **2.** *Mus:* **ornaments,** ornements.
ornament² ['ɔ:nəment], *v.tr.* orner, ornementer, décorer (une chambre, etc.); agrémenter, embellir (une robe, etc.); orner (son style) (**with,** de).
ornamental [ɔ:nə'mentl], *a.* ornemental, -aux; d'ornement, d'ornementation, d'agrément; décoratif; **o. tree, plant,** *s.* **o.,** arbre *m*, plante *f*, d'ornement; **o. addition,** enjolivement *m*, enjolivure *f*; *Aut: O:* **o. radiator cap,** bouchon *m* artistique de radiateur; *Phot:* **o. mask,** cache *m* artistique.
ornamentalist [ɔ:nə'mentəlist], *s.* ornemaniste *m.*
ornamentally [ɔ:nə'mentəli], *adv.* **1.** pour servir d'ornement. **2.** décorativement.
ornamentation [ɔ:nəmen'teiʃ(ə)n], *s.* **1.** ornementation *f*, embellissement *m*, décoration *f.* **2.** ornements *mpl*, embellissements, décorations.
ornamenter ['ɔ:nəmentər], *s.* embellisseur, -euse; décorateur, -trice.
ornamentist [ɔ:nə'mentist], *s. Art: Arch:* ornemaniste *m.*
ornate [ɔ:'neit], *a.* orné, chamarré; surchargé d'ornements; **o. style,** style orné, imagé, fleuri.
ornately [ɔ:'neitli], *adv.* avec une surabondance d'ornements; en style trop fleuri.
ornateness [ɔ:'neitnis], *s.* ornementation exagérée.
Orneodidae [ɔ:ni'ɔdidi:], *s.pl. Ent:* ornéodidés *m.*
ornery ['ɔ:nəri], *a. NAm: F:* (*a*) de qualité inférieure; (*b*) désagréable; (*c*) d'humeur maussade; rouspéteur.
ornis ['ɔ:nis], *s. Orn:* avifaune *f*, faune avienne.
ornithic [ɔ:'niθik], *a.* ornithique.
ornithin(e) ['ɔ:niθin, -i:n], *s. Ch:* ornithine *f.*
Ornithischia [ɔ:ni'θiskiə], *s.pl. Paleont:* ornithopodes *m.*
Ornithodelphia [ɔ:niθə'delfiə], *s.pl. Z:* ornithodelphes *m.*
ornithodelphian [ɔ:niθə'delfiən], *a. & s. Z:* ornithodelphe (*m*).
ornithodelphic [ɔ:niθə'delfik], **ornithodelphous** [ɔ:niθə'delfəs], *a.* ornithodelphe.
ornithogalum [ɔ:ni'θɔgələm], *s. Bot:* ornithogale *m.*
ornithoid ['ɔ:niθɔid], *a. Z:* ornithoïde.
ornithological [ɔ:niθə'lɔdʒikl], *a.* ornithologique.
ornithologist [ɔ:ni'θɔlədʒist], *s.* ornithologue *mf*, ornithologiste *mf.*
ornithology [ɔ:ni'θɔlədʒi], *s.* ornithologie *f.*
ornithomancy [ɔ:'niθəmænsi], *s.* ornithomancie *f.*
ornithomantic [ɔ:niθə'mæntik], *a.* ornithomantique.
ornithophilous [ɔ:ni'θɔfiləs], *a.* **1.** ornithophile. **2.** *Bot:* ornithogame.
ornithophily [ɔ:ni'θɔfili], *s.* **1.** ornithophilie *f.* **2.** *Bot:* ornithogamie *f.*
ornithopod [ɔ:'niθəpɔd], *s. Paleont:* ornithopode *m.*
Ornithopoda [ɔ:ni'θɔpədə], *s.pl. Paleont:* ornithopodes *m.*
ornithopodous [ɔ:ni'θɔpədəs], *a. Paleont:* ornithopode.
ornithopter [ɔ:ni'θɔptər], *s. A.Av:* ornithoptère *m.*
ornithoptera [ɔ:ni'θɔptərə], *s. Ent:* ornithoptère *m.*
ornithorhynchus [ɔ:niθou'riŋkəs], *s. Z:* ornithoryngue *m*; *F:* bec-d'oiseau *m*, *pl.* becs-d'oiseau.
ornithoscopic [ɔ:niθou'skɔpik], *a.* ornithoscopique.
ornithoscopy [ɔ:ni'θɔskəpi], *s.* ornithoscopie *f.*
ornithosis [ɔ:ni'θousis], *s. Med:* ornithose *f.*
ornithotic [ɔ:ni'θɔtik], *a. Med:* ornithotique.
ornithotomic [ɔ:ni'θɔtəmik], *a.* ornithotomique.
ornithotomist [ɔ:ni'θɔtəmist], *s.* ornithotomiste *mf.*
ornithotomy [ɔ:ni'θɔtəmi], *s.* ornithotomie *f.*
Ornithurae ['ɔ:niθjuəri:], *s.pl. Paleont:* ornithurés *m.*
ornithuric [ɔ:ni'θju:rik], *a. Ch:* ornithurique.
Orobanchaceae [ɔrəbæŋ'keisii:], *s.pl. Bot:* orobanchacées *f.*
orobanchaceous [ɔrəbæŋ'keiʃəs], *a. Bot:* orobanché.
orobanche [ɔrə'bæŋki], *s. Bot:* orobanche *f.*
orobus ['ɔrəbəs], *s. Bot:* orobe *m or f.*
orogenesis [ɔrou'dʒenisis], *s. Geol:* orogénèse *f.*
orogenic [ɔrou'dʒenik], **orogenetic** [ɔrədʒi'netik], *a. Geol:* orogénique.
orogeny [ɔ'rɔdʒini], *s. Geol:* orogénie *f.*
orographic(al) [ɔrə'græfik(l)], *a.* (carte, pluie) orographique.
orography [ɔ'rɔgrəfi], *s.* orographie *f.*
oroide ['ɔ:rouid], *s.* similor *m*, chrysocale *m.*
orological [ɔrə'lɔdʒikl], *a.* orologique.
orologist [ɔ'rɔlədʒist], *s.* orologiste *mf.*
orology [ɔ'rɔlədʒi], *s.* orologie *f.*
orometer [ɔ'rɔmitər], *s.* oromètre *m.*
orometric [ɔrə'metrik], *a.* orométrique.
orometry [ɔ'rɔmitri], *s.* orométrie *f.*
Orontes (the) [θiɔ'rɔnti:z]. *Pr.n. Geog:* l'Oronte *m.*
oropendola [ɔ:rou'pendələ], *s. Orn:* cassique *m.*
Oropesa [ɔ:rou'pi:zə], *Pr.n. Navy:* **O. float,** (sorte *f* de) flotteur *m* de drague de mines.
Orosius [ɔ'rousjəs], *Pr.n.m. Ecc.Hist:* Orose.
orotund ['ɔrətʌnd], *a.* **1.** (style, discours) sonore, mâle. **2.** (style) emphatique, ampoulé.
orphan¹ ['ɔ:fən]. **1.** *s.* orphelin, -ine; **to be left an o.,** rester, devenir, orphelin; *Adm:* **orphans in care** = pupilles *mf* de l'État; **war o.,** pupille *mf* de la Nation; *U.S:* **orphans' court,** tribunal *m* des tutelles et des successions. **2.** *a.* **an o. child,** un(e) orphelin(e).
orphan², *v.tr.* (*usu. in pass.*) rendre (qn) orphelin, -ine; **he was orphaned at an early age, and brought up by his uncle,** orphelin en bas âge, il fut élevé par son oncle; **orphaned of both parents,** orphelin de père et (de) mère.
orphanage ['ɔ:fənidʒ], *s.* **1.** orphelinat *m.* **2.** *A:* orphelinage *m*, état *m* d'orphelin.
orphanhood ['ɔ:fənhud], *s.* orphelinage *m*, état *m* d'orphelin.
Orphean [ɔ:'fi(:)ən], *a.* (lyre, etc.) d'Orphée; (doctrine, etc.) orphique.
Orpheus ['ɔ:fju:s], *Pr.n.m. Myth:* Orphée.
Orphic ['ɔ:fik], *a.* **1.** *Gr.Ant:* (doctrine, mystère, etc.) orphique; **the O. poems,** les Orphiques *m*; **the O. festivities,** les Orphiques *f.* **2.** (*a*) (*of music, etc.*) ravissant, enchanteur, -eresse; (*b*) mystérieux, ésotérique. **3.** *Art:* **O. cubism,** orphisme *m.*
Orphism ['ɔ:fizm], *s. Gr.Ant: Art:* orphisme *m.*
orphrey ['ɔ:fri], *s. Ecc.Cost:* orfroi *m*, parement *m* (de chasuble).
orpiment ['ɔ:pimənt], *s. Miner:* orpiment *m*, orpin *m*; sulfure *m* jaune d'arsenic.
orpin(e) ['ɔ:pin], *s. Bot:* grand orpin, orpin reprise; *F:* herbe *f* à la coupure, aux charpentiers.
orra ['ɔrə], *a. Scot:* dépareillé; **an o. job,** un emploi occasionnel, supplémentaire.
orrery ['ɔrəri], *s. Astr:* planétaire *m.*
orris¹ ['ɔris], *s.* passementerie *f*; galon *m* d'or.
orris², *s. Bot:* iris *m* (de Florence); *Pharm:* **o. root,** racine *f* d'iris; **o. powder,** poudre *f* d'iris.
orseille [ɔ:'seil], *s. Bot: Dy:* orseille *f.*
orsellic [ɔ:'selik], **orsellinic** [ɔ:'selinik], *a. Ch:* orsellique.
orthicon ['ɔ:θikən], *s. T.V:* orthicon(oscope) *m.*

orthite ['ɔːθait], *s. Miner:* orthite *f.*
ortho- ['ɔːθə, ɔːθou, ɔː'θɔ], *pref.* ortho-.
orthobasic [ɔːθou'beisik], *a. Ch:* orthobasique.
orthocarbonic [ɔːθoukɑː'bɔnik], *a. Ch:* (acide, ester) orthocarbonique.
orthocentre [ɔːθə'sentər], *s. Mth:* orthocentre *m.*
orthocentric [ɔːθə'sentrik], *a. Mth:* orthocentrique.
orthoceras [ɔː'θɔsərəs], *s. Paleont:* orthoceras *m*, orthocère *m.*
orthochlorite [ɔːθou'klɔːrait], *s. Miner:* orthochlorite *f.*
orthochromatic [ɔːθoukrə'mætik], *a. Phot:* orthochromatique.
orthochromatism [ɔːθou'kroumətizm], *s. Phot:* orthochromatisme *m.*
orthochromatization [ɔːθoukroumətai'zeiʃ(ə)n], *s. Phot:* orthochromatisation *f.*
orthochromatize [ɔːθou'kroumətaiz], *v.tr. Phot:* orthochromatiser.
orthoclase ['ɔːθəkleis], *s. Miner:* orthoclase *f*, orthose *m.*
orthodiagonal [ɔːθoudai'ægən(ə)l], *s. Cryst:* orthodiagonale *f.*
orthodiagram [ɔːθou'daiəgræm], *s. Med:* orthodiagramme *m.*
orthodiagraphic [ɔːθoudaiə'græfik], *a. Med:* orthodiagraphique.
orthodiagraphy [ɔːθoudai'ægrəfi], *s. Med:* orthodiagraphie *f.*
orthodont ['ɔːθədɔnt], *a. Anthr:* orthodonte.
orthodontia [ɔːθə'dɔntiə], *s. Dent:* orthodontie *f.*
orthodontic [ɔːθə'dɔntik], *a. Dent:* orthodontique.
orthodontics [ɔːθə'dɔntiks], *s.pl.* (*usu. with sg. const.*) *Dent:* orthodontie *f*; orthopédie dento-faciale; **corrective o.,** orthodontie corrective, réductrice; **interceptive o.,** orthodontie modificatrice; **preventive o.,** orthodontie préventive.
orthodontist [ɔːθə'dɔntist], *s. Dent:* orthodontiste *mf.*
orthodox ['ɔːθədɔks], *a.* **1.** *Ecc:* (théologien, dogme, etc.) orthodoxe; **the O. Church,** l'Église *f* orthodoxe; **O. Judaism,** judaïsme rabbinique; *s.* **the o.,** les orthodoxes *mpl.* **2.** (historien, etc.) orthodoxe, traditionaliste; (politicien, etc.) bien pensant; (méthode, opinion, etc.) orthodoxe; classique.
orthodoxly ['ɔːθədɔksli], *adv.* orthodoxement.
orthodoxy ['ɔːθədɔksi], *s.* **1.** orthodoxie; conformisme *m* (d'une doctrine, des opinions de qn, etc.). **2.** *Jew.Rel:* judaïsme *m* rabbinique.
orthodromic [ɔːθə'drɔmik], *a. Nav:* (navigation, etc.) orthodromique.
orthodromics [ɔːθə'drɔmiks], *s.pl.* (*usu. with sg. const.*) *Nau:* orthodromie *f.*
orthodromy [ɔː'θɔdrəmi], *s. Nau:* orthodromie *f.*
orthoepic(al) [ɔːθou'epik(l)], *a.* orthoépique.
orthoepically [ɔːθou'epikəli], *adv.* selon l'orthoépie.
orthoepist [ɔːθou'epist], *s.* orthoépiste *mf.*
orthoepy ['ɔːθouepi], *s.* orthoépie *f*; orthophonie *f.*
orthoformic [ɔːθə'fɔːmik], *a. Ch:* (acide) orthoformique; **o. ester,** orthoformiate *m* d'éthyle.
orthogenesis [ɔːθə'dʒenisis], *s. Biol:* orthogénèse *f.*
orthogenetic ['ɔːθoudʒi'netik], **orthogenic** [ɔːθə'dʒenik], *a. Biol:* (forme, etc.) orthogénétique.
orthogeotropism ['ɔːθoudʒiːou'trɔpizm], *s. Bot:* orthogéotropisme *m.*
orthognathism, orthognathy [ɔː'θɔgnəθizm, -θi], *s. Anthr:* orthognathisme *m*, orthognathie *f.*
orthognathous [ɔː'θɔgnəθəs], *a. Anthr:* orthognathe.
orthogneiss ['ɔːθənais], *s. Geol:* gneiss *m* ortho.
orthogonal [ɔː'θɔgənl], *a. Mth:* orthogonal, -aux; orthographique; **o. projection,** projection orthogonale, orthographique; orthographie *f*; **o. set,** système *m* de coordonnées orthogonales; **o. system,** réseau orthogonal.
orthogonally [ɔː'θɔgənəli], *adv. Mth:* orthogonalement; à angle droit.
orthograde ['ɔːθəgreid], *a. Z:* (animal) qui marche debout.
orthograph ['ɔːθəgræf], *s. Arch:* orthographie *f.*
orthographer, orthographist [ɔː'θɔgrəfər, -fist], *s.* orthographiste *mf.*
orthographic(al) [ɔːθə'græfik(l)], *a.* **1.** *Gram:* orthographique. **2.** *Mth:* = ORTHOGONAL.
orthographically [ɔːθə'græfik(ə)li], *adv.* orthographiquement.
orthography [ɔ'θɔgrəfi], *s.* **1.** *Gram:* orthographe *f.* **2.** *Mth: Arch:* projection orthogonale, perpendiculaire; coupe *f* perpendiculaire; orthographie *f.*
orthohydrogen [ɔːθou'haidrədʒən], *s. Ch:* orthohydrogène *m.*
orthometric [ɔːθou'metrik], *a.* orthométrique; (cristal) orthoédrique.
orthometry [ɔː'θɔmitri], *s. Pros: Med:* orthométrie *f.*
orthomorphic [ɔːθou'mɔːfik], *a. Mth:* (projection, etc.) orthomorphique, conforme.
orthomorphism [ɔːθou'mɔːfizm], *s. Mth: etc:* orthomorphisme *m*, conformité *f.*
orthonormal [ɔːθou'nɔːm(ə)l], *a. Mth:* **o. base,** base orthonormée.
orthop(a)edic [ɔːθə'piːdik], *a. Med:* **1.** (traitement, appareil) orthopédique; **o. surgeon,** chirurgien *m* orthopédiste. **2.** (enfant) difforme.
orthop(a)edically [ɔːθə'piːdikəli], *adv.* (traité) par l'orthopédie.
orthop(a)edics [ɔːθə'piːdiks], *s.pl.* (*usu. with sg. const.*) *Med:* orthopédie *f.*
orthop(a)edist [ɔːθə'piːdist], *s. Med:* orthopédiste *mf.*
orthop(a)edy [ɔːθə'piːdi], *s.* orthopédie *f.*
orthophonic [ɔːθə'fɔnik], *a. Med:* orthophonique.
orthophony [ɔː'θɔfəni], *s. Med:* orthophonie *f.*
orthophoria [ɔːθə'fɔːriə], *s. Opt:* orthophorie *f.*
orthophosphate [ɔːθou'fɔsfeit], *s. Ch:* orthophosphate *m.*
orthophosphoric [ɔːθoufɔs'fɔrik], *a. Ch:* orthophosphorique.
orthophyre ['ɔːθoufaiər], *s. Geol:* orthophyre *m.*
orthophyric [ɔːθou'firik], *a. Geol:* orthophyrique.
orthopinacoid [ɔːθou'pinəkɔid], *s. Cryst:* orthopinacoïde *m.*
orthopn(o)ea [ɔː'θɔpni(ː)ə], *s. Med:* orthopnée *f.*
orthopn(o)eic [ɔː'θɔpniik], *a. Med:* orthopnoïque.
orthoposit(r)onium ['ɔːθoupɔzi't(r)ounjəm], *s. Atom.Ph:* orthoposit(r)onium *m.*
orthopter [ɔː'θɔptər], *s. Ent: A.Av:* orthoptère *m.*
orthopteral [ɔ'θɔptərəl], *a. Ent:* orthoptère.
orthopteran [ɔː'θɔptərən], *a. & s. Ent:* orthoptère (*m*).
orthopteroid [ɔː'θɔtərɔid], *a. & s. Ent:* orthoptéroïde (*m*).
Orthopteroidea [ɔːθɔptə'rɔidiə], *s.pl. Ent:* orthoptéroïdes *m.*
orthopterological [ɔː'θɔptərə'lɔdʒik(ə)l], *a. Ent:* orthoptérologique.
orthopterologist [ɔːθɔptə'rɔlədʒist], *s. Ent:* orthoptérologiste *mf.*
orthopterology [ɔːθɔptə'rɔlədʒi], *s. Ent:* orthoptérologie *f.*
orthopteron, *pl.* **-a** [ɔː'θɔptərən, -ə], *s. Ent:* orthoptère *m*; **the Orthoptera,** les orthoptères.
orthopterous [ɔː'θɔptərəs], *a. Ent:* orthoptère.
orthoptia [ɔː'θɔpsiə], *s. Med:* orthoptie *f.*
orthoptic [ɔː'θɔptik], *a. Med: Mth:* orthoptique.
orthoptics [ɔː'θɔptiks], *s.* (*usu with sg. const.*) *Med:* orthoptie *f.*
orthoptist [ɔː'θɔptist], *s. Med:* orthoptiste *mf.*
orthoradioscopy [ɔːθoureidi'ɔskəpi], *s. Med:* orthoradioscopie *f.*
Orthor(r)hapha [ɔːθou'ræfə], *s.pl. Orn:* orthor(h)aphes *m.*
orthorhombic [ɔːθou'rɔmbik], *a. Cryst:* (prisme, etc.) orthorhombique; **o. system,** système *m* (ortho)rhombique, terbinaire.
orthoscope ['ɔːθəskoup], *s. Med: Opt:* orthoscope *m.*
orthoscopic [ɔːθə'skɔpik], *a. Phot:* (objectif) orthoscopique.
orthose ['ɔːθouz], *s. Miner:* orthose *f*, orthoclase *f.*
orthoselection ['ɔːθousi'lekʃ(ə)n], *s. Biol:* orthosélection *f.*
orthosilicate [ɔːθou'silikeit], *s. Ch:* orthosilicate *m.*
orthosilicic [ɔːθousi'lisik], *a. Ch:* orthosilicique.
orthostat ['ɔːθəstæt], *s. Arch:* orthostate *m.*
orthostatic [ɔːθou'stætik], *a. Med:* orthostatique.
orthostatism [ɔːθou'stætizm], *s. Anat:* orthostatisme *m.*
orthostereoscope [ɔːθou'stiːriəskoup], *s. Opt:* orthostéréoscope *m.*
orthostereoscopic [ɔːθoustiːriə'skɔpik], *a. Opt:* orthostéréoscopique.
orthostichy [ɔː'θɔstiki], *s. Bot:* orthostique *f.*
orthotonus [ɔː'θɔtənəs], *s. Med:* orthotonos *m.*
orthotropic [ɔːθou'trɔpik], *a.* (*of timber, etc.*) orthotrope.
orthotropism [ɔːθou'trɔpizm], *s. Bot:* orthotropisme *m.*
orthotropous [ɔː'θɔtrəpəs], *a. Bot:* (ovule) orthotrope.
orthoxylene [ɔː'θɔksiliːn], *s. Ch:* orthoxylène *m.*
ortive ['ɔːtiv], *a. Astr:* (amplitude) ortive *f.*
ortol ['ɔːtɔl], *s. Phot:* ort(h)ol *m.*
ortolan ['ɔːtələn], *s. Orn:* **1. o. bunting,** ortolan *m*; jardinière *f.* **2.** *NAm:* dolichonyx *m*, bobolink *m*; *Fr.C:* goglu *m.*
orts [ɔːts], *s.pl. A:* restes *m*, bribes *m*, reliefs *m* (de viande, etc.); *Fig:* **to make o. of sth.,** faire peu de cas de qch.
ortstein ['ɔːtstain], *s. Geol:* ortstein *m.*
orval ['ɔːv(ə)l], *s. Bot: A:* orvale *f*, sauge *f* sclarée.
orycteropus [ɔrik'terəpəs], *s. Z:* oryctérope *m.*
oryssid [ɔ'risid], *s. Ent:* orysse *m.*
Oryssidae [ɔ'risidiː], *s.pl. Ent:* oryssidés *m.*
oryx ['ɔriks], *s. Z:* oryx *m*; antilope *f* à sabre; **scimitar-horned o.,** oryx algazelle.
oryzomys [ɔː'rizəmis], *s. Z:* oryzomys *m.*
oryzopsis [ɔːri'zɔpsis], *s. Bot:* oryzopsis *m.*
os, *pl.* **osar** [ous, 'ousər], *s. Geol:* os *m*, ôs *m*; esker *m.*
Osage [ɔ'seidʒ]. **1.** *Ethn:* (*a*) *a.* osage; (*b*) *s.* Osage *mf*; Indien, -ienne, osage. **2.** *s. Ling:* osage *m.* **3.** *a. Bot:* **O. orange,** toxylon *m*; orange *f* des Osages.
osazone ['ousəzoun], *s. Ch:* osazone *f.*
Oscan ['ɔskən]. **1.** *A.Geog:* (*a*) *a.* osque; (*b*) *s.* Osque *mf.* **2.** *s. Ling:* osque *m.*
Oscar ['ɔskər]. **1.** *Pr.n.m.* Oscar; *Tp:* **(O for) O.,** O comme Oscar. **2.** *s. Cin: etc:* Oscar *m.*
oscillate ['ɔsileit]. **1.** *v.i.* (*a*) osciller; (*of indicator needle*) **to o. violently,** s'affoler; *Fig:* **to o. between two opinions,** osciller, balancer, hésiter, entre deux opinions; (*b*) *Ph: W.Tel:* (i) osciller; **to make a valve o.,** faire osciller une lampe; (ii) (*of radio listener*) laisser osciller le poste. **2.** *v.tr.* balancer, faire osciller.
oscillating[1] ['ɔsileitiŋ], *a.* oscillant, oscillatoire; oscillateur, -trice; (*a*) **o. motion,** mouvement oscillant, oscillatoire, d'oscillation, de va-et-vient; *Atom.Ph:* **o. electron,** électron oscillateur; (*b*) *El: Elcs:* **o. coil,** bobine oscillante, oscillatrice; bobinage oscillateur; **o. current,** courant oscillant, oscillatoire, d'oscillation; **o. field,** champ *m* oscillatoire; *W.Tel:* **o. tube, valve,** lampe oscillatrice; oscillateur *m* (à lampe); **(self-)o. transmitter,** oscillateur auto-entretenu, à auto-oscillation; (*c*) *Mch: O:* **o. cylinder,** cylindre oscillant; **o. engine,** machine oscillante, à cylindre oscillant; (*d*) *Navy:* **o. mine,** mine *f* ludion.
oscillating[2], *s.* oscillation *f*; *W.Tel:* **o. voltage,** tension *f* d'oscillation; **o. point,** limite *f* d'accrochage.
oscillation [ɔsi'leiʃ(ə)n], *s.* oscillation *f*; (*a*) **o. of a pendulum, pendular o.,** oscillation d'un pendule, pendulaire; **double o.,** oscillation complète (d'un pendule); **violent o.,** oscillation brutale, affolement *m* (de l'aiguille aimantée d'une boussole, etc.); **o. frequency,** fréquence *f* d'oscillations; *Atom.Ph:* **betatron, synchrotron o.,** oscillation bêtatron, synchrotron; (*b*) *Elcs: W.Tel:* **damped o.,** oscillation amortie; **continuous, (self-)sustained, undamped, o.,** oscillation entretenue; **o. generator,** oscillateur *m*; (*c*) *Geog:* **o. of the tide,** mouvement *m* de la marée.
oscillator ['ɔsileitər], *s.* **1.** *Elcs: W.Tel:* (i) oscillateur *m*; (bobine) oscillatrice (*f*); (ii) lampe oscillatrice; **autodyne, feedback, o.,** oscillateur à réaction; **booster o.,** oscillateur d'appoint; **crystal o.,** oscillateur à quartz; **linear o.,** oscillateur linéaire; **local o.,** oscillateur local; **beat frequency o.,** oscillateur à battements; **self-excited o.,** oscillateur à auto-excitation; **valve o., vacuum tube o.,** oscillateur à lampe, à tube électronique; **master o.,** oscillateur pilote; **o. coil,** bobine oscillatrice; **o. valve, tube,** lampe oscillatrice; tube à vide oscillateur, tube électronique. **2.** *Cin:* **mirror o.,** miroir oscillant (pour enregistrement de la piste sonore).
oscillatoria [ɔsilə'tɔːriə], *s. Algae:* oscillaire *f*; oscillaria *m.*
oscillatory ['ɔsileit(ə)ri], *a. Elcs: W.Tel:* (circuit) oscillant, oscillatoire; **o. discharge,** décharge oscillante.
oscillatron [ɔ'silətrɔn], *s. Atom.Ph:* tube *m* cathodique.
oscillogram [ɔ'siləgræm], *s. Ph: El: Elcs:* oscillogramme *m.*
oscillograph [ɔ'siləgræf], *s. Ph: El: Elcs:* oscillographe *m*; **cathode-ray o.,** oscillographe cathodique.
oscillographic [ɔsilə'græfik], *a. Ph: El: Elcs:* oscillographique; *Cin:* **o. recording apparatus,** appareil *m* d'enregistrement oscillographique; équipage *m* oscillographique.
oscillography [ɔsi'lɔgrəfi], *s. Ph: El: Elcs:* oscillographie *f.*
oscillometer [ɔsi'lɔmitər], *s. Med: Nau: etc:* oscillomètre *m.*
oscillometric [ɔsilə'metrik], *a. Med: Nau: etc:* oscillométrique.
oscillometry [ɔsi'lɔmitri], *s. Med: Nau: etc:* oscillométrie *f.*
oscilloscope [ɔ'siləskoup], *s. El:* oscilloscope *m*; **cathode-ray o.,** oscilloscope à rayons cathodiques; **projection o.,** oscilloscope à projection.
oscilloscopic [ɔsilə'skɔpik], *a. El:* oscilloscopique.
oscine ['ɔsiːn], **oscinine** ['ɔsinain], *Orn:* **1.** *a.* oscine. **2.** *s.pl.* **Oscines,** oscines *m.*
oscitancy ['ɔsitənsi], **oscitation** [ɔsi'teiʃ(ə)n], *s. Med:* oscitation *f*; bâillement *m.*
osculant ['ɔskjulənt], *a. Nat.Hist:* (espèces, genres) qui se touchent, qui ont des caractères communs.
oscular ['ɔskjulər], *a.* **1.** (*a*) *Anat:* (muscle, etc.) os-

culaire; (*b*) *Hum:* **o. demonstrations,** épanchements *m* en embrassades. **2.** *Mth:* osculateur, -trice.

osculate [ˈɔskjuleit], *v.i.* **1.** *Mth:* **curve that osculates with a line,** courbe osculatrice à, qui a un contact d'ordre supérieur avec, une ligne (**at a point,** en un point). **2.** *Nat.Hist:* (*of genera, species*) avoir des traits en commun; avoir des traits communs (**with,** avec). **3.** *Hum:* (*of pers.*) s'embrasser.

osculating [ˈɔskjuleitiŋ], *a.* (*of curve, circle, etc.*) osculateur, -trice.

osculation [ɔskjuˈleiʃ(ə)n], *s.* **1.** *Mth:* osculation *f*; **point of o.,** point *m* d'attouchement. **2.** *Hum:* *A:* embrassement *m*; baisers *mpl.*

osculatory[1] [ˈɔskjulət(ə)ri], *a.* **1.** *Mth:* osculateur, -trice. **2.** *Hum:* *A:* **o. demonstrations,** épanchements *m* en embrassades.

osculatory[2], *s. Ecc:* paix *f.*

osculum, *pl.* **-a** [ˈɔskjuləm, -ə], *s. Z:* oscule *m* (d'éponge, etc.).

ose [ouz], *s. Ch:* (*esp. in comb.fm.*) ose *m.*

oside [ˈousaid], *s. Ch:* (*esp. in comb.fm.*) oside *m.*

osier [ˈouziər, ˈouʒər], *s.* (*a*) *Bot:* osier *m*; **common, velvet, o.,** osier blanc, vert; saule *m* des vanniers; **golden o.,** osier jaune; **red, purple, o.,** osier rouge, pourpre; **o. bed, holt, land,** oseraie *f*; **o. cultivation,** osiériculture *f*; **o. grower,** osiériculteur, -trice; osiériste *mf*; **o.-producing,** (région, etc.) osiéricole; (*b*) (brin *m* d')osier; **o. basket,** panier *m* d'osier; **o. seller,** osiériste; **o. stripper,** pèle-osier *m inv*; **o. tie,** pleyon *m.*

osiery [ˈouʒəri], *s.* **1.** oseraie *f.* **2.** vannerie *f.*

os innominatum [ˈɔsinɔmiˈneitəm], *s. Anat:* os innominé; os iliaque.

Osirian [ɔˈsairiən], *a. Ant:* osirien.

osiride [ɔˈsairid], *a. Arch:* **o. pillar,** pilier *m* osiriaque.

Osiris [ɔˈsairis], *Pr.n.m. Myth:* Osiris.

Osler [ˈouzlər], *Pr.n.m. Med:* **Osler's disease,** maladie *f* d'Osler, endocardite maligne lente.

Osman [ˈɔzmən], **Osmanli** [ɔzˈmænli]. *Hist:* **1.** *a.* osmanli. **2.** *s.* Osmanli, -ie; Turc, Turque, d'Europe.

osmate [ˈɔzmeit], **osmiate** [ˈɔzmieit], *s. Ch:* osmiate *m.*

osmatic[1] [ɔzˈmætik], *a. Ch:* = OSMIC.

osmatic[2], *a. Nat.Hist:* qui s'oriente par l'odorat.

osmia [ˈɔzmiə], *s. Ent:* osmie *f.*

osmic [ˈɔzmik], *a. Ch:* osmique; **o. acid,** tétraoxyde *m* d'osmium.

osmidrosis [ɔzmiˈdrousis], *s. Med:* osmi(hi)drose *f.*

osmious [ˈɔzmiəs], *a. Ch:* osmieux.

osmiridium [ɔzmiˈridiəm], **osmi-iridium** [ɔzmiiˈridiəm], *s. Miner:* osmiridium *m.*

osmium [ˈɔzmiəm], *s. Ch:* osmium *m*; **o. alloy,** osmiure *m*; **iridium o. alloy,** osmiure d'iridium; **o. lamp,** lampe *f* à osmium; **o.-bearing,** osmiuré.

osmograph [ˈɔzmougræf], *s. Ph:* osmomètre *m.*

osmol [ˈɔzmoul], *s. Bio-Ch:* osmole *f.*

osmolarity [ɔzmouˈlæriti], *s. Bio-Ch:* osmolarité *f.*

osmometer [ɔzˈmɔmitər], *s. Ph:* osmomètre *m.*

osmometric [ɔzmouˈmetrik], *a. Ph:* osmométrique.

osmometry [ɔzˈmɔmitri], *s. Ph:* osmométrie *f.*

osmondite [ˈɔzməndait], *s. Miner:* osmondite *f.*

osmophore [ɔzmouˈfɔər], *s. Ch:* osmophore *m.*

osmophoric [ɔzməˈfɔrik], *a. Ch:* osmophorique.

osmoregulation [ɔzmouregjuˈleiʃ(ə)n], *s. Biol:* régulation *f* de la pression osmotique.

osmosis [ɔzˈmousis], **osmose** [ˈɔzmous], *s. Ch: Physiol:* osmose *f.*

osmotaxis [ɔzmouˈtæksis], *s. Biol:* osmotactisme *m.*

osmotic [ɔzˈmɔtik], *a. Ch: Physiol:* (pression) osmotique.

osmund [ˈɔzmənd], *s. Bot:* osmonde *f*; **o. royal,** osmonde royale; fougère fleurie.

osmunda [ɔzˈmʌndə], *s. Bot:* osmondée *f.*

Osmundaceae [ɔzmʌnˈdeisii:], *s.pl. Bot:* osmondacées *f.*

osmundaceous [ɔzmʌnˈdeiʃəs], *a. Bot:* osmondacé.

osone [ˈousoun], *s. Ch:* osone *f.*

osphresiology [ɔsfri:ziˈɔlədʒi], *s. Physiol:* osphrésiologie *f.*

osphresiophilia [ɔsfri:zioˈfiliə], *s. Psy:* osphrésiophilie *f.*

Osphromenidae [ɔsfrouˈmenidi:], *s.pl. Ich:* osphroménidés *m.*

osphromenus [ɔsfrouˈmi:nəs], *s. Ich:* osphroménus *m.*

osprey [ˈɔspri, -prei], *s.* **1.** *Orn:* balbuzard pêcheur, fluviatile; *Fr.C:* aigle pêcheur. **2.** *A.Cost:* aigrette *f.*

Ossa [ˈɔsə], *Pr.n. A.Geog:* Ossa *m*; *Lit:* **to pile Pelion on O.,** entasser Pélion sur Ossa.

ossature [ˈɔsətjər], *s.* ossature *f* (d'un comble, d'une voûte, etc.); **the o. of the earth,** l'ossature terrestre.

ossein [ˈɔsiin], *s. Ch:* osséine *f*, ostéine *f.*

osselet [ˈɔs(ə)lit], *s. Vet:* osselet *m* (du boulet, etc.).

osseous [ˈɔsiəs], *a.* **1.** (système, tissu, etc.) osseux. **2.** *Geol:* (terrain) osseux, à ossements (fossiles). **3.** *Ich:* (poisson) osseux, téléostéen.

Osset [ˈɔsit], *s. Ethn:* Ossète *m*, Osse *m.*

Ossete [ˈɔsi:t], *s.* **1.** *Ethn:* Ossète *m*, Osse *m.* **2.** *Ling:* osse *m*, ossète *m.*

Ossetian [ɔˈsi:ʃ(j)ən]. **1.** *a. Ethn:* ossète. **2.** *s.* (*a*) *Ethn:* Ossète *m*, Osse *m*; (*b*) *Ling:* osse *m*, ossète *m.*

Ossetic [ɔˈsetik]. **1.** *a. Ethn:* ossète. **2.** *s. Ling:* ossète *m.*

Ossianesque [ɔsiəˈnesk], *a. Lit:* (style, etc.) ossianesque; qui rappelle les poésies d'Ossian.

Ossianic [ɔsiˈænik], *a. Lit:* ossianique.

Ossianism [ˈɔsiənizm], *s. Lit:* ossianisme *m.*

Ossianist [ˈɔsiənist], *s. Lit:* ossianiste *mf.*

ossicle [ˈɔsikl], *s. Anat:* ossicule *m*; **the ossicles of the ear,** les osselets *m* de l'oreille.

ossicular [ɔˈsikjulər], *a.* ossiculaire.

ossicusp [ˈɔsikʌsp], *s. Z:* épiphyse osseuse du frontal, *F:* corne *f* (de la girafe, de l'okapi).

Ossie [ˈɔzi]. *P:* **1.** *a.* australien. **2.** *s.* Australien, -ienne.

ossiferous [ɔˈsifərəs], *a.* ossifère.

ossific [ɔˈsifik], *a.* ossifique.

ossification [ɔsifiˈkeiʃ(ə)n], *s.* **1.** ossification *f* (d'un cartilage, etc.). **2.** *Fig:* sclérose *f* (du gouvernement, etc.).

ossified [ˈɔsifaid], *a.* **1.** (cartilage, etc.) ossifié. **2.** *Fig:* (esprit, gouvernement, etc.) sclérosé. **3.** *P:* ivre; raide.

ossifluent [ˈɔsifluənt], *a. Med:* (abcès) ossifluent.

ossifrage [ˈɔsifridʒ], *s. Orn:* **1.** = OSPREY. **2.** gypaète barbu, vautour barbu.

ossify [ˈɔsifai]. **1.** *v.i.* (*a*) (*of cartilage, etc.*) s'ossifier; (*b*) *Fig:* (*of pers.*) se cantonner dans des idées arriérées; se fossiliser; (*of government, etc.*) se scléroser. **2.** *v.tr.* (*a*) ossifier (un cartilage, etc.); (*b*) *Fig:* amener, entraîner, la sclérose dans (le gouvernement, etc.).

ossuary [ˈɔsjuəri], *s.* ossuaire *m.*

ostariophysan [ɔstæriouˈfaisən], *s. Ich:* ostariophysaire *m.*

Ostariophyseae, Ostariophysi [ɔstæriouˈfaisii:, -faisail], *s.pl.* ostariophysaires *m.*

osteal [ˈɔstiəl], *a.* ostéal, ostéique.

ostealgia [ɔstiˈældʒiə], *s. Med:* ostéalgie *f.*

ostearthritis [ɔstiɑ:ˈθraitis], *s. Med:* ostéo-arthrite *f.*

Osteichthyes [ɔstiˈikθii:z], *s.pl. Ich:* ostéichthyens *m.*

ostein [ˈɔstiin], *s. Ch:* ostéine *f*, osséine *f.*

osteitis [ɔstiˈaitis], *s. Med:* ostéite *f*; **o. deformans,** ostéite déformante; maladie *f* de Paget.

Ostend [ɔsˈtend], *Pr.n. Geog:* Ostende.

ostensible [ɔsˈtensibl], *a.* prétendu; qui sert de prétexte; soi-disant; feint; **the o. object of the project,** le but avoué du projet; **he went out with the o. object of posting a letter,** il est sorti sous prétexte de mettre une lettre à la poste; **my o. purpose was to get provisions,** j'étais censé être à la recherche de provisions.

ostensibly [ɔsˈtensibli], *adv.* en apparence; censément; **he is living in Nice o. for his health,** il est en séjour à Nice, soi-disant pour sa santé; **he went out o. to buy some tobacco,** il sortit sous prétexte d'acheter du tabac, censément pour, soi-disant pour, acheter du tabac.

ostension [ɔsˈtenʃ(ə)n], *s. Ecc:* ostension *f* (du saint Sacrement).

ostensive [ɔsˈtensiv], *a.* ostensible, manifeste.

ostensory [ɔsˈtensəri], *s. Ecc:* ostensoir *m.*

ostentation [ɔstenˈteiʃ(ə)n], *s.* ostentation *f*, faste *m*, apparat *m*; parade *f*; gros luxe.

ostentatious [ɔstenˈteiʃəs], *a.* fastueux; plein d'ostentation; *Lit:* ostentatoire; (luxe) affichant; **an o. person,** un paradeur, une paradeuse; **to show o. generosity,** afficher la générosité; faire montre de générosité; **less o. in appearance,** plus modeste d'apparence.

ostentatiously [ɔstenˈteiʃəsli], *adv.* avec ostentation; avec faste; *Lit:* ostentatoirement; **to display sth. o.,** faire ostentation de qch.; **o. acquitted,** acquitté avec éclat.

ostentatiousness [ɔstenˈteiʃəsnis], *s.* ostentation *f.*

osteo-arthritis [ˈɔstiouɑ:ˈθraitis], *s. Med:* ostéo-arthrite *f.*

osteoarthropathy [ˈɔstiouɑ:ˈθrɔpəθi], *s. Med:* ostéo-arthropathie *f.*

osteoblast [ˈɔstioublæst], *s. Biol:* ostéoblaste *m.*

osteochondritis [ɔstioukɔnˈdraitis], *s. Med:* ostéochondrite *f.*

osteochondroma [ɔstioukɔnˈdroumə], *s. Med:* ostéochondrome *m.*

osteochondromatosis [ˈɔstioukɔndrouməˈtousis], *s. Med:* ostéochondromatose *f.*

osteoclasis [ɔstiouˈkleisis], *s. Surg:* *A:* ostéoclasie *f.*

osteoclast [ˈɔstiouklæst], *s. Biol: Surg:* ostéoclaste *m.*

osteocolla [ɔstiouˈkɔlə], *s. Miner:* ostéocolle *f*; calcaire tufacé.

osteocranium [ɔstiouˈkreiniəm], *s. Z:* crâne osseux.

osteocyte [ˈɔstiousait], *s. Biol:* cellule osseuse.

osteodentine [ˈɔstiouˈdenti:n], *s. Anat:* ostéodentine *f.*

osteoderm [ˈɔstioudə:m], *s. Med:* production *f* ostéodermique.

osteodermal, osteodermic, osteoderm(at)ous [ɔstiouˈdə:m(ə)l, -mik, -m(ət)əs], *a. Med:* ostéodermique.

osteogenesis [ˈɔstiouˈdʒenisis], **osteogeny** [ɔstiˈɔdʒini], *s. Biol:* ostéogénèse *f*, ostéogénie *f.*

osteogenetic [ɔstioudʒiˈnetik], **osteogenic** [ɔstiouˈdʒenik], *a. Biol:* ostéogénique.

osteogenous [ɔstiˈɔdʒinəs], *a. Biol:* ostéogène.

osteoglossid [ɔstiouˈglɔsid], *a. & s. Ich:* (poisson) ostéoglosside (*m*).

Osteoglossidae [ɔstiouˈglɔsidi:], *s.pl. Ich:* ostéoglossidés *m.*

osteographic [ɔstiouˈgræfik], *a. Anat:* ostéographique.

osteography [ɔstiˈɔgrəfi], *s.* ostéographie *f.*

osteoid [ˈɔstiɔid], *a.* **1.** *Med:* (tumeur, etc.) ostéoïde. **2.** *Physiol:* (poisson, etc.) osseux.

osteolepid [ɔstiouˈlepid], *a. & s. Paleont:* ostéolépide (*m*).

Osteolepidae [ɔstiouˈlepidi:], *s.pl. Paleont:* ostéolépidés *m.*

osteolite [ˈɔstioulait], *s. Miner:* ostéolite *f.*

osteologic(al) [ɔstiouˈlɔdʒik(l)], *a.* ostéologique.

osteologist [ɔstiˈɔlədʒist], *s.* ostéologiste *m.*

osteology [ɔstiˈɔlədʒi], *s.* **1.** (*science*) ostéologie *f.* **2.** structure osseuse (d'un animal, du crâne, etc.).

osteolysis [ɔstiˈɔlisis], *s. Med:* ostéolyse *f.*

osteoma, *pl.* **-as, -omata** [ɔstiˈoumə, -əz, -ˈoumətə], *s. Med:* ostéome *m.*

osteomalacia [ˈɔstiouməˈleisiə], *s. Med:* ostéomalacie *f.*

osteomyelitis [ˈɔstioumaiiˈlaitis], *s. Med:* ostéomyélite *f.*

osteonecrosis [ˈɔstiouneˈkrousis], *s. Med:* ostéonécrose *f.*

osteopath [ˈɔstiəpæθ]; *NAm:* **osteopathist** [ɔstiˈɔpəθist], *s. Med:* praticien manipulateur des os et des articulations; (médecin) ostéopathe *m.*

osteopathic [ɔstiəˈpæθik], *a. Med:* ostéopathique.

osteopathy [ɔstiˈɔpəθi], *s. Med:* **1.** (*malady*) ostéopathie *f.* **2.** traitement *m* des affections de la santé par la manipulation des os et des articulations. **3.** théorie médicale qui préconise ce mode de traitement.

osteoperiosteal [ˈɔstiouperiˈɔstiəl], *a. Med:* ostéopériostique.

osteoperiostitis [ɔstiouperiouˈstaitis], *s. Med:* ostéopériostite *f.*

osteopetrosis [ɔstioupeˈtrousis], *s. Med:* ostéopétrose *f.*

osteophone [ˈɔstioufoun], *s. Med:* ostéophone *m.*

osteophyte [ˈɔstiəfait], *s. Med:* ostéophyte *m*; *F:* bec-de-perroquet *m.*

osteophytic [ɔstiouˈfitik], *a. Med:* ostéophytique.

osteoplastic [ɔstiouˈplæstik], *a. Surg:* ostéoplastique.

osteoplasty [ɔstiouˈplæsti], *s. Surg:* ostéoplastie *f.*

osteoporosis [ɔstioupɔˈrousis], *s. Med:* ostéoporose *f.*

osteosarcoma [ˈɔstiousɑ:ˈkoumə], *s. Med:* ostéosarcome *m.*

osteosclerosis [ˈɔstiouskliˈrousis], *s. Med:* ostéosclérose *f.*

osteosclerotic [ˈɔstiouskliˈrɔtik], *a. Med:* ostéosclérotique.

osteosynthesis [ɔstiouˈsinθisis], *s. Surg:* ostéosynthèse *f.*

osteotome [ˈɔstioutoum], *s. Surg:* ostéotome *m.*

osteotomist [ɔstiˈɔtəmist], *s. Surg:* ostéotomiste *mf.*

osteotomy [ɔstiˈɔtəmi], *s. Surg:* ostéotomie *f.*

Ostia [ˈɔstiə], *Pr.n. Geog:* Ostie.

Ostiak [ˈɔstiæk], *a. & s. Ethn: Ling:* = OSTYAK.

ostiary [ˈɔstiəri], *s. R.C.Ch:* portier *m.*

ostiate [ˈɔstieit], *a. Nat.Hist:* muni d'un ostium, d'ostiums.

ostinato [ɔstiˈnɑ:tou], *a. & s. Mus:* (**basso**) **o.,** basse contrainte.

ostiolate [ˈɔstiouleit], *a. Nat.Hist:* ostéolé.

ostiole [ˈɔstioul], *s. Nat.Hist:* ostiole *m.*

ostium [ˈɔstiəm], *s.* **1.** *Anat:* ostium *m* (du cœur, etc.); orifice *m* (de la trompe de Fallope). **2.** *Spong:* pore inhalant.

ostler [ˈɔslər], *s.m.* valet d'écurie; garçon d'écurie; garçon d'attelage; palefrenier.

ostomy [ˈɔstəmi], *s. Surg:* création *f* d'un anus artificiel.

ostr(ae)acea [ɔstr(i:)eiʃiə], *s.pl. Moll:* ostracés *m.*

ostracean [ɔˈstreiʃ(ə)n], *a. & s. Moll:* ostracé (*m*).

ostraceous [ɔˈstreiʃəs], *a.* ostracé.

ostracion [ɔˈstreisiən], *s. Ich:* ostracion *m*, coffre *m.*

ostracism [ˈɔstrəsizm], *s.* ostracisme *m.*

ostracize [ˈɔstrəsaiz], *v.tr.* **1.** *Gr.Ant:* ostraciser, exiler, bannir. **2.** ostraciser; frapper (qn) d'ostracisme; mettre (qn) au ban de la société.

ostracod [ˈɔstrəkɔd], *s. Crust:* ostracode *m.*

Ostracoda [ɔstrəˈkoudə], *s.pl. Crust:* ostracodes *m.*

ostracoderm [ɔs'trækoudə:m], *a. & s. Paleont:* ostracoderme (*m*).

Ostracodermi [ɔstrəkou'də:mi], *s.pl. Paleont:* ostracodermes *m*.

ostreger ['ɔstridʒər], *s. Ven:* autoursier *m*.

ostreiculture ['ɔstriikʌltjər], *s.* ostréiculture *f*.

ostreiculturist [ɔstrii'kʌltjərist], *s.* ostréiculteur, -trice.

Ostreidae [ɔ'stri:idi:], *s.pl. Moll:* ostréidés *m*.

ostreiform [ɔ'stri:ifɔ:m], *a.* ostréiforme.

ostrich [ɔ'stritʃ], *s.* autruche *f*; **young o.,** autruchon *m*; *Fig:* **o. policy,** politique *f* d'autruche; **to have the digestion of an o.,** avoir un estomac d'autruche; **o. farm,** autrucherie *f*; **o. farming,** élevage *m* des autruches; **o. feather,** plume *f* d'autruche; **o. plume,** (i) plume d'autruche; (ii) (faisceau *m* de) plumes d'autruche.

Ostrogoth ['ɔstrəgɔθ]. *Hist:* **1.** *a.* ostrogot(h). **2.** *s.* Ostrogot(h), -e.

Ostrogothic [ɔstrə'gɔθik], *a. Hist:* ostrogothe.

Ostyak ['ɔstiæk]. **1.** *Ethn:* (*a*) *a.* ostiaque, ostiak; (*b*) *s.* Ostiaque *mf*, Ostiak *m*. **2.** *s. Ling:* l'ostiak *m*.

otacariasis [outəkæri'eisis], *s. Vet:* otacariose *f*.

otalgia [ou'tældʒiə], *s. Med:* otalgie *f*; douleur *f* d'oreille.

otalgic [ou'tældʒik], *a. Med:* otalgique.

otaria [ou'tɑ:riə], *s. Z:* otarie *f*.

Otariidae [outə'raiidi:], *s.pl. Z:* otaridés *m*.

otary ['outəri], *s. Z:* otarie *f*; lion marin.

other ['ʌðər]. **1.** *a.* autre; (*a*) **the o. one,** l'autre; **every o. day, week, night,** un jour, une semaine, une nuit, sur deux; tous les deux jours, semaines, nuits; de deux jours, semaines, nuits, l'un(e); **I saw him the o. day,** je l'ai vu l'autre jour; **the o. side,** (i) l'autre côté (de la rue, etc.); (ii) *Jur:* la partie adverse (dans un procès); (iii) *Com: St.Exch:* la contre-partie (dans un marché); *F:* **if he doesn't like it, he can, must, do the o. thing,** si cela ne lui plaît pas, ne lui va pas, tant pis pour lui; (*b*) **the o. four,** les quatre autres; **the o. two hundred francs,** les deux cents autres francs; **potatoes and (all) o. vegetables,** les pommes de terre et autres légumes; **o. things being equal,** toutes choses égales (d'ailleurs); (*c*) **potatoes and (some) o. vegetables,** les pommes de terre et d'autres légumes; **o. people have seen it,** d'autres l'ont vu; **o. people's property,** le bien d'autrui; **any o. book,** tout autre livre; **I have no o. friends,** je n'ai pas d'autres amis; **no one o. than he knows it,** nul autre que lui, personne d'autre, ne le sait; il n'y a que lui qui le sache; il est seul à le savoir; **somebody o. than me, you, him,** quelqu'un d'autre; **all verbs o. than those in -er,** tous les verbes autres que ceux en -er; *Prov:* **o. days, o. ways,** autres temps, autres mœurs; (*d*) (*different*) **I do not wish him o. than he is,** je ne le souhaite pas autre qu'il n'est; je ne souhaite pas qu'il soit autrement qu'il n'est; **a film is something o. than a play,** un film diffère d'une pièce de théâtre; **he is far o. from the Martin I knew as a boy,** il est bien différent du Martin que j'ai connu quand j'étais petit; **quite o. reasons induced me to give in,** des raisons tout autres m'ont engagé à céder. **2.** *pron.* autre; (*a*) **one after the o.,** l'un après l'autre; (*b*) *pl.* **the others,** les autres, le reste; **all the others are there,** tous les autres sont là; **what about the others?** eh bien, et les autres? (*c*) **some . . . others . . .,** les uns . . . les autres . . .; **have you any others?** (i) en avez-vous encore? (ii) en avez-vous d'autres? **there are three others,** (i) il y en a encore trois; (ii) il y en a trois autres; **I have no o.,** je n'en ai pas d'autre; **since then I have used no o.,** depuis lors je ne me suis servi d'aucun autre; **for this reason, if for no o.,** pour cette raison, à défaut d'une autre; **he and no o. told me so,** lui et nul autre me l'a dit; **no o. than he,** nul autre que lui; **it was no o. than the President,** c'était le Président lui-même, en personne; **one or o. of us will see to it,** l'un de nous y veillera; **I don't want to add one o. to the list of failures,** je ne voudrais pas ajouter encore un nom à la liste des ratés; **this day of all others,** ce jour entre tous; (*d*) *pl.* (*of pers.*) **others,** d'autres; (*in oblique cases also*) autrui *m*; **they prefer you to all others,** ils vous préfèrent à tout autre; **I find my happiness in that of others,** je trouve mon bonheur dans celui d'autrui; **let us do unto others as we would be done by,** faisons pour autrui ce que nous voudrions qu'on fît pour nous; (*e*) **I could not do o. than smile, I could do no o. than smile,** (i) je n'ai pu faire autrement que sourire; (ii) je n'ai pu m'empêcher de sourire; **he cannot be o. than amused,** cela ne laissera pas de le divertir. **3.** *adv.* autrement; **I could not do it o. than hurriedly,** je n'ai pu le faire qu'à la hâte.

otherness [ʌðənis], *s.* différence *f*; *Phil:* altérité *f*.

otherwhere ['ʌðəwɛər], *adv. Lit:* ailleurs.

otherwise ['ʌðəwaiz], *adv. & a.* **1.** autrement (**than,** que); **to see things o. than (as) they are,** voir les choses autrement qu'elles ne sont; **in this way he explained the affinity, o. inexplicable,** de cette manière il a expliqué cette affinité autrement inexplicable; **he could not do o.,** il n'a pas pu faire autrement; **it cannot be o. than harmful,** cela ne peut être que nuisible; **I do not remember him o. that with a beard,** je ne me le rappelle pas autrement que barbu; **should it be o.,** dans le cas contraire; s'il en était autrement; **to think o.,** penser autrement; être d'un autre avis, d'une autre opinion; **I could have wished it o.,** j'aurais préféré qu'il en fût autrement; **if he's not o. engaged,** s'il n'est pas occupé à autre chose; **except where o. stated,** sauf indication contraire; **except where o. expressly provided,** sauf disposition expressément contraire; **improvements profitable and o.,** améliorations profitables et peu profitables; **all people rich or o.,** tout le monde, riches et pauvres; **Poquelin o. Molière,** Poquelin autrement (dit) Molière. **2.** autrement; sans quoi, sans cela; dans le cas contraire; **do what I tell you, o. everything will go wrong,** faites ce que je vous dis, autrement, sans cela, tout ira de travers; **work, o. you shall not eat,** travaille, sans quoi tu ne mangeras pas; **o. we will take legal proceedings against you,** faute de quoi nous vous poursuivrons en justice. **3.** sous d'autres rapports; **wrong dates given by a historian o. worthy of credence,** date fausse donnée par un historien par ailleurs digne de foi; **o. he is quite sane,** à d'autres égards, à part cela, il est complètement sain d'esprit.

otherworld [ʌðə'wə:ld], *s.* **the o.,** l'autre monde *m*, l'au-delà *m*; *attrib.* ['ʌðəwə:ld], **she heard o. voices,** elle entendait des voix qui venaient de l'au-delà, qui n'étaient pas de ce monde.

otherworldliness [ʌðə'wə:ldlinis], *s.* détachement *m* de ce monde.

otherworldly [ʌðə'wə:ldli], *a.* détaché de ce monde.

Otho ['ouθou], *Pr.n.m.* Othon.

otic ['outik], *a. Anat:* (nerf, ganglion) otique; **o. bone,** os pétreux; rocher *m*; **the o. bones,** les osselets *m* de l'oreille.

Otididae [ou'tididi:], *s.pl. Orn:* otididés *m*; outardes *f*.

otiorhynchid [ouʃiou'riŋkid], *a. & s. Ent:* otiorhynque (*m*).

otiose ['outious], *a.* **1.** inutile, superflu, oiseux; **o. epithet,** épithète oiseuse. **2.** *occ.* oisif, fainéant.

otiosely ['outiousli], *adv.* **1.** inutilement, sans profit. **2.** *occ.* oisivement.

otioseness ['outiousnis], *s.* superfluité *f*; inutilité *f* (d'une démarche, etc.).

otitis [ou'taitis], *s. Med:* otite *f*; **o. media,** otite moyenne.

otocyon [outou'saiən], *s. Z:* otocyon *m*; *F:* chien oreillard.

otocyst ['outousist], *s. Z: Moll:* otocyste *m*.

otolite, otolith ['outəlait, -liθ], *s. Anat: Biol:* otolit(h)e *f*.

otolithus [outou'liθəs], *s. Ich:* otolithe *m*.

otologic(al) [outə'lɔdʒik(l)], *a. Med:* otologique.

otologist [ou'tɔlədʒist], *s. Med:* otologiste *mf*.

otology [ou'tɔlədʒi], *s. Med:* otologie *f*.

Otomi ['outəmi], *s. Ethn:* Otomi(te) *m*.

otopiesis [outəpai'i:sis], *s. Med:* otopiésis *f*.

otoplasty ['outouplæsti], *s. Surg:* otoplastie *f*.

otorhinolaryngologist [outourainoulærin'gɔlədʒist], *s. Med:* oto-rhino-laryngologiste *mf*.

otorhinolaryngology [outourainoulærin'gɔlədʒi], *s. Med:* oto-rhino-laryngologie *f*.

otorrhagia [outou'reidʒiə], *s. Med:* otorrhagie *f*.

otorrhoea [outə'rii:ə], *s. Med:* otorrhée *f*.

otosclerosis [outouskliə'rousis], *s. Med:* otosclérose *f*.

otosclerotic [outouskliə'rɔtik], *a. Med:* otosclérotique.

otoscope [outou'skoup], *s. Med:* otoscope *m*.

otoscopic [outou'skɔpik], *a. Med:* otoscopique.

otoscopy [ou'tɔskəpi], *s. Med:* otoscopie *f*.

otospongiosis [outəuspɔndʒi'ousis], *s. Med:* otospongiose *f*.

Otranto [ɔ'træntou], *Pr.n. Geog:* Otrante.

ottava rima [ɔtɑ:və'ri:mə], *s. Pros:* huitain composé de six vers à rimes alternées suivis de deux rimés.

otter ['ɔtər], *s.* **1.** *Z:* loutre *f*; **sea o.,** loutre de mer, marine; *attrib.* **o. hound,** chien *m* pour la chasse aux loutres; *Breed:* otterhound *m*; **o. hunter,** loutreur *m*, loutrier *m*; **o. spear,** lance *f* de loutrier; *Com:* **o. skin,** loutre; **o.-skin cap,** casquette *f* en loutre; *Z:* **o. civet,** cynogale *m*; **o. shrew,** potamogale *m*; *Moll:* **o. shell,** lutraire *m*, *F:* pied *m* de sabot. **2.** *Fish:* **o. (board),** otter *m*; **o. trawl,** chalut *m* de mer à double panneau; otter trawl *m*. **3.** *Navy:* (paravane *m* genre) otter.

otto[1] ['ɔtou], *s.* **o. of roses,** essence *f* de roses.

Otto[2], *Pr.n.m.* **1.** Othon. **2.** *I.C.E:* **O. cycle,** cycle *m* à quatre temps.

Ottoman[1] ['ɔtəmən]. *Hist:* **1.** *a.* ottoman. **2.** *s.* Ottoman, -ane.

ottoman[2], *s.* **1.** *Furn:* divan *m*; ottomane *f*; **box o.,** divan-coffre *m*, *pl.* divans-coffres. **2.** *Tex:* ottoman *m*.

ottrelite ['ɔtrəlait], *s. Miner:* ottrélite *f*.

ouabain [wə'baiin], *s. Ch:* ouabaïne *f*.

oubliette [u:bli'et], *s. Hist:* oubliettes *fpl*.

ouch[1] [autʃ], *int.* (*expr. pain*) aïe!

ouch[2] [outʃ], *s.* (i) boucle, (ii) broche, (ornée de bijoux).

Oudh [aud], *Pr.n. Geog:* l'Oude *f*.

ought[1] [ɔ:t], *v.aux.* (*with present and past meaning; inv. except for A:* **oughtest** *or* **oughtst; o. not** *is frequently abbreviated to* **oughtn't**) (*parts of*) devoir, falloir. **1.** (*obligation*) **one o. never to be unkind,** il ne faut, on ne doit, jamais être malveillant; **this o. to have been done before,** on aurait dû, il aurait fallu, le faire auparavant; **to behave as one o.,** se conduire comme il convient; **if he had done as he o.,** s'il avait fait ce qu'il devait faire; **to drink more than one o.,** boire plus que de raison; **I thought I o. to let you know about it,** j'ai cru devoir vous en faire part; **we o. to inform you that there has been an increase in price,** nous croyons devoir vous faire savoir qu'il y a eu une augmentation de prix; **cars are parked where they o. not, oughtn't, to be,** les voitures stationnent où ce n'est pas licite; **coffee o. to be drunk hot,** il faut boire le café chaud; le café aime à être bu chaud; **I know the law, or at least I o. to,** je connais la loi; je l'ai assez pratiquée. **2.** (*vague desirability or advantage*) **you o. to go and see the Exhibition,** vous devriez aller voir l'Exposition; **you o. to have helped yourself,** vous auriez dû vous servir vous-même; **you o. not,** *P:* **you didn't, hadn't, o. to have waited,** il n'aurait pas fallu attendre; vous n'auriez pas dû attendre; **o. you to have been so blunt?** auriez-vous dû être si brusque? **he o. to have been a doctor,** c'est un médecin manqué; *F:* **I o. to be going,** il est temps que je parte; **you o. to have seen it!** il fallait voir ça! **3.** (*probability*) **your horse o. to win,** votre cheval a de grandes chances de gagner; **that o. to do,** je crois que cela suffira; **there o. to be some fun at tomorrow's meeting,** je pense qu'on s'amusera à la réunion de demain; *F:* **you o. to know,** vous êtes bien placé pour le savoir.

ought[2], *s. A: & Lit:* (= AUGHT) quelque chose *m*; quoi que ce soit; **for o. I care,** pour ce qui m'importe; *still used occ. in* **for o. I know,** (pour) autant que je sache; à ce que je sache.

ought[3], *s. F:* (= NAUGHT) **1.** rien *m*, néant *m*. **2.** *Mth:* zéro *m*.

Ouija ['wi:dʒɑ:], *s. R.t.m: Psychics:* **O. (board),** oui-ja *m*.

ounce[1] [auns], *s. Meas:* once *f*; (*a*) (mesure de poids) **avoirdupois o.** = 28,35 g.; **Troy o.** = 31,1035 g.; *F:* **he hasn't an o. of courage,** il n'a pas pour deux sous de courage; (*b*) (mesure de capacité) **fluid o.** = 28,4 cm³.

ounce[2], *s.* **1.** *Z:* once *f*; léopard *m*, panthère *f*, des neiges; irbis *m*. **2.** *A: & Lit:* lynx *m*.

our ['auər], *poss.a.* notre, *pl.* nos; **o. house and garden,** notre maison et notre jardin; **o. friends,** nos ami(e)s; **o. father and mother,** notre père et notre mère; nos père et mère; **o. two,** les deux nôtres; **o. George,** mon, notre, frère Georges; mon, notre, fils Georges; **this is one of o. books,** (i) ce livre nous appartient, est à nous; (ii) c'est nous qui avons écrit ce livre; (iii) c'est notre maison qui a publié ce livre; **furniture of o. own make,** meubles de notre propre fabrication; **let's look after o. own,** (i) soignons le nôtre; (ii) occupons-nous des nôtres; *Com:* **o. Mr Martin,** M. Martin de notre maison.

ours ['auəz], *poss.pron.* (*a*) le nôtre, la nôtre, les nôtres; **your house is larger than o.,** votre maison est plus grande que la nôtre; **this is o.,** ceci est à nous; ceci nous appartient; **provinces that have become o. again,** provinces redevenues nôtres; **o. is a nation of travellers,** nous sommes une nation de voyageurs; **o. is a day of rapid changes,** les choses changent rapidement à notre époque; **a friend of o.,** un(e) de nos ami(e)s; un(e) ami(e) à nous; **this book is one of o.,** (i) ce livre nous appartient, est à nous; (ii) c'est nous qui avons écrit ce livre; (iii) c'est notre maison qui a publié ce livre; **it's no business of o.,** ce n'est pas notre affaire; cela ne nous regarde pas; **no effort of o. would alter it,** aucun effort de notre part ne le changerait; *F: Pej:* **that gardener of o.,** notre sacré jardinier; *Mil: O:* **Major de Vere of o.,** le commandant de Vere de notre régiment, des nôtres; (*b*) **it is not o. to object,** ce n'est pas à nous, il ne nous appartient pas, de faire des objections.

ourself [auə'self], *pers.pron.* **1.** (*said by monarch, editor, etc.*) nous-même; **we o. are convinced that the report is accurate,** nous sommes nous-même convaincu que le reportage est exact. **2. none of us can know the effect such a thing would have on o.,** personne ne peut savoir les effets qu'une telle chose aurait sur soi-même.

ourselves [auə'selvz], *pers.pron.pl.* (*a*) (*emphatic*) nous-mêmes; **we did it o.,** nous l'avons fait nous-mêmes; **we o. do not believe it,** nous, pour notre part, ne le croyons pas; **we want everybody to be as happy as o.,** on voudrait que chacun soit heureux comme soi; (*b*) (*reflexive*) nous; **we are enjoying o. very much,** nous nous amusons bien; **we had to laugh, we couldn't help o.,** nous ne pouvions nous empêcher de rire; (*c*) (*after preposition*) nous, nous-mêmes; **we say to o.,** nous nous disons; **we brought it on o.,** nous nous le sommes attiré; **we have no confidence in o.,** nous nous défions de nous-mêmes; **we shouldn't talk about o.,** on ne doit pas parler de soi; **we all have the right to think first of o.,** nous avons tous le droit de penser d'abord à soi(-même); (*reciprocal*) **instead of fighting among o.,** au lieu de se battre entre nous.

ousel ['u:zl], *s. Orn:* = OUZEL.

oust [aust], *v.tr.* **1.** (*a*) *Jur:* déposséder, évincer (qn) (of, de); (*b*) **to o. s.o. from his post,** déloger qn de son poste. **2.** prendre la place de (qn); évincer, supplanter, déplacer (qn); *F:* débusquer, dégotter, dégommer (qn).

ouster ['austər], *s. Jur:* & *NAm:* éviction *f*; dépossession illégale.

out[1] [aut], *adv., int., a., s. & prep.*

I. *adv.* (*the uses of* **out** *as an adjunct to verbs, such as:* **call o., hold o.,** *etc., are illustrated under the respective verbs.*) **1.** dehors; (*a*) (*with motion*) **to go o., walk o.,** sortir; **to skip o.,** sortir en gambadant; **to run o.,** sortir en courant; courir dehors; **where are you going?—o.,** où allez-vous?—dehors; je sors; **o. you go!** hors d'ici! allez, hop! vous pouvez prendre le chemin de la porte! **put him o.! o. with him!** mettez-le dehors! emmenez-le! à la porte! **to go in at one door and o. at the other,** entrer par une porte et sortir par l'autre; **the voyage o.,** l'aller *m*; **voyage o. and home,** voyage *m* d'aller et retour; **to insure a ship o. and home,** assurer un navire pour l'aller et le retour; *Golf:* **to go o. in 35 (shots),** faire les neuf premiers trous en trente-cinq coups; (*b*) (*without motion*) **my father is o.,** mon père est sorti; **my daughter is o. a great deal,** ma fille sort beaucoup; **I was o. with some friends yesterday,** (i) j'ai fait une sortie, (ii) j'étais sorti, avec des amis hier; **I am dining o. this evening,** je dine dehors, en ville, au restaurant, chez des amis, ce soir; **they are o. shooting,** ils sont partis à la chasse; **he is o. and about again,** il est de nouveau sur pied; *A:* **day o.,** jour *m* de sortie (d'une domestique, etc.); **to have one day o. a week,** avoir un jour de libre par semaine; **this is my night o.,** ce soir je suis de sortie; *F:* **we had a night o. on Saturday,** (i) nous sommes sortis samedi soir; (ii) samedi, nous avons passé la nuit à faire la bombe; **to be o. on business,** être en course(s); être sorti pour affaires; (*of commercial traveller*) **to be o.,** être en tournée, en route; **the mob was o.,** la populace était descendue dans la rue; **the workmen are o.,** les ouvriers sont en grève; **the troops are o.,** les troupes sont sur pied; **a well-known duellist, who had been o. several times,** duelliste bien connu, qui avait été plusieurs fois sur le terrain, qui plus d'une fois s'était aligné sur le terrain; **he does not live far o. (of the town),** il ne demeure pas loin de la ville; **once the tooth is o.,** dès que la dent sera arrachée; **the jury was o. for two hours,** le jury s'est retiré pendant deux heures pour délibérer; **o. at sea,** en mer, au large; **four days o. from Liverpool,** à quatre jours de Liverpool; **anchored some way o., not far o.,** mouillé à quelque distance, pas loin, de la côte; **o. in America,** en Amérique; **o. there,** là-bas; **we live right o. in the country,** nous habitons dans un trou perdu à la campagne; **the tide is o.,** la marée est basse; **(library) books o.,** livres *m* en lecture; *Fin:* **money o. (on loan),** argent prêté; prêts *mpl*; *Fish:* **our lines were o.,** nos lignes étaient dehors; (*c*) *F:* **way o., far o.,** d'une originalité poussée à l'extrême; très avant-garde; **I'm not conventional but this is a bit too far o. for me,** je ne suis pas conventionnel, mais ceci est quand même un peu trop pour moi. **2.** (*a*) en dehors; **to turn one's toes o.,** tourner les pieds en dehors; (*b*) au dehors; **to lean o. (of the window),** se pencher au dehors; **to jut o. beyond the building,** faire saillie hors du bâtiment; **his shirt was o.,** sa chemise pendait au dehors (de son pantalon); (*of garment*) **to be o. at elbow(s),** être troué, percé, aux coudes; (*of pers.*) **to look o. at elbow(s),** avoir l'air miteux, déguenillé. **3.** (*a*) au clair; découvert, exposé; (*of secret*) échappé, éventé; (*of bird*) éclos; (*of sword*) tiré, au clair; **the sun is o.,** il fait du soleil; **the stars were not o.,** les étoiles n'étaient pas visibles; *F:* **the best game o.,** le meilleur jeu qui soit; **the book is o., is already o., is just o.,** le livre est paru, a déjà paru, vient de paraître; **the secret is o.,** le secret est connu, éventé; **a warrant is o. against him,** un mandat d'amener est lancé contre lui; *A:* **girl who is o.,** jeune fille qui a fait son entrée dans le monde; **servant who has never been o. before,** domestique qui n'a jamais été en service, en place; (*b*) (*with motion*) **to whip o. a revolver,** tirer, sortir, vivement un revolver; *P:* **he o. with a knife,** il tira, sortit, un couteau; *F:* **o. with it!** achevez donc! racontez-nous cela! allons, dites-le! expliquez-vous! *P:* allons, accouche! *Prov:* **truth, murder, will o.,** tôt ou tard la vérité se fait jour; la vérité, le crime, se découvre, se trahit, toujours; (*c*) (*of sail, etc.*) déployé; (*of flower, etc.*) épanoui; **the may is o.,** l'aubépine *f* est en fleur; **the rope is o. to its full length,** tout le cordage est filé; (*d*) *F:* **to be o. after s.o., sth.,** être à la recherche de qn, de qch.; **he's simply o. for money,** tout ce qui l'intéresse c'est l'argent; **I'm not o. for compliments,** je ne suis pas en quête de compliments; **I am not o. to reform the world,** je n'ai pas entrepris, je n'ai pas à tâche, mon but n'est pas, de réformer le monde; **to go (all) o. for sth.,** mettre toute son énergie, se donner corps et âme, pour faire aboutir qch.; tendre tous ses efforts vers un but; mettre tout en œuvre, se démener, ne pas s'épargner, pour obtenir qch.; **I'm (going) o. for big results,** je vise aux grands résultats; **he's going all o. for a headship,** il met tout en œuvre pour se faire nommer directeur; **I'm all o. for reform,** je suis entièrement pour les réformes; (*e*) *Sp: etc:* **all o.,** à toute vitesse, à toute allure, à fond de train, à plein rendement; *Sp:* **to start all o.,** partir à fond; **boat that can do thirty knots when she is going all o.,** bateau qui fait trente nœuds à toute vapeur; *Aut:* **she does 80 (when she's going) all o.,** elle fait du 130 quand on la laisse filer, quand on met tous les gaz; (*f*) **o. loud,** tout haut, à haute voix; **to tell s.o. sth. straight o., right o.,** dire qch. à qn carrément, franchement, sans détours, sans ambages. **4. shoulder o. (of joint),** épaule luxée; **I'm o. of practice,** je n'ai plus la main; j'ai perdu le tour de main; je suis rouillé; *Pol:* **the party that's o.,** le parti qui n'est pas au pouvoir; **long skirts are o. this year,** les jupes longues sont hors de mode cette année; **this style is o.,** cette mode est passée; **these two projects are now definitely o.,** il n'est plus possible de considérer ces deux projets; **the players who are o. (of the game),** les joueurs qui sont hors jeu, éliminés; *Cr:* **the batsmen o.,** les joueurs hors jeu; **not o.,** encore au guichet (à la fin de l'innings, de la journée); **the side is all o.,** toute l'équipe est hors jeu; (*of boxer*) **to be o. for seven seconds,** être sur le plancher pendant sept secondes; *F:* **to be o. on one's feet,** tomber, tituber, de fatigue; **to be fifty pounds o. (of pocket),** être en perte de cinquante livres; *O:* **to be o. with s.o.,** être fâché, brouillé, en bisbille, avec qn. **5.** dans l'erreur; **to be o. in one's calculations,** être loin de compte; avoir dépassé ses prévisions; **to be o. in one's reckoning,** s'être trompé dans son calcul; **he is five pounds o. (in his accounts),** il a une erreur de cinq livres dans ses comptes; **I was not far o.,** je ne me trompais pas de beaucoup; **you are quite o.,** vous n'y êtes pas du tout; **watch that is ten minutes o.,** montre qui est en avance, en retard, de dix minutes; **you have put me o.,** vous m'avez dérouté; **the measurements were a millimetre o.,** il y avait une erreur d'un millimètre dans les mesures; **the shot was only a centimetre o.,** le coup n'a manqué, raté, le but que d'un centimètre. **6. the fire, gas, is o.,** le feu, le gaz, est éteint; *Mil:* **lights o.,** extinction *f* des feux; *Nau:* **to steam with all lights o.,** naviguer avec tous les feux masqués. **7.** (*a*) à bout, achevé; **my patience is o.,** ma patience est à bout; **the crew was rowed o. at the finish,** à la fin de la course l'équipe était à bout; **my pipe is smoked o.,** j'ai fini ma pipe; **the lease is o.,** le bail est expiré; **before the week is o.,** avant la fin de la semaine; avant que la semaine soit achevée; (*at dominoes*) **to be o.,** faire domino; *W.Tel:* **o.!** terminé! (*b*) jusqu'au bout; **hear me o.,** entendez-moi jusqu'à la fin, jusqu'au bout; **to have one's sleep o.,** finir de dormir; finir son somme; dormir tout son soûl. **8.** (*a*) *adv.phr.* **this is o. and away the best,** c'est de beaucoup, sans comparaison, sans contredit, le meilleur; (*b*) **o. and o.,** (i) complètement, absolument, sans restriction; **to oppose sth. o. and o.,** s'opposer à qch. avec la dernière énergie; **to be beaten o. and o.,** être battu à plate couture; (ii) (*preceding noun*) (républicain, etc.) outrancier, convaincu, intransigeant, enragé; à tout crin; (adulateur, etc.) à (toute) outrance; (menteur) fieffé, accompli, achevé; (sot, etc.) renforcé; **o. and o. rogue,** franc coquin. **9.** *prep.phr.* **from o. (of) the open window came bursts of laughter,** par la fenêtre ouverte arrivaient des éclats de rire. **10.** *prep.phr.* **out of:** (*a*) hors de, au dehors de, en dehors de; **animal that is not found o. of Europe,** animal qu'on ne trouve pas hors de l'Europe, qui ne se trouve qu'en Europe; **that is o. of our power,** cela n'est pas en notre pouvoir; **o. of danger,** (i) hors de danger; (ii) à l'abri du danger; **o. of sight,** hors de vue; **to live o. of the world,** vivre retiré du monde; **o. of doors** = OUTDOORS; **hardly were the words o. of my mouth,** à peine avais-je prononcé ces mots; **are you o. of your time?** avez-vous fini votre apprentissage? **he is o. of all his troubles** (*i.e., dead*), il a laissé derrière lui les tribulations de ce monde; *F:* **I'm glad I'm o. of the whole business,** je suis content d'en être quitte; **he's well o. of the whole business,** il en est quitte, il s'en est tiré, à bon marché; **to be o. of it,** (i) n'être pas de la partie (de plaisir, de chasse, etc.); (ii) n'être pas de connivence; (iii) être laissé à l'écart; **you're absolutely o. of it!** vous n'y êtes pas du tout! **to feel o. of it,** se sentir dépaysé, en dehors du mouvement; se sentir de trop; (*b*) **o. of season,** hors de saison; **o. of date,** suranné, vieilli; passé de mode, démodé; **to become o. of date,** passer de mode; **my passport is o. of date,** mon passeport est périmé; **o.-of-date theories,** théories désuètes; **o.-of-date methods,** méthodes périmées, dépassées; **o. of fashion,** démodé, passé de mode; *A:* **times o. of number,** maintes et maintes fois; **o. of measure,** outre mesure; **to be o. of one's mind,** avoir perdu la raison; **o. of spirits,** mal en train; **o. of health,** malade; (*c*) (*with motion*) **to go o. of the house,** sortir de la maison; **is there a way o. of it?** y a-t-il (un) moyen d'en sortir? **to throw sth., to leap, o. of the window,** jeter qch., sauter, par la fenêtre; **to jump o. of bed,** sauter à bas du lit; **to turn s.o. o. of the house,** mettre, flanquer, qn à la porte; **to get the cart o. of the ditch,** faire sortir la charrette du fossé; **to get money o. of s.o.,** obtenir de l'argent de qn; soutirer, extorquer, de l'argent à qn; **I got ten pounds o. of it,** j'y ai gagné dix livres; (*d*) *Breed:* **Gladiator by Monarch o. of Gladia,** Gladiatour par Monarch et Gladia; (*e*) dans, à, par; **to drink o. of a glass,** boire dans un verre; **to drink o. of the bottle,** boire à (même) la bouteille; **to eat o. of the same dish,** manger au même plat; **to copy sth. o. of a book,** copier qch. dans un livre; **steps cut o. of the solid rock,** escalier taillé à même la pierre; **you will pay yourself o. of what remains over,** vous vous payerez sur le surplus; **the firemen are paid o. of the rates,** on paie les pompiers sur le budget de la ville; (*f*) parmi, d'entre; **choose one o. of these ten,** choisissez-en un parmi les dix; **one fact o. of a thousand,** un seul fait entre mille; **it happens once o. of a thousand times,** cela arrive une fois sur mille; **three days o. of four,** trois jours sur quatre; **one o. of every three,** un sur trois, de trois l'un; (*g*) **hut made o. of a few old planks,** cabane faite de quelques vieilles planches; **to build sth. o. of nothing,** bâtir qch. à partir de rien; (*h*) **o. of respect for you,** par respect pour vous; **to do sth. o. of friendship, o. of curiosity,** faire qch. par amitié, par curiosité; **to act o. of fear,** agir sous le coup de la peur; (i) **to be o. of tea,** ne plus avoir de thé; être à court de thé; manquer de thé; **o. of cash,** démuni d'argent; *Com:* **I am o. of this article,** je suis démuni, désassorti, de cet article.

II. *int.* (*a*) *A:* & *Lit:* **o. upon him!** fi de lui! haro! **o. upon you!** fi du vilain! (*b*) **o. (with you)!** sortez!

III. *a.* (*preceding a noun*) **1.** extérieur, à l'extérieur; (*a*) **o. parish,** (i) paroisse *f* extra-muros; (ii) paroisse écartée; *Hist:* **o. voter,** électeur, -trice, qui ne résidait pas dans la circonscription (mais qui avait le droit d'y venir voter en tant que propriétaire foncier); (*b*) *Rail: etc:* **o. porter,** commissionnaire messager; *Adm: A:* **o. relief,** secours *mpl* à domicile. **2.** vers l'extérieur; (*a*) **the o. door,** la (porte de) sortie; *Min:* **o. take,** puits *m* de sortie; (*b*) *Com: etc:* **o. (tray),** (corbeille *f* à courrier) sorties *fpl*; *Book-k:* **o. book,** livre *m* du dehors; (*c*) *Arch:* **o. thrust,** poussée *f* en dehors; (*d*) *Cmptr:* **o. tape,** bande *f* sortie.

IV. *s.* **1.** *Typ:* bourdon *m*; **to make an o.,** sauter un mot. **2.** *pl. Med: F:* **outs,** le service de consultations externes. **3.** (*a*) *pl. Pol: etc.: F:* **the outs,** ceux qui ne sont pas au pouvoir; (*b*) *Ind:* pièce *f* de rebut; *Cin:* prise *f* de vues à écarter. **4.** *Fin: etc: F:* **outs,** débits *m*; *esp.* prélèvement fiscal. **5.** *F:* (*a*) **to find an o.,** se ménager une porte de sortie, une échappatoire; se débrouiller; (*b*) *NAm:* **to make a poor o.,** se mal acquitter. **6.** *NAm: F:* **to be at outs with s.o.,** être fâché, brouillé, en bisbille, avec qn. **7.** *Ten:* balle *f* (qui tombe) en dehors des limites.

V. *prep. F:* **to go o. the door,** sortir par la porte; **to look o. the window,** regarder par la fenêtre.

out[2], *v.tr.* **1.** (*a*) *Box:* mettre (un boxeur) knockout; knockouter; (*b*) *F:* (i) assommer, (ii) faire perdre connaissance à (qn). **2.** *F:* (i) mettre (qn) à la porte; (ii) chasser (le parti au pouvoir, etc.). **3.** *F:* éteindre (le feu, etc.).

out-act [aut'ækt], *v.tr.* éclipser le jeu de (qn) (sur la scène).

outage ['autidʒ], *s. NAm:* **1.** panne *f* (d'une machine); perturbation *f* (dans le fonctionnement d'un appareil); coupure *f* (d'électricité); dérangement *m* (du téléphone, etc.). **2.** (*a*) pertes *fpl* (des liquides pendant le transport); (*b*) *Av:* consommation *f* de combustible (pendant un vol).

out-and-outer ['autnd'autər], *s. F:* **1.** (*pers.*) (*a*) outrancier, -ière; (*b*) fripon accompli; *F:* salaud *m*. **2.** *O:* (*a*) mensonge effronté; (*b*) chef-d'œuvre *m, pl.* chefs-d'œuvre.

out-argue [aut'ɑ:gju:], *v.tr.* vaincre (qn) dans un débat; mettre (qn) à bout d'arguments.

outback, *a. & s. Austr:* **1.** *s.* ['autbæk], **the o.,** l'intérieur *m.* **2.** *adv.* [aut'bæk], à l'intérieur.

outbalance [aut'bæləns], *v.tr.* l'emporter sur (qch.); être plus important que (qch.).

outbent [aut'bent], *a.* tourné en dehors.

outbid [aut'bid], *v.tr.* (*p.t.* **outbid;** *p.p.* **outbid, -bidden** ['bidn]) **1.** (*at auction*) (r)enchérir, surenchérir, sur (qn); mettre sur (qn); faire une surenchère sur (qn). **2.** surpasser; **to o. s.o. in generosity,** surpasser qn en générosité; renchérir sur qn.

outbidder [aut'bidər], *s.* surenchérisseur, -euse, renchérisseur, -euse.

outbidding [aut'bidiŋ], *s.* surenchère *f.*

outblaze [aut'bleiz], *v.tr.* surpasser (qn, qch.) en éclat.

outboard ['autbɔ:d]. **1.** *a. & s.* (*a*) *Nau:* (*of rigging, etc.*) extérieur, hors bord, en abord; **o. (motor),** moteur *m* hors bord; **o. (motorboat),** hors-bord *m inv;* **o. cabin,** cabine extérieure, *Navy:* chambre extérieure; (*b*) *Av:* extérieur (au fuselage); (*c*) *Mec.E: etc:* (tuyau, etc.) qui va vers l'extérieur; (*d*) *Mec.E:* (pièce) qui se prolonge hors du centre de gravité; **o. bearing,** palier *m* à chevalet isolé, palier en porte-à-faux, palier extérieur. **2.** *adv.* (*a*) *Nau:* (attaché, etc.) au dehors, hors bord; (jeter qch.) par-dessus bord; (*b*) *Av:* (i) à l'extérieur, au dehors (du fuselage); (ii) (*of internal fitment, etc.*) **o. of sth.,** à l'extérieur de qch.; (*c*) vers l'extérieur.

outbound ['autbaund], *a.* (*a*) (navire) en partance; (avion, train) en partance, au départ; (*b*) (navire, avion) effectuant un voyage d'aller; (*c*) **o. freight,** fret *m* de sortie.

outbreak ['autbreik], *s.* **1.** éruption *f* (volcanique, etc.); début *m*, commencement *m*, ouverture *f* (des hostilités, etc.); débordement *m* (des sentiments); **o. of temper,** explosion *f* de rage; bouffée *f*, accès *m*, de colère; déchaînement *m* de colère; sortie violente; **the o. of an epidemic,** la première manifestation d'une épidémie; **at the o. of an epidemic,** lorsqu'une épidémie se déclare; **an o. of influenza,** une épidémie de la grippe; **precautions against an o. of typhus,** précautions contre le typhus; **o. of pimples,** poussée *f* de boutons; éruption; **o. of fire,** incendie *m;* **new o.,** recrudescence *f* (d'une épidémie, du feu, etc.); nouveau foyer (d'incendie); **at the o. of war,** quand la guerre éclata. **2.** révolte *f*, émeute *f.* **3.** *Geol: Min:* affleurement *m* (d'un filon).

outbreeding ['autbri:diŋ], *s. Breed:* élevage *m* sans consanguinité.

outbuilding ['autbildiŋ], *s.* bâtiment extérieur; annexe *f;* **the outbuildings,** les communs *m*, dépendances *f.*

outburst ['autbə:st], *s.* **1.** éruption *f*, explosion *f;* élan *m* (de générosité); déchaînement *m* (de la haine, etc.); **o. of temper,** accès *m*, bouffée *f*, éclat *m*, de colère; sortie violente; mouvement *m* d'humeur, algarade *f* (**against s.o.,** contre qn). **2.** *Geol:* affleurement *m* (d'un filon).

out-by(e) [aut'bai], *adv.phr. Scot:* dehors.

outcast ['autkɑ:st], *a. & s.* expulsé, -ée, exilé, -ée, proscrit, -ite, banni, -ie; **an o. of society,** un déchet, un(e) réprouvé(e), de la société; un paria; **social outcasts,** le rebut, les déchus *m*, de la société; **the outcasts of fortune,** les déshérités *m.*

outcaste[1] ['autkɑ:st]. **1.** *a.* qui n'appartient à aucune caste; hors caste. **2.** *s.* hors-caste *mf, inv;* paria *m.*

outcaste[2] [aut'kɑ:st], *v.tr.* mettre (qn) hors caste.

outclass [aut'klɑ:s], *v.tr.* surclasser (un concurrent).

out-clearer ['autkliərər], *s. Fin: Bank:* commis chargé du livre du dehors.

out-clearing ['autkliəriŋ], *a. Fin: Bank:* **o.-c. book,** livre *m* du dehors.

outcome ['autkʌm], *s.* issue *f*, résultat *m*, conséquence *f*, aboutissement *m*, dénouement *m;* **the o. of our labours,** le fruit de nos travaux; **atheism is the logical o. of this doctrine,** l'athéisme est le terme logique de cette doctrine; **I don't know what the o. will be,** je ne sais pas ce qui en résultera.

outcrop[1] ['autkrɔp], *s.* **1.** *Geol: Min:* affleurement *m*, pointement *m; Geol:* tranche *f* de couche; *Psy:* **o. of the unconscious,** affleurement de l'inconscient. **2. the recent o. of violent crimes,** l'éruption récente de crimes de violence.

outcrop[2], *v.i.* (**outcropped**) *Geol: Min:* (*of seam*) affleurer.

outcropping[1] ['autkrɔpiŋ], *a. Geol: Min:* (filon) affleurant au jour, à la surface.

outcropping[2], *s.* = OUTCROP[1] 1.

outcross[1] ['autkrɔs], *s.* mélange *m* d'individus sans consanguinité.

outcross[2] [aut'krɔs], *v.tr.* croiser (un individu avec un autre qui n'est pas consanguin).

outcry ['autkrai], *s.* cri *m*, cris (de réprobation, d'indignation); clameur *f;* **to raise an o. against s.o.,** crier haro, tollé, sur qn; (*of proposal, etc.*) **to raise a general o.,** soulever des réclamations indignées, un tollé général.

outcurve ['autkə:v], *s. Sp:* (*baseball*) balle *f* qui fait une courbe latérale vers la gauche (du batteur).

outdare [aut'dɛər], *v.tr.* **1.** braver, défier (le danger). **2.** surpasser (qn) en intrépidité; se montrer plus hardi que (qn).

outdate [aut'deit], *v.tr.* rendre démodé, désuet, périmé, suranné; **outdated ideas,** idées surannées, démodées, vieux jeu.

outdistance [aut'distəns], *v.tr.* distancer, dépasser (un concurrent).

outdo [aut'du:], *v.tr.* (**outdid** [aut'did], **outdone** [aut'dʌn]) surpasser (**s.o. in sth.,** qn en qch.); l'emporter, renchérir, sur (qn); vaincre (un concurrent); **to o. s.o. in kindness,** enchérir sur la bonté de qn; surpasser qn en bonté; **they are all anxious to o. each other,** c'est à qui fera le mieux; **they tried to o. each other in generosity,** ils faisaient assaut de générosité.

outdoor ['autdɔ:r], *a.* **1.** (*a*) extérieur; à l'extérieur; au dehors; (vie, jeux, etc.) au grand air, en plein air, de plein air; (essai, expérience) à l'air libre; **o. (air) temperature,** température extérieure; **o. work,** travail (à l')extérieur, au dehors, en plein air; **o. photography,** photographie à l'extérieur; **o. portrait,** portrait en extérieur; *Cin:* **o. scenes, shots,** extérieurs *m; Adm:* **o. staff, establishment,** personnel extérieur, de service actif; (le) service actif; *W.Tel:* **o. aerial,** antenne extérieure; (*b*) **o. clothes,** vêtements *m* de ville, de sortie; **I must put on my o. clothes,** il faut que je m'habille pour sortir. **2.** (*a*) (*of patient, etc.*) externe; (*b*) *Hist:* **o. relief,** secours *mpl* à domicile.

outdoors [aut'dɔ:z]. **1.** *adv.* dehors; hors de la maison; au dehors; en plein air; **to live o.,** vivre au grand air; **to sleep o.,** coucher à la belle étoile; **seen from o.,** vu de dehors; *Av:* **craft o.,** avions *m* hors, à l'extérieur, des hangars; avions en piste; *Hort:* **to sow o.,** semer en pleine terre. **2.** *s.* **the o.,** la vie en plein air.

outdrive [aut'draiv], *v.tr.* (**outdrove, -driven** [aut'drouv, -driv(ə)n]) *Golf:* dépasser (son adversaire) (du premier coup de crosse); avoir la crossée plus longue que (qn).

outer ['autər]. **1.** *a.* extérieur, externe; (*of boundary, etc.*) circonférentiel; **o. darkness,** les ténèbres extérieures; **recluse who knows nothing about the o. world,** reclus qui ne sait rien du monde extérieur; **the o. man,** (i) le corps; (ii) l'extérieur (d'un homme), l'homme extérieur; **o. garments,** vêtements *m* de dessus; *Arch:* **o. door,** avant-portail *m, pl.* avant-portails; *Mil: etc:* **o. wall,** contre-mur *m, pl.* contre-murs; (*of wheeling line*) **o. flank,** aile marchante; *Elcs:* **o. layer, shell,** couche (électronique) externe, superficielle; **o.(-shell) electron,** électron *m* périphérique; **o. space,** l'espace intersidéral. **2.** *s.* (*in range shooting*) (*a*) cercle extérieur (de la cible); (*b*) balle *f* dans le cercle extérieur.

outermost ['autəmoust], *a.* **1.** extérieur, -eure; le plus à l'extérieur; le plus en dehors. **2.** le plus écarté; extrême; **to the o. parts of the earth,** jusqu'aux extrémités de la terre.

outfall ['autfɔ:l], *s.* embouchure *f* (d'une rivière, d'une vallée); déversoir *m*, déchargeoir *m*, décharge *f*, débouché *m* (d'un égout, etc.); **o. sewer,** égout de décharge.

outfeed ['autfi:d], *s. Cmptr:* côté *m* sortie.

outfield ['autfi:ld], *s.* **1.** *Cr:* terrain éloigné des guichets; (*baseball*) extra-champ *m.* **2.** *Cr:* (les) joueurs éloignés des guichets; (*baseball*) (les trois) joueurs dans l'extra-champ.

outfielder ['autfi:ldər], *s.* **1.** *Cr:* joueur éloigné des guichets. **2.** (*baseball*) joueur dans l'extra-champ.

outfighting ['autfaitiŋ], *s.* **1.** *Box:* combat *m* à bras tendus. **2.** *Navy:* combats d'avant-garde.

outfit ['autfit], *s.* **1.** appareil *m*, appareillage *m*, équipement *m*, équipage *m;* attirail *m* (de chasse, etc.); *Nau:* armement *m* (d'un navire); **o. of tools,** ensemble *m* d'outils; jeu *m* d'outils; outillage *m;* **first aid o.,** trousse *f* de premiers secours; boîte *f* de secours; **repair(ing) o.,** nécessaire *m*, trousse, de réparation, à réparations. **2.** (*of clothes*) trousseau *m;* effets *mpl;* ensemble *m* des articles de vêtement; *Mil:* équipement *m;* **scout's o.,** uniforme *m* de boy-scout; **o. allowance,** indemnité *f*, gratification *f*, de première mise, d'équipement. **3.** *NAm:* (*a*) établissement *m*, organisation *f* (agricole, etc.); *P:* **what's he doing in that o.?** que diable fait-il dans cette galère? (*b*) *F:* équipe *f* d'ouvriers; *Mil: F:* (i) compagnie *f;* (ii) bataillon *m.*

outfitter ['autfitər], *s. Com:* **1.** fournisseur, -euse, d'articles d'habillement; confectionneur, -euse; ensemblier *m;* **men's o.,** marchand *m* de confections et chemisier *m;* **law and university o.,** costumier *m.* **2.** fournisseur (d'une expédition, etc.).

outfitting ['autfitiŋ], *s.* **1.** équipement *m;* armement *m* (d'un navire). **2.** *Com:* **o. department,** rayon *m* de confection *f* (pour hommes, enfants).

outflank [aut'flæŋk], *v.tr.* **1.** *Mil:* déborder, tourner, prendre à revers (l'ennemi, une position adverse); **outflanking movement,** mouvement débordant, tournant. **2.** circonvenir (qn).

outflow[1] ['autflou], *s.* **1.** (*a*) écoulement *m*, échappement *m* (d'un liquide, gaz, etc.); coulée *f* (de lave); sortie *f* (de matières, etc.); décharge *f* (d'un égout, bief, etc.); *Fin:* **o. of gold, exchange,** sortie d'or, de devises; (*b*) **o. per hour,** débit *m* par heure. **2.** épanchement *m* (de sentiments).

outflow[2] [aut'flou], *v.i.* s'écouler, sortir, s'échapper.

outflowing[1] ['autflouiŋ], *a.* (courant, etc.) effluent, de sortie; **o. stream,** émissaire *m.*

outflowing[2], *s.* = OUTFLOW[1].

outfly [aut'flai], *v.tr.* (**outflew** [aut'flu:]; **outflown** [aut'floun]) dépasser (qn, etc.) au vol; voler plus vite, plus haut, plus loin, que (qn, etc.).

outfoot [aut'fut], *v.tr.* courir plus vite que (qn); dépasser (qn) à la course.

outfox [aut'fɔks], *v.tr.* se montrer plus malin, habile, que (qn); duper (qn).

outgas [aut'gæs], *v.tr.* (**outgassed**) *U.S:* dégazer (un tube à vide, etc.).

outgassing [aut'gæsiŋ], *s. U.S:* dégazage *m* (d'un tube à vide, etc.).

outgate ['autgeit], *s. Metall:* (trou *m* d')évent *m.*

outgeneral [aut'dʒen(ə)rəl], *v.tr.* (**outgeneralled**) surpasser (qn) en tactique; l'emporter sur (qn) en tactique.

outgiving ['autgiviŋ], *s. NAm:* annonce *f* (publique).

outgo ['autgou], *s. NAm:* **1.** sortie *f.* **2.** dépenses *fpl*, sorties de fonds.

outgoer ['autgouər], *s.* sortant, -ante.

outgoing[1] ['autgouiŋ], *a.* **1.** (*a*) (locataire, fonctionnaire, etc.) sortant; **o. crowd,** foule qui sort (d'une salle de spectacle, etc.); **o. ministry,** ministère sortant, démissionnaire; *Ind: etc:* **o. shift,** équipe sortante, relevée; (*b*) partant; (avion, navire, train) en partance; **o. mail,** courrier *m* (i) à expédier, (ii) au départ; **o. traffic,** *Tp:* trafic *m* au départ; *Cmptr:* trafic en émission; (*c*) *El:* **o. cable,** câble *m* de sortie, de départ; *Tp:* **o. call,** communication *f* de sortie; (*d*) **o. tide,** marée descendante. **2.** (*of pers.*) sociable, qui se lie facilement, extraverti.

outgoing[2], *s.* **1.** sortie *f* (de qn, qch.); **o. inventory,** inventaire *m* de sortie (lorsqu'on quitte un immeuble). **2.** *pl.* **outgoings,** dépenses *f*, débours *m;* sorties de fonds; **the outgoings exceed the incomings,** les dépenses excèdent les recettes.

outgrow [aut'grou], *v.tr.* (**outgrew** [aut'gru:]; **outgrown** [aut'groun]) **1.** croître plus vite que (qn, qch.), devenir plus grand que (qn, qch.); dépasser (d'autres plantes, etc.) en hauteur. **2.** (*a*) devenir trop grand pour (ses vêtements, etc.); **to o. one's strength,** grandir trop vite; (*b*) **to o. a habit,** perdre une habitude avec le temps, en grandissant, en vieillissant; se défaire d'une habitude; **to o. an opinion,** se défaire d'une opinion; revenir sur une opinion.

outgrowth ['autgrouθ], *s.* **1.** excroissance *f; Geol:* apophyse (éruptive). **2.** conséquence naturelle, résultat *m* (de certains faits, etc.).

outguard ['autgɑ:d], *s. Mil:* garde avancée.

outguess [aut'ges], *v.tr.* déjouer les intentions, les menées, de (qn); se montrer plus malin que (qn).

outgun [aut'gʌn], *v.tr.* **1.** *Navy:* porter des canons d'un plus grand calibre que (les bâtiments ennemis, etc.). **2.** *Fig:* être plus fort que, l'emporter sur (qn).

outhaul ['authɔ:l], *s. Nau:* drisse *f;* **jib o.,** hale-dehors *m inv.*

out-herod [aut'herəd], *v.tr.* **to o.-h. Herod,** (i) se montrer plus violent qu'Hérode; surhéroder Hérode; être plus royaliste que le roi; (ii) *F:* dépasser les bornes; passer toute mesure; être plus royaliste que le roi.

outhouse ['authaus], *s.* (*a*) bâtiment extérieur; dépendance *f;* (*b*) appentis *m*, hangar *m*, toit *m;* (*c*) *NAm:* lieux *mpl* d'aisance.

outing ['autiŋ], *s.* **1.** (*a*) promenade *f;* (*b*) excursion *f*, sortie *f*, partie *f* de plaisir; **day's o. (in a car, etc.),** randonnée *f;* **to have a nice o.,** faire une belle promenade (à pied, à cheval, en voiture); **to go for an o. on Sundays,** faire une sortie le dimanche; (*c*) *Sp:* match *m*, concours *m.* **2.** *Tex:* **o. flannel,** flanelle *f* de coton et de laine.

outjockey [aut'dʒɔki], *v.tr.* l'emporter sur (qn) (en ruse); rouler, duper (qn).

outland ['autlænd], *s. NAm:* **1.** pays étranger. **2. outlands,** (i) terres écartées (d'un domaine); (ii) régions écartées (d'un pays).

outlander ['autlændər], *a. & s.* **1.** étranger, -ère. **2.** *Hist:*

Outlander, Uitlander (*m*).

outlandish [aut'lændiʃ], *a.* **1.** qui semble étranger. **2.** (*a*) (*of manner, dress, etc.*) baroque, incongru, bizarre, étrange; (*of language*) barbare; (*b*) (*of place*) retiré, écarté; **to live in an o. place,** habiter au bout du monde, dans un coin perdu, un pays perdu.

outlandishness [aut'lændiʃnis], *s.* bizarrerie *f*, étrangeté *f* (de manières, de costume).

outlast [aut'lɑ:st], *v.tr.* durer plus longtemps que (qch.); survivre à (qn).

outlaw[1] ['autlɔ:], *s.* **1.** *Hist:* hors-la-loi *m inv*; proscrit, -e; banni, -e. **2.** *NAm:* cheval *m* indomptable; **o. strike,** grève non officielle.

outlaw[2], *v.tr.* **1.** *Hist:* mettre (qn) hors la loi; proscrire (qn). **2.** proscrire, bannir (un usage, etc.).

outlawry ['autlɔ:ri], *s. Hist:* mise *f* hors la loi; proscription *f*.

outlay ['autlei], *s.* débours *mpl*, frais *mpl*, dépenses *fpl*; *Ind: etc:* **first, initial, capital, o.,** première mise de fonds, frais de premier établissement, dépenses d'établissement; **national o. on armaments,** effort financier qu'un État consacre à ses armements; **to get back, recover, one's o.,** rentrer dans ses fonds, dans ses débours, dans ce qu'on a déboursé; **without any great o., considerable o.,** (i) sans grande mise de fonds; (ii) à peu de frais.

outlet ['autlet], *s.* **1.** (*a*) orifice *m* d'émission; issue *f* (de tunnel, etc.); sortie *f*, départ *m* (d'air, de gaz); échappement *m* (de vapeur); débouché *m* (de tuyau); sortie (de mine); *Hyd.E:* dégorgeoir *m*, épanchoir *m*, bonde *f*, émissaire *m* (d'un lac); **air, water, steam, o.,** sortie d'air, d'eau, de vapeur; **to give sth. an o.,** donner issue à qch.; **to provide an o. for the smoke,** ménager un passage pour la fumée; *Hyd.E:* **o. pipe, drain,** tuyau *m* d'écoulement, colateur *m*; **discharge o.,** émissaire, débouché (d'un égout, etc.); **o. works of a reservoir,** éjecteur *m* d'un réservoir; **o. velocity, temperature,** vitesse *f*, température *f*, à la sortie; (*b*) **to find an o. for one's energy, for one's anger,** trouver une issue, un déversoir, pour son trop-plein d'énergie, un exutoire à sa colère; (*c*) *Com:* (i) débouché (pour marchandises); (ii) **retail o.,** magasin *m*. **2.** *El: NAm:* prise *f* de courant.

outlier ['autlaiər], *s.* **1.** (*a*) *Geol:* massif détaché; lambeau *m* de recouvrement; butte *f*; témoin *m*; butte témoin; (*b*) annexe *f* (d'une institution quelconque). **2.** (*a*) *Ven: etc:* bête *f* solitaire, qui gîte au loin; (*b*) *NAm:* personne qui demeure loin de son lieu de travail.

outline[1] ['autlain], *s.* **1.** (*a*) **outline(s),** contour(s) *m*, profil *m* (d'une colline, etc.); configuration *f* (de la terre); galbe *m*, gabarit *m* (d'un monument, etc.); silhouette *f* (de qn, d'un édifice); linéature *f* (des traits, du visage, etc.); **elegant o. of a car,** galbe élégant, ligne élégante, d'une voiture; *Arch:* **(proportion and) outlines of a cornice,** modénature *f* d'une corniche; (*b*) dessin *m* au trait; tracé *m*; **vase drawn in o.,** vase dessiné au trait; **o. plan,** plan *m* schématique, d'ensemble; (*c*) argument *m*, canevas *m* (d'une pièce, d'un roman); **main outlines, general o., broad outlines, of a scheme,** grandes lignes, données générales, aperçu *m*, d'un projet; **to give a general o. of sth.,** décrire qch. à grands traits; **I am only giving you an o.,** je ne vous donne que les grandes lignes; **an o. of French history,** un résumé de l'histoire de France; **outlines of astronomy,** éléments *m* d'astronomie; *Art: Lit:* **rough o.,** premier jet. **2.** (*shorthand*) sténogramme *m*. **3.** *Fish:* ligne flottante, dormante.

outline[2], *v.tr.* **1.** contourner, silhouetter (le profil de qch.); **the mountains are outlined against the sky,** les montagnes se dessinent, se profilent, sur le ciel; **the castle turrets are outlined against the horizon,** le château découpe ses tourelles sur l'horizon. **2.** exposer à grands traits, dans ses lignes générales (une théorie, etc.); esquisser (un roman, un projet); tracer les grandes lignes (d'un projet, etc.); ébaucher, indiquer (un plan d'action). **3.** *Draw: etc:* tracer, esquisser à grands traits, délinéer (un dessin, etc.).

outlining ['autlainiŋ], *s.* **1.** contournement *m* (du profil de qch., etc.). **2.** exposition *f* (d'un projet, etc.); ébauchage *m* (d'un roman, etc.). **3.** *Draw:* traçage *m*, délinéation *f* (d'un dessin).

outlive [aut'liv], *v.tr.* survivre à (qn, une défaite, etc.); **he will o. us all,** il nous enterrera tous, il nous mettra tous au tombeau; **the patient will not o. the winter,** le malade ne passera pas l'hiver; (*of ship*) **to o. a storm,** survivre à une tempête; sortir indemne d'une tempête; **to o. one's day,** se survivre.

outlook ['autluk], *s.* **1.** guet *m*; **to be on the o.,** être aux aguets; **to be on the o. for sth.,** guetter qch. **2.** (*a*) vue *f*, perspective *f*; **the o. is none too promising,** la perspective n'est pas des plus rassurantes; **the political o. is darkening,** l'horizon *m* politique se rembrunit; (*b*) façon *f* de voir les choses; **o. (up)on life,** conception *f* de la vie; **to have a melancholy o. on life,** voir les choses en noir; **to share s.o.'s o.,** partager, entrer dans, les idées de qn; **breadth of o.,** largeur *f* de vues. **3.** *NAm:* belvédère *m*.

outlying ['autlaiiŋ], *a.* éloigné, écarté; (*of rock, island, etc.*) isolé; d'en dehors; **o. quarter,** quartier *m* excentrique; **o. areas,** régions *f* périphériques; **o. building,** annexe *f*; **o. farm buildings,** dépendances *f*; *Nau:* **o. tackle (of fishing boat),** appareil immergé, qui déborde; *Navy:* **o. station,** point *m* d'appui.

outmanoeuvre [autmə'nu:vər], *v.tr.* **1.** l'emporter sur (l'ennemi) en tactique. **2.** déjouer (les plans de) (qn); rouler (qn).

outmarch [aut'mɑ:tʃ], *v.tr.* **1.** battre (un régiment, etc.) à la marche. **2.** devancer, dépasser (l'ennemi, etc.).

outmatch [aut'mætʃ], *v.tr. Sp: etc:* surpasser, battre (qn); se montrer supérieur à (qn); **to o. one's competitors,** devancer ses rivaux.

outmode [aut'moud], *v.tr. NAm:* démoder.

outmoded [aut'moudid], *a.* démodé; passé de mode.

outmost ['autmoust]. **1.** *a.* = OUTERMOST. **2.** *s. A:* **to the o.,** au plus haut degré; **at the o.,** au maximum.

outnumber [aut'nʌmbər], *v.tr.* l'emporter en nombre sur, surpasser en nombre, être plus nombreux que (l'ennemi, etc.).

out-of-pocket [autəv'pɔkit], *a.* **o.-of-p. expenses,** menues dépenses; débours *m*.

out-of-round [autəv'raund], *a.* ovalisé.

out-of-roundness [autəv'raundnis], *s.* ovalisation *f*.

out-of-school [autəv'sku:l], *a.* **o.-of-s. activities,** activités *f* extra-scolaires.

out-of-service [autəv'sə:vis], *a. Cmptr:* **o.-of-s. time,** temps *m* de non-disponibilité, d'immobilisation.

out-of-the-way [autəvðə'wei], *a.* **1.** (*of place, house, etc.*) écarté; perdu; **o.-of-t.-w. spot,** endroit peu fréquenté, loin de tout et de tous; **little o.-of-t.-w. place,** (petit) trou perdu. **2.** peu ordinaire, peu commun, insolite; (prix) excessif, exorbitant.

out-of-the-world [autəvðə'wə:ld], *a.* = OUT-OF-THE-WAY 1.

out-of-towner [autəv'taunər], *s. NAm:* **to be an o.-of-t.,** demeurer hors de la ville.

outpace [aut'peis], *v.tr.* dépasser, distancer (un concurrent, etc.); gagner (qn) de vitesse; **the demand has outpaced production,** la demande a dépassé la production.

outpatient ['autpeiʃənt], *s.* malade *mf* qui vient consulter à l'hôpital, à la clinique; **outpatients' department,** service *m* des consultations externes.

outplay [aut'plei], *v.tr.* jouer mieux que (qn); *Sp:* **to o. the other side,** dominer la partie; *Fig:* **to be outplayed,** trouver son maître.

outpoint [aut'pɔint], *v.tr.* **1.** *Y:* courir plus près du vent que (son concurrent). **2.** *Sp:* gagner plus de points que (qn); battre (qn) aux points.

outport ['autpɔ:t], *s.* **1.** port *m* de mer (d'une ville). **2.** port de partance. **3.** avant-port *m*, *pl.* avant-ports. **4.** *Can:* petit village de pêcheurs (de Terre-Neuve).

outpost ['autpoust], *s.* **1.** *Mil: etc:* avant-poste *m*, *pl.* avant-postes; poste avancé. **2. o. of Empire,** poste colonial éloigné.

outpouring ['autpɔ:riŋ], *s.* épanchement *m*, effusion *f* (de sentiments); débordement *m* (d'injures); **outpourings of the heart,** effusions de cœur.

output[1] ['autput], *s.* **1.** (*a*) production *f*, rendement *m* (d'une exploitation, d'une mine, d'un travailleur); **literary o. of an author,** production littéraire d'un auteur; **daily o. of a worker,** production journalière, rendement journalier, d'un ouvrier; **o. per hour,** production horaire, à l'heure; **maximum, peak, o.,** production maximale, maximum; rendement maximal, maximum; (production, rendement) record (*m*); **o. bonus,** prime *f* de rendement; **to reduce, curtail, o.,** réduire la production; (*b*) débit *m*, rendement (d'une machine-outil, etc.); débit, refoulement *m* (d'une pompe); *El:* débit (d'une génératrice); **machine with a large o.,** machine à grand débit, à grand rendement; *W.Tel:* **aerial o.,** énergie rayonnée par l'antenne. **2.** *Mec.E: etc:* puissance *f*, rendement (d'un moteur, etc.); *Av:* **take-off o.,** puissance au décollage; *El:* **o. (power), power o.,** puissance débitée, de sortie; **rated o.,** puissance de sortie nominale; **o. circuit, current,** circuit *m*, courant *m*, de sortie; **o. response,** gain *m*; **o. terminal,** borne *f* de sortie; **o. valve, lamp,** lampe *f*, tube *m* (à vide), de sortie; **o. voltage,** tension *f* de sortie. **3.** *Cmptr:* (i) sortie (de données, de renseignements); (ii) résultat(s) *m(pl.)* (d'un traitement de données); **o. area, block, section,** zone *f* de sortie, d'extraction; **o. card,** carte sortie, carte résultat; **o. device, unit,** appareil *m* périphérique de sortie; **o. equipment,** matériel *m* périphérique de sortie; **o. file,** fichier *m* sortie, fichier résultat; **o. tape,** bande *f* de sortie; bande réceptrice (en duplication); **o. magazine,** magasin *m* de réception; **o. pocket, stacker,** case *f* de réception; **o. spool,** bobine réceptrice.

output[2], *v.tr.* (*p.p. & p.t.* **output, outputted**) **1.** produire, rendre, débiter. **2.** *Cmptr:* sortir (des informations).

outrage[1] ['autreidʒ], *s.* **1.** (*a*) outrage *m*, atteinte *f*; **to commit an o. on, against, s.o., sth.,** faire outrage à qn, à qch.; **o. against society, against humanity,** crime *m* de lèse-société, de lèse-humanité; **what an o.!** quelle indignité! *Jur:* **o. against morals,** outrage aux (bonnes) mœurs; attentat *m* à la pudeur; (*b*) **plastic bomb o.,** attentat au plastic. **2.** *NAm:* indignation *f* (**at,** de, contre).

outrage[2], *v.tr.* **1.** outrager, faire outrage à (la religion, etc.); violenter, faire outrage à (une femme); **to o. nature, the law,** outrager la nature, la loi; **to o. common sense,** aller à l'encontre du bon sens. **2.** *NAm:* faire éclater l'indignation de (qn).

outrageous [aut'reidʒəs], *a.* (*a*) (*of cruelty, etc.*) immodéré, indigne; (*of price*) excessif, exorbitant; (*b*) (*of statement, accusation*) outrageant, outrageux; (*of conduct, etc.*) outrageux, atroce, indigne, révoltant, scandaleux; *F:* (*of trick, etc.*) pendable; **o. insult,** insulte sanglante; **o. injustice,** injustice flagrante, criante, révoltante; **it's o.!** c'est indigne! c'est une indignité! cela dépasse toutes les bornes! **the o. part of it was that we were asked to pay,** ce qu'il y a de plus violent c'est qu'on nous a demandé un paiement; (*c*) *F:* **an o. get-up,** une toilette impossible; **what o. shoes!** quelles horreurs ces chaussures!

outrageously [aut'reidʒəsli], *adv.* (*a*) immodérément, outre mesure; **they spoil him o.,** on le gâte abominablement; **o. expensive,** horriblement cher; **to charge o. for sth.,** demander un prix exorbitant pour qch.; (*b*) d'une façon scandaleuse, indigne.

outrageousness [aut'reidʒəsnis], *s.* **1.** caractère outrageant, outrageux (d'un soupçon, etc.). **2. the o. of his conduct,** l'indignité *f* de sa conduite; **the o. of his prices,** l'exorbitance *f* de ses prix.

outrange [aut'reindʒ], *v.tr.* **1.** *Ball:* (*a*) (*of gun, missile, etc.*) dépasser en portée, avoir une portée supérieure à, plus grande que (l'artillerie ennemie, etc.); **we were outranged,** les canons ennemis avaient une portée supérieure aux nôtres; (*b*) **to o. the enemy's artillery,** se mettre hors de portée de l'artillerie ennemie. **2.** surpasser (**s.o. in sth.,** qn en qch.).

outrank [aut'ræŋk], *v.i.* **1.** être supérieur en grade à (qn). **2.** avoir, prendre, le pas sur (qch.); **wheat now outranks rye as the chief crop,** le froment remplace maintenant le seigle comme principale culture.

outreach[1] ['autri:tʃ], *s.* portée *f* (d'une grue de levage, etc.); étendue *f* (d'une inondation, etc.).

outreach[2] [aut'ri:tʃ], *v.tr.* **1.** *Box:* avoir une allonge supérieure à (son adversaire). **2.** (*a*) dépasser (qn, qch.), aller au-delà de (qch.); (*b*) duper (qn).

outride [aut'raid], *v.tr.* (**outrode** [aut'roud]; **outridden** [aut'ridn]) **1.** chevaucher plus vite que (qn); dépasser, devancer, (qn) à cheval; **he outrode all his pursuers,** il distança tous ceux qui étaient à sa poursuite. **2.** *Nau:* étaler (une tempête).

outrider ['autraidər], *s.* (*a*) *Hist:* piqueur *m*, jockey *m* (de carrosse, de diligence); (*b*) **motor-cycle o.,** motard *m* d'escorte.

outrig ['autrig], *s. Nau:* épatement *m* (des haubans).

outrigged [aut'rigd], *a. Nau:* **1.** (*of shrouds*) épaté. **2.** (*of boat*) à porte-nages en dehors.

outrigger ['autrigər], *s.* **1.** *Nau:* espar *m* en saillie; arc-boutant *m*, *pl.* arcs-boutants; tangon *m*. **2.** *Row:* (*a*) porte-nage *m inv*; en dehors; porte-en-dehors *m inv*; dame *f* de nage; (*b*) (*boat*) outrigger *m*. **3.** balancier *m* (d'un prao); **o. canoe,** pirogue *f* à balancier. **4.** *Av:* (i) longeron-support *m*, *pl.* longerons-supports (de gouverne); (ii) arc-boutant; **tail o.,** longeron-support du plan fixe; poutre *f* de liaison, de réunion.

outright ['aut'rait], *adv. & a.*

I. *adv.* **1.** (*a*) complètement; **to buy sth. o.,** acheter qch. comptant, à forfait, à un prix forfaitaire; **to buy rights o.,** acquérir des droits en bloc; (*b*) du premier coup; sur le coup; **to kill s.o. o.,** tuer qn raide; **he was killed o.,** il fut tué net, sur le coup. **2.** sans ménagement; franchement, carrément; **to give one's opinion o.,** donner carrément son opinion; **to laugh o. (at s.o.),** partir d'un franc rire (au nez de qn), éclater de rire; **to refuse o.,** refuser tout net.

II. *a.* (*before noun* ['autrait]) **1.** (*a*) **o. sale,** vente *f* à forfait; **o. purchase,** marché *m* forfaitaire; **o. gift,** don pur et simple; (*b*) **it's o. wickedness,** c'est de la pure méchanceté, de la méchanceté pure. **2.** (*of manner*) franc, *f.* franche; carré.

outrightness [aut'raitnis], *s.* franchise (un peu brutale).

outrival [aut'raiv(ə)l], *v.tr.* (**outrivalled**) surpasser, devancer (qn); l'emporter sur (qn).

outrun [aut'rʌn], *v.tr.* (*p.t.* **outran** [aut'ræn]; *p.p.* **outrun**; *pr.p.* **outrunning**) **1.** dépasser, gagner, (qn) de vitesse; distancer (un concurrent); *B:* **the other disciple did o. Peter,** l'autre disciple, courait plus vite que Pierre. **2. his zeal outruns his discretion,** son ardeur l'emporte sur son jugement; **his imagination outruns the facts,** son imagination outrepasse les faits; **to o. one's income,** dépenser plus que son revenu; *F: A:* **to o. the constable,** dépenser au delà de ses moyens.

outrunner ['autrʌnər], *s. Hist:* piqueur *m*; avant-coureur *m, pl.* avant-coureurs (d'un carrosse, etc.).

outrush ['autrʌʃ], *s.* jaillissement *m*; fuite *f* (d'eau, de gaz).

outsail [aut'seil], *v.tr.* gagner (de vitesse), dépasser (un navire); *Y:* distancer (un concurrent).

outsell [aut'sel], *v.tr.* (**outsold,** [aut'sould]) **1.** (*of goods*) (i) se vendre en plus grande quantité que, être plus demandé que (qch.); (ii) se vendre plus cher que (qch.). **2.** l'emporter sur (qn) (en ventes, comme vendeur).

outset ['autset], *s.* **1.** commencement *m*; **at the o.,** au départ, au début; tout d'abord; du, au, premier coup d'œil; **from the o.,** dès le début, dès le premier jour, dès l'origine, dès l'abord, dès le principe; **at, from, the o. of his career,** au début, dès le début, de sa carrière. **2.** courant *m* qui coule vers le large.

outshine [aut'ʃain], *v.tr.* (**outshone** [aut'ʃɔn]) **1.** surpasser (qch.) en éclat. **2.** surpasser, éclipser, dépasser (qn, qch.); **he has had pupils who outshone him,** il a eu des élèves qui l'ont surpassé.

outside [aut'said, 'autsaid]. **1.** *s.* (*a*) extérieur *m*, dehors *m* (d'une maison, d'un livre, etc.); **to judge sth. by the o.,** juger qch. sur, d'après, son extérieur; **on the o. of sth.,** au dehors, en dehors, à l'extérieur, de qch.; *F:* **to be on the o. looking in,** ne pas faire partie d'une société, d'un groupe; ne pas être de la partie, du métier; **to open a door from the o.,** ouvrir une porte du dehors; **the house, looked at from the o., was pleasant,** la maison, à la voir de l'extérieur, était agréable; **the window opens to the o.,** la fenêtre s'ouvre (de dedans) en dehors; **to turn a skin o.-in,** retourner une peau (de lapin, etc.); (*b*) **at the o.,** tout au plus; au maximum; **it is twelve o'clock at the o.,** c'est tout au plus s'il est midi; **he gets £2,000 at the o.,** s'il a deux mille livres de traitement c'est le bout du monde; (*c*) *A:* (i) impériale *f* (d'un omnibus); banquette *f* (d'un coche, d'une diligence); (ii) voyageur, -euse, de l'impériale; (*d*) *Cu:* rissolé *m* (d'un mets); (*e*) *Fb:* ailier *m*; **o. left, o. right,** ailier gauche, droit; (*f*) *Paperm:* **outsides,** papier cassé (à l'extérieur de la rame). **2.** *attrib.a.* ['autsaid] (*a*) du dehors, extérieur, -eure; **o. cal(l)ipers,** compas *m* d'extérieur; **o. diameter,** diamètre extérieur (d'un tuyau, etc.); *Const:* **o. measurements,** dimensions hors d'œuvre; **o. seat,** (i) *A:* (*on omnibus*) banquette sur, de, l'impériale; (ii) (*of row of seats*) siège *m*, place *f*, du bout; (*b*) **o. work,** travail extérieur, à l'extérieur, au dehors, au grand air, en plein air; *W.Tel:* **o. aerial,** antenne extérieure; **o. broadcast,** production extérieure; **o. porter,** commissionnaire messager; (*c*) **recluse who knows nothing about the o. world,** reclus qui ne sait rien du monde extérieur; **o. interests,** intérêts en dehors de son travail, de sa famille, etc.; **we are too busy to take on o. work,** nous avons trop à faire pour entreprendre du travail pour autrui; **o. worker,** ouvrier, -ière, à domicile; **to get an o. opinion,** obtenir une opinion du dehors, un avis étranger; **o. man,** homme qui n'est pas du métier; *F:* profane; **strike aggravated by o. agitators,** grève aggravée par des agitateurs externes; (*of theft, etc.*) **it was an o. job,** les voleurs, etc., étaient étrangers à la maison; *St.Exch:* **o. market,** coulisse *f*; **o. broker,** coulissier *m*; **o. transactions,** transactions coulissières; *Turf:* **o. bookmaker,** bookmaker *m* qui n'est pas membre du Tattersall's; (*d*) **o. prices,** prix maximums, maxima; les plus hauts prix; *F:* **it's the o. edge,** ça c'est un peu fort (de café), après ça il faut tirer l'échelle; (*e*) *F:* **it's an o. chance,** il y a tout juste une chance (de réussir). **3.** *adv.* (*a*) dehors, à l'extérieur, en dehors; **I've left my dog o.,** j'ai laissé mon chien dehors, à la porte; **the taxi is o.,** le taxi vous attend à la porte; **to put s.o. o.,** mettre qn dehors; **seen from o.,** vu de dehors; **government controlled by influence from o.,** gouvernement sous l'empire d'influences extérieures; **vase that is black o. and in,** vase qui est noir au dehors et au dedans, à l'extérieur et à l'intérieur; *A:* **to ride o.,** voyager sur l'impériale; **to sit o. (at a café),** s'asseoir à la terrasse; *P:* **come o.!** réglons ça dehors! si tu es un homme . . .! *P:* **when he's o.,** lorsqu'il n'est pas en prison; (*b*) *prep.phr. F:* **o. of,** (i) hors de, à l'extérieur de, en dehors de; **o. of a good horse,** monté sur un bon cheval; **to get o. of a good dinner,** s'envoyer un bon dîner; **get o. of that and you'll feel a different man,** avale-moi ça, ça te remontera; (ii) **o. of a few intimates nobody knows anything about it,** sauf quelques amis intimes, personne n'en sait rien. **4.** *prep.* en dehors de, hors de, à l'extérieur de; **o. my bedroom,** (i) à la porte de ma chambre; (ii) sous les fenêtres de ma chambre; **I'll meet you o. the cinema,** je vous rencontrerai devant le cinéma; **garden lying o. my grounds,** jardin extérieur à ma propriété; **ship lying o. the harbour,** navire mouillé au large du port; **o. the town,** en dehors de la ville; extra-muros; **they are o. my circle of friends,** ils sont en dehors de mon cercle d'amis; **occupation o. my office work,** occupation *f* en dehors de mon travail de bureau; **o. the Conference,** en marge du Congrès; **that's o. the question,** c'est en dehors du sujet; **phrase little used o. the business letter,** locution peu employée en dehors des lettres d'affaires; (*of writer, artist*) **to go o. his range,** sortir de son talent; **parsons shouldn't stand o. things,** le clergé ne doit pas se tenir à l'écart, ne doit pas se tenir en dehors du mouvement; **these questions lie o. the scope, o. the purpose, of my address,** ces questions *f* dépassent la portée, le but, de mon discours.

outsider [aut'saidər], *s. F:* **1.** étranger, -ère, profane *mf*; **he's an o.,** (i) il n'est pas du métier, de la partie; (ii) il n'est pas de notre monde; **he's a rank o.,** c'est un intrus dans notre monde; c'est un pleutre. **2.** *St.Exch:* courtier marron; courtier libre; coulissier *m*. **3.** *Turf:* cheval non classé; outsider *m*. **4.** *Fb:* ailier *m*.

outsize ['autsaiz], *s. Com:* **1.** (i) dimension *f*, (ii) pointure *f*, hors série; taille exceptionnelle; dimensions spéciales; (*in men's clothes*) très grand patron. **2.** *attrib.* (*a*) **o. dress,** robe en taille exceptionnelle; **o. shoes,** pointure hors série; (*b*) *F:* **an o. parcel,** un paquet géant, énorme. **3.** personne *f* de taille exceptionnelle; **for outsizes,** pour les grandes tailles.

outsized ['autsaizd], *a.* de taille exceptionnelle; géant, énorme.

outskirts ['autskə:ts], *s.pl.* **1.** limites *f*, (a)bords *m*; lisière *f* (d'une forêt); faubourgs *m* (d'une ville); banlieue *f*, périphérie *f* (d'une grande ville); **the o. of society,** le demi-monde. **2.** approches *f* (d'une ville, etc.).

outsmart [aut'sma:t], *v.tr. F:* surpasser (qn) en finesse; damer le pion à (qn).

outsole ['autsoul], *s. Bootm:* semelle extérieure.

outspan[1] ['autspæn], *s.* (*S. Africa*) **1.** dételage *m*. **2.** campement *m* d'étape.

outspan[2] [aut'spæn], *v.* (**outspanned**) (*S. Africa*) **1.** *v.i.* (*a*) dételer; (*b*) camper à l'étape. **2.** *v.tr.* dételer (les bœufs).

outspoken [aut'spouk(ə)n], *a* (*of pers.*) franc, *f.* franche; carré, rond; **to be o.,** avoir son franc-parler; parler franc; ne pas mâcher ses mots; **he is an o. man,** il aime son franc-parler; **o. criticism,** critique franche.

outspokenly [aut'spouk(ə)nli], *adv.* franchement, carrément, rondement.

outspokenness [aut'spoukənnis], *s.* franchise *f* un peu brusque; franc-parler *m*.

outspread[1] [aut'spred], *a.* étendu, étalé, déployé; **with wings o., with o.** ['autspred] **wings,** les ailes déployées; **with o. sails,** toutes (les) voiles au vent.

outspread[2] ['autspred], *s.* étendue *f*, étalage *m*, déploiement *m*.

outstanding [aut'stændiŋ], *a.* **1.** (*a*) (*of detail, feature, etc.*) saillant; qui fait saillie; (*b*) (*of pers., incident*) marquant; (*of artist, etc.*) hors ligne, éminent; **o. features of a race,** traits dominants d'une race; **there were no o. events in his life,** aucun événement ne marqua dans sa vie; **man of o. personality, of o. merit,** homme au-dessus du commun, de première valeur; **man of o. bravery,** homme brave parmi les braves; **matter of o. importance,** affaire de la première importance. **2.** (*a*) (affaire) en suspens, en cours de règlement; **o. problem,** problème pas encore résolu; (*in election*) **there are three results o.,** il y a encore trois résultats qui ne sont pas connus; (*b*) (compte, etc.) impayé, dû, à recouvrer, à percevoir, en suspens; (paiement) arriéré, en retard; (intérêt) échu, arriéré; **o. debts (due to us),** créances *f* à recouvrer, recouvrements *m*, actifs *m*, créances; **total of bills o. at any time,** encours *m*; **the o. debt,** l'encours de la dette; **o. coupons,** coupons *m* en souffrance; **o. shares,** titres non amortis; **o. notes,** billets effectivement en circulation; **there is nothing o.,** tout est réglé.

outstandingly [aut'stændiŋli], *adv.* éminemment; **he's not o. intelligent,** il n'a pas une intelligence hors ligne.

outstare [aut'stɛər], *v.tr.* fixer (qn) jusqu'à ce qu'il détourne son regard; faire baisser les yeux à (qn).

outstation ['autsteiʃ(ə)n], *s.* station écartée, éloignée; poste éloigné, écarté.

outstay [aut'stei], *v.tr.* **1.** rester plus longtemps que (qn). **2. to o. an invitation,** prolonger sa visite au delà du moment prévu; **to o. one's welcome,** lasser l'amabilité de ses hôtes.

outstep [aut'step], *v.tr.* (**outstepped**) franchir, dépasser, outrepasser (les bornes de qch.).

outstretched [aut'stretʃt], *a.* déployé, étendu; (bras) tendu; **with arms o., with o.** ['autstretʃt] **arms,** les bras ouverts, étendus.

outstrip [aut'strip], *v.tr.* (**outstripped**) (*a*) devancer, dépasser (qn à la course); gagner (qn) de vitesse; *Sp:* distancer (un concurrent); (*b*) surpasser (qn) (en générosité, etc.).

outstroke ['autstrouk], *s. NAm: Mch:* course *f* aller, course avant (du piston).

outswinger ['autswiŋər], *s. Cr:* balle déviante qui s'écarte du batteur.

out-take ['autteik], *s.* **1.** évent *m* (pour fumées, etc.). **2.** coupure (faite dans une narration, etc.).

out-talk [aut'tɔ:k], *v.tr.* (*a*) parler plus que (qn); (*b*) l'emporter sur (qn) (dans un débat).

out-to-out ['auttu'aut], *a. Const: etc:* (dimensions) hors d'œuvre; **o.-to-o. diameter,** diamètre extérieur (d'un tuyau, etc.).

out-turn ['auttə:n], *s.* **1.** production *f* (d'une mine, etc.); rendement net. **2.** résultat *m*.

outvalue [aut'vælju], *v.tr.* surpasser (qch.) en valeur; valoir plus que (qch.).

outvie [aut'vai], *v.tr.* **1.** surpasser (qn en splendeur, etc.); l'emporter sur (un concurrent). **2. they o. each other in studying,** ils rivalisent d'ardeur à l'étude; ils étudient à qui mieux mieux.

outvote [aut'vout], *v.tr.* (*usu. in pass.*) obtenir une majorité sur, l'emporter sur (qn); **we were outvoted,** la majorité des voix a été contre nous; nous fûmes mis en minorité.

outwalk [aut'wɔ:k], *v.tr.* dépasser, devancer, (qn) en marchant; faire preuve de plus d'endurance à la marche que (qn); être meilleur marcheur que (qn).

outward ['autwəd]. **1.** *a.* (*a*) (*of direction, etc.*) en dehors; *Nau:* pour l'étranger; **o. voyage, o. cargo,** voyage *m* d'aller; cargaison *f*, chargement *m*, d'aller; **the o. and the homeward voyages,** l'aller *m* et le retour; **we had a fair wind on the o. passage,** nous avons eu bon vent à l'aller; **o. freight,** fret *m* de sortie; *Rail: etc:* **o. half (of ticket),** billet *m* d'aller; (*b*) extérieur, de dehors; **o. form,** extérieur *m*, dehors *m*; **o. things,** affaires du dehors; *Pharm:* **for o. application,** pour l'usage externe; **to o. seeming,** apparemment; **the o. man,** (i) le corps; (ii) *F:* les vêtements *m*. **2.** *adv.* = OUTWARDS; *Nau:* **o.-bound,** (navire) (i) sur son départ, en partance, sortant; (ii) en route, faisant route, pour l'étranger; *Sch: etc:* **o.-bound course,** école *f* d'endurcissement (en plein air). **3.** *s.* extérieur *m*, dehors *m*.

outwardly ['autwədli], *adv.* **1.** à l'extérieur, extérieurement, au dehors. **2.** en apparence.

outwardness ['autwədnis], *s.* **1.** objectivité *f* (d'un jugement, etc.). **2.** extériorité *f*.

outwards ['autwədz], *adv.* au dehors; vers l'extérieur; **to turn one's feet o.,** tourner les pieds en dehors; **the window opens o.,** la fenêtre s'ouvre en dehors.

outwash ['autwɔʃ], *s.* eaux *fpl* de fusion (d'un glacier); **o. plains,** plaines *f* de lavage proglaciaire.

outwear [aut'wɛər], *v.tr.* (**outwore** [aut'wɔ:r]; **outworn** [aut'wɔ:n]) **1.** user complètement; **outworn doctrine,** doctrine désuète, périmée, vieux jeu. **2.** durer plus longtemps que (qch.); faire plus d'usage que (qch.).

outweigh [aut'wei], *v.tr.* **1.** peser plus que (qch.). **2.** avoir plus d'influence, plus de poids, que (qn); l'emporter sur (qch.).

outwit [aut'wit], *v.tr.* (**outwitted**) **1.** circonvenir (qn); déjouer les intentions, les menées, de (qn); surpasser (qn) en finesse; se montrer plus malin que (qn). **2.** (*of hunted animal or pers.*) dépister (les chiens, la police); mettre (les chiens, la police) en défaut.

outwork[1] ['autwə:k], *s.* **1.** (*a*) *Fort:* ouvrage avancé; travail, -aux *m*, de défense; (*b*) *Arch: Const:* hors-d'œuvre *m inv.* **2.** *Ind: Com:* (*also* **out work**) travail fait à domicile.

outwork[2] [aut'wə:k], *v.tr.* travailler mieux, plus vite, que (qn).

ouzel ['u:zl], *s. Orn:* **1. ring o.,** merle *m* à plastron, à collier; **Alpine ring o.,** merle à plastron des Alpes; **water o.,** cincle plongeur, merle d'eau; **brook o.,** râle *m* d'eau. **2.** *A: & Lit:* merle (noir).

oval ['ouv(ə)l]. **1.** *a.* ovale; en ovale; **o. knob,** bouton à olive; *Anat:* **o. foramen,** trou *m* ovalaire; **to make sth. o.,** ovaliser qch. (*of piston*) **to wear o.,** s'ovaliser. **2.** *s.* ovale *m*; *Mth:* **ovals of Cassini,** ovales de Cassini; **Cartesian ovals,** ovales de Descartes; **o. of a letter,** panse *f* d'une lettre; *Cr:* **the O.,** terrain *m* de cricket à Kennington, Londres.

ovalbumin [ou'vælbjumin], *s. Bio-Ch:* ovalbumine *f.*
ovality [ou'væliti], *s.* forme ovale.
ovalization [ouvəlai'zeiʃ(ə)n], *s.* ovalisation *f,* faux rond (d'un cylindre de moteur, etc.).
ovalize ['ouvəlaiz]. **1.** *v.tr.* ovaliser. **2.** *v.i.* s'ovaliser.
ovalized ['ouvəlaizd], *a.* (cylindre, etc.) ovalisé; **to become o.,** s'ovaliser.
ovally ['ouvəli], *adv.* en ovale.
ovalness ['ouvəlnis], *s.* forme ovale.
ovarian [ou'vɛəriən], *a. Anat: Bot:* ovarien.
ovariectomized [ouvəri'ektəmaizd], *a. Med:* (femme) qui a subi une ovariectomie.
ovariectomy [ouvəri'ektəmi], *s. Surg:* ovariectomie *f.*
ovariole [ou'vɛərioul], *s. Biol:* ovariole *f.*
ovariotomy [ouvəri'ɔtəmi], *s. Surg:* ovariotomie *f.*
ovaritis [ouvə'raitis], *s. Med:* ovarite *f.*
ovary ['ouvəri], *s. Anat: Bot:* ovaire *m*; *Bot:* **inferior, superior, o.,** ovaire infère, supère.
ovate[1] ['ouveit], *a. Nat.Hist:* ové, ovale.
ovate[2] [ɔvət], *s.* **1.** *Rel.H:* eubage *m,* ovate *m.* **2.** (*in Wales, Brittany*) barde *m*; poète, poétesse.
ovation [ou'veiʃ(ə)n], *s.* ovation *f*; **to give s.o. an o.,** faire une ovation, un triomphe, à qn; **to receive an o.,** être l'objet d'une ovation.
oven ['ʌv(ə)n], *s.* **1.** *Dom.Ec:* four *m*; **electric o.,** four électrique; **to put sth., to be, in the o.,** mettre qch., être, au four; **to cook sth. in a slow, quick, o.,** cuire qch. à (un) feu doux, vif; (*of poultry, etc.*) **o. ready,** prêt à rôtir; *Mil:* **field o.,** four de campagne; *F:* **it's like an o. in here, this room's like an o.,** il fait chaud comme dans un four; on se croirait dans un four; cette pièce est une véritable fournaise. **2.** *Ind:* **drying o.,** étuve *f,* four de séchage; **enamelling o.,** étuve, four, à émailler; **japanning o.,** four à vernir; *Metall:* **heat-treat o.,** four de traitement thermique; **reducing o.,** four de réduction.
oven-baked ['ʌv(ə)nbeikt], *a. Ind:* cuit au four; **o.-b. enamel,** émail (cuit) au four.
ovenbird ['ʌv(ə)nbə:d], *s. Orn:* (*a*) *NAm:* fauvette (d'Amérique) couronnée; (*b*) (*S. America*) fournier *m.*
ovenman, *pl.* **-men** ['ʌv(ə)nmən], *s.m. Ind:* fournier.
ovenproof ['ʌv(ə)npru:f], *a.* (plat) allant au four.
ovenware ['ʌv(ə)nwɛər], *s.* vaisselle *f* allant au four.
over ['ouvər], *prep., adv. & s.* (*the uses of* **over** *as an adjunct to verbs such as:* **run over, turn over,** *etc., are illustrated under the respective verbs*)

I. *prep.* **1.** (*a*) sur, dessus, par-dessus; **to spill ink o. the table,** répandre de l'encre sur la table; **to spill ink o. it,** répandre de l'encre dessus, par-dessus; **to spread a cloth o. sth.,** étendre une toile sur, par-dessus, qch.; (*b*) **all o. the north of England,** sur toute l'étendue du nord de l'Angleterre; **famous all o. the world,** célèbre dans le monde entier, par tout le monde; **he has travelled all o. the world,** il a voyagé par le monde entier; *F:* il a visité les quatre coins du monde; **have you been o. the house?** avez-vous visité la maison? **to glance o. sth.,** parcourir qch. des yeux, du regard; **measured o. its widest part,** mesuré sur la partie la plus large; **length o. all,** longueur *f* hors tout, longueur totale; *N.Arch:* longueur de tête en tête; *F:* **to be all o. s.o.,** faire l'empressé auprès de qn, faire des grâces à qn; (*c*) **o. (the top of) sth.,** par-dessus (qch.); **to throw sth. o. the wall,** jeter qch. par-dessus le mur; **to get o. sth.,** passer par-dessus qch.; **we're o. the worst,** le plus mauvais moment est passé; **to read o. s.o.'s shoulder,** lire par-dessus l'épaule de qn; **with his coat o. his shoulder,** le pardessus sur l'épaule; **we heard voices o. the wall,** nous avons entendu des voix de l'autre côté du mur; **to fall o. a cliff,** tomber du haut d'une falaise; **to stumble, trip, o. sth.,** buter contre qch., s'achopper à, contre, qch.; trébucher sur qch. **2.** (*a*) **jutting out o. the street,** faisant saillie sur la rue, au-dessus de la rue; **a court with a glazed roof o. it,** une cour avec un vitrage au-dessus; **his name is o. the door,** il a son nom au-dessus de la porte; **hanging o. our heads,** suspendu au-dessus de, sur, nos têtes; **with his hat o. his eyes,** le chapeau enfoncé jusqu'aux yeux; **his hat o. one ear,** le chapeau sur l'oreille; **to be o. one's ankles in water,** avoir de l'eau par-dessus la cheville; *Mth:* **a o. b.,** a divisé par b; (*b*) **to have an advantage o. s.o.,** avoir un avantage sur qn; **to reign o. a land,** régner sur un pays; **to prevail o. s.o.,** l'emporter sur qn; **he is o. me in the office,** il est au-dessus de moi (au bureau); (*c*) **bending o. his work,** courbé sur son travail; **sitting o. the fire,** assis tout près du feu; couvant le feu; **to have a chat o. a glass of wine,** causer tout en buvant, en prenant, un verre de vin; **story told o. the port** = histoire racontée au moment des liqueurs; **how long will you be o. it?** cela vous prendra combien de temps? quand aurez-vous fini? **to go to sleep o. one's work,** s'endormir sur son travail; **to laugh o. sth.,** rire de qch.; **there was disagreement o. the agenda,** on n'était pas d'accord au sujet de l'ordre du jour; **we had trouble o. the tickets,** nous avons eu des ennuis au sujet des billets. **3.** (*across*) (*a*) **to cross o. the road,** traverser la rue; **the house o. the way,** la maison d'en face; la maison vis-à-vis; **the people from o. the way,** les gens d'en face; **o. the border,** au delà de la frontière; **to live o. the river, the hill,** demeurer de l'autre côté de la rivière, de la colline; **from o. the seas,** de par delà les mers; (*b*) **the bridge o. the river,** le pont qui traverse, le pont sur, la rivière; (*c*) (i) *O:* **to hear sth. o. the radio,** entendre qch. à la radio; (ii) **to order sth. o. the phone,** commander qch. au, par, téléphone. **4.** (*in excess of*) **numbers o. a hundred,** numéros au-dessus de cent; **o. fifty pounds,** plus de cinquante livres; *Post:* **not o. 250 gr.,** jusqu'à 250 gr.; **our company numbered rather o. forty,** nous étions quarante et quelques; **the figures show a decrease of 10% o. last year's,** les chiffres accusent une baisse de 10% sur ceux de l'année dernière; **children o. five (years of age), the o. fives,** les enfants au-dessus de cinq ans; **he's o. fifty,** il a (dé)passé la cinquantaine; **he spoke for o. an hour,** il a parlé pendant plus d'une heure; *prep.phr.* **he receives tips o. and above his wages,** il reçoit des pourboires indépendamment de ses gages, en sus de ses gages; **o. and above what he owes me,** en plus de ce qu'il me doit. **5. o. the last three years wages have diminished,** au cours des trois dernières années les salaires ont diminué; **o. the summer,** pendant tout l'été; **can you stay o. Sunday?** pouvez-vous rester jusqu'à lundi? jusqu'après dimanche?

II. *adv.* **1.** (*a*) sur toute la surface; partout; **studded o. with spangles,** parsemé de paillettes; **to search all o. Paris,** chercher par tout Paris; **famous (all) the world o.,** célèbre dans le monde entier, par tout le monde; **to be all o. dust, mud,** être tout couvert de poussière, de boue; **to ache all o.,** avoir mal partout; souffrir de partout; être courbaturé; **he's French all o.,** il est français jusqu'au bout des ongles; **that's you all o.,** je vous reconnais bien là; (*b*) d'un bout à l'autre; **to read a letter o.,** lire une lettre en entier; **I've had to do it all o. again,** j'ai dû le refaire d'un bout à l'autre, le faire de nouveau, encore une fois, à nouveau; **we've had that story o. before,** il nous a déjà raconté cette histoire tout au long; (*c*) (*repetition*) **ten times o.,** dix fois de suite; **twice o.,** à deux reprises; **o. and o. (again),** à plusieurs, maintes, reprises; maintes et maintes fois; mille fois; à n'en plus finir. **2.** par-dessus (qch.); **to look o. into a garden,** regarder dans un jardin par-dessus le mur; **the ball went o. into the road,** la balle a passé par-dessus la haie, le mur, et est tombée dans la rue; **the milk boiled o.,** le lait s'est sauvé. **3.** (*a*) **to knock sth. o.,** renverser qch.; **a slight knock would send it o.,** un coup léger le renverserait; **and o. I went,** et me voilà par terre; (*b*) **please turn o.!** voir au dos! tournez s'il vous plaît! **to turn sth. o. and o.,** tourner et retourner qch.; **to bend sth. o.,** replier qch.; (*c*) *Nau:* **hard o.!** la barre toute! *Aut:* **to put the wheel hard o.,** braquer jusqu'à la dernière limite. **4.** (*across*) **he led me o. to the window,** il m'a conduit à la fenêtre; **to cross o.,** (i) traverser (la rue, etc.); (ii) faire la traversée (de la Manche, etc.); **to take the ferry o. to the island,** prendre le bac pour aller à l'île; **o. there, o. yonder,** là-bas; **when I was o. there,** quand j'étais là-bas, de l'autre côté; **o. here,** ici; de ce côté; **o. against sth.,** vis-à-vis de qch.; en face de qch.; **o. in France they think otherwise,** en France on est d'une autre opinion; **he is o. from France,** il vient de France; il est en Angleterre, à Londres, etc., en ce moment (venant de France); **ask him o.,** demandez-lui de venir (chez nous); **our friends are coming o. tomorrow,** nos amis vont venir nous voir demain; **to deliver, hand, sth. o. to s.o.,** remettre qch. à qn, entre les mains de qn; *Cr:* **o.!** changez! (c.-à-d. changez de places pour attaquer l'autre guichet); **o. to you,** (i) *W.Tel:* (*usu.* **o.!**) répondez! à vous! (ii) (*on office memorandum, etc.*) à votre attention; (iii) c'est votre tour, c'est à vous. **5.** en plus, en excès; (*a*) **cook for an hour, but allow five minutes o.,** faire cuire pendant une heure, mais ajoutez-y cinq minutes; **children of fourteen and o.,** les enfants qui ont quatorze ans et davantage, et au delà; **three into seven goes twice and one o.,** sept divisé par trois donne deux, et (il reste) un; **nineteen divided by five makes three, and four o.,** dix-neuf divisé par cinq, je pose trois, reste quatre; **he is six foot and a bit o.,** il a six pieds et le pouce; **difference o. or under,** différence en plus ou en moins; (*b*) **you will keep what is (left) o.,** vous garderez l'excédent, le surplus; **I have a card o.,** j'ai une carte de trop, en trop; **I have one card left o.,** il me reste encore une carte; *adv.phr.* **o. and above, he is younger than you,** en outre, et d'ailleurs, il est moins âgé que vous; *St.Exch:* **sellers o.,** excès *m* de vendeurs; *Publ:* **o. copies,** exemplaires *m* de passe; (*c*) **he didn't look o. cheerful,** il n'était pas d'une gaieté folle; **we're not o. busy,** nous n'avons pas trop à faire; (*d*) (*until later*) **to hold o.,** remettre (à plus tard) (une décision); différer (une question); réserver (une coupe en forêt, etc.); **bills held o.,** effets *m* en souffrance, en suspens; *NAm:* **I was invited to stay o.,** on m'a invité à prolonger mon séjour. **6.** fini, achevé; **the storm, danger, is o.,** l'orage est passé, est dissipé; le danger est passé; **the rain is o.,** la pluie a cessé; **the game is o.,** la partie est finie; **the holidays are o.,** les vacances sont terminées; **winter was just o.,** on sortait de l'hiver; **the war was just o.,** la guerre venait de finir; **when dinner, the sermon, is o.,** à l'issue du dîner, du sermon; **when the play is, was, o.,** à la sortie du théâtre; **it is all o.,** c'est fini; tout est fini; **all that is o. long ago,** il y a longtemps que tout cela a pris fin; **it is all o. with me,** c'en est fait de moi; **youthful follies, that's all o.,** les folies de jeunesse, c'est fini, tout ça; **that's o. and done with,** voilà qui est fini et bien fini; *F:* adieu, paniers, vendanges sont faites.

III. *s.* **1.** *Cr:* **six-ball, eight-ball, o.,** série *f* de six, huit, balles. **2.** (*a*) *Com:* **o. in the cash,** excédent *m* dans l'encaisse; **shorts and overs,** déficits et excédents; (*b*) **overs,** (i) *Typ:* main *f* de passe, simple passe *f*; *Publ:* exemplaires *m* de passe; *Typ:* **double overs,** double passe. **3.** *Artil:* coup long. **4.** *Knit: A:* augmentation *f*; **single, double, o.,** jeté *m* simple, double.

overabound [ouvərə'baund], *v.i.* surabonder.
overabounding [ouvərə'baundiŋ], *a.* surabondant.
overabundance [ouvərə'bʌndəns], *s.* surabondance *f.*
overabundant [ouvərə'bʌndənt], *a.* surabondant.
overact [ouvər'ækt]. **1.** *v.tr.* outrer, charger, exagérer (un rôle, sa colère, etc.). **2.** *v.i.* exagérer; *F:* forcer la note.
overacting [ouvər'æktiŋ], *s.* charge *f* (d'un rôle); exagération *f* (dans l'interprétation d'un rôle, dans l'expression de ses sentiments).
overactive [ouvər'æktiv], *a.* trop actif.
overactivity [ouvəræk'tiviti], *s.* suractivité *f.*
overage[1] [ouvər'eidʒ], *a.* (*of pers.*) trop âgé; (*of equipment, etc.*) vétuste; trop vieux, trop usagé, pour servir.
overage[2] ['ouvəridʒ], *s. U.S:* excédent *m,* surplus *m.*
overall ['ouvərɔ:l]. **1.** *a.* (*a*) hors tout; total, -aux; **o. length,** longueur totale, hors tout; **o. dimensions,** dimensions extérieures, hors tout; encombrement *m* (d'une voiture, etc.); (*b*) général -aux, global, -aux, total; **o. efficiency,** (i) efficacité totale; (ii) rendement global; **o. plan,** plan *m* d'ensemble; *El:* **o. amplification, gain,** gain total; **o. loss,** affaiblissement général (du courant). **2.** *s.* (*a*) blouse *f,* sarrau *m, pl.* -aus, -aux, salopette *f*; (*woman's*) tablier *m* blouse; **coat o.,** blouse paletot; (*b*) *pl.* **overalls,** combinaison *f* (de travail); salopette; cotte (bleue), *F:* bleus *mpl* (de mécanicien, etc.).
overanxiety [ouvəræŋ'zaiiti], *s.* **1.** vives inquiétudes, inquiétude extrême, angoisse *f.* **2.** excès *m* de zèle.
overanxious [ouvər'æŋ(k)ʃəs], *a.* **1.** extrêmement, trop, inquiet; angoissé. **2.** exagérément zélé; qui fait des excès de zèle.
overarm ['ouvərɑ:m], *a. & adv.* **1.** (*a*) *Swim:* **o. stroke,** brasse indienne, nage indienne, nage à l'indienne, coupe (indienne); (*b*) *Cr:* **o. bowling,** service *m,* lancement *m,* de la balle au-dessus de la tête; *Ten:* **o. service,** service au-dessus de la tête; **to serve o.,** servir par le haut; (*c*) *Box:* **o. blow,** coup croisé. **2.** *Mec.E:* **o. bracket,** support *m* en porte-à-faux.
overassessment [ouvərə'sesmənt], *s.* surtaux *m.*
overawe [ouvə'rɔ:], *v.tr.* intimider (qn); en imposer à (qn); **overawed admiration,** admiration mêlée de crainte.
overbalance[1] ['ouvəbæləns], *s.* excédent *m* (de poids, de valeur); *Av:* **aerodynamic o.,** (i) charge aérodynamique excessive; (ii) inversion *f* de la charge aérodynamique.
overbalance[2] [ouvə'bæləns]. **1.** *v.tr.* (*a*) peser plus que (qch.); (*b*) surpasser, l'emporter sur (qch.); (*c*) renverser (qch.). **2.** *v.i.* (*a*) (*of pers.*) perdre l'équilibre; *F:* faire la bascule; (*b*) (*of thg*) se renverser; tomber.
overbank ['ouvəbæŋk], *a. Artil:* **o. fire,** tir *m* en barbette.
overbear [ouvə'bɛər], *v.* (**overbore** [ouvə'bɔ:r]; **overborne** [ouvə'bɔ:n]) **1.** *v.tr.* (*a*) renverser, terrasser, passer sur le corps de (son adversaire); (*b*) (i) **to o. s.o.,** **s.o.'s will,** ne tenir aucun compte de qn, des volontés de qn; passer outre aux volontés de qn; (ii) intimider (qn); (*c*) surpasser, l'emporter sur (qch.), avoir plus d'importance que (qch.). **2.** *v.i.* (*of fruit tree, etc.*) porter trop de fruits; (*of animal*) se reproduire trop (souvent).
overbearing [ouvə'bɛəriŋ], *a.* arrogant, impérieux, autoritaire, arbitraire, dictatorial, -aux; **in an o. manner,** avec arrogance, avec raideur, autoritairement, arbitrairement.
overbearingly [ouvə'bɛəriŋli], *adv.* avec arrogance; autoritairement.

overbearingness [ouvə'beəriŋnis], *s.* arrogance *f.*

overbid[1] ['ouvəbid], *s.* (*a*) surenchère *f*, suroffre *f*; (*b*) enchère, offre, exagérée.

overbid[2] [ouvə'bid], *v.* (**overbid; overbidden** [ouvə'bidn]) **1.** *v.tr.* (*a*) enchérir sur (qn, un prix offert); (*b*) *Cards:* forcer sur l'annonce de (qn). **2.** *v.i.* (*a*) (*at sale*) faire one offre exagérée; (*b*) *Cards:* annoncer au-dessus de ses moyens.

overbidder ['ouvə'bidər], *s.* surenchérisseur, -euse.

overbite ['ouvəbait], *s. Dent:* supraclusion *f* (des dents).

overblowing ['ouvəblouiŋ], *s. Metall:* sursoufflage *m.*

overblown[1] [ouvə'bloun], *a.* (*of storm*) passé, dissipé.

overblown[2], *a.* (*of flower*) trop épanoui.

overboard ['ouvəbɔ:d], *adv.* **1.** *Nau:* hors du bord; pardessus (le) bord; **to be washed o.,** être enlevé par une lame; **to heave, throw, sth., s.o., o.,** (i) jeter qch. pardessus (le) bord, à la mer; (ii) *F:* abandonner, lâcher, délaisser (un projet, etc.); (iii) abandonner, trahir (qn); **to fall o.,** tomber à la mer; **man o.!** un homme à la mer! **2.** *F:* **to go o.,** s'emporter; s'emballer (**on sth., for s.o.,** pour qch., qn).

overbook [ouvə'buk], *v.tr. & i.* **to o.** (**a flight, etc.**), louer plus de places qu'il n'y en a de disponibles.

overboot ['ouvəbu:t], *s.* couvre-chaussure *m*, *pl.* couvre-chaussures.

overbought ['ouvəbɔ:t], *a. St.Exch:* (marché) surévalué.

overbridge ['ouvəbridʒ], *s.* passage *m* en dessus, passage supérieur, saut-de-mouton *m*, *pl.* sauts-de-mouton.

overbuild [ouvə'bild], *v.* (**overbuilt** [ouvə'bilt]) **1.** *v.tr.* (*a*) surbâtir, trop bâtir, dans (une localité); (*b*) couvrir (un lot, etc.) de bâtiments. **2.** *v.i.* construire trop de bâtiments; trop bâtir.

overbuilt [ouvə'bilt], *a.* **o. areas,** localités aux constructions trop denses.

overburden[1] ['ouvəbə:d(ə)n], *s.* **1.** surcharge *f* (de travail, etc.). **2.** *Geol: Min:* terrain(s) *m* (*pl*) de couverture, de recouvrement; *Min:* morts-terrains *m* de recouvrement; cosse *f* (d'une carrière d'ardoise); **to remove the o.,** pratiquer la découverte; **thickness of o.,** hauteur *f* stérile.

overburden[2] [ouvə'bə:d(ə)n], *v.tr.* surcharger, accabler (**with,** de); *Fig:* **not overburdened with principles,** peu encombré de principes; **he's not overburdened with brains,** ce n'est pas l'intelligence qui l'écrase, l'étouffe.

overbuy [ouvə'bai], *v.tr.* (**overbought** [ouvə'bɔ:t]) acheter au delà de (i) ses moyens, (ii) ce qu'on pourra écouler; **fear of a shortage made people o.,** la peur d'une disette a amené le public à trop acheter.

overby [ouvə'bai], *adv. Scot:* là-bas.

overcalcine [ouvə'kælsain], *v.tr. Ch: etc:* surcalciner.

overcall[1] ['ouvəkɔ:l], *s. Cards:* (*at bridge*) annonce *f* qui force sur une autre.

overcall[2] [ouvə'kɔ:l], *v.tr. Cards:* (*at bridge*) **1.** forcer sur l'annonce de (qn). **2. to o. one's hand,** *v.i.* **to o.,** annoncer au-dessus de ses moyens.

overcapacity [ouvəkə'pæsiti], *s. Pol.Ec:* surcapacité *f.*

overcapitalization ['ouvəkæpitəlai'zeiʃ(ə)n], *s. Fin:* surcapitalisation *f.*

overcapitalize ['ouvə'kæpitəlaiz], *v.tr. Fin:* surcapitaliser (une société).

overcast[1] ['ouvəkɑ:st], *s.* **1.** *Needlew:* surjet *m.* **2.** *Meteor:* nébulosité *f.*

overcast[2] [ouvə'kɑ:st], *v.tr.* (**overcast**) **1.** obscurcir, assombrir (le ciel, l'esprit); couvrir (le ciel). **2.** *Needlew:* surjeter, surfiler; **to o. a seam,** faire un surjet.

overcast[3] ['ouvəkɑ:st], *a.* **1.** (*a*) *O:* couvert, obscurci, assombri (**with,** de); **his face was o.,** il avait le visage assombri; (*b*) **o. sky,** ciel couvert, sombre, nuageux, obnubilé, assombri; **o. weather,** temps bouché; **the weather is becoming o.,** le ciel se charge, s'assombrit; le temps se couvre. **2.** *Needlew:* **o. stitch,** (point *m* de) surjet *m.*

overcharge[1] ['ouvətʃɑ:dʒ], *s.* **1.** surcharge *f* (d'une mine, d'un accumulateur, etc.). **2.** (*a*) survente *f*; prix excessif; prix surfait; majoration excessive du prix; **to make an o. on sth.,** survendre qch.; *St.Exch:* **fraudulent o.,** extorsion *f*; (*b*) **o. on an account,** majoration d'un compte.

overcharge[2] [ouvə'tʃɑ:dʒ], *v.tr.* **1.** (*a*) surcharger (une mine, un canon, une batterie d'accus); (*b*) **to o. a book with quotations,** surcharger un livre de citations; (*c*) exagérer, charger (un portrait). **2.** (*a*) survendre, surfaire (des marchandises); (*b*) faire payer trop cher un article à (qn); **you have overcharged me two pounds for it,** vous me l'avez surfait de deux livres; **he always overcharges (his customers),** il écorche ses clients; (*c*) **to o. on an account,** majorer une facture; compter qch. en trop sur une facture; **you are overcharging me,** vous me comptez trop.

overcheck ['ouvətʃek], *s. Tex:* (étoffe *f*) à carreaux superposés.

overclothe [ouvə'klouð], *v.tr.* (*p.t.* **overclothed;** *p.p.* **overclothed, overclad** [ouvə'klæd]) surcharger (un enfant, etc.) de vêtements; **to be overclothed,** être trop couvert, trop vêtu.

overcloud [ouvə'klaud]. **1.** *v.tr.* (*a*) couvrir de nuages; (*b*) obscurcir, assombrir; **care had overclouded his brow,** les soucis lui avaient assombri le front. **2.** *v.i.* (*a*) (*of the sky*) se couvrir de nuages; (*b*) s'obscurcir, s'assombrir.

overcoat ['ouvəkout], *s.* **1.** pardessus *m*, paletot *m*; *Mil:* capote *f*; *P:* **wooden o.,** cercueil *m*, *P:* paletot de sapin, dernier paletot. **2.** *Paint:* couche *f* de finition.

overcome[1] [ouvə'kʌm], *v.tr.* (*p.t.* **overcame** [ouvə'keim]; *p.p.* **overcome**) triompher de, vaincre, mettre bas (ses adversaires, etc.); venir à bout de, avoir raison de (qn, qch.); dominer, maîtriser, surmonter (son émotion, etc.); **to o. s.o.'s resistance,** venir à bout de la résistance de qn; **to o. an obstacle,** triompher d'un obstacle, surmonter, vaincre, un obstacle.

overcome[2], *a.* (*a*) **to be o. with, by (sth.),** être accablé de (douleur, etc.); être paralysé par (l'effroi, etc.); être transi de (peur); être gagné par (le sommeil, les larmes); succomber à (l'émotion); **to be o. by a spectacle,** être fortement ému par un spectacle; **I was o. with fatigue,** je n'en pouvais plus; j'étais éreinté; **to be o. by temptation,** se laisser vaincre par la tentation; (*b*) **to be o. by fumes,** être asphyxié par des gaz; **to be o. by the heat,** succomber à la chaleur, être assommé par la chaleur.

overcompensate [ouvə'kɔmpenseit]. **1.** *v.tr.* surcompenser (une inégalité, etc.). **2.** *v.i. Psy:* présenter une surcompensation.

overcompensation ['ouvəkɔmpen'seiʃ(ə)n], *s. Tchn: Psy:* surcompensation *f.*

overcompensatory ['ouvəkɔmpen'seit(ə)ri], *a. Tchn: Psy:* surcompensateur, -trice; surcompensatoire.

overcompound [ouvəkəm'paund], *v.tr. El.E:* hypercompounder.

overcompounding [ouvəkəm'paundiŋ], *s. El.E:* hypercompoundage *m.*

overcompress [ouvəkəm'pres], *v.tr.* surcomprimer.

overconfidence [ouvə'kɔnfidəns], *s.* **1.** confiance exagérée (**in,** en). **2.** suffisance *f*, présomption *f*, témérité *f.*

overconfident [ouvə'kɔnfidənt], *a.* **1.** trop confiant (**in s.o.,** en qn). **2.** suffisant, présomptueux, téméraire.

overcongested [ouvəkən'dʒestid], *a.* (*of street, etc.*) surencombré.

overcongestion [ouvəkən'dʒestʃ(ə)n], *s.* surencombrement *m* (d'une voie, etc.).

overconsumption [ouvəkən'sʌm(p)ʃ(ə)n], *s.* surconsommation *f.*

overcool [ouvə'ku:l], *v.tr.* surrefroidir, trop refroidir.

overcorrect [ouvəkə'rekt], *v.tr. Opt: etc:* surcorriger.

overcorrection [ouvəkə'rekʃ(ə)n], *s. Opt: etc:* surcorrection *f* (chromatique).

overcover ['ouvəkʌvər], *s.* **1.** couvert *m*; **beneath an o. of trees,** sous une voûte d'arbres. **2.** gaine *f*, fourreau *m*, manchon *m* (de protection).

overcritical [ouvə'kritikl], *a.* qui outre la critique; **to be o.,** (i) chercher la petite bête; (ii) se montrer d'un rigorisme exagéré.

overcrop [ouvə'krɔp], *v.tr.* (**overcropped**) *Agr:* épuiser (un champ).

overcrossing ['ouvəkrɔsiŋ], *s.* passage *m* en dessus, passage supérieur (d'une route, d'un chemin de fer); saut-de-mouton *m*, *pl.* sauts-de-mouton.

overcrowd [ouvə'kraud], *v.tr.* (*a*) trop remplir (un autobus, etc.); **to o. a shelf with ornaments,** surcharger un rayon d'ornements; *W.Tel: O:* **to o. the ether,** embouteiller l'éther; (*b*) surpeupler (une ville, une forêt); (*c*) entasser (des voyageurs, etc.).

overcrowded [ouvə'kraudid], *a.* (*a*) trop rempli (**with,** de); (appartement, autobus) bondé (**with people,** de monde); **flat o. with furniture,** appartement encombré, surchargé, de meubles; *Sch:* **o. form,** classe surchargée, pléthorique; **the hall was o.,** la salle regorgeait de monde; (*b*) (*of town*) surpeuplé; (*of forest*) trop dense, surpeuplé.

overcrowding [ouvə'kraudiŋ], *s.* **1.** remplissage excessif, surcharge *f* (d'un autobus, etc.); encombrement *m* (d'une salle, etc.); *W.Tel: O:* **o. of the ether,** embouteillage *m* de l'éther. **2.** surpeuplement *m* (d'une ville, forêt).

overcurrent ['ouvəkʌrənt], *s. El:* surintensité *f*; **o. tripping,** déclenchement *m* à surintensité; **o. relay,** relais *m* à maxima.

overcut[1] ['ouvəkʌt], *s. For:* abattage excessif.

overcut[2] [ouvə'kʌt], *v.tr.* **1.** *For:* trop éclaircir (une forêt). **2.** *Rec:* graver (un disque) trop profondément.

overcutting ['ouvəkʌtiŋ], *s.* **1.** *For:* abattage excessif (dans une forêt). **2.** *Rec:* gravure (de disque) trop profonde.

overdamping [ouvə'dæmpiŋ], *s. Ph:* suramortissement *m* (des oscillations, etc.).

overdecorate [ouvə'dekəreit], *v.tr.* trop fleurir (son style); apporter trop de décorations à (une maison, etc.).

overdeepening [ouvə'di:p(ə)niŋ], *s. Geol:* surcreusement *m* (par les glaciers).

overdetermined [ouvədi'tə:mind], *a.* **1.** trop résolu, trop volontaire. **2.** *Psy:* (*of symbol, etc.*) surdéterminé.

overdevelop [ouvədi'veləp], *v.tr.* **1.** développer à l'excès; trop développer; *Phot:* **overdeveloped negative,** négatif trop poussé. **2.** *Pol.Ec:* surdévelopper.

overdevelopment [ouvədi'veləpmənt], *s.* **1.** développement excessif; *Phot:* excès *m* de développement. **2.** *Pol.Ec:* surdéveloppement *m.*

overdischarge [ouvədis'tʃɑ:dʒ], *v.tr. El:* décharger (une batterie) jusqu'à épuisement; mettre (un accu) à plat.

overdo [ouvə'du:], *v.tr.* (**overdid** [ouvə'did]; **overdone** [ouvə'dʌn]. **1.** outrer (les choses); charger (un rôle, etc.); *F:* **to o. it, things,** forcer la note; exagérer; dépasser la mesure; **type of advertisement that has been overdone,** genre d'annonces dont on a abusé, dont le public est fatigué. **2.** excéder de fatigue, surmener, éreinter (un cheval, etc.); **to o. oneself,** *F:* **to o. it, things,** se fatiguer outre mesure; se surmener; **don't o. it!** pas de zèle! **3.** *Cu:* trop cuire (de la viande).

overdone [ouvə'dʌn], *a.* **1.** outré, excessif, exagéré; dont on abuse. **2.** fourbu, éreinté. **3.** (*of meat, etc.*) trop cuit, surcuit. **4. to be o. with sth.,** avoir trop de qch.

overdoor ['ouvədɔ:r], *s.* dessus *m* de porte.

overdosage [ouvə'dousidʒ], *s.* dosage excessif; surdosage *m.*

overdose[1] ['ouvədous], *s.* trop forte dose; surdose *f*; dose (i) nuisible, (ii) mortelle.

overdose[2] [ouvə'dous], *v.tr.* (*a*) administrer à (qn) des remèdes à trop forte(s) dose(s); **to o. oneself,** prendre des médicaments à trop fortes doses; (*b*) surdoser (un médicament).

overdraft ['ouvədrɑ:ft], *s. Bank:* découvert *m*, solde débiteur; **to allow s.o. an o. of £1,000,** accorder à qn un découvert de £1,000; **to grant a firm o. facilities,** consentir des facilités de caisse à une maison.

overdraught ['ouvədrɑ:ft], *s. NAm:* **1.** = OVERDRAFT. **2.** (*a*) courant d'air descendant; (*b*) *Mch:* courant d'air au-dessus du feu.

overdraw [ouvə'drɔ:], *v.tr.* (**overdrew** [ouvə'dru]; **overdrawn** [ouvərdrɔ:n]) **1.** charger (le portrait de qn); trop colorer (un récit). **2.** *Bank:* **to o. (one's account),** mettre son compte à découvert; tirer à découvert; **overdrawn account,** compte découvert, désapprovisionné; **to be overdrawn at the bank,** avoir un découvert à la banque.

overdress[1] ['ouvədres], *s. Cost:* robe *f* qui se porte pardessus un tricot, etc.

overdress[2] [ouvə'dres], *v.tr. & i.* habiller (qn) avec trop de recherche; **to o. (oneself),** faire trop de toilette; **she's rather overdressed for the occasion,** sa toilette manque de simplicité et de bon ton.

overdrive[1] ['ouvədraiv], *s. Aut:* vitesse surmultipliée, entrainement surmultiplié; surmultiplication *f*; **in o.,** en surmultipliée.

overdrive[2] [ouvə'draiv], *v.tr.* (**overdrove** [ouvə'drouv]; **overdriven** [ouvə'drivn]) **1.** surmener (qn), écraser (un employé) de travail; surmener, éreinter (un cheval); surmener, fatiguer, surcharger (une machine); *El:* surcharger (un amplificateur, etc.), surexciter (un électroaimant, etc.). **2.** *Golf:* dépasser (son adversaire, la pelouse d'arrivée) du premier coup de crosse.

overdue [ouvə'dju:], *a.* (*a*) (*of account*) arriéré, échu, en retard, en souffrance; **interest on o. payments,** intérêts *m* moratoires; **the interest is o.,** l'intérêt n'a pas été payé à l'échéance; (*b*) **the train is (ten minutes) o.,** le train est en retard (de dix minutes); **he's long o.,** il devrait être là depuis longtemps; (*c*) **o. baby,** bébé tardif; (*d*) **o. reforms,** réformes dont le besoin se fait sentir, qui auraient dû être faites, depuis longtemps.

overeat [ouvə'ri:t], *v.i.* (**overate** [ouvə'ret]; **overeaten** [ouvə'ri:tn]) manger avec excès; trop manger.

overeating [ouvə'ri:tiŋ], *s.* excès *mpl* de nourriture, de table.

overelaborate[1] [ouvəri'læb(ə)rət], *a.* trop compliqué; (style littéraire) trop fouillé, trop poussé, tourmenté, tarabiscoté.

overelaborate[2] ['ouvəri'læbəreit], *v.tr.* élaborer (un argument) outre mesure; trop pousser (son style).

overemphasis [ouvər'emfəsis], *s.* accentuation excessive; **to give o. to sth.,** trop appuyer, insister, sur qch.; faire ressortir qch. à l'excès.

overemployment [ouvərim'plɔimənt], *s.* suremploi *m.*

overenthusiastic [ouvərinθjuzi'æstik], *a.* (par) trop enthousiaste; **he's not o. about the plan,** il n'est pas chaud pour le projet.

overequip [ouvəri'kwip], *v.tr.* suréquiper (une usine, etc.).

overequipment [ouvəri'kwipmənt], *s.* suréquipement *m.*

overestimate[1] [ouvər'estimət], *s.* surestimation *f* (du prix, etc.); majoration *f* (de l'actif).

overestimate[2] [ouvər'estimeit], *v.tr.* surestimer, surévaluer (le coût de qch., les talents de qn, etc.); exagérer (le danger, etc.); trop présumer de (ses forces); *Com:* majorer (son actif); **to o. one's own importance,** s'en faire accroire; *Artil:* **to o. the distance, the range,** apprécier long.

overexcite [ouvərek'sait], *v.tr.* surexciter; surexalter (l'imagination, les esprits).

overexcitement [ouvə'rek'saitmənt], *s.* surexcitation *f*; *Med:* surexaltation.

overexert [ouvəreg'zə:t], *v.tr.* surmener, fatiguer outre mesure; **to o. oneself,** se fatiguer; abuser de ses forces; se surmener.

overexertion [ouvəreg'zə:ʃ(ə)n], *s.* surmenage *m*; abus *m* de ses forces.

overexpansion [ouvəreks'pænʃ(ə)n], *s.* expansion excessive.

overexploitation [ouvəreksplɔi'teiʃ(ə)n], *s.* surexploitation *f.*

overexpose [ouvəreks'pouz], *v.tr.* *Phot:* surexposer; donner trop de pose à (un cliché, etc.).

overexposure [ouvəreks'pouʒər], *s.* *Phot:* surexposition *f*; excès *m* de pose; exagération *f* de pose.

overextend [ouvər'ekstend], *v.tr.* étendre, étirer, démesurément; **to o. oneself,** prendre des engagements en excès de ses moyens (financiers).

overextension [ouvəreks'tenʃ(ə)n], *s.* surextension *f.*

overface [ouvə'feis], *v.tr.* *F:* farder, maquiller (un panier de fruits).

overfacing [ouvə'feisiŋ], *s.* *F:* fardage *m* (d'un panier de fruits).

overfall ['ouvəfɔ:l], *s.* (*a*) raz *m* de courant causé par les hauts fonds; (*b*) *Hyd.E:* déversoir *m*, dégorgeoir *m* (d'un étang).

overfamiliar [ouvəfə'miljər], *a.* **to be o. with s.o.,** se montrer trop familier avec qn; prendre des libertés, privautés, avec qn.

overfatigue[1] [ouvəfə'ti:g], *s.* fatigue excessive; surmenage *m.*

overfatigue[2], *v.tr.* surmener, éreinter (qn).

overfault ['ouvəfɔ:lt], *s.* *Geol:* pli-faille *m* inverse (*pl.* plis-failles).

overfed [ouvə'fed], *a.* **1.** suralimenté. **2.** *F:* pansu, ventru.

overfeed[1] ['ouvəfi:d], *a.* *Ind:* **o. stoker,** foyer *m* automatique à alimentation par en dessus.

overfeed[2] [ouvə'fi:d], *v.* (**overfed** [ouvə'fed]) **1.** *v.tr.* suralimenter, surnourrir. **2.** *v.i.* & *pr.* trop manger; se nourrir trop abondamment.

overfeeding [ouvə'fi:diŋ], *s.* suralimentation *f.*

overfish [ouvə'fiʃ], *v.tr.* épuiser (un cours d'eau) par des pêches excessives; faire des pêches excessives dans (des fonds de pêche).

overfishing [ouvə'fiʃiŋ], *s.* épuisement *m* (d'un cours d'eau) par des pêches excessives; surexploitation *f* (des fonds de pêche).

overflight ['ouvəflait], *s.* *Av:* survol *m.*

overfloat [ouvə'flout], *v.tr.* surnager.

overflow[1] ['ouvəflou], *s.* **1.** (*a*) débordement *m*, épanchement *m* (d'un liquide); (*b*) eau débordée; inondation *f.* **2.** (*a*) trop-plein *m inv*; **o. pipe,** (tuyau *m* de) trop-plein; tuyau d'écoulement; déversoir *m* (d'une citerne); dégorgeoir *m* (d'un étang); **float type o.,** trop-plein à flotteur; *Hyd.E:* **o. sill, weir,** vanne *f*; **o. arm of a river,** fausse rivière; (*b*) surplus *m* (de population, etc.); **annexe to accommodate the o. of guests,** annexe pour loger les clients en surplus; (*c*) **o. meeting,** réunion *f* supplémentaire (pour ceux qui ont trouvé salle comble). **3.** *Cmptr:* (i) dépassement *m* de capacité; (ii) débordement *m*; **o. area,** zone *f* de débordement; **o. indicator,** indicateur *m* de dépassement de capacité; **o. record,** article *m* en débordement. **4.** *Pros:* enjambement *m*, rejet *m.*

overflow[2] [ouvə'flou]. **1.** *v.tr.* (*a*) (*of liquid*) déborder de (la coupe, etc.); (*b*) (*of river, etc.*) inonder (un champ); **the river overflowed its banks,** la rivière est sortie de son lit. **2.** *v.i.* (*a*) (*of cup, heart, etc.*) déborder; **room overflowing with people,** salle qui regorge de monde; **cafés overflowing on to the pavement,** cafés débordant sur le trottoir; **to o. with riches,** surabonder de, en, richesses; (*b*) (*of liquid*) déborder, s'épancher; (*of gutter, stream*) dégorger; **the guests overflowed into the other rooms,** les invités se répandaient dans les autres pièces.

overflowing[1] [ouvə'flouiŋ], *a.* débordant; plein à déborder; (*of kindness*) surabondant; **o. wit,** débordement *m* d'esprit; **her o. activity,** son activité débordante; *Th: etc:* **o. house,** salle *f* comble.

overflowing[2], *s.* débordement *m*; **full to o.,** plein à déborder.

overfly [ouvə'flai], *v.tr.* (**overflew** [ouvə'flu:]; **overflown** [ouvə'floun]) (*of hawk, aircraft*) survoler (la proie, une région).

overfold ['ouvəfould], *s.* *Geol:* pli renversé; pli déversé; pli de charriage, de chevauchement; chevauchement *m.*

overfraught [ouvə'frɔ:t], *a.* surchargé (**with,** de).

overfree [ouvə'fri:], *a.* trop familier (**with,** avec); **to be o. in one's conduct,** se conduire trop librement.

overfreight ['ouvəfreit], *s.* **1.** poids *m* en excès. **2.** (*price*) surfret *m.*

overfuelling [ouvə'fjuəliŋ], *s.* *Mch:* suralimentation *f* (en combustible).

overfull [ouvə'ful], *a.* trop plein (**of, with,** de); **o. production,** production *f* excédentaire.

overgeared [ouvə'giəd], *a.* *Aut:* **1. o. fourth,** quatrième vitesse surmultipliée. **2.** (automobile) dont les multiplications sont trop fortes pour la puissance du moteur.

overglaze ['ouvəgleiz], *s.* *Cer:* deuxième glaçure *f.*

overgrow [ouvə'grou], *v.tr.* (**overgrew** [ouvə'gru:]; **overgrown** [ouvə'groun]) **1.** (*of plants, etc.*) couvrir, recouvrir (un mur, etc.); envahir (un terrain, etc.). **2.** (*of child, etc.*) devenir trop grand pour (ses habits, etc.); **to o. oneself,** grandir trop vite.

overgrown [ouvə'groun], *a.* **1.** couvert (**with sth.,** de qch.); **garden, road, o. with weeds,** jardin envahi, recouvert, par les mauvaises herbes; route mangée d'herbes; **o. with ivy,** tapissé de lierre; **path o. with brambles,** sentier encombré de ronces. **2.** (*of child*) trop grand pour son âge; qui a grandi trop vite; **the headmaster was just an o. schoolboy,** le directeur n'était qu'un élève âgé.

overgrowth ['ouvəgrouθ], *s.* **1.** surcroissance *f*; croissance excessive. **2.** couverture *f* (d'herbes, de ronces, de poils, etc.). **3.** *For:* étage supérieur.

overhair ['ouvəhɛər], *s.* jarre *m* (d'une fourrure); **free of, from, o.,** éjarré.

overhand ['ouvəhænd], *a.* **1.** = OVERARM 1. **2.** *Nau:* **o. knot,** demi-nœud *m*, *pl.* demi-nœuds; nœud *m* simple. **3.** *Min:* **o. stopes,** gradins renversés.

overhang[1] ['ouvəhæŋ], *s.* surplomb *m*; porte-à-faux *m inv*; saillie *f*; *Nau:* élancement *m* (de l'accastillage); *Const:* **to have an o.,** porter à faux.

overhang[2] [ouvə'hæŋ], *v.* (**overhung** [ouvə'hʌŋ]) **1.** *v.tr.* surplomber; faire saillie au-dessus de (qch.); avancer, déborder, sur (qch.); pencher sur (qch.); **steep rocks overhung the river banks,** des rochers escarpés surplombaient les bords du fleuve; **ivy overhangs the ruins,** le lierre retombe sur les ruines; **eyes overhung with heavy brows,** yeux surplombés par des sourcils touffus; **a slight mist overhung the forest,** une brume légère flottait sur la forêt; **the threat that overhung us,** la menace qui était suspendue sur nos têtes. **2.** *v.i.* surplomber, faire saillie; **girder that overhangs,** poutrelle qui avance en porte-à-faux.

overhanging[1] [ouvə'hæŋiŋ], *a.* surplombant, en surplomb, en porte-à-faux; (mur) déversé; **o. foliage,** feuillage ombreux; *Civ.E:* **o. footway,** trottoir *m* en encorbellement.

overhanging[2], *s.* surplombement *m*; débordement *m* (au-dessus de qch.); porte-à-faux *m.*

overhaul[1] ['ouvəhɔ:l], *s.* **1.** (*a*) révision *f* (d'une machine etc.); visite *f* (d'une machine, etc., pour réparations); **complete, major, o.,** révision complète, détaillée, générale; (*b*) *Med:* examen détaillé (de qn). **2.** remise *f* en état (d'un véhicule, d'une machine).

overhaul[2] [ouvə'hɔ:l], *v.tr.* **1.** (*a*) examiner en détail, réviser, visiter, démonter (une machine, etc.), vérifier (les machines, contacts, etc.); *Nau:* **to o. the lifeboats,** faire la visite des canots de sauvetage; **to o. the seams,** parcourir les coutures (d'un navire); **to o. the rigging,** repasser le gréement; (*b*) remettre en état, au point, réparer, réfectionner (une machine, etc.); arranger (une montre); **car just overhauled,** auto qui vient d'être révisée. **2.** *Nau:* rattraper, gagner de vitesse, dépasser (un autre navire). **3.** *Nau:* affaler, reprendre (un palan).

overhauling [ouvə'hɔ:liŋ], *s.* **1.** = OVERHAUL[1]. **2.** *Nau:* dépassement *m* (d'un autre navire).

overhead [ouvə'hed]. **1.** *adv.* au-dessus (de la tête); en haut, en l'air; **the planes were flying o.,** les avions volaient au-dessus de nos têtes; **the clouds o.,** les nuages qui flottaient sur nos têtes; **our neighbours o.,** nos voisins *m* d'au-dessus, d'en haut. **2.** *a.* (*a*) aérien; **o. cable,** câble aérien; **o. (cable) transport,** transport *m* par trolley; téléphérage *m*; **o. system,** système suspendu; *Rail:* **o. railway,** chemin de fer aérien; **o. runway, trackway,** monorail aérien, chemin de fer suspendu; **o. contract wire, line,** caténaire *f*; (*b*) *Civ.E: Rail:* **o. crossing,** croisement supérieur; (*c*) *I.C.E:* **o. valves,** soupapes *f* en dessus, en tête; **o.-valve cylinder,** cylindre *m* à soupapes, à arbre à cames, en tête; (*d*) *Metalw:* **o. welding,** soudure *f* en plafond; (*e*) *Art: Phot:* **o. lighting,** éclairage vertical; (*f*) *Ten:* **o. volley,** volley pris au-dessus de la tête. **3.** *a.* & *s.* *Com:* (*a*) **o. expenses, charges, overhead(s),** frais généraux; (*b*) **o. price,** prix *m* forfaitaire. **4.** *a.* *Cmptr:* **o. bit,** bit *m* supplémentaire. **5.** *s.* *Nau:* plafond *m* (d'une cabine).

overhear [ouvə'hiər], *v.tr.* (**overheard** [ouvə'hə:d]) surprendre (une conversation, etc.); **I overheard a few words,** j'ai surpris quelques mots.

overhearing [ouvə'hiəriŋ], *s.* *Tp:* diaphonie *f*, interférence *f.*

overheat [ouvə'hi:t]. **1.** *v.tr.* (*a*) surchauffer, trop chauffer (un four, etc.); (*b*) **to o. oneself,** s'échauffer (trop). **2.** *v.i.* (*with passive force*) (*of engine, etc.*) chauffer.

overheated [ouvə'hi:tid], *a.* (*of engine, etc.*) surchauffé; **to get o.,** (i) (*of pers.*) s'échauffer, prendre chaud; (ii) (*of engine, etc.*) chauffer; **o. brakes,** freins qui chauffent.

overheating [ouvə'hi:tiŋ], *s.* **1.** surchauffe *f*, surchauffage *m*; *Pol.Ec:* **o. of the economy,** surchauffe économique. **2.** *Mec.E:* échauffement (anormal); chauffe *f*, chauffage *m*; *Mch:* **local o.,** coup *m* de feu.

overhung ['ouvəhʌŋ], *a.* **1.** (*a*) en surplomb; surplombant; en saillie; protubérant; (*of crank, etc.*) en porte-à-faux; **o. girder,** poutre *f* en encorbellement, en console; (*b*) avec attaches en dessus. **2.** *Cu:* (*of game*) trop faisandé.

overimpression [ouvərim'preʃ(ə)n], *s.* *Typ:* excès *m* de foulage.

overindulge [ouvərin'dʌldʒ]. **1.** *v.tr.* (*a*) montrer trop d'indulgence envers (qn); gâter (qn); (*b*) se laisser aller trop librement à (une passion, etc.). **2.** *v.i.* **to o. in metaphor,** abuser, faire abus, des métaphores; **to o. in wine,** trop boire.

overindulgence [ouvərin'dʌldʒəns], *s.* **1.** indulgence excessive (**of s.o.,** envers qn). **2. o. in wine,** abus *m* du vin; **o. in food,** excès *mpl* de table.

overindustrialization ['ouvərindʌstriəlai'zeiʃ(ə)n], *s.* surindustralisation *f.*

overinflate [ouvərin'fleit], *v.tr.* distendre (un ballon); trop gonfler (un pneu).

overinflation [ouvərin'fleiʃ(ə)n], *s.* distension *f*; gonflage excessif (d'un pneu).

overinsurance [ouvərin'ʃuərəns], *s.* surassurance *f.*

overinsure [ouvərin'ʃuər], *v.tr.* surassurer.

overinvest [ouvərin'vest], *v.tr.* *Fin:* surinvestir.

overinvestment [ouvərin'vestmənt], *s.* *Fin:* surinvestissement *m.*

overissue[1] ['ouvərisju:], *s.* *Fin:* surémission *f*, émission excessive (de papier-monnaie, etc.).

overissue[2] [ouvər'isju:], *v.tr.* *Fin:* faire une surémission de (papier-monnaie).

overjet ['ouvədʒet], *s.* *Dent:* avancée *f*, surplomb *m* (des incisives supérieures).

overjoy [ouvə'dʒɔi], *v.tr.* transporter (qn) de joie; combler (qn) de joie; ravir (qn).

overjoyed [ouvə'dʒɔid], *a.* transporté de joie; **to be o.,** nager dans la joie; être au comble de la joie, rempli de joie; *F:* sauter au plafond (de joie); **to be o. to see s.o.,** être ravi de voir qn; **I was o. at the news,** cette nouvelle me remplit de joie, me transporta de joie, me mit au comble de la joie; **she was o. that he was coming with her,** elle était tout heureuse qu'il l'accompagnât, de ce qu'il l'accompagnait.

overjumper ['ouvədʒʌmpər], *s.* tricot porté par-dessus d'un corsage, d'une robe.

overkill[1] ['ouvəkil], *s.* *Mil:* (*a*) surmortalité *f*; (*b*) surcapacité *f* de tuer; sursaturation *f* d'armes.

overkill[2] [ouvə'kil], *v.tr.* *Mil:* sursaturer (un objectif).

overlabour [ouvə'leibər], *v.tr.* élaborer (un argument) outre mesure.

overladen [ouvə'leidn], *a.* surchargé (**with,** de).

overland[1]. **1.** *adv.* [ouvə'lænd], par voie de terre. **2.** *a.* ['ouvəlænd], qui voyage par voie de terre; **o. route,** (i) voie *f* de terre; (ii) *Av:* trajet survolant la terre.

overland[2] ['ouvəlænd], *v.tr.* & *i.* *Austr:* conduire (le bétail) à de longues distances.

overlander ['ouvəlændər], *s.* *Austr:* conducteur *m* de bestiaux (qui fait de longs parcours).

overlap[1] ['ouvəlæp], *s.* **1.** recouvrement *m*; (*a*) *Const:* chevauchement *m*, (en)chevauchure *f*, imbrication *f* (des tuiles, etc.); *Geol:* recouvrement (des couches); **to lay tiles with an o.,** enchevaucher, embrocher, des tuiles; **this coat has not enough o.,** cet habit ne croise pas assez; *Carp:* **o. joint,** joint *m* à recouvrement; *Geol:* **o. fault,** faille *f* inverse; *Dent:* **horizontal o.,** débordement *m*, surplomb *m* (des dents supérieures); **vertical o.,** surocclusion *f*; *Mapm: Phot:* **side o.,** recouvrement latéral (des feuilles, des clichés); (*b*) empiètement *m*, chevauchement (d'une opération sur une autre); *Cmptr:* recouvrement, simultanéité *f* d'exécution. **2.** partie chevauchante, débordante.

overlap[2] [ouvə'læp], *v.tr. & i.* (**overlapped** [ouvə'læpt]) **1.** (*a*) recouvrir (partiellement); (*of tiles, slates*) **to o. (one another),** chevaucher; (*b*) (*of roofer*) enchevaucher, embroncher (les tuiles, etc.). **2.** dépasser, outrepasser (l'extrémité de qch.); **cover that overlaps (the edges),** couverture *f* (de livre) qui déborde. **3.** (*of categories, etc.*) se chevaucher; **catalogue that overlaps another,** catalogue qui empiète sur un autre; **aesthetics partly overlaps (with) ethics,** les domaines de l'esthétique et de l'éthique se chevauchent; l'esthétique et l'éthique se confondent en partie.

overlapping[1] [ouve'læpiŋ], *a.* chevauchant, imbriqué, imbriquant; (dents, etc.) qui chevauchent; *Av:* **o. plane,** plan débordant.

overlapping[2], *s.* **1.** = OVERLAP[1]. **2.** *I.C.E:* **o. of explosions,** chevauchement *m* des explosions. **3. o. of two jobs,** chevauchement, empiètement *m*, de deux emplois.

overlay[1] ['ouvəlei], *s.* **1.** (*a*) matelas *m* (de lit); (*b*) (i) couvre-lit *m*, *pl.* couvre-lits; (ii) napperon *m*. **2.** *Min: Geol:* cosse *f*. **3.** *Typ:* hausse *f*, béquet *m*. **4.** (*a*) calque superposé (à une carte, etc., portant des indications supplémentaires); (*b*) *Draw:* cache *m*. **5.** *Cmptr:* (i) segment *m* de recouvrement; (ii) recouvrement *m*.

overlay[2] [ouvə'lei], *v.tr.* (**overlaid**) **1.** (*a*) recouvrir, couvrir (**with,** de); **overlaid with mud,** enduit (d'une couche) de boue; (*b*) *Const:* **to o. a wall,** incruster un mur. **2.** = OVERLIE 2. **3.** *Typ:* mettre des hausses sur (le tympan).

overlaying [ouvə'leiiŋ], *s.* **1.** (*a*) recouvrement *m*; (*b*) *Const:* incrustation *f* (d'un mur). **2.** *Metall:* acérage *m* (de l'acier). **3.** = OVERLYING[2] 2.

overleaf [ouvə'li:f], *adv.* au dos (de la page); **see o.!** voir au verso!

overleap [ouvə'li:p], *v.tr.* (*p.p. & p.t.* **overleaped** [ouvə'li:pt] *or* **overleapt** [ouvə'lept]) **1.** sauter par-dessus (qch.); *Fig:* franchir, dépasser (les bornes de qch.). **2.** *v.i.* sauter trop loin, dépasser son but.

overlie [ouvə'lai], *v.tr.* (**overlay** [ouvə'lei]; **overlain** [ouvə'lein]) **1.** recouvrir, couvrir; *Her:* **charge overlying another,** pièce *f* qui broche sur une autre. **2.** suffoquer (par mésaventure un bébé couché dans le même lit).

overlighting ['ouvəlaitiŋ], *s.* *Phot: etc:* excès *m* d'éclairage.

overload[1] ['ouvəloud], *s.* **1.** (poids *m* en) surcharge *f* (d'un véhicule, plancher, etc.). **2.** (*a*) *Mch: etc:* **o. running,** marche *f* en surcharge; **sudden o.,** à-coup *m* (brusque) de surcharge; coup *m* de collier; *I.C.E:* **o. knock,** cognement dû à une charge excessive; *Cmptr:* **o. level,** puissance *f* limite admissible; (*b*) *El:* surcharge; surélévation *f* d'intensité; **o. capacity,** capacité *f* de surcharge; **o. current,** surintensité *f*; **o. relay,** relais *m* à maxima. **3.** *I.C.E:* excès *m* d'injection, de richesse.

overload [ouvə'loud], *v.tr.* surcharger. **1. roof that overloads the walls,** toiture qui charge trop les murs. **2.** surmener (une machine, le moteur).

overloading [ouvə'loudiŋ], *s.* **1.** surchargement *m*, surcharge *f*. **2.** surmenage *m* (du moteur, etc.).

overlong [ouvə'lɔŋ]. **1.** *adv.* trop longtemps. **2.** *a.* trop long, *f.* longue.

overlook [ouvə'luk], *v.tr.* **1.** (*a*) *A:* regarder par-dessus (une haie, etc.); (*b*) avoir vue sur (qch.); (*of building, etc.*) dominer, commander (un vallon, etc.); (*of window*) donner sur (la rue, etc.); **room overlooking the garden,** chambre sur le jardin; **we are overlooked by our neighbours,** nos voisins ont vue sur nous. **2.** (*a*) oublier, laisser passer (l'heure, etc.); négliger, laisser échapper (une occasion); **I overlooked the fact,** ce fait m'a échappé; **I shall not o. this assurance,** je tiendrai compte de cette promesse; (*b*) fermer les yeux sur (qch.), passer sur (qch.), laisser passer (une erreur); **o. it this time,** passez-le-moi cette fois. **3.** surveiller (un travail); avoir l'œil sur (qn). **4.** jeter le mauvais œil à (qn); jeter un sort sur (qn).

overlooker ['ouvəlukər], *s.* surveillant, -ante; *Ind: O:* contremaître, -tresse.

overlord ['ouvəlɔ:d], *s.m.* suzerain; *Hist:* **Operation O.,** campagne interalliée pour la libération de la France (1944).

overlordship [ouvə'lɔ:dʃip], *s.* suzeraineté *f*.

overly ['ouvəli], *adv.* *Scot: NAm:* trop; à l'excès, excessivement.

overlying[1] [ouvə'laiiŋ], *a.* superposé; (*of stratum*) surjacent; *Her:* brochant.

overlying[2], *s.* **1.** recouvrement *m*. **2.** suffocation *f* (par mésaventure d'un bébé couché dans le même lit).

overman[1], *pl.* **-men** ['ouvəmæn, -men], *s.* **1.** *Ind:* contremaître, -tresse; *Min:* maître-mineur *m*, *pl.* maîtres-mineurs; porion *m*. **2.** *Phil:* surhomme *m* (de Nietzsche).

overman[2] [ouvə'mæn], *v.tr.* **to be overmanned,** avoir un personnel, *Nau:* un équipage, trop nombreux.

overmantel ['ouvəmæntl], *s.* étagère *f* de cheminée.

overmature ['ouvəmətjuər], *a.* trop mûr; (fromage) trop fait.

overmodulation [ouvəmɔdju'leiʃ(ə)n], *s.* *Elcs: W.Tel:* surmodulation *f*.

overmuch [ouvə'mʌtʃ]. **1.** *adv.* (par) trop; à l'excès; outre mesure; **this author has been praised o.,** on a surfait cet auteur; **to exert oneself o.,** se dépenser à l'excès; **I don't care for him o.,** il ne m'est guère sympathique. **2.** *a.* **it's o. work for a child,** c'est un travail excessif pour un enfant. **3.** *s.* *NAm:* excès *m*; (le) trop.

overnice [ouvə'nais], *a.* **1.** (*of pers.*) trop exigeant, dégoûté, renchéri; **to be o.,** (i) trop faire le délicat; (ii) être trop scrupuleux. **2. o. distinction,** distinction vétilleuse, subtile.

overnicety [ouvə'naisiti], *s.* vétillerie *f*, subtilité *f*.

overnight. 1. *adv.* [ouvə'nait], (*a*) la veille (au soir); (*b*) (pendant) la nuit; **the produce arrives o.,** les arrivages ont lieu pendant la nuit; **to stay o.,** rester jusqu'à demain, jusqu'au lendemain; passer la nuit; (*of food*) **to keep o.,** se conserver jusqu'au lendemain; (*c*) **he became famous o.,** il devint célèbre du jour au lendemain. **2.** *a.* ['ouvənait], (*a*) de la veille; (*b*) d'une nuit (de durée); **o. guest,** ami(e) qui passe la nuit (chez qn); client(e) qui passe la nuit (à un hôtel); **o. bag,** sac *m* de voyage; **o. case,** mallette *f*; **o. stay,** séjour *m* d'une nuit, (*in hotel*) nuitée *f*; **o. stop,** arrêt *m* pour la nuit; *Fin:* **o. loans,** prêts *m* du jour au lendemain; (*c*) **o. success,** succès soudain.

overoptimism [ouvər'ɔptimizm], *s.* excès *m* d'optimisme; optimisme béat.

overoptimistic [ouvərɔpti'mistik], *a.* excessivement, par trop, optimiste.

overoxidize [ouvər'ɔksidaiz], *v.tr.* *Ch:* suroxyder.

overpaint [ouvə'peint], *v.tr.* **1.** mettre trop de peinture sur (qch.). **2.** exagérer, charger (une description, etc.).

overparticular [ouvəpə'tikjulər], *a.* (par) trop exigeant, trop méticuleux.

overpass[1] ['ouvəpɑ:s], *s.* *Civ.E:* (i) enjambement *m*; (ii) passage supérieur.

overpass[2] [ouvə'pɑ:s], *v.tr.* **1.** surmonter, vaincre (un obstacle). **2.** surpasser (**s.o. in sth.,** qn en qch.). **3.** outrepasser (les bornes de qch.). **4.** *A:* fermer les yeux sur, laisser passer, sous silence (une erreur, etc.).

overpay [ouvə'pei], *v.tr.* (**overpaid** [ouvə'peid]) surpayer; trop payer (qn); **overpaid workmen,** ouvriers trop payés; **it appears that I am overpaid,** il paraît que je suis payé au-dessus de ce que je vaux, du taux normal.

overpayment [ouvə'peimənt], *s.* **1.** surpaie *f*; paiement *m* en trop; plus-payé *m*, *pl.* plus-payés; (*of taxes*) trop-perçu *m*, *pl.* trop-perçus. **2.** rémunération, rétribution, excessive (d'un employé, etc.).

overpeopled [ouvə'pi:pld], *a.* surpeuplé.

overpitch [ouvə'pitʃ], *v.tr.* **1.** *Cr:* lancer (la balle) trop longue. **2.** outrer, exagérer (ses griefs, etc.).

overpitched [ouvə'pitʃt], *a.* (toit) à pente trop raide.

overplacement [ouvə'pleismənt], *s.* (*a*) superposition *f*; (*b*) *Geol:* terrains *mpl* de (re)couvrement.

overplay [ouvə'plei], *v.tr.* **1. to o. one's hand,** (i) *Cards:* annoncer au-dessus de ses moyens; (ii) *Fig:* essayer de faire quelque chose au-dessus de ses moyens; viser trop haut. **2.** *Golf:* dépasser (la pelouse d'arrivée).

overplus ['ouvəplʌs], *s.* **1.** excédent *m*, surplus *m*, excès *m*. **2.** *Const:* balèvre *f* (d'une assise de maçonnerie). **3.** *Typ:* main *f* de passe; simple passe *f*.

overpolite [ouvəpə'lait], *a.* trop poli; (gens) qui font des embarras, *F:* à chichis.

overpopulated [ouvə'pɔpjuleitid], *a.* surpeuplé.

overpopulation [ouvəpɔpju'leiʃ(ə)n], *s.* surpeuplement *m*, surpopulation *f*.

overpot [ouvə'pɔt], *v.tr.* *Hort:* planter dans un pot trop grand.

overpower [ouvə'pauər], *v.tr.* **1.** maîtriser, dominer, vaincre, subjuguer (un bandit, ses passions); **overpowered with grief,** accablé de douleur; **to be overpowered by superior numbers, by fumes,** succomber sous le nombre, sous l'effet des gaz; être écrasé sous le nombre; **your kindness overpowers me,** je suis confus de vos bontés. **2.** fournir à (une voiture, etc.) une puissance excessive.

overpowering [ouvə'pauəriŋ], *a.* (*of emotion, etc.*) accablant; (*of desire, etc.*) tout-puissant, irrésistible; **o. forces,** forces écrasantes; **o. heat,** chaleur accablante; **o. fumes,** vapeurs suffocantes; **I find her o.,** c'est une femme par trop imposante.

overpraise [ouvə'preiz], *v.tr.* trop louer; outrer l'éloge de (qn); surfaire (un auteur, etc.).

overpressure ['ouvəpreʃər], *s.* surpression *f*; surtension *f* (de la vapeur); surmenage (intellectuel); accumulation *f* (des affaires).

overprint[1] ['ouvəprint], *s.* **1.** (*a*) *Typ:* impression *f* en surcharge; repiquage *m*; surcharge *f* (sur un timbre-poste, etc.); (*b*) *Phot: Cin:* surimpression *f*. **2.** timbre-poste surchargé; **he specializes in overprints,** il fait sa spécialité de timbres-poste surchargés.

overprint[2] [ouvə'print], *v.tr.* **1.** (*a*) *Typ:* imprimer (une rectification, etc.) en surcharge; repiquer (un imprimé, etc.); surcharger (un timbre-poste, etc.); (*b*) *Phot: Cin:* tirer en surimpression. **2.** *Typ:* tirer trop d'exemplaires, un excédent, de (qch.). **3.** *Phot:* surexposer, trop pousser (une épreuve positive).

overprinting ['ouvəprintiŋ], *s.* **1.** (*a*) *Typ:* impression *f* (d'une rectification, etc.) en surcharge; (*b*) *Phot: Cin:* (tirage *m* en) surimpression *f*. **2.** *Typ:* impression, tirage, d'un excédent d'exemplaires. **3.** *Phot:* surexposition *f* (d'une épreuve positive).

overproduce [ouvəprə'dju:s], *v.tr. & i.* surproduire.

overproduction [ouvəprə'dʌkʃ(ə)n], *s.* surproduction *f*.

overproof ['ouvəpru:f], *a.* (*of spirits*) au-dessus de preuve.

overpunch [ouvə'pʌn(t)ʃ], *v.tr.* *Cmptr:* perforer en hors texte; superposer une perforation hors texte à (une fiche).

overpunch(ing) [ouvə'pʌnt(ʃ)iŋ], *s.* *Cmptr:* (i) perforation *f* (d'une fiche) hors texte; (ii) perforation hors texte, double perforation.

overqualified [ouvə'kwɔlifaid], *a.* **to be o.,** avoir plus de qualités, de diplômes, qu'il n'en faut (pour un poste, etc.).

overquire ['ouvəkwaiər], *s.* *Typ:* main *f* de passe; simple passe.

overrate [ouvə'reit], *v.tr.* **1.** surévaluer, surestimer, surfaire (qn, qch.); faire trop de cas de (qch.); exagérer (les qualités de qn); **to o. one's strength,** trop présumer de ses forces; **overrated restaurant,** restaurant surfait. **2.** *Adm:* surtaxer (un contribuable à l'impôt foncier).

overreach [ouvə'ri:tʃ], *v.tr.* **1.** dépasser. **2.** tromper, duper (qn). **3. to o. oneself,** (i) se donner un effort; (ii) trop présumer de ses forces; (iii) être victime *f* de sa propre fourberie. **4.** *v.i.* (*of horse*) forger, (s')attraper, se nerférer.

overreacher [ouvə'ri:tʃər], *s.* *Farr:* cheval *m* qui forge.

overreact [ouvəri'ækt], *v.i.* réagir trop vivement (**to,** à; **against,** contre).

overrefine [ouvəri'fain], *v.tr.* **1.** suraffiner (un métal); suraffiner (le pétrole, etc.). **2.** alambiquer, fignoler (son style, etc.).

overrefinement [ouvəri'fainmənt], *s.* (*a*) afféterie *f*, affectation *f*; (*b*) alambiquage *m*, préciosité *f* (du style).

overridable [ouvə'raidəbl], *a.* (*a*) (*of decision, etc.*) qui peut être annulé; (*b*) *Cmptr:* non prioritaire.

override [ouvə'raid], *v.tr.* (**overrode** [ouvə'roud]; **overridden** [ouvə'ridn]) **1.** (*a*) (*of mounted troops*) ravager, dévaster (une région ennemie); (*b*) passer (à cheval) sur le corps de (qn). **2.** (*a*) outrepasser (ses ordres, etc.); passer outre à (la loi); fouler aux pieds (les droits de qn); **to o. one's commission,** outrepasser ses pouvoirs; commettre un abus de pouvoir, d'autorité; (*b*) avoir plus d'importance que, avoir la priorité sur (qch.); **considerations that o. all others,** considérations qui l'emportent sur toutes les autres; **decision that overrides a former decision,** arrêt qui annule, casse, un arrêt antérieur. **3.** surmener, outrer, harasser (un cheval); **overridden horse,** cheval usé. **4.** *Mec.E: Tch:* (i) occélérer, aller au delà de, dépasser; *El:* survolter; (ii) détourner; brancher (une canalisation, etc.) en dérivation; *El:* dériver, shunter (un circuit). **5.** *v.i.* (*of ends of fractured bone, etc.*) chevaucher.

overrider ['ouvəraidər], *s.* *Aut:* sabot *m* (de pare-choc); barrette (verticale); *F:* banane *f*.

overriding [ouvə'raidiŋ], *a.* principal, -aux; **the o. consideration,** la considération qui prime toutes les autres; **o. principle,** principe premier, auquel il ne saurait être dérogé; *Jur:* **o. clause,** clause *f* dérogatoire.

overrig [ouvə'rig], *v.tr.* (**overrigged**) *Nau:* gréer (un yacht, etc.) au delà de ce qu'il doit porter de voilure.

overripe [ouvə'raip], *a.* trop mûr; (*of cheese*) trop fait;

(*of fruit*) blet, *f.* blette.

overripeness [ouvə'raipnis], *s.* bletture *f* (des fruits).

overrule [ouvə'ru:l], *v.tr.* **1.** *O:* gouverner, diriger (avec une autorité supérieure). **2.** (*a*) décider contre (qn, l'avis de qn); (*b*) *Jur:* annuler, casser (un arrêt, etc.); rejeter (une réclamation); (*c*) passer outre à (une difficulté); passer à l'ordre du jour sur (une objection). **3.** être plus fort que (qn, qch.); l'emporter sur (qn); **fate overruled him,** le destin fut plus fort que lui.

overrun[1] ['ouvərʌn], *s.* **1.** *Typ:* (*at end of line*) chasse *f*; (*at end of page*) report *m*; ligne(s) *f* à reporter. **2.** *Av:* prolongement *m* de piste. **3.** *Aut:* **when the car is on the o.,** lorsque le moteur est entraîné par le véhicule. **4.** *NAm:* **o. (costs),** dépassement *m* du coût estimé.

overrun[2] [ouvə'rʌn], *v.* (**overran** [ouvə'ræn]; **overrun; overrunning**)

I. *v.tr.* **1.** (*a*) (*of invaders*) (i) se répandre sur, envahir (un pays); (ii) dévaster, ravager (un pays); **to o. the land,** faire des incursions dans tout le pays; **the district was overrun with bandits,** toute la région était courue par des bandits; (*b*) **these eastern towns were overrun with soldiers,** ces villes de l'est grouillaient de soldats; **garden o. with weeds,** jardin envahi par les mauvaises herbes; **house o. with mice,** maison infestée de souris; (*c*) (*of floods*) inonder (un champ, etc.). **2.** dépasser, aller au delà de (la limite); **the lecturer overran his time,** le conférencier a dépassé le temps prévu; *Rail:* **to o. a signal,** brûler un signal; **to o. oneself,** être emporté trop loin par son élan; *F: O:* **to o. the constable,** dépenser au-dessus de ses moyens. **3.** (*a*) surmener, fatiguer (une machine); *El:* survolter, surmener (une lampe); (*b*) **to o. oneself,** se surmener (en courant). **4.** *Typ:* reporter (un mot) à la ligne ou à la page suivante; remanier (les lignes); **words that o. the line,** mots qui chassent.

II. *v.i.* **1.** (*a*) *Aut:* (*of car*) (i) rouler plus vite que le moteur; (ii) rouler à roue libre; (*b*) **the bobbin tends to o. after the machine has stopped,** la bobine a une tendance à continuer de tourner après l'arrêt de la machine. **2.** (*of liquid, river*) déborder. **3.** *Typ:* **words that o. (into the margin),** mots qui sortent, chassent.

overrunner [ouvə'rʌnər], *s.* envahisseur *m.*

overrunning ['ouvərʌniŋ], *s.* **1.** (*a*) incursions *fpl*; envahissement *m*, dévastation *f*; (*b*) inondation *f.* **2.** *El:* survoltage *m.* **3.** *Typ:* report *m*; remaniement *m* (des lignes).

oversailing ['ouvəseiliŋ], *a.* (*of course of masonry*) débordant.

overscrupulous [ouvə'skru:pjuləs], *a.* scrupuleux jusqu'à l'excès.

overseas. 1. *a.* ['ouvəsi:z] (colonie, commerce, etc.) d'outre-mer; **o. debt,** dette extérieure. **2.** *adv.* [ouvə'si:z] par delà les mers; **from o.,** d'outre-mer, de par delà les mers.

oversee [ouvə'si:], *v.tr.* (**oversaw** [ouvə'sɔ:]; **overseen** [ouvə'si:n]) surveiller, avoir l'œil sur (un atelier, etc.).

overseer ['ouvəsiər], *s.* **1.** surveillant, -ante; inspecteur, -trice; *Ind:* contremaître, -tresse; chef *m* d'atelier; *Civ.E:* brigadier *m*; *Typ:* prote *m*; **case o.,** prote à la composition; **o. of the machine room,** prote aux machines. **2.** *Hist:* **o. of the poor** = directeur *m* du Bureau de bienfaisance.

oversell [ouvə'sel], *v.tr.* **1.** vendre trop de (qch.); *St.Exch:* vendre plus de (qch.) qu'on ne peut livrer. **2.** exagérer les mérites de, surfaire (qch.).

oversensitive [ouvə'sensitiv], *a.* hypersensible.

oversensitiveness [ouvə'sensitivnis], *s.* hypersensibilité *f.*

overset [ouvə'set], *v.* (*p.t. & p.p.* **overset**) **1.** *v.tr.* (*a*) *A:* renverser (un vase); faire verser (une voiture); (faire) chavirer (un canot); culbuter (qn); (*b*) mettre à bas (un tyran, etc.); renverser (le gouvernement). **2.** *v.i. A:* (*of vase, etc.*) se renverser; (*of vehicle*) verser.

oversew ['ouvəsou], *v.tr.* (**oversewn** ['ouvəsoun]) *Needlew:* surjeter; assembler (deux pièces) au point de surjet; surfiler (un bord).

oversexed [ouvə'sekst], *a.* à tendances sexuelles exagérées.

overshadow [ouvə'ʃædou], *v.tr.* **1.** ombrager; couvrir de son ombre; **clouds that o. the sky,** nuages qui obscurcissent le ciel. **2.** éclipser (qn); surpasser (qch., qn) en éclat.

overshoe ['ouvəʃu:], *s.* couvre-chaussure *m, pl.* couvre-chaussures; galoche *f*; **rubber overshoes,** caoutchoucs *m.*

overshoot[1] ['ouvəʃu:t], *s.* **1.** = OVERSHOOTING 1. **2.** *Hyd.E:* déversoir *m.* **3.** *Elcs: W.Tel:* suroscillation(s) *f(pl)*; **o. distortion,** distorsion *f* par surmodulation.

overshoot[2] [ouvə'ʃu:t], *v.tr.* (*p.t. & p.p.* **overshot** [ouvə'ʃɔt]) **1.** dépasser, outrepasser (le point d'arrêt); (*of shot, gun*) porter au delà de (qch.); **to o. the mark,** (i) dépasser le but, aller au delà du but; (ii) *Fig:* dépasser les bornes; *Av:* **to o. the runway,** *v.i.* **to o.,** (i) atterrir, se présenter, trop long (sur la piste); (ii) remettre les gaz (au lieu d'atterrir); *Fig:* **to o. oneself,** être victime de sa propre fourberie. **2.** trop chasser sur (une terre); dépeupler (une chasse).

overshooting [ouvə'ʃu:tiŋ], *s.* **1.** dépassement *m* (d'un point d'arrêt, etc.); *Artil: etc:* tir long; *Av:* (i) présentation trop longue (sur la piste); (ii) remise *f* de gaz. **2.** chasse excessive (du gibier); dépeuplement *m* (d'un terrain de chasse).

overshot ['ouvəʃɔt]. **1.** *a.* (*a*) *Hyd.E:* **o. wheel,** roue *f* (à augets) en dessus; roue à auges, augets, godets; (*b*) *Tex:* **o. pick,** duite *f* d'endroit; (*c*) (chien) dont la mâchoire supérieure fait saillie. **2.** *s. Min:* souricière *f.*

overside. 1. *adv.* [ouvə'said], *Nau:* **to load, unload, a vessel o.,** charger, décharger, un bâtiment par allèges. **2.** *a.* ['ouvəsaid], **o. loading,** chargement *m* par allèges; **o. delivery,** livraison *f* sous palan.

oversight ['ouvəsait], *s.* **1.** oubli *m*, omission *f*, bévue *f*, inadvertance *f*; **through, by, an o.,** par mégarde; par étourderie; par inadvertance; par oubli; par négligence. **2.** surveillance *f*; **rights of o. of a commission,** droits de tutelle *f* d'une commission.

oversimplification ['ouvəsimplifi'keiʃ(ə)n], *s.* simplification excessive.

oversimplify [ouvə'simplifai], *v.tr.* trop simplifier (un problème).

oversize ['ouvəsaiz], *s.* **1.** *Mec.E: etc:* (i) surdimension *f*; (ii) surépaisseur *f*; **o. in tyres,** surprofil *m* de bandages; **o. tyre,** bandage surprofilé; *I.C.E:* **o. piston,** piston surprofilé; piston à cote de réalésage. **2.** refus *m* de crible.

oversized ['ouvəsaizd], *a.* au-dessus des dimensions normales.

overskirt ['ouvəskə:t], *s.* jupe extérieure.

overslaugh[1] ['ouvəslɔ:], *s.* **1.** *Mil:* exemption *f* de service (d'un soldat affecté à un service plus urgent). **2.** *NAm:* allaise *f* (qui entrave la navigation).

overslaugh[2], *v.tr.* **1.** *Mil:* exempter (un soldat) de service en l'affectant à un autre service. **2.** *NAm:* passer par-dessus le dos, faire un passe-droit, à (qn).

oversleep [ouvə'sli:p], *v.i. & pr.* (*p.t. & p.p.* **overslept** [ouvə'slept]) **to o. (oneself),** dormir trop longtemps; s'éveiller après l'heure.

oversleeve ['ouvəsli:v], *s.* fausse manche; manchette *f*; manche en lustrine; garde-manche *m, pl.* garde-manches.

oversolicitous [ouvəsə'lisitəs], *a.* trop occupé (**about,** de).

oversoul ['ouvəsoul], *s. Rel:* (l')âme universelle.

oversow [ouvə'sou], *v.tr.* (*p.t.* **oversowed** [ouvə'soud]; *p.p.* **oversowed, oversown** [ouvə'soun]) sursemer (un champ, une graine).

overspecialization [ouvəspeʃəlai'zeiʃ(ə)n], *s.* spécialisation excessive.

overspeed[1], *s.* excès *m* de vitesse; vitesse excessive; *Mec.E: etc:* survitesse *f*; **o. gear,** modérateur *m* de vitesse; **o. test,** essai *m* de survitesse.

overspeed[2] [ouvə'spi:d], *v.i.* (*of vehicle*) rouler en survitesse; (*of engine*) tourner en survitesse.

overspeeding [ouvə'spi:diŋ], *s.* excès *m* de vitesse; allure, vitesse, excessive.

overspend [ouvə'spend], *v.tr.* (*p.t. & p.p.* **overspent** [ouvə'spent]) dépenser au delà de (ses moyens, etc.); **to o. one's income by £1,000,** dépenser £1,000 de plus que le montant de ses revenus; *Fin:* **amount overspent,** découvert *m.*

overspill ['ouvəspil], *s.* surplus *m*, déversement *m*, de population; **Siberia was an o. area for the western cities,** la Sibérie était un déversoir pour les grandes villes de l'ouest; **o. town,** ville *f* servant à décongestionner une agglomération surpeuplée.

overspread [ouvə'spred], *v.tr.* (*p.t. & p.p.* **overspread**) **1.** *Lit:* (re)couvrir (**with,** de); **the snow o. the plain,** la neige recouvrait la plaine; **jealousy o. with hatred,** jalousie doublée de haine; **contempt o. with blandness,** mépris caché sous l'affabilité. **2.** se répandre, s'étendre, sur (qch.); (*of floods, light, etc.*) inonder (qch.); **a mist o. the forest,** une brume planait sur la forêt.

overspun ['ouvəspʌn], *a. Mus:* **o. string,** corde filée.

overstaffed [ouvə'sta:ft], *a.* qui a un personnel trop nombreux, du superflu de main-d'œuvre.

overstate [ouvə'steit], *v.tr.* exagérer (les faits, etc.); **I am neither overstating nor understating the case,** je n'exagère ni dans un sens ni dans l'autre; **overstated argument,** argument outré.

overstatement [ouvə'steitmənt], *s.* **1.** exagération *f*; hyperbole *f.* **2.** récit exagéré; affirmation exagérée.

overstay [ouvə'stei], *v.tr.* dépasser (son congé, etc.).

oversteer [ouvə'stiər], *v.i. Aut:* survirer.

overstep [ouvə'step], *v.tr.* (**overstepped** [ouvə'stept]) franchir, outrepasser, dépasser (les bornes de qch., etc.); **to o. the truth,** outrepasser les bornes de la vérité; *F:* **don't o. the mark,** n'y allez pas trop fort.

overstimulation ['ouvəstimju'leiʃ(ə)n], *s. Med: etc:* surexcitation *f.*

overstitch ['ouvəstitʃ], *s. Needlew:* point *m* de surjet.

overstock[1] ['ouvəstɔk], *s.* surabondance *f*; encombrement *m*, surcharge *f* (de marchandises); *Com:* surstock *m.*

overstock[2] [ouvə'stɔk], *v.tr.* (*a*) encombrer (le marché, etc.) (**with,** de); (*b*) trop meubler (une ferme) de bétail; entretenir un cheptel au delà de ce que (la ferme) peut nourrir; surcharger (un étang) de poissons; **to o. a shop,** encombrer un magasin de stocks.

overstocked [ouvə'stɔkt], *a.* encombré, surchargé (**with,** de); (peuplement forestier) trop dense.

overstocking [ouvə'stɔkiŋ], *s.* encombrement *m* (de marchandises); approvisionnement exagéré.

overstoping [ouvə'stoupiŋ], *s. Min:* abattage *m* en gradins renversés.

overstrain[1] ['ouvəstrein], *s.* **1.** *Mec.E: etc:* tension excessive; surtension *f.* **2.** surmenage *m* (de qn).

overstrain[2] [ouvə'strein], *v.tr.* **1.** surtendre (un câble, etc.). **2.** (*a*) outrer; surmener (qn, un cheval); **to o. oneself with working,** se surmener (à travailler); (*b*) **to o. an argument,** pousser trop loin un argument; **to o. the truth,** donner une entorse à la vérité.

overstress[1] ['ouvəstres], *s. Mec.E:* surcharge *f.*

overstress[2] [ouvə'stres], *v.tr.* **1.** *Mec.E:* surcharger (une transmission, etc.). **2.** trop insister sur (un détail, etc.).

overstride [ouvə'straid], *v.tr.* (**overstrode** [ouvə'stroud]; **overstridden** [ouvə'stridn]) enjamber (qch.).

overstrung, *a.* **1.** [ouvə'strʌŋ] (*of pers.*) surexcité, énervé; dans un état de surexcitation nerveuse. **2.** ['ouvəstrʌŋ], **o. piano,** piano *m* oblique (à cordes croisées).

oversubscribe [ouvəsəb'skraib], *v.tr. Fin:* surpasser, sursouscrire (une émission).

oversubscription [ouvəsəb'skripʃ(ə)n], *s. Fin:* **o. of a loan,** sursouscription *f* à un emprunt, dépassement *m* d'un emprunt.

overswarm [ouvə'swɔ:m]. **1.** *v.tr.* (*of troops, etc.*) se répandre sur (un pays). **2.** *v.i.* (*of bees*) essaimer au delà de la capacité de la ruche.

overswing ['ouvəswiŋ], *s. Ph:* suroscillation *f* (de l'aiguille aimantée).

overswollen [ouvə'swoulən], *a.* **1.** (cœur) gonflé. **2.** (fleuve) enflé.

overt [ou'və:t], *a.* patent, évident, manifeste; *Jur:* **o. act,** acte *m* manifeste; **market o.,** marché public.

overtake [ouvə'teik], *v.tr.* (**overtook** [ouvə'tuk]; **overtaken** [ouvə'teikn]) **1.** (*a*) rattraper, atteindre (qn); **to hurry (in order) to o. s.o.,** allonger le pas pour rejoindre qn; **to o. arrears of work,** rattraper le retard dans son travail; se remettre au courant; **demand has overtaken supply,** la demande a rattrapé l'offre; (*b*) doubler, dépasser, devancer, gagner de vitesse, *F:* gratter (un concurrent, une voiture, un bateau). **2.** (*of accident*) arriver à (qn); (*of evil fate, etc.*) s'abattre sur (qn); **the calamity that has overtaken us,** le malheur qui nous frappe; **the catastrophe overtook many people,** la catastrophe atteignit beaucoup de gens; **overtaken by a storm,** surpris par un orage; **darkness overtook us,** la nuit nous gagna. **3.** *F: A:* **overtaken in drink,** ivre.

overtaking [ouvə'teikiŋ], *s.* dépassement *m*; **o. signal,** signal *m* pour dépasser; *Aut:* **o. lane,** piste *f* de doublage; *P.N:* **no o.,** défense de doubler.

overtask [ouvə'ta:sk], *v.tr.* surcharger, accabler, (qn) de travail; surmener (qn); **to o. one's strength,** se surmener (à marcher, à travailler, etc.), abuser de ses forces.

overtax [ouvə'tæks], *v.tr.* **1.** (*a*) pressurer (le peuple); accabler (la nation) sous les impôts; (*b*) surcharger (qn); **to o. one's strength,** se surmener; abuser de ses forces; **to o. a horse's strength,** trop exiger (des forces) d'un cheval; *F:* **he doesn't o. his brains,** il ne se fatigue pas les méninges. **2.** *Adm:* surtaxer, surimposer (qn).

overtaxation [ouvətæk'seiʃ(ə)n], *s.* surchargement *m* d'impôts, surimposition *f.*

over-the-counter ['ouvəðə'kauntər], *a.* **o.-t.-c. sales,** ventes *f* au comptant; **o.-t.-c. medicines,** médicaments vendus sans ordonnance; *NAm:* **o.-t.-c. shares,** titres *m* hors cote.

overthrow[1] ['ouvəθrou], *s.* **1.** subversion *f*, chute *f*, renversement *m* (d'un empire); ruine *f*, défaite *f* (de qn, d'un projet); déroute *f* (des projets de qn). **2.** *Cr:* balle *f* qui dépasse le guichet.

overthrow[2] [ouvə'θrou], *v.tr.* (**overthrew** [ouvə'θru:]; **overthrown** [ouvə'θroun]) **1.** renverser (une table, etc.); abattre, enfoncer (un adversaire). **2.** défaire, vaincre (qn); abattre, mettre à bas (un empire); mettre par terre, renverser, culbuter, démolir (un ministère, etc.); ruiner, réduire à néant (les projets de qn).

overthrower [ouvə'θrouər], *s.* vainqueur *m*, renverseur, -euse, démolisseur, -euse (d'un empire, d'un ministère, etc.).

overthrust[1] ['ouvəθrʌst], *s. Geol:* chevauchement *m*, recouvrement *m*; **o. fault,** faille *f* de chevauchement, de charriage.

overthrust[2] [ouvə'θrʌst], *v.i.* (*p.t. & p.p.* **overthrust**) *Geol:* (*of strata*) chevaucher.

overthrusting [ouvə'θrʌstiŋ], *s. Geol:* chevauchement *m*, charriage *m*.

overtime[1] ['ouvətaim]. **1.** *s. Ind:* (*a*) heures *fpl* supplémentaires (de travail); surtemps *m*; **an hour of o., an hour's o.,** une heure supplémentaire; (*b*) **wages, including o.,** le salaire, y compris le paiement d'heures supplémentaires; **all o. will be paid weekly,** tous les frais de travail hors d'heures seront payés par semaine; (*c*) *Sp:* prolongation *f* (en cas de match nul). **2.** *adv.* **to work o.,** faire des heures supplémentaires.

overtime[2] [ouvə'taim], *v.tr.* surestimer le temps de (cuisson, pose photographique, etc.); *Phot:* surexposer (un cliché, etc.).

overtire [ouvə'taiər], *v.tr.* surmener (qn); **to o. oneself,** se fatiguer outre mesure; se surmener.

overtly [ou'və:tli], *adv.* manifestement, ouvertement, sans se cacher; à découvert.

overtness [ou'və:tnis], *s.* franchise *f*.

overtone[1] ['ouvətoun], *s.* **1.** *Mus:* harmonique *m*; **harmonic overtones,** harmoniques supérieurs. **2. the phrase bears an o. of disparagement,** la phrase comporte un soupçon, un rien, de dénigrement; **there are overtones of sadness in his poems,** il y a des nuances de tristesse dans ses poèmes.

overtone[2] [ouvə'toun], *v.tr. Phot:* pousser trop avant, trop pousser, le virage (d'une épreuve).

overtop [ouvə'tɔp], *v.tr.* (**overtopped** [ouvə'tɔpt]) **1.** s'élever au-dessus de (qn, qch.); dépasser (qn, qch.) en hauteur; dominer (qch.); **he will soon have overtopped his father,** il aura bientôt dépassé son père; il sera bientôt plus grand que son père. **2.** surpasser (qn); l'emporter sur (qn).

overtrain [ouvə'trein], *v.tr. & i. Sp:* surentraîner (qn); (s')épuiser par un entraînement trop sévère.

overtraining [ouvə'treiniŋ], *s. Sp:* surentraînement *m*.

overtrick ['ouvətrik], *s. Cards:* levée *f* en plus de la demande.

overtrump [ouvə'trʌmp], *v.tr. & i. Cards:* surcouper; (*of player*) **to be overtrumped,** être en surcoupe.

overtrumping [ouvə'trʌmpiŋ], *s. Cards:* surcoupe *f*.

overture ['ouvətjuər], *s.* **1.** ouverture *f*, offre *f*; **to make overtures to s.o.,** faire des ouvertures à qn; **overtures of peace,** ouvertures de paix; **his overtures met with no response,** on ne répondit pas à ses initiatives *f*, à ses propositions *f*. **2.** *Mus:* ouverture (d'opéra, etc.).

overturn [ouvə'tə:n]. **1.** *v.tr.* (*a*) renverser (une table, etc.); mettre (qch.) sens dessus dessous; faire verser (une voiture); faire chavirer (un canot); **easily overturned,** versable; (*b*) abattre, mettre à bas (un empire); renverser, mettre par terre, culbuter, démolir (un ministère); ruiner, réduire à néant (les projets de qn). **2.** *v.i.* (*a*) se renverser; (*of vehicle*) verser; (*of boat*) chavirer; (*b*) (*turn turtle*) *Aut: Av: Nau:* capoter; faire capot(age). **3. to o. a screw,** forcer une vis.

overturning [ouvə'tə:niŋ], *s.* **1.** renversement *m* (d'une table, voiture, etc.); chavirement *m*, chavirage *m* (d'un canot). **2.** capotage *m* (d'une voiture, d'un canot, d'un avion).

overtype ['ouvətaip], *a. El:* (armature, dynamo) (du) type supérieur; *Mch:* **o. engine,** machine superposée.

overuse[1] [ouvə'ju:s], *s.* emploi excessif (**of,** de).

overuse[2] [ouvə'ju:z], *v.tr.* faire un emploi excessif de (qch.).

overvaluation ['ouvəvælju'eiʃ(ə)n], *s.* **1.** *Com:* surestimation *f*, surévaluation *f*; majoration *f* (de l'actif, etc.). **2.** trop haute idée (des mérites de qn, etc.).

overvalue[1] ['ouvəvælju:], *s.* survaleur *f* (des monnaies).

overvalue[2] [ouvə'vælju:], *v.tr.* **1.** *Com:* surestimer, majorer (l'actif, etc.); estimer (un objet) au-dessus de sa valeur. **2.** faire trop de cas de (la capacité de qn).

overvoltage ['ouvəvoultidʒ], *s. El:* surtension *f*; **o. tripping,** fonctionnement *m* à surtension; **o. protection,** protection *f* contre les surtensions.

overwater[1] ['ouvəwɔ:tər], *a. Av:* (vol, etc.) au-dessus de l'eau.

overwater[2] [ouvə'wɔ:tər], *v.tr. Hort:* arroser à l'excès.

overweening [ouvə'wi:niŋ], *a.* (*of pers.*) outrecuidant, présomptueux, suffisant; **o. ambition,** ambition excessive, sans bornes.

overweight[1]. **1.** *s.* ['ouvəweit], (*a*) surpoids *m*; poids *m* en excès; poids fort; (*b*) excédent *m* (de bagages). **2.** *a.* [ouvə'weit], (*a*) au-dessus du poids réglementaire; **parcel 50 gr. o.,** colis qui excède, dépasse, de 50 gr. le poids réglementaire; qui a un excédent de 50 gr.; **o. luggage,** excédent *m* de bagages; *Num:* **o. coin,** pièce forte; (*b*) au-dessus du poids normal; **he's rather o.,** il pèse trop; il a de l'embonpoint.

overweight[2] [ouvə'weit], *v.tr.* surcharger (un bateau, mulet, etc.) (**with,** de); **to o. a book with details,** surcharger un livre de détails; **the tower, by its height, overweights the main building,** la tour, par sa hauteur, écrase le corps de bâtiment; **the author has overweighted the economic problem,** l'auteur a donné trop d'importance au problème économique.

overwhelm [ouvə'(h)welm], *v.tr.* **1.** ensevelir (une ville dans la lave, etc.); submerger (un champ, etc.); **Pompeii was overwhelmed by dust and ashes,** Pompéi fut ensevelie sous les poussières et les cendres. **2.** (*a*) écraser, accabler (l'ennemi, etc.); (*b*) **to be overwhelmed with work,** être accablé, débordé, de travail; (*c*) combler (qn de bontés, etc.); confondre (qn de honte, etc.); **you o. me with your praises,** vous me confondez par vos louanges; **I am overwhelmed by your kindness,** je suis confus de vos bontés; **they were overwhelmed at the news,** cette nouvelle les a atterrés; **overwhelmed with joy,** au comble de la joie.

overwhelming[1] [ouvə'(h)welmiŋ], *a.* irrésistible; accablant; **o. misfortune,** malheur anéantissant, atterrant; **o. majority,** majorité écrasante.

overwhelming[2], *s.* **1.** ensevelissement *m* (sous la lave, etc.). **2.** écrasement *m*.

overwhelmingly [ouvə'(h)welmiŋli], *adv.* irrésistiblement; **o. polite,** d'une politesse accablante.

overwind[1] [ouvə'waind], *v.tr.* (*p.t. & p.p.* **overwound** [ouvə'waund]) **1. to o. a watch,** trop remonter une montre; trop tendre le grand ressort. **2.** *Min:* **to o. the cage,** envoyer la cage aux molettes.

overwind[2] ['ouvəwaind], **overwinding** [ouvə'waindiŋ], *s. Min:* envoi *m*, mise *f*, aux molettes; **overwind gear,** évite-molettes *m inv*.

overwinder [ouvə'waindər], *s. Min:* évite-molettes *m inv*.

overwinter [ouvə'wintər], *v.i.* (*of bird, etc.*) hiverner.

overwork[1] ['ouvəwə:k, ouvə'wə:k], *s.* **1.** surmenage *m*; travail *m* outre mesure; **he has broken down through o.,** il s'est détraqué la santé à force de travailler; **he died of o.,** il s'est tué de travail; *Med:* **suffering from o.,** très fatigué. **2.** *occ.* travail *m* en plus.

overwork[2] [ouvə'wə:k]. **1.** *v.tr.* (*a*) surmener (qn); outrer (un cheval, etc.); surcharger (qn) de travail; **he doesn't o. himself,** *F:* il ne se foule pas la rate; il ne se casse rien; (*b*) **to o. a literary device,** se servir trop souvent d'un effet de style; abuser d'un truc. **2.** *v.i.* se surmener; travailler outre mesure. **3.** *v.tr. Art: etc:* orner la surface de (qch.).

overworking [ouvə'wə:kiŋ], *s.* **1.** surmenage *m*. **2.** ornementation *f* de la surface (de qch.).

overwrite [ouvə'rait], *v.tr.* **1.** écrire sur (une écriture); *Cmptr:* superposer une écriture à, recouvrir (des informations périmées). **2.** (*a*) **this subject has been overwritten,** on a trop écrit sur ce sujet; (*b*) **author who has overwritten himself,** auteur qui a trop écrit, a épuisé sa veine, son talent.

overwrought [ouvə'rɔ:t], *a.* **1.** trop travaillé; (*of literary work*) tourmenté. **2.** (*of pers.*) excédé (de fatigue); surmené; **o. senses,** sens surexcités.

overzealous [ouvə'zeləs], *a.* trop zélé; **to be o.,** pécher par excès de zèle.

ovibos ['ouvibɔs], *s. Z:* ovibos *m*; bœuf musqué.

ovibovine [ouvi'bouvain], *a. Z:* oviboviné, ovibosiné.

ovicapsule [ouvi'kæpsju:l], *s. Nat.Hist:* ovicapsule *f*.

ovicell ['ouvisel], *s. Biol:* ovicelle *f*.

Ovid ['ɔvid], *Pr.n.m. Lt.Lit:* Ovide.

Ovidae ['ouvidi:], *s.pl. Z:* ovidés *m*.

Ovidian [ɔ'vidiən], *a. Lt.Lit:* ovidien.

oviducal, oviductal [ouvi'dju:kl, -'dʌktl], *a. Nat.Hist:* de l'oviducte.

oviduct ['ouvidʌkt], *s. Nat.Hist:* oviducte *m*.

oviferous [ou'vifərəs], *a. Nat.Hist:* ovifère, ovigère.

oviform ['ouvifɔ:m], *a.* oviforme, ovoïde.

ovigenous [ou'vidʒinəs], *a. Nat.Hist:* ovigène.

ovigerous [ou'vidʒərəs], *a. Nat.Hist:* ovigère, ovifère.

Ovinae ['ouvini:], *s.pl. Z:* ovinés *m*.

ovine ['ouvain], *a.* (animal, etc.) ovin.

oviparity [ouvi'pæriti], *s. Biol:* oviparité *f*, oviparisme *m*.

oviparous [ou'vipərəs], *a. Nat.Hist:* ovipare.

oviparously [ou'vipərəsli], *adv.* (se reproduire) par oviparité.

oviposit [ouvi'pɔzit], *v.tr. Ent:* pondre.

oviposition [ouvipə'ziʃ(ə)n], *s. Ent:* oviposition *f*; ponte *f*.

ovipositor [ouvi'pɔzitər], *s. Ent:* ovipositeur *m*, pondoir *m*.

ovisac ['ouvisæk], *s. Nat.Hist:* ovisac *m*.

oviscapt ['ouviskæpt], *s. Ent:* oviscapte *m*.

ovism ['ouvizm], *s. Biol:* ovisme *m*.

ovo- ['ouvou], *comb.fm. Biol:* ovo-.

ovocentre ['ouvousentər], *s. Biol:* ovocentre *m*.

ovocyte ['ouvousait], *s. Biol:* ovocyte *m*.

ovogenesis [ouvou'dʒenisis], *s. Biol:* ovogénèse *f*, ovogénie *f*.

ovoid ['ouvɔid]. **1.** *a.* ovoïde. **2.** *s.* (*a*) figure *f* ovoïde; (*b*) *pl. Com:* **ovoids,** boulets *m* (de charbon).

ovoidal [ou'vɔidl], *a.* ovoïdal, -aux.

ovolo, *pl.* **-li** ['ouvəlou, -li:], *s. Arch:* **1.** ove *m*; (*small*) ovicule *m*. **2.** boudin *m* (de base de colonne); quart-de-rond *m*, *pl.* quarts-de-rond; échine *f* (de chapiteau dorique); *Tls:* **o. plane,** boudin; quart-de-rond.

ovology [ou'vɔlədʒi], *s.* ovologie *f*.

ovomucoid [ouvou'mju:kɔid], *s. Bio-Ch:* ovomucoïde *m*.

Ovonic [ou'vɔnik], *a. Elcs:* **O. device,** ovonic *m*.

ovotestis [ouvou'testis], *s. Biol:* ovotestis *m*.

ovoviviparity [ouvouvivi'pæriti], *s. Biol:* ovoviviparité *f*.

ovoviviparous [ouvouvi'vipərəs], *a. Biol:* ovovivipare.

ovular ['ouvjulər], *a. Biol:* ovulaire.

ovulate[1] ['ouvjuleit], *v.i. Biol:* pondre des ovules.

ovulate[2], *a. Biol:* ovulé.

ovulation [ouvju'leiʃ(ə)n], *s. Biol:* ovulation *f*; ponte *f* ovarique.

ovulatory ['ouvjulətri], *a. Biol:* de l'ovulation.

ovule ['ouvju:l], *s. Biol:* ovule *m*.

ovuliferous [ouvju'lifərəs], *a. Biol:* ovuligère.

ovum, *pl.* **ova** ['ouvəm, 'ouvə], *s.* **1.** (*a*) *Biol:* ovule *m*, œuf *m*; (*b*) *pl. Pisc:* œufs (pour la reproduction). **2.** *Arch:* ove *m*.

ow [au], *int.* aïe!

owe [ou], *v.tr.* (*p.p. & p.t.* **owed** [oud], *A:* **ought**) devoir. **1.** (*a*) **to o. s.o. sth., to o. sth. to s.o.,** devoir qch. à qn; **the sum owed (to) her by her brother,** la somme qui lui est due par son frère; **he still owes me a pound,** il me redoit une livre; il m'est redevable d'une livre; **I still o. you for the petrol,** je vous dois encore l'essence; j'ai encore à vous payer l'essence; *F:* **this old suit doesn't o. me anything,** ce vieux complet m'en a donné pour mon argent; *v.i.* **he owes for three months' rent,** il doit trois mois de loyer; (*b*) **to o. respect to one's father,** devoir du respect à son père; **the duties that I o. him,** les devoirs auxquels je suis tenu envers lui; **to o. allegiance, obedience, to s.o.,** devoir son obéissance à qn; **I o. you an apology,** vous avez droit à mes excuses; **their idols are owed only the scantiest reverence,** ils n'apportent à leurs idoles qu'une médiocre vénération; **you o. it to yourself to do your best,** vous vous devez à vous-même de faire de votre mieux; **I o. it to my friends to spare them this sorrow,** je dois à mes amis de leur éviter ce chagrin; (*c*) *Sp:* rendre (tant de points à son adversaire); *Ten:* **o. fifteen, love,** moins quinze à rien. **2. I o. my life to you,** je vous suis redevable de ma vie; je vous dois la vie; **she owes her happiness to you,** c'est à vous qu'elle doit son bonheur; **he owes his ability to his mother,** il tient sa capacité de sa mère; **he owes his misfortunes to himself,** il est l'artisan de ses malheurs; **to whom, to what, do I o. this honour?** à qui suis-je redevable de cet honneur? qu'est-ce qui me vaut cet honneur?

Owen ['ouin], *Pr.n.m.* Ouen.

Owenism ['ouinizm], *s. Pol.Ec:* owénisme *m*.

owing ['ouiŋ]. **1.** *a.* dû; **all the money o. to me,** tout l'argent qui m'est dû; **there are still twenty pounds o. to me,** il m'est redû vingt livres; *Com:* **the moneys o. to us,** nos créances *f*; les créances envers nous; **the rent o.,** l'arriéré *m* du louer. **2.** *prep.phr.* **o. to,** à cause de, par suite de, en raison de; **I am giving up the journey o. to the expense,** je renonce au voyage à cause de la dépense; **o. to the heat I shall travel by night,** vu la chaleur je voyagerai de nuit; **o. to a recent bereavement,** en raison d'un deuil récent; **o. to his wound,** par suite de sa blessure; **all this is o. to your carelessness,** tout cela vient, provient, de votre négligence; **it's o. to you that I haven't succeeded,** c'est à cause de vous que je n'ai pas réussi.

owl [aul], *s.* (*a*) *Orn:* hibou *m*, -oux; **the owls,** les strigiens *m*, les strigidés *m*; **wood owl,** (i) *or* **brown o.,** *or* **tawny o.,** chouette *f* hulotte, hulotte *f* chat-huant; (ii) *or* **long-eared o.,** hibou moyen-duc, *Fr.C:* hibou à aigrettes longues; (iii) *or* **barred o.,** *Fr.C:* chouette rayée; **screech o.,** (i) *or* **barn o.,** (chouette) effraie *f*, chouette des clochers; (ii) *Fr.C:* petit duc; **flammulated screech o.,** *Fr.C:* duc nain; **white o.,** (i) (chouette) effraie, chouette des clochers; (ii) *or* **snowy o.,** chouette harfang, harfang *m* des neiges; **little o.,** (chouette) chêveche *f*; **sparrow o.,** (i) (chouette) chêveche; (ii) chêvechette *f, Fr.C:* chouette naine; **burrowing o.,** chouette des terriers, *Fr.C:* chouette de terrier; **(Asian) fish o.,** hibou kétupa; **(African) fishing o.,** chouette pêcheuse; **great grey o., Lapland o.,** *NAm:* **great gray o.,** chouette lapone, *Fr.C:* chouette cendrée; **horned o.,** duc *m*; **great horned o.,** (i) *or* **eagle o.,** grand-duc *m* (d'Europe); (ii) grand-duc de Virginie, *Fr.C:* grand-duc; **desert eagle o.,** grand-duc ascalaphe; **hawk o.,** chouette épervière; **(African) marsh o.,** hibou du Cap; **pygmy o.,** chevêchette, *Fr.C:* chouette naine; **saw-whet o.,** *Fr.C:* petite nyctale; **scops o.,** scops *m*, hibou petit-duc; **short-eared o.,** hibou des marais, hibou brachyote; **spotted o.,** *Fr.C:* chouette tachetée; **Tengmalm's o.,** *NAm:* **Richardson's o.,** chouette de Tengmalm, *Fr.C:* nyctale boréale; **Ural o.,** chouette de l'Oural; (*b*) *Orn:* **fern o.,** engoulevent *m* (d'Europe); *N.Z:* **o. parrot,** strigops *m*; kakapo *m*; perroquet-hibou *m, pl.* perroquets-hiboux; (*c*) *Z:* **o. monkey,** nyctipithèque *m*, douroucouli *m*, singe *m* nocturne; *Ent:* **o. moth,** cordon bleu; (*d*) **a wise old o.,** un vieux sage; *F:* **to look like a stuffed o.,** avoir l'air d'un hibou empaillé; **drunk as an o.,** soûl comme une bourrique; (*e*) *Scout:* **Brown O.,** cheftaine *f* (de ronde, de Jeannettes); **Tawny O.,** assistante *f*; (*f*) **o. light,** (le) crépuscule; *NAm:* **o. train,** train *m* de nuit.

owlery ['auləri], *s.* repaire *m*, nid *m*, de hiboux.

owlet ['aulit], *s.* (*a*) *Orn:* petit hibou, jeune hibou; (*b*) *Ent:* **o. moth,** noctuelle *f*.

owl-eyed ['aul'aid], *a.* aux yeux de hibou; **to look o.-e. at s.o.,** regarder qn solennellement.

owlish ['auliʃ], *a.* de hibou; **he looks o.,** il a des yeux de hibou; il a un air de faux sage; il a l'air de tomber de la lune.

owlishly ['auliʃli], *adv.* (regarder qn, etc.) avec des yeux de hibou, solennellement.

own[1] [oun], *v.tr.* **1.** posséder; **in the days when I owned a boat,** du temps que j'étais possesseur d'un bateau, du temps que j'avais un bateau à moi; **who owns this land?** quel est le propriétaire de cette terre? **he behaves as if he owned the place,** il se conduit comme en pays conquis; **state-owned company,** compagnie qui appartient à l'état, étatisée. **2.** reconnaître; (*a*) **to o. a child, a poor relation,** avouer un enfant, un parent pauvre; **he had never owned the child,** il n'avait jamais reconnu l'enfant; **dog nobody will o.,** chien que personne ne réclame, que personne ne veut admettre comme sien; **to o. s.o. as one's brother,** avouer qn pour frère; (*b*) avouer (qch.); convenir de (qch.); **I o. I was wrong,** j'ai eu tort, je l'avoue, j'en conviens, je le reconnais; **he owns he was lying,** il convient qu'il a menti; **she owned that she was unhappy,** elle avouait être malheureuse; **to o. oneself beaten,** se reconnaître vaincu; (*c*) reconnaître (l'autorité, la suzeraineté, de (qn); **they refused to o. the King,** ils refusaient de reconnaître le Roi. **3.** *v.ind.tr.* **to o. to a mistake,** reconnaître, avouer, une erreur; convenir d'une erreur; **to o. to being mistaken,** reconnaître s'être trompé; **to o. to disliking s.o.,** avouer qu'on n'aime pas qn; **she owns to being thirty,** (i) elle admet qu'elle a trente ans; (ii) elle se donne trente ans; **to o. up to a crime,** faire l'aveu d'un crime; **he owned up to the deed,** il se déclara l'auteur du méfait; **to o. up to having done sth.,** avouer avoir fait qch.; *v.i. F:* **to o. up,** faire des aveux; s'attabler; manger le morceau.

own[2]. **1.** *a.* (*a*) *attrib.* propre; **her o. money,** son propre argent; son argent à elle; **I saw it with my o. eyes,** je l'ai vu de mes propres yeux; **it's what in my o. mind I call unscrupulousness,** c'est ce que j'appelle en mon particulier un manque de scrupules; **o. brother, sister,** frère germain, sœur germaine; **one of my o. children,** un de mes enfants; **one of my o. friends,** un de mes amis; un mien ami; **I had my o. table,** j'avais ma table à part; **the company is opening its o. bank,** la société va ouvrir sa banque à elle; *Cmptr:* **o. code, coding,** séquence (écrite par l')utilisateur; **I do my o. cooking,** je fais la cuisine moi-même; je fais ma propre cuisine; **she makes her o. dresses,** elle fait ses robes elle-même; **to make, roll, one's o. cigarettes,** rouler ses cigarettes; (*b*) le mien, le tien, etc.; à moi, à toi, etc.; **the house is my o.,** la maison est à moi; la maison m'appartient (en propre); **to make sth. one's o.,** s'approprier qch.; **your interests are my o.,** vos intérêts sont (les) miens; **my money and your o.,** mon argent et le vôtre; **his ideas are his o.,** ses idées lui sont propres; **my time is my o.,** mon temps est à moi; mon temps m'appartient; je suis maître, libre, de mon temps; **there are moments when my time is not my o.,** il y a des heures où je ne m'appartiens pas. **2.** *s.* **my o., his o., one's o., etc.;** (*a*) le mien, le sien, etc.; **to look after one's o.,** soigner le sien; **I have money of my o.,** j'ai de l'argent à moi; **she has a hundred thousand francs of her o.,** elle a cent mille francs vaillant; **he has nothing of his o.,** il n'a rien à lui; **I have no resources of my o.,** je n'ai pas de ressources qui me soient propres; **a child of his o.,** un enfant à lui; un de ses enfants; **a small thing, but my o,** une bagatelle, mais qui est de moi; **he has a copy of his o.,** il a un exemplaire à lui, en propre; **I have a house of my o.,** je suis propriétaire; **for reasons of his o.,** pour des raisons particulières, à lui connues; **a style of one's o., all one's o.,** un style original; **the landscape has a wild beauty of its o.,** le paysage a une beauté sauvage qui lui est propre; **I have a shampoo of my o.,** je me sers d'un shampooing de ma composition; **I am not adding anything of my o.,** je n'y mets rien du mien; **may I have it for my (very) o.?** est-ce que je peux l'avoir pour moi seul? **there's not a thing here that I can call my o.,** il n'y a pas ici un objet qui m'appartienne en propre; **to come into one's o.,** (i) entrer en possession de son bien; (ii) recevoir sa récompense; **to claim, take back, one's o.,** réclamer, reprendre, son bien; (*b*) *coll.* les miens, les siens, etc.; *B:* **his o. received him not,** les siens ne l'ont point reçu; (*c*) **my o. (sweetheart)!** ma chérie! (*d*) *adv.phr.* **to do sth. on one's o.,** faire qch. (i) de sa propre initiative, de son chef, (ii) indépendamment, à soi tout seul; **to be, work, on one's o.,** être établi à son propre compte; **I am (all) on my o. today,** je suis seul aujourd'hui; **as an organizer he stands on his o.,** comme organisateur il n'a pas son pareil.

owner ['ounər], *s.* **1.** propriétaire *mf*; possesseur *m*; patron, -onne (d'une maison de commerce); **rightful o.,** possesseur légitime; *Jur:* ayant *m* droit; **sole o.,** propriétaire unique; **absolute o.,** propriétaire incommutable; **bare o.,** nu propriétaire; **cars parked here at the owner's risk,** parc *m* pour autos aux risques et périls de leurs propriétaires; *Aut:* **o. driver,** conducteur *m* propriétaire; propriétaire conducteur; **o. farm,** exploitation *f* en faire-valoir direct; **o.-built, o.-occupied,** construit, occupé, par le propriétaire; **o. occupier,** propriétaire-occupant *m, pl.* propriétaires-occupants. **2.** *Nau:* (*a*) **the owners (of a ship),** les armateurs *m*, l'armement *m*; **o. charterer,** armateur affréteur; (*b*) *esp. Navy:* **the o.,** le capitaine, le commandant.

ownerless ['ounəlis], *a.* sans propriétaire; **o. dog,** chien *m* sans maître; *Adm:* chien épave.

ownership ['ounəʃip], *s.* **1.** (droit *m* de) propriété *f*; possession *f*; *Jur:* **bare o.,** nue propriété; **common o.,** collectivité *f*; **change of o.,** mutation *f*; *Com:* changement *m* de propriétaire; *P.N:* *Com:* **change of o.,** changement de propriétaire; *Jur:* **claim of o.,** action *f* pétitoire. **2. during his o. of the property,** pendant qu'il possédait la propriété.

ownsome ['ounsəm], **ownio** ['ouniou], *s. P:* **to be on one's o.,** être tout seul.

owt [aut], *s. Dial: P:* n'importe quoi; quelque chose.

owyheeite [ou'waiiait], *s. Miner:* owyhéeite *f*.

ox, *pl.* **oxen** [ɔks, 'ɔks(ə)n], *s.* bœuf *m*; **humped ox,** zébu *m*; **Indian ox,** zébu de l'Inde; **Cambodian forest ox,** kouprey *m*; **wild oxen,** bovidés *m* sauvages; *Cu:* **o. heart, tongue,** cœur *m*, langue *f*, de bœuf; *Lit:* **the black ox hath trod on his foot,** (i) il est tombé dans le malheur; (ii) il n'est plus jeune; **ox cart, waggon,** char *m* à bœufs; **ox fence,** haie bordée d'une palissade; *Z:* **o. antelope,** bubale *m*.

oxalacetic [ɔksələ'setik], *a. Ch:* oxalacétique.

oxal(a)emia [ɔksə'li:miə], *s. Med:* oxalémie *f*.

oxalate ['ɔksəleit], *s. Ch:* oxalate *m*; **o. of iron, ferrous o., ferric o.,** oxalate de fer; *Com:* **acid potassium o.,** sel *m* d'oseille.

oxalic [ɔk'sælik], *a. Ch:* oxalique.

Oxalidaceae [ɔksæli'deisii:], *s.pl. Bot:* oxalid(ac)ées *f*.

oxalidaceous [ɔksæli'deiʃəs], *a. Bot:* oxalidacé.

oxalis ['ɔksəlis, ɔk'sælis], *s. Bot:* oxalis *m*, oxalide *f*.

oxaloacetic [ɔksælouə'si:tik], *a. Ch:* oxalo-acétique.

oxaluria [ɔksə'ljuːriə], *s. Med:* oxalurie *f*.

oxaluric [ɔksə'ljuːrik], *a. Ch:* oxalurique.

oxalyl ['ɔksəlil], *s. Ch:* oxalyle *m*.

oxalylurea [ɔksæli'ljuːriə], *s. Ch:* oxalylurée *f*, oxalyluréide *f*; acide *m* parabanique.

oxamic [ɔk'sæmik], *a. Ch:* oxamique.

oxamide ['ɔksəmaid], *s. Ch:* oxamide *m*.

oxammite ['ɔksəmait], *s. Miner:* oxammite *f*.

oxanilic [ɔksənə'nilik], *a. Ch:* oxanilique.

oxanilide [ɔk'sænilaid], *s.* oxanilide *m*.

oxazine ['ɔksəzain], *s. Ch:* oxazine *f*.

oxazole ['ɔksəzoul], *s. Ch:* oxazole *m*.

oxbird ['ɔksbəːd], *s. Orn:* bécasseau *m*.

oxblood ['ɔksblʌd], *a. & s.* rouge sang (*m*) *inv*.

oxbow ['ɔksbou], *s.* **1.** collier *m* de bœuf. **2.** *Geog:* **o. (lake),** délaissé *m*, bras mort (d'un cours d'eau).

Oxbridge ['ɔksbridʒ]. *Pr.n. F:* les universités d'Oxford et de Cambridge.

oxer ['ɔksər], *s.* haie bordée d'une palissade.

oxetone ['ɔksitoun], *s. Ch:* oxétone *f*.

oxeye ['ɔksai], *s.* **1.** œil *m* de bœuf. **2.** *Arch:* œil-de-bœuf *m, pl.* œils-de-bœuf. **3.** *Bot:* (*a*) **o. daisy, white o.,** marguerite *f* des champs; grande marguerite; chrysanthème *m* des prés, œil-de-bœuf; **yellow o.,** marguerite dorée; **o. camomile,** camomille *f* œil-de-bœuf; (*b*) buphtalme *m*. **4.** *Orn:* (mésange *f*) charbonnière *f*; mésangère *f*.

ox-eyed ['ɔksaid], *a.* aux yeux de bœuf.

Oxford ['ɔksfəd], *Pr.n. Geog:* Oxford; **O. blue,** bleu foncé *inv*; *Sch:* **O. man, woman,** membre *m* de l'Université d'Oxford; *Rel.H:* **the O. Movement,** le mouvement d'Oxford; le puseyisme; **O. shoes, oxfords,** souliers *m* de ville; souliers richelieu; richelieux *m*; *Tail: F:* **O. bags,** pantalon *m* très large, pattes d'éléphant; *Tex:* **O. mixture,** drap *m* de laine gris foncé; **O. shirting,** oxford *m*; *Typ:* **O. border,** encadrement *m* à croisillons; **O. (picture) frame,** cadre *m* à croisillons.

Oxfordian [ɔks'fɔːdiən], *a. & s. Geol:* oxfordien (*m*).

oxheart ['ɔkshɑːt], *s. Hort:* **o. (cherry),** cœur-de-bœuf *m*, *pl.* cœurs-de-bœuf.

oxherd ['ɔkshəːd], *s.* bouvier, -ière.

oxhide ['ɔkshaid], *s.* cuir *m* de bœuf.

oxhorn ['ɔkshɔːn], *s.* corne *f* de bœuf.

oxidability [ɔksaidə'biliti], *s. Ch:* oxydabilité *f*.

oxidable [ɔk'saidəbl], *a. Ch:* oxydable.

oxidant ['ɔksidənt], *s. Ch:* oxydant *m*; (*for rockets*) comburant *m*.

oxidase ['ɔksideis], *s. Bio-Ch:* oxydase *f*.

oxidation [ɔksi'deiʃ(ə)n], *s. Ch:* oxydation *f*; *Metall:* calcination *f*; **o. number,** indice *m* d'oxydation; **o. reduction,** oxydoréduction *f*; **o.-reduction reactions,** réactions *f* d'oxydoréduction; **o. state,** état *m* d'oxydation; *Physiol:* **to destroy by o.,** brûler.

oxidative ['ɔksideitiv], *a. Bio-Ch:* (enzyme, etc.) d'oxydation.

oxide ['ɔksaid], *s. Ch:* oxyde *m*; **magnesium, molybdenum, o.,** oxyde de magnésium, de molybdène; **cupric o.,** oxyde de cuivre; **o. coating, film, skin,** pellicule *f* d'oxyde; *El:* **o.-coated cathode,** cathode à oxyde.

oxidizability [ɔksidaizə'biliti], *s. Ch:* oxydabilité *f*.

oxidizable ['ɔksidaizəbl], *a. Ch:* oxydable.

oxidization [ɔksidai'zeiʃ(ə)n], *s. Ch:* oxydation *f*.

oxidize ['ɔksidaiz]. **1.** *v.tr. Ch: etc:* oxyder, *Metall:* calciner. **2.** *v.i.* s'oxyder.

oxidizer ['ɔksidaizər], *s. Ch:* oxydant *m*.

oxidizing[1] ['ɔksidaiziŋ], *a.* oxydant; **o. agent,** oxydant *m*.

oxidizing[2], *s.* oxydation *f*.

oxidoreduction [ɔksidouri'dʌkʃ(ə)n], *s.* oxydoréduction *f*.

oxim(e) ['ɔksim, -iːm], *s. Ch:* oxime *f*.

oximation [ɔksi'meiʃ(ə)n], *s. Ch:* oximation *f*.

oximeter [ɔk'simitər], *s. Ch: Physiol:* oxymètre *m*.

oximetric [ɔksi'metrik], *a. Ch: Physiol:* oxymétrique.

oximetry [ɔk'simitri], *s. Ch: Physiol:* oxymétrie *f*.

oxisalt ['ɔksisɔːlt], *s. Ch:* oxysel *m*.

oxlip ['ɔkslip], *s. Bot:* primevère élevée; primevère à grandes fleurs.

Oxonian [ɔk'souniən]. **1.** *a. Geog:* oxfordien, -ienne; oxonien, -ienne. **2.** *s.* membre *m* de l'Université d'Oxford; **he's an old O.,** c'est un ancien étudiant de l'Université d'Oxford.

oxonium [ɔk'souniəm], *s. Ch:* oxonium *m*.

oxpecker ['ɔkspekər], *s. Orn:* pique-bœuf *m*, *pl.* pique-bœufs; buphage *m*.

oxtail ['ɔksteil], *s. Cu:* queue *f* de bœuf; **o. soup,** crème *f* de queue de bœuf.

oxter ['ɔkstər], *s.* **1.** *Dial:* aisselle *f*. **2.** *N.Arch:* **o. plate,** tôle *f* de voûte.

oxtongue ['ɔkstʌŋ], *s. Bot:* picride *f* (échioïde).

ox(y)- ['ɔks(i)], *comb.fm.* ox(y)-.

oxyacetylene ['ɔksiə'setiliːn], *a.* (*of gas, welding*) oxyacétylénique; **o. cutting out,** oxycoupage *m*; découpage *m* au chalumeau; **o. torch,** chalumeau *m* oxyacétylénique de découpage; oxycoupeur *m*.

oxyacid ['ɔksi'æsid], *s.* oxacide *m*, oxyacide *m*.

oxyaena [ɔksi'iːnə], *s. Paleont:* oxyaena *m*.

oxycalcium ['ɔksi'kælsiəm], *a.* **o. light,** lumière *f* oxhydrique.

oxycellulose ['ɔksi'seljulous], *s. Ch:* oxycellulose *f*.

oxycephalic ['ɔksisi'fælik], **oxycephalous** ['ɔksi'selfələs], *a.* oxycéphale.

oxycephaly ['ɔksi'sefəli], *s.* oxycéphalie *f*.

oxychloride ['ɔksi'klɔːraid], *s. Ch:* oxychlorure *m*.

oxycrate ['ɔksikreit], *s.* oxycrat *m*.

oxycutting ['ɔksikʌtiŋ], *s.* oxycoupage *m*; découpage *m* au chalumeau (oxyacétylénique, oxhydrique); **o. torch,**

(chalumeau) oxycoupeur *m.*

oxycyanide ['ɔksi'saiənaid], *s. Ch:* oxycyanure *m.*

oxydactyl ['ɔksi'dæktil], *a. Z:* oxydactyle.

oxydant ['ɔksidənt], *s. Ch:* oxydant *m.*

oxyfluoride ['ɔksi'flu:əraid], *s. Ch:* oxyfluorure *m.*

oxygen ['ɔksidʒən], *s. Ch:* oxygène *m*; **o. bottle, cylinder,** bouteille *f* d'oxygène; **o. (breathing) apparatus, equipment,** inhalateur *m* d'oxygène; **o. mask, tent,** masque *m*, tente *f*, à oxygène; *Med:* **o. treatment,** oxygénothérapie *f*; *Metalw:* **o. cutting,** oxycoupage *m.*

oxygenate ['ɔksidʒineit, ɔk'si-], *v.tr.* oxygéner.

oxygenation [ɔksidʒi'neiʃ(ə)n], *s. Ch:* oxygénation *f.*

oxygenator ['ɔksidʒineitər], *s.* oxygénateur *m.*

oxygenizable [ɔksidʒi'naizəbl], *a. Ch:* oxygénable.

oxygenize ['ɔksidʒinaiz], *v.tr. Ch:* oxygéner.

oxygnathous [ɔk'signəθəs], *a.* oxygnathe.

oxyhaemoglobin ['ɔksihi:mə'gloubin], *s. Physiol:* oxyhémoglobine *f.*

oxyhydrogen ['ɔksi'haidrədʒən], *a.* (chalumeau, lumière, etc.) oxhydrique.

oxymel ['ɔksimel], *s. Pharm:* oxymel *m.*

oxymoron [ɔksi'mɔ:rən], *s. Rh:* oxymoron *m.*

oxyopia [ɔksi'oupiə], *s.* oxyopie *f.*

oxyphosphate [ɔksi'fɔsfeit], *s. Ch:* oxyphosphate *m.*

oxyrhynch ['ɔksiriŋk], *s.* **1.** *Crust:* oxyrhynque *m.* **2.** = OXYRHYNCHUS.

Oxyrhyncha [ɔksi'riŋkə], *s.pl. Crust:* oxyrhynques *m.*

oxyrhynchid [ɔksi'riŋkid], *s.* oxyrhynque *m.*

oxyrhynchous [ɔksi'riŋkəs], *a. Crust:* oxyrhynque.

oxyrhynchus, *pl.* **-chi** [ɔksi'riŋkəs, -kai], *s. Ent: Ich:* oxyrhynque *m.*

oxysalt ['ɔksisɔ:lt], *s. Ch:* oxysel *m.*

oxysulphide ['ɔksi'sʌlfaid], *s. Ch:* oxysulfure *m.*

oxytetracycline ['ɔksitetrə'saikli:n], *s. Ch:* oxytétracycline *f.*

oxytocic [ɔksi'tousik], *a. Obst:* ocytocique.

oxytocin [ɔksi'tousin], *s. Physiol:* ocytocine *f.*

oxytone ['ɔksitoun], *a. & s. Gram:* oxyton (*m*).

oxytonesis [ɔksitou'ni:sis], *s. Ling:* oxytonisme *m.*

oxyuriasis [ɔksiju'raiəsis], *s. Med:* oxyurose *f.*

oxyuris [ɔksi'juəris], *s. Ann:* oxyure *f.*

oxywelding [ɔksi'weldiŋ], *s. Metalw:* soudure *f* au chalumeau (oxyacétylénique, oxhydrique).

oyapok [ɔ'jæpɔk], *s. Z:* yapo(c)k *m* chironecte *m.*

oyer ['ɔiər], *s. Jur: A:* (*a*) **o. (and terminer),** audition *f* et jugement *m* (d'une cause criminelle); (*b*) autorisation accordée aux juges en tournée d'entendre les cas au criminel.

oyez! oyez! [ou'jes], *int.* oyez! (interjection par laquelle le crieur public réclame le silence).

oyster ['ɔistər], *s.* **1.** (*a*) *Moll:* huître *f*; **pearl o.,** (huître) perlière *f*; perle *f* mère; mère perle; **native o.,** huître du pays; **rock o.,** chame *f*, chamidé *m*, came *f*; **o. bed, bank,** huîtrière *f*; (i) banc *m* d'huîtres; (ii) parc *m* à huîtres; **o. breeder, farmer, culturist,** ostréiculteur, -trice; parqueur, -euse (d'huîtres), parquier *m*; **o. breeding, farming, the o. industry,** ostréiculture *f*; l'industrie huîtrière, ostréicole; **o. dealer, seller,** écailler, -ère; marchand, -ande, d'huîtres; **o. farm, park,** parc *m* à huîtres; clayère *f*; **o. fishing,** pêche *f* aux huîtres; **o. knife, sheller,** couteau *m* à huîtres, écaillère *f*, ouvre-huître(s) *m inv*; **o. opener,** (i) (*pers.*) écailleur, -euse; (ii) = **o. knife** (*see above*); **o. shell,** écaille *f* d'huître; *F:* **he's a regular o.,** il est très taciturne; **he's as close as an o.,** il sait garder un secret; jamais il ne jase; (*b*) *Bot:* **o. nut,** telfairia *m*, kouème *m*; **o. plant,** salsifis (blanc). **2.** *Cu:* **o. (piece),** sot-l'y-laisse *m inv* (d'une volaille). **3.** *P:* crachat *m*; *P:* huître.

oysterage ['ɔistəridʒ], *s.* huîtrière *f*; parc *m* à huîtres.

oystercatcher ['ɔistəkætʃər], *s. Orn:* huîtrier(-pie) *m*, *pl.* huîtriers-pies; pie *f* de mer; bec-de-hache *m*, *pl.* becs-de-hache.

oysterman, *pl.* **-men** ['ɔistəmən], *s.m.* écailler, marchand d'huîtres.

oysterwoman, *pl.* **-women** ['ɔistəwumən, -wimin], *s.f.* écaillère; marchande d'huîtres.

oz(a)ena [ou'zi:nə], *s. Med:* ozène *m*; *F:* punaisie *f.*

ozobrome ['ouzəbroum], *s. Phot:* ozobromie *f*; **o. process,** procédé *m* ozobrome.

ozokerite [ou'zoukərait], **ozocerite** [ou'zɔsərait], *s. Miner:* ozocérite *f*, ozokérite *f*; cire minérale.

ozone [ou'zoun], *s. Ch:* ozone *m*; **o. apparatus,** ozoniseur *m*; **o. generator,** ozonateur *m*; *Meteor:* **o. layer,** ozonosphère *f*; *Med:* **o. treatment,** ozonothérapie *f.*

ozoner [ou'zounər], *s. NAm: F:* cinéma *m* en plein air auquel on assiste en voiture.

ozonide ['ouzounaid], *s. Ch:* ozonide *m.*

ozonium [ou'zouniəm], *s. Fung:* ozonium *m.*

ozonization [ouzənai'zeiʃ(ə)n], *s. Ch:* ozonisation *f*, ozonation *f.*

ozonize ['ouzənaiz], *v.tr.* ozoniser, ozoner.

ozonizer ['ouzənaizər], *s. Ch:* ozonateur *m*; ozoniseur *m*, ozoneur *m.*

ozonolysis [ouzə'nɔlisis], *s. Ch:* ozonolyse *f.*

ozonometer [ouzə'nɔmitər], *s. Ph:* ozonomètre *m.*

ozonometric [ouzənə'metrik], *a.* ozonométrique.

ozonometry [ouzə'nɔmitri], *s.* ozonométrie *f.*

ozonoscope [ou'zounəskoup], *s. Ch:* ozonoscope *m.*

ozonoscopic [ouzənə'skɔpik], *a. Ch:* ozonoscopique.

ozonosphere [ou'zounəsfi:ər], *s. Meteor:* ozonosphère *f.*

ozotype ['ouzətaip], *s. Phot:* ozotype *m*; **o. process,** procédé *m* ozotype; ozotypie *f.*

ozotypic ['ouzətaipik], *a. Phot:* ozotypique.

P

P, p [piː], *s.* **1.** (la lettre) P, p *m*; *Tp:* **P for Peter,** P comme Pierre; *F:* **to mind one's P's and Q's,** (i) se surveiller; (ii) faire bien attention aux détails. **2.** *F:* penny *m*, *pl.* pence; **25 p each,** 25 pence la pièce; **a 10 p stamp,** un timbre de 10 pence; **a half p,** un demi-penny; *Com:* **1 p off,** baisse d'un penny.

pa [pɑː], *s.m. F: O:* papa.

pabulum ['pæbjuləm], *s. Lit:* aliment *m*, nourriture *f*; **mental p.,** nourriture, aliment, de l'esprit.

paca ['pɑːkə], *s. Z:* paca *m.*

pace[1] [peis], *s.* **1.** pas *m*; **ten paces off,** à dix pas de distance; *Mil: etc:* **one p. forward!** un pas en avant! **2.** (*a*) (*gait*) allure *f*; **to put a horse through its paces,** faire parader un cheval; faire passer un cheval à la montre; faire montre d'un cheval; **to put s.o. through his paces,** mettre qn à l'épreuve; **to ruin a horse's paces,** détraquer un cheval; *Mil:* **p. setter,** homme, etc. (en tête d'une colonne) chargé de régler l'allure; (*b*) amble *m* (d'un cheval, d'un ours, etc.). **3.** (*a*) (*speed*) vitesse *f*, train *m*, allure; **to walk at a good, quick, smart, p.,** marcher rapidement, à vive allure; **at a slow p.,** au petit pas; **at a walking p.,** au pas; **to keep p. with s.o.,** marcher du même pas, suivre la même allure, que qn; marcher de pair avec qn; **I can't keep p. with you,** je ne peux pas vous suivre; **she can't keep p. with her children,** ses enfants la dépassent; **I can't keep p. with my work,** je suis débordé de travail; **supply is keeping p. with demand,** l'offre suit la demande; *Sp:* **even p.,** train soutenu; **at the p. you are going,** au train dont vous allez; **to quicken one's p.,** hâter, presser, le pas; **to force the p.,** forcer le pas, l'allure, la vitesse; **to slacken the p.,** ralentir le pas, la marche, l'allure; *Mus:* **to press the p.,** presser la mesure; **to set the p.,** donner le pas (à qn); *Sp:* donner, régler, l'allure; mener le train; *F:* **to go the p.,** (i) mener la vie à grandes guides; (ii) mener un train d'enfer, une vie de bâton de chaise; **he (really) goes the p.,** c'est un viveur; (*b*) rythme *m.*

pace[2]. **1.** *v.i.* (*a*) aller au pas; marcher à pas mesurés; **to p. up and down,** faire les cent pas; **to p. up and down a room,** arpenter une pièce; (*b*) (*of horse, etc.*) ambler, aller l'amble. **2.** *v.tr.* (*a*) arpenter (une rue, une pièce, etc.); (*b*) **to p. (off) a distance,** mesurer une distance au pas; (*c*) *Sp:* entraîner (qn).

pacemaker ['peismeikər], *s.* **1.** (*a*) *Sp:* (i) meneur *m* de train; (ii) entraîneur *m* (d'un coureur); *Cy:* pacemaker *m*; (*b*) animateur *m*, chef *m* de file (d'un mouvement politique, etc.); celui, celle, qui règle la cadence de travail d'une équipe. **2.** (*a*) *Anat:* nœud sinusal cardiaque, nœud sinusal de Keith et Flack, d'Archoff et Tawara; pacemaker; (*b*) *Med:* (*device*) stimulateur *m*, pacemaker.

pacemaking ['peismeikiŋ], *s.* **1.** *Sp:* règlement *m* de l'allure. **2.** *Med:* excitation cardiaque artificielle.

pacer ['peisər], *s.* **1.** *Sp:* entraîneur *m.* **2.** cheval ambleur, jument ambleuse.

pacha ['pɑːʃə, 'pæʃə], *s.* pacha *m.*

pachnolite ['pæknoulait], *s. Miner:* pachnolite *f.*

pachyblepharon [pæki'blefərɔn], *s. Med:* pachyblépharose *f.*

pachycephalia, pachycephaly [pækise'feiliə, '-sefəli], *s. Med:* pachycéphalie *f.*

pachyderm ['pækidəːm], *s. Z:* pachyderme *m.*

pachydermal, pachydermatous, pachydermic, pachydermous [pæki'dəːməl, -'dəːmətəs, -'dəːmik, -'dəːməs], *a.* pachyderme, pachydermique, à la peau épaisse.

Pachydermata [pæki'dəːmətə], *s.pl. Z:* pachydermes *m.*

pachydermia [pæki'dəːmiə], *s. Med:* pachydermie *f.*

pachylosis [pæki'lousis], *s. Med:* pachylose *f.*

pachymeningitis [pækimenin'dʒaitis], *s. Med:* pachyméningite *f.*

pachymeter [pæ'kimitər], *s. Ph: etc:* pachomètre *m.*

pachypleuritis [pækipluːraitis], *s. Med:* pachypleurite *f.*

pachyrhizus [pæki'raizəs], *s. Bot:* pachyrhize *f.*

pachysalpingitis [pækisælpin'dʒaitis], *s. Med:* pachysalpingite *f.*

pachytene ['pækitiːn], *a. & s. Biol:* (*state*) pachytène (*m*).

pachyvaginitis [pækivædʒi'naitis], *s. Med:* pachyvaginite *f.*

pacific [pə'sifik], *a.* **1.** (*a*) pacifique; (*b*) paisible. **2.** *Geog:* **the P. (Ocean),** l'océan *m* Pacifique; le Pacifique; **the P. coast,** le littoral du Pacifique; (*US:*) **the P. States,** les États qui bordent le Pacifique.

pacifically [pə'sifik(ə)li], *adv.* pacifiquement; paisiblement.

pacification [pæsifi'keiʃ(ə)n], *s.* pacification *f* (d'un pays, etc.); apaisement *m* (de qn).

pacificatory [pæsifi'keitəri], *a.* pacificateur, -trice.

pacifier ['pæsifaiər], *s.* **1.** (*pers.*) pacificateur, -trice. **2.** *esp. NAm:* (*for babies*) sucette *f*, tétine *f.*

pacifism ['pæsifizm], *s. Pol:* pacifisme *m.*

pacifist ['pæsifist], *s. & a.* pacifiste (*mf*).

pacify ['pæsifai], *v.tr.* pacifier (une foule, un pays, etc.); apaiser, adoucir, calmer (qn, la colère de qn).

pacifying[1] ['pæsifaiiŋ], *a.* pacificateur, -trice.

pacifying[2], *s.* **1.** pacification *f.* **2.** apaisement *m.*

pacing ['peisiŋ], *s.* **1.** (*a*) marche *f*; (*b*) mesurage *m* au pas. **2.** *Sp:* entraînement *m* (d'un cycliste, etc.).

pack[1] [pæk], *s.* **1.** (*a*) paquet *m*, ballot *m* (de linge, de marchandises, etc.); balle *f* (de coton, etc.); ballot (de colporteur); **p. wool,** laine *f* en balles; **p. cloth,** toile *f* d'emballage; **p. goods,** marchandises *f* en balle(s); (*b*) *Mil:* (i) sac *m* (porté sur le dos); (ii) paquetage *m*; **put on packs!** sac au dos! **packs off!** sac à terre! **p. drill,** exercice *m* en tenue de campagne (à titre de punition), *P:* le bal; *F:* **no names no p. drill,** pas de nom, pas de démon; (*c*) bât *m* (de bête de somme); cacolet *m* (pour transporter un blessé, etc.); **p. animal,** animal *m* de bât, de charge; bête *f* (de somme); sommier *m*; **p. mule,** mulet *m* (i) de bât, (ii) de cacolet; **p. train,** convoi *m* de bêtes de somme; **p. road, trail,** chemin muletier; piste muletière; *Mil:* **p. artillery,** artillerie *f* de bât; (*d*) *Av:* **(parachute) p.,** (i) parachute (plié et prêt à servir); (ii) enveloppe *f*, sac, de parachute; **back p.,** parachute dorsal; **chest p.,** parachute de poitrine; **lap p.,** parachute ventral; **seat p.,** parachute siège; (*e*) *T.V:* **p. shot,** plan-paquet *m*, *pl.* plans-paquets; (*f*) **a p. of lies,** un tissu, un tas, de mensonges; **a p. of nonsense,** un tas de sottises. **2.** (*a*) bande *f* (de loups); volée *f* (de gibier); presse *f* (de gens); **p. of thieves,** bande de voleurs; **p. of fools,** tas d'imbéciles; (*b*) *Ven:* (*of foxhounds*) meute *f*; (*of staghounds*) équipage *m*; (*of buckhounds*) harde *f*; (*of boarhounds, wolfhounds*) vautrait *m*; **to lay on the p.,** laisser courre; (*c*) *Scout:* meute (de Louveteaux, de Louvettes); ronde *f* (de Jeannettes); (*d*) *Rugby Fb:* **the p.,** le pack. **3.** (*a*) jeu *m* (de cartes, de dominos); paquet (de cartes; *esp. U.S:* paquet (de cigarettes); (*b*) *Cmptr:* paquet (de cartes); **disc p.,** chargeur *m* (de disques). **4.** (*a*) *Min:* remblai *m* (de terre); (*b*) *Oc:* **(ice) p.,** embâcle *m* de glaçons; **packs of ice,** amas *m* de glace. **5.** (*a*) *Med:* **wet p., cold p.,** drap humide, mouillé; enveloppement humide, froid; (*b*) *Med: Toil:* emplâtre *m*; **surgical p.,** pansement chirurgical.

pack[2], *v.*

I. *v.tr.* **1.** (*a*) emballer, empaqueter (des objets); mettre (ses effets) dans sa valise, sa malle; **I won't p. this dress until the last minute,** je ne mettrai cette robe dans ma valise qu'à la dernière minute; (*with passive force*) **dress that packs well,** robe qui sort impeccable d'une valise; **tent that packs easily,** tente facile à emballer, qui s'emballe facilement; *F:* **I've decided to p. it in,** j'y renonce! *U.S: F:* **to p. a pistol,** porter un revolver; (*b*) *Com:* conserver (de la viande) en boîtes; embariller, encaquer (des harengs, etc.); baguer (des marchandises périssables); (*c*) *Med:* **to p. a patient,** envelopper un malade dans un drap mouillé; faire un enveloppement froid à un malade. **2.** (*a*) tasser (de la terre dans un trou, etc.); entasser, serrer (des voyageurs dans une voiture, etc.); *Cmptr:* comprimer, tasser (des données); **we were packed (in) like sardines,** nous étions serrés, pressés, comme des harengs (en caque), comme des sardines; **p. it in!** (i) *F:* trouve quand même un peu de place pour ça! (ii) *P:* assez! la ferme! *P:* **to p. a punch,** cogner dur; (*b*) *Nau:* **to p. on all sail,** mettre toutes voiles dehors; faire force de voiles. **3.** remplir, bourrer **(sth. with sth.,** qch. de qch.); *Civ.E: Min: etc:* remblayer (un fossé, etc.); **to p. one's case,** faire sa valise; *Aut:* **when I've packed the boot we can start,** dès que j'aurai mis les bagages dans le coffre on pourra se mettre en route; **the train was packed,** le train était bondé; **the hall was packed,** la salle était comble, archipleine, pleine à craquer; **book packed with information,** livre bourré de faits; *Mec.E:* **to p. a cup with grease,** remplir, bourrer, un graisseur de graisse. **4.** (*a*) *Mec.E: Mch:* garnir, étouper (un gland, etc.); fourrer (un assemblage); garnir (un piston); (*b*) **to p. a pipe in cork,** garnir un tuyau de liège; *Typ:* **to p. a cylinder,** habiller un cylindre. **5.** bâter (un mulet, etc.). **6.** (*a*) **to p. a jury,** se composer un jury favorable; **to p. a meeting, the house,** faire la salle; s'assurer un nombre prépondérant de partisans à une réunion; (*b*) *Cards:* **to p. the cards,** apprêter les cartes. **7.** *Ven:* ameuter (les chiens). **8.** (*a*) **to p. a child off to bed,** envoyer un enfant au lit; **his father packed him off to America,** son père l'a expédié en Amérique, l'a embarqué pour l'Amérique; (*b*) *F:* **to send s.o. packing,** envoyer promener, balader, qn; faire déguerpir qn.

II. *v.i.* **1.** faire sa valise, ses valises. **2.** (*of earth, etc.*) se tasser; (*of snow, etc.*) **to p. down hard,** se tasser dur. **3.** (*a*) (*of wolves*) s'assembler en bande; (*of birds*) s'assembler en compagnie; (*b*) (*of people*) s'attrouper, se presser (ensemble); (*c*) (*of runners, etc.*) se former en peloton; (*d*) *Rugby Fb:* former le pack.

III. (*compound verb*) **pack up,** *v.tr. & i.* (*a*) emballer (ses effets); ranger (ses livres, etc.); faire ses valises; **let's p. up and go,** (i) rangeons nos affaires, (ii) faisons nos valises, et partons; *F:* **to p. up one's traps,** faire ses valises; plier bagage; (*b*) *F:* (*at end of day*) cesser le travail; (*c*) *F:* (*of machine, etc.*) tomber en panne; **my car's packed up,** ma voiture ne marche plus; (*d*) *P:* **p. it up!** assez! la ferme!

package[1] ['pækidʒ], *s.* **1.** empaquetage *m*, emballage *m*. **2.** (*a*) paquet *m*, colis *m*; ballot *m*; *Tex:* moche *f* (de soie filée); (*b*) *Cmptr:* collection *f* de programmes; (*c*) *U.S:* **p. store,** débit *m* où on vend des boissons à emporter. **3.** emballage (les caisses et papiers, etc.). **4. p. deal,** (i) compromis *m*; (ii) *Com: etc:* contrat global; **p. tour,** voyage *m* à prix forfaitaire.

package[2], *v.tr. Com: etc:* empaqueter; emballer; conditionner.

packaged [p'ækidʒd], *a. Com:* préemballé; préconditionné.

packager ['pækidʒər], *s.* conditionneur, -euse.

packaging ['pækidʒiŋ], *s.* (*a*) *Com: etc:* empaquetage *m*; emballage *m*; conditionnement *m*; (*b*) *Cmptr:* **p. density,** densité *f* d'enregistrement (des données).

packed [pækt], *a.* (*a*) *Com: etc:* empaqueté, emballé; conditionné; **p. consignment,** envoi *m* à couvert; (*b*) *Cmptr:* **in p. form, format,** en condensé; (*c*) **p. lunch,** panier-repas *m*, *pl.* paniers-repas; pique-nique *m*, *pl.* pique-niques.

packer ['pækər], *s.* **1.** (*pers.*) (*a*) *Com: etc:* emballeur, -euse; empaqueteur, -euse; conditionneur, -euse; (*b*) fabriquant *m* de conserves en boîtes; (*c*) *U.S:* entrepreneur *m* de transport par bêtes de somme; transporteur *m* sur bêtes de somme. **2.** *Austr:* animal *m* de bât, bête *f* de somme, sommier *m*. **3.** (*device*) (*a*) machine *f* à emballer, à empaqueter, à conditionner; (*b*) bourroir *m*; instrument *m* pour bourrer (une matière dans un moule, etc.); (*c*) *Atom.Ph:* chargeur *m*; (*d*) *Min:* remblayeur *m*.

packet ['pækit], *s.* **1.** (*a*) paquet *m* (de lettres, etc.); pochette *f* (de papier, etc.); **p. of needles,** sachet *m* d'aiguilles; **p. of tea, of biscuits,** paquet de thé, de biscuits; **p. soup,** bouillon *m*, potage *m*, en sachet; (*b*) **(postal) p.,** colis (postal), paquet poste; (*c*) *F:* **to catch, get,** *P:* **cop, a p.,** écoper; attraper un coup; être atteint par une balle; **to make a p.,** gagner un argent fou; **he's dropped a p.,** il a perdu un paquet; **that'll cost a p.,** ça va coûter les yeux de la tête. **2.** *O:* **p. (boat),** paquebot *m*.

packfong ['pækfɔŋ], *s. Metall:* pacfung *m*, packfond *m*, packfong *m*; cuivre blanc, cuivre chinois, maillechor(t) *m*.

pack-harden ['pækhɑːd(ə)n], *v.tr. Metalw:* tremper en paquet.

packhorse ['pækhɔːs], *s.* cheval *m* (*pl.* chevaux) de bât, de somme, de suite; sommier *m*.

packing ['pækiŋ], *s.*

I. 1. (*action of wrapping, enveloping*) (*a*) *Com: etc:* emballage *m*; empaquetage *m*; colisage *m*; **p. charges,** frais *m* d'emballage; **p. included, p. extra,** emballage compris, en sus; **p. list,** liste *f* de colisage; **p. case,** caisse *f*, boîte *f*, d'emballage; **p. crate,** cadre *m* d'emballage; **p. cloth, canvas,** toile *f* d'emballage; **p. needle,** carrelet *m*; aiguille *f* d'emballage, d'emballeur; **p. paper,** papier d'emballage, papier gris; **p. room,** salle *f* d'emballage; **p. agent,** emballeur *m*; **p. hook,** crochet *m* de pliage (d'un parachute); (*b*) *Nau:* arrimage *m* (de la cargaison); (*c*) **to do one's p.,** faire sa valise, ses valises; (*d*) embarillage *m* (des harengs, etc.); mise *f* en conserve (de la viande, etc.); **p. house,** conserverie *f*; (*e*) *Med:* enveloppement *m* (dans un drap mouillé); **p. sheet,** drap mouillé; enveloppement froid, humide. **2.** (*material used*) (*a*) matériel *m* d'emballage; **non-returnable p.,** emballage perdu; (*b*) *Med:* pansement *m*.
II. 1. (*action of insertion, of pressing* (*down*)) (*a*) *Civ.E: etc:* remblayage *m*, comblement *m* (d'un fossé, etc.); (*b*) tassement *m*, agglomération *f* (de la terre, etc.); (*c*) *Atom.Ph:* tassement (des particules); **p. fraction,** coefficient *m*, fraction *f*, de tassement; (*d*) *Cmptr:* tassement (de données); **p. density,** densité *f* d'enregistrement; (*e*) *Mch: etc:* bourrage *m*, étoupage *m*, garnissage *m* (d'un joint, etc.); garnissage (d'un piston); *Typ:* habillage *m* (d'un cylindre); *Mch:* **p. box,** presse-étoupe *m inv*; **p. gland, washer,** chapeau *m*, bague *f*, de presse-étoupe; *Mec.E: etc:* **p. disc,** rondelle *f* de joint, de calage; **p. bolt,** boulon *m* de serrage; **p. flange,** bride *f* de garniture, d'étanchéité; **p. block,** presse-garnitures *m inv*; cale *f* d'épaisseur; cale, billot *m* (pour cric); **p. tow,** étoupe *f*, tresse *f*, pour garniture (de joint, etc.); **p. extractor,** tire-bourrage *m inv*; **p. strip,** bande *f* antifriction pour rattraper l'usure; cale, lardon *m*, d'ajustage; **p. piece,** (i) *Mec.E: etc:* cale d'appui, d'épaisseur; (ii) *Rail:* semelle *f* (d'arrêt); *Rail:* **p. plate,** selle *f* d'appui, d'arrêt; **p. ring,** (i) *Mec.E:* rondelle, bague, de garniture; garniture *f* annulaire; bague de fond (d'un cylindre); collet *m* (de presse-étoupe); anneau *m* d'obturation; cercle *m* d'étoupe; (ii) *Mch:* segment *m*, bague, garniture (de piston); (*f*) *Med:* tamponnement *m*; **p. of the pharynx,** tamponnement du pharynx; *Dent:* **denture p.,** bourrage *m* d'une prothèse; remplissage *m* d'un moufle (à prothèse); (*g*) *Pej:* manipulation *f* (du choix des membres d'un jury, d'un comité, etc.). **2.** (*material object, added or inserted; result of pressing* (*down*)) (*a*) *Civ.E: etc:* remblai *m* (pour combler un fossé, etc.); (*b*) *Atom.Ph:* masse (spécifique apparente); **p. fraction,** défaut *m* de masse relatif; **p. loss,** défaut de masse; (*c*) *Mec.E: etc:* garniture (d'un joint, d'un piston, etc.); joint *m* (d'un gland, etc.); fourrure *f* (d'un assemblage); **asbestos p.,** garniture en amiante; **felt, hemp, p.,** garniture en feutre, en chanvre; **watertight p.,** joint étanche à l'eau; **oil p.,** segment *m* d'étanchéité; (*d*) *Med:* tampon *m*.

packman, *pl.* **-men** ['pækmən], *s.m. A:* colporteur, porteballe.

packsaddle ['pæksædl], *s.* bât *m*.

packthread ['pækθred], *s.* fil *m* d'emballage; ficelle *f*.

pact [pækt], *s.* pacte *m*, convention *f*, contrat *m*; *Hist:* **the Locarno P.,** le pacte de Locarno; **four-power p.,** pacte à quatre; **to make a p. with s.o.,** faire, signer, un pacte, *Pej:* pactiser, avec qn; **to make a suicide p.,** prendre l'engagement *m* de se suicider ensemble.

Pactolus(the) [ðəpæk'touləs], *Pr.n. A.Geog:* le Pactole.

pad[1] [pæd], *s.* **1.** *P: A:* chemin *m*, route *f*; *P:* trimard *m*; **gentleman, knight, of the p.,** voleur *m* de grand chemin; **to be on the p.,** vagabonder; être sur le trimard; trimarder. **2. p. (nag),** cheval *m* (*pl.* chevaux) à l'allure aisée; cheval de promenade; bidet *m*. **3.** bruit sourd des pas d'une bête (chien, loup, etc.); bruit de pas feutrés.

pad[2], *v.tr. & i.* **(padded)** (*a*) *P: A:* aller à pied; **to p. the road,** cheminer à pied; parcourir la route à pied; vagabonder; **to p. it, to p. the hoof,** trimarder; (*b*) (*of dog, camel, etc.*) **to p. (along),** trotter à pas sourds; (*of pers.*) **to p. about the room,** aller et venir à pas feutrés, à pas de loup.

pad[3], *s.* **1.** (*a*) bourrelet *m*, coussinet *m*; **(porter's) carrying p.,** (i) surdos *m*; (ii) torche *f*, tortillon *m* (pour la tête); *Sp:* **ankle p.,** protège-cheville *m inv*; **shin pads,** *Cr:* **batting pads,** jambières *fpl*; (*b*) tampon *m* (d'ouate, etc.); *Med:* tampon, compresse *f*; **polishing p.,** bichon *m*, tampon à reluire (pour chaussures, etc.); **inking p.,** tampon encreur; **self-inking p.,** tampon perpétuel, inépuisable; **stamp p.,** tampon à timbrer; *Mec.E:* **p. lubricator,** tampon graisseur; *Mus:* **key p.,** tampon de clef (de flûte, etc.); *Artil:* **obturator p.,** coussinet d'obturation, galette *f*; *Toil:* **hair p.,** crépon *m*; (*c*) *Harn:* (i) sellette *f* (de cheval de trait); (ii) coussinet (de selle, de collier); (iii) *A:* selle *f* sans arçon; (*d*) *Fenc:* plastron *m*. **2.** (*a*) pelote digitale (de certains animaux); pulpe *f* (du doigt, de l'orteil); pelote adhésive (d'insecte); (*b*) (i) patte *f*, (ii) empreinte *f* (de renard, de lièvre, etc.); (*c*) *Anat:* **gum p.,** grête gingivale, alvéolaire. **3.** bloc *m* (de papier à écrire, etc.); sous-main *m inv*; **memo p., scribbling p.,** bloc-notes *m*, *pl.* blocs-notes; *Mil: etc:* **one-time p., p. cypher,** carnet *m* de clefs-blocs (pour chiffrement). **4.** *Tls:* (*a*) mandrin *m* (de vilebrequin); (*b*) manche *m* porte-outils. **5.** *Mec.E:* (*a*) semelle *f*, support *m* (de moteur, etc.); patin *m* (d'appui); **jacking p.,** patin de levage; **spring p.,** patin de ressort; *Metalw:* **blanking p.,** support de découpage; (*b*) patin (de butée), amortisseur *m*; **bumper p.,** tampon amortisseur, tampon de butée; *Aut:* (*of disc brake*) **brake p.,** plaquette *f*; garniture *f*; (*c*) bride *f*, patte *f*; **mounting p.,** bride de fixation, de montage; (*d*) *Cin:* patin, étouffoir *m*, glissière *f* (de la bande); **pressure p.,** patin presseur, de pression (de la fenêtre de l'image). **6.** (*a*) *Av:* aire *f* de décollage et d'atterissage (pour hélicoptères); **(warm(ing) up) p.,** aire de point fixe (pour avions); (*b*) *Ball:* **launching p.,** aire, plate-forme *f*, de lancement (d'une fusée, d'un mis sile). **7.** (*a*) *Tp:* **(artificial extension) p.,** ligne artificielle d'équilibre, de complément; complément *m*; (*b*) *W.Tel: etc:* atténuateur *m* (d'amplitude) non réglable. **8.** *P:* (*a*) logement *m*, piaule *f*; (*b*) lit *m*, pieu *m*; **to hit the p.,** se coucher, se pieuter.

pad[4], *v.tr.* **(padded) 1.** bourrer, rembourrer (un coussin, etc.); matelasser (une porte, etc.); capitonner, ouater (un meuble); ouater (un vêtement); coussiner (le collier d'un cheval); bouler (les cornes d'un taureau); *Nau:* larder (un paillet, etc.); *Tail:* **to p. the shoulders of a coat,** garnir les épaules d'un manteau. **2.** *F:* (*a*) délayer (un discours, etc.); cheviller (un vers); **to p. (out) a book,** ajouter des pages de remplissage dans un livre; (*b*) *U.S:* gonfler (un budget, un relevé de dépenses, etc.).

pad[5], *s. Com:* bourriche *f*.

padauk [pə'dɔːk], *s.* =PADOUK.

padded ['pædid], *a.* rembourré; garni de bourre; matelassé; **p. cell,** cellule matelassée, capitonnée; cabanon *m*; *Nau:* **p. mat,** paillet lardé.

padding ['pædiŋ], *s.* **1.** (*a*) remplissage *m*, rembourrage *m*; garnissage *m* (avec de la bourre, de la ouate, etc.); ouatage *m*, ouatinage *m*; (*b*) *Cmptr:* remplissage (de positions inutilisées); garnissage; (*c*) *W.Tel: etc:* **p. condenser, p. capacitor,** condensateur additionnel en série; condensateur-série *m* d'équilibrage, *pl.* condensateurs-série d'équilibrage. **2.** (*a*) bourre *f*, ouate *f*, rembourrage (d'un coussin, etc.); *Com:* fer *m* à meubles; **to remove the p. of an armchair,** débourrer un fauteuil; (*b*) coussinet *m*, matelassure *f* (d'une selle, d'un collier de cheval de trait, etc.); matelassure (d'un siège, etc.). **3.** *F:* délayage *m* (d'un discours); remplissage, délayage (dans une œuvre littéraire); cheville *f* (dans un vers); *F:* bla-bla-bla *m*; **this essay's mostly p.,** cette dissertation est remplie de choses qui n'ont rien à voir avec le sujet.

paddle[1] ['pædl], *s.* **1.** pagaie *f*; **double p.,** pagaie à double pale. **2.** (*a*) aube *f*, pale *f*, palette *f* (de roue hydraulique, de bateau à roues); jantille *f*, volet *m* (de roue hydraulique); palette (de pompe à huile, etc.); *O:* **p. boat,** bateau *m*, vapeur *m*, à aubes, à roues; (*b*) **p. (wheel),** roue *f* à aubes, à palettes; (*c*) vannelle *f* (de porte d'écluse); (*d*) (*for beating clothes in running water*) battoir *m* (à linge); (*e*) *Glassm: Tan:* moulinet *m*. **3.** *Z: etc:* nageoire *f* (de cétacé, de manchot, de tortue); aileron *m* (de requin); aile *f* (de manchot); patte *f* (de canard); palette (de cténophore).

paddle[2], *s. Row:* (*a*) allure douce; **to row at a p.,** tirer en douce; (*b*) promenade *f* (en canot) à allure douce.

paddle[3], *v.tr.* **1.** (*a*) pagayer; **to p. one's own canoe,** aller son chemin; arriver par soi-même; se débrouiller (tout seul); (*b*) *v.i. Row:* tirer en douce. **2.** (*of horse*) faucher. **3.** *Tan:* mouliner (des peaux). **4.** (*a*) battre (le linge, avec le battoir); (*b*) *NAm: F:* donner une fessée à, fesser (un enfant).

paddle[4], *s.* barbotage *m*; (*of child*) **to go for a p.,** aller barboter dans la mer, dans la rivière.

paddle[5], *v.i.* **1.** barboter; se promener (dans l'eau, etc.); patauger, patouiller (dans la boue, etc.); **paddling pool,** bassin *m* à patauger. **2.** *A:* **to p. about sth., with sth., on sth.,** tripoter, patouiller, qch. **3.** *O:* (*toddle*) trottiner; **to p. about the house,** trottiner par la maison.

paddlefish ['pædlfiʃ], *s. Ich:* spatule *f*.

paddler ['pædlər], *s.* **1.** pagayeur, -euse (de canoë, de périssoire). **2.** *Cost:* **paddlers,** barboteuse *f* (d'enfant).

paddock[1] ['pædək], *s.* **1.** (*a*) parc *m*, enclos *m*, pré *m* (pour chevaux); paddock *m*; **to put a horse in the p.,** parquer un cheval; (*b*) *Turf:* pesage *m*, paddock; (*c*) *Austr:* champ *m*. **2.** *Min:* chantier *m* à ciel ouvert.

paddock[2], *s. A: & Scot:* (*a*) grenouille *f*; (*b*) crapaud *m*.

Paddy[1] ['pædi]. **1.** (*a*) *Pr.n.* (*dim.*) (i) *m*; Patrice, Patrick; (ii) *f*. Patricia; (*b*) *Pr.n.m.* (*nickname*) Irlandais; (*c*) *s. F: NAm:* **p. wagon,** panier *m* à salade. **2.** *s. F:* **to be, get, in a p.,** être, se mettre, en colère, en rage, en rogne. **3.** *s. Civ.E:* excavateur *m* à vapeur.

paddy[2], *s. Com:* paddy *m* (riz non décortiqué); **p. field,** rizière *f*; plantation *f* de riz.

paddymelon ['pædimel(ə)n], *s.* = PADEMELON.

paddywhack ['pædi(h)wæk], *s. F: O:* **1.** raclée *f*, rossée *f*, fessée *f*. **2.** = PADDY[1] 2.

pademelon ['pædimel(ə)n], *s. Z:* thylogale *m*; kangourou *m* de petite taille.

padlock[1] ['pædlɔk], *s.* cadenas *m*.

padlock[2], *v.tr.* cadenasser; fermer (une porte, etc.) au cadenas.

padouk [pə'duːk], *s. Com:* padouk *m*; bois *m* de corail.

padre ['pɑːdrei, 'pædrei], *s.m.* (*a*) prêtre; (*b*) aumônier (militaire).

padsaw ['pædsɔː], *s. Carp:* scie *f* à guichet démontable; scie à manche.

Padua ['pædjuə], *Pr.n. Geog:* Padoue *f*.

Paduan ['pædjuən]. *Geog:* (*a*) *a.* padouan; (*b*) *s.* Padouan, -ane.

paduasoy ['pædjuəsɔi], *s. Tex: A:* pou-de-soie *m*, *pl.* poux-de-soie.

paean ['piːən], *s.* péan *m*, pæan *m*.

paederast, *etc.* = PEDERAST, etc.

paedobaptism [piːdou'bæptizm, ped-], *s. Rel:* pédobaptisme *m*.

paedogenesis [piːdou'dʒenisis, 'ped-], *s. Biol:* paedogénèse *f*, pédogénèse *f*.

paedogenetic [piːdoudʒe'netik, ped-], *a. Biol:* paedogénétique, pédogénétique.

paedologic(al) [piːdou'lɔdʒik(l), ped-], *a. Med:* pédologique.

paedologist [piː'dɔlədʒist, ped-], *s. Med:* pédologue *mf*.

paedology [piː'dɔlədʒi, ped-], *s. Med:* pédologie *f*.

paedophilia [pi:dou'filiə, ped-], *s. Psy:* pédophilie *f.*

paeon ['pi:ən], *s. Pros:* péon *m.*

paeonic [pi:'ɔnik], *a. Pros:* péonique.

pagan ['peigən], *a. & s.* païen, -ïenne.

paganism ['peigənizm], *s.* paganisme *m.*

paganize ['peigənaiz], *v.tr. & i.* paganiser; rendre païen; vivre en païen.

page[1] [peidʒ], *s.* **1.** (*a*) *A:* petit laquais; (*b*) (*attending person of rank*) page *m*; **p. of honour,** page du roi, de la reine; (*c*) (*at wedding*) page (d'honneur). **2.** jeune chasseur (d'hôtel). **3.** *A. Cost:* page, relève-jupe *m inv.*

page[2], *v.tr.* **1.** *Hist:* servir (qn) comme laquais, comme page. **2.** envoyer chercher (qn) par un chasseur; appeler (qn) par haut-parleur, par radio portative.

page[3], *s.* page *f*; **first p., front p.,** recto *m* (d'une feuille de papier); **right-hand p.,** (i) recto (d'une page de livre, de journal); (ii) *Typ:* belle page; **left-hand p.,** (i) verso *m* (d'une page de livre, de journal); (ii) *Typ:* fausse page; **at the back of the p.,** au dos, au verso, de la page, de la feuille; **on p. 6,** à la page 6; *Journ: etc:* **continued on p. 6, on back p.,** suite *f* (en) page 6, en dernière page; *Typ:* **p. setting,** mise *f* en pages; **p. proofs,** épreuves *f* en pages; **p. printing set,** appareil *m* à imprimer en page; **p. teleprinter,** téléimprimeur *m* par page; **p. copy,** copie *f,* exemplaire *m,* sur page (de téléimprimeur); *Cmptr:* **p. (-at-a-time) printer,** imprimante *f* page par page; **p. break, p. change,** changement *m* de feuillet; **p. directory,** index *m* de pages; **p. ejection,** saut *m* de feuillet; **p. reader,** lecteur *m* de page.

page[4], *v.tr.* **1.** numéroter (les feuilles); paginer, folioter (un livre); chiffrer les pages (d'un registre, etc.). **2.** *Typ:* mettre (la composition) en pages.

pageant ['pædʒ(ə)nt], *s.* **1.** (*a*) spectacle pompeux; (*b*) **an empty p.,** du spectacle, sans plus. **2.** (*a*) cortège *m* ou cavalcade *f* historique; (*b*) grand spectacle historique donné en costume (avec ou sans chœurs, déclamation, etc.). **3. air p.,** fête *f* d'aviation; fête aéronautique.

pageantry ['pædʒəntri], *s.* apparat *m,* pompe *f.*

pageboy ['peidʒbɔi], *s.* **1.** petit chasseur (d'hôtel). **2.** *attrib. Hairdr:* **p. style** coiffure *f* à l'ange, à la page.

pagehood ['peidʒhud], *s. Hist:* condition *f* de page; **out of p.,** hors de page.

Paget ['pædʒit]. *Pr.n. Med:* **Paget's disease,** (i) maladie de la peau de Paget; (ii) maladie (osseuse) de Paget, ostéite déformante.

paginal ['pædʒin(ə)l], *a.* **1. p. references,** renvois *m* à la page. **2.** (*of reprint, etc.*) reproduit, copié, page à page.

paginate ['pædʒineit], *v.tr.* paginer (un livre); numéroter, folioter, les pages (d'un livre).

pagination [pædʒi'neiʃ(ə)n], *s.* pagination *f*; numérotage *m,* foliotage *m* (des pages); **mistake in p.,** faute *f* de pagination.

paging[1] ['peidʒiŋ], *s.* (*in hotel, etc.*) recherche *f* de personnes.

paging[2], *s.* **1.** numérotage *m* des pages; pagination *f,* foliotage *m*; **p. machine,** machine *f* à numéroter; folioteuse *f.* **2.** *Typ:* mise *f* en pages.

Pagliacci [pæli'ɑ:tʃi]. *Pr.n. Th:* Paillasse *m* (opéra de Leoncavallo).

pagne [pɑɲ], *s.* pagne *m* (des indigènes des pays chauds).

pagoda [pə'goudə], *s.* **1.** (*a*) *Arch:* pagode *f*; (*b*) *Cost:* **p. sleeves,** manches *f* pagode. **2.** *Num: A:* pagode. **3.** *Bot:* **p. tree,** (i) sophora *m* du Japon; (ii) figuier *m* des Banians. **4.** *Miner:* **p. stone,** pagodite *f.*

pagodite ['pægədait, pə'goudait], *s. Miner:* pagodite *f.*

pagoscope ['pægouskoup], *s. Ph:* pagoscope *m.*

pagrus ['pægrəs], *s. Ich:* pagre *m.*

pagurian [pæ'gju:riən], *s. Crust:* pagure *m*; *F:* bernard-l'ermite *m.*

pah [pɑ:], *int.* pouah!

Pahlavi ['pɑ:ləvi], *s. Ling:* pehlvi *m.*

paiche ['paitʃei], *s. Ich:* paiche *m,* pirarucu *m.*

paid [peid], *a.* **1.** appointé, payé, rétribué, rémunéré, salarié; **p. assistant,** aide rétribué(e); **p. holidays,** congés payés; **p. work,** travail rémunéré, rétribué, salarié; **p. worker,** travailleur salarié, rétribué. **2.** (*a*) *Com:* (*of goods, freight, etc.*) payé; **p. bills,** rentrées *fpl*; **p. cash book,** main courante de dépenses, de sortie; (*b*) *Fin:* **p. up,** (i) (*of capital*) versé; (ii) (*of shares*) libéré.

pail [peil], *s.* **1.** seau *m*; (*wooden*) seille *f*; *Nau:* baille *f*; **household p.,** seau de ménage; **tar p.,** baille à brai; **milking p.,** seille à traire. **2. a p. of water,** un seau d'eau.

pailful ['peilful], *s.* (plein) seau (de lait, etc.); **to bring a p. of water,** apporter (plein) un seau d'eau.

paillasse [pæl'jæs], *s.* paillasse *f.*

paillette [pai'jet], *s. Cost: etc:* paillette *f.*

pain[1] [pein], *s.* **1.** (*a*) douleur *f,* souffrance *f*; (*mental*) peine *f*; **to give s.o. p.,** (i) (*of tooth, etc.*) faire mal à qn, faire souffrir qn; (ii) (*of incident, etc.*) faire de la peine à qn; **it gives me much p. to . . .,** il me peine beaucoup de . . .; **to be in (great) p.,** souffrir beaucoup; **is he in p.?** souffre-t-il? **to cry out with p.,** pousser un cri, des cris, de douleur; **to be out of p.,** avoir cessé de souffrir; **to put a wounded animal out of its p.,** achever un animal blessé, donner le coup de grâce à un animal; (*b*) **shooting pains,** élancements *m,* douleurs lancinantes; **a p. in the side,** une douleur dans le côté; un point de côté; **to have a p. in the head, in one's head, to suffer from pains in the head,** avoir mal à la tête; souffrir de la tête; **p. reliever,** calmant *m,* analgésique *m,* antalgique *m*; *F:* **he's, he gives me, a p. in the neck,** il me tape sur le système; il est enquiquinant, emmerdant; c'est un casse-pieds; **it gives me a p. in the neck,** ça me débecte. **2.** *pl.* **pains:** (*a*) peine; **to take pains, be at great pains, to do sth.,** prendre, se donner, de la peine, beaucoup de peine, pour faire qch.; se donner du mal pour faire qch.; s'appliquer, mettre tous ses soins, mettre un soin infini, à faire qch.; **to take pains over sth.,** s'appliquer à qch.; **to have one's labour for one's pains, to have one's pains for nothing, to have nothing for one's pains,** en être pour sa peine, pour ses frais; (i) perdre, (ii) avoir perdu, sa peine; *F:* travailler pour le roi de Prusse; **they are fools for their pains,** ils en sont pour leur peine; **you will only get laughed at for your pains,** vous n'en rapporterez que des moqueries; (*b*) travail *m* d'enfant; douleurs *fpl* de l'enfantement. **3.** *A:* châtiment *m*; *still so used in* **on p. of (death, etc.),** sous peine de (mort, etc.); **pains and penalties,** châtiments et peines.

pain[2], *v.tr.* faire souffrir (qn); (*physically*) faire mal à (qn); (*mentally*) faire de la peine à (qn), peiner, affliger (qn); **my arm pains me, my arm is paining,** mon bras me fait souffrir; **it pains me to see him,** cela me fait (du) mal de le voir; **it pains me to say so,** cela me coûte à dire; il m'en coûte de le dire.

pained [peind], *a.* (*a*) attristé, peiné (**at,** de); (*b*) **p. expression,** air affligé, peiné; **in p. surprise,** d'un air de surprise affligée.

painful ['peinf(u)l], *a.* **1.** (*of wound, part of the body*) douloureux; **I find walking p.,** je souffre à marcher; (*of limb, etc.*) **to become p.,** s'endolorir; **my knee was getting p.,** mon genou, le genou, commençait à me faire mal. **2.** (*of spectacle, effort*) pénible; **p. subject,** sujet *m* pénible; **it is p. to hear him,** on souffre, cela fait peine, de l'entendre; **misery that is p. to see,** misère *f* qui fait peine à voir; **it is p. for me to have to say so,** cela me coûte de le dire. **3.** *A:* (travail) laborieux, pénible.

painfully ['peinfuli], *adv.* **1.** douloureusement, péniblement. **2.** *A:* laborieusement.

painfulness ['peinfulnis], *s.* nature douloureuse, pénible (**of,** de); pénibilité *f.*

painkiller ['peinkilər], *s.* calmant *m,* antalgique *m.*

painkilling ['peinkiliŋ], *a.* calmant, antalgique.

painless ['peinlis], *a.* **1.** indolore; (extraction *f,* etc.) sans douleur. **2. p. tumour,** tumeur indolente, indolore.

painlessness ['peinlisnis], *s.* absence *f* de douleur; indolence *f* (d'une tumeur).

painstaking[1] ['peinzteikiŋ], *a.* soigneux, assidu; **p. pupil,** élève travailleur, appliqué; **p. work,** travail soigné.

painstaking[2], *s.* **with a little p. you will manage it,** en vous donnant un peu de peine vous y arriverez.

paint[1] [peint], *s.* **1. to give sth. a p.,** peindre qch.; passer une couche de peinture sur qch.; **this door needs a p.,** il nous faut repeindre cette porte. **2.** (*a*) peinture *f*; **coat of p.,** couche de peinture; **glossy p.,** peinture brillante, laquée; **mat(t) p.,** peinture mate; **acid-resisting p.,** peinture résistant aux acides; **aluminium p.,** peinture (à l') aluminium; **anticorrosive p.,** peinture anticorrosive; **antirust p.,** peinture antirouille; **cellulose p.,** peinture cellulosique; **emulsion p.,** peinture à émulsion; **luminous p.,** peinture lumineuse; **metallic p.,** peinture métallique; **oil p.,** peinture, couleur *f,* à l'huile; **priming p.,** peinture d'apprêt; **red-lead p.,** peinture au minium; **thin p.,** bruine *f* (pour peindre au pistolet); **water p.,** peinture à l'eau; **white-lead p.,** peinture à la céruse; **disrupted p.,** peinture bigarrée, en zébrures (pour camouflage); *Nau:* **antifouling p.,** peinture antiparasites; **(ship) bottom p.,** peinture de carène, sous-marine; **fireproof p.,** peinture ignifuge; **pot of p.,** pot *m* de peinture; **p. pot,** pot à peinture; **p. gun, spray(er),** pistolet *m* à peindre, à peinture; **p. roller,** rouleau *m* à peindre, à peinture; **p. thinner,** solvant *m* pour peinture; **p. remover,** décapant *m* pour peinture; **p. shop,** (i) magasin *m* de couleurs; (ii) *Ind:* atelier *m* de peinture; *P.N:* **wet p.! mind the p.!** attention, prenez garde, à la peinture! peinture fraîche! (*b*) *Art:* couleur; **box of paints,** boîte *f* de couleurs, de peinture, d'aquarelle; **tube of p.,** tube *m* de peinture, de couleurs; (*c*) *Med:* badigeon *m*; (*d*) *F: A:* fard *m*; **she puts p. on her face,** elle se farde.

paint[2], *v.tr.* peindre. **1.** (*a*) **to p. a portrait in oils,** peindre un portrait à l'huile; **to p. a sunset,** peindre un coucher de soleil; **to p. the passions,** dépeindre les passions; **to p. everything in rosy colours,** peindre tout en beau; (*b*) *v.i.* faire de la peinture; **to p. in water-colours, in gouache,** faire de l'aquarelle, de la gouache. **2.** dépeindre; **what words can p. the scene?** comment dépeindre cette scène? **3.** (*a*) enduire, couvrir, de peinture; **to p. a room,** peindre une pièce; **the kitchen needs painting,** il faut faire repeindre la cuisine; **to p. a door green,** peindre une porte en vert; *Th:* **to p. the scenery for a play,** brosser les décors d'une pièce; **to p. an escutcheon heraldically,** blasonner un écu; *F:* **to p. the town red,** faire une orgie, une noce, à tout casser; *Lit:* **spring paints the fields with a thousand hues,** le printemps diapre les champs de mille couleurs; (*b*) *F: A:* **to p. one's face,** se farder; se peindre; *F:* se plâtrer (le visage); se mettre du fard aux joues; (*c*) *Med:* badigeonner (la gorge, etc.).

paintable ['peintəbl], *a.* qui peut être peint; **she's very p.,** c'est un beau sujet de peinture.

paintbox ['peintbɔks], *s.* boîte *f* de couleurs, d'aquarelle.

paintbrush ['peintbrʌʃ], *s.* **1.** pinceau *m*; brosse *f* à peinture. **2.** *Bot:* **(Indian) p.,** castillèje *f.*

painted ['peintid], *a.* peint; *Bot:* **p. cup,** castillèje *f*; **p. grass,** phalaride *m,* phalaris *m*; *Ent:* **p. lady,** belle-dame *f, pl.* belles-dames.

painter[1] ['peintər], *s.* **1.** (*a*) *Art:* peintre *m*; **the p. of the picture,** l'auteur *m* du tableau; **she was a famous p.,** elle fut un peintre célèbre; **p. of animals,** animalier *m*; **ivory p., china p.,** peintre sur ivoire, sur porcelaine; **heraldic p.,** peintre de blason; **landscape p.,** paysagiste *m*; (*b*) coloriste *mf* (de cartes postales, de jouets). **2. (house) p.,** peintre en bâtiments, en décor; peintre décorateur; *Med:* **painter's colic,** colique(s) *f(pl)* de plomb, colique(s) saturnine(s).

painter[2], *s. Nau:* bosse *f* (d'embarcation, de lof); **to slip the p.,** (i) filer la bosse; (ii) *F:* mourir; **to cut the p.,** couper, trancher, l'amarre.

painting ['peintiŋ], *s.* **1.** peinture *f*; (*a*) **to study p.,** étudier la peinture; (*b*) **(house) p.,** peinture (de bâtiments, etc.). **2.** peinture, tableau *m* (à l'huile, à l'aquarelle).

paintwork ['peintwə:k], *s.* (*house building*) les peintures *f.*

pair[1] [pɛər], *s.* **1.** (*a*) paire *f* (de chaussures, de vases, de ciseaux, de jambes, etc.); **two pair(s) of scissors,** deux paires de ciseaux; **arranged in pairs,** arrangés deux par deux, par paires, par couples; **the p. of you,** vous deux; **the two of them are a pretty p.,** les deux font la paire; *Mec.E:* **p. of brasses,** jeu *m* de coussinets; **p. of gears,** couple *m* d'engrenages; (*b*) **a p. of trousers, of pants,** un pantalon, un caleçon; *O:* **a p. of scales,** une balance; (*c*) attelage *m* (de deux chevaux); **carriage and p.,** voiture *f* à deux chevaux; **p. of oxen,** couple *f* de bœufs; (*d*) (*man and wife*) couple *m*; **the happy p.,** les deux conjoints *m*; **p. of pigeons (cock and hen),** couple de pigeons; (*e*) (*match*) **these two pictures are a p.,** ces deux tableaux se font pendant; **stockings that are not a p.,** bas *m* disparates, qui ne vont pas ensemble; (*f*) **where is the p. of this glove?** où se trouve l'autre gant de cette paire? (*g*) *Row:* deux *m*; (*h*) **p. royal,** (i) *Cards:* brelan *m*; (ii) (*dice*) rafle *f*; (*i*) *Atom.Ph:* **electron, ion, p.,** paire d'électrons, d'ions; **electron-posit(r)on p.,** paire électron-positron; **energy expended per ion p.,** perte *f* d'énergie par paire d'ions; **ion-p. yield,** rendement *m* en paires d'ions; **yield per ion p.,** rendement par paire d'ions; **p. conversion,** conversion *f* d'une paire; **p. creation, p. formation,** création *f* d'une paire, de paires; **p. emission,** émission *f* d'une paire, de paires; **p. production,** production *f* de paires; (*j*) *Tp:* **telephone p.,** paire téléphonique; **coaxial p.,** paire coaxiale; **shielded p.,** paire blindée; **twisted p.,** paire torsadée. **2.** *O:* **p. of stairs,** escalier *m* (en deux volées); étage *m*; **I had to go down two p. of stairs,** il me fallait descendre deux étages; *A:* **to lodge on the three-p. front, on the three-p. back,** loger au troisième (étage) sur la rue, sur la cour; *O:* **p. of steps,** marchepied (volant), escabeau *m.* **3.** *Parl:* (*a*) paire de membres de partis adverses qui se sont pairés pour un vote ou pour une période déterminée; (*b*) **to apply for a p.,** demander aux chefs de partis de désigner un membre du parti adverse avec qui l'on puisse se pairer.

pair[2], *v.*

I. 1. *v tr.* (*a*) appareiller, apparier, assortir (des gants, etc.); (*b*) accoupler, apparier (des oiseaux, etc.). **2.** *v.i.* (*a*) faire la paire (**with s.o., sth.,** avec qn, qch.); **two vases that p.,** deux vases *m* qui (se) font pendant; (*b*) (*of birds, etc.*) s'accoupler, s'apparier (**with,** avec); (*c*) *Parl:* **to p.,** se pairer (**with s.o.,** avec qn); s'absenter après entente avec un adversaire qui désire aussi s'absenter (de façon que la majorité parlementaire reste la même).

II. (*compound verb*) **pair off;** (*a*) *v.tr.* arranger, distribuer, (des personnes, des objets) deux par deux; (*b*) *v.i.* s'en aller, se disperser, défiler, deux par deux, deux à deux, en couples.

pair[3], *s.* **au p.,** au pair; **au p. (student),** étudiant(e) au pair; **she's staying with them au p.,** elle est chez eux au pair.

paired ['pɛəd], *a.* (*a*) deux par deux, par paires, par couples; (*of guns, machines*) jumelés, conjugués; *I.C.E:* **p. cylinders,** cylindres accouplés; *Artil:* **guns p. in turret,** canons jumelés en tourelle; *Av: etc:* **p. engines,** moteurs jumelés; **p. floats,** flotteurs (disposés) en catamaran; (*b*) *Tp:* **p. cable,** câble *m* à paires; (*c*) apparéillé, apparié; *Atom: Ph:* **p. lattices,** réseaux appariés.

pairing ['pɛəriŋ], *s.* (*a*) appariement *m* (de chaussures, etc.); jumelage *m*, conjugaison *f* (de machines, des canons); appareillement *m* (de bœufs pour le joug); (*b*) appariement, accouplement *m* (d'animaux mâle et femelle); **p. season, time,** saison *f* des amours; (*of birds*) pariade *f*; (*c*) *Parl:* pairage *m*; (*d*) *T.V:* pairage; (*e*) *Tp:* câblage *m* par paires; *Atom.Ph:* **p. energy,** énergie *f* de création d'une paire (d'ions).

Paisley ['peizli]. *Pr.n. Tex:* **P. pattern,** (dessin *m*) cachemire *m*.

pajamas [pə'dʒæməz], *s.pl. NAm:* pyjama *m*.

pakfong ['pækfɔŋ], **paktong** ['pæktɔŋ], *s.* = PACKFONG.

Pakistan [pæki'stɑːn]. *Pr.n. Geog:* Pakistan *m*.

Pakistani [pæki'stɑːni]. *Geog:* (*a*) *a.* pakistanais; (*b*) *s.* Pakistanais, -aise.

pal[1] [pæl], *s. F:* camarade *mf*; copain, *f.* copine; **we're great pals,** nous sommes bons copains; **to make a p. of s.o.,** se faire un camarade de qn.

pal[2], *v.i.* **(palled)** *F:* **to p. up with s.o.,** se lier (d'amitié) avec qn; nouer amitié avec qn; se prendre d'amitié pour qn; devenir copain avec qn.

palace ['pælis], *s.* **1.** palais *m*; **Buckingham P.,** Buckingham Palace; **the P. of Versailles,** le palais de Versailles; **Bishop's p.,** évêché *m*; palais épiscopal; **Archbishop's p.,** archevêché *m*; palais archiépiscopal; *Pol:* **p. revolution,** révolution *f* de palais. **2.** (*hotel, etc.*) palace *m*; *O:* **picture p.,** cinéma *m*; *F: O:* **gin p.,** bar *m* de basse classe (aux décors somptueux mais de mauvais goût).

paladin ['pælədin], *s.* paladin *m*.

Palaemon [pæ'liːmən]. **1.** *Pr.n.m. Myth:* Palémon. **2.** *s. Crust:* palémon *m*, bouquet *m*; grande crevette salicoque.

palaeo- ['pæliou, pæli'ɔ], *comb.fm.* = PALEO- (*e.g. for* **palaeobotany** *see* PALEOBOTANY).

Palaeologus [pæli'ɔləgəs]. *Pr.n. Hist:* (Michel, etc.) Paléologue.

palaestra [pæ'liːstrə], *s. Gr.Ant:* palestre *f*.

palaestral [pæ'liːstr(ə)l], *a.* palestrique.

palafitte ['pæləfit], *s. Prehist:* palafitte *m*.

palais de danse ['pælidə'dɑːns], *s. O:* dancing *m*.

palaite ['pæleiait], *s. Miner:* palaïte *f*.

Palamedes [pælə'miːdiːz]. *Pr.n.m. Gr.Myth:* Palamède.

palank ['pælæŋk], *s. Fort:* palanque *f*.

palanquin [pælən'kiːn], *s.* palanquin *m*.

palatability [pælətə'biliti], *s.* sapidité *f*.

palatable ['pælətəbl], *a.* (*a*) d'un goût agréable; agréable au palais, au goût; sapide; **p. wine,** vin *m* qui se laisse boire; **p. fruit,** fruit *m* qui se laisse manger; (*b*) (*of doctrine, etc.*) agréable **(to,** à); **truth is seldom p. to kings,** il est rare que la vérité soit agréable aux rois.

palatal ['pælətl]. **1.** *a. Anat: Ling:* palatal, -aux; *Anat:* palatin; **p. l,** l mouillée. **2.** *s. Ling:* palatale *f*.

palatality [pælə'tæliti], *s. Ling:* mouillure *f* (d'une consonne).

palatalization [pælətəlai'zeiʃ(ə)n], *s. Ling:* palatalisation *f*.

palatalize ['pælətəlaiz], *v.tr. Ling:* palataliser; mouiller (une **l,** la combinaison **gn**).

palate ['pælət], *s.* **1.** (*a*) *Anat:* palais *m*; **hard p.,** palais (dur), voûte *f* du palais, voûte palatine; **soft p.,** voile *m* du palais; **cleft p.,** palais fendu; (*b*) **to have a delicate p.,** avoir le palais fin; **depraved p.,** dépravation *f* du goût; **to have no p. for coarse jokes,** ne pas goûter, ne pas savourer, les plaisanteries corsées. **2.** *Bot:* palais (de la corolle du muflier, etc.).

palatial [pə'leiʃ(ə)l], *a.* (édifice) qui ressemble à un palais, magnifique, grandiose.

palatic [pə'lætik], *a. Anat:* palatal, -aux.

palatinate [pə'lætineit], *s.* **1.** palatinat *m*; *Hist:* **the P.,** le Palatinat. **2.** *Sch:* **p. purple,** pourpre *f* (i) des robes académiques, (ii) des insignes sportifs, de l'université de Durham; **to get one's p.,** être choisi comme membre de l'équipe universitaire.

palatine[1] ['pælətain], *a.* & *s.* **1.** *Hist:* palatin, -ine. **2.** *Geog:* **the P. (Hill),** le (mont) Palatin. **3.** *A.Cost:* **p. (tippet),** palatine *f*.

palatine[2]. **1.** *a. Anat:* palatal, -aux, palatin; du palais. **2.** *s.pl.* **palatines,** (os) palatins; la voûte palatine.

palatodental [pælətou'dentəl], *a. Ling:* palato-dental, -aux.

palatoglossal [pælətou'glɔsəl], *a. Anat:* palato-glosse, *pl.* palato-glosses.

palatoglossus, *pl.* **-i** [pælətou'glɔsəs, -ai], *s. Anat:* (muscle *m*) palato-glosse *m*.

palatogram ['pælətougræm], *s. Med:* palatogramme *m*.

palatographic [pælətou'græfik], *a. Med:* palatographique.

palatography [pælə'tɔgrəfi], *s. Med:* palatographie *f*.

palato-pharyngeal [pælətoufærin'dʒiːəl], *a. Ling: Anat:* palato-pharyngien, *pl.* palato-pharyngiens.

palatopharyngitis [pælətoufærin'dʒaitis], *s. Med:* palatopharyngite *f*.

palatoplastic [pælətou'plæstik], *a. Surg:* palatoplastique.

palatoplasty [pælətou'plæsti], *s. Surg:* palatoplastie *f*.

palatorrhaphic [pælətɔ'ræfik], *a. Surg:* palatorrhapique.

palatorrhaphy [pælətɔ'ræfi], *s. Surg:* palatorrhapie *f*.

palaver[1] [pə'lɑːvər], *s.* **1.** palabre *f*; **after a long p.,** après de longues palabres. **2.** *F:* (*a*) *O:* cajoleries *fpl*; flagornerie *f*; (*b*) embarras *mpl*; **what's all the p. about?** qu'est-ce qu'il y a qui cloche?

palaver[2]. **1.** *v.i.* palabrer. **2.** *v.tr. F: O:* entortiller (qn) par de belles paroles; amadouer, cajoler, flagorner (qn).

pale[1] [peil], *s.* **1.** pieu *m* (de clôture); pale *f*; pal *m*, *pl.* pals; *F:* palis *m*. **2.** (*a*) *A:* bornes *fpl*, limites *fpl*; *still so used in* **outside the p. of society, beyond the p.,** au ban de la société, de l'humanité; **within the p. of the Church,** dans le giron, dans le sein, de l'Église; **to be outside the p. (of the Church),** être hors de l'arche; **within the p. of reason,** accessible à la raison; (*b*) *Hist:* **the (English) P. (in Ireland),** la Pale (la région sous la juridiction de l'Angleterre); **the English P. in France,** le territoire de Calais. **3.** *Her:* pal; **party per p.,** parti.

pale[2], *v.tr.* **to p. (in) a field,** palissader, clôturer, un champ.

pale[3], *a.* (*a*) pâle, blême; sans couleur; (*of complexion*) délavé; **her face was p. and sad,** son visage décoloré était empreint de tristesse; **p. as death, deadly p., ghastly p.,** pâle comme la mort, comme un mort; d'une pâleur mortelle; blême; **p. as ashes,** blanc comme un linge; **to grow, become, p.,** pâlir; **to turn p. with fright,** pâlir de terreur; **this dress makes you look p.,** cette robe vous pâlit; (*b*) (*of colour*) pâle, clair; **p. blue dress,** robe *f* d'un bleu pâle; robe bleu clair; (*c*) **a p. and watery sun,** un soleil pâle qui annonce la pluie; un soleil blafard; **by the p. light of the moon,** à la lumière blafarde de la lune.

pale[4]. **1.** *v.i.* (*a*) pâlir, blêmir; (*b*) **my adventures p. beside yours, before yours,** mes aventures *f* pâlissent auprès des vôtres; *A:* **his star is paling,** son étoile *f* pâlit. **2.** *v.tr.* faire pâlir; pâlir; **fever had paled him,** la fièvre l'avait pâli.

pale[5], *s. Bot:* paléa *f*; préfeuille *f*; glumelle supérieure (d'une graminacée).

palea, *pl.* **-eae** ['peiliə, -iiː], *s. Bot:* paléa *f*; préfeuille *f*; glumelle supérieure (d'une graminacée); paillette *f* (d'une composacée, d'une graminacée).

paleaceous [peili'eiʃəs], *a. Bot:* paléacé.

palearctic [pæli'ɑːktik], *a.* paléarctique.

paled [peild], *a.* palissadé, à palissade.

paleface ['peilfeis], *s.* visage *m* pâle (blanc, *f.* blanche, dans le parler des Peaux-Rouges).

pale-faced ['peilfeist], *a.* au visage, au teint, pâle ou blême; à face pâle.

palely ['peilli], *adv.* pâlement; sans éclat.

paleness ['peilnis], *s.* pâleur *f*.

paleo- ['pæliou, pæli'ɔ], *comb.fm.* paléo-.

paleoanthropological [pæliouænθrəpə'lɔdʒikl], *a.* paléoanthropologique.

paleoanthropologist [pæliouænθrə'pɔlədʒist], *s.* paléoanthropologiste *mf*, paléoanthropologue *mf*.

paleoanthropology [pæliouænθrə'pɔlədʒi], *s.* paléoanthropologie *f*.

paleoarchaeologic(al) [pæliouɑːkiə'lɔdʒik(l)], *a.* paléoarchéologique.

paleoarchaeologist [pæliouɑːki'ɔlədʒist], *s.* paléoarchéologue *mf*.

paleoarchaeology [pæliouɑːki'ɔlədʒi], *s.* paléo-archéologie *f*.

paleobiological [pælioubaiə'lɔdʒikl], *a.* paléo-biologique.

paleobiologist [pælioubai'ɔlədʒist], *s.* paléobiologiste *mf*.

paleobiology [pælioubai'ɔlədʒi], *s.* paléobiologie *f*.

paleobotanical [pælioubə'tænikl], *a.* paléobotanique.

paleobotanist [pæliou'bɔtənist], *s.* paléobotaniste *mf*.

paleobotany [pæliou'bɔtəni], *s.* paléobotanique *f*.

Paleocene ['pæliousiːn], *a.* & *s. Geol:* paléocène (*m*).

Paleo-Christian [pæliou'kristjən], *a.* & *s.* paléochrétien, -ienne.

paleoclimate [pæliou'klaimət], *s.* paléoclimat *m*.

paleoclimatological [pæliouklaimətə'lɔdʒikl], *a.* paléoclimatologique.

paleoclimatology [pæliouklaimə'tɔlədʒi], *s.* paléoclimatologie *f*.

paleocrystic [pæliou'kristik], *a. Geol:* paléocrystique.

Paleodictyoptera [pælioudikti'ɔptərə], *s.pl. Ent:* paléodictyoptères *m*.

paleoecologic(al) [pælioui:kə'lɔdʒik(l)], *a.* paléoécologique.

paleoecologist [pælioui:'kɔlədʒist], *s.* paléoécologiste *mf*.

paleoecology [pælioui:'kɔlədʒi], *s.* paléoécologie *f*.

paleoethnological [pælioueθnə'lɔdʒikl], *a.* paléoethnologique.

paleoethnologist [pælioueθ'nɔlədʒist], *s.* paléoethnologue *mf*.

paleoethnology [pælioueθ'nɔlədʒi], *s.* paléoethnologie *f*.

paleogene ['pælioudʒiːn], *a.* & *s. Geol:* paléogène (*m*).

paleogeographer [pælioudʒiː'ɔgrəfər], *s.* paléogéographe *mf*.

paleogeographic(al) [pælioudʒiːə'græfik(l)], *a.* paléogéographique.

paleogeography [pælioudʒiː'ɔgrəfi], *s.* paléogéographie *f*.

paleographer [pæli'ɔgrəfər], *s.* paléographe *mf*.

paleographic(al) [pæliou'græfik(l)], *a.* paléographique.

paleography [pæli'ɔgrəfi], *s.* paléographie *f*.

paleohistological [pæliouhistə'lɔdʒikl], *a.* paléohistologique.

paleohistologist [pæliouhis'tɔlədʒist], *s.* paléohistologiste *mf*.

paleohistology [pæliouhis'tɔlədʒi], *s.* paléohistologie *f*.

paleolith ['pæliouliθ], *s.* vestige *m*, outil *m*, objet *m*, du paléolithique.

paleolithic [pæliou'liθik], *a.* paléolithique; **the P. age,** le paléolithique, l'âge *m* de la pierre taillée.

paleologist [pæli'ɔlədʒist], *s.* paléologue *mf*.

paleology [pæli'ɔlədʒi], *s.* paléologie *f*.

paleomagnetic [pælioumæg'netik], *a.* paléomagnétique.

paleomagnetism [pæliou'mægnitizm], *s.* paléomagnétisme *m*.

paleometabolic [pælioumetə'bɔlik], *a. Biol:* paléométabolique.

paleometabolism [pælioume'tæbəlizm], *s. Biol:* paléométabolisme *m*, paléométabolie *f*.

paleometabolous [pælioume'tæbələs], *a. Biol:* paléométabole.

paleontological [pæliɔntə'lɔdʒikl], *a.* paléontologique.

paleontologist [pæliɔn'tɔlədʒist], *s.* paléontologiste *mf*, paléontologue *mf*.

paleontology [pæliɔn'tɔlədʒi], *s.* paléontologie *f*.

paleopathology [pælioupæ'θɔlədʒi], *s.* paléopathologie *f*.

paleophytograph [pæliou'faitougræf], *s. Bot:* paléophytogramme *m*.

paleophytographer [pælioufai'tɔgrəfər], *s. Bot:* paléophytographe *mf*.

paleophytographical [pælioufaitou'græfikl], *a. Bot:* paléophytographique.

paleophytography [pælioufai'tɔgrəfi], *s. Bot:* paléophytographie *f*.

paleophytology [pælioufai'tɔlədʒi], *s. Bot:* paléophytologie *f*.

paleoplain ['pæliouplein], *s. Geol:* paléoplaine *f*.

paleopsychic(al) [pæliou'saikik(l)], *a.* paléopsychique.

paleopsychology [pæliousai'kɔlədʒi], *s.* paléo-psychologie *f*.

paleopter [pæli'ɔptər], *s. Ent:* paléoptère *m*.

Paleoptera [pæli'ɔptərə], *s.pl. Ent:* paléoptères *m*.

paleopteran [pæli'ɔptərən], *a. Ent:* (aile) paléoptère.

paliothere ['pæliouθiər], **paleotherium** [pæliou'θiəriəm], *s.* paléothérium *m*.

paleotropical [pæliou'trɔpikl], *a.* paléotropical, -aux.

paleovolcanic [pæliouvɔl'kænik], *a.* paléovolcanique.

paleozoic [pæliou'zouik], *a. Geol:* paléozoïque.

paleozoological [pæliouzouə'lɔdʒikl], *a.* paléozoologique.

paleozoologist [pæliouzou'ɔlədʒist], *s.* paléozoologiste *mf*.

paleozoology [pæliouzou'ɔlədʒi], *s.* paléozoologie *f*.

Palermitan [pə'ləːmit(ə)n]. *Geog:* (*a*) *a.* palermitain; (*b*) *s.* Palermitain, -aine.

Palermo [pə'ləːmou]. *Pr.n. Geog:* Palerme.

Palestine ['pælistain]. *Pr.n.* Palestine *f*.

Palestinian [pælis'tiniən], (*a*) *a.* palestinien; (*b*) *s.*

Palestinien, -ienne.
palestra [pæ'lestrə], *s.*, **palestral** [pæ'lestr(ə)l], *a.* = PALAESTRA, PALAESTRAL.
paletot ['pæltou], *s. Cost:* paletot *m.*
palette ['pælit], *s.* **1.** *Art:* palette *f*; **to set, lay out, one's p.,** faire, charger, sa palette; **p. knife,** couteau *m* à palette; amassette *f.* **2.** *Tls:* conscience *f*, plastron *m* (d'un porte-foret).
palfrey ['pɔːlfri], *s. A: & Lit:* palefroi *m.*
Pali ['pɑːli], *s. Ling:* pali *m.*
palikar ['pælikɑːr], *s. Gr.Hist:* palicare *m*, palikare *m*, pallikare *m.*
palimpsest ['pælimpsest], *a. & s.* palimpseste (*m*).
palindrome ['pælindroum], *s.* palindrome *m.*
palindromia [pælin'droumiə], *s. Med:* palindromie *f.*
palindromic [pælin'drɔmik], *a.* **1.** *Lit: Mth:* palindrome. **2.** *Med:* palindromique.
paling[1] ['peiliŋ], *s.* **1.** (*fencing; also* **palings**) clôture *f* à claire-voie; palissade *f*, palis *m*; échalier *m.* **2.** = PALE[1] 1.
paling[2], *s.* pâlissement *m.*
palingenesia [pælindʒi'niːsiə], **palingenesis** [pælin'dʒenisis], **palingenesy** [pælin'dʒenisi], *s.* (*a*) *Biol:* palingénésie *f*; reproduction *f* des mêmes traits, des mêmes évolutions; régénération *f*; (*b*) *Phil:* palingénésie, retour *m* à la vie, renaissance *f*; (*c*) *Geol:* palingénèse *f.*
palingenetic [pælindʒi'netik], *a.* (*a*) *Biol: Geol:* (*also* **palingenic**) palingénésique; (*b*) *Phil:* palingénésique, palingénésiaque.
palinode ['pælinoud], *s. Lit: etc:* palinodie *f.*
palinodic [pæli'noudik], *a.* palinodique.
palinodist ['pælinoudist], *s.* palinodiste *mf.*
palinurid [pæli'njuːrid], *s. Crust:* palinure *m.*
Palinuridae [pæli'njuːridiː], *s.pl. Crust:* palinuridés *m.*
Palinuro [pæli'njuːrou], *Pr.n. Geog:* **Cape P.,** le cap Palinure.
Palinurus [pæli'njuːrəs]. **1.** *Pr.n.m. Lit. Lit:* Palinure. **2.** *s. Crust:* palinure *m.*
palisade[1] [pæli'seid], *s.* (*a*) palissade *f*; **p. tree,** arbre *m* en espalier; (*b*) *Bot:* **p. tissue,** tissu *m* palissadique; (*c*) *Ann:* **p. worm,** strongle géant.
palisade[2], *v.tr.* palissader.
palisading [pæli'seidiŋ], *s.* palissadement *m*; fortification *f* au moyen de palissades; érection *f* d'un enclos palissadé.
palisander [pæli'sændər], *s. Com:* (*wood*) palissandre *m*, jacaranda *m.*
palish ['peiliʃ], *a.* (*a*) un peu pâle; pâlot, -otte; (*b*) décoloré; (*of light*) blafard.
palissé ['pælisi], *a. Her:* palissé.
pall[1] [pɔːl], *s.* **1.** *Ecc:* (*a*) poêle *m*; drap *m* funéraire, mortuaire; **p. bearer,** porteur *m* (d'un cordon du poêle); **the p. bearers were . . .,** les cordons du poêle étaient tenus par . . .; (*b*) = PALLA; (*c*) = PALLIUM 1. **2.** manteau *m* (de neige, etc.); voile *m* (de fumée, etc.). **3.** *Her:* (**cross**) **p.,** pairle *m*, pallium *m.*
pall[2], *v.tr.* couvrir d'un poêle; voiler.
pall[3]. **1.** *v.i.* s'affadir; devenir fade, insipide (**on s.o.,** pour qn); **these pleasures p.,** on se blase de ces plaisirs; **happiness that never palls,** bonheur *m* dont je ne me suis jamais rassasié; **food, literature, that palls,** nourriture dont on se dégoûte vite; littérature fastidieuse à la longue; **sustained eloquence palls,** l'éloquence continue ennuie; **even pleasure palls on one,** l'accoutumance *f* diminue le plaisir même; **it never palls,** on ne s'en dégoûte jamais. **2.** *v.tr.* blaser, émousser (les sens); rassasier (l'appétit).
palla ['pælə], *s. Ecc:* pale *f.*
Palladian [pə'leidiən], *a. Arch:* palladien.
palladic [pə'lædik], *a. Ch:* palladique.
palladium[1] [pə'leidiəm], *s. Myth: etc:* palladium *m.*
palladium[2], *s. Ch:* palladium *m.*
pallasite ['pæləsait], *s. Geol:* pallasite *f.*
palleal ['pæliəl], *a. Moll:* palléal, -aux; **p. chamber,** cavité palléale.
pallet[1] ['pælit], *s.* (*a*) paillasse *f*; (*b*) grabat *m.*
pallet[2], *s.* **1.** palette *f* (de doreur, de potier, etc.). **2.** *Art:* = PALETTE 1. **3.** *Mec.E:* cliquet *m*; *Clockm:* palette (de l'arbre). **4.** *Com:* palette (de manutention). **5.** *Mus:* (*organ*) soupape *f* (de sommier).
pallet[3], *s. Her:* vergette *f.*
palletization [pælitai'zeiʃ(ə)n], *s. Com:* palettisation *f* (des marchandises).
palletize ['pælitaiz], *v.tr. Com:* palettiser (des marchandises); mettre (des marchandises) sur palette(s); **palletized goods,** marchandises palettisées, sur palette(s).
palletizing ['pælitaiziŋ], *s. Com:* palettisation *f.*
palliasse ['pæljæs], *s.* paillasse *f.*
palliate ['pælieit], *v.tr.* pallier (la misère, une faute, une maladie, etc.); lénifier (une maladie); pallier, atténuer (un vice, etc.).
palliating ['pælieitiŋ], *a.* qui pallie; (*of medicine*) lénitif; **p. circumstances,** circonstances atténuantes.
palliation [pæli'eiʃ(ə)n], *s.* palliation *f* (de la misère, d'une maladie, d'une faute, etc.); atténuation *f* (d'une faute).
palliative ['pæliətiv]. **1.** *a.* = PALLIATING. **2.** *s.* palliatif *m*, lenitif *m*, anodin *m.*
palliator ['pælieitər], *s.* palliateur, -trice.
palliatory ['pæliət(ə)ri], *a.* palliateur, -trice.
pallid ['pælid], *a.* (*a*) pâle, décoloré; (*b*) (*of light, moon, etc.*) blafard; (*c*) (*of face*) blême.
pallidly ['pælidli], *adv.* pâlement.
pallidness ['pælidnis], *s.* pâleur *f*; pâlissement *m.*
pallium, *pl.* **-ia** ['pæliəm, -iə], *s.* **1.** *Gr.Ant: Ecc:* pallium *m.* **2.** manteau *m* (de mollusque, de brachiopode).
pall-mall ['pel'mel, 'pæl'mæl], *s. A:* (*a*) (jeu *m* de) mail *m*; (*b*) terrain *m* de mail.
pallor ['pælər], *s.* pâleur *f.*
pallwise ['pɔːlwaiz], *adv. Her:* en pairle.
pally ['pæli], *a. F: O:* **1.** qui se lie facilement (d'amitié); liant. **2. to be p. with s.o.,** être lié, être copain, avec qn.
palm[1] [pɑːm], *s.* **1.** (*a*) **p.** (**tree**), palmier *m*; **date p.,** dattier *m*; **Bourbon p.,** latanier *m* de Bourbon; **Moriche p., Ita p.,** palmier Bâche; **royal p.,** palmier royal; **troolie p.,** manicaria *m*; **oil p.,** éléis *m* de Guinée, palmier à huile; **dwarf p.,** palmette *f*; **p. grove, plantation,** palmeraie *f*; **p. house,** palmarium *m*; **p. leaf,** feuille *f* de palmier; *Arch:* **p. leaf** (**moulding**), palmette; (*b*) **p. marrow,** palmite *m*; **p. oil,** huile *f* de palme, de palmier; pumicin *m*; **p. wax,** cire *f* de palme; **p. butter,** beurre *m* de palmier, de palme; **p. sugar,** sucre *m* de palme; **p. wine,** vin *m* de palme; (*c*) **p. cabbage,** (chou *m*) palmiste *m*; (*d*) *Z:* **p. civet, p. cat,** (i) paradoxure *m*; (ii) nandini *f*; **p. squirrel,** rat *m* palmiste; *Orn:* **p. chat,** jaseur *m* des palmes, *F:* oiseau-palmiste *m*; *Ent:* **p. worm, grub, borer,** ver *m* palmiste; **p. weevil,** calandre *f* palmiste. **2.** (*branch*) (*a*) palme *f*; *Ecc:* rameau *m*, buis (béni); **P. Sunday,** le Dimanche des Rameaux, *F:* les Rameaux; *Fig:* **to bear, win, the p.,** remporter la palme; **to yield, assign, the p. to s.o.,** céder, décerner, la palme à qn; (*b*) branche *f* de saule marceau.
palm[2], *s.* **1.** (*a*) paume *f* (de la main); *F:* **to grease, oil, tickle, s.o.'s p.,** graisser la patte à qn; *F:* **to hold s.o. in the p. of one's hand,** avoir qn sous sa coupe; (*b*) empaumure *f* (d'un gant). **2.** *A.Meas:* palme *m.* **3.** *Nau:* (*a*) patte, oreille *f* (d'ancre); (*b*) *Tls:* paumelle *f*, paumet *m* (de voilier). **4.** *Ven:* (em)paumure *f* (de bois de cerf).
palm[3], *v.*
I. *v.tr.* **1.** manier, tripoter, patiner (qch., qn). **2. to p. a card,** empalmer, escamoter, une carte; filer la carte. **3.** *F: O:* graisser la patte de, à (qn).
II. (*compound verb*) **palm off,** *v.tr.* faire passer, *F:* colloquer, refiler (**sth.** (**up**)**on s.o.,** qch. à qn); (*conjuring*) **to p. off a card,** filer la carte; **to p. off old stock on a client,** refiler des rossignols à un client; **to p. off a bad coin on s.o.,** (re)passer, refiler, une fausse pièce à qn; **to p. off sth. as a genuine article,** faire passer une contrefaçon pour un article d'origine; **they've palmed off pebbles on you for diamonds,** on vous a fait prendre du quartz pour des diamants.
palmaceous [pɑː'meiʃəs], *a. Bot:* de la famille, de la nature, du palmier.
Palma Christi ['pælmə'kristi], *s. Bot:* Palma-christi *m inv*; ricin *m.*
palmar ['pælmər], *a. & s. Anat:* palmaire (*m*); **p. arch,** arcade *f* palmaire; **p. nerve,** nerf *m* palmaire.
palmate ['pælmeit], *a. Nat.Hist:* palmé.
palmatifid [pæl'mætifid], *a. Bot:* palmatifide, palmifide.
palmatiflorate [pælmæti'flɔːreit], *a. Bot:* palmatiflore, palmiflore.
palmatifoliate [pælmæti'foulieit], *a. Bot:* palmatifolié, palmifolié.
palmatilobate, palmatilobed [pælmæti'loubeit, -'loubd], *a. Bot:* palmatilobé, palmilobé.
palmatinerved [pælmæti'nəːvd], *a. Bot:* palmatinervé, palminervé.
palmation [pæl'meiʃ(ə)n], *s. Nat.Hist:* palmure *f*, palmature *f.*
palmatipartite [pælmæti'pɑːtait], *a. Bot:* palmiparti(te), palmatiparti(te).
palmatisect [pæl'mætisekt], *a. Bot:* palmiséqué, palmatiséqué.
palmature ['pɑːmətjər], *s. Med:* palmature *f.*
palmed [pɑːmd], *a. Nat.Hist:* palmé.
palmer[1] ['pɑːmər], *s.* **1.** (*a*) pèlerin *m* de retour de la Terre Sainte (en foi de quoi il portait un rameau); *A:* paumier *m*; (*b*) pèlerin. **2.** (*a*) **p.** (**worm**), chenille poilue, velue; (*b*) *Fish:* (mouche *f*) araignée *f* (d'hameçon).
palmer[2], *s. O:* prestidigitateur *m.*
palmette [pæl'met], *s. Arch:* palmette *f.*
palmetto [pæl'metou], *s. Bot:* (*a*) palmier nain; palmette *f*; **bristly p.,** palmier nain sétigère; (*b*) (chou *m*) palmiste *m.*
palmierite ['pælmiərait], *s. Miner:* palmiérite *f.*
palmiform ['pælmifɔːm], *a. Bot:* palmiforme.
palmilobate [pælmi'loubeit], *a. Bot:* palmilobé.
palming ['pɑːmiŋ], *s.* empalmage *m* (d'une carte).
palmiped ['pælmiped], *a. & s. Orn:* palmipède (*m*).
palmist ['pɑːmist], *s.* chiromancien, -ienne.
palmistry ['pɑːmistri], *s.* chiromancie *f.*
palmitate ['pælmiteit], *s. Ch:* palmitate *m.*
palmitic [pæl'mitik], *a. Ch:* (acide) palmitique.
palmitin ['pælmitin], *s. Ch:* palmitine *f.*
palmitone ['pælmitoun], *s. Ch:* palmitone *f.*
palmy ['pɑːmi], *a.* **1.** (*of plain, etc.*) couvert de palmiers. **2. p. days,** jours heureux; époque florissante (d'une nation, etc.); **in his p. days,** dans ses beaux jours.
Palmyra [pæl'maiərə]. **1.** *Pr.n. A.Geog:* Palmyre *f.* **2.** *s. Bot:* rondier *m.*
Palmyrene [pælmai'riːn]. *A.Geog:* (*a*) *a.* palmyrien; (*b*) *s.* Palmyrien, -ienne.
palnut ['pælnʌt], *s. Mec.E:* contre-écrou *m*, *pl.* contre-écrous.
palp [pælp], *s. Nat.Hist:* palpe *f*, barbillon *m* (d'insecte); palpe (d'annélide).
palpability [pælpə'biliti], **palpableness** ['pælpəb(ə)lnis], *s.* **1.** palpabilité *f.* **2.** évidence *f* (d'un fait, etc.).
palpable ['pælpəbl], *a.* **1.** palpable; que l'on peut toucher. **2.** palpable, manifeste, clair, évident; **p. lie,** mensonge évident; **p. difference,** différence *f* sensible.
palpably ['pælpəbli], *adv.* palpablement, manifestement; sensiblement.
palpate [pæl'peit], *v.tr.* palper.
palpation [pæl'peiʃ(ə)n], *s.* palpation *f.*
palpebra, *pl.* **-ae** ['pælpibrə, -iː], *s. Anat:* paupière *f.*
palpebral ['pælpibr(ə)l], *a. Anat:* palpébral, -aux.
palpicorn ['pælpikɔːn], *a. Ent:* palpicorne.
palpigerous [pæl'pidʒərəs], *a. Ent:* palpigère.
palpitate ['pælpiteit], *v.tr. & i.* palpiter.
palpitating ['pælpiteitiŋ], *a.* palpitant.
palpitation [pælpi'teiʃ(ə)n], *s.* palpitation *f.*
palpus, *pl.* **-i** ['pælpəs, -ai], *s. Nat.Hist:* = PALP.
palsgrave ['pɔːlzgreiv], *s.m. Hist:* comte palatin.
palsgravine ['pɔːlzgrəviːn], *s.f. Hist:* comtesse palatine.
palsied ['pɔːlzid], *a. A:* paralysé, paralytique.
palsy ['pɔːlzi], *s. Med: O:* paralysie *f*; **shaking p.,** paralysie agitante.
palter ['pɔːltər], *v.i.* **1. to p.** (**with s.o.**), chercher des faux-fuyants, biaiser, feindre (avec qn); tergiverser; **to p. with one's honour,** transiger sur, avec, l'honneur. **2.** marchander (**with s.o. about sth.,** qch. avec qn); marchandailler, barguigner; **to p. with s.o.,** marchander qn. **3. to p. with a question,** jouer, badiner, avec une question; traiter une question à la légère.
palterer ['pɔːltərər], *s.* **1.** chercheur, -euse, d'équivoques; individu *m* de mauvaise foi. **2.** marchandeur, -euse; marchandailleur, -euse; barguigneur, -euse. **3.** baguenaudier *m*; velléitaire *mf.*
paltering[1] ['pɔːltəriŋ], *a.* **1.** (individu *m*) de mauvaise foi. **2.** marchandeur, -euse; barguigneur, -euse.
paltering[2], *s.* **1.** compromission *f*; faux-fuyants *mpl.* **2.** marchandage *m*, barguignage *m.*
paltriness ['pɔːltrinis], *s.* mesquinerie *f* (d'un cadeau, etc.).
paltry ['pɔːltri], *a.* misérable, mesquin; **for a p. two thousand pounds,** pour deux pauvres mille livres; **I had lost a p. five-franc piece,** j'avais perdu une malheureuse pièce de cinq francs; **p. excuses,** plates excuses; pauvres excuses; **p. reason,** raison chétive.
paludal [pæ'ljuːdl], *a.* marécageux; (*of plain, fever*) paludéen, -enne; (plante, animal) des marais.
paludicolous [pælju'dikələs], *a.* paludicole.
paludina [pælju'dainə], *s. Moll:* paludine *f.*
paludism ['pæljudizm], *s. Med:* paludisme *m*, impaludisme *m.*
palustral, palustrine [pæ'lʌstr(ə)l, -'lʌstrain], *a.* (terrain, plante) palustre.
paly ['peili], *a. Her:* palé; vergeté.
palynological [pælinou'lɔdʒikl], *a. Bot:* palynologique.
palynology [pæli'nɔlədʒi], *s. Bot:* palynologie *f*, pollénographie *f.*
pam [pæm], *s. Cards:* mistigri *m*; valet *m* de trèfle; (*at poker*) **p.-flush,** flush terminé par le valet de trèfle.
pamé ['pæmi], *a. Her:* (dauphin) pâmé.
Pamela ['pæmələ]. *Pr.n.f.* Paméla.
pampa ['pæmpə], *s. Geog:* pampa *f*; **the Pampa(s),** la Pampa; **pampas grass,** gynérion argenté, herbe *f* des pampas.
Pampean [pæm'piːən, 'pæmpiən], *a. & s. Ethn:*

pampéro (*m*); Indien, -ienne, des pampas.

Pampeluna [pæmpi'lu:nə]. *Pr.n. Geog:* Pampelune *f.*

pamper ['pæmpər], *v.tr.* **1.** choyer, dorloter, mignoter, mitonner, douilleter (un enfant); flatter, charmer, délecter (l'esprit, la vanité de qn). **2.** *A:* gorger (qn) de bonne chère.

pampered ['pæmpəd], *a.* choyé, dorloté, mignoté, mitonné; **p. tastes,** goûts difficiles, exigeants, luxueux.

pampero [pæm'pɛərou]. **1.** *a. & s.* = PAMPEAN. **2.** *s.* (*wind*) pamper *m*; pampéro *m.*

pamphlet ['pæmflit], *s.* brochure *f*; (*literary, scientific*) opuscule *m*; (*libellous or scurrilous*) pamphlet *m*; *Publ:* **stabbed p.,** brochure à piqûre métallique; piqûre *f.*

pamphleteer[1] [pæmfli'tiər], *s.* auteur *m* de brochures; (*scurrilous*) pamphlétaire *m.*

pamphleteer[2], *v.i. O: usu. Pej:* écrire des pamphlets; se livrer à une guerre de pamphlets.

Pamphylia [pæm'filiə]. *Pr.n. A.Geog:* Pamphylie *f.*

pampiniform [pæm'pinifɔ:m], *a. Anat:* pampiniforme.

Pamplona [pæm'plounə]. *Pr.n. Geog:* Pampelune *f.*

pampre ['pæmpər], *s. Arch: Art:* pampre *m.*

pamprodactyl [pæmprou'dæktil]. *Orn:* **1.** *a.* pamprodactyle. **2.** *s.* oiseau pamprodactyle.

pamprodactylous [pæmprou'dæktiləs], *a. Orn:* pamprodactyle.

pan[1] [pæn], *s.* **1.** (*a*) *Dom.Ec:* casserole *f*; poêlon *m*; plat *m*; **frying p.,** poêle *f*; **oven p.,** plat à rôtir, à four; **pots and pans,** batterie *f* de cuisine; (*b*) **perfume p.,** cassolette *f,* brûle-parfums *m inv*; (*c*) **settling p.,** bac *m* de décantation; *Art:* **moist colours in pans,** couleurs *f* moites en godets; *Med:* **douche p.,** bock laveur; (*d*) *P:* visage *m*, binette *f,* museau *m.* **2.** (*a*) (i) plateau *m*, plat, (ii) bassin *m* (d'une balance); (*b*) *Mec.E: etc:* carter *m*, tôle inférieure, cuvette *f* (de moteur, etc.); faux carter; (*c*) **lavatory p.,** cuvette *f* de W.C.; (*d*) *Min:* (*gold*) bat(t)ée *f,* gamelle *f,* écuelle *f,* sébile *f*; (*small*) augette *f.* **3.** (**priming**) **p.,** bassinet *m* (d'un fusil). **4.** *Geol: etc:* (*a*) cuvette; bassin de déposition, de sédimentation; **diamond p.,** gisement diamantifère; **salt p.,** marais salant; saline *f,* salin *m*; (*for salt*) **evaporating p.,** œillet *m*; (*b*) **iron p.,** croûte ferrugineuse, alios *m*; **lime p.,** croûte calcaire.

pan[2], *v.* (**panned**) **1.** *v.tr. Min:* (*gold*) **to p.** (**out, off**), laver (le gravier, etc.) à la batée. **2.** *v.i.* (*a*) **to p. out at so much,** rendre tant à la batée; (*b*) **it didn't p. out well,** cela n'a pas réussi, n'a pas donné; **things didn't p. out as he intended,** les choses ne se sont pas passées comme il l'aurait voulu, n'ont pas donné ce qu'il espérait; (*c*) *F:* **to p. out about sth.,** s'étendre sur un sujet.

pan[3] [pɑ:n], *s.* bétel *m* (masticatoire).

pan[4], *v.tr.* (**panned**) *F:* exécuter, rabaisser, ravaler, décrier, éreinter (qn, qch.).

Pan[5], *Pr.n.m. Myth:* (le dieu) Pan; **Pan's pipes,** flûte *f* de Pan.

pan[6], *v.tr.* (**panned**) *Cin: F:* panoramiquer (une vue).

pan-, *comb.fm.* pan-.

panacea [pænə'siə], *s.* panacée *f*; remède universel.

panache [pə'næʃ], *s.* **1.** panache *m* ((i) de casque, (ii) *Arch:* de pendentif). **2.** panache, ostentation *f.*

panada [pæ'nɑ:də], *s. Cu:* panade *f.*

pan-African [pæn'æfrikən], *a.* panafricain.

pan-Africanism [pæn'æfrikənizm], *s.* panafricanisme *m.*

Panama [pænə'mɑ:]. **1.** *Pr.n. Geog:* Panama *m.* **2.** *s.* **p.** (**hat**), panama.

Panamanian [pænə'meiniən]. *Geog:* (*a*) *a.* panaméen; (*b*) *s.* Panaméen, -éenne.

pan-American [pænə'merikən], *a.* panaméricain.

pan-Americanism [pænə'merikənizm], *s.* panaméricanisme *m.*

pan-Arab [pæn'ærəb], *a.* panarabe.

pan-Arabism [pæn'ærəbizm], *s.* panarabisme *m.*

panary ['pænəri], *a.* **p. fermentation,** fermentation *f* panaire.

pan-Asian, pan-Asiatic [pæn'eiʃən, -eizi'ætik], *a.* panasiatique.

pan-Asianism [pæn'eiʃənizm], *s.* panasiatisme *m.*

panatella [pænə'telə], *s.* (cigare *m*) panatel(l)a *m.*

panathenaea [pænəθi'ni(:)ə], *s.pl. Gr.Ant:* panathénées *f.*

panathenaean [pænəθi'ni(:)ən], **panathenaic** [pænəθi'neiik], *a. Gr.Ant:* panathénaïque.

panax ['pænæks], *s. Bot:* panax *m.*

pancake[1] ['pænkeik], *s.* **1.** *Cu:* crêpe *f*; **to toss a p.,** faire sauter une crêpe; **p. day,** mardi gras. **2.** *Nau:* **p. ice,** gâteaux *mpl* de glace; glace *f* en fragments. **3.** *W.Tel:* **p. coil,** galette *f.* **4.** *Av:* **p.** (**landing**), atterrissage brutal, à plat.

pancake[2], *v.i. Av:* plaquer à l'atterrissage, faire un atterrissage brutal.

pancaking ['pænkeikiŋ], *s. Av:* atterrissage brutal, à plat.

pancarditis [pænkɑ:'daitis], *s. Med:* pancardite *f.*

panchromatic [pænkrou'mætik], *a. Phot:* (plaque *f*) panchromatique.

panchromatism [pæn'kroumətizm], *s. Phot:* panchromatisme *m.*

pancosmic [pæn'kɔzmik], *a. Phil:* pancosmique.

pancosmism [pæn'kɔzmizm], *s. Phil:* pancosmisme *m.*

Pancras ['pæŋkrəs]. *Pr.n.m. Rel.Hist:* Pancrace.

pancrati(a)st ['pænkrətist, -'krætiæst], *s. Gr.Ant:* pancratiaste *m.*

pancratic [pæn'krætik], *a.* **1.** *Gr.Ant:* du pancrace. **2.** *Opt:* pancratique.

pancratium [pæn'kreiʃiəm], *s. Gr.Ant:* pancrace *m.*

pancreas ['pæŋkræs], *s. Anat:* pancréas *m.*

pancreatectomy [pæŋkriə'tektəmi], *s. Surg:* pancréatectomie *f.*

pancreatic [pæŋkri'ætik], *a. Anat: Physiol:* pancréatique; **p. duct, juice,** canal *m*, suc *m*, pancréatique.

pancreaticoduodenal [pæŋkri'ætikoudjuou'di:nəl], *a. Anat:* pancréatico-duodénal, -aux.

pancreatin ['pæŋkriətin], *s. Ch: Pharm:* pancréatine *f.*

pancreatitis [pæŋkriə'taitis], *s. Med:* pancréatite *f.*

pancreatomy [pæŋkri'ætəmi], *s. Surg:* pancréatotomie *f.*

pancreatotomy [pæŋkriə'tɔtəmi], *s. Surg:* pancréatotomie *f.*

panda ['pændə], *s. Z:* panda *m*; **giant p.,** panda géant, grand panda; **small Himalayan p.,** petit panda.

Pandaean [pæn'di:ən], *a. Myth:* de Pan; **P. pipe,** flûte *f* de Pan.

Pandanaceae [pændə'neisii:], *s.pl. Bot:* pandanacées *f.*

pandanaceous [pændə'neiʃəs], *a. Bot:* pandacé, pandané.

pandanus [pæn'deinəs], *s. Bot:* pandanus *m.*

pandarus ['pændərəs], *s. Crust:* pandare *m.*

Pandean [pæn'di:ən], *a. Myth:* de Pan.

pandects ['pændekts], *s.pl. Rom.Jur:* pandectes *f.*

pandemia [pæn'di:miə], *s. Med:* pandémie *f.*

pandemic [pæn'demik]. *Med:* **1.** *a.* pandémique. **2.** *s.* pandémie *f*; épidémie généralisée.

pandemonium [pændi'mouniəm], *s.* pandémonium *m*; **it's p.,** c'est une vraie tour de Babel; **a fearful p.,** un bruit infernal, un bacchanal de tous les diables; une scène de désordre indescriptible.

pander[1] ['pændər], *s.* entremetteur *m*, proxénète *m*, *P:* maquereau *m.*

pander[2], *v.i.* servir de proxénète à qn; **to p. to s.o.,** encourager bassement qn; **to p. to a vice,** se prêter, conniver, à un vice; **to p. to a taste,** flatter bassement un goût.

panderer ['pændərər], *s.* **to be a p. to s.o.'s vices,** encourager les vices de qn; servir les vices de qn avec une basse complaisance.

panderess ['pændəres], *s.f. A:* procureuse, proxénète, entremetteuse.

pandermite [pæn'də:mait], *s. Miner:* pandermite *f.*

pandiculation [pændikju'leiʃ(ə)n], *s. Physiol:* pandiculation *f.*

pandit ['pændit], *s.* (*Indian title*) pandit *m.*

Pandora[1] [pæn'dɔ:rə]. **1.** *Pr.n.f. Gr.Hist:* Pandore; **Pandora's box,** la boîte, le coffret, de Pandore. **2.** *s. Moll:* pandore *f.*

pandora[2], **pandore** [pæn'dɔər], *s. A.Mus:* pandore *f.*

Pandoridae [pæn'dɔ:ridi:], *s.pl. Moll:* pandoridés *m.*

pane[1] [pein], *s.* **1.** vitre *f,* carreau *m* (de fenêtre); *Glassm:* plat *m* (de verre). **2.** carreau (d'un tissu à carreaux). **3.** pan *m* (d'un mur, d'un écrou).

pane[2], *s.* panne *f* (d'un marteau); **p. hammer,** marteau à panne.

panegyric [pæni'dʒirik], *a. & s.* panégyrique (*m*).

panegyrical [pæni'dʒirik(ə)l], *a.* panégyrique; élogieux.

panegyrist [pæni'dʒirist], *s.* panégyriste *m.*

panegyrize ['pænidʒiraiz], *v.tr.* panégyriser (qn); faire le panégyrique de (qn); prononcer ou écrire l'éloge de (qn).

panel[1] [pænl], *s.* **1.** (*a*) panneau *m*; placard *m* (de porte); caisson *m* (de plafond); **p. of a roof,** pan *m* de comble; **sunk p.,** panneau en retrait; arrière-corps *m inv*; **wainscot p.,** panneau de lambris; **folding p.,** panneau, vantail, -aux *m*; **glass p.,** panneau vitré, en verre; **sliding p.,** panneau mobile; *Av: etc:* **escape p.,** panneau d'échappée, d'évacuation; *Mec.E: etc:* **access p., inspection p.,** panneau d'accès, de visite; *Carp:* **p. work,** lambrissage *m*; lambris *mpl*, boiseries *fpl*; **p. strip,** couvre-joint *m*, *pl.* couvre-joints; *Aut: etc:* **p. beater,** tôlier *m*; (*b*) *Dressm:* panneau; (*shaped*) volant *m*; (*c*) (i) *Arch: Civ.E:* entre-deux *m inv*; **p. filling,** masque *m*; (ii) *Bookb:* entre-nerf(s) *m*; (iii) *Av:* section *f,* travée *f* (d'aile); **inner wing p.,** aile médiane; **outer wing p.,** aile extrême; **skin p.,** élément *m* de revêtement (du fuselage, etc.); (*d*) *Aut: Av:* **instrument p.,** *Rec:* **control, front, p.,** tableau *m* de bord; **p. light,** lampe *f,* éclairage *m*, de tableau de bord; *El:* **contactor p., fuse, p.,** panneau de contacteurs, de fusibles; **switch p.,** tableau de distribution; *Tp:* **distribution p.,** tableau de distribution; **jack p.,** panneau de commutation, de jacks; **p. switch,** sélecteur *m* à panneau; *Cmptr:* **control p.,** pupitre *m*, tableau, de commande; **jack p., patch p.,** tableau de connexion; *Com:* **advertisement p.,** panneau d'affichage, de publicité; panneau-réclame *m*, *pl.* panneaux-réclame; (*e*) *Av: Mil: etc:* **code p., p. signal, signalling p.,** panneau de signalisation; **ground-air** (**liaison**) **p.,** panneau de signalisation sol-air; **identification p.,** panneau d'identification; **marking p.,** panneau de jalonnement; **p. code,** code *m* de signalisation par panneaux; **p. display ground,** aire *f,* emplacement *m*, de signalisation par panneaux, de déploiement des panneaux de signalisation. **2.** *Min:* panneau; chambre isolée; **p. work,** exploitation *f* par chambres. **3.** *Harn:* (*a*) panneau, coussinet *m* (d'une selle); (*b*) *A:* selle *f* sans arçon. **4.** (*a*) *Jur:* (i) tableau, liste *f,* du jury; (ii) **the p.,** le jury; (iii) *Scot:* l'accusé; les accusés; **on the p.,** en jugement; (*b*) *A:* = liste des médecins conventionnés; **p. doctor** = médecin conventionné; **p. patient** = malade assuré social, affilié à la sécurité sociale; (*c*) (i) liste des membres d'un comité, d'une commission; (ii) comité, commission (d'enquête, etc.); groupe *m* de travail; table ronde; **p. discussion,** discussions *fpl*, débats *mpl*, en comité, du comité; *T.V: etc:* discussion de groupe, débat; **p. of experts,** comité, commission, d'experts; *T.V: etc:* (*F:* **the p.**) l'équipe *f,* le jury.

panel[2], *v.tr.* (**panelled**) **1.** (*a*) diviser (un mur, etc.) en panneaux; construire (un mur) à panneaux; (*b*) recouvrir de panneaux; lambrisser (une paroi); plaquer (une surface); (*c*) **to p. a sheet of metal,** estamper une tôle. **2.** *Min:* exploiter (une mine) par chambres isolées. **3.** *Dressm:* garnir (une robe) de panneaux.

panelled ['pænəld], *a.* (*of room*) boisé, lambrissé; (*of wall*) revêtu de boiseries; **oak p.,** à panneaux de chêne; lambrissé de chêne; **p. ceiling,** plafond à caissons, lambrissé; **p. door,** porte *f* à placard, à panneaux.

panelling ['pænəliŋ], *s.* **1.** (*a*) division *f* (d'un mur) en panneaux; panneautage *m* (d'une surface); (*b*) lambrissage *m* (d'une pièce); (*c*) *Min:* exploitation *f* par chambres isolées. **2.** (*a*) lambris *m* de hauteur, boiserie *f*; placage *m*, panneautage; **oak p.,** panneaux *mpl* de chêne; lambris *mpl* de chêne; (*b*) (*wood for panelling*) aubage *m.*

panentheism [pæn'enθi:izm], *s. Theol:* panenthéisme *m.*

panful ['pænful], *s.* terrinée *f,* bassinée *f,* poêlée *f.*

pang [pæŋ], *s.* angoisse *f,* douleur *f*; serrement *m* de cœur; **the pangs of death,** l'agonie *f* (de la mort); les affres *fpl*, angoisses, de la mort; **pangs of love,** blessures *f* de l'amour; **pangs of jealousy,** tourments *m* de la jalousie; **to feel a p.,** sentir une petite pointe au cœur; **to feel the pangs of hunger,** entendre crier ses entrailles; avoir faim.

pangene ['pændʒi:n], *s. Biol:* pangène *m.*

pangenesis [pæn'dʒenisis], *s. Biol:* pangénèse *f.*

pan-German [pæn'dʒə:mən], **pan-Germanic** [pændʒə:'mænik], *a. Hist:* pangermanique.

pan-Germanism [pæn'dʒə:mənizm], *s. Hist:* pangermanisme *m.*

pangolin [pæŋ'goulin], *s. Z:* pangolin *m*; **three-cusped p.,** pangolin à écailles tricuspides; **Chinese p.,** pangolin pentadactyle.

panhandle[1] ['pænhændl], *s. NAm:* enclave *f,* territoire *m* (en forme de queue de casserole).

panhandle[2], *v.i. NAm: F:* mendier.

panhead ['pænhed], *s.* tête *f* cylindrique (de rivet).

panhellenic [pænhe'li:nik], *a.* panhellénique, panhellénien.

panhellenism [pæn'helinizm], *s.* panhellénisme *m.*

panic[1] ['pænik], *a. & s.* **p.** (**terror**), (terreur *f*) panique *f*; affolement *m*; **p. on the Stock Exchange,** panique en Bourse; **to create a p.,** causer une panique; **to throw the crowd into a p.,** affoler la foule; **they fled in a p.,** pris de panique ils s'enfuirent; **p. press,** presse *f* alarmiste; **p. measures,** mesures dictées par la panique.

panic[2], *v.* (**panicked**) **1.** *v.tr.* remplir de panique; affoler (la foule, etc.); *F:* paniquer (qn). **2.** *v.i.* être pris de panique; perdre la tête; s'affoler.

panic[3], *s. Bot:* **p.** (**grass**), panic *m* (d'Italie); panis *m*; millet *m* des oiseaux.

panicky ['pæniki], *a. F:* (*of feelings*) panique; (*of pers.*) sujet à la panique; (*of market, etc.*) enclin à la panique; (*of newspaper, etc.*) alarmiste; **don't get p.,** ne vous impressionnez pas; ne vous frappez pas; ne prenez pas les choses au tragique.

panicle ['pænikl], *s. Bot:* panicule *f.*

panicled ['pænikld], *a. Bot:* paniculé.

panicmonger ['pænikmʌŋgər], *s.* semeur, -euse, de panique; *F:* paniquard *m.*

paniconographic [pænaikɔnou'græfik], *a.* paniconographique.

paniconography [pænaikɔ'nɔgrəfi], *s.* pan(é)iconographie *f.*

panicstricken, panicstruck ['pænikstrikn, -strʌk], *a.* pris de panique; affolé.

paniculate [pæ'nikjuleit], *a. Bot:* paniculé.

panification [pænifi'keiʃ(ə)n], *s.* panification *f.*

panisc, panisk ['pænisk], *s. Myth:* panisque *m.*

Pan-Islam [pæn'izlɑːm], *s.* le monde panislamique.

Pan-Islamic [pæniz'læmik], *a.* panislamique.

Pan-Islamism [pæn'izləmizm], *s.* panislamisme *m.*

Pan-Islamist [pæn'izlæmist], *s.* panislamiste *mf.*

Panjab (the) [ðəpʌn'dʒɑːb]. *Pr.n. Geog:* le Pendjab.

panjandrum [pən'dʒændrəm], *s. F: O:* gros bonnet; grand personnage; **grand p.,** mamamouchi *m,* grand Manitou.

panka(h) ['pæŋkə], *s.* panca *m,* panka *m.*

panlogical [pæn'lɔdʒikl], *a. Phil:* panlogique.

panlogism ['pænlɔdʒizm], *s. Phil:* panlogisme *m.*

panlogist ['pænlɔdʒist], *s. Phil:* panlogiste *mf.*

panmeristic [pænmə'ristik], *a. Biol:* panméristique.

panmixia, panmixis, panmixy [pæn'miksiə, -'miksis, -'miksi], *s. Biol:* panmixie *f.*

pannage ['pænidʒ], *s.* **1.** *Jur:* panage *m,* paisson *m.* **2.** glandée *f.*

panne [pæn], *s. Tex:* panne *f.*

panniculitis [pænikju'laitis], *s. Med:* panniculite *f.*

panniculus [pæ'nikjuləs], *s. Anat:* pannicule *m;* **p. adiposus,** pannicule adipeux.

pannier ['pæniər], *s.* **1.** *(a) (basket)* panier *m; (b)* panier de bât (d'une bête de somme); *Husb:* verveux *m; (c)* hotte *f,* benne *f* (de vendangeur); *(d) Med:* pharmacie portative. **2.** *Dressm:* **dress with panniers,** robe *f* à paniers.

pannikin ['pænikin], *s.* écuelle *f,* gobelet *m* (en fer blanc).

panning[1] ['pæniŋ], *s.* lavage *m* (des graviers).

panning[2], *s. F:* éreintement *m* (de la critique).

panning[3], *s. Cin:* panoramique *m;* survol *m.*

Pannonia [pæ'nouniə], *Pr.n. Geog:* la Pannonie.

Pannonian [pæ'nouniən], *a. Geog:* pannonien; **P. basin,** bassin pannonien.

Pannonic [pæ'nɔnik], *a. Geog:* pannonien.

Pano ['pænou], *s. Ethn:* Pano.

Panoan [pæ'nouən]. **1.** *a. Ethn:* pano. **2.** *s. Ling:* pano *m.*

panoplied ['pænəplid], *a.* armé de pied en cap.

panoply ['pænəpli], *s.* **1.** panoplie *f.* **2.** *A: & Lit:* **pomp and p.,** grand apparat.

panoptical [pæn'ɔptikl], *a. Arch: Opt:* panoptique.

panopticon [pæn'ɔptikən], *s. (a) Arch:* panoptique *m; (b) Opt:* lunette *f* panoptique.

panorama [pænə'rɑːmə], *s.* panorama *m.*

panoramic [pænə'ræmik], *a.* (photographie, vue, etc.) panoramique; **p. restaurant,** restaurant *m* panoramique; *Aut:* **p. mirror,** rétroviseur *m* panoramique.

panoramist [pænə'ræmist], *s.* peintre *m* de panoramas.

panorthodox [pæn'ɔːθədɔks], *a.* panorthodoxe.

panpsychism [pæn'saikizm], *s. Phil:* panpsychisme *m.*

panscraper, panscrubber ['pænskreipər, -skrʌbər], *s.* tampon *m* à récurer (les casseroles, etc.).

pan-Serbian [pæn'səːbiən], *a. Hist:* panserbe.

pansinusitis [pænsain(j)u'saitis], *s. Med:* pansinusite *f.*

Pan-Slav [pæn'slɑːv], *a.* panslave, panslaviste.

Pan-Slavism [pæn'slɑːvizm], *s.* panslavisme *m.*

Pan-Slavist [pæn'slɑːvist], panslaviste *mf.*

pansophy ['pænsəfi], *s.* pansophie *f,* science universelle.

panspermia, panspermy [pæn'spəːmiə, -'spəːmi], *s. Biol:* panspermie *f,* panspermisme *m.*

panspermic [pæn'spəːmik], *a. Biol:* panspermique.

pansy ['pænzi], *s.* **1.** *Bot:* pensée *f;* **wild p.,** petite jacée. **2.** *F: (a)* pédéraste *m,* tapette *f; (b)* homme efféminé, femmelette *f.*

pant[1] [pænt], *s.* souffle pantelant, haletant; halètement *m;* battement *m* (du cœur).

pant[2], *v.i.* **1.** *(a)* panteler; *(of animal)* battre du flanc; *(of heart)* palpiter; *(b)* haleter, ahaner; **to p. for breath,** chercher à reprendre haleine; être à court de souffle; **he panted out a few words,** il a dit quelques mots en haletant, d'une voix entrecoupée. **2.** *F:* **I'm panting to do it,** j'ai tellement envie de le faire; *O:* **to p. for, after, sth.,** soupirer après, pour, qch. **3.** *Nau: (of ship's sides)* travailler.

pantagraph ['pæntəgræf], *s.* = PANTOGRAPH.

pantagruelian [pæntəgru'eliən], **pantagruelic** [pæntəgru'elik], *a.* pantagruélesque, pantagruélique.

pantagruelism [pæntə'gruəlizm], *s.* pantagruélisme *m.*

pantagruelist [pæntə'gruəlist], *s.* pantagruéliste *mf.*

pantaleon [pæn'tæliən], *s. A.Mus:* pantaléon *m.*

pantalettes [pæntə'lets], *s.pl. A:* **1.** pantalon *m* (de femme ou d'enfant, ruché aux chevilles). **2.** *Hum:* culotte *f* cycliste (de femme).

Pantaloon [pæntə'luːn], *s.* **1.** *A. Th: (pers.)* Pantalon *m,* cassandre *m.* **2.** *Cost: A:* **(pair of) pantaloons,** pantalon.

pantaloonery [pæntə'luːnəri], *s. A.Th:* pantalonnade *f.*

pantaphobia [pæntə'foubiə], *s. Psy:* pantaphobie *f.*

pantechnicon [pæn'teknikən], *s.* **1.** garde-meuble *m, pl.* garde-meubles; dépôt *m* pour les meubles. **2. p. (van),** fourgon *m,* voiture *f,* de déménagement.

pantees ['pæntiz], *s.pl. F:* culotte *f* (de femme).

pantelegraph [pæn'telifræf], *s. Tg:* pantélégraphe *m.*

pantheism ['pænθi(ː)izm], *s.* panthéisme *m.*

pantheist ['pænθi(ː)ist], *a. & s.* panthéiste *(mf).*

pantheistic(al) [pænθi(ː)'istik(l)], *a.* panthéiste, panthéistique.

pantheon ['pænθiən], *s.* panthéon *m.*

panther ['pænθər], *s.* **1.** *Z:* panthère *f* (mâle); **mountain p.,** once *f;* léopard *m* des neiges. **2.** *Z: U.S:* couguar *m,* puma *m.* **3.** *Ich:* **p. fish,** poisson-panthère *m, pl.* poissons-panthères.

pantheress ['pænθəris], *s.* panthère *f* (femelle).

pantherine ['pænθərain], *a.* panthérin; **p. bound,** bond *m* de panthère.

pantie ['pænti], *s. Cost:* **panties,** culotte *f* (de femme, de bébé); **p. girdle,** gaine-culotte *f, pl.* gaines-culottes; **p. hose,** bas-slip *m, pl.* bas-slip; collant *m.*

pantile ['pæntail], *s.* **1.** tuile flamande, en S; panne *f.* **2.** *pl. A:* **pantiles,** dallage *m* en carreaux hollandais.

panting[1] ['pæntiŋ], *a. (a)* pantelant; *(of heart)* palpitant; *(of bosom)* bondissant; *(b)* haletant.

panting[2], *s. (a)* essoufflement *m,* halètement *m; (b)* palpitation *f* (du cœur).

pantler ['pæntlər], *s. A:* panetier *m,* crédencier *m;* **pantler's office,** paneterie *f.*

panto- ['pæntou, pæn'tɔ], *comb.fm.* panto-.

panto ['pæntou], *s. Th: F:* = PANTOMIME[1] 2*(b).*

Pantocrator [pæn'tɔkrətər], *a. & s.m. (a) Ecc: Art:* **(Christ) P.,** (Christ) Pantocrator; *(b) Myth:* **Zeus p.,** Zeus pantocrator.

pantodon ['pæntoudɔn], *s. Ich:* pantodon *m.*

pantograph ['pæntəgræf], *s.* **1.** *Draw:* pantographe *m,* singe *m.* **2.** *El:* pantographe (de locomotive électrique, etc.).

pantographic(al) [pæntə'græfik(l)], *a.* pantographique.

pantographically [pæntə'græfik(ə)li], *adv.* pantographiquement.

pantometer [pæn'tɔmitər], *s. Mth: Surv:* pantomètre *m.*

pantometric [pæntə'metrik], *a.* pantométrique.

pantomime[1] ['pæntəmaim], *s. Th:* **1.** *Rom.Ant: (pers.)* pantomime *m,* mime *m.* **2.** *(a) (dumb show)* pantomime *f; (b)* revue-féerie à grand spectacle (représentée aux environs de la Noël).

pantomime[2]. **1.** *v.tr.* mimer (un rôle, etc.). **2.** *v.i.* s'exprimer en pantomime.

pantomimic [pæntə'mimik], *a. (a)* pantomimique; *(b)* de féerie; à transformations féeriques, dignes d'une féerie.

pantomimist ['pæntəmaimist], *s.* **1.** pantomime *m.* **2.** acteur, -trice, de féerie.

panton ['pæntɔn], *s. Farr:* **p. (shoe),** (fer *m* à) pantoufle *f.*

pantophobia [pæntou'foubiə], *s. Psy:* pantophobie *f.*

Pantopoda [pæn'tɔpədə], *s.pl. Arach:* pantopodes *m.*

pantoscope ['pæntəskoup], *s. Phot:* pantoscope *m.*

pantothenic [pæntou'θiːnik], *a. Bio-Ch:* pantothénique.

pantoum ['pæntoum], *s. Lit:* pantoum *m,* pantoun *m.*

pantry ['pæntri], *s. (a)* dépense *f;* (grand) placard à provisions; **(butler's) p.,** office *m;* sommellerie *f;* **p. maid,** fille *f* d'office; *(b) Av:* bar *m.*

pantryman, *pl.* **-men** ['pæntrimən], *s.m. A:* **1.** sommelier. **2.** *Nau:* matelot de l'office.

pants [pænts], *s.pl. (a)* caleçon *m* (d'homme, *F:* de femme); *(b) F:* pantalon *m; (c) F:* **a kick in the p.,** un coup de pied au derrière, *P:* au cul; **to be caught with one's p. down,** être pris en mauvaise posture, dans une situation fort embarrassante.

panty ['pænti], *s. U.S:* = PANTIE.

pantywaist ['pæntiweist], *s. U.S: (a) Cost:* culotte courte d'enfant (boutonnée au maillot de corps); *(b) F:* homme efféminé, enfantin.

pap[1] [pæp], *s.* **1.** *A: & Dial:* mamelon *m,* tétin *m,* bout *m* de sein. **2.** *Geog:* mamelon, piz *m,* pis *m* (de montagne); **the Paps of Jura,** les pitons *m* de l'île de Jura.

pap[2], *s. (a)* bouillie *f;* **fed on p.,** nourri de bouillies; *(b)* pulpe *f,* pâte *f* (très liquide).

pap[3], *v.tr.* **(papped)** mettre (qch.) en bouillie.

pap[4], *s.m. U.S: F:* papa *m.*

papa [pə'pɑː], *s.m. F: O:* papa.

papacy ['peipəsi], *s.* **1.** papauté *f;* **to aspire to the p.,** aspirer à la tiare. **2.** = POPERY.

papaia [pæ'paiə], *s.* = PAPAW **1.**

papain [pæ'paiin], *s. Ch:* papaïne *f.*

papal ['peip(ə)l], *a.* papal, -aux; apostolique; **p. legate,** légat *m* du Pape; **the P. States,** les États *m* de l'Église; les États Pontificaux.

papalize ['peipəlaiz]. **1.** *v.i.* tourner au catholicisme (de Rome). **2.** *v.tr.* convertir au catholicisme, à la foi catholique.

papaver [pæ'peivər], *s. Bot:* papaver *m,* pavot *m.*

Papaveraceae [pæpeivə'reisiiː], *s.pl. Bot:* papavéracées *f.*

papaveraceous [pæpeivə'reiʃəs], *a. Bot:* papavéracé.

papaverin(e) [pæ'peivər(a)in], *s. Pharm:* papavérine *f.*

papaverous [pæ'peiv(ə)rəs], *a.* **1.** qui ressemble au pavot; *Bot:* papavéracé. **2.** soporifique.

papaw [pə'pɔː], *s. Bot:* **1.** *(a)* papaye *f; (b)* **p. (tree),** papayer *m.* **2.** *(in America) (a)* asimine *f; (b)* asiminier *m.*

papelonné [pæpi'lɔnei], *a. Her:* papelonné.

paper[1] ['peipər], *s.* **1.** papier *m; (a)* **hand-made p.,** papier à la main, papier cuve; **machine-made p.,** papier mécanique; **p. in rolls, continuous fanfold p.,** papier (en) continu; **laid p.,** papier vergé; **alfa, esparto, p.,** papier d'alfa; **rag p.,** papier chiffon; **rice p.,** papier de Chine, de riz; **manila p.,** papier bulle; **vellum p.,** papier vélin; **India p.,** papier bible, papier pelure; **featherweight p.,** papier bouffant; **blotting p.,** (papier) buvard *m;* **carbon p.,** papier carbone; **sized p.,** papier collé; **waxed p.,** papier paraffiné; **art p.,** **(surface-)coated p., baryta p.,** papier couché; **crepe p.,** papier crêpe; **glassine, translucent, p.,** papier cristal; **emery p.,** papier émeri; **glass p.,** papier abrasif, papier de verre; **tar p., bituminized p.,** papier goudronné, bitumé; **brown p., wrapping p.,** papier gris; **filter p.,** papier filtre; papier laboratoire; papier joseph; **butter p.,** papier sulfurisé; **greaseproof p.,** papier beurre, papier jambon, papier parcheminé; **glossy, glazed, p.,** papier brillant; **semi-matt p.,** papier demi-brillant; **matt, unglazed, dull-finish, p.,** papier mat, non-satiné; **cigarette p.,** papier à cigarettes; *Phot:* **sensitized p.,** papier sensible; **bromide p.,** papier au bromure (d'argent); **soft p.,** papier pour effets doux; **self-toning p.,** papier autovireur; **tracing p.,** papier calque, à calquer; **writing p.,** papier à écrire; **letter p.,** papier à lettres; **cambric p.,** papier (à lettres) toile; **typing p.,** papier pour machine à écrire, *F:* papier machine; **drawing p.,** papier à dessin; **exercise p.,** papier écolier; **rough p., scribbling p.,** papier brouillon; **ruled, lined, p.,** papier réglé; **squared p.,** papier quadrillé, à carreaux; **blank p.,** papier vierge; **packing, wrapping, p.,** papier d'emballage; **toilet p., lavatory p.,** *F:* **loo p.,** papier hygiénique, papier toilette; *(b)* **a sheet, a piece, of p.,** une feuille, un morceau de papier; *Com: A:* **p. of pins,** carte *f* d'épingles; *Toil: A:* **curl papers,** papillotes *f; attrib.* **p. bag,** sac *m* de, en, papier; **p. parcel,** paquet enveloppé de papier; *(c)* papier peint; **have you chosen the new p. for the bedroom?** avez-vous choisi le nouveau papier pour la chambre? **p. hanging,** collage *m,* pose *f,* de papiers peints, de papier tenture; **p. hanger,** tapissier *m,* poseur *m* de papiers peints; *(d)* **the p. industry,** l'industrie papetière; la papeterie; **p. mill,** papeterie, moulin *m* à papier, fabrique *f* de papier; **p. manufacturer,** fabricant *m* de papier; **p. merchant,** marchand *m* de papier; **p. cutter, p. knife, p. trimmer,** coupe-papier *m inv;* massicot *m; Bookb:* plioir *m; Cmptr: etc:* **p. track,** chemin *m* du papier; **p. tractor,** entraîneur *m* de papier; **p. shredder,** machine *f* à détruire les documents (par lacération); *(e)* **to put sth. down on p.,** mettre qch. sur papier; coucher qch. par écrit; **to explain sth. on p.,** expliquer qch. par écrit; **the scheme's a good one on p.,** ce projet est excellent en théorie; **on p. he's the better man,** (i) il a de meilleurs diplômes; (ii) il s'exprime mieux par écrit; **p. profits,** profits fictifs; **p. strength,** force *f* (d'une armée) sur le papier; *Sp:* **form on p.,** forme fictive (d'une équipe de football, etc.); **to bet on form on p.,** jouer le papier; *(f) Th: F:* billets *mpl* de faveur; **the house is full, but half of it is p.,** la salle est pleine, mais la moitié des places sont à l'œil. **2.** *(a)* écrit *m,* document *m,* pièce *f;* **family papers,** papiers, documents, de famille; **private, personal, papers,** papiers personnels; **old papers,** vieux papiers; paperasses *f;* **p. clip, fastener,** attache *f* métallique; trombone *m;* **papers of a firm,** écritures *f* d'une entreprise; **we have handed the papers to our solicitor** = nous avons remis les documents, les pièces, chez notre notaire; **identity papers,** papiers d'identité; **naturalization papers,** papiers, documents, de naturalisation; **relevant papers,** pièces justificatives; **ship's papers,** papiers, documents, de bord; **clearance papers,** papiers d'expédition; *Mil: etc:* **call-up papers,** ordre *m* d'appel (sous les drapeaux); **officer's papers,**

dossier personnel d'un officier; **to send, hand, in one's papers,** donner sa démission; (*b*) *Fin: etc:* valeurs *fpl*, papier(s); **accommodation p.,** papier de complaisance; **bankable, unbankable, p.,** papier banquable, non banquable; **commercial, mercantile, trade, p.,** papier, document, commercial, de commerce; **guaranteed p.,** papier fait; **long, short, p.,** papier à long terme, à court terme; **negotiable p.,** papier négociable, commerciable; **p. securities,** papiers valeurs, titres *m* fiduciaires; (*c*) billets *m* (de banque); **p. money, currency,** papier-monnaie *m*, *pl.* papiers-monnaie; (*d*) **voting p.,** bulletin *m* de vote; (*e*) *Parl:* papiers, documents (relatifs à une affaire) communiqués à la Chambre. **3.** *Sch:* **examination p.,** (i) questions *fpl* d'examen; (ii) copie *f*; **to set a p.,** choisir le sujet, les sujets, pour un examen; **to correct, mark, papers,** corriger l'écrit; **he did a good p. in French,** il a fait un bon écrit en français. **4.** étude *f*, mémoire *m* (sur un sujet scientifique, etc.); **to read a p.,** (i) faire une communication (à une société savante, etc.); (ii) faire une conférence, un exposé, *F:* lire un papier. **5.** journal, -aux *m*; **it's in the p.,** c'est dans le journal; **daily p.,** journal, quotidien *m*; **weekly p.,** hebdomadaire *m*; **Sunday p.,** journal du dimanche; **fashion p.,** journal de modes; **to write for the papers,** faire du journalisme; **p. boy,** (i) vendeur *m*, (ii) livreur *m*, de journaux. **6.** (*a*) *Bot:* **p. bark,** mélaleuque *m* leucadendron; cajeput *m*; niaouli *m*; **p. mulberry,** mûrier *m* à papier, de Chine; arbre *m* à papier; broussonétie *f* à papier; (*b*) *Ent:* **p. wasp,** mouche papetière; (guêpe) cartonnière *f*.

paper², *v.tr.* **1.** (*a*) (i) empaqueter (qch.) dans une feuille de papier; (ii) encarter (des épingles); (*b*) doubler (une boîte) de papier; (*c*) tapisser (une chambre); **room papered in blue,** pièce tapissée d'un papier bleu, tapissée de bleu; pièce tendue de (papier) bleu; *F:* **to p. over the cracks,** déguiser les défauts (de qch.). **2.** *Th: F:* remplir (la salle) de billets de faveur. **3.** émeriser (qch.); passer (qch.) à la toile d'émeri, au papier de verre.

paperback ['peipəbæk], *s. Publ:* livre *m* de poche.

paperbacked ['peipəbækt], *a. Bookb:* broché.

paperer ['peipərər], *s.* tapissier *m*, poseur *m* de papiers peints.

paperweight ['peipəweit], *s.* presse-papiers *m inv*; **ornamental glass p.,** sulfure *m*.

paperwork ['peipəwəːk], *s.* écriture *f*; travail *m* d'employé de bureau; *Sch:* exercices écrits; **VAT makes a lot of p. for shopkeepers,** la TVA complique les écritures des commerçants.

papery ['peipəri], *a.* semblable au papier; mince comme le papier; *Nat.Hist:* papyracé.

Paphian ['peifiən]. **1.** *a. & s. A.Geog:* Paphien, -ienne; **the P. Goddess,** la déesse de Paphos; Vénus. **2.** *s.f. A:* courtisane.

Paphlagonia [pæflæ'gouniə], *Pr.n. A.Geog:* Paphlagonie *f*.

Paphlagonian [pæflæ'gouniən]. *A.Geog:* (*a*) *a.* paphlagonien; (*b*) *s.* Paphlagonien, -ienne.

papier mâché ['pæpjei'mæʃei], *s.* carton-pâte *m*; papier-pierre *m*; pâte *f* de carton.

Papilionaceae [pæpiliə'neisiiː], *s.pl. Bot:* papilionacées *f*.

papilionaceous [pæpiliə'neiʃəs], *a. Bot:* papilionacé; **p. plant,** papilionacée *f*.

Papilionidae [pæpili'ɔnidiː], *s.pl. Ent:* papilionidés *m*.

papilla, *pl.* **-ae** [pə'pilə, -iː], *s. Nat.Hist:* papille *f*; *Anat:* **(circum)vallate p.,** papille caliciforme; **gustatory p.,** papille gustative, papille du goût; **lingual p.,** papille linguale; **p. salivaris,** papille salivaire; **sublingual p.,** papille, caroncule, sublinguale.

papillary [pə'piləri], *a. Nat.Hist:* papillaire.

papillate(d) ['pæpileit(id)], *a.* papillé, papillaire.

papillectomy [pæpi'lektəmi], *s. Surg:* papillectomie *f*.

Papillifera [pæpi'lifərə], *s.pl. Mol:* papillifères *m*.

papilliferous [pæpi'lifərəs], *a. Nat.Hist:* papillifère.

papilliform [pæ'pilifɔːm], *a.* papilliforme.

papillitis [pæpi'laitis], *s. Med:* papillite *f*.

papilloma [pæpi'loumə], *s. Med:* papillome *m*.

papillomatosis [pæpiloumæ'tousis], *s. Med:* papillomatose *f*.

papillomatous [pæpi'loumətəs], *a. Med:* papillomateux.

papillose ['pæpilous], *a. Nat.Hist:* papilleux, papillé.

papio ['pæpiou], *s. Z:* papion *m*.

papism ['peipizm], *s.* papisme *m*.

papist ['peipist], *s.* papiste *mf*.

papistic(al) [pə'pistik(l)], *a. Pej:* qui sent le papisme; papiste; *A:* papalin.

papistry ['peipistri], *s. Pej:* papisme *m*.

papolater [pə'pɔlətər], *s. Pej:* papolâtre *mf*.

papolatrous [pə'pɔlətrəs], *a. Pej:* papolâtre.

papolatry [pə'pɔlətri], *s. Pej:* papolâtrie *f*.

papoose [pə'puːs], *s.* enfant *mf* en bas âge (des Indiens de l'Amérique du Nord).

pappiferous [pæ'pifərəs], *a. Bot:* pappifère.

pappose [pæ'pous], *a. Bot:* pappeux.

pappus ['pæpəs], *s. Bot:* pappe *m*, aigrette *f*.

pappy ['pæpi], *a.* **1.** pâteux, pulpeux. **2.** *F: O:* (*of character*) mou, *f.* molle; flasque.

paprica, paprika ['pæprikə], *s.* paprika *m*.

Papua ['pæpjuə], *Pr.n. Geog:* Papouasie *f*.

Papuan ['pæpjuən]. *Geog:* (*a*) *a.* papou; (*b*) *s.* Papou, -oue.

papula, *pl.* **-ae** ['pæpjulə, -iː], **papule** ['pæpjuːl], *s. Med: Bot:* papule *f*.

papulose, papulous ['pæpjulous, -ləs], *a.* papuleux.

papyraceous [pæpi'reiʃəs], *a. Nat.Hist:* papyracé.

papyrological [pæpirou'lɔdʒikl], *a.* papyrologique.

papyrologist [pæpi'rɔlədʒist], *s.* papyrologue *mf*.

papyrology [pæpi'rɔlədʒi], *s.* papyrologie *f*.

papyrus, *pl.* **-ri** [pə'paiərəs, -rai], *s. Bot: Pal:* papyrus *m*.

par¹ [pɑːr], *s.* pair *m*, égalité *f*; (*a*) **to be on a p. with s.o., sth.,** être au niveau de, aller de pair avec, qn, qch.; être l'égal de qn; (*b*) *Fin:* **p. of exchange,** pair du change; **above p., below p.,** au-dessus, au-dessous, du pair; **value at p., p. value,** valeur *f* du pair; valeur au pair; **repayable at p.,** remboursable au pair; **exchange at p.,** change *m* à (la) parité; (*c*) moyenne *f*; **on a p.,** en moyenne; **below p.,** au-dessous du commun, de la moyenne; médiocre; *F:* **to feel below p.,** ne pas être dans son assiette; être mal en train; (*d*) *Golf:* par *m*.

par², *s.* (*paragraph*) **1.** *Journ:* entrefilet *m*; fait-divers *m*, *pl.* faits-divers; **writer of pars, p. writer,** courriériste *m*, échotier *m*; fait-diversier *m*, *pl.* fait-diversiers. **2.** paragraphe *m*; alinéa *m*.

Para¹ ['pɑːrə], *Pr.n. Geog:* Para *m*; **P. rubber,** para *m*; *Bot:* **P. rubber plant,** hevé *m*.

para², *s. Num:* para *m*.

para- ['pærə, pə'ræ], *comb.fm.* para-.

para-axial [pærə'æksiəl], *a. Opt:* para-axial, -aux.

parabanic [pærə'bænik], *a. Ch:* parabanique; **p. acid,** oxalylurée *f*.

parabasis, *pl.* **-ses** [pə'ræbəsis, -siːz], *s. Gr.Th:* parabase *f*.

parabenzene [pærə'benziːn], *s. Ch:* parabenzène *m*.

parabiosis, *pl.* **-ses** [pærəbai'ousis, -siːz], *s. Biol:* parabiose *f*.

parablast ['pærəblæst], *s. Biol:* parablaste *m*; feuillet *m* vasculaire.

parable ['pærəbl], *s.* parabole *f*; **to speak in parables,** parler par, en, paraboles.

parabola [pə'ræbələ], *s. Mth:* parabole *f*.

parabolic [pærə'bɔlik], *a.* **1. p. teaching,** enseignement *m* parabolique, en paraboles. **2.** (*a*) *Mth: etc:* **p. curve,** courbe *f* parabolique; **p. cylinder,** cylindre *m* parabolique; **p. mirror, reflector,** miroir *m*, réflecteur *m*, parabolique; *T.V: etc:* **p. aerial, antenna,** antenne *f* parabolique; (*b*) *Space:* **p. velocity,** vitesse *f* de libération (de l'attraction terrestre, etc.); vitesse parabolique.

parabolically [pærə'bɔlik(ə)li], *adv.* paraboliquement.

parabolicness [pærə'bɔliknis], *s.* parabolicité *f*.

parabolist [pə'ræbəlist], *s.* paraboliste *mf*.

parabolize [pə'ræbəlaiz], *v.tr. Opt:* paraboliser.

paraboloid [pə'ræbəlɔid], *s. Mth:* paraboloïde *m*; **p. of revolution,** paraboloïde de révolution.

paraboloidal [pəræbə'lɔidl], *a. Mth:* paraboloïdal, -aux; paraboloïde.

parabulia [pærə'buːliə], *s. Psy:* paraboulie *f*.

paracarp ['pærəkɑːp], *s. Bot:* paracarpe *m*.

paracasein [pærə'keisiːn], *s. Bio-Ch:* paracaséine *f*.

Paracelsus [pærə'selsəs]. *Pr.n.m. Med.Hist:* Paracelse.

paracentesis [pærəsen'tiːsis], *s.* paracentèse *f*.

paracentral [pærə'sentr(ə)l], *a. Anat:* (lobe, etc.) paracentral, -aux.

paracentric [pærə'sentrik], *a. Mth: Mec:* (courbe, mouvement) paracentrique.

paracephalus [pærə'sefələs], *s. Ter:* paracéphale *m*.

parachor ['pærəkɔːr], *s. Ch:* parachor *m*.

parachronism [pæ'rækrənizm], *s.* parachronisme *m*; erreur *f* de date (trop tardive).

parachute¹ ['pærəʃuːt], *s.* (*a*) parachute *m*; **back-pack p., back(-type) p.,** parachute dorsal; **seat-pack p., seat-type p.,** parachute à siège; **lap-pack p.,** parachute ventral; **pilot p.,** parachute d'extraction; **manually-operated p.,** parachute commandé à la main, à ouverture commandée à la main; **self-opening p.,** parachute (à ouverture) automatique; **p. static line,** sangle *f* d'ouverture automatique de parachute; **p. harness,** ceinture *f*, harnais *m*, de parachute; **p. vent,** fente radiale, soupirail *m*, de parachute; **p. jump, descent,** saut *m*, descente *f*, en parachute; **delayed p. jump,** saut en parachute avec ouverture retardée; **to make a p. jump,** sauter en parachute; **to drop s.o., sth., by p.,** larguer qn, qch., par parachute; parachuter qn, qch.; **p. troops, unit,** troupes *f*, unité *f*, parachutiste; **p. tower,** tour *f* d'instruction de parachutistes; (*b*) **brake p., landing p., tail p., p. brake,** parachute de freinage (à l'atterrissage); parachute de queue; **p. flare, p. light,** fusée (éclairante) à parachute.

parachute². **1.** *v.i.* **to p. (down),** descendre en parachute. **2.** *v.tr.* parachuter (qn, qch.); larguer (qn, qch.) par parachute.

parachuting ['pærəʃuːtiŋ], *s.* **1.** (*a*) descente *f* en parachute; (*b*) le parachutisme. **2.** parachutage *m* (de qn, de qch.); largage *m* (de qn, de qch.) par parachute.

parachutist ['pærəʃuːtist], *s.* parachutiste *mf*.

Paraclete (the) [ðə'pærəkliːt], *s.* le Paraclet, le Saint-Esprit.

paracresol [pærə'kriːsɔl], *s. Ch:* paracrésol *m*.

paracusia [pærə'kjuːziə], *s. Med:* paracousie *f*.

paracyanogen [pærəsai'ænoudʒen], *s. Ch:* paracyanogène *m*.

paracyst ['pærəsist], *s.* paracyste *m*.

parade¹ [pə'reid], *s.* **1.** parade *f*; **to make a p. of one's poverty,** faire parade, ostentation, étalage, de sa pauvreté; afficher sa pauvreté; **to make a p. of learning,** faire étalage, faire parade, d'érudition. **2.** *Mil:* (*a*) rassemblement *m*; **p. under arms,** prise *f* d'armes; **church p.,** (i) *Mil:* rassemblement du bataillon, etc., pour assister à l'office du dimanche; (ii) *F: A:* promenade *f* du beau monde après l'office; tour *m* de plage, du parc, après l'office; (*b*) exercice *m*; **on p.,** à l'exercice; **guard-mounting p.,** parade; **to go on p.,** parader; **to march as if on p.,** marcher au pas de parade; **p. ground,** terrain *m* de manœuvres; place *f* d'armes; (*c*) *Fenc:* parade. **3.** (*a*) procession *f*, défilé *m*; (*b*) **mannequin p., fashion p.,** défilé de mannequins; présentation *f* de collections; (*c*) **beauty p.,** concours *m* d'élégance. **4.** esplanade *f*; promenade publique; boulevard *m* (le long d'une plage, etc.).

parade². **1.** *v.tr.* (*a*) faire parade, ostentation, étalage, de (ses richesses, ses connaissances, etc.); **to p. one's poverty,** afficher sa pauvreté; **he is fond of parading his knowledge,** il aime à faire parade de ses connaissances; (*b*) *Mil:* faire l'inspection (des troupes); rassembler (un bataillon); faire parader, faire défiler (les troupes); **after church he would p. his whole family in the park,** après l'office il promenait fièrement toute sa famille dans le parc. **2.** *v.i.* (*a*) *Mil:* se rassembler; faire la parade; parader (pour l'exercice, pour l'inspection); **to p. under arms,** prendre les armes; (*b*) **to p. (through) the streets,** marcher en procession dans les rues; défiler dans les rues; **to p. on the pier,** se pavaner, parader, sur la jetée.

paradesmose [pærə'dezmous], *s. Biol:* paradesmose *f*.

paradichlorobenzene [pærədaiklɔːrou'benziːn], *s. Ch:* paradichlorobenzène *m*.

paradigm ['pærədaim], *s. Gram:* paradigme *m*; modèle *m* (de conjugaison, etc.).

paradigmatic [pærədig'mætik], *a.* paradigmatique.

Paradisaeidae [pærədi'siːidiː], *s.pl. Orn:* paradiséidés *m*, paradisiers *m*.

paradisaic(al) [pærədi'zeiik(l)], *a.* paradisiaque.

paradise ['pærədais], *s.* **1.** paradis *m*; **the Earthly P.,** le Paradis terrestre; **an earthly p.,** un paradis sur terre; un jardin de délices; **to go to p.,** aller en paradis; **the joys of p.,** les joies *f* paradisiaques. **2.** *Orn:* (*a*) **bird of p.,** paradisier *m*, oiseau de paradis; **Emperor of Germany's bird of p.,** paradisier de l'Empereur Guillaume; **greater bird of p.,** paradisier apode; **king bird of p.,** manucode *m* royal; **King of Saxony's bird of p.,** ptéridophore *m*; **lesser bird of p.,** petit paradisier jaune; **long-tailed bird of p.,** épimaque *f*; **magnificent bird of p.,** paradisier magnifique; **Prince Rudolph's bird of p.,** paradisier du Prince Rodolphe; **six-wired bird of p.,** sifflet *m* à six brins; **standard-wing bird of p.,** sémioptère *m*, paradisier de Wallace; **superb bird of p.,** lophorine *f*, paradisier superbe; **twelve-wired bird of p.,** ptéridophore, paradisier multifil; **Wilson's bird of p.,** paradisier républicain, de Wilson; (*b*) **p. crane,** grue *f* de paradis; **p. crow,** lycocorax *m*; **p. magpie,** astrapie *f*. **3.** *Ich:* **p. fish,** paradisier, macropode *m*; gourami *m*. **4.** *Hort:* **p. (apple),** paradis.

paradisiac [pærə'diziæk], **paradisiacal** [pærədi'zaiəkl], **paradisial** [pærə'diziəl], *a.* paradisiaque.

parados ['pærədɔs], *s. Fort:* parados *m*.

paradox ['pærədɔks], *s.* paradoxe *m*; antinomie *f*; *Ph:* **the hydrostatic p.,** le paradoxe hydrostatique.

paradoxical [pærə'dɔksikl], *a.* paradoxal, -aux; antinomique.

paradoxically [pærə'dɔksik(ə)li], *adv.* paradoxalement.

Paradoxides [pærə'dɔksidiːz], *s. Paleont:* paradoxides *m*.

paradoxology [pærədɔk'sɔlədʒi], *s.* paradoxologie *f*.

paradoxure [pærə'dɔksjər], *s. Z:* paradoxure *m.*
paradrop[1] ['pærədrɔp], *s.* parachutage *m* (de qn, de qch.); largage *m* (de qn, de qch.) par parachute.
paradrop[2], *v.tr.* (**paradropped**) parachuter (qn, qch.); larguer (qn, qch.) par parachute.
paraesthesia, paraesthesis [pæres'θi:ziə, -'θi:sis], *s. Med:* paresthésie *f.*
paraffin[1], *A:* **paraffine** ['pærəfin, -fi:n], *s.* paraffine *f*; **the p. series,** les paraffènes *m*; **crude p.,** graisse minérale; **p. hydrocarbons,** carbures *m* paraffiniques; **p. distillate,** distillat paraffineux; **p. wax,** paraffine solide; **to coat with p.,** paraffiner; **p. (oil),** pétrole (lampant), kérosène *m,* kérosine *f*; **p. lamp,** lampe *f* à pétrole; *Pharm:* **liquid p.,** huile *f* de vaseline; vaseline *f* liquide; huile de paraffine.
paraffin[2], *v.tr.* (*a*) paraffiner; (*b*) pétroler (un marais, etc.).
paraffinic [pærə'finik], *a.* paraffinique.
parafoil ['pærəfɔil], *s.* parachute ascensionnel.
paraform ['pærəfɔ:m], **paraformaldehyde** [pærəfɔ:'mældihaid], *s. Ch:* paraformaldéhyde *m,* paraforme *m.*
paragenesis [pærə'dʒenisis], *s. Biol:* paragénésie *f*; *Biol: Geol:* paragénèse *f.*
paraglossa [pærə'glɔsə], *s. Ent:* paraglosse *m.*
paragneiss [pærə'nais], *s. Geol:* paragneiss *m.*
paragnosia [pæræg'nouziə], *s. Med:* paragnosie *f.*
paragoge [pærə'goudʒi], *s. Gram:* paragoge *m.*
paragogic [pærə'gɔdʒik], *a. Gram:* paragogique.
paragon[1] ['pærəgən], *s.* **1.** modèle *m* (de beauté, de vertu, etc.); phénix *m.* **2.** *Lap:* (diamant *m*) parangon *m.*
paragon[2], *v.tr. A:* **1.** citer (qch., qn) comme parangon. **2.** comparer (**with,** à, avec).
paragonite [pæ'rægənait], *s. Miner:* paragonite *f.*
paragraph[1] ['pærəgræf], *s.* **1.** paragraphe *m,* alinéa *m*; **the last p. of article 6,** le dernier alinéa de l'article 6; (*when dictating*) **new p.,** à la ligne; *Typ:* **p. (mark),** pied *m* de mouche. **2.** *Journ:* entrefilet *m.*
paragraph[2], *v.tr.* **1.** diviser, mettre, en paragraphes, en alinéas. **2.** *Journ:* écrire un entrefilet sur (qn, qch.); **much paragraphed actress,** actrice très en vedette (dans les journaux).
paragrapher, paragraphist ['pærəgræfər, -græfist], *s.* journaliste *mf* qui rédige les entrefilets.
paragraphia [pærə'græfiə], *s. Med:* paragraphie *f.*
Paraguay ['pærəgwai]. **1.** *Pr.n. Geog:* Paraguay *m.* **2.** *attrib.* **P. tea,** maté *m.*
Paraguayan [pærə'gwaiən]. *Geog:* (*a*) *a.* paraguayen; (*b*) *s.* Paraguayen, -enne.
parahydrogen [pærə'haidrədʒin], *s. Ch:* parahydrogène *m.*
parakeet ['pærəki:t], *s. Orn:* perruche *f*; **blossom-headed p.,** perruche à tête prune; **ground p.,** perruche terrestre, pézopore; **hanging p.,** loricule *m,* suspenseur *m*; **monk p.,** perruche souris; **rose-banded p.,** perruche Alexandre; **rosella p.,** perruche platycerque, omnicolore; **blue-bonnet p.,** perruche *f* à bonnet bleu; **Bourke's p.,** perruche de Bourke; **Brown's p.,** perruche de Brown; **grass p.,** perruche platycerque; **hooded p.,** perruche à capuchon noir; **large Indian p.,** perruche Alexandre; **Pennant's p.,** perruche élégante, perruche de Pennant; **redrump p.,** perruche à croupion rouge; **ring-necked p.,** perruche à collier; **Stanley p.,** perruche de Stanley.
parakeratosis [pærəkerə'tousis], *s. Med:* parakératose *f.*
parakinesia, parakinesis [pærəkai'ni:ziə, -'ni:sis], *s. Med:* parakinésie *f.*
paralalia [pærə'leiliə], *s. Med:* paralalie *f.*
paralaurionite [pærə'lɔ:riənait], *s. Miner:* paralaurionite *f.*
paraldehyde [pæ'rældihaid], *s. Ch:* paraldéhyde *m.*
paralexia [pærə'leksiə], *s. Med:* paralexie *f.*
Paralipomena (the) [ðəpærəlai'pominə], *s.pl. B.Lit:* les Paralipomènes *m.*
paral(e)ipsis [pærə'lipsis], *s. Rh:* paralipse *f,* prétérition *f.*
parallactic [pærə'læktik], *a. Astr:* parallactique.
parallax ['pærəlæks], *s. Astr: Opt:* parallaxe *f*; **correction for p.,** correction *f* de (la) parallaxe; **diurnal, geocentric, p.,** parallaxe diurne; **horizontal p.,** parallaxe horizontale; **p. in altitude,** parallaxe en altitude; *T.V:* **time p.,** parallaxe de temps; *Opt:* **p. free,** sans parallaxe.
parallel[1] ['pærəlel], *a. & s.*
I. *a.* parallèle (**to, with, sth.,** à qch.). **1.** (*a*) *Mth: etc:* **p. curves, lines, planes,** courbes *f,* lignes *f,* plans *m,* parallèles; *Mec:* **p. forces,** forces *f* parallèles; **to be p. to sth.,** être parallèle à qch.; **in a p. direction with sth.,** parallèlement à qch.; **draw a line p. to the edge of the paper,** tirer, tracer, une ligne parallèle au bord de la feuille; **streets running p. to the boulevard,** rues parallèles, collatérales, au boulevard; **walls built p.,** murs construits parallèlement; **p. rule(r),** règle *f* à (tracer des) parallèles; parallèle *m*; (*b*) *Pol.Ec: etc:* **p. sequencing,** ordonnancement *m* (de la production) en parallèle; **to follow a p. course,** suivre un cours parallèle; (*c*) *Tls: etc:* **p. file,** lime *f* parallèle; **p. pliers,** pince *f* (à serrage) parallèle; **p. vice,** étau *m* parallèle; **p. lathe,** tour *m* parallèle; (*d*) **p. motion,** (i) *Mec:* parallélogramme *m* de Watt; (ii) *Mch:* parallélogramme (articulé); *Mch:* **p. rod,** bielle *f* d'accouplement; *Av:* **p. floats,** flotteurs (disposés) en catamaran; (*e*) *El:* **p. circuits,** circuits *m* parallèles; **p. connection,** couplage *m,* montage *m,* en parallèle, en dérivation; **to connect two cells in p.,** accoupler deux piles en parallèle, en dérivation; **p. feed,** alimentation *f* parallèle; *W.Tel: etc:* **p. feeders,** descente *f* d'antenne double; (*f*) *Cmptr:* **p. computer,** calculateur *m* parallèle; **p. feed,** alimentation ligne à ligne; **p. printer,** imprimante *f* parallèle; **p. processing,** traitement *m* (des données) en simultané; **p. running, storage,** exploitation *f,* enregistrement *m,* en parallèle. **2.** pareil, semblable; (cas) analogue (**to, with, sth.,** à qch.).
II. *s.* **1.** (*a*) (ligne *f*) parallèle *f*; **to draw a p. to a straight line,** tracer une parallèle à une droite; (*b*) *Geog: Astr:* parallèle *m* (de latitude, de déclinaison); **p. of altitude,** parallèle de hauteur; **the 49th p. forms the frontier between Canada and the United States,** le 49e parallèle forme la frontière entre le Canada et les États-Unis; *Astr:* **twilight p.,** cercle *m* crépusculaire; *Nau:* **p. sailing,** navigation *f* sur un parallèle; (*c*) *Fort:* (tranchée *f*) parallèle *f*; (*d*) *Typ:* **parallels,** barres *f*; (*e*) *Tls:* calibre *m* d'épaisseur. **2.** *El:* (*of dynamo*) **out of p.,** déphasé, hors de phase, hors de synchronisme. **3.** parallèle *m,* comparaison *f,* analogue *m*; **to draw a p. between two things,** établir un parallèle, une comparaison, entre deux choses; **wickedness without p.,** méchanceté sans pareille; **there is no p. to this catastrophe,** il n'y a rien de comparable, rien que l'on puisse comparer, à cette catastrophe.
parallel[2], *v.tr.* (**paralleled**) **1.** (*a*) placer parallèlement, paralléliser (des objets); **the two machine guns were paralleled on their tripods,** les deux mitrailleuses furent mises sur leur trépied et placées parallèlement; (*b*) *El:* mettre (deux circuits, deux piles, etc.) en parallèle; synchroniser (deux dynamos); (*c*) *NAm:* être parallèle à (qch.); longer parallèlement (qch.); **the road parallels the railroad,** la route longe parallèlement la voie ferrée. **2.** mettre (deux choses) en parallèle; comparer (deux choses). **3.** (*a*) trouver un parallèle à (qch.); (*b*) égaler (qch.); être égal, pareil, à (qch.); **greed that has never been paralleled,** avidité sans pareille.
parallelepiped [pærəlelə'paiped], *s. Mth:* parallélépipède *m.*
parallelepipedal, parallelepipedic [pærəlelə'paipedl, -paipedik], *a.* parallélépipédique.
parallelinervate, parallelinerved [pærəleli'nə:veit, -'nə:vd], *a. Bot:* parallélinervé.
parallelism ['pærəlelizm], *s.* **1.** parallélisme *m* (entre qch. et qch., de qch. à qch.); **p. between the axis of the tail stock and the runner,** parallélisme de l'axe de la contre-pointe à la glissière (d'un tour). **2.** *Phil:* parallélisme.
parallelist ['pærəlelist], *s. Phil:* paralléliste *mf.*
parallelistic [pærəle'listik], *a. Phil:* paralléliste.
parallelization [pærəlelai'zeiʃ(ə)n], *s.* parallélisation *f.*
parallelize ['pærəlelaiz], *v.tr.* paralléliser, rendre parallèle.
parallelogram [pærə'leləgræm], *s.* parallélogramme *m*; *Mec:* **p. of forces, of velocities,** parallélogramme des forces, des vitesses.
parallelogrammatic [pærəleləugrə'mætik], *a.* parallélogrammatique.
parallelopiped [pærəlelou'paiped], *s. Mth:* parallélépipède *m.*
parallel-veined [pærəlel'veind], *a. Bot:* parallélinervé.
paralogism [pə'rælədʒizm], *s. Log:* paralogisme *m*; faux raisonnement.
paralogize [pə'rælədʒaiz], *v.i. Log:* commettre un paralogisme; raisonner à faux.
paralogy [pə'rælədʒi], *s. Gram:* paralogie *f.*
paraluminite [pærə'lu:minait], *s. Miner:* paraluminite *f.*
paralysation [pærəlai'zeiʃ(ə)n], *s.* immobilisation *f* (de l'industrie, de la circulation, etc.).
paralyse ['pærəlaiz], *v.tr.* paralyser; (*a*) **paralysed in one leg, in both arms,** paralysé d'une jambe, des deux bras; (*b*) **laws that p. industry,** lois *f* qui paralysent l'industrie; **paralysed with fear,** paralysé par l'effroi; glacé d'effroi; transi de peur; **I was paralysed by the news,** cette nouvelle m'a suffoqué.
paralyser ['pærəlaizər], *s.* agent paralysateur.
paralysing ['pærəlaiziŋ], *a.* paralysant; paralysateur, -trice; **it had a p. effect on me,** cela m'a complètement paralysé.
paralysis [pə'rælisis], *s.* **1.** *Med:* paralysie *f*; **general p.,** paralysie générale; diaplégie *f*; **bilateral p.,** paralysie bilatérale; displégie *f*; **facial p.,** paralysie faciale; **pseudobulbar p.,** paralysie pseudo-bulbaire; **creeping p.,** paralysie progressive; **Bell's p., histrionic p.,** paralysie de Bell; **p. agitans,** paralysie agitante, maladie *f* de Parkinson; *F: A:* **infantile p.,** paralysie infantile, poliomyélite *f.* **2.** paralysie, impuissance *f*; **the war caused a p. of trade,** le commerce a été paralysé à cause de la guerre; **industry seems to be moving towards p.,** l'industrie semble marcher vers une paralysie générale; **faced with this new problem he was affected by a sort of p.,** il se trouvait impuissant, paralysé, en face de ce nouveau problème.
paralytic [pærə'litik]. **1.** *a.* (*a*) *Med:* paralytique; **p. stroke,** attaque *f* de paralysie; (*b*) *F:* **he's (completely) p.,** il est soûl comme un Polonais. **2.** *s.* paralytique *mf.*
paralyze ['pærəlaiz], *v.tr.* = PARALYSE.
paramagnetic [pærəmæg'netik], *a. Ph:* paramagnétique; **nuclear p. resonance,** résonance *f* paramagnétique nucléaire.
paramagnetism [pærə'mægnitizm], *s.* paramagnétisme *m.*
paramastitis [pærəmæs'taitis], *s. Med:* paramastite *f.*
Paramatta [pærə'mætə]. **1.** *Pr.n. Geog:* Paramatta *m.* **2.** *s. Tex:* paramatta *m.*
paramecium [pærə'mi:siəm], *s. Prot:* paramécie *f.*
paramelaconite [pærəme'lækənait], *s. Miner:* paramélaconite *f.*
paramere ['pærəmiər], *s. Ent:* paramère *f.*
parameter [pə'ræmitər], *s. Mth: etc:* paramètre *m*; **design parameters,** paramètres d'étude; **preset p.,** paramètre prédéfini; **state p.,** paramètre d'état; *Atom.Ph:* **impact p.,** paramètre d'impact; *Geol:* **crystal p.,** paramètre cristallin; *Cmptr:* **p. card, word,** carte *f,* mot *m,* paramètre.
parameterization [pærəmi:tərai'zeiʃ(ə)n], *s. Mth:* paramétrisation *f*; paramétrage *m.*
parameterize [pærə'mi:təraiz], *v.tr. Mth:* paramétriser.
parametral [pə'ræmitrəl], **parametric** [pærə'metrik], *a. Mth:* paramétrique; **p. transformation,** paramétrage *m*; *Elcs:* **p. amplification,** amplification *f* paramétrique.
parametritis [pærəme'traitis], *s. Med:* paramétrite *f.*
parametrium [pærə'metriəm], *s. Anat:* paramètre *m.*
paramilitary [pærə'milit(ə)ri], *a.* paramilitaire; **p. organizations,** formations *f* paramilitaires; **p. police force,** police *f* paramilitaire.
paraminia [pærə'miniə], *s. Med:* paraminie *f.*
paraminophenol [pæ'ræminoufenɔl], *s. Ch:* paraminophénol *m,* paramidophénol *m.*
paramnesia [pæræm'ni:ziə], *s. Med:* paramnésie *f.*
paramorph ['pærəmɔ:f], *s. Miner: Biol:* structure *f* paramorphe.
paramorphic, paramorphous [pærə'mɔ:fik, -'mɔ:fəs], *a. Miner:* paramorphe.
paramorphosis, paramorphism [pærə'mɔ:fəsis, -'mɔ:fizm], *s. Biol:* paramorphose *f*; *Miner:* paramorphisme *m.*
paramount ['pærəmaunt], *a.* **1.** éminent, souverain; *A:* **lord, lady, p.,** suzerain, -aine. **2.** suprême; de la plus haute importance; **duty is p. with him,** chez lui le devoir prime tout, l'emporte sur tout, vient avant tout; **p. necessity,** nécessité *f* de toute première urgence.
paramour ['pærəmuər], *s. A:* (*a*) amant *m*; (*b*) amante *f,* maîtresse *f.*
paramyotonia [pærəmaiou'touniə], *s. Med:* paramyotonie *f.*
parang [pɑ:'ræŋ], *s.* couteau malais.
paranoia [pærə'nɔiə], *s. Med:* paranoïa *f.*
paranoiac [pærə'nɔiæk], *a. & s.* paranoïque *mf.*
paranoid ['pærənɔid], *a. Med:* paranoïde.
paranthelion [pæræn'θi:liən], *s.* parenthélie *f.*
paranthropus [pæ'rænθrəpəs], *s.* paranthrope *m.*
paranucleus [pærə'nju:kliəs], *s. Biol:* paranucléus *m.*
parapet ['pærəpet], *s.* (*a*) *Fort:* parapet *m*; berge *f* (de tranchée); *Artil:* **to fire over the p.,** tirer en barbette; (*of machine gun*) **p. mounting,** affût *m* de rempart; (*b*) parapet; garde-fou *m, pl.* garde-fous; garde-corps *m inv* (d'un pont, etc.).
parapeted ['pærəpetid], *a.* (pont, etc.) à garde-fous.
paraph[1] ['pæræf], *s.* paraphe *m,* parafe *m.*
paraph[2], *v.tr.* parapher, parafer.
paraphasia [pærə'feiziə], *s. Med:* paraphasie *f.*
paraphasic [pærə'feizik], *a. Med:* paraphasique.
paraphernal [pærə'fə:n(ə)l], *a. Jur: A:* paraphernal, -aux.
paraphernalia [pærəfə'neiliə], *s.pl.* **1.** *Jur: A:* biens paraphernaux. **2.** (*a*) effets *m*; affaires *f*; **all the p.,**

tous les effets, *F:* tout le bataclan; (*b*) attirail *m*, accessoires *m*.

paraphimosis [pæræfi'mousis], *s. Med:* paraphimosis *m*.

paraphonia [pærə'founiə], *s. A.Gr.Mus: Med:* paraphonie *f*.

paraphonic [pærə'fɔnik], *a.* (*a*) *A.Gr.Mus:* paraphonique; (*b*) *Med:* paraphone.

paraphrase[1] ['pærəfreiz], *s.* paraphrase *f*.

paraphrase[2], *v.tr.* paraphraser.

paraphraser ['pærəfreizər], *s.* paraphraseur, -euse.

paraphrast ['pærəfræst], *s.* paraphraste *m*.

paraphrastic [pærə'fræstik], *a.* paraphrastique.

paraphrenia [pærə'fri:niə], *s. Psy:* paraphrénie *f*.

paraphysis, *pl.* **-ses** [pærə'faisis, -si:z], *s. Fung:* paraphyse *f*.

paraplasm ['pærəplæzm], *s. Biol:* paraplasme *m*.

paraplegia [pærə'pli:dʒiə], *s. Med:* paraplégie *f*; **spastic p.**, paraplégie spasmodique.

paraplegic [pærə'pli:dʒik], *a.* & *s. Med:* paraplégique (*mf*).

parapraxia [pærə'præksiə], *s. Med:* parapraxie *f*.

parapsychological [pærəsaikə'lɔdʒikl], *a.* parapsychique, métapsychique.

parapsychology [pærəsai'kɔlədʒi], *s.* parapsychologie *f*; parapsychisme *m*; métapsychique *f*.

parasceve ['pærəsi:v], *s.* (*a*) *Jew.Rel:* parascève *f*; (*b*) *R.C.Ch:* parascève, vendredi saint.

paraselene, *pl.* **-nae** [pærəsi'li:ni, -ni:], *s. Astr:* parasélène *f*.

parasexuality [pærəseksju'æliti], *s.* parasexualité *f*.

parasite ['pærəsait], *s.* (*a*) parasite *m*; *Biol:* **accidental, permanent, p.,** parasite accidentel, permanent; **secondary, tertiary, p.,** hyperparasite *m*; **to be a p. on sth.,** être parasite de qch.; (*b*) (*of pers.*) **to live as a p.,** vivre en parasite; (*c*) *Av:* **p. drag,** traînée *f* de forme, de profil, et de frottement.

parasit(a)emia [pærəsi'ti:miə], *s. Med:* parasitémie *f*.

parasitic [pærə'sitik], *a.* (insecte, plante) parasite (**on,** de); **p. life,** vie *f* pararasitaire; **p. weeds,** herbes gourmandes; **p. disease,** maladie *f* parasitique, parasitaire; *Atom.Ph:* **p. capture of neutrons,** capture *f* parasite des neutrons; *Elcs: etc:* **p. noise,** bruit *m* parasite; **p. oscillation,** oscillation *f* parasite; **p. resonance,** résonance *f* parasitaire; **p. suppressor,** éliminateur *m* de parasites, dispositif *m* antiparasites; (*of pers.*) **p. activities,** activités *f* parasitaires.

parasiticide [pærə'sitisaid], *a.* & *s.* parasiticide (*m*).

parasitism ['pærəsaitizm], *s.* parasitisme *m*.

parasitize ['pærəsitaiz], *v.tr.* vivre en parasite; parasiter.

parasitologist [pærəsai'tɔlədʒist], *s.* parasitologiste *mf*.

parasitology [pærəsai'tɔlədʒi], *s.* parasitologie *f*.

parasitosis [pærəsai'tousis], *s. Med:* parasitose *f*.

parasol ['pærəsɔl], *s.* **1.** (*a*) ombrelle *f*; (*b*) **p. pine,** pin *m* parasol; **p. mushroom,** coulemelle *f*. **2.** *Av: A:* parasol *m*.

parasymbiosis [pærəsimbai'ousis], *s.* parasymbiose *f*.

parasympathetic [pærəsimpə'θetik]. *Physiol:* **1.** *a.* parasympathique; **p. nerve,** parasympathique *m*. **2.** *s.* parasympathique.

parasympathomimetic [pærəsimpæθoum(a)i'metik], *a. Med:* parasympathomimétique.

parasynapsis [pærəsi'næpsis], *s. Biol:* parasynapsis *f*.

parasynthesis [pærə'sinθəsis], *s. Ling:* dérivation *f* parasynthétique.

parasynthetic [pærəsin'θetik], *a. Ling:* parasynthétique.

parasyphilitic [pærəsifi'litik], *a. Med:* parasyphilitique.

paratactic [pærə'tæktik], *a. Gram:* paratactique.

paratartaric [pærəta:'tærik], *a. Ch:* paratartarique.

parataxis [pærə'tæksis], *s. Gram:* parataxe *f*.

parathormone [pærə'θɔ:moun], *s. Bio-Ch:* parathormone *f*.

parathyroid [pærə'θairɔid]. *Physiol:* **1.** *a.* (*also* **parathyroidal**) parathyroïde, parathyroïdien. **2.** *s.* parathyroïde *f*.

parathyroidectomy [pærəθairɔi'dektəmi], *s. Surg:* parathyroïdectomie *f*.

paratrooper ['pærətru:pər], *s.* (soldat) parachutiste *m*.

paratroops ['pærətru:ps], *s.pl.* (soldats) parachutistes *m*.

paratuberculosis [pærətjubəkju'lousis], *s. Vet:* paratuberculose *f*.

paratuberculous [pærətju'bə:kjuləs], *a.* paratuberculeux.

paratyphoid [pærə'taifɔid], *s. Med:* paratyphoïde *f*.

paravane ['pærəvein], *s. Nau:* paravane *m*; appareil *m* pare-mines; **to get in, out, the paravanes,** rentrer, mettre à l'eau, les paravanes.

paraviparous [pærə'vipərəs], *a. Z:* paravipare.

paraxial [pæ'ræksiəl], *a. Anat: Opt:* paraxial, -aux.

paraxylene [pæ'ræksili:n], *s. Ch:* paraxylène *m*.

parboil ['pa:bɔil], *v.tr. Cu:* faire cuire à demi (dans l'eau); faire bouillir à demi; blanchir (des légumes, etc.).

parbuckle[1] ['pa:bʌkl], *s. Nau:* trévire *f*.

parbuckle[2], *v.tr. Nau:* trévirer (un ballot, un canon, etc.).

Parcae (the) [ðə'pa:ki:], *Pr.n.f.pl. Rom.Myth:* les Parques.

parcel[1] ['pa:s(ə)l], *s.* **1.** (*a*) *A:* partie *f*; (*b*) pièce *f*, morceau *m*, parcelle *f* (de terrain); (*c*) *St.Exch: etc:* **p. of shares,** paquet *m* d'actions, de titres; **p. of goods,** (i) lot *m*, (ii) envoi *m*, de marchandises; *Min:* **p. of ore,** lot de minerai; *P: O:* **to make a p.,** arrondir sa pelote; faire son magot; **p. of lies,** tas *m* de mensonges. **2.** (*a*) paquet, colis *m*; **to make, do up, a p.,** faire un paquet; **to do up goods into parcels,** empaqueter des marchandises; **p. post,** service *m* (i) des colis postaux, (ii) de messageries; **to send sth. by p. post,** envoyer qch. comme, par, colis postal; **registered p.,** paquet, colis, recommandé; **insured p.,** colis de valeur déclarée; **cash on delivery p.,** colis contre remboursement; **parcel(s) delivery,** livraison *f*, remise *f*, de colis à domicile; factage *m*, service de messageries; **parcel(s) office,** bureau *m* des messageries; messageries *fpl*; **p. rates,** tarif *m* (de la) messagerie; **p. to be called for,** colis restant; (*b*) *typ:* **p. of type,** paquet (de composition).

parcel[2], *v.tr.* (**parcelled**) **1.** (*a*) **to p. (out),** parceller, partager (un héritage); morceler (**into,** en); lotir (des terres, etc.); répartir (des vivres, etc.); *Com:* **to p. out goods,** lotir des marchandises; (*b*) empaqueter (du thé, etc.); **to p. up a consignment of books,** mettre en paquets, emballer, un envoi de livres. **2.** *Nau:* (*a*) limander (un cordage); (*b*) aveugler (une couture).

parcellary [pa:'seləri], *a.* (plan *m*, etc.) parcellaire.

parcelling ['pa:səliŋ], *s.* **1.** partage *m*, parcellement *m*, lotissement *m*; morcellement *m*, répartition *f* (**into,** en). **2.** *Nau:* limande *f*.

parcenary ['pa:sənəri], *s. Jur:* **1.** copartage *m* (d'une succession); indivision *f*. **2.** copropriété *f*.

parcener ['pa:sənər], *s. Jur:* copartageant, -ante; cohéritier, -ière; propriétaire indivis.

parch [pa:tʃ]. **1.** *v.tr.* (*a*) rôtir, griller, sécher (des céréales, etc.); (*b*) (*of fever*) brûler (qn); (*of sun, etc.*) dessécher (une plaine, etc.); **grass parched (up) by the wind,** herbe desséchée par le vent; **food that parches the mouth,** mets *m* qui altère; **to be parched with thirst,** avoir une soif ardente, dévorante; avoir la bouche sèche; étrangler de soif. **2.** *v.i.* se dessécher.

parched [pa:tʃt], *a.* desséché; (désert *m*) aride; **p. tongue,** langue sèche.

parching[1] ['pa:tʃiŋ], *a.* (vent, etc.) desséchant, brûlant.

parching[2], *s.* **1.** rôtissage *m*, grillage *m*, séchage *m* (de céréales, etc.). **2.** dessèchement *m*.

parchment ['pa:tʃmənt], *s.* **1.** (*a*) parchemin *m*; **p. manuscript,** manuscrit *m* sur parchemin; (*b*) **p. paper, vegetable p., imitation p., cotton p.,** papier parchemin; papier parcheminé; papier sulfurisé; papier pergamine. **2.** parchemin (du café).

pard[1] [pa:d], *s. A:* & *Poet:* léopard *m*.

pard[2], *s. U.S: P:* (*a*) camarade *m*, copain *m*; (*b*) associé *m*.

pardalote ['pa:dəlɔt], *s. Orn:* pardalote *m*.

pardon[1] ['pa:d(ə)n], *s.* **1.** pardon *m*; **I beg your p. for the liberty I am taking,** je vous demande pardon de la liberté que je prends; **I beg your p.!** je vous demande pardon! mille fois pardon! mille pardons! **I beg your p.?** plait-il? *F:* comment (dites-vous)? **2.** *Ecc:* indulgence *f*. **3.** *Jur:* (*a*) **free p.,** grâce *f*; (*of monarch*) **to grant s.o. a free p.,** faire grâce à qn; **the right of p.,** le droit de grâce; **to receive the King's, Queen's, p.,** être gracié; **general p.,** amnistie *f*; (*b*) lettre *f* de grâce.

pardon[2], *v.tr.* **1.** pardonner, excuser, passer (une faute, etc.); **p. the liberty I am taking,** pardonnez la liberté que je prends; **p. my contradicting you, p. me for contradicting you,** pardonnez(-moi) si je vous contredis. **2.** (*a*) **to p. s.o.,** pardonner à qn; *P:* **p. me!** faites excuse! mille pardons! (*b*) **to p. s.o. sth.,** absoudre qn de qch.; **to p. s.o. an offence,** remettre une offense à qn; **to p. s.o. for having done sth.,** pardonner à qn d'avoir fait qch.; excuser qn d'avoir fait qch. **3.** *Jur:* faire grâce à (qn); gracier, amnistier (qn).

pardonable ['pa:dənəbl], *a.* **1.** pardonnable, excusable. **2.** *Jur:* graciable.

pardonableness ['pa:dənəb(ə)lnis], *s.* **1.** excusabilité *f* (d'une faute). **2.** *Jur:* nature graciable (d'un délit).

pardonably ['pa:dənəbli], *adv.* excusablement.

pardoner ['pa:dənər], *s.* **1.** pardonneur, -euse. **2.** *Ecc.Hist:* (prêtre ou moine des ordres mendiants) vendeur *m* d'indulgences.

pare [pεər], *v.tr.* **1.** rogner (ses ongles, etc.); parer (le bois, le fer); doler, délarder (le bois); ébarber (la tranche d'un livre); *Leath:* doler, bouter (les peaux); *Farr:* parer, rénetter (le sabot d'un cheval); **to p. one's nails to the quick,** se rogner les ongles jusqu'au vif; **his claws have been pared,** on lui a rogné les griffes. **2.** éplucher; peler (un fruit). **3.** *Agr:* dégazonner (un terrain).

paregoric [pæri'gɔrik], *a.* & *s. Pharm:* parégorique (*m*).

pareira [pæ'rεərə], *s. Bot:* pareire *f*, cissampélos *m*.

parelectronomy [pærilek'trɔnəmi], *s. Physiol:* parélectronomie *f*.

parella [pæ'relə], *s. Bot:* parelle *f*.

parenchyma [pə'reŋkimə], *s. Anat: Bot:* parenchyme *m*.

parenchymal [pə'reŋkim(ə)l], *a. Anat: Bot:* parenchymal, -aux.

parenchymatous [pæreŋ'kimətəs], *a. Anat: Bot:* parenchymateux.

parent ['pεərənt], *s.* **1.** père *m*, mère *f*; *pl.* parents *m*, les père et mère; **our first parents,** nos premiers parents; **parents and relations,** les ascendants directs et les collatéraux; *Adm:* **pension to parents (of servicemen),** pension *f* d'ascendants; *Sch:* **p.-teacher association,** association *f* de parents d'élèves. **2.** origine *f*, source *f*, mère (d'un événement, d'un phénomène, etc.); souche *f* (d'une famille); *Atom.Ph:* **nuclear p.,** parent nucléaire; *attrib.* **p. branch (of a tree),** branche mère; **p. rock,** roche mère; **p. state (of colonies),** mère patrie, métropole *f*; *Com:* **p. company, establishment, house,** société mère, maison mère; *Mil:* **p. unit,** unité *f* d'origine; *Navy:* **p. ship,** navire *m*, bâtiment *m*, de soutien logistique; (bâtiment) ravitailleur *m* (de sous-marins, etc.); *Atom.Ph:* **p. atom,** atome original, primitif; atome mère; **p. element,** élément original, primitif; élément mère; **p. nucleus,** noyau original, primitif, précurseur; **p. nuclide,** nuclide *m* mère; précurseur radioactif; **p. substance,** substance mère; (*welding*) **p. metal,** métal *m* de base.

parentage ['pεərəntidʒ], *s.* parentage *m*, origine *f*, naissance *f*, extraction *f*; **born of humble p.,** né de parents humbles; d'humble naissance.

parental [pə'rent(ə)l], *a.* (autorité *f*, etc.) des parents, des père et mère; (pouvoir) paternel; **we were forbidden by p. authority to continue,** nos parents nous défendirent de continuer.

parentally [pə'rentəli], *adv.* comme des parents; (agir) en père, en mère.

parenteral [pə'rentərəl], *a. Med:* (*of injection, etc.*) parentéral, -aux.

parenthesis, *pl.* **-theses** [pə'renθəsis, -i:z]. **1.** parenthèse *f*; **in parentheses,** entre parenthèses. **2.** intermède *m*; intervalle *m*.

parenthesize [pə'renθəsaiz], *v.tr.* (*a*) mettre (des mots) entre parenthèses; (*b*) mentionner (qch.) par parenthèse; intercaler (une observation).

parenthetic(al) [pæren'θetik(l)], *a.* **1.** entre parenthèses. **2.** *Gram:* **p. clause,** incidente *f*.

parenthetically [pæren'θetik(ə)li], *adv.* par parenthèse, en manière de parenthèse.

parenthood ['pεərənthud], *s.* paternité *f*, maternité *f*.

parentless ['pεərəntlis], *a.* sans père ni mère; orphelin.

pareo [pə'reiou], *s. Cost:* paréo *m*.

parer ['pεərər], *s.* **1.** rogneur, -euse. **2.** *Tls:* rognoir *m*; *Leath:* paroir *m*, doloir *m*.

parergon, *pl.* **-ga** [pæ'rə:gɔn, -gə], *s.* **1.** *Art:* hors-d'œuvre *m inv.* **2.** travail *m* supplémentaire.

paresis [pæ'ri:sis], *s. Med:* parésie *f*; **(general) p.,** paralysie générale.

paresthesia [pæres'θi:ziə], *s. Med:* paresthésie *f*.

paretic [pæ'ri:tik], *a.* & *s. Med:* parétique (*mf*).

pargasite ['pa:gəsait], *s. Miner:* pargasite *f*.

parget[1] ['pa:dʒit], *s. Const:* **1.** plâtre *m*. **2.** crépi *m*, crépissure *f*.

parget[2], *v.tr.* **1.** recouvrir (un mur) d'une couche de plâtre. **2.** crépir.

pargeting ['pa:dʒitiŋ], *s.* **1.** (*a*) plâtrage *m*; (*b*) crépissage *m*. **2.** = PARGETRY.

pargetry ['pa:dʒitri], *s.* **1.** plâtres *mpl*; plâtrage *m*; couche *f* de plâtre. **2.** crépi *m*, crépissure *f*.

parheliacal [pa:hi:'laiək(ə)l], **parhelic** [pa:'hi:lik], *a. Meteor:* par(h)élique.

parhelion, *pl.* **-ia** [pa:'hi:liən, -iə], *s. Meteor:* par(h)élie *m*; faux soleil.

pariah [pə'raiə], *s.* (*a*) paria *m*; (*b*) **p. dog,** chien pariah, chien métis des Indes; (*c*) *Orn:* **p. kite,** milan *m* brahme.

Parian ['pεəriən]. **1.** *a. Geog:* parien; **P. marble,** marbre *m* de Paros; *Cer:* **P. (biscuit),** parian *m*. **2.** *s. Geog:* Parien, -ienne.

Paridae ['pæridi:], *s.pl. Orn:* paridés *m*.

parietal [pə'raiət(ə)l], *s. Anat: Bot:* pariétal, -aux; **p. bone,** pariétal *m*.

Parietales [pærie'teili:z], *s.pl. Bot:* pariétales *f*.

Parietaria [pærie'tεəriə], *s.pl. Bot:* pariétaires *f*.

paring ['pεəriŋ], *s.* **1.** (*a*) rognage *m*, rognement *m* (des ongles, etc.); parage *m* (du bois, du fer); ébarbage *m*, ébarbement *m* (d'un livre); *Leath:* dolage *m* (des peaux); (*b*) épluchage *m*, épluchement *m* (de fruits, etc.); (*c*) *Agr:* dégazonnage *m*. **2.** *usu.pl.* (*a*) rognures *f*; **parings of metal,** cisaille *f*; *Tchn:* **parings of leather,** parure *f* de cuir; (*b*) épluchures *f*, pelures *f* (de légumes, etc.). **3.** *attrib.* **p. knife,** (i) (*also* **p. iron**) rognoir *m*; paroir *m*; *Bootm:* tranchet *m*; *Farr:* rénette *f*, reinette *f*, boutoir *m*, rogne-pied *m inv*; (ii) couteau *m* de cuisine.

pari passu [pæri'pæsu:]. *Lt.phr:* **to go p. p. with . . .,** marcher de pair avec . . .; **here stock raising goes p. p. with agriculture,** ici l'élevage est en fonction de l'agriculture.

paripinnate [pæri'pineit], *a. Bot:* paripenné.

Paris[1] ['pæris]. *Pr.n. Geog:* Paris *m*; **the P. basin,** le bassin parisien; *Com:* **P. goods,** articles *m* de Paris; **P. white,** blanc *m* de Paris; *Dressm: A:* **P. doll,** mannequin *m*; *Hort:* **P. green,** vert *m* de Scheele (employé comme insecticide).

Paris[2]. *Pr.n.m. Gr.Lit:* Pâris.

parish ['pæriʃ], *s.* (*a*) *Ecc:* paroisse *f*; **p. church,** église paroissiale; *F:* la paroisse; **p. register,** registre paroissial, paroissien; (*b*) **civil p.,** commune *f*; **p. council** = conseil municipal (d'une petite commune); **p. councillor,** conseiller municipal; **p. school,** école communale; *A:* **p. boy,** enfant trouvé, assisté; *A:* **to come, go, on the p.,** tomber à la charge de la commune; tomber dans l'indigence; devenir un indigent; **p. pump politics,** politique *f* de clocher.

parishioner [pə'riʃənər], *s.* (*a*) paroissien, -ienne; (*b*) habitant, -ante, de la commune.

Parisian [pə'riziən], (*a*) *a.* parisien; (*b*) *s.* Parisien, -ienne.

parison ['pæriz(ə)n], *s. Glassm:* paraison *f*; **p. mould,** moule *m* de paraison; moule mesureur.

parisyllabic [pærisi'læbik], *a.* parisyllabe; parisyllabique.

parity ['pæriti], *s.* **1.** (*a*) égalité *f* (de rang, etc.); parité *f*; (*b*) analogie *f*, comparaison *f*; **p. of reasoning,** raisonnement *m* analogue; analogie de raisonnement. **2.** (*a*) *Atom.Ph:* **p. operator,** opérateur *m* de parité; **p. selection rule,** loi *f* de sélecteur par parité; (*b*) *Cmptr:* **(even) p.,** parité; **(even) p. check,** contrôle *m*, vérification *f*, de parité; **odd p.,** imparité *f*; **odd p. check,** contrôle, vérification, d'imparité. **3.** *Fin:* **exchange at p.,** change *m* à (la) parité, au pair; **exchange parities,** parités de change; **fixed p.,** parité fixe; **stable and unified parities,** parités (monétaires) stables et homogènes; **p. table,** table *f* des parités; **p. value,** valeur *f* au pair. **4.** *Mth: A:* (*evenness*) parité (d'un nombre).

park[1] [pɑ:k], *s.* **1.** (*a*) parc (clôturé); *Ven:* réserve *f*; **deer p.,** parc (clôturé) réservé à cerfs; **national p.,** parc national; (*b*) **public p.,** jardin public; parc; **p. keeper, officer,** gardien *m* de parc; *F:* **the P.,** Hyde Park (à Londres); (*c*) dépendances *fpl* d'un château. **2.** (*a*) **car p.,** parc de stationnement pour voitures, garage *m* pour voitures; **car p. attendant,** gardien de parc de stationnement; (*b*) *Mil: O:* **ammunition p.,** parc à munitions; **artillery p.,** parc d'artillerie; **engineer p.,** parc du génie.

park[2], *v.tr.* **1.** (*a*) enfermer (des moutons, etc.) dans un parc; parquer (des moutons); (*b*) mettre (de l'artillerie, etc.) en parc. **2.** (*a*) parquer, garer (une voiture); *F: O:* **to p. one's hat in the hall,** laisser son chapeau dans le vestibule (en entrant faire une visite); **p. it over there,** mets-le là-bas; (*b*) *v.i.* (*of car, aircraft, etc.*) stationner, être en stationnement, se garer; (*c*) *F:* **to p. oneself,** s'installer, se planquer (quelque part); **his mother-in-law came and parked herself on him,** sa belle-mère s'est installée chez lui; *O:* **I'll p. myself here till he sees me,** je ne bouge pas d'ici avant qu'il m'accorde une entrevue.

parka ['pɑ:kə], *s. Cost:* parka *f*.

parked [pɑ:kt], *a.* **1.** parqué. **2.** (*of car, aircraft, etc.*) en stationnement.

parkerize ['pɑ:kəraiz], *v.tr. Metalw:* parkériser (un métal ferreux).

parkerizing ['pɑ:kəraiziŋ], *s.* parkérisation *f*.

parkin ['pɑ:kin], *s. Cu:* croquet *m* (de farine d'avoine et de mélasse).

parking ['pɑ:kiŋ], *s.* **1.** parcage *m* (d'animaux, d'huîtres, etc.). **2.** parcage, (mise *f* en) stationnement *m* (de véhicules, d'avions, etc.); **p. area,** aire *f* de stationnement, parking *m*; *Aut:* **p. lights,** feux *m* de position; **p. meter,** parcomètre *m*; **p. attendant,** gardien *m* de parc de stationnement, gardien de voitures, d'autos; **no p. here, p. prohibited,** défense *f* de stationner; stationnement, parcage, interdit; **p. place,** (endroit *m* de) stationnement; **p. brake,** frein *m* (à main) de secours, de stationnement; **angle p.,** stationnement en oblique; **parallel p.,** stationnement parallèle à la route; **off street p. (area),** parc de stationnement en retrait de la rue; zone *f* de stationnement; **double p.,** stationnement en double file; **p. fees,** tarif *m* de stationnement; *U.S:* **bilateral p.,** stationnement bilatéral; **p. lot,** parcage, parking; **p. lane,** voie *f* de stationnement, de parcage; **p. line,** bande *f* délimitant un parc de staionnement; **p. stall,** emplacement réservé au stationnement d'un véhicule; **employee p.,** terrain *m* de stationnement pour les employés. **3.** *Space:* **p. orbit,** orbite *f* d'attente.

parkinsonia [pɑ:kin'souniə], *s. Bot:* parkinsonia *m*.

parkinsonian [pɑ:kin'souniən], *a. Med:* parkinsonien.

parkway ['pɑ:kwei], *s. NAm:* = route *f* touristique; **belt p.,** boulevard *m* périphérique, de ceinture, d'encerclement.

parky ['pɑ:ki], *a. F:* (*of weather*) frisquet; un peu froid; **the p. morning air,** l'air vif du matin.

parlance ['pɑ:ləns], *s.* langage *m*, parler *m*; **in common p.,** dans la langue familière, en langage courant, en langage ordinaire; **in legal p.,** en langage, en termes, de pratique.

parley[1] ['pɑ:li], *s.* conférence *f*, parlementage *m*; *Mil:* pourparlers *mpl* (avec l'ennemi); **to hold a p.,** parlementer (**with,** avec); **we had been in p. for an hour,** nous parlementions depuis une heure; *Mil: A:* **to beat, sound, a p.,** battre la chamade.

parley[2]. **1.** *v.i.* être, entrer, en pourparlers; parlementer; engager, entamer, des négociations (**with the enemy,** avec l'ennemi). **2.** *v.tr. A:* & *Hum:* parler (une langue étrangère).

parleyvoo[1] ['pɑ:li'vu:], *s. Hum: A:* **1.** le français. **2.** un Français, une Française.

parleyvoo[2], *v.i. Hum: A:* parler français.

parliament ['pɑ:ləmənt], *s.* le Parlement; les Chambres *f*; **p. was prorogued on the 24th,** le Parlement a été prorogé le 24; **the Houses of P.,** le Palais, les Chambres, du Parlement; les Chambres; **in p.,** au parlement.

parliamentarian [pɑ:ləmen'teəriən]. **1.** *s.* (*a*) parlementaire *m*, membre *m* du Parlement; **skilled p.,** député rompu aux débats de la Chambre; politicien expérimenté; (*b*) *Eng.Hist:* parlementaire (au cours de la guerre civile). **2.** *a.* parlementaire.

parliamentarianism [pɑ:ləmen'teəriənizm], **parliamentarism** [pɑ:lə'mentərizm], *s.* parlementarisme *m*.

parliamentary [pɑ:lə'ment(ə)ri], *a.* (régime *m*, gouvernement *m*) parlementaire; **p. election,** élection législative; **p. candidate,** candidat *m* à la Chambre des Communes; (*in Fr.*) candidat à la députation; **an old p. hand,** un vétéran de la politique; un politicien expérimenté; **p. eloquence,** éloquence *f* de la tribune; **p. agent,** conseiller juridique attitré auprès des Chambres représentant une corporation intéressée à un projet de loi; **p. language,** langage parlementaire, courtois; *A:* **p. train,** train *m* à prix minimum; train omnibus.

parlour ['pɑ:lər], *s.* (*a*) parloir *m* (d'un couvent); (*b*) *O:* & *NAm:* salon *m*; **back p.,** petit salon (à l'arrière de la maison); **p. games,** petits jeux de salon, de société; *F:* **p. tricks,** (i) arts *m* d'agrément; (ii) talents *m* de société; (*c*) **beauty p.,** salon de beauté; *NAm:* **beer p.,** bar *m* (où on sert la bière); *O:* **bar p.,** arrière-salle *f* (d'un café); *U.S:* **funeral p.,** bureau *m* d'un entrepreneur de pompes funèbres; *NAm: Rail:* **p. car,** wagon-salon *m*, *pl.* wagons-salons; (*d*) *Sch: A:* **p. boarder,** pensionnaire *mf* habitant avec la famille du directeur, de la directrice.

parlourmaid ['pɑ:ləmeid], *s.f.* bonne (affectée au service de table).

parlous ['pɑ:ləs]. **1** *a.* (*a*) *Lit:* périlleux, précaire, dangereux; **the p. state of the finances,** l'état alarmant des finances; (*b*) *A:* & *Dial:* (*of pers.*) malin, -igne; madré; fourbe; (*c*) *A:* & *Dial:* (*intensive*) terrible; fameux (coquin); rude (surprise). **2.** *adv. A:* & *Dial:* (*intensive*) extrêmement, terriblement; joliment, rudement.

parlously ['pɑ:ləsli], *adv.* **1.** dangereusement. **2.** *A:* = PARLOUS 2.

Parma ['pɑ:mə], *Pr.n. Geog:* (*a*) la duché de Parme; (*b*) (la ville de) Parme.

parmelia [pɑ:'mi:liə], *s. Moss:* parmélie *f*.

Parmenio [pɑ:mi:niou], *Pr.n.m. Gr.Hist:* Parménion.

Parmesan [pɑ:mi'zæn]. **1.** *Geog:* (*a*) *a.* parmesan; (*b*) *s.* Parmesan, -ane. **2.** *s.* **P. (cheese),** parmesan.

parnas(s) [pɑ:'næs], *s. Jew.Rel:* parnassin *m*.

Parnassian [pɑ:'næsiən], *a.* & *s.* parnassien, -ienne; **the P. school (of poetry),** le Parnasse.

Parnassus [pɑ:'næsəs]. *Pr.n. Geog: Gr.Ant:* le Parnasse.

Parnellite ['pɑ:nəlait], *s. Hist:* parnelliste *m*.

parochial [pə'roukiəl], *a.* (*a*) *Ecc:* paroissial, -aux; **the p. hall,** la salle d'œuvres de la paroisse; (*b*) (*of civil parish*) communal, -aux; (*c*) *Pej:* provincial, -aux; **p. outlook,** esprit *m* de clocher.

parochialism [pə'roukiəlizm], *s.* esprit *m* de clocher; patriotisme *m* de clocher.

parodist ['pærədist], *s.* parodiste *mf*; pasticheur, -euse; travestisseur, -euse.

parodontal [pærə'dɔntəl], *a. Anat:* **p. tissue,** parodonte *m*.

parodontitis [pærədɔn'taitis], *s. Med:* périodontite *f*, parodontite *f*.

parody[1] ['pærədi], *s.* parodie *f*, pastiche *m*; **a p. of justice,** un travestissement de la justice.

parody[2], *v.tr.* parodier, pasticher; travestir (la justice, etc.).

paroemiographer [pærimi'ɔgrəfər], *s.* parémiographe *mf*.

paroemiography [pærimi'ɔgrəfi], *s.* parémiographie *f*.

paroemiologist [pærimi'ɔlədʒist], *s.* parémiologue *mf*.

paroemiology [pærimi'ɔlədʒi], *s.* parémiologie *f*.

parol ['pærəl]. **1.** *s.* parole *f*; *used only in Jur:* **by p.,** verbalement. **2.** *a. Jur:* **p. contract,** contrat verbal, *pl.* contrats verbaux; **p. evidence,** témoignage verbal.

parole[1] [pə'roul], *s.* **1.** parole *f* (d'honneur); parole donnée; **prisoner on p.,** (i) *Mil:* prisonnier *m* sur parole, sur sa foi; (ii) *Jur:* prisonnier (de droit commun) libéré conditionnellement; **to be put on p.,** être libéré sur parole; **to break one's p.,** manquer à sa parole. **2.** *A:* mot *m* d'ordre.

parole[2], *v.tr.* libérer (un prisonnier) (i) sur parole, (ii) conditionnellement.

paroli ['pɑ:rəli], *s.* (*at faro, etc.*) paroli *m*.

paronomasia [pærənə'meiziə], *s.* paronomase *f*; jeu *m* de mots.

paronychia [pærə'ni:kiə], *s.* **1.** *Med:* panaris *m*. **2.** *Bot:* paronychia *m*, paronyque *m*.

paronym ['pærənim], *s. Ling:* paronyme *m*.

paronymous [pə'rɔniməs], *a. Ling:* paronymique.

paronymy [pə'rɔnimi], *s.* paronymie *f*.

paroptic [pæ'rɔptik], *a.* paroptique.

parosmia [pæ'rɔzmiə], *s. Med:* parosmie *f*.

Parotia [pæ'routə], *s. Orn:* parotie *f*.

parotic [pə'rɔtik], *a. Anat:* parotique.

parotid [pə'rɔtid]. *Anat:* **1.** *a.* (glande *f*) parotide; (canal) parotidien. **2.** *s.* (glande) parotide *f*.

parotidean [pərɔti'di:ən], *a.* = PAROTID 1.

parotidectomy [pərɔti'dektəmi], *s. Surg:* parotidectomie *f*.

parotitis [pærou'taitis], *s. Med:* parotidite *f*; *F:* oreillons *mpl*.

Parousia [pə'ru:ziə], *s. Theol:* Parousie *f*; second avènement.

paroxysm ['pærəksizm], *s.* (*a*) *Med:* paroxysme *m* (d'une fièvre, etc.); (*b*) crise *f* (de fou rire, de rage, etc.); accès *m* (de fureur); **p. of tears,** crise de larmes.

paroxysmal, paroxysmic [pærək'sizm(ə)l, -'sizmik], *a.* paroxysmique; paroxysmal, -aux; paroxystique.

paroxytone [pə'rɔksitoun], *a.* & *s. Gr.Gram:* paroxyton (*m*).

parpen ['pɑ:pin], *s. Const:* parpaing *m*; **p. wall,** cloison *f* mince en briques; mur *m* de parpaing.

parquet ['pɑ:kei], *s.* **1. p. (floor),** parquet *m* (en parquetage); **p. flooring,** parquetage *m*. **2.** *Th: U.S:* premiers rangs du parterre.

parqueted ['pɑ:kitid], *a.* parqueté.

parquetry ['pɑ:kitri], *s.* parquetage *m*, parqueterie *f*.

par(r) [pɑ:r], *s. Ich:* saumon *m* d'un an; saumoneau *m*, parr, *m*, tacon *m*.

parrel ['pærəl], *s. Nau: O:* racage *m*, matagot *m*.

parricidal [pæri'said(ə)l], *a.* parricide.

parricide[1] ['pærisaid], *s.* (*pers.*) parricide *mf*.

parricide[2], *s.* (crime *m* de) parricide *m*.

Parridae ['pæridi:], *s.pl. Orn:* parridés *m*.

parrot[1] ['pærət], *s.* **1.** *Orn:* perroquet *m*; **hen p.,** perruche *f*, perroquet femelle; **grass p., turquoise p., turquoisine p., chestnut-shouldered p.,** turquoisine *f*, perruche *f* d'Edwards; **Amazon p.,** amazone *m*; **African grey p.,** jaco *m*; **hawk-headed p.,** perroquet accipitrin, maillé; (*Austr.*) **night p.,** perruche nocturne; (*N.Z.*) **owl p.,** perroquet-hibou *m*, kakapo *m*; **timneh p.,** perroquet timneh; **brush-tongued p.,** trichoglosse *m*, loriquet *m*; **she's a mere p.,** elle parle comme un perroquet. **2.** *Ich:* **p. fish,** scare *m*; poisson *m* perroquet.

parrot[2], *v.tr.* (**parroted**) **1.** répéter (qch.) comme un perroquet; *v.i.* parler comme un perroquet. **2.** seriner (**sth. to s.o.,** qch. à qn).

parrotbill ['pærətbil], *s. Orn:* paradoxornis *m*.

parrotlet ['pærətlet], *s. Orn:* perruche *f* moineau.

parrotry ['pærətri], *s.* psittacisme *m*.

parry[1] ['pæri], *s. Fenc: Box:* parade *f*.

parry[2]. **1.** *v.tr.* (*a*) *Box: Fenc: etc:* parer, détourner (un coup); *Box:* **to p. a blow,** *Fenc:* **to p. a cut,** parer un coup; *Fenc:* **to p. a thrust,** parer une botte; (*b*) détourner, éviter (un danger); tourner, éviter (une difficulté); parer (une question). 2. *v.i.* **to p. and thrust, to p. and riposte,** (i) *Fenc:* parer et tirer; (ii) *Fig:* riposter, répondre du tac au tac.

parse [pɑːz], *v.tr.* faire l'analyse (grammaticale) (d'un mot); analyser (grammaticalement) (une phrase).

parsec [pɑː'sek], *s. Astr.Meas:* parsec *m.*

Parsee ['pɑːsiː, pɑː'siː]. 1. (*a*) *a.* parsi; parse; (*b*) *s.* Parsi, -ie; Parse *mf.* 2. *s. Ling:* parsi *m*, parse *m.*

Parseeism ['pɑːsiizm], *s.* parsisme *m.*

Parsifal ['pɑːsifæl]. *Pr.n.m. Lit:* Parsifal.

parsimonious [pɑːsi'mouniəs], *a.* parcimonieux; économe, *F:* regardant; *Pej:* pingre.

parsimoniously [pɑːsi'mouniəsli], *adv.* parcimonieusement.

parsimony ['pɑːsiməni], *s.* parcimonie *f*; épargne *f*; *Pej:* pingrerie *f.*

parsing ['pɑːziŋ], *s.* analyse grammaticale.

parsley ['pɑːsli], *s.* (*a*) *Bot:* persil *m*; **p. fern,** fougère *f* femelle; **p. piert,** alchémille des champs; *Cu:* **p. sauce,** sauce *f* au persil; (*b*) *Amph:* **p. frog,** pélodyte *m*, (grenouille *f*) persillée *f.*

parsnip ['pɑːsnip], *s.* panais *m.*

parson ['pɑːs(ə)n], *s. Ecc:* 1. titulaire *m* d'un bénéfice. 2. ecclésiastique *m*; prêtre *m*; pasteur *m*; *F: A:* **parson's week,** congé *m* de treize jours. 3. *Orn:* **p. bird,** prosthémadère *m* (de la Nouvelle-Zélande).

parsonage ['pɑːsənidʒ], *s.* = presbytère *m*; cure *f.*

part[1] [pɑːt], *s. & adv.*

I. *s.* 1. partie *f*; (*a*) **to cut sth. into two parts,** couper qch. en deux parties; **p. of the house is to let,** une portion de la maison est à louer; **p. of the paper is damaged,** une partie du papier est avariée; **p. of my money,** une partie de mon argent; **good in parts,** bon en partie; **it's not bad in parts,** il y a des parties qui ne sont pas mauvaises, qui ne sont pas mal; **the pathetic parts of the story,** les endroits *m*, les passages *m*, pathétiques de l'histoire; **the funny, odd, p. about it is that . . .,** le comique de l'histoire, ce qu'il y a de comique, d'étrange, c'est que . . .; **in the early p. of the week,** dans les premiers jours de la semaine; **he spends p. of the year in Paris,** il est à Paris pendant une partie de l'année; **the greater p. of the population,** la plus grande partie, la plupart, de la population; **to be, form, p. of sth.,** faire partie de qch.; **as p. of this expansion programme,** dans le cadre de ce programme d'expansion; **it is p. and parcel of . . .,** c'est une partie intégrante, essentielle, de . . .; **it is p. of his job to . . .,** il lui appartient de . . .; **it forms no p. of my intentions to . . .,** il n'entre pas dans mes intentions de . . .; **to pay in p.,** payer partiellement; **to contribute in p. to the expenses,** contribuer pour partie aux frais; (*b*) **ten parts of water to one of milk,** dix parties d'eau pour une partie de lait; *O:* **three parts,** les trois quarts; *F: O:* **three parts drunk,** aux trois quarts ivre; (*c*) **the parts of the body,** les parties du corps; (*d*) *Ind: etc:* pièce *f*, organe *m*, élément *m*; **engine, machine, parts,** pièces, éléments, de moteur, de machine; **moving parts,** organes, parties, en mouvement; **replacement parts, spare parts,** pièces détachées, de rechange; (*e*) *Cmptr:* exemplaire *m* (de liasse); **seven-p. set,** liasse *f* à sept exemplaires; **five-p. tag,** étiquette *f* à cinq colets; **fixed-point p.,** mantisse *f*; (*f*) *Gram:* **parts of speech,** parties du discours; **principal parts (of a verb),** temps principaux (d'un verbe); (*g*) *Mth:* (*calculus*) **parts of a fraction,** petites parties d'une fraction; (*h*) *Publ:* fascicule *m*, livraison *f* (d'un ouvrage); **to buy a work in parts,** acheter un ouvrage par fascicules; (i) **in that p. of the world, in those parts,** dans cette partie du monde; dans cette région; **in my p. of the world,** par chez moi; **they are not from our p. of the world,** ils ne sont pas de chez nous; **we are from the same p. of the world,** nous sommes du même pays, du même endroit; **he doesn't belong to these parts,** il n'est pas d'ici; **what are you doing in these parts?** qu'est-ce que vous faites ici, dans ces parages? (*j*) *attrib.* **p. truth,** vérité approximative; **p. owner,** copropriétaire *mf*; *Nau:* coarmateur *m*; **p. ownership,** (i) copropriété *f*; indivision *f*; (ii) *Nau:* quirat *m*; **to work p. time,** travailler à temps partiel, à mi-temps; **to be on p. time,** être en chômage partiel; **p.-time worker, p. timer,** ouvrier, -ière, employé, -ée, (i) qui travaille à temps partiel, à mi-temps, (ii) en chômage partiel; *Nau:* **p. shipment,** expédition partielle, chargement partiel; **p. cargo charter,** affrètement partiel; *Rail:* **p. truck load,** wagon incomplet; changement partiel (de wagon). 2. part *f*; (*a*) **to take (a) p. in sth.,** prendre part à, participer à, qch.; apporter son appoint à qch.; **to take p. in the conversation,** prendre part à, se mêler à, la conversation; *Mil: etc:* **to take p. in the action,** participer à l'engagement, prendre part à l'action; *T.V: etc:* **those taking p. were . . .,** avec le concours de . . .; **to take no p. in sth.,** se désintéresser de qch.; **without my taking any p. in it,** sans ma participation; **I had no p. in it,** cela s'est fait en dehors de moi, sans mon concours; je n'y suis pour rien; *Lit:* **to have neither art nor p., p. nor lot, no p. or lot, in sth.,** n'avoir aucune part dans qch.; (*b*) *Th: etc:* rôle *m*; personnage *m*; **supporting p.,** second rôle; **small p., bit p.,** petit rôle, *pl.* utilités *f*; **to play one's p.,** jouer, remplir, son rôle; **he's playing a p.,** il joue la comédie; c'est une comédie qu'il nous fait; **in all this imagination plays a large p.,** dans tout ceci l'imagination entre pour beaucoup; **he played no p. in the business,** il n'a joué aucun rôle dans l'affaire; il ne s'est pas mêlé de l'affaire; (*c*) *Mus:* **orchestral parts,** parties d'orchestre; **p. music,** musique *f* d'ensemble; **p. song,** chant *m*, chanson *f*, à plusieurs voix; **p. singing,** chant à plusieurs voix. 3. (*a*) côté *m*; *O:* **on the one p. . . ., on the other p. . . .,** d'un côté . . ., de l'autre . . .; d'une part . . ., d'autre part . . .; (*b*) parti *m*; **to take s.o.'s p.,** prendre parti pour qn; prendre fait et cause pour qn; (*c*) **an indiscretion on the p. of. . .,** une indiscrétion de la part de . . .; **he was subjected to much criticism on the p. of his supporters,** il était l'objet de beaucoup de critique de la part de ses partisans; **I presume an intention of fraud on the p. of the tenant,** je présume chez le locataire une intention de fraude; **we should be grateful for our p. if you would do this,** de notre côté nous vous serions très reconnaissants de bien vouloir faire ceci; **for my p.,** quant à moi; pour ce qui est de moi; en ce qui me concerne; **for my p., I am willing,** (quant à) moi, je veux bien. 4. **to take sth. in good p., in bad p.,** prendre qch. en bonne part, en mauvaise part; prendre qch. du bon côté, du mauvais côté. 5. *pl.* moyens *m*, facultés *f*; **man of parts,** homme bien doué, de valeur, de talent; **man of many parts,** homme à facettes. 6. *NAm:* raie *f* (dans les cheveux).

II. *adv.* partiellement; en partie; **p. eaten,** partiellement mangé; mangé en partie; **p. silk p. cotton,** mi-soie mi-coton; **p. one and p. the other,** moitié l'un moitié l'autre.

part[2]. 1. *v.tr.* (*a*) séparer en deux; (*of island*) diviser (un cours d'eau); (*of pers.*) faire une trouée dans (une foule, etc.); fendre (la foule); **to p. one's hair,** se faire une raie (dans les cheveux); **to p. one's hair in the middle, at the side,** faire, porter, la raie au milieu, sur le côté; *Her:* **shield parted per pale,** écu mi-parti; **shield parted per bend sinister,** écu taillé; (*b*) séparer (**sth. from sth.,** qch. de qch.); séparer, déprendre (deux boxeurs, etc.); (*c*) rompre (une amarre, etc.); *Nau:* **to p. one's cable,** casser sa chaîne; rompre son amarre, sa touée; (*d*) *Ch:* départir (des métaux); (*e*) *A:* partager, répartir. 2. *v.i.* (*a*) (*of crowd, etc.*) se diviser; se ranger de part et d'autre; (*b*) (*of two pers.*) se quitter, se séparer; (*of two thgs*) se séparer; (*of roads*) diverger; **to p. good friends,** se quitter bons amis; *Prov:* **the best of friends must p.,** il n'y a si bonne compagnie qui ne se sépare; **to p. from s.o.,** quitter qn; se séparer de, d'avec, qn; **to p. with (sth.),** céder (qch.); se dessaisir, se défaire, se départir, de (qch.); *Jur:* aliéner (un droit, un bien); **he hates to p. with his money,** il n'aime pas à débourser; (*c*) (*of cable, etc.*) rompre, se rompre, partir, céder; **the frigate parted amidships,** la frégate se cassa en deux; (*d*) *A:* s'en aller; partir.

partake [pɑː'teik], *v.* (**partook** [pɑː'tuk]; **partaken** [pɑː'teikən]) 1. *v.tr.* partager (le sort de qn, etc.); prendre part à (un sentiment général, etc.). 2. *v.i.* (*a*) **to p. in, of, sth.,** prendre part, participer, à qch. (**with s.o.,** avec qn); *O:* **to p. of a meal,** (i) partager le repas de qn; prendre un repas (avec d'autres); (ii) prendre un repas; *O:* **to p. of a dish,** goûter, manger, un mets; *Ecc:* **to p. of the Sacrament,** s'approcher des sacrements.

partaker [pɑː'teikər], *s.* participant, -ante (**in sth.,** à qch.); partageant, -ante (**in sth.,** de qch.); *Ecc:* **to be a regular p. of the Sacrament,** fréquenter les sacrements.

parterre [pɑː'tɛər], *s.* 1. *Hort:* parterre *m.* 2. *Th: A: & NAm:* parterre.

parthenocarpic, parthenocarpous [pɑːθənou'kɑːpik, -'kɑːpəs], *a. Bot:* parthénocarpique.

parthenocarpy [pɑːθənou'kɑːpi], *s. Bot:* parthénocarpie *f.*

parthenogenesis [pɑːθənou'dʒenisis], *s. Biol:* parthénogénèse *f*; **thelytokous p.,** parthénogénèse thélytoque; **arrhenotokous p.,** parthénogénèse arrhénotoque.

parthenogenetic [pɑːθənoudʒə'netik], **parthenogenic** [pɑːθənou'dʒenik], **parthenogenous** [pɑːθə'nɔdʒənəs], *a. Biol: Ent:* parthénogénétique, parthénogénésique.

parthenogenetically [pɑːθənoudʒə'netik(ə)li], *adv.* parthénogénétiquement, parthénogénésiquement.

Parthenon (the) [ðə'pɑːθənən], *s. Gr.Ant:* le Parthénon.

parthenospore ['pɑːθənouspɔːr], *s. Bot:* parthénospore *f.*

Parthia ['pɑːθiə], *Pr.n. A.Geog:* Parthie *f.*

Parthian ['pɑːθiən], *a. & s. A.Geog:* 1. *a.* parthe; de Parthe; parthique; **a P. shot, shaft,** la flèche du Parthe. 2. *s.* Parthe *mf.*

partial ['pɑːʃ(ə)l], *a.* 1. (*a*) partial, -aux (envers qn); injuste; (*b*) *F:* **to be p. to s.o., sth.,** avoir un faible, une prédilection, pour qn, qch.; avoir un penchant pour qn; **I am p. to a pipe after dinner,** je fume volontiers une pipe après dîner. 2. partiel, -ielle; en partie; **p. board,** demi-pension *f*; **p. clean-up,** nettoyage partiel (d'une machine, etc.); **p. eclipse,** éclipse partielle; *Phot:* **p. mask,** cache partiel; **p. damage to goods,** avarie *f* d'une partie de la marchandise; **p. loss,** perte partielle, sinistre partiel; *Com:* **p. acceptance of a bill,** acceptation partielle d'une traite; (*of pers.*) **p. disability,** incapacité partielle; *Mth:* **p. derivative,** dérivée partielle; **p. differences,** différences partielles; **p. differential equation,** équation *f* aux dérivées partielles; **p. product,** produit partiel; **p. fractions,** petites parties d'une fraction; *Ph:* **p. vacuum,** vide partiel imparfait; **p. wave,** onde partielle.

partialist ['pɑːʃəlist], *s.* 1. partialiste *mf.* 2. *Theol:* particulariste *mf.*

partiality [pɑːʃi'æliti], *s.* 1. (*a*) partialité *f* (**for, to,** pour, envers); injustice *f*; (*b*) favoritisme *m*; **a mother's p. for her children,** la faiblesse d'une mère pour ses enfants. 2. prédilection *f*, préférence marquée, faible *m* (**for,** pour); **to have a p. for sth.,** marquer de la prédilection pour qch.; **a p. for the bottle,** un penchant pour la boisson.

partially ['pɑːʃəli], *adv.* 1. partialement; avec partialité. 2. partiellement; en partie.

participant [pɑː'tisipənt], *a. & s.* participant, -ante (**in,** à).

participate [pɑː'tisipeit]. 1. *v.tr. A:* **to p. sth. with s.o.,** partager qch. avec qn; prendre part à (la joie, etc.) de qn. 2. *v.i.* (*a*) **to p. in sth.,** prendre part, participer, s'associer, à qch.; **to p. in the conversation,** prendre part à la conversation; **to p. in s.o.'s joy, work,** s'associer à la joie, aux travaux, de qn; **he did not p. in the plot,** il n'a eu aucune participation au complot; (*b*) (*of thg*) participer, tenir (**of sth.,** de qch.).

participation [pɑːtisi'peiʃ(ə)n], *s.* participation *f* (**in sth.,** à qch.); *Bank: Ins:* **p. loan,** crédit syndical.

participative [pɑː'tisipeitiv], *a.* participatif, -ive.

participator [pɑː'tisipeitər], *s.* participant, -ante (**in, de**); **to be a p. in a crime,** (i) s'associer à un crime; (ii) avoir trempé dans un crime; avoir participé à un crime.

participial [pɑːti'sipiəl], *a. Gram:* participial, -aux; **p. adjective,** adjectif participial; **p. phrase,** proposition *f* participe.

participle ['pɑːtisipl], *s. Gram:* participe *m*; **present, past, p.,** participe présent, passé; **misrelated, unrelated, wrongly related, p.,** participe isolé, indépendant, sans soutien.

particle ['pɑːtikl], *s.* 1. (*a*) particule *f*, parcelle *f*, infime quantité *f* (de matière); paillette *f* (de métal); gouttelette *f* (de liquide); **a p. of sand,** une particule, un grain, de sable; **there's not a p. of truth in this story,** il n'y a pas l'ombre, pas une once, de vérité dans ce récit; **without a p. of malice,** sans un grain, sans la moindre parcelle, de méchanceté; **not a p. of evidence against the accused,** pas la moindre preuve, pas un semblant de preuve, contre le prévenu; (*b*) *Atom.Ph:* particule, corpuscule *m*; **accelerated p.,** particule accélérée; **alpha, beta, p.,** particule alpha, bêta; **bombarded, struck, p.; target p.,** particule bombardée, particule cible; **charged p.,** particule chargée; **colliding, incident, p.,** particule bombardante, incidente; particule projectile; **ejected, emitted, p.,** particule émise; **elementary, fundamental, subatomic, p.,** particule élémentaire, fondamentale, subatomique; **free, unbound, p.,** particule libre; **high-energy, low-energy, p.,** particule de grande, de faible, énergie; **initial, original, p.,** particule primitive, originale; **neutral, uncharged, p.,** particule neutre, non chargée; **relativistic p.,** particule relativiste; **scattered p.,** particule diffusée; **p. acceleration,** accélération *f* de particules; **p. accelerator,** accélérateur *m* de particules; **p. bombardment,** bombardement *m* de particules; **p. size,** grosseur *f* des particules, de la particule; **p.-size distribution,** granulométrie *f*; **p. velocity,** vitesse *f* corpusculaire. 2. (*a*) *Gram:* particule; (*b*) **the nobiliary p.,** la particule nobiliaire.

parti-coloured ['pɑːtikʌləd], *a.* 1. mi-parti. 2. bigarré, bariolé, panaché, versicolore.

particular [pə'tikjulər], *a. & s.*

I. *a.* 1. (*a*) particulier; spécial, -aux; **that p. book,** ce livre-là; ce livre-ci; ce livre en particulier; **a p. object,** un objet déterminé; **p. branch** (*of a service*), spécialité *f*; **my own p. feelings,** mes sentiments particuliers; mes propres sentiments; mes sentiments personnels; **I can't** attribute the article to any p. person, je serais incapable d'attribuer l'article à tel ou tel; *Theol:* **p. election,** grâce particulière; *Rel.H:* **p. Baptists,** Baptistes *m* particularistes; (*b*) **a p. friend of mine,** un ami intime; un de mes bons, meilleurs, amis; **to take p. care over doing sth.,** faire qch. avec un soin particulier; **I have called on p. business,** je viens pour une affaire spéciale; **I have a p. dislike for him,** il me répugne; **I left for no p. reason,** je suis parti sans raison précise, sans raison bien définie; **to have nothing p. to do,** n'avoir rien de particulier à faire; **I didn't notice anything p.,** je n'ai rien remarqué de particulier; (*c*) *adv.phr.* **in p.,** en particulier; notamment, nommément; **the influence of climate and in p. of rainfall,** l'influence du climat et nommément, notamment, celle de la pluie. **2.** (*of account, etc.*) détaillé, circonstancié. **3.** (*of pers.*) méticuleux, minutieux, soigneux; pointilleux, vétilleux, exigeant, regardant, renchéri; **to be p. about one's food,** être difficile, exigeant, sur la nourriture; **to be p. about one's dress,** soigner sa mise, sa tenue; **p. on points of honour,** délicat sur le point d'honneur; pointilleux sur l'honneur; **he is p. in his choice of friends,** il est difficile dans le choix, quant au choix, de ses relations; **to be very p. about having things done methodically,** s'attacher à ce que tout se fasse avec ordre; **don't be too p.,** ne vous montrez pas trop exigeant; **he's not so p. as all that,** il n'y regarde pas de si près. **4.** *P:* **I'm not p. (about it),** je n'y tiens pas plus que ça. **II.** *s.* **1.** détail *m*, particularité *f*; **alike in every p.,** semblables en tout point; **to give particulars of sth.,** donner les détails de qch.; particulariser (un projet); entrer dans les détails; **to give full particulars,** donner les menus détails, tous les détails; **to ask for fuller particulars about sth.,** demander des précisions *f*, des indications *f* supplémentaires, sur qch.; **he asked me for particulars about her,** il m'a demandé des renseignements *m* sur elle; **for further particulars apply to . . .,** pour plus amples détails, pour plus amples renseignements, s'adresser à . . .; **without entering into particulars,** sans entrer dans les détails; *Adm:* **particulars on the postmark,** mentions *f* du cachet d'oblitération; *Com:* **particulars of sale,** description *f* de la propriété à vendre; cahier *m* des charges; *Jur:* **particulars of charge,** chef *m* d'accusation; *Book-k:* **the particulars of an entry,** le libellé d'un article, d'une écriture (comptable). **2.** *F: A:* **a London p.,** un de ces brouillards comme on n'en voyait qu'à Londres.

particularism [pə'tikjulərizm], *s. Pol: Theol: etc:* particularisme *m*.

particularist [pə'tikjulərist], *a. & s. Pol: Theol:* particulariste (*mf*).

particularistic [pətikjulə'ristik], *a.* particulariste.

particularity [pətikju'læriti], *s.* **1.** particularité *f.* **2.** méticulosité *f*; minutie *f* (d'une description, etc.). **3.** *pl.* soins assidus (**to s.o.,** auprès de qn); assiduités *f* (auprès de qn).

particularization [pətikjulərai'zeiʃ(ə)n], *s.* particularisation *f.*

particularize [pə'tikjuləraiz], (*a*) *v.tr.* particulariser, spécifier; (*b*) *v.i.* entrer dans les détails; préciser; **certain members, I do not wish to p.,** certains membres, je ne nomme personne, je ne précise pas.

particularly [pə'tikjuləli], *adv.* particulièrement, spécialement; en particulier; **note p. that . . .,** notez en particulier que . . .; **I want this p. for tomorrow,** il me le faut absolument pour demain; **I asked him p. to be careful,** je l'ai prié particulièrement, instamment, de faire attention; **I asked him to be p. careful,** je lui ai demandé de faire particulièrement soin; **to refer p. to sth.,** faire ressortir qch.; **not p.,** pas particulièrement, spécialement, tellement; **he's not p. rich,** il n'est pas tellement riche.

particulate [pɑː'tikjuleit]. **1.** *a. Ph:* particulaire. **2.** *s. Atom.Ph:* macroparticule *f.*

parting[1] ['pɑːtiŋ], *a.* **1.** séparant, qui sépare. **2.** *A:* partant, s'en allant; *Lit:* **the p. day,** le jour qui tombe.

parting[2], *s.* **1.** (*a*) séparation *f*; (*of waters*) partage *m*; **p. line,** ligne *f* de séparation; **to be at the p. of the ways,** (i) se trouver là où deux routes se séparent, s'écartent; (ii) être au carrefour, à la croisée des chemins; (*b*) **the bitterness of p.,** l'amertume *f* du départ, de la séparation; **p. kiss,** baiser *m* d'adieu; **p. shot,** riposte (lancée en partant); **he gave me some p. advice,** avant mon départ il m'a donné quelques recommandations, quelques conseils; (*c*) *Ch:* départ *m* (des métaux); (*d*) **p. bead, p. strip,** baguette *f* (de panneaux, de carrosserie); **p. tool,** outil *m* à tronçonner, à saigner; gouge *f* triangulaire; carrelet *m*; burin *m* (à bois). **2.** rompement *m*, rupture *f* (d'un câble, etc.). **3.** (*a*) (*of the hair*) raie *f*; **p. on the left,** raie à gauche; **p. in the middle,** raie médiane; **p. of a horse's name,** épi *m* de la crinière; (*b*) *Min:* entre-deux *m inv.*

partisan[1] [pɑːti'zæn], *s.* **1.** partisan, -ane; **to act in a p. spirit,** faire preuve (i) d'esprit de parti, (ii) de parti pris. **2.** partisan; soldat *m*, officier *m*, d'une troupe irrégulière.

partisan[2] ['pɑːtizən], *s. A:* **1.** *Arms:* pertuisane *f.* **2.** (*soldier*) pertuisanier *m*.

partisanship [pɑːti'zænʃip], *s.* partialité *f*; esprit *m* de parti; sectarisme *m* (politique, etc.).

partita [pɑː'tiːtə], *s. Mus:* partita *f.*

partite ['pɑːtait], *a. Bot:* parti, -i(t)e.

partition[1] [pɑː'tiʃ(ə)n], *s.* **1.** (*a*) partage *m*; répartition *f* (d'un héritage entre héritiers, etc.); morcellement *m* (d'une terre, etc.); démembrement *m* (d'un empire); division *f*, découpage *m* (en plusieurs parties); *Cmptr:* segmentation *f* (d'un programme); *Atom.Ph:* division, mode *m* de partage (de l'atome, etc.); **p. coefficient,** coefficient *m*, rapport *m*, de partage, de division; *Ins:* **p. of average,** répartition d'avaries; *Hist:* **the p. of Poland,** le partage de la Pologne; **the P. Treaties,** les traités de partage de la Succession d'Espagne (1698, 1700); (*b*) *Hort:* éclatage *m* (des racines). **2.** (*a*) cloison *f*, cloisonnage *m*; paroi *f*; entre-deux *m inv*; *Min:* serrement *m* (pour retenir l'eau); **p. quartering the kernel of a nut,** zeste *m* d'une noix; *Const:* **internal p., p. wall,** mur *m* de refend, de séparation; **wooden p.,** pan *m* de bois; **framed p.,** hourdis *m* de pan de bois; **brick p.,** cloison de briques; galandage *m*; **glass p.,** vitrage *m*; (*in vehicle*) glace *f* de séparation; (*b*) compartiment *m* (de cale, etc.); section *f*; (*c*) *Her:* partition *f* (de l'écu). **3.** *Mus: A:* partition.

partition[2], *v.tr.* **1.** (*a*) partager, répartir (un héritage, etc.); morceler (une terre); morceler, démembrer (une propriété); partager, démembrer (un pays vaincu); diviser, découper (qch. en plusieurs parties); *Cmptr:* segmenter (un programme); *Atom.Ph:* partager, diviser (l'atome, etc.); (*b*) *Hort:* éclater (des racines). **2. to p. (off) a room,** cloisonner une pièce; séparer une pièce par une cloison.

partitioned [pɑː'tiʃənd], *a.* cloisonné; à compartiments.

partitioning [pɑː'tiʃəniŋ], *s.* **1.** = PARTITION[1] 1. **2.** cloisonnage *m*; compartimentage *m*.

partitive ['pɑːtitiv], *a. & s. Gram:* partitif (*m*).

partizan[1,2], *s.* = PARTISAN[1,2].

partly ['pɑːtli], *adv.* partiellement; en partie; **wholly or p.,** en tout ou en partie; **p. by force p. by persuasion,** moitié de force moitié par persuasion; *Fin:* **p. paid up,** (action) non (complètement) libérée; (capital) non entièrement versé.

partner[1] ['pɑːtnər], *s.* **1.** (*a*) associé, -ée (**with s.o. in sth.,** de qn dans qch.); **to be s.o.'s p. in a crime,** être associé à qn, être l'associé de qn, dans un crime; *Com: etc:* **senior p.,** associé principal; **full p.,** associé à part entière; **general p.,** associé en nom collectif; **sleeping p., silent p., secret p., latent p.,** (associé) commanditaire *m*; associé à responsabilité limitée; bailleur *m* de fonds; **active p.,** (associé) commandité *m*; *Jur:* **contracting p.,** contractant, -ante; *O:* **p. in life,** époux, -ouse; conjoint, -ointe; (*b*) partenaire *mf* (au tennis, aux cartes, etc.); *Cards:* **to cut, draw, for partners** = faire les rois; (*c*) *Danc:* cavalier, -ière; **my p.,** mon danseur, ma danseuse. **2.** *attrib. Biol:* (*of plant, insect, etc.*) associé (à autre) par symbiose.

partner[2], *v.tr.* **1.** (*a*) être associé, s'associer, à (qn), avec (qn); (*b*) *Games: etc:* être le partenaire de (qn). **2. to p. s.o. with s.o.,** (i) donner qn à qn comme associé, comme partenaire; (ii) faire danser deux personnes ensemble.

partnership ['pɑːtnəʃip], *s.* **1.** (*a*) association *f* (**in sth. with s.o.,** avec qn dans qch.); **p. in crime,** association dans le crime; (*b*) *Com: etc:* **to enter, go into, p. with s.o.,** entrer en association avec qn; s'associer avec qn; **to take up a p. in a business,** s'intéresser dans une affaire; **to take s.o. into p.,** prendre qn comme associé; **particular, special, p.,** association en participation; **to dissolve a p.,** dissoudre une association; **deed, articles, of p.,** contrat *m*, acte *m*, de société, d'association. **2.** *Com: etc:* société *f*; **general p.,** société commerciale en nom collectif; **limited p., sleeping p.,** (société en) commandite *f* (simple); **p. limited by shares,** (société en) commandite par actions; **industrial p.,** participation *f* des travailleurs aux bénéfices.

partridge ['pɑːtridʒ], *s.* **1.** *Orn:* (*pl.* **partridges,** *Ven: Cu:* **partridge**) perdrix *f*; *Cu:* perdreau *m*; **p. poult, young p.,** perdreau; **common p., grey p.,** perdrix grise; **red (-legged) p.,** perdrix rouge; **hill p., tree p.,** perdrix percheuse; **wood p.,** perdrix des bois; **crested wood p.,** roulroul *m*; **rock p.,** (perdrix) bartavelle *f*; **bamboo p.,** perdrix des bambous; **Barbary p.,** perdrix gambra, de Barbarie; **bobwhite p.,** colin *m*; **American, Guianan, p.,** colin de Virginie, de Guyane; **black p.,** francolin *m*; **snow p.,** lerwa *m*; *NAm: F:* **ice p.,** mouette sénateur, *Fr.C:* mouette blanche; **p. net,** tomberelle *f*; **a brace of p.,** une couple de perdrix; **p. are scarce this year,** les perdrix sont rares cette année; **as plump as a p.,** dodu comme une caille. **2.** *Bot:* **p. berry,** gaulthérie *f* du Canada. **3.** *Com:* **p. wood,** bois *m* d'angelin.

partschinite ['pɑːtʃinait], *s. Miner:* partschine *f.*

parturient [pɑː'tjuːriənt]. **1.** *a.* (*a*) en parturition; à son terme; (*of woman*) sur le point d'accoucher; (*of animal*) sur le point de mettre bas; (*b*) *Lit:* (*of mind*) en train de faire naître (une idée, etc.). **2.** *s.f.* parturiente.

parturition [pɑːtju'riʃ(ə)n], *s.* parturition *f*; (*of woman*) travail *m*; (*of animal*) mise *f* bas.

party[1] ['pɑːti], *s.* **1.** (*faction*) parti *m*; *Pol:* **the Labour P., the Democratic P.,** le parti travailliste, démocratique; **p. leader,** chef *m* de parti; **p. warfare,** guerre *f* de partis; **p. quarrels,** querelles partisanes; **p. man,** homme de parti; **p. politics,** politique *f* de parti; **to have no p. spirit,** manquer d'esprit de parti; **to follow,** *F:* **toe the p. line,** obéir aux directives du parti; **to desert one's p.,** abandonner son parti; **to join s.o.'s p.,** se ranger sous la bannière de qn; **to win s.o. over to one's p.,** attirer qn à sa cause; **they form a p. of their own,** ils font secte, bande, à part. **2.** (*a*) **pleasure p., shooting p.,** partie *f* de plaisir, de chasse; **will you join our p.?** voulez-vous être des nôtres? **we're a small p.,** nous sommes peu nombreux, ne sommes pas nombreux; **I was one of the p.,** j'étais de la partie; (*b*) réunion (privée, intime); réception *f*; **evening p.,** soirée *f*; **dinner p.,** dîner *m*; **tea p.,** (i) thé *m*; (ii) (**also children's p.**), goûter *m* d'enfants; (iii) *P:* réunion pour fumer la marijuana; **to give a p.,** donner une réception; recevoir (du monde); (*of child*) **may I wear my p. dress, frock?** puis-je mettre ma belle robe? *F:* **he's caught the p. spirit,** il s'est abandonné aux joies de la fête. **3.** (*a*) groupe *m*, bande *f* (de touristes, etc.); **the official p.,** le groupe des officiels, les officiels *m*; **he joined a p. to visit Paris,** il a visité Paris en excursion organisée, *F:* avec un groupe; **p. ticket,** billet collectif; (*b*) brigade *f*, équipe *f*, groupe (de mineurs, etc.); atelier *m* (d'ouvriers, etc.); **a p. of prisoners,** un groupe de prisonniers; **rescue p.,** équipe de secours; *Adm: etc:* **working p.,** comité *m* d'étude; (*c*) *Mil: etc:* détachement *m*; **the advance p.,** les éléments *m* d'avant-garde; **water p., ration p.,** corvée *f* d'eau, de vivres; **firing p.,** peloton *m* d'exécution; **landing p.,** compagnie *f* de débarquement; (*d*) *Mil:* parti (détaché pour battre la campagne). **4.** (*a*) *Jur:* **p. (to a suit, to a dispute),** partie; **the parties to the case,** les parties en cause; **to be p. to a suit,** être en cause; **to become p. to an action,** se rendre partie dans un procès; **the belligerent parties,** les parties belligérantes; (*b*) *Com: etc:* **to become a p. to an agreement,** signer un contrat; **parties to a bill of exchange,** intéressé(e)s à une lettre de change; **a third p.,** un tiers, une tierce personne; **to deposit a sum in the hands of a third p.,** déposer une somme en main tierce; **for the account of a third p.,** pour compte d'autrui; **payment on behalf of a third p.,** paiement *m* par intervention; **to become a third p. to an agreement,** intervenir à un contrat; **third p. risks,** risques *m* de préjudice au tiers; **third p. insurance,** assurance *f* au tiers; (*c*) **to be, to become, (a) p. to a crime,** être, se rendre, complice d'un crime; prendre part à un crime; **I would never be (a) p. to such a thing,** je ne donnerais jamais mon consentement, je ne m'associerais jamais, à chose pareille; (*d*) *P:* individu *m*, type *m*; **a p. by the name of Martin,** un nommé Martin; un type du nom de Martin; **a funny old p.,** un drôle de bonhomme, de bonne femme.

party[2], *a. Her:* **p. per pale,** parti; **p. per bend,** tranché; **p. per fesse,** coupé; **p. per bend sinister,** taillé; **p. per saltire,** écartelé en sautoir.

Parulidae [pæ'ruːlidiː], *s.pl. Orn:* parulidés *m*.

parvenu ['pɑːvənjuː], *s.* parvenu, -ue.

parvifolious, parvifoliate [pɑːvi'fouliəs, -'foulieit], *a. Bot:* parvifolié.

parvis ['pɑːvis], *s.* parvis *m* (d'une cathédrale, etc.).

parvoline ['pɑːvoul(a)in], *s. Ch:* parvoline *f.*

pasan(g) ['pɑːsən, -əŋ], *s. Z:* pasan *m*, pasang *m*, paseng *m*; chèvre *f* aegagre, à bézoard.

pascal ['pæskəl], *s. Ph.Meas:* pascal *m*.

Pasch [pɑːsk], *s. A:* **1.** la Pâque. **2.** Pâques *m*.

paschal ['pɑːsk(ə)l], *a.* pascal, -aux.

pascoite ['pæskouait], *s. Miner:* pascoïte *f.*

paseng ['pɑːseŋ], *s. Z:* = PASAN(G).

pash [pæʃ], *s. F:* **to have a p. for, on, s.o.,** être entiché, toqué, de qn; avoir le béguin pour qn, être mordu pour qn.

pasha ['pɑːʃə, 'pæʃə], *s.* pacha *m*.

Pashto ['pæʃtou], *s. Ling:* pachto *m*, pouchtou *m*, poushtou *m*.

Pasiphae [pə'sifai]. *Pr.n.f. Gr.Hist:* Pasiphaé.

pasqueflower ['pæskflauər], *s. Bot:* (anémone *f*) pulsatille *f*; fleur *f* de Pâques; herbe *f* du vent; passe-fleur *f*, *pl.* passe-fleurs; œil-de-Dieu *m*, *pl.* œils-de-Dieu.

pasquinade[1] [pæskwi'neid], *s. Lit.Hist:* pasquin *m*, pasquinade *f*.

pasquinade[2], *v.tr. A:* pasquiner, pasquiniser (qn).

pass[1] [pɑːs], *s.* **1.** col *m*, défilé *m*, passage *m* (de montagne); *Hist:* **the P. of Thermopylae,** le Pas des Thermopyles; **to hold the p.,** (i) *Mil:* tenir le défilé; (ii) tenir la clef d'une position; **to sell the p.,** trahir son pays ou son parti. **2.** *Nau:* passe *f* (entre des hauts-fonds). **3. fish p.,** passage à poissons; échelle *f* à poissons (dans un barrage).

pass[2], *s.* **1.** (*a*) *A: & Lit:* **to come to p.,** arriver, avoir lieu; **it came to p. that . . .,** or il arriva, il advint, il se passa, il se fit, que . . .; (*b*) **things have come to a pretty p.,** les choses sont dans un bel état; les choses sont dans une mauvaise passe; voilà donc où en sont les choses! **things came to such a p. that . . .,** les choses en vinrent à ce point, à tel point, au point, que . . .. **2.** *Sch:* (*in examination*) **to obtain, get, a p.,** être reçu; **he got a bare p.,** il a été reçu tout juste; **p. mark,** moyenne *f*; **p. degree** = *approx.* licence *f* libre. **3.** (*a*) passe *f* (de magnétiseur, de prestidigitateur); (*in card tricks*) **to make the p.,** faire sauter la coupe; (*b*) *Fenc:* passe, passade *f*, botte *f*; **to make a p. at s.o.,** (i) porter une botte à qn; (ii) *F:* flirter avec qn; faire du gringue à qn. **4.** *Metalw:* (*a*) passe, passage *m* (du métal dans le laminoir); **final p.,** passe finale; **finishing p.,** passe de finissage; **roughing p.,** passe de dégrossissage; (*b*) cannelure *f* (du laminoir); **rail p.,** cannelure à rail. **5.** permis *m*, passe, permission *f*, laissez-passer *m inv*; *Mil: etc:* permission de courte durée; **day p., night p.,** permission de la journée, de la nuit; **(free) p.,** (i) *Rail: etc:* titre *m*, carte *f*, de circulation; (ii) *Th: etc:* billet gratuit, de faveur; carte d'entrée; **p. check, ticket,** contremarque *f* (de sortie); **police p.,** coupe-file *m inv*; **customs, custom-house, p.,** laissez-passer de douane; **p. duty,** droits *mpl* de passe-debout; **p. key,** (clef *f*) passe-partout *m inv*; *Bank: O:* **p. book,** carnet *m*, livret *m*, de banque. **6.** (*a*) *Fb: etc:* passe; **back p.,** passe en arrière; (*b*) **the aircraft made two low passes over the village,** l'avion a effectué deux passages à basse altitude au-dessus du village; (*c*) *W.Tel: etc:* **high p., low p., filter,** filtre *m* passe haut, passe bas.

pass[3], *v.*

I. *v.i.* passer. **1.** (*a*) **as we were passing,** comme nous passions; **I'll look in next time I'm passing,** je ferai un saut chez vous quand je repasserai; **the tourists passed into the dining hall,** les touristes ont défilé dans le réfectoire; **the land passed into the hands of a nephew,** la terre passa entre les mains d'un neveu; **words passed between them,** il y a eu un échange d'injures, de propos désobligeants; **after all the correspondence that passed between us,** après tout cet échange de lettres; *Mil:* **to p. from one formation to another,** passer d'une formation à une autre; **to p. from a war to a peace footing,** passer du pied de guerre au pied de paix; **p. friend!** avance à l'ordre! *B:* **let this cup p. from me,** éloignez de moi ce calice; (*b*) **to p. along a street,** passer par une rue; **the procession passed (by) slowly,** le cortège passa, se déroula, défila, lentement; **I'm waiting for the postman to p.,** j'attends le passage du facteur; **he passed right in front of me without seeing me,** il a passé juste devant moi sans me voir; **everyone smiles as he passes,** tout le monde sourit à son passage; **he passed (by) on the other side of the street,** il a passé de l'autre côté de la rue; **he passed by, under, my window,** il est passé, a passé, devant, sous, ma fenêtre; **the motorway passes close to the village,** l'autoroute passe tout près du village; **the road passes alongside the river,** la route longe la rivière; **to let s.o. pass, allow s.o. to p.,** livrer passage à qn; laisser passer qn; **may I p., please?** excusez-moi, s'il vous plaît! *Rail: etc:* **p. along, down, the car!** avancez! dégagez la portière! **to p. unobserved,** passer inaperçu; **let it, that, p.!** passe pour cela! glissons là-dessus! **I'd like to say in passing,** soit dit en passant; (*c*) *Aut:* doubler; **no passing,** défense de doubler; (*d*) *Cards:* passer, renoncer, passer parole; (*at dominoes*) bouder; *Cards:* **p.!** parole! **2.** (*of time*) **to p. (by),** (se) passer, s'écouler; **a fortnight passed (by),** quinze jours se sont écoulés; **when five minutes had passed,** au bout de cinq minutes; **how time passes!** que le temps passe vite! **he let the opportunity p.,** il a laissé passer l'occasion. **3. water passes from a liquid to a solid state when it freezes,** l'eau se transforme de liquide en solide quand il gèle; **many quotations from Shakespeare have passed into everyday language,** beaucoup de citations de Shakespeare ont trouvé leur place dans la langue de tous les jours. **4.** (*a*) disparaître; (*of clouds, etc.*) se dissiper; **to p. into nothingness,** rentrer dans le néant; **beauty that will soon p.,** beauté *f* qui passera, disparaîtra, bientôt; (*b*) *A:* mourir. **5.** *O:* arriver, avoir lieu, se passer; **I know what has passed,** je sais ce qui s'est passé. **6.** (*a*) **it would p. in certain circles,** ça passerait dans certains milieux; **that won't p.!** (i) cela est inacceptable! (ii) ça ne prend pas! *F:* **you'd p. in a crowd!** tu n'es pas si mal que ça! (*b*) **she passes for a great beauty,** elle passe pour une beauté, pour être très belle; **to p. for a liberal,** (i) passer, (ii) se faire passer, pour un libéral; **to p. by, under, the name of Thomas,** être connu sous le nom de Thomas; (*c*) (*of pers. of mixed blood*) se faire passer pour cent pour cent de race blanche.

II. *v.tr.* **1.** (*a*) passer devant, près de (qn, la fenêtre, etc.); **to p. s.o. on the stairs,** croiser qn dans l'escalier; **they often p. each other in the street,** ils se croisent souvent dans la rue; (*b*) passer (sans s'arrêter); dépasser (le but); outrepasser (les bornes de qch.); **to p. the place where one ought to have stopped,** dépasser l'endroit où il fallait s'arrêter; *Aut:* **to p. the red light,** brûler le feu rouge; (*of train*) **to p. a station,** (i) ne pas s'arrêter à une gare; (ii) brûler une gare; (*c*) *esp. U.S: Com: etc:* **to p. a dividend,** conclure un exercice sans payer de dividende; (*d*) passer, franchir (une frontière, etc.); *Nau:* **to p. a headland,** dépasser, doubler, un cap; **that passes my comprehension,** cela dépasse ma compréhension; cela me dépasse; *F:* **to have passed the fifty mark,** avoir doublé le cap de la cinquantaine; (*e*) surpasser (qn); gagner (qn) de vitesse; dépasser, rattraper (qn, un autre navire, etc.); doubler (une autre voiture); *Sp: etc:* devancer (un concurrent); (*f*) **to p. a test,** subir une épreuve avec succès; **to p. an exam(ination),** être reçu, admis, à un examen; **to p. the written examination,** être reçu à l'écrit; être admissible; **to pass the oral (examination),** être reçu à l'oral; (*g*) **bill that has passed the House of Commons,** projet *m* de loi qui a été voté par la Chambre des Communes; **if the bill is passed,** si le projet de loi est voté; si la loi passe; (*h*) **to p. the censor, the customs,** être accepté par la censure, par la douane. **2.** approuver; (*a*) **to p. an invoice,** approuver, admettre, apurer, une facture; **to p. an item of expenditure,** allouer une dépense; (*of company*) **to p. a dividend of 5%,** approuver un dividende de 5%; **boiler passed by the surveyors,** chaudière certifiée par la commission de surveillance; chaudière timbrée; **the censor has passed the play,** le censeur a accordé le visa; (*b*) *Sch:* **to p. a candidate,** recevoir un candidat; admettre un candidat (à un examen); (*c*) *Parl: etc:* **to p. a bill, a resolution,** passer, voter, adopter, un projet de loi, une résolution; (*d*) *Mil: etc:* **to be passed fit,** être reconnu apte. **3.** (*a*) transmettre; donner; **to p. sth. from hand to hand,** passer qch. de main en main; **to p. sth. up, down,** monter, descendre, qch.; **p. it over!** donnez-le-moi! **to p. sth. out of the window,** sortir, passer, qch. par la fenêtre; **p. me the salt, please,** donnez-moi le sel, s'il vous plaît; **to p. the cakes, the wine, round,** faire passer les gâteaux; faire circuler le vin; *Fb: etc:* **to p. the ball,** passer le ballon; faire une passe, des passes; *A:* **to p. one's word,** donner, engager, sa parole; (*b*) *Book-k:* **to p. an item to current account,** passer, porter, un article en compte courant; (*c*) (faire) passer, écouler, *F:* refiler (un faux billet de banque, etc.). **4.** mettre; glisser; **to p. one's hand between the bars,** glisser, passer, sa main à travers les barreaux; **to p. a rope round sth.,** passer une corde autour de qch.; **to p. vegetables through a sieve,** passer des légumes; **to p. the cotton through the eye of the needle,** passer le fil dans le trou de l'aiguille; **to p. a sponge over sth.,** passer l'éponge sur qch. **5.** *Mil:* **to p. troops in review,** passer des troupes en revue. **6.** *Nau:* **to p. a stopper,** fouetter une bosse. **7.** (*a*) *O:* **to p. the spring abroad,** passer le printemps à l'étranger; **to p. a few days with s.o.,** passer quelques jours chez qn; (*b*) **to p. (away) the time,** passer le temps; **to p. one's time painting,** passer son temps à peindre; s'amuser à faire de la peinture. **8.** (*a*) *Jur:* **to p. sentence,** prononcer le jugement; (*b*) **to p. criticism on sth.,** faire la critique de qch.; **to p. remarks (on sth.),** faire des commentaires, des observations (sur qch.). **9.** *Physiol:* **to p. water,** uriner; *Med:* **to p. sth. with the stools,** rendre qch. avec, dans, les selles; **to p. blood,** être affecté d'hématurie, *F:* pisser du sang.

III. (*compound verbs*) **1. pass away,** *v.i.* (*a*) disparaître; (*of empire*) périr; (*b*) mourir; rendre le dernier soupir.

2. pass off, (*a*) *v.i.* (i) (*of pain, etc.*) se passer; disparaître; (ii) **everything passed off well,** tout s'est bien passé; (*b*) *v.tr.* (i) **to p. sth. off on s.o.,** repasser, refiler, qch. à qn; **to p. off one's goods as those of another make,** faire passer ses propres produits pour ceux d'une autre marque; (ii) **to p. oneself off as an artist,** se faire passer pour artiste; (iii) **to p. sth. off as a joke,** (α) prendre qch. en riant; (β) dire qu'on a fait qch. comme plaisanterie.

3. pass on, (*a*) *v.i.* (i) continuer son chemin, sa route; **to p. on to another subject,** passer à un nouveau sujet; (ii) mourir, passer à la vie éternelle; (*b*) *v.tr.* faire circuler (qch.); (faire) passer (qch. à qn); **to p. on an order, etc.,** passer, transmettre, un ordre, etc.; **read this and p. it on,** lisez ceci et faites circuler; *F:* **we've passed it on,** on se l'est dit.

4. pass out, *v.i.* (*a*) sortir (d'une salle, etc.); (*b*) **this estate must not p. out of your hands,** il ne faut pas que ce domaine passe à d'autres; **don't let this document p. out of your hands,** gardez soigneusement ce document; ne transmettez pas ce document à d'autres; (*c*) *Sch: etc:* (*after final examination*) sortir; **cadets passing out,** élèves sortants; **passing-out list,** classement *m* de sortie; (*d*) *F:* s'évanouir, tomber dans les pommes.

5. pass over, (*a*) *v.i.* (i) traverser, franchir (une rivière, etc.); franchir, passer sur (un obstacle); passer (qch.) sous silence; passer sur, glisser sur, couler sur (une difficulté, une erreur, etc.); (ii) **to p. over to the enemy,** passer à l'ennemi; (iii) (*of storm*) se dissiper, finir; (iv) mourir; (*b*) *v.tr.* (*in making a promotion*) **to p. s.o. over,** passer par-dessus le dos à qn; faire un passe-droit.

6. pass through, *v.i.* (*a*) **as we were passing through northern France,** comme nous traversions le nord de la France; **he was (only) passing through Paris,** il était de passage à Paris; (*b*) **to p. through difficult times,** passer par de rudes épreuves; **to p. through a crisis,** traverser une crise.

7. pass up, *v.tr.* refuser, renoncer à (qch.); **to p. up an opportunity,** négliger, laisser passer, une occasion.

passable ['pɑːsəbl], *a.* **1.** (*a*) (rivière, bois, etc.) traversable, franchissable; (route) praticable, carrossable; (*b*) (monnaie) ayant cours. **2.** passable, assez bon, *F:* potable; **it's p.,** ce n'est pas si mauvais, trop mal; *F:* **she's p.,** elle n'est pas mal.

passably ['pɑːsəbli], *adv.* passablement, assez; **he plays p.,** il ne joue pas trop mal; **she's p. goodlooking,** elle n'est pas mal; elle est assez jolie.

passacaglia [pæsə'kɑːliə], *s. Mus:* passacaille *f*.

passade [pæ'seid, -'sɑːd], *s.* **1.** *Equit:* passade *f*. **2.** (*love affair*) passade.

passage[1] ['pæsidʒ], *s.* **1.** passage *m*; (*a*) **p. of an electric current,** passage d'un courant électrique; **p. of a ray of light through a prism,** passage, trajet *m*, d'un rayon (de lumière) à travers un prisme; **p. of neutrons through matter,** passage, trajet, des neutrons à travers la matière; **p. of birds,** passage d'oiseaux; **bird of p.,** oiseau *m* de passage; **the p. of the herrings,** le passage des harengs; *Tex:* **p. of the shuttle,** trajet de la navette; *Surg:* **false p.,** fausse-route *f*, *pl.* fausses-routes; **the p. of time,** le temps qui passe; (*b*) *esp. Nau:* passage, traversée *f*; **to have a bad, rough, p.,** avoir, faire, une mauvaise traversée, une traversée mouvementée; **that was a rough p.!** ça nous a créé des difficultés! **can you give me a p. in your boat?** pouvez-vous me donner un passage, me prendre, dans votre bateau? **to book a p. on a boat, on an aircraft,** prendre passage, retenir son passage, une place, sur un bateau, sur un avion; **to pay for one's p.,** payer son passage, son billet; **to work one's p.,** gagner son passage (en travaillant à bord); **p. money,** prix *m* du passage, de la traversée, du voyage; (*c*) **to force a p.,** se frayer un passage par la force; *Jur:* **right of p.,** droit *m* de passage; (*d*) *Pol:* **p. of a bill,** adoption *f* d'un projet de loi; (*e*) **a sudden p. from heat to cold,** un passage brutal, une transition abrupte, du chaud au froid. **2.** (*a*) couloir *m*, corridor *m*; *N.Arch:* coursive *f*; **underground p.,** passage souterrain; *Prehist:* **p. grave,** allée couverte; dolmen *m* à galerie; (*b*) passage, ruelle *f*; (*at end of street*) échappée *f*; (*c*) *Geog:* **the North-West, North-East, P.,** le passage Nord-Ouest, Nord-Est. **3.** (*a*) *Mec.E: etc:* canalisation *f*, conduit *m*, conduite *f*; **air p.,** conduit d'aérage, conduit(e) à air; **cored p.,** canalisation venue de fonderie; **drilled p.,** canalisation forcée; **steam p.,** conduite, tubulure *f*, de vapeur; (*b*) *Anat:* **air passages,** voies aériennes, aérifères; *F:* **the front p.,** l'urètre *m*; **the back p.,** le rectum. **4.** (*a*) **passages,** rapports (amoureux, etc.); relations *f* intimes; **confidential passages,** échange *m* de secrets; (*b*) **p. of arms, at arms,** (i) *A:* pas *m* d'armes; (ii) passe *f* d'armes; échange de mots vifs; *F:* prise *f* de bec. **5.** passage (d'un livre, d'un morceau de musique); **an obscure p. in Virgil,** un passage obscur de Virgile: **the love passages,** les scènes *f* d'amour: **the most touching p. in the book,** l'endroit le plus touchant du livre; **selected passages,** morceaux choisis; *Mus:* **melodic p.,** trait *m*. **6.** *Equit:* passage, passège *m*.

passage[2]. *Equit:* **1.** *v.i.* (*of horse*) passager, passéger. **2.**

v.tr. passager, passéger, appuyer (un cheval); porter (un cheval) de côté.

passageway ['pæsidʒwei], *s.* **1.** (*way for passage*) passage *m*; **to leave a p.,** laisser le passage libre. **2.** (*a*) passage, ruelle *f*; (*b*) (*in house*) couloir *m*, corridor *m*.

Passalidae [pæ'sælidi:], *s.pl. Ent:* passalidés *m*.

passant ['pæsənt], *a. Her:* passant; **lion p. gardant,** lion léopardé.

passé ['pɑ:sei], *a.* (*a*) qui n'est plus à la mode; (*b*) défraîchi; fané; (femme) qui a perdu sa beauté.

passegarde ['pɑ:sgɑ:d], *s. N.Arm:* passe-garde *f inv*.

passementerie [pɑ:s'mɑ̃təri], *s.* passementerie *f*.

passenger ['pæsəndʒər], *s.* (*a*) voyageur, -euse; (*on ship, aircraft*) passager, -ère; (*on bus*) **the inside, upper-deck** (*A:* **outside**), **passengers,** les voyageurs de l'intérieur, de l'impériale; **standing passengers downstairs only!** les voyageurs debout doivent rester en bas! **p. train,** train *m* de voyageurs; **to send goods by p. train,** expédier des marchandises en régime accéléré; **p. coach, carriage,** *NAm:* **car,** voiture *f*, wagon *m*, à voyageurs; *Nau:* **first-class, tourist-class, p.,** passager de première classe, de classe touriste; **steerage p.,** passager d'entrepont; (*on car ferry, hovercraft*) **foot passengers are requested to remain seated while the car passengers rejoin their vehicles,** les voyageurs à pied sont priés de rester assis pendant que les automobilistes, les occupants des voitures, rejoignent leurs véhicules; *Aut:* **p. seat,** le siège à côté du conducteur; **the passengers in the car escaped injury,** les occupants de la voiture n'ont pas été blessés; (*b*) *F:* non-valeur *f*, *pl.* non-valeurs; poids mort; **we can't take passengers,** on ne peut pas embarquer des poids morts; il faut que tout le monde y mette du sien; (*c*) *Orn:* **p. pigeon,** pigeon migrateur.

passe-partout [pɑ:spɑ:'tu:], *s.* **1.** (clef *f*) passe-partout *m inv*; *Typ:* **p.-p. plate, block,** passe-partout. **2.** ruban *m* de bordure (de photographie sous verre, etc.); bande gommée; **p.-p. framing,** encadrement *m* sous verre.

passer-by [pɑ:sə'bai], *s.* (*pl.* **passers-by**) passant, -ante.

Passeres ['pæsəri:z], **Passeriformes** [pæsəri'fɔ:mi:z], *s.pl. Orn:* passereaux *m*.

passerina [pæsə'rainə], *s. Orn:* passerine *f*.

passerine ['pæsərain]. *Orn:* **1.** *a.* des passereaux. **2.** *s.* passereau *m*.

passible ['pæsibl], *a. esp. Theol:* passible; capable d'éprouver la douleur ou le plaisir; **saints with bodies of flesh p.,** saints revêtus d'une chair passible.

passiflora [pæsi'flɔ:rə], *s. Bot:* passiflore *f*.

Passifloraceae [pæsiflɔ'reisii:], *s.pl. Bot:* passifloracées *f*, passiflorées *f*.

passim ['pæsim]. *Lt. adv.* passim.

passimeter [pæ'simitər], *s. Rail:* tourniquet-compteur *m*, *pl.* tourniquets-compteurs.

passing[1] ['pɑ:siŋ]. **1.** *a.* (*a*) passant; **a p. cyclist,** un cycliste qui passait; **p. remark,** remarque *f* en passant; *Ten:* **p. shot,** passing-shot *m*; (*b*) passager, éphémère; **p. whim,** lubie *f*; **p. desire, fancy,** désir fugitif; **the p. hour,** l'heure fugitive. **2.** *adv. A:* & *Lit:* extrêmement, fort (riche, etc.); **p. fair,** de toute beauté; beau, belle, comme le jour, comme un ange.

passing[2], *s.* **1.** (*a*) passage *m* (d'un train, d'oiseaux, etc.); (*b*) (*overtaking*) dépassement *m*, doublement *m* (d'une autre voiture); **p. place,** (i) *Rail:* voie *f* d'évitement, de dédoublement; (ii) *A:* gué *m*; endroit *m* où l'on peut passer en bac; **single track road with p. places,** voie unique avec garages; (*c*) *adv.phr.* **in p.,** à propos; entre parenthèses. **2.** (*a*) écoulement *m* (du temps); *O:* disparition *f* (de la beauté de qn, etc.); (*b*) mort *f* (de qn); *Lit:* **the p. of Arthur,** la mort, le trépas, d'Arthur; **p. bell,** glas *m*. **3.** *Sch: etc:* admission *f* (d'un candidat). **4.** *Jur:* prononcé *m* (du jugement). **5.** (*a*) *Pol: etc:* adoption *f* (d'une résolution, etc.); vote *m* (d'une loi); (*b*) *Fin: Com:* approbation *f* (des comptes); passation *f* (d'un dividende). **6.** (*a*) **p. (on),** transmission *f* (d'un message, etc.); (*b*) *Fb: etc:* passe *f* (du ballon). **7.** *Mus:* **p. note,** note *f* de passage.

passion ['pæʃ(ə)n], *s.* **1.** (*a*) **the P. (of Christ),** la Passion (de Jésus-Christ); **P. Sunday,** le dimanche de la Passion; **P. Week,** (i) la semaine de la Passion; (ii) la semaine sainte; *Mus:* **the Saint Matthew P.,** la Passion selon saint Matthieu; (*b*) *Lit:* **p. play,** mystère *m* de la Passion. **2.** passion; **to overcome one's passions,** dominer ses passions; **ruling p.,** passion dominante; **a p. for the truth,** la passion de la vérité; **to have a p. for music, for painting,** avoir la passion de la musique, de la peinture; **he has a p. for gambling,** il a la rage du jeu; **p. for work,** acharnement *m* au travail, pour le travail; **to have a p. for doing sth.,** avoir la passion de, s'acharner à, faire qch. **3.** accès *m* de colère, de fureur; colère *f*, emportement *m*; **to be in a p.,** être furieux, pris de colère; **that put him into a p., made him fly into a p.,** cela l'a emporté, l'a rendu furieux. **4.** amour *m*, passion; **to have a p. for s.o.,** aimer qn passionnément, à la folie. **5.** *A:* accès, transport *m* (de douleur, etc.); crise *f* (de larmes).

passional[1] ['pæʃən(ə)l], *a. Phil:* (sentiment) passionnel; (attraction) passionnelle.

passional[2], **passionary** ['pæʃənəri], *s. Ecc:* passionnaire *m*.

passionate ['pæʃənət], *a.* **1.** emporté, irascible; (discours) véhément. **2.** passionné, ardent; **p. embrace,** étreinte passionnée, ardente.

passionately ['pæʃənətli], *adv.* **1.** passionnément; ardemment; avec passion; **to be p. in love with s.o.,** aimer qn passionnément, à la folie; éprouver une grande passion pour qn; **to be p. fond of (doing) sth.,** être passionné de qch.; avoir la passion de faire qch.; **a p. interesting job,** un métier passionnant. **2.** avec colère, avec emportement.

passionateness ['pæʃənətnis], *s.* **1.** passion *f*, ardeur *f*. **2.** véhémence *f*, emportement *m*.

passionflower ['pæʃənflauər], *s. Bot:* passiflore *f*; passionnaire *f*; fleur *f* de la Passion.

passionfruit ['pæʃənfru:t], *s.* fruit *m* de la grenadille.

Passionist ['pæʃənist], *s. Ecc:* passionniste *m*.

passionless ['pæʃənlis], *a.* sans passion, dépourvu de passion; impassible.

passionlessly ['pæʃənlisli], *adv.* sans passion; d'un air, d'un ton, impassible.

Passiontide ['pæʃəntaid], *s. Ecc:* la semaine de la Passion et la semaine sainte.

passivate ['pæsiveit], *v.tr.* passiver.

passivation [pæsi'veiʃ(ə)n], *s.* passivation *f*.

passive ['pæsiv]. **1.** *a.* passif; (*a*) **p. resistance,** résistance passive, inerte; **the nation remained p.,** la nation ne réagissait pas; (*b*) *Com:* **p. debts,** dettes *f* ne portant pas d'intérêt; (*c*) *Lacem:* **p. bobbins,** fuseaux *m* de la chaîne; (*d*) **p. iron,** fer passivé; (*e*) *El:* **p. electrode,** électrode passive; **p. network,** réseau passif; *Elcs:* **p. transducer,** transducteur passif; *Rad:* **p. responder,** récepteur passif. **2.** *a.* & *s. Gram:* **the p. (voice),** la voix passive, le passif; **verb in the p.,** verbe *m* au passif.

passively ['pæsivli], *adv.* passivement; sans réagir.

passiveness ['pæsivnis], **passivity** [pæ'siviti], *s.* passivité *f* (de l'esprit, d'un métal, etc.); inertie *f*.

Passover ['pɑ:souvər], *s.* (*a*) la Pâque; (*b*) **to eat the p.,** manger la pâque, l'agneau pascal.

passport ['pɑ:spɔ:t], *s.* (*a*) passeport *m*; **ship's p.,** permis *m* de navigation; (*b*) **money is a p. to anything,** l'argent est un bon passe-partout.

password ['pɑ:swə:d], *s.* mot *m* de passe; mot d'ordre; mot de ralliement.

past[1] [pɑ:st]. **1.** *a.* (*a*) passé, ancien; **those days are p.,** ces jours sont passés; **p. event,** événement passé; **in p. times, times p.,** autrefois, *Lit:* au temps jadis; **p. chairman,** (i) président sortant; (ii) ancien président; **p. master,** (i) *A:* passé maître, maître passé (d'un corps de métier); (ii) ancien maître (d'une loge de francs-maçons); (iii) ancien président (d'une des corporations de la Cité); (iv) expert *m*; **he's a p. master at (doing) it,** il est expert dans la matière; il est passé maître dans l'art de le faire; (*b*) *Gram:* **p. participle,** participe passé; *a.* & *s.* **in the p. (tense),** au passé; (*c*) (*of the immediate past*) passé, dernier; **the p. week,** la semaine dernière, passée; **the p. few years,** ces dernières années; **for some time p.,** depuis quelque temps. **2.** *s.* (*a*) **the p.,** le passé; **in the p.,** au temps passé; autrefois; **the old plan is a thing of the p.,** l'ancien projet (i) n'existe plus, (ii) est périmé; **to live in the p.,** vivre dans le passé; **this is no longer the England of the p.,** ce pays n'est plus l'Angleterre d'autrefois, des temps passés; (*b*) **town with a p.,** ville *f* historique; (*c*) (*of pers.*) antécédents *mpl*; **woman with a p.,** femme qui a eu des aventures, avec un passé (qu'il vaut mieux taire).

past[2]. **1.** *prep.* au delà de; (*a*) **a little p. the bridge,** un peu plus loin que le pont; **to walk p. s.o., p. the house,** passer qn, la maison; passer devant qn, devant la maison; **the train ran p. the signal,** le train brûla, dépassa, le signal; **I had some difficulty in getting p. the sentry,** j'ai eu du mal pour passer devant le factionnaire, pour forcer la consigne du factionnaire; (*b*) plus de; **he is p. eighty,** il a plus de quatre-vingts ans; il a quatre-vingts ans passés; **it is p. four (o'clock),** il est passé quatre heures; il est quatre heures passées; il est plus de quatre heures; **a quarter p. four,** quatre heures et quart; quatre heures un quart; **ten (minutes) p. four,** quatre heures dix; **half p. four,** quatre heures et demie; **half p. twelve,** (i) midi et demi, (ii) minuit et demi; **we will wait until half p.,** nous attendrons jusqu'à la demie; **it is half p.,** il est la demie; **every hour at half p., every thirty minutes p. the hour,** toutes les heures à la demie; (*c*) **p. all understanding,** hors de toute compréhension; **p. endurance,** qui ne peut être supporté plus longtemps; insupportable; **malady p. cure,** maladie *f* inguérissable, incurable; **that's p. all belief,** cela n'est pas à croire; **to be p. one's work,** être trop vieux pour travailler, n'être plus en état de travailler; **I'm p. dancing, p. work,** je ne suis plus d'âge à danser, à travailler; **to be p. child bearing,** avoir passé l'âge d'avoir des enfants; **to be p. caring for sth.,** être revenu de qch.; *F:* **he's p. it,** il est trop vieux pour travailler, pour jouer au tennis, etc.; il n'est plus à la hauteur de sa tâche; *F:* **he's, it's, p. praying for,** (il n'y a) rien à faire; *F:* **I wouldn't put it p. him,** il en est bien capable; je ne l'en crois pas incapable. **2.** *adv.* **to walk p., go p.,** passer; **to run p.,** passer en courant; **to march p.,** défiler.

pasta ['pæstə], *s. Cu:* pâtes *f* (alimentaires).

paste[1] [peist], *s.* **1.** *Cu:* pâte *f* (à pâtisserie). **2.** pâte; (*a*) *Cer:* **hard, soft, p.,** pâte dure, tendre; *El:* **accumulator p.,** empâtage *m* pour grilles d'accumulateur; *Ind:* **grinding p.,** pâte abrasive; **soldering p.,** pâte à souder, fondant *m* en pâte; (*b*) *Comest:* **anchovy p.,** beurre *m* d'anchois; **bloater p.,** beurre de harengs; **turkey p.** = mousse *f* de dindon. **3.** colle *f* (de pâte); **starch p.,** colle d'amidon; **p. pot,** pot *m* à colle. **4.** *Lap:* stras(s) *m*; faux brillants; **it's only p.,** c'est en toc. **5.** *Miner:* pâte (d'une roche).

paste[2], *v.tr* **1.** coller; (*a*) **to p. (up) an advertisement,** coller une affiche; **to p. (up) a notice,** afficher un avis; (*b*) **to p. a screen with pictures,** coller des images sur un écran. **2.** empâter (une plaque d'accumulateur, etc.); **pasted plate,** plaque empâtée, tartinée. **3.** *F:* battre, rosser (qn); flanquer une raclée, une rossée, à (qn).

pasteboard ['peistbɔ:d], *s.* **1.** (*a*) carton *m* (de collage); carton-pâte *m*; *Pej:* **p. house,** maison *f* en carton-pâte; bâtisse *f*; (*b*) *F:* *O:* (i) carte *f* (de visite); (ii) carte(s) à jouer; (iii) billet *m* (de chemin de fer, etc.). **2.** *U.S:* planche *f* à pâtisserie.

pastel[1] ['pæst(ə)l], *s. Art:* (crayon *m*) pastel *m*; **p. drawing, drawing in p.,** (dessin *m* au) pastel; **to draw in p.,** dessiner en pastel; **p. blue,** bleu pastel; **p. shades,** couleurs *f* tendres, tons pastel.

pastel[2], *s. Bot: Dy:* pastel *m*, guède *f*.

pastel(l)ist ['pæstəlist], *s. Art:* pastelliste *mf*.

paste-on ['peistɔn], *s.* (*a*) *Typ:* becquet *m*, béquet *m*; (*b*) *attrib.* **p.-on label,** applique *f*.

pastern ['pæstən], *s. Z:* paturon *m*; **small p.,** os *m* coronaire; **p. joint,** boulet *m*; **horse short in the p.,** (*also* **short-pasterned horse),** cheval court-jointé; **long in the p.** (*also* **long-pasterned),** haut-jointé, long-jointé.

pasteurella [pæstə'relə], *s. Bac:* pasturella *f*.

pasteurellosis [pæstəre'lousis], *s. Vet:* pasteurellose *f*.

Pasteurian [pæs'tə:riən], *a.* pasteurien, pastorien, de Pasteur.

pasteurization [pæst(j)ərai'zeiʃ(ə)n], *s.* pasteurisation *f*.

pasteurize ['pæst(j)əraiz], *v.tr.* pasteuriser; **pasteurized milk,** lait pasteurisé.

pasteurizer ['pæst(j)əraizər], *s.* pasteurisateur *m* (de lait, etc.).

pastiche[1] [pæs'ti:ʃ], *s.* pastiche *m*.

pastiche[2], *v.tr.* pasticher.

pastille ['pæstil, pæs'ti:l], *s.* (*a*) *Comest: Pharm:* pastille *f*; **fruit pastilles** = pâtes *f* de fruits; (*b*) pastille à brûler.

pastime ['pæstaim, 'pɑ:-], *s.* passe-temps *m inv*, distraction *f*, divertissement *m*.

pastiness ['peistinis], *s.* **1.** nature pâteuse, consistance pâteuse (du pain, etc.). **2.** (*of face*) teint *m* pâle (et aspect malsain); pâleur terreuse.

pasting ['peistiŋ], *s.* **1.** (*a*) collage *m* (d'affiches, etc.); (*b*) empâtage *m* (de plaques d'accumulateurs). **2.** *F:* rossée *f*, raclée *f*; **to give the enemy a good p.,** écraser l'ennemi; *Sp:* **to get a p.,** être battu à plates coutures.

pastor ['pɑ:stər], *s.* **1.** *A:* pasteur *m*, berger *m*, pâtre *m*. **2.** *Ecc:* pasteur. **3.** *Orn:* **rose-coloured p.,** (martin) roselin *m*, merle *m* rose.

pastoral ['pɑ:stərəl]. **1.** *a.* pastoral, -aux; (*a*) **p. tribes,** tribus pastorales; peuples pasteurs; **p. land,** (terre *f* en) pâturages *mpl*; (*b*) **p. epistles (of St Paul),** épîtres pastorales; *Ecc:* **p. letter,** *s.* **pastoral,** (lettre) pastorale *f*; instruction pastorale; mandement *m* (de l'évêque); **the p. ring,** l'anneau pastoral. **2.** *s.* pastorale *f*; (*a*) *Lit:* poème pastoral; bergerie *f*; églogue *f*; pastourelle *f*; *a. Mus:* **p. song,** pastourelle; bergerette *f* champêtre; (*b*) *Art:* scène pastorale; (*c*) *Th:* pièce pastorale.

pastorale, *pl.* **-li** [pɑ:stə'rɑ:li, -li:], *s. Mus: Th:* pastorale *f*.

pastoralist ['pɑ:stərəlist], *s.* **1.** *esp. Austr:* éleveur *m* de bétail. **2.** *Th: Mus:* pastoraliste *mf*.

pastorally ['pɑ:stərəli], *adv. Ecc:* pastoralement.

pastorate ['pɑ:stəreit], *s. Ecc:* (*a*) pastorat *m*; (*b*) *coll.* les pasteurs *m*.

pastruga [pæs'truːgə], *s. Ich:* (esturgeon *m*) pastruga *f.*

pastry ['peistri], *s.* (*a*) pâte *f*; **short p.,** pâte brisée; **flaky, puff, p.,** pâte feuilletée; **chou p.,** pâte à chou; **she's got a light hand for p.,** elle fait de la bonne pâtisserie; **p. board,** planche *f* à pâtisserie; **p. brush,** pinceau *m* à pâte; doroir *m*; **p. wheel,** rouleau *m*; **p. cutter,** emporte-pièce *m inv*; (*b*) (*cake*) pâtisserie; **you can buy wonderful pastries there,** on peut y acheter des pâtisseries de premier ordre.

pastrycook ['peistrikuk], *s.* pâtissier, -ière.

pasturage ['pɑːstjuridʒ]. **1.** (*a*) pâturage *m*, pacage *m* (des bestiaux, du cheptel); (*b*) *Jur: Scot:* droit *m* de pacage. **2.** = PASTURE[1] 1.

pasture[1] ['pɑːstjər], *s.* **1. p. (ground, land),** lieu *m* de pâture; pré *m*; pâturage *m*, pâtis *m*, herbage *m*; gagnage *m*, pacage *m*; (*for deer*) viandis *m*; **forest p.,** pâturage en forêt; **to take cattle out to p.,** mener des bêtes en pâture; **common p.,** vaine pâture; *F:* **to be put out to p.,** être mis à la retraite, au vert. **2.** = PASTURAGE 1; **right of p.,** droit *m* de parcours et vaine pâture.

pasture[2]. **1.** (*of animals*) (*a*) *v.i.* paître, pâturer, pacager; (*b*) *v.tr.* paître (l'herbe); pâturer (un pré). **2.** *v.tr.* (*of shepherd*) (*a*) (faire) paître, mener paître (les bêtes); (*b*) pâturer (un pré).

pasturing ['pɑːstjəriŋ], *s.* pacage *m.*

pasty[1] ['peisti], *a.* **1.** empâté; pâteux. **2. p. complexion,** teint terreux, brouillé; teint colle de pâte; **p. face,** visage terreux; *F:* figure de papier mâché.

pasty[2] ['pæsti], *s. Cu:* = (petit) pâté en croûte (cuit sans moule); **Cornish p.,** pâté (en croûte) qui contient du bœuf, des pommes de terre et d'autres légumes.

pat[1] [pæt], *s.* **1.** (*a*) coup *m* de patte; coup léger; petite tape; (*b*) caresse *f*; **to give a dog a p.,** caresser un chien; **to give s.o. a p. on the back,** (i) donner une tape à qn dans le dos; (ii) féliciter qn. **2.** bruit sourd (de pas, etc.); pas feutrés. **3.** (*a*) rondelle *f*, médaillon *m*, coquille *f* (de beurre); (*b*) motte *f*, pain *m* (de beurre). **4.** palette *f*.

pat[2], *v.tr.* **(patted)** (*a*) taper, tapoter; **to p. one's hair,** se tapoter les cheveux; (*b*) caresser, faire des caresses à (un animal, etc.); flatter (qn, un animal, etc.) de la main; **he patted my cheek, patted me on the cheek,** il m'a tapoté la joue, il m'a donné une petite tape sur la joue; **to p. a dog on the back,** flatter le dos d'un chien; **to p. s.o. on the back,** (i) donner une tape à qn dans le dos; (ii) encourager qn; **to p. oneself on the back,** se féliciter (de qch.); s'enorgueillir (d'avoir fait qch.).

pat[3]. **1.** *adv.* à propos; à point; **to answer s.o. p.,** répondre sur-le-champ, sans hésiter; donner la réplique à qn; **his answer came p.,** il a répondu sur-le-champ, du tac au tac; **to know sth. off p.,** savoir qch. exactement, par cœur; **to stand p.,** (i) *Cards:* jouer d'autorité; (ii) *NAm:* refuser de bouger. **2.** *a.* (*a*) apte; à propos; **p. answer,** (i) réponse bien tapée; (ii) réponse faite sans hésiter; (*b*) *Cards:* (*poker*) **p. hand,** jeu *m* dont on ne veut rien écarter.

Pat[4], *Pr.n.* (*dim.*) **1.** *m.* Patrice, Patrick. **2.** *f.* Patricia.

patagium, *pl.* **-ia** [pætə'dʒaiəm, -aiə], *s. Rom.Ant: Nat.Hist:* patagium *m.*

Patagonia [pætə'gouniə], *Pr.n. Geog:* Patagonie *f.*

Patagonian [pætə'gouniən]. *Geog:* (*a*) *a.* patagon; (*b*) *s.* Patagon, -one.

patball ['pætbɔːl], *s. Games:* (*a*) balle *f* au camp; (*b*) tennis mal joué; jeu faiblard, de petites pensionnaires.

patch[1] [pætʃ], *s.* **1.** (*a*) pièce *f* (pour raccommoder un vêtement); **to put a p. on a garment,** rapiécer un vêtement; *F:* **she's not a p. on him,** elle n'est pas de taille avec lui; elle ne lui arrive pas à la cheville; **his last novel isn't a p. on the others,** son dernier roman est loin de valoir les autres; (*b*) pièce rapportée; *Nau:* placard *m*, renfort *m* de voile; *Tail: etc:* **p. pocket,** poche rapportée, appliquée, plaquée; *Aer:* **rigging p.,** placard pour le raccordement du cordage; (*c*) *El: Tp:* **p. board, p. panel,** tableau *m* de commutation (à cordon); **p. cord,** cordon *m* de commutation; **p. plug,** fiche *f* de connexion; (*d*) emplâtre *m* (pour réparer un tuyau souple, etc.); *Aut: etc:* **(rubber) p.,** (i) (*for inner tube*) pastille *f*, rustine *f* (*R.t.m.*); (ii) (*for outer cover*) emplâtre, guêtre *f*; (*e*) emplâtre, pansement adhésif (sur une plaie); **eye p.,** couvre-œil *m*, *pl.* couvre-œils; (*f*) *Toil: A:* mouche (assassine), assassin *m*; **p. box,** boîte *f* à mouches; (*g*) *Cmptr:* correction *f* (de programme); **p. card,** carte *f* de correction; **p. routine,** sous-programme *m* de correction. **2.** (*a*) tache *f* (de couleur, de lumière, etc.); **dark p. on the horizon,** tache sombre à l'horizon; **p. of blue sky,** pan *m*, coin *m*, échappée *f*, de ciel bleu; **p. of fog,** bouchon *m* de brume; **darkness broken, relieved, by patches of light,** obscurité mouchetée de taches lumineuses, trouée de réveillons; **a p. of light in the sky showed that we were nearing the station,** la gare s'annonçait par un halo sur le ciel; **p. of oil,** flaque *f* d'huile; **p. of snow,** flaque, plaque *f*, de neige; **p. of ice,** plaque (i) de glace (flottante), (ii) de verglas; (*on wood, metal, etc.*) **rough patches,** aspérités *f*; **book that is good in patches,** livre *m* qui contient de bons passages; **he had two red patches on his cheeks,** il avait deux taches, deux plaques, rouges sur les joues; *Med:* **mucous p.,** plaque muqueuse; **opaline p.,** plaque opaline, syphilide opaline; **p. test,** test *m* épidermique; *F:* **to strike a bad p.,** être en guigne, en déveine; (*b*) morceau *m*, coin; lopin *m*, parcelle *f* (de terre); carré *m*, plant *m* (de légumes); (*c*) *F:* (*of police*) secteur *m*; (*of criminal, etc.*) **keep off my p.!** ça c'est mon territoire (à moi)! (*d*) *Orn:* **brooding patches,** plaques incubatrices.

patch[2], *v.*

I. *v.tr.* **1.** (*a*) mettre une pièce à, rapiécer, raccommoder (un vêtement, etc.); poser une pastille à (une chambre à air); mettre une pièce à (un pneu); (*b*) placarder (une voile); (*c*) **to p. the fragments of sth. together,** réunir les fragments de qch.; (*d*) *Typ:* **to p. the blanket,** coller un béquet au blanchet; (*e*) *Cmptr:* corriger (un programme). **2.** *usu.passive* tacheter (qch.).

II. (*compound verb*) **patch up,** *v.tr.* (*a*) rapetasser, rafistoler (qch.); arranger, ajuster, *F:* rabibocher, replâtrer (une querelle); *Med: F:* **I've been patched up,** on m'a retapé; (*b*) *Pej:* bâcler (un travail).

patcher ['pætʃər], *s.* **1.** (*a*) raccommodeur, -euse, rapetasseur, -euse; (*b*) **p.-up,** badigeonneur *m* (de meubles, etc.). **2. p. up,** bâcleur, -euse; bousilleur, -euse.

patchiness ['pætʃinis], *s.* (*a*) effet *m* de teintes, de couleurs, mal fondues, mal venues; (*b*) manque *m* d'harmonie (d'un paysage, etc.); **p. of a book,** manque d'unité d'un livre.

patching ['pætʃiŋ], *s.* **1.** (*a*) rapiéçage *m*, rapiècement *m*, raccommodage *m*; (*b*) *Cmptr:* correction *f* (de programme). **2.** *El: etc:* raccordement *m* (de fils électriques, etc.). **3. p. up,** (i) rapetassage *m*, rafistolage *m*; (ii) bâclage *m*; (iii) *Typ:* montage *m.*

patchouli ['pætʃuli], *s. Bot: Toil:* patchouli *m*; **p. oil,** essence *f* de patchouli.

patchwork ['pætʃwəːk], *s.* ouvrage fait de pièces et de morceaux, de pièces de rapport, de pièces disparates; *F:* (*of literary composition, etc.*) marqueterie *f*; **p. of fields,** campagne bigarrée; **book that is mere p.,** livre *m* qui n'est qu'un rapiéçage, qu'un placage; **p. quilt,** couverture paysanne, couvre-pied *m* à combinaisons enchevêtrées.

patchy ['pætʃi], *a.* (*a*) (*of paint, etc.*) qui offre des taches, qui manque de fondu; inégal, -aux; (*b*) (*of book, etc.*) inégal; qui manque d'unité.

pate [peit], *s. A: & F:* tête *f*, *F:* caboche *f.*

pâté ['pætei], *s. Cu:* pâté *m*; **liver p.,** pâté de foie; **I'll have some of your special p.,** je prendrai du pâté maison.

patella, *pl.* **-ae** [pə'telə, -iː], *s.* **1.** *Rom.Ant:* patelle *f.* **2.** *Anat:* (*pl.* **-ae** *or* **-as**) rotule *f* (du genou). **3.** *Moll:* patelle. **4.** patelle (de lichen).

patellar [pə'telər], *a. Anat:* (ligament, etc.) rotulien, patellaire; **p. reflex,** réflexe *m* patellaire.

patellate [pə'teleit], *a. Nat.Hist:* patellé, patelliforme.

patellid, patellidan [pə'telid, -'telidən], *a. & s. Moll:* patellidé (*m*).

Patellidae [pə'telidiː], *s.pl. Moll:* patellidés *m.*

patelliform [pə'telifɔːm], **patelline** ['pætəlain], **patelloid** [pə'telɔid], *a.* patelliforme.

paten ['pæt(ə)n], *s. Ecc:* patène *f.*

patency ['peitənsi], *s.* **1.** évidence *f* (d'un fait, etc.). **2.** état ouvert, inobstrué (d'une entrée, etc.).

patent[1] ['peit(ə)nt, 'pæt-], *a. & s.*

I. *a.* **1.** *Jur:* **letters p.,** (i) lettres patentes, de nobilité; (ii) lettres patentes, brevet *m* d'invention, d'inventeur. **2.** breveté; **p. goods,** articles brevetés; **p. medicine,** spécialité pharmaceutique, médicale; **p. food,** spécialité alimentaire; **p. fuel,** briquettes *fpl*, boulets *mpl*, agglomérés *mpl*, etc.; **p. leather,** cuir verni; **p.-leather shoes,** souliers vernis; *A:* **to have a p. way of doing sth.,** avoir une façon à soi de faire qch. **3.** (*a*) *A:* (*of door*) ouvert; (*of passage*) inobstrué, libre; (*b*) *Bot:* (*of petals, leaves, etc.*) étalé. **4.** (fait, etc.) patent, manifeste, clair, évident; **how can we deny p. facts?** comment nier l'évidence même? *Jur:* **p. offence,** délit constant; **p. and established crime,** crime avéré.

II. *s.* **1.** (*a*) lettres patentes; **p. of nobility,** lettres d'anoblissement, de noblesse; *A:* **p. of gentility,** marque *f*, signe *m*, de gentillesse; (*b*) *A:* privilège *m* (de vente, de fabrication). **2.** (*a*) brevet *m* d'invention; **p. relating to improvements,** brevet de perfectionnement; **to take out a p.,** prendre un brevet; se faire breveter par le gouvernement; **to take out a p. for an invention,** faire breveter une invention; **to grant a p. to s.o.,** délivrer un brevet à qn; breveter (qn); **p. applied for,** une demande de brevet a été déposée; **infringement of a p.,** contrefaçon *f*; **invention the p. of which has expired,** invention tombée dans le domaine public; **commissioner of patents,** directeur *m* de brevets; **p. agent,** agent *m* en brevets (d'invention); **p. engineer,** ingénieur *m* conseil (en matière de propriété industrielle); **p. office,** bureau *m* des brevets; office national de la propriété industrielle; **p. rights,** propriété industrielle; **p. rolls,** registres *m* portant nomenclature des brevets d'invention; (*b*) invention, fabrication, brevetée.

patent[2], *v.tr.* protéger par un brevet, faire breveter (une invention); prendre un brevet pour (une invention).

patentability [peitəntə'biliti, pæt-], *s.* brevetabilité *f.*

patentable ['peitəntəbl, 'pæt-], *a.* brevetable.

patented ['peitəntid, 'pæt-], *a.* breveté.

patentee [peitən'tiː, pæt-], *s.* détenteur, -trice, concessionnaire *mf*, titulaire *mf*, d'un brevet.

patenting ['peitəntiŋ, 'pæt-], *s.* **1.** brevetage *m.* **2.** *Metall:* patentage *m.*

patently ['peitəntli], *adv.* manifestement; clairement.

pater ['peitər], *s.m. F: O:* papa, le paternel.

patera, *pl.* **-ae** ['pætərə, -iː], *s. Rom.Ant: Arch:* patère *f.*

paterfamilias [peitəfə'miliæs], *s.m.* (*a*) *Rom.Hist:* pater familias; (*b*) père de famille; chef de maison.

paternal [pə'təːn(ə)l], *a.* paternel; **p. authority,** autorité paternelle; **the p. roof,** la maison paternelle; **the p. side,** le côté paternel; le côté du père (dans la descendance).

paternalism [pə'təːnəlizm], *s.* paternalisme *m.*

paternalist(ic) [pə'təːnəlist, pətəːnə'listik], *a.* paternaliste.

paternally [pə'təːnəli], *adv.* paternellement.

paternity [pə'təːniti], *s.* (*a*) paternité *f*; (*b*) paternité, origine *f.*

paternoite ['pætənoit], *s. Miner:* paternoïte *f.*

paternoster ['pætə'nɔstər], *s.* **1.** (*a*) patenôtre *f*; pater *m*; **to say five paternosters,** dire cinq paters; **devil's p.,** pater récité à l'envers; (*b*) **p. (bead),** pater *m* (de rosaire). **2.** *Fish:* **p. (line),** pater-noster *m inv*; arondelle *f.* **3.** *Hyd.E: Min: Arch:* patenôtre; **p. pump,** pompe *f* à chapelet, à godets; chapelet *m* hydraulique.

path, *pl.* **paths** [pɑːθ, pɑːðz], *s.* **1.** (*a*) chemin *m*, sentier *m*; (*in forest*) laie *f*, layon *m*; (*in garden*) allée *f*; **mountain p.,** sentier de montagne; **mule p.,** sentier muletier; **the p. of glory,** le chemin de la gloire; **to follow the p. of duty,** suivre le chemin du devoir; (*b*) trottoir *m*; (*c*) *Rac:* piste *f*; **cinder p.,** piste cendrée; *Cy:* **p. racing,** course *f* sur piste; (*d*) *Nau:* **swept p.,** chemin, chenal, passage, dragué. **2.** cours *m*, trajet *m*, course (d'un corps en mouvement); trajectoire *f* (d'un mobile, d'un projectile, *Atom.Ph:* d'une particule); passage, trajet (d'un rayon de lumière); trajectoire (d'un astre); trajectoire, orbite *f* (d'une planète); route *f* (du soleil); course (d'une manivelle); *Cmptr:* (i) chemin (de la carte); (ii) circuit *m* (de l'information); (iii) branche *f* (de l'organigramme); *Ph:* **p. of free fall,** trajectoire (d'un corps tombant) en chute libre; **p. of lines of force,** trajet, flux *m*, des lignes de force; **p. of wave propagation,** trajet de la propagation des ondes; *Ball:* **p. of a bullet,** (i) (*through the air*) trajectoire, (ii) (*through the body*) trajet, sillon *m*, d'une balle; *Av:* **flight p.,** ligne *f* de vol; **glide p.,** axe *m* de descente, trajectoire d'atterrissage; *Atom.Ph:* **p. length,** parcours *m* (d'une particule); **p.-length difference,** différence *f* de parcours; *Meteor:* **p. of a storm,** trajectoire d'une dépression; *El:* **armature p.,** circuit d'induit; *Anat:* **condyle p.,** trajet condylien; **occlusal p.,** trajet articulaire (des mandibules).

Pathan [pə'tɑːn, -'θɑːn]. *Ethn:* (*a*) *a.* pat(h)an; (*b*) *s.* Pat(h)an, -ane.

pathetic [pə'θetik]. **1.** *a.* (*a*) pathétique, touchant, attendrissant; **p. story,** histoire pathétique, touchante; **this p. Queen of Scots,** cette malheureuse reine d'Écosse; **she's a p. creature,** c'est une créature pitoyable; **you're p.!** tu me fais pitié! **how p.! it's p.! isn't it p.?** (i) c'est tout de même lamentable, malheureux! (ii) que c'est pitoyable, indigne! (*b*) *Anat:* **p. muscle,** muscle *m* pathétique (de l'œil); grand oblique de l'œil; (*c*) qui a rapport aux émotions. **2.** *s.* (*a*) **the p.,** le pathétique; pathétisme *m*; (*b*) **pathetics,** (i) sentiments *m* pathétiques; étalage *m* de sensiblerie; (ii) étude *f* du pathétique.

pathetically [pə'θetik(ə)li], *adv.* pathétiquement.

pathfinder ['pɑːθfaindər], *s.* **1.** pionnier *m*; *Mil: etc:* orienteur *m.* **2.** avion éclaireur.

pathless ['pɑːθlis], *a.* sans chemin frayé, battu; (terrain) vierge.

patho- ['pæθou, pæ'θɔ], *comb.fm.* patho-.

pathogen ['pæθoudʒen], *s.* microbe *m* pathogène.

pathogenesis [pæθou'dʒenisis], *s. Med:* pathogénie *f*, pathogénèse *f*, pathogénésie *f.*

pathogenetic [pæθoudʒi'netik], **pathogenic**

[pæθou'dʒenik], **pathogenous** [pæ'θɔdʒinəs], *a. Med:* pathogène, pathogénique.
pathognomic [pæθɔg'nɔmik], **pathognomonic** [pæθɔgnou'mɔnik], *a. Med:* pathognomonique.
pathognomy [pæ'θɔgnəmi], *s. Med:* pathognomonie *f.*
pathological [pæθə'lɔdʒikl], *a.* pathologique.
pathologically [pæθə'lɔdʒik(ə)li], *adv.* pathologiquement.
pathologist [pə'θɔlədʒist], *s.* (*a*) pathologiste *mf*; (*b*) médecin *m* légiste.
pathology [pə'θɔlədʒi], *s.* pathologie *f*; **plant p.,** phytopathologie *f,* pathologie végétale; **gross p.,** pathologie clinique.
pathomania [pæθou'meiniə], *s. Med:* pathomanie *f.*
pathomimesis [pæθoum(a)i'mi:sis], *s. Psy:* pathomimie *f.*
pathophobia [pæθou'foubiə], *s. Psy:* pathophobie *f.*
pathopoietic [pæθoupɔi'i:tik], *a.* pathopoétique.
pathos ['peiθɔs], *s.* pathétique *m*; **told with p.,** raconté d'une façon touchante.
pathway ['pɑ:θwei], *s.* sentier *m.*
patience ['peiʃ(ə)ns], *s.* **1.** patience *f*; **the p. of Job,** une patience d'ange; l'endurance *f* de Job; **to try, tax, s.o.'s p.,** mettre la patience de qn à l'épreuve; éprouver, exercer, la patience de qn; **his p. was severely tried,** sa patience a été mise à une rude épreuve; **to exhaust s.o.'s p.,** mettre la patience de qn à bout; lasser la patience de qn; mettre qn à bout de patience; **my p. is exhausted, is at an end,** ma patience est à bout; je suis à bout de patience; **to show p. with s.o.,** prendre patience avec qn; **have p.!** (prenez) patience! ayez de la patience! **to lose p., to get out of p.,** perdre patience; **he lost p.,** il a perdu patience; **I lost all p. with him,** il m'a mis hors de moi; il a mis ma patience à bout; **out of (all) p.,** à bout de patience; énervé, excédé; **to make s.o. lose p.,** faire perdre patience à qn; **to be out of p. with s.o.,** être à bout de patience avec qn; **I've no p. with him,** il m'impatiente; il a mis ma patience à bout; **I have no p. with all your foolishness,** vous m'impatientez avec vos folies; **to possess one's soul in p., to exercise p.,** patienter; prendre patience; s'armer, se munir, de patience. **2.** *Cards:* réussite *f*; **Russian p.,** nigaud *m*; **to play p.,** faire des réussites. **3.** *Bot:* **p. (dock),** patience; oseille-épinard *f, pl.* oseilles-épinards.
patient ['peiʃ(ə)nt]. **1.** *a.* (*a*) patient, endurant; **to be p.,** patienter; prendre patience; **one should be p. with young children,** il faut avoir de la patience avec les jeunes enfants; **p. in adversity,** qui sait supporter, endurer, l'adversité; qui prend l'adversité en patience; (*b*) *A:* **word p. of misconstruction,** mot *m* qui prête à de fausses interprétations; mot susceptible d'être mal interprété. **2.** *s.* malade *mf*; (*surgical case*) patient, -ente; **a doctor and his patients,** un médecin et ses clients; **two nurses were looking after the patients after their operations,** deux infirmières soignaient les opéré(e)s; **in p.,** malade hospitalisé(e); **out p.,** malade qui vient consulter à l'hôpital, à la clinique.
patiently ['peiʃəntli], *adv.* patiemment; **to bear sth. p.,** prendre, supporter, qch. avec patience; **to wait (for s.o., for sth.) p.,** attendre (qn, qch.) avec patience; patienter.
patina ['pætinə]. **1.** patine *f*; (*of bronze*) **to take on a p.,** se patiner; **to give a p. to bronze, etc.,** patiner le bronze, etc. **2.** *Ecc: A:* = PATEN.
patinate ['pætineit], **patine** ['pæti:n], *v.tr.* patiner.
patinated ['pætineitid], *a.* couvert d'une patine; (bronze) patiné.
patination [pæti'neiʃ(ə)n], *s.* patinage *m* (du bronze, etc.).
patio ['pætiou], *s.* **1.** *Arch:* patio *m.* **2.** *Min:* chantier *m* de lavage.
Patmos ['pætmɔs]. *Pr.n. Geog:* Patmos *m.*
patness ['pætnis], *s.* à-propos *m* (d'une observation, etc.).
patriarch ['peitriɑ:k], *s.* (*a*) *Anthr: Ecc: etc:* patriarche *m*; (*b*) (*oldest member*) **the village p.,** le patriarche du village; *Pol:* **the party patriarchs,** les anciens *m* du parti; (*c*) fondateur *m* (d'une organisation, etc.).
patriarchal [peitri'ɑ:kl], *a.* patriarcal, -aux.
patriarchally [peitri'ɑ:kəli], *adv.* patriarcalement; en patriarche.
patriarchate ['peitriɑ:kət], *s. Ecc:* patriarcat *m.*
patriarchy ['peitriɑ:ki], *s.* (*a*) patriarchie *f*; (*b*) patriarcat *m,* système patriarcal.
patrician [pə'triʃ(ə)n]. **1.** *a.* & *s. Rom.Hist: etc:* patricien, -ienne; **the order of the patricians,** le patriciat. **2.** (*later Rom. Empire*) (*a*) *a.* patricial, -aux; (*b*) *s.* patrice *m.*
patriciate [pə'triʃieit], *s.* patriciat *m.*
patricide ['pætrisaid], *s.* = PARRICIDE[1,2].
Patrick ['pætrik]. *Pr.n.m.* Patrice, Patrick.
patriclan ['pætriklæn], *s. Anthr:* patriclan *m.*
patrilineage [pætri'liniidʒ], *s.* descendance *f* par la ligne paternelle.
patrilineal, patrilinear [pætri'liniəl, -'liniər], *a.* patrilinéaire; (descendance) par la ligne paternelle; **p. clan,** patriclan *m.*
patrimonial [pætri'mouniəl], *a.* patrimonial, -aux.
patrimonially [pætri'mouniəli], *adv.* patrimonialement.
patrimony ['pætriməni], *s.* **1.** patrimoine *m.* **2.** biens-fonds *mpl,* renvu *m,* d'une église; *A:* patrimoine. **3.** *Hist:* **the P. of St. Peter,** le Patrimoine de Saint-Pierre.
Patriofelis [pætriou'fi:lis], *s. Paleont:* patriofelis *m.*
patriot ['peitriət, 'pæ-], *s.* patriote *mf.*
patriotic [peitri'ɔtik, pæ-], *a.* **1.** (*of pers.*) patriote. **2.** (*of speech, etc.*) patriotique.
patriotically [peitri'ɔtik(ə)li, pæ-], *adv.* patriotiquement; en patriote.
patriotism ['peitriətizm, 'pæ-], *s.* patriotisme *m.*
patristic [pə'tristik]. *Theol:* **1.** *a.* patristique; des Pères de l'Église. **2.** *s.pl.* (*usu. with sg. const.*) **patristics,** patristique *f,* patrologie *f.*
patroclinic, patroclinous [pætrou'klinik, -'klainəs], *a. Biol:* patrocline.
Patroclus [pæ'trɔkləs], *Pr.n.m. Gr.Lit:* Patrocle.
patrol[1] [pə'troul], *s.* patrouille *f*; (*a*) *Mil:* **contact p.,** patrouille de contact; **member of a p.,** homme *m* de patrouille, patrouilleur *m*; **moving p.,** patrouille mobile; **p. leader,** chef *m* de patrouille; **p. of six men,** patrouille de six hommes; **reconnoitring, scouting, p.,** patrouille de reconnaissance, de découverte; **security p.,** patrouille de sûreté, de protection; **standing p.,** patrouille fixe, statique; **to be on p.,** être en patrouille, patrouiller; (*b*) *Av: Nau:* **long-range p.,** patrouille à grand rayon d'action; *Av:* **fighter p.,** patrouille de chasse; **p. aircraft,** (avion *m*) patrouilleur *m*; **p. bomber,** patrouilleur de bombardement, bombardier *m* patrouilleur; *Navy:* **p. craft, vessel,** patrouilleur; vedette *f* de surveillance; **ice p. service,** service *m* de surveillance des glaces; **p. helicopter, p. seaplane,** hélicoptère *m,* hydravion *m,* de surveillance; (*c*) (*of police*) patrouille (de surveillance); ronde *f*; **police officer's p.,** ronde de police; **traffic p.,** patrouille de la circulation (routière); **p. car,** voiture *f* de reconnaissance, de liaison policière; **p. wagon,** voiture, fourgon *m,* cellulaire; (*d*) **A.A. p.,** (i) patrouilleur, (ii) voiture de patrouille, de l'Automobile Association; (*e*) *Scout:* patrouille.
patrol[2], *v.* **(patrolled) 1.** *v.i.* patrouiller, aller en patrouille; faire une ronde; faire la patrouille. **2.** *v.tr.* faire la patrouille dans (un quartier, etc.); **at night the streets were patrolled,** la nuit des patrouilles parcouraient les rues, faisaient des rondes.
patrolling [pə'trouliŋ], *s.* (*a*) *Mil: etc:* service *m* de patrouille; (*b*) (*of police*) service de ronde, de surveillance.
patrolman, *pl.* **-men** [pə'troulmən], *s.m.* (*a*) patrouilleur; (*b*) *NAm:* agent de police (en service de ronde).
patrology [pæ'trɔlədʒi], *s. Theol:* patrologie *f,* patristique *f.*
patron ['peitrən], *s.* **1.** (*a*) protecteur *m,* ami *m,* mécène *m* (des artistes, des arts, etc.); patron *m* (d'une œuvre de charité, etc.); (*b*) *Ecc:* **p. saint,** patron, -onne; saint patronal, sainte patronale (d'une église, de qn); **p. saint's day,** fête patronale (d'une localité); (*c*) *Ecc:* patron, collateur *m,* présentateur *m* (d'un bénéfice); (*d*) *Rom.Ant:* patron. **2.** *Com:* client, -ente (d'un magasin); habitué, -ée (d'un cinéma, etc.); **the patrons of the drama, of the cinema,** le public du théâtre, du cinéma.
patronage ['pætrənidʒ], *s.* **1.** (*a*) protection *f*; encouragement *m* (des arts, etc.); mécénat *m*; patronage *m*; **concert under the p. of . . .,** concert honoré d'une souscription de . . .; (*b*) *Pej:* air protecteur (envers qn); condescendance *f.* **2.** clientèle *f* (d'un hôtel, etc.). **3.** *Ecc:* droit *m* de présentation (à un bénéfice).
patronal [pə'troun(ə)l], *a. Ecc:* patronal, -aux.
patronate ['pætrəneit], *s. Rom.Ant: etc:* patronat *m.*
patroness ['peitrənis], *s.f.* **1.** protectrice (des arts, etc.); (dame) patronnesse (d'une œuvre de charité). **2.** *Ecc:* collateur *m,* patronne (d'un bénéfice).
patronite ['pætrənait], *s. Miner:* patronite *f.*
patronize ['pætrənaiz], *v.tr.* **1.** (*a*) patronner, protéger (un artiste, etc.); favoriser, encourager (un art); appuyer, patronner (une société, etc.); subventionner (un hôpital, etc.); souscrire pour, à (une œuvre de bienfaisance); (*b*) traiter (qn) d'un air protecteur, avec condescendance, de haut en bas; traiter (qn) de son haut. **2.** accorder sa clientèle à (une maison); **to p. a cinema,** être un habitué d'un cinéma; fréquenter un cinéma.
patronizer ['pætrənaizər], *s.* protecteur, -trice.
patronizing ['pætrənaiziŋ], *a.* (*a*) protecteur, -trice; (*b*) **p. tone, air,** ton *m,* air *m* de condescendance; **p. nod,** petit signe de tête protecteur; **to become p.,** prendre un air protecteur.
patronizingly ['pætrənaiziŋli], *adv.* d'un air protecteur; d'un air de condescendance.
patronym ['pætrənim], *s.* patronyme *m.*
patronymic [pætrə'nimik]. **1.** *a.* patronymique. **2.** *s.* patronyme *m,* nom *m* patronymique.
patsy ['pætsi], *s. U.S: F:* dupe *f,* jobard *m.*
patten ['pæt(ə)n], *s.* **1.** claque *f,* socque *m,* patin *m* (pour garantir les chaussures contre la boue). **2.** *Arch:* socle *m* (de colonne); patin (de mur, de fondement).
patter[1] ['pætər], *s.* **1.** (*a*) argot *m* (des voleurs, etc.); (*b*) boniment *m* (de prestidigitateur, de charlatan); bagout *m*; (*c*) bavardage *m,* jaserie *f,* caquet *m.* **2.** parlé *m* (dans une chansonnette, etc.).
patter[2]. **1.** *v.tr.* marmotter, expédier (ses prières, etc.); parler tant bien que mal (le français, etc.). **2.** *v.i.* bavarder sans arrêt; jaser, caqueter.
patter[3], *s.* petit bruit (de pas précipités, etc.); trottinement *m*; crépitement *m* (de la grêle, etc.); fouettement *m* (de la pluie); **a p. of feet,** un bruit de pas précipités.
patter[4], *v.i.* (*a*) trottiner, marcher à petits pas rapides; (*of hail, rain*) crépiter, fouetter; (*b*) **to p. about,** trottiner çà et là; **she pattered away, out, off,** elle s'en est allée à petits pas pressés.
pattern[1] ['pæt(ə)n], *s.* **1.** modèle *m,* exemple *m,* type *m,* schéma *m*; **to take s.o. as a p., to take p. by s.o.,** se modeler sur qn; prendre exemple, modèle, sur qn; prendre qn pour modèle; suivre l'exemple de qn; s'inspirer de qn; **to be a p. of virtue,** être un exemple, un modèle, de vertu. **2.** (*a*) modèle, dessin *m,* maquette *f*; **garments of different patterns,** vêtements de coupes différentes; **machines all built to one p.,** machines construites, fabriquées, toutes sur le même modèle; *Ind:* **p. designer,** dessinateur, -trice, de modèles; **p. shop,** atelier *m* de modelage; atelier des modèles; *Mil:* **regulation p.,** modèle réglementaire; *Dent: etc:* **wax p.,** (modèle, maquette, en) cire *f*; *T.V:* **p. generator,** générateur *m* de mire; **(test) p.,** mire *f* de réglage (i) *T.V:* de l'image, (ii) *Phot:* de la lampe, de l'agrandisseur; (*b*) *Dressm: etc:* patron *m* (en papier, etc.); **to cut out a shirt to, from, on, a p.,** tailler une chemise sur un patron; **to take a p.,** relever un patron; (*c*) *Metall:* **casting p.,** modèle, gabarit *m,* calibre *m* (de fonderie); **p. moulder,** mouleur *m* (de fonderie); **p. drawing machine,** démouleuse *f* (de fonderie). **3.** *Com:* échantillon *m*; **not to be up to p.,** ne pas être conforme à l'échantillon; **p. book,** livre *m* d'échantillons; **p. card,** carte *f* d'échantillons. **4.** (*a*) dessin, motif *m* (de papier peint, etc.); *Tex:* broché *m* (d'un tissu); (*b*) grille *f* (de mots croisés); (*c*) **streets arranged in an orderly p.,** rues établies suivant un plan ordonné; **they looked down from the aircraft at the p. of fields,** ils regardaient de l'avion la disposition géométrique des champs; **the p. of history,** la trame de l'histoire; **the normal p. of trade,** la tendance normale du marché; *Meteor:* **temperature p.,** régime *m* thermique; *Opt:* **diffraction p.,** figure *f* de diffraction; (*d*) *Ball:* groupement *m* (des points d'impact de projectiles sur une cible, sur le sol, etc.); gerbe *f* (d'un fusil tirant des cartouches à plombs); *Mil.Av:* **bombfall p.,** groupement, répartition *f,* des points d'impact de bombes (sur un objectif, etc.); **p. bombing,** bombardement *m* systématique; *Mil:* **weapon deployment p.,** plan *m* d'implantation, de déploiement, des armes; (*e*) *Cmptr:* **p. of holes, of punches,** combinaison *f* de perforations; (*f*) *Ph:* **beam p.,** diagramme directionnel de rayonnement; **diffraction p.,** diagramme, figures, de diffraction; **flow p.,** diagramme d'écoulement; *Physiol:* **growth p.,** diagramme de croissance (d'un organe, d'un os, etc.); (*g*) *Av:* **(traffic) p.,** circuit *m,* figure, de procédure; **landing p.,** circuit de procédure à l'atterrissage.
pattern[2], *v.tr.* **1.** (*a*) **to p. sth. after, (up)on, sth.,** modeler qch. sur qch.; faire qch. d'après le modèle de qch.; (*b*) *Ling:* structurer. **2.** tracer des dessins, des motifs, sur (qch.); orner (qch.) de motifs; **patterned fabrics,** tissus imprimés, à dessins.
patterning ['pætəniŋ], *s. Ling:* structuration *f.*
patternmaker ['pætənmeikər], *s.* **1.** *Ind:* modeleur, -euse; **patternmaker's lathe,** tour *m* de modeleur. **2.** *Dressm: etc:* modéliste *mf,* modelliste *mf*; *Tex: etc:* patronnier, -ière.
patternmaking ['pætənmeikiŋ], *s.* **1.** *Ind:* modelage *m,* fabrication *f* de(s) modèles. **2.** *Dressm: etc:* création *f* de(s) modèles.
patting ['pætiŋ], *s.* tapotement *m*; caresses *fpl.*
pattinsonization [pætinsənai'zeiʃ(ə)n], *s. Metall:* pattinson(n)age *m* (du plomb argentifère).
pattinsonize ['pætinsənaiz], *v.tr. Metall:* pattinson(n)er

(le plomb argentifère).

patty ['pæti], *s. Cu:* petit pâté (en croûte); bouchée *f* à la reine; **oyster patties,** bouchées aux huîtres; **p. tin,** petit moule à pâté.

pattypan ['pætipæn], *s. Cu:* petit moule à pâté, à gâteau.

patulous ['pætjuləs], *a.* **1.** (orifice) ouvert, bâillant. **2.** *(a)* (arbre) ombreux, à rameaux déployés; *(b) Bot:* étalé.

paty ['pæti], *a. Her:* patté.

pauciflorous [pɔːsi'flɔːrəs], *a. Bot:* pauciflore.

paucity ['pɔːsiti], *s.* manque *m*, disette *f*; rareté *f*; **p. of new plays,** indigence *f* de la production théâtrale; **there is a p. of news,** il y a disette de nouvelles; **p. of money,** manque d'argent, pénurie *f* d'argent; rareté de l'argent.

Paul [pɔːl]. *Pr.n.m.* Paul; *Danc:* **P. Jones,** boulangère *f.*

Paula ['pɔːlə]. *Pr.n.f.* Paule, Paula.

Paulician [pɔː'liʃən], *s. Rel.H:* Paulicien *m.*

Pauline[1] ['pɔːliːn], *Pr.n.f.* Pauline.

Pauline[2] ['pɔːlain]. **1.** *a. Ecc:* paulinien; **the P. Epistles,** les épîtres *f* de saint Paul. **2.** *s. Sch:* (i) élève, (ii) ancien élève, de *St Paul's School.*

Paulinian [pɔː'liniən], *s. Rel.H:* paulinien, -ienne.

Paul(in)ism ['pɔːl(in)izm], *s. Rel.H:* paulinisme *m.*

Paulinist ['pɔːlinist], *s. Rel.H:* pauliniste *m.*

Paulinus [pɔː'lainəs]. *Pr.n.m. Rel.H:* Paulin.

Paulist ['pɔːlist], *s. R.C.Ch:* pauliste *m.*

paulownia [pɔː'ləvniə, -'louniə], *s. Bot:* paulownia *m.*

Paulus ['pɔːləs]. *Pr.n.m. Rom.Hist:* **Aemilius P.,** Paul-Émile.

paunch[1] [pɔːnʃ], *s.* **1.** *(a)* panse *f*, ventre *m*, abdomen *m*, *F:* bedaine *f* (de qn); *(b)* panse, herbier *m*, rumen *m* (des ruminants). **2.** *Nau:* paillet *m*, baderne *f* (de protection).

paunch[2], *v.tr.* éventrer, étriper (un animal, etc.); *Cu:* **to p. a rabbit,** vider un lapin.

paunched [pɔːnʃt], **paunchy** ['pɔːnʃi], *a.* pansu.

paunchiness ['pɔːnʃinis], *s.* corpulence *f.*

pauper ['pɔːpər], *s.* **1.** *(a)* indigent, -ente; *A:* **p. children,** enfants assistés; **p. asylum,** hôpital *m*, hospice *m*, des pauvres; **indoor p.,** hospitalisé, -ée; *(b) Jur:* indigent admis à l'assistance judiciaire. **2.** *Pej:* mendiant, -ante; pauvre, -esse.

pauperdom ['pɔːpədəm], *s.* **1.** indigence *f.* **2.** *coll.A:* les indigents *m.*

pauperism ['pɔːpərizm], *s.* paupérisme *m.*

pauperization [pɔːpərai'zeiʃ(ə)n], *s.* réduction *f* à l'indigence; *Pol.Ec:* paupérisation *f* (d'une population).

pauperize ['pɔːpəraiz], *v.tr.* réduire (qn) à l'indigence; amener (une population) au paupérisme.

paurometabolous [pɔːroume'tæbələs], *a.* **p. insect,** (insecte) paurométabole *(m).*

pauropod ['pɔːroupɔd], *s. Myr:* pauropode *m.*

Pauropoda [pɔː'rɔpədə], *s.pl. Myr:* pauropodes *m.*

pauropodous [pɔː'rɔpədəs], *a. Myr:* pauropode.

pause[1] [pɔːz], *s.* **1.** *(a)* pause *f*, arrêt *m*; **to make a p.,** faire une pause; **there was a p. in the conversation,** la conversation s'est arrêtée; il y a eu un silence; *(b) Rec:* blanc *m* sonore; silence; *(c) A:* **to give p. to s.o.,** faire hésiter qn; arrêter l'élan de qn. **2.** *Pros:* repos *m*; césure *f.* **3.** *Mus:* point *m* d'orgue; repos; *(over a rest)* point d'arrêt; **to make a p. on a note,** tenir une note. **4.** *Typ:* **p. dots,** points de suspension.

pause[2], *v.i.* **1.** faire une pause; s'arrêter un instant; marquer un temps; **he paused at the door to say to me . . .,** il s'est arrêté à la porte pour me dire . . .; **to p. at every shop window,** s'arrêter devant toutes les vitrines. **2.** hésiter; **to make s.o. p.,** faire hésiter qn; donner à réfléchir à qn. **3. to p. on a word,** s'arrêter, pauser, sur un mot; *Mus:* **to p. on a note,** tenir une note.

paussid ['pɔːsid], *s. Ent:* paussidé *m.*

Paussidae ['pɔːsidiː], *s.pl. Ent:* paussidés *m.*

pauxi ['pɔːksi], *s. Orn:* pauxi *m.*

pavan(e) [pæ'væn], *s. Danc:* pavane *f.*

pave [peiv], *v.tr.* paver (une rue, etc.); carreler (une cour, etc.); **wood-paved,** pavé en bois; **to p. the way,** préparer le terrain; frayer la voie; **to p. the way to fame for s.o.,** frayer à qn le chemin des honneurs.

pavement ['peivmənt], *s.* **1.** *(a)* pavé *m*, pavage *m*, dallage *m*, carrelage *m*; **marble p.,** pavement *m* de marbre; **wood p., brick p.,** pavé en bois, en briques; **cobblestone, cobbled, p.,** empierrement *m* en cailloux; **glass p.,** pavé en verre; **flexible p.,** revêtement *m* souple; **p. light,** dallage éclairant, en verre; verre *m* dalle; verdal *m, pl.* -als; *(b)* trottoir *m*; **p. artist,** artiste *mf* de trottoir; *F:* **to be on the p.,** être sur le pavé; se trouver (i) sans asile, (ii) sans emploi; *(c) NAm:* chaussée *f*; *(d) Anat:* **p. epithelium,** épithélium pavimenteux. **2.** *Min:* sole *f* (d'une galerie); mur *m* (d'une couche de houille).

paver ['peivər], *s.* **1.** paveur *m*; dalleur *m*, carreleur *m.* **2.** pierre *f* à paver; pavé *m.*

pavia[1] ['peiviə], *s. Bot:* pavier *m*; marronnier *m* à fleurs rouges.

Pavia[2] [pə'viːə], *Pr.n. Geog:* Pavie *f.*

pavilion[1] [pə'viliən], *s.* **1.** *A:* pavillon *m*, tente *f*; *Her:* pavillon. **2.** *(a) Sp: etc:* pavillon; *(b) Mus:* **Chinese p.,** chapeau chinois. **3.** *Arch:* pavillon; **p. roof,** comble *m* en pavillon. **4.** *Anat:* pavillon (de l'oreille). **5.** *Lap:* pavillon (de diamant).

pavilion[2], *v.tr. A:* **1.** abriter (une fête, etc.) sous un pavillon, sous des tentes. **2.** dresser des pavillons sur (un champ, etc.).

paving ['peiviŋ], *s.* **1.** pavage *m*; dallage *m*; carrelage *m*; **p. stone,** pierre *f* à paver; pavé *m*; cadette *f*; **rough, dressed, p. stone,** pavé brut, piqué; **p. tile,** carreau *m* (de pavage); *Tls:* **p. beetle,** hie *f*, dame *f*, demoiselle *f.* **2.** pavé, dalles *fpl.*

paviour ['peivjər], *s.* paveur *m*; dalleur *m*; carreleur *m*; **paviour's hammer,** marteau *m* de carreleur, de paveur.

pavis(e) ['pævis], *s. A.Arm:* pavois *m.*

Pavlovian [pæv'louviən], *a. Physiol:* pavlovien; **P. theories, system,** pavlovisme *m.*

Pavlovism ['pævlouvizm], *s.* pavlovisme *m.*

Pavo ['pɑːvou]. *Pr.n. Astr:* le Paon.

pavonazzo [pævou'nætsou], *a. & s.* **p. (marble),** pavonazzo *m*; œil-de-paon *m.*

pavonine ['pævənain]. **1.** *a.* *(a)* (démarche, etc.) de paon; *(b)* irisé. **2.** *s. Miner:* iris *m.*

paw[1] [pɔː], *s. F:* **1.** *(a)* patte *f* (d'animal onguiculé); *(b) F:* main *f*, patte (de qn); **paws off!** bas les pattes! **2.** piaffement *m* (de cheval).

paw[2], *v.tr.* **1.** *(a) (of animal)* donner des coups de patte, de griffe, à (qn, qch.); *(b) (of horse)* **to p. the ground,** *v.i.* **to p.,** piaffer; gratter (la terre) du pied; battre la poussière. **2.** *(of pers.)* *(a) F:* patiner, tripoter, tripotailler (qn, qch.); **don't p. me like that,** ne me tripotez pas comme ça; *(b) P:* peloter, patouiller, tripatouiller (une femme).

pawing [pɔːiŋ], *s.* **1.** piaffement *m* (de cheval). **2.** *F:* patinage *m* (de qn, qch.); pelotage *m* (de qn).

pawkiness ['pɔːkinis], *s. Scot:* **1.** malice *f*, finasserie *f.* **2.** humour *m* de pince-sans-rire.

pawky ['pɔːki], *a. Scot:* **1.** rusé, malicieux, finaud. **2. a p. fellow,** un pince-sans-rire *inv*; **a p. answer,** une réponse normande.

pawl[1] [pɔːl], *s. Mec.E: etc:* linguet *m*, ginguet *m* (de cabestan, etc.); cliquet *m* (d'arrêt), chien *m* (d'arrêt), arrêtoir *m*; doigt *m* d'encliquetage; **disengaging p.,** cliquet de débrayage; **driving p.,** linguet d'entraînement; **to let fall the p.,** décliqueter; **p. and ratchet wheel, motion,** roue *f*, encliquetage *m*, à rochet; *Sm.a:* **rotating p.,** barrette *f* (de revolver); **p. head,** butoir *m* (du cabestan); **p. rim,** couronne *f* des linguets (du cabestan).

pawl[2], *v.tr. Mec.E: etc:* mettre les linguets à (un cabestan, etc.); fournir (qch.) d'un cliquet, d'un chien d'arrêt.

pawn[1] [pɔːn], *s.* **1.** gage *m*, nantissement *m.* **2. in p.,** en gage; chez le prêteur; **to put one's watch in p.,** mettre sa montre en gage; engager sa montre; déposer sa montre au crédit municipal; **to take sth. out of p.,** dégager, désengager, qch.; **p. office,** bureau *m* de prêteur sur gages; maison *f* de prêt; = crédit municipal; **p. ticket,** reconnaissance *f* (de dépôt de gage).

pawn[2], *v.tr.* *(a)* mettre (qch.) en gage; engager (qch.); *(b) St.Exch:* **pawned stock,** titres *mpl* en pension; *(c) A:* **to p. one's life, one's word, one's honour,** engager sa vie, sa parole, son honneur.

pawn[3], *s. Chess:* pion *m*; **ringed p.,** pion coiffé; *F: O:* **to be s.o.'s p.,** être le jouet de qn.

pawnable ['pɔːnəbl], *a.* engageable.

pawnbroker ['pɔːnbroukər], *s.* prêteur, -euse, sur gage(s); commissionnaire *m* au crédit municipal; **article at the pawnbroker's,** article *m* en gage.

pawnbroking ['pɔːnbroukiŋ], *s.* prêt *m* sur gage(s).

pawnee[1] [pɔː'niː], *s. Jur:* détenteur *m* du gage; créancier *m* sur gage.

Pawnee[2], *s. Ethn:* Paunie *mf*, Pawnee *mf.*

pawner ['pɔːnər], *s. Jur:* emprunteur, -euse, sur gage(s).

pawning ['pɔːniŋ], *s.* mise *f* en gage; engagement *m.*

pawnshop ['pɔːnʃɔp], *s.* bureau *m* de prêt sur gage(s); maison *f* de prêt; = crédit municipal.

pawpaw ['pɔːpɔː], *s. Bot:* = PAPAW.

pax [pæks]. **1.** *s.* *(a)* **p. romana,** la paix romaine; *(b) Ecc:* (i) paix; (ii) baiser *m* de paix. **2.** *int. Sch: F:* pouce!

paxillus [pæk'siləs], *s. Fung:* paxille *m.*

paxwax ['pækswæks], *s. Anat: F:* ligament cervical.

pay[1] [pei], *s.* **1.** paie *f*; salaire *m* (d'un ouvrier, etc.); appointements *mpl*; gages *mpl* (d'un domestique); traitement *m* (d'un fonctionnaire); indemnité *f* (d'un parlementaire); *Mil: etc:* solde *f*; **rate of p.,** taux *m* de salaire, etc.; **basic p.,** salaire, traitement, de base; **take-home p.,** salaire, etc., reçu (moins impôt retenu à la source, etc.); **back p.,** arrérages *mpl*, rappel *m*, de traitement, de salaire; **equal p.,** égalité *f* des salaires, des appointements (entre hommes et femmes); **holidays with p.,** congés payés; **severance p.,** indemnité *f* de cessation d'emploi; **unemployment p.,** allocation *f* de chômage; *Mil: etc:* solde de non-activité; *Mil: etc:* **p. and allowances,** solde et indemnités; **to allot, assign, part of one's p. to one's wife,** déléguer une partie de sa solde à sa femme; **to earn one's p.,** bien gagner son argent, son salaire; **to draw one's p.,** toucher son salaire, son traitement, son mois, sa solde; **p. day,** jour *m* de paie, *F:* la Sainte-Touche; **p. slip,** bulletin *m*, feuille *f*, de paie; **p. cheque,** chèque *m* de règlement de traitement, de salaire; **p. envelope** = salaire (payé en espèces); *Mil: etc:* **p. book,** livret *m* de solde; **p. voucher,** pièce justificative de solde; **p. parade,** rassemblement *m* pour le paiement de la solde; **to be in s.o.'s p.,** (i) être dans l'emploi de qn; (ii) être à la solde, aux gages, de qn. **2.** *attrib.* *(deriving from vb.* **to pay)** **p. desk,** caisse *f*; *Th: etc:* guichet *m*; **p. office,** (i) caisse; guichet; (ii) *Mil: etc:* bureau *m* de l'officier payeur, du trésorier; **p. gate,** tourniquet *m*; **p. bed,** lit *m* pour malade payant (dans un hôpital); *esp U.S:* **p. school,** école payante; *NAm:* **p. station, p. phone** = cabine *f* téléphonique; taxiphone *m*; **p. dirt,** (i) *Min:* minerai *m* exploitable; *(for gold)* alluvion exploitable, rémunérateur; (ii) *F:* projet, etc., rémunérateur, qui paie.

pay[2], *v.* *(p.t. & p.p.* **paid** [peid])

I. *v.tr. & i.* payer; *(a)* **to p. s.o. £100,** payer £100 à qn; **she paid him £100 for it,** elle le lui a payé £100; **how much do you p. for tea?** combien payez-vous le thé? **you have paid too much for it,** vous l'avez payé trop cher; *F:* **you've paid through the nose for it,** on vous a volé, salé, écorché; **the meat has been paid for,** la viande a été payée; **his uncle paid for his schooling,** son oncle a subvenu aux frais de ses études; **£1000 to be paid in four instalments,** £1000 payable en quatre termes; **how much is there to p.?** c'est combien? ça fait combien? *NAm: F:* **what's to p.?** qu'est-ce qui se passe? **how much did you (have to) p. for me?** combien avez-vous payé, dépensé, pour moi? je vous dois combien? **I'll p. (for you),** je payerai (votre billet, votre consommation, etc.); **p. at the gate, at the door,** entrée payante; **to p. cash (down), spot cash, ready money,** payer (argent) comptant, payer au comptant; **to p. in advance,** payer d'avance, par anticipation; **to p. in full,** payer intégralement, en totalité; *P.N:* *(on bus)* **p. as you enter,** (i) payez le conducteur en entrant; (ii) (utilisez le) distributeur automatique de billets (à l'intérieur); **p. as you earn,** *NAm:* **as you go,** retenue *f* (de l'impôt sur le revenu) à la base, à la source; *NAm:* **to p. as you go,** (i) payer ses factures promptement; (ii) ne jamais dépenser plus que l'on ne gagne; **could you lend me £5? I'll p. you back tomorrow,** peux-tu me prêter £5? je te rembourserai demain; **advance to be paid back within a year,** avance *f* restituable dans un an; **to p. s.o. back in his own coin,** rendre la pareille à qn; payer qn de la même monnaie; **to p. sth. down, on account,** verser une (somme à titre de) provision; verser des arrhes; *(b) Com: Fin: etc:* **to p. at maturity, at due date,** payer à échéance; **to p. on demand, on presentation,** payer à vue, à présentation; **dividend paid out of capital,** dividende prélevé sur le capital; **p. to the order of . . .,** payez à l'ordre de . . .; *(on cheque)* **p. self, p. cash,** payez (à l'ordre de) moi-même; **to p. in a cheque,** faire porter, verser, un chèque à son compte; **to p. money into s.o.'s account,** verser de l'argent au compte de qn; *Jur:* **to p. a sum of money into court,** cantonner une somme; *(c)* payer (ses employés, etc.); **to be paid by the hour, by the week,** être payé à l'heure, à la semaine; **we're paid on Fridays,** nous sommes payés le vendredi; **badly paid job,** situation mal payée, mal rémunérée; **he's not very well paid,** il n'est pas très bien payé; il ne gagne pas gros; **to p. for services,** rémunérer des services; **to p. s.o. for his trouble,** dédommager qn de sa peine; **to p. s.o. to do sth.,** payer qn pour faire qch.; **I wouldn't do it if you paid me, even if I were paid for it,** je ne le ferais pas même si on me payait; on me payerait que je ne le ferais pas; **we shall have to p. him to hold his tongue,** il va falloir acheter son silence; *(d)* **to p. a fine,** payer une amende; **to p. (off) a debt,** payer, solder, liquider, régler, acquitter (une dette); **to p. (off) a creditor,** rembourser, désintéresser, un créancier; **to p. off a mortgage,** purger une hypothèque; **to p. a bill,** (i) *(also* **an account),** payer, régler, acquitter, un compte, une facture; s'acquitter d'un compte; (ii) payer une traite, un effet; *(on receipted bill)* **paid,** pour acquit; *F:* **that's put paid to his account,** il a son compte; on lui a réglé son compte; **carriage to be paid by sender,**

Dom.Ec: éplucheur *m*; **vegetable p.,** (i) machine *f* à

carriage paid, le port est à la charge, aux frais, de l'expéditeur; *Cust:* **to p. (the) duty on sth.,** payer, acquitter, les droits sur qch.; (*e*) (i) **to p. tribute, homage, to s.o.,** faire honneur, hommage, à qn; *Mil:* **to p. honours to s.o.,** rendre les honneurs à qn; **to p. one's respects to s.o.,** présenter ses respects à qn; **to p. a visit to s.o.,** faire, rendre, une visite à qn; **please p. attention to what you are doing,** faites attention, s'il vous plaît, à ce que vous faites; (ii) **to p. for one's folly,** être victime de sa propre folie; **he paid for his rashness with his life,** il a payé sa témérité de sa vie; **to p. dearly for one's happiness,** payer cher son bonheur; **to p. dearly for one's experience,** acquérir de l'expérience à ses propres dépenses; **he paid for it up to the hilt,** il a expié durement sa faute; *F:* **he'll p. for this! I'll make him p. for this!** il me le payera cher! je le lui ferai payer! il ne l'emportera pas en paradis! (*f*) **it will p. you to do it,** c'est dans votre intérêt de le faire, vous y gagnerez à le faire; **it won't p. me,** je n'en tirerai aucun avantage; **business that doesn't p.,** affaire *f* qui ne rapporte pas, qui ne paie pas, qui n'est pas rentable; **his business isn't paying,** il ne fait pas ses affaires; **it wouldn't p.,** cela ne rapporterait pas, ne serait pas intéressant; **it will p. for itself,** cela s'amortira tout seul; **it pays to advertise,** la publicité rapporte; pas d'affaires sans réclame.

II. (*compound verbs*) **1. pay off,** *v.tr. & i.* (*a*) congédier (des ouvriers, etc.); licencier (des troupes); débarquer, mettre en congé (des marins); désarmer (un navire); (*b*) *Nau:* abattre sous le vent; laisser arriver; **to p. off the ship's head,** laisser arriver le navire; **to p. off on the right tack, on the wrong tack,** abattre de bon bord, à contre-bord; (*to small boat*) **p. off!** (restez) au large! (*c*) **the business seems to be paying off well,** l'affaire semble être très rentable; **all these years of work have paid off at last,** toutes ces années de travail sont enfin couronnées de succès.

2. pay out, *v.tr. & i.* (*a*) payer, verser, débourser; **I'm always having to p. out,** j'ai toujours la main à la poche; je suis toujours à débourser; (*b*) *F:* se venger (de qn, sur qn); rendre (à qn) la pareille; **I'll p. you out for that!** je vous revaudrai cela! (*c*) (*p.t.* **payed**) *Nau:* (laisser) filer (un câble, une touée); *Cin: etc:* débiter, dérouler (la bande de film, etc.).

3. pay up, *v.tr. & i.* payer, *F:* s'exécuter; se libérer (de ses dettes, etc.); **I finally made him p. up,** j'ai finalement réussi à le faire payer, débourser, *F:* casquer.

pay³, *v.tr.* (*p.t. & p.p.* **payed**, *occ.* **paid**) *Nau:* enduire (un navire) de goudron, de brai, de suif; goudronner, espalmer, brayer, suiffer (un navire).

payable ['peiəbl], *a.* **1.** payable, acquittable; **rates p. by the tenant** = impôts *m* à la charge du locataire; *Com:* **p. at sight, to order, to bearer,** payable à vue, à ordre, au porteur; **p. on presentation,** payable au comptant, à présentation; **p. on delivery,** payable à la livraison; **the amount that would have been p.,** le montant qui aurait été dû; **bill p. in one month, two months,** lettre *f* de change à une usance, à deux usances, à trente jours, à soixante jours; **p. on the 15th prox.,** valeur au 15 prochain; **to make an expense p. out of public funds,** assigner une dépense sur le trésor public; **to make a bill p. to s.o.,** faire un billet à l'ordre de qn; **cheque p. to bearer,** chèque *m* au porteur; **bonds made p. in francs,** bons libellés en francs; **bills p.,** *s. U.S:* **payables,** factures *f* à payer; *Book-k:* **bills p. book,** échéancier *m*. **2.** *Min:* (*of seam, etc.*) rémunérateur, exploitable.

paycheck ['peitʃek], *s. NAm:* chèque *m* de règlement de traitement, de salaire.

payee [pei'i:], *s.* (*a*) preneur, -euse, bénéficiaire *mf* (d'un bon de poste, etc.); **payable at address of p.,** payable à domicile; (*b*) *Com:* porteur *m* (d'un effet).

payer ['peiər], *s.* payeur, -euse, payant, -ante; **he's a good, a prompt, p.,** c'est un bon payeur; **he's a bad, a slow, p.,** il paie mal; *St.Exch:* **p. of contango,** reporté *m*.

paying¹ ['peiiŋ], *a.* **1.** (élève, etc.) payant; **p. guest,** pensionnaire *mf*. **2.** (*of business, etc.*) rémunérateur, -trice, lucratif, profitable; qui rapporte.

paying², *s.* **1.** paiement *m*, versement *m* (d'argent). **2.** (*a*) **p. back,** remboursement *m*, restitution *f* (d'un emprunt); (*b*) versement *m* (d'argent à la banque, etc.); **p.-in slip,** bulletin *m*, feuille *f*, de versement, de paiement; **p.-in book,** carnet *m* de versements; (*c*) **p. off,** (i) liquidation *f*, règlement *m*, amortissement *m* (d'une dette); purge *f* (d'une hypothèque); (ii) congédiement *m* (des ouvriers, etc.); licencement *m* (de troupes); débarquement *m* (de marins); désarmement *m* (d'un navire); *Navy:* **p. off pendant,** flamme *f* de fin de campagne; (*d*) **p. out,** (i) (*also* **p. up**) déboursement *m*; (ii) déroulement *m*, déroulage *m*, *Nau:* filage *m* (d'un câble, etc.); **p.-out reel,** dérouleuse *f*; *F:* **p. out, p. up, isn't his strong point,** il n'aime pas débourser, casquer.

paying³, *s.* goudronnage *m*; suiffage *m*; **p. stuff,** suif *m*.

payload ['peiloud], *s.* charge payante, commerciale, utile (d'un véhicule); charge utile (d'une fusée, d'un missile); *Av:* poids *m* utile.

paymaster ['peima:stər], *s.* trésorier *m*; *Mil: etc:* officier trésorier; *Navy:* commissaire *m* (de la Marine); **assistant p.,** sous-commissaire *m*, *pl.* sous-commissaires.

payment ['peimənt], *s.* **1.** (*act or fact of paying*) paiement *m*, versement *m* (d'argent); paiement, règlement *m*, acquittement *m* (d'une dette, etc.); remboursement *m* (d'un créancier); **subject to p.,** à titre onéreux, moyennant paiement; **without p.,** à titre gracieux; à titre bénévole; **terms of p.,** conditions *f* de paiement; **cash p.,** paiement (au) comptant, paiement argent comptant; **cash payments,** paiements effectués par la caisse; **p. in cash,** paiement en espèces, en numéraire; **p. by cheque,** paiement par chèque; **to present a cheque for p.,** présenter un chèque au paiement, à l'encaissement; **to stop p. on a cheque,** faire opposition sur un chèque, frapper un chèque d'opposition; **p. in full,** (i) paiement intégral, en totalité; (ii) liquidation *f* (d'un compte); *St.Exch:* **p. in full on allotment,** libération *f* (d'actions) à la répartition; **p. in full discharge,** paiement libératoire; **p. of balance,** paiement pour solde; **p. of interest,** paiement des intérêts; **p. by instalments,** paiement par acomptes, paiement échelonné; **(hire purchase) p.,** traite *f*; **down p.,** premier versement; **p. on account,** (i) paiement partiel; (ii) versement à titre d'acompte; acompte *m*; à-valoir *m inv*; **on p. of £100,** contre paiement de £100, moyennant (le paiement de) £100; **p. in advance,** paiement d'avance, par anticipation; **deferment of p.,** ajournement *m* de, du, paiement; **deferred p.,** paiement différé, retardé; **to defer, extend, the term of p.,** prolonger, différer, le paiement; **non p.,** défaut *m* de paiement; **to stop payments,** cesser, suspendre, les paiements; (*of bank*) fermer ses guichets; **capital payments,** mouvement *m* des capitaux; **p. schedule,** programme *m* de(s) paiements; **to order, authorize, p., to issue an order for p.,** autoriser le paiement (d'un compte); *Adm:* ordonnancer; *Jur:* **p. into court** = offre réelle consignée à la Caisse des Dépôts et Consignations; **to present a bill for p.,** présenter un effet au paiement, à l'encaissement; **in p. of your latest consignment,** en paiement de votre dernier envoi de marchandises. **2.** paiement, rémunération *f*; rétribution *f*; **as (a) p. for your services,** en rémunération de vos services; **my only p. was a thorough soaking,** pour toute récompense j'ai été trempé jusqu'aux os.

paynim ['peinim], *s. A: & Lit:* païen, -enne (musulman(e)); infidèle *mf*.

pay-off ['peiɔf], *s. NAm:* (*a*) paiement *m*, règlement *m*; (*b*) bénéfice *m*; récompense *f*; *F:* règlement de comptes; (*c*) facteur décisif, conclusif; **p.-o. test,** test final, décisif; (*d*) *F:* le dénouement, le fin mot (de l'histoire).

payroll ['peiroul], *s.* feuille *f* des appointements, des salaires; *Mil: etc:* feuille, état *m*, de solde; **to be on the p.,** émarger au budget.

pea¹ [pi:], *s.* **1.** (*a*) pois *m*; **climbing p.,** pois à rames; **marrowfat p.,** pois carré; **field p.,** pois des champs, pois gris; pisaille *f*; **dwarf p.,** pois nain; **sugar p.,** pois gourmand, (pois) mange-tout *m inv*; **p. pod, shell,** cosse *f*, gousse *f*, de pois; **p. sheller,** (i) (*pers.*) écosseur, -euse; (ii) (*device*) *U.S:* **p. huller,** écosseuse *f*; *U.S:* **p. vine,** plant *m* de petit pois; (*b*) *Cu:* **(green) peas,** petits pois; **split peas,** pois cassés; **p. soup,** soupe *f*, potage *m*, crème *f*, aux pois (cassés); (*thick*) purée *f* de pois; *F:* **p. souper,** purée de pois, brouillard *m* (jaune) à couper au couteau; (*c*) **sweet p.,** gesse odorante, pois de senteur; **everlasting p.,** gesse; pois vivace, pois de Chine; **bush p.,** thermopside *f*, thermopsis *m*; (*d*) *Ent:* **p. beetle, bug, weevil,** bruche *f* de pois, cosson *m*; *Crust:* **p. crab,** pinnothère *m*; (*e*) *a. & s.* **p. green,** vert feuille (*m*) *inv*; (*f*) **(conjuror's) p.,** muscade *f*; (*g*) *A.Med:* **issue p.,** pois à cautère. **2.** *Min:* **p. ore,** minerai *m* pisiforme; *Com:* **peas,** houille fine, fines *f*.

pea², *s. Nau:* bec *m* d'ancre.

peace [pi:s], *s.* **1.** (*a*) paix *f*; **country at p. with its neighbours,** pays en paix avec ses voisins; **in time of p.,** en temps de paix; **to make p. with a country,** faire la paix avec un pays; **to make (one's) p. with s.o.,** faire la paix, se réconcilier, avec qn; **to keep the p. between two people,** faire vivre en paix deux personnes; **patched-up p.,** paix plâtrée; **p. at any price,** la paix à tout prix; **p. with honour,** une paix honorable; **if you want p. prepare for war,** si tu veux la paix, tiens-toi prêt à la guerre, prépare la guerre; **p. treaty,** traité *m* de paix; **to broach, enter into, p. negotiations,** entamer des pourparlers de paix; **to make overtures for p.,** faire des ouvertures de paix; **to sue for p.,** demander, solliciter, la paix; **p. offering,** (i) *Jew.Rel:* sacrifice *m* de prospérités, de propitiation, d'actions de grâces; (ii) cadeau *m* de réconciliation; (*b*) traité de paix; **the P. of Amiens,** la Paix d'Amiens. **2. p. and order,** la paix et l'ordre public; le repos public; **to keep the p.,** (i) ne pas troubler l'ordre public; (ii) maintenir la concorde; veiller à l'ordre public; **to break, disturb, the p.,** troubler, violer, l'ordre public; troubler la tranquillité publique, la paix du pays; (*at night*) faire du tapage nocturne; **disturber of the p.,** violateur, -trice, de l'ordre public; tapageur, -euse; **justice of the p.** = juge *m* de paix; **to be sworn of the p.,** être nommé juge de paix; être nommé magistrat. **3.** (*a*) tranquillité *f* (de l'âme, etc.); **to live in p.,** vivre en paix; **for the sake of p. and quiet,** pour avoir la paix; **I'd like to be able to sleep in p.,** mon seul désir est de pouvoir dormir en paix; **to leave s.o. in p.,** laisser qn en paix, en repos; laisser qn tranquille; **he doesn't give me any p.,** il ne me donne ni paix ni trêve; **he gave me no p. until . . .,** il ne m'a pas laissé la paix tant que . . .; **my conscience is at p.,** ma conscience est en paix; **the p. of the evening, of the woods,** la tranquillité du soir, des bois; **p. be with you!** la paix soit avec vous! **p. to his memory!** paix à ses cendres! **go in p.!** allez en paix! **God rest his soul in p.!** que Dieu donne le repos à son âme! (*b*) *A:* **to hold one's p.,** se taire; garder le silence.

peaceable ['pi:səbl], *a.* **1.** pacifique; qui aime la paix; **p. man,** homme de paix. **2.** = PEACEFUL 2.

peaceableness ['pi:səbəlnis], *s.* caractère *m* pacifique (de qn).

peaceably ['pi:səbli], *adv.* **1.** pacifiquement. **2.** en paix.

peaceful ['pi:sful], *a.* **1.** paisible, calme, tranquille; **the p. countryside,** les campagnes paisibles, silencieuses; **p. death,** mort *f* tranquille. **2.** pacifique; qui porte la paix; qui ne trouble pas la paix; **p. settlement of a dispute,** règlement *m* pacifique d'un litige; règlement à l'amiable.

peacefully ['pi:sfuli], *adv.* **1.** paisiblement; (*a*) tranquillement; (*b*) en paix; *Jur:* **p. at home,** clos et coi. **2.** pacifiquement.

peacefulness ['pi:sfulnis], *s.* tranquillité *f*, paix *f*.

peacekeeping ['pi:ski:piŋ], *s.* maintien *m* de la paix.

peace-loving ['pi:slʌviŋ], *a.* (nation *f*) pacifique, qui aime la paix; (mari *m*, etc.) qui aime sa tranquillité.

peacemaker ['pi:smeikər], *s.* **1.** pacificateur, -trice, conciliateur, -trice; médiateur, -trice, de la paix; *B:* **blessed are the peacemakers,** bienheureux sont ceux qui procurent la paix. **2.** *P:* revolver *m*.

peach¹ [pi:tʃ], *s.* (*a*) pêche *f*; (*b*) **p. (tree),** pêcher *m*; *Ent:* **p. fly,** puceron *m* du pêcher; (*c*) *s. & a.* **p. (colour),** (couleur *f*) fleur de pêcher *inv*; (*d*) **p. palm,** péjiboie *m*; (*e*) *F:* **she's a p.,** elle est belle à croquer; c'est une jolie pépée, un beau brin de fille, une belle petite caille; **it's a p.,** c'est magnifique; c'est une perle.

peach², *v.i. P: O:* cafarder, moucharder; vendre la mèche; manger le morceau; **he peached to the boss,** il a rapporté ça au patron; **to p. on, against, s.o.,** dénoncer (un copain).

peachblossom ['pi:tʃblɔsəm], *s.* fleur *f* de pêcher.

peachblow ['pi:tʃblou], *s.* (couleur *f*) fleur de pêcher *inv*.

peachick ['pi:tʃik], *s. Orn:* paonneau *m*; jeune paon.

peachy ['pi:tʃi], *a.* (*a*) (*of skin, etc.*) velouté (comme une pêche); (*b*) *F:* agréable, jojo, juteux.

peacock¹ ['pi:kɔk], *s.* **1.** (*a*) *Orn:* paon *m*; **black-winged p.,** paon nigripenne; **Congo p.,** paon du Congo; **green, Java, p.,** paon spicifère; **Indian p.,** paon commun, bleu; **p. pheasant,** éperonnier *m*; (*b*) **to screech like a p.,** pousser des cris de paon; **as proud as a p.,** fier comme un paon; *Her:* **p. in its pride,** paon rouant; (*c*) **p. (blue),** bleu paon *m inv*; **p. (blue) ribbons,** des rubans bleu paon; (*d*) *Ent:* **p. butterfly,** paon (du jour); *Ich:* **p. fish,** paon de mer; *Algae:* **peacock's tail,** padine *f*; *Ann:* **p. worm,** sabelle *f*; (*e*) **p. coal,** houille miroitante. **2.** *Astr:* **the P.,** le Paon.

peacock², *v.i. O:* **to p. (about), to p. it,** se pavaner; paonner.

peafowl ['pi:faul], *s.* paon *m*, paonne *f*.

peahen ['pi:hen], *s.* paonne *f*.

peajacket ['pi:dʒækit], *s. Nau:* caban *m*.

peak¹ [pi:k], *s.* **1.** (*a*) visière *f* (de casquette, etc.); (*b*) bec *m* (d'une selle de bicyclette, d'une ancre, etc.); (*c*) pointe *f* (de barbe, de toit, etc.); **widow's p.,** pointe de cheveux sur le front; (*d*) *A:* bec (d'oiseau). **2.** *Nau:* (*a*) coqueron *m* (de la cale); **after p.,** coqueron arrière; arrière-bec *m* (d'un ponton); (*b*) pic *m*, corne *f*, empointure *f* (de voile); penne *f* (d'antenne); **gaff-sail p.,** point *m* de drisse; **p. halyard,** drisse *f* de pic; **with the flag at the p.,** le pavillon à la corne. **3.** (*a*) pic, cime *f*, sommet *m* (de montagne); **the highest peaks,** les plus hauts sommets; les points culminants; (*b*) pointe, apogée *m* (d'une courbe, d'une charge); *Med:* pointe, poussée *f* (d'une fièvre); *Ph:* sommet *m* (d'une courbe); crête *f* (d'une onde); **p. load,** charge maximum; débit *m* maximum (d'un générateur); **p. intensity,** intensité maximale, maximum; **p. to p. deviation,** déviation *f* de crête en crête; **p. to valley ratio,** taux *m* d'amplitude (d'une onde); *Atom.Ph:* **diffraction p.,** diffraction maximale, maximum; pic de diffraction; **photo p.,** pic photoélectrique; **resonance p.,** crête, pic, de résonance; *El: etc:* **p. current,** courant *m* de pointe, de crête; **p. power, p. voltage,** puissance *f*, tension *f*, de pointe, de crête; **p. load,** charge de pointe; **p.-load station,** centrale *f* de pointe; **p. voltmeter,** voltmètre *m* de pointe, de crête; **p. response,** réponse *f* de pointe (d'un transducteur); **p. limiter,** limiteur *m* d'amplitude; écrêteur *m*; **p. limiting,** limitation *f* d'amplitude; écrêtage *m*; **to cope with p. consumption,** couvrir, faire face à, la consommation de pointe; *Ind: etc:* **p. output,** (niveau *m*) record *m* de production; **p. year,** année *f* record; **prosperity was at its p.,** la prospérité était à son apogée, à son maximum; *El: Trans: T.V: etc:* **p. hours, period,** heures *f* de pointe; heures d'affluence; **off-p. hours, time,** heures creuses; temps mort (dans l'utilisation d'un matériel, etc.); **off-p. fare, tariff,** tarif *m* hors pointe, en dehors des périodes d'affluence.

peak², *v.* **1.** *v.tr. Nau:* apiquer (une vergue); **to p. the yard,** faire la penne; **to p. oars,** mâter les avirons. **2.** *v.i.* (*of whale*) plonger (à pic). **3.** *v.i.* (*of curve, load, etc.*) passer par son apogée.

peak³, *v.i.* (*a*) *A:* dépérir; s'étioler; (*b*) **to p. and pine,** tomber en langueur; tomber dans le marasme.

peaked [pi:kt], *a.* **1.** (*a*) (casquette) à visière; (*b*) **p. beard,** barbe *f* en pointe; (*c*) **high-p. hat,** chapeau (haut et) pointu; (*d*) *F:* **p. features,** traits tirés, hâves. **2.** (montagne *f*) à pic.

peakiness ['pi:kinis], *s. F:* pâleur *f*; air *m* malingre.

peaking ['pi:kiŋ], *s.* **1.** *Nau:* apiquage *m* (d'une vergue). **2.** *Ph: El: etc:* **p. coil,** bobine *f* de crête.

peaky ['pi:ki], *a. F:* pâlot, malingre, maigrelet, souffreteux; **to look p.,** avoir les traits tirés; être pâlot.

peal¹ [pi:l], *s.* (*a*) **p. of bells,** carillon *m*; **to ring a p.,** sonner un carillon; carillonner; **full p. of the bells,** volée *f* de cloches; **the bells are in full p.,** les cloches *f* sonnent à toute volée; (*b*) retentissement *m*; grondement *m* (du tonnerre, de l'orgue); coup *m* (de tonnerre); **a loud p. at the bell,** un coup de sonnette retentissant; **the organ was in full p.,** l'orgue *m* donnait de toutes ses anches; (*c*) **peals of laughter,** éclats *m* de rire.

peal². **1.** *v.i.* (*a*) (*of bells*) (i) carillonner; (ii) sonner à toute volée; (*b*) (*of thunder, of the organ*) retentir, gronder; (*of laughter*) résonner. **2.** *v.tr.* (*a*) sonner (les cloches) à toute volée; (*b*) carillonner (un air).

pean¹ [pi:n], *s. Her:* sable semé d'hermines d'or.

pean², *s. Tls:* panne *f* (de mareau); **soldering p.,** panne de fer à souder.

peanut ['pi:nʌt], *s.* (*a*) arachide *f*; *Com:* cacah(o)uète *f*, cacahouette *f*; **p. oil,** huile *f* d'arachide; **p. butter,** beurre *m* d'arachide; (*b*) *F:* **peanuts,** une bagatelle; deux fois rien; **this salary's peanuts compared with . . .,** ces appointements sont dérisoires à côté de . . .; (*c*) *P:* barbiturique *m*.

pear ['pɛər], *s.* **1.** (*a*) poire *f*; **butter p.,** beurré *m*; **musk p.,** muscat *m*, poire musquée; **choke p.,** poire d'angoisse, d'étranguillon; *Ent:* **p. midge,** cécidomyie *f* des poirettes; (*b*) (*tree*) poirier *m*; (*c*) **avocado p.,** poire d'avocat; (*tree*) avocatier *m*; **prickly p.,** figue *f*, figuier *m*, de Barbarie; **garlic p.,** crataeva *m* gynandra; (*d*) *Echin:* **sea p.,** bolténie *f*; (*e*) *El:* **p. switch,** (interrupteur *m* à) poire.

pearceite ['pi:əsait], *s. Miner:* pearcéite *f*, pearixte *f*.

peardrop ['pɛədrɔp], *s.* bonbon parfumé à la poire.

pearl¹ [pə:l], *s.* **1.** perle *f*; **real p.,** perle fine, naturelle; **virgin p.,** perle vierge; **p. of a fine water,** perle d'une belle eau; **cultured p.,** perle cultivée, de culture; perle japonaise; **imitation p.,** perle fausse, artificielle, d'imitation; **p. necklace,** collier *m* de perles; **p. diving, fishing,** pêche *f* des perles, des huîtres perlières; **p. diver, fisher,** pêcheur *m* de perles; **p.(-bearing) oyster,** huître perlière; **p. mussel,** mulette perlière; **p. grey,** gris *m* de perle *inv*; gris perle *inv*; **p. white,** d'une blancheur de perle; **to cast pearls before swine,** jeter des perles devant les, aux, pourceaux; *Her:* **coronet set with pearls,** couronne grêlée; *F:* **she's a p.,** c'est une perle, un trésor. **2.** (*a*) **mother of p.,** nacre *f* (de perle); **p. button,** bouton *m* de nacre; **p. shell,** coquille nacrée; (*b*) *Miner:* **p. opal,** cacholong *m*; **p. spar,** spath perlé; **p. mica,** margarite *f*; (*c*) *El:* **p. bulb,** ampoule opale. **3.** (*a*) **p. barley, tapioca,** orge, tapioca perlé; *Cu:* **to bring sugar to the p.,** cuire le sucre au perlé; (*b*) *Pharm:* perle, globule *m*; (*c*) *Med:* **epithelial p.,** perle épidermique; *Vet:* **p. disease,** tuberculose bovine; (*d*) **pearls of dew,** perles de rosée; *Bot:* **p. grass,** brize *f*, amourette *f*; *Algae:* **p. moss,** mousse perlée, d'Irlande; carragheen *m*; (*e*) *Com:* **p. ash,** carbonate de potasse brut; (cendre *f*) gravelée *f*; perlasse *f*. **4.** *Typ:* parisienne *f*, corps *m*. **5.** *Ven:* pierrure *f*, perlure *f* (de la meule d'un cerf).

pearl². **1.** *v.i.* (*a*) (*of moisture, etc.*) perler; former des gouttelettes; (*of sugar*) faire la perle; (*b*) pêcher des perles; (*c*) (*of the sky, etc.*) se nacrer. **2.** *v.tr.* (*a*) perler (de l'orge); (*b*) *Cu:* cuire (le sucre) au perlé; *Lit:* **dawn was pearling the sky,** l'aurore nacrait le ciel.

pearl³, *s. Lacem:* picot *m*, engrêlure *f* (de dentelle); **p. edge,** bordure *f* à picots.

pearled [pə:ld], *a.* **1.** perlé; à surface perlée, granitée. **2.** *Cu:* (sucre) concentré au filé, au perlé.

pearler ['pə:lər], *s.* **1.** pêcheur *m* de perles. **2.** bateau perlier.

pearliness ['pə:linis], *s.* **1.** teint perlé. **2.** tons nacrés.

pearling ['pə:liŋ], *s.* pêche *f* de perles.

pearlite ['pə:lait], *s. Metall:* perlite *f*.

pearlstone ['pə:lstoun], *s. Miner:* perlite *f*.

pearlweed, pearlwort ['pə:lwi:d, -wə:t], *s. Bot:* sagine *f*.

pearly ['pə:li]. **1.** *a.* (*a*) perlé; nacré; **p. (white) teeth,** dents perlées, de perle; *Moll:* **p. nautilus,** nautile *m*, nautilus *m*; *Vet:* **p. disease,** tuberculose bovine; (*b*) *A:* qui renferme des perles; (mer) où abondent les perles; (*c*) **p. king,** marchand *m* des quatre saisons de Londres (qui porte les jours de fête un costume couvert de boutons de nacre); **p. queen,** (i) femme, (ii) héritière, d'un *pearly king*. **2.** *s.* (*a*) *F:* bouton *m* de nacre; (*b*) **pearlies,** costume de *pearly king*, etc.; (*c*) membre *m* d'une famille de *pearly kings*.

pearmain ['pɛəmein], *s. Arb:* **p. (apple),** permaine *f*.

pear-shaped ['pɛəʃeipt], *a.* en forme de poire; piriforme.

peasant ['pez(ə)nt], *s.* paysan, -anne; campagnard, -arde; *Pej:* rustre *mf*; *Hist:* **the Peasants' War,** la Guerre des Paysans; (*b*) petit fermier; (*c*) ouvrier, -ière, agricole.

peasantry ['pezəntri], *s. Hist:* le paysannat, la paysannerie, les paysans *m*.

pease [pi:z], *s.* (*a*) *A:* pois *mpl*; (*b*) **p. pudding,** purée *f* de pois (cassés).

peasecod ['pi:zkɔd], *s. A:* cosse *f*, gousse *f*, de pois.

pea-shaped ['pi:ʃeipt], *a.* pisiforme.

peashooter ['pi:ʃu:tər], *s.* petite sarbacane.

peastone ['pi:stoun], *s. Miner:* pisolithe *f*.

peat [pi:t], *s.* (*a*) tourbe *f*; cendrière *f*; **p. bog, p. moor, p. moss,** tourbière *f*; marais tourbeux; **p. cutting, digging,** tourbage *m*; **p. cutter,** tourbier *m*; **p. spade,** louchet *m*; **p. drag,** puchette *f*; **to dig, cut, p.,** extraire de la tourbe; tourber; (*b*) **(turf, sod, block, of) p.,** motte *f* de tourbe; **to put a p. on the fire,** mettre une motte de tourbe sur le feu; (*c*) **p. reek,** (i) fumée de tourbe; (ii) *F:* whisky (chauffé à la tourbe et qui a le goût de la fumée); (*d*) *Bot:* **p. moss,** sphaigne *f*.

peatery ['pi:təri], *s.* tourbière *f*.

peaty ['pi:ti], *a.* **1.** tourbeux; **p. soil,** sol tourbeux, sol tourbier. **2.** (goût *m*) de fumée de tourbe.

peav(e)y, peavie ['pi:vi], *s. For:* grappin *m*.

pebble¹ ['pebl], *s.* **1.** (*a*) caillou, -oux *m*; **p. beach,** plage *f* de galets; *F:* **you're not the only p. on the beach,** vous n'êtes pas unique au monde; il n'y a pas que vous sur la terre; *Anthr:* **p. culture,** civilisation *f* de galet aménagé; (*b*) *Lap:* **Scotch p.,** agate *f* (de ruisseaux d'Écosse); **Egyptian p.,** caillou d'Égypte; (*c*) *Const:* **p. dash,** crépi (moucheté); cailloutage *m*; **p.-dash finish,** crépissure *f*; **p.-dash paper,** papier chagriné; **to give a p.-dash finish to a wall,** crépir un mur; **p. dashing,** crépissage *m*; **p. paving,** cailloutage; **p. work,** cailloutage, caillout *m*; (*d*) *Exp: Ball:* **p. powder,** poudre *f* à gros grains. **2.** *Opt:* (*a*) cristal *m* de roche; (*b*) lentille *f* en cristal de roche; *F:* **p. lensed spectacles,** lunettes *f* à verres très épais. **3.** *Leath:* maroquinage (communiqué au cuir); **p. leather,** cuir crépi, maroquiné. **4.** *Tex:* **p. weave,** granité *m*.

pebble², *v.tr. Leath:* crépir, maroquiner (le cuir); **pebbled paper,** papier chagriné.

pebble-dash ['pebldæʃ], *v.tr. Const:* crépir (un mur).

pebbling ['pebliŋ], *s.* crépissage *m*; *Leath:* maroquinage *m*.

pebbly ['pebli], *a.* caillouteux; (plage *f*) à galets.

pebrine [pe'bri:n], *s. Ser:* pébrine *f*.

pebrinous ['pebrinəs], *a. Ser:* pébrineux.

pecan ['pi:kən, 'pe-; pi'kæn], *s. Bot:* (*a*) **p. (nut),** pacane *f*, (noix) pecan *m*; (*b*) **p. (tree),** pacanier *m*.

peccability [pekə'biliti], *s. Theol:* peccabilité *f*.

peccable ['pekəbl], *a.* peccable.

peccadillo [pekə'dilou], *s.* peccadille *f*; faute légère; **to punish a child for a p.,** punir un enfant pour une vétille; **it's a mere p.,** il n'y a pas là de quoi fouetter un page, un chat.

peccancy ['pekənsi], *s. Theol:* **1.** nature *f* coupable; état *m* de péché, de faute. **2.** péché *m*, faute *f*, offense *f*.

peccant ['pekənt], *a.* **1.** coupable; en faute. **2.** *A.Med:* **p. humours,** humeurs peccantes.

peccary ['pekəri], *s. Z:* pécari *m*; cochon noir, cochon des bois; sanglier *m* d'Amérique.

peccavi [pe'kɑ:vi:, pe'keivai], *s.* & *int.* peccavi (*m*); **to cry p.,** faire son mea-culpa.

peck¹ [pek], *s.* **1.** (*a*) coup *m* de bec; (*b*) *F:* (*kiss*) bécot *m*; **to give s.o. a p.,** bécoter qn. **2.** (*mark*) **fruit covered with pecks,** fruit couvert de picotures *f*. **3.** *P: A:* boustifaille *f*, mangeaille *f*, becquetance *f*.

peck². **1.** *v.tr.* (*a*) (*of bird*) picoter, becqueter, béqueter (qch., qn); donner un coup de bec à (qn); (*of bird*) **to p. a hole in sth.,** faire un trou dans qch. (avec le bec); percer qch. à coups de bec; **fruit that has been pecked,** fruit couvert de picotures; **to p. to death,** tuer à coups de bec; (*b*) *F:* (*kiss*) bécoter, baisoter (qn). **2.** *v.i.* & *ind.tr.* **to p. (at sth.),** picoter (qch.); donner des coups de bec (à qch.); *F:* manger du bout des dents; **to p. at one's food,** pignocher, mangeotter, son repas; *F:* **don't keep pecking at me!** ne me taquine pas comme ça! **to p. out s.o.'s eyes,** crever les yeux de qn à coups de bec.

peck³, *s.* (*a*) *A.Meas:* = 9,09 litres; (*b*) picotin *m* (d'avoine, etc.); *A:* **to eat a p. of salt with s.o.,** manger un minot de sel avec qn; vivre longtemps ensemble; (*c*) tas *m* (de poussière, etc.); foule *f* (de malheurs); **she's had a p. of trouble,** elle a eu bien des malheurs; **you'll have to eat a p. of dirt before you die,** avaler un grain de poussière ne vous fera pas de mal.

pecker ['pekər], *s.* **1.** *Orn:* *F:* pic vert. **2.** *Tls:* pioche *f*, piochon *m*. **3.** *P:* (*a*) nez *m*, bec *m*; (*b*) *F:* courage *m*; cran *m*; **to keep one's p. up,** ne pas se laisser abattre; **keep your p. up!** ne vous découragez pas! ne perdez pas courage! du courage! ne calez pas!

peckhamite ['pekəmait], *s. Miner:* peckhamite *f*.

pecking ['pekiŋ], *s.* **1.** becquetage *m*; **p. order,** *Orn:* hiérarchie du becquetage; *F:* hiérarchie sociale. **2.** piochage *m*.

peckish ['pekiʃ], *a. F:* **to be, feel, p.,** se sentir le ventre creux.

Pecksniff ['peksnif], *s.m.* faux saint; pharisien; hypocrite (du personnage de Dickens).

pecopteris [pe'kɔptəris], *s. Paleont:* pécoptéris *m*.

pectase ['pekteis], *s. Ch:* pectase *f*.

pectate ['pekteit], *s. Ch:* pectate *m*.

pecten, *pl.* **pectines** ['pektən, 'pektini:z], *s.* **1.** *Nat.Hist:* peigne *m* (d'œil d'oiseau, de patte de scorpion, etc.). **2.** *Moll:* coquille *f* Saint-Jacques; peigne, pèlerine *f*; (*genus*) pecten *m*.

pectic ['pektik], *a. Ch:* pectique.

pectin ['pektin], *s. Ch:* pectine *f*.

Pectinacea [pekti'neisiə], *s.pl. Moll:* pectinacés *m*.

pectinacean [pekti'neisiən], *s. Moll:* pectinacé *m*.

pectinaceous [pekti'neiʃəs], *a. Moll:* pectinacé.

pectinal ['pektinəl], *a. Nat.Hist:* pectiné.

pectinate(d) ['pektineit(id)], *a. Nat.Hist:* pectiné; *Ent:* **p. antenna,** antenne pectinée; *Ich:* **p. branchiae,** branchies pectinées; *Bot:* **p. leaf,** feuille pectinée.

pectination [pekti'neiʃ(ə)n], *s. Nat.Hist:* structure pectinée.

pectineal [pekti'niəl], *a. Anat:* pectinéal, -aux.

pectinibranch ['pektinibræŋk], **pectinibranchian, pectinibranchiate** [pektini'bræŋkiən, -'bræŋkieit], *a.* & *s. Moll:* pectinibranche (*m*).

Pectinibranchia(ta) [pektini'bræŋkiə, -bræŋki'eitə], *s.pl. Moll:* pectinibranches *m*.

pectinid ['pektinid], *s. Moll:* pectinidé *m*.

Pectinidae [pek'tinidi:], *s.pl. Moll:* pectinidés *m*.

pectinite ['pektinait], *s. Paleont:* pectinite *f*.

pectizable [pek'taizəbl], *a. Ch:* pectisable.

pectization [pektai'zeiʃ(ə)n], *s. Ch:* pectisation *f*.

pectize ['pektaiz], *v.tr. Ch:* pectiser.

pectolite ['pektəlait], *s. Miner:* pectolite *f*.

pectoral ['pektərəl]. **1.** *a. Anat: Med: etc:* pectoral, -aux; **(Bishop's) p. cross,** croix pectorale; *Ich:* **p. fin,** nageoire pectorale. **2.** *s.* (*a*) *Jew.Rel:* pectoral *m*; (*b*) *Anat:* (muscle) pectoral; (*c*) *Pharm:* pectoral.

pectoriloquy [pektəriləkwi], *s. Med:* pectoriloquie *f*.

pectose ['pektous], *s. Ch:* pectose *f*.

pectous ['pektəs], *a.* pecteux, -euse.

peculate ['pekjuleit]. **1.** *v.i.* commettre des malversations; détourner des fonds; voler l'État. **2.** *v.tr.* détourner (des fonds, les deniers publics).

peculation [pekju'leiʃ(ə)n], *s.* péculat *m*, malversation *f*, déprédation *f*; détournement *m* de fonds; *Jur:* vol public; prévarication *f*.

peculator ['pekjuleitər], *s.* déprédateur, -trice; concussionnaire *mf*; péculateur *m*; prévaricateur, -trice.

peculiar [pi'kju:liər]. **1.** *a.* (*a*) particulier; **I have my own p. reasons for wishing it,** j'ai des raisons particulières pour le désirer; **this gait is p. to him,** cette façon de marcher lui est particulière, lui est propre; **smell p. to an animal,** odeur *f* spécifique d'un animal; **the condor**

is **p. to the Andes,** le condor est particulier aux Andes; **privilege p. to military men,** privilège réservé aux militaires; *U.S: Hist:* **p. institution,** esclavage *m* (dans les États du Sud); (*b*) special, -aux; particulier; **of p. interest,** d'un intérêt tout particulier; *Typ:* **p. sorts,** sortes spéciales; *Theol:* **the p. people,** le peuple élu; *Rel.H:* **the P. People,** secte religieuse qui pratique la thérapeutique fondée sur la prière; (*c*) (*of thg*) étrange; (*of pers.*) bizarre, singulier; original, -aux; **p. flavour,** goût *m* insolite; **well, that's p.,** voilà qui est singulier, qui est bizarre! **a p. girl,** une drôle de fille; **he, she, is a little p.,** c'est un(e) excentrique; **to be p. in one's dress,** s'habiller singulièrement. **2.** *s.* (*a*) propriété particulière; privilège particulier; (*b*) *Ecc:* paroisse *f* ou église *f* hors de la juridiction de l'ordinaire.

peculiarity [pikju:li'æriti], *s.* **1.** trait distinctif; particularité *f*; **a p. of his was that he couldn't spell,** il se distinguait par sa mauvaise orthographe; il avait ceci de particulier qu'il manquait complètement d'orthographe; *Adm: A:* (*on passport*) **special peculiarities,** signes particuliers. **2.** bizarrerie *f*, singularité *f*; originalité *f*, excentricité *f*.

peculiarize [pi'kju:liəraiz], *v.tr.* singulariser.

peculiarly [pi'kju:liəli], *adv.* (*a*) personnellement; (*b*) particulièrement; d'une façon toute particulière; (*c*) étrangement; bizarrement, singulièrement; d'une façon bizarre ou excentrique.

peculium [pi'kju:liəm], *s. Rom.Ant:* pécule *m*.

pecuniary [pi'kju:niəri], *a.* pécuniaire; **p. difficulties,** embarras financiers; ennuis *m* d'argent; *Jur:* **for p. gain,** dans un but lucratif; **p. offence,** délit puni d'une amende.

pedagogic(al) [pedə'gɔdʒik(l)], *a.* pédagogique.

pedagogically [pedə'gɔdʒikəli], *adv.* pédagogiquement.

pedagogics [pedə'gɔdʒiks], *s.pl.* (*usu. with sg. const.*) la pédagogie.

pedagogism ['pedəgɔdʒizm], *s. Pej:* pédagogisme *m*.

pedagogist ['pedəgɔdʒist], *s.* pédagogue *mf*, éducateur, -trice.

pedagogue ['pedəgɔg], *s. Pej:* pédagogue *mf*, pédant, -ante.

pedagogy ['pedəgɔdʒi], *s.* pédagogie *f*.

pedal[1] ['ped(ə)l, 'pi:-], *a.* du pied; *Anat:* pédieux, -ieuse; **p. ganglion, p. muscle,** ganglion, muscle, pédieux.

pedal[2] ['ped(ə)l], *s.* **1.** pédale *f* (de machine, de véhicule, de bicyclette, d'instrument de musique, etc.); (*a*) *Aut: Mch: etc:* **accelerator p.,** pédale d'accélérateur; **control p.,** pédale de commande; **p. control,** commande *f* par pédale; **clutch p.,** pédale de débrayage, d'embrayage; **gear(-change) p.,** pédale de changement de vitesse; **brake p.,** pédale de frein; *Cy:* **rat-trap p.,** pédale à scies; *Av:* **rudder p.,** pédale de direction, de palonnier; **p. linkage,** attelage *m*, tringlage *m*, de pédale; **p. pull-rod,** tringle *m* de traction, de pédale; **p. fulcrum,** axe *m* (d'articulation) de pédale; **p. stroke,** course *f* de la pédale; **p. clearance,** course morte de la pédale; **p. return spring,** ressort *m* de rappel de pédale; **to depress the p.,** agir sur la pédale; **to release the p.,** lâcher la pédale; *Cy:* **to cycle up a hill standing on one's pedals,** monter une côte en danseuse; *Mec.E:* **p. lathe,** tour *m* à pédale; *Dom.Ec:* **p. bin,** poubelle *f* à pédale; (*b*) (*of piano*) **soft p.,** petite pédale; **loud, damper, p.,** grande pédale; (*of organ*) **swell p.,** pédale expressive; **composition p.,** pédale de combinaison; **p. board,** pédalier *m*; clavier *m* de pédales; **p. point,** point *m* d'orgue. **2.** *Mus:* **p. (note),** (note) fondamentale *f*; pédale.

pedal[3], *v.i.* (**pedalled**) **1.** *Cy: etc:* pédaler. **2.** *Mus:* (*a*) (*organ*) jouer sur le pédalier; toucher les pédales; pédalier; (*b*) (*piano*) mettre la pédale.

pedal[4] ['ped(ə)l], *s. Hatm:* **1. Tuscan pedals,** paille *f* de Toscane. **2. five-, seven-end p.,** tresse *f* de cinq, sept, brins.

pedalcar ['ped(ə)lkɑ:r], *s.* **1.** vélocar *m*. **2.** voiture *f* à pédales.

pedalcraft ['ped(ə)lkrɑ:ft], *s.* pédalo *m*.

pedalfer [pe'dælfər], *s. Geol:* pedalfer *m*.

pedalia [pe'deiliə], *s. Bot:* pédalie *f*.

Pedaliaceae [pedeili'eisii:], *s.pl. Bot:* pédaliacées *f*.

pedaliaceous [pedeili'eiʃəs], *a. Bot:* pédaliacé.

pedalier [pedə'liər], *s.* (*of organ*) pédalier *m*; clavier *m* de pédales.

pedaline ['pedəlain], *s. Hatm:* pédaline *f*.

pedalist, pedal(l)er ['pedəlist, -ər], *s. O:* cycliste *mf*; pédaleur, -euse.

pedalo ['pedəlou], *s.* pédalo *m*.

pedal-operated [pedəl'ɔpəreitid], *a. Mec.E: etc:* commandé, mu, par pédale(s); **p.-o. countershaft,** renvoi *m* de mouvement avec débrayage par pédale.

pedal pusher ['pedəlpuʃər], *s. F:* **1.** cycliste *mf*; pédaleur, -euse. **2.** *Cost: U.S:* **pedal pushers,** pantalon *m* corsaire.

pedant ['pedənt], *s.* pédant, -ante.

pedantic [pi'dæntik], *a.* pédant; pédantesque.

pedantically [pi'dæntik(ə)li], *adv.* pédantesquement; en pédant.

pedanticism [pi'dæntisizm], *s.* pédanterie *f*.

pedantism, pedantry ['pedəntizm, -tri], *s.* pédantisme *m*, pédanterie *f*.

pedantize ['pedəntaiz], *v.i.* pédantiser.

pedantocracy [pedæn'tɔkrəsi], *s.* pédantocratie *f*.

pedantocratic [pedæntou'krætik], *a.* pédantocratique; **p. government,** pédantocratie *f*.

Pedata [pe'deitə], *s.pl. Z:* pédates *m*.

pedate ['pedeit], *a.* **1.** *Bot:* (*of leaf*) palmilobé, pédalé. **2.** *Z: etc:* qui a des pieds, des pattes.

peddle ['ped(ə)l]. **1.** *v.i.* (*a*) faire le colportage; (*b*) *O:* **to p. (about, around),** baguenauder, musarder; s'occuper de futilités. **2.** *v.tr.* (*a*) colporter (des marchandises); **to p. drugs,** trafiquer en stupéfiants; faire le trafic des stupéfiants; (*b*) *O:* répartir (qch.) parcimonieusement, avec parcimonie.

peddler ['pedlər], *s.* colporteur *m*.

peddling[1] ['pedliŋ], *a. F:* (*a*) (*of pers.*) (i) chipotier; (ii) musard; (*b*) (*of thg*) futile, mesquin, insignifiant; **p. attitude (of mind),** esprit gagne-petit.

peddling[2], *s.* colportage *m*.

pederast ['pedəræst, 'pi:-], *s.m.* pédéraste.

pederastic ['pedəræstik, 'pi:-], *a.* pédérastique.

pederasty ['pedəræsti, 'pi:-], *s.* pédérastie *f*.

pedesis [pe'di:sis], *s. Ph:* pédèse *f*; mouvement brownien.

pedestal ['pedist(ə)l], *s.* **1.** *Arch: Sculp: etc:* piédestal, -aux *m*; socle *m*; (*small*) piédouche *m*; **to put s.o. on a p.,** mettre qn sur un piédestal, sur le chandelier. **2.** (*a*) socle (de pompe, etc.); support *m*, colonne *f* (de projecteur, etc.); table-support *f*, *pl.* tables-supports; *Av:* **jet p.,** support de turboréacteur; *Furn:* **p. table,** guéridon *m*; table *f* à pied central; **p. writing table,** bureau *m* ministre; *Artil:* **p. mounting,** affût *m* à piédestal, à pivot central; *Dom.Ec:* **p. washbasin,** lavabo *m* à pied; (*b*) *Mec.E:* palier *m*, chaise *f*, chevalet *m* (de coussinet); chandelier *m* (de chaudière); **p. box,** (i) boîte *f* des coussinets; (ii) *Rail:* boîte d'essieu, de graissage (d'une locomotive); (*c*) *Rail:* plaque *f* de garde (de locomotive); (*d*) *Atom.Ph:* plaque convertisseuse. **3.** cuvette *f* (d'une harpe). **4.** *T.V:* signal *m*, impulsions *fpl*, de suppression; **p. level,** niveau *m* de noir; **p. mixer,** mélangeur *m* des impulsions de suppression.

pedestalled ['pedist(ə)ld], *a.* à piédestal, à socle, à piédouche; (*of table*) à pied central.

pedestrian [pi'destriən]. **1.** *a.* (*a*) pédestre; (*b*) (style, etc.) prosaïque, terre à terre. **2.** *s.* (*a*) piéton *m*; **p. crossing,** passage pour piétons, passage clouté; (*b*) *Sp: A:* pédestrien, -ienne.

pedestrianism [pi'destriənizm], *s.* **1.** *Sp: A:* pédestrianisme *m*. **2.** *Lit:* prosaïsme *m*; style *m* terre à terre.

pedetid [pe'detid], *a. & s. Z:* pédétidé (*m*).

Pedetidae [pe'detidi:], *s.pl. Z:* pédétidés *m*.

pediatrician [pi:diə'triʃ(ə)n], **pediatrist** [pi:di'ætrist], *s. Med:* pédiatre *mf*.

pediatrics [pi:di'ætriks], **pediatry** ['pi:diætri], *s. Med:* pédiatrie *f*.

pedicab ['pedikæb], *s.* cyclo-pousse *m*, vélo-pousse *m*, *pl.* cyclo-, vélo-pousses.

pedicel ['pedisel], *s.* **1.** *Bot:* pédicelle *m*. **2.** *Nat.Hist:* pédicelle, pédoncule *m*, pédicule *m*.

pedicellaria, *pl.* **-iae** [pedise'lɛəriə, -ii:], *s. Echin:* pédicellaire *m* (d'oursin).

pedicellate [pedi'seleit], *a.* **1.** *Bot:* pédicellé. **2.** *Nat.Hist:* pédicellé, pédonculé, pédiculé.

pedicellina [pedise'lainə], *s. Nat.Hist:* pédicelline *f*.

Pedicellinidae [pedise'linidi:], *s.pl. Nat.Hist:* pédicellinidés *m*.

pedicle ['pedikl], *s. Nat.Hist:* = PEDICEL 2.

pedicled ['pedikld], *a. Nat.Hist:* pédiculé.

pedicular [pe'dikjulər], *a.* (maladie, etc.) pédiculaire.

pediculate, *s. Ich:* pédiculé *m*.

pediculate(d) [pe'dikjuleit(id)], *a.* = PEDICELLATE 2.

Pediculati [pedikju'leitai], *s.pl. Ich:* pédiculates *m*.

pedicule ['pedikjul], *s. Nat.Hist:* pédicule *m*; *Ven:* pivot *m*.

Pediculidae [pedi'kju:lidi:], *s.pl. Ent:* pédiculidés *m*.

pediculosis [pedikju'lousis], *s. Med:* pédiculose *f*, phtiriase *f*, maladie *f* pédiculaire.

pediculous [pe'dikjuləs], *a.* (*a*) pédiculaire; (*b*) (*of pers.*) pouilleux.

pedicure[1] ['pedikjuər], *s.* **1.** (*pers.*) (*also* **pedicurist**) pédicure *mf*. **2.** soins *mpl*, traitement *m*, pédicure.

pedicure[2], *v.tr.* pédicurer.

pedigree[1] ['pedigri:], *s.* **1.** arbre *m* généalogique. **2.** (*a*) ascendance *f*, généalogie *f* (de qn); (*b*) *Breed:* certificat *m* d'origine, pedigree *m* (d'un chien, etc.); **p. dog, bull,** chien, taureau *m*, de (pure) race, de bonne lignée, de bonne souche, qui a de la race; **p. sire,** reproducteur *m* d'élite. **3.** origine *f*, dérivation *f* (d'un mot).

pedigree[2], *v.tr.* fournir le pedigree (d'un chien, etc.).

pedimanous [pe'dimənəs], *a. Z:* pédimane.

pediment ['pedimənt], *s.* **1.** *Arch:* fronton *m*; (*small*) fronteau *m*. **2.** *Geol:* **(rock) p.,** pédiment *m*.

pedimental [pedi'ment(ə)l], *a. Arch:* de fronton.

pedimentation [pedimen'teiʃ(ə)n], *s. Geol:* pédimentation *f*.

pedimented ['pedimentid], *a. Arch:* à fronton.

pedipalp(id) ['pedipælp, pedi'pælpid], *s. Arach:* pédipalpe *m*.

Pedipalpida [pedi'pælpidə], *s.pl. Arach:* pédipalpes *m*.

pepdipalpous [pedi'pælpəs], *a. Arach:* pédipalpe.

pedipalpus, *pl.* **-i** [pedi'pælpəs, -ai], *s. Arach:* pédipalpe *m*.

pediplain, pediplane ['pediplein], *s. Geol:* pédiplaine *f*.

pediplanation [pediplə'neiʃ(ə)n], *s. Geol:* pédiplanation *f*.

pedlar ['pedlər], *s.* colporteur *m*; marchand ambulant, (marchand) forain *m*; **drug p.,** trafiquant, ante, en stupéfiants.

pedobaptism [pi:dou'bæptizm], *s. Rel:* pédobaptisme *m*.

pedobaptist [pi:dou'bæptist], *s. Rel:* pédobaptiste *mf*.

pedocal ['pedoukæl], *s. Geol:* pédocal *m*.

pedogenesis[1] [pedou'dʒenisis], *s. Geol:* pédogénèse *f*.

pedogenesis[2] [pi:dou'dʒenisis], *s. Biol:* paedogénèse *f*, pédogénèse *f*.

pedogenetic [pi:doudʒe'netik], *a. Biol:* paedogénétique, pédogénétique.

pedogenic [pedou'dʒenik], *a. Geol:* pédogénétique.

pedologic(al)[1] [pedou'lɔdʒik(l)], *a. Geol:* pédologique.

pedologic(al)[2] [pi:dou'lɔdʒik(l)], *a. Med:* pédologique.

pedologist[1] [pe'dɔlədʒist], *s. Geol:* pédologue *mf*.

pedologist[2] [pi:'dɔlədʒist], *s. Med:* pédologue *mf*.

pedology[1] [pe'dɔlədʒi], *s. Geol:* pédologie *f*.

pedology[2] [pi:'dɔlədʒi], *s. Med:* pédologie *f*.

pedometer [pe'dɔmitər], *s.* pédomètre *m*, podomètre *m*, odomètre *m*, compte-pas *m inv*.

pedophilia [pi:dou'filiə], *s. Psy:* pédophilie *f*.

pedrail ['pedreil], *s. Mec.E:* **p. chain,** chaîne *f* sans fin à patins (de tracteur).

peduncle [pe'dʌŋkl], *s.* **1.** *Bot:* pédoncule *m*, scape *m*; hampe florale. **2.** *Nat.Hist:* pédicelle *m*, pédoncule *m*, pédicule *m*.

peduncular [pe'dʌŋkjulər], *a.* pédonculaire.

pedunculate [pe'dʌŋkjuleit], *a.* pédonculé; **p. oak,** chêne pédonculé; (chêne) rouvre *m*.

pee[1] [pi:], *v.i. F:* faire pipi.

pee[2], *s. F:* pipi *m*; **to go and have a p.,** aller faire pipi.

peek[1] [pi:k], *s.* regard furtif; coup d'œil (furtif).

peek[2], *v.i.* jeter un regard furtif, un coup d'œil furtif (sur qn, qch.); risquer un coup d'œil.

peekaboo ['pi:kəbu:]. **1.** *int.* coucou! **2.** *s. attrib.* (*a*) *Cost:* (corsage, etc.) (i) d'un tissu transparent, en mousseline, en voile; (ii) avec, en, broderie(s) ajourée(s); (*b*) *Cmptr:* **p. system,** système *m* de recherches documentaire à cartes perforées.

peel[1] [pi:l], *s. Hist:* **p.(-house, -tower),** petite tour carrée (construite sur la frontière écossaise).

peel[2], *s.* **1.** pelleron *m*, rondeau *m* (de boulanger); **oven p.,** pelle *f* à four, à enfourner. **2.** *Typ:* ferlet *m*.

peel[3], *s.* pelure *f* (de pomme, etc.); écorce *f*, peau *f*, *Cu:* zeste *m* (de citron, d'orange); **candied p.,** zeste confit, zeste d'Italie; écorces confites; **candied orange p.,** zeste d'orange confit; orangeat *m*; **candied lemon p.,** zeste de citron confit; citronnat *m*.

peel[4]. **1.** *v.tr.* (*a*) peler (un fruit); éplucher (des pommes de terre, des crevettes); décortiquer (un chêne, des amandes); écorcer (un bâton, etc.); (*with passive force*) **apples that p. easily,** pommes qui se pèlent facilement; **to p. (off) the bark, the skin,** enlever l'écorce, la peau; excorier la peau (de qn); *O:* **I've peeled my shin,** je me suis enlevé la peau du devant de la jambe; *Cu:* **to p. the outer skin off a lemon,** zester un citron; *Ind:* **to p. timber (into thin plates),** dérouler des troncs de bois. **2.** *v.i.* (*a*) **to p. (off),** (*of paint, etc.*) s'écailler, s'écaler; (*of skin*) peler, s'excorier, *Med:* se desquamer; (*b*) (*of the nose, etc.*) peler; se dépouiller de sa peau; (*of tree*) se décortiquer; (*of wall*) se décrépir; (*of tyre*) se déchaper; (*c*) *Sp: F:* se déshabiller; (*of boxer*) se mettre le torse à nu; (*of runner*) se mettre en maillot; **to p. for a fight,** mettre bas la jaquette pour se battre; tomber la veste; (*d*) **to p. off,** se détacher (de la formation).

peel[5], *s. Ich: Dial:* **(salmon) p.,** saumoneau *m*.

peeler[1] ['pi:lər], *s.* **1.** (*pers.*) (*a*) éplucheur, -euse; (*b*) *F:* strippeuse *f*. **2.** *Tls:* (*a*) *Ind: etc:* éplucheur *m*; (*b*)

Dom.Ec: éplucheur *m*; **vegetable p.,** (i) machine *f* à éplucher les légumes; (ii) rasoir *m* à légumes; **orange, lemon, p.,** zesteur *m*, zesteuse *f*.

peeler[2], *s. Bak:* enfourneur *m*, défourneur *m*.

peeler[3], *s. F: A:* (*policeman*) sergent *m* de ville; sergot *m*.

peeling ['pi:liŋ], *s.* **1.** (*a*) épluchage *m*, épluchement *m*; écorçage *m*, écorcement *m*; *Ind:* **wood p., veneer p.,** déroulage *m*; **wood-p. machine,** dérouleuse *f*; (*b*) **p. (off),** écaillement *m*; *Med:* desquamation *f* (de l'épiderme); (*c*) déchapage *m* (d'un pneu). **2. peelings,** (i) épluchures *f* (de pommes de terre, etc.); (ii) *Med: etc:* écailles *f*.

Peelite ['pi:lait], *s. Eng. Hist:* peeliste *m*; partisan *m* de Sir Robert Peel.

peen[1] [pi:n], *s. Tls:* panne *f* (de marteau); **ball p.,** panne ronde, sphérique, bombée; **cross p.,** panne en travers; **straight p.,** panne en long; **p. hammer,** marteau *m* à panne; **ball-p. hammer,** marteau à panne rode, sphérique; marteau de mécanicien.

peen[2], *v.tr. Metalw:* marteler; rabattre; mater; panner.

peening ['pi:niŋ], *s. Metalw:* martelage *m*; **shot p.,** granaillage *m*.

peep[1] [pi:p], *s.* piaulement *m*, pépiement *m* (d'oiseau); cri *m* (de souris); *F:* **if I hear so much as a p. out of you,** si vous faites le moindre bruit.

peep[2], *v.i.* (*of bird*) piauler, pépier; (*of mouse*) crier.

peep[3], *s.* **1.** coup d'œil (furtif, par l'entre-bâillement de la porte, par le trou de la serrure, etc.); **to have, take, a p. at sth.,** jeter un regard furtif sur qch.; **to get a p. at sth.,** entrevoir qch. **2.** filtrée *f* (de lumière); petite flamme (de gaz); **at p. of day, at p. of dawn,** au point du jour; dès l'aube.

peep[4], *v.i.* **1. to p. at s.o., sth.,** regarder qn, qch., à la dérobée; jeter un coup d'œil furtif sur qn, qch.; **to p. into a room,** jeter un regard furtif dans une pièce (par l'entre-bâillement de la porte, par la fenêtre, etc.); **to p. round the corner, through the door,** glisser un œil, risquer un coup d'œil, *F:* un œil, au coin de la rue, par la porte; **I saw you peeping through the keyhole,** je vous ai vu regarder par le trou de la serrure; **to p. out,** risquer un œil. **2. to p. (out),** se laisser entrevoir, se montrer; (*of flower, mental qualities, etc.*) percer, pointer; **her curls peeped out from under her hat,** ses boucles *f* ressortaient de dessous son chapeau; **violets peeping (up) from the grass,** violettes *f* qui émergent au milieu de l'herbe.

peep-bo ['pi:pbou]. **1.** *int.* coucou! **2.** *s.* **to play at p.-bo,** jouer à cache-cache (avec un enfant).

peeper ['pi:pər], *s.* **1.** curieux, -euse; indiscret, -ète. **2.** *P:* **peepers,** yeux *m*, mirettes *f*, quinquets *m*.

peephole ['pi:phoul], *s.* **1.** judas *m*. **2.** *Mec.E: etc:* (trou *m* de) regard *m*; regard, orifice *m*, de visite. **3.** *Sm.a:* œilleton *m* (d'une hausse).

peeping[1] ['pi:piŋ], *s.* = PEEP[1].

peeping[2], *a.* **1.** qui regarde à la dérobée; **P. Tom,** curieux *m*, indiscret *m*. **2.** (*of flower, etc.*) perçant, pointant.

peepshow ['pi:pʃou], *s.* optique *f*; vues *fpl* stéréoscopiques.

peepsight ['pi:psait], *s. Sm.a:* hausse *f* à trou, à œilleton; hausse de combat.

peepul ['pi:pəl], *s. Bot:* **p. (tree),** arbre *m* des conseils.

peer[1] [piər], *s.* **1.** pair *m*; pareil, -eille, égal, -ale; **you will not find his, her, p.,** vous ne trouveriez pas son pareil, sa pareille; il n'y en a pas deux comme lui, comme elle. **2. p. of the realm,** pair du Royaume-Uni; **life p.,** pair à vie.

peer[2]. *Lit:* **1.** *v.tr.* égaler (qn); être l'égal de (qn). **2.** *v.i.* **to p. with s.o., sth.,** égaler qn, qch.

peer[3], *v.i.* **1.** (*a*) **to p. at s.o., sth.,** scruter qn, qch., du regard (avec une attention soutenue); **to p. into s.o.'s face,** scruter le visage de qn; dévisager qn; **to p. into a chasm,** sonder un gouffre des yeux; plonger le regard dans un gouffre; **he peered (out) into the night,** il cherchait à percer l'obscurité; (*b*) **to p. round the corner, over the wall,** risquer un coup d'œil au coin de la rue, par-dessus le mur. **2.** *A:* apparaître.

peerage ['piəridʒ], *s.* **1.** pairie *f*; **life p.,** pairie personnelle; **to confer a p. on s.o., to raise s.o. to the p.,** conférer une pairie à qn; élever qn à la pairie; **conferment of a p. on s.o.,** anoblissement *m* de qn; élévation *f* de qn à la pairie. **2.** *coll.* **the p.,** les pairs *m*. **3. p. (book),** almanach *m* nobiliaire; nobiliaire *m*.

peeress ['piəres], *s.f.* pairesse; **p. in her own right,** pairesse de son propre chef.

peering ['piəriŋ], *a.* (regard, etc.) curieux, scrutateur, inquisiteur.

peerless ['piəlis], *a. Lit:* sans pareil, sans pair, sans second; hors de pair; inimitable, incomparable; **p. beauty,** beauté à nulle autre seconde.

peerlessly ['piəlisli], *adv. Lit:* incomparablement, inimitablement.

peeve[1] [pi:v], *v.tr. F:* fâcher, irriter, barber (qn).

peeve[2], *s. F:* ennui *m*, grief *m*, barbe *f*, emmerdement *m*.

peeved [pi:vd], *a. F:* fâché, irrité, ennuyé.

peevish ['pi:viʃ], *a.* atrabilaire, irritable, quinteux, geignard; *F:* gnan-gnan; **p. child,** enfant maussade, pleurnicheur.

peevishly ['pi:viʃli], *adv.* maussadement; d'un air chagrin, maussade; avec humeur.

peevishness ['pi:viʃnis], *s.* maussaderie *f*, grognonnerie *f*; mauvaise humeur; hargne *f*.

peewit ['pi:wit], *s. Orn:* **1.** vanneau (huppé). **2. p. (gull),** mouette rieuse.

peg[1] [peg], *s.* **1.** (*a*) cheville *f* (en bois), (*small*) chevillette *f*; fiche *f*; fausset *m*, fosset *m* (d'un tonneau); *Mec.E:* (i) cheville, clavette *f*, goupille *f*; (ii) goujon *m*, ergot *m*; *Const:* **slate p.,** pointe *f* à ardoise; *Games:* **cribbage p.,** fiche; (*b*) ranche *f*, enture *f* (d'échelier); (*c*) **hat p., coat p.,** patère *f*; **clothes off the p.,** vêtements *m* de confection; (*d*) **clothes p.,** pince *f* à linge; (*e*) piquet *m* (de tente, etc.); *Surv:* jalonnette *f*; (*croquet*) **starting p., finishing p.,** piquet de départ, d'arrivée; (*f*) *Mus:* cheville (de violon, etc.); bouton *m* (de corde de harpe); **p. box,** chevillier *m*; (*g*) *F:* **he's a square p. in a round hole,** il n'est pas à sa place, à son affaire; il n'est pas dans son emploi; il n'est pas taillé pour cela; **to take s.o. down a p. (or two),** remettre qn à sa place; faire baisser qn de ton; faire baisser le ton à qn; rabattre le caquet à qn; faire mettre de l'eau dans son vin à qn; **that's a p. to hang a grievance on,** voilà un prétexte de plainte. **2.** (*a*) pointe, fer *m* (de toupie); pied *m*, pique *f* (de violoncelle); **p. top,** toupie *f*; *A.Cost:* **p.-top trousers, p.-tops,** pantalon *m* à la hussarde; (*b*) *P: O:* jambe *f*, quille *f*; **not to stir a p.,** ne pas bouger d'une semelle; (*c*) *O:* **p. leg,** jambe de bois. **3.** doigt *m* (de whisky, etc.); **to mix oneself a stiff p.** = se faire un grog bien tassé.

peg[2], *v.* **(pegged)**

I. *v.tr.* **1.** cheviller (un assemblage, deux choses l'une à l'autre); brocher (des peaux); **to p. clothes on the line,** accrocher du linge sur la corde (avec des épingles); *Bootm:* **pegged soles,** semelles chevillées, brochées. **2.** *Games:* marquer (des points). **3.** *St.Exch: Fin:* **to p. the market, the exchange,** stabiliser le marché, le cours du change (en achetant et en vendant à tout venant); maintenir le marché ferme; *esp.* maintenir le cours du change. **4.** *Mil: P: O:* **to be pegged,** être accusé d'un délit.

II. (*compound verbs*) **1. peg away,** *v.i. F:* **to p. away (at sth.),** travailler ferme, travailler assidûment (à qch.); piocher, bûcher (un sujet); **you must keep pegging away,** il faut persévérer, il faut continuer.

2. peg down, *v.tr.* (*a*) fixer, assujettir, (un filet, etc.) avec des piquets; **pegged down by regulations,** entravé par des règlements; (*b*) *F:* **you can never p. him down,** impossible de le faire (i) prendre une décision, (ii) répondre oui ou non.

3. peg out, (*a*) *v.tr.* **to p. out a claim,** piqueter, jalonner, (a)borner, une concession; **to p. out a line,** jalonner une ligne; *Const:* **to p. out the ground plan,** implanter le tracé des fondations; (*b*) *v.i.* (i) (*croquet*) toucher le piquet final (et se retirer de la partie); **ball pegged out,** balle vagagonde; (ii) *P:* mourir; casser sa pipe; passer l'arme à gauche; lâcher la rampe.

pegamoid ['pegəmɔid], *s. R.t.m:* pégamoïd *m*.

peganite ['pegənait], *s. Miner:* péganite *f*.

Pegasus ['pegəsəs], (*a*) *Pr.n. Gr.Myth: Astr:* Pégase *m*; *Lit:* **to mount one's P.,** monter sur Pégase; enfourcher Pégase; (*b*) *s. Ich:* **p. (fish),** pégase.

pegboard ['pegbɔ:d], *s.* (*a*) *Cmptr:* pegboard *m*; (*b*) *U.S:* table *f* à trous (de solitaire, etc., pour y planter les chevilles).

pegging ['pegiŋ], *s.* **1.** chevillage *m*; *Bootm:* **p. awl,** broche *f*. **2.** *Sp:* **it's still level p.,** ils sont encore à égalité. **3.** *St.Exch: Fin:* stabilisation *f* (du marché, etc.); blocage *m* (de la livre sterling, etc.).

Peggy ['pegi]. *Pr.n.f.* (*dim. of Margaret*) = Margot.

pegmatite ['pegmətait], *s. Miner:* pegmatite *f*.

pegmatoid ['pegmətɔid], *a. Miner:* pegmatoïde.

pegomancy ['pegoumænsi], *s.* pégomancie *f*.

peignoir ['peinwɑ:r], *s. Cost:* peignoir *m*.

pejoration [pedʒə'reiʃ(ə)n], *s.* péjoration *f*.

pejorative [pe'dʒɔrətiv, pi-; 'pi:dʒ-]. **1.** *a.* péjoratif. **2.** *s.* (mot) péjoratif *m*.

pejoratively [pe'dʒɔrətivli, pi-], *adv.* péjorativement.

pekan ['pek(ə)n], *s. Z:* pékan *m*; martre *f* du Canada, martre du Pennaut.

peke [pi:k], *s. F:* (chien) pékinois *m*.

peke-faced ['pi:kfeist], *a.* (chat) à museau aplati (comme un pékinois).

Pekin [pi:'kin]. **1.** *Pr.n. Geog:* Pékin; *Anthr:* **P. man,** homme de Pékin, homme de Chine, sinanthrope *m*; *Husb:* **P. (duck),** canard *m* (de) pékin; pékin *m*. **2.** *s. Tex:* pékin.

Pekinese, Pekingese [pi:ki'ni:z, -ki'ŋi:z]. **1.** *a. Geog:* pékinois. **2.** *s.* (*a*) *Geog:* Pékinois, -oise; (*b*) (chien *m*) pékinois *m*; **p. bitch,** pékinoise *f*.

Peking [pi:'kiŋ]. *Pr.n. Geog:* Pékin.

pekoe ['pi:kou], *s.* **p. (tea),** péko(ë) *m*; **orange p.,** péko orange.

pelada [pi'lɑ:də], **pelade** [pi'leid], *s. Med:* pelade *f*.

pelage ['pelidʒ], *s.* pelage *m*; robe *f* (du cheval); toison *f* (du mouton).

Pelagia [pi'leidʒiə], *Pr.n.f. Rel.H:* Pélagie.

Pelagian[1] [pi'leidʒiən], *a. & s. Rel.H:* pélagien, -ienne.

pelagian[2], *a.* = PELAGIC.

Pelagianism [pi'leidʒiənizm], *s. Rel.H:* pélagianisme *m*.

pelagic [pi'lædʒik], *a. Oc:* pélagien, pélagique; **p. zone,** région *f* pélagique; **p. deposit,** dépôt *m* pélagique.

Pelagius [pi'leidʒiəs]. *Pr.n.m. Rel.H:* Pélage.

Pelagothuria [pelægou'θju:riə], *s. Echin:* pelagothuria *f*.

pelamid, pelamyd ['peləmid], *s. Ich:* (*a*) pélamide *f*, pélamyde *f*; (*b*) jeune thon *m*.

pelargonate [pe'lɑ:gəneit], *s. Ch:* pélargonate *m*.

pelargonic [pelɑ:'gɔnik], *a. Ch:* pélargonique.

pelargonium [pelɑ:'gouniəm], *s. Bot:* pélargonium *m*, *F:* géranium *m*; *Hort:* **trailing p.,** géranium lierre.

Pelasgi [pi'læzgai], *Pr.n.pl. Gr.Hist:* Pélasges *m*.

Pelasgian [pe'læzgiən]. *Gr.Hist:* **1.** *a.* = PELASGIC. **2.** *s.* Pélasge *m*.

Pelasgic [pe'læzgik], *a. Gr.Hist:* pélasgien, pélasgique.

Pelé ['pelei]. *Pr.n. Geol:* **Pelé's hair,** cheveux *mpl* de Pélée.

Pelea [pe'li:ə], *s. Z:* péléee *f*.

Pelean [pe'li:ən], *a. Geol:* péléen; **P. eruption,** éruption péléenne.

Pelecanidae [peli'kænidi:], *s.pl. Orn:* pélécanidés *m*, les pélicans *m*.

Pelecaniformes [pelikæni'fɔ:mi:z], *s.pl. Orn:* pélécaniformes *m*.

Pelecanoides [pelikæ'nɔidi:z], *s. Orn:* pélécanoïde *m*.

Pelecanoididae [pelikæ'nɔididi:], *s.pl. Orn:* pélécanoïdidés *m*.

pelecypod [pe'lesipɔd], *a. & s. Moll:* pélécypode (*m*).

Pelecypoda [pele'sipədə], *s.pl. Moll:* pélécypodes *m*.

pelerine ['peləri:n], *s. A.Cost:* pèlerine *f*.

Peleus ['pi:lju:s]. *Pr.n.m. Gr.Myth:* Pélée.

Pelew [pe'lju:]. *Pr.n. Geog:* **the P. Islands,** les Palaos *f*.

pelf [pelf], *s. Pej:* richesses *fpl*, lucre *m*.

pelham ['peləm], *s. Harn:* pelham *m*.

pelican ['pelikən], *s.* **1.** *Orn:* pélican *m*; **Dalmatian p.,** pélican frisé; **white p.,** pélican blanc. **2.** *Her:* **p. in her piety,** pélican avec sa piété. **3.** (*a*) **p. fish,** eurypharynx *m*; (*b*) *Moll:* **pelican's foot,** pied *m* de pélican.

peliom ['peliəm], *s. Miner:* péliom *m*.

Pelion ['pi:liən]. *Pr.n. A.Geog:* Pélion *m*.

pelisse [pe'li:s], *s. A.Cost:* **1.** pelisse *f* (de femme, d'enfant). **2.** *Mil:* **Hussar p.,** pelisse, dolman *m*.

pelite ['pi:lait], *s. Miner:* pélite *f*.

pelitic [pe'litik], *a. Geol:* pélitique.

pellagra [pe'lægrə, -'lei-], *s. Med:* pellagre *f*.

pellagrin [pe'lægrin, -'lei-], *s. Med:* pellagreux, -euse.

pellagroid [pe'lægrɔid, -'leigrɔid], *a. Med:* pellagroïde.

pellagrous [pe'lægrəs, -'leigrəs], *a. Med:* pellagreux.

pellet ['pelit], *s.* (*a*) boulette *f* (de papier, etc.); pelote *f* (d'argile, etc.); pastille *f* (de matière plastique); (*b*) *Sm.a: etc:* grain *m* de plomb; projectile *m* (de pistolet à bouchon, de sarbacane); **airgun pellets,** plombs *m* pour carabine à air comprimé; *Artil:* **striker p.,** concuteur *m* à bille (d'une fusée d'obus); (*c*) *Pharm:* pilule *f*, grain *m*, bol *m*; *Med:* pellet *m*; *Dent:* **gold p.,** coussinet *m* d'or; (*d*) *Orn:* **pellets,** pelotes de réjection, boulettes d'aliments régurgités (par les hiboux, etc.); ingluvie *f* (des oiseaux de proie); (*e*) *Husb:* granulé *m*; (*f*) *Metall:* boulette; *Ch:* boulette, bâtonnet *m*, anneau *m*, tube *m*; (*g*) *Her:* tourteau *m* de sable.

pelletierine [pe'letiəri:n, -ain], *s. Pharm:* pelletiérine *f*.

pelletization [pelitai'zeiʃ(ə)n], *s.* pelletisation *f*; réduction *f* en boulettes.

pelletize ['pelitaiz], *v.tr.* pastiller; réduire en boulettes.

pelletizer ['pelitaizər], *s.* **1.** (*pers.*) pastilleur, -euse. **2.** machine *f* à pastiller, pastilleur *m*, pastilleuse *f*.

pellicle ['pelikl], **pellicule** ['pelikju:l], *s.* (*a*) pellicule *f*; (*b*) membrane *f*.

pellicular, pelliculate [pe'likjulər, -leit], *a.* (*a*) pelliculaire; (*b*) membraneux.

pellitory ['pelitəri], *s. Bot:* **1. p. of Spain,** pyrèthre *m*, anacycle *m*. **2. wall-p., p. of the wall,** pariétaire *f*; *F:* casse-pierre(s) *m inv*; perce-muraille *f*, *pl.* perce-murailles.

pell-mell ['pel'mel]. **1.** *adv.* pêle-mêle; (courir, etc.) à la débandade. **2.** *a.* mis pêle-mêle; en confusion, en désordre. **3.** *s.* pêle-mêle *m*, confusion *f*.

pellucid [pe'lju:sid], *a. Lit:* (*a*) pellucide, transparent, translucide; (*b*) (style *m*, etc.) lucide, limpide; (*c*) (esprit) clair, lucide.

pellucidity [pelju'siditi], **pellucidness** [pe'lju:sidnis], *s. Lit:* (*a*) transparence *f*, translucidité *f*; (*b*) lucidité *f*, limpidité *f* (du style, etc.).

Pelmanism ['pelmənizm], *s.* le système mnémotechnique de Pelman.

Pelmatozoa [pelmætou'zouə], *s.pl. Echin:* pelmatozoaires *m.*

pelmatozoan [pelmætou'zouən], *a.* & *s. Echin:* pelmatozoaire (*m*).

pelmatozoic [pelmætou'zouik], *a. Echin:* pelmatozoaire.

pelmet ['pelmit], *s. Furn:* lambrequin *m.*

pelobatid [pelou'bætid], *a.* & *s. Amph:* **p. (toad),** pélobate *m.*

Pelobatidae [pelou'bætidi:], *s.pl. Amph:* pélobatidés *m.*

pelodytes [pe'lɔditi:z], **pelodytid** [pelou'di:tid], *s. Amph:* pélodyte *m.*

Pelomedusidae [peloumi'dju:sidi:], *s.pl. Rept:* pélomédusidés *m.*

pelopaeus [pelou'pi:əs], *s. Ent:* pélopée *m*, scéliphron *m.*

Peloponnese, Peloponnesus (the) [ðəpeləpə'ni:z, -'ni:səs], *Pr.n. Geog:* le Pélopon(n)èse.

Peloponnesian [peləpə'ni:ʃən]. **1.** *a. Geog:* pélopon(n)ésien; *A.Hist:* **the P. War,** la Guerre du Pélopon(n)èse. **2.** *s. Geog:* Pélopon(n)ésien, -ienne.

peloria [pe'lɔ:riə], *s. Bot:* pélorie *f.*

pelorian, peloriate, peloric [pe'lɔ:riən, -'lɔ:rieit, -'lɔ:rik], *a. Bot:* pélorié.

pelorism ['pelɔrizm], *s. Bot:* pélorisme *m.*

pelorization [pelərai'zeiʃ(ə)n], *s. Bot:* pélorisation *f.*

pelorize ['peləraiz], *v.tr. Bot:* péloriser.

pelorus [pe'lɔ:rəs], *s. Nau:* alidade *f*; taximètre *m.*

pelota [pə'loutə], *s. Games:* pelote *f* basque; **p. player,** pelotari *m.*

pelt[1] [pelt], *s.* **1.** peau *f*, dépouille *f*, fourrure *f* (de mouton ou de chèvre); **p. wool,** avalies *fpl.* **2.** *Tan:* (i) (*with hair on*) peau verte; (ii) (*without hair*) peau en tripe.

pelt[2], *v.tr.* écorcher (un animal); écorcer (un bâton); **pelted ash,** bâtons de frêne dépouillés de leur écorce.

pelt[3], *s.* **1.** grêle *f* (de pierres); fracas *m* (de la pluie). **2.** *adv.phr.* **(at) full p.,** (courir, s'enfuir) à toute vitesse, à toutes jambes, ventre à terre, à la galope. **3.** *Dial: F:* explosion *f* de colère; **to be in a p.,** être en colère.

pelt[4]. **1.** *v.tr.* **to p. s.o. with stones, to p. stones at s.o.,** lancer, jeter, des pierres à qn; lapider qn; **to p. s.o. with snowballs,** lancer des boules de neige à qn; **he was pelted with invitations,** il a été accablé d'invitations; **he pelted abuse at them,** il les a criblés d'injures. **2.** *v.i.* (*a*) (*of rain, etc.*) **to p. (down),** tomber à verse, à seaux; (*b*) **invitations came pelting in,** on a été inondé d'invitations; (*c*) (*of pers.*) **to p. off,** partir à toute vitesse; se sauver à toutes jambes.

pelta ['peltə], *s. Gr.Ant:* pelta *f*, pelte *f.*

peltandra [pel'tændrə], *s. Bot:* peltandra *m.*

peltast ['peltæst], *s. A.Gr.Mil:* peltaste *m.*

peltate ['pelteit], *a. Nat.Hist:* pelté; en forme de bouclier.

Peltier ['peltiei]. *Pr.n. El:* **P. effect,** effet *m* Peltier.

peltiform ['peltifɔ:m], *a. Nat.Hist:* pelté, peltiforme.

peltigera [pel'tidʒərə], *s. Moss:* peltigera *m*, peltigère *f.*

pelting[1] ['peltiŋ], *a.* **p. rain,** pluie battante.

pelting[2], *s.* = PELT[3] 1.

Pelton ['peltən]. *Pr.n. Hyd.E:* **P. wheel,** turbine tangentielle; turbine, roue *f*, Pelton.

peltry ['peltri], *s.* pelleterie *f*; peausserie *f*; peaux *fpl.*

peludo [pe'lu:dou], *s. Z:* peludo *m*; tatou pelu, velu; poyou *m*; encoubert *m.*

pelure [pe'ljuər], *s.* **p. (paper),** papier *m* pelure (d'oignon).

pelvetia [pel'vi:ʃiə], *s. Algae:* pelvetia *f*, goémon noir.

pelvic ['pelvik], *a. Anat:* pelvien; **p. cavity,** cavité pelvienne; **p. girdle,** ceinture pelvienne; **p. bone,** os *m* du bassin; **p. limb,** membre pelvien; **p. index,** indice pelvien; *Ich:* **p. fins,** pelviennes *f.*

pelviform ['pelvifɔ:m], *a.* pelviforme.

pelvimeter [pel'vimitər], *s.* pelvimètre *m.*

pelvimetry [pel'vimitri]. *s.* pelvimétrie *f.*

pelviotomy [pelvi'ɔtəmi], *s. Obst:* pelviotomie *f.*

pelviperitonitis [pelviperitə'naitis], *s. Med:* pelvipéritonite *f.*

pelvis ['pelvis], *s. Anat:* (*a*) bassin *m*; **false p.,** pelvis *m*; (*b*) bassinet *m* (du rein).

pelycosaur ['pelikousɔər], *s. Paleont:* pélycosaure *m*, pélycosaurien *m.*

Pelycosauria [pelikou'sɔ:riə], *s.pl. Paleont:* pélycosauriens *m.*

pelycosaurian [pelikou'sɔ:riən], *a.* & *s. Paleont:* pélicosaurien (*m*).

pemmican ['pemikən], *s.* pemmican *m.*

pemphigoid ['pemfigɔid], *a. Med:* pemphigoïde.

pemphigous ['pemfigəs], *a. Med:* (*a*) qui tient du pemphigus; (*b*) atteint de pemphigus.

pemphigus ['pemfigəs], *s.* **1.** *Med:* pemphigus *m*; maladie vésiculeuse (de la peau); **p. vulgaris,** pemphigus vrai, vulgaire. **2.** *Ent:* pemphigus.

pemphredon [pem'fri:dən], *s. Ent:* pemphredon *m.*

pen[1] [pen], *s.* **1.** (*a*) parc *m*, enclos *m* (à moutons, etc.); **chicken p.,** (i) poulailler *m*; (ii) cage *f* à poules; **bull p.,** toril *m*; **pig p.,** *U.S:* **hog p.,** porcherie *f*; **to let the cattle out of the p.,** déparquer les bestiaux; (*b*) *Nau:* cage. **2.** *Const:* **lime-slacking p.,** bassin *m* pour éteindre la chaux. **3.** *Navy:* **submarine p.,** abri *m* de sous-marins; (*of destroyers*) **to go in the pens,** aller aux appontements; *Av:* **revetted p.,** alvéole *f* de départ; abri alvéolé. **4.** (*in W. Indies*) (*farm*) élevage *m.*

pen[2], *v.tr.* **(penned) to p. (up, in),** parquer (des moutons, etc.); (r)enfermer, confiner (qn dans une chambre, etc.); **house in which one feels penned up,** maison *f* où on se sent parqué comme des moutons, où on se sent à l'étroit; **to p. oneself up in one's office,** s'enfermer, se claquemurer, dans son bureau.

pen[3], *s.* **1.** (*a*) plume *f* (d'oiseau); (*b*) **p. feather,** penne *f*, rémige *f*; *A:* **the pens,** les rémiges. **2.** (*a*) plume (pour écrire); **fountain p.,** stylo *m*; **ball(-point) p.,** stylo à bille, stylo-bille *m*; **felt p.,** crayon *m* feutre; **quill p.,** plume (d'oie); **drawing p., mapping p.,** plume à dessin; **p. (-and-ink) drawing,** dessin *m* à la plume, à l'encre; **p. rest,** pose-plumes *m inv*; **p. box,** plumier *m*; **p. tray,** plumier (plat); **stroke of the p.,** trait *m* de plume; **to put p. to paper,** prendre la plume (en main); écrire; **p. friend,** correspondant, -ante (épistolaire); **to earn one's living by one's p.,** vivre de sa plume; **p. name,** nom *m* de plume; pseudonyme *m*; (*of journalist*) nom de guerre; *F: Pej:* **p. pusher,** gratte-papier *m inv*; scribouillard, -arde; (*b*) **p. (nib),** plume; **steel p.,** plume métallique, d'acier; (*c*) **p. compass,** compas *m* à tire-ligne; **wheel p.,** tire-ligne *m* (*pl.* tire-lignes) à pointiller; **bow p.,** balustre *m* à encre; **drop p.,** balustre à pompe; **p. recorder,** enregistreur *m* à plume. **3.** (*a*) *Moll:* plume (de calmar, d'encornet); (*b*) *Moll:* **p. shell,** pinne marine; (*c*) *Coel:* **sea p.,** plume marine, de mer.

pen[4], *v.tr.* **(penned)** écrire, rédiger (une lettre, etc.).

pen[5], *s. Orn:* cygne *m* femelle.

pen[6], *s. NAm: F:* prison *f*, taule *f.*

penal ['pi:n(ə)l], *a.* (*of laws, code*) pénal, -aux; (*of offence*) qui comporte, entraîne, une pénalité; **p. servitude,** travaux forcés (d'une durée minimum de trois ans, sans transportation); **seven years' p. servitude,** *F:* **seven years' p.,** sept ans de travaux forcés, *F:* de bagne; **p. servitude for life,** travaux forcés à perpétuité; *A:* **p. colony, p. settlement,** colonie *f* pénitentiaire; colonie de déportation.

penalization [pi:nəlai'zeiʃ(ə)n], *s.* infliction *f* d'une peine **(of s.o.,** à qn); *Sp:* pénalisation *f.*

penalize ['pi:nəlaiz], *v.tr.* **1.** sanctionner (un délit) d'une peine, d'une pénalité; attacher une peine à (un délit). **2.** (*a*) infliger une peine à (qn); (*b*) *Sp:* pénaliser (un concurrent, un joueur); déclasser (un coureur); **to p. a competitor 10 points,** pénaliser un concurrent de dix points; (*c*) *Sp:* handicaper.

penally ['pi:nəli], *adv.* pénalement.

penalty ['penəlti], *s.* **1.** (*a*) peine *f*, pénalité *f*; *Com:* amende *f* (pour retard de livraison, etc.); *Adm:* sanction (pénale); **to impose penalties,** prendre des sanctions; (*in contract*) **p. clause,** clause pénale (de dommages-intérêts); **p. for non-performance of contract,** peine contractuelle; dédit *m*; **torts subject to p.,** fautes *f* dommageables; **the death p., the extreme, the ultimate, p.,** la peine de mort, le dernier supplice, la peine capitale; **the p. of the lash,** le supplice du fouet; **on, upon, under, p. of death,** sous peine de mort; sous peine de la vie; **to pay the p. of one's foolishness,** subir les conséquences de sa sottise; être puni de sa sottise; (*b*) désavantage *m*; **the p. of progress,** la rançon du progrès; **to pay the p. of fame,** payer la rançon de la gloire. **2.** *Sp:* (*a*) pénalisation *f*, amende, pénalité, penalty *m*, *pl.* penaltys; *Golf:* **p. stroke,** coup *m* d'amende; *Fb:* **p. (kick),** coup de pied de réparation, de pénalité; penalty *m*; **a p. taken by X,** un penalty botté par X; **p. area, p. spot,** surface *f*, point *m*, de réparation, de pénalité, de pénalisation; (*b*) handicap *m*. **3.** *Post: U.S:* **p. mail,** courrier officiel; courrier, correspondance *f*, en franchise (au service de l'État).

penance[1] ['penəns], *s.* (*a*) *Theol:* **the sacrament of p.,** le sacrement de la pénitence; (*b*) **to do p. for one's sins,** faire pénitence de, pour, ses péchés; **to do sth. as a p.,** faire qch. par pénitence; **works of p.,** œuvres pénitentielles.

penance[2], *v.tr.* infliger une pénitence à (qn); punir (qn).

penannular [pen'ænjulər], *a.* à peu près annulaire; approximativement en forme d'anneau.

penates [pe'neiti:z, -'nɑ:ti:z], *s.pl. Rom.Ant:* pénates *m*; *Lit:* **to set up one's p.,** établir ses pénates.

pencatite ['penkətait], *s. Miner:* pencatite *f.*

pence [pens], *s.pl. See* PENNY.

pencil ['pens(ə)l], *s.* **1.** *Art: A:* pinceau *m*; (*still so used in*) **to have a bold, a delicate, p.,** avoir le pinceau hardi, délicat. **2.** crayon *m*; (*a*) **lead p.,** crayon à mine de plomb; **coloured p.,** crayon de couleur; **indelible p.,** crayon (à encre) indélébile, crayon violet; **propelling p.,** porte-mine *m inv* réglable, à vis; stylomine *m*; *Art:* **charcoal p., carbon p.,** fusain *m*; **chinagraph p.,** crayon pour porcelaine; **ball-point p.,** crayon à bille; **p. box, case,** plumier *m*; **p. sharpener,** taille-crayon(s) *m inv*; **p. compass,** compas *m* à porte-crayon; **p. mark,** trait *m*, marque *f*, au crayon; **to mark sth. in p., with a p.,** marquer qch. au crayon; **to make p. marks on sth.,** crayonner qch.; **p. stroke,** coup de crayon; **written in p.,** écrit au crayon; **p. sketch,** croquis *m*; **drawing in p., p. drawing,** (dessin *m* au) crayon; crayonnage *m*; **he's clever with his p.,** il dessine bien; *Av:* **p.-shaped fuselage,** fuselage *m* filiforme; (*b*) **slate p.,** crayon d'ardoise; *Miner:* **p. stone,** pyrophyllite *f* (à crayon); (*c*) **carbon p. (of arc lamp),** crayon (d'une lampe à arc); (*d*) *Toil:* **eyebrow p.,** crayon à sourcils. **3.** (*a*) *Opt:* **p. of light rays, light p.,** (i) faisceau lumineux; faisceau de lumière, de rayons; (ii) aigrette lumineuse; houppe *f*; **tip of the light p.,** spot lumineux; *Rad:* **p. beam,** faisceau étroit; **p. marker,** crayon gras pour repérage (des échos sur l'écran); (*b*) *Ball:* **p. of trajectories,** gerbe *f* de trajectoires; (*c*) *Mth:* faisceau (de courbes, etc.); **geodesic p.,** faisceau géodésique; *Cmptr:* **conductor p.,** crayon conducteur; (*d*) *Nat.Hist:* houppe. **4.** *Med: F: O:* **p. and tassel,** les parties viriles (chez l'enfant). **5.** *Ich:* **p. fish,** poisson *m* crayon.

pencil[2], *v.tr.* **(pencilled) 1.** (*a*) faire une marque au crayon sur (qch.); marquer (qch.) au crayon; (*b*) dessiner, esquisser, (une figure) au crayon; (*c*) **to p. one's eyebrows, one's eyes,** se faire les sourcils, les yeux (au crayon). **2.** (*a*) **to p. a note,** crayonner un billet; (*b*) **to p. down a note,** noter une remarque au crayon; faire une note au crayon; (*c*) *Turf:* inscrire (un cheval) au carnet de paris.

pencilled ['pensəld], *a.* **1.** écrit au crayon. **2.** marqué au crayon; **p. eyebrows,** sourcils tracés au crayon; **delicately p. eyebrows,** sourcils d'un tracé délicat. **3.** *Nat.Hist:* à houppe.

pencilling ['pensəliŋ], *s.* crayonnage *m.*

pencraft ['penkrɑ:ft], *s.* **1.** calligraphie *f.* **2.** art *m* d'écrire.

pendant[1] ['pendənt], *s.* **1.** (*a*) pendentif *m* (de collier); breloque *f* (de bracelet); pendeloque *f* (de lustre); **ear p.,** pendant *m* d'oreille; (*b*) *Clockm:* pendant, anneau *m* (de montre); (*c*) *Arch:* clef pendante; cul-de-lampe *m*, *pl.* culs-de-lampe; (*d*) **electric light p.,** lustre *m* (électrique). **2.** *Nau:* (*a*) (*rope*) pantoire *f*, pendeur *m*; **Burton p.,** pendeur de candelette; **mooring p.,** itague *f* de corps-mort; **rudder p.,** sauvegarde *f*; (*b*) ['penənt] (*flag*) flamme *f*, guidon *m*. **3.** (*also* [pɑ̃dɑ̃]) pendant (d'un tableau, d'un ornement); **to make a p. to sth.,** faire pendant à qch.; faire le pendant de qch.

pendant[2], *a.* = PENDENT[1].

pendeloque ['pendəlɔk], *s. Lap: etc:* pendeloque *f.*

pendency ['pendənsi], *s. Jur:* litispendance *f.*

pendent[1] ['pendənt], *a.* **1.** (*of plants, etc.*) pendant; (*of draperies, etc.*) retombant; (*of rocks, etc.*) surplombant, en surplomb; *Mec.E:* **p. bearing,** chaise pendante. **2.** *Jur:* (procès) pendant, en instance; **negotiations p. between two countries,** négociations en cours, pendantes, entre deux pays. **3.** *Gram:* **p. sentence,** phrase incomplète.

pendent[2], *s.* = PENDANT[1].

pendentive [pen'dentiv], *s. Arch:* pendentif *m*, trompe *f.*

pending ['pendiŋ]. **1.** *a.* (procès) pendant, en instance; (négociations) en cours; *Adm: Com:* **p. tray,** documents *mpl* en attendant, en attente, en instances; instances *fpl.* **2.** *prep.* en attendant (le retour de qn, etc.); **p. further news,** en attendant de plus amples nouvelles; **p. a decision of the court on . . .,** en attendant que le tribunal ait décidé, ait statué, sur . . .; **all my plans are hung up p. decision of this lawsuit,** ce procès a mis tous mes projets en souffrance.

pendragon [pen'drægən], *s. Welsh Hist:* prince *m*, chef *m*, pendragon *m.*

pendular ['pendjulər], *a.* (mouvement *m*) pendulaire.

pendulate ['pendjuleit], *v.i.* (*a*) osciller, balancer; avoir un mouvement pendulaire; (*b*) *O:* (*of pers.*) vaciller (entre deux opinions, etc.).

penduline ['pendjulain]. *Orn:* **1.** *a.* qui construit un nid suspendu; penduline (*only the f. form is used*); **p. tit(mouse),** rémiz penduline. **2.** *s.* penduline *f*, rémiz *f.*

pendulous ['pendjuləs], *a.* **1.** (*of branch, lip, etc.*) pendant; **dog with p. ears,** chien *m* aux oreilles pendantes. **2.** balançant, oscillant; (mouvement) pendulaire.

pendulum ['pendjuləm], *s. Ph: Clockm:* pendule *m*; balancier *m*; **ballistic p.,** pendule balistique; **compensated, compensation, p.,** pendule, balancier, compensé, compensateur; **dummy p.,** pendule passif; **free p.,** pendule libre; **geodetic p.,** pendule géodésique; **motor p.,** balancier moteur; **torsion p.,** pendule de torsion; **p. clock,** horloge *f* à pendule, à balancier; **p. ball, bob,** lentille *f* de pendule, de balancier; **p. rod,** pendillon *m*; **p. effect, motion, stability,** effet *m*, mouvement *m*, stabilité *f*, pendulaire; mouvement de va-et-vient; *Bill:* **p. stroke,** carambolage *m* va-et-vient.

peneid [pe'ni:id], *a. & s. Crust:* pénéidé (*m*).

Peneidae [pe'ni:idi:], *s.pl. Crust:* pénéidés *m*.

Penelope [pi'neləpi]. **1.** *Pr.n.f.* Pénélope; *Gr.Lit:* **Penelope's web,** le travail de Pénélope. **2.** *Orn:* pénélope *f*.

peneplain[1], **peneplane**[1] ['pi:niplein], *s. Geol:* pénéplaine *f*.

peneplain[2], **peneplane**[2], *v.tr. Geol:* pénéplaner.

peneplanation [pi:niplə'neiʃ(ə)n], *s. Geol:* pénéplanation *f*.

penetrability [penitrə'biliti], *s.* pénétrabilité *f*; *Petr:* **worked, unworked, p.,** pénétrabilité (d'une graisse) après, sans, malaxage.

penetrable ['penitrəbl], *a.* pénétrable.

penetrableness ['penitrəb(ə)lnis], *s.* pénétrabilité *f*.

penetralia [peni'treiliə], *s.pl.* partie la plus reculée (d'un temple, etc.); sanctuaire *m*.

penetrameter [peni'træmitər], *s.* = PENETROMETER.

penetrance ['penitrəns], *s. Biol:* pénétrance *f*.

penetrant ['penitrənt], *a.* = PENETRATING.

penetrate ['penitreit]. **1.** *v.tr.* (*a*) pénétrer, percer; **the shell penetrated the hull,** l'obus *m* a pénétré la coque; **darkness that the eye could not p.,** ténèbres que l'œil ne pouvait percer; (*b*) **to p. a secret,** pénétrer, percer, un secret; **to p. s.o.'s mind,** voir clair dans l'esprit de qn; pénétrer la pensée de qn; (*c*) *Lit:* **to p. s.o. with a feeling,** pénétrer qn d'un sentiment. **2.** *v.i.* pénétrer; **the bayonet penetrated to the lung,** la baïonnette a pénétré jusqu'au poumon; **the water is penetrating everywhere,** l'eau s'introduit partout; **to p. through sth.,** passer à travers qch.; **to p. through the enemy's lines,** faire une trouée dans les lignes ennemies; **to p. into a forest,** pénétrer dans une forêt.

penetrated ['penitreitid], *a. Ph: etc:* pénétré, imprégné.

penetrating ['penitreitiŋ], *a.* (*a*) pénétrant; (vent, froid) pénétrant, mordant; (son) mordant; (*of bullet, shell*) perforant; **p. power,** pouvoir pénétrant, de pénétration; *Ball:* puissance de pénétration (d'un projectile); *Atom.Ph:* **p. particle,** particule pénétrante; *Mec.E:* **p. oil,** dégrippant *m*; **to have a p. eye,** avoir des yeux perçants, de lynx; avoir un regard d'aigle; (*b*) (esprit) clairvoyant, pénétrant, perspicace.

penetration [peni'treiʃ(ə)n], *s.* pénétration *f*; (*a*) **p. of foreign markets,** pénétration des marchés étrangers; *Pol:* **peaceful p.,** pénétration pacifique; *Mil: etc:* **p. of enemy territory,** pénétration (d'éléments) dans des territoires ennemis; **multiple p.,** pénétration en plusieurs points; *Mil.Av:* **p. fighter,** chasseur *m* de pénétration; (*b*) venue *f* (de gaz, etc.); entrée *f* (d'air dans un ballon, etc.); *Atom.Ph:* pénétration (des radiations dans un corps); **p. factor,** facteur *m*, coefficient *m*, de pénétration; **p. probability,** probabilité *f* de pénétration; *El:* **p. frequency,** fréquence *f* critique; (*c*) *Cryst:* **p. twin,** macle *f* par pénétration, par entrecroisement; (*d*) pénétration (de l'esprit), perspicacité *f*, clairvoyance *f*.

penetrative ['penitrətiv], *a.* pénétrant.

penetrator ['penitreitər], *s.* **1.** celui, celle, qui pénètre. **2.** avion *m* de pénétration.

penetrometer [peni'trɔmitər], *s. Tchn:* pénétromètre *m*, pénétramètre *m*.

Peneus [pe'ni:əs]. **1.** *Pr.n. Geog:* **the (river) P.,** le Pénée. **2.** *s. Crust:* pénée *m*.

penfieldite ['penfi:ldait], *s. Miner:* penfieldite *f*.

penful ['penful], *s.* plumée *f* (d'encre).

penguin ['peŋgwin], *s. Orn:* manchot *m*, gorfou *m*; *F:* (*incorrectly*) pingouin *m*; **big-crested p.,** gorfou huppé; **emperor p.,** manchot empereur; **gentoo p.,** manchot papou; **jackass p.,** manchot du Cap; **king p.,** manchot royal; **Adélie p.,** manchot d'Adélie; **macaroni p.,** gorfou doré; **rock-hopper p.,** gorfou sauteur; **royal p.,** gorfou à joues blanches.

penholder ['penhouldər], *s.* **1.** porte-plume *m inv*. **2.** pose plume(s) *m inv*, plumier *m*.

penial ['pi:niəl], *a.* **1.** *Anat:* pénien. **2.** *Z:* (fourreau, etc.) de la verge.

penicillate [peni'sileit], *a. Nat.Hist:* pénicillé.

penicilliform [peni'silifɔ:m], *a. Z:* pénicilliforme.

penicillin [peni'silin], *s.* pénicilline *f*; **p. resistant,** pénicillino-résistant, *pl.* pénicillino-résistants.

penicillinase [peni'silineis], *s. Bac:* pénicillinase *f*.

penicillium [peni'siliəm], *s. Fung:* pénicillium *m*.

penile ['pi:nail], *a. Anat:* pénien.

peninsula [pi'ninsjulə], *s. Geog:* péninsule *f*; presqu'île *f*; **the Iberian P.,** la péninsule Ibérique; *Hist:* (1914–18) **the P.,** la péninsule de Gallipoli.

peninsular [pi'ninsjulər], *a.* péninsulaire; *Hist:* **the P. War,** la guerre d'Espagne.

penis, *pl.* **-nes** ['pi:nis, -ni:z], *s. Anat: Z:* pénis *m*, verge *f*; membre viril.

penitence ['penit(ə)ns], *s.* pénitence *f*, repentir *m*, contrition *f*.

penitent ['penit(ə)nt]. **1.** *a.* pénitent, repentant, contrit. **2.** *s.* (*a*) (*pers. doing penance*) pénitent, -ente; *Ecc:* **the p. form,** le banc des pénitents; (*b*) *R.C.Ch:* (*member of a Penitent order*) pénitent, -ente.

penitential [peni'tenʃ(ə)l]. **1.** *a.* pénitentiel, de pénitence, de contrition; **p. robe,** robe *f* de pénitent; **p. good works,** œuvres pénitentielles; **p. psalms,** psaumes *m* de la pénitence; psaumes pénitentiaux. **2.** *s.* (*book*) pénitentiel *m*.

penitentiary [peni'tenʃəri]. **1.** *a.* (*a*) *Ecc:* **p. priest,** pénitencier *m*; (*b*) **p. house,** maison *f* pénitentiaire; (*c*) *U.S:* **p. offense,** délit puni de réclusion dans une maison pénitentiaire. **2.** *s.* (*a*) *R.C.Ch:* (*pers.*) pénitencier; **Grand P., High, Chief, Great, P.,** Grand Pénitencier; (*b*) *R.C.Ch:* (*tribunal*) pénitencerie *f*; (*c*) *Adm: A:* maison pénitentiaire; pénitencier *m*; maison de correction; (*d*) *NAm:* prison *f*.

penitentiaryship [peni'tenʃəriʃip], *s. R.C.Ch: A:* pénitencerie *f*; charge *f* de pénitencier.

penitently ['penitəntli], *adv.* d'un air contrit.

penknife, *pl.* **-knives** ['pennaif, -naivz], *s.* canif *m*.

penman, *pl.* **-men** ['penmən], *s.m.* **1.** écrivain; homme de plume; auteur. **2.** (*a*) *A:* (*scrivener*) écrivain (public); (*b*) **good p., expert p.,** calligraphe.

penmanship ['penmənʃip], *s.* **1.** l'art *m* d'écrire. **2.** calligraphie *f*.

pennant ['penənt], *s.* **1.** *Nau:* flamme *f*, guidon *m*; **broad p.,** guidon de commandement, guidon du chef de division; **answering p.,** pavillon *m* d'aperçu; **paying-off p.,** flamme de fin, de retour, de campagne; **ship's pennants,** numéro *m* du bâtiment. **2.** *A.Mil:* pennon *m*.

pennate ['peneit], *a.* **1.** *Bot:* penné, pinné. **2.** *Nat.Hist:* penniforme.

pennatifid [pe'nætifid], *a. Bot:* pennatifide.

pennatilobate [penəti'loubeit], *a. Bot:* pennatilobé.

pennatisect(ed) [penəti'sekt(id)], *a. Bot:* pennatiséqué.

pennatula [pe'nætjulə], *s. Coel:* pennatule *f*, plume *f* de mer.

Pennatulacea [penætju'leisiə], *s.pl. Coel* pennatulacés m.

pennatulacean [penætju'leisiən], *a. & s. Coel:* pennatulacé (*m*).

pennatulaceous [penætju'leiʃəs], *a. Coel:* pennatulacé.

pennatularian [penætju'lɛəriən], *a. & s. Coel:* pennatulaire (*m*).

Pennatulidae [penə'tju:lidi:], *s.pl. Coel:* pennatulidés *m*.

penniform ['penifɔ:m], *a. Nat.Hist: Anat:* penniforme.

penniless ['penilis], *a.* sans le sou; sans ressources; **to be p.,** n'avoir pas le sou, pas un sou vaillant; avoir la poche vide; **to leave s.o. p.,** laisser qn sans le sou; mettre qn sur la paille; **to leave oneself p.,** se dépouiller de ses biens; *s.pl.* **the p.,** les sans-le-sou *m*, les misérables *m*.

pennine[1] ['penain], *a. Geog:* **1. the P. Alps,** les (Alpes) Pennines. **2. the P. Chain,** *s.* **the Pennines,** la chaîne Pennine.

pennine[2] ['pen(a)in], **penninite** ['peninait], *s. Miner:* pennine *f*.

pennon ['penən], *s.* flamme *f*, banderole *f*; *A.Mil:* pennon *m*; *Sp:* fanion *m*.

pennoned ['penənd], *a.* à flamme, à banderole, *A.Mil:* à pennon.

penn'orth ['penəθ], *s. F: O:* = PENNYWORTH.

Pennsylvania [pensil'veiniə]. *Pr.n. Geog:* Pen(n)sylvanie *f*.

Pennsylvanian [pensil'veiniən]. *Geog:* (*a*) *a.* pen(n)sylvanien; (*b*) *s.* Pen(n)sylvanien, -ienne.

penny ['peni], *s.* **1.** (*coin*) (*pl. usu.* **pennies**) (= £$\frac{1}{100}$, *A:* £$\frac{1}{240}$) penny *m*; **he gave me the change in pennies,** il m'a donné la monnaie en petites pièces; **a ten pence, fifty pence, piece,** une pièce de dix pence, de cinquante pence; **they haven't a p. (to their name, to bless themselves with),** *A:* **they haven't a p. piece,** ils n'ont pas le sou, ils sont sans le sou, sans un sou vaillant; **pennies from heaven,** une aubaine; **to watch, look twice at, count, every p.,** regarder, prendre garde à, un sou; compter ses sous; **to come back like a bad p.,** revenir comme un mauvais sou; **he's a bad p.,** c'est un mauvais sujet; *O:* **market p.,** sou du franc; **the penny's dropped,** (i) le sou est tombé (dans la machine); le mécanisme est déclenché; (ii) *F:* j'y suis, il y est, etc.; voilà qu'il comprend (la plaisanterie, etc.); *F:* **to spend a p.,** aller faire pipi. **2.** (*pl.* **pence** [pens]) (*a*) (*value*) **I paid 60 pence for it,** je l'ai payé 60 pence; **eighteen pence,** (i) *A:* un shilling et six pence; (ii) dix-huit pence; **it could be worth anything from fifty pence to fifty pounds,** cela vaut cinquante livres comme quelques sous; **they're two a p. nowadays,** c'est monnaie courante à l'heure actuelle; **a p. for your thoughts,** *F:* **for them,** à quoi rêvez-vous, pensez-vous? **nobody was a p. the worse,** (i) cela n'a fait tort à personne; (ii) il n'y a pas eu de blessé; tout le monde s'en est tiré sans une égratignure; **nobody was a p. the better,** personne n'en a profité; **I'm not a p. the wiser,** je n'en sais pas plus qu'avant; *Prov:* **in for a p. in for a pound,** quand le vin est tiré il faut boire; qui a dit A doit dire B; *O:* **p. bun,** gâteau *m* de deux sous; *Fung: F:* **p. bun (mushroom),** cèpe *m*; **p. post,** (i) *Hist:* la poste à deux sous; (ii) *Bot:* hydrocotyle américain; **p. whistle,** (i) flûteau *m*, flûtiau *m*; (ii) (*toy*) mirliton *m*; *A:* **p. bank,** caisse *f* d'épargne qui acceptait des versements d'un penny; *F:* **p. dreadful,** feuilleton *m* à gros effets; roman *m* à deux sous, à sensation; **in p. numbers,** en petites quantités; *Prov:* **take care of the pence, pennies, and the pounds will take care of themselves,** les petites économies font les bonnes maisons; il n'y a pas de petites économies; **to be p. wise,** faire des économies de bouts de chandelle; lésiner; **to be p. wise and pound foolish,** économiser les sous et prodiguer les louis; (*b*) **that'll cost a pretty p.,** cela coûtera cher; **£10,000 is a pretty p.!** dix mille livres, c'est un prix! **to come in for a pretty p.,** hériter d'une jolie fortune; **to make a pretty p. out of sth.,** tirer une petite fortune de qch.; **to earn, turn, an honest p.,** gagner honnêtement sa vie. **3.** (*a*) *B:* denier *m*; (*b*) *NAm:* cent *m*.

penny-a-liner [peniə'lainər], *s. F: A:* écrivailleur *m*, journaliste *m* à deux sous la ligne.

pennycress ['penikres], *s. Bot:* **(field) p.,** thlaspi *m*, tabouret *m*, des champs; monnayère *f*.

penny-farthing [peni'fɑ:ðiŋ], *s. F: A:* vélocipède *m*.

penny-in-the-slot [peniinðə'slɔt], *attrib.* (machine *f*) à sous.

pennyroyal [peni'rɔiəl], *s. Bot:* pouliot *m*.

pennyweight ['peniweit], *s. A.Meas: approx.* = un gramme et demi.

pennywort ['peniwə:t], *s. Bot:* **1. wall p.,** cotylédon *m*; nombril *m* de Vénus; gobelets *mpl*. **2. marsh p., water p.,** hydrocotyle *f*; écuelle *f* d'eau.

pennyworth ['peniwə:θ], *s.* (*a*) ce qu'on peut acheter pour un penny; **to buy ten p. of sweets,** acheter pour dix pence de bonbons; *A:* **it's a good p.,** on en a pour ses (quatre) sous; (*b*) très petite quantité; **I haven't a p. left,** il ne m'en reste pour ainsi dire rien.

penologist [pi:'nɔlədʒist], *s.* **1.** criminologiste *mf*. **2.** spécialiste *mf* de l'étude des régimes pénitentiaires.

penology [pi:'nɔlədʒi], *s.* **1.** criminologie *f*. **2.** pénologie *f*, étude *f* des régimes pénitentiaires.

pensile ['pensail, -sil], *a.* **1.** (*a*) suspendu, pendant; (*b*) *Lit:* **p. gardens,** jardins suspendus. **2.** (oiseau *m*) qui bâtit un nid pendant, un nid suspendu.

pension[1], *s.* **1.** ['penʃ(ə)n], (*a*) pension *f*; retraite *f*; **government p.,** pension sur l'État; **retirement, old age, p.,** pension de retraite; retraite de la vieillesse; **widow's p.,** pension de veuve, de réversion; **graduated p. scheme** = retraite des cadres; **p. fund,** caisse *f* de retraite; **service that counts towards a p.,** service *m* comptant pour la retraite; **to retire on a p.,** prendre sa retraite; *Mil: etc:* **to be discharged with a p.,** être mis à la retraite; **to commute a p.,** liquider une pension; (*b*) *A:* gages *mpl* (d'un agent secret, etc.). **2.** ['pɑ̃sjɔ̃] pension de famille; (*at hotel*) **en p.,** en pension.

pension[2] ['penʃ(ə)n], *v.tr.* **1.** pensionner (qn); fournir une pension à (qn); faire une rente à (qn); **to p. s.o. off,** mettre qn à la retraite. **2.** *A:* soudoyer (des spadassins, etc.).

pensionable ['penʃənəbl], *a.* **1.** (*of pers.*) qui mérite une pension; qui a droit à une pension, à sa retraite. **2.** (*of injury, etc.*) qui donne droit à une pension; **p. age,** âge *m* de la mise à la retraite. **3.** (emploi) donnant droit à pension; **p. emoluments,** traitement soumis à retenue.

pensionary ['penʃənəri]. **1.** *a.* (*a*) (droit, etc.) à une pension, à sa retraite; (*b*) (*of pers.*) pensionné ou retraité; (*c*) *A:* (spadassin *m*, etc.) à gages. **2.** *s.* (*a*) pensionnaire *mf*, pensionné, -ée; (*b*) *Hist:* **the Grand P.,** le Grand Pensionnaire (de Hollande); (*c*) = PENSIONER 2 (*b*).

pensioner ['penʃənər], *s.* **1.** titulaire *mf* d'une pension; pensionné, -ée; retraité, -ée; **army p.,** (i) militaire retraité, en retraite; (ii) (*in institution*) invalide *m*; **civil**

pensioners, invalides civils; **state p.**, retraité de l'État. **2.** *A:* (*a*) **gentleman p.**, gentilhomme *m* de la garde; (*b*) créature *f*, âme damnée (de qn); **to be s.o.'s p.**, être à la solde de qn. **3.** *Sch:* (*at Cambridge*) étudiant *m* ordinaire (qui n'a ni bourse ni subvention).

pensioning ['penʃəniŋ], *s.* mise *f* à la retraite.

pensive ['pensiv], *a.* pensif, méditatif, rêveur, songeur.

pensively ['pensivli], *adv.* pensivement, d'un air pensif; soucieusement.

pensiveness ['pensivnis], *s.* air pensif; songerie *f.*

penstemon [pen'sti:mən], *s. Bot:* penstémon *m.*

penstock ['penstɔk], *s. Hyd.E:* **1.** vanne *f* de tête d'eau. **2.** canal *m* d'amenée, de dérivation; conduite forcée; bief *m* d'amont; buse *f*, bée *f*. **3.** barillet *m* (de pompe).

pent [pent], *a.* **1. p. (in, up)**, renfermé; parqué; **p. up in a small space,** resserré, (r)enfermé, dans un étroit espace. **2. p. up emotion,** émotion refoulée, contenue; **p. up tears,** larmes refoulées; **to be p. up,** être sous pression.

penta- ['pentə, pen'tæ], *comb.fm.* penta-.

pentabromide [pentə'broumaid], *s. Ch:* pentabromure *m.*

pentachloride [pentə'klɔ:raid], *s. Ch:* pentachlorure *m.*

pentachord ['pentəkɔ:d], *s. Mus:* pentacorde *m.*

pentacle ['pentəkl], *s.* = PENTAGRAM.

Pentacrinidae [pentə'krinidi:], *s.pl. Paleont:* pentacrinidés *m.*

pentacrinite [pen'tækrinait], *s. Paleont:* pentacrine *m.*

pentacrinoid [pen'tækrinɔid], *a. Paleont:* pentracrinoïde.

Pentacrinus [pen'tækrinəs], *s. Paleont:* pentacrine *m.*

pentad ['pentæd], *s.* **1.** (*a*) pentade *f*; groupe *m* de cinq; (*b*) période *f* de cinq ans. **2.** *Ch:* corps pentavalent.

pentadactyl(e) [pentə'dæktil], *a. & s. Nat.Hist:* pentadactyle (*m*).

pentadecagon [pentə'dekəgɔn], *s. Mth:* pentadécagone *m*, pentédécagone *m.*

pentaerythritol [pentəɛə'riθritɔl], *s. Ch:* pentaérythrite *f*, pentaérythritol *m.*

pentagon ['pentəgən], *s.* **1.** *Mth:* pentagone *m.* **2.** *Mil:* **the P.,** le Pentagone.

pentagonal [pen'tægənəl], *a. Mth:* pentagonal, -aux; pentagone.

pentagram ['pentəgræm], *s.* pentagramme *m*, pentacle *m*, pentalpha *m.*

pentagrid ['pentəgrid], *attrib.a. W.Tel:* **p. lamp, valve,** lampe *f*, tube *m*, pentagrille, à cinq grilles; **p. converter,** heptode changeuse de fréquence.

pentagynia [pentə'dʒiniə], *s. Bot:* pentagynie *f.*

pentagynian [pentə'dʒiniən], **pentagynous** [pen'tædʒinəs], *a. Bot:* pentagyne.

pentahedral [pentə'hi:drəl, -'hed-], *a. Mth:* pentaèdre.

pentahedron [pentə'hi:drən, -'hed-], *s. Mth:* pentaèdre *m.*

pentail ['penteil], *s. Z:* ptilocerque *m.*

pentalpha [pen'tælfə], *s.* = PENTAGRAM.

Pentamera [pen'tæmərə], *s.pl. Ent:* pentamères *m.*

pentameral, pentamerous [pen'tæmərəl, -'tæmərəs], *a. Ent: Bot:* pentamère, quinaire.

pentameran [pen'tæmərən], *s. Ent:* pentamère *m.*

pentamerid [pen'tæmərid], *s. Paleont:* pentamère *m.*

Pentameridae [pentə'meridi:], *s.pl. Paleont:* pentamérides *m.*

pentamerism [pen'tæmərizm], *s. Nat.Hist:* pentamérisme *m.*

Pentamerus [pen'tæmərəs], *s. Paleont:* pentamère *m.*

pentameter [pen'tæmitər], *s. Pros:* pentamètre *m.*

pentamethylene [pentə'meθili:n], *s. Ch:* pentaméthylène *m.*

pentamethylenediamine [pentə'meθili:n'daiəmain], *s. Ch:* pentaméthylènediamine *m.*

pentametric [pentə'metrik], *a. Pros:* pentamétrique.

pentandria [pen'tændriə], *s. Bot:* pentandrie *f.*

pentandrous [pen'tændrəs], *a. Bot:* pentandre; à cinq étamines.

pentane ['pentein], *s. Ch:* pentane *m.*

pentanoic [pentə'nouik], *a. Ch:* **p. acid,** pentanoïque *m.*

pentanol ['pentənɔl], *s. Ch:* pentanol *m.*

pentanone ['pentənoun], *s. Ch:* pentanone *f.*

pentapetalous [pentə'petələs], *a. Bot:* pentapétale; à cinq pétales.

pentaploid(ic) ['pentəplɔid, pentə'plɔidik], *s. Biol:* pentaploïde *m.*

pentapody [pen'tæpədi], *s. Pros:* pentapodie *f.*

pentapolis [pen'tæpəlis], *s. A.Hist:* pentapole *f.*

pentarch ['pentɑ:k], *s.* pentarque *m.*

pentarchical [pen'tɑ:kikl], *a.* pentarchique.

pentarchy ['pentɑ:ki], *s.* pentarchie *f.*

pentastome ['pentəstoum], *s. Ent:* pentastome *m*, linguatule *f.*

Pentastomida [pentə'stoumidə], *s.pl. Ent:* pentastomides *m*, linguatules *f.*

pentastom(o)id [pentə'stoum(ɔ)id], *a. & s. Ent:* pentastome (*m*).

pentastyle ['pentəstail], *a. Arch:* pentastyle.

pentastylos [pentə'stailəs], *s. Arch:* pentastyle *m.*

pentasulphide [pentə'sʌlfaid], *s. Ch:* pentasulfure *m.*

pentasyllabic [pentəsi'læbik], *a.* pentasyllabe.

pentasyllable [pentə'siləbl], *s.* pentasyllabe *m.*

Pentateuch (the) [ðə'pentətju(:)k], *s. B:* le Pentateuque.

pentathionate [pentə'θaiəneit], *s. Ch:* pentathionate *m.*

pentathionic [pentəθai'ɔnik], *a. Ch:* pentathionique.

pentathlete [pen'tæθli:t], *s.* (*a*) *Gr.Ant:* pentathle *m*; (*b*) (*modern Olympic Games*) pentathlonien, -ienne.

pentathlon [pen'tæθlɔn], *s.* (*a*) *Gr.Ant:* pentathle *m*; (*b*) (*modern Olympic Games*) pentathlon *m*, pentathle.

pentatomic [pentə'tɔmik], *a. Ch:* pentatomique.

pentatomid [pentə'tɔmid], *s. Ent:* pentatome *m.*

Pentatomidae [pentə'tɔmidi:], *s.pl. Ent:* pentatomidés *m.*

pentatonic [pentə'tɔnik], *a. Mus:* (gamme) pentatonique.

pentavalence [pentə'veiləns], *s. Ch:* pentavalence *f.*

pentavalent [pentə'veilənt], *a. Ch:* pentavalent.

Pentecost ['pentikɔst], *s. Ecc:* la Pentecôte.

pentecostal [penti'kɔstl], *a. Ecc:* de la Pentecôte.

Pentelic [pen'telik], *a.* (marbre) pentélique.

Pentelicus [pen'telikəs]. *Pr.n. Geog:* **Mount P.,** le Pentélique.

pentene ['penti:n], *s. Ch:* pentène *m.*

Penthesilia [penθesi'li:ə]. *Pr.n.f. Gr.Myth:* Penthésilée.

Pentheus ['penθiəs]. *Pr.n.m. Gr.Myth:* Penthée.

penthiophene ['penθiaufi:n], *s. Ch:* penthiofène *m*, penthiophène *m.*

penthorum ['penθərəm], *s. Bot:* penthore *m.*

penthouse ['penthaus], *s. Const:* **1.** (*a*) appentis *m*; abrivent *m*; hangar *m*; (*b*) (*over the door, window*) auvent *m*; abat-vent *m inv*; (*c*) *Ten: A:* toit *m.* **2.** (*a*) *A.Mil:* **ram p.,** tour bélière; (*b*) appartement *m* (de) terrasse, construit sur le toit d'un immeuble.

pentite, pentitol ['pentait, -titɔl], *s. Ch:* pentite *f*, pentitol *m*, penta(a)lcool *m.*

pentlandite ['pentlændait], *s. Miner:* pentlandite *f.*

pentode ['pentoud], *s. W.Tel:* pent(h)ode *f*; lampe *f* à cinq électrodes.

pentolite ['pentoulait], *s. Exp:* pentolite *f.*

pentosan ['pentousæn], *s. Ch:* pentosane *m.*

pentose ['pentous], *s. Ch:* pentose *m.*

pentosid(e) ['pentousaid], *s. Ch:* pentoside *m.*

pentosuria [pentou'sju:riə], *s. Med:* pentosurie *f.*

pentoxide [pen'tɔksaid], *s. Ch:* **nitrogen p.,** anhydride *m* azotique; **antimony p.,** anhydride antimonique.

pentryl ['pentril], *s. Exp:* pentryl *m.*

pentstemon [pent'sti:mən], *s. Bot:* pen(t)stémon *m.*

pentyl ['pentil], *s. Ch:* pentyle *m.*

penult(imate) [pe'nʌlt(imət)]. **1.** *a.* pénultième; avant-dernier. **2.** *s.* pénultième *f*; avant-dernière syllabe.

penumbra [pe'nʌmbrə], *s.* pénombre *f.*

penurious [pe'nju:riəs], *a.* **1.** (*a*) (terrain, etc.) maigre, stérile; (*b*) pauvre. **2.** (*a*) avare, parcimonieux; (*b*) mesquin.

penuriously [pe'nju:riəsli], *adv.* **1.** pauvrement. **2.** (*a*) avarement, parcimonieusement; (*b*) mesquinement.

penuriousness [pe'nju:riəsnis], *s.* (*a*) avarice *f*, parcimonie *f*; (*b*) mesquinerie *f.*

penury ['penjuri], *s.* pénurie *f.* **1.** indigence *f*; dénuement *m*, misère *f*; **to live in p.,** vivre dans l'indigence, dans la misère. **2.** manque *m*, disette *f*, pauvreté *f* (**of,** de).

penwiper ['penwaipər], *s.* essuie-plume(s) *m inv.*

peon ['pi:ən], *s.* **1.** *A:* (*in India*) péon *m*; soldat *m* à pied. **2.** (*in Mexico*) péon.

peonage ['pi:ənidʒ], *s.* péonage *m.*

peony ['pi:əni], *s. Bot:* pivoine *f*; rose *f* de Notre-Dame; **as red as a p.,** rouge comme une pivoine.

people[1] ['pi:pl], *s.* (*coll. with pl. const. except for* **I** *where pl. is usu.* **peoples**) **1.** peuple *m*, nation *f*; **the French p.,** la nation française; les Français *m*; **English-speaking people(s),** peuples, nations, de langue anglaise; les anglophones *m*; **a warlike p.,** un peuple guerrier, une nation guerrière. **2.** (*a*) peuple, habitants *mpl*; **country p.,** les populations rurales; les gens *m* de la campagne; (*b*) **a king and his p.,** un roi et ses sujets, et son peuple; **I'll get one of my p. to do it,** un de mes employés, de mes ouvriers, de mes gens, le fera; (*c*) parents *mpl*; famille *f*; **my wife's p.,** ma belle-famille; **how are your p.?** comment va votre famille? **my p. are abroad,** mes parents sont à l'étranger; **I must introduce you to my p.,** il faut que je vous présente à ma famille; (*d*) *Ecc:* ouailles *fpl*; fidèles *mpl.* **3.** (*a*) citoyens *mpl* (d'un État); **people's democracy, republic,** démocratie *f*, république *f*, populaire; **government by the p.,** gouvernement par le peuple; **the will of the p.,** la volonté du peuple; **the p. as a whole,** le grand public; (*b*) **the (common) p.,** le peuple; la populace; **a man of the p.,** un homme sorti du peuple. **4.** (*a*) gens; **young p.,** jeunes gens; **old p.,** les vieilles gens; les vieux; **old people's home,** maison *f* de retraite pour personnes âgées; **society p.,** gens du monde; **thousands of p.,** des milliers de gens; **there were not many p.,** il n'y avait pas beaucoup de monde; **most p.,** la plupart des gens, du monde; **they are pleasant p.,** ce sont des gens aimables; **p. here say . . .,** les gens d'ici disent . . .; **who are these p.?** quels sont ces gens? **p. are so hard to please,** les gens sont si difficiles; on ne peut pas contenter tout le monde; **he's one of those p. who . . .,** il est de ceux qui . . .; c'est un homme qui . . .; **all honest p.,** tous ceux qui sont honnêtes; **what do you p. think?** qu'en pensez-vous, vous autres? (*b*) personnes *fpl*; **there were five p. in the room,** il y avait cinq personnes dans la pièce; **I applied to several p.,** je me suis adressé à plusieurs personnes; **it's a question of knowing the right p., the p. who matter,** il faut avoir des relations; **there were 400 p. at the meeting,** quatre cents personnes ont assisté à la réunion; **we're having p. to dinner tonight,** nous aurons des invités, du monde, à dîner ce soir; (*c*) (*indefinite*) on; **p. say that. . .,** on dit que. . .; (*d*) *Myth:* **the little p., the good p.,** les fées *f.*

people[2], *v.tr.* peupler (**with,** de); **densely peopled country,** pays très peuplé; **thinly peopled,** peu peuplé.

pep[1] [pep], *s. F:* entrain *m*, fougue *f*; **full of p.,** plein de sève, d'allant; **to put a bit of p. into s.o.,** ragaillardir qn; **p. talk,** petit discours émoustillant, d'encouragement; **p. pill,** excitant *m*, stimulant *m.*

pep[2], *v.tr.* (**pepped**) *F:* **to p. s.o. up,** ragaillardir qn; **to p. up a dance,** donner de l'entrain à un bal; **to p. up a play,** corser une pièce.

peperino [pepə'ri:nou], *s. Geol:* péperin(o) *m.*

Pepin ['pepin], *Pr.n.m. Hist:* **P. the Short,** Pépin le Bref.

peplis ['peplis], *s. Bot:* péplide *f.*

peplum ['pepləm], *s. Gr.Cost:* péplum *m.*

pepo ['pepou], *s. Bot:* pépon *m*, péponide *f.*

pepper[1] ['pepər], *s.* (*a*) poivre *m*; **p. (plant),** poivrier *m*; *Cu:* **black p.,** poivre noir, gris; **white p.,** poivre blanc; **green p.,** poivre vert; **whole p.,** poivre en grains; **ground p.,** poivre moulu; **p. mill,** moulin *m* à poivre; **p. pot,** (i) poivrière *f*; (ii) (*in W. Indies*) ragoût assaisonné de poivre de Cayenne; (*b*) **long p., Spanish p.,** poivre long, poivre d'Espagne; **Cayenne p.,** poivre de Cayenne, d'Amérique; cayenne *m*; **Guinea p., malaguetta p.,** poivre de Guinée, d'Éthiopie; malaguette *f*; **Jamaica p.,** poivre de la Jamaïque, piment *m*; **Java p., cubeb p.,** poivre à queue; **sweet p.,** piment doux, poivron *m*; (*c*) **p. tree,** faux-poivrier *m*, *pl.* faux-poivriers; mollé *m*; **p. grass,** (i) cresson alénois; passerage *f*; (ii) pilulaire *f*; **water p.,** poivre d'eau.

pepper[2], *v.tr.* **1.** poivrer (de la viande, etc.). **2.** (*a*) cribler (l'ennemi, etc.) de balles; **to p. the enemy with machine-gun fire,** mitrailler l'ennemi; (*b*) *F: A:* rosser (qn); flanquer une tannée à (qn).

pepper-and-salt ['pepərən(d)'sɔ:lt], (*a*) *a. & s. Tex:* marengo (*m inv*); (*b*) *attrib.* (*of hair, etc.*) poivre et sel.

pepperbox ['pepəbɔks], *s.* **1.** poivrière *f.* **2.** *Arch:* **p. (turret),** poivrière.

peppercorn ['pepəkɔ:n], *s.* **1.** grain *m* de poivre. **2.** *Jur:* **p. rent,** loyer nominal, insignifiant, payable pour la forme.

peppered ['pepəd], *a.* (*a*) poivré; (*b*) *Ent:* **p. moth,** géomètre *f* du bouleau.

pepperiness ['pepərinis], *s.* **1.** goût poivré (**of,** de). **2.** *F:* irascibilité *f.*

peppermint ['pepəmint], *s.* **1.** menthe poivrée; menthe anglaise; **oil of p.,** essence *f* de menthe poivrée. **2. p. drop,** bonbon *m* à la menthe; **p. lozenge,** pastille *f* à la menthe. **3.** *Bot:* **p. (tree),** eucalyptus poivré.

pepperwort ['pepəwə:t], *s. Bot:* passerage *f.*

peppery ['pepəri], *a.* **1.** (*of dish, etc.*) poivré. **2.** *F:* (*of pers.*) irascible, emporté, coléreux, colérique.

peppy ['pepi], *a. F:* **1.** (*of pers.*) plein de sève, d'allant; vigoureux. **2.** (moteur) nerveux; (publicité) piquante, originale.

pepsin ['pepsin], *s. Ch: Physiol:* pepsine *f.*

pepsis ['pepsis], *s. Ent:* pepsis *m.*

peptic ['peptik]. **1.** *a. Physiol:* peptique, pepsique, gastrique; **p. glands,** glandes *f* gastriques, à pepsine; *Med:* **p. ulcer,** ulcère *m* simple de l'estomac. **2.** *s.* (*a*) *Pharm:* digestif *m*; (*b*) *F:* **the peptics,** les organes digestifs.

peptidase ['peptideis], *s. Bio-Ch:* peptidase *f.*

peptide ['pept(a)id], *s. Bio-Ch:* peptide *m.*

peptizable [pep'taizəbl], *a. Ch:* peptisable.

peptization [pept(a)i'zeiʃ(ə)n], *s. Ch:* peptisation *f.*

peptogen ['peptoudʒen], *s. Med:* peptogène *m.*

peptogenic [peptou'dʒenik], *a. Med:* peptogène.

peptonate ['peptəneit], *s. Bio-Ch:* peptonate *m.*

peptone ['peptoun], *s. Bio-Ch:* peptone *f.*

peptonizable [peptə'naizəbl], *a. Ch:* peptonisable.

peptonization [peptənai'zeiʃ(ə)n], *s. Physiol: etc:* peptonisation *f.*

peptonize ['peptənaiz], *v.tr. Physiol: etc:* peptoniser.

peptonuria [peptə'nju:riə], *s. Med:* peptonurie *f.*

per [pə:r], *prep. Com: etc:* (*a*) par; **sent p. carrier,** envoyé par messageries; **p. Messrs Martin & Co.,** par l'entremise, par l'intermédiaire, de MM. Martin et Cie; (*b*) **as p. invoice,** suivant facture; selon, d'après, facture; **as p. sample,** conformément à l'échantillon; **credited as p. contra,** crédité ci-contre, en contre-partie; *P: O:* **as p. usual,** comme d'ordinaire, comme d'habitude; (*c*) **p. pro(curationem),** par procuration; (*d*) **p. cent,** pour cent; **ten francs p. kilo,** dix francs le kilo; **100 km p. hour,** cent kilomètres par heure; (*e*) **p. annum,** par an; **p. week,** par semaine; **p. day, p. diem,** par jour; *NAm:* **the p. diem,** le salaire journalier.

per- [pə(:)r], *pref. Ch:* per-.

Peracarida [pəræ'kæridə], *s.pl. Crust:* peracarides *f.*

peracetic [pərə'si:tik], *a. Ch:* peracétique.

peracid [pə:'ræsid], *s. Ch:* peracide *m.*

peracute [pə:rə'kju:t], *a. Med:* (*of inflammation, etc.*) suraigu, -uë.

peradventure [pə:rəd'ventjər], *adv. A:* **1.** (*when used with 'if,' 'unless,' 'lest,' 'that'*) par aventure, d'aventure, par hasard; **if p. the knight met a dragon . . .,** si par aventure le chevalier rencontrait un dragon . . .. **2.** peut-être; **p. he is mistaken,** il a pu se tromper; **p. he will not come,** il se peut qu'il ne vienne pas. **3.** *s.* **without p.,** sans faute; sans l'ombre d'un doute; **beyond p.,** à n'en pas douter.

Peraea [pə'ri(:)ə]. *Pr.n. A.Geog:* Pérée *f.*

perambulate [pə'ræmbjuleit], *v.tr.* **1.** parcourir, se promener dans (son jardin, etc.). **2.** *O:* visiter, inspecter (une forêt, etc.). **3.** promener (un enfant) dans sa voiture.

perambulation [pəræmbju'leiʃ(ə)n], *s.* **1.** promenade *f,* tournée *f.* **2.** *O:* visite *f,* inspection *f,* pérambulation *f.*

perambulator [pə'ræmbjuleitər], *s.* **1.** voiture *f* d'enfant; voiture landau. **2.** *Cin:* pied-chariot *m* (de caméra), *pl.* pieds-chariots; caméra-voyage *f, pl.* caméras-voyage.

perameles, peramelid [peræ'mi:li:z, -'mi:lid], *s. Z:* péramèle *m,* péramélidé *m.*

Peramelidae [peræ'mi:lidi:], *s.pl. Z:* péramélidés *m.*

perborate ['pə:bɔreit], *s. Ch:* perborate *m.*

perbromide [pə:'broumaid], *s. Ch:* perbromure *m.*

percale [pə:'keil, -'kɑ:l], *s. Tex:* percale *f.*

percaline ['pə:kəli:n, pə:kə'li:n], *s. Tex:* percaline *f.*

percarbonate [pə:'kɑ:bəneit], *s. Ch:* percarbonate *m.*

perceivable [pə'si:vəbl], *a.* (*of sound, etc.*) percevable (**to the ear,** à l'oreille); perceptible; **no p. difference,** aucune différence sensible.

perceivably [pə:'si:vəbli], *adv.* perceptiblement, sensiblement.

perceive [pə'si:v], *v.tr. esp. Lit:* **1.** percevoir (la vérité, etc.); **to p. the futility of . . .,** se rendre compte de la futilité de . . .. **2.** percevoir (un son, une odeur). **3.** s'apercevoir de (qch.); **he perceived that he was being watched,** il s'aperçut qu'on l'observait. **4. to p. s.o.,** apercevoir qn.

perceiving [pə:'si:viŋ], *a.* percepteur, -trice.

percentage [pə'sentidʒ], *s.* **1.** pourcentage *m;* **p. of profit,** pourcentage de bénéfice; **directors' p. of profits,** tantièmes *mpl* des administrateurs; **to allow a p. on all transactions,** allouer un tant pour cent, un tantième, sur toutes opérations; **to get a good p. on one's outlay,** retirer un gros intérêt de sa mise de fonds; **only a small p. of the pupils were successful,** la proportion des élèves admis a été faible; *Ph:* **p. of elongation,** allongement *m* pour cent. **2. p. of acid, of alcohol, etc.,** teneur *f* en acide, en alcool, etc.; **p. of alcohol in a wine,** proportion d'alcool dans un vin; teneur en alcool d'un vin; **composition of tar expressed in percentages,** composition centésimale du goudron.

percentile [pə:'sentail], *s.* percentile *m.*

percept ['pə:sept], *s. Phil:* **1.** l'objet perçu (par les sens). **2.** la perception de l'objet. **3.** *Psy:* **percepts,** (*also* **perceptor**) percepta *m.*

perceptibility [pəsepti'biliti], *s.* perceptibilité *f.*

perceptible [pə'septibl], *a.* (*a*) perceptible (à l'esprit); *Phil:* cognoscible; **p. difference,** différence *f* sensible; (*b*) **p. to the eye,** apercevable; visible; **p. to the ear,** perceptible à l'oreille; audible.

perceptibly [pə'septibli], *adv.* perceptiblement, sensiblement.

perception [pə'sepʃ(ə)n], *s.* **1.** (*a*) perception *f;* extériorisation *f* des sensations; **organs of p.,** organes percepteurs; (*b*) sensibilité *f* (aux impressions extérieures); faculté perceptive; intellection *f;* (*c*) chose perçue. **2.** *Jur:* perception (d'un loyer); recouvrement *m* (d'impôts).

perceptive [pə'septiv], *a.* **1.** perceptif; **the p. organs,** les organes *m* de la perception; **p. faculties,** facultés perceptives. **2.** perspicace; sensible.

perceptiveness [pə'septivnis], **perceptivity** [pə:sep'tiviti], *s.* perceptivité *f;* faculté perceptive.

perceptual [pə:'septjuəl], *a. Phil:* perceptif.

perch[1] [pə:tʃ], *s.* **1.** perchoir *m;* (*in cage*) bâton *m;* (*of bird*) **to take, get on, its p.,** se percher; *F:* **to knock s.o. off his p.,** détrôner, déjucher, dégotter, dégommer, qn. **2.** *A: Meas:* perche *f* (de $5\frac{1}{2}$ yards, *approx.* = 5 m.). **3.** *A: Veh:* flèche *f.* **4.** *Tan:* chevalet *m* d'étirage.

perch[2]. **1.** (*a*) *v.i.* (*of bird, F: of pers.*) percher, se percher (**on,** sur); gîter; (*of poultry*) jucher; (*b*) *v.pr.* se percher, se jucher (**on,** sur). **2.** *v.tr.* (*a*) **castle perched on a hill,** château perché sur (le sommet d')une colline; *F:* **to p. a vase on top of a cupboard,** percher un vase sur une armoire; **they'd perched me at the top of the house,** on m'avait juché au dernier étage; (*b*) *Tan:* étirer (les peaux).

perch[3], *s. Ich:* perche *f;* **Nile p.,** perche du Nil; **climbing p.,** perche grimpeuse; anabar grimpeur; souris *f;* **giant p.,** latès *m;* **the p. family,** les percidés *m;* **the American perches,** les centrarchidés *m.*

perchance [pə'tʃɑ:ns], *adv. A:* = PERADVENTURE.

percher ['pə:tʃər], *s. Orn:* percheur *m;* **the perchers,** les percheurs, les passereaux *m.*

perching[1] ['pə:tʃiŋ], *a.* (oiseau) percheur; **the lark is not a p. bird,** l'alouette n'est pas percheuse.

perching[2], *s. Orn:* perchage *m.*

perchlorate [pə:'klɔ:reit], *s. Ch:* perchlorate *m.*

perchloric [pə:'klɔrik], *a. Ch:* perchlorique.

perchloride [pə:'klɔ:raid], *s. Ch:* perchlorure *m.*

perchlorinate [pə:'klɔ:rineit], *v.tr. Ch:* perchlorer.

perchromate [pə:'kroumeit], *s. Ch:* perchromate *m.*

perchromic [pə:'kroumik], *a. Ch:* perchromique.

percid ['pə:sid], *s. Ich:* percidé *m.*

Percidae ['pə:sidi:], *s.pl. Ich:* percidés *m.*

percipience, percipiency [pə:'sipiəns, -ənsi], *s.* capacité *f* de percevoir (les sentiments d'autrui, etc.); perception *f* (du mystérieux, etc.).

percipient [pə'sipiənt]. **1.** *a.* percepteur, -trice (de sensations, etc.); conscient; **to be p. of a sensation,** percevoir une sensation. **2.** *s.* sujet *m* télépathique.

percoid ['pə:kɔid], *a. & s. Ich:* percoïde (*m*).

Percoidea [pə:'kɔidiə], *s.pl. Ich:* percoïdes *m.*

percoidean [pə:'kɔidiən], *a. Ich:* percoïde.

percolate ['pə:kəleit]. **1.** *v.i.* s'infiltrer; (*of coffee, etc.*) filtrer, passer; **ideas that take a long time to p.,** idées qui s'infiltrent lentement. **2.** *v.tr.* (*a*) (*of liquid*) passer à travers, filtrer à travers, s'infiltrer dans (le sable); (*b*) (*of pers., filter, etc.*) filtrer (un liquide); **to p. the coffee,** passer le café; **coffee must be percolated very slowly,** il faut que le café passe très lentement.

percolation [pə:kə'leiʃ(ə)n], *s.* **1.** infiltration *f;* *Petr: etc:* percolation *f.* **2.** filtration *f,* filtrage *m.*

percolator ['pə:kəleitər], *s.* (*a*) filtre *m;* percolateur *m;* (*b*) cafetière *f* automatique, russe.

percomorph ['pə:koumɔ:f], *s. Ich:* percomorphe *m.*

Percomorphi [pə:kou'mɔ:fai], *s.pl. Ich:* percomorphes *m.*

percuss [pə'kʌs], *v.tr. Med:* percuter (la poitrine, etc.).

percussion [pə:'kʌʃ(ə)n], *s.* percussion *f;* choc *m;* (*a*) **p. gun,** fusil *m* à percussion; **p. fire,** tir percutant; *Artil:* **p. fuse,** fusée percutante, à percussion; **p. pin,** rugueux *m* (de fusée); (*b*) *Petr:* **p. drilling,** forage *m* à, par, percussion; (*c*) *Mus:* **p. instruments,** instruments *m* de, à, percussion; **p. player,** percussionniste *mf;* (*d*) *Med:* percussion (d'un organe).

percussive [pə'kʌsiv], *a.* percutant; à, de, par, percussion; *Petr:* **p. boring,** forage *m* à, par, percussion; *Metalw:* **p. welding,** soudage *m* par percussion.

percutaneous [pə:kju:'teiniəs], *a. Med:* percutané; (*of injection, etc.*) hypodermique; sous-cutané; **p. reaction,** percuti-réaction *f.*

percutient [pə'kju:ʃiənt], *a.* = PERCUSSIVE.

percylite ['pə:silait], *s. Miner:* percylite *f.*

perdition [pə:'diʃ(ə)n], *s.* perte *f,* ruine *f;* *Theol:* perdition *f;* *A:* **p. take him!** que le diable l'emporte!

perdu [pə:'dju:], *a. A.Mil:* perdu, caché; **to lie p.,** se cacher, s'embusquer; être posté en sentinelle perdue.

perdurable [pə:'dju:rəbl], *a. A: & Lit:* (*of friendship, etc.*) durable; (*of peace, etc.*) durable, stable, permanent; (*of granite, etc.*) résistant; *Theol:* (*of life, bliss, etc.*) éternel.

perdure [pə:'djuər], *v.i. A: & Lit:* durer, persister; se perpétuer.

peregrinate ['perigrineit], *v.i. A: & Hum:* faire des pérégrinations; pégréginer, voyager.

peregrination [perigri'neiʃ(ə)n], *s.* pérégrination *f,* voyage *m.*

peregrinator ['perigrineitər], *s. A:* pérégrinateur, -trice; voyageur, -euse.

peregrine ['perigrin], *a. & s.* **1.** *A:* pérégrin (*m*); étranger, -ère. **2.** *Orn:* **p. (falcon),** (faucon) pèlerin (*m*).

peremptorily [pə'rem(p)tərili], *adv.* (*a*) péremptoirement, absolument, définitivement; (*b*) dictatorialement, impérieusement.

peremptoriness [pə'rem(p)t(ə)rinis], *s.* **1.** caractère péremptoire, dictatorial, absolu (d'un ordre, etc.); intransigeance *f.* **2.** ton absolu, tranchant.

peremptory [pə'rem(p)təri], *a.* péremptoire; (*a*) *Jur:* **p. writ,** mandat *m* de comparaître en personne; **p. defence,** défense *f* au fond; **p. exception of jurymen,** exception *f* péremptoire, récusation *f,* des jurés; **p. call to do sth.,** mise en demeure formelle de faire qch.; (*b*) (*of refusal, etc.*) péremptoire, absolu, décisif; **p. necessity,** nécessité absolue; (*c*) (*of tone*) tranchant, dogmatique, impératif, absolu, dictatorial; (*of pers.*) impérieux, autoritaire, intransigeant.

perennating ['perəneitiŋ], *a. Bot:* pérennant.

perennial [pə'reniəl]. **1.** *a.* (*a*) éternel, perpétuel; pérenne; **p. spring,** (i) source *f* intarissable, pérenne; (ii) *Poet:* printemps perpétuel; (*b*) *Bot:* vivace, persistant. **2.** *s.* plante *f* vivace.

pereniality [pəreni'æliti], *s.* pérennité *f.*

perennially [pə'reniəli], *adv.* à perpétuité; éternellement.

perennibranch [pə'renibræŋk], **perennibranchiate** [pəreni'bræŋkieit], *a. & s. Amph:* pérennibranche (*m*).

Perennibranchiata [pərenibræŋki'eitə], *s.pl. Amph:* pérennibranches *m.*

perfect[1] ['pə:fikt], *a.* **1.** parfait; (*a*) **God alone is p.,** Dieu seul est parfait; (*b*) **p. happiness is not of this world,** le bonheur parfait n'est pas sur la terre; **p. love,** parfait amour; **p. specimen, example,** spécimen, exemple, parfait; **a p. piece of work,** un travail achevé; **p. master of a game,** parfaitement maître d'un jeu; **p. actress,** actrice consommée; **p. type of the old aristocrat,** type achevé du vieil aristocrate; **his English is p.,** son anglais est impeccable; **to be p.,** (i) avoir toutes les perfections; (ii) (*also* **to be in p. condition**) être intact, sans défaut; **this wine is in p. condition,** ce vin est arrivé à la perfection; **to have a p. knowledge of sth.,** savoir qch. à fond; **engine with a p. performance,** moteur qui marche à perfection; **this will be p. for the job,** voilà exactement ce qu'il me faut pour ce travail; **p.!** parfait! voilà juste ce qu'il faut! (*c*) **in p. sincerity,** en parfaite, en toute, sincérité; **he's a p. stranger to me,** il m'est tout à fait, complètement, inconnu; il m'est parfaitement étranger; *F:* **he's a p. idiot,** c'est un parfait imbécile; **she's a p. fright,** c'est un véritable épouvantail; **that's p. nonsense,** ça ne rime à rien; ça c'est complètement ridicule. **2.** (*a*) *Mth:* **p. number,** nombre parfait; **p. group,** ensemble parfait; **p. square,** carré parfait; (*b*) *Mus:* **p. interval,** intervalle *m* juste; **p. fourth, fifth,** quarte *f,* quinte *f,* juste; **p. chord,** accord parfait; **p. cadence,** cadence parfaite; (*c*) **p. flower,** fleur parfaite; **p. insect,** insecte parfait; (*d*) **p. gas,** gaz parfait; **p. liquids,** liquides parfaits; (*e*) *Bookb:* **p. binding,** reliure *f* arraphique, sans couture. **3.** *a. & s. Gram:* **the p. (tense),** le parfait, le passé composé; **future p.,** futur antérieur; **verb in the p.,** verbe au parfait.

perfect[2] [pə:'fekt], *v.tr.* **1.** achever, parachever, accomplir (une besogne, etc.). **2.** rendre parfait, perfectionner, parfaire (une méthode, etc.); **to p. a measure, an invention,** mettre une mesure, une invention, au point. **3.** *Typ:* imprimer, mettre, (une feuille) en retiration.

perfectibility [pə:fekti'biliti], *s.* perfectibilité *f.*

perfectible [pə:'fektibl], *a.* perfectible; parachevable.

perfecting [pə:'fektiŋ], *s.* **1.** achèvement *m,* accomplissement *m.* **2.** perfectionnement *m;* mise *f* au point (d'un dessin, d'un projet, etc.). **3.** *Typ:* (impression *f* en) retiration *f;* **p. machine, press,** machine *f,* presse *f,* à réaction, à retiration, à double impression.

perfection [pə:'fekʃ(ə)n], *s.* **1.** *O:* perfection *f;* (*a*) achèvement *m,* accomplissement *m* (d'une tâche); (*b*) perfectionnement *m* (d'un travail, etc.). **2.** (*a*) **p. itself,** la perfection même; **to attain p.,** toucher, arriver, à la perfection; **to bring sth. to p.,** parachever qch.; **to do sth. to p.,** faire qch. à la perfection; **p. of detail,** achevé *m* (d'un objet d'art, etc.); (*b*) développement complet (d'une plante, d'un insecte); **in this climate certain fruits never come to p.,** dans ce climat certains fruits n'arrivent jamais à la maturité.

perfectionism [pə:'fekʃənizm], *s.* **1.** *Rel:* perfectionnisme *m.* **2.** *often Pej:* perfectionnisme; manie *f* de la perfection.

perfectionist [pə:'fekʃənist], *s.* **1.** *Rel:* perfectionniste *mf.* **2.** *often Pej:* perfectionniste; maniaque *mf* de la perfection.

perfective [pə:'fektiv], *a. Gram:* (temps) perfectif; (aspect) perfectif (du verbe).

perfectly ['pə:fiktli], *adv.* parfaitement; **to know sth. p.,**

savoir qch. à fond; *Th:* **to know one's part p.,** savoir son rôle par cœur; **to do sth. p.,** faire qch. à la perfection; **she's p. right,** elle a parfaitement raison; **you know p. well that . . .,** vous savez parfaitement que . . .; **it's p. ridiculous,** c'est parfaitement ridicule, d'un ridicule achevé; c'est tout ce qu'il y a de plus ridicule.

perfecto [pəː'fektou], *s.* cigare effilé aux deux bouts.

perfervid [pəː'fəːvid], *a. Lit:* chaleureux, ardent, exalté.

perfidious [pəː'fidiəs], *a.* perfide; traître, traîtresse; *Lit:* **p. Albion,** la perfide Albion.

perfidiously [pəː'fidiəsli], *adv.* perfidement; traîtreusement.

perfidiousness [pəː'fidiəsnis], **perfidy** ['pəːfidi], *s.* perfidie *f*; traîtrise *f.*

perfoliate [pəː'foulieit], *a.* **1.** *Bot:* perfolié, perfeuillé. **2.** *Ent:* perfolié.

Perforata [pəːfə'reitə], *s.pl. Z:* perforés *m.*

perforate[1] ['pəːfəreit]. **1.** *v.tr.* (*a*) perforer, percer, transpercer; **the bullet had perforated the lung,** la balle avait perforé le poumon; (*b*) poinçonner (une tôle, un billet, etc.); (*c*) grillager (une plaque, etc.); (*d*) *Tchn:* perforer (un papier, etc.) en pointillé; réaliser (dans du papier, etc.) un moletage par perforations en pointillé. **2.** *v.i.* (*a*) pénétrer (**into,** dans); **to p. through sth.,** perforer qch.; (*b*) *Med:* (*of ulcer*) déterminer une perforation.

perforate[2], *a. Her:* percé.

perforated ['pəːfəreitid], *a.* perforé, percé, troué; à trous, ajouré, grillagé; *Tchn:* (papier, etc.) perforé en pointillé; *Cmptr:* **p. tape,** bande perforée; *Anat:* **p. space,** espace perforé (du cerveau); *Const:* **p. brick,** brique creuse.

perforating[1] ['pəːfəreitiŋ], *a.* (*of muscle, ulcer, etc.*) perforant; **p. wound,** plaie pénétrante.

perforating[2], *s.* perforation *f*; **p. machine,** (i) *Dressm: etc:* machine à piquer; (ii) *Mec.E: etc:* machine à perforer; perforateur *m*; perforatrice *f*; (iii) *Cin:* perforeuse *f.*

perforation [pəːfə'reiʃ(ə)n], *s.* **1.** perforation *f*; perforage *m*, perçage *m*, percement *m*; *Cmptr:* **chadless p.,** perforation partielle; **chad-type p.,** perforation complète. **2.** (*a*) petit trou; *Anat:* orifice *m*; *Med:* perforation; (*b*) *coll.* trous *mpl*, ajours *mpl*, perforation(s); (*for counterfoils, etc.*) (perforation(s) en) pointillé *m*; (*of detached postage stamp*) dentelure *f*; **p. gauge,** (i) *Cin: etc:* pas *m* de la perforation de la bande; (ii) *Cin:* (*also* **p. comb**) peigne *m* à calibrage; (iii) (*philately*) odontomètre *m.*

perforative ['pəːfərətiv], *a.* perforant, perforatif; perforateur, -trice.

perforator ['pəːfəreitər], *s.* **1.** machine *f* à perforer; perforateur *m*; *Min:* perforatrice *f.* **2.** *Surg:* tréphine *f*; foret *m*; pince *f* à percer. **3.** *Cmptr: Tg: etc:* **(tape-)p.,** perforateur, perforatrice, *Cmptr:* de bande, *Tg:* de ruban; **keyboard p.,** *Cmptr:* perforatrice à clavier, *Tg:* compositeur *m*; *Tg:* **receiving p.,** perforateur d'arrivée. **4.** *Archeol:* perçoir *m.*

perforce [pəː'fɔːs], *adv. Lit:* forcément; par nécessité.

perform [pəː'fɔːm], *v.tr.* **1.** célébrer (un rite); remplir (son devoir); **the whole operation is performed in five seconds,** l'opération entière s'accomplit en cinq secondes; *Surg:* **to p. an operation on s.o.,** opérer qn. **2.** *Th: etc:* (*a*) jouer, représenter (une pièce); exécuter (une danse); exécuter, jouer (un morceau de musique); tenir, remplir (un rôle); (*b*) *v.i.* **to p. in a play,** tenir un rôle, jouer, dans une pièce; **to p. on the flute,** jouer de la flûte.

performance [pəː'fɔːməns], *s.* **1.** exécution *f* (d'un contrat, d'un opéra); accomplissement *m* (d'une tâche); célébration *f* (d'un rite); **p. bond,** garantie *f* de bonne exécution. **2.** (*a*) acte *m*, exploit *m*; **to make a great p. of doing sth.,** faire qch. avec beaucoup de brio; *F:* **what a p.!** quelle histoire! quel spectacle! (*b*) *Sp:* performance *f*; **to put up a good p.,** accomplir une performance; (*c*) *Ind:* cadence *f* (de travail d'un ouvrier); **average incentive p.,** seuil *m* de prime; (*d*) *Mec.E:* (i) fonctionnement *m*, marche *f* (d'une machine); (ii) rendement *m*, performance (d'un avion, d'un appareil, d'un moteur, etc.); (iii) comportement *m*, tenue *f* (d'un matériel); **best, optimum, p.,** meilleur rendement; rendement maximum, optimum; maximum *m* de rendement; **p. curve,** diagramme *m* de marche (d'une machine); **p. rating,** rendement effectif; (*e*) *Cmptr:* **p. analysis,** tableau comparatif de performances; **p. evaluation,** analyse *f* des performances. **3.** *Th: etc:* représentation *f* (d'une pièce); séance *f* (de cinéma); **charity p.,** représentation à bénéfice; **first p.,** première *f*; **farewell p.,** représentation d'adieu; *Cin:* **continuous p.,** spectacle permanent; **there is no p. tonight,** il y a relâche ce soir; **play that has run for a hundred performances,** pièce qui a eu cent représentations.

performer [pəː'fɔːmər], *s.* **1.** *Mus:* exécutant, -ante; artiste *mf*; musicien, -ienne; **incompetent p.,** mauvais joueur. **2.** *Th:* acteur, -trice; artiste.

performing[1] [pəː'fɔːmiŋ], *a.* **p. dog, p. fleas,** chien savant, puces savantes.

performing[2], *s.* **1.** accomplissement *m*, exécution *f* (**of,** de). **2.** *Th: etc:* représentation *f* (d'une pièce); interprétation *f* (d'un rôle); **p. rights,** droit(s) *m* (i) *Th:* de représentation, (ii) *Mus:* d'exécution.

perfume[1] ['pəːfjuːm], *s.* parfum *m*; (*a*) odeur *f* agréable; senteur *f*; (*b*) **bottle of p.,** flacon *m* de parfum.

perfume[2] [pə'fjuːm], *v.tr.* parfumer; *Lit:* **the scent of roses perfumed the air,** l'air était embaumé de roses.

perfumer [pə'fjuːmər], *s.* parfumeur, -euse.

perfumery [pə'fjuːməri], *s.* parfumerie *f.*

perfunctorily [pə'fʌŋkt(ə)rili], *adv.* par manière d'acquit, superficiellement, pour la forme; **to do sth. p.,** bâcler qch.

perfunctoriness [pə'fʌŋkt(ə)rinis], *s.* négligence *f*; manque *m* de soin, peu de soin (**in doing sth.,** apporté à faire qch.).

perfunctory [pə'fʌŋkt(ə)ri], *a.* **1.** (*of inquiry, etc.*) fait pour la forme; de pure forme; superficiel; **the examination was p.,** l'examen a été une pure formalité; **p. work,** travail fait par-dessous la jambe, fait à la diable, fait à la hâte; **p. look,** coup d'œil superficiel; **p. inquiry,** (i) enquête peu poussée; (ii) renseignements pris par manière d'acquit. **2.** (*of pers.*) négligent; peu zélé.

perfuse [pəː'fjuːz], *v.tr.* **1.** *Lit:* (*a*) asperger (**sth. with water, etc.,** qch. d'eau, etc.); **to p. sth. with colour, light,** répandre de la couleur, de la lumière, sur qch.; **perfused with light,** noyé de lumière; (*b*) inonder. **2.** filtrer (un liquide) (**through,** à travers).

perfusion [pə'fjuːʒ(ə)n], *s.* **1.** *Lit:* aspersion *f* (**of sth. with sth.,** de qch. avec qch.). **2.** *Physiol:* perfusion *f.*

Pergamene ['pəːgəmiːn], **Pergamenian** [pəːgə'miːniən]. *A.Geog:* (*a*) *a.* pergaménien; (*b*) *s.* Pergaménien, -ienne.

pergameneous [pəːgə'miːniəs], *a. Nat.Hist:* pergamentacé.

Pergamos, Pergamum ['pəːgəməs, -məm]. *Pr.n. A.Geog:* Pergame.

pergelisol [pə'dʒelisɔl], *s. Geol:* pergélisol *m*, permafrost *m.*

pergola ['pəːgələ], *s.* pergola *f*, pergole *f*; treille *f* à l'italienne; tonnelle *f.*

Pergolese, Pergolesi [pəːgɔ'leizi]. *Pr.n.m. Mus.Hist:* Pergolèse.

perhaps [pə'hæps, præps], *adv.* peut-être; **p. so, p. not,** peut-être (bien) que oui, que non; **p. we shall come back tomorrow,** peut-être reviendrons-nous demain; peut-être que nous reviendrons demain; **p. I have it,** il se peut que je l'aie; **I'm giving up this work but p. I'll take it up again later,** j'abandonne ce travail, quitte à le reprendre plus tard; **there were p. a dozen people, not more,** il y avait peut-être une douzaine de personnes, pas davantage; **I'll do it unless, p., you want to do it yourself,** je vais le faire, à moins que par hasard vous ne désiriez le faire vous-même; **p. you would like to try it on,** vous voudriez peut-être l'essayer.

perhydride [pəː'haidraid], *s. Ch:* perhydrure *m.*

peri ['piəri], *s. Myth:* péri *m & f*; **as fair as a p.,** d'une beauté divine.

peri- ['peri], *pref.* péri-.

periadenitis [periædə'naitis], *s. Med:* périadénite *f.*

perianal [peri'einəl], *a. Anat:* périanal, -aux.

Periander [peri'ændər]. *Pr.n.m. Gr.Hist:* Périandre.

perianth ['periænθ], *s. Bot:* périanthe *m.*

periapsis [peri'æpsis], *s. Space:* périastre *m.*

periapt ['periæpt], *s.* périapte *m*, amulette *f*, talisman *m.*

periarteritis [periɑːtə'raitis], *s. Med:* périartérite *f.*

periarthritis [periɑː'θraitis], *s. Med:* périarthrite *f.*

periarticular [periɑː'tikjulər], *a. Anat:* périarticulaire.

periastron [peri'æstrɔn], *s. Astr:* périastre *m.*

periblast ['periblæst], *s. Biol:* périblaste *m.*

periblastula [peri'blæstjulə], *s. Biol:* périblastula *f.*

periblem ['periblem], *s. Bot:* périblème *m.*

peribolos, peribolus [pe'ribələs, -ləs], *s. Arch:* péribole *m.*

pericardectomy [perikɑː'dektəmi], *s. Surg:* péricardectomie *f.*

pericardial [peri'kɑːdiəl], *a. Anat:* péricardique.

pericardiotomy [perikɑːdi'ɔtəmi], *s. Surg:* péricardiotomie *f.*

pericarditis [perikɑː'daitis], *s. Med:* péricardite *f.*

pericardium [peri'kɑːdiəm], *s. Anat:* péricarde *m.*

pericarp ['perikɑːp], *s. Bot:* péricarpe *m.*

pericarpial, pericarpic [peri'kɑːpiəl, -pik], *a. Bot:* péricarpique; péricarpien; péricarpial, -aux.

pericemental [perisi'ment(ə)l], *a. Anat:* pericémentaire; paradontal, -aux.

pericementitis [perisimen'taitis], *s. Med:* péricémentite *f*, périodontite *f.*

pericementum [perisi'mentəm], *s. Anat:* périodonte *m*, desmodonte *m.*

perichondritis [perikɔn'draitis], *s. Med:* périchondrite *f.*

perichondrium [peri'kɔndriəm], *s. Anat:* périchondre *m.*

periclase ['perikleis], **periclasite** [peri'kleisait], *s. Miner:* périclase *m.*

Pericles ['perikliːz]. *Pr.n.m. Gr.Hist:* Périclès.

periclinal [peri'klain(ə)l], *a. Geol:* périclinal, -aux.

pericline ['periklain], *s. Miner: Geol:* péricline *f.*

pericolitis [perikə'laitis], *s. Med:* péricolite *f.*

pericope ['perikoup], *s. Ecc: etc:* péricope *f.*

Pericopidae [peri'kɔpidiː], *s.pl. Ent:* péricopides *m.*

pericranium [peri'kreiniəm], *s. Anat:* péricrâne *m.*

pericrocotus [perikrɔ'koutəs], *s. Orn:* péricrocote *m*, minivet *m.*

pericycle ['perisaikl], *s. Bot:* péricycle *m.*

pericystitis [perisis'taitis], *s. Med:* péricystite *f.*

periderm ['peridəːm], *s. Nat.Hist:* périderme *m.*

peridermal, peridermic [peri'dəːm(ə)l, -mik], *a. Nat.Hist:* péridermique.

peridesm ['peridezm], *s. Bot:* péridesme *m.*

peridesmic [peri'dezmik], *a. Bot:* péridesmique.

peridinian [peri'diniən], *s. Algae:* péridinien *m.*

Peridiniidae [peridi'niːidiː], *s.pl. Algae:* péridinidés *m.*

peridinium [peri'diniəm], *s. Algae:* péridinium *m.*

peridium [pe'ridiəm], *s. Bot:* péridium *m.*

peridot ['peridɔt], *s. Miner:* péridot *m.*

peridotite [peri'doutait], *s. Miner:* péridotite *f.*

periesophageal [periisɔfə'dʒi(ː)əl], *a. Anat:* périœsophagien.

periesophagitis [periisɔfə'dʒaitis], *s. Med:* périœsophagite *f.*

perifolliculitis [perifɔlikju'laitis], *s. Med:* périfolliculite *f.*

perigee ['peridʒiː], *s. Astr:* périgée *m*; **the moon is in p.,** la lune est dans son périgée, est périgée.

periglacial [peri'gleisiəl], *a. Geog:* périglaciaire.

perigone ['perigoun], **perigonium** [peri'gouniəm], *s. Bot:* périgone *m.*

Perigordian [peri'gɔːdiən], *a. & s. Prehist:* périgordien (*m*).

perigynous [pe'ridʒinəs], *a. Bot:* périgyne.

perihelion [peri'hiːliən], *s. Astr:* périhélie *m*; **star in p.,** astre (au) périhélie.

perihepatitis [perihepə'taitis], *s. Med:* périhépatite *f.*

perijove ['peridʒouv], *s. Astr:* périjove *m.*

peril[1] ['peril], *s.* péril *m*, danger *m*; **in p.,** en danger, en péril; **in p. of one's life,** en danger de mort; **to do sth. at one's (own) p.,** faire qch. à ses risques et périls; **touch him at your p.,** gare à vous si vous le touchez; *M.Ins:* **peril(s) of the sea,** fortune *f* de mer; risque(s) *m* de mer.

peril[2], *v.tr.* **(perilled)** *O: & Lit:* mettre (qch., qn) en péril, en danger.

perilla [pe'rilə], *s. Bot:* pérille *f.*

perilous ['periləs], *a.* périlleux, dangereux; **p. climb,** ascension périlleuse.

perilously ['periləsli], *adv.* périlleusement, dangereusement; **he came p. near breaking his neck,** il s'en est fallu de peu qu'il ne se soit cassé le cou.

perilousness ['periləsnis], *s.* caractère dangereux (de qch.); danger *m* (d'une entreprise).

perilune ['periluːn], *s.* périlune *m*; périgée *m* de la lune.

perilymph ['perilimf], *s. Anat:* périlymphe *f.*

perimeter [pə'rimitər], *s.* **1.** périmètre *m*; circonférence *f*; *Hyd:* **wet p.,** périmètre mouillé; *El: etc:* **p. cable,** câble *m* périphérique, de ceinture; *Sp: Av: etc:* **p. track,** piste *f* périphérique; *Mil:* **p. defence,** défense *f* périphérique. **2.** *Opt:* (*device*) campimètre *m.*

perimetric [peri'metrik], *a.* périmétrique; périmétral, -aux.

perimetritis [perime'traitis], *s. Med:* périmétrite *f.*

perimetry [pe'rimitri], *s. Opt:* périmétrie *f.*

perimorphism [peri'mɔːfizm], *s. Cryst:* périmorphose *f.*

perimysium [peri'maisiəm], *s. Anat:* périmysium *m.*

perin(a)eum [peri'niːəm], *s. Anat:* périnée *m.*

perinatal [peri'neit(ə)l], *a. Med:* périnatal, -als.

perineal [peri'niːəl], *a. Anat:* périnéal, -aux.

perineoplasty [periniou'plæsti], *s. Surg:* périnéoplastie *f.*

perineorrhaphy [periniː'ɔrəfi], *s. Obst:* périnéorraphie *f.*

perineotomy [periniː'ɔtəmi], *s. Surg:* périnéotomie *f.*

perinephric [peri'nefrik], *a. Anat:* périnéphrétique.

perinephritis [perini'fraitis], *s. Med:* périnéphrite *f.*

perineuritis [perinju'raitis], *s. Med:* périnévrite *f.*

perineurium [peri'njuːriəm], *s. Anat:* périnèvre *m.*

period ['piəriəd], *s.* **1.** (*a*) période *f*; durée *f*, délai *m*; **for a p. of three months,** pendant une période de trois mois; **p. of availability of a ticket,** durée de validité d'un billet; **authors' rights are protected for a p. of fifty years,** la protection des droits d'auteur s'étend sur une période de cinquante ans; **to discharge a liability within the agreed p.,** liquider une créance dans les délais convenus; *Bank:* **deposit for a fixed p.,** dépôt *m* à terme fixe; (*b*) *Sch:* heure *f* de cours; (*for pupil*) **free p., prep. p.,** heure d'étude; (*for teacher*) **free p.,** heure libre; *Meteor:* **fair periods,** éclaircies *f*; **p. of drought,** période de sécheresse; **a p. of training,** une période d'entraînement; (*of a mechanism, etc.*) **p. of rest,** (i) *Mec.E:* période, intervalle *m*, de repos; (ii) *Elcs:* période, intervalle, entre deux balayages; *Aut: etc:* **running-in p.,** période de rodage; *Med:* **incubation p.,** période d'incubation; **p. of latency,** période latente; *Physiol:* **(monthly) p.,** menstrues *fpl*, règles *fpl*; (*c*) *Astr: etc:* cycle *m*, période (de la révolution d'un planète); *Ph:* **p. of a wave, of an alternating current,** période d'une onde, d'un courant alternatif; **half p.,** demi-période *f, pl.* demi-périodes; **p. of oscillation, of vibration,** période d'oscillation, de vibration; **vibrational p.,** période vibratoire; **natural p.,** période propre; *Elcs: Cmptr:* **scan p.,** période de balayage; **regeneration p.,** période de régénération; **charging p.,** période de taxation; (*d*) *Atom.Ph:* période (d'un corps radioactif, d'un réacteur); **accelerating p.,** période d'accélération; **counting p.,** période de comptage; **p. of decay,** période de désintégration. **2.** (*a*) époque *f*, âge *m*; ère *f*; **the Victorian p.,** la période, l'ère, victorienne; **at certain periods of his life,** durant certaines périodes de sa vie; **attitude typical of the p.,** attitude *f* caractéristique (i) de l'époque (en question), (ii) de notre époque; **p. play, novel,** comédie *f*, roman *m*, historique; **p. dress,** robe *f* de style; **p. costume,** toilette *f* d'époque; **p. furniture,** meubles *mpl* de style, d'époque; (*b*) *Com: etc:* **p. of an account,** période, époque, d'un compte courant; **accounting p.,** exercice *m*; **p. under review,** exercice écoulé. **3.** (*a*) *Lit:* phrase *f*; **well rounded periods,** phrases, périodes, bien tournées; (*b*) *Mus:* phrase complète. **4.** *Gram: Typ:* point *m* (de ponctuation); *F:* **p.!** un point, c'est tout! **he's no good at maths!—he's no good, p.!** il est nul en math!—il est nul, tout court! **she talks too much about her health!—she talks too much, p.!** elle parle trop de sa petite santé!—tu veux dire qu'elle parle trop.

periodate [pəː'raiədeit], *s. Ch:* periodate *m.*

periodic[1] [piəri'ɔdik], *a.* **1.** périodique; **p. wind,** vent *m* périodique; *Ph:* **p. point,** nœud *m* de vibration; **p. wave,** onde *f* périodique; *El:* **p. current, voltage,** courant *m*, tension *f*, périodique; *W.Tel:* **p. aerial,** antenne accordée; *Ch:* **p. law,** loi *f* périodique (des éléments); *Mth:* **p. function,** fonction *f* périodique; *Med:* **p. fever,** fièvre *f* périodique. **2.** *Lit:* **p. style,** style périodique, ample, fourni, riche en périodes.

periodic[2], **per-iodic** [pəːrai'ɔdik], *a. Ch:* periodique.

periodical [piəri'ɔdikl]. **1.** *a.* périodique. **2.** *s.* (publication *f*) périodique *m*; journal *m*; **learned p.,** journal savant.

periodicalist [piəri'ɔdikəlist], *s. Journ:* périodiste *mf.*

periodically [piəri'ɔdik(ə)li], *adv.* périodiquement; de temps en temps; à intervalles réguliers.

periodicity [piəriə'disiti], *s.* **1.** périodicité *f* (d'une comète, etc.). **2.** *El:* fréquence *f* (d'un courant alternatif).

periodide [pəː'raiədaid], *s. Ch:* periodure *m.*

periodontal [periou'dɔntəl], *a. Anat:* périodontique, parodontaire, parodontal, -aux; **p. tissue,** parodonte *m*, périodonte *m.*

periodontia, periodontics [periou'dɔnʃiə, -'dɔntiks], *s. Dent:* parodontologie *f.*

periodontist [periou'dɔntist], *s. Dent:* spécialiste *mf* en parodontologie.

periodontitis [perioudɔn'taitis], *s. Med:* périodontite *f.*

periodontium [periou'dɔnʃiəm], *s. Anat:* parodonte *m.*

periodontology [perioudɔn'tɔlədʒi], *s. Dent:* parodontologie *f.*

periodontosis [perioudɔn'tousis], *s. Med:* parodontose *f.*

perioeci [peri'iːsai], *s.pl. Geog:* périœciens *m.*

periœsophageal [periiːsɔfə'dʒi(ː)əl], *a. Anat:* périœsophagien.

periœsophagitis [periiːsɔfə'dʒaitis], *s. Med:* périœsophagite *f.*

periophthalmus [periɔf'θælməs], *s. Ich:* périopht(h)alme *m.*

periople ['periouplj], *s. Vet:* périople *m.*

perioplic ['periɔplik], *a. Vet:* périoplique.

periosteal [peri'ɔstiəl], *a. Anat:* périostique; périostéal, -aux.

periosteum [peri'ɔstiəm], *s. Anat:* périoste *m.*

periostitis [periɔs'taitis], *s. Med:* périostite *f.*

periostosis [periɔs'tousis], *s. Med:* périostose *f.*

periovular [peri'ouvjulər], *a. Anat:* périovulaire.

peripatetic [peripə'tetik]. **1.** *a.* (*a*) *A.Phil:* péripatéticien, péripatétique; (*b*) ambulant, itinérant; **p. teacher,** professeur qui enseigne dans plusieurs collèges. **2.** *s.* (*a*) *A.Phil:* péripatéticien *m*; (*b*) *O:* marchand ambulant.

peripatetically [peripə'tetik(ə)li], *adv.* péripatétiquement.

peripateticism [peripə'tetisizm], *s.* péripatétisme *m.*

peripatus [pe'ripətəs], *s. Nat.Hist:* péripate *m.*

peripet(e)ia [peripe'tiːə], *s. Gr.Th: etc:* péripétie *f.*

peripheral [pə'rifərəl]. **1.** *a.* (*also* **peripheric** [peri'ferik]) périphérique; circonférentiel; tangentiel; (*a*) *Atom.Ph:* **p. electron,** électron *m* périphérique; **p. layer,** couche *f* périphérique; **p. region,** région *f* périphérique; (*b*) *Mec:* **p. force,** force tangentielle; **p. speed,** vitesse périphérique, circonférentielle, tangentielle; **p. tension,** tension circonférentielle; (*c*) *Opt:* **p. vision,** vision *f* périphérique. **2.** *a. & s. Cmptr:* périphérique (*m*); **p. assignment table,** table *f* d'affectation des périphériques; **p. computer,** ordinateur *m* satellite; **p. device, p. unit,** appareil *m*, élément *m*, organe *m*, périphérique; **p. equipment,** matériel *m* périphérique; périphériques *mpl*; **p. equipment operator,** mécanographe *mf*; **p. transfer,** transfert *m* entre périphériques; **p. buffer,** tampon *m* de périphérique; **p. bound, limited,** limité par la vitesse des périphéries.

periphery [pə'rifəri], *s.* périphérie *f*, circonférence *f*, pourtour *m*, périmètre *m*; **on the p. of. . .,** en bordure de. . ..

periphlebitis [perifli'baitis], *s. Med:* périphlébite *f.*

periphrase[1] ['perifreiz], *s.* = PERIPHRASIS.

periphrase[2]. **1.** *v.tr.* exprimer (une idée, etc.) par périphrase. **2.** *v.i.* user de périphrases; périphraser.

periphrasis, *pl.* **-es** [pə'rifrəsis, -iːz], *s.* périphrase *f*; circonlocution *f.*

periphrastic [peri'fræstik], *a.* (style *m*, etc.) périphrastique; *Gram:* **p. tenses,** temps composés; temps périphrastiques.

periphrastically [peri'fræstik(ə)li], *adv.* par périphrase.

periplasm ['periplæzm], *s. Nat.Hist:* périplasme *m.*

periplus ['periplʌs], *s. Lit:* périple *m*, circumnavigation *f.*

peripneustic [peri(p)'njuːstik], *a. Ent:* péripneustique.

periproct ['periprɔkt], *s. Echin:* périprocte *m.*

periprostatic [periprɔs'tætik], *a. Anat:* périprostatique.

periprostatitis [periprɔstæ'taitis], *s. Med:* périprostatite *f.*

peripteral [pə'riptərəl], *a. Arch:* (temple) périptère.

peripteros, periptery [pə'riptərɔs, -təri], *s. Arch:* périptère *m.*

periradicular [perirræ'dikjulər], *a. Anat:* périradiculaire.

perirectitis [perirek'taitis], *s. Med:* périrectite *f.*

perirenal [peri'riːnəl], *a. Anat:* périnéphrétique.

perisarc ['perisɑːk], *s. Z:* périsarc *m*, périsarque *m.*

periscii [pe'risiai], *s.pl. Geog:* périsciens *m.*

periscope ['periskoup], *s.* périscope *m*; **submarine p.,** périscope de sous-marin; *Mil:* **trench p.,** périscope de tranchée; **turret p.,** périscope de tourelle; *Nau:* **at p. depth,** en plongée périscopique.

periscopic [peri'skɔpik], *a.* (*of lens, etc.*) périscopique.

perish[1] ['periʃ]. **1.** *v.i.* (*a*) (*of pers.*) périr, mourir; **to p. by the sword,** périr par l'épée; **to p. from starvation, from cold,** mourir, périr, d'inanition, de froid; **I shall do it or p. in the attempt,** je le ferai ou j'y perdrai la vie; **p. the thought!** loin de nous cette pensée! *F:* **I'm perishing (with cold),** je meurs de froid; (*b*) (*of rubber, etc.*) se détériorer, se gâter, s'altérer; (*of leather, etc.*) s'avachir. **2.** *v.tr.* (*a*) détériorer, altérer, gâter; **oil soon perishes the tyres,** l'huile *f* amène vite la détérioration des pneus; (*b*) (*of frost, etc.*) faire mourir, brûler, griller (la végétation).

perish[2], *s. Austr: F:* **to do a p.,** être sur le point de mourir de faim (dans la brousse).

perishable ['periʃəbl]. **1.** *a.* (*a*) périssable; sujet à s'altérer, à se détériorer; *Nau:* **p. cargo,** denrées *f* périssables; chargement *m* périssable; (*b*) *A:* (*of glory, beauty, etc.*) de courte durée, éphémère. **2.** *s.pl.* **perishables,** marchandises *f* périssables.

perishableness ['periʃəbəlnis], *s.* (*a*) nature *f* périssable; (*b*) nature transitoire, éphémère (de la renommée, etc.).

perished ['periʃt], *a.* **1.** (*a*) péri; (*b*) (*of rubber, etc.*) détérioré, gâté, abîmé; (*of metal, etc.*) corrodé, corrompu. **2.** *F:* **to be p. (with cold),** être transi de froid; **my feet are p.,** mes pieds sont gelés; j'ai les pieds gelés.

perisher ['periʃər], *s.* **1.** *P:* sale type *m*, saligaud *m.* **2.** *Austr: F:* **to do a p.,** être sur le point de mourir de faim (dans la brousse).

perishing[1] ['periʃiŋ], *a.* **1.** *A:* transitoire, passager. **2.** destructif, fatal; *F:* **it's p.,** il fait un froid de loup. **3.** *P:* **p. idiot,** sacré idiot.

perishing[2], *s.* altération *f* (du caoutchouc); avachissement *m* (du cuir).

perisigmoiditis [perisigmɔi'daitis], *s. Med:* périsigmoïdite *f.*

perisperm ['perispəːm], *s. Bot:* périsperme *m.*

perispermal, perispermic [peri'spəːməl, -mik], *a. Bot:* périspermatique.

Perisphinctidae [peri'sfiŋ(k)tidiː], *s.pl. Paleont:* périsphinctidés *m.*

perisplenitis [perisple'naitis], *s. Med:* périsplénite *f.*

perispore ['perispɔːr], *s. Fung:* périspore *m.*

Perisporiaceae [perispɔːri'eisiiː], *s.pl. Fung:* périsporiacées *f.*

Perisporiales [perispɔːri'eiliːz], *s.pl. Fung:* périsporiales *f.*

perissodactyl [perisou'dæktil], *s. Z:* périssodactyle *m.*

Perissodactyla [perisou'dæktilə], *s.pl. Z:* périssodactyles *m.*

perissodactylous [perisou'dæktiləs], *a. Z:* périssodactyle, imparidigité.

peristalsis [peri'stælsis], *s. Physiol:* péristaltisme *m*; mouvement(s) *m* péristaltique(s); péristole *f.*

peristaltic [peri'stæltik], *a. Physiol:* péristaltique.

peristerite [pe'ristərait], *s. Miner:* péristérite *f.*

peristeronic [peristə'rɔnik], *a.* (société *f*) péristéronique, colombophile.

peristole ['peristoul], *s. Physiol:* péristole *f.*

peristomal [peri'stouməl], *a. Nat.Hist:* péristomal, -aux.

peristomatic [peristou'mætik], *a. Nat.Hist:* péristomique.

peristome ['peristoum], **peristomium** [peri'stoumiəm], *s. Anat: Bot:* péristome *m.*

peristomial [peri'stoumiəl], *a. Nat.Hist:* péristomal, -aux.

peristylar [peri'stailər], *a. Arch:* péristyle.

peristyle ['peristail], *s. Arch:* péristyle *m.*

perisystole [peri'sistəli], *s. Physiol:* périsystole *f.*

perisystolic [perisis'tɔlik], *a. Physiol:* périsystolique.

peritectic [peri'tektik], *a.* péritectique.

perithecium [peri'θiːsiəm], *s. Fung:* périthèce *m.*

perithoracic [periθɔ'ræsik], *a. Anat:* périthoracique.

peritomy [pe'ritəmi], *s.* péritomie *f*, circoncision *f.*

peritoneal [peritə'niːəl], *a. Anat:* péritonéal, -aux.

peritoneoscopy [peritəni'ɔskəpi], *s. Med:* péritonéoscopie *f.*

peritoneum [peritə'niːəm], *s. Anat:* péritoine *m.*

peritonitis [peritə'naitis], *s. Med:* péritonite *f.*

peritracheal [peritræ'kiːəl], *a. Ent:* péritrachéen.

peritrich ['peritrik], *s. Prot:* péritriche *m.*

Peritricha [pe'ritrikə], *s.pl. Prot:* péritriches *m.*

peritrichous [pe'ritrikəs], *a. Prot: Bac:* péritriche.

peritrophic [peri'trɔfik], *a. Ent:* péritrophique.

perityphlitis [periti'flaitis], *s. Med:* pérityphlite *f.*

periureteritis [perijuritə'raitis], *s. Med:* périurétérite *f.*

periuterine [peri'juːtərain], *a. Anat:* périutérin.

perivascular [peri'væskjulər], *a. Anat:* périvasculaire.

perivisceral [peri'visərəl], *a. Anat:* périviscéral, -aux.

perivisceritis [perivisə'raitis], *s. Med:* périviscérite *f.*

periwig ['periwig], *s. A:* perruque *f.*

periwigged ['periwigd], *a. A:* coiffé d'une perruque; en perruque; emperruqué.

periwinkle[1] ['periwiŋkl], *s. Bot:* (*genus*) vinca *f*; (petite) pervenche; **great p., large p.,** grande pervenche; bergère *f*; petit pucelage; **p. (blue),** bleu pervenche *inv.*

periwinkle[2], *s. Moll:* **1.** bigorneau *m*; *F:* vignot *m*, vigneau *m*; limaçon *m* de mer; **common p.,** bigorneau noir; **dwarf p.,** bigorneau jaune; **rough p.,** bigorneau rugueux. **2.** *Austr:* trochidé *m.*

perjure ['pəːdʒər], *v.pr.* **to p. oneself,** (i) se parjurer; *Jur:* porter faux témoignage; (ii) commettre un parjure; violer son serment.

perjurer ['pəːdʒərər], *s.* parjure *mf.*

perjurious [pəː'dʒuəriəs], *a.* menteur, -euse; faux, fausse.

perjury ['pəːdʒəri], *s.* **1.** (*as a moral offence*) parjure *m.* **2.** *Jur:* (*a*) faux serment; **to commit p.,** faire un faux serment; (*b*) faux témoignage; **subornation of p.,** subornation *f* de témoin.

perk[1] [pəːk]. **1.** *v.i. F:* **to p. (up),** (i) se rengorger; redresser la tête; (ii) se raviver; se ranimer; reprendre sa gaieté; (iii) (*after illness*) se requinquer, se ravigoter. **2.** *v.tr.* (*a*) (i) **to p. up one's head,** redresser la tête (d'un air crâneur ou guilleret); (ii) (*of dog*) **to p. up its ears,** dresser les oreilles; (*b*) *F:* **to p. s.o. up,** (i) parer, orner, requinquer, qn; (ii) (*of drink, etc.*) ravigoter qn.

perk[2], *v.tr. & i. F:* faire (le café) dans une cafetière automatique; (*of coffee*) se faire.

perkily ['pəːkili], *adv. F:* (*a*) d'un air éveillé, malin, déluré; (*b*) d'un air dégagé, désinvolte.

perkiness ['pəːkinis], *s. F:* **1.** allure(s) dégagée(s), désinvolte(s); présomption *f.* **2.** air éveillé, alerte; ton guilleret.

perks [pə:ks], *s.pl. F:* petits profits; gratte *f.*

perky ['pə:ki], *a.* (*a*) éveillé, guilleret, déluré; (*b*) outrecuidant, suffisant; (ton) dégagé, désinvolte.

perleche [pə:'leʃ], *s. Med:* perlèche *f,* pourlèche *f.*

perlid ['pə:lid], *s. Ent:* perlide *m.*

Perlidae ['pə:lidi:], *s.pl. Ent:* perlides *m,* perlidés *m.*

perlite ['pə:lait], *s. Miner:* perlite *f.*

perlitic [pə:'litik], *a. Geol:* perlitique.

perloir ['pə:lwɑ:r], *s. Metalw:* perloir *m.*

perm[1] [pə:m], *s. Hairdr: F:* (ondulation) permanente *f*; **home p.,** permanente à froid; permanente chez soi.

perm[2], *v.tr. Hairdr: F:* **to have one's hair permed,** se faire faire une permanente.

perm[3], *s.* (*in football pool*) permutation *f.*

permafrost ['pə:məfrɔst], *s. Geol:* pergélisol *m,* permafrost *m.*

Permalloy ['pə:məlɔi], *s. Metall: R.t.m:* permalloy *m.*

permanence ['pə:mənəns], *s.* permanence *f.*

permanency ['pə:mənənsi], *s.* **1.** permanence *f.* **2.** emploi permanent.

permanent ['pə:mənənt], *a.* permanent; **p. establishment,** établissement *m* à demeure; **p. assembly,** assemblée permanente, en permanence; **p. residence, address,** résidence *f,* adresse *f,* fixe; **p. job,** situation permanente; *Fin:* **p. assets,** actif immobilisé; capital immobilisé; *Ph:* **p. magnet,** aimant permanent; *Atom.Ph:* **p. disposal,** élimination permanente, définitive (des déchets); *Mec:* **p. set,** déformation permanente, plastique (d'un matériau); *Rail: etc:* **p. work, structure,** ouvrage *m* d'art; *Rail:* **p. way,** voie (ferrée); superstructure *f*; **unballasted p. way,** superstructure sans ballast; **p. way department,** service *m* de la voie; **p.-way man, engineer,** ouvrier *m,* ingénieur *m,* de la voie; *Rad:* **p. echo,** écho fixe, permanent; *Cmptr:* **p. data,** données constantes; **p. fault,** panne franche; *a. & s. Hairdr:* **p. (wave),** (ondulation) permanente *f.*

permanently ['pə:mənəntli], *adv.* d'une façon permanente; **do you mean to live in France p.?** avez-vous l'intention de vous établir définitivement en France? **p. appointed,** nommé à titre définitif; **p. attached to a firm,** attaché en permanence à une maison; **part p. fixed to a machine,** organe fixé à demeure à une machine; *Cmptr:* **p. stored,** implanté en permanence (en mémoire).

permanganate [pə:'mæŋgəneit], *s. Ch:* permanganate *m*; **potassium p., p. of potash,** permanganate de potassium.

permanganic [pə:mæŋ'gænik], *a. Ch:* permanganique.

permatron ['pə:mətrɔn], *s. Elcs:* permatron *m.*

permeability [pə:miə'biliti], *s.* perméabilité *f*; pénétrabilité *f*; **the p. of porous rocks,** la perméabilité des roches poreuses; **magnetic p.,** perméabilité magnétique; **p. under low magnetizing,** perméabilité à faible aimantation; *El:* **absolute, relative, p.,** perméabilité absolue, relative; **normal p.,** perméabilité normale; **p. tuning,** accord *m* par variation de perméabilité.

permeable ['pə:miəbl], *a.* perméable; pénétrable.

permeameter [pə:mi'æmitər], *s.* perméamètre *m,* perméabilimètre *m.*

permeance ['pə:miəns], *s.* **1.** = PERMEATION. **2.** *Magn:* perméance *f* magnétique.

permeate ['pə:mieit], *v.tr. & ind.tr.* **to p. (through) sth.,** filtrer à travers, passer à travers, percer, qch.; **ideas that have permeated (through, into, among) the people,** idées qui se sont infiltrées, qui se sont répandues, qui ont pénétré, dans le peuple; **water permeates everywhere,** l'eau s'insinue partout; **the soil was permeated with water,** le sol était saturé d'eau, imprégné d'eau.

permeation [pə:mi'eiʃ(ə)n], *s.* (*a*) pénétration *f,* infiltration *f,* imprégnation *f*; (*b*) *Med:* perméation *f.*

Permian ['pə:miən], *a. & s. Geol:* permien (*m*).

permissible [pə:'misibl], *a.* admissible, acceptable, tolérable; *Mec.E:* **p. clearance,** jeu *m* admissible, tolérable; **p. defects,** tolérances *f*; *Civ.E:* **p. explosives,** explosifs autorisés; *Atom.Ph:* **p. dose,** dose *f* admissible; **p. exposure,** irradiation *f* admissible; **would it be p. to say that . . .,** serait-il permis de dire, serait-on fondé à dire, que . . ..

permissibly [pə:'misibli], *adv.* par tolérance.

permission [pə:'miʃ(ə)n], *s.* permission *f*; autorisation *f*; **written p.,** autorisation écrite, par écrit; **to ask, give, s.o. p. to do sth.,** demander, donner, à qn la permission, l'autorisation, de faire qch.; **with your p.,** avec votre permission, votre autorisation; si vous voulez bien me le permettre; si je puis me le permettre.

permissive [pə:'misiv], *a.* **1. p. legislation,** législation facultative; **these laws are p. rather than mandatory,** ces lois constituent de simples facultés et ne sont pas impératives. **2.** (*a*) permis, toléré; **p. morals,** morale *f* commode; **p. society,** société *f* à la morale commode, qui se croit tout permis; (*b*) *Rail:* **p. blocking,** bloc permissif; (*c*) *Jur:* **p. waste,** défaut *m* d'entretien (d'un immeuble, etc.).

permissively [pə:'misivli], *adv.* avec autorisation; à bon droit.

permissiveness [pə:'misivnis], *s.* **1.** légalité *f* (d'une action). **2.** morale *f* commode (d'une société).

permit[1] ['pə:mit], *s.* **1.** (*a*) permis *m*; permission *f,* autorisation *f*; **to take out a p.,** se faire délivrer un permis; **building p.,** permission, autorisation, permis, de construire; **work p.,** permis de travail; (*b*) permis de circuler; laissez-passer *m inv.* **2.** *Cust:* acquit-à-caution *m, pl.* acquits-à-caution; passavant *m*; **export p.,** autorisation d'exporter; **loading, discharging, p.,** permis de chargement, de déchargement.

permit[2] [pə:'mit], *v.* (**permitted**) **1.** *v.tr.* permettre; **shooting is not permitted here,** ici la chasse n'est pas permise; **no smoking permitted,** défense de fumer; **to p. s.o. to do sth.,** permettre à qn de faire qch.; autoriser qn à faire qch.; **if I may be permitted,** si vous me le permettez; **I cannot p. such behaviour!** je ne puis pas permettre, tolérer, une telle conduite! (*angrily*) **p. me to tell you . . .!** laissez-moi vous dire . . .! *Adm:* **permitted hours,** heures légales de la vente des boissons alcooliques. **2.** *v.ind.tr.* **tone which permitted of no reply,** ton qui n'admettait pas de réplique; **matters that p. of no delay,** affaires qui ne souffrent pas de retard. **3.** *v.i.* **if time permits,** si j'ai, nous avons, le temps; **weather permitting,** si le temps le permet; **I drove as quickly as the road permitted,** j'ai conduit aussi vite que la route le permettait.

permittivity [pə:mi'tiviti], *s. El:* permittivité *f*; constante *f* diélectrique.

Permocarboniferous [pə:mouka:bə'nifərəs], *a. & s. Geol:* permo-carbonifère (*m*), *pl.* permo-carbonifères.

permonosulphuric [pə:mɔnousʌl'fju:rik], *a. Ch:* permonosulfurique.

permutability [pə:mju:tə'biliti], *s.* permutabilité *f.*

permutable [pə:'mju:təbl], *a.* permutable.

permutation [pə:mju'teiʃ(ə)n], *s. Mth: Ling:* permutation *f*; *Mth:* **permutations and combinations,** permutations et combinaisons; **permutations of *n* things taken *r* at a time** ($_nP_r$), permutations, arrangements *m,* de *n* objets *r* à *r.*

permutator ['pə:mjuteitər], *s. El:* permutatrice *f,* commutatrice *f.*

permute [pə:'mju:t], *v.tr.* **1.** *Ling: Mth:* permuter; *Ling:* **permuted consonants,** consonnes permutées. **2.** *Log:* retourner (une proposition).

pern [pə:n], *s. Orn:* bondrée *f.*

Pernambuco [pə:næm'b(j)u:kou]. **1.** *Pr.n. Geog:* Pernambouc *m.* **2.** *s.* **P. wood,** pernambouc.

pernettya [pə:'netiə], *s. Bot:* pernettya *m.*

pernicious [pə:'niʃəs], *a.* pernicieux; (*of doctrine, etc.*) malsain, délétère; *F:* **he's absolutely p.!** quelle horreur! quelle plaie!

perniciously [pə:'niʃəsli], *adv.* pernicieusement.

perniciousness [pə:'niʃəsnis], *s.* perniciosité *f*; effet pernicieux.

pernickety [pə:'nikiti], *a. F:* (*a*) tatillon, vétilleux, pointilleux; **to be p. about one's food,** être difficile sur sa nourriture; manger du bout des dents, pignocher; (*b*) (*of job*) délicat, minutieux; exaspérant (à cause du temps que ça prend).

pernio, *pl.* **-ones** ['pə:niou, -'ouni:z], *s. Med:* pernion *m.*

pernitrate [pə:'naitreit], *s. Ch:* perazotate *m,* pernitrate *m.*

pernitric [pə:'naitrik], *a. Ch:* perazotique, pernitrique.

pernoctation [pə:nɔk'teiʃ(ə)n], *s. Ecc:* veillée *f* (de toute la nuit); nuit passée en prières.

pero ['perou], *s. Breed:* co(c)quard *m,* coquart *m*; faisan bâtard.

peroba [pe'roubə], *s. Bot:* **ipé p.,** peroba *m* jaune; **p. rosa,** peroba rose.

Perognathus [pə'rɔgnəθəs], *s. Z:* perognathe *m.*

Peromyscus [perou'miskəs], *s. Z:* péromysque *m.*

peroneal [perou'ni:əl], *a. Anat:* (muscle, etc.) péronier.

peroneotibial [perouniou'tibiəl], *a. Anat:* péronéotibial, -iaux.

peroneus, *pl.* **-nei** [perou'ni:əs, -'ni:ai], *s. Anat:* (muscle *m*) péronier *m.*

peronospora [perə'nɔspərə], *s. Fung:* péronospora *m.*

Peronosporaceae [perɔnouspɔ:'reisii:], *s.pl. Fung:* péronosporacées *f,* péronosporées *f.*

Peronosporales [perɔnouspɔ:'reili:z], *s.pl. Fung:* péronosporales *f.*

peroral [pər'ɔ:rəl], *a. Med:* **p. administration,** administration *f* per os, par la bouche, par voie buccale.

perorate ['perəreit], *v.i.* **1.** faire la péroraison; conclure son discours. **2.** pérorer; discourir longuement.

peroration [perə'reiʃ(ə)n], *s.* **1.** péroraison *f.* **2.** discours prolongé, de longue haleine.

per os [pə'rous], *adv.phr. Med:* per os.

perosis [pə'rousis], *s. Vet:* pérose *f.*

perovskite [pə'rɔvskait], *s. Miner:* perovskite *f,* perowskite *f.*

peroxidase [pə'rɔksideis], *s. Bio-Ch:* peroxydase *f.*

peroxidate [pə'rɔksideit], *v.tr.* = PEROXIDIZE.

peroxidation [pərɔksi'deiʃ(ə)n], *s.* péroxydation *f.*

peroxide[1] [pə'rɔksaid], *s. Ch:* peroxyde *m*; **hydrogen p.,** eau oxygénée; **manganese p.,** peroxyde de manganèse; **red p. of iron,** colcotar *m*; *F: Pej:* **p. blonde,** fausse blonde.

peroxide[2], *v.tr. Pej:* faire blondir (ses cheveux) à l'eau oxygénée; **peroxided hair,** cheveux oxygénés.

peroxidize [pə'rɔksidaiz], *v.tr. Ch:* peroxyder; suroxyder.

peroxy [pə'rɔksi], *a. Ch:* **p. acid,** peroxyacide *m*; **p. salt,** peroxysel *m.*

peroxydisulphuric [pərɔksidaisʌl'fju:rik], *a. Ch:* perdisulfurique.

peroxydization [pərɔksidai'zeiʃ(ə)n], *s. Ch:* suroxydation *f.*

perpend [pə:'pend], *v.tr. & i. A:* peser (ses paroles); considérer (qch.); méditer.

perpendicular [pə:pən'dikjulər]. **1.** *a.* (*a*) perpendiculaire; (*of wall, cliff, etc.*) vertical, -aux; à plomb; (*of cliff*) à pic; **line p. to another,** ligne perpendiculaire à, sur, une autre; (*b*) *a. & s. Eng.Arch:* (style *m*) (gothique) perpendiculaire; (*c*) *F: O:* (*of pers.*) debout. **2.** *s.* (*a*) niveau *m* à plat; fil *m* à plomb; **out of (the) p.,** hors d'aplomb; hors d'équerre; (*b*) *Mth:* perpendiculaire *f*; *N.Arch:* **forward, after, p.,** perpendiculaire avant, arrière; **length between perpendiculars,** longueur *f* entre perpendiculaires.

perpendicularly [pə:pən'dikjuləli], *adv.* perpendiculairement; verticalement; d'aplomb; à pic.

perpetrate ['pə:pitreit], *v.tr.* commettre, perpétrer (un crime); **who on earth perpetrated this blunder, this terrible joke?** qui diable a pu être l'auteur de cette gaffe, de cette mauvaise plaisanterie?

perpetration [pə:pi'treiʃ(ə)n], *s.* perpétration *f* (d'un crime, etc.).

perpetrator ['pə:pitreitər], *s.* auteur *m* (d'un crime, d'une farce, etc.).

Perpetua [pə:'petjuə], *Pr.n.f. Rel.H:* Perpétue.

perpetual [pə:'petjuəl], *a.* (*a*) perpétuel, éternel; **p. motion,** mouvement perpétuel; **p. calendar,** calendrier perpétuel; (*b*) sans fin, continuel, incessant; **he's a p. grumbler,** c'est un éternel mécontent.

perpetually [pə:'petjuəli], *adv.* (*a*) perpétuellement, à perpétuité, éternellement; (*b*) sans cesse; incessamment, continuellement.

perpetuate [pə:'petjueit], *v.tr.* (*a*) perpétuer, éterniser; **this is how abuses are perpetuated,** c'est ainsi que les abus s'éternisent; (*b*) **to p. s.o.'s memory,** préserver le nom de qn de l'oubli.

perpetuation [pə:petju'eiʃ(ə)n], *s.* (*a*) perpétuation *f,* éternisation *f*; (*b*) préservation *f* de l'oubli.

perpetuator [pə:'petjueitər], *s.* celui, celle, qui assure, qui a assuré, la perpétuité (**of,** de).

perpetuity [pə:pe'tju:iti], *s.* **1.** perpétuité *f*; **in, to, for, p.,** à perpétuité. **2.** *Jur:* (*a*) jouissance *f* (d'un bien) à perpétuité; (*b*) **(rent in) p.,** rente constituée en perpétuel; rente perpétuelle.

perplex [pə:'pleks], *v.tr.* **1.** embarrasser (qn); mettre (qn) dans la perplexité; laisser (qn) perplexe; troubler l'esprit de (qn). **2.** *A:* emmêler, embrouiller, compliquer (une question, son style, etc.).

perplexed [pə:'plekst], *a.* perplexe, embarrassé; (regard) confus.

perplexedly [pə:'pleksidli], *adv.* d'un air embarrassé, perplexe; avec perplexité.

perplexing [pə:'pleksiŋ], *a.* (*of problem, etc.*) embarrassant, troublant; (*of book, pers., etc.*) difficile (à comprendre); **it's very p.,** on n'y comprend rien; on s'y perd facilement.

perplexity [pə:'pleksiti], *s.* **1.** perplexité *f,* embarras *m.* **2.** *A:* confusion *f,* enchevêtrement *m.*

perquisite ['pə:kwizit], *s.* (*a*) profit éventuel; bénéfice *m*; casuel *m*; revenant-bon *m, pl.* revenants-bons; (*b*) **perquisites,** (i) avantages *m* en nature; (ii) petits profits, *esp.* pourboires *m*; (iii) *Jur:* revenu casuel.

perquisition [pə:kwi'ziʃ(ə)n], *s. Jur:* perquisition *f* (à domicile).

perrhenate [pə:'ri:neit], *s. Ch:* perrhénate *m.*

perrhenic [pə:'ri:nik], *a. Ch:* perrhénique.

perrier ['periər], *s. A.Arms:* perrière *f.*

perron ['perən], *s. Arch:* perron *m.*

perry ['peri], *s.* poiré *m,* cidre *m* de poire.

persalt [pə:'sɔlt], *s.* persel *m.*

persecute ['pə:sikju:t], *v.tr.* (*a*) persécuter (des hérétiques, etc.); (*b*) tourmenter, harceler, importuner (qn); brimer (des recrues, des nouveaux élèves, etc.).

persecuting ['pə:sikju:tiŋ], *a.* persécuteur, -trice; persécutant; tourmentant, qui tourmente.

persecution [pə:si'kju:ʃ(ə)n], *s.* persécution *f*; **p. mania,** délire *m,* manie *f,* de la persécution.

persecutor ['pə:sikju:tər], *s.* persécuteur, -trice.

Perseids ['pə:siidz], *s.pl. Astr:* perséides *f.*

perseite ['pə:siait], **perseitol** [pə:'si:itɔl], *s. Ch:* perséite *f,* perséitol *m.*

Persephone [pə:'sefəni]. *Pr.n.f. Gr.Myth:* Perséphone.

Persepolis [pə:'sepəlis]. *Pr.n. A.Geog:* Persépolis *f.*

perseulose [pə:'si:julous], *s. Ch:* perséulose *m.*

Perseus ['pə:siəs]. *Pr.n.m. Gr.Myth:* Persée.

perseverance [pə:si'viərəns], *s.* persévérance *f*; assiduité *f*; constance *f* (dans le travail).

perseverate [pə:'sevəreit], *v.i. Psy:* (*of idea*) revenir spontanément à intervalles fréquents.

perseveration [pə:sevə'reiʃ(ə)n], *s. Psy:* persévération *f*; persistance *f,* hantise *f* (d'une image, d'un air de chanson, etc.).

persevere [pə:si'viər], *v.i.* persévérer (dans son travail, à faire qch.).

persevering [pə:si'viəriŋ], *a.* persévérant; assidu.

perseveringly [pə:si'viəriŋli], *adv.* avec persévérance; assidûment; avec constance.

Persia ['pə:ʃə]. *Pr.n. Geog:* Perse *f.*

Persian ['pə:ʃən]. **1.** *a.* persan; *A.Hist:* perse; **the P. Gulf,** le Golfe persique; *Arch:* **P. order,** ordre *m* persique; **P. carpet,** tapis *m* de Perse; **P. cat,** chat persan; **P. horse,** (cheval) persan *m*; *Bot:* **P. berry,** graine *f* de Perse, baie *f* de nerprun; *Hyd.E:* **P. wheel,** roue *f* à sabots. **2.** *s.* (*pers.*) Persan, -ane; *A.Hist:* Perse *mf.* **3.** *s. Ling:* perse *m.*

persicaria [pə:si'kɛəriə], *s. Bot:* persicaire *f.*

persicot ['pə:sikou, -kɔt], *s. Dist:* persicot *m.*

persimmon [pə:'simən, 'pəsimən], *s. Bot:* (*a*) plaqueminе *f*; **(Chinese) p.,** kaki *m*; figue-caque *f, pl.* figues-caques; (*b*) **p. (tree),** plaqueminier *m* (de Virginie), persimmon *m*; **(Chinese) p. (tree),** plaqueminier kaki.

persist [pə:'sist], *v.i.* persister. **1. to p. in one's opinion,** persister, s'obstiner, dans son opinion; **to p. in doing sth.,** persister, s'obstiner, à faire qch.; **I still p. in saying . . .,** j'en reviens toujours à dire . . .. **2.** continuer, durer; **childish traits which p. in adults,** traits enfantins qui persistent, qui subsistent, chez les adultes; **the fever persists,** la fièvre persiste, persévère, continue.

persistence, persistency [pə:'sist(ə)ns, -tənsi], *s.* persistance *f* **(in doing sth.,** à faire qch.). **1.** opiniâtreté *f,* ténacité *f,* obstination *f.* **2.** continuité *f*; **p. of vision,** persistance des impressions lumineuses, des images; **p. of matter,** persistance, permanence *f,* de la matière.

persistent [pə:'sist(ə)nt], *a.* persistant. **1.** opiniâtre, tenace; **p. thought,** pensée importune; **p. rain,** pluie *f* qui s'obstine; **p. in his intention to . . .,** toujours ferme dans son dessein de . . .. **2.** continu; *Com:* **p. demand for . . .,** demande suivie pour . . .; *Ph:* **p. beat,** oscillation persistante. **3.** *Bot:* **p. leaves,** feuillage persistant.

persistently [pə:'sistəntli], *adv.* avec persistance; opiniâtrement, avec ténacité.

Persius ['pə:siəs], *Pr.n.m. Lt.Lit:* Perse.

persnickety [pə:'snikiti], *a. F: esp. U.S:* = PERNICKETY.

person ['pə:s(ə)n], *s.* **1.** (*a*) (*pl. usu.* **people**) personne *f,* individu *m*; **the p. of whom I was speaking,** la personne dont je parlais; **the efficiency of the method depends on the p. who applies it,** l'efficacité de la méthode dépend de la personne qui l'applique; **he's a very cheerful p.,** c'est un homme très gai; il est toujours de bonne humeur; **I wouldn't have believed it of a p. of his intelligence,** je n'aurais jamais cru que quelqu'un d'aussi intelligent que lui aurait fait cela; **private p.,** simple particulier *m*; **to act through a third p.,** passer par une tierce personne, par personne interposée; **without exception of persons,** sans exception de personnes; **to be no respecter of persons,** ne pas faire cas de personnalités; **there is no p. of that name here,** il n'y a ici personne de ce nom; *Jur:* **some p. or persons unknown,** un certain quidam; **the said persons,** lesdits quidams; *F: A:* **what is a p. to do?** qu'est-ce que vous voulez qu'on fasse? **a p. doesn't like to be treated like that,** on n'aime pas à être traité ainsi; (*b*) *Pej:* individu, type *m*; **who is this p.?** quel est cet individu? **there's a p. wanting to speak to you,** une personne demande à vous parler; (*c*) **in (one's own) p.,** en (propre) personne; **he came in p.,** il est venu en personne; **to be delivered to the addressee in p.,** à remettre en main(s) propre(s); **he found a friend in the p. of his uncle,** il a trouvé un ami dans la personne de son oncle; **to carry weapons on one's p.,** porter des armes sur soi; (*d*) *A:* **to have a fine p.,** être bien de sa personne; être beau, belle; **he was attracted not by her p. but by her fortune,** il fut attiré non pas par sa personne mais par sa fortune; (*e*) *Jur:* **natural p.,** personne physique, naturelle; **artificial p.,** personne, personnalité, morale, civile, juridique; (*f*) personnage *m* (d'un roman, etc.). **2. (one) God in three Persons,** un (seul) Dieu en trois personnes. **3.** *Gram:* **verb in the first p.,** verbe à la première personne; **the second p. plural,** la deuxième personne du pluriel.

personable ['pə:sənəbl], *a.* bien (fait) de sa personne; beau, belle; **he's very p.,** il présente bien.

personage ['pə:sənidʒ], *s.* (*a*) personnage *m*; personnalité *f*; (*b*) *Th: O:* personnage.

personal ['pə:sən(ə)l], *a.* personnel. **1.** (*a*) **p. liberty,** liberté individuelle; **p. rights,** droits *m* du citoyen; **p. equation,** equation personnelle; **p. friend,** ami(e) personnel(le); **to give a p. touch to sth.,** personnaliser qch.; **p. issue,** question personnelle; **it's a p. matter,** c'est une affaire privée, personnelle; **I want it for my p. use,** j'en ai besoin pour mon usage personnel; *Cust:* **articles for p. use,** effets usagers; **it suits his p. convenience,** cela répond à, cadre avec, ses convenances personnelles; *Bank:* **p. account,** compte (en banque) personnel, particulier; *Adm:* **p. income,** revenu *m* des personnes physiques; *Com:* **p. selling,** vente directe au consommateur; **p. action at law,** action personnelle; **p. accident insurance,** assurance *f* contre les accidents corporels, contre les accidents à personnes; **to be careless about one's p. appearance,** négliger sa tenue; (*on letter*) **personal,** personnelle; *Journ:* **p. column,** petites annonces; (*b*) **p. remark,** allusion personnelle; **don't be p., don't make p. remarks,** ne faites pas des allusions personnelles; *s. Journ: NAm:* **personals,** chronique mondaine, mondanités *f,* échos *m*; (*c*) **p. enquiry,** enquête personnelle; **to make a p. appearance,** venir, paraître, en personne; **to have a p. interview with s.o.,** avoir une entrevue personnelle avec qn; parler personnellement à qn; **to make a p. application (for a job),** se présenter en personne, poser personnellement sa candidature (à un poste); **I have p. experience of this kind of problem,** j'ai une expérience personnelle de ce genre de difficulté. **2.** *Jur:* **p. estate, property,** biens personnels, biens meubles, biens mobiliers; **p. effects,** effets personnels; **p. action,** action mobilière; **heir to p. estate,** héritier mobilier. **3.** *Gram:* **p. pronoun,** pronom personnel.

personalia [pə:sə'neiliə], *s.pl.* **1.** ana *mpl.* **2.** objets personnels.

personalism ['pə:sənəlizm], *s. Phil:* personnalisme *m.*

personalist ['pə:sənəlist], *s. Phil:* personnaliste *mf.*

personality [pə:sə'næliti], *s.* **1.** (*a*) personnalité *f*; personnage *m*; (*b*) caractère *m* propre (de qn); **he's got no p.,** il manque de personnalité; *F:* **he's quite a p.,** c'est vraiment quelqu'un. **2.** (*a*) caractère personnel (d'une remarque, etc.); (*b*) **to indulge in personalities,** faire des allusions personnelles, des allusions blessantes.

personalization [pə:sənəlai'zeiʃ(ə)n], *s.* personnalisation *f*; personnification *f.*

personalize ['pə:sənəlaiz], *v.tr.* (*a*) personnaliser; personnifier; (*b*) *Com:* **personalized sales technique,** publicité personnalisée; **a personalized shirt, etc.,** une chemise, etc., personnalisée, avec vos initiales; **personalized letter,** lettre personnelle.

personally ['pə:sən(ə)li], *adv.* personnellement; **p. I think . . .,** pour ma part, pour moi, je pense . . .; quant à moi, je pense . . .; **p., I am willing,** moi, je veux bien; je veux bien, moi; **that belongs to me p.,** cela m'appartient en propre; **don't take that remark p.,** ne prenez pas cette remarque pour vous; **to deliver sth. to s.o. p.,** remettre qch. à qn en main(s) propre(s); **to intervene p.,** intervenir de son propre chef, en personne; **p. conducted tour,** voyage organisé sous la direction personnelle d'un guide.

personalty ['pə:sənəlti], *s. Jur:* **1.** objet mobilier. **2.** biens meubles, biens mobiliers, fortune mobilière; **to convert realty into p.,** ameublir un bien; **conversion of realty into p.,** ameublissement *m* d'un bien.

personate[1] ['pə:səneit], *v.tr.* **1.** *Th: A:* représenter, jouer (un personnage). **2.** *Jur:* se faire passer pour, contrefaire (qn); usurper l'état civil de (qn).

personate[2], *a. Bot:* (*of flower*) personé.

personation [pə:sə'neiʃ(ə)n], *s.* (*a*) *Th:A:* représentation *f* (d'un personnage); (*b*) *Jur:* **(false) p.,** usurpation *f* de nom, d'état civil.

personator ['pə:səneitər], *s.* (*a*) *Th: A:* joueur, -euse (d'un rôle); (*b*) personne *f* qui se fait passer pour quelqu'un d'autre; imposteur *m.*

personification [pə:sɔnifi'keiʃ(ə)n], *s.* personnification *f.*

personify [pə:'sɔnifai], *v.tr.* personnifier; **he's meanness personified,** il est, c'est, l'avarice même, l'avarice en personne.

personnel [pə:sə'nel], *s. Ind: etc:* personnel *m*; **p. department,** service *m* du personnel; **p. manager,** directeur *m* du personnel; *Mil:* **armoured p. carrier,** véhicule blindé de transport de personnel; **anti-p. mine,** mine *f* antipersonnel.

perspective [pə:'spektiv]. **1.** *s.* (*a*) *Mth: Art:* perspective *f*; **parallel p.,** perspective en vue de face; **angular, oblique, p.,** perspective en vue oblique; **aerial p.,** perspective aérienne; **drawing in p.,** dessin en perspective; **the p. of a picture,** les fuyants *m* d'un tableau; **picture out of p.,** tableau qui manque de perspective, dont la perspective est fausse; **to see a matter in its true p.,** voir une affaire sous son vrai jour; (*b*) **stage p.,** optique *f* du théâtre; (*c*) vue *f*; **a fine p. opened out before his eyes,** une belle perspective, une belle vue, s'ouvrit devant ses yeux; (*d*) **with a long p. of happy days before us,** avec devant nous une longue perspective de jours heureux. **2.** *a.* (dessin, etc.) perspectif, en perspective; **p. lines of a picture,** fuyants d'un tableau; **p. grid,** quadrillage perspectif; **p. projection,** projection perspective.

perspectivism [pə'spektivizm], *s. Phil:* perspectivisme *m.*

perspectivist [pə:'spektivist], *a.* & *s. Phil: Art:* perspectiviste *mf.*

perspectograph [pə:'spektougræf], *s. Surv:* perspectographe *m.*

perspicacious [pə:spi'keiʃəs], *a.* (*of pers.*) perspicace; fin, discernant; clairvoyant; (*of the mind*) perçant, pénétrant.

perspicaciously [pə:spi'keiʃəsli], *adv.* d'une manière perspicace; avec perspicacité; avec pénétration.

perspicacity [pə:spi'kæsiti], *s.* perspicacité *f*; pénétration *f,* discernement *m*; clairvoyance *f.*

perspicuity [pə:spi'kju:iti], *s.* perspicuité *f*; clarté *f,* netteté *f,* lucidité *f* (du style, etc.).

perspicuous [pə:'spikjuəs], *a.* clair, net, lucide.

perspicuously [pə:'spikjuəsli], *adv.* clairement, nettement, lucidement.

perspicuousness [pə:'spikjuəsnis], *s.* = PERSPICUITY.

perspiration [pə:spə'reiʃ(ə)n], *s.* (*a*) transpiration *f*; *Med:* sudation *f*; **fetid p.,** bromidrose *f*; **to be in (a) p.,** être en transpiration, en sueur; **to break into p.,** entrer en moiteur; **medicine that brings on p.,** remède *m* sudorifique, qui fait transpirer; (*b*) sueur *f*; **beads of p.,** gouttes *f* de sueur; **streaming with, bathed in, p.,** trempé de sueur; en nage.

perspiratory [pə:'spairət(ə)ri], *a.* **1.** (*of glands, etc.*) sudorifère, sudoripare. **2.** *Med:* sudorifique.

perspire [pə:'spaiər]. **1.** *v.i.* transpirer; suer; **my feet don't p.,** je ne transpire pas des pieds. **2.** *v.tr.* (*of plant, etc.*) transpirer (un liquide visqueux, etc.).

persuadable [pə:'sweidəbl], *a.* persuasible.

persuade [pə:'sweid], *v.tr.* persuader, convaincre (qn); **he persuaded me that he was telling the truth, of the truth of his statement,** il m'a convaincu, persuadé, qu'il disait la vérité; **I am persuaded that . . .,** je suis persuadé, convaincu, que . . .; **to p. s.o. that he ought to do sth.,** persuader à qn qu'il doit faire qch.; **they will not p. him to accept, into accepting,** ils ne l'amèneront pas à accepter, ne le persuaderont pas d'accepter; **p. your brother to come!** décidez votre frère à venir! **to p. s.o. not to do sth.,** déconseiller à qn, dissuader qn, de faire qch.

persuader [pə:'sweidər], *s.* conseilleur, -euse.

persuasibility [pə:sweisi'biliti], *s.* caractère *m* persuasible.

persuasible [pə:'sweisibl], *a.* persuasible.

persuasion [pə:'sweiʒ(ə)n], *s.* **1.** persuasion *f*; **power of p.,** force *f* de persuasion; **the art of p.,** l'art *m* de persuader; **he wants to collectivize agriculture by p.,** il veut collectiviser l'agriculture par la douceur. **2.** (*a*) *O:* conviction *f*; **it's my p. that he is mad,** je suis persuadé, convaincu, j'ai la conviction, qu'il est fou; (*b*) **(religious) p.,** (i) religion *f,* foi *f,* confession *f*; croyances religieuses; (ii) secte *f,* communion *f*; **they are of the same p.,** ils ont la même religion; **the Methodist p.,** la secte méthodiste; le méthodisme; (*c*) **(political) p.,** opinions *fpl* en matière de politique; idéologie *f*; (*d*) *F: A:* genre *m,* espèce *f*; **the male p.,** le sexe mâle.

persuasive [pə:'sweiziv, -siv], *a.* persuasif; persuadant; **p. salesman,** vendeur persuasif, qui sait inciter ses clients à acheter.

persuasively [pə:'sweizivli, -siv-], *adv.* d'un ton persuasif, de persuasion.

persuasiveness [pə:'sweizivnis, -siv-], *s.* force persuasive; persuasion *f.*

persulphate [pə:'sʌlfeit], *s. Ch:* persulfate *m*; **am-**

monium p., persulfate d'ammoniaque.
persulphide [pə:'sʌlfaid], *s. Ch:* persulfure *m.*
persulphuric [pə:sʌl'fjuərik], *a. Ch:* persulfurique.
pert [pə:t], *a.* **1.** mutin, moqueur, -euse; effronté, hardi; répliqueur, -euse. **2.** *NAm:* guilleret; gaillard; bien en train.
pertain [pə:'tein], *v.i.* appartenir (à qch.); concerner, regarder (qch.); **matters pertaining to man and his environment,** ce qui concerne, regarde, l'homme et son environnement; **the house and the land pertaining to it,** la maison et le terrain qui fait partie de la propriété, qui y appartient; **we had a turkey and everything else that pertains to Christmas,** nous avons eu une dinde et toutes les autres choses qu'on associe avec les fêtes de Noël.
perthite ['pə:θait], *s. Miner:* perthite *f.*
pertinacious [pə:ti'neiʃəs], *a.* obstiné, opiniâtre; (*of disease*) persistant.
pertinaciously [pə:ti'neiʃəsli], *adv.* obstinément, opiniâtrement.
pertinaciousness, pertinacity [pə:ti'neiʃəsnis, -'næsiti], *s.* obstination *f*, opiniâtreté *f* (à faire qch.).
pertinence, pertinency ['pə:tinəns(i)], *s.* pertinence *f* (d'une raison); à-propos *m*, justesse *f* (d'une remarque, etc.).
pertinent ['pə:tinənt]. **1.** *a.* (*a*) pertinent, approprié, à propos, juste; **to say sth. p.,** dire qch. à propos; (*b*) **books p. to the question,** livres *m* qui ont rapport à la question; **some questions p. to the matter in hand,** quelques questions qui relèvent de l'affaire qui nous occupe. **2.** *s.pl. Jur: Scot:* **pertinents,** appartenances *f*, dépendances *f.*
pertinently ['pə:tinəntli], *adv.* d'une manière pertinente; pertinemment; à propos; avec à-propos.
pertly ['pə:tli], *adv.* **1.** avec mutinerie, d'un ton mutin; d'un air effronté, hardi. **2.** *NAm:* d'un ton, d'un air, guilleret.
pertness ['pə:tnis], *s.* **1.** mutinerie *f*; effronterie *f.* **2.** *NAm:* air guilleret.
perturb [pə:'tə:b], *v.tr.* **1.** jeter le désordre, la perturbation, dans (un royaume, etc.). **2.** (*a*) *Astr:* dévier (un astre); (*b*) *Ph:* affoler (l'aiguille d'une boussole, le compas). **3.** troubler, inquiéter, agiter; jeter le trouble dans (l'esprit, etc.).
perturbation [pə:tə:'beiʃ(ə)n], *s.* **1.** perturbation *f*, commotion *f*, désordre *m*, bouleversement *m.* **2.** (*a*) *Astr:* perturbation; (*b*) affolement *m* (de l'aiguille aimantée); (*c*) *Elcs:* parasite *m.* **3.** agitation *f*, inquiétude *f*, trouble *m* (de l'esprit).
perturbative [pə:'tə:bətiv], *a.* (*of force, etc.*) perturbateur, -trice.
perturbed [pə'tə:bd], *a.* **1.** (*of thgs*) en désordre. **2.** *Ph:* **p. field,** champ *m* variable. **3.** (*of pers., of the mind*) agité, troublé, inquiet, -ète; **he was p.,** il était agité; il montrait de l'inquiétude; **he was not at all p.,** il restait calme, impassible; il ne s'est pas laissé démonter.
Peru [pə'ru:], *Pr.n. Geog:* Pérou *m*; *Pharm:* **balsam of P.,** baume *m* du Pérou.
Perugia [pə'ru:dʒiə], *Pr.n. Geog:* Pérouse *f.*
Perugian [pə'ru:dʒiən]. *Geog:* (*a*) *a.* pérugin; (*b*) *s.* Pérugin, -ine.
Perugino [peru'dʒi:nou], *Pr.n.m. Hist: of Art:* le Pérugin.
peruke [pə'ru:k], *s. A:* perruque *f*; **p. maker,** perruquier *m.*
perula ['peru:lə], *s. Bot:* pérule *f.*
perusal [pə'ru:zəl], *s.* lecture *f*; (*of document*) **for p.,** en communication; **to be deep in the p. of a document,** être plongé dans la lecture d'un document; **careful p.,** lecture attentive; examen attentif.
peruse [pə'ru:z], *v.tr.* (*a*) lire attentivement, prendre connaissance de (qch.); **to p. a book,** lire un livre (d'un bout à l'autre); (*b*) *A:* considérer (qch.); regarder (qch.) attentivement; **to p. s.o.'s countenance,** dévisager qn.
Peruvian [pə'ru:viən], *Geog:* (*a*) *a.* péruvien; **P. bark,** quinquina *m*; **P. balsam,** baume *m* du Pérou; (*b*) *s.* Péruvien, -ienne.
pervade [pə:'veid], *v.tr.* s'infiltrer dans, se répandre dans (qch.); **the feeling of revolt that pervades the whole book,** le sentiment de révolte qui anime tout ce livre; **a feeling of Sunday afternoon boredom pervaded the streets,** un sentiment de cet ennui d'après-midi de dimanche se répandait dans les rues; **the scent of pine trees pervaded the air,** l'air était embaumé de l'odeur des pins.
pervading [pə:'veidiŋ], *a.* **(all-)p.,** qui se répand partout; (*of influence, etc.*) régnant, dominant; **p. smell,** odeur persistante, pénétrante.
pervasion [pə'veiʒ(ə)n], *s.* infiltration *f*, pénétration *f.*
pervasive [pə:'veisiv], *a.* qui se répand partout; pénétrant; (parfum, etc.) subtil.
pervasiveness [pə:'veisivnis], *s.* puissance *f* de pénétration; tendance *f* à se répandre.
perveance ['pə:viəns], *s. Elcs:* pervéance *f.*
perverse [pə:'və:s], *a.* (*a*) pervers, perverti, méchant; (*b*) opiniâtre, dans l'erreur, dans le mal; (*c*) contrariant, désobligeant; (*d*) revêche, chagrin, bourru, acariâtre; (*e*) *Jur:* **p. verdict,** verdict *m* qui va à l'encontre des témoignages, des directives énoncées par le juge; verdict rendu de mauvaise foi.
perversely [pə:'və:sli], *adv.* (*a*) perversement, avec perversité, méchamment; (*b*) d'une manière contrariante; avec l'intention de contrarier (qn).
perverseness, perversity [pə:'və:snis, -'və:siti], *s.* (*a*) perversité *f*, méchanceté *f*; (*b*) esprit contraire, contrariant; (*c*) caractère *m* revêche; acariâtreté *f.*
perversion [pə:'və:ʃ(ə)n], *s.* **1.** action *f* de pervertir; pervertissement *m.* **2.** perversion *f*; **a p. of the truth,** un travestissement de la vérité; *Med:* **p. of the appetite,** perversion, dépravation *f*, de l'appétit; **sexual perversions,** inversions sexuelles.
perversive [pə:'və:siv], *a.* qui tend à pervertir; (*of doctrine, etc.*) mauvais, malsain, dépravant.
pervert[1] ['pə:və:t], *s.* **1.** (*a*) perverti, -ie; (*b*) apostat *m.* **2.** *Psy:* **sexual p.,** inverti, -ie.
pervert[2] [pə:'və:t], *v.tr.* **1.** détourner (qch. de son but); **to p. the course of justice,** égarer la justice. **2.** pervertir (qn); dépraver (le goût, l'appétit). **3.** fausser, altérer, dénaturer (les faits, les mots de qn); pervertir (le sens d'un passage).
perverted [pə:'və:tid], *a.* **1.** perverti. **2.** dénaturé, faussé.
perverter [pə:'və:tər], *s.* pervertisseur, -euse.
pervertible [pə:'və:tibl], *a.* pervertissable.
perverting [pə:'və:tiŋ], *s.* **1.** pervertissement *m.* **2.** altération *f.*
pervious ['pə:viəs], *a.* **1.** *A:* accessible (**to,** à); traversable (par qn). **2.** perméable (à l'eau, au gaz, etc.); **p. soil,** sol perméable.
perviousness ['pə:viəsnis], *s.* **1.** *A:* accessibilité *f* (d'un pays, etc.). **2.** perméabilité *f* (d'une roche, etc.).
perylene ['perili:n], *s. Ch:* pérylène *m.*
pesade [pə'zeid], *s. Equit:* pesade *f.*
peseta [pə'seitə], *s. Num:* peseta *f.*
pesky ['peski], *a. NAm: F:* maudit, exécrable, sacré.
peso ['peisou], *s. Num:* peso *m.*
pessary ['pesəri], *s. Med:* pessaire *m.*
pessimism ['pesimizm], *s.* pessimisme *m.*
pessimist ['pesimist], *s.* pessimiste *mf.*
pessimistic [pesi'mistik], *a.* pessimiste.
pessimistically [pesi'mistik(ə)li], *adv.* d'une manière pessimistique; avec pessimisme.
pest [pest], *s.* **1.** (*a*) *Med: A:* peste *f*; **p. house,** hôpital *m* (-aux) pour les pestiférés; lazaret *m*; **p. cart,** tombereau *m* des pestiférés; (*b*) *F:* **to avoid s.o. like the p.,** fuir qn comme un pestiféré. **2.** (*a*) insecte *m*, plante *f*, nuisible; **rabbits are a p. here,** ici les lapins sont un fléau; **p. control,** (service de) dératisation *f*, désinsectisation *f*, etc.; (*b*) *F:* peste, fléau; **he's a perfect p.!** c'est un véritable casse-pieds! **that child's a p.!** quelle peste, quel fléau, que cet enfant!
pester ['pestər], *v.tr.* **1.** (*of insects, etc.*) infester (un pays); harceler, tourmenter (qn). **2.** *F:* tourmenter, importuner, ennuyer, tenailler, tirailler (qn); *F:* être comme une tique après (qn); **to p. s.o. with questions,** importuner, assommer, harceler, qn de (ses) questions; assiéger qn de questions; **to p. s.o. to do sth.,** importuner qn pour lui faire faire qch.; **to p. s.o. for money,** bombarder qn de demandes d'argent, harceler qn pour obtenir de l'argent; **he's always pestering me for something,** ce sont des quémanderies sans fin.
pesterer ['pestərər], *s. F:* tourmenteur, -euse; importun, -une.
pestering ['pestəriŋ], *a. F:* importun.
pesticidal [pesti'saidl], *a.* antiparasite, pesticide.
pesticide ['pestisaid], *s.* pesticide *m*, antiparasitaire *m.*
pestiferous [pes'tifərəs], *a.* (*a*) (*of air, etc.*) pestifère, pestilent; (*b*) (*of insects, etc.*) nuisible; (*c*) (*of doctrine, etc.*) pestifère, pernicieux; (*d*) *F:* ennuyant, enquiquinant.
pestilence ['pestiləns], *s.* peste *f*, *esp.* peste bubonique.
pestilent ['pestilənt], *a.* (*a*) pestilent, malsain, nocif; (*b*) *O:* (*of doctrine, etc.*) pestilentiel; corrupteur, -trice; pernicieux; (*c*) *F:* assommant, exécrable, maudit, empoisonnant.
pestilential [pesti'lenʃ(ə)l], *a.* (*a*) (*of disease*) pestilentiel, contagieux, pestifère; (*b*) (*of smell*) infect; (*c*) *O:* (*of doctrine, etc.*) pernicieux; corrupteur, -trice; (*d*) *F:* assommant, empoisonnant.
pestilentially [pesti'lenʃəli], *adv. F:* exécrablement; d'une manière assommante, empoisonnante.
pestle[1] ['pesl], *s.* pilon *m* (pour mortier).
pestle[2], *v.tr.* piler, broyer (au mortier).
pestology [pes'tɔlədʒi], *s.* étude *f* des insectes nuisibles.
pet[1] [pet], *s.* **1.** (*a*) animal familier; oiseau *m*, chien *m*, etc., d'appartement; **p. lamb,** agneau favori; **to make a p. of an animal,** choyer un animal; (*in block of flats, etc.*) **no pets,** pas de bêtes; **p. shop,** boutique *f* où l'on vend des animaux familiers; **p. food,** nourriture *f* pour chiens, chats, etc.; (*b*) mignon, -onne; enfant gâté; **mother's p., teacher's p.,** le chouchou de sa mère, du professeur; **my p.!** mon chéri! mon chouchou! mon petit chat! ma petite chatte! mon bijou! ma mignonne! ma douce! (*c*) *attrib.* **p. subject,** sujet *m* de prédilection; dada *m*; **p. name,** (i) diminutif *m*; (ii) nom *m* d'amitié; **my p. aversion,** ma bête noire. **2.** *Tchn:* **p. cock,** (i) *Mch:* robinet *m* de purge, purgeur *m* (de vapeur); (ii) *I.C.E:* robinet de décompression, de dégommage; vis-robinet *f* (*pl.* vis-robinets) de contrôle; *Mch:* **p. valve,** soupape *f* d'évent.
pet[2], *v.tr.* **(petted)** (*a*) choyer, dorloter, mignoter, chouchouter (qn); (*b*) caresser, câliner (qn); *Pej:* peloter (qn).
pet[3], *s. F: O:* accès *m* de mauvaise humeur; **to get into a p., to take the p.,** se fâcher, prendre la bisque, la mouche; se dépiter; **to be in a p.,** bouder; être de mauvaise humeur.
petal ['petl], *s. Bot:* pétale *m*; (*of flower*) **to shed its petals,** s'effeuiller.
petaline ['petəlain], *a. Bot:* pétalin, pétaliforme, pétaloïde, pétalaire.
petalism ['petəlizm], *s. Gr.Ant:* pétalisme *m*; bannissement *m* de cinq ans.
petalite ['petəlait], *s. Miner:* pétalite *f.*
petalled ['petəld], *a. Bot:* (*a*) pétalé; (*b*) **three p., six p.,** à trois, à six, pétales; **blue p.,** à pétales bleus.
petalocerous [petə'lɔsərəs], *a. Ent:* pétalocère.
petalodic [petə'loudik], *a. Bot:* pétalodé.
petalodont ['petəloudɔnt], *s. Paleont:* pétalodonte *m.*
Petalodontidae [petəlou'dɔntidi:], *s.pl. Paleont:* pétalodontidés *m.*
petalody ['petəloudi], *s. Bot:* pétalodie *f.*
petaloid ['petəlɔid], *a. Nat.Hist:* pétaloïde.
Petalostemon [petəlou'sti:mən], *s. Bot:* petalostemon *m*, petalostemum *m.*
petalous ['petələs], *a. Bot:* pétalé.
petard [pe'tɑ:d], *s.* **1.** *Mil.A:* pétard *m.* **2.** *Pyr:* pétard.
petasus ['petəsəs], *s. Gr.Cost:* pétase *m.*
petaurist [pe'tɔ:rist], *s. Z:* pétauriste *m*; écureuil volant marsupial.
petaurista [petɔ:'ristə], *s. Z:* taguan *m*; écureuil volant (asiatique).
petauroides [petɔ:'rɔidi:z], *s. Z:* pétauroïde *m.*
petaurus [pe'tɔ:rəs], *s. Z:* pétaure *m.*
petechiae [pi'tikii:], *s.pl. Med:* pétéchies *f*, marques *f* d'ecchymoses sous-épidermiques.
Peter ['pi:tər]. **1.** *Pr.n.m.* Pierre; *R.C.Ch:* **Peter's penny, P. penny, Peter's pence,** le denier de Saint-Pierre. **2.** *s. Nau:* **Blue P.,** pavillon *m* de partance, de départ; signal *m* de départ. **3.** *s. P:* (*a*) coffre-fort *m*, coffiot *m*; (*b*) cellule *f* de prison.
Peterkin ['pi:təkin], *Pr.n.m.* (*dim. of Peter*) Pierrot.
peterman, *pl.* **-men** ['pi:təmən], *s. P:* casseur *m* de coffres-forts, de coffiots.
peter out [pi:tə'raut], *v.i.* (*a*) *Min: etc:* (*of seam*) mourir; (*of deposit*) s'épuiser; (*b*) (*of stream*) disparaître (sous terre); (*of path*) s'arrêter, disparaître; (*c*) (*of scheme, etc.*) tomber à l'eau; venir à rien; se perdre dans les sables; s'arrêter en fumée; (*d*) *Aut:* (*of engine*) s'arrêter (faute d'essence); *F:* flancher.
petersham ['pi:təʃəm], *s. Tex:* **1.** gros drap (à pardessus); ratine *f.* **2. p. (ribbon),** ruban *m* gros grain.
pethidine ['peθidi:n], *s. Pharm:* péthidine *f.*
petiolar ['petioulər], *a. Bot:* pétiolaire.
Petiolata [petiou'leitə], *s.pl. Ent:* pétiolés *m.*
petiolate(d) ['petiouleit(id)], *a. Bot:* pétiolé.
petiole ['petioul], *s. Bot:* pétiole *m.*
petiolular [peti'ɔljulər], *a. Bot:* pétiolulaire.
petiolulate [peti'ɔljuleit], *a. Bot:* pétiolulé.
petiolule ['petiɔlju:l], *s. Bot:* pétiolule *m.*
petite [pə'ti:t], *a.* (*of woman*) petite (et svelte).
petition[1] [pi'tiʃ(ə)n], *s.* (*a*) prière *f*, supplication *f* (à Dieu); (*b*) pétition *f*, supplique *f*, placet *m*, requête *f*; **to grant a p.,** faire droit à une pétition; *Hist:* **the P. of Rights,** la Pétition des droits; (*c*) *Jur:* **p. for a reprieve,** recours *m* en grâce; **p. for mercy,** recours en grâce; **p. for a divorce,** demande *f* en divorce; **p. in bankruptcy,** (i) requête des créanciers; (ii) requête du négociant insolvable; (*d*) *Jur: A:* **p. of right,** procédure par laquelle on intentait une action contre la Couronne.
petition[2], *v.tr.* adresser, présenter, une pétition, une requête, à (la cour, un souverain, etc.); supplier (le souverain) (**to do sth.,** de faire qch.); *v.i.* pétitionner; **to p. the court for sth.,** réclamer, demander, qch. au

tribunal; **to p. s.o. to do sth.**, supplier, prier, qn de faire qch.; **to p. for sth.**, demander, requérir, solliciter, qch.; **to p. for mercy**, se pourvoir, recourir, en grâce.

petitionary [pi'tiʃən(ə)ri], *a.* (*attitude, etc.*) de suppliant, de pétition.

petitioner [pi'tiʃənər], *s.* suppliant, -ante; pétitionnaire *mf*; solliciteur, -euse; *Jur:* requérant, -ante.

petit nègre [pəti'nɛgr], *s. Ling: F:* petit nègre.

petitory ['petitəri], *a. Jur: Scot:* **p. suit**, action *f* pétitoire; pétitoire *m*; action en revendication de propriété.

petit point [pəti'pwɛ̃], *s. Needlew:* petit point.

petiveria [peti'viəriə], *s. Bot:* petiveria *m.*

Petrarch ['petrɑ:k], *Pr.n.m. Lit:* Pétrarque.

petrel ['petrəl], *s.* **1.** *Orn:* pétrel *m*; **black-capped p.**, pétrel diablotin, *Fr.C:* diablotin errant; **Bulwer's p.**, pétrel de Bulwer; **fork-tailed storm p.**, *NAm:* **fork-tailed p.**, pétrel à queue fourchue; **giant p.**, pétrel géant; ossifrage *m*; **Kermadec p.**, pétrel de Kermadec; **Leach's p.**, pétrel cul-blanc; **Madeiran p.**, *NAm:* **Madeira p.**, *U.S:* **Harcourt's storm p.**, pétrel de Castro, *Fr.C:* pétrel de Madère; **pintado p.**, pétrel damier; **snow p.**, pétrel des neiges; **storm p., stormy p.**, pétrel tempête; **white-chinned p.**, pétrel équinoxial; **white-winged, collared, p.**, pétrel à ailes blanches; *U.S:* **white-faced p.**, pétrel frégate; **Wilson's p.**, pétrel océanite, pétrel de Wilson, *Fr.C:* pétrel océanique; **diving p.**, pélécanoïde *m*; **silver-grey p.**, fulmar *m* antarctique. **2. stormy p.**, semeur *m* de discorde.

petricola [pe'trikələ], *s. Moll:* pétricole *f.*

Petricolidae [petri'kɔlidi:], *s.pl. Moll:* pétricolidés *m.*

petricolous [pe'trikələs], *a. Moll:* pétricole.

petrifaction, petrification [petri'fækʃ(ə)n, -fi'keiʃ(ə)n], *s.* pétrification *f.*

petrifactive [petri'fæktiv], *a.* pétrifiant; pétrificateur, -trice.

petrified ['petrifaid], *a.* (*a*) (bois, etc.) pétrifié; (*b*) **p. with fear**, pétrifié, paralysé, de terreur.

petrify ['petrifai]. **1.** *v.tr.* (*a*) pétrifier (le bois, etc.); (*b*) pétrifier, méduser, paralyser (qn). **2.** *v.i.* se pétrifier.

petrifying ['petrifaiiŋ], *a.* pétrifiant; (puits) incrustant; (fontaine) incrustante; **p. silence**, silence paralysant, pétrifiant.

Petrine ['pi:train], *a.* de Saint Pierre; **the P. liturgy**, la liturgie romaine.

petrissage ['petrisɑ:ʒ], *s. Med:* pétrissage *m.*

petrochemical [petrou'kemikl]. **1.** *a.* pétrochimique, pétroléochimique; **the p. industry**, l'industrie *f* pétrochimique; la pétrochimie; **p. engineer**, pétrochimiste *mf.* **2.** *s.pl.* **petrochemicals**, produits *m* pétrochimiques, pétroléochimiques.

petrochemistry [petrou'kemistri], *s.* pétrochimie *f*, pétroléochimie *f.*

petrogale [pe'trɔgəli], *s. Z:* pétrogale *m.*

petrogenesis [petrou'dʒenəsis], *s. Geol:* pétrogénèse *f.*

petroglyph ['petrouglif], *s.* **1.** *Geol:* pétroglyphe *f.* **2.** *Archeol:* pétroglyphe, inscription *f* rupestre.

Petrograd ['petrougræd], *Pr.n. Hist:* Pétrograd *m.*

petrographer [pe'trɔgrəfər], *s.* pétrographe *mf.*

petrographic(al) [petrou'græfik(l)], *a.* pétrographique.

petrography [pe'trɔgrəfi], *s.* pétrographie *f.*

petrol ['petrəl], *s. Ch:* essence (minérale); *Aut:* essence, *Sw.Fr:* benzine *f*; *Ch:* **high-octane p.**, essence à haut indice d'octane; **straight-run p.**, essence de premier jet; **sweet p.**, essence adoucie, désulfurisée; **wild p.**, essence très volatile, non stabilisée; **synthetic p.**, essence synthétique; *I.C.E:* **anti-knock p.**, essence antidétonante; **high-grade, premium-grade, branded, four-star, p.** = supercarburant *m*, *F:* super *m*; **to fill up with p.**, faire le plein; **p. tank**, réservoir *m* à essence; **p. pump**, (i) (*in car*) pompe *f* à essence; (ii) distributeur *m* d'essence; **p. pump indicator**, volucompteur *m*; **p. can**, bidon *m* à essence; **p. lorry**, camion-citerne *m*, *pl.* camions-citernes.

petrolatum [petrou'leitəm], *s.* **1.** *Pharm:* pétrolatum *m*, vaseline officinale. **2.** *Ind:* graisse verte.

petrolen(e) ['petrouli(:)n], *s. Ch:* pétrolène *m.*

petroleum [pe'trouliəm], *s.* pétrole *m*; huile minérale (naturelle); huile de roche; **crude p.**, pétrole brut; **refined, rectified, p.**, pétrole raffiné, rectifié; **the p. industry**, l'industrie pétrolière; **p. engineer**, ingénieur *m* des pétroles; pétrolier *m*; **p. coke**, coke *m* de pétrole; **p. ether**, éther *m* de pétrole; **p. gas**, gaz *m* de pétrole; **p. oil**, huile *f* de pétrole; **p. jelly**, gelée *f* de pétrole, vaseline *f*; **p. products**, produits pétroliers.

petrolic [pe'trɔlik], *a. Ch:* **p. ether**, éther *m* de pétrole.

petroliferous [petrə'lifərəs], *a.* pétrolifère.

petrolization [petrəlai'zeiʃ(ə)n], *s.* pétrolage *m* (d'un étang, etc.).

petrolize ['petrəlaiz], *v.tr.* pétroler (un étang, etc.).

petrologic(al) [petrə'lɔdʒik(l)], *a.* pétrologique.

petrology [pe'trɔlədʒi], *s.* pétrologie *f.*

Petromyidae [petrou'maiidi:], *s.pl. Z:* pétromyidés *m.*

Petromyzon(t)idae [petroumai'zɔn(t)idi:], *s.pl. Ich:* pétromyzon(t)idés *m.*

petronel ['petrounel], *s. A.Arms:* pétrinal, -aux *m.*

Petronilla [petrou'nilə]. *Pr.n.f. Rel.H:* Pétronille.

Petronius [pe'trouniəs]. *Pr.n.m. Lt.Lit:* Pétrone.

petrosal [pe'trous(ə)l], *a. Anat:* pétreux; *a. & s.* **p. (bone)**, os pétreux; rocher *m.*

petrosilex [petrou'saileks], *s. Miner:* pétrosilex *m.*

petrous ['petrəs], *a.* (*a*) pierreux; (*b*) *Anat:* (nerf, etc.) pétreux.

petticoat ['petikout], *s.* **1.** (*a*) *A:* jupe *f*, cotte *f*, cotillon *m*; **a Napoleon in petticoats**, un Napoléon en jupons; *F: O:* **to be always after a p.**, courir le cotillon; être porté sur la bagatelle; **p. government**, régime *m* de cotillons; **he's under p. government**, c'est sa femme qui porte la culotte; (*b*) jupon *m*; (*c*) *A:* (*for small boys*) jupon, *A:* jaquette *f*; **he was still in petticoats**, il portait encore le jupon. **2.** *El:* cloche *f* (d'isolateur). **3.** *Mch: O:* **p. (pipe)**, éjecteur *m* tronconique (pour activer le tirage).

pettifog ['petifɔg], *v.i.* (**pettifogged**) **1.** avocasser. **2.** chicaner.

pettifogger ['petifɔgər], *s.* **1.** avocassier *m*; homme *m* d'affaires à l'esprit retors; procédurier, -ière; suppôt *m* de chicane. **2.** chicanier *m.*

pettifoggery [peti'fɔgəri], *s.* = PETTIFOGGING².

pettifogging¹ ['petifɔgiŋ], *a.* **1.** avocassier, procédurier, retors; **p. lawyer, p. attorney**, avocassier *m*; homme *m* de loi de bas étage. **2.** chicanier; **p. objections**, objections *f* de pure chicane.

pettifogging², *s.* **1.** avocasserie *f.* **2.** chicane *f*, chicanerie *f.*

pettily ['petili], *adv.* mesquinement; avec mesquinerie.

pettiness ['petinis], *s.* petitesse *f*, mesquinerie *f.*

petting ['petiŋ], *s.* caresses (données à un chat, etc.); *F:* badinage amoureux, pelotage *m.*

pettish ['petiʃ], *a.* de mauvaise humeur, maussade; irritable.

pettishly ['petiʃli], *adv.* de mauvaise humeur; d'un ton, d'un geste, irritable.

pettishness ['petiʃnis], *s.* mauvaise humeur; irritabilité *f*; maussaderie *f.*

pettitoes ['petitouz], *s.pl. F:* **1.** *Cu:* pieds *m* de porc. **2.** *A:* petits petons (d'un bébé).

petty ['peti], *a.* **1.** (*a*) petit, insignifiant, sans importance; **p. prince(ling)**, petit prince; **p. monarch**, roitelet *m*; **these are only p. differences**, ce ne sont que des différences insignifiantes, sans importance; **p. annoyances**, (i) coups *m* d'épingle; (ii) petits ennuis (de la vie journalière); (*b*) *Jur:* **p. offences**, contraventions *f*; délits *m* de peu d'importance; **p. larceny**, vol *m* simple; vol minime; **p. jury**, petit jury; jury de jugement; (*c*) *Com:* **p. cash**, petite caisse; menue monnaie; **p. cash book**, livre *m* de petite caisse; (*d*) **p.(-minded)**, mesquin; à l'esprit petit; **things that make men p. and vindictive**, ce qui rend les hommes mesquins et rancuniers; **don't be so p.!** tâchez d'avoir des vues plus larges! **2.** *Navy:* **p. officer**, officier marinier; sous-officier *m*, *pl.* sous-officiers; gradé *m*; **chief p.-officer**, (i) maître principal; (ii) premier maître; (iii) maître; (**second class**) **p. officer**, second maître.

petty-mindedness [peti'maindidnis], *s.* petitesse *f*; mesquinerie *f.*

petulance ['petjuləns], *s.* irritabilité *f*; susceptibilité *f*; vivacité *f*; **in an outburst of p.**, dans un accès de mauvaise humeur, d'irritation.

petulant ['petjulənt], *a.* irritable; susceptible; vif.

petulantly ['petjuləntli], *adv.* avec irritation; d'un ton irrité, énervé.

petunia [pi'tju:niə], *s. Bot:* pétunia *m.*

petun(t)se, petuntze [pe'tʌn(t)si, -zi], *s. Cer:* pétunsé *m*, pétunzé *m.*

peucedanum [pju:'sedənəm], *s. Bot:* peucédan *m.*

peulven ['pə:lven], *s. Prehist:* peulven *m.*

pew¹ [pju:], *s.* banc *m* d'église; **churchwarden's p.**, banc d'œuvre; **p. rent**, abonnement *m* à un banc d'église; *O:* **p. opener**, bedeau *m*; *F:* **take a p.!** assieds-toi! asseyez-vous!

pew², *v.tr. O:* fournir (une église) de bancs.

pewage ['pju:idʒ], *s.* **1.** *coll.* bancs *mpl* (d'une église); **p. for 600 worshippers**, bancs pour 600 fidèles. **2.** abonnement *m* à un banc d'église.

pewee ['pi:wi:], *s. Orn:* **wood p., eastern wood p.**, moucherolle *m* pioui; **western wood p.**, moucherolle de Richardson.

pewit ['pi:wit], *s.* = PEEWIT.

pewter ['pju:tər], *s.* **1.** étain *m*, potin *m*; **grey p.**, potin gris; **plate p.**, potin d'assiettes; **p. (ware)**, poterie *f* d'étain; vaisselle *f* d'étain. **2.** (*a*) pot *m* d'étain; (*b*) *Sp: F: A:* coupe *f.* **3.** *P: A:* argent *m*, galette *f*; **to stump up the p.**, payer, éclairer.

pewterer ['pju:tərər], *s.* potier *m* d'étain.

peyote, peyotl [pei'outi, -outl], *s. Bot:etc:* peyotl *m.*

peziza [pə'zaizə], *s. Fung:* pézize *f.*

pfennig ['(p)fenig], *s. Num:* pfennig *m.*

phacochoerus [fækə'ki:rəs], **phacoch(o)ere** ['fækəkiər], *s. Z:* phacochère *m.*

phacometer [fæ'kɔmitər], *s. Opt:* phacomètre *m.*

Phaeacian [fi:'eiʃ(ə)n], *s. Gr.Lit:* Phéacien, -ienne.

Phaedo ['fi:dou], *Pr.n.m. Gr.Ant:* Phédon.

Phaedra ['fi:drə], *Pr.n.f. Gr.Myth:* Phèdre.

Phaedrus ['fi:drəs], *Pr.n.m. Cl.Lit:* Phèdre.

phaeomelanin [fiou'melənin], *s. Bio-Ch:* phæmélanine *f*, phéomélanine *f.*

Phaeophyceae [fiou'faisii:], *s.pl. Algae:* phéophycées *f.*

Phaethon ['feiθən], *Pr.n.m. Gr.Myth:* Phaéton.

phaeton ['feitən], *s. A.Veh:* phaéton *m.*

phage [feidʒ], *s. Bac:* (bactério)phage *m*; **p. typing**, lysotypie *f*; **enteric p. typing**, lysotypie entérique; **p. type**, lysotype *m.*

phaged(a)ena [fædʒə'di:nə, fæg-], *s. Med:* phagédénisme *m.*

phaged(a)enic [fædʒə'di:nik, fæg-], *a. Med:* phagédénique.

phagocyte¹ ['fægəsait], *s. Biol:* phagocyte *m.*

phagocyte², *v.tr. Biol:* phagocyter.

phagocytic [fægou'sitik], *a. Biol:* phagocytaire.

phagocytize, phagocytose [fægousai'taiz, -'touz], *v.tr. Biol:* phagocyter.

phagocytosis [fægousai'tousis], *s. Biol:* phagocytose *f*, phagocytisme *m.*

phagolysis [fæ'gɔlisis], *s. Biol:* phagolyse *f.*

Phalacrocoracidae [fæləkrokɔ'reisidi:], *s.pl. Orn:* phalacrocoracidés *m*, les cormorans *m.*

phalaena [fæ'li:nə], *s. Ent:* phalène *f.*

phalange ['fælændʒ], *s. Anat:* phalange *f.*

phalangeal [fæ'lændʒiəl], *a. Anat:* phalangien.

phalanger [fæ'lændʒər], *s. Z:* phalanger *m*; couscou *m*; **flying p.**, écureuil volant marsupial; pétauriste *m.*

Phalangeridae [fælæn'dʒeridi:], *s.pl. Z:* phalangéridés *m.*

phalangette [fælæn'dʒet], *s. Anat:* phalangette *f.*

phalangian [fæ'lændʒiən], *a. & s. Arach:* phalangien (*m*).

phalangid [fæ'lændʒid]. *Arach:* **1.** *a.* phalangien. **2.** *s.* phalangide *m*, phalangien *m.*

Phalangid(e)a [fæ'lændʒidə, fælæn'dʒidiə], *s.pl. Arach:* phalangides *m*, phalangiens *m.*

phalangiform [fæ'lændʒifɔ:m], *a.* phalangiforme.

Phalangistidae [fælæn'dʒistidi:], *s.pl. Z:* phalangéridés *m.*

phalangite ['fælændʒait], *s. A.Mil:* phalangiste *m.*

phalansterian [fælæn'stiəriən], *a. Hist:* phalanstérien.

phalanstery ['fælænstəri], *s. Hist:* phalanstère *m.*

phalanx ['fælæŋks], *s.* **1.** (*pl. usu.* **phalanxes** ['fælæŋksiz]) (*a*) *A.Mil:* phalange *f*; (*b*) *Hist: occ.* = PHALANSTERY. **2.** *Anat: Bot:* (*pl. usu.* **phalanges** [fæ'lændʒi:z]) phalange; **ungual p.**, phalangette *f*; phalange unguéale.

phalarica [fæ'lærikə], *s. Ant:* falarique *f.*

phalaris ['fæləris], *s. Bot:* phalaris *m*, phalaride *m.*

phalarope ['fæləroup], *s. Orn:* phalarope *m*; **red-necked p.**, *NAm:* **northern p.**, phalarope à bec étroit, phalarope hyperboré; **grey p.**, *NAm:* **red p.**, phalarope à bec large, phalarope platyrhynque, *Fr.C:* phalarope roux; **Wilson's p.**, phalarope de Wilson.

phalera, *pl.* **-ae** ['fælərə, -i:], *s.* **1.** *Ant:* phalère *f.* **2.** *Ent:* phalère.

Phalerum [fæ'liərəm], *Pr.n. A.Geog:* Phalère.

phallic ['fælik], *a.* phallique; **p. symbol**, emblème *m* phallique.

phall(ic)ism ['fæl(is)izm], *s.* phallisme *m.*

phalloid ['fælɔid]. *Fung:* **1.** *a.* phalloïde. **2.** *s.* phallus *m.*

phalloidin(e) [fæ'lɔid(a)in], *s. Fung: Ch:* phalline *f.*

phallus ['fæləs], *s.* phallus *m.*

phanatron ['fænətrɔn], *s. Elcs:* phanotron *m.*

phanerocrystalline [fænərou'kristəlain], *a. Miner:* phanérocristallin.

phanerogam ['fænərougæm], *s. Bot:* phanérogame *f.*

Phanerogamia [fænərou'geimiə], *s.pl. Bot:* phanérogames *f.*

phanerogamic [fænərou'gæmik], **phanerogamous** [fænə'rɔgəməs], *a. Bot:* phanérogame.

phanerogamy [fænə'rɔgəmi], *s. Bot:* phanérogamie *f.*

Phaneroglossa [fænərou'glɔsə], *s.pl. Amph:* phanéroglosses *m.*

phanerophyte ['fænəroufait], *s. Bot:* phanérophyte *f.*

phanotron ['fænətrɔn], *s. Elcs:* phanotron *m.*

phantasm ['fæntæzm], *s.* **1.** (*a*) chimère *f*, illusion *f*; (*b*) *A:* fantôme *m*, spectre *m.* **2.** (*a*) *Med:* phantasme *m*, fantasme *m*; (*b*) *Psychics:* apparition *f.*

phantasmagoria, phantasmagory [fæntæzmæ'gɔriə, -'mægəri], *s.* fantasmagorie *f.*

phantasmagoric [fæntæzmæ'gɔrik], *a.* fantasmagorique.

phantasmal, phantasmic [fæn'tæzm(ə)l, -mik], *a.* fantômal, -als, -aux; fantomatique; spectral, -aux.

phantastron [fæn'tæstrɔn], *s. Elcs:* phantastron *m.*

phantasy ['fæntəsi], *s.* fantaisie *f.*

phantom ['fæntəm], *s.* fantôme *m*, spectre *m*; **p. ship,** vaisseau *m* fantôme; **manœuvres against a p. army,** manœuvres *f* contre une armée imaginaire; *Tp: Tel:* **p. circuit,** circuit *m* fantôme; *Med:* **p. limb,** membre *m* fantôme.

Pharaoh ['fɛərou], *s.* **1.** *A.Hist:* pharaon *m*; **the Pharaoh's wife,** la pharaone; **the tombs of the Pharaohs,** les tombeaux des pharaons. **2.** (*a*) *Orn:* **Pharaoh's hen, chicken,** néophron *m*; (*b*) *Z:* **Pharaoh's rat, mouse,** rat *m* de pharaon, d'Égypte; ichneumon *m*; (*c*) *Pyr:* **Pharaoh's serpent,** serpent *m* de pharaon.

Pharaonic [fɛə'rɔnik], *a.* pharaonien, pharaonique.

Pharetrones [færi'trouni:z], *s.pl. Spong:* pharétrones *f.*

pharisaic(al) [færi'seiik(l)], *a.* pharisaïque.

pharisaically [færi'seiik(ə)li], *adv.* pharisaïquement; en pharisien.

pharisaism ['færiseiizm], *s.* pharisaïsme *m.*

pharisee ['færisi:], *s.* pharisien, -ienne.

phariseeism ['færisi:izm], *s.* pharisaïsme *m.*

pharmaceutic(al) [fɑ:mə'sju:tik(l)], *a.* pharmaceutique.

pharmaceutics [fɑ:mə'sju:tiks], *s.pl.* (*usu. with sg. const.*) la pharmaceutique; la pharmacie.

pharmacist ['fɑ:məsist], *s.* pharmacien, -ienne.

pharmacodynamic [fɑ:məkoudai'næmik], *a.* pharmacodynamique.

pharmacodynamics [fɑ:məkoudai'næmiks], *s.pl.* (*usu. with sg. const.*) pharmacodynamie *f.*

pharmacognosy [fɑ:mə'kɔgnəsi], *s.* pharmacognosie *f.*

pharmacolite [fɑ:'mækoulait], *s. Miner:* pharmacolit(h)e *f.*

pharmacological [fɑ:məkə'lɔdʒikl], *a.* pharmacologique.

pharmacologist [fɑ:mə'kɔlədʒist], *s.* pharmacologiste *mf,* pharmacologue *mf.*

pharmacology [fɑ:mə'kɔlədʒi], *s.* pharmacologie *f.*

pharmacomania [fɑ:məkou'meiniə], *s. Psy:* pharmacomanie *f.*

pharmacopoeia [fɑ:məkou'pi:ə], *s.* (*a*) pharmacopée *f*; codex *m* (pharmaceutique); (*b*) (*medicine chest*) pharmacie *f.*

pharmacotherapy [fɑ:məkou'θerəpi], *s.* pharmacothérapie *f.*

pharmacy ['fɑ:məsi], *s.* **1.** pharmacie *f*; pharmaceutique *f.* **2.** pharmacie; magasin *m* de pharmacien.

Pharsalia [fɑ:'seiliə]. *Pr.n.* (*a*) *Geog:* Pharsale *f*; *Rom.Hist:* **Battle of P.,** bataille *f* de Pharsale; (*b*) *Lt.Lit:* **the P.,** la Pharsale (de Lucain).

Pharsalus ['fɑ:sələs], *Pr.n. A.Geog:* Pharsale.

pharyngal [fə'riŋgəl], **pharyngeal** [færin'dʒi:əl], *a.* **1.** *Anat:* pharyngien, pharyngé. **2.** *Ling:* pharyngal, -aux.

pharyngitis [færin'dʒaitis], *s. Med:* pharyngite *f,* syndrome pharyngo-laryngé.

pharyngoglossal [færiŋgou'glɔs(ə)l], *a. Anat:* pharyngoglosse.

pharyngoglossus [færiŋgou'glɔsəs], *s. Anat:* muscle *m* pharyngoglosse.

pharyngognath [fæ'riŋgɔgnæθ], *a. & s. Ich:* pharyngognate (*m*).

Pharyngognathi [færiŋ'gɔgnəθi], *s.pl. Ich:* pharyngognates *m.*

pharyngognathous [færiŋ'gɔgnəθəs], *a. Ich:* pharyngognate.

pharyngolaryngitis [færiŋgoulærin'dʒaitis], *s. Med:* pharyngo-laryngite *f.*

pharyngoscope [fæ'riŋgouskoup], *s. Med:* pharyngoscope *m.*

pharyngoscopic [færiŋgou'skɔpik], *a. Med:* pharyngoscopique.

pharyngoscopy [færiŋ'gɔskəpi], *s. Med:* pharyngoscopie *f.*

pharyngostomy [færiŋ'gɔstəmi], *s. Surg:* pharyngostomie *f.*

pharyngotomy [færiŋ'gɔtəmi], *s. Surg:* pharyngotomie *f.*

pharynx ['færiŋks], *s. Anat:* pharynx *m.*

phascogale [fæs'kɔgəli], *s. Z:* phasco(lo)gale *m.*

phascolarctos [fæskou'lɑ:ktɔs], *s. Z:* phascolarcte *m.*

Phascolomidae, Phascolomydae [fæskou'lɔmidi:], *s.pl. Z:* phascolomidés *m.*

phascolomis, phascolomys [fæskou'loumis], *s. Z:* phascolome *m.*

phascolosoma [fæskoulə'soumə], *s. Ann:* phascolosome *m.*

phase[1] [feiz], *s.* **1.** phase *f* (d'un phénomène, d'un processus, etc.); (*a*) **initial, starting, p.,** phase initiale; **intermediate p.,** phase intermédiaire; **final p.,** phase finale, dernière phase; **labour has two phases,** l'accouchement *m* s'effectue en deux temps; **phases of an attack, of a battle,** phases d'une attaque, d'une bataille; **phases of an illness,** phases, stades *m,* d'une maladie; **to enter upon a new p.,** entrer dans une nouvelle phase; (*b*) *Astr:* phase (d'une planète); (*c*) *Ch:* phase (d'un système chimique); **p. diagram of the hydrogen-oxygen system,** diagramme *m* de phase du système hydrogène-oxygène; **p. rule,** règle *f* des phases. **2.** (*a*) *Ph: Mec:* **in p.,** en phase; **in opposite p.,** en opposition de phase; **out of p.,** hors de phase, déphasé, décalé; *W.Tel:* **waves out of p.,** ondes décalées; **p. adjustment,** mise *f* en phase; **p. angle,** angle *m* de phase; **p. constant,** constante *f* de phase; **p. difference, difference in p.,** différence *f,* décalage *m,* de phase; (angle de) déphasage *m*; **p. displacement,** décalage de phase, déphasage; **p. distortion,** distorsion *f* de phase; **p.-contrast microscope,** microscope *m* à contraste de phase; **p. jump,** changement *m* brusque de phase; **p. lag,** (i) retard *m* de phase, (ii) *Mec.E:* (*of servo-control*) retard à la réponse; **p. lead,** avance *f* de phase; **to lead, lag, in p.,** être en avance, en retard, de phase; **angle of lead in p.,** angle d'avance de phase; **p. space,** espace *m* de phase, extension *f* en phase; **p. velocity,** vitesse *f* de phase (d'une onde); (*b*) *El:* **p. conductor, p. wire,** conducteur *m,* fil *m,* de phase; **p. current,** courant *m* de phase; **single-p. current,** courant monophasé; **two-p. current,** courant biphasé, diphasé; **three-p. current,** courant triphasé; **four-p. current,** courant tétraphasé; **p. inversion, reversal,** inversion *f* de phase; **p. transformer,** transformateur *m* de phase; **p. voltage,** tension *f* de phase; **to differ in p. from the current,** être décalé en phase, déphasé, sur le courant; (*c*) *El: Elcs:* **p. advancer,** avanceur *m,* régulateur *m,* de phase; **p. shift,** déphasage; **p. converter, shifter,** déphaseur *m*; **p. modulation,** modulation *f* de phase; *Cmptr:* **p.-modulation recording,** enregistrement *m* en modulation de phase; **p. recorder,** phasemètre enregistreur.

phase[2], *v.*

I. *v.tr.* **1.** faire (qch.) par phases, par stades, progressivement; développer (un projet) en phases successives; échelonner (un programme de fabrication, etc.). **2.** *El: etc:* mettre en phases; caler en phase; *Cin:* **to p. the shutter,** mettre l'obturateur en phase; caler l'obturateur.

II. (*compound verbs*) **1. phase in,** *v.tr.* adopter, introduire, progressivement (de nouvelles méthodes, etc.); mettre en place progressivement (de nouvelles installations, etc.).

2. phase out, *v.tr.* éliminer progressivement (de vieilles méthodes, etc.); éliminer, retirer, progressivement (de vieux équipements, etc.).

phased [feizd], *a.* **1.** par phases, par stades; progressif; échelonné; **p. withdrawal,** évacuation *f* par échelons, par étapes; *Mil:* **p. progression,** progression *f* par phases successives. **2.** *El:* phasé; *Ph:* **p. light,** lumière cohérente.

phaselin ['feisilin], *s. Bio-Ch:* phaséline *f.*

phasemeter ['feizmi:tər], *s. El:* phasemètre *m.*

phaseolin [fei'si:əlin], *s. Bio-Ch:* phaséoline *f.*

phaseolunatin [feizioulu:'neitin], *s. Ch:* phaséolunatine *f.*

phase-shift ['feizʃift], *v.tr. Ph: El:* déphaser.

phasianella [feiziə'nelə], *s. Moll:* phasianelle *f.*

Phasianidae [feizi'ænidi:], *s.pl. Orn:* phasianidés *m,* les faisans *m.*

phasic ['feizik], *a. El:* de phase.

phasing ['feiziŋ], *s.* **1.** exécution par phases, par stades, progressive (de qch.); échelonnement *m* (d'un programme de fabrication, etc.); **p. of a withdrawal,** échelonnement d'une évacuation; **p. in,** adoption, introduction, progressive (de nouvelles méthodes, etc.); mise en place progressive (de nouvelles installations, etc.); **p. out,** élimination progressive (de vieilles méthodes, etc.); retrait progressif (de vieux équipements, etc.). **2.** *El: etc:* mise *f* en phase; calage *m* en phase; **p. relay,** relais *m* de mise en phase; (*facsimile*) **p. line,** signal *m* de cadrage.

phasis, *pl.* **-es** ['feisis, -i:z], *s. Astr:* phase *f.*

phasitron ['feizitrɔn], *s. Elcs:* phasitron *m.*

phasma ['fæzmə], *s. Ent:* phasme *m.*

Phasmatidae [fæz'mætidi:], *s.pl. Ent:* phasmidés *m.*

phasmid ['fæzmid], *s. Ent:* phasmidé *m.*

Phasmidae ['fæzmidi:], *s.pl. Ent:* phasmidés *m.*

Phasmoptera [fæz'mɔptərə], *s.pl. Ent:* phasmoptères *m.*

pheasant ['feznt], *s.* **1.** *Orn:* (*a*) faisan *m*; **cock p.,** (coq *m*) faisan; **hen p.,** (poule) faisane *f*; **young p., p. poult,** faisandeau *m*; (*b*) **p.** (*Phasianus colchicus*), *NAm:* **ring-necked p.,** faisan de chasse; *Fr.C:* faisan à collier; **Chinese ring-necked p.,** faisan de chasse de Chine; **argus p.,** argus *m*; **blood p.,** ithagine *m or f*; **cheer p.,** faisan de Wallich; **copper p.,** faisan de Sommering; **eared p.,** hoki *m*; faisan oreillard; **fireback p.,** lophure *m*; faisan pyronote; **golden p.,** faisan doré; **green p.,** faisan versicolore; **horned p.,** tragopan *m*; **impeyan, monal, p.,** lophophore *m*; **kalij p.,** faisan leucomèle; **koklas p.,** pucrasie *f,* eulophe *m*; **Lady Amherst's p.,** faisan d'Amherst; **long-tailed p.,** faisan vénéré; **peacock p.,** éperonnier *m*; **Siamese fireback p.,** faisan prélat; **silver p.,** faisan argenté; **wattled p.,** faisan de Bulwer; **snow p.,** tétraogalle *m*; **swamp p.,** coucal *m*; (*c*) **p. preserve,** faisanderie *f*; **p. shooting,** chasse *f* au faisan. **2.** *Bot:* **pheasant's eye,** (i) adonis *f,* goutte-de-sang *f, pl.* gouttes-de-sang; (ii) narcisse *m* des poètes, œillet *m* de Pâques, œil-de-faisan *m, pl.* œils-de-faisan. **3.** *Moll:* **p. shell,** phasianelle *f.*

pheasantry ['fezntri], *s.* faisanderie *f.*

Phebe ['fi:bi]. **1.** *Pr.n.f.* Phébé. **2.** *s. Orn:* = PHOEBE.

phellandrene [fe'lændri:n], *s. Ch:* phellandrène *m.*

phelloderm ['feloudə:m], *s. Bot:* phelloderme *m.*

phellogen ['feloudʒən], *s. Bot:* phellogène *m.*

phellogenetic [feloudʒə'netik], **phellogenic** [felou'dʒenik], *a. Bot:* phellogène.

phenacetin [fə'næsitin], *s. Ch.Pharm:* phénacétine *f.*

phenaceturic [fenæsə'tjurik], *a. Ch:* phénacéturique.

phenacite ['fenəsait], *s. Miner:* phénacite *f.*

phenacyl ['fenəsil], *s. Ch:* phénacyle *m.*

phenakistiscope [fenə'kistiskoup], *s. Opt:* phénakistiscope *m.*

phenakite ['fenəkait], *s. Miner:* phénacite *f.*

phenanthrene [fə'nænθri:n], *s. Ch:* phénanthrène *m.*

phenanthridine [fə'nænθridi:n], *s. Ch:* phénanthridine *f.*

phenanthridone [fə'nænθridoun], *s. Ch:* phénanthridone *f.*

phenanthrol [fə'nænθrɔl], *s. Ch:* phénanthrol *m.*

phenanthroline [fə'nænθrəli:n], *s. Ch:* phénanthroline *f.*

phenazine ['fenəzi:n], *s. Ch:* phénazine *f.*

phenazone ['fenəzoun], *s. Ch:* phénazone *f.*

phenetidine [fə'netidi:n], *s. Ch:* phénétidine *f.*

phenetole ['fenətoul], *s. Ch:* phénétole *m.*

phengite ['fendʒait], *s. Miner:* phengite *f.*

phenic ['fi:nik, 'fen-], *a.* phénique; **p. acid,** phénol *m.*

phenobarbital, phenobarbitone [fi:nou'bɑ:bit(ə)l, -'bɑ:bitoun], *s. Pharm:* phénobarbital *m.*

phenocryst ['fi:nəkrist], *s. Geol:* phénocristal *m.*

phenogenetic [fi:noudʒə'netik], *a. Biol:* phénogénétique.

phenol ['fi:nɔl], *s. Ch:* phénol *m*; acide *m* phénique.

phenolate ['fi:nəleit], *s. Ch:* phénate *m,* phénolate *m.*

phenolic [fə'nɔlik], *a. Ch:* phénolique.

phenology [fə'nɔlədʒi], *s. Meteor:* phénologie *f.*

phenolphthalein [fi:nɔl'θæli:in], *s. Ch:* phénolphtaléine *f.*

phenolsulphonic [fi:nɔlsʌl'fɔnik], *a. Ch:* phénolsulfonique.

phenomenal [fi'nɔminl], *a.* **1.** *Phil:* phénoménal, -aux. **2.** extraordinaire, remarquable, prodigieux; **a p. piece of stupidity,** une bêtise phénoménale.

phenomenalism [fi'nɔminəlizm], *s. Phil:* phénoménalisme *m,* phénoménisme *m.*

phenomenalist [fi'nɔminəlist], *s. Phil:* phénoméniste *mf.*

phenomenally [fi'nɔminəli], *adv.* phénoménalement, extraordinairement, remarquablement, prodigieusement; **to be p. stupid,** être d'une bêtise extrême.

phenomenism [fi'nɔmənizm], *s. Phil:* phénoménisme *m.*

phenomenist [fi'nɔmənist], *s. Phil:* phénoméniste *mf.*

phenomenologic(al) [finɔminə'lɔdʒik(l)], *a. Phil:* phénoménologique, phénoménologue.

phenomenologist [finɔmi'nɔlədʒist], *s. Phil:* phénoménologue *mf.*

phenomenology [finɔmi'nɔlədʒi], *s. Phil:* phénoménologie *f.*

phenomenon, *pl.* **-mena** [fi'nɔminən, -minə], *s.* **1.** (*a*) *Phil:* phénomène *m*; (*b*) **atmospheric p.,** phénomène météorologique; météore *m.* **2.** phénomène; chose *f* remarquable; (*of pers.*) prodige *m*; **infant p.,** jeune phénomène; enfant *mf* prodige.

phenoplast ['fi:nəplæst], *s. Ch:* phénoplaste *m.*

phenosafranine [fi:nou'sæfrəni:n], *s. Ch:* phénosafranine *f.*

phenothiazine [fi:nou'θaiəzi:n], *s. Ch:* thiodiphénylamine *f,* phénothiazine *f.*

phenotype ['fi:noutaip], *s. Biol:* phénotype *m.*

phenotypic(al) [fi:nou'tipik(l)], *a.* phénotypique.

phenoxazine [fi:'nɔksəzi:n], *s. Ch:* phénoxazine *f.*

phenoxide [fi:'nɔksaid], *s. Ch:* phénolate *m.*

phenyl ['fenil], *s. Ch:* phényle *m*; **p. alcohol,** phénol *m.*

phenylacetaldehyde [fenilæset'ældəhaid], *s. Ch:* phénylacétaldéhyde *m.*

phenylacetamide [fenilæ'setəmaid], *s. Ch:* phénylacétamide *m.*
phenylacetic [fenilæ'si:tik], *a.* phénylacétique.
phenylalanine [feni'læləni:n], *s. Ch:* phénylalanine *f.*
phenylamine [fenilæ'mi:n], *s. Ch:* phénylamine *f.*
phenylene ['fenili:n], *s. Ch:* phénylène *m.*
phenylethylene [fenil'eθili:n], *s. Ch:* phényléthylène *m.*
phenylhydrazine [fenil'haidrəzi:n], *s. Ch:* phénylhydrazine *f.*
phenylic [fə'nilik], *a. Ch:* phénilique.
pheon ['fi:ɔn], *s. Her:* phéon *m.*
pherecratean [ferikrə'ti:ən], **pherecratic** [feri'krætik], *a. Pros:* (vers) phérécratéen, phérécratien.
phew [fju:], *int.* **1.** pffft! pouf! **2.** (*disgust*) pouah!
phi [fai], *s. Gr.Alph:* phi *m.*
phial ['faiəl], *s.* (*a*) fiole *f*, flacon *m*, ampoule *f*; (*b*) (*for samples*) topette *f.*
Philadelphia [filə'delfiə]. *Pr.n. Geog:* Philadelphie *f*; *U.S:* **P. lawyer,** avocat habile, avisé, retors; **this will need a dozen P. lawyers,** c'est une question très complexe, difficile à résoudre.
Philadelphian [filə'delfiən]. *Geog:* **1.** *a.* philadelphien. **2.** *s.* Philadelphien, -ienne.
philadelphus [filə'delfəs], *s. Bot:* philadelphus *m*; *Hort:* seringa(t) *m.*
philander[1] [fi'lændər], *s.* **1.** *O:* flirt *m*, flirtage *m.* **2.** *Z:* philander *m*; opossum laineux.
philander[2], *v.i. O:* flirter; **to p. with s.o.,** flirter avec qn; conter fleurette à (une femme).
philanderer [fi'lændərər], *s.* flirteur *m*; galant *m.*
philanthid [fi'lænθid], *s. Ent:* philanthe *m.*
philanthropic(al) [filən'θrɔpik(l)], *a.* philanthropique; (*pers.*) philanthrope.
philanthropically [filən'θrɔpikəli], *adv.* d'une manière philanthropique; philanthropiquement; avec philanthropie.
philanthropism [fi'lænθrəpizm], *s.* philanthropisme *m.*
philanthropist [fi'lænθrəpist], *s.* philanthrope *mf.*
philanthropy [fi'lænθrəpi], *s.* philanthropie *f.*
philanthus [fi'lænθəs], *s. Ent:* philanthe *m.*
philatelic [filə'telik], *a.* philatélique, philatéliste.
philatelist [fi'lætəlist], *s.* philatéliste *mf.*
philately [fi'lætəli], philatélie *f*, philatélisme *m.*
Philemon [fi'li:mɔn]. *Pr.n.m.* Philémon.
philepitta [filə'pitə], *s. Orn:* philépitte *f.*
Philepittidae [filə'pitidi:], *s.pl. Orn:* philépittidés *m.*
philharmonic [fil(h)ə'mɔnik]. **1.** *a.* philharmonique. **2.** *s.* philharmonique *f.*
philhellene [fil'heli:n], *a. & s.* philhellène (*mf*).
philhellenic [filhe'li:nik], *a.* philhellène.
philhellenism [fil'helinizm], *s.* philhellénisme *m.*
philhellenist [fil'helinist], *a. & s.* philhellène (*mf*).
philine [fi'laini:], *s. Moll:* philine *f.*
Philip ['filip]. *Pr.n.m.* Philippe; *Hist:* **P. the Good,** Philippe le Bon; **P. the Fair,** Philippe le Bel (de France); **P. the Handsome,** Philippe le Beau (d'Espagne); **P. the Bold (of Burgundy), P. the Rash (of France),** Philippe le Hardi; **P. Augustus,** Philippe-Auguste (de France).
Philippa ['filipə]. *Pr.n.f. Hist:* **P. of Hainault,** Philippine de Hainaut.
Philippi ['filipai]. *Pr.n. A.Geog:* Philippes.
Philippian [fi'lipiən], *s. A.Geog:* Philippien, -ienne; *B:* **Epistle of St. Paul to the Philippians,** épître de saint Paul aux Philippiens.
philippic [fi'lipik], *s. Lit:* (*a*) **the Philippics,** les Philippiques *f* (de Démosthène, de Cicéron); (*b*) philippique.
Philippine ['filipi:n]. *Geog:* (*a*) *a.* philippin; *Vet:* **P. fowl disease,** pseudo-peste *f*, maladie *f* de Newcastle; (*b*) *Pr.n.* **the Philippines,** les (îles) Philippines *f.*
philipstadite [filip'stɑ:dait], *s. Miner:* philipstadite *f.*
Philistine ['filistain]. **1.** *s. B:* **the Philistines,** les Philistins *m.* **2.** *a. & s. Art: Lit:* philistin (*m*); **he's a bit of a P.,** il est un peu philistin.
philistinism ['filistinizm], *s. Lit:* philistinisme *m.*
phillipsite ['filipsait], *s. Miner:* phillipsite *f.*
Philo ['failou]. *Pr.n.m. Phil:* **P. (Judaeus),** Philon le Juif.
Philocrates [fi'lɔkrəti:z]. *Pr.n.m. Gr.Hist:* Philocrate.
Philoctetes [filɔk'ti:ti:z]. *Pr.n.m. Gr.Lit:* Philoctète.
philologer [fi'lɔlədʒər], *s. A:* philologue *m.*
philological [filə'lɔdʒik(ə)l], *a.* philologique.
philologically [filə'lɔdʒikəli], *adv.* philologiquement.
philologist [fi'lɔlədʒist], *s.* philologue *mf.*
philology [fi'lɔlədʒi], *s.* philologie *f.*
philomathic [filə'mæθik], *a.* philomathique.
Philomel ['filəmel]. *Pr.n. Lit:* philomèle *m*, rossignol *m.*
Philomela [filou'mi:lə]. *Pr.n.f.* **1.** *Gr.Myth:* Philomèle. **2.** = PHILOMEL.
philopterid [fi'lɔptərid], *s. Ent:* philoptère *m.*
Philopteridae [filɔp'teridi:], *s.pl. Ent:* philoptéridés *m.*
philosopher [fi'lɔsəfər], *s.* (*a*) philosophe *mf*; **idealist, materialist, p.,** philosophe idéaliste, matérialiste; *A:* **natural p.,** philosophe de la nature; (*b*) *Alch:* **the philosopher's stone,** la pierre philosophale; le Grand Œuvre.
philosophic(al) [filə'sɔfik((ə)l)], *a.* **1.** philosophique. **2.** (*of pers.*) philosophe, calme, modéré.
philosophically [filə'sɔfikəli], *adv.* philosophiquement; **to take a misfortune p.,** supporter un malheur en philosophe, avec philosophie.
philosophize [fi'lɔsəfaiz]. **1.** *v.i.* (*a*) philosopher; (*b*) *Pej:* philosophailler. **2.** *v.tr.* (*a*) traiter (une religion, etc.) en philosophe; réduire (une religion) à une philosophie, la concilier avec une philosophie; (*b*) **to p. oneself out of one's fears,** se prouver par le raisonnement que ses craintes sont mal fondées.
philosophizer [fi'lɔsəfaizər], *s. usu. Pej:* philosophâtre *m.*
philosophizing [fi'lɔsəfaiziŋ], *s. Pej:* philosophaillerie *f.*
philosophy [fi'lɔsəfi], *s.* (*a*) philosophie *f*; **moral p., ethical p.,** philosophie morale, éthique; **natural p.,** sciences *fpl* de la nature; **mental p.** = sciences humaines; **p. of history,** philosophie de l'histoire; (*b*) **one of those personal philosophies,** une de ces philosophies personnelles; **one's own p. about sth.,** sa conception personnelle d'une chose; (*c*) **to take one's troubles with p.,** supporter ses malheurs avec philosophie, en philosophe.
Philostratus [fi'lɔstrətəs]. *Pr.n.m. Gr.Lit:* Philostrate.
philotechnic [filə'teknik], *a.* philotechnique.
philtre ['filtər], *s.* philtre *m.*
phimosis [fai'mousis], *s. Med:* phimosis *m.*
Phine(h)as ['finiæs]. *Pr.n.m. B:* Phinée(s).
Phineus ['fainiu:s]. *Pr.n.m. Gr.Myth:* Phinée.
phiz [fiz], **phizog** ['fizɔg], *s. F: O:* visage *m*, binette *f*, frimousse *f.*
phlebectasia [flebek'teiʒiə], *s. Med:* phlébectasie *f.*
phlebectomy [fle'bektəmi], *s. Surg:* phlébectomie *f.*
phlebitis [fli'baitis], *s. Med:* phlébite *f.*
phlebographic(al) [flebou'græfik(əl)], *a.* phlébographique.
phlebography [fle'bɔgrəfi], *s. Med:* phlébographie *f.*
phlebolith ['flebəliθ], *s. Med:* phlébolithe *f.*
phlebology [fle'bɔlədʒi], *s. Med:* phlébologie *f.*
phleborrhagia [flebou'reidʒiə], *s. Med:* phléborragie *f.*
phlebosclerosis [flebouskliə'rousis], *s. Med:* phlébosclérose *f.*
phlebotomize [fli'bɔtəmaiz], *v.tr. A:* saigner, phlébotomiser (qn).
phlebotomus, *pl.* **-mi, -muses** [fli'bɔtəməs, -mai, -məsiz], *s. Ent:* phlébotome *m*; *Med:* **p. fever,** fièvre *f* à phlébotome, fièvre à pappataci.
phlebotomy [fli'bɔtəmi], *s. A.Med:* phlébotomie *f*, saignée *f.*
phlegm [flem], *s.* **1.** flegme *m*; pituite (bronchiale); **to cough up p.,** tousser gras. **2.** flegme, calme *m*, patience *f*, impassibilité *f.*
phlegma ['flegmə], *s. Brew:* flegme *m.*
phlegmasia [fleg'meiziə], *s. Med:* phlegmasie *f*; **p. dolens,** leucophlegmasie *f*, phlegmatia *f* alba dolens.
phlegmatic [fleg'mætik], *a.* flegmatique.
phlegmatically [fleg'mætikəli], *adv.* flegmatiquement.
phlegmon ['flegmɔn], *s. Med:* phlegmon *m*, flegmon *m.*
phlegmonic [fleg'mɔnik], **phlegmonous** ['flegmənəs], *a. Med:* phlegmoneux, flegmoneux.
phlegmy ['flemi], *a. Med:* flegmatique, pituiteux; **p. cough,** toux grasse.
phleum ['fli:əm], *s. Bot:* fléole *f.*
phlobaphene ['flɔbəfi:n], *s. Ch:* phlobaphène *m.*
phloem ['flouem], *s. Bot:* phloème *m*, liber *m.*
phlogistic [flɔ'dʒistik], *a. A.Ch:* phlogistique.
phlogiston [flɔ'dʒistən], *s. A.Ch:* phlogistique *m.*
phlogopite ['flɔgəpait], *s. Miner:* phlogopite *f.*
phloretic [flɔ'ri:tik], *a. Ch:* phlorétique.
phloretin [flɔ'ri:tin], *s. Ch:* phlorétine *f.*
phlorizin, phlor(r)hizin ['flɔrizin, flɔ'raizin], **phloridzin** [flɔ'ridzin], *s. Ch:* phlori(d)zine *f.*
phloroglucin(ol) [flɔ:rou'glu:sin(ɔl)], *s. Ch:* phloroglucine *f*, phloroglucinol *m.*
phlox [flɔks], *s. Bot:* phlox *m.*
phlyct(a)ena, *pl.* **-t(a)enae** [flik'ti:nə, -'ti:ni:], *s. Med:* phlyctène *f*, ampoule *f.*
phlyctenoid [flik'ti:nɔid], *a. Med:* phlycténoïde.
phlyct(a)enula, *pl.* **-lae** [flik'tenjulə, -'ti:julə, -li:], **phlyctenule** [flik'tenju:l], *s. Med:* phlycténule *f.*
phlyctenular [flik'tenjulər], *a. Med:* phlycténulaire.
phobia ['foubiə], *s.* phobie *f.*
phobiac ['foubiæk], *s. Med:* phobique *mf.*
phobic ['foubik], *a. & s. Med:* phobique (*mf*).
phobism ['foubizm], *s. Med:* phobisme *m.*
Phocaea [fou'si(:)ə]. *Pr.n. A.Geog:* Phocée *f.*
Phocaean [fou'si(:)ən]. *A.Geog:* **1.** *a.* phocéen. **2.** *s.* Phocéen, -éenne.
phocaena [fou'si:nə], *s. Z:* phocène *f.*
Phocian ['fouʃiən]. *Geog:* **1.** *a.* phocidien. **2.** *s.* Phocidien, -ienne.
Phocidae ['fousidi:], *s.pl. Z:* phocidés *m.*
Phocis ['fousis]. *Pr.n. Geog:* Phocide *f.*
phocomelia [foukou'mi:liə], *s. Ter:* phocomélie *f.*
phocomelic [foukou'mi:lik], *a. Ter:* phocomèle.
phocomelus [fou'kɔmələs], *s. Ter:* phocomèle *m.*
Phoebe ['fi:bi]. **1.** *Pr.n.f. Myth: Astr:* Phébé. **2.** *s. Orn:* **eastern p.,** moucherolle *m* phébi; **Say's p.,** moucherolle à ventre roux.
Phoebean ['fi:biən], *a.* phébéen, -éenne.
Phoebus ['fi:bəs], *Pr.n.m. Myth:* Phébus.
Phoenicia [fi'ni:ʃə], *Pr.n. A.Geog:* Phénicie *f.*
Phoenician [fi'ni:ʃən]. **1.** *A.Geog:* (*a*) *a.* phénicien; (*b*) *s.* Phénicien, -ienne. **2.** *s. Ling:* le phénicien. **3.** *s.* [fi:'niʃən], *U.S:* habitant, -ante, de Phoenix, Arizona.
phoenicite ['fi:nisait], *s. Miner:* phoenicite *f*, phénicite *f.*
phoenicochroite [fi:ni'kɔkrouait], *s. Miner:* phoenicochroïte *f*, phénicochroïte *f.*
Phoenicopteridae [fi:nikɔp'teridi:], *s.pl. Orn:* phoenicoptéridés *m*, phénicoptéridés *m*; les flamants *m.*
phoenix ['fi:niks], *s.* **1.** *Myth:* phénix *m.* **2.** *Bot:* phoenix *m.* **3.** *Husb:* **p. fowl,** phénix.
phokomelia [foukou'mi:liə], *s. Ter:* phocomélie *f.*
Pholadidae [fou'lædidi:], *s.pl. Moll:* pholadidés *m.*
pholas, *pl.* **-ades** ['foulæs, -ədi:z], *s. Moll:* pholade *f.*
Pholcidae ['fɔlsidi:], *s.pl. Arach:* pholcidés *m.*
Pholidota [fɔli'doutə], *s.pl. Z:* pholidotes *m*, les pangolins *m.*
pholiota [fouli'outə], *s. Fung:* pholiote *f.*
phoma ['foumə], *s. Fung:* phoma *m.*
phon [fɔn], *s. Ac.Meas:* phone *m*; **p. meter,** phonemètre *m.*
phonal ['founəl], *a. Physiol:* vocal, -aux; (*of organ*) phonateur, -trice.
phonate ['founeit], *v.tr. Physiol: Ling:* émettre, produire, des phonèmes.
phonation [fou'neiʃ(ə)n], *s. Physiol: Ling:* phonation *f.*
phonatory ['founət(ə)ri], *a.* phonatoire.
phonautograph [fou'nɔ:təgræf], *s. Ph:* phonautographe *m.*
phone[1] [foun], *s. Ling:* phonème *m.*
phone[2], *s.* téléphone *m*; **to be on the p.,** (i) être au téléphone; (ii) être abonné au téléphone; **are you on the p.?** avez-vous le téléphone? **who answered the p.?** qui a répondu au téléphone? **p. call,** coup *m* de téléphone; **to give a piece of news on the p., by p.,** téléphoner une nouvelle; **to speak to s.o. on the p.,** parler à qn au téléphone, par téléphone; **p. book,** annuaire *m* téléphonique, du téléphone; **p. box,** cabine *f* téléphonique; (*of police*) **to tap s.o.'s p.,** employer la table d'écoute; **p. tapping,** emploi *m* de la table d'écoute.
phone[3], *v.tr. & i.* **to p. s.o.,** téléphoner à qn; appeler qn au téléphone; donner un coup de téléphone à qn; **I'll p. you,** je vous téléphonerai; **to p. for sth.,** demander qch. par téléphone; **to p. for a taxi,** appeler un taxi; **I phoned the doctor to come at once,** j'ai téléphoné au docteur de venir tout de suite; **I'll p. for the leg of mutton,** je vais faire venir le gigot par téléphone; **to p. a piece of news,** téléphoner une nouvelle.
phonematic [founə'mætik], *a. Ling:* phonématique.
phonematics [founə'mætiks], *s.pl.* (*usu. with sg. const.*) *Ling:* phonématique *f.*
phoneme ['founi:m], *s. Ling:* phonème *m.*
phonemic [fou'ni:mik], *a. Ling:* phonémique.
phonemics [fou'ni:miks], *s.pl.* (*usu. with sg. const.*) phonématique *f.*
phonendoscope [fou'nendəskoup], *s. Med:* phonendoscope *m.*
phonendoscopy [founen'dɔskəpi], *s. Med:* phonendoscopie *f.*
phonetic [fə'netik], *a.* phonétique; **p. spelling,** écriture *f* phonétique; **p. alphabet,** alphabet *m* phonétique.
phonetically [fə'netik(ə)li], *adv.* phonétiquement.
phonetician [founə'tiʃ(ə)n], **phoneticist** [fə'netisist], *s.* phonéticien, -ienne; phonétiste *mf.*
phonetics [fə'netiks], *s.pl.* (*usu. with sg. const.*) phonétique *f.*
phonetist ['founətist], *s.* phonétiste *mf*; phonéticien, -ienne.
phoney ['founi]. *F:* **1.** *a.* **(phonier, phoniest)** faux, *f.* fausse; factice; (bijouterie *f*) en toc; **the p. war,** la drôle de guerre (1939–40); **a p. baron,** un prétendu baron; **he's p.,** il est faux comme un jeton. **2.** *s.* imposteur *m*; prétendu, faux artiste, intellectuel, etc.; **he's a p.,** il est faux comme un jeton.
phoniatric [founi'ætrik], *a. Med:* **p. specialist,** phoniatre *mf.*
phoniatrics [founi'ætriks], *s.pl.* (*usu. with sg. const.*),

phoniatry ['founiætri], *s. Med:* phoniatrie *f.*

phonic ['fɔnik, 'founik], *a.* phonique; *Tg:* **p. wheel,** roue *f* phonique.

phonics ['fɔniks], *s.pl.* (*usu. with sg. const.*) phonique *f.*

phonily ['founili], *adv. F:* faussement.

phoniness ['founinis], *s. F:* fausseté *f*; **of obvious p.,** manifestement faux.

phonocardiogram [founou'kɑ:diougræm], *s. Med:* phonocardiogramme *m.*

phonocardiography [founoukɑ:di'ɔgrəfi], *s. Med:* phonocardiographie *f.*

phonogram ['founəgræm], *s.* **1.** phonogramme *m* (d'enregistrement sonore). **2.** *Tg: Tp:* télégramme téléphoné; **p. circuit,** circuit *m* pour télégrammes téléphonés; **p. position,** position *f* de transmission des télégrammes téléphonés. **3.** sténogramme *m.*

phonograph ['founəgræf], *s. NAm:* phonographe *m.*

phonographic [founə'græfik], *a.* **1.** phonographique. **2.** sténographique.

phonography [fə'nɔgrəfi], *s.* **1.** phonographie *f*; orthographe *f* phonétique. **2.** sténographie *f.*

phonolite ['founəlait], *s. Miner:* phonolit(h)e *f.*

phonolitic [founə'litik], *a. Geol:* phonolit(h)ique; de phonolite; **p. dyke,** dyke *m* de phonolite; suc *m.*

phonologic(al) [founə'lɔdʒik((ə)l)], *a.* phonologique.

phonologist [fə'nɔlədʒist], *s. Ling:* phonologue *mf.*

phonology [fə'nɔlədʒi], *s.* phonologie *f*; phonétique *f* historique.

phonometer [fə'nɔmitər], *s. Ph:* phonomètre *m.*

phonometric [founə'metrik], *a. Ph:* phonométrique.

phonometry [fə'nɔmətri], *s. Ph:* phonométrie *f.*

phonon ['founɔn], *s. Ph:* phonon *m.*

phonoscope ['founəskoup], *s. Ph:* phonoscope *m.*

phoney ['founi], *a. & s.* = PHONEY.

phonyness ['founinis], *s.* = PHONINESS.

phooey ['fu:i], *int.* peuh!

phooka ['pu:kə], *s. Irish Myth:* = loup-garou *m.*

phoresia [fə'ri:ziə], **phoresis** [fə'ri:sis], **phoresy** ['fɔ(:)rəsi], *s. Biol:* phorésie *f.*

Phoridae ['fɔridi:], *s.pl. Ent:* phorides *m.*

phormium ['fɔ:miəm], *s. Bot:* phormium *m*; *F:* lin *m* de la Nouvelle-Zélande.

phorone ['fouroun], *s. Ch:* phorone *f.*

phoronid [fə'rɔnid], *s. Nat.Hist:* phoronidien *m.*

Phoronida [fə'rɔnidə], **Phoronidea** [fɔ:rə'nidiə], *s.pl. Nat.Hist:* phoronidiens *m.*

phosgene ['fɔzdʒi:n], *s. Ch:* phosgène *m*; oxychlorure *m* de carbone; chlorure *m* de carbonyle; *Mil:* (*1914–1918*) **p. (gas),** gaz *m* phosgène.

phosgenite ['fɔzdʒinait], *s. Miner:* phosgénite *f*; plomb corné.

phospham ['fɔsfæm], *s. Ch:* phospham *m.*

phosphataemia [fɔsfə'ti:miə], *s. Med:* phosphatémie *f.*

phosphatase ['fɔsfəteis], *s. Ch:* phosphatase *f.*

phosphate[1] ['fɔsfeit], *s. Ch:* phosphate *m*; **p. of lime, calcium p.,** phosphate de chaux; **organic p.,** phosphate organique; **p. miner, miner of p. rock,** phosphatier *m*; **p. mine, p. works,** phosphaterie *f*; **p. treatment** (*of soil, of wine*), phosphatage *m*; *Nau:* **p. carrier,** phosphatier.

phosphate[2], *v.tr. Agr: Metalw:* phosphater.

phosphated ['fɔsfeitid], *a.* phosphaté.

phosphatemia [fɔsfə'ti:miə], *s. Med:* phosphatémie *f.*

phosphatic [fɔs'fætik], *a.* phosphatique; phosphaté.

phosphatide ['fɔsfətaid], *s. Bio-Ch:* phosphatide *m*; phospholipide *m.*

phosphatidic [fɔsfə'tidik], *a. Bio-Ch:* phosphatidique.

phosphating ['fɔsfeitiŋ], *s. Agr: etc:* phosphatage *m.*

phosphatize ['fɔsfətaiz], *v.tr.* **1.** convertir en phosphate. **2.** traiter au phosphate; phosphater.

phosphaturia [fɔsfə'tju:riə], *s. Med:* phosphaturie *f.*

phosphaturic [fɔsfə'tju:rik], *a. Med:* phosphaturique.

phosphene ['fɔsfi:n], *s. Physiol:* phosphène *m.*

phosphenyl [fɔs'fenil], *s. Ch:* phosphényle *m.*

phosphide ['fɔsfaid], *s. Ch:* phosphure *m.*

phosphine ['fɔsfi:n], *s. Ch:* phosphine *f.*

phosphite ['fɔsfait], *s. Ch:* phosphite *m.*

phosphoaminolipid(e) [fɔsfouəmi:nou'lip(a)id], *s. Bio-Ch:* phosphoaminolipide *m.*

phospholipase [fɔsfou'l(a)ipeis], *s. Bio-Ch:* phospholipase *f.*

phospholipid(e) [fɔsfou'lip(a)id], *s. Bio-Ch:* phospholipide *m*; phosphatide *m.*

phosphomolybdic [fɔsfoumə'libdik], *a. Ch:* phosphomolybdique.

phosphonium [fɔs'founiəm], *s. Ch:* phosphonium *m.*

phosphor ['fɔsfər], *s. Ch:* phosphore *m*; *Metall:* **p. bronze,** bronze phosphoreux, phosphoré.

phosphorate ['fɔsfəreit], *v.tr.* phosphorer.

phosphoresce [fɔsfə'res], *v.i.* être phosphorescent; luire par phosphorescence; entrer en phosphorescence; (*of sea*) lamper.

phosphorescence [fɔsfə'resəns], *s.* phosphorescence *f.*

phosphorescent [fɔsfə'resənt], *a.* phosphorescent.

phosphoret(t)ed ['fɔsfəretid], *a. Ch:* phosphuré; **p. hydrogen,** hydrogène phosphoré, hydrure *m* de phosphore.

phosphoric [fɔs'fɔrik], *a. Ch:* phosphorique; **p. anhydride,** anhydride *m* phosphorique, hémipentaoxyde *m* de phosphore.

phosphorism ['fɔsfərizm], *s. Med:* phosphorisme *m.*

phosphorite ['fɔsfərait], *s. Miner:* phosphorite *f.*

phosphoritic [fɔsfə'ritik], *a.* phosphoritique.

phosphorize ['fɔsfəraiz], *v.tr.* phosphoriser, phosphorer.

phosphorogen ['fɔsfəroudʒen], *s.* phosphorogène *m.*

phosphorogenic [fɔsfərou'dʒenik], *a.* phosphorogène.

phosphorographic [fɔsfərou'græfik], *a.* phosphorographique.

phosphorography [fɔsfə'rɔgrəfi], *s.* phosphorographie *f.*

phosphoroscope ['fɔsfərəskoup], *s.* phosphoroscope *m.*

phosphorous ['fɔsfərəs], *a.* phosphoreux.

phosphorus ['fɔsfərəs], *s. Ch:* phosphore *m*; **red p.,** phosphore rouge; **yellow p.,** phosphore blanc; **p. pentachloride,** pentachlorure *m* de phosphore; **p. matches,** allumettes *f* au phosphore; **p. necrosis,** nécrose phosphorée (de la mâchoire).

phosphoryl ['fɔsfəril], *s. Ch:* phosphoryle *m.*

phosphotungstate [fɔsfou'tʌŋsteit], *s. Ch:* phosphotungstate *m.*

phosphuranylite [fɔsfjə'rænəlait], *s. Miner:* phosphuranylite *f.*

phosphuret(t)ed ['fɔsfjəretid], *a.* = PHOSPHORET(T)ED.

phossy jaw ['fɔsidʒɔ:], *s. F: A:* nécrose phosphorée (de la mâchoire).

phot [fɔt, fout], *s. Opt.Meas:* phot *m* (= 10,000 lux).

Photian ['fouʃ(ə)n], *s. Rel.H:* adhérent, -ente, de Photius.

photic ['foutik], *a.* **p. region, zone,** zone *f* photique (de la mer).

Photinus [fou'tainəs]. *Pr.n.m. Rel.H:* Photin.

photism ['foutizm], *s. Biol:* photisme *m.*

photo ['foutou], *s. F:* photo *f*; **p. cover,** couverture *f* photo(graphique) (d'une région); **p. reconnaissance,** reconnaissance *f* photographique; *Sp:* **p. finish,** photo à l'arrivée; décision *f* par photo; photo-finish *f inv*; **p.-finish camera,** photo-finish.

photo- ['foutou, fə'tɔ], *comb.fm.* photo-.

photobacterium [foutoubæk'tiəriəm], *s.* photobactérie *f.*

photocatalysis [foutoukæ'tælisis], *s. Ch:* photocatalyse *f.*

photocathode [foutou'kæθoud], *s. Elcs:* photocathode *f.*

photocell ['foutousel], *s.* photocellule *f.*

photoceramic [foutousə'ræmik], *a.* photocéramique.

photoceramics [foutousə'ræmiks], *s.pl.* (*usu. with sg. const.*) photocéramique *f.*

photochemical [foutou'kemikl], *a.* photochimique; **p. cell,** cellule *f* photovoltaïque.

photochemistry [foutou'kemistri], *s.* photochimie *f.*

photochrom(at)ic [foutou'kroumik, -krou'mætik], *a.* photochromique.

photochromy ['foutəkroumi], *s.* photochromie *f.*

photocinesis [foutousi'ni:sis], *s. Biol:* photokinésie *f.*

photocleistogamous [foutouklai'stɔgəməs], *a. Bot:* photocléistogame.

photocollography [foutoukɔ'lɔgrəfi], *s.* photocollographie *f.*

photocomposition [foutoukɔmpə'ziʃ(ə)n], *s. Typ:* photocomposition *f.*

photoconductance [foutoukən'dʌkt(ə)ns], *s. Elcs:* photoconductivité *f*, photoconductibilité *f.*

photoconduction [foutoukən'dʌkʃ(ə)n], *s. Elcs:* photoconduction *f.*

photoconductive [foutoukən'dʌktiv], *a. Elcs:* photoconducteur, -trice; photoconductif; **p. cell,** cellule photoconductrice, photoconductive; **p. effect,** photoconduction *f*; effet *m* photoélectrique interne.

photoconductivity [foutoukɔndʌk'tiviti], *s. Elcs:* photoconductivité *f*, photoconductibilité *f.*

photoconductor [foutoukən'dʌktər], *s. Elcs:* photoconducteur *m*; couche photoconductrice.

photocopier ['foutoukɔpiər], *s.* photocopieur *m.*

photocopy[1] ['foutoukɔpi], *s.* photocopie *f.*

photocopy[2], *v.tr.* photocopier.

photocurrent ['foutoukʌrənt], *s. Elcs:* photocourant *m.*

photodermatosis [foutoudə:mə'tousis], *s. Med: Vet:* photodermatose *f.*

photodiode [foutou'daioud], *s. Elcs:* photodiode *f.*

photodisintegration [foutoudisinti'greiʃ(ə)n], *s. Atom.Ph:* photodésintégration *f.*

photodissociation [foutoudisousi'eiʃ(ə)n], *s. Ch:* photodissociation *f.*

photodynamic [foutoudai'næmik], *a.* photodynamique.

photoelasticity [foutouelæs'tisiti], *s.* photo(-)élasticité *f.*

photoelectric [foutoui'lektrik], *a.* photoélectrique; **p. cell,** cellule *f* photoélectrique; **p. current,** courant *m* photoélectrique; **p. effect,** effet *m* photoélectrique; **p. emission,** émission *f* photoélectrique; photoémission *f*; *T.V:* **p. tube,** tube *m* photoélectrique; **p. mosaic,** mosaïque *f* photoélectrique; **p. threshold,** seuil *m* photoélectrique.

photoelectricity [foutoutelek'trisiti], *s.* photoélectricité *f.*

photoelectron [foutoui'lektrɔn], *s.* photoélectron *m.*

photoemission [foutoui'miʃ(ə)n], *s. Elcs:* photoémission *f.*

photoemissive [foutoui'misiv], *a. Elcs:* photoémissif; **p. cell,** cellule photoémissive; **p. effect,** effet *m* photoélectrique interne; photoémission *f.*

photoemittent [foutoui'mitənt], *a. Elcs:* photoémetteur, -trice.

photoengraver [foutouin'greivər], *s.* photograveur *m.*

photoengraving [foutouin'greiviŋ], *s.* photogravure *f.*

photoetching [foutou'etʃiŋ], *s. Elcs:* photogravure *f.*

photofission [foutou'fiʃ(ə)n], *s. Atom.Ph:* photofission *f.*

photofluorography [foutoutfljuə'rɔgrəfi], *s.* radiophotographie *f.*

photogenesis [foutou'dʒenəsis], *s.* photogénèse *f.*

photogenetic [foutoudʒə'netik], *a.* photogène.

photogenic [foutou'dʒenik], *a.* photogénique.

photogeology [foutoudʒi'ɔlədʒi], *s.* photogéologie *f.*

photoglyphy ['foutouglifi], *s.* photoglyptie *f.*

photoglyptic [foutou'gliptik], *a.* photoglyptique.

photogram ['foutougræm], *s.* photogramme *m.*

photogrammetric [foutougræ'metrik], *a.* photogrammétrique.

photogrammetrist [foutou'græmətrist], *s.* photogrammètre *m.*

photogrammetry [foutou'græmitri], *s.* photogrammétrie *f.*

photograph[1] ['foutəgræf], *s.* photographie *f*; **aerial p.,** photographie aérienne; **oblique p.,** photographie oblique; **panoramic p.,** photographie panoramique; **to take s.o.'s p.,** prendre une photographie de qn; **he had his p. taken,** il s'est fait photographier; **satellite that transmits, returns, photographs of the earth,** satellite *m* qui transmet des photographies de la terre.

photograph[2], *v.tr.* **1.** photographier; prendre une photographie de (qn, qch.). **2.** (*with passive force*) (*of pers.*) **to p. well,** être photogénique; **she does not p. well,** ses photographies ne lui rendent pas justice.

photographer [fə'tɔgrəfər], *s.* photographe *mf*; **street p.,** photostoppeur, -euse; *Journ:* **press p., staff p.,** reporter *m* photographe, photographe de presse; **to take some photographs to the photographer's to be developed,** porter des photos à développer chez un photographe.

photographic [foutə'græfik], *a.* (procédé, papier, description, etc.) photographique; **p. image,** image *f* photographique; **p. interpretation,** interprétation *f* des photographies; **p. reconnaissance,** reconnaissance *f* photographique; **p. survey(ing),** levé *m*, lever *m*, photographique; photographie *f*; **p. club,** société *f* de photographie.

photographically [foutə'græfik(ə)li], *adv.* photographiquement.

photography [fə'tɔgrəfi], *s.* photographie *f*; **aerial p.,** photographie aérienne; **underwater p.,** photographie subaquatique, sous-marine; **colour p.,** photographie en couleurs; **street p.,** photostop *m*; **high-speed p.,** photographie ultra-rapide; **infra-red p.,** photographie infrarouge; **endoscopic, stereoscopic, stroboscopic, p.,** photographie endoscopique, stéréoscopique, stroboscopique.

photogravure [foutougrə'vjuər], *s.* photogravure *f.*

photogravurist [foutougrə'vju:rist], *s.* photograveur *m.*

photoheliograph [foutou'hi:liougræf], *s.* photohéliographe *m.*

photo-ionization [foutouaiənai'zeiʃ(ə)n], *s.* photo-ionisation *f.*

photokinesis [foutouki'ni:sis], *s. Biol:* photokinésie *f.*

photolithograph[1] [foutou'liθəgræf], *s.* photolithographie *f*; gravure *f* photolithographique.

photolithograph[2], *v.tr.* photolithographier.

photolithographer [foutouli'θɔgrəfər], *s.* photolithographe *m.*

photolithographic [foutouliθə'græfik], *a.* photolithographique; **p. transfer,** report *m* photolithographique.

photolithography [foutouli'θɔgrəfi], *s.* photolithographie *f*; gravure *f* photolithographique.

photology [fou'tɔlədʒi], *s.* photologie *f.*

photoluminescence [foutoulu:mi'nes(ə)ns], *s.* photoluminescence *f.*
photoluminescent [foutoulu:mi'nesənt], *a.* photoluminescent.
photolysis [fou'tɔlisis], *s. Biol:* photolyse *f.*
photolytic [foutə'litik], *a. Biol:* photolytique.
photomacrograph [foutou'mækrougræf], *s.* photomacrographie *f.*
photomacrography [foutoumæ'krɔgrəfi], *s.* photomacrographie *f.*
photomagnetic [foutoumæg'netik], *a.* photomagnétique.
photomap[1] ['foutoumæp], *s.* carte photographique (aérienne); photocarte *f.*
photomap[2], *v.tr. & i.* (**photomapped**) faire une carte photographique, une photocarte (d'une région).
photomechanical [foutoumi'kænikl], *a.* photomécanique.
photomeson [foutou'mi:zɔn], *s. Atom.Ph:* photoméson *m.*
photometer[1] [fou'tɔmitər], *s. Ph:* photomètre *m;* **automatic-scanning p.,** photomètre à balayage, à exploration, automatique; **Bunsen, grease-spot, p.,** photomètre (de) Bunsen, photomètre à tache d'huile; **electronic p.,** photomètre électronique; **flicker p.,** photomètre à éclats, à papillotement; **integrating p.,** photomètre à intégration; **photocell p.,** photomètre à cellule photoélectrique; **polarization p.,** photomètre à polarisation; **recording p.,** photomètre enregistreur; **Rumford, shadow, p.,** photomètre (de) Rumford, photomètre à ombre.
photometer[2], *v.tr. Ph:* photométrer.
photometric [foutou'metrik], *a.* photométrique; **p. constant,** constante *f* photométrique; **p. bench,** banc *m* photométrique.
photometry [fou'tɔmitri], *s. Ph:* photométrie *f;* **astronomical, heterochromatic, p.,** photométrie astronomique, hétérochrome.
photomicrograph [foutou'maikrougræf], *s.* photomicrographie *f.*
photomicrographic [foutoumaikrou'græfik], *a.* photomicrographique.
photomicrography [foutoumai'krɔgrəfi], *s.* photomicrographie *f.*
photomontage [foutoumɔn'tɑ:ʒ], *s.* photomontage *m,* montage *m* photographique.
photomorphosis [foutou'mɔ:fəsis], *s. Biol:* photomorphose *f.*
photomultiplier [foutou'mʌltiplaiər], *s. Elcs:* photomultiplicateur *m.*
photon ['foutɔn], *s. Opt: Meas:* photon *m.*
photonastic ['foutounæstik], *a. Bot:* photonastique.
photonasty ['foutounæsti], *s. Bot:* photonastie *f.*
photonegative [foutou'negətiv], *a. Biol:* photonégatif.
photoneutron [foutou'nju:trɔn], *s. Atom.Ph:* photoneutron *m.*
photonic [fou'tɔnik], *a. Ph:* photonique.
photonuclear [foutou'nju:kliər], *a.* photonucléaire.
photoperiod ['foutoupiəriəd], *s. Biol:* photopériode *f.*
photoperiodism [foutou'piəriədizm], *s. Bot:* photopériodisme *m.*
photophile ['foutoufail], **photophilic** [foutou'filik], **photophilous** [fou'tɔfiləs], *a. Nat.Hist:* photophile.
photophobia [foutou'foubiə], *s. Med:* photophobie *f.*
photophobic [foutou'foubik], *a. Med:* photophobe.
photophone ['foutoufoun], *s. Hist.ofTp:* photophone *m.*
photophore ['foutoufɔ:r], *s. Med:* photophore *m;* endoscope *m.*
photophoresis [foutoufɔ'ri:sis], *s. Ph:* photophorèse *f.*
photopic [fou'tɔpik], *a. Opt:* photopique.
photopolymerization [foutoupɔlimərai'zeiʃ(ə)n], *s. Ch:* photopolymérisation *f.*
photopositive [foutou'pɔzitiv], *a. Biol:* photopositif.
photoproton [foutou'proutɔn], *s. Atom.Ph:* photoproton *m.*
photopsia [fou'tɔpsiə], **photopsy** ['foutɔpsi], *s. Med:* photopsie *f.*
photoreaction [foutouri'ækʃ(ə)n], *s. Ch:* photoréaction *f.*
photoresistance [foutouri'zistəns], *s.* photorésistance *f;* photorésistivité *f.*
photoresistive [foutouri'zistiv], *a.* photorésistant.
photoresistivity [foutourezis'tiviti], *s.* photorésistivité *f.*
photoscopic [foutou'skɔpik], *a.* photoscopique.
photosensing [foutou'sensiŋ], *s. Elcs:* lecture *f,* détection *f,* photoélectrique.
photosensitive [foutou'sensitiv], *a.* photosensible.
photosensitivity [foutousensi'tiviti], *s.* photosensibilité *f.*
photosensitization [foutousensitai'zeiʃ(ə)n], *s.* photosensibilisation *f.*

photosensor [foutou'sensər], *s. Elcs:* détecteur *m* photoélectrique.
photosphere ['foutousfiər], *s. Astr:* photosphère *f.*
photostat[1] ['foutoustæt], *s.* photostat *m.*
photostat[2], *v.tr. & i.* (**photostatted**) faire des copies photostatiques.
photostereograph [foutou'stiəriougræf], *s.* stéréogramme *m.*
photostereographic [foutoustiəriou'græfik], *a.* stéréophotographique; **p. survey(ing),** photostéréotopographie *f.*
photosurvey [foutou'sə:vei], *s.* phototopographie *f.*
photosurveying [foutousə:'veiiŋ], *s.* phototopographie *f.*
photosynthesis [foutou'sinθisis], *s.* photosynthèse *f.*
photosynthetic [foutousin'θetik], *a.* photosynthétique.
phototactism [foutou'tæktizm], *s. Biol:* phototactisme *m.*
phototaxis, phototaxy [foutou'tæksis, -'tæksi], *s. Biol:* phototaxie *f.*
phototelegram [foutou'teligræm], *s.* phototélégramme *m.*
phototelegraph [foutou'teligræf], *s.* phototélégraphe *m.*
phototelegraphic [foutouteli'græfik], *a.* phototélégraphique.
phototelegraphy [foutouti'legrəfi], *s.* phototélégraphie *f.*
phototherapeutic [foutouθerə'pju:tik], *a. Med:* photothérapeutique; **p. bath,** bain photothérapeutique.
phototherapeutics [foutouθerə'pju:tiks], *s.pl.* (*usu. with sg. const.*) photothérapie *f.*
phototherapy [foutou'θerəpi], *s. Med:* photothérapie *f.*
phototimer ['foutoutaimər], *s. Phot:* compte-pose *m* photoélectrique.
phototopography [foutoutə'pɔgrəfi], *s.* phototopographie *f.*
phototransfer [foutou'trænsfər], *s. Lith:* report *m* photo(graphique).
phototransistor [foutoutræn'zistər], *s.* phototransistor *m,* phototransistron *m.*
phototrophic [foutou'trɔfik], *a. Nat.Hist:* phototrophe; phototropique.
phototropism [foutou'trɔpizm], *s. Nat.Hist:* phototropisme *m;* héliotropisme *m;* actinotropisme *m.*
phototropy [fou'tɔtrəpi], *s.* phototropie *f.*
phototype ['foutoutaip], *s.* phototype *m;* photocalque *m.*
phototypographic [foutoutaipou'græfik], *a.* phototypographique.
phototypography [foutoutai'pɔgrəfi], *s.* phototypographie *f.*
phototypogravure [foutoutaipougræ'vjuər], *s.* phototypogravure *f.*
phototypy ['foutoutaipi], *s.* phototypie *f.*
photovoltaic [foutouvɔl'teiik], *a.* photovoltaïque; **p. cell,** cellule *f* photovoltaïque, à couche d'arrêt; photopile *f;* **p. effect,** effet *m* photovoltaïque.
photozincography [foutouziŋ'kɔgrəfi], *s.* photozincographie *f.*
phrase[1] [freiz], *s.* **1.** (*a*) locution *f,* expression *f;* tournure *f,* tour *m,* de phrase; **neat p.,** tour élégant; **you use that p. too often,** vous abusez de cette expression; **I'm trying to find a polite p. to . . .,** je cherche une formule de politesse pour . . .; **p. book,** recueil *m* de locutions, d'idiotismes; (*b*) *Lit: O:* phraséologie *f;* style *m;* **felicity of p.,** phraséologie heureuse, bonheur *m* d'expression; (*c*) *Gram:* locution (adverbiale, prépositive, etc.); membre *m* de phrase. **2.** *Mus:* phrase, période *f.* **3.** *Fenc:* phrase d'armes.
phrase[2], *v.tr.* **1.** exprimer (sa pensée, etc.); donner un tour à (sa pensée); **well-phrased letter,** lettre bien rédigée, bien tournée; **that is how he phrased it,** voilà comment il s'est exprimé; voilà l'expression qu'il a employée. **2.** *A:* désigner, nommer, appeler. **3.** *Mus:* phraser.
phraseogram ['freiziougræm], *s.* sténogramme *m* (qui représente une locution, un groupe de mots).
phraseological [freiziə'lɔdʒikl], *a.* phraséologique.
phraseology [freizi'ɔlədʒi], *s.* phraséologie *f.*
phrasing ['freiziŋ], *s.* **1.** (*a*) expression *f* (de la pensée); rédaction *f* (d'un document); (*b*) phraséologie *f.* **2.** *Mus:* phrasé *m.*
phratry ['freitri], *s. Gr.Ant: etc:* phratrie *f.*
phreatic [fri'ætik], *a. Geol:* phréatique; **p. water,** nappe *f* phréatique.
phreatophyte [fri'ætoufait], *s. Bot:* phréatophyte *f.*
phrenic ['frenik], *a. Anat:* (nerf, artère) phrénique.
phrenicectomy [freni'sektəmi], *s. Surg:* phrénicectomie *f.*
phrenicotomy [freni'kɔtəmi], *s. Surg:* phrénicotomie *f.*
phrenitis [fre'naitis], *s. Med:* phrénitis *m.*

phrenocardia [frenou'kɑ:diə], *s. Med:* phrénocardie *f.*
phrenological [frenə'lɔdʒikl], *a.* phrénologique.
phrenologist [fre'nɔlədʒist], *s.* phrénologiste *mf,* phrénologue *mf.*
phrenology [fre'nɔlədʒi], *s.* phrénologie *f.*
phronima ['frɔnimə], *s. Crust:* phronime *f.*
phryganea [fri'geiniə], *s. Ent:* phrygane *f.*
Phrygia ['fridʒiə], *Pr.n. A.Geog:* Phrygie *f.*
Phrygian ['fridʒiən]. **1.** *a. A.Geog:* phrygien; *Hist:* **P. cap,** bonnet phrygien; *Mus:* **P. mode,** mode phrygien. **2.** *s. A.Geog:* Phrygien, -ienne.
Phrynosoma [frainou'soumə], *s. Rept:* phrynosome *m.*
phthalate ['θæleit], *s. Ch:* phtalate *m.*
phthalein ['θæliin], *s. Ch:* phtaléine *f.*
phthalic ['θælik], *a. Ch:* (acide) phtalique.
phthalide ['θælaid], *s. Ch:* phtalide *m.*
phthalimide ['θælimaid], *s. Ch:* phtalimide *m.*
phthalin ['θælin], *s. Ch:* phtaline *f.*
phthalocyanine [θælou'saiənain], *s. Ch:* phtalocyanine *f;* **platinum p.,** phtalocyanine du platine.
phthanite ['θænait], *s. Miner:* phtanite *f.*
phthiriasis [θaiəri'eisis], *s. Med:* phtiriase *f,* maladie *f* pédiculaire.
phthisical ['tizikl], *a. Med:* phtisique.
phthisiogenesis [θiziou'dʒenəsis, tiz-], *s. Med:* phtisiogénèse *f.*
phthisiogenic [θiziou'dʒenik, tiz-], *a. Med:* phtisiogénique.
phthisiologist [θizi'ɔlədʒist, tiz-], *s. Med:* phtisiologue *mf.*
phthisiology [θizi'ɔlədʒi, tiz-], *s. Med:* phtisiologie *f.*
phthisiotherapy [θiziou'θerəpi, tiz-], *s. Med:* phtisiothérapie *f.*
phthisis ['θaisis], *s. Med:* phtisie *f.*
phugoid ['fju:gɔid], *a. Av:* **p. oscillation,** oscillation longitudinale à longue période.
phut [fʌt]. *F:* **1.** *s.* bruit sourd (de deux objets qui se heurtent, etc.). **2.** *adv. F:* (*of business, engine, etc.*) **to go p.,** claquer; (*of rope, etc.*) céder; se casser; **my car's gone p.,** ma voiture ne marche plus; **the light went p.,** nous avons eu une panne d'électricité.
phycoerythrin [faikou'eriθrin], *s. Algae:* phycoérythrine *f.*
phycologist [fai'kɔlədʒist], *s.* phycologue *mf,* phycologiste *mf.*
phycology [fai'kɔlədʒi], *s.* phycologie *f.*
Phycomyceteae, Phycomycetes [faikoumai'si:tii:, -'si:ti:z], *s.pl. Fung:* phycomycètes *m.*
phylactery [fi'læktəri], *s.* **1.** *Jew.Rel:* phylactère *m; Lit:* **they make broad their phylacteries,** ils font ostentation de leurs sentiments religieux. **2.** *Art:* phylactère; banderole *f* à inscription.
Phylactolaemata [filæktouli:'meitə], *s.pl. Z:* phylactolémates *m.*
phylarch ['failɑ:k], *s. Gr.Hist:* phylarque *m.*
phylarchy ['failɑ:ki], *s. Gr.Hist:* phylarchie *f.*
phyletic [fai'letik], *a.* phylétique.
Phyllis ['filis]. *Pr.n.f.* Philis, Phyllis.
phyllite ['filait], *s. Miner:* phyllite *f.*
phyllo- ['filou, fi'lɔ], *comb.fm. Bot:* phyllo-.
phyllocactus [filou'kæktəs], *s.* phyllocactus *m.*
phylloclade ['filoukleid], *s. Bot:* phylloclade *m.*
phyllode ['filoud], *s. Bot:* phyllode *f.*
phyllogenetic [filoudʒe'netik], **phyllogenous** [fi'lɔdʒənəs], *a. Bot:* phyllogène.
phylloid ['filɔid], *a. Nat.Hist:* phylloïde, foliacé.
phyllophagan [fi'lɔfəgən], *a. & s. Ent:* phyllophage (*m*).
phyllophagous [fi'lɔfəgəs], *a. Ent:* phyllophage.
phyllopod ['filəpɔd], *s. Crust:* phyllopode *m.*
phyllopodous [fi'lɔpədəs], *a. Crust:* phyllopode.
phyllopteryx [fi'lɔptəriks], *s. Ich:* phylloptéryx *m.*
phyllorhine ['filɔrain], *s. Z:* **p. (bat),** phyllorhine *m.*
phyllosoma [filou'soumə], *s. Crust:* phyllosome *m.*
phyllostachys [fi'lɔstəkis], *s. Bot:* phyllostachys *m.*
Phyllostom(at)idae [filoustou'mætidi:, -'stoumidi:], *s.pl. Z:* phyllostomidés *m.*
phyllotaxis [filou'tæksis], *s. Bot:* phyllotaxie *f.*
phylloxera [fi'lɔksərə], *s. Ent: Vit:* phylloxéra *m.*
phylloxeran [fi'lɔksərən], *a. Vit:* phylloxérien, phylloxérique.
phylloxerized [fi'lɔksəraizd], *a.* (*of vine*) phylloxéré.
phylo- ['failou, fai'lɔ], *comb.fm.* phylo-.
phylogenesis [failou'dʒenəsis], **phylogeny** [fai'lɔdʒəni], *s. Biol:* phylogénèse *f,* phylogénie *f.*
phylogenetic, phylogenic [failoudʒe'netik, -'dʒenik], *a. Biol:* phylogénétique, phylogénique; phylétique.
phylogenist [fai'lɔdʒənist], *s.* phylogéniste *mf.*
phylum ['failəm], *s. Nat.Hist:* phylum *m.*
Phymatidae [fai'mætidi:], *s.pl. Ent:* phymatidés *m.*
physa ['faisə], *s. Moll:* physe *f.*
physalia [fai'seiliə], *s. Cœl:* physalie *f.*

Physalis ['faisəlis], *s. Bot:* physalis *m.*
physalite ['faisəlait], *s. Miner:* physalite *f.*
Physalospora [faisəlou'spɔ:rə], *s. Fung:* physalospore *m.*
physic[1] ['fizik], *s. O:* médecine *f,* médicament *m,* remède *m.*
physic[2], *v.tr.* (**physicked**) *O:* (*a*) administrer un médicament à (qn); (*b*) purger (qn).
physical ['fizikl], *a.* physique. **1. p. body,** corps matériel; **p. impossibility,** impossibilité physique, matérielle; **p. geography,** géographie physique; **p. features,** topographie *f*; *Ph:* **p. point,** point matériel; *Tp:* **p. line,** ligne réelle; *U.S:* **p. inventory,** inventaire *m* (du matériel, des marchandises, etc.). **2. p. sciences,** sciences *f* physiques; **p. chemistry,** chimie *f* physique; **p. optics,** optique *f* physique; optique ondulatoire; **p. laws,** lois *f* de la physique; **p. analysis,** analyse physique; **p. atomic weight,** poids *m* atomique physique; **p. property, quantity,** propriété *f,* grandeur *f,* physique. **3.** (*a*) *Med:* (*of symptoms, etc.*) somatique; (*b*) **p. strength,** force *f* physique; **p. fitness,** aptitude *f* physique; **p. examination,** examen médical, d'aptitude physique (pour un emploi, etc.); **p. exercise,** exercice physique, corporel; **p. culture, p. education,** culture *f,* éducation *f,* physique; **p. culturist,** expert *m* en, amateur *m* de, culture physique; **p. exercises, p. training,** *F:* **p. jerks,** exercices physiques, d'assouplissement.
physicalism ['fizikəlizm], *s.* physicalisme *m.*
physically ['fizik(ə)li], *adv.* **1.** physiquement, matériellement; **p. impossible,** matériellement impossible. **2. p. fit,** en bonne santé; apte physiquement (à faire qch.).
physician [fi'ziʃ(ə)n], *s.* médecin *m*; **consulting p.,** médecin consultant.
physicism ['fizisizm], *s. Phil:* physicisme *m,* matérialisme *m.*
physicist ['fizisist], *s.* **1.** physicien, -ienne. **2.** *Phil:* adhérent, -ente, du physicisme.
physico- ['fizikou], *comb.fm.* physico-.
physicochemical [fizikou'kemikl], *a.* physico-chimique, *pl.* physico-chimiques.
physicochemist [fizikou'kemist], *s.* physico-chimiste *mf, pl.* physico-chimistes.
physicochemistry [fizikou'kemistri], *s.* chimie *f* physique.
physicomathematical [fizikoumæθi'mætikl], *a.* physico-mathématique, *pl.* physico-mathématiques.
physicomechanical [fizikoumi'kænikl], *a.* physico-mécanique, *pl.* physico-mécaniques.
physicotheological [fizikouθi:ə'lɔdʒikl], *a.* physico-théologique, *pl.* physico-théologiques.
physicotherapeutic [fizikouθerə'pju:tik], *a. Med:* physicothérapeutique.
physicotherapy [fizikou'θerəpi], *s. Med:* physicothérapie *f.*
physics ['fiziks], *s.pl.* (*usu. with sg. const.*) la physique; **applied p.,** physique appliquée; **atomic p.,** physique atomique; **electron p.,** physique électronique; **experimental p.,** physique expérimentale; **fundamental p., pure p.,** physique fondamentale, pure, générale; **molecular p.,** physique moléculaire; **neutron p.,** physique neutronique; **nuclear p.,** physique nucléaire; **p. of fission,** physique de fission.
physio- [fizi'ɔ, fiziə, 'fiziou], *comb.fm.* physio-.
physiocracy [fizi'ɔkrəsi], *s. Pol.Ec:* physiocratie *f.*
physiocrat ['fizioukræt], *s. Pol.Ec:* physiocrate *m.*
physiocratic [fiziou'krætik], *a.* physiocratique.
physiogenesis [fiziou'dʒenəsis], *s.* physiogénèse *f.*
physiogeny [fizi'ɔdʒəni], *s.* physiogénie *f.*
physiognomic(al) [fiziou'nɔmik(l)], *a.* **1.** physionomique. **2.** physiognomonique.
physiognomist [fizi'ɔnəmist], *s.* **1.** physionomiste *mf.* **2.** physiognomoniste *mf.*
physiognomy [fizi'ɔnəmi], *s.* **1.** physionomie *f.* **2.** physiognomonie *f.*
physiographer [fizi'ɔgrəfər], *s.* physiographe *mf.*
physiographical [fiziə'græfikl], *a.* physiographique.
physiography [fizi'ɔgrəfi], *s.* physiographie *f.*
physiological [fiziə'lɔdʒikl], *a.* physiologique; *Bio-Ch:* **p. salt solution,** solution *f,* sérum *m,* physiologique.
physiologically [fiziə'lɔdʒik(ə)li], *adv.* physiologiquement.
physiologist [fizi'ɔlədʒist], *s.* physiologiste *mf,* physiologue *mf.*
physiology [fizi'ɔlədʒi], *s.* physiologie *f*; **plant p.,** physiologie végétale.
physiopathology [fizioupə'θɔlədʒi], *s. Med:* physiopathologie *f.*
physiotherapeutic [fiziouθerə'pju:tik], *a. Med:* physiothérapeutique.
physiotherapeutist [fiziouθerə'pju:tist], *s. Med:* physiothérapeute *mf.*
physiotherapist [fiziou'θerəpist], *s.* physiothérapiste *mf,* physiotherapeute *mf.*
physiotherapy [fiziou'θerəpi], *s.* physiothérapie *f.*
physique [fi'zi:k], *s.* (*a*) physique *m* (de qn); structure *f* du corps; **fine p.,** beau physique; **to have a poor p.,** être d'apparence malingre; **he hasn't the p. for it,** il manque les aptitudes physiques à faire cela; (*b*) plastique *f* (d'une actrice, d'une danseuse).
physoclist ['faisouklist], *s. Ich:* physocliste *m.*
Physoclisti [faisou'klisti], *s.pl. Ich:* physoclistes *m.*
physoclistic [faisou'klistik], *a. Ich:* physocliste.
physogastry [faisou'gæstri], *s. Z:* physogastrie *f.*
physostegia [faisou'stedʒiə], *s. Bot:* physostegia *m,* dracocéphale *m* de Virginie.
physostigma [faisou'stigmə], *s. Bot:* physostigma *m,* fève *f* de Calabar.
physostigmine [faisou'stigmain], *s. Ch:* physostigmine *f.*
physostomatous [faisou'stoumətəs], *a. Ich:* physostome.
physostome ['faisoustoum], *s. Ich:* physostome *m.*
Physostomi [fai'sɔstəmai], *s.pl. Ich:* physostomes *m.*
phytelephas [fai'teləfæs], *s. Bot:* phytéléphas *m.*
phytic ['faitik], *a. Ch:* **p. acid,** acide *m* phytique.
phytin ['faitin], *s. Ch:* phytine *f.*
phytobezoar [faitou'bi:zouər], *s. Physiol:* phytobézoard *f.*
phytobiological [faitoubaiə'lɔdʒik(ə)l], *a.* phytobiologique.
phytobiology [faitoubai'ɔlədʒi], *s.* phytobiologie *f.*
phytochemistry [faitou'kemistri], *s.* phytochimie *f.*
phytocoenosis, *pl.* **-ses** [faitousi:'nousis, -si:z], *s. Bot:* phytocénose *f*; association végétale.
phytoecological [faitoui:kə'lɔdʒik(ə)l], *a.* phytoécologique.
phytoecology [faitoui'kɔlədʒi], *s.* phytoécologie *f.*
phytoflagellate [faitou'flædʒəleit], *s. Nat.Hist:* phytoflagellé *m.*
phytogenesis [faitə'dʒenəsis], *s. Biol:* phytogénésie *f,* phytogénèse *f.*
phytogenetic(al) [faitoudʒi'netik((ə)l)], *a.* phytogénétique.
phytogenic [faitou'dʒenik], *a. Geol: Miner:* phytogène.
phytogeographer [faitoudʒi:'ɔgrəfər], *s.* phytogéographe *mf.*
phytogeographic(al) [faitoudʒi:ə'græfik((ə)l)], *a.* phytogéographique.
phytogeography [faitoudʒi'ɔgrəfi], *s.* phytogéographie *f.*
phytography [fai'tɔgrəfi], *s.* phytographie *f.*
phytohormone [faitou'hɔ:moun], *s. Bot:* phytohormone *f.*
phytoid ['faitɔid], *a.* phytoïde.
phytol ['faitɔl], *s. Bio-Ch:* phytol *m.*
phytolacca [faitə'lækə], *s. Bot:* phytolacca *m.*
Phytolaccaceae [faitoulæ'keisii:], *s.pl. Bot:* phytolaccacées *f.*
phytology [fai'tɔlədʒi], *s.* phytologie *f*; botanique *f.*
Phytomonadina [faitoumonə'dainə], *s.pl. Prot:* phytomonadines *f.*
phytoparasite [faitou'pærəsait], *s.* phytoparasite *m.*
phytopathological [faitoupæθə'lɔdʒik(ə)l], *a.* phytopathologique.
phytopathologist [faitoupə'θɔlədʒist], *s.* phytopathologiste *mf.*
phytopathology [faitoupə'θɔlədʒi], *s.* phytopathologie *f.*
Phytophaga [fai'tɔfəgə], *s.pl. Ent:* phytophages *m.*
phytophagous [fai'tɔfəgəs], *a. Nat.Hist:* phytophage.
phytopharmacological [faitoufɑ:məkə'lɔdʒik(ə)l], *a.* phytopharmaceutique.
phytopharmacology [faitoufɑ:mə'kɔlədʒi], *s.* phytopharmacie *f.*
phytophthora [fai'tɔfθərə], *s. Fung:* phytophthora *m.*
phytoplankter [faitou'plæŋktər], *s.* plante *f* planctonique.
phytoplankton [faitou'plæŋktɔn], *s.* phytoplancton *m*; **natural p. community,** essaim *m* de plancton.
phytoptid [fai'tɔptid], **phytoptus** [fai'tɔptəs], *s. Arach:* phytopte *m.*
Phytosauria [faitou'sɔ:riə], *s.pl. Paleont:* phytosauriens *m.*
phytosociology [faitousousi'ɔlədʒi], *s. Bot:* phytosociologie *f.*
phytosterol [fai'tɔstərɔl], *s. Ch:* phytostérol *m.*
phytotechny [faitou'tekni], *s.* phytotechnie *f.*
phytotherapy [faitou'θerəpi], *s.* phytothérapie *f.*
phytotoma [faitə'toumə], *s. Orn:* phytotome *m,* rara *m.*
Phytotomidae [faitə'tɔmidi:], *s.pl. Orn:* phytotomidés *m.*
phytotomy [fai'tɔtəmi], *s.* phytotomie *f*; anatomie *f* des plantes.
phytozoon, *pl.* **-zoa** [faitou'zouən, -'zouə], *s.* phytozoaire *m,* zoophyte *m.*
pi[1] [pai], *s. Gr.Alph:* pi *m.*
pi[2], *a. F: O:* pieux, bondieusard.
pia ['paiə], *s. Bot:* pia *m.*
Piacenza [piə'tʃentsə], *Pr.n. Geog:* Plaisance *f.*
piacular [pai'ækjulər], *a. Lit:* (*a*) piaculaire, expiatoire; (*b*) qui demande une expiation.
piaffe[1] [pi'æf], *s. Equit:* piaffé *m.*
piaffe[2], *v.i. Equit:* piaffer.
pia mater [paiə'meitər], *s. Anat:* pie-mère *f, pl.* pies-mères.
pian ['paiən], *s. Med:* pian *m.*
pianette, pianino [piæ'net, -'ninou], *s. Mus:* pianino *m.*
pianissimo [piə'nisimou], *adv. & s. Mus:* pianissimo (*m*).
pianist ['piənist], *s.* pianiste *mf.*
pianistic [piə'nistik], *a. Mus:* pianistique.
piano[1] [pi'ɑ:nou], *adv. & s. Mus:* piano *m*; doucement.
piano[2] [pi'ænou], **pianoforte** [piænou'fɔ:rti], *s.* (*instrument*) (*a*) piano *m*; **grand p.,** piano à queue; **upright p.,** piano droit; **to play the p.,** jouer du piano; **to strum on the p.,** pianoter; **sonata for p. and violin,** sonate *f* pour piano et violon; **p. key,** touche *f* de piano; *El: Elcs:* **p.-key control, switch,** commande *f,* commutateur *m,* à touches; **p. wire,** corde *f* à piano; **p. stool,** tabouret *m* de piano; **p. tuner,** accordeur *m* de pianos; (*b*) **p. player,** pianola *m*; **p. organ,** piano mécanique des rues (à cylindre).
Piarist ['paiərist], *s. Ecc:* piariste *m.*
piassaba, piassava [piə'sɑ:bə, -'sɑ:və], *s. Bot:* piassava *m,* piassave *f*; attalea *f*; *Com:* **p. brush, broom,** balai *m* en piassava.
piastre [pi'æstər], *s. Num:* piastre *f.*
piazza [pi'ætsɑ:], *s.* (*a*) (*esp. in Italy*) place (publique); (*b*) *N Am:* véranda *f*; terrasse *f.*
pibroch ['pi:brɔχ], *s. Scot:* pibroch *m,* pibrock *m* (air de cornemuse).
pica[1] ['paikə], *s. Typ:* pica *m,* cicéro *m,* corps *m* 12; **small p.,** cicéro approché, corps 11; **double p.,** gros parangon, corps 22; **three-line p.,** trismégiste *m,* corps 36; **two-line double p.,** gros canon, corps 42.
pica[2], *s. Med: Vet:* pica *m.*
picador ['pikədɔər], *s.* picador *m.*
Picardy ['pikədi], *Pr.n. Geog:* Picardie *f.*
picarel ['pikərəl], *s. Ich:* picarel *m*; mendole *f.*
picaresque [pikə'resk], *a.* (roman) picaresque.
picaroon [pikə'ru:n], *s. A:* **1.** brigand *m.* **2.** pirate *m,* corsaire *m.*
picayune [pikə'ju:n]. *N.Am:* **1.** *s.* (*a*) *Num:* pièce *f* de cinq cents; (*b*) bagatelle *f,* rien *m.* **2.** *a.* pauvre, mesquin.
piccalilli [pikə'lili], *s. Comest:* pickles *mpl* à la moutarde.
pic(c)aninny [pikə'nini], *s. F:* (*a*) négrillon, -onne; *Austr:* petit(e) aborigène; (*b*) *U.S: O:* mioche *mf.*
piccolo ['pikəlou], *s. Mus:* (*a*) piccolo *m*; petite flûte; (*b*) **p. (player),** joueur, -euse, de piccolo.
piccoloist ['pikəlouist], *s.* joueur, -euse, de piccolo.
pice [pais], *s. Num: A:* pice *f.*
pichiciago [piʃisi'ɑ:gou], *s. Z:* chlamydophore *m.*
Picidae ['pisidi:], *s.pl. Orn:* picidés *m,* les pics *m.*
Piciformes [pisi'fɔ:mi:z], *s.pl. Orn:* piciformes *m.*
pick[1] [pik], *s.* (*a*) pic *m,* pioche *f*; *Min:* rivelaine *f*; *Stonew:* picot *m*; **double p.,** pic à deux pointes; **stonedressing p.,** pic de tailleur de pierre; **miner's p.,** pic à main; **tamping p.,** pioche à bourrer; **p. hammer,** picot; **p. and shovel man,** terrassier *m*; **p. and shovel work,** (i) terrassement *m*; (ii) travail *m* pénible; recherche patiente et laborieuse; (*b*) **lobster p.,** fourchette *f* à homard.
pick[2], *s.* **1.** coup *m* de pioche, de pic. **2.** cueillage *m,* cueillaison *f* (des fruits, etc.). **3.** choix *m,* élite *f*; **the p. of the basket, of the bunch,** le dessus du panier; la fleur des pois; le meilleur de tous; *F:* le gratin (du gratin); **that's the p. of the bunch,** c'est celui-là le meilleur; **the p. of the army,** la (fine) fleur de l'armée.
pick[3], *v.*
I. *v.tr.* **1.** (*a*) piocher (la terre, etc.); (*b*) **to p. a hole in sth.,** faire un trou dans qch., à qch. (avec une pioche, ses ongles, etc.); *F:* **to p. holes in sth.,** critiquer, trouver à redire à, qch.; chercher la petite bête; (*c*) *F:* **to p. on, at, s.o.,** chercher querelle, noise, à qn; **why p. on me?** pourquoi m'accuser, moi? **2.** (*a*) **to p. one's nose, one's teeth, etc.,** se curer le nez, les dents, etc.; **to p. a pimple, a scab,** gratter un bouton, une croûte (du bout de l'ongle); (*b*) *N Am:* **to p. a guitar,** pincer de la guitare. **3.** épailler, échardonner (de la laine); époutier (un tissu); plumer (une volaille); **to p. a bone,** (i) ôter, enlever, la chair d'un os; (ii) ronger un os; *F:* **to have a bone,** *A:* **a crow, to p. with s.o.,** avoir maille à partir avec qn, un

compte à régler avec qn; en devoir à qn. **4.** (*of birds*) picoter, becqueter (le blé, etc.); *F:* (*of pers.*) **to p. at one's food,** manger du bout des dents; faire la petite bouche; pignocher; **to p. at sth.,** grignoter qch. **5.** (*a*) choisir; sélectionner; **to p. a book from the shelves,** choisir un livre dans la bibliothèque; **to p. one's words,** choisir ses mots; **to p. the least deserving candidate,** choisir le candidat le moins méritant; **to p. the winners,** repérer les gagnants; *F:* **you've really picked a winner!** tu as vraiment bien choisi! **to p. and choose,** se montrer difficile; faire le, la, difficile; **stop picking and choosing!** ne fais pas le difficile! *Games:* **to p. sides,** tirer les camps; (*b*) trier (du minerai, etc.). **6.** (*a*) cueillir (des fleurs, des fruits, etc.); **to p. the strawberries,** faire la cueillette des fraises; (*b*) **to p. rags,** chiffonner. **7.** (*a*) **to p. s.o.'s pocket,** prendre, voler, qch. dans la poche de qn; **to p. and steal,** commettre le vol et le larcin; voler de droite et de gauche; (*b*) crocheter (une serrure); **to p. s.o.'s brains,** exploiter l'intelligence, les connaissances, de qn; **may I p. your brains?** pouvez-vous m'aider (à résoudre ce problème, etc.)? **8.** mettre (qch.) en pièces; défaire, détisser, effilocher (des chiffons, etc.)

II. (*compound verbs*) **1. pick off,** *v.tr.* (*a*) enlever, ôter (les fleurs mortes d'une plante, etc.); (*b*) descendre, abattre un à un (des soldats ennemis, etc.).

2. pick out, *v.tr.* (*a*) extirper, enlever (qch.); ôter (qch.) (avec les doigts, etc.); (*b*) faire le tri de (qch.); **he picked out the best peaches,** il a choisi les meilleures pêches; **to p. s.o. out in a crowd,** repérer qn parmi la foule; (*in identification parade*) **to p. out a criminal,** identifier un criminel; **the searchlight picked out the aircraft,** le projecteur a repéré l'avion; **to p. out a tune on the piano,** (i) tapoter un air au piano; (ii) déchiffrer lentement un air au piano; (*c*) *Paint:* réchampir; **blue panels picked out with black,** panneaux bleus réchampis en noir; **picked out in gold,** à filets d'or.

3. pick over, *v.tr.* trier (des fruits, etc.).

4. pick up, (*a*) *v.tr.* (i) prendre; ramasser, relever (qch. par terre); **to p. sth. up again,** reprendre qch.; **to p. up a penny,** ramasser un penny (par terre); **to p. up the odd penny or two, the odd pound or two,** gagner un peu d'argent; **to p. up a child,** (*α*) prendre un enfant dans les bras; (*β*) relever en enfant (qui est tombé); **I'll call and p. up the letters,** je passerai prendre les lettres; **to p. up the receiver,** décrocher le récepteur, le téléphone; **to p. s.o. up on the way,** prendre qn en passant; **I'll p. you up at the station,** je viendrai vous chercher à la gare; **the train stops to p. up passengers,** le train s'arrête pour prendre des voyageurs; *Navy:* **to p. up a torpedo,** repêcher une torpille; **to p. up a telegraph cable,** relever un câble; **to p. up a buoy,** prendre un coffre d'amarrage; *Knit:* **to p. up a stitch,** relever une maille; *Cards:* **to p. up a trick,** (*α*) ramasser les cartes; (*β*) faire une levée inattendue; *Golf:* **to p. up (one's ball),** ramasser sa balle; renoncer au trou; (ii) apprendre (un tour, etc.); **to p. up a language,** s'initier rapidement à une langue; **where did you p. up that news?** où avez-vous recueilli ces nouvelles? **to p. up information about s.o., sth.,** glaner des renseignements sur qn, qch.; **to p. up scraps of knowledge,** ramasser des bribes de connaissances; (iii) trouver, retrouver; **the narrative switches back to p. up the major characters,** le récit fait un retour en arrière pour retrouver les personnages principaux; **in this chapter the author picks up the story of his hero again,** dans ce chapitre l'auteur reprend l'histoire de son héros; **we soon picked up the road again,** nous avons vite retrouvé notre chemin; **to p. sth. up cheap,** trouver, acheter, qch. bon marché; **she's good at picking up bargains,** elle a du flair pour les bonnes affaires; **where did you p. that up?** où avez-vous pêché ça? **you can't p. them up easily,** il ne s'en trouve pas à la douzaine; **it's difficult to p. up all the misprints,** il est difficile de relever toutes les fautes d'impression; (iv) *F:* faire la connaissance de (qn); ramasser (qn); (*of prostitute*) **to p. up a client,** raccrocher un client; **to p. up the pieces,** repartir à zéro; recoller les restes; (v) *El:* prendre, capter (le courant); *W.Tel:* capter (des ondes); accrocher (un poste); capter, recevoir (un message); recueillir (des sons); **we picked up Moscow,** nous avons eu Moscou; (*of searchlight*) **to p. up an aircraft,** repérer un avion; (vi) **to p. s.o. up sharply,** reprendre qn vertement; (vii) *Aut: etc:* **to p. up speed,** reprendre de la vitesse; **this engine picks up well,** ce moteur a de bonnes reprises, reprend bien; **to p. up speed downhill,** gagner de vitesse dans une descente; (viii) (*of pers.*) **to p. up strength,** reprendre des forces; **that will p. you up,** voilà qui vous remettra; (*b*) *v.i.* (i) (*of pers.*) retrouver la santé, ses forces; se rétablir; **business is picking up,** les affaires reprennent; **the weather looks like picking up,** le temps a l'air de s'arranger; (ii) *Sp: etc:* **to p. up on s.o.,** gagner de l'avance sur qn; rattraper qn.

pick[4], *s. Tex:* **1.** chasse *f* (de la navette). **2.** duite *f.*

pick[5]. **1.** *v.tr. Dial: A:* jeter, lancer. **2.** *v.i. Tex:* chasser, lancer, la navette.

pick-a-back ['pikəbæk]. **1.** *adv.* sur le dos; sur les épaules; **I carried her across the river p.-a-b.,** je lui ai fait traverser la rivière sur mon dos; **to ride p.-a-b. on s.o.,** monter à dos sur qn. **2.** *s.* **to give s.o. a p.-a-b.,** porter qn sur le dos.

pickable ['pikəbl], *a.* **1.** (*of fruit, etc.*) récoltable; prêt à être cueilli; **our strawberries will be p. tomorrow,** on pourra faire la cueillette des fraises demain. **2.** (serrure) crochetable.

pickaninny [pikə'nini], *s.* = PIC(C)ANINNY.

pickaxe[1] ['pikæks], *s.* (*NAm: also* **pickaxe**) *Tls:* pioche *f,* pic *m; Min:* hoyau *m.*

pickaxe[2], *v.tr. & i.* piocher.

picked [pikt], *a.* **1.** (*of fruit, etc.*) cueilli. **2.** choisi; trié; **p. men,** hommes de choix, d'élite; **p. ore,** minerai trié. **3. p. oakum,** étoupe démêlée.

picker[1] ['pikər], *s.* **1.** (*pers.*) (*a*) éplucheur, -euse (de laine, etc.); démêleur, -euse (de coton, etc.); (*b*) cueilleur, -euse (de fleurs, de fruits, etc.); récolteur, -euse (de fruits, etc.); **grape p.,** vendangeur, -euse; **hop p.,** cueilleur, -euse, de houblon; (*c*) trieur, -euse (de minerai); (*d*) **pickers and stealers,** voleurs *m* et filous *m;* (*e*) **p. up (of unconsidered trifles),** ramasseur, -euse, collectionneur, -euse (de bibelots, etc.). **2.** (*device*) (*a*) machine *f* à éplucher; (*b*) *Farr:* cure-pied *m, pl.* cure-pieds; (*c*) *Cmptr:* **p. belt,** courroie *f* d'alimentation; **p. knife,** couteau *m* d'alimentation, d'entraînement.

picker[2], *s. Tex:* **1.** tacot *m,* taquet *m,* chasse-navettes *m inv* (de métier à tisser). **2.** batteur *m* (de coton, etc.) (dans un métier à tisser).

pickerel ['pik(ə)rəl], *s. Ich:* brocheton *m.*

picket[1] ['pikit], *s.* **1.** (*a*) piquet *m; Surv: etc:* jalon *m;* **p. man,** jalonneur *m;* (*b*) *Surv: Const:* repère *m;* (*c*) pieu *m* (d'une clôture, etc.); **p. fence,** palis *m,* palissade *f;* (*d*) piquet d'attache (pour chevaux, chèvres, etc.); **p. rope,** attache *f,* longe *f* (de cheval, etc.). **2.** (*a*) *Mil: etc:* (i) piquet (d'hommes); (ii) poste *m* de surveillance; **fire p.,** piquet d'incendie; **police p.,** garde *f* de police, piquet en armes; **inlying p.,** piquet de sécurité; **outlying p.,** poste de surveillance (avancé); **p. line,** éléments *mpl* de sûreté rapprochée; **p. commander,** (i) chef *m,* commandant *m,* du piquet (d'incendie, etc.); (ii) chef de poste de surveillance; **p. guard,** piquet en armes, piquet de sécurité; **to be on p.,** être de piquet; (*b*) *Ind: etc:* (i) piquet (de grévistes); **strike pickets,** piquets de grève; **to put strikers on p. duty,** mettre des grévistes en faction; (ii) gréviste *mf* en faction; factionnaire *m;* (*c*) **p. boat,** vedette *f;* (*d*) **(radar) p.,** piquet radar.

picket[2], *v.tr.* (**picketed**) **1.** mettre (des chevaux) au(x) piquet(s), à la corde; attacher (une chèvre). **2.** entourer (un terrain) de piquets, de pieux; palissader (un terrain). **3.** *Mil:* détacher (des soldats) en grand-garde. **4. to p. a factory,** (i) installer des piquets de grève; (ii) se tenir en faction, aux abords d'une usine (pour en interdire l'accès).

picketing ['pikitiŋ], *s.* **1.** mise *f* (des chevaux) au piquet; **p. rope,** longe *f.* **2.** *Ind: etc:* constitution *f* de piquets de grève; entrave *f* à la liberté du travail. **3.** *NAm:* (*a*) palissadement *m;* (*b*) palissade *f,* palis *m.*

picking[1] ['pikiŋ], *s.* **1.** (*a*) épluchage *m,* épluchement *m,* échardonnage *m,* épaillage *m* (de la laine, etc.); époutiage *m* (des étoffes); (*b*) triage *m* (du minerai, etc.); **hand p.,** triage à la main; **p. belt,** toile *f* de triage, de transport (du charbon); (*c*) cueillette *f,* cueillage *m* (de fruits, de fleurs, etc.); **p. season,** cueillette; (*d*) **p. and stealing,** grappillage *m;* (*e*) crochetage *m* (d'une serrure); (*f*) démêlage *m,* démêlement *m* (de l'étoupe). **2. pickings,** (i) épluchures *f,* restes *m,* rognures *f;* (ii) bénéfices *m,* gratte *f,* glanes *f.*

picking[2], *s. Tex:* (*a*) lancement *m,* chasse *f* (de la navette); **p. stick,** fouet *m,* épée *f,* de chasse; (*b*) battage *m* (du coton, etc.).

pickle[1] ['pikl], *s.* **1.** marinade *f,* saumure *f,* vinaigre *m;* **in p.,** en conserve; en train de mariner. **2. pickles,** pickles *m;* conserves *f* au vinaigre; **mixed pickles,** variantes *f.* **3.** *F:* (*a*) **to be in a (nice, fine, sad, sorry) p.,** être dans de beaux draps, dans le pétrin, dans les choux; **what a p. you're in!** comme vous voilà fait! (*b*) enfant *mf* terrible; petit diable. **4.** (*a*) *Metalw:* solution *f* de décapage, de dérochage; (*b*) *Leath:* jusée *f.*

pickle[2], *v.tr.* **1.** mariner, saumurer; conserver (au vinaigre, à la saumure). **2.** *Metalw:* décaper, dérocher, nettoyer.

pickle[3], *s. Dial:* grain *m* (de blé, de poussière, etc.).

pickled ['pik(ə)ld], *a.* (*a*) mariné, saumuré; confit (au vinaigre); **p. cabbage,** chou *m* rouge au vinaigre; **p. pork,** porc *m* en saumure; **p. herrings,** harengs marinés; (*b*) *F:* (*of pers.*) ivre, gris, émêché.

pickling ['pikliŋ], *s.* **1.** marinage *m,* saumurage *m;* conservation *f* au vinaigre; **p. onions,** petits oignons. **2.** (*a*) *Metalw:* décapage *m,* dérochage *m;* **gas, jet, p.,** décapage au gaz, au jet; **p. tank,** bac *m* de décapage; **p. acid,** décapant *m;* (*b*) *Leath:* mise *f* en jusée, piklage *m.*

picklock[1] ['piklɔk], *s.* **1.** (*pers.*) crocheteur *m* de serrures. **2.** crochet *m* (de serrurier); rossignol *m* (de cambrioleur).

picklock[2], *a. & s.* **p. (wool),** laine *f* mère, laine prime.

pickman, *pl.* **-men** ['pikmən], *s.m. Civ.E: etc:* piocheur; terrassier.

pick-me-up ['pikmiʌp], *s. F:* remontant *m,* stimulant *m;* **that's a good p.-me-up!** voilà qui vous remonte!

pick-off ['pikɔf], *attrib. Mec.E:* **p.-o. gear,** engrenage sélectif; *Mch.Tls:* **p.-o. gear system,** tête *f* de cheval.

pickpocket ['pikpɔkit], *s.* voleur, -euse, à la tire; pickpocket *m;* fouilleur, -euse, de poches.

pickpocketing ['pikpɔkitiŋ], *s. F:* vol *m* à la tire.

pick-up ['pikʌp], *s.* **1.** ramassage *m,* ramassement *m* (de qch.); *Elcs: W.Tel:* captage *m* (des ondes, d'un signal); *T.V:* prise *f* (de son); *Cmptr:* prise (de carte); *Atom.Ph:* rapt *m* (de particules); *Mec.E:* **p.-up points,** points *m* de fixation. **2.** (*thing picked up*) (*a*) *Min:* pépite *f* (d'or); (*b*) (*bargain*) occasion *f;* (*c*) client, -ente (d'un chauffeur de taxi en maraude); (*d*) connaissance *f* de rencontre, de raccroc. **3.** (*a*) reprise *f* (des affaires, etc.); (*b*) *I.C.E:* reprise (du moteur). **4.** (*a*) *Rec:* lecteur *m* (phonographique); pick-up *m inv;* **crystal p.-up,** pick-up piézoélectrique, à cristal; **electromagnetic p.-up,** pick-up électromagnétique; **p.-up adapter, attachment,** prise pour pick-up; **p.-up arm,** bras *m* de pick-up; (*b*) *Elcs: etc:* capteur *m,* détecteur *m* (d'ondes, de vibrations); **p.-up coil,** bobine exploratrice; **p.-up voltage,** tension *f* de capteur; **p.-up factor,** sensibilité effective (d'un récepteur); (*c*) *Cin:* **sound p.-up,** (i) lecteur de son, lecteur phonique; (ii) lecture *f* sonore (d'un film). **5.** *Veh:* pick-up; camionnette *f* à ridelles basses, à plateau. **6.** *F:* rencontre *f* de fortune; femme dont on fait connaissance dans la rue.

picky ['piki], *a. F:* difficile, délicat.

picnic[1] ['piknik], *s.* (*a*) pique-nique *m, pl.* pique-niques; **p. basket,** panier garni (pour pique-niques); mallette *f* de camping; (*b*) **we'll take a p. (lunch) with us,** nous emporterons un pique-nique; (*c*) **the Korean campaign was no p.,** la campagne de Corée n'a guère été une partie de plaisir.

picnic[2], *v.i.* (**picnicked**) pique-niquer; faire un pique-nique; *F:* saucissonner.

picnicker ['piknikər], *s.* pique-niqueur, -euse; *F:* saucissonneur, -euse.

picnometer [pik'nɔmitər], *s. Ph:* pycnomètre *m.*

pico- ['paikou], *comb.fm. Meas:* pico-.

picofarad [paikou'færæd], *s. El.Meas:* picofarad *m.*

picoline ['pikəli:n], *s. Ch:* picoline *f.*

picosecond [paikou'sekənd], *s.* picoseconde *f.*

picot[1] ['pi:kou], *s. Needlew: Lacem:* **p. (stitch),** picot *m;* **p. edge,** engrêlure *f;* **p.-stitch hand,** picoteuse *f.*

picot[2], *v.tr.* (**picoted** ['pi:koud]) *Needlew: Lacem:* picoter; engrêler (une dentelle).

picotee [pikə'ti:], *s. Hort:* œillet tiqueté; œillet jaspé.

picotite ['pikətait], *s. Miner:* picotite *f.*

picramic [pi'kræmik], *a. Ch:* (acide *m*) picramique.

picrate ['pikreit], *s. Ch:* picrate *m; Exp:* **ammonium p.,** picrate d'ammonium.

picrated ['pikreitid], *a. Ch:* picraté.

picric ['pikrik], *a. Ch:* (acide *m*) picrique.

picris ['pikris], *s. Bot:* picris *m,* picride *f.*

picrite ['pikrait], *s. Miner:* picrite *f.*

picrol ['pikrɔl], *s. Ch:* picrol *m.*

picrolite ['pikrəlait], *s. Miner:* picrolite *f.*

picromerite [pi'krɔmərait], *s. Miner:* picroméride *f,* picromérite *f.*

picrotoxin [pikrou'tɔksin], *s. Pharm:* picrotoxine *f.*

picry ['pikri:], *s. Bot:* arbre *m* à la gale, à la puce, à poison; sumac vénéneux.

picryl ['pikril], *s. Ch:* picryle *m.*

Pict [pikt], *s. Ethn: Hist:* Picte *mf.*

Pictish ['piktiʃ], *a. Ethn:* pictique, picte.

pictogram, pictograph ['piktəgræm, -græf], *s.* pictogramme *m;* pictographe *m;* diagramme *m* à images.

pictographic [piktə'græfik], *a.* pictographique.

pictography [pik'tɔgrəfi], *s.* pictographie *f.*

pictorial [pik'tɔ:riəl]. **1.** *a.* (*a*) (talent, etc.) pictural, -aux; (*b*) (écriture) en images; (*c*) (périodique, etc.) illustré; (*d*) graphique; *Av:* **p. computer,** traceur *m* de route; **p. deviation indicator,** indicateur *m* graphique de déviation, d'écart. **2.** *s.* périodique illustré; journal illustré.

pictorially [pik'tɔ:riəli], *adv.* par images, au moyen d'illustrations.

picture[1] ['piktʃər], *s.* (*a*) tableau *m*, peinture *f*; **to paint a p.,** faire, peindre, un tableau; **wall hung with pictures,** mur orné de tableaux; **p. cord,** cordon *m* pour suspendre les tableaux; **p. rail,** rail *m*, moulure *f*, pour accrocher les tableaux; **p. wire,** fil *m* pour suspendre les tableaux; fil à suspendre; **p. dealer,** marchand *m* de tableaux; **p. gallery,** musée *m* de peinture; **p. restorer,** restaurateur *m* de tableaux; **p. hat,** chapeau *m* gainsborough; **my garden is a p.,** mon jardin est à mettre en peinture; **she's a perfect p.,** elle est à peindre; *F:* **to be in the p.,** être au courant, au fait, à la page, dans la course; **put me in the p.,** mets-moi au courant; **it doesn't come into the p.,** cela n'entre pas en ligne de compte, en considération; *Turf:* **his horse wasn't in the p.,** son cheval ne s'est pas classé, est resté dans les choux; (*b*) (*in book, etc.*) image *f*, gravure *f*, illustration *f*, photographie *f*; **p. book,** livre *m* d'images, album *m*; **p. postcard,** carte postale illustrée; **p. puzzle,** rébus *m*; **p. writing,** pictographie *f*; *Cards:* **p. card,** figure *f*; *Jur:* **composite p.,** portrait *m* robot; (*c*) (i) image, portrait; **he's the p. of his father,** c'est (tout) le portrait de son père; *F:* c'est son père décalqué, tout craché; **he's the p. of health,** il respire la santé; **a perfect p. of misery,** le malheur personnifié; (ii) **p. of the morals of the period,** peinture des mœurs de l'époque; **this book gives a more accurate p. of the general,** ce livre offre un portrait plus fidèle du général; **to get a mental p. of sth.,** se représenter qch.; (*d*) *Med:* **clinical p.,** facies *m*, tableau, clinique; (*e*) *T.V:* image; **p. element,** élément *m* d'image; **p. frequency,** fréquence *f* d'image; **p. receiver,** récepteur *m* d'images; **p. signal,** signal *m* vidéo; **p. tube,** tube *m* à rayons cathodiques; (*f*) *Cin: O:* film *m*; **to go to the pictures,** aller au cinéma.

picture[2], *v.tr.* peindre, dépeindre, représenter (qn, qch.); (*b*) **to p. (to oneself),** s'imaginer, se figurer, se représenter (qch.); **p. my surprise,** figurez-vous, représentez-vous, mon étonnement.

picturesque [piktjə'resk], *a.* pittoresque; **p. style,** style pittoresque, imagé; **p. phrases,** expressions *f* qui font image; **in a p. style,** pittoresquement.

picturesquely [piktjə'reskli], *adv.* pittoresquement.

picturesqueness [piktjə'resknis], *s.* pittoresque *m*.

piculet ['pikjulet], *s. Orn:* picumne *m*, picule *m*.

piddle[1] ['pidl], *v.i.* **1.** *O:* **to p. about, around,** baguenauder, musarder; s'occuper de futilités. **2.** *F:* faire pipi.

piddle[2], *s. F:* pipi *m*; **to have a p.,** aller faire pipi.

piddling ['pidliŋ], *a. F:* mesquin, insignifiant; futile; **if you think one can live on such a p. salary,** si vous pensez qu'on peut vivre avec une pitance comme ça.

piddock ['pidək], *s. Moll: F:* pholade *f*.

pidgin ['pidʒin], *s.* **1.** pidgin *m*; **p. (English, French, etc.)** = petit nègre; (*in S. Pacific*) bichlamar *m*, bêche-de-mer *m*. **2. that's my p.,** ça c'est mon affaire.

pi-dog ['paidɔg], *s.* chien errant (de l'Orient).

pie[1] [pai], *s. Orn:* **1.** pie *f*. **2. French p.,** pic-vert *m*, *pl.* pics-verts; pivert *m*. **3.** pigeon *m* pie.

pie[2], *s.* (*a*) **(veal and ham, etc.) p.** = pâté *m* en croûte; **chicken p.** = croustade *f* de volaille; **cottage p., shepherd's p.,** *F:* **resurrection p.** = hachis parmentier; **fish p.** = timbale *f* de poissons; **(apple, etc.) p.** = (i) tourte *f*, (ii) *esp. NAm:* tarte *f* (aux pommes); **custard p.** = tarte à la crème; *F:* **p. in the sky,** le miel de l'autre monde; (*b*) *F:* **as easy as p.,** simple comme bonjour; (*c*) **p. chart,** diagramme *m* en secteurs.

pie[3], *s. Typ:* (composition tombée en) pâte *f*; pâté *m*; **to make p.,** laisser tomber en pâte un paquet de composition; faire un mastic.

pie[4], *v.tr.* **(pied; pieing)** *Typ:* mettre (la composition) en pâte; **to p. a take,** laisser tomber en pâte un paquet de composition.

pie[5], *s. Num:* pie *f*; douzième *m* d'anna.

piebald ['paibɔ:ld]. **1.** *a.* (*a*) (cheval *m*, etc.) pie; **p. horses,** des chevaux pie(s), des pies *mf*; (*b*) **p. skin,** vitiligo *m* (des noirs); (*c*) bigarré, disparate. **2.** *s.* (cheval) pie *m*.

piece[1] [pi:s], *s.* pièce *f*. **1.** (*a*) morceau *m* (de papier, de pain, etc.); bout *m* (de ruban, de ficelle, de route, etc.); parcelle *f* (de terrain); tranche *f* (de gâteau); tronçon *m* (de serpent, d'anguille); **pieces of cloth, of meat,** coupons *m* de drap; débris *m* de viande; **p. by p.,** pièce à pièce; (*b*) fragment *m*, éclat *m* (de verre, etc.); **to break sth. in pieces,** briser qch.; mettre qch. en morceaux; **to fall, go, to pieces,** s'en aller en morceaux; se désagréger; (*of machinery, etc.*) se détraquer, se démantibuler; (*of house, etc.*) se délabrer; crouler; (*of business, engine, etc.*) claquer; **my clothes are falling, coming, to pieces,** mes habits s'en vont, tombent, en lambeaux; **garment falling to pieces,** vêtement *m* qui ne tient plus (ensemble); **things are going to pieces,** tout se disloque; tout se désorganise; *F:* (*of pers.*) **to go (all) to pieces,** (i) perdre tout empire sur soi-même; (ii) perdre son sang-froid; (iii) perdre tous ses moyens; **in the second half our team went all to pieces,** dans la seconde mi-temps notre équipe s'est effondrée, a perdu toute cohésion, était entièrement à bout de souffle; **under cross examination he went to pieces,** le contre-interrogatoire a démoli son histoire; (*of barrel*) **to drop to pieces,** tomber en javelle; **to burst, fly, to pieces,** voler en éclats; **to pick sth. to pieces,** mettre qch. en pièces, en miettes *f*; *F:* **to pick s.o. to pieces,** déchirer qn à belles dents; bêcher qn; éreinter qn; **to pull, tear, to pieces,** déchirer, lacérer, défaire (qch.); mettre, réduire, (qch.) en pièces; mettre (qch.) en quartiers; déchirer (du papier) en menus morceaux; dépecer (un poulet, etc.); mettre (de l'étoffe) en lambeaux; déchirer (une proie) à belles dents; *F:* **they'll tear you to pieces,** vous allez vous faire écharper; **to tear an argument to pieces,** démolir un argument; *F:* **to pull s.o. to pieces,** critiquer qn sévèrement; éreinter qn; **to pull an author, a play, to pieces,** éreinter, bêcher, critiquer sévèrement, dépiauter, un auteur, une pièce. **2.** partie *f*, pièce (d'une machine, etc.); **to take a machine to pieces,** démonter une machine; **machine that takes to pieces,** machine démontable, qui se démonte; **to take a dress to pieces,** défaire une robe. **3.** *Com:* pièce (de drap, de vin, etc.); rouleau *m* (de papier peint); **to sell sth. by the p.,** vendre qch. à la pièce; *Tex:* **p. goods,** marchandises *f*, tissus *m*, à la pièce; **p. dyeing,** teinture *f* en pièces; *Ind:* **p. work,** travail *m* à la tâche, à la pièce, aux pièces; **p. rate,** salaire *m* à la tâche, à la pièce, aux pièces; **to be paid p. rates,** *esp. NAm:* **by the p.,** être payé à la tâche, à la pièce, aux pièces; *Typ:* **p. hand,** paquetier *m*. **4. wheel forming one p. with another,** roue solidaire d'une autre; **all in one p.,** tout d'une pièce; d'une seule pièce; **lands all of a p.,** terres toutes d'une tenue; terres d'une seule tenue; **the hangings are of a p. with the furniture,** les tentures *f* sont à l'avenant du mobilier; *F:* (*of pers.*) **they are all of a p.,** ils sont tous du même acabit; *Metall:* **to cast cylinders in one p.,** couler des cylindres d'un seul jet, en bloc; **cast, pressed, made, in one p.,** monobloc *inv*; **forged, cast, in one p. with . . .,** venu de forge, de fonte, de coulée, avec . . .; **mast in one p.,** mât *m* d'un seul brin. **5.** (*a*) **a p. of work,** un travail; un ouvrage; **a p. of my work,** un spécimen, un échantillon, de mon travail; **p. of water,** pièce d'eau; lac *m*, étang *m*; **p. out of a book,** passage *m* d'un livre; (*b*) **p. of bravery, of folly,** acte *m* de bravoure, de folie; **p. of wit,** trait *m* d'esprit; **p. of good luck,** coup *m* de chance; (*c*) **what a p. of luck!** quelle chance! **a p. of advice,** un conseil; **a p. of extravagance,** une extravagance; **a p. of impertinence,** une impertinence; **a p. of insolence, of cheek,** une insolence; **a p. of injustice,** une injustice; **a p. of carelessness,** une étourderie; **a ridiculous p. of affectation,** une affectation ridicule; **a p. of cruelty,** une cruauté; **a p. of nonsense,** une sottise; **a p. of news,** une nouvelle; **a p. of bad news,** une mauvaise nouvelle; **various pieces of news,** diverses nouvelles; **a p. of luggage,** une valise, etc.; **a p. of furniture,** un meuble; **a p. of clothing,** un vêtement; **a complicated p. of mechanism,** un mécanisme compliqué; *F:* **she's a pretty p.,** c'est un beau brin de fille. **6.** (*a*) *Artil:* pièce (d'artillerie); (ii) *Mil: A:* fusil *m*; **to load one's p.,** charger son fusil; (iii) **fowling p.,** fusil de chasse; (*b*) *Metall:* **punched p.,** pièce estampée; **shaped p.,** pièce profilée; **hollow-drawn p.,** pièce emboutie creuse; (*c*) pièce (de monnaie); **five-shilling p.,** pièce de cinq shillings; *A:* **p. of eight,** peso *m*. **7.** (*a*) morceau *m* (de musique, de poésie); *Journ:* article *m*, papier *m*; **to say one's p.,** (i) *O:* réciter son morceau; (ii) *F:* prononcer son discours; **the best pieces in his collection,** les plus belles pièces de sa collection; (*b*) instrument *m* de musique; **three-p. ensemble,** trio *m*. **8.** (*a*) (*backgammon*) dame *f*; (*dominoes*) domino *m*, dé *m*; *Draughts:* pion *m*; (*b*) *Chess:* **pieces and pawns,** pièces et pions. **9.** *Her:* pièce; **barry of ten pieces,** burelé de dix pièces.

piece[2], *v.tr.* **1.** rapiécer, raccommoder; mettre une pièce à (un habit, etc.). **2.** joindre, unir **(one thing to another,** une chose à une autre); **to p. ropes, etc.,** joindre, assembler, des cordages, etc.; **to p. facts together,** coordonner des faits. **3.** *Tex:* rattacher (les fils cassés).

piece-dye ['pi:sdai], *v.tr. Tex:* teindre (les tissus) en pièces.

piecemeal ['pi:smi:l]. **1.** *adv.* (*a*) par morceaux, pièce à pièce; peu à peu; **to learn sth. p.,** apprendre qch. par bribes; **the collection was sold p.,** les pièces de la collection ont été vendues séparément; (*b*) *A:* **to break sth. p.,** mettre qch. en pièces, en morceaux. **2.** *a.* (*a*) parcellaire; **p. information, news,** nouvelles *f* fragmentaires; (*b*) fait pièce à pièce; **to work on a p. plan,** travailler sans méthode, sans organisation.

piecer ['pi:sər], *s.* **1.** *Tail:* ap(p)iéceur, -euse. **2.** *Tex:* (*also* **piecener**) rattacheur, -euse.

piecing ['pi:siŋ], *s.* **1.** rapiéçage *m*, rapiècement *m*; raccommodage *m*. **2.** *Tex:* rattachage *m* (des fils cassés). **3. p. (together),** assemblage *m*; coordination *f* (des faits, etc.).

piecrust ['paikrʌst], *s.* croûte *f*, chapeau *m*, de pâte (en croûte), de tourte.

pied [paid], *a.* (*a*) mi-parti; bariolé, bigarré, panaché; (*b*) diapré (de fleurs, etc.).

pied-à-terre [pje(i)də'tɛ:r], *s.* pied-à-terre *m inv*.

piedish ['paidiʃ], *s.* (*a*) terrine *f* (pour pâtés à croûte); (*b*) tourtière *f*.

Piedmont ['pi:dmɔnt]. **1.** *Pr.n. Geog:* (*a*) le Piémont; (*b*) le Piedmont (U.S.A.). **2.** *s.m.* **p. (plain),** plaine *f* de piedmont, de piémont; **p. glacier,** glacier de piedmont, de piémont.

Piedmontese [pi:dmɔn'ti:z]. *Geog:* (*a*) *a.* piémontais; (*b*) *s.* Piémontais, -aise.

piedmontite ['pi:dmɔntait], *s. Miner:* piémontite *f*, manganépidote *f*.

pie-dog ['paidɔg], *s.* chien errant (de l'Orient).

piedouche [pjei'du:ʃ], *s.* piédouche *m*.

piedroit ['pjeidrwɑ:], *s. Arch:* pied-droit *m*, *pl.* pieds-droits; piédroit *m*.

pie-eyed ['paiaid], *a. F:* ivre, éméché.

pieman, *pl.* **-men** ['paimən], *s.m. A:* marchand de petits pâtés.

pier ['piər], *s.* **1.** (*a*) (*of stone*) jetée *f*, môle *m*, digue *f*; (*b*) (*on piles*) estacade *f*; (*in river, harbour*) appontement *m*; **landing p.,** embarcadère *m*, débarcadère *m*, quai *m*; **p. dues,** droits *m* de quai, de jetée; (*c*) **floating p.,** ponton *m*, embarcadère flottant; (*d*) (*at seaside resort*) (i) jetée promenade; (ii) estacade. **2.** *Civ.E:* pilier *m* (de maçonnerie); pile *f* (en pierre), palée *f* (en bois) (d'un pont); piédroit *m*, pied-droit *m*, *pl.* pieds-droits (d'un arc, d'un pont). **3.** *Arch:* (*a*) pilastre *m*, dosseret *m*, pied-droit (de porte); (*b*) jambe *f* (sous poutre); chaîne *f* de liaison; (*c*) trumeau *m*; entre-fenêtre *m*, *pl.* entre-fenêtres; *Furn:* **p. glass,** trumeau; glace *f* en trumeau; **p. table,** console *f*. **4.** *Dent:* **bridge p.,** pilier de bridge.

pierage ['piəridʒ], *s.* droits *mpl* de jetée.

pierce ['piəs]. **1.** *v.tr.* (*a*) percer, transpercer, pénétrer; **to have one's ears pierced,** se faire percer les oreilles; **a thorn pierced his finger,** une épine lui est entrée dans le doigt; **to p. a cask,** mettre un tonneau en perce; **to p. a hole,** percer un trou; (*of light*) **to p. the darkness,** percer les ténèbres; **to p. the air with one's cries,** percer l'air de ses cris; **to p. s.o. to the heart,** transpercer le cœur à qn; transpercer qn de douleur; (*b*) *Metall:* épingler (un moule, l'âme). **2.** *v.i.* **to p. into, through, the enemy's lines,** pénétrer les lignes de l'ennemi.

pierced [piəst], *a.* percé; (*of battlements, etc.*) à jour; *Ethn:* **p.-nose Indians,** Nez-percés *m*.

piercer ['piəsər], *s.* **1.** perceur, -euse. **2.** *Tls:* perçoir *m*, perce *f*, poinçon *m*, vrille *f*.

piercing[1] ['piəsiŋ], *a.* (outil, regard, cri, etc.) aigu, perçant, pénétrant; (froid) pénétrant, saisissant; (son) éclatant, mordant; **p. wind,** vent pénétrant.

piercing[2], *s.* **1.** (*a*) perçage *m*, percement *m*, perforation *f*; **p. saw,** scie *f* à découper, à repercer; bocfil *m*; (*b*) *Metall:* épinglage *m* (d'un moule, de l'âme). **2.** trou *m*, perforation; ajour *m*.

piercingly ['piəsiŋli], *adv.* d'une manière perçante, pénétrante; **to fix one's eye p. on s.o.,** fixer qn d'un regard perçant.

pierhead ['piəhed], *s.* **1.** extrémité *f* de la jetée; musoir *m*. **2.** avant-bec *m*, *pl.* avant-becs (d'une pile de pont).

Pieria [pai'iəriə]. *Pr.n. Geog:* la Piérie.

Pierian [pai'iəriən], *a. Myth: Geog:* piérien; des Muses; **to drink of, at, the P. Spring,** boire les eaux de l'Hippocrène; **the P. Maids,** les Muses *f* de l'Hélicon.

Pieridae [pai'eridi:], *s.pl. Ent:* piérides *f*, piéridés *m*.

Pierides (the) [ðəpai'eridi:z]. *Pr.n.f.pl. Myth:* les Piérides, les Muses.

pierrette [piə'ret], *s.f. Th:* pierrette.

pierrot ['piərou], *s.m. Th:* pierrot.

pietà [pi'eitɑ:], *s. Art:* pietà *f*.

pietism ['paiətizm], *s.* **1.** *Rel.H:* piétisme *m*. **2.** piété *f* sincère; dévotisme *m*.

pietist ['paiətist], *s.* **1.** *Rel.H:* piétiste *mf.* **2.** personne *f* d'une piété (i) sincère, (ii) outrée.
pietistic [paiə'tistik], *a.* **1.** *Rel.H:* piétiste. **2.** d'une piété sincère.
piety ['paiəti], *s.* piété *f.*
piezo [pai'i:zou, pi:'eizou], *a.* piézoélectrique; **p. resonator,** oscillateur *m* piézoélectrique.
piezochemistry [paii:zou'kemistri], *s.* piézochimie *f.*
piezocrystallization [paii:zoukristəlai'zeiʃ(ə)n], *s.* piézocristallisation *f.*
piezodynamography [paii:zoudainə'mɔgrəfi], *s. Ph:* piézodynamographie *f.*
piezoelectric [paii:zoui'lektrik], *a.* piézoélectrique; **p. effect,** effet *m* piézoélectrique; **inverse p. effect,** électrostriction *f*; **p. oscillator,** oscillateur *m* piézoélectrique, piloté par quartz; **p. pick-up,** pick-up *m* piézoélectrique; **p. vibration pick-up,** capteur *m* de vibrations piézoélectrique; **p. pressure gauge,** capteur piézoélectrique.
piezoelectricity [paii:zouilek'trisiti], *s.* piézoélectricité *f.*
piezograph [pai'i:zougræf], *s.* piézographe *m.*
piezoid ['paii:zɔid], *s. Miner:* quartz taillé.
piezometer [paii:'zɔmitər], *s. Ph:* piézomètre *m.*
piezometric(al) [paii:zə'metrik(l)], *a. Ph:* piézométrique.
piezometry [paii:'zɔmətri], *s. Ph:* piézométrie *f.*
piffle[1] ['pifl], *s. F:* futilités *fpl,* bêtises *fpl,* niaiseries *fpl,* sottises *fpl,* balivernes *fpl*; **to talk p.,** dire des futilités.
piffle[2], *v.i. F: O:* **1.** dire des niaiseries, des sottises. **2.** s'occuper à des futilités; baguenauder.
piffling ['pifliŋ], *a. F:* futile; (discours, etc.) creux; **to do p. jobs,** s'occuper à des futilités.
pig[1] [pig], *s.* **1.** *(a)* porc *m,* cochon *m*; pourceau *m*; *NAm:* cochonnet *m,* porcelet *m,* goret *m*; **sow in p.,** truie pleine; *P:* **to be in p.,** être enceinte; **suck(l)ing p.,** cochon de lait; **roast p.,** rôti *m* de porc; **p. farm,** porcherie *f*; **p. breeding,** élevage *m* de porcs; l'industrie porcine; **p. bucket, pail, tub,** seau *m,* baquet *m,* aux déchets de cuisine, aux eaux grasses; *F:* **to buy a p. in a poke,** acheter chat en poche; *Com: F:* **p. on pork,** effet creux, papier creux; *F:* **to bring one's pigs to the wrong market,** faire une mauvaise affaire; rater son affaire; *F:* **when pigs begin to fly,** à, dans, la semaine des quatre jeudis; quand les poules auront des dents; *F:* **to bleed like a stuck p.,** saigner comme un veau; **to eat like a p., to make a p. of oneself,** manger gloutonnement; être comme un cochon à l'auge; *(b)* **wild p.,** sanglier *m*; *NAm:* marcassin *m,* jeune sanglier; **sea p.,** (i) marsouin *m*; pourceau, cochon, de mer; (ii) dauphin *m*; (iii) dugong *m,* vache marine; **water p.,** cabiai *m*; **p. deer,** babiroussa *m*; *(c) (pers.)* (i) *F:* goinfre *m,* glouton *m*; (ii) *F:* sale type *m*; vache *f*; grossier personnage; abruti *m*; (iii) *P:* agent *m* de police, flic *m,* perdreau *m*; **you dirty little p.!** petit cochon! **he's a greedy p.,** il est goulu comme un dindon; **you're an obstinate p.!** tu es têtu comme un mulet! **what a selfish p.!** quel égoïste! **don't be a p.!** voyons, sois chic! **2.** *Metall:* *(a)* gueuse *f* (de fonte); saumon *m* (de plomb, d'étain, etc.); **conversion, converter, p.,** fonte *f* d'affinage; **Swedish p.,** fonte suédoise; **p. metal,** métal *m* en gueuses, en saumons; **p. (iron),** fer *m* de première coulée; fonte brute, en gueuses; fer en fonte, en gueuse, en saumon; gueuse de fer, de fonte; saumon de fer; **basic p. (iron),** fonte basique; **forge p. (iron),** fer puddlé; **grey p. (iron),** fonte grise; **malleable p. (iron),** fonte malléable; **p. lead,** plomb *m* en saumons; *(b)* **p. (mould),** moule *m* pour gueuses, à saumons; gueuse; **p. bed,** moule pour gueuses; aire *f* de coulée.
pig[2], *v.i.* **(pigged) 1.** *(of sow)* mettre bas, cochonner. **2.** *F: (of pers.)* *(a)* se goinfrer, manger comme un cochon; *(b)* **to p. it,** vivre comme un cochon.
pig[3], *s. Scot:* cruchon *m,* cruche *f,* bouteille *f* en grès; *(in bed)* moine *m.*
pig[4], *s. F:* quartier *m* (d'orange); gousse *f* (d'ail).
pigboat ['pigbout], *s. Nau: F:* sous-marin *m.*
pigeon ['pidʒin], *s.* **1.** pigeon *m*; *(a)* **cock p.,** pigeon mâle; **hen p.,** pigeonne *f*; pigeon femelle; **young p.,** pigeonneau *m*; *(b)* **domestic p.,** pigeon domestique, pigeon de volière; **fantail p.,** pigeon paon; **pouter p.,** pigeon (à) grosse gorge, (pigeon) boulant *m*; **tambourine p.,** pigeon tambour; **tumbler p.,** pigeon culbutant; **homing p., racing p.,** pigeon voyageur; **carrier p.,** pigeon voyageur, pigeon messager; *(c)* **p. breeder,** colombophile *mf*; éleveur *m* de pigeons (de consommation); **p. breeding,** colombophilie *f*; l'industrie pigeonnière; **p. fancier,** colombophile *mf*; **p. fancying,** colombophilie *f*; **p. house, p. loft,** colombier *m,* pigeonnier *m,* trie *f*; **p. run,** volière *f*; **p. post,** transport *m* de dépêches par pigeons voyageurs; *Sp:* **p. shooting,** tir *m* aux pigeons; **clay p.,** pigeon (d'argile); **clay p. shooting,** ball-trap *m*; *(d) Orn:* **the p. family,** les columbidés *m*; **rock p.,** biset *m*; **wood p.,** (pigeon) ramier *m*; **bleeding-heart p.,** colombe poignardée; **bronze-wing p.,** phaps *m*; **crowned p.,** goura *m*; **fruit p.,** ptilope *m*; **green p.,** colombar *m*; **imperial p.,** carpophage *m*; **kelp p.,** chionis *m*; **tooth-billed p.,** didunculе *m*; **white-crowned p.,** pigeon à couronne blanche; **band-tailed p.,** pigeon à queue barrée, *Fr.C:* pigeon du Pacifique; **passenger p.,** pigeon migrateur, ectopiste *m,* *Fr.C:* tourte *f*; *(e) NAm:* **p. hawk,** faucon *m* émerillon; *(f)* **Cape p.,** pigeon du Cap, pétrel *m* damier. **2.** *F: O:* pigeon, dupe *f*; dindon *m* de la farce. **3.** (= PIDGIN) **that's my p.,** ça c'est mon affaire.
pigeon-breasted, -chested [pidʒin'brestid, -'tʃestid], *a.* qui a la poitrine en saillie, en bréchet; bossu par devant.
pigeonhole[1] ['pidʒinhoul], *s.* **1.** boulin *m* (de colombier). **2.** *(a)* case *f* (de bureau, etc.); **set of pigeonholes,** casier *m*; *(b)* case, compartiment *m* (de l'esprit, de la mémoire).
pigeonhole[2], *v.tr.* *(a)* caser, classer (des papiers, etc.); *(b)* classer (une réclamation, etc.); **my application has been pigeonholed,** ma demande dort, est restée, dans les casiers; *(c)* reléguer (qch.) dans sa mémoire.
pigeonholing ['pidʒinhouliŋ], *s.* classement *m* (de papiers, etc.).
pigeonite ['pidʒinait], *s. Miner:* pigeonite *f.*
pigeon-toed [pidʒin'toud], *a.* qui marche les pieds tournés en dedans; (cheval) cagneux.
pig-eyed ['pigaid], *a.* à petits yeux (de porc).
pig-faced ['pigfeist], *a.* à tête de cochon.
piggery ['pigəri], *s.* **1.** *(a)* porcherie *f*; étable *f* à porcs, à cochons; toit *m* à porcs; *(b) F:* endroit *m* sale; vrai bouge; vraie bauge. **2.** = PIGGISHNESS.
piggin ['pigin], *s. Dial:* petit seau; *Nau:* gamelot *m.*
piggish ['pigiʃ], *a. F: (of pers.)* *(a)* sale, malpropre; grossier; *(b)* goinfre, goulu; *(c)* égoïste; désagréable; entêté.
piggishness ['pigiʃnis], *s. F:* *(a)* saleté *f,* malpropreté *f*; grossièreté *f*; *(b)* goinfrerie *f*; *(c)* égoïsme *m*; entêtement *m.*
piggy ['pigi]. *F:* **1.** *s.* *(a)* cochonnet *m,* petit cochon, porcelet *m,* goret *m*; *(nursery talk)* **come and see the p. wiggies,** viens voir les petits cochons; *(b)* **p. bank,** (cochon) tirelire *f.* **2.** *a. (of pers.)* goinfre, goulu.
piggyback[1] ['pigibæk]. **1.** *adv. & s.* = PICK-A-BACK. **2.** *s.* *NAm:* ferroutage *m.*
piggyback[2], *v.tr. NAm:* ferrouter.
pigheaded [pig'hedid], *a.* obstiné, opiniâtre, entêté; têtu comme un mulet.
pigheadedly [pig'hedidli], *adv.* obstinément; avec entêtement.
pigheadedness [pig'hedidnis], *s.* obstination *f*; opiniâtreté *f*; entêtement *m.*
piglet, pigling ['piglit, -liŋ], *s.* cochonnet *m,* porcelet *m,* goret *m.*
pigman[1], *pl.* **-men** ['pigmən], *s.m.* porcher.
pigman[2], *s. Scot:* marchand *m* de pots de grès; colporteur *m* de vaisselle.
pigmeat ['pigmi:t], *s.* **1.** porc *m*; jambon *m*; charcuterie *f.* **2.** *P:* prostituée *f.*
pigment[1] ['pigmənt], *s.* **1.** *Art: Paint:* couleur *f,* colorant *m,* pigment *m*; **earth p.,** couleur terreuse; **ground p.,** couleur, colorant, en poudre; **organic p..** couleur, colorant, organique; **p. volume,** volume *m* pigmentaire. **2.** *Physiol:* pigment; **p. cell,** cellule *f* pigmentaire.
pigment[2] [pig'ment], *v.tr. & i.* (se) colorer; (se) pigmenter; teindre (qch.).
pigmentary ['pigmənt(ə)ri], *a.* **1.** colorant. **2.** *Physiol: etc:* pigmentaire.
pigmentation [pigmən'teiʃ(ə)n], *s.* pigmentation *f.*
pigmented [pig'mentid], *a.* pigmenté.
pigmentophage [pig'mentoufeidʒ], *s. Anat:* pigmentophage *m.*
pigmentous ['pigməntəs], *a.* pigmentaire, pigmenteux.
pigmy ['pigmi], *s.* = PYGMY.
pignoration [pignə'reiʃ(ə)n], *s. Jur:* pignoration *f,* engagement *m*; mise *f* en gage.
pignorative ['pignərətiv], *a. Jur:* pignoratif.
pignut ['pignʌt], *s. Bot:* **1.** arachide *f.* **2.** *U.S:* fruit *m* du carya.
pigskin ['pigskin], *s. Leath:* **1.** peau *f* de porc, de truie; **imitation p.,** cuir *m* façon porc; *attrib.* **p. purse,** bourse *f* en peau de porc. **2.** *(a) Turf: P: O:* selle *f*; *(b) Fb: F: O:* ballon *m.*
pigsticking ['pigstikiŋ], *s.* **1.** chasse *f* au sanglier (à courre courre avec épieu); *(b)* égorgeur *m,* saigneur *m,* de porcs. **2.** *(a)* épieu *m* de chasse; *(b) F:* gros couteau, coutelas *m,* eustache *m,* coupe-choux *m inv.*
pigsticking ['pigstikiŋ], *s.* **1.** chasse *f* au sanglier (à courre et à l'epieu). **2.** égorgement *m* de porcs.
pigsty ['pigstai], *s.* **1.** porcherie *f*; étable *f* à porcs; bauge *f.* **2.** *F:* (sale) taudis *m*; **the room's a real p.,** la pièce est d'une saleté incroyable, est une vraie écurie.
pigswill ['pigswil], *s.* = PIGWASH.
pigtail ['pigteil], *s.* **1.** *(a)* tabac *m* en corde, en carotte; *(b) El:* connexion tressée, toronnée, en queue de cochon; **p. resistor,** résistance *f* en queue de cochon; *Tchn:* **p. hook,** crochet *m* en queue de cochon. **2.** queue *f,* natte *f* (de cheveux).
pigtailed ['pigteild], *a.* **1.** à queue de porc; **p. monkey,** singe *m* cochon. **2.** *(of girl)* qui porte les cheveux en nattes; *(of wig, etc.)* à queue.
pigwash ['pigwɔʃ], *s.* **1.** pâtée *f* pour les porcs; eaux grasses (de cuisine). **2.** *F:* mauvaise soupe; lavasse *f*; *(of food)* de la cochonnerie.
pigweed ['pigwi:d], *s. Bot:* **1.** ansérine *f.* **2.** berce *f* branc-ursine; angélique *f* sauvage. **3.** renouée *f* des oiseaux; herbe *f* à cochon. **4.** consoude *f.*
pi-jaw[1] ['paidʒɔ:], *s. F: O:* prêchi-prêcha *m*; exhortations morales ou religieuses.
pi-jaw[2], *v.tr. F: O:* sermonner (qn); tenir à (qn) un discours édifiant.
pika ['paikə], *s. Z:* pika *m,* ochotone *m,* ogotone *m.*
pike[1] [paik], *s.* **1.** *(a) A.Arms:* pique *f,* haste *f*; **p. bearer,** piquier *m*; *(b)* pointe *f* (de bâton ferré, etc.). **2.** *Dial:* *(a) Agr:* fourche *f*; *(b) Min:* pic *m,* pioche *f.* **3.** *Geog:* *(in the Lake District)* pic (de montagne).
pike[2], *v.tr. A:* transpercer (qn) d'une pique.
pike[3], *s. Ich:* brochet *m*; **small p.,** brocheton *m*; **(Danubian) p. perch,** sandre *f.*
pike[4], *s. Dial: & NAm:* *(a)* barrière *f* de péage; *(b)* péage *m*; *(c)* route *f* à péage.
pike[5], *s.* *(a) (diving)* plongeon carpé; *(b) Gym:* mouvement carpé.
piked [paikt], *a.* *(a)* pointu, en pointe; *(b)* à pointe(s); *Z:* **p. whale,** balénoptère *m* à bec; *(c) Gym: etc:* carpé.
pikelet[1] ['paiklit], *s. Cu:* (sorte de) crêpe (servie rôtie et beurrée).
pikelet[2], *s. Ich:* lanceron *m.*
pikeman[1], *pl.* **-men** ['paikmən], *s.m.* **1.** *Hist:* piquier. **2.** *Dial: Min:* piqueur.
pikeman[2], *pl.* **-men,** *s.m. Dial: & NAm:* péager.
piker ['paikər], *s. NAm: P:* **1.** *(a)* une non-valeur; un gringalet; *(b)* poule mouillée; caneur *m.* **2.** *(a) Gaming:* joueur mesquin, sans audace; *(b) St.Exch:* boursicoteur *m,* boursicotier *m.*
pikestaff ['paikstɑ:f], *s.* **1.** bois *m,* hampe *f,* de pique. **2.** bâton *m* à pointe de fer.
pilaf(f) ['pi:læf], *s. Cu:* pilaf *m,* pilau *m,* pilaw *m.*
pilar ['pailər], **pilary** ['pailəri], *a. Anat:* pilaire.
pilaster [pi'læstər], *s. Arch:* pilastre *m.*
pilastered [pi'læstəd], *a.* supporté par des pilastres; bâti sur pilastres.
Pilate ['pailət], *Pr.n.m. Hist:* **Pontius P.,** Ponce Pilate.
Pilatus [pi'lɑ:təs], *Pr.n. Geog:* Mont *m* Pilate.
pilau, pilaw ['pi:lau, -lou, -lɔ:], *s. Cu:* = PILAF(F).
pilbarite ['pilbərait], *s. Atom.Ph:* pilbarite *f.*
pilch [piltʃ], *s. O:* couche-culotte *f, pl.* couches-culottes (de bébé).
pilchard ['piltʃəd], *s. Ich:* pilchard *m,* célerin *m,* sardine *f.*
pilcorn ['pilkɔ:n], *s. Bot:* avoine nue; avoine de Tartarie.
pile[1] [pail], *s.* **1.** *Civ.E: Const:* pieu *m,* pilot *m*; **tubular p.,** pieu creux; **screw p.,** pieu, pilot, à vis; **disc p.,** pieu à disque; **sheet p., p. plank,** palplanche *f*; **p. planking,** palplanches; **foundation p.,** pieu pilot, de fondation, de soutènement; **batter p.,** pieu (de fondation) incliné; **bridge p.,** pilot de pont; **bearing p.,** pilot de support; **filling p.,** pilot de remplage; **row of piles,** pilotis *m,* palée *f*; **to drive in a p.,** enfoncer, battre, un pieu; **to drive piles,** enfoncer des pieux, piloter; **to drive piles home,** enfoncer des pieux, piloter, jusqu'à refus (de mouton); **to drive piles into the ground, into sand,** enfoncer des pieux dans le sol, dans le sable; piloter (le sol), piloter le sable; **built on piles,** bâti sur pilotis; **p. cap,** chapeau *m,* coiffe *f,* de pieu; **p. helmet,** casque *f* de battage; avant-pieu *m, pl.* avant-pieux; **p. shoe,** sabot *m* de pilot; lardoire *f*; **p. hoop,** frette *f* de pilot; **p. driver,** (i) sonnette *f,* batterie *f,* bélier *m,* mouton *m*; **hand p. driver,** sonnette à bras, (sonnette à) tiraude *f*; **floating p. driver,** sonnette flottante; (ii) *Nau: F:* bateau *m* canard; canardeur *m*; (iii) *F:* coup *m* d'assommoir; *Fb:* shot, shoot, vigoureux; **p. driving,** battage *m,* enfonçage *m,* de pilots; pilotage *m*; **p. driving machine, apparatus,** machine *f* à battre, à enfoncer, des pieux; sonnette; **p. drawer,** arrache-pieux *m inv*; **p. extractor,** machine à arracher les pilotis; *(for boat)* **p. mooring,** pieu, poteau *m,* d'amarrage; duc *m* d'Albe; **p. foundation,** fondation *f* sur pilotis; *Prehist:* **p. dwelling,** habitation *f* lacustre. **2.** *Her:* pile, pointe, renversée. **3.** *(a)* tête *f,* pointe, fer *m* (de flèche); *(b) A.Arms:* pilum *m.*

pile[2], *v.tr. Civ.E: Const:* (a) soutenir (un édifice) au moyen de pilots; consolider (un édifice) avec un pilotis; (b) piloter (un terrain); affermir (le sol) avec des pilotis; palifier (le sol).

pile[3], *s.* 1. (a) (*heap*) tas *m* (de bois, de pierres, de minerai, etc.); monceau *m* (d'or, de morts, de détritus, etc.); amas *m*, amoncellement *m*, empilement *m*, entassement *m* (d'objets, de marchandises, etc.); meule *f* (de charbon de bois); pile *f* (de pièces de monnaie, d'assiettes, de linge, de documents, etc.); *Civ.E:* **gauged p. (of road metal),** toise *f*; **pile of shells,** pile, tas, d'obus; *A:* **p. of shot(s),** pyramide *f* de boulets; **piles of corpses,** des monceaux de cadavres; des corps entassés; **funeral p.,** bûcher *m* (funéraire); **an incredible p. of packing cases,** un empilement invraisemblable de caisses d'emballage; **to put in(to) a p.,** mettre en tas, empiler; (b) *Mil:* faisceau *m* (d'armes); (c) *Metall:* paquet *m* (de fer ébauché); **piles for railway rails,** paquets pour fabriquer des rails de chemin de fer; (d) *F:* fortune *f*, magot *m*; **to make one's p.,** faire fortune; faire son magot, sa pelote; **as soon as I've made my p.,** quand j'aurai fait fortune; après avoir fait fortune; une fois fortune faite, (je . . .); quand j'en aurai suffisamment. 2. (a) *El:* **(electric) p.,** pile (électrique); **dry p.,** pile sèche; **galvanic p., voltaic p., Volta's p.,** pile galvanique, voltaïque, de Volta; **thermoelectric p.,** pile thermoélectrique; (b) *Atom.Ph:* **(atomic) p.,** pile, réacteur *m* (atomique); **chain-reacting p.,** pile à réaction en chaîne; **disturbed p.,** pile perturbée; **enriched p.,** pile enrichie; **graphite-moderated p.,** pile modérée au graphite; **heavy-water p.,** pile à eau lourde; **high-power, low-power, p.,** pile génératrice de grande, de petite, énergie; **p. oscillator,** oscillateur *m* de pile. 3. (a) masse *f* (d'un édifice); (b) édifice.

pile[4], *v.*

I. *v.tr.* 1. (a) **to p. (up),** (i) entasser, amonceler (de la terre, etc.); amasser (une fortune, etc.); mettre (des objets) en tas; (ii) empiler (du bois, du charbon, des livres, etc.), mettre (des objets) en pile; **to p. up money,** amasser de l'argent; thésauriser des capitaux; **ship piled up on the rocks,** navire échoué sur les rochers; **to p. up mistakes,** accumuler faute sur faute; **to p. on the coal,** entasser du charbon sur le feu; **to p. up, on, the expenses,** faire monter les frais; **to p. up, on, the agony,** accumuler les détails pénibles; *F:* **to p. it on,** (i) exagérer, charrier, cherrer; (ii) surfaire ses clients; saler la note; **don't p. it on,** n'en jetez plus; (b) *Mil:* **to p. arms,** former les faisceaux; (c) *Metall:* paqueter (le fer ébauché); (d) *F:* **to p. up one's plane, a car,** bousiller son appareil, une voiture. 2. **to p. a table with dishes,** charger une table de plats.

II. *v.i.* 1. **to p. up,** s'amonceler, s'entasser, s'empiler; (*of cars*) caramboler; *Typ:* (*of ink*) plaquer; **his money was piling up at the bank,** son argent s'accumulait à la banque; **the clouds are piling up,** les nuages s'amoncellent. 2. **seven of them piled into the car,** sept d'entre eux se sont empilés dans la voiture; **fifteen piled out of the compartment,** ils sont descendus quinze du compartiment.

pile[5], *s.* 1. poil *m* (de chameau, etc.); laine *f* (de mouton). 2. *Tex:* poil (d'un tapis, etc.); **velvet with silk p.,** velours *m* en poil soie naturelle; **p. fabrics,** tissus *m* à poil; **p. warp,** chaîne *f* à poil.

pile[6], *s. Med: F:* 1. hémorroïde *f*; **to remove a p.,** faire l'ablation d'une hémorroïde; *Surg:* **p. clamp,** pince *f* à hémorroïdes. 2. *pl.* **piles,** hémorroïdes; **bleeding piles,** hémorroïdes fluentes; **bleeding of piles,** flux hémorroïdal; **blind piles,** hémorroïdes sèches.

pileate ['pailiit], **pileated** ['pailieitid], *a. Fung:* à pileus; à chapeau.

piled[1] [paild], *a. Const:* bâti sur pilotis.

piled[2], *a.* entassé, empilé; en tas, en monceau, en pile.

piled[3], *a. Tex:* à poils; (*of carpet*) velouté; **three-p.,** à trois poils.

pileorhiza [pailiou'raizə], *s. Bot:* pilorhize *f*; coiffe *f* de la racine.

pile-up ['pailʌp], *s.* (a) *Aut: F:* carambolage *m*, emboutissage *m*; téléscopage *m* en série; (b) *Atom.Ph:* empilement *m* (dans un appareil de comptage).

pileum ['pailiəm], *s. Orn:* pileum *m*, capuchon *m*.

pileus ['pailiəs], *s. Bot:* pileus *m*.

pilework ['pailwə:k], *s. Civ.E:* 1. pilotage *m*. 2. pilotis *m*, palée *f*.

pilewort ['pailwə:t], *s. Bot:* ficaire *f*; petite éclaire; éclairette *f*; petite chélidoine; herbe *f* de fic; herbe aux hémorroïdes.

pilfer ['pilfər], (a) *v.tr.* chaparder, chiper, marauder, dérober, escamoter (**sth. from s.o.,** qch. à qn); (b) *v.i.* chaparder, grappiller, picorer.

pilferage ['pilfəridʒ], *s.* petits vols; larcins *mpl*; chapardage *m*, maraude *f*.

pilferer ['pilfərər], *s.* chapardeur, -euse, chipeur, -euse; maraudeur, -euse, grappilleur, -euse.

pilfering[1] ['pilfəriŋ], *a.* (enfant) voleur; **p. servant,** domestique pilleur, -euse.

pilfering[2], *s.* = PILFERAGE.

pilgarlic [pil'gɑ:lik], *s. A:* 1. homme chauve, teigneux. 2. *F:* teigneux *m*, gueux *m*.

pilgrim ['pilgrim], *s.* 1. pèlerin, -ine; **pilgrim('s) bottle,** gourde *f* de pèlerin. 2. (a) *Hist:* **the P. Fathers,** les (pères) Pèlerins; (b) *U.S:* colon *m*; nouveau débarqué, nouvelle débarquée.

pilgrimage ['pilgrimidʒ], *s.* (a) pèlerinage *m*; **to go on (a) p.,** aller en pèlerinage; faire un pèlerinage; **p. town,** (ville *f* de) pèlerinage; (b) long voyage.

piliferous [pai'lifərəs], *a. Bot:* pilifère.

piliform ['pailifɔ:m], *a. Nat.Hist:* piliforme, capilliforme.

piling[1] ['pailiŋ], *s.* 1. (a) consolidation *f* (d'un édifice) avec un pilotis; (b) pilotage *m*, palification *f* (d'un terrain); (c) *Sm.a: A:* **p. pin,** quillon *m* (du fusil Lebel); **p. swivel,** anneau *m* de battant d'embouchoir. 2. *coll.* pilotis, pilotage; **steel p.,** pilotis d'acier.

piling[2], *s.* 1. **p. (up),** (i) amoncellement *m*, entassement *m*; (ii) empilage *m*, empilement *m*; mise *f* en pile, en tas; (iii) *Typ:* **p. up of ink,** plaquage *m* de l'encre (au blanchet); (iv) *Metall:* paquetage *m*. 2. *coll. Civ.E:* **side p. (of a road),** cavalier *m*.

pill[1] [pil], *s.* 1. (a) pilule *f*; *F:* **the p.,** la pilule; **the p. and birth control,** la pilule et la limitation des naissances; **she's on the p.,** elle prend la pilule; *Pharm:* **(sugar coated) p.,** dragée *f*; **sleeping p.,** pilule, cachet *m*, pour dormir; somnifère *m*; **laxative p.,** dragée purgative; **small p.,** globule *m*; **blue p.,** pilule mercurielle; **p. machine,** pilulier *m*; *Med:* **radio p.,** pile chercheuse, radioélectronique; **it's a bitter p. (to swallow),** la dragée est amère; **to swallow the (bitter) p.,** avaler la pilule, la dragée; **it's a hard p. to swallow,** la couleuvre est de taille (à avaler); **to gild, sugar, the p.,** dorer la pilule; (b) *Ent:* **p. beetle,** byrrhe *m*; *Crust:* **p. bug,** cloporte *m*. 2. *F:* (a) *A:* boulet *m* (de canon); (b) *O:* balle *f* (de tennis, de golf, etc.); ballon *m* (de football); (c) *O:* **game of pills,** partie *f* de billard.

pill[2], *v.tr. P: O:* blackbouler (qn).

pill[3], *v.tr. Tex:* égruger (le lin).

pill[4], *v.i. U.S:* (*of wool garment*) boulocher.

pillage[1] ['pilidʒ], *s.* 1. pillage *m*. 2. *A:* butin *m*.

pillage[2], (a) *v.tr.* piller, saccager; mettre (une ville) au pillage, à sac; faire main basse sur (une ville); (b) *v.i.* se livrer au pillage; piller.

pillager ['pilidʒər], *s.* pilleur, -euse; pillard, -arde; saccageur, -euse.

pillaging ['pilidʒiŋ], *a.* pillard.

pillar[1] ['pilər], *s.* 1. (a) pilier *m*, colonne *f*, colonnette *f*; *Arch:* **arch p.,** pilier d'arche, de voûte; **supporting p.,** pilier de soutènement; **Corinthian, Doric, p.,** colonne corinthienne, dorique; **plain p.,** colonne lisse; **fluted p.,** colonne cannelée; *Rel.H:* **p. saint,** stylite *m*; (*of pers.*) **a p. of the Church,** un pilier, une colonne, de l'Église; **to drive s.o. from p. to post,** renvoyer qn de Caïphe à Pilate, d'un endroit à l'autre; ballotter qn de l'un à l'autre; *B:* **she became a p. of salt,** elle devint une statue de sel; *Geog: A:* **the Pillars of Hercules,** les Colonnes d'Hercule; (b) *Min:* pilier, stappe *m*; **chain p.,** pilier (de protection) de galerie; **shaft p.,** pilier (de protection) de puits; **barrier p.,** massif *m* de protection; **p. and stall system,** méthode *f* de piliers et galeries; (c) *Furn:* pied central (d'une table, d'un guéridon); *Surv: etc:* borne *f*, colonne (de démarcation, de signalisation, etc.); **boundary p.,** borne frontière; (*in street*) **p. box,** boîte *f* aux lettres (en forme de borne); boîte-borne *f*, *pl.* boîtes-bornes; **p. box red** = rouge-drapeau *m*; **p. box red ribbons,** rubans *m* rouge-drapeau; (d) **p. of fire, of smoke,** colonne de feu, de fumée; (e) *Anat:* **p. of the diaphragm, of the fauces,** pilier du diaphragme, du voile du palais. 2. (a) *Mec.E:* colonne, montant *m* (d'une machine-outil); (*small and round*) chandelle *f*; **p. drilling machine,** perceuse *f* à colonne; **p. mounting,** montage *m* sur colonne(tte); *Artil:* **p. mount,** affût-pivot *m*, *pl.* affûts-pivots; *Tls:* **p. file,** lime plate à côtés lisses; (b) *Aut:* **door p.,** montant de porte; *O:* **steering p.,** colonne de direction; (c) *Cy:* **saddle p.,** tige *f* de selle; (d) *Clockm:* (*between two plates of clock movement*) pilier, colonne; (e) *N.Arch:* épontille *f*; **head, heel, of p.,** tête *f*, pied, d'épontille; **hollow, solid, p.,** épontille creuse, massive; **hold p.,** épontille de cale; **middle deck p.,** épontille d'entrepont; **quarter p.,** épontille latérale; (f) *Cin: T.V:* portant *m*; *El:* **brush p.,** pivot *m* de porte-balai.

pillar[2], *v.tr.* soutenir, consolider, (qch.) avec des piliers.

pillared ['piləd], *a.* (a) à piliers, à colonnes; hypostyle; (b) en pilier, en colonne.

pillaring ['piləriŋ], *s.* 1. *Arch: Civ.E:* ensemble *m*, série *f*, groupe *m*, de piliers. 2. *N.Arch:* épontillage *m*.

pillarist ['pilərist], *s. Rel.H:* stylite *m*.

pillbox ['pilbɔks], *s.* 1. boîte *f* à pilules, pilulier *m*. 2. *Cost:* **p. (hat),** petit chapeau rond sans bord. 3. *Mil:* casemate (bétonnée ou blindée, pour mitrailleuse ou pièce antichar); blockhaus *m*. 4. *F: O:* espace restreint; toute petite pièce; **p. house,** vraie maison de poupée.

pilling ['piliŋ], *s. Tex:* égrugeage *m*.

pillion ['piljən], *s.* 1. *Harn:* (a) selle *f* de femme; (b) coussinet *m* de cheval; **to ride (on the) p.,** monter en croupe. 2. (*on motor cycle*) **p. (seat),** siège *m* arrière; selle de passager; selle tandem; tan-sad *m*, *pl.* tan-sads; **to ride p.,** monter derrière; **p. rider,** passager, -ère (de derrière).

pillorize ['pilɔraiz], *v.tr.* = PILLORY[2].

pillory[1] ['piləri], *s.* pilori *m*; *A:* **to put s.o. in the p.,** mettre qn au pilori; pilorier qn.

pillory[2], *v.tr.* (**pilloried**) pilorier (qn); mettre, clouer, (qn) au pilori; **to p. an abuse,** dénoncer un abus.

pillow[1] ['pilou], *s.* 1. (a) oreiller *m*; **p. fight,** combat *m*, bataille *f*, à coups d'oreillers, à coups de polochon(s); *A:* **p. book,** livre *m* de chevet; (b) *Lacem:* **(lace) p.,** carreau *m*, coussin *m* (pour dentelle); oreiller (pour dentelle aux fuseaux); **p. lace,** dentelle *f* aux fuseaux, au coussin(et); guipure *f*. 2. *Mec.E:* (a) **p. (bush),** coussinet, grain *m*, dé *m*; (*for upright shaft*) crapaudine *f*; **conical p.,** coquille *f* de coussinet; (b) (corps *m* de) palier *m*; **p. cap,** chapeau *m* de palier. 3. *Nau:* (a) coussin (de beaupré); (b) pomme *f* (de mât).

pillow[2]. 1. *v.tr.* **to p. one's head on one's arms,** reposer sa tête sur ses bras; se faire un oreiller de ses bras. 2. *v.i.* (*of the head*) reposer (**on,** sur).

pillowcase, pillowslip ['piloukeis, -slip], *s.* taie *f* d'oreiller; **housewife style p.,** taie portefeuille.

pillowy ['piloui], *a.* doux, *f.* douce, comme un oreiller; moelleux.

pillwort ['pilwə:t], *s. Bot:* pilulaire *f*.

pilobolus [pai'lɔbələs], *s. Fung:* pilobole *m*.

pilocarpidine [pailou'kɑ:pidi:n], *s. Ch:* pilocarpidine *f*.

pilocarpine [pailou'kɑ:pi:n], *s. Ch:* pilocarpine *f*.

pilocarpus [pailou'kɑ:pəs], *s. Bot:* pilocarpe *m*, pilocarpus *m*.

pilori [pi'louri:], *s. Z:* pilori *m*.

pilose ['pailous], *a. Nat.Hist:* pileux, poilu.

pilosebaceous [pailousi'beiʃəs], *a. Physiol:* pilo-sébacé.

pilosis [pai'lousis], *s. Anat:* pilosisme *m*.

pilosism ['pailousizm], *s. Bot:* pilosisme *m*.

pilosity [pai'lɔsiti], *s.* pilosité *f*.

pilot[1] ['pailət], *s.* 1. (a) *Nau:* pilote *m*; *A: & Poet:* nautonier *m*, nocher *m*; **sea p.,** pilote de mer, pilote hauturier; **river p.,** pilote de rivière, pilote fluvial; **inshore p., coasting p., hobbling p., branch p.,** pilote côtier; lamaneur *m*; **dock p., harbour p., mud p.,** pilote de port; **bar p.,** pilote de barre; **p. master,** pilote major; chef *m*, inspecteur *m*, du pilotage; **licensed p.,** pilote breveté; **pilot's licence,** brevet *m* de pilote; **p. waters,** zone *f* de pilotage; **p. boat, p. cutter,** bateau-pilote *m*, *pl.* bateaux-pilotes; **p. flag,** pavillon *m* de, du, pilote; **p. ladder,** échelle *f* de pilote; **p. office,** bureau *m* de pilotage; *Tex:* **p. cloth,** drap *m* pilote; **p. coat, p. jacket,** jaquette *f* de drap pilote; vareuse *f*, caban *m*; **p. bread,** biscuit *m* de mer; (b) *Av:* **(air, aircraft) p.,** pilote (aviateur, d'avion); **airline p.,** pilote de ligne; **ferry p.,** pilote convoyeur, de convoyage; **prototype p.,** pilote de prototype; **test p.,** pilote d'essais; **aerobatic p.,** pilote d'acrobatie; **p. trainee,** élève *m* pilote; **licensed p.,** *Mil.Av:* **qualified p.,** *U.S:* **certified p.,** pilote breveté; **p. in command,** pilote commandant de bord; **first, senior, p.,** premier pilote, chef pilote; **second p.,** second pilote, copilote *m*; *Mil.Av:* **fighter p.,** pilote de chasse; **bomber p.,** pilote de bombardier; **p. officer,** sous-lieutenant *m* (aviateur); (*W.R.A.F.*) = troisième classe; **acting p. officer,** aspirant *m*; *A:* **non-commissioned p., sergeant p.,** sous-officier *m* pilote; *Aer:* **balloon p.,** aéronaute *m*, aérostier *m* (de ballon libre); *Space:* **lunar module p.,** pilote de module lunaire; (c) guide *m*, mentor *m*. 2. (a) *Av: etc:* **automatic p.,** pilote automatique; *Rail:* **p. (engine),** locomotive *f* estafette; locomotive pilote; **p. wheel,** roue porteuse avant (de locomotive, etc.); (b) *Rail: U.S:* chasse-bestiaux *m inv*. 3. (a) *Mec.E:* guide *m*; axe-guide *m*, *pl.* axes-guides; **aligning p.,** guide de montage; **buffer p.,** guide d'amortisseur; **cutter p.,** porte-fraise *m inv*; **p. bar,** barre-guide *f*, *pl.* barres-guides; *Mch.Tls:* **p. wheel,** volant *m* à pignées radiales; *Cin:* **p. claw of the feeding motion,** griffe *f* d'ajustage de l'entraînement de la bande; (b) **p. light, flame, jet, burner,** veilleuse *f* (de bec de gaz, etc.); *El: etc:* **p. light, lamp,** lampe *f* témoin, lampe pilote; voyant lumineux; témoin *m* de contrôle; **p. bulb,** veilleuse; **p. cell,** élément *m* témoin; **p. circuit,** circuit *m* pilote; **p.**

relay, relais *m* pilote; **p. fuse,** fusible indicateur; **p. exciter,** excitatrice *f* pilote; **p. wire,** fil *m* pilote, fil témoin; câble *m* auxiliaire (pour télécommande); **p. wire controlled,** télécommandé par câble auxiliaire; *Tp:* **p. wire regulator,** compensateur *m* thermique; **p. bell,** sonnerie *f* pilote; *W.Tel:* **p. signal,** signal *m* d'identification; **p. channel,** voie principale; *Elcs:* **p. loudspeaker,** haut-parleur *m* pilote; **p. oscillator,** oscillateur *m* pilote, maître oscillateur; **p.-operated,** à asservissement; *Ph:* **p. wave,** onde *f* pilote, onde de Broglie; *Atom.Ph:* **p. reactor,** réacteur *m* pilote; *I.C.E:* **p. needle,** aiguille *f* de ralenti; **p. jet,** gicleur *m* du, de, ralenti; **p. burner,** injecteur *m* de départ; *Phot:* **p. print,** épreuve *f* témoin; *Av: etc:* **p. parachute,** parachute extracteur; *Meteor:* **p. balloon,** ballon-sonde *m*, *pl.* ballons-sondes; (*c*) **p. factory, p. plant,** usine *f* pilote; installation *f* d'essai; *Ind: Com:* **p. run, p. series,** présérie *f*; **p. sample,** échantillon *m* pilote; *Cin: T.V:* **p. film,** film *m* d'essai. **4.** *Ich:* **p. fish,** poisson *m* pilote; pilote (de requin); gouverneur *m* (de baleine); *Z:* **p. whale,** globicéphale *m*; *Orn:* **p. bird,** pluvier argenté, varié.

pilot[2], *v.tr.* **1.** (*a*) piloter (un navire, un avion, une auto de course, etc.); *Nau:* **to p. a ship in, out,** piloter un navire à l'entrée, à la sortie; (*b*) mener, conduire (qn à travers des obstacles, etc.); *Parl:* **to p. a bill through the House,** guider les débats sur un projet de loi. **2.** *Mec.E: etc:* **to p. the drill,** guider la mèche.

pilotage ['pailətidʒ], *s.* **1.** *Nau:* (*a*) pilotage *m*; **inward p., outward p.,** pilotage d'entrée, de sortie; **inshore p., coastal p.,** pilotage côtier; lamanage *m*; **free, compulsory, p.,** pilotage libre, obligatoire; **on p. duty,** en service de pilotage; (*b*) **p. (dues),** (droits *m*, frais *m*, de) pilotage. **2.** *Av:* pilotage; navigation observée.

piloted ['pailətid], *a.* (*of aircraft, etc.*) piloté; avec pilote; **remotely p. vehicle,** véhicule (spatial, etc.) télécommandé.

pilothouse ['pailəthaus], *s. Nau:* kiosque *m* de veille, de navigation; (kiosque de) timonerie *f*.

piloting ['pailətiŋ], *s.* **1.** pilotage *m*. **2.** guidage *m*.

pilotless ['pailətlis], *a.* sans pilote; **p. aircraft,** avion téléguidé, avion robot.

pilous ['pailəs], *a. Nat.Hist:* pileux, poilu.

pilpul ['pilpu:l], *s. Jew.Rel:* pilpoul *m*.

pilular ['piljulər], *a. Pharm: etc:* pilulaire.

pilule ['pilju:l], *s.* petite pilule.

pilum ['pailəm], *s. A.Arms:* pilum *m*, javelot *m*.

pimaric [pi'mærik], *a. Ch:* (acide *m*) pimarique.

pimelic [pi'melik], *a. Ch:* (acide *m*) pimélique.

pimelite ['piməlait], *s. Miner:* pimélite *f*.

piment [pi'ment], *s. A:* piment *m*.

pimento [pi'mentou], *s.* **1.** *Bot:* piment *m*; poivre *m* de la Jamaïque; toute-épice *f*, *pl.* toutes-épices; poivron *m*. **2.** *Cu:* (i) poivron; (ii) piment; **to season with p.,** pimenter; **p. sauce,** pimentade *f*.

pi-meson [pai'mezɔn], *s. Atom.Ph:* pi *m*, pion *m*.

pimp[1] [pimp], *s.* entremetteur, -euse; souteneur *m*; proxénète *mf*; *P:* maquereau *m*, barbeau *m*, marlou *m*.

pimp[2], *v.i.* exercer le métier de proxénète.

pimpernel ['pimpənel], *s. Bot:* anagallide *f*, anagallis *f*; **scarlet p.,** mouron *m* rouge, des champs; faux mouron; morgeline *f*, menuchon *m*; anagallide des champs; **yellow p.,** lysimaque *f*, lysimachie *f*; **false p., bastard p.,** centenille *f*; **water p.,** (i) cresson *m* de cheval; (ii) samole *m* aquatique; mouron d'eau; pimprenelle *f* aquatique.

pimpinella [pimpi'nelə], *s. Bot:* boucage *m*; pied-de-chèvre *m*, *pl.* pieds-de-chèvre.

pimping[1] ['pimpiŋ], *s.* maquerellage *m*, proxénétisme *m*.

pimping[2], *a.* mesquin, misérable, chétif.

Pimpla ['pimplə], *s. Ent:* pimple *m*.

pimple ['pimp(ə)l], *s.* bouton *m*, pustule *f*, phlyctène *f*; (*on the lip*) babouin *m*; **to break out, come out, in pimples,** boutonner, bourgeonner; avoir une poussée de boutons.

pimpled ['pimp(ə)ld], **pimply** ['pimpli], *a.* pustuleux, boutonneux; bourgeonné, couvert de boutons; **to get p.,** boutonner, bourgeonner; se couvrir de boutons.

pin[1] [pin], *s.* **1.** (*a*) épingle *f*; **brass p., steel p.,** épingle en laiton, en acier; **safety p.,** épingle de nourrice; **blanket p.,** (i) drapière *f*; (ii) *Typ:* ardillon *m*; **fixing of sth. with a p.,** épinglage *m* de qch.; **p. case,** étui *m* pour épingles; **p. tray,** (i) porte-épingles *m inv*; (ii) *A.Furn:* vide-poche(s) *m inv*; *Ind:* **p. shank,** hanse *f* (d'épingle); *Dressm:* **p. tuck,** nervure *f*; **p. money,** (i) *A:* (*α*) épingles *fpl* (d'une femme); (*β*) argent (donné à une femme, à une jeune fille) pour ses frais de toilette; somme prévue (par contrat de mariage) pour les dépenses personnelles de la femme; (ii) argent de poche; **no larger than a pin's head,** pas plus gros qu'une tête d'épingle; **you could have heard a p. drop,** on aurait entendu voler une mouche; **there isn't a p. to choose between them,** il n'y a aucune, pas la moindre, différence entre eux; l'un vaut l'autre; **for two pins I'd punch his face,** pour un rien je lui casserais la figure; *Prov:* **he that will steal a p. will steal a pound,** qui vole un œuf vole un bœuf; **to be on pins and needles,** être, marcher, sur des épines, sur des charbons (ardents), sur le gril; (*b*) **pins and needles,** fourmillements *m*; **I've got pins and needles in my feet,** j'ai des fourmillements, des fourmis, dans les pieds; j'ai des picotements aux pieds; (*c*) *O:* **(knitting) p.,** aiguille *f* à tricoter; (*d*) *Hairdr:* (i) épingle; (ii) pince *f* (pour mise en plis); **bobby p.,** pince (à cheveux); **p. curl,** boucle plate; **hair set in p. curls,** mise en plis bouclée. **2.** (*a*) *Mec.E:* axe *m* (de fixation, de guidage, de repérage), goupille *f*, clavette *f*; **guide p.,** axe guide; axe, tenon *m*, de guidage; **indexing, locating, p.,** ergot *m* de repérage, de centrage; goupille de montage; **taper p.,** goupille conique; **axle p.,** clavette d'essieu; **attaching p., fixing p.,** axe, goupille, de fixation; broche *f* d'attache; *Rail:* **coupling p., draw p.,** cheville, broche, d'attelage; **check p., stop p., detent p.,** axe, goupille, d'arrêt; ergot de butée; étoquiau *m*; **short p., p. not passing through,** cheville *f* à bout perdu; **set p.,** goupille de calage, goupille à demeure; prisonnier *m*; **safety p.,** (i) goupille, clavette, de sûreté (d'un mécanisme); (ii) *Mil:* goupille (de sûreté) (d'une grenade, d'une fusée d'obus, etc.); **p. coupling,** accouplement *m* par cheville, par goupille; **p. chain,** chaîne *f* à fuseau; **p. extractor,** tire-goupille *m*, *pl.* tire-goupilles; *Mch:* **wrist p.,** axe, bouton *m*, maneton *m*, soie *f* (de manivelle); **crosshead p.,** axe, tourillon *m*, de traverse, de tête de piston; axe de pied de bielle; **knuckle p.,** (i) axe d'articulation; (ii) axe de pied de bielle secondaire; **the p. won't enter, goes the wrong way,** la cheville refoule; **to take the p. out of sth.,** dégoupiller qch.; (*b*) pivot *m* (d'une grue, d'une plaque tournante, etc.); axe, verge *f* (de girouette); axe, essieu *m* (de poulie); **centre p.,** pivot central, cheville ouvrière (de bogie); **centre p. of a compass,** pivot d'un compas; **fulcrum p.,** axe d'articulation (de levier, etc.); **main p.,** (i) *Aut:* pivot de roue avant; (ii) cheville ouvrière, pivot central (de bogie, etc.); **pivot p., swivel p.,** axe de pivotement; **catch p.,** doigt *m*, goupille, toc *m*, d'entraînement (du plateau-toc d'un tour); (*c*) broche (de clef, de serrure, de cartouche de fusil); broche, cheville, fiche *f*, lacet *m*, rivure *f* (d'une charnière); gond *m* (de penture, de pommelle); tourillon (de porte); *Mus:* fiche (de corde de piano, de clavecin); bouton (de harpe); pointeau *m* (de valve de pneu, de valve de chambre à air); style *m* (de cadran solaire); *El:* fiche (de prise de courant); **banana p.,** fiche banane; **connector p.,** broche mâle (de prise de courant); **p. insulator,** (i) isolateur *m* rigide; (ii) isolateur pourvu de sa tige verticale; **p. type insulator,** isolateur à tige, à console, verticale; *Elcs:* **base p.,** broche de support (de tube électronique); **p. connections,** brochage *m* (d'un tube électronique); *Tg:* **insulator p.,** porte-isolateur *m*, *pl.* porte-isolateurs; console verticale; *Tp:* **p. jack,** jack *m* miniature, jack de très petit diamètre; *Mec.E:* **p. valve,** robinet *m*, soupape *f*, vanne *f*, à pointeau; **firing p.,** percuteur *m* (d'une arme à feu); (*d*) clou *m*, pointe *f*; *Surg:* broche, clou (pour fracture); *Metall:* **moulding p.,** pointe de mouleur; (*e*) *Carp: Join:* tenon *m* (en queue d'aronde, etc.); **wooden p.,** cheville, fiche, en bois; fenton *m*; **drawbore p.,** cheville (pour assujettir un tenon dans une mortaise); (*f*) *Nau:* tolet *m*, dame *f* (d'embarcation); **jack p.,** cabillot *m* de râtelier. **3.** *Cu:* **(rolling) p.,** rouleau *m* à pâtisserie, à pâte. **4.** (*a*) *Surv:* **(chain) p.,** fiche d'arpenteur; *Civ.E:* **line p.,** fiche à barrages; (*b*) *Golf:* drapeau *m* de trou. **5.** *Cmptr:* picot *m* (d'entraînement de bande); **p. feed,** entraînement *m* (des étiquettes, etc.) par picots; **p. feed hole,** perforation *f* d'entraînement: **p. feed margin,** bande marginale d'entraînement; **p. feed tractor,** entraîneur *m* à picots; **p.-fed label,** étiquette entraînée par picots. **6.** (*a*) (*at ninepins*) quille *f*; *Bill:* **p. pool,** partie *f* de quilles (sur table); **p. table,** billard chinois, japonais; (*b*) *O:* **p. (leg),** jambe *f* de bois, pilon *m*; (*c*) *pl. F:* jambes; guibolles *f*, flûtes *f*, quilles; fumerons *m*. **7.** *Tls:* (*a*) têton *m* (d'une mèche à aléser, à forer, etc.); **p. spanner, p. wrench,** clef *f* à griffes; **p. bit, p. drill,** foret *m* à têton cylindrique; **p. punch, p. driver, p. drift,** chasse-goupilles *m inv*; **p. vice,** étau *m* à main, à queue; *Fish:* **netting p.,** moule *m* pour filets; (*b*) *Metall:* broche, mandrin *m*, de coulée.

pin[2], *v.tr.* **(pinned) 1.** (*a*) épingler; attacher, fixer, avec une épingle, des épingles; **to p. a label to a sample,** épingler une étiquette à, sur, un échantillon; **to p. a shawl over one's shoulders,** épingler un châle sur ses épaules; attacher un châle sur ses épaules avec une épingle; (*of woman*) **to p. on one's hat,** fixer, assujettir, son chapeau avec des épingles; épingler son chapeau; **to p. clothes on a line,** épingler du linge sur une corde; **to p. a map to, on, the wall,** fixer une carte au mur (avec des punaises); **to p. the paper to the board,** fixer le papier sur la planchette (avec des punaises); **to p. up one's hair, a hem,** épingler ses cheveux, rabattre un ourlet avec des épingles; **to p. up a stray wisp of hair,** rattacher une mèche avec une épingle; **to p. up one's skirt,** retrousser sa jupe; (*b*) *Mec.E: etc:* cheviller, goupiller; mettre une goupille à (qch.); (*with a cotter*) claveter; (*with a bolt*) boulonner. **2.** fixer, clouer; **to p. s.o. against a wall,** clouer, plaquer, qn contre un mur; **to p. s.o. by the throat,** saisir qn à la gorge, empoigner qn par la gorge; **to p. s.o.'s arms to his sides,** (i) coller, plaquer, les bras de qn au corps; (ii) ficeler les bras de qn au corps; ligoter qn; **to be pinned (down) under a fallen tree,** se trouver pris, coincé, sous un arbre déraciné; *Mil:* **to p. down the enemy,** clouer l'ennemi (au sol); **to be pinned down by fire,** être cloué au sol par le feu de l'ennemi; **to p. s.o. (down) to his word,** obliger qn à tenir ses promesses, à tenir parole; **to p. s.o. (down) to facts,** obliger qn à s'en tenir aux faits, à reconnaître les faits; **to p. s.o. (down) to do sth.,** obliger, contraindre, qn à faire qch.; **to p. oneself (down) to do sth.,** s'engager formellement à faire qch.; **without pinning himself down to anything,** sans s'engager à rien; sans rien préciser; **to p. sth. on s.o.,** rendre qn responsable; mettre qch. sur le compte, sur le dos, de qn; **to p. one's hopes on s.o., sth.,** mettre tous ses espoirs en qn, dans qch.; *Chess:* **to p. a piece,** clouer une pièce. **3.** étayer, étançonner (un mur, etc.).

pinaceae [pai'neisii:], *s.pl. Bot:* pinacées *f*.

pinacoid ['pinəkɔid], *s. Cryst:* pinacoïde *m*.

pinacoidal [pinə'kɔid(ə)l], *a. Cryst:* pinacoïde.

pinacol, pinacone ['pinəkɔl, -koun], *s. Ch:* pinacol *m*.

pinacolic [pinə'kɔlik], *a. Ch:* pinacolique.

pinacolone, pinacolin(e) [pi'nækəloun, -in, -i:n], *s. Ch:* pinacoline *f*.

pinafore ['pinəfɔ:r], *s.* **1.** tablier *m* (d'enfant, etc.); **I knew her when she was in pinafores,** je l'ai connue toute petite. **2. p. dress,** robe *f* à bretelles, robe chasuble, *Fr.C:* jumper *m*.

pinafored ['pinəfɔ:d], *a.* en tablier.

pinakiolite [pi'nækiəlait], *s. Miner:* pinaciolite *f*.

Pinakothek [pinəkə'teik], *s.* **the Munich P.,** la pinacothèque de Munich.

pinascope ['pinəskoup], *s.* pinascope *m*.

pinaster [pai'næstər], *s. Bot:* pinastre *m*; pin *m* maritime; pin de Bordeaux.

pinatype ['pinətaip], *s. Phot:* pinatypie *f*.

pinball ['pinbɔ:l], *s.* billard *m* électrique; flipper *m*; **p. machine, game, table,** billard chinois, japonais.

pince-nez ['pɛ̃snei], *s.inv.* pince-nez *m inv*.

pincers ['pinsəz], *s.pl.* **1.** *Tls:* **(pair of) p.,** pince *f*, tenaille(s) *f(pl)*; **bit p.,** tenailles à chanfrein; **straight p.,** pinces plates; *Carp: Farr:* tricoise(s) *f(pl)*; **cutting p.,** pince coupante. **2.** *Nat.Hist:* pince (de crustacé, d'insecte). **3.** *Mil:* **pincer(s) movement,** mouvement *m*, manœuvre *f*, en tenailles.

pinch[1] [pinʃ], *s.* **1.** (*a*) action *f* de pincer; pincement *m*, pinçure *f*, pinçade *f*; **to give s.o. a p.,** pincer qn; (*b*) **the p. of hunger,** la morsure de la faim; *F:* **to feel the p.,** tirer le diable par la queue; (*c*) **at a p.,** au besoin; **when it comes to the p.,** au moment décisif; **it was a close p.,** il était moins cinq. **2.** pincée *f* (de sel, etc.); prise *f* (de tabac); **to take a p. of snuff,** humer une prise. **3.** *Geol:* serrement *m*, étranglement *m* (d'un filon, etc.); airure *f*. **4.** *Atom.Ph:* pincement, resserrement, striction *f* (magnétique); **p. effect,** (i) effet *m* de pincement, de resserrement, de striction (magnétique); (ii) *Elcs:* rhéostriction *f*; *Cmptr: etc:* **p. roller,** rouleau presseur, entraîneur, pinceur. **5.** *Tls:* **p. (bar),** pince *f* de manœuvre; levier *m* à griffe, à pince; arcanseur *m*, anspect *m*; pied-de-biche *m*, *pl.* pieds-de-biche; *Mec.E:* **p. nut,** contre-écrou *m*, *pl.* contre-écrous.

pinch[2], *v.tr.* **1.** (*a*) (*nip*) pincer; **to p. s.o.'s nose,** pincer le nez à qn; **to p. one's nose to avoid a bad smell,** se pincer le nez pour ne pas sentir une odeur; **her grandfather pinched her cheek,** son grand-père lui a pincé la joue; *F:* **he pinched her bottom,** il lui a pincé les fesses; **to p. one's finger in the door,** se pincer le doigt dans la porte; **to p. sth. off,** enlever qch. en le pinçant (avec les ongles, etc.); *Hort:* **to p. off a bud,** épincer un bourgeon; *Aut: Cy:* **pinched inner tube,** chambre à air pincée, cisaillée, pliée; **shoe that pinches,** chaussure qui blesse, qui serre, qui est trop étroite; **that's where the shoe pinches,** c'est là que le bât (le) blesse; (*b*) *Rac:* presser (un cheval). **2.** (*restrict*) (*a*) serrer, gêner; **to p. s.o. for food,** mesurer la nourriture à qn; **to p. (oneself),** se priver (du nécessaire); se serrer le ventre; **to p. and scrape,** faire de petites économies, vivre avec parcimonie; regarder à la dépense; gratter le pavé; (*b*) *v.i. Geol:* (*of lode, etc.*)

se rétrécir, se resserrer; (*c*) *Y:* faire courir (un yacht) au plus serré, au plus près; chicaner; (*d*) *v.i. U.S:* (*of land, etc.*) **to p. in on, upon, sth.,** empiéter sur qch. **3.** *F:* **to p. sth. from, out of, s.o.,** extorquer qch. à qn. **4.** *F:* (*a*) chiper, chauffer, choper, chaparder, barboter, faucher, kidnapper (qch.); **to p. sth. from s.o.,** chiper, refaire, qch. à qn; **someone has pinched my matches,** on m'a chauffé mes allumettes; **I've had my purse pinched,** on m'a refait mon porte-monnaie; (*b*) arrêter, agrafer, pincer, piger, coincer, chauffer (un voleur, etc.); **to get pinched,** se faire pincer, chauffer, choper, épingler.

pinchbeck ['pinʃbek], *s.* **1.** *Metall:* chrysocal(e) *m*, chrysoc(h)alque *m*, similor *m*, potin *m*, pinchbeck *m*, pinsbeck *m*. **2.** *attrib.* (*a*) en chrysocal(e), en similor; (*b*) simili, en toc; **a p. Napoleon,** un Napoléon de pacotille; **p. hero,** héros *m* d'occasion.

pinchcock ['pinʃkɔk], *s. Ch: etc:* pince *f* d'arrêt.

pinche ['pi:nʃei], *s. Z:* tamarin *m*.

pinched [pinʃt], *a.* **1.** (*of face, etc.*) tiré, hâve, amaigri; *Med:* **p. features,** traits grippés; grippement *m* de la face; **p. by the cold,** pincé par le froid; **to be p. with hunger,** être tenaillé par la faim; **his face p. with hunger,** ses traits tirés par la faim. **2.** étroit; **in p. circumstances,** à court d'argent; dans la gêne; **to be (a bit) p. (for money, time, etc.),** être à court d'argent, de temps, etc.; **to be p. for room,** être à l'étroit. **3.** *Needlew:* **p. tuck,** nervure *f*.

pinchers ['pinʃəz], *s.pl. Dial: P:* = PINCERS 1.

pinchfist, pinchgut, pinchpenny ['pinʃfist, -gʌt, -peni], *s.* avare *mf*; ladre, *f.* ladresse; pingre *mf*; grippe-sou *m*, *pl.* grippe-sou(s).

pinching[1] ['pinʃiŋ], *a.* **1.** qui pince; (*of shoe, etc.*) qui gêne, étroit. **2.** (froid, etc.) cuisant, âpre. **3.** parcimonieux, avare.

pinching[2], *s.* **1.** pincement *m*, pinçure *f*; *Aut: etc:* **p. of the inner tube,** pincement, cisaillement *m*, écrasement *m*, de la chambre à air; *Hort:* **p. off (of buds),** épinçage *m*, pinçage *m*, pincement (de bourgeons). **2.** parcimonie *f*. **3.** *F:* chapardage *m*, barbotage *m*.

pinch-out ['pinʃaut], *s. Geol:* airure *f*.

pincushion ['pinkuʃ(ə)n], *s.* pelote *f* à épingles, à aiguilles.

Pindar ['pindər], *Pr.n.m. Gr.Lit:* Pindare.

Pindaric [pin'dærik]. **1.** *a.* pindarique, pindaresque. **2.** *s.* ode *f* pindarique; **Pindarics,** vers *m* pindariques.

Pindus ['pindəs]. *Pr.n. A.Geog:* le Pinde.

pine[1] [pain], *s.* (*a*) *Bot:* **p. (tree),** pin *m*; **Aleppo p.,** pin d'Alep, de Jérusalem; **American p.,** pin, sapin *m*, d'Amérique; **black p.,** pin noir; pin d'Autriche; **broom p., longleaf, long-leaved, p., Georgia p., rosemary p.,** pin à longues feuilles, pin à balais; **shortleaf (yellow) p., short-leaved p., rosemary p.,** pin à feuilles courtes; **ponderosa p., heavy(-wooded) p., bull p., western (white, yellow) p.,** pin à bois lourd; **Cembra p., Swiss (stone) p., arolla p., Siberian p., yellow p.,** (pin) cembro *m*; tinier *m*; **maritime p., cluster p., sea p., star p.,** pin maritime, de Bordeaux; pinastre *m*; **dwarf p.,** pin nain; **scrub p.,** pin de Virginie; **mountain p.,** pin de montagne, pin à crochets; **Norway p.,** pin sylvestre, suisse; pin de Genève, de Russie; pin à mâtures; pinasse *f*; **parasol p., stone p., umbrella p.,** pin (en) parasol; pin pignon; **Weymouth p., white p.,** pin de (lord) Weymouth; sapin blanc; **Douglas p., Oregon p.,** sapin, pseudotsuga *m*, de Douglas; **Swiss p., silver p.,** sapin argenté, blanc, pectiné; sapin des Vosges; *U.S:* **silver p.,** sapin baumier; **Scotch p.,** sapin du Nord, de la Baltique, d'Écosse; **stiff-leaved p., (long-leaf) yellow p., pitch p.,** pitchpin *m*; faux sapin; pin à trochets; **Chile p.,** araucaria *m*, araucarie *f*; **screw p.,** arbre indécent, impudique; **p. grove, p. plantation,** pinède *f*; **p. forest,** forêt de pins, pinède; **p. kernel,** pigne *f*, pignon *m*; **p. needle,** aiguille *f* de pin; **p. blister,** rouille *f* du pin; (*b*) (bois *m* de) pin; (*c*) *Ent:* **p. beauty,** noctuelle *f* piniperde, du pin; **p. beetle, p. borer,** hylésine *m* piniperde; **p. sawfly,** lophyre *m* du pin; **p. weevil,** hylobie *m* du sapin; charançon *m* du pin.

pine[2], *s. A:* ananas *m*.

pine[3], *v.i.* **1. to p. (away),** languir, se consumer, dépérir; tomber en langueur; mourir de langueur; sécher sur pied; **to p. with grief,** languir, se consumer, de tristesse. **2. to p. for s.o., for sth.,** languir pour, après, qn, qch.; soupirer après qn, qch.; **he's pining for home,** il a la nostalgie du foyer.

pineal ['piniəl], *a. Anat:* pinéal, -aux; **p. gland, p. body,** glande pinéale.

pinealoma [piniə'loumə], *s. Med:* pinéalome *m*.

pineapple ['painæpl], *s.* **1.** ananas *m*. **2.** *Mil: F: O:* grenade *f* à main.

pinecone ['painkoun], *s.* (*a*) pomme *f*, cône *m*, de pin; pigne *f*; (*b*) *Ich:* **p. fish,** poisson *m* pomme de pin.

pinene ['paini:n], *s. Ch:* pinène *m*.

pinery[1] ['painəri], *s. For:* pinède *f*.

pinery[2], *s.* (*a*) serre *f* à ananas; (*b*) champ *m* d'ananas.

pinesap ['painsæp], *s. Bot:* monotrope *m*.

pinetum [pai'ni:təm], *s.* pinède *f*.

pinewood ['painwud], *s.* **1.** (bois *m* de) pin *m*. **2.** pinède *f*.

pin-eyed ['pinaid], *a. Bot:* (primevère) longistyle.

pinfeather ['pinfeðər], *s. Orn:* plume naissante, couton *m*.

pinfeathered ['pinfeðəd], *a.* (oiseau) aux plumes naissantes.

pinfire ['pinfaiər], *a. Sm.a: A:* (cartouche *f*, fusil *m*) à broche.

pinfold[1] ['pinfould], *s. O:* (*a*) fourrière *f*; (*b*) parc *m* (à moutons, etc.).

pinfold[2], *v.tr. O:* (*a*) mettre (un animal) en fourrière; (*b*) parquer (du bétail, etc.).

ping[1] [piŋ], *s.* (*a*) cinglement *m*, fouettement *m* (d'une balle de fusil, etc.); (*b*) *I.C.E:* détonation *f*; cognement *m*; (*c*) *Rad:* impulsion *f* sonar.

ping[2], *v.i.* (*a*) (*of bullet, etc.*) cingler, fouetter; (*b*) *I.C.E:* (*of engine*) **to p. slightly,** faire entendre un léger cognement.

pinger ['piŋər], *s.* (*a*) *Rad:* émetteur *m* d'impulsion (sonar); (*b*) *Dom.Ec: F:* compte-minutes *m inv*.

pingo ['piŋgou], *s. Geol:* pingo *m*, hydrolaccolithe *m*.

ping-pong[1] ['piŋpɔŋ], *s.* (*a*) *R.t.m.* ping-pong *R.t.m. m*; tennis *m* de table; **p.-p. set,** jeu *m* de ping-pong; (*b*) *Cmptr:* travail *m* en bascule (du dérouleur, etc.).

ping-pong[2], *v.tr. Cmptr:* transférer (une donnée) de la mémoire auxiliaire à la mémoire centrale (ou vice versa).

pinguecula [piŋ'gwekjulə], **pinguicula**[1] [piŋ'gwikjulə], *s. Med:* pinguécula *f*, pinguicula *f*.

pinguicula[2], *s. Bot:* pinguicule *f*, pinguicula *m*; *F:* grassette *f*.

pinguid ['piŋgwid], *a.* gras, graisseux.

pinguite ['piŋgwait], *s. Miner:* pinguite *f*.

pinhead ['pinhed], *s.* (*a*) tête *f* d'épingle; (*b*) *attrib. Tex:* (drap) pointillé; (*c*) *F: O:* **what a p.!** quelle andouille! quel idiot!

pinheaded ['pinhedid], *a.* (*a*) à tête d'épingle; (*b*) *F: O:* stupide; **p. remark,** réflexion idiote; (*c*) *Bot:* (primevère) longistyle.

pinhole ['pinhoul], *s.* **1.** trou *m* de cheville, de goujon. **2.** (*a*) trou d'épingle; (*b*) *Opt:* très petite ouverture (dans un écran, etc.); *Phot:* sténopé *m*; *Cmptr:* perforation *f* d'entraînement; **p. source of light,** source *f* de lumière punctiforme; **lamp giving a p. beam of light,** lampe ponctuelle; **p. photography,** photographie *f* sans objectif; sténopéphotographie *f*; **p. camera,** sténoscope *m*; (*c*) *Phot:* piqûre (sur le cliché, due aux poussières); picoture *f*; tour d'aiguille; bouillon *m* d'air.

pinic ['painik], *a. Ch:* pinique.

pinicolous [pai'nikələs], *a. Nat.Hist:* pinicole.

piniferous [pai'nifərəs], *a.* pinifère.

piniform ['painifɔ:m], *a.* en forme de pomme de pin.

pining ['painiŋ], *s.* **1.** langueur *f*, languissement *m*, dépérissement *m*. **2.** désir ardent, grande envie (**for sth.,** de qch.).

pinion[1] ['pinjən], *s.* **1.** (*a*) bout *m* d'aile; aileron *m*; (*b*) *Poet:* aile *f*. **2.** penne *f*, rémige *f*.

pinion[2], *v.tr.* **1.** rogner les ailes à, éjointer (un oiseau). **2.** (*a*) lier les bras à, ligoter, garrotter (qn); **to p. s.o.'s arms to his sides,** lier les bras de qn; (*b*) lier (**s.o. to a tree, etc.,** qn à un arbre, etc.).

pinion[3], *s. Mec.E:* pignon *m*; (*mounted on shaft*) tympan *m*; **bevel p., mitre p.,** pignon conique, pignon d'angle; **camshaft p.,** pignon d'arbre à cames; **crown-wheel and p.,** pignon et couronne d'entraînement; **differential p., planet, p.,** pignon satellite; **double-toothed p.,** pignon à double denture; **drive p., driving p.,** pignon d'attaque, de commande, d'entraînement; **sliding p.,** pignon baladeur, coulissant; **spider p., sun p.,** pignon planétaire; **spur p.,** pignon droit; **timing p., half-time p.,** pignon de distribution; **rack and p.,** crémaillère *f* et pignon; *Aut:* **gear p.,** pignon de boîte de vitesses; *Mec. E:* **p. carrier,** porte-pignon *m*, *pl.* porte-pignon(s); support *m de satellites;* **p. wheel,** roue *f* à pignon.

pinioned ['piniənd], *a.* **1.** (*a*) *Lit:* ailé; (*b*) (oiseau) éjointé, à ailes rognées. **2.** lié, ligoté.

pinite ['pinait], *s. Miner:* pinite *f*.

pink[1] [piŋk]. **1.** *s.* (*a*) *Bot:* œillet *m*; **garden p.,** (œillet) mignardise *f*; **sea p.,** œillet maritime; **Indian p.** = PINKROOT; (*b*) **the p. of perfection,** la perfection même; le modèle, la crème, de la perfection; **in the p. of condition,** en excellente, parfaite, santé; (*of racehorse, etc.*) entraîné à fond; *O:* (*of pers.*) **to be in the p.,** se porter à merveille, comme un charme. **2.** *a.* & *s.* (*a*) (couleur *f* de) rose *m*; **salmon p.,** rose saumon *inv*; **shocking p.,** rose bonbon, vif; **p. cheeks,** joues roses; (*of albino rabbit, etc.*) **p. eyes,** yeux rouges; **p. gutta percha,** gutta-percha *m* incarnadine; *Pol: F:* **to be a bit p.,** (i) être libéral; (ii) être socialiste modéré, à l'eau de rose; (*b*) (**hunting**) **p.,** rouge (*m*), écarlate (*m*); (*c*) *P: O:* **strike me p.!** pas possible!

pink[2], *v.tr.* **1.** percer, toucher (son adversaire). **2.** *Dressm: etc:* (i) (denteler, hocher, découper, les bords (de qch.); (ii) travailler à jour, évider (le cuir, etc.); (iii) piquer (la soie).

pink[3], *s. Ich:* **1.** saumoneau *m*. **2.** véron *m*, vairon *m*.

pink[4], *v.i. I.C.E:* (*of engine*) cliqueter.

pinked [piŋkt], *a. Dressm: etc:* (*a*) cranté, dentelé; découpé aux bords; (*b*) percé; travaillé à jour; évidé; **p. tape,** bande crantée, dentelée.

pinkeye ['piŋkai], *s.* **1.** *Med:* conjonctivite aiguë contagieuse. **2.** *Vet:* (*a*) fièvre *f* typhoïde du cheval; (*b*) gourme *f*; (*c*) ophtalmie contagieuse (des bovins); (*d*) pasteurellose *f* des ruminants.

pink-eyed ['piŋkaid], *a.* aux yeux rouges, roses.

pinkie ['piŋki]. *Scot: F:* **1.** *a.* petit, menu. **2.** *s.* petit doigt; auriculaire *m*.

pinking[1] ['piŋkiŋ], *s. Dressm: etc:* crantage *m*, dentelure *f*; découpage *m*, découpure *f* (sur les bords); évidage *m*, vidure *f*; **p. shears,** ciseaux *m* à cranter, à denteler; **p. iron,** emporte-pièce *m inv*; découpoir *m* à figures; *Leath:* fer *m* à découper.

pinking[2], *s.* cliquetis (produit par les auto-allumages).

pinkish ['piŋkiʃ], *a.* rosâtre; rosé.

pinkness ['piŋknis], *s.* (couleur *f*) rose *m*.

pinkroot ['piŋkru:t], *s. Bot:* **Maryland p.,** spigélie *f* de Maryland; **Demerara p.,** spigélie anthelminthique; brinvillière *f*.

pinkster ['piŋkstər], *s. U.S: F:* la Pentecôte; **p. flower,** azalée *f* rose.

pinkwood ['piŋkwud], *s. Bot:* dicypellion *m*.

pinky ['piŋki], *a. F:* rosâtre; rosé; **p. grey,** gris rosâtre *inv*.

pinlay ['pinlei], *s. Dent:* onlay *m* à crampons.

pinlock ['pinlɔk], *s.* serrure *f* à broche.

pinmaker ['pinmeikər], *s.* épinglier, -ière; fabricant *m* d'épingles.

pinna ['pinə], *s. Moll:* pinne (marine), *F:* jambonneau *m*.

pinnace ['pinəs], *s. Nau:* **1.** pinasse *f*, péniche *f*. **2.** grand canot.

pinnacle ['pinəkl], *s.* **1.** *Arch:* (*a*) pinacle *m*, clocheton *m*; (*b*) couronnement *m* (de faite, etc.). **2.** (*a*) cime *f* (d'une montagne, etc.); pic *m*; (*b*) **rock p.,** pénitent *m*, dame *f*; **snow p.,** pénitent; **ice p.,** sérac *m*; (*c*) *Oc:* aiguille *f*. **3. the p. of glory,** le faîte de la gloire; **on the highest p. of fame,** à l'apogée *m*, au comble, au sommet, de la gloire.

pinnacled ['pinəkld], *a.* **1.** *Arch:* à pinacle(s); à clochetons; à couronnement. **2.** mis sur le pinacle; porté au pinacle.

pinnate(d) ['pineit(id)], *a. Nat.Hist:* penné, pinné; **odd p.,** imparipenné; **bluntly p.,** paripenné.

pinnately ['pineitli], *adv. Bot:* **p. lobed,** pennatilobé, pinnatilobé; **p. cleft,** pennatifide, pinnatifide.

pinnatifid [pi'nætifid], *a. Bot:* pennatifide, pinnatifide.

pinnatilobate [pinæti'loubeit], *a. Bot:* pennatilobé, pinnatilobé.

pinnatiped [pi'nætiped], *a.* & *s. Orn:* pinnatipède (*m*).

pinnatisect [pi'nætisekt], *a. Bot:* pennatiséqué, pinnatiséqué.

pinner ['pinər], *s.* **1.** *A.Cost:* coiffe *f* à barbes. **2.** *Dial:* tablier *m* à bavette.

Pinnidae ['pinidi:], *s.pl. Moll:* pinnidés *m*.

pinning ['piniŋ], *s.* **1.** (*a*) **p. (on, up),** épinglage *m*; (*b*) *Mec.E:* chevillage *m*, goupillage *m*, clavetage *m*, boulonnage *m*. **2.** (*a*) fixage *m*, clouage *m*, clouement *m*; (*b*) *Surg:* enclouage *m* (d'un os).

pinniped ['piniped], *a.* & *s. Z:* pinnipède (*m*).

Pinnipedia [pini'pi:diə], *s.pl. Z:* pinnipèdes *m*.

pinnoite ['pinɔit], *s. Miner:* pinnoïte *f*.

pinnotherid [pinou'θiərid], *s. Crust:* pinnothère *m*.

pinnule ['pinjul], *s.* **1.** pinnule *f* (d'une alidade). **2.** (*a*) *Z:* pinnule; (*b*) *Bot:* pinnule, foliole *f*.

pinny ['pini], *s. F:* tablier *m*.

pinochle, pinocle ['pi:nɔkl], *s. Cards:* jeu *m* de cartes ressemblant à la belote.

pinocytosis [pinousai'tousis], *s. Biol:* pinocytose *f*.

Pinoideae [pi'nɔidii:], *s.pl. Bot:* pinoïdées *f*.

pinonic [pi'nɔnik], *a. Ch:* pinonique.

pinpoint[1] ['pinpɔint], *s.* (*a*) pointe *f* d'épingle; *Anat:* **p. pupil,** pupille *f* en pointe d'épingle; (*b*) point infime, infinitésimal, minuscule; **to turn the gas down to a p.,** mettre le gaz en veilleuse; **p. flame,** (i) flamme *f* minuscule, à peine perceptible; (ii) source ponctuelle de chaleur; **at night the sky was studded with pinpoints of light,** la nuit des points lumineux parsemaient, saupoudraient, le ciel; (*c*) (i) point repéré, point désigné (au sol, etc.); (ii) point de repère; (ii) *Mil:* objectif ponctuel; **p. accuracy,** haute précision; **p. localization,** localisation exacte, précise; **p. observation,** repérage précis, de précision; *Mil:* **p. bombing, firing,** bombardement *m*, tir *m*, de précision; **p. target,** objectif ponctuel; *Opt:* **p. lens,** verre ponctuel.

pinpoint[2], *v.tr.* (*a*) indiquer exactement, mettre le doigt sur (qch.); localiser, repérer, désigner (qch.) avec exactitude, avec précision; photographier (qch. de petite dimension, un objectif ponctuel); mettre en évidence, souligner (un fait); (*b*) *Mil:* viser (un objectif) avec précision; effectuer un tir, un bombardement de précision, sur (un objectif); bombarder, tirer sur (un objectif ponctuel, de petite dimension).

pinpointing ['pinpɔintiŋ], *s.* (*a*) localisation *f*, désignation *f*, exacte, précise (de qch.); repérage précis, de précision; photographie *f*, prise *f* de vue (de qch. de petite dimension, d'un objectif ponctuel); mise *f* en évidence (d'un fait); (*b*) *Mil:* visée précise, de précision; tir *m*, bombardement (i) de précision, (ii) ponctuel.

pinprick ['pinprik], *s.* (*a*) piqûre *f* d'épingle; (*b*) *F:* **pinpricks,** picoterie(s) *f*, tracasseries *f*; coups *m* d'épingle.

pinstripe ['pinstraip], *s. Tex:* filet *m* (de couleur dans un tissu).

pint [paint], *s. Meas:* pinte *f* (= 0,568 litre; *U.S:* = 0,473 litre); (*in Eng.*) **imperial p.,** pinte légale; **reputed p.,** bouteille *f*, etc., d'environ une pinte; **p. bottle,** bouteille d'une pinte; *F:* **p.-size(d), half-p.,** minuscule; **he's only p.-sized,** il est tout riquiqui.

pinta[1] ['pintə], *s. Med:* pinta *m*.

pinta[2] ['paintə], *s. F:* **a p. milk,** une pinte de lait.

pintado [pin'tɑːdou], *s. Orn:* **1.** pintade *f*. **2. p. petrel,** pétrel *m* damier, pigeon *m* de Cap.

pintadoite [pin'tɑːdouait], *s. Miner:* pintadoïte *f*.

pintail ['pinteil], *s. Orn:* **1.** pilet *m*. **2.** (*a*) ganga *m* cata; (*b*) tétras *m* à longue queue, *Fr.C:* gelinotte *f* à queue fine.

pintailed ['pinteild], *a. Orn:* **p. duck,** pilet *m*; **p. grouse, p. sandgrouse,** ganga *m* cata; **p. chicken,** tétras *m* à longue queue, *Fr.C:* gelinotte *f* à queue fine.

pintle ['pintl], *s.* (*a*) pivot central; *Veh: Artil:* cheville ouvrière; (*b*) broche *f*, goujon *m*, lacet *m*, rivure *f* (d'une charnière); bourdonnière *f* (d'un chardonnet de porte); tête *f* (de gond); *Nau:* gond *m* (de penture de sabord); (*c*) broche (de serrure); (*d*) *Nau:* aiguillot *m*, vitonnière *f* (de gouvernail); (*e*) **p. chain,** chaîne *f* à fuseau.

pinto[1] ['pintou], *a. & s. U.S:* (cheval) pie (*m*).

pinto[2], *s. Med:* pinta *m*.

pinup ['pinʌp], *a. & s. F:* **p. (girl),** pin-up *f inv*.

pinwheel ['pin(h)wiːl], *s.* **1.** *Clockm:* roue *f* des chevilles. **2.** *Cmptr:* roue à picots; **p. feed,** entraînement *m* à picots. **3.** *Pyr:* soleil *m*.

pinworm ['pinwəːm], *s. Med:* oxyure *f* vermiculaire.

piolet ['piːəlei], *s.* piolet *m* (d'alpiniste).

Piombi (the) [ðə'pjɔmbi], *s.pl. Hist:* les Plombs *m* (de Venise).

pion ['paiɔn], *s. Atom.Ph:* pion *m*, méson *m* pi.

pioneer[1] [paiə'niər], *s.* pionnier *m*.

pioneer[2]. **1.** *v.tr.* (*a*) parcourir (un pays, etc.), frayer (un chemin), en pionnier; (*b*) servir de guide, de pionnier à (qn). **2.** *v.i.* faire œuvre de pionnier; frayer le chemin.

pious ['paiəs], *a.* pieux; **p. fraud,** (i) pieux mensonge; (ii) *F:* (*pers.*) hypocrite *mf*.

piously ['paiəsli], *adv.* pieusement; avec piété.

piousness ['paiəsnis], *s.* piété *f*.

pip[1] [pip], *s.* **1.** *Husb:* pépie *f* (de la volaille). **2.** *F:* **to have the p.,** avoir le cafard; broyer du noir; **to give s.o. the p.,** donner, flanquer, le cafard à qn; embêter qn.

pip[2], *s.* **1.** point *m* (d'une carte, d'un dé, etc.); **two pips,** le deux. **2.** *Bot:* fleuron *m* (d'une composée). **3.** *Mil: F:* **to get one's third p.** = recevoir sa troisième ficelle. **4.** *Elcs:* pointe *f* (de tube électronique). **5.** *W.Tel:* top *m*; *Rad:* top d'écho; *W.Tel:* **the pips,** les (six) points musicaux; le signal horaire (par points musicaux); **at the sixth p. it will be nine o'clock,** au sixième top il sera exactement neuf heures.

pip[3], *v.tr.* **(pipped)** *F:* **1.** (*a*) blackbouler (qn); (*b*) *Sch: O:* refuser, recaler, retoquer (un candidat). **2.** *O:* vaincre, battre (qn). **3.** *O:* (*a*) atteindre (qn) d'une balle (de fusil); (*b*) tuer (qn) d'un coup de fusil.

pip[4], *s.* pépin *m* (de fruit).

pip[5], *v.* **(pipped) 1.** *v.i.* (*of chick*) piauler. **2.** *v.tr.* (*of chick*) casser, briser (sa coquille).

pip[6], *s. Mil: Tg. & Tp: A:* (la lettre) p; *F: O:* **p. emma** (= **p.m.**), (six heures, etc.) du soir.

pipa ['piːpə], *s. Amph:* pipa *m*.

pipage ['paipidʒ], *s.* **1.** transport *m* (de l'eau, etc.) par conduites, par canalisation. **2.** *coll.* tubulures *fpl*, conduites *fpl*, canalisation *f*. **3.** (pose *f* d'une) canalisation.

pipal ['piːpəl], *s. Bot:* **p. (tree),** arbre *m* des conseils, figuier *m* des pagodes.

pipe[1] [paip], *s.* **1.** (*a*) tuyau *m*, tube *m*; tubulure *f*; conduit *m*, conduite *f*, canalisation *f*; **water p.,** tuyau, conduite, d'eau; **gas p.,** tuyau, conduite, de gaz; **air p.,** (i) tuyau d'air; (ii) *Min:* buse *f* d'aérage; **main p., trunk p.,** tuyau principal; conduite, canalisation, principale; **pipes and fittings,** tuyauterie *f* et accessories de tuyauterie; **to lay pipes,** poser, installer, des tuyaux, des canalisations; **admission p., intake p.,** tuyau, tubulure, d'admission, d'amenée, d'aspiration; **suction p.,** tuyau d'aspiration; **rainwater p., down p., fall p.,** tuyau de descente (d'une maison); **overflow p.,** tuyau de trop-plein; **discharge p.,** tuyau d'évacuation; **blow-down, blow-off, blow-out, p.,** tuyau d'extraction, de vidange; (*of cesspool*) **blow-off p.,** tuyau d'évent; **blow-through p.,** tuyau de purge; **connecting p.,** tuyau de communication; raccord *m*; **delivery p.,** (i) tuyau de distribution (de gaz, etc.); (ii) tuyau, conduite, de refoulement (de pompe); **distributing p.,** tuyau distributeur, tubulure de distribution; **extension p.,** (tube) rallonge *f*; **angle p., elbow p.,** coude *m*; tuyau coudé, cintré; raccord coudé; **screen p.,** tube filtre; **spacer p.,** tube entretoise; *Hyd.E:* **weir p.,** (tuyau) déversoir *m*; *Min:* **drill p.,** tige *f*, tube, de forage; *Metall:* **leg p.,** coude du porte-vent (d'un haut fourneau); **p. bending,** cintrage *m* des tuyaux; **p. connection, p. coupling, p. union,** raccord de tuyauterie; **p. clamp,** (i) *Plumb: etc:* collier *m* d'assemblage pour tuyaux; (ii) *Min:* collier, frein *m*, de retenue (pour descendre les tubages de puits); **p. clip,** bride *f*, collier, de fixation (de tube, de tuyau); **p. cutter,** coupe-tube(s) *m inv*; coupe-tuyaux *m inv*; **p. twister, p. wrench,** clef *f* à tubes; **p. key,** clef forée; **p. flange,** collet *m*, bride *f*, de tuyau; flasque *f* (de fixation) de tuyau; **p. joint,** (i) *Plumb: etc:* joint *m*, assemblage *m*, de tuyauterie; (ii) *W.Tel:* raccord de guide d'ondes; **p. tongs,** pince *f* serre-tubes; **p. grab,** accroche-tube *m inv*; **p. threader,** machine *f* à tarauder, à fileter, les tuyaux; **p. tap,** (i) taraud *m* pour tuyauteries; (ii) prise *f* de tuyauterie; **p. dog,** arrache-tuyau(x) *m inv*; **p. fitter,** tuyauteur *m*; **p. fitter's vice,** étau *m* de tuyauteur; **p. manufacturer,** fabricant *m* de tuyaux; (*b*) *Anat: F: O:* tube, *esp.* tube respiratoire; **it's my pipes!** j'ai les bronches malades; (*c*) entre(-)nœud *m* (d'un brin de paille); (*d*) forure *f*, canon *m* (d'une clef). **2.** (*a*) *Mus:* (i) pipeau *m*, chalumeau *m*; **the pipes,** la cornemuse; *Mil:* **p. major,** cornemuse-chef *m*; (ii) **p. organ,** grand orgue; **organ p.,** tuyau d'orgue; **p. stop,** jeu *m* de fond (de l'orgue); **reed p.,** tuyau à anche; (*b*) *Nau:* sifflet *m* (du maître d'équipage); (*c*) (filet *m* de) voix *f*; chant *m* (d'oiseau). **3.** pipe *f*; **to smoke a p.,** fumer une pipe; **I smoke a p., I'm a p. smoker,** je fume la pipe; **how about a p.?** si on fumait une pipe? **p. of peace, peace p.,** calumet *m* de (la) paix; *F:* **put that in your p. and smoke it!** mettez ça dans votre pipe! mettez ça dans votre poche, dans votre sac, et votre mouchoir pardessus! *F: A:* **the King's, Queen's, P.,** le grand incinérateur du port de Londres (où la douane brûlait les déchets de tabac); **p. cleaner,** cure-pipe *m*, *pl.* cure-pipes; goupillon *m* nettoie-pipes; furet *m*; **p. case,** écrin *m*, étui *m*, de pipe; **p. rack,** râtelier *m* à pipes; porte-pipes *m inv*; **p. manufacturer,** fabricant de pipes; pipier *m*; **p. dream,** rêve *m* (chimérique); projet *m* illusoire; **one of my favourite p. dreams,** un de mes rêves les plus chers; **p. dreamer,** rêveur, -euse; bâtisseur *m* de chimères. **4.** (*a*) *Geol:* cheminée *f* de volcan; (*b*) *Min:* **p. vein, p. of ore,** colonne *f* de richesse; coulée *f* de minerai; (*c*) *Metall:* retassure *f*. **5.** pipe (de vin); grande futaille.

pipe[2], *v.*

I. *v.i.* (*a*) jouer (i) *A: & Lit:* du chalumeau, de la flûte, (ii) du fifre, de la cornemuse; (*b*) (*of bird, etc.*) siffler; gazouiller; (*of pers.*) parler d'une voix flûtée; (*c*) *Navy:* donner un coup de sifflet.

II. *v.tr.* **1.** (*a*) installer, poser une canalisation, des canalisations, dans (une maison, etc.); canaliser (l'eau, le pétrole, etc.); capter (l'eau); **piped water,** eau courante; **to p. oil to a refinery,** amener le pétrole à une raffinerie par oléoduc, par pipeline; (*b*) *Min:* abattre (de la terre, etc.) par la méthode hydraulique; (*c*) *F:* transmettre (de la musique) (par radio); (*d*) *F: O:* **to p. one's eye(s),** (i) pleurer; pleurnicher; (ii) y aller de sa larme. **2.** (*a*) jouer (un air) (i) *A: & Lit:* au chalumeau, sur la flûte, (ii) sur le fifre, sur la cornemuse; **to p. the troops to the barracks,** conduire les troupes à la caserne au son du fifre, de la cornemuse; (*in Scot.*) **to p. in the guests, the haggis,** jouer de la cornemuse en tête de la procession (lors de l'entrée solonelle des invités, du haggis); (*b*) chanter (un air) d'une voix flûtée; (*c*) *Navy:* siffler (un commandement); **to p. all hands down,** siffler en bas tout le monde; **to p. dinner,** siffler à dîner; **to p. the side,** rendre les honneurs au sifflet. **3.** *Hort:* bouturer (des œillets). **4.** (*a*) *Laund:* tuyauter (un jabot, etc.); (*b*) *Dressm: etc:* liserer, ganser, passepoiler (une robe, etc.); (*c*) *Cu:* décorer (un gâteau avec une douille).

III. (*compound verbs*) **1. pipe down,** *v.i. F:* (*a*) changer de ton; (*b*) se taire, la boucler; **p. down!** boucle-la! (*c*) mettre une sourdine, filer doux.

2. pipe up, (*a*) *v.i.* (i) se mettre à jouer sur la cornemuse, etc.; (ii) *F:* se mettre à chanter, à parler; **a little voice piped up,** une petite voix s'est fait entendre; (*b*) *v.tr.* **to p. up a tune,** commencer à jouer un air (sur la cornemuse, etc.).

pipeclay[1] ['paipklei], *s.* **1.** terre *f* de pipe; blanc *m* de terre à pipe (pour astiquage). **2.** *F: A:* formalisme *m* dans l'administration de l'armée.

pipeclay[2], *v.tr.* passer (des buffleteries, etc.) à la terre de pipe; astiquer (qch.) au blanc de terre à pipe.

pipecoline [pai'pekəlain], *s. Ch:* pipécoline *f*.

piped [paipt], *a.* **1.** (*a*) à tuyau(x); à tube(s); tubulé; (*b*) *F:* **p. music,** musique transmise par la radio, etc. **2.** *Dressm:* liseré, passepoilé. **3.** *esp. U.S: P:* ivre, gris.

pipefish ['paipfiʃ], *s. Ich:* syngnathe *m*; serpent *m*, vipère *f*, de mer; aiguille *f* (de mer); trompette *f*; siphonostome *m*.

pipeful ['paipful], *s.* pipe *f* (de tabac).

pipelayer ['paipleiər], *s.* poseur *m* de tuyaux, de canalisation.

pipelaying ['paipleiiŋ], *s.* pose *f* de tuyaux.

pipeline[1] ['paiplain], *s.* **1.** canalisation *f*, conduite *f*; (*for gas*) conduite de gaz naturel, gazoduc *m*; (*for petrol*) oléoduc *m*, pipeline *m*; **conveyor p.,** canalisation d'acheminement, de transport; **p. proper,** tube *m*, tubage *m*, tuyauterie *f*; **p. routing,** tracé *m* de pipeline, d'oléoduc, de gazoduc; **p. stocks,** stocks *m* en cours d'acheminement (par pipeline); **port p.,** pipeline, oléoduc, gazoduc, portuaire. **2.** canal *m*, voie *f*, d'acheminement (des nouvelles, du matériel, etc.); *Mil:* **logistics p.,** canal d'acheminement logistique; *F:* **it's in the p.,** ce sera bientôt prêt; vous l'aurez bientôt.

pipeline[2], *v.tr.* canaliser (l'eau, le pétrole).

piper ['paipər], *s.* **1.** joueur *m* de chalumeau, de fifre, de cornemuse; cornemuseur *m*; *F:* **to pay the p.,** payer les violons, la danse, les pots cassés; éclairer la dépense; **he pays the p. while the others call the tune,** il paie les violons et les autres dansent; **he who pays the p. calls the tune,** qui paie a bien le droit de choisir. **2.** *Vet:* cheval siffleur. **3.** *Min:* soufflard *m* de grisou.

Piperaceae [pipə'reisiiː], *s.pl. Bot:* pipéracées *f*.

piperaceous [pipə'reiʃəs], *a. Bot:* pipéracé.

Piperales [pipə'reiliːz], *s.pl. Bot:* pipérales *f*.

piperazine ['pipərəzain], *s. Ch:* pipérazine *f*.

piperic [pi'perik], *a. Ch:* pipérique.

piperideine [pipə'ridiain], *s. Ch:* pipéridéine *f*.

piperidine [pi'peridain], *s. Ch:* pipéridine *f*.

piperine ['pipərain], *s. Ch:* pipérine *f*, pipérin *m*.

piperonal [pi'perənəl], *s. Ch:* pipéronal *m*.

pipestone ['paipstoun], *s. Miner:* catlinite *f*.

pipette [pi'pet], *s. Ch: etc:* pipette *f*; *Pharm:* compte-gouttes *m inv*; **graduated p.,** pipette graduée.

pipework ['paipwəːk], *s.* tuyauterie *f*, tuyautage *m*, canalisation *f*.

Pipidae ['pipidiː], *s.pl. Amph:* pipidés *m*.

piping[1] ['paipiŋ]. **1.** *a.* (*a*) qui joue du chalumeau, de la flûte, de la cornemuse; *Lit:* **p. times of peace,** heureuse époque de paix; (*b*) (son) aigu, sifflant; **p. voice,** voix flûtée; (*c*) *Orn:* **p. crow,** gymnorhine *m*; *NAm:* **p. plover,** pluvier siffleur; *Z:* **p. hare,** pika *m*. **2.** *adv.* **p. hot,** tout chaud, tout bouillant; **p. hot day,** journée de grande chaleur; **the coffee was p. hot,** le café était tout bouillant.

piping[2], *s.* **1.** (*a*) installation *f*, pose *f*, de tuyaux, de canalisations (dans un immeuble, etc.); (*b*) canalisation *f*, amenée *f*, transport *m*, par canalisation(s) (de l'eau, du gaz, du pétrole, etc.), par gazoduc (du gaz), par oléoduc, par pipeline (du pétrole); (*c*) *coll.* conduites *fpl*, conduits *mpl*, tuyaux *mpl*, tuyautage *m*, tuyauterie(s) *f(pl)*; **induction p., inlet p.,** tubulure *f*, tuyauterie, d'admission; **outlet p.,** tubulure, tuyauterie, de sortie; **p. system,** réseau *m* de canalisations; *Nau:* **ballast p.,** tuyautage de ballast; **bilge p.,** tuyautage de cale; **oil p.,** tuyautage de mazout; (*d*) *Min:* abattage *m* (de la terre, etc.) par la méthode hydraulique; (*e*) *Metall:* retassure *f*. **2.** (*a*) son *m* du chalumeau, du fifre, de la cornemuse; (*b*) sifflement *m* (du vent, etc.); gazouillement *m*, gazouillis *m*, ramage *m* (d'oiseaux); (*c*) *Navy:* commandement *m* au sifflet. **3.** (*a*) *Laund:* tuyautage; (*b*) *Dressm: etc:* (i) liserage *m*; **p. cord,** ganse *f*; (ii) liseré *m*, passepoil *m*, nervure *f*; (*on trousers*) baguette *f*; (*c*) *Cu:* décoration (d'un gâteau, etc.) faite avec une douille; **p. nozzle, tube,** douille; **p. bag,** poche *f* à douilles, sac *m* à dresser.

pipistrel(le) [pipi'strel], *s. Z:* pipistrelle *f*.

pipit ['pipit], *s. Orn:* pipit *m*; **tawny p.,** pipit rousseline;

meadow p., pipit des prés; **Indian tree p.,** pipit indien; **Pechora p.,** pipit de la Petchora; **red-throated p.,** pipit à gorge rousse; **Richard's p.,** pipit de Richard; **rock p.,** pipit maritime, pipit obscur; **Scandinavian rock p.,** pipit des rivages; **Sprague's p.,** pipit des prairies; **tree p.,** pipit des arbres; **water p., alpine p.,** *NAm:* **American p.,** pipit spioncelle, *Fr.C:* pipit commun.

pipkin ['pipkin], *s.* casserole *f* en terre; capucine *f*; poêlon *m*; (marmite *f*) huguenote *f*.

pipless ['piplis], *a.* sans pépins.

pippin ['pipin], *s. Hort:* (pomme *f*) reinette *f*.

Pipridae ['pipridi:], *s.pl. Orn:* pipridés *m*.

pipsqueak ['pipskwi:k], *s. F:* **1.** (*pers.*) petit bonhomme de rien du tout; gringalet *m*. **2.** *O:* (*a*) petit obus (à note aiguë); (*b*) petite moto (à note aiguë); petit tacot, petite bagnole, etc., de peu d'apparence.

pipul ['pi:pəl], *s. Bot:* arbre *m* des conseils.

piquancy ['pi:kənsi], *s.* **1.** goût piquant, relevé (d'un mets). **2.** sel *m*, piquant *m* (d'un conte, etc.); **the p. of the situation,** ce qu'il y a de piquant dans l'affaire; le piquant de l'affaire.

piquant ['pi:kənt], *a.* (*of flavour, beauty, anecdote, etc.*) piquant; **p. satire,** satire piquante, mordante; *Cu:* **p. sauce,** sauce piquante.

piquantly ['pi:kəntli], *adv.* avec du piquant; d'une manière piquante.

pique[1] [pi:k], *s.* pique *f*, ressentiment *m*; **in a fit of p.,** dans un accès de pique; **to act in a p.,** agir par pique; **feeling of p.,** sentiment *m* de rancune.

pique[2], *v.tr.* **1.** piquer, offenser, dépiter (qn); **to p. s.o.'s pride,** piquer, blesser, qn dans son orgueil. **2.** piquer, exciter (la curiosité de qn). **3. to p. oneself on sth.,** se piquer de qch.; se glorifier, être fier, de qch.; **to p. oneself on one's generosity,** se piquer de générosité.

pique[3], *s. Cards:* (*at piquet*) pic *m*.

pique[4], *v.i. Cards:* (*at piquet*) faire pic; passer de trente à soixante.

piqué ['pi:kei], *s. Tex:* piqué *m*.

piquet[1] [pi'ket], *s. Cards:* piquet *m*; **to play a hand of p.,** faire, jouer, un piquet.

piquet[2] ['pikit], *s. Mil:* = PICKET[1] 2.

piracy ['paiərəsi], *s.* **1.** piraterie *f*, flibusterie *f*. **2.** atteinte *f* au droit d'auteur; contrefaçon *f* (d'un livre, etc.); pillage *m*, vol *m* (des idées, etc.).

Piraeus (the) [ðəpai'ri:əs], *Pr.n. Geog:* le Pirée.

piragua [pi'rægwə], *s.* pirogue *f*.

piranha, piraña [pi'rɑ:n(j)ə], *s. Ich:* piranha *m*, piraya *m*.

pirarucu [pi'rɑ:rəku:], *s. Ich:* pirarucu *m*, paiche *m*.

pirate[1] ['paiərət], *s.* **1.** (*a*) pirate *m*; forban *m*, flibustier *m*; écumeur *m* (de mer); *Cost:* **p. pants,** pantalon corsaire; (*b*) navire *m* pirate; (*c*) *W.Tel:* **p. station,** poste *m*, émetteur *m*, pirate. **2.** contrefacteur *m*, démarqueur *m* (d'un ouvrage littéraire, d'une œuvre musicale, etc.); voleur *m*, pilleur *m* (d'idées, etc.).

pirate[2]. **1.** *v.i.* (*a*) pirater, flibuster; faire de la piraterie; (*b*) faire de la contrefaçon littéraire ou artistique; faire du démarquage. **2.** *v.tr.* (*a*) saisir (un navire) en pirate, en flibustier; (*b*) s'approprier, voler (une invention, etc.); contrefaire (une marque de fabrique); **to p. a book,** (i) republier un livre sans autorisation; (ii) contrefaire, démarquer, un livre.

piratic(al) [paiə'rætik(l)], *a.* **1.** de pirate, de flibustier. **2.** de contrefacteur; de contrefaçon.

piratically [paiə'rætik(ə)li], *adv.* **1.** en pirate, en flibustier. **2.** en contrefacteur; par contrefaçon.

piratinera [paiərəti'niərə], *s. Bot:* piratinère *m*, piratinera *m*.

pirating ['paiərətiŋ], *s.* **1.** piraterie *f*, flibusterie *f*. **2.** (*a*) saisie *f* (d'un navire) par des pirates; (*b*) contrefaçon *f*; vol *m* (littéraire, etc.); démarquage *m*.

piriform ['pirifɔ:m], *a.* piriforme.

Pirithous [pai'riθouəs], *Pr.n.m. Gr.Myth:* Pirithoos, Pirithoüs.

pirn [pə:n], *s. Scot:* **1.** *Tex:* cannette *f*, sépoule *f*. **2.** bobine *f* (de fil à coudre, etc.).

pirogue [pi'roug], *s.* pirogue *f*.

piroplasm ['pirouplæzm], **piroplasma** [pirou'plæzmə], *s. Prot:* piroplasme *m*.

piroplasmosis, *pl.* **-ses** [pirouplæz'mousis, -si:z], *s. Vet:* piroplasmose *f*.

pirouette[1] [piru'et], *s. Danc:* pirouette *f*.

pirouette[2], *v.i.* pirouetter.

Pirquet ['piəkei]. *Pr.n. Med:* **Pirquet('s) test, Pirquet('s) reaction,** cuti-réaction *f*.

pirssonite ['pə:sənait, 'piə-], *s. Miner:* pirssonite *f*.

Pisa ['pi:zə]. *Pr.n. Geog:* Pise *f*.

Pisan ['pi:zən]. *Geog:* (*a*) *a.* pisan; de Pise; (*b*) *s.* Pisan, -ane.

piscary ['piskəri], *s.* **1.** *Jur:* **common of p.,** droit *m* de pêche. **2.** pêcherie *f*.

piscatorial [piskə'tɔ:riəl], **piscatory** ['piskət(ə)ri], *a.* qui se rapporte à la pêche; (instruments, etc.) de pêche.

Pisces ['piski:z, 'paisi:z], *Pr.n.pl. Astr:* les Poissons *m*.

piscicola [pi'sikələ], *s. Ann:* piscicole *f*.

piscicultural [pisi'kʌltjərəl], *a.* piscicole.

pisciculture ['pisikʌltjər], *s.* pisciculture *f*.

pisciculturist [pisi'kʌltjərist], *s.* pisciculteur *m*.

pisciform ['pisifɔ:m], *a.* pisciforme.

piscina, *pl.* **-as, -ae** [pi'si:nə, -əz, -i:], **piscine**[1] ['pisi:n], *s.* **1.** *Rom.Ant: Ecc:* piscine *f*. **2.** vivier *m*.

piscine[2] ['pisain], *a.* ayant rapport aux poissons; de poisson.

piscivorous [pi'sivərəs], *a.* piscivore.

pisé ['pi:zei], *s. Const:* pisé *m*; **p. built,** en pisé.

Pisgah ['pizgə]. *Pr.n. B:* Pisga.

pish [piʃ], *int. A:* **1.** fi! zut! bah! **2.** pouah!

Pisidia [pai'sidiə]. *Pr.n. A.Geog:* Pisidie *f*.

pisidium [pi'sidiəm], *s. Moll:* pisidie *m*.

pisiform ['paisifɔ:m, 'pizi-]. **1.** *a.* pisiforme. **2.** *s.Anat:* os *m* pisiforme.

Pisistratus [pai'sistrətəs]. *Pr.n.m. Gr.Hist:* Pisistrate.

pisolite ['paisoulait], *s. Miner:* pisolit(h)e *f*; calcaire *m* pisolit(h)ique.

pisolitic [paisou'litik], *a. Geol:* pisolit(h)ique.

piss[1] [pis], *s. P:* pisse *f*, pipi *m*; (*of animals*) pissat *m*; **it's (just) cat's p.,** c'est de la lavasse.

piss[2]. *P:* **1.** *v.i.* (*a*) pisser, faire pipi; (*b*) **p. off!** fous le camp! **2.** *v.tr.* (*a*) pisser (du sang, etc.); (*b*) **to p. out the fire,** éteindre le feu en pissant dessus; (*c*) *U.S:* **money to p. away,** de l'argent à jeter par-dessus la haie.

pissasphalt ['pisæsfælt], *s. Miner:* pissasphalte *m*.

pissed [pist], *a. P:* (*a*) soûl; (*b*) **p. (off),** furieux, en rogne.

pistachio [pis'tɑ:ʃiou], *s. Bot:* (*a*) **p. (nut),** pistache *f*; **p. green,** (vert *m*) pistache (*m*) *inv*; (*b*) **p. (tree),** pistachier *m*.

pistacite ['pistəsait], *s. Miner:* pistacite *f*, pistazite *f*.

pistil ['pistil], *s. Bot:* pistil *m*; gynécée *m*, dard *m*.

pistillary [pis'tiləri], *a. Bot:* pistillaire.

pistillate ['pistileit], *a. Bot:* pistillé, pistillifère; (fleur *f*) femelle.

pistol[1] ['pist(ə)l], *s.* **1.** (*a*) *Sm.a:* pistolet *m*; **air p.,** pistolet à air comprimé; **automatic p.,** pistolet automatique; **cap p.,** pistolet à amorces; **duelling p.,** pistolet de combat; **p. shot,** coup *m* de pistolet; **within p. shot,** à portée de pistolet; **to hold a p. to s.o.'s head,** (i) tenir un pistolet braqué contre la tempe, la nuque, de qn; (ii) *Fig:* mettre à qn le pistolet sous la gorge; **to return p.,** remettre, rengainer, le pistolet; (*b*) *Artil:* **firing p.,** pistolet de tir; (*c*) *Mil: Nau:* **flare p., rocket p.,** pistolet lance-fusées; **signal(ling) p.,** pisolet signaleur, de signalisation. **2.** pistolet (d'un outil pneumatique, etc.); **(paint spraying) p.,** pistolet à peindre; **p. grip,** poignée pistolet (d'un outil); **p.-grip saw,** scie *f* à poignée pistolet.

pistol[2], *v.tr.* (**pistolled**) abattre (qn) d'un coup de pistolet.

pistole [pis'toul], *s. Num:* pistole *f*.

pistoleer [pistə'liər], *s. A.Mil:* pistolier *m*.

piston ['pistən], *s.* (*a*) *Mec.E: Mch: etc:* piston *m*; **air, water, p.,** piston à air, à eau; **floating, free, p.,** piston flottant, libre; **trunk p.,** piston à fourreau; **steam p.,** piston (de machine) à vapeur; **balance, balancing, p.,** piston compensateur, d'équilibre; **valve p.,** piston de soupape; piston à clapet(s); **disc p.,** piston à plateau; **shock-absorber p., dashpot p.,** piston d'amortisseur; **gas-cylinder p.,** piston de cylindre à gaz; **p. engine,** machine *f*, moteur *m*, à pistons; **p. pin,** axe *m* de piston; **p.-pin chamfer, plug,** embout *m* d'axe de piston; **p. displacement,** cylindrée *f*; **p. head,** tête *f*, fond *m*, haut *m*, du piston; **p. ring,** segment *m*, bague *f*, de piston; cercle *m* de contact; **oil-scraper p. ring,** segment racleur d'huile; **taper-faced p. ring,** segment biseauté; **wedge-type p. ring,** segment conique; **p. rod,** tige *f*, verge *f*, de piston; **p. stroke,** (i) course *f* du piston; (ii) coup *m* de piston; **p. clearance,** espace mort, libre, vent *m* (du piston); **p. slap,** claquement *m* du piston; **p. barrel, body,** corps *m* de piston; **p. skirt,** jupe *f* de piston; **full-skirt type p.,** piston à jupe pleine; **p. chamber,** barillet *m* (de pompe); **p. packing,** garnitures *fpl* de piston; **to pack a p.,** garnir un piston; (*b*) *Mus:* piston (d'instrument à vent en cuivre).

pit[1] [pit], *s. NAm:* noyau *m* (de cerise, etc.).

pit[2], *v.tr.* (**pitted**) *NAm:* dénoyauter (des cerises, etc.).

pit[3], *s.* **1.** (*a*) fosse *f*, trou *m*; excavation *f*; (*roughly dug*) fouille *f*; **to dig a p.,** creuser une fosse; *Ind:* **erecting p.,** puits *m* de montage; **settling p.,** fosse de repos; *Metall:* **casting p.,** fosse de coulée (de fonderie); bassin *m* de coulée (d'aciérie); **setting-up p.,** fosse, fouille, de remoulage; **tan p.,** cuve *f*, fosse, à tanner; *Aut: etc:* **inspection p.,** fosse de visite; *Rail:* **working p.,** fosse de travail; *Husb:* **(storage) p.,** silo *m* (de betteraves fourragères, etc.); *Mil:* **machine-gun p.,** épaulement *m* pour mitrailleuse; **rifle p.,** trou individuel de tirailleur; (*b*) *A:* fosse, tombe *f*; **the p.,** l'enfer *m*, les enfers; (*c*) piège *m*, trappe *f*, fosse (à attraper les animaux); *Lit:* **to dig a p. for s.o.,** tendre un piège à qn; (*d*) *Min:* (i) puits *m* (de mine); (ii) mine *f* (de houille); (iii) carrière *f* (à chaux, etc.); **p. prop,** poteau *m*, étai *m*, de mine; chandelle *f*, butte *f*, étançon *m*; **p. boy,** galibot *m*; **p. pony,** cheval *m* de mine; **to work in the pits,** être mineur (de fond); (*e*) *Tls:* **p. saw,** scie *f* de long; (h)arpon *m*, hansard *m*; **p. sawyer,** scieur *m* de long. **2.** (*a*) arène *f*, parc *m* (de combat de coqs); fosse (à ours); (*b*) *Th:* parterre *m*; **orchestra p.,** fosse d'orchestre; (*c*) *NAm:* marché *m* (à la Bourse); **wheat p.,** Bourse des blés; (*d*) *Rac:* **the pits,** les stands *m* de ravitaillement. **3.** (*a*) petite cavité, piqûre *f*, alvéole *m* or *f* (dans un métal, etc.); ponctuation *f*; *Bot: etc:* favéole *f*; *Hort:* **p. sowing,** semis *m* en poquets; (*b*) *Med:* cicatrice *f*, marque *f* (de la petite vérole). **4.** *Anat:* (*a*) pertuis *m*, puits; **buccal p.,** puits vestibulaire; (*b*) **the p. of the stomach,** le creux de l'estomac; l'épigastre *m*. **5.** *Games: O:* (*marbles*) **to play at pits,** jouer au pot, à la bloquette; **the pits,** le pot, la bloquette.

pit[4], *v.tr.* (**pitted**) **1.** mettre (qch.) dans une fosse; *Husb:* ensil(ot)er (l'herbe, etc.). **2.** (*a*) mettre (deux coqs) en parc; faire jouter (des coqs); (*b*) **to p. s.o. against s.o.,** mettre qn aux prises avec qn; opposer qn à qn; **to p. oneself against s.o.,** se mesurer contre qn; **to be pitted against s.o.,** avoir qn comme adversaire. **3.** (*a*) (*of acids, etc.*) piquer, trouer, ronger (le métal, etc.); (*b*) *Med:* (*of smallpox*) grêler, marquer (le visage). **4.** *v.i.* (*of metals*) se piquer.

pita ['pi:tə], *s. Bot:* agave *m* d'Amérique; **p. fibre, p. hemp, p. thread,** fibre *f* d'agave.

Pitangus [pi'tæŋgəs], *s. Orn:* pitangue *m*.

pit-a-pat ['pitə'pæt]. **1.** *adv.* **to go p.-a-p.,** (*of rain, etc.*) crépiter; (*of feet*) trottiner; (*of the heart*) battre, palpiter; faire toc-toc; battre la breloque; **the sound of feet going p.-a-p.,** le bruit de petits pas trottinants. **2.** *s.* crépitement *m* (de la pluie); battement *m* (du cœur); **the p.-a-p. of horses' hoofs,** le bruit rythmé des sabots des chevaux. **3.** *v.i.* **to p.-a-p. about the house,** trottiner, marcher à pas de souris, par la maison.

pitch[1] [pitʃ], *s.* poix *f*; (*from coal-tar*) brai *m*; **mineral p., Jew's p.,** bitume *m* de Judée; spalt *m*; asphalte minéral; **Burgundy p.,** poix de Bourgogne; **navy p.,** goudron *m* à calfater; **p. mop,** penne *f* à brai; guipon *m*; *Nau: F:* **the p. pot,** le pot au noir; *Prov:* **he who touches p. shall be defiled,** d'un sac à charbon ne peut sortir blanche farine; **p. coal,** (i) houille bitumineuse; (ii) *O:* jais *m*; **p. coke,** coke *m* de brai; *Com:* **p. paper,** emballage gras; **p. dark, p. black,** noir comme poix, comme dans un four; **it's p. dark, black,** il fait nuit noire.

pitch[2], *v.tr.* brayer; enduire (qch.) de poix, de brai.

pitch[3], *s.* **1.** lancement *m*, jet *m* (d'une pierre, etc.); *Cr:* **full p.,** balle qui arrive sur le guichet sans avoir rebondi sur le sol; **the ball came full p. at my head,** la balle est venue droit à ma tête; *Games: O:* **p. and toss,** jeu *m* de pile ou face. **2.** (*a*) place *f*, emplacement *m* (dans un marché, etc.); place habituelle (d'un marchand forain, d'un mendiant, etc.); (*b*) *Fish:* **(baited) p.,** coup *m*; (*c*) *Cr:* terrain *m* entre les guichets; **to water the p.,** (i) arroser le terrain; (ii) *Fig:* préparer le terrain; prédisposer qn (en faveur de qch.); (*d*) *NAm:* annonce *f*, émission *f*, publicitaire. **3.** (*a*) *A:* hauteur *f* (à laquelle s'élève un faucon); **to fly at a higher p. than s.o.,** surpasser qn; (*b*) *Arch:* hauteur (du plafond); hauteur sous clef (d'un arc); (*c*) *Mus:* hauteur (d'un son); diapason *m* (d'un instrument); **p. pipe,** diapason à bouche; **he has absolute, perfect, p.,** il a l'oreille absolue; **to give the orchestra the p.,** donner l'accord à un orchestre; **to raise the p. of the piano by a quarter tone,** monter un piano d'un quart de ton; **to rise in p.,** monter de ton; (*of voice, instrument*) **to go off p.,** dérailler; *Ling:* **p. accent,** accent *m* de hauteur; (*d*) degré *m* (d'insolence, etc.); **to such a p. that . . .,** à tel point que . . .; à ce point que . . .; au point que . . .; **to the highest p.,** au plus haut degré; au dernier point; à son comble. **4.** (*a*) pente *f* (d'une colline); pente, rampant *m* (d'un toit, d'un comble, d'un escalier); chute *f*, inclinaison *f* (d'un toit, d'un comble); **p. of the roof rafters,** pente, rampant, des chevrons; *Min:* **p. of a lode,** plongement *m* d'un filon; (*b*) *Tls:* inclinaison, basile *m* (d'un fer de rabot). **5.** (i) tangage *m*, (ii) coup *m* de tangage (d'un navire, d'un avion); **angle of p., p. angle,** angle *m* de tangage; **p. axis,** axe *m* de tangage; *Av:* **p. (attitude),** inclinaison (longitudinale); **p.-attitude indicator,** indicateur *m* de piqué; **p. and bank command,** commande *f* d'assiette et d'inclinaison latérale; **p.-trim control,** réglage *m* d'assiette. **6.** (*a*) espacement *m*, écartement *m* (des rivets); **p. of holes,** écartement des trous; **p. of rivet, hole, centres,** écartement des rivets, des trous, d'axe en axe; (*b*) *Cmptr:* espacement, pas *m* (des perforations d'une carte, etc.); **feed p.,** pas d'entraînement; **row p.,** pas longitudinal; **track p.,** pas transversal; (*c*) pas (d'une roue dentée, d'une scie, d'un engrenage); **p. line,** ligne primitive; ligne d'engrenage, d'engrènement (d'une roue dentée); **p. circle,** cercle primitif; ligne d'engrènement (d'une roue); **p. point,** point *m* de contact des cercles primitifs (d'une denture); **p. surface,** surface primitive (d'une denture); **p. of gear,** pas de la denture; **p. of teeth,** écartement des dents; **arc p., circular p., circumferential p.,** pas circulaire, circonférentiel; **p. arc,** arc *m* d'engrènement, de prise; **p. wheel,** roue d'engrenage; **diametr(ic)al p.,** pas diamétral; module *m*; **bevel-gear p.,** cône primitif d'un pignon conique; **p. of a chain,** pas d'une chaîne; **p. of the track,** pas de la chenille (d'un véhicule chenillé, d'un tracteur); (*d*) *Atom.Ph:* **lattice p.,** pas du réseau; (*e*) *El:* **brush p.,** écartement (angulaire) des balais; **commutator p.,** pas du collecteur (d'une dynamo); **grid p.,** pas de la grille; **pole p.,** pas polaire; **p. of turns,** pas des spires (d'une bobine); **twist p.,** pas de câblage; **winding p.,** d'enroulement, de bobinage; (*f*) pas (d'une vis, d'un boulon); **p. of thread,** pas du filet; **odd p., bastard p.,** pas bâtard; **even p.,** pas exact; **Congress p.,** pas du Congrès; **fine p.,** pas fin; **fine-p. screw,** vis à pas fin; **linear p.,** pas linéaire; **long p., coarse p., quick p.,** pas allongé, rapide; **metric p.,** pas métrique; (*g*) pas (des aubes d'une turbine); pas (d'une hélice, d'un rotor d'hélicoptère); **p. (diameter) ratio,** pas relatif (de l'hélice); **constant, uniform, p.,** pas constant; **nominal p.,** pas nominal; **variable p.,** pas variable; *Nau:* **increasing p.,** pas croissant; **axially increasing p.,** pas croissant axial; **radially increasing p.,** pas croissant radial; *Av:* **(geometric) p.,** avancement *m* (d'une hélice); **coarse p., high p.,** grand pas; **effective p.,** pas effectif; **fine p., low p.,** petit pas; **zero-thrust p., experimental p.,** pas de traction nulle, pas théorique; (*of helicopter rotor*) **collective p.,** pas collectif; **cyclic p.,** pas cyclique; *Av:* **p. setting,** calage *m* du pas (de l'hélice); **p. control,** commande *f* de pas; **p. change,** changement *m* de pas; **p. reversing,** inversion *f* du pas.

pitch[4], *v.*

I. *v.tr.* **1.** (*a*) tendre, dresser, asseoir (une tente); asseoir, établir (un camp); (*b*) *Cr:* planter, dresser (les guichets); **wickets pitched at two o'clock,** la partie commence à deux heures. **2.** *O:* placer, mettre; **to p. a ladder against a building,** poser une échelle contre un bâtiment; **village pitched on a hill,** village perché sur une colline. **3.** *O:* exposer (des marchandises) en vente. **4.** *Civ.E:* (*a*) (i) empierrer, (ii) paver (une chaussée); (*b*) établir la fondation (d'une route). **5.** (*a*) *Mus:* jouer, écrire (un morceau) dans une clef donnée; **these songs are pitched too high, too low, for me,** ces chansons montent trop haut, descendent trop bas, pour ma voix; **to p. one's voice higher, lower,** hausser, baisser, le ton de sa voix; **to p. one's voice correctly,** se mettre dans le ton; bien poser la voix; (*b*) arrêter, déterminer; **to p. an estimate too low,** arrêter trop bas un devis estimatif; **to p. one's aspirations too high,** viser trop haut; *Games:* **to p. sides,** choisir les camps. **6.** jeter, lancer (une balle); (*at baseball*) lancer; **to p. the hay on to the cart,** jeter le foin sur la charrette; charger le foin; *Cr:* **full-pitched ball,** balle *f* à toute volée; *O:* **to be pitched off one's horse,** être désarçonné; **to be pitched about,** être ballotté. **7.** *F:* raconter, débiter (une histoire); **to p. it strong,** exagérer, charger, y aller fort; **you'll have to p. it strong at the meeting,** il faudra leur parler carrément à la réunion; *O:* **to p. it straight to s.o.,** avouer la vérité à qn.

II. *v.i.* **1.** tomber; **to p. onto one's head,** tomber sur sa tête, sur la tête; **the ball pitched on a stone,** le ballon a rebondi sur une pierre. **2.** (*a*) *Nau:* (*of ship*) tanguer; plonger du nez; renvoyer; **to p. heavily astern,** acculer; (*b*) (*of aircraft*) tanguer. **3.** *Mec. E:* (*of cogwheel*) s'engrener (**into,** avec). **4.** (of coal seam, etc.) s'incliner; prendre de la pente; plonger. **5. to p. on sth.,** se décider pour qch.; arrêter son choix sur qch.; choiser qch.; faire choix de qch.; *F:* **to p. in,** (i) se mettre à la besogne; (ii) *U.S:* payer son écot.

III. (*compound verbs*) **1. pitch into,** *v.i. F:* (*a*) (i) taper sur (qn); s'attaquer à (qn); faire une sortie à, contre (qn); tomber (à bras raccourcis) sur (qn); rentrer dedans à (qn); (ii) dire son fait à (qn); **p. into him!** tapez dessus! (*b*) tomber la tête la première dans (une mare, etc.).

2. pitch over, *v.i. F:* (*of pers.*) tomber à la renverse; faire la culbute.

pitchblende ['pitʃblend], *s. Miner:* pechblende *f*, péchurane *m*.

pitched [pitʃt], *a.* **1. p. battle,** bataille rangée. **2.** (*of road*) (i) empierré; (ii) (*with square setts*) pavé.

pitcher[1] ['pitʃər], *s.* **1.** (*a*) cruche *f* (de grès); broc *m*, pichet *m*; *Prov:* **little pitchers have long ears,** les petits enfants ont l'oreille fine; les enfants entendent tout; **the p. goes so often to the well that at last it breaks,** tant va la cruche à l'eau qu'à la fin elle se brise; (*b*) *esp. NAm:* cruchette *f*, cruchon *m*, pot *m* (à lait, etc.). **2.** *Bot: F:* (*a*) ascidie *f*; **p. shaped,** ascidiforme, urcéolé; (*b*) **p. plant,** (i) népenthe *m*, népenthacée *f*; (ii) sarracénie *f*, sarracéniacée *f*; (iii) **(Australian) p. plant,** céphalote *m*.

pitcher[2], *s.* **1.** (*pers.*) (*a*) (*baseball*) lanceur *m* (de la balle); (*hay making*) broqueteur *m*; (*b*) *Com: O:* vendeur, -euse, à l'étalage; étalagiste *mf*; marchand, -ande, en plein air. **2.** pierre *f* à paver; pavé *m* (en grès); caillou, -oux *m* (d'empierrement).

pitcherful ['pitʃəful], *s.* cruchée *f*, plein broc.

pitchfork[1] ['pitʃfɔ:k], *s. Mus:* diapason *m* (en acier).

pitchfork[2], *s. Agr:* fourche *f* (à foin); fouine *f*; (*two-pronged*) bident *m*.

pitchfork[3], *v.tr.* **1.** lancer (une gerbe, etc.) avec la fourche. **2.** *F:* bombarder (qn dans un poste).

pitching[1] ['pitʃiŋ], *a.* **p. ship,** navire qui tangue.

pitching[2], *s.* **1.** dressage *m*, assiette *f* montage *m* (d'une tente); établissement *m* (d'un camp). **2.** (*a*) mise *f* (de qch. dans une position quelconque); (*b*) *O:* mise en vente (des marchandises). **3.** (*a*) (*action*) (i) pavage *m*; (ii) empierrement *m*; (iii) pose *f* de la fondation (d'une chaussée); (*b*) (*result*) (i) pavage, pavé *m*; (ii) empierrement, perré *m*; (iii) fondation. **4.** lancement *m*, jet *m* (*d'une pierre, etc.*); **pitching about,** ballottement *m*. **5.** chute *f*; rebond *m* (d'une balle). **6.** tangage *m* (d'un navire, d'un avion); (*of ship*) **p. by the stern,** acculement *m*; *Av:* **p. stability,** stabilité longitudinale. **7.** *Min:* descente *f*, inclinaison *f* (d'un filon). **8.** *Mec.E:* engrenage *m*, engrénement *m*, prise *f* (de deux pignons).

pitchstone ['pitʃstoun], *s. Miner:* pechstein *m*; rétinite *f*.

pitchy ['pitʃi], *a.* **1.** poisseux, poissé. **2.** noir comme poix.

piteous ['pitiəs], *a.* **1.** *A:* compatissant (**of,** pour). **2.** pitoyable, piteux, apitoyant, misérable, triste.

piteously ['pitiəsli], *adv.* **1.** *A:* avec compassion. **2.** pitoyablement, piteusement, misérablement, tristement.

piteousness ['pitiəsnis], *s.* **1.** *A:* compassion *f*. **2.** état piteux; tristesse *f* (d'une situation, etc.).

pitfall ['pitfɔ:l], *s.* trappe *f*, fosse *f*; piège *m*, attrapoire *f*; **the pitfalls of the English language, of the law,** les traquenards *m*, les pièges, de la langue anglaise, de la procédure.

pith[1] [piθ], *s.* **1.** (*a*) *Bot: Anat:* moelle *f*; *Bot:* médulle *f*; **palm-tree p.,** cervelle *f* de palmier; *Arb:* **p. ray,** rayon *m* médullaire; **p. helmet,** casque (colonial) en sola; (*b*) peau blanche (d'une orange, etc.); (*c*) *A:* moelle épinière. **2.** (*a*) vigueur *f*, force *f*, sève *f*, ardeur *f*; **the p. and marrow of the country,** la force du pays; (*b*) moelle, essence *f*, âme *f*, suc *m* (d'un livre, etc.); piquant *m* (d'une histoire); **to get the p. (and marrow) out of a book,** extraire la moelle (substantifique), la quintessence, d'un livre.

pith[2], *v.tr.* abattre (un bœuf) par énervation.

pithead ['pithed], *s.* bouche *f* de puits; gueulard *m* de mine; carreau *m* (de mine); **p. stock,** stock *m* (de charbon) sur le carreau; **p. price,** prix *m* (du charbon) sur le carreau; **p. baths,** bains *m*, douches *f*, lavabo *m* (à proximité d'une mine).

pithecanthrope, pithecanthropus [piθi'kænθroup, -'kænθrəpəs], *s. Paleont:* pithécanthrope *m*.

pithecism ['piθisizm], *s.* pithécisme *m*.

pithecoid ['piθikɔid], *a. Z:* pithécoïde, simiesque.

pithiatic [piθi'ætik], *a. Med:* pithiatique.

pithiatism ['piθiətizm], *s. Med:* pithiatisme *m*.

pithily ['piθili], *adv.* en un style nerveux, condensé, concis; avec concision.

pithiness ['piθinis], *s.* concision *f*; style nerveux.

pithing ['piθiŋ], *s.* énervation *f* (d'un bœuf).

pithless ['piθlis], *a.* (*a*) (*of orange, etc.*) sans peau blanche; (*b*) mou, *f.* molle; flasque; qui manque de moelle.

pithy ['piθi], *a.* **1.** (*of stem, etc.*) moelleux; à moelle; (*of orange, etc.*) rempli de peau blanche. **2.** (*of style, etc.*) (i) nerveux, concis, succinct, condensé; vigoureux; (ii) substantiel; **p. phrase,** phrase *f* lapidaire.

pitiable ['pitiəbl], *a.* pitoyable, piteux, déplorable; digne de pitié; (*of appearance, objects, furniture*) minable, lamentable; **it's p.!** c'est à faire pitié; **he was in a p. state,** il était dans un état à faire pitié.

pitiableness ['pitiəb(ə)lnis], *s.* état *m* lamentable, pitoyable.

pitiably ['pitiəbli], *adv.* pitoyablement, lamentablement; à faire pitié.

pitiful ['pitiful], *a.* **1.** *O:* compatissant; plein de pitié. **2.** (*a*) pitoyable, lamentable, apitoyant; **it's p. to see him,** il fait pitié; **isn't it p.!** si c'est pas malheureux de voir ça! (*b*) *Pej:* lamentable; à faire pitié.

pitifully ['pitifuli], *adv.* **1.** avec compassion, avec pitié. **2.** (*a*) pitoyablement, piteusement, misérablement; **to cry p.,** pleurer à fendre l'âme; (*b*) *Pej:* lamentablement; à faire pitié.

pitifulness ['pitifulnis], *s.* **1.** compassion *f*, pitié *f*. **2.** = PITIABLENESS.

pitiless ['pitilis], *a.* impitoyable; sans pitié; (vent, froid) cruel.

pitilessly ['pitilisli], *adv.* impitoyablement; sans pitié.

pitilessness ['pitilisnis], *s.* caractère *m* impitoyable; manque *m* de pitié; dureté *f* de cœur; cruauté *f*.

pitman, *pl.* **-men** ['pitmən], *s.* **1.** *Min:* mineur *m*, *esp.* houilleur *m*. **2.** scieur *m* de long. **3.** *Mch: U.S:* (*pl.* **pitmans**) bielle *f*; *Aut:* **p. head,** tête *f* de bielle; **steering p. arm,** levier *m* de commande de direction.

pitometer [pi'tɔmitər], *s. Nau:* **p. (log),** pitomètre *m*.

piton ['pi:tɔ̃], *s. Mount:* piton *m*; **to plant pitons,** pitonner; **p. hammer,** marteau-piolet *m*, *pl.* marteaux-piolets.

Pitot ['pi:tou]. *Pr.n. Av: Nau:* **P. pressure,** pression *f* dynamique; **P. (static) tube,** tube *m* de Pitot; *Av:* **P. venturi airspeed indicator,** indicateur *m* de vitesse Pitot à tube venturi.

pitpan ['pitpæn], *s. U.S:* pirogue *f*.

pitpat ['pitpæt]. = PIT-A-PAT.

pitta ['pitə], *s. Orn:* brève *f*, grive *f* superbe; **blue-banded p.,** brève à ceinture bleue; **New Guinea p., black-headed p.,** brève de Nouvelle-Guinée.

pittance ['pit(ə)ns], *s.* maigre salaire *m*; **to work for a p.,** travailler pour une maigre rétribution, pour un salaire dérisoire; **to be reduced to a mere p.,** être réduit à la portion congrue.

pitted ['pitid], *a.* **1.** (*of metal, etc.*) piqué, troué, gravé, rongé, corrodé, alvéolé (par un acide, etc.); *Biol: Bot:* favéolé; **p. gun,** fusil chambré; **p. bearing,** roulement piqué. **2.** (*of pers.*) grêlé, marqué, picoté, cousu, criblé (par la petite vérole).

pitter-patter[1] ['pitəpætər], *s.* = PATTER[3].

pitter-patter[2], *v.i.* = PATTER[4].

pitticite ['pitisait], *s. Miner:* pittizite *f*.

Pittidae ['pitidi:], *s.pl. Orn:* pittidés *m*.

pitting ['pitiŋ], *s.* **1.** piqûre *f* (d'un métal, etc., par un acide, etc.). **2.** *coll.* marques *fpl* (de la petite vérole sur la peau).

pittinite ['pitinait], *s. Atom.Ph:* pittinite *f*.

pittizite ['pitizait], *s. Miner:* pittizite *f*.

Pittosporaceae [pitouspɔ'reisii:], *s.pl. Bot:* pittosporacées *f*.

pittospore ['pitouspɔər], **pittosporum** [pitou'spɔ:rəm], *s. Bot:* pittosporum *m*.

Pittsburg(h)er ['pitsbə:gər], *s.* habitant, -ante, de Pittsburgh.

pituitary [pi'tju:it(ə)ri], *a. Anat:* pituitaire; **p. gland, body,** hypophyse *f*; glande *f* pituitaire.

pituitous [pi'tju:itəs], *a. Med:* pituiteux.

pity[1] ['piti], *s.* pitié *f*; (*a*) compassion *f*, apitoiement *m*; attendrissement *m*; **to take p. on s.o.,** prendre qn en pitié; prendre pitié de qn; **have p. on us!** ayez pitié de nous! **to feel p. for s.o.,** éprouver de la compassion pour qn; s'apitoyer sur qn; **to move s.o. to p.,** exciter la compassion de qn; apitoyer qn; **to do sth. out of p. for s.o.,** faire qch. par pitié pour qn; **to excite public p.,** exciter la commisération publique; **for pity's sake,** par pitié; de grâce; (*b*) dommage *m*; **what a p.!** quel dommage! quel malheur! **what a p. I didn't know of it!** quel malheur que je ne l'aie pas su! **it's a great p. that. . . ,** il est bien malheureux, il est bien dommage, que . . . .

pity[2], *v.tr.* plaindre (qn); avoir pitié de, s'apitoyer sur, être compatissant pour (qn); **he is to be pitied,** il est à plaindre; il fait pitié; **he's in no mood to be pitied,** il n'est pas en humeur d'être plaint.

pitying ['pitiiŋ], *a.* compatissant; **p. glance,** regard de pitié.

pityingly ['pitiiŋli], *adv.* avec compassion, avec pitié.

pitylus ['pitiləs], *s. Orn:* pityle *m*.

pityriasic [pitiri'æsik], *a. Med:* pityriasique.

pityriasis [piti'raiəsis], *s. Med:* pityriasis *m*; dartres farineuses.

Pius ['paiəs], *Pr.n.m.* Pie.

pivalic [pai'veilik], *a. Ch:* pivalique.

pivot[1] ['pivət], *s.* **1.** pivot *m*; (*a*) *Mec.E: etc:* pivot, axe *m* (de rotation); pivot (d'une grue, etc.); axe (d'articulation); tourillon *m*; **ball p.,** (i) pivot à rotule, tourillon sphérique; (ii) tourillon à billes; **p. bearing,** crapaudière *f*; palier *m* de pied (d'arbre vertical); **p. pin,** axe de pivot, de pivotement; goupille-pivot *f*, *pl.* goupilles-pivots; **p. joint,** (i) *Mec.E:* articulation *f* à pivot; (ii) *Anat:* diarthrose *f* rotatoire; (*b*) pivot, crampon *m* (de dent artificielle); **p. tooth, crown,** dent *f* à pivot; (c) *Mil:* **p. of manœuvre,** pivot de manœuvre; **Verdun was the p. of a wide outflanking movement,** Verdun fut le pivot d'un vaste mouvement débordant. **2.** (*pers.*) pivot, cheville ouvrière (d'une entreprise, etc.); *Mil:* **p. (man),** pivot, guide *m*, homme de base (d'un mouvement d'ordre serré).

pivot², *v.* **(pivoted) 1.** *v.tr.* (a) monter (une pièce) sur pivot; (b) **to p. a fleet,** faire pivoter une flotte. **2.** *v.i.* pivoter, tourner (**on sth.,** sur qch.).

pivotal ['pivətl], *a.* (a) pivotal, -aux; **p. connection,** assemblage *m* à pivot; (b) **p. position, point,** point pivotal, cardinal; position *f* clef.

pivoted ['pivətid], *a.* monté sur pivot; articulé; **p. slipper,** patin (de crosse de piston) articulé.

pivoting¹ ['pivətiŋ], *a.* pivotant; à pivot; *N.Arch:* **p. point,** point *m* giratoire (d'un navire).

pivoting², *s.* (a) pivotement *m*, pivotation *f*; (b) *Dent:* pose *f* d'un crampon, d'un pivot, d'une dent à pivot.

pixie, pixy ['piksi], *s.* (a) lutin *m*, farfadet *m*; (b) fée *f*.

pixil(l)ated ['piksileitid], *a.* **1.** *esp. U.S:* **countryside with a p. charm,** paysage féerique. **2.** *F:* (a) confus, désorienté; (b) un peu fou, cinglé; (c) éméché, rétamé.

Pizarro [pi'zɑ:rou]. *Pr.n. Hist:* Pizarre.

pizza ['pi:tsə], *s.* pizza *f*.

pizzicato [pitsi'kɑ:tou], *a., adv. & s. Mus:* pizzicato (*m*), pincé (*m*).

pizzle ['pizl], *s.* **1.** verge *f* (d'un taureau, etc.). **2.** (*weapon*) **bull's p.,** nerf *m* de bœuf.

placability [plækə'biliti], **placableness** ['plækəbəlnis], *s.* facilité *f* d'humeur; douceur *f*.

placable ['plækəbl], *a.* facile à apaiser; doux; *f.* douce à l'humeur facile.

placard¹ ['plækɑ:d], *s.* écriteau *m*; affiche *f*, placard *m*.

placard², *v.tr.* **1.** couvrir (un mur, etc.) d'affiches; placarder (un mur). **2.** placarder, afficher (une annonce, etc.). **3.** faire de la réclame par affiches pour (qch.); annoncer (une vente, etc.) par affiches.

placarding ['plækɑ:diŋ], *s.* affichage *m*, placardage *m*.

placate [plə'keit], *v.tr.* apaiser, calmer, concilier (qn).

placating [plə'keitiŋ], *a.* = PLACATORY.

placation [plə'keiʃ(ə)n], *s.* apaisement *m*, conciliation *f*.

placatory [plə'keitəri], *a.* conciliatoire, propitiatoire.

place¹ [pleis], *s.* **1.** (a) lieu *m*, endroit *m*; **a pleasant p.,** un endroit agréable; **when we find a quiet p.,** quand nous trouverons un endroit tranquille; **this would be an ideal p. for a picnic,** voilà un endroit idéal pour piqueniquer; **this is the p.!** nous voilà (arrivés)! c'est là! **finally we came to a p. where . . .,** nous sommes arrivés enfin à un endroit, un lieu, où . . .; **before I leave this p.,** avant de partir d'ici; **to move from one p. to another,** se déplacer d'un lieu, d'un endroit, à un autre; **to move from p. to p.,** aller de-ci, de-là; se déplacer souvent; *F:* **to go places,** (i) sortir beaucoup; (ii) voir du pays et du monde; (iii) réussir (dans la vie); **in another p.,** (i) dans un autre endroit, lieu; autre part, ailleurs; (ii) *Parl: F:* (α) à la Chambre des Lords; (β) à la Chambre des Communes; **in any other p.,** n'importe où ailleurs; dans n'importe quel autre endroit; *Sch: F:* **the other p.,** (i) (*at Oxford*) Cambridge; (ii) (*at Cambridge*) Oxford; *F: A:* **to go to one's p.,** *O:* **to go to the other p.,** mourir, aller ad patres; **p. of refuge,** lieu de refuge; **p. of arrival,** point *m* d'arrivée; **in proper time and p.,** en temps et lieu; **one can't be in two places at once,** on ne peut pas être à deux endroits à la fois; on ne peut pas être à la fois au four et au moulin; **all over the p.,** partout; **he leaves his things all over the p.,** il laisse traîner ses affaires partout, dans tous les coins, de tous les côtés; **they've been looking for you all over the p.,** on vous a cherché partout; (b) **p. of amusement,** lieu de divertissement; **p. of worship,** église *f*; temple *m*, etc.; **my p. of work,** l'endroit où je travaille; mon bureau, etc.; **market p.,** place *f* du marché; **meeting p.,** (lieu de) rendez-vous *m inv*; (c) localité *f*; ville *f*, village *m, etc.;* **p. name,** nom *m* de lieu; **a little country p.,** un petit village, coin, rustique; **seaside p.,** plage *f*; station *f* balnéaire; **Whitstable is a great p. for oysters,** Whitstable est un grand centre pour les huîtres, est très réputé pour ses huîtres; **interesting places, places of interest,** des endroits intéressants; des ville intéressantes; des monuments intéressants; **a p. well worth a visit, well worth visiting, that you ought to see,** un endroit, une ville, qui vaut la visite; **the p. we live in,** (i) la ville, le village, où nous habitons; (ii) notre maison, notre appartement; (d) maison *f*, etc.; **p. of residence,** résidence *f*; demeure *f*; domicile (réel); **he has a p. in Kent,** il a une résidence, un manoir, un château, une maison de campagne, dans le Kent; **a little p. in the country,** une petite maison à la campagne; *F:* **come round to my p.,** venez (jusque) chez moi; **p. of ill repute,** endroit mal famé, mal fréquenté; **this is no p. for you,** vous n'avez que faire ici; **we must find a less expensive p.,** il nous faut trouver un endroit, un hôtel, un magasin, etc., moins cher; *F:* **his usual p. of call,** son café, bistro, préféré; *Mil:* **fortified p.,** place forte, place de guerre; (e) (*in street names*) cour *f*, passage *m*, rue *f*, ruelle *f*; (f) *Fin: Bank:* place; **p. of payment,** lieu de paiement; *St.Exch:* (*in quotation*) **place: London, Paris,** devises: Londres, Paris. **2.** place; (a) **a p. for everything and everything in its p.,** une place pour chaque chose et chaque chose à sa place; **to find a p. for sth.,** trouver une place pour qch.; **I can't find a p. for this new chest of drawers,** je n'arrive pas à caser cette nouvelle commode; **to hold sth. in p.,** tenir qch. en place; assujettir qch.; **this book is out of p., not in its (proper) p.,** ce livre est déplacé, n'est pas à sa place; **put it back in its p.,** remettez-le à sa place; **you've put it back in the wrong p.,** vous ne l'avez pas remis à sa place; **this remark is out of p.,** cette observation est déplacée, est hors de propos, mal à propos; (*of pers.*) **to look out of p.,** avoir l'air dépaysé; (b) **to book a p.,** réserver une place; **if I get there first I'll keept a p. for you,** si j'y arrive le premier je te garderai une place; **please take my p.!** prenez ma place, je vous en prie; **to change places with s.o.,** changer de place avec qn; *Sch: A:* **free p.** = bourse *f* (d'études); **there isn't enough p. for five in our car,** il n'y a pas assez de place pour cinq personnes dans notre voiture; **radio has given p. to television,** la radio a cédé la place à la télévision; **his anger gave p. to pity,** sa colère a fait place à un sentiment de pitié; (c) (*at table*) **p. (setting),** couvert *m*; **to lay an extra p.,** mettre un couvert supplémentaire; (*to frequent guest*) **you know your p.,** prenez votre place habituelle; **p. mat** = napperon (individuel); **p. card,** carte portant le nom du convive; (d) (*situation*) **put yourself in my p.,** mettez-vous à ma place; **if I were in your p. I should go,** à votre place, j'irais; (e) **to take p.,** avoir lieu; se passer; arriver; se produire; se faire; **the marriage will not take p.,** le mariage ne se fera pas; **many changes have taken p.,** il y a eu beaucoup de changements; **it took p. ten years ago,** cela s'est passé il y a dix ans; **the demonstration took p. without disturbance,** la manifestation s'est déroulée sans désordre; **while this was taking p.,** tandis que cela se passait; sur ces entrefaites; **the collision took p. at midnight,** la collision a eu lieu à minuit; **a struggle was taking p. in his mind,** il luttait dans son esprit. **3.** (a) place, rang *m*; **to hold the first p.,** tenir, occuper, le premier rang; **he has taken his p. among the famous writers of the century,** il a pris rang, il compte, parmi les écrivains célèbres de ce siècle; **his name has a p. in history,** son nom a pris place dans l'histoire; **to keep s.o. in his p.,** garder les distances avec qn; éviter des familiarités; *O:* **to keep one's p., to know one's p.,** observer les distances; *F:* **I'll put him in his p.!** je vais le remettre à sa place! je vais lui rabattre le caquet! (b) **in the first p.,** d'abord, en premier lieu; **in the second p.,** en second lieu; **in the next p.,** ensuite, puis; *Turf:* **to back a horse for a p.,** jouer un cheval placé; (c) *Mth:* **to three places of decimals,** à trois décimales; **correct to five places of decimals, to five decimal places,** exact jusqu'à la cinquième décimale. **4.** (a) *A:* place, poste *m*, emploi *m*, situation *f*; (b) **to take s.o.'s p.,** remplacer qn; remplir les fonctions de qn; **it's not my p. to do it,** ce n'est pas à moi de le faire. **5.** (a) endroit; **damp p.,** tache *f* d'humidité (sur un mur, etc.); **weak p. in a beam,** endroit défectueux d'une poutre; **a sore p. (on one's arm, etc.),** (i) un endroit sensible, douloureux, (ii) une plaie, *F:* un bobo (sur le bras, etc.); **in places,** par endroits; **let's hope the audience will laugh in the right places,** espérons que les spectateurs riront au bon endroit; (b) *Rugby Fb:* **p. kick,** coup de pied placé; (c) (*in a book*) **to lose, find, one's p.,** perdre, retrouver, la page.

place², *v.tr.* **1.** placer, mettre; (a) **to p. a board, a gun, in position,** mettre une planche, une pièce (d'artillerie), en position; **to p. a book back on a shelf,** remettre un livre (en place) sur un rayon; **to p. concrete,** couler du béton (en place); **to p. one's seal on a document,** apposer son sceau à un document; **to p. an amount (of money) to s.o.'s credit,** placer une somme au crédit de qn; **this exhibit is badly placed,** cet objet est mal exposé; **the house is well, badly, placed,** la maison est bien, mal, située; **strategically placed airfields,** des champs d'aviation stratégiquement situés; (b) (*of pers.*) **to be awkwardly placed,** être dans une situation délicate, difficile; **you can see how I'm placed,** vous voyez, comprenez, ma situation; (c) **to p. a book with a publisher,** faire accepter un livre par un éditeur; **my play is placed,** ma pièce est acceptée; *Com: Fin:* **to p. goods, shares,** placer, vendre, des marchandises, des actions; **difficult to p.,** de vente, d'écoulement, difficile; difficile à vendre, à écouler; **to p. an order (for goods),** placer, passer, une commande; **to p. a loan,** placer, négocier, un emprunt; **to p. £10,000 in bonds,** placer £10,000 en obligations; **to p. a contract,** adjuger, concéder, un contrat; **to p. a bet,** faire un pari; (d) confier; **to p. a matter in s.o.'s hands,** mettre une affaire dans les mains de qn; confier une affaire à qn; **I'll p. myself at your disposal,** je me mets à votre service, à votre disposition; **this placed me in his power,** cela m'a mis à sa merci; **he has been placed in command,** on lui a confié le commandement; **to p. a child in s.o.'s care,** confier un enfant à la garde, aux soins, de qn; **to p. a child with foster parents,** placer un enfant chez des parents adoptifs. **2.** donner un emploi à (qn); **I could p. her as a typist,** je pourrais la prendre, la caser, comme dactylo; **after we had placed two more men on the job,** après avoir mis deux ouvriers supplémentaires à la tâche. **3. I would p. him among the outstanding biographers of the century,** je le mettrais, le classerais, parmi les meilleurs biographes du siècle; *Sch: Sp: etc:* **to be placed third,** se classer troisième; *Turf:* **placed horse,** cheval placé. **4.** (a) assigner une date à (qch.); **details which enable us to p. this tomb at the beginning of the tenth century B.C.,** détails qui nous permettent de dater ce tombeau du commencement du dixième siècle avant Jésus-Christ; (b) **to p. a sound,** localiser un son; établir d'où vient un son; (c) **I know his face but I can't p. him,** je le reconnais de vue mais je ne sais pas où je l'ai rencontré, je ne sais pas qui c'est, comment il s'appelle; je ne peux pas le remettre.

placebo [plæ'si:bou], *s.* **1.** *Med:* placebo *m*, remède *m* factice. **2.** *R.C.Ch:* vêpres *fpl* pour les morts.

placeman, *pl.* **-men** ['pleismən], *s.m. O: usu. Pej:* (a) fonctionnaire, homme en place (qui ne cherche que son propre intérêt); (b) arriviste.

placement ['pleismənt], *s. esp. U.S:* placement *m* (de qch., de qn, *Fin:* des capitaux, *Sp:* d'une balle).

placenta [plə'sentə], *s.* (a) *Bot:* placenta *m*, trophosperme *m*; (b) *Anat:* placenta; gâteau *m* placentaire.

placental [plə'sent(ə)l]. **1.** *a. Bot: Anat:* placentaire; *Z:* **p. barrier,** barrière placentaire; **p. murmur,** murmure *m* placentaire; **p. vessels,** vaisseaux *m* placentaires. **2.** *s. Z:* placentaire *m*.

Placentalia [plæsen'teiliə], *s.pl. Z:* placentaires *m*.

placentary [plə'sentəri], *a. & s. Bot: Anat:* placentaire (*m*).

placentation [plæsen'teiʃ(ə)n], *s. Bot: Anat:* placentation *f*.

placentiferous [plæsen'tifərəs], *a.* placentifère.

placentiform [plə'sentifɔ:m], *a.* placentiforme.

placentography [plæsen'tɔgrəfi], *s. Med:* placentographie *f*.

placentoma [plæsen'toumə], *s. Med:* placentome *m*.

placer ['pleisər], *s. Geol: Min:* placer *m*; gisement alluvial, *esp.* gisement aurifère; *Min:* **placers,** chantier *m* de lavage.

placet ['plæset], *s. Sch: O:* assentiment *m*, sanction *f*.

placid ['plæsid], *a.* placide, calme, tranquille, serein.

placidity [plæ'siditi], **placidness** ['plæsidnis], *s.* placidité *f*, calme *m*, tranquillité *f*, sérénité *f*.

placidly ['plæsidli], *adv.* placidement; tranquillement.

Placidus ['plæsidəs]. *Pr.n.m. Rel.H:* Placide.

placing ['pleisiŋ], *s.* **1.** (a) placement *m*, mise *f* en place (de qch.); (b) **p. of concrete,** coulage *m* (en place) du béton; **p. by gravity,** coulage par gravité. **2.** placement *m*, écoulement *m*, vente *f* (de marchandises, d'actions); placement (d'un emprunt).

placket ['plækit], *s. Dressm:* **1. p. (hole),** fente *f* de jupe. **2.** poche *f*, pochette *f* (de jupe).

placoderm ['plækoudə:m], *s. Paleont:* placoderme *m*.

Placodermi [plækou'də:mi], *s.pl. Paleont:* placodermes *m*.

placodont ['plækoudɔnt], *s. Paleont:* placodonte *m*.

Placodontia [plækou'dɔnʃiə], *s.pl. Paleont:* placodontes *m*.

placoid ['plækɔid], *a. & s. Ich:* placoïde (*m*).

placuna [plæ'kju:nə], *s. Moll:* placune *f*.

plagal ['pleigəl], *a. Mus:* plagal, -aux; **p. cadence,** cadence plagale; **the p. modes,** les modes plagaux (du plain-chant).

plagiarism ['pleidʒiərizm], *s.* **1.** (habitude *f* du) plagiat; démarquage *m*. **2.** plagiat; larcin *m* littéraire.

plagiarist ['pleidʒiərist], *s.* plagiaire *mf*; démarqueur *m*.

plagiarize ['pleidʒiəraiz], *v.tr.* plagier (une œuvre, un auteur); faire un plagiat à, contrefaire (une œuvre); *v.i.* se livrer à des plagiats; **preacher who plagiarizes Bossuet,** prédicateur *m* plagiaire de Bossuet.

plagiary ['pleidʒiəri], *s.* **1.** *A:* = PLAGIARIST. **2.** = PLAGIARISM.

plagiocephalic, plagiocephalous [pleidʒiouse'fælik, -'sefələs], *a. Med:* plagiocéphale.

plagiocephaly [pleidʒiou'sefəli], *s. Med:* plagiocéphalie *f*.

plagioclase ['pleidʒioukleis], *s. Miner:* plagioclase *f.*
Plagiostomata [pleidʒiou'stoumətə], *s.pl. Ich:* plagiostomes *m.*
plagiostome ['pleidʒioustoum], *s. Ich:* plagiostome *m*; sélacien *m.*
Plagiostomi(a) [pleidʒi'ɔstəmi, pleidʒiou'stoumiə], *s.pl. Ich:* plagiostomes *m.*
plagiotropic, plagiotropous [pleidʒiou'trɔpik, pleidʒi'ɔtrəpəs], *a. Bot:* plagiotrope.
plagiotropism [pleidʒi'ɔtrəpizm], *s. Bot:* plagiotropisme *m.*
plagiotropy [pleidʒi'ɔtrəpi], *s. Bot:* plagiotropie *f.*
plague[1] [pleig], *s.* **1.** fléau *m*; **the ten plagues of Egypt,** les dix plaies *f* d'Égypte; *B:* **as many as had plagues,** tous ceux qui étaient affligés de quelque mal; *F:* **what a p. that child is!** c'est une peste que cet enfant! **mosquitoes are the p. of our lives here,** ici les moustiques sont un fléau, les moustiques empoisonnent l'existence. **2.** peste *f*; **p. bacillus,** bacille pesteux; **p.-bearing rat,** rat pesteux; **p. spot,** (i) lésion, tache, occasionnée par la peste; (ii) foyer *m* d'infection; **p.-stricken,** (i) (pays, etc.) frappé de la peste, dévasté par la peste; (ii) (*of pers.*) pestiféré; *Vet:* **cattle p.,** peste bovine; *F:* **to avoid s.o. like the p.,** fuir qn comme la peste, comme un pestiféré; *A:* **a p. on him! p. take him!** la (male)peste soit de lui! diantre soit de lui!
plague[2], *v.tr.* **1.** *A:* frapper (qn, un pays) d'un fléau; *B:* **the Lord plagued Pharaoh and his house with great plagues,** l'Eternel frappa de grandes plaies Pharaon et sa maison. **2.** *F:* tourmenter, harceler, tirailler, embêter, raser, bassiner, asticoter (qn); **to p. s.o.'s life,** être le fléau de qn; empoisonner l'existence de qn; **to p. s.o. with questions,** harceler, assommer, qn de questions.
plaguesome ['pleigsəm], *a.* = PLAGUY.
plaguily ['pleigili], *adv. O:* diablement, rudement.
plaguing ['pleigiŋ], *s.* harcèlement *m.*
plaguy ['pleigi], *a. A:* maudit, fâcheux, assommant; **his p. scruples,** ses diables de scrupules; *adv.* **a p. long time,** rudement longtemps, diablement longtemps.
plaice [pleis], *s. Ich:* carrelet *m*; plie (franche).
plaid [plæd, *Scot:* pleid], *s.* **1.** (*a*) *Scot: Cost:* plaid *m*; couverture *f* servant de manteau; (*b*) couverture de voyage en tartan. **2.** *Tex:* tartan *m*, écossais *m.*
plaided ['plædid, *Scot:* 'plei-], *a.* (*a*) (*of pers.*) portant un plaid; enveloppé dans un plaid; (*b*) (vêtement) fait de tartan.
plain [plein], *a., adv. & s.*
I. *a.* **1.** *A:* plat, plan; **p. ground,** terrain plat. **2.** (*a*) clair, évident, distinct; **to make sth. p. to s.o.,** faire comprendre qch. à qn; **it's (all) perfectly p.,** c'est tout à fait, parfaitement, clair; **as p. as (p.) can be, as p. as daylight, as p. as a pikestaff,** *F:* **as p. as the nose on your face,** c'est on ne peut plus clair; c'est clair comme le jour, comme l'eau de roche; **it was p. that he didn't want to do it,** il était clair, évident, qu'il ne voulait pas le faire; **to make one's meaning perfectly p.,** se faire bien comprendre; mettre les points sur les i; **in (good) p. English,** en bon anglais; **I thought I was speaking p. English, I thought I was making my meaning p.,** je croyais que je m'exprimais (assez) clairement; **don't you understand p. English?** tu ne comprends pas quand je parle anglais? *Com:* **marked in p. figures,** marqué en chiffres connus; (*b*) (*not in code*) **p. text,** texte *m* en clair; *s.* **in p.,** en clair. **3.** (*a*) (style) simple, uni; (mobilier) simple; (cigarettes) sans filtre; **p. (post)card,** carte *f* de correspondance; **under p. cover,** sous pli discret; **p. drawing,** dessin *m* au trait; **p. wood,** bois cru; **p. dress,** robe simple; **in p. clothes,** en civil; **p.-clothes policeman,** agent *m* en civil; *Knit:* **one p. (stitch), one purl,** une maille à l'endroit, une maille à l'envers; **p. knitting,** (i) point *m* jersey; (ii) point mousse; (*b*) uni; lisse; **p. surface,** surface lisse, unie; **p. paper,** papier non réglé; *Tex:* **p. material,** tissu (i) uni, (ii) (de teinte) uni(e); **p. velvet,** velours plain, uni; *Arch:* **p. column,** colonne *f* lisse; *Mec.E:* **p. bearing,** portée lisse; **p. tube,** tube *m* lisse; **p. barrel,** (i) *Artil:* tube lisse; (ii) *Sm.a:* canon *m* lisse; **p. roll(er),** cylindre *m* lisse (de laminoir, etc.); **p. flange,** joint plat; (*c*) **p. sewing,** couture *f* simple; **p. cooking,** cuisine simple, bourgeoise; **I like my cooking p.,** j'aime une cuisine simple; **she's an excellent p. cook,** elle fait une cuisine bourgeoise excellente; **p. boiled beef,** bœuf bouilli nature, au naturel; **p. cake,** (i) = gâteau *m* de Savoie; (ii) = quake quarts *m*; **p. chocolate,** chocolat *m* à croquer; chocolat fondant; **p. black coffee,** café noir (sans sucre); **p. bread and butter,** des tartines simplement beurrées; **p. living,** vie simple; **I haven't any other names, just p. David,** je n'ai pas d'autres prénoms; je m'appelle David tout court; (*d*) **the p. truth,** la franche, pure, simple, vérité; la vérité brutale; **I'll be quite p. with you,** je vais vous parler franchement, sans détours; **to give a p., unvarnished account of sth., to stick to the p. facts,** raconter qch. tel quel, simplement, sans broder, sans l'enjoliver; s'en tenir à la stricte réalité, à la réalité pure et simple; **p. answer,** réponse carrée; **that's a p. (enough) answer,** voilà qui est net; **p. speech, p. speaking,** le franc-parler; **to be p. (spoken) with s.o.,** être franc, carré; user d'une franchise (brutale) (avec qn); **it's p. common sense,** c'est du gros bon sens; **p. dealing,** procédés *m* honnêtes; franchise; sincérité *f*; **I'm a p. man,** je ne fais pas de cérémonies; je dis ce que je pense; (*e*) **p. country people,** de simples campagnards; **the p. man,** l'homme ordinaire. **4.** (*of pers.*) sans beauté; **to be p.,** manquer de beauté; (*of woman*) **p. but attractive,** sympathique sans être belle; **she looks plainer than ever,** elle a enlaidi; **a p. Jane,** une jeune fille au visage plutôt quelconque.
II. *adv. F:* **1.** clairement, distinctement; **I can't speak any plainer,** je ne peux pas m'exprimer plus clairement; **you're not speaking p. enough,** je ne vous comprends pas. **2.** franchement; **to speak p.,** parler franc, sans détours.
III. *s.* **1.** *Geog:* (i) plaine *f*; (ii) prairie *f*; **high plains,** les hautes plaines; **in the open p.,** en rase campagne; **base-level p.,** plaine de niveau de base; **piedmont p.,** plaine de piedmont; **alluvial p.,** plaine alluviale; (*of river*) **flood p.,** plaine d'inondation; **the Great Plains,** la Prairie (américaine). **2.** *Fr.Hist:* **the P.,** la Plaine.
plainchant ['pleintʃɑ:nt], *s.* = PLAINSONG.
plainly ['pleinli], *adv.* **1.** clairement; manifestement; distinctement; évidemment; **to see sth. p.,** voir qch. distinctement, nettement; **I can see p. that . . .,** il est évident, cela saute aux yeux, que . . .; **to speak p.,** parler distinctement, clairement; **p. I was not wanted,** il était évident, clair, que j'étais de trop; **it is p. your duty to do it,** il est évident que c'est votre devoir de le faire. **2.** (*a*) simplement; **to live p.,** (i) vivre modestement, simplement; (ii) se contenter d'une cuisine simple; **to dress p.,** s'habiller simplement, sans recherche; (*b*) franchement, carrément, sans détours; **to speak p.,** parler carrément; user de franchise, du franc-parler; **it is better to speak p.,** mieux vaut nommer les choses par leur nom; **to put it p., you refuse,** tranchons le mot, pour parler clairement, carrément, vous refusez.
plainness ['pleinnis], *s.* **1.** clarté *f* (de langage); netteté *f* (des objets lointains); évidence *f* (des preuves). **2.** (*a*) simplicité *f* (de vie, etc.); **p. of furniture,** simplicité de mobilier; **p. of dress,** absence *f* de recherche dans la toilette; simplicité de mise; (*b*) franchise *f*, rondeur *f* (de langage). **3.** manque *m* de beauté.
plainsman, *pl.* **-men** ['pleinzmən], *s.m.* homme, habitant, de la plaine.
plainsong ['pleinsɔŋ], *s. Mus:* plain-chant *m*, *pl.* plains-chants.
plaint [pleint], *s.* **1.** *Jur:* plainte *f.* **2.** *Poet:* plainte, lamentation *f*, gémissement *m.*
plaintiff ['pleintif], *s. Jur:* demandeur, -eresse; poursuivant, -ante; plaignant, -ante; partie plaignante, requérante.
plaintive ['pleintiv], *a.* plaintif.
plaintively ['pleintivli], *adv.* plaintivement; d'un ton plaintif.
plaintiveness ['pleintivnis], *s.* ton plaintif.
plait[1] [plæt], *s.* **1.** *A: usu.* [pli:t] = PLEAT[1]. **2.** (*a*) natte *f*, tresse *f* (de cheveux, de paille, etc.); ganse *f* (de cheveux); **hair braided in small plaits,** cheveux tressés en cordelettes; (*b*) *Med:* **Polish p.,** plique polonaise.
plait[2], *v.tr.* **1.** *A: usu.* [pli:t] = PLEAT[2]. **2.** natter, tresser (les cheveux, de la paille, etc.); *Hatm:* ourdir (la paille).
plaited ['plætid], *a.* **1.** *A:* = PLEATED. **2.** natté, tressé; en natte(s), en tresse(s).
plaiting ['plætiŋ], *s.* **1.** *A:* = PLEATING. **2.** (*a*) nattage *m*, tressage *m*; *Hatm:* ourdissage *m*; (*b*) (i) natte *f*, tresse *f*; (ii) *coll.* nattes, tresses.
plan[1] [plæn], *s.* **1.** (*a*) plan *m* (d'un bâtiment, d'une installation, etc.); **p. and elevation,** plan et élévation *f*; **ground p.,** plan géométral; **sketch p.,** plan sommaire; croquis *m*; **to draw a p.,** tracer, dessiner, un plan; *Mch: etc:* **erection p.,** plan d'assemblage; *N.Arch:* **lines p.,** plan des formes; **body p.,** plan des couples, plan latitudinal; **half-breadth p.,** projection horizontale, plan des lignes d'eau; **sheer p.,** plan longitudinal; **capacity p.,** plan des capacités; (*b*) *Surv:* plan, levé *m* (d'un terrain); **town p.,** plan de ville, plan urbain; **street p.,** plan des rues; (*c*) cadre *m*, plan (d'un roman, etc.); **to work out the p. of a speech,** faire le plan d'un discours; (*d*) *For:* **this year's felling p.,** l'assiette *f* des coupes de cette année. **2.** projet *m*, dessein *m*, plan; **general p.,** plan d'ensemble; **preliminary p.,** avant-projet *m*, *pl.* avant-projets; **p. of attack, of battle,** plan d'attaque, de bataille; **p. of campaign,** plan de campagne; *F:* **what's the p. of campaign for today?** quels sont les projets pour aujourd'hui? qu'est-ce que nous allons faire aujourd'hui? *Mil: etc:* **logistic p.,** plan logistique; **p. of manœuvre,** plan de manœuvre; *Fin:* **investment p.,** plan d'investissement; *Pol.Ec:* **economic p.,** plan économique; **five year p.,** plan quinquennal; *Adm:* **development p.,** plan d'aménagement; **zoning p.,** plan de servitudes; *Av:* **flight p.,** plan de vol; *esp. NAm:* (*hotel reservation*) **European p.,** chambre *f* (sans pension); **American p.,** pension complète; **to draw up, work out, a p.,** faire, établir, un plan, un projet; **to carry out a p.,** exécuter un plan, un projet; mettre un plan, un projet, à exécution, en application; **to change one's plans,** changer de dessein; **to have no fixed plan(s),** ne pas avoir de plan, de projet, bien déterminé; **everything went according to p.,** tout a marché, s'est déroulé, selon les prévisions, comme prévu; **the best p. would be to . . .,** le mieux serait de . . .; **it's not a bad p.,** ce n'est pas une mauvaise idée; **it would be a good p. to . . .,** ce serait une bonne idée, on ferait bien, de . . .; **what are your plans for the summer?** quels sont vos projets pour cet été? qu'est-ce que vous allez faire cet été? **your suggestions do not fit in with our plans,** vos propositions ne cadrent pas avec nos plans, nos projets.
plan[2], *v.* **(planned) 1.** *v.tr.* (*a*) faire, tracer, dessiner, le plan de (qch.); **the school was planned for 500 pupils,** l'école a été prévue pour 500 élèves; (*b*) faire, établir, élaborer, le plan de (son nouveau roman, etc.); **to p. a piece of work,** faire le plan d'un travail; (*c*) *Pol.Ec:* planifier (la production, etc.). **2.** *v.tr.* projeter (un voyage, etc.); combiner (une attaque, une évasion, etc.); comploter, tramer (un crime); **to p. to do sth.,** former le projet de faire qch.; **I'm planning to go,** *F:* **I p. going, to Paris in May,** j'espère aller à Paris en mai; **to p. everything ahead,** tout arranger d'avance; **he had planned it all (out),** il en avait établi tous les détails; **to p. one's time,** établir son emploi du temps; **they were planning to rob a bank,** ils faisaient des plans pour voler une banque; **we had planned for you to stay until tomorrow,** nous pensions, nous avions dans l'idée, que vous alliez rester jusqu'à demain. **3.** *v.i.* faire des projets; **to p. for the future,** (i) faire des projets pour l'avenir; (ii) songer à l'avenir.
planar ['pleinər], *a. Mth:* planaire; **p. co-ordinates,** coordonnées *f* planaires; **p. graph,** graphe *m* planaire.
Planaria [plə'nɛəriə], *s.pl. Ann:* planaires *f.*
planarian [plə'nɛəriən], *s. Ann:* planaire *f.*
planariform [plə'nɛərifɔ:m], *a. Ann:* planariforme.
planarioid [plə'nɛərioid], *a. Ann:* planarioïde.
planarity [plə'næriti], *s. Mth:* planarité *f.*
planation [plæ'neiʃ(ə)n], *s. Geol:* arasement *m*; aplanissement *m* de la terre (par l'érosion).
planchéite ['plænʃeiait], *s. Miner:* planchéite *f.*
planchet ['plænʃit], *s. Num:* flan *m.*
planchette [plæn'ʃet], *s.* planchette *f*; oui-ja *m.*
Planck [plæŋk]. *Pr.n. Ph:* **Planck('s) constant,** constance *f* de Planck; **Planck('s) radiation law, distribution law,** loi *f* de radiation, de rayonnement, de Planck.
planctivorous [plæŋk'tivərəs], *a. Nat.Hist:* planctonophage.
plancton ['plæŋktən], *s. Nat.Hist:* plancton *m.*
plane[1] [plein], *a.* (*a*) plan, uni; égal, -aux; plat; **p. surface,** surface plane; *Nau:* **p. chart,** carte plane, plate; (*b*) *Mth: etc:* **p. curve,** courbe plane; **p. angle,** angle plan, rectiligne; **p. triangle,** triangle plan, rectiligne; **p. geometry,** géométrie plane; **p. trigonometry,** trigonométrie rectiligne; **p. vector,** vecteur *m* planaire; (*c*) *Ph:* **p. flow,** écoulement plan (d'air); **p. wave,** onde plane; **p. mirror,** miroir plan; *Atom.Ph:* **p. source,** source plane, émetteur plan (de neutrons); *W.Tel:* **p. reflector antenna,** antenne *f* à réflecteur plan.
plane[2], *s.* **1.** (*a*) *Mth: etc:* plan *m*; **axial p.,** plan axial; **geometric p., ground p.,** plan géométrique; **horizontal p.,** plan horizontal; **vertical p.,** plan vertical; **mid p.,** plan médian; **cutting p.,** plan sécant; **perpendicular p., tangent p.,** plan perpendiculaire, tangent; **p. of projection,** plan de projection; *Mec:* **p. of spin,** plan de rotation; *Draw: etc:* **perspective p.,** plan perspectif; **picture p., p. of delineation,** (plan du) tableau *m*; *Surv:* **datum p.,** plan de référence; *Astr:* **p. of the ecliptic,** plan de l'écliptique; **p. of the celestial equator,** plan de l'équateur céleste; *Opt: etc:* **image p.,** plan image (d'une lentille); **p. of incidence,** plan d'incidence; **p. of reflection, of refraction,** plan de réflexion, de réfraction; **focal p.,** plan focal; *Magn:* **p. of polarization,** plan de polarisation; **p. polarization,** polarisation *f* rectiligne, dans un plan; **p. polarized,** polarisé dans un plan, rectilignement; *Ball:* **p. of defilade,** plan de défilement; **p. of fire,** plan de tir; **p. of sight,** plan de visée, de site; **p. of site,** plan de site; (*b*) *Geol:* **bedding**

p., p. of stratification, plan de stratification; fault p., plan de faille; joint p., plan de diaclase, de séparation; thrust p., plan de charriage, de poussée; p. of fracture, plan de cassure, de fracture; *Miner:* p. of a crystal, plan d'un cristal; cleavage p., plan de clivage; slip p., gliding p., plan de glissement; twinning p., plan d'hémitropie; p. of symmetry, plan de symétrie; (*c*) *Anat:* orbital p., plan orbital; sagittal p., plan sagittal; *Dent:* occlusal p., plan occlusal, d'occlusion; *Art:* planes that build up the face, méplats *m* du visage; (*d*) on the economic p., sur le plan économique; a higher p. of intelligence, un niveau intellectuel plus élevé, supérieur. 2. (*a*) *Mec:* inclined p., plan incliné; (*b*) *Arch:* curved p., rampe hélicoïdale (d'accès, etc.); (*c*) *Min:* galerie *f* de roulage. 3. *Av:* (*a*) plan; aile *f*; supporting p., surface portante; hanging p., plan débordant; stub p., amorce *f* d'aile, emplanture *f*; tail p., plan fixe horizontal; variable-camber p., plan à courbure variable; (*b*) avion *m*; I came by p., je suis venu en avion.

plane[3], *v.i.* 1. (*a*) (*of bird, aircraft*) planer; to p. down, descendre en vol plané, en planant; (*b*) (*of hydroplane*) to p. along the water, courir le redan; (*c*) (*of submarine*) to p. down, up, descendre, s'élever (en plongée).

plane[4], *s. Tls:* 1. rabot *m*; rough p., rabot à corroyer; compass p., round p., rabot cintré, rond; double-iron p., rabot à contre-fer; smoothing p., rabot à repasser; tongue p., rabot à languette; tooth(ing) p., rabot denté, à dents, à coller; grooving p., bouvet *m* femelle, à rainure; rabot à languette; feuilleret *m*, guimbarde *f*; match p., bouvet à joindre; tonguing p., bouvet mâle, à languette; plough p., bouvet à approfondir; guimbarde; rabbet(ting) p., feuilleret, guillaume *m*; bullnose(d) p., guillaume; fluting p., guillaume à canneler; mitre p., guillaume à onglet; filleting p., tire-filets *m inv*; hollow p., gorget *m*; ogee p., bouvement *m*, doucine *f*; reeding p., doucine (à baguettes); try(ing) p., varlope *f*, rabot à corroyer, jointout *m*; jack p., riflard *m*; demi-varlope *f*, *pl.* demi-varlopes; long p., grande varlope; galère *f*; shooting p., varlope à équarrir; (cooper's) p., chimb p., chime p., colombe *f* (de tonnelier); barrel p., gouge *f*; p. iron, fer *m*, mèche *f*, de rabot; p. stock, fût *m*, bois *m*, corps *m*, de rabot. 2. *Mec.E:* marbre *m* à redresser.

plane[5], *v.tr.* 1. raboter (le bois); aplanir, planer, dresser, surfacer (le bois, le métal); dégauchir (le bois); (*with trying plane*) varloper; to rough p., corroyer; to p. down, away, the irregularities, enlever les irrégularités avec un rabot; to p. down a board, (i) araser, (ii) alléger, blanchir, amincir, menuiser, une planche. 2. *A:* aplanir. 3. *Typ:* to p. (down) a form, taquer une forme.

plane[6], *s. Bot:* p. (tree), platane *m*.

planer ['pleinər], *s.* 1. (*pers.*) raboteur *m*; rough p., corroyeur *m*. 2. (*a*) *Tls:* machine *f* à raboter, à dresser, à dégauchir; machine de planage; raboteuse *f*, planeuse *f*; varlopeuse *f*; rough p., machine à corroyer; edge p., chanfreineuse *f*; (*b*) *Typ:* taquoir *m*.

planet[1] ['plænit], *s.* 1. *Astr:* planète *f*; the p. Neptune, la planète Neptune; major, minor, planets, grandes, petites, planètes; secondary p., planète secondaire; satellite *m*; the inner planets, les planètes intérieures, terrestres (Mercure et Vénus); the outer planets, les planètes extérieures; to be born under a lucky p., être né sous une bonne étoile. 2. *Mec.E:* p. spindle, arbre *m* à mouvement planétaire; p. pinion, wheel, (roue *f*) satellite; p. gear, engrenage *m* planétaire, à satellites.

planet[2], *s. Ecc:* chasuble *f*.

plane table [plein'teibl], *s. Surv:* planchette *f*; p.-t. survey(ing), levé *m* à la planchette; p.-t. traverse, traversing, cheminement *m* à la planchette.

plane-table, *v.i. & tr. Surv:* faire, effectuer, un levé à la planchette (de . . .).

plane tabling [plein'teibliŋ], *s.* levé(s) *m(pl)* à la planchette.

planetarium [plæni'tɛəriəm], *s. Astr:* (*a*) planétaire *m*; (*b*) planétarium *m*.

planetary ['plænit(ə)ri], *a.* 1. (*a*) *Astr:* (système, heure, mouvement) planétaire; p. nebula, nébuleuse *f* planétaire; (*b*) *Atom.Ph:* p. electron, électron *m* planétaire, satellite; (*c*) *Mec.E:* p. gear(ing), engrenage *m* planétaire, satellite; p. reduction gear, réducteur *m* à engrenages planétaires, à satellites; p. transmission, transmission *f* planétaire; p. hoist, palan différentiel. 2. terrestre, sublunaire. 3. *A:* p. life, vie errante, vagabonde.

planetoid ['plænitɔid], *s. Astr:* planétoïde *m*, astéroïde *m*; planète *f* télescopique; petite planète; p. ring, zone *f* des petites planètes.

planeze [plæ'nez], *s. Geol:* planèze *f*.

plangency ['plæn(d)ʒənsi], *s. Lit:* 1. retentissement *m*, résonance *f*, stridence *f* (d'un son). 2. caractère plaintif (d'un son).

plangent ['plæn(d)ʒənt], *a. Lit:* 1. retentissant, sonnant, strident. 2. plaintif.

plani- ['plæni, plə'ni, 'pleini], *comb.fm.* plani-.

planidium, *pl.* -ia [plə'nidiəm, -iə], *s. Ent:* planidium *m*.

planiform ['pleinifɔ:m], *a.* planiforme.

planigraph ['plænigræf], *s.* planigraphe *m*.

planimeter [plæ'nimitər], *s. Mth:* planimètre *m*; polar p., planimètre polaire.

planimetric(al) [plæni'metrik(l)], *a. Mth:* planimétrique.

planimetry [plæ'nimitri], *s. Mth:* planimétrie *f*.

planing ['pleiniŋ], *s. Join: etc:* rabotage *m*, rabotement *m*, planage *m*; aplanissage *m*; angle p., rabotage oblique; circular p., rabotage circulaire; rough p., corroyage *m*; p. file, lime *f* à planer; p. machine = PLANER 2(*a*); p. shop, atelier *m* de rabotage, de rabotement.

Planipennia [plæni'peniə], *s.pl. Ent:* planipennes *m*.

planirostral [pleini'rɔstrəl], *a.* planirostre.

planish ['plæniʃ], *v.tr.* 1. (*a*) planer, aplaner (le bois); dresser au marteau, égaliser, aplanir (le métal); (*b*) *Num:* laminer (les lingots). 2. polir; *Phot:* glacer, satiner (une épreuve).

planisher ['plæniʃər], *s.* 1. (*pers.*) planeur *m*. 2. *Tls:* (*a*) plane *f* (de tour); (*b*) planeuse *f*, machine *f* à planer.

planishing ['plæniʃiŋ], *s.* (*a*) *Join: etc:* planage *m*; p. machine, planeuse *f*; machine à planer, à raboter; (*b*) *Metalw:* dressage *m* au marteau; planage (à chaud); aplanissement *m*; p. hammer, marteau *m* à planer, à dresser, à aplanir (le métal); p. machine, planeuse, machine à planer; p. roll, cylindre polisseur; (cylindre) espatard *m*.

planisphere ['plænisfiər], *s.* planisphère *m*; mappemonde *f* céleste.

plank[1] [plæŋk], *s.* 1. (*a*) planche (épaisse); madrier *m*; wood in planks, bois (débité) en planches, en madriers; bois méplat; loose p., planche mobile; *U.S:* p. house, cabane *f*, hutte *f*, en planches; *Nau:* dunnage planks, planches, bois, de fardage, d'arrimage; *A:* to walk the p., passer à la planche; (*b*) *N.Arch:* inner p., vaigre *f*; outside planks, bordage extérieur. 2. *esp. U.S: Pol:* p. in the party platform, article *m* du programme du parti.

plank[2], *v.tr.* 1. planchéier (un plancher, etc.); *N.Arch:* vaigrer (l'intérieur); border (l'extérieur); *Min:* coffrer (une galerie, etc.). 2. *Hatm:* fouler (le feutre). 3. *F:* (*a*) to p. sth. down, déposer qch. (brusquement); he planked himself down on a bench, il s'est campé sur un banc; (*b*) to p. down the money (for sth.), payer, casquer (qch.); (*c*) *esp. U.S:* to p. down for sth., se déclarer en faveur de qch.

planking ['plæŋkiŋ], *s.* 1. (*a*) *Const:* planchéiage *m*; roof p., voligeage *m*; (*b*) *N.Arch:* bordage *m*; vaigrage *m*; (*c*) *Min:* coffrage *m*; (*d*) *Hatm:* foulage *m* (du feutre). 2. *coll.* (*a*) planches *fpl*, madriers *mpl*; revêtement *m* de planches; to remove the p. from sth., déplancher qch.; (*b*) *N.Arch:* bordé *m*, vaigrage; carvel p., bordé à franc-bord; clinker p., bordé à clins; to rip off the p., déborder; déclinquer (un navire bordé à clins).

planktivorous [plæŋk'tivərəs], *a. Nat.Hist:* planctonophage.

planktologist [plæŋk'tɔlədʒist], *s.* planctonologiste *mf*.

planktology [plæŋk'tɔlədʒi], *s.* planctonologie *f*.

plankton ['plæŋktən], *s.* plancton *m*, plankton *m*; p. feeder, planctonophage *m*.

planktonic [plæŋk'tɔnik], *a. Nat.Hist:* planctonique.

planktonology [plæŋktə'nɔlədʒi], *s.* planctonologie *f*.

planned [plænd], *a.* (*a*) conçu, imaginé, projeté; élaboré, préparé, organisé; well p., badly p., bien, mal, conçu; (complot, crime) bien, mal, concerté, préparé, organisé; p. demonstration, manifestation organisée; (*b*) *Pol.Ec: etc:* planifié; p. economy, économie dirigée, planifiée; dirigisme *m* économique; p. obsolence, p. waste, désuétude calculée.

planner ['plænər], *s.* (*a*) projeteur, -euse; auteur *m* (d'un crime, etc.); he's a p., c'est un homme qui ne laisse rien au hasard, un homme de méthode; (*b*) *Pol.Ec:* planificateur, -trice; town p., urbaniste *mf*.

planning ['plæniŋ], *s.* 1. tracé *m* (d'un plan); town p., architecture urbaine; urbanisme *m*, aménagement *m* des villes; country p., aménagement des campagnes, du territoire. 2. conception *f*, organisation *f* (d'un projet, d'un complot, etc.). 3. *Pol.Ec: etc:* dirigisme *m*, planification *f*; *F:* planning *m*; economic p., planification économique; *Mil:* force p., planification des forces: operational p. and control, planification et conduite *f* des opérations; *Cmptr:* p. board, tableau *m* de charge; *Pej:* p. mania, folie *f* planiste. 4. family p., limitation *f*, planification, des naissances; planning familial.

plano-concave [pleinou'kɔnkeiv], *a. Opt:* plan-concave, *pl.* plan-concaves.

plano-convex [pleinou'kɔnveks], *a. Opt:* plan-convexe, *pl.* plan-convexes.

plano-cylindrical [pleinousi'lindrik(ə)l], *a. Opt:* plan-cylindrique, *pl.* plan-cylindriques.

planograph ['plænougræf], *s. Lith:* planographie *f*.

planographic [plænou'græfik], *a. Lith:* planographique.

planography [plæ'nɔgrəfi], *s. Lith:* planographie *f*.

planomania [plænou'meiniə], *s. Psy:* planomanie *f*.

planometer [plæ'nɔmitər], *s.* planomètre *m*; marbre *m* à dresser.

planometry [plæ'nɔmitri], *s.* planométrie *f*.

planomiller ['pleinoumilər], *s. Mch.Tls:* fraiseuse-raboteuse *f*, *pl.* fraiseuses-raboteuses.

planomilling [pleinou'miliŋ], *s.* fraisage-rabotage *m*; p. machine = PLANOMILLER.

planorbid [plæ'nɔ:bid], *s. Moll:* planorbe *f*.

Planorbidae [plæ'nɔ:bidi:], *s.pl. Moll:* planorbidés *m*.

plant[1] [plɑ:nt], *s.* 1. (*a*) plante *f*; herbaceous p., plante herbacée; flowering p., plante à fleurs; (indoor) pot p., house p., plante d'appartement; hothouse p., plante à serre; (*b*) bedding p., plant *m* à repiquer; (*c*) cup p., silphium *m*; ice p., ficoïde cristalline, glaciaire; (*d*) p. physiology, physiologie végétale; p. biology, phytobiologie *f*; p. life, (i) vie végétale; (ii) flore *f* (d'une région); p. wax, cire végétale; (*e*) *Ent:* p. beetle, chrysomèle *f*; p. bug, capse *m*; p. louse, aphis *m*, puceron *m*; p. lice, aphidés *mpl*, aphidiens *mpl*; (*f*) *Orn:* p. cutter, (i) rara *m*, phytotome *m*; (ii) touraco *m*; (*g*) (*of plants*) croissance *f*; in p., croissant; (*h*) récolte *f* (de navets, etc.). 2. manière *f* de se camper; pose *f*, attitude *f*, assiette *f*; to get a firm p. on the ground, trouver une bonne assiette de pied sur le terrain; se planter solidement, bien d'aplomb, sur le terrain. 3. *Ind:* (*a*) appareil(s) *m(pl)*, appareillage *m*, outillage *m*; équipement *m*, matériel *m* (industriel); the p., l'outillage, les machines *f*, le matériel; cooling p., appareil de refroidissement; heavy p., grosses machines, gros matériel; stationary p., matériel fixe; p. engineer, ingénieur (chargé de la mise en œuvre et de l'entretien) du matériel; to equip with p., outiller; (*b*) installation (industrielle); usine *f*; p. layout, schéma *m* d'installation; cement p., cimenterie *f*; concrete mixing p., centrale *f* à béton; (electric) power p., generating p., centrale électrique; peak-load p., installation(s) d'appoint; p. peak load, pointe *f* de centrale (d'énergie, etc.); printing p., imprimerie *f*; refrigerating p., installation frigorifique; standby p., installation(s) de secours. 4. *P:* (*a*) coup monté; (*b*) coup, cambriolage *m*, à faire. 5. *P:* (*a*) agent *m* de la police secrète; mouchard *m*; (*b*) fabrication *f* de faux témoignage.

plant[2], *v.tr.* 1. (*a*) *Hort: Agr:* planter (un arbre, un champ, etc.); enterrer (des oignons); to p. a field with wheat, mettre une terre en blé; to p. land with fruit trees, affruiter un terrain; to p. (out), repiquer, dépoter (des semis); décaisser (un arbuste, etc.); (*b*) *P: A:* enterrer (qn). 2. (*a*) planter (un piquet dans la terre, etc.); *Nau:* mouiller (une mine); *Mil:* to p. a bomb, poser, déposer, une bombe; to p. a battery on a height, installer une batterie sur une hauteur; *F:* to find oneself planted on a desert island, se trouver délaissé sur une île déserte; to p. an idea in s.o.'s mind, implanter une idée dans l'esprit de qn; (*b*) *F:* to p. a bullet in the target, loger une balle dans la cible; a well planted blow, un coup bien asséné, bien appliqué, bien dirigé; (*c*) *F:* to p. one's foot on s.o.'s chest, poser le pied en plein sur la poitrine de qn; to p. oneself in front of s.o., se planter, se camper, devant qn; to p. oneself on s.o., s'implanter chez qn. 3. *F:* (*a*) aposter, planter (un espion chez qn); (*b*) to p. incriminating evidence on s.o., substituer les preuves d'un délit sur un tiers; fabriquer de faux témoignages contre qn; (*c*) mettre en sûreté, planquer (des objets volés); (*d*) monter (un coup, un cambriolage); (*e*) *Min:* saler (une mine); (*f*) before the conference many of the questions were planted by the press attaché, avant la conférence nombre de questions avaient été suggérées par l'attaché de presse. 4. *P: O:* planter là (un ami, une femme); plaquer (une femme).

plantable ['plɑ:ntəbl], *a.* propre à la plantation.

Plantagenet [plæn'tædʒənet]. *Pr.n. Hist:* Plantagenet.

Plantaginaceae [plæntædʒi'neisii:], *s.pl. Bot:* plantaginacées *f*.

plantaginaceous [plæntædʒi'neiʃəs], *a. Bot:* plantaginacé, plantaginé.

plantain[1] ['plæntin], *s. Bot:* 1. plantain *m*, plantago *m*; greater p., grand plantain; buckhorn p., buck's horn p., corne *f* de cerf; ribwort p., plantain lancéolé, herbe *f* aux cinq coutures. 2. water p., plantain d'eau; alisma *m*, alisme *m*; wiesnérie *f*, flûteau *m*; pain *m* de grenouille.

plantain[2], *s. Bot:* 1. banane *f*, *esp.* banane des Antilles, plantanier *m*; *Com: F:* gros michel. 2. p. (tree), bananier *m*, *esp.* bananier du paradis, figuier *m* d'Adam. 3. *Orn:* **p. eater,** touraco *m*, musophage *m*.

plantar ['plæntər], *a. Anat:* plantaire; **p. artery,** artère *f* plantaire; plantaire *f*; **p. fascia,** aponévrose *f* plantaire; **p. nerve,** nerf *m* plantaire; **p. reflex,** réflexe *m* plantaire.

plantation [plæn'teiʃ(ə)n], *s.* 1. *A:* (*a*) établissement *m*, fondation *f* (d'une colonie); colonisation *f* (d'un pays); (*b*) colonie *f*; (*c*) **to send s.o. to the plantations,** envoyer qn dans une colonie pénitentiaire. 2. (*a*) *For:* plantation *f*, pépinière *f*, peuplement *m* (d'arbres); (*b*) plantation (de coton, etc.); **p. song,** chanson *f* de noirs (des plantations).

planter ['plɑːntər], *s.* 1. (*a*) planteur *m* (de choux, etc.); cultivateur *m*; (*b*) (*in colonies*) planteur; propriétaire *m* d'une plantation; **tea p., coffee p.,** planteur de thé, de café; (*c*) *A:* fondateur *m*; (d'une colonie, etc.); colonisateur *m* (d'un pays); (*d*) *Irish Hist:* occupant (anglais ou écossais) d'une ferme dont le propriétaire avait été dépossédé. 2. *Tls:* planteuse *f*.

plantigrade ['plæntigreid], *a. & s. Z:* plantigrade (*m*).

planting ['plɑːntiŋ], *s.* 1. *Hort: Agr:* plantage *m*, plantation *f* (d'un arbre, etc.); **p. out,** repiquage *m*, dépotage *m*; **p. bed,** planche *f* (de semis, de jeunes plantes). 2. installation *f* (d'une batterie, etc.); établissement *m* (d'une colonie, etc.); *Nau:* mouillage *m* (d'une mine). 3. *F:* (*a*) apostement *m* (d'un espion, etc.); (*b*) salage *m* (d'une mine).

plantlet ['plɑːntlit], *s. Bot:* 1. plantule *f*. 2. petite plante.

plantlike ['plɑːntlaik], *a.* qui ressemble à une plante; *Nat.Hist:* **p. flagellate,** flagellé végétal, phytoflagellé *m*.

planula, *pl.* **-ae** ['plænjulə, -iː], *s. Coel:* planula *f*.

plaque [plɑːk, plæk], *s.* 1. plaque *f* (de bronze, de marbre, etc.). 2. plaque (d'un ordre de chevalerie, etc.); décoration *f*. 3. *Med: Dent:* plaque; tache de rougeur; **bacterial p.,** plaque bactérienne, microbienne; **mucinous, mucoid, p.,** plaque de mucine; **mucous p.,** plaque muqueuse; **psoriatic p.,** plaque psoriasique.

plaquette [plæ'ket], *s.* plaquette *f*.

plash[1] [plæʃ], *s.* 1. mare *f*. 2. flaque *f* d'eau.

plash[2], *s.* 1. (*a*) clapotement *m*, clapotis *m*, clapotage *m* (des vagues); bruissement *m* (de la pluie); (*b*) flac *m* (d'un corps qui tombe dans l'eau). 2. tache *f* (de boue, de couleur, etc.); éclaboussure *f*.

plash[3]. 1. *v.tr.* (*a*) plonger (qch. dans l'eau) avec un flac; (*b*) éclabousser (**with,** de). 2. *v.i.* (*a*) (*of liquids*) clapoter, faire un clapotis; (*of stream*) bruire, babiller; (*b*) faire flac (sur l'eau); (*c*) **to p. through the water, through the mud,** patauger dans l'eau, dans la boue.

plash[4], *v.tr.* entrelacer, enlacer, tresser (les branches d'une haie).

plashing[1] ['plæʃiŋ], *a.* clapotant; (*of rain*) bruissant; (*of stream*) babillant.

plashing[2], *s.* 1. clapotage *m*, clapotement *m*; bruissement *m* (de la pluie). 2. éclaboussement *m*.

plashing[3], *s.* entrelacement *m*, tressage *m* (des branches d'une haie, etc.).

plashy ['plæʃi], *a.* (terrain) bourbeux, couvert de flaques d'eau.

plasm [plæzm], *s.* = PLASMA 1 (*b*).

plasma ['plæzmə], *s.* 1. (*a*) plasma *m* (sanguin, etc.); **p. expander,** succédané *m*, substitut *m*, de plasma sanguin; **p. cell,** plasmocyte *m*; (*b*) protoplasme *m*, protoplasma *m*. 2. *Ph:* (*ionized gas*) plasma; **electron p.,** plasma électronique; **p. diode,** diode *f* à plasma; **p. engine, p. rocket,** moteur *m*, fusée *f*, à plasma; **p. propulsion,** propulsion *f* par plasma. 3. *Miner:* plasma; calcédoine *f* vert foncé.

plasmaph(a)eresis, plasmaphoresis [plæzməfə'riːsis], *s. Med:* plasmaphérèse *f*.

plasm(at)ic [plæz'mætik, 'plæzmik], *a.* plasmatique.

plasmin ['plæzmin], *s. Bio-Ch:* plasmine *f*.

plasmocyte ['plæzmousait], *s. Biol:* plasmocyte *m*.

plasmodi(a)eresis [plæzmoudai'iərisis], *s. Biol:* plasmodiérèse *f*.

plasmodiophora [plæzmoudai'ɔfərə], *s. Fung:* plasmodiophore *m*.

plasmodium, *pl.* **-ia** [plæz'moudiəm, -iə], *s.* plasmodie *f*, plasmodium *m*.

plasmogamic [plæzmou'gæmik], *a. Biol:* plasmogamique, plastogamique.

plasmogamy [plæz'mɔgəmi], *s. Biol:* plasmogamie *f*, plastogamie *f*.

plasmogony [plæz'mɔgəni], *s. Biol:* 1. abiogénèse *f*. 2. plasmogamie *f*.

plasmology [plæz'mɔlədʒi], *s. Biol:* plasmologie *f*.

plasmolysis [plæz'mɔlisis], *s. Biol:* plasmolyse *f*.

plasmolytic [plæzmou'litik], *a. Biol:* plasmolytique.

plasmopara [plæz'mɔpərə], *s. Fung:* plasmopara *m*.

plasmophagous [plæz'mɔfəgəs], *a. Z:* plasmophage.

plasmophagy [plæz'mɔfədʒi], *s. Z:* plasmophagie *f*.

plasmosoma [plæzmə'soumə], **plasmosome** ['plæzməsoum], *s. Biol:* 1. plasmosome *m*. 2. microsome *m*.

plasmotherapy [plæzmou'θerəpi], *s. Med:* plasmothérapie *f*.

plaster[1] ['plɑːstər], *s.* 1. *Med:* emplâtre *m*; **adhesive p., sticking p.,** pansement adhésif, sparadrap *m*; **corn p.,** emplâtre, pansement, cor(r)icide; emplâtre contre, pour, les cors; *A:* **court p.,** taffetas gommé, d'Angleterre; **lead p.,** (emplâtre) diachylon *m*. 2. (*a*) *Const: etc:* plâtre *m*; **p. kiln,** four *m* à plâtre; plâtrière *f*; **hard p.,** plâtre dur; **quick-setting, slow-setting, p.,** plâtre à prise rapide, à prise lente; **wall p.,** enduit *m* de mur, plâtre des murs; **there was p. falling from the ceiling,** le plafond se déplâtrait; **p. of Paris,** plâtre de Paris, plâtre de moulage, plâtre fin, plâtre cuit; **to put a leg in p.,** plâtrer une jambe; (*b*) **dentist's p.,** plâtre de dentiste; **impression p.,** plâtre à empreinte(s).

plaster[2], *v.tr.* 1. *Med:* mettre un emplâtre sur (une plaie, etc.). 2. (*a*) **to p. (over, up) a wall,** plâtrer, ravaler, un mur; enduire un mur de plâtre; **wall plastered with advertisements,** mur tapissé d'affiches; **to p. (up) a crack,** plâtrer, boucher, une fente; *F:* **to p. over the cracks,** déguiser les défauts (de qch.); dissimuler les désaccords; (*of pers.*) **plastered with mud,** plâtré, tout couvert, de boue; *F:* **plastered with medals,** chamarré de décorations; (*b*) *F:* **to p. the enemy,** bombarder l'ennemi; (*c*) *P:* **to get plastered,** se soûler; **to be plastered,** être soûl. 3. (*a*) plâtrer (le vin); (*b*) *Agr:* plâtrer (un champ, etc.).

plasterboard ['plɑːstəbɔːd], *s. Const:* plasterboard *m*; Placoplâtre *m* (*R.t.m.*).

plasterer ['plɑːstərər], *s.* plâtrier *m*, ravaleur *m*.

plastering ['plɑːst(ə)riŋ], *s.* 1. (*a*) *Med:* pose *f* d'un emplâtre; (*b*) plâtrage *m*, ravalement *m* (d'un mur, etc.); (*c*) travaux *mpl* de plâtrerie. 2. enduit *m* de plâtre; plâtrage *m*. 3. (*a*) plâtrage (du vin); (*b*) *Agr:* plâtrage (d'un champ). 4. *F:* (*a*) **to give the enemy a p.,** bombarder (sévèrement) l'ennemi; (*b*) volée *f* de coups.

plasterstone ['plɑːstəstoun], *s. Miner:* pierre *f* à plâtre; gypse *m*.

plasterwork ['plɑːstəwəːk], *s.* plâtrage *m*, plâtrerie *f*; (*esp. on walls and ceilings*) les plâtres *m*.

plastic ['plæstik]. 1. *a.* plastique; (*a*) **p. movement,** mouvement plastique; **the p. arts,** les arts plastiques; **p. surgery,** chirurgie *f* (i) plastique, (ii) esthétique; **p. surgeon,** plasticien *m*; chirurgien *m* esthétique; (*b*) (*qui se laisse modeler, mouler*) **p. material, substance,** matière *f* plastique; **p. compound,** composé *m* plastique; **p. clay,** argile *f* plastique, terre *f* à modeler; **p. sulphur,** soufre mou; **p. wood,** bois *m* plastique; *Fig:* **p. nature,** caractère *m* malléable; (*c*) (*qui se laisse déformer sans se rompre*) **p. deformation, p. flow,** déformation *f* plastique; **p. stability,** stabilité *f* plastique; **p. buckling,** flambage *m* plastique; (*d*) **p. explosive,** explosif *m* plastique; plastic *m*; **p. bomb attack,** plastiquage *m*; **the terrorists attacked the house with a p. bomb,** les terroristes ont plastiqué la maison; (*e*) *Biol:* **p. lymph, tissue,** lymphe *m*, tissu *m*, plastique. 2. *s.* (*a*) plastique *m*; matière *f* plastique; **acrylic p.,** plastique acrylique; **cellulosic p.,** plastique cellulosique; **phenolic p.,** plastique phénolique; **vinyl p.,** plastique vinylique; **laminated p.,** (plastique) stratifié *m*, lamifié *m*; **moulded p.,** plastique moulé; **foam p., p. foam, expanded p.,** mousse *f* de plastique; **a p. cup,** une tasse en (matière) plastique; **the plastics industry,** l'industrie *f* des plastiques; (*b*) *Exp:* plastic *m*.

plasticine ['plæstisiːn], *s.* pâte *f* à modeler; **p. set,** boîte *f* de modelage.

plasticity [plæs'tisiti], *s.* (*a*) plasticité *f*; (*b*) *Art: Cin:* relief *m* (d'une image); effet *m* plastique.

plasticization [plæstisai'zeiʃ(ə)n], *s.* plastification *f*.

plasticize ['plæstisaiz], *v.tr.* (*a*) plasticiser; (*b*) *Tchn:* boudiner; **plasticizing machine,** boudineuse *f*.

plasticizer ['plæstisaizər], *s.* (agent *m*) plastifiant *m*.

plastid ['plæstid], *s. Nat.Hist:* plaste *m*, plastide *m*.

plastidular [plæs'tidjulər], *a. Nat.Hist:* plastidulaire.

plastidule ['plæstidjuːl], *s. Nat.Hist:* plastidule *f*.

plastification [plæstifi'keiʃ(ə)n], *s.* plastification *f*.

plastify ['plæstifai], *v.tr.* plastifier.

plastigel ['plæstidʒel], *s.* plastigel *m*.

plastin ['plæstin], *s. Ch:* plastine *f*.

plastisol ['plæstisɔl], *s.* plastisol *m*.

plastogamic [plæstou'gæmik], *a. Bot:* plastogamique, plasmogamique.

plastogamy [plæs'tɔgəmi], *s. Bot:* plastogamie *f*, plasmogamie *f*.

plastomer ['plæstoumər], *s. Ch:* plastomère *m*.

plastometer [plæs'tɔmitər], *s.* plastomètre *m*.

plastotype ['plæstoutaip], *s. Typ:* plastotype *f*.

plastron ['plæstrən], *s.* 1. (*a*) *Fenc:* plastron *m*; (*b*) *Arm:* plastron (de cuirasse); (*c*) *Cost: A:* plastron (de chemise). 2. plastron, bouclier inférieur (de tortue).

plat[1] [plæt], *s.* 1. *A:* coin *m* de terre; morceau *m*, *F:* bout *m* (de terrain, etc.); plant *m* (de pommes de terre, etc.); **p. sowing,** semis *m* par planches. 2. *NAm:* plan *m* (d'un terrain, d'un immeuble, etc.).

plat[2], *v.tr.* (**platted**) *NAm:* dresser un plan de (qch.).

plat[3,4], *s. & v.tr.* = PLAIT[1] 2, [2]2.

Plataea [plæ'tiːə], *Pr.n. A.Geog:* Platée *f*.

Plataleidae [plætə'liːidiː], *s.pl. Orn:* plataléidés *m*, les spatules *m*.

platan ['plætən], *s. Bot:* platane *m*.

platanist ['plætənist], *s. Z:* plataniste *m*, sousouc *m*.

platband ['plætbænd], *s. Arch:* plate-bande *f*, *pl.* plates-bandes.

plate[1] [pleit], *s.* 1. (*a*) (petite) plaque, (petite) lame, lamelle *f* (de métal, de verre, de matière plastique, etc.); **small p.,** plaquette *f*; **thin p.,** feuillet *m*; **stone that splits into plates,** pierre *f*, minéral *m*, qui se fend en lamelles; (*b*) *Anat:* plaque (osseuse, etc.); **cribriform p.,** plaque criblée; (*c*) (i) **dental p., denture p.,** plaque de prothèse; **clasp p.,** plaque à crochets; **suction p.,** plaque à succion; **retention p.,** plaque de contention; (ii) *F:* dentier *m*. 2. (*a*) *Metall:* plaque; (grande) feuille (de métal); tôle *f*; **cast iron p.,** plaque de, en, fonte; taque *f*; **iron p.,** plaque de, en, fer; **p. iron,** tôle (de fer); tôlerie *f*; **p. brass,** laiton *m* en feuilles; **chequered p.,** tôle gaufrée, striée; *N.Arch:* tôle à empreintes; **dished p.,** tôle emboutie; **fashioned p.,** tôle façonnée; **flanged p.,** tôle à bord tombé; **heavy p.,** grosse tôle, tôle forte; **medium p.,** tôle moyenne; **thin p.,** tôle mince; **perforated, punched, p.,** tôle, plaque. perforée; **ribbed p.,** tôle à nervures; **rolled p.,** tôle laminée; **tinned p.,** tôle étamée; **to shear a p.,** cisailler une tôle; **p. roll(er),** cylindre *m* à tôle; **p. bending,** cintrage *m* des tôles; **p.-bending machine, rolls, rollers,** machine à cintrer, à couder, les tôles; **p. cutting,** cisaillement *m*, découpage *m*, des tôles; **p. cutting machine,** cisaille *f* à tôles; machine *f* à découper les tôles; **p. shears,** cisailles à tôles; **p. hoist,** lève-tôles *m inv*; **p. mill, works,** laminoir *m* à tôle, train *m* à tôle; (train de) tôlerie *f*; **p. metal,** (i) fonte affinée; (ii) potin *m* d'assiettes; **p. armour,** (plaque de) blindage *m*; (*b*) plaque, plate *f* (d'armure); **p. armour,** armure *f* à plates; (*c*) *N.Arch:* **bilge p.,** tôle de bouchain; **boss p.,** tôle de bossage; **bulkhead p.,** tôle de cloison; **bulwark p.,** tôle de pavois; **ceiling p.,** vaigre *f*; **counter p.,** tôle de voûte; **deck p.,** tôle de pont; **horseshoe p.,** plaque de jaumière; **oxter p., tuck p.,** tôle de sommier; **transom p.,** tôle d'arcasse; (*d*) *Mec.E: etc:* **assembly p.,** plaque de montage; **backing p., stiffening p.,** plaque, tôle, de renfort; **blanking p.,** plaque d'obturation, plaque obturatrice (d'une canalisation, etc.); **base p., bed p., bottom p., foundation p.,** (i) *Mch:* plaque d'assise, de base, de fondation (d'une machine, etc.); (ii) *Metall:* plaque de fond, du dessous (d'un moule de fonderie); **top p.,** plaque du dessus (d'un moule de fonderie, etc.); **covering p.,** plaque de fermeture; plaque, tôle, de recouvrement; tôle d'enveloppe (d'un organe de machine, etc.); *Mch.Tls:* **ejector p., stripper p.,** plaque d'éjection (d'une emboutisseuse, etc.); **thrust p.,** plaque de butée, de choc (d'une emboutisseuse, etc.); **friction p., chafing p., wear p.,** plaque de friction, de frottement; *Mec.E:* **p. nut,** écrou prisonnier; *Const:* **gusset p.,** plaque de jonction; **lining p.,** plaque, tôle, de revêtement; **manhole p.,** plaque d'trou d'homme, de visite; plaque de regard (d'égout, etc.); **match p., pattern p.,** plaque modèle (de fonderie); **protective p.,** plaque de protection, plaque protectrice; **spacer p.,** plaque entretoise; **support(ing) p.,** plaque (de) support; *Artil:* **base p.,** plaque de base (du mortier); *Sm.a:* **butt p.,** plaque de couche (de fusil); (*e*) plateau *m* (de machine-outil, de balance, etc.); table *f* (d'enclume, de marteau); platine *f* (de montre); platine, palastre *m*, palâtre *m* (de serrure); contre-heurtoir *m*, *pl.* contre-heurtoirs (de marteau de porte); paumelle *f* (de gond de porte); *Mec.Tls:* **chuck p., face p.,** plateau de tour; **index p.,** plateau de division; plateau diviseur, indicateur; **feed index p.,** plateau indicateur des avances; **work p.,** plateau porte-pièce; *Mec.E:* **p. coupling,** accouplement *m* à plateaux; *Aut:* **clutch p.,** disque *m*, plateau, d'embrayage; **p. clutch,** embrayage *m* à disque, à plateau; **multiple p. clutch,** embrayage à disques multiples; **p. wheel,** roue pleine, à voile; **wheel-guard p.,** plaque d'appui; *Sm.a:* **lock p.,** platine (d'arme à feu); *Dom.Ec:* **hot p.,** (i) plaque chauffante (de cuisinière); (ii) réchaud *m* (électrique, à gaz); (iii) chauffe-assiettes *m inv*; (*f*) **door p.,** plaque de porte; **name p.,** (i) plaque de porte; (ii) plaque indicatrice (de rue); (iii) plaque d'identification, de série (d'une machine); plaque de constructeur; *Mil: etc:* **identification p.,** plaque d'identité; *Aut: etc:* **number p.,** plaque d'immatriculation, de police; plaque minéralogique; (*g*) *Farr:* (i) fer *m* à bœufs; (ii) fer à cheval léger (pour courses); (*h*) *Rail:* (i) *A:* rail *m*; (ii) **p. rail,** rail méplat; (*i*) (*baseball*) base *f* (du lanceur, du batteur); (*j*) *Ch:* plateau (de colonne de distillation); **bubble p.,** plateau à coupelles; **p. column, p. tower,** colonne *f* à plateaux; (*k*) *Paperm:* **p. glazer,** lamineur *m*. **3.** (*a*) *El:* plaque, lame (de batterie, etc.); **accumulator p.,** plaque d'accummulateur; **capacitor, condenser, p.,** plaque, lame, armature *f*, de condensateur; **crystal p.,** lame piézo-électrique; **grid p.,** plaque à grille, grillage *m*, grille *f* (d'accumulateur); **pasted p.,** plaque empâtée; **p. battery,** batterie *f* anodique; **p. core,** plaque à âme; (*b*) *Elcs:* plaque, anode *f* (de tube électronique); **baffle p., deflecting p.,** plaque de déviation; **p. circuit,** circuit *m* de plaque, circuit anodique; **p. current,** courant *m* anodique; **p. dissipation,** dissipation *f* anodique; **p. impedance,** impédance *f* de plaque; *W.Tel:* **p. modulation,** modulation *f* dans l'anode; **p. neutralization,** neutralisation *f* du circuit anodique; **p. potential,** potentiel *m* anodique; **p. pulsing,** impulsion *f* sur la plaque; **p. resistance,** résistance *f* de plaque; **p. voltage,** tension *f* de plaque, tension anodique; (*c*) *Atom.Ph:* **fuel p.,** plaque de combustible, plaque active; **lattice p.,** plaque de réseau; **accelerator p.,** plaque accélératrice. **4.** (*a*) *Phot:* **(photographic) p.,** plaque (photographique); **anti-halo, anti-halation, p.,** plaque antihalo; **autochrome p.,** plaque autochrome; **contrast p.,** plaque contraste; **dry p.,** plaque sèche; **sensitive, sensitized, p.,** plaque sensible; **whole p.,** plaque et format *m* 16cm5 × 21cm5; **half p.,** plaque et format 12cm × 16cm5; **quarter p.,** plaque et format 8cm2 × 10cm8; **p. holder,** (i) châssis (négatif); porte-plaque *m*, *pl.* porte-plaques; (ii) intermédiaire *m* pour plaques; **p. tester,** opacimètre *m*; **p. adapter,** adapteur *m* de plaques; adapte-plaques *m inv*; (*b*) *Engr: Typ:* plaque; **deep-etched p.,** plaque d'offset en creux; **key p.,** plaque de trait (pour offset en couleurs); **machine p., press p.,** plaque machine; **p. holding frame,** châssis *m* porte-plaque; **p. cylinder,** cylindre *m* de plaque; **p. coating,** couchage *m* des plaques; **p. coating machine,** tournette *f*; **to fix, put on, the p.,** caler la plaque; (*c*) *Engr: Phot: etc:* cliché *m* (photographique ou imprimant); cliché (de photogravure); **half-tone p.,** cliché de similigravure; *Typ:* **(stereotype) p.,** cliché; **p. marker,** clicheur *m*; (*d*) *Engr:* planche *f*; **second p.,** contre-planche *f*, *pl.* contre-planches; **p. mark,** coup *m* de planche; **p. marking,** estampage *m* des épreuves; (*e*) *Engr:* planche, gravure *f*, estampe *f*; **full-page p.,** hors-texte *m inv*. **5.** *Const:* (poutre *f*) sablière *f*; panne *f*; **ridge p.,** panne faîtière; **roof p.,** sablière de comble; **sole p.,** semelle *f*, patin *m*, couchis *m* (d'une fondation); **wall p.,** (i) plaque d'assise (de poutre); lambourde *f*, ligneul *m* (pour les solives du plancher); (ii) sablière de comble; **p.(-web) girder,** poutre (métallique) à âme pleine; *Plumb:* **bed p.,** plaque d'appui. **6.** (*a*) orfèvrerie *f*; vaisselle plate; vaisselle d'or, d'argent; (*b*) **it's (only) p.,** c'est de l'argenté, du plaqué; (*c*) *Rac:* coupe (d'or, d'argent) (donnée en prix); (*d*) *Her:* besant *m* d'argent. **7.** (*a*) assiette *f*; **dinner p.,** assiette plate; **soup p.,** assiette creuse; *F:* **to have enough, a lot, on one's p.,** avoir du pain sur la planche; *F:* **to hand s.o. sth. on a p.,** le servir sur un plateau; l'offrir tout rôti; **p. warmer,** chauffe-assiettes *m inv*; **p. rack,** (i) porte-assiettes *m inv*; (ii) égouttoir *m*; **p. basket,** ramasse-couverts *m inv*; (*b*) *Ecc: etc:* **(collection) p.,** plat *m*, plateau, de quête; **to pass round, take round, the p.,** faire la quête.

plate[2], *v.tr.* **1.** (*a*) blinder; recouvrir, garnir, (qch.) de plaques; *N.Arch:* **to p. a ship,** border un navire en fer, en acier; (*b*) *Farr:* ferrer (i) un bœuf, (ii) un cheval pour une course. **2.** métalliser; plaquer en or, en argent; argenter par galvanoplastie; étamer (une glace); **to p. with gold, silver, tin, nickel,** dorer, argenter, étamer, nickeler; **to p. a medal with gold,** fourrer une médaille d'or. **3.** *Ven:* **to p. a gun,** essayer la gerbe de dispersion d'un fusil de chasse. **4.** *Typ:* clicher (les pages).

Plate[3]. *Pr.n. Geog:* **the (river) P.,** la Rio de la Plata.

plateau, *pl.* **-eaux, -eaus** ['plætou, -ouz], *s.* **1.** *Geog:* plateau *m*; **tectonic p.,** plateau structural; **residual p.,** plateau d'érosion. **2.** plateau, plat (décoratif); assiette (décorative). **3.** *Ph:* palier *m* (d'une courbe d'instrument enregistreur); **relative p. slope,** pente relative de palier.

plated ['pleitid], *a.* **1.** recouvert, garni, de plaques; **(armour) p.,** blindé. **2.** plaqué; **gold p.,** doublé d'or; **nickel p.,** nickelé; **silver p.,** argenté; **chromium p.,** chromé.

platée ['plætei], *a. Her:* besanté d'argent.

plateful ['pleitful], *s.* assiettée *f*, pleine assiette (de qch.); *F:* **you've got a p. there!** vous avez de quoi faire! voilà du pain sur la planche!

platelayer ['pleitleiər], *s. Rail:* (*a*) poseur *m*, metteur *m*, de rails, de voie; (*b*) ouvrier *m* de la voie; **foreman p.,** piqueur *m* de voie.

platelaying ['pleitleiiŋ], *s. Rail:* pose *f* de voies.

platelet ['pleitlit], *s.* **blood platelets,** plaquettes sanguines, hématoblastes *m*.

platen ['plætən], *s.* **1.** *Mec.E:* plateau *m*, table *f* (de machine-outil, etc.); **p. feed,** avance *f* de table. **2.** (*of printing press*) platine *f*. **3.** *Typewr:* rouleau *m* porte-papier.

plater ['pleitər], *s.* **1.** *Metalw:* plaqueur *m*; **tin p.,** étameur *m*; **silver p.,** argenteur *m*; **gold p.,** doreur *m*. **2.** *Turf:* (*a*) cheval *m* à réclamer; (*b*) cheval de second ordre.

plateresque [plætə'resk], *a. Arch:* plateresque.

platform ['plætfɔ:m], *s.* **1.** (*a*) terrasse *f*; *Fort: etc:* plate-forme *f*, *pl.* plates-formes (en terre); (*b*) *Geog:* **(wave-cut) p.,** plate-forme d'abrasion (marine). **2.** (*a*) plate-forme; tablier *m* (de bascule, de pont, etc.); passerelle *f* (de grue); *Ind: etc:* **handling p.,** pont *m* de chargement; **swinging p.,** pont-levis *m*, *pl.* ponts-levis; *Artil:* **gun p.,** plate-forme de pièce, de tir; **machine-gun p.,** plate-forme de mitrailleuse; **range-finder p.,** plate-forme de télémétrie; *Ball:* **launching, firing, p.,** plate-forme de lancement, de tir (de missiles); *Navy:* **flying(-off) p.,** plate-forme d'envol (pour avions); **landing p.,** plate-forme d'atterrissage, d'apontage; *Petr:* **(oil-)drilling p.,** plate-forme de forage pétrolier (sous-marin); derrick flottant; **travelling p.,** (i) (*also* **p. truck**) (chariot *m*) transporteur *m*, transbordeur *m*; (ii) *Cin:* travelling *m*; *NAm:* **p. elevator,** monte-charge *m inv*; plate-forme élévatrice; *Rail: NAm:* **p. car,** (wagon *m*) plate-forme; *Nau:* **p. sling,** plateau *m* à caissage; (*b*) *Nau:* parquet *m*, plancher *m*; plate-forme (de cale, de soute); **engine-room p., stockhold p.,** parquet de la machine, de la chaufferie; **compass p.,** passerelle de navigation; (*c*) *Rail:* quai *m*; **arrival, departure, p.,** quai d'arrivée, de départ; *Mil:* **entraining, detraining, p.,** quai d'embarquement, de débarquement; **loading, unloading, p.,** quai de chargement, de déchargement; **which p. does the train start, leave, from?** de quel quai part le train? le train part de quel quai? **3.** (*a*) estrade *f*, plate-forme, tribune *f* (de réunion publique); (*b*) *Pol:* plate-forme, programme *m* (d'un parti).

Platforming ['plætfɔ:miŋ], *s. R.t.m: Petr:* reformage *m*, réformation *f* au platine, reforming *m*.

Plathelminthes [plæthel'minθi:z], *s.pl. Ann:* plathelminthes *m*.

platinate[1] ['plætineit], *s. Ch:* platinate *m*.

platinate[2], *v.tr. Metall:* platin(is)er.

plating ['pleitiŋ], *s.* **1.** (*a*) revêtement *m* en tôle; armature *f* (de four, de fourneau, etc.); *N.Arch:* (*outside*) bordage *m*; (*inside*) vaigrage *m*; **(steel, armour) p.,** blindage *m*; (*b*) (*plates*) tôles *fpl*; *N.Arch:* (*outside*) bordé *m* (en fer); (*inside*) vaigres *fpl*; **deck p.,** bordé de pont; **side p.,** bordé de côté, de muraille. **2.** placage *m*; **(immersion) p.,** galvanoplastie *f*; électroplastie *f*; **copper p.,** cuivrage *m*; **nickel p.,** nickelage *m*, nickelure *f*; **silver p.,** argentage *m*, argenture *f*; **gold p.,** dorage *m*, dorure *f*; **p. balance,** balance *f* galvanoplastique; **p. generator,** génératrice *f* de galvanoplastie; **p. rack,** support *m* de cathode (pour galvanoplastie); **p. rectifier,** redresseur *m* pour galvanoplastie. **3.** *Typ:* clichage *m*. **4.** *Turf:* courses *fpl* à réclamer.

platinic [plə'tinik], *a. Ch:* platinique.

platiniferous [plæti'nifərəs], *a.* platinifère.

platiniridium [plætini'ridiəm], *s.* = PLATINO-IRIDIUM.

platinite ['plætinait], *s. Miner:* platinite *f*.

platinization [plætinai'zeiʃ(ə)n], *s. Metalw:* platinage *m*.

platinize ['plætinaiz], *v.tr. Metalw:* platin(is)er.

platinochloride [plætinou'klɔ:raid], *s. Ch:* platinochlorure *m*.

platinocyanide [plætinou'saiənaid], *s. Ch:* plat(in)ocyanure *m*; **barium p.,** platinocyanure de barium.

platinode ['plætinoud], *s. El:* pôle négatif (de pile).

platinoid ['plætinɔid], *a. & s. Metall:* platinoïde (*m*).

platino-iridium [plætinoui'ridiəm], *s.* platiniridium *m*; platine iridié; iridium platiné.

platinotype ['plætinoutaip], *s. Phot:* (*a*) platinotypie *f*; (*b*) épreuve tirée en platinotypie.

platinous ['plætinəs], *a. Ch:* platineux.

platinum ['plætinəm], *s.* platine *m*; **native p.,** platine natif; **p. foil, sheet,** feuille *f*, lame *f*, de platine; platine laminé; **p. sponge,** éponge *f*, mousse *f*, de platine; **p. wire,** fil *m* de platine; **p. black,** noir *m* de platine; **p. metals,** métaux *m* de la mine de platine; **p. plated,** platiné, platinisé; **p. tipped,** (à bout) platiné; **p. gold,** or platiné; **p. steel,** acier *m* au platine; *Aut:* **p. contact, p. point, p.-tipped screw,** vis platinée; **p. blond (hair),** (cheveux) platinés; **she's a p. blonde,** c'est une blonde platinée.

platitude ['plætitju:d], *s.* **1.** platitude *f*, insipidité *f* (d'un discours, du style, etc.). **2.** platitude; lieu commun; banalité *f*; vérité *f* de la Palisse; lapalissade *f*.

platitudinarian [plætitjudi'nɛəriən]. **1.** *s.* débiteur, -euse, de platitudes. **2.** *a.* plat; insipide.

platitudinize [plæti'tju:dinaiz], *v.i.* débiter des platitudes, des banalités, des lieux communs.

platitudinous [plæti'tju:dinəs], *a.* (style, etc.) plat, banal.

Plato ['pleitou], *Pr.n.m.* Platon.

Platonic [plə'tɔnik], *a.* (*a*) (philosophe, etc.) platonicien; *Chr:* **P. year,** année *f* platonique; (*b*) (amour) platonique.

platonically [plə'tɔnik(ə)li], *adv.* d'une manière platonique; platoniquement.

Platonism ['pleitənizm], *s. Phil:* platonisme *m*.

Platonist ['pleitənist], *s. Phil:* platonicien, -ienne.

platonize ['pleitənaiz], *v.i. & tr. Phil: etc:* platoniser.

platoon [plə'tu:n], *s. Mil:* (*a*) *A:* (i) peloton *m*; (ii) salve *f*, volée *f*, feu *m*, de peloton; (*b*) (i) section *f* (dans l'infanterie); (ii) peloton (dans les blindés, le train); **leading p.,** section, peloton, de tête; **machine-gun p.,** section de mitrailleuses; **mortar p.,** section de mortiers; **p. commander, p. leader,** chef *m* de section, de peloton; **p. drill, p. training,** école de section, de peloton; **rifle p.,** section de voltigeurs; **weapons p.,** section lourde (d'une compagnie de voltigeurs); *U.S:* **p. sergeant,** sergent-chef *m*, *pl.* sergents-chefs.

platter ['plætər], *s.* **1.** *A:* plat *m* (de bois); écuelle *f*. **2.** *Rec:* (*a*) (*on record player*) plateau *m*; (*b*) *U.S: F: O:* disque *m*.

platy[1] ['plæti], *s. Ich:* platy *m*.

platy[2], *a. Her:* besanté d'argent.

platy- ['plæti], *comb.fm.* platy-.

platybasic [plæti'beisik], *a.* platybasique.

platycephalic [plætise'fælik], **platycephalous** [plæti'sefələs], *a.* platycéphale.

Platycephalidae [plætise'fælidi:], *s.pl. Ich:* platycéphalidés *m*.

platycephalus [plæti'sefələs], *s. Ich:* platycéphale *m*.

platycephaly [plæti'sefəli], *s. Med: etc:* platycéphalie *f*.

platycerium [plæti'siəriəm], *s. Bot:* platycérium *m*.

platycnemia [plætik'ni:miə], *s. Anthr:* platycnémie *f*.

platycnemic [plætik'ni:mik], *a. Anthr:* platycnémique; **p. index,** indice *m* platycnémique.

platydactylous [plæti'dæktiləs], *a.* platydactyle.

platyhelminth [plæti'helminθ], *s. Ann:* plat(y)helminthe *m*.

platymeria [plæti'miəriə], *s. Anthr:* platymérie *f*.

platymeric [plæti'miərik], *a. Anthr:* platymérique; **p. index,** indice *m* platymérique.

platypetalous [plæti'petələs], *a. Bot:* platypétale.

Platypoda [plæti'poudə], *s.pl. Moll:* platypodes *m*.

platypodia [plæti'poudiə], *s. Med:* platypodie *f*.

platypus ['plætipəs], *s. Z:* ornithor(h)ynque *m*.

Platyr(r)hina [plæti'rainə], *s.pl. Z:* platyr(r)hiniens *m*.

platyr(r)hine ['plætirain], **platyr(r)hinian** [plæti'rainiən], *a. & s. Z:* (singe) platyr(r)hinien *m*.

platyr(r)hiny ['plætiraini], *s. Z:* platyr(r)hinie *f*.

platysma [plæ'tizmə], *s. Anat:* (muscle *m*) peaucier *m*.

plaudits ['plɔ:dits], *s.pl. esp. Lit:* (salve *f* d') applaudissements *mpl*.

plausibility [plɔ:zi'biliti], *s.* plausibilité *f*; (i) vraisemblance *f* (d'une excuse, etc.); (ii) spécieux *m* (d'un argument, etc.).

plausible ['plɔ:zibl], *a.* **1.** (*a*) (*of argument, excuse, etc.*) plausible, vraisemblable; **that makes the theory p.,** cela rend plausible la théorie; **it's quite a p. reason,** c'est une raison comme une autre; (*b*) (prétexte, etc.) spécieux. **2.** (*of pers.*) captieux; enjôleur; aux belles paroles.

plausibly ['plɔ:zibli], *adv.* **1.** plausiblement; (i) vraisemblablement; (ii) spécieusement. **2.** captieusement.

Plautus ['plɔ:təs]. *Pr.n.m. Lt.Lit:* Plaute.

play[1] [plei], *s.* **1.** (*a*) jeu *m*, reflets *mpl* (de lumière); chatoiement *m*, reflets (de couleurs); irisation *f*; **the p. of light and shadow on the snow,** le jeu de la lumière et des ombres sur la neige; **p. of light on a jewel,** chatoiement d'un bijou; **a dazzling p. of colours,** un chatoiement de couleurs éblouissantes, une étincelante irisation; *Th: etc:* **p. of features,** jeux de physionomie; (*b*) maniement *m*, manipulation *f* (d'une arme); jeu (d'un escrimeur, d'un épéiste); **to make p. with one's stick,** s'escrimer avec sa canne; (*c*) jeu, mouvement *m*, activité *f*; *Anat:* **the p. of muscles in physical effort,** le jeu des muscles dans l'effort physique; **to come into p.,** entrer en jeu, en action; intervenir; **the passions that come into p. in this drama,** les passions qui s'agitent, qui se déchaînent, dans ce drame; **the motives that come into p. in such a case,** les motifs qui interviennent en pareille circonstance; **to bring, call, put, sth. into p.,** mettre qch. en jeu, en œuvre, en action; exercer (ses facultés); **to bring the guns into p.,** faire donner, faire intervenir, l'artillerie; *U.S:* **to make a p. for sth.,** mettre tout en œuvre, jouer le grand jeu, pour obtenir qch.; **in full p.,** en pleine action, en plein essor; **to hold, keep, s.o. in p.,** (i) tenir qn en haleine; (ii) amuser, occuper, qn; **p. of fancy,** (i) cours *m,* divagation *f,* essor, de la fantaisie; (ii) fantaisie; (iii) illusion *f;* **to give, allow, full p. to one's imagination,** donner libre cours, libre carrière, à son imagination; (*d*) *Mch:* course *f,* jeu (du piston d'un moteur, d'une pompe, etc.); (*e*) *Mec.E: etc:* jeu, chasse *f* (d'un boulon, d'une pièce de mécanisme, etc., dans son logement); **admissible, permissible, p.,** jeu admis(sible), permis; **angular p.,** jeu angulaire; **diametrical, radial, p.,** jeu diamétral, radial, vertical; **side p.,** jeu latéral; **free from p.,** sans jeu; **too much p.,** trop de jeu; **tenon that has too much p. in its mortise,** tenon trop gai dans sa mortaise; **to give p. to a part,** donner du jeu à un organe; **to have p.,** avoir du jeu; **to let the belt, the rope, have some p.,** donner du mou à la courroie, à la corde; détendre la courroie, la corde; **to leave p.,** laisser du jeu; **to remove p.,** reprendre le jeu; *Veh: etc:* **p. in the wheels,** flottement *m* des roues. **2.** *Rec: F:* **this stylus should be good for a great number of plays,** ce saphir doit pouvoir servir pour un très grand nombre de tours; **this record got scratched after a few plays,** ce disque s'est éraillé après avoir joué un petit nombre de fois. **3.** (*a*) jeu, amusement *m;* **to be at p.,** être en train de jouer; **schoolboys at p.,** élèves en récréation; **p. world,** monde *m* imaginaire (des enfants); (*b*) **to say sth. in p.,** dire qch. en riant, en plaisantant, pour rire, pour plaisanter; **out of mere p.,** par pur badinage; **child full of p.,** enfant enjoué, folâtre; **p. on words,** calembour *m,* jeu de mots; équivoque *f;* (*c*) badinage amoureux, échange *m* de caresses, flirt *m;* (*of cock birds, male animals*) danse, parade, nuptiale; (*d*) *Ind: A:* chômage *m.* **4.** (*a*) jeu (de hasard); **to lose at p.,** perdre au jeu; **to be ruined by p.,** s'être ruiné au jeu; **high p., low p.,** gros jeu, petit jeu; **the p. runs high,** on joue gros jeu; (*b*) *Games:* **to win a match by good p.,** gagner une partie par l'excellence de son jeu; **p. began at one o'clock,** la partie a commencé, on a commencé la partie, à une heure; **ball in p., out of p.,** ballon *m* en jeu; ballon hors jeu, ballon mort; **to bring the ball into p.,** mettre la balle en jeu; *Golf:* **stroke p., medal p.,** concours par coups; (*c*) *Pol.Ec: etc:* jeu (des hypothèses, des combinaisons); **open, closed, p.,** jeu ouvert, fermé; *Mil:* **pre-exercise p.,** jeu préparatoire à un exercice. **5.** (*a*) pièce *f* (de théâtre); **short p.,** piécette *f,* saynète *f;* **Shakespeare's plays,** le théâtre de Shakespeare; **to give a p.,** représenter, donner, une pièce; (*b*) *O:* spectacle *m;* **to go to the p.,** aller au spectacle, au théâtre.

play[2], *v.*

I. *v.i.* **1.** se mouvoir vivement; (*of animals*) folâtrer, gambader, s'ébattre; (*of light, colour*) se jouer, chatoyer; **specks of dust playing in the sunbeams,** des atomes de poussière qui dansent dans les rayons de soleil; **butterflies playing among the flowers,** papillons voltigeant autour des fleurs; **her hair played in the breeze,** ses cheveux flottaient, ondoyaient, dans la brise; **the sun is playing on the water,** le soleil se joue sur l'eau. **2.** (*a*) (*of fountain*) jouer; **the fountains will p. on Sunday,** les eaux joueront dimanche; (*b*) **the organ is playing,** les orgues donnent, jouent, retentissent; **a band is playing in the park,** une musique joue dans le parc; **a romantic waltz was being played on the radio,** la radio diffusait, jouait, une valse romantique; *v.tr.* **the organ played the people in, out,** l'orgue a joué (pour) l'entrée, la sortie; **the band played the troops past,** la musique a accompagné le défilé des troupes; les troupes ont défilé en musique; **they played the bride and bridegroom home,** ils ont accompagné, conduit, les nouveaux mariés chez eux en musique; (*c*) (*of part of mechanism, organ, etc.*) jouer, fonctionner, se mouvoir (librement); (*of bolt, tenon, etc.*) avoir du jeu. **3.** (*a*) jouer, s'amuser, se divertir; **children playing in the garden,** enfants qui jouent, qui s'amusent, dans le jardin; **child fond of playing,** enfant joueur; **to p. (at) soldiers,** jouer aux soldats; **to p. at keeping shop, at keeping house,** jouer à la marchande, au ménage; **the children were playing at running across the street,** les enfants s'amusaient à traverser la rue en courant; **(only) to p. at doing sth.,** faire qch. en amateur; **run away and p.!** déguerpissez, fichez le camp, et allez jouer! allez jouer, allez vous amuser (et laissez-moi tranquille, et fichez-moi la paix)! **to p. with a child, with a doll,** jouer, s'amuser, faire joujou, avec un enfant, avec une poupée; (*b*) **to p. with one's glasses, with a fan,** jouer (distraitement) avec ses lunettes, jouer de l'éventail; (*c*) **to p. with fire,** jouer avec le feu; **don't p. with water, children!** ne jouez pas avec l'eau, les enfants! **don't p. with your health,** ne jouez pas, ne plaisantez pas, avec votre santé; **to p. with ideas,** se forger des idées; **to p. with s.o.'s affections,** jouer avec l'affection de qn; **to p. with love,** badiner avec l'amour; **he's not a man to be played with,** ce n'est pas un homme avec qui on plaisante; (*d*) **to p. on words,** jouer sur les mots, équivoquer; user d'équivoques; (*e*) (i) (*of man and woman*) se comporter en amoureux, échanger des caresses, flirter; se peloter; *U.S:* avoir des relations sexuelles, coucher ensemble; **girls playing about with sailors,** des filles qui frayent, qui flirtent, *U.S:* qui couchent, avec des matelots; (ii) (*of cock bird*) faire la roue devant la femelle; (*of cock bird, male animal*) exécuter la danse, la parade, nuptiale; (*f*) *Ind: A:* chômer.

II. *v.tr. or ind.tr.* **1. to p. billiards, football, chess, cards,** jouer au billard, au football, aux échecs, aux cartes; **to p. (at) ball,** jouer à la balle, au ballon; **p.!** y êtes-vous? prêt(e)? prêt(e)s? *F:* **what d'you think you're playing at?** que diable fais-tu là? **to p. fair,** jouer franc jeu; agir loyalement; **to p. for money,** jouer pour de l'argent; **to p. high, for high stakes,** jouer gros (jeu); **to p. low,** jouer petit (jeu); *F:* **to p. into s.o.'s hands,** jouer, faire, le jeu de qn; fournir à qn des armes contre soi, des armes pour se faire battre; **they p. into each other's hands,** ils sont de connivence, d'intelligence. **2.** (*a*) **to p. (on) the piano, the flute,** jouer du piano, de la flûte; **she was playing the harmonium,** elle tenait l'harmonium; **to p. a piece, a tune,** jouer un morceau, un air; **to p. a tune on the piano, on the flute,** jouer un air au piano, sur la flûte; **won't you p. for us?** voudriez-vous nous faire un peu de musique, nous jouer qch.? **p. us a tune,** jouez-nous un air; **p. me sth. by Chopin,** jouez-moi du Chopin, qch. de Chopin; **she plays well,** elle joue bien; elle est bonne musicienne; (*b*) **to p. the record player,** faire marcher le tourne-disques; écouter des disques; **to p. a record, a tape,** passer un disque, une bande.

III. *v.tr.* **1.** *Th: Cin:* (*a*) **to p. a part, a rôle,** jouer un rôle; **to p. Macbeth,** jouer, tenir, le rôle de Macbeth; **to p. an important part, a questionable rôle, in a matter,** jouer un rôle important, équivoque, dans une affaire; *v.i.* (*of actor*) **to p. on the stage,** jouer, se produire, sur la scène, sur les planches; **to p. in a film,** jouer, tourner, dans un film; *F:* **to p. the fool,** faire l'idiot, l'imbécile; **to p. the man,** se conduire en homme, faire preuve de courage; **to p. the hero,** jouer les héros; *F:* **don't p. the martyr, the tough guy,** ne jouez pas les martyrs, les durs; (*b*) **to p. a tragedy,** jouer, représenter, une tragédie; **an old comedy is being played,** on donne, on joue, une vieille comédie; (*with passive force*) **piece that plays well,** pièce qui rend bien à la scène; **production, film, now playing at . . .,** pièce, film, que l'on donne, qui passe, actuellement à . . .. **2. to p. a joke, a trick, on s.o.,** jouer un tour à qn. **3.** (*a*) *Cards:* **to p. a card,** jouer une carte; **to p. clubs, spades,** jouer trèfle, pique; *v.i.* **to p. high, low,** jouer une forte, basse, carte; **to p. a piece,** jouer, *Chess:* une pièce, (*draughts*) un pion, (*backgammon*) une dame, (*dominoes*) un domino; *Turf:* **to p. the favourite,** jouer le favori; *F:* **to p. a hunch,** jouer, agir, par intuition; (*b*) *Games:* **to p. a stroke,** jouer un coup; **to p. a ball,** jouer une balle (au tennis, etc.); jouer une boule (au jeu de boules); *Bill:* **to p. one's ball into the pocket,** envoyer sa bille dans la blouse; *v.i.* **who plays first?** à qui de commencer, d'entamer? (*at bowling*) à qui la boule? *Golf:* à qui l'honneur? **4.** (*a*) **to p. a game of tennis,** jouer une partie de tennis; **to p. a match,** disputer un match; (*b*) **to p. s.o. at chess,** faire une partie d'échecs avec qn; **to p. s.o. for a championship,** jouer contre qn dans un championnat; disputer un championnat à qn; **I'll p. you for the drinks,** je vous joue les consommations; (*c*) *Fb: etc:* **to p. left back, goalkeeper,** jouer arrière *m* gauche, gardien *m* de but; (*d*) *Sp:* inclure (qn) dans son équipe; **the team was playing two reserves,** l'équipe jouait avec deux réserves. **5.** *esp. Lit:* **to p. s.o. false,** trahir qn, agir déloyalement envers qn; **to p. s.o. fair,** agir loyalement avec qn. **6.** *Fish:* **to p. a fish,** épuiser, manœuvrer, noyer, un poisson. **7.** manier avec dextérité, avec habileté (un bâton, une arme, un instrument, etc.). **8.** diriger (**upon, over,** sur); **to p. a torchlight full in s.o.'s face,** diriger, braquer, la lumière d'une torche électrique en plein visage de qn; **to p. water on the fire,** diriger de l'eau sur l'incendie; **to p. a hose on the fire,** diriger la lance sur le feu; **to p. the guns on sth.,** appliquer, diriger, le feu des pièces sur qch.; *v.i.* **the fire engine played on the house,** la pompe à incendie arrosait la maison, déversait son eau sur la maison; **the guns played on the town,** les canons bombardaient la ville, tiraient sur la ville; **to p. on s.o.'s feelings,** agir, faire pression, sur les sentiments de qn; prendre qn par les sentiments; **the dreariness of the place played upon my mood,** la tristesse du lieu se reflétait, jouait, sur mon état d'âme; **to p. on s.o.'s credulity,** abuser de la crédulité de qn; **to p. on the dissension within the opposition,** profiter, tirer parti, des dissensions au sein de l'opposition.

IV. (*compound verbs*) **1. play back,** *v.tr. Rec:* (faire) repasser (une bande); **p. the last sentence back,** faites repasser la dernière phrase.

2. play down, *v.tr.* minimiser (l'importance de qch.).

3. play in, *v.pr. Sp:* **to p. oneself in,** s'accoutumer, se faire, au jeu.

4. play off, *v.tr.* (*a*) (i) **to p. s.o. off against s.o.,** opposer qn à qn; (ii) montrer (qn) sous un jour désavantageux; (iii) **to p. sth. off as sth. (else),** faire passer qch. pour qch.; (*b*) *Sp:* rejouer (un match nul).

5. play out, *v.tr.* (*a*) jouer (une pièce de théâtre) jusqu'au bout; (*b*) *Cr:* **to p. out time,** faire durer la partie pour obtenir match nul; (*c*) *F:* **played out,** (i) très fatigué, vanné, éreinté, **this man is played out,** c'est un homme vidé; c'est un homme qui montre la corde; (ii) vieux jeu, démodé; **this theory is played out,** cette théorie a fait son temps; (iii) banal, usé, rebattu.

6. play up, (*a*) *v.i.* (i) *Sp:* jouer de son mieux; faire de son mieux; y mettre du sien; en mettre; **p. up!** allez-y! (ii) **to p. up to s.o.,** (α) soutenir qn; donner la réplique à qn; (β) *F:* flatter, aduler, qn; flatter la marotte de qn; lécher les bottes à qn; (iii) (*of child, horse, etc.*) faire des siennes; (*b*) *v.tr. F:* (i) **to p. s.o. up,** agacer, asticoter, enquiquiner, qn; **she plays him up,** elle le fait marcher; **my rheumatism is playing me up,** mes douleurs me font mal; **my heart is playing me up,** mon cœur bat la breloque; (ii) faire ressortir (qch.); exploiter (un incident, un scandale); tirer parti de (qch.); monter (qch.) en épingle.

playact ['pleiækt], *v.i. Th: & F:* faire du théâtre, jouer la comédie.

playacting ['pleiæktiŋ], *s.* (*a*) *Th:* fait *m* de faire du théâtre, de jouer la comédie; (*b*) *F:* **it's just p.,** c'est de la comédie; il fait semblant; c'est une comédie qu'il nous joue.

playactor, *f.* **playactress** ['pleiæktər, -æktris], *s. A:* acteur, -trice; artiste *mf* (dramatique).

playback ['pleibæk], *s. Rec: etc:* play-back *m;* (*of tape recorder*) lecture *f* sonore; *Cin:* postsonorisation *f;* *T.V:* présonorisation *f,* surjeu *m;* (*geophysics*) rejeu *m;* *Cmptr:* **p. head,** tête *f* de lecture.

playbill ['pleibil], *s.* affiche *f* (de théâtre); annonce *f* de spectacle.

playbook ['pleibuk], *s.* recueil *m* de pièces de théâtre.

playbox ['pleibɔks], *s.* coffre *m* à jouets, à ustensiles de sport.

playboy ['pleibɔi], *s.* (*a*) garçon *m,* individu *m,* qui manque de sérieux; (*b*) playboy *m,* noceur *m.*

playday ['pleidei], *s.* jour *m* de congé, de récréation.

player ['pleiər], *s.* **1.** joueur, -euse; *Mus:* musicien, -ienne; exécutant, -ante; artiste *mf;* **trombone p.,** joueur de trombone; **cornet p.,** cornettiste *mf;* **p. piano,** piano *m* mécanique (à rouleau); Pianola *m* (*R.t.m.*). **2.** *Th:* acteur, -trice; artiste (dramatique); interprète *mf* (d'un rôle). **3.** *Sp:* (*a*) équipier, -ière; (*b*) joueur professionnel; **gentlemen versus players,** amateurs contre professionnels. **4.** *Cards:* **card p.,** joueur aux cartes; **first p., last p.,** premier, -ière, dernier, -ière, en cartes. **5.** (*a*) *Rec:* **record p.,** tourne-disques *m inv;* **cassette p.,** magnétophone *m* à cassettes; (*b*) *Tchn:* **maximizing, minimizing, p.,** joueur du maximum, du minimum.

playfellow ['pleifelou], *s. O:* = PLAYMATE.

playfield ['pleifi:ld], *s. esp. U.S:* terrain *m* de jeux, de sports.

playful ['pleiful], *a.* enjoué, badin, folâtre, gai; **p. style,** style badin.

playfully ['pleifuli], *adv.* gaiement, en badinant, avec enjouement.

playfulness ['pleifulnis], *s.* enjouement *m,* badinage *m,* folâtrerie *f,* gaieté *f.*

playgoer ['pleigouər], *s.* habitué, -ée, des spectacles; fréquenteur, -euse, de théâtres.

playground ['pleigraund], *s.* **1.** (*a*) *Sch:* cour *f* (de récréation); **covered p.,** préau *m;* (*b*) **nursery p.,** parc *m* à bébés. **2.** lieu *m* de divertissement; **Switzerland is the p. of Europe,** toute l'Europe va en Suisse pour s'amuser.

playhouse ['pleihaus], *s. A:* théâtre *m;* salle *f* de spectacles.

playing ['pleiiŋ], *s.* **1.** jeu *m;* **p. card,** carte *f* à jouer; **p. card maker,** cartier *m;* **p. field,** terrain *m* de jeux, de sports. **2.** *Th:* (*a*) interprétation *f* (d'un rôle); jeu (d'un acteur); (*b*) représentation *f* (d'une pièce). **3.** *Mus:* exécution *f* (d'un morceau de Chopin, etc.).

playlet ['pleilit], *s.* piécette *f*, saynète *f*.

playmate ['pleimeit], *s.* camarade *mf*, compagnon, *f.* compagne, (de jeu(x)); copain, *f.* copine; **old p.,** ami, -ie, de jeunesse, d'enfance.

play-off ['pleiɔf], *s. Sp:* second match nécessité par un match nul; match de barrage.

playpen ['pleipen], *s.* parc *m* à bébé, pour enfants; **folding p.,** parc repliable (pour enfant).

playroom ['pleiru:m], *s.* salle *f* de jeux.

playschool ['pleisku:l], *s.* = (école) maternelle *f*.

playspell ['pleispel], *s. Sch: U.S:* récréation *f*.

playsuit ['pleisju:t], *s. Cost:* costume *m* de plage.

plaything ['pleiθiŋ], *s.* jouet *m*, joujou *m*; **as a p.,** pour servir d'amusette; **the children treat the dog like a p.,** le chien sert de jouet aux enfants.

playtime ['pleitaim], *s. Sch:* (moment *m*, heure *f*, de la) récréation; heures de récréation, de détente.

playwhite ['plei(h)wait], *s.* mulâtre *mf* (d'Afrique du Sud) qui a franchi la barre de couleur.

playwright ['pleirait], *s.* auteur *m* dramatique; dramaturge *m*.

plea [pli:], *s.* **1.** *Jur:* (*a*) *A:* & *Scot:* procès *m*; action *f* en justice; *Eng.Hist:* **Court of Common Pleas,** Cour *f* des Plaids Communs; (*b*) conclusions *fpl*, moyens *mpl* (de défense); défense *f*, allégations *fpl*; (*c*) **incidental p.,** exception *f*; **defendant's p.,** première exception; **foreign p.,** exception déclinatoire; non-lieu *m*; **p. in bar, special p.,** exception péremptoire; fin *f* de non-recevoir; **to put in a p. in bar of trial,** réclamer l'incompétence; **to put in a p. of alienism,** alléguer sa qualité d'étranger; **his counsel will put forward a p. of insanity,** son défenseur va plaider la folie; **to establish a p. of . . .,** exciper de . . .; **to submit the p. that . . .,** plaider que + *ind.*; **p. of necessity,** défense fondée sur l'impossibilité de faire autrement; **to urge the p. of necessity,** (i) alléguer, plaider, l'impossibilité de faire autrement; (ii) se retrancher derrière la force des choses. **2.** (*a*) excuse *f*, prétexte *m*, justification *f* (**for doing sth.,** pour faire qch.); *Jur:* **to offer a p.,** exciper d'une excuse; **on the p. of . . .,** sous prétexte de . . .; **if you apply to him he will put up a p. of impossibility,** si vous vous adressez à lui il alléguera l'impossible; (*b*) **p. for mercy,** appel *m* à la clémence.

pleach [pli:tʃ], *v.tr.* entrelacer, enlacer, enchevêtrer.

plead [pli:d], *v.i.* & *tr.* (**pleaded,** *occ.* **pled** [pled]) **1.** *v.i.* (*a*) *Jur:* plaider (**for,** pour; **against,** contre); (*b*) **to p. with s.o. for s.o., sth.,** intervenir, intercéder, plaider, auprès de qn pour, en faveur de, qn, qch.; **they were pleading with him to stop,** ils le suppliaient de s'arrêter; (*c*) *Jur:* **to p. guilty,** plaider coupable; s'avouer coupable; **to p. not guilty,** plaider non coupable; se dire, se proclamer, innocent, non coupable; nier sa culpabilité. **2.** *v.tr.* (*a*) *Jur:* plaider (une cause); **he was not allowed to p. his cause,** on lui a interdit tout plaidoyer; **to p. s.o.'s cause with s.o.,** intercéder pour qn auprès de qn; plaider la cause de qn auprès de qn; (*b*) *Jur:* **to p. one's good faith,** exciper de sa bonne foi; **his counsel will p. insanity,** son défenseur va plaider la folie; **to p. the prisoner's youth,** plaider la jeunesse de l'accusé; (*c*) invoquer, alléguer, faire valoir (une excuse); **to p. ignorance,** alléguer, prétexter, l'ignorance; **to p. difficulties in regard to sth.,** objecter des difficultés à qch.; **to p. fatigue,** prétexter la fatigue; invoquer la fatigue comme excuse.

pleadable ['pli:dəbl], *a.* **1.** *Jur:* plaidable. **2.** (excuse, etc.) invocable, alléguable.

pleader ['pli:dər], *s.* **1.** avocat (plaidant); défenseur *m*; **special p.,** (i) *Jur:* avocat consultant; (ii) plaideur *m* pour son saint; casuiste *m*. **2.** intercesseur *m* (**for s.o.,** en faveur de qn).

pleading[1] ['pli:diŋ], *a.* implorant; (regard, ton) de prière.

pleading[2], *s.* **1.** l'art *m* de plaider. **2.** *Jur:* (*a*) plaidoyer *m*; plaidoirie *f*; (*b*) *pl.* **the pleadings,** (i) les débats *m*; (ii) l'exposé *m* des chefs d'accusation ou des moyens de défense; les conclusions (échangées avant l'audience); (*c*) **special p.,** (i) défense fondée sur ce que la cause offre de spécial; (ii) arguments spécieux, fallacieux. **3.** prières *fpl*, intercession *f* (**for,** en faveur de).

pleadingly ['pli:diŋli], *adv.* d'un ton de prière; d'un ton suppliant.

pleasance ['plez(ə)ns], *s. A:* & *Poet:* **1.** plaisir *m*, délice *m*. **2.** jardin *m* d'agrément.

pleasant ['plez(ə)nt], *a.* **1.** agréable, charmant, aimable; doux, *f.* douce; **it's p. to look at, p. to the eye,** cela fait plaisir à voir, cela flatte les yeux; **p. smile,** doux sourire; **things p. to hear,** choses agréables à entendre; **p. news,** douce nouvelle; **story that makes p. reading,** histoire *f* agréable à lire; **p. breeze,** brise douce; **p. perfumes,** de savoureux parfums; **p. to the taste,** agréable au goût; **to keep a p. memory of s.o.,** garder un doux souvenir de qn; **p. society,** charmante société; société agréable; **life is p. here,** il fait bon vivre ici; **my life has been a p. one,** j'ai eu la vie douce; **it's a p. day,** il fait bon aujourd'hui; **it's a p. day for walking,** il fait bon se promener aujourd'hui; **to have a p. day,** passer agréablement la journée; **it's very p. to take a walk on the beach,** il est très agréable de se promener sur la plage; **goodnight, p. dreams,** bonne nuit, faites de beaux rêves; **it's pleasanter here,** il fait meilleur ici; *s.* **to combine the p. with the useful,** joindre l'utile à l'agréable. **2.** (*of pers.*) gai, plaisant; **a man p. to deal with,** un homme d'humeur facile; homme facile à vivre; **to make oneself p., to be p. (to s.o.),** faire l'agréable (auprès de qn), faire l'aimable (avec qn); **he was very p.,** il a été charmant; il s'est montré très affable, très gentil.

pleasantly ['plez(ə)ntli], *adv.* **1.** agréablement; **the room was p. warm,** il régnait dans la pièce une chaleur agréable. **2.** d'une manière agréable, charmante, affable; avec affabilité.

pleasantness ['plezəntnis], *s.* **1.** agrément *m*, charme *m* (d'un endroit, etc.). **2.** (*of pers.*) (*a*) gaieté *f*, enjouement *m*; (*b*) affabilité *f*; gentillesse *f*.

pleasantry ['plezəntri], *s.* **1.** *A:* gaieté *f*, enjouement *m*. **2.** plaisanterie *f*.

please [pli:z], *v.tr.* **1.** (i) plaire à (qn); faire plaisir à (qn); (ii) contenter (qn); **nothing pleases him,** rien ne lui plaît; il n'est jamais content de rien; **to p. s.o. greatly,** faire grand plaisir à qn; **you can't p. everybody,** on ne peut plaire à tout le monde; **to be easily pleased,** s'arranger de tout; **there's no pleasing him,** il n'y a pas moyen de lui plaire; **he's hard to p.,** il est difficile (à contenter); **in order to p. s.o.,** par complaisance pour qn; pour faire plaisir à qn; **to p. one's boss,** donner satisfaction à son chef; **wine that pleases the palate,** vin *m* agréable au palais, qui chatouille le palais; **music that pleases the ear,** musique qui flatte l'oreille; **I dress to p. myself,** je m'habille à mon gré, à ma guise; **I play the piano to p. myself,** je joue du piano pour mon plaisir; **p. yourself! do as you p.!** faites comme il vous plaira, comme vous voudrez; faites à votre guise; *v.i.* **works intended merely to p.,** ouvrages de pur agrément; **to lay oneself out to p.,** se mettre en frais pour plaire; faire des frais; **to set out to p. s.o.,** chercher à plaire à qn; **she tries to p. him,** elle cherche à lui plaire; **anything to p.!** à tes ordres! **2.** (*a*) *impers. A:* & *Lit:* **if it so p. you,** si tel est votre plaisir; **may it p. your Majesty,** plaise, n'en déplaise, à votre Majesté; **p. God!** plaise à Dieu! Dieu le veuille! (*b*) (**if you**) **p.,** s'il vous plaît; s'il te plaît; **come in, p.,** entrez, s'il vous plaît; entrez, je vous prie; **p. don't cry,** de grâce ne pleurez pas; **p. turn over,** tournez (la page), s'il vous plaît; **p. tell me . . .,** ayez la bonté de me dire . . .; veuillez me dire . . .; **p. be so kind as to . . ., p. have the kindness to . . .,** veuillez (bien) . . .; **may I?—p. do!** vous permettez?—je vous en prie! faites donc! **p. sit down, p. take a seat,** veuillez (donc) vous asseoir; vous plairait-il de vous asseoir? **p. don't interrupt!** veuillez bien ne pas nous interrompre; pas d'interruptions, s'il vous plaît! **will you p. shut up!** voulez-vous me faire le plaisir de vous taire! **p. return this book,** prière de retourner ce livre; **p. don't answer me back,** pas d'insolences, s'il vous plaît; *P.N:* **p. do not walk on the grass,** prière de ne pas marcher sur l'herbe; *Sch:* **p., sir!** pardon, monsieur! *Iron:* **and then if you p. he blamed me for it!** et puis il a dit que c'était de ma faute, s'il vous plait! **3.** *v.i.* **to do as one pleases,** agir à sa guise, à son gré; **do as you p.,** faites comme vous voudrez, comme vous l'entendez, comme bon vous semblera, comme il vous plaira; faites ce qui vous semble bon, ce que bon vous semblera; **he will do just as he pleases, he will only do as he pleases,** il n'en fera qu'à sa guise, qu'à sa tête; *F:* **just as you p.,** c'est, ce sera, comme vous voudrez; **when you p.,** quand vous voudrez; quand il vous plaira; **I'll do it if I p.,** je le ferai si cela me plaît, si bon me semble.

pleased [pli:zd], *a.* **1.** satisfait, content, heureux; **p. smile,** sourire *m* de satisfaction; **to be p. with sth.,** être satisfait de qch.; se louer de qch.; approuver qch.; **I'm p. with anything,** je m'accommode de tout; **he's very p., highly p., with himself,** il est très content, fort satisfait, de sa petite personne; **your father will not be p.,** votre père ne sera pas content; *B:* **this is my beloved Son, in whom I am well p.,** c'est ici mon Fils bien-aimé, en qui j'ai mis toute mon affection; **I'm p. at the news,** je suis heureux d'apprendre cette nouvelle; **I'm very p. he's coming,** cela me fait grand plaisir, je suis très content, qu'il vienne; **to be anything but p.,** ne pas être du tout content; *F:* **he's as p. as Punch,** (i) il est heureux comme un roi; (ii) il en est fier comme Artaban; **to be p. to do sth.,** faire qch. avec plaisir, se faire un plaisir de faire qch.; **I'll be p. to come,** j'aurai grand plaisir à venir; **he'll be very p. to do it,** il le fera volontiers; **I'm very p. to see you,** je suis très content de vous voir; cela me fait grand plaisir de vous voir; **I'm p. to say that . . .,** j'ai, je prends, plaisir à constater que . . .; je suis heureux, charmé, enchanté, de pouvoir vous dire que . . .; cela me fait plaisir de vous apprendre que . . .; *Com:* **I am p. to inform you that . . .,** je m'empresse de vous aviser que . . .. **2. His Majesty has been graciously p. to . . .,** il a plu à sa gracieuse Majesté de . . .; **the King was p. to accept . . .,** le roi voulut bien accepter . . .; le roi daigna accepter . . .; **be p. to accept these few flowers,** daignez accepter ces quelques fleurs; *Iron:* **you are p. to say so,** cela vous plaît à dire.

pleasing ['pli:ziŋ], *a.* agréable; **p. face,** figure *f* sympathique; **p. figure,** silhouette gracieuse; physique *m* agréable; **p. manner,** abord *m* agréable; prévenance *f*; **a p. memory,** un doux souvenir; un souvenir agréable; **a p. view,** un spectacle riant, qui flatte les yeux.

pleasingly ['pli:ziŋli], *adv.* agréablement.

pleasingness ['pli:ziŋnis], *s.* agrément *m*, charme *m*; nature *f* agréable, aspect riant (**of,** de).

pleasurable ['pleʒərəbl], *a.* agréable.

pleasurableness ['pleʒərəblnis], *s.* agrément *m*, charme *m*.

pleasurably ['pleʒərəbli], *adv.* agréablement.

pleasure[1] ['pleʒər], *s.* **1.** plaisir *m*; **to take, find, (a) p. in doing sth.,** éprouver du plaisir, prendre, avoir, (du) plaisir, se (com)plaire, à faire qch.; **to take p. in music,** prendre du plaisir à la musique; **I derive great p. from music,** je prends grand plaisir à la musique; la musique me procure de grands plaisirs; **I shall have great p. in seeing you again,** j'aurai beaucoup de plaisir à vous revoir; **I have p. in informing you that . . .,** je suis heureux, j'ai le plaisir, de vous apprendre que . . .; je prends plaisir, j'ai plaisir, à vous faire savoir que . . .; **it is our p. to inform you that . . .,** nous avons le plaisir, l'honneur, de vous faire savoir que . . .; **it will be a p. to go with you,** je me ferai un plaisir, je serai très heureux, ce sera pour moi un grand plaisir, de vous accompagner; **it gave me great p.,** cela m'a fait grand plaisir; **it gave me great p. to see him again,** cela m'a fait plaisir de le revoir; **it would give me the greatest p.,** cela me ferait le plus grand plaisir; **it is a great p. to me to be present,** c'est pour moi un grand plaisir d'être présent; **it is a real p. to learn that . . .,** c'est un réel plaisir d'apprendre que . . .; **it's a real p. to see you looking so cheerful,** cela me fait (infiniment de) plaisir de vous voir si gai; **it was a p. to hear him,** c'était (un) plaisir de l'entendre; **it is a p. to listen to him,** il y a plaisir à l'écouter; **I haven't the p. of knowing him, of his acquaintance,** je n'ai pas le plaisir, l'avantage, de le connaître; **I'm so glad to meet you—the p. is mine,** je suis très heureux de faire votre connaissance—mais c'est moi qui suis enchanté; **Mr X requests the p. of the company of Miss Y at . . .,** M. X prie Mlle Y de lui faire le plaisir d'assister à . . .; **they request the p. of your company to dinner,** ils vous prient de leur faire le plaisir de dîner avec eux; **with p.,** avec plaisir; volontiers; de bon cœur; de grand cœur; **with great p.,** avec grand plaisir; **with the greatest (of) p.,** avec le plus grand plaisir. **2.** (*a*) plaisir(s), jouissances *fpl*; **to be fond of p.,** aimer le plaisir; **life given up to p., life of p.,** vie adonnée au plaisir; **to take one's p.,** s'amuser, se divertir; **if you take your pleasures in that way,** si cela vous amuse; **to take one's pleasures sadly,** s'amuser en faisant une figure d'enterrement; **to travel for p.,** voyager pour son plaisir; **place with no opportunities for p.,** endroit *m* sans distractions; **p. seeker,** jouisseur, -euse; personne *f* en quête de plaisirs; **p. seeking,** recherche *f* des plaisirs; **he's always been p. loving, p. seeking,** il a toujours été amoureux des plaisirs; il a toujours aimé le(s) plaisir(s); **p. trip,** partie *f* de plaisir; *O:* **p. resort,** ville *f* de plaisir; **p. boat,** bateau *m* de plaisance, plaisancier *m*; *U.S:* (*pers.*) **p. boater,** plaisancier; **p. ground,** parc *m*, jardin *m*, d'agrément; lieu *m* de plaisance; (*b*) **sensual p.,** volupté *f*, débauche *f*; *A:* **a woman of p.,** fille de joie; **man of p.,** débauché *m*. **3.** volonté *f*; bon plaisir; *A:* **without consulting my p.,** sans me consulter; **at p.,** à volonté; **at s.o.'s p.,** au gré de qn; au bon plaisir de qn; **office held during p.,** emploi *m* amovible; **during the King's p.,** pendant le bon plaisir du roi; (*of king*) **it is our p. to . . .,** il nouse a plu de . . .; *O:* **what's your p., madam?** qu'y a-t-il pour votre service, madame?

pleasure[2], *v. A:* **1.** *v.tr.* faire plaisir à (qn). **2.** *v.i.* se plaire, prendre plaisir (**in sth., in doing sth.,** à qch., à faire qch.).

pleat[1] [pli:t], *s.* (*a*) *Dressm: etc:* pli *m*; **pleats,** plis; plissé *m*; **box p., inverted p.,** pli creux, rentré, inverti; double pli; **knife pleats,** plis cassants; **flat pleats,** plis couchés, plats; **to take the pleats out of material,** déplisser une étoffe; (*b*) *Hairdr:* (**French**) **p.,** banane *f.*

pleat[2], *v.tr.* (*a*) plisser, faire des plis à (une jupe, etc.); (*b*) bâtonner (du linge).

pleated ['pli:tid], *a.* (*of skirt, etc.*) plissé; **accordion-p. skirt,** jupe à plis d'accordéon; **box-p. skirt,** jupe à doubles plis, à plis creux; **permanently p.,** indéplissable.

pleater ['pli:tər], *s.* plisseur, -euse.

pleating ['pli:tiŋ], *s.* **1.** plissage *m*; **p. machine,** plisseuse *f.* **2.** *coll.* plissé(s) *m(pl).*

pleb [pleb], *s.* (*a*) *F:* plébéien, -ienne; prolétaire *mf*; prolo *m*; (*b*) **the plebs,** (i) *Rom.Hist:* la plèbe; (ii) *F:* le peuple; le prolétariat; la plèbe.

plebe [pli:b], *s. U.S: F:* élève *m* de première année (dans une école militaire ou navale).

plebeian [pli'bi:ən]. **1.** *s.* (*a*) *Rom.Hist:* plébéien, -ienne; (*b*) homme, femme, du bas peuple; plébéien; prolétaire *mf;* roturier, -ière. **2.** *a.* plébéien, vulgaire; du peuple; **p. name,** nom bourgeois; nom de roturier; *Pej:* **to speak with a p. accent,** parler avec l'accent du peuple.

plebeianism [pli'bi:ənizm], *s.* plébéianisme *m;* vulgarité *f*; caractère plébéien (d'une œuvre, etc.).

plebeianize [pli'bi:ənaiz], *v.tr.* **1.** rendre commun, grossier, vulgaire; vulgariser. **2.** mettre (une littérature, etc.) au niveau du peuple; prolétariser (une œuvre, etc.).

plebification [plebifi'keiʃ(ə)n], *s.* (*a*) fait de rendre grossier, vulgaire; **the popularization of art often leads to its p.,** la vulgarisation de l'art le fait souvent tomber dans la vulgarité; (*b*) prolétarisation *f.*

plebiscitary [pli'bisit(ə)ri], *a.* plébiscitaire.

plebiscite ['plebisit], *s.* plébiscite *m.*

Plecoptera [pli'kɔptərə], *s.pl. Ent:* plécoptères *m.*

plecopteran, plecopterous [pli'kɔptərən, -rəs], *a. Ent:* plécoptère.

plecopterid [pli'kɔptərid], *a. & s. Ent:* plécoptère (*m*).

plectognath ['plektəgnæθ], *a. & s. Ich:* plectognathe (*m*).

Plectognathi [plek'tɔgnəθai], *s.pl. Ich:* plectognathes *m.*

plectognathous [plek'tɔgnəθəs], *a. Ich:* plectognathe.

Plectoptera [plek'tɔptərə], *s.pl. Ent:* plectoptères *m.*

plectopteran [plek'tɔptərən], *a. & s. Ent:* plectoptère (*m*).

Plectroptera [plek'trɔptərə], *s.pl. Orn:* plectroptères *m.*

plectropteran [plek'trɔptərən], *a. & s. Orn:* plectroptère (*m*).

plectrum ['plektrəm], *s. Mus:* plectre *m*, médiator *m.*

pledge[1] [pledʒ], *s.* **1.** gage *m*, nantissement *m*; **additional p.,** complément *m* de gage; **depreciation of the p.,** dépréciation *f* du gage; **p. holder,** détenteur, -trice, de gage(s); (créancier *m*) gagiste *m*; **p. of movables,** gage mobilier; **p. of real property,** gage immobilier; **realization of a p.,** réalisation *f* d'un gage; **setting aside as p.,** affectation *f* en gage; **unredeemed p.,** gage non retiré; **valuation of a p.,** estimation *f* d'un gage; **value as p.,** valeur *f* en gage; **to borrow on p.,** emprunter sur gage; **to give, put, sth. in p.,** donner, mettre, qch. en gage; **to hold in p.,** (dé)tenir en gage, en nantissement; **to keep sth. as a p.,** conserver qch. en gage; **to realize a p.,** réaliser un gage; **to redeem a p.,** retirer un gage; **to set aside as a p.,** affecter en gage; **to supplement a p.,** suppléer à un gage; **to take sth. as a p.,** prendre qch. en gage; **to take sth. out of p.,** dégager qch. **2. p. of good faith,** garantie *f* de bonne foi. **3.** *A:* gage d'amour; enfant *mf.* **4.** (*a*) promesse *f*, engagement *m*, vœu *m*; parole *f* d'honneur; **I am under a p. of secrecy,** j'ai fait vœu de garder le secret; je me suis engagé à garder le secret; (*b*) **to take, sign, the p.,** promettre de s'abstenir d'alcool. **5.** toast *m*; santé (portée à qn).

pledge[2], *v.tr.* **1.** donner, mettre (qch.) en gage; déposer (qch.) en gage, en nantissement; donner (qch.) en garantie; engager, gager (qch.); **to p. one's property,** engager, gager, son bien; **to p. securities,** engager, gager, nantir, des titres, des valeurs; déposer, remettre, des titres, des valeurs, en gage, en garantie, en nantissement; **to p. shares as security for money advanced,** gager, nantir, des titres, des valeurs, en garantie de fonds avancés; **to p. securities as collateral,** gager des titres, des valeurs, en garantie, en nantissement. **2.** engager (sa parole, etc.); **to p. oneself, one's word, to do sth.,** s'engager à faire qch.; prendre l'engagement de faire qch.; **on my pledging not to say anything about it,** quand j'ai promis de n'en rien dire; **to p. oneself for sth.,** se porter garant de qch.; **I p. myself that . . .,** je me porte garant que + *ind.*; **to p. s.o. (to do sth.),** lier qn par un engagement (à faire qch.); **to be pledged to do sth.,** avoir pris l'engagement de faire qch.; **to p. one's honour, one's word,** engager sa parole; donner sa parole d'honneur; s'engager sur l'honneur; jurer sa foi; **to p. one's honour to do sth.,** s'engager d'honneur à faire qch.; **I p. you my word that . . .,** je vous garantis, je vous donne ma parole, que . . .; **I would not p. my word that . . .,** je n'affirmerais pas que . . .; **to p. one's allegiance to the king,** vouer obéissance au roi. **3.** (*a*) boire à la santé de (qn), porter un toast à (qn); (*b*) *A:* faire raison à (qn).

pledgee [ple'dʒi:], *s. Jur:* (créancier *m*) gagiste *m*; prêteur, -euse, sur gage(s).

pledger ['pledʒər], *s.* emprunteur, -euse, sur gage(s); débiteur, -trice, sur gages.

pledget ['pledʒit], *s.* **1.** *Surg:* (*a*) compresse *f*, tampon *m* (d'ouate, etc.); bourdonnet *m*; (*b*) *A:* plumasseau *m*, sindon *m.* **2.** *Tchn:* bouchon *m*, tampon (d'étoupe); *Nau:* cordon *m* d'étoupe; quenouillon *m.*

pledging ['pledʒiŋ], *s.* **1.** engagement *m*; mise *f* en gage; nantissement *m.* **2.** garantissement *m.*

pleiad, *pl.* **-ads, -ades** ['plaiəd, -ədz, -ədi:z], *s.* **1.** *Lit:* pléiade *f.* **2. the Pleiads, the Pleiades,** (*a*) *Myth:* les Pléiades, les Atlantides *f*; (*b*) *Astr:* les Pléiades.

plein air [plein'ɛər]. *Art:* **1.** *s.* le plein air (en peinture). **2.** *a.* relatif (i) à la peinture de plein air, (ii) *Hist:* à l'école française de peinture en plein air; **p. a. painter,** peintre *m* (i) de plein air, (ii) *Hist:* de l'école française de peinture en plein air.

pleinairism [plein'ɛərizm], *s. Art:* (i) la peinture de plein air; (ii) *Hist:* la théorie, l'œuvre *f*, de l'école française de peinture en plein air; pleinairisme *m.*

pleinairist(e) [plein'ɛərist, -'ri:st], *s. Art:* peintre *m* (i) de plein air, (ii) *Hist:* appartenant à l'école française de peinture en plein air; pleinairiste *mf.*

pleiomerous [plai'ɔmərəs], *a. Bot:* pléiomère.

pleiomery [plai'ɔməri], *s. Bot:* pléiomérie *f.*

pleiotropic [plaiou'trɔpik], *a. Biol:* pléiotropique.

pleiotropism [plai'ɔtrəpizm], *s. Biol:* pléiotropisme *m.*

pleiotropy [plai'ɔtrəpi], *s. Biol:* pléiotropie *f.*

pleistocene ['plaistousi:n], *a. & s. Geol:* pléistocène (*m*).

plenarily ['pli:nərili], *adv.* pleinement, complètement, entièrement; plénièrement.

plenary ['pli:nəri], *a.* complet, -ète, entier; **p. power,** pouvoir absolu; plein pouvoir; **p. court, assembly,** cour, assemblée, plénière.

plenipotentiary [plenipə'tenʃ(ə)ri], *a. & s.* plénipotentiaire (*m*); **minister p.,** ministre *m* plénipotentiaire (**to,** auprès de).

plenish ['pleniʃ], *v.tr. Scot:* (*a*) remplir (**with,** de); (*b*) garnir, meubler (une maison, une métairie).

plenishing ['pleniʃiŋ], *s. Scot:* (*a*) mobilier *m* (d'une maison); matériel *m* et cheptel *m* (d'une ferme); (*b*) apport *m* de mobilier en mariage (par la femme).

plenism ['pli:nizm], *s. Phil:* plénisme *m.*

plenist ['pli:nist], *s. Phil:* pléniste *mf.*

plenitude ['plenitju:d], *s.* plénitude *f.*

plenteous ['plentiəs], *a. Poet:* **1.** abondant, copieux. **2.** fertile, riche (**in sth.,** en qch.).

plenteously ['plentiəsli], *adv. Poet:* en abondance.

plenteousness ['plentiəsnis], *s.* abondance *f.*

plentiful ['plentiful], *a.* abondant, copieux, ample; **p. harvest,** moisson abondante; **p. dinner,** dîner copieux, plantureux; **to be p.,** abonder, affluer; **money is p. with him,** l'argent afflue chez lui.

plentifully ['plentifuli], *adv.* abondamment; en abondance; copieusement, amplement.

plentifulness ['plentifulnis], *s.* abondance *f.*

plenty ['plenti]. **1.** *s.* (*a*) abondance *f*; **he has p. of everything,** il a tout en abondance; il a de tout à, en, suffisance; **p. of money, money in p.,** une ample provision d'argent; une ample fortune; de l'argent en abondance; **to have p. of courage,** ne pas manquer de courage; **you've got p. of time,** vous avez bien, amplement, largement, grandement, le temps; vous avez du temps de reste; ce n'est pas le temps qui vous manque; **to arrive in p. of time,** arriver de bonne heure; **to fix a dress with p. of pins,** ajuster une robe à grand renfort d'épingles; **for landscape work six tubes of paint are p.,** pour le paysage, c'est assez de six tubes de couleur; **to have p. to live on,** avoir grandement de quoi vivre; **there are p. (of) other books upstairs,** il ne manque pas d'autres livres en haut; (*b*) **to live in p.,** vivre à l'aise; vivre dans l'abondance; **land of p.,** pays *m* de cocagne, de bénédiction; **year of p.,** année *f* d'abondance. **2.** *adv. F:* **it's p. big enough,** c'est bien assez gros; **it's p. good enough,** ça suffit grandement. **3.** *a. A: & U.S:* abondant, copieux, ample; **money is p. but labour is scarce,** l'argent abonde mais on manque de main-d'œuvre.

plenum ['pli:nəm], *s.* **1.** *Ph:* plein *m*; **p. method of ventilation,** ventilation *f* mécanique par insufflation; *Mec.E:* **p. chamber,** chambre *f* de tranquillisation. **2.** *A:* assemblée plénière; salle pleine.

pleochroic, pleochroous [pli:ou'krouik, pli:'ɔkrouəs], *a. Cryst:* pléochroïque, polychroïque.

pleochroism [pli:'ɔkrouizm], *s. Cryst:* pléochroïsme *m*, polychroïsme *m.*

pleomorphic, pleomorphous [pli:ou'mɔ:fik, -'mɔ:fəs], *a. Biol: Ch:* pléomorphe, polymorphe.

pleomorphism, pleomorphy [pli:ou'mɔ:fizm, 'pli:oumɔ:fi], *s. Biol: Ch:* pléomorphisme *m*, polymorphisme *m.*

pleonasm ['pli:ənæzm], *s.* pléonasme *m.*

pleonast ['pli:ənæst], *s. Miner:* pléonaste *m.*

pleonastic [pli:ə'næstik], *a.* pléonastique, redondant; (*of word*) **to be p.,** faire pléonasme.

pleonastically [pli:ə'næstik(ə)li], *adv.* d'une manière pléonastique; par pléonasme.

pleospora [pli:'ɔspərə], *s. Fung:* pléospore *m.*

pleroma [pli'roumə], *s. A.Phil:* plérome *m.*

plerome ['pliəroum], *s. Bot:* plérome *m.*

plesiosaur, plesiosaurus, *pl.* **-ri** ['pli:siəsɔ:r, 'sɔ:rəs, -rai], *s. Paleont:* plésiosaure *m.*

plethodon ['pleθədɔn], *s. Amph:* pléthodon *m.*

plethodont(id) ['pleθədɔnt, -'dɔntid], *a. & s. Amph:* pléthodontidé (*m*).

Plethodontidae [pleθou'dɔntidi:], *s.pl. Amph:* pléthodontidés *m.*

plethora ['pleθərə], *s.* **1.** *Med:* pléthore *f.* **2.** pléthore, surabondance *f* (de bien, etc.).

plethoric [pli'θɔrik], *a.* pléthorique; **p. condition (of body),** réplétion *f.*

plethron ['pleθrɔn], *s. A.Meas:* plèthre *m.*

plethysmogram [pli'θizməgræm], *s. Med:* pléthysmogramme *m.*

plethysmograph [pli'θizməgræf], *s. Med:* pléthysmographe *m.*

plethysmographic [pliθizmə'græfik], *a. Med:* pléthysmographique.

plethysmography [pleθiz'mɔgrəfi], *s. Med:* pléthysmographie *f.*

pleura, *pl.* **-ae** ['pluərə, -i:], *s. Anat:* plèvre *f*; **pulmonary p.,** feuillet viscéral de la plèvre; **costal p., parietal p.,** feuillet pariétal de la plèvre.

Pleuracanthus [pluərə'kænθəs], *s. Paleont:* pleuracanthe *m*, pleuracanthus *m.*

pleural ['pluərəl], *a. Anat:* pleural, -aux.

pleurectomy [pluə'rektəmi], *s. Surg:* pleurectomie *f.*

pleurisy ['pluərisi], *s. Med:* pleurésie *f*; **dry p.,** pleurésie sèche; pleurite *f*; **wet p.,** pleurésie avec épanchement; **p. patient,** pleurétique *mf.*

pleuritic [pluə'ritik], *a.* pleurétique.

pleurocarpous [pluərou'kɑ:pəs], *a. Bot:* pleurocarpe.

pleurodont ['pluəroudɔnt], *a. & s. Z:* pleurodonte (*m*).

pleurodynia [pluərou'diniə], *s. Med:* pleurodynie *f*; fausse pleurésie.

pleurodynic [pluərou'dinik], *a. Med:* pleurodynique.

pleuromorph ['pluəroumɔ:f], *s. Miner:* pleuromorphe *m.*

pleuromorphosis [pluəroumɔ:'fousis], *s. Ph:* pleuromorphose *f.*

pleuronectid [pluərou'nektid], *s. Ich:* pleuronecte *m.*

Pleuronectidae [pluərou'nektidi:], *s.pl. Ich:* pleuronectidés *m.*

pleuropericarditis [pluərouperikɑ:'daitis], *s. Med:* pleuropéricardite *f.*

pleuropneumonia [pluərounju:'mouniə], *s. Med:* pleuropneumonie *f*, pneumopleurésie *f*; *Vet:* **contagious bovine p.,** péripneumonie *f.*

pleuropneumonic [pluərounju:'mɔnik], *a. Med:* pleuropneumonique.

pleuroscope ['pluərəskoup], *s. Med:* pleuroscope *m.*

pleuroscopic [pluərə'skɔpik], *a. Med:* pleuroscopique.

pleuroscopy [pluə'rɔskəpi], *s. Med:* pleuroscopie *f.*

pleurothotonos [pluərou'θɔtənəs], *s. Med:* pleurothotonos *m.*

pleurotomy [pluə'rɔtəmi], *s. Surg:* pleurotomie *f.*

Pleurotremata [pluərou'tremətə], *s.pl. Ich:* pleurotrèmes *m.*

pleurotus [pluə'routəs], *s. Fung:* pleurote *m.*

plexalgia [plek'sældʒiə], *s. Med:* plexalgie *f.*

plexiform ['pleksifɔ:m], *a. Anat:* plexiforme.

Plexiglass ['pleksiglɑ:s], *s. R.t.m:* Plexiglas *m.*

pleximeter [plek'simitər], *s. Med:* plessimètre *m.*

plexor ['pleksɔ:r], *s. Med:* percuteur *m.*

plexus ['pleksəs], *s.* **1.** *Anat:* plexus *m*; **solar p.,** plexus solaire; **coeliac p.,** plexus cœliaque; **cardiac p.,** plexus cardiaque; **gastric p.,** plexus hypogastrique; **mesenteric p.,** plexus mésentérique; **dental p.,** plexus dentaire; **nerve p.,** plexus nerveux. **2.** enchevêtrement *m*, dédale *m* (de rues, etc.).

pliability [plaiə'biliti], *s.* (*a*) flexibilité *f*, souplesse *f* (d'une tige, etc.); (*b*) docilité *f*, souplesse, tractabilité *f*, malléabilité *f*, facilité *f* (de caractère).

pliable ['plaiəbl], *a.* **1.** (*a*) pliable, pliant, flexible; (cuir) souple; **steel is more p. than iron,** l'acier *m* obéit mieux que le fer; (*b*) (voix, etc.) flexible. 2. (caractère, etc.) docile, malléable, souple, accommodant, complaisant; **p. character,** caractère de cire.

pliancy ['plaiənsi], *s.* = PLIABILITY.

pliant ['plaiənt], *a.* = PLIABLE.

pliantly ['plaiəntli], *adv.* (*a*) souplement; avec souplesse; (*b*) d'une manière docile, accommodante; docilement.

plica, *pl.* **-ae** ['plaikə, 'plikə, -i:], *s.* 1. (*a*) *Anat:* pli *m*, repli *m* (de la peau, etc.); **plicae palantinae transversae,** crêtes palatines; **p. sublingualis,** repli sublingual; (*b*) *Bot:* repli longitudinal (d'une feuille de muscinée, d'un sporange). 2. *Med:* **p. (polonica),** plique (polonaise). 3. *A.Mus:* liaison *f*.

plicate(d) ['plaikeit(id), 'pli-], *a. Bot:* (*of leaf, etc.*) plicatif; *Geol:* (*of stratum*) plissé, replié.

plicatile ['plaikətail, 'pli-], *a. Nat.Hist:* plicatile.

plication [plai'keiʃ(ə)n, pli-], *s. Geol:* plissement *m* (de couches).

plié ['pli:ei], *s. Danc:* plié *m*.

pliers ['plaiəz], *s.pl.* (*a*) *Tls:* pince(s) *f(pl)*, tenaille(s) *f(pl)*; **bent nose p.,** pince à bec de corbin; **roundnose(d) p.,** pince(s) à bec rond, à mors rond; pinces rondes; **flat (nose) p.,** pinces plates; **long nose p.,** pince(s) à long bec; **needle nose p.,** pince(s) à bec effilé; **duckbill p.,** pince à bec de canard; **smooth p.,** pince(s) à mors lisse; **(five position) adjustable p.,** pince multiprise (à cinq positions); **insulated p.,** pince(s) isolante(s), pinces d'électricien; **bending p.,** pince(s) à cintrer, à courber; **contouring p.,** pince(s) à bouteroller; **crimping p.,** pince(s) à sertir; **(fixed die, removable die) riveting p.,** pince(s) à river (à bouterolle fixe, à bouterolle interchangeable); **sealing p.,** pince(s) à plomber; **soldering p.,** pince(s) à souder; **combination p.,** pinces universelles; **gas p.,** pinces à gaz, pinces de plombier; **punch p.,** pince à emporte-pièce; *El:* **stripping p.,** pince(s) à dénuder (les fils); **universal p.,** pinces universelles; (*b*) *Surg:* **cotton p.,** pince, précelles *fpl*, à coton; **dressing p.,** pince à pansement; **surgical p.,** pince(s) chirurgicale(s).

plight[1] [plait], *s.* (*a*) *A:* condition *f*, situation *f*, état *m*; (*b*) **to be in a sorry p., in a sad p.,** (i) être en mauvaise passe, en fâcheuse posture; être dans de beaux draps, (ii) être dans un triste état; **what a p. you're in!** comme vous voilà fait.

plight[2], *s. Lit:* engagement *m*, gage *m* (de sa foi, de son amour, etc.); serments (échangés); **he to whom I gave my p.,** celui à qui j'ai promis ma foi.

plight[3], *v.tr. Lit:* engager, promettre (sa foi, etc.); faire un serment de (fidélité, etc.); **to p. oneself, one's troth,** promettre, engager, sa foi; **to p. one's troth to s.o.,** donner sa foi à qn.

plighted ['plaitid], *a. Lit:* **p. faith,** foi promise, jurée; **p. word,** parole donnée, engagée; **to be p. to s.o.,** être fiancé, promis, à qn; **p. lovers,** fiancés *m*.

Plimsoll ['plimsəl]. 1. *Pr.n. Nau:* **P. line, P. mark,** ligne *f* de Plimsoll; ligne de flottaison en charge. 2. *s.pl.* **plimsolls,** chaussures *f* de gymnastique, de tennis, etc.

Plinian ['pliniən], *a. Geol:* plinien; **P. eruption,** éruption plinienne.

plinth [plinθ], *s.* (*a*) *Arch:* plinthe *f*; socle *m* (d'une statue, d'une colonne); (*b*) *Const:* **p. (course) of rubble wall,** plinthe d'un mur en moellon; (*c*) escabelon *m* (d'une coupe en argent, d'un buste, etc.).

Pliny ['plini], *Pr.n.m. Lt.Lit:* **P. the Elder, the Younger,** Pline l'Ancien, le Jeune.

pliocene ['plaiəsi:n], *a. & s. Geol:* pliocène (*m*).

pliodynatron [plaiou'dainətrɔn], *s. Ph:* pliodynatron *m*.

Pliopithecus [plaiou'piθikəs], *s. Paleont:* pliopithèque *m*.

Ploceidae [plou'si:idi:], *s.pl. Orn:* plocéidés *m*, les tisserins *m*.

plod[1] [plɔd], *s.* 1. (*a*) marche lourde, pénible; (*b*) pas pesant. 2. travail *m* pénible, rebutant, de longue durée; travail assidu.

plod[2], *v.i.* **(plodded)** 1. marcher lourdement, péniblement; **to p. along, to p. one's way,** cheminer, avancer, aller marcher, d'un pas pesant, en traînant la jambe; suivre péniblement son chemin; **to p. along through life,** passer sa vie à peiner; **to p. on,** continuer courageusement son chemin; continuer sa marche pénible; persévérer; **to p. on in the rain,** cheminer sous la pluie. 2. **to p. (away),** travailler laborieusement, assidûment; peiner, trimer **(at,** à); bûcher, piocher; **to p. through a book,** lire assidûment un livre d'un bout à l'autre.

plodder ['plɔdər], *s.* travailleur, -euse, persévérant, -ante; bûcheur, -euse; piocheur, -euse; laborieux, -euse; **he's a p.,** il est courageux au travail; c'est un bœuf au travail.

plodding[1] ['plɔdiŋ], *a.* (*a*) qui marche lourdement, péniblement; (pas) pesant, lourd; (*b*) qui travaille laborieusement; persévérant.

plodding[2], *s.* 1. marche lourde, pénible. 2. labeur assidu.

plonk[1] [plɔŋk], *s.* bruit sourd.

plonk[2], *v.tr. F:* poser (qch.) lourdement et sans façons.

plonk[3], *s. F:* vin *m* ordinaire; pinard *m*.

plop[1] [plɔp], *a. & adv.* 1. flac (*m*), floc (*m*), plouf (*m*) (de qch. tombant dans l'eau). 2. pouf (*m*).

plop[2], *v.i.* **(plopped** [plɔpt]**)** 1. faire flac; tomber (dans l'eau) en faisant flac, plouf. 2. tomber en faisant pouf; **to p. down in an armchair,** se laisser tomber, s'affaler, dans un fauteuil.

plosive ['plousiv], *a. & s. Ling:* (consonne) explosive, plosive.

plot[1] [plɔt], *s.* 1. (parcelle *f*, lot *m*, de) terrain *m*; coin *m*, lopin *m*, quartier *m* (de terre); **building p.,** terrain à bâtir, lotissement *m*; (*in garden*) **vegetable p.,** coin des légumes. 2. intrigue *f*, action *f*, trame *f*, plan *m*, argument *m*, affabulation *f* (d'une pièce de théâtre, d'un roman, etc.); **subordinate p.,** intrigue secondaire; **the p. thickens,** l'intrigue se noue, se complique; l'affaire *f* se corse; **unravelling of the p.,** dénouement *m* de l'action, de l'intrigue; *Cin:* **to accept a play from an outline of the p.,** recevoir une pièce sur scénario. 3. *Mth: etc:* tracé *m*; graphe *m*, graphique *m*, diagramme *m*; courbe *f* (d'un point mobile, etc.); *Surv:* relèvement *m*; point *m*, position *f*; *Av: Nau:* tracé, graphe (de la route d'un avion, d'un navire, etc.); *Rad:* pointé *m*, relevé *m*, tracé; **p. telling,** transmission *f* des pointés de radar; marquage *m*; *Mth:* **logarithmic p.,** diagramme logarithmique. 4. complot *m*, conjuration *f*, conspiration *f*; **communist plots,** menées *f* communistes; **to lay, hatch, a p.,** tramer, ourdir, un complot; **to defeat, frustrate, a p.,** déjouer une machination, un complot.

plot[2], *v.* **(plotted)**

I. *v.tr.* 1. *Surv: etc:* (*a*) dresser, lever, le plan de, faire le levé, le relevé, de, lever, relever (un terrain, etc.); restituer (une photographie aérienne, un stéréogramme); **to p. a point of the ground,** calculer, relever, un point du terrain; **to p. the longitudinal section of a site,** lever les profils en long d'un emplacement; *v.i.* **to p. by alignment, by successive stations,** faire un levé par alignement, par cheminement; (*b*) tracer, rapporter (une figure géométrique, un levé topographique); **to p. an angle,** rapporter un angle; (*c*) marquer, tracer, repérer, situer, pointer (sur une carte); *Rad:* marquer, relever, enregistrer (un pointé de radar); **to p. a point on a map,** repérer, situer, un point sur une carte; **to p. a bearing,** tracer un gisement; **to p. a course,** relever, tracer, une route (d'avion, de navire, etc.); *Av: Nau:* **to p. the position,** faire le point, porter le point sur la carte. 2. *Mth: Ph:* tracer, faire le graphe, le graphique, de, figurer graphiquement (une courbe, etc.); **to p. a diagram, a graph,** tracer, relever, un diagramme, un graphe; **to p. the graph of an equation,** tracer le graphique d'une équation; **to p. the abscissa, the ordinate, of a point,** porter un point en abscisse, en ordonnée; **to p. viscosity against temperature,** faire la courbe de la viscosité en fonction de la température. 3. comploter, combiner, manigancer, ourdir, tramer, préparer en secret (le meurtre, la ruine, de qn); **what mischief are you plotting between you?** qu'est-ce que vous êtes en train de comploter, de manigancer, de mijoter? **to p. a coup d'état,** ourdir, tramer, préparer en secret, un coup d'État.

II. *v.i.* comploter, conspirer **(against s.o.,** contre qn).

Plotinian [plou'tiniən], *a. Phil:* plotinien.

Plotinism ['ploutinizm], *s. Phil:* plotinisme *m*.

Plotinist ['ploutinist], *s. Phil:* plotiniste *mf*.

Plotinus [plɔ'tainəs]. *Pr.n.m. Hist:* Plotin.

plotter ['plɔtər], *s.* 1. (*a*) (*pers.*) traceur, -euse; *Surv:* restituteur *m* (de photographies aériennes, de stéréogrammes); *Rad:* marqueur, -euse, plotteur *m* (de pointés de radar); (*b*) (*device*) abaque *m*; appareil *m* à tracer; traceur (de courbes); table traçante; **photographic p.,** photocartographe *m*; **stereoscopic p.,** stéréocomparateur *m*; *Cmptr:* **X-Y p.,** traceur de courbes. 2. conspirateur, -trice; conjuré, -ée; comploteur *m*.

plotting ['plɔtiŋ], *s.* 1. *Surv: etc:* (*a*) report *m* (d'un point repéré sur le terrain); levé *m* (d'un terrain, etc.); planimétrage *m*; restitution *f* (d'une photographie aérienne, d'un stéréogramme); **p. of details,** levé des détails; **p. by alignment, by successive stations,** levé par alignement, par cheminement; **p. scale,** échelle *f* de réduction; règle graduée à l'échelle; (*b*) pointage *m* (d'une carte); (*c*) report (des cotes, des points relevés, sur un appareil enregistreur, sur un instrument de mesure, etc.); **method of p.,** méthode *f* de report; *Mch:* **pressure p.,** relevé *m* des pressions; **p. machine,** appareil de restitution (de photographies aériennes, de stéréogrammes); (*d*) *Rad:* report, marquage *m* (des pointés de radar); plotting *m*. 2. représentation *f* graphique; tracé *m* (d'une courbe, d'un diagramme); *Av: Nau:* tracé (de la route); traçage *m*, construction *f* (d'une courbe, d'une figure géométrique, etc.); **p. board, p. table,** table traçante, traceur *m* de courbes; **p. paper,** papier millimétré, papier diagramme. 3. complots *mpl*, conjurations *fpl*, conspirations *fpl*, manigances *fpl*.

plough[1] [plau], *s.* 1. (*a*) charrue *f*; **balance p.,** charrue (à) balance; **disc p.,** charrue à disques; **turnwrest p., oneway p.,** brabant *m* double; **sulky p.,** charrue tilbury; **trenching p.,** (charrue) défonceuse *f*; **seeding p.,** charrue-semoir *f*, *pl.* charrues-semoirs; **vineyard p.,** charrue vigneronne; **subsoil p.,** fouilleuse *f*; sous-soleuse *f*, *pl.* sous-soleuses; coutrier *m*; **single (furrow) p.,** normande *f*, monosoc *m*; **double (furrow) p.,** bi(s)soc *m*; **multiple p., gang p.,** polysoc *m*; **p. beam,** age *m*, flèche *f*, de charrue; **p. line,** guide *f* de cheval de charrue; **p. stock,** mancheron *m* de charrue; **p. tail,** mancherons *mpl* de charrue; **he was bred at the p. (tail), he has followed the p. (tail),** il a conduit la charrue; **to drive the p.,** mener, pousser, la charrue; charruer; **to put the p. over a field,** faire passer la charrue dans, sur, un champ; **to put one's hand to the p.,** mettre la main à la charrue; **to follow the p.,** être laboureur; **P. Monday,** lundi de l'Épiphanie; **p. shaped,** aratriforme; en forme de charrue; (*b*) *Ven: F:* terres *fpl* de labour; labours *mpl*. 2. *Astr:* **the P.,** la Grande Ourse; le Chariot. 3. *Bookb: etc:* couteau *m*, presse *f*, à rogner. 4. *Tls:* **p. (plane),** bouvet *m* à approfondir; guimbarde *f*. 5. *El:* frotteur souterrain, chariot, sabot *m*, de prise de courant. 6. *Min:* **coal p.,** rabot *m*. 7. *Sch: F: O:* échec *m* (à un examen), recalade *f*, recalage *m*.

plough[2], *v.*

I. *v.tr.* 1. (*a*) labourer, verser, donner un labour à (un champ, etc.); tracer, creuser (un sillon); **to p. the soil,** retourner la terre (à la charrue); *v.i.* **to p.,** labourer la terre; **to p. deeply,** biloquer; **ploughed land,** terres *fpl* de labour; labours *mpl*; (*with passive force*) **land that ploughs easily,** terre qui se laboure facilement; **to p. (one's way) through the snow,** avancer péniblement, se frayer difficilement un chemin, dans la neige; **to p. through a book,** lire laborieusement un livre jusqu'au bout; **a bullet ploughed into his thigh,** une balle lui est entrée profondément dans la cuisse; (*b*) (*of ship*) fendre, sillonner (les flots); (*c*) **as negotiations p. on,** pendant que les négociations continuent avec difficulté. 2. *Bookb:* rogner (le papier). 3. *Join:* bouveter; **ploughed and feathered joint,** assemblage *m* à fausse languette; **to p. out a groove,** enlever une rainure au bouvet. 4. *Sch: F: O:* **to p. an exam, to be, get, ploughed in an exam,** échouer, être recalé, collé, à un examen. 5. *Com: Fin:* **profits ploughed back into the business,** bénéfices reversés dans l'affaire; **ploughing back of profits,** autofinancement *m*.

II. (*compound verbs*) 1. **plough down,** *v.tr.* déraciner (des plantes, etc.) en labourant.

2. **plough in,** *v.tr.* enterrer, enfouir (le fumier, etc.) dans le sol en labourant.

3. **plough up,** *v.tr.* (*a*) (i) faire passer la charrue dans, sur (un champ); **meadow ploughed up by moles,** pré que les taupes ont labouré; (ii) (*of shells, etc.*) effondrer, défoncer (le terrain); (*b*) déraciner, arracher, extirper, (des mauvaises herbes, etc.) avec la charrue.

ploughboy ['plaubɔi], *s.m.* garçon de charrue.

ploughing ['plauiŋ], *s.* 1. labourage *m*, labour *m*; charrue *f*, charruage *m*; **first p.,** versage *m*; **second p.,** binage *m*. 2. *Carp:* travail *m* au bouvet. 3. *Sch: F: O:* échec *m* (à un examen), recalade *f*, recalage *m*.

ploughland ['plaulænd], *s.* 1. (*a*) terre labourée, cultivée; terres *fpl* de labour; labours *mpl*; (*b*) terre arable, labourable; labourage *m*. 2. *A.Agr: Meas:* charruage *m* (= *approx.* 48 hectares).

ploughman, *pl.* **-men** ['plaumən], *s.m.* (*a*) laboureur; (*b*) paysan, campagnard; (*c*) **ploughman's lunch,** déjeuner de pain, de beurre et de fromage arrosé de bière.

ploughshare ['plauʃεər], *s.* 1. soc *m* de charrue. 2. *Anat:* **p. bone,** vomer *m*.

plover ['plʌvər], *s.* 1. *Orn:* pluvier *m*; **golden p.,** pluvier doré; **American golden p.,** pluvier doré américain; **Asiatic golden p.,** pluvier doré asiatique; **Caspian p.,** pluvier asiatique; **mountain p.,** pluvier montagnard; **great p., Norfolk p.,** grand pluvier; courlis *m* de terre; arpenteur *m*; **black-bellied p.,** pluvier à ventre noir; **grey,** *U.S:* **black-bellied, p.,** pluvier argenté, varié; **white-tailed p.,** pluvier à queue blanche; **wattled p.,** pluvier à caroncules; **piping p.,** pluvier siffleur; **sociable p.,** pluvier sociable; **Wilson's p.,** pluvier de Wilson; **greater sand p.,** gravelot mongol; **killdeer p.,** gravelot à double collier, *Fr.C:* pluvier kildir; **Kentish p.,** *NAm:* **snowy p.,** gravelot à collier interrompu, *Fr.C:* pluvier neigeux; **ringed p.**, *Can:* **semipalmated p.**, grand gravelot, grand pluvier à collier, *Fr.C:* pluvier à collier; **little ringed p.**, petit gravelot; **bastard p.**, vanneau *m*; **green p.**, vanneau (huppé); **spur-winged p.**, vanneau éperonné; **stilt p.**, échasse *f*; **wrybill p.**, **crooked-bill p.**, anarhynche *m*; **upland p.**, bartramie *f* à longue queue, *Fr.C:* maubèche *m* des champs; **crab p.**, dromas *m*, drome *m*; **plover('s) page**, bécasseau *m* cincle; cocorli *m*; **p. snipe**, pressirostre *m*. **2.** *Cu:* **plovers' eggs**, œufs *m* de vanneau.

plow[1,2] [plau], *s. & v. NAm:* = PLOUGH[1,2].

ploy[1] [plɔi], *s.* **1.** occupation *f*, passe-temps *m inv.* **2.** *Scot:* espièglerie *f*; tour *m*; fredaine *f*. **3.** démarche *f*.

ploy[2], *v.tr. Mil: A:* ployer (des troupes).

ployment ['plɔimənt], *s. Mil: A:* ploiement *m* (de troupes).

pluck[1] [plʌk], *s.* **1. to give a p. at sth.**, tirer qch. d'un petit coup sec; **he gave my sleeve a p.**, il m'a tiré la manche. **2.** *Sch: F: O:* échec *m* (à un examen), recalade *f*, recalage *m*. **3.** *Cu:* fressure *f* (de veau, etc.); levée *f* (d'agneau). **4.** courage *m*, cran *m*; **he's got plenty of p.**, il a du cran, de l'estomac; il a du cœur au ventre; **he lacks p.**, il manque de cran; **his p. failed him**, il a manqué de courage.

pluck[2], *v.*

I. *v.tr.* **1.** arracher (des cheveux, des plumes, etc.); cueillir (une fleur); *v.ind.tr.* **to p. at, out, one's hair**, s'arracher les cheveux. **2.** *(a)* **to p. (at) s.o.'s sleeve, to p. s.o. by the sleeve**, tirer qn par la manche; *(b)* **to p. a guitar**, pincer de la guitare. **3.** *Sch: F: O:* **to be plucked (in an exam)**, échouer, être recalé, collé (à un examen). **4.** *(a)* plumer (une volaille); *F: O:* **to p. a pigeon**, rouler qn; *(b)* éplucher (la laine); *(c)* **to p. one's eyebrows**, épiler ses sourcils; *(d)* éjarrer (une fourrure).

II. *(compound verbs)* **1. pluck off**, *v.tr.* détacher (une feuille d'une plante).

2. pluck up, *v.tr.* *(a)* arracher, déraciner (une plante, etc.); *(b)* **to p. up (one's) courage to do sth.**, prendre son courage à deux mains, s'armer de courage, faire appel à tout son courage, pour faire qch.; s'enhardir à faire qch.; *v.i.* **he had plucked up**, il avait repris courage.

plucker ['plʌkər], *s.* plumeur, -euse (de volaille); éjarreur, -euse (de fourrure).

pluckily ['plʌkili], *adv.* courageusement; avec courage; sans se laisser abattre.

pluckiness ['plʌkinis], *s. O:* courage *m*.

plucking ['plʌkiŋ], *s.* **1.** arrachage *m*; cueillage *m* (d'une fleur, etc.). **2.** pincement *m* (de la guitare). **3.** *Sch: F: O:* recalage *m* (d'un candidat). **4.** *(a)* plumage *m* (d'une volaille, etc.); *(b)* épluchage *m* (de la laine, etc.); *(c)* épilage *m*, épilation *f* (des sourcils); *(d)* éjarrage *m* (de fourrure).

plucky ['plʌki], *a.* **1.** courageux; **to be p.**, avoir du courage, du cran; **a p. young fellow**, un garçon qui a du cran. **2.** *Phot:* **p. negative**, cliché vigoureux.

plug[1] [plʌg], *s.* **1.** *(a)* bouchon *m*, tampon *m*; bonde *f*, crapaudine *f* (de bassin, de réservoir, etc.); **waste p.**, tampon, soupape *f* (de baignoire, de lavabo, de réservoir); bouchon, tampon (d'évier); **drain(ing) p.**, bouchon de vidange; **filling p.**, **filler p.**, bouchon de remplissage; **overflow p.**, bouchon de trop-plein; **sealing p.**, **obturating p.**, bouchon, tampon, obturateur; *Metall:* **clay p.**, tampon, bouchon, d'argile; **p. of fireclay**, tampon, bouchon, réfractaire; *Metalw:* **p. welding**, soudage *m* en bouchon; *Aut: etc:* **drain p.**, **drawoff p.**, **sump p.**, bouchon de vidange (de carter d'huile); bouchon de puisard; *Mch:* **safety p.**, **fusible p.**, bouchon, rondelle *f*, fusible; fusible *m* (de chaudière); **lubricating p.**, bouchon de graissage; **oil drain p.**, bouchon de vidange d'huile; **swirl p.**, bouchon atomiseur; **breather p.**, bouchon de reniflard; *Mec.E: etc:* **expansion p.**, bouchon extensible; **fouling, non-fouling, p.**, bouchon encrassable, inencrassable; **threaded p.**, bouchon fileté; **p. gauge**, tampon-calibre *m*, *pl.* tampons-calibres; tampon-jauge *m*, *pl.* tampons-jauges; **p. valve**, robinet *m* à boisseau conique; *Nau:* **(boat, docking, draining) p.**, (bouchon, tampon, de) nable *m*; **ballast tank plugs**, nables de ballasts; *Navy:* **gun p.**, tape *f* de canon; *(b)* *Surg: Dent:* tampon (d'ouate, de coton); **(antiseptic) p.**, bourdonnet *m*; *(c)* *Artil:* **adapter p.**, bouchon d'œil de projectile, bouchon d'obus; **fuse p.**, **primer p.**, bouchon allumeur, bouchon d'amorce; *Sm.a: A:* rondelle, bourre *f* (de cartouche); *(d)* *Geol:* culot *m* volcanique; *(e)* *Cost: NAm: F:* **p. hat**, (chapeau *m*) haut-de-forme *m*, *pl.* hauts-de-forme. **2.** *(a)* cheville *f*, coin *m*, fiche *f*; *El:* fiche (mâle); prise *f* de courant; broche *f* (de lampe, etc.); **fuse p.**, bouchon de fusible; **coaxial p.**, fiche coaxiale; **connecting p.**, fiche de commutateur; **coupler p.**, fiche de connecteur, de raccordement; **short circuit p.**, fiche de court-circuit; **throw-over p.**, fiche de commutation; **two-pin, three-pin, p.**, fiche à deux, à trois, broches; **multiple p.**, prise, fiche, multiple; **power p.**, prise de courant force; **floor p.**, prise de courant (de parquet); **wall p.**, prise de courant (murale); **p. switch**, prise de courant à fiches; commutateur *m*, interrupteur *m*, à fiches; **p. socket**, prise de courant (femelle); **flush p. socket**, prise de courant encastrée; **three-contact p. socket**, prise de courant à trois plots; **p. and socket**, prise de courant (ordinaire); **p. connector**, prise de courant (à fiche); prise (de courant) mâle; **p. connection**, accouplement *m* à fiche; **p. contact**, contact *m* à fiche; **p. wire**, fil *m* de connexion; **p. cord**, (i) cordon *m* de fiche; (ii) *Cmptr:* fil de connexion; **p. key**, fiche à manette; clef *f*, cheville, broche; *Tp:* **answering, calling, p.**, fiche d'écoute, d'appel; **test p.**, fiche d'essai; **jack p.**, fiche de jack; **duct p.**, bouchon d'obturation (d'une canalisation téléphonique); *(b)* *(for nail, screw, in wall)* fiche; tampon (de scellement); scellement *m*; *(c)* *Min: etc:* platcoin *m*, *pl.* plats-coins; coin demi-rond; coin (à pierre), quille *f*; **p. and feather**, aiguille-coin *f*, *pl.* aiguilles-coins; **p. and feathering**, bosseyage *m*; *(d)* *Rail:* cale *f*, coin (pour coussinet de rail); *(e)* *I.C.E:* **spark(ing) p.**, **ignition p.**, bougie *f* d'allumage, de démarrage; **screened, shielded, p.**, bougie blindée; **unshielded p.**, bougie non blindée; **p. body**, corps *m*, culot, de bougie; **p. core**, axe *m* de bougie; **p. electrode, p. point**, électrode *f*, pointe *f*, de bougie; **p. fouling**, encrassement *m* de la bougie; **p. gap**, écartement *m* des électrodes, des pointes, de la bougie; **p. setting**, réglage *m* de l'écartement des électrodes, des pointes, de la bougie; **p. wire**, fil de bougie; *W.Tel:* **radio shielded p.**, bougie antiparasite; *(f)* clef, canillon *m*, noix *f* (de robinet); opercule *m* (de vanne); **p. cock**, robinet à clef. **3.** *(a)* **fire hydrant p.**, bouche *f* d'eau; prise d'eau; bouche d'incendie; *(b)* *Plumb:* chasse *f* d'eau (de cabinet d'aisances); **to pull the p.**, tirer la chaîne. **4.** *O:* **p. tobacco**, tabac *m* en carotte, en barre; **p. of tobacco**, chique *f*, manoque *f*, de tabac; carotte *f*. **5.** *F:* *(a)* *NAm:* vieux cheval, canasson *m*, bourrin *m*; *(b)* *Publ: U.S:* ouvrage *m* qui se vend lentement; *(c)* *Com:* réclame (tapageuse); battage *m*. **6.** *P:* coup *m* de poing; **I gave him a p. (in the earhole)**, je lui ai donné une beigne, une baffe.

plug[2], *v.* **(plugged)**

I. *v.tr.* **1. to p. (up) (an opening, a pipe)**, boucher, obturer (une ouverture, un tuyau), tamponner (une ouverture); *Nau:* taper (un écubier, etc.); *Dent:* obstruer (une cavité dentaire); *(of pipe, etc.)* **to get plugged (up)**, se boucher, s'obstruer, super; **to p. a wound**, tamponner une plaie. **2.** *(a)* enfoncer des chevilles dans, tamponner (un mur, etc.); *(b)* *Min:* enferrer; **to p. and feather**, bosseyer; **p. and feathering machine**, bosseyeuse *f*; *(c)* **to p. in**, (i) *v.tr. El:* brancher (une lampe, un appareil électrique); connecter; *Tp:* enficher; (ii) *v.i.* mettre une fiche dans une prise de courant; établir la connexion. **3.** *P:* *(a)* tirer un coup de fusil, de revolver, sur (qn); fusiller, flinguer (qn); *(b)* frapper (qn) à coups de poing; flanquer un coup à (qn); **p. him one in the earhole**, donne-lui une beigne. **4.** *F:* *(a)* faire l'article, faire de la réclame, faire du battage, pour (un produit, etc.); *(b)* *(of disc jockey)* **to p. a record**, faire à un disque une publicité enragée.

II. *v.i.* *(a)* se boucher, s'obstruer; *(b)* *F:* **to p. along**, continuer péniblement son chemin; **to p. away**, persévérer, s'acharner; bûcher; *Box:* **to p. away at s.o. with one's left**, bourrer qn de coups du gauche.

plugboard ['plʌgbɔ:d], *s. El: Cmptr:* tableau *m* de connexion; **p. wiring**, connexions *fpl* de tableau.

pluggable ['plʌgəbl], *a. Cmptr: etc:* enfichable, embrochable.

plugger ['plʌgər], *s.* **1.** *Tls:* perforatrice percutante à main. **2.** *Dent:* fouloir *m*; **automatic p.**, fouloir automatique; **hand p.**, fouloir à main; **reverse p.**, fouloir pour traction. **3.** *F:* agent *m* de publicité.

plugging ['plʌgiŋ], *s.* **1.** bouchage *m*, obturation *f*, tamponnement *m* (d'un trou, d'une ouverture); obturation (d'un tuyau, d'une cavité dentaire); **p. bar**, chasse-tampon *m inv*; **p. tool**, tamponnoir *m*. **2.** *Min:* enferrure *f*; **p. agent**, colmatant *m* (pour boues de forage). **3.** *El: etc:* connexion(s) *f(pl)*; **p. chart**, schéma *m* de(s) connexion(s); *Tp:* **p. up**, transfert *m* d'une ligne en dérangement sur des appareils de vérification.

plughole ['plʌghoul], *s.* bonde *f*; trou *m* d'écoulement (d'évier, de baignoire); *Nau:* nable *m* (d'embarcation).

plug-in ['plʌgin], *s. El:* connexion *f*; *Tp:* enfichage *m*; **p.-in battery**, batterie *f* à prises; **p.-in coil, condenser**, bobine *f*, condensateur *m*, interchangeable; **p.-in relay**, relais *m* à fiches; *Cmptr:* **p.-in unit**, unité *f* enfichable, embrochable.

plug-ugly ['plʌgʌgli], *s. NAm: F:* *(a)* gangster *m*; *(b)* un mur, un vaurien.

plum [plʌm], *s.* **1.** *(a)* prune *f*; **Java p.**, **jambolan p.**, jamelongue *f*; **bunch p.**, cornouiller *m* du Canada; **p. orchard**, prunelaie *f*; **p. jam**, confiture *f* de prunes; prunelée *f*; **p. brandy**, eau-de-vie *f* de prunes; **a glass of p. brandy**, un verre de prune; **brandy plums**, prunes à l'eau-de-vie; *(b)* **p. (tree)**, prunier *m*; **wild p.**, (i) prunier sauvage; (ii) *(sloe)* prunellier *m*; **Spanish p. tree**, rheedia *m*; **Japanese p. tree**, prunier trilobé, du Japon. **2.** *A:* raisin sec; *Cu:* **p. cake**, cake *m*, gâteau *m* aux raisins; **p. duff**, pudding *m* aux raisins; **p. pudding**, (i) pudding aux raisins fait à la graisse de bœuf; (ii) pudding de Noël; *Miner:* **p. pudding stone**, poudingue *m*, conglomérat *m*. **3. p.(-coloured)**, (de couleur) prune *inv*; **p. ribbons**, rubans *m* prune. **4.** *F:* *(a)* travail facile, bien rétribué; assiette *f* au beurre; **to have a p. job**, avoir une place en or; *(b)* fin morceau, morceau de choix; **you got the p.**, vous avez trouvé le filon. **5.** *P: A:* cent mille livres sterling.

plumage ['plu:midʒ], *s.* plumage *m*; *Ven:* pennage *m* (d'un oiseau de proie); **summer p.**, **winter p.**, plumage d'été, d'hiver; **courting p.**, robe *f* de noces; **birds of p.**, oiseaux à beau plumage.

plumaged ['plu:midʒd], *a.* à plumes; à plumage.

plumassier [plu:mə'siər], *s.* plumassier, -ière.

plumatella [plu:mə'telə], *s. Z:* plumatelle *f*.

plumb[1] [plʌm], *s.* **1. p. (bob)**, plomb *m* (d'un fil à plomb). **2.** aplomb *m*; **to take the p. of a wall**, prendre l'aplomb d'un mur; **out of p.**, hors d'aplomb; dévoyé; (mur) qui porte à faux; **to get out of p.**, déverser; prendre coup; faire coup; **p. line, p. bob**, (i) fil à plomb; (ii) verticale *f*; **deviation of the p. line**, déviation *f* de la verticale; **p. point**, point *m* à la verticale; nadir *m*; *Phot: Surv:* **(ground) p. point**, pied *m* de la verticale (au sol, sur le terrain); **p. rule, p. level**, niveau vertical; niveau de maçon; niveau à plomb. **3.** *(a)* *Nau:* **p. (line, bob)**, (ligne *f* de) sonde *f*; *(b)* *Fish:* plomb, balle *f* (d'une ligne de pêche).

plumb[2], **1.** *v.tr.* sonder (la mer, etc.); *Lit:* **to have plumbed the depths of shame**, avoir toute honte bue. **2.** *v.tr.* *(a)* vérifier l'aplomb de (qch.); plomber (un mur, etc.); *(b)* remettre d'aplomb (un socle, etc.). **3.** *v.i.* *Plumb:* *(a)* effectuer un travail de plomberie; *(b)* être plombier, faire le plombier.

plumb[3]. **1.** *a.* *(a)* droit; vertical, -aux; d'aplomb; *(b)* *NAm: F:* *(intensive)* **p. nonsense**, pure sottise. **2.** *adv.* perpendiculairement **(with sth.**, à qch.); à la verticale, à l'aplomb **(with sth.**, de qch.); **p. above, below, sth.**, à la verticale et au-dessus, et au-dessous, de qch.; *F:* **p. in the centre**, juste au milieu, en plein dans le milieu; *F:* **p. crazy**, complètement fou, dingue.

Plumbaginaceae [plʌmbædʒi'neisii:], *s.pl. Bot:* plombaginacées *f*, plumbaginacées *f*.

plumbaginous [plʌm'bædʒinəs], *a.* graphiteux, graphitique.

plumbago [plʌm'beigou], *s.* **1.** graphite *m*. **2.** *Bot:* dentelaire *f*, malherbe *f*, plumbago *m*.

plumbate ['plʌmbeit], *s. Ch:* plombate *m*.

plumbeous ['plʌmbiəs], *a. Ch:* plombeux, plumbeux.

plumber ['plʌmər], *s.* plombier *m*; **plumber's shop**, plomberie *f*.

plumbery ['plʌməri], *s.* plomberie *f* (atelier ou travail).

plumbic ['plʌmbik], *a.* **1.** *Ch:* plombique. **2.** *Med:* **p. poisoning**, saturnisme *m*; coliques *fpl* de plomb.

plumbiferous [plʌm'bifərəs], *a.* plombifère.

plumbing ['plʌmiŋ], *s. Plumb:* **1.** plomberie *f*, plombage *m*, bloc-eau *m*, *pl.* blocs-eaux; **p. wrench**, clef *f* de plombier. **2.** *coll.* tuyauterie *f*; tuyaux *mpl*. **3.** *F:* installations *fpl* sanitaires; le sanitaire; **to have a look at the p.**, aller faire pipi.

plumbism ['plʌmbizm], *s. Med:* saturnisme *m*.

plumbite ['plʌmbait], *s. Ch:* plombite *m*.

plumbless ['plʌmlis], *a.* (abîme *m*) insondable.

plumb-line ['plʌmlain], *v.tr.* **1.** plomber (un mur, etc.); vérifier la verticalité (d'un mur, etc.) au fil à plomb. **2.** *Nau:* sonder.

plumboferrite [plʌmbou'ferait], *s. Miner:* plumboferrite *f*.

plumbojarosite [plʌmbou'dʒærousait], *s. Miner:* plumbojarosite *f*.

plumbous ['plʌmbəs], *a. Ch:* plombeux, plumbeux.

plumcot ['plʌmkɔt], *s. Hort:* prune-abricot *f*, *pl.* prunes-abricots.

plume[1] [plu:m], *s.* **1.** *A: & Lit:* plume *f*. **2.** panache *m*, aigrette *f*; plumet *m* (de casque). **3.** *Bot:* **p. nutmeg**, athérosperme *m*; **p.-of-Navarre**, habenaria *m*; *Ent:* **p. moth**, alucite *f*.

plume[2]. **1.** *v.tr.* *(a)* orner, garnir, de plumes; **black-plumed**, aux plumes noires; *(b)* garnir d'un panache; empanacher (un casque). **2.** *v.pr.* *(a)* *(of bird)* **to p. itself**, se lisser les plumes; *(b)* *(of pers.)* *O:* **to p. oneself on sth.**, se glorifier, se flatter, se piquer, de qch.

plumelet ['plu:mlit], *s.* **1.** petite plume. **2.** *Bot:* plumule *f.*
plumelike ['plu:mlaik], *a.* semblable à des plumes; plumeux.
plumetty ['plu:məti], *a. Her:* (champ) plumeté.
plumicorn ['plu:mikɔ:n], *s.* aigrette *f* (du hibou).
plumiera [plu:'miərə], *s. Bot:* frangipanier *m.*
plummer ['plʌmər], *s.* **p. (block, box),** (i) *Mch:* palier *m* (d'arbre); palier d'appui; palier-support *m, pl.* paliers-supports; **p. block with swivel bearing,** palier à rotule; **self-lubricating p. block,** palier graisseur; (ii) *Metalw:* empoise *f* (de laminoir).
Plummer-Vinson [plʌmə'vinsən]. *Pr.n. Med:* **P.-V. syndrome,** syndrome *m* de Plummer-Vinson.
plummet[1] ['plʌmit], *s.* **1.** (*a*) plomb *m* (de fil à plomb, de sonde, de ligne de pêche); (*b*) *A:* poids *m,* entrave *f;* boulet *m.* **2.** (*a*) fil *m* à plomb; perpendicule *m;* (*b*) *Nau:* sonde *f.*
plummet[2], *v.* **1.** *v.tr. Nau:* sonder. **2.** *v.i.* (*a*) plonger, tomber, verticalement, comme une pierre; **the aircraft plummeted to the ground,** l'avion s'est écrasé au sol en chute libre; (*b*) (*of prices, etc.*) s'effondrer; (*of blood pressure, etc.*) diminuer, tomber, soudainement; **the birth rate has plummeted since 1948,** le taux des naissances a fortement baissé depuis 1948.
plummy ['plʌmi], *a.* **1.** riche en raisins, en prunes. **2.** *F:* (travail) agréable, bien payé. **3.** (*a*) (goût) de prunes; (*b*) (*colour*) prune *inv;* (*c*) (*of voice*) profond, caverneux.
plumose ['plu:mous], *a. Nat.Hist: Miner:* plumeux.
plumosite ['plu:məsait], *s. Miner:* plumosite *f,* federerz *m,* hétéromorphite *f.*
plump[1] [plʌmp], *a.* (*of pers.*) rebondi, grassouillet, dodu, boulot; *P:* (*of woman*) gironde; (*of fowl*) dodu; (*of chicken or pers.*) bien en chair; **p. little woman,** petite femme rebondie; **p. shoulders,** épaules rondelettes; **p. little hands,** petites mains potelées; **p. cheeked,** joufflu.
plump[2]. **1.** *v.tr.* (*a*) engraisser, faire grossir, rendre dodu; (*b*) *Tan:* gonfler (les peaux); (*c*) **to p. up (a pillow),** secouer, brasser (un oreiller). **2.** *v.i.* **to p. (out, up),** devenir dodu; engraisser; s'arrondir; **she had plumped out,** elle avait perdu sa maigreur (de jeune fille); elle avait grossi.
plump[3]. **1.** *s.* (*a*) bruit sourd (de chute); floc *m,* plouf *m;* **to fall with a p.,** tomber en faisant plouf; (*b*) *esp. Scot:* **summer p.,** ondée *f.* **2.** *adv.* (*a*) **to fall p. into the mud,** tomber dans la boue avec un floc; **he sat down p. on his hat,** il s'est laissé tomber en plein sur son chapeau; (*b*) **to say sth. p.,** dire qch. brusquement, carrément, catégoriquement, tout net. **3.** *a.* **p. denial,** dénégation *f* catégorique.
plump[4]. **1.** *v.tr.* jeter brusquement, flanquer; **to p. oneself into an armchair,** se laisser tomber, s'affaler, dans un fauteuil; **to p. out a remark,** lâcher brusquement une remarque; **to p. s.o. down between two strangers,** faire asseoir qn (sans façon), colloquer qn, entre deux étrangers; **he plumped down my suitcase and walked off,** il a déposé ma valise, sans plus de façons, et s'en est allé. **2.** *v.i.* (*a*) tomber lourdement, comme une masse; tomber avec un floc; faire plouf; (*b*) **to p. for a candidate,** accorder toutes ses voix à un candidat (au lieu de les partager entre plusieurs candidats); *F:* **to p. for sth.,** choisir qch.
plump[5], *s. A:* **p. of spears,** troupe *f* de chevaliers.
plumper ['plʌmpər], *s.* **1.** (*a*) électeur, -trice, qui accorde toutes ses voix à un seul candidat; (*b*) vote accordé à un seul candidat. **2.** *F: O:* gros mensonge; craque *f.*
plumping[1] ['plʌmpiŋ], *s. Tan:* gonflement *m,* bassage *m,* bassement *m,* basserie *f,* passerie *f.*
plumping[2], *a. F: O:* immense; colossal, -aux; **p. majority,** majorité écrasante.
plumpish ['plʌmpiʃ], *a.* (*of pers.*) rondelet.
plumpness ['plʌmpnis], *s.* embonpoint *m,* rondeur *f.*
plumula, plumule ['plu:mjulə, -ju:l], *s. Bot:* plumule *f,* gémule *f,* blaste *m; Orn:* plumule.
plumulaceous [plu:mju'leiʃəs], *a. Bot:* plumulacé.
plumular ['plu:mjulər], *a. Nat.Hist:* plumulaire.
plumularia [plu:mju'lɛəriə], *s. Z:* plumulaire *f.*
plumularian [plu:mju'lɛəriən], *a. & s. Z:* plumulaire (*f*).
Plumulariidae [plu:mjulə'raiidi:], *s.pl. Z:* plumularidés *m.*
plumulose ['plu:mjulous], *a. Nat.Hist:* plumuleux.
plumy ['plu:mi], *a. Lit:* (*a*) couvert de plumes, emplumé; (*b*) (*of helmet*) empanaché; (*c*) plumeux.
plunder[1] ['plʌndər], *s.* **1.** pillage *m;* mise *f* à sac (d'une ville, etc.). **2.** (*a*) butin *m;* (*b*) *F:* petits bénéfices; gratte *f.*
plunder[2], *v.tr.* (*a*) piller, mettre à sac, dépouiller (un pays, etc.); dépouiller (qn); (*b*) **to p. a ship,** détourner des marchandises à bord d'un navire; (*c*) *v.i. F:* brigander.
plunderage ['plʌndəridʒ], *s.* **1.** pillage *m.* **2.** *Jur:* (*a*) pillage, détournement *m,* de marchandises à bord d'un navire; (*b*) marchandises détournées; butin *m.*
plunderer ['plʌndərər], *s.* pillard, -arde; pilleur, -euse.
plundering ['plʌndəriŋ], *s.* (*a*) pillage *m;* (*b*) dépouillement *m* (de qn).
plunge[1] [plʌndʒ], *s.* plongeon *m;* **to take a p.,** faire un plongeon, plonger (**into,** dans); *F:* **to take the p.,** (i) prendre le taureau par les cornes, plonger au large; (ii) se marier; **to be about to take the p.,** être sur le tremplin; *Swim:* **p. (dive),** coulée *f;* **p. board,** plongeoir *m,* tremplin; **p. bath,** piscine *f.*
plunge[2]. **1.** *v.tr.* (*a*) plonger, immerger (le linge dans la lessive, etc.); **to p. a dagger into s.o.'s heart, into s.o.'s breast,** plonger un poignard dans le cœur, dans le sein, de qn; **to p. one's hands into one's pockets,** enfoncer ses mains dans ses poches; **plunged in darkness,** plongé dans l'obscurité; **to p. s.o. into despair, into grief, into poverty,** précipiter, plonger, qn dans le désespoir; plonger qn dans la douleur, dans la misère; (*b*) *Hort:* **to p. pots,** mettre des pots (de fleurs) en pleine terre; (*c*) *Metalw:* tremper (l'acier, etc.). **2.** *v.i.* (*a*) plonger, se jeter (la tête la première); se plonger (dans la méditation); s'enfoncer, s'engouffrer (dans un bois, etc.); se perdre (dans la foule); se jeter (à corps perdu) (dans une affaire, dans le plaisir, etc.); *Geol:* (*of stratum*) plonger; **to p. (headlong) into a description,** se lancer (à fond) dans une description; (*b*) **to p. forward,** s'élancer en avant; **to p. into the room,** se précipiter dans la salle; entrer en coup de vent; (*c*) (*of horse*) (se cabrer et) ruer; (*d*) (*of ship*) tanguer, canarder; piquer du nez; (*e*) *Gaming:* jouer, parier, sans compter; jouer gros jeu; *St.Exch:* risquer de grosses sommes.
plunger ['plʌndʒər], *s.* **1.** (*pers.*) (*a*) plongeur, -euse; (*b*) *F:* joueur, -euse effréné(e); parieur, -euse, effréné, -ée; *St.Exch:* (spéculateur, -trice) risque-tout *m inv.* **2.** (*device*) (*a*) plongeur (de pompe, de presse hydraulique); heuse *f,* chopine *f* (de pompe); **p. piston,** (piston) plongeur; piston plein; **leather p.,** plongeur en cuir; **grease gun p.,** piston compresseur de pompe de graissage; **p. pump,** pompe *f* à piston plongeur; (*b*) *Husb:* batte *f* à beurre (de baratte); **p. churn,** baratte *f* ordinaire; (*c*) **p. of a hydraulic hoist,** colonne *f* d'un monte-charge hydraulique; **p. elevator,** élévateur *m,* monte-charge *m inv, U.S:* ascenseur *m,* à piston plongeur, hydraulique; (*d*) *Sm.a: Artil:* percuteur *m; Navy:* **p. of a mine,** plongeur; (*e*) *Mec.E:* noyau *m* mobile; (noyau) poussoir *m* (de ressort, etc.); (*f*) *Dom.Ec:* **rubber p.,** débouchoir *m* (à ventouse), ventouse *f.*
plunging[1] ['plʌndʒiŋ], *a.* plongeant; **p. neckline,** décolleté plongeant; *Artil:* **p. fire,** tir plongeant, feu fichant.
plunging[2], *s.* **1.** (*a*) plongée *f,* plongement *m,* immersion *f,* enfoncement *m;* (*b*) *Metalw:* trempe *f.* **2.** tangage *m* (d'un bateau). **3.** *Cards: etc:* jeu effréné.
plunk[1] [plʌŋk], *s.* **1.** son pincé (de la guitare, du banjo); son aigu. **2.** *U.S: F:* bonne beigne. **3.** *U.S: P:* dollar *m.*
plunk[2], *v.* **1.** *v.tr.* (*a*) pincer les cordes (d'un banjo, etc.); *F:* (*b*) laisser tomber lourdement qch.; **to p. a stone at s.o.,** lancer raide une pierre à qn; *NAm:* **he plunked down four thousand dollars for the car,** il a payé quatre mille dollars pour la voiture; (*c*) *U.S: P:* donner une beigne à (qn); fusiller, flinguer (qn). **2.** *v.i.* (*a*) produire un son aigu; (*b*) *F:* **to p. (down),** tomber raide.
pluperfect [plu:'pə:fikt], *a. & s. Gram:* plus-que-parfait (*m*); **in the p.,** au plus-que-parfait.
plural ['pluərəl]. **1.** *a. & s. Gram:* pluriel (*m*); **in the p.,** au pluriel; **sign of the p.,** signe *m* de la pluralité. **2.** *a.* (*a*) *Pol:* **p. vote,** vote plural; (*b*) *Ecc:* **p. livings,** bénéfices détenus par cumul.
pluralism ['pluərəlizm], *s.* **1.** (*a*) *Ecc:* cumul *m,* pluralité *f,* de bénéfices; (*b*) cumul de fonctions (quelconques). **2.** *Phil: etc:* pluralisme *m.*
pluralist ['pluərəlist]. **1.** *s.* (*a*) *Ecc:* détenteur *m* de plusieurs bénéfices; (*b*) cumulard *m.* **2.** *a. & s. Phil: etc:* pluraliste (*mf*).
pluralistic [pluərə'listik], *a.* **1.** (*of office, etc.*) cumulatif. **2.** *Phil: etc:* pluraliste.
pluralistically [pluərə'listik(ə)li], *adv.* cumulativement.
plurality [pluə'ræliti], *s.* **1.** pluralité *f.* **2. p. of offices,** *Ecc:* **of livings,** cumul *m* de fonctions, *Ecc:* de bénéfices; **to hold a p. of offices,** cumuler des fonctions. **3.** *Ecc:* bénéfice détenu par cumul. **4.** (*a*) majorité *f* (des voix); (*b*) *NAm:* majorité relative.
pluralization [pluərəlai'zeiʃ(ə)n], *s.* pluralisation *f.*
pluralize ['pluərəlaiz]. **1.** *v.tr. Gram:* pluraliser; mettre au pluriel. **2.** *v.i.* détenir plusieurs bénéfices, plusieurs fonctions.
plurally ['pluərəli], *adv.* **1.** au pluriel. **2.** par cumul.
pluricellular [pluəri'seljulər], *a. Biol:* pluricellulaire.
plurilocular [pluəri'lɔkjulər], *a. Bot:* (pistil) pluriloculaire.
pluripresence ['pluəriprez(ə)ns], *s. Theol:* omniprésence *f,* ubiquité *f.*
pluriserial, pluriseriate ['pluərisiəriəl, -'siərieit], *a.* plurisérié.
plurisyllable ['pluərisiləbl], *a. Gram:* polysyllabique.
plurivalence ['pluəriveil(ə)ns], *s. Ch:* plurivalence *f.*
plurivalent ['pluəriveil(ə)nt], *a. Ch:* plurivalent, polyvalent.
plurivalve ['pluərivælv], *a. Z:* plurivalve, multivalve.
plus [plʌs]. **1.** *prep.* plus; **seven p. nine p. one,** sept plus neuf plus un; **two floors p. an attic,** deux étages plus un grenier; **courage p. sense,** le courage plus le bon sens; le bon sens ajouté au courage. **2.** *a.* (*a*) (*of quantity, number, electric charge, etc.*) positif; (*b*) **on the p. side of the account,** à l'actif du compte; **p. value,** plus-value *f, pl.* plus-values; *Jur:* **p. petitio,** plus-pétition *f, pl.* plus-pétitions; (*c*) *Sp:* **p. player,** (i) *Ten:* joueur, -euse, qui rend des points; (ii) *Golf:* joueur, -euse, dont le handicap lui fait rendre des coups sur la normale du parcours; *Cost:* **p. fours,** culotte (bouffante) de golf; knickerbocker *m;* **to be in p. fours,** être en tenue, en costume, de golf; (*d*) *F:* **fifteen p.,** au-dessus de quinze ans. **3.** *s.* (*pl.* **plus(s)es** ['plʌsiz]) (*a*) plus *m;* signe *m* de l'addition; (*b*) quantité positive.
plush[1] [plʌʃ], *s. Tex:* **1.** peluche *f,* panne *f;* **bouclé p.,** peluche bouclée; **loop p.,** peluche à brides. **2.** *A:* **plushes,** culotte *f* de valet de pied.
plush[2], *a.* **1.** en peluche. **2.** *F:* (appartement, etc.) somptueux, luxueux.
plushy ['plʌʃi], *a.* **1.** peluché. **2.** rupin.
plusia ['plu:ziə, 'plu:ʒiə], *s. Ent:* plusie *f,* phytomètre *f.*
Plutarch ['plu:tɑ:k]. *Pr.n.m. Gr.Lit:* Plutarque.
plutarchy ['plu:tɑ:ki], *s.* ploutocratie *f.*
pluteus ['plu:tiəs], *s. Echin:* plutéus *m* (d'oursin).
Pluto ['plu:tou]. *Pr.n.m. Myth: Astr:* Pluton.
plutocracy [plu:'tɔkrəsi], *s.* ploutocratie *f.*
plutocrat ['plu:təkræt], *s.* ploutocrate *m.*
plutocratic [plu:tə'krætik], *a.* ploutocratique.
Plutonian, Plutonic [plu:'touniən, -'tɔnik], *a. Myth:* *Geol:* plutonien, plutonique; *Geol:* **plutonic rocks,** *s.* **plutonics,** roches *f* d'intrusion, de profondeur; roches abyssales; **the plutonic hypothesis,** l'hypothèse vulcanienne.
plutonism ['plu:tənizm], *s. Geol:* plutonisme *m.*
plutonist ['plu:tənist], *s. Geol:* plutoniste *m.*
plutonium [plu:'touniəm], *s. Ch: Atom.Ph:* plutonium *m;* **enriched p.,** plutonium enrichi; **foil-covered p.,** plutonium gainé; **fuel-grade p.,** plutonium combustible; **p. core,** cœur *m* (de réacteur) en plutonium; **p. pile, p. reactor,** pile *f,* réacteur *m,* au plutonium; **p. recycle,** recyclage *m* du plutonium; **p. producing reactor,** réacteur plutonigène.
plutonomy [plu:'tɔnəmi], *s.* ploutonomie *f;* économie *f* politique.
pluvial ['plu:viəl]. **1.** *a.* (*a*) *Geol: etc:* pluvial, -iaux; (*b*) (temps) pluvieux. **2.** *s. Ecc.Cost: A:* chape *f,* pluvial *m.*
pluviograph ['plu:viougræf], *s. Meteor:* pluviographe *m,* pluviométrographe *m,* pluviomètre enregistreur.
pluviographic [plu:viou'græfik], *a. Meteor:* pluviographique.
pluviography [plu:vi'ɔgrəfi], *s. Meteor:* pluviographie *f.*
pluviometer [plu:vi'ɔmitər], *s. Meteor:* pluviomètre *m,* udomètre *m.*
pluviometric(al) [plu:viou'metrik(əl)], *a.* pluviométrique, udométrique.
pluviometry [plu:vi'ɔmitri], *s. Meteor:* pluviométrie *f.*
pluvioscope ['plu:viouskoup], *s. Meteor:* pluvioscope *m.*
pluvious ['plu:viəs], *a.* pluvieux.
ply[1] [plai], *s.* **1.** (*a*) pli *m* (de tissu appliqué en plusieurs plis); (*b*) placage *m,* pli, épaisseur *f* (de contre-plaqué); pli (d'un pneu); **inner p., outer p.,** pli intérieur, pli extérieur; **five-p. wood,** contre-plaqué *m* en cinq épaisseurs; (*c*) *Cmptr:* exemplaire *m* (de liasse); **six-p. form,** liasse *f* de six exemplaires. **2.** brin *m,* fil *m* (de corde, de laine); toron *m* (de corde); **three-p. wool,** laine *f* trois fils.
ply[2]. **1.** *v.tr.* (*a*) manier vigoureusement; **to p. the oars,** (i) ramer; manier les avirons; (ii) faire force de rames; *A:* **to p. the distaff,** filer la quenouille; **to p. the needle,** faire courir l'aiguille; **to p. a spade, a shovel,** manier une bêche, une pelle; **to p. the bottle,** faire des libations; (*b*) **to p. a trade,** exercer un métier; **there are too many people plying that trade already,** ils sont déjà trop dans ce métier; (*c*) **to p. s.o. with questions,** presser, harceler, accabler, qn de questions; **to p. s.o. with drink,** verser force rasades à qn; faire boire qn sans arrêt; arroser (un client); **to p. s.o. with food,** bourrer qn de nourriture. **2.** *v.i.* (*a*) (*of ship, bus, etc.*) faire le service, la navette, le va-et-vient (**between . . . and . . .,** entre . . . et . . .); (*of taxi, etc.*) **to p. for hire,** prendre des voyageurs; travailler (dans les rues); faire des courses

rétribuées; (*b*) (*of taxi, etc.*) stationner; se tenir à la disposition des clients; (*c*) *Nau:* **to p. to windward,** louvoyer, bouliner.

plyers ['plaiəz], *s.pl.* = PLIERS.

Plymouth ['plɪməθ], *Pr.n. Rel:* **the P. Brethren,** les Frères *m* de Plymouth; les darbystes *m*.

plywood ['plaiwud], *s.* (bois) contre-plaqué *m*; **p. construction,** contre-placage *m*.

pneodynamics [nioudai'næmiks], *s.pl.* (*usu. with sg. const.*) pnéodynamique *f*.

pneometer [ni'ɔmitər], *s. Med: etc:* pnéomètre *m*.

pneuma ['nju:mə], *s. Gr.Phil:* pneuma *m*.

pneumarthrosis [nju:mɑ:'θrousis], *s. Med:* pneumarthrose *f*.

pneumatic [nju:'mætik]. **1.** *a.* pneumatique; **p. engine, tool,** machine *f*, outil *m*, pneumatique; **p. drill,** marteau *m* pneumatique, piqueur; **p. pick,** pic *m* pneumatique; pic à air comprimé; *Min:* marteau-piqueur *m*, *pl.* marteaux-piqueurs; **p. tyre,** pneumatique *m*, pneu *m*; **p. spring, p. shock absorber,** ressort *m*, amortisseur *m*, à air comprimé; **p. plant,** installation *f* à air comprimé. **2.** *s. A:* (*a*) pneumatique, pneu; (*b*) bicyclette *f* à pneus.

pneumatically [nju:'mætik(ə)li], *adv.* **p. operated,** (appareil) à marche pneumatique, à air comprimé; **p. controlled,** à frein pneumatique.

pneumaticity [nju:mə'tisiti], *s.* pneumaticité *f*.

pneumaticohydraulic [nju:mætikouhai'drɔ:lik], *a.* pneumaticohydraulique.

pneumatics [nju:'mætiks], *s.pl.* (*usu. with sg. const.*) *Ph:* pneumatique *f*.

pneumatization [nju:mətai'zeiʃ(ə)n], *s. Med:* pneumatisation *f*.

pneumatocele [nju:'mætousi:l], *s. Med:* pneumatocèle *f*.

pneumatocyst [nju:'mætousist], *s. Nat.Hist:* poche *f* pneumatique (d'oiseau, etc.); *Bot:* pneumatophore *m*; *Algae:* pneumatocyste *m*; *Coel:* pneumatophore (de siphonophore).

pneumatograph [nju:'mætougræf], *s. Med:* pneumatographe *m*.

pneumatological [nju:mətə'lɔdʒik(ə)l], *a. Phil: Theol:* pneumatologique.

pneumatologist [nju:mə'tɔlədʒist], *s. Phil: Theol:* pneumatologiste *mf*, pneumatologue *mf*.

pneumatology [nju:mə'tɔlədʒi], *s. Phil: Theol:* pneumatologie *f*.

pneumatolysis [nju:mə'tɔlisis], *s. Geol:* pneumatolyse *f*.

pneumatolytic [nju:mətə'litik], *a. Geol:* pneumatolytique.

pneumatometer [nju:mə'tɔmitər], *s. Med:* pneumatomètre *m*.

pneumatophore ['nju:mətoufɔ:r], *s. Bot: Z:* pneumatophore *m*.

pneumatophorous [nju:mə'tɔfərəs], *a. Bot: Z:* pneumatophore.

pneumatosis [nju:mə'tousis], *s. Med:* pneumatose *f*.

pneumaturia [nju:mə'tjuəriə], *s. Med:* pneumaturie *f*.

pneumectomy [nju:'mektəmi], *s. Surg:* pneum(on)ectomie *f*.

pneumobacillus, *pl.* **-i** [nju:moubə'siləs, -ai], *s. Bac:* pneumobacille *m*.

pneumocele ['nju:mousi:l], *s. Med:* pneumocèle *f*.

pneumococcemia [nju:moukɔk'si:miə], *s. Med:* pneumococcémie *f*.

pneumococcia [nju:mou'kɔksiə], *s. Med:* pneumococcie *f*.

pneumococcus, *pl.* **-i** [nju:mou'kɔkəs, -'kɔksai], *s. Bac:* pneumocoque *m*.

pneumoencephalitis [nju:mouensefə'laitis], *s. Med:* pneumoencéphalite *f*; *Vet:* **avian p.,** pseudo-peste *f*, maladie *f* de Newcastle.

pneumoencephalogram [nju:mouen'sefəlougræm], *s. Med:* pneumoencéphalogramme *m*.

pneumoencephalograph [nju:mouen'sefəlougræf], *s. Med:* pneumoencéphalographe *m*.

pneumoencephalographic [nju:mouensefəlou'græfik], *a. Med:* pneumoencéphalographique.

pneumoencephalography [nju:mouensefə'lɔgrəfi], *s. Med:* pneumoencéphalographie *f*.

pneumoenteritis [nju:mouentə'raitis], *s. Med:* pneumoentérite *f*.

pneumogastric [nju:mou'gæstrik]. *Anat:* **1.** *a.* pneumogastrique. **2.** *s.* **the p.** le (nerf) pneumogastrique.

pneumograph ['nju:mougræf], *s. Med:* pneumographe *m*.

pneumography [nju:'mɔgrəfi], *s. Med:* pneumographie *f*.

pneumolith ['nju:mouliθ], *s. Med:* pneumolithe *m*.

pneumology [nju:'mɔlədʒi], *s. Med:* pneumologie *f*.

pneumonectomy [nju:mou'nektəmi], *s. Surg:* pneum(on)ectomie *f*.

pneumonia [nju:'mouniə], *s. Med:* pneumonie *f*; congestion *f* pulmonaire; **catarrhal p., lobular p.,** pneumonie lobulaire; **interstitial p.,** pneumonie franche, lobaire, fibrineuse; **acute p.,** pneumonie lobaire; pneumonie franche lobaire aiguë; **single p.,** pneumonie d'un seul poumon; **double p.,** pneumonie double.

pneumonic [nju:'mɔnik], *a. Med:* pneumonique.

pneumonitis [nju:mou'naitis], *s. Med:* pneumonite *f*.

pneumo(no)coniosis, pneumo(no)koniosis [nju:mou(nou)kouni'ousis], *s. Med:* pneumoconiose *f*.

pneumonopathy ['nju:mənoupæθi], *s. Med:* pneumo(no)pathie *f*.

pneumopericardium [nju:mouperi'kɑ:diəm], *s. Med:* pneumopéricarde *m*.

pneumoperitonitis [nju:mouperitə'naitis], *s. Med:* pneumopéritoine *m*.

pneumor(r)hagia [nju:mou'reidʒiə], *s. Med:* pneumorragie *f*.

pneumoserosa [nju:mousi'rousə], *s. Med:* pneumoséreuse *f*.

pneumotherapy [nju:mou'θerəpi], *s. Med:* pneumothérapie *f*.

pneumothorax [nju:mou'θɔ:ræks], *s. Med:* pneumothorax *m*; **artificial p.,** pneumothorax artificiel.

pneumotomy [nju:'mɔtəmi], *s. Surg:* pneumotomie *f*.

pneumotoxin [nju:mou'tɔksin], *s. Bac:* pneumotoxine *f*.

pneumotyphoid [nju:mou'taifɔid], *s. Med:* pneumotyphoïde *f*.

po[1] [pou], *s. F:* pot *m* de chambre, Jules *m*; **po-faced,** avec une figure d'enterrement.

Po[2], *Pr.n. Geog:* le Pô.

poa ['pouə], *s. Bot:* pâturin *m*; **wood p.,** pâturin des bois.

Poaceae [pou'eisii:], *s.pl. Bot:* poacées *f*.

poach[1] [poutʃ], *v.tr. Cu:* pocher (des œufs).

poach[2], *v.tr.* **1.** (*a*) (*of horse, ox, etc.*) **to p. (up) the ground,** labourer la terre (de ses sabots); piétiner la terre; (*b*) *v.i.* (*of land*) devenir bourbeux; passer à l'état de fondrière. **2.** (*a*) braconner dans (un bois, etc.); (*b*) braconner (le gibier, un saumon, etc.); (*c*) *v.i.* braconner; **to p. on s.o.'s preserves,** (i) braconner sur la chasse réservée de qn; chasser sur les terres de qn; (ii) *Fig:* empiéter sur les prérogatives de qn; marcher sur les plates-bandes de qn; (*d*) *Ten:* braconner; **to p. a ball,** chiper une balle à son partenaire.

poached [poutʃt], *a.* (œuf) poché.

poacher[1] ['poutʃər], *s. Dom.Ec:* pocheuse *f* (à œufs).

poacher[2], *s.* **1.** braconnier *m*; panneauteur *m*; *Tail:* **poacher's pocket,** poche *f* carnier (de costume de chasse). **2.** *Ten: F:* chipeur, -euse.

poachiness ['poutʃinis], *s.* état bourbeux (de la terre, etc.).

poaching[1] ['poutʃiŋ], *s. Cu:* pochage *m* (d'un œuf).

poaching[2], *s.* braconnage *m*.

poachy ['poutʃi], *a.* (terrain) bourbeux.

pochard ['poutʃəd], *s. Orn:* fuligule *f* milouin; milouin *m*; **red-crested p.,** nette rousse; **white-eyed p.,** fuligule nyroca.

pochette [pɔ'ʃet], *s.* pochette *f* (de dame).

pock [pɔk], *s. Med:* pustule *f* (de la petite vérole).

pocket[1] ['pɔkit], *s.* **1.** (*a*) poche *f* (de vêtement); **p. flap,** patte *f* de poche; **p. hole,** (fente *f* de) poche; **trouser p.,** poche de pantalon, de culotte; **waistcoat p.,** gousset *m*; **small p.,** pochette *f*; **hat that rolls up for the p.,** chapeau qui se met dans la poche; **p. comb,** peigne *m* de poche; **p. handkerchief,** mouchoir *m* de poche; **p. pistol,** (i) pistolet *m* de poche; (ii) gourde *f* de poche (pour eau-de-vie); *A:* **p. piece,** (pièce de monnaie) porte-bonheur *m inv*; *F:* **you could put him in your p.,** vous le mettriez dans votre poche; **to have empty pockets,** avoir la poche vide; être sans le sou; *F:* **to line one's pockets,** faire sa pelote; **to put sth. in(to) one's p.,** mettre qch. dans sa poche; empocher qch.; **to put one's hands in one's pockets,** mettre ses mains dans ses poches; **to go through s.o.'s pockets,** faire les poches à qn; *F:* **to have s.o. in one's p.,** faire marcher qn comme on veut; avoir qn dans sa manche; **he has two newspapers in his p.,** il a deux journaux sous sa coupe; **to be always in s.o.'s p.,** être toujours tout près de qn; **p. money,** argent *m* de poche; *Jur:* **p. agreement,** contre-lettre *f*, *pl.* contre-lettres; **p. dictionary,** dictionnaire *m* de poche; **p. edition,** édition *f* de poche; *Bookb:* **p. size,** format *m* de poche; *A:* **p. violin,** pochette; **p. case of maths instruments,** pochette de compas; **p. camera,** appareil *m* de poche; **p. radio,** récepteur *m* de poche; *Navy:* **p. battleship, p. submarine,** cuirassé *m*, sous-marin *m*, de poche; (*b*) **prices to suit every p.,** des prix à la portée de tout le monde; *F:* **to suffer in one's p.,** en être de sa poche; **he's a good friend until you touch his p.,** il est ami jusqu'à la bourse; **he's always got his hand in his p.,** il a toujours la main à la poche; il est toujours à débourser; **to pay s.o. from one's own p.,** payer qn de sa poche; **to be in p.,** être en bénéfice, en gain; **to be £10 in p.,** avoir £10 de gain, de bénéfice; gagner £10; **to be out of p. (over a transaction),** être en perte; ne pas retrouver son argent; ne pas rentrer dans ses fonds; **to be £10 out of p.,** être en perte de £10; en être de sa poche pour £10; **I'm out of p. by it,** j'y suis de ma poche; **you won't be out of p. by it,** vous n'y perdrez pas. **2.** (*a*) sac *m* (de houblon, de laine); (*b*) *Bill:* blouse *f*; **p. table,** billard *m* à blouses; (*c*) *Aut:* (*in door, etc.*) **car p.,** poche intérieure; (*d*) **pockets under the eyes,** poches sous les yeux. **3.** (*a*) *Mec.E:* retrait *m* (pour recevoir un organe, etc.); *I.C.E:* chambre *f*, chapelle *f* (de soupape); *El:* **p. of an accumulator grid,** alvéole *f* d'un grillage; **p. valve,** soupape latérale; (*b*) *Anat:* cul-de-sac *m*, *pl.* culs-de-sac; **infrabony p.,** cul-de-sac infra-osseux; **suprabony p.,** cul-de-sac supra-osseux, extra-osseux; (*c*) *Cmptr:* case *f* de réception, récepteur *m* (de cartes); case, pochette, de tri. **4.** (*a*) *Min:* poche, nid *m*, sac (de minerai); (*b*) poche (d'eau, de gaz); poche, nid (de grisou); **dead water p.,** poche d'eau stagnante; retenue *f* d'eau; (*c*) **(air) p.,** (i) *Av:* trou *m* d'air; (ii) *Hyd. E: etc:* cantonnement *m*, poche, d'air (dans une canalisation); (iii) collecteur *m* à air; poche à air.

pocket[2], *v.tr.* **(pocketed) 1.** (*a*) empocher (qch.); mettre (qch.) dans sa poche; **to p. the money,** mettre l'argent dans sa poche; (*b*) *Pej:* soustraire (de l'argent); chiper (qch.); **he used to p. half the takings,** il mettait la moitié de la recette dans sa poche; **someone's pocketed my matches,** on m'a chipé mes allumettes. **2.** avaler, empocher, encaisser (un affront, une insulte, etc.). **3.** faire taire (ses sentiments); refouler (sa colère). **4.** *Bill:* blouser (la bille); **to p. one's own ball (by mistake),** se blouser; **to p. one's opponent's ball,** bloquer la bille de son adversaire. **5.** *Rac:* (*of group of runners*) entraver la marche (d'un concurrent); gêner, coincer (un concurrent). **6.** *Mec.E: etc:* ménager un retrait pour (un organe); monter (un organe) en retrait.

pocketable ['pɔkitəbl], *a.* portatif, de poche.

pocketbook ['pɔkitbuk], *s.* (*a*) carnet *m* de poche; calepin *m*; **p. diary,** agenda *m* de poche; (*b*) portefeuille *m*, porte-billets *m inv*; (*c*) *NAm:* livre *m* de poche.

pocketed ['pɔkitid], *a.* (électrode, soupape, etc.) en retrait.

pocketful ['pɔkitful], *s.* pleine poche; pochée *f*, pochetée *f*; **pocketfuls of sweets,** des pleines poches de bonbons.

pocketing ['pɔkitiŋ], *s.* **1.** action *f* d'empocher (un objet, une insulte, etc.). **2.** *Bill:* mise *f* en blouse (de la bille). **3.** *Mec.E: etc:* montage *m* en retrait. **4.** *Cmptr:* envoi *m* (d'une carte) dans une case.

pocketknife ['pɔkitnaif], *s.* couteau *m* de poche.

pockety ['pɔkiti], *a.* **1.** *Min:* poché. **2.** *Av:* (parcours) plein de trous d'air.

pockmark ['pɔkmɑ:k], *s.* marque *f*, stigmate *m*, de la petite vérole; grain *m*.

pockmarked ['pɔkmɑ:kt], *a.* marqué, picoté, de la petite vérole; **p. face,** visage grêlé, gravé; **countryside p. with bungalows,** paysage défiguré par des bungalows.

pockwood ['pɔkwud], *s.* (bois *m* de) gaïac *m*.

pococurante [poukoukjuə'rænti], *a. & s.* insouciant, -ante; sans-souci (*mf*) *inv*; indifférent, -ente.

pococurantism [poukoukjuə'ræntizm], *s.* insouciance *f*, indifférence *f*.

pod[1] [pɔd], *s. Tls:* mandrin *m* (de vilebrequin).

pod[2], *s.* **1.** (*a*) cosse *f*, gousse *f* (de fèves, de pois, etc.); écale *f* (de pois); silique *f* (des crucifères); *P:* **to be in p.,** être enceinte; (*b*) **senna pods,** follicules *m* de séné. **2.** cocon *m* (de ver à soie); coque *f* (d'œufs de sauterelle). **3.** *Fish:* nasse *f* (pour anguilles). **4.** *Geol: Miner:* lentille allongée de minerai. **5.** *Av:* nacelle *f*, fuseau *m* (de réacteur, etc.); **engine, jet, p.,** nacelle-moteur *f*, *pl.* nacelles-moteur; nacelle-réacteur *f*, *pl.* nacelles-réacteur; **gun p.,** nacelle-canon *f*, *pl.* nacelles-canon; nacelle porte-canon; **rocket p.,** (nacelle) lance-roquettes *m inv*; **the engines are mounted in underwing, in wing tip, pods,** les réacteurs sont installés dans des nacelles sous la voilure, en bout d'aile.

pod[3], *v.* **(podded) 1.** *v.i.* (*of plant*) former des cosses, des gousses. **2.** *v.tr.* écosser, écaler (des pois, etc.).

pod[4], *s.* petite bande (de baleines, de phoques).

pod[5], *v.tr.* **(podded)** rassembler (des baleines, des phoques) (pour les tuer).

podagra [pɔ'dægrə], *s. Med:* podagre *f*, goutte *f*.

podagral, podagric, podagrous [pɔ'dægr(ə)l, -rik, -rəs], *a. Med:* podagre, goutteux.

podal ['poudl], *a.* pédieux; du pied.

podalic [pou'dælik], *a. Obst:* **p. version,** version *f* podalique.

Podargidae [pɔ'dɑ:dʒidi:], *s.pl. Orn:* podargidés *m*, les podarges *m*.

podded ['pɔdid], *a.* **1.** (*of seeds, etc.*) à cosses; en cosses.

2. *F:* (*of pers.*) cossu; riche.

podge [pɔdʒ], *s. F:* individu gros; bouboule *m*, boulot, -otte; **fat p. (of a boy),** gros boulot.

podger ['pɔdʒər], *s. Tls:* broche *f* à visser.

podginess ['pɔdʒinis], *s.* embonpoint *m*, rondeur *f*.

podgy ['pɔdʒi], *a.* boulot, -otte, replet, -ète; **what a p. little boy!** quel gros pâté que ce petit! **he was a p. little man,** il était rond comme une boule; **p. fingers,** doigts boudinés, rondelets.

podiatrist [pɔ'daiətrist], *s.* pédicure *mf*.

podiatry [pɔ'daiətri], *s.* chirurgie *f* pédicure.

Podicipitidae [pɔdisi'pitidi:], *s.pl. Orn:* podicipitidés *m*, les grèbes *m*.

podium, *pl.* **-ia** ['poudiəm, -iə], *s. Rom.Ant: etc:* podium *m*.

podobranch ['pɔdoubræŋk], **podobranchia,** *pl.* **-ae** [pɔdou'bræŋkiə, -i:], *s. Crust:* podobranchie *f*.

podobranchial, podobranchiate [pɔdou'bræŋkiəl, -'bræŋkieit], *a. Crust:* podobranche.

podocarpic [pɔdou'kɑ:pik], *a. Ch:* podocarpique.

podolite ['poudəlait], *s. Miner:* podolite *f*.

podological [pɔdou'lɔdʒik(ə)l], *a. Med:* podologique.

podology [pɔ'dɔlədʒi], *s. Med:* podologie *f*.

Podophthalmia, Podophthalma(ta) [pɔdɔf'θælmiə, -'θælmə(tə)], *s.pl. Crust:* podophtalmes *m*, podophtalmaires *m*.

podophthalmian [pɔdɔf'θælmiən], *a. & s. Crust:* podophtalmaire (*m*).

podophthalmic, podophthalmous [pɔdɔf'θælmik, -məs], *a. Crust:* podophtalmaire; aux yeux pédonculés.

podophyllin [pɔdou'filin], *s. Pharm:* podophylline *f*, podophyllin *m*.

podophyllum [pɔdou'filəm], *s. Bot:* podophylle *m*.

podostemon [pɔdou'sti:mən], *s. Bot:* podostémon *m*.

Podostem(on)aceae [pɔdousti:mə'neisii:, -sti'meisii:], *s.pl. Bot:* podostémonacées *f*.

podostem(on)aceous [pɔdousti:mə'neiʃəs, -sti'meiʃəs], *a. Bot:* podostémon(ac)é.

podzol, podsol ['pɔdzɔl, -sɔl], *s. Geol:* podzol *m*, podsol *m*.

podzolic, podsolic [pɔd'zɔlik, -sɔl-], *a. Geol:* podzolique, podsolique.

podzolization, podsolization [pɔdzəlai'zeiʃ(ə)n, -səl-], *s. Geol:* podzolisation *f*, podsolisation *f*.

podzolize, podsolize ['pɔdzəlaiz, -səl-], *v.tr. Geol:* podzoliser, podsoliser.

poë ['poui], *s. Orn:* **p. (bird),** prosthémadère *m* (de la Nouvelle-Zélande).

poecile ['pi:sili:], *s. Gr.Ant:* pécile *m*, pœcile *m*.

Poeciliidae [pi:si'laiidi:], *s.pl. Ich:* pœciliidés *m*.

poecilotherm ['pi:silouθə:m], *s. Z:* poïkilotherme *m*, pœcilotherme *m*.

poecilothermal [pi:silou'θə:ml], *a. Z:* poïkilotherme, pœcilotherme, hétérotherme.

poem ['pouim], *s.* poème *m*; poésie *f*; **prose p.,** poème en prose.

poesy ['pouizi], *s. A: & Lit:* poésie *f*.

poet ['pouit], *s.* poète *m*; **woman p.,** femme poète; poétesse *f*; *A:* **courtier p.,** poète de cour; *Bot:* **poet's cassia,** rouvet *m*.

poetaster [poui'tæstər], *s.* mauvais poète; poét(r)aillon *m*; poétereau *m*; poétastre *m*; rimailleur *m*.

poetess ['pouitis], *s.f.* femme poète; poétesse; **Mrs X is a distinguished p.,** Mme X est un poète distingué, une poétesse distinguée.

poetic(al) [pou'etik(əl)], *a.* poétique; **a poetic soul,** une âme de poète; **the poetical works of. . .,** les œuvres *f* poétiques de . . .

poetically [pou'etik(ə)li], *adv.* poétiquement.

poeticize [pou'etisaiz], *v.tr. & i.* poétiser.

poeticizing [pou'etisaiziŋ], *s.* poétisation *f*.

poetics [pou'etiks], *s.pl.* (*usu. with sg. const.*) **1.** (*treatise on poetry*) poétique *f*. **2.** l'art *m* poétique.

poetize ['pouitaiz]. **1.** *v.tr.* (*a*) poétiser (son style, un sentiment, etc.); (*b*) mettre en vers (un événement, etc.). **2.** *v.i.* faire des vers.

poetry ['pouitri], *s.* poésie *f*; **to write p.,** écrire des vers; **piece of p.,** poésie; **the art of p.,** l'art *m* poétique.

pogonia [pɔ'gouniə], *s. Bot:* pogonie *f*, pogonia *f*.

Pogonophora [pougə'nɔfərə], *s.pl. Z:* pogonophores *m*.

pogrom ['pɔgrəm], *s.* pogrom(e) *m*.

pogromist ['pɔgrəmist], *s.* pogromiste *m*.

pogy ['pougi], *s. Ich: U.S:* menhaden *m*.

poignancy ['pɔinjənsi], *s.* (*a*) *A:* piquant *m* (d'une sauce, etc.); âpreté *f* (d'un parfum, etc.); mordant *m* (d'une satire, etc.); (*b*) violence *f*, caractère poignant (d'une émotion, etc.); acuité *f* (d'une douleur).

poignant ['pɔinjənt], *a.* (*a*) *A:* **p. scent,** parfum âpre; **p. sauce,** sauce relevée; (*b*) (*of feeling, emotion*) poignant, vif; (*of regret, etc.*) amer; (*of pain*) cuisant, aigu; (*of reply, etc.*) mordant, caustique; **of all his thoughts this was the most p.,** de toutes ses pensées, celle-ci était la plus angoissante.

poignantly ['pɔinjəntli], *adv.* d'une façon poignante.

poikilotherm [pɔi'kilouθə:m], *s. Z:* poïkilotherme *m*, pœcilotherme *m*.

poikilothermal, -thermic, -thermous [pɔikilou'θə:ml, -'θə:mik, -'θə:məs], *a. Z:* poïkilotherme, pœcilotherme.

poinciana [pɔinsi'ɑ:nə], *s. Bot:* poinciana *f*.

poind[1] [pɔind, pind], *s. Jur: Scot:* **1.** contrainte *f*; saisie-exécution *f*, *pl.* saisies-exécutions. **2.** biens saisis.

poind[2], *v.tr. Jur: Scot:* saisir (les biens de qn).

poinding ['pɔindiŋ, 'pindiŋ], *s. Jur: Scot:* saisie *f*, exécution *f*.

poinsettia [pɔin'setiə], *s. Bot:* poinsettie *f*, poinsettia *f*.

point[1] [pɔint], *s.*

I. point *m*. **1.** (*a*) *Gram:* **full p.,** point (de ponctuation); (*b*) *Ling:* point (dans les langues sémitiques pour indiquer une voyelle, différencier une consonne, marquer un accent); point (d'alphabet Braille); *Hebrew Gram:* **vowel p.,** point-voyelle *m*, *pl.* points-voyelles; *Mth:* **decimal p.,** virgule *f* (décimale); **three p. five (3·5)** = trois virgule cinq (3,5); *Cmptr:* **binary p.,** virgule binaire; *Atom.Ph:* **p. lattice,** réseau *m* de points; *Ph:* **p. lamp, p. source of light,** source ponctuelle (de lumière); *Mil:* **p. defence,** défense ponctuelle; **p. target,** objectif ponctuel; **p. light,** (i) *Opt: Cin:* source lumineuse ponctuelle; lampe ponctuelle; (ii) *Av:* feu ponctuel; **p. process,** processus ponctuel; **p. set,** ensemble ponctuel; **her pupil contracted to a mere p.,** sa pupille s'est contractée jusqu'à n'apparaître que comme un simple point; **points of light sprinkled the darkness,** des points lumineux parsemaient les ténèbres. **2.** (*point in space*) (*a*) **p. of arrival, of departure,** point d'arrivée, de départ; **loading, unloading, p.,** point de chargement, de déchargement; **disembarking, landing, p.,** point de débarquement; **embarking p.,** point d'embarquement; **assembly p.,** point, lieu *m*, de rassemblement; **rallying p.,** point de ralliement; **observation p.,** point d'observation; **orientation, orientating, p.,** point d'orientation; *Tp: etc:* **p.-to-p. link,** relayage *m*; **p.-to-p. network,** réseau de trafic fixe; **p.-to-p. (race),** (i) *A:* course *f* au clocher; (ii) steeple-chase *m*, *pl.* steeple-chases; *Mil:* **defence of critical, of weak, points,** défense des points sensibles; **key points,** points vitaux, points d'importance stratégique ou tactique; **p. of direction,** point de direction; **to take up points in marching,** jalonner une direction, un itinéraire; **initial p.,** point initial (d'une marche); **dispersal p.,** point de dispersion (d'une colonne, d'un convoi, etc.); *Artil:* **predicted p.,** point futur; *Ball:* **aiming p., p. (to be) aimed at, (to be) fired at,** point de visée, de pointage; point visé; **p. of fall,** point de chute, d'arrivée (d'un projectile); **p. of impact,** point d'impact; **mean p. of impact, of a grouping,** point moyen d'un groupement (de points d'impact); **sighting p.,** point de mire; *Av:* **drop p.,** point de largage (du personnel, du matériel); **(bomb) release p.,** point de largage (des bombes); **way p.,** point de survol, point en route; **re-entry p.,** point de retour; *Aedcs:* **separation p.,** point de décollement; *Mth:* **p. of convergence, of intersection, of tangency,** point de concours (ou de convergence), d'intersection, de tangence; **p. pair AB,** intervalle *m* AB; **the line intersects the circle at points A and B,** la ligne coupe le cercle aux points A et B; **intersection, intersected, p.,** point d'intersection, point intersecté; **geodetic p.,** point géodésique; **trig(onometrical) p.,** point trigonométrique; **trig p. booklet,** carnet *m* de points; **zero p.,** point origine; **conjugate p.,** point conjugué; **to give the coordinates of a p.,** donner les coordonnées d'un point; **to plot a p.,** calculer, relever, un point; **plotted p.,** point relevé; *Surv:* **conspicuous, outstanding, p. of the ground,** point caractéristique, remarquable, saillant, du terrain; *Mec.E:* **lubricating p.,** point de graissage; *El:* **neutral p.,** point mort, point neutre; *Nau:* **lighting p.,** point lumineux; *Mec: Ph:* **attach(ment) p.,** point de fixation; **datum p.,** point de repère; **fixed p.,** point fixe; **dead p.,** point mort (d'un arbre moteur, etc.); (*of gear*) **pitch p.,** point de contact; **p. of application, working p.,** point d'application (d'une force); **p. of equilibrium,** point d'équilibre; **points of support,** points d'appui, de soutien (d'une poutre, etc.); **suspension p.,** point de suspension; **tie p., anchor p.,** point d'amarrage, d'ancrage; **contact p., p. of contact,** point de contact; **branch p.,** point de connexion; **set p.,** point de réglage; **check p.,** point de contrôle, de reprise; **index p.,** point machine; **re-run p., re-start p.,** point de reprise; **cardinal p.,** point cardinal; **intercardinal p., quarantal p.,** point intercardinal, quarantal; **astronomical p.,** point astronomique; **equinoctial p.,** point équinoxial; *Astr:* **first p. of Aries,** point gamma; *Hyd:* **non-perennial water p.,** point d'eau intermittent; *Med:* **bleeding p.,** point hémorragique; *Anat:* **cephalometric, craniometric, p.,** point céphalométrique, crâniométrique; *Sculp:* **points of a statue,** points d'une statue (que l'on veut reproduire); *Her:* **the nine points of the shield,** les neuf points de l'écu; **armed at all points,** armé de toutes pièces, de pied en cap; **at all points,** en tous points, sous tous rapports; (*b*) **p. of view,** point de vue; **to consider sth. from all points of view,** considérer qch. sous tous ses aspects; **from the international p. of view,** du point de vue international. **3.** (*a*) point, détail *m* (d'un raisonnement, etc.); **the main p.,** le point capital; **the chief p. of an argument,** le point capital, l'important *m*, l'essentiel *m* d'un raisonnement; **figures that give p. to his argument,** chiffres qui ajoutent du poids à sa thèse; **to differ on a p.,** ne pas être d'accord sur un point, sur un détail, sur un chapitre; **on that p. we disagree,** là-dessus nous ne sommes pas d'accord; **to be right in every p.,** avoir raison en tout point; **I see your p.,** je vois ce que vous voulez dire; **to pursue one's p.,** poursuivre son idée; **to maintain one's p.,** maintenir son dire; **to make a p.,** faire ressortir un argument; **I saw by their faces that he had made his p.,** je me suis rendu compte à leurs visages que son plaidoyer avait porté; **having made this p. . . .,** sous le bénéfice de cette observation . . .; **to catch s.o.'s p.,** saisir le raisonnement de qn; **points to be remembered,** considérations *f* à se rappeler; considérations qu'il ne faut pas perdre de vue; **and here is another p.,** bien plus . . .; **her p. is that . . .,** d'après elle . . ., selon elle . . .; **a p. of conscience,** un cas de conscience; **to make a p. of doing sth.,** se faire un devoir, un scrupule, une règle, une loi, de faire qch.; avoir grand soin, avoir bien soin, avoir le souci, ne pas manquer, de faire qch.; s'attacher à faire qch.; prendre à tâche de faire qch.; **to make a p. of accuracy,** avoir le scrupule de l'exactitude; **I am making a p. of telling you,** je tiens à vous le dire; **p. of grammar, of law,** question *f* de grammaire, de droit; point de droit; **on a p. of law,** au point de vue du droit; légalement parlant; **in p. of fact,** par le fait; au fait; en fait; en vérité; **we are the stronger in p. of numbers,** nous sommes les plus forts comme nombre; nous l'emportons par le nombre; **superior in p. of quality,** supérieur sous le rapport de la qualité; **sensitive on points of honour,** sensible sur l'article de l'honneur; **to make it a p. of honour not to yield,** mettre son point d'honneur à ne pas céder; (*b*) **the p.,** le sujet, la question; **the p. is (that). . .,** c'est que . . .; **here's the p.,** je vais vous dire ce que c'est; voici ce dont il s'agit; **that's the p.,** c'est là le point; **that's not the p.,** ce n'est pas là la question; il ne s'agit pas de cela; ce n'est pas de cela qu'il s'agit; **off the p.,** à côté de la question; hors de propos; **on this p.,** à cet égard; à ce propos; **this is very much to the p.,** c'est bien parlé; c'est bien dit; **argument off the p.,** argument qui porte à faux; **speak to the p.,** ne vous écartez pas de la question; parlez sans ambages; **your remark isn't to the p.,** votre observation manque d'à-propos; **to wander from the p.,** s'écarter, sortir, de la question; **I would draw your attention to this p.,** j'attire votre attention sur ce point; (*c*) **what would be the p. (of doing sth.)?** à quoi bon (faire qch.)? **I see no p. in relating . . .,** je juge, j'estime, inutile de raconter . . .; **there is no p. in denying that . . .,** cela ne servirait à rien de nier que . . .; **I can't see the p. of your writing to him,** je ne vois pas pourquoi vous lui écririez; **I don't see the p. of the story,** je ne vois pas où cette histoire veut en venir; (*d*) caractère *m*; trait distinctif; **p. of interest,** particularité intéressante; détail intéressant; **to have one's good points,** avoir ses qualités; (*of thg*) **to have its good points,** avoir ses bons côtés. **4.** (*a*) (*precise moment*) **to be on the p. of doing sth.,** être sur le point de faire qch.; **at, on, the p. of death,** sur le point de mourir; à l'article de la mort; **to be on the p. of departure,** être sur le point, être près, de partir; être sur son départ; **I was on the p. of jumping,** j'étais au moment de sauter; j'allais sauter; **p. of no return,** point limite de retour, point de non-retour; **critical p.,** point critique; *Av:* **commit p.,** moment d'engagement; *Cmptr:* **break p.,** point d'arrêt, d'interruption; *Book-k:* **break-even p.,** point mort; (*b*) **I've got to the p. of speaking to him,** j'en suis venu à lui parler; **matters are at such a p. that. . .,** les choses en sont là que . . .; **to come to the p.,** arriver au fait; **when it came to the p.,** quand le moment critique est arrivé; **up to a (certain) p.,** jusqu'à un certain point, dans une certaine mesure; **severe to the p. of cruelty,** sévère jusqu'à la cruauté; **the highest p. of glory, of eloquence,** le plus haut point, degré, de la gloire, de l'éloquence; **the culminating p. of the drama,** le moment, le point, culminant du drame. **5.** *Games:* **to score so many points,** marquer, faire, tant de points; **to play ten pence a p.**, jouer à dix pence le point; **what points shall we play?** (i) en combien jouons-nous la partie? (ii) à combien le point? **to play a game of one hundred points at piquet,** jouer un cent de piquet; *Box:* **to win on points,** gagner aux points; **beaten on points,** battu aux points; *Ten:* **one p.,** une balle; **match p., set p.,** balle de match, de set; **to need one p. for a game,** être à une balle du jeu; **to give points to s.o.,** donner, rendre, des points à qn; **he can give both of you points,** il vous rend des points à tous les deux. **6.** (*measure*) (*a*) **the thermometer went up, went down, two points,** le thermomètre a, est, monté, a baissé, est descendu, de deux degrés, de deux divisions; **freezing p.,** point de congélation; **melting p., fusion p.,** point de fusion; **boiling p.,** point d'ébullition; **burning p.,** point de combustion; **saturation p.,** point de saturation; **setting p.,** point de solidification; **dew p.,** point de rosée; **flash p.,** point éclair, point d'inflammabilité; *Ch:* **cloud p.,** point de nuage; *Elcs:* **Curie p.,** point de Curie; **transition p.,** point de transition; **isoelectric p.,** point isoélectrique; *St.Exch:* (*of price*) **to decline, lose, one p.,** baisser d'un point; **to gain, rise, one p.,** gagner un point, hausser d'un point; **rise, fall, of one p.,** hausse *f*, baisse *f*, d'un point; **silver p.,** silver-point *m*; **silver import p.,** silver-point d'entrée; **silver export p.,** silver-point de sortie; (*b*) *Typ:* point; **ten-p. type,** caractères *mpl* de dix points; corps *m* dix points; philosophie *f*; **five-p. type,** perle *f*; **seven-p. type,** mignonne *f*; **set up in twelve-p. (body),** composé en corps douze. **7.** *A.Adm:* (*rationing*) coupon *m*, ticket *m*, d'alimentation; **cereal products are on points,** on demande des tickets pour les produits à base de céréales.

II. pointe *f*. **1.** (*a*) pointe (d'une aiguille, d'une épingle, d'un clou, d'une épée, d'un outil, etc.); bec *m* (d'une plume à écrire); **at the p. of the sword,** le couteau sur la gorge; *Mus:* **p. of the bow,** pointe de l'archet; *Box:* **blow to the p.,** coup *m* à la pointe de la mâchoire; **points of the toes,** pointe des pieds; *Danc:* **to dance on points,** faire des pointes; **on (full) p.,** sur la pointe; **on demi-p.,** sur la demi-pointe; **p. work,** pointes; **p. shoes,** chaussons *m* (de danse à pointes renforcées); **p. of a drill,** mouche *f* d'un foret; *Surg:* **sharp p. of a probe,** extrémité pointue d'une sonde; *Mec.E:* **p. of a gear tooth,** saillie *f*, tête *f*, d'une dent d'engrenage; *Carp:* **p. of a wedge,** tranchant *m* d'un coin; *Av:* **p. drag,** résistance *f* à la pointe (de l'avion); **five-p. star,** étoile *f* à cinq branches; **to end in a p.,** aller, se terminer, en pointe; **to give a p. to a pencil, to a stick,** appointer, tailler en pointe, un crayon, un bâton; **to give a p. to a tool,** appointer, aiguiser, un outil; **p. of a joke,** piquant *m*, sel *m*, d'une plaisanterie; **to give p. to an epigram,** donner du mordant à une épigramme, acérer une épigramme; **to take the p. out of an anecdote,** enlever tout le sel à une anecdote, affadir une anecdote; (*b*) *Nau:* (*end of a rope*) queue-de-rat *f*, *pl.* queues-de-rat; (*c*) **bay horse with black points,** cheval bai aux extrémités noires; **to describe the points of a hound,** décrire les caractéristiques d'un chien courant; (*d*) *pl. Ven:* cors *m* (du cerf); **buck of ten points,** cerf (de) dix cors; (*e*) *Mil:* pointe (d'avant-garde); (*f*) *Geog:* pointe, promontoire *m*; *Nau:* **to double a p.,** doubler une pointe; (*g*) *Ling:* **p. consonant,** dentale *f*; **p. r,** r cacuminal. **2.** *Tls:* pointe, poinçon *m*; **abrasive p.,** pointe abrasive; **diamond p.,** (i) pointe de diamant, diamant *m* (de vitrier); (ii) pointe diamantée (d'un outil); *Dent:* **polishing p.,** pointe à polir. **3.** *El:* (*a*) **platinum p.,** contact platiné; (*b*) (point de) prise *f* de courant (sur le secteur); **power of points,** pouvoir *m* des pointes; **power p.,** prise de courant (force); **we'll put in ten (power) points,** nous allons installer dix prises de courant; (*c*) *I.C.E:* **eight-p. distributor,** distributeur *m* (d'allumage) à huit plots; *F:* **(contact) points,** vis platinées. **4.** (*a*) *Rail:* (*of a switchblade*) pointe; **p. of crossing,** cœur *m* de croisement; **points,** aiguillage *m*; aiguille *f* de raccordement; changement *m*, branchement *m*, de voie; **cross points,** pointe de croisement; **p. rail,** (i) (lame *f* d')aiguille; rail *m* mobile; (ii) pointe de croisement; **to shift, throw over, the points,** aiguiller; changer l'aiguille; **wrong setting of the points,** erreur *f* d'aiguillage; (*of train*) **to take the points,** franchir l'aiguille; **the trains collided at the points,** les deux trains se sont pris d'écharpe; (*b*) **p. duty,** service *m* de la circulation; **to be on p. duty,** être de service à la circulation; **policeman on p. duty,** agent *m* de service à la circulation, agent de circulation. **5.** *Typ:* **tympan points,** pointures *f*. **6. the points of the compass,** les aires *f* du vent; **p. of the compass,** quart *m* (de vent), r(h)umb *m* (= 11° 15'); **half p.,** demi-quart *m*, *pl.* demi-quarts (de la rose des vents); **to alter (the) course two points to the east,** changer la route de deux quarts vers l'est; **to alter course 16 points,** venir de 16 quarts; **to cast off one p.,** abattre d'un quart; **the wind has changed to the opposite p.,** le vent a changé cap pour cap; **p. of sailing,** allure *f* (du bateau); **ships standing on opposite points,** navires qui courent à contre-bord. **7.** *Games:* (*backgammon*) flèche *f*, pointe, case *f*. **8.** (*a*) *Lacem:* **p. (lace),** dentelle *f* à l'aiguille; point *m*; guipure *f*; **French p. lace,** point d'Alençon; **Irish p.,** point, dentelle, d'Irlande; (*b*) *Tex:* **p. paper,** carte *f*; **to put, prick, a design on p. paper,** mettre un dessin en carte. **9.** *A.Cost:* aiguillette *f*. **10.** (*a*) *Cr:* (i) station *f* à droite dans le prolongement du guichet; (ii) joueur stationné à droite et près du guichet (pour attraper la balle); (*b*) (*lacrosse position, player*) arrière *m* fixe; **cover p.,** arrière volant.

III. 1. action *f* de montrer du doigt; **he added with a smile and a p. at his wife,** il ajouta en souriant, et en désignant sa femme du doigt. **2.** *Ven:* **dog making a p., coming to a p.,** chien qui tombe en arrêt, qui se met en arrêt.

point², *v.*

I. *v.tr.* **1.** (*a*) marquer (qch.) de points, mettre des points sur (les i, etc.); (*b*) *Gram:* ponctuer (une phrase); (*c*) *Mth:* **to p. decimals off,** séparer les décimales par une virgule; (*d*) mettre les points-voyelles (dans un texte sémitique); *Ecc:* **to p. the psalms,** mettre les points-repères au-dessus du texte des psaumes (pour en faciliter le chant d'après la liturgie anglicane). **2.** (*a*) faire une pointe à (une tige de fer, etc.); tailler en pointe (un bâton, etc.); affûter, acérer, aiguiser (un outil, etc.); tailler (un crayon); affiner, empointer, appointer (un clou, une aiguille, un pieu, etc.); **stick pointed with steel,** canne ferrée, à bout d'acier; *Nau:* **to p. a rope,** faire une queue-de-rat à un cordage; **pointed(-up) rope end,** queue-de-rat, *pl.* queues-de-rat; (*b*) *Danc: etc:* **to p. the toe, the foot,** pointer, tendre, le pied; (*c*) donner du piquant à (des remarques, etc.); **to p. an epigram,** aiguiser, acérer, une épigramme; **to p. a moral,** inculquer une leçon (en soulignant la conclusion de l'histoire); (*d*) *Nau:* **to p. a sail,** mettre les garcettes de ris à une voile. **3.** (*a*) **to p. a gun, a telescope,** pointer, braquer, un canon; diriger, orienter, braquer, une longue-vue (**at,** sur); **to p. a rifle at s.o.,** (i) braquer un fusil sur qn; coucher qn en joue, viser qn avec un fusil; (ii) diriger son fusil vers qn; (*b*) *Nau:* **to p. (up) a mast,** présenter un mât. **4. to p. the way,** indiquer, montrer, le chemin (**to s.o.,** à qn; **to a place,** vers un endroit). **5.** *Const:* jointoyer, ficher, gobeter, liaisonner, bloquer (un mur). **6.** *Ven:* (*of hound*) arrêter (le gibier); *v.i.* tomber en arrêt. **7.** *Sculp:* mettre (une statue) aux points.

II. *v.i.* **1. to p. at s.o.,** (i) montrer, désigner, qn du doigt, du bout de sa canne, etc.; (ii) (*in scorn or reproach*) montrer qn au doigt. **2.** (*a*) **to p. to a direction,** (i) (*of pers.*) désigner le chemin à prendre; (ii) (*of thg*) être dirigé, tourné, orienté, dans une direction; **the magnetic needle always points north,** l'aiguille aimantée est toujours tournée vers le nord, regarde toujours le nord; **pointing upwards,** dirigé vers le haut; **the clock pointed to ten,** la pendule marquait dix heures; (*b*) **this points to the fact that . . .,** cette circonstance (i) laisse supposer que . . ., (ii) fait ressortir que . . .; **everything seems to p. to success,** tout semble annoncer, indiquer, faire prévoir, le succès; **everything points to him as the culprit,** tout indique que c'est lui le coupable; toutes les preuves sont contre lui. **3.** *Med:* (*of abscess*) mûrir, aboutir.

III. (*compound verbs*) **1. point in,** *v.tr. Hort:* enterrer légèrement (le fumier) avec la pointe de la bêche.

2. point out, *v.tr.* (*a*) **to p. out sth. to s.o. (with one's finger),** désigner, montrer, qch. du doigt à qn; (*b*) (i) **to p. out sth. to s.o.,** attirer l'attention de qn sur qch.; signaler, faire remarquer, faire observer, qch. à qn; **to p. out the mistakes,** signaler, relever, les fautes, les erreurs; **to p. out a fact,** faire ressortir, faire valoir, un fait; **he had had the difficulty pointed out to him,** on lui avait signalé cette difficulté; **to p. out to s.o. his error, his duty,** remontrer à qn son erreur, son devoir; **to p. out to s.o. that he is wrong,** remontrer à qn qu'il a tort; **to p. out to s.o. the advantages of sth.,** représenter à qn les avantages de qch.; **might I p. out that . . .,** permettez-moi de vous faire observer que . . .; (ii) **he has been pointed out to me as a capable man,** on me l'a signalé comme un homme capable.

3. point up, *v.tr. NAm:* monter (qch.) en épingle.

point-black ['point'blæŋk]. **1.** *a.* (*a*) *Artil: etc:* (tir) direct, sans corrections, à bout portant; (*b*) *F:* (question) faite de but en blanc; (refus) net, catégorique. **2.** *adv.* **to fire p.-b. at s.o.,** tirer sur qn à bout portant, de but en blanc; *F:* **to tell s.o. sth. p.-b.,** dire qch. à qn à brûle-pourpoint; **he asked me p.-b. whether . . .,** il m'a demandé de but en blanc si . . .; **to refuse p.-b.,** refuser catégoriquement, carrément, (tout) net.

point-device [pɔintdi'vais]. *A:* **1.** *adv.* avec une extrême précision, très exactement. **2.** *a.* parfait; à souhait; impeccable; **p.-d. in his dress,** tiré à quatre épingles.

pointe [pɔint, pwænt], *s. Danc:* **on p.,** sur la pointe; **p. work,** pointes; **to dance on p.,** faire des pointes.

pointed ['pɔintid], *a.* **1.** pointu; à pointe; *Tchn:* alêné; **p. beard,** barbe *f* en pointe. **2.** (*a*) (réflexion) sarcastique, caustique, mordante; (*b*) (allusion) peu équivoque, peu voilée. **3.** (*in composition*) **single-p.,** à une seule pointe; **six-p. star,** pentacle *m*.

pointedly ['pɔintidli], *adv.* (*a*) sarcastiquement; d'un ton mordant, caustique; (*b*) explicitement, ouvertement, nettement; (*c*) d'une manière marquée; **not too p.,** sans y appuyer.

pointedness ['pɔintidnis], *s.* **1.** mordant *m* (d'une remarque, etc.); piquant *m* (du style, etc.). **2.** caractère *m* explicite (d'une allusion).

pointer ['pɔintər], *s.* **1.** (*pers.*) (*a*) *Ind:* (em)pointeur, -euse (d'aiguilles, etc.); (*b*) *Sculp:* metteur, -euse, aux pointes. **2.** *Z:* chien *m* d'arrêt; pointer *m*. **3.** (*a*) aiguille *f* (d'horloge, de manomètre); aiguille, languette *f*, index *m* (d'une balance); indicateur *m* (d'un baromètre, etc.); **p. knob,** bouton *m* à index; **p. instrument,** instrument *m* à lecture directe; (*b*) *Elcs: Space:* **sun p., star p.,** pointeur solaire, stellaire; (*c*) *Sch:* baguette *f* (du tableau noir). **4.** *Tls:* pointe *f* (de maçon, etc.). **5.** *Astr:* **the Pointers,** les Gardes *f* (de la Grande Ourse). **6.** *F:* renseignement *m*, conseil *m*; tuyau *m*.

pointful ['pɔintful], *a.* (histoire, remarque) qui a de l'à-propos.

pointillism(e) ['pwæntilizm], *s. Art:* pointillisme *m*.

pointillist(e) ['pwænulist], *s. Art:* pointilliste *mf*.

pointillistic [pwænti'listik], *a. Art:* pointilliste.

pointing ['pɔintiŋ], *s.* **1.** (*a*) mise *f* des points (sur les i, etc.); ponctuation *f* (d'une phrase); (*b*) *Sculp:* mise aux points (d'une statue que l'on veut reproduire); **p. machine,** pointomètre *m*. **2.** (*a*) appointage *m*, taillage *m* en pointe; affûtage *m*; affinage *m* (des aiguilles); (*b*) *Nau:* mise de garcettes de ris (à une voile). **3.** pointage *m*, direction *f*, braquage *m* (d'un canon, d'une longue-vue, etc.). **4.** *Const:* (*a*) jointoiement *m*, gobetage *m* (d'un mur); **p. towel,** fiche *f* (de maçon); (*b*) (*cement*) gobetis *m*. **5. p. at s.o.,** désignation *f* de qn du doigt. **6.** *Ven:* arrêt *m* (d'un chien). **7.** *Med:* aboutissement *m* (d'un abcès).

pointless ['pɔintlis], *a.* **1.** épointé, émoussé. **2.** (*a*) (*of story, etc.*) insignifiant, insipide; (plaisanterie) fade, sans sel; (*b*) (observation etc.) qui n'a rien à voir à la question.

pointlessness ['pɔintlisnis], *s.* **1.** fadeur *f* (d'une plaisanterie, etc.). **2.** manque *m* d'à-propos (d'une observation, etc.).

pointsman, *pl.* **-men** ['pɔintsmən], *s.m. Rail:* aiguilleur.

poise¹ [pɔiz], *s.* **1.** (*a*) **(equal, even, just) p.,** équilibre *m*, aplomb *m*; **at p.,** en équilibre; (*of question, etc.*) **to hang at p.,** être en suspens, en balance; (*b*) **treatment that tends to restore p. of mind,** traitement qui favorise le rééquilibre mental; (*of pers.*) **to have p.,** (i) avoir de la prestance; (ii) avoir l'esprit bien équilibré; **a man of p.,** un homme pondéré. **2.** port *m* (de la tête, du corps). **3.** *Ph:* **air p.,** aéromètre *m*.

poise². **1.** *v.tr.* (*a*) équilibrer; (*b*) tenir, porter, (qch.) en équilibre; balancer (un javelot); **to p. sth. in the hand,** soupeser qch.; **we were listening with poised forks,** nous écoutions la fourchette en l'air. **2.** *v.i.* **to p. in the air, in mid air,** planer en l'air; *Ven:* (*of hawk*) se bloquer.

poise³ [poiz, pwæz], *s. Ph.Meas:* poise *m*; **1/10 p.,** poiseuille *m*.

poiser ['pɔizər], *s. Ent:* haltère *m*, balancier *m*, aileron *m* (de diptère).

poison¹ ['pɔizən], *s.* (*a*) poison *m*, toxique *m*; **p. effect,** effet *m* d'empoisonnement, effet toxique; **to take p.,** s'empoisonner; **to die of p.,** mourir empoisonné; **to give s.o. a dose of p.,** empoisonner qn; *F:* **name your p., what's your p.?** qu'est-ce que tu veux boire? **p. pen letter,** lettre malicieuse anonyme; **(writer of) p. pen (letters),** corbeau *m*; (*b*) *Bot:* **p. ivy, p. oak,** toxicodendron *m*; sumac vénéneux; arbre *m* à la gale, à la puce, à poison; **p. nut,** noix *f* vomique; **p. tree,** arbre vénéneux; *Z:* **p. gland,** glande *f* à venin; **p.-bearing gland,** glande vénénifère; *Mil: etc:* **p. gas,** gaz toxique, asphyxiant; **p. gas attack from the air,** attaque *f* aérochimique; (*c*) *Ch:* **(catalyst) p.,** poison; *Atom.Ph:* **fission p.,** poison de fission; **nuclear p.,** poison nucléaire.

poison², *v.tr.* (*a*) empoisonner (qn, le sang, une flèche, etc.); intoxiquer (qn); **poisoned wound,** plaie envenimée; (*b*) corrompre, pervertir (l'esprit); **to p. s.o.'s mind against s.o.,** empoisonner l'esprit de qn contre qn; **to p. s.o.'s life,** empoisonner la vie de qn.

poisoner ['pɔizənər], *s.* empoisonneur, -euse.

poisoning ['pɔizəniŋ], *s.* (*a*) empoisonnement *m*; intoxication *f*; **mercurial p.,** mercurialisme *m*; **food p.,** intoxication alimentaire; (*b*) corruption *f* (de l'esprit).

poisonous ['pɔizənəs], *a.* (*a*) toxique, intoxicant; empoisonné; (*of animal*) venimeux; (*of plant*) vénéneux, vireux; **p. effect,** effet *m* d'empoisonnement, effet toxique; **p. water,** eau empoisonnée; **p. gas,** gaz *m* asphyxiant, toxique, délétère; (*b*) **a p. play,** une pièce empoisonnante; **p. doctrine,** doctrine pernicieuse, empoisonnée; **she has a p. tongue,** elle a une langue de vipère.

poisonousness ['pɔizənəsnis], *s.* toxicité *f* (d'un suc végétal, etc.); caractère pernicieux (d'une doctrine).

Poisson ['pwæsɔn]. *Pr.n. Ph: etc:* **P. distribution,** distribution *f* de Poisson; **Poisson's constant, number,** constante *f,* nombre *m,* de Poisson; **Poisson's ratio,** coefficient *m* de Poisson; **P. type process,** processus poissonnien.

poke[1] [pouk], *s. Dial:* sac *m,* poche *f.*

poke[2], *s. Bot:* phytolaque *m*; raisin *m* d'Amérique; épinard *m* de Virginie; **Indian p.,** ellébore blanc, vératre *m* (d'Amérique).

poke[3], *s.* **1.** poussée *f*; (*nudge*) coup *m* de coude; (*with the finger*) coup du bout du doigt; (*with a poker*) coup de tisonnier; (*with one's stick*) coup du bout de sa canne; **to give s.o. a p. in the ribs,** enfoncer son doigt, son coude, dans les côtes de qn; cogner qn du coude; **he gave me a p. in the ribs with his stick,** du bout de sa canne il m'a donné une bourrade dans les côtes. **2.** *Husb:* tribart *m* (au cou d'un veau, d'un porc, etc.). **3.** *A.Cost:* bord *m* (de chapeau capote); **p. (bonnet),** chapeau *m* capote (à bord évasé); cabas *m.*

poke[4], *v.*

I. *v.tr.* **1.** (*a*) pousser (qn, qch.) du bras, du coude; piquer (qch.) du bout (d'un bâton); **to p. s.o. in the ribs,** donner une bourrade (amicale) à qn; chatouiller les côtes à qn; (*b*) **to p. a hole in sth.,** faire un trou dans qch.; crever qch. (avec le doigt, etc.); enfoncer un bâton, etc., dans qch. **2.** tisonner, attiser, remuer, fourgonner (le feu); ringarder (un fourneau). **3.** (*a*) **to p. sth. up the chimney, down a pipe,** passer qch. dans la cheminée, dans un tuyau; **to p. one's head round the corner,** porter la tête en avant pour regarder au coin; passer la tête au coin de la rue; (*b*) **to p. one's head,** s'engoncer, arrondir les épaules. **4. to p. rubbish into a corner,** fourrer des saletés dans un coin; **I poked fifty pence into his hand,** je lui ai mis cinquante pence dans la main. **5. to p. fun at s.o.,** (i) plaisanter amicalement qn; (ii) tourner qn en ridicule; se moquer de qn; se payer la tête de qn.

II. *v.i.* **1. to p. at sth.,** tâter qch. du bout du doigt, d'un bâton, etc. **2.** (*a*) **to p. (about) in every corner,** fouiller, farfouiller, fureter, fourgonner, dans tous les coins; (*b*) **to p. into other people's business,** fourrer son nez dans les affaires d'autrui.

III. (*compound verbs*) **1. poke out,** (*a*) *v.tr.* **to p. s.o.'s eye out,** éborgner qn; **to p. the fire out,** (i) éteindre le feu à coups de tisonnier, avec sa canne, etc.; (ii) éteindre le feu à trop le fourgonner; (*b*) **to p. one's head out (of the window),** passer, sortir, la tête par la fenêtre.

2. poke up, *v.tr.* (*a*) tisonner, fourgonner, raviver (le feu); (*b*) **to be poked up in a tiny house,** être enfermé à l'étroit, être confiné, dans une petite maison.

pokeberry ['poukberi], *s. Bot:* phytolaque *m*; raisin *m* d'Amérique, épinard *m* de Virginie.

poker[1] ['poukər], *s.* **1.** tisonnier *m*; *Ind:* fourgon *m*; (*for furnace*) ringard *m,* pique-feu *m inv*; cure-feu *m, pl.* cure-feu(x); *F:* **he looks as if he's swallowed a p.,** il est raide comme un pieu, comme un manche à balai. **2.** pointe *f* métallique (pour pyrogravure); **p. work,** pyrogravure *f.* **3.** *Bot:* **red-hot p.,** tritoma *m.*

poker[2], *s. Cards:* poker *m*; **p. dice,** poker dice, poker d'as; *F:* **p. face,** visage qui ne trahit aucune émotion (comme celui du joueur de poker); visage impassible; figé; **p.-faced,** au visage impassible, figé.

pokeroot ['poukru:t], *s. Bot:* **(Indian) p.,** ellébore blanc, vératre *m* (d'Amérique).

pokeweed ['poukwi:d], *s. Bot:* phytolaque *m.*

pokey ['pouki], *s. NAm: F:* prison *f.*

poking ['poukiŋ], *s.* **1.** tisonnage *m,* attisage *m* (du feu). **2.** intervention *f* (dans les affaires d'autrui). **3. p. fun at s.o.,** dérision *f* de qn; moqueries *fpl.*

poky ['pouki], *a.* (*of room*) exigu; misérable; **to live in a p. little place,** être logé à l'étroit, étroitement, petitement; **a p. little room,** une petite pièce de rien du tout.

polacca [pou'lækə], *s.* (*a*) *Danc: Mus:* polonaise *f*; (*b*) *A.Nau:* polacre *f.*

Polack ['poulæk], *s.* (*a*) *Hist:* Polaque *m,* Polacre *m*; (*b*) *NAm: P: Pej:* Polonais, -aise; Pola(c)k *m,* Polaque.

Poland ['poulənd]. *Pr.n. Geog:* Pologne *f.*

polar ['poulər]. **1.** *a.* (*a*) *Astr: Geog:* polaire; du pôle, des pôles; **in the p. regions,** dans les régions polaires; **p. lights,** aurore boréale, australe; **p. altitude,** hauteur *f* polaire; **p. cap,** calote *f* polaire (d'une planète); **p. circle,** cercle *m* polaire; **p. ice,** glace *f* polaire; *Meteor:* **p. front,** front *m* polaire; **p. front depression,** dépression *f* du front polaire; (*b*) *Mth: Ph:* polaire; **p. axis,** axe *m* polaire; **p. co-ordinates,** coordonnées *f* polaires; **p. curve,** (i) courbe *f* polaire; (ii) *Av:* polaire *f* (d'une aile); **p. distance,** distance *f* polaire; **p. equation,** équation *f* polaire; **p. expression,** notation *f* polaire; **p. triangle, radius,** triangle *m,* rayon *m,* polaire; **p. vector,** vecteur *m* polaire; *Mapm:* **p. projection,** projection *f* polaire; *Biol:* **p. body,** globule *m* polaire. **2.** *s. Mth:* polaire *m.*

polarimeter [poulə'rimitər], *s. Opt:* polarimètre *m.*

polarimetric [poulæri'metrik], *a. Ph:* polarimétrique.

polarimetry [poulə'rimitri], *s. Ph:* polarimétrie *f.*

polaris [pou'lɑ:ris], *s.* **1.** *Astr:* l'étoile *f* polaire. **2.** *Ball: Navy:* **p. missile,** missile *m,* fusée *f,* polaris; **p. submarine,** sous-marin lanceur de missiles, de fusées, polaris.

polariscope [pou'læriskoup], *s. Opt:* polariscope *m.*

polariscopic [poulæri'skɔpik], *a. Opt:* polariscopique.

polarity [pou'læriti], *s. Ph:* polarité *f* (optique ou magnétique); **straight p.,** polarité normale; **change of p., p. reversal,** inversion *f* de polarité; **reverse(d) p.,** polarité inversée; **to change, reverse, the p.,** inverser la polarité; **p. reversing switch,** inverseur *m* de polarité; **p. indicator,** indicateur *m* de polarité.

polarizability [pouləraizə'biliti], *s. Ph:* polarisabilité *f.*

polarizable ['pouləraizəbl], *a. Ph:* polarisable; **non p.,** impolarisable.

polarization [pouləraі'zeiʃ(ə)n], *s. Ph:* polarisation *f*; **p. of light, of a medium,** polarisation de la lumière, d'un milieu; **anodic, cathodic, p.,** polarisation anodique, cathodique; **circular, rotary, elliptic, p.,** polarisation circulaire, rotatoire, elliptique; **horizontal, vertical, electrostatic, erratic, p.,** polarisation horizontale, verticale, électrostatique, irrégulière; **p. current, energy,** courant *m,* énergie *f,* de polarisation; **p. error,** erreur due à la polarisation; **plane of p.,** plan *m* de polarisation; **plane p.,** polarisation dans un plan; **reversal of p.,** inversion *f* de la polarisation.

polarize ['pouləraiz], *v.tr.* **1.** (*a*) polariser (la lumière, une barre de fer, etc.); (*b*) (*with passive force*) se polariser. **2.** (*a*) inverser (le sens d'une expression, etc.); (*b*) donner une direction unique à (des efforts, l'opinion, etc.).

polarized ['pouləraizd], *a. Ph:* polarisé; **elliptically, horizontally, vertically, p.,** polarisé elliptiquement, horizontalement, verticalement; **p. radiation,** radiation polarisée; **p. wave,** onde polarisée; *Atom.Ph:* **p. neutron, nucleus,** neutron, noyau, polarisé; *El:* **p. relay,** relais polarisé.

polarizer ['pouləraizər], *s. Opt:* polariseur *m.*

polarizing[1] ['pouləraiziŋ], *a.* polarisant; polarisateur, -trice; **p. angle,** angle *m* de polarisation; **p. current,** courant *m* de polarisation; *Opt:* **p. microscope,** microscope polarisant; **p. nicol, prism,** nicol, prisme, polarisateur.

polarizing[2], *s.* polarisation *f.*

polarogram [pou'lærougræm], *s. Ch:* polarogramme *m.*

Polarograph [pou'lærougræf], *s. Ch: R.t.m:* polarographe *m.*

polarographic [poulærou'græfik], *a. Ch:* polarographique.

polarography [poulə'rɔgrəfi], *s. Ch:* polarographie *f.*

Polaroid ['poulərɔid], *s. Opt: R.t.m:* Polaroïd *m.*

polatouche ['poulətu:ʃ], *s. Z:* polatouche *m* (de Sibérie); écureuil volant.

polder ['pouldər], *s. Geog:* polder *m.*

pole[1] [poul], *s.* **1.** (*a*) perche *f* (à houblon); échalas *m,* rame *f*; mât *m,* écoperche *f* (d'échafaudage); hampe *f* (d'un drapeau); trabe *f* (d'une bannière); balancier *m* (de funambule); *Hort:* **p. bean,** haricot *m* à rame; *For:* **p. plantation,** perchis *m*; **tent p.,** mât de tente; **p. of a boathook,** manche *m* de gaffe; **telegraph, telephone, p.,** poteau *m* télégraphique, téléphonique; **A p.,** poteau en A; **anchoring p.,** poteau de rappel; **coupled, twin, poles,** poteaux jumelés; *Tg: Tp:* **p. mounting,** montage *m* (des fils) sur poteau(x); **p. line,** ligne *f* sur poteaux; **p. line cable,** fil *m* de ligne (sur poteaux); **p. climbers,** griffes *f* (pour grimper aux poteaux); *Min:* **p. drill,** perforatrice *f* (de sonde); *Const:* **p. plate,** panne sablière; semelle *f* de comble; *Fish:* **p. trawl,** chalut *m* à vergue; **p. boat,** bateau conduit à la perche; *Sp:* **(vaulting) p.,** perche de saut; **p. vault(ing), jump(ing),** saut *m* à la perche; **to p.-vault,** sauter à la perche; **p. vaulter,** sauteur, -euse, à la perche; perchiste *mf*; *Turf: etc:* **to have the p. (position),** tenir la corde; *F:* **to be up the p.,** (i) être timbré, toqué; (ii) être dans le pétrin; (iii) *A:* être soûl; (*b*) timon *m,* flèche *f* (de voiture); bras *m* (de civière); barre *f* (d'écurie); fléau *m* (de coolie); **p. tip,** mouflette *f*; (*of horse*) **to get a leg over the p.,** s'embarrer; **p. horse,** cheval *m* de timon; timonier *m*; *Harn:* **p. chain,** mancelle *f*; (*c*) **curtain p.,** monture *f,* bâton *m,* tube *m,* pour rideaux; (*d*) *Nau:* flèche (de mât); **p. mast,** mât à pible; mât de flèche. **2.** *A.Meas:* (*a*) perche; (*b*) perche carrée.

pole[2], *s.* pôle *m*; (*a*) *Geog:* **North P.,** pôle nord, arctique, boréal; **South P.,** pôle sud, antarctique, austral; **magnetic p.,** pôle magnétique; **true p.,** pôle géographique; **terrestrial p.,** pôle terrestre; *Astr:* **celestial poles,** pôles célestes; **p. of the ecliptic, of the equator, of the horizon,** pôle de l'écliptique, de l'équateur, de l'horizon; **to be poles apart, as far apart as the poles,** être aux antipodes l'un de l'autre; **their views are poles apart,** leurs opinions sont diamétralement opposées; *Mth:* **poles of a circle (of a sphere),** pôles d'un cercle (tracé sur une sphère); **reciprocal p.,** antipôle *m*; (*b*) *Magn:* **p. of a magnet,** pôle d'un aimant; **north(-seeking) p., red p.,** pôle nord; **south (-seeking) p., blue p.,** pôle sud; **consequent poles,** pôles conséquents; **salient p.,** pôle saillant; **like poles,** pôles de même nom; **opposite poles,** pôles de nom contraire; **p. strength,** intensité *f* de pôle; (*c*) *El:* **positive p.,** pôle positif, anode *f,* électrode positive; **negative p.,** pôle négatif, cathode *f,* électrode négative; **commutating, commutation, p.,** pôle de commutation; **field p.,** pôle inducteur; **double-p., two-p., switch,** interrupteur *m* bipolaire; **p. field,** champ *m* polaire; **p. horns, tips,** cornes *f* polaires (d'un inducteur de champ); **p. core,** noyau *m* polaire, magnétique; **p. piece,** masse *f,* pièce *f,* polaire (d'une dynamo); **p. shoe,** épanouissement *m* polaire (d'une dynamo); **p. shoe angle,** angle *m* d'épanouissement polaire; **p. paper,** papier *m* cherche-pôles; **p. pitch,** pas *m* polaire, distance *f* entre pôles; **p. distance,** distance entre pôles; **p. spacing,** écartement *m* des pôles; **p. changer,** inverseur *m* de pôle; **p. changing,** inversion *f* de pôle; (*d*) *Cryst:* **analagous, antilogous, p.,** pôle analogue, antilogue; (*e*) *Atom.Ph:* pôle, dent *f* (de magnétron à cavités); **p. gap,** entrefer *m* (de cyclotron).

Pole[3], *s. Geog:* Polonais, -aise.

poleax(e)[1] ['poulæks], *s.* **1.** *A.Arms:* hache *f* d'armes. **2.** *A:* (*a*) hallebarde *f*; (*b*) *Nau:* hache d'abordage. **3.** merlin *m.*

poleax(e)[2], *v.tr.* assommer; abattre (un animal) avec un merlin.

poleaxing ['poulæksiŋ], *s.* abattage *m* (des bœufs).

polecat ['poulkæt], *s.* **1.** *Z:* (*a*) putois *m*; (*b*) putois d'Amérique; **Patagonian p.,** lyncodon *m* de Patagonie; **African p.,** zorilla *f,* zorille *f.* **2.** *Pej: A:* (*a*) vil personnage; (*b*) putain *f.*

poled [pould], *a.* **1.** (*with num. adj. prefixed*) **three-p. marquee,** pavillon *m* à trois mâts. **2.** (bœuf) assommé.

polemarch ['polimɑ:k], *s. Gr.Ant:* polémarque *m.*

polemic [pə'lemik]. **1.** *a.* polémique. **2.** *s.* (*a*) polémique *f*; (*b*) (*pers.*) polémiste *mf.*

polemical [pə'lemik(ə)l], *a.* polémique.

polemi(ci)st [pə'lemisist, 'polimist], *s.* polémiste *mf.*

polem(ic)ize [pə'lemisaiz, 'pɔlimaiz], *v.i.* polémiquer.

polemics [pə'lemiks], *s.pl. Theol:* polémique *f.*

Polemoniaceae [pɔlimouni'eisii:], *s.pl. Bot:* polémoniacées *f.*

polemoniaceous [pɔlimouni'eiʃəs], *a. Bot:* polémoniacé.

polemonium [pɔli'mouniəm], *s. Bot:* polémoine *f,* polémonie *f,* polémonium *m.*

polenta [pou'lentə], *s. Cu:* polenta *f.*

polewood ['poulwud], *s. For:* perchis *m.*

polianite ['pouliənait], *s. Miner:* polianite *f.*

Polianthes [pɔli'ænθi:z], *s. Bot:* polianthe *m.*

police[1] [p(ə)'li:s], *s.inv.* (*a*) (*usu. with sg. const.*) police *f*; **city with an efficient p.,** ville qui a une police compétente; **p. inspector,** (i) inspecteur *m* de police; (ii) (*in the C.I.D.*) commissaire *m* de police; **p. constable,** agent *m* de police; **p. spies,** agents de la police; **p. station,** poste *m,* commissariat *m,* de police; **to take s.o. to the p. station,** conduire qn au poste, au commissariat; **to contravene p. regulations,** contrevenir aux règlements de police; **p. supervision,** surveillance *f* (de police); **p. van,** (i) voiture *f* cellulaire; panier *m* à salade; (ii) car *m* de police; **p. dog,** chien policier; **p. state,** état policier; (*b*) (*with pl. const.*) **the p. (force),** la police; **twenty p. were on duty,** vingt agents étaient de service; **municipal, country, p.,** police municipale, rurale; **the United Nations p. (force),** force *f* de police des Nations Unies; **military p.,** police militaire; **traffic p.,** police de la circulation, de la route; **river p.,** (agents de) la police fluviale; **to be a member of the p. force, to be in the p.,** être de, dans, la police; **to denounce s.o. to the p.,** dénoncer qn à la police; **the p. are after you,** la police est à vos trousses.

police[2], *v.tr.* **1.** policer; assurer la police de (l'État, etc.); maintenir l'ordre dans (le pays, etc.). **2.** *Mil: NAm:* mettre de l'ordre dans (un camp, une caserne).

policeman, *pl.* **-men** [p(ə)li:smən], *s.m.* agent (de police); (*in town*) gardien de la paix; **traffic p.,** agent de la circulation; **mounted p.,** agent à cheval, agent monté; **motor cycle p.,** agent motocycliste: motard; **rural, country, p.,** garde champêtre; **river p.,** garde-rivière, *pl.* gardes-rivière.

policewoman, *pl.* **-women** [p(ə)'li:swumən, -wimin], *s.f.* femme-agent (de police), *pl.* femmes-agents; auxiliaire féminine (de la police).

policing [pə'li:siŋ], *s.* police *f* (des mers, de la route, etc.); maintien *m* de l'ordre (dans un pays, etc.).

policlinic [pɔli'klinik], *s. Med:* policlinique *f,* clinique *f.*

policy[1] ['pɔlisi], *s.* **1.** politique *f*; ligne *f* de conduite; tactique *f,* but *m,* plan *m*; **foreign p.,** politique étrangère, extérieure; **home p.,** politique intérieure; **economic p.,** politique économique; **financial p.,** politique financière; **exchange p.,** politique en matière de change; **p. of deflation, of inflation,** politique de déflation, d'inflation; politique déflationniste, inflationniste; **prices and incomes, and wage, p.,** politique des prix et des salaires; **free-trade p.,** politique de libre échange; **agricultural p.,** politique agricole; **full-employment p.,** politique du plein emploi; **to adopt a p.,** adopter une ligne de conduite, un plan, une tactique; **our p. is to satisfy our customers,** notre but, notre politique, est de satisfaire nos clients; **cyclical p.,** politique de conjoncture, politique conjoncturelle; *Com:* **product p.,** politique de lancement d'un produit (sur le marché); **sales p.,** méthodes *fpl* de vente; *Jur:* **public p.,** l'intérêt, l'ordre, public; **contrary to public p.,** contraire à l'ordre public. **2.** *A:* diplomatie *f*; **to deem it p. to . . .,** considérer comme de bonne politique, juger prudent, de . . .. **3.** *Scot:* terres *fpl,* propriété *f,* parc *m* (entourant un château).

policy[2], *s.* **(insurance) p.,** police *f* (d'assurance); **(fully) comprehensive, all-risks, p.,** (police) omnium *m,* police tous risques; **life insurance, life assurance, p.,** police d'assurance (sur la) vie; **fire insurance p.,** police d'assurance (contre l')incendie; **dowry insurance p., portion (insurance) p.,** police (d'assurance) dotale; **standard p.,** police type; **joint p.,** police conjointe; **floating p., open p.,** police d'abonnement, police flottante, police ouverte; **time p.,** police à temps, à terme; **p. for a specific amount,** police à forfait; **p. to bearer,** police au porteur; **p. to a named person,** police à bénéficiaire désigné, police nominative; **war risks p.,** police sur risques de guerre; **p. holder,** porteur, -euse, titulaire *mf,* détenteur, -trice, d'une police d'assurance; assuré, -ée; **to draw up, make out, a p.,** établir une police; **to take out a p.,** prendre une police; *M.Ins:* **marine insurance p.,** police d'assurance maritime; **non-marine p.,** police terrestre; **named (ship) p.,** police à navire dénommé; **cargo p.,** police sur facultés; **hull, ship, p.,** police sur corps; **round p.,** police à l'aller et au retour; **voyage p.,** police au voyage.

poling ['pouliŋ], *s.* **1.** *Civ.E: etc:* (*a*) étayage *m* avec des perches; (*b*) blindage *m*; (*c*) *Min:* enfilage *m,* poussage *m*; **p. board,** bois *m* d'enfilage, de poussage. **2.** *Metall:* perchage *m.* **3.** conduite *f* (d'un bateau) à la perche.

polio ['pouliou], *s. F:* polio *f,* poliomyélite *f*; **p. vaccination,** vaccination *f* antipoliomyélite.

polioencephalitis [poulioueensefə'laitis], *s. Med:* polioencéphalite *f.*

poliomyelitic [poulioumaiə'litik], *a. Med:* poliomyélitique.

poliomyelitis [poulioumaiə'laitis], *s. Med:* poliomyélite *f*; paralysie spinale (infantile ou des adultes).

poliosis [pouli'ousis], *s. Med:* poliose *f.*

polish[1] ['pɔliʃ], *s.* **1.** poli *m,* brillant *m,* lustre *m* (d'une surface, etc.); brunissure *f* (des métaux); **high p.,** poli brillant; **mirror-like p.,** poli de glace, poli spéculaire; **wood that takes a high p.,** bois qui prend un beau poli; **to lose its p.,** se dépolir; **to take the p. off sth.,** dépolir, ternir, qch. **2.** crème *f,* pâte *f,* produit *m,* à polir; *Com:* **household polishes,** produits d'entretien ménagers; **boot, shoe, p.,** cirage *m,* crème, pour chaussures; **floor p.,** encaustique *f,* cire *f,* à parquet; **metal p.,** pâte, produit, à polir les métaux; nettoie-métaux *m inv*; **liquid metal p., brass p.,** liquide *m* à polir les métaux, eau *f* de cuivre; **wax leather p.,** cirage à base de cire; **nail p.,** vernis *m* à ongles; *A:* **stove p.,** pâte à fourneaux. **3.** belles manières, éducation *f,* savoir-vivre *m inv,* vernis; **to have a certain p.,** avoir un certain vernis, avoir l'usage du monde; **to put a p. on s.o.,** donner à qn un certain vernis, l'usage du monde; styler qn; **he has acquired, taken on, p.,** il a acquis un certain vernis, un certain savoir-vivre; **he lacks p.,** il manque de formes, d'éducation, de savoir-vivre. **4. writer of great p.,** écrivain au style châtié, impeccable.

polish[2] ['pɔliʃ], *v.*

I. *v.tr.* **1.** polir (le bois, le fer, etc.); brunir (l'or, l'argent); adoucir (le métal, le verre); cirer (des chaussures); astiquer (le cuir, etc.); lisser (une pierre, etc.); encaustiquer, faire reluire (les meubles, les dalles); cirer (le parquet); glacer, polir (le riz); éclaircir (des épingles); **to p. a cylinder with emery,** roder un cylindre à l'émeri; (*with passive force*) **marble that polishes well,** marbre qui prend bien le poli. **2.** polir, civiliser, dégrossir (qn, les mœurs).

II. (*compound verbs*) **1. polish off,** *v.tr.* (*a*) (i) terminer vite, expédier, dépêcher, bâcler (un travail); (ii) vider (un verre); ne rien laisser (d'un plat); achever, nettoyer (un plat); trousser (un repas); (iii) régler le compte de, en finir avec (qn); **she soon polished off her washing,** elle a bientôt torché sa lessive; (*b*) donner le coup de fion à, mettre la dernière main à (un travail).

2. polish up, *v.tr.* (*a*) faire reluire (qch.); astiquer, brunir, lustrer, blanchir (des objets en cuivre); (*b*) **to p. up one's French,** dérouiller son français; **to p. up a poem, etc.,** polir, passer le rabot sur, un poème, etc.; **to p. up a piece of work,** donner le coup de fion à un travail; **to p. up one's style,** châtier, raboter, son style.

Polish[3] ['pouliʃ]. **1.** *a. Geog:* polonais. **2.** *s. Ling:* polonais *m.*

polished ['pɔliʃt], *a.* **1.** poli; **p. oak,** chêne ciré; **p. parts,** parties brillantes (d'une machine, etc.). **2. p. manners,** manières polies, distinguées; **to become more p.,** devenir plus affiné; s'affiner. **3. p. style,** style châtié, raffiné.

polisher ['pɔliʃər], *s.* **1.** (*pers.*) polisseur, -euse, brunisseur, -euse (de métaux, etc.); astiqueur, -euse (de cuivre, etc.); adoucisseur, -euse (de verre, de marbre, etc.); lustreur, -euse (de glaces, etc.); *Cer:* useur, -euse; *Opt: etc:* **(precision) p.,** surfaceur, -euse (de précision); **(floor) p.,** cireur, -euse, de parquet; **shoe p.,** cireur de chaussures. **2.** *Tls:* instrument *m* à polir, polissoir *m*; brunissoir *m* (pour métaux); lustreuse *f* (pour glaces, etc.); **(electric floor) p.,** cireuse *f* (électrique à parquet); *Toil:* **nail p.,** polissoir à ongles.

polishing ['pɔliʃiŋ], *s.* (*a*) polissage *m,* brunissage *m* (des métaux, etc.); adoucissage *m* (des glaces, du marbre, etc.); lustrage *m* (des glaces, etc.); brillantage *m* (du cuir, des métaux); *Opt:* **(precision) p.,** surfaçage *m* (de précision); **electrolytic p.,** polissage électrolytique; **emery p.,** polissage à l'émeri; *Ind:* **p. shop,** atelier *m* de polissage; polissoire *f*; **p. machine,** machine *f* à polir, à roder; polisseuse *f*; surfaceuse *f*; polissoir *m*; **p. disc, wheel,** disque polisseur; meule *f* à polir; meule polissoire (de coutelier); polisseuse; **p. iron,** (i) *Tls:* polissoir; (ii) *Bootm:* fer *m* à déformer; **p. stone,** (i) *Tls:* meule polissoire; meule adoucissante; (ii) *Metalw:* sanguine *f* à brunir; **p. stick,** asti(c) *m*; (*b*) cirage *m* (des chaussures); encaustiquage *m* (des meubles, des parquets); astiquage *m* (des cuirs, des cuivres, etc.); **p. cloth,** chiffon *m* à reluire; **p. brush (for shoes),** brosse *f* à reluire, à chaussures; **p. powder,** poudre *f* à polir; **p. cream, paste,** crème *f* à astiquer, à lustrer, à nettoyer; pâte *f* à polir; *Mil:* asti(c).

polistes [pou'listi:z], *s.inv. Ent:* poliste *f.*

politburo, politbureau ['pɔlitbjuərou], *s.* politburo *m,* politbureau *m.*

polite [pə'lait], *a.* **1. p. society,** (i) le beau monde; (ii) les gens instruits, cultivés; *Lit: etc:* **p. letters, p. learning,** belles-lettres *fpl.* **2.** poli, courtois, complaisant, honnête (**to s.o.,** envers, avec, qn); **the Japanese are a p. race,** les Japonais sont un peuple poli; **a p. letter,** une lettre courtoise, aimable; **p. refusal,** refus poli; **to be p.,** être poli; **to be extremely p.,** être, se montrer, d'une politesse extrême; **he was just about p. to me,** il a été tout juste poli avec moi.

politely [pə'laitli], *adv.* poliment; avec politesse; d'une manière polie; honnêtement; **to greet, treat, s.o. p.,** faire des politesses à qn.

politeness [pə'laitnis], *s.* politesse *f,* courtoisie *f,* civilité *f*; **it is only common p. to . . .,** la politesse la plus élementaire exige que . . ..

politic ['pɔlitik], *a.* **1.** (*of pers., conduct*) (*a*) politique, avisé; (*b*) adroit, habile; (*c*) *Pej:* rusé, astucieux. **2. the body p.,** le corps politique; le corps social; l'État *m.*

political [pə'litik(ə)l], *a.* **1.** politique; **p. parties,** partis politiques; **p. manœuvring,** politicaille(rie) *f*; **p. prisoner,** (prisonnier *m*) politique *m*; **p. geography,** géographie *f* politique; **p. science,** sciences *fpl* politiques; **p. scientist,** spécialiste *mf* des sciences politiques; politicologue *mf.* **2.** *Gr.Pros:* **p. verse,** versification *f* populaire.

politically [pə'litik(ə)li], *adv.* politiquement.

politicaster [pə'litikæstər], *s. Pej:* politicailleur *m,* politicard *m.*

politician [pɔli'tiʃ(ə)n], *s.* **1.** (homme) politique *m.* **2.** *esp. NAm: Pej:* politicien *m,* politicard *m*; **notions entertained by politicians,** idées politiciennes.

politicize [pə'litisaiz]. **1.** *v.i.* faire de la politique; parler politique. **2.** *v.tr.* politiser. **3.** *v.i. Pej:* politicailler.

politicizing [pə'litisaiziŋ], *s.* politisation *f.*

politicly ['pɔlitikli], *adv.* (*a*) politiquement; avec sagacité; (*b*) d'une manière adroite; avec habileté; (*c*) avec astuce.

politico [pə'litikou], *s.* politicard *m.*

politico-economical [pəlitikoui:kə'nɔmik(ə)l], *a.* politico-économique.

politicomania [pəlitikou'meiniə], *s.* politicomanie *f.*

politics ['pɔlitiks], *s.pl.* (*usu. with sg. const.*) **1.** la politique; **to talk p.,** parler politique; **to study p.,** étudier la politique; **to dabble in p.,** politicailler; se mêler de politique; **foreign p.,** politique extérieure, étrangère; **internal p.,** politique intérieure; **power p.,** politique de force; **to go into p.,** se jeter, se lancer, dans la politique; **to enter p.,** naître à la vie politique; **what are his p.?** quelles sont ses opinions politiques? **such a scheme is not practical p.,** un tel projet n'est pas d'ordre pratique. **2.** *U.S: Pej:* **playing p., peanut p.,** politicaille(rie) *f*; **to play p.,** politicailler.

politique [pɔli'ti:k], *s. Hist:* politique *m.*

politization [pɔlitai'zeiʃ(ə)n], *s.* politisation *f.*

polity ['pɔliti], *s.* **1.** administration *f* politique. **2.** (*a*) constitution *f* politique; forme *f* de gouvernement; régime *m*; **a system of positive p.,** un système de politique positive; (*b*) État *m.*

polje ['poujei], *s. Geog:* poljé *m,* polje *m, pl.* poljé(s), polje(s).

polka ['pɔlkə], *s. Danc: Mus:* polka *f*; *Tex:* **p. dot,** pois *m*; **blue p. dot tie,** cravate bleue à pois (blancs).

poll[1] [poul], *s.* **1.** *A: Dial:* (*a*) tête *f* (d'une personne, d'un animal); **per p.,** par tête, par personne; *Hist:* **p. tax,** capitation *f*; taille capitale; (*b*) sommet *m,* haut *m,* de la tête (d'une personne, d'un oiseau, etc.); nuque *f* (d'un cheval); *Vet:* (*of horse*) **p. evil,** mal *m* de taupe, de nuque; dermite *f*; **grey p.,** tête grise. **2.** (i) votation *f* par tête; (ii) vote *m* (par bulletins); scrutin *m*; **constituency p.** = scrutin d'arrondissement; **Gallup p.,** (sondage *m*) Gallup *m*; **public opinion p.,** sondage d'opinion; **a p. was demanded,** on a demandé le (vote par) scrutin; **the day before the p.,** la veille du scrutin, des élections; **to go to the p.,** aller voter; **to go to the polls,** aller aux urnes; **there will have to be a second p.,** il y aura ballottage; **to declare the p.,** déclarer, proclamer, le résultat du vote, du scrutin; **to head the p.,** arriver en tête de scrutin; venir en tête de liste; **how does the p. stand?** où en est le scrutin? **heavy p., small p.,** nombre *m* considérable, peu considérable, de votants; forte, faible, participation électorale.

poll[2] [poul], *v.*

I. *v.tr.* **1.** (*a*) *A:* tondre (qn); couper ras les cheveux de (qn); (*b*) *Arb:* étêter, écimer (un arbre); (*c*) écorner, décorner (un taureau, etc.). **2.** (*a*) (*of polling clerk*) faire voter (qn); recueillir le bulletin de vote de (qn); (*b*) (*of candidate*) réunir (tant de voix); (*c*) **to p. a vote for s.o.,** donner sa voix, voter, pour qn.

II. *v.i.* voter (à une élection); **Brighton polls next Wednesday,** mercredi prochain Brighton votera, ira aux urnes.

poll[3] [poul], *s.* **p. (ox, cow, sheep),** bœuf *m,* vache *f,* mouton *m,* sans cornes.

poll[4] [poul], *a. Jur:* **p. deed,** acte unilatéral; contrat *m* à titre gratuit.

Poll[5] [pɔl], *Pr.n.f.* (*dim. of Mary*) *F:* **1.** Marie, Mariette. **2. P. (parrot), (pretty) P.,** perroquet *m,* Jacquot *m.*

pollack ['pɔlæk], *s. Ich:* lieu *m*; merlan *m* jaune; **green p.,** colin *m.*

pollakiuria [poulæki'juəriə], *s. Med:* pollakiurie *f.*

pollan ['pɔlən], *s. Ich:* lavaret *m.*

pollard[1] ['pɔləd], *s.* **1.** (*a*) *Arb:* têtard *m*; arbre étêté; **p. willow,** saule étêté; (*b*) *Husb:* animal, -aux *m* sans cornes. **2.** *Mill:* (*a*) recoupe *f*; (*b*) repasse *f.*

pollard[2], *v.tr. Arb:* étêter, écimer (un arbre).

pollarding ['pɔlədiŋ], *s. Arb:* étêtement *m,* étêtage *m,* écimage *m* (d'un arbre).

polled [pould], *a.* (*of ox, etc.*) **1.** sans cornes. **2.** décorné.

pollen ['pɔlən], *s. Bot:* pollen *m*; **p. grain,** grain *m* de pollen; **p. sac,** sac *m* pollinique; **p. tube,** tube *m* pollinique; **p. chamber,** chambre *f* pollinique; **p. mass,** pollini(d)e *f*; *Ent:* **p. basket, plate,** corbeille *f* (à pollen) (d'abeille); **p. count,** taux *m* du pollen; *Archeol:* **p. analysis,** palynologie *f*; **p.-analytical,** (techniques, etc.) de la palynologie.

pollex ['pɔleks], *s. Anat:* pollex *m.*
pollical ['pɔlikəl], *a. Anat:* pollicial, -aux.
pollicitation [pɔlisi'teiʃ(ə)n], *s. Jur:* pollicitation *f.*
pollinate ['pɔlineit], *v.tr. Bot:* transporter, émettre, du pollen sur (les stigmates); polliniser.
pollinated ['pɔlineitid], *a. Bot:* **wind p.,** pollinisé par le vent; anémophile; **water p.,** hydrophile; **animal p.,** zoïdophile; **bat p.,** pollinisé par les chauves-souris; **bird p.,** pollinisé par les oiseaux; ornithophile; **insect p.,** pollinisé par les insectes; entomophile.
pollinating ['pɔlineitiŋ], *a. Bot:* pollinisateur, -trice; **(flower-)p. birds,** oiseaux pollinisateurs.
pollination [pɔli'neiʃ(ə)n], *s. Bot:* pollinisation *f*, fécondation *f*; **self p.,** pollinisation directe; **cross p.,** pollinisation croisée, indirecte; **below the water p.,** pollinisation hyphydrogame; **p. by wind, water, animals,** pollinisation anémophile, hydrophile, zoïdophile; **p. by birds,** ornithogamie *f.*
polling ['pouliŋ], *s.* **1.** *Arb:* étêtement *m*, étêtage *m*, écimage *m* (d'un arbre). **2.** vote *m*; élections *fpl*; **p. district,** circonscription électorale; **p. station,** bureau *m* de vote; **p. booth,** isoloir *m*; **p. clerk,** secrétaire *mf* du scrutin.
pollinic [pɔ'linik], *a. Bot:* pollinique.
polliniferous [pɔli'nifərəs], *a. Bot:* pollinifère.
pollinium, *pl.* **-ia** [pɔ'liniəm, -iə], *s. Bot:* pollini(d)e *f.*
pollinization [pɔlinai'zeiʃ(ə)n], *s. Bot:* pollinisation *f.*
pollinosis [pɔli'nousis], *s. Med:* pollinose *f*, pollinosis *m.*
polliwog, pollywog ['pɔliwɔg], *s. Amph: NAm:* têtard *m.*
pollster ['poulstər], *s. NAm:* enquêteur, -euse, organisateur, -trice, d'un sondage Gallup.
pollutant [pə'lu:tənt], *s.* agent *m* de pollution.
pollute [pə'lu:t], *v.tr.* **1.** polluer, souiller, rendre impur, corrompre; **polluted water,** eau corrompue; eau qui n'est plus potable. **2.** profaner, violer (un lieu saint, etc.).
polluter [pə'lu:tər], *s.* **1.** corrupteur, -trice; **the polluters of the stream,** ceux qui déversent des impuretés, des eaux vannes, etc., dans le cours d'eau. **2.** profanateur, -trice (d'un temple, etc.).
pollution [pə'lu:ʃ(ə)n], *s.* (*a*) pollution *f*, souillure *f*; **atmospheric p., p. of the atmosphere,** pollution atmosphérique, de l'air; **river p.,** pollution des cours d'eau; (*b*) *Med:* pollution; (*c*) profanation *f.*
Pollux ['pɔləks], *Pr.n.m. Gr.Myth: Astr:* Pollux.
Polly ['pɔli]. *F:* **1.** *Pr.n.f.* (*dim. of Mary*) (*a*) Marie, Mariette; (*b*) (*parrot*) **(pretty) P.,** Jacquot *m.* **2.** *s. O:* (eau minérale d')Apollinaris *f.*
polo ['poulou], *s. Sp:* polo *m*; **p. stick, mallet,** maillet *m*; **p. player,** poloïste *m*; *Cost:* **p. neck,** col roulé; **p.-neck(ed) jumper,** chandail *m* à col roulé.
polocyte ['poulousait], *s. Biol:* globule *m* polaire.
polonaise [pɔlə'neiz], *s. Mus: Danc: & A.Cost:* polonaise *f.*
Polonia [pə'louniə]. *Pr.n. Hist:* Pologne *f.*
Polonian [pə'louniən]. *Hist:* (*a*) *a.* polonais; (*b*) *s.* Polonais, -aise.
Polonism ['poulənizm], *s. Ling:* polonisme *m.*
Polonist ['poulənist], *s. Ling:* poloniste *mf*; polonisant, -ante.
polonium [pə'louniəm], *s. Ch:* polonium *m.*
polonization [poulənai'zeiʃ(ə)n], *s.* polonisation *f.*
polonize ['poulənaiz], *v.tr.* poloniser.
polony [pə'louni], *s.* **p. (sausage),** (petit) saucisson; cervelas *m* (sans ail).
poltergeist ['pɔltəgaist], *s. Psychics:* esprit frappeur.
poltroon [pɔl'tru:n], *s. A:* poltron *m*, lâche *m.*
poltroonery [pɔl'tru:nəri], *s. A:* poltronnerie *f*, lâcheté *f.*
poly ['pɔli], *s. F:* École professionnelle d'enseignement technique.
poly- ['pɔli, pə'li], *comb.fm.* poly-.
polyacid ['pɔliæsid], *a. & s. Ch:* polyacide (*m*).
polyacrylate [pɔli'ækrileit], *s. Ch:* polyacrylate *m.*
polyacrylic [pɔliə'krilik], *a. Ch:* polyacrylique.
polyadenia [pɔliə'di:niə], *s. Med:* polyadénite *f.*
polyadenoma [pɔliædə'noumə], *s. Med:* polyadénome *m.*
polyadic [pɔli'ædik], *a. Ch:* polyadique.
polyalcohol [pɔli'ælkəhɔl], *s. Ch:* polyalcool *m.*
polyamide [pɔli'æmaid], *s. Ch:* polyamide *m.*
polyandria [pɔli'ændriə], *s. Bot:* polyandrie *f.*
polyandric [pɔli'ændrik], *a.* polyandrique.
polyandrous [pɔli'ændrəs], *a. Bot: etc:* polyandre.
polyandry ['pɔliændri], *s.* polyandrie *f.*
polyanthus [pɔli'ænθəs], *s. Bot:* primevère *f* des jardins.
polyarchic(al) [pɔli'ɑ:kik(əl)], *a.* polyarchique.
polyarchy ['pɔliɑ:ki], *s.* polyarchie *f.*
polyargyrite [pɔli'ɑ:dʒirait], *s. Miner:* polyargyrite *f.*
polyarticular [pɔliɑ:'tikjulər], *a. Med:* polyarticulaire.
polyatomic [pɔliə'tɔmik], *a. Ch:* polyatomique.
polybasic [pɔli'beisik], *a. Ch:* polybasique.
polybasite [pɔli'beisait], *s. Miner:* polybasite *f.*
Polybius [pɔ'libiəs], *Pr.n.m. Gr.Lit:* Polybe.
Polybranchi(at)a [pɔlibræŋki'ɑ:tə, -'bræŋkiə], *s.pl. Moll:* polybranches *m.*
polycarpellary, polycarpellate [pɔlikɑ:'peləri, -'kɑ:pileit], *a. Bot:* polycarpellé.
polycarpic, polycarpous [pɔli'kɑ:pik, -pəs], *a. Bot:* polycarpique, polycarpien.
polycellular [pɔli'seljulər], *a. Biol:* polycellulaire.
polycentric [pɔli'sentrik], *a. Biol:* polycentrique.
polycephalous [pɔli'sefələs], *a. Ter:* polycéphale.
Polychaeta [pɔli'ki:tə], *s.pl. Ann:* polychètes *f.*
polychord ['pɔlikɔ:d], *a. A.Mus:* polycorde.
polychroic [pɔli'krouik], *a. Cryst:* polychroïque.
polychroism [pɔli'krouizm], *s. Cryst:* polychroïsme *m.*
polychrom(at)ic [pɔlikrou'mætik, -'kroumik], *a.* polychrome.
polychromatophilia [pɔlikroumətou'filiə], *s. Med:* polychromatophilie *f.*
polychrome ['pɔlikroum]. (*a*) *a.* polychrome; (*b*) *s.* polychromie *f.*
polychromism [pɔli'kroumizm], *s.* polychromisme *m.*
polychromy ['pɔlikroumi], *s.* polychromie *f.*
Polycladida [pɔli'klædidə], *s.pl. Z:* polyclades *m.*
polyclinic [pɔli'klinik], *s. Med:* polyclinique *f.*
polycondensation [pɔlikɔnden'seiʃ(ə)n], *s. Ch:* polycondensation *f.*
polyconic [pɔli'kɔnik], *a. Mth:* polyconique; **p. projection,** projection *f* polyconique.
polycotyledonous [pɔlikɔti'li:dənəs], *a. Bot:* polycotylédone.
Polycrates [pə'likrəti:z], *Pr.n.m. Gr.Hist:* Polycrate.
polycrystal ['pɔlikristl], *s. Miner:* polycristal, -aux *m.*
polycrystalline [pɔli'kristəlain], *a. Miner:* polycristallin.
polycyclic [pɔli'saiklik], *a. Ch: Ph:* polycyclique.
polycystic [pɔli'sistik], *a. Med:* polykystique.
polycyth(a)emia [pɔlisai'θi:miə], *s. Med:* polycythémie *f.*
polydactyl [pɔli'dæktil], *a. & s. Z:* polydactyle (*mf*).
polydactylism, polydactyly [pɔli'dæktilizm, -'dæktili], *s.* polydactylie *f*, polydactylisme *m.*
polydimensional [pɔlidai'menʃənəl], *a.* multidimensionnel.
polydipsia [pɔli'dipsiə], *s. Med:* polydipsie *f.*
polyembryony [pɔli'embriəni], *s. Biol:* polyembryonie *f.*
polyene ['pɔlii:n], *s. Ch:* polyène *m.*
polyenergetic [pɔlienə'dʒetik], *a. Ph:* polyénergétique.
polyenic [pɔli'i:nik], *a. Ch:* polyénique.
polyergus [pɔli'ə:gəs], *s. Ent:* polyergue *m.*
polyester [pɔli'estər], *s. Ch:* polyester *m.*
polyesterification [pɔliestərifi'keiʃ(ə)n], *s. Ch:* polyestérification *f.*
polyethylene [pɔli'eθili:n], *s. Ch:* polyéthylène *m*, polythène *m.*
polyfunctional [pɔli'fʌŋ(k)ʃən(ə)l], *a. Ch:* polyfonctionnel.
polygala [pə'ligələ], *s. Bot:* polygala *m*, polygale *m.*
Polygalaceae [pɔligə'leisii:], *s.pl. Bot:* polygal(ac)ées *f.*
polygalaceous [pɔligə'leiʃəs], *a. Bot:* polygalé.
polygamist [pə'ligəmist], *s.* polygame *mf.*
polygamous [pə'ligəməs], *a.* (personne, animal, plante) polygame.
polygamy [pə'ligəmi], *s.* polygamie *f.*
polygenetic [pɔlidʒi'netik], *a. Ch:* polygénétique; *Geol:* polygénique.
polygenic [pɔli'dʒenik], *a. Anthr:* polygénique.
polygenism [pə'lidʒinizm], *s.* polygénisme *m.*
polygenist [pə'lidʒinist], *s.* polygéniste *mf.*
polygeny [pə'lidʒini], *s.* polygénie *f.*
polyglobulia [pɔliglɔb'ju:liə], *s. Med:* polyglobulie *f.*
polyglot ['pɔliglɔt], *a. & s.* polyglotte (*mf*); **p. Bible,** polyglotte *f.*
polyglottal, polyglottic, polyglottous [pɔli'glɔtl, -tik, -təs], *a.* polyglotte.
polyglottism ['pɔliglɔtizm], *s.* polyglottisme *m.*
polygon ['pɔligən], *s. Mth:* polygone *m*; *Mec:* **p. of forces,** polygone des forces; *El:* **p. connection,** montage *m* en polygone; *Geol:* **p. soil,** sol polygonal.
Polygonaceae [pɔligə'neisii:], *s.pl. Bot:* polygonales *f*, polygonacées *f.*
polygonaceous [pɔligə'neiʃəs], *a. Bot:* polygoné.
polygonal [pə'ligənl], *a. Mth: etc:* polygonal, -aux; *Const:* **p. rubble,** appareil polygonal.
polygonation [pɔligə'neiʃ(ə)n], *s.* polygonation *f.*
polygonatum [pɔli'gɔnətəm], *s. Bot:* polygonatum *m*, polygonate *m.*
polygonum [pə'ligənəm], *s. Bot:* polygonum *m*, renouée *f.*
polygraph ['pɔligræf], *s.* (*a*) (*pers.*) polygraphe *m*; (*b*) (*machine*) *Med:* détecteur *m* de mensonge.
polygraphic [pɔli'græfik], *a.* polygraphique.
polygraphy [pə'ligrəfi], *s.* polygraphie *f.*
polygyny [pə'lidʒini], *s.* polygynie *f.*
polyhalite [pɔli'hælait], *s. Miner:* polyhalite *f.*
polyhedral, polyhedric [pɔli'hi:drəl, -'hi:drik], *a. Mth:* polyédrique, polyèdre.
polyhedron [pɔli'hi:drən], *s. Mth:* polyèdre *m.*
polyhybrid [pɔli'haibrid], *s. Biol:* polyhybride *m.*
polyhybridism [pɔli'haibridizm], *s. Biol:* polyhybridisme *m.*
Polyhymnia [pɔli'himniə]. *Pr.n.f. Myth:* Polymnie.
polyisoprene [pɔli'aisoupri:n], *s. Ch:* polyisoprène *m.*
polymastia [pɔli'mæstiə], **polymasty** ['pɔlimæsti], *s. Ter:* polymastie *f.*
polymastic [pɔli'mæstik], *a. Ter:* polymastique.
Polymastida [pɔli'mæstidə], *s.pl. Prot:* polymastigines *f*, trichomonadines *m.*
Polymastig(in)a [pɔlimæsti'dʒi:nə, -'mæstigə], *s.pl. Prot:* polymastigines *f*, trichomonadines *m.*
polymath ['pɔlimæθ]. (*a*) *a.* polymathique; (*b*) *s.* polymathe *m.*
polymathic [pɔli'mæθik], *a.* polymathique.
polymathy [pə'liməθi], *s.* polymathie *f.*
polymelia [pɔli'mi:liə], **polymely** [pə'liməli], *s. Ter:* polymélie *f.*
polymelian [pɔli'mi:liən], *a. & s. Ter:* polymèle (*mf*).
polymenorrh(o)ea [pɔlimenə'riə], *s. Med:* polyménorrhée *f.*
polymer ['pɔlimər], *s. Ch:* polymère *m*; **acryloid p.,** polymère acryloïde; **ethylene p.,** polymère éthylénique.
polymeric [pɔli'merik], *a. Ch:* polymère.
polymerism [pə'limərizm], *s. Ch: Biol:* polymérie *f*; *Nat.Hist:* polymérisme *m.*
polymerization [pɔlimərai'zeiʃ(ə)n], *s. Ch:* polymérisation *f.*
polymerize ['pɔliməraiz], *v.tr. Ch:* polymériser.
polymethylene [pɔli'meθili:n], *s. Ch:* polyméthylène *m.*
polymicrobial, polymicrobic [pɔlimai'kroubiəl, -'kroubik], *a.* polymicrobien.
Polymnia [pə'limniə]. **1.** *Pr.n.f. Myth:* Polymnie. **2.** *s. Bot:* polymnia *m.*
polymolecular [pɔlimə'lekjulər], *a. Ph:* polymoléculaire.
polymorphic, polymorphous [pɔli'mɔ:fik, -'mɔ:fəs], *a. Biol: Ch:* polymorphe, polymorphique; *Cmptr:* **polymorphic system,** système *m* polymorphe.
polymorphism [pɔli'mɔ:fizm], *s. Biol: Ch:* polymorphisme *m*, polymorphie *f.*
polymyositis [pɔlimaiou'saitis], *s. Med:* polymyosite *f.*
polymyxin [pɔli'miksin], *s. Med:* polymyxine *f.*
polynemid [pɔli'ni:mid], *s. Ich:* polynémidé *m.*
Polynemidae [pɔli'nemidi:], *s.pl. Ich:* polynémidés *m.*
polynemus [pɔli'ni:məs], *s. Ich:* polynème *m.*
Polynesia [pɔli'ni:ziə]. *Pr.n. Geog:* Polynésie *f.*
Polynesian [pɔli'ni:ziən]. *Geog:* (*a*) *a.* polynésien; (*b*) *s.* Polynésien, -ienne.
polyneuritis [pɔlinjuə'raitis], *s. Med:* polynévrite *f.*
Polynices [pɔli'naisi:z]. *Pr.n.m. Gr.Lit:* Polynice.
polynoid ['pɔlinɔid], *a. & s. Ann:* polynoé (*f*).
polynomial [pɔli'noumiəl], *s. Mth:* polynôme *m.*
polynuclear [pɔli'nju:kliər], *a. Biol:* polynucléaire, polynucléé.
polynucleosis [pɔlinju:kli'ousis], *s. Med:* polynucléose *f.*
Polyodon ['pɔlioudɔn], *s. Ich:* polydon *m*, spatulaire *m.*
polyodontia [pɔliou'dɔnʃiə], *s. Dent:* hypergénèse *f* dentaire.
Polyodontidae [pɔliou'dɔntidi:], *s.pl. Ich:* polyodontidés *m*, spatularidés *m.*
polyonychia [pɔliou'nikiə], *s. Med:* polyonychie *f.*
polyopia [pɔli'oupiə], *s. Opt:* polyopie *f.*
polyopsia [pɔli'ɔpsiə], **polyopsy** ['pɔliɔpsi], *s. Opt:* polyopsie *f.*
polyose ['pɔlious], *s. Bio-Ch:* polyoside *m*, polyholoside *m*, polyose *m.*
polyoxymethylene [pɔliɔksi'meθili:n], *s. Ch:* polyoxyméthylène *m.*
polyp ['pɔlip], *s. Coel: Med:* polype *m.*
polypary ['pɔlipəri], *s. Coel:* polypier *m.*
Polypedates [pɔlipi'deiti:z], *s. Amph:* rhacophore *m.*
polypeptide [pɔli'peptaid], *s. Bio-Ch:* polypeptide *m.*
polypetalous [pɔli'petələs], *a. Bot:* polypétale.
Polyphaga [pə'lifəgə], *s.pl. Ent:* polyphages *m.*
polyphagia [pɔli'feidʒiə], *s. Med:* polyphagie *f.*
polyphagous [pə'lifəgəs], *a. Z:* polyphage.
polypharmacy [pɔli'fɑ:məsi], *s.* polypharmacie *f.*
polypharyngeal [pɔlifə'rindʒiəl], *a. Ann:* polypharyngé.

polypharyngy [pɔlifə'rindʒi], *s. Ann:* polypharyngie *f.*
polyphase ['pɔlifeiz], *a.* polyphasé; *El:* **p. circuit, current,** circuit, courant, polyphasé; **p. motor,** moteur polyphasé; **p. supply,** distribution polyphasée; *Cmptr:* **p. sort,** tri polyphasé.
Polyphemus [pɔli'fi:məs], *Pr.n.m. Myth:* Polyphème.
polyphenol [pɔli'fi:nɔl], *s. Ch:* polyphénol *m.*
polyphonic [pɔli'fɔnik], *a. Mus: Ling:* polyphone, polyphonique.
polyphony [pə'lifəni], *s. Mus: Ling:* polyphonie *f.*
polyphylogeny [pɔlifai'lɔdʒini], *s. Biol:* polyphylogénèse *f.*
polyphyly ['pɔlifaili], *s. Biol:* polyphylétisme *m.*
polyphyodont [pɔli'faioudɔnt], *a. & s. Z:* polyphyodonte (*m*).
polypide ['pɔlipaid], *s. Prot:* polypide *m.*
Polyplacophora [pɔliplə'kɔfərə], *s.pl. Moll:* polyplacophores *m.*
polyploid ['pɔliplɔid], *a. & s. Biol:* polyploïde (*m*); **p. cell, complex, series,** cellule *f,* complexe *m,* série *f,* polyploïde.
polyploidic [pɔli'plɔidik], *a. Biol:* polyploïdique.
polyploidization [pɔliplɔidai'zeiʃ(ə)n], *s. Biol:* polyploïdisation *f.*
polyploidize ['pɔliplɔidaiz], *v.tr. & i. Biol:* polyploïdiser.
polyploidy ['pɔliplɔidi], *s. Biol:* polyploïdie *f.*
polypn(o)ea [pɔlip'ni:ə], *s. Med:* polypnée *f.*
polypod ['pɔlipɔd], *a. & s. Z:* polypode (*m*).
polypodia [pɔli'poudiə], *s. Ter:* polypodie *f.*
Polypodiaceae [pɔlipoudi'eisii:], *s.pl. Bot:* polypodiacées *f.*
polypodium [pɔli'poudiəm], *s. Bot:* polypode *m.*
polypody ['pɔlipoudi], *s. Bot:* polypode *m.*
polypoid ['pɔlipɔid], *a. Z: Med:* polypoïde.
polyporus [pə'lipərəs], *s. Fung:* polypore *m.*
polyposis [pɔli'pousis], *s. Med:* polypose *f.*
polypotome [pə'lipoutoum], *s. Surg:* polypotome *m.*
polypous ['pɔlipəs], *a. Z: Med:* polypeux, -euse.
polyprene ['pɔlipri:n], *s. Ch:* polyprène *m.*
Polyprotodontia [pɔliproutou'dɔnʃiə], *s.pl. Z:* polyprotodontes *m.*
polypterus [pə'liptərəs], *s. Ich:* polyptère *m.*
polyptych ['pɔliptik], *s. Art:* polyptique *m.*
polypus ['pɔlipəs], *s. Med:* polype *m.*
polysaccharide [pɔli'sækəraid], *s. Ch:* polysaccharide *m.*
polyscope ['pɔliskoup], *s. Opt:* polyscope *m.*
polysemous [pɔli'si:məs], *a. Ling:* polysémique.
polysemy ['pɔlisi:mi], *s. Ling:* polysémie *f.*
polysepalous [pɔli'sepələs], *a. Bot:* polysépale.
polyserositis [pɔliserou'saitis], *s. Med:* polysérite *f.*
polysilicate [pɔli'silikət], *s. Miner:* polysilicate *m.*
polysilicic [pɔlisi'lisik], *a. Miner:* polysilicique.
Polysiphonia [pɔlisai'founiə], *s. Algae:* polysiphonia *f.*
polysomic [pɔli'soumik], *a. & s. Biol:* polysomique (*m*).
polysomy ['pɔlisoumi], *s. Biol:* polysomie *f.*
polyspermia [pɔli'spə:miə], **polyspermy** ['pɔlispə:mi], *s. Biol:* polyspermie *f.*
polyspermic [pɔli'spə:mik], *a. Biol:* polyspermique; **p. fertilization,** fécondation *f* polyspermique.
polyspored ['pɔlispɔ:d], **polysporic** [pɔli'spɔ:rik], *a. Bot:* polyspore.
polystelic [pɔli'sti:lik], *a. Bot:* polystélique.
polystely ['pɔlisti:li], *s. Bot:* polystélie *f.*
polystemonous [pɔli'sti:mənəs], *a. Bot:* polystémone.
polystichoid [pə'listikɔid], *a. Bot:* polystichoïde.
polystichous [pə'listikəs], *a. Nat.Hist:* polystique.
Polystichum [pə'listikəm], *s. Bot:* polystic *m,* polystichum *m.*
polystomatous [pɔli'stoumətəs], **polystome** ['pɔlistoum], *a. Z:* polystome.
polystyle ['pɔlistail]. *Arch:* **1.** *a.* polystyle. **2.** *s.* temple *m,* salle *f,* polystyle.
polystyrene [pɔli'stairi:n], *s. Ch: etc:* polystyrène *m.*
polysulphide [pɔli'sʌlfaid], *s. Ch:* polysulfure *m.*
polysyllabic [pɔlisi'læbik], *a.* polysyllabe, polysyllabique.
polysyllabism [pɔli'siləbizm], *s.* polysyllabisme *m.*
polysyllable ['pɔlisiləbl], *s.* polysyllabe *m.*
polysyllogism [pɔli'silədʒizm], *s. Log:* polysyllogisme *m.*
polysyllogistic [pɔlisilou'dʒistik], *a. Log:* polysyllogistique.
polysyndeton [pɔli'sindətɔn], *s. Rh:* polysyndéton *m,* polysyndète *m.*
polysynthesis [pɔli'sinθisis], *s. Ling:* polysynthèse *f.*
polysynthesism, polysynthetism [pɔli'sinθisizm, -'sinθitizm], *s. Ling:* polysynthétisme *m.*
polysynthetic [pɔlisin'θetik], *a. Ling:* polysynthétique.
polytechnic [pɔli'teknik]. **1.** *a.* polytechnique. **2.** *s.* École professionnelle d'enseignement technique.

polyterpene [pɔli'tə:pi:n], *s. Ch:* polyterpène *m.*
polytheism ['pɔliθi:izm], *s.* polythéisme *m.*
polytheist ['pɔliθi:ist], *a. & s.* polythéiste (*mf*).
polytheistic [pɔliθi:'istik], *a.* polythéiste.
polythelia [pɔli'θi:liə], *s. Ter:* polythélie *f.*
polythene ['pɔliθi:n], *s.* polyéthylène *m,* polythène *m.*
polytomous [pə'litəməs], *a.* polytome.
polytomy [pə'litəmi], *s.* polytomie *f.*
polytonal [pɔli'toun(ə)l], *a. Mus:* polytonal.
polytonalism [pɔli'tounəlizm], *s. Mus:* polytonalisme *m.*
polytonalist [pɔli'tounəlist], *s. Mus:* polytonaliste *mf.*
polytonality [pɔlitou'næliti], *s. Mus:* polytonalité *f.*
polytone ['pɔlitoun], *a. Ac:* polytone.
Polytrichum [pə'litrikəm], *s. Moss:* polytric *m.*
polytypic [pɔli'tipik], *a. Cryst:* polytypique.
polyunsaturated [pɔliʌn'sætjureitid], *a. Ch:* polyinsaturé; **p. fatty acids,** acides gras polyinsaturés.
polyuresis [pɔlijuə'ri:sis], **polyuria** [pɔli'juəriə], *s. Med:* polyurie *f.*
polyurethan(e) [pɔli'juəriθein, -θæn], *s. Ch: etc:* polyuréthane *m.*
polyuric [pɔli'juərik], *a. Med:* polyurique.
polyvalence, polyvalency [pɔli'veiləns, -'veilənsi], *s. Ch:* polyvalence *f.*
polyvalent [pɔli'veilənt], *a. Ch:* polyvalent.
polyvinyl [pɔli'vainil], *s. Ch:* polyvinyle *m*; **p. acetate,** acétate *m* de polyvinyle; **p. alcohol,** alcool *m* polyvinylique; **p. chloride,** chlorure *m* de polyvinyle; **p. resin,** résine *f* (poly)vinylique.
polyvoltine [pɔli'voulti:n], *a.* (ver à soie) polyvoltin.
Polyxena [pə'liksinə]. *Pr.n.f. Gr.Lit:* Polyxène.
Polyzoa [pɔli'zouə], *s.pl. Z:* bryozoaires *m.*
polyzoic [pɔli'zouik], *a. Z:* polyzoïque.
pom[1] [pɔm], *s. Z: F:* loulou *m* de Poméranie.
Pom[2], *s. Austr: F:* Anglais, -aise.
pomace ['pʌmis], *s.* **1.** (*cider making*) (*a*) pulpe *f* de pommes; (*b*) marc *m* de pommes. **2.** (*a*) pulpe; (*b*) tourteau *m* (de poisson, etc.).
pomaceous [pɔ'meiʃəs], *a. Bot:* pomacé, piré.
pomade[1] [pɔ'mɑ:d], *s. Toil:* pommade *f.*
pomade[2], *v.tr. & i.* (se) pommader.
pomaderris [pɔmə'deris], *s. Bot:* pomaderris *m.*
pomander [pə'mændər], *s.* pomme *f* d'ambre.
pomatum [pɔ'meitəm], *s. Toil:* pommade *f.*
pombe ['pɔmbi], *s.* (*African beer*) pombé *m.*
pome [poum], *s.* **1.** *Bot:* fruit *m* à pépins. **2.** *Poet:* pomme *f.* **3.** *Hist:* globe *m,* monde *m* (insigne de royauté).
pomegranate ['pɔm(i)grænit], *s. Bot:* **1.** grenade *f*; **p. syrup,** sirop *m* de grenadine. **2. p. (tree),** grenadier *m.*
pomelo ['pɔmilou], *s. Bot:* pomelo *m*; pamplemousse *m.*
Pomerania [pɔmə'reiniə], *Pr.n. Geog:* Poméranie *f.*
Pomeranian [pɔmə'reiniən]. **1.** *Geog:* (*a*) *a.* poméranien; (*b*) *s.* Poméranien, -ienne. **2.** *a. & s.* **P. (dog),** loulou *m* (de Poméranie).
pomey ['poumei], *s. Her:* tourteau *m* de sinople.
pomfret[1] ['pɔmfrit], *s. Ich:* **1.** stromatée *m.* **2.** brama *m* raii; *F:* brame *m*; castagnole *f*; brème *f* de mer.
Pomfret[2] ['pʌmfrit], *Pr.n.* (*a*) *Geog: A:* = PONTEFRACT; (*b*) **p. cakes,** pastilles *f* de réglisse.
pomiferous [pɔ'mifərəs], *a. Bot:* pomifère.
pomiform ['pɔmifɔ:m], *a. Bot:* pomiforme.
pommel[1] ['pʌm(ə)l], *s.* **1.** pommeau *m* (d'épée). **2.** *Harn:* arçon *m* de devant; pommeau (de selle).
pommel[2], *v.tr.* **(pommelled)** battre, rosser, gourmer (qn); bourrer (qn) de coups.
pommelly ['pɔməli], *a. Her:* pommeté.
pommetty ['pɔmiti:], *a. Her:* pommeté.
pommie, pommy ['pɔmi], *s. Austr: F:* Anglais, -aise.
pomological [pɔmə'lɔdʒik(ə)l], *a.* pomologique.
pomologist [pɔ'mɔlədʒist], *s.* pomologue *mf,* pomologiste *mf.*
pomology [pɔ'mɔlədʒi], *s.* pomologie *f.*
Pomona [pə'mounə]. **1.** *Pr.n.f. Rom.Myth:* Pomone. **2. P. green,** vert pomme *inv.*
pomp [pɔmp], *s.* pompe *f,* éclat *m,* faste *m,* splendeur *f,* appareil *m,* apparat *m*; **to like p.,** aimer le cérémonial; **to escort s.o. with great p.,** escorter qn en grande cérémonie; **p. and circumstance,** (grand) apparat; parade *f*; *Lit:* **to renounce the pomps and vanities of this wicked world,** renoncer aux pompes du siècle.
pompadour ['pɔmpədu:ər]. **1.** *a.* (style) pompadour. **2.** *s.* coiffure relevée.
Pompeian [pɔm'peiən], *a. Geog:* pompéien.
Pompeii [pɔm'peii]. *Pr.n. Geog:* Pompéi.
Pompey ['pɔmpi]. *Pr.n.* **1.** (*a*) *Rom.Hist:* Pompée *m*; (*b*) *F: A:* domestique *m* nègre. **2.** *Navy: F:* (l'arsenal *m* de) Portsmouth.
pompilid ['pɔmpilid], *s. Ent:* pompile *m.*
Pompilidae [pɔm'pilidi:], *s.pl. Ent:* pompilidés *m.*

pom-pom ['pɔmpɔm], *s. Artil:* canon-revolver *m, pl.* canons-revolvers; canon-mitrailleuse *m, pl.* canons-mitrailleuses (système Maxim).
pompom, pompon ['pɔmpɔm, -pɔn], *s.* **1.** *Cost: etc:* pompon *m.* **2.** *Hort:* (*a*) rose *f* pompon; (*b*) chrysanthème, dahlia, etc., nain.
pomposity [pɔm'pɔsiti], *s.* emphase *f,* suffisance *f.*
pompous ['pɔmpəs], *a.* **1.** pompeux, fastueux. **2.** (*a*) **a p. man,** un homme suffisant, qui fait l'important, qui se donne de grands airs; **she was p. but good-natured,** ses grands airs ne l'empêchaient pas d'être une brave femme; (*b*) **p. style,** style emphatique, ampoulé, empanaché, pompeux.
pompously ['pɔmpəsli], *adv.* pompeusement; avec suffisance; avec emphase.
pompousness ['pɔmpəsnis], *s.* **1.** pompe *f,* faste *m.* **2.** emphase *f,* suffisance *f.*
ponce[1] [pɔns], *s. P:* souteneur *m,* marlou *m, pl.* marlous; barbeau *m,* poisson *m.*
ponce[2], *v. P:*
I. *v.i.* être souteneur.
II. (*compound verb*) **ponce off,** *v.i.* partir, foutre le camp.
ponceau ['pɔnsou], *a. & s.* (rouge) ponceau *m inv.*
poncelet ['pɔns(ə)lit], *s. Mec.Meas:* poncelet *m* (= 100 kilogrammètres par seconde).
poncho, *pl.* **-os** ['pɔn(t)ʃou, -ouz], *s. Cost:* poncho *m.*
pond[1] [pɔnd], *s.* (*a*) étang *m*; bassin *m,* pièce *f* d'eau (de parc); mare *f,* abreuvoir *m* (de village); vivier *m,* réservoir *m* (pour le poisson); réservoir (de moulin); **p. life,** vie animale des eaux stagnantes; *Moll:* **p. snail,** hélice *f* aquatique; (*b*) *Ind:* **cooling p.,** bac *m* de refroidissement.
pond[2]. **1.** *v.tr.* **to p. back, p. up, a stream,** barrer un cours d'eau; établir une retenue sur un cours d'eau. **2.** *v.i.* (*of water*) **to p. (up),** former un étang, une mare; s'accumuler.
pondage ['pɔndidʒ], *s.* **1.** accumulation *f* de l'eau (d'une rivière, etc.). **2.** capacité *f* (d'une retenue).
ponder ['pɔndər]. **1.** *v.tr.* réfléchir sur (une question); considérer, peser (un avis); méditer (sur) (la situation); ruminer (une idée). **2.** *v.i.* méditer; **to p. on, over, sth.,** réfléchir à, méditer sur, spéculer sur, qch.
ponderability [pɔnd(ə)rə'biliti], **ponderableness** ['pɔnd(ə)rəbəlnis], *s.* pondérabilité *f.*
ponderable ['pɔnd(ə)rəbl], *a.* pondérable; (gaz) pesant.
ponderal ['pɔndərəl], *a.* pondéral, -aux; *Ch:* **p. analysis,** analyse pondérale; *Ph:* **p. index,** indice pondéral.
ponderation [pɔndə'reiʃ(ə)n], *s.* pondération *f* (d'une idée).
pondering[1] ['pɔnd(ə)riŋ], *a.* (*of pers.*) méditatif.
pondering[2], *s.* méditation *f.*
ponderingly ['pɔnd(ə)riŋli], *adv.* en méditant; d'un air réfléchi; d'un air absorbé.
ponderosity [pɔndə'rɔsiti], *s.* **1.** lourdeur *f*; *Ph:* pondérosité *f.* **2.** *A:* importance *f* (d'un événement, etc.). **3.** lourdeur (de style).
ponderous ['pɔnd(ə)rəs], *a.* **1.** massif, lourd, pesant. **2.** *A:* (*of business, etc.*) important, grave. **3.** (travail) laborieux. **4.** (style) lourd, pesant, ampoulé.
ponderously ['pɔnd(ə)rəsli], *adv.* lourdement; avec lourdeur.
ponderousness ['pɔnd(ə)rəsnis], *s.* = PONDEROSITY.
Pondicherry [pɔndi'tʃeri]. *Pr.n. Geog:* Pondichéry *m.*
pondweed ['pɔndwi:d], *s. Bot:* potamot luisant; *F:* épi *m* d'eau.
pone[1] [poun, 'pouni], *s. Cards:* premier *m* en main (ou son partenaire).
pone[2] [poun], *s. U.S:* **1.** pain *m* de maïs. **2.** pain de fantaisie.
poney ['pouni], *s.* = PONY.
pong[1] [pɔŋ], *s. P:* puanteur *f*; **what a p.!** comme ça pue, ça schlingue!
pong[2], *v.i. P:* puer, schlinguer.
pongee [pɔn'dʒi:], *s. Tex:* pongé(e) *m*; **Japanese p.,** pongé(e) du Japon.
pongid ['pɔndʒid], *s. Z:* pongidé *m.*
Pongidae ['pɔndʒidi:], *s.pl. Z:* pongidés *m.*
pongo ['pɔŋgou], *s. Navy: P: O:* soldat *m.*
poniard[1] ['pɔnjɑ:d], *s.* poignard *m.*
poniard[2], *v.tr.* poignarder (qn).
ponor ['pounɔər], *s. Geog:* ponor *m,* entonnoir *m.*
pons asinorum ['pɔnzæsi'nɔ:rəm], *s. F:* le pont aux ânes ((i) la cinquième proposition du premier livre d'Euclide; (ii) difficulté quelconque).
pons Varolii ['pɔnzvæ'rouliai], *s. Anat:* pont *m* de Varole, de Varoli; protubérance cérébrale.
pontage ['pɔntidʒ], *s.* pontonnage *m*; péage *m* (pour la traversée d'un pont).
pontederia [pɔnti'diəriə], *s. Bot:* pontédérie *f.*
Pontederiaceae [pɔntidiəri'eisii:], *s.pl. Bot:*

pontédériacées *f*.

pontederiaceous [pɔntidiəri'eiʃəs], *a. Bot:* pontédériacé.

Pontefract ['pɔntifrækt]. *Pr.n.* Pontefract (ville du Yorkshire); **P.** (['pɔmfrit]) **cakes,** pastilles *f* de réglisse.

Pontic[1] ['pɔntik], *a. A.Geog:* pontique; du Pont; **the P. Sea,** le Pont-Euxin.

pontic[2], *s. Dent:* intermédiaire *m* de bridge.

ponticello [pɔnti'tʃelou], *s. Mus:* chevalet *m* (d'instrument à corde); *esp. in the phr.* **sul p.,** sur le chevalet.

pontifex, *pl.* **pontifices** ['pɔntifeks, pɔn'tifisiːz], *s. Rom.Ant:* pontife *m*; **p. maximus,** grand pontife.

pontiff ['pɔntif], *s.* pontife *m*. **1.** *Rom.Ant:* = PONTIFEX. **2.** *Ecc:* évêque *m*, prélat *m*; *esp.* **the sovereign p.,** le souverain pontife, le pape.

pontifical [pɔn'tifik(ə)l]. **1.** *a.* pontifical, -aux; épiscopal, -aux; *Pej:* **p. airs,** airs *m* de pontife. **2.** *s.* pontifical *m* (livre du rituel des évêques). **3.** *s. pl.* **pontificals,** vêtements, ornements, sacerdotaux.

pontificate[1] [pɔn'tifikeit], *s.* pontificat *m*.

pontificate[2], *v.i.* **1.** pontifier; officier en qualité de pontife ou d'évêque. **2.** *Pej:* pontifier; faire l'important; parler avec une solennité de pontife, avec emphase.

pontify ['pɔntifai], *v.i. Pej:* = PONTIFICATE[2] 2.

pontil ['pɔntil], *s. Glassm:* pontil *m* (la barre de fer).

Pontine ['pɔntain], *a. Geog:* **the P. Marshes,** les Marais Pontins.

Pontius Pilate ['pɔnʃəs'pailət]. *Pr.n.m. B.Hist:* Ponce Pilate.

Pontocaspian [pɔntou'kæspiən], *a. Geog:* pontocaspien.

pontoneer, pontonier [pɔntə'niər], *s. Mil:* pontonnier *m*.

pontoon[1] [pɔn'tuːn], *s.* **1.** ponton *m*, bac *m*. **2.** *Mil:* bateau *m*, nacelle *f*, ponton (d'un pont de bateaux); **p. bridge,** pont de bateaux, pont flottant; pont d'équipage; *A:* **p. corps,** corps *m* de pontonniers; *Nau: etc:* **p. crane,** ponton-grue *m*, *pl.* pontons-grues; (*b*) flotteur *m* (d'hydravion); **inflatable p.,** flotteur gonflable.

pontoon[2], *v.tr.* **1.** traverser (une rivière) sur un pont de bateaux. **2.** jeter des pontons, un pont de bateaux, sur (une rivière).

pontoon[3], *s. Cards:* vingt-et-un.

Pontus ['pɔntəs]. *Pr.n. A.Geog:* **1.** le Pont. **2. P. Euxinus,** le Pont-Euxin.

ponty ['pɔnti], *s. Glassm:* pontil *m*, pontis *m*.

pony[1] ['pouni], *s.* **1.** (*a*) poney *m*; **p. mare,** ponette *f*; **p. carriage, p. trap,** attelage *m* à poney; **p. trekking,** randonnées *fpl* à dos de poney; (*b*) *U.S:* petit cheval de l'Ouest, *esp.* mustang *m*; **cow p.,** cheval de ranch; (*c*) *U.S: F:* **ponies,** chevaux de course; (*d*) *P: A:* **Jerusalem p.,** (i) âne *m*, baudet *m*, bourrique *f*; (ii) clergyman pauvre. **2.** *P:* vingt-cinq livres sterling. **3.** *Sch: U.S: F:* traduction *f* (juxtalinéaire). **4.** petit verre (sans pied). **5. p. engine,** (i) *Nau: etc:* moteur démarreur; (ii) *Rail:* locomotive *f* de manœuvre; *Rail: O:* **p. truck,** bissel *m* (de locomotive).

pony[2], *v.i. esp. U.S: P:* **to p. up,** payer, casquer.

ponyskin ['pouniskin], *s. Com:* (fourrure *f*) poulain *m*.

ponytail ['pouniteil], *s. Hairdr:* queue *f* de cheval.

pooch [puːtʃ], *s. P:* chien *m*, clebs *m*, cabot *m*, clébard *m*; **come on, p.!** viens, toutou!

pood [puːd], *s. Russian Meas:* poud *m*.

poodle[1] ['puːdl], *s.* caniche *mf*, barbet, -ette.

poodle[2], *v.tr.* tondre (un caniche).

poodle-faker ['puːdlfeikər], *s.m. F: O:* (*Anglo-Indian*) greluchon, gigolo.

pooh [puː], *int.* bah! peuh! *F:* ça pue! **p., is that all!** la belle affaire!

Pooh-Bah ['puː'bɑː], *s. F: Pej:* cumulard *m*; *F:* homme-orchestre *m*; (personnage du *Mikado* de W. S. Gilbert).

pooh-pooh ['puː'puː], *v.tr.* traiter légèrement, tourner en ridicule, ridiculiser (une idée, une théorie, etc.); se moquer, faire peu de cas (d'une idée, d'un avertissement); repousser (un conseil) avec mépris.

pooka ['puːkə], *s. Irish:* = loup-garou *m*.

pool[1] [puːl], *s.* **1.** (*a*) (*of running water*) fontaine *f*; calme *m*; (*in river*) trou *m* d'eau; **the P. (of London),** le mouillage sur la Tamise en aval de London Bridge; (*b*) (*stagnant*) mare *f*; (*ornamental*) pièce *f* d'eau; (*left on sandy beach at low tide*) bâche *f*; **rock p.,** mare (dans les rochers au bord de la mer); (*c*) **swimming p.,** piscine *f*; **paddling p.,** bassin *m* à patauger; (*d*) flaque *f* (d'eau, d'encre, de sang); **lying in a p. of blood,** baignant dans son sang. **2.** (*a*) **mercury p.,** bain *m* de mercure; (*b*) *El:* **p. cathode,** cathode *f* à bain, à liquide; **p. rectifier,** soupape *f* à cathode liquide.

pool[2], *v.tr. Min:* haver, sou(s)chever (une roche, etc.).

pool[3], *s.* **1.** (*a*) *Games:* poule *f*, cagnotte *f*; (*b*) *Bill: Fenc: etc:* poule; (*c*) **football p. (competitions),** *F:* **the pools,** concours *m* de pronostics de matchs de football. **2.** (*a*) groupe *m* (de travail); équipe *f* (de journalistes); **typing p.,** service général de dactylographie; central *m* dactylographique; *F:* pool *m* de dactylos; (*b*) *Com: etc:* groupement *m* (pour opérations en commun); syndicat *m* de placement, de répartition (de marchandises, de commandes, etc.); (*c*) *Pol.Ec: etc:* fonds commun, *F:* pool.

pool[4], *v.tr.* (*a*) mettre en commun (ses capitaux, ses bénéfices, etc.); grouper (ses moyens); **we pooled our resources,** nous avons fait bourse commune; (*b*) *Com: etc:* mettre en syndicat, grouper (les commandes); répartir l'exploitation de (qch.).

pooling ['puːliŋ], *s.* mise *f* en commun (de fonds, etc.); *Com: etc:* groupement *m* (des intérêts, des commandes, etc.).

poon [puːn], *s. Bot:* **p. (tree),** calophylle *m* inophylle, calophyllum *m*.

Poona ['puːnə]. *Pr.n. Geog:* Poona *m*, Pouna *m*; *A:* **P. painting,** gouache *f* sur papier de Chine.

poop[1] [puːp], *s. Nau:* **1.** poupe *f*. **2. p. (deck),** (pont *m* de) dunette *f*, gaillard *m* d'arrière; **full p.,** dunette pleine; **p. break,** fronteau *m* de dunette; **p. rail,** lisse *f*, rambarde *f* de dunette.

poop[2], *v.tr. Nau:* (*of wave*) **to p. a ship,** balayer la poupe d'un navire; **to be pooped,** être capelé, embarquer une vague par l'arrière.

poop[3]. **1.** *v.tr.* tirer (un canon); faire partir (un coup de canon). **2.** *v.i.* (*of guns*) tonner.

pooped [puːpt], *a.* **high-p.,** (navire) à haute poupe.

poor [puər], *a.* pauvre. **1.** (*a*) besogneux, malheureux, *Adm: O:* indigent; **a p. man,** un pauvre; **a p. woman,** une pauvre femme; **the poorer classes,** les classes pauvres; **p. whites,** pauvres, petits, blancs; **as p. as a church mouse, as Job,** *U.S:* **as Job's cat,** gueux comme un rat d'église, pauvre comme Job; **I'm poorer by a thousand francs,** j'en suis pour mille francs; *F:* **p. man's oysters,** les moules *f*; (*b*) *s.pl.* **the p.,** les pauvres, les malheureux, les indigents; **to help the p.,** secourir les pauvres; *Ecc:* **p. box,** tronc *m* pour les pauvres; *A:* **p. law,** lois *fpl* sur l'assistance publique; **p. rate,** taxe *f* des pauvres; **p. relief,** aide *f*, assistance *f*, aux pauvres, aux indigents. **2.** de mauvaise, de piètre, qualité; médiocre; **p. soil,** sol maigre, peu fertile, improductif; **p. harvest,** mauvaise récolte; **the potatoes were p. this year,** (i) nous avons eu une mauvaise récolte de pommes de terre cette année; (ii) les pommes de terre étaient de mauvaise qualité cette année; **p. cattle,** bétail *m* maigre; **p. wine,** vin pauvre, *F:* piquette *f*; **p. blood,** sang vicié; **p. health,** santé débile; mauvaise santé; **p. food, fare,** maigre chère *f*; cuisine *f* médiocre; mets peu appétissants; **p. quality,** qualité inférieure; mauvaise qualité; **that's p. (quality) stuff,** c'est de la camelote; **p. excuse,** mauvaise, piètre, excuse; **I've a p. memory,** je n'ai pas de mémoire; j'ai peu de mémoire; **a p. looking house,** une maison minable, de piètre apparence; **a p. horse,** un mauvais cheval; une rosse; **she's p. spirited, a p. creature,** elle est faible, sans énergie, sans courage; c'est une femme qui n'a pas de ressort; **to cut a p. figure,** faire piètre figure; **the patient's had a p. night,** le malade a passé une mauvaise nuit; **p. reception,** (i) mauvais accueil; (ii) *W.Tel: etc:* mauvaise transmission; *Th:* **there was a p. house,** la salle était plutôt dégarnie; **he's a p. driver,** c'est un mauvais conducteur; **he's p. at maths,** il est faible, nul, en math(s); **my students are p. this year,** cette année mes étudiants sont médiocres, ne sont pas brillants. **3.** (*a*) (*to be pitied*) **p. creature! p. thing!** (*to child, animal*) **p. little chap!** pauvre petit! pauvre petite! **I'm so sorry for the p. man,** je le plains bien, le pauvre homme; *O:* **p. (little) me!** pauvre de moi! (*b*) (*of pers. who has died*) **when p. Alice was alive,** du vivant de la, notre, pauvre Alice.

poorhouse ['puəhaus], *s. A:* hospice *m*; asile *m* des pauvres.

poorly ['puəli]. **1.** *adv.* pauvrement, médiocrement, maigrement; **p. dressed,** pauvrement vêtu; **p. furnished room,** pièce minable, mal meublée; **p. lit streets,** rues mal éclairées; **the potatoes did p. this year,** (i) nous avons eu une mauvaise récolte de pommes de terre cette année; (ii) les pommes de terre étaient de mauvaise qualité cette année; **he did p. in his exams,** il a eu de mauvais résultats aux examens. **2.** *a.* (*of pers.*) souffrant, indisposé; **he's looking p.,** il a mauvaise mine; **I'm feeling p.,** je ne me porte pas bien; *F:* ça ne va pas, je ne suis pas dans mon assiette.

poorness ['puənis], *s.* **1.** pauvreté *f*, insuffisance *f*, manque *m* (d'imagination, etc.); **p. of the soil,** pauvreté, maigreur *f*, stérilité *f*, du sol. **2.** infériorité *f*, peu *m* de valeur; mauvaise qualité.

poorwill ['puəwil], *s. Orn:* engoulevent *m* de Californie, de Nuttall.

pop[1] [pɔp]. **1.** *int.* crac! pan! **to go p.,** éclater, crever; **p. goes the cork!** paf! le bouchon saute; on entend péter le bouchon. **2.** *s.* (*a*) bruit sec, soudain (de bouchon qui saute, etc.); (*b*) *F:* boisson pétillante, gazeuse, mousseuse; *esp.* champagne *m*; (*c*) *P:* (*of watch, etc.*) **to be in p.,** être au clou, chez ma tante.

pop[2], *v.* **(popped)**

I. *v.tr. & i.* **1.** *v.i.* (*a*) faire entendre une petite explosion; éclater, péter; (*of cork*) sauter, péter; (*of toy balloon*) crever; **they were popping away at the pheasants,** ils tiraient sur, canardaient, les faisans; (*b*) *U.S:* (*of enamel, etc.*) se soulever, s'écailler; (*c*) *F:* **to p. over, across, down, up, to the grocer's,** faire un saut (jusque) chez l'épicier; **I popped upstairs for a handkerchief,** je suis monté vite chercher un mouchoir; **I'm going to p. into town,** *NAm:* **to p. downtown,** je vais faire un saut en ville; **to p. into bed,** se glisser dans son lit; **I saw him p. out of the house,** je l'ai vu sortir; **I'll p. round at six,** je viendrai à six heures; **this question has popped up again,** cette question est revenue sur le tapis. **2.** *v.tr.* (*a*) crever (un ballon); faire sauter (un bouchon); **to p. corn,** faire éclater le maïs; (*b*) *P:* **to p. one's watch,** mettre sa montre en gage, au clou, chez ma tante; accrocher sa montre; (*c*) *F:* **to p. sth. behind a screen,** fourrer qch. derrière un écran; **he popped it down on the table,** il l'a jeté, déposé, sur la table; **to p. sth. into a drawer, into one's pocket,** mettre, fourrer, qch. dans un tiroir, dans sa poche; **to p. one's head out of the window,** sortir (tout à coup) sa tête par la fenêtre; **p. your coat on,** mets ton manteau; (*d*) *F:* **they kept popping questions at the speaker,** ils bombardaient l'orateur de questions; **then he popped the question (to her),** alors il lui a demandé de l'épouser.

II. (*compound verbs*) **1. pop in,** *v.i. F:* entrer à l'improviste; entrer en passant, pour un instant (chez qn); **I've just popped in,** je ne fais qu'entrer et sortir.

2. pop off, *v.i.* (*a*) *F:* filer, déguerpir, décamper; (*b*) *P:* mourir (subitement); faire le grand saut.

3. pop out, *v.i. F:* sortir; **I'm just popping out for a minute,** je sors pour quelques minutes; **his eyes were popping out of his head,** les yeux lui sortaient de la tête.

pop[3], *s. esp. NAm: F:* papa *m*.

pop[4] (*abbr. for* popular) *F:* **1.** *a.* (*a*) **p. song,** chanson *f* en vogue, chanson pop; **p. singer,** chanteur, -euse, de pop; **p. music,** musique *f* pop; (*b*) **p. art,** pop'art *m*, pop *m*. **2.** *s.* (*a*) *O:* concert *m* populaire; (*b*) musique pop.

popcorn ['pɔpkɔːn], *s.* maïs grillé et éclaté, *F:* pop-corn *m*.

pope[1] [poup], *s.* **1.** pape *m*; le Saint-Père; **P. Joan,** (i) la papesse Jeanne; (ii) *Cards:* le Nain jaune; *Ecc:* **the Pope's seal,** l'anneau *m* du pêcheur; *Cu:* **Pope's eye,** noix *f* (de veau, de gigot); **Pope's head,** (i) *Bot:* mélocacte *m*, mélocactus *m*; (ii) *Dom.Ec:* tête-de-loup *f*, *pl.* têtes-de-loup. **2.** *Ich:* perche goujonnière; gremille *f* vulgaire.

pope[2], *s.* pope *m* (de l'Église orthodoxe).

popedom ['poupdəm], *s.* papauté *f*.

popery ['poupəri], *s. Pej:* papisme *m*; romanisme *m*.

popeyed ['pɔpaid], *a. F:* (*a*) aux yeux protubérants; (*b*) aux yeux en boules de loto.

popeyes ['pɔpaiz], *s.pl. F:* (*a*) yeux protubérants; (*b*) yeux en boules de loto.

popgun ['pɔpgʌn], *s. Toys:* canonnière *f*, pétoire *f*; pistolet *m* à bouchon; *F:* (*of rifle*) **it's only a p.,** ce n'est qu'une pétoire.

popinjay ['pɔpindʒei], *s.* **1.** *A:* (*a*) perroquet *m*; (*b*) *Sp:* papegai *m*. **2.** *A:* fat *m*, freluquet *m*. **3.** *Orn: Dial:* pivert *m*; pic-vert *m*, *pl.* pics-verts.

popish ['poupiʃ], *a. Pej:* papiste; (*of thg*) de papiste; qui sent le papisme.

poplar ['pɔplər], *s. Bot:* **1.** peuplier *m*; **white p., silver p.,** peuplier blanc, de Hollande; ypréau *m*, ipréau *m*, abèle *m*; **grey p.,** peuplier gris; grisard *m*; grisaille *f*; **black p.,** peuplier noir, franc; **black Italian p.,** peuplier suisse; **Lombardy p.,** peuplier d'Italie; **balsam p.,** peuplier baumier. **2.** *U.S:* **tulip p.,** tulipier *m* (de Virginie).

poplin ['pɔplin], *s. Tex:* popeline *f*; **end-on-end p.,** popeline fil à fil.

popliteal [pɔ'plitiəl], *a. Anat:* poplité; du jarret; **p. artery,** artère poplitée.

popliteus [pɔ'plitiəs], *s. Anat:* **p. (muscle),** muscle poplité.

popover ['pɔpouvər], *s.* **1.** *Cu:* (espèce de) pâte cuite au four. **2.** *Cost:* robe *f* jumper (pour enfant).

poppa ['pɔpə], *s.m. esp. NAm: F:* papa.

Poppaea [pɔ'piːə]. *Pr.n.f. Rom.Hist:* Poppée.

popper ['pɔpər], *s. F:* bouton-pression *m*, *pl.* boutons-pression.

poppet ['pɔpit], *s.* **1.** (*a*) *A:* poupée *f*; marionnette *f*; (*b*) *F:* **she's a p.,** elle est charmante, exquise; **my p.,** mon chéri; ma chérie; mon petit poupon. **2.** *Nau:* (*a*) colombier *m* (de lancement); (*b*) (**rowlock**) **poppets,** portières *f* de dames; montants *m* de dames; porte-tolet *m inv* (d'un canot); (*c*) barre *f* (de cabestan); **p. holes,** logements *m* des barres. **3.** *Mec.E:* **p. (head),** poupée *f* (de tour); **sliding p.,** poupée mobile; contre-poupée *f, pl.* contre-poupées; *Min:* **p. head,** chevalement *m* (d'un puits de mine); châssis *m* à molettes; *I.C.E:* **p. valve,** (i) soupape soulevante, à manchon, à déclic; clapet *m*; (soupape en) champignon *m*; (ii) distributeur soulevant, à soupape; **p. valve gear,** distribution à soupape.

popping ['pɔpiŋ], *s.* **1.** bruit sec (des bouchons qui sautent). **2.** *Cr:* **p. crease,** ligne blanche, à quatre pieds du guichet (limite dans laquelle doit se tenir le batteur).

popple[1] ['pɔpl], *s.* clapotement *m* (de l'eau).

popple[2], *v.i.* (*a*) (*of water, stream*) clapoter, s'agiter; (*b*) (*of floating object*) danser sur l'eau.

poppy ['pɔpi], *s. Bot:* **1.** pavot *m*; **corn p., field p.,** coquelicot *m*, ponceau *m*; pavot rouge; pavot des moissons; **opium p.,** pavot somnifère; œillette *f*; **oriental p.,** pavot de Tournefort; **horn p., yellow horned p., sea(side) p.,** glaucienne *f* jaune; pavot cornu; **Iceland p.,** pavot d'Islande; **blue p.,** méconopsis *m*; **Californian p.,** (i) platystémon *m*; (ii) eschscholtzie *f*; **Mexican p.,** argémone *f* du Mexique; *Hort:* **Shirley p.,** coquelicot anglais à grandes fleurs simples; **p. oil,** huile *f* d'œillette, de pavot; **oil p.,** œillette; **p. (coloured), p. red,** rouge coquelicot *inv*; ponceau *inv*; *F:* **p. day,** (i) *A:* le onze novembre; (ii) le dimanche le plus près du onze novembre. **2. frothy p.,** silène enflé; béhen blanc; **plume p.,** bocconia *f*.

poppycock ['pɔpikɔk], *s. F:* bêtises *fpl*, inepties *fpl*, fadaises *fpl*.

poppyhead ['pɔpihed], *s.* **1.** tête *f* de pavot. **2.** *Ecc.Arch:* finial *m* (de stalle).

poppyseed ['pɔpisi:d], *s.* graine(s) *f(pl)* de pavot, d'œillette; **p. oil,** huile *f* d'œillette, de pavot.

popshop ['pɔpʃɔp], *s. P: O:* maison *f* de prêt sur gages; *P:* clou *m*; **her rings are at the p.,** ses bagues sont au clou, chez ma tante.

popsy ['pɔpsi], *s. F:* pépée *f*.

populace ['pɔpjuləs], *s.* **the p.,** (i) le peuple, la foule; (ii) *Pej:* la populace.

popular ['pɔpjulər], *a.* **1.** populaire; (*a*) du peuple; *Pol:* **p. sovereignty,** souveraineté *f* du peuple; (*b*) à la mode, goûté du public; qui a de la vogue, qui a une vogue, qui est en vogue; (opéra) très couru; **p. music,** musique *f* populaire, en vogue; **p. song,** chanson *f* populaire, en vogue; **p. concert,** concert *m* populaire; **p. lectures,** conférences très suivies; *Sp:* **p. event,** réunion sportive très courue; **p. king, general,** roi, général, populaire; **to make oneself p.,** se rendre populaire; **his cheerfulness makes him p.,** sa gaieté le popularise; **officer p. with his men,** officier très aimé par ses hommes; (*c*) **p. work, treatise,** ouvrage *m* de vulgarisation; **to write for the p. market,** écrire pour le grand public; **with a p. appeal,** qui plaît au peuple, au grand public; **p. prices,** prix *m* à la portée de tous; **p.-priced car,** voiture de type économique; (*d*) **p. error,** erreur courante. **2.** *Jur:* **action p.,** action publique.

popularity [pɔpju'læriti], *s.* popularité *f*; succès *m* (d'un produit, etc.) auprès du (grand) public.

popularization [pɔpjulərai'zeiʃ(ə)n], *s.* popularisation *f*; vulgarisation *f* (d'une science, etc.); **p. at a high level,** haute vulgarisation.

popularize ['pɔpjuləraiz], *v.tr.* (*a*) populariser (une idée, une science), vulgariser (des connaissances, etc.); propager (une méthode, etc.); (*b*) rendre (qn) populaire; (*c*) mettre (une mode, etc.) en vogue.

popularizer ['pɔpjuləraizər], *s.* vulgarisateur, -trice (d'une science, etc.).

popularly ['pɔpjuləli], *adv.* populairement; **it is p. believed that. . .,** les gens croient, on croit, que . . ..

populate ['pɔpjuleit], *v.tr.* peupler; **densely, thickly, populated country,** pays très peuplé; **sparsely populated areas,** régions à faible peuplement, population.

population [pɔpju'leiʃ(ə)n], *s.* (*a*) population *f*; **p. between one and two million,** population comprise entre un et deux millions; **fall in p.,** décroissance *f* de la population, décroissance démographique; dépopulation *f*; **increase in p.,** accroissement *m* de la population; accroissement, poussée *f*, démographique; **p. explosion,** explosion *f* démographique; **p. policy,** politique *f* démographique; **p. statistics,** statistique(s) *f(pl)* démographique(s); **the adult male, female, p.,** la population mâle, féminine, adulte; **working p.,** (i) population active; (ii) population laborieuse, classes laborieuses; **a floating p. of seasonal workers,** une population flottante, un effectif fluctuant, de travailleurs saisonniers; (*b*) peuplement *m*; **to encourage the p. of lands reclaimed from the marshes,** encourager le peuplement des terres conquises sur les marais.

populin ['pɔpjulin], *s. Ch:* populine *f*.

populism ['pɔpjulizm], *s. Hist: etc:* populisme *m*.

populist ['pɔpjulist], *a. & s. Hist: etc:* populiste (*mf*).

populous ['pɔpjuləs], *a.* populeux; très peuplé.

populousness ['pɔpjuləsnis], *s.* densité *f* de population (d'une région).

pop-up [pɔp'ʌp], *a. Dom.Ec:* **p.-up toaster,** grille-pain *m* automatique.

popweed ['pɔpwi:d], *s. Bot:* utriculaire *f*.

porbeagle ['pɔ:bi:gl], *s. Ich:* lamie *f* long-nez; *F:* chien-dauphin *m, pl.* chiens-dauphins; requin *m* marsouin; taupe *f* de mer.

porcelain ['pɔ:slin], *s.* (*a*) porcelaine *f*; **hard-paste p.,** porcelaine dure; **soft-paste p., artificial p.,** porcelaine tendre; *El:* **dark-glazed p.,** basalte *m*; *Miner:* **p. jasper,** porcelanite *f*; **p. manufacturer,** porcelainier *m*; (*b*) **p. paper,** papier *m* porcelaine (pour cartes de Noël, etc.); (*c*) *Crust:* **p. crab,** porcellane *f*, porcellanidé *m*; **hairy p. crab,** petit crabe velu; *Moll:* **p. shell,** porcelaine *f*, cyprée *f*; *F:* coquille *f* de Vénus.

porcellana [pɔ:sə'leinə], *s. Crust:* (crabe *m*) porcellane *f*.

porcellaneous [pɔ:si'leiniəs], **porcellanic** [pɔ:si'lænik], *a.* porcelanique.

porcellanite ['pɔ:s(ə)linait], *s. Miner:* porcelanite *f*.

porch [pɔ:tʃ], *s.* **1.** (*a*) porche *m*, portique *m*; (*b*) (**glass**) **p.,** marquise *f* (d'hôtel, etc.); (*c*) **p. roof,** auvent *m*. **2.** *Gr.Phil:* **the P.,** le Portique. **3.** *NAm:* véranda *f*; terrasse *f*.

porcine ['pɔ:sain], *a.* de porc; (race) porcine.

porcupine ['pɔ:kjupain], *s.* **1.** *Z:* porc-épic *m, pl.* porcs-épics; **tree p.,** coendou *m*; **brush-tailed p.,** athérure *m*; *F:* **he's as prickly as a p.,** il est aimable comme un chardon. **2.** *Ich:* **p. fish,** diodon *m*; hérisson *m* de mer, orbe épineux; poisson *m* boule. **3.** (*a*) *Tex:* peigneuse-enleveuse *f, pl.* peigneuses-enleveuses; (*b*) *Civ.E:* **p. roller,** hérisson. **4.** *Med:* **p. disease,** ichtyose *f*.

pore[1] [pɔ:r], *s. Anat: Bot: etc:* pore *m*.

pore[2], *v.i.* **to p. over a book,** s'absorber dans la lecture, dans l'étude, d'un livre; être plongé dans un livre; passer des heures courbé, penché, sur un livre; **he's always poring over his books,** il est toujours absorbé dans, courbé sur, ses livres; **to p. over a problem,** méditer longuement un problème.

porencephalia [pɔ:rense'feiliə], *s. Med:* porencéphalie *f*.

porgy ['pɔ:gi], *s. Ich:* pagre *m*.

poricidal [pɔ:ri'saidəl], *a. Bot:* poricide.

porifer ['pɔ:rifər], *s. Spong:* spongiaire *m*.

Porifera [pɔ:'rifərə], *s.pl. Spong:* spongiaires *m*.

poriform ['pɔ:rifɔ:m], *a.* poriforme.

porism ['pɔ:rizm], *s. Mth:* porisme *m*.

porismatic [pɔ:riz'mætik], **poristic** [pɔ:'ristik], *a. Mth:* poristique.

porite ['pɔ:rait], *s. Coel:* porite *m*.

pork [pɔ:k], *s.* **1.** (viande *f* de) porc *m*; **salt p.,** porc salé; **roast (of) p.,** rôti *m* de porc; **p. chop,** côtelette *f* de porc; **p. sausage,** (i) (*for frying*) saucisse *f*; (ii) (*for eating cold*) = saucisson *m* (pur porc); **p. barrel,** baril *m* de porc salé; saloir *m*; **p. pie,** pâté *m* de porc en croûte; **p.-pie hat,** chapeau de feutre rond à forme aplatie; **p. rind,** couenne *f*; **p. butcher** = charcutier *m*; **p. butcher's** = charcuterie *f*. **2.** *U.S: F:* entreprises grassement rétribuées dont l'allocation dépend du gouvernement, d'un député, etc.; **the p. barrel** = l'assiette *f* au beurre.

porker ['pɔ:kər], *s.* porcelet, jeune porc, engraissé, destiné à la boucherie.

porkling ['pɔ:kliŋ], *s.* goret *m*, porcelet *m*, cochonnet *m*.

porky ['pɔ:ki], *a.* **1.** qui tient du porc. **2.** *F:* gras, obèse.

porn [pɔ:n], *s. F:* pornographie *f*; **soft p., hard p.,** (livre, etc.) légèrement, grossement, obscène.

pornocracy [pɔ:'nɔkrəsi], *s. Hist:* pornocratie *f*.

pornographer [pɔ:'nɔgrəfər], *s.* pornographe *mf*.

pornographic [pɔ:nə'græfik], *a.* pornographique.

pornography [pɔ:'nɔgrəfi], *s.* pornographie *f*.

Porocephalidae [pɔ:rouse'fælidi:], *s.pl. Ann:* porocéphalidés *m*.

porocyte ['pɔ:rousait], *s. Spong:* porocyte *m*.

porogamic [pɔ:rou'gæmik], *a. Bot:* porogamique.

porogamy [pɔ:'rɔgəmi], *s. Bot:* porogamie *f*.

porokeratosis [pɔ:roukerə'tousis], *s. Med:* porokératose *f*.

poroscope ['pɔ:rəskoup], *s.* poroscope *m*.

poroscopic [pɔ:rə'skɔpik], *a.* poroscopique.

poroscopy [pɔ:'rɔskəpi], *s.* poroscopie *f*.

porosimeter [pɔ:rou'simitər], *s.* porosimètre *m*.

porosis [pɔ:'rousis], *s. Med:* porose *f*.

porosity [pɔ:'rɔsiti], *s.* porosité *f*; **p. test,** essai *m* d'étanchéité (d'une suture, d'un joint, etc.).

porous ['pɔ:rəs], *a.* poreux, perméable; **non-p.,** non-poreux; anti-poreux.

porousness ['pɔ:rəsnis], *s.* = POROSITY.

porphin(e) ['pɔ:fin, -fain], *s. Ch:* porphine *f*.

porphyria [pɔ:'firiə], *s. Med:* porphyrie *f*.

Porphyrian [pɔ:'firiən], *a. Gr.Phil:* porphyrien.

porphyrin ['pɔ:firin], *s. Bio-Ch:* porphyrine *f*.

porphyrinuria [pɔ:firi'nju:riə], *s. Med:* porphyrinurie *f*.

porphyrite ['pɔ:firait], *s. Miner:* porphyrite *f*.

porphyritic [pɔ:fi'ritik], *a. Miner:* porphyrique, porphyritique.

Porphyrius [pɔ:'firiəs], *Pr.n.m. Gr.Phil:* Porphyre.

porphyroblast ['pɔ:firoublæst], *s. Miner:* porphyroblaste *m*.

porphyropsin [pɔ:fi'rɔpsin], *s. Bio-Ch:* porphyropsine *f*.

porphyry ['pɔ:firi], *s.* **1.** *Miner:* porphyre *m*; **hornstone p.,** porphyre kératique. **2.** *Pharm:* **p. muller,** porphyre.

porpoise[1] ['pɔ:pəs], *s.* **1.** *Z:* marsouin *m*; phocène *f*; *F:* cochon *m* de mer; pourceau *m* de mer. **2.** *F:* (*of pers.*) gros ventru.

porpoise[2], *v.i. Av: Nau:* marsouiner.

porpoising ['pɔ:pəsiŋ], *s. Av: Nau:* marsouinage *m*.

porraceous [pɔ'reiʃəs], *a. A:* vert poireau *inv*; porracé; *Med:* **p. vomiting,** vomissements porracés.

porrection [pɔ'rekʃ(ə)n], *s. Ecc:* porrection *f*.

porridge ['pɔridʒ], *s.* **1.** bouillie *f* d'avoine, porridge *m*. **2.** *P:* **to do p.,** purger sa peine en prison, être mis au frais.

porriginous [pɔ'ridʒinəs], *a. Med:* porrigineux.

porrigo [pɔ'raigou], *s. Med:* porrigo *m*.

porringer ['pɔrindʒər], *s.* écuelle *f* (pour *porridge*, etc.); jatte *f*.

port[1] [pɔ:t], *s.* port *m*; (*a*) **the Channel, Mediterranean, ports,** les ports de la Manche, de la Méditerranée; **the p. of London, of Antwerp,** le port de Londres, d'Anvers; **inland p.,** port intérieur; **river p.,** port fluvial; **artificial, prefabricated, p.,** port artificiel, préfabriqué; **in p.,** au port; **to put into p.,** relâcher; **to come safe into p., to reach p. safely,** arriver à bon port; **to call at a p.,** faire escale à un port; **p. of call,** (i) port d'escale, de relâche; (ii) *F:* bistro(t) *m*; **p. of necessity, of refuge,** port de relâche forcée, de refuge; *F:* **any p. in a storm,** nécessité n'a pas de loi; **p. authority,** autorité *f* portuaire; **p. installations,** installations *f* portuaires; **p. capacity,** capacité *f* portuaire; **p. charges, dues,** droits *m* de port; (*b*) **fishing p.,** port de pêche; **commercial p.,** port de commerce, port marchand; **oil p.,** port pétrolier; *Com:* **free p.,** port franc; **open p.,** port ouvert; **naval p.,** port de guerre, port militaire; **p. of registry,** *U.S:* **p. of documentation,** port d'armement; **home p., p. of commission,** port d'attache; *Navy:* **home p.,** (i) (*for sailors*) port d'immatriculation; (ii) (*for ships*) port d'affectation; **the home ports,** les ports de la métropole; **p. Admiral** = préfet maritime.

port[2], *s.* **1.** *Scot:* porte *f* (d'une ville, d'une forteresse). **2.** (*a*) *Nau:* (i) sabord *m*; (ii) **p.(-lid),** mantelet *m*, panneau *m*, volet *m*, de sabord; contre-sabord *m, pl.* contre-sabords; contre-hublot *m, pl.* contre-hublots; contre-tape *f, pl.* contre-tapes; **half p.,** mantelet brisé (de hublot); **air p., ventilation p.,** sabord d'aération; **freeing p.,** sabord de dégagement; **gangway p.,** sabord de coupée; (*b*) **sighting p.,** fenêtre *f* de visée (d'un blockhaus, d'une tourelle, etc.); *Cin:* **observation p.,** fenêtre d'observation (de la cabine de projection). **3.** *Mch:* orifice *m*, lumière *f* (d'un cylindre, etc.); **discharge p., eduction p.,** lumière, orifice, de décharge, d'échappement; **water p.,** orifice d'eau; **p. bridge,** barrette *f* du tiroir; *I.C.E:* **admission p., inlet p., intake p.,** orifice, pipe *f* d'admission; **valve p.,** orifice de soupape. **4.** *Harn:* liberté *f* de langue (du mors).

port[3], *s. Nau:* **p. (side),** bâbord *m*; **land to p., on the p. side!** la terre par bâbord! **on the p. bow,** par bâbord devant; **hard a-p.!** bâbord toute! bâbord la barre! **to be on the p. tack,** être bâbord amures; **p. watch,** bordée *f* de bâbord; bâbordais *m*.

port[4]. *Nau: A:* **1.** *v.tr.* **to p. the helm,** mettre la barre à tribord; **p. (the helm)!** venez sur tribord! **2.** *v.i.* (*of ship*) venir sur bâbord.

port[5], *s.* **1.** *A:* port *m*, allure *f*, maintien *m*. **2.** *A:* train *m* de maison. **3.** *Mil:* **at the p.,** au port d'armes; **to charge at the high p.,** charger en croisant la baïonnette, charger la baïonnette haute.

port[6], *v.tr. Mil:* **to p. arms,** présenter les armes (obliquement) pour l'inspection; porter (le sabre).

port[7], *s.* (*a*) vin *m* de Porto; porto *m*; (*b*) **p.-wine mark,** tache *f* de vin (sur le corps, datant de la naissance).

porta ['pɔ:tə], *s. Anat:* **1.** hile *m* du foie; sillon transversal (du foie). **2.** (veine *f*) porte (*f*).

portability [pɔ:tə'biliti], *s.* portabilité *f*.

portable ['pɔ:təbl]. **1.** (*a*) *a.* portatif; transportable; mobile; roulant; **p. plant,** matériel *m* mobile, outillage portatif; **p. building,** construction *f* démontable; **p. forge,** forge portative, *Mil:* forge de campagne; *Nau:* **p.**

deadlight, tape *f* amovible de hublot; **p. winch,** cabestan volant; (*b*) *a. & s.* **p. (typewriter, radio, etc.),** machine à écrire portative, poste de radio portatif, etc. **2.** *A:* (mal *m*, etc.) supportable.

portableness ['pɔːtəb(ə)lnis], *s.* portabilité *f.*

portage[1] ['pɔːtidʒ], *s.* **1.** transport *m*, port *m* (de marchandises). **2.** frais *mpl* de port, de transport. **3.** *A:* pacotille *f* (de marin). **4.** portage *m* (de bateaux, etc., entre deux cours d'eau, ou d'un point navigable à un autre d'un même cours d'eau).

portage[2]. **1.** *v.tr.* faire le portage de (son canot, etc.). **2.** *v.i.* faire un portage, *Fr.C:* portager.

portal[1] ['pɔːtəl], *s.* (*a*) *Arch:* portail *m* (de cathédrale); **outer p.,** avant-portail *m, pl.* avant-portails; (*b*) entrée *f* (de tunnel); (*c*) portique *m.*

portal[2], *a. Anat:* portal, -aux; **p. vein,** veine *f* porte.

portamento [pɔːtə'mentou], *s. Mus:* glissade *f* (sur le violon, etc.); portée *f* de voix, port *m* de voix.

portative ['pɔːtətiv], *a.* **1.** *A:* (orgue, etc.) portatif. **2.** sustentateur, -trice; portant; **p. force of a magnet,** force portante d'un aimant.

portcrayon [pɔːt'kreiən], *s. Art:* porte-fusain *m, pl.* porte-fusains; porte-crayon *m, pl.* porte-crayons.

portcullis [pɔːt'kʌlis], *s. A.Fort:* herse *f*; sarrasine *f*; porte coulante.

Porte [pɔːt], *s. Hist:* **the (Sublime) P., the Ottoman P.,** la sublime Porte, la Porte ottomane.

ported ['pɔːtid], *a. Mec.E: etc:* (disque, plateau) à orifices, à lumières.

portend [pɔː'tend], *v.tr.* présager, augurer, faire pressentir (qch.); **they believe that eclipses p. evil,** ils croient que les éclipses présagent le malheur; **dark clouds that p. a storm,** nuages sombres qui annoncent un orage.

portent ['pɔːtent], *s.* **1.** présage *m* de malheur; mauvais augure. **2.** prodige *m.*

portentous [pɔː'tentəs], *a.* **1.** de mauvais présage, de mauvais augure; menaçant, funeste. **2.** prodigieux. **3.** solennel.

portentously [pɔː'tentəsli], *adv.* **1.** sinistrement. **2.** prodigieusement, extraordinairement, étonnamment. **3.** solennellement.

porter[1] ['pɔːtər], *s.* (*a*) portier *m*, concierge *m* (de musée, etc.); concierge (d'un immeuble); tourier *m* (d'un monastère); **porter's lodge,** (i) conciergerie *f*, loge *f* de, du, de la, concierge; (ii) maisonnette *f*, pavillon *m*, du portier (à l'entrée d'une grande propriété); (*b*) *Rail: NAm:* garçon *m* (de wagon-lit, etc.).

porter[2], *s.* **1.** porteur *m* (de bagages, etc.); portefaix *m*, crocheteur *m* (de fardeaux lourds); chasseur *m*, garçon *m* (d'hôtel); garçon (de magasin); **bank p.,** garçon de recette. **2.** *Metall:* ringard *m* (de pièce à forger). **3.** bière brune (anglaise); porter *m.*

porterage ['pɔːtəridʒ], *s.* **1.** (*a*) transport *m*, manutention *f*, factage *m* (de marchandises, de colis); **p. facilities,** service *m* de porteurs; (*b*) *Bank:* déplacement *m*, portage *m* (de documents) par un commissaire spécial. **2.** prix *m* de transport; factage.

porteress ['pɔːtəres], *s.f.* (*a*) portière, tourière (de couvent); (*b*) *NAm:* portière, concierge.

porterhouse ['pɔːtəhaus], *s.* (*a*) *A:* taverne(-restaurant) *f*; (*b*) *Cu:* **p. steak** = châteaubriant *m.*

portering ['pɔːtəriŋ], *s.* métier *m* de portefaix.

portfire ['pɔːtfaiər], *s.* (*a*) *Min: etc:* étoupille *f*; (*b*) *Artil: A:* boutefeu *m*, lance *f* à feu.

portfolio [pɔːt'fouliou], *s.* **1.** (*a*) serviette *f* (pour documents, etc.); (*b*) chemise *f* de carton; garde-notes *m inv*; carton *m* (à dessins, à estampes); **p. stand,** porte-cartons *m inv*; **book in p. form,** livre *m* en carton; (*c*) **minister's p.,** portefeuille *m* de ministre; maroquin *m*; **minister without p.,** ministre *m* sans portefeuille; (*d*) *Com:* portefeuille d'assurances. **2.** *Fin: etc:* **securities in p.,** valeurs *f* en portefeuille.

porthole ['pɔːthoul], *s.* **1.** *Nau:* sabord *m*, hublot *m*; *Ind:* **p. fan,** ventilateur aspirateur mural. **2.** *Mch:* = PORT[2] 3.

portia tree ['pɔːʃətriː], *s. Bot:* thespesia *m*, faux bois de rose.

portico, *pl.* **-o(e)s** ['pɔːtikou, -ouz], *s. Arch:* portique *m*; *Hist. of Phil:* **the P.,** (i) le Portique (à Athènes); (ii) le Portique; la philosophie de Zénon; le stoïcisme.

portion[1] ['pɔːʃ(ə)n], *s.* **1.** (*a*) partie *f*; part *f* (dans un partage); lot *m* (de terre); extrait *m* (d'un livre); **a p. of my money,** une partie de mon argent; (*on ticket*) **this p. to be given up,** côté *m* à détacher; *Fin:* **p. of shares,** tranche *f* d'actions; (*b*) portion *f*, ration *f* (de viande); quartier *m*, tranche (de gâteau); (*c*) *Jur:* **p. (of inheritance),** (i) part d'héritage (d'un enfant); (ii) avancement *m* d'hoirie; **p. (of inheritance) that must devolve upon the heirs,** réserve légale; (*d*) **(marriage) p.,** dot *f*; (*e*) *Rail:* rame *f*, tranche *f* (de wagons, de voitures); **the through p. for Aberdeen,** la rame directe pour Aberdeen; **the rear p. of the train,** le groupe de queue; la rame de queue. **2.** *A: & Lit:* destinée *f*, destin *m*, sort *m*, lot; **suffering is our p. here below,** la souffrance est notre part, notre lot, ici-bas; c'est notre destin de souffrir ici-bas.

portion[2], *v.tr.* **1.** **to p. (out),** partager (un bien, etc.); répartir (une somme); distribuer (les parts); **the estates portioned to the eldest son,** les terres échues en partage au fils aîné. **2.** *A:* doter (sa fille).

portioner ['pɔːʃənər], *s. Jur:* portionnaire *mf* (d'un héritage).

portionless ['pɔːʃənlis], *a. A:* sans dot; **she is p.,** elle n'a pas de dot.

Portland ['pɔːtlənd]. *Pr.n. Geog:* Portland *m*; **P. cement,** ciment *m* de Portland, portland *m*; **P. stone,** pierre *f* de Portland, de liais; calcaire portlandien.

Portlandian [pɔːt'lændiən], *a. & s. Geol:* portlandien (*m*).

portliness ['pɔːtlinis], *s.* **1.** prestance *f*, port majestueux; air imposant. **2.** corpulence *f*, embonpoint *m.*

portly ['pɔːtli], *a.* **1.** majestueux; de noble prestance; **p. matron,** matrone imposante. **2.** corpulent, ventru.

portmanteau, *pl.* **-eaus, eaux** [pɔːt'mæntou, -ouz], *s.* **1.** valise *f*; **p. word,** (i) mot qui combine le son et le sens de deux autres; mots télescopés (*p. ex.* **motel** = motor-hotel; **smog** = smoke + fog); (ii) mot passe-partout. **2.** *A:* portemanteau *m*, patères *fpl.*

portolan ['pɔːtəlæn], *s. Geog: A:* portulan *m.*

portor ['pɔːtɔːr], *s. Geol:* portor *m*, porte-or *m.*

Porto Rican [pɔːtou'riːkən], *a. & s.* = PUERTO RICAN.

Porto Rico [pɔːtou'riːkou], *Pr.n. Geog:* PUERTO RICO.

portrait ['pɔːtreit], *s.* portrait *m*; **full-length, half-length, p.,** portrait en pied, en buste; **p. painter,** portraitiste *mf*; **p. painting,** l'art du portrait; **p. gallery,** galerie *f* de portraits; *Sculp:* **p. bust,** (portrait en) buste (*m*); **to have one's p. painted, to sit for one's p.,** se faire peindre; **to make a sketch p.,** esquisser un portrait (de qn); **to make a p. of s.o.,** faire le portrait de qn; **p. in words,** portrait en prose; *Phot:* **p. attachment (to camera),** bonnette *f*, lentille *f*, à portrait.

portraitist ['pɔːtrətist], *s.* portraitiste *mf.*

portraiture ['pɔːtrətjər], *s.* **1.** portrait *m*. **2.** art *m* du portraitiste, du portrait. **3.** peinture *f*, description *f* (d'une société, etc.).

portray [pɔː'trei], *v.tr.* **1.** *A: & Lit:* peindre (qn); faire le portrait de (qn); **the painter has not portrayed you well,** le peintre a mal rendu vos traits, a tracé de vous une image infidèle. **2.** dépeindre, décrire (une scène, etc.); tracer le tableau (d'une scène, etc.); **to p. character,** peindre les caractères; **man difficult to p.,** homme difficile à définir; homme d'une personnalité difficile à rendre.

portrayal [pɔː'treiəl], *s.* **1.** portrait *m*. **2.** peinture *f*, représentation *f*, description *f* (d'une scène, des mœurs d'une époque, etc.).

portrayer [pɔː'treiər], *s.* peintre *m* (des événements, etc.); **a faithful p. of the life of his period,** un peintre fidèle des mœurs de son époque.

portreeve ['pɔːtriːv], *s. A:* bailli *m*; maire *m.*

portress ['pɔːtris], *s.f.* (*a*) portière, tourière (de couvent); (*b*) *NAm:* portière, concierge.

Portugal ['pɔːtjug(ə)l]. *Pr.n. Geog:* Portugal *m.*

Portuguese [pɔːtju'giːz]. **1.** *Geog:* (*a*) *a.* portugais; (*b*) *s.* Portugais, -aise. **2.** *s. Ling:* portugais *m.*

portulaca [pɔːtju'leikə], *s. Bot:* portulaca *m*, pourpier *m.*

Portulacaceae [pɔːtjulə'keisiiː], *s.pl. Bot:* portulacacées *f.*

portulan ['pɔːtjulæn], *s. Geog: A:* portulan *m.*

Portunidae [pɔː'tjuːnidiː], *s.pl. Crust:* portunidés *m.*

Portunus ['pɔːtjunəs], *s. Crust:* portune *m.*

posaune [pou'zaunə], *s. Mus:* (*of organ*) (jeu *m* de) trombone *m.*

pose[1] [pouz], *s.* **1.** pose *f*, attitude *f* (du corps); pose (d'un modèle); **she can't hold the p.,** elle ne sait pas garder la pose. **2.** pose, affectation *f*; **his socialism is a mere p.,** son socialisme n'est que de la pose; il est socialiste par snobisme; **without p.,** sans affectation. **3.** *Games:* pose (aux dominos).

pose[2], *v.*

I. *v.tr.* **1.** (*a*) poser (un problème); (*b*) émettre, énoncer (une opinion); citer (un exemple). **2.** *Art:* faire prendre une pose à (qn) (pour son portrait); poser (un modèle); **all the subjects are well posed,** tous les personnages sont bien campés. **3.** *Games:* poser (le premier domino).

II. *v.i.* **1.** (*a*) poser (pour son portrait); poser (comme modèle); (*b*) *F:* poser; se donner des airs (affectés, prétentieux); **she is always posing,** elle est toujours en attitude. **2.** **to p. as a Frenchman,** se faire passer pour Français; **to p. as a socialist,** se poser en socialiste; poser au socialiste; faire profession de socialisme.

pose[3], *v.tr. A:* réduire (qn) à quia; interloquer (qn); embarrasser (qn) par une question; *F:* coller (qn).

posé ['pouzei], *a. Her:* (lion) posé.

poser ['pouzər], *s. F:* question embarrassante, colle *f*; **to give s.o. a p.,** poser une colle à qn.

poseur, *f.* **-euse** [pou'zɔːr, -əːz], *s.* poseur, -euse.

posh[1] [pɔʃ], *a. F:* chic, bath, chouette; **it looks p.,** ça fait bien.

posh[2], *v.tr. F:* **to p. oneself up,** se faire beau, belle; s'attifer; **all poshed up,** sur son trente et un.

posidonia [pɔzi'douniə], *s. Algae:* posidonie *f.*

Posilipo [pɔsi'liːpou]. *Pr.n. Geog:* (le) Pausilippe.

posing ['pouziŋ], *s.* pose *f.*

posit ['pɔzit], *v.tr.* **1.** *Phil: etc:* avancer (une proposition); énoncer (un postulat, etc.); poser en principe **(that,** que). **2.** *Lit:* situer (qch. dans un endroit).

position[1] [pə'ziʃ(ə)n], *s.* **1.** (*a*) position *f*; posture *f*, attitude *f* (du corps, etc.); **horizontal, vertical, p.,** position horizontale, verticale; *Anat: etc:* **rest p.,** position de repos (d'un membre, etc.); **prone p.,** position couchée; **obstetrical p.,** position (i) gynécologique, (ii) obstétricale; *Med:* **knee-chest p.,** position genupectorale; **to be in a cramped p.,** être à l'étroit, dans une position étriquée; être dans une fausse position; *Danc:* **the five positions of the feet,** les cinq positions des jambes; *Mil:* **firing p.,** position (i) du tir, (ii) du tireur; **aiming p.,** position en joue; (*b*) position; attitude, disposition *f* (de l'esprit); **to adopt a definite p., to take up a p., on a question,** prendre position sur une question; **to take up an uncompromising p. (about sth.),** prendre une attitude, une position, intransigeante (à l'égard de qch.). **2.** (*a*) position; place *f* (d'un objet, etc.); situation *f* (d'une ville, etc.); **in p.,** en place; **to put sth. in p., to get sth. into p.,** mettre qch. en place; **this exhibit is out of p., in a poor p.,** cet objet n'est pas à sa place, est mal exposé; **the shop has a good p. in the centre of the town,** le magasin est bien situé au centre de la ville; **let's look for a p. where we shall be able to see the procession over the heads of the crowd,** cherchons un endroit, une position, d'où on pourra voir le cortège par-dessus les têtes de la foule; *Nau:* **to take up p. ahead, astern,** prendre poste en tête, derrière; *Mus:* (*of stringed instrument*) **second, third, p.,** deuxième, troisième, position; **to know one's positions,** savoir son manche; *Cmptr:* **storage p.,** position de mémoire; **code p., punch p.,** position de perforation; *Atom.Ph:* **lattice p.,** position du réseau; **vacant lattice positions,** positions du réseau dépourvues de barreaux; (*b*) *Post: Bank:* guichet *m*; **p. closed,** guichet fermé; (*c*) *Av: Nau: etc:* position (d'un avion, d'un navire); **angle of p.,** angle *m* de route; **dead reckoning p., estimated p.,** point estimé; **p. by bearing,** position (obtenue) par relèvement; **p. by land bearing,** point en vue de terre; **p. by observation,** point observé; **to fix, work out, one's p.,** faire le point; (*of convoy*) **break-off p.,** point de rupture; **rendezvous p.,** point de ralliement; **p. error,** erreur *f* dans le calcul de la position; **p.-error grid,** grille *f* de correction; **p. finding,** (i) orientation *f*; (ii) *Artil:* goniométrie *f*; **p. finder, indicator,** indicateur *m* de position; radiocompas *m*; radiogoniomètre *m*; *Artil:* goniomètre *m*; **p. astronomy,** astronomie *f* de position; (*d*) *Mil:* emplacement *m*, position; **to move into p.,** gagner ses emplacements, ses positions; se mettre en place, en position; **to bring guns into p.,** mettre des pièces en batterie, en position; **p. artillery,** artillerie lourde de campagne; **p. warfare,** guerre *f* de position; **advance p.,** position avancée; **covering p.,** position de couverture; **defensive p.,** position défensive, de défense; **supporting p.,** position de soutien; **to capture a p.,** s'emparer d'une position; **to storm the enemy's positions,** prendre d'assaut les positions ennemies. **3.** (*a*) état *m*, situation *f*; **in order to understand the p. properly,** pour bien comprendre la situation; **to be in an awkward p.,** se trouver dans une situation difficile, dans une impasse, *F:* dans une drôle de situation; **to be in a strong p.,** être en bonne passe, bien placé; **put yourself in my p.,** mettez-vous à ma place; **this is a nice p. to be in!** voilà une belle situation! me voilà bien loti, dans de beaux draps! **to be in a p. to do sth.,** être à même, en mesure, en situation, en état, de faire qch.; **I'm not in a p. to do anything,** je ne puis rien faire; **you're in a better p. to judge,** vous êtes mieux placé que moi, que lui, etc., pour en juger; **financial p.,** situation financière; **I'm worried about the p. of my account,** je m'inquiète de l'état de mon compte; je crains de ne pas avoir assez d'argent dans mon compte, à la banque; **the cash p. is not good,** la situation de la caisse laisse à désirer; **what is the p. of the firm?** quelle est la situation (financière) de cette maison? (*b*) condition *f*, état, rang social; **to keep up one's p.,** tenir son rang. **4.** (*a*) *O:* emploi *m*, situation; (*b*) **to work one's way up to a good p.,** se faire une belle situation; **key p.**, position clef; **p. of trust**, poste *m* de confiance. **5.** *Phil: etc:* (*a*) énonciation *f*, mise *f* en avant (d'une proposition, d'un principe); (*b*) proposition *f*; principe posé; assertion *f*.

position², *v.tr.* **1.** mettre (qch.) en place, en position; mettre, placer, (qch.) dans une position (déterminée); *Tchn:* positionner (qch.); **to p. troops**, mettre des troupes en place, en position; *Mil.Av:* **the controller positioned the aircraft over the target**, le contrôleur a guidé l'avion sur l'objectif; *Cmptr:* **to p. a tape**, positionner une bande; *Mec.E: etc:* **to p. open**, mettre en position ouverte; ouvrir. **2.** déterminer la position de (qch.); situer (un lieu sur la carte, etc.).

positionable [pə'ziʃənəbl], *a. Cmptr:* **p. read-write head**, tête *f* de lecture-écriture positionnable.

positional [pə'ziʃən(ə)l], *a.* de position; **p. accuracy**, (i) *Mec.E: etc:* précision *f* de mise en place, de placement; (ii) *Av:* braquage précis (d'une gouverne); *U.S:* **p. warfare**, guerre *f* de position; *Cmptr:* **p. notation, representation**, représentation positionnelle.

positioner [pə'ziʃən(ə)r], *s. Tchn:* positionneur *m*; *Mec.E:* **valve p.**, indicateur *m* de fermeture de soupape.

positioning [pə'ziʃəniŋ], *s.* mise *f* en place, en position; *Tchn:* positionnement *m*; *T.V:* orientation *f* (de l'antenne); *Mec.E:* **p. of the engine**, mise en place du moteur; **p. angle**, cornière *f* de mise en place, de centrage; *Cmptr:* **p. arm**, bras *m* de positionnement, de lecture-écriture; *Mil:* **p. and deployment of the covering forces**, mise en place des forces de couverture; *Gram: etc:* (*of verb, significant word, etc.*) **end p.**, rejet *m*.

positive ['pɔzitiv], *a. & s.* **1.** *a.* (*a*) positif; affirmatif; **p. proof**, preuve positive, patente, manifeste; **p. statement**, témoignage formel; **p. order**, ordre formel, catégorique; **p. law**, droit positif; **p. laws**, lois positives; *Med: etc:* **p. reaction**, réaction positive; **p. blood test**, analyse positive, examen positif, du sang; (*b*) authentique, indiscutable; **a p. fact**, un fait authentique, indiscutable, patent; **a p. miracle**, un véritable, un pur, miracle; *F:* **he's a p. nuisance!** c'est une vraie peste! il est empoisonnant! **it's a p. shame**, c'est une véritable honte. **2.** *a.* (*a*) convaincu, persuadé, assuré, certain, sûr (**of**, de); **he is p. of his facts**, il est sûr de ses faits; il est certain de ce qu'il avance; **I'm p. on that point**, là-dessus je n'ai aucun doute; je n'ai aucun doute à ce sujet; **I'm p. (that) I saw him**, je suis certain que je l'ai vu; **I feel p. that you will succeed**, je suis convaincu, certain, sûr, que vous réussirez; (*b*) (*of pers.*) trop assuré; suffisant; **he's so p.!** il tranche sur tout; **don't be so p.**, ne soyez pas si péremptoire, si sûr de ce que vous dites; **p. tone of voice**, ton tranchant, péremptoire, absolu. **3.** (*a*) *a.* **p. philosophy**, philosophie positive; (*b*) *a.* **p. suggestion**, proposition constructive; **p. help**, aide constructive, concrète, positive; (*c*) *s.* le positif, le réel, la réalité. **4.** (*a*) *a. Mth:* **p. number**, nombre positif; **p. quantity**, quantité positive; (*b*) *a. El: etc:* **p. charge**, charge positive; **p. wire**, fil positif; **p. terminal**, borne positive; **p. pole**, (i) pôle positif; (ii) *Magn:* pôle nord, pôle austral; **p. electrode**, électrode positive; **p. feedback**, réaction positive; **p. booster**, survolteur *m*; **p.-negative booster**, survolteur-dévolteur *m*, *pl.* survolteurs-dévolteurs; *T.V:* **p. transmission**, transmission positive; **p. (light) modulation**, modulation positive; (*c*) *a. Ph: etc:* **p. rays**, rayons positifs; **p. particle**, particule positive; **p. ion**, ion positif; **p. electron**, électron positif; posit(r)on *m*; **p. valency**, valence positive; **p. dilation**, dilation positive; *Atom.Ph:* **p. absorption**, absorption positive; **p. excess**, excédent positif; *Opt:* **p. optical system**, système optique positif, convergent; **p. lens**, lentille positive, convergente; **p. eyepiece**, oculaire positif, oculaire de Ramsden; (*d*) *a. & s. Phot:* **p. (print)**, positif; épreuve positive; **p. (plate)**, positif sur verre; *Phot.Engr:* **direct p.**, phototype positif; (*e*) *a. Mec.E: etc:* **p. movement**, mouvement commandé; mouvement desmodromique; **p. drive**, commande directe, positive; commande desmodromique; **p. feed**, entraînement positif; **p. blower**, ventilateur positif, soufflant; **p. stress**, effort *m* de compression; **p. stagger**, décalage *m* en avant (d'une pièce mécanique, etc.). **5.** *a. & s. Gram:* **p. (degree)**, (degré) positif (d'un adjectif, d'un adverbe). **6.** *a. & s. Mus: A:* **p. (organ)**, positif (d'un grand orgue).

positively ['pɔzitivli], *adv.* **1.** (*a*) positivement; affirmativement; (*b*) **he p. refused to leave**, il a absolument refusé de partir; *P.N: U.S:* **p. no smoking**, interdiction absolue de fumer. **2.** (*a*) assurément, certainement, sûrement; **I can't speak p.**, je ne puis rien affirmer; **p. the best cake I ever ate**, assurément le meilleur gâteau que j'aie jamais mangé; (*b*) d'un ton tranchant, absolu; péremptoirement. **3.** *Mec.E:* **p. connected**, solidarisé; à liaison rigide; **p. driven**, à commande directe, desmodromique.

positiveness ['pɔzitivnis], *s.* **1.** certitude *f*, assurance *f*. **2.** ton décisif, tranchant, péremptoire.

positivism ['pɔzitivizm], *s. Phil:* positivisme *m*; **logical p.**, néo-positivisme *m*.

positivist ['pɔzitivist], *a. & s. Phil:* positiviste (*mf*).

posit(r)on ['pɔzit(r)ɔn], *s. Atom.Ph:* positon *m*, positron *m*; **p. emission**, émission *f* de positons, émission positogène; **p. decay, p. disintegration**, désintégration *f* positogène.

positronium [pɔzi'trouniəm], *s. Atom.Ph:* posit(r)onium *m*.

posologic(al) [pɔsə'lɔdʒik(l)], *a. Med:* posologique.

posology [pə'sɔlədʒi], *s. Med:* posologie *f*.

posse ['pɔsi], *s.* **1.** (*a*) détachement *m* (d'agents de police); (*b*) troupe *f*, bande *f* (de personnes). **2.** *Phil:* **in p.**, en puissance.

possess [pə'zes], *v.tr.* **1.** (*a*) posséder (un bien); être possesseur, être en possession, de (qch.); **all I p.**, tout mon avoir; **to p. certain rights**, avoir la jouissance de certains droits; (*b*) avoir, posséder (une qualité, une faculté). **2.** (*a*) *Lit:* **to p. oneself of sth.**, (i) se mettre en possession, se rendre maître, s'emparer, de qch.; (ii) s'approprier qch.; (*b*) **to be possessed of a property**, posséder un bien. **3. to be possessed**, se posséder, se contenir; **to p. one's soul in peace**, posséder son âme en paix; **to p. one's soul in patience**, se munir de patience. **4.** (*of evil spirit*) posséder, dominer (qn); *B:* **possessed with, of, a devil**, possédé d'un démon, démoniaque; **possessed by fear**, sous le coup de l'effroi; **possessed with doubt**, en proie au doute; **what possessed you to do that?** qu'est-ce qui vous a pris de faire cela? **to be possessed with an idea**, être obsédé, coiffé, imbu, d'une idée; avoir une idée en tête; **to scream like one possessed**, crier comme un possédé. **5.** posséder (une femme).

possession [pə'zeʃ(ə)n], *s.* **1.** possession *f*, jouissance *f* (**of**, de); **to have sth. in one's p.**, avoir qch. en sa possession; **to take p. of an estate, to come, enter, into p. of an estate**, entrer en possession, en jouissance, d'un bien; **to take, get, p. of sth.**, s'emparer de qch.; **to regain, resume, p. of sth.**, (i) rentrer en possession, en jouissance, d'un bien, etc.; (ii) reprendre possession de qch.; *Jur:* **to resume p. of one's domicile**, réintégrer son domicile; **to remain in p. of the field**, rester maître du champ de bataille; **this move put them in p. of the village**, ce coup leur livra le village; **to keep papers in one's p.**, garder des papiers par devers soi; **to come into p. of a large fortune**, hériter d'une grande fortune; **we are already in p. of data on . . .**, on possède déjà des données sur . . .; **the information in my p.**, les renseignements dont je dispose; **in p. of a passport**, nanti d'un passeport; **in full p. of his faculties**, en pleine possession, dans la pleine possession, de toutes ses facultés; jouissant, maître, de toutes ses facultés; *Pol: etc:* **to be in p. of the House**, avoir la parole; *Jur:* **to put s.o. in p. of an inheritance**, saisir qn d'un héritage; **actual p.**, possession de fait; **right of p.**, possessoire *m*; **prevention of p.**, privation *f*, trouble *m*, de jouissance; **vacant p.**, libre possession (d'un immeuble); **house to let with vacant p.**, maison *f* à louer clefs en main, avec jouissance immédiate; *Prov:* **p. is nine points of the law**, possession vaut titre. **2.** possession (par le démon). **3.** (*a*) objet possédé; possession; **a valued p. of my father's**, un objet auquel mon père attache beaucoup de prix; (*b*) **possessions**, (i) possessions, biens, avoir *m*; (ii) possessions, colonies *f*; **overseas possessions**, possessions d'outre-mer.

possessional [pə'zeʃən(ə)l], *a. Jur:* possessionnel.

possessive [pə'zesiv], *a.* **1.** possessif; (*of pers.*) accapareur, -euse; qui a le désir de posséder entièrement; **a p. mother**, une mère abusive, possessive. **2.** *Gram:* **p. adjective, pronoun**, adjectif, pronom, possessif; *a. & s.* **the p. (case)**, le (cas) possessif.

possessor [pə'zesər], *s.* possesseur *m*; propriétaire *m*, *Jur:* possesseur; **to be the p. of a large fortune**, être en possession d'une grande fortune.

possessory [pə'zesəri], *a. Jur:* possessoire; **p. action**, action *f* possessoire; **p. right**, possessoire *m*.

posset ['pɔsit], *s. A:* posset *m* (boisson chaude au lait caillé).

possibilist [pɔ'sibilist], *s. & a. Pol:* possibiliste (*mf*).

possibility [pɔsi'biliti], *s.* **1.** possibilité *f*; **to consider the p. of sth. happening**, considérer l'éventualité d'un événement; **the p. of severe penalties**, la perspective de peines graves; **I admit the p. of your being right**, j'admets que vous n'avez peut-être pas tort; **have you considered the p. of his being dead?** avez-vous envisagé la possibilité qu'il soit mort? **he doesn't believe in the p. of its being useful**, il ne croit pas à la possibilité que cela soit utile; **there is no p. of my going there**, il n'est pas possible que j'y aille; **if by any p. I am not there**, si par hasard, par impossible, je n'y étais pas; s'il arrive que je ne sois pas là; **within the range, the bounds, of p.**, dans l'ordre des choses possibles; dans la limite du possible. **2.** (*a*) événement *m* possible, éventualité *f*; **to foresee all the possibilities**, envisager tout ce qui peut arriver, toutes les éventualités; **to allow for all possibilities**, parer à toute éventualité; (*b*) *pl.* possibilités de succès; chances *f* de succès; **life is full of possibilities**, tout est possible dans la vie; la vie offre des occasions à tous les instants; **the subject is full of possibilities**, c'est un sujet qui prête; **the plan has possibilities**, ce projet offre des possibilités, des chances de succès.

possible ['pɔsibl]. **1.** *a.* (*a*) possible; **it's p.**, c'est possible; cela se peut bien; **it's just p.**, il y a une chance; **that's quite p.**, c'est très possible, fort possible; **everything is p. to him who has the will**, tout est possible à celui qui veut; **it is p. for you to do this**, il vous est possible de faire cela; **it is p. that he will come**, il se peut qu'il vienne; **is it p. that you know nothing about it?** se peut-il que vous n'en sachiez rien? **is it p. to see him?** y a-t-il moyen de le voir? **how is it p. to get out of it?** le moyen d'en sortir? **to give as many details as p., all p. details**, donner le plus de détails possible, le plus possible de détails, tous les détails possibles; **the best style p.**, le meilleur style possible; **to live in the simplest p. way**, vivre le plus simplement du monde; **what p. interest can you have in it?** quel diable d'intérêt cela peut-il avoir pour vous? **there is no p. check on his administration**, sa gestion échappe à tout contrôle; **if p.**, (i) (*if feasible*) si possible; (ii) (*if imaginable*) si c'est possible; **as far as p.**, dans la mesure du possible; dans la plus large mesure possible; **as early as p.**, le plus tôt possible; **orders carried out as well as p.**, commandes exécutées au mieux; (*b*) **as a p. event**, à titre éventuel; **to provide for the p. nomination of . . .**, pourvoir à la nomination éventuelle de . . .; **to insure against p. accidents**, s'assurer contre des accidents éventuels; (*c*) *F:* (*of pers.*) tolérable, supportable, acceptable; **they're p.**, on peut les fréquenter. **2.** *s.* (*a*) **to do one's p.**, faire son possible (**to**, pour); (*b*) (*shooting*) **to score a p.**, faire le maximum; (*c*) (*pers.*) candidat *m* possible, acceptable.

possibly ['pɔsibli], *adv.* **1. I can't p. do it**, il ne m'est pas possible de le faire; **how can I p. do it?** comment pourrais-je le faire? le moyen de le faire? **it can't p. be true!** pas possible! **it can't p. do him any harm**, ça ne peut pas lui faire de mal; **I'll do all I p. can**, je ferai tout mon possible; je ferai de mon mieux; **I'll come if I p. can**, je ferai tout mon possible pour venir; **I come as often as I p. can**, je viens aussi souvent que possible. **2.** peut-être (bien); **he has p. heard of you**, peut-être a-t-il entendu parler de vous; il se peut, il est possible, qu'il ait entendu parler de vous; **p.!** c'est possible; cela se peut.

possum ['pɔsəm], *s. F:* (*a*) *Z:* opossum *m*; **honey p.**, souris *f* à miel, tarsipède *m*; (*b*) **to play p.**, faire le mort; se tenir coi; cacher son jeu.

post¹ [poust], *s.* **1.** (*a*) poteau *m*; pieu *m*; montant *m*; pilier *m*; (*small*) potelet *m*; **finger p., direction p.**, poteau indicateur; **telegraph p.**, poteau télégraphique; *Rail:* **distance p.**, poteau kilométrique; **grade p., gradient p.**, poteau indicateur de pente; **he stood there like a p.**, il était planté là comme un piquet, comme une borne; (*b*) *Const: etc:* poteau, pilier; (*of door, window*) montant, jambage *m*; poteau d'huisserie; *Min:* chandelle *f*; butte *f* (de boisage); **corner p.**, poteau cornier, d'angle; **middle p.**, poinçon *m* de comble; *Min:* **headache p.**, pieu de sécurité; (*c*) **(bed) p.**, colonne *f* de lit; (*d*) arbre *m*, fût *m* (de grue); *Min:* colonne (d'un trépan); **Samson p.**, support *m* de balancier; *Aut:* **steering p.**, colonne de direction. **2.** *El:* borne *f* (à vis); **battery p.**, borne d'accumulateur; **binding p.**, serre-fils *m inv*; **coil p.**, borne de bobine. **3.** *Min:* pilier, massif *m*, lopin *m* (de houille). **4.** *Nau:* **(stern) p.**, étambot *m*. **5.** *Turf: etc:* (*a*) **(starting) p.**, (poteau de) départ *m*; barrière *f*; **(winning) p.**, (poteau d')arrivée *f*; **to go to the p.**, prendre part à la course; (*of horse*) **to refuse to leave the p.**, rester au poteau; **to be left at the p.**, manquer au départ; **to win at the p.**, gagner de justesse; gagner au poteau; **to leave s.o. at the p.**, laisser qn loin derrière soi; (*b*) jalon *m* (de la piste); **to be on the wrong side of the p.**, faire fausse route, se fourvoyer.

post², *v.tr.* **1.** (*a*) **to p. (up)**, placarder, coller (des affiches, etc.); afficher (un avis, etc.); **the market rates are posted (up) at the town hall**, les cours sont affichés à la mairie; *P.N:* **p. no bills**, défense d'afficher; (*b*) **to p. (up) a wall**, couvrir un mur d'affiches; placarder un mur. **2.** (*a*) inscrire, porter (qn) sur une liste; *M.Ins:* porter (un navire) disparu; *Sch:* (*at Cambridge*) inscrire, porter, (un candidat) sur la liste des refusés; **to be posted for night duty,** être sur la liste (du personnel) de service de nuit; **to be posted missing,** être porté disparu; (*b*) (*at a club, etc.*) **to p. a member,** afficher le nom d'un membre en défaut.

post[3], *s.* **1.** *A:* (*a*) (*relay of horses*) poste *f*; **p. horse,** cheval *m* de poste, postier *m*; **to travel ten posts,** faire, parcourir, dix postes; (*b*) **p. coach,** malle-poste *f, pl.* malles-poste(s); **p. chaise,** chaise *f* de poste, coucou *m*; **p. horn,** trompe *f* (de la malle-poste); **p. road,** route *f* de malle-poste; à relais de poste; **to travel p.,** (i) voyager en poste; (ii) aller un train de poste; **to go p. haste,** courir la poste. **2.** (*a*) courrier *m*; **by return of p.,** par retour du courrier; **it's p. time,** c'est l'heure du courrier; **when does the next p. go?** à quelle heure est la prochaine levée? **to miss the p.,** manquer la levée, le courrier; **the first p.,** la première distribution; *A:* **the general p. (delivery),** la distribution principale; **the p. has come,** le courrier est arrivé; le facteur est passé; **there's no p. today,** pas de courrier, pas de lettres, aujourd'hui; *Games:* **general p.,** chassé-croisé *m, pl.* chassés-croisés; **there's been a general p. in the Cabinet,** il y a eu un chassé-croisé au Ministère; (*b*) la poste; **the P. Office** = les Postes et Télécommunications; **to send sth. by p.,** envoyer qch. par la poste; (*c*) **p. (office),** (bureau *m* de) poste; **to take a letter to the p.,** porter une lettre à la poste; **general p. office,** la grande poste; le bureau central (des postes); **sub p. office, branch p. office,** bureau auxiliaire (des postes); recette *f* auxiliaire; bureau de quartier; **p.-office clerk,** employé, -ée, des postes; **p.-office directory,** annuaire *m* des postes; **p.-office box,** boîte postale; case postale; *El:* **p.-office bridge,** pont *m* de mesure modèle des postes. **3. p. (paper)** = *approx.* papier *m* écu; **bank p.,** papier poste; papier coquille; coquille anglaise; **small p.,** (papier) couronne *f*.

post[4], *v.* **1.** *v.tr.* (*a*) *A:* voyager par relais, en poste; (*b*) courir la poste, aller un train de poste; (*c*) *Equit: NAm:* trotter à l'anglaise; faire du trot enlevé. **2.** *v.tr.* (*a*) **to p. (a letter),** mettre (une lettre) à la poste, à la boîte; poster (une lettre); **I'll p. it to you,** je vous l'enverrai par la poste; (*b*) *Book-k:* **to p. (up) the books,** passer les écritures; **to p. an entry,** passer écriture d'un article; **to p. an item in the ledger, to p. up an item,** porter, inscrire, passer, reporter, rapporter, transcrire, un article au grand-livre; **to p. up the ledger,** arrêter le grand-livre; mettre le grand-livre au courant, à jour; **my books are posted up,** mes livres (de comptes) sont au courant, sont à jour; *F:* **I'll keep you posted,** je vous tiendrai au courant.

post[5], *s.* **1.** *Mil: etc:* (*a*) faction *f*; **to be on p.,** être de, en, faction; être en sentinelle; **to come off p.,** quitter la faction, le service de sentinelle; **to go on p.,** prendre la faction, le service de sentinelle; (*b*) poste *m* (de combat, etc.); **take p.! to your posts!** à vos postes! **to be at one's p.,** être à son poste; **to stick to one's p.,** être fidèle au poste; **to die at one's p.,** mourir à son poste; **to be absent, away, from one's p.,** ne pas être à son poste; **to leave, quit, abandon, one's p.,** abandonner, déserter, son poste; **desertion of p. before the enemy,** abandon *m* de poste devant l'ennemi; (*c*) (*group of men at a post, place where they are stationed*) poste; **advanced, outlying, p.,** poste avancé; **collecting p.,** poste de recueil (des traînards, etc.); **detached p.,** poste détaché; **lookout p.,** poste de guet, d'observation, de surveillance; *U.S:* **command p.,** poste de commandement; **control p.,** poste de contrôle (de la circulation, etc.); **frontier p.,** poste frontière; (*d*) *U.S:* (i) camp *m*, fort *m* (servant de lieu de garnison); garnison *f*; **p. exchange,** coopérative *f* militaire, coopérative de garnison; **p. hospital,** hôpital *m* militaire, hôpital de garnison; (ii) **p. of the American Legion** = groupement de province, groupement local, de la Légion Américaine. **2.** (*a*) *Hist:* **trading p.,** comptoir *m*, établissement *m* (aux Indes, au Canada, etc.); (*b*) *Av:* **air staging p.,** escale aérienne. **3.** (*a*) poste, emploi *m*; **to take up one's p.,** entrer en fonction, prendre ses fonctions; (*b*) *Navy: Hist:* **p. captain,** capitaine *m* de vaisseau; commandant *m* d'un navire d'au moins 20 canons.

post[6], *v.tr.* **1.** poster, placer (qn à un endroit); poster, placer, mettre en faction (une sentinelle); aposter (un espion); **they posted an accomplice at the entrance to the bank,** ils ont posté un complice à l'entrée de la banque; **she posted herself at the window,** elle s'est postée à la fenêtre, a pris position près de la fenêtre; **to p. a sentry at a door,** mettre, placer, une sentinelle, un factionnaire, devant une porte. **2.** *Mil: etc:* (*a*) désigner (qn) à un commandement; **to be posted to a unit, to a ship,** recevoir une affectation, être affecté, à une unité, à un navire; (*b*) **to be posted missing,** être porté manquant; **to be posted as a deserter,** être porté déserteur.

post[7], *s. Mil:* **first p.,** première partie (de la sonnerie) de la retraite; **last p.,** (i) dernière partie (de la sonnerie); (ii) (la) sonnerie aux morts; **to sound the last p. (over the grave),** rendre les honneurs par la sonnerie aux morts.

post- [poust], *pref.* post-; après.

postabdomen [poust'æbdəmən], *s. Ent:* postabdomen *m*.

postabdominal [poustæb'dɔmin(ə)l], *a. Ent: Z:* postabdominal, -aux.

postabortal [poustə'bɔːt(ə)l], *a. Obst:* **p. period,** post-abortum *m*.

postage ['poustidʒ], *s.* affranchissement *m*, port *m* (d'une lettre, etc.); **postages,** frais *m* d'envoi, de port; **p. rates,** tarifs postaux; (*on insufficiently stamped letter*) **additional p.,** surtaxe (postale); **p.-due stamp,** timbre *m* taxe; **p. included,** port compris; **p. paid,** port payé, port perçu, franc de port.

postal ['poust(ə)l], *a.* postal, -aux; **p. authorities,** l'Administration *f* des Postes; **p. charges,** frais *mpl* d'envoi, port *m* (d'une lettre, etc.); **p. receipt,** récépissé postal; **p. services,** les services postaux, les Postes *f* et Télécommunications; les postes; **p. transfer,** virement postal; **p.-transfer form,** mandat *m* de virement; **p. transport contractor,** courrier *m* d'entreprise; **p. union,** union postale; *U.S:* **p. card,** *s.* **postal,** carte postale; **p. code,** code postal.

postatomic [poustə'tɔmik], *a. Ph: etc:* post-atomique.

postbag ['poustbæg], *s.* sac postal, de dépêches.

post-Biblical [poust'biblik(ə)l], *a.* postbiblique.

postbox ['poustbɔks], *s.* boîte *f* aux lettres.

postboy ['poustbɔi], *s.m.* **1.** courrier, messager. **2.** *A:* postillon.

postcard ['poustkɑːd], *s.* carte postale; **picture p.,** carte postale illustrée.

post-classical [poust'klæsikl], *a.* postérieur à l'époque classique; post-classique.

postcode ['poustkoud], *s.* code postal.

postcommunion [poustkə'mjuːniən], *s. Ecc:* postcommunion *f*.

postdate[1] ['poustdeit], *s.* postdate *f*.

postdate[2] [poust'deit], *v.tr.* postdater (un chèque, un document).

postdental [poust'dent(ə)l], *a. Ling:* postdental.

postdiluvial, postdiluvian [poustdai'luːviəl, -'luːviən], *a. Geol: etc:* post-diluvien.

post-dorsal [poust'dɔːs(ə)l], *a. Anat:* post-dorsal.

post-edit [poust'edit], *v.tr. Cmptr:* mettre en forme (des résultats).

postembryonal, postembryonic [poust'embriən(ə)l, poustembri'ɔnik], *a.* postembryonnaire.

postentry ['poustentri], *s.* **1.** *Book-k:* écriture postérieure, subséquente. **2.** *Cust:* déclaration additionnelle.

poster ['poustər], *s.* **1.** (*pers.*) afficheur *m* (d'un avis, etc.); colleur *m* d'affiches. **2.** affiche murale; placard *m* (de publicité); **picture p.,** affiche illustrée; **p. designer, artist,** affichiste *mf*; **p. boarding,** panneau *m* d'affichage; **p. stamp,** timbre *m* vignette.

poste restante [poust'restɑ̃nt], *s.* poste restante.

posterior [pɔs'tiəriər]. **1.** *a.* postérieur (**to,** à). **2.** *s. F:* le postérieur, le derrière (de qn).

posteriority [pɔstiəri'ɔriti], *s.* postériorité *f*.

posteriorly [pɔs'tiəriəli], *adv.* postérieurement; (vu) de derrière.

posterity [pɔs'teriti], *s.* postérité *f*. **1. to leave a large p.,** laisser une postérité nombreuse. **2. p. will be grateful to him,** la postérité lui sera reconnaissante.

postern ['poustəːn], *s.* **1.** *Fort:* poterne *f*. **2.** *A: & Lit:* **p. (door),** porte *f* de derrière, de service, de piétons; porte dérobée.

post-extraction [pousteks'trækʃən], *attrib. Dent:* post-opératoire.

postface ['poustfeis], *s.* postface *f* (d'un livre).

postfix[1] ['poustfiks], *s. Ling:* suffixe *m*.

postfix[2] [poust'fiks], *v.tr. Ling:* ajouter en suffixe (une terminaison, etc.).

postform [poust'fɔːm], *v.tr. Metalw: etc:* postformer.

postformable [poust'fɔːməbl], *a. Metalw: etc:* postformable.

postforming [poust'fɔːmiŋ], *s. Metalw: etc:* postformage *m*.

postfrontal [poust'frʌnt(ə)l], *a. Anat:* postfrontal, *pl.* -aux.

postglacial [poust'gleisiəl], *a. Geol:* postglaciaire.

postgraduate [poust'grædjuət], *a.* post-universitaire; **p. student** = licencié(e) qui continue ses études; **p. studies** = études supérieures (après la licence).

post-haemorrhage [poust'hemərid ʒ], *s. Med:* hémorragie *f* postopératoire.

posthaste [poust'heist], *adv.* en toute hâte; dare-dare; **to ride, travel, p.,** courir la poste; aller un train de poste, à franc étrier.

posthitis [pɔs'θaitis], *s. Med:* posthite *f*.

posthole ['pousthoul], *s. Min:* potelle *f*.

post-Homeric [pousthou'merik], *a. Gr.Lit:* posthomérique.

posthouse ['pousthaus], *s. A:* maison *f* de relais (de la malle-poste).

posthumous ['pɔstjuməs], *a.* (enfant, œuvre) posthume.

posthumously ['pɔstjuməsli], *adv.* posthumement; (paru) après la mort de l'auteur.

posthypophyseal [pousthaipou'fiːziəl], *a.* posthypophysaire.

posthypophysis [pousthai'pɔfisis], *s. Anat:* posthypophyse *f*.

postiche [pɔs'tiːʃ], *s.* postiche *m*.

posticous [pɔs'tiːkəs], *a. Bot:* (*of anther, etc.*) postérieur, extrorse.

postil ['pɔstil], *s.* postille *f*, glose littérale (sur l'Ancien Testament, etc.).

postil(l)ion [pɔs'tiliən], *s.* postillon *m*.

post-impressionism [poustim'preʃənizm], *s. Art:* post-impressionnisme *m*.

post-impressionist [poustim'preʃənist], *a. & s. Art:* post-impressionniste (*mf*).

posting[1] ['poustiŋ], *s.* (*a*) affichage *m*, collage *m*; (*b*) inscription *f*.

posting[2], *s.* **1.** (*a*) *A:* voyage(s) *m* en poste; (*b*) *Equit: NAm:* trot *m* à l'anglaise; trot enlevé. **2.** (*a*) envoi *m* (d'une lettre) par la poste; mise *f* à la poste (d'une lettre); postage *m*; (*b*) *Book-k:* passation *f* (d'écritures); report *m*, entrée *f* (au grand-livre); transcription *f* (du journal); (*c*) *Cmptr:* inscription *f*, enregistrement *m*, écriture *f*; **p. card,** carte *f* de mouvement; **p. interpreter,** reporteuse *f*; **p. machine,** machine *f* d'enregistrement.

posting[3], *s.* **1.** *Mil:* mise *f* en faction (de sentinelles, etc.). **2.** affectation *f* (à un poste, etc.); *Mil:* **cross p.,** affectation d'unité en unité.

postliminium [poustli'miniəm], **postliminy** [poust'limini], *s. Jur:* postliminium *m*.

postlude ['poustluːd], *s. Mus:* postlude *m*.

postluminescence [poustluːmi'nesəns], *s. El: etc:* luminescence résiduelle.

postman, *pl.* **-men** ['poustmən], *s.m.* **1.** facteur *m*, *Adm:* préposé (des postes); (*on mail train*) courrier convoyeur; **postman's knock,** jeu *m* de salon pour enfants. **2.** *Navy:* vaguemestre.

postmark[1] ['poustmɑːk], *s.* cachet *m* de la poste; (cachet d')oblitération *f*; timbre *m* (i) de départ, (ii) d'arrivée; **letter bearing the London p.,** lettre timbrée de Londres, portant le timbre de Londres.

postmark[2], *v.tr.* timbrer (une lettre); **the letter was postmarked London,** la lettre était timbrée (au départ) de Londres; **must be postmarked not later than . . .** = le cachet de la poste fera foi; **date as p.,** date *f* de la poste (faisant foi).

postmaster[1] ['poustmɑːstər], *s.m.* receveur (des postes); *A: & Can:* **P. General** = ministre *m* des Postes et Télécommunications.

postmaster[2], *s.m. Sch:* boursier (de Merton College, Oxford).

postmastership ['poustmɑːstəʃip], *s.* recette *f* des Postes.

post-medication [poustmedi'keiʃ(ə)n], *s. Med:* médication *f* post-opératoire.

postmeridian [poustmə'ridiən], *a.* postméridien, de l'après-midi, du soir.

post meridiem [poustmə'ridiəm]. *Lt.phr.* de l'après-midi, du soir.

post-mill ['poustmil], *s.* moulin *m* (à vent) à corps tournant.

postmistress ['poustmistris], *s.f.* receveuse des Postes.

postmortem[1] [poust'mɔːtəm]. **1.** (*a*) *a. & s.* **p. (examination),** autopsie *f* (d'un cadavre); **to hold a p. (examination),** faire une autopsie sur un cadavre; autopsier un cadavre; **the p. revealed no traces of poison,** l'autopsie n'a révélé aucune trace de poison; (*b*) *s. Fig:* autopsie; analyse rétrospective, après coup; (*c*) *s. Cmptr:* **p. dump,** vidage *m* d'autopsie; **p. program(me),** (sous-)programme *m* d'autopsie. **2.** *adv.* (*usu. 2 words*) après la mort; **the beard had grown p.,** la barbe avait poussé après la mort.

postmortem[2], *v.tr. & i. F:* autopsier.

postnatal [poust'neitl], *a.* postérieur à la naissance; (*of medical case, etc.*) postnatal, -als.

postnuptial [poust'nʌpʃəl], *a.* postérieur au mariage.

post-obit [poust'oubit], *a. & s.* **p.-o. (bond),** contrat *m* exécutoire, obligation *f* réalisable, effet *m* payable, après le décès d'un tiers.

postocular [poust'ɔkjulər], *a. Anat:* post-oculaire.
postoperative [poust'ɔpərətiv], *a. Med:* (maladie, etc.) postopératoire; **p. care,** soins postopératoires; **p. shock,** choc postopératoire.
postoral [poust'ɔrəl], *a. Anat:* postoral, -aux.
postpaid ['poust'peid], *a.* affranchi; port payé.
postpalatal [poust'pælətl], *a. Ling:* postpalatal, -aux; (consonne) vélaire.
postpalatine [poust'pælətain], *a. Anat:* post-palatin.
postpartum [poust'pɑːtəm], *s. & a. Obst:* post-partum *m inv;* (période) qui suit l'accouchement; **p. fever,** fièvre puerpérale.
post-Pliocene [poust'plaiousiːn], *a. & s. Geol:* postpliocène (*m*).
postponable [poust'pounəbl], *a.* ajournable.
postpone [poust'poun], *v.tr.* (*a*) remettre, ajourner, renvoyer à plus tard, reporter à plus tard, différer, reculer (un départ, un projet, etc.); **to p. a matter for a week,** remettre, renvoyer, une affaire à huitaine; **to p. it until next week,** le remettre à la semaine prochaine; **to p. a payment,** différer, arriérer, un paiement; **to p. a burial,** surseoir à une inhumation; **postponed action, trial,** cause remise; **the sale has been postponed,** il a été sursis à la vente; (*b*) *O:* **to p. sth. to sth.,** subordonner qch. à qch.; faire passer qch. après qch.
postponement [poust'pounmənt], *s.* (*a*) remise *f* à plus tard; ajournement *m* (d'une réunion, d'une cause); renvoi *m* (d'une cause); sursis *m;* (*b*) *O:* subordination (de qch. à qch.).
postposition [poustpə'ziʃ(ə)n], *s. Gram:* **1.** postposition *f* (de l'adjectif, etc.). **2.** postposition; particule *f* enclitique.
postpositive [poust'pɔzitiv], *a. & s. Gram:* postpositif (*m*).
postprandial [poust'prændiəl], *a. usu. Hum:* postprandial, -aux; après le repas.
postpunch ['poustpʌntʃ], *attrib. Cmptr:* **p. station,** poste *m* après perforation.
postpuncher [poust'pʌntʃər], *s. Min:* haveuse *f* à pic sur affût colonne.
postread [poust'riːd], *a. Cmptr:* **p. station,** poste *m* après lecture.
postremogeniture [pɔs'triːmɔdʒenitjər], *s.* ultimogéniture *f.*
postscript(um) ['pous(t)skript, pous(t)'skriptəm], *s.* **1.** post-scriptum *m inv;* **by way of p.,** en post-scriptum. **2.** postface *f* (d'un écrit).
postslew[1] [poust'sluː], *s. Cmptr:* saut *m* (du papier) après impression.
postslew[2], *v.i. Cmptr:* (*of paper*) faire un saut après impression.
postsynchronization [poustsiŋkrənai'zeiʃ(ə)n], *s. Cin:* postsynchronisation *f.*
postsynchronize [poust'siŋkrənaiz], *v.tr. Cin:* postsynchroniser.
postulant ['pɔstjulənt], *s. Ecc:* postulant, -ante.
postulate[1] ['pɔstjulət], *s. Mth: Log:* postulat *m;* **Euclid's p.,** le postulat(um) d'Euclide; **to formulate the postulates of a law,** formuler les conditions d'une loi.
postulate[2] ['pɔstjuleit]. **1.** *v.tr. & i.* **to p. (for) sth.,** postuler, demander, réclamer, qch. **2.** *v.tr. Mth: Log:* postuler (qch.); poser (qch.) en postulat; considérer (qch.) comme admis, établi, possible. **3.** *v.tr. Ecc:* postuler (un tel pour évêque).
postulation [pɔstju'leiʃ(ə)n], *s.* **1.** sollicitation *f,* demande *f.* **2.** *Log:* supposition *f;* postulat *m.* **3.** *Ecc:* postulation *f.*
postulator ['pɔstjuleitər], *s. Ecc:* postulateur *m.*
postural ['pɔstjər(ə)l], *a.* postural, -aux; *Med:* **p. reflex,** réflexe *m* de posture; **p. albuminuria,** albuminurie *f* orthostatique, de posture.
posture[1] ['pɔstjər], *s.* (*a*) posture *f,* pose *f,* attitude *f* (du corps); **easy p.,** posture, position *f,* commode; (*b*) position, situation *f,* état *m* (des choses); *Mil:* **the strategic p. of the forces,** le dispositif stratégique des forces.
posture[2]. **1.** *v.tr.* poser (un modèle); mettre (ses membres, etc.) dans une certaine position, une certaine posture. **2.** *v.i.* prendre une posture, une pose, une position; prendre une attitude (affectée).
posturing ['pɔstjəriŋ], *s.* pose *f.*
postvelar [poust'viːlər], *a. Ling:* postvélaire; **p. phoneme,** postvélaire *f.*
postverbal [poust'vəːb(ə)l], *a. Ling:* postverbal, -aux.
postwar [poust'wɔːr], *a.* d'après-guerre; **the p. period,** l'après-guerre *m inv.*
posy ['pouzi], *s.* petit bouquet.
pot[1] [pɔt], *s.* **1.** (*a*) pot *m;* **flower p.,** pot à fleurs; **coffee p.,** cafetière *f;* **chamber p.,** pot de chambre, vase *m* de nuit; **beer p.,** pot à bière; *F: O:* **I could do with a p.,** si on prenait une bière! *El:* **battery p.,** bac *m* de pile; **coil p.,** pot pour bobinage; (*b*) marmite *f;* **pots and pans,** batterie *f* de cuisine; **p. herb,** herbe potagère; **p. roast,** morceau de viande cuit à l'étouffé; **to take p. luck,** manger à la fortune du pot; *F:* **to go to p.,** aller à la ruine, (s'en) aller à vau-l'eau; **he's gone to p.,** il est fichu; *Prov:* **the p. calls, it's the p. calling, the kettle black,** la pelle se moque du fourgon; *F:* **to take a p. shot at sth., (at s.o.),** (i) (*also* **to take a p.**), lâcher à l'aveuglette un coup de fusil à qch., (à qn); (ii) faire qch. au petit bonheur; (*c*) *Ind:* **melting p.,** creuset *m; Fig:* **to be in the melting p.,** (i) être en pleine réorganisation; (ii) être en pleine révolution sociale; **to put everything back into the melting p.,** tout remettre en question; *Metall:* **p. furnace,** four *m* à creusets; four potager; **p. steel,** acier *m* au creuset; **annealing p.,** creuset de recuit, à recuire; **p. scrap,** débris *mpl* de fonte; bocage *m,* vieilles fontes, de poterie; *Mec.E:* **air p.,** amortisseur *m* à air; **p. magnet,** aimant *m* en pot; *Gasm:* **seal p.,** pot d'évacuation; (*plastics*) **transfer p.,** pot d'injection; *Elcs:* **p. oscillator,** oscillateur *m* à cavités résonnantes; *Ch:* **p. retort,** cornue *f* de distillation d'amalgame; **p. still,** alambic chauffé directement par la flamme; *Rail:* **p. sleeper,** cloche *f;* (*d*) *Sp: F:* coupe (remportée en prix). **2.** *Fish:* casier *m* (à homards, etc.). **3.** *F:* (*a*) **pots, a p., of money,** des tas *m* d'argent; **to make pots of money,** gagner gros; ramasser l'argent à la pelle; **to have pots of money,** être colossalement riche; avoir le sac; (*b*) *Cards:* **the p.,** la cagnotte; (*c*) *Turf: etc:* **to put the p. on,** parier gros; parier la forte somme. **4.** *F:* (*pers.*) **a big p.,** un gros bonnet, un grand manitou, *P:* une grosse légume. **5.** *Paperm:* **p. (paper),** papier *m* pot. **6.** *P:* (i) marijuana *f,* thé *m,* pot; (ii) hachisch *m,* fée verte.
pot[2], *v.tr.* **(potted) 1.** (*a*) mettre en pot, conserver (le beurre, la viande salée, etc.); (*b*) *Hort:* mettre en pot, empoter (une plante); (*c*) mettre (un bébé) sur son pot (de chambre); (*d*) *Bill:* blouser (une bille). **2.** *F:* (*a*) tirer, tuer, abattre (du gibier, etc.); (*b*) *v.i.* **to p. at (game, the enemy, etc.),** lâcher un coup de fusil à (une pièce de gibier); descendre (un faisan, etc.); tirailler contre (l'ennemi); canarder (l'ennemi).
pot[3], *s. Elcs: F:* potentiomètre *m.*
potability [poutə'biliti], *s.* potabilité *f.*
potable ['poutəbl], *a.* potable, buvable.
potalia [pɔ'teiliə], *s. Bot:* potalia *m,* potalie *f.*
potamic [pɔ'tæmik], *a.* potamique, fluvial, -aux.
potamochoerus [pɔtəmou'kəːrəs], *s. Z:* potamochère *m.*
potamodromous [pɔtə'mɔdrəməs], *a. Ich:* potamotoque.
Potamogalidae [pɔtəmou'gælidiː], *s.pl. Z:* potamogalidés *m.*
potamogeton [pɔtəmou'ʒiːtɔn], *s. Bot:* potamogéton *m.*
Potamogetonaceae [pɔtəmouʒiːtə'neisiː], *s.pl. Bot:* potamogétonacées *f.*
potamology [pɔtə'mɔlədʒi], *s. Geog:* potamologie *f.*
potamoplankton [pɔtəmou'plæŋktən], *s. Biol:* potamoplancton *m.*
potash ['pɔtæʃ], *s.* potasse *f;* **p. mine,** mine *f* de potasse; **the p. industry,** l'industrie potassière; **p. fertilizer,** engrais *m* potassique; **p. salts,** sels *m* potassiques; **carbonate of p.,** carbonate *m* de potasse; **caustic p.,** potasse caustique; hydroxyde *m* de potassium; **sulphate of p.,** sulfate *m* de potasse; potasse sulfatée; *Ch:* **p. bulb,** tube *m* à potasse.
potassic [pɔ'tæsik], *a. Ch:* potassique.
potassium [pə'tæsiəm], *s. Ch:* potassium *m;* **p. bromide,** bromure *m* de potassium; **p. carbonate, chlorate,** carbonate *m,* chlorate *m,* de potasse; **p. chloride, cyanide, hydroxide, sulphate,** chlorure *m,* cyanure *m,* hydroxyde *m,* sulfate *m,* de potassium; **p. salt,** sel *m* potassique.
potation [pou'teiʃ(ə)n], *s.* (*a*) boisson *f* (*esp.* boisson alcoolique); (*b*) action de boire; *pl.* libations *f.*
potato, *pl.* **-oes** [p(ə)'teitou, -ouz], *s.* **1.** (*a*) pomme *f* de terre; *F:* patate *f;* **new potatoes,** pommes de terre nouvelles; **p. apple,** (tubercule *m* de) pomme de terre; **p. disease, rot, mildew, blight,** maladie *f,* mildiou *m,* de la pomme de terre; *Bot:* **p. canker,** gangrène *f* de la pomme de terre; **p. crinkle,** frisolée *f* (de la pomme de terre); **p. mosaic,** mosaïque *f,* bigarrure *f* (de la pomme de terre); **p. scab,** galle *f* (de la pomme de terre); **p. wilt,** verticilliose *f* (de la pomme de terre); **to dig up, lift, potatoes,** arracher des pommes de terre; *Tls: Agr:* **p. lifter,** arrachoir *m,* arracheur *m,* arracheuse *f* (de pommes de terre); *Cu:* **roast potatoes,** pommes de terre au four; **boiled potatoes,** pommes de terre à l'eau, à l'anglaise; **steamed potatoes,** pommes nature; **chipped potatoes, French fried potatoes,** pommes (de terre) frites, *F:* frites *fpl;* **p. crisps,** *U.S:* **p. chips,** pommes chips; **mashed potatoes, p. purée,** purée *f* (de pommes de terre), pommes mousseline; **potatoes baked in their skins, in their jackets,** pommes de terre en robe de chambre, en robe des champs; **p. straws,** pommes paille; **sauté, soufflé, potatoes,** pommes sautées, soufflées; **p. spirit,** eau-de-vie *f* de pommes de terre; *Dom.Ec:* **p. chipper,** (i) coupe-frites *m inv.* (ii) friteuse *f;* **p. peeler,** (i) (*machine*) éplucheuse *f,* (ii) (*knife*) éplucheur *m,* (de pommes de terre); (*b*) *F:* (grand) trou (dans un bas); (*c*) *F:* **hot p.,** affaire épineuse; **to drop s.o. like a hot p.,** laisser tomber qn; (*d*) *F:* **small potatoes,** personne, chose, insignifiante. **2. sweet p., Spanish p.,** patate; **Indian p.,** igname *f.*
potbellied [pɔt'belid], *a. F:* ventru, pansu; **he's (very) p.,** c'est un gros poussah, un pot à tabac; **he's getting p.,** il commence à bedonner.
potbelly ['pɔtbeli], *s. F:* gros ventre, panse *f,* bedon *m,* bedaine *f.*
potboiler ['pɔtbɔilər], *s. F:* **1.** œuvre *f* alimentaire, qui fait bouillir la marmite; **to write potboilers,** écrire de la littérature alimentaire. **2.** écrivain, peintre, besogneux, qui travaille pour faire bouillir la marmite.
potbound ['pɔtbaund], *a.* (plante) dont le pot est trop petit.
potboy ['pɔtbɔi], *s.m. O:* garçon de café.
poteen [pɔ'tiːn], whisky irlandais distillé en fraude; **p. maker,** bouilleur (de whisky) non patenté; bouilleur clandestin, de contrebande.
potence ['poutəns], *s. Clockm:* potence *f.*
potency ['poutənsi], *s.* **1.** puissance *f,* pouvoir *m,* autorité *f* (du monarque, etc.) **2.** force *f,* puissance (d'un argument); efficacité *f,* activité *f* (d'un médicament); force, degré *m* (d'une boisson alcoolique). **3.** virilité sexuelle.
potent ['pout(ə)nt], *a.* **1.** *Lit: Poet:* puissant; **most p., grave and reverend signors,** très puissants, très graves et respectables seigneurs. **2.** (*of drug, etc.*) efficace, puissant, actif; (*of motive, etc.*) convaincant, décisif; plein de force; **p. drink,** boisson très forte; **p. poison,** poison violent. **3.** *Her:* potencé.
potentate ['poutənteit], *s.* potentat *m.*
potential [pə'tenʃəl]. **1.** *a.* (*a*) en puissance; virtuel; latent; **p. danger,** danger possible, latent; **p. enemy,** ennemi *m* en puissance; **p. criminals,** individus susceptibles de devenir malfaiteurs; criminels *m* en puissance; **p. customers,** clients éventuels; **p. manager** = futur cadre; (*b*) potentiel; **the p. resources of Africa,** les ressources potentielles de l'Afrique; **p. value of a mineral deposit,** valeur virtuelle, potentielle, d'un gîte métallifère; (*c*) *Mth: etc:* **p. equation,** équation potentielle; **p. function,** fonction potentielle; *Ph:* **p. attractive force,** force d'attraction potentielle; potentiel *m* d'attraction; **p. energy,** énergie potentielle; **p. flow,** courant, écoulement, potentiel; *Atom.Ph:* **p. scattering,** diffusion potentielle; *Meteor:* **p. instability,** instabilité potentielle; *Med:* **p. cautery,** cautère potentiel. **2.** *a. & s. Gram:* **the p. (mood),** le potentiel. **3.** *s.* (*a*) **human p.,** potentiel humain; **to reach one's p.,** atteindre son maximum; *Med:* **evoked p.,** potentiel évoqué; **membrane p.,** potentiel de membrane; **industrial p.,** potentiel industriel; *Petr:* **open flow p.,** potentiel maximal (d'un puits); **rated p.,** potentiel nominal; *Mil:* **kill p.,** potentiel de destruction; **ideal kill p.,** potentiel théorique de destruction; **military p.,** potentiel militaire; **(military) nuclear p.,** potentiel nucléaire (militaire); **war p.,** potentiel de guerre; (*b*) *Ph:* **electric, magnetic, p.,** potentiel électrique, magnétique; **equilibrium p.,** potentiel d'équilibre; **ionization p.,** potentiel d'ionisation; **p. barrier,** barrière *f* de potentiel; **p. gradient,** gradient *m* de potentiel; **p. hole, p. trough, p. well,** cuvette *f,* puits *m,* de potentiel; **p. plateau,** plateau *m* de potentiel; **reaction p.,** potentiel de réaction; **zero p.,** potentiel zéro; (*c*) *El:* tension *f,* potentiel; **charging p.,** tension de charge; **earth p.,** *U.S:* **ground p.,** potentiel de la masse, de la terre; **operating p.,** tension de fonctionnement, de service, d'utilisation; voltage *m* de régime; **p. antinode, p. loop,** ventre *m* de tension; **p. difference,** différence *f* de potentiel; **p. divider,** diviseur *m* de tension; **p. drop, p. fall,** chute *f* de potentiel, de tension; **p. equalizer,** stabilisateur *m* de tension; **p. pulse,** impulsion *f* de tension; **p. transformer,** transformateur *m* de tension; *W.Tel:* **grid p.,** potentiel de grille.
potentiality [pətenʃi'æliti], *s.* potentialité *f;* virtualité *f;* **military potentialities,** potentiel *m* militaire; **situation full of potentialities,** situation *f* (i) où tout devient possible, (ii) qui promet.
potentialize [pə'tenʃəlaiz], *v.tr. Mec:* convertir (de l'énergie actuelle) en énergie potentielle.
potentially [pə'tenʃəli], *adv.* potentiellement; virtuellement; d'une manière latente; en puissance.
potentiate [pə'tenʃieit], *v.tr.* **1.** donner de la force à (qch.). **2.** rendre (qch.) possible. **3.** *Pharm:*

potentialiser.

potentiation [pətenʃi'eiʃ(ə)n], *s. Pharm:* potentialisation *f.*

potentilla [poutən'tilə], *s. Bot:* potentille *f.*

potentiometer [pətenʃi'ɔmitər], *s. Elcs:* potentiomètre *m*; **composition p.,** potentiomètre non bobiné; **inductive p.,** potentiomètre bobiné; **logarithmic p.,** potentiomètre à variation logarithmique; **slidewire p.,** potentiomètre à contact glissant; **straight-line p.,** potentiomètre à variation linéaire; **to measure an electromotive force through a p.,** mesurer une force électromotrice au moyen d'un potentiomètre; **p. recorder,** potentiomètre enregistreur; **p. rheostat,** rhéostat *m* en pont; **p. stud,** *U.S:* **p. step,** plot *m* de potentiomètre.

potentiometric [pətenʃiə'metrik], *a. Elcs:* potentiométrique.

potentiometry [pətenʃi'ɔmitri], *s. Elcs:* potentiométrie *f.*

poterium [pɔ'tiəriəm], *s. Bot:* potérium *m*, pimprenelle *f.*

potestative [pə'testətiv], *a. Jur:* potestatif.

pothead ['pɔthed], *s. El:* tête *f* de câble.

potheen [pɔ'θi:n], *s.* = POTEEN.

pother[1] ['pɔðər], *s. O:* **1.** nuage *m* de fumée, de poussière; **to kick up a p.,** soulever un nuage de poussière. **2.** (*a*) agitation *f*, confusion *f*; (*b*) tapage *m*, tumulte *m*, vacarme *m*, tohu-bohu *m*; (*c*) tracas *m*, embarras *mpl*, histoires *fpl*; **to make, kick up, a p.,** faire des histoires; **all this p. about nothing!** tant d'histoires à propos de rien!

pother[2]. *O:* **1.** *v.tr.* (*a*) tourmenter, tracasser, cramponner (qn); (*b*) agiter l'esprit de (qn). **2.** *v.i.* (*a*) faire des histoires (**about,** à propos de); (*b*) se tourmenter.

pothole ['pɔthoul], *s.* (*a*) *Geol:* marmite torrentielle, de géants; (*in glacier*) moulin *m*; (*b*) (*in road*) trou *m*; nid-de-poule *m*, *pl.* nids-de-poule.

potholer ['pɔthoulər], *s. F:* spéléologue *mf.*

potholing ['pɔthouliŋ], *s. F:* spéléologie *f.*

pothook ['pɔthuk], *s.* **1.** crémaillère *f* (de foyer). **2.** *Sch: A:* bâton *m*, jambage *m* (de premier modèle d'écriture).

pothos ['pɔθɔs], *s. Bot:* pothos *m.*

pothouse ['pɔthaus], *s. A:* cabaret *m*, taverne *f.*

pothunter ['pɔthʌntər], *s. F:* (*a*) chasseur *m* qui tire sur n'importe quoi; (*b*) *Sp:* coureur, -euse, de prix.

potichomania [pɔtikou'meiniə], *s.* potichomanie *f.*

Potidaea [pɔti'di:ə], *Pr.n. A.Geog:* Potidée *f.*

potion ['pouʃ(ə)n], *s.* potion *f*; dose *f*; **love p.,** philtre *m* d'amour.

Potiphar ['pɔtifɑ:r], *Pr.n.m. B:* Putiphar.

potman, *pl.* **-men** ['pɔtmən], *s.m. O:* garçon de café.

potomania [pɔtou'meiniə], *s. Med:* potomanie *f.*

potometer [pɔ'tɔmitər], *s. Bot:* potomètre *m.*

potoo [pə'tou], *s. Orn:* ibijau *m.*

potoroo [pɔtə'ru:], *s. Z:* potoroo *m*, potorou *m.*

pot pourri [pou pu:'ri:], *s.* pot-pourri *m*, *pl.* pots-pourris.

potsherd ['pɔtʃə:d], *s. Archeol: & Lit:* tesson *m* (de pot cassé); fragment *m* de vaisselle.

potstone ['pɔtstoun], *s. Miner:* pierre *f* ollaire, chloritoschiste *m*, potstone *m.*

pott[1] [pɔt], *s. Paperm:* papier *m* pot.

Pott[2]. *Pr.n. Med:* **Pott's disease,** mal *m* de Pott, spondylite tuberculeuse.

pottage ['pɔtidʒ], *s. A:* potage (épais); potée *f* (de viande et de légumes); *B:* **mess of p.** = plat *m* de lentilles.

potted ['pɔtid], *a.* **1.** (*a*) (conservé) en pot, en terrine; **p. meat,** terrine *f* de porc, etc.; **p. head,** fromage *m* de tête; **p. shrimps,** crevettes en conserve cuites avec du beurre; (*b*) *F:* **p. music,** musique enregistrée, en cassette(s); (*c*) *F:* abrégé, condensé. **2.** *El:* **p. plug,** prise *f* à fiches noyées.

potter[1] ['pɔtər], *s.* (*a*) potier *m*; **potter's clay,** terre *f* de potier, à potier; terre glaise; argile *f* plastique; **potter's lead, potter's ore,** alquifoux *m*; **potter's lathe,** tour *m* de potier; **potter's wheel,** (i) roue *f* de potier, tour de potier; (ii) disque *m* (du tour); (*b*) *Ent:* **p. bee,** abeille maçonne.

potter[2], *v.i.* **1.** s'occuper de bagatelles; s'amuser à des riens; **to p. away the time,** passer son temps à ne rien faire; **to p. about (at odd jobs),** bricoler. **2.** traîner, traînasser; flâner; *Aut: etc:* **to p. along,** aller doucement; rouler à la papa; **to p. about the house,** trottiner par la maison.

potterer ['pɔtərər], *s.* bricoleur, -euse; flâneur, -euse.

pottering ['pɔtəriŋ], *s.* **1.** flânerie *f*; bricolage *m.* **2.** *Aut:* allure *f* à la papa.

pottery ['pɔtəri], *s.* (*a*) poterie *f*, l'art *m* du potier; **p. industry, trade,** industries *f* céramiques; faïencerie *f*; (*b*) (*works, studio*) poterie; faïencerie; (*c*) vaisselle *f* de terre; faïence *f*; **a piece of p.,** (i) une poterie; (ii) une céramique; (*not porcelain*) **it's only p.,** ce n'est que de la faïence.

potting ['pɔtiŋ], *s.* mise *f* en pot (des plantes, de la viande, etc.); *Hort:* **p. shed,** serre *f* de bouturages.

pottle ['pɔtl], *s. A:* **1.** *Meas:* demi-gallon *m.* **2.** petite corbeille (à fruits).

potto ['pɔtou], *s. Z:* **1.** pérodictique *m*, potto *m.* **2.** kinkajou *m.*

potty[1] ['pɔti], *a. F:* **1.** (*a*) insignifiant, minable; **a p. little state,** un petit état de rien du tout; (*b*) **a p. little job,** une petite tâche trop facile, qui ne vaut pas la peine. **2.** (*a*) toqué, timbré, maboule; **to go p.,** devenir fou, maboule; (*b*) **to be p. on, over, s.o., sth.,** être mordu pour, toqué de, qn, qch.

potty[2], *s. F:* pot *m* de chambre (d'enfant).

potwalloper ['pɔtwɔləpər], *s.* **1.** *Hist: F:* électeur *m* en vertu d'être propriétaire ou locataire d'une maison. **2.** *F: A:* (*a*) marmiton *m*; (*b*) maître-coq *m* (à bord d'un baleinier). **3.** *P: A:* pilier *m* de taverne; ivrogne *m.*

pouch[1] [pautʃ], *s.* **1.** (*a*) (petit) sac; bourse *f*; **tobacco p.,** blague *f* à tabac; (*b*) *Dipl:* valise *f* diplomatique; *Post:* **postal express p.,** ramasse-plis *m inv.* **2.** *Nat.Hist:* bourse, sac, poche ventrale (des marsupiaux); marsupium *m* (de certains insectes); poche, sac (du pélican); sac (de plante); **cheek p.,** abajoue *f*, salle *f* (d'un singe, etc.); *Anat:* **p. of Douglas,** cul-de-sac *m* de Douglas.

pouch[2]. **1.** *v.tr.* (*a*) empocher; (*b*) (*of fish, penguin, etc.*) avaler; **the monkey pouched the nut,** le singe s'est fourré la noisette dans l'abajoue; (*c*) *Dressm:* faire former une poche à, faire bouffer (un vêtement); (*d*) *F: A:* donner un pot-de-vin à (qn). **2.** *v.i.* (*of dress*) former une poche, bouffer.

pouched [pautʃt], *a.* (*a*) *Nat.Hist:* à sac, à poche; (singe) à abajoues; (*b*) *Dressm:* bouffant.

pouchy ['pautʃi], *a.* (*a*) bouffant; (*b*) bouffi.

poudrette [pu:'dret], *s. Agr:* poudrette *f.*

pouf(fe) [pu:f], *s. Furn:* pouf *m.*

poulard ['pu:lɑ:d], *a.* **p. wheat,** (blé) poulard *m.*

poulard(e) ['pu:lɑ:d], *s. Cu:* poularde *f.*

poulp(e) [pu:lp], *s. Moll:* poulpe *m*, pieuvre *f.*

poult [poult], *s.* (*a*) dindonneau *m*; (*b*) pouillard *m*, faisandeau *m*; (*c*) pouillard, perdreau *m*; (*d*) (jeune) poulet *m.*

poult-de-soie [pu:də'swɑ:], *s. Tex:* pou(l)t-de-soie *m*, *pl.* pou(l)ts-de-soie.

poulterer ['poultərər], *s.* marchand, -ande, de volaille; volailler, -ère; volailleur, -euse.

poultice[1] ['poultis], *s. Med:* cataplasme *m*; *Vet:* charge *f*; *F:* **p. on a wooden leg,** cautère *m* sur une jambe de bois.

poultice[2], *v.tr.* mettre, appliquer, un cataplasme sur (qch.).

poultry ['poultri], *s. coll.* volaille *f*; oiseaux *mpl* de basse-cour; **p. farming,** aviculture *f*, élevage *m* avicole, de volaille; **p. house,** poulailler *m*; **p. show,** concours *m* d'aviculture; **p. yard,** basse-cour *f*, *pl.* basses-cours.

poultryman, *pl.* **-men** ['poultrimən], *s.m.* **1.** marchand de volaille. **2.** aviculteur.

pounce[1] [pauns], *s.* **1.** serre *f*, griffe *f* (d'oiseau de proie). **2. to make a p. on sth.,** (i) (*of bird, beast*) fondre, s'abattre, sur (sa proie); (ii) *F:* (*of pers.*) s'élancer pour saisir qch.; se jeter sur qch.

pounce[2]. **1.** *v.tr. Ven:* (*of hawk, etc.*) fondre sur (la proie); saisir (la proie) dans ses serres. **2.** *v.i.* (*a*) (*of bird, beast*) **to p. on the prey,** fondre, s'abattre, sur la proie; (*b*) *F:* (*of pers.*) se précipiter, se jeter (**on,** sur); sauter, bondir (sur une faute).

pounce[3], *s.* **1.** (poudre *f* de) sandaraque *f.* **2.** ponce *f*; *Needlew: etc:* poncette *f.*

pounce[4], *v.tr.* **1.** poncer; polir, frotter, (qch.) à la ponce. **2.** reproduire, copier, calquer, (un dessin) à la ponce; poncer (un dessin); *Needlew:* **to p. the pattern on the material,** poncer, décalquer, le dessin sur le tissu; **pounced drawing,** poncif *m.*

pound[1] [paund], *s.* **1.** livre *f* (de 453, 6 grammes); **to sell sth. by the p.,** vendre qch. à la livre; **40 pence a p.,** quarante pence la livre; *Cu:* **p. cake** = quatre-quarts *m inv.* **2. p. (sterling),** livre (sterling); **p. note,** billet *m*, coupure *f*, d'une livre; **five-p. note,** billet de cinq livres; (*of bankrupt*) **to pay 50 pence in the p.,** payer cinquante pence par livre.

pound[2], *v.tr.* (*at the Mint*) vérifier le poids (des monnaies).

pound[3], *s.* **1.** (*a*) fourrière *f* (pour animaux errants, pour voitures saisies par la police); (*b*) parc *m* (à moutons, etc.); (*c*) **to bring a boar into a p.,** acculer un sanglier; *O:* **to bring s.o. into a p.,** mettre qn au pied du mur. **2.** *Fish:* compartiment *m* (d'un filet à cœur); **p. net,** filet à cœur, paradière *f.* **3.** *Hyd.E:* (*a*) bassin *m*, retenue *f*, réservoir *m*; **p. lock,** écluse *f* à sas; (*b*) bief *m*, retenue (entre deux écluses).

pound[4], *v.tr.* **1.** (*a*) mettre (des animaux) en fourrière; (*b*) **to p. s.o. up,** enfermer qn; (*c*) *Ven:* (*of hedge, etc.*) **to p. the field,** opposer une barrière infranchissable à la chasse; (*of rider*) **to get pounded,** se fourrer dans une impasse. **2. to p. (back) the water,** retenir l'eau; établir un barrage sur un cours d'eau.

pound[5]. **1.** *v.tr.* (*a*) broyer, piler, concasser (des pierres, etc.); égruger (du sel, du sucre); casser, briser (des mottes de terre); écraser (des pommes); pilonner (la terre, une drogue); **pounded sugar,** sucre *m* en poudre; *U.S: F:* **to p. the asphalt,** battre le pavé; (*b*) battre, rosser (qn); bourrer (qn) de coups de poing; taper sur (qn); *Mil:* **to p. a position,** pilonner, marteler, une position; (*c*) **to p. sth. to atoms, to pieces,** réduire qch. en miettes, en morceaux. **2.** *v.i.* (*a*) **to p. at, on, sth., to p. away at sth.,** cogner dur, frapper ferme, frapper à bras raccourcis, sur qch.; **to p. on the door,** donner de grands coups dans la porte; frapper à la porte à coups redoublés; **feet were heard pounding on the stairs,** on entendait résonner lourdement des pas sur l'escalier; **to p. away on the piano,** martyriser le piano; **the guns were pounding away,** les canons tapaient dur, étaient engagés dans un feu nourri; (*b*) **to p. along,** (i) marcher, (ii) chevaucher, d'un pas lourd (sur la route); (iii) (*of steamer*) fendre les vagues avec difficulté; piquer (du nez) dans la lame; (*c*) *I.C.E:* (*of engine*) cogner, marteler; (*d*) *Veh: etc:* **the axle is pounding against the body,** l'essieu *m* talonne; **the ship was pounding on the bottom,** le navire talonnait; **the hull was pounding on the rocks,** la coque se broyait, s'écrasait, sur les récifs.

poundage[1] ['paundidʒ], *s.* **1.** (*a*) *Hist:* poundage *m*; (*b*) (droit *m* de) commission *f*; remise *f* de tant par livre (sterling). **2.** taux *m* de tant par livre (de poids).

poundage[2], *s.* **1.** mise *f* en fourrière. **2.** frais *mpl* de fourrière.

poundal ['paundl], *s. Mec.Meas:* pied-livre *m*, *pl.* pieds-livres.

pounder[1] ['paundər], *s.* pilon *m*; (**concrete**) **p.,** pilon, dame *f*; (**paviour's**) **p.,** demoiselle *f*, hie *f.*

pounder[2], *s.* (*with num. prefixed*) **two p., three p.,** de deux, de trois, livres (de poids); *Artil:* **thirty p.,** canon *m*, pièce *f*, de trente.

pounding ['paundiŋ], *s.* **1.** (*a*) broyage *m*, broiement *m*; pilage *m*; concassage *m* (de pierres, etc.); égrugeage *m* (du sel); écrasage *m* (des pommes); (*b*) martellement *m* (de qch.); réduction *f* en miettes. **2.** (*a*) marche pesante; (*b*) (*of engine, etc.*) cognement *m*; (*c*) (*of ship, etc.*) talonnement *m*; (*d*) bruit *m* de quelque chose qui se broie.

pour[1] [pɔ:r], *s.* **1.** *A:* pluie abondante; torrent *m*, déluge *m*, de pluie. **2.** *Metall:* coulée *f* (de métal).

pour[2], *v.*

I. *v.tr. & i.* **1.** *v.tr.* (*a*) verser (qch. dans qch., de qch.); **she poured some tea into the cup,** elle a versé du thé dans la tasse; **he poured me some more wine,** il m'a reversé du vin, m'a versé encore du vin; **to p. (down) blessings on s.o.,** verser, répandre, des bienfaits sur qn; (*b*) *Metall:* couler (le métal); (*with passive force*) **metal that pours well,** métal qui se coule bien, facilement. **2.** *v.i.* (*a*) **it's pouring, the rain's pouring (down),** il pleut à verse, la pluie tombe à torrents; **water was pouring into the cellar,** l'eau entrait à flots dans la cave; **the water from the melting snow was pouring into the lake,** l'eau de la fonte se jetait, se déversait, dans le lac; **water was pouring from the roof,** l'eau ruisselait du toit; (*b*) **tourists were pouring into, out of, the palace,** des touristes entraient dans le château, sortaient du château, en foule, à flots; **light pouring through the window,** lumière entrant à flots par la fenêtre.

II. (*compound verbs*) **1. pour in.** (*a*) *v.tr.* **to p. in a broadside,** lâcher, envoyer, une bordée; (*b*) *v.i.* **the crowd came pouring in,** on entrait à flots, en foule; on arrivait de toutes parts; **invitations came pouring in,** il nous pleuvait des invitations; ce fut une avalanche d'invitations.

2. pour out, *v.tr. & i.* (*a*) verser le thé, le café; (*b*) répandre (sa colère); donner libre cours à (ses sentiments); épancher (ses chagrins); **the chimney was pouring out smoke,** la cheminée vomissait des nuages de fumée; **to p. out a torrent of abuse on s.o.,** déverser, faire pleuvoir, un torrent d'injures sur qn; (*c*) (*of people*) sortir en foule.

pourer ['pɔ:rər], *s.* **1.** (*a*) verseur *m*; (*b*) **this teapot isn't a good p.,** cette théière verse mal. **2.** *Metall:* (*pers.*) couleur *m.*

pouring[1] ['pɔ:riŋ], *a.* **p. rain,** pluie torrentielle, battante; **a p. wet evening,** une soirée ruisselante.

pouring[2], *s.* (*a*) *Metall:* coulée *f*; **top p.,** coulée à la descente; **side p.,** coulée à talon; **bottom p.,** coulée en source; **p. ladle,** cuillère *f* de fondeur; (*b*) *attrib.* **p. bottle,** flacon verseur; **collodion p. bottle,** carafe *f* à collodion; **p. point,** point *m* de fluage, température *f* de présolidification (d'une huile de graissage, etc.); (*c*) **p. out,** émission *f*, crachement *m*, vomissement *m*, projection *f* (de fumée, de vapeur); déversement *m*, épanchement *m*, émission (d'un liquide); épanchement (de ses chagrins).

pourpoint ['puəpɔint], *s. A.Cost:* pourpoint *m.*

pout[1] [paut], *s. Ich:* (**whiting**) **p.**, tacaud *m*; (**eel**) **p.**, lotte *f.*

pout[2], *s.* (*a*) moue *f*; (*b*) *O:* **to have the pouts,** bouder.

pout[3], *v.i.* **1.** (*a*) faire la moue, la lippe; (*b*) bouder. **2.** (*of pigeon*) gonfler, enfler, le jabot; faire jabot.

pouter ['pautər], *s.* **1. p. (pigeon),** pigeon *m* grosse-gorge, (pigeon) boulant *m.* **2.** *Ich:* tacaud *m.*

pouting[1] ['pautiŋ], *a.* (*a*) qui fait la moue; (*b*) boudeur, -euse; (*c*) **p. lips,** lèvres proéminentes, qui avancent.

pouting[2], *s.* (*a*) moue *f*; (*b*) bouderie *f.*

poverty ['pɔvəti], *s.* **1.** pauvreté *f*; pénurie *f*; *Adm:* indigence *f*; **extreme p., abject p.,** misère *f*; **to live in p.,** vivre pauvrement, dans la gêne, dans la misère; **to be reduced to p.,** être réduit à la misère; **to die in abject p.,** mourir sur un grabat, sur la paille; **to cry p.,** pleurer misère; *Prov:* **p. is no disgrace, no crime, no sin, no vice,** pauvreté n'est pas vice. **2.** disette *f*, manque *m*, pénurie (de denrées, etc.); stérilité *f*, pauvreté (du sol); **p. of ideas,** pauvreté, pénurie, dénuement *m*, d'idées; **p. of the soil,** pauvreté du sol; **p. of blood,** viciation *f* du sang; *I.C.E:* **p. of the mixture,** pauvreté du mélange.

poverty-stricken ['pɔvətistrik(ə)n], *a.* (*a*) (*of pers.*) indigent; réduit à la misère; (*b*) (*of dwelling, etc.*) misérable.

powder[1] ['paudər], *s.* poudre *f*; (*a*) **to reduce sth. to p.,** (i) réduire qch. en poudre, pulvériser qch.; (ii) *Fig:* réduire qch. en poussière, en miettes; réduire qch. à néant, anéantir qch.; **abrasive p., grinding p.,** poudre abrasive; **brazing p., welding p.,** poudre à souder; **cementing p., cementatory p.,** poudre à cémenter, poudre cémentatoire; **chalk p.,** (i) craie pulvérisée, craie en poudre; (ii) blanc *m* d'Espagne; **fluorescent p.,** poudre fluorescente; **magnetic p.,** poudre magnétique; *Metall:* **smelting p.,** poudre de fusion; **p. metallurgy,** métallurgie *f* des poudres; *Tp:* **p. microphone,** microphone *m* à poudre de charbon; *Tchn:* **p. diffraction,** diffraction *f* par poudre; **p.(-diffraction) method,** procédé *m* de Debye-Scherrer; **p. camera,** chambre *f* Debye-Scherrer; **p. pattern,** diagramme *m* d'une diffraction par poudre; **p. blue,** (i) *Laund: O:* bleu anglais (en poudre); (ii) (*colour*) bleu clair *inv*; *O:* **p. post,** pourriture sèche (du bois); **p.-post beetle,** lycte *m*; (*b*) poudre, explosif *m*; **black p.,** poudre noire; **chlorate p.,** poudre chloratée; **coarse-grained, large-grain(ed), p.,** poudre à gros grains; **fine-grain(ed) p.,** poudre à grains fins, poudre fine; **flashless p.,** poudre anti-lueur; **fulminating p.,** poudre fulminante; **mealed p.,** pulvérin *m*; **nitrate p., nitrogen p.,** poudre au nitrate, poudre azotée; **nitrocellulose p.,** poudre à la nitrocellulose; **non-hygroscopic p.,** poudre non hygroscopique; **priming p.,** amorce *f*, fulminate *m*, pulvérin *m*; **progressive p.,** poudre progressive, explosif progressif; **pyro p.,** poudre pyroxylée; **quick-burning p.,** poudre vive; **slow-burning p.,** poudre lente; **smokeless p.,** poudre sans fumée; **service p.,** poudre de guerre; **sheet p., strip p.,** poudre, explosif, en lamelles, en plaquettes; **p. factory, mill, works,** poudrerie *f*; fabrique *f* d'explosifs; **p. depot,** dépôt *m* d'explosifs; poudrière *f*; **p. train,** traînée *f* de poudre; *Mil: A:* **p. chest,** caisson *m* à poudre; **p. horn,** poire *f*, flasque *f*, cornet *m*, à poudre; *Artil: etc:* **p. chamber,** chambre *f* à poudre, à charge; **p. charge,** charge *f* de poudre, d'explosif; **p. bag,** gargousse *f*; *Nau: A:* **p. boy,** *F:* **p. monkey,** moussaillon gargoussier; *Mec.E:* (*of tool, etc.*) **p. actuated,** actionné, mû, par explosif; **to smell p. for the first time,** recevoir le baptême du feu; **to keep one's p. dry,** se tenir prêt à parer à toute éventualité, à tenir le coup; **it's not worth p. and shot,** cela ne vaut pas la peine; **he's not worth p. and shot,** il ne vaut pas la corde pour le pendre; **to waste (one's) p. and shot,** perdre son temps et sa peine; tirer sa poudre aux moineaux; *F: O:* **blow with no p. behind it,** coup sans vigueur, sans énergie; (*c*) *Toil:* (**face**) **p.,** poudre (de riz); **talcum p.,** (poudre de) talc *m*; **tooth p., dental p.,** poudre dentifrice; **p. box, bowl, compact,** poudrier *m*; boîte *f* à poudre; **p. puff,** houppe *f*, houppette *f*, pompon *m* (à poudre); *A:* **p. closet,** cabinet *m* de toilette (où l'on se poudrait les cheveux); (*in hotel, etc.*) **p. room,** toilette *f* pour dames; (*d*) *Pharm:* poudre; **purgative p.,** poudre purgative; **worm p.,** poudre vermifuge; *P:* **to take a p.,** prendre la poudre d'escampette.

powder[2], *v.* **1.** (*a*) *v.tr.* saupoudrer (un gâteau de sucre, etc.); **landscape powdered with snow,** paysage saupoudré de neige; *Her:* **shield powdered with fleurs-de-lis,** écu semé de fleurs de lis; (*b*) *v.tr. & i. Typ:* poudrer, talquer (le blanchet); (*of ink*) poudrer. **2.** *v.tr. & i.* poudrer (à blanc), blanchir (les cheveux); **to p. (one's face),** se poudrer (le visage); *F:* **to go and p. one's nose,** aller aux cabinets, à la toilette. **3.** (*a*) *v.tr.* réduire (qch.) en poudre; pulvériser (qch.); (*b*) *v.i.* se pulvériser; se réduire en poudre, en poussière; tomber en poussière.

powdered ['paudəd], *a.* **1.** (*of face, hair*) poudré. **2.** en poudre, pulvérisé; **p. milk,** lait *m* en poudre; **p. carbon,** poudre *f* de charbon; **p. coal,** charbon pulvérisé; **p. ore,** farine minérale, farine de brocard; *El:* **p. iron core,** noyau de fer divisé, de fer pulvérulent.

powderiness ['paud(ə)rinis], *s.* pulvérulence *f.*

powdering ['paud(ə)riŋ], *s.* **1.** poudrage *m*, saupoudrage *m*; (*for pickling*) **p. tub,** saloir *m.* **2.** pulvérisation *f* (de qch.).

powdery ['paud(ə)ri], *a.* (*a*) poudreux; (*b*) friable.

powellite ['pauəlait], *s. Miner:* powellite *f*, molybdoscheelite *f.*

power[1] ['pauər], *s.* **1.** (*a*) pouvoir *m*; **I'll do everything in my p.,** je ferai tout ce qui est dans mon pouvoir, tout mon possible; **as far as lies within my p.,** dans la mesure où cela m'est, me sera, possible; **to the utmost of my p.,** de tout mon pouvoir, dans toute la mesure de mes possibilités; **by every means in his p.,** par tous les moyens en son pouvoir; **it's beyond my p.,** cela dépasse mes possibilités, ne m'est pas possible; **the p. of suggestion,** l'action *f*, la puissance, de la suggestion; **the p. of reason,** la puissance de la raison; **he has no p. to hold the interest of his audience,** il n'est pas capable de retenir l'intérêt de son auditoire; (*b*) faculté *f*, capacité *f*, talent *m*; **mental powers,** facultés intellectuelles, de l'esprit; **man of great intellectual powers,** homme de hautes facultés; **his powers are failing,** ses facultés baissent; **p. of speech,** la parole; **p. of observation,** faculté, dons *mpl*, d'observation; (*c*) *Ph: Ch: etc:* **p. of absorption, absorbent, absorptive, p.,** pouvoir absorbant; capacité *f* d'absorption; **heating p.,** pouvoir, puissance, calorifique, de chauffage; *Atom.Ph:* **ionizing p.,** pouvoir ionisant; **scattering p.,** pouvoir de diffusion; *El:* **inductive, insulating, p.,** pouvoir inducteur, isolant; *Mec:* **braking p.,** puissance de freinage, pouvoir freinant; (*d*) *Pol.Ec:* **purchasing p.,** pouvoir d'achat. **2.** vigueur *f*, force *f*, énergie *f* (physique); *F:* **more p. to your elbow!** (i) allez-y! (ii) bonne chance! **3.** (*a*) puissance (d'une machine, d'un microscope, etc.); force (d'un aimant, d'une chute d'eau, etc.); **magnifying p.,** pouvoir grossissant, grossissement *m* (d'une lentille); **refractive p.,** pouvoir réfractif, réfringent; **attractive p.,** force d'attraction; **accelerating p.,** force accélératrice; **lifting p.,** (i) force élévatrice, portante (d'un aimant); (ii) force ascensionnelle (d'un ballon); (iii) *Av:* force de sustentation; *Mec: etc:* **absolute p.,** puissance absolue; **full p.,** pleine puissance, puissance maximale; **p. delivered,** puissance développée; **p.-to-weight ratio, p. per unit of mass,** puissance massique; *Elcs: etc:* **audio-frequency, radio-frequency, p.,** puissance basse fréquence, haute fréquence; **p. amplifier, amplification,** amplificateur *m*, amplification *f*, de puissance; (*b*) énergie *f* (électrique, hydraulique, etc.); **nuclear p.,** énergie nucléaire, atomique; **sources of p., p. supply,** sources *f* d'énergie; ressources *f* énergétiques; **p. consumption,** consommation *f* d'énergie, énergie consommée; *Mec: etc:* **motive, driving, p.,** force motrice; mobile *m*; *El:* **p. conductor,** conducteur *m* d'énergie; **p. load,** (i) charge *f* (d'un réseau); (ii) consommation *f* (d'une machine en énergie électrique); **p. house,** (i) centrale *f* électrique; (ii) *F:* homme vigoureux et dynamique; source *f* d'énergie et de dynamisme; **p. station,** centrale électrique; **p. plant,** (i) centrale électrique; (ii) *Av: etc:* (groupe) moteur *m*, groupe (moto)propulseur, motoréacteur, réactopropulseur; **p. cut, failure,** panne *f* de courant; *Atom.Ph:* **p. reactor, p. pile,** génératrice *f* nucléaire; pile *f*, réacteur *m*, d'énergie, de puissance; **p. breeder,** réacteur régénérateur de puissance; réacteur surgénérateur; **p. drift,** dérive *f* de puissance; **p. excursion,** saute *f* de puissance; *El: etc:* **p. factor,** facteur *m* de puissance; (*c*) *El: F:* la force; **p. rate,** tarif *m* force; **p. point,** prise *f* de courant (force); (*d*) la machine, le machinisme; **p. has revolutionized industry,** la machine a révolutionné l'industrie; *Ind:* **p. press,** presse *f* mécanique; **p. loom,** métier *m* mécanique; *Mec.E:* **p. driven, propelled,** à entraînement, à propulsion, mécanique; à moteur; *Av:* **p. drive,** piqué *m* avec moteur, à pleins gaz; (*e*) *Mec: O:* **the mechanical powers,** les machines simples. **4.** (*a*) pouvoir, influence *f*, autorité *f*; **absolute p.,** pouvoir absolu; **executive, legislative, p.,** pouvoir exécutif, législatif; **to come into p.,** arriver au pouvoir; **assumption of p.,** prise *f* de pouvoir; **to be in p.,** être au pouvoir, détenir le pouvoir; *Pol:* **the party in p.,** le parti au pouvoir; **Black P.,** pouvoir noir; **Spain was then at the height of her p.,** l'Espagne était alors à l'apogée de sa puissance; **p. of life and death,** droit *m* de vie et de mort; **to have s.o. in one's p.,** avoir du pouvoir sur qn; **to be in s.o.'s p.,** être sous l'emprise, à la merci, de qn; (*b*) **to act with full powers,** agir de pleine autorité; **to ask for powers to conclude peace,** demander des pouvoirs pour conclure la paix; **this lies beyond his powers,** cela ne rentre pas dans ses attributions; **definite powers of a court,** attributions précises d'une cour; (*c*) *Jur:* procuration *f*, mandat *m*, pouvoir; **delegation of powers,** délégation *f* de pouvoirs; **blank p.,** procuration en blanc; **joint p.,** pouvoir, mandat, collectif; procuration collective; **to furnish s.o. with full powers,** donner pleins pouvoirs à qn; munir qn de pleins pouvoirs; (*d*) *Jur:* **p. of appointment,** pouvoir (donné à l'usufruitier) de désigner celui qui bénéficiera d'un legs. **5.** (*a*) (*pers., etc.*) puissance; **the powers that be,** les autorités constituées, les puissances établies; **the press is a p. in the state,** la presse est une puissance (avec laquelle il faut compter) dans le pays; *Theol:* **the (angelic) powers,** les puissances; **the powers of darkness,** les puissances des ténèbres; *A:* **merciful powers!** grands dieux! (*b*) (*country*) **world p.,** puissance mondiale; **the great powers,** les grandes puissances. **6.** (*a*) *A:* armée *f*, force; (*b*) *F: O:* **a p. of people,** une masse, un tas, de gens; **that'll do you a p. of good,** ça vous fera énormément de bien. **7.** *Mth:* puissance (d'un nombre); **to the nth p.,** à la nième puissance; **three to the p. of ten** (3^{10}), trois (à la puissance dix, à la dixième puissance; trois exposant dix.

power[2], *v.tr.* fournir de l'énergie, de l'électricité, à (une machine); actionner; motoriser; **powered by two engines,** actionné par deux moteurs.

power-assisted [pauərə'sistid], *a. Aut:* (*of steering*) assisté.

power-dive ['pauədaiv], *v.i. Av:* piquer à pleins gaz.

powered ['pauəd], *a.* (*a*) actionné mécaniquement; **p. vehicle,** véhicule *m* à moteur; **p. glider,** planeur *m* à moteur, aviette *f*; **p. controls,** commandes asservies; (*b*) **atomic p., nuclear p.,** à propulsion atomique, nucléaire; **rocket p.,** propulsé par fusée; (*of car, etc.*) **high p., low p.,** de haute, de faible, puissance.

powerful ['pauəf(u)l], *a.* **1.** (*a*) puissant; **to become more p.,** augmenter en puissance; (*of state*) s'agrandir; **to have to deal with a p. adversary,** avoir affaire à forte partie; (*b*) (*of physical strength*) fort, vigoureux; (*of blow*) vigoureux; **p. remedy,** remède *m* énergique, efficace; **p. dose,** forte dose (d'un médicament). **2.** *P: O:* (*a*) **a p. lot of people,** une masse, un tas, de gens; **a p. lot of trouble,** énormément de peine; (*b*) *adv. esp. U.S:* **I was p. tired,** j'étais rudement fatigué.

powerfully ['pauəf(u)li], *adv.* puissamment; fortement; **p. built man,** homme puissamment charpenté.

powerfulness ['pauəf(u)lnis], *s.* **1.** puissance *f.* **2.** force *f*, vigueur *f* (musculaire); **p. of a drug,** action *f* énergique d'une drogue.

powerless ['pauəlis], *a.* **1.** sans puissance; impuissant; **p. to act,** sans le pouvoir, la possibilité, d'agir; **I am p. to help you,** je ne puis rien faire pour vous aider. **2.** inefficace.

powerlessness ['pauəlisnis], *s.* **1.** impuissance *f.* **2.** inefficacité *f.*

pow-wow[1] [pau'wau], *s.* **1.** devin *m*, sorcier *m*, guérisseur *m* (chez les Peaux-Rouges). **2.** cérémonie *f* (avec rites magiques); assemblée *f*, orgie *f* (des Peaux-Rouges). **3.** *F:* palabre *f*; réunion *f* (où on discute beaucoup de choses); **we must have a p.-w. about this,** il faut parler de ça.

pow-wow[2]. **1.** *v.i.* (*of N. American Indians*) (*a*) pratiquer la sorcellerie; (*b*) tenir une assemblée; se livrer à une orgie. **2.** *v.i. F:* se réunir pour discuter qch.; palabrer; **to p.-w. about sth.,** discuter qch. **3.** *v.tr.* traiter (un malade) par la sorcellerie.

pox [pɔks], *s.* **1.** (*a*) *Med: P:* **the p.,** la syphilis; **to get the p.,** se faire plomber; (*b*) *F: A:* **a p. on him!** qu'il aille au diable! **2.** *Vet:* **cow p.,** vaccine *f*, variole *f* des vaches, cow-pox *m*; **sheep p.,** clavelée *f*, claveau *m*; rougeole *f*, variole, des moutons; **horse p.,** variole équine.

poxed [pɔkst], *a. P:* syphilitique, plombé.

poyou ['pɔiju:], *s. Z:* tatou *m* poyou, encoubert *m.*

pozz(u)olana [pɔts(u)ou'lɑ:nə], *s. Miner:* po(u)zzolane *f.*

Pozzuoli [pɔtsu'ouli]. *Pr.n. Geog:* Pouzzoles.

praam [prɑ:m], *s. Nau: A:* prame *f.*

practicability [præktikə'biliti], *s.* praticabilité *f.*

practicable ['præktikəbl], *a.* **1.** praticable; faisable; entreprenable; **to make a rule p.,** réduire une règle en pratique; **this method is not so p.,** cette méthode n'est pas, du point de vue pratique, aussi satisfaisante. **2.** (*a*) (*of road, ford*) praticable; **road p. for vehicles,** chemin *m* carrossable; (*b*) *Th:* **p. door, window,** porte *f*, fenêtre *f*, praticable.

practical ['præktikl], *a.* **1.** (*a*) pratique; **p. application,** mise *f* en pratique (d'une théorie, etc.); réalisation *f* (pratique) (d'une invention, etc.); **p. suggestion,** proposition *f* réalisable, d'ordre pratique; **of no p. value, useless for p. purposes,** inutilisable dans la pratique; **from a p. point of view,** pratiquement parlant; **p. mechanics, chemistry,** mécanique, chimie, appliquée; *Sch: p.* **work,** *s. F:* **practical,** travaux *mpl* pratiques; **the examination will be p., written and oral,** l'examen comprendra des épreuves pratiques, écrites et orales; *s.* **we must confine ourselves to the p.,** il nous faut nous limiter à ce qui est pratique; (*b*) *O:* **p. tradesman,** artisan *m*; (*c*) **he's very p.,** il a beaucoup de bon sens; ce n'est pas un homme à poursuivre des chimères; **it appeals to p. minds,** cela plaît aux esprits positifs; (*d*) (outil, etc.) pratique; **p. range of a weapon,** portée réelle d'une arme. **2. with p. unanimity,** d'un consentement presque unanime.

practicality [prækti'kæliti], **practicalness** ['præktik(ə)lnis], *s.* **1.** nature *f* pratique; caractère *m* pratique. **2.** sens *m*, esprit *m*, pratique.

practically ['præktik(ə)li], *adv.* **1.** pratiquement, en pratique; **p. speaking,** pratiquement parlant; **p. speaking, he's the boss,** il est le patron en fait (sinon en droit). **2.** pour ainsi dire; **there has been p. no snow,** il n'y a presque pas eu de neige; **there is p. nothing left,** il ne reste pour ainsi dire, presque, plus rien; **p. cured,** presque guéri; **I'm p. ruined,** c'est la ruine, ou peu s'en faut; **elected by a p. unanimous vote,** élu à la quasi-unanimité; **p. the whole of the audience,** la quasi-totalité de l'auditoire; presque tous les assistants; **the conditions amount p. to a refusal,** les conditions équivalent, en fait, à un refus; **p. the same temperature,** sensiblement la même température.

practice[1] ['præktis], *s.* **1.** (*a*) pratique *f*; exercice *m* (d'une profession, etc.); **to put one's ideas into p.,** mettre ses idées en pratique, donner suite à ses idées; **in p. one finds that . . .,** en, dans la, pratique, on constate que . . .; (*of doctor, etc.*) **to be in p.,** pratiquer, exercer; être en exercice; **he's no longer in p.,** il n'exerce plus; (*b*) (*of doctor, etc.*) pratique, clientèle *f*; (*of solicitor*) étude *f*; **to buy a p.,** acheter une clientèle, un cabinet, une étude; **private p.,** clientèle privée, cabinet (médical, etc.) privé; **group p.,** cabinets groupés; groupement médical, dentaire. **2.** (*a*) habitude *f*, coutume *f*, usage *m*; **to make a p. of doing sth.,** se faire une habitude, une règle, de faire qch.; **it's the usual p.,** c'est l'usage; c'est une pratique, une habitude, courante; (*b*) *Ind: etc:* technique *f*; méthodes *fpl*; **shop p.,** technique d'atelier; *Jur:* **the p. of the courts,** la procédure, la pratique, du Palais. **3.** (*a*) exercice(s); *Sp: etc:* entraînement *m*; **it can be learnt only by p.,** cela ne s'apprend que par l'usage; **it takes years of p.,** cela demande des années de pratique; **stroke that needs a lot of p.,** coup qui demande beaucoup d'application, de travail; **exercise that is good p. for swimming,** exercice qui est un bon entraînement pour la natation; **to do sth. for p.,** faire qch. pour s'exercer; **to keep in p.,** se maintenir en forme; **to get out of p.,** perdre l'habitude, la main; se rouiller; *Sp:* **p. match,** match *m* d'entraînement; *Mus:* **choir p.,** répétition (chorale); (*to child*) **have you done your p.?** as-tu fait tes exercices (au piano, etc.)? *Prov:* **p. makes perfect,** c'est en forgeant qu'on devient forgeron; usage rend maître; on se perfectionne par la pratique; (*b*) *Mil:* tir *m* (d'entraînement); *Artil:* école *f* à feu; **battle, combat, p.,** (i) exercice de combat, entraînement au combat; (ii) tir de combat; **target p.,** tir à la cible, au but; *Av:* **p. flight,** vol *m* d'entraînement. **4.** *usu. pl.* agissements *m*, manigances *f*, pratiques, menées *f*, intrigues *f*. **5.** *Mth: A:* méthode des parties aliquotes.

practice[2], *v. NAm:* = PRACTISE.

practician [præk'tiʃ(ə)n], *s.* praticien, -ienne.

practise ['præktis], *v.* **1.** *v.tr.* pratiquer (une vertu, etc.); suivre (une méthode); mettre en pratique, en action (un principe, etc.); **to p. deceit,** user de supercherie; **to p. what one preaches,** montrer l'exemple; prêcher d'exemple. **2.** (*a*) *v.tr.* pratiquer, exercer (une profession); exercer (la médecine); faire (du journalisme); (*b*) *v.i.* (*of doctor*) exercer; faire de la clientèle. **3.** (*a*) *v.tr.* étudier (le piano, etc.); **to p. the flute, fencing,** s'exercer sur la flûte, à l'escrime; **to p. scales, exercises (on the piano),** faire des gammes, jouer des exercices (au piano); *Ten: Bill: etc:* **to p. a shot,** s'exercer à un coup; **to p. one's French (on s.o.),** essayer son français (sur qn); (*b*) *v.i. Mus: etc:* s'exercer; faire des exercices. **4.** *v.tr.* entraîner (une équipe, etc.). **5.** *v.ind.tr. O:* **to p. (up)on s.o.,** exploiter, duper, qn.

practised ['præktist], *a.* exercé, expérimenté; (joueur, etc.) expérimenté, averti; (orateur, etc.) habile.

practising[1] ['præktisiŋ], *a.* **1.** qui exerce, praticien; (*of doctor, etc.*) praticien, exerçant; (*of solicitor, etc.*) exerçant, en exercice. **2.** (chrétien, catholique) pratiquant.

practising[2], *s.* (*a*) pratique *f* (de la vertu); entraînement *m* (pour un sport); exercice *m* (d'une profession, etc.); (*b*) *Mus:* répétitions *fpl* (d'ensemble); exercices (au piano).

practitioner [præk'tiʃənər], *s.* **medical p.,** médecin *m*; **general p.,** médecin de médecine générale; (médecin) généraliste *mf*; omnipraticien, -ienne; **dental p.,** dentiste praticien.

praedial ['pri:diəl], *a.* = PREDIAL.

praemunire [pri:mju'nairi], *s. Eng.Hist:* **statutes of p.,** statuts contre les empiétements de la juridiction ecclésiastique sur le pouvoir civil; **writ of p.,** mandat *m* sommant un délinquant de répondre à l'accusation de *praemunire*.

Praeneste [pri:'nesti:]. *Pr.n. A.Geog:* Préneste.

praenomen [pri:'noumen], *s. Rom.Ant:* prénom *m*.

Praesidium [pri'sidiəm], *s. Pol:* (*in U.S.S.R.*) praesidium *m*.

praetor ['pri:tər], *s. Rom.Hist:* préteur *m*.

praetorial [pri'tɔ:riəl], *a. Rom.Hist:* prétorial, -aux.

praetorian [pri'tɔ:riən], *a. & s. Rom.Hist:* prétorien (*m*).

praetorium [pri'tɔ:riəm], *s. Rom.Ant:* prétoire *m*.

praetorship ['pri:təʃip], *s. Rom.Hist:* préture *f*.

pragmatagnosia [prægmætæg'nousiə], *s. Med:* pragmatagnosie *f*.

pragmatic [præg'mætik], *a.* **1.** *Hist: Phil:* pragmatique; *Hist:* **p. sanction,** *s.* **p.,** pragmatique sanction *f*; pragmatique *f*. **2.** = PRAGMATICAL.

pragmatical [præg'mætikl], *a.* **1.** *A:* officieux, importun. **2.** (*a*) suffisant, important, infatué de soi-même; (*b*) dogmatique, dictatorial, -aux, doctrinaire. **3.** *Phil:* pragmatique.

pragmatically [præg'mætik(ə)li], *adv.* **1.** *Phil:* pragmatiquement. **2.** *A:* officieusement, avec importunité. **3.** d'un ton suffisant, dogmatique, dictatorial, doctrinaire; d'un ton positif.

pragmaticism [præg'mætisizm], *s. Phil:* pragmaticisme *m*.

pragmatism ['prægmətizm], *s.* **1.** *Phil:* pragmatisme *m*. **2.** *A:* officiosité *f*; suffisance *f*. **3.** pédantisme *m*, pédanterie *f*.

pragmatist ['prægmətist], *s. Phil:* pragmatiste *mf*.

pragmatize ['prægmətaiz], *v.tr.* matérialiser, rationaliser (un mythe, etc.).

prairie ['prɛəri], *s.* prairie *f* (de l'Amérique du Nord); **the Prairies,** la Prairie; **the P. States,** la Prairie américaine; **the P. Provinces,** la Prairie canadienne; *Z:* **p. dog,** cynomys *m*, chien *m* de prairie; **p. wolf,** coyote *m*; *Orn:* **p. chicken,** tétras *m* cupidon, cupidon *m* des prairies, *Fr.C:* poule *f* des Prairies; *Bot:* **p. clover,** petalostemon *m*; *Hist:* **p. schooner,** chariot *m* dont se servaient les premiers colons américains; *F:* **p. oyster, p. cocktail,** œuf cru à gober.

praisable ['preizəbl], *a.* louable.

praise[1] [preiz], *s.* (i) (*deserved*) éloge(s) *m(pl)*; (ii) (*adulatory or of worship*) louange(s) *f(pl)*; **in p. of s.o., of sth.,** à la louange de qn, de qch.; **to speak in p. of s.o.,** faire l'éloge de qn; **it must be said in his p. that . . .,** il faut dire à son mérite, à son éloge, que . . .; **to sing the praises of sth., of s.o.,** chanter, célébrer, les louanges de qch., de qn; **to sing one's own praises,** faire son propre éloge; **he is not given to p.,** il est peu flatteur; il n'est pas enclin à la louange; il n'est pas louangeur; **I have nothing but p. for him,** je n'ai rien pour lui que des louanges; **his conduct is beyond all p.,** sa conduite est au-dessus de tout éloge; **this is the highest p. one can give him,** c'est le plus bel éloge à lui faire; **to the p. of God,** à la gloire de Dieu; à la louange de Dieu; **p. be to God!** Dieu soit loué!

praise[2], *v.tr.* **1.** louer, faire l'éloge de (qn, qch.); **to be praised by all,** être loué de tous. **2. to p. God,** glorifier Dieu; chanter, célébrer, les louanges de Dieu.

praiseworthy ['preizwə:ði], *a.* digne d'éloges; louable; (travail) méritoire.

praising ['preiziŋ], *s.* (*a*) louange *f*, éloge *m*; (*b*) glorification *f* (de Dieu); célébration *f* des louanges (de Dieu).

praiss [preis], *s.* praiss *m*.

praline ['præli:n], *s. Cu:* praline *f*.

pram[1] [præ:m], *s. Nau:* **1.** *A:* prame *f*. **2.** plate *f*; youyou *m*; prame.

pram[2], *s. F:* **1.** voiture *f* d'enfant. **2.** *A:* voiture à bras de laitier.

prance[1] [prɑ:ns], *v.i.* **1.** (*of horse*) fringuer; piaffer; **to p. about,** caracoler; **to p. and curvet,** caracoler et faire des courbettes. **2.** (*of pers.*) **to p. (about),** se pavaner; se carrer; **to p. in, out,** entrer, sortir, d'un pas dégagé.

prance[2], *s.* = PRANCING[2].

prancer ['prɑ:nsər], *s.* cheval fringant.

prancing[1] ['prɑ:nsiŋ], *a.* (*of horse*) fringant, qui caracole; (*of pers.*) fringant, qui se pavane.

prancing[2], *s.* (*of horse*) allure fringante; caracoles *fpl*; (*of pers.*) allure dégagée.

prandial ['prændiəl], *a.* (*a*) *Med:* prandial, -aux; (*b*) *Hum:* du repas; **p. excesses,** excès *m* de table.

prang[1] [præŋ], *v.tr. F: O:* (*a*) *Av:* atteindre (son objectif); (*b*) bousiller (son avion, sa voiture).

prang[2], *s. F: O:* (*a*) bombardement *m* (d'un objectif); (*b*) collision *f*; accident *m*.

prangos ['prængɔs], *s. Bot:* prangos *m*.

prank[1] [præŋk], *s.* **1.** escapade *f*, folie *f*, frasque *f*, fredaine *f*; **to play all sorts of pranks,** faire les cent coups. **2.** tour *m*, farce *f*, plaisanterie *f*, espièglerie *f*; **to play pranks on s.o.,** jouer des tours, des farces, à qn.

prank[2]. *A:* **1.** *v.tr.* parer, orner, décorer; attifer; **field pranked with flowers,** champ (par)semé, émaillé, de fleurs; **to p. oneself out, up,** se parer de ses plus beaux atours. **2.** *v.i.* se pavaner; prendre des airs.

prankish ['præŋkiʃ], *a.* espiègle, malicieux, folâtre, capricieux.

prase [preiz], *s. Miner:* prase *m*.

praseodymium [preiziou'dimiəm], *s. Ch:* praséodyme *m*.

praseolite [preisioulait], *s. Miner:* praséolite *f*.

prat [præt], *s.* **1.** *esp. U.S: P:* derrière *m*, fesses *fpl*. **2.** *F:* **you silly p.!** espèce d'idiot, d'andouille!

prate [preit], *v.i.* (*a*) dire, débiter, des riens, des niaiseries, des absurdités (d'un air important); jaser, bavarder, jacasser; (*b*) laisser échapper des secrets; jaser.

prater ['preitər], *s.* bavard, -arde; jaseur, -euse.

pratfall ['prætfɔ:l], *s. F:* (*a*) chute *f* (sur le derrière); (*b*) échec humiliant.

praties ['preitiz], *s.pl. Dial:* (*in Ireland*) pommes *f* de terre.

pratincole ['prætiŋkoul], *s. Orn:* **(collared) p.,** glaréole *f* à collier; **black-winged p.,** glaréole à ailes noires.

pratincolous [præ'tiŋkələs], *a. Nat.Hist:* pratincole; **p. ants,** fourmis pratincoles.

prating[1] ['preitiŋ], *a.* bavard; jaseur, -euse.

prating[2], *s.* débitage *m* de niaiseries, de balivernes; jaserie *f*, bavardage *m*.

pratique [præ'ti:k], *s. Nau:* libre pratique *f*; **to have p.,** avoir libre pratique; **to admit a ship to p.,** donner libre pratique à un navire; lever la quarantaine.

prattle[1] ['prætl], *s.* (*a*) babil *m*, babillage *m* (d'enfants); gazouillis *m* (des enfants, des oiseaux); (*b*) bavardage *m*, caquet *m* (de commères).

prattle[2], *v.i.* (*a*) (*of children*) babiller; (*of birds, children, water*) gazouiller; (*b*) (*of women*) jaser, bavarder, caqueter.

prattler ['prætlər], *s.* (*a*) babillard, -arde; (*b*) jaseur, -euse; bavard, -arde.

prattling[1] ['prætliŋ], *a.* (*a*) (enfant) babillard, babillant; **p. brook,** ruisseau *m* qui gazouille; (*b*) bavard; jaseur, -euse.

prattling[2], *s.* (*a*) babillage *m*, gazouillement *m*, ramage *m*; (*b*) bavardage *m*, caquetage *m*.

prau [prau], *s. Nau:* prao *m* (malais).

prawn[1] [prɔ:n], *s. Crust:* crevette *f* rose; bouquet *m*; (grande crevette) salicoque *f*; **Dublin Bay p.,** langoustine *f*; **freshwater p.,** crevette d'eau douce; **burrowing p.,** callianasse *f*; *Cu:* **p. cocktail,** crevettes (à la) mayonnaise.

prawn[2], *v.i.* (*a*) faire la pêche à la crevette; (*b*) pêcher (le saumon) à la crevette.

prawning ['prɔ:niŋ], *s.* (*a*) pêche *f* à la crevette; (*b*) pêche du saumon avec des crevettes comme appât.

praxeology, praxiology [præksi'ɔlədʒi], *s.* praxéologie *f*.

praxinoscope ['præksinouskoup], *s. A:* praxinoscope *m*.

praxis ['præksis], *s.* **1.** (*a*) pratique *f*, coutume *f*; usage établi; (*b*) *Phil:* praxis *m*. **2.** *A:* (*a*) exemple *m*, exercice *m*, modèle *m* (de grammaire); (*b*) recueil *m* d'exemples.

Praxiteles [præk'sitəli:z]. *Pr.n.m. Hist. of Art:* Praxitèle.

pray [prei], *v.tr. & i.* **1.** prier, implorer, supplier (**s.o. to do sth.,** qn de faire qch.); **to p. (to) God,** prier Dieu; **to p. for s.o.,** prier pour qn; **he had been prayed for twice daily,** on avait fait deux fois par jour des prières à son intention; **to p. for sth.,** prier le Seigneur qu'il nous accorde qch.; prier pour avoir qch.; **to p. for peace,** prier pour la paix; **I'm praying (to God) I won't have to do it,** je prie Dieu, je supplie Dieu, que je ne serai, sois, pas obligé de le faire; **to p. for s.o.'s soul,** prier pour (le repos de) l'âme de qn; *F:* **he's past praying for,** (i) il est perdu sans retour; (ii) il est incorrigible, impossible; **it's past praying for,** c'est fichu, perdu, sans remède. **2.** *A:* **(I) p. (you),** je vous (en) prie; de grâce; **what good will that do, p.?** à quoi bon, je vous demande un peu? **p. be**

seated, donnez-vous la peine de vous asseoir; veuillez (bien) vous asseoir; *Jur:* **to p. for an injunction,** demander un arrêt de suspension.

prayer [prɛər], *s.* **1.** (*a*) prière *f* (à Dieu); oraison *f*; **the Lord's P.,** l'oraison dominicale; le Pater; **p. for the dead,** prière pour les morts; **p. for forgiveness,** déprécation *f*; **to offer (up a) p.,** faire une prière; **to say one's prayers,** faire, dire, réciter, ses prières; faire ses dévotions; **remember me in your prayers,** je me recommande à vos prières; **to be at one's prayers,** être en prières; **to be at prayers,** être à la prière (en commun); *Ch. of Eng:* **Morning P., Evening P.,** office *m* du matin, du soir; **the Book of Common P., the P. Book,** le rituel de l'Église anglicane; **p. book,** livre *m* de prières; livre d'office; **family prayers were at nine o'clock,** la prière en commun se faisait à neuf heures; *Sch:* **prayers,** la prière du matin en commun; **p. meeting,** réunion *f* pour prières en commun; office de la semaine; **p. mat,** tapis *m* à prières; **p. mill, wheel,** moulin *m* à prières (des Bouddhistes); (*b*) *A:* demande instante; prière; **he did it at my p.,** il l'a fait à ma prière. **2.** (*thg prayed for*) **his p. was granted,** sa prière fut exaucée.

prayerful ['prɛəf(u)l], *a.* porté à la prière; pieux; dévot.

praying[1] ['preiiŋ], *a.* en prières; *Ent:* **p. mantis,** mante religieuse; prie-Dieu *m inv.*

praying[2], *s.* prière *f*, supplication *f*.

pre- [pri(:)], *pref.* (*a*) pré-; (*b*) avant, antérieur, préalable; (faire qch.) d'avance, au préalable.

preach [pri:tʃ], *v.* prêcher. **1.** *v.i.* prononcer le sermon; **to p. to the converted,** prêcher un converti; **it's no use preaching to a hungry man,** ventre affamé n'a pas d'oreilles; **to p. against s.o.,** prêcher contre qn; **to p. at s.o.,** faire des allusions à qn (dans un sermon); diriger un sermon contre qn (qui est présent, mais sans nommer personne); *F:* **he's always preaching at me,** il est toujours à me sermonner. **2.** *v.tr.* (*a*) **to p. a sermon,** prononcer un sermon; (*b*) **to p. the gospel,** annoncer l'Évangile; **to p. a new doctrine,** se faire l'évangéliste d'une doctrine nouvelle.

preacher ['pri:tʃər], *s.* **1.** (*a*) prédicateur *m*; **he's a poor p.,** il prêche mal; ses sermons sont peu intéressants; (*b*) *Pej:* prêcheur, -euse; (*c*) *U.S: F: O:* pasteur *m*. **2.** *B:* **the P.,** l'Ecclésiaste *m*.

preachify ['pri:tʃifai], *v.i. F:* sermonner; faire de la morale.

preaching[1] ['pri:tʃiŋ], *a. Ecc:* qui prêche; prédicateur; *Hist:* **P. friar,** frère prêcheur; religieux *m* de l'ordre de Saint-Dominique.

preaching[2], *s.* **1.** prédication *f*; **vocation for p.,** vocation *f* pour la chaire; *Hist:* **the p. of the Cross,** la prédication de la Croix. **2.** *Pej:* prêcherie *f*; prêchi-prêcha *m*.

pre-acquaint [pri:ə'kweint], *v.tr.* informer (qn) au préalable, d'avance (**with,** de).

pre-acquaintance [pri:ə'kweintəns], *s.* connaissance *f* préalable (de qch.).

preactivation [pri:ækti'veiʃ(ə)n], *s. Mil:* dispositions *fpl*, mesures *fpl*, préalables à la mise sur pied (d'une unité).

preadamic [pri:ə'dæmik], *a.*, **preadamite** [pri:'ædəmait], *a.* & *s.*, **preadamitic** [pri:ædə'mitik], *a.* préadamite (*mf*).

preadamitism [pri:'ædəmaitizm], *s. Hist:* préadamisme *m*.

preadaptation [pri:ædæp'teiʃ(ə)n], *s. Biol:* préadaptation *f*.

preadmission [pri:əd'miʃ(ə)n], *s. Mch:* admission prématurée, anticipée (de la vapeur, etc.).

preadmonition [pri:ædmə'niʃ(ə)n], *s.* avis *m*, avertissement *m*, préalable.

preadolescence [pri:ædə'les(ə)ns], *s.* préadolescence *f*.

preadolescent [pri:ædə'les(ə)nt]. **1.** *a.* (problèmes, etc.) de la préadolescence. **2.** *s.* préadolescent, -ente.

preamble[1] ['pri:æmbl], *s.* **1.** (*a*) préambule *m*; introduction *f*, préface *f*; (*b*) préliminaires *mpl* (d'un traité, etc.). **2.** *Jur:* (*a*) exposé *m* des motifs (d'un projet de loi); **p. of a decree,** les attendus *m* d'un arrêt; (*b*) exposé (d'un brevet).

preamble[2]. **1.** *v.tr.* rédiger le préambule, l'exposé des motifs de (qch.). **2.** *v.i.* faire des observations préliminaires.

preamp ['pri:æmp], *s. Rec: F:* préampli *m*.

preamplification [pri:æmplifi'keiʃ(ə)n], *s. Ph: Elcs:* préamplification *f*.

preamplifier [pri:'æmplifaiər], *s. W.Tel:* préamplificateur *m*.

preanaesthesia [pri:ænəs'θi:ziə], *s. Med:* préanesthésie *f*.

preanaesthetic [pri:ænəs'θetik], *s.* préanesthésique *m*.

preanalysis [pri:ə'nælisis], *s. Cmptr: etc:* analyse *f* préparatoire.

preapprehension [pri:æpri'henʃ(ə)n], *s.* **1.** appréhension *f*, pressentiment *m* (**of,** de). **2.** idée préconçue.

prearrange [pri:ə'rein(d)ʒ], *v.tr.* arranger au préalable, d'avance.

prearrangement [pri:ə'rein(d)ʒmənt], *s.* **1.** arrangement *m* préalable; disposition(s) *f*(*pl*) préalable(s). **2.** accord *m*, entente *f*, préalable.

preassembled [pri:ə'sembld], *a. Const: etc:* préfabriqué; tout monté.

preatomic [pri:ə'tɔmik], *a.* préatomique; **the p. age,** l'ère *f*, la période, préatomique; **p. weapons,** armes *f* préatomiques.

prebend ['prebənd], *s. Ecc:* **1.** prébende *f*. **2.** = PREBENDARY.

prebendal [pri'bendl], *a. Ecc:* attaché à la prébende; **p. stall,** stalle canoniale; **p. services,** offices canoniaux.

prebendary ['prebənd(ə)ri], *s. Ecc:* prébendier *m*, chanoine *m*.

prebilling [pri:'biliŋ], *s. Cmptr:* préfacturation *f*.

Precambrian [pri:'kæmbriən], *a.* & *s. Geol:* précambrien (*m*).

precancerosis [pri:kænsə'rousis], *s. Med:* état *m* précancéreux, conditions précancéreuses.

precancerous [pri:'kænsərəs], *a. Med:* précancéreux.

precapitalist(ic) [pri:kæpitə'list(ik)], *a. Pol.Ec:* précapitaliste.

precarious [pri'kɛəriəs], *a.* **1.** *Jur:* (possession *f*, tenure *f*) précaire; **to enjoy the p. use of sth.,** jouir de qch. par précaire. **2.** (*a*) précaire, incertain; **to make a p. living,** gagner sa vie précairement; **p. inference,** conclusion douteuse, risquée; (*b*) **p. life,** vie périlleuse.

precariously [pri'kɛəriəsli], *adv.* précairement; d'une manière précaire.

precariousness [pri'kɛəriəsnis], *s.* précarité *f*, incertitude *f* (dans la possession); état *m* précaire (de la santé).

precarium [pri'kɛəriəm], *s. Jur:* précaire *m*.

precast[1] ['pri:kɑ:st], *a. Const: etc:* (*of concrete*) prémoulé.

precast[2], *v.tr. Const: etc:* prémouler (du béton).

precative ['prekətiv], *a. Gram:* (mot) précatif.

precatory ['prekətəri], *a.* **1.** *Gram:* précatif. **2.** *Jur:* **p. words,** mots *m* d'où l'on peut déduire la volonté du testateur; **p. trust,** legs précatif.

precaution [pri'kɔ:ʃ(ə)n], *s.* (*a*) précaution *f*; **to take precautions against sth.,** prendre ses précautions, se précautionner, se prémunir, contre qch.; obvier, parer, à qch.; **precautions to be taken to prevent accidents,** précautions à prendre pour éviter les accidents; **to take due precautions, every p.,** prendre toutes précautions utiles; **air-raid precautions,** défense passive; (*b*) prévoyance *f*; **as a p., by way of p.,** par mesure de précaution, de prévoyance, de prudence; à titre de précaution; par précaution, par prudence.

precautionary [pri'kɔ:ʃən(ə)ri], *a.* de précaution, préventif; **p. measures,** mesures *f* de précaution, mesures préventives (**against,** contre).

precede [pri'si:d], *v.tr.* **1.** (*a*) précéder; **the calm that precedes the storm,** le calme qui précède la tempête; **the advanced guard precedes the main body (of troops),** l'avant-garde *f* précède le gros de l'armée; **formalities that p. the debate,** formalités *f* préalables aux débats; **for a week preceding this occasion,** pendant une semaine avant cette occasion; (*b*) faire précéder; **the conference was preceded by a reception,** une réception a eu lieu avant la conférence. **2.** avoir le pas, la préséance, sur (qn).

precedence ['presidəns], *s.* (*a*) préséance *f*; priorité *f*; **to have, take, p. of s.o.,** avoir le pas, la préséance, sur qn; prendre le pas sur qn; avoir l'honneur du pas sur qn; **ladies take p.,** les dames passent avant; **to contend for p. with s.o.,** disputer le pas à qn; **to yield p. to s.o.,** céder le pas à qn; s'effacer devant qn; **duty that takes p. of all others,** devoir *m* qui prime tout; (*b*) (ordre *m* de) priorité; *Cmptr:* **p. table,** table *f* des priorités; *Mil:* **p. of troops,** ordre de bataille; (*c*) droit *m* de priorité (pour la proposition d'une loi, etc.); degré *m* de priorité (d'un message, etc.).

precedent[1] ['presidənt], *s.* **1.** précédent *m*; **to create a p.,** créer un précédent; **this constitutes a p.,** ceci constitue un précédent; **there's no p. for it,** il n'y en a point d'exemple; **according to p.,** suivant la coutume; conformément à la tradition. **2.** *Jur:* décision *f* judiciaire faisant jurisprudence; **to set p.,** faire jurisprudence; **precedents of a case,** jurisprudence *f* d'un cas de droit.

precedent[2] [pri'si:dənt], *a. A:* précédent.

precedential [presi'denʃ(ə)l], *a.* **1.** qui constitue un précédent. **2.** préliminaire.

preceding [pri'si:diŋ], *a.* précédent; **the p. day,** la veille; le jour précédent; **the p. year,** l'année d'auparavant; **in the p. article,** dans l'article ci-dessus.

precentor [pri(:)'sentər], *s. Ecc:* **1.** (*a*) grand-chantre *m*, *pl.* grands-chantres; premier chantre; (*b*) maître *m* de chapelle. **2.** *A:* chef *m* du chœur (dans l'église réformée).

precentorship [pri(:)'sentəʃip], *s. Ecc:* maîtrise *f*, préchantrerie *f*.

precept ['pri:sept], *s.* **1.** précepte *m*; commandement *m* (de Dieu); **example is better than p.,** l'exemple vaut mieux que le précepte. **2.** (*a*) ordre *m* de convocation; (*b*) *Jur:* mandat *m* d'amener, d'arrêt, de dépôt; (*c*) *Adm:* (i) sommation *f* d'avoir à payer; (ii) feuille *f* d'impôt, de contribution.

preceptor [pri'septər], *s.* précepteur, -trice.

preceptorial [pri:sep'tɔ:riəl], *a.* préceptoral, -aux; (fonctions) de précepteur, -trice.

preceptorship [pri'septəʃip], *s.* préceptorat *m*.

preceptory [pri'septəri], *s. Hist:* = commanderie *f* de l'Ordre du Temple.

preceptress [pri'septris], *s.f.* préceptrice.

precession [pri'seʃ(ə)n], *s. Astr:* précession *f* (des équinoxes).

precessional [pri'seʃən(ə)l], *a. Astr:* de précession.

pre-checking [pri:'tʃekiŋ], *s. Cmptr:* précontrôle *m*.

pre-Christian [pri:'kristjən]. **1.** *a.* préchrétien. **2.** *s.* préchrétien, -ienne.

precinct ['pri:siŋkt], *s.* **1.** (*a*) enceinte *f*, enclos *m*; **pupils are forbidden to leave the school precincts,** il est interdit aux élèves de sortir; (*b*) **precincts,** pourtour *m* (d'une cathédrale, etc.); environs *mpl* (d'un endroit); (*c*) **pedestrian p.,** zone piétonnière; **shopping p.,** centre commercial (fermé à la circulation automobile). **2.** limite *f* (du pourtour). **3.** *U.S:* circonscription électorale; circonscription administrative urbaine.

preciosity [preʃi'ɔsiti, -si-], *s. Lit:* préciosité *f*.

precious ['preʃəs]. **1.** *a.* (*a*) précieux; de grand prix, de grande valeur; **p. blood,** précieux sang (de Notre Seigneur); **p. metals,** métaux précieux; **p. stones,** pierres précieuses; **p. garnet, opal,** grenat *m*, opale *f*, noble; **my p. child,** mon enfant chéri; **this privilege is p. to him,** ce privilège lui est précieux; **this ring is p. to me because of its associations,** cette bague m'est précieuse pour les souvenirs qu'elle évoque; **we wasted a lot of p. time,** nous avons perdu beaucoup d'heures précieuses; (*b*) *F:* fameux, fier, beau; **a p. pair,** une belle paire (de vauriens, etc.); **he's a p. fool,** c'est un fameux imbécile, un bel idiot; **she's always worrying about her p. health,** elle s'inquiète toujours de sa petite santé; **you and your p. dictionary!** toi et ton sacré dictionnaire! **he thinks a p. sight too much of himself,** il est trop fier de sa petite personne; il est par trop suffisant; (*c*) *Lit: etc:* (style) précieux, affecté, (trop) recherché. **2.** *s.* (*term of endearment*) **my p.!** mon trésor! mon amour! ma vie! **3.** *adv. F:* **there are p. few of them,** il n'y en a guère; **there's p. little hope,** il n'y a guère d'espoir; **you'd better take p. good care of it!** tu en feras rudement bien soin! **it's p. cold,** il fait diablement, rudement, froid.

preciously ['preʃəsli], *adv.* (*a*) précieusement; (*b*) *F:* fameusement, joliment, extrêmement; (*c*) *Lit: etc:* avec préciosité, avec affectation; d'un style précieux.

preciousness ['preʃəsnis], *s.* **1.** haute valeur (de qch.). **2.** *Lit: etc:* préciosité *f*.

precipice ['presipis], *s.* escarpement abrupt; paroi *f* à pic; **to fall over a p.,** tomber dans un précipice; **to rescue s.o. from the edge of a p.,** sauver qn sur le bord d'un précipice, de l'abîme.

precipitability [prisipitə'biliti], *s. Ch: Ph:* précipitabilité *f*.

precipitable [pri'sipitəbl], *a. Ch: Ph:* précipitable.

precipitance, precipitancy [pri'sipitəns, -ənsi], *s.* (*a*) précipitation *f*, empressement; (*b*) précipitation, manque *m* de réflexion, irréflexion *f*.

precipitant [pri'sipitənt], *s. Ch: Ph:* précipitant *m*.

precipitate[1] [pri'sipiteit], *s.* **1.** *Ch:* précipité *m*; **electrolytic p.,** précipité électrolytique; *Pharm:* **white p.,** mercure précipité blanc; **to form a p.,** (se) précipiter. **2.** *Meteor:* eau *f* de condensation.

precipitate[2] [pri'sipitət], *a.* **1.** précipité, fait à la hâte; **p. flight,** fuite précipitée. **2.** précipité, trop empressé; irréfléchi; **if only I had been less p.,** si j'avais réfléchi avant d'agir.

precipitate[3] [pri'sipiteit]. **1.** *v.tr.* (*a*) précipiter (qn, qch.) (dans qch.); (*b*) *Ch:* précipiter (une substance solide); *Meteor:* condenser, faire tomber (la rosée, etc.); (*c*) accélérer, hâter, précipiter (un événement); **to p. matters,** brusquer les choses. **2.** *v.i. Ch: Ph:* (se) précipiter; *Meteor:* se condenser; (*of salt, etc.*) **to p. out,** se séparer par précipitation.

precipitated [pri'sipiteitid], *a. Ch: etc:* précipité.

precipitately [pri'sipitətli], *adv.* **1.** précipitamment, avec précipitation, en toute hâte. **2.** avec précipitation, sans réfléchir.

precipitating [pri'sipiteitiŋ], *a.* **p. agent,** précipitant *m*.

precipitation [prisipi'teiʃ(ə)n], *s.* **1.** (*a*) *Ch: Ph:*

précipitation *f*; **p. by means of acids, with barium chloride,** précipitation au moyen d'acides, par le chlorure de barium; **electric, electrostatic, p.,** précipitation électrique, électrostatique; **anodic p.,** précipitation à l'anode; *Atom.Ph:* **p. with carrier,** précipitation avec entraîneur; **settling p.,** précipitation, déposition *f*, sédimentation *f* (d'un résidu); **p. hardening,** durcissement structural; **p. box, tank, vat,** caisse *f*, bac *m*, cuve *f*, de précipitation; (*b*) *Meteor:* précipitation; **p. in the form of snow,** chute *f* de neige; **annual p.,** précipitation annuelle. **2. to act with p.,** agir avec précipitation, précipitamment; (i) montrer trop de hâte; (ii) manquer de reflexion.

precipitator [pri'sipiteitər], *s. Ch:* **1.** (*a*) précipitateur *m*; (*b*) précipitant *m*. **2.** bac *m*, cuve *f*, de précipitation.

precipitin [pri'sipitin], *s. Bio-Ch:* précipitine *f*.

precipitous [pri'sipitəs], *a.* **1.** escarpé, abrupt; à pic. **2.** précipité.

precipitously [pri'sipitəsli], *adv.* **1.** (monter, descendre) à pic. **2.** précipitamment.

précis[1], *pl.* **précis** ['preisi:, 'preisi:z], *s.* précis *m*, analyse *f*, résumé *m*, abrégé *m*; **to make a p. of a document,** analyser un dossier; **I'll give you a p. of what he said,** je vous ferai un résumé de ce qu'il a dit; *Sch:* **p. writing,** compte-rendu *m* de lecture.

précis[2], *v.tr.* faire un précis, une analyse, un résumé, un compte-rendu, de (qch.).

precise[1] [pri'sais], *a.* **1.** (*a*) précis, exact; **to give p. orders,** donner des ordres précis; **p. work,** travail précis, toujours exact; **p. movements,** mouvements exécutés avec précision; *Equit:* mouvements écoutés; **(in order) to be p.,** pour préciser; (*b*) **at the p. moment when . . .,** au moment précis où . . .; juste au moment où . . .. **2.** (*of pers.*) méticuleux; formaliste, pointilleux, scrupuleux; rigide, rigoriste; **he's very p.,** (i) il est très formaliste; (ii) il est extrêmement méticuleux, d'une exactitude remarquable.

precise[2] [pri'saiz], *v.tr.* préciser.

precisely [pri'saisli], *adv.* **1.** (*a*) avec précision; **to state the facts p.,** préciser les faits; **that's p. the truth,** c'est la plus stricte vérité; (*b*) **at six (o'clock) p.,** à six heures précises; **two minutes to three p.,** trois heures moins deux, deux heures cinquante-huit, heure précise. **2.** précisément! parfaitement! exactement!

preciseness [pri'saisnis], *s.* **1.** précision *f*. **2.** (*a*) méticulosité *f*; (*b*) formalisme *m*.

precisian [pri'siʒən], *s.* **1.** formaliste *mf*. **2.** *Rel.H:* rigoriste *mf*.

precisianism [pri'siʒənizm], *s.* **1.** formalisme *m*. **2.** *Rel.H:* rigorisme *m*.

precision [pri'siʒ(ə)n], *s.* **1.** précision *f*, exactitude *f*, justesse *f*; **lack of p.,** manque *m* de précision; imprécision *f*; **with mathematical p.,** avec une précision (toute) mathématique; *Ball:* **p. of a firearm,** précision d'une arme à feu; **lateral p.,** précision en direction; **p. range,** précision en portée; *attrib.* **p. work, p. engineering,** travail *m*, mécanique *f*, de précision; **p. instruments,** instruments *m* de précision. **2.** précision; méticulosité *f*; rigorisme *m*.

precisionist [pri'siʒənist], *s.* puriste *mf*.

preclude [pri'klu:d], *v.tr.* empêcher, prévenir, exclure (d'avance), écarter (une objection, un malentendu, etc.); **in order to p. any misunderstanding,** pour prévenir tout malentendu.

precocial [pri:'kouʃəl], *a. Orn:* nidifuge.

precocious [pri'kouʃəs], *a.* (*of plant*) précoce, hâtif; **p. child,** enfant précoce.

precociously [pri'kouʃəsli], *adv.* précocement; avec précocité.

precociousness, precocity [pri'kouʃəsnis, -'kɔsiti], *s.* précocité *f*.

precoded [pri:'koudid], *a. Cmptr:* pré-programmé.

precognition [pri:kɔg'niʃ(ə)n], *s.* **1.** *Phil: etc:* préconnaissance *f*; connaissance anticipée, antérieure. **2.** *Jur: Scot:* (*a*) instruction *f* (d'une affaire criminelle); interrogatoire *m* préliminaire (des témoins); (*b*) déposition *f* d'un témoin (à l'instruction).

precognosce [pri:kɔg'nɔs], *v.tr. Jur: Scot:* instruire (une affaire criminelle); interroger (les témoins) à l'instruction.

pre-Columbian [pri:kə'lʌmbiən], *a.* précolombien.

precombustion [pri:kəm'bʌstʃ(ə)n], *s.* précombustion *f*; **p. engine,** moteur Diesel à chambre de précombustion; **p. chamber,** antichambre *f* de combustion.

preconceive [pri:kən'si:v], *v.tr.* préconcevoir; **preconceived idea,** idée préconçue.

preconception [pri:kən'sepʃ(ə)n], *s.* **1.** préconception *f*. **2.** (*a*) idée, opinion, préconçue; (*b*) préjugé *m*; **to free oneself from all preconceptions,** se libérer de toute opinion préconçue, de tout préjugé.

preconceptual [pri:kɔn'septjuəl], *a. Phil:* préconceptif.

preconcerted [pri:kən'sə:tid], *a.* convenu, arrangé, concerté, d'avance; **p. plan,** plan arrêté.

precondemn [pri:kən'dem], *v.tr.* condamner d'avance.

preconization [pri:kənai'zeiʃ(ə)n], *s. R.C.Ch:* préconisation *f* (d'un nouvel évêque).

preconize ['pri:kənaiz], *v.tr.* **1.** *A: & Lit:* préconiser, vanter, louer (qn, qch.). **2.** sommer (les membres d'un comité, etc.) nominativement. **3.** *R.C.Ch:* préconiser (un nouvel évêque).

preconscious [pri:'kɔnʃəs], *a. & s. Psy:* préconscient (*m*).

preconsciously [pri:'kɔnʃəsli], *adv. Psy:* de manière préconsciente.

preconsonantal [pri:kɔnsə'næntəl], *a. Ling:* préconsonantique.

preconstruction [pri:kən'strʌkʃ(ə)n], *s.* préconstruction *f*.

precontract[1] [pri:'kɔntrækt], *s.* contrat antérieur, préalable (au mariage, etc.).

precontract [pri:kən'trækt], *v.tr.* **1.** engager (qn) par un contrat préalable, antérieur (au mariage, etc.). **2.** contracter (une habitude) au préalable.

precook [pri:'kuk], *v.tr.* précuire.

precool [pri:əku:l], *v.tr.* préréfrigérer.

precooler [pri:'ku:lər], *s.* refroidisseur *m* préliminaire; préréfroidisseur *m*.

precooling [pri:'ku:liŋ], *s.* préréfrigération *f*.

precordial [pri:'kɔ:diəl], *a. Anat: Med:* précordial, -aux.

precordialgia [pri:kɔ:di'ældʒiə], *s. Med:* précordialgie *f*.

precursive [pri'kə:siv], *a.* = PRECURSORY.

precursor [pri'kə:sər], *s.* précurseur *m*; devancier, -ière; avant-coureur *m*, *pl.* avant-coureurs; avant-courrier, -ière, *pl.* avant-courriers, -ières.

precursory [pri'kə:səri], *a.* (*a*) précurseur; (symptôme) avant-coureur, *pl.* avant-coureurs; (*b*) **p. remarks,** observations *f* préliminaires.

predacious [pri'deiʃəs], *a.* = PREDATORY.

predacity [pri'dæsiti], *s.* instinct, caractère, prédateur, de rapine, de bête de proie.

predate [pri:'deit], *v.tr.* **1.** antidater (un document). **2.** venir avant (un fait historique, etc.).

predation [pri'deiʃ(ə)n], *s.* action prédatrice; déprédation *f*, pillage *m*, rapine *f*.

predator ['predətər], *s.* (*a*) prédateur, -trice; bête *f* de proie; (*b*) (*pers.*) pillard, -arde; pilleur, -euse; ravageur, -euse.

predatory ['predət(ə)ri], *a.* prédateur, -trice; (animal) rapace; (bête) de proie; (*of pers.*) pillard; **p. instincts,** instincts *m* de pillage, de rapine, de bête de proie; **he has p. eyes,** il a les yeux d'un oiseau de proie.

predecease[1] [pri:di'si:s], *s.* prédécès *m*.

predecease[2], *v.tr.* prédécéder, mourir avant (qn).

predeceaser [pri:di'si:sər], *s. Jur:* prémourant *m*.

predecessor ['pri:disesər], *s.* **1.** prédécesseur *m*; devancier, -ière (d'un dignitaire, etc.); **scheme that is no improvement on its p.,** projet qui n'est nullement supérieur à celui qui l'a devancé. **2.** ancêtre *m*; aïeul *m*, *pl.* aïeux.

predefine [pri:di'fain], *v.tr.* prédéfinir.

predella [pri'delə], *s. Art:* prédelle *f*.

predestinate[1] [pri:'destineit], *a. & s.* prédestiné, -ée.

predestinate[2], *v.tr.* prédestiner.

predestination [pri:desti'neiʃ(ə)n], *s.* prédestination *f*.

predestinator [pri:'destineitər], *s.* prédestinateur *m*.

predestine [pri:'destin], *v.tr.* destiner d'avance (**to,** à); *Theol:* prédestiner (à); *Theol:* **predestined to damnation,** prédestiné à l'enfer.

predeterminate [pri:di'tə:minət], *a. Theol: etc:* prédéterminé.

predetermination [pri:ditəmi'neiʃ(ə)n], *s.* prédétermination *f*.

predetermine [pri:di'tə:min], *v.tr.* **1.** déterminer, arrêter, d'avance. **2.** *Theol: Phil:* prédéterminer; préordonner; **motives that p. man's actions,** mobiles *m* qui (pré)déterminent les actions de l'homme.

predeterminism [pri:di'tə:minizm], *s. Phil:* prédéterminisme *m*.

predetonation [pri:detə'neiʃ(ə)n], *s.* détonation prématurée (d'une bombe, etc.).

predial ['pri:diəl], *a.* (*of tithe, servitude*) prédial, -aux; réel; (*of property*) foncier; *Hist:* **p. serf,** serf attaché à la glèbe.

prediastolic [pri:daiəs'tɔlik], *a. Physiol:* prédiastolique.

predicable [pri'dikəbl]. *Log:* **1.** *a.* prédicable. **2.** *s.* catégorème *m*; **the five predicables,** les universaux *m*.

predicament [pri'dikəmənt], *s.* **1.** *Phil: Log:* prédicament *m*, catégorie *f*, catégorème *m*. **2.** situation difficile, fâcheuse; malheureuse conjoncture; **to be in an awkward p.,** être en mauvaise passe; *Iron:* **we're in a fine p.!** nous voilà dans de beaux draps! nous voilà propres! nous voilà dans une jolie passe! **I'm in the same p.,** je suis logé à la même enseigne; nous pouvons nous donner la main.

predicant ['predikənt]. *Ecc:* (*a*) *a.* (frère) prêcheur; (*b*) *s.* prédicant *m*.

predicate[1] ['predikət], *s. Log: Gram:* prédicat *m*; attribut *m*.

predicate[2] ['predikeit], *v.tr.* affirmer.

predication [predi'keiʃ(ə)n], *s.* **1.** *A:* (*a*) prédication *f* (de l'Évangile, etc.); (*b*) sermon *m*. **2.** *Log:* affirmation *f*, assertion *f* (de qch. concernant le sujet); *Gram:* **verb of incomplete p.,** verbe attributif.

predicative [pri'dikətiv], *a.* affirmatif; *Gram: Log:* prédicatif.

predicatory [predi'keitəri], *a. Ecc:* (frère) prêcheur.

predict [pri'dikt], *v.* **1.** (*a*) *v.tr.* prédire (un événement); (*b*) *v.i.* prophétiser. **2.** *v.tr.* (*a*) *Artil:* calculer à l'avance (les éléments de tir); **predicted firing,** (i) tir calculé à l'avance; tir d'après la carte; (ii) tir au passage; (*b*) *Ball:* extrapoler; **to p. where the missile will have to point,** extrapoler la direction dans laquelle il faut pointer le missile; **to p. a fuse,** régler, extrapoler, une fusée.

predictable [pri'diktəbl], *a.* qui peut être prédit, annoncé d'avance; **their victory was anything but p.,** personne n'aurait jamais pensé qu'ils remporteraient la victoire.

predictably [pri'diktəbli], *adv.* **the Labour party p. won the seat,** le parti travailliste a, comme de raison, comme on s'y attendait, remporté la victoire; **p. the time will come when . . .,** le jour viendra à coup sûr, j'en suis sûr, où . . ..

predicting [pri'diktiŋ], *s.* **1.** prédiction *f* (d'un événement). **2.** (*a*) *Artil:* calcul *m* à l'avance (des éléments de tir); tir *m* d'après la carte; (*b*) *Ball:* extrapolation *f*.

prediction [pri'dikʃ(ə)n], *s.* **1.** prédiction *f* (d'un événement). **2.** *Ball:* extrapolation *f*; **p. data,** (i) éléments extrapolés; (ii) paramètres *m* de tir; **gunnery p. calculation,** élaboration *f* des paramètres de tir. **3.** *Mth:* **predictions,** valeurs théoriques calculées.

predictive [pri'diktiv], *a.* prophétique; prédictif.

predictor [pri'diktər], *s.* **1.** (*pers.*) prédiseur, -euse (d'un événement); prophète, prophétesse. **2.** *Ball:* pointeur *m* automatique; télépointeur *m*; poste *m* de conduite de tir.

predigest [pri:dai'dʒest], *v.tr.* prédigérer.

predigested [pri:dai'dʒestid], *a.* prédigéré.

predigestion [pri:dai'dʒestjən], *s.* prédigestion *f*.

predilection [pri:di'lekʃ(ə)n], *s.* prédilection *f*.

predispose [pri:dis'pouz], *v.tr.* prédisposer; (*a*) **to p. s.o. in s.o.'s favour,** prédisposer qn en faveur de qn; **to p. s.o. to do sth.,** incliner qn à faire qch.; (*b*) **this life had predisposed him to gout,** cette vie l'avait prédisposé à la goutte.

predisposition [pri:dispə'ziʃ(ə)n], *s.* prédisposition *f*; **p. to arthritis,** prédisposition à l'arthritisme.

predistillation [pri:disti'leiʃ(ə)n], *s. Ch:* prédistillation *f*; **p. column,** colonne *f* de prédistillation.

prednisolone [pred'nisəloun], *s. Pharm:* prednisolone *f*.

prednisone ['prednisoun], *s. Pharm:* prednisone *f*.

predominance [pri'dɔminəns], *s.* prédominance *f*.

predominant [pri'dɔminənt], *a.* prédominant, prévalent.

predominantly [pri'dɔminəntli], *adv.* d'une manière prédominante; **this race is p. blue-eyed,** chez cette race les yeux bleus prédominent.

predominate [pri'dɔmineit], *v.i.* **1.** prédominer; **in business interest predominates,** dans les affaires c'est l'intérêt qui prédomine, qui l'emporte; **men in whom good predominates over evil,** hommes chez qui le bon l'emporte sur le mauvais. **2.** l'emporter par le nombre, par la quantité; prédominer.

predominating [pri'dɔmineitiŋ], *a.* prédominant.

predorsal [pri'dɔ:s(ə)l], *a. Anat:* prédorsal, -aux.

predynastic [pri:di'næstik], *a.* prédynastique.

pre-elect [pri:i'lekt], *v.tr.* **1.** *Ecc:* prédestiner au salut. **2.** choisir d'avance.

pre-election [pri:i'lekʃ(ə)n]. **1.** *s.* (*a*) *Ecc:* prédestination *f* (au salut); (*b*) *A:* élection anticipée. **2.** *a. Pol:* préélectoral, -aux; antérieur aux élections; **p.-e. campaign,** campagne préélectorale; **p.-e. promises,** promesses préélectorales, de candidature.

pre-eminence [pri'eminəns], *s.* prééminence *f*.

pre-eminent [pri'eminənt], *a.* (*a*) prééminent; (*b*) remarquable.

pre-eminently [pri'eminəntli], *adv.* (*a*) d'une manière prééminente; à un degré prééminent; **he is p. a jurist,** il est juriste avant tout, en premier lieu; (*b*) souverainement, remarquablement, extraordinairement, par excellence.

pre-emphasis [pri'emfəsis], *s. Ph:* expansion *f* des contrastes; *Elcs: etc:* préaccentuation *f*.

pre-empt [pri'em(p)t], *v.tr.* **1.** (*a*) acquérir (une terre) en usant d'un droit de préemption; (*b*) *U.S:* occuper (un terrain) afin d'obtenir un droit d'achat préférentiel. **2.** acquérir (un monopole, etc.) au préalable, d'avance. **3.** *v.i. Cards:* (*at bridge*) faire une ouverture préventive.

pre-emption [pri'em(p)ʃ(ə)n], *s. Jur:* (droit *m* de) préemption *f*; **to obtain by p.-e.,** préempter (un terrain, un privilège, etc.).

pre-emptive [pri'em(p)tiv], *a.* **1. p.-e. right,** droit *m* de préemption. **2.** *Cards:* (*at bridge*) **p.-e. bid,** appel élevé (pour s'assurer l'enchère); ouverture préventive.

pre-emptor [pri'em(p)tər], *s.* acquéreur, -euse, en vertu d'un droit de préemption.

preen [pri:n], *v.tr.* (*a*) (*of bird*) lisser, nettoyer (ses plumes) avec le bec; (*attrib. use*) **p. gland,** glande uropygienne; (*b*) (*of pers.*) **to p. oneself,** (i) faire soigneusement sa toilette; se faire beau, belle; (ii) prendre un petit air satisfait; (*of woman*) faire ses grâces.

pre-establish [pri:is'tæbliʃ], *v.tr.* préétablir; *Phil:* **pre-established harmony,** harmonie préétablie.

pre-exist [pri:ig'zist], *v.i.* préexister.

pre-existence [pri:ig'zist(ə)ns], *s.* préexistence *f.*

pre-existent [pri:ig'zist(ə)nt], *a.* préexistant; préexistentiel.

prefab ['pri:fæb], *s. F:* maison préfabriquée; préfabriqué *m.*

prefabricate [pri'fæbrikeit], *v.tr.* préfabriquer; **prefabricated house,** maison préfabriquée.

prefabrication [prifæbri'keiʃ(ə)n], *s.* préfabrication *f.*

preface[1] ['prefəs], *s.* **1.** préface *f*; avant-propos *m inv* (d'un livre); **to write a p. to, for, s.o.'s work,** préfacer l'ouvrage de qn. **2.** introduction *f*, exorde *m*, préambule *m* (d'un discours). **3.** *Ecc:* préface (precédant le canon); **proper prefaces,** préfaces propres.

preface[2], *v.tr.* **1.** écrire une préface pour (un ouvrage); préfacer (un ouvrage). **2.** (*a*) préluder à (un discours); **to p. one's remarks with an anecdote,** faire précéder ses remarques d'une anecdote; débuter par une anecdote; (*b*) **the events that prefaced the crisis,** les événements qui ont précédé la crise, qui ont préludé à la crise.

prefacer, prefacist ['prefəsər, -sist], *s.* préfacier *m.*

prefatory ['prefətəri], *a.* (remarque) préliminaire, d'introduction; (page(s)) liminaire(s), servant d'avant-propos; **a few p. words,** quelques mots d'introduction, à titre de préface.

prefect ['pri:fekt], *s.* **1.** *Rom.Ant: Fr.Adm:* préfet *m.* **2.** (*in Catholic colleges*) **p. of discipline,** préfet de discipline. **3.** *Sch:* élève choisi parmi les grands pour aider au maintien de la discipline; "préfet."

prefector(i)al [pri'fektərəl, pri:fek'tɔriəl], *a. Rom.Ant: Fr.Adm:* préfectoral, -aux.

prefectship ['pri:fektʃip], *s. Rom.Ant: Fr.Adm:* préfecture *f.*

prefecture ['pri:fektjər], *s.* **1.** *Rom.Ant: Fr.Adm:* préfecture *f.* **2.** *R.C.Ch:* **p. apostolic,** préfecture apostolique.

prefer [pri'fə:r], *v.tr.* (**preferred**) **1.** nommer, élever (qn à un emploi, à une dignité); **to be preferred to an office,** être promu à un emploi. **2.** émettre (une prétention); intenter (une action en justice); **to p. a complaint,** déposer, porter, plainte (**against,** contre); **to p. a petition,** adresser une pétition. **3. to p. sth. to sth.,** préférer qch. à qch.; aimer mieux qch. que qch.; **I p. sitting to standing,** j'aime mieux être assis que de rester debout; **I p. meat well done,** je préfère la viande bien cuite; **I p. that nothing should be said about it,** j'aimerais mieux qu'on n'en dise rien; **I would p. to go without rather than pay so dearly for it,** j'aimerais mieux m'en passer que de le payer si cher.

preferable ['prefərəbl], *a.* préférable; **it would be p. to establish a guarantee fund,** il serait préférable que l'on constituât un fonds de garantie.

preferably ['prefə'rəbli], *adv.* préférablement, par préférence, de préférence.

preference ['prefər(ə)ns], *s.* **1.** préférence *f*; **what is your p.?** que préférez-vous? lequel, laquelle, préférez-vous? **my p. is for beef rather than lamb,** je préfère le bœuf à l'agneau; j'aime mieux le bœuf que l'agneau; **to give sth. p. (over sth.),** donner, accorder, la préférence à qch. (sur qch.); **in p. to . . .,** de préférence, préférablement, à . . .; **in p. to any other,** de, par, préférence à tout autre; **I would choose David in p. to Martin,** je choisirais David plutôt que, de préférence à, Martin; **in order of p.,** par ordre de préférence; **p. voting,** vote *m* par ordre de préférence (sur une liste de candidats). **2.** (*thg preferred*) **this is my p.,** voilà celui que je préfère; **I have no p.,** je n'ai pas de préférence; je les aime également. **3.** *Pol.Ec:* tarif *m*, régime *m*, de faveur; traitement préférentiel; préférence; **imports entitled to p.,** importations ayant droit à un régime de faveur; *Hist:* **imperial p.,** préférence impériale. **4.** droit *m* de priorité; *Fin:* **p. stock, shares,** actions privilégiées, de priorité; **liquidity p.,** préférence pour la liquidité; *Jur:* **p. clause,** pacte *m* de préférence; **p. legacy,** prélegs *m*; **to bequeath sth. as a p. legacy,** préléguer qch.

preferential [prefə'renʃ(ə)l], *a.* **1.** (*a*) (traitement, etc.) préférentiel; *Com:* **p. price,** prix *m* de faveur; (*b*) *Cust:* **p. tariff,** tarif préférentiel, de faveur. **2.** *Jur:* **p. claim, p. right,** privilège *m*; **in a bankruptcy, wages constitute a p. claim,** dans une faillite, les salaires constituent un privilège; **creditor's p. claim,** privilège de créancier; **p. creditor,** créancier privilégié; **p. debt,** créance privilégiée; **p. dividend,** dividende privilégié, dividende de priorité.

preferment [pri'fə:mənt], *s.* avancement *m*; promotion *f* (**to an office,** à une fonction); appel *m* à de hautes fonctions, à un bénéfice.

preferred [pri'fə:d], *a. Fin:* **p. stock,** actions privilégiées, de priorité.

prefiguration [pri:fig(j)ə'reiʃ(ə)n], *s.* préfiguration *f.*

prefigure [pri:'figər], *v.tr.* préfigurer.

prefigurement [pri:'figəmənt], *s.* préfiguration *f.*

prefinancing [pri:fai'nænsiŋ], *s.* préfinancement *m.*

prefix[1] ['pri:fiks], *s.* **1.** *Gram: etc:* préfixe *m.* **2.** (*a*) *Tg: W.Tel: etc:* **priority p.,** préfixe de priorité; *Cmptr:* **p. notation,** notation préfixée; (*b*) *Tp:* indicatif (départemental, etc.). **3.** titre *m* (précédant un nom propre).

prefix[2], *v.tr.* **1.** mettre (un chapitre, etc.) comme introduction à (un livre). **2** préfixer; mettre un préfixe à (un mot).

prefixal [pri:'fiks(ə)l], *a. Gram:* préfixal, -aux.

prefixation [pri:fik'seiʃ(ə)n], *s. Gram:* préfixation *f.*

prefixion [pri:'fikʃ(ə)n], *s. Gram:* emploi *m* d'un préfixe.

prefixture [pri:'fikstjər], *s. Gram:* **1.** emploi *m* du préfixe. **2.** préfixe.

pre-flight [pri:'flait], *a. Av:* **p. check, inspection,** vérification *f*, inspection *f*, avant vol; **p. training,** entraînement *m*, formation *f* (d'un pilote) avant vol.

prefloration [pri:flɔ'reiʃ(ə)n], *s. Bot:* préfloraison *f*; estivation *f.*

prefoliation [pri:fouli'eiʃ(ə)n], *s. Bot:* préfoliation *f*; vernation *f.*

preform[1] [pri:'fɔ:m], *v.tr. Tchn:* préformer, préfaçonner; *Cost:* **preformed brassière,** soutien-gorge préformé.

preform[2], *s. Tchn:* préforme *f.*

preformant, preformative [pri:'fɔ:mənt, -mətiv], *a. Ling:* préformant.

preformation [pri:fɔ:'meiʃ(ə)n], *s.* préformation *f.*

preformationism [pri:fɔ:'meiʃənizm], *s. Biol:* préformationnisme *m.*

preformative [pri:'fɔ:mətiv], *a.* (*a*) préformatif; (*b*) préformant.

preforming [pri:'fɔ:miŋ], *s.* préformage *m*, préfaçonnage *m.*

preformism [pri:'fɔ:mizm], *s.* préformisme *m.*

prefractionator [pri:'frækʃəneitər], *s. Petr:* préfractionnateur *m.*

prefrontal [pri:'frʌnt(ə)l], *a.* (*a*) *Anat:* préfrontal, -aux; *a. & s.* **p. (bone),** (os) préfrontal *m*; **p. lobe,** lobe préfrontal; *Surg:* **p. lobotomy, leucotomy,** lobotomie, leucotomie, préfrontale; (*b*) *Meteor:* **p. thunderstorm,** orage préfrontal.

pregenital [pri:'dʒenit(ə)l], *a.* prégénital, -aux.

preggers ['pregəz], *a.f. P:* enceinte.

preglacial [pri:'gleisiəl], *a. Geol:* préglaciaire.

pregnable ['pregnəbl], *a. O: & Lit:* (forteresse) prenable; (opinion) attaquable.

pregnancy ['pregnənsi], *s.* **1.** grossesse *f*, gestation *f*; gravidité *f*; **phantom p.,** fausse grossesse; grossesse nerveuse; **extra-uterine p.,** grossesse extra-utérine; **twin p.,** grossesse gémellaire. **2.** *Lit:* fécondité *f*, fertilité *f* (de l'esprit); richesse *f* de sens (d'un mot); grande portée (d'un événement).

pregnant ['pregnənt], *a.* **1.** (*a*) (*of woman*) enceinte, grosse; (*of animal*) pleine, grosse, gravide; **she has been p. for three months, she's three months p.,** elle est enceinte de trois mois; (*b*) *Ch:* **p. liquor,** liqueur féconde; **p. solution,** solutionmère *f, pl.* solutionsmères. **2.** (*a*) fécond, fertile (**with,** en); d'une grande portée; **p. with consequences,** gros de conséquences; **p. with meaning,** chargé de sens; suggestif, riche en suggestions; (*b*) *Gram:* **p. construction,** construction prégnante.

preheat [pri:'hi:t], *v.tr.* préchauffer; (ré)chauffer d'avance.

preheater [pri:'hi:tər], *s. I.C.E: etc:* préchauffeur *m*; dégourdisseur *m*; réchauffeur *m* (du mélange, etc.).

preheating [pri:'hi:tiŋ], *s.* préchauffage *m*; réchauffage *m* préalable; *I.C.E: etc:* dégourdissage *m.*

prehensile [pri'hensail], *a.* préhensile; préhenseur; **with a p. tail,** caudimane; à queue prenante.

prehension [pri'henʃ(ə)n], *s. Lit:* **1.** préhension *f*, prise *f.* **2.** appréhension *f* (d'une idée, etc.).

prehensive, prehensory [pri'hensiv, -'hensəri], *a.* préhensile.

prehistorian [pri:his'tɔriən], *s.* préhistorien, -ienne.

prehistoric [pri:his'tɔrik], *a.* préhistorique.

prehistory [pri:'hist(ə)ri], *s.* préhistoire *f.*

prehnite ['preinait], *s. Miner:* prehnite *f.*

prehnitene ['preiniti:n], *s. Ch:* préhnitène *m.*

prehnitic [prei'nitik], *a. Ch:* préhnitique.

prehominid [pri:'hɔminid], *s. Paleont:* préhominien *m.*

Prehominidae [pri:hɔ'minidi:], *s.pl. Paleont:* préhominiens *m.*

prehuman [pri:'hju:m(ə)n], *a.* préhumain.

pre-ignition [pri:ig'niʃ(ə)n], *s. I.C.E: etc:* préallumage *m*; allumage prématuré.

prejudge [pri:'dʒʌdʒ], *v.tr.* **1.** préjuger (une question, etc.). **2.** condamner (qn) d'avance.

prejudice[1] ['predʒudis], *s.* **1.** préjudice *m*, tort *m*, dommage *m*; *Jur:* **without p. (to my rights),** réservation faite de tous mes droits; sans préjudice de mes droits; **without p. to any claim they may otherwise have on the characters,** sans préjudice pour tous les droits et recours qu'ils pourraient avoir sur les affréteurs; **without p. to the solution of the question,** sans préjuger la solution de la question; **to accept an order without p. to the measures already taken,** accepter un décret sans préjudice des mesures déjà prises; **without p.,** sous toutes réserves; **to the p. of. . .,** au préjudice de. . .. **2.** préjugé *m*, prévention *f*, préconception *f* (contre, en faveur de, qn, qch.); parti pris *m*; **racial p.,** racisme *m*; **I have a p. against that sort of thing,** je suis contre, j'ai des préjugés contre, de telles choses, une conduite pareille.

prejudice[2], *v.tr.* **1.** (*a*) nuire, faire tort, porter préjudice, préjudicier, à (une réputation, etc.); **without prejudicing my rights,** sans préjudice de mes droits; (*b*) **this will not p. the decisions that may have to be taken,** cela ne constituera aucun précédent pour les décisions à prendre; **this does not p. the solution of the question,** cela ne préjuge pas la solution de la question. **2.** prévenir, prédisposer (qn contre qn, en faveur de qn).

prejudiced ['predʒudist], *a.* prévenu, prédisposé; à préjugés; **to be p.,** avoir des préjugés.

prejudicial [predʒu'diʃ(ə)l], *a.* préjudiciable, nuisible (**to,** à); **to be p. to s.o.'s interests,** porter, faire, préjudice aux intérêts de qn; **it might be p. to us,** cela pourrait nous nuire.

pre-judicial [pri:dʒu'diʃ(ə)l], *a. Jur:* préjudiciel.

prejudicially [predʒu'diʃəli], *adv.* d'une manière préjudiciable; nuisiblement.

prelacy ['preləsi], *s.* **1.** (*a*) prélature *f*, épiscopat *m*; (*b*) *coll.* **the p.,** les prélats *m*; le corps des évêques; l'épiscopat. **2.** *Pej:* hiérarchisation *f* de l'Église; gouvernement *m* par les prélats.

prelate ['prelət], *s.* prélat *m.*

prelatic(al) [pre'lætik(l)], *a.* de prélat; épiscopal, -aux.

prelim [pri'lim], *s. F:* (*a*) examen *m* préliminaire; (*b*) *Typ:* **prelims,** pages *f* de départ.

preliminary [pri'liminəri]. **1.** *a.* préliminaire, préalable, préparatoire; **to take p. steps for the establishment of . . .,** préparer la création de . . .; **payable without p. advice,** payable sans avis préalable; **after a few p. remarks,** après quelques avant-propos; *Sch:* **p. examination,** examen *m* préliminaire; *Jur:* **p. investigation,** instruction *f* (d'une affaire); *Typ:* **p. matter,** feuilles *f* liminaires; *Civ.E: etc:* **p. scheme, plan,** avant-projet *m, pl.* avant-projets; *Min:* **p. work,** travaux *mpl* de premier établissement. **2.** *s.* (*a*) prélude *m* (à une conversation, etc.); **by way of, as a, p.,** préliminairement; à titre de mesure préalable; (*b*) **preliminaries,** préliminaires *m* (d'un traité, etc.); **the preliminaries to peace, the peace preliminaries,** les préliminaires de (la) paix.

prelude[1] ['prelju:d], *s.* **1.** prélude *m*; proème *m* (**to,** de); **a few skirmishes, the p. to the battle,** quelques escarmouches, prélude de la bataille. **2.** *Mus:* prélude; **to play a p.,** préluder; jouer un prélude.

prelude[2]. **1.** *v.i. Mus: etc:* (*a*) préluder; jouer un prélude; (*b*) servir d'introduction, préluder (**to,** à). **2.** *v.tr.* (*a*) faire présager (un événement, etc.); (*b*) précéder.

preludize ['preljudaiz], *v.i. Mus:* préluder; jouer un prélude.

prelumbar [pri:'lʌmbər], *a. Anat:* prélombaire.

prelusive, prelusory [pri'lju:siv, -'lju:səri], *a.* de prélude; préliminaire.

premandibular [pri:mæn'dibjulər], *a. Anat:* prémandibulaire.

premarital [pri:'mærit(ə)l], *a.* prématrimonial, -aux; avant le mariage; *U.S: Jur:* **p. agreement,** contrat *m* de mariage.

premature ['premətjər], *a.* prématuré; **p. birth,** accouchement prématuré, avant terme; **p. old age,**

vieillesse prématurée; **it is p. to discuss this business,** il est prématuré de, trop tôt pour, discuter cette affaire; *F:* **you're being a bit p.!** tu vas trop vite!

prematurely ['prematjə:li], *adv.* prématurément; avant le temps; *Obst:* avant terme.

prematureness ['prematjə:nis], **prematurity** [premə'tju:riti], *s.* prématurité *f.*

premedical [pri:'medikl], *a.* **p. studies,** études *f* préparatoires en médecine.

premedication [pri:medi'keiʃ(ə)n], *s. Med:* prémédication *f,* médication *f* préopératoire.

premeditate [pri:'mediteit], *v.tr.* préméditer (un coup, etc.).

premeditated [pri'mediteitid], *a.* prémédité; (crime) réfléchi; **p. insolence,** insolence calculée.

premeditation [primedi'teiʃ(ə)n], *s.* préméditation *f.*

premenstrual [pri:'menstruəl], *a. Physiol:* prémenstruel; **p. tension,** syndrome prémenstruel.

premier ['pri:miər, 'prem-]. **1.** *a.* premier. **2.** *s.* premier ministre.

première[1] ['prəmiεər, 'prem-], *s.* **1.** première *f* (d'une pièce de théâtre, d'un film); **world p.,** première mondiale. **2.** (*woman*) vedette *f* (qui joue le rôle principal).

première[2], *v.tr.* donner la première (d'une pièce de théâtre, d'un film).

premiership ['pri:miəʃip, 'prem-], *s.* fonctions *fpl* de premier ministre.

premilitary [pri:'milit(ə)ri], *a.* (formation, etc.) prémilitaire.

premise[1] ['premis], *s.* **1.** *Log:* (*also* **premiss**) prémisse *f.* **2.** *Jur:* **premises,** intitulé *m* (d'un document). **3. the premises,** le local, les locaux; l'immeuble *m;* **business premises,** locaux commerciaux; **shop premises,** (locaux à usage de) magasin(s) *m;* **the police visited the premises,** la police s'est transportée sur les lieux; **these are private premises,** c'est ici un terrain privé, un immeuble privé, etc.; **drinks to be consumed on, off, the premises,** boissons à consommer dans, hors de, l'établissement.

premise[2] [pri'maiz], *v.tr.* **1.** (*a*) *Log:* poser (un fait) en prémisse; poser en prémisse (**that,** que + *ind.*); (*b*) poser en principe (**that,** que). **2.** *A:* & *Lit:* faire remarquer, citer, (qch.) par avance, en guise d'introduction; **to p. a speech with a few general remarks,** faire précéder un discours de, par, quelques remarques générales. **3.** *Med: Surg: A:* commencer une opération, un traitement, par (qch.).

premium ['pri:miəm], *s.* **1.** prime *f,* prix *m,* récompense *f; Ind: etc:* **to give a p. for increased output,** donner une prime pour une augmentation du rendement; **to put a p. on laziness,** donner une prime à, encourager, la paresse. **2.** (*a*) prix convenu, indemnité *f* (pour l'apprentissage à une profession libérale); (*b*) (**insurance**) **p.,** prime (d'assurance); **annual p.,** prime annuelle; **low-p. insurance,** assurance *f* à prime réduite; (*c*) droit *m,* redevance *f* (à payer au début d'un bail); **flat to let, no p.,** appartement à louer sans reprise; (*d*) *U.S:* **p. loan,** emprunt *m* à prime. **3.** *Fin: etc:* (*a*) (**exchange**) **p.,** agio *m;* prix, prime, du change; **p. on gold,** agio sur l'or; **the (quoted) p. or discount,** le déport ou le report; (*b*) **to issue shares at a p.,** émettre des actions au-dessus du pair, de leur valeur nominale; **p. on redemption,** prime à remboursement; **p. bonds,** (i) obligations *f* à primes; (ii) bons *m* à lots; **to sell sth. at a p.,** vendre qch. à prime, à bénéfice; **antiques are at a p.,** les antiquités (i) sont très recherchées, (ii) se vendent à prix d'or. **4.** *attrib.* **p. grade petrol** = supercarburant *m, F:* super *m.*

premolar [pri:'moulər], *a.* & *s. Anat:* (dent *f*) prémolaire *f;* petite molaire.

premonition [pri:mə'niʃ(ə)n], *s.* prémonition *f,* indice *m;* avertissement *m* préalable; pressentiment *m* (de malheur, etc.); **premonitions,** indices précurseurs; *Med:* signes avant-coureurs.

premonitory [pri'mɔnitəri], *a.* prémonitoire; prémoniteur, -trice; **p. sign,** signe avant-coureur, indice précurseur; *Med:* **p. diarrhoea,** diarrhée *f* prémonitoire (de choléra).

Premonstrant [pri'mɔnstrənt], **Premonstratensian** [primɔnstrə'tensiən], *a.* & *s. Ecc.Hist:* prémontré, -ée.

premorse [pri'mɔ:s], *a. Bot: Ent:* tronqué.

pre-motoring [pri:'moutəriŋ], *a.* **in the p.-m. days,** avant l'ère de l'automobile.

pre-mundane [pri:'mʌndein], *a.* d'avant le monde.

prenatal [pri:'neit(ə)l], *a.* prénatal, -als, -aux.

prentice[1] ['prentis], *s. A:* apprenti, -ie; **p. hand,** main *f* de novice; main inhabile, inexpérimentée.

prentice[2], *v.tr. A:* mettre (qn) en apprentissage (chez qn).

prenumbering [pri:'nʌmb(ə)riŋ], *s. Cmptr:* immatriculation *f.*

prenuptial [pri:'nʌpʃəl], *a.* prénuptial, -aux.

preoccupancy [pri:'ɔkjupənsi], *s.* préoccupation *f,* occupation antérieure (d'un territoire, etc.).

preoccupant [pri:'ɔkjupənt], *s.* occupant antérieur.

preoccupation [pri:ɔkju'peiʃ(ə)n], *s.* **1.** (*a*) préoccupation *f* (de l'esprit); (*b*) préoccupation (**with,** de); **my greatest p.,** ma plus grande préoccupation; mon premier souci. **2.** = PREOCCUPANCY.

preoccupied [pri:'ɔkjupaid], *a.* préoccupé; absorbé (par un souci); **to be p.,** être dans la préoccupation; **to be p. with sth.,** se préoccuper de qch.

preoccupy [pri'ɔkjupai], *v.tr.* **1.** préoccuper, absorber (l'esprit). **2.** occuper (un territoire) antérieurement, par avance.

preoperative [pri:'ɔpərətiv], *a.* préopératoire.

preopercle [pri:'ɔpəkl], **preoperculum** [pri:ɔ'pəækjuləm], *s. Ich:* préopercule *m.*

preopercular [pri:ɔ'pə:kjulər], *s. Ich:* préoperculaire *m.*

preoral [pri:'ɔrəl], *a. Z:* préoral, -aux.

preorbital [pri:ɔ:bit(ə)l], *a.* & *s. Anat:* préorbital (*m*).

preordain [pri:ɔ:'dein], *v.tr.* **1.** ordonner, régler, d'avance. **2.** préordonner, prédéterminer; **it was preordained,** c'était préordonné, prédestiné, cela devait être.

prep [prep]. *Sch: F:* **1.** *s.* étude *f* (du soir); devoirs *mpl* (du soir); **p. room,** (salle *f* d')étude; **work done in p.,** travail fait à l'étude; **p. period,** (heure de) permanence. **2.** *a.* **p. school,** école préparatoire (pour élèves de 8 à 13 ans).

prepack, prepackage [pri:'pæk, pri:'pækidʒ], *v.tr.* préconditionner, préemballer.

prepaid ['pri:peid], *a.* payé d'avance; (*of letter, etc.*) affranchi; **carriage p.,** port payé; franc de port, franc de poste; franco *inv; Tg:* **p. answer,** réponse payée.

prepalatal [pri:'pælət(ə)l], *a. Ling:* prépalatal, -aux.

preparation [prepə'reiʃ(ə)n], *s.* **1.** (*a*) préparation *f* (de la nourriture, d'un médicament, etc.); accommodage *m* (d'un mets); apprêt *m* (du drap, etc.); rédaction *f* (d'un document, etc.); (*of meal, etc.*) **to be in p.,** se préparer; **the samples are in p.,** les échantillons *m* sont en préparation; **in course of p.,** en cours d'élaboration, de préparation; **to do sth. without (any) p.,** faire qch. sans apprêts, sans s'y être préparé, sans aucun préparatif; faire qch. au pied levé; (*b*) mise *f* en état (de fonctionner, d'être utilisé); préparation; *Const:* appareillage *m* (des pierres à bâtir); *Tchn:* apprêt (du cuir, des tissus, etc.); *Ecc:* **p. for mass,** préparation à la messe; *Sch:* **p. for an examination,** préparation à un examen; *Med:* **p. of a patient for an operation,** préparation d'un patient en vue d'une opération; **surgical p.,** soins *mpl* préparatoires (à une opération); *Sp:* **p. of a team for a match,** entraînement, préparation, d'une équipe à un match; **they broke the news to her without any p.,** ils lui ont annoncé la (mauvaise) nouvelle sans aucune préparation, ils lui ont annoncé brutalement la nouvelle. **2.** *usu.pl.* préparatifs *mpl;* apprêts; **preparations for war,** préparatifs de guerre; **to make (one's) preparations for sth.,** prendre ses mesures, ses dispositions, faire des préparatifs, en vue de qch.; **to make preparations for a journey,** se préparer à, pour, un voyage; faire ses préparatifs de voyage; **to make preparations for a meal,** faire les préparatifs d'un repas; **to make preparations for guests,** se préparer à recevoir les invités. **3.** *Sch:* étude *f* (du soir); devoirs *m* (du soir). **4. pharmaceutical p.,** préparation pharmaceutique; **anatomical p.,** préparation anatomique; **p. mounted on a microscope slide,** préparation (microscopique) sur lamelle.

preparative [pri'pærətiv]. **1.** *a.* préparatoire. **2.** *s.* (*a*) acte *m,* signal *m,* préparatoire; (*b*) **preparatives,** préparatifs *m.*

preparatory [pri'pærətəri], *a.* préparatoir, préalable (**to,** à); **p. school,** école préparatoire (aux grandes écoles secondaires); *For: Ind:* **p. period,** période d'attente.

prepare [pri'pεər]. **1.** *v.tr.* (*a*) préparer (un repas, etc.); accommoder, confectionner (un mets); dresser, rédiger (un document); monter, préparer, amorcer (une attaque, etc.); **to p. s.o. for an examination,** préparer qn à un examen; **to p. a patient for an operation,** préparer un patient pour une opération; **I must p. you for some bad news,** je regrette que j'ai une mauvaise nouvelle à vous annoncer; **I must p. the room for my guests,** il me faut préparer la chambre (d'amis) pour mes invités; **to p. a surprise for s.o.,** ménager une surprise à qn; **to p. the way for negotiations,** amorcer des négociations; (*b*) mettre (qch.) en état (de fonctionner, d'être utilisé); préparer (qch.); appareiller (des pierres à bâtir); apprêter (le cuir, des tissus, etc.); (*c*) **I am (quite) prepared to . . .,** je suis prêt, disposé, à . . .; **I am not prepared to . . .,** je ne suis pas disposé à . . .; je refuse de . . .; **your room is being prepared,** on vous prépare une chambre; **to be prepared for anything, for everything,** être prêt, s'attendre, à toute éventualité; **be prepared to start at eleven,** tenez-vous prêt pour partir à onze heures; *Scouting:* **be prepared,** soyez toujours prêt; ne vous laissez jamais prendre au dépourvu. **2.** *v.i.* se préparer, se disposer, s'apprêter (**for sth., to do sth.,** à qch., à faire qch.); se mettre en devoir (**to do sth.,** de faire qch.); **to p. for departure,** faire ses préparatifs de départ; **to p. for the struggle,** s'apprêter à la lutte; **to p. for an examination,** préparer un examen; *Mil:* **to p. for action,** se préparer au combat, à combattre; **p. for action!** dispositions de combat! **p. to move!** dispositions de route! *Nau:* **to p. to meet a squall,** parer à un grain.

prepared [pri'pεəd], *a.* (*a*) préparé; **well p. dish,** mets bien préparé; (*of food*) **I bought it ready p.,** je l'ai acheté tout préparé, prêt pour la table; (*b*) en état; apprêté; **p. timber,** bois refait.

preparedness [pri'pεər(i)dnis], *s.* état *m* de préparation; **everything was in a state of p.,** (i) tout était prêt; (ii) on était paré; *Mil:* **to be in a state of p.,** être en état d'alerte (préventive).

preparer [pri'pεərər], *s.* préparateur, -trice; *Ind:* apprêteur, -euse.

preparietal [pri:pə'raiət(ə)l], *a. Anat:* prépariétal, -aux.

prepay [pri:'pei], *v.tr.* (*p.t.* & *p.p.* **prepaid**) payer, régler, (qch.) d'avance; affranchir (une lettre, etc.); **to send sth. carriage prepaid,** envoyer qch. port payé, franc de port, franco.

prepayment [pri:'peimənt], *s.* paiement *m* d'avance; paiement par anticipation; affranchissement *m* (d'une lettre, etc.).

prepense [pri'pens], *a. Jur:* prémédité; fait avec intention, de propos délibéré; **with, of, through, malice p.,** avec intention criminelle; avec préméditation; de propos délibéré.

preperceptive [pri:pə'septiv], *a. Psy:* préperceptif.

preponderance [pri'pɔndərəns], *s.* prépondérance *f* (**over,** sur).

preponderant [pri'pɔndərənt], *a.* prépondérant.

preponderantly [pri'pɔndərəntli], *adv.* à un degré prépondérant.

preponderate [pri'pɔndəreit], *v.i.* peser davantage; emporter la balance (**over,** sur); **reasons that p. over all others,** raisons qui l'emportent sur toutes les autres.

preponderating [pri'pɔndəreitiŋ], *a.* prépondérant.

preposition[1] [prepə'ziʃ(ə)n], *s. Gram:* préposition *f;* **employed as a p.,** employé prépositivement; faisant fonction de préposition.

preposition[2] [pri:pə'ziʃ(ə)n], *v.tr. Cmptr: etc:* prépositionner.

prepositional [prepə'ziʃən(ə)l], *a.* prépositionnel, prépositif; **p. phrase,** locution prépositive.

prepositionally [prepə'ziʃən(ə)li], *adv.* (employé) comme préposition.

prepositive [pri'pɔzitiv], *a. Gram:* prépositif.

prepossess [pri:pə'zes], *v.tr.* **1.** pénétrer (qn) (**with,** de); **to be prepossessed with an idea,** être pénétré d'une idée; être inspiré par une idée. **2.** (*of idea, etc.*) accaparer, posséder (qn); prendre possession de l'esprit de (qn). **3.** prévenir (qn); **his way of talking prepossessed me in his favour,** sa conversation m'a prévenu en sa faveur.

prepossessing [pri:pə'zesiŋ], *a.* (visage) agréable, prévenant; **p. appearance,** aspect engageant, attrayant, avenant; mine avantageuse, bonne mine; (*of pers.*) sympathique; **he has a p. face,** son visage prévient en sa faveur.

prepossessingly [pri:pə'zesiŋli], *adv.* d'une manière prévenante, attrayante, engageante.

prepossessingness [pri:pə'zesiŋnis], *s.* caractère engageant.

prepossession [pri:pə'zeʃ(ə)n], *s.* prévention *f;* préjugé *m.*

preposterous [pri'pɔst(ə)rəs], *a.* irrationnel; contraire au bon sens; absurde; **p. claim,** prétention déraisonnable; **p. story,** histoire absurde, qui ne tient pas debout; **p. questions,** questions saugrenues; **that's simply p.!** voilà qui est fort! c'est le monde renversé! cela n'ai ni queue ni tête!

preposterously [pri'pɔst(ə)rəsli], *adv.* d'une façon absurde.

preposterousness [pri'pɔst(ə)rəsnis], *s.* absurdité *f.*

prepotence [pri'poutəns], *s.* = PREPOTENCY 1.

prepotency [pri'poutənsi], *s.* **1.** prépotence *f,* prédominance *f.* **2.** *Biol:* prépotence.

prepotent [pri'poutənt], *a.* **1.** prédominant. **2.** *Biol:* (caractère) dominant.

preprandial [pri:'prændiəl], *a. Med:* préprandial, -aux; avant le déjeuner, le repas; **p. pains,** douleurs préprandiales; *F: Hum:* **p. drink,** apéritif *m* (de midi).

preprint[1] ['pri:print], *s. Typ:* **1.** prétirage *m.* **2.** épreuve(s) *f* avant tirage.

preprint[2], *v.tr. Typ:* préimprimer; prétirer.

prepuber(t)al [pri:'pju:bər(t)əl], **prepubescent** [pri:pju:'besənt], *a. Physiol:* prépubertaire.

prepuberty [pri:'pju:bəti], *s. Physiol:* prépuberté *f.*
prepubian, prepubic [pri:'pju:biən, -'pju:bik], *a. Anat:* prépubien.
prepubis [pri'pju:bis], *s. Anat:* prépubis *m.*
prepuce ['pri:pju:s], *s. Anat:* prépuce *m.*
prepunch[1] [pri:'pʌn(t)ʃ], *v.tr. Cmptr:* préperforer.
prepunch[2] ['pri:pʌn(t)ʃ], *attrib. Cmptr:* **p. station,** poste *m* avant perforation.
prepunching [pri:'pʌn(t)ʃiŋ], *s. Cmptr:* préperforation *f.*
preputial [pri:'pju:ʃ(ə)l], *a. Anat:* préputial, -aux.
Pre-Raphaelite [pri:'ræf(i)əlait], *a. & s. Art:* préraphaélite (*m*).
Pre-Raphael(it)ism [pri:'ræf(i)əl(ait)izm], *s. Art:* préraphaél(it)isme *m.*
prerecord [pri:ri'kɔ:d], *v.tr.* préenregistrer; enregistrer au préalable; *Cin:* présynchroniser.
prerecorded [pri:ri'kɔ:did], *a.* préenregistré; (bande) avec enregistrement préalable; *Cin:* présynchronisé; **p. broadcast,** émission *f* en différé.
prerecording [pri:ri'kɔ:diŋ], *s.* préenregistrement *m*; enregistrement préalable; *Cin:* présynchronisation *f*; *W.Tel: T.V:* le différé.
prerelease [pri:ri'li:s], *s.* avant-première *f* (d'un film); présentation *f* (d'un film) avant la mise en circulation.
prerequisite [pri:'rekwizit]. **1.** *a.* préalablement nécessaire, indispensable. **2.** *s.* préalable *m*; nécessité *f*, condition *f*, préalable.
prerogative [pri'rɔgətiv]. **1.** *s.* prérogative *f*, privilège *m*; **it is our p. (to do it),** nous avons la prérogative, c'est notre prérogative, il nous appartient (de le faire); **the royal p.,** la prérogative royale; **to exercise the royal p.,** faire acte souverain; **the p. of pardon,** le droit de grâce. **2.** *a.* (*a*) *Rom.Ant:* (centurie, tribu) prérogative; (*b*) privilégié.
pre-Roman [pri:'roumən], *a.* préromain.
preromanesque [pri:roumə'nesk], *a. Arch: etc:* préroman.
preromantic [pri:rou'mæntik], *a. Lit: etc:* préromantique.
preromanticism [pri:rou'mæntisizm], *s. Lit: etc:* préromantisme *m.*
presage[1] ['presidʒ], *s. Lit:* (*a*) présage *m*, auspice *m*, augure *m*; (*b*) pressentiment *m*; **p. of evil,** (i) présage, (ii) pressentiment, de malheur.
presage[2] ['presidʒ, pri'seidʒ]. *Lit:* **1.** *v.tr.* (*a*) (*of omen, etc.*) présager, annoncer (une catastrophe, etc.); (*b*) (*of pers.*) augurer, prédire (qch.). **2.** *v.i.* **sign that presages well for the future,** signe qui est de bon augure pour l'avenir.
presanctified [pri:'sæŋktifaid], *a. Ecc:* **the Mass of the P.,** la Messe des présanctifiés.
presbyacousia, presbyacusia, presbycusis [prezbiə'ku:ziə, -ə'kju:ziə, -'kju:sis], *s. Med:* presbyacousie *f.*
presbyope ['prezbioup], *s. Med:* presbyte *mf.*
presbyophrenia [prezbiou'fri:niə], *s. Med:* presbyophrénie *f.*
presbyopia [prezbi'oupiə], *s. Med:* presbytie *f*, presbytisme *m.*
presbyopic [prezbi'ɔpik], *a. Med:* (vue) presbytique; (personne) presbyte.
presbyter ['prezbitər], *s.* **1.** *Presbyterian Ch:* ancien *m.* **2.** *Episcopal Ch:* prêtre *m.*
presbyteral [prez'bitərəl], *a. Ecc:* (*of office, duty, etc.*) presbytéral, -aux; de prêtre.
presbyterial [prezbi'tiəriəl], *a. Ecc:* qui a rapport aux anciens (de l'Église primitive ou presbytérienne); presbytéral, -aux.
Presbyterian [prezbi'tiəriən], *a. & s. Rel:* presbytérien, -ienne.
Presbyterianism [prezbi'tiəriənizm], *s. Rel:* presbytérianisme *m.*
presbytery ['prezbit(ə)ri], *s.* **1.** *Ecc.Arch:* sanctuaire *m*, chœur *m.* **2.** *R.C.Ch:* presbytère *m*, cure *f.* **3.** *Presbyterian Ch:* consistoire *m.*
presbytia [prez'bitiə], *s. Med:* presbytie *f*, presbytisme *m.*
presbytic [prez'bitik], *a. Med:* presbyte, presbytique.
prescience ['presiəns], *s.* prescience *f*, prévision *f.*
prescient ['presiənt], *a.* prescient, prévoyant.
prescientific [pri:saiən'tifik], *a.* préscientifique.
prescribe [pri'skraib]. **1.** *v.tr.* (*a*) prescrire, ordonner; **to p. regulations,** établir un règlement, des règles; **to p. a line of action,** indiquer, imposer, une ligne de conduite; **prescribed task,** tâche imposée; **in the prescribed time,** dans le délai prescrit, réglementaire; en temps utile; *Sch:* **the subjects prescribed,** les matières (inscrites) au programme; (*b*) *Med:* **to p. sth. for s.o.,** prescrire, ordonner, qch. à qn; donner qch. en traitement à qn; faire une ordonnance pour qn. **2.** *v.i. Jur:* (*a*) **to p. to, for, a right,** prescrire un droit; acquérir un droit par prescription; (*b*) *Scot:* (*of right, etc.*) se prescrire, périmer par prescription.
prescript ['pri:skript], *s.* prescription *f*, ordonnance *f*, précepte *m*; *Phil:* prescript *m.*
prescriptibility [priskripti'biliti], *s. Jur:* prescriptibilité *f.*
prescriptible [pri'skriptibl], *a.* prescriptible.
prescription [pri'skripʃ(ə)n], *s.* prescription *f.* **1.** (*a*) ordre *m*, précepte *m*; (*b*) *Med:* ordonnance *f*; **to write, make out, a p. for s.o.,** rédiger une ordonnance pour qn; **to dispense,** *U.S:* **to fill, a p.,** préparer une ordonnance; **available only on (a doctor's) p.,** délivré seulement sur ordonnance. **2.** *Jur:* (*a*) **negative p., extinctive p.,** prescription extinctive; **positive p., acquisitive p.,** prescription acquisitive; (*b*) droit consacré par l'usage; coutume *f*; usage *m.*
prescriptive [pri'skriptiv], *a.* **1.** (*a*) ordonnateur, -trice; réglementaire; (*b*) normatif; **p. grammar,** grammaire normative. **2.** consacré par l'usage, par la coutume.
preselect [pri:si'lekt], *v.tr.* choisir à l'avance; *Tchn:* présélectionner.
preselection [pri:si'lekʃ(ə)n], *s.* présélection *f.*
preselective [pri:si'lektiv], *a.* présélectif; **p. gear change,** changement *m* de vitesse présélectif.
preselector [pri:si'lektər], *s.* présélecteur *m.*
presence ['prez(ə)ns], *s.* présence *f.* **1.** (*a*) **your p. is requested at . . .,** (i) on vous prie, vous êtes prié, d'assister à . . .; (ii) *Adm:* vous êtes convoqué à . . .; **in the p. of . . .,** en présence de . . .; **say nothing about it in his p.,** n'en dites rien, n'en parlez pas, devant lui, en sa présence; *Theol:* **real p.,** présence réelle; réalité *f*; (*b*) **to be admitted to the p.,** être admis en présence du roi, etc.; **in such an august p.,** en présence d'un si auguste personnage; **p. chamber,** salle *f* d'audience; *P: A:* **saving your p.,** sauf votre respect. **2. p. of mind,** présence d'esprit; **to keep one's p. of mind,** conserver sa tête, son sang-froid. **3.** (*of pers.*) air *m*, mine *f*, extérieur *m*, maintien *m*; **to have a good p.,** représenter bien; avoir du maintien; être d'un aspect imposant.
presenile [pri:'si:nail], *a. Psy:* présénile.
presensitized [pri:'sensitaizd], *a. Phot: etc:* présensibilisé.
present[1] ['prez(ə)nt], *a. & s.*
I. *a.* **1.** (*a*) présent (et non absent); **to be p. at a ceremony,** être présent, assister, à une cérémonie; **any other person p.,** toute autre personne présente; **all p. heard it,** toute l'assistance l'a entendu; **some of you p. here,** quelques-uns d'entre vous, ici présents; **nobody else was p.,** nul autre n'était là; **minerals which are p. in the solution,** minéraux qui sont présents, qui se rencontrent, se trouvent, dans la solution; **p. to the mind,** présent à l'esprit; (*b*) *A:* d'un accès facile; *B:* **a very p. help in trouble,** un secours qui ne manque jamais dans la détresse. **2.** (*a*) actuel; **p. fashions,** modes actuelles, d'aujourd'hui; **the p. king,** le roi actuel; **p. year,** année courante; **at the p. time,** à présent; (i) en ce moment; (ii) à l'époque actuelle; aujourd'hui; **up to the p. time,** jusqu'ici; **p. value,** valeur actuelle; **question of p. interest,** question actuelle; *Com:* **p. capital,** capital appelé; (*b*) en question; que voici; **the p. volume,** le volume en question; ce volume; **in the p. case,** dans le cas qui nous occupe; *O:* **the p. writer,** l'auteur (de ce livre, de cet article) (c.-à-d. moi); *Com: O:* **on receipt of the p. letter,** au reçu de la présente; (*c*) *Gram:* **p. tense,** *s.* **the present,** le (temps) présent; **in the p.,** au présent; **p. participle,** participe présent; **p. subjunctive,** présent du subjonctif.
II. *s.* **1.** présent *m*; **the p.,** le présent; le temps présent; **up to the p.,** jusqu'à présent; jusqu'à ce moment; jusqu'à maintenant; jusqu'ici; **at p.,** (i) à présent; maintenant; actuellement; (ii) (*referring to past time*) alors; **no more at p.,** rien de plus pour le moment; **as things are at p.,** (i) au point où en sont les choses; (ii) par le temps qui court; **for the p.,** pour le moment, pour l'heure. **2.** *Jur:* **by these presents,** par la présente; **know all men by these presents that . . .,** savoir faisons par ces présentes que . . ..
present[2] ['prez(ə)nt], *s.* don *m*, cadeau *m*; présent *m*; **to send s.o. sth. as a p.,** envoyer qch. en cadeau à qn; **to make s.o. a p. of sth., to give sth. to s.o. as a p.,** faire présent, faire cadeau, de qch. à qn; **to make a p. to s.o.,** faire un cadeau à qn; (*when buying*) **it's for a p.,** c'est pour offrir.
present[3] [pri'zent], *v.tr.* présenter. **1.** (*a*) **to p. s.o. to s.o.,** présenter qn à qn; **to p. s.o. at court,** présenter qn à la cour; **she has not yet been presented,** elle n'a pas encore été présentée à la cour; **to p. s.o. as candidate,** présenter qn comme candidat; *Ecc:* **to p. s.o. (to the bishop, for a benefice),** recommander, désigner, qn pour un bénéfice; *Th:* (*of company, etc.*) **to p. a play,** présenter, donner, une pièce; **to p. oneself at, for, an examination,** se présenter à, pour, un examen; (*b*) **writer who is good at presenting his characters,** écrivain qui introduit bien ses personnages; **business that presents some difficulty,** affaire qui présente des difficultés; **a good opportunity presents itself (for doing sth.),** une bonne occasion se présente (de faire qch.); **the matter was presented in a new light,** l'affaire se présentait sous un jour nouveau; (*c*) **to p. a pistol at s.o.'s head,** présenter un pistolet à, braquer un pistolet sur, la tête de qn; *Mil: A:* **present!** joue! **2.** (*a*) donner; **to p. sth. to s.o.; to p. s.o. with sth.,** donner qch. à qn; faire présent, faire cadeau, de qch. à qn; (*b*) **to p. one's compliments to s.o.,** présenter ses compliments à qn. **3.** (*a*) *Com:* **to p. a bill for payment,** présenter un billet à l'encaissement; **to p. a bill for acceptance,** présenter une traite à l'acceptation; (*b*) *Jur:* déposer (une plainte, etc.); **to p. a plea,** introduire une instance; (*c*) *Parl:* **to p. a bill,** présenter, introduire, un projet de loi. **4. to p. sth. to the authorities,** attirer l'attention des autorités sur qch.; **to p. a plan to a meeting,** soumettre un plan à une assemblée. **5.** *Mil:* **to p. arms,** présenter les armes; rendre les honneurs à qn; **p. arms!** présentez armes! **6.** *v.i. Obst:* se présenter; **the child presents badly,** l'enfant se présente mal.
present[4] [pri'zent], *s. Mil: A:* **arms at the p.,** l'arme en joue.
presentable [pri'zentəbl], *a.* (*of pers., thg*) présentable; (*of garment*) portable, *F:* mettable; *F:* **I've nothing p. (to put on),** je n'ai rien de mettable, de sortable; *F:* **he's not p.,** il n'est pas sortable.
presentation [prezən'teiʃ(ə)n], *s.* **1.** (*a*) présentation *f* (de qn à la cour, etc.); *Ecc:* **(Feast of) the P.,** la Présentation de la Vierge; (*b*) *Ecc:* présentation (de qn à un bénéfice); (*c*) présentation, représentation *f* (d'une pièce de théâtre); (*d*) présentation (d'une théorie, etc.); (*e*) *Com:* **payable on p. of the coupon,** payable contre remise du coupon; **on p. of the invoice,** sur le vu de la facture; (*f*) *Pol:* **bill on the eve of p.,** proposition *f* de loi en instance; (*g*) *Rad:* présentation (des informations); *T.V:* aspect *m* de l'image. **2.** *Obst:* présentation (du fœtus); **breech p., face p.,** présentation par le siège, par la face. **3.** (*a*) remise *f*, présentation (d'un cadeau, d'un souvenir, à qn); *Mil:* remise (des drapeaux); **to make a p. to s.o.,** offrir un cadeau, un souvenir, à qn; *Publ:* **p. copy,** (i) exemplaire envoyé gracieusement, à titre gracieux, par l'éditeur; (ii) exemplaire offert à titre d'hommage (par l'auteur); (*b*) cadeau, souvenir (offert à qn). **4.** *Ecc:* collation *f* (d'un bénéfice).
presentative [pri'zentətiv], *a.* **1.** *Ecc:* (bénéfice) collatif. **2.** *Phil: etc:* (*a*) suggestif; (*b*) perceptif.
present-day [prezənt'dei], *a.* actuel; d'aujourd'hui; **p.-d. problems,** problèmes *m* d'actualité.
presentee [prezən'ti:], *s.* **1.** (*a*) personne présentée (pour un office, etc.); (*b*) débutante *f* (à la cour); (*c*) *Ecc:* collataire *m.* **2.** donataire *mf*; bénéficiaire *mf* (d'un chèque, etc.).
presenter [pri'zentər], *s.* (*a*) présentateur, -trice; présenteur, -euse; marraine *f* (d'une débutante); (*b*) *Ecc:* présentateur (à un bénéfice).
presentiment [pri'zentimənt], *s.* pressentiment *m*; **to have a p. of sth.,** avoir le pressentiment de qch., pressentir qch.
presently ['prezəntli], *adv.* **1.** *A:* aussitôt, tout de suite. **2.** bientôt; plus tard. **3.** actuellement, maintenant, à présent.
presentment [pri'zentmənt], *s.* **1.** (*a*) *Lit:* présentation *f* (d'une idée, etc.); représentation *f* (de qch. en peinture, d'une pièce de théâtre); *Com:* **p. of a bill (for acceptance),** présentation d'une traite à l'acceptation; (*b*) *Lit:* tableau *m*, image *f* (de qch.); description *f.* **2.** (*a*) *Jur:* déclaration *f* émanant du jury; (*b*) *Ecc:* plainte, réclamation, faite au diocésain.
preservable [pri'zə:vəbl], *a.* susceptible d'être conservé; qui se conserve bien.
preservation [prezə'veiʃ(ə)n], *s.* **1.** (*a*) conservation *f*; naturalisation *f* (d'une fleur, d'un spécimen); **in a state of good p., in a good state of p.,** en bon état de conservation; bien conservé; **p. of peace,** maintien *m* de la paix; **p. society,** société *f* de sauvegarde; (*b*) (*of goods, etc.*) traitement *m* avant stockage. **2.** préservation *f* (d'un danger, etc.).
preservative [pri'zə:vətiv]. **1.** *a.* (*a*) préservatif, -ive; préservateur, -trice; (*b*) (*assurant la conservation*) conservateur, -trice. **2.** *s.* (*a*) préservatif *m* **(against,** contre); (*b*) agent conservateur, de conservation; *Comest:* **without artificial colouring or preservatives,** sans colorant ni conservateur.
preserve[1] [pri'zə:v], *s.* **1.** (*often pl.*) **(apricot, etc.) preserve(s),** confiture *f* (d'abricots, etc.). **2.** (*a*) *For:* réserve *f*; (*b*) **game p.,** réserve *f*; chasse gardée; tiré *m*;

varenne *f*; **fish p.,** vivier *m*; (*c*) *esp. U.S:* **wildlife p.,** réserve zoologique; (*d*) (*of place, sphere of activity, etc.*) **he considers it his private p.,** il considère que c'est son territoire à lui.

preserve[2], *v.tr.* **1. to p. s.o. from sth.,** préserver, garantir, qn de qch.; soustraire qn à (un danger, etc.). **2.** (*a*) conserver (un bâtiment, une coutume, la mémoire de qn, etc.); maintenir (la paix, etc.); garder, observer (le silence, etc.); **bodies which p. heat,** corps *m* qui retiennent la chaleur; **to p. appearances,** sauver les apparences, les dehors; **certain traditions are preserved in the family,** dans la famille se gardent certaines traditions; (*b*) conserver, mettre en conserve (des fruits, de la viande, etc.); confire (des fruits); (*c*) naturaliser (un spécimen botanique). **3.** (*a*) élever (du gibier) dans une réserve, (des poissons) dans un vivier; (*b*) garder (une rivière, une chasse). **4.** (*with passive force*) se conserver.

preserved [pri'zəːvd], *a.* **1.** conservé; **p. ginger,** gingembre confit; **p. food,** conserves *fpl*; **p. meat,** conserve de viande; viande *f* de conserve. **2. well p., badly p.,** (bâtiment *m*, etc.) en bon, mauvais, état de conservation; **well p. woman,** femme bien conservée.

preserver [pri'zəːvər], *s.* **1.** (*pers.*) (*a*) préservateur, -trice; sauveur *m*; **God, the creator and p. of all mankind,** Dieu, créateur et sauveur de l'humanité; (*b*) conservateur, -trice (d'un bien, etc.). **2.** (*thg*) **dress p.,** dessous *m* de bras; sous-bras *m inv*; **life p.,** assommoir *m*, nerf *m* de bœuf.

preserving [pri'zəːviŋ], *s.* **1.** préservation *f*, garantissement *m* (**from,** de); **wood p. plant,** usine d'injection *f* des bois. **2.** (*a*) = PRESERVATION; (*b*) conservation *f* (des aliments); **fruit p.,** confiserie *f* des fruits; *Dom.Ec:* **p. pan,** bassine *f* à confitures.

preset[1] [priː'set], *v.tr.* (*p.t. & p.p.* **preset;** *pr.p.* **presetting**) **1.** *Mec: Elcs:* prérégler (le fonctionnement d'un mécanisme, etc.). **2.** prépositionner (un index indicateur); affecter une valeur de référence (à un compteur); initialiser à zéro, à dix, etc. **3.** prédéfinir (un paramètre).

preset[2] ['priːset], *a.* **1.** *Mec: Elcs:* préréglé; *Elcs:* **p. wave,** onde préréglée. **2.** (*of index*) prépositionné; (*of counter*) affecté d'une valeur de référence; initialisé (à zéro, à dix, etc.). **3.** (*of parameter*) prédéfini.

presettable [priː'setəbl], *a.* préréglable.

presetting [priː'setiŋ], *s.* **1.** *Mec: Elcs:* préréglage *m* (du fonctionnement d'un mécanisme, etc.). **2.** prépositionnement *m* (d'un index indicateur); affectation *f* d'une valeur de référence (à un compteur); initialisation *f* (d'un compteur à zéro, à dix, etc.). **3.** (*of parameter*) prédéfinition *f*.

preshrink [priː'ʃriŋk], *v.tr.* (**preshrank** [-'ʃræŋk], **preshrunk** [-'ʃrʌŋk]) rendre (un tissu) irrétrécissable; **preshrunk material,** tissu rétréci en cours de fabrication.

preside [pri'zaid], *v.i.* présider; (*a*) **to p. at, over, a meeting,** présider une réunion; **the town council is presided over by the mayor,** le conseil municipal est présidé par le maire; **justice should p. over policy,** la justice doit présider à la politique; *O:* **to p. at the organ, at the piano,** tenir l'orgue, le piano; (*b*) exercer les fonctions de président; occuper le fauteuil présidentiel; présider (à table, etc.).

presidency ['prezidənsi], *s.* **1.** présidence *f*; (*a*) **to assume the p.,** prendre possession du fauteuil présidentiel; **during my p.,** pendant ma présidence; (*b*) *Hist:* (*district*) présidence (du Bengale, de Madras, de Bombay). **2.** *Sch:* directorat *m*, rectorat *m* (d'un collège).

president ['prezidənt], *s.* **1.** président *m* (d'une république, etc.); *NAm:* président (d'une société anonyme, etc.); président, -ente (d'une réunion, etc.); *Adm: A:* **P. of the Board of Trade** = Ministre *m* du Commerce; **Lord P. of the Council,** président du Conseil privé du Roi, de la Reine; **P. of a trade union** = Secrétaire général d'un syndicat. **2.** *Sch:* directeur *m*, recteur *m* (d'un collège, *U.S:* d'une université).

presidential [prezi'denʃ(ə)l], *a.* présidentiel; **p. elections,** (élections) présidentielles *fpl*; *U.S:* **p. year,** année *f* des élections présidentielles.

presidentship ['prezidəntʃip], *s.* **1.** présidence *f*. **2.** *Sch:* directorat *m*, rectorat *m* (d'un collège, *U.S:* d'une université).

presidial [pri'sidiəl], *a. & s. Hist:* présidial, -aux (*m*).

presidiary [pri'sidiəri], *a. Hist:* (troupes, etc.) de garnison.

presiding [pri'zaidiŋ], *a.* qui préside; **p. examiner,** surveillant, -ante (à un examen écrit); **p. officer,** président *m* du scrutin (à une élection).

presidium [pri'sidiəm, -'zid-], *s. Pol:* présidium *m*.

preslew[1] ['priːsluː], *s. Cmptr:* saut *m* (du papier) avant impression.

preslew[2] [priː'sluː], *v.i. Cmptr:* (*of paper*) faire un saut avant impression.

presort [priː'sɔːt], *v.tr.* trier préalablement.

presphygmic [priː'sfigmik], *a. Physiol:* présphygmique.

press[1] [pres], *s.* **1.** (*a*) pression *f* (sur qch.); **with a p. of the hand,** avec un serrement de main; **give it a slight p.!** appuyez légèrement là-dessus! (*b*) *O:* **the p. of modern life,** l'activité fiévreuse, la fièvre, de la vie moderne; **the p. of business,** la presse, le tourbillon, le poids, des affaires; (*c*) foule *f*; mêlée *f* (de la bataille); **to force one's way through the p.,** fendre la foule; se frayer un chemin à travers la foule; **in the thick of the p.,** au cœur, au plus fort, de la mêlée; (*d*) *Nau:* **to carry a p. of sail,** faire force de voiles. **2.** (*a*) **wine p.,** pressoir *m*; **cider p.,** pressoir à cidre; **oil p.,** pressoir à huile; **p. house, room,** pressoir; **botanist's p.,** coquette *f*; **(tennis) racquet p.,** presse à raquette; **trouser p.,** presse pour pantalons; presse-pantalon *m, pl.* presse-pantalons; *A:* **letter p., copying p.,** presse à copier; (*b*) **linen p., clothes p.,** armoire *f* à linge; (*c*) *Ind: etc:* **hydraulic p.,** presse hydraulique; **forging p.,** presse à forger; **drop-forging p.,** presse hydraulique à estamper; **p. forging,** emboutissage *m*; **p. forger,** emboutisseur *m*; **p. forged,** embouti; **power p.,** presse mécanique; **screw p.,** presse à vis; **fly p.** presse à balancier; **coining p.,** balancier *m* monétaire; presse à frapper (la monnaie); *Glassm: etc:* **mould(ing) p.,** serre *f*; machine à mouler sous pression; (*for plastics*) **injection moulding p.,** presse à injection; **p. mould,** moule *m* pour moulage sous pression; (*d*) *Typ:* **printing p.,** presse à imprimer, d'imprimerie; **hand p.,** presse à bras; **platen p.,** presse à platine; **rotary p.,** presse rotative; **lithographic p.,** presse lithographique; **offset p.,** presse offset; **perfecting p.,** presse à double impression; **proof p.,** presse à épreuves; **reversing p.,** presse à contre-épreuves; **p. blanket,** blanchet *m*; **p. stone,** marbre *m* (d'une presse); **book in the p.,** livre sous presse, à l'impression; **to go to p.,** mettre sous presse; **ready for p.,** prêt à mettre sous presse; **to pass a proof for p.,** donner le bon à tirer; **in time for p.,** à temps pour l'impression; (*e*) (*in name of firm*) imprimerie *f*; **the XYZ P.,** (i) l'Imprimerie XYZ; (ii) Éditions XYZ. **3. the p.,** la presse, les journaux; **the liberty, freedom, of the p.,** la liberté de la presse; **the p. exerts a great influence,** l'influence de la presse est très étendue; **p. attaché,** attaché *m* de presse; **p. conference,** conférence *f* de presse; **p. campaign,** campagne *f* de presse; **p. agency, bureau,** agence *f*, bureau *m*, de presse; **p. agent,** agent *m* de publicité (d'un artiste, etc.); **to have a good, bad, p.,** avoir bonne, mauvaise, presse; **p. cutting,** coupure *f* de journal, de presse; **p.-cutting agency,** argus *m* de la presse; *Publ:* **p. copy,** exemplaire *m* de publicité, de service de presse; **to write for the p.,** écrire pour les journaux; faire du journalisme; **p. photographer,** photographe *mf* de presse.

press[2], *v.*

I. *v.tr.* **1.** (*a*) appuyer sur (qch.); **p. the button,** appuyez sur le bouton; *Tp:* enfoncez le bouton; **he pressed the drawing pin into the board,** il a enfoncé la punaise sur la planche; **his face was pressed against the window,** il avait le visage collé à la vitre; **p. the key down,** abaissez la manette; **you must p. the pedal right down,** il faut enfoncer la pédale (à fond); (*b*) (*squeeze*) serrer; **he pressed my hand in his,** il a serré ma main dans la sienne; **to p. (the juice out of) a lemon,** exprimer le jus d'un citron; presser un citron (pour en extraire le jus). **2.** (*a*) mettre (qch.) sous presse; *Metalw:* matricer, estamper, emboutir (le métal); *Rec:* matricer, presser (un disque); *Paperm:* satiner, calandrer (le papier); *Tex:* calandrer, catir (un tissu); *Tan:* fouler (les peaux); *Glassm: etc:* mouler (le verre, le plastique); (*b*) pressurer, fouler (le raisin); pressurer (des pommes, etc.); presser, pressurer (le fromage); (*c*) *Laund:* repasser, donner un coup de fer à (un vêtement); **to p. (down) a seam,** rabattre une couture. **3.** (*a*) **to p. the enemy hard, closely,** serrer l'ennemi de près; talonner l'ennemi; **to p. the enemy back,** refouler l'ennemi; **to p. s.o. hard,** mettre qn aux abois, à la dernière extrémité; poursuivre qn l'épée dans les reins; **don't p. him too hard,** il ne faut pas lui mettre l'épée dans les reins; il ne faut pas trop le tourmenter; **pressed by one's creditors,** pressé, harcelé, par ses créanciers; **to be pressed for time, money,** être à court de temps, d'argent; (*b*) **to p. s.o. to do sth.,** presser qn de faire qch.; **he didn't need much pressing,** il ne s'est pas trop fait prier; **to p. s.o. for a debt,** réclamer une dette à qn; **to p. for an answer,** réclamer une réponse immédiate; insister pour avoir une réponse immédiate; **the Liberals are pressing for a decision (to be made),** les Libéraux demandent instamment, avec instance, que l'on prenne une décision; (*c*) **to p. a point,** insister sur un point; **he needn't p. the argument,** il est inutile d'insister; **to p. a claim,** insister sur une demande; (*d*) **to p. a gift on s.o.,** forcer qn à accepter un cadeau.

II. *v.i.* **1.** (*a*) appuyer; exercer une pression; **a bone was pressing on a nerve,** un os pressait, exerçait une pression, sur un nerf; **don't p. too hard,** n'appuyez pas trop fort; **you're pressing too hard on your pencil,** tu appliques ton crayon trop fort sur le papier; (*b*) **the crowd was pressing forward towards the exit,** la foule se pressait pour gagner la sortie; **to p. close against s.o.,** se serrer contre qn. **2. time's pressing,** le temps presse; **nothing presses,** rien ne presse, il n'y a rien d'urgent.

III. (*compound verb*) **press on,** *v.i.* presser, forcer, le pas; se presser, se hâter; continuer (rapidement) son chemin; **to p. on with one's work,** activer, hâter, son travail, s'activer à son travail; *F:* **p. on, regardless!** allons-y et tant pis!

press[3], *s. Nau: Mil: A:* presse *f* (de matelots, etc.); enrôlement forcé; **p. gang,** (détachement *m* de la) presse; **p. warrant,** autorisation *f* de faire la presse; **p. money,** prime versée comme avance (à un marin, à un soldat).

press[4], *v.tr.* (*a*) *Nau: A:* enrôler de force (un matelot); prendre (qn) par la presse; (*b*) *Mil: A:* réquisitionner (des mulets, etc.); (*c*) **to p. s.o. into service,** enrôler, faire appel à, qn; **even the farm carts were pressed into service for the occasion,** on a réquisitionné même les charrettes.

pressboard ['presbɔːd], *s.* **1.** *Bookb:* ais *m*. **2.** *El:* Presspahn *m* (*R.t.m.*).

pressbutton ['presbʌt(ə)n], *s.* **1.** (bouton *m*) poussoir *m*; *Tg: etc:* touche *f* (de clavier); **p. switch,** clef *f* de commutation à poussoir. **2.** = PRESS-STUD.

pressed [prest], *a.* (*a*) pressé, serré, comprimé; **p. cotton, hay,** coton *m*, foin *m*, en balles; *Cu:* **p. beef,** bœuf salé, bouilli et moulé en forme; (*b*) *Metalw:* embouti, matricé, estampé; **p. steel frame,** châssis *m* en tôle d'acier emboutie; (*c*) **p. oil,** huile *f* de presse; *Petr:* **p. distillate,** distillat *m* de presse.

presser ['presər], *s.* **1.** *Ind:* (*pers.*) presseur, -euse. **2.** presse *f* (à viande, etc.); **vegetable p.,** presse-purée *m inv*.

press-forge ['presfɔːdʒ], *v.tr. Metalw:* emboutir.

pressing[1] ['presiŋ], *a.* (danger) pressant; (travail) pressé, urgent; **p. debt,** dette criarde; **to have nothing more p. than to . . .,** n'avoir rien de plus pressé que de . . .; **the case is p.,** il y a urgence; **p. invitation,** invitation instante, pressante; **since you are so p.,** puisque vous insistez.

pressing[2], *s.* **1.** (*a*) pression *f* (sur qch.); mise *f* en balle (du coton, etc.); pressage *m* (d'un fruit pour en extraire le jus); expression *f* (du jus d'un citron, etc.); pressurage *m*, foulage *m* (du raisin); pressurage (des pommes, etc.); pressage, pressurage (des fromages); (*b*) *Metalw:* emboutissage *m*, estampage *m*, matriçage *m*; *Rec:* matriçage, pressage (des disques); moulage *m* (du verre, du plastique, etc.); (*c*) *Tex:* calandrage *m*, catissage *m* (des tissus); *Paperm:* calandrage, satinage *m* (du papier); *Tan:* foulage *m* (des peaux); (*d*) *Laund:* repassage *m* (des vêtements); **steam p.,** repassage à la vapeur, *Com:* pressing *m*. **2.** (*a*) *Metalw:* pièce matricée, emboutie; **sheet steel p.,** tôle emboutie; (*b*) *usu.pl.* **pressing(s),** pressée *f*, pressis *m* (de pommes, etc.). **3.** insistance *f* (sur un point); réclamation *f* (d'une dette, etc.).

pressing[3], *s. A:* presse *f*; enrôlement forcé (de matelots, etc.).

pressingness ['presiŋnis], *s.* urgence *f* (d'un travail, etc.).

pressirostral [presi'rɔstrəl], *a. Orn:* pressirostral, -aux.

Pressirostres [presi'rɔstriːz], *s.pl. Orn:* pressirostres *m*.

pressman, *pl.* **-men** ['presmən], *s.m.* **1.** presseur; pressureur. **2.** *Typ:* pressier. **3.** journaliste, reporter.

pressmark ['presmɑːk], *s.* cote *f* (d'un livre dans une bibliothèque).

pressroom ['presruːm], *s.* **1.** *Typ:* salle *f* de la presse; atelier *m* des machines. **2.** *Num:* salle des balanciers. **3.** *Wine-m:* pressoir *m*.

pressrun ['presrʌn], *s. Typ:* tirage *m* (en une seule fois); **p. of 5000,** tirage à, de, en, 5000 exemplaires.

press-stud ['presstʌd], *s.* bouton *m* (à) pression (de vêtement).

press-up ['presʌp], *s. Gym:* **to do press-ups,** faire des tractions, *F:* des pompes.

pressurage ['preʃəridʒ], *s. Wine-m:* pressurage *m*.

pressure[1] ['preʃər], *s.* **1.** (*a*) pression (exercée sur qch.); **it needs a bit more p.,** il faut appuyer plus fort; **I felt the slight p. of his hand on my arm,** j'ai senti la légère pression de sa main sur mon bras; *Typ:* **p. cylinder,** cylindre *m* de pression; *Mec.E: etc:* **p. roller,** galet de pression, galet presseur (d'une courroie de transport, etc.); *Metalw:* **p. diecast,** pièce moulée en coquille sous pression; **p. plate,** (i) plaque *f,* plateau *m,* face *f,* de pression; (ii) *Aut:* disque *m* de pression (d'un frein); *Med:* **p. bandage,** bandage compressif; **p. dressing,** pansement compressif; (*b*) **to bring p. to bear, to put p., on s.o.,** exercer une pression, son influence, sur qn; *Pol: etc:* **p. group,** groupe *m* de pression; *Sp:* **sustained p.,** forcing *m*; **to act under p.,** agir sous la contrainte, sous la pression des circonstances; **the p. of circumstances,** la pression des circonstances; **financial p.,** embarras financiers; **the p. of poverty,** le poids, les rigueurs *f,* de la pauvreté, de la misère; **p. of business, of work,** le poids, la presse, des affaires, du travail; **to work at high p.,** travailler fiévreusement, au plus fort; **population p.,** pression démographique; *esp. U.S:* **the hunting p. (on animals),** l'impact *m* de la chasse (sur les animaux). **2.** (*a*) *Ph: Mec: etc:* pression; poussée *f* (d'un fluide, d'un corps pesant); **absolute p.,** pression absolue; **active, actual, effective, p.,** pression effective; **back p., negative p.,** pression inverse; contre-pression *f*; **zero-point p.,** pression au zéro absolu; **dynamic, impact, p.,** pression dynamique; **equalized p.,** pression équilibrée; **equalizing p.,** pression de compensation; **differential p.,** différence *f* de pression; **critical p.,** pression critique; **specific p., unit p.,** pression spécifique, unitaire; **static p.,** pression statique; **suction p.,** pression d'aspiration; **surface p.,** pression de surface; **p. at a point,** pression en un point; **p. centre,** centre *m* de pression; **p. coefficient,** coefficient *m* de pression; **p. control, regulation,** contrôle *m,* régulation *f,* de la pression; **p. controller, regulator, governor,** régulateur *m* de pression; pressostat *m*; **gas p.,** pression du gaz, pression gazeuse; **elastic p. of gases,** force *f* élastique des gaz; **p. gas,** gaz pauvre par pression; **hydrostatic p.,** pression hydrostatique; **water p.,** charge *f* d'eau; pression, poussée, de l'eau; *Bot:* **osmotic p.,** pression osmotique; *Meteor:* **atmospheric p.,** pression atmosphérique; **barometric p.,** pression barométrique; **high-p. area,** aire *f,* zone *f,* anticyclonique, de hautes pressions; **low-p. area,** aire, zone, cyclonique, de basses pressions; **wind p.,** pression, poussée, du vent; **blast p.,** (i) *Metall:* pression du vent (dans un haut fourneau); (ii) *Atom.Ph:* pression de souffle (d'un réacteur); *Mch:* **p. stage,** étage *m* de pression (d'une turbine); **p. turbine,** turbine à pression, à réaction; *Mch: Mec.E:* **actuating, driving, p.,** pression motrice; **intake p.,** pression d'admission; **initial p.,** pression initiale; **rated p.,** pression nominale; **working p.,** (i) pression effective; (ii) pression de fonctionnement, de marche, de régime; pression normale; (iii) (*of boiler*) (pression du) timbre *m*; **test p.,** pression, surcharge *f,* d'épreuve, d'essai; **p. test,** épreuve *f,* essai, de pression; **p. feed,** alimentation *f* sous pression; *I.C.E: Av:* **boost p.,** pression de suralimentation; **oil p.,** pression d'huile; **high-p., low-p., engine,** machine *f* à haute, à basse, pression; *Aut: etc:* **tyre p.,** pression des pneus; **table of tyre pressures,** table *f,* tableau *m,* de gonflage; *Artil: etc:* **bore p.,** pression (des gaz de la poudre) dans l'âme; *Petr:* **open p.,** pression d'écoulement (du pétrole en jaillissement); **p. drilling,** forage *m* sous pression; *Mec.E: etc:* **p. chamber,** réservoir *m* d'air comprimé; **p. tank,** réservoir de, sous, pression; *Av:* **p. cabin,** cabine pressurisée; *Av: Space:* **p. suit,** vêtement pressurisé; combinaison pressurisée; *N.Arch:* **p. hull,** coque intérieure, résistante (d'un sous-marin); **p. pump,** pompe *f* à pression; pompe de mise en pression; pompe foulante ou refoulante; *Dom.Ec:* **p. cooker,** autocuiseur *m*; marmite *f* à, sous, pression; marmite autoclave; (*b*) *Physiol:* **(arterial) blood p.,** pression artérielle, sanguine; tension artérielle (du sang); **venous blood p.,** pression veineuse; **high blood p.,** hypertension, hypertonie (artérielle); **low blood p.,** hypotension, hypotonie (artérielle); **to suffer from high blood p.,** *F:* **to have blood p.,** avoir de l'hypertension, *F:* de la tension; **pulse p.,** pression différentielle; différentiel *m*; (*c*) *El:* pression (électrique), tension, voltage *m*; **working p.,** tension de régime, de service, d'utilisation; **drop in p.,** chute *f* de tension.

pressure², *v.tr. esp. U.S:* **1.** exercer une pression, faire pression, sur (qn). **2.** pressuriser (la cabine d'un avion, etc.). **3.** *Cu:* (faire) cuire sous pression, dans un autocuiseur.

pressure-cook ['preʃəkuk], *v.tr. Cu:* (faire) cuire sous pression, dans un autocuiseur.

pressure-sealed ['preʃəsi:ld], *a.* autoclave.

pressurization [preʃərai'zeiʃ(ə)n], *s.* pressurisation *f*; mise *f,* maintien *m,* en, sous, pression; **p. system,** dispositif *m* de mise, de maintien, en, sous, pression; circuit *m* de mise en, sous, pression.

pressurize ['preʃəraiz], *v.tr.* (*a*) pressuriser; mettre, maintenir, en, sous, pression; **to p. at ten atmospheres,** mettre, maintenir, sous pression de dix atmosphères; (*b*) = PRESSURE² 1.

pressurized ['preʃəraizd], *a.* pressurisé; en pression; (mis) sous pression; *Av:* **p. cabin,** cabine pressurisée; **p. fuel tank,** réservoir de combustible pressurisé; **p. suit,** vêtement pressurisé, combinaison pressurisée; *Atom.Ph:* **p. casing,** gaine *f* en pression; **p. water reactor,** pile *f,* réacteur *m,* à eau sous pression; *Mec.E:* **p. operation,** fonctionnement *m* en pression.

pressurizer ['preʃəraizər], *s. Mec.E:* générateur *m* de pression; dispositif *m* de mise en, sous, pression.

pressurizing ['preʃəraiziŋ], *s. Mec.E:* pressurisation *f*; mise *f,* maintien *m,* en, sous, pression; **p. valve,** valve *f* de mise en pression; *Av: etc:* **fuel p.,** mise du combustible sous pression.

presswork ['preswə:k], *s.* **1.** *Metalw:* étampage *m,* emboutissage *m.* **2.** *Typ:* tirage *m,* impression *f.* **3.** journalisme *m,* reportage *m.*

prestation [pres'teiʃ(ə)n], *s.* prestation *f.*

Prester John ['prestə'dʒɔn], *Pr.n.m. Hist:* Prêtre-Jean.

prestidigitation [prestididʒi'teiʃ(ə)n], *s.* prestidigitation *f.*

prestidigitator [presti'didʒiteit(ə)r], *s.* prestidigitateur *m.*

prestige [pres'ti:ʒ], *s.* prestige *m*; **the p. which he owes to his position,** la considération que lui vaut sa position; **to ruin the p. of a country,** ruiner le crédit d'un pays; **loss of p.,** perte *f* de prestige; **it would mean loss of p.,** ce serait déchoir, déroger; **p. advertising,** publicité *f* de prestige; **p. flats,** appartements *m* de grand standing.

prestigious [pres'tidʒəs], *a.* prestigieux.

prestissimo [pres'tisimou], *a., adv. & s. Mus:* prestissimo (*m*).

presto¹ ['prestou], *a., adv. & s. Mus:* presto (*m*).

presto², *int.* **hey p.!** passez muscade!

prestocking [pri:'stɔkiŋ], *s.* préstockage *m.*

prestore [pri:'stɔər], *v.tr. Cmptr:* **1.** préenregistrer. **2.** initialiser.

prestress¹ [pri:'stres], *s. Const:* précontrainte *f.*

prestress², *v.tr. Const:* précontraindre (le béton).

prestressed [pri:'strest], *a. Const:* (béton) précontraint.

prestressing [pri:'stresiŋ], *s. Const:* précontrainte *f.*

presumable [pri'zju:məbl], *a.* présumable.

presumably [pri'zju:məbli], *adv.* **p. he will come,** il est à croire, il y a lieu de croire, qu'il viendra; **he is p. dead,** il est vraisemblablement mort; **p. you told him that . . .,** je suppose, il est à supposer, que vous lui avez dit que . . .; **he's p. gone by now,** il est déjà parti, n'est-ce pas?

presume [pri'zju:m]. **1.** *v.tr.* (*a*) présumer; **to p. s.o. innocent,** présumer qn innocent, que qn est innocent; **he was presumed dead,** (i) on le croyait mort; (ii) on l'a porté mort; **let us p. that . . .,** supposons que + *sub.*; **you are Mr X, I p.,** vous êtes M. X, je suppose; **I p. you've written to him,** je suppose que vous lui avez écrit; vous lui avez écrit, n'est-ce pas? **I p. that a decision has been reached,** je présume, il est à croire, qu'on a pris une décision; **you p. too much,** vous allez trop vite; vous présumez trop; **you don't expect me to go with you, I p.,** vous n'attendez pas, je l'espère, que je vous accompagne; (*b*) prendre la liberté, présumer, avoir la présomption (de faire qch.); **I wouldn't p. to question his decision,** je n'oserais pas mettre en question sa décision; **if I may p. to advise you,** si je puis me permettre de vous conseiller. **2.** *v.i.* (*a*) **to p. too much,** présumer trop de soi; (*b*) se montrer présomptueux; prendre des libertés (avec qn); (*c*) **to p. on one's friendship with s.o.,** abuser de l'amitié de qn; **to p. on one's birth, one's wealth,** se prévaloir de sa naissance, de sa richesse.

presumed [pri'zju:md], *a.* présumé; prétendu.

presumedly [pri'zju:midli], *adv.* vraisemblablement; d'après ce qu'on croit.

presuming¹ [pri'zju:miŋ], *a.* (*a*) présomptueux; (*b*) indiscret, -ète.

presuming², *s.* présomption *f.*

presumption [pri'zʌm(p)ʃ(ə)n], *s.* **1.** présomption *f*; **the natural p. is that . . .,** la conclusion naturelle est que . . .; **the p. is that he is dead,** on présume, il est à présumer, qu'il est mort; **p. in favour of s.o.,** préjugé *m* en faveur de qn; **there is a strong p. against the truth of the news,** il y a tout lieu de croire que la nouvelle est fausse; *Jur:* **p. of law,** présomption légale; **p. of fact,** présomption de fait; (*of one person to another in a catastrophe*) **p. of survival,** présomption de survie. **2.** présomption, arrogance *f,* suffisance *f*; **forgive my p.,** excusez mon audace.

presumptive [pri'zʌmptiv], *a. Jur: etc:* **p. evidence,** (preuve *f* par) présomption *f*; *Ins:* **the ship is a p. loss,** il y a présomption de perte; **heir p.,** héritier présomptif.

presumptively [pri'zʌmptivli], *adv.* par présomption; présomptivement.

presumptuous [pri'zʌmptjuəs], *a.* présomptueux, outrecuidant.

presumptuously [pri'zʌmptjuəsli], *adv.* présomptueusement.

presumptuousness [pri'zʌmptjuəsnis], *s.* présomption *f,* outrecuidance *f.*

presuppose [pri:sə'pouz], *v.tr.* présupposer.

presupposition [pri:sʌpə'ziʃ(ə)n], *s.* présupposition *f.*

presystole [pri:'sistoul], *s. Physiol:* présystole *f.*

presystolic [pri:sis'tɔlik], *a. Physiol:* présystolique.

pretemporal [pri:'tempərəl], *a. Anat:* prétemporal, -aux.

pretence [pri'tens], *s.* **1.** (faux) semblant; simulation *f,* affectation *f,* prétexte *m*; **p. of repentance,** semblants *mpl* de repentir; **to make a p. of doing sth.,** faire semblant de faire qch.; **he makes a p. of protecting you,** en apparence il vous protège; **his work is mere p.,** il fait seulement semblant de travailler; **it was all p.,** c'était pour rire; **under the p. of friendship, of religion,** sous prétexte, sous couleur, d'amitié; sous le manteau de la religion; **under the p. that . . .,** sous prétexte que + *ind.* **under, on, the p. of consulting me,** sous prétexte de me consulter; **to ring for the servants on the smallest p.,** sonner les domestiques sous le moindre prétexte; *Jur:* **false pretences,** faux semblant; présentation mensongère (en vue d'escroquer); **to obtain sth. by, on, under, false pretences,** obtenir qch. par fraude *f,* par des moyens frauduleux; **to gain admittance under false pretences,** s'introduire chez qn sous de fausses apparences. **2.** (*a*) prétention *f,* vanité *f*; **devoid of all p.,** sans aucune prétention; (*b*) **he makes no p. to wit,** il ne prétend pas à l'esprit; il n'a aucune prétention à l'esprit.

pretend¹ [pri'tend]. **1.** *v.tr.* (*a*) feindre, simuler (qch.); **to p. ignorance,** simuler l'ignorance; faire l'ignorant; **to p. to be ill,** faire le malade; **to p. to do sth.,** faire semblant, faire le simulacre, feindre, affecter, de faire qch.; **he pretends to be very busy,** il fait celui qui est très affairé; il fait l'affairé; **they p. to be friends, to be friendly,** ils font semblant d'être amis; **he pretended to be angry,** il fit mine d'être fâché; **don't p. you don't understand,** ne faites pas semblant de ne pas comprendre; ne faites pas l'innocent; **they pretended that nothing had happened,** ils faisaient comme si rien ne s'était passé; **it's no use pretending (that) I'm still young,** ce n'est pas la peine de me faire l'illusion que je suis encore jeune; **he pretended he was a doctor,** il s'est fait passer pour médecin; **let's pretend we're kings and queens,** faisons semblant d'être des rois et des reines; jouons au roi et à la reine; **to play at** ***let's pretend,*** jouer à faire semblant; **he went off, pretending that he was coming back,** il est parti, soi-disant pour revenir; **pretending that he had a lot of work to do, he left early,** sous prétexte d'avoir beaucoup de travail à faire, il est parti de bonne heure; (*b*) prétendre; **he does not p. to be artistic,** il ne prétend pas être artiste; il n'a pas de prétentions artistiques; **I can't p. to advise you,** je ne prétends pas vous conseiller, je n'ai pas la prétention de vous conseiller; **he is not so virtuous as he pretends (to be),** il n'est pas si vertueux qu'il en a la prétention. **2.** *v.ind.tr. A:* **to p. to sth.,** prétendre à qch.; revendiquer son droit à qch.; **to p. to intelligence,** avoir des prétentions, prétendre, à l'intelligence; **to p. to s.o.'s hand, to s.o.,** prétendre à la main de qn. **3.** *v.i.* faire semblant; jouer la comédie; **stop pretending, please!** finissez de jouer la comédie, je vous en prie!

pretend², *s. F:* **it was only p.!** mais on faisait semblant! c'était pour rire!

pretended [pri'tendid], *a.* (*a*) (*of quality, emotion, etc.*) feint, simulé, faux; (*b*) (*of pers.*) soi-disant, supposé, prétendu.

pretender [pri'tendər], *s.* **1.** simulateur, -trice. **2.** prétendant *m* (to, à); *Hist:* **the Old P.,** le Prétendant; **the Young P.,** le Jeune Prétendant.

pretension [pri'tenʃ(ə)n], *s.* **1.** prétention *f* (to, à); désir ambitieux (de); **to have no pretensions to the first rank,** n'avoir aucune prétention au premier rang; n'avoir aucun désir d'occuper le premier rang; **pretensions to dictatorship,** prétention à la dictature; **man of no pretension(s),** homme sans prétentions; **to have pretensions to literary taste,** se piquer de littérature; **to have social pretensions,** vouloir arriver. **2.** droit *m,* titre *m*; prétention justifiée. **3.** PRETENTIOUSNESS.

pretentious [pri'tenʃəs], *a.* prétentieux; (*of display, etc.*) ostentateur, -trice; **p. man,** homme à prétentions; **he's so p.,** il a ce petit air prétentieux; **p. style,** style apprêté, prétentieux; **they entertain in such a p. way,** ils reçoivent avec trop d'ostentation.

pretentiously [pri'tenʃəsli], *adv.* prétentieusement; avec ostentation.

pretentiousness [pri'tenʃəsnis], *s.* prétention *f*; ostentation *f*; air prétentieux.

preterhuman [pri:tə'hju:mən], *a.* surhumain.

preterite ['pretərit], *a. & s. Gram:* **p.** (tense), (temps) passé (*m*); prétérit (*m*); **in the p.,** au passé, au prétérit.

preterition [pri:tə'riʃ(ə)n], *s.* **1.** = PRETERMISSION 1. **2.** *Theol:* omission *f* (d'une âme) de parmi les élus.

pretermission [pri:tə'miʃ(ə)n], *s.* **1.** (*a*) *Lit:* prétérition *f*, omission *f* (de qch. dans un récit); (*b*) *Rh:* prétérition, prétermission *f*; (*c*) *Rom.Jur:* prétérition (d'un héritier). **2.** *Lit:* interruption *f*, suspension *f*, cessation momentanée; **without p.,** sans interruption.

pretermit [pri:tə'mit], *v.tr.* (**pretermitted**) *Lit:* **1.** (*a*) passer (qch.) sous silence; omettre (qch.); (*b*) négliger, oublier (de faire qch.). **2.** interrompre, suspendre (un cours, etc.); (*b*) (*erroneously*) cesser (qch.) (définitivement).

preternatural [pri:tə'nætjərəl], *a.* préternaturel; surnaturel.

preternaturalism [pri:tə'nætjərəlizm], *s. Theol:* surnaturalisme *m.*

preternaturally [pri:tə'nætjərəli], *adv.* surnaturellement.

pretest[1] [pri:'test], *s. Com: etc:* prétest *m*, prétesting *m*; préenquête *f.*

pretest[2], *v.tr. Com: etc:* prétester; préenquêter sur (qch.).

pretesting [pri:'testiŋ], *s.* = PRETEST[1].

pretext[1] ['pri:tekst], *s.* prétexte *m*; **to give sth. as a p.,** alléguer qch. comme prétexte; **to find a p. for refusing, for a refusal,** trouver un prétexte pour refuser; trouver prétexte à un refus; **he came under, on, the p. of consulting his brother,** il est venu sous prétexte de consulter son frère; **under the p. of calling on s.o.,** sous le couvert d'une visite à rendre.

pretext[2] [pri'tekst], *v.tr.* alléguer (qch.) comme prétexte; prétexter (qch.).

pretonic [pri:'tɔnik], *a. Ling:* prétonique.

pretreat [pri:'tri:t], *v.tr. Tchn:* prétraiter.

pretreatment [pri:tri:'tmənt], *s. Tchn:* prétraitement *m.*

prettify ['pritifai], *v.tr.* enjoliver.

prettily ['pritili], *adv.* joliment; gentiment; agréablement; (*of girl*) **p. dressed,** joliment habillée; *P.N:* (*outside hotel, etc.*) **please park p.,** prière de stationner convenablement.

prettiness ['pritinis], *s.* (*a*) joliesse *f*, gentillesse *f*; (*b*) afféterie *f*; mignardise *f* (de style, etc.).

pretty ['priti]. **1.** *a.* (*a*) (*of woman, child*) jolie; gentille; mignonne; **as p. as a picture,** jolie comme un cœur; gentille, jolie, mignonne, comme tout; **my p.,** ma mignonne; **what a p. child, kitten!** quel amour d'enfant, de chaton! (*to child*) **go and make yourself p.!** va te faire beau, belle! (*b*) (*of thg*) joli; gentil; **a p. thatched cottage,** une jolie chaumière; **it makes a p. picture, a p. scene,** c'est vraiment attrayant; (*with Pej: nuance*) **p. picture, p. song,** joli petit tableau, jolie petite chanson (sans avoir de vraie valeur artistique); **to make p. speeches,** dire des gentillesses; (*c*) adroit, habile; **a p. wit,** un bel esprit; *Sp:* **that was p. play,** c'était bien joué; (*d*) *Iron:* **a p. state of affairs! a p. mess!** (i) en voici une belle! c'est du joli, du beau, du propre! (ii) nous voilà dans de beaux draps! **that's a p. way to talk!** c'est du joli que de parler comme ça! **I've heard some p. tales about you!** j'ai entendu de belles sur votre compte! **that'll cost me a p. penny!** ça va me coûter cher! **2.** *adv.* (*a*) assez, passablement; **I'm p. well,** je ne me porte pas, ça ne va pas, trop mal; **p. good,** (i) passablement bon; (ii) magnifique, superbe; **it's p. difficult,** c'est plutôt difficile; ce n'est pas exactement facile; **p. nearly, p. much, p. well, the same,** à peu près la même chose; presque la même chose; **p. nearly new,** neuf, à peu de chose près; **you're p. nearly right,** vous n'êtes pas loin du compte; c'est à peu près ça; **they're p. much alike,** ils sont assez semblables; ils se ressemblent beaucoup; (*b*) *F:* **to be sitting p.,** être bien placé; avoir la bonne place. **3.** *s.* (*a*) *A:* ornement *m*, bibelot *m*; **to fill one's glass up to the p.,** remplir son verre jusqu'à la dentelle; (*b*) *F: A:* **pretties,** lingerie fine; (*c*) *Bot: U.S:* **p. by night,** belle-de-nuit *f*, *pl.* belles-de-nuit; merveille *f* du Pérou.

pretty-pretty ['pritipriti], *a. Pej:* affété; mignard.

pretubercular, pretuberculous [pri:tju'bə:kjulər, -kjuləs], *a. Med:* prétuberculeux.

pretzel ['pretzl], *s. Comest:* bretzel *m.*

prevail [pri'veil], *v.i.* **1.** prévaloir; avoir l'avantage; réussir; **to p. over, against, s.o., sth.,** prévaloir sur, contre, qn, qch.; avoir l'avantage, l'emporter, sur qn; dominer qn, qch.; **the strong hand of the law prevailed,** force est restée à la loi. **2. to p. on s.o. to do sth.,** amener, déterminer, décider, qn à faire qch.; conduire qn à faire qch.; obtenir de qn qu'il fasse qch.; **to p. on s.o. to consent,** arracher son consentement à qn; **he was prevailed (up)on by his friends to . . .,** il se laissa persuader par ses amis de . . . **3.** prédominer, régner; **the theory prevails that . . .,** la théorie domine, est répandue, a cours que . . .; **calm prevails,** le calme règne; **the conditions prevailing in France,** les conditions *f* qui règnent en France; **the conditions now prevailing in the country,** l'état actuel du pays.

prevailing [pri'veiliŋ], *a.* (*a*) (pré)dominant; **p. winds,** vents dominants; **the p. opinion,** l'opinion prédominante, la plus répandue; **the p. tints of a landscape,** les teints dominants d'un paysage; (*b*) **the p. cold,** le froid qui règne en ce moment; **p. fashions,** la mode actuelle; **the p. depression,** le malaise actuel.

prevailingly [pri'veiliŋli], *adv.* à un degré prépondérant, prédominant; d'une manière prédominante.

prevalence ['prevələns], *s.* prédominance *f* (d'une opinion, etc.); **p. of bribery,** généralité *f* de la corruption; **p. of typhus,** fréquence *f* des cas de typhus.

prevalent ['prevələnt], *a.* (pré)dominant, répandu, général; (*of wind, disease, etc.*) régnant; **disease that is p. in a place,** maladie qui est très répandue, qui règne, dans un lieu; **the p. idea on the question,** l'idée qu'on se fait généralement de l'affaire.

prevalently ['prevələntli], *adv.* généralement; d'une manière prédominante.

prevaricate [pri'værikeit], *v.i.* (*a*) équivoquer; user d'équivoques; tergiverser; répondre évasivement; (*b*) mentir.

prevaricating [pri'værikeitiŋ], **prevarication** [priværi'keiʃ(ə)n], *s.* (*a*) équivoques *fpl*; tergiversation *f*; réponse(s) évasive(s); (*b*) mensonge(s) *m*(*pl*).

prevaricator [pri'værikeitər], *s.* (*a*) tergiversateur, -trice; (*b*) menteur, -euse.

prevelar [pri:'vi:lər], *a. Ling:* prévélaire.

prevenient [pri'vi:njənt], *a.* **1.** *Lit:* (événement, etc.) préalable, antécédent (**to,** à). **2.** (traitement médical, etc.) préventif (**of,** de). **3.** *Theol:* **p. grace,** grâce prévenante.

prevent [pri'vent], *v.tr.* **1.** empêcher, mettre obstacle à (un mariage, etc.); **to p. the exercise of a right,** porter atteinte à l'exercice d'un droit; **to p. s.o. (from) doing sth., to p. s.o.'s doing sth.,** empêcher qn de faire qch.; empêcher que qn ne fasse qch.; arrêter qn de faire qch.; **he has been prevented by a previous engagement from taking the chair,** une promesse antérieure l'empêche d'occuper le fauteuil, de présider; **there is nothing to p. our doing so,** il n'y a rien qui nous en empêche; **to be unavoidably prevented from doing sth.,** être dans l'impossibilité matérielle de faire qch.; **I cannot p. him,** je ne peux pas l'en empêcher; **what is to p. you?** qu'est-ce qui vous retient? qu'est-ce qui vous en empêche? **2.** (*a*) prévenir, détourner (un malheur, etc.); parer à (un accident, etc.); **to take steps to p. accidents,** prendre des mesures préventives contre les accidents; **I cannot p. it,** je ne peux pas l'empêcher; **could I have prevented it?** pouvais-je faire que cela n'arrivât pas? **to p. any scandal . . .,** pour obvier à tout scandale . . .; (*b*) **the police prevented the murderer from being lynched,** la police a évité à l'assassin d'être lynché. **3.** *A:* prévenir (les désirs de qn); *Theol:* **that Thy grace may always p. and follow us,** que ta grâce nous prévienne et nous accompagne toujours.

preventable [pri'ventəbl], *a.* évitable; obviable; qui peut être empêché.

preventative [pri'ventətiv], *a.* & *s.* = PREVENTIVE.

preventer [pri'ventər], *s.* **1.** (*a*) (*pers.*) empêcheur, -euse; (*b*) empêchement *m*, obstacle *m*. **2.** *Nau:* **p. (stay, rope),** faux étai; attrape *f*; **p. brace,** faux-bras *m inv*; **p. sheet,** fausse écoute; **p. shroud,** pataras *m*; hauban *m* de fortune; **p. tack,** fausse amure.

preventible [pri'ventibl], *a.* = PREVENTABLE.

prevention [pri'venʃ(ə)n], *s.* **1.** empêchement *m*; **in case of p.,** en cas d'empêchement. **2. p. of accidents,** mesures préventives, précautions *fpl*, contre les accidents; prévention *f* des accidents (de la circulation); **p. of disease,** mesures préventives contre la maladie; prévention de la maladie; prophylaxie *f*; **rust p.,** protection *f* contre la rouille; **society for the p. of cruelty to children, to animals,** société protectrice des enfants, des animaux; *Prov:* **p. is better than cure,** mieux vaut prévenir que guérir.

preventionism [pri'venʃənizm], *s. Med: etc:* préventologie *f.*

preventionist [pri'venʃənist], *s. Med: etc:* préventologue *mf.*

preventive [pri'ventiv]. **1.** *a.* (*a*) (médicament, etc.) préventif; **p. medicine,** médecine préventive; prophylaxie *f*; préventologie *f*; **p. measures,** mesures préventives, de précaution; *Mil: etc:* **p. attack,** attaque préventive; *Jur:* **p. detention,** détention préventive; (*b*) **P. Service,** service *m* des gardes-côtes (douaniers); **P. officer,** officier *m* de la douane. **2.** *s.* (*a*) empêchement *m*; mesure préventive; (*b*) médicament préventif; (*c*) **rust p.,** antirouille *m.*

preventively [pri'ventivli], *adv.* préventivement; à titre préventif.

preventorium [preven'tɔ:riəm], *s. Med:* préventorium *m.*

prevertebral [pri:'və:tibrəl], *a. Anat:* prévertébral, -aux.

preview[1] ['pri:vju:], *s.* (*a*) exhibition *f* préalable; (*b*) *Cin: etc:* avant-première *f*, *pl.* avant-premières; (*c*) *esp. U.S: Cin:* film *m* annonce.

preview[2], *v.tr. Cin: etc:* voir en avant-première.

previous ['pri:viəs]. **1.** *a.* (*a*) préalable; antérieur, antécédent (**to,** à); précédent; **the p. day,** le jour précédent; le jour d'avant; la veille; **the p. night,** la nuit d'avant; la veille au soir; **p. engagement,** engagement antérieur; **without p. notice,** sans avertissement préalable; *Pol: etc:* **to move the p. question,** demander la question préalable; (*b*) *F:* **you're a bit (too) p.!** vous êtes trop pressé! vous allez trop vite! **to be a bit p. in forming a plan,** dresser ses plans prématurément. **2.** *adv.* **p. to my departure,** préalablement, antérieurement, à mon départ; avant mon départ, avant de partir.

previously ['pri:viəsli], *adv.* préalablement, au préalable; précédemment; antérieurement; **p. to my departure,** avant mon départ; avant de partir.

previousness ['pri:viəsnis], *s.* **1.** antériorité *f*; priorité *f*. **2.** *F:* précipitation *f*; manque *m* de délibération.

previse [pri'vaiz], *v.tr.* **1.** prévoir. **2.** prévenir (**that,** que).

prevision [pri'viʒ(ə)n], *s.* prévision *f.*

prevocalic [pri:vou'kælik], *a. Ling:* prévocalique.

prewar [pri:'wɔ:r]. **1.** *a.* d'avant-guerre; **p. prices,** prix d'avant-guerre; **the p. period,** l'avant-guerre *m*; **in the p. period,** avant la guerre. **2.** *adv.* avant la guerre.

prewiring [pri:'waiəriŋ], *s. Cmptr: etc:* précâblage *m.*

prey[1] [prei], *s.* proie *f*; (*a*) **birds of p.,** oiseaux *m* de proie; rapaces *m*; **beasts of p.,** bêtes *f* féroces, bêtes de proie; carnassiers *m*; (*b*) (*of beast*) **to pursue its p.,** poursuivre sa proie; **to be a p. to sth.,** (i) être la proie de qch.; (ii) être en proie à, être dévoré, travaillé, par (la peur, etc.); **to fall a p. to temptation,** tomber en proie aux tentations; se laisser vaincre par les tentations; devenir la proie des tentations.

prey[2], *v.i.* **to p. (up)on sth., s.o.,** faire sa proie de qch., de qn; **something is preying on his mind,** il y a quelque chose qui le travaille, le tourmente.

preying ['preiiŋ], *a.* (oiseau) de proie; (animal) féroce, carnassier.

priacanthus [priə'kænθəs], *s. Ich:* priacanthe *m.*

priapic [prai'æpik], *a.* (culte, etc.) priapique.

priapism ['praiəpizm], *s.* **1.** *Med:* priapisme *m*. **2.** lasciveté *f.*

Priapuloidea [praiæpju'lɔidiə], *s.pl. Ann:* priapuliens *m.*

Priapus [prai'eipəs]. **1.** *Pr.n.m. Cl.Myth:* Priape. **2.** *s.* phallus *m*, priape *m.*

price[1] [prais], *s.* (*a*) prix *m*; **cost p.,** prix coûtant, prix de revient; **to sell under cost p.,** vendre à perte; **full p.,** prix fort; **discount p.,** prix modéré, faible; **manufacturer's p.,** prix de fabrique; **trade p.,** prix marchand, prix de demi-gros; **wholesale p.,** prix de, en, gros; prix de demi-gros; **marked p.,** prix marqué; **catalogue p., list p.,** prix (de) catalogue; prix de nomenclature; (*of book*) **published p.,** prix de catalogue, prix fort; **cash p., p. for cash,** prix (au) comptant; **net p.,** prix net; **inclusive p.,** prix tout compris, tous frais compris; **low, high, p.,** bas, haut, prix; **to buy sth. at a low p., at a fair p.,** acheter qch. à bas prix, à juste prix; *Rail: Th: etc:* **half p.,** demi-place *f*; **to travel (at) half p.,** voyager à demi-place; **to sell sth. (at) half p.,** vendre qch. à moitié prix; **lowest p.,** prix le plus bas, dernier prix; **rock-bottom p.,** prix le plus bas, tout dernier prix; **moderate p.,** prix modique, modéré; **recommended p.,** prix conseillé, recommandé, (plan de fabricant); **(at a) high, low, p.,** (à un) haut, bas, prix; (à un) prix élevé, peu élevé; **at a reduced p.,** à prix réduit, au rabais; **p. cutting, slashing,** forte réduction de prix; **advantageous, attractive, p.,** prix avantageux, intéressant; **unbeatable p.,** prix compétitif, imbattable; **p. range,** écart *m*, éventail *m*, ciseaux *mpl*, des prix; **p. list,** liste *f*, barème *m*, des prix; prix-courant *m*, *pl.* prix-courants; tarif *m*; **market p. list,** mercuriale *f*; **p. current,** prix-courant; **p. tag,** étiquette *f*; *Pol.Ec: etc:* **fixed p.,** prix fixe; prix fait; **agreed p., fixed p.,** prix à forfait, prix forfaitaire; **administered p., agreed fair p.,** prix imposé; **to agree on a p.,** convenir d'un prix; **p. agreed,** prix convenu, prix fait; **actual p.,** prix réel; **basic p.,** prix de base; **ceiling p.,** prix plafond; **floor p.,** prix plancher; **current p.,** prix actuel, courant, pratiqué; prix en vigueur; prix du jour; **firm, steady, p.,** prix ferme; **direct p.,** prix de, en, gros, **shadow p.,** prix fictif, fantôme; **pegged, supported, standby, p.,** prix de soutien; **p. freezing, pegging,** blocage *m* des prix; **p. regulation,** réglementation *f* des prix; **p. control,** contrôle *m*, régulation *f* des prix; **p. index,** indice *m* des prix; **p. inquiry,** demande *f* de prix; **p. mechanism, system,** régime *m* des prix; **p. war,** guerre *f* des prix; **standard p. of wheat (as fixed by the authorities),** prix officiel, taux *m*, du blé; **to sell sth. above, under, the established p.,** vendre qch. au-dessus, au-dessous, du prix fixé; (*of goods*) **to advance, rise, increase, in p.,** augmenter de prix; renchérir; **to force up, push up, prices,** faire monter les prix; pousser à la hausse; **to force down, depress, prices,** faire baisser les prix; pousser à la baisse; **cut in prices,** forte réduction des prix; **all at one p., 50p,** prix unique, 50p; 50p, au choix; **one-p. store,** magasin à prix unique; **what p. is that article?** quel est le prix de cet article? **to ask a p. for an article,** demander un prix pour un article; **his p. for this sideboard is £300,** il demande £300 pour ce buffet; **I'll let you have it at a fair p.,** je vous le céderai, le laisserai, à, pour, un prix raisonnable; **he charges reasonable prices,** il pratique des prix raisonnables; **to quote, name, a p.,** faire le prix; **I haven't the p. of my ticket,** je n'ai pas le prix de mon billet; **his pictures fetch huge prices,** ses tableaux se vendent à prix d'or; **to be above p., beyond p., without p.,** (d'un prix) inestimable; hors de prix, sans prix; ne pas avoir de prix; **furs at extravagant prices,** fourrures à des prix astronomiques; fourrures hors de prix; **you can buy it, get it, at a p.,** vous pouvez l'acheter, vous le procurer, en y mettant le prix; **this must be done at any p.,** il faut que cela se fasse à tout prix, coûte que coûte; **not at any p.,** à aucun prix; pour rien au monde; **the p. paid for progress,** la rançon du progrès; **to fix the p. of, set a p. on, an article,** fixer le prix d'un article; **to set a high p. on sth.,** attacher un grand prix à qch., faire grand cas de qch.; **to put, set, a p. on s.o.'s head,** mettre à prix la tête de qn; **there is a p. (set) on his head,** sa tête est, a été, mise à prix; **he had put a p. on every man's conscience,** il avait tarifé les consciences; **every man has his p.,** (i) il n'y a pas d'homme qu'on ne puisse acheter, qui ne soit à vendre, qui ne soit vénal; (ii) chaque homme a sa valeur propre, vaut son prix; (*b*) *Turf:* cote *f*; **long p., short p.,** forte, faible, cote; *F:* **what p. my chances of being appointed?** quelles sont mes chances d'être nommé? **what p. my new bike?** et ma nouvelle bécane, qu'est-ce que tu en dis? **well, what p. his theories now?** eh bien, à quoi servent ses théories maintenant? eh bien, qu'est-ce que vous pensez maintenant de ses théories? **what p. glory!** pour ce qu'elle rapporte la gloire! la voilà bien la gloire! (*c*) *Bank: Fin:* **p. of money,** taux, loyer *m*, de l'argent; **p. of allotment,** taux d'attribution (des actions); **issue p.,** taux d'émission (des titres, etc.); **collapse of prices, slump in prices,** effondrement *m* des prix, des cours; (*esp. of gold*) **prices fell out of bed,** il y avait une chute catastrophique des prix; **prices are easing off,** les prix s'effritent; **p. ring,** coalition *f* de vendeurs, de marchands; monopole *m* de prix; *St.Exch:* **closing p.,** cours *m* de clôture; **opening p.,** cours (i) d'introduction, (ii) d'ouverture; **market p.,** cours du marché, de la bourse; **at current market prices,** suivant le cours du marché; **marking-up p.,** cours de compensation; **p. bid,** cours demandé; **p. for the account,** cours à terme; **p. of call,** cours du dont; **p. of option, option p.,** cours de la prime; **p. of put,** cours de l'ou; **put and call p.,** cours de l'option; **spot p.,** cours du comptant; **to make a p.,** fixer, spécifier, un cours (d'achat, de vente); *Cmptr: etc:* **p. performance ratio,** rapport *m* performance(s)-prix; **p. card,** carte *f* barème; **p. file,** fichier *m* barème.

price², *v.tr.* **1.** mettre un prix à (qch.); fixer un prix pour (qch.); **the book is priced at £4 net,** le livre se vend au prix net de £4. **2.** estimer, évaluer; **to p. sth. high, low,** attacher un grand prix, peu de prix, à qch.; faire grand, peu de, cas de qch. **3.** s'informer du prix de (qch.). **4.** *Com:* **to p. competitors out of the market,** fixer des prix si bas que les concurrents ne peuvent continuer à vendre; **we shall be priced out of the markets,** nos prix (trop élevés) nous feront perdre les marchés; **to p. oneself out of the market,** perdre sa clientèle en demandant des prix inabordables. **5.** *Cmptr: Pol.Ec:* valoriser (une quantité).

priced [praist], *a.* **1. high-p.,** de haut prix. **2.** marqué d'un prix, chiffré; **everything in the window is p.,** à l'étalage tous les prix sont marqués; **p. catalogue,** catalogue *m* avec prix; tarif-album *m, pl.* tarifs-albums; **p. schedule,** inventaire chiffré, nomenclature chiffrée.

priceite ['praisait], *s. Miner:* pricéite *f*.

priceless ['praislis], *a.* (*a*) hors de prix; inestimable; (*b*) *F:* (*of joke, pers., etc.*) très amusant, impayable.

pricelessness ['praislisnis], *s.* valeur *f* inestimable (**of,** de).

pricewise ['praiswaiz], *adv. F:* en matière de prix.

pricey ['praisi], *a. F:* cher, coûteux; **too p.,** trop cher.

pricing ['praisiŋ], *s.* fixation *f* du prix (**of sth.,** de qch.); évaluation *f*.

prick¹ [prik], *s.* **1.** (*a*) piqûre *f* (d'une aiguille, etc.); **pricks of conscience,** remords *m* de conscience; **p. ears,** oreilles pointues (d'un chien, *Hist: F:* des têtes rondes); *Needlew: etc:* **p. wheel,** roulette *f*; (*b*) *Farr:* enclouure *f*; (*c*) *A:* piqûre; point (marqué sur une liste). **2.** *A:* aiguillon *m*; *Lit:* **the pricks of remorse,** l'aiguillon du remords; *B:* **to kick against the pricks,** regimber contre les aiguillons. **3.** *V:* (*a*) queue *f*, verge *f*; (*b*) (*pers.*) vaurien *m*, couillon *m*.

prick², *v.*

I. *v.tr.* **1.** (*a*) piquer (qch., qn), dégonfler (qch.); faire une piqûre à (qch.); **to p. s.o. with a pin,** piquer qn avec une aiguille; **to p. one's finger,** se piquer au, le, doigt; **to p. a blister,** crever, ponctionner, une ampoule; **to p. a balloon,** crever, percer, un ballon; **to p. the bubble,** désabuser qn; *Farr:* **to p. a horse,** enclouer un cheval (en le ferrant); **his conscience pricks him,** sa conscience l'aiguillonne, le tourmente; il a des remords; (*b*) **to p. a hole in sth.,** faire un trou d'épingle dans qch.; **to p. pins into a pincushion,** piquer des épingles dans une pelote; **to p. (off, out) a design on sth.,** piquer, reproduire, tracer, un dessin sur qch.; *Lacem:* **to p. the card,** piqueter le carton; (*c*) *Nau:* **to p. the seam of a sail,** renforcer la couture d'une voile; (*d*) *Hort:* **to p. seedlings in, out, off,** repiquer des plants. **2. to p. (off) names on a list,** piquer, pointer, marquer, des noms sur une liste; *A:* **to be pricked as Sheriff,** être choisi, désigné, pour shériff; *Nau:* **to p. a bearing on the chart,** porter un relèvement sur la carte; **to p. off the ship's position on the chart,** porter le point sur la carte; **to p. the chart,** pointer, compasser, la carte; faire le point; *A:* **to p. (down) music, a tune,** copier de la musique, noter un air. **3.** *Mch:* nettoyer, fourgonner, décrasser (la grille d'un fourneau); **p. bar,** ringard *m*, attisoir *m*. **4.** éperonner (un cheval); piquer (un cheval) de l'éperon; **to p. one's horse with the spur,** appuyer l'éperon à son cheval; (*lightly*) picoter son cheval. **5. to p. (up) one's ears,** (i) (*of animal*) dresser les oreilles; (ii) (*of pers.*) tendre, dresser, l'oreille; ouvrir de grandes oreilles; **at these words he pricked up his ears,** à ces mots il est devenu attentif; **with pricked ears,** l'oreille aux aguets.

II. *v.i.* **1.** (*of the skin, of nerves, etc.*) avoir des picotements; picoter; fourmiller. **2.** (*of horseman*) avancer au galop; piquer des deux. **3.** (*of wine, beer*) se piquer.

prick-eared ['prikiːəd], *a.* **1.** (chien) aux oreilles droites, pointues. **2.** (*of pers.*) (*a*) aux oreilles dressées; les oreilles aux aguets; *Hist: F:* **p.-e. rascal,** tête ronde; (*b*) *A:* suffisant.

pricker ['prikər], *s.* **1.** (*pers.*) *Ven: etc:* piqueur *m*. **2.** *Tls:* (*a*) poinçon *m*, pointe *f*; *Mch:* aiguille *f* à décrasser; *Lacem:* aiguille à piqueter, piqueur; débouche-becs *m inv* (pour lanterne à acétylène, etc.); *Leath:* épée *f*; tire-point *m, pl.* tire-points; *Exp: O:* épinglette *f*; *Metall: Mch:* dégorgeoir *m*, ringard *m*, fourgon *m*, attisoir *m*, pique-feu *m inv*, cure-feu *m, pl.* cure-feu(x); (*b*) tire-ligne *m, pl.* tire-lignes, à pointiller; (*c*) *Draw:* piquoir *m*; *Needlew: etc:* roulette *f*; (*d*) aiguillon *m*; (*e*) mouchettes *fpl*.

pricket ['prikit], *s.* **1.** *Ven:* brocard *m* (d'un an); daguet *m*. **2.** broche *f* (de chandelier, de herse à cierges).

pricking¹ ['prikiŋ], *a.* piquant; (*of pain*) lancinant; **p. sensation,** picotement *m*, fourmillement *m*.

pricking², *s.* **1.** (*a*) piquage *m*; *Med:* ponction *f* (d'une ampoule); *Farr:* enclouage *m*; *Needlew: etc:* **p. wheel,** roulette *f*; (*b*) pointage *m* (d'une liste); *Nau:* pointage, compassement *m* (de la carte); (*c*) *Mch:* nettoyage *m*, nettoiement *m*, décrassage *m*, décrassement *m* (d'une grille de fourneau); (*d*) *Hort:* **p. out,** repiquage *m*, repiquement *m* (de plants). **2.** (*a*) **prickings of conscience,** remords *mpl* (de conscience); (*b*) picotement *m*, fourmillement *m* (de la peau, des nerfs).

prickle¹ ['prikl], *s.* (*a*) piquant *m* (de plante, d'animal); épine *f*, aiguillon *m* (de plante); (*b*) picotement *m*.

prickle². **1.** *v.tr.* piquer, picoter, aiguillonner. **2.** *v.i.* (*of parts of body*) fourmiller; avoir des picotements.

prickleback ['priklbæk], *s. Ich:* épinoche(tte) *f*.

prickliness ['priklinis], *s.* hérissement *m* (d'une plante, etc.).

prickling¹ ['prikliŋ], *a.* (sensation) de picotement, de fourmillement.

prickling², *s.* picotement *m*, fourmillement *m*.

prickly ['prikli], *a.* **1.** (*a*) (*of plant, animal*) hérissé, armé de piquants; (*of plant*) aiguillonné, épineux; *Nat.Hist:* échinulé; *Bot:* **p. pear,** (i) figuier *m* de Barbarie; raquette *f*, oponce *m*; (ii) figue *f* de Barbarie; **p. ash,** xanthoxylum *m*; (*b*) (*of question, etc.*) épineux; *F:* **he's very p. today,** il est très irritable aujourd'hui. **2.** (sensation) de picotement, de fourmillement.

prickspur ['prikspəːr], *s. A.Equit:* éperon *m* à ergot, à pointe.

prickwood ['prikwud], *s. Bot:* fusain *m*.

pride¹ [praid], *s.* **1.** orgueil *m*; (*a*) fierté *f*, morgue *f*; **the sin of p.,** le péché d'orgueil; **to be bursting with p.,** crever d'orgueil; **puffed up, blown up, with p.,** bouffi d'orgueil; **she's eaten up with p.,** l'orgueil la dévore; **it's just out of p. that she refuses,** elle refuse par pur orgueil; **p. of birth,** l'orgueil de la naissance; **false p.,** vanité *f*; **to take an empty p. in sth.,** faire vanité, tirer vanité, de qch.; **to take p. in one's knowledge,** tirer vanité de ses connaissances; *Prov:* **p. comes, goes, before a fall, p. will have a fall,** de grande montée grande chute; (*b*) **proper p.,** orgueil légitime; amour-propre *m*; **to hurt, wound, s.o.'s p.,** blesser l'amour-propre, l'orgueil, de qn; **to take (a) p. in sth., in doing sth.,** être fier, se faire gloire, de qch.; mettre son orgueil à faire qch.; **to take p. in one's work,** mettre son amour-propre dans son travail; **he takes great p. in his son's achievements,** il est très fier des succès de son fils. **2.** (*a*) **he is the p. of the family,** il fait l'orgueil de la famille; **the p. of the fleet,** l'orgueil de la flotte; (*b*) *Bot:* **p. of India, of China,** azédarach *m*, margousier *m*; arbre saint, arbre à chapelets; faux sycomore. **3.** (*a*) *Lit:* faste *m*, ostentation *f*, pompe *f*; (*b*) *Her:* **peacock in his p.,** paon rouant; paon qui fait la roue. **4.** comble *m*, apogée *m*; **to have p. of place,** avoir, tenir, la place d'honneur; *Lit:* **May was in its p.,** le mois de mai était dans toute sa splendeur; **in the p. of years,** à la fleur de l'âge. **5.** *A:* fougue *f*, ardeur *f* (d'un cheval). **6. p. of lions,** troupe *f*, bande *f*, de lions.

pride², *v.pr.* **to p. oneself (up)on (doing) sth.,** s'enorgueillir, se piquer, se faire gloire, se glorifier, se vanter, se targuer, de (faire) qch.; être fier, tirer vanité, de (faire) qch.; **to p. oneself on one's knowledge of literature, on being punctual,** se piquer de littérature, de ponctualité; **to p. oneself on one's knowledge of English,** tirer vanité de sa connaissance de l'anglais.

prideful ['praidful], *a. esp. Scot:* fier, orgueilleux, arrogant.

pridefully ['praidfuli], *adv.* fièrement, orgueilleusement avec arrogance.

pridefulness ['praidfulnis], *s. esp. Scot:* fierté *f*, orgueil *m*, arrogance *f*.

prier ['praiər], *s.* curieux, -euse; fureteur, -euse.

priest [priːst], *s.* **1.** *s.m.* (*a*) prêtre; **the priests,** le clergé; **bishops, priests and deacons,** évêques, prêtres et diacres; *R.C.Ch:* **parish p.** = curé; **assistant p.,** vicaire; **p. in charge,** desservant (d'église succursale); **p. vicar,** chanoine qui n'est pas membre du chapitre; **priest('s) hole,** cachette *f* d'un prêtre (à l'époque des persécutions religieuses); **high p.,** grand prêtre; *Jewish Rel:* grand sacrificateur; **the high priests of politics,** les pontifes *m* de la politique; **p.-ridden,** sous l'empire, sous la coupe, des prêtres; tyrannisé par les prêtres; **then the p. shall recite . . .,** alors l'officiant récitera . . .; **to become a p.,** se faire prêtre; prendre la soutane; **I'll mention it to the p.,** j'en parlerai à monsieur l'abbé; (*b*) prêtre (de temple païen). **2.** *Fish:* assommoir *m*.

priestcraft ['priːstkrɑːft], *s.* (*a*) connaissances professionnelles d'un prêtre; (*b*) *Pej:* artifices *mpl* de la prêtrise; intrigues sacerdotales; cléricalisme *m*.

priestess ['priːstis], *s.f.* prêtresse.

priesthood ['priːsthud], *s.* **1.** prêtrise *f*, sacerdoce *m*; **to enter the p.,** se faire prêtre. **2.** *coll.* **the p.,** le clergé.

priestling ['priːstliŋ], *s. F:* prestolet *m*.

priestly ['priːstli], *a.* sacerdotal, -aux; ecclésiastique; de prêtre.

prig¹ [prig], *s.* **1.** (*a*) poseur *m*, formaliste *mf*, pédant, -ante; suffisant *m*, fat *m*; **don't be a p.!** ne fais pas ta sainte nitouche; (*b*) poseur à la vertu; (*of boy*) **he's a real little p.,** il fait toujours le petit saint. **2.** *A: F:* chipeur, -euse; chapardeur, -euse.

prig², *v.tr.* **(prigged)** *F: A:* chiper, chaparder.

priggery ['prigəri], *s.* = PRIGGISHNESS.

priggish ['prigiʃ], *a.* (*a*) poseur, formaliste, pédant, suffisant; **he's unbearably p.,** il est d'une suffisance insupportable; (*b*) collet monté *inv*; bégueule.

priggishly ['prigiʃli], *adv.* d'une manière suffisante.

priggishness ['prigiʃnis], *s.* (*a*) pose *f*, formalisme *m*; pédanterie *f*; (*b*) bégueulerie *f*.

prim¹ [prim], *a.* (*a*) (*of pers.*) collet monté *inv*; compassé dans ses manières; (*of manner*) guindé, affecté, compassé; **p. smile,** sourire pincé; (*b*) **p. garden,** jardin méticuleusement entretenu.

prim², *v.tr.* **(primmed) 1. to p. (up) one's mouth, one's lips,** *v.i.* **to p. (up),** prendre un air pincé, pincer les lèvres. **2.** *O:* **to p. oneself (up),** se parer; faire un brin, un bout, de toilette; **to p. up a room,** mettre une pièce en ordre.

prima ['priːmə], *a.* **p. donna,** prima donna *f*; **p. ballerina,** première danseuse étoile.

primacy ['praiməsi], *s.* **1.** primauté *f*, prééminence *f*, primat *m*; premier rang. **2.** *Ecc:* primatie *f.*

primaeval [prai'mi:v(ə)l], *a.* = PRIMEVAL.

prima facie [praimə'feiʃii:]. **1.** *adv.* de prime abord, à première vue. **2.** *a.* de prime abord; *Jur:* **p. f. case,** affaire qui d'après les premiers témoignages paraît bien fondée.

primage[1] ['praimidʒ], *s. Nau: Com:* chapeau *m* (du capitaine, de mérite); primage *m.*

primage[2], *s. Mch:* primage *m.*

primal ['praim(ə)l], *a.* **1.** primitif, originel. **2.** (*of duty, etc.*) principal, -aux; essentiel; fondamental, -aux.

primally ['praiməli], *adv.* **1.** primitivement, originairement. **2.** principalement, essentiellement.

primarily [prai'mərili, *esp. U.S:* prai'mεərili], *adv.* **1.** primitivement, originairement, primordialement; dans le principe. **2.** principalement, essentiellement.

primariness ['praimərinis], *s.* primarité *f.*

primary[1] ['praiməri], *a.* **1.** premier, primitif, originel; **p. meaning of a word,** sens premier, primitif, d'un mot; signification originelle d'un mot; **p. colours,** couleurs fondamentales, primaires, primitives; *Geol:* **p. era,** (ère *f*) primaire *m*; **p. rocks,** roches *f* primaires; **p. soils,** terrains primitifs, primaires; **p. forest,** forêt primitive; *Petr:* **p. cracking,** précraquage *m*; **p. product,** produit *m* de base, matière première, produit brut; *Gram:* **p. tenses,** temps primitifs; *Surg:* **p. amputation,** amputation *f* primaire; *Med:* **p. infection,** primo-infection *f, pl.* primo-infections; **p. lesion,** lésion *f,* accident *m,* primaire; **p. vaccination,** primovaccination *f*; **p. teeth,** premières dents, dents temporaires, caduques; *Psy:* **test of p. mental abilities,** test *m* des aptitudes mentales primaires; *Sch:* **p. education, school,** enseignement *m,* école *f,* primaire; *El:* **p. battery,** batterie *f* de piles; **p. coil, winding,** bobine *f,* enroulement *m,* primaire; **p. wire,** fil conducteur; **p. cell,** élément *m* de pile; **p. armature,** induit *m* primaire; **p. current, network,** courant *m,* réseau *m,* primaire; *Elcs:* **p. emission (of vacuum tube),** émission *f* (électronique) primaire; **p. radar,** radar *m* primaire; **p. tuning,** accord *m* primaire; *Atom.Ph:* **p. electron, particle,** électron *m,* particule *f,* primaire; **p. radiation,** radiation *f,* rayonnement *m,* primaire; *I.C.E:* **p. air,** (i) (*in turbojet engine*) air carburé; (ii) (*in turbo-fan engine*) air primaire; **p. airstream,** flux *m* d'air primaire; *Mch: etc:* **p. coolant circuit,** circuit *m* primaire de refroidissement; **p. shaft,** arbre *m* primaire; *Pol:* **p. assembly,** assemblée *f* primaire; *Pol: U.S:* **p. election,** (élection *f*) primaire *f*; *Pol.Ec:* **p. industries,** secteur *m* primaire. **2.** premier, principal, -aux; essentiel; **p. cause,** cause première; *Astr:* **p. planet,** planète principale, primaire; grande planète; **p. circle,** cercle *m* de base (de la sphère céleste); *Cmptr:* **p. key,** indicatif majeur; **p. storage, store,** mémoire centrale; *Nau:* **p. port,** port principal (de destination); *Orn:* **p. quills,** rémiges *f.*

primary[2], *s.* **1.** *Astr:* (*a*) planète principale, planète primaire, grande planète; (*b*) étoile *f* de magnitude; primaire *f*; (*c*) partie la plus lumineuse d'une étoile double. **2.** *El:* bobine *f* primaire. **3.** *Ph:* couleur fondamentale, primaire, primitive. **4.** (*a*) *Orn:* rémige *f*; (*b*) *Ent:* aile antérieure (d'un insecte); élytre *m* (d'un orthoptère). **5.** *Pol:* (*a*) assemblée *f* primaire; (*b*) *U.S:* (élection *f*) primaire *f.*

primate ['praim(e)it], *s.* **1.** *Ecc:* (*a*) primat *m*; (*b*) **the P. of England,** l'archevêque *m* d'York; **the P. of All England,** l'archevêque de Cantorbéry. **2.** *Z:* primate *m.*

Primates ['praimeits, prai'meiti:z], *s.pl. Z:* primates *m.*

primateship ['praim(e)itʃip], *s. Ecc:* primatie *f.*

primatial, primatical [prai'meiʃ(ə)l, -'mætik(ə)l], *a. Ecc:* primatial, -aux.

Primaticcio [pri:mæ'ti:tʃiou]. *Pr.n. Art:* le Primatice.

primavera [pri:mə'verə], *s. Bot:* primavera *m.*

prime[1] [praim], *a.* **1.** premier, principal, -aux; de premier ordre; **p. minister,** premier ministre; **of p. importance,** d'importance capitale, de (toute) première importance; **p. necessity,** nécessité primordiale, première; **p. motive,** principal mobile (**of,** de); **p. mover,** (i) *Mec:* source *f* d'énergie; générateur *m,* génératrice *f,* de force motrice; moteur *m* primaire; (ii) (véhicule *m,* camion *m*) tracteur *m* (d'une remorque, etc.); (iii) (*pers.*) âme *f,* principal animateur, cheville ouvrière, inspirateur, -trice, instigateur, -trice (d'un complot, etc.); *Mec:* **p. power,** puissance *f* immédiatement disponible; *Const: Ind:* **p. contractor,** maître *m* d'œuvre. **2.** excellent, de qualité supérieure, de première qualité; **p. quality meat,** viande *f* de première qualité, de premier choix; viande surchoix; **p. cut (of meat),** morceau *m* de (premier) choix; *Tex:* **p. wool,** prime *f*; *Fin:* **p. bills,** papier *m* de haut commerce; **p. bond,** obligation *f* de premier ordre. **3.** premier, originel, primitif; de base; *Mth:* **p. number,** nombre premier; **two is p. to five, two and five are relatively p.,** deux et cinq sont premiers entre eux; **p. meridian of Greenwich,** méridien *m* (d')origine de Greenwich; **p. vertical,** premier vertical (d'un lieu); *Opt:* **p. stimulus,** lumière *f* de référence. **4.** *A:* lubrique, luxurieux.

prime[2], *s.* **1.** (*a*) perfection *f*; **p. of perfection,** comble *m* de la perfection; **p. of youth,** fleur *f* de la jeunesse; **in the p. of beauty,** dans l'éclat de sa beauté; dans toute sa fleur; **in the p. of life, in one's p.,** dans la force, dans la vigueur, de l'âge; à, dans, la fleur de l'âge; **to be past one's p.,** avoir passé le bel âge; (*b*) le choix, le meilleur (d'un rôti, d'un panier de fruits, etc.). **2.** (*a*) commencement *m,* premiers jours (de qch.); (*b*) commencement, origine *f,* du monde; origine des temps. **3.** (*a*) *Ecc:* prime *f*; **to say, sing, the p.,** dire, chanter, prime; (*b*) *A:* **at p.,** à l'aube, au point du jour. **4.** *Fenc:* prime. **5.** *Mth:* nombre premier. **6.** *Ch:* atome *m* simple. **7.** *Mus:* (*a*) son fondamental; (*b*) **superfluous p.,** demi-ton *m* chromatique. **8.** *Mth:* prime; **n p.,** *n* prime; n'; **n double p.,** *n* seconde; n''.

prime[3], *v.tr.* **1.** (*a*) amorcer (un obus, une cartouche de mine, *I.C.E:* un moteur, *Hyd:* une pompe, etc.); allumer (une pompe); *I.C.E:* enrichir le mélange au départ; injecter du carburant au départ; *A.Artil:* étoupiller (un canon); *Mch:* **to p. the boilers,** faire le plein des chaudières; (*b*) (*with passive force*) (*of boiler*) **to p.,** primer, avoir des projections d'eau, entraîner de l'eau (dans les cylindres). **2.** (*a*) faire la leçon à (qn); souffler aux oreilles de (qn); **to p. s.o. for a speech,** préparer qn à faire son discours; mettre qn au fait de ce qu'il devra dire; (*b*) **to be well primed (with alcohol),** être bien parti; avoir son plumet; être mûr. **3.** (*a*) *Paint:* apprêter, imprimer, donner l'apprêt à, passer un enduit préalable à (la surface à peindre); (*b*) maroufler (la toile).

prime[4], *v.i. Astr:* (*of tide*) primer.

primeness ['praimnis], *s.* excellence *f*; bonne qualité (de la viande, etc.).

primer[1] ['praimər], *s.* **1.** (*pers.*) (*a*) *A:* amorceur, -euse (d'un canon, etc.); (*b*) apprêteur, -euse (de toiles d'artiste, de boiseries, etc.). **2.** (*a*) *I.C.E:* amorceur *m*; enrichisseur *m* (du mélange au départ); injecteur *m* (de départ); **p. line,** canalisation *f* d'enrichissement, d'injection, (au) départ; **p. nozzle,** buse *f* d'injection; **p. pump,** pompe *f* d'injection (de départ); **p. valve,** soupape *f* d'injection départ; (*b*) *Pyr:* amorce (fulminante), étoupille *f*; **p. box, casing, tube,** boîte *f* d'amorce; **p. cap, cover,** couvre-amorce *m, pl.* couvre-amorces; **p. pouch,** sac *m* à étoupilles; **p. cup,** cuvette *f* (d'amorce); **p. detonator,** amorce-détonateur *f, pl.* amorces-détonateurs; détonateur *m* primaire; **p. holder, spindle,** porte-amorce *m inv*; **p. mixture, composition,** mélange *m* d'amorçage, composition (fulminante) d'amorce. **3.** *Paint:* (couche *f* d')apprêt *m,* enduit *m* préalable; peinture *f* de fond.

primer[2] ['praimər, 'primər], *s.* **1.** (*a*) premier livre de lecture; alphabet *m,* abécédaire *m*; (*b*) introduction *f* (à l'étude des mathématiques, etc.); **p. of geography,** premier cours de géographie; premiers éléments de géographie. **2.** *Ecc: A:* livre de prières (pour les laïques); livre d'heures. **3.** *Typ:* **great p.,** gros romain; gros texte; corps 16; **long p.,** philosophie *f*; corps 10; **two-line long p.,** petit parangon; corps 20.

primeval [prai'mi:v(ə)l], *a.* primitif, primordial, -aux; des premiers âges (du monde); **p. forest,** forêt primitive.

primine ['praimi:n], *s. Bot:* primine *f* (de l'ovule).

priming[1] ['praimiŋ], *s.* **1.** (*a*) *Hyd:* amorçage *m* (d'une pompe); **p. cock,** amorceur *m*; **p. pipe,** fourreau *m* (de pompe); (*b*) *I.C.E:* amorçage (du carburateur, du moteur); enrichissement (du mélange au départ); injection *f* (de carburant au départ); **automatic, self, p.,** amorçage automatique; **p. jet,** injecteur *m*; **p. nozzle,** buse *f* d'injection; (*c*) *El:* **p. grid voltage,** tension *f* de grille à l'amorçage; **p. pulse,** impulsion *f* d'amorçage; **p. voltage, potential,** tension d'amorçage; **p. illumination,** pré-illumination *f, pl.* pré-illuminations (d'une cellule photoélectrique); (*d*) *Pyr:* **p. (powder),** amorce *f*; **p. charge,** charge *f* d'amorçage; **p. explosive,** explosif *m* d'amorçage; **percussion p.,** amorce à percussion; *Sm.a. Artil: A:* **p. pan,** bassinet *m*; **p. wire, iron,** dégorgeoir *m,* épinglette *f*; **p. hole,** lumière *f* (d'une arme à feu). **2.** (*a*) apprêtage *m,* impression *f* (d'une toile, de boiserie, etc.); (*b*) couche *f,* apprêt *m*; première couche; couche d'impression, de première impression; imprimure *f* (de boiserie, etc.); empreinte *f* (de toile d'artiste). **3.** *Mch:* primage *m*; (*of water in a boiler*) écumage *m*; **p. valve,** soupape *f* de sûreté (du cylindre).

priming[2], *s.* accélération *f* diurne de la marée.

primipara [prai'mipərə], *s.* primipare *f.*

primiparous [prai'mipərəs], *a.* primipare.

primipilar [prai'mipilər], *s. A.Mil:* primipilaire *m,* primipile *m.*

primitive ['primitiv]. **1.** *a.* (*a*) primitif, primaire; **p. language,** langue primitive; **p. word,** mot primitif; *Gram:* **p. tenses,** temps primitifs; *Log:* **p. concept,** concept primitif; *Geol:* **p. rocks,** roches primitives, primaires; *Mth:* **p. figure,** figure première; *Mec.E:* **p. circle (of gearing),** (cercle) primitif *m*; **the P. Church,** l'église primitive; *Hist:* **P. Methodist,** méthodiste primitif, -ive; (*b*) (*of method, custom, etc.*) primitif, rude, grossier; rudimentaire; **the plumbing is very p.,** les installations sanitaires sont rudimentaires. **2.** *s.* (*a*) *Art:* (peintre, tableau) primitif *m*; **the primitives,** les (peintres) primitifs; (*b*) *Anthr:* primitif, -ive; (*c*) *Rel.H:* méthodiste primitif, -ive; (*d*) *Mth:* primitive *f.*

primitively ['primitivli], *adv.* primitivement.

primitiveness ['primitivnis], *s.* caractère primitif; (*of manners, etc.*) primitivité *f*; rudesse *f* (d'un peuple, etc.).

primitivism ['primitivizm], *s.* primitivisme *m.*

primitivist ['primitivist], *a. & s. Art: etc:* primitiviste (*mf*).

primitivistic [primiti'vistik], *a. Art: etc:* primitiviste.

primly ['primli], *adv.* d'un air collet monté.

primness ['primnis], *s.* (*a*) air *m* collet monté; **the p. of her manners,** ses manières compassées; l'afféterie *f* de ses manières; (*b*) arrangement méticuleux (d'un jardin, etc.); ordre parfait.

primogenital, primogenitary [praimou'dʒenitl, -'dʒenitəri], *a.* de, par, primogéniture; relatif à la primogéniture; **p. rules,** règles *f* régissant le droit de primogéniture, le droit d'aînesse; **p. succession,** succession *f* par primogéniture.

primogenitor [praimou'dʒenitər], *s.* (*a*) premier ancêtre; (*b*) ancêtre; aïeul *m, pl.* aïeux; aïeule *f.*

primogenitorship [praimou'dʒenitəʃip], *s.* droit *m* d'aînesse, de primogéniture.

primogeniture [praimou'dʒenitʃər], *s.* primogéniture *f*; **(right of) p.,** droit d'aînesse.

primordial [prai'mɔ:diəl], *a.* primordial, -aux; (*a*) premier, originel, primitif; *Geol:* **p. stratum,** étage primordial; (*b*) fondamental, -aux; essentiel.

primordially [prai'mɔ:diəli], *adv.* primordialement; (*a*) primitivement, originellement; (*b*) fondamentalement, essentiellement.

primp [primp]. *Dial:* **1.** *v.tr.* parer, orner; attifer. **2.** *v.i. & pr.* **to p. (oneself) up,** se parer; s'attifer; se mettre sur son trente et un.

primrose ['primrouz], *s. Bot:* primevère *f* à grandes fleurs; **bird's eye p.,** primevère farineuse; **evening p.,** œnothère *m,* onagre *f,* onagraire *f*; herbe *f* aux ânes; **pin-eyed p.,** primevère longistyle; **thrum-eyed p.,** primevère brévistyle; **Cape p.,** streptocarpus *m*; **the p. path,** le chemin de velours; *Pol:* **P. Day,** anniversaire (le 19 avril) de la mort de Disraeli; **P. League,** association conservatrice destinée à perpétuer la politique de Disraeli.

primula ['primjulə], *s. Bot:* primula *f,* primevère *f.*

Primulaceae [primju'leisii:], *s.pl. Bot:* primulacées *f.*

primuline ['primjuli(:)n], *s. Ch:* primuline *f.*

primum mobile ['praiməm'moubili], *s. A.Astr: & Fig:* premier mobile.

primus[1] ['praiməs]. **1.** *a. Sch: A:* **Martin p.,** Martin (l')aîné. **2.** *s. Scot: Episcopal Church:* évêque élu à la présidence.

primus[2], *Dom.Ec: R.t.m:* **p. (stove),** fourneau, réchaud portatif à pétrole vaporisé sous pression; primus *m.*

prince [prins], *s.m.* **1.** (*a*) prince; **p. of the blood,** prince du sang; **p. regent** (*pl.* **p. regents),** prince régent; **p. consort,** (*pl.* **princes consort),** prince consort; **p. charming,** prince charmant; *Hist:* **the Black P.,** le Prince Noir; **p. elector,** électeur; **the Princes of the Church,** les Princes de l'Église; *A.Cost: NAm:* **P. Albert (coat),** redingote *f*; *Jur:* **restraint of princes,** le fait du prince; (*b*) **the very p. of poets,** le prince des poètes; **the princes of this world,** les grands de ce monde; **the P. of darkness, of this world,** le prince des ténèbres, de ce monde; le diable. **2.** *Metall:* **Prince's metal,** métal *m* du prince Rupert; métal de prince. **3.** *Bot:* **prince's feather,** amarante élégante.

princedom ['prinsdəm], *s.* principauté *f*; dignité *f* de prince.

princelet ['prinslit], **princeling** ['prinsliŋ], *s.m.* principicule.

princely ['prinsli], *a.* princier; royal, -aux; splendide; **p. fees,** honoraires princiers; **of p. birth,** de naissance princière; **a p. gift,** un cadeau royal, magnifique; **he gets a p. salary,** il est payé princièrement; **to treat s.o. in a p. manner,** traiter qn en prince, princièrement, royalement.

princess ['prinsis, prin'ses], *s.f.* princesse; **p. royal,**

princesse royale; *Cost:* **p. dress,** robe *f* princesse, *pl.* robes princesse; *A:* **p. petticoat, slip,** combinaison-jupon *f, pl.* combinaisons-jupons.

principal ['prinsip(ə)l], *a. & s.*
I. *a.* principal, -aux; **the p. citizens of a town,** les principaux *m* d'une ville; **p. events in one's life,** événements capitaux de la vie; *Th:* **p. part (in a play),** rôle principal; (*in pantomime*) **p. boy,** rôle du héros (toujours joué par une femme); *Cu:* **p. dish,** pièce *f* de résistance; **p. branch of a stream,** branche maîtresse, branche principale, d'un cours d'eau; *Const:* **p. member,** maîtresse poutre (d'une charpente); **p. rafter (of a roof),** *s.* **p.,** chevron *m* de ferme; arbalétrier *m*; *Mth:* **p. axis of a curve,** axe principal d'une courbe; *Surv:* **p. contour,** courbe maîtresse; *Gram:* **p. clause,** proposition principale.
II. *s.* **1.** (*pers.*) (*a*) directeur *m* (de fabrique, d'école, etc.); chef *m*, patron *m* (d'une maison de commerce); principal *m*, -aux, directrice *f* (d'école, de collège); patronne *f* (d'une maison de commerce); *Adm:* **assistant p.** = secrétaire *m* d'administration; (*b*) *Com: Jur:* (*in transaction*) mandant *m*, commettant *m*; (*in purchase*) command *m*; *St.Exch:* donneur *m* d'ordre; *Jur:* **p. and agent,** employeur *m* et mandataire *m*; commettant et préposé *m*; **declaration of p. (by agent),** déclaration *f* de command; (*c*) *Jur:* auteur *m* (d'un crime); **p. in the first degree,** auteur principal; **p. in the second degree,** complice *m*; (*d*) **principals in a duel,** combattants *m*, adversaires *m*, dans un duel; **the second and his p.,** le témoin et son client; (*e*) *Mus:* soliste *mf*; (*f*) *Th:* (i) (acteur, -trice, qui joue le) rôle principal; (ii) chef *m* d'emploi. **2.** *Com:* capital *m*, principal *m* (d'une dette); **p. and interest,** principal, capital, et intérêts. **3.** *Mus:* prestant *m* (de l'orgue).

principality [prinsi'pæliti], *s.* **1.** principauté *f*; dignité *f* de prince. **2.** principauté (régie par un prince); **the P.,** la principauté de Galles. **3.** *Theol:* **the Principalities,** les Principautés.

principally ['prinsip(ə)li], *adv.* principalement; pour la plupart; surtout.

principalship ['prinsip(ə)lʃip], *s.* directorat *m* (d'école, etc.); principalat *m* (de collège).

principate ['prinsipət], *s. Rom.Hist:* principat *m*.

principial [prin'sipiəl], *a.* fondamental, de base.

principium [prin'sipiəm], *s.* **1.** *Phil:* principe fondamental, fondement *m*, base *f*. **2.** *A.Mil:* principium *m*.

principle ['prinsipl], *s.* **1.** (*a*) principe *m*; **fundamental p.,** principe premier, fondamental; principe mère; **the p. of life,** le principe de la vie; la source même de la vie; la cause première de la vie; (*b*) **first principles of geometry,** premiers principes, principes fondamentaux, de la géométrie; **the Archimedean p.,** le principe d'Archimède; **to lay sth. down as a p.,** poser qch. en principe; **to reach an agreement in p.,** aboutir à un accord de principe; **machines that work on the same p.,** machines qui fonctionnent sur, d'après, le même principe; **the major principles upon which the project was based,** les grandes lignes du projet. **2.** (*a*) principe, règle *f*; **guiding p.,** principe directeur; **moral principles,** principes moraux; **to have high principles,** avoir des principes; **man of high principles,** homme de haute moralité; **man of no principles,** homme sans principes; **relaxing of p.,** relâchement *m* des principes; **on p.,** par principe; **to do sth. on p., to make it a matter of p. to do sth.,** avoir pour principe de faire qch.; faire qch. par principe; **to stick to one's principles,** rester fidèle à ses principes; **as a general p.,** en thèse générale; **upon all principles I am bound to approve of this plan,** tous les principes établis me somment d'approuver ce projet. **3.** *Ch:* **fatty, bitter, active, p.,** principe gras, amer, actif. **4.** *Phil: etc:* loi *f*; **p. of absorption,** loi d'absorption; **p. of causality,** loi, principe, de causalité; **p. of excluded middle,** loi du tiers exclu; *Biol: etc:* **p. of acceleration,** loi, principe, d'accélération.

principled ['prinsipld], *a.* **1.** (*of pers.*) qui a tels ou tels principes; **a most highly p. woman,** une femme aux principles très stricts; **(high-)p., low-p.,** qui a de bons, de mauvais, principes. **2.** (*of art etc.*) fondé sur des pricipes.

prink [priŋk]. **1.** *v.tr.* (*a*) **to p. (up),** attifer, parer, orner (qn); (*b*) (*of bird*) **to p. its feathers,** se nettoyer, se lisser, les plumes. **2.** *v.i.* prendre des airs. **3.** *v.i. & pr.* **to p. (oneself) up,** s'attifer; se mettre sur son trente et un.

print¹ [print], *s.* **1.** (*a*) empreinte *f*, impression *f*; marque *f*, trace *f* (du pied); **thumb p.,** empreinte du pouce; (*b*) **butter p.,** (i) moule *m* à beurre, moule-beurre *m inv*; (ii) rond *m* de beurre. **2.** *Typ:* (*a*) matière imprimée; **he likes to see himself in p.,** il aime à se faire imprimer, à se voir imprimé; **to appear in p.,** (i) (*of writings*) paraître sous forme imprimée; (ii) (*of author*) se faire imprimer; **I have never seen this story in p.,** je ne savais pas que cette histoire avait jamais été imprimée; **the book is in p.,** le livre est imprimé; **edition in p.,** édition en vente (courante); édition disponible; **out of p.,** épuisé; **to rush into p.,** (i) publier à la légère; (ii) envoyer une lettre indignée à un journal; **these speeches are not very interesting in cold p.,** à la lecture ces discours n'intéressent guère; (*b*) caractères *mpl*; **large p., small p.,** gros, petits, caractères; **p. letters, p. hand,** caractères, écriture *f*, qui imite(nt) les caractères d'imprimerie; (*c*) édition, impression; (*d*) feuille imprimée; imprimé *m*; *NAm:* journal *m*; (*e*) *Cmptr:* **p. bar,** barre *f* d'impression, barre à caractères; **p. drum,** tambour *m* d'impression; **p. hammer,** marteau *m* d'impression; **p. member,** élément *m* porte-caractères; **p. roll,** cylindre *m* d'impression; **p. span,** largeur *f* de la ligne d'impression; **p. unit,** unité *f* d'impression; **p. wheel,** roue *f* d'impression, roue à caractères; **p. yoke,** bloc *m* d'impression; bloc-tambour *m, pl.* blocs-tambours. **3.** estampe *f*, gravure *f*, image *f*; (*in library, museum*) **p. room,** cabinet *m* d'estampes. **4.** *Phot:* (*a*) épreuve *f*; photographie *f*; copie *f*; **to take a p. from a negative,** tirer une épreuve d'un cliché; **contact p.,** épreuve, copie, par contact; **reduction p.,** copie par réduction; **projection p.,** épreuve par projection; **p. cutter,** coupeuse *f*; **double-edged p. cutter,** déchiqueteuse *f*; **p. trimmer,** massicot *m*; **p. glazer,** glaceuse *f*; **p. meter,** photomètre *m* de tirage; (*b*) *Ind:* **black p., brown p.,** tirage *m* en noir, en brun. **5.** *Tex:* indienne *f*, cotonnade *f*, rouennerie *f*; **p. dress,** robe *f* d'indienne; **(cotton) p.,** imprimé *m*. **6.** *Metall:* portée *f* (de moulage); porte-noyau *m inv*.

print², *v.tr.* **1.** empreindre; imprimer; faire une empreinte de (qch. sur qch.); marquer (qch.) d'une empreinte; **to p. a seal upon wax,** empreindre un sceau dans la cire; imprimer un sceau sur la cire; **incidents that p. themselves on the memory, on the mind,** incidents qui se gravent dans la mémoire; incidents qui s'impriment, s'empreignent, sur l'esprit; **to p. one's footsteps in the sand,** imprimer la trace de ses pas sur le sable. **2.** (*a*) *Typ:* imprimer (un livre, etc.); **to p. down (on metal plate),** copier sur métal; **to p. close to paper,** imprimer sec; **to p. (off) a newspaper,** imprimer, tirer, un journal; **the book is printed off,** le livre est achevé d'imprimer; (*of author*) **to p. a book, to have a book printed,** faire imprimer un livre; livrer un ouvrage à l'impression; se faire imprimer; **a limited number only were printed,** l'ouvrage a été tiré à un petit nombre d'exemplaires, a fait l'objet d'un tirage limité; (*with passive force*) **the book is now printing,** le livre est à l'impression, à l'imprimerie, est en cours d'impression, est actuellement sous presse, s'imprime actuellement; *Post:* **printed matter,** imprimés *mpl*; **printed paper rate,** papiers *mpl* d'affaires; tarif *m* imprimés; (*b*) mouler (des lettres); **to p. an address,** écrire une adresse en lettres moulées. **3.** *Phot:* **to p. (off, out) a negative,** tirer une épreuve d'un cliché; (*passive use*) **negative that prints well,** cliché qui rend bien, qui donne de bonnes épreuves; **paper that prints out by artificial light,** papier à tirage en lumière artificielle. **4.** *Tex:* imprimer (du coton, etc.); **printed cotton,** indienne imprimée.

printability [printə'biliti], *s.* imprimabilité *f*.

printable ['printəbl], *a.* imprimable.

printer ['printər], *s.* **1.** *Typ: etc:* (*a*) (*pers.*) (i) imprimeur *m* (typographique), typographe *m*; (ii) ouvrier *m* typographe; tireur *m* (d'une feuille, d'une estampe, etc.); **letterpress p.,** imprimeur typographe; **p. and publisher,** imprimeur-libraire *m, pl.* imprimeurs-libraires; **printers and stationers,** imprimeurs *mpl* et fournitures *fpl* de bureau; **printer's error,** faute *f* d'impression; coquille *f*; **printer's reader,** correcteur, -trice, d'épreuves; **printer's block,** cliché *m* d'imprimerie; (*b*) (*machine*) (i) *Cmptr: etc.* imprimante *f*, imprimeuse *f*; **character(-at-a-time) p.,** imprimante caractère par caractère; **dot p., matrix p., mosaic p., stylus p.,** imprimante par points; **(hit-)on-the-fly p., hit-on-the-run p.,** imprimante à la volée; **line(-at-a-time) p.,** imprimante ligne par ligne; **ink jet p.,** imprimante à jet d'encre; (ii) *Tg:* téléimprimeur *m*, téléscripteur *m*, télétype *m*; **multiplex p.,** téléscripteur multiplex. **2.** *Phot:* (*a*) (*pers.*) tireur, -euse, d'épreuves; (*b*) (*machine*) tireuse *f*. **3.** *Tex:* imprimeur (de cotonnade, etc.); **cotton p.,** imprimeur d'indiennes.

printery ['printəri], *s. U.S:* **1.** imprimerie *f* (typographique). **2.** imprimerie (pour tissus).

printing ['printiŋ], *s.* **1.** (*a*) impression *f*, tirage *m* (d'un livre); **direct p.,** impression directe; **offset p.,** impression offset; **gelatine p.,** impression à la gélatine; **p. number,** chiffre *m* de tirage; **p. paper,** papier *m* d'impression; (*b*) (*art of printing*) imprimerie *f*, typographie *f*; **p. and kindred trades,** industries *f* polygraphiques; **p. office,** *A:* **p. house,** imprimerie; **p. apparatus,** appareil *m* imprimant; imprimante *f*, imprimeuse *f*; **p. machine,** machine *f* à imprimer; presse *f* mécanique; imprimeuse; **p. ink,** encre *f* d'impression, d'imprimerie; **p. drum,** cylindre imprimant, imprimeur; **p. telegraph,** téléimprimeur *m*, téléscripteur *m*, télétype *m*; (*c*) écriture *f* en caractères moulés, en moulé; (*d*) *Cmptr:* **dot p.,** impression par points; **on-the-fly p.,** impression à la volée; **page p.,** impression page par page. **2.** *Phot:* **p. (out),** tirage; **daylight p.,** tirage par noircissement direct, tirage au jour; insolation *f*; **p. (out) paper,** (i) papier aristotypique; papier à image apparente, à noircissement direct, au citrate (d'argent); (ii) *Ind:* (*for plans, etc.*) papier héliographique; **p. machine, box,** tireuse *f*; **p. frame,** châssis (positif); châssis-presse *m, pl.* châssis-presses; **p. mask,** cache *m*. **3.** *Tex:* **cotton p.,** impression du, sur, coton.

printseller ['printselər], *s.* marchand, -ande, d'estampes, de gravures.

printshop ['printʃɔp], *s.* magasin *m* d'estampes.

printworks ['printwə:ks], *s.pl.* imprimerie *f* pour étoffes.

priodont ['praioudɔnt], *a. & s. Z:* priodonte (*m*).

Priodontes [praiou'dɔnti:z], *s.pl. Z:* les priodontes *m*.

prion ['praiɔn], *s. Orn:* prion *m*.

prionid [prai'ounid], *s. Ent:* prionien *m*.

Prionidae [prai'ɔnidi:], *s.pl. Ent:* prioniens *m*.

prionops ['praiənɔps], *s. Orn:* prionops *m*.

prior¹ ['praiər]. **1.** *a.* préalable, précédent; antérieur (**to sth.,** à qch.); **to have a p. claim,** être le premier en date; **p. sequel,** continuation *f* qui traite d'une période antérieure. **2.** *adv.* **p. to my departure,** antérieurement à mon départ; avant mon départ, avant de partir; **p. to any discussion,** préalablement à toute discussion; **p. to his appointment,** avant sa nomination.

prior², *s.m. Ecc:* prieur.

prioral ['praiər(ə)l], *a. Ecc:* prieural, -aux.

priorate ['praiərət], *s. Ecc:* **1.** (*place*) prieuré *m*. **2.** (*office*) prieuré, priorat *m*.

prioress ['praiəris], *s.f. Ecc:* prieure.

priorite ['praiərait], *s. Miner:* priorite *f*.

priority [prai'ɔriti], *s.* priorité *f*, antériorité *f*; **p. of invention,** antériorité d'invention; **to have p.,** être prioritaire; **to have p. over s.o.,** primer qn; avoir le pas sur qn; avoir la préséance, la priorité, sur qn; **to have p. over s.o. (in claim on mortgaged property),** primer qn en hypothèque; **to rank in p., with, to, s.o.,** avoir droit de priorité sur qn; **subject to the priorities attached to the loan,** abstraction faite des rangs de priorité attribués à l'emprunt; **according to p.,** selon l'ordre de priorité; (*on message*) **p.,** urgent; **preemptive, non-preemptive, p.,** priorité absolue, relative; *Jur:* **p. of a creditor,** privilège *m*, préférence *f*, d'un créancier; **right of p.,** droit *m* d'antériorité; **p. rights,** droits de priorité, de préférence; droits prioritaires; **p. of claim,** priorité; **p. holder,** prioritaire *mf*; *St.Exch:* **p. share,** action privilégiée; *Adm:* **p. fee,** droit *m* de prompte expédition; **p. index,** indice *m* de priorité; *Cmptr:* **p. processing,** traitement *m* par priorités; **p. programme, project,** programme *m*, projet *m*, prioritaire; *Aut:* **p. road,** route *f* à priorité; *Mil:* **p. target,** objectif *m* prioritaire.

priorship ['praiəʃip], *s. Ecc:* prieuré *m* (dignité de prieur); priorat *m*.

priory ['praiəri], *s. Ecc:* prieuré *m* (le couvent).

Priscian ['priʃiən]. *Pr.n.m. Rom.Hist:* Priscien.

Priscilla [pri'silə]. *Pr.n.f.* Priscille.

Priscillian [pri'siliən], *Rel.H:* **1.** *Pr.n.m.* Priscillien. **2.** *s.* priscillianiste *mf*.

Priscillianism [pri'siliənizm], *s. Rel.H:* priscillianisme *m*.

Priscillianist [pri'siliənist], *a. & s. Rel.H:* priscillianiste (*mf*).

prise¹,² [praiz], *s. & v.tr.* = PRIZE⁵,⁶.

prism ['priz(ə)m], *s.* **1.** prisme *m*; *Mth:* **right p.,** prisme droit; **oblique p., slanting p.,** prisme oblique; *Opt:* **reversing p., erecting p.,** prisme redressant les images; prisme redresseur; **dispersing p.,** prisme à dispersion; **reflecting p.,** prisme réflecteur; **total reflection p.,** prisme à réflexion totale; **deflecting p.,** prisme de renvoi; **polarizing p., Nicol p.,** prisme de Nicol; nicol *m*; **p. binoculars,** jumelle(s) *f* à prismes; jumelles prismatiques; *Ph:* **p. spectrum,** spectre *m* prismatique; **dove p.,** prisme basculant; *Astr:* **solar p.,** hélioscope *m*; **polarizing solar p.,** hélioscope de polarisation; *W.Tel:* **p. aerial,** antenne *f* prismatique; *Surv:* **laying p.,** collimateur *m*. **2.** (*a*) spectre *m* (solaire); (*b*) **prisms,** couleurs *f* prismatiques. **3.** *Dent:* **enamel p.,** prisme (de l'émail).

prismatic [priz'mætik], *a.* (forme, couleur, etc.) prismatique; (cristal) prismé, orthorhombique; **p. lens,** lentiprisme *m*; **p. sight,** viseur *m* à prisme; **p. binoculars,** jumelle(s) *f* à prisme(s); *Opt:* **p. condenser,** condensateur *m* prismatique, de Fresnel; *Cin:* **p. eye,**

viseur à prisme; *Surv:* **p. compass,** boussole *f* topographique à prisme; *Geol:* **p. jointing,** division *f* en crayons d'ardoise, en bâtonnets; *Cryst:* **p. system,** système *m* terbinaire, système (ortho)rhombique; *Exp:* **p. powder,** *s.* **p.,** poudre *f* prismatique.

prismatization [prizmətai'zeiʃ(ə)n], *s.* prismatisation *f.*

prismatize ['prizmətaiz], *v.tr.* prismatiser.

prismatoid ['prizmətɔid], *s. Mth:* prismatoïde *m.*

prismoid ['prizmɔid], *s. Mth:* prismoïde *m.*

prismy ['priz(ə)mi], *a. Lit:* aux nombreuses couleurs; prismatique.

prisometer [prai'zɔmitər], *s. Civ.E:* prisographe *m.*

prison[1] ['priz(ə)n], *s.* prison *f*; maison *f* d'arrêt; **state p.,** (i) prison politique; (ii) *U.S:* prison d'État; *Nau:* **floating p.,** cayenne *f*; **to send s.o. to p.; to put, throw, s.o. into p.; to have s.o. sent to p.,** mettre, jeter, qn en prison; (faire) emprisonner, incarcérer, qn; **to be sent to p.,** être incarcéré, emprisonné; **to go to p.,** aller en prison; **to be put in p.,** être mis en prison; **to be,** *A:* **lie, in p.,** être en prison, faire, tirer, de la prison, garder la prison, être emprisonné; **he's been in p.,** il a été en prison, il a fait de la prison; **to be kept three months in p. awaiting trial,** faire trois mois de prévention; **p. is not the right punishment for these crimes,** la détention n'est pas la punition qui convient à ces crimes; **detention in an open p.,** détention dans un établissement ouvert; **p. camp,** camp *m* de prisonniers (de guerre); **to break p.,** s'échapper, s'évader, de prison; **p. breaker,** échappé, -ée, de prison; évadé, -ée, de prison; **p. breaking,** (i) évasion *f,* (ii) *Jur:* bris *m,* de prison; **p. yard,** préau *m,* cour *f,* de prison; **p. van,** voiture *f* cellulaire; *F:* panier *m* à salade.

prison[2], *v.tr. Poet:* emprisonner.

prisoned ['prizənd], *a.* emprisonné, incarcéré, en prison, captif.

prisoner ['priz(ə)nər], *s.* **1.** prisonnier, -ière; **State p., p. of State,** prisonnier d'État; détenu, -ue, politique; **p. of war,** prisonnier de guerre; **p. of war camp,** camp *m* de prisonniers (de guerre); **to take s.o. p.,** faire qn prisonnier; **they were taken p.,** ils ont été faits prisonniers; **he took ten thousand men p.,** il fit dix mille prisonniers; **Murat routed Klenau and took ten thousand of his men p.,** Murat mit Klenau en déroute et lui fit dix mille prisonniers; **the prisoners taken from the Spanish,** les prisonniers qu'on avait faits sur les Espagnols; **to be a p. to one's room, to one's chair,** être cloué à sa chambre, à sa chaise. **2.** *Jur:* détenu; (*a*) **p. at the bar,** prévenu, -ue; accusé, -ée; **p. under common law,** prévenu de droit commun; (*b*) (*after sentence*) détenu; prisonnier; coupable *mf.* **3.** *Games:* **prisoners' base, prisoners' bars,** (jeu *m* de) barres *fpl.*

prissy ['prisi], *a.* (*a*) chichiteux; collet monté; (*b*) efféminé.

Pristidae ['pristidi:], *s.pl. Ich:* pristidés *m.*

pristine ['pristain, -i:n], *a.* (*a*) premier, primitif; ancient; d'antan; de jadis; **p. simplicity,** simplicité primitive; (*b*) propre, sans tache; à l'état (de) neuf.

pristiophorus [pristiou'fɔ:rəs], *s. Ich:* pristiophore *m.*

prithee ['priði], *int. A:* je te prie, je t'en prie; de grâce.

privacy ['praivəsi, 'pri-], *s.* **1. the p. of one's home,** l'intimité *f* du chez-soi; **to live in p.,** mener une vie privée; être retiré des affaires; vivre dans la retraite; **in the p. of his room he wrote . . .,** enfermé, retiré, dans sa chambre, il écrivait . . .; **desire for p.,** désir de se cacher aux regards indiscrets, de se tenir à l'écart de la société; **to disturb s.o.'s p.,** faire intrusion chez qn; **there is no p. here,** ça manque d'intimité, on est complètement exposé aux regards indiscrets; **to be married in strict p.,** se marier dans la plus stricte intimité. **2.** secret *m*; **lack of p.,** manque *m* de secret (dans une affaire); *Tg: Tp:* **p. system,** cryptographie *f.*

private ['praivit], *a.* & *s.*

I. *a.* **1.** privé, particulier; **p. citizen,** simple particulier, simple citoyen *m*; **p. persons,** particuliers; **to do sth. in a p. capacity,** faire qch. à titre particulier; **the p. life of an actor,** la vie privée d'un acteur; **in p. life,** dans le particulier, dans la vie privée, dans le privé, dans l'intimité *f*; **p. charity,** la charité privée; *Pol:* **p. member,** simple député; *Mil:* **p. soldier,** simple soldat *m*; *Jur:* **p. law,** droit privé; **p. wrong,** atteinte *f* aux droits d'un individu. **2.** secret, -ète; **to keep a matter p.,** empêcher qu'une affaire ne s'ébruite; tenir une affaire secrète; **he is very p. about his affairs,** il est très réservé au sujet de ses affaires; **p. entrance,** (i) entrée secrète, dérobée; (ii) entrée particulière. **3.** (*p. to oneself*) **p. study,** études particulières; **p. plans,** projets *m* intimes; **for my p. use,** pour mon usage personnel; **p. motives,** motifs personnels, particuliers; **p. parts,** parties génitales, naturelles; *F:* les parties (honteuses). **4.** (*confidential*) intime; **p. and confidential,** secret et confidentiel; **p. conversation,** conversation *f* intime; aparté *m*; **p. interview,** (i) entretien *m* à huis clos; (ii) entretien privé; **to be received in p. audience,** être reçu en audience particulière; **to mark a letter** *p.,* marquer sur une lettre *confidentiel, personnel;* **the news comes through p. channels,** les nouvelles nous parviennent de source privée; **p. information,** renseignements privés; **this is for your p. ear,** je vous le dis confidentiellement; ceci est pour vous seul; **p. arrangement,** accord *m* à l'amiable; **by p. arrangement,** de gré à gré; *Jur:* **p. agreement, contract,** acte *m* sous seing privé; sous-seing *m, pl.* sous-seings; *A:* & *Jur:* **p. letter,** lettre missive. **5.** (*a*) (*not business*) **p. house,** maison particulière; **p. car,** voiture particulière, privée; **p. plane, aircraft,** avion *m* de tourisme; **p. flying,** aviation privée; (*b*) (*reserved for private use*) **p. bus,** bus réservé; **p. chauffeur,** chauffeur *m* de maître; **p. room (in hotel, etc.),** salon réservé; **p. bathroom,** salle de bain(s) particulière; **p. office,** cabinet particulier; **p. staircase,** escalier particulier, privé, dérobé; (*c*) (*to which public are not admitted*) **p. dance,** bal *m* sur invitation; **p. performance,** (i) *A:* représentation *f* en privé, comédie *f* de salon; (ii) (*in theatre*) représentation à bureaux fermés; **p. party,** (i) réunion privée, intime; (ii) groupe *m* de particuliers; **p. sitting,** séance privée; séance à huis clos; **p. wedding,** mariage *m* dans l'intimité; **the funeral will be p.,** les obsèques auront lieu dans la plus stricte intimité; (*d*) (*as opposed to public*) **p. education,** (i) enseignement *m* libre; (ii) enseignement par un précepteur; **p. trader,** marchand établi à son propre compte; **p. detective, investigator,** *F:* **p. eye,** détective privé; **p. (as opposed to nationalized) industry,** le privé; (*e*) **p. nursing home,** clinique privée; (*in hospital*) **p. room,** chambre particulière; **p. practice,** clientèle privée, cabinet (médical, etc.) privé. **6. p. income, money, means,** rentes *fpl*; fortune personnelle; **p. exchange,** standard *m* d'abonné; installation téléphonique privée; **p. line,** ligne intérieure; *P.N:* **p.,** entrée interdite au public, défense d'entrer; **p. property,** propriété privée; **p. road,** chemin privé, particulier; **p. fishing,** pêche réservée. **7.** (*of place*) isolé; loin des regards indiscrets; retiré.

II. *s.* **1.** *adv.phr.* (*a*) **in p.,** dans la vie privée, dans le privé; dans l'intimité; **married in p.,** marié dans l'intimité; (*b*) (*of assembly*) **to sit in p.,** se réunir en séance privée; *Jur:* **to hear a case in p.,** juger une affaire à huis clos; **to speak to s.o. in p.,** parler à qn en particulier, en privé, sans témoins. **2.** *Mil:* (*pers.*) soldat *m* de 2e classe, simple soldat, homme du rang; **fall out P. Martin!** soldat Martin, sortez des rangs! **the privates and the N.C.O's,** la troupe et les gradés. **3. privates,** parties génitales; *F:* les parties (honteuses).

privateer[1] [praivə'tiər], *s. Hist:* **1.** (bâtiment armé en) corsaire *m*; bâtiment armé en course. **2.** (*pers.*) corsaire; capitaine *m* à la course.

privateer[2], *v.i. Nau:* aller en course, faire la course.

privateering [praivə'tiəriŋ], *s. Hist:* (guerre *f* de) course *f*; **to go p.,** aller en course; faire la guerre de course; **to fit out a ship for p.,** armer un navire en course.

privateersman, *pl.* **-men** [paivə'tiəzmən], *s.m. Hist:* (*pers.*) corsaire.

privately ['praivitli], *adv.* **1.** en simple particulier; **p. owned,** qui appartient à un particulier. **2.** en particulier; **to speak to s.o. p.,** parler à qn en particulier; **to hear sth. p.,** entendre qch. en secret, à titre confidentiel; **p. sold,** vendu à l'amiable, de gré à gré; **match played p.,** match joué dans le privé. **3.** en personne; **to benefit p. from sth.,** bénéficier personnellement, en particulier, de qch. **4.** (*of treatment at doctor's, dentist's, etc.*) **I had it done p.,** je l'ai fait faire à mes frais.

privation [prai'veiʃ(ə)n], *s.* (*a*) perte *f,* absence *f,* manque *m* (**of,** de); (*b*) **to live in p.,** vivre dans la privation, vivre de privations.

privative ['pr(a)ivətiv], *a.* **1.** (défaut, etc.) négatif. **2.** *Gram:* (*of particle, etc.*) privatif.

privet ['privit], *s.* **1.** *Bot:* (*a*) troène *m*; (*b*) **Egyptian p.,** henné *m.* **2.** *Ent:* **p. hawkmoth,** sphinx *m* du troène.

privilege[1] ['privilidʒ], *s.* **1.** privilège *m,* prérogative *f*; **that is a p. of old age,** c'est là un privilège de la vieillesse; **the privileges of the nobility,** les privilèges de la noblesse; **to grant s.o. certain privileges,** octroyer certains avantages à qn; **to invade s.o.'s privileges,** violer les privilèges de qn; **to enjoy the p. of doing sth.,** jouir du privilège, avoir le privilège, de faire qch.; **it was a p. to hear him speak,** c'était un vrai plaisir de l'entendre parler. **2.** *Jur:* immunité *f* contre les poursuites en diffamation (accordée aux juges, avocats et témoins); **parliamentary p.,** prérogative, immunité, parlementaire; **writ of p.,** mandat *m* ordonnant la mise en liberté d'un privilégié qui a été arrêté.

privilege[2], *v.tr.* **1.** privilégier (qn); **to p. s.o. to do sth.,** accorder à qn le privilège de faire qch. **2.** *R.C.Ch:* privilégier (un autel).

privileged ['privilidʒd], *a.* privilégié; **the p. class,** la classe des privilégiés; **the p. classes,** les classes privilégiées; **a p. few,** quelques privilégiés; **p. from sth.,** exempté de qch. par privilège; **to be p. to do sth.,** jouir du privilège, avoir le privilège, de faire qch.

privily ['privili], *adv.* en secret; en cachette; secrètement.

privity ['priviti], *s.* **1.** connaissance *f* (**to a plan,** d'un plan); **it was done with the p. of his mother,** cela s'est fait au su de sa mère. **2.** *Jur:* (*a*) lien *m* (du sang, etc.); rapport contractuel (entre employé et employeur, etc.); (*b*) obligation *f*; lien de droit; **p. in deed,** obligation contractuelle; **without p.,** sans lien de droit.

privy ['privi], *a.* & *s.*

I. *a.* **1. to be p. to sth.,** avoir connaissance de qch., être instruit de qch.; être dans le secret; tremper dans (un complot). **2.** privé; (*a*) *A:* secret, caché; **p. parts,** parties génitales, naturelles; (*b*) **the P. Council,** le Conseil privé (du souverain); **P. Councillor,** conseiller privé; **the P. purse,** la cassette du souverain; **(Keeper of the) P. Purse,** trésorier *m* de la maison du souverain; **Lord P. Seal,** *A:* **Keeper of the P. Seal,** Garde *m* du petit sceau; *A:* **the p. seal,** le petit sceau.

II. *s.* **1.** *Jur:* (*pers.*) (*a*) partie intéressée; contractant *m*; ayant droit *m,* ayant cause *m, pl.* ayants droit, ayants cause; (*b*) complice *mf.* **2.** (*a*) *A:* lieux *mpl* d'aisances; latrine *f*; (*b*) *NAm:* cabinets *mpl* (souvent en dehors de la maison).

prix [pri:], *pl.* [pri:(z)], *s.inv. Rac:* **Grand P.,** grand prix (automobile); **he has won 14 grands p.,** il a gagné 14 grands prix.

prize[1] [praiz], *s.* **1.** prix (remporté); **consolation p.,** prix de consolation; **the Nobel p.,** le prix Nobel; **a Nobel p. winner,** un prix Nobel; *Sch:* **p. for good work and progress,** prix d'encouragement; **to take, win, the history p.,** remporter le prix d'histoire; **p. list,** palmarès *m*; **p. book,** livre *m* de prix; **to win, carry off, the p.,** remporter le prix; **to award a p. to a bull (at a show),** primer un taureau; **p. ox,** bœuf primé, médaillé; bœuf gras; **p. novel,** roman couronné (dans un concours); **p. money,** prix en espèces; **p. packet, package,** surprise *f* (à une distribution de jouets, etc.); *Box:* **p. ring,** ring *m* des professionnels; **the prizes of life,** les récompenses *f* de la vie. **2.** (*in a lottery*) lot *m*; **to draw the first p.,** gagner le gros lot.

prize[2], *v.tr.* évaluer, estimer, priser; **to p. sth. highly,** faire grand cas de qch., tenir à qch.

prize[3], *s.* **1.** (*a*) *Navy:* prise *f,* capture *f*; **to make p. of a ship,** capturer un navire; **to be (a) lawful p.,** être de bonne prise; **to bring the p. into port,** amener la prise dans le port; **p. money,** part *f* de prise; **p. law,** droit *m* de prise; **p. court,** cour *f,* conseil *m,* des prises; **p. master,** officier *m* qui commande la prise; **p. crew,** équipage *m* de prise; **to put a p. crew on board a vessel,** amariner une prise; (*b*) butin *m* de guerre. **2.** *Fig. O:* aubaine *f,* trouvaille *f.*

prize[4], *v.tr.* capturer (un navire).

prize[5], *s.* **1.** force *f* de levier; pesée *f* (au moyen d'un levier, d'une pince). **2.** point *m* d'appui (pour le levier, pour exercer une pesée).

prize[6]. **1.** *v.tr.* **to p. sth. up,** soulever qch. à l'aide d'un levier; **to p. a lid open,** forcer, ouvrir, un couvercle avec un levier, avec une pince; **to p. a horse's mouth open,** ouvrir de force la bouche d'un cheval. **2.** *v.i.* **to p. against sth.,** faire levier sur qch.; exercer une pesée sur (une porte, etc.).

prized [praizd], *a.* estimé; **his most p. possession,** l'objet dont il fait le plus de cas, auquel il tient le plus, qu'il prise au-dessus de tout.

prizefight ['praizfait], *s.* match *m* de boxe pour un prix en espèces.

prizefighter ['praizfaitər], *s.* boxeur professionnel.

prizefighting ['praizfaitiŋ], *s.* boxe *f* pour des prix en espèces; boxe professionnelle.

prizegiving ['praizgiviŋ], *s.* (*a*) distribution *f* de prix; (*b*) (jour *m* de) la distribution des prix.

prizeman, *pl.* **-men** ['praizmən], *s. Sch: etc:* gagnant, -ante, d'un prix; lauréat, -ate.

prizewinner ['praizwinər], *s.* gagnant, -ante, d'un prix; lauréat, -ate.

prizewinning ['praizwiniŋ], *a.* **p. novel,** roman primé.

pro[1] [prou]. **p. and contra,** *F:* **p. and con,** (i) *adv.* & *prep.phr.* pour et contre; **evidence p. and con,** témoignages *mpl* pour et contre; (ii) *s.pl.* **the pros and cons,** le pour et le contre.

pro[2], *s. Sp: etc: F:* pro *m inv.*

pro- [prou], *pref.* pro-.

proa ['prouə], *s. Nau:* prao *m,* praw *m* (malais).

proaction ['prouækʃ(ə)n], *s. Psy:* proaction *f.*

proamnion [prou'æmniən], *s. Biol:* proamnios *m.*

probabiliorism [prɔbə'biliərizm], *s. Theol:*

probabiliorisme *m.*

probabiliorist [prɔbə'biliərist], *s. Theol:* probabilioriste *mf.*

probabilism ['prɔbəbilizm], *s. Phil: Theol:* probabilisme *m.*

probabilist ['prɔbəbilist], *s. Phil: Theol:* probabiliste *mf.*

probability [prɔbə'biliti], *s.* probabilité *f*; vraisemblance *f*; **beyond the bounds of p.,** au delà du vraisemblable; **dramatic p.,** vraisemblance dramatique; **in all p.,** selon toute probabilité, selon toute vraisemblance; **the p. is that he won't come,** il est très probable qu'il ne viendra pas; il y a de grandes chances (pour) qu'il ne vienne pas; **there is no p. of his coming,** il n'y a aucune probabilité qu'il vienne; *Mth:* **calculation of probabilities, calculus of p.,** calcul *m* des probabilités; **p. curve,** courbe *f* de probabilité, courbe de la cloche; **p. (density) function,** fonction *f* (de distribution) de probabilité; *Log: etc:* **p. theory,** théorie *f* des probabilités, des chances; **p. laws,** lois *f* de probabilité; **p. process,** processus *m* aléatoire; **prior p.,** probabilité a priori; **posterior p.,** probabilité a posteriori; **equal p.,** équiprobabilité *f*; *Mil:* **p. of a hit,** *NAm:* **hit p.,** probabilité d'atteinte, de coup au but, de succès.

probable ['prɔbəbl]. **1.** *a.* (*a*) probable; **it's p. that he'll come,** il est probable, vraisemblable, qu'il viendra; *Rac:* **p. starters,** partants *m* probables; **p. candidates,** candidats *m* (i) probables, (ii) qui ont les meilleures chances; *Mth:* **p. error,** erreur *f* probable; (*b*) **p. story, excuse,** histoire *f*, excuse *f*, vraisemblable; **a hardly p. story,** une histoire peu vraisemblable. **2.** *s.* (*a*) *esp. U.S:* chose *f*, circonstance *f*, événement *m*, probable; probabilité *f*; **certainties and probables,** certitudes *f* et probabilités; (*b*) *esp. U.S:* avion, etc., probablement détruit, endommagé; **reported ten hits, probables six,** signalés dix coups au but, probables six; (*c*) candidat, participant *m*, (i) probable, (ii) qui a les meilleures chances.

probably ['prɔbəbli], *adv.* probablement; vraisemblablement.

probang ['proubæŋ], *s. Med: Vet:* sonde œsophagienne; *Vet:* dépommoir *m.*

probate[1] ['proub(e)it], *s. Jur:* **1. (grant of) p.,** validation *f*, vérification *f*, homologation *f*, (d'un testament); **to apply for p.,** ouvrir une succession; **to take out, to obtain, p. (of a will),** faire homologuer, faire valider, un testament; **to grant p. (of a will),** homologuer un testament; *Hist:* **the P. Court,** la division de la Haute Cour de justice qui connaissait des testaments et successions; *NAm:* **p. court, court of p.,** tribunal *m* des successions et des tutelles; *Hist: & NAm:* **p. duty,** droits *mpl* de succession (par testament). **2.** testament revêtu de la formule exécutoire; copie *f* authentique.

probate[2] ['proubeit], *v.tr.* **1.** *NAm:* homologuer, valider (un testament). **2.** *U.S:* mettre (un condamné) en liberté surveillée.

probation [prə'beiʃ(ə)n], *s.* **1.** épreuve *f*, stage *m*; *Ecc:* probation *f* (d'un novice); **to be on p.,** être en stage, être à l'épreuve; faire son stage; **officer on p.,** officier *m* stagiaire; **period of p.,** période *f* stagiaire; stage; **to engage s.o. on p.,** engager qn à l'essai. **2.** *Jur:* probation; **p. system,** régime *m* de la mise en liberté surveillée; **five years' p. with a suspended sentence of two years,** deux ans de prison avec sursis de cinq ans sous surveillance de la police; **on p.,** en liberté surveillée; **p. officer,** agent *m* de probation.

probationary [prə'beiʃən(ə)ri], *a.* (période, etc.) d'épreuve, de stage; (période) stagiaire; *Ecc:* **p. period,** (période *f* de) probation *f*.

probationer [prə'beiʃənər], *s.* **1.** (*a*) stagiaire *mf*; (*b*) *Ecc:* novice *mf*; (*c*) *Ecc:* (*in the Protestant Church*) suffragant *m* qui aspire à la charge de pasteur. **2.** *Jur:* jeune délinquant, -ante, en liberté surveillée.

probative ['proubətiv], *a.* (*of evidence, etc.*) probant, probatoire.

probe[1] [proub], *s.* **1.** *Med: Surg:* (*a*) sonde *f*, stylet *m*; **blunt p.,** sonde mousse; **calibrated, metered, p.,** sonde graduée; **sharp p.,** sonde pointue; (*b*) coup *m* de sonde. **2.** (*a*) nettoie-becs *m inv*, débouche-becs *m inv* (pour lampe à acétylène); *Min:* lance *f*, tête *f*, de sonde; *Tchn:* **p. feeler,** tige exploratrice, sensible; *Elcs:* **coupling p.,** sonde de couplage; **sensing p.,** détecteur *m*; **ultrasonic p.,** palpeur *m*; *El.E:* **p. coil,** bobine exploratrice; *Atom.Ph:* **beta-gamma p.,** sonde à rayons bêta-gamma; **dosimetry p.,** sonde de mesure; **electron, neutron, p.,** sonde électronique, neutronique; **p. unit,** tête de détection, sonde; (*b*) *Av: etc:* perche *f*; **in-flight refuelling p.,** perche, prise *f*, de ravitaillement en vol; **nose p.,** perche, aiguille *f*, de nez (de fuselage); **incidence p.,** antenne *f* d'incidence; **tank p.,** sonde de réservoir; (*c*) *Space:* (fusée *f*) sonde; **space p.,** sonde spatiale. **3.** enquête *f*, investigation *f*, sondage *m.*

probe[2], *v.tr.* **1.** *Med:* sonder, explorer (une plaie, etc.); introduire une sonde dans (une plaie); **to p. a wound with one's finger,** insinuer le doigt dans une plaie. **2.** (*a*) sonder (qn); tâter (les défenses, etc.); (*b*) approfondir, fouiller (un mystère, etc.); **to p. the evidence,** scruter les témoignages. **3.** *v.i.* **to p. into the past,** sonder le passé; **he has probed deep into the matter,** il a examiné l'affaire de près; il sait le fonds et le tréfonds de l'affaire; (*of novelist, etc.*) **to p. deeply into the human heart,** pénétrer profondément dans le cœur humain.

prober ['proubər], *s.* sondeur, -euse (d'une plaie, etc.); fouilleur, -euse (d'un mystère, etc.).

probing[1] ['proubiŋ], *a.* (*a*) **p. procedure,** procédé *m* d'investigation, d'expérimentation; (*b*) (*of question, study, etc.*) pénétrant; approfondi, qui va au fond des choses; **p. interrogation,** interrogatoire serré.

probing[2], *s.* (*a*) *Med:* sondage *m*, exploration (d'une plaie); introduction *f* d'une sonde dans (un organe); **p. with a catheter,** cathétérisme *m*; (*b*) enquête *f*, investigation *f*, sondage.

probity ['proubiti], *s.* probité *f*; honnêteté *f*.

problem ['prɔbləm], *s.* (*a*) problème *m* (de mathématiques, etc.); *Cmptr:* **check p.,** problème test; *Mil: Navy:* **map p.,** thème *m* d'exercice sur la carte; (*b*) **present day problems,** les problèmes actuels, les questions d'actualité; les problèmes qui nous occupent aujourd'hui; **political problems,** problèmes politiques; **social problems,** difficultés sociales, problèmes sociaux; **the housing p.,** le problème, la question, la crise, du logement; **the problems discussed at the meeting,** les questions débattues à la réunion; **have you got a p., any problems?** avez-vous une difficulté quelconque? avez-vous un problème, des problèmes? **your friend's a real p. to me,** votre ami est pour moi un vrai problème; **it's a p. to know what to do,** il est bien difficile, bien embarrassant, de savoir quoi faire; **that's a p.,** cela pose des problèmes; **p. child,** enfant d'un caractère difficile, difficile à élever; (enfant) caractériel, -elle; **p. area,** source *f* de difficultés, d'incidents (techniques); *Th:* **p. novel, p. play,** roman *m*, pièce *f*, à thèse.

problematic(al) [prɔbli'mætik(əl)], *a.* **1.** (question, opinion, résultat, etc.) problématique; douteux, incertain; **p. gain,** profit *m* aléatoire. **2.** (*a*) *Log:* qui n'est pas nécessairement vrai; (*b*) (question) discutable.

problematically [prɔbli'mætik(ə)li], *adv.* problématiquement.

problemist ['prɔblimist], *s. Chess: etc:* composeur, -euse, de problèmes.

proboscidate [prou'bɔsideit], *a.* (*a*) *Ent:* lécheur; (*b*) *Z:* proboscidé.

Proboscidea [proubou'sidiə], *s.pl. Z:* proboscidiens *m.*

proboscidean, -ian [proubou'sidiən], *a. & s. Z:* proboscidien (*m*).

proboscis, *pl.* **proboscises, -ides** [prə'bɔsis, prə'bɔsisiz, -idi:z], *s.* **1.** (*a*) trompe *f* (d'éléphant, de tapir); *Z:* **p. monkey,** nasique *m*; guenon *f* à long nez; (*b*) *Ent:* proboscide *f*; **without p.,** élingué. **2.** *Hum: O:* nez *m.* **3.** *Av:* aiguille *f*, perche *f*, de nez (de fuselage).

procacity [prə'kæsiti], *s. A:* impertinence *f*.

procaine ['proukein], *s. Ch:* procaïne *f*.

procathedral [proukə'θi:dr(ə)l], *s.* église *f* qui tient lieu de cathédrale.

procedural [prə'si:djərəl], *a.* **1.** *Jur:* procédural, -aux. **2.** de marche à suivre, de mode opératoire; *W.Tel:* de procédure; *Cmptr:* **p. step,** phase *f* de traitement; **p. error,** erreur due à un défaut de conception du problème.

procedure [prə'si:djər], *s.* **1.** procédé *m*; **the correct p.,** la (vraie) marche à suivre; la bonne méthode. **2.** (mode *m* de) procédure *f* (d'une réunion, etc.); *Adm:* disposition(s) *f(pl)* réglementaire(s); **the p. for doing this,** les modalités *fpl* de cette opération; **rules, order, of p.,** règlement intérieur (d'une assemblée); règles *fpl* de procédure; **p. of a court,** fonctionnement *m* d'une cour; **code of criminal p.,** code *m* d'instruction criminelle; **the established p.,** les formes établies; **standard (operating) p.,** dispositions réglementaires, instructions permanentes; **reporting p.,** dispositions réglementaires pour l'établissement des comptes rendus; **flaw in p.,** vice de procédure. **3.** (*a*) *Tchn:* méthode, mode, opératoire; manière *f* de procéder; marche à suivre; **design p.,** procédé d'étude; *Med:* **diagnostic p.,** méthode d'établissement d'un diagnostic; *W.Tel: etc:* **p. line,** ligne *f* de service; **p. signal,** signal *m* (i) de service, (ii) réglementaire; **p. message,** message *m* réglementaire; (*b*) *Cmptr:* traitement *m*, procédure; **p.-oriented language,** langage orienté vers le traitement.

proceed [prə'si:d], *v.i.* **1.** (*a*) **to p. (on one's way),** continuer son chemin; poursuivre sa route, sa course; se (re)mettre en route; **before we p. any further,** avant d'aller plus loin; (*b*) **to p. to(wards) a place,** aller, se rendre, à un endroit; se diriger vers un endroit; s'acheminer sur, vers, un endroit; **to p. in an easterly direction,** se diriger vers l'est; (*of ship*) **to p. at a high speed, at twenty knots,** filer à grande vitesse, à vingt nœuds; **to p. to Dover in ballast,** aller sur lest à Douvres; **to p. head on to the sea,** aller debout à la mer; (*c*) agir; **to p. with caution, to p. methodically,** agir, procéder, avec prudence, avec méthode; **how shall we p.?** comment nous y prendrons-nous? quelle est la marche à suivre? **we shall p. as directed,** nous nous conformerons à nos instructions; (*d*) **to p. to do sth.,** (i) se mettre à faire qch.; (ii) s'y prendre pour faire qch.; **he then proceeded to unlock the safe,** puis il se mit en devoir d'ouvrir le coffre; (*at meeting, etc.*) **to p. to business,** passer aux affaires; se mettre à la besogne; **I will now p. to another matter,** je passe maintenant à une autre question; *Jur:* **to p. to blows,** en venir aux voies de fait; **to p. to violence,** recourir à la violence; *Sch:* **to p. to the degree of M.A.,** prendre le grade de maîtrise (ès lettres); passer la maîtrise (ès lettres). **2.** (*a*) (se) continuer, se poursuivre; **the letter proceeds thus,** la lettre se poursuit, (se) continue, en ces termes; **they sat down and the dinner proceeded in silence,** ils s'assirent et le dîner se déroula en silence; **the play proceeded without further interruption,** la pièce se poursuivit, se continua, sans nouvelle interruption; **"in any case", he proceeded, "she doesn't live there any more",** en tout cas, continua-t-il, elle n'y habite plus; (*b*) **negotiations are now proceeding,** des négociations sont en cours; **things are proceeding as usual,** les choses suivent leur cours normal; **to pay as the work proceeds,** payer au fur et à mesure de l'ouvrage; (*c*) **to p. with sth.,** poursuivre, continuer (ses études, etc.); **p.!** continuez! allez toujours! **3.** (*a*) *A:* **to p. severely with s.o.,** traiter sévèrement qn; agir envers qn avec sévérité; (*b*) *Jur:* **to p. against s.o.,** procéder contre qn; poursuivre qn (en justice); intenter un procès à qn. **4.** (*a*) **sounds proceeding from a room,** bruits qui sortent, proviennent, d'une pièce; **his conduct proceeds from most noble principles,** sa conduite découle, procède, des plus nobles principes; **war and all the evils that p. from it,** la guerre et tous les maux qui en découlent; (*b*) *Ecc:* **the Holy Ghost, who proceeds from the Father and the Son,** l'Esprit Saint qui procède du Père et du Fils.

proceeding [prə'si:diŋ], *s.* **1.** façon *f* d'agir; **the best way of p.,** la meilleure marche à suivre. **2.** (*a*) procédé *m*, fait *m*, acte *m*, action *f*; *pl.* faits et gestes *m*; **suspicious proceedings,** démarches suspectes; **the whole proceedings were disgraceful,** toute l'affaire a été menée d'une façon indigne; **to note proceedings,** noter ce qui se passe; (*b*) *pl.* débats *m* (d'une assemblée); **proceedings of a society,** (i) délibérations *f*, transactions *f*, travaux *m*, d'une société; (ii) (*document*) compte rendu, procès-verbaux *m*, des séances d'une société; **to conduct the proceedings,** diriger les débats; **the proceedings will begin at 8 p.m.,** la séance, la cérémonie, commencera à 20 h; **the proceedings were orderly,** la réunion s'est déroulée dans le calme; **the proceedings ended with the national anthem,** à la fin de la réunion, de la soirée, on a chanté l'hymne national; (*c*) *Jur:* **(legal) proceedings, proceedings at law,** procès *m* (*sing.*); poursuites *f* judiciaires, en justice; **to take, institute, proceedings against s.o.,** intenter une action, un procès, à, contre, qn; engager, intenter, faire, diriger, entamer, initier, (faire) commencer, exercer, des poursuites (judiciaires) contre qn; introduire une instance; avoir recours aux moyens légaux, aux voies de droit; recourir à la justice; agir contre qn; faire (ses) diligence(s) contre qn; **to begin legal proceedings,** ouvrir une information; **to order proceedings to be taken against s.o.,** instrumenter contre qn.

proceeds ['prousi:dz], *s.pl.* produit *m*, montant *m* (d'une vente, etc.); bénéfices *mpl* (d'une œuvre de charité).

Procellariidae [prouselə'raiːidi:], *s.pl. Orn:* procellariidés *m.*

Procellariiformes [prouseləraii'fɔ:miz], *s.pl. Orn:* procellariiformes *m.*

procephalic [prousi'fælik], *a.* (apophyse) procéphalique (d'un crustacé).

process[1] ['prouses], *s.* **1.** (*a*) processus *m*; développement *m*; **when ice turns into water the p. is gradual,** lorsque la glace se transforme en eau le phénomène est progressif; **the evolutionary p.,** le processus de l'évolution; **the p. is always the same,** le processus est toujours le même; **processes of the mind,** opérations *f* de l'esprit; **the principles that guide the processes of human thought,** les principes qui guident la marche de la pensée humaine; **it's a slow p.,** c'est un long travail;

cela prend du temps; *Mth: etc:* **probability p., random p.,** processus aléatoire; **vector, multivariate, p.,** processus vectoriel; **point p.,** processus ponctuel; **recurrent, recursive, p.,** processus récurrent; (*b*) cours *m*, progrès *m*, avancement *m*; marche *f* (des événements); **to be in the p. of doing sth.,** être en train de faire qch.; **during the p. of dismantling,** au cours du démontage, du démantèlement; **in p. of development,** en voie de développement; **in p. of disappearing,** en passe de disparaître. **2.** (*a*) *Ind:* procédé (industriel, etc.); méthode *f*, technique *f*; opération *f*, traitement *m*; réaction *f* (chimique); **manufacturing p.,** procédé de fabrication; **operating p.,** procédé de travail, mode *m* d'opération; **processes of recovery,** opérations de récupération; **p. water,** eaux *f* résiduaires; **p. gas,** gaz *m* de traitement, gaz utilisé (dans une opération); **p. timer,** compte-pose *m*, *pl.* compte-poses; *Metall:* **Bessemer p.,** procédé Bessemer; *Metalw:* **basic p.,** procédé basique; *Ch:* **dry, wet, p.,** voie sèche, voie humide; **p. of crude oil,** traitement du pétrole brut; (*b*) *Typ: Phot.Engr: etc:* procédés photomécaniques; *esp.* similigravure *f*, simili *f*; **three-colour p.,** procédé trichrome, trichromie *f*; **four-colour p.,** procédé quadrichrome, quadrichromie *f*; **rolling-up p.,** guillotage *m*; **colour screen p.,** similigravure en couleur; **p. block, plate,** (i) cliché *m* en simili(gravure); (ii) cliché photomécanique (à demi-teintes); **p. engraving,** similigravure; **p. engraver, worker,** (i) similigraveur *m*; (ii) photograveur *m*; **p. work,** (i) (*half-tone*) similigravure; simili; (ii) *Lith:* photolithographie *f*, phototypie *f*; héliogravure *f*; (*c*) *Cmptr:* procédé, opération, traitement; **assembly p.,** assemblage *m*; **iterative p.,** processus itératif, itération *f*; **p. control,** automatisme industriel; **p. (control) computer,** calculateur industriel; **p.-bound, p.-limited,** asservi au traitement. **3.** *Jur:* (*a*) procès *m*; action *f* en justice; (*b*) sommation *f* de comparaître; **p. server,** huissier (exploitant); (*c*) **first p.,** introduction *f* d'instance; (*d*) *NAm:* **by due p. of law,** par voies légales, par voie de droit. **4.** (*a*) éminence *f*, prolongement *m* (d'une montagne, etc.); (*b*) *Anat:* excroissance *f*, processus, procès; (*of bone*) apophyse *f*; **ciliary processes,** procès ciliaires; **vermiform processes of the cerebellum,** éminences vermiformes du cervelet; **jugal, zygomatic, p.,** apophyse zygomatique; **odontoid p.,** apophyse odontoïde; (*c*) *Bot:* proéminence *f*.

process[2], *v.tr.* **1.** (*a*) *Ind:* traiter, transformer (une matière première, un produit); préparer, confectionner, industriellement (des aliments); *Tex:* apprêter; *Dent:* cuire, polymériser, (une prothèse); *Cmptr:* traiter (une information, etc.); **processed food,** aliment(s) industriel(s); plat(s) cuisiné(s) industriellement; **process(ed) cheese,** fromage industriel, fromage fondu, crème *f* (de gruyère, etc.); **processed butter,** beurre industriel; (*b*) *Adm: esp. U.S:* faire l'analyse préalable (i) des documents, etc., (ii) des candidats à un poste; acheminer (des documents); exploiter (un renseignement). **2.** *Jur:* intenter un procès à (qn); poursuivre (qn). **3.** *Typ:* reproduire (un cliché) par un procédé photomécanique, par similigravure.

process[3] [prə'ses], *v.i. F:* défiler en cortège.

processability [prousesə'biliti], *s. Cmptr:* possibilité(s) *f(pl)* de traitement (de l'information).

processable [prou'sesəbl], *a. Cmptr:* (information) traitable.

processing ['prousesiŋ], *s.* **1.** (*a*) traitement *m*, travail *m*, transformation *f* (d'une matière première, d'un produit); opérations *fpl* (d'une fabrication); confection, préparation, industrielle (d'aliments); **p. industry,** industrie *f* de transformation; **food p. industry,** l'industrie alimentaire; **chemical p.,** traitement chimique; **p. cycle,** cycle *m* d'opérations; *Mch.Tls:* **p. machine,** machine *f* à transfert; (*b*) *Dent:* polymérisation *f* (d'une prothèse, etc.); (*c*) *Phot:* développement *m*, traitement (d'un film, d'un papier, etc., photographique); (*d*) *Cmptr:* **computer p.,** traitement sur ordinateur; **background, foreground, p.,** traitement des programmes non prioritaires, prioritaires; **batch p.,** traitement par lots, par trains; traitement différé, groupé; **digital p.,** traitement numérique; **in-line p.,** traitement direct, immédiat; **off-line p.,** traitement en différé; **parallel p.,** traitement en simultanéité; **central p. unit,** unité *f* de traitement, unité centrale; **data p., information p.,** traitement (des données, de l'information); informatique *f*; mécanographie *f*; **data p. machine, system,** ordinateur *m*; **data p. run,** phase *f* de traitement (de l'information); **data p. card,** carte *f* mécanographique, carte perforée; **data p. consultant,** ingénieur-conseil *m* en informatique; *Elcs:* **p. of raw data,** manipulation *f* de données brutes; (*e*) *Mil: etc:* **p. of mail,** acheminement *m* du courrier; (*f*) *Adm: esp. U.S:* examen *m* préalable (i) de documents, etc., (ii) de candidats à un poste; acheminement *m* (de documents).

procession[1] [prə'seʃ(ə)n], *s.* **1.** cortège *m*; défilé *m*; (*religious, etc.*) procession *f*; **funeral, bridal, p.,** cortège funèbre, nuptial; **to go, walk, in p.,** aller en cortège, en procession; défiler; *Ecc: A:* **p. week,** la semaine des Rogations; **p. of cars,** procession, défilé, file *f*, de voitures; *Ent:* **p. moth,** bombyx *m* du chêne. **2.** *Theol:* **the P. of the Holy Spirit,** la Procession du Saint-Esprit.

procession[2]. **1.** *v.i.* défiler en cortège, *Ecc:* en procession; processionner. **2.** *v.tr.* parcourir (les rues, etc.) en cortège, en procession.

processional [prə'seʃən(ə)l]. **1.** *a.* processionnel. **2.** *s.* (*a*) (*book*) processionnal *m*, -aux; (*b*) hymne processionnel.

processionally [prə'seʃən(ə)li], *adv.* processionnellement; en cortège; à pas comptés; *Ecc:* en procession.

processionary [prə'seʃənəri], *a. Ent:* **p. caterpillar,** (chenille *f*) processionnaire *f*, chattepeleuse *f*; **p. moth,** bombyx *m* du chêne.

processionist [prə'seʃənist], *s.* membre *m* du cortège, de la procession.

processor ['prousesər], *s.* **1.** (*a*) *Ind:* spécialiste *mf* préposé(e) au traitement d'un produit; personne qui travaille dans une industrie de transformation; préparateur, -trice, (d'aliments industriels); (*b*) photographe *mf* (spécialiste) de laboratoire; (*c*) *Cmptr:* (*machine*) organe *m* de traitement, processeur *m*; **(central) p.,** unité centrale; **language p.,** programme *m* de traitement de langage, compilateur *m*; **data p.,** (i) ordinateur *m*; (ii) (*pers.*) informaticien, -ienne; (*d*) *Adm: esp. U.S:* personne chargée de l'examen préalable (i) de documents, etc., (ii) de candidats à un poste.

processual [prou'sesjuəl], *a.* processuel.

Prochorda(ta) [proukɔ:'deitə, -'kɔ:də], *s.pl. Algae:* proc(h)ordés *m*, protochordés *m*.

prochromosome [prou'krouməsoum], *s. Biol:* prochromosome *m*.

prochronism ['proukrənizm], *s.* prochronisme *m*.

proclaim [prə'kleim], *v.tr.* **1.** (*a*) **to p. s.o. king,** proclamer, déclarer, qn roi; **to p. s.o. leader,** (faire) reconnaître qn pour chef; (*b*) **to have sth. proclaimed through the town,** faire annoncer, faire crier, qch. par la ville; **to p. war,** déclarer la guerre; **his face proclaimed his guilt,** son visage trahissait sa culpabilité; (*c*) *v.pr.* **Hitler proclaimed himself dictator,** Hitler se proclama dictateur. **2.** *A:* (*a*) mettre (par proclamation) (qn) au ban, hors la loi; (*b*) **to p. a meeting,** interdire une réunion; (*c*) **to p. a district,** mettre une région sous un régime spécial de police.

proclaimer [prə'kleimər], *s.* proclamateur, -trice; déclarateur, -trice.

proclamation [prɔklə'meiʃ(ə)n], *s.* **1.** proclamation *f*; déclaration *f* (publique); publication *f* (des bans, etc.); **to make, issue, a p.,** faire une proclamation; **to make sth. known by public p.,** annoncer qch. à cri public; *Ecc:* **p. of a fast,** indiction *f* d'un jeûne. **2.** *A:* (*a*) (*of pers.*) mise *f* au ban, mise hors la loi; (*b*) interdiction *f* (d'une assemblée, etc.); (*c*) (*of district*) mise sous le coup d'une ordonnance de police.

proclisis ['prouklisis], *s. Ling:* proclise *f*.

proclitic [prou'klitik], *a. & s. Ling:* proclitique (*m*).

proclivity [prou'kliviti], *s.* penchant *m*, tendance *f*, propension *f*, inclination *f* (**to sth.,** à qch.); disposition *f* (pour qch.).

Procne ['prɔkni]. *Pr.n.f. Gr.Myth:* Progné, Procné.

procoelous [prou'si:ləs], *a. Anat:* procœlique.

proconsul [prou'kɔnsəl], *s. Hist:* proconsul *m*.

proconsular [prou'kɔnsjulər], *a.* proconsulaire.

proconsulate [prou'kɔnsjulət], *s. Hist:* **1.** proconsulat *m*. **2.** province *f* proconsulaire.

proconsulship [prou'kɔnsəlʃip], *s. Hist:* proconsulat *m*.

Procopius [prou'koupiəs]. *Pr.n.m. Gr.Lit:* Procope.

procrastinate [prou'kræstineit], *v.i.* remettre les affaires au lendemain, à plus tard; temporiser, atermoyer.

procrastination [proukræsti'neiʃ(ə)n], *s.* remise *f* des affaires à plus tard; procrastination *f*; temporisation *f*, inaction *f*; *Prov:* **p. is the thief of time,** ne remettez pas au lendemain ce que vous pouvez faire le jour même.

procrastinative [prou'kræstineitiv], *a.* temporisant; temporisateur; (*of tactics, etc.*) dilatoire.

procrastinator [prou'kræstineitər], *s.* temporisateur, -trice.

procreate [proukri'eit], *v.tr.* procréer, engendrer.

procreation [proukri'eiʃ(ə)n], *s.* procréation *f*, engendrement *m*.

procreative [proukri'eitiv], *a.* procréateur, -trice.

procreativeness [proukri'eitivnis], *s.* pouvoir procréateur.

Procrustean [prou'krʌstiən], *a.* **a P. bed,** un lit de Proc(r)uste.

Procrustes [prou'krʌsti:z], *Pr.n.m. Gr.Myth:* Proc(r)uste; **the bed of P.,** le lit de Procuste.

procrypsis [prou'kripsis], *s. Nat.Hist:* homochromie *f*.

procryptic [prou'kriptik], *a. Nat.Hist:* homochrome, mimétique.

proctalgia [prɔk'tældʒiə], *s. Med:* proctalgie *f*.

proctitis [prɔk'taitis], *s. Med:* proctite *f*.

proctocele ['prɔktousi:l], *s. Med:* proctocèle *f*; hernie *f*, chute *f*, du rectum.

proctocolitis [prɔktoukɔ'laitis], *s. Med:* recto-colite *f*.

proctologist [prɔk'tɔlədʒist], *s. Med:* proctologue *mf*.

proctology [prɔk'tɔlədʒi], *s. Med:* proctologie *f*.

proctoptosis [prɔktɔp'tousis], *s. Med:* proctoptose *m*.

proctor ['prɔktər], *s.* **1.** *Sch:* (*at Oxford, Cambridge, etc.*) membre exécutif du conseil de discipline; censeur *m*; **senior, junior, p.,** premier, second, censeur. **2.** *Jur:* (*a*) avoué *m* (devant une cour ecclésiastique); (*b*) **Queen's, King's, p.,** procureur *m* de la reine, du roi (devant certaines cours). **3.** *Ecc:* procureur. **4.** *Hist:* **(tithe) p.,** dimier *m*.

proctorial [prɔk'tɔ:riəl], *a.* **1.** *Sch:* (*at Oxford, Cambridge, etc.*) qui relève des membres exécutifs du conseil de discipline; censorial, -iaux. **2.** (*a*) qui relève des avoués (devant les cours ecclésiastiques); (*b*) qui relève d'un procureur.

proctorize ['prɔktəraiz], *v.tr. Sch:* (*at Oxford, Cambridge, etc.*) soumettre (un étudiant) à la discipline de l'université; le réprimander; le mettre aux arrêts; lui infliger une amende.

proctoscope ['prɔktəskoup], *s. Med:* rectoscope *m*.

proctotrupid, -trypid [prɔktou'tru:pid, -'tripid], *s. Ent:* proctotrupe *m*, proctotrype *m*, proctotrypidés *m*.

Proctotrupidae, -trypidae [prɔktou'tru:pidi:, -'tripidi:], *s.pl. Ent:* proctotrupides *m*.

procumbent [prou'kʌmbənt], *a.* **1.** (*of pers.*) couché sur le ventre, la face contre terre. **2.** *Bot:* (*of plant*) procombant, rampant.

procurable [prə'kju:rəbl], *a.* procurable.

procuracy ['prɔkjurəsi], *s. Ecc:* procure *f*.

procural [prə'kju:rəl], *s.* obtention *f*, acquisition *f* (de qch.).

procurance [prə'kju:rəns], *s.* obtention *f*, acquisition *f* (de qch.).

procuration [prɔkju'reiʃ(ə)n], *s.* **1.** *Jur:* procuration *f*; **letters of p.,** procuration, mandat *m*; **p. signature,** signature *f* par procuration; (*in purchase*) **act of p.,** commandement *m*; **to act by p.,** agir (i) par procuration, (ii) (*in sale*) en vertu d'un commandement. **2.** *Ecc:* procuration. **3.** (*a*) acquisition *f*, obtention *f* (de qch., pour qn); négociation *f* (d'un emprunt); entremise *f* d'un(e) proxénète; (*b*) commission payée (à un agent) pour l'obtention d'un prêt. **4.** proxénétisme *m*.

procurator ['prɔkjureitər], *s.* **1.** *Hist:* procurateur *m*; **the P. of Judaea,** le procurateur de Judée. **2.** *Jur:* fondé *m* de pouvoir(s); agent *m*, procureur *m*; *Scot:* **p. fiscal,** procureur général.

procuratorial [prɔkjurə'tɔ:riəl], *a.* **1.** procuratorial, -aux. **2.** *Hist:* procuratorien.

procuratorship ['prɔkjureitəʃip], *s.* **1.** *Rom.Hist:* procuratèle *f*. **2.** *Ital.Hist:* procuratie *f*.

procuratory ['prɔkjurət(ə)ri], *s. Jur:* **(letters of) p.,** (lettres *f* de) procuration *f*; pouvoir *m*.

procuratrix [prɔkju'reitriks], *s.f. Hist: Ecc:* procuratrice; (sœur) économe.

procure [prə'kjuər], *v.tr.* **1.** (*a*) obtenir, procurer; **to p. sth. for s.o.,** procurer qch. à qn; (*b*) **to p. sth. (for oneself),** se procurer qch. **2.** *A: & Lit:* amener (un résultat, etc.); **to p. s.o.'s death,** amener, causer, occasionner, la mort de qn. **3.** (*a*) embaucher (une femme) en vue de la prostitution, aux fins de débauche; (*b*) *v.i.* faire le métier de proxénète, d'entremetteur, d'entremetteuse.

procurement [prə'kjuəmənt], *s.* **1.** (*a*) obtention *f*, acquisition *f* (**of,** de); *Ind:* équipement *m*; *Ind: Pol.Ec:* **p. costs,** dépenses *f* (i) d'acquisition, (ii) d'équipement; (*b*) *Adm: U.S:* approvisionnement *m* (d'un service); service des approvisionnements, des fournitures; **emergency p.,** approvisionnement d'urgence; **p. (lead) time,** délai *m* d'approvisionnement; (*c*) *Com:* **p. staff,** acheteurs *mpl*. **2.** embauchage *m*, embauchement *m* (d'une femme) aux fins de débauche; proxénétisme.

procurer [prə'kju:rər], *s.* **1.** (i) acquéreur, -euse; (ii) personne *f* qui procure (qch. pour qn). **2.** entremetteur, -euse, proxénète *mf*.

procuress [prə'kju:ris], *s.f.* entremetteuse, proxénète, procureuse.

procuring [prə'kju:riŋ], *s.* = PROCUREMENT.

procursive [prou'kə:siv], *a. Med:* **p. epilepsy,** épilepsie procursive.

Procyon ['prousiɔn]. **1.** *Pr.n. Astr:* Procyon *m.* **2.** *s. Z:* procyon *m,* raton *m.*

Procyonidae [prousi'ɔnidi:], *s.pl. Z:* procyonidés *m.*

prod[1] [prɔd], *s.* **1.** coup (donné du bout du doigt, etc.); **he gave me a p. in the ribs,** il m'a enfoncé son coude dans les côtes; **to give s.o. a p. with a stick,** donner un coup de bâton à qn; *F:* **give him a p.,** aiguillonnez-le un peu. **2.** instrument pointu; aiguillon *m,* poinçon *m; Metall:* broche *f* (de moule en terre).

prod[2], *v.tr. & ind.tr.* **(prodded) 1. to p. (at) s.o., sth. (with sth.),** tâter, pousser, qn, qch. (du bout de qch.); **to p. s.o. in the ribs with one's finger,** enfoncer son doigt dans les côtes de qn; **prodding tool,** poinçon *m.* **2.** *F:* aiguillonner, stimuler, pousser **(s.o. into doing sth.,** qn à faire qch.); **to p. s.o. on,** presser qn; serrer les côtes à qn.

prodder ['prɔdər], *s.* = PROD[1] 2.

prodelision [proudi'liʒ(ə)n], *s. Ling:* élision *f* d'une voyelle initiale.

prodigal ['prɔdig(ə)l], *a. & s.* prodigue *(mf)*; dissipateur, -trice; dilapidateur, -trice; gaspilleur, -euse; *B:* **the P. Son,** l'enfant *m* prodigue; **p. administration,** administration dissipatrice; **to be p. of sth.,** être prodigue de qch.; prodiguer qch.

prodigality [prɔdi'gæliti], *s.* prodigalité *f.*

prodigalize ['prɔdigəlaiz], *v.tr.* prodiguer (qch.); être prodigue de (qch.); dépenser (son argent) sans compter.

prodigally ['prɔdig(ə)li], *adv.* prodigalement; en prodigue; **to give p.,** donner à pleines mains.

prodigious [prə'didʒəs], *a.* prodigieux; merveilleux, extraordinaire; énorme; phénoménal, -aux.

prodigiously [prə'didʒəsli], *adv.* prodigieusement; merveilleusement, extraordinairement; énormément.

prodigiousness [prə'didʒəsnis], *s.* merveille *f*; énormité *f*; *Lit:* prodigiosité *f.*

prodigy ['prɔdidʒi], *s.* prodige *m;* merveille *f*; **child p.,** enfant *mf* prodige.

prodromal, prodromic ['prɔdrəm(ə)l, prou'drɔmik], *a.* *(a) Med:* prodromique; *(b) (of sign, etc.)* avant-coureur; *(of remark, etc.)* préliminaire.

prodrome, prodromus, *pl.* **-mi** ['proudroum, 'prɔdrəməs, -mai], *s.* **1.** prodrome *m;* préambule *m,* introduction *f* (à un livre, etc.). **2.** *Med:* prodrome.

produce[1] ['prɔdju:s], *s.* **1.** *(a)* rendement *m* (d'un champ de blé, des minerais, etc.); *(b)* produit *m,* résultat *m.* **2.** *coll.* produits, denrées *fpl*; **home, inland, p.,** produits du pays, produits indigènes; **foreign p.,** produits étrangers, exotiques; **p. intended for export,** produits destinés à l'exportation; **raw p.,** matières premières; **natural p.,** produit(s) naturel(s); **agricultural p.,** produits agricoles; **farm p.,** produits de ferme, produits fermiers; **garden p.,** produits du jardinage; **market garden p.,** produits maraîchers, productions maraîchères. **3.** *Mil: etc:* matériel réformé; **to bring scrapped stores to p.,** liquider, mettre en vente, du matériel réformé.

produce[2] [prə'dju:s], *v.tr.* **1.** *(a)* présenter, exhiber (son billet, son passeport, etc.); *Jur:* présenter, produire (des documents); **to p. accounts for inspection,** présenter, montrer, les écritures pour l'inspection; **I can p. the documents,** je peux fournir les documents; **to p. a rabbit out of a hat.** faire sortir un lapin d'un chapeau; **he produced a little doll from his pocket,** de sa poche il a tiré, sorti, une petite poupée; **to p. reasons,** donner des raisons; **to p. a witness,** produire, faire comparaître, un témoin; *(b)* **to p. a play,** mettre une pièce en scène; produire, représenter, une pièce; **badly produced play,** pièce mal montée; **to p. an actress, a singer,** produire, lancer, une actrice, une cantatrice; *(c)* éditer (un livre); produire (un film); mettre en ondes (une émission de radio). **2.** *(a)* créer; **to p. a vacuum,** produire, faire, le vide; *El:* **to p. a spark,** faire jaillir une étincelle; **current produced by a battery,** courant engendré, produit, par une pile; **this writer has produced about thirty novels,** cet auteur a donné une trentaine de romans; *(b) Ind:* fabriquer (des marchandises); *(c)* produire, causer, provoquer (un effet, etc.); **to p. a sensation,** faire sensation. **3.** rapporter, rendre (un profit, etc.); **tree that produces a lot of fruit,** arbre qui produit beaucoup de fruits; **shares that p. five per cent,** actions qui rapportent cinq pour cent. **4.** *Mth:* prolonger (une ligne).

producer [prə'dju:sər], *s.* **1.** *(pers.) (a)* producteur, -trice; fabricant *m* **(of, de); producers' co-operative,** coopérative *f* de production; **p. goods,** biens *mpl* de production, d'équipement; *(b) Th:* metteur *m* en scène; *Cin:* (i) producteur *m,* société productrice (de films); (ii) metteur en scène, directeur *m* de production; réalisateur, -trice; *(c)* metteur en ondes, réalisateur (d'une émission de radio); **television p.,** téléaste *mf.* **2.** *Ind:* **(gas) p.,** gazogène *m;* (appareil *m*) gazifère *m;* **p. gas,** gaz *m* pauvre; gaz de gazogène.

producible [prə'dju:sibl], *a.* **1.** productible; présentable; facile à fabriquer, à produire, à réaliser. **2.** *Mth: (of line)* prolongeable.

producing[1] [prə'dju:siŋ], *a.* producteur, -trice; productif; **p. centre,** centre *m* de production; **p. capacity,** capacité *f* de production, productivité *f.*

producing[2], *s.* = PRODUCTION 1.

product ['prɔdʌkt], *s.* **1.** produit *m;* **the p. of ten years' work,** le produit de dix années de travail; *Pol.Ec:* **gross national p.,** produit national brut; *Ind:* **basic p.,** produit de base; **end p., finished p.,** produit fini; **secondary p.,** produit secondaire; sous-produit *m, pl.* sous-produits; **semi-manufactured p.,** produit semi-ouvré; **waste products,** produits de rejet; *Atom.Ph:* **reaction, fission, p.,** produit de la réaction, de fission; **decay p.,** produit de désintégration; **final p.,** produit final, terminal; **p. material,** produit; **p. particle,** particule produite. **2.** *(a) Mth:* produit; **p. of x into y,** produit de x par y; **twice the p. of ten and six,** le double produit de dix et six; **p. quantity,** grandeur *f* scalaire; *(b) Book-k:* **red p.,** nombre *m* rouge.

production [prə'dʌkʃ(ə)n], *s.* **1.** *(a)* production *f,* représentation *f,* communication *f* (de documents); présentation *f* (d'un billet, etc.); **on p. of an identity card,** sur présentation, sur production, d'une carte d'identité; *Jur:* **p. of a witness,** production d'un témoin; *(b)* mise *f* en scène, représentation (d'une pièce de théâtre); réalisation *f* (d'un film, d'une émission de radio); mise en ondes (d'une émission de radio); *(of film, etc.)* **spectacular p.,** production à grand spectacle. **2.** *(a) Ph: etc:* production, génération *f* (d'énergie, de vapeur, etc.); **study of the p. of sound,** étude de la production du son; *Atom.Ph:* **fission p. of neutrons,** production de neutrons par fission; **p. reactor,** réacteur producteur, pile productrice, de matière fissile; *(b)* production, fabrication *f* (de marchandises, etc.); **mass p.,** production en masse; production, fabrication, en grandes, grosses, séries; **quantity p.,** production, fabrication, en série; **p. to order,** production sur commande; **planned p.,** production dirigée, planifiée; **allowable p.,** contingent *m* de production; **restricted p.,** restriction *f* de production; **rate of p.,** taux *m* de production; **drop in p.,** chute *f,* baisse *f,* de la production; **p. surplus,** excédent *m,* surplus *m,* de production; **p. plant,** usine *f*; **p. unit,** (i) unité *f,* (ii) équipe *f,* de production; **p. line,** chaîne *f* de montage, de fabrication, de production; **to work on a p. line,** travailler à la chaîne; **p. line system,** production, travail *m,* à la chaîne; **p. engineering,** organisation *f* de la production; **p. control,** gestion *f* de la production; **p. costs,** coûts *m,* frais *m,* de production; **p. car, aircraft,** voiture *f,* avion *m,* de série; *(c) Cmptr:* exécution *f,* production (d'un programme); **p. programme,** programme exécutable; **p. run,** phase *f* d'exécution; **p. running,** phase d'exploitation.

productive [prə'dʌktiv], *a.* **1.** *(a)* (i) générateur, -trice **(of sth.,** de qch.); productif; *(of tree, capital, mine, etc.)* en plein rapport, en plein rendement; (ii) profitable, utile; *Hyd:* **p. head,** chute *f* utile; *Cmptr:* **p. time,** temps *m* d'exploitation, temps utile; *(b) (of land, etc.)* fécond; **p. artist,** artiste fécond. **2.** *(a) Pol.Ec:* (travail, etc.) productif; *(b)* **p. period of an author,** années productives d'un auteur. **3.** fertile, riche (of, en).

productively [prə'dʌktivli], *adv.* **1.** avec fertilité. **2.** profitablement.

productiveness [prə'dʌktivnis], **productivity** [prɔdʌk'tiviti], *s.* productivité *f*; **land in full p.,** terres en plein rapport, en plein rendement; *Ind:* **p. of an enterprise,** productivité financière, rentabilité *f,* rapport *m,* d'une entreprise; **productivity drive,** campagne *f* de productivité; **productivity bargaining,** négociation des contrats de productivité.

Productus [prə'dʌktəs], *s. Paleont:* productus *m.*

proem ['prouem], *s.* proème *m;* préface *f,* avant-propos *m inv,* préambule *m* (d'un ouvrage); exorde *m* (d'un discours).

proembryo [prou'embriou], *s. Biol:* proembryon *m.*

proembryonic [prouembri'ɔnik], *a. Biol:* proembryonnaire.

proemial [prou'i:miəl], *a.* introductoire; en forme de proème, de préface.

proenzyme [prou'enzaim], *s. Bio-Ch:* proenzyme *f,* proferment *m,* prozymase *f.*

prof [prɔf], *s. F:* prof *m* (de faculté).

profanation [prɔfə'neiʃ(ə)n], *s.* profanation *f.*

profane[1] [prə'fein], *a.* **1.** *(a)* (histoire, etc.) profane; **things sacred and p.,** le sacré et le profane; *(b) (of pers.)* profane; non initié. **2.** (rite, etc.) païen, impie. **3.** *(a)* (acte) profane; (langage) impie, blasphématoire; *(b) (of pers.)* grossier; qui blasphème à tout propos.

profane[2], *v.tr.* profaner (une chose sainte, un talent, etc.); polluer (une église); **to p. the name of God,** blasphémer le saint nom de Dieu; *O:* **to p. the Sabbath (day),** violer le (jour du) sabbat; violer le repos dominical.

profanely [prə'feinli], *adv.* **1.** d'une manière profane; avec impiété. **2.** en jurant, en blasphémant.

profaneness [prə'feinnis], *s.* = PROFANITY 1.

profaner [prə'feinər], *s.* profanateur, -trice; violateur, -trice **(of,** de).

profanity [prə'fæniti], *s.* **1.** *(a)* nature *f* profane (d'un écrit, etc.); *(b)* impiété *f* (d'une action, etc.). **2. to utter profanities,** dire des blasphèmes, lâcher des jurons.

proferment [proufə'ment], *s. Bio-Ch:* proferment *m.*

profert ['proufət], *s. Jur: A:* production *f,* représentation *f,* communication *f* (d'un document).

profess [prə'fes], *v.tr.* **1.** *(a)* professer, faire profession de (sa foi, etc.); déclarer; **to p. oneself satisfied,** se déclarer satisfait; **to p. oneself a socialist,** se déclarer socialiste; faire profession de socialisme; *(b) (often falsely)* **to p. a great esteem for s.o.,** professer une grande estime pour qn, faire profession d'une grande estime pour qn; **she professed an interest in my future,** elle a déclaré s'intéresser à mon avenir; **to p. (oneself) to be a social reformer,** se dire, se faire passer pour, réformateur social; **I do not p. to be a scholar,** je ne prétends pas être savant; **she professes to be thirty,** elle se donne trente ans. **2.** *Ecc:* *(a)* **to p. oneself (in an order),** faire profession (dans un ordre); *(b)* recevoir (un moine) dans un ordre. **3.** *(a)* exercer (un métier, etc.); *(b) Sch:* professer (l'histoire, etc.).

professed [prə'fest], *a.* **1.** *(of monk, nun)* profès, -esse; **p. house,** maison professe. **2.** *(a)* **p. enemy of the government,** ennemi déclaré du gouvernement; **p. Marxist,** marxiste avéré; *(b)* prétendu, soi-disant; **a p. scientist,** un prétendu scientifique. **3.** professionnel; de profession.

professedly [prə'fesidli], *adv.* **1.** de son propre aveu; ouvertement; ostensiblement; **he is p. ignorant on the subject,** il avoue son ignorance à ce sujet. **2.** soi-disant.

profession [prə'feʃ(ə)n], *s.* **1.** profession *f,* déclaration *f*; **atheist in fact if not in p.,** athée de fait sinon avéré; **p. of faith,** profession de foi; *Ecc:* **to make one's p.,** faire profession (dans un ordre). **2.** *(a)* profession, métier *m,* carrière *f*; **the teaching p.,** le corps professoral, le professorat; **the (learned) professions,** les professions libérales; **to follow, practise, pursue, a p.,** exercer une profession; exercer, faire, un métier; *A:* **to take up the p. of arms, the military p.,** embrasser la carrière des armes, la carrière militaire; adopter, choisir, le métier des armes, le métier militaire; **the p. of medicine,** la profession de médecin; **writer by p.,** écrivain professionnel; **he is a doctor by p.,** il est médecin de (sa) profession; il exerce la médecine; *(b)* **the p.,** (i) (les membres *m* de) la profession; les gens *m* du métier; *esp.* (ii) *F:* le théâtre; **to belong to the p.,** faire du théâtre; **in the p.,** dans les milieux professionnels; **the oldest p.,** la prostitution.

professional [prə'feʃən(ə)l]. **1.** *a.* professionnel; *(a)* **p. practices,** usages *m* de la profession, du métier; **conduct that is not p.,** conduite contraire aux usages de la profession (de médecin, etc.); **to take p. advice on a matter,** (i) consulter une personne du métier, un professionnel, sur qch.; (ii) consulter un avocat, un médecin; *(b)* de profession, de métier, de son état; **p. qualifications,** aptitudes, connaissances, professionnelles; **the p. army,** l'armée de métier; **p. soldier, diplomat,** soldat, diplomate, de carrière; **p. agitator,** agitateur professionnel; **p. dancer,** danseur, -euse, de profession; *Sp:* **p. player,** joueur professionnel, de profession; **p. football,** le football professionnel; *(c)* qui a reçu une instruction professionnelle; expert; **p. engineer,** ingénieur diplômé; *(d)* **p. man, woman,** homme, femme, qui exerce une des professions libérales; intellectuel, -elle; **the p. classes,** les membres *m* des professions libérales. **2.** *s.* *(a)* professionnel, -elle; personne de métier, expert *m;* **professionals,** professionnels, gens *m* de, du, métier; *(b) Sp: etc:* professionnel; *esp.* golfeur professionnel, golfeuse professionnelle; **a rugby p.,** un professionnel de rugby; **to turn, go, p.,** se faire professionnel.

professionalism [prə'feʃənəlizm], *s.* **1.** caractère professionnel. **2.** *Sp: etc:* professionnalisme *m.*

professionality [prəfeʃə'næliti], *s.* caractère professionnel **(of,** de).

professionalize [prə'feʃənəlaiz], *v.tr.* *(a)* faire un métier de (qch.); *(b)* livrer (un sport, etc.) au professionnalisme.

professionally [prə'feʃən(ə)li], *adv.* professionnellement; **to do sth. p.,** faire qch. en homme, femme, du métier; **to consult s.o. p.,** consulter qn pour affaires; **to act p.,** agir dans l'exercice de sa profession; agir en médecin, etc.; **p. trained,** ayant reçu une instruction professionnelle.

professor [prə'fesər], *s.* **1.** *Ecc: etc:* adepte *mf* (d'une doctrine, etc.). **2.** *Sch:* professeur *m* (de faculté); **P. Martin,** Monsieur le Professeur Martin; **she is p. of English,** elle est professeur d'anglais.

professorate [prə'fesərit], *s.* **1.** = PROFESSORSHIP. **2.** = PROFESSORIATE 1.

professorial [prɔfi'sɔːriəl], *a.* professoral, -aux.

professorially [prɔfi'sɔːriəli], *adv.* d'un ton professoral; d'une manière professorale.

professoriate [prɔfi'sɔːriit], *s.* **1.** corps professoral. **2.** = PROFESSORSHIP.

professorship [prə'fesəʃip], *s.* professorat *m;* chaire *f* (de l'enseignement supérieur); **to be appointed to a p.,** être nommé à une chaire; être nommé professeur (of, de).

proffer[1] ['prɔfər], *s. Lit:* offre *f,* proposition *f.*

proffer[2], *v.tr.* (**proffered**) offrir, présenter; **to p. one's hand,** tendre la main (à qn); **to p. one's arm to a lady,** offrir son bras à une dame.

profferer ['prɔfərər], *s. A:* offrant, -ante; (*at sale*) **the best p.,** le plus offrant.

proficiency [prə'fiʃ(ə)nsi], *s.* capacité *f,* compétence *f,* force *f* (**in a subject,** en une matière); **to reach, attain, (a stage of) p.,** arriver à la compétence; *Mil:* **p. pay,** prime *f* de spécialité.

proficient [prə'fiʃ(ə)nt]. **1.** *a.* capable, compétent; versé (**in,** dans); **to be p. in German,** être fort en allemand; bien connaître l'allemand; **p. in book-keeping,** versé dans la comptabilité; expert en comptabilité. **2.** *s.* personne *f* capable; expert *m,* connaisseur *m.*

proficiently [prə'fiʃ(ə)ntli], *adv.* avec compétence.

profile[1] ['proufail], *s.* **1.** (*a*) (i) profil *m* (de qn, du visage); (ii) silhouette *f;* **half p. portrait,** portrait *m* de trois quarts; **drawn in p.,** dessiné, esquissé, de profil; **cut out in p.,** silhouetté; (*b*) *Journ: etc:* profil (psychologique), portrait (de qn); *Psy:* psychogramme *m;* (*c*) (*of pers.*) **to keep a low p.,** se tenir coi; (*d*) *Tchn:* profil (du terrain, d'une aile d'avion, etc.); configuration *f* (des ailes d'un avion, etc.); tracé *m; Arch: etc:* coupe *f* perpendiculaire; **to project in p.,** projeter en profil; *Tls:* **p. cutter,** fraise profilée, fraise à profiler; *Aedcs:* **p. drag,** traînée *f* de profil; (*e*) graphique *m,* courbe *f;* **operation p.,** (i) graphique des opérations; (ii) calendrier *m* d'exploitation; (*f*) *Carp: etc:* chantournement *m; Mec.E:* **cam p.,** rampe *f* de came; (*g*) *Th:* ferme *f* (de décor). **2.** *Cer: etc:* calibre *m* (de tourneur, etc.); **to turn the clay with a p.,** calibrer la pâte; **turning with a p.,** calibrage *m.*

profile[2], *v.tr.* **1.** (*a*) dessiner, esquisser, montrer, (qch.) de profil; dessiner, tracer, le contour de (qch.); silhouetter (qch.); *Arch: etc:* dessiner (qch.) en coupe perpendiculaire, tracer la coupe perpendiculaire de (qch.); (*b*) **the trees are profiled against the horizon,** les arbres se profilent sur l'horizon. **2.** *Ind:* profiler, contourner, chantourner; *Carp:* moulurer; *Metalw:* fraiser (une pièce) en bout.

profiler ['proufailər], *s. Metalw:* (*a*) machine *f* à profiler; profileur *m;* (*b*) (*pers.*) ouvrier *m* qui travaille sur une machine à profiler.

profiling ['proufailiŋ], *s.* profilage *m,* contournement *m; Carp:* moulurage *m,* moulure *f; Metalw:* fraisage *m* en bout; **p. machine,** machine *f* à profiler, profileur *m.*

profilograph [prou'filəgræf], *s. Civ.E: etc:* profilographe *m.*

profit[1] ['prɔfit], *s.* profit *m,* bénéfice *m;* (*a*) avantage *m,* gain *m,* fruit *m;* **to turn sth. to p.,** tirer profit, tirer bénéfice, de qch.; **what p. will that be to you?** qu'est-ce que vous y gagnerez? (*b*) *Com:* **gross p.,** bénéfice brut; **net (operating) profit(s),** bénéfice net (d'exploitation); **£100 clear p.,** £100 de bénéfice net; **capital profits,** plus-value *f, pl.* plus-values (sur réalisation de biens corporels); **p. on a transaction,** rendement *m* d'une opération; **profits on an estate,** revenu *m* d'une terre; **to bring in, yield, show, a p.,** donner un bénéfice; **to sell sth. at a p.,** vendre qch. à profit, à bénéfice; **to work a mine at a p.,** exploiter une mine avec profit; **to make a p. on a sale,** faire un profit, un bénéfice, sur une vente; profiter, bénéficier, sur une vente; **to make huge profits,** gagner gros; réaliser de gros bénéfices; **to derive (a) p. from sth.,** retirer un profit de qch.; **a small p.,** un léger bénéfice; **the year's trading shows a p.,** l'exercice *m* est bénéficiaire; **p. amount,** montant *m* des bénéfices; **p. margin,** marge *f* bénéficiaire; **p. and loss,** profits et pertes; **loss of p.,** manque *m* à gagner; **p. balance,** solde *m* bénéficiaire; **p. graph,** courbe *f* de rentabilité; **p.-earning,** rentable; **p.-earning (capacity),** rentabilité *f;* **p. making,** réalisation *f* de bénéfices; **p.-making association,** association à but lucratif; **p.-seeking,** (i) (*of pers.*) intéressé; (ii) (*of company*) à but lucratif; **p. taking,** prise *f,* réalisation *f,* de bénéfices; **p. taker,** profiteur, -euse; *Ind: etc:* **p.-sharing (scheme),** partage *m* des bénéfices; participation *f* aux bénéfices; intéressement *m;* **p. sharing by the workers,** coparticipation *f* des travailleurs dans les bénéfices; **p.-sharing employee,** employé intéressé; **p.-sharing bond,** obligation participante; *Pol.Ec:* **p. system,** économie basée sur le profit, économie de libre entreprise.

profit[2], *v.* (**profited**) **1.** *v.tr.* bénéficier; profiter à (qn); faire du bien à (qn); être avantageux à (qn); **what will it p. you to go there?** à quoi (cela) vous profitera-t-il, cela vous servira-t-il, d'y aller? **2.** *v.i.* **to p. by sth.,** profiter, bénéficier, de qch.; faire (son) profit de qch.; tirer profit de qch.; **to p. by, from, s.o.'s advice,** mettre à profit le conseil de qn; **to p. largely by dealings in rubber,** réaliser de gros bénéfices en spéculant sur le caoutchouc; **you don't p. by it,** on n'y trouve pas son compte.

profitability [prɔfitə'biliti], *s.* rentabilité *f.*

profitable ['prɔfitəbl], *a.* profitable, avantageux; (*of speculation, etc.*) lucratif, fructueux, rémunérateur, -trice; rentable; (emploi, etc.) d'un bon rapport; **it is highly p. to do it,** il y a un grand profit à le faire; **it will be more p. for us to sell it,** nous aurons plus d'avantage à le vendre; il nous profitera plus de le vendre.

profitableness ['prɔfitəblnis], *s.* nature *f* profitable, nature avantageuse; profit *m,* avantage *m;* rentabilité *f.*

profitably ['prɔfitəbli], *adv.* profitablement, avantageusement, lucrativement; **to use one's time p.,** employer utilement son temps.

profiteer[1] [prɔfi'tiər], *s.* profiteur, -euse; affairiste *mf;* rabioteur, -euse; **war profiteers,** profiteurs de guerre; mercantis *m* de guerre.

profiteer[2], *v.i.* faire des bénéfices excessifs.

profiteering [prɔfi'tiəriŋ], *s.* mercantilisme *m;* affairisme *m.*

profiterole [prə'fitəroul], *s. Cu:* profiterole *f.*

profitless ['prɔfitlis], *a.* sans profit; **p. deal,** affaire blanche; **engaged in a p. task,** travailler pour un profit nul, pour rien.

profligacy ['prɔfligəsi], *s.* **1.** débauche *f,* libertinage *m;* dévergondage *m;* **the p. that was rampant under the Regency,** le dérèglement des passions sous la Régence. **2.** prodigalité *f;* (*a*) folle dépense; (*b*) abondance *f,* profusion *f;* **a real p. of pictures,** une vraie orgie de tableaux.

profligate ['prɔfligit], *a.* & *s.* **1.** débauché, -ée; libertin, -ine; dissolu, -ue; dévergondé, -ée; (personne) aux mœurs dépravées. **2.** (homme, femme) prodigue, dissipateur, -trice.

profligately ['prɔfligitli], *adv.* (vivre, etc.) dans la débauche; (vivre) sans mœurs.

pro forma [prou'fɔːmə]. **1.** *adv.phr.* pour la forme. **2.** *adj.phr. Com:* **p. f. invoice, s. p. f.,** facture simulée, fictive, de complaisance; facture pro forma.

profound [prə'faund]. **1.** *a.* profond; (*a*) **p. bow,** révérence profonde; (*b*) **p. secret,** secret absolu; **p. scholar,** érudit accompli, profond; **p. study of a subject,** étude approfondie, pénétrante, approfondissement *m,* d'un sujet; **there is a p. difference,** il y a une profonde différence; **to take a p. interest in sth.,** s'intéresser profondément à qch.; **to listen to s.o. with p. interest,** écouter qn avec un intérêt profond. **2.** *s. A:* & *Lit:* profondeurs *fpl* (de la mer, de l'âme, etc.).

profoundly [prə'faundli], *adv.* profondément.

profoundness [prə'faundnis], **profundity** [prə'fʌnditi], *s.* profondeur *f* (d'un abîme, d'une pensée, etc.).

profunda [prə'fʌndə], *s. Anat:* vaisseau profond.

profuse [prə'fjuːs], *a.* **1.** prodigue; **to be p. in one's apologies,** se montrer prodigue d'excuses; se confondre, se répandre, en excuses; **to be p. in one's praises,** donner des louanges à profusion; **to be p. of praise,** être prodigue de louanges; prodiguer les louanges. **2.** (*of thg*) profus, abondant, excessif; **p. bleeding,** hémorragie abondante; **p. gratitude,** remerciements abondants, excessifs.

profusely [prə'fjuːsli], *adv.* profusément, excessivement, abondamment; **to apologize p.,** se confondre en excuses; **to praise s.o. p.,** donner à qn des louanges à profusion; se répandre en louanges sur qn; **to perspire p.,** transpirer abondamment.

profuseness [prə'fjuːsnis], *s.* profusion *f,* prodigalité *f.*

profusion [prə'fjuːʒ(ə)n], *s.* **1.** profusion *f,* abondance *f.* **2.** prodigalité *f;* **to have everything in p.,** avoir tout à profusion; **everywhere flowers in p.,** partout des fleurs à profusion, à foison.

prog[1] [prɔg], *s. Sch: F:* (*at Oxford, Cambridge*) censeur *m.*

prog[2], *v.tr.* (**progged**) *Sch: F:* (*at Oxford, Cambridge*) **to be progged,** (i) être pincé en rupture de discipline; (ii) se voir infliger une peine disciplinaire.

progamous ['prɔgəməs], *a. Biol:* progamique.

progenitor [prou'dʒenitər], *s.* **1.** (*a*) aïeul *m, pl.* aïeux; aïeule *f;* ancêtre *m;* (*b*) **the p. of the revolution,** le précurseur de la révolution. **2.** original *m* (d'un manuscrit).

progenitress, progenitrix [prou'dʒenitris, -triks], *s.f.* aïeule.

progeniture [prou'dʒenitʃər], *s.* **1.** génération *f,* engendrement *m.* **2.** progéniture *f;* (*of man*) enfants *mpl;* (*of animal*) petits *mpl.*

progeny ['prɔdʒini], *s.* **1.** = PROGENITURE 2. **2.** (*a*) descendants *mpl,* lignée *f,* postérité *f;* (*b*) descendants (d'une plante); (*c*) *Husb:* **p. test,** test *m* de la descendance; **to p.-test an animal,** tester un animal.

progeria [prou'dʒiəriə], *s. Med:* progérie *f.*

progesterone [prou'dʒestəroun], *s. Bio-Ch:* progestérone *f.*

progestogen [prou'dʒestədʒən], *s. Bio-Ch:* progestatif *m.*

proglottid, proglottis [prou'glɔtid, -is], *s. Ann:* proglottis *m.*

prognathic, prognathous [prɔg'næθik, -'neiθəs], *a. Anthr:* prognathe.

prognathism ['prɔgnəθizm], **prognathy** ['prɔgnəθi], *s. Anthr:* prognathisme *m,* prognathie *f.*

Progne ['prɔgni]. *Pr.n.f. Gr.Myth:* Progné, Procné.

prognose [prɔg'nouz], *v.tr. Med: O:* pronostiquer.

prognosis, *pl.* **-oses** [prɔg'nousis, -ousiːz], *s.* **1.** *Med:* (*a*) pronostic *m;* **to give a very serious p.,** pronostiquer au plus grave; (*b*) (*the art*) prognose *f.* **2.** prévision(s) *f(pl),* pronostic; analyse prévue.

prognostic [prɔg'nɔstik]. **1.** *a.* (essai, etc.) de pronostic; *Med:* **p. sign,** signe *m* pro(g)nostique; symptôme *m;* **signs p. of sth.,** signes qui pronostiquent, présagent, prédisent, annoncent, qch.; signes annonciateurs, avant-coureurs, de qch. **2.** *s.* (*a*) pronostic *m,* présage *m,* prédiction *f,* auspice *m;* (*b*) *Med:* signe pro(g)nostique; symptôme.

prognosticate [prɔg'nɔstikeit], *v.tr.* (*of pers., sign, etc.*) pronostiquer, présager, prédire (qch.).

prognostication [prɔgnɔsti'keiʃ(ə)n], *s.* **1.** (*a*) pronostication *f,* prédiction *f;* (*b*) pressentiment *m.* **2.** = PROGNOSTIC 2 (*a*).

prognosticative [prɔg'nɔstikeitiv], *a.* **p. of sth.,** qui pronostique, prédit, présage, qch.

prognosticator [prɔg'nɔstikeitər], *s.* pronostiqueur, -euse.

prognosticatory [prɔg'nɔstikeitəri], *a.* symptomatique; **p. of sth.,** qui pronostique, présage, prédit, qch.

programmable [prou'græməbl], *a. Cmptr: etc:* programmable.

programmatic [prougrə'mætik], *a. Cmptr: etc:* relatif à la programmation.

programmatics [prougrə'mætiks], *s.pl.* (*usu. with sg. const.*) programmatique *f.*

programme[1] ['prougræm], *s.* **1.** programme *m* (de spectacle, de recherche, politique, etc.); *A:* **ball, dance, p.,** carnet *m* de bal; *Th: etc:* **p. seller,** vendeur, -euse, de programmes; ouvreuse *f;* **to draw up, arrange, a p.,** arrêter un programme, dresser un emploi du temps; *F:* **what's the p. for today?** quel est le programme, qu'est-ce qu'on va faire, aujourd'hui? **training p.,** programme d'instruction, de formation, d'entraînement; **time p.,** horaire *m;* **television p.,** (i) programme, (ii) émission *f,* de télévision; **dramatized p.,** (émission) dramatique *f;* **sponsored p.,** programme offert par une initiative privée; **p. transmission,** relais *m* de télévision; **radio p.,** émission de radio; **p. music,** musique (i) descriptive, (ii) de genre; *Cin:* **supporting p.,** film(s) d'appoint, film(s) bouche-trou *inv.* **2.** *Cmptr:* **computer p.,** programme machine; **master p.,** programme principal; **control p.,** programme de gestion; **operational p.,** programme au point, exécutable; **stored p.,** programme enregistré; **utility p.,** sous-programme *m, pl.* sous-programmes, de service; **self-triggered, self-triggering, p.,** programme à lancement automatique; **tracing p.,** programme d'analyse; **branching p.,** programme ramifié; **p. card,** carte *f* programme; **p. tape,** bande-programme *f, pl.* bandes-programmes; **p. sheet,** feuille *f* de programmation; **p. chart,** organigramme *m;* **p. language,** langage *m* de programmation; **p. package,** ensemble *m,* lot *m,* de programmes; **p. scheduling,** planification *f* de programme; **p. flow,** déroulement *m* du programme; **p. storage,** zone *f* d'implantation du programme (en mémoire); **p. writer,** rédacteur *m* du programme, de programmes; **p. write-up,** description *f* de programme.

programme[2], *v.tr. Cmptr: etc:* programmer; **programmed check,** contrôle programmé; **p. teaching, learning,** enseignement programmé, séquentiel.

programmer ['prougræmər], *s. Cmptr: etc:* (*a*) (*pers.*) programmeur, -euse; programmateur, -trice; **trainee p.,** élève-programmeur, -euse, *pl.* élèves-programmeurs, -euses; **junior p.,** mécanographe *mf*; (*b*) (*machine*) programmateur *m.*

programming ['prougræmiŋ], *s. Cmptr: T.V: etc:* programmation *f*, mise *f* en programme (**of sth.,** de qch.); **p. department,** service *m* (de la) programmation; **p. manager,** chef *m* du service (de) programmation; **p. staff,** personnel chargé de la programmation; **p. chart,** organigramme *m* de programmation; **p. unit,** (appareil *m*) programmateur *m*; *Cmptr:* **automatic p.,** programmation automatique; **multiple p.,** multiprogrammation *f*; **optimum p.,** programmation optimale; **prior p.,** programmation préalable; **serial p.,** programmation (en) série.

progress[1] ['prougres], *s.* (*no pl.*) **1.** (*a*) marche *f* (du temps, d'un astre, d'une maladie, etc.); cours *m*; avancement *m* (d'un travail, etc.); étapes successives (de la vie, d'un voyage); **to stop, check the p. of the locusts,** arrêter la marche des sauterelles; *Ind:* **p. of the work through the different departments,** cheminement *m* des pièces à travers les différents services; **p. chart,** diagramme *m* de l'avancement des travaux, du déroulement des opérations; **p. of thought,** cheminement, marche, de la pensée; **the p. of events,** le cours des événements; *Chess:* **the knight's p.,** la marche du cavalier; **in p. of time,** avec le temps; **in the p. of centuries,** dans la suite des siècles; **the work is now in p.,** le travail est en voie, en cours, d'exécution; l'œuvre est en accomplissement; **the negotiations in p.,** les négociations en cours; **the harvesting is in full p.,** la moisson bat son plein; (*b*) progrès *m*; **age of p.,** siècle de progrès; **to make p. in one's studies,** faire des progrès dans ses études; **to make slow p.,** n'avancer que lentement; **to make great, astonishing, p.,** avancer à pas de géant, brûler les étapes; faire de grands progrès, des progrès étonnants; **industry that has made great p.,** industrie *f* qui a pris un grand essor; **negotiations are making good p.,** les négociations sont en bonne voie; **he has made good p.,** il a fait de grands progrès; **I am satisfied with his p.,** je suis satisfait de son avancement, de ses progrès. **2.** *A:* (*a*) voyage *m*; (*b*) tournée *f* (d'un juge, etc.); **royal p.,** visite royale; voyage officiel (de la reine, du roi).

progress[2] [prə'gres], *v.i.* **1.** (*a*) s'avancer; **to p. towards a place,** s'approcher d'un endroit (par étapes successives); **as the inquiry progresses,** à mesure que l'enquête avance; au cours de l'enquête; **as the year progresses,** au cours de l'année; (*b*) faire des progrès; progresser, avancer; **to p. with one's studies,** faire des progrès dans ses études; avancer dans ses études; **industry is progressing,** l'industrie est en progrès; **the patient is progressing favourably, satisfactorily,** le malade fait des progrès satisfaisants. **2.** *A:* (*of official, etc.*) faire une tournée.

progression [prə'greʃ(ə)n], *s.* **1.** progression *f*; marche *f* (d'un astre); *Mil:* avance *f*; **to slow down the enemy's p.,** ralentir l'avance de l'ennemi. **2.** *Mth:* **arithmetical p.,** progression arithmétique, par différence; **geometrical p.,** progression géométrique, par quotient; **harmonic p.,** progression harmonique. **3.** *Mus:* marche (des parties); progression; **harmonic p.,** progression harmonique; marche d'harmonie.

progressional [prə'greʃən(ə)l], *a.* progressif; progressionnel.

progressionism [prə'greʃənizm], *s. Pol:* progressisme *m.*

progressionist, progressist [prə'greʃənist, -'gresist], *a. & s. Pol:* progressiste (*mf*).

progressive [prə'gresiv]. **1.** *a.* (*a*) **p. movement,** mouvement progressif, en avant; **by p. stages,** par degrés; *Med:* **p. disease,** maladie progressive; *Phot.Engr:* **set of p. proofs,** gamme d'épreuves trichromes; **p. increase in taxation,** progressivité *f* (de l'impôt); *Fin:* (*of interest*) **at a p. rate,** à taux progressif; *Elcs:* **p. scanning,** analyse par lignes contiguës; *Cmptr: etc:* **p. total,** total cumulé; cumul *m*; (*b*) **p. age,** siècle de progrès; **to be p.,** avoir des idées avancées; **p. literature, music,** littérature, musique, d'avant-garde; *Pol:* **p. principles,** principes progressifs; **p. ideas,** idées avancées, progressistes; **the p. party,** le parti progressiste; le parti de l'extrême-gauche; (*c*) *Gram:* **the p. form,** la forme progressive, le duratif. **2.** *s.* progressiste *mf.*

progressively [prə'gresivli], *adv.* progressivement; au fur et à mesure.

progressiveness [prə'gresivinis], *s.* progressivité *f.*

prohibit [prə'hibit], *v.tr.* **1.** prohiber, défendre, interdire (qch.); **smoking is prohibited,** il est défendu, interdit, de fumer; défense de fumer; **prohibited flying area,** zone de survol interdit; **this zone remains a prohibited area for all military works,** cette zone reste interdite à toute installation militaire; **marriage within the prohibited degrees,** mariage entre degrés prohibés; **to p. s.o. from doing sth.,** défendre, prohiber, interdire, à qn de faire qch.; *Jur:* **the parties are prohibited from** + *ger.*, défenses et inhibitions sont faites de . . .. **2.** empêcher (**s.o. from doing sth.,** qn de faire qch.).

prohibition [prou(h)i'biʃ(ə)n], *s.* **1.** (*a*) prohibition *f*, interdiction *f*, défense *f* (**from doing sth.,** de faire qch.); (*b*) *U.S: Hist:* interdiction de vendre, de consommer, les boissons alcooliques; prohibitionnisme *m*; régime sec; **p. law,** loi de prohibition; **p. party,** parti prohibitionniste. **2.** *Jur:* défense de statuer adressée par une cour supérieure à une cour inférieure.

prohibitionism [prou(h)i'biʃənizm], *s. Pol.Ec: etc:* prohibitionnisme *m* (en matière de boissons alcooliques).

prohibitionist [prou(h)i'biʃənist], *a. & s. Pol.Ec: etc:* prohibitionniste (*mf*); **p. countries,** pays secs.

prohibitive [prə'hibitiv], *a.* prohibitif; **p. price,** prix prohibitif, inabordable; **the price of caviare is p.,** le caviar est hors de prix; *Cust: etc:* **p. duties,** droits prohibitifs.

prohibitory [prə'hibit(ə)ri], *a.* (*a*) (*of law, etc.*) prohibitif; *Aut: U.S:* **p. sign,** signal d'interdiction; (*b*) *Jur:* prohibitoire.

project[1] ['prɔdʒekt], *s.* (*a*) projet *m*; plan (conçu, envisagé); **to form, carry out, upset, a p.,** former, accomplir, renverser, un projet; (*b*) *Sch:* étude pratique (individuelle ou collective); (*c*) *U.S: Civ.E:* ouvrage d'art (projeté, réalisé); travaux *mpl* (d'assèchement, d'irrigation, etc.).

project[2] [prə'dʒekt].

I. *v.tr.* **1.** **to p. a plan, a journey,** projeter un plan, un voyage; **projected motorway,** autoroute projetée, en projet. **2.** (*a*) projeter, lancer, (qch.) en avant; (*b*) *Ch:* **to p. a powder into a crucible,** verser une poudre dans un creuset. **3.** (*a*) **to p. a picture on(to) a screen,** projeter une image, un film, sur un écran; **form projected against, on, the sky,** forme dessinée, projetée, sur le ciel; *Art:* **projected shadow,** ombre portée; (*b*) *Mth:* **to p. a plan, a line, a figure,** projeter un plan, une ligne, une figure; tracer la projection d'un plan, etc.; **projected angle, segment,** angle, segment, projeté. **4.** extrapoler (des résultats); **to p. oneself into the past, into the future,** se transporter dans le passé, dans l'avenir; (*of author*) **to p. oneself into a character in a novel,** se portrayer dans un roman.

II. *v.i.* faire saillie, faire ressaut; déborder, dépasser, (s')avancer, sortir, forjeter; (*of balcony, etc.*) porter à faux; **stone that projects from the wall,** pierre qui sort du mur; **the balcony projects over the pavement,** le balcon surplombe le trottoir; **to p. beyond the building line,** déborder, dépasser, l'alignement; **a strip of land projects into the sea,** une langue de terre s'avance dans la mer.

projectile [prə'dʒektail], *a. & s.* **1.** *a.* (*a*) **p. force,** force impulsive, projective; (*b*) **p. motion,** mouvement par impulsion; (*c*) **p. weapons,** armes de jet. **2.** *s.* projectile *m*; **atomic, nuclear, p.,** projectile atomique, nucléaire; **smoke p.,** projectile fumigène; **hand p.,** projectile à main.

projecting[1] [prə'dʒektiŋ], *a. Arch: etc:* saillant, en saillie; hors d'œuvre, en porte-à-faux; **p. part of a roof,** avance *f* d'un toit; **p. forehead,** front bombé; **large p. ears,** de grandes oreilles décollées; **p. teeth,** dents saillantes, qui débordent les lèvres; *Veh:* **p. axle,** essieu en porte-à-faux.

projecting[2], *s.* = PROJECTION 1 (*a*) & (*b*).

projection [prə'dʒekʃ(ə)n], *s.* **1.** (*a*) projection *f* (d'eau, de débris, d'un rayon de lumière, etc.); **p. of an image on a screen,** projection d'une image sur un écran; *Cin: etc:* **p. room, booth,** cabine *f* de projection; **p. screen,** écran de projection; **p. port,** fenêtre *f*, lucarne *f*, de projection; **p. lens,** lentille *f*, objectif *m*, de projection; **p. period,** phase *f* d'éclairement, de projection; **rear p.,** projection par transparence; *T.V:* **p. receiver,** récepteur *m* à projection; *Phot:* **p. print,** épreuve *f* par projection; (*b*) départ *m*, lancement *m* (d'un projectile); *Ball:* **angle of p.,** angle de départ; (*c*) conception *f* (d'un projet, etc.). **2.** (*a*) *Mapm:* **gnomonic p.,** projection centrale, gnomonique; **conical, polyconical, p.,** projection conique, polyconique; **conformal, orthomorphic, p.,** projection conforme, orthomorphique; **Lambert conformal cylindrical p.,** projection cylindrique conforme de Lambert; **Mercator's p.,** projection de Mercator; **secant conical p.,** projection conique sécante; **equal area p.,** projection équivalente; **perspective p.,** projection perspective; **zenithal p.,** projection zénithale; **zenithal, azimuthal, equidistant p.,** projection zénithale équidistante; (*b*) *Mapm:* planisphère *m*; (*c*) projection concrète d'une image mentale. **3.** saillie *f*; (*a*) avancement *m* (en dehors); prolongement *m*; (*b*) *Arch:* partie *f* qui fait saillie; ressaut *m*, projecture *f*, forjet *m*; porte-à-faux *m inv*; portée *f* (d'un balcon, etc.); avant-corps *m inv* (de façade); (*in masonry*) orillon *m*; (*c*) (*on wheel, etc.*) mentonnet *m*; téton *m*; *Metalw:* **p. welding,** soudure *f* par projection, par bossage.

projectional [prə'dʒekʃən(ə)l], *a. Mth: Psy: etc:* de projection, projectif.

projectionist [prə'dʒekʃənist], *s. Cin: etc:* projectionniste *mf*; opérateur, -trice, de cabine.

projective [prə'dʒektiv], *a.* **1.** *Arch: etc:* saillant, en saillie, débordant. **2.** *Mth:* **p. plane,** plan de projection; **p. geometry,** géométrie projective; **p. properties,** propriétés projectives; **p. relativity,** (théorie de la) relativité projective; **p. transformation,** transformation projective (de l'espace géométrique). **3.** *Psy:* (*a*) (*of imagination*) porté, tendant, à s'extérioriser; **a p. imagination,** une imagination prompte à s'extérioriser; (*b*) révélateur, -trice, de la subjectivité, de la personnalité; subjectif; **p. tests,** tests projectifs, subjectifs.

projectivity [proudʒek'tiviti], *s.* (*a*) caractère projectif; *Mth:* (i) projectivité *f* (d'une figure); (ii) transformation projective (de l'espace géométrique); (*b*) *Psy:* (*of imagination*) aptitude *f* à s'extérioriser; **p. of a test,** efficacité *f* d'un test à révéler la subjectivité, la personnalité (de qn).

projector [prə'dʒektər], *s.* **1.** (*a*) celui, celle, qui forme un projet (de voyage, etc.); (*b*) *A:* promoteur, -trice, fondateur, -trice (d'une compagnie). **2.** (*a*) *Ball:* **pyrotechnic, rocket, p.,** projecteur *m* lance-fusée; (*b*) *Cin: etc:* (**cinema**) **p.,** projecteur (de cinéma, cinématographique); **slide, transparency, p.,** projecteur de diapositives; **overhead p.,** rétroprojecteur *m*; **sound p.,** projecteur sonore; **stereo p.,** projecteur stéréoscopique.

projecture [prə'dʒektʃər], *s. Arch:* projecture *f.*

prolactin [prou'læktin], *s. Bio-Ch:* prolactine *f.*

prolamin [prou'læmin], *s. Bio-Ch:* prolamine *f.*

prolan ['proulæn], *s. Bio-Ch:* prolan *m.*

prolapse[1] ['proulæps], **prolapsus** [prou'læpsəs], *s. Med:* prolapsus *m*, procidence *f*, descente *f*, abaissement *m* (de l'utérus, etc.); chute *f* (du rectum).

prolapse[2], *v.i. Med:* (*of organ*) descendre, tomber.

prolapsed ['proulæpst], *a. Med:* prolabé.

prolate ['prouleit], *a.* **1.** *Mth:* (ellipsoïde) allongé, prolongé. **2.** *Fig:* largement répandu.

prolative [prou'leitiv], *a. Gram:* **p. infinitive,** infinitif *m* régime sans préposition.

proleg ['prouleg], *s. Ent:* patte membraneuse; fausse patte.

prolegomena [proule'gɔminə], *s.pl. Lit: etc:* prolégomènes *m*; introduction *f* (à un ouvrage).

prolepsis [prou'lepsis], *s. Rh: Gram:* prolepse *f*, anticipation *f.*

proleptic [prou'leptik], *a.* **1.** (signe, etc.) proleptique, avant-coureur. **2.** *Chr:* **p. year,** année proleptique. **3.** *Med:* **p. fever,** fièvre proleptique, subintrante.

proletarian [prouli'tɛəriən]. **1.** *a.* prolétarien, prolétaire. **2.** *s.* prolétaire *mf.*

proletarianism [prouli'tɛəriənizm], *s.* **1.** prolétariat *m.* **2.** opinions *f* politiques du prolétariat.

proletarianization [proulitɛəriənai'zeiʃ(ə)n], *s.* prolétarisation *f.*

proletarianize [prouli'tɛəriənaiz], *v.tr.* prolétariser.

proletariat(e) [prouli'tɛəriət], *s.* prolétariat *m.*

proliferate [prə'lifəreit], *v.i. & tr. Nat.Hist:* proliférer; (*of human beings*) se multiplier.

proliferation [prəlifə'reiʃ(ə)n], *s. Nat.Hist:* prolifération *f*; *Pol:* **nuclear non-p. treaty,** traité *m* de non-prolifération des armes nucléaires.

proliferative [prə'lifərətiv], *a. Nat.Hist:* (*a*) capable de proliférer; fécond; (*b*) en cours de prolifération.

proliferous [prə'lifərəs], *a. Nat.Hist:* prolifère; *Med:* **p. cyst,** kyste proligère, prolifère.

prolific [prə'lifik], *a.* prolifique; fécond, fertile (**in, of,** en).

prolificacy [prə'lifikəsi], *s.* fécondité *f*, fertilité *f*; qualité *f* prolifique.

prolifically [prə'lifik(ə)li], **prolificly** [prə'lifikli], *adv.* abondamment; fécondement, fertilement.

prolification [prəlifi'keiʃ(ə)n], *s.* **1.** (*a*) procréation *f*, génération *f*; (*b*) fécondité *f*, fertilité *f*. **2.** (*a*) *Nat.Hist:* prolifération *f*; (*b*) *Bot:* prolification *f.*

prolificity [prouli'fisiti], *s.* prolificité *f.*

prolificness [prə'lifiknis], *s.* = PROLIFICACY.

proligerous [prə'lidʒərəs], *a.* **1.** *Nat.Hist:* proligère. **2.** *Bot:* (*of plant, etc.*) prolifère.

prolin(e) ['prouli(:)n], *s. Bio-Ch:* proline *f.*

prolix ['prouliks], *a.* **1.** prolixe, diffus; (style) délayé. **2.** *A:* long.

prolixity [prou'liksiti], *s.* **1.** prolixité *f.* **2.** *A:* longueur *f.*
prolixly ['prouliksli], *adv.* prolixement.
prolocutor [prou'lɔkjutər], *s.* **1.** président *m* (d'une assemblée ecclésiastique, etc.). **2.** porte-parole *m inv.*
prolocutorship [prou'lɔkjutəʃip], *s.* présidence *f* (d'une assemblée ecclésiastique, etc.).
prologue[1] ['proulɔg], *s.* prologue *m* (**to,** de).
prologue[2], *v.tr.* faire précéder (une pièce, etc.) d'un prologue.
prolong [prə'lɔŋ], *v.tr.* prolonger (la vie, un entretien, etc.); continuer, prolonger (une ligne); *Mus:* **to p. a stroke of the bow,** allonger un coup d'archet.
prolongation [proulɔŋ'geiʃ(ə)n], *s.* **1.** = PROLONGING 2; **in p. of. . .,** sur le prolongement de. . . . **2.** prolongation *f*; délai accordé.
prolonge [prou'lɔndʒ], *s. A.Artil:* prolonge *f.*
prolonged [prə'lɔŋd], *a.* prolongé; **p. applause,** acclamations nourries.
prolonger [prə'lɔŋər], *s.* celui, celle, qui prolonge, qui a prolongé (le mur, les négociations, etc.).
prolonging [prə'lɔŋiŋ], *s.* **1.** (*in time*) prolongation *f* (de la durée de qch.); *Fin: Com:* prorogation *f,* atermoiement *m* (d'une échéance, etc.). **2.** (*in space*) prolongement *m* (d'un mur, etc.).
prom [prɔm], *s. F:* **1.** = PROMENADE[1] 2, 3. **2.** concert-promenade *m, pl.* concerts-promenade.
pro(-)market ['proumɑ:kit], *a.* (personne) qui est en faveur de l'adhésion de la Grande-Bretagne au Marché Commun.
pro(-)marketeer [proumɑ:ki'tiər], *s.* personne qui est pour l'adhésion de la Grande-Bretagne au Marché Commun.
promenade[1] ['prɔmənɑ:d], *s.* **1.** *O:* promenade *f* (dans un lieu public). **2.** (*a*) (lieu de) promenade; (*at seaside*) front *m* de mer, promenade du bord de mer; *Nau:* **p. deck,** pont-promenade *m, pl.* ponts-promenades; (*b*) *Th:* promenoir *m,* pourtour *m* (du parterre); **p. concert,** concert-promenade *m, pl.* concerts-promenade. **3.** *NAm:* bal *m* d'étudiants, *pl.* bals.
promenade[2]. **1.** *v.i.* se promener, parader (à pied, en voiture, etc.); déambuler; **to p. on the pier,** faire un tour de jetée (en grande tenue). **2.** *v.tr.* (*a*) se promener dans (une salle, etc.); se promener sur (les boulevards, etc.); (*b*) promener (qn) (pour lui montrer la ville, etc.); (*c*) faire parade de (sa famille, etc.); exhiber (qn, qch.).
promenader ['prɔmənɑ:dər], *s.* promeneur, -euse.
Promethean [prə'mi:θiən], *a.* prométhéen.
Prometheus [prə'mi:θiəs]. *Pr.n.m. Gr.Myth:* Prométhée; *Lit:* **P. bound, unbound,** Prométhée enchaîné, délivré.
promethium [prə'mi:θiəm], *s. Ch:* prométhéum *m.*
prominence ['prɔminəns], *s.* **1.** (*a*) proéminence *f*; relief *m*; (*b*) saillie *f,* protubérance *f*; proéminence (du sol); **solar p.,** protubérance solaire. **2.** éminence *f*; **to bring sth. into p., to give sth. p.,** faire ressortir qch.; **the son's part is not given enough p.,** le rôle du fils ne ressort pas assez; **to give p. to certain incidents,** mettre en avant, monter en épingle, certains incidents; **to come into p.,** (*of pers.*) percer; arriver à un rang éminent; (*of thg*) devenir plus important; (*of idea, etc.*) se faire jour.
prominency ['prɔminənsi], *s.* = PROMINENCE 2.
prominent ['prɔminənt], *a.* **1.** saillant; en saillie; proéminent; (*of ears*) décollé; **p. cheekbones,** pommettes saillantes; **p. nose,** nez prononcé. **2.** (*a*) saillant; remarquable; **p. features,** traits prononcés, saillants (d'un paysage, d'un caractère, etc.); (*of idea, characteristic, etc.*) **to be p.,** ressortir; être en évidence; **in a p. position,** très en vue; **to hold a p. position,** occuper une position très importante; (*b*) éminent; **p. people,** personnages de marque.
prominently ['prɔminəntli], *adv.* éminemment; d'une manière marquée; **to bring sth. more p. into view,** mettre qch. plus en vue, plus en évidence; **to display a sign p.,** mettre une affiche bien en vue.
promiscuity [prɔmis'kju:iti], *s.* **1.** promiscuité *f,* mélange *m,* confusion *f.* **2.** promiscuité (entre les deux sexes).
promiscuous [prə'miskjuəs], *a.* **1.** confus, mêlé; chaotique; **p. crowd,** foule *f* hétérogène; **p. massacre,** massacre général; **p. hospitality,** hospitalité offerte à n'importe qui, à tous venants. **2.** (*a*) fortuit, occasionnel; casuel; (*b*) **she is completely p.,** elle couche avec n'importe qui.
promiscuously [prə'miskjuəsli], *adv.* **1.** (*a*) confusément, au hasard, au petit bonheur; en promiscuité; **things thrown p. together,** choses jetées ensemble pêle-mêle; **p. furnished,** meublé de bric et de broc; (*b*) sans distinction de classe, de race, etc.; sans discrimination; sans distinction; **they were sentenced p.,** ils furent condamnés en bloc. **2.** fortuitement, occasionnellement; casuellement.
promise[1] ['prɔmis], *s.* promesse *f*; (*a*) **to make a p.,** faire une promesse; **to keep one's p.,** tenir sa promesse; tenir parole; **to break one's p.,** manquer à, violer, sa promesse; manquer de parole; **to release s.o. from his p.,** rendre sa parole à qn; **he surrendered on the p. that his life would be spared,** il se rendit sous promesse de vie sauve; **a p. is a p.,** chose promise, chose due; *int.* **promises, promises!** rien que des promesses! **empty promises,** promesses vaines; **p. of marriage,** promesse de mariage; *B:* **the Land of P.,** la Terre promise; **the children of the p.,** les enfants de la promesse; (*b*) **child who shows p. of a fine future, child full of p.,** enfant qui promet (un bel avenir); enfant plein de promesses; **to show great p.,** donner de belles espérances; **pupil of great p.,** élève de beaucoup d'avenir, d'un grand avenir; **young man with every p. of a brilliant future,** jeune homme promis à un brillant avenir; **not that the book is without p.,** non que le livre ne contienne des promesses; **to hold out a p. to s.o. of sth.,** faire espérer qch. à qn; **there is a p. of warm weather,** le temps promet de la chaleur.
promise[2], *v.tr.* (*a*) **to p. s.o. sth.,** promettre qch. à qn; **she's been promised a wedding present by, from, her boss,** son patron lui a promis un cadeau de noces; *O:* **to p. s.o. one's daughter in marriage,** promettre sa fille en mariage à qn; **to p. (s.o.) to do sth.,** promettre (à qn) de faire qch.; s'engager à faire qch.; **he promised me he'd do it,** il m'a promis qu'il le ferait; il m'a promis de le faire; **to p. oneself sth.,** se promettre qch.; *F:* **you'll be sorry, I p. you,** vous le regretterez. je vous le promets, je vous en réponds; **I'll wait for you, (I) p.,** je t'attendrai, je te promets; **I'll wait for you—(do you) p.?** je t'attendrai—tu le promets? *Prov:* **it's one thing to p. and another to perform,** promettre et tenir sont deux; (*b*) **this promises trouble in the future,** cela laisse prévoir des ennuis pour l'avenir; **it promises to be hot,** le temps promet d'être chaud; le temps s'annonce chaud, promet de la chaleur; *v.i.* **the scheme promises well,** le projet s'annonce bien, donne de belles espérances; l'affaire promet.
promised ['prɔmist], *a.* promis; *B:* **the P. Land,** la Terre promise; la Terre de Promission; *A:* **p. husband, bride,** promis, -ise.
promisee [prɔmi'si:], *s. Jur:* celui, celle, à qui une promesse a été faite; détenteur, -trice, de la promesse.
promiser ['prɔmisər], *s.* celui, celle, qui a fait une promesse.
promising ['prɔmisiŋ], *a.* plein de promesses; **p. young man,** jeune homme qui promet; jeune homme de beaucoup d'avenir, de grande espérance; **she's made a p. start,** elle a fait des débuts prometteurs; **p. undertaking,** entreprise qui promet, pleine de promesses; **the future, the harvest, looks p.,** l'avenir, la moisson, s'annonce bien; l'avenir, la moisson, promet; **the future doesn't look (too) p.,** l'avenir s'annonce mal; **that looks p.!** ça promet!
promisingly ['prɔmisiŋli], *adv.* d'une manière pleine de promesses, qui promet.
promisor ['prɔmisɔ:r], *s. Jur:* celui, celle, qui a fait une promesse; l'engagé, -ée.
promissory ['prɔmisəri], *a.* (*of oath, etc.*) promissoire, de promesse; **p. of sth.,** qui promet qch.; *Com: etc:* **p. note,** billet *m* simple; promesse *f*; **p. note made out to order,** billet à ordre; **p. note made out to bearer,** billet au porteur.
promontoried ['prɔməntərid], *a.* (baie, côte, etc.) à promontoire.
promontory ['prɔmənt(ə)ri], *s.* **1.** *Geol:* promontoire *m,* cap élevé. **2.** *Anat:* promontoire (du tympan, etc.); protubérance *f.*
promotable [prə'moutəbl], *a.* (fonctionnaire) promouvable.
promote [prə'mout], *v.tr.* **1.** (*a*) promouvoir (qn); donner de l'avancement à (qn); **to p. s.o. to an office,** promouvoir qn à un poste; **to be promoted to (the rank of) captain,** être nommé, promu (au grade de) capitaine; passer capitaine; **to be promoted,** être promu; avancer; recevoir de l'avancement; (*of official*) monter en grade; (*b*) *Chess:* échanger (un pion) contre une pièce prise. **2.** (*a*) encourager (les arts, un projet); favoriser (le succès, etc.); faciliter (le progrès); avancer (les intérêts de qn, etc.); amener, contribuer à (un résultat, etc.); mettre (un projet) en œuvre; servir (une cause); **to p. good feeling between nations,** encourager l'amitié entre les nations; (*b*) **to p. a company,** lancer, fonder, monter, une société anonyme; *Pol:* **to p. a bill,** prendre l'initiative d'un projet de loi; (*c*) *Com:* (i) lancer (un produit); (ii) stimuler la vente (d'un produit); (*d*) *Ch:* **to p. a reaction,** amorcer, provoquer, une réaction.
promoter [prə'moutər], *s.* instigateur, -trice, auteur *m* (d'un projet, etc.); monteur *m,* lanceur *m* (d'affaires); metteur *m* en œuvre (de la paix, d'une guerre civile); *Sp: etc:* promoteur, -trice; **company p.,** promoteur, fondateur *m,* de sociétés anonymes; *Pej:* affairiste *m*; *Fin:* **promoters' shares,** parts *f* de fondateurs; *Com:* **sales p.,** promoteur de ventes.
promoting [prə'moutiŋ], *s.* **1.** promotion *f,* avancement *m.* **2.** (*a*) encouragement *m* (de l'amitié, etc.); avancement (des intérêts de qn, etc.); (*b*) fondation *f,* lancement *m* (d'une société anonyme); *Ch:* amorçage *m* (d'une réaction).
promotion [prə'mouʃ(ə)n], *s.* **1.** promotion *f,* avancement *m*; *Mil: etc:* nomination *f* à un grade supérieur; **to get p.,** être promu; obtenir de l'avancement; **p. by seniority, by selection,** l'avancement à l'ancienneté, au choix; **p. list, roster,** tableau d'avancement; **he's been recommended for p.,** il a été proposé pour l'avancement. **2.** (*a*) fondation *f,* lancement *m* (d'une société anonyme); **p. money,** frais *mpl* de fondation (d'une société anonyme); frais d'établissement; coût *m* de premier établissement; (*b*) *Com:* lancement (d'un produit); **sales p.,** promotion des ventes; stimulation *f* de la vente.
promotional [prə'mouʃən(ə)l], *a. Com: etc:* promotionnel; **p. campaign, sale,** campagne, vente, promotionnelle.
promotive [prə'moutiv], *a.* **to be p. of sth.,** amener, encourager, favoriser, avancer, qch.
prompt[1] [prɔmpt], *a.* **1.** prompt; (*a*) vif, rapide; diligent; **p. service,** service rapide; **to be p. in action, to act,** être prompt à agir; (*b*) immédiat, instantané; **to take p. action,** prendre des mesures immédiates; agir promptement, sur-le-champ; **p. decision,** décision prompte, immédiate; **p. reply,** (i) réplique *f*; prompte réponse; (ii) réponse par retour du courrier; (*c*) *Atom.Ph:* **p. gammas,** rayons gamma immédiats; **p. neutron,** neutron immédiat, instantané; **p. poison(ing) of a reactor,** empoisonnement instantané d'un réacteur; (*d*) *adv.* **at three o'clock p.,** à trois heures précises; **to arrive p. to the minute,** arriver à l'heure exacte, *F:* à l'heure pile. **2.** *Com:* (*a*) *a.* **p. cotton, p. sugar,** coton, sucre, livrable sur-le-champ et comptant; (*b*) *s.* terme *m* (de paiement); délai *m* limite; **p. note,** mémoire *m* de vente (avec indication du délai de paiement).
prompt[2], *s.* (*a*) suggestion *f*; inspiration *f*; (*b*) *Th:* **to give an actor a p.,** souffler un acteur; souffler la réplique, etc., à un acteur; **p. box,** trou *m* du souffleur; **p. side,** côté *m* de la scène à la gauche, *U.S:* à la droite, des acteurs; côté jardin; **p. copy,** exemplaire *m,* manuscrit *m,* du souffleur.
prompt[3], *v.tr.* **1. to p. s.o. to sth.,** suggérer qch. à qn; **to p. s.o. to do sth.,** pousser, porter, convier, inciter, qn à faire qch.; suggérer à qn de faire qch.; **what prompted you to come?** qu'est-ce qui vous a donné l'idée de venir? **he felt prompted to speak,** il se sentit poussé à prendre la parole; **to be prompted by a feeling of pity,** être mû, animé, par un sentiment de pitié; **feeling prompted by hatred,** sentiment inspiré, dicté, par la haine. **2.** souffler (un acteur, un élève, etc.); rappeler qch. à la mémoire de qn; **to p. a witness,** suggérer des jalons à un témoin; **to p. s.o. with an answer,** suggérer une réponse à qn.
promptbook ['prɔmptbuk], *s. Th:* exemplaire *m,* manuscrit *m,* du souffleur.
prompter ['prɔmptər], *s.* **1.** instigateur, -trice (d'un crime, etc.). **2.** *Th:* souffleur, -euse; **opposite p.,** côté *m* de la scène à la droite, *U.S:* à la gauche, des acteurs; côté cour; **prompter's box,** trou *m* du souffleur.
prompting ['prɔmptiŋ], *s.* **1.** suggestion *f*; impulsion *f*; incitation *f* (**to do sth.,** à faire qch.); instigation *f* (de qn); **the promptings of conscience,** l'aiguillon *m* de la conscience. **2.** action *f* de souffler (un acteur, un élève); *Sch:* **no p.!** ne soufflez pas! laissez-le répondre tout seul.
promptitude ['prɔmptitju:d], **promptness** ['prɔmptnis], *s.* promptitude *f,* empressement *m*; rapidité *f*; **p. in obeying,** promptitude à obéir.
promptly ['prɔmptli], *adv.* promptement; (*a*) avec empressement, avec rapidité; diligemment; **your orders will be carried out p.,** vos commandes seront exécutées avec la plus grande diligence; (*b*) sur-le-champ, immédiatement; **to pay p.,** (i) payer argent comptant; (ii) payer ponctuellement; *F:* **she screamed, and p. dropped the tray,** elle jeta un cri, et du coup laissa tomber le plateau; **he p. went and told everybody,** il est allé immédiatement le raconter à tout le monde.
promptuary ['prɔmptjuəri], *s. A:* manuel *m,* abrégé *m.*
promulgate ['prɔməlgeit], *v.tr.* **1.** promulguer (une loi, un édit). **2.** disséminer, répandre (une idée, une doctrine); proclamer, répandre (une nouvelle).
promulgation [prɔməl'geiʃ(ə)n], *s.* **1.** promulgation *f* (d'une loi, d'un édit). **2.** dissémination *f* (d'une idée,

d'une doctrine); proclamation *f* (d'une nouvelle, etc.).

promulgator ['prɔməlgeitər], *s.* **1.** promulgateur, -trice (d'une loi, d'un édit). **2.** diffuseur *m*, propagateur, -trice (d'une idée, d'une doctrine).

promycelium [proumai'si:liəm], *s. Fung:* promycélium *m*.

pronaos [prou'neiɔs], *s. Gr.Ant:* pronaos *m*.

pronate ['prouneit], *v.tr. Physiol:* mettre (la main, etc.) en pronation.

pronation [prou'neiʃ(ə)n], *s. Physiol:* pronation *f*.

pronator [prou'neitər], *s. Anat:* (muscle) pronateur *m*.

prone[1] [proun], *a.* **1.** *(a) (of hand, etc.)* en pronation; *(b) (of pers., animal, etc.)* couché sur le ventre; étendu face à terre; **to fall p.,** tomber face contre terre; **p. position,** (i) décubitus ventral; (ii) *Mil: etc:* position du tireur couché, position couchée. **2.** *A: (of land, etc.)* en pente, incliné. **3. to be p. to sth., to do sth.,** être enclin, porté, à qch., à faire qch.; **p. to laziness,** sujet à la paresse; **to be p. to a disease,** être prédisposé à une maladie; **to be p. to accidents, to be accident p.,** être enclin aux accidents.

prone[2], *s. Ecc:* prône *m*, homélie *f*.

proneness ['prounnis], *s.* disposition *f*, inclination *f*, propension *f* **(to,** à); **p. to accidents,** prédisposition *f* aux accidents.

pronephros [prou'nefrɔs], *s. Z: Anat:* pronephros *m*.

prong[1] [prɔŋ], *s.* **1.** fourchon *m*, dent *f*, branche *f* (de fourche); griffe *f* (de mandrin, etc.); pointe *f* (d'andouiller, etc.). **2.** *Dial:* fourche *f*, fourchet *m*. **3.** *NAm:* embranchement *m* (d'un cours d'eau).

prong[2], *v.tr.* **1.** transpercer (avec une fourche). **2.** retourner, remuer (le fumier, etc.) à la fourche; fourcher (la terre, etc.).

prongbuck ['prɔŋbʌk], *s.* = PRONGHORN.

pronged [prɔŋd], *a.* à fourchons, à dents, à pointes; **two-p. fork,** fourchette à deux dents, à deux fourchons.

pronghorn ['prɔŋhɔ:n], *s.* (*also* **pronghorned antelope**) *Z:* **p. (antelope),** antilocapre (nord-américain); antilocapra *f*.

pronograde ['prounougreid], *a. Z:* qui marche à quatre pattes.

pronominal [prou'nɔmin(ə)l], *a. Gram:* pronominal, -aux.

pronominally [prou'nɔmin(ə)li], *adv. Gram:* pronominalement.

pronotum [prou'noutəm], *s. Ent:* pronotum *m*.

pronoun ['prounaun], *s. Gram:* pronom *m*.

pronounce [prə'nauns], *v.tr.* **1.** *(a)* déclarer; **to p. s.o. (to be) a genius,** déclarer que qn est un génie; *(b) Jur:* prononcer (une sentence, un arrêt, un jugement); rendre (un arrêt); **meanwhile judgement had been pronounced,** dans l'intervalle il était intervenu un jugement. **2.** *v.i.* **to p. on a subject,** prononcer sur un sujet; *(of tribunal)* statuer sur une question; **to p. for s.o., in favour of s.o., against s.o.,** se prononcer, se déclarer, pour, contre, qn. **3.** prononcer; articuler (un mot, etc.); **difficult word to p.,** mot difficile à prononcer; **this letter is not pronounced,** cette lettre ne se prononce pas; *v.i.* **to p. well, badly,** bien, mal, prononcer; avoir une bonne, une mauvaise, articulation.

pronounceable [prə'naunsəbl], *a.* prononçable.

pronounced [prə'naunsd], *a.* prononcé, marqué; **p. features,** traits accusés; **p. taste of garlic,** goût d'ail très prononcé; très fort goût d'ail; **the change is becoming more p.,** le changement s'accentue.

pronouncedly [prə'naunsidli], *adv.* d'une manière prononcée, marquée, très accusée.

pronouncement [prə'naunsmənt], *s.* prononcement *m*, déclaration *f*; **before any p. is made on the subject,** avant de se prononcer à ce sujet.

pronouncing [prə'naunsiŋ], *s.* **1.** *(a)* déclaration *f* (d'une opinion, etc.); *(b) Jur:* prononciation *f* (d'un jugement, d'une sentence). **2.** prononciation (d'un mot, etc.); **p. dictionary,** dictionnaire de prononciation, (de) phonétique.

pronto ['prɔntou], *adv. F:* sur-le-champ; presto, illico.

pronucleus [prou'nju:kliəs], *s. Biol:* pronucléus *m*.

pronunciamento [prənʌnsiə'mentou], *s.* pronunciamento *m*; manifeste *m* (d'un parti révolutionnaire, etc.).

pronunciation [prənʌnsi'eiʃ(ə)n], *s.* prononciation *f* (d'un mot, d'une langue).

proof[1] [pru:f], *s.* **1.** preuve *f*; **positive p., p. positive,** preuve patente; **cast-iron p.,** preuve rigide; **clear p. of guilt,** preuve évidente de culpabilité; **to give p. of sth.,** faire preuve de (qch.); donner des preuves de (sa nationalité, etc.); annoncer (l'intelligence); **to give, show, p. of goodwill,** faire acte, témoigner, de bonne volonté; donner (à qn) une marque de bienveillance; **to give p. of one's gratitude to s.o.,** témoigner sa reconnaissance à qn; **if p. is needed for these statements,** s'il faut une preuve à ces affirmations; **this is p. that he is lying,** cela prouve qu'il ment; **by way of p. he mentioned that . . .,** comme preuve, il nous a fait observer que . . .; **the p. being that . . .,** à telles enseignes que . . .; **in p. of, as a p. of, one's good faith,** en preuve, pour preuve, en témoignage, de sa bonne foi; **and in p. of this . . .,** et la preuve c'est que . . .; **capable of p.,** susceptible de preuve, de démonstration; **to await p. of sth.,** attendre la confirmation de qch.; **to produce p. to the contrary,** fournir la preuve contraire; *Jur:* **the onus, the burden, of p. lies with . . .,** le soin, l'obligation, de faire la preuve incombe à . . .; **p. of a right, of one's identity,** justification *f*, constatation *f*, d'un droit; justification de son identité; preuve d'identité; **to pay s.o. a sum upon submission of p. of identity,** verser une somme à qn contre légitimation; **p. by documentary evidence,** notoriété de droit; **p. by the evidence of witnesses,** notoriété de fait; **written p.,** preuve par écrit; acte *m*; **document in p. (of sth.),** pièce justificative; justificatif *m*. **2.** *(a)* épreuve *f*; **to bring, put, sth. to the p.,** mettre qch. à l'épreuve; **it has stood the p.,** cela a résisté à l'épreuve; *Prov:* **the p. of the pudding is in the eating,** à l'œuvre on connaît l'artisan; la qualité se révèle à l'usage; *Exp:* **p. of powder,** épreuve des poudres; *Artil:* **p. to bursting,** épreuve d'outrance; **p. charge,** charge *f* d'épreuve; **p. shot,** coup *m* d'épreuve, d'essai; *A:* **armour of p.,** armure éprouvée; *(b)* teneur *f* en alcool (d'un spiritueux); **p. vinegar,** vinaigre *m* de première qualité; *(c) Ch: (test tube)* éprouvette *f*. **3.** *(a) Typ:* **(printer's) p.,** épreuve (d'imprimerie); **galley p.,** (épreuve en) placard *m*; **page proofs,** épreuves en page; **revised p.,** épreuve de révision, de lecture en second; deuxième épreuve; **p. correcting,** correction *f* sur épreuves; **to read proofs,** corriger les, des, épreuves; **to pass the proofs,** donner le bon à tirer; **to read a book in p. (form),** lire un livre sur épreuves; *(b) Engr:* **p. before letters, p. engraving,** épreuve avant la lettre; **letter p.,** épreuve avec la lettre; **signed p.,** épreuve signée; **smoke p., blockmaker's p.,** fumé *m*; **black p.,** épreuve en noir; **colour p.,** épreuve en couleur(s); **reversed p.,** contre-épreuve *f*, *pl.* contre-épreuves. **4.** *Bookb:* témoins *mpl*; **to leave p.,** laisser les témoins (non rognés).

proof[2], *a.* **p. against sth.,** résistant à qch.; peu sensible à qch.; à l'épreuve de qch.; à l'abri de qch.; **p. against damp,** imperméable, étanche, à l'eau, à l'humidité; hydrofuge; **drip p.,** étanche aux chutes d'eau verticales; **evaporation p.,** à l'abri de l'évaporation; **organism p. against poison,** organisme *m* réfractaire au poison; **to be p. against danger, against disease,** être à l'abri du danger, immunisé contre la maladie; **p. against temptation, against flattery,** inaccessible, insensible, à la tentation, à la flatterie; **the poet's creativeness seemed to be p. against years,** la puissance créatrice du poète paraissait défier les années.

proof[3], *v.tr.* **1.** *Typ: Engr:* tirer une épreuve de (la page, l'estampe, etc.). **2.** *(a)* imperméabiliser (un tissu, etc.); *(b)* rendre (qch.) étanche (à la poussière, etc.); *(c)* rendre (qch.) résistant, inattaquable (aux acides, etc.).

proofing ['pru:fiŋ], *s.* **1.** imperméabilisation *f*. **2.** enduit *m* imperméable.

proofmark ['pru:fmɑ:k], *s. Sm.a:* poinçon *m* d'essai.

proofread ['pru:fri:d], *v.tr. & i. Typ:* corriger les épreuves (d'un livre).

proofreader ['pru:fri:dər], *s. Typ:* correcteur, -trice (d'épreuves).

proofreading ['pru:fri:diŋ], *s. Typ:* correction *f* sur épreuves.

prop[1] [prɔp], *s.* **1.** appui *m*, support *m*, soutien *m*, étai *m*, cale *f*; *Const: etc:* chandelle *f*, étançon *m*; pointal *m*, -aux; chevalement *m*; jambe *f* de force (de mur, etc.); étrésillon *m*; *N.Arch:* accore *m*, béquille *f*, épontille *f*; *Min: O:* **to withdraw the props (from a gallery, etc.),** déboiser (une galerie, etc.); *Rugby: Fb:* **p. (forward),** pilier *m* (de mêlée). **2.** échalas *m*, paisseau *m*, pesseau *m*, (de vigne, etc.); tuteur *m* (d'un plant); rame *f* (pour les haricots, etc.); écuyer *m* (d'un arbre). **3. he was the p. of his father's old age,** c'était lui qui soutenait son père âgé.

prop[2], *v.tr.* **(propped)** *(a)* **to p. (up),** appuyer, soutenir; **to p. up a patient against, on, his pillow,** appuyer un malade sur son oreiller; adosser un malade à son oreiller; **to p. a ladder (up) against a wall,** appuyer une échelle contre un mur; **to p. up a piece of furniture,** placer des hausses sous les pieds d'un meuble; **to p. oneself firmly against sth.,** se caler contre qch.; *(b) Const:* étayer, chandeller, chevaler, étançonner, arc-bouter, assurer, accoter, accorer (un mur, etc.); *Civ.E:* étrésillonner (une tranchée, etc.); *Min:* boiser, buter (une mine); *N.Arch:* épontiller (des baux, etc.); *(c)* échalasser, paisseler, pesseler (des vignes, etc.); *Hort:* ramer (des haricots, des pois); tuteurer (un arbuste, etc.).

prop[3], *s. F: A:* proposition *f* (d'Euclide).

prop[4], *s. F:* (= PROPELLER) hélice *f*.

propadiene [proupə'daii:n], *s. Ch:* propadiène *m*.

propaedeutic [proupi'dju:tik]. **1.** *a. & s.* propédeutique *(m)*. **2.** *s.pl. (usu. with sg. const.)* **propaedeutics,** propédeutique *f*.

propaedeutical [proupi'dju:tikl], *a.* propédeutique.

propaganda [prɔpə'gændə], *s.* **1.** *R.C.Ch:* **the P.,** la Propagande; l'Œuvre *f* de la Propagation de la foi. **2.** propagande; **p. film,** film *m* de propagande; **to make p. out of an incident,** se servir d'un incident pour faire de la propagande; **this is only p.,** cela c'est un argument de mauvaise foi.

propagandism [prɔpə'gændizm], *s.* propagandisme *m*.

propagandist [prɔpə'gændist], *s.* **1.** *R.C.Ch:* missionnaire *m* de la Propagation de la foi. **2.** propagandiste *mf*.

propagandize [prɔpə'gændaiz]. **1.** *v.tr.* soumettre (qn, un pays) à la propagande; essayer de convertir (qn) par la propagande. **2.** *v.i.* faire de la propagande.

propagate ['prɔpəgeit]. **1.** *v.tr. (a)* propager, faire reproduire (des animaux, une plante, etc.); **to p. plants by cuttings,** bouturer des plantes; **disease propagated from generation to generation,** maladie transmise de génération en génération; *(b)* propager, répandre, disséminer, transmettre; **to p. light,** propager, répandre, la lumière; **light is propagated in a straight line,** la lumière se propage en ligne droite; **to p. ideas,** répandre, disséminer, propager, des idées. **2.** *v.i. (of animal, plant)* se propager, se reproduire, se multiplier; *(of discontent, etc.)* se propager.

propagation [prɔpə'geiʃ(ə)n], *s.* **1.** propagation *f* (d'une espèce, etc.); reproduction *f*, multiplication *f* (des animaux, etc.); *(of plants by cuttings)* bouturage *m*. **2.** *(a) Ph:* propagation (de la lumière, du son, etc.); **free space p.,** propagation en espace libre; **ground p.,** propagation par le sol; **hop p.,** propagation par relais successifs; **ionospheric p.,** propagation dans l'atmosphère; **p. coefficient, p. constant,** constante *f* de propagation; **p. factor, p. ratio,** facteur *m* de propagation; **p. path,** parcours de l'onde, des ondes; *(b)* propagation, diffusion *f*, dissémination *f* (d'une doctrine, des idées, etc.).

propagative ['prɔpəgeitiv], *a.* propagateur, -trice.

propagator ['prɔpəgeitər], *s.* **1.** propagateur, -trice. **2.** *Hort:* germoir *m*.

propagule ['prɔpəgju:l], **propagulum,** *pl.* **-a** [prɔ'pægjuləm, -ə], *s. Moss:* propagule *f*.

propane ['proupein], *s. Ch:* propane *m*; *Nau:* **p. carrier,** propanier *m*.

propanoic [proupə'nouik], *a. Ch:* propanoïque.

propanol ['proupənɔl], *s. Ch:* propanol *m*, alcool *m* propylique.

propanone ['proupənoun], *s. Ch:* propanone *f*.

proparoxytone [proupæ'rɔksitoun], *s. Gr.Gram:* proparoxyton *m*.

propel [prə'pel], *v.tr.* **(propelled)** *(a)* propulser; pousser en avant; donner une impulsion à (qch.); mouvoir; faire avancer; **mechanically propelled vehicle,** véhicule *m* à propulsion mécanique, à traction mécanique; *(b)* **propelled by ambition,** poussé, animé, par l'ambition.

propellant, propellent [prə'pelənt]. **1.** *a.* propulseur *(no fem.)*; propulsif; *Ball: etc:* **p. charge,** charge propulsive. **2.** *s.* propulseur *m*; combustible *m*; carburant *m*; ergol *m*, propergol *m* (pour fusées); **liquid, solid, (rocket) p.,** propergol liquide, solide; **hybrid p.,** propergol hybride; lithergol *m*.

propeller, propellor [prə'pelər], *s.* **1.** propulseur *m*; *Ind: etc:* **air p.,** aérateur *m*; *Aut: etc:* **p. shaft,** arbre longitudinal, de propulsion, de transmission; arbre à cadran. **2.** *Nau: Av:* hélice *f*; **controllable-pitch p.,** hélice à pas commandé, à pas réglable; **variable-pitch p.,** hélice à pas variable; **solid p.,** hélice monobloc, d'une seule pièce; **reversible p.,** hélice réversible; **three-bladed p.,** hélice à trois pales; **p. blade,** pale *f*, aile *f*, d'hélice; **p. pitch,** pas *m* de l'hélice; **p. modulus,** coefficient *m* d'avance, argument *m* de similitude, de l'hélice; *Nau:* **built-up p.,** hélice à ailes rapportées; **constant-pitch p.,** hélice à pas constant; **in-turning, out-turning, propellers,** hélices supracONVergentes, supradivergentes; **tunnel screw p.,** hélice sous voûte; **folding-blade p.,** hélice rabattable; **p. shaft,** arbre *m* porte-hélice; **p. post,** étambot *m* avant; *Av:* **braking p.,** hélice frein; **co-axial p.,** hélice coaxiale; **contrarotating propellers,** hélices contrarotatives; **feathered p.,** hélice en drapeau; **(quick) feathering p.,** hélice à mise en drapeau (rapide); **geared p.,** hélice démultipliée; **p. gear,** démultiplicateur *m* d'hélice; **p. gear ratio,** rapport *m* de réduction de l'hélice; **pusher, tractor, p.,** hélice propulsive, tractive; **p. clearance,** (angle *m* de) garde *f* de l'hélice; **p. race,** souffle *m*, vent *m*, de l'hélice.

propelling [prə'peliŋ], *a.* propulseur (*no fem.*); propulsif; moteur, -trice; **p. power, force,** force propulsive, motrice; **p. charge,** charge propulsive (d'un projectile); (*in jet engine*) **p. nozzle,** tuyère propulsive.

propenoic [proupə'nuik], *s. Ch:* propénoïque *m*.

propense [prou'pens], *a. A: & Lit:* porté, enclin, disposé (à qch., à faire qch.).

propensity [prə'pensiti], *s.* propension *f*, penchant *m*, inclination *f*, tendance *f* (à, vers, qch.; à faire qch.); **great p. for lying,** grand penchant pour le mensonge; **to have a p. for running into debt,** être sujet à s'endetter.

propenyl ['proupənil], *s. Ch:* propényle *m*.

propenylic [proupə'nilik], *a. Ch:* propénylique.

proper ['prɔpər], *a. & s.*

I. *a.* propre. **1.** *A:* **with my own p. eyes,** de mes propres yeux. **2.** (*a*) **p. to sth.,** propre, particulier, à qch.; **p. to tropical climates,** propre aux climats tropicaux; (*b*) **in his p. colours,** sous son vrai jour; **p. use of a drug,** emploi rationnel d'un remède; **to put sth. to its p. use,** utiliser rationnellement qch.; **that's not the p. tune for that song,** cela n'est pas l'air authentique de cette chanson; *Ecc:* **p. psalms,** psaumes *m* du jour; *Astr:* **p. motion,** mouvement *m* propre (d'un astre); (*c*) *Gram:* **p. noun,** nom *m* propre; (*d*) *Her:* **argent a lion p.,** d'argent à un lion naturel. **3.** (*a*) vrai, juste; approprié; **the p. word,** le mot juste, propre; **p. meaning of a word,** signification *f* propre d'un mot; **what's its p. name?** quel est son nom correct? **architecture p.,** l'architecture proprement dite; **Greece p.,** la Grèce propre; (*b*) *Mth:* **p. fraction,** fraction *f* moindre que l'unité. **4.** (*a*) *F:* **a p. cold,** un rhume soigné, carabiné; **we're in a p. mess!** nous voilà dans de beaux draps! **he's a p. fool, a p. idiot,** c'est un parfait imbécile, une vraie andouille; **a p. tomboy,** un garçon manqué; *P:* **he's a p. bastard,** c'est un beau salaud; (*b*) *adv. P:* **to feel p. poorly,** se sentir tout patraque; ne pas être dans son assiette; **they got it good and p.,** ils ont reçu ce qu'ils méritaient. **5.** (*a*) convenable; **at the p. time,** en temps opportun; en temps utile; à l'heure qu'il faut; au moment convenable, voulu; quand il y aura lieu; **he's never got his work finished at the p. time,** il n'a jamais fini son travail au moment voulu, quand il le faut; **to apply to the p. person,** s'adresser à qui de droit; **to think p. to . . .,** juger à propos, juger bon, de . . .; **I think it only p. to warn you that . . .,** je crois bon de vous avertir que . . .; **do as you think p.,** faites comme bon vous semblera; *Jur:* **to be used as may be thought p.,** pour valoir ce que de raison; *F:* **to do the p. thing by s.o.,** agir honnêtement, loyalement, avec qn; **the p. measures to take,** les mesures *f* qui s'imposent; **the p. way to do it,** la meilleure façon de le faire; **the p. tool to use,** le bon outil; l'outil approprié; **that's not the p. way to use it,** ce n'est pas comme ça qu'on s'en sert; **the p. use of the subjunctive,** l'emploi correct du subjonctif; **p. receipt,** quittance régulière; **paid at the p. rate,** payé au taux, au prix, convenable; **in p. condition,** en bon état; (*b*) convenable, comme il faut; **a very p. old lady,** une vieille dame (i) très comme il faut, (ii) très digne; *O:* **it's not the p. thing to do, that sort of thing isn't p.,** cela ne se fait pas; *A:* **it isn't p. for a girl to show her ankles,** une jeune fille bien élevée ne montre pas ses chevilles; (*to child*) **that's not the p. way to behave!** en voilà des manières! tiens-toi plus convenablement!

II. *s. Ecc:* **P. of Saints,** Propre *m* des Saints.

properdin ['proupədin], *s. Physiol:* properdine *f*.

properispomenon [prouperi'spouminɔn], *s. Gr.Gram:* propérispomène *m*.

properly ['prɔpəli], *adv.* **1.** (*a*) **word p. used,** mot employé proprement, correctement; **p. speaking,** proprement dit; à proprement parler; (*b*) bien, de la bonne façon; **do it p. or not at all,** faites-le bien, comme il faut, ou pas du tout. **2.** *F:* (*intensive*) **he was p. drunk,** il était complètement soûl; **to tell s.o. off p.,** rembarrer vertement qn; arranger qn de la belle manière; *Sp: etc:* **we were p. beaten,** ils nous ont battus à plate(s) couture(s). **3.** (*a*) convenablement; comme il faut; **to behave p.,** se conduire comme il faut; (*b*) **he very p. refused,** il a refusé, comme il le fallait. **4.** *Jur:* (agir) de bon droit.

propertied ['prɔpətid], *a.* possédant; **the p. classes,** les possédants, les classes possédantes.

Propertius [prou'pə:ʃiəs]. *Pr.n.m. Lt.Lit:* Properce.

property ['prɔpəti], *s.* **1.** (droit *m* de) propriété *f*; **to retain the p. in one's estate,** conserver la propriété de ses biens; **literary p.,** propriété littéraire. **2.** (*a*) propriété, biens *mpl*, avoir(s) *m*(*pl*); **private, public, p.,** propriété privée, publique; *Jur:* **funded p.,** biens en rentes; **to come into public p.,** rentrer en domaine public; **that's my p.,** cela m'appartient; **personal p.,** biens personnels, mobiliers; effets personnels; **damage to p.,** dommages matériels; **to make free with other peoples' p.,** (i) faire des largesses avec l'argent d'autrui; (ii) traiter comme le sien ce qui appartient à d'autres; **lost p. office,** service *m* des objets trouvés; (*b*) immeuble(s) *m*(*pl*); propriété (foncière), terre *f*; **a small p. in the country,** une petite propriété à la campagne; **p. for sale,** immeuble, maison *f*, à vendre; *Hist:* **p. qualification,** cens (électoral); quotité de propriété requise pour l'exercice d'une fonction; (*c*) *Mil: etc:* matériel *m* (appartenant à l'État); **p. book,** registre *m* du matériel. **3.** *Th: etc:* **properties,** accessoires *m*; réserve *f* de décors, de costumes, etc.; **p. sword,** épée *f* de scène; **p. horse,** cheval-jupon *m*, *pl.* chevaux-jupons; **p. man,** accessoiriste *m*; **p. room,** magasin *m* des accessoires. **4.** qualité *f* (propre), propriété; **(inherent) p.,** attribut *m*; **the properties of matter,** les propriétés des corps; **plants with healing properties,** plantes qui ont la vertu de guérir; **a magnet has the p. of attracting iron,** un aimant a la faculté d'attirer le fer.

prophage ['proufeidʒ], *s. Bac:* prophage *m*.

prophase ['proufeiz], *s. Biol:* prophase *f*.

prophecy ['prɔfisi], *s.* **1.** prophétie *f*; **the gift of p.,** le don de prophétie. **2.** prophétie, prédiction *f*; **the p. was fulfilled,** la prophétie s'est accomplie.

prophesier ['prɔfisaiər], *s.* prophète, -étesse; *Pej:* vaticinateur, -trice.

prophesy ['prɔfisai]. **1.** *v.i.* (*a*) parler en prophète; rendre des prophéties; prophétiser; *Pej:* vaticiner; **he prophesied correctly,** il s'est montré bon prophète; **to p. of things to come,** émettre des prophéties sur l'avenir; (*b*) *Ecc:* *A:* interpréter, commenter, les Écritures; (*c*) *Ecc:* *A:* prêcher l'Évangile. **2.** *v.tr.* prophétiser, prédire (un événement).

prophesying ['prɔfisaiiŋ], *s.* (*a*) prophéties *fpl*; prédiction *f*; (*b*) *Ecc: A:* prédication *f*.

prophet ['prɔfit], *s.* **1.** prophète *m*; *B.Hist:* **the major, minor, prophets,** les grands, petits, prophètes; *Mohamm.Rel:* **the P.,** le Prophète (Mahomet); **p. of evil,** prophète de malheur; prêche-malheur *m inv*; cassandre *f*; **she had shown herself a true p.,** elle avait prophétisé vrai; *Prov:* **no man is a p. in his own country,** nul n'est prophète en son pays. **2.** *Turf: F:* donneur *m* de tuyaux.

prophetess ['prɔfites], *s.f.* prophétesse.

prophetic(al) [prə'fetik(l)], *a.* prophétique; **these deeds were p. of his future greatness,** ces actions annonçaient sa grandeur à venir.

prophetically [prə'fetik(ə)li], *adv.* prophétiquement.

prophetism ['prɔfitizm], *s.* prophétisme *m*.

prophylactic [prɔfi'læktik], *a. & s. Med:* prophylactique (*m*).

prophylaxis [prɔfi'læksis], *s. Med:* prophylaxie *f*.

prophyll ['proufil], **prophyllum,** *pl.* **-a** [prou'filəm, -ə], *s. Bot:* bractéole *f*.

propine ['proupain], *s. Ch:* propyne *m*.

propinquity [prə'piŋkwiti], *s.* **1.** proximité *f* (de lieu); voisinage *m*. **2.** (proche) parenté *f*. **3.** affinité *f* **(of ideas,** entre les idées).

propiolic [proupi'ɔlik], *a. Ch:* propiolique.

propionate ['proupiəneit], *s. Ch:* propionate *m*.

propione ['proupioun], *s. Ch:* propione *f*.

propionic [proupi'ɔnik], *a. Ch:* propionique.

propionitrile [proupiou'naitril], *s. Ch:* propionitrile *m*.

propionyl ['proupiənil], *s.* propionyle *m*.

propithecus [proupi'θi:kəs], *s. Z:* propithèque *m*.

propitiate [prə'piʃieit], *v.tr.* **1.** rendre propice, favorable; **to p. the gods,** se rendre les dieux favorables. **2.** apaiser (qn que l'on a offensé); se faire pardonner par (qn).

propitiation [prəpiʃi'eiʃ(ə)n], *s.* **1.** propitiation *f*. **2.** apaisement *m* (des dieux courroucés, etc.). **3.** (*a*) expiation *f*; (*b*) *A:* offrande *f*, sacrifice *m* expiatoire; *B:* **and he is the p. for our sins,** car c'est lui qui est la victime de propitiation pour nos péchés.

propitiative [prə'piʃieitiv], *a.* (*of statement, action, etc.*) expiatoire.

propitiator [prə'piʃieitər], *s.* propitiateur, -trice.

propitiatory [prə'piʃiət(ə)ri], *a. & s.* propitiatoire (*m*); expiatoire.

propitious [prə'piʃəs], *a.* propice, favorable (à qn, à une entreprise); **the planets were p.,** les planètes *f* étaient propices.

propitiously [prə'piʃəsli], *adv.* d'une manière propice; favorablement.

propitiousness [prə'piʃəsnis], *s.* nature *f* propice.

propjet ['prɔpdʒet], *s. I.C.E: Av:* turbopropulseur *m*.

propliopithecus [proupliou'piθikəs], *s. Paleont:* propliopithecus *m*.

propodite ['prɔpədait], *s. Crust:* propodite *m*.

propolis ['prɔpəlis], *s. Ap:* propolis *f*.

propolization [prɔpəlai'zeiʃ(ə)n], *s. Ap:* propolisation *f*.

proponent [prə'pounənt], *s. NAm:* **1.** proposeur, -euse (d'une motion). **2.** auteur *m*, défenseur *m* (d'une doctrine).

Propontis [prou'pɔntis]. *Pr.n. A.Geog:* la Propontide.

proportion[1] [prə'pɔ:ʃ(ə)n], *s.* **1.** partie *f* (d'une surface); portion *f*; part *f*; **to divide expenses in equal proportions,** répartir les frais par parts égales; **to pay one's p. of the expenses,** verser sa quote-part, sa quotité, des dépenses; **a certain p. of the profits will be assigned to you,** on vous assignera un quantum, un tantième, sur les bénéfices; **p. of an ingredient in a mixture,** proportion *f*, dose *f*, d'un ingrédient dans un mélange; **alloy containing nickel in small proportions,** alliage *m* contenant du nickel dans des proportions restreintes. **2.** rapport *m*, proportion; (*a*) **p. of the net load to the gross load,** rapport du poids utile au poids mort; *Ch:* **law of multiple proportions,** loi *f* des proportions multiples; **friction in p. to the load,** frottement *m* en fonction de, par rapport à, la charge; **in a fixed p. to each other,** dans un rapport constant (entre eux); (*b*) **in p. to . . .,** à, en, proportion de . . .; proportionnellement à . . .; en fonction, en raison, de . . .; **out of all p. to . . .,** sans mesure avec . . .; **his short legs are out of p. to the rest of his body,** ses jambes courtes ne sont pas en proportion avec le reste de son corps; **each man's pay will be in p. to the work done,** chaque homme sera payé selon le travail fourni; **the payment is out of all p. to the work involved,** la rétribution n'a aucun rapport avec le travail requis, est disproportionnée au travail requis; (*c*) *Arch: etc:* **in perfect p.,** en parfaite harmonie; **out of p.,** mal proportionné; **the two doors are in admirable p.,** les deux portes sont d'une symétrie admirable; **a Greek temple of classical proportions,** un temple grec d'une harmonie classique, aux lignes classiques; **to have an eye for p.,** avoir du coup d'œil, un coup d'œil juste; **he has no sense of p.,** il n'a pas le sens des proportions; **to lose all sense of p.,** ne garder aucune mesure; oublier toute mesure; (*d*) *Mth:* (i) **arithmetical, geometrical, p.,** proportion arithmétique, géométrique; **inverse p.,** rapport inverse; **the p. of** *x* **to** *y*, la proportionnalité entre *x* et *y*; (ii) *A:* règle *f* de trois, de proportion; (*e*) *Mus:* **harmonical p.,** proportion harmonique. **3.** *pl.* proportions (d'un édifice, du corps humain, etc.); dimensions *f* (d'une machine, etc.); **proportions of an organ pipe,** étalon *m* d'un tuyau d'orgue; **horse that has good proportions,** cheval qui a de l'ensemble.

proportion[2], *v.tr.* **1.** proportionner, mesurer (la punition au crime, etc.); **to p. one's expenditure to one's profits,** mesurer sa dépense sur ses profits. **2.** doser (des ingrédients, un mélange); *Min:* **to p. the shots,** compasser les feux. **3.** *Ind:* (*a*) déterminer les dimensions (d'une pièce); (*b*) coter (un dessin).

proportionable [prə'pɔ:ʃənəbl], *a.* en proportion; proportionné.

proportionably [prə'pɔ:ʃənəbli], *adv.* *A:* = PROPORTIONALLY.

proportional [prə'pɔ:ʃən(ə)l]. **1.** *a.* proportionnel; en proportion (to, de); proportionné (to, à); **p. scale,** échelle proportionnelle; **compensation p. to the damage,** compensation proportionnelle au dommage subi; **the weight is directly p. to the volume,** le poids est en raison directe du volume; **inversely p. to . . .,** inversement proportionnel à . . .; en raison inverse de . . .; *Pol:* **p. representation,** représentation proportionnelle; *Adm:* **p. assessment,** coéquation *f*; *Atom.Ph:* **p. band, limit,** bande *f*, limite *f*, de proportionnalité; **p. counter,** compteur proportionnel. **2.** *s. Mth:* proportionnelle *f*; **mean p.,** moyenne proportionnelle.

proportionalism [prə'pɔ:ʃənəlizm], *s. Pol:* théorie *f* de la représentation proportionnelle.

proportionalist [prə'pɔ:ʃənəlist], *s. Pol:* proportionnaliste *mf*, partisan, -ane, de la représentation proportionnelle.

proportionally [prə'pɔ:ʃənəli], *adv.* en proportion, proportionnément, proportionnellement (to, à).

proportionate [prə'pɔ:ʃənət], *a.* proportionné (to, à); **the result was not p. to the effort made,** le résultat était disproportionné à l'effort fourni.

proportioned [prə'pɔ:ʃənd], *a.* **well, badly, p.,** bien, mal, proportionné.

proportioning [prə'pɔ:ʃəniŋ], *s.* **1.** dosage *m* (des ingrédients); *Min:* compassement *m* (des feux); *Atom.Ph:* **p. pump,** pompe doseuse. **2.** détermination *f* des dimensions (d'une machine, etc.).

proportionment [prə'pɔ:ʃənm(ə)nt], *s.* distribution proportionnelle, au prorata.

proposal [prə'pouzl], *s.* **1.** (*a*) proposition *f*, offre *f*; **to make a p.,** faire, formuler, une proposition; **proposals for . . .,** propositions relatives à . . .; **p. of peace,** proposition de paix; (*b*) demande *f* en mariage; offre de mariage; (*c*) *U.S:* soumission *f* (pour un travail, etc.);

p. bond, caution *f* de participation à une adjucation. **2.** dessein *m*, projet *m*.

proposant [prə'pouzənt], *s. Ecc:* proposant *m*.

propose [prə'pouz]. **1.** *v.tr. O:* proposer, poser (une question à résoudre, une énigme). **2.** *v.tr.* (*a*) **I should like to p. that. . ., may I p. that. . .,** puis-je proposer, suggérer, exprimer, l'avis, que . . .; **he proposed that they should offer £10,000 for it,** il a proposé qu'on en fasse une offre de £10.000; *v.i.* **man proposes, God disposes,** l'homme propose et Dieu dispose; (*b*) **to p. a candidate, a motion,** proposer un candidat, une motion; **I p. Mr X as president,** je propose, je présente, M. X à la présidence; **will you p. me for your club?** voulez-vous me présenter à votre cercle? **to p. a toast, s.o.'s health,** porter un toast (en l'honneur, à la santé, de qn); **I p. our president,** je vous invite à boire à la santé de notre président; (*c*) **to p. to do sth., doing sth.,** se proposer, avoir l'intention, de faire qch.; **what do you p. to do now?** que comptez-vous, qu'est-ce que vous aller, faire maintenant? **3.** *v.i.* faire une demande en mariage; **he proposed to her,** il lui a demandé de l'épouser.

proposed [prə'pouzd], *a.* proposé; **p. translation,** essai *m* de traduction.

proposer [prə'pouzər], *s.* auteur *m* d'une offre, d'une proposition; proposeur, -euse; (*at club, etc.*) parrain, marraine (d'un candidat); **p. of a motion,** motionnaire *m*.

proposing [prə'pouziŋ], *s.* (*a*) proposition *f*, offre, *f*; (*b*) demande *f* en mariage.

proposition[1] [prɔpə'ziʃ(ə)n], *s.* **1.** (*a*) proposition *f*, offre *f*; (*b*) *F:* affaire *f*; **it's a big p.,** c'est une grosse affaire; **paying p.,** affaire rentable, qui rapporte; **it's a tough p.,** c'est une question difficile à résoudre, un cas embarrassant; **he's a tough p.,** il est peu commode; on ne sait pas par où le prendre; *Sp:* **the Australians will be a tough p.,** on aura du mal à battre l'équipe australienne; (*c*) *P:* proposition indécente (faite à une femme). **2.** (*a*) *Log:Gram:* proposition; *Log:* **axiomatic p.,** thèse *f* axiomatique; (*b*) *Mth: A:* proposition, théorème *m*. **3.** *Mus:* proposition (d'une fugue).

proposition[2], *v.tr.* (*a*) *F:* proposer un projet à (qn); (*b*) *P:* faire des propositions indécentes à (une femme).

propositional [prɔpə'ziʃən(ə)l], *a. Log:* propositionnel, de la proposition; **the two p. terms,** les deux prémisses *f*; **p. theology,** théologie *f* par syllogismes.

propound [prə'paund], *v.tr.* **1.** proposer (une énigme, un traité de paix); émettre (une idée); poser (une question, un problème); exposer (un programme). **2.** *Jur:* soumettre (un testament) à la validation; demander l'homologation (d'un testament).

propounder [prə'paundər], *s.* personne *f* qui propose, qui pose (un problème); auteur *m* (d'une théorie, d'une proposition).

propping ['prɔpiŋ], *s.* (*a*) soutènement *m*; (*b*) étayage *m*, étaiement *m*, étançonnement *m*, accorage *m*, étrésillonnement *m*; *N.Arch:* épontillage *m* (des baux, etc.); *Min:* **p. of a roof,** consolidation *f* d'un ciel; (*c*) échalassage *m*, échalassement *m*.

propraetor [prou'pri:tər], *s. Rom.Hist:* propréteur *m*.

propraetorship [prou'pri:təʃip], *s. Rom.Hist:* propréture *f*.

proprietary [prə'praiət(ə)ri]. **1.** *a.* (*a*) de propriété, de propriétaire; **the p. rights of the Crown,** les droits *m* de propriété de la Couronne; (*b*) *O:* **p. classes,** classes possédantes; (*c*) **p. chapel,** chapelle particulière, privée; **p. insurance company,** compagnie d'assurance à primes; *Com:* **p. article,** spécialité *f*, article breveté; **p. medicines,** spécialités pharmaceutiques. **2.** *s.* (*a*) droit *m* de propriété; **peasant p.,** propriété paysanne; (*b*) *coll. O:* classe *f* des propriétaires; **the landed p.,** les propriétaires fonciers.

proprietor [prə'praiətər], *s.* propriétaire *mf*; **p. of a hotel,** propriétaire, patron *m*, d'un hôtel; **landed p.,** propriétaire foncier.

proprietorship [prə'praiətəʃip], *s.* **1.** droit *m* de propriété. **2.** propriété *f*, possession *f*.

proprietress [prə'praiətris], *s.f.* propriétaire; patronne (d'un hôtel, etc.).

propriety [prə'praiəti], *s.* **1.** (*a*) propriété *f*, justesse *f*, à-propos *m inv*, convenance *f* (d'une expression, etc.); correction *f* (de langage, de manières); rectitude *f* (de conduite); **I doubt the p. of refusing it,** je me demande s'il convient de le refuser; **I persuaded him of the p. of resigning,** je l'ai persuadé que sa démission s'imposait; (*b*) opportunité *f* (d'une action, d'une démarche). **2.** (*a*) bienséance *f*, décence *f*; **conventional p.,** les convenances admises; **breach of, lack of, p.,** manque *m* de savoir-vivre; *O:* **to throw p. to the winds,** se moquer de toutes les convenances; *F:* (*of woman*) jeter son bonnet par-dessus les moulins; (*b*) **to observe the proprieties,** observer les convenances.

proprioception [proupriou'sepʃ(ə)n], *s. Physiol:* proprioception *f*.

proprioceptive [proupriou'septiv], *a. Physiol:* proprioceptif.

proprioceptor [proupriou'septər], *s. Physiol:* propriocepteur *m*.

props [prɔps], *s. Th: etc: F:* **1.** *pl.* accessoires *f*. **2.** (*pers.*) accessoiriste *mf*.

propulsion [prə'pʌlʃ(ə)n], *s.* **1.** *Mec.E:* propulsion *f*, mise *f* en mouvement, traction *f*; **means of p.,** moyen(s) *m*(*pl*), mode *m*, de propulsion; **mechanical p.,** propulsion mécanique; **jet p.,** propulsion par réaction; **rocket p.,** propulsion par fusée(s); **cycloidal p.,** propulsion cycloïdale; **Diesel-electric p.,** propulsion Diesel-électrique; **hydraulic p.,** propulsion hydraulique; **p. engine,** (i) moteur *m* de propulsion, de traction; (ii) *Av:* moteur, réacteur *m*, de propulsion; **p. unit,** groupe moteur, motopropulseur; ensemble moteur; moteur; **p. turbine,** turbine *f* de propulsion; **p. jet,** réacteur de propulsion; *Av:* **p./lift engine,** réacteur de propulsion et de sustentation; *Atom.Ph:* **p. reactor,** réacteur (nucléaire) de propulsion (d'un sous-marin, d'un navire de surface). **2.** *Cin:* entraînement *m* (du film).

propulsive [prə'pʌlsiv], *a.* propulsif; propulseur (*no f.*); (mouvement *m*, effort *m*) de propulsion; (force) motrice; **p. coefficient,** coefficient *m* de propulsion; **p. efficiency,** rendement propulsif; (*of jet engine*) **p. duct,** tuyère propulsive; *Ball: Mec:* **p. power,** puissance de propulsion, puissance propulsive (d'un explosif, d'un moteur, etc.).

propyl ['proupil], *s. Ch:* propyle *m*; **p. alcohol,** alcool *m* propylique.

propylaeum, *pl.* **-aea** [prɔpi'li:əm, -iə], *s. Gr.Ant:* propylée *m*.

propylamine [proupil'æmain], *s. Ch:* propylamine *f*.

propylene ['proupili:n], *s. Ch:* propylène *m*.

propylic [prou'pilik], *a. Ch:* propylique.

propylite ['prɔpilait], *s. Miner:* propylite *f*.

propyne ['proupain], *s. Ch:* propyne *m*.

propynoic [proupi'nɔik], *a. Ch:* propynoïque.

proquaestor [prou'kwi:stər], *s. Rom.Hist:* proquesteur *m*.

pro rata [prou'rɑ:tə, -'reitə], *adv. & adj.phr.* au pro rata; au marc le franc; **paid p. r. to the debts owing to them,** payés au marc le franc de leurs créances.

prorate [prou'reit], *v.tr. Fin: etc:* partager proportionnellement.

prorogate ['prourougeit], *v.tr.* **1.** proroger. **2.** *Jur: Scot:* faire une extension *ad hoc* de la compétence d'un tribunal.

prorogation [prourou'geiʃ(ə)n], *s.* **1.** prorogation *f* (du Parlement). **2.** *Jur: Scot:* extension *f ad hoc* de la compétence d'un tribunal.

prorogue [prou'roug]. **1.** *v.tr.* proroger (le Parlement). **2.** *v.i.* (*of Parliament, etc.*) se proroger.

proroguing[1] [prou'rougiŋ], *a.* prorogatif.

proroguing[2], *s.* prorogation *f*.

prosaic(al) [prou'zeiik(l)], *a.* (style, esprit, etc.) prosaïque, positif, banal, -aux.

prosaically [prou'zeiik(ə)li], *adv.* prosaïquement.

prosaic(al)ness [prou'zeiik(əl)nis], *s.* prosaïsme *m* (de la vie, etc.); banalité *f* (du style, etc.).

prosaicism [prou'zeiisizm], **prosaism** ['prouzeiizm], *s.* prosaïsme *m*; banalité *f* (de style).

prosaist ['prouzeiist], *s.* **1.** prosateur *m*. **2.** personne *f* prosaïque; esprit terre à terre, positif, dépourvu de poésie.

proscenium [prou'si:niəm], *s. Th:* (*a*) *Ant:* proscenium *m*; (*b*) *esp. Ant:* scène *f*; (*c*) avant-scène *f*, *pl.* avant-scènes; **p. arch,** manteau *m* (d'Arlequin).

proscribe [prous'kraib], *v.tr.* proscrire. **1.** mettre (un criminel, etc.) hors la loi; **to p. s.o. from a society,** proscrire, bannir, qn d'une société. **2.** interdire, défendre (une pratique, un usage, etc.); **to p. a religion,** proscrire, interdire, une religion.

proscriber [prous'kraibər], *s.* proscripteur *m*.

proscript ['prouskript], *s.* proscrit, -ite; hors-la-loi *m inv*.

proscription [prous'kripʃ(ə)n], *s.* proscription *f*; (i) mise *f* (de qn) hors la loi; (ii) interdiction *f* (d'une religion, d'une pratique, etc.).

proscriptive [prous'kriptiv], *a.* **1.** (lois, etc.) de proscription. **2.** (décret, arrêt, etc.) prohibitif.

prose[1] [prouz], *s.* **1.** prose *f*; **selected Victorian p. writings,** morceaux choisis des prosateurs de l'ère victorienne; **p. works of Milton,** œuvres en prose de Milton; **p. poem, poem in p.,** poème *m* en prose; **p. writer,** prosateur *m*; **great p. stylist,** grand prosateur. **2.** *Ecc:* prose (chantée avant l'Évangile). **3.** *Sch:* **Latin p., French p.,** thème latin, français. **4.** *O:* prosaïsme *m* (de la vie, etc.). **5.** (*a*) *O:* discours fastidieux, ennuyeux; (*b*) *A:* entretien familier; (*c*) *A:* personne ennuyante, fatigante.

prose[2]. **1.** *v.tr.* mettre en prose (un passage en vers); récrire (qch.) en prose. **2.** *v.i. F:* tenir des discours fastidieux, ennuyeux; **he went prosing on,** il continuait son rabâchage.

prosecretin [prou'si:kritin], *s. Physiol:* prosécrétine *f*.

prosecutable [prɔsi'kju:təbl], *a.* **1.** (*of pers.*) poursuivable. **2.** (*of action*) que l'on peut intenter; (*of claim*) que l'on peut déposer.

prosecute ['prɔsikju:t], *v.tr.* **1.** (*a*) poursuivre (qn) (en justice répressive); traduire (qn) en justice; engager ou exercer des poursuites contre (qn); agir au criminel contre (qn); **to be prosecuted for exceeding the speed limit,** attraper une contravention pour excès de vitesse; *v.i.* **to decide to p.,** décider d'engager des poursuites judiciaires; (*b*) **to p. an action,** intenter une action; poursuivre un procès; **to p. a claim,** poursuivre une réclamation. **2.** *A:* (*a*) effectuer (un voyage); (*b*) poursuivre (des études, une enquête, etc.); mener (une enquête); (*c*) exercer (un métier, etc.).

prosecution [prɔsi'kju:ʃ(ə)n], *s.* **1.** *Jur:* (*a*) poursuites *fpl* (en justice répressive); poursuites judiciaires; **you are making yourself liable to p. by the Council,** vous vous exposez à des poursuites de la part du Conseil; **before calling for a p.,** avant de déclencher des poursuites judiciaires; **to start a p. against s.o.,** engager des poursuites contre qn; (*b*) accusation *f*, action publique; **Director of Public Prosecutions** = le procureur de la République; (*c*) **the p.,** les plaignants *m*; (*in Crown case*) = le Ministère public; **witness for the p.,** témoin *m* à charge. **2.** *A:* (*a*) continuation *f* (d'études, etc.); (*b*) exercice *m* (d'un métier, etc.).

prosecutor ['prɔsikjutər], *s. Jur:* **1.** plaignant *m*, poursuivant *m*, demandeur *m*. **2. the Public P.** = le procureur de la République; *Hist:* accusateur public (du Tribunal révolutionnaire).

prosecutrix ['prɔsikjutriks], *s.f. Jur:* plaignante; demanderesse.

proselyte[1] ['prɔsilait], *s.* prosélyte *mf*; *Jew.Rel:* **p. of the covenant, of righteousness,** prosélyte de justice; **p. of the gate,** prosélyte de la porte.

proselyte[2], *v.i.* faire des prosélytes.

proselytical [prɔsi'litikl], *a.* prosélytique.

proselytism ['prɔsilitizm], *s.* prosélytisme *m*.

proselytize ['prɔsilitaiz]. **1.** *v.tr.* convertir (qn); faire un prosélyte de (qn). **2.** *v.i.* faire des prosélytes.

proselytizer ['prɔsilitaizər], *s.* personne animée de prosélytisme.

proselytizing ['prɔsilitaiziŋ], *a.* prosélytique.

prosenchyma [prɔ'seŋkimə], *s. Bot:* prosenchyme *m*.

Proserpine ['prɔsəpain], **Proserpina** [prɔ'sə:pinə]. *Pr.n.f. Myth:* Proserpine.

prosify ['prouzifai], *v. Pej:* **1.** *v.tr.* proser, prosaïser, banaliser. **2.** *v.i.* écrire de la prose ennuyeuse.

prosily ['prouzili], *adv.* fastidieusement.

Prosimii [prou'simii:], *s.pl. Z:* prosimiens *m*, lémuroïdes *m*.

prosiness ['prouzinis], *s.* prosaïsme *m* (d'une conversation, etc.); terre à terre *m inv* (du style); verbosité *f* (d'une personne); banalité *f*.

prosiphon [prou'saifən], *s. Moll:* prosiphon *m*.

Prosobranchi(at)a [prɔsou'bræŋkiə, -bræŋki:'eitə], *s.pl. Moll:* prosobranches *m*.

prosodiac(al) [prɔsə'daiək(l)], *a.* prosodiaque.

prosodic(al) [prə'sɔdik(l)], *a.* prosodique.

prosodist ['prɔsədist], *s.* **he's a competent Latin p.,** il sait bien la prosodie latine.

prosody ['prɔsədi], *s.* prosodie *f*.

prosoma [prou'soumə], *s. Arch:* prosoma *m*.

prosopite ['prɔsəpait], *s. Miner:* prosopite *f*.

prosopopoeia [prɔsoupə'pi:ə], *s. Rh:* prosopopée *f*.

prospect[1] ['prɔspekt], *s.* **1.** vue *f*; point *m* de vue; perspective *f*; paysage *m*; **wide p.,** horizon très étendu. **2.** (*a*) perspective, expectative *f*; **a sad p.,** une triste expectative; **to open up a new p. to s.o.,** ouvrir une nouvelle perspective à qn; **to have sth. in p.,** avoir qch. en perspective, en vue; (*b*) **there is very little p. of it,** on ne peut guère y compter; **there is no p. of their leaving,** il n'y a rien qui fasse prévoir leur départ; **no p. of agreement,** aucune perspective d'accord. **3.** *Min:* (*a*) prélèvement *m* d'essai (d'un terrain aurifère); (*b*) teneur *f* en or du prélèvement. **4.** *pl.* avenir *m*, espérances *fpl*; **future prospects of an undertaking,** perspectives d'avenir d'une entreprise; **the prospects of a mine,** l'avenir d'une mine; les espérances que donne une mine; **the prospects of the harvest are excellent,** la récolte s'annonce excellente; **prospects of success,** chances *f* de succès; **his prospects are brilliant,** son avenir est brillant; un brillant avenir s'ouvre devant lui; **to have fine prospects before one,** avoir un bel avenir devant soi. **5.** *Com:* client éventuel, possible.

prospect[2] [prə'spekt]. **1.** *v.i. Min: etc:* aller à la découverte; explorer; prospecter; **to p. for gold,** chercher de l'or. **2.** *v.tr.* prospecter (un terrain, une mine).

prospecting [prə'spektiŋ], *s.* (*a*) prospection *f*, recherche(s) *f*(*pl*); **oil p.,** recherches pétrolières, prospection pétrolière; **gold p., p. for gold,** prospection de l'or; **p. level,** (i) *Min:* galerie *f* de recherches, de prospection; (ii) *Geol: Archeol:* niveau *m*, étage *m*, de recherches, de prospection; **p. pit,** trou *m* de prospection; **p. shaft, p. tunnel,** puits *m*, tunnel *m*, de recherches, de prospection; **p. licence,** permis *m* de recherches, de prospection; (*b*) *Atom.Ph:* **p. audio-indicator,** radiophone *m* de prospection; audio-signaleur *m*, *pl.* audio-signaleurs; (*c*) **biological p.,** prospection biologique.

prospection [prə'spekʃ(ə)n], *s.* **1.** *Min: etc:* prospection *f*, recherche(s) *f*(*pl*). **2.** *Lit:* prévision *f*; prospective *f*.

prospective [prə'spektiv], *a.* **1.** qui ne regarde que l'avenir; **this law is only p.,** cette loi ne produira ses effets que dans l'avenir; **p. obligation,** obligation future; *For: etc:* **p. value,** valeur *f* d'avenir. **2.** en perspective; à venir; futur; **p. majority,** majorité *f* en perspective; **my p. son-in-law,** mon gendre en perspective; le fiancé de ma fille; **p. buyer,** acheteur éventuel.

prospector [prə'spektər], *s.* (*pers.*) prospecteur, -trice; (*for gold*) chercheur *m* d'or; **oil p.,** chercheur de pétrole, pétrolier *m*.

prospectus, *pl.* **-tuses** [prə'spektəs, -təsiz], *s.* (*a*) *Com:* prospectus *m*; réclame *f*; (*b*) *Fin:* appel *m* à la souscription publique.

prosper ['prɔspər]. **1.** *v.i.* prospérer, réussir; venir à bien; **his business is not prospering,** il est au-dessous de ses affaires; ses affaires ne vont pas. **2.** *v.tr. A: & Lit:* faire prospérer, faire réussir; favoriser; **(may) God p. you!** Dieu vous fasse prospérer! **each one gives as God has prospered him,** chacun donne selon ses moyens.

prosperity [prɔs'periti], *s.* prospérité *f*.

prosperous ['prɔspərəs], *a.* **1.** prospère, florissant, heureux; **p. look,** air *m* de prospérité; air prospère. **2.** favorable, propice; **p. winds,** vents *m* favorables.

prosperously ['prɔspərəsli], *adv.* heureusement, prospèrement.

prosperousness ['prɔspərəsnis], *s.* prospérité *f*; succès *m* (d'une entreprise).

prostaglandin [prɔstə'glændin], *s. Bio-Ch:* prostaglandine *f*.

prostate ['prɔsteit], *s. Anat:* prostate *f*.

prostatectomy [prɔstə'tektəmi], *s. Surg:* prostatectomie *f*.

prostatic [prɔs'tætik], *a. Anat:* prostatique.

prostatitis [prɔstə'taitis], *s. Med:* prostatite *f*.

prostatorrhea [prɔstætə'ri:ə], *s. Med:* prostatorrhée *f*.

prosternum [prou'stə:nəm], *s. Ent:* prosternum *m*.

prosthesis ['prɔsθisis], *s.* **1.** *Gram:* prosthèse *f*. **2.** *Surg: etc:* prothèse *f*; **dental p.,** prothèse dentaire.

prosthetic [prɔs'θetik]. **1.** *a. Gram:* prosthétique. **2.** *Surg: Dent:* (*a*) *a.* prothétique; (*b*) *s.pl.* (*usu. with sg. const.*) **prosthetics,** prothèse *f*.

prosthion ['prɔsθiən], *s. Anat:* prosthion *m*.

prosthodontia [prɔsθou'dɔnʃiə], *s.* prothèse *f* dentaire; appareil *m* (dentaire); **complete, partial, p.,** prothèse dentaire complète, partielle.

prosthodontist [prɔsθou'dɔntist], *s.* prothésiste *mf* dentaire.

prostitute[1] ['prɔstitju:t], *s.* prostituée *f*; **common p.,** professionnelle de la prostitution; *Jur:* **accused of living on a prostitute's earnings,** accusé de vagabondage spécial.

prostitute[2], *v.tr.* (*a*) prostituer (son corps, son honneur, son talent, etc.); (*b*) **to p. oneself,** se prostituer.

prostitution [prɔsti'tju:ʃ(ə)n], *s.* prostitution *f*; **male p.,** prostitution masculine.

prostitutor ['prɔstitju:tər], *s.* prostituteur *m* (de son talent, de son honneur).

prostrate[1] ['prɔstreit], *a.* **1.** prosterné; couché (à terre); étendu; **to lie p.,** être prosterné. **2.** abattu, accablé; *Med:* prostré; **p. with grief,** terrassé, anéanti, par le chagrin; effondré dans la douleur; **utterly p.,** dans l'anéantissement; **the patient is completely p. today,** le malade est très abattu aujourd'hui. **3.** *Bot:* (*of stem*) procombant.

prostrate[2], *v.tr.* **1.** coucher, étendre (à terre); **to p. oneself before s.o.,** se prosterner devant qn; tomber aux pieds de qn. **2.** abattre, renverser; *Med:* abattre; mettre dans un état de prostration; **prostrated by the heat, by fever,** accablé par la chaleur, par la fièvre.

prostration [prɔs'treiʃ(ə)n], *s.* **1.** prosternation *f*, prosternement *m*. **2.** abattement *m*, anéantissement *m*; *Med:* prostration *f*, affaissement *m*, accablement *m*, adynamie *f*; **in a state of complete p.,** dans un état d'effondrement complet.

prostyle ['proustail], *a. & s. Arch:* prostyle (*m*).

prosy ['prouzi], *a. F:* (*a*) (style) prosaïque, fastidieux, terre à terre; (*b*) *O:* (*of pers.*) verbeux, ennuyeux; rasant, assommant; (*of life*) monotone, fastidieux.

prosyllogism [prou'silədʒizm], *s.* prosyllogisme *m*.

protactinium [proutæk'tiniəm], *s. Ch:* protactinium *m*.

protagon ['proutəgɔn], *s. Ch: Physiol:* protagon *m*.

protagonism [prou'tægənizm], *s.* défense *f* (d'une doctrine, etc.).

protagonist [prɔ'tægənist], *s.* (*a*) *Gr.Th: etc:* protagoniste *m*; (*b*) protagoniste (d'une théorie, etc.).

protalization [proutəlai'zeiʃ(ə)n], *s. Metall:* protalisation *f* (de l'aluminium, etc.).

protalize ['proutəlaiz], *v.tr. Metall:* protaliser (l'aluminium, etc.).

protalized ['proutəlaizd], *a. Metall:* protalisé.

protamin(e) ['proutəm(a)in], *s. Bio-Ch:* protamine *f*.

protandric [prou'tændrik], *a. Z:* protandrique, protérandrique; *Bot:* protandre.

protandrous [prou'tændrəs], *a. Bot:* protandre.

protandry [prou'tændri], *s. Bot:* protandrie *f*.

protarsus [prou'ta:səs], *s. Ent: Arach:* protarse *m*.

protasis, *pl.* **-ases** ['prɔtəsis, -əsi:z], *s. Gr.Th: Gram:* protase *f*.

protatic [prou'tætik], *s. Gr.Th:* (personnage *m*, etc.) protatique.

protea ['proutiə], *s. Bot:* protée *f*.

Proteaceae [prouti'eisii:], *s.pl. Bot:* protéacées *f*.

protean ['proutiən], *a.* protéen, de Protée; protéiforme, protéique, changeant.

protease ['proutieis], *s. Ch:* protéase *f*.

protect [prə'tekt], *v.tr.* **1.** (*a*) protéger; **to p. s.o., sth., from sth., against sth.,** préserver, défendre, garder, abriter, garantir, qn, qch., de qch.; **straw to p. plants against the frost,** de la paille pour protéger les plantes du gel; **this tree will p. us from the rain,** cet arbre va nous servir d'abri, nous abriter, de la pluie; **well protected against the cold,** bien protégé du froid; **to p. s.o. against s.o.'s anger,** soustraire qn à la colère de qn; **to plant a hedge to p. oneself from one's neighbours,** planter une haie pour se protéger des regards indiscrets des voisins; *Mil:* **to p. a position from enfilade,** défiler un emplacement; **to p. a position from view,** mettre une position à l'abri des vues (de l'ennemi); *Rail:* (*with signals, etc.*) **to p. a train,** couvrir un train; (*b*) sauvegarder (les intérêts de qn, etc.); *St.Exch:* **to p. a book,** défendre une position; *Com:* **to p. a bill of exchange,** garantir le bon accueil d'une lettre de change; faire provision pour une lettre de change. **2.** *O:* protéger, patronner (qn); tenir (qn) en tutelle. **3.** *Pol.Ec:* protéger (une industrie).

protected [prə'tektid], *a.* protégé; **p. area,** zone protégée; **p. screw,** vis cachée; *Navy:* **p. cruiser,** croiseur protégé; *El:* **p. contacts,** contacts protégés; *Cmptr:* **p. locations,** positions réservées (en mémoire); *Cards:* **p. king,** roi gardé.

protecting[1] [prə'tektiŋ], *a.* protecteur, -trice; de protection, de garde; **p. wall,** mur *m*, paroi *f*, de protection; muraille *f* de défense; *El:* **p. resistor,** résistance *f* de protection.

protecting[2], *s.* = PROTECTION 1(*a*).

protection [prə'tekʃ(ə)n], *s.* **1.** (*a*) protection *f*, défense *f* (**against,** contre); sauvegarde *f* (des intérêts de qn, etc.); (*b*) **to be under s.o.'s p.,** être sous la protection, la sauvegarde, de qn; **under police p.,** sous la protection de la police; **under the p. of the law,** sous la tutelle des lois; **to claim the p. of the law,** demander la protection de la loi; **society for the p. of birds,** société protectrice des oiseaux; *Mil:* **p. (duty),** service *m* de sûreté; **p. on the march,** sûreté *f* en marche; (*c*) *O:* patronage *m* (d'un auteur, etc.). **2.** (*a*) *Pol.Ec:* protectionnisme *m*; protection; (*b*) *F:* **p. (racket),** chantage *m* (sous prétexte de protéger les commerçants, etc., contre le gangstérisme). **3.** (*a*) abri *m*, protection; **to erect a p. against the wind,** construire un abri contre le vent; (*b*) blindage *m*. **4.** sauf-conduit *m*, *pl.* sauf-conduits.

protectionism [prə'tekʃənizm], *s. Pol.Ec:* protectionnisme *m*.

protectionist [prə'tekʃənist], *a. & s. Pol.Ec:* protectionniste (*mf*).

protective [prə'tektiv], *a.* protecteur, -trice; **p. clothing,** vêtements protecteurs, de protection (contre la radiation, etc.); **p. screen,** écran protecteur; **p. steel plate,** plaque *f* de protection en acier; *Paint: etc:* **p. coating,** couche protectrice, enduit protecteur; **p. belt,** (i) *For:* rideau forestier; (ii) *Fort:* ceinture protectrice; *Mil:* **p. troops,** troupes *f* de couverture; éléments *m* de protection; *Pol.Ec:* **p. tariff,** tarif protecteur; *El:* **p. relay, tube,** relais, tube, protecteur; *Nat.Hist:* **p. colouring, coloration,** mimétisme *m* des couleurs; **p. resemblance,** mimétisme des formes.

protector [prə'tektər], *s.* **1.** (*pers.*) (*a*) protecteur, -trice; (*b*) *O:* patron, -onne, mécène *m* (des arts, etc.); (*c*) *Hist:* **the Lord P.,** le Protecteur (Oliver Cromwell). **2.** (dispositif) protecteur (d'une machine, d'un appareil, etc.); **boot p.,** ferrure *f* pour bottes; **lung p.,** protège-poumons *m inv*; **ear p.,** protège-oreilles *m inv*; *Dent:* **mouth p.,** prothèse protectrice.

protectorate [prə'tektərət], *s.* **1.** *Pol:* protectorat *m*, pays *m* sous protectorat. **2.** protectorat, fonction *f* de protecteur. **3.** gouvernement *m* sous un protecteur; *Eng.Hist:* **the P.,** le Protectorat (1653–59).

protectress [prə'tektris], *s.f.* protectrice.

protégé ['prɔti(d)ʒei, 'prɔteʒe], *s.* protégé, -ée.

Proteidae [prou'ti:idi], *s.pl. Amph:* protéidés *m*.

proteiform [prou'ti:ifɔ:m], *a.* protéiforme.

protein ['prouti:n], *s.* protéine *f*; **crude p.,** protéine brute; **p. therapy,** protéinothérapie *f*.

proteinate ['prouti:neit], *s. Pharm:* **silver p.,** protéinate *m* d'argent.

proteinuria [prouti:'njuəriə], *s. Med:* protéinurie *f*.

Protelytroptera [prouteli'trɔptərə], *s.pl. Ent: Paleont:* protélytroptères *m*.

pro tempore (*F:* **pro tem**) [prou'tem(pəri)]. **1.** *adv.* temporairement. **2.** *a.* temporaire.

proteolysis [prouti'ɔlisis], *s. Bio-Ch:* protéolyse *f*.

proteolytic [proutiou'litik], *a. Bio-Ch:* protéolytique.

proteose ['proutious], *s. Bio-Ch:* protéose *f*.

proterandry ['proutərændri], *s. Bot:* protérandrie *f*.

proteroglyph ['proutərouglif], *s. Rept:* protéroglyphe *m*.

Proteroglypha [proutərou'glifə], *s.pl. Rept:* protéroglyphes *m*.

proteroglyphic [proutərou'glifik], *a. Rept:* protéroglyphe.

proterogynous [proutə'rɔdʒinəs], *a. Bot:* protogyne, protérogyne.

proterogyny [proutə'rɔdʒini], *s. Biol:* protérogynie *f*.

proterosaurian, proterosaurus [proutərou'sɔ:riən, -'sɔ:rəs], *s. Paleont:* protérosaurus *m*.

Proterozoic [proutərou'zouik], *a. & s. Geol:* protérozoïque (*m*).

Protesilaus [proutesi'leiəs]. *Pr.n.m. Gr.Myth:* Protésilas.

protest[1] ['proutest], *s.* **1.** protestation *f*; **to make a p.,** protester; faire des représentations; **to make no p.,** ne pas protester; **to raise a strong p.,** élever des protestations énergiques; **his whole life is one p. against . . .,** sa vie entière proteste contre . . .; **general p. of the people,** soulèvement *m* du peuple; (*of action*) **to give rise to protests,** soulever des protestations; **p. meeting,** réunion *f* de protestation; *Jur:* **p. in writing,** réserve *f*; **under p.,** (i) (signer, etc.) sous réserve; (ii) (faire qch.) à son corps défendant, en protestant; *Jur:* **to act under p.,** protester de violence. **2.** *Com:* protêt *m*; **certified p.,** protêt authentique; **p. for non-acceptance,** protêt faute d'acceptation; **non-payment and p.,** protêt faute de paiement; **to make a p.,** lever, faire, protêt. **3. ship's p.,** rapport *m* de mer; déclaration *f* d'avaries; procès-verbal *m* des avaries; **to note a p.,** faire un rapport de mer.

protest[2] [prə'test]. **1.** *v.tr.* (*a*) protester; **to p. one's innocence, one's good faith,** protester de son innocence, de sa bonne foi; (*b*) *Com:* **to p. a bill,** (faire) protester un effet, une lettre de change; lever protêt d'une lettre de change; (*c*) *NAm:* protester contre, réclamer contre, dénoncer (qch.). **2.** *v.i.* protester, réclamer, s'élever (**against,** contre); **to p. loudly,** pousser les hauts cris.

protestable [prə'testəbl], *a. Com:* (effet, etc.) protestable.

protestant ['prɔtist(ə)nt], *a. & s.* **1.** *Rel:* (*usu. cap.* **P**) protestant, -ante; **the P. church,** l'église protestante; = l'église réformée. **2.** (*also* [prə'test(ə)nt]) protestateur, -trice; protestataire *mf*.

protestantism ['prɔtistəntizm], *s. Rel:* protestantisme *m*.

protestantize ['prɔtistəntaiz], *v.tr. Rel:* convertir (qn) au protestantisme.

protestation [prɔtes'teiʃ(ə)n], *s.* **1.** protestation *f* (**against,** contre). **2.** protestation, déclaration *f* (de sa foi, etc.); **to make a solemn p. that . . .,** protester solennellement que . . .; **solemn protestations of friendship, of good faith,** protestations solennelles d'amitié, de bonne foi.

protested [prə'testid], *a. Com:* (effet, etc.) protesté.

protester, protestor [prə'testər], *a.* **1.** protestateur, -trice; protestataire *mf*. **2.** *Com:* débiteur *m* qui a fait protester un effet.

protesting[1] [prə'testiŋ], *a.* (voix, etc.) de protestation.

protesting[2], *s.* protestation(s) *f*(*pl*).

protestingly [prə'testiŋli], *adv.* en protestant.
Proteus ['proutiəs]. **1.** *Pr.n.m. Myth:* Protée. **2.** *s.* (*a*) *Rept:* protée *m*; (*b*) *Bac:* proteus *m.*
prothalamion, prothalamium [prouθə'leimiən, -miəm], *s. Lit:* prothalame *m.*
prothallium, prothallus [prou'θæliəm, -'θæləs], *s. Bot:* prothallium *m*, prothalle *m.*
prothesis ['prɔθisis], *s.* **1.** *Ecc:* (*a*) prothèse *f* (des éléments); (*b*) autel *m* de la prothèse; crédence *f.* **2.** = PROSTHESIS 1.
prothetic [prou'θetik], *a.* = PROSTHETIC 1.
prothonotary [prouθou'noutəri], *s.* = PROTONOTARY.
prothoracic [prouθɔ'ræsik], *a. Ent:* prothoracique.
prothorax [prou'θɔ:ræks], *s. Ent:* prothorax *m.*
prothrombin [prou'θrɔmbin], *s. Physiol:* prothrombine *f.*
protid(e) ['prout(a)id], *s.* protide *m.*
protist, *pl.* **protista** ['proutist, prou'tistə], *s. Biol:* protiste *m.*
protistology [proutis'tɔlədʒi], *s.* protistologie *f.*
Protium[1] ['proutiəm], *s. Bot:* protium *m.*
protium[2], *s. Ch:* protium *m.*
proto- ['proutou], *comb.fm.* proto-.
protoactinium [proutouæk'tiniəm], *s. Ch:* protactinium *m.*
Protoascomycetes ['proutouæskoumai'si:ti:z], *s.pl. Fung:* protoascomycètes *m.*
proto-Attic [proutou'ætik], *a. Cer:* proto-attique, *pl.* proto-attiques.
Protobasidiomycetes [proutoubæ'sidioumai'si:ti:z], *s.pl. Fung:* protobasidiomycètes *m.*
protoblast ['proutoublæst], *s. Biol:* protoblaste *m.*
Protoblattoptera [proutoublæ'tɔptərə], *s.pl. Ent: Paleont:* protoblattoptères *m.*
protocanonical [proutoukæ'nɔnik(ə)l], *a. B:* protocanonique.
protoceratops [proutou'serətɔps], *s. Rept: Paleont:* protoceratops *m.*
protochlorophyll [proutou'klɔ:rəfil], *s. Bot:* protochlorophylle *f.*
Protochordata [proutoukɔ:'deitə], *s.pl. Nat.Hist:* protoc(h)ordés *m.*
protococcus, *pl.* **-cocci** [proutou'kɔkəs, -'kɔksai], *s. Bot:* protocoque *m*, protococcus *m.*
protocol ['proutəkɔl], *s.* **1.** *Dipl: etc:* protocole *m.* **2.** *Jur: etc:* protocole (d'une charte, etc.).
protocolar ['proutəkɔlər], *a.* protocolaire.
protoconch ['proutoukɔŋk], *s. Moll:* protoconque *f.*
protocone ['proutoukoun], *s. Anat:* protocone *m.*
proto-Corinthian [proutoukə'rinθiən], *a. Arch: etc:* protocorinthien.
Protodonata [proutoudə'neitə], *s.pl. Ent: Paleont:* protodonates *m.*
proto-Doric [proutou'dɔrik], *a. Arch:* protodorique.
Protoephemeroptera [proutouifemə'rɔptərə], *s.pl. Ent: Paleont:* protéphémères *m.*
protogenic [proutou'dʒi:nik], *a.* protogène.
proto-Germanic [proutoudʒə:'mænik], *a. & s. Ling:* protogermanique (*m*).
protogine ['proutoudʒ(a)in], *s. Geol:* protogine *m.*
protogynic, protogynous [proutou'dʒainik, -'dʒainəs], *a. Nat.Hist:* protogynique.
protogyny [prou'tɔdʒini], *s. Nat.Hist:* protogynie *f.*
Protohemiptera [proutouhe'miptərə], *s.pl. Ent: Paleont:* protohémiptères *m.*
protohippus [proutou'hipəs], *s. Paleont:* protohippus *m.*
protohistorian [proutouhi'stɔ:riən], *s.* protohistorien, -ienne.
protohistoric [proutouhi'stɔrik], *a.* protohistorique.
protohistory [proutou'hist(ə)ri], *s.* protohistoire *f.*
protolysis [prou'tɔlisis], *s. Ch:* protolyse *f.*
protoma, protome [prou'toumə, -'toumi], *s. Arch: etc:* protomé *m.*
protomartyr [proutou'mɑ:tər], *s.* protomartyr *m.*
proto-Mycenean [proutoumai'si:niən], *a.* protomycénien.
proton ['proutɔn], *s. Atom.Ph:* proton *m*; **cosmic ray p.,** proton (de rayonnement) cosmique; **negative p.,** proton négatif; **recoil p.,** proton de recul; **p. synchrotron,** synchrotron *m* à protons; **p. accelerator,** accélérateur *m* de protons; **p. beam, cloud,** faisceau *m*, nuage *m*, de protons; **p. emitter, generator,** émetteur *m*, générateur *m*, de protons; **p. microscope,** microscope *m* protonique; **p. resonance,** résonance *f* protonique; **p. wave, spectrum,** onde *f*, spectre *m*, protonique; **p. scattering,** diffusion *f* des protons.
protonema, *pl.* **-nemata** [proutou'ni:mə, -'nemətə], *s. Moss:* protonéma *m.*
protonic [prou'tɔnik], *a. Atom.Ph:* protonique.
protonotary [proutou'nɔtəri], *s. Ecc: Jur: A:* protonotaire *m*; **p. apostolic(al),** protonotaire apostolique.
protopathic [proutou'pæθik], *a. Psy:* protopathique.
protopathy ['proutoupæθi], *s. Psy:* protopathie *f.*
protophosphide [proutou'fɔsfaid], *s. Ch:* protophosphure *m.*
Protophyta [prou'tɔfitə], *s.pl. Nat.Hist:* protophytes *m.*
protophyte ['proutoufait], *s. Nat.Hist:* protophyte *m.*
protoplasm ['proutouplæzm], *s. Biol:* protoplasme *m*, protoplasma *m.*
protoplasmic [prou'touplæzmik], *a. Biol:* protoplasmique.
protoplast ['proutouplæst], *s.* **1.** *A:* prototype *m.* **2.** *Biol:* protoplaste *m.*
protopterus [prou'tɔptərəs], *s. Ich:* protoptère *m.*
Protorthoptera [proutɔ:'θɔptərə], *s.pl. Ent: Paleont:* protorthoptères *m.*
protospore ['proutouspɔ:ər], *s. Biol:* protospore *f.*
protosulphide [proutou'sʌlfaid], *s. Ch:* protosulfure *m.*
Prototheria [proutou'θiəriə], *s.pl. Z:* protothériens *m.*
prototropic [proutou'trɔpik], *a. Atom.Ph:* prototropique.
prototropy [prou'tɔtrəpi], *s. Atom.Ph:* prototropie *f.*
prototypal [proutou'taip(ə)l], *a.* prototypique.
prototype ['proutətaip], *s.* (*a*) prototype *m*; *Ind:* **p. series,** présérie *f*; **p. aircraft, car,** avion *m*, voiture *f*, prototype; **exhibit p.,** prototype de démonstration; **p. tests,** essais *m* d'homologation, de qualification; **the war chariot of antiquity may be considered as the p. of the modern tank,** le char utilisé dans les guerres de l'Antiquité peut être considéré comme l'ancêtre, le précurseur, de notre char moderne; (*b*) *Meas:* étalon *m*, prototype; **the p. metre,** le mètre étalon.
prototypic(al) [proutou'tipik(l)], *a.* prototypique.
protoxide [prou'tɔksaid], *s. Ch:* protoxyde *m.*
Protozoa [proutə'zouə], *s.pl.* protozoaires *m.*
protozoal, protozoic [proutə'zouəl, -ik], *a.* protozoaire.
protozoan, protozoon [proutə'zouən, -ɔn], *s.* protozoaire *m.*
protozoology [proutouzou'ɔlədʒi], *s.* protozoologie *f.*
protract [prə'trækt], *v.tr.* **1.** prolonger, allonger; faire durer; traîner (une affaire) en longueur. **2.** *Surv:* relever (un terrain); faire le tracé (d'un terrain, etc.) à l'échelle.
protracted [prə'træktid], *a.* prolongé; **p. stay,** séjour prolongé.
protractedly [prə'træktidli], *adv.* longuement.
protractile [prou'træktail], *a.* protractile; extensile.
protraction [prə'trækʃ(ə)n], *s.* **1.** prolongation *f* (d'un procès, etc.); longueur *f* (d'une procédure, etc.); *Atom.Ph:* **p. dose,** étalement *m* de dose (d'irradiation). **2.** *Anat:* (*a*) protraction *f* (d'un muscle); (*b*) **p. of the mandible,** prognathie mandibulaire, inférieure; **p. of the maxilla,** protrusion *f* du maxillaire supérieur, prognathie supérieure. **3.** *Surv:* levé *m* (d'un terrain, etc.) à l'échelle; réduction *f* à l'échelle.
protractive [prə'træktiv], *a.* qui se prolonge; qui dure.
protractor [prə'træktər], *s.* **1.** *Mth:* rapporteur *m*; **circular p.,** rapporteur cercle entier, à limbe complet; **semi-circular p.,** rapporteur demi-cercle; **bevel p.,** rapporteur d'atelier; sauterelle graduée; **bubble p.,** rapporteur à niveau. **2.** *Anat:* **p. (muscle),** (muscle) protracteur (*m*).
protrude [prə'tru:d]. **1.** *v.tr.* (*a*) (faire) sortir, pousser en avant, avancer; *O:* **to p. one's tongue,** tirer la langue; (*b*) *Lit:* importuner. **2.** *v.i.* s'avancer, faire saillie, déborder; **the tall buildings that p. from, above, the hillsides,** les grands bâtiments qui font saillie sur les collines; **his teeth p. (too far),** il a les dents proéminentes.
protruding [prə'tru:diŋ], *a.* en saillie; saillant; **p. forehead,** front bombé; **p. chin,** menton *m* en saillie; **p. eyes,** yeux exorbités, saillants; **p. lips,** grosses lèvres; lèvres épaisses, lippues; **p. teeth,** dents proéminentes.
protrusile [prou'tru:sail], *a.* protractile; extensile.
protrusion [prə'tru:ʒ(ə)n], *s.* **1.** sortie *f*, saillie *f*; poussée *f* en avant. **2.** saillie, protubérance *f*; *Anat:* protrusion *f*; **mandibular p.,** prognathie mandibulaire, inférieure; **maxillary p.,** prognathie supérieure, protrusion du maxillaire supérieur; **double p.,** prognathie bimaxillaire.
protrusive [prə'tru:siv], *a.* saillant; en saillie; proéminent; qui avance; *Anat:* **p. jaw,** mâchoire *f* prognathe.
protuberance [prə'tju:bərəns], *s.* protubérance *f*; protrusion *f*, saillie *f*; *Anat:* **mental p.,** éminence mentonnière; **bony p.,** protubérance osseuse.
protuberant [prə'tju:bərənt], *a.* protubérant.
protuberantial [proutju:bə'rænʃəl], *a. Astr:* protubérantiel.
Protura [prou'tju:rə], *s.pl. Ent:* protoures *m.*
proud [praud], *a.* **1.** (*a*) fier, orgueilleux; hautain, altier; **as p. as Lucifer, as a peacock, as Punch,** fier comme Artaban, comme un coq; il est glorieux, fier, comme un paon; le roi n'est pas son cousin; (*b*) **too p. to fight, to complain,** trop fier pour se battre, pour se plaindre; **to be proud of sth., of having done sth.,** être fier, s'enorgueillir, se glorifier, de qch., d'avoir fait qch.; **to be unduly p. of sth.,** tirer vanité de qch.; (*c*) **to be p. to do sth.,** se faire honneur de faire qch.; **I shall be p. to help,** je ne demande pas mieux que de vous aider; **the proudest day of my life,** le plus beau jour de ma vie; *F:* **to do s.o. p.,** (i) faire beaucoup d'honneur à qn, flatter qn; (ii) se mettre en frais pour qn; **to do oneself p.,** se bien soigner; ne se priver de rien. **2.** *Lit:* (*a*) altier, hautain, superbe; **a p. steed,** un fier coursier; **a p. beauty,** une beauté orgueilleuse; (*b*) (*of view, city, etc.*) beau, noble, imposant, magnifique, superbe. **3.** (*a*) **p. waters,** grosses eaux; (*b*) **p. flesh,** (i) *Med:* chair fongueuse, baveuse; tissu bourgeonnant; fongosité *f*; (ii) *Surg: Vet:* bouillon *m*; (*c*) **p. nail, rivet,** clou *m*, rivet *m*, qui dépasse, qui fait saillie; (*of condenser*) **p. mica,** lame de mica désaffleurante. **4.** *adv. P:* **you've done me p.,** vous m'avez régalé.
proudly ['praudli], *adv.* fièrement, orgueilleusement; avec fierté; altièrement, d'un air altier.
Proustian ['pru:stiən], *a. Lit:* proustien.
proustite ['pru:stait], *s. Miner:* proustite *f.*
provable ['pru:vəbl], *a.* que l'on peut prouver; prouvable, démontrable.
prove [pru:v], *v.* (*p.p.* **proved,** *esp. NAm: Scot: also* **proven** ['pru:v(ə)n, 'prou-])
I. *v.tr.* **1.** (*a*) *A: & Tchn:* éprouver; faire l'essai de; mettre à l'épreuve; essayer (l'or, un cheval, une arme à feu); **to p. a beam (to see if it is sound),** sonder une poutre; **proved remedy,** remède éprouvé; **to p. the patience of s.o.,** mettre à l'épreuve la patience de qn; **to be proved by adversity,** passer par le creuset de l'adversité; *B:* **this he said to prove him,** or il disait cela pour l'éprouver; (*b*) *Mth: O:* **to p. a sum,** vérifier un calcul; faire la preuve d'un calcul; (*c*) (*freemasonry*) tuiler (un frère); (*d*) *Min:* reconnaître (la nature d'un terrain, etc.); (*e*) *Typ: Engr:* tirer une épreuve d'essai (de la matière, d'une planche, d'un cliché). **2.** (*a*) prouver, démontrer, établir, faire foi de (la vérité de qch., etc.); constater (un fait); **it remains to be proved,** cela n'est pas encore prouvé; **to p. one's identity,** justifier de son identité; **to p. one's goodwill,** témoigner de sa bonne volonté; **to p. my case,** comme preuve à l'appui; *Jur:* **proved damages,** préjudice justifié; **all the evidence goes to p. that . . .,** les témoignages concourent à prouver que . . .; **the plaintiff proved that he could not find . . .,** le plaignant a justifié ne pas pouvoir trouver . . .; **this letter proves him to be still alive,** cette lettre prouve qu'il est encore en vie; *Lit:* **this hope is already proven a dream,** il apparaît déjà que cet espoir n'était qu'un rêve; *Jur: Scot:* **not proven,** (verdict *m* de) culpabilité non avérée; (verdict de) non-lieu *m* faute de preuves; *Prov:* **the exception proves the rule,** l'exception confirme la règle; **he spoils his case who tries to prove too much,** qui veut trop prouver ne prouve rien; (*b*) *Jur:* **to p. a will,** homologuer un testament; établir la validité d'un testament; **to p. claims in bankruptcy and liquidation,** produire à une liquidation, à une faillite; (*c*) **to p. oneself,** faire ses preuves.
II. *v.i.* se montrer, se trouver, être; **to p. useful,** se trouver, être reconnu, utile; **if what you say proves (to be) true,** si ce que vous dites est vrai, se confirme; **many of his observations have proved correct,** beaucoup d'entre ses observations se sont affirmées justes; **the news proved false,** la nouvelle s'est avérée fausse; **the document proved to be a forgery,** on a découvert que le document était un faux; **the undertaking is proving unproductive,** l'entreprise s'avère, se révèle, improductive; **to p. unequal to one's task,** se révéler, se montrer, au-dessous de sa tâche.
III. (*compound verbs*) **1. prove out,** *v.i. U.S:* donner satisfaction.
2. prove up, *v.i. U.S:* (*a*) donner satisfaction; (*b*) **to p. up on a claim,** faire valoir ses droits à une revendication; **to p. up on a concession,** accomplir toutes les formalités requises pour obtenir une concession.
provection [prou'vekʃ(ə)n], *s. Ling:* **1.** mutation *f* consonantique. **2.** agglutination *f* d'une consonne finale avec le mot suivant.
proven ['pru:v(ə)n, 'prou-], *a.* confirmé; éprouvé; *Jur: Scot:* (*of verdict*) **non p.,** de culpabilité non avérée faute de preuves; *Cmptr:* (*of programme, etc.*) **field p.,** rodé, au point.
Provençal [prɔvɑ̃:sɑ:l]. **1.** *Geog:* (*a*) *a.* provençal, -aux;

(*b*) *s.* Provençal, -ale. **2.** *s. Ling:* provençal *m.*

Provence [prɔ'vɑ̃:s], *Pr.n. Geog:* Provence*f.*

provender ['prɔvindər], *s.* (*a*) *Husb:* fourrage *m*, affourragement *m*, provende *f*; (*b*) *O:* nourriture *f.*

prover ['pru:vər], *s.* **1.** *Tex:* (*machine*) (**linen, etc.**) **p.**, compte-fils *m inv.* **2.** *Typ:* (*pers.*) tireur *m* d'épreuves.

proverb ['prɔvə:b], *s.* proverbe *m*; **to have the force of a p.**, **to become a p.**, passer en proverbe; *B:* **the Book of Proverbs**, le Livre des Proverbes.

proverbial [prə'və:biəl], *a.* proverbial, -aux; passé en proverbe; **his meanness is p.**, son avarice est proverbiale, est passée en proverbe.

proverbially [prə'və:biəli], *adv.* proverbialement; **he's p. mean, stupid**, son avarice, sa bêtise, est passée en proverbe.

provide [prə'vaid]. **1.** (*a*) *v.i.* **to p. against sth.**, se pourvoir, se prémunir, se précautionner, prendre des mesures, contre (une attaque, etc.); **to p. against a danger**, aller au-devant d'un danger; parer à un danger; **to p. against accidents**, parer à l'imprévu; obvier aux éventualités; **to p. for an eventuality**, pourvoir à, prévoir, une éventualité; prendre des mesures en vue d'une éventualité; **expenses provided for in the budget**, dépenses prévues au budget; **to p. for urgent needs**, parer aux besoins urgents; **this has been provided for**, on y a pourvu; *Ins:* **this risk is not provided for in the policy**, ce risque n'est pas prévu dans la police; *Com:* **to p. for a bill**, faire provision pour une lettre de change; (*b*) *v.tr.* stipuler (**that,** que + *ind.*); **the contract provides that cases of dispute shall go to arbitration**, il est stipulé que tout cas contentieux sera soumis à l'arbitrage; **the law provides that. . .**, la loi porte, dispose, que . . .. **2.** (*a*) *v.tr.* fournir; **to p. s.o. with sth.**, fournir qch. à qn; pourvoir, munir, fournir, approvisionner, qn de qch.; **to p. an exit**, (i) (*of passage, etc.*) fournir une sortie; (ii) (*of architect*) ménager une sortie; **to p. a regular bus service to the airport**, assurer un service régulier d'autobus pour l'aéroport; **to p. an opportunity for s.o. to do sth.**, ménager à qn l'occasion de faire qch.; *Com:* **to p. a bill with acceptance**, revêtir un effet de l'acceptation; (*b*) *v.i.* **to p. for s.o.**, (i) pourvoir aux besoins, à l'entretien, de qn; subvenir aux besoins de qn; (ii) mettre qn à l'abri du besoin; assurer le sort de qn; **to p. for oneself**, se suffire; **to be provided for**, être bien nanti; être à l'abri du besoin; avoir son pain assuré; **to be well, amply, provided for**, avoir grandement de quoi vivre; **to be poorly provided for**, être réduit à la portion congrue; (*c*) *v.i.* **he provided for everything**, il a subvenu à tout; **the Lord will p.**, Dieu y pourvoira, nous viendra en aide. **3.** *v.tr. Ecc: A:* **to p. an incumbent to a benefice**, désigner un ecclésiastique à un bénéfice.

provided [prə'vaidid]. **1.** *a. A:* **p. school**, école communale. **2.** *conj.* **p. (that)**, pourvu que (+ *sub.*); à condition que (+ *ind. or sub.*); sous (la) réserve que (+ *ind.*); en admettant que (+ *sub.*); si seulement (+ *ind.*); **p. there is enough**, pourvu qu'il y ait, si seulement il y a, assez; **you may stay p. you keep quiet**, vous pouvez rester à condition de garder le silence; **a 5% discount p. (that) you pay cash**, une remise de 5% à condition que vous payiez comptant; **you will get better p. you take a few precautions**, vous vous rétablirez moyennant quelques précautions.

providence ['prɔvid(ə)ns], *s.* **1.** (*a*) prévoyance *f*, prudence *f*; sagesse *f*; (*b*) économie *f*, épargne *f.* **2.** (*a*) providence (divine); **there is a special p. for . . .**, il y a une providence particulière qui veille sur . . .; (*b*) **by a special p.**, par une intervention providentielle.

provident ['prɔvid(ə)nt], *a.* **1.** prévoyant; **p. society**, société *f* de prévoyance. **2.** économe, frugal, -aux.

providential [prɔvi'denʃ(ə)l], *a.* (secours, etc.) providentiel.

providentialism [prɔvi'denʃəlizm], *s.* providentialisme *m.*

providentially [prɔvi'denʃəli], *adv.* providentiellement; par une intervention providentielle.

providently ['prɔvidəntli], *adv.* avec prévoyance; d'une manière prévoyante.

provider [prə'vaidər], *s.* pourvoyeur, -euse; fournisseur, -euse; **the family p.**, le gagne-pain de la famille; (*of husband*) **he's a good p.**, il pourvoit bien aux besoins de sa famille.

providing [prə'vaidiŋ], *conj.* **p. (that)** = PROVIDED 2.

province ['prɔvins], *s.* **1.** province *f* (d'un pays, d'un archevêque, etc.); **in the provinces**, en province. **2.** *Jur: etc:* juridiction *f*, ressort *m*, compétence *f* (d'un tribunal); sphère *f* d'action (de qn); **that is not (within) my p.**, ce n'est pas, cela sort, de mon domaine, de mon ressort, de ma compétence; cela n'est pas dans ma juridiction; cela ne rentre pas dans mes attributions.

provincial [prə'vinʃ(ə)l]. **1.** *a. & s.* provincial, -ale, *pl.* -aux, -ales; **p. theatre**, théâtre *m* de province; **he's a real p.**, il est bien de sa province. **2.** *s.m. Ecc:* provincial.

provincialate [prə'vinʃəleit], *s. Ecc:* provincialat *m.*

provincialism [prə'vinʃəlizm], *s.* provincialisme *m.*

provinciality [prəvinʃi'æliti], *s.* provincialité *f*; caractère provincial.

provincialize [prə'vinʃəlaiz], *v.tr.* rendre provincial; **to become provincialized**, se provincialiser.

provincially [prə'vinʃəli], *adv.* provincialement.

provine [prou'vain], *v.tr. Vit:* provigner.

proving ['pru:viŋ], *s.* **1.** (*a*) épreuve *f*; essai *m* (de bon fonctionnement); *Tchn:* **p. bench**, banc *m* d'épreuve, d'essai; **p. ground**, (i) terrain *m* d'essai, d'expériences (de matériel roulant, etc.); (ii) *Artil:* polygone *m* d'essai, d'expériences; (iii) *Av:* aérodrome *m* d'essai; (*b*) *Mth: O:* vérification *f* (d'un calcul); (*c*) *Min:* reconnaissance *f* (d'un terrain); (*d*) *Typ:* tirage *m* d'une épreuve d'essai. **2.** (*a*) preuve *f*, démonstration *f*, établissement *m* (de la vérité de qch.); constatation *f* (d'un fait); (*b*) *Jur:* homologation *f* (d'un testament).

provining [prou'vainiŋ], *s. Vit:* provignage *m*, provignement *m.*

provirus [prou'vaiərəs], *s. Bac:* provirus *m.*

provision[1] [prə'viʒ(ə)n], *s.* **1.** (*a*) **p. for sth., against sth.**, prise *f* des dispositions nécessaires pour assurer qch., pour parer à qch.; **p. for the education of one's children is a duty**, c'est un devoir d'assurer l'éducation de ses enfants; **to make p. for sth., to secure sth.**, pourvoir à qch.; prendre les dispositions *f* nécessaires pour assurer qch.; **no p. has been made for it**, on n'y a pas pourvu; **the law makes no p. for a case of this kind**, la loi n'a pas prévu un cas semblable; **we have made provisions to this effect**, nous avons pris des dispositions dans ce sens; **to make p. for one's family**, (i) pourvoir aux besoins, (ii) assurer l'avenir, de sa famille; **to make p. against sth.**, se pourvoir, prendre des mesures, prendre des précautions, contre qch.; **to make a p. for s.o.**, assurer une pension à qn; (*b*) **p. of the necessities of life**, fourniture *f* des nécessités de la vie; **p. and issue of coins**, frappe *f* et émission *f* de monnaies; **p. of ammunition**, ravitaillement *m* en munitions; *Com:* **p. of capital**, prestation *f* de capitaux. **2.** (*a*) *Com:* provision *f*, réserve *f*; **p. for depreciation of investments**, prévision *f* pour moins-value de portefeuille; (*b*) **provisions**, provisions (de bouche), comestibles *m*; *Nau: etc:* **to lay in a store of provisions**, faire des vivres *m*; **wholesale p. business**, maison *f* d'alimentation en gros; *A:* **p. dealer**, marchand, -ande, de comestibles; *Nau:* **p. room**, cambuse *f.* **3.** article *m* (d'un traité); clause *f*, stipulation *f* (d'un contrat); **provisions of a convention**, dispositions d'une convention; **matter that comes within the provisions of the act**, question *f* qui rentre dans les dispositions du décret; **there is no p. to the contrary**, il n'y a pas de clause contraire; **to come within the provisions of the law**, tomber sous le coup de la loi; *Hist:* **the Provisions of Oxford**, les Provisions d'Oxford (1258).

provision[2], *v.tr.* approvisionner, ravitailler (une armée, un navire, etc.).

provisional [prə'viʒən(ə)l], *a.* provisoire; *Jur:* provisionnel; **p. judgment**, jugement *m* par provision; sentence *f* provisoire; **p. duty**, fonctions *f* intérimaires, temporaires; **p. government**, gouvernement *m* provisoire; intérimat *m*; *Pol:* **P. I.R.A.**, I.R.A. provisoire.

provisionally [prə'viʒən(ə)li], *adv.* provisoirement, par provision, intérimairement; *Jur:* provisionnellement; **appointed p.**, nommé à titre provisoire; **to sign an agreement p.**, signer un engagement sous condition; *Mil:* **conscript exempted p.**, conscrit *m* en sursis; sursitaire *m.*

provisioning [prə'viʒəniŋ], *s.* = PROVISIONMENT.

provisionment [prə'viʒənmənt], *s. A:* approvisionnement *m*; amunitionnement *m* (d'une armée, etc.); alimentation *f* (d'un marché, d'une ville).

proviso, *pl.* **-oes** [prə'vaizou, -ouz], *s.* clause conditionnelle; condition *f* (d'un contrat); stipulation *f*; **with the p. that . . .**, à condition que . . .; **subject to this p. I agree with you**, cette restriction faite je suis d'accord avec vous.

provisory [prə'vaizəri], *a.* **1.** (*of clause, etc.*) qui énonce une stipulation; conditionnel. **2.** (gouvernement *m*) provisoire. **3.** (soin *m*) qui pare à toute éventualité.

provitamin [prou'vitəmin], *s. Biol:* provitamine *f.*

provo ['prɔvou], *s. Pol: F:* membre *m* de l'I.R.A. provisoire.

provocation [prɔvə'keiʃ(ə)n], *s.* (*a*) provocation *f*; **he gets angry on, at, the slightest p.**, il se fâche à la moindre provocation, à la moindre incitation; **to act under p.**, agir sous le coup de la colère; **he struck the blow under great p.**, il a frappé, mais il avait été provoqué; (*b*) agacerie *f.*

provocative [prə'vɔkətiv]. **1.** *a.* (*a*) provocateur, -trice; provocant; (*b*) (sourire, etc.) aguichant. **2.** *s.* stimulant *m*; *esp.* aphrodisiaque *m.*

provoke [prə'vouk], *v.tr.* **1.** (*a*) provoquer, pousser, inciter (**s.o. to do sth.**, qn à faire qch.); **to p. s.o. to anger**, mettre qn en colère; (*b*) irriter, fâcher, impatienter, contrarier, agacer, exaspérer (qn); mettre (qn) en colère; **to p. a dog**, exciter un chien. **2.** exciter, faire naître (la curiosité, etc.); provoquer (la gaieté); stimuler (l'appétit); soulever (une passion, l'indignation); **to p. a smile**, faire naître un sourire; faire sourire les auditeurs.

provoker [prə'voukər], *s.* provocateur, -trice.

provoking [prə'voukiŋ], *a.* (*a*) irritant, contrariant, impatientant; **a p. child**, un enfant insupportable, exaspérant; **how p. you are!** que vous êtes agaçant, énervant, exaspérant! (*b*) (sourire, etc.) provocant.

provokingly [prə'voukiŋli], *adv.* d'une manière irritante, contrariante, exaspérante; **he was p. polite**, sa politesse me donnait sur les nerfs.

provost, *s.* **1.** ['prɔvəst], (*a*) *Sch:* (*at Oxford, Cambridge*) principal *m* (de certains collèges universitaires); (*b*) *Scot:* maire *m*; **the Lord P. of Edinburgh**, le Lord Maire d'Édimbourg; (*c*) *Hist: Ecc: A:* prévôt *m*; **Grand P. of France, of the Household**, Grand Prévôt de France, de l'Hôtel. **2.** ['prɔvou]. *Mil:* **p. marshal**, grand prévôt; **assistant p. marshal**, prévôt; **p. sergeant**, sergent *m* de police (militaire); **p. duty**, service prévôtal; prévôté *f.*

provostry ['prɔvəstri], *s. Hist:* prévôté *f.*

provostship ['prɔvəstʃip], *s.* **1.** (*a*) *Sch:* principalat *m* (de certains collèges universitaires); (*b*) *Scot:* mairie *f*; charge *f* de maire. **2.** *Hist:* prévôté *f.*

prow [prau], *s.* proue *f*, avant *m* (d'un navire).

prowess ['prauis], *s. Lit:* **1.** prouesse *f*, vaillance *f*; **deeds of p.**, prouesses, exploits *m.* **2.** exploit.

prowl[1] [praul], *s.* (*a*) action *f* de rôder (en quête de proie); (*of lion, etc.*) **to go on the p.**, partir en chasse; *F:* (*of pers.*) **to be always on the p.**, être toujours à rôder; être toujours en quête de bonnes fortunes; (*b*) *U.S: F:* **p. car**, voiture *f* de patrouille (de police).

prowl[2]. **1.** *v.i.* (*a*) (*of animal*) rôder en quête de proie; (*b*) **to p. about the streets**, rôder par toute la ville. **2.** *v.tr.* **to p. the streets**, rôder les rues.

prowler ['praulər], *s.* rôdeur, -euse.

prox. [prɔks], *adv. Com: O:* = PROXIMO.

proximal ['prɔksim(ə)l], *a.* proximal, -aux.

proximate ['prɔksimət], *a.* **1.** proche, prochain, immédiat; *Ch:* **p. analysis**, analyse immédiate; *Phil:* **p. cause**, cause prochaine. **2.** approximatif.

proximately ['prɔksimətli], *adv.* **1.** immédiatement; sans intermédiaire. **2.** approximativement.

proximity [prɔk'simiti], *s.* proximité *f.* **1. its p. to London**, sa situation à proximité de Londres; **p. to the station is an advantage**, le voisinage de la gare est un avantage; **in the p. of a town**, à proximité d'une ville; **in p. to**, à proximité de; près de. **2. p. of blood**, proximité du sang; proche parenté. **3.** *Artil:* **p. fuse**, fusée *f* à influence; fusée de proximité.

proximo ['prɔksimou], *adv. Com: O:* (du mois) prochain; **on the third p.**, le trois (du mois) prochain.

proxy ['prɔksi], *s. Jur:* **1.** procuration *f*; délégation *f* de pouvoirs; pouvoir *m*; mandat *m*; **to vote by p.**, voter par procuration; **p. signature**, signature *f* par procuration; **special p.**, (i) pouvoir, mandat, spécial; (ii) pouvoir, mandat, impératif. **2.** mandataire *mf*; fondé *m* de pouvoir(s); délégué, -ée; **to send a p.**, se faire représenter; **to make s.o. one's p.**, constituer qn procureur. **3.** voix donnée par mandataire (à une assemblée d'actionnaires).

prude [pru:d], *s.f.* prude; **don't be such a p.!** ne soyez pas si prude, si pudibonde!

prudence ['pru:d(ə)ns], *s.* prudence *f*; sagesse *f.*

prudent ['pru:d(ə)nt], *a.* prudent; sage.

prudential [pru:'denʃ(ə)l]. **1.** *a.* (*a*) *O:* de prudence; dicté, commandé, par la prudence; **p. measure**, mesure *f* de prudence; (*b*) *U.S:* **p. committee**, comité *m* de surveillance (d'une municipalité, d'une société). **2. prudentials**, (i) *A:* considérations *f* de prudence; (ii) *U.S:* questions *f* d'administration locale.

prudentialism [pru:'denʃəlizm], *s. O:* (*a*) prudence exagérée; (*b*) conduite, politique, fondée sur la prudence.

prudently ['pru:dəntli], *adv.* prudemment, avec prudence; sagement.

prudery ['pru:dəri], *s.* pruderie *f*; pudibonderie *f.*

prudish ['pru:diʃ], *a.* prude; pudibond.

prudishness ['pru:diʃnis], *s.* = PRUDERY.

pruinescence, pruinosity [prui'nes(ə)ns, -'nɔsiti], *s. Bot:* (*a*) pruinescence *f*; (*b*) pruinosité *f*, pruine *f.*

pruinose, pruinous ['pru:inous, -əs], *a. Bot:* pruineux, pruiné.

prulaurasin [pru:'lɔrəsin], *s. Ch:* prulaurasine *f.*

Prunaceae [pru:'neisii:], *s.pl. Bot:* prunées *f.*

prune[1] [pru:n], *s.* **1.** (*a*) pruneau *m*; (*b*) **prunes and prisms,** manière affétée de parler; affectation *f.* **2.** (*a*) *A:* prune *f*; (*b*) **p. (purple),** (couleur) prune *m inv.*

prune[2], *v.tr.* **1.** (*a*) tailler (un rosier, un arbre fruitier); rafraîchir (les racines d'un arbre); châtrer (une plante); **you've pruned it too much, too hard,** vous l'avez taillé trop sévèrement; (*b*) émonder, égayer, rajeunir, habiller, esserter (un arbre forestier); **to p. (off, away) a branch,** élaguer une branche; **to dry p. a tree,** élaguer les branches mortes d'un arbre. **2.** *F:* faire des coupures, des amputations, dans (un article, etc.); émonder, élaguer (un article, etc.).

prunella[1] [pru:'nelə], *s. Tex:* prunelle *f.*

prunella[2], *s.* **1.** *Med: A:* affection *f* de la gorge; angine *f*, muguet *m*, etc. **2.** *Bot:* prunelle *f*, brunelle *f.*

pruner ['pru:nər], *s.* (*pers.*) tailleur *m* d'arbres; élagueur *m*, émondeur *m.*

pruning ['pru:niŋ], *s.* **1.** (*a*) taille *f* (d'un rosier, etc.); ciselage *m*, cisellement *m* (d'une vigne); (*b*) émondage *m*, habillage *m* (d'un arbre forestier); élagage *m* (d'une branche); **dry p.,** élagage des branches mortes; (*c*) **p. hook,** émondoir *m*, ébranchoir *m*; **p. knife,** serpette *f*, cernoir *m*, émondoir; **p. saw,** scie *f* à émonder, de jardinier; **p. shears,** (i) sécateur *m*; (ii) cisailles *fpl*; taille-buissons *m inv.*

prurience, pruriency ['pruəriəns, -iənsi], *s.* **1.** *A:* démangeaison *f.* **2.** lasciveté *f*, lubricité *f.*

prurient ['pruəriənt], *a.* (à l'esprit) lascif.

pruriginous [pruə'ridʒinəs], *a. Med:* prurigineux.

prurigo [pruə'raigou], *s. Med:* prurigo *m.*

pruritus [pruə'raitəs], *s. Med:* prurit *m.*

Prussia ['prʌʃə]. *Pr.n. Geog: Hist:* Prusse *f*; **East P.,** la Prusse orientale.

Prussian ['prʌʃ(ə)n]. **1.** *a.* prussien; **P. blue,** bleu *m* de Prusse, de Berlin. **2.** *s.* Prussien, -ienne.

Prussianism ['prʌʃənizm], *s. Hist:* prussianisme *m.*

Prussianize ['prʌʃənaiz], *v.tr. Hist:* prussianiser.

prussiate ['prʌʃieit], *s. Ch:* prussiate *m*; **p. of potash,** prussiate de potasse; cyanure *m* de potassium.

prussic ['prʌsik], *a. Ch:* (acide) prussique, cyanhydrique.

pry[1] [prai], *s.* curieux, -euse; indiscret, -ète; **a Paul P.,** un curieux; un furet.

pry[2], *v.i.* (**pried**) fureter; fouiller, chercher à voir (dans qch.); fourrer son nez partout; **to p. into a secret,** chercher à pénétrer un secret.

pry[3], *v.tr.* (**pried**) soulever, mouvoir, à l'aide d'un levier; **to p. a door open,** exercer des pesées sur une porte; forcer une porte avec un levier; **the box had been pried open,** on avait forcé la serrure, etc., du coffret; **to p. loose,** décoller, détacher.

prying ['praiiŋ], *a.* curieux; indiscret, -ète; fureteur; **p. look,** regard inquisiteur; **p. eyes,** yeux fureteurs; **safe from p. eyes,** à l'abri des regards indiscrets.

pryingly ['praiiŋli], *adv.* indiscrètement; en indiscret; avec une curiosité indiscrète.

prytaneum [pritə'ni:əm], *s. Gr.Ant:* prytanée *m.*

prytanis ['pritənis], *s.m. Gr.Ant:* prytane.

psalm [sɑ:m], *s.* psaume *m*; **p. book,** livre *m* de psaumes; psautier *m.*

psalmist ['sɑ:mist], *s.* psalmiste *m.*

psalmodic [sæl'mɔdik], *a.* psalmodique.

psalmodize ['sɑ:mədaiz], *v.i.* psalmodier.

psalmody ['sɑ:mədi], *s.* psalmodie *f.*

psalter ['sɔ:ltər], *s.* psautier *m.*

psaltery ['sɔ:lt(ə)ri], *s. A.Mus:* psaltérion *m.*

Psammetichus [psæ'metikəs]. *Pr.n.m. A.Hist:* (*a*) Psammétique; (*b*) Psammétik.

psammite ['(p)sæmait], *s. Miner:* psammite *m.*

psammitic [(p)sæ'mitik], *a. Miner:* psammitique.

psammoma [sæ'moumə], *s. Med:* psammome *m.*

psammophile ['sæmoufail], *a. & s.* (reptile *m*, plante *f*) psammophile.

psammophilous [sæ'mɔfiləs], *a.* psammophile.

psammophyte ['sæmoufait], *s. Bot:* psammophyte *m.*

psammophytic [sæmou'fitik], *a. Bot:* psammophyte.

pschent [(p)skent], *s. Egyptian Ant:* pschent *m.*

Pselaphidae [se'læfidi], *s.pl. Ent:* psélaphidés *m.*

psephology [se'fɔlədʒi], *s. Journ: etc:* l'étude *f* de l'orientation des élections.

pseud [sju:d], *s. F:* **he's a p.,** il est faux comme un jeton; c'est un charlatan.

pseud(a)esthesia [sju:des'θi:ziə], *s. Med:* pseudesthésie *f.*

pseudarthrosis [sju:dɑ:'θrousis], *s. Surg:* pseudarthrose *f.*

pseudepigraph [sju:'depigræf], *s.* pseudépigraphe *m.*

pseudepigraphic [sju:depi'græfik], *a.* pseudépigraphique.

pseudepigraphy [sju:de'pigrəfi], *s.* pseudépigraphie *f.*

pseudo ['sju:dou], *a.* faux; *Cmptr:* **p. code,** pseudo-code *m.*

pseudoadiabatic [sju:doueidiə'bætik], *a. Meteor:* pseudo-adiabatique.

pseudo-alloy [sju:dou'æləi], *s. Metall:* pseudo-alliage *m*, *pl.* pseudo-alliages.

pseudo-anodont [sju:dou'ænoudɔnt], *a. Z:* pseudo-anodonte, *pl.* pseudo-anodontes.

pseudo-anodontia [sju:douænou'dɔnʃiə], *s.* pseudo-anodontie *f.*

pseudoarthrosis [sju:douɑ:'θrousis], *s. Surg:* pseudarthrose *f.*

pseudobulb [sju:doubʌlb], *s. Bot:* pseudo-bulbe *m.*

pseudobulbar [sju:dou'bʌlbər], *a. Med:* (paralysie *f*, etc.) pseudo-bulbaire.

pseudocarp ['sju:doukɑ:p], *s. Bot:* pseudocarpe *m.*

pseudocarpous [sju:dou'kɑ:pəs], *a. Bot:* pseudocarpien.

pseudochrysalis [sju:dou'krisəlis], *s. Ent:* pseudo-chrysalide *f*, pseudo-nymphe *f.*

pseudocumene [sju:dou'kju:mi:n], *s. Ch:* pseudo-cumène *m.*

pseudodementia [sju:doudi'menʃiə], *s. Med:* pseudo-démence *f.*

pseudodont ['sju:doudɔnt], *a. Z:* pseudodonte.

pseudodontia [sju:dou'dɔnʃiə], *s. Z:* pseudodontie *f.*

pseudogalena [sju:dougə'li:nə], *s. Miner:* fausse galène.

pseudogamy [sju:'dɔgəmi], *s. Bot:* pseudogamie *f.*

pseudoglanders [sju:dou'glændəz], *s. Vet:* lymphangite ulcéreuse.

pseudo-gothic [sju:dou'gɔθik], *a. Arch:* pseudo-gothique.

pseudograph ['sju:dougræf], *s.* pseudographe *m.*

pseudographic(al) [sju:dou'græfik(l)], *a.* pseudographique.

pseudography [sju:'dɔgrəfi], *s. A:* pseudographie *f.*

pseudogyne ['sju:doudʒain], *s. Ent:* pseudogyne *f.*

pseudohaemophilia ['sju:douhi:mə'filiə], *s. Med:* hémogénie *f.*

pseudohalide [sju:dou'hælaid], *s. Ch:* pseudo-halogénure *m*, *pl.* pseudo-halogénures.

pseudohallucination ['sju:douhəlu:si'neiʃ(ə)n], *s. Med:* pseudo-hallucination *f.*

pseudohalogen [sju:dou'hælədʒen], *a. & s. Ch:* pseudohalogène (*m*).

pseudohermaphrod(it)ism [sju:douhə:'mæfrəd-(ait)izm], *s.* pseudohermaphrodisme *m*; androgynie *f.*

pseudo-instruction [sju:douin'strʌkʃ(ə)n], *s. Cmptr:* pseudo-instruction *f.*

Pseudolamellibranchi(at)a ['sju:doulæmeli'bræŋkiə, -bræŋki'eitə], *s.pl. Moll:* pseudo-lamellibranches *m.*

pseudomalachite [sju:dou'mæləkait], *s. Miner:* pseudo-malachite *f*, lunnite *f.*

pseudomembrane [sju:dou'membrein], *s. Med:* pseudo-membrane *f*; fausse membrane.

pseudomembranous [sju:dou'membrənəs], *a.* pseudo-membraneux.

pseudomeningitis [sju:doumenin'dʒaitis], *s. Med:* pseudo-méningite *f.*

pseudomer ['sju:doumə:r], *s. Ch:* pseudomère *m.*

pseudomeric [sju:dou'merik], *a. Ch:* pseudomérique.

pseudomerism [sju:'dɔmərizm], *s. Ch:* pseudomérie *f.*

pseudomorph ['sju:doumɔ:f], *s. Miner:* pseudomorphe *m.*

pseudomorphic, pseudomorphous [sju:dou'mɔ:fik, -fəs], *a. Miner:* (cristal, etc.) pseudomorphe.

pseudomorphosis [sju:dou'mɔ:fəsis, -mɔ:'fousis], *s. Miner:* pseudomorphose *f.*

pseudonitrole [sju:dou'naitroul], *s. Ch:* pseudonitrol *m.*

pseudonym ['sju:dənim], *s.* pseudonyme *m.*

pseudonymous [sju:'dɔniməs], *a.* pseudonyme.

pseudo-nymph [sju:dou'nimf], *s. Ent:* pseudo-nymphe *f.*

pseudoparasite [sju:dou'pærəsait], *s.* pseudo-parasite *m.*

pseudoparasitism [sju:dou'pærəs(a)itizm], *s.* pseudo-parasitisme *m.*

pseudoperiodic [sju:doupiəri'ɔdik], *a. Mth: etc:* pseudopériodique.

pseudo-pocket [sju:dou'pɔkit], *s. Anat:* faux cul-de-sac, *pl.* culs-de-sac.

pseudopod ['sju:doupɔd], **pseudopodium** [sju:dou'poudiəm], *s. Prot: Moss:* pseudopode *m.*

pseudoporphyritic [sju:doupɔ:fi'ritik], *a. Geol:* porphyroïde.

pseudorabies [sju:dou'reibi:z], *s. Vet:* pseudo-rage *f.*

pseudo-random [sju:dou'rændəm], *a.* (nombre, etc.) pseudo-aléatoire, *pl.* pseudo-aléatoires.

pseudo-rheumatism [sju:dou'ru:mətizm], *s. Med:* pseudo-rhumatisme *m.*

pseudo-scalar [sju:dou'skeilər], *a.* pseudo-scalaire, *pl.* pseudo-scalaires.

pseudoscorpion [sju:dou'skɔ:piən], *s. Arach:* pseudo-scorpion *m.*

Pseudoscorpionida ['sju:douskɔ:pi'ɔnidə], *s.pl. Arach:* pseudo-scorpions *m*, pseudo-scorpionidés *m.*

pseudosmia [sju:'dɔzmiə], *s. Med:* pseudosmie *f.*

pseudosphere ['sju:dousfiər], *s. Mth:* pseudo-sphère *f.*

pseudospherical [sju:dou'sferikl], *a.* pseudo-sphérique.

pseudospore ['sju:douspɔ:r], *s. Nat.Hist:* pseudo-spore *f.*

Pseudosuchia [sju:dou'sju:kiə], *s.pl. Paleont:* pseudosuchiens *m.*

pseudosuchian [sju:dou'sju:kiən], *s. Paleont:* pseudosuchien *m.*

pseudotsuga [sju:dou'tsju:gə], *s. Bot:* pseudosuga *m*; sapin *m* de Douglas, douglas *m.*

pseudotuberculosis [sju:doutju:bə:kju'lousis], *s. Med: Vet:* pseudo-tuberculose *f.*

pseudo-vector [sju:dou'vektər], *s. Mth:* pseudo-vecteur *m*; **p.-v. field,** champ pseudo-vectoriel.

pseudovelocity [sju:douvi'lɔsiti], *s.* pseudo-vitesse *f.*

pseudovolcanic [sju:douvɔl'kænik], *a. Geol:* pseudo-volcanique.

pseudovolcano [sju:douvɔl'keinou], *s. Geol:* pseudo-volcan *m*, *pl.* pseudo-volcans.

pshaw [(p)ʃɔ:], *int.* (*indicating disgust, disdain, impatience*) peuh! (ça) quand-même! allons donc! c'en est assez!

psi [psai], *s. Gr.Alph:* psi *m.*

psila ['sailə], *s. Ent:* psile *f.*

psiloceran, psiloceras [sai'lɔsərən, -ræs], *s. Paleont:* psiloceras *m.*

psilomelane [sailou'melein], *s. Miner:* psilomélane *f.*

psilophyton [sai'lɔfitɔn], *s. Paleont:* psilophyton *m.*

psilosis [sai'lousis], *s.* **1.** *Ling:* psilose *f.* **2.** *Med:* (*a*) psilose, alopécie *f*; (*b*) psilosis *m*, sprue *m.*

Psilotaceae [sailou'teisii:], *s.pl. Bot:* psilotacées *f.*

Psittacidae [si'tæsidi:], *s.pl. Orn:* psittacidés *m.*

Psittaciformes [sitæsi'fɔ:mi:z], *s.pl. Orn:* psittaciformes *m.*

Psittacinae [sitə'saini:], *s.pl. Orn:* psittacinés *m.*

psittacine ['sitəsain], *a. & s. Orn:* psittacin (*m*), psittaciné (*m*).

psittacinite ['sitəsinait], *s. Miner:* psittacinite *f.*

psittacism ['sitəsizm], *s.* psittacisme *m.*

psittacosis [sitə'kousis], *s. Med: Vet:* psittacose *f.*

psoas ['souəs], *s. Anat:* psoas *m*; **p. magnus, p. parvus,** grand, petit, psoas.

psoatic [sou'ætik], *a. Anat:* **p. muscle,** psoas *m.*

psocid ['sousid], *s. Ent:* psoque *m*; pou *m* de bois.

Psocidae ['sousidi:], *s.pl. Ent:* psocidés *m.*

Psocoptera [sou'kɔptərə], *s.pl. Ent:* psocoptères *m.*

Psocopteroidea [soukɔptə'rɔidiə], *s.pl. Ent:* psocoptéroïdes *m.*

psoitis [sou'aitis], *s. Med:* psoïtis *m.*

psophometer [sou'fɔmitər], *s. Tp: Tg:* psophomètre *m.*

psora ['sɔ:rə], *s. Med:* psore *f*, psora *f.*

psoriasis [sɔ:'raiəsis], *s. Med:* psoriasis *m.*

psoriatic [sɔ:ri'ætik], *a. Med:* psorias(ist)ique.

psoric ['sɔ:rik], *a. Med:* psorique.

psoroptic [sɔ'rɔptik], *a. Ent: Vet:* psoroptique; **p. mange,** gale *f* psoroptique.

psst [pst], *int.* (*a*) (*to attract attention*) psitt! pst! (*b*) chut!

psychagogic [saikə'gɔdʒik], *a.* psychagogique.

psychagogy ['saikəgɔdʒi], *s.* psychagogie *f.*

psychalgia [sai'kældʒiə], *s. Med:* psychalgie *f.*

psychasthenic [saikæs'θi:nik], *a.* psychasthénique.

Psyche ['(p)saiki]. **1.** *Pr.n.f. Gr.Myth:* Psyché. **2.** *s.* (*a*) *Ent:* psyché *f*; (*b*) *Furn:* psyché (grande glace sur pivots); (*c*) psyché, psyché *f*, psychisme *m.*

psychedelic [saikə'delik], *a.* psychédélique.

psychedelism ['saikədelizm], *s. Psy:* psychédélisme *m.*

psychiater [sai'kaiətər], *s. A:* psychiatre *m.*

psychiatric [saiki'ætrik], *a.* psychiatrique.

psychiatrist [sai'kaiətrist], *s.* psychiatre *mf.*

psychiatry [sai'kaiətri], *s.* psychiatrie *f.*

psychic ['saikik]. **1.** *a.* (*a*) psychique; (phénomène *m*, etc.) métapsychique; (pouvoir) médiumnique; (*b*) *Cards:* **p. bid,** annonce *f* psychique. **2.** *s.* médium *m.*

psychics ['saikiks], *s.pl.* (*usu. with sg. const.*) la métapsychique.

psychid ['saikid], *s. Ent:* psychidé *m.*

Psychidae ['saikidi:], *s.pl. Ent:* psychidés *m.*

psychism ['saikizm], *s.* psychisme *m.*

psychist ['saikist], *s.* psychiste *mf*; métapsychiste *mf.*

psycho ['saikou], *a. & s. F:* psychopathe (*mf*).

psychoanalyse [saikou'ænəlaiz], *v.tr.* psychanalyser (qn).

psychoanalysis [saikouə'nælisis], *s.* psychanalyse *f*,

psychoanalyse *f.*
psychoanalyst [saikou'ænəlist], *s.* psychanalyste *mf.*
psychoanalytic(al) [saikouænə'litik(l)], *a.* psychanalytique; **p. novelist,** romancier psychanalyste.
psychobiological [saikoubaiə'lɔdʒikl], *a.* psychobiologique.
psychobiology [saikoubai'ɔlədʒi], *s.* psychobiologie *f.*
psychodrama ['saikoudrɑ:mə], *s. Psy: Med:* psychodrame *m.*
psychodramatic [saikoudrə'mætik], *a.* psychodramatique.
psychogalvanic [saikougæl'vænik], *a.* **p. reflex,** réflexe psychogalvanique.
psychogenesis [saikou'dʒenisis], *s. Med:* psychogénie *f*, psychogénèse *f.*
psychogenetic [saikoudʒə'netik], *a.* psychogénétique.
psychogenic [saikou'dʒenik], *a. Psy:* psychogène; *Med:* (affection *f*) psychogénique.
psychogram ['saikougræm], *s. Psychics:* psychogramme *m.*
psychographer [sai'kɔgrəfər], *s. Psychics:* psychographe *mf.*
psychography [sai'kɔgrəfi], *s.* psychographie *f.*
psychoid ['saikɔid], *a.* psychoïde.
psycholeptic [saikou'leptik], *a.* psycholeptique.
psycholinguistics [saikouliŋ'gwistiks], *s.pl.* (*usu. with sg. const.*) psycholinguistique *f.*
psychological [saikə'lɔdʒik(ə)l], *a.* psychologique; **the p. moment,** le moment psychologique; **p. novel,** roman *m* d'analyse.
psychologically [saikə'lɔdʒikəli], *adv.* psychologiquement.
psychologism [sai'kɔlədʒizm], *s.* psychologisme *m.*
psychologist [sai'kɔlədʒist], *s.* psychologue *mf.*
psychologistic [saikɔlə'dʒistik], *a.* psychologiste.
psychology [sai'kɔlədʒi], *s.* psychologie *f*; **clinical p.,** psychologie clinique; **genetic p.,** psychologie génétique; **depth p.,** psychologie en profondeur, psychologie abyssale; **applied p., individual p.,** psychologie appliquée.
psychomachy [sai'kɔməki], *s.* psychomachie *f.*
psychomancy ['saikoumænsi], *s.* psychomancie *f.*
psychometer [sai'kɔmitər], *s.* psychomètre *m.*
psychometric [saikou'metrik], *a.* psychométrique.
psychometrician [saikoume'triʃ(ə)n], **psychometrist** [sai'kɔmətrist], *s.* psychométricien, -ienne.
psychometry [sai'kɔmətri], *s.* psychométrie *f.*
psychomotor ['saikoumoutər], *a.* psychomoteur, -trice.
psychoneurosis [saikounju:'rousis], *s. Med:* psychonévrose *f.*
psychoneurotic [saikounju:'rɔtik], *a. Med:* psychonévrosique, psychonévrotique; **p. child,** (enfant) caractériel.
psychopath ['saikoupæθ], *s. Psy:* psychopathe *mf*; caractériel, -ielle.
psychopathic [saikou'pæθik], *a. & s.* psychopathe (*mf*); (état, personnalité) psychopathique.
psychopathological [saikoupæθə'lɔdʒik(ə)l], *a.* psychopathologique.
psychopathology [saikoupə'θɔlədʒi], *s.* psychopathologie *f.*
psychopathy [sai'kɔpəθi], *s. Med:* psychopathie *f.*
psychopharmacological [saikoufɑ:məkə'lɔdʒikl], *a.* psychopharmacologique.
psychopharmacologist [saikoufɑ:mə'kɔlədʒist], *s.* psychopharmacologiste *mf.*
psychopharmacology [saikoufɑ:mə'kɔlədʒi], *s.* psychopharmacologie *f.*
psychophysical [saikou'fizikl], *a.* psychophysique.
psychophysicist [saikou'fizisist], *s.* psychophysicien, -ienne.
psychophysics [saikou'fiziks], *s.pl.* (*usu. with sg. const.*) psychophysique *f.*
psychophysiologist [saikoufizi'ɔlədʒist], *s.* psychophysiologiste *mf*, psychophysiologue *mf.*
psychophysiology [saikoufizi'ɔlədʒi], *s.* psychophysiologie *f.*
psychosensorial [saikousen'sɔ:riəl], *a.* psychosensoriel.
psychosexual [saikou'seksjuəl], *a.* psychosexuel.
psychosis, *pl.* **-oses** [sai'kousis, -ousi:z], *s. Med:* psychose *f*; **involutional p.,** psychose d'involution.
psychosocial [saikou'souʃiəl], *a.* psychosocial.
psychosomatic [saikousə'mætik], *a. Med:* psychosomatique.
psychosomatics [saikousə'mætiks], *s.pl.* (*usu. with sg. const.*) psychosomatique *f.*
psychosurgery [saikou'sə:dʒəri], *s.* psychochirurgie *f.*
psychotechnical [saikou'teknikl], *a.* psychotechnique.
psychotechnician [saikoutek'niʃ(ə)n], *s.* psychotechnicien, -ienne.
psychotechnics [saikou'tekniks], *s.pl.* (*usu. with sg. const.*) psychotechnie *f*, psychotechnique *f.*
psychotechnology [saikoutek'nɔlədʒi], *s.* psychotechnie *f*, psychotechnique *f.*
psychotherapeutic [saikouθerə'pju:tik], *a.* psychothérapeutique.
psychotherapeutics [saikouθerə'pju:tiks], *s.pl.* (*usu. with sg. const.*) psychothérapeutique *f.*
psychotherapist [saikou'θerəpist], *s.* psychothérapeute *mf.*
psychotherapy [saikou'θerəpi], *s.* psychothérapie *f.*
psychotic [sai'kɔtik], *a. & s. Med:* psychotique (*mf*), psychosé, -ée.
psychotrine ['saikɔtri:n], *s. Ch:* psychotrine *f.*
psychotropic [saikou'trɔpik], *a.* psychotrope.
psychrometer [sai'krɔmitər], *s. Meteor:* psychromètre *m.*
psychrometric [saikrou'metrik], *a. Meteor:* psychrométrique; **p. chart,** carte *f* psychrométrique.
psychrometry [sai'krɔmitri], *s. Meteor:* psychrométrie *f.*
psychrophile ['saikroufail], **psychrophilic** [saikrou'filik], **psychrophilous** [sai'krɔfiləs], *a. Biol:* psychrophile.
psylla, psyllid ['silə, -lid], *s. Ent:* psylle *f.*
Psyllidae ['silidi:], *s.pl. Ent:* psyllidés *m.*
psyllium ['siliəm], *s. Pharm:* psyllium *m.*
ptarmigan ['tɑ:migən], *s. Orn:* **p.,** *NAm:* **rock p.,** lagopède muet, ptarmigan *m, Fr.C:* lagopède des rochers; **white-tailed p.,** lagopède à queue blanche; **willow p.,** lagopède des saules.
Ptenoglossa [tenou'glɔsə], *s.pl. Moll:* pténoglosses *m.*
pteranodon [tə'rænoudɔn], *s. Paleont:* ptéranodon *m.*
pteridine ['teridi:n], *s. Ch: Ent:* ptérine *f*, ptéridine *f.*
pteridology [teri'dɔlədʒi], *s. Bot:* étude *f* des fougères.
Pteridophyta [teri'dɔfitə], *s.pl. Bot:* ptéridophytes *f.*
Pteridospermaphyta [teridouspə:mə'faitə], *s.pl. Paleont:* ptéridospermales *f*, ptéridospermées *f.*
pterin ['terin], *s. Ch: Ent:* ptérine *f*, ptéridine *f.*
pterion ['teriɔn], *s. Anat:* ptéréon *m*, ptérion *m.*
ptero- ['terou], *comb.fm.* ptéro-.
Pterobranchia [terou'bræŋkiə], *s.pl. Nat.Hist:* ptérobranches *m.*
pterocarpous [terou'kɑ:pəs], *a. Bot:* ptérocarpe.
Pterocletidae [terou'kletidi:], **Pteroclididae** [terou'klididi:], *s.pl. Orn:* ptéroclididés *m*, les gangas *m.*
pterodactyl [terou'dæktil], *s. Paleont:* ptérodactyle *m.*
Pterodactylidae [teroudæk'tilidi:], *s.pl. Paleont:* ptérodactylidés *m.*
pterodactyloid, pterodactylous [terou'dæktilɔid, -tiləs], *a.* ptérodactyle.
pteromalid [terou'mælid], *s. Ent:* ptéromale *m*, ptéromalide *m.*
Pteromalidae [terou'mælidi:], *s.pl. Ent:* ptéromalides *m.*
pterophorid [terou'fɔrid], *s. Ent:* ptérophoridé *m.*
Pterophoridae [terou'fɔridi:], *s.pl. Ent:* ptérophoridés *m.*
pteropod ['teroupɔd], *s. Moll:* ptéropode *m.*
Pteropoda [terou'poudə], *s.pl. Moll:* ptéropodes *m.*
pterosaur ['terousɔ:r], *s. Paleont:* ptérosaurien *m.*
pterygium [te'ridʒiəm], *s. Med:* ptérygion *m*, onglet *m.*
pterygode ['terigoud], **pterygodum** [te'rigədəm], *s. Ent:* ptérygode *m.*
pterygoid ['terigɔid]. *Anat:* **1.** *a.* ptérygoïdien, ptérygoïde; **p. muscle,** muscle ptérygoïdien; **p. nerve,** nerf ptérygoïdien; **p. process,** apophyse *f* ptérygoïde. **2.** *s.* ptérygoïde *f*; ptérygoïdien *m.*
pterygomaxillary [terigoumæk'siləri], *a. Anat:* ptérygo-maxillaire.
pterygopalatine [terigou'pælətain], *a. Anat:* ptérygopalatin.
pterygopodia [terigou'poudiə], *s.pl. Ich:* ptérygopodes *m* (de la raie mâle).
Pterygota [teri'goutə], *s.pl. Ent:* ptérygotes *m.*
pterygotus [teri'goutəs], *s. Paleont:* pterygotus *m.*
pteryla ['terilə], *s. Orn:* ptéryle *f.*
pterylography [teri'lɔgrəfi], *s. Orn:* ptérylographie *f.*
pterylosis [teri'lousis], *s. Orn:* ptérylose *f.*
ptilinum ['tilinəm], *s. Ent:* ptiline *f.*
Ptilonorhynchidae [tilənou'riŋkidi:], *s.pl. Orn:* ptilonorhynchidés *m.*
ptinid ['tinid], *s. Ent:* ptine *m.*
Ptinidae ['tinidi:], *s.pl. Ent:* ptinidés *m.*
Ptolemaic [tɔlə'meiik], *a.* **1.** *A.Hist:* ptolémaïque; des Ptolémées. **2.** *Astr:* **P. system,** système de Ptolémée; système ptoloméen, ptoléméen; *Mapm:* **P. projection,** projection *f* de Ptolémée.
Ptolemy ['tɔləmi], *Pr.n.m. A.Hist:* **1.** (Claude) Ptolémée (l'astronome). **2.** Ptolémée (roi d'Egypte); **the Ptolemies,** les Lagides; **P. Euergetes** [ju'ə:giti:z], Ptolémée Évergète.
ptomaine ['toumein], *s. Ch:* ptomaïne *f*; **p. poisoning,** intoxication *f* alimentaire (par les ptomaïnes).
ptosis ['tousis], *s. Med:* (*a*) ptosis *f* (de la paupière); (*b*) ptôse *f* (des viscères).
ptyalagogic [taiælə'gɔdʒik], *a. Med:* ptyalagogue, sialagogue.
ptyalagogue [tai'ælәgɔg], *s. Med:* sialagogue *m.*
ptyalolithiasis [taiælouli'θaiəsis], *s. Med:* lithiase *f* salivaire.
ptyalorrhea [taiælɔ'ri:ə], *s. Med:* sialorrhée *f.*
ptyalin ['taiəlin], *s. Physiol: Ch:* ptyaline *f.*
ptyalism [taiəlizm], *s. Physiol:* ptyalisme *m*, salivation *f.*
pub [pʌb], *s. F:* = café *m*, bistro(t) *m* (où on sert aussi souvent des repas simples); **p. lunch, p. food, grub,** déjeuner *m* simple (viandes froides, sandwichs, saucisses, steaks, etc.) (servis dans un *pub*); **p. crawl,** tournée *f* des bistro(t)s; **p. crawler,** coureur *m* de bistro(t)s.
pub-crawl ['pʌbkrɔ:l], *v.i.* faire la tournée des bistro(t)s.
puberty ['pju:bəti], *s. Physiol:* puberté *f.*
pubes ['pju:bi:z], *s. Anat:* région pubienne; pubis *m.*
pubescence [pju:'bes(ə)ns], *s.* **1.** *Bot:* pubescence *f.* **2.** *Physiol:* puberté *f.*
pubescent [pju:'bes(ə)nt], *a.* **1.** *Bot:* pubescent; velu. **2.** *Physiol:* pubère.
pubic ['pju:bik], *a. Anat:* pubien.
pubiotomy [pju:bi'ɔtəmi], *s. Surg:* pubiotomie *f.*
pubis ['pju:bis], *s.m. Anat:* (*a*) (os) pubien *m*; (*b*) pubis *m.*
public ['pʌblik]. **1.** *a.* public, *f.* publique; (*a*) **p. authorities,** pouvoirs publics; **p. building,** bâtiment, édifice, public; **p. service, p. welfare,** la chose publique; **to work for the p. good,** travailler pour le bien public; **to restore p. confidence,** rétablir la confiance publique, du public, du pays; **p. finance,** finances publiques; **at the p. expense,** aux frais du contribuable; **p. utility (service),** service public; **p. transport,** transports *m* en commun; *Pol:* **p. bill,** projet *m* de loi d'intérêt public; **p. opinion poll,** sondage *m* d'opinion publique; **p. holiday,** fête légale; **p. indecency,** outrage public à la pudeur; **p. enemy,** ennemi public; *F:* **p. enemy number 1,** ennemi public numéro 1; (*b*) **p. garden,** jardin public; **p. library,** bibliothèque municipale, communale, de la ville; **p. call box,** cabine (téléphonique) publique; **p. lavatory,** toilettes publiques; **p. house** = débit *m* de boissons; café *m*; **p. lecture,** conférence publique; (*c*) **to make sth. p.,** rendre qch. public; publier (une nouvelle, etc.); **to make a p. protest,** protester publiquement; **to make a p. appearance,** paraître en public; **p. relations,** relations publiques; *Pol: etc:* **p. image,** image *f* de marque; **p. address system,** système *m* de (diffusion par) hauts-parleurs; sonorisation *f* pour diffusion en public; *F:* (*of firm*) **to go p.,** émettre, placer, des actions dans le public; (*d*) **p. life,** vie publique; **men in p. life,** les hommes publics; **p. spirit,** patriotisme *m*; civisme *m*; amour *m* du bien public; **p. spirited,** dévoué au bien public; (*e*) **p. law,** droit public, international. **2.** *s.* (*a*) **the (general) p.,** le (grand) public; **the p. is requested to . . .,** le public est prié de . . .; **the reading p.,** le public qui lit; le public ami des livres; **book that appeals to a large p.,** livre qui s'adresse à un public très étendu; *Fin:* **to issue shares to the p.,** émettre, placer, des actions dans le public; (*b*) **in p.,** en public; publiquement; (*c*) *F: O:* = débit *m* de boissons, bistro(t) *m.*
publican ['pʌblikən], *s.* **1.** *Rom.Hist:* publicain *m*; fermier *m* des deniers publics; *B:* **a friend of publicans and sinners,** un ami des publicains et des pécheurs. **2.** = débitant, -ante, de boissons.
publication [pʌbli'keiʃ(ə)n], *s.* **1.** (*a*) publication *f*; parution *f*, apparition *f* (d'un livre); **to read a book on first p.,** lire un livre dans sa primeur; (*b*) publication (d'une nouvelle, des bans, etc.); promulgation *f* (d'une ordonnance, d'un décret); *Journ:* **for p. in your columns,** prière d'insérer; **the above constitutes legal p.,** dont acte. **2.** ouvrage publié; publication.
publicist ['pʌblisist], *s.* **1.** publiciste *m*, expert *m* en droit international. **2.** *O:* journaliste *mf.* **3.** publicitaire *m.*
publicity [pʌb'lisiti], *s.* **1.** publicité *f*; **to give unfortunate p. to a private matter,** donner une regrettable publicité à une affaire privée. **2.** *Com:* publicité, réclame *f*; **p. campaign,** campagne *f* de publicité; **advance p.,** publicité d'amorçage; **p. (department),** (i) *Com:* la publicité; (ii) *Publ:* le service de presse; **p. man,** publicitaire *m*; **p. manager,** chef *m* de publicité; **p. bureau, agency,** bureau *m*, agence *f*, de publicité.
publicize ['pʌblisaiz], *v.tr.* faire connaître au public; faire de la publicité, de la réclame, pour (un produit).
publicly ['pʌblikli], *adv.* publiquement; en public.
publish ['pʌbliʃ], *v.tr.* **1.** (*a*) publier (un édit, des bans de mariage, etc.); (*b*) publier, révéler, divulguer (une

nouvelle, etc.). 2. (a) *Jur:* mettre, offrir (un livre, etc.) en vente; (b) (*of publisher*) éditer, publier, faire paraître, un livre; (*of book*) **just published,** vient de paraître; **as soon as published,** dès parution; **the volumes already published,** les volumes déjà parus; **it will be published by XYZ,** il sera publié, paraîtra, chez XYZ, dans les éditions XYZ.

published ['pʌbliʃt], *a.* **p. books, works,** publications *f*; ouvrages *m* en librairie.

publisher ['pʌbliʃər], *s.* 1. éditeur *m.* 2. *U.S:* propriétaire *m* d'un journal.

publishing ['pʌbliʃiŋ], *s.* 1. publication *f* (des bans, etc.). 2. publication, mise *f* en vente (d'un livre); **date of p.,** date *f* de mise en vente; **the p. trade,** l'édition *f*; **p. house, firm,** maison *f* d'édition; **to be in p.,** (i) être éditeur; (ii) travailler dans une maison d'édition, chez un éditeur.

puccinia [puk'siniə], *s. Fung:* puccinia *m.*

puccoon [pʌ'ku:n], *s. Bot:* **(red) p.,** sanguinaire *f*; **yellow p.,** hydraste *m* du Canada.

puce [pju:s], *a. & s.* (couleur *f*) puce *m inv.*

Puck[1] [pʌk]. 1. *Pr.n.m.* (le lutin) Puck. 2. *s.* (a) lutin, farfadet *m*; (b) *A:* petit espiègle.

puck[2], *s.* (a) *Orn: Dial:* engoulevent *m*; (b) maladie du bétail attribuée à l'engoulevent.

puck[3], *s. Sp:* galine *f*, palet *m* en caoutchouc (pour le hockey sur glace).

pucker[1] ['pʌkər], *s.* ride *f*, pli *m* (du visage); fronce *f*, fronçure *f*, faux pli, poche *f*, godet *m*, godure *f* (d'un tissu); grigne *f* (dans le feutre).

pucker[2]. 1. *v.tr.* rider (le visage); plisser, froncer, faire goder (un tissu); faire des fronces à (une feuille de papier, etc.); *Nau:* faire boire (une couture de voile); **to p. (up) one's brows, one's lips,** froncer les sourcils; plisser les lèvres. 2. *v.i.* (a) (*of garment*) **to p. (up),** faire des plis, des fronces; se froncer; (*of material*) goder, gripper; (*of felt*) grigner; (b) **his face puckered up,** sa figure s'est crispée.

puckered ['pʌkəd], *a.* (*of brow, material*) plissé, froncé; (*of skin*) ridé; **p. face,** figure (i) toute ratatinée, (ii) crispée (par la douleur, etc.).

puckering ['pʌk(ə)riŋ], *s.* 1. plissement *m* (du visage); froncement *m* (des sourcils, d'un tissu); godage *m* (d'un tissu); formation *f* de faux plis. 2. (a) *Geol: etc:* gaufrage *m* (d'une couche); (b) *Ph:* **puckerings in the Einsteinian space,** rides *f* de l'espace einsteinien.

puckie ['pʌki], *s. U.S: P:* **that's a lot of p.,** tout ça c'est de la foutaise.

puckish ['pʌkiʃ], *a.* de lutin; malicieux, capricieux, espiègle, comme un lutin.

puckishness ['pʌkiʃnis], *s.* malice *f*, espièglerie *f*, de lutin.

pud[1] [pʌd], *s. F:* (a) patte *f* (d'animal); (b) menotte *f* (de bébé).

pud[2] [pud], *s. F:* pudding *m*; entremets sucré.

pudding[1] ['pudiŋ], *s.* 1. *Cu:* (a) **(suet) p.,** pudding *m*, pouding *m*; **steak (and kidney) p., apple p., etc.,** pâte molle faite avec de la graisse de bœuf (et du sucre quand on y met des fruits), fourrée de viande, de pommes, etc., et cuite dans un bol au bain-marie; **p. basin,** moule *m* à puddings; (b) **milk p.,** entremets sucré au lait; crème *f*; **rice p.,** (i) (*milky*) riz *m* au lait; (ii) (*solid*) gâteau *m* de riz; **tapioca p.,** pudding au tapioca à l'anglaise; (c) **black p.,** *O:* **blood p.,** boudin (noir); **white p.,** boudin blanc. 2. *Nau:* (a) (*also* **puddening**) emboudinure *f*; (b) **p. (fender),** bourrelet *m* de défense; boudin, tampon *m*, ballon *m*.

pudding[2], *v.tr. Nau:* emboudiner (une ancre, un câble, etc.).

puddingface ['pudiŋfeis], *s. F:* visage empâté; pleine lune.

puddingfaced ['pudiŋfeist], *a. F:* au visage empâté.

puddinghead ['pudiŋhed], *s. F:* idiot, -ote; tête *f* vide; andouille *f*; **he's a p.,** il est bête comme ses pieds.

puddingstone ['pudiŋstoun], *s. Miner:* poudingue *m.*

puddingwife, *pl.* **-wives** ['pudiŋwaif, -waivz], *s. Ich:* vieille *f*; perroquet *m* de mer, des coraux.

puddle[1] ['pʌdl], *s.* 1. (a) flaque *f* d'eau, d'huile; (b) petite mare; (c) *F:* **the dog's made a p. on the carpet,** le chien a fait pipi sur le tapis. 2. *F: A:* gâchis *m*; **to be in a pretty p.,** être dans un beau pétrin. 3. *Hyd.E:* corroi *m*, glaise *f*; braye *f* (d'argile); **to line with p.,** corroyer (un bassin, un canal, etc.). 4. *attrib. Metall:* **p. steel,** acier puddlé; **p. bar,** ébauché *m* de puddlage, fer ébauché; **p. ball,** loupe *f*; balle *f*, boule *f*, de puddlage; **p. train,** train *m*, laminoir *m*, ébaucheur, de puddlage.

puddle[2]. 1. *v.i.* **to p. (about),** (i) patauger, barboter (dans la boue); (ii) *F: A:* faire du gâchis, de la mauvaise besogne. 2. *v.tr.* (a) rendre (l'eau) boueuse; troubler (l'eau); (b) corroyer, malaxer (l'argile); (c) corroyer, glaiser (un bassin, etc.); (d) *Metall:* puddler, brasser, corroyer (le fer); (e) (*ram down*) tasser, damer (un plancher en terre, etc.).

puddled ['pʌdld], *a.* 1. (*of water*) trouble, bourbeux. 2. *Hyd.E:* **p. clay,** argile corroyée; pisé *m*, glaise *f*. 3. *Metall:* puddlé.

puddler ['pʌdlər], *s. Metall:* 1. (*pers.*) puddleur *m*, brasseur *m.* 2. (a) brasseur mécanique; (b) four *m* à puddler, de puddlage.

puddling ['pʌdliŋ], *s.* 1. (a) corroyage *m* (de l'argile); (b) *Metall:* puddlage *m*, brassage *m* (du fer); **p. forge, furnace,** forge *f*, four *m*, à puddler, de puddlage; **p. slag,** scorie *f* de four à puddler. 2. corroi *m*, glaise *f*; braye *f* (d'argile).

puddly ['pʌdli], *a.* rempli, couvert, de flaques d'eau.

puddock ['pʌdək], *s. A:* (a) grenouille *f*; (b) crapaud *m.*

pudency ['pju:dənsi], *s. Lit:* pudicité *f.*

pudenda [pju:'dendə], *s.pl. Anat:* organes génitaux externes.

pudge [pʌdʒ], *s. F:* (*pers.*) boulot, -otte; patapouf *m.*

pudgy ['pʌdʒi], *a. F:* (*of pers.*) rondelet, dodu; boulot; pansu.

pudicity [pju:'disiti], *s. Lit:* pudicité *f.*

pudu ['pu:du:], *s. Z:* pudu *m.*

puerile ['pjuərail], *a.* puéril; (a) *Med:* **p. breathing,** respiration puérile (chez l'adulte); (b) *Pej:* puéril, enfantin; **to ask p. questions,** poser des questions puériles.

puerileness ['pjuərailnis], **puerility** [pjuə'riliti], *s.* puérilité *f.*

puerilism ['pjuərilizm], *s. Med:* puérilisme *m.*

puerperal [pju:'ə:pərəl], *a. Med:* puerpéral, -aux.

puerperium [pjuə'piəriəm], *s. Obst:* puerpéralité *f.*

Puerto Rican [pwεətou'ri:kən]. *Geog:* (a) *a.* portoricain; (b) *s.* Portoricain, -aine.

Puerto Rico [pwεətou'ri:kou], *Pr.n. Geog:* Puerto Rico, Porto Rico.

puff[1] [pʌf], *s.* 1. (a) souffle *m* (de la respiration, d'air); bouffée *f* (d'air, de fumée); échappement soudain (de vapeur); **the least p. would knock it over,** on le renverserait d'un souffle, au moindre souffle; **to take a p. at one's pipe,** tirer une bouffée de sa pipe; (b) *F:* respiration *f*; **out of p.,** essoufflé, à bout de souffle; (c) *Rept:* **p. adder,** vipère heurtante; *Ich:* **p. fish,** triodon *m.* 2. (a) bouillon *m* (de robe); bouffant *m* (d'une manche); **p. sleeves,** manches bouffantes; (b) bouffette *f* (de ruban); chou *m*, *pl.* choux; (c) *U.S:* édredon *m.* 3. **powder p.,** houppe *f*, houpette *f* (à poudre). 4. *Cu:* **p. pastry,** pâte feuilletée; **jam p.,** puits *m* d'amour; bouchée *f* aux confitures; **cream p.,** (i) feuilleté *m* à la crème; (ii) *P:* (*pers.*) mollasson *m.* 5. *F: O:* réclame (tapageuse).

puff[2], *v.*

I. *v.i. & tr.* 1. *v.i.* (a) souffler; émettre des bouffées d'air; **to p. at the embers,** souffler sur la braise; **to puff and blow,** haleter; **to p. (and blow) like a grampus,** souffler comme un phoque, comme un bœuf; (b) lancer des bouffées (de fumée, de vapeur); émettre des jets (de vapeur); **to p. (away) at one's pipe,** tirer sur sa pipe; tirer des bouffées de sa pipe; *O:* **the engine puffed out of the station,** la locomotive quitta la gare en haletant, en lançant des jets de vapeur; (c) *F: O:* (*at sale*) pousser les enchères (pour faire monter les prix). 2. *v.tr.* (a) émettre, lancer (des bouffées de fumée, d'air, etc.); **to p. smoke into s.o.'s face,** lancer de la fumée à la figure de qn; (b) **to p. a cigar,** tirer à petits coups sur un cigare; fumer un cigare par petites bouffées; (c) gonfler (le riz, etc.); (d) *F: O:* prôner, pousser, vanter, faire mousser (ses marchandises).

II. (*compound verbs*) 1. **puff out,** (a) *v.tr.* (i) gonfler (les joues); faire ballonner (une manche); **to p. out one's skirt,** faire bouffer, faire ballonner, sa jupe; (ii) émettre, lancer (des bouffées de fumée); (b) *v.i.* (*of skirt*) bouffer. 2. **puff up,** *v.tr.* (a) gonfler (les joues); (b) **to be puffed up (with pride),** être bouffi, gonflé, d'orgueil; se rengorger.

puffball ['pʌfbɔ:l], *s. F:* 1. *Fung:* vesse-de-loup *f*, *pl.* vesses-de-loup. 2. *Bot:* boule *f* de pissenlit, chandelle *f*, voyageur *m.*

puffbird ['pʌfbə:d], *s. Orn:* tamatia *m*, barbacou *m*, trappiste *m*, paresseux *m.*

puffed [pʌft], *a.* 1. (a) **p. sleeves,** manches bouffantes; (b) *Cu:* **p. rice,** riz gonflé. 2. *F:* (*of pers.*) essoufflé; à bout de souffle; hors d'haleine. 3. (a) **p. out,** ballonné; (b) **p. up,** (i) (*of face, etc.*) enflé, bouffi; (ii) (*of pers.*) gonflé (d'orgueil).

puffer ['pʌfər], *s.* 1. *F: O:* (*child's language*) (= **train**) teuf-teuf *m inv.* 2. *Com: A:* (a) réclamiste *m*, puffiste *m*; (b) compère *m* (à une vente aux enchères); faux enchérisseur. 3. *Ich:* **p. (fish),** orbe épineux; poisson-boule *m*, *pl.* poissons-boules; triodon *m.*

puffin ['pʌfin], *s. Orn:* macareux *m*; **Atlantic p.,** macareux moine, *Fr.C:* macareux arctique; **horned p.,** macareux cornu; **tufted p.,** macareux huppé.

puffiness ['pʌfinis], *s.* boursouflure *f*, enflure *f*, vultuosité *f*, bouffissure *f* (du visage); **p. round the eyes,** bouffissure des yeux.

puffing[1] ['pʌfiŋ], *a.* 1. (a) soufflant, haletant; (b) *Z: U.S:* **p. pig,** marsouin *m.* 2. *Com: A:* (*of adverisement*) tapageux.

puffing[2], *s.* (a) émission *f* (de fumée, de vapeur) par bouffées; souffle *m* (d'une locomotive); halètement *m* (de la respiration); (b) *A:* réclames tapageuses (de marchandises); puff *m*, puffisme *m.*

puff-puff ['pʌfpʌf], *s. F: O:* (*child's language*) teuf-teuf *m inv.*

puffy ['pʌfi], *a.* 1. (vent) qui souffle par bouffées. 2. (*of pers.*) (i) à l'haleine courte; poussif; (ii) hors d'haleine. 3. (a) bouffi, boursouflé; (*of dress*) bouffant; **p. face,** visage bouffi, soufflé; *Med:* visage vultueux; **p. eyes,** yeux gonflés; **eyes p. with sleep,** yeux bouffis de sommeil; **to be p. under the eyes,** avoir les yeux bouffis; avoir des poches sous les yeux; (b) *F: O:* (*of pers.*) adipeux, obèse.

pug[1] [pʌg], *s.* 1. (a) **p. (dog),** carlin *m*, petit dogue; roquet *m*; *F:* **p. face,** visage *m*, tête *f*, de dogue; **p. nose,** nez épaté, écrasé, camus; **p.-nosed,** au nez écrasé; camus, camard; (b) *A:* singe *m*; (c) *F: A:* **the pugs,** les principaux domestiques; (d) *F: A:* **P.,** Maître Renard. 2. *A:* **p. (engine),** locomotive *f* de manœuvre.

pug[2], *s. Brickm: etc:* argile malaxée; glaise *f*; **p. mill,** (i) *Brickm:* broyeur *m*, malaxeur *m* (à palettes), pétrin *m*; (ii) *Cer:* patouillet *m*; (*pers.*) **p. miller,** (i) broyeur, malaxeur; (ii) patouilleur *m.*

pug[3], *v.tr.* **(pugged)** 1. *Brickm: etc:* malaxer, pétrir (l'argile). 2. (a) *Const:* hourder (un plancher, une cloison); (b) corroyer, glaiser (un bassin, etc.).

pug[4], *s.* (*in India*) empreinte *f* (des pattes d'un tigre, etc.); **to follow the pugs of a tiger,** suivre la trace, la piste, d'un tigre.

pug[5], *v.tr.* **(pugged)** (*in India*) suivre (un tigre, etc.) à la piste, à la trace.

pug[6], *s. P:* pugiliste *m*, boxeur *m.*

puggaree ['pʌgəri], *s.* 1. turban *m* (d'Indien). 2. voile *m* (de casque colonial).

pugger ['pʌgər], *s.* (a) *Const:* terrasseur *m*; (b) *Cer:* patouilleur *m.*

pugging ['pʌgiŋ], *s.* 1. corroyage *m* (de l'argile). 2. hourdis *m*, hourdage *m* (de plancher, de cloison); glaise *f.*

pugilism ['pju:dʒilizm], *s.* pugilisme *m*, la boxe.

pugilist ['pju:dʒilist], *s.* pugiliste *m*; boxeur *m.*

pugilistic [pju:dʒi'listik], *a.* pugilistique; de boxeur.

pugnacious [pʌg'neiʃəs], *a.* querelleur, -euse; batailleur, -euse.

pugnaciously [pʌg'neiʃəsli], *adv.* d'une manière querelleuse, batailleuse.

pugnaciousness, pugnacity [pʌg'neiʃəsnis, -'næsiti], *s.* pugnacité *f*; caractère querelleur, batailleur; humeur querelleuse, batailleuse.

puisne ['pju:ni]. *Jur:* 1. *a. & s.* **p. (judge),** (juge) conseiller *m* (à une cour); juge subalterne (d'une cour). 2. *a.* postérieur (en date) **(to,** à); subséquent.

puissant ['pwisənt], *a. A: & Lit:* puissant.

puke[1] [pju:k], *s. A: or P:* vomissement *m*, *P:* dégobillage *m.*

puke[2], *v.tr. & i. A: or P:* vomir, *P:* dégobiller.

pukka ['pʌkə], *a. O:* (*Anglo-Indian*) vrai, authentique; accompli, parfait; **a p. Englishman,** un vrai Anglais d'Angleterre; **a p. sahib,** un vrai gentleman.

pukras ['pʌkrəs], *s. Orn:* **p. (pheasant),** pucrasie *f.*

Pulcheria [pul'tʃiəriə]. *Pr.n.f. A.Hist:* Pulchérie.

pulchritude ['pʌlkritju:d], *s. Lit:* beauté *f.*

pule [pju:l], *v.i.* (*of child, chicken*) piauler, piailler; (*of child*) criailler; vagir; (*of bird*) pépier.

pulicaria [pju:li'kεəriə], *s. Bot:* pulicaire *f.*

Pulicidae [pju:'lisidi:], *s.pl. Ent:* pulicidés *m.*

puling[1] ['pju:liŋ], *a.* (enfant) (i) vagissant, (ii) piaulard, piailleur, criailleur.

puling[2], *s.* piaulement *m*, piaillement *m* (d'enfant, de poussin); vagissement *m*, criaillement *m* (d'enfant); piaulis *m*, pépiement *m* (d'oiseau).

pull[1] [pul], *s.* 1. (a) tirage *m*; traction *f*; **to give a p. at the bell,** tirer sur la sonnette; **p. bell,** sonnette à cordon; **bell p.,** cordon *m* de sonnette; **give it a hard p.!** tirez fort! **p. on the trigger,** pression *f* sur la détente, sur la gâchette; (b) force *f* d'attraction, appel *m*, sollicitation *f* (d'un aimant); **gravitational p.,** gravitation *f*; (c) effort *m* de traction; tension *f*, tirage (d'une courroie, etc.); **uphill p.,** effort à la montée; **it was a stiff p. to the top (of the hill),** il a fallu un grand effort pour arriver au sommet; *Veh:* **p. bar,** barre *f* de tirage, de tension; crochet *m* de traction, d'attelage (d'une locomotive); *Mec.E:* **p. rod,** tige *f*, tringle *f*, de traction; **p. handle,** tirette *f*; (d) *Row:* coup *m*, palade *f* (d'aviron); **we had a hard p.,** il nous a fallu ramer, souquer, ferme; (*e*) *Turf: etc:* manœuvre *f* (pour retenir un cheval). **2.** *Golf: etc:* longue crossée à gauche; coup tiré. **3.** avantage *m*; **to have plenty of p.,** (i) avoir un avantage marqué; (ii) *F:* avoir le bras long; avoir de l'influence, du piston. **4.** *F:* (*a*) gorgée *f*, lampée *f* (de bière, etc.); (*b*) **to take a p. at one's pipe,** tirer une bouffée de sa pipe. **5.** *Typ: Engr:* première épreuve.

pull[2], *v.*

I. *v.tr. & i.* **1.** (*a*) *v.tr.* tirer (une corde, les cheveux de qn, etc.); **to p. a muscle,** se déchirer un muscle; **pulled muscle,** élongation *f*; **to p. the trigger,** presser sur la détente, la gâchette; *F:* **to p. a gun,** sortir un revolver; **to p. a gun on s.o.,** tirer un coup de revolver à qn; **to p. the alarm bell,** tirer sur la sonnette d'alarme; **to p. the door to,** tirer, fermer, la porte; *v.i. Equit:* **horse that pulls,** cheval qui gagne à la main, qui résiste au mors, qui se braque; (*b*) *Row: v.i.* ramer; nager, souquer; *v.tr.* manier (un aviron); **to p. a stroke,** donner un coup de rame; souquer un coup; **to p. hard,** souquer ferme; **p. away!** avant! souquez! **to p. for the shore,** se diriger, nager, vers la terre, vers le rivage; **boat that pulls eight oars,** canot *m* à huit avirons; (*c*) *v.tr. Turf: etc:* retenir, tirer (un cheval); (*d*) *v.i.* **to p. on, at, a rope,** tirer sur un cordage, un cordon; **to p. at one's pipe,** tirer sur sa pipe; **to p. at a bottle,** boire un coup à même la bouteille. **2.** (*a*) *v.tr. & i.* traîner, tirer (une charrette, etc.); **the engine was pulling thirty trucks,** la locomotive traînait trente wagons; **the train was pulling into, out of, the station,** le train entrait en gare, sortait de la gare; *Aut:* **to p. out from behind a vehicle,** sortir de la file pour doubler; **horse that pulls well,** cheval qui tire bien; *Aut: etc:* **the engine is pulling heavily,** le moteur fatigue, peine; **to p. unevenly,** marcher irrégulièrement; (*of pers., car, etc.*) **to p. slowly up the hill,** gravir péniblement la côte; monter lentement (et avec difficulté); *Sp:* **two runners were pulling ahead,** deux coureurs se détachaient du peloton; **dress that pulls,** robe qui gêne; (*of pers.*) **they're pulling in different directions, they're not pulling together,** ils ne s'entendent pas, ne sont pas d'accord; *A:* **to p. caps,** se disputer; *Lit:* **it's p. devil, p. baker,** (i) ils se disputent; il faut les laisser se débrouiller; (ii) la lutte est égale; *Ph: etc:* **body pulled by a force,** corps sollicité, (r)appelé, par une force; (*b*) *v.tr. & i. Com: etc:* attirer (la clientèle); avoir de l'influence; exercer son influence; (*c*) *v.tr.* **to p. sth. apart, to pieces,** déchirer qch., mettre qch. en petits morceaux; **to p. s.o. to pieces,** critiquer sévèrement qn; **to p. sth. away from sth., from s.o.,** arracher qch. de qch., des mains de qn; **to p. sth. off sth., down from sth.,** tirer sur qch. pour le faire descendre; **to p. one's hat (down) over one's eyes,** renfoncer, rabattre, son chapeau sur ses yeux; **to p. sth. back into position,** ramener qch. en position; **p. it a bit further back,** reculez-le un peu; **p. your chair up to, nearer, the fire,** approchez votre fauteuil du feu; **we must try to p. it up a bit higher,** il faut essayer de le remonter, de le hisser, plus haut; *v.i. Gym:* **to p. up to the bar,** faire une traction; **to p. (one's car) in to, over to, up at, alongside, the kerb,** se ranger près du trottoir; **to p. sth. out of sth.,** tirer, sortir, qch. de qch.; **to p. s.o. out of a difficulty,** tirer qn d'une difficulté, d'une mauvaise situation; *F:* **to p. out all the stops,** donner le maximum, mettre le paquet; **p. it (over) nearer to you,** tirez-le plus près de vous. **3.** *v.tr.* **to p. a face,** faire une grimace. **4.** *v.tr.* **to p. a cork,** déboucher une bouteille; **to p. (up) a plant,** déraciner, arracher, une plante; **to p. (out) a tooth,** extraire, arracher, une dent; *F:* **to p. a fast one on s.o.,** avoir qn; *O:* **to p. a yarn,** débiter une histoire peu vraisemblable. **5.** *v.tr. Typ: Engr:* tirer (une épreuve). **6.** *v.tr. & i. Sp:* **to p. (the ball),** renvoyer la balle d'un coup tiré à gauche; *Golf:* faire un coup tiré.

II. (*compound verbs*) **1. pull about,** *v.tr.* (*a*) tirailler (qch.); (*b*) malmener, houspiller (qn).

2. pull back, *v.i.* hésiter; refuser à continuer (un projet, etc.); *Mil:* décrocher.

3. pull down, *v.tr.* (*a*) baisser, faire descendre (un store, etc.); descendre (sa jupe); (*b*) démolir, abattre (une maison, etc.); défaire (une cloison); (*c*) (*of illness*) abattre, affaiblir (qn); (*of circumstances*) décourager (qn).

4. pull in, (*a*) *v.tr.* (i) rentrer (un filet, etc.); (ii) retenir (son cheval); tirer les rênes de (son cheval); (iii) **to p. oneself in,** se serrer la taille; (iv) *F:* (*of police*) arrêter (un suspect); (v) attirer (le public); (*b*) *v.i.* (i) s'arrêter, faire étape (à un restaurant, etc.); (ii) *Turf:* couper un concurrent (en prenant la corde); *NAm: F:* **to be pulled in (for speeding),** être arrêté, sifflé (pour excès de vitesse).

5. pull off, *v.tr.* (*a*) détacher (qch. de qch.); (*with passive force*) **the lid simply pulls off,** il faut tirer pour enlever le couvercle; (*b*) *F:* gagner, remporter, décrocher (un prix); **to p. off a deal,** réussir une opération, boucler une affaire; **I wonder whether he'll p. it off,** je me demande s'il réussira, s'il en viendra à bout.

6. pull out, *v.i.* (*a*) *F:* partir, se retirer; **to p. out of the fire,** sauver la partie; (*b*) *F:* se dérober, tirer son épingle du jeu; (*c*) *Av:* faire une ressource.

7. pull over, (*a*) *v.i. Aut:* se ranger (pour laisser passer une autre voiture); (*b*) *v.tr.* **you'll p. me over,** tu vas me faire tomber, perdre l'équilibre.

8. pull round, (*a*) *v.tr.* remettre (qn) sur pied; ranimer (qn); (*b*) *v.i.* se remettre (d'une maladie); se ranimer.

9. pull through, (*a*) *v.tr.* tirer (qn) d'embarras, d'affaire; (*of doctor, etc.*) remettre (qn) sur pied; (*b*) *v.i.* se tirer d'affaire; s'en tirer; surmonter ses difficultés; (*of sick pers.*) guérir; **I'm afraid he won't p. through,** il ne guérira pas, n'en reviendra pas.

10. pull together, (*a*) *v.tr.* **to p. oneself together,** se reprendre; se remettre; reprendre ses esprits; **p. yourself together!** voyons, remettez-vous! (*b*) *v.i.* agir ensemble; s'entendre, s'accorder; *Row:* **p. together!** avant partout! nage d'accord!

11. pull up, (*a*) *v.tr.* (i) hausser, lever (un store, etc.); retrousser, relever (sa jupe); **to p. one's socks up,** (α) tirer, remonter, ses chaussettes; (β) *F:* se remuer, s'activer; remonter la pente; faire mieux que ça; faire appel à toute son énergie; (ii) arracher, déraciner, extirper (les mauvaises herbes); (iii) arrêter, parer (un cheval); **to p. oneself up,** s'arrêter (quand on est sur le point de faire, de dire, qch. d'indiscret); (iv) *F:* réprimander, rembarrer (qn); *Aut:* **to be pulled up (by the police),** se faire arrêter, siffler (par l'agent); (*b*) *v.i.* (i) s'arrêter; **he pulled up at the traffic lights,** il s'est arrêté au feu rouge; **we'll p. up at the next restaurant,** nous allons nous arrêter au prochain restaurant; (ii) *Sp: etc:* **to p. up on another competitor,** réduire la distance qui vous sépare d'un autre concurrent; **we'll p. up,** nous allons remonter ça.

pullback ['pulbæk]. **1.** *a.* **p. spring,** ressort *m* de rappel (de frein, etc.); *a. & s. Bill:* **p. (stroke),** effet *m* rétrograde; rétro *m*. **2.** *s.* (*a*) dispositif *m* de rappel; (*b*) entrave *f*. **3.** *s. U.S:* retrait *m* (de troupes).

puller ['pulər], *s.* **1.** (*pers.*) (*a*) tireur, -euse; arracheur, -euse; (*b*) rameur, -euse. **2.** (*a*) (*of horse*) **to be a good p.,** tirer à plein collier; (*b*) *Equit:* cheval fort en bouche, qui n'a pas de bouche, qui a la bouche forte, qui tire à la main. **3.** *Tls:* outil *m* de démontage; appareil démonteur; **ball-bearing p.,** extracteur *m* pour roulements à billes; **bushing p.,** arrache-bague *m, pl.* arrache-bagues; **gear p.,** arrache-engrenage *m, pl.* arrache-engrenages; arrache-pignon *m, pl.* arrache-pignons; **universal p.,** arrache-tout *m inv*; extracteur universel. **4.** *U.S:* (*a*) attraction *f*; *Th:* pièce *f* qui fait recette; **to be a good p.,** attirer un grand public; (*b*) *Com: A:* **p.-in,** employé *m* qui fait l'article sur le trottoir; aboyeur *m*.

pullet ['pulit], *s.* **1.** *Husb:* poulette *f*; **fattened p.,** poularde *f*; **corn-fed p.,** poulet *m* de grain. **2.** *Moll: F:* **p. shell,** palourde *f*.

pulley ['puli], *s.* (*a*) poulie *f*; *Min:* molette *f*, poulie (de chevalement); **grooved p.,** poulie à gorge; **chain p.,** poulie à empreintes pour chaînons; barbotin *m*; **frame p.,** poulie à chape; **cheek p., flange p.,** poulie à joues; **p. brace, bracket,** porte-poulie *m inv*; **p. housing,** carter *m* de poulie; **p. lathe,** tour *m* à poulies; (*b*) **band p., belt p.,** poulie à courroie; **cable p.,** roue à corde; **tension p.,** poulie tendeur; galet *m* tendeur; **driven p.,** poulie conduite, menée, réceptrice; **driving p.,** poulie menante, conductrice; poulie de commande, d'attaque; pignon *m* de commande; **fixed p.,** poulie fixe; **loose p., dead p.,** poulie folle; galopin *m*; **movable p.,** poulie mobile; **follow-up p.,** poulie d'asservissement; **return p.,** poulie de renvoi, de retour; **step p.,** poulie à gradins; **band-saw p.,** volant *m* porte-lame; (*c*) **p. block,** (i) moufle *m or f*; poulie mouflée; arcasse *f*; (ii) palan *m*; **differential p. block,** palan différentiel; **chain, rope, p. block,** palan à chaîne, à corde; **worm (geared) p. block,** palan (à engrenage) à vis sans fin; **travelling p. block,** palan roulant; **three-strand p. block,** moufle à trois brins; (*d*) **p. wheel,** réa *m*, rouet *m*; (*c*) *Nat.Hist:* **p.-shaped,** trochléen.

pull-in ['pulin], *s.* (*a*) parking *m* (*esp.* près d'un restaurant); (*b*) = restaurant pour routiers.

pulling ['puliŋ], *s.* **1.** tirage *m*; traction *f*; (*a*) *Typ: Engr:* tirage (d'épreuve(s)); **transfer p.,** tirage d'épreuve(s) à report; (*b*) *Mec.E:* **p. strain,** effort *m*, force *f*, de traction; (*c*) *Cmptr:* **p. file,** fichier *m* d'extraction; (*d*) *Row: O:* **p. race,** course *f* à l'aviron. **2.** *W.Tel:* glissement *m* (de fréquence); **p. figure,** indice *m* de glissement (aval).

Pullman ['pulmən], *a. & s. Rail:* **P. (car),** voiture *f* Pullman; *Aut:* **P. (coach),** autocar *m* Pullman.

pull-off ['pulɔf]. **1.** *s. Sm.a:* (*of trigger*) **light, hard, p.-o.,** détente douce, dure. **2.** *a.* **p.-o. spring,** ressort *m* de rappel; **p.-o. lid,** couvercle *m* à glissière; *Rail:* **p.-o. cable,** câble *m* de suspension (de caténaire).

pull-on ['pulɔn], *a.* (vêtement) qui s'enfile, que l'on se passe par-dessus la tête.

pullorum [pu'lɔːrəm], *s. Vet:* **p. disease,** pullorose *f*.

pull-out ['pulaut]. **1.** *a.* **p.-o. slide,** tablette *f* à coulisse, tirette *f* (de table, de bureau); rallonge *f* à l'italienne (de table); **p.-o. handle,** poignée *f* de traction. **2.** *s.* (*a*) *Av:* (*from dive*) ressource *f*; (*b*) *Journ:* supplément *m* (qu'on peut détacher de la revue).

pullover ['pulouvər], *s. Cost:* pull-over *m, pl.* pull-overs; *F:* pull *m*.

pull-through ['pulθruː], *s. Sm.a:* ficelle *f* (de nettoyage); ramoneuse *f*.

pull-to ['pultuː], *a. Aut: etc:* **p.-to handle,** poignée *f* de tirage (d'une portière).

pullulate ['pʌljuleit], *v.i.* (*a*) (*of seed*) germer; (*of bud*) pousser; (*b*) (*of rats, heresy, etc.*) pulluler; (*of opinions, etc.*) proliférer; (*c*) (*of vermin*) grouiller.

pullulation [pʌlju'leiʃ(ə)n], *s.* (*a*) germination *f* (d'une graine); pousse *f* (des bourgeons, etc.); (*b*) pullulation *f* (des rats, etc.); prolifération *f* (d'une doctrine).

pull-up ['pulʌp], *s.* **1.** (*a*) arrêt *m* (d'une voiture, etc.); *Mil:* à-coup *m* (dans une colonne, etc.); (*b*) = restaurant *m* pour routiers; **good p.-up for carmen,** rendez-vous des routiers. **2.** (*a*) *Mount:* tirée *f*; (*b*) *Gym:* rétablissement *m*; (*c*) *Sp:* **a good p.-up,** une belle remontée.

pully-haul ['pulihɔːl], *v.tr.* tirer à force de bras.

pulmobranchiate [pʌlmou'bræŋkieit], *a. Moll:* pulmobranche.

pulmometer [pʌl'mɔmitər], *s. Med:* spiromètre *m*.

pulmonaria [pʌlmə'nɛəriə], *s. Bot:* pulmonaire *f*.

pulmonary ['pʌlmənəri], *a.* **1.** *Anat:* pulmonaire; **p. artery, vein,** artère *f*, veine *f*, pulmonaire; **p. circulation,** circulation *f* pulmonaire; **p. disease,** maladie *f* pulmonaire, des poumons; **p. emphysema,** emphysème *m* pulmonaire. **2.** *O:* (*of pers.*) poitrinaire, pulmonique. **3.** *Z:* (animal) poumoné, pourvu de poumons.

Pulmonata [pʌlmə'neitə], *s.pl. Moll:* pulmonés *m*.

pulmonate ['pʌlməneit]. **1.** *a. Z:* poumoné; *Moll:* pulmoné. **2.** *s. Moll:* pulmoné *m*.

pulmonic [pʌl'mɔnik]. **1.** *a.* pulmonaire; pulmonique. **2.** *s. Med:* pulmonique *mf*; poitrinaire *mf*.

Pulmotor ['pʌlmoutər], *s. R.t.m: U.S:* poumon artificiel; réanimateur *m* électrique.

pulp[1] [pʌlp], *s.* (*a*) pulpe *f*, chair *f* (des fruits); pulpe (des doigts); **dental p.,** pulpe dentaire; **devitalized p.,** pulpe dévitalisée; **necrotic p.,** pulpe nécrosée; **vital, non-vital, p.,** pulpe vitale, avitale; (*b*) **beet p.,** pulpe de betterave; **paper p.,** pâte *f*, pulpe, à papier; *Paperm:* **mineral p.,** fines *fpl* de minerai; **strong p.,** pâte dure, solide, écrue; *U.S:* **p. fiction, p. novels,** romans *m* de, à, quatre sous; **to reduce sth. to a p.,** réduire qch. en pulpe; *Pharm:* pulper qch.; *F:* **I reduced him to a p.,** je l'ai mis en bouillie, en marmelade; j'en ai fait de la charpie; je l'ai écrabouillé; **to have one's arm crushed to p.,** avoir le bras complètement écrasé.

pulp[2]. **1.** *v.tr.* (*a*) réduire en pulpe, en pâte; *Pharm:* pulper; **to p. (books, etc.),** mettre (des livres) au pilon; mettre au papier (une fin d'édition, etc.); (*b*) décortiquer (des graines, des grains de café). **2.** *v.i.* devenir charnu, pulpeux.

pulpboard ['pʌlpbɔːd], *s.* carton-bois *m inv*; carton-pâte *m inv*.

pulpectomy [pʌl'pektəmi], *s. Dent:* pulpectomie *f*.

pulped [pʌlpt], *a. Ind:* mâché; *Publ:* mis au pilon.

pulper ['pʌlpər], *s. Tls: etc:* dépulpeur *m*.

pulpiness ['pʌlpinis], *s.* nature pulpeuse, charnue (d'un fruit, etc.).

pulping ['pʌlpiŋ], *s.* **1.** réduction *f* en pulpe, en pâte; pulpage *m*, pulpation *f*; *Paperm: etc:* **p. machine,** pilon *m*; **this book is fit only for p.,** voilà un livre à mettre au pilon. **2.** décorticage *m*, décortication *f*.

pulpit ['pulpit], *s.* **1.** (*a*) chaire *f* (du prédicateur); **to mount the p.,** monter en chaire; **to express an opinion from the p.,** exprimer une opinion en (pleine) chaire; **p. oratory,** éloquence *f* de la chaire; éloquence sacrée; (*b*) *Lit:* les orateurs *m* de la chaire; la prédication; **the influence of the p.,** l'influence de la chaire. **2.** vigie *f* (de surveillant d'usine, etc.).

pulpiteer [pulpi'tiər], *s. Pej:* prêcheur *m*.

pulpiteering [pulpi'tiəriŋ], *s. Pej:* prêcherie *f*.

pulpitis [pʌl'paitis], *s. Med:* pulpite *f*; **acute p., chronic p.,** pulpite aiguë, chronique; **suppurative p., ulcerative p.,** pulpite purulente, ulcéreuse.

pulpless ['pʌlplis], *a.* (*of tooth*) dépulpé, sans pulpe.

pulpotomy [pʌl'pɔtəmi], *s. Dent:* pulpotomie *f*, dépulpation *f*.

pulpous ['pʌlpəs], *a.* pulpeux, pultacé, charnu.

pulpwood ['pʌlpwud], *s. Paperm:* bois *m* de papeterie.

pulpy ['pʌlpi], *a.* **1.** pulpeux, pultacé, charnu. **2.** *F:* mou, *f.* molle; flasque.

pulque ['pulki], *s. Dist:* pulque *m.*

pulsar ['pʌlsər], *s. Astr:* pulsar *m.*

pulsatance ['pʌlsətəns], *s. El:* pulsation *f*; *Ph:* vitesse *f* angulaire.

pulsate [pʌl'seit]. **1.** *v.i.* (*a*) (*of heart, etc.*) battre; (*b*) palpiter; vibrer; (*c*) (*of elastic fluid*) avoir des pulsations; entrer en vibration. **2.** *v.tr. Min:* cribler au berceau (des alluvions diamantifères).

pulsatile ['pʌlsətail], *a.* **1.** *Med:* (tumeur *f*, etc.) pulsatile. **2.** *Mus:* (instrument *m*) de percussion.

pulsatilla [pʌlsə'tilə], *s. Bot:* pulsatille *f*; passe-fleur *f*, *pl.* passe-fleurs; fleur *f* de Pâques; coquelourde *f.*

pulsating [pʌl'seitiŋ], *a.* (*a*) *Physiol:* (*of heart, etc.*) battant, palpitant; (*b*) *El:* (courant, tension, etc.) pulsatoire; (*c*) *Av:* **p. de-icer,** dégivreur *m* à impulsions; (*d*) *Astr:* **p. star,** étoile pulsante, variable; céphéide *f*; (*e*) *Nat.Hist:* **p. vacuole,** vacuole *f* contractile.

pulsation [pʌl'seiʃ(ə)n], *s.* (*a*) *Physiol:* pulsation *f*, battement *m* (du cœur, des artères, etc.); (*b*) pulsation, vibration *f* (d'un moteur, etc.); *Ph:* **sound pulsations,** pulsations sonores; **p. damper,** amortisseur *m* de pulsations; (*c*) *El:* pulsation (du courant); *Elcs:* impulsion *f*; **high frequency pulsations,** impulsions (à) haute fréquence; **p. generator, p. transformer,** générateur *m*, transformateur *m*, d'impulsions; (*d*) *Astr:* pulsation (d'une étoile variable).

pulsative ['pʌlsətiv], *a.* pulsatif.

pulsator [pʌl'seitər], *s.* **1.** *Min:* crible *m* à grille mobile; berceau *m* (pour alluvions diamantifères). **2.** *Ind:* pulsomètre *m.*

pulsatory ['pʌlsətəri], *a.* pulsatoire, pulsatif; *El:* (courant) pulsatoire.

pulse[1] [pʌls], *s.* **1.** *Physiol:* pouls *m*; **low p.,** pouls faible; **quick p.,** pouls fréquent, précipité; **irregular p.,** pouls intermittent; **to feel, take, s.o.'s p.,** prendre le pouls à qn; **let's feel your p.,** voyons votre pouls; **p. rate,** fréquence *f* du pouls; **p. pressure,** pression différentielle. **2.** (*a*) pulsation *f*, battement *m* (du cœur, d'une artère); (*b*) *Ph:* vibration *f* (de la lumière, du son, etc.); **p. number,** indice *m* de pulsation; (*c*) *Elcs: W.Tel:* impulsion *f*; **calibration p.,** impulsion étalon; **difference p.,** impulsion différentielle; **drive p., driving p.,** impulsion de commande; **input, output, p.,** impulsion d'entrée, de sortie; **potential, voltage, p.,** impulsion de tension; **recurrent p.,** impulsion périodique; **p. amplifier,** amplificateur *m* d'impulsion; **p. carrier,** train porteur (d'impulsions); **p. decay,** affaiblissement *m*, amortissement *m*, de l'impulsion; **p. height,** hauteur *f*, amplitude *f*, d'impulsion; **p. height analyser,** analyseur *m* d'amplitude (d'impulsions); **p. power,** puissance pulsée, puissance de crête; **p. rate, p. ratio,** taux *m* d'impulsions; **p. modulated,** (i) modulé par impulsions; (ii) à modulation *f* d'impulsion; *Rad:* **strobe p.,** impulsion de fixation; **under p. conditions,** en régime impulsionnel; *Cmptr:* **digit p.,** impulsion d'information; **enable p., inhibit p.,** impulsion de validation, de blocage; **read(ing) p.,** impulsion (de commande) de lecture; **write p., writing p.,** impulsion d'écriture; (*d*) *Pros: Mus:* cadence *f*, rythme *m*, mouvement *m* (rythmique). **3.** *Mec.Meas:* pied-livre-seconde *m.*

pulse[2]. **1.** *v.i.* avoir des pulsations; battre; palpiter; (*of blood*) **to p. through the arteries,** circuler dans les artères par pulsations rythmées; **exercise sends the blood pulsing through the veins,** l'exercice *m* fouette le sang, active la circulation du sang; **the life pulsing through a great city,** la vie qui anime une grande ville. **2.** *v.tr. El: etc:* moduler (un courant) en impulsions; **pulsed waves,** ondes fonctionnant, travaillant, en régime d'impulsions.

pulse[3], *s. coll.* plantes légumineuses; légumes *mpl* à gousse.

pulsed [pʌlst], *a.* (*a*) pulsé; *Atom.Ph:* **p. column,** colonne pulsée; **p. neutron source,** source *f* de neutrons pulsés; (*b*) *Elcs: W.Tel:* **p. frequency modulation,** modulation *f* de fréquence par impulsions; **p. oscillator,** oscillateur *m* à impulsions; *Av: etc:* **p. altimeter,** radar *m* altimétrique à impulsions; **p. glide-path,** atterrissage *m* par impulsions.

pulser ['pʌlsər], *s. Elcs: W.Tel:* oscillateur *m* à impulsions.

pulsimeter [pʌl'simitər], *s. Med:* pulsimètre *m*, sphygmomètre *m.*

pulsing ['pʌlsiŋ]. **1.** *a. El:* (circuit) pulsant; *Rail:* **p. shoe,** frotteur *m*, patin *m*, pulsant. **2.** *s. Elcs: W.Tel:* émission *f* d'impulsions.

pulsion ['pʌlʃ(ə)n], *s.* pulsion *f.*

pulsometer [pʌl'sɔmitər], *s.* **1.** *Ind:* pulsomètre *m.* **2.** *Med:* pulsimètre *m.*

pulsus paradoxus ['pʌlsəspærə'dɔksəs], *s. Med:* pouls paradoxal.

pultaceous [pʌl'teiʃəs], *a.* pultacé, pulpeux.

pulverizable [pʌlvə'raizəbl], *a.* pulvérisable.

pulverization [pʌlvərai'zeiʃ(ə)n], *s.* pulvérisation *f.*

pulverize ['pʌlvəraiz]. **1.** *v.tr.* (*a*) pulvériser, réduire en poudre; broyer (le charbon); *Pharm:* porphyriser; **to p. s.o.,** démolir qn, le discours de qn; pulvériser (l'orateur, etc.); (*b*) atomiser (de la peinture liquide, de l'eau de Cologne, etc.); *I.C.E:* vaporiser, atomiser (l'essence). **2.** *v.i.* (*a*) tomber en poussière; se pulvériser; (*b*) se vaporiser.

pulverizer ['pʌlvəraizər], *s.* (*device*) pulvérisateur *m*; vaporisateur *m* (d'essence, etc.); *Ind:* broyeur *m* (de charbon).

pulverizing ['pʌlvəraiziŋ], *s.* **1.** pulvérisation *f*; broyage *m* (du charbon); *Pharm:* porphyrisation *f.* **2.** vaporisation *f.*

pulverulence [pʌl'verjuləns], *s.* pulvérulence *f*; état poudreux.

pulverulent [pʌl'verjulənt], *a.* pulvérulent; poudreux.

pulvimixer ['pʌlvimiksər], *s. Civ.E:* tritureuse *f.*

pulvinar [pʌl'vainɑːr], *s.* pulvinar *m.*

pulvinate ['pʌlvineit], *a. Bot: Ent: etc:* pulviné.

pulvino [pʌl'vainou], *s. Arch:* sommier *m* de voûte.

puma ['pjuːmə], *s. Z:* puma *m*, couguar *m.*

pumice[1] ['pʌmis], *s.* **p. (stone),** (pierre *f*) ponce *f.*

pumice[2], *v.tr.* poncer; passer (une surface) à la pierre ponce; polir à la ponce.

pumiced ['pʌmist], *a. Vet:* **p. foot,** pied *m* comble; fourmilière *f.*

pumiceous [pjuː'miʃəs], *a.* ponceux, pumiqueux.

pummel[1] ['pʌm(ə)l], *s.* = POMMEL[1].

pummel[2], *v.tr.* **(pummelled)** battre, rosser; bourrer (qn) de coups de poing.

pummelling ['pʌməliŋ], *s.* volée *f* de coups; **to give s.o. a good p.,** bourrer qn de coups.

pump[1] [pʌmp], *s.* **1.** pompe *f*; (*a*) *Ph: Mec.E:* **suction p., lift p.,** pompe aspirante; **force p.,** pompe (re)foulante; **lift-and-force p.,** pompe aspirante et foulante; **induction p.,** pompe à induction; **jet p.,** pompe à jet; **reciprocating p.,** pompe à mouvement alternatif; **continuous-action p.,** pompe à mouvement continu; **single-acting p., double-acting p.,** pompe à simple effet, à double effet; **rotary p.,** pompe rotative; **centrifugal p.,** pompe centrifuge; **turbo p.,** pompe centrifuge à diffuseur; **main p., auxiliary p., booster p.,** pompe principale, secondaire, auxiliaire; **hand p.,** pompe à bras, à main; **foot p.,** pompe à pied; **motor p., steam p.,** pompe à moteur, à vapeur; **electric p.,** pompe (à commande) électrique; **wind p.,** pompe éolienne, pompe à vent; **p. spindle,** axe *m* de pompe; **p. body, barrel, cylinder,** corps *m*, cylindre *m*, de pompe; **one-throw, three-throw, p.,** pompe à un, à trois, corps; **p. stage,** étage *m* de pompe; **one-stage, two-stage, p.,** pompe à un étage, à deux étages; **multi-stage p.,** pompe à plusieurs étages, pompe multicellulaire; **p. pack, gland,** garniture *f*, presse-étoupe *m*, de pompe; **packless, glandless, p.,** pompe sans garniture, sans presse-étoupe; **p. connection,** raccord *m*, tuyauterie *f*, de pompe; **p. governor,** régulateur *m* de pompe; **p. house, room, compartment,** bâtiment *m*, chambre *f*, compartiment *m*, des pompes; (*at spa*) **p. room,** pavillon *m* (où l'on prend les eaux); **vane p.,** pompe à ailette, à palette; **(flap-)valve p.,** pompe à clapet; **valveless p.,** pompe sans clapet; **diaphragm p.,** pompe à diaphragme, à membrane; **gear p.,** pompe à engrenage; **piston, plunger, p.,** pompe à piston, à plongeur; **hollow-piston, solid-piston, p.,** pompe à piston creux, à piston plein; **propeller p.,** pompe à hélice; **turbine p., impeller p.,** pompe à turbine; **stirrup p.,** pompe à étrier; **screw p.,** pompe à vis; (*b*) **air p., pneumatic p.,** pompe à air, pompe pneumatique; **mercurial air p.,** pompe à mercure; **vacuum p.,** pompe à vide; **high-vacuum p.,** pompe à vide élevé; **compression p.,** pompe de compression; **booster p.,** pompe de sur(com)pression; **bicycle p.,** pompe à bicyclette; *Nau: Civ.E:* **diver's p.,** pompe de scaphandre; (*c*) *Hyd:* **hydraulic p., water p.,** pompe hydraulique, à eau; **the village p.,** la pompe du village; **p. water,** eau *f* de pompe; *Min:* eau de puits; *F:* **hair as straight as a yard of p. water,** cheveux *m* raides comme la justice, comme des baguettes de tambour; **irrigating p.,** pompe d'arrosage; **mining p.,** pompe de mine; **drainage, draining, p.,** pompe d'épuisement, d'exhaure; **sinking p.,** pompe de fonçage, d'avaleresse; **fire p.,** pompe à incendie, d'incendie; **priming, primer, p.,** pompe d'amorçage; **self-priming p.,** pompe à amorçage automatique; **constant-flow p.,** pompe à débit constant; **variable-flow, variable-delivery, adjustable-discharge, p.,** pompe à débit variable; *Nau:* **water-service p.,** pompe de service; **sanitary p.,** pompe sanitaire; *Mch: Ind: etc:* **feed p., donkey p.,** pompe alimentaire; **electric, steam, feed p.,** pompe d'alimentation électrique, à vapeur; **water feed p.,** pompe d'alimentation en eau; **boiler feed p.,** pompe d'alimentation de chaudière; **discharge p.,** *Av:* **scavenger p.,** pompe d'épuisement, d'extraction; *Nau:* **main p.,** pompe royale; **bilge p.,** pompe de cale; **ballast p.,** pompe de ballast; **dredging p.,** pompe de dragage; (*of tanker*) **cargo p.,** pompe de chargement, de déchargement; **stripping p., stripper p.,** pompe d'assèchement; (*d*) *Mch: I.C.E:* **(water, fuel, oil) circulating, circulation, p.,** pompe de circulation (d'eau, de combustible, d'huile); **lubricating p.,** pompe à graisse, de graissage; **oil p.,** pompe à huile; *Aut:* **accelerating p.,** pompe de reprise; **petrol p.,** (i) (*of engine*) pompe à essence; (ii) (*at garage*) poste *m* d'essence; distributeur *m* (automatique) (d'essence); **(petrol) p. attendant,** pompiste *mf*; **fuel p.,** pompe à carburant, à combustible; **fuel-feed p.,** pompe d'alimentation en combustible; **(fuel) booster p.,** pompe de suralimentation, de gavage (en combustible); (*of diesel engine*) **(fuel) injection p.,** pompe d'injection (de carburant); **direct-injection p.,** pompe d'injection directe; *Av:* **wobble p.,** pompe à main, à plateau oscillant; (*e*) *Atom.Ph:* **conduction p.,** pompe de transfert; **coolant p.,** pompe des circuits de réfrigérant; **proportioning p.,** pompe de dosage; **ionic, ionization, p.,** pompe ionique, d'ionisation; (*f*) *Med:* **stomach p.,** pompe stomacale; **breast p.,** pompe à sein; **saliva p.,** pompe à salive; (*g*) *Sm.a:* **p. gun,** fusil *m* à magasin tubulaire. **2.** **to give (sth.) a p.,** donner un coup de pompe à (qch.).

pump[2]. **1.** *v.tr.* (*a*) **to p. (out, up) water,** (i) pomper, extraire, de l'eau; (ii) épuiser l'eau à la pompe; **to p. out a vacuum tube,** vider, faire le vide dans, un tube électronique; **to p. out a boat,** agréner une embarcation; *Nau:* **to p. out the holds,** assécher les cales; *F:* **to p. a secret out of s.o.,** arracher un secret à qn; tirer un secret de qn; **to p. up a tyre,** gonfler un pneu; (*b*) **to p. a well dry,** assécher un puits; **to p. ship,** (i) *Nau:* pomper l'eau de la cale; mettre l'équipage aux pompes; (ii) *P: A:* pisser; *F:* **to p. s.o.,** sonder qn; pomper qn (pour avoir des renseignements); cuisiner qn; (*c*) **to p. water into a boiler, air into a mine,** refouler de l'eau dans une chaudière, de l'air dans une mine; **to p. air into s.o.'s lungs,** insuffler de l'air dans les poumons de qn. **2.** *v.i.* (*of heart, machine, etc.*) pomper.

pump[3], *s. Cost:* (*a*) = ballerine *f*; (*b*) *A: & NAm:* escarpin *m*, chaussure décolletée.

pumped [pʌmpt], *a.* (*a*) pompé; asséché; *Elcs:* (*of vacuum tube*) **p. (out),** vidé; **p. rectifier,** redresseur *m* à vide entretenu; (*b*) *F:* (*of pers.*) essoufflé; **p. (out),** épuisé, éreinté, pompé.

pumper ['pʌmpər], *s.* **1.** ouvrier chargé des pompes; *Min:* ouvrier à l'exhaure. **2.** *F:* questionneur astucieux.

pump-handle ['pʌmphændl], *v.tr. F:* **to p.-h. s.o.,** serrer vigoureusement la main à qn.

pumping ['pʌmpiŋ], *s.* **1.** (*a*) pompage *m*, extraction *f* (de l'eau, etc.); **p. (out),** épuisement *m* (des eaux dans une mine, etc.); exhaure *f*; asséchage *m* (d'un puits); **back-crank p.,** pompage par commande excentrique; **p. engine,** pompe *f* d'extraction, d'épuisement; *Min:* épuise *f*; **p. station,** station *f* de pompage, d'épuisement, des pompes; *Min:* **p. shaft,** puits *m* d'exhaure, d'épuisement; (*b*) gonflage *m* (d'un pneu). **2.** *F:* interrogation *f*, cuisinage *m* (de qn).

pumpkin ['pʌmpkin], *s. Hort:* potiron *m*; citrouille *f*; courge *f.*

pumpkinhead ['pʌmpkinhed], *s. U.S: F:* idiot, -ote; nouille *f*, andouille *f.*

pumpkinseed ['pʌmpkinsiːd], *s. Ich:* perche *f* soleil.

pun[1] [pʌn], *s.* calembour *m*, jeu *m* de mots.

pun[2], *v.i.* **(punned)** faire des calembours, des jeux de mots; jouer sur les mots.

pun[3], *v.tr.* damer, pilonner, piler (la terre, le pisé); tasser, consolider (le béton coulé).

puna ['puːnə], *s.* (*a*) *Geog:* puna *f* (des Andes); (*b*) *Med:* puna, mal *m* des montagnes.

punch[1] [pʌntʃ], *s.* **1.** *Tls: etc:* (*a*) poinçon *m*; (*for piercing*) perçoir *m*, perce *f*; **rivet(t)ing p.,** poinçon à river; bouterolle *f*; **(ticket, etc.) p.,** poinçon (de contrôleur de chemin de fer, etc.); pince *f* de contrôle; **number p.,** poinçon à chiffrer; **centre p., centring p.,** pointeau *m* (de mécanicien); amorçoir *m*; **p. mark,** coup *m* de pointeau; repère *m*; **nail p., brad p.,** chasse-clous *m inv*; chasse-pointes *m inv*; **bookbinder's p.,** petit fer; (*b*) (*machine*) poinçonneuse *f*; **p. press,** presse *f* à découper, à l'emporte-pièces; **p. pressing,** découpage *m* à l'emporte-pièces; **bear p.,** poinçonneuse portative; (*c*) **hollow p.,** emporte-pièce *m inv*, découpoir *m*;

(**paper**) **p.**, perforateur *m* à papier; *Cmptr:* **card p.**, **tape p.**, perforateur de cartes, de bande; **automatic p.**, perforateur automatique; **automatic feed p.**, perforateur à alimentation automatique; **spot p.**, **hand p.**, poinçonneuse manuelle, trou par trou; perforateur manuel; (*pers.*) **p. operator**, perforateur, -trice; perforeur, -euse; **p. card** = **punched card** (*see* PUNCHED). 2. *Cmptr:* perforation *f*; **digit p.**, perforation numérique; **zone p.**, perforation hors-texte.

punch², *v.tr.* (*a*) percer, découper (à l'emporte-pièce); poinçonner (un trou, une barre de fer, un billet); perforer (le cuir, etc.); **to p. a nail in**, enfoncer un clou au poinçon; **to p. out**, chasser (une goupille); (*b*) **to p. an iron plate**, estamper, étamper, une plaque de fer; (*c*) *Cmptr:* perforer (une carte, une bande); sortir (un document) sur perforateur; (*d*) *v.i. Ind:* **to p. in, out**, pointer à l'entrée, à la sortie.

punch³, *s.* **1.** (*a*) coup *m* de poing; **to give s.o. a p. in the face**, flanquer, coller, son poing sur la figure de qn; donner à qn un coup de poing à la figure; (*b*) *Box:* coup de poing, punch *m*; **to pack a good p.**, (i) cogner dur; (ii) *F:* (*of drink*) être corsé; **to pull a p.**, retenir, adoucir, un coup; **he didn't pull his punches**, (i) il n'a pas ménagé l'adversaire; (ii) *F:* il n'a pas mâché ses mots; il n'y est pas allé par quatre chemins. **2.** *F:* force *f*, énergie *f*; *Sp:* punch; **style that has p.**, style incisif, énergique, nerveux; **p. line**, pointe *f* (d'une plaisanterie); **the team lacked p.**, l'équipe *f* manquait de punch.

punch⁴, *v.tr.* (*a*) donner un coup de poing à (qn); cogner sur (qn); **to p. s.o. on the nose**, flanquer, coller, son poing sur le nez de qn; **to p. s.o.'s head**, flanquer des taloches à qn; *F:* **he's got a face you'd like to p.**, il a une tête de massacre; *Sp:* **he was punching the ball**, il s'entraînait au punching-ball; (*b*) *NAm:* **to p. cattle**, être cowboy.

punch⁵, *s.* (*drink*) punch *m*; **milk p.**, lait *m* au rhum.

Punch⁶. *Pr.n.m.* = Polichinelle; Guignol; **P. and Judy show** = (théâtre *m* de) Guignol.

punch⁷. **1.** *s.* **Suffolk p.**, cheval *m* de gros trait du Suffolk. **2.** *a.* & *s. Dial: F:* (homme) trapu.

punchball ['pʌnʃbɔ:l], *s. Box:* punching(-ball) *m*.

punchbowl ['pʌnʃboul], *s.* **1.** bol *m* à punch. **2.** *Geog:* cuvette *f* (entre collines).

punchdrunk ['pʌnʃdrʌŋk], *a. F: esp. Box:* abruti, stupéfié (de coups).

punched [pʌʃt], *a.* (*a*) perforé, percé; poinçonné; *Metalw:* **p. piece**, pièce estampée; (*b*) *Cmptr:* **p. card**, carte perforée, fiche *f* mécanographique; **p. card file**, fichier *m* mécanographique, sur cartes perforées; (*device*) **p. card reader**, lecteur *m* de cartes perforées; **p. card machine operator**, mécanographe *mf*.

puncheon¹ ['pʌnʃ(ə)n], *s.* **1.** *Min:* (*a*) cale *f*, tasseau *m*; (*b*) poteau *m* d'étayage. **2.** *Const: U.S:* tronçon fendu. **3.** *Tls:* poinçon *m*.

puncheon², *s. Meas:* tonneau *m* (de 72 à 120 gallons); **p. of rum**, pièce *f* de rhum.

puncher¹ ['pʌnʃər], *s.* **1.** (*pers.*) (*a*) poinçonneur *m*, perceur *m* (de tôle, etc.); poinçonneur (de billets, etc.); (*b*) *Cmptr:* perforateur, -trice, perforeur, -euse (de cartes, de bandes); (*c*) *Metalw:* estampeur *m*, frappeur *m*. **2.** (*device*) (*a*) poinçonneuse *f*; perforateur *m*; emporte-pièce *m inv*; (*b*) découpeuse *f*; (*c*) *Cmptr:* perforateur (de cartes, de bandes); (*d*) *Min:* haveuse *f* à pic.

puncher², *s.* (*a*) *Box:* puncheur *m*; (*b*) (**cow**) **p.**, cowboy *m*.

Punchinello [pʌnʃi'nelou]. **1.** *Pr.n.m. Th:* Polichinelle. **2.** *s. F: O:* personne grosse et courte; personne boulotte; homme courtaud, trapu, ragot.

punching¹ [pʌnʃiŋ], *s.* **1.** (*a*) perçage *m*, poinçonnage *m*; **p. (out)**, découpage *m* (à l'emporte-pièce); **p. press**, machine *f* à découper; découpeuse *f*; **p. machine**, poinçonneuse *f*; machine à poinçonner; (*b*) poinçonnement *m*, poinçonnage (des billets, etc.); *Ind: etc:* **p. in, out**, pointage *m* à l'entrée, à la sortie; (*c*) *Cmptr:* perforation *f* (des cartes, des bandes); **double p.**, double frappe *f*; **lace p.**, (perforation en) grille *f*; **multiple p.**, multiperforation *f*; **zone p.**, perforation (en) hors-texte; **p. unit**, perforateur *m*; **p. machine**, perforatrice *f*. **2.** (*a*) *Metalw:* pièce étampée; (*b*) **punchings**, (i) perforations; (ii) confetti *mpl* de perforation.

punching², *s.* **1.** coups *mpl* de poing; *Box:* **p. ball**, punching(-ball) *m*; **p. bag**, punching-bag *m*. **2.** *NAm:* conduite *f* (des bestiaux) à l'aiguillon; **to go cow p.**, travailler comme cowboy.

punchless ['pʌnʃlis], *a. Cmptr: etc:* sans perforation(s); non perforé.

punch-mark ['pʌnʃmɑ:k], *v.tr.* repérer au poinçon.

punch-up ['pʌnʃʌp], *s. F:* bagarre *f*.

punctate ['pʌŋkteit], *a. Nat.Hist:* pointillé, ponctulé.

punctiform ['pʌŋktifɔ:m], *a.* ponctulé, punctiforme.

punctilio [pʌŋk'tiliou], *s.* **1.** pointillerie *f*; formalisme exagéré. **2.** point *m* d'étiquette.

punctilious [pʌŋk'tiliəs], *a.* **1.** (*a*) pointilleux, méticuleux, formaliste; qui s'attache à des vétilles, à des minuties; (*b*) **he is p. on every point of honour**, il est chatouilleux sur tous les points d'honneur; **loyal and p. to a high degree**, loyal et scrupuleux au suprême degré. **2. to be very p.**, se soucier beaucoup du protocole; s'attacher à un formalisme exagéré; être très cérémonieux.

punctiliously [pʌŋk'tiliəsli], *adv.* (*a*) pointilleusement; scrupuleusement; (*b*) cérémonieusement.

punctiliousness [pʌŋk'tiliəsnis], *s.* **1.** pointillerie *f*; scrupule *m* des détails. **2.** souci *m* du protocole; **diplomats must always act with extreme p.**, les diplomates doivent toujours agir avec une extrême délicatesse, avec beaucoup de tact.

punctual ['pʌŋktjuəl], *a.* **1.** (*a*) ponctuel; **he's always p.**, il est toujours à l'heure, toujours ponctuel; (*b*) *A:* ponctuel, exact, régulier; pointilleux, méticuleux. **2.** *Mth:* **p. co-ordinates**, coordonnées *f* d'un point.

punctuality [pʌŋktju'æliti], *s.* (*a*) ponctualité *f*; (*b*) *A:* ponctualité, exactitude *f*.

punctually ['pʌŋktjuəli], *adv.* (*a*) ponctuellement; (*b*) *A:* ponctuellement, exactement, assidûment.

punctuate ['pʌŋktjueit], *v.tr.* **1.** ponctuer (une phrase, etc.). **2.** ponctuer (ses mots en parlant); donner plus de force à, accentuer (une remarque, etc.); ponctuer, souligner, scander (une phrase) de (soupirs, etc.); **speech punctuated with anecdotes**, discours agrémenté d'anecdotes.

punctuation [pʌŋktju'eiʃ(ə)n], *s.* ponctuation *f*; **p. mark**, signe *m* de ponctuation.

punctulated ['pʌŋktjuleitid], *a. Nat.Hist:* pointillé, ponctulé.

punctum, *pl.* -a ['pʌŋktəm, -ə], *s. Biol: etc:* point *m*.

puncture¹ ['pʌŋktjər], *s.* **1.** (*a*) *Surg:* ponction *f* (d'une ampoule, d'un abcès); **lumbar p.**, ponction lombaire; (*b*) crevaison *f*, perforation *f* (d'un pneu, d'un abcès). **2.** (*hole*) (*a*) piqûre *f*, perforation; (*b*) (*in tyre*) crevaison; **p. patch**, pastille adhésive (pour réparer un pneu); Rustine *f* (*R.t.m.*); **p. sealant**, auto-obturant *m*, *pl.* auto-obturants. **3.** *El:* claquage *m*, percement *m*, perforation *f* (d'un câble, d'un isolant); **p. test**, essai *m* de claquage, de perforation; **p. voltage**, tension *f* de percement.

puncture², **1.** (*a*) *v.tr.* ponctionner (une ampoule, un abcès); (*b*) *v.tr.* crever, perforer (un pneu); (*c*) *v.i.* (*of tyre*) crever; avoir une crevaison. **2.** *v.tr. El:* claquer, percer, perforer (un câble, etc.).

punctured ['pʌŋktjəd], *a.* **1.** (abcès, etc.) crevé, perforé; (pneu) crevé. **2.** fait, composé, de piqûres; *Typ:* **p. blanket**, blanchet piqué de trous. **3.** *El:* (*of cable, etc.*) claqué, percé, perforé.

puncturing ['pʌŋktjəriŋ], *s.* perforage *m* (d'un abcès, etc.); crevaison *f* (d'un pneu).

pundit ['pʌndit], *s.* **1.** (*in India*) pandit *m*. **2.** pontife *m* (de la politique, etc.); critique *m*; *F:* ponte *m*.

pungency ['pʌndʒənsi], *s.* **1.** goût piquant (d'une épice, etc.); odeur forte, piquante (d'un parfum). **2.** (*a*) acuité *f* (d'une douleur); âcreté *f*, aigreur *f* (de paroles); piquant *m*, mordant *m* (d'un sarcasme); (*b*) saveur *f* (d'un récit, du style); causticité *f* (du style, d'une épigramme).

pungent ['pʌndʒənt], *a.* **1.** *Bot:* piquant, épineux. **2.** (*of pain, etc.*) cuisant; aigu, -uë; (*of sorrow, etc.*) poignant. **3.** (*of style, sarcasm, etc.*) mordant, caustique; **p. words**, paroles aigres. **4.** (*of smell, etc.*) fort, âcre, piquant, irritant; (*of taste*) piquant; **p. mustard**, moutarde forte, qui monte au nez; **p. sauce**, sauce relevée, épicée.

pungently ['pʌndʒəntli], *adv.* d'une manière piquante; avec causticité.

Punic ['pju:nik], *a. Hist:* punique; **the P. Wars**, les guerres puniques; **P. faith**, la foi punique; perfidie *f*.

Punicaceae [pjuni'keisii:], *s.pl. Bot:* punicacées *f*.

puniness ['pju:ninis], *s.* (*a*) chétiveté *f*; (*b*) petitesse *f*.

punish ['pʌniʃ], *v.tr.* **1.** punir (un malfaiteur, une faute); châtier (qn); corriger (un enfant); **to p. s.o. with death, with imprisonment**, punir qn de mort, de prison; **to p. s.o. for a crime, for a lie**, punir qn d'un crime, pour un mensonge; **to p. s.o. for his impudence**, châtier l'impudence de qn; **to p. s.o. for having done sth., for doing sth.**, punir qn d'avoir fait qch., pour avoir fait qch.; **he is punished for my weakness**, il subit les conséquences de ma faiblesse; *Jur:* **to p. s.o. by, with, a fine**, frapper qn d'une amende; infliger une amende à qn. **2.** *Sp: etc: F:* taper dur sur (qn); malmener (un adversaire); *Box: etc:* **he was severely punished**, il a encaissé; **to p. a horse (in a race)**, fouetter, malmener, un cheval; *Aut: etc:* **to p. the engine**, fatiguer, forcer, le moteur; **we punished his port**, nous avons largement bu de son porto.

punishable ['pʌniʃəbl], *a.* punissable; *Jur:* délictueux; **p. by a fine**, passible d'amende.

punisher ['pʌniʃər], *s.* **1.** punisseur, -euse. **2.** *Box: F:* boxeur *m* qui frappe dur.

punishing¹ ['pʌniʃiŋ], *a. F:* qui frappe dur; (coup) violent; **p. game**, jeu rude; **p. race**, course épuisante; **p. work**, travail épuisant, éreintant.

punishing², punition *f*, correction *f*.

punishment ['pʌniʃmənt], *s.* **1.** punition *f*, correction *f*, châtiment *m*; *Jur:* peine *f*; **corporal p.**, châtiment corporel; punition corporelle; **capital p.**, peine capitale; **eternal p.**, les supplices éternels; **as a p.**, par, pour, punition; **as a p. for sth.**, en punition de qch.; **to inflict a p. on s.o.**, donner, infliger, une punition, un châtiment, à qn; **law providing p. for . . .**, loi qui comporte des sanctions pénales pour . . .; **to be brought to p. for one's crimes**, être puni de ses crimes; **to escape p.**, échapper à la punition; **to make the p. fit the crime**, proportionner la punition à l'offense; *Mil:* **summary p.**, sanction disciplinaire. **2.** *Sp: etc: F:* **to inflict severe p. on a team**, administrer une cruelle défaite, une raclée, à une équipe; *Box:* **to take a lot of p.**, l'encaisser; **man who can stand, take, p.**, homme dur à l'encaisse, qui sait encaisser.

punitive ['pju:nitiv], **punitory** ['pju:nit(ə)ri], *a.* répressif; (*of taxation*) très sévère; *Jur:* **p. justice**, justice répressive, vindicative; *Mil:* **p. expedition**, expédition punitive.

Punjab [pʌn'dʒɑ:b]. *Pr.n. Geog:* le Pen(d)jab.

Punjabi [pʌn'dʒɑ:bi]. **1.** *a.* & *s.* (originaire *mf*, habitant, -ante) du Pend(j)ab. **2.** *s. Ling:* pendjabi *m*.

punk¹ [pʌŋk], *s.* **1.** (*a*) bois pourri; (*b*) amadou *m*. **2.** *F:* (*a*) (qch. de) toc *m*; camelote *f*; **he's talking a load of p.**, il débite des sottises; **it's all p.**, ça ne vaut pas tripette; (*b*) vaurien *m*, crapule *f*; (*c*) débutant, -ante, novice *mf*. **3.** *Mus: F:* punk *m*. **4.** *U.S: P:* tapette *f*.

punk², *a.* **1.** (bois) pourri. **2.** *F:* (*a*) (*of pers.*) qui ne vaut rien; misérable; (*b*) (*of thg*) mauvais, moche, toc(ard).

punka(h) ['pʌŋkə], *s.* (*in India*) panca *m*, panka *m*, punka *m*; éventail *m*; *A:* **p. boy, wallah**, tireur de panca.

punkie, punky¹ ['pʌŋki], *s. U.S: F:* moucheron *m*.

punkwood ['pʌŋkwud], *s.* bois entamé par la pourriture; bois pourri.

punky ['pʌŋki]², *a.* (bois) entamé par la pourriture; (bois) pourri.

punner ['pʌnər], *s. Civ.E: etc:* hie *f*, pilon *m*, demoiselle *f*, dame *f*.

punnet ['pʌnit], *s.* maniveau *m*; petit panier (à fraises, etc.).

punning ['pʌniŋ], *s.* calembours *mpl*; jeux *mpl* de mots.

punster ['pʌnstər], *s.* faiseur, -euse, de calembours, de jeux de mots; calembouriste *mf*, calembourdier, -ière.

punt¹ [pʌnt], *s.* **1.** (*a*) bateau plat (de rivière, conduit à la perche); **p. pole**, perche (pour la conduite d'un bateau plat); (*b*) bac *m*, bachot *m*; *Navy:* **harbour p.**, **dockyard p.**, ras *m* de carène; *Ven:* **p. shooting**, chasse *f* en barque; **p. gun**, canardière *f*. **2.** poussée *f*; coup *m* de perche.

punt², *v.tr.* (*a*) conduire (un bateau) à la perche; pousser du fond; (*b*) transporter (qn) dans un bateau plat, dans un bachot.

punt³, *s. Fb:* & *Rugby Fb:* coup *m* (de pied) de volée; **to have a p. (about)**, faire quelques coups de pied (en attendant le commencement de la partie).

punt⁴, *v.tr. Fb:* & *Rugby Fb:* envoyer (le ballon) d'un coup de pied de volée; *v.i.* donner un coup de pied de volée; **to p. the ball about**, faire quelques coups de pied (en attendant le commencement de la partie).

punt⁵, *s.* (*Cards:*) (*a*) (*pers.*) ponte *m*; (*b*) (*at faro*) point *m*.

punt⁶, *v.i.* **1.** *Cards:* ponter; **to p. high**, ponter gros. **2.** (*a*) *Turf: F:* parier; (*b*) *St.Exch:* boursicoter.

punter¹ ['pʌntər], *s.* canotier *m* qui conduit à la perche.

punter², *s.* **1.** *Cards:* ponte *m*. **2.** (*a*) *Turf:* parieur *m*; (*b*) *St.Exch:* boursicoteur *m*, boursicotier *m*.

punty ['pʌnti], *s. Glassm:* pontil *m*.

puny ['pju:ni], *a.* **1.** petit, menu; **p. shrub**, arbuste chétif. **2.** (*of pers.*) chétif, faible, débile, souffreteux, malingre, maigrelet; **a p. little fellow**, un petit gringalet; *Pej:* un avorton.

pup¹ [pʌp], *s.* **1.** (*a*) petit chien, jeune chien; chiot *m*; **a bitch and her pups**, une chienne et ses petits; (*of bitch*) **to be in p.**, être pleine; *F:* **to sell s.o. a p.**, rouler, blouser, filouter, qn; **you've been sold a p., you've bought a p.**, on vous a refilé un rossignol; on vous a refait; (*b*) jeune phoque *m*, louveteau *m*, raton *m*, etc. **2.** *F:* (*of pers.*) freluquet *m*, fat *m*; **a young p.**, un blanc-bec, *pl.* blancs-becs; **insolent young p.**, jeune suffisant *m*.

pup[2], *v.tr. & i.* (**pupped**) (*of bitch, etc.*) mettre bas (des petits).

pupa, *pl.* **-ae** ['pju:pə, -i:], *s. Ent:* nymphe *f*, chrysalide *f*, pupe *f*; **burrowing p.,** nymphe souterraine; **p. case,** chrysalide, pupe.

pupal ['pju:p(ə)l], *a. Ent:* de nymphe, de chrysalide, de pupe; nymphal, -aux.

pupate ['pju:peit], *v.i. Ent:* se métamorphoser en nymphe, en chrysalide; se chrysalider.

pupation [pju:'peiʃ(ə)n], *s. Ent:* nymphose *f*, pupation *f*, pupaison *f*.

pupil[1] ['pju:p(i)l], *s.* **1.** *Sch:* élève *mf*; écolier, -ière. **2.** *Jur:* pupille *mf*; mineur, -eure.

pupil[2], *s.* pupille *f* (de l'œil).

pupil(l)age ['pju:pilidʒ], *s.* **1.** *Jur:* (*a*) minorité *f*; (*b*) pupillarité *f*; **child in p.,** enfant en pupille, en tutelle; **child out of its p.,** enfant hors de tutelle; **industry still in its p.,** industrie encore à l'état d'enfance. **2.** état *m* d'élève; **in the period of my p.,** lorsque j'étais écolier, élève.

pupil(l)arity [pju:pi'læriti], *s. Jur:* pupillarité *f*.

pupil(l)ary[1] ['pju:piləri], *a.* **1.** *Jur:* pupillaire. **2.** d'élève, d'écolier.

pupil(l)ary[2], *a. Anat:* pupillaire.

pupillometry [pju:pi'lɔmitri], *s. Med:* pupillométrie *f*.

pupilloscopy [pjupi'lɔskopi], *s. Med:* pupilloscopie *f*.

Pupin ['pju:pin]. *Pr.n. Tp:* **P. coil,** bobine *f* Pupin.

Pupipara [pju:'pipərə], *s.pl. Ent:* pupipares *m*.

pupiparous [pju:'pipərəs], *a. Ent:* pupipare.

puppet ['pʌpit], *s.* **1.** (*a*) marionnette *f* (à fils); fantoche *m*; **glove, hand, p.,** marionnette à gaine; **p. show, play,** (spectacle *m* de) marionnettes; **p. theatre,** (théâtre *m* de) marionnettes; **p. player,** marionnettiste *mf*, montreur, -euse, joueur, -euse, de marionnettes; **to pull the puppet(s') strings,** tirer les fils, les ficelles, des marionnettes; (*b*) (*of pers.*) marionnette; **mere p.,** pantin *m*; **his characters are mere puppets,** ses personnages sont de purs fantoches; **p. government,** gouvernement fantoche. **2.** *Mec.E:* poupée *f* (de tour); *I.C.E:* **p. valve,** (i) soupape soulevante, à manchon, à déclic; clapet *m*; (soupape en) champignon *m*; (ii) distributeur soulevant, à soupape.

puppeteer [pʌpi'ti:ər], *s.* marionnettiste *mf*, montreur, -euse, joueur, -euse, de marionnettes.

puppetry ['pʌpitri], *s.* **1.** *A:* mômerie *f*. **2.** (i) fabrication *f* de marionnettes; (ii) représentation *f* des spectacles de marionnettes. **3.** *esp. Lit:* monde *m* de fantoches, de pantins.

puppy ['pʌpi], *s.* **1. p. (dog),** jeune chien *m*; chiot *m*; **p. love,** premier amour, amour juvénile; les premières amours; **p. fat,** adiposité *f* d'enfance, d'adolescence. **2.** (*of pers.*) freluquet *m*, fat *m*; petit impertinent; **a young p.,** un jeune suffisant.

puppyish ['pʌpiiʃ], *a.* impertinent, fat, outrecuidant.

Purana [pu'rɑ:nə], *s. Lit:* Purâna *m*, Pourâna *m*.

Puranic [pu'rɑ:nik], *a. Lit:* des Purânas, des Pourânas.

purblind ['pə:blaind], *a.* **1.** (*a*) presque aveugle; qui ne voit pas clair; (*b*) myope; qui a la vue basse. **2.** à l'esprit épais, obtus, sans vision; **p. policy,** politique aveugle.

purblindness ['pə:blaindnis], *s.* **1.** (*a*) quasi-cécité *f*; (*b*) myopie *f*; vue basse. **2.** manque *m* d'intelligence, de vision.

purchasable ['pə:tʃəsəbl], *a.* achetable.

purchase[1] ['pə:tʃəs], *s.* **1.** (*a*) achat *m*, acquisition *f*, emplette *f*; **cash p., p. for cash,** achat au comptant; **credit p., p. on credit,** achat à crédit, à terme; **fixed p.,** achat ferme; **local p.,** achat sur place; **p. by contract,** achat de gré à gré, achat à forfait; **to make some purchases,** faire des achats, des emplettes; **p. money,** prix *m* d'achat; somme dépensée; **p. price,** prix d'achat, d'acquisition; prix coûtant; **p. deed,** contrat *m*, acte *m*, d'achat; *Book-k:* **p. book,** facturier *m* d'entrée; journal *m* des achats; livre *m* d'achat; **p. return,** rendu *m* sur achat; *Hist:* **p. tax,** taxe *f* à la production, à l'achat, de consommation; (*b*) *St.Exch:* **p. contract,** bordereau *m* d'achat; **bull p.,** achat à découvert; **p. for the settlement,** achat à terme; (*c*) *Hist:* achat (des grades militaires, etc.). **2.** loyer *m*; **sold at 20 years' p.,** vendu moyennant 20 ans de loyer; **his life would not be worth an hour's p.,** on ne lui donnerait pas, il n'aurait pas, une heure à vivre. **3.** *Jur:* acquisition des biens immobiliers (non hérités). **4.** (*a*) force *f* mécanique; abattage *m*; (*b*) prise *f*; **to get, secure, a p. on sth.,** trouver prise à qch.; (*c*) point *m* d'appui; appui *m*; **to take p. on sth.,** prendre appui sur qch. **5.** (*a*) palan *m*, moufle *m or f*; appareil *m* de levage; **double p.,** palan à deux poulies simples, palan double; **twofold p.,** palan à deux réas, à deux poulies doubles; **p. block,** moufle à estrope double; **p. fall,** courant *m* de palan; (*b*) *Nau:* caliorne *f*; gros apparaux; **threefold, fourfold, p.,** caliorne à trois, à quatre, réas; **launch p.,** apparaux de chaloupe; **p. for masting,** appareil pour mâter; **union p.,** (manœuvre en) colis volant.

purchase[2], *v.tr.* **1.** acheter, acquérir; faire l'acquisition de (qch.); **to p. an estate from a neighbour,** acquérir une terre d'un voisin; **to p. for cash, on credit,** acheter (au) comptant, à crédit; *Lit:* **to p. freedom with one's blood,** acquérir la liberté au prix de son sang; *v.i.* **now is the time to p.,** c'est maintenant qu'il faut acheter. **2.** (*a*) lever (qch.) à l'aide, au moyen, d'un palan; (*b*) *Nau:* lever (l'ancre) à l'aide du cabestan.

purchaser ['pə:tʃəsər], *s.* (*a*) acheteur, -euse, acquéreur, -euse; (*at auction*) adjudicataire *mf*; **purchasers' association,** coopérative *f* d'achats; (*b*) *Com:* preneur, -euse; **to have found a p. for sth.,** avoir (trouvé) preneur pour qch.

purchasing[1] ['pə:tʃəsiŋ], *a.* **p. party,** acquéreur, -euse; (*at auction*) partie *f* adjudicataire.

purchasing[2], *s.* **1.** achat *m*, acquisition *f*; **p. costs,** frais *m* de passation de commande; *Pol.Ec:* **p. power,** pouvoir *m* d'achat; *Mil:* **p. and contract officer,** officier chargé des achats et marchés; *Com: U.S:* **p. agent,** acheteur, -euse. **2.** levage *m* (de l'ancre, etc.).

purdah ['pə:dɑ:], *s. Muslim Rel:* (*a*) rideau destiné à soustraire les femmes à la vue; (*b*) système qui astreint les femmes à une vie retirée; (*c*) *F:* **to go into p.,** se retirer, ne voir personne.

pure[1] ['pjuər], *a.* **1.** (*a*) (*free from foreign elements*) pur; **p. gold,** or pur; **p. copper,** cuivre pur, rouge; **p. colour,** couleur pure; **a p. green,** un vert franc; **p. water,** eau pure; **p. alcohol,** alcool rectifié; **p. silk, p. wool,** pure soie, pure laine; **p. Basque,** Basque pur sang, Basque de pure race, de race pure; **p. Arab (horse),** (cheval) arabe *m* de race pure; **p. vowel,** voyelle pure; *Mus:* **p. tone,** son pur; *Ch:* **p. substance,** corps pur; *Ph:* **p. spectrum,** spectre pur; *El:* **p. direct current,** courant parfaitement continu; *W.Tel:* **p. wave,** onde sinusoïdale; *Ins:* **p. premium,** prime nette; (*b*) **p. mathematics,** les mathématiques pures; **p. mechanics,** la mécanique rationnelle; *Phil:* **p. reason,** la raison pure; (*c*) **p. chance,** par pur hasard; **the p. and simple truth,** la vérité pure et simple; **it's p. obstinacy,** c'est de l'entêtement tout pur; **it's a p. waste of time,** c'est tout simplement du temps perdu; c'est une pure perte de temps; **this rumour is a p. fabrication,** ce bruit est une pure invention; **out of p. malice,** par pure malice; **from p. necessity,** par pure nécessité. **2.** (*free from taint*) (*a*) **p. air,** air pur; **p. style, p. taste,** style, goût, pur; **p. English,** l'anglais pur; (*b*) innocent, chaste; sincère; **p.-minded,** pur d'esprit; chaste; **p.-mindedness,** pureté *f* d'esprit; chasteté *f*; *B:* **blessed are the p. in heart,** bienheureux ceux qui ont le cœur pur.

pure[2], *v.tr. Tan:* chiper (les peaux).

pure(-)blood, *a. & s.*, **pure(-)blooded**, *a.* ['pjuə'blʌd(id)] (*of pers., animal*) de sang (pur), de race (pure); (cheval) de pur sang, racé; pur-sang (*m inv*).

purebred ['pjuəbred], *a. & s.* (chien, taureau) de race (pure), de sang (pur).

purée[1] ['pjuərei], *s. Cu:* purée *f*; **potato p.,** purée (de pommes de terre).

purée[2], *v.tr. Cu:* mettre en purée.

purely ['pjuəli], *adv.* **1.** purement; avec pureté. **2.** purement, simplement; **the invitation is p. formal,** l'invitation est de pure forme.

pureness ['pjuənis], *s.* pureté *f*.

purfle[1] ['pə:fl], *s. Cost: A:* bordure brodée; liseré *m*.

purfle[2], *v.tr.* **1.** *A:* orner (une robe, etc.) d'une bordure brodée; liserer. **2.** *Arch:* orner, embellir (un bâtiment de crochets, etc.).

purfling ['pə:fliŋ], *s.* filet *m* (de violon).

purgation [pə:'geiʃ(ə)n], *s.* **1.** *Med:* purge *f* (de l'intestin). **2.** *Theol:* purgation de l'âme (au purgatoire). **3.** *Hist:* **canonical p.,** purgation canonique; justification *f* devant un juge ecclésiastique; **vulgar p.,** purgation vulgaire, par les épreuves de combat, etc.

purgative ['pə:gətiv]. **1.** *a. & s. Med:* purgatif (*m*). **2.** *a. Lit:* purifiant.

purgatorial [pə:gə'tɔ:riəl], *a. Theol:* (*a*) du purgatoire; (*b*) de purification; purificateur, -trice; purifiant.

purgatory[1] ['pə:gət(ə)ri], *s. Theol:* purgatoire *m*; **the souls in p.,** les âmes du purgatoire, les âmes en peine; **to live a life of p., to go through p. in one's lifetime,** faire son purgatoire sur terre, en ce monde; souffrir les peines du purgatoire de son vivant.

purgatory[2], *a.* purificateur, -trice; purificatoire, purifiant; de purification.

purge[1] [pə:dʒ], *s.* **1.** *Med: Pharm:* purgatif *m*, purge *f*. **2.** (*a*) purgation *f*; (*b*) épuration *f*, purge, nettoyage *m* (d'un parti politique, etc.). **3.** (*a*) vidange *f* (d'une chaudière, etc.); **p. cock,** (robinet) purgeur *m*, robinet de vidange, de purge; (*b*) *Cmptr:* élimination (d'un article périmé du fichier, etc.); **p. date,** date de péremption, de fin de validité.

purge[2], *v.tr.* **1.** *Med:* purger (qn). **2.** nettoyer (un égout); purger, vidanger (un réservoir, un circuit hydraulique, etc.); purifier, clarifier (un liquide, etc.); épurer (les mœurs, un parti politique, etc.); *Sug.-R:* purger, clarifier (le sucre); *Cmptr:* éliminer (des articles périmés d'un fichier, etc.); **to p. the finances of a country,** assainir les finances d'un pays; *Theol:* **to p. oneself of, from, sin,** se laver de ses péchés. **3. to p. away, p. out, one's sins,** purger ses péchés; expier ses fautes. **4.** *Jur:* (*a*) *A:* **to p. a charge,** se purger par serment; (*b*) **to p. oneself of a charge,** se disculper, se justifier. **5.** *Jur:* (*a*) **to p. an offence,** expier une offense; purger sa peine; (*b*) **to p. one's contempt,** faire amende honorable (pour outrage aux magistrats).

purger ['pə:dʒər], *s.* **1.** purificateur, -trice. **2.** (*device*) (*a*) épurateur *m*, purgeur *m*; **gas p.,** épurateur de gaz; (*b*) nettoyeur *m*.

purgery ['pə:dʒəri], *s. Sug.-R:* purgerie *f*.

purging[1] ['pə:dʒiŋ], *a. Med:* purgatif; *Bot:* **p. flax,** lin purgatif.

purging[2], *s.* **1.** *Med: etc:* purge *f*, purification *f* (du corps). **2.** (*a*) nettoyage *m* (d'un égout); purification, clarification *f* (d'un liquide); épuration *f* (des mœurs, d'un parti politique, etc.); assainissement *m* (des finances publiques, etc.); *Sug.-R:* clarification (du sucre); *Cmptr:* élimination *f* (d'un article périmé du fichier, etc.); (*b*) purgeage *m*, vidange *f* (d'un réservoir, d'un circuit hydraulique, etc.); **p. cock,** (robinet) purgeur *m*; robinet de vidange, de purge.

purificant [pjuə'rifikənt], *s. Ch: etc:* agent purificateur.

purification [pjuərifi'keiʃ(ə)n], *s.* **1.** purification *f*; épuration *f* (du gaz, de l'huile, etc.); assainissement *m* (des finances publiques, etc.); *Cmptr:* **data p.,** contrôle *m*, vérification *f*, des données avant traitement. **2.** *Ecc:* (*a*) **p. of the chalice after communion,** la purification; (*b*) **Feast of the P. (of the Virgin Mary),** (fête de) la Purification.

purificator ['pju:rifikeitər], *s. Ecc:* purificatoire *m*.

purificatory ['pju:rifikeitəri], *a.* purificatoire; purificateur, -trice.

purifier ['pju:rifaiər], *s.* **1.** (*pers.*) purificateur, -trice. **2.** (*device*) épurateur *m* (de gaz, d'huile, etc.); **air p.,** assainisseur *m* d'air.

puriform ['pju:rifɔ:m], *a. Med:* (crachat, etc.) puriforme.

purify ['pju:rifai]. **1.** *v.tr.* purifier (l'air, etc.); épurer (le gaz, l'huile, une langue, etc.); dépurer (le sang); clarifier, rendre limpide (un liquide); sublimer (le cœur, l'esprit, etc.); *Sug.-R: Pharm:* déféquer (une liqueur, etc.); **to p. a metal,** dépurer un métal; **to p. s.o. of, from, his sins,** purger qn de ses péchés. **2.** *v.i.* se purifier, s'épurer; (*of liquid*) se dépurer, se clarifier.

purifying[1] ['pju:rifaiiŋ], *a.* purifiant, purificatoire, purificateur, -trice.

purifying[2], *s.* purification *f*; épuration *f*; dépuration *f* (du sang, etc.); clarification *f* (d'un liquide); *Sug.-R:* défécation *f* (du sucre); **air p. machine,** assainisseur *m* d'air; *Hyd.E:* **p. tank,** purgeoir *m*.

Purim ['pjuərim], *s. Jew.Rel:* purim *m*, pourim *m*.

purine ['pju:ri:n], *s. Ch:* purine *f*; **p. base,** base purique.

puring ['pju:riŋ], *s. Tan:* chipage *m* (des peaux).

purism ['pju:rizm], *s.* purisme *m* (de langue, style, etc.).

purist ['pju:rist], *s.* puriste *mf*.

puristical [pju'ristik(ə)l], *a.* puriste.

Puritan ['pju:rit(ə)n], *a. & s.* (*a*) *Hist:* puritain, -aine; (*b*) **p.,** puritain, -aine, rigoriste *mf*.

puritanical [pju'ri'tænik(ə)l], *a.* (de) puritain; rigoriste.

puritanically [pju:ri'tænik(ə)li], *adv.* à la manière des puritains, en puritain; puritainement.

puritanism ['pju:ritənizm], *s.* puritanisme *m*; rigorisme *m* (des mœurs).

purity ['pju:riti], *s.* pureté *f*; **degree of p.,** (i) (degré de) pureté (de l'eau, etc.); (ii) titre *m* (de l'or).

Purkinje [pə:'kindʒi:]. *Pr.n. Physiol:* **P. afterimage,** image *f* de Purkinje; **P. cell,** cellule *f* de Purkinje; **P. phenomenon, shift, effect,** phénomène *m* de Purkinje.

Purkinjean [pə:'kindʒiən], *a.* de Purkinje.

purl[1] [pə:l], *s.* **1.** *Needlew:* cannetille *f* (à broder). **2.** picot *m*, engrêlure *f* (de dentelle, etc.). **3.** *Knit:* **p. stitch,** maille *f* à l'envers.

purl[2], *v.tr.* **1.** engrêler (de la dentelle, etc.). **2.** *Knit:* tricoter des mailles à l'envers; **knit one, p. one,** une maille à l'endroit, une maille à l'envers.

purl[3], *s. Lit:* doux murmure, gazouillement *m*, gazouillis *m* (d'un ruisseau, etc.).

purl[4], *v.i. Lit:* (*of brook, etc.*) murmurer, gazouiller; couler en murmurant.

purl[5], *s. A:* mélange épicé de bière chaude et de genièvre ou d'armoise.

purl[6], *s.* = PURLER.

purler ['pə:lər], *s. F:* chute *f* la tête la première; **to come,**

take, a p., piquer une tête; ramasser une bûche, une pelle; prendre un gadin.

purlieu ['pəːljuː], *s.* **1.** *Hist:* confins *mpl* (d'une forêt) soumis au régime du domaine forestier. **2.** (*a*) limites *fpl*, bornes *fpl* (de qn); (*b*) lieu fréquenté (par qn). **3.** **purlieus,** alentours *mpl*, environs *mpl*, voisinage *m*, abords *mpl* (d'une gare, etc.).

purlin ['pəːlin], *s. Const:* panne *f*, ventrière *f*; **eaves p.,** panne sablière; **ridge p.,** panne faîtière; **p. post, support,** jambette *f*, chevron, *m* de comble; **p. cleat,** chantignole *f*.

purling[1] ['pəːliŋ], *a.* (ruisseau, etc.) murmurant, gazouillant.

purling[2], *s.* murmure *m*, gazouillement *m* (d'un ruisseau, etc.).

purloin [pəː'lɔin], *v.tr.* voler, dérober.

purloiner [pəː'lɔinər], *s.* voleur, -euse, dérobeur, -euse.

purloining [pəː'lɔiniŋ], *s.* vol *m*.

purple[1] ['pəːpl].

I. *a.* (*a*) *A:* pourpre, pourpré; (*b*) violet; **a pale p. dress,** une robe mauve; **he turned, went, p. (with rage, etc.),** il est devenu cramoisi, pourpre, violet (de rage, etc.); **face p. with cold,** visage violacé par le froid, violet de froid; *Lit:* **p. passage, patch,** morceau de bravoure; *Bot:* **p. wood,** palissandre *m*; *Med: F:* **royal p. disease,** porphyrie *f*; *F:* **p. heart,** comprimé violet de drinamyl en forme de cœur; bleuet *m*; *U.S:* **P. Heart,** décoration remise à un blessé de guerre.

II. *s.* **1.** (*a*) *Dy:* pourpre *f*; **Tyrian p.,** pourpre de Tyr, pourpre tyrienne; **madder p.,** purpurine *f*; (*b*) violet *m*; **reddish p.,** zinzolin *m*; **material of a nice p.,** tissu d'un beau violet; **materials of episcopal p.,** tissus violet évêque; **p. bronze (varnish),** purpurine; (*c*) **born in the p.,** né dans la pourpre; *Gr.Ant:* porphyrogénète; **raised to the p.,** élevé à la pourpre (romaine); élevé à la pourpre, à la dignité de cardinal; (*d*) *Physiol:* **visual p.,** pourpre rétinien. **2.** *Moll:* **p. (fish),** pourpre *m*, pourprier *m*. **3. purples,** (*a*) *Med:* purpura *m*; (*b*) *Vet:* rouget *m* (du porc); (*c*) *Agr:* nielle *f* (du blé).

purple[2], *esp. Lit:* **1.** *v.tr.* rendre pourpre, violet; empourprer (le ciel, le visage). **2.** *v.i.* devenir pourpre, cramoisi; s'empourprer.

purplish ['pəːpliʃ], **purply** ['pəːpli], *a.* violacé, violâtre; pourpré, purpurin; amarante *inv*; (*of the face*) cramoisi, vultueux; **p. red,** rouge violacé; **p. blue,** hyacinthe *inv*.

purport[1] ['pəːpɔːt, -pət], *s.* **1.** (*a*) sens *m*, signification *f* (d'un document); (*b*) portée *f*, valeur *f*, force *f* (d'un argument, etc.). **2.** but *m*, objet *m*.

purport[2] [pə'pɔːt], *v.tr.* **1. to p. to be sth.,** avoir la prétention d'être qch.; être donné, présenté, comme étant qch.; **his story purports to be an autobiography,** son récit vise à être autobiographique, a la prétention d'être autobiographique; **a letter purporting to be written by you,** une lettre censée être de votre main. **2.** impliquer; tendre à démontrer, à établir (un fait).

purpose[1] ['pəːpəs], *s.* **1.** (*a*) dessein *m*, objet *m*; but *m*, fin *f*, intention *f*; **with honesty of p.,** dans des intentions honnêtes; **fixed p.,** dessein bien arrêté; **to gain, achieve, effect, one's p.,** en venir à ses fins; accomplir son dessein; toucher au but; **for, with, the p. of doing sth.,** dans le but de, dans l'intention de, afin de, faire qch.; **for the mere p. of . . .,** à seule fin de . . .; **to do sth. on p.,** faire qch. exprès, à dessein, de propos délibéré; **on p. to do sth.,** en vue de faire qch.; dans l'intention expresse de faire qch.; **of set p.,** de propos délibéré, de parti pris; (*b*) résolution *f*; **man of p.,** homme résolu, décidé, assuré; **steadfastness of p.,** ténacité de caractère; détermination *f*. **2. intended p.,** destination *f*, affectation *f* (d'un bâtiment, d'une somme d'argent, etc.); **to answer, serve, various purposes,** servir à plusieurs usages, à plusieurs fins; **to answer, serve, no p.,** ne servir à rien; être sans utilité; **to answer the p.,** répondre au but; **this will suit, answer, serve, your p.,** cela vous accommodera, vous arrangera; cela fera votre affaire; **serving a double p.,** à deux fins; **for this, that, p.,** dans cette intention, dans ce dessein; à cette fin, à cet effet; pour cela; **made for that very p.,** fait tout exprès; **for whatever p. it may serve,** à toutes fins utiles; **for all purposes,** à toutes fins, à tous usages; **for all necessary purposes,** pour tout ce qui est nécessaire; **general p. vehicle,** véhicule tous usages, toutes fins; **general p. formula,** formule passe-partout; **p.-built offices,** bureaux construits et aménagés en vue d'un usage déterminé; **p.-made tool,** outil façonné pour un usage précis; outil spécial; **intended for practical purposes,** destiné à des usages pratiques; **expropriation for public purposes,** expropriation pour cause d'utilité publique; **to set up a commission for the p. of investigation,** former un comité à des fins d'enquête; **to retain a portion for purposes of analysis,** en prélever une partie aux fins d'analyse; *Jur:* **for the p. of this convention . . .,** pour l'application de la présente convention . . .; **for the p. of this article . . .,** au sens du présent article . . .. **3. to speak to the p.,** parler à propos; **very much to the p.,** fort à propos; **we're (talking) at cross purposes,** il y a malentendu (entre nous); **we were at cross purposes the whole time,** nous n'avons fait que nous contrarier tout du long; **not to the p.,** hors de propos; **it is nothing to the p.,** cela ne fait rien à l'affaire; cela ne signifie rien; **to come to the p.,** venir au fait. **4. to work, study, to good p.,** travailler, étudier, avec profit; **to some p.,** utilement, avantageusement, efficacement; **the efforts I made served little p.,** mes efforts n'ont pas abouti à grand-chose; **to intervene to little p.,** s'entremettre sans grande utilité; **all that is to no p.,** tout cela ne sert à rien, est sans intérêt, sans utilité; **I've spent my money to no p.,** j'ai gaspillé mon argent; **to talk to no p.,** parler en l'air.

purpose[2], *v.tr. A:* **1. to p. doing sth., to do sth.,** se proposer, avoir (dans) l'intention, avoir le dessein, avoir en vue, de faire qch.; **we never knew what he purposed to do,** nous n'avons jamais su ce qu'il voulait faire, ce qu'il comptait faire, ce qu'il avait dans l'idée. **2. to be purposed to do sth.,** (i) être déterminé, décidé, résolu, à faire qch.; (ii) avoir l'intention de faire qch.

purposeful ['pəːpəsful], *a.* (*a*) prémédité; intentionnel; (*b*) (*of pers.*) réfléchi, avisé; tenace.

purposefully ['pəːpəsfuli], *adv.* dans un but précis.

purposefulness ['pəːpəsfulnis], *s.* **1.** discernement *m*. **2.** ténacité *f*.

purposeless ['pəːpəslis], *a.* sans but; inutile.

purposelessness ['pəːpəslisnis], *s.* inutilité *f*; manque *m* de but.

purposely ['pəːpəsli], *adv.* **1.** (faire qch.) à dessein, intentionnellement, de propos délibéré. **2.** exprès; **I came p. to see him,** je suis venu exprès pour le voir, dans le seul but de le voir.

purposive ['pəːpəsiv], *a.* **1.** (*of thg*) qui répond à un but; qui remplit une fonction. **2.** (*of action, etc.*) intentionnel, fait de propos délibéré. **3.** (*of pers.*) résolu; qui a des intentions arrêtées; qui agit dans un but arrêté.

purpura ['pəːpjurə], *s.* **1.** *Med:* purpura *m*. **2.** *Moll:* pourprier *m*.

purpure ['pəːpjuər], *s. Her:* pourpre *m*.

purpuric [pəː'pjuːrik], *a.* **1.** *Med:* purpuracé; **p. fever,** purpura *m*. **2.** *Ch:* **p. acid,** acide purpurique.

purpurin ['pəːpjurin], *s. Ch:* purpurine *f*.

purpurite ['pəːpjuərait], *s. Miner:* purpurite *f*.

purpurogenous [pəːpju'rɔdʒinəs], *a. Nat.Hist:* purpurigène, purpurifère.

purpuroxanthin [pəːpjurɔk'zænθin], *s. Ch:* purpuroxanthine *f*.

purr[1] [pəːr], *s.* **1.** ronron *m*, ronronnement *m* (de chat). **2.** ronflement *m*, ronron (d'une machine); ronronnement, vrombissement *m* (d'un moteur, etc.).

purr[2], *v.i.* (*a*) (*of cat, pers., engine*) ronronner; (*of cat*) faire ronron; (*of car, etc.*) ronfler; (*of engine*) vrombir; (*b*) *v.tr.* **cat purring its contentment,** chat ronronnant de satisfaction.

purree ['pʌri], *s.* jaune indien naturel.

purring[1] ['pəːriŋ], *a.* (chat) qui ronronne, qui fait ronron; (moteur) vrombissant, qui vrombit; *Med:* **p. thrill, p. tremor,** frémissement *m* cataire (du cœur).

purring[2], *s.* = PURR[1].

purse[1] [pəːs], *s.* **1.** (*a*) bourse *f*, porte-monnaie *m inv*; *NAm:* sac *m* à main; **net p.,** bourse en filet; *A:* **chain, belt, p.,** aumônière *f*; escarcelle *f*; *F:* **heavy p., long p., well-lined p.,** bourse bien garnie; bourse ronde; **to have a well-lined p.,** avoir le sac; **light p.,** bourse plate, légère; **to be p.-proud,** être orgueilleux de sa fortune, de son argent; **his prices are beyond my p.,** ses prix ne sont pas abordables; *F:* **she holds the p. strings,** c'est elle qui tient les cordons de la bourse; **to keep a tight hold on the p. strings,** tenir serrés les cordons de la bourse; *Prov:* **little and often fill the p.,** petit à petit l'oiseau fait son nid; les petits ruisseaux font les grandes rivières; **you cannot make a silk p. out of a sow's ear,** on ne saurait faire d'une buse un épervier; on ne peut tirer de la farine d'un sac de son; tout bois n'est pas bon à faire flèche; (*b*) **the public p.,** les finances *f* de l'État; le Trésor; **p. bearer,** (i) trésorier *m*; (ii) officier *m* du sceau, porte-sceau *m* (du Grand Chancelier); (*c*) *Sp:* **to give, put up, a p.,** constituer et offrir une somme d'argent, une bourse, pour une rencontre sportive, pour un match de boxe. **2.** (*a*) *Nat.Hist: etc:* sac *m*, bourse, poche *f*; (*b*) *Anat: A:* scrotum *m*, bourses testiculaires; (*c*) *Crust:* **p. crab,** crabe *m* des cocotiers; (*d*) **sea p.,** (i) *Ich:* œuf *m* de la raie; (ii) *Coel:* alcyon palmé; (iii) *U.S:* (*along beach*) remous *m*, tourbillon *m*. **3.** (*a*) *Fish:* bourse; **p. seine, p. net,** senne *f*, seine *f* (à poche); aissaugue *f*; (*b*) *Ven:* **p. net,** bourse (que l'on place devant le terrier pour prendre les lapins). **4.** *A:* (*in Turkey*) **p. of gold,** bourse d'or (de 10 000 piastres); **p. of silver,** bourse d'argent (de 500 piastres).

purse[2], *v.tr.* **1.** plisser (le front); froncer (les sourcils); **to p. (up) one's lips,** pincer les lèvres; faire la moue; **with pursed lips,** les lèvres pincées. **2.** *A:* mettre (de l'argent) dans sa bourse, dans sa poche.

purser ['pəːsər], *s. Nau:* commissaire *m* (de la marine (marchande)); **purser's mate,** cambusier *m*.

purslane ['pəːslin], *s. Bot:* **1.** pourpier *m*. **2. water, marsh, p.,** pourpier des marais, pourpière *f*; **sea p.,** (i) pourpier de mer; (ii) sabline *f*; **rock p.,** calandrinia *f*.

pursuable [pə'sjuːəbl], *a.* poursuivable.

pursuance [pə'sjuːəns], *s.* action *f* de poursuivre; **in p. of your instructions, of our intention,** conformément à vos instructions; suivant notre intention; **in p. of this decree,** en vertu, par suite, en conséquence, de ce décret; **in p. of this article,** aux stipulations de cet article.

pursuant [pə'sjuːənt]. **1.** *a. & s. Lit: & Jur: A:* poursuivant (*m*). **2.** *adv.* **p. to your instructions,** conformément à vos instructions; en conséquence, par suite, de vos instructions.

pursuantly [pə'sjuːəntli], *adv.* = PURSUANT 2.

pursue [pə'sjuː], *v.tr.* **1.** (*a*) poursuivre (qn); être à la poursuite de (qn); prendre (qn) en chasse; **to be pursued by misfortune,** être talonné par le malheur; **he is pursued by remorse,** le remords le suit partout; (*b*) rechercher (le plaisir); aspirer à (un but); courir après (le bonheur); être à la poursuite (du bonheur). **2.** continuer, suivre (son chemin); donner suite à, poursuivre (une enquête, une politique); **to p. a new course,** suivre une nouvelle voie; **to p. a line of conduct,** suivre une ligne de conduite; **to p. a profession,** faire, suivre, exercer, un métier; **to p. one's studies to the end,** pousser ses études jusqu'au bout; **the subject was pursued no further,** on ne s'attacha pas davantage à débattre ce sujet; *v.i.* **he was the only one who dared p.,** il fut seul à oser continuer la poursuite.

pursuer [pə'sjuːər], *s.* **1.** poursuivant, -ante. **2.** *Scot: Jur:* plaignant, -ante; demandeur, -eresse; poursuivant, -ante; requérant, -ante.

pursuit [pə'sjuːt], *s.* **1.** (*a*) poursuite *f*; **pack in eager, hot, p.,** meute acharnée à la poursuite; **to set out in p. of s.o.,** se mettre à la poursuite de qn; **in p. of his aim he discovered . . .,** en poursuivant son but il découvrit . . .; *Mil: Av:* **p. plane,** chasseur *m*, avion *m* de chasse; *Cy:* **p. race,** (course *f*) poursuite *f*; (*b*) recherche *f* (du bonheur, etc.); **in p. of happiness,** à la poursuite, à la recherche, en quête, du bonheur; **the p. of wealth,** la poursuite des richesses; **in his p. of knowledge,** dans ses efforts pour s'instruire. **2.** (*a*) visée *f*; **ambitious pursuits,** visées ambitieuses; (*b*) carrière *f*, profession *f*; études *fpl*; **to engage in scientific pursuits,** (i) adopter, embrasser, la carrière des sciences; (ii) s'adonner à des recherches scientifiques; **literary pursuits,** travaux *m* littéraires; (*c*) occupation *f*; passe-temps *m inv*; **hunting is his favourite p.,** la chasse est son occupation favorite, son passe-temps favori.

pursuivant ['pəːswivənt], *s.* **1.** *Her:* **p. (of, at, arms),** poursuivant *m* d'armes. **2.** *A: & Lit:* suivant *m*; **his pursuivants,** les gens *m* de sa suite; sa suite.

pursy[1] ['pəːsi], *a.* **1.** poussif; à l'haleine courte. **2.** gros, corpulent, bedonnant.

pursy[2], *a.* **1. p. mouth,** bouche pincée; **p. eyes,** yeux bridés. **2.** (*a*) à la bourse bien remplie; riche, cossu; (*b*) (homme) orgueilleux de sa fortune.

purtenance ['pəːtənəns], *s. A:* fressure *f* (d'un animal).

purulence ['pjuːrələns], *s. Med:* **1.** purulence *f*. **2.** pus *m*.

purulency ['pjuːrələnsi], *s.* = PURULENCE 1.

purulent ['pjuːrələnt], *a. Med:* purulent.

purvey [pə'vei], *v.tr.* fournir (des provisions); *v.i.* **to p. for s.o., the army, etc.,** être le fournisseur, le pourvoyeur, de qn, de l'armée, etc.

purveyance [pə'veiəns], *s.* **1.** fourniture *f* de provisions; approvisionnement *m*. **2.** *Hist:* **(right of) p.,** droit *m* de pourvoirie; droit de prise et de réquisitionnement (prérogative royale).

purveying [pə'veiiŋ], *s.* = PURVEYANCE 1.

purveyor [pə'veiər], *s.* **1.** fournisseur, -euse; pourvoyeur, -euse (de provisions); approvisionneur, -euse. **2.** *Hist:* officier *m* de bouche (de la Maison du roi).

purview ['pəːvjuː], *s.* **1.** *Jur:* corps *m*, dispositif *m*, texte *m*, articles *mpl* (d'un statut). **2.** (*a*) limites *fpl*, portée *f*, (d'un projet, d'un livre, etc.); **questions outside the p. of our enquiry,** questions hors des limites de notre enquête; (*b*) vue *f*, perspective *f*; champ *m* (d'observation); **to lie, come, within the p. of s.o.,** (i) être à portée de la vue de qn; (ii) être du ressort de qn, de la compétence de qn; être dans le domaine de qn.

pus [pʌs], *s. Med:* pus *m*; sanie *f*.

Puseyism ['pju:ziizm], *s. Rel.H: Pej:* puseyisme *m.*

Puseyite ['pju:ziait], *s. Rel.H: Pej:* puseyiste *mf.*

push[1] [puʃ], *s.* **1.** *(a)* poussée *f,* impulsion *f;* **to give a p. to sth.,** pousser qch.; **at, with, one p.,** d'un seul coup; *F:* **to give s.o. the p.,** flanquer qn à la porte; sa(c)quer qn; donner son congé à qn; **to get the p.,** recevoir son congé; se faire dégommer; **to give s.o. a p.,** (i) donner une poussée à qn; (ii) pistonner qn; *(b) F:* **p. bike,** bicyclette *f,* bécane *f* (sans moteur); *Rail:* **p. car,** pousse-wagon *m inv; Nau:* **p. boat,** pousseur *m;* **to give a car a p. start,** faire démarrer une voiture en la poussant; *(c) Civ.E:* poussée (d'une voûte). **2.** *(a)* coup d'estoc; coup de corne (d'une bête); *(b) Bill:* **p. (stroke),** coup queuté; queutage *m;* **to play a p. stroke,** queuter. **3.** *(a)* effort *m;* coup de collier; *(b) Mil:* attaque *f* en masse; **p. all along the line,** poussée en avant sur toute la ligne; *(c)* énergie *f,* hardiesse *f;* initiative *f;* **to have plenty of p.,** (i) avoir beaucoup d'initiative, d'énergie; (ii) être un arriviste. **4.** moment *m* difficile; circonstance *f* critique; **at a p.,** dans une extrémité; en cas de besoin; au besoin; **when it comes to the p.,** au moment critique; quand il est question d'agir. **5.** *El:* **p. button,** bouton *m* de contact; poussoir *m;* bouton-poussoir *m, pl.* boutons-poussoirs; *(of doorbell)* bouton de sonnerie, de sonnette, d'appel; **p.-button switch,** interrupteur *m,* commutateur *m,* à poussoir; **p.-button operation,** fonctionnement *m* automatique; **p.-button war,** la guerre presse-bouton; **p. piece, p. button,** poussoir (d'une montre à répétition). **6.** *P: esp. Austr:* bande *f,* clique *f* (de voyous, de pickpockets); bande de voleurs à l'esbrouffe.

push[2], *v.*

I. *v.tr.* pousser. **1.** *(a)* **to p. a wheelbarrow,** pousser une brouette; **to p.-start a car,** faire démarrer une voiture en la poussant; *(b)* **he pushed the gate,** il a poussé la grille; **to p. a button,** appuyer sur un bouton; **to p. a pin through a piece of cardboard,** transpercer un carton d'une épingle. **2.** *(a)* **to p. s.o. with one's hand,** pousser qn de la main; **to p. s.o. into the room,** pousser qn (pour le faire entrer) dans la pièce; **to p. s.o. in the crowd,** bousculer qn dans la foule; **don't p. (me)!** ne (me) poussez pas! ne (me) bousculez pas! **to p. s.o. out of the way,** faire écarter qn; forcer qn à se ranger; *F:* **we're sick and tired of being pushed around,** nous en avons marre d'être menés par le bout du nez, d'être bousculés; *(b)* **to p. oneself (forward),** (i) se mettre en avant; (ii) faire de l'arrivisme; (iii) se pousser dans le monde; faire son chemin. **3.** *(a)* étendre (son influence); *(b)* **to p. an attack home,** pousser à fond une attaque; *O: F:* **to p. one's luck,** aller un peu fort; *(c)* pousser la vente de (sa marchandise); lancer (une mode, un article); activer (un commerce); **to p. one's wares,** faire l'article; **to p. drugs,** vendre, fournir, fourguer, des drogues; *(d)* **to p. one's demands,** revendiquer ses droits; *(e) St.Exch:* **to p. shares,** placer des valeurs douteuses. **4. to p. s.o. into doing sth.,** pousser qn à faire qch.; **to p. s.o. for payment,** presser, importuner, qn pour se faire payer; **I don't want to p. you,** je ne voudrais pas vous importuner, vous forcer; **don't p. him too far,** ne le poussez pas à bout; **we are pushed for an answer,** on nous presse de répondre; **I'm terribly pushed (for time),** le temps me manque; je suis très pressé; tout mon temps est pris; **to be pushed for money,** être à court d'argent. **5.** *F: O:* **he's pushing sixty,** il frise la soixantaine.

II. *v.i.* **1.** avancer (avec difficulté); **the army had pushed a long way into the forest,** l'armée avait pénétré à l'intérieur de la forêt; **to p. as far as Paris,** pousser jusqu'à Paris; **to p. (one's way) through the crowd,** se frayer, s'ouvrir, un chemin à travers la foule; **he had pushed his way into the meeting,** il s'était faufilé dans la réunion; **to p. one's way into a job,** s'ingérer dans un emploi. **2.** pousser; exercer une pression; **to p. against sth.,** pousser, s'appuyer, sur qch. **3.** *Bill:* queuter; pousser tout.

III. *(compound verbs)* **1. push aside,** *v.tr.* écarter (d'une poussée).

2. push away, *v.tr.* repousser, éloigner (qn, qch.).

3. push back, *(a) v.tr.* repousser; faire reculer; **he pushed back the shutters,** il a repoussé les volets; **the police pushed back the crowd,** la police a fait reculer la foule; *(b) v.i.* reculer.

4. push forward, *(a) v.tr.* pousser en avant, (faire) avancer; *(b) v.i.* avancer; se porter en avant; **to p. forward to the attack,** prendre l'offensive, pousser une pointe.

5. push in, *(a) v.tr.* enfoncer, refouler, repousser (qch.); *F:* **to p. s.o.'s face in,** casser la gueule à qn; *(b) v.i.* entrer à toute force; resquiller.

6. push off, *v.i. Nau:* pousser au large; *F:* **time to p. off!** il est temps de se mettre en route, de partir; *P:* **p. off!** fiche le camp! file!

7. push on, *(a) v.tr.* pousser (en avant); faire avancer; **to p. on a horse,** lancer, presser, un cheval; **to p. s.o. on to do sth.,** pousser, exciter, qn à faire qch.; *Min:* **to p. on the levels,** pousser les galeries; *(b) v.i.* (i) **to p. on to, as far as, a place,** pousser jusqu'à un endroit; (ii) **it's time to p. on,** il est temps de nous remettre en route; (iii) **to p. on with the work,** pousser, hâter, accélérer, presser, les travaux.

8. push out, *v.tr.* (i) pousser dehors; faire sortir; expulser, chasser; mettre (qn) à la porte; (ii) **to p. a boat out,** mettre une embarcation à l'eau; *F:* **to p. the boat out,** faire la fête; (iii) *(of plant)* pousser (des racines, etc.); *(of snail)* **to p. out its horns,** sortir ses cornes.

9. push over, *v.tr.* faire tomber (qn, qch.).

10. push through, *(a) v.tr.* (i) faire passer (qch.) à travers (qch.); (ii) mener à bien, parvenir à terminer (un travail); (iii) faire accepter (un projet de loi, etc.); *(b) v.i.* se frayer un chemin à travers.

11. push to, *v.tr.* pousser, fermer (la porte, les volets).

12. push up, *v.tr.* *(a)* **to p. up one's spectacles,** relever ses lunettes (sur son front); *(b)* aider (qn) à monter (en le poussant).

push-and-pull ['puʃənd'pul], *a. O:* = PUSH-PULL.

pushbike ['puʃbaik], *s. F:* vélo *m.*

pushcar [puʃka:r] *s.* poussette *f,* voiture *f* d'enfant.

pushcart ['puʃka:t], *s.* voiture *f* à bras; charrette *f* à bras.

pushchair ['puʃtʃɛə:r], *s.* poussette *f,* voiture *f,* d'enfant.

pusher ['puʃər], *s.* **1.** *(a)* personne *f* qui pousse (une voiture, etc.); *(b) Min:* **tool p.,** surveillant *m* de forage, contremaître *m.* **2.** *Rail:* machine *f* de renfort (en queue de rame); machine pour la montée des côtes. **3. p. aircraft,** avion *m* à hélice propulsive, à hélice arrière; **p. propeller,** hélice propulsive. **4.** *(a)* ambitieux, -euse; arriviste *mf;* *(b)* personne qui pousse la vente de qch.; fournisseur *m,* fourgueur *m* (de drogues); trafiquant *m* en stupéfiants. **5. (baby's) p.,** raclette *f.*

pushing[1] ['puʃiŋ], *a.* *(a)* entreprenant, hardi, énergique; **he's a p. man,** c'est un arriviste, un ambitieux; il aime à se pousser dans le monde; il sait se faire valoir; *(b)* indiscret.

pushing[2], *s.* **1.** *(a)* poussée *f;* **no p.!** ne poussez pas! *(b) Bill:* queutage *m; Nau: Rail:* poussage *m.* **2.** *(of pers.)* *(a)* arrivisme *m;* *(b)* indiscrétion *f;* intrusion *f;* importunité *f.* **3.** vente *f* (de marchandises); fournissement *m* (de drogues, etc.). **4.** *(compound nouns)* **p. aside,** écartement *m;* **p. away, p. back,** repoussement *m,* éloignement *m;* **p. down,** (i) renversement *m;* (ii) enfoncement *m;* **p. forward,** poussée (en avant); avancement *m;* **p. out,** expulsion *f;* **p. on,** poussée en avant; avancement; **p. on of the work,** accélération *f* des travaux.

Pushkin ['puʃkin]. *Pr.n.m. Lit:* Pouchkine.

pushover ['puʃouvər], *s.* **1.** *F:* chose facile à faire, à obtenir; **it's a p.,** c'est donné, c'est du gâteau. **2.** *(a) F:* adversaire *m* facile à vaincre; *(b) P:* femme facile, Marie-couche-toi-là; *(c) NAm: F:* personne crédule, poire *f,* blanc-bec *m, pl.* blancs-becs.

pushpin ['puʃpin], *s.* **1.** *Games:* poussette *f.* **2.** *U.S:* punaise *f* (pour planche à dessin).

push-push ['puʃpuʃ], *attrib. a. Elcs:* **p.-p. circuit,** circuit *m inv;* **p.-p. circuit,** circuit *m,* montage *m,* symétrique; circuit push-pull; **p.-p. amplifier,** amplificateur *m* push-pull; amplificateur symétrique; *El:* **p.-p. button,** bouton *m* tirette; **p.-p. switch,** commutateur *m,* interrupteur *m,* à tirage.

push-push ['puʃpuʃ], *attrib.a. Elcs:* **p.-p. circuit,** circuit *m* push-push.

pushrod ['puʃrɔd], *s. I.C.E:* poussoir *m;* tige-poussoir *f, pl.* tiges-poussoirs.

Pushtu ['puʃtu:], *s. Ling:* pouchtou *m,* pouktou *m,* pachtou *m.*

push-up ['puʃʌp], *s. Gym:* **to do p.-ups,** faire des tractions, des pompes.

pushy ['puʃi], *a. F:* arriviste, poseur, plastronneur; **he's a very p. man,** c'est un ambitieux; il sait se pousser dans le monde.

pusillanimity [pju:silə'nimiti], *s.* pusillanimité *f;* manque *m* de courage.

pusillanimous [pju:si'læniməs], *a.* pusillanime.

pusillanimously [pju:si'læniməsli], *adv.* avec pusillanimité.

puss [pus], *s.* **1.** minet *m,* minette *f;* minou *m;* mimi *m;* **P. in Boots,** le Chat botté; **to play (at) p. in the corner,** jouer aux quatre coins. **2.** *Ven: F:* le lièvre. **3.** *F:* **p.! p.!** que tu es rosse! *(to little girl)* **you little p.!** petite coquine! petite friponne! petite rusée! **4.** *Ent:* **p. moth,** dicranure *f* vinule; queue-fourchue *f, pl.* queues-fourchues.

pussy ['pusi], *s.* **1.** *(a)* **p. (cat),** minet *m,* minette *f;* minou *m;* mimi *m;* *U.S:* **to play p. wants a corner,** jouer aux quatre coins; *(b) F:* **p.! p.!** que tu es rosse! **2.** *P:* les génitaux *m* (externes) de la femme. **3.** *F:* chaton *m* (du saule, etc.).

pussyfoot[1] ['pusifut], *s.* **1.** patte-pelue *mf, pl.* pattes-pelues. **2.** *U.S:* prohibitionniste *m.*

pussyfoot[2], *v.i.* **1.** marcher à pas étouffés, sur la pointe des pieds. **2.** faire patte de velours. **3.** ne pas se mouiller; demeurer sur la réserve; **he's going to p.,** il ne s'engagera à rien (sur une question).

pussyfooted ['pusifutid], *a.* **1.** qui marche à pas étouffés. **2.** cauteleux; réservé.

pussyfooter ['pusifutər], *s.* celui, celle, qui ne veut pas se compromettre.

pussyfooting ['pusifutiŋ], *s. F:* l'art *m* de ne pas se mouiller; **to speak out with no p.,** se déclarer sans réserve.

pustular ['pʌstjulər], *a. Med: Bot:* pustuleux, pustulé.

pustulate ['pʌstjuleit], *v.i. Med: Bot:* se former en pustules; se couvrir de pustules.

pustule ['pʌstju:l], *s. Med: Vet:* pustule *f;* **malignant p. (of anthrax),** pustule maligne (du charbon).

pustulous ['pʌstjuləs], *a. Med:* pustuleux, pustulé.

put[1] [put], *s.* **1.** *Sp:* lancer *m,* lancement *m* (du poids). **2.** *St.Exch:* **p. (option),** prime *f* comportant le droit de livrer; prime pour livrer; prime vendeur; option *f* de vente; **p. of more,** la demande de plus; l'encore autant *m;* **p. and call,** double option; doubles primes; stellage *m.*

put[2], *v.* *(p.t. & p.p.* **put,** *pr.p.* **putting)**

I. *v.tr* mettre. **1.** *(a) (place in a spot)* **p. it on the table,** mettez-le, placez-le, posez-le, sur la table; **p. all that on the floor,** mettez tout cela par terre; **p. it in the dustbin,** mettez-le à la poubelle; **to p. an advertisement in the paper,** insérer une annonce dans le journal; **to p. milk in one's tea,** mettre du lait dans son thé; **to p. a patch on a garment,** mettre une pièce à un vêtement; **to p. one's ear to the door,** mettre l'oreille contre la porte; **to p. one's glass to one's lips,** porter son verre à ses lèvres; **to p. one's lips to one's glass,** tremper ses lèvres dans son verre; **to p. sth. into s.o.'s hands,** mettre, glisser, qch. dans la main à qn; *F:* **p. it there!** (= **shake hands**) touchez là! **to p. oneself into s.o.'s hands,** s'en remettre à qn; **to p. a matter into s.o.'s hands,** confier une affaire à qn; **to p. sth. to dry in front of the fire,** mettre sécher qch. au feu; mettre qch. à sécher devant le feu; **to p. dishes to drain in the rack,** mettre égoutter de la vaisselle; mettre de la vaisselle à égoutter; **to p. s.o. in his place,** remettre qn à sa place; rembarrer qn; **to p. the horse to the cart,** mettre le cheval à la voiture; atteler la voiture; **to p. bull to cow,** accoupler le taureau et la vache; **to p. a tick against s.o.'s name,** faire une croix devant le nom de qn; **to p. one's signature to sth.,** apposer sa signature sur, à, qch.; **to p. numbers on packages,** apposer des numéros sur des paquets; **he p. an ace on my king,** il a joué un as sur mon roi; *Book-k:* **to p. an amount in the receipts, in the expenditure,** employer une somme en recette, en dépense; **to p. honour before riches,** préférer l'honneur à l'argent; *(b) (put in state or condition)* **to p. s.o. in the wrong,** prendre qn en faute; **to p. a matter right,** (i) arranger une affaire; (ii) remettre les choses au point; **to p. s.o. out of suspense,** tirer qn de doute; **to p. s.o. out of patience,** mettre à bout la patience de qn; **to p. s.o. against s.o.,** monter qn contre qn; **to p. the law into operation,** appliquer la loi; **to p. s.o. in the right way,** montrer son chemin à qn; (re)mettre qn sur la voie; **to p. a field under wheat, to p. a field to wheat,** mettre une terre en blé; planter un champ en blé; **to p. an article on the market,** mettre un article en vente, sur le marché; **to p. a new article on the market,** lancer une marchandise; *St.Exch:* **to p. stock at a certain price,** délivrer, fournir, des actions à un certain prix; **to p. a play on the stage,** monter une pièce; *(c)* **to p. a passage into Greek,** mettre, traduire, un passage en grec; **to p. one's thoughts into words,** traduire ses pensées par des mots; *(d)* **to p. money into an undertaking,** verser des fonds dans une affaire; **to p. one's money into land,** placer son argent en terres; **to p. money on a horse,** miser, parier, sur un cheval; *Cards: F:* **to p. a bit on (the game),** intéresser le jeu; **to p. energy into finishing a job,** mettre de l'énergie à achever une tâche. **2.** *(a)* **to p. a question to s.o.,** poser, faire, une question à qn; **to p. a case before s.o.,** soumettre un cas à qn; **to p. a resolution to the meeting,** présenter une résolution à l'assemblée; **I shall p. your proposal to the Board,** je porterai votre proposition à la connaissance du conseil d'administration; **I p. it to you whether . . .,** je vous demande un peu si . . .; *Jur:* **I p. it to you that you were not there at the time,** n'est-il pas vrai que vous étiez absent à ce moment-là? **I p. it to him that it would be advantageous to . . .,** je lui ai représenté qu'il y aurait avantage à . . .; **p. it to him nicely,** présentez-lui la chose gentiment; **when I p. it to him he. . .,** à l'exposé de ce projet il. . .; **p. it that you are right . . .,** supposons, mettons, que vous ayez raison . . .; (*b*) **to p. the case clearly,** exposer clairement la situation; **to p. things in a clearer light,** présenter les choses plus clairement; **to p. it bluntly,** pour parler franc; pour parler sans ambages; **as Horace puts it,** comme dit Horace; selon l'expression d'Horace; **if one may p. it in that way,** si l'on peut s'exprimer ainsi; **you p. things in such a way that you seem to be right,** vous tournez les choses de telle manière qu'il semble que vous ayez raison; **p. it so as not to offend him,** présentez-lui la chose de manière à ne pas l'offenser; **neat way of putting things,** phrase adroite; **I don't know how to p. it,** je ne sais comment dire; **all that can be p. in two words,** tout cela tient en deux mots; **to p. it otherwise,** pour m'exprimer autrement. **3. to p. the population at 10,000,** estimer, évaluer, la population à 10 000; **I p. her fur at £1000,** j'évalue sa fourrure à £1000; **to p. no value on s.o.'s advice,** n'attacher aucun prix aux conseils de qn. **4. to p. an end, a stop, to sth.,** mettre fin à qch.; **to p. an end to one's life, to oneself,** mettre fin à sa vie. **5.** (*a*) **to p. s.o. to do sth.,** faire faire qch. à qn; désigner qn pour faire qch.; **he is p. to every kind of work,** on lui fait faire toutes sortes de besognes; *Mil:* **to p. a man on extra fatigue,** appointer un homme de corvée; **p. him to a trade,** apprenez-lui un métier; **to p. s.o. to bed,** mettre qn au lit; coucher (un enfant); **to p. sth. to a good use,** employer qch. à un bon usage; **to p. a horse to, at, a fence,** diriger un cheval vers une barrière; faire sauter une barrière à un cheval; **to p. s.o. through an examination,** faire passer, faire subir, un examen à qn; **to p. s.o. through an ordeal,** faire subir une rude épreuve à qn; *F:* **to p. s.o. through it,** faire passer un mauvais quart d'heure à qn; (*of police*) passer (un accusé) à tabac; **to p. s.o. to the test,** soumettre qn à l'épreuve; **to p. a resolution to the vote,** mettre une résolution aux voix; **to p. s.o. to torture,** mettre qn à la torture; (*b*) **to p. the enemy to flight,** mettre l'ennemi en fuite, en déroute; **to p. s.o. to sleep,** endormir qn; *F:* **to p. a dog to sleep,** faire piquer un chien; **I am putting you to a lot of trouble,** je vous donne beaucoup d'embarras. **6.** (*a*) **to p. a bullet through s.o.'s head,** loger une balle dans la tête de qn; **to p. one's fist through the window,** enfoncer la fenêtre d'un coup de poing: **to p. one's pen through a word,** rayer, barrer, biffer, un mot; (*b*) *Sp:* **to p. the weight, to p. the shot,** lancer le poids; (*c*) *Min:* pousser, trainer (des wagonnets).

II. *v.i. Nau:* **to p. (out) to sea,** mettre à la voile, à la mer; prendre la mer, le large; **to p. into port,** relâcher; faire relâche; **to p. into harbour,** relâcher pour se mettre à l'abri.

III. (*compound verbs*) **1. put about,** *v.tr.* (*a*) faire circuler (un bruit); (*b*) déranger (qn); inquiéter (qn); (*c*) *P:* **she puts it about,** elle accorde ses faveurs à tout venant; (*d*) *Nau:* **to p. a ship about,** *v.i.* **to p. about,** virer de bord.

2. put across, *v.tr. F:* **to p. a deal across,** faire accepter un marché; boucler une affaire; **you can't p. that across (on) me,** on ne me la fait pas.

3. put aside, *v.tr.* mettre (de l'argent, etc.) de côté.

4. put away, *v.tr.* (*a*) ranger (qch.); remettre (qch.) à sa place; **I'll p. the car away,** je vais garer la voiture; *Ten: etc: F:* **he doesn't p. the ball away,** il ne fait pas le point; (*b*) *P:* mettre (qn) en prison, coffrer (qn); (*c*) *P: O:* mettre (qch.) au clou, chez ma tante; (*d*) *F:* bouffer, expédier (de la nourriture); (*e*) *A:* répudier (sa femme); (*f*) tuer, assassiner (qn); **we had to p. the dog away,** il nous a fallu faire piquer le chien.

5. put back, (*a*) *v.tr.* (i) remettre (qch.) à sa place; (ii) retarder (une pendule, etc.); **we p. the clocks back next Saturday,** samedi prochain il faut retarder les pendules d'une heure; **this decision has p. the clock back,** cette décision nous a ramenés en arrière; *Sch:* **his absence has p. him back,** son absence l'a retardé dans ses études; (*b*) *v.i. Nau:* retourner, revenir, rentrer, au port.

6. put by, *v.tr* mettre de côté (de l'argent); mettre en réserve (des provisions, etc.); **to have sth. p. by,** avoir (i) des économies, (ii) des réserves.

7. put down, *v.tr.* (*a*) poser, déposer; **to p. sth. down on the ground,** déposer qch. par terre; **p. it down!** (i) posez-le! (ii) laissez cela! n'y touchez pas! *Tp:* **to p. down the receiver,** raccrocher; *Cards:* **to p. down one's hand,** abattre ses cartes, son jeu; (*of bus, etc.*) **to p. down passengers,** débarquer, déposer, laisser descendre, des voyageurs; *Nau:* **to p. down a buoy,** mouiller une bouée; *Mil:* **to p. down a smoke screen,** faire un rideau, un écran, de fumée; *Min:* **to p. down boreholes,** pratiquer des sondages; (*b*) supprimer, réprimer, apaiser (une révolte); vaincre l'opposition; supprimer, faire cesser, mettre fin à (un abus); (*c*) fermer (un parapluie); (*d*) noter (sur papier); mettre, coucher, par écrit; **to p. down one's name,** inscrire son nom; s'inscrire; se faire inscrire (**for,** pour); **p. me down for £10,** inscrivez-moi pour £10; **p. it down to me, to my account,** inscrivez-le, mettez-le, à, sur, mon compte; **I should p. her down at, as, thirty-five,** je lui donne trente-cinq ans; **to p. down sth. to s.o., to sth.,** mettre qch. au compte de qn; attribuer, imputer, qch. à qn, à qch.; **I p. his success down to luck,** j'attribue son succès à la chance; **he couldn't p. down the money,** il ne pouvait pas payer comptant; (*e*) *F:* tuer, abattre (un animal); **to have a dog p. down,** faire piquer un chien; (*f*) *v.i. Av:* atterrir.

8. put forward, *v.tr.* (*a*) avancer, proposer, mettre en avant, faire valoir (une théorie, un projet, etc.); émettre (une prétention); **to p. oneself forward,** (i) se mettre en avant, en évidence; (ii) s'imposer; **to p. one's best foot forward,** (i) presser le pas; (ii) se mettre en devoir de faire de son mieux; (*b*) avancer (la pendule, l'heure d'une réunion, etc.).

9. put in, (*a*) *v.tr.* (i) **to p. one's head in at the window,** passer sa tête par la fenêtre; (ii) planter (un arbre); semer (du grain); greffer (un écusson); (iii) *Jur:* **to p. in a bailiff,** installer un huissier (dans le domicile d'un saisi); **to p. in a distraint, an execution,** opérer, faire pratiquer, une saisie; (iv) **to p. a word in,** placer un mot (dans la conversation); **to p. in a good word for s.o.,** dire un mot en faveur de qn; (v) *Jur:* présenter, produire, fournir (un document, un témoin); **to p. in a claim,** présenter une réclamation; *Sch:* **to p. pupils in for an examination,** présenter des élèves à un examen; (vi) passer (le temps); **to p. in an hour's work,** faire une heure de travail; travailler pendant une heure; (vii) *Turf:* (*of horse*) **to p. all in,** faire tout son possible; (*b*) *v.i.* (i) *Nau:* **to p. in at a port,** entrer, relâcher, dans un port; faire escale dans un port; (ii) **to p. in for an election, for a job,** poser sa candidature à une élection, à un poste; **to p. in for two days' leave,** demander un congé, *Mil:* une permission, de 48 heures.

10. put off, (*a*) *v.tr.* (i) remettre, différer, ajourner, renvoyer; **to p. off a payment,** arriérer, différer, reculer, un paiement; **to p. a plan off for the moment,** mettre un projet en veilleuse; **to p. off doing sth.,** différer de faire qch.; remettre qch. à plus tard; **don't keep putting things off,** ne remettez pas à l'infini; **we shall have to p. our guests off,** il va falloir contremander nos invités; **the sale has been p. off,** il a été sursis à la vente; (ii) **to p. s.o. off,** donner le change à qn; **to p. s.o. off with an excuse,** se débarrasser de qn, renvoyer qn, avec une excuse; **I won't be p. off with a promise,** je ne me contenterai pas d'une promesse; (iii) déconcerter, dérouter, troubler (qn); **these interruptions p. me off,** ces interruptions me déroutent, me dérangent; (iv) **the cooking in this hotel puts me off,** la cuisine de cet hôtel me dégoûte, me coupe l'appétit; **the mere smell of that cheese puts me off,** la seule odeur de ce fromage suffit à m'écœurer; **his stupidity puts me off,** sa stupidité me rebute; (*b*) *v.i. Nau:* déborder du quai; pousser au large; **to p. off from the shore,** quitter la côte.

11. put on, *v.tr.* (*a*) (i) **to p. the kettle on,** mettre la bouilloire à chauffer; **to p. on a record, a tape,** passer un disque, une bande; (ii) **to p. on a play,** monter une pièce de théâtre; **to p. on a train,** mettre un train en service; (iii) **to p. on the brake,** freiner; serrer le frein; (iv) **to p. on a button,** recoudre un bouton; (*b*) (i) mettre (ses vêtements); revêtir (un pardessus); enfiler (son pantalon); chausser (ses pantoufles, ses lunettes, ses éperons); **p. on your hat,** (re)mettez votre chapeau; couvrez-vous; **to p. one's coat on again,** remettre, rendosser, son manteau; **to p. on a dinner jacket,** se mettre en smoking; **to p. on one's shoes,** se chausser; (ii) **to p. on an air of injured innocence,** affecter, prendre, se donner, un air innocent; **to p. on an act,** faire la comédie; *F:* **you're putting it on!** tout ça c'est (i) de l'affectation, de la pose, (ii) du chiqué; (*c*) (i) **to p. on weight,** grossir; prendre du poids; **I've p. on five kilos,** j'ai grossi de cinq kilos; (ii) *F:* **they know how to p. it on,** ils s'entendent à saler la facture; (iii) **to p. on speed,** prendre de la vitesse; **to p. on full speed,** mettre à toute vitesse; (iv) *Turf: etc:* **to p. on £1,** miser £1; (*d*) **to p. on the light,** mettre la lumière; allumer; **to p. the gas on,** allumer le gaz; **to p. on the radio, the television,** faire marcher, allumer, la radio, la télévision; (*e*) avancer (la pendule); **we p. the clocks on next Saturday,** samedi prochain il faut avancer les pendules d'une heure; (*f*) **to p. s.o. on to do a job,** donner un travail à qn; désigner qn pour faire un travail; (*g*) *F:* **to p. s.o. on to sth.,** indiquer qch. à qn; tuyauter qn; **who p. you on to it?** qui est-ce qui vous a donné le tuyau? **who p. you on to this wine?** qui est-ce qui vous a recommandé ce vin? (*h*) *Tp:* **would you p. me on to Mr X?** voulez-vous me passer à M. X?

12. put out, *v.tr.* (*a*) avancer, tendre (la main); allonger, étendre (le bras); *O:* (*traffic signal*) **to p. out one's arm,** étendre, sortir, le bras; (*b*) mettre dehors; **to p. the cat out,** mettre le chat dehors; **to p. the clothes out to dry,** mettre le linge à sécher (dans le jardin); **I've p. your clothes out (on the bed),** j'ai mis tes vêtements sur le lit; tes vêtements sont préparés sur le lit; *Nau:* **to p. out a boat,** mettre un canot à l'eau; **to p. one's head out of the window,** passer sa tête par la fenêtre; sortir la tête à la fenêtre; **to p. out one's tongue,** tirer la langue; **the snail p. out its horns,** l'escargot a sorti ses cornes; (*c*) **to p. one's shoulder out,** se démettre, se déboîter, l'épaule; **to p. one's jaw out,** se décrocher la mâchoire; (*d*) (i) éteindre (une bougie, le feu, la lumière); fermer (le gaz); *Mch:* **to p. out the fires,** jeter bas les feux; **to p. out a fire in its early stages,** étouffer un commencement d'incendie; étouffer un incendie dès le commencement; (ii) **to p. s.o.'s eyes out,** crever les yeux à qn; aveugler qn; **you're going to p. my eye out with your umbrella,** tu vas m'éborgner avec ton parapluie; (*e*) (i) déconcerter, décontenancer, interloquer, interdire, embarrasser, troubler, démonter (qn); brouiller les idées à (qn); faire perdre le fil de ses idées à (qn); **nothing ever puts him out,** il ne se laisse jamais démonter; **I was very much p. out by the news,** la nouvelle m'a beaucoup déconcerté, inquiété; (ii) ennuyer, fâcher, contrarier (qn); **to be p. out about sth.,** être mécontent de qch.; (iii) déranger, incommoder, gêner (qn); **I hope that this won't p. you out,** j'espère que cela ne vous dérangera pas; **you mustn't p. yourself out for me,** il ne faut pas vous déranger, vous mettre en frais, pour moi; (*f*) (i) **to p. a baby out to nurse,** mettre un bébé en nourrice; **to p. a cow out to grass,** mettre une vache en pâture; (ii) **to p. money out (to interest),** placer de l'argent (à intérêt).

13. put over, *v.tr. F:* (*a*) = PUT ACROSS; (*b*) *U.S:* = POSTPONE.

14. put through, *v.tr.* (*a*) mener à bien, faire aboutir (un projet); faire accepter (un marché); (*b*) *Tp:* **to p. s.o. through to s.o.,** donner à qn la communication avec qn; **I'll p. you through to him,** je vous le passerai.

15. put to, *v.tr.* (*a*) atteler (un cheval); mettre (les chevaux) à la voiture; (*b*) **to be hard p. to it to do sth.,** avoir beaucoup de mal, un mal extrême, à faire qch.

16. put together, *v.tr.* (*a*) assembler, mettre ensemble (les parties d'un tout); monter, assembler (une machine, etc.); **now we shall have to p. it together again,** il faut maintenant le remonter; (*b*) *F:* **to p. two and two together,** tirer ses conclusions; **he can't p. two and two together,** il est bête comme ses pieds; (*c*) **I'll just p. a few things together (in my bag),** je vais faire rapidement ma valise; (*d*) mettre (deux choses) côte à côte; rapprocher, comparer (des faits).

17. put up, *v.tr.* (*a*) (i) relever (ses cheveux, le col de son manteau); ouvrir (un parapluie); dresser (une échelle); fixer, accrocher (un tableau); poser (un rideau); **p. up your hands!** (α) *Sch:* levez la main! (β) haut les mains! (ii) coller (une affiche); afficher (un avis); (iii) **I'm going to p. my feet up for a few minutes,** je vais me reposer un peu; (*b*) *Turf:* faire courir (un jockey); donner une monte à (un jockey); (*c*) *Ven:* (faire) lever, faire envoler, faire partir (une perdrix, etc.); (*d*) augmenter, (faire) hausser, majorer (les prix); (*e*) proposer, présenter (un candidat aux élections); *v.i.* (*of candidate*) **to p. up for the council,** poser sa candidature comme conseiller; (*f*) **to p. sth. up for sale,** mettre qch. en vente; **to p. a picture up for auction,** mettre une peinture aux enchères; (*g*) fournir (une somme d'argent); **to p. up the money for an undertaking,** fournir les fonds d'une entreprise; (*h*) **my wife will p. us up some sandwiches,** ma femme va nous faire un paquet de sandwichs; *Com:* **p. up in tubes,** présenté en tubes; **p. up in capsules,** délivré en capsules; (*i*) remettre (son épée) au fourreau; rengainer (son épée); (*j*) offrir, opposer (une résistance); **to p. up no resistance,** ne pas se défendre; (*k*) loger (qn); héberger (qn); donner un lit à (qn); **I can't p. you up,** je ne puis pas vous coucher; *v.i.* **to p. up at a(n) hotel,** (i) descendre, (ii) séjourner, à un hôtel; **to p. up with friends,** séjourner chez des amis; (*l*) *v.i.* **to p. up with sth.,** s'accommoder, s'arranger, de qch.; se résigner à qch.; supporter, souffrir (qch.); **we must p. up with it,** il faut nous en contenter; il faut l'accepter, nous y résigner; **he can p. up with anything,** il s'arrange de tout; **I'll have to p. up with him,** il me faut m'accommoder de lui, me résigner à sa présence; (*m*) *F:* **to p. s.o. up to sth.,** (i) *O:* mettre qn au courant de qch.; (ii) inciter qn à faire qch.; (iii) tuyauter qn; **who p. you up to it?** qui vous a fait faire ça? (*n*) construire, bâtir (une maison, etc.); ériger (un monument); installer, monter (un échafaudage). **18. put upon,** *v. ind.tr. F:* **to p. upon s.o.,** en imposer à qn; abuser de qn; exploiter qn; **he's easily p. upon,** il se laisse mener facilement, s'en laisse imposer; **I won't be p. upon,** je refuse qu'on abuse de moi, se joue de moi, se fiche de moi.

putative ['pju:tətiv], *a. Jur:* (mariage, père) putatif.

putatively ['pju:tətivli], *adv. Jur:* putativement.

putlog[1] ['pʌtlɔg], *s. Const:* boulin *m*; bois *m* de support (d'échafaudage); **p. hole,** ope *m*, boulin.

putlog[2], *v.tr.* **(putlogged)** ficher (une poutrelle) en boulin.

put-off ['putɔf], *s. F:* **1.** retard *m*; remise *f* à plus tard. **2.** excuse *f*, prétexte *m*; faux-fuyant *m*, *pl.* faux-fuyants; échappatoire *f*, défaite *f*.

put-on ['putɔn], *a.* (air) affecté; (élégance) empruntée, d'emprunt; (joie) feinte, de mauvais aloi.

putrefaction [pju:tri'fækʃ(ə)n], *s.* putréfaction *f*.

putrefactive [pju:tri'fæktiv], *a.* putréfactif, putréfiant; de putréfaction; **p. fermentation,** fermentation *f* putride.

putrefiable [pju:tri'faiəbl], *a.* putréfiable, pourrissable.

putrefy ['pju:trifai]. **1.** *v.tr.* putréfier, corrompre, pourrir. **2.** *v.i.* (*a*) (*of carrion, etc.*) se putréfier, se corrompre; pourrir; (*b*) (*of living tissue*) (i) suppurer, s'envenimer; (ii) se gangrener.

putrefying ['pju:trifaiiŋ], *a.* en putréfaction; en pourriture; putrescent.

putrescence [pju:'tres(ə)ns], *s.* putrescence *f*.

putrescent [pju:'tres(ə)nt], *a.* putrescent; en putréfaction; en pourriture.

putrescibility [pju:tresi'biliti], *s.* putrescibilité *f*.

putrescible [pju:'tresibl], *a.* putrescible; pourrissable.

putrescine ['pju:tresi:n], *s. Bio-Ch:* putrescine *f*.

putrid ['pju:trid], *a.* **1.** (*a*) putride, corrompu; en putréfaction; infect; **to become p.,** tomber en pourriture; se corrompre; (*b*) *Med: A:* **p. fever,** typhus *m*; fièvre *f* putride; **p. sore throat,** pharyngite gangreneuse. **2.** *F: O:* au-dessous de tout.

putridness ['pju:tridnis], **putridity** [pju:'triditi], *s.* putridité *f*, pourriture *f*, corruption *f*.

putsch [putʃ], *s.* putsch *m*.

putt[1] [pʌt], *s. Golf:* putt *m*; **to hole a long p.,** rentrer un long putt.

putt[2], *v.tr. & i. Golf:* poter (la balle); putter.

puttee [pʌ'ti], *s. A.Mil.Cost:* bande molletière.

putter[1] ['pʌtər], *s. Golf:* **1.** (*club*) poteur *m*, putter *m*. **2.** (*pers.*) (*a*) *Sp:* lanceur *m* (du poids lourd); (*b*) *Golf:* poteur, putter; **good, bad, p.,** joueur, -euse, qui pote bien, mal.

putter[2], *v.i. U.S:* = POTTER[2].

putting[1] ['putiŋ], *s.* **1.** (*a*) mise *f*, pose *f*; *Tchn:* mettage *m*; apposition *f* (d'une signature); (*b*) **p. under wheat,** semailles *fpl* en blé; (*c*) *St.Exch:* délivrement *m* (d'actions). **2.** présentation *f* (d'un argument); mise, soumission *f* (d'une résolution). **3.** *Sp:* **p. the weight,** lancement du poids. **4. p. to sea,** mise à la mer; appareillage *m*; **p. about,** virement *m* de bord; **p. back,** retour *m*, rentrée *f*, au port; **p. in,** (r)entrée *f* au port. **5. p. away,** rangement *m* (des livres, etc.); **p. by,** mise *f* à côté (de l'argent); **p. down,** (i) suppression *f* (d'une révolte); (ii) abattage *m* (d'un animal); **p. together,** assemblage *m* (de morceaux); montage *m* (d'une machine, etc.).

putting[2] ['pʌtiŋ], *s. Golf:* **to practise p.,** s'exercer à poter la balle, à putter; **p. iron,** poteur *m*, putter *m*; **p. green,** putting(-green) *m*; pelouse d'arrivée; le vert; *F:* **to be made as welcome as a dog on a p. green,** être reçu comme un chien dans un jeu de quilles.

putto, *pl.* **putti** ['putou, -ti:], *s. Paint: Sculp:* putto *m*, *pl.* putti.

putty[1] ['pʌti], *s.* **1.** (*a*) mastic *m*, enduit *m*, lut *m*; **glazier's p.,** mastic à vitres; lut de vitrier; **to fill a hole with p.,** mastiquer un trou; **p. knife,** spatule *f* de vitrier; couteau *m* à palette; couteau à mastiquer; **p.-coloured,** couleur mastic; **p.-faced,** (*of pers.*) au visage de papier mâché; (*b*) **plasterer's p.,** pâte *f* de chaux. **2. jeweller's p., p. of tin, p. powder,** potée *f* (d'étain).

putty[2], *v.tr.* **to p. (up) a hole,** mastiquer un trou; boucher un trou au mastic.

puttying ['pʌtiiŋ], *s.* masticage *m*.

put-up ['putʌp], *a.* **1.** *F:* **a p.-up job,** une affaire machinée à l'avance; un coup monté; une affaire bricolée, maquignonnée; **it's a p.-up job,** ils se sont donné le mot; il y a un micmac, là-dedans; c'est du chiqué. **2.** (*at auction*) **p.-up price,** mise *f* à prix.

puzzle[1] ['pʌzl], *s.* **1.** embarras *m*, perplexité *f*. **2.** question embarrassante, troublante; énigme *f*; **your friend is a real p. to me,** je ne comprends pas du tout votre ami. **3.** (*a*) (*manual*) casse-tête *m inv*; **Chinese p.,** casse-tête chinois; **jigsaw p.,** jeu *m* de patience (en bois chantourné); puzzle *m*; (*b*) (*mental*) devinette *f*, problème *m*; **pictorial p.,** rébus *m*; **crossword p.,** (problème de) mots croisés; (*c*) **p. lock,** (i) serrure *f* à combinaisons; (ii) cadenas *m* à secret.

puzzle[2], *v.tr.* embarrasser, intriguer, déconcerter; **puzzled look,** air hébété, perdu; **I was puzzled,** je ne savais que penser; **I was puzzled how to answer,** j'étais embarrassé pour répondre; **he was puzzled about what to do,** il se demandait ce qu'il fallait faire.

puzzlement ['pʌzlmənt], *s.* embarras *m*, confusion *f*, perplexité *f*.

puzzler ['pʌzlər], *s. F:* **that's a p.!** voilà une question embarrassante!

puzzling ['pʌzliŋ], *a.* embarrassant, intrigant, troublant.

puzzolana [pʌtsou'lɑ:nə], *s.* = POZZOLANA.

pyaemia [pai'i:miə], *s. Med:* py(o)hémie *f*, pyémie *f*.

pyaemic [pai'i:mik], *a. Med:* py(o)hémique.

pyarthrosis [paiɑ:'θrousis], *s. Med:* pyarthrose *f*.

pycnid ['piknid], **pycnidium,** *pl.* **-ia** [pik'nidiəm, -iə], *s. Fung:* pycnide *f*.

pycnidiospore [pik'nidiouspɔ:r], *s. Fung:* pycnidiospore *f*.

pycniospore ['pikniouspɔ:r], *s. Fung:* pycnospore *f*.

pycnite ['piknait], *s. Miner:* pycnite *f*.

Pycnodonti [piknou'dɔntai], *s.pl. Paleont:* pycnodontes *m*.

pycnogonid [pik'nɔgənid], *s. Nat.Hist:* pycnogonide *m*.

Pycnogonida [piknou'gɔnidə], *s.pl. Nat.Hist:* pycnogonides *m*.

pycnometer [pik'nɔmitər], *s. Ph:* pycnomètre *m*; flacon *m* à densité.

pycnometry [pik'nɔmitri], *s. Ph:* pycnométrie *f*.

Pycnonotidae [piknou'nɔtidi:], *s.pl. Orn:* pycnonotidés *m*.

pycnosis [pik'nousis], *s. Med:* pycnose *f*.

pycnospore ['piknouspɔ:r], *s. Fung:* pycnospore *f*.

pycnosporic [piknou'spɔ:rik], *a. Fung:* pycnosporé.

pycnostyle ['piknoustail], *a. & s. Arch:* pycnostyle (*m*).

pye-dog ['paidɔg], *s.* chien errant (de l'Orient).

pyelic [pai'elik], *a. Anat:* pyélique.

pyelitis [paii'laitis], *s. Med:* pyélite *f*.

pyelography [paii'lɔgrəfi], *s. Med:* pyélographie *f*.

pyelonephritis [paiiloune'fraitis], *s. Med:* pyélonéphrite *f*.

pyeloscopy [paii'lɔskəpi], *s. Med:* pyéloscopie *f*.

pyelotomy [paii'lɔtəmi], *s. Surg:* pyélotomie *f*.

pyemia [pai'i:miə], *s.* = PYAEMIA.

pygmy ['pigmi]. **1.** *s.* pygmée *m*. **2.** *a.* pygmée, pygméen; *Orn:* **p. owl,** chevêchette *f*; *Z:* **p. hippopotamus,** hippopotame nain.

Pygopodes [pai'gɔpədi:z], *s.pl. Orn:* pygopodes *m*.

Pygopodidae [paigou'pɔdidi:], *s.pl. Rept:* pygopodidés *m*.

pygopus ['paigəpəs], *s. Rept:* pygope *m*.

pygostyle ['paigoustail], *s. Orn:* pygostyle *m*.

pyjama [pə'dʒɑ:mə], *s. Cost:* **(pair of) pyjamas,** pyjama *m*; **to sleep in pyjamas,** dormir en pyjama; **to wear pyjamas,** porter des pyjamas; **beach pyjamas,** pyjamas de plage; **p. trousers, p. jacket,** pantalon *m*, veste *f*, de pyjama; **p. cord,** ceinture *f* de pyjama.

pyknic ['piknik], *a.* pycnique.

pyknolepsy ['piknəlepsi], *s. Med:* pycnolepsie *f*, pyknolepsie *f*.

Pylades ['pilədi:z]. *Pr.n.m. Gr.Lit:* Pylade.

pylephlebitis [pailefli'baitis], *s. Med:* pyléphlébite *f*.

pylethrombosis [paileθrɔm'bousis], *s. Med:* pyléthrombose *f*.

pylon ['pailən], *s.* **1.** *Arch:* pylône *m*. **2.** *Civ.E: El.E: etc:* pylône (en charpente métallique; en béton armé).

pylorectomy [pailou'rektəmi], *s. Surg:* pylorectomie *f*.

pyloric [pai'lɔrik], *a. Anat:* pylorique.

pyloroplasty [pai'lɔ:rəplæsti], *s. Surg:* pyloroplastie *f*.

pylorospasm [pai'lɔ:rəspæzm], *s. Med:* pylorospasme *m*.

pylorus [pai'lɔ:rəs], *s. Anat:* pylore *m*.

pyobacillosis [paioubæsi'lousis], *s. Vet:* pyobacillose *f*.

pyoctanin [pai'ɔktənin], *s. Pharm:* pyoktanine *f*.

pyocyanin [paiou'saiənin], *s. Bio-Ch:* pyocyanine *f*.

pyocyte ['paiousait], *s. Med:* pyocyte *m*.

pyodermatitis [paioudə:mə'taitis], *s. Med:* pyodermite *f*.

pyogenesis [paiou'dʒenisis], *s. Med:* pyogénie *f*, pyogénèse *f*.

pyogenic [paiou'dʒenik], *a. Med:* pyogène.

pyoid ['paiɔid], *a. Med:* pyoïde.

pyolabyrinthitis [paioulæbərin'θaitis], *s. Med:* pyolabyrinthite *f*.

pyonephrosis [paioune'frousis], *s. Med:* pyonéphrose *f*.

pyophagia [paiou'feidʒiə], *s. Med:* pyophagie *f*.

pyophthalmia [paiɔf'θælmiə], *s. Med:* pyophtalmie *f*.

pyopneumothorax [paiounju:mou'θɔ:ræks], *s. Med:* pyopneumothorax *m*.

pyorrhea [paiə'riə], *s. Med:* pyorrhée *f*; **p. (alveolaris),** pyorrhée alvéolo-dentaire; gingivite expulsive.

pyorrheal, pyorrheic, pyorrhetic [paiə'ri:əl, -'ri:ik, -'retik], *a. Med:* pyorrhéique.

pyosis [pai'ousis], *s. Med:* suppuration *f*.

pyothorax [paiou'θɔ:ræks], *s. Med:* pyothorax *m*, empyème *m*.

pyracanth ['paiərəkænθ], **pyracantha** [paiərə'kænθə], *s. Bot:* pyracanthe *f*; buisson ardent, arbre *m* de Moïse.

Pyralidae [pi'rælidi:], **Pyralididae** [pirə'lididi:], *s.pl. Ent:* pyralides *f*, pyralidés *m*, pyralididés *m*.

pyralis, *pl.* **-ides** ['pirəlis, pi'rælidi:z], *s. Ent:* pyrale *f*.

pyramid ['pirəmid], *s.* (*a*) pyramide *f*; **stepped p.,** pyramide à degrés; **to stack in a p.,** arranger (qch.) en pyramide; *Anat:* **Malphigian p.,** pyramide de Malphigi; (*b*) arbre taillé en pyramide.

pyramidal [pi'ræmid(ə)l]. **1.** *a.* pyramidal, -aux; pyramidé; *Anat:* **p. bone,** os pyramidal; **p. cell,** cellule pyramidale. **2.** *s. Anat:* os pyramidal.

Pyramidellidae [pirəmi'delidi:], *s.pl. Moll:* pyramidellidés *m*.

pyramidical [pirə'midikl], *a.* pyramidal -aux.

pyramidion, *pl.* **-ia** [pirə'midiən, -iə], *s. Arch:* pyramidion *m* (d'un obélisque, etc.).

Pyramus ['pirəməs], *Pr.n.m. Lit:* Pyrame.

pyran ['paiəræn], *s. Ch:* pyran(ne) *m*.

pyranometer [paiəræ'nɔmitər], *s. Ph:* pyranomètre *m*.

pyrargyrite [paiə'rɑ:dʒirait], *s. Miner:* pyrargyrite *f*, argent rouge antimonial.

pyrausta [paiə'rɔ:stə], *s. Ent:* pyrauste *f*.

pyrazin(e) ['pirəzi(:)n], *s. Ch:* pyrazine *f*.

pyrazol(e) ['pirəzoul, -zɔl], *s. Ch:* pyrazol(e) *m*.

pyrazolin(e) [pi'ræzouli(:)n], *s. Ch:* pyrazoline *f*.

pyrazolone [pi'ræzouloun], *s. Ch:* pyrazolone *f*.

pyre ['paiər], *s.* bûcher *m* (funéraire).

pyrene[1] ['paiəri:n], *s. Ch:* pyrène *m*.

pyrene[2], *s. Bot:* pyrène *f*, nucule *f*.

Pyrenean [pirə'ni:ən], *a. Geog:* pyrénéen; des Pyrénées; **P. mountain dog,** Saint-Bernard des Pyrénées.

Pyrenees (the) [ðəpirə'ni:z]. *Pr.n.pl. Geog:* les Pyrénées *f*; *Z: NAm:* **Great Pyrenees,** Saint-Bernard des Pyrénées.

pyrenin [paiə'ri:nin], *s. Biol:* pyrénine *f*.

pyrenoid [paiə'ri:nɔid], *a. Bot:* pyrénoïde.

pyrenolichen [paiəri:nou'laikən], *s. Fung:* pyrénolichen *m*.

pyrenomycete [paiəri:nou'maisi:t], *s. Fung:* pyrénomycète *m*.

Pyrenomycetes [paiəri:noumai'si:ti:z], *s.pl. Fung:* pyrénomycètes *m*.

pyrethrin [paiə'ri:θrin], *s. Pharm:* pyréthrine *f*.

pyrethrum [paiə'ri:θrəm], *s. Bot:* pyrèthre *m*; **p. powder,** poudre *f* insecticide de pyrèthre.

pyretic [paiə'retik], *a. Med:* pyrétique.

pyretogenetic [paiəri:toudʒə'netik], *a.* pyrétogène.

pyretology [paiərə'tɔlədʒi], *s. Med:* pyrétologie *f*.

pyretotherapy [paiəri:tou'θerəpi], *s. Med:* pyrétothérapie *f*.

Pyrex ['paiəreks], *s. Glassm: R.t.m:* Pyrex *m*.

pyrexia [paiə'reksiə], *s. Med:* pyrexie *f*.

pyrexial [paiə'reksiəl], **pyrexic** [paiə'reksik], *a. Med:* pyrexique.

pyrgeometer [paidʒi:'ɔmitər], *s. Ph:* pyrgéomètre *m*.

pyrheliometer [paiəhi:li'ɔmitər], *s. Ph:* pyrhéliomètre *m*.

pyrheliometric [paiəhi:liou'metrik], *a. Ph:* pyrhéliométrique.

pyridazin(e) [paiə'ridəzi(:)n], *s. Ch:* pyridazine *f*.

pyridic [paiə'ridik], *a. Ch:* pyridique.

pyridin(e) ['paiəridi(:)n], *s. Ch:* pyridine *f*.

pyridone ['piridoun], *s. Ch:* pyridone *f*.

pyridoxin(e) [piri'dɔksi(:)n], *s. Bio-Ch:* pyridoxine *f*.

pyriform ['pirifɔ:m], *a. Bot:* pyriforme.

pyrimidin(e) [pi'rimidi(:)n], *s. Ch:* pyrimidine *f*.

pyrites [paiə'raiti:z], *s.inv. in pl. Miner:* pyrite *f*; **arsenical p.,** mispickel *m*; **copper p.,** chalcopyrite *f*; cuivre pyriteux; **magnetic p.,** pyrrhotine *f*; magnétopyrite *f*; **iron p.,** sulfure *m* de fer; fer sulfuré; **white iron p.,** marcassite *f*.

pyritic [paiə'ritik], *a. Miner:* pyriteux.

pyritiferous [paiəri'tifərəs], *a. Miner:* pyritifère.

pyritous ['paiəritəs], *a. Miner:* pyriteux.

pyro- ['paiərou, paiə'rɔ], *comb.fm.* pyro-.

pyro ['paiərou], *s. Phot: F:* pyrogallol *m*; acide *m* pyrogallique.

pyroacid [paiərou'æsid], *s. Ch:* acide pyrogéné.

pyroarsenate [paiərou'ɑ:səneit], *s. Ch:* pyroarséniate *m*.

pyroboric [paiərou'bɔ(:)rik], *a. Ch:* pyroborique.

pyrocatechin [paiərou'kætitʃin, -kin], *s. Ch: Phot:* pyrocatéchine *f*.

pyrocatech(in)ol [paiərou'kætik(in)oul, -tʃ(in)oul], *s. Ch: Phot:* pyrocatéchol *m.*
pyrochlore ['paiəroukl ɔ:r], *s. Miner:* pyrochlore *m.*
pyroclastic [paiərou'klæstik], *a. Geol:* pyroclastique.
pyrocollodion [paiəroukə'loudiən], *s.* pyrocollodion *m.*
pyroelectric [paiəroui'lektrik], *a.* pyroélectrique.
pyroelectricity [paiərouilek'trisiti], *s.* pyroélectricité *f.*
pyrogallate [paiərou'gæleit], *s. Ch:* pyrogallate *m.*
pyrogallic [paiərou'gælik], *a. Ch:* **p. acid,** acide *m* pyrogallique; pyrogallol *m.*
pyrogallol [paiərou'gæləl], *s. Ch:* pyrogallol *m.*
pyrogenation [paiərɔdʒi'neiʃ(ə)n], *s. Ch: Ph:* pyrogénation *f.*
pyrogenesis [paiərou'dʒenəsis], *s.* pyrogénèse *f.*
pyrogenetic [paiəroudʒi'netik], *a. Ph:* pyrogénétique, pyrogénésique.
pyrogen-free ['paiərədʒənfri:], *a.* apyrogène.
pyrogenic [paiərou'dʒenik], **pyrogenous** [paiə'rɔdʒinəs], *a.* **1.** *Geol: etc:* pyrogène. **2.** *Ch:* (huile, résine) pyrogénée.
pyrognostic [paiərɔg'nɔstik], *a.* pyrognostique.
pyrograph[1] ['paiərəgræf], *s.* pyrogravure *f.*
pyrograph[2], *v.tr. & i.* pyrograver.
pyrographer [paiə'rɔgrəfər], *s.* pyrograveur, -euse.
pyrography [paiə'rɔgrəfi], **pyrogravure** ['paiərougrəvjuər], *s.* pyrogravure *f.*
pyrola ['pirələ], *s. Bot:* pyrole *f.*
Pyrolaceae [pirou'leisii:], *s.pl. Bot:* pyrolacées *f.*
pyrolator [paiə'rɔlətər], *s.* pyrolâtre *mf.*
pyrolatry [paiə'rɔlətri], *s.* pyrolâtrie *f.*
pyroligneous [paiərou'ligniəs], *a. Ch:* (acide) pyroligneux.
pyrolignite [paiərou'lignait], *s. Ch:* pyrolignite *f.*
pyrolusite [paiərou'lu:sait], *s. Miner:* pyrolusite *f.*
pyrolysis [paiə'rɔlisis], *s. Ch:* pyrolyse *f.*
pyromagnetic [paiəroumæg'netik], *a.* pyromagnétique.
pyromancy ['paiəroumænsi], *s.* pyromancie *f.*
pyromania [paiərou'meiniə], *s. Psy:* pyromanie *f.*
pyromaniac [paiərou'meiniæk], *s.* pyromane *mf.*
pyromeconic [paiəroumi'kɔnik], *a.* (acide) pyroméconique.
pyromellitic [paiəroumi'litik], *a. Ch:* pyromellique.
pyrometamorphism [paiəroumetə'mɔ:fizm], *s. Geol:* pyrométamorphisme *m.*
pyrometer [paiə'rɔmitər], *s. Ph: Metall:* pyromètre *m*; **dial p.,** pyromètre à cadran; **optical p.,** pyromètre à lunette; **radiation p.,** pyromètre à radiation totale; *Cer:* **p. cone,** cône *m* pyrométrique.
pyrometric(al) [paiərou'metrik(əl)], *a. Ph:* pyrométrique; *Cer:* **pyrometric cone,** cône *m* pyrométrique.
pyrometry [paiə'rɔmitri], *s. Ph:* pyrométrie *f*; **p. wire,** fil *m* pyrométrique.
pyromorphite [paiərou'mɔ:fait], *s. Miner:* pyromorphite *f.*
pyromucic [paiərou'mju:sik], *a.* (acide) pyromucique.
pyrone ['paiəroun], *s. Ch:* pyrone *f.*
pyrope ['paiəroup], *s. Miner:* pyrope *m*; grenat magnésien.
pyrophanite [paiə'rɔfənait], *s. Miner:* pyrophanite *f.*
pyrophanous [paiə'rɔfənəs], *a.* pyrophane.
pyrophoric [paiərou'fɔrik], *a. Ch:* pyroforique; *Metall: etc:* pyrophorique; **p. alloy,** alliage *m* pyrophorique.
pyrophorus [paiə'rɔfərəs], *s. Ch: Ent:* pyrophore *m.*
pyrophosphate [paiərou'fɔsfeit], *s. Ch:* pyrophosphate *m.*
pyrophosphoric [paiəroufɔs'fɔrik], *a. Ch:* pyrophosphorique.
pyrophosphorous [paiərou'fɔsfərəs], *a. Ch:* pyrophosphoreux.
pyrophyllite [paiərou'filait], *s. Miner:* pyrophyllite *f.*
pyrophysalite [paiərou'fisəlait], *s. Miner:* pyrophysalite *f.*
pyrophyte ['paiəroufait], *s. Bot:* pyrophyte *m.*
pyroscope ['paiərəskoup], *s. Ph: Metall:* pyroscope *m.*
pyroscopy [paiə'rɔskɔpi], *s. Ph: Metall:* pyroscopie *f.*
pyrosis [paiə'rousis], *s. Med:* pyrosis *m.*
pyrosmalite [paiə'rɔzməlait], *s. Miner:* pyrosmalite *f.*
pyrosoma [paiərou'soumə], **pyrosome** ['paiərousoum], *s. Moll:* pyrosome *m.*
pyrosphere ['paiərousfiər], *s. Geol: A:* pyrosphère *f.*
pyrostat ['paiəroustæt], *s.* pyrostat *m.*
pyrostilpnite [paiərou'stilpnait], *s. Miner:* pyrostilpnite *f.*
pyrosulphate [paiərou'sʌlfeit], *s. Ch:* pyrosulfate *m.*
pyrosulphite [paiərou'sʌlfait], *s. Ch:* pyrosulfite *m.*
pyrosulphuric [paiərousʌl'fju:rik], *a. Ch:* pyrosulfurique.
pyrosulphuryl [paiərou'sʌlfjuril], *s. Ch:* pyrosulfuryle *m.*
pyrotartaric [paiəroutɑ:'tærik], *a. Ch:* pyrotartrique.
pyrotechnic(al) [paiərou'teknik(əl)], *a.* pyrotechnique; **p. display,** feu *m* d'artifice.
pyrotechnics [paiərou'tekniks], *s.pl.* (*usu. with sg. const.*) pyrotechnie *f*, pyrotechnique *f*; (*of oratory, etc.*) un vrai feu d'artifice.
pyrotechnist [paiərou'teknist], *s.* artificier *m*; pyrotechnicien, -ienne.
pyrotechny ['paiərouteknі], *s.* pyrotechnie *f*, pyrotechnique *f.*
pyrotherium [paiərou'θiəriəm], *s. Paleont:* pyrotherium *m.*
pyroxene ['paiərɔksi:n], *s. Miner:* pyroxène *m.*
pyroxenic [paiərɔk'senik], *a. Miner:* pyroxéneux.
pyroxenite [paiə'rɔksinait], *s. Miner:* pyroxénite *f.*
pyroxyle [paiə'rɔksil], *s. Ch: Exp:* pyroxyle *m*, pyroxyline *f.*
pyroxylic [paiərɔk'silik], *a. A.Ch:* pyroxylique; pyroligneux.
pyroxylin [paiə'rɔksilin], *s. Ch: Exp:* pyroxyle *m*, pyroxyline *f*; *attrib.* pyroxylé.
pyrrhic[1] ['pirik], *a. & s.* **1.** *Gr.Ant:* (danse) pyrrhique (*f*). **2.** *Pros:* (pied) pyrrhique (*m*).
Pyrrhic[2], *a. Rom.Hist:* de Pyrrhus; **P. victory,** victoire *f* à la Pyrrhus; victoire désastreuse.
Pyrrho ['pirou]. *Pr.n.m. Gr.Phil:* Pyrrhon.
pyrrhocorid [pirou'kɔrid], *s. Ent:* pyrrhocore *m*, pyrrhocoris *m.*
Pyrrhocoridae [pirou'kɔridi:], *s.pl. Ent:* pyrrhocoridés *m.*
Pyrrhonist ['pirənist], *a. & s. Gr.Phil:* pyrrhonien (*m*).
pyrrhotine, pyrrhotite ['pirətain, -tait], *s. Miner:* pyrrhotine *f*, pyrrhotite *f*, magnétopyrite *f.*
Pyrrhus ['pirəs]. *Pr.n.m. Hist:* Pyrrhus.
pyrrol(e) ['piroul], *s. Ch:* pyrrol(e) *m.*
pyrrolidin(e) [pi'roulidi(:)n], *s. Ch:* pyrrolidine *f.*
pyrrolin(e) ['pirəli(:)n], *s. Ch:* pyrroline *f.*
pyruvic [paiə'ru:vik], *a. Ch:* pyruvique.
Pythagoras [pai'θægərəs]. *Pr.n.m. Gr.Phil:* Pythagore; **Pythagoras' theorem,** théorème *m* de Pythagore.
Pythagorean [paiθægə'ri:ən]. **1.** *a.* pythagoricien, pythagorique, pythagoréen; *Mth:* **the P. proposition,** le théorème de Pythagore; **P. table,** table *f* de Pythagore. **2.** *s.* pythagoricien *m.*
Pythagorism [pai'θægərizm], **Pythagoreanism** [paiθægə'riənizm], *s.* pythagorisme *m.*
Pytheas ['piθiæs]. *Pr.n.m. Gr.Hist:* Pythéas.
Pythia ['piθiə]. *Gr.Ant:* **1.** *Pr.n.f.* la Pythie. **2.** *s.pl.* les jeux pythiens.
Pythiad ['piθiæd], *s. Gr.Ant:* pythiade *f.*
Pythian ['piθiən], *a. & s.* (oracle, etc.) pythien; **P. games,** jeux pythiens, jeux pythiques; *Gr.Lit:* **the Pythians, the P. Odes** (*of Pindar*), les Pythiques *f.*
python ['paiθ(ə)n], *s. Gr.Myth: Rept:* python *m*; **rock p.,** python(-)tigre *m*; **Indian p.,** (python) molure *m*; **reticulate p.,** python réticulé.
pythoness ['paiθənes], *s.f. Gr.Ant:* pythonisse; pythie.
pyuria [pai'juəriə], *s. Med:* pyurie *f.*
pyx [piks], *s.* **1.** *Ecc:* ciboire *m*; **p. cloth,** custode *f.* **2.** (*at London Mint*) boîte *f* des monnaies d'or et d'argent destinées au contrôle; **trial of the p.,** essai *m* des monnaies; contrôle.
pyxidium, *pl.* **-ia** [pik'sidiəm, -iə], *s. Bot:* pyxide *f.*
pyxis, *pl.* **-ides** ['piksis, -idi:z], *s.* **1.** *Bot:* pyxide *f.* **2.** *Anat:* cavité *f* cotyloïde.

Q

Q, q [kju:], *s.* (la lettre) Q, q *m*; *Tp:* **Q for Queenie,** Q comme Quintal; *Nav.Hist:* **Q ship, Q boat,** bateau-piège *m*, *pl.* bateaux-pièges; *El.Meas:* **Q meter,** Q-mètre *m*; *Elcs:* **Q factor,** facteur *m* Q, de qualité; *Telecom:* **Q signal,** code *m* Q; *Med:* **Q fever,** fièvre *f* Q; *F:* **on the q.t.** [kju:'ti:] (= *quiet*), discrètement; en confidence; sans en parler à personne; **on the strict q.t.,** en cachette, en secret, en tapinois; sans bruit; en douce; **I'm telling you that on the q.t.,** je vous dis ça entre quat'z yeux.

q'at, qat [kæt], *s. Bot:* kat *m*, qat *m*.

qua [kwei, kwɑ:]. *Lt.adv.* en tant que; considéré comme; **men q. men,** les hommes en tant qu'hommes.

quack[1] [kwæk]. **1.** *int.* **q., q.!** coin-coin! **2.** *s.* (*a*) cri *m* du canard; coin-coin *m inv*; (*b*) *F:* (*nursery*) **q.-q.,** canard *m*.

quack[2], *v.i.* **1.** (*of ducks*) crier; cancaner; faire coin-coin. **2.** *F:* (*of pers.*) bavarder.

quack[3], *s.* (*a*) **q. (doctor),** charlatan *m*; banquiste *m*; **q. remedy,** remède *m* de charlatan; **q. powder,** poudre *f* de perlimpinpin; (*b*) *F:* médecin *m*, toubib *m*.

quack[4]. **1.** *v.i. F:* faire le charlatan, le mariol. **2.** *v.tr. A:* **to q. sth. up,** vanter, prôner (un remède, etc.).

quackery ['kwækəri], *s.* **1.** charlatanisme *m*; empirisme médical. **2.** charlatanerie *f*, hâblerie *f*.

quacking ['kwækiŋ], *s.* coin-coin *m inv* (du canard).

quackish ['kwækiʃ], *a.* de charlatan, charlatanesque.

quad[1] [kwɔd], *s. Sch: F:* = QUADRANGLE 2.

quad[2], *a. & s. Rec: F:* **q. (effect),** tétraphonie *f*.

quad[3], *s. Typ: F:* = QUADRAT.

quad[4], *v.tr.* **(quadded)** *Typ:* **1. to q. a line,** remplir une ligne de cadrats. **2. to q. out a line,** insérer des cadrats dans la ligne.

quad[5], *a.* (= QUADRUPLE[1]) **1.** *Paperm:* **q. crown** = double jésus *m*; **q. demy** = quadruple carré; **q. royal** = quadruple raisin. **2.** *El:* quarte *f*; **spiral q.,** quarte torsadée; **star q.,** quarte en étoile; **q. cable,** câble *m* à quartes; **multiple twin q.,** quarte D.M.

quad[6], *s. F:* = quadruplé, -ée.

quad[7], *s. & v.tr. P:* = QUOD[1,2].

quadded ['kwɔdid], *a. El:* (câble *m*) à quartes.

quadding ['kwɔdiŋ], *s. El:* fabrication *f* d'une paire, d'une quarte.

quadra ['kwɔdrə], *s.* cadre *m* (d'un bas-relief, d'une tapisserie, d'une glace).

quadrable ['kwɔdrəbl], *a. Mth:* dont on peut effectuer la quadrature; qui peut se réduire à un carré équivalent.

quadragenarian [kwɔdrədʒə'nɛəriən], *a. & s.* quadragénaire (*mf*).

Quadragesima [kwɔdrə'dʒesimə], *s. Ecc:* **Q. (Sunday),** (le dimanche de) la Quadragésime.

quadragesimal [kwɔdrə'dʒesim(ə)l], *a.* quadragésimal, -aux.

quadrangle ['kwɔdræŋgl], *s.* **1.** (*a*) *Mth:* figure *f* quadrangulaire; quadrilatère *m*; tétragone *m*; (*b*) *Palmistry:* quadrangle *m*. **2.** cour (carrée) (d'un palais, d'une école, etc.); **main q.,** cour d'honneur (d'une école, etc.).

quadrangular [kwɔ'dræŋgjulər], *a.* quadrangulaire, quadrangulé, tétragone.

quadrangularly [kwɔ'dræŋgjuləli], *adv.* quadrangulairement.

quadrant ['kwɔdrənt], *s.* **1.** (*a*) *Astr: Mth:* quart *m* de cercle; quadrant *m*; *Nau:* octant *m*; **q. compasses,** compas *m* quart de cercle; *El:* **q. electrometer,** électromètre *m* à quadrants; (*b*) *Artil:* niveau *m* (de pointage); **gunner's q.,** niveau de pointage en hauteur; **elevation q.,** niveau de hausse; **q. angle, q. elevation,** angle *m* au niveau, angle de tir; **quadrant twenty-five!** niveau vingt-cinq! **2.** (*a*) *Mec.E: Mch:* secteur *m*; (*of steam engine*) secteur Stephenson; **notched, toothed, q.,** secteur denté, crénelé; **control q.,** secteur de commande; **q.-type lever,** levier *m* se déplaçant sur secteur; **ratchet-toothed q.,** secteur denté de cliquet; *Aut:* **q. of the handbrake,** secteur du frein; *Mch:* **q. guide,** guide *m* de secteur; *Nau:* **rudder q., steering q.,** secteur de barre, de gouvernail; *Aut:* **steering q.,** secteur de direction; **skylight q.,** secteur de claire-voie; (*b*) *Mch.Tls:* **q. (plate),** lyre *f*, cavalier *m*, tête *f* de cheval (de tour à fileter). **3.** *Arch: Carp:* quart-de-rond *m*, *pl.* quarts-de-rond.

quadrantal [kwɔ'drænt(ə)l], *a.* quadrantal, -aux; (*a*) *Mth:* **q. triangle,** triangle quadrantal; (*b*) **q. corrector,** globe compensateur (de compas); **q. deviation,** déviation quadrantale (de l'aiguille aimantée); **q. error,** erreur quadrantale; **q. points,** points intercardinaux; (*c*) *Av:* **q. altitude,** altitude quadrantale.

quadraphonic [kwɔdrə'fɔnik], *a. Rec:* **q. effect, sound,** tétraphonie *f*.

quadraphony [kwɔ'drɔfəni], *s. Rec:* tétraphonie *f*.

quadrat ['kwɔdrət], *s. Typ:* cadrat *m*, quadrat *m*; **em-q.,** cadratin *m*; **en-q.,** demi-cadratin *m*.

quadrate[1] ['kwɔdreit], *a. & s. Anat:* **q. (muscle),** (muscle) carré *m*; *Orn: Rept:* **q. (bone),** (os) carré (de la tête).

quadrate[2] [kwɔ'dreit]. **1.** *v.tr.* (*a*) *Mth:* réduire (une surface, une expression) au carré équivalent; **to q. the circle,** faire la quadrature du cercle; (*b*) faire cadrer **(sth. with, to, sth.,** qch. avec qch.). **2.** *v.i.* cadrer **(with,** avec).

quadratic [kwɔ'drætik]. **1.** *a.* (*a*) *Mth:* **q. equation,** équation *f* quadratique, du second degré; **q. forms,** formes *f* quadratiques; **q. mean,** moyenne *f* quadratique; (*b*) *Elcs:* **q. detector,** détecteur *m* quadratique; *Cmptr:* **q. programming,** programmation *f* quadratique. **2.** *a. Miner:* quadratique, tétragonal; **q. crystal,** cristal *m* quadratique; **q. system,** système *m* quadratique, quaternaire. **3.** *s. Mth:* équation quadratique, du second degré.

quadratrix, *pl.* **-trices** [kwɔ'dreitriks, -trisi:z], *s. Mth:* quadratrice *f*.

quadrature ['kwɔdrətjər], *s.* **1.** *Mth:* quadrature *f*; **q. of the circle,** quadrature du cercle. **2.** *Astr:* quadrature; (aspect *m*) quadrat *m*; **the moon is now in q. to the sun,** la lune est maintenant en quadrature avec le soleil. **3.** *Ph: El:* **q. booster,** survolteur-déphaseur *m*, *pl.* survolteurs-déphaseurs; **q. current,** courant déwatté; **q. transformer,** transformateur *m* d'intensité déphaseur.

quadrennial [kwɔ'dreniəl], *a.* quadriennal, -aux; quatriennal, -aux.

quadrennially [kwɔ'dreniəli], *adv.* tous les quatre ans.

quadri- ['kwɔdri], *comb.fm.* quadri-.

quadribasic [kwɔdri'beisik], *a. Ch:* quadribasique.

quadric ['kwɔdrik], *a. & s. Mth:* quadrique (*f*).

quadricapsular [kwɔdri'kæpsjulər], *a.* quadricapsulaire.

quadricentennial [kwɔdrisen'teniəl], *s.* quadricentenaire *m*.

quadriceps ['kwɔdriseps], *s. Anat:* quadriceps *m*.

quadricipital [kwɔdri'sipit(ə)l], *a. Anat:* quadriceps.

quadricuspid [kwɔdri'kʌspid], **quadricuspidate** [kwɔdri'kʌspideit], *a.* quadricuspidé.

quadricycle ['kwɔdrisaik(ə)l], *s. Veh:* quadricycle *m*.

quadridentate [kwɔdri'denteit], *a. Bot:* quadridenté.

quadridigitate [kwɔdri'didʒiteit], *a. Z:* quadridigité.

quadrifid ['kwɔdrifid], *a. Bot:* (feuille, calice) quadrifide.

quadrifoliate [kwɔdri'foulieit], *a. Bot:* quadrifolié.

quadriform ['kwɔdrifɔ:m], *a. Cryst:* quadriforme.

quadriga [kwɔ'draigə], *s. Rom.Ant:* quadrige *m*.

quadrigeminal [kwɔdri'dʒemin(ə)l], *a. Anat:* **the q. bodies,** les tubercules quadrijumeaux (de la moelle allongée).

quadrijugate [kwɔdri'dʒu:geit], *a.* quadrijugué.

quadrilateral [kwɔdri'læt(ə)rəl]. **1.** *a.* quadrilatéral, -aux; quadrilatère. **2.** *s. Mth: etc:* quadrilatère *m*, tétragone *m*; **complete q.,** quadrilatère complet; **skew q.,** quadrilatère gauche; *Veh:* **Ackerman q. system,** quadrilatère articulé; *Hist:* **the Q.,** le Quadrilatère vénitien.

quadrilingual [kwɔdri'liŋgwəl], *a.* (écrit) en quatre langues; qui parle quatre langues.

quadriliteral [kwɔdri'lit(ə)rəl], *a. Ling:* quadrilitère.

quadrille[1] [kwə'dril], *s. Cards: A:* quadrille *m*.

quadrille[2], *s.* **1.** *Danc: Mus:* quadrille *m*; contredanse *f*; **to dance a set of quadrilles,** danser un quadrille. **2.** (*bullfighting*) quadrille *f*.

quadrillé [kwə'drili], **quadrille**[3] [kwə'dril], *a.* (papier) quadrillé.

quadrilled [kwə'drild], *a. Tex:* quadrillé.

quadrillion [kwɔ'driliən], *s.* **1.** quatrillion *m*, quadrillion *m* (10^{24}). **2.** *U.S:* mille billions (10^{15}).

quadrilobate [kwɔdri'loubeit], *a. Bot:* quadrilobé.

quadrinomial [kwɔdri'noumiəl], *a. Mth:* quadrinôme.

quadripartite [kwɔdri'pɑ:tait], *a. Nat.Hist: Arch: Pol:* quadriparti, quadripartite.

quadripartition [kwɔdripɑ:'tiʃ(ə)n], *s. Nat.Hist: Arch: Pol:* quadripartition *f*.

quadriplegia [kwɔdri'pli:dʒiə], *s. Med:* quadriplégie *f*.

quadriplegic [kwɔdri'pli:dʒik], *a. & s. Med:* quadriplégique (*mf*).

quadripolar [kwɔdri'poulər], *a.* quadripolaire.

quadripole ['kwɔdripoul], *s. El:* quadripôle *m*.

quadrireme ['kwɔdriri:m], *s.f. A.Nau:* quadrirème.

quadrisyllabic [kwɔdrisi'læbik], *a.* quadrisyllabique.

quadrisyllable [kwɔdri'siləbl], *s.* quadrisyllabe *m*.

quadrivalence [kwɔdri'veiləns], *s. Ch:* quadrivalence *f*, tétravalence *f*.

quadrivalent [kwɔdri'veilənt], *a. Ch:* quadrivalent, tétravalent.

quadrivalve ['kwɔdrivælv], **quadrivalvular** [kwɔdri'vælvjulər], *a. Bot: etc:* quadrivalve.

quadrivium [kwɔ'driviəm], *s. Sch: A:* quadrivium *m*.

quadroon [kwɔ'dru:n], *a. & s. Ethn:* quarteron, -onne.

quadrual ['kwɔdruəl], *s. Ling:* quadriel *m*.

quadrumane, *pl.* **-mana** ['kwɔdrumein, kwɔ'dru:mənə], *s.* quadrumane *m*.

quadrumanous [kwɔ'dru:mənəs], *a.* quadrumane.

quadruped ['kwɔdruped], *a.* & *s.* quadrupède (*m*).
quadrupedal [kwɔ'dru:pid(ə)l], *a.* quadrupède.
quadruplane ['kwɔdruplein], *s. Av:* quadriplane *m.*
quadruplator ['kwɔdrupleitər], *s. Rom.Hist:* quadruplateur *m.*
quadruple[1] ['kwɔdrupl], *a.* & *s.* quadruple (*m*); **profits q. those, (the) q. of those, of the previous year,** bénéfices quadruples, au quadruple, de ceux de l'année précédente; *Hist:* **the Q. Alliance,** la Quadruple Alliance.
quadruple[2]. **1.** *v.tr.* quadrupler. **2.** *v.i.* (se) quadrupler.
quadruplet ['kwɔdruplet], *s.* **1.** quadruplé(e); *pl. Biol:* quadruplets, -ettes; **birth of quadruplets,** accouchement *m* quadrigémellaire. **2.** bicyclette *f* à quatre places; quadruplette *f.* **3.** *Mus:* quartolet *m.*
quadruplex ['kwɔdrupleks], *a.* & *s. Tg:* (télégraphe) quadruplex *m.*
quadruplicate[1] [kwɔ'dru:plikət], *a.* quadruplé, quadruple; **q. copies,** *s.* **quadruplicates,** quatre exemplaires *m*; **in q.,** en quatre exemplaires.
quadruplicate[2] [kwɔ'dru:plikeit], *v.tr.* **1.** quadrupler; multiplier par quatre. **2.** faire, tirer, quatre exemplaires (d'une lettre, etc.).
quadruplication [kwɔdru:pli'keiʃ(ə)n], *s.* quadruplication *f.*
quadrupling [kwɔ'dru:p(ə)liŋ], *s.* quadruplement *m.*
quadruply ['kwɔdrupli], *adv.* quadruplement.
quadrupole ['kwɔdrupoul], *s. El:* quadrupôle *m.*
quaestor ['kwi:stər], *s.* **1.** *Rom.Hist:* questeur *m.* **2.** *A.Jur:* quésiteur *m.*
quaestorial [kwi:s'tɔ:riəl], *a. Rom.Hist:* questorien.
quaestorship ['kwi:stəʃip], *s. Rom.Hist:* questure *f.*
quaff[1] [kwɑ:f], *s. Lit:* trait *m,* gorgée *f.*
quaff[2], *v.tr. Lit:* (*a*) boire (du vin) à longs traits, à plein verre; (*b*) vider (une coupe) d'un trait.
quaffer ['kwɑ:fər], *s.* grand buveur.
quag [kwæg, kwɔg], *s.* = QUAGMIRE.
quagga ['kwægə], *s. Z:* couagga *m.*
quaggy ['kwægi, 'kwɔgi], *a.* marécageux.
quagmire ['kwægmaiər, 'kwɔg-], *s.* fondrière *f*; marécage *m*; *Fig: O:* mauvaise passe.
quaich, quaigh [kweiχ], *s. A:* coupe écossaise (en bois cerclé).
quail[1] [kweil], *s.* (*Ven: inv. in pl.*) **1.** *Orn:* caille *f* (des blés); *Fr.C:* colin *m*; **bobwhite q.,** colin de Virginie; **California q., valley q.,** colin de Californie; **painted q.,** caille peinte, caille naine; **mountain q.,** colin des montagnes; **bustard q., button q.,** tridactyle *m,* turnix *m,* hémipode *m*; **young q.,** cailleteau *m*; **q. call, q. pipe,** courcaillet *m.* **2.** *U.S: P: A:* étudiante *f.*
quail[2], *v.i. Lit:* (*of pers.*) fléchir, reculer, faiblir (**before,** devant); **his heart quailed,** son cœur défaillit; **his courage, spirit, quailed,** son courage fléchit.
quaint [kweint], *a.* étrange, bizarre, fantasque; suranné; **q. tale,** histoire étrange, bizarre; **q. ideas,** idées (i) un peu surannées, (ii) baroques, cocasses; **q. costume,** costume qui fait sourire; **q. sight,** chose curieuse à voir; spectacle curieux; **q. style,** (i) style singulier, original; (ii) style d'un archaïsme piquant; *F:* **isn't she q.!** quelle drôle de petite bonne femme!
quaintly ['kweintli], *adv.* étrangement, bizarrement, pittoresquement; d'une manière originale.
quaintness ['kweintnis], *s.* étrangeté *f,* bizarrerie *f,* singularité *f*; pittoresque suranné.
quake[1] [kweik], *s.* (*a*) tremblement *m*; (*b*) *F:* tremblement de terre.
quake[2], *v.i.* **1.** (*of thg*) trembler, branler; **the earth quaked under our feet,** la terre tremblait sous nos pas. **2.** (*of pers.*) trembler, frémir, frissonner (**for, with, fear,** de crainte); **to q. in one's shoes,** trembler dans sa peau.
Quaker ['kweikər], *s. Rel.H:* quaker *m,f.* quakeresse; **Q. meeting,** office *m* des quakers; **Q. (gun),** faux canon; *Orn:* **q. bird,** albatros brun; albatros fuligineux; *Bot: U.S:* **q. ladies,** houstonia *f*; **q. buttons,** noix *f* vomiques.
Quakeress ['kweikəres], *s.f.* quakeresse.
Quakerish ['kweikəriʃ], *a.* de quaker, des quakers; **Q. dress,** costume sobre digne d'un quaker.
Quakerism ['kweikərizm], *s.* quakerisme *m.*
quaking[1] ['kweikiŋ], *a.* tremblant; *Bot:* **q. grass,** (i) briza *f*; (ii) glycérie *f.*
quaking[2], *s.* **1.** tremblement *m* (de la terre). **2.** tremblement, frémissement *m* (de qn).
quaky ['kweiki], *a. O:* tremblant; **to feel q.,** être en proie à un vague sentiment de crainte; avoir de la peine à ne pas trembler.
qualifiable ['kwɔlifaiəbl], *a.* qualifiable.
qualification [kwɔlifi'keiʃ(ə)n], *s.* **1.** réserve *f,* restriction *f*; **to accept without q.,** accepter (i) sans réserve, (ii) sans conditions; **remark that requires q.,** remarque qui demande des restrictions, des modifications; **I make only one q.,** je n'ai qu'une réserve à faire; **agreement subject to many qualifications,** consentement sous bien des réserves. **2.** aptitude *f,* compétence *f,* talent *m,* capacité *f*; **to have the necessary qualifications for a job,** avoir la compétence nécessaire pour remplir une fonction; avoir les qualités requises, posséder les titres *m,* les qualifications nécessaires, pour un poste; **to have the necessary qualifications (to exercise a right),** avoir capacité (pour exercer un droit); être habilité (à exercer un droit); **professional qualifications,** qualification professionnelle; **qualifications for membership of a club,** titres d'éligibilité à un cercle; *Hist:* **property q.** (to vote), cens électoral; **applicants must bring their qualifications with them,** les candidats devront apporter leurs titres justificatifs, leurs papiers. **3.** (*description*) qualification (**of s.o. as sth.,** de qn de qch.).
qualificative ['kwɔlifikeitiv], *a.* & *s. Gram:* qualificatif (*m*).
qualificator ['kwɔlifikeitər], *s. Ecc:* qualificateur *m.*
qualificatory ['kwɔlifikeitəri], *a.* qualificatif.
qualified ['kwɔlifaid], *a.* **1.** (*a*) qui a les qualités requises (pour un poste, etc.); **to be q. to do sth.,** être apte, propre, à faire qch.; avoir les capacités pour faire qch.; avoir qualité pour faire qch.; **I am certainly q. to speak about it,** je suis certainement qualifié pour en parler; **badly q. for a task,** mal préparé à une tâche; **q. expert,** expert diplômé; **q. persons,** personnes compétentes; **q. seaman,** matelot breveté; (*b*) autorisé; *Jur:* capable (**to,** de); **to be q. to vote,** avoir qualité d'électeur; **to be q. to speak,** avoir voix au chapitre; *Jur:* **q. to inherit,** habile à succéder. **2.** (*a*) restreint, mitigé, modéré; **q. approval,** approbation modérée; **to give a q. no,** refuser à moins de certaines conditions; **in a q. sense,** dans un sens restreint; dans un certain sens; *Com:* **q. acceptance,** acceptation conditionnelle, sous condition (d'une traite, etc.); (*b*) *F:* **you q. idiot!** sacré idiot!
qualifier ['kwɔlifaiər], *s.* **1.** modification *f,* restriction *f,* réserve *f.* **2.** *Gram:* qualificatif *m.* **3.** *Sp:* qualifié(e).
qualify ['kwɔlifai], *v.*
I. *v.tr.* **1.** (*a*) **to q. s.o., sth., as sth.,** qualifier qn, qch., de qch.; (*b*) *Gram:* qualifier. **2.** **to q. s.o. for (doing) sth., to do sth.,** donner à qn les qualités requises pour (faire) qch.; rendre qn apte, propre, à (faire) qch.; *Jur:* donner qualité à qn pour (faire) qch.; autoriser qn à faire qch.; **to q. oneself for a job,** acquérir les capacités, les titres, nécessaires pour remplir un emploi; se qualifier pour un emploi; **my knowledge qualifies me to undertake this work,** mes connaissances me qualifient à entreprendre cet ouvrage; *Sp:* **a second place in the French championships qualifies for the Olympic Games,** la seconde place aux championnats de France qualifie pour les Jeux Olympiques. **3.** (*a*) apporter des réserves à (un consentement, etc.); modifier, atténuer, restreindre (une affirmation); (*b*) modérer, diminuer, tempérer (un plaisir). **4.** (*a*) étendre, couper (une boisson); (*b*) *F: O:* fortifier (une boisson) (**with,** de).
II. *v.i.* acquérir les qualités, l'expérience, les connaissances, requises, se préparer, se qualifier (**for sth.,** pour qch.); *Sp:* obtenir sa qualification; **to q. for the civil service,** subir avec succès l'examen d'admissibilité aux emplois de l'État; être admissible à être fonctionnaire; **to q. as (a) doctor,** être reçu médecin; **to q. as a pilot,** obtenir son brevet de pilote.
qualifying ['kwɔlifaiiŋ], *a.* **1.** *Gram:* (adjectif) qualificatif; (adverbe) modificatif. **2.** (*a*) **q. examination,** (i) examen pour certificat d'aptitude; (ii) examen d'entrée (à une école, etc.); **q. certificate,** certificat de capacité; (*b*) *Fin:* **q. shares,** actions statutaires; (*c*) *Sp:* **q. round,** série *f* éliminatoire. **3.** modificateur, -trice; **q. statement,** déclaration, phrase, corrective.
qualitative ['kwɔlitətiv], *a. Gram: Ch:* qualitatif; *Ch:* **q. analysis,** analyse qualitative.
quality ['kwɔliti], *s.* qualité *f.* **1.** (*a*) (*degree of excellence*) **of good, high, poor, q.,** de bonne qualité; de qualité supérieure, inférieure; **of the best q.,** de première qualité; de premier choix; **goods of sterling q.,** marchandises de bon aloi, du meilleur aloi; **q. matters more than quantity,** la qualité importe plus que la quantité; *Tex:* **first q. cotton, wool,** fleuret *m* de coton, de laine; (*b*) *Mch:* **q. of (wet) steam,** titre *m* de la vapeur; *Elcs:* **q. factor,** facteur *m* Q, de qualité; (*c*) (*excellence*) **wine that has q.,** vin qui a de la qualité; *Com:* **q. goods,** marchandises de qualité; **q. (news)paper,** journal sérieux; *Prov:* **q. will tell in the end,** le bon grain finit toujours par lever. **2.** (*a*) (*of pers.*) qualité, trait *m*; **moral qualities, intellectual qualities,** qualités morales, intellectuelles; **he has many (good) qualities,** il a beaucoup de qualités; **he has many bad qualities,** il a beaucoup de défauts; **he has the q. of inspiring confidence,** il a le don d'inspirer la confiance; (*b*) **heating q. of a fuel,** pouvoir *m,* valeur *f,* calorifique d'un combustible; **that will give you an idea of his q.,** cela vous donnera une idée de sa valeur. **3.** *A:* noblesse *f*; distinction *f*; **person of q.,** personne de qualité; homme, femme, du monde; **the q.,** la petite noblesse. **4.** **to act in the q. of. . .,** agir en qualité, en caractère, de . . .. **5.** qualité, timbre *m* (d'un son, de la voix). **6.** *Log:* qualité logique (d'une proposition).
qualm [kwɑ:m, kwɔ:m], *s.* **1.** soulèvement *m* de cœur; nausée *f,* malaise *m*; haut-le-cœur *m inv.* **2.** (*a*) scrupule *m,* remords *m*; **qualms of conscience,** (i) angoisses *fpl* de conscience; retour *m* de conscience; (ii) scrupules de conscience; **to have, feel, a q.,** avoir un scrupule; **to feel some qualms (about sth.),** avoir des remords; **to have no qualms about doing sth.,** ne pas se faire le moindre scrupule de faire qch.; (*b*) pressentiment *m* de malheur; **to feel some qualms about the future,** éprouver des inquiétudes *f* au sujet de l'avenir.
qualmish ['kwɑ:miʃ, 'kwɔ:-], *a.* **1.** qui a mal au cœur; qui a des nausées; sujet aux nausées. **2.** mal à l'aise; inquiet, -ète.
qualmishness ['kwɑ:miʃnis, 'kwɔ:-], *s.* **1.** soulèvement *m* de cœur; nausées *fpl.* **2.** scrupules exagérés.
quandary ['kwɔnd(ə)ri], *s.* situation embarrassante; difficulté *f*; **to be in a q.,** (i) se trouver dans une impasse; être dans l'embarras; (ii) ne pas trop savoir que faire; **to be in a great q.,** être au pied du mur; être à quia.
Quango ['kwæŋgou], *s. F:* société nationale de service public.
quant[1] ['kwɔnt], *s.* perche *f* de bachot (à bout en rondelle, pour les fonds vaseux du Norfolk).
quant[2], *v.tr.* conduire (un bateau) à la perche (en enfonçant la perche et en marchant le long du bateau avant de la retirer).
quantic ['kwɔntik]. **1.** *a.* **q. physics,** physique *f* quantique. **2.** *s. Mth:* fonction *f* homogène à plusieurs variables; forme *f.*
quantifiable ['kwɔntifaiəbl], *a.* quantifiable.
quantification [kwɔntifi'keiʃ(ə)n], *s. Log:* quantification *f* (du prédicat).
quantifier ['kwɔntifaiər], *s. Log: Mth:* quantificateur *m*; **universal q.,** quantificateur universel; **existential q.,** quantificateur existentiel.
quantify ['kwɔntifai], *v.tr.* **1.** *Log:* quantifier (le prédicat). **2.** déterminer la quantité de (qch.); mesurer, évaluer, avec précision.
quantitative ['kwɔntitətiv], *a.* **1.** quantitatif; *Ch:* **q. analysis,** analyse quantitative. **2.** **q. prosody,** prosodie fondée sur la quantité.
quantitatively ['kwɔntitətivli], *adv.* quantitativement.
quantity ['kwɔntiti], *s.* **1.** (*a*) quantité *f*; **a small q. of,** une petite quantité de; **a (large) q. of,** une (grande) quantité de; **to buy sth. in large quantities,** acheter qch. par quantités considérables, en quantité considérable, en grande quantité; **in (great) quantities,** en grande quantité; en abondance; **how many can I have?—any q.,** combien puis-je en avoir?—autant que vous désirez; *Cust:* **the q. permitted,** la tolérance, la quantité, permise (de tabac, etc.); *Ind:* **q. production,** (i) production *f* en quantité, en masse; (ii) fabrication *f* en série; (*b*) *Const:* **to survey a building for quantities,** faire le toisé d'un immeuble; **bill of quantities,** devis *m*; *Civ.E:* **to take out the quantities (for earthworks, etc.),** relever le cubage (d'un terrassement, etc.); **q. surveyor,** métreur *m* (vérificateur); **q. surveying,** métrage *m*; métré *m*; toisé *m*; (*c*) *El:* **connected in q.,** couplé en quantité, en parallèle. **2.** *Mth:* quantité; **unknown q.,** inconnue *f*; **he's an unknown q.,** c'est un élément imprévisible; **negligible q.,** quantité négligeable; *F:* **he's a negligible q.,** il n'a pas la moindre importance; il est tout à fait négligeable; c'est une quantité négligeable. **3.** *Pros:* quantité; **false q.,** faute *f* de quantité; **q. mark,** signe *m* de quantité. **4.** *Log:* quantité (d'une proposition); **extensive q.,** extension *f*; **intensive q.,** compréhension *f.* **5.** *Pol.Ec:* **q. theory,** théorie quantitative; **q. theorist,** quantitativiste *mf.*
quantization [kwɔntai'zeiʃ(ə)n], *s. Ph:* quantification *f*; **q. distortion,** distorsion *f* de quantification.
quantize ['kwɔntaiz], *v.tr. Ph:* quantifier; exprimer (l'énergie) en quanta.
quantum, *pl.* **-a** ['kwɔntəm, -ə], *s.* quantum *m.* **1.** **each has his q. of wisdom,** chacun a sa part de sagesse. **2.** *Ph:* **q. theory,** théorie *f* des quanta, théorie quantique; **q. mechanics, optics, electrodynamics, statistics,** mécanique *f,* optique *f,* électrodynamique *f,* statistique *f,* quantique; **virtual q.,** quantum virtuel; **q. number,** nombre *m* quantique; **first q. number,** nombre quantique principal; **nuclear spin q. number,** nombre quantique de spin nucléaire; **orbital q. number,** nombre quantique secondaire; **q. energy,** énergie *f* quantique; **q. efficiency, yield,** rendement *m* quantique; **q. jump, q.**

transition, saut *m* quantique; **q. potential, voltage,** potentiel *m* quantique; **q. state,** état *m* quantique. **3.** *Mil:* **the q. of forces,** les effectifs *mpl.*

quantum-mechanical ['kwɔntəmmi'kænik(ə)l], *a.* (mécanique) quantique; **q.-m. theory of nuclear motion,** théorie *f* quantique du mouvement nucléaire; **q.-m. wavelength,** longueur *f* d'onde quantique.

quaquaversal [kweikwə'vəːs(ə)l], *a. Geol:* **q. dip,** pente *f* du terrain dans tous les sens.

quarantinable [kwɔrən'tiːnəbl], *a.* quarantenaire.

quarantine[1] ['kwɔrəntiːn], *s.* **1.** quarantaine *f*; **to be in q.,** faire (la) quarantaine; **to go into q.,** se mettre en quarantaine; *Nau:* **to be out of q.,** avoir libre pratique; **to break the q. regulations,** violer, forcer, la quarantaine; **the q. service,** le service de santé; **the q. flag,** le pavillon de quarantaine; le pavillon Q. **2.** *Jur:* période de quarante jours pendant laquelle la veuve a le droit d'occuper la maison de son mari après le décès de celui-ci.

quarantine[2], *v.tr.* mettre (qn, un navire) en quarantaine.

quark [kwɑːk, kwɔːk], *s. Atom.Ph:* quark *m.*

quarrel[1] ['kwɔrəl], *s.* **1.** *A.Arms:* carreau *m*, matras *m* (d'arbalète). **2.** *Arch: A:* carreau de vitrail. **3.** *Tls:* (*a*) diamant *m* de vitrier; (*b*) *Engr:* burin *m* losange; (*c*) burin de tailleur de pierres.

quarrel[2], *s.* (*a*) querelle *f*, dispute *f*, brouille *f*, *F:* attrapade *f* (entre deux personnes); **groundless q.,** querelle d'Allemand; **to pick a q. with s.o.,** faire (une) querelle à qn; **to try to pick a q. with s.o.,** chercher querelle, chercher dispute, chercher chicane, chercher noise, à qn; **they have had a q.,** ils sont fâchés, brouillés; **it takes two to make a q.,** il ne peut y avoir de querelle quand l'une des parties refuse de se fâcher; **to make up a q.,** (r)accommoder un différend; (*b*) motif *m* de plainte; **I have no q. with, against, him,** je n'ai rien à lui reprocher; **our q. is not with you,** nous n'en avons pas après vous; (*c*) **to take up s.o.'s q., to fight s.o.'s q. for him,** épouser, embrasser, la querelle, la cause, de qn.

quarrel[3], *v.i.* **(quarrelled) 1.** se quereller, se disputer (**with s.o. over, about, sth.,** avec qn à propos de qch.); se brouiller (**with s.o.,** avec qn); *F:* batailler; **they've been quarrelling,** il y a de la brouille entre eux; **he's bent on quarrelling,** il ne rêve que plaies et bosses; **to q. about precedence,** soulever des querelles de préséance; **to q. openly with s.o.,** rompre en visière à, avec, qn; **two dogs quarrelling over, for, a bone,** deux chiens qui se disputent un os; **they are quarrelling as to who should have the biggest share,** ils se disputent à qui aura le plus gros morceau. **2. to q. with s.o. for doing sth.,** reprocher à qn de faire qch.; **to q. with sth.,** trouver à redire à qch.; se plaindre de qch.

quarreller ['kwɔrələr], *s.* querelleur, -euse.

quarrelling[1] ['kwɔrəliŋ], *a.* querelleur, -euse.

quarrelling[2], *s.* querelle(s) *f(pl)*, dispute(s) *f(pl).*

quarrelsome ['kwɔrəlsəm], *a.* querelleur; batailleur; **he's very q.,** c'est un mauvais coucheur; **in a q. mood,** d'humeur batailleuse, querelleuse.

quarrelsomeness ['kwɔrəlsəmnis], *s.* humeur querelleuse.

quarrier ['kwɔriər], *s.* = QUARRYMAN.

quarry[1] ['kwɔri], *s. Ven:* **1.** proie *f*; gibier (poursuivi à courre); (*of pers.*) **he became the q. of the police of a whole continent,** il se vit traqué par la police de tout un continent. **2.** *A:* curée *f*; **to blow the q.,** sonner la curée.

quarry[2], *v.tr.* **(quarried)** *Ven:* chasser (la bête) à courre; traquer ou acculer (la bête).

quarry[3], *s.* (*a*) carreau *m* (de céramique); (*b*) *A:* carreau (de verre); **heraldic q.,** carreau armorié.

quarry[4], *s.* carrière *f* (de pierres, d'ardoises, etc.); **open q.,** carrière à ciel ouvert; **q. stone,** moellon *m*; **stone fresh from the q.,** pierre verte; **q. owner,** maître carrier.

quarry[5], *v.tr.* **(quarried) 1.** extraire, tirer, (la pierre) de la carrière; *v.i.* exploiter une carrière; **to q. information from books,** puiser des renseignements dans les livres; *v.i.* **to q. among old documents,** fouiller dans de vieux documents. **2.** creuser une carrière dans (une colline).

quarrying ['kwɔriiŋ], *s.* exploitation *f* de carrières; abattage *m* en carrières; **q. of stone,** extraction *f*, tirage *m*, de la pierre; **open q.,** travail *m* à ciel ouvert.

quarryman, *pl.* **-men** ['kwɔrimən], *s.m.* (ouvrier) carrier; (*in sandstone quarry*) grésier; **(slate) q.,** perrayeur, perrier.

quart[1] [kwɔːt], *s. Meas:* un quart de *gallon* (**English q.** = 1 litre 136; **American liquid q.** = 0 litre 946; **American dry q.** = 1 litre 101); **you can't make a q. fit in a pint pot,** on ne peut pas faire l'impossible.

quart[2] [kɑːt], *s.* **1.** *Fenc:* quarte *f*; **to parry in q.,** parer en quarte; **to practise q. and tierce,** faire des exercices d'escrime. **2.** *Cards:* quatrième *f.*

quartan ['kwɔːt(ə)n], *a. & s. Med: A:* **q. (fever), q. ague,** fièvre quarte, quartaine; **double q.,** fièvre double quarte.

quartation [kwɔː'teiʃ(ə)n], *s. Metall:* quartation *f*, inquartation *f*, inquart *m.*

quarte [kɑːt], *s.* = QUART[2] 1.

quarter[1] ['kwɔːtər], *s.* **1.** (*a*) quart *m* (de pomme, de cercle, de siècle, etc.); **to divide sth. in(to) quarters,** diviser qch. en quatre; **three quarters,** trois quarts; **three and a q.,** trois et un quart; **a q. (of a pound) of coffee,** un quart (de livre) de café; **bottle one, a, q. full,** bouteille au quart pleine; **the bottle is only three quarters full,** la bouteille n'est qu'aux trois quarts pleine; **I am not a q. finished with my work,** je ne suis pas au quart de mon travail; **a q. cheaper,** d'un quart meilleur marché; **it is (only) a q. as long,** c'est quatre fois moins long; **I can buy it for a q. (of) the price, for q. the price,** je peux l'avoir au quart du prix, quatre fois moins cher; **the sea covers three quarters of the globe,** la mer couvre les trois quarts du globe; **to give a screw a q. turn,** donner un quart de tour à une vis; *Mec.E:* **q. turn belt, drive,** courroie tordue au quart; courroie semi-croisée; *Sp:* **q. final,** quart de finale; *Aut:* **q. light,** (i) glace *f* de custode; (ii) lampe *f* de coin arrière; *Bookb:* **q. binding, leather,** demi-reliure *f*; *Mil:* **q. left, right,** oblique *f* à gauche, à droite; *Plumb:* **q. bend,** coude *m* en équerre; *U.S:* **q.(-)blood,** quarteron, -onne; (*b*) (i) *Cu:* quartier *m* (de bœuf, d'agneau); **fore q., hind q.,** quartier de devant, de derrière; (ii) **(hind) quarters,** arrière-train *m*, train *m* de derrière (d'une bête); arrière-main *m or f* (du cheval); *Vet:* **q. crack,** (seime) quarte *f*; *Hist:* **quarters,** membres dépecés (d'un condamné); (*c*) *Her:* quartier, franc-quartier *m*, *pl.* francs-quartiers; écart *m*, partition *f* (de l'écu); (*d*) *N.Arch: Nau:* hanche *f*; **lee q.,** hanche sous le vent; **on the q.,** par la hanche; sur l'arrière du travers; en retraite; **to fire on the q.,** tirer en retraite; **wind on the q., q. wind,** vent grand largue, vent de la hanche; **q. block,** poulie *f* de retour; **q. line,** ligne *f* de relèvement, de gisement; **double q. line,** angle *m* de chasse; (*e*) *Bootm:* quartier (de chaussure); (*f*) *Farr:* quartier (de sabot); (*g*) loge *f*, tranche *f* (d'orange, etc.); (*h*) **to cut timber on the q.,** débiter un tronc d'arbre sur quartier, sur maille *f*; **cutting on the q.,** débit *m* sur quartier; **q. girth measurement,** cubage *m* au quart; (*i*) *Const:* **winding q., q. pace,** quartier tournant (d'un escalier); (*j*) *Arch:* **q. round,** quart-de-rond *m*, *pl.* quarts-de-rond; échine *f* de chapiteau; (*k*) *Mus:* **q. (note),** noire *f.* **2.** (*a*) *A.Meas:* (i) quarter *m* (= 2,909 hectolitres); (ii) quarter (= 12 kilogrammes 7, *U.S:* = 11 kilogrammes 34); **q. cask,** quartaut *m*; (iii) *Nau:* quart de brasse (457 mm); **a q. less ten,** dix brasses moins un quart; **and a q. ten,** dix brasses et un quart; (*b*) trimestre *m*; terme *m* (de loyer); **to be paid by the q.,** être payé par trimestre; **a quarter's rent,** un terme, un trimestre (de loyer); **q. day,** (jour *m* de) terme; *Jur:* **q. sessions,** assises trimestrielles; cour trimestrielle de comté; (*c*) quartier de la lune; **moon at the first q., at three quarters,** lune au premier quartier, au dernier quartier; **moon in its last q.,** lune sur son décroît; (*d*) **a q. to six,** six heures moins le quart; **it's a q. to,** il est moins le quart; **the clock has struck the q. to,** l'horloge a sonné l'avant-quart; **it is not the q. (to), a q. to, yet,** il n'est pas encore (moins) le quart; **a q. past six,** six heures et quart; **he went at a q. past,** il est parti au quart; **it has gone the q. (past),** il est plus du quart; **every q. of an hour, q. hourly,** tous les quarts d'heure; **clock that strikes the q. hours, the quarters,** pendule qui sonne les quarts; *Clockm:* **q. repeater,** pièce *f* des quarts; **q. bell,** timbre qui sonne les quarts; appeau *m*; (*e*) *U.S:* pièce *f* de vingt-cinq cents; quart de dollar; (*f*) *Sp:* (course *f* d'un) quart de mille. **3.** (*a*) *Nau:* (i) quart d'aire de vent (= 2° 48′ 45″); (ii) aire *f* de vent, quart, côté *m*; **what q. is the wind in?** de quel côté, de quelle direction, de quel quartier, souffle le vent? de quel bord dépend le vent? **the wind is in the right q.,** le vent vient du bon côté; (*b*) (*of a wood, etc.*) **fair weather q.,** côté exposé au soleil; **stormy q.,** côté exposé aux intempéries; (*c*) région *f*, partie *f*, côté; **the four quarters of the globe,** les quatre parties du globe; **they pour in from all four quarters of the globe,** ils affluent des quatre points du monde; **the four quarters of the heavens,** les quatre coins du ciel; **they arrived from all quarters,** ils arrivaient de tous côtés, de toutes parts; **news from all quarters,** nouvelles de partout; **what is he doing in these quarters?** que fait-il dans ces parages? **I expect no more trouble from, in, that q.,** je n'attends plus aucune difficulté de ce côté-là; **to have received news from another q.,** savoir une nouvelle par ailleurs; **in high quarters,** en haut lieu; chez les grands; **an order from high quarters,** un ordre d'en haut; **it is rumoured in certain quarters that . . .,** le bruit court dans certaines sphères que . . .; **in responsible quarters,** dans les milieux autorisés; **information from a reliable q.,** informations *f* de source certaine; **to apply to the proper q.,** s'adresser à qui de droit; **from whatever q.,** d'où que cela vienne; **I hear it from all quarters,** je l'entends dire à droite et à gauche, de droite et de gauche. **4.** quartier (d'une ville); **the slum q.,** le quartier des taudis; **the residential q.,** le quartier d'habitation, des maisons bourgeoises. **5.** *pl.* (*a*) **living quarters,** appartements *m* (domestiques); **to shift one's quarters,** changer de résidence *f*; (*b*) *Mil:* quartier, cantonnement *m*, stationnement *m*, logement *m*; **free quarters,** droit *m* au logement; **to take up one's quarters,** prendre ses quartiers; **to return to quarters,** rentrer au quartier; *Aer:* **crew's quarters,** locaux affectés au personnel du bord; *Navy:* **sailors' quarters,** poste *m* d'équipage. **6.** *pl. Navy:* (*a*) postes de combat; **to beat, pipe, to quarters,** battre, sonner, le branle-bas; **all hands to quarters!** tout le monde à son poste! (*b*) **morning quarters, evening quarters,** branle-bas du matin, du soir; **general quarters,** branle-bas de combat. **7.** (*clemency in battle*) quartier, merci *f*; **to give q.,** faire quartier; accorder merci; **to ask for, to cry, q.,** demander quartier; crier merci; **to give no q.,** ne pas faire de quartier.

quarter[2]. **1.** *v.tr.* (*a*) diviser (une pomme, etc.) en quatre; diviser (un bœuf, etc.) par quartiers; équarrir (un bœuf); *Min:* quarter; **quartered oak,** chêne en quartier; chêne débité en quart de rond; **quartered logs (of firewood),** bois *m* de quartier; (*b*) *A:* écarteler (un condamné); (*c*) *Her:* (i) écarteler (l'écu); (ii) **to q. one's arms on the shield,** disposer ses armes sur les quartiers alternes de l'écu; **he quarters such and such arms,** il écartèle de telles et telles armes; (*d*) *Ven:* (*of dogs*) **to q. (the ground),** bricoler, quêter; (*e*) *Mec.E: etc:* caler à 90°. **2.** *v.tr.* (*a*) *Mil:* cantonner, caserner, loger (des troupes); **to q. the troops on the inhabitants,** loger les troupes chez l'habitant, chez les habitants; **to be quartered with s.o.,** loger chez qn; (*b*) *Navy:* désigner leurs postes (aux hommes). **3.** *v.i.* (*of the moon*) entrer dans un nouveau quartier.

quarterage ['kwɔːtəridʒ], *s.* (*a*) paiement trimestriel; (*b*) loyer trimestriel; terme *m.*

quarterdeck ['kwɔːtədek], *s.* **1.** *Nau:* gaillard *m* (d')arrière; *Navy:* plage *f* arrière; *N.Arch:* **raised q.,** demi-dunette *f*, *pl.* demi-dunettes; *A:* **to walk the q.,** être officier. **2.** *coll. Navy:* **the q.,** les officiers *m.*

quartering[1] ['kwɔːtəriŋ], *a. Nau:* **q. wind,** vent grand largue.

quartering[2], *s.* **1.** (*a*) division *f* en quatre; **q. of a log,** équarrissage *m* d'un tronc d'arbre; (*b*) *A:* écartèlement *m* (d'un malfaiteur); (*c*) *Mec.E: etc:* calage *m* à 90°. **2.** (*a*) *Mil:* logement *m*, cantonnement *m*, stationnement *m* (de troupes); (*b*) *Navy:* désignation *f* des postes (de combat, etc.). **3.** *Her:* écartelure *f*, quartier *m* (d'un écusson). **4.** *Ven:* (*of dogs*) quête *f.* **5.** *Carp:* bois *m* à chevrons; chevron *m.* **6.** *Petr: Min:* échantillonnage *m* du minerai.

quarterly ['kwɔːtəli]. **1.** *a.* trimestriel; **q. salary,** appointements trimestriels; **q. subscription,** abonnement *m* au trimestre. **2.** *s.* publication trimestrielle. **3.** *adv.* (*a*) trimestriellement; par trimestre; tous les trois mois; (*b*) *Her:* (disposé) (i) dans les quartiers alternes, (ii) dans les quartiers (d'un écu).

quartermaster ['kwɔːtəmɑːstər], *s.* **1.** *Nau:* maître *m* de timonerie. **2.** *Mil:* officier chargé des vivres et des fournitures; *U.S:* **Q. Corps,** service *m* de l'Intendance; **Q. General** = Directeur *m* de l'Intendance (militaire); **q. sergeant,** fourrier *m*; (*women's services, W.R.A.C.*) troisième catégorie *f*; **senior q. sergeant,** sergent *m* major.

quartern ['kwɔːtən], *s.* **1.** *Meas:* quart *m* (de pinte, de *stone*, d'once). **2. q. loaf,** pain *m* de quatre livres.

quarter-saw ['kwɔːtəsɔː], *v.tr.* débiter (un chêne) en quartier.

quarterstaff ['kwɔːtəstɑːf], *s. Sp:* **1.** bâton *m* (à deux bouts); **to fence with quarterstaffs,** jouer du bâton; **q. player, fencer,** bâtonniste *m.* **2.** escrime *f* au bâton.

quartet(te) [kwɔː'tet], *s.* **1.** *Mus:* quatuor *m*; **string q.,** quatuor à cordes; **jazz q.,** quartette *f.* **2.** *Biol:* quartette.

quartic ['kwɔːtik], *s. Mth:* quartique *f.*

quartile ['kwɔːtil]. **1.** *a. & s. Astrol:* **q. (aspect),** (aspect *m*) quadrat *m*, quartile aspect (de deux astres); astres *m* à 90°. **2.** *s. Stat:* quartile *m*; **division into quartiles,** quartilage *m.*

quarto ['kwɔːtou], *a. & s.* in-quarto *(m)inv.*

quartz [kwɔːts], *s. Miner:* quartz *m*; cristal *m* de roche; **smoky q.,** quartz enfumé; **rutilated q.,** flèches *fpl* d'amour; **blue q.,** pseudo-saphir *m*; **rose q.,** pseudo-rubis *m*; rubis *m* de Bohême; **mother q.,** quartz naturel; **flamboyant q.,** quartz aventuriné; **q. crystal,** cristal de quartz; **q.-crystal watch,** montre *f* à quartz; **q. lamp,** lampe *f* (à vapeur de mercure) à tube de quartz; *Min:* (*gold*) **free-milling q.,** quartz à or libre; **q. rock,** quartzite *f*; **q. sand,** sable quartzeux; sable de quartz; **q. diorite,** diorite *f* quartzifère; **q. mill,** moulin *m* à quartz; **q. mining,** exploitation minière du quartz; *Cmptr:* **q. delay line,** ligne *f* à retard à quartz.

quartzic ['kwɔːtsik], *a.* quartzique.

quartziferous [kwɔːt'sifərəs], *a.* quartzifère.

quartzine ['kwɔːtsin], *s. Miner:* quartzine *f*.

quartzite ['kwɔːtsait], *s. Miner:* quartzite *f*.

quartzose ['kwɔːtsous], **quartzous** ['kwɔːtsəs], **quartzy** ['kwɔːtsi], *a. Miner:* quartzeux.

quasar ['kweizɑːr, -s-], *s. Astr:* quasar *m*.

quash [kwɔʃ], *v.tr.* **1.** *Jur:* casser, infirmer, annuler (un jugement, une décision); invalider (une élection); **to q. proceedings, an action,** arrêter les poursuites. **2.** étouffer (un sentiment, un projet); écraser, étouffer (une révolte).

quashing ['kwɔʃiŋ], *s.* **1.** *Jur:* cassation *f*, infirmation *f*, annulation *f* (d'un jugement); invalidation *f* (d'une élection). **2.** écrasement *m* (d'une révolte).

quasi ['kweisai, 'kwɑːzi]. **1.** *pref.* quasi, presque; **q. contract,** quasi-contrat *m*, *pl.* quasi-contrats; **q. delict,** quasi-délit *m*, *pl.* quasi-délits; **q. expert,** quasi-expert; **q. public,** quasi-public; soi-disant public; *Psy:* **q. need,** quasi-besoin *m*; *Jur:* **q. easement,** quasi-possession *f*. **2.** *conj.* (*introducing etymological note*) c'est-à-dire . . .; autant dire . . ..

quassia ['kwɔʃiə, 'kwɔsiə], *s.* **1.** *Bot:* **q. (tree),** quassier *m*, quassia *m* (amara); **Jamaica q.,** quassier de la Jamaïque. **2.** *Pharm: etc:* quassia; **q. chips,** quassia en copeaux.

quassin ['kwæsin], *s. Ch:* quassine *f*.

quat [kæt], *s. Bot:* kat *m*, qat *m*.

quatercentenary [kwætəsen'tiːnəri], *s.* quatrième centenaire *m*.

quaterfoil ['kætəfɔil], *s.* = QUATREFOIL.

quatern ['kwɔːtən], *s. A:* quaterne *m*; *Bak:* **q. loaf,** pain *m* de quatre livres.

quaternary [kwə'təːnəri]. **1.** *a. Ch: Mth:* quaternaire. **2.** *a. & s. Geol:* **the Q. (era),** le quaternaire. **3.** *s. Mus: A:* **the Pythagorean q.,** le quaternaire sacré de Pythagore.

quaternate [kwə'təːnət], *a. Bot:* **with q. leaves,** aux feuilles quaternées; quaternifolié.

quaternion [kwə'təːniən], *s.* **1.** cahier *m* de quatre feuilles; quaternion *m*. **2.** *Mth:* quaternion. **3.** = QUATERNARY 3.

quatorze [kə'tɔːz], *s. Cards:* (*at piquet*) quatorze *m*.

quatrain ['kwɔtrein], *s. Pros:* quatrain *m*.

quatrefoil ['kætəfɔil], *s.* (*a*) *Arch: Her:* quatre-feuilles *m inv*; quadrilobe *m*; **q. tracery,** remplage *m* en quatre feuilles; (*b*) *Her:* quartefeuille *f*.

quattrocentist [kwætrou'tʃentist]. *Art: Lit:* **1.** *s.* quattrocentiste *m*. **2.** *a.* des quattrocentistes; de l'Italie du XVe siècle.

quattrocento [kwætrou'tʃentou], *s. Art: Lit:* quattrocento *m*.

quaver[1] ['kweivər], *s.* **1.** *Mus:* croche *f*. **2.** (*a*) *Mus:* trille *m*, tremolo *m*; (*b*) tremblement *m*, chevrotement *m* (de la voix); **to have a q. in one's voice,** avoir des tremolos dans la voix; parler d'une voix mal assurée.

quaver[2]. **1.** *v.i.* (*a*) (*of singer*) faire des trilles; faire un tremolo; triller; (*b*) (*of voice*) chevroter, trembloter; *Mus:* trembler. **2.** *v.tr.* (*a*) **to q. (out) a tune,** trembloter, chevroter, un air; (*b*) *Mus:* triller (une note, un passage).

quavering[1] ['kweivəriŋ], *a.* **q. voice,** voix tremblotante, chevrotante; voix mal assurée.

quavering[2], *s.* = QUAVER[1] 2(*b*).

quaveringly ['kweivəriŋli], *adv.* d'une voix mal assurée; en chevrotant.

quay [kiː], *s.* quai *m*; appontement *m*; **alongside the q.,** à quai; **q. berth,** place *f* à quai; **q. wall,** (mur *m*) bajoyer *m*; *Com:* (*of goods*) **ex-q.,** à prendre, livrable, à quai.

quayage ['kiːidʒ], *s.* **1.** quayage *m*; droit(s) *m(pl)* de quai, de wharf, de bassin. **2.** quais *mpl*.

quayside ['kiːsaid], *s.* (terrain au bord du) quai; **q. worker, crane,** ouvrier *m*, grue *f*, de quai.

quean [kwiːn], *s.f.* **1.** *F: A:* coquine, gueuse. **2.** *Scot:* jeune fille.

queasiness ['kwiːzinis], *s.* **1.** malaise *m*; nausées *fpl*. **2.** scrupules *mpl* de conscience.

queasy ['kwiːzi], *a.* **1.** (*a*) (*of pers.*) sujet à des nausées; qui éprouve facilement des nausées; **I feel q.,** j'ai mal au cœur; **q. stomach,** estomac délicat; (*b*) **q. conscience,** conscience scrupuleuse à l'excès. **2.** (*of food*) nauséabond; dégoûtant.

Quebec [kwi'bek], *Pr.n. Geog:* Québec *m*.

Quebec(k)er [kwi'bekər], *s. Geog:* Québecois, -oise.

quebrachitol [kei'brætʃitɔl], *s. Ch:* québrachite *f*.

quebracho [kei'brætʃou], *s. Bot:* quebracho *m*.

Quechua ['ketʃwa], *s.* **1.** *Ethn:* Quechua *mf*. **2.** *Ling:* quechua, quichua *m*.

queen[1] [kwiːn], *s.f.* **1.** reine; (*a*) **the q. of Spain,** la reine d'Espagne; **Q. Anne,** la reine Anne; *F:* **Q. Anne's dead,** c'est connu; c'est vieux comme le Pont-Neuf, cette histoire-là! **she was q. to Henry VIII,** elle fut l'épouse de Henri VIII; **the kings and queens of England,** les souverains *m* britanniques; **Q. regnant,** reine régnante; **Q. regent,** reine régente; **q. mother,** reine mère; **q. dowager,** reine douairière; **beauty q.,** reine de beauté, du village, de la fête, etc.; *F: A:* **Queen's weather,** temps *m* superbe; (*b*) **Q. of heaven,** reine du ciel; **Q. of hearts,** reine des cœurs; **she is the q. of my heart,** elle règne dans mon cœur; **the rose is the q. of flowers,** la rose est la reine des fleurs; *Com:* **the q. of washing machines,** la merveille des machines à laver; *Cu:* **q. of puddings,** pudding au pain couronné de méringue; **q. cake,** petit cake aux raisins, parfois en forme de cœur; (*c*) *Bot:* **q. of the meadows,** reine des prés; **queen's cushion,** saxifrage *f* cotylédon; **q. of the night,** (cactus *m*) reine de la nuit; **Q. Anne's lace, queen's lace,** faux chervis, carotte *f* sauvage; **queen's pincushion,** boule-de-neige *f*, *pl.* boules-de-neige; (*d*) *Const:* **q. post,** clef pendante latérale; **q. (post) truss,** arbalète *f* à deux poinçons. **2.** (*a*) *Cards:* dame *f*; (*b*) *Chess:* dame, reine; **Queen's knight,** cavalier *m* de la reine; (*of pawn*) **to go to q.,** aller à dame. **3.** (*a*) chatte *f*; (*b*) *Ent:* reine (des fourmis, etc.); **q. substance,** ectohormone *f*, phérormone *f*; **q. bee,** (i) abeille mère, reine des abeilles; (ii) maîtresse femme; présidente active. **4.** *Moll:* vanneau *m*. **5.** *P:* pédale *f*.

queen[2]. **1.** *v.tr.* (*a*) faire (qn) reine; (*b*) *Chess:* damer (un pion). **2.** *v.i.* (*a*) *F:* **to q. it,** faire la reine; (*b*) *Chess:* (*of pawn*) aller à dame.

queenhood ['kwiːnhud], *s.* dignité *f* de reine; qualité *f* de reine; souveraineté *f*.

queening ['kwiːniŋ], *s. Hort:* (pomme *f*) calville *m* or *f*.

queenlike ['kwiːnlaik], **queenly** ['kwiːnli], *a.* de reine; digne d'une reine.

queenliness ['kwiːnlinis], *s.* majesté *f*.

queenship ['kwiːnʃip], *s.* = QUEENHOOD.

Queensland ['kwiːnzlənd]. *Pr.n. Geog:* Queensland *m*; *Bot:* **Q. nut,** (i) noix *f*, noisette *f*, (ii) noyer *m*, du Queensland.

queer[1] ['kwiər], *a.* **1.** (*a*) bizarre, étrange, singulier, drôle, falot; **q.-sounding name,** nom aux consonances bizarres; **a q.-looking chap,** une drôle de tête; **q. ideas,** idées bizarres, *F:* idées biscornues; *F:* **q. in the head,** toqué, falot, timbré; **he's had some q. experiences,** il en a vu de(s) raides; *F:* **to be in Q. Street,** être dans une situation (financière) embarrassée; (*b*) suspect; *U.S:* **q. (money),** fausse monnaie; **on the q.,** par des moyens peu honnêtes; par des moyens louches; (*c*) *P:* homosexuel; *s.* **a q.,** une pédale. **2.** (*a*) *F:* mal à l'aise; **I feel very q.,** je suis tout je ne sais comment; je me sens tout chose, tout drôle, tout patraque; je ne suis pas dans mon assiette; (*b*) *P:* **to come over, to be taken, q.,** tomber malade; (*c*) *P: A:* ivre, gris.

queer[2], *v.tr. F:* déranger, détraquer; gâcher; **to q. the pitch for s.o., to q. s.o.'s pitch,** bouleverser, faire échouer, les plans de qn; contrecarrer qn; entraver les opérations de qn; *Th:* **they did all they could to q. her entry, her scene,** ils ont fait tout ce qu'ils ont pu pour lui faire rater son entrée, pour lui faire manquer sa scène.

queerish ['kwiəriʃ], *a. F:* **1.** un peu bizarre; assez drôle; tant soit peu singulier. **2.** **to feel q.,** se sentir un peu souffrant, mal en train, plutôt patraque.

queerly ['kwiəli], *adv.* étrangement, bizarrement, singulièrement.

queerness ['kwiənis], *s.* **1.** étrangeté *f*, bizarrerie *f*, singularité *f*. **2.** *F:* malaise *m*.

quelea ['kwiːliə], *s. Orn:* quelea *m*.

quell [kwel], *v.tr. esp. Lit:* réprimer, étouffer (une révolte, une émotion); dompter (qn, une passion); calmer (un orage).

quelling ['kweliŋ], *s.* répression *f*, étouffement *m* (d'une révolte, d'une émotion).

quench[1] [kwen(t)ʃ], *s. Metalw:* trempe *f*, refroidissement *m* brusque; **differential q.,** trempe différentielle; **free fall q.,** trempe au bain de sel; **step q.,** trempe en bains de sel par étapes; **hot q.,** trempe à haute température; **slack q.,** trempe martensitique incomplète; **time q., interrupted q.,** trempe interrompue; **pot q.,** trempe en vase clos.

quench[2], *v.tr.* **1.** éteindre (un feu, une flamme). **2.** (*a*) *Metalw:* tremper, éteindre, (le métal); **quenched in oil, in water,** refroidi à l'huile, à l'eau; (*b*) **to q. s.o.'s enthusiasm,** refroidir l'enthousiasme de qn. **3.** (*a*) réprimer, étouffer (un désir); arrêter (un mouvement); (*b*) **to q. one's thirst,** étancher, éteindre, assouvir, sa soif; se désaltérer; (*c*) *El:* (i) étouffer (une étincelle); **quenched spark,** étincelle étouffée; (ii) amortir (des oscillations).

quenchable ['kwen(t)ʃəbl], *a.* (incendie, soif) qu'on peut éteindre.

quencher ['kwen(t)ʃər], *s. F:* boisson *f*, consommation *f*; **let's have a q.,** on va prendre quelque chose; *P:* on va se rincer la dalle.

quenching ['kwen(t)ʃiŋ], *s.* **1.** (*a*) extinction *f* (du feu); (*b*) assouvissement *m*, étanchement *m* (de la soif). **2.** (*a*) *Metalw:* trempe *f* (à l'eau, à l'huile); **q. and hardening,** trempe et revenu; **q. bath,** bain *m* de trempe; (*b*) *Petr:* quench *m*.

quenchless ['kwen(t)ʃlis], *a. Lit:* inextinguible.

quenelle [kə'nel], *s. Cu:* quenelle *f*.

quenouille-trained [kə'nuːj'treind], *a. Arb:* **q.-t. fruit-tree,** quenouille *f*; arbre *m* en fuseau.

quenselite ['kwensəlait], *s. Miner:* quensélite *f*.

quenstedtite ['kwenstetait], *s. Miner:* quenstedtite *f*.

quercetin, quercitin ['kwəːsitin], *s. Ch:* quercétine *f*.

quercitol ['kwəːsitɔl], *s. Ch:* quercite *f*, quercitol *m*.

quercitrin ['kwəːsitrin], *s. Ch: Bot:* quercitrin *m*, quercitrine *f*.

quercitron ['kwəːsitrən], *s. Bot:* quercitron *m*.

querimony ['kwerimәni], *s. Ecc:* quérimonie *f*.

querist ['kwiərist], *s.* questionneur, -euse.

quern [kwəːn], *s.* **1.** moulin *m* à bras (pour céréales); **q. stone,** meule *f*. **2.** **pepper q.,** moulin à poivre.

querulent ['kwer(j)ulənt], *a. & s. Psy:* quérulent, -ente.

querulous ['kwer(j)uləs], *a.* plaintif et maussade; qui se plaint toujours; chagrin, grognon; récriminateur, -trice; **q. tone,** ton plaintif, dolent.

querulously ['kwer(j)uləsli], *adv.* en se plaignant; d'un ton plaintif, dolent.

querulousness ['kwer(j)uləsnis], *s.* disposition *f* à se plaindre; habitude *f* de se plaindre; humeur chagrine; ton plaintif, dolent.

query[1] ['kwiːəri], *s.* **1.** (*a*) question *f*, interrogation *f*; **to settle a q.,** résoudre une question (de méthode, de routine, etc.); (*b*) **q.: was the money ever paid?** reste à savoir si la somme a jamais été versée; (*in margin of document, etc.*) **q.: is this accurate?** s'assurer de l'exactitude de cette déclaration. **2.** *Gram: Typ:* point *m* d'interrogation.

query[2], *v.tr.* **1.** **to q. if, whether . . .,** s'informer si. . . .. **2.** (*a*) marquer (qch.) d'un point d'interrogation; (*b*) mettre (une affirmation) en question, en doute; contester (qch.); **I q. whether he ever said any such thing,** je doute fort qu'il ait jamais rien dit de la sorte.

quest[1] [kwest], *s.* **1.** *A: & Dial:* (*a*) enquête *f*; (*b*) jury chargé d'une enquête. **2.** (*a*) *Ven:* quête *f* (par les chiens); (*b*) recherche *f*; **to go in q. of s.o.,** se mettre, aller, partir, à la recherche de qn, en quête de qn; **it's a hopeless q.,** on a beau chercher; *Lit:* **the Q. for the Holy Grail,** la quête du Graal.

quest[2]. **1.** *v.i.* (*a*) *Ven:* (*of dogs*) quêter; (*b*) *Lit:* (*of pers.*) **to q. after, for, sth.,** être, aller, à la recherche de qch. **2.** *v.tr. Poet:* **to q. out sth.,** (re)chercher qch.

question[1] ['kwestʃ(ə)n], *s.* question *f*. **1.** (*questioning*) (*a*) interrogation *f*; (*b*) *A:* (*torture*) **the common q.,** la question ordinaire; **the q. extraordinary,** la question extraordinaire; **to put s.o. to the q.,** mettre qn à la question; appliquer la question à qn. **2.** (*raising of doubt*) doute *m*; mise *f* en doute; **without q.,** sans aucun doute; sans contredit; sans conteste; **to allow sth. without q.,** permettre qch. sans poser de questions, sans discussion; **to obey without q.,** obéir aveuglément; **beyond all q., past q.,** hors de doute; incontestable; incontestablement; **courage beyond q.,** courage *m* indiscutable, au-dessus de toute discussion; **that is beyond q.,** cela ne peut être mis en question; cela n'est pas discutable; c'est incontestable; **to call, bring, sth. in q.,** mettre qch. en question, en doute; révoquer qch. en doute; contester, discuter, qch.; **his honesty has never been in q.,** sa probité reste hors cause; **to make no q. of sth.,** ne pas douter de qch.; **there is no q. about it,** il n'y a pas de doute là-dessus, cela ne fait pas question. **3.** (*a*) **the matter, person, in q.,** l'affaire, la personne, en question; l'affaire dont il s'agit; **the case in q.,** le cas en litige; **there was some q. of . . .,** il a été question de . . .; **there is no q. of his returning so soon,** il n'est pas question qu'il revienne si promptement; (*of thg*) **to come into q.,** surgir; (*b*) (*subject of discussion*) **that's the q.,** c'est là la question; **that's another q. altogether,** ça, c'est une autre affaire; **that is not the q., that is beside the q.,** ce n'est pas là la question; il ne s'agit pas de cela; cela est hors de cause; **what is the q. in hand?** de quoi s'agit-il? **to state a q.,** poser une question; **the q. arose whether . . .,** on a soulevé la question de savoir si. . .; on s'est demandé si. . .; **the q. is whether . . .,** il s'agit de savoir si . . .; **it's a q. whether he'll come,** je doute qu'il vienne; **the q. as to when he would return,** la question de savoir quand il reviendrait; **it is out of the q.,** c'est impossible; il ne faut pas y songer; jamais de la vie! **the scheme is out of the q.,** ce projet est absolument impraticable, inadmissible; **it is quite out of the q. for us to . . .,** il ne saurait être question pour nous de . . .; **it is not out of the q. that . . .,** il n'est pas exclu que . . .; (*at meeting*) **to move the previous q.,** demander la question préalable; **to put the q.,** (i) mettre la question aux voix; (ii) *F:* demander qn en mariage; **q.!** (i) au fait! revenez au fait! (ii) c'est à savoir! ce n'est pas prouvé! (*c*) (*problem*) **the Eastern q.,** la question d'Orient; **a difficult, a vexed, q.,** une question difficile, souvent débattue; **a q. of life or death,** une question de vie ou de mort; **simply a q. of money,** une simple question d'argent; **success is merely a q. of time,** le succès n'est qu'une question de temps; **it is only a q. of doing . . .,** il ne s'agit que de faire . . .. **4.** (*interrogative sentence*) interrogation *f*; *Typ:* **q. mark,** point *m* d'interrogation; *Gram:* **direct, indirect, q.,** question directe, indirecte; **to ask s.o. a q., to ask a q. of s.o., to put a q. to s.o.,** poser, adresser, une question à qn; *Parl:* adresser une interpellation à qn; **he's fond of asking questions,** c'est un questionneur; *Sch: etc:* **list, set, of questions,** questionnaire *m*; **multiple choice questions,** questions à choix multiples; **question(s) and answer(s),** demandes *f* et réponses *f*; **what a q. to ask!** la belle question! la belle demande! **he disappeared, but no questions were asked,** il a disparu, mais personne ne s'en est inquiété.

question[2], *v.tr.* **1.** (*a*) questionner, interroger (qn); **to q. s.o. closely,** soumettre qn à un interrogatoire serré; presser qn de questions; **to be questioned,** subir un interrogatoire; *Sch:* **to q. a candidate on chemistry,** interroger un candidat en chimie, sur la chimie; (*b*) *A:* **they questioned what crime he had done,** ils demandèrent quel crime il avait commis. **2.** (*a*) mettre (qch.) en question, en doute, en cause; révoquer (qch.) en doute; douter de, suspecter (qch.); contester (qch.); **to q. a right,** mettre un droit en contestation; **to q. the value of sth.,** contester la valeur de qch.; (*b*) **I q. whether he will come,** je doute qu'il vienne; **I q. whether it would not be better . . .,** je me demande, je ne sais pas trop, s'il ne vaudrait pas mieux . . .; **it is not to be questioned that . . .,** il n'y a pas de doute que . . ..

questionable ['kwestʃənəbl], *a.* **1.** contestable, discutable, douteux, incertain, problématique; (*of document, etc.*) **of q. authenticity,** d'une authenticité (fort) douteuse. **2.** *Pej:* (*of conduct, etc.*) suspect, équivoque; **in q. taste,** d'un goût douteux.

questionableness ['kwestʃənəblnis], *s.* **1.** caractère douteux (**of,** de); contestabilité *f.* **2.** caractère équivoque (**of,** de).

questionably ['kwestʃənəbli], *adv.* **1.** d'une manière incertaine, contestable. **2.** *Pej:* d'une manière équivoque, qui prête aux soupçons, à la critique.

questionary ['kwestʃənəri], *s. A:* questionnaire *m.*

questioner ['kwestʃənər], *s.* questionneur, -euse; interrogateur, -trice.

questioning[1] ['kwestʃəniŋ], *a.* (regard, etc.) interrogateur; **to give s.o. a q. look,** interroger qn du regard.

questioning[2], *s.* questions *fpl*, interrogation *f*; *Mil: etc:* interrogatoire *m* (de prisonniers).

questioningly ['kwestʃəniŋli], *adv.* d'un air interrogateur; **to look q. at s.o.,** diriger sur qn un regard interrogateur; interroger qn du regard.

questionless ['kwestʃənlis], *a. A:* **1.** hors de doute, incontestable. **2.** (foi) qui ne pose pas de questions.

question(-)master ['kwestʃənmɑ:stər], *s. W.Tel: T.V: etc:* animateur, -trice, meneur *m* de jeu (d'un jeu-concours).

questionnaire [kwestʃə'nɛər, kestjə'nɛər], *s.* questionnaire *m.*

questor ['kwestər], *s. Fr.Adm:* questeur *m.*

quetsch [kwetʃ], *s. Dist:* quetsche *f.*

quetsche [kwetʃ], *s. Hort:* quetsche *f*; **q. plum tree,** quetschier *m.*

quetzal ['ketsəl], *s.* **1.** *Orn:* quetzal *m, pl.* quetzals; couroucou *m* du Guatemala. **2.** (*pl.* **quetsales** [ket'sɑ:leis]) *Num:* quetzal, *pl.* quetzales.

queue[1] [kju:], *s.* **1.** queue *f* (de cheveux, de perruque). **2.** queue (de personnes, de voitures); **to form a q., to stand in a q.,** faire (la) queue; **to join the q.,** prendre la file.

queue[2]. **1.** *v.tr.* attacher (les cheveux de qn) en forme de queue. **2.** *v.i.* **to q. (up),** faire (la) queue; se mettre à la queue; (*of taxis*) prendre la file.

queue-barge ['kju:bɑ:dʒ], **queue-jump** ['kju:dʒʌmp], *v.i. F:* resquiller, carotter.

queue-barger, -jumper ['kju:bɑ:dʒər, -dʒʌmpər], *s. F:* resquilleur, -euse, carotteur, -euse.

quibble[1] ['kwibl], *s.* **1.** *A:* (*play on words*) calembour *m*; jeu *m* de mots. **2.** (*evasion*) argutie *f*; chicane *f* de mots; faux-fuyant *m, pl.* faux-fuyants; évasion *f.*

quibble[2], *v.i.* (*a*) (*equivocate*) ergoter; chicaner sur les mots; user d'équivoque, de subterfuge; sophistiquer; (*b*) (*split hairs*) chipoter, chicaner, vétiller, discutailler.

quibbler ['kwiblər], *s.* ergoteur, -euse; chicaneur, -euse; casuiste *mf*; sophistiqueur, -euse.

quibbling[1] ['kwibliŋ], *a.* (*of pers.*) ergoteur, -euse; chicaneur, -euse; argutieux, -euse; (*of argument, etc.*) évasif.

quibbling[2], *s.* arguties *fpl*, évasions *fpl*; chicane *f* de mots; chicanerie *f*; ergoterie *f.*

quibinary [kwi'bainəri], *a. Cmptr:* (code) quibinaire.

quica ['ki:kə], *s. Z:* quiça *f*, sarigue *mf.*

quiche[1] [ki:ʃ], *s. Cu:* quiche *f.*

Quiche[2] ['ki:tʃei], *s. Ling:* quiché *m.*

Quichua ['ki:tʃwə], *s. Ling:* quichua *m.*

quick [kwik]. **1.** *a.* (*a*) (*of movement, growth, etc.*) rapide; **at a q. pace,** d'un pas rapide; **to walk with short q. steps,** marcher à petits pas pressés; trotter dru et menu; **the quickest way there,** le chemin le plus court (pour y arriver); **a q. way of doing sth.,** une manière rapide de faire qch.; **q. recovery (from illness),** prompt rétablissement (d'une maladie); **q. sale,** prompt débit; vente *f* facile; **to have a q. lunch,** déjeuner sur le pouce; *F:* **let's have a q. one,** viens prendre un petit verre; *Cards:* **q. trick,** levée assurée; **five q. tricks,** cinq levées franches; **as q. as lightning, as thought,** aussi vite que l'éclair; comme un éclair; à toute vitesse; en un clin d'œil; rapide comme la pensée; en un coup d'éclair; (*of pers.*) **to be q. about, over, sth.,** faire qch. vite; **be q. (about it)!** faites vite! dépêchez-vous! que cela ne traîne pas! plus vite que ça! **q.!** dépêchons! dépêche-toi! vite! allons vite! faites vite! **he is q. in all he does,** il est prompt dans tout ce qu'il fait; **try to be a little quicker,** tâchez d'y aller un peu plus vite; (*b*) vif; **a q. child,** un enfant vif, éveillé, qui a l'esprit prompt; **he's q.,** il a de la facilité; il apprend facilement; **q. wits, q. mind,** esprit prompt, vif, agile; **q. wit,** esprit prompt à la repartie; **q. sight, q. eye,** œil vif; **q. ear, q. hearing,** oreille fine, subtile; **q. temper,** tempérament emporté; irascibilité *f*; **she has a q. temper,** elle s'emporte facilement; elle a la tête chaude; **q. to act,** prompt à agir; **q. to anger, q. to answer back,** prompt, vif, à se fâcher, à répliquer; **man q. to anger,** homme emporté; **to be q. of understanding,** être intelligent; avoir l'esprit ouvert; avoir la compréhension facile; **q. of foot,** agile, leste, preste; *F:* **you're a bit q., aren't you?** vous ne vous faites pas prier! (*c*) *Mus:* vite, animé, vif; **quicker,** animez; plus vite; (*d*) *A:* vif, vivant; **q. hedge,** haie vive; *s. Ecc:* **the q. and the dead,** les vivants et les morts; (*e*) (i) *Obst:* (fœtus) dont les mouvements actifs sont perceptibles; (ii) *A: & Lit:* **q. with child,** enceinte; *esp.* dans un état de grossesse assez avancé. **2.** *s.* (*a*) vif *m*; chair vive; **to bite one's nails to the q.,** ronger ses ongles jusqu'au vif; **to sting, cut, s.o. to the q.,** blesser, piquer, qn au vif; **it cut me to the q. to see them,** cela me fendait le cœur de les voir; **stung to the q.,** piqué au vif; **English to the q.,** anglais jusqu'à la moelle des os; (*b*) = QUICKSET 1. **3.** (*a*) *F: adv.* vite, rapidement; **as q. as possible,** aussi vite que possible; **to run quicker,** courir plus vite; **he just wants to get rich q.,** il ne pense qu'à s'enrichir à tout prix; (*b*) **q.-acting, q.-action,** (mécanisme) à action rapide, immédiate; *Med: etc:* (drogue, médicament) à réaction rapide; *El:* **q.-break switch,** interrupteur instantané; **q.-firing rifle,** fusil *m* à tir rapide; **q.-growing,** (plante, etc.) à croissance rapide; *Artil: A:* **q.-match,** mèche *f* d'artilleur; *Mec.E:* **q.-return(ing),** à retour rapide; *Const: Cu: etc:* **q.-setting,** (mortier, gelée) à prise rapide.

quickbeam ['kwikbi:m], *s. Bot:* sorbier *m* sauvage.

quick-change ['kwik'tʃeindʒ], *a.* **1.** *Th:* **q.-c. artist,** artiste à transformations rapides; **q.-c. part,** rôle à travestissements. **2.** *Aut: etc: O:* **q.-c. gear device,** système de changement rapide des engrenages; *Tls: etc:* **q.-c. part,** pièce interchangeable.

quicken[1] ['kwik(ə)n], *s. Bot:* **1.** sorbier *m* sauvage. **2.** sorbier.

quicken[2]. **1.** *v.tr.* (*a*) *Lit:* donner la vie à, (r)animer, vivifier, raviver (les hommes, les plantes); (*b*) animer, stimuler, exciter (qn); exciter, stimuler, aiguiser (le désir, l'appétit); animer (la conversation); (*c*) hâter, presser, accélérer (**one's pace,** le pas); hâter (son départ); *Med:* accélérer (le pouls); *Mus:* **to q. the tempo,** presser la mesure; *Rac:* **to q. the pace,** activer l'allure; (*d*) *Tchn:* activer, accélérer (la combustion, le tirage). **2.** *v.i.* (*a*) (*of nature, hope, etc.*) s'animer, se ranimer; (*of offspring in womb*) donner des signes de vie; (*of pregnant woman*) sentir les premiers mouvements du fœtus; (*b*) (*of pace, etc.*) devenir plus rapide; s'accélérer.

quickener ['kwiknənər], *s.* **1.** animateur, -trice. **2.** principe vivifiant; stimulant *m.*

quickening[1] ['kwikəniŋ], *a.* **1.** animateur, -trice, vivifiant; **a q. force,** une force vive. **2.** (*a*) qui s'anime, qui se ranime; (*b*) (pas) qui s'accélère.

quickening[2], *s.* **1.** (*a*) retour *m* à la vie (de la nature, etc.); (*b*) *Obst:* premiers mouvements du fœtus. **2.** accélération *f* (du pas, du pouls).

quick-freeze [kwik'fri:z], *v.tr.* congeler, surgeler.

quick-freezing [kwik'fri:ziŋ], *s.* quick-freezing *m*, sur(con)gélation *f.*

quickie ['kwiki], *s. F:* (*a*) chose faite à la hâte, à la six-quatre-deux; (*b*) consommation prise sur le pouce; **have a q.?** tu prendras vite quelque chose? (*c*) *U.S:* grève soudaine.

quicklime ['kwiklaim], *s.* chaux vive.

quickly ['kwikli], *adv.* vite, rapidement, vivement, prestement; **retaliation q. followed,** les représailles furent promptes, ne tardèrent pas.

quickness ['kwiknis], *s.* **1.** vitesse *f*, rapidité *f*; vivacité *f*; fréquence *f* (du pouls). **2.** acuité *f* (de vision); finesse *f* (d'oreille); promptitude *f*, vivacité (d'esprit); **q. of temper,** caractère emporté, irascible.

quicksand ['kwiksænd], *s.* (*a*) sable(s) mouvant(s) (du bord de la mer); lise *f*; **to get caught in a q., in the quicksands,** s'enliser; (*b*) *Min: Civ.E: etc:* **quicksands,** sables flottants, boulants, mouvants.

quickset ['kwikset]. **1.** *s.* bouture *f*, plançon *m* (d'aubépine, etc.). **2.** *a. & s.* **q. (hedge),** haie vive.

quicksilver[1] ['kwiksilvər], *s.* (*a*) *O:* vif-argent *m*, mercure *m*; (*b*) **he's, she's, just like q.,** c'est du vif-argent.

quicksilver[2], *v.tr. O:* étamer (une glace).

quicksilvering ['kwiksilvəriŋ], *s. O:* **1.** étamage *m* (d'une glace). **2.** tain *m.*

quickstep ['kwikstep], *s.* **1.** *Mil:* pas accéléré; pas redoublé; pas cadencé. **2.** *Mus:* pas redoublé; *Danc:* fox-trot *m* rapide.

quick-tempered [kwik'tempəd], *a.* emporté, colérique, coléreux, irascible; *F:* qui a la tête près du bonnet; **she is (rather) q.-t.,** elle a l'humeur (un peu) vive; elle a le sang chaud; *F:* elle s'emporte comme une soupe au lait.

quickthorn ['kwikθɔ:n], *s. Bot:* aubépine *f.*

quick-witted [kwik'witid], *a.* à l'esprit prompt; vif, éveillé; d'esprit vif.

quick-wittedness [kwik'witidnis], *s.* vivacité *f* d'esprit.

quid[1] [kwid], *s.* (*usu. inv. in pl.*) *P:* livre *f* (sterling); **five q.,** cinq livres; **we're quids in,** on a trouvé le filon.

quid[2], *s.* chique *f* (de tabac).

quidam ['kwaidæm], *s.* quidam *m.*

quiddity ['kwiditi], *s.* **1.** *Phil:* quiddité *f*; essence *f.* **2.** argutie *f*, chicane *f.*

quidnunc ['kwidnʌŋk], *s.* curieux, -euse; chercheur, -euse, de nouvelles; nouvelliste *mf.*

quid pro quo ['kwidprou'kwou], *s.* **1.** *A:* quiproquo *m.* **2.** (*a*) équivalent *m*, compensation *f*; *Pol.Ec:* contrepartie *f*; (*b*) **to return a q. p. q.,** rendre la pareille à qn.

quiescence [kwai'es(ə)ns], *s.* **1.** repos *m*, quiétude *f*, tranquillité *f.* **2.** *Hebrew Gram:* quiescence *f* (d'une consonne).

quiescent [kwai'es(ə)nt], *a.* **1.** en repos; tranquille. **2.** *Hebrew Gram:* quiescent.

quiet[1] ['kwaiət], *s.* (*a*) tranquillité *f*, repos *m*, calme *m*, quiétude *f*; **period of q. (in illness, etc.),** accalmie *f*; **to enjoy perfect peace and q.,** jouir d'une parfaite tranquillité; (*b*) tranquillité, silence *m*; **the q. of the night,** le calme, la tranquillité, de la nuit.

quiet[2], *a.* **1.** (*with little sound or motion*) tranquille, calme, silencieux, reposé; **q. sea,** mer calme, immobile; **q. waters,** eaux tranquilles; **q. footsteps,** pas légers; **q. running of a machine,** marche silencieuse d'une machine; **q. engine,** moteur silencieux; **the wind grew q.,** le vent s'est apaisé; **q. worker,** travailleur silencieux; **q. neighbours,** voisins *m* tranquilles; **to keep q.,** se tenir, rester, tranquille; se tenir coi, en repos; **we must keep q. about it,** il ne faut pas en parler; **to keep a child q.,** faire taire un enfant; **how q. we all are!** comme nous sommes tous silencieux! **be q.!** tais-toi! taisez-vous! laissez-moi tranquille! **q., please!** silence, s'il vous plaît! **2.** (*gentle*) doux *f.* douce; **q. disposition,** caractère doux, calme; **q. horse,** cheval doux, tranquille, sage. **3.** (*subdued*) (*a*) (*of dress, colours, etc.*) simple; discret, -ète; sobre; **q. style,** style *m* simple, sans apparat; style sobre; **q. dinner,** dîner *m* intime; **q. wedding,** mariage célébré dans l'intimité; **in his q. way he is very proud of his daughter,** bien que peu démonstratif il est très fier de sa fille; (*b*) **q. irony,** ironie voilée; **q. resentment,** rancune sourde; **I had a q. suspicion that . . .,** je soupçonnais à part moi que . . .; **to have a q. dig at s.o.,** faire une allusion discrète à qn; **we had a q. laugh over it,** nous en avons ri entre nous; **keep it q.,** pas un mot; *s. F:* **to do sth. on the q.,** faire qch. en cachette, à la dérobée, clandestinement; faire qch. sous le manteau (de la cheminée); faire qch. sans avois l'air de rien; **to drink on the q.,** boire à la dérobée; **I'm telling you that on the q.,** je vous dis ça entre nous, en confidence. **4.** (*a*) (*undisturbed*) calme, tranquille, paisible; **q. mind,** esprit *m* tranquille; **to lead a q. life,** mener une vie calme; *F:* **anything for a q. life!** tout ce que tu voudras, mais fiche-moi la paix! **to have a q. meal,** prendre son repas en toute tranquillité; **he's had a q. sleep,** il a dormi tranquillement; **to spend a q. evening,** passer une soirée tranquille; **we're having a q. day,** on ne fait rien aujourd'hui; **to have a q. cigar,** fumer un cigare tranquillement; **all q. on the western front,** à l'ouest rien de nouveau; *Com:* **q. market,** marché calme; **business is very q.,** les affaires sont très calmes; *St.Exch:* **oils are q.,** les pétroles sont calmes; (*b*) *A:* sans inquiétude; **you may be q. on that score,** quant à cela vous pouvez être tranquille.

quiet[3], **quieten** ['kwaiət(ə)n]. **1.** *v.tr.* (*a*) apaiser, calmer; tranquilliser (qn, sa conscience); faire taire (un enfant); (*b*) apaiser, calmer (un tumulte); dissiper (les craintes, les soupçons); assoupir (une douleur, les sens). **2.** *v.i.* **to q. down,** s'apaiser, se calmer.

quieting[1] ['kwaiətiŋ], *a.* apaisant, calmant, tranquillisant.

quieting[2], *s.* apaisement *m* (du tumulte); dissipation *f* (des soupçons).

quietism ['kwaiətizm], *s. Phil: Rel.H:* quiétisme *m.*

quietist ['kwaiətist], *a. & s. Phil: Rel.H:* quiétiste (*mf*).

quietly ['kwaiətli], *adv.* **1.** (*a*) tranquillement, doucement; (*said by police*) **come q.!** pas d'histoires! (*b*) silencieusement, sans bruit; **to slip q. away,** s'éloigner en tapinois, à pas feutrés; **she took the news q.,** elle a appris la nouvelle avec calme. **2.** (vêtu, etc.) simplement, discrètement, sobrement; **to get married q.,** se marier sans cérémonie, sans éclat, dans l'intimité; **we live very q.,** nous menons une vie très simple.

quietness ['kwaiətnis], *s.* **1.** tranquillité *f*, repos *m*, calme *m*, quiétude *f*; **q. of a horse,** tranquillité, sagesse *f*, d'un cheval. **2.** sobriété *f* (de tenue, etc.).

quietude ['kwaiətju:d], *s.* quiétude *f.*

quietus [kwai'i:təs], *s.* **1.** *A:* quittance *f*, quitus *m.* **2.** *O:* coup *m* de grâce; **to give s.o. his q.,** régler son compte à qn; envoyer qn dans l'autre monde.

quiff [kwif], *s.* **q. (of hair),** toupet *m.*

quill[1] [kwil], *s.* **1.** (*a*) tuyau *m* (de plume); (*b*) *Orn:* **q. (feather),** penne *f*; (*c*) **q. (pen),** plume *f* d'oie (pour écrire); (*d*) cure-dent(s) *m* (en plume d'oie); (*e*) *Fish:* plume, flotteur *m* (de ligne). **2.** piquant *m* (de porc-épic, etc.). **3.** *Tex:* bobine *f*, cannette *f* (de tisserand). **4.** *Mec.E:* arbre creux tournant autour d'un arbre plein; fourreau *m*; manche *f*; arbre d'entraînement. **5.** *Laund:* tuyau. **6.** *Mus:* pipeau *m*, chalumeau *m.* **7.** *Com: Pharm:* tuyau (de quinquina, de cannelle).

quill[2], *v.tr.* **1.** tuyauter, rucher, cisailler (un ruban, une dentelle). **2.** *A:* bobiner (le coton, etc.).

quillai [ki'lei], **quillaia** [kwi'leiə], *s. Bot:* quillaja *m*; **quillai(a)bark,** écorce *f* de quillaja; bois *m* de Panama.

quill-driver ['kwildraivər], *s. F: A:* gratte-papier *m inv*; plumitif *m*; gratteur *m* de papier; noircisseur *m* de papier; rond-de-cuir *m*, *pl.* ronds-de-cuir.

quill-driving ['kwildraiviŋ], *s. F: A:* métier *m* de gratte-papier; écritures *fpl.*

quilled [kwild], *a.* **1.** *Com:* (écorce *f*) en forme de tuyaux. **2.** (ruban, linge) tuyauté, ruché. **3.** *Bot:* (chrysanthème *m*, etc.) tubuliflore.

quillet ['kwilit], *s. A:* argutie *f*, subtilité *f.*

quilling ['kwiliŋ], *s.* **1.** tuyautage *m* (du linge, etc.). **2.** ruche *f.*

quillon ['ki:jɔn], *s. Mil:* quillon *m.*

quillwort ['kwilwə:t], *s. Bot:* isoète *m.*

quilt[1] [kwilt], *s.* **1.** couverture piquée, ouatée; édredon piqué; couvre-pied *m*, *pl.* couvre-pieds; **continental q.,** duvet *m.* **2.** *A.Cost:* rembourrage *m* (de pourpoint); pourpoint rembourré, capitonné.

quilt[2], *v.tr.* **1.** piquer, contre-pointer, capitonner, ouater, ouatiner (un vêtement, etc.). **2.** (*a*) piquer (deux morceaux d'étoffe); (*b*) *F:* faire (un livre) à coups de ciseaux. **3.** *P: A:* rosser (qn).

quilted ['kwiltid], *a.* piqué, capitonné, ouaté, ouatiné, rembourré; **q. coat,** douillette *f.*

quilting ['kwiltiŋ], *s.* **1.** piquage *m*, rembourrage *m*, capitonnage *m*, ouatinage *m.* **2.** piqué *m*; étoffe ouatée; ouatine *f.*

quin [kwin], *s. F:* quintuplé, -ée.

quinaldic [kwi'nældik], **quinaldinic** [kwinæl'dinik], *a. Ch:* (acide) quinaldinique.

quinaldine [kwi'nældain], *s. Ch:* quinaldine *f*, quinophtalone *f.*

quinalizarin [kwinə'lizərin], *s. Ch:* quinalizarine *f.*

quinarius, *pl.* -ii [kwi'nɛəriəs, -iai], *s. Rom.Ant: Num:* quinaire *m.*

quinary ['kwainəri], *a. Mth:* quinaire.

quinate ['kwaineit], *a. Bot:* **1. q. leaflets,** folioles quinées. **2.** (feuille *f*) à cinq folioles.

quince [kwins], *s. Bot:* **1.** coing *m*; **q. jelly,** gelée *f* de coings; **q. cheese, jelly,** pâte *f* de coings; **q. marmalade,** cotignac *m*; **q. wine,** cotignelle *f.* **2. q. (tree),** cognassier *m.*

quincentenary [kwinsen'ti:nəri], **1.** *a.* de cinq cents ans, de cinq siècles, cinq fois centenaire. **2.** *s.* cinquième centenaire *m.*

quincuncial [kwin'kʌnʃ(ə)l], *a.* quinconcial, -aux, en quinconce.

quincunx ['kwinkʌŋks], *s.* quinconce *m*; *For:* **q. planting,** plantation *f* en quinconce; **trees planted in q.,** arbres plantés en quinconce.

quindecagon [kwin'dekəgən], *s.* pentadécagone *m*, pentédécagone *m*, quindécagone *m.*

quindecemvir [kwindi'semvər], *s.m. Rom.Ant:* quindécemvir.

quindecemvirate [kwindi'semvəreit], *s. Rom.Ant:* quindécemvirat *m.*

quindecennial [kwindi'senjəl], *a.* quindécennal, -aux.

quinhydrone [kwin'haidroun], *s. Ch:* quinhydrone *f.*

quinia ['kwiniə], *s. Ch:* = QUININE.

quinic ['kwinik], *a. Ch:* (acide *m*) cinchonique.

quinidine ['kwinidain], *s. Ch:* quinidine *f.*

quinine [kwi'ni:n], *s. Ch:* quinine *f*; *Pharm:* **(sulphate of) q.,** sulfate *m* de quinine; *A:* **q. wine,** (vin de) quinquina *m.*

quininism [kwi'ni:nizm], *s. Med:* quin(in)isme *m.*

quinitol ['kwinitɔl], *s. Ch:* quinite *f.*

quinizarin [kwi'nizərin], *s. Ch:* quinizarine *f.*

quinnat ['kwinət], *s. Ich:* quinnat *m.*

quinoa [ki:'nouə], *s. Bot:* quinoa *m.*

quinoid ['kwinɔid], *a. Ch:* quinonique.

quinol ['kwinɔl], *s. Ch: Phot:* hydroquinone *f.*

quinoline ['kwinoulain], *s. Ch:* quinoléine *f.*

quinolinic [kwinou'linik], *a. Ch:* quinoléique.

quinone ['kwinoun, kwi'noun], *s. Ch:* quinone *f.*

quinonoid [kwi'nounɔid], *a. Ch:* quinonique.

quinoxalin(e) [kwi'nɔksəli(:)n], *s. Ch:* quinoxaline *f.*

quinquagenarian [kwiŋkwədʒə'nɛəriən], *a. & s.* quinquagénaire (*mf*).

Quinquagesima [kwiŋkwə'dʒesimə], *s. Ecc:* **Q. (Sunday),** (le dimanche de) la Quinquagésime.

quinquangular [kwiŋ'kwæŋgjulər], *a. Mth:* quinquangulaire.

quinquefoliate [kwiŋkwi'foulieit], *a. Bot:* quinquéfolié.

quinquelateral [kwiŋkwi'lætər(ə)l], *a.* à cinq côtés.

quinquenniad [kwiŋ'kweniæd], *s.* quinquennat *m.*

quinquennial [kwiŋ'kweniəl]. **1.** *a.* quinquennal, -aux. **2.** *s.* quinquennium *m*; quinquennalité *f.*

quinquennium [kwiŋ'kweniəm], *s.* quinquennium *m.*

quinquepartite [kwiŋkwi'pɑ:tait], *a. Nat.Hist:* quinquéparti, -ite.

quinquereme ['kwiŋkwiri:m], *s. A.Nau:* quinquérème *f.*

quinquevalence [kwiŋkwi'veiləns], *s. Ch:* pentavalence *f.*

quinquevalent [kwiŋkwi'veilənt], *a.* quintivalent, pentavalent.

quinquina [kiŋ'ki:nə, kwiŋ'kwainə], *s. Bot: Pharm:* quinquina *m.*

quinsy ['kwinzi], *s. Med:* esquinancie *f*; angine (laryngée); amygdalite aiguë; *Bot:* **q. berry,** cassis *m.*

quint [kwint], *s.* **1.** *Mus:* quinte *f.* **2.** *Cards:* (*at piquet*) [*also* kint] quinte; **q. major,** quinte majeure. **3.** *Fenc:* = QUINTE.

quintain ['kwint(ə)n], *s. A:* **1.** *Pros:* quintain *m.* **2. to tilt at the q.,** courir la quintaine.

quintal ['kwint(ə)l], *s. Meas:* **1.** *A:* quintal, -aux *m* (de 112 livres = 50 kg 802; ou de 100 livres = 45 kg 35). **2.** quintal métrique (de 100 kg).

quintan ['kwintən], *a. & s. Med: A:* fièvre quint(an)e.

quintaton ['kwintətoun], *s. Mus:* quintaton *m.*

quinte [kɛ̃:t], *s. Fenc:* quinte *f*; **to parry in q.,** parer en quinte.

quintessence[1] [kwin'tes(ə)ns], *s.* quintessence *f.*

quintessence[2], *v.tr.* quintessencier.

quintessential [kwinti'senʃ(ə)l], *a.* quintessenciel, quintessencié.

quintessentialize [kwinti'senʃəlaiz], *v.tr.* quintessencier.

quintet(te) [kwin'tet], *s. Mus:* quintette *m.*

quintile ['kwintil], *a. Astrol:* **q. aspect,** quintil aspect; planètes *fpl* à 72°.

Quintilian [kwin'tiljən], *Pr.n.m. Lt.Lit:* Quintilien.

quintillion [kwin'tiljən], *s.* **1.** quintillion *m* (10^{30}). **2.** *U.S:* trillion *m* (10^{18}).

quintole(t) ['kwintoul(et)], *s. Mus:* quintolet *m.*

quinton ['kwintən], *s. Mus:* quinton *m.*

quintroon [kwin'tru:n], *s. & a. Ethn:* quinteron, -onne.

quintuple[1] ['kwintjupl], *a. & s.* quintuple (*m*).

quintuple[2]. **1.** *v.tr.* quintupler. **2.** *v.i.* (se) quintupler.

quintuplet [kwin'tju:plit, 'kwintjuplit], *s.* **1.** groupe *m* de cinq; *Mus:* quintolet *m.* **2.** quintuplé, -ée; **birth of quintuplets,** accouchement *m* quintigémellaire.

quinuclidine [kwi'nju:klidi:n], *s. Ch:* quinuclidine *f.*

quinze [kwinz], *s. Cards:* quinze *m.*

quip [kwip], *s.* **1.** sarcasme *m*, repartie *f*; raillerie *f*; mot piquant. **2.** *A:* = QUIBBLE[1] 2.

quire[1] ['kwaiər], *s.* **1. q. of paper (24 sheets),** *approx.* = main *f* de papier (25 feuilles); **half a q.** = demi-main *f*; **quarter of a q.,** cahier *m*; **over q.,** main de passe, simple passe *f.* **2.** *Typ:* **in quires,** en feuilles.

quire[2,3], *s. & v. A:* = CHOIR[1,2].

Quirinal (the) [ðə'kwirin(ə)l], *s.* **1.** le (mont) Quirinal. **2.** (*a*) le palais du Quirinal; (*b*) *Hist: F:* le gouvernement italien.

quiritarian [kwiri'tɛəriən], *a. Rom.Jur:* quiritaire.

quirk[1] [kwə:k], *s.* **1.** *O:* = QUIP. **2.** (*a*) *A:* tour *m*, caprice *m*; (*b*) bizarrerie *f* de caractère. **3.** *A:* faux-fuyant, *pl.* faux-fuyants; défaite *f*; manigance *f*; équivoque *f*; **there's sure to be a q. in it,** on va encore être dupés. **4.** (*a*) trait *m* de plume; arabesque *f*, fioriture *f*; (*b*) parafe *m.* **5.** (*a*) *Arch:* gorge *f*, gorgerin *m*; (*b*) *Carp:* carré *m*; **q. ogee, ovolo,** doucine *f*, boudin *m*, à carré.

quirk[2], *s. MilAv: F: O:* recrue *f*, apprenti *m*, novice *m.*

quirky ['kwə:ki], *a.* **1.** (*a*) qui se plaît aux arguties, aux faux-fuyants; (*b*) (*of sense of humour, etc.*) bizarre. **2.** (*a*) (*of road, etc.*) sinueux, plein de détours; (*b*) peu franc; où il y a un traquenard.

quirt[1] [kwə:t], *s. U.S:* cravache *f* à longue mèche en cuir tressé.

quirt[2], *v.tr. U.S:* cingler avec le *quirt*; fouetter.

quisling ['kwizliŋ], *s.* quisling *m.*

quit[1] [kwit], *a.* quitte, libéré; **to be q. for a fine,** en être quitte pour une amende; **to be q. of s.o., of sth.,** être débarrassé de qn, de qch.

quit[2], *v.tr. & i.* (*p.t. & p.p.* **quitted,** *Dial: & U.S:* **quit;** *pr.p.* **quitting**) **1.** (*a*) quitter (qn, un endroit); vider les lieux; déménager; s'en aller; **I've had my notice to q.,** (i) on m'a donné mon congé; (ii) je sais bien que je vais mourir (bientôt); (*b*) **to q. office,** se démettre de ses fonctions; **to q. (one's job),** quitter son emploi; démissionner; (*c*) **to q. hold of sth.,** lâcher qch.; lâcher prise; (*d*) **to q. doing sth.,** cesser de faire qch.; **to q. (work),** cesser le travail; rentrer chez soi; (*e*) céder; baisser pavillon; mettre les pouces. **2.** *A:* (*acquit*) **q. you like men,** comportez-vous vaillamment; conduisez-vous, agissez, en hommes. **3.** *A:* récompenser; payer; venger.

quitch [kwitʃ], *s. Bot:* **q. (grass),** chiendent *m.*

quitclaim[1] ['kwitkleim], *s. Jur:* acte *m* de renonciation (à un droit, etc.).

quitclaim[2], *v.tr. Jur:* renoncer à, abandonner (un droit, une possession).

quite [kwait], *adv.* **1.** (*entirely*) tout à fait; entièrement, complètement; **q. new,** tout nouveau; **q. finished,** tout à fait fini; **q. covered,** entièrement couvert; **q. recovered,** complètement rétabli; **q. the best story of its kind,** sans exception la meilleure histoire de ce genre; **it is q. five days ago,** il y a bien cinq jours de cela; **q. as much,** tout autant; **q. enough,** bien assez; **it is q. enough to have forgiven you once,** c'est déjà assez de vous avoir pardonné une fois; **q. right,** très bien; (*of sum*) parfaitement juste; (*of clock*) bien à l'heure; **you are q. right,** vous avez bien raison, tout à fait raison; **q. so!** parfaitement! d'accord! vous l'avez dit! **q. so, I did see him,** en effet, je l'ai vu; **not q.,** pas tout à fait; **I do not q. know what he will do,** je ne sais pas trop ce qu'il fera; **I q. see that . . .,** je vois bien que . . .; **I q. understand,** j'ai bien compris; je me rends parfaitement compte; **in q. another tone,** sur un tout autre ton. **2. they are q. young,** (i) ils sont tout jeunes, elles sont toutes jeunes; (ii) ils, elles, sont encore assez jeunes; **she is q. happy,** (i) elle est tout à fait heureuse; (ii) elle est plus ou moins heureuse; **it is q. interesting,** cela ne manque pas d'intérêt; **q. a miracle,** un véritable miracle; **q. a beauty,** une vraie beauté; **his story is q. a romance,** son histoire est tout un roman; **it was q. a surprise,** c'était une véritable surprise; *F:* **it's been q. a day,** quelle journée! **she's q. a girl,** elle est formidable; **q. a number of people,** un assez grand nombre de personnes; **q. like him,** je l'aime assez bien; **I (can) q. believe that. . .,** je crois bien que . . .; je veux bien croire que . . ..

quitrent ['kwitrent], *s.* redevance *f* (minime); (*feudal*) cens *m.*

quits [kwits], *a.* quitte(s); **to be q.,** être quittes; **to cry q.,** demander l'aman; **we'll cry q.! now we're q.!** nous voilà quittes! nous voilà quitte à quitte! *Games:* **double**

or q., quitte ou double; **I'll be q. with him yet,** je lui rendrai la pareille; il me le paiera.

quittance ['kwit(ə)ns], *s.* **1.** quittance *f*, décharge *f*, acquit *m*, reçu *m.* **2.** *A:* récompense *f*, représailles *fpl*; revanche *f*.

quitter[1] ['kwitər], *s. F:* lâcheur, -euse.

quitter[2], *s. Vet: A:* javart *m.*

quiver[1] ['kwivər], *s.* carquois *m*; **to have an arrow, a shaft, left in one's q.,** n'être pas à bout de ressources; *A:* **to have one's q. full,** avoir beaucoup d'enfants, une famille nombreuse.

quiver[2], *s.* tremblement *m*; (i) frisson *m*; (ii) frémissement *m*; (iii) palpitation *f*; **with a q. in his voice,** d'une voix frémissante, mal assurée; **a q. went through him,** il a frémi par tout son corps; **q. of the eyelid,** battement *m* de paupière.

quiver[3]. **1.** *v.i.* (*of pers.*) trembler, frémir, tressaillir, frissonner; (*of leaves, lips*) trembler; (*of voice, light*) trembloter; (*of flesh*) palpiter; **to q. with fear, with impatience,** frémir de crainte, d'impatience; **voice quivering with emotion,** voix vibrante d'émotion; **I felt the earth q.,** j'ai senti trembler la terre. **2.** *v.tr.* (*of bird*) **to q. its wings,** agiter ses ailes.

quiverful ['kwivəful], *s.* carquois plein; plein carquois (de flèches); *A:* **q. of children,** famille nombreuse.

quivering[1] ['kwivəriŋ], *a.* tremblant, frissonnant, frémissant, tressaillant, palpitant; **flesh still q.,** chair encore pantelante.

quivering[2], *s.* tremblement *m*, frémissement *m*, tressaillement *m*, frissonnement *m*, palpitation *f*; **q. of the eyelids,** battement *m* de paupières.

quiveringly ['kwiv(ə)riŋli], *adv.* en tremblant; avec un frémissement.

qui vive ['kiː'viːv], *s. used in the phr.* **to be on the q. v.,** être sur le qui-vive.

Quixote (Don) [dɔn'kwiksout], *Pr.n.m. Lit:* Don Quichotte.

quixotic [kwik'sɔtik], *a.* de Don Quichotte; (*a*) exalté, visionnaire; (*b*) donquichottesque, par trop chevaleresque.

quixotically [kwik'sɔtik(ə)li], *adv.* en Don Quichotte.

quixotism, quixotry ['kwiksətizm, -tri], *s.* (Don)quichottisme *m.*

quiz[1] [kwiz], *s.* **1.** *A:* mystification *f*, plaisanterie *f*, farce *f*, attrape *f.* **2.** *A:* (*a*) personne *f* ridicule; une drôle de figure; original *m*; (*b*) railleur, -euse; persifleur, -euse; gouailleur, -euse. **3.** (*a*) *Sch: U.S: F:* examen oral; colle *f*; **q. kid,** enfant prodige; (*b*) *W.Tel: T.V: etc:* jeu-concours *m*; **q. master,** animateur *m*, meneur *m* de jeu; **let's play a q. game,** jouons aux devinettes *f.*

quiz[2], *v.tr.* (**quizzed**) **1.** *A:* railler, persifler (qn). **2.** *A:* (*a*) lorgner, reluquer (qn); (*b*) regarder (qn) d'un air narquois. **3.** (*a*) questionner; (*b*) *U.S:* faire passer l'oral à (un candidat).

quizzical ['kwizik(ə)l], *a.* **1.** *A:* risible, cocasse. **2.** (*a*) *A:* railleur, -euse, plaisant; (*b*) **a q. look,** un regard interrogateur. **3.** *U.S:* à l'esprit critique.

quizzically ['kwizik(ə)li], *adv.* (*a*) railleusement, d'un air railleur, moqueur; (*b*) d'un air interrogateur.

quizzing ['kwiziŋ], *s.* **1.** raillerie *f*, persiflage *m.* **2.** *A:* lorgnerie *f*; **q. glass,** (i) lorgnon *m*; face-à-main, *m, pl.* faces-à-main; (ii) monocle *m.* **3.** interrogation *f.*

quod[1] [kwɔd], *s. P:* prison *f*, taule *f*, boîte *f*, bloc *m*, ballon *m*; **in q.,** en prison; au bloc; en cage; sous les verrous; à l'ombre.

quod[2], *v.tr.* (**quodded**) *P:* mettre (qn) en prison; fourrer (qn) au bloc; mettre (qn) à l'ombre.

quodlibet ['kwɔdlibet], *s.* quo(d)libet *m.*

quoin[1] [kɔin], *s.* **1.** *Const:* pierre *f* d'angle; coin *m* (de mur); encoignure *f*; **rectangular q.,** angle *m* (de mur) rectangulaire; **obtuse q.,** angle obtus; **squint q.,** angle aigu; *Const:* **q. stone,** pierre d'angle, d'arête; *Hyd.E:* **q. post,** poteau-tourillon *m, pl.* poteaux-tourillons (d'une porte d'écluse). **2.** (*a*) *Mec.E:* coin (pour caler); *Artil:* coussin *m*; coin de mire; *Typ:* coin, cale *f*; (*b*) *Arch: A:* voussoir *m*, vousseau *m*, claveau *m.*

quoin[2], *v.tr.* caler, coincer; **to q. up,** soulever avec des cales, avec une cale.

quoining ['kɔiniŋ], *s.* calage *m*, coinçage *m.*

quoit [kɔit], *s. Games:* palet *m*; **to play (at) quoits,** jouer au palet.

quondam ['kwɔndæm], *a. A:* ci-devant, ancien, d'autrefois; **q. manager,** ancien gérant; **my q. friends,** mes amis d'autrefois, de jadis.

quorum ['kwɔːrəm], *s.* quorum *m*; quantum *m*; nombre suffisant; nombre voulu; **to form, have, a q.,** être en nombre; constituer un quorum.

quota ['kwoutə], *s.* (*a*) quote-part *f, pl.* quotes-parts; quotité *f*; cotisation *f*; **to contribute one's q.,** payer, apporter, sa quote-part; *Adm:* **taxable q.,** quotité imposable; (*b*) contingent *m*, quota *m*; **full q. of troops, of immigrants,** plein contingent de troupes, d'immigrants; (*c*) **electoral q.,** quotient électoral; **q. sampling,** sondage *m* par quota; (*d*) *War Adm:* attribution *f* (d'essence, de sucre, etc.); *Cin: etc:* taux *m* de contingentement (des films, etc.); **q. system (of distribution),** contingentement *m*; **to apportion, fix, quotas for an import,** contingenter une importation; déterminer les contingents d'importation.

quotable ['kwoutəbl], *a.* **1.** citable. **2.** *St.Exch:* cotable.

quotation [kwou'teiʃ(ə)n], *s.* **1.** citation (empruntée à un auteur, etc.); *Typ:* **q. marks,** guillemets *m*; **to put in the q. marks at the beginning, at the end, of a passage,** ouvrir les guillemets; fermer les guillemets; **to put a word, a passage, in q. marks,** guillemeter un mot, un passage. **2.** (*a*) *Com: St.Exch:* cotation *f*, cote *f*, cours *m*, prix *m*; **the latest quotations,** les derniers cours faits; **actual quotations,** cours effectifs; prix effectifs cotés; **stock admitted to q.,** valeurs admises à la cote officielle; (*b*) *Ind:* **q. for plant,** prix pour matériel. **3.** *Typ:* **q. (quadrat),** cadrat creux.

quote[1] [kwout], *s. F:* **1.** citation *f.* **2.** *pl.* guillemets *m.*

quote[2], *v.tr.* **1.** (*a*) citer (un auteur, un passage); **to q. from an author, from a book,** tirer une citation, des citations, d'un auteur, d'un livre; **he said—and I q.,** et voici exactement ce qu'il a dit; *F:* **can I q. you on that?** est-ce que je puis vous citer? (*b*) alléguer, citer (une autorité, une preuve); **to q. an instance of sth.,** fournir un exemple de qch.; **to q. s.o. as an example,** citer qn pour, en, exemple; (*c*) *Adm: Com:* **in reply please q. this number,** prière de rappeler ce numéro. **2.** (*a*) *Com:* établir, faire (un prix); **to q. s.o. a price for sth.,** fixer à qn un prix pour qch.; **this is the best price I can q. you,** il m'est impossible de vous faire un meilleur prix; (*b*) *St.Exch:* coter (une valeur); **shares quoted at 90p,** actions *f* qui se cotent à 90 pence; **stock officially quoted,** valeur admise à la cote officielle. **3.** *Typ: etc:* guillemeter (un mot, un passage); **words quoted,** mots entre guillemets.

quoteworthy ['kwoutwəːði], *a.* digne d'être cité.

quoth [kwouθ], *v.tr. def.* (*found only in p.t. with sbs. and prons. of 1st and 3rd pers., with inversion*) *A:* **'no,' q. I,** 'non,' dis-je; **'very well,' q. Thomas,** 'très bien,' dit, fit, Thomas.

quotha ['kwouθə], *int. A:* (= *quoth he*) **1.** dit-il; *F:* qu'il dit. **2.** vraiment.

quotidian [kwɔ'tidiən]. **1.** *a.* (*a*) quotidien, journalier; (*b*) banal, -als; de tous les jours. **2.** *s. Med: A:* fièvre quotidienne.

quotient ['kwouʃ(ə)nt], *s. Mth:* quotient *m*; *Physiol:* **respiratory q.,** quotient respiratoire; *Psy:* **intelligence q.,** quotient d'intelligence, intellectuel.

quotity ['kwɔtiti], *s.* quotité *f.*

R

R, r [ɑːr], *s.* (la lettre) R, r *f or m; Ling:* **point, dental, r,** r cacuminale; **uvular r.,** r vélaire; *Tp:* **R for Robert,** R comme Raoul; *F:* **the r months,** les mois en r (c.-à-d. septembre à avril où les huîtres sont de saison); *F:* **the three R's** (*Reading, (w)Riting and (a)Rithmetic*), l'enseignement *m* primaire (c.-à.-d. la lecture, l'écriture et l'arithmétique).

Ra [rɑː, rɔː], *Pr.n.m. Myth:* Râ, Rê.

raad [rɑːd], *s. Ich:* malaptérure *m.*

rabanna [rəˈbænə], *s. Tex:* rabane *f.*

rabat(te) [rəˈbæt], *v.tr. Mth:* rabattre (un plan).

rabbet[1] [ˈræbit], *s.* **1.** *Carp: N.Arch:* feuillure *f*, rainure *f*; *N.Arch:* râblure *f*; (*at junction of double doors, windows*) battant *m*; **r. joint,** assemblage *m* à feuillure; *Tls:* **r. plane,** feuilleret *m*, guillaume *m*; **r. iron,** fer *m* de guillaume. **2.** *Metall: etc:* rabat *m* (de marteau-pilon).

rabbet[2], *v.tr. Carp: etc:* (*a*) faire une feuillure à, feuiller (une planche, etc.); tailler (qch.) en feuillure; (*b*) assembler (deux planches) à feuillure; **rabbeted joint,** assemblage *m* à feuillure; **rabbeted lock,** serrure encastrée.

rabbeting [ˈræbitiŋ], *s. Carp:* assemblage *m* à feuillure; *Tls:* **r. plane,** feuilleret *m*, guillaume *m.*

rabbi [ˈræbai], *s. Jew.Rel:* rabbin *m*; (*as voc. case and as title*) rabbi *m*; **chief r.,** grand rabbin.

rabbinate [ˈræbinət], *s. Jew.Rel:* rabbinat *m.*

rabbinic(al) [ræˈbinik(əl)], *a.* rabbinique; **Rabbinic Hebrew,** hébreu *m* rabbinique, talmudique.

rabbinics [ræˈbiniks], *s.pl.* (*usu. with sg. const.*) études *f* rabbiniques; *Pej:* rabbinage *m.*

rabbinism [ˈræbinizm], *s.* rabbinisme *m.*

rabbinist [ˈræbinist], *s.* rabbiniste *m.*

rabbins [ˈræbinz], *s.pl. Jew.Rel:* rabbins *m.*

rabbit[1] [ˈræbit], *s.* **1.** lapin *m*; **to produce a r. out of a hat,** (i) (*of conjuror*) faire sortir un lapin d'un chapeau; (ii) *F:* trouver, annoncer, une solution inattendue, épatante (à un problème); **buck r.,** lapin mâle; **doe r.,** lapine *f*; **young r.,** lapereau *m*; **tame r.,** lapin domestique, (lapin de) clapier *m*; **wild r.,** lapin de garenne; **thicket r.,** lapin buissonnier; **rock r.,** pika *m*; **r. breeder,** cuni(culi)culteur *m*; **r. breeding,** élevage *m* de lapins; cuni(culi)culture *f*; *T.V:* **r. ears,** antenne *f* double d'intérieur; **r. farm,** élevage de lapins; **r. farmer,** cuni(culi)culteur; *Med:* **r. fever,** tularémie *f*; *F:* **r. food,** salade *f*; = crudités *fpl*; **r. hutch,** cabane *f*, cage *f*, à lapins; clapier, lapinière *f*; *Box: etc:* **r. punch,** coup *m* lapin; **r. warren,** (i) garenne, lapinière, clapier; (ii) enchevêtrement *m* de petites rues, de ruelles; agglomération *f* de petites habitations; tas *m* de petits logements. **2.** *Cu:* (*a*) **stewed r.,** = civet *m* de lapin; (*b*) **Welsh r.,** welsh rabbit *m*; rôtie de pain dorée au fromage; rôtie anglaise. **3.** *F:* (*a*) personne *f* faible, malingre, sans caractère; (*b*) *Sp:* mazette *f*; novice *mf.* **4.** *Atom.Ph:* cartouche *f*, furet *m.*

rabbit[2], *v.i.* faire la chasse au lapin; chasser le lapin.

rabbit[3], *v.tr. P: A:* **(odd) r. it!** nom d'un nom! **(odd) r. him!** que le diable l'emporte!

rabbiter [ˈræbitər], *s.* chasseur *m* de lapins.

rabbit-faced [ˈræbitfeist], *a. F:* à profil de lapin.

rabbiting [ˈræbitiŋ], *s.* chasse *f* au lapin.

rabbity [ˈræbiti], *a.* **1.** (goût, etc.) de lapin. **2.** *F:* (*a*) (jeune personne) (i) malingre, (ii) timide; (*b*) *Sp:* (jeu) de novice.

rabble[1] [ˈræbl], *s.* **1.** cohue *f*; foule (confuse, en désordre); tourbe *f.* **2. the r.,** la populace, la canaille, la racaille; **r. rouser,** agitateur, -trice, fomentateur, -trice (de troubles); **r. rousing,** incitation *f* à la violence, au désordre.

rabble[2], *s. Metall:* crochet *m*, ringard *m*, râble *m.*

rabble[3], *v.tr. Metall:* brasser, ringarder (le fer puddlé).

rabbler [ˈræblər], *s. Metall:* = RABBLE[2].

rabble-rousing [ˈræblrauziŋ], *a.* (démagogue, etc.) qui incite au désordre.

rabbling [ˈræbliŋ], *s. Metall:* brassage *m* (du fer puddlé).

Rabelaisian [ræbəˈleiziən], *a. & s.* rabelaisien, -ienne.

rabic [ˈræbik], *a. Med:* (virus, etc.) rabique.

rabid [ˈræbid], *a.* **1.** (*a*) furieux, féroce; **r. hate,** haine *f* farouche; **to be a r. enemy of s.o.,** être acharné contre, après, qn; **r. disease,** maladie virulente; **r. hunger,** faim dévorante; (*b*) (démagogue, etc.) outrancier, à outrance; **to be r. on a subject,** être violent sur un sujet; **he had become a r. free trader,** il était devenu un libre-échangiste enragé. **2.** *Vet:* (*a*) (chien) enragé; (*b*) **r. virus,** virus *m* rabique.

rabidity [ræˈbiditi], **rabidness** [ˈræbidnis], *s.* **1.** violence *f* (des passions, opinions). **2.** rage *f* (d'un animal).

rabidly [ræbidli], *adv.* furieusement, violemment.

rabies [ˈreibiːz], *s. Med: Vet:* rage *f*, hydrophobie *f*; **dumb, mute, r.,** rage mue.

raccoon [rəˈkuːn], *s. Z:* raton laveur.

race[1] [reis], *s.* **1.** (*a*) (*in sea, river*) raz *m*, ras *m*, de courant; (*b*) *Aer:* remous *m* d'air. **2.** (*a*) cours *m*, course *f* (du soleil); (*b*) *A:* carrière *f* (de qn); **his r. is run,** il est arrivé au terme de sa vie, la course; *B:* **let us run with patience the r. that is set before us,** nous devons courir avec patience l'épreuve qui nous est proposée. **3.** (*a*) *Hyd.E:* canal *m*, -aux; rigole *f*, bief *m*; (*b*) *Mch:* **flywheel r.,** puits *m*, fosse *f*, du volant; (*c*) **r. trough,** coulisseau *m* (pour chargement de voitures, etc.); (*d*) *Leath: etc:* **r. knife,** rénette *f.* **4.** (*a*) *Mec.E:* **(ball) r.,** (i) chemin *m*, voie *f*, cuvette *f*, bague *f*, de roulement (pour billes); (ii) cage *f* à billes; **wheel r.,** cage de roue; (*b*) *Tex:* **shuttle r., lay r.,** (i) course de la navette; (ii) *also* **r. board,** seuil *m*, seuillet *m*, verguette *f.* **5.** (*a*) *Sp:* course (de personnes, de chevaux, de bateaux, etc.); course, match *m* (d'aviron); **to run a r.,** prendre part à, disputer, une course; lutter à la course; **hundred metres r.,** course sur cent mètres; **long distance r.,** course de (grand) fond; **medium distance r.,** course de demi-fond; **foot r.,** course à pied; **bicycle r.,** course de bicyclettes; **r. against the clock, watch, against time,** course contre la montre; **horse r.,** course de chevaux; **point-to-point r.,** course au clocher; steeple-chase *m*, *pl.* steeple-chases; *F:* steeple *m*; **no r.,** course nulle; *Turf:* **to go to the races,** aller aux courses; **r. card,** programme *m* des courses; **r. meeting,** réunion *f* de courses (de chevaux); (*b*) **the arms r.,** la course aux armements.

race[2], *v.i. & tr.*

I. *v.i.* **1.** (*a*) lutter de vitesse, faire une course (**with,** avec); (*b*) courir à toute vitesse, galoper; **to r. over the ground,** parcourir le terrain à grande vitesse, au grand galop; **to r. down the street,** dévaler la rue à toute vitesse; **the stream races down the valley,** le ruisseau dévale; **to r. past a competitor,** brûler, griller, un concurrent; **their pens raced over the paper,** leurs plumes couraient sur le papier. **2.** (*a*) (*of athlete*) courir; *Turf:* (*of rider*) monter en course; faire de l'hippisme; *Aut:* **to r. for a firm,** courir pour une maison; (*b*) *Turf:* (i) (*of owner*) faire courir des chevaux; (ii) parier aux courses. **3.** (*a*) (*of engine*) s'emballer, s'emporter; (*of propeller*) s'affoler; (*b*) (*of pulse*) être fréquent; battre la fièvre; **my heart is racing,** mon cœur bat la breloque.

II. *v.tr.* **1.** (*a*) lutter de vitesse avec (qn); **I'll r. you!** la course à deux!; **I'll r. you home!** au premier arrivé (de nous deux) à la maison! (*b*) faire courir (un cheval); **he used to r. his camel against our horses,** il faisait lutter de vitesse son méhari et nos chevaux; (*c*) **to r. s.o. through the country,** faire parcourir le pays à qn à toute vitesse, en brûlant les étapes; *F:* **he used to r. me off my feet,** il me faisait courir, trotter, à une vitesse impossible, insoutenable. **2.** *I.C.E: etc:* **to r. the engine (without a load),** emballer le moteur (à vide).

III. (*compound verbs*) **1. race about,** *v.i.* parcourir le pays, la maison, etc., au grand galop.

2. race along, (*a*) *v.i.* aller, courir, à toute vitesse; (*b*) *v.tr.* entraîner (qn) à toute vitesse, au grand galop.

3. race away, (*a*) *v.i.* (*also* **race off**) partir à toute vitesse, au grand galop; (*b*) *v.tr.* **to r. away a fortune,** perdre une fortune aux courses.

race[3], *s.* race *f.* **1.** (*a*) **the Mongolian r.,** la race mongole; **r. conflict,** guerre *f* de races; **r. consciousness,** racisme *m*; **r. discrimination,** discrimination raciale; **r. relations,** rapports *m* entre des races différentes (dans le même pays); **r. riot,** bagarre, émeute, raciale; (*b*) **the human r.,** la race humaine; *Fig:* **the feathered r.,** la race ailée; *Hum:* la gent ailée; **the present r. of poets,** les poètes de la génération actuelle. **2.** (*a*) descendance *f*; **to be of Jewish r.,** être de race juive; **of noble r.,** de sang noble; (*of horse, dog, etc.*) **true to r.,** fortement racé; (*b*) lignée *f.*

race[4], *s.* racine *f* (de gingembre); **r. ginger,** racines de gingembre.

racecourse [ˈreiskɔːs], *s.* terrain *m*, champ *m*, de courses; piste *f*; hippodrome *m*; *F:* turf *m.*

racegoer [ˈreisgouər], *s.* turfiste *mf*; habitué, -ée, du turf; *F:* pelousard, -arde.

racehorse [ˈreishɔːs], *s.* cheval *m*, -aux, de course; coureur *m.*

racemate [ˈræsimeit], *s. Ch:* racémate *m.*

raceme [ræˈsiːm], *s. Bot:* racème *m*, grappe *f.*

racemic [ræˈsemik, -ˈsiːmik], *a. Ch:* (acide, etc.) racémique; **r. compounds,** racémiques *m.*

racemization [ræsimaiˈzeiʃ(ə)n], *s. Ch:* racémisation *f.*

racemize [ˈræsimaiz], *v.tr. Ch:* racémiser.

racemose [ˈræsimous], *a. Bot: etc:* racémeux; *Anat:* **r. glands,** glandes *f* en grappes.

racer [ˈreisər], *s.* **1.** (*pers.*) (*a*) coureur, -euse; **road r.,** *Cy:* routier *m*; *Aut:* coureur; (*b*) *Turf:* **(horse) r.,** (i) propriétaire *mf* de chevaux de course; (ii) jockey *m*; turfiste *mf.* **2.** (*a*) cheval *m*, -aux, de course; racer *m*; (*b*) bicyclette *f*, automobile *f*, motocyclette *f*, de course, de piste; machine *f* de piste; yacht *m* de course, racer. **3.** *Artil: Navy:* circulaire *f* (pour affût de canon); **emplacement r.,** épi *m* courbe (d'artillerie lourde sur rails).

racetrack ['reistræk], *s.* (*a*) piste *f* (pour autos, motos, etc.); (*b*) *esp. NAm:* champ *m* de courses.
raceway ['reiswei], *s.* **1.** (*a*) *esp. NAm:* canal *m*, -aux; rigole *f*, bief *m*; (*b*) *El.E:* caniveau *m* guide-fils; tube *m* guide-fils. **2.** *NAm:* piste *f* (d'hippodrome).
Rachel ['reitʃəl], *Pr.n.f.* Rachel.
rachialgia [ræki'ældʒiə], *s. Med:* rachialgie *f*.
rachianaesthesia [rækiænis'θi:ziə], *s. Med:* rachianesthésie *f*.
rachianalgesia [rækiænæl'dʒiziə], *s. Med:* rachianalgésie *f*.
rachidian [rə'kidiən], *a. Nat.Hist:* rachidien.
Rachiglossa [reiki'glɔsə], *s.pl. Moll:* rachiglosses *m*.
rachis, *pl.* **-ides** ['reikis, -idi:z], *s. Nat.Hist:* rachis *m*.
rachischisis [rei'kiskisis], *s. Med:* rachischisis *m*, spina-bifida *m*.
rachitic [ræ'kitik], *a. Med:* rachitique.
rachitis [ræ'kaitis], *s. Med: Bot:* rachitisme *m*.
rachitogenic ['rækitou'dʒenik], *a. Med:* rachitigène.
rachitome ['rækitoum], *s. Surg:* rachitome *m*.
Rachmanism ['rækmənizm], *s.* exploitation *f* de locataires par des propriétaires sans scrupules.
racial ['reiʃl], *a.* de (la) race; racial, -aux; **r. discrimination,** discrimination raciale; **r. minority,** race en minorité, minoritaire.
racialism ['reiʃəlizm], *s.* racisme *m*.
racialist ['reiʃəlist], *a.* & *s.* raciste (*mf*).
racially ['reiʃəli], *adv.* au, du, point de vue de la race.
racily ['reisili], *adv.* d'une manière piquante; avec verve.
raciness ['reisinis], *s.* **1.** (*of wine, fruit*) goût *m* de terroir; (*of wine*) bouquet *m*. **2.** (*of writing, style*) piquant *m*, verve *f*.
racing[1] ['reisiŋ], *a.* **1.** (*a*) qui court vite; (*b*) qui prend part à des courses; **r. cyclist,** coureur *m* cycliste; **r. driver,** coureur automobile; pilote *m* (de course). **2.** (*of engine*) emballé; (*of propeller*) affolé; (*of pulse*) précipité, fréquent.
racing[2], *s.* **1.** courses *fpl*; lutte *f* à la course; (*a*) **foot r.,** la course à pied; **road r.,** courses sur route; **motor r.,** courses d'automobiles; **boat r.,** courses d'aviron, de bateaux; **yacht r.,** courses de yachts; **r. bicycle,** vélo *m* de course, de piste; **r. car,** voiture *f* de course; **r. yacht,** yacht *m* de course; racer *m*; **r. path, track,** piste *f* (de vitesse), anneau *m* de vitesse; (*b*) **(horse) r.,** les courses (de chevaux); l'hippisme *m*; **r. people, the r. world,** le monde des courses; **r. man,** turfiste *m*; **r. stable,** écurie *f* de courses; **to keep a r. stable, stud,** faire courir. **2.** emballement *m* (d'un moteur); affolement *m* (d'une hélice).
racism ['reisizm], *s.* racisme *m*.
rack[1] [ræk], *s.* **(cloud) r.,** légers nuages chassés par le vent; diablotins *mpl*.
rack[2], *v.i.* (*of clouds*) fuir devant, être chassé par, le vent.
rack[3], *s. only in the phr.* **to go to r. and ruin,** aller à la ruine; tomber en ruine; (s'en) aller à vau-l'eau; (*of house, etc.*) se délabrer.
rack[4], *s.* **1.** (*a*) *Husb:* râtelier *m* (d'écurie, d'étable); *A:* **to live at r. and manger,** vivre dans l'abondance, *F:* comme un coq en pâte; (*b*) (i) râtelier; casier *m*; (*set of shelves*) étagère *f*; **bottle r.,** casier à bouteilles; porte-bouteilles *m inv* (*s.a.* (ii) *below*); **bicycle r.,** soutien-vélos *m inv*, support *m* pour vélos; **glass r.,** verrier *m*; **hat-and-coat r.,** porte-habits *m inv*, portemanteau *m*, vestiaire *m*; **key r.,** tableau *m* (pour clefs); **letter r.,** porte-lettres *m inv*; **luggage r.,** porte-bagages *m inv*; porte-paquet(s) *m inv*; filet *m* (à bagages); *Aut:* **roof (luggage) r.,** galerie *f* porte-bagages; **music r.,** classeur *m* à musique; **newspaper r.,** porte-journaux *m inv*, porte-revues *m inv*; **paper r.,** classeur à papiers; **pipe r.,** râtelier à pipes; porte-pipes *m inv*; **record r.,** (chevalet *m*) porte-disques *m inv*; **test tube r.,** support d'éprouvettes; **toast r.,** porte-rôties *m inv*, porte-toasts *m inv*; **tool r.,** porte-outils *m inv*; **vegetable r.,** casier, resserre *f*, à légumes; *Av:* **wing, fuselage, r.,** dispositif *m* d'arrimage d'aile, de fuselage; *Mil.Av:* **bomb r.,** lance-bombes *m inv*; *Nau:* **bucket r.,** râtelier à seaux; *Sm.a:* **arm r.,** râtelier d'armes; (ii) **draining r.,** égouttoir *m*; **bottle (draining) r.,** égouttoir à bouteilles; if *m*, hérisson *m*; **plate r., dish r.,** égouttoir; range-assiettes *m inv*; (iii) *Cmptr:* châssis *m*; (*c*) *Husb:* **fruit (drying) r.,** claie *f*, clayette *f*; (*d*) *Mch:* grille *f* (de turbine); (*e*) *Veh:* ridelle *f* (de charrette). **2.** *Mec.E:* crémaillère *f*; **segmental r.,** arc denté; **r. and pinion,** crémaillère (et pignon); **r. (-and-pinion) gearing,** engrenage *m* à crémaillère; *Phot:* **focusing r.,** crémaillère de mise au point; **r. adjustment,** monture *f* à crémaillère; **r. bar,** crémaillère; *Rail:* **r. rail,** crémaillère; **r. (and pinion) railway,** chemin *m* de fer à crémaillère; **r. wheel,** roue dentée, à dents; **r. work,** mécanisme *m* à crémaillère; *Navy: Artil:* **training r.,** circulaire *f* de pointage. **3.** *NAm: F:* **to come up to the r.,** (i) supporter les conséquences de son action; (ii) prendre sa part du fardeau; *F:* y mettre du sien.
rack[5], *v.tr.* **1.** *Husb:* **to r. up a horse,** (i) remplir le râtelier pour un cheval; (ii) attacher un cheval au râtelier. **2.** *Mec.E: etc:* déplacer (le chariot d'un pont roulant, etc.) au moyen de la crémaillère. **3.** mettre (le fruit, etc.) sur les claies, sur les clayettes. **4.** *NAm:* **to r. up a good score,** marquer, faire, un bon nombre de points.
rack[6], *s.* (*a*) *Hist:* chevalet *m* (de torture); **to put, submit, s.o. to the r.,** appliquer la question à qn; mettre qn à la torture, à la question; (*b*) **to be on the r.,** être à la torture; être dans les tourments; être au supplice; être sur des charbons ardents; **to keep s.o. on the r.,** faire mourir qn à petit feu.
rack[7], *v.tr.* **1.** (*a*) *Hist:* faire subir le supplice du chevalet à (qn); (*b*) (*of disease, pain, etc.*) tourmenter, torturer (qn); faire souffrir le martyre à (qn); mettre (qn) à la torture; **the cough seemed to r. his whole frame,** la toux semblait le secouer tout entier; **to r. a machine to pieces,** tourmenter, détraquer, une machine; **the sea racked the ship,** le navire était tourmenté par la mer; (*c*) **to r. one's brains,** se casser la tête (à se rappeler qch.). **2.** (*a*) extorquer (un loyer); pressurer (un locataire); imposer un loyer exorbitant à (un locataire); (*b*) *NAm: P:* engueuler (qn); passer un savon à (qn); savonner (la tête à) qn; (*c*) épuiser (le sol, etc.). **3.** *Leath:* étirer (les peaux).
rack[8], *s. Dist:* arack *m*; **r. punch,** punch *m* à l'arack.
rack[9], *s. Equit:* traquenard *m*; amble rompu.
rack[10], *v.i.* (*of horse*) aller le traquenard; traquenarder.
rack[11], *v.tr.* **to r. (off),** soutirer (le vin, le cidre, pour le séparer du marc).
rack[12], *v.tr.* **1.** *Nau:* genoper, brider (deux cordages). **2. to r. down,** guinder, brêler (les planches d'un pont); brider (une charge, etc.).
racker[1] ['rækər], *s.* **1.** (*a*) *Hist:* bourreau *m*; (*b*) *F:* **a real brain r.,** un vrai casse-tête. **2.** *Leath:* étireur, -euse (de peaux).
racker[2], *s. Equit:* cheval *m*, -aux, qui va le traquenard; traquenard *m*.
racket[1] ['rækit], *s.* **1.** (*a*) raquette *f* (de tennis, etc.); **r. press,** presse-raquette *m*, *pl.* presse-raquettes; (*b*) *pl.* (*usu. with sg.const.*) *Games:* **rackets,** rackets *m*. **2.** raquette (pour la marche sur la neige).
racket[2], *s. F:* **1.** (*a*) fracas *m*, tapage *m*, vacarme *m*; tintamarre *m*, boucan *m*; **to kick up a r.,** faire du boucan; faire les cent (dix-neuf), les quatre cents, coups; **to kick up an infernal r., no end of a r.,** faire un bruit infernal; faire un charivari, un bacchanal, un sabbat, de tous les diables; (*b*) **to stand the r.,** (i) subir les conséquences; payer les pots cassés; (ii) affronter la critique, la tempête; (iii) subvenir aux dépenses; **I'll have to stand the r.,** tout ça retombera sur moi; **the new manager won't be able to stand the r.,** le nouveau gérant ne tiendra pas le coup; **the r. of modern life,** la tension de la vie moderne. **2.** *O:* gaieté tapageuse; dissipation *f*; vie mouvementée; **to go on the r.,** (i) s'adonner au plaisir; (ii) tirer une bordée; faire la bombe, la noce; **to be on the r.,** être en bombe, en bordée. **3.** (*a*) (i) métier *m*, genre *m* d'affaires, spécialité *f* (d'un escroc, gangster); **the blackmail r.,** l'escroquerie *f* au chantage; (ii) métier (légitime); **what's his r.?** quel est son métier, son boulot? **he's got a cushy r.,** il l'a pépère; (*b*) entreprise *f* de gangsters; coup *m*; combine *f* louche; racket *m*; affaire véreuse; **do you want to be in on this r.?** voulez-vous être de la bande? (*c*) supercherie *f*; **it's a r.,** c'est une escroquerie, du vol; **the South Sea Bubble r.,** l'affaire *f* des Mers du Sud.
racket[3], *v.i. F: O:* **1. to r. (about),** faire du tapage, du boucan. **2.** faire la vie, la noce; faire la bombe.
racketeer[1] [ræki'tiər], *s.* gangster *m*; combinard *m*; racketter *m*, racketteur *m*.
racketeer[2], *v.i.* faire du gangstérisme.
racketeering [ræki'tiəriŋ], *s.* escroquerie *f*; gangstérisme *m*.
rackety ['rækiti], *a. F:* **1.** tapageur, bruyant; charivarique. **2.** *O:* noceur, coureur; qui fait la vie; **to lead a r. life,** mener une vie de bâton de chaise; mener une vie de patachon, de fêtard; faire la noce, la bombe.
racking[1] ['rækiŋ], *a.* **1.** (*of pain, etc.*) atroce, déchirant; **r. headache,** mal de tête fou; **r. toothache,** rage *f* de dents. **2.** (impôt, loyer) exorbitant.
racking[2], *s.* **1.** *Hist:* supplice *m* du chevalet. **2.** *Leath:* étirage *m* (des peaux); **second r.,** retenage *m*.
racking[3], *a. Equit:* **r. gait, pace,** amble rompu; traquenard *m*; **r. horse,** traquenard.
racking[4], *s. Dist:* soutirage *m*.
racking[5], *s.* **1.** *Nau:* genope *f*, bridure *f*. **2.** brêlage *m* (des planches d'un pont); bridage *m* (d'une charge).
racking[6], *s. Const:* empattement *m* (de mur) à gradins; déliaison *f*; **r. (effect),** effet *m* de déliaison transversale.
rack-lash ['rækla̧ʃ], *v.tr. Mil.E: etc:* guinder, brêler (les planches d'un pont); brider (une charge).
rack-lashing ['ræk'læʃiŋ], *s.* guindage *m*, brêlage *m* (d'un pont de bateaux); bridage *m* (d'une charge).
rack rent[1] ['rækrent], *s.* loyer excessif, exorbitant; loyer porté au maximum.
rack-rent[2], *v.tr.* **1.** louer (une propriété) à un loyer exorbitant. **2.** extorquer un loyer exorbitant à (qn).
rack renter ['rækrentər], *s.* **1.** propriétaire *mf* qui extorque des loyers exorbitants. **2.** locataire *mf* qui paie un loyer exorbitant.
racon ['reikən], *s.* racon *m*, balise *f* radar.
raconteur, -euse [rækɔn'tə:r, -ə:z], *s.* raconteur, -euse.
racoon [rə'koun], *s. Z:* raton laveur; **crab-eating r.,** crabier *m*.
racquet ['rækit], *s.* = RACKET[1].
racy ['reisi], *a.* **1.** (*a*) (vin) qui a de la race; (*b*) (*of character, etc.*) **to be r. of the soil,** sentir le terroir. **2.** (*a*) **r. story,** (i) anecdote savoureuse; (ii) anecdote corsée; (*b*) (*of pers., etc.*) vif, piquant, plein de verve; **r. style,** (i) style plein de verve, de mouvement; (ii) style de terroir. **3.** (animal) de race.
rad[1] [ræd], *s. Pol: F: O:* radical *m*, -aux.
rad[2], *s. Rad.-A:* rad *m*.
radar ['reida:r], *s.* radar *m*; **continuous wave r.,** radar à ondes entretenues; **frequency modulated r.,** radar à modulation de fréquence; **diversity r.,** radar diversité; **Doppler r.,** radar Doppler; **pulse r.,** radar à impulsions; **sound r.,** radar acoustique; **airborne, aircraft, r.,** radar de bord, d'avion; **ship(borne) r.,** radar de bord; **airport r.,** radar d'aérodrome; **air-traffic control r.,** radar de contrôle de la circulation aérienne; **approach r.,** radar d'approche; **anticollision r.,** radar anticollision; **terrain avoidance r.,** radar détecteur d'obstacles; **terrain-following r.,** radar de navigation de très basse altitude; **landing r.,** radar d'atterrissage; *Navy:* radar d'appontage; **navigation(al) r.,** radar de navigation; **acquisition r.,** radar d'acquisition, de désignation d'objectif; **locator, locating, r.,** radar de localisation; **search r., surveillance r., watch r.,** radar de détection, de surveillance, de veille; **sideways-looking r.,** radar à balayage latéral; **tracking r.,** radar de poursuite; *Meteor:* **balloon r.,** radar sonde; **weather r.,** radar de météorologie; *F:* radar météo; *Mil:* **plan position indicator r.,** radar panoramique; *Artil:* **gun-laying r.,** radar de pointage, radar pointeur; *Ball:* **homing r.,** radar d'autoguidage; **r. installation, station,** installation *f*, station *f*, radar; **r. data,** renseignements *mpl*, données *fpl*, radar; **r. echo,** écho *m* radar; **r. equation,** équation *f* radar; **r. picture,** image *f* radar; **r. navigation,** navigation *f* au radar; **r. operator,** radariste *mf*; opérateur radar; **r. scan,** balayage *m* radar; *Artil:* **r. gun-layer,** radar de pointage, radar pointeur; **r. bombing,** bombardement *m* au radar; **r. homing,** (i) guidage *m* des missiles par radar; (ii) *Av:* ralliement *m* par radar; **r. camouflage,** protection *f* antiradar; **r.(-) monitored,** contrôlé, dirigé, guidé, par radar; **r.-operated,** actionné, commandé, par radar.
radarscope ['reidə:skoup], *s.* écran *m* (de) radar.
raddle[1] ['rædl], *s.* ocre *f* rouge.
raddle[2], *v.tr.* (*a*) peindre, marquer, à l'ocre; (*b*) farder (grossièrement) (le visage); **raddled old harridan,** vieille mégère mal fardée, au maquillage grossier.
radial[1] ['reidiəl]. **1.** *a.* (*a*) *Mec.E: Mth: etc:* radial, -aux; **r. arm,** bras radial; **r. wires,** câbles radiaux; **r. stones of a well,** pierres radiales d'un puits; **r. drilling machine,** machine à percer radiale; **r. spoke,** rayon droit (de roue de bicyclette, etc.); *I.C.E:* **r. engine,** moteur *m* en étoile; *Veh:* **r. axle,** essieu pivotant, à déplacement radial; *Aut:* **r. (ply) tyre,** pneu radial, à carcasse radiale; *Rail:* **r. truck,** bog(g)ie *m*; *Mec:* **r. force,** force centrifuge, radiale; *Town P:* **r. road,** radiale *f*; (*b*) *Anat:* radial; du radius. **2.** *s.* (*a*) **radials,** *pl.* lignes radiales, réseau radial, lignes de rayonnement; (*b*) *I.C.E:* moteur en étoile; **double-row, twin-row, r.,** moteur en double étoile; **multibank r.,** moteur en étoile à plusieurs rangées de cylindres; (*c*) *Anat:* (muscle, nerf) radial (*m*); (veine, artère) radiale (*f*).
radial[2], *a. Ch:* du radium.
radiale [reidi'a:li], *s. Anat:* os *m* naviculaire.
radialized ['reidiəlaizd], *a.* arrangé radialement, en étoile; radiaire.
radially ['reidiəli], *adv.* radialement.
radian ['reidiən], *s. Mth:* radian(t) *m*.
radiance ['reidiəns], *s.* **1.** rayonnement *m*, éclat *m*, splendeur *f*, lustre *m*; **in the full r. of her beauty,** dans tout l'éclat de sa beauté. **2.** *Ph:* rayonnement, radiation *f*, radiance *f*. **3. r. of glory,** auréole *f* de gloire.
radiancy ['reidiənsi], *s. Lit: Poet:* = RADIANCE 1.
radiant ['reidiənt]. **1.** *a.* (*a*) radiant, rayonnant; **r. heat,** *Ph:* chaleur radiante, chaleur rayonnante; *Med:* chaleur radiante; **r. density,** densité *f* de rayonnement;

r. energy, énergie *f* de rayonnement; **r. point,** point radiant; **r. flux,** flux *m* énergétique; (*b*) (soleil, visage, etc.) radieux; **he was r. with joy,** il rayonnait de joie; **face r. with smiles,** visage souriant et radieux; **r. with youth,** brillant de jeunesse; **r. joy, eyes,** joie rayonnante; yeux rayonnants de joie; (*c*) *Bot:* (stigmate, etc.) rayonnant; (*d*) *Her:* rayonné. **2.** *s.* (*a*) *Ph:* point radiant; foyer lumineux; foyer de rayonnement; (*b*) élément chauffant (de radiateur de gaz, électrique); (*c*) *Astr:* radiant *m.*

radiantly ['reidiəntli], *adv.* d'un air radieux; **r. happy,** rayonnant de joie.

radiary ['reidiəri], *s. Z: A:* radiaire *m.*

Radiata ['reidieitə], *s.pl. Z: A:* radiaires *m*, rayonnés *m.*

radiate[1] ['reidiət], **radiated** [reidi'eitid], *a.* **1.** *Nat.Hist: etc:* radié, rayonné; *Bot:* (composée) à fleurs rayonnantes. **2.** *Her:* **radiate crown,** couronne rayonnée, à l'antique.

radiate[2] ['reidieit]. **1.** *v.i.* rayonner, irradier; (*a*) jeter, émettre, des rayons; **the heat that radiates from the sun,** la chaleur qui irradie du soleil; **happiness radiates from her eyes,** ses yeux sont rayonnants de bonheur; le bonheur brille dans ses yeux; (*b*) (*of lines, roads, etc.*) partir d'un même centre; **six avenues r. from the square,** six avenues rayonnent, forment une étoile, autour de la place. **2.** *v.tr.* (*a*) émettre, radier, dégager (de la chaleur, de la lumière); **orator who radiates enthusiasm,** orateur qui dégage l'enthousiasme; **she radiates happiness wherever she goes,** elle répand le bonheur partout où elle va; (*b*) *W.Tel:* émettre, (radio)diffuser, transmettre (un programme); **radiated field,** champ rayonné; **radiated power,** puissance émise, rayonnée.

radiating[1] ['reidieitiŋ], *a.* **1.** radiant, rayonnant; **r. surface,** (i) (*of heater*) surface *f* de chauffe; (ii) (*of cooler*) surface de refroidissement. **2.** radié, rayonné, rayonnant, radiaire; *Bot:* **r. umbel,** ombelle rayonnante.

radiating[2], *s.* radiation *f*, rayonnement *m*; **r. capacity,** pouvoir rayonnant, radiant (d'une source de lumière, etc.).

radiation [reidi'eiʃ(ə)n], *s.* **1.** irradiation *f*, rayonnement *m*; **r. of light,** rayonnement lumineux. **2.** *Ph: etc:* radiation *f*, rayonnement; **caloric, heat, thermal, r.,** radiation, rayonnement, thermique; **black-body r., Planckian r.,** rayonnement d'un corps noir; **high-level, low-level, r.,** rayonnement de grande, faible, énergie; **scattered r.,** rayonnement diffusé; **perturbing, spurious, stray, r.,** rayonnement parasite; **cosmic r.,** rayonnement, radiation, cosmique; *Ch:* **ionizing, non-ionizing, r.,** radiation ionisante, non-ionisante; rayonnement ionisant, non-ionisant; *Elcs:* **high-frequency r.,** radiation (de) haute fréquence; **Cerenkov r.,** rayonnement de Cerenkov; *W.Tel:* **r. zone,** zone *f* de radiation; *Atom.Ph:* **alpha, beta, gamma, r.,** radiation, rayonnement, alpha, bêta, gamma; **nuclear r.,** rayonnement nucléaire, atomique; **neutron r.,** radiation, rayonnement, neutronique; **initial, residual, induced, r.,** radiations instantanées, résiduelles, induites; rayonnement instantané, résiduel, induit; **r. counter, survey meter,** compteur *m*, indicateur *m*, de radiation; **r. detector, monitor,** détecteur *m* de rayonnements, de radiations; **r. measurement,** mesure *f* des radiations; **r. hazard,** danger *m* des radiations; *Med:* **r. sickness,** troubles dus aux radiations.

radiative ['reidieitiv], *a.* radiatif; *Astr:* **r. equilibrium,** équilibre radiatif; *Atom.Ph:* **r. capture,** capture radiative.

radiator ['reidieitər], *s.* **1.** (*a*) radiateur *m* (pour chauffage); *Fr.C:* calorifère *m*; **hot-water r.,** radiateur à eau chaude; **oil-filled r.,** radiateur à circulation d'huile; **electric r.,** radiateur électrique; (*b*) *I.C.E:* radiateur, refroidisseur *m*; *Av:* **secondary surface r.,** radiateur à lamelles; *Aut:* **fan-cooled r.,** radiateur refroidi par ventilateur; **gilled, ribbed, r.,** radiateur à nervures, à ailettes; **r. cap,** bouchon *m* du radiateur; **r. grille, fender,** protège-radiateur *m inv*; **r. muff,** couvre-radiateur *m*, *pl.* couvre-radiateurs. **2.** *Atom.Ph:* émetteur *m*; **alpha r.,** émetteur alpha. **3.** *W.Tel:* antenne *f* d'émission.

radical ['rædik(ə)l]. **1.** *a.* radical, -aux; (*a*) **a r. error,** une erreur radicale; **to make a r. alteration in sth.,** changer qch. radicalement; **r. principle,** principe fondamental; principe premier; **r. diversity,** diversité radicale, foncière; **r. surgery,** chirurgie radicale; (*b*) aux idées avancées; (opinions) hardies; *Hist:* **the R. party,** le parti radical; les Gauches *m*; (*c*) *Bot:* **r. leaf,** feuille radicale; (*d*) *Ling:* **r. word,** mot radical, primitif; **r. letter,** lettre radicale; (*e*) *Mth:* **r. axis, centre,** axe, centre, radical; **r. sign,** (signe) radical (*m*). **2.** *s.* (*a*) *Pol:* radical, -ale; (*b*) *Ch: Ling: Mth:* radical; (*c*) *Phil:* principe premier, fondamental.

radicalism ['rædikəlizm], *s. Pol:* radicalisme *m.*

radically ['rædik(ə)li], *adv.* radicalement; foncièrement, fondamentalement.

radicant ['rædikənt], **radicating** ['rædikeitiŋ], *a. Bot:* radicant.

radication [rædi'keiʃ(ə)n], *s. Bot:* radication *f.*

radicel ['rædisel], *s. Bot:* radicelle *f.*

radicicolous [rædi'sikələs], *a. Bot:* radicicole.

radicivorous [rædi'sivərəs], *a. Z:* radicivore.

radicle ['rædikl], *s.* **1.** *Bot:* (*a*) radicule *f* (de l'embryon, d'une bryophyte); (*b*) radicelle *f*; petite racine. **2.** *Ch:* radical *m*, -aux.

radicular [ræ'dikjulər], *a. Bot:* radiculaire.

radiculitis [rædikju'laitis], *a. Med:* radiculite *f.*

radiculose [ræ'dikjulous], *a. Bot:* (*of bryophyte*) radiculeux.

radiesthesia [reidiis'θi:ziə], *s.* radiesthésie *f.*

radiesthesist [reidiis'θi:zist], *s.* radiesthésiste *mf*; sourcier, -ière.

radiferous [rei'difərəs], *a. Miner:* radifère.

radio[1] ['reidiou], *s.* **1.** (*a*) *W.Tel:* la radio(télégraphie); **r. communication,** liaison(s) *f*(*pl.*) radio(électrique(s)); télécommunications *fpl*; radiocommunications *fpl*; **r. waves,** ondes radioélectriques, hertziennes; ondes radio; **r. link,** câble, faisceau, radiotéléphonique, hertzien; **r. relay system,** réseau hertzien; **r. relay set,** station *f* relais de câble hertzien; **r. bearing, fix,** relèvement *m* radio(goniométrique); **r. bearing station,** poste *m*, station, de relèvement, radiogoniométrique; **r. aid,** moyen *m*, aide *f*, radio(goniométrique); **r. control,** radioguidage *m*, radiocommande *f*, téléguidage *m*; **r. flying,** radionavigation *f*; **r. guidance,** radioguidage *m*; **r. channel,** canal *m*, -aux, de radiocommunication; bande *f* de fréquences; **r. beam,** faisceau dirigé; *Av: Ball:* faisceau de guidage; **r. conductor,** radioconducteur *m*; cohéreur *m*; **r. receiver,** radiorécepteur *m*; récepteur *m* radio; **r. set,** appareil *m* radio, poste radio; **r. transmitter,** (poste) émetteur *m* radio; **r. station,** poste (i) radiotélégraphique, (ii) radiophonique; **r. amateur,** radio(-)amateur *m*; **r. specialist, technician, electrician,** radioélectricien, -ienne; **r. engineer,** ingénieur radio(électricien); **r. engineering,** technique *f* radio(électrique); radiotechnique *f*; **r. operator,** (opérateur *m* de) radio *m*; opérateur de T.S.F.; radiotélégraphiste *mf*; **r. officer,** officier radio; **r. call,** appel *m* radio; **r. car,** voiture-radio *f*, *pl.* voitures-radio; **r. taxi,** radio-taxi, *m*, *pl.* radio-taxis; **r. compass,** radiocompas *m*; **r. interferometer,** radio-interféromètre *m*, *pl.* radio-interféromètres; **r. telescope,** radio-télescope *m*, *pl.* radio-télescopes; *Nau:* **r. room,** poste radio, central *m*, -aux, radio, de bord; **r. watch,** (service *m* de) veille *f* radio; (service d')écoute *f* radio; (*b*) **r. (set),** (poste de) radio; radiorécepteur; **table, portable, r.,** poste portatif; **A.C.-D.C. r.,** radio tous courants; (*c*) **r. broadcasting,** radiodiffusion *f*; radio(phonie) *f*; **the French r.,** la radiodiffusion française; **R. Moscow,** Radio Moscou; **he was on the r. last night,** il a parlé, passé, à la radio hier soir; **r. announcement,** annonce *f* radiophonique; annonce à la radio; **r. advertising,** publicité *f* radiophonique; radiopublicité *f*; publicité à la radio; **r. news (bulletin),** radio-journal *m*; **r. play,** pièce *f* radiophonique; **r. theatre,** radiothéâtre *m*; **r. serial,** radioroman *m*. **2.** *Med:* (i) radiographie *f*; (ii) radiologie *f.*

radio[2], *v.tr.* **1.** envoyer (un message) par la radio; radiotélégraphier (un message); **to r. (to) s.o.,** radiotélégraphier à qn. **2.** *Med:* radiographier (qn).

radio- ['reidiou, reidi'ɔ, 'reidiə], *comb.fm. Anat: Ph: Med:* radio-.

radioacoustics [reidiouə'koustiks], *s.pl.* (*usu. with sg.const.*) acoustique *f* radiophonique.

radioactinium [reidiouæk'tiniəm], *s. Ch:* radioactinium *m.*

radioactivate [reidiou'æktiveit], *v.tr. Atom.Ph:* (radio)activer.

radioactivation [reidiouækti'veiʃ(ə)n], *s.* radioactivation *f.*

radioactive [reidiou'æktiv], *a.* radioactif; **r. body,** corps radioactif; radiocorps *m*; **r. constant,** constante radioactive, de désintégration; **r. equilibrium,** équilibre radioactif; **r. material,** matière radioactive; **r. series,** famille, série, radioactive; **r. waste,** déchets radioactifs.

radioactivity [reidiouæk'tiviti], *s.* radioactivité *f*; **airborne r.,** radioactivité dans l'air; **environmental r.,** radioactivité ambiante; **r. detection,** détection *f* de la radioactivité; **r. meter,** radioactivimètre *m*; **r. monitor,** détecteur *m* de radioactivité; **r. standard,** étalon radioactif.

radioaltimeter [reidiou'æltimitər], *s.* radioaltimètre *m*, radiosonde *f.*

radio astronomer [reidiouəs'trɔnəmər], *s.* radioastronome *m.*

radio astronomy [reidiouəs'trɔnəmi], *s.* radioastronomie *f.*

radiobiological [reidioubaiə'lɔdʒik(ə)l], *a.* radiobiologique.

radiobiology [reidioubai'ɔlədʒi], *s.* radiobiologie *f.*

radiocalcium [reidiou'kælsiəm], *s.* calcium radioactif.

radiocarbon [reidiou'kɑ:bən], *s.* radiocarbone *m*; **r. dating,** datation *f* par radiocarbone.

radio-carpal [reidiou'kɑ:p(ə)l], *a. Anat:* radiocarpien.

radiochemical [reidiou'kemik(ə)l], *a.* radiochimique.

radiochemist [reidiou'kemist], *s.* radiochimiste *mf.*

radiochemistry [reidiou'kemistri], *s.* chimie radioactive; radiochimie *f.*

radiochronologist [reidioukrə'nɔlədʒist], *s.* expert *m* en datation par radiocarbone.

radiocinematographic [reidiousinimætə'græfik], *a.* radiocinématographique.

radiocinematography [reidiousinimə'tɔgrəfi], *s.* radiocinématographie *f.*

radiocobalt [reidiou'koubɔ:lt], *s.* radiocobalt *m*, cobalt radioactif.

radiocolloid [reidiou'kɔlɔid], *s.* radiocolloïde *m.*

radio-control [reidioukən'troul], *v.tr.* radioguider, radiocommander, téléguider; **radio-controlled,** (atterrissage) radioguidé; (missile) radioguidé, téléguidé; *Mil:* **radio-controlled mine,** mine télécommandée.

radiodensity [reidiou'densiti], *s. Ph:* radio-opacité *f*, *pl.* radio-opacités.

radiodermatitis [reidioudə:mə'taitis], *s. Med:* radiodermite *f.*

radiodetection [reidioudi'tekʃ(ə)n], *s.* radiodétection *f.*

radiodetector [reidioudi'tektər], *s.* radiodétecteur *m.*

radiodiagnosis [reidioudaiəg'nousis], *s. Med:* radiodiagnostic *m.*

radiodiascopy [reidioudai'æskəpi], *s.* radiodiascopie *f.*

radiodontia [reidiou'dɔnʃiə], *s.*, **radiodontics** [reidiou'dɔntiks], *s.pl.* (*usu. with sg. const.*) radiologie *f* dentaire.

radiodontist [reidiou'dɔntist], *s.* spécialiste *mf* en radiologie dentaire.

radioecology [reidioui'kɔlədʒi], *s.* radioécologie *f.*

radioelectric [reidioui'lektrik], *a.* radioélectrique.

radioelectricity [reidiouilek'trisiti], *s.* radioélectricité *f.*

radioelement [reidiou'elimənt], *s. Atom.Ph:* radioélément *m.*

radiofluorine [reidiou'fluə:ri:n], *s.* fluor radioactif.

radiofrequency ['reidiou'fri:kwənsi], *s.* radiofréquence *f*; fréquence *f* radioélectrique; **r. amplifier, circuit, current, field, etc.,** amplificateur *m*, circuit *m*, courant *m*, champ *m*, etc., haute fréquence; **r. keying,** manipulation *f* dans la haute fréquence; **r. resistance,** résistance *f* en haute fréquence; *Med:* **r. treatment,** arsonvalisation *f.*

radiogene ['reidiədʒi:n], *s. Med:* appareil *m* radiogène.

radiogenic [reidiə'dʒenik], *a.* **1.** (appareil, etc.) radiogène. **2.** *W.Tel:* (personne, etc.) radiogénique, qui rend bien à la radio.

radiogoniometer [reidiougouni'ɔmitər], *s. W.Tel:* radiogoniomètre *m.*

radiogoniometric(al) [reidiougouniou'metrik(l)], *a.* radiogoniométrique.

radiogoniometry [reidiougouni'ɔmitri], *s.* radiogoniométrie *f.*

radiogram ['reidiəgræm], *s.* **1.** *W.Tel:* radiogramme *m*; *F:* radio *m*. **2.** *Med:* = RADIOGRAPH[1]. **3.** (*also* **radiogramophone** ['reidiou'græməfoun]) combiné *m* (radio-électrophone, radio-pick-up).

radiograph[1] ['reidiougræf], *s. Med: etc:* radiogramme *m*, skiagramme *m*, radiographie *f.*

radiograph[2], *v.tr. Med: etc:* radiographier.

radiographer [reidi'ɔgrəfər], *s. Med: etc:* technicien, -ienne, assistant(e) d'un radiologue; manipulateur, -trice, radiographe.

radiographic [reidiou'græfik], *a.* radiographique.

radiography [reidi'ɔgrəfi], *s.* **1.** *Med:* radiographie *f*, skiagraphie *f*; *F:* radio *f*; **flash r.,** radiographie éclair; **mass r.,** radiographie collective; **follow-up r.,** radiographie de contrôle. **2.** radiotélégraphie *f.*

radiohumeral [reidiou'hju:mər(ə)l], *a. Anat:* radiohuméral, -aux.

radio-iodine [reidiou'aiədi:n], *s. Ch:* radio-iode *m.*

radioisomer [reidiou'aisəmər], *s. Ch:* radioisomère *m.*

radioisotope [reidiou'aisətoup], *s.* radioisotope *m*; isotope radioactif; **r. concentration,** concentration *f* radioisotopique; **r. production,** production *f* de radioisotopes.

Radiolaria [reidiou'lɛəriə], *s. pl. Prot:* radiolaires *m.*

radiolarian [reidiou'lɛəriən], *a. & s. Prot:* radiolaire (*m*);

Geol: **r. ooze,** vase *f* à radiolaires; **r. cherts,** radiolarites *f.*
radiolarite [reidiou'lɛərait], *s. Geol:* radiolarite *f.*
radiole ['reidioul], *s. Echin:* radiole *f,* piquant *m* (d'oursin).
radiolite[1] ['reidioulait], *s. Moll:* radiolite *m.*
radiolite[2], *s. Miner:* radiolite *f.*
radiolocation ['reidioulou'keiʃ(ə)n], *s.* radiorepérage *m;* radiolocation *f,* radiolocalisation *f.*
radiological [reidiou'lɔdʒikl], *a. Med: etc:* radiologique; *Mil:* **r. warfare,** guerre *f* radiologique.
radiologist [reidi'ɔlədʒist], *s. Med:* radiologue *mf,* radiologiste *mf.*
radiology [reidi'ɔlədʒi], *s. Med:* radiologie *f.*
radiolucency [reidiou'lu:s(ə)nsi], *s. Ph:* radiotransparence *f.*
radiolucent [reidiou'lu:s(ə)nt], *a. Ph:* radioclair, radiotransparent.
radioluminescence [reidioulu:min'es(ə)ns], *s. Ph:* radioluminescence *f.*
radioluminescent [reidioulu:min'es(ə)nt], *a.* radioluminescent.
radiolysis [reidi'ɔlisis], *s. Ch:* radiolyse *f.*
radioman, *pl.* **-men** ['reidiouman], *s.m. NAm:* (*a*) *W.Tel:* opérateur; (*b*) employé d'une compagnie de radiodiffusion; (*c*) employé utilisant une voiture munie de radio pour détecter les défauts des installations électriques.
radiometallography [reidioumetə'lɔgrəfi], *s.* radiométallographie *f.*
radiometer [reidi'ɔmitər], *s. Ph:* radiomètre *m.*
radiometric [reidiou'metrik], *a.* radiométrique.
radiometry [reidi'ɔmitri], *s. Ph:* radiométrie *f.*
radiomicrograph [reidiou'maikrəgræf], *s.* microradiographie *f.*
radiomicrographic [reidioumaikrə'græfik], *a.* microradiographique.
radiomicrography [reidioumai'krɔgrəfi], *s.* (la) microradiographie.
radiomicrometer [reidioumai'krɔmitər], *s.* radiomicromètre *m.*
radiomuscular [reidiou'mʌskjulər], *a. Anat:* radiomusculaire.
radiomutation [reidioumju'teiʃ(ə)n], *s.* radiomutation *f.*
radionecrosis [reidioune'krousis], *s. Med:* radionécrose *f.*
radionuclide [reidiou'nju:klaid], *s.* radionucl(é)ide *m.*
radiopacity [reidiou'pæsiti], *s.* radio-opacité *f.*
radiopaque [reidiou'peik], *a.* radio-opaque.
radiopathology [reidioupə'θɔlədʒi], *s.* radiopathologie *f.*
radiophare [reidioufɑ:r], *s. W.Tel:* radiophare *m.*
radiopharmaceutical [reidioufɑ:mə'sju:tikl], *s.* produit pharmaceutique radioactif.
radiophone ['reidioufoun], *s. Ph: etc:* radio(télé)phone *m.*
radiophonic [reidiə'fɔnik], *a.* radio(télé)phonique.
radiophony [reidi'ɔfəni], *s.* radio(télé)phonie *f.*
radiophosphorus [reidiou'fɔsfərəs], *s. Ch:* radiophosphore *m.*
radiophoto(graph) [reidiou'foutou(græf)], *s.* **1.** *Med:* radiophotographie *f, F:* radiophoto *f.* **2.** photographie transmise par la radio.
radioprotection [reidioupra'tekʃ(ə)n], *s.* radioprotection *f.*
radioprotective [reidiouprə'tektiv], *a.* (écran, etc.) de radioprotection.
radio-range [reidiou'reindʒ], *a.* **r.-r. beacon,** radiophare directionnel, à alignement fixe; radioborne *f;* **r.-r. leg, beam,** faisceau *m* de radioalignement; **r.-r. transmitter,** émetteur *m* de radioalignement; **r.-r. airway,** radioalignement *m;* **r.-r. navigation,** navigation *f* par radioalignement.
radioresistance [reidiouri'zistəns], *s. Ph:* résistance *f* à la radiation, aux radiations.
radioresistant [reidiouri'zistənt], *a. Ph:* résistant à la radiation, aux radiations.
radioscope ['reidiəskoup], *s.* radioscope *m.*
radioscopic [reidiou'skɔpik], *a. Med: etc:* radioscopique.
radioscopy [reidi'ɔskəpi], *s. Med: etc:* radioscopie *f.*
radiosensitive [reidiou'sensitiv], *a. Biol: Med:* radiosensible; *Med:* radiolabile.
radiosensitivity [reidiousensi'tiviti], *s.* radiosensibilité *f.*
radiosensitize [reidiou'sensitaiz], *v.tr. Med:* rendre (un cancer, etc.) radiosensible.
radiosodium [reidiou'soudiəm], *s. Ch:* radiosodium *m;* sodium radioactif.
radiosondage [reidiou'sɔndɑ:ʒ], *s. Meteor:* radiosondage *m.*
radiosonde [reidiou'sɔnd], *s. Meteor:* radiosonde *f.*
radiostereoscopy [reidioustiəri'ɔskəpi], *s.* radiostéréoscopie *f.*
radiostrontium [reidiou'strɔntiəm], *s. Ch:* radiostrontium *m,* strontium radioactif.
radiosymmetrical [reidiousi'metrikl], *a. Bot:* symétrique par rapport à un axe actinomorphe.
radiotechnology [reidioutek'nɔlədʒi], *s.* radiotechnique *f.*
radiotelegram [reidiou'teligræm], *s.* radiotélégramme *m,* radiogramme *m; F:* radio *m.*
radiotelegraph [reidiou'teligræf], *s.* appareil *m* de radiotélégraphie *f.*
radiotelegraphic [reidiouteli'græfik], *a.* radiotélégraphique.
radiotelegraphist [reidiouti'legrəfist], *s.* radiotélégraphiste *mf; F:* radio *m.*
radiotelegraphy [reidiouti'legrəfi], *s.* radiotélégraphie *f;* radio *f.*
radiotelephone[1] [reidiou'telifoun], *s.* radiotéléphone *m.*
radiotelephone[2], *v.tr. & i.* radiotéléphoner.
radiotelephony [reidiouti'lefəni], *s.* radiotéléphonie *f;* téléphonie *f* sans fil; T.S.F. *f.*
radioteletype [reidiou'telitaip], *s.* radiotéléimprimeur *m.*
radiotherapeutic [reidiouθerə'pju:tik], *Med:* **1.** *a.* radiothérapique. **2.** *s.pl.* (*usu. with sg. const.*) **radiotherapeutics,** radiothérapie *f.*
radiotherapeutist [reidiouθerə'pju:tist], **radiotherapist** [reidiou'θerəpist], *s.* radiothérapeute *mf.*
radiotherapic [reidiou'θerəpik], *a.* radiothérapique.
radiotherapy [reidiou'θerəpi], *s.* radiothérapie *f.*
radiothermics [reidiou'θə:miks], *s.pl.* (*usu. with sg. const.*) *El:* chauffage *m* haute fréquence.
radiothermy [reidiou'θə:mi], *s. El:* diathermie *f* haute fréquence.
radiothorium [reidiou'θɔ:riəm], *s. Ch:* radiothorium *m.*
radiotoxicity [reidioutɔk'sisiti], *s.* radiotoxicité *f.*
radiotoxicology [reidioutɔksi'kɔlədʒi], *s.* radiotoxicologie *f.*
radiotracer [reidiou'treisər], *s. Atom.Ph:* radiotraceur *m,* traceur radioactif.
radiotranslucency [reidioutrænz'lu:sənsi], *s. Ph:* radiotranslucence *f.*
radiotransparent [reidioutræns'pærənt], *a.* transparent aux rayons X.
radiotropism [reidi'ɔtrəpizm], *s. Ph:* radiotropisme *m.*
radish ['rædiʃ], *s.* radis *m;* **r. dish,** ravier *m.*
radium ['reidiəm], *s. Ch:* radium *m;* **r. paint,** incrustation *f* de radium; *Med:* **r. treatment,** radiumthérapie *f; Ph:* **r. emanation,** émanation *f* du radium; radon *m.*
radiumize ['reidiəmaiz], *v.tr. Med:* traiter (un cancer, etc.) au radium.
radiumtherapist [reidiəm'θerəpist], *s. Med:* radiumthérapeute *m.*
radiumtherapy [reidiəm'θerəpi], *s.* radiumthérapie *f;* curiethérapie *f.*
radius, *pl.* **-ii** ['reidiəs, -iai], *s.* **1.** rayon *m;* (*a*) *Mth:* **r. of a circle,** rayon de cercle; **r. of curvature,** rayon de courbure; **r. vector,** rayon vecteur; *Ph:* **r. of gyration,** rayon de giration; (*b*) **r. of a crane jib,** portée *f* d'une grue; *Aut:* **steering, turning, r.,** rayon de courbure, de braquage; **r. of action of an aircraft, a submarine, etc.,** rayon d'action, autonomie *f,* d'un avion, sous-marin, etc.; *Av: etc:* **cruising r.,** rayon d'action, autonomie, à vitesse économique; **within a r. of ten miles of Dover,** dans un rayon de dix milles autour de Douvres; (*c*) *attrib. Mec.E: etc:* **r. arm, link, rod,** (i) bielle *f,* tringle *f,* de poussée; (ii) tendeur *m,* jambe *f* de force; *Av:* bielle de relevage, contrefiche articulée (du train d'atterrissage); **r. bar,** (i) tige *f* de parallélogramme; (ii) *Mch:* bielle du tiroir; (iii) *Nau: Surv:* alidade *f.* **2.** *Anat:* radius *m* (de l'avant-bras); *Ent:* radius (de l'aile). **3.** *Bot:* rayon (de fleur composée, etc.).
radix, *pl.* **-ices** ['reidiks, -isi:z], *s.* **1.** *Mth:* base *f* (d'un système de logarithmes, etc.); *Cmptr:* **diminished r. complement, r. minus one complement,** complément restreint, complément à base diminuée (de un); **mixed r. notation,** numération *f* à base multiple, à plusieurs bases; **r. notation,** indication *f* de la base; **r. point,** emplacement *m* de la virgule. **2.** racine *f,* source *f* (d'un mal).
radome ['reidoum], *s. Av:* radôme *m;* carter *m* d'antenne de radar.
radon ['reidɔn], *s. Atom.Ph:* radon *m;* émanation *f* du radium.
radula, *pl.* **-ae** ['rædjulə, -i:], *s. Moll:* radula *f,* radule *f.*
raffia ['ræfiə], *s. Bot:* raphia *m;* **r. mat,** carpette *f* en raphia.
raffinate ['ræfineit], *s. Ch: Ind:* produit *m* de raffinage.
raffinose ['ræfinous], *s. Ch:* raffinose *m.*
raffish ['ræfiʃ], *a.* bravache, esbrouffeur; (air, etc.) de casseur d'assiettes.
raffishly ['ræfiʃli], *adv.* d'un air bravache, de casseur d'assiettes.
raffle[1] ['ræfl], *s.* loterie *f* (pour une œuvre de bienfaisance, etc.).
raffle[2]. **1.** *v.tr.* mettre (qch.) en loterie. **2.** *v.i.* prendre part à une loterie; prendre un billet (**for sth.,** pour qch.).
raffle[3], *s.* **1.** rebut *m;* fatras *m.* **2.** *A:* lie *f* (du peuple).
rafflesia [ræ'fli:ziə], *s. Bot:* rafflesia *m,* rafflésie *f.*
Rafflesiaceae [ræflizi:eisii:], *s.pl. Bot:* rafflésiacées *f.*
raffling ['ræfliŋ], *s.* **1.** mise *f* en loterie (**of,** de). **2.** **r. is controlled by law,** les loteries sont réglementées.
raft[1] [rɑ:ft], *s.* **1.** radeau *m;* (**inflatable, rubber**), **life r.,** radeau (pneumatique) de sauvetage; **emergency r.,** radeau de fortune; *Mil:* **bridge r.,** radeau, portière *f,* de pont; **r. bridge,** pont flottant, sur portières; **pontoon r.,** bac *m* à ponton; *Nau:* **repairing r.,** ras *m* de carène; **r. port,** sabord *m* de charge. **2.** (*a*) (**timber**) **r.,** *NAm:* **lumber r.,** train *m* de bois, de flottage; accolure *f;* **r. wood,** bois flotté; bois de flottage; (*b*) masse flottante (de glace, etc.); grand assemblement (d'oiseaux aquatiques) sur l'eau; (*c*) *NAm: F:* grand nombre (de choses); **there are rafts of it,** il y en a des tas. **3.** *Const:* **foundation r.,** radier *m;* châssis *m* de fondation.
raft[2]. **1.** *v.tr.* (*a*) transporter (des marchandises, etc.) sur un radeau; (*b*) faire un radeau avec (des rondins); (*c*) passer (une rivière, etc.) sur un radeau. **2.** *v.i.* (*a*) **to r. across the river, down the river,** traverser, descendre, le fleuve sur un radeau; (*b*) *esp. NAm:* (*of river ice*) s'amasser, s'amonceler.
rafter[1] ['rɑ:ftər], *s.* **1.** *Const:* (**common**) **r.,** chevron *m* (d'un comble); **main r.,** arbalétrier *m;* **jack r.,** empannon *m;* chevron de croupe; **valley r.,** arêtier *m* de noue; **the rafters of a roof,** le chevronnage d'un comble. **2.** *Orn:* **r. (bird),** gobe-mouches *m inv* gris.
rafter[2], *v.tr.* **1.** chevronner (un comble). **2.** *Agr:* labourer (un champ) en billes.
rafter[3], *s.* = RAFTSMAN.
raftered ['rɑ:ftəd], *a.* à chevrons.
raftering ['rɑ:ftəriŋ], *s.* **1.** *Const:* chevronnage *m.* **2.** *Agr:* labour *m* en billons.
rafting ['rɑ:ftiŋ], *s.* flottage *m* (de bois) en trains.
raft(s)man, *pl.* **-men** ['rɑ:ft(s)mən], *s.m. NAm:* flotteur (de bois); voiturier par eau; radeleur, radelier.
rag[1] [ræg], *s.* **1.** chiffon *m;* lambeau *m;* **to clean sth. with a r.,** nettoyer qch. avec un chiffon; **my dress looks like a r.,** ma robe est toute en tapon; *O:* **I feel like a r.,** je me sens (mou) comme une chiffe; je suis comme une loque; **with every r. of sail set,** couvert de toile; avec tout dessus; **to tear sth. to rags,** mettre qch. en lambeaux; **my dress is worn to rags,** ma robe tombe en lambeaux; **meat cooked to rags,** viande réduite en bouillie, en lambeaux (à force de cuire); viande cuite et recuite; *Meteor:* **flying rags of cloud,** diablotins *m;* **r. baby, doll,** poupée *f* en chiffons, en étoffe; **r. book,** livre d'images imprimé sur toile (pour jeunes enfants); **r. collector, gatherer, picker,** chiffonnier, -ière; **r. picking,** ramassage *m,* collectage *m,* de chiffons; *A:* chiffonnerie *f;* **r.-picking trade,** commerce *m* des chiffons; *F:* chiffe *f.* **2.** (*a*) *pl.* **rags (and tatters),** haillons *m,* guenilles *f,* loques *f;* **to be in rags,** être en guenilles, en haillons; être dépenaillé, déguenillé; **all in rags and tatters,** tout déguenillé, tout en loques; **to rise from rags to riches,** faire son chemin de la pauvreté à la richesse; (*b*) **r. fair,** marché *m* aux vieux habits; *F:* marché aux puces; *F:* **the r. trade,** le commerce de confection. **3.** *Com: Paperm:* **rag(s),** chiffons, drilles *f;* peilles *f;* **r. merchant,** marchand *m* de chiffons, chiffonnier *m,* en gros; peill(i)er, -ère; peillereau *m; Paperm:* **r. pulp,** pâte *f* de chiffons; **r. paper,** papier *m* de chiffons; **r. picker, sorter,** chiffonnier; trieur, -euse, de chiffons; **r. picking,** triage *m* de chiffons; **r. cutting,** effilochage *m* des chiffons; **r.-cutting machine,** machine *f* à pâte de chiffons; délisseuse *f* mécanique; dérompoir *m;* **r. engine,** pile défileuse. **4.** *F:* (*a*) (*newspaper*) (i) *Pej:* feuille *f* de chou; **I don't read that r.,** je ne lis pas ce canard-là; (ii) **the local r.,** le journal du pays; (*b*) *P:* (**nose**) **r.,** mouchoir *m.* **5.** *P: O:* **to lose one's r.,** se fâcher tout rouge, sortir de ses gonds. **6.** peau blanche (d'une orange, etc.). **7.** *Mus:* (*a*) = RAGTIME; (*b*) morceau *m* de musique dans le style du *ragtime.* **8.** *Metalw:* barbe *f,* bavure *f;* **r. bolt,** boulon *m* de scellement à crans; boulon barbelé; cheville barbelée.
rag[2], *s. Sch: F:* **1.** brimade *f,* mauvais tour; farce *f.* **2.** chahut *m;* bacchanal *m* (*no pl.*); **students' r.** (i) canular *m;* (ii) carnaval *m, pl.* -als (surtout pour œuvre de charité); **it was only a r.,** c'était les étudiants qui s'amusaient.
rag[3], *v.tr.* (**ragged**) *F:* **1.** brimer, faire des brimades à (un camarade). **2.** chahuter (un professeur, etc.);

monter une scie à (un professeur); taquiner, faire endêver, faire endiabler (qn); asticoter (qn); chambarder les effets (d'un étudiant); *v.i.* chahuter, bahuter; faire du chahut. **3.** *A:* gronder, tancer (qn).

rag[4], *s.* **1.** *Geol:* calcaire *m* oolithique. **2.** *Const:* forte ardoise (de toiture).

ragamuffin ['rægəmʌfin], *s.* **1.** (*a*) gueux *m*; va-nu-pieds *m inv*; loqueteux, -euse; (*b*) mauvais garnement. **2.** gamin *m* des rues; **a little r., a young r.,** un petit déguenillé; un petit galopin; **you little r.!** petit polisson!

rag-and-bone ['rægn(d)'boun], *a.* **r.-a.-b. man,** chiffonnier *m*.

ragbag ['rægbæg], *s.* **1.** sac *m* aux chiffons. **2.** femme fagotée, mal attifée.

rage[1] [reidʒ], *s.* **1.** rage *f*, fureur *f*, furie *f*, emportement *m*; **fit of r.,** accès *m* de fureur; déchaînement *m* de colère; **to be in a r.,** être furieux, être en fureur; rager; **to be in a r. with s.o.,** être furieux contre qn; **to get, fly, into a r.,** se mettre en colère; entrer en fureur; s'emporter; **to put s.o. into a r.,** mettre qn en fureur; faire rager qn; **mad with r.,** fou de rage, fou de colère. **2.** fureur, furie (des vents, de la mer, des flammes). **3.** *O:* manie *f*, toquade *f*; **to have a r. for sth.,** être enragé pour qch.; avoir la rage, la manie, de qch.; avoir une toquade pour qch. (*of thg*) **to be (all) the r.,** faire fureur, faire rage; **it's all the r.,** c'est la grande vogue, c'est le grand chic, à l'heure actuelle.

rage[2], *v.i.* **1.** (*of pers.*) **to r. (and fume),** être furieux; rager; être dans une colère bleue; *Lit:* jeter feu et flamme; **to r. against, at, s.o.,** être furieux, tempêter, contre qn. **2.** (*of wind*) faire rage, être furieux; (*of sea*) être en furie; (*of fire, storm*) faire rage; (*of war, epidemic*) sévir, régner; faire des ravages.

ragged ['rægid], *a.* **1.** (*a*) (*of garment, etc.*) en lambeaux, en loques; (*b*) (*of pers.*) en haillons, en guenilles; déguenillé, dépenaillé, loqueteux; (*c*) *Hist:* **r. school,** école communale (des quartiers pauvres). **2.** (*a*) (rocher, nuage) déchiqueté; (rocher) ébréché; (plante) en broussailles; (terrain) raboteux, rocailleux; **r. wound,** plaie mâchée; **r. pencil line,** trait de crayon imprécis; (*b*) **r. sentence,** (i) phrase hachée; (ii) phrase mal faite, sans syntaxe; **r. voice,** voix *f* rude; **work done in a r. fashion,** ouvrage qui manque de fini; (*of crew*) **to row a r. stroke,** manquer d'ensemble; *Mus:* **the execution is r.,** l'exécution manque d'ensemble; *Mil:* **r. fire,** feu désordonné, confus; (*c*) *F:* **to run oneself r.,** s'épuiser; *F:* s'éreinter; (*d*) *Bot:* **r. lady,** cheveux *mpl* de Vénus; **r. robin,** lychnide *f* des prés; œillet *m* des prés; (fleur *f* de) coucou *m*; véronique *f* des jardiniers; véronique amourette; lampette *f*; (*e*) *Her:* **r. staff,** écot *m*.

raggedly ['rægidli], *adv.* **1.** (vêtu) de guenilles, de haillons. **2. the grass grew r.,** l'herbe poussait irrégulièrement; (*of team*) **to play r.,** (*of crew*) **to row r.,** manquer d'ensemble.

raggedness ['rægidnis], *s.* **1.** déguenillement *m*, guenilles *fpl* (de qn); délabrement *m* (d'un vêtement). **2.** (*a*) inégalités *fpl*, rugosités *fpl*; (*b*) inégalité, rudesse *f* (d'un ouvrage, etc.); manque *m* d'ensemble (d'une équipe, d'un orchestre, de l'exécution).

ragger ['rægər], *s.* *F:* **1.** chahuteur *m*. **2.** moqueur *m*; *P:* chineur *m*.

ragging ['rægiŋ], *s.* **1.** brimades *fpl*. **2.** chahutage *m*.

raggle-taggle ['rægltægl], *a.* **1.** (*of pers.*) déguenillé. **2.** (*of thgs*) dépareillé; **r.-t. assortment of old clothes,** ramassis de vieux habits.

raging[1] ['reidʒiŋ], *a.* furieux, en fureur; **r. lion,** lion furieux; **to be in a r. temper,** être furieux; **r. tempest,** tempête furieuse; **r. sea,** mer furieuse, déchaînée, démontée; *Lit:* mer en courroux; **r. fever,** fièvre ardente, brûlante; fièvre de cheval; **r. thirst,** soif ardente; **r. headache,** mal de tête fou, affreux; **r. toothache,** rage *f* de dents.

raging[2], *s.* **1.** rage *f*, fureur *f*, furie *f* (de qn). **2.** fureur, furie (de la mer, de la tempête).

ragingly ['reidʒiŋli], *adv.* avec fureur; furieusement, rageusement.

raglan ['ræglən], *s. & a.* **r. (overcoat),** raglan *m*; **r. sleeves,** manches *f* raglan.

raglanite ['ræglənait], *s.* *Miner:* raglanite *f*.

raglet ['ræglit], *s.* *Plumb:* rainure *f* (dans un mur pour encastrer une lame de plomb).

ragman, *pl.* **-men** ['rægmən], *s.m.* **1.** (*also* **ragpicker**) chiffonnier; *F:* biffin. **2.** (*merchant*) marchand de chiffons; chiffonnier; *Paperm:* peill(i)er, peillereau.

ragout ['rægu:], *s.* *Cu:* ragoût *m*.

ragstone ['rægstoun], *s.* **1.** *Geol:* calcaire *m* oolithique. **2.** *Const:* pierre bourrue; bourru *m*; souchet *m* (de carrière).

ragtag ['rægtæg], *s.* **the r.-t. and bobtail,** la canaille; **what a r.-t. and bobtail show it was!** quelle cohue que cette procession!

ragtime ['rægtaim], *s.* *Mus:* ragtime *m*; *F:* **r. army,** armée indisciplinée; armée pour rire.

raguly ['rægjuli], *a.* *Her:* contre-écoté.

Ragusa [ræ'gu:zə], *Pr.n. Hist:* Raguse *f*.

ragweed ['rægwi:d], *s.* *Bot:* **1.** = RAGWORT. **2.** *NAm:* ambrosie *f*.

ragwheel ['ræg(h)wi:l], *s.* **1.** *Mec.E:* pignon *m* de chaîne; poulie *f* à chaînes; hérisson *m*, bouc *m*. **2.** *Metalw: etc:* disque *m* en drap.

ragworm ['rægwə:m], *s.* *Ann:* néréis *m*, néréide *f*.

ragwort ['rægwə:t], *s.* *Bot:* herbe *f* de saint-Jacques.

rah [rɑ:], *int. U.S:* hourra!

rahat lakoum ['rɑ:hætlə'ku:m], *s.* (rahat-)lo(u)koum *m*.

rah-rah ['rɑ:rɑ:], *a.* *NAm:* (étudiant) enthousiaste (et stupide).

raid[1] [reid], *s.* **1.** (*a*) razzia *f* (de bandits, etc.); **pirate r.,** descente *f* de pirates (sur la côte); **r. on a bank,** attaque *f* d'une banque; *F:* **the children made a r. on the store cupboard,** les enfants ont pillé l'armoire à provisions; (*b*) **police r.,** (i) descente de police (dans une boîte de nuit, etc.); rafle *f* (dans un quartier mal famé, etc.). **2.** (*a*) *Mil: Av: Navy:* raid *m* (**on,** sur, contre); incursion *f*, attaque *f*; *Mil:* coup *m* de main; action *f* de commando; *Av:* **daylight, night, r.,** attaque (aérienne) de jour, de nuit; (*b*) *Fig:* **to make a r. into s.o.'s domain,** faire une incursion dans le domaine de qn. **3. r. on the market,** razzia sur le marché; *St.Exch:* **r. on the bears,** chasse *f* du découvert.

raid[2]. **1.** *v.i.* faire une razzia, des razzias; *Mil:* faire un raid, des raids. **2.** *v.tr.* (*a*) razzier (une tribu, une côte, etc.); (*b*) (*of police*) faire une descente dans (une boîte de nuit, un quartier, etc.); faire une rafle dans (un quartier); (*c*) **to r. orchards,** marauder des fruits dans les vergers; **the children raided the store cupboard,** les enfants ont pillé l'armoire à provisions; (*d*) **to r. a bank,** attaquer une banque; (*e*) **to r. the market,** faire une razzia sur le marché; *St.Exch:* **to r. the bears, the shorts,** (pour)chasser le découvert.

raider ['reidər], *s.* **1.** (*pers.*) (*a*) maraudeur *m*, pillard *m*; **bank r.,** voleur *m* à main armée; (*b*) *Mil:* soldat *m* en razzia; aviateur *m* en, de, raid; (*c*) *Nau: A:* corsaire *m*. **2.** (*a*) avion *m* de, en, raid; *raiders past* **signal,** signal *m* de fin d'alerte; (*b*) *Navy:* navire *m* de course.

rail[1] [reil], *s.* **1.** (*a*) barre *f*, barreau *m* (de barrière, clôture, etc.); barreau, bâton *m* (de chaise); **hat r.,** porte-chapeaux *m inv*; **(post and) r. fence,** clôture *f* à barres horizontales; **r. splitter,** fendeur *m* des bois (pour barreaux); (*b*) barre d'appui; garde-fou *m*, *pl.* garde-fous; parapet *m* (de pont, etc.); balustrade *f* (de balcon); accoudoir *m*, appui *m*, allège *f* (de fenêtre); rampe *f* (d'escalier); **r. post,** potelet *m* (de balustrade, etc.); (*c*) *Veh:* ridelle *f* (de charrette); (*upper*) trésaille *f*; (*d*) *Carp:* (barre de) traverse *f* (d'une porte, etc.); **middle r.,** traverse du milieu. **2. rails,** (*iron*) grille *f*; (*wood*) clôture *f*, palissade *f*, balustrade; *Rac:* **the rails,** la corde; **to have got on the rails,** tenir la corde; (*of horse*) **to be driven on the rails,** être coincé à la corde. **3.** *N.Arch:* (*a*) lisse *f*; garde-corps *m inv*; **to lower the lifeboats to the r.,** amener les embarcations à hauteur de lisse; **rails of the head,** lisses de l'éperon; **over the r.,** par-dessus bord; (*b*) *pl.* bastingages *m* (d'un paquebot); **leaning over the rails,** accoudé aux bastingages. **4.** (*at abattoir*) **killing r.,** chaîne *f* d'abattage. **5.** *Rail: etc:* (*a*) rail *m*; **adhesion r.,** rail à adhérence; **tram r., grooved r.,** rail à gorge, à ornière, creux, plat; **bullhead(ed), double-headed, r.,** rail à double champignon; **flange, flat-bottom(ed), flat-footed, foot, Vignoles, r.,** rail à patin, rail Vignoles; **flat r.,** rail méplat; **sunken r.,** rail noyé; **raised r., edge r.,** rail saillant; **main, line, stock, r.,** (rail) contre(-)aiguille (*m*), *pl.* contre(-)aiguilles; **switch, point, tongue, r.,** lame *f*, rail mobile (d'aiguillage); **safety, check, r.,** contre-rail, *pl.* contre-rails; **crossing r., r. for turn-out,** rail d'évitement; *El.Rail:* **conductor, contact, live, r.,** rail de, du, courant, de contact, conducteur, électrisé, sous tension; **collector, third, r.,** rail de prise de courant; **fourth r.,** rail de retour; **middle r.,** rail central; **r. bond,** câble *m* de liaison (de) rails; railbond *m*; **r. bond tester,** vérificateur *m* de connexions rails; **r. bonding,** railbondage *m*; (*of train*) **to run off, jump, leave, the rails,** dérailler; quitter les rails, sortir des rails; *Fig:* (*of pers.*) **to go off the rails,** (i) dérailler; s'écarter du bon sens; (ii) s'écarter du droit chemin; mener une vie déréglée; **the whole system is off the rails,** tout le système est détraqué; **the train kept the rails,** le train n'a pas déraillé, n'a pas quitté la voie; **r. guard,** chasse-pierres *m inv* (d'une locomotive); **r.-laying machine,** machine à poser les rails; **r. lifter,** relève-rails *m inv*; **r. plate,** serre-rails *m inv*; *El.Rail:* **r. drop,** chute *f* de tension de ligne; *Civ.E: etc:* **r. wheel,** galet *m* de roulement; roue *f* de translation (de pont roulant); (*b*) chemin *m* de fer; voie ferrée; **r. over road, road under r., crossing,** passage *m* en dessous; **road over r. crossing,** passage en dessus; **to travel by r.,** voyager en, par le, chemin de fer; voyager par voie ferrée; **r. transport,** transport *m* par voie ferrée, par fer; **co-ordination of r. and road transport,** coordination *f* du rail et de la route; coordination rail-route; **r. communications,** communications ferroviaires; *Com:* **price on r.,** prix *m* sur le wagon; (*c*) *St.Exch:* **rails,** valeurs *f* de chemins de fer; chemins (de fer).

rail[2]. **1.** *v.tr.* (*a*) **to r. sth. in,** fermer (un jardin, etc.) avec une grille, une palissade; griller, palissader (un enclos, etc.); **to r. sth. round,** entourer (une pelouse, un tombeau, etc.) d'une grille, d'une palissade; **railed off from the road,** séparé de la rue par une grille; (*b*) transporter, envoyer (des marchandises, etc.) par (le) chemin de fer; (*c*) munir (un endroit dangereux, etc.) d'un garde-fou, d'un garde-corps, d'une barre d'appui. **2.** *v.i.* aller, voyager, en chemin de fer.

rail[3], *s.* *Orn:* râle *m*; **water r.,** râle d'eau; *NAm:* **black r.,** râle noir; **clapper r.,** râle gris; **king r.,** râle élégant; **sora r.,** marouette *f* de la Caroline; *Fr.C:* râle de la Caroline; **Virginia r.,** râle de Virginie; **wood r.,** aramide *m*; grand râle de la Cayenne; **yellow r.,** râle jaune.

rail[4], *v.i.* se répandre en plaintes, en injures; **to r. at, against, s.o.,** crier, criailler, invectiver, épancher sa bile, contre qn; s'en prendre à qn; se répandre en reproches, en invectives, contre qn; **to r. at fate,** s'en prendre au sort; se révolter contre le sort; se plaindre du sort.

railage ['reilidʒ], *s.* fret *m* de chemin de fer.

railbird ['reilbə:d], *s.* *Rac: P:* pelousard, -arde, assidu(e) (qui se tient toujours près de la barrière).

railcar ['reilkɑ:r], *s.* *Rail:* automotrice *f*; autorail *m*.

railed [reild], *a.* **1. r.(-in, -off) space,** espace entouré d'une grille; espace séparé (de la rue, etc.) par une grille. **2.** *Rail:* **single-r., double-r.,** (ligne *f*) à une seule voie, à deux voies.

railer ['reilər], *s.* **1.** criailleur, -euse. **2.** détracteur, -trice (**at, against,** de); mauvaise langue.

railhead ['reilhed], *s.* **1.** *Rail:* champignon *m* de rail; champignon de roulement. **2.** (*a*) *Rail: etc:* tête *f* de ligne; (*b*) *Mil:* gare *f* de ravitaillement.

railing[1] ['reiliŋ], *s.* **1. railing(s),** (*a*) clôture *f* à claire-voie; grille *f*, palissade *f*; **iron railings,** clôture en fer; grille; (*b*) garde-fou *m*, *pl.* garde-fous; garde-corps *m inv*; parapet *m* (de pont); balustrade *f* (de balcon); rampe *f* (d'escalier); (*c*) *Rad:* brouillage *m* en palissade. **2.** *Veh:* **top r.,** galerie *f* de toit (de taxi, etc.). **3.** bois *m*, fer *m*, pour barres.

railing[2], *a.* criailleur, railleur.

railing[3], *s.* criailleries *fpl*; injures *fpl*, invectives *fpl*.

raillery ['reiləri], *s.* raillerie *f*.

railless ['reillis], *a.* **1.** (escalier, etc.) sans rampe, sans balustrade. **2.** (pays, région) sans chemin de fer.

railman, *pl.* **-men** ['reilmən], *s.m.* employé des chemins de fer.

railroad[1] ['reilroud], *s.* *A: & NAm:* chemin *m* de fer; **r. pass,** carte *f* de circulation.

railroad[2]. *NAm:* **1.** *v.tr.* (*a*) expédier (des marchandises, etc.) par (le) chemin de fer; (*b*) *Pol: F:* **to r. a bill,** faire voter en vitesse un projet de loi; faire avaler un projet de loi à la Chambre; (*c*) *F:* envoyer (qn) en prison à l'aide de faux témoignages; (*d*) fournir (une région) de chemins de fer. **2.** *v.i.* (*a*) voyager en chemin de fer; (*b*) être employé aux chemins de fer.

railroader ['reilroudər], *s.* *NAm:* employé *m* des chemins de fer; cheminot *m*.

railway ['reilwei], *s.* **1. r. (line),** (ligne *f* de) chemin *m* de fer; voie ferrée; **local r.,** chemin de fer d'intérêt local; **narrow-gauge, light, r.,** chemin de fer à voie étroite; **mountain r.,** (i) chemin de fer de montagne; (ii) (*also* **scenic r.**), montagnes *f* russes; **circle r.,** chemin de fer de ceinture; **electric r.,** chemin de fer électrique; **portable r.,** chemin de fer à voie démontable, transportable; chemin de fer du type Decauville; **the main r. lines,** les grandes lignes (ferroviaires); **r. network, system,** réseau ferré, ferroviaire, de chemin de fer; **r. station,** gare *f*; (*small*) station *f* (de chemin de fer); *Com:* **delivery at r. station,** livraison *f* (en) gare; **r. bridge, carriage, company,** pont *m*, wagon *m*, compagnie *f*, de chemin de fer; **r. engineer,** ingénieur des chemins de fer; *Mil:* sapeur *m* des chemins de fer (du génie); **r. engineering,** ingénierie *f*, technique *f*, des chemins de fer; **r. contractor,** entrepreneur *m* de chemins de fer; **r. cutting,** (voie en) déblai (*m*); **r. embankment,** (voie en) remblai (*m*); **r. accident,** accident *m* de chemin de fer, ferroviaire; **r. guide, timetable,** indicateur *m* des chemins de fer; **r. traffic,** trafic *m* ferroviaire; **r. transport,** transport *m* par chemin de fer; **works with r. facilities,** usine avec facilités d'accès, avec raccordement, au réseau ferroviaire; **r. parcels,**

articles *m* de messagerie; **r. parcels service,** (service *m* des) messageries *f*; *Mil:* **r. artillery,** artillerie *f* sur voie ferrée; **r. operating battalion** = groupe *m* de chemin de fer en campagne; **r. shop battalion** = compagnie *f* de réparation de chemin de fer; **r. transport, traffic,** *U.S:* **r. transportation, officer,** commissaire *m* de gare. **2.** *NAm:* chemin de fer (i) d'intérêt local, (ii) à voie étroite. **3.** *Ind:* **overhead r.,** pont roulant (pour le service des ateliers).

railwayman, *pl.* **-men** ['reilweimən], *s.m.* employé des chemins de fer; cheminot.

raiment ['reimənt], *s. A: & Poet:* habillement *m*, vêtement(s) *m(pl)*; *Jur:* **food and r.,** la nourriture et le vêtement.

rain[1] [rein], *s.* pluie *f.* **1.** *(a)* **fine r.,** pluie fine; **heavy r.,** forte, grosse, grande, pluie; pluie abondante; **pelting r., driving r.,** pluie battante; **soaking r.,** pluie pénétrante; **thunder r.,** pluie d'orage; **freezing r.,** verglas *m*; **it looks like r., as if we are going to have r.,** le temps est à la pluie, menace la pluie; le temps a l'air d'être à la pluie; il a l'air de vouloir pleuvoir; nous allons avoir de la pluie; **it is turning to r.,** le temps se met à la pluie; **sign of r.,** signe pluvieux; signe de pluie; **a walk in the r.,** une promenade sous la pluie; **they came in torrential r.,** ils sont venus par une pluie torrentielle, diluvienne; **r. or shine he worked in his garden,** par tous les temps, par n'importe quel temps, il travaillait dans son jardin; **r. or shine I'll be there,** qu'il pleuve ou qu'il fasse beau temps, j'y serai; **to stay out in the r.,** rester à la pluie; **come in out of the r.!** entrez donc, ne restez pas à la pluie! *F:* **to keep out of the r.,** éviter des ennuis; se tenir à l'écart; **r. cloud,** nuage *m* de pluie; nuage pluvieux; nimbus *m*; **r. shower,** averse *f*; **r. band,** bande *f* de pluie (dans le spectre); **r. chart,** carte *f* pluviométrique; **r. gauge,** pluviomètre *m*, udomètre *m*, ombromètre *m*; **recording, self-registering, r. gauge,** pluviographe *m*; *F:* **r. glass,** baromètre *m* (à cadran); **r. forest,** forêt (tropicale) humide; *Geog:* **r. shadow,** région *f* sous le vent (dans les montagnes); *NAm: Sp: etc:* **r. check,** billet *m* valable pour une réunion remise à cause de la pluie; *F:* **I'll take a r. check on that,** impossible, mais invitez-moi pour une autre fois; *Com: F:* **to give a r. check for sale goods that cannot be supplied,** s'engager à offrir plus tard des soldes qu'on ne peut pas fournir; *Const:* **r. cap,** parapluie *m* (de cheminée); **r. pipe,** (tuyau *m* de) descente *f*; *Th:* **r. box,** appareil *m* à faire la pluie; *Orn: Dial:* **r. pie,** pic-vert *m, pl.* pics-verts; pivert *m*; *(b)* (chute *f* de) pluie; **the winds and rains of March,** les tempêtes et les pluies du mois de mars; **we need a good r.,** nous avons besoin d'une pluie abondante; *(c) Fig:* **r. of fire, bullets,** pluie de feu, de balles; **r. of tears,** débordement *m*, flot *m*, de larmes; **there was a r. of congratulations,** les félicitations pleuvaient; *(d) pl.* **the rains,** la saison des pluies, pluviale, pluvieuse (sous les tropiques). **2. golden r.,** (i) *Pyr:* pluie d'or; (ii) *Bot:* cytise *f.* **3.** *Cin:* pluie (d'un film rayé).

rain[2]. **1.** *v.impers.* pleuvoir; **it rains, it is raining,** il pleut; il tombe de l'eau, de la pluie; **it is raining hard, fast,** il pleut à verse; il pleut fort; *F:* **it is raining cats and dogs,** *NAm:* **pitchforks, it is raining in torrents, in sheets, in buckets,** il pleut des hallebardes; il pleut à seaux, à torrents; *F:* il tombe de la flotte; **it is raining again,** voilà qu'il repleut; **it has rained itself out,** la pluie a cessé; le ciel s'est vidé; **it rained presents that day,** il pleuvait des cadeaux ce jour-là; *B:* **it rained fire from heaven,** il tomba du ciel une pluie de feu; *Prov:* **it never rains but it pours,** un malheur, un bonheur, ne vient jamais seul; jamais deux sans trois; quand on reçoit une visite, une lettre, on en reçoit dix. **2.** *v.i.* **blows rained upon him,** les coups pleuvaient sur lui; **tears rained down her cheeks,** ses joues ruisselaient de larmes; une pluie de larmes coulait sur ses joues; **misfortunes have rained thick on me,** les malheurs ont grêlé sur ma tête; **invitations are raining on us,** il nous pleut des invitations. **3.** *v.tr.* **to r. blows on s.o.,** faire pleuvoir des coups sur qn; frapper qn à coups pressés; **to r. benefits on s.o.,** faire tomber sur qn une pluie de bienfaits. **4.** *(of match, etc.)* **to be rained off, out,** être annulé à cause de la pluie.

rainbird ['reinbə:d], *s. Orn:* **1.** pic-vert *m, pl.* pics-verts; pivert *m.* **2.** tacco *m*; vieillard *m*; oiseau *m* de pluie.

rainbow ['reinbou], *s.* **1.** arc-en-ciel *m, pl.* arcs-en-ciel; **sea r.,** arc-en-ciel marin; *F:* **all the colours of the r.,** toutes les couleurs de l'arc-en-ciel, du spectre; *Fig:* **to chase a r.,** se nourrir d'illusions; **r.-hued, -tinted,** irisé; *Metall: Miner:* **r. colours,** iris *m*; *Ich:* **r. (trout),** truite *f* arc-en-ciel. **2.** *pl. P:* **rainbows,** barbiturique *m*, tricolore *m.*

raincoat ['reinkout], *s.* imperméable *m*; manteau *m* de pluie; *F:* imper *m.*

raindrop ['reindrɔp], *s.* goutte *f* de pluie.

rainfall ['reinfɔ:l], *s.* **1.** *Meteor:* *(a)* précipitation *f* (atmosphérique); *(b)* quantité *f* d'eau tombée; hauteur *f* pluviométrique; pluviosité *f* (d'une région); **annual r.,** précipitations annuelles; **average r.,** hauteur moyenne des chutes de pluie. **2.** averse *f.*

raininess ['reininis], *s.* caractère pluvieux; disposition *f* à la pluie; pluviosité *f*; **the r. of the weather,** le temps pluvieux.

rainless ['reinlis], *a.* sans pluie; (pays) dépourvu de pluie; **r. storm,** orage sec.

rainlessness ['reinlisnis], *s.* manque *m* de pluie; impluviosité *f.*

rainproof[1] ['reinpru:f]. **1.** *a.* *(a)* imperméable (à la pluie); *(b)* inaltérable par la pluie. **2.** *s.* imperméable *m*; manteau *m* de pluie; *F:* imper *m.*

rainproof[2], *v.tr.* imperméabiliser (un tissu, etc.).

raintight ['reintait], *a.* imperméable (à la pluie).

rain tree ['reintri:], *s.* pithecolobium *m.*

rainwash ['reinwɔʃ], *s. Geog:* *(a)* (transport *m* par) ruissellement *m*; *(b) (material transported)* peloux *m.*

rainwater ['reinwɔ:tər], *s.* eau *f* de pluie; eaux pluviales; **r. pipe,** (tuyau *m* de) descente *f*; **r. head,** dalle *f.*

rainwear ['reinwɛər], *s.* vêtements *mpl* de pluie.

rainworm ['reinwə:m], *s. Ann:* ver *m* de terre.

rainy ['reini], *a.* **1.** *(a)* pluvieux; **r. weather,** temps pluvieux, à la pluie; **r. season,** saison des pluies; saison pluviale, pluvieuse; **the r. season has set in,** les pluies ont commencé; **r. day,** journée de pluie; **what do you do on r. days?** que faites-vous les jours où il pleut? **we must lay, put, something by for a r. day; we must provide against a r. day,** il faut mettre de côté pour les mauvais jours; il faut garder une poire pour la soif; qui garde son dîner il a mieux à souper; **it is r.,** le temps est à la pluie, à l'eau; **it is a r. wind,** le vent souffle à la pluie; *(b)* (trottoir, etc.) mouillé par la pluie. **2.** *Cin:* (film) rayé.

raise[1] [reiz], *s.* **1.** *(a) NAm: & F:* augmentation *f* (de salaire, d'enjeu, etc.); *(b) Cards: (at poker)* relance *f.* **2.** rue montante; route montante.

raise[2], *v.tr.* **1.** *(a) (erect)* dresser, mettre debout (une échelle, un mât); guinder (un mât); **to r. (up) sth. that has fallen over,** relever qch. qui est tombé; **to r. a flag,** planter un drapeau; **to r. the standard of revolt,** lever, arborer, l'étendard de la révolte; **to r. the hair of a fur,** éveiller le poil d'une fourrure; **to r. (up) a patient to a sitting position,** soulever un malade sur son séant; *Tex:* **to r. (the nap of) the cloth,** carder, rebourser, garnir, aplaigner, lainer, gratter, le drap; *(of bird)* **to r. its feathers,** hérisser ses plumes; *(b) (make stand up)* **to r. (up) s.o. from the dead,** ressusciter qn des morts, d'entre les morts; **the dead are raised (up),** les morts ressuscitent; *(c)* **to r. game,** lever du gibier; **to r. the country, the people,** soulever, exciter, le peuple; mettre le pays en émoi **(against,** contre). **2.** bâtir, élever (un palais); ériger (une statue). **3.** élever (une famille); cultiver (des légumes); élever (du bétail); faire l'élevage (du bétail); **to r. wine,** élever du vin. **4.** *(a)* produire; **to r. a blister, a bump,** occasionner, faire naître, une ampoule; faire une bosse; **these shoes always raise blisters,** ces souliers me donnent toujours des ampoules; **to r. steam,** produire de la vapeur; chauffer une chaudière, une locomotive; pousser les feux; chauffer; **to r. a storm,** faire naître, exciter, une tempête; **to r. a storm of laughter,** déchaîner l'hilarité, une tempête de rires; **to r. astonishment, a smile,** provoquer l'étonnement, un sourire; **to r. a blush, a laugh,** faire rougir, faire rire; **to r. a hope, a suspicion,** faire naître une espérance, un soupçon; **there's nothing like walking for raising a thirst,** il n'y a rien de tel que la promenade pour donner soif; *(b)* **to r. a cry,** faire entendre, pousser, un cri; **to r. a song, a hymn,** entonner une chanson, un cantique; **no one raised his voice,** personne ne souffla mot; *(c)* **to r. a question,** soulever une question; **two new points were raised,** deux nouvelles questions ont été mises en avant; **protests were raised against this measure,** des protestations s'élevèrent contre cette mesure; cette mesure fut l'objet de protestations; *(d)* **to r. (up) enemies,** se faire des ennemis; **God raised up prophets,** Dieu suscita des prophètes. **5.** *(elevate)* *(a) (lift)* lever (le bras, les yeux); soulever (un poids); **to r. one's glass to one's lips,** porter son verre à ses lèvres; **to r. one's glass to s.o.,** lever son verre à la santé de qn; **to r. an anchor,** lever une ancre; **to r. a mine, a submarine,** relever une mine, un sous-marin; **to r. a ship,** relever, renflouer, un navire; **to r. coal (to the pithead),** remonter, extraire, le charbon; *Austr:* **to r. the colour,** trouver de l'or; **to r. the workmen (from a mine),** monter, remonter, les ouvriers; **to r. the water (from a mine),** extraire, épuiser, l'eau; **submarine that can be raised,** sous-marin relevable; *(b) (promote)* élever; **to r. s.o. to power,** élever qn au pouvoir; **to r. s.o. to a higher rank,** élever qn à un rang plus élevé; donner de l'avancement à qn; **to r. s.o. to noble rank,** anoblir qn; **raised to the peerage,** élevé à la pairie; *Mil:* **to r. a soldier from the ranks,** donner un grade, du galon, à un soldat; **to be raised to the episcopate,** être promu à l'épiscopat; *(c)* **to r. (up) s.o. from poverty,** tirer qn de la pauvreté; **I raised him from nothing,** je l'ai tiré de rien; **to r. the soul,** exalter l'âme; **to r. s.o.'s hopes,** exalter l'espoir de qn; **to r. s.o.'s spirits,** relever le courage de qn; relever, remonter, le moral de qn; faire reprendre courage à qn; **to r. s.o. in s.o.'s estimation,** faire monter qn dans l'estime de qn; **to r. one's reputation,** relever, rehausser, sa réputation; ajouter à sa réputation. **6.** *(a)* hausser, relever (un store); **to r. the window,** (i) relever le châssis; (ii) *Veh:* relever la glace; *Aut:* **to r. the bonnet,** soulever le capot; **to r. the hood,** relever la capote; **to r. one's veil,** relever son voile; **to r. a corner of the veil that hides the future,** soulever le voile qui cache l'avenir; *(b)* **to r. camp,** lever le camp; *(c)* **to r. (the height of) a building,** surélever un immeuble; **to r. a wall three feet,** surélever, (ex)hausser, un mur de trois pieds; *(d)* **to r. (the pitch of) a piano by a quarter tone,** monter un piano d'un quart de ton; **to r. one's voice,** élever, hausser, la voix; **he never once raised his voice at his wife,** il n'a jamais dit un mot plus haut que l'autre à sa femme; **one could hear voices raised in anger,** on entendait des éclats de voix; *(e) (increase)* **to r. a tariff,** relever un tarif; **to r. the price of goods,** élever, (re)hausser, augmenter, relever, le prix des marchandises; (r)enchérir des marchandises; **to r. the value of the franc,** relever le cours du franc; **to r. production to maximum,** porter la production au maximum; **to r. s.o.'s salary,** relever le salaire de qn; augmenter (les appointements de) qn; **if you could r. the sum to a thousand pounds,** si vous pouviez porter la somme à mille livres; *Cards: (bridge)* **to r. a call,** *v.i.* **to r.,** forcer (sur une annonce); *(poker)* **to r. the stake,** *v.i.* **to r.,** relancer; *NAm:* **to r. a cheque,** augmenter (frauduleusement) le montant d'un chèque; **to r. the temperature,** élever la température; **to r. the temperature to 100°,** porter la température à 100°; **to r. a colour,** relever une couleur; *Mth:* **to r. a number to the ninth power,** élever un nombre à la neuvième puissance; *(f)* **to r. dough, the bread,** faire lever la pâte, le pain. **7.** *(a)* **to r. an army,** lever, assembler, réunir, mettre sur pied, une armée; *(b)* **to r. money,** trouver, se procurer, de l'argent; **how much can you r.?** combien d'argent avez-vous de disponible? **to r. funds by subscription,** réunir des fonds par souscription; **to r. money for an industry,** procurer des capitaux à une industrie; **to r. money on an estate, one's watch,** emprunter de l'argent sur une terre, sa montre; *F:* **if we can r. a taxi,** si nous pouvions dénicher, dégot(t)er, un taxi; *esp. U.S:* **I couldn't r. you this morning,** je ne pouvais pas (i) vous trouver, *F:* dénicher, (ii) vous joindre au téléphone, ce matin; **I can't r. the office,** je ne peux pas établir la communication (au téléphone) avec le bureau; **to r. a tear,** y aller de sa larme; **I couldn't r. a smile,** je ne pouvais pas esquisser un sourire; *(c)* **to r. taxes,** lever des impôts; *(of the State)* **to r. a loan,** contracter, émettre, un emprunt. **8. to r. a spirit,** évoquer un esprit; *F:* **to r. hell, Cain,** (i) faire un bruit, un fracas, de tous les diables; (ii) faire une scène monumentale. **9.** *Nau:* **to r. the land,** voir se lever la terre; **to r. a coast, a lighthouse,** élever une côte, un phare. **10. to r. a siege, a blockade,** (i) lever, (ii) faire lever, un siège, un blocus; **to r. an embargo, a ban,** lever un embargo, une interdiction.

raised[1] [reizd], *a.* **1.** *(a) (of arm, etc.)* levé; *(of head)* relevé; *(b)* **r. deck,** pont surélevé; **r. floor,** faux plancher; **r. signal box,** cabine surélevée; *Geog:* **r. beaches,** plages soulevées. **2.** *(a)* saillant, en relief; **r. work,** ouvrage relevé en bosse; **r. rail,** rail saillant; **r. letter,** caractère *m* en relief; **r. print,** impression *f* anaglyptique (pour les aveugles); **r. map,** carte *f* en relief; *(b)* **r. plan,** élévation *f.* **3. r. voice,** voix élevée. **4.** *Cu:* **r. pie** = pâté *m* en croûte.

raised[2], *a. Tex:* **r. velvet,** velours frappé.

raiser ['reizər], *s.* **1.** *(a)* souleveur *m* (d'un poids, etc.); *(b)* auteur *m* (d'une tempête, d'un tumulte); souleveur (d'une révolte); *(c)* éleveur *m* (de bestiaux); cultivateur *m* (de plantes). **2.** *(a)* levain *m*; *(b)* **condition raisers for horses,** aliments engraissants pour chevaux; *(c) Mil: etc: F:* **morale r.,** facteur *m* qui relève le moral. **3.** *(a) Anat:* élévateur *m*; *(b) Aut:* **window r.,** lève-glace(s) *m inv.* **4.** *Carp:* contre-marche *f* (d'escalier).

raisin ['reizn], *s.* raisin sec; **r. wine,** vin *m* de raisins secs; *Bot:* **Japanese r. tree,** hovenia *m.*

raising ['reiziŋ], *s.* **1.** *(a)* relèvement *m* (d'un objet tombé); *Nau:* guindage *m* (d'un mât); *Tex:* garnissage *m*, grattage *m*, lainage *m*, cardage *m*, aplaignage *m* (du drap); (*b*) résurrection *f*, ressuscitation *f* (des morts). **2.** élévation *f*; érection *f* (d'un monument). **3.** élevage *m* (du bétail); culture *f* (des plantes); **tobacco of my own r.,** tabac de ma propre culture. **4.** production *f* (de la vapeur, etc.). **5.** relevage *m* (d'un sous-marin, etc.); extraction *f* (du charbon); *Min:* remontée *f* (des ouvriers, etc.). **6.** (*a*) relèvement (d'un mur, etc.); surélévation *f* (d'un immeuble); exhaussement *m* (de terrain, etc.); *Const:* **r. piece, plate,** sablière *f*; (*b*) élévation *f* (de la voix); rehaussement *m* (de réputation); relèvement (des tarifs, des prix); élévation (des prix); augmentation *f* (des prix, des salaires); hausse *f* (des loyers); **r. of the bank rate,** relèvement du taux officiel de l'escompte; **r. of the school-leaving age,** prolongation *f* de la scolarité. **7.** évocation *f* (des esprits). **8.** levée *f* (des troupes, des impôts). **9.** levée (d'un siège, d'un blocus).

raj [rɑːdʒ], *s.* (*Anglo-Indian*) souveraineté *f*, autorité *f*; **under the British r.,** sous l'empire britannique.

raja(h) ['rɑːdʒə], *s.m.* raja(h).

Rajidae ['rædʒidiː], *s.pl. Ich:* rajidés *m.*

Rajput, Rajpoot ['rɑːdʒput], *s.* Rajpoute *m*, Rajput *m.*

Rajputana [rɑːdʒpu'tɑːnə], *Pr.n. Geog:* le Rajp(o)utana.

rake[1] [reik], *s. Tls:* **1.** *Agr: Hort:* râteau *m*; **hay r.,** râteau, fauchet *m*; *Const:* **plasterer's r.,** râble *m* de plâtrier. **2.** (*a*) fourgon *m*, rouable *m*, râble (de boulanger); tire-braise *m inv*; (*b*) ringard *m* (à crochet), crochet *m* à feu (de forgeron, etc.). **3.** *Toil:* **r.(comb),** démêloir *m.*

rake[2], *v.*

I. *v.tr.* **1. to r. the leaves (up, together),** râteler, ratisser, les feuilles; rassembler, amasser, les feuilles au râteau; **to r. the hay,** râteler le foin. **2.** (*a*) râteler (le sol); ratisser (une allée); **to r. a path clean, a surface level,** nettoyer une allée, niveler une surface, au râteau; *F:* **the police raked the district for the criminals,** la police a fouillé (dans) tout le quartier pour trouver les criminels; **to r. history for examples,** scruter toute l'histoire pour trouver des exemples; **to r. one's memory,** fouiller (dans) ses souvenirs; *v.i.* **to r. (about) among old documents,** fouiller, fureter, dans de vieux documents; (*b*) gratter, racler, égratigner (une surface). **3. to r. a ship, a trench,** enfiler, prendre en enfilade, un navire, une tranchée; **to r. the enemy with machine-gun fire,** mitrailler l'ennemi. **4.** *NAm: F:* **to r. s.o. (over the coals),** réprimander, semoncer, qn.

II. (*compound verbs*) **1. rake away,** *v.tr.* enlever (les feuilles, etc.) au râteau.

2. rake down, *v.tr. NAm:* ratisser (les mises).

3. rake in, *v.tr.* (*a*) *Agr: Hort:* enfouir (des engrais, etc.) au râteau, avec un râteau; (*b*) (*at casino*) ratisser (les mises); (*c*) *F:* amasser (de l'argent).

4. rake off, *v.tr.* (*a*) enlever (des feuilles, etc.) au râteau; (*b*) *F:* prélever (une somme d'argent, un tantième).

5. rake out, *v.tr.* (*a*) **to r. out the fire,** (i) retirer, enlever, les cendres du feu; dégager la grille du foyer; détiser le feu; (ii) *Mch: Ind:* faire tomber le feu; (*b*) *Const:* **to r. out the joints (of brickwork),** nettoyer les joints.

6. rake over, *v.tr.* (*a*) égratigner (le sol); (*b*) **to r. over a path,** repasser une allée; (*c*) fouiller (dans) (le passé).

7. rake up, *v.tr.* rassembler, attiser (le feu); *F:* **to r. up an old quarrel,** attiser, faire revivre, une ancienne querelle; **to r. up evidence,** exhumer des preuves; **to r. up the past,** revenir sur le passé; **don't r. up the past,** ne remuez pas le passé; **to r. up s.o.'s past,** rechercher les vieux péchés de qn; fouiller dans le passé de qn; **to r. up an old slander,** remémorer, rééditer, une calomnie; **to r. up old grievances,** rappeler d'anciens griefs.

rake[3], *s. Min:* rame *f*, train *m* (de wagons).

rake[4], *s.* viveur *m*, roué *m*, coureur *m*, noceur *m*; **old r.,** vieux marcheur; **a rake's progress,** la décadence progressive d'un libertin.

rake[5], *s.* **1.** inclinaison *f* (d'un mât, d'un toit; *Aut:* de la colonne de direction, d'un dossier de siège); *Nau:* **r. of the stem, of the stern-post,** élancement *m* de l'étrave; quête *f* de l'étambot; **ship masted with a r.,** navire mâté en frégate; *Veh:* **r. of the axle pin,** carrossage *m* de la fusée de l'essieu. **2. r. of a tool,** (i) inclinaison (sur l'horizontale) d'un outil; (ii) dépouille *f*, affranchissement *m*, dégagement *m*, d'un outil; **angle of r.,** angle *m* d'attaque, pente *f* (d'une machine-outil); **propeller r.,** angle d'attaque de la pale de l'hélice. **3.** *Th:* pente (du parterre, du plateau).

rake[6]. **1.** *v.i.* **to r., to be raked,** (*of mast, etc.*) pencher, être incliné; (*of roof, floor*) être en pente. **2.** *v.tr.* incliner (vers l'arrière), faire pencher (un mât, etc.).

rakeful ['reikful], *s.* râtelée *f* (de foin, etc.).

rake-off ['reikɔf], *s. F:* pourcentage *m* (illicite ou non); commission *f*, ristourne *f*; *F:* gratte *f*; **to get a r.-o. on all business introduced to the firm,** toucher une commission, *F:* une guelte, sur toutes les affaires qu'on amène à la maison; **the police were accused of getting a r.-o.,** on accusa la police d'avoir fait de la gratte.

raker ['reikər], *s.* **1.** (*pers.*) (*a*) râteleur, -euse; (*b*) fureteur, -euse. **2.** *Tls:* (*a*) racloir *m*, grattoir *m*; (*b*) *Agr:* râteau *m* mécanique. **3.** *Austr: P:* **to go a r.,** chuter; *F:* ramasser une pelle.

raki ['rɑːki], *s.* raki *m.*

raking[1] ['reikiŋ], *a. Mil:* (feu) d'enfilade; (tir) en enfilade.

raking[2], *s.* (*a*) râtelage *m*, ratissage *m*; (*b*) **rakings,** râtelures *f.*

raking[3], *a.* **1.** (*a*) (mât) incliné vers l'arrière; (*b*) *N.Arch:* (avant) élancé. **2.** (toit, plancher) en pente.

rakish[1] ['reikiʃ], *a.* **1.** (*of pers.*) libertin, dissolu. **2. r. appearance, air,** (i) air crâne, bravache, cavalier, effronté, désinvolte, polisson; (ii) air de bambocheur; **to wear one's hat at a r. angle,** (i) porter avec désinvolture son chapeau sur l'oreille; (ii) porter son chapeau en casseur d'assiettes.

rakish[2], *a.* (*a*) *N.Arch:* (avant, etc.) élancé; (navire *m*) à formes élancées; (*b*) *Hist:* (navire) aux allures de corsaire, de pirate.

rakishly ['reikiʃli], *adv.* **1.** en libertin; dissolument. **2.** crânement, avec crânerie, cavalièrement, effrontément; **hat tilted r.,** chapeau à la cavalière; chapeau sur l'oreille.

rakishness ['reikiʃnis], *s.* **1.** libertinage *m*; mœurs déréglées. **2.** crânerie *f*, effronterie *f*; air crâne, cavalier.

râle [rɑːl], *s. Med:* râle *m*; **bubbling r.,** râle bulleux; **moist r.,** râle humide; **sonorous r.,** ronchus *m.*

rallentando [rælən'tændou], *adv. Mus:* rallentando; en ralentissant; "cédez".

Rallidae ['rælidiː], *s.pl. Orn:* rallidés *m.*

ralline ['rælain], *a. Orn:* des rallidés; semblable aux rallidés.

rally[1] ['ræli], *s.* **1.** (*a*) ralliement *m* (de troupes, partisans); (*b*) réunion *f*, assemblée *f*, en masse; grand rassemblement, grand concours, de gens; (*c*) **boy scouts' r.,** réunion de boy-scouts; (*d*) *Aut:* **(car) r.,** rallye *m* d'automobiles, rallye automobile; *NAm:* **r. master,** organisateur *m*, chef *m*, de rallye. **2.** (*a*) *Mil:* reprise *f* en main; *Sp:* dernier effort pour gagner le match; retour *m* d'énergie; (*b*) (i) reprise des forces; retour à la santé; (ii) mieux momentané; (*c*) *Com:* reprise (des prix); reprise des affaires. **3.** *Box:* reprise. **4.** *Ten:* (belle) passe de jeu.

rally[2]. **1.** *v.tr.* (*a*) rallier (des troupes, ses partisans) **(round,** autour de); (*b*) battre le rappel de (ses partisans); rassembler, réunir (des hommes, etc.); (*c*) ranimer (qn); rappeler (qn) à la vie; (*d*) **to r. one's strength,** avoir un retour d'énergie; faire appel à toutes ses forces; **to r. one's spirits,** reprendre courage. **2.** *v.i.* (*a*) (*of troops*) se reformer, se rallier; (*b*) se rallier **(to a party, to s.o.'s opinion,** à un parti, à l'opinion de qn); **his partisans rallied round him,** ses partisans se sont groupés autour de lui; **my party is rallying round me again,** mes partisans me reviennent; (*c*) reprendre des forces; se reprendre à la vie; se ranimer; **to r. from an illness,** se remettre d'une maladie; prendre le dessus; **his flagging powers rallied,** il surmonta son abattement; ses forces défaillantes se ranimèrent; (*d*) (*of team, etc.*) avoir un retour d'énergie; se reprendre; (*e*) *St.Exch:* **shares, prices, rallied,** les actions se sont redressées; (*f*) (*of pers. at a rally*) se rassembler, se réunir.

rally[3], *v.tr. A:* railler **(s.o. on sth.,** qn de qch.); se gausser de (qn).

rallying[1] ['ræliiŋ], *a.* (*of demonstrators, etc.*) (i) en train de se rassembler; (ii) assistant à un rassemblement.

rallying[2], *s.* **1.** ralliement *m*; **r. point,** point *m* de ralliement; **r. cry,** cri *m* de guerre (d'un parti, etc.). **2.** reprise *f* des forces, retour *m* à la santé.

rallying[3], *a.* qui prend part à un rallye.

rallying[4], *a. A:* railleur, narquois.

rallying[5], *s. A:* raillerie *f.*

rallyingly ['ræliiŋli], *adv.* en raillant; d'un ton moqueur, narquois.

rallyist ['ræliist], *s. NAm:* compétiteur, -trice, dans un rallye.

Ralph [reif, rælf, rɑːf], *Pr.n.m.* Raoul, Ralph, Rodolphe.

ralstonite ['rɔːlstənait], *s. Miner:* ralstonite *f.*

ram[1] [ræm], *s.* **1.** (*a*) *Z:* bélier *m*; **ram's horn,** (i) corne *f* de bélier; (ii) *Moll:* planorbe *f*; (*b*) *Astr:* **the R.,** le Bélier; (*c*) *P:* individu porté sur le sexe; *P:* chaud lapin. **2.** (*a*) **(battering) r.,** bélier; (*b*) *Ind:* défourneuse *f* (de four à coke). **3.** *Navy:* navire *m* à éperon; navire éperonné; navire bélier. **4.** (*a*) *Hyd.E:* piston *m*, piston plongeur, piston plein (de pompe refoulante); piston, pot *m* (de presse); **r. pump,** pompe (re)foulante; pompe à plongeur; (*b*) *Navy:* **hydraulic elevating r.,** presse *f* de pointage en hauteur; (*c*) *Mec.E:* vérin *m* (hydraulique, pneumatique). **5.** (*a*) dame *f*, damoir *m*, demoiselle *f*, pilon *m*, hie *f*, blin *m* (de paveur); (*b*) *Civ.E: Mec.E:* mouton *m* (de sonnette); bélier à pilotage; (*c*) mouton, pilon (de marteau-pilon). **6.** *Mec.E:* chariot *m* porte-outil; trompette *f* (d'étau limeur). **7.** *Min:* bourre *f* (d'argile) (de trou de mine). **8.** (*a*) *Ph:* surpression *f*, surpuissance *f* (aérodynamique, hydraulique); *Av:* **r. effect,** effet *m* de surpuissance, effet (aéro)dynamique; **r. air,** air en surpuissance; air (de pression) aérodynamique; (*b*) *Hyd:* **hydraulic r.,** bélier hydraulique.

ram[2], *v.* **(rammed)**

I. *v.tr.* **1.** (*a*) battre, damer, tasser (le sol); damer, pilonner (une allée); *Metall:* fouler (le sable, etc.); *Const:* **rammed earth,** pisé *m* de terre; (*b*) bourrer (une arme à feu, une pipe); remplir, bourrer **(sth. with sth.,** qch. de qch.); *Min:* **to r. the charge home,** bourrer, refouler, la charge; *F:* **to r. one's clothes into one's suitcase,** fourrer ses vêtements dans sa valise; (*c*) enfoncer, damer (un pieu); *F:* **to r. sth. into s.o. (by repeating it),** faire entrer qch. dans la tête de qn (à force de le répéter); *Artil:* **to r. home the projectile,** refouler le projectile à poste; *F:* **to r. an argument home,** pousser un argument à fond; *Fig:* **he's always ramming it down my throat,** il m'en rabat toujours les oreilles. **2.** (*a*) *Nau:* aborder (un navire) à l'éperon; éperonner un navire; (*b*) *Aut:* **to r. a car,** tamponner une voiture; (*c*) heurter, cogner **(sth. against sth.,** qch. contre qch.); **he rammed his head against the wall,** il s'est heurté la tête contre le mur; il a donné de la tête contre le mur. **3.** *P:* coïter avec, aiguiller (une femme).

II. (*compound verbs*) **1. ram down,** *v.tr.* (*a*) tasser (la terre); (*b*) (r)enfoncer (un pieu); bliner, hier (les pavés); **to r. one's hat down on one's head,** enfoncer son chapeau sur sa tête.

2. ram in, *v.tr.* (r)enfoncer (un pieu, etc.).

3. ram up, *v.tr.* boucher (un trou).

ram[3], *s. N.Arch:* longueur *f* (d'un navire) de tête en tête.

Rama ['rɑːmə], *Pr.n.m. Hindu Myth:* Râma(-Tchandra).

Ramadan [ræmə'dɑːn], *s. Moslem Rel:* ramad(h)an *m*, ramazan *m*, ramdame *m.*

ramal ['reim(ə)l], *a. Bot:* ramaire.

Raman ['rɑːmən], *Pr.n.m. Ph:* **R. effect,** effet *m* Raman.

ramble[1] ['ræmbl], *s.* **1.** excursion *f*, grande promenade (sans itinéraire bien arrêté); **to go for a r.,** *F:* faire une balade, partir en balade. **2.** discours incohérent.

ramble[2], *v.i.* **1.** (*a*) errer à l'aventure; se promener; vagabonder; rôder de-ci de-là; **to r. through the streets, over the country,** parcourir les rues au hasard de la promenade; vagabonder dans la campagne; (*b*) faire des excursions à pied. **2.** divaguer; parler sans suite; causer à bâtons rompus; (*in delirium*) battre la campagne; **to r. on,** dire mille inconséquences; passer sans suite d'un sujet à l'autre. **3.** (*of plant*) s'étendre; **there was ivy rambling all over the ruins,** le lierre rampait sur les ruines.

rambler ['ræmblər], *s.* **1.** (*a*) promeneur, -euse, (sans but); (*b*) excursionniste *mf* (à pied). **2.** divagateur, -trice; radoteur, -euse. **2.** *Hort:* rosier sarmenteux; rosier grimpant.

rambling[1] ['ræmbliŋ], *a.* **1.** errant, vagabond; **r. life,** vie errante, vagabonde. **2.** (récit, discours) décousu, sans suite, incohérent, inconséquent; **r. thoughts,** pensées vagabondes; **r. talk,** propos incohérents, divagations *fpl*; **r. conversation,** conversation à bâtons rompus. **3. r. plant,** plante rampante ou grimpante; plante sarmenteuse. **4. r. house,** maison aux nombreux corridors, maison pleine de coins et de recoins; **r. street,** rue irrégulière, tortueuse.

rambling[2], *s.* **1.** (*a*) vagabondage *m*; promenades *fpl* à l'aventure; **r. propensity,** penchant *m* à vagabonder, à errer à l'aventure; (*b*) excursions *fpl* à pied. **2.** divagations *fpl*; **ramblings of old age,** radotages *m.*

ramblingly ['ræmbliŋli], *adv.* **1.** en vagabondant; d'une manière vagabonde. **2.** en divaguant; (parler) d'une manière décousue; (causer) à bâtons rompus.

rambunctious [ræm'bʌŋ(k)ʃəs], *a. U.S: F:* turbulent; tapageur, -euse, bruyant; chahuteur, -euse.

rambunctiousness [ræm'bʌŋ(k)ʃəsnis], *s. U.S: F:* turbulence *f.*

rambutan [ræm'buːtən], *s. Bot:* ramboutan *m*, litchi chevelu.

ramee ['ræmi], *s. Bot:* ramie *f.*

ramekin, ramequin ['ræmikin], *s. Dom.Ec:* ramequin *m.*

ramentaceous [ræmən'teiʃəs], *a. Bot:* ramentacé.

ramentum, *pl.* **-a** [rə'mentəm, -ə], *s. Bot:* ramentum *m.*

Rameses ['ræmisiːz], *Pr.n.m. Hist:* Ramsès.

ramet ['ræmit], *s. Biol:* individu *m* faisant partie d'un clone.

ramicorn ['ræmikɔːn], *a. Ent:* ramicorne.

ramie ['ræmi], *s. Bot:* ramie *f.*

ramification [ræmifi'keiʃ(ə)n], *s.* **1.** (*a*) ramification *f* (d'un arbre, d'une tige); (*b*) ramification (des artères, etc.). **2. the ramifications of a plot,** les ramifications d'un complot.

ramiflorous [ræmi'flɔ:rəs], *a. Bot:* ramiflore.

ramify ['ræmifai]. **1.** *v.tr.* ramifier (un réseau de chemins de fer, etc.). **2.** *v.i.* se ramifier.

ramisection ['ræmisekʃ(ə)n], **ramisectomy** [ræmi'sektəmi], *s. Surg:* ramisection *f.*

Ramism ['reimizm], *s. Phil:* ramisme *m.*

ramjet ['ræmdʒet], *s. Av:* **r. (engine),** statoréacteur *m.*

rammelsbergite [ræməlz'bə:dʒait], *s. Miner:* rammelsbergite *f.*

rammer ['ræmər], *s.* **1.** (*a*) pilon *m*, bourroir *m*; **pneumatic r.,** pilon à air comprimé; (*b*) dame *f*, damoir *m*, demoiselle *f*, pilon, hie *f*, blin *m* (de paveur); (*c*) *Metall:* fouloir *m*, batte *f* (de mouleur). **2.** *Artil:* refouloir *m*. **3.** mouton *m* (pour pieux); bélier *m* à pilotage. **4.** *Tls:* (*pin drift*) repoussoir *m.*

ramming ['ræmiŋ], *s.* **1.** (*a*) damage *m*, battage *m*, tassement *m*, compression *f* (du sol); *Metall:* foulement *m* (du sable, etc.); (*b*) bourrage *m*. **2.** *Nau:* abordage *m* à l'éperon. **3.** *Ph:* surpression *f* aérodynamique; *Av:* **r. effect,** effet *m* de pression extérieure.

rammish ['ræmiʃ], *a. Dial:* à odeur forte; à odeur d'aisselles; **to smell r.,** sentir le bouc, le bouquin, *A:* le gousset.

ramose ['ræmous], *a. Nat.Hist:* rameux, branchu.

ramous ['ræməs], *a.* (*a*) rameux, branchu; (*b*) semblable à un rameau.

ramp[1] [ræmp], *s.* **1.** (*a*) *Civ.E: Rail: Fort:* rampe *f*, pente *f*, talus *m*; **approach r. of a bridge,** rampe d'accès d'un pont; **ramps of a cloverleaf,** rampes d'un échange; *NAm:* **r. garage,** garage *m* en étages; *Rail:* **unloading r.,** rampe de déchargement, de débarquement; **end loading r.,** rampe terminus inclinée pour chargement; (*b*) **portable r.,** rampe mobile; **retractable r.,** rampe relevable; *Ball:* **launching r.,** rampe de lancement; (*c*) **garage repair r.,** pont élévateur; *Rail:* **re-railing r.,** sabot *m* de remise. **2.** (*a*) *Arch:* dénivellement *m* (des pieds-droits d'un arc rampant); (*b*) *P.N:* **(beware) r.!** dénivellement! **3.** *Av:* **illuminated landing r.,** rampe lumineuse d'atterrissage.

ramp[2]. **1.** *v.i.* (*a*) *Her:* (*of lion*) se dresser sur ses pattes de derrière; (*b*) *F:* (*of pers.*) rager, tempêter, être furieux; **to r. and rave,** crier comme un énergumène; (*c*) (*of plant*) ramper; (*d*) *Arch: Fort:* (*of wall*) ramper, suivre une pente déterminée. **2.** *v.tr.* construire (un mur) en rampe, en pente.

ramp[3], *s. F:* **1.** supercherie *f*; **the whole thing's a r.,** c'est un coup monté. **2.** majoration exorbitante des prix; **the housing r.,** le scandale des loyers.

rampage[1] [ræm'peidʒ], *s. F:* **to be on the r.,** en avoir après tout le monde; ne pas décolérer; se comporter comme un fou; **to go on the r.,** (i) tomber dans une folie furieuse; (ii) (*of hooligan, etc.*) se livrer à des actes de violence.

rampage[2], *v.i.* **to r. (about),** se conduire en énergumène, comme un fou; en avoir après tout le monde; se livrer à des actes de violence.

rampageous [ræm'peidʒəs], *a.* **1.** violent, furieux, rageur. **2.** tapageur, -euse.

rampageously [ræm'peidʒəsli], *adv.* **1.** avec violence; avec fureur. **2.** tapageusement.

rampageousness [ræm'peidʒəsnis], *s.* **1.** violence *f*, rage *f.* **2.** conduite tapageuse.

rampancy ['ræmpənsi], *s.* **1.** violence *f.* **2.** (*a*) exubérance *f*, excès *m*, surabondance *f*; (*b*) **the r. of vice,** l'extension *f* du vice; l'effrénement *m* du vice.

rampant ['ræmpənt], *a.* **1.** *Her:* (lion) rampant, acculé. **2.** (*of pers., etc.*) violent, déchaîné, effréné; **r. anarchy,** anarchie effrénée; **famine is r. in the land,** la famine sévit dans le pays; **vice is r.,** le vice s'étale. **3.** (*of plant, growth*) exubérant, luxuriant. **4.** *Arch:* (*of arch*) rampant.

rampantly ['ræmpəntli], *adv.* **1.** violemment, sans frein. **2.** surabondamment.

rampart[1] ['ræmpɑ:t], *s.* **1.** *Fort:* rempart *m*; **r. walk,** chemin *m* de ronde; *Lit:* **the ramparts of liberty,** les remparts de la liberté. **2.** *Can: Geog:* escarpement *m* (d'une gorge).

rampart[2], *v.tr.* entourer (une place, etc.) d'un rempart, de remparts.

rampion ['ræmpiən], *s. Bot:* raiponce *f.*

ramrod ['ræmrɔd], *s.* **1.** baguette *f* (de fusil); *Artil:* écouvillon *m*; **as straight as a r.,** droit comme un i, un jonc, un cierge. **2.** *F:* personne raide, inflexible.

Ramsden ['ræmzdən], *Pr.n. Opt:* **R. eyepice,** oculaire *m* de Ramsden.

Ramses ['ræmsi:z], *Pr.n.m. Hist:* Ramsès.

ramshackle ['ræmʃækl], *a.* délabré; qui tombe en ruines; *F:* qui ne tient ni à fer ni à clou; **r. old house,** vieille maison délabrée; **r. old conveyance,** vieille guimbarde; **r. staircase,** escalier branlant; **r. furniture,** meubles boiteux; **r. empire,** empire délabré, croulant, qui menace ruine.

ramson ['ræmsən], *s.* (*usu. pl.*) *Bot:* ail *m* des ours; ail des bois.

ramtil ['ræmtil], *s. Bot:* guizotia *f.*

ramulus ['ræmjuləs], *s. Bot:* ramule *m.*

ramus, *pl.* **-i** ['reiməs, -ai], *s.* **1.** *Anat:* branche *f*, rameau *m*; **mandibular r.,** branche montante du maxillaire inférieur. **2.** *Orn:* barbe *f* (d'une plume).

ranatra ['rænətrə], *s. Ent:* ranâtre *f.*

rance [ræns], *s. Const:* rance *f.*

ranch[1] [rɑ:n(t)ʃ], *s. NAm:* **1.** (*a*) ranch *m*, prairie *f* d'élevage (de bétail, de chevaux, d'ovins); *Aut:* **r. wagon,** break *m*; (*b*) (ferme *f* d')élevage *m* (de visons, etc.); **fruit r.,** ferme, culture, fruitière. **2. r. (house),** maison *f* sans étage et avec peu de cloisons.

ranch[2]. **1.** *v.i.* (*a*) tenir, avoir, un ranch; exploiter un ranch; faire de l'élevage; (*b*) être employé de ranch. **2.** *v.tr.* exploiter (des prairies, etc.) en ranch(s).

rancher ['rɑ:n(t)ʃər], **ranchman**, *pl.* **-men** ['rɑ:n(t)ʃmən], *s. NAm:* **1.** propriétaire *m* d'un ranch. **2.** employé *m* de ranch.

rancherie ['rɑ:n(t)ʃəri:], *s. Can:* campement *m* d'Indiens.

rancho ['rɑ:n(t)ʃou], *s.* ranch *m.*

rancid ['rænsid], *a.* rance; **to smell r.,** sentir le rance; **to become, grow, r.,** rancir.

rancidity [ræn'siditi], **rancidness** ['rænsidnis], *s.* rancidité *f*, rancissure *f.*

rancorous ['ræŋkərəs], *a.* rancunier, haineux; **r. criticism,** critique fielleuse, pleine de fiel.

rancorously ['ræŋkərəsli], *adv.* avec haine, rancune; haineusement.

rancour ['ræŋkər], *s.* rancune *f*, rancœur *f*, haine *f*; **full of r.,** (*of pers.*) plein d'aigreur; (*of remark, etc.*) plein de fiel.

rand [rænd], *s.* **1.** bord *m*, marge *f*; bande *f*; *Bootm:* couche-point *m*, *pl.* couche-points. **2.** (*in S. Africa*) (*a*) *Geog:* arête *f* (de montagne); **the R.,** le Rand; (*b*) *Num:* rand *m.*

randan[1] [ræn'dæn]. **1.** *adv.* **to row r.,** ramer, nager, à trois (l'homme du milieu nageant en couple). **2.** *a. & s.* **r. (gig),** canot conduit par trois rameurs dont un en couple et deux en pointe.

randan[2], *s. P: O:* **to go on the r.,** faire la fête, la bombe.

randanite [ræn'dænait], *s. Miner:* randanite *f.*

randem ['rændəm]. **1.** *adv.* **to drive r.,** conduire à trois chevaux en flèche. **2.** *s.* voiture *f* à trois chevaux en flèche.

Randolph ['rændɔlf], *Pr.n.m.* Randolphe.

random ['rændəm]. **1.** *s.* **at r.,** (choisir, etc.) au hasard; (errer, etc.) à l'aventure; **to speak at r.,** parler à tort et à travers; parler en l'air; ne pas mesurer ses paroles; **to fire at r.,** tirer à coup(s) perdu(s); **to hit out at r.,** lancer des coups à l'aveuglette. **2.** *a.* (*a*) aléatoire; (i) (fait) au hasard; **r. choice,** choix *m* au hasard; **r. shot,** coup tiré au hasard, coup perdu, balle perdue; **r. order, sequence,** ordre *m* au hasard, quelconque; **r. sampling,** échantillonnage *m* au hasard; **r. check,** contrôle *m* par sondage(s); *Cmptr:* **r. processing,** traitement non ordonné; *Mth:* **r. number,** *Cmptr:* **r. digit,** nombre *m* aléatoire; **r. factor,** facteur *m* aléatoire; **r. function,** fonction *f* aléatoire; *Cmptr:* **r. access,** accès aléatoire, sélectif; **r. access device,** appareil *m* à accès sélectif, direct; **r. access memory, storage, store,** mémoire *f* à accès sélectif, direct; (ii) erratique, chaotique; **r. noise,** *Ac:* bruit *m* aléatoire, complexe; *W.Tel: Elcs:* parasite intermittent; bruit erratique; **r. variations, fluctuations,** variations *f* erratiques, aléatoires; *Cmptr:* **r. failure,** défaillance *f* erratique, imprévisible; *Stat:* **r. error,** erreur *f* aléatoire; *Atom.Ph:* **r. walk,** marche *f* au hasard, mouvement *m* chaotique, erratique (des molécules); (*b*) *Com: etc:* **r. lengths,** longueurs *f* tout-venant; *Const:* **r. ashlar work,** maçonnerie *f* en moellons bruts.

randomization [rændəmi'zeiʃ(ə)n], *s.* (*a*) *Stat:* randomisation *f*, probabilisation *f*; (*b*) *Cmptr:* rangement *m* à une adresse calculée; randomisation.

randomize ['rændəmaiz], *v.tr.* (*a*) *Stat:* randomiser, probabiliser; (*b*) *Cmptr:* ranger à une adresse calculée; randomiser.

randomizer ['rændəmaizər], *s. Cmptr:* programme *m* de calcul d'adresse.

randomizing[1] ['rændəmaiziŋ], *s.* (*a*) *Stat:* (procédé, etc.) de randomisation, de probabilisation; (*b*) *Cmptr:* (programme, etc.) de calcul d'adresse.

randomizing[2], *s.* = RANDOMIZATION.

randomly ['rændəmli], *adv.* au hasard; **r. arranged,** disposé au hasard, dans un ordre quelconque; *Atom.Ph:* **r. moving molecules,** molécules se déplaçant, se mouvant, d'une façon erratique.

randomness ['rændəmnis], *s.* aspect *m*, caractère *m*, aléatoire, erratique.

randy ['rændi], *a.* **1.** *Scot:* grossièrement importun; à la langue grossière. **2.** (taureau) farouche; (cheval) rétif. **3.** *P:* (*of pers.*) (*a*) lascif; paillard; (*b*) émoustillé, allumé, excité.

ranee [rɑ:'ni:], *s.f.* rani.

Raney ['rɑ:ni:], *Pr.n. Metall:* **R. nickel,** nickel *m* de Raney.

range[1] [reindʒ], *s.* **1.** (*a*) rangée *f* (de bâtiments, etc.); profilée *f* (de colonnes, etc.); enfilade *f* (de salles, etc.); **a long r. of arches and bridges,** toute une profilée d'arcs et de ponts; **a fine r. of cliffs,** une belle ligne de falaises; (*b*) chaîne *f* (de montagnes). **2.** direction *f*, alignement *m*; **in r. with two markers,** à l'alignement de deux repères; *Nau: Av:* **r. beacon,** balise *f* de direction; **r. light,** feu *m* d'alignement; **r. station,** poste *m*, station *f*, de radioalignement; *Surv:* **r. post,** jalon *m*. **3.** (*a*) champ *m* libre; **he has free r. of the house,** la maison lui est ouverte; **to give free r. to one's imagination,** donner libre cours, carrière, à son imagination; (*b*) *NAm:* grand pâturage non clôturé; (*c*) *Nat.Hist:* aire *f* de répartition (d'une espèce, etc.); (*d*) *For:* cantonnement *m*. **4.** (*a*) étendue *f*, portée *f*, champ, domaine *m*; **wide r.,** champ très étendu; **r. of knowledge, of thought,** étendue des connaissances, de la pensée; **r. of a science, of an art,** domaine, champ, d'une science, d'un art; **r. of action,** champ d'activité; **r. of a musical instrument,** étendue, clavier *m*, d'un instrument de musique; **r. of voice,** étendue, diapason *m*, registre *m*, de la voix; **r. of vision,** étendue, portée, de la vue; portée visuelle; **r. of a telescope,** portée d'une lunette; **r. of audibility,** champ d'audibilité; *Phot:* **r. of contrast,** intervalle *m* de contraste; **the whole r. of politics,** le champ entier de la politique; **unlimited r. of speculation,** vaste champ d'hypothèses; **the r. of my observation,** mon champ d'observation; le cercle de mes observations; **the r. of our ideas,** le cercle de nos idées; **r. of expression,** variété *f* de moyens d'expression; **within my r., beyond my r.,** à ma portée; hors de ma portée; **not within my r.,** pas dans mes moyens; (*of writer, artist*) **to go outside his r.,** sortir de son talent; (*b*) **r. of the barometer,** variation *f* du baromètre; **r. of tide,** amplitude *f* de la marée; **mean r. of tide,** amplitude moyenne, niveau moyen, de la marée; **increase of r. between two tides,** rapport *m* de marée; **r. of temperature,** amplitude thermique; **mean annual r. of temperature,** amplitude thermique moyenne annuelle; (*c*) gamme *f*, assortiment *m* (de couleurs, etc.); **r. of sizes,** éventail *m*, série *f*, de dimensions; *Const:* assortiment de tailles; **wide r. of patterns,** ample, grand, assortiment, grand choix, d'échantillons; **salary r.,** éventail des salaires; **wide r. of speeds,** grand éventail, grand écart, de vitesses; *Aut:* **steering r.,** braquage *m* à maximum; *Phot:* **film with a wide r. of exposure,** film qui admet des écarts de pose; *Pharm:* **wide-r. remedy,** remède *m* à haute polyvalence; (*d*) **the whole r. of events,** la série complète des événements; (*e*) *Ph: etc:* gamme, bande *f*, plage *f*, zone *f*; **operating r.,** plage de fonctionnement; **usable r.,** plage d'utilisation; **energy r.,** bande, gamme, d'énergie; **r. of power,** gamme, plage, de puissance; *Aedcs:* **transonic r.,** zone, région *f*, d'écoulement transonique; *W.Tel:* **r. of audible frequencies, audible r., speech frequency r.,** gamme des fréquences audibles; **audio r.,** gamme de fréquences acoustiques; **transmission r.,** bande passante; **volume r.,** gamme de puissances sonores; **wave r.,** gamme d'ondes; *Cmptr:* **error r.,** plage d'erreurs. **5.** (*a*) distance *f* franchissable, rayon *m* d'action, autonomie *f* (d'un avion, sous-marin, char, etc.); **cruising r.,** autonomie à vitesse de croisière; **long-r., medium-r., short-r., aircraft,** long-, moyen(s)-, court(s)-, courrier(s); (*b*) *Atom.Ph:* parcours *m*, portée (des particules); **short-r. neutron,** neutron à parcours réduit; **r. straggling,** fluctuation *f* de parcours. **6.** (*a*) *Ball:* distance *f* (de tir), portée, tir *m*; **at a r. of 1000 metres,** à une distance de mille mètres; **within a r. of twenty kilometres of London,** dans un rayon de vingt kilomètres, à vingt kilomètres à la ronde, de Londres; **at close, short, r.,** à petite distance, à courte portée; **at mean, medium, r.,** à moyenne distance, à moyenne portée; **at long r.,** à grande distance, à longue portée; *Meteor:* **long-r. forecast,** prévision *f* à longue échéance; *Artil:* **high r.!** grande hausse! **low r.!** petite hausse! **estimation of r.,** appréciation *f* des distances; **fighting r.,** *U.S:* **combat r.,** distance de combat; **firing r.,** distance de tir; **ground r.,** distance sur le terrain, distance topographique; **map r.,** distance sur la carte; **to**

take key ranges, repérer des distances; **to correct the r.**, rectifier le tir; **to increase, lengthen, the r.**, allonger le tir, augmenter la portée; **to reduce, shorten, the r.**, raccourcir le tir, diminuer la portée; *Navy:* **to set the r. of a torpedo**, régler le parcours, la course, d'une torpille; *attrib.* **r. card**, planchette *f*; **r. dial**, cadran *m* de pointage; **r. finder, taker**, télémètre *m*; indicateur *m* de distance; **r. finding, taking**, télémétrie *f*; **r.-finding, -taking, calculator**, calculateur *m* télémétrique; **r. table**, table *f* de tir; (*b*) *Ball:* portée (d'une arme à feu, d'une arme de jet); **rifle that has a r. of a thousand metres**, fusil qui a une portée de mille mètres, qui porte à mille mètres; **throwing r.**, portée de jet (d'une grenade à main, d'un javelot, etc.); **effective r.**, portée efficace; **extreme r., maximum r.**, portée maximale, portée maximum; **horizontal r.**, portée horizontale; **true r.**, vraie portée; **beyond r., out of r.**, hors de portée, hors d'atteinte; **beyond the r. of the guns**, hors de portée des canons, de l'artillerie; **within r.**, à portée de tir; **within rifle r.**, à portée de fusil; *Navy:* **ship within torpedo r.**, navire *m* à portée, à distance, de lancement de torpille; (*c*) portée (d'un phare d'un projecteur, d'un radar, d'un sonar, etc.); **long-r. radar**, radar *m* à longue portée. **7.** (*a*) *Mil: etc:* **(shooting) r.**, champ *m* de tir, stand *m* (de tir); **experimental r.**, polygone *m* d'essais; **field firing r.**, champ de tir de campagne; **miniature r.**, stand de tir réduit; **rifle r.**, champ, stand, de tir au fusil; **torpedo r.**, polygone *m* de réglage des torpilles; (*b*) *NAm:* **golf r.**, terrain *m* d'exercice pour le golf. **8.** *Nau:* (*a*) *A:* bitture *f* (de câble); (*b*) **the ranges**, les bittes *f*; **r. heads**, bittes du cabestan. **9.** *Dom.Ec:* **(kitchen) r.**, fourneau *m*, cuisinière *f* (à charbon); *A:* **gas r.**, fourneau, cuisinière, à gaz; *NAm:* **(electric) r.**, fourneau, cuisinière, électrique.

range[2], *v.*

I. *v.tr.* **1.** (*a*) ranger, aligner (des troupes, etc.); disposer (des objets) en ordre, en ligne; *Typ:* **to r. the type**, aligner les caractères, les lignes; **line that needs ranging**, ligne sortante; *Nau:* **to r. the cable**, élonger la chaîne (de l'ancre); **they ranged themselves along the kerb**, ils se sont alignés, rangés, le long du trottoir; (*b*) ranger, classer; **to r. oneself with s.o., against s.o.**, se ranger du côté de qn, contre qn; **to r. s.o. among great men**, ranger qn au nombre des grands hommes, parmi les grands hommes; **to r. timber**, triquer, trier, les bois. **2.** parcourir (une ville, forêt, etc.); rôder dans (une forêt). **3.** braquer (un télescope). **4.** *NAm:* élever, (faire) paître, (du bétail) dans un grand pâturage non clôturé.

II. *v.i.* **1.** (*a*) s'étendre **(from one place to another, between two places)**, d'un endroit à un autre, entre deux endroits); **houses that r. along the railway**, maisons qui longent la voie; **the frontier ranges from north to south**, la frontière va, s'étend, du nord au sud; (*b*) *A:* **our house ranges with the next building**, notre maison est à l'alignement du bâtiment voisin; **books that r. well with one another**, livres qui s'alignent bien. **2.** (*a*) courir, errer; **to r. over the country**, parcourir le pays; rôder à travers le pays; **his eyes ranged over the audience**, ses yeux se promenaient sur l'auditoire; il parcourut des yeux l'auditoire; **researches ranging over a wide field**, recherches qui s'étendent sur un vaste terrain; **to r. far and wide (in a speech)**, discourir à perte de vue; (*b*) **latitudes between which a plant ranges**, latitudes entre lesquelles on trouve une plante; latitudes limites de la répartition d'une plante. **3. strip that ranges from two to three cm in width**, bande qui varie de deux à trois cm en largeur; **temperatures ranging from ten to thirty degrees**, températures comprises, s'échelonnant, entre dix et trente degrés; **incomes ranging from £5000 to £6000**, revenus de l'ordre de £5000 à £6000. **4.** *Artil:* (*a*) (*of projectile*) porter **(over a given distance**, à une distance donnée); **these guns r. over six miles**, ces pièces ont une portée de six milles; (*b*) (*of gun crew*) régler le tir; **to r. for elevation, for line**, régler en hauteur, en direction; **to r. for fuse**, régler la hauteur d'éclatement (du projectile).

ranger ['reindʒər], *s.* **1.** (*a*) *A:* rôdeur *m*, vagabond *m*; (*b*) *Ven:* chien courant; limier *m*. **2.** (*a*) conservateur *m* des forêts; garde forestier; (*b*) grand maître des parcs royaux. **3.** *Mil:* (*a*) **rangers**, (i) *A:* chasseurs *m* (à cheval); (ii) troupes montées faisant fonction de gendarmerie; gardes montés; gendarmerie montée. **4.** *Scout:* guide aînée.

rangership ['reindʒəʃip], *s.* charge *f* du grand maître des parcs royaux.

ranging ['reindʒiŋ], *s.* **1.** rangement *m*, alignement *m* (des troupes); disposition *f* (des objets) en ordre; *Typ:* alignement (des caractères); *Surv:* **r. rod, pole**, jalon *m*. **2.** *Artil:* (*a*) réglage *m* du tir; **smoke r.**, réglage par fumigène; **r. fire**, tir de réglage; (*b*) repérage *m*; **flash r.**, repérage aux lueurs; **r. mark**, point *m* de repère; **r.** stake, piquet *m* de mire. **3.** *Nau:* élongement *m* (d'une chaîne).

Rangoon [ræŋ'gu:n]. **1.** *Pr.n. Geog:* Rangoon, Rangoun. **2.** *s. P:* haschich *m*; marihuana *f*.

rangy ['reindʒi], *a.* **1.** (animal) enclin à errer; errant. **2.** (*a*) (animal, homme) bien membré; bien découplé; de grande taille; (*b*) (animal) effilé; (homme) élancé. **3.** (pays) montueux, montagneux. **4.** *NAm:* (projet, etc.) de grande envergure.

Ranidae ['rænidi:], *s.pl. Amph:* ranidés *m*.

raniform ['rænifɔ:m], *a.* raniforme, ranin.

ranina [rə'nainə], *s. Crust:* ranine *f*.

ranine ['reinain], *a.* **1.** *Amph:* ranin. **2.** *Anat:* **r. vein, artery**, veine, artère, ranine.

Raninidae [rə'nainidi:], *s.pl. Crust:* raninidés *m*.

ranivorous [rə'nivərəs], *a. Nat.Hist:* ranivore.

rank[1] [ræŋk], *s.* **1.** *Mil:* (*a*) rang *m*; **front r.**, premier rang; **rear r.**, (i) second rang, (ii) dernier rang; (*of troops*) **to break ranks**, rompre les rangs; (*of man*) **to break r.**, quitter les rangs, sortir des rangs; **to close the ranks**, serrer les rangs; **to keep r.**, rester dans les rangs, en rangs; **to return to the r.**, rentrer, revenir, dans les rangs; **to fall, form, into r.**, se mettre, se rassembler, en rangs; former les rangs; **to pass down the ranks**, passer sur le front des troupes; (*b*) **the ranks**, les hommes du rang, les hommes de troupe, les simples soldats, les hommes, le rang; **to serve in the ranks**, servir comme simple soldat; **officer promoted, risen, from the ranks**, officier sorti du rang; **to have risen from the ranks**, (i) *Mil:* avoir passé par les cadres, par la filière; (ii) être parti de rien; **to reduce an N.C.O. to the ranks**, casser un gradé; **reduction to the ranks**, cassation *f*, dégradation *f* (d'un officier, d'un sous-officier); **to return to the ranks**, redevenir simple soldat, retomber dans le rang; (*c*) **the r. and file**, (i) *Mil:* (les hommes de) troupe (simples soldats et gradés); **ten officers and two hundred r. and file**, dix officiers et deux cents hommes; (ii) **the r. and file of men**, le commun des mortels; monsieur Tout-le-Monde; **the r. and file of union members**, le commun des syndiqués; **the r. and file of the workers**, la piétaille du monde ouvrier. **2.** (*a*) rang (social), classe *f*; **high r.**, rang élevé; **people of all ranks**, gens de tous les rangs, de toutes les classes de la société; **person of (high) r.**, personne de haut rang, de qualité, de condition; **to rise to high r.**, s'élever au sommet de la hiérarchie, aux dignités; **the r. and fashion**, la haute société; *F:* la haute; le gratin; **according to one's r.**, selon son rang; **to take r. with s.o.**, prendre rang avec qn; avoir le rang de qn; **dancer of the first r.**, danseur, -euse, de premier plan, *F:* de la première volée; **artist of second r., second-r. artist**, artiste de second plan; **the higher ranks of the civil service**, les hauts fonctionnaires; les grands commis; (*b*) *Mil: Navy: etc:* grade *m*; **all ranks**, (i) les militaires *m* de tous grades; officiers, sous-officiers et troupe; (ii) tous sans exception; **badge of r.**, insigne *m* de grade; **date of r.**, date *f* de promotion; **officer's r.**, grade, rang, d'officier; **officer of high r.**, officier de grade élevé, de haut grade; **officers and other ranks**, officiers et personnel(s) non officier(s); officiers et troupe; **to be promoted to the r. of captain**, être promu (au grade de) capitaine; **to hold the r. of colonel**, avoir rang de colonel; **he is above me in r.**, il est mon supérieur hiérarchique; *F:* **to pull r.**, user et abuser de son rang; **to reduce in r.**, rétrograder (un officier, un sous-officier); **reduction in r.**, rétrogradation *f*; **to resign one's r.**, démissionner de son grade, *F:* rendre ses galons; **acting r.**, grade intérimaire; **substantive, permanent, r.**, grade à titre définitif; **temporary, provisional, r.**, grade à titre temporaire. **3.** (*a*) *Fin: etc:* rang (d'une créance, d'une hypothèque, etc.); **to assign a r. to a debt**, assigner un rang à une créance; *Stat:* **r. order statistics**, méthodes *f* statistiques de rang; (*b*) *Mth:* rang (d'un système de vecteurs); (*c*) *Min:* **ranks of coal**, stades *m* de la houille. **4. (taxi, cab) r.**, (i) station *f* (de taxis), stationnement *m* (pour taxis); (ii) les taxis en station; **the taxi at the head of the r.**, le taxi en tête de file.

rank[2]. **1.** *v.tr.* (*a*) *Mil:* ranger (des troupes); (*b*) **to r. s.o. among the great writers**, ranger, compter, qn parmi les grands écrivains; mettre qn au rang, placer qn au nombre, des grands écrivains; **I don't r. him very high**, je ne lui assigne qu'une valeur médiocre; (*c*) *Jur:* **to r. creditors (in bankruptcy)**, colloquer les créanciers; (*d*) *NAm:* occuper un rang supérieur à (qn); avoir le pas sur (qn); **to r. s.o. in age**, être l'aîné de qn. **2.** *v.i.* (*a*) (*of pers.*) se ranger, être classé, placé **(among**, parmi); **to r. among the best**, compter parmi les meilleurs; **to r. high**, *NAm:* **to r.**, avoir un rang élevé; **to r. third**, venir au, en, troisième rang; **to r. as a citizen**, avoir qualité de citoyen; **to r. with s.o.**, avoir le même rang que qn; aller de pair avec qn; **corporals will r. with sergeants for this duty**, les caporaux sont assimilés aux sergents pour ce service; **to r. above, below, s.o.**, occuper un rang supérieur, inférieur, à qn; être (hiérarchiquement, socialement) supérieur, inférieur, à qn; (*of creditor, claimant, etc.*) **to r. after s.o.**, prendre rang, avoir rang, passer, après qn; **to r. before s.o.**, prendre rang, avoir rang, passer, avant qn; **to r. equally with s.o.**, prendre, avoir, le même rang que qn; passer en même temps que qn; (*b*) (*of thg*) (i) *Jur:* (*of claim in bankruptcy*) être accepté à la vérification des créances; (ii) **to r. after sth.**, (*of mortgage*) prendre rang après, (*of share*) être primé par, qch.; **to r. before sth.**, (*of mortgage*) prendre rang avant, (*of share*) primer, qch.; **to r. equally with sth.**, prendre le même rang que qch.; **preference shares of all issues shall r. equally**, les actions de toutes les émissions prendront (le) même rang; **shares that r. first in dividend rights**, actions qui priment en fait de dividende; **the shares will r. for the July dividend**, les actions prendront part à la distribution de dividendes en juillet; (*c*) *Mil:* **to r. past**, défiler; *A:* **to r. off**, partir en marche.

rank[3], *a.* **1.** (*too luxuriant*) (trop) luxuriant; prolifique; (trop) fort; exubérant, dru; **r. vegetation**, végétation luxuriante; **r. grass**, herbe haute et touffue; herbe drue; **the rankest weeds**, les mauvaises herbes les plus vigoureuses; **land too r. for corn**, sol trop fort, trop riche, trop gras, pour le blé; (*of grass, etc.*) **to grow r.**, croître trop rapidement, trop dru; (*of weeds*) pulluler. **2.** (*a*) (*smelling, tasting, foul*) rance; fort (en odeur), fétide; **to smell r.**, sentir fort; (*b*) (*loathsome, gross*) grossier, répugnant. **3.** (*thorough*) complet, -ète, absolu; **r. poison**, (i) vrai poison; (ii) poison violent; **r. idolatry**, pure idolâtrie; **r. injustice**, injustice criante; **r. malice**, malice noire; **r. lie**, mensonge grossier; mensonge odieux; **r. stupidity**, stupidité grossière; **r. impostor**, imposteur fieffé; **r. swindler**, pur escroc; **r. fool**, parfait imbécile.

ranker ['ræŋkər], *s.* **1.** simple soldat *m*; *A:* **gentleman r.**, fils de famille qui s'est engagé dans les rangs. **2.** officier sorti du rang.

Rankine ['ræŋkin], *Pr.n. Ph:* **R. cycle**, cycle *m* de Rankine; **R. scale**, échelle *f* (thermométrique) Rankine; **R. temperature**, température *f* Rankine.

ranking[1] ['ræŋkiŋ], *a.* **1. (high) r.**, qui a un rang élevé; de premier rang; **the r. economists of the period**, les économistes éminents de l'époque. **2.** *NAm:* **r. officer**, supérieur *m* hiérarchique.

ranking[2], *s.* **1.** rang *m*; *Jur:* **r. of a creditor**, collocation *f* utile. **2.** hiérarchie *f*; *Pol.Ec:* **essentiality r.**, hiérarchies d'essentialité.

rankle ['ræŋkl], *v.i.* **1.** (*a*) *A:* (*of wound, sore*) s'envenimer, s'enflammer; s'ulcérer ou être ulcéré; (*b*) **the wound still rankles**, c'est une plaie qui saigne encore. **2.** (*of feelings, events*) **to r. (in s.o.'s mind, heart)**, rester sur le cœur de qn; **this refusal rankles in his mind**, ce refus lui reste, lui demeure, sur le cœur; il garde de ce refus une rancœur; il n'a pas digéré ce refus; **it rankled with her**, cela lui tenait au cœur.

rankling[1] ['ræŋkliŋ], *a.* **1.** (*a*) *A:* (*of wound*) envenimé, enflammé; (*b*) (*of hatred*) envenimé, venimeux. **2.** (*of injustice, etc.*) qui laisse une rancœur.

rankling[2], *s.* **1.** *A:* inflammation *f*, ulcération *f* (d'une blessure). **2.** rancœur (laissée par une injustice, etc.).

rankly ['ræŋkli], *adv.* **1.** fortement, avec exubérance, surabondamment, dru. **2.** avec une odeur fétide. **3.** grossièrement; **r. cheated**, grossièrement abusé.

rankness ['ræŋknis], *s.* **1.** luxuriance *f*, exubérance *f*, surabondance *f* (de la végétation, des mauvaises herbes). **2.** goût fort et désagréable; odeur forte; fétidité *f*. **3.** grossièreté *f* (d'une insulte, d'un mensonge).

ransack ['rænsæk], *v.tr.* **1.** fouiller (une bibliothèque, un tiroir, les poches de qn); fouiller dans (sa mémoire); **they had ransacked the room to find the letter**, on avait retourné la pièce pour trouver la lettre. **2.** dévaliser, faire le sac de, saccager, piller (une maison, etc.).

ransacking ['rænsækiŋ], *s.* **1.** fouille *f* (d'une bibliothèque, des poches de qn, etc.). **2.** pillage *m*.

ransom[1] ['rænsəm], *s.* **1.** (*a*) rachat *m* (d'un captif); *Hist:* **the Order of Our Lady of R.**, l'ordre *m* de Notre-Dame de la Merci; **to hold s.o. to r.**, mettre qn à rançon; rançonner qn; (*b*) *Jur:* **r. of cargo**, rachat de cargaison; (*c*) *Theol:* rachat (de l'humanité par Jésus-Christ). **2.** rançon *f*; **to pay r.**, payer rançon; **to exact a r. from s.o.**, rançonner qn; *F:* **it will cost a king's r.**, cela coûtera une rançon de roi; **to obtain sth. at a r. price**, obtenir qch. à prix d'or; **furs at r. prices**, fourrures *f* hors de prix; *Hist:* **r. bill, bond**, engagement *m* à payer par la suite la rançon demandée.

ransom[2], *v.tr.* **1.** (*a*) racheter (qn); payer la rançon de (qn); payer rançon pour (qn); (*b*) racheter, expier (qch.). **2.** (*a*) mettre (qn) à rançon; rançonner (qn);

faire payer rançon à (qn); (b) *Hist:* faire payer rançon à (un navire capturé en course).

ransomer ['rænsəmər], *s.* celui qui paie la rançon (de qn, *Hist:* d'une capture).

ransoming ['rænsəmiŋ], *s.* **1.** rachat *m* (de qn, d'un navire, mis à rançon). **2.** mise *f* à rançon; rançonnement *m.*

ransomite ['rænsəmait], *s. Miner:* ransomite *f.*

rant[1] [rænt], *s.* **1.** déclamation extravagante (d'un acteur, orateur). **2.** discours creux; rodomontades *fpl*; discours d'énergumène.

rant[2]. **1.** *v.i.* faire l'énergumène; déclamer avec extravagance; tenir un langage déclamatoire; **to r. and rave,** tempêter, extravaguer. **2.** *v.tr.* déclamer (un rôle, discours) avec extravagance.

rantan ['ræn'tæn], *s. F: A:* noce *f,* bombe *f*; **to be, go, on the r.,** faire la noce.

ranter ['ræntər], *s.* déclamateur, -trice; énergumène *mf*; harangueur *m.*

ranting[1] ['ræntiŋ], *a.* (style, etc.) déclamatoire; (orateur, etc.) tonitruant; (discours, etc.) d'énergumène.

ranting[2], *s.* = RANT[1].

rantus ['ræntəs], *s. Ent:* rhantus *m.*

ranula ['rænjulə], *s. Med:* ranule *f,* grenouillette *f* (sous la langue).

Ranunculaceae [rænʌŋkju'leisii:], *s.pl. Bot:* renonculacées *f.*

ranunculus, *pl.* **-uses, -i** [ræ'nʌŋkjuləs, -əsiz, -ai], *s. Bot:* renoncule *f,* ranunculus *m.*

Ranvier ['rænviər], *Pr.n. Anat:* **Ranvier's node,** commissure *f,* nœud *m,* de Ranvier.

ranz-des-vaches [rɑ̃:sdei'væʃ], *s. Mus: Sw.Fr:* ranz *m* des vaches.

Raoult ['rault], *Pr.n. Ch:* **Raoult's law,** loi *f* de Raoult.

rap[1] [ræp], *s.* **1.** petit coup sec et dur; **to give s.o. a r. on, over, the knuckles,** (i) donner sur les doigts à qn; (ii) remettre qn à sa place; **to give s.o. a r. on the head,** donner une calotte, une taloche, à qn; **r. at the door,** coup (frappé) à la porte; **there was, came, a r. on the door,** on a frappé à la porte. **2.** (a) *F:* punition *f*; **to take the r.,** se faire taper sur les doigts; payer les pots cassés; **to take the r. for s.o.,** se laisser punir pour protéger qn; *NAm:* **to beat the r.,** s'en tirer; échapper au châtiment; (b) *NAm: P:* peine *f* de prison; (c) *NAm: P:* accusation *f* (de meurtre, parjure, etc.).

rap[2], *v.* **(rapped) 1.** *v.tr.* (a) frapper (qch.), donner un coup sec à (qch.); **the chairman rapped the table to call the meeting to order,** *NAm:* **rapped the meeting to order,** le président a frappé sur la table pour rappeler l'assemblée à l'ordre; **to r. s.o.'s knuckles, to r. s.o. on, over, the knuckles,** (i) donner sur les doigts à qn; (ii) tancer qn; (b) *NAm:* **to r. s.o.,** (i) *F:* critiquer qn vivement, bêcher qn; (ii) *P:* arrêter, *P:* épingler (qn); (iii) *P:* tuer, buter (qn); (c) *Metall:* ébranler, ballotter (un moule avant de le retirer). **2.** *v.i.* **to r. at the door, on the table,** frapper un coup, donner un coup sec, à la porte, sur la table; cogner, frapper, sur la table; *Psychics:* **rapping spirits,** esprits frappeurs. **3.** *v.tr.* (a) **to r. out an oath,** lâcher, lancer, décocher, un juron; **to r. out one's words,** parler sec; (b) *Psychics:* (*of spirit*) **to r. out a message,** faire une communication au moyen de coups frappés.

rap[3], *s.* **1.** (a) *Hist:* petite pièce fausse d'un demi-farthing, qui avait cours en Irlande; (b) *F: A:* sou *m,* liard *m.* **2.** *F:* **not a r.,** rien du tout; **it isn't worth a r.,** ça ne vaut pas tripette, chipette.

rap[4], *s. Tex:* échevette *f* (de fil).

rap[5], *s. NAm: F:* conversation *f,* bavardage *m*; bavette *f,* causette *f.*

rap[6], *v.i.* **(rapped)** *NAm: F:* bavarder.

rapacious [rə'peiʃəs], *a.* (oiseau, avare, etc.) rapace; (marchand, etc.) voleur, -euse; (*of pers.*) **to be r.,** avoir les ongles, les doigts, crochus; avoir les mains crochues.

rapaciously [rə'peiʃəsli], *adv.* avec rapacité.

rapaciousness [rə'peiʃəsnis], **rapacity** [rə'pæsiti], *s.* rapacité *f.*

rapakivi [rɑ:pə'ki:vi:], *s. Geol:* rapakiwi *m.*

rape[1] [reip], *s.* **1.** *Lit:* rapt *m,* enlèvement *m,* ravissement *m*; **the r. of the Sabines, of Helen,** l'enlèvement des Sabines; le ravissement d'Hélène. **2.** *Jur:* viol *m*; **assault with intent to commit r.,** tentative *f* de viol; *U.S:* **statutory r.,** viol commis sur une personne au-dessous de l'âge nubile.

rape[2], *v.tr.* **1.** *Lit:* ravir (une femme); enlever de force (une femme). **2.** *Jur:* violer (une femme).

rape[3], *s. Hist:* district administratif (du comté de Sussex).

rape[4], *s. Bot:* **1.** (i) **(summer) r.,** colza *m*; (ii) navette *f*; *Husb:* **r. cake,** tourteau *m* de colza; **r. seed,** graine *f* de colza; **r. (seed) oil,** (i) huile *f* de colza; (ii) (huile de) navette. **2. wild r.,** sénevé *m* sauvage, moutarde *f* des champs.

rape[5], *s.* **1.** (*usu. pl.*) marc *m* de raisin; râpe *f.* **2.** *A:* **r. (wine),** râpé *m,* criquet *m.*

Raphael ['ræfeiəl], *Pr.n.m.* Raphaël.

Raphaelesque [ræfəlesk], *a. Art:* raphaëlesque.

Raphaelite ['ræfəlait], *s. Art:* disciple *m* de Raphaël.

raphania [rə'feiniə], *s. Agr:* raphanie *f.*

raphanus ['ræfənəs], *s. Bot:* raphanus *m.*

raphe ['reifi], *s. Anat: Bot:* raphé *m*; *Anat:* **palatine r.,** raphé du palais; **pterygomandibular r.,** ligament *m* ptérygo-mandibulaire.

raphia ['ræfiə], *s. Bot:* raphia *m*; **r. mat,** carpette en raphia.

Raphidae ['ræfidi:], *s.pl. Orn:* raphidés *m.*

raphide ['reifid], **raphis** ['reifis], *s. Bot:* raphide *f.*

raphidian [ræ'fidiən], **raphidiid** [ræ'fidiid], *s. Ent:* raphidie *f.*

rapid ['ræpid]. **1.** *a.* rapide; (a) **r. movement,** mouvement *m* rapide; *Physiol:* **r. eye movements,** mouvements oculaires rapides; **to make r. progress,** faire des progrès rapides; *El:* **r. drop in voltage,** chute *f* brusque de tension; *Atom.Ph:* **r. shutdown,** arrêt *m* brusque (d'une réaction en chaîne); *Artil:* **r. fire,** feu accéléré, continu; **r.-fire, r.-firing, gun,** canon *m* à tir rapide; **r. fire of questions,** bombardement *m* de questions; (b) **r. slope,** pente *f* rapide, raide. **2.** *s.* (*usu. pl.*) *Geog:* rapide *m* (d'un fleuve); **to shoot the rapids,** franchir les rapides (en canoë).

rapidity [rə'piditi], *s.* rapidité *f* (d'un courant, d'un objectif, etc.).

rapidly ['ræpidli], *adv.* rapidement; à grands pas.

rapier ['reipiər], *s.* rapière *f*; **r. thrust,** (i) coup *m* d'estoc, de pointe; (ii) *Fig:* trait *m* (de satire, etc.).

rapine ['ræpain], *s.* rapine *f*; **to live by r.,** vivre de rapine.

rappee [ræ'pi:], *s.* tabac râpé.

rappel [rə'pel], *s. Mount:* rappel *m.*

rapper ['ræpər], *s.* **1.** (a) frappeur, -euse; (b) acheteur, -euse, d'antiquités (dans les campagnes, etc.); antiquaire *m* qui fait des tournées. **2.** (a) marteau *m* (de porte); (b) *Min:* marteau avertisseur.

rapping ['ræpiŋ], *s.* **1.** coups frappés (à la porte, etc.). **2.** *Metall:* ébranlage *m* (d'un moule avant de le retirer).

rapport [ræ'pɔ:r], *s.* (a) sympathie *f*; rapport *m,* affinité *f*; **there was an instant r. between them,** ils ressentirent une sympathie immédiate; (b) *Psy:* rapport *m*; (c) (*spiritualism*) communication *f* par l'intermédiaire d'un médium.

rapporteur [ræpɔ:'tɜ:r], *s.* rapporteur *m* (d'une conférence).

rapprochement [ræ'prɔʃmɑ̃], *s.* rapprochement *m* (entre deux pays hostiles, etc.).

rapscallion [ræp'skæliən], *s.m.* homme de rien; vaurien; propre à rien; canaille *f.*

rapt [ræpt]. **1.** *p.p.* (a) enlevé; **r. (away, up) into heaven,** transporté au ciel; (b) ravi, enchanté, extasié **(by,** par); (c) occupé profondément; absorbé **(in,** dans); **r. in contemplation,** plongé dans la contemplation; recueilli. **2.** *a.* (*of attention, interest*) profond, enthousiaste; **to listen to s.o. with r. attention,** écouter qn avec une attention profonde; être suspendu aux lèvres de qn.

raptly ['ræptli], *adv.* (écouter) avec une attention profonde.

raptor ['ræptɔ:r], *s. Orn:* oiseau *m* rapace; *A:* **the Raptores** [ðəræp'tɔ:ri:z], les rapaces *m,* raptores *m.*

raptorial [ræp'tɔ:riəl], *a.* **1.** (oiseau *m*) de proie. **2.** (griffes, etc.) d'animal, d'oiseau, rapace.

rapture ['ræptjər], *s.* ravissement *m,* extase *f,* transport *m,* ivresse *f*; **to dance with r.,** danser avec ivresse; *Poet:* **the r. of strife,** la griserie de la lutte; **to be in raptures,** être ravi, enchanté **(with, over,** de); être dans le ravissement, être en extase; **in raptures of admiration, of delight,** transporté d'admiration, de joie; **to go into raptures,** s'extasier **(over,** sur); tomber en extase, se pâmer de joie; **to throw s.o. into raptures,** ravir, transporter, enthousiasmer, faire s'extasier, qn; *Med:* **r. of the deep,** ivresse *f* des profondeurs.

raptured ['ræptjə:d], *a. O:* ravi; transporté (d'admiration, etc.).

rapturous ['ræptʃjərəs], *a.* **1.** (cris) de ravissement, d'extase, d'enthousiasme; (joie) frénétique; **r. applause,** applaudissements *m* enthousiastes, frénétiques. **2.** ravi, transporté; en extase.

rapturously ['ræptʃərəsli], *adv.* avec transport, avec enthousiasme, avec frénésie; avec ravissement; d'un air ravi.

raptus ['ræptəs], *s. Psy:* raptus *m.*

rara avis ['rɛərə'eivis]. *Lt.phr. Fig:* oiseau rare; rara avis.

rare[1] ['rɛər], *a.* **1.** (atmosphère) rare, peu dense. **2.** rare; **very r., extremely r.,** très rare; rarissime; **r. object, occurrence,** objet, événement, rare; rareté *f*; **to grow r., rarer,** se raréfier; **it is r., it is a r. thing, for him to do that,** il est rare qu'il fasse cela; **r. courage,** courage rare; rare courage; *Ch:* **r. gas,** gaz *m* rare; **r. earths,** terres *f* rares; **r.-earth metals, elements,** métaux *m* des terres rares. **3.** *F: O:* excellent, fameux, fier; **you gave me a r. fright,** tu m'as fait une fière peur; **a r. thrashing,** une raclée soignée; **we had r. fun,** on s'est fameusement, richement, amusé; **we had a r. old time,** on s'en est donné à cœur joie; **I'm a r. one for a swim,** je suis enragé de la nage; **he's a r. one to fight, for a fight,** il est toujours prêt à se battre.

rare[2], *a.* peu cuit; (bifteck) saignant, bleu.

rarebit ['ræbit, 'rɛəbit], *s. Cu:* **Welsh r.,** welsh rabbit *m*; rôtie *f* de pain dorée au fromage; rôtie anglaise.

raree-show ['rɛəri:ʃou], *s. A:* spectacle forain de curiosités; petit spectacle ambulant (porté dans une boîte); optique *f.*

rarefaction [rɛəri'fækʃ(ə)n], *s.* raréfaction *f*; *Med:* **r. of bone,** raréfaction osseuse.

rarefactive [rɛəri'fæktiv], *a. Ph:* raréfiant.

rarefiable ['rɛərifaiəbl], *a. Ph:* raréfiable.

rarefied ['rɛərifaid], *a.* (air) raréfié; **r. state,** subtilité *f* (de l'air); **to become r.,** se raréfier; *Fig:* **to live in a r. atmosphere,** vivre dans une atmosphère détachée de ce monde.

rarefy ['rɛərifai]. **1.** *v.tr.* (a) raréfier (l'air, un gaz); (b) affiner (le goût); subtiliser (une idée). **2.** *v.i.* (*of the air, of a gas, Med: of bone*) se raréfier.

rarefying[1] ['rɛərifaiiŋ], *a.* raréfiant.

rarefying[2], *s.* raréfaction *f.*

rarely ['rɛəli], *adv.* **1.** rarement; **one r. sees him,** il est rare qu'on le voie; on ne le voit que rarement; **I r. ever see him,** je ne le vois que très rarement. **2.** *F: O:* (s'amuser) fameusement, merveilleusement.

rareness[1] ['rɛənis], *s.* **1.** rareté *f* (de l'atmosphère). **2.** (a) rareté (d'un objet); (b) *Lit:* excellence *f.*

rareness[2], *s.* état saignant (d'un biftek).

raring ['rɛəriŋ], *a. P:* **to be r. to go,** trépigner d'impatience.

rarity ['rɛəriti], *s.* **1.** = RARENESS[1]. **2.** objet *m* rare; événement *m* rare; **museum full of rarities,** musée plein de raretés; **here a fine day is a r.,** ici les belles journées sont rares.

ras [rɑ:s], *s.* (*in Ethiopia*) ras *m.*

rasant ['reiz(ə)nt], *a. Mil:* **r. fortification,** fortification rasante.

rasbora [ræz'bɔ:rə], *s. Ich:* rasbora *m.*

rascal ['rɑ:skəl]. **1.** *s.* (a) coquin *m,* gredin *m,* pendard *m,* fripon *m*; mauvais sujet; *F:* **you little r.!** petit coquin! **(you) lucky r.!** veinard! **that r. of a nephew of mine,** mon polisson de neveu; (b) *Cmptr:* variété *f* d'ordinateur numérique; (c) *Cu:* **Jersey rascals, fat rascals** = oreillettes *f.* **2.** *a. A:* du bas peuple; vulgaire; **the r. rout,** le vulgaire, la canaille.

rascally ['rɑ:skəli], *a.* **1.** de coquin, de gredin; canaille; (homme de loi) retors; **those r. barrow boys,** ces canailles de marchands des quatre-saisons; **r. trick,** méchant tour; friponnerie *f.* **2.** misérable, ignoble.

rasceta [rə'si:tə], *s.pl. Anat:* rascettes *f.*

rascette [ræ'set], *s.* (*palmistry*) rascette *f.*

rase [reiz], *v.tr.* = RAZE.

rash[1] [ræʃ], *s.* **1.** *Med:* éruption *f,* rash *m,* exanthème *m*; efflorescences *fpl* (de la rougeole); **teething r., tooth r.,** gourme *f,* strophulus *m*; **the r. comes out at the end of three days,** l'éruption paraît au bout de trois jours. **2.** *Fig:* **a r. of labour troubles,** une explosion de troubles ouvriers; **r. of customers' complaints,** inondation *f* de plaintes par la clientèle.

rash[2], *a.* téméraire; irréfléchi, étourdi; inconsidéré, impétueux; **r. words,** paroles inconsidérées, imprudentes; **r. person,** personne téméraire, imprudente; **r. act,** coup *m* de tête; **r. measures,** mesures inconsidérées; **r. judgment, statement,** jugement *m,* affirmation *f,* téméraire.

rasher ['ræʃər], *s.* tranche *f* de lard.

rashly ['ræʃli], *adv.* témérairement; inconsidérément, imprudemment, impétueusement, follement; **to speak r.,** parler à la légère; **to act r.,** agir sans raison, à l'étourdie.

rashness ['ræʃnis], *s.* témérité *f*; précipitation *f,* étourderie *f*; imprudence *f*; **to pay for one's r.,** payer sa témérité; *F:* payer la folle enchère.

rasp[1] [rɑ:sp], *s.* **1.** *Tls:* râpe *f*; **r.-file,** écouane *f*; grosse lime; lime mordante; **triangular r.,** trois-quarts *m inv*; **wood r.,** râpe pour bois. **2.** *Equit:* obstacle *m* difficile à franchir (à la chasse à courre). **3.** bruit *m* de râpe; crissement *m,* grincement *m*; **the r. in his voice,** le ton âpre, rauque, de sa voix.

rasp[2], *v.*

I. *v.tr.* **1.** râper (le bois, etc.); chapeler (du pain). **2.** racler, frotter (une surface); écorcher (la peau); **wine that rasps the throat,** vin qui racle, écorche, le gosier. **3.**

to **r. s.o., s.o.'s feelings,** froisser qn; produire une impression désagréable sur qn; *F:* taper sur les nerfs à qn.
II. *v.i.* **1.** grincer, crisser; (*of sound*) **to r. on the ears,** écorcher l'oreille; *F:* **to r. on the violin,** racler du violon. **2.** parler d'une voix âpre, sèche.
III. (*compound verbs*) **1. rasp away, off,** *v.tr.* enlever (qch.) à la râpe, en rapant; *Cu:* **to r. away the crust (of the bread),** chapeler la croûte.
2. rasp out, *v.tr.* dire (qch.), lâcher (une insulte), d'une voix âpre, rauque, sèche.

raspatory ['rɑ:spətəri], *s. Tls:* râpe *f*; *Surg:* raspatoire *m*, rugine *f*.

raspberry ['rɑ:zb(ə)ri], *s.* **1.** (*a*) framboise *f*; **r. jam,** confiture *f* de framboises; **r. vinegar,** vinaigre framboisé, à la framboise; **r. (flavoured),** framboisé; **r. (coloured),** framboise *inv*; (*b*) **r. (bush),** framboisier *m*; **r. cane,** tige *f* de framboisier; **r. bed, field,** framboiseraie *f*, framboisière *f*. **2.** *P:* bruit *m* des lèvres à l'imitation d'un pet; **to blow s.o. a r., to give s.o. the r.,** faire nargue à qn; = envoyer chier qn; **to get the r.,** (i) essuyer une rebuffade; (ii) se faire engueuler; **to get a r. from s.o.,** se faire rabrouer par qn.

rasper ['rɑ:spər], *s.* **1.** (*pers.*) râpeur, -euse. **2.** *Tls:* râpe *f*. **3.** *Equit:* obstacle *m* difficile à franchir (à la chasse à courre).

rasping[1] ['rɑ:spiŋ], *a.* (son)grinçant, irritant; **r. voice,** voix rauque, âpre, sèche; *F:* voix de crécelle.

rasping[2]. **1.** (*a*) râpage *m*; (*b*) travail *m* à la râpe; raclage *m*. **2. r. (sound),** bruit *m* de frottement; *Med:* **r. (murmur),** bruit de scie, de râpe; râpe *f* (du cœur). **3. raspings,** râpure(s) *f*(*pl*).

raspingly ['rɑ:spiŋli], *adv.* d'un ton, d'une voix, rauque, âpre; *F:* avec une voix de crécelle.

raspite ['ræspait], *s. Miner:* raspite *f*.

rasputitsa [ræspu'titsə], *s. Meteor:* rasputitsa *f*.

raspy ['rɑ:spi], *a.* **1.** (bruit) de râpe, de scie; (voix) âpre, rauque. **2.** (*of surface*) râpeux. **3.** (personne) de mauvaise humeur.

rasse ['ræsi, ræs], *s. Z:* genette *f* rasse, civette *f* rasse.

raster ['ræstər], *s. T.V:* trame *f*.

rat[1] [ræt], *s.* **1.** *Z:* rat *m*; (*a*) **black r.,** rat noir; **grey, brown, Norway, r.,** (rat) surmulot *m*; **water r.,** rat d'eau; campagnol nageur; **sewer r.,** rat d'égout; **female (of the) r., she r.,** femelle *f* du rat; *O:* rate *f*; **r. chinchilla,** abrocome *m*, rat chinchilla; **cotton r.,** rat des cotonniers; **multimamillate r.,** rat à mamelles multiples; **pencil-tailed r.,** octodonte *m*; **rice r.,** rat de rizière; **rock r.,** pétromys *m*; **spiny r.,** rat hérissé; échimys *m*; **striped r.,** rat rayé; **Brazilian tree r.,** rat arboricole du Brésil; **wood r.,** néotome *m*; (*b*) **bush-tailed marsupial r.,** phascolo(lo)gale *m*; **r. shrew,** gymnure *m*; **r. kangaroo,** bettongie *f*, potorou *m*, kangourou-rat *m*, *pl.* kangourous-rats; (*c*) **to clear a place of rats,** dératiser un endroit; **extermination of rats,** dératisation *f*; **r. week,** semaine *f* de dératisation; **r. poison,** (i) raticide *m*; (ii) *P:* mauvaise boisson; (*beer*) bibine *f*; (*wine*) vinasse *f*; (*spirits*) casse-gueule *m inv*; (*in ship, etc.*) **r. colony,** ratage *m*; *F:* **to live in a rat's nest,** vivre dans un nid à rats; **to smell a r.,** se douter de, subodorer, quelque chose; soupçonner anguille sous roche; **I smelt a r. at once,** cela m'a mis la puce à l'oreille; **to die like a r. in a hole,** mourir dans son trou, sans secours; **to be caught like a r. in a trap,** être pris comme un rat au piège; être fait comme un rat; *F:* **the r. race,** la curée des places, la foire d'empoigne, la course au biftek; *F:* **rats!** allons donc! pas possible! va-t'en voir (s'ils viennent)! tu rêves! *F: O:* **to have rats in the upper storey, in the attic,** avoir une araignée dans le plafond; *F:* **to have the rats,** (i) être rogne, hargneux; (ii) être en proie au delirium tremens; voir les rats bleus. **2.** *F:* (*a*) sale type *m*, salopard *m*; (*b*) traître *m*; *Pol:* transfuge *m*, renégat *m*; *Ind:* gâte-métier *m*; (*strike breaker*) jaune *m*, faux frère; (*c*) indicateur *m*, mouchard *m*; (*d*) **a little r. of a man,** un petit homme chétif, malingre.

rat[2], *v.i.* **(ratted) 1.** (*of pers.*) faire la chasse aux rats; attraper des rats; (*of dog*) tuer des rats. **2.** *F:* (*a*) passer à l'ennemi; faire défection; *Pol:* abandonner son parti; tourner casaque, retourner sa veste, changer de chemise; (re)virer de bord; (*b*) *Ind:* (*of man refusing to strike*) faire le jaune; (*c*) **to r. on s.o.,** (i) abandonner, planter là, qn; (ii) vendre, dénoncer, qn; **to r. on a promise, an obligation,** manquer à une promesse, obligation.

rat[3], *v.tr.* (*used only in third pers. sg. sub.*) *A:* **r. me if I allow it,** que le diable m'emporte si je le permets.

rata ['rɑ:tə], *s. N.Z: Bot:* métrosidère *m*, metrosideros *m*.

ratable ['reitəbl], *a.* = RATEABLE.

ratafia [rætə'fiə], *s.* **1.** (*liqueur*) ratafia *m*. **2. r. biscuit,** petit gâteau sec à pâte d'amandes.

ratal ['reit(ə)l], *s. Adm:* valeur locative imposable (d'un immeuble); évaluation cadastrale (d'un terrain à bâtir).

rataplan ['rætəplæn], *s. Onomat:* rataplan *m*.

rat-a-tat ['rætətæt], *s. Onomat:* rat(-tat)-tat *m*.

ratatouille [rɑtɑ'tu:j], *s. Cu:* ratatouille *f*.

ratbag ['rætbæg], *s. P:* (*a*) salaud *m*, salopard *m*; (*applied to woman*) chameau *m*, chipie *f*; (*b*) (*esp. Austr: & N.Z:*) drôle *m* de type; original, -ale, -aux.

ratbite ['rætbait], *a. Med:* **r. fever,** sodoku *m*.

ratcatcher ['rætkætʃər], *s.* **1.** preneur *m* de rats. **2.** (*of fox-hunter*) **to wear a r.,** porter un veston d'équitation en tweed.

ratch[1] [rætʃ], *s.* **1.** cliquet *m*, doigt *m* d'encliquetage. **2.** roue *f* d'encliquetage, à cliquet.

ratch[2], *v.tr.* **1.** munir (une roue, etc.) d'un encliquetage. **2.** denter, endenter (une roue).

ratchet ['rætʃit], *s.* (*a*) **r. (wheel),** roue *f* d'encliquetage, encliquetée, à rochet, à chien, à cliquet; *Aut:* **hand-brake r.,** secteur *m* du frein; (*b*) cliquet *m*; chien *m* d'arrêt; doigt *m* d'encliquetage; **r. stop,** bouton *m*, tête *f*, à friction (d'un palmer); (*c*) **r. (and pawl) mechanism, motion,** encliquetage *m* à rochet; **driving r.,** rochet *m* d'entraînement; entraîneur *m*; **r. lever, spanner, wrench,** levier *m*, clef *f*, à cliquet, à rochet; cliquet simple; **r. drill,** drille *f* à rochet, à levier; cliquet à canon, à percer, cliquet porte-foret.

rate[1] [reit], *s.* **1.** nombre proportionnel, quantité proportionnelle; **r. of failure, breakdown,** taux *m* de défaillance (d'un mécanisme, etc.); **r. per cent,** pourcentage *m*; **birth, death, marriage, r.,** (taux de la) natalité, mortalité, nuptialité. **2.** (*a*) taux, raison *f*; **at the r. of ten per minute,** à raison de dix par minute; **r. of speed,** degré *m* de vitesse; *Hyd.E: etc:* **r. of flow,** vitesse *f* d'écoulement; débit moyen; *I.C.E: etc:* **r. of air delivery,** débit de l'air; **at the present r. of consumption,** au taux actuel de la consommation; à raison de la consommation actuelle; *El:* **r. of charging,** taux, régime *m*, intensité *f*, de chargement (d'un accumulateur); **high charging r.,** haut régime de charge; **low-r. discharge,** décharge à faible régime; **r. meter,** intensimètre *m*; **linear, logarithmic, r. meter,** intensimètre linéaire, logarithmique; (*b*) allure *f*, vitesse, train *m*, cadence *f*; **to go at a great r.,** aller à grande allure; aller (à) grand train; **at the r. of a mile a minute,** à la vitesse d'un mille par minute; *Nau:* **at the r. of twenty knots,** à l'allure de vingt nœuds; *F:* **he ran off at the r. of knots,** il se sauva à toute vitesse; **at that r. he won't get home today,** à ce train-là il n'arrivera pas chez lui aujourd'hui; **he was going at a tremendous r.,** il allait d'un train d'enfer; **he dealt with this business at a marvellous r.,** il a conclu cette affaire avec une célérité merveilleuse; **at the r. you are going,** du train dont vous allez; **at the r. (at which) things are progressing,** au train où marchent les choses; **to talk away at a great r.,** parler avec une volubilité extrême; **unemployment is increasing at a fearful r.,** le chômage augmente avec une rapidité effrayante; *Artil:* **to increase, slacken, the r. of fire,** augmenter, diminuer, la cadence du tir; *Nau:* **daily r. of a chronometer,** marche *f* diurne d'un chronomètre; *Med:* **pulse r.,** fréquence *f* du pouls; *Cmptr:* **perforation, punching, r.,** vitesse, cadence, de perforation; **modulation r.,** rapidité *f* de modulation; vitesse télégraphique; *Av:* **r. gyro(scope),** indicateur *m* gyroscopique de vitesse de virage; gyromètre *m*. **3.** *Com: Adm: Fin:* taux; (*a*) **to pay s.o. at the r. of £100 per week,** payer qn au taux, au tarif, sur le pied de £100 par semaine; **at the r. of £2 an hour,** au taux, à raison, de deux livres l'heure; **standard wage r.,** taux du salaire de base; **rates of wages,** taux, barème *m*, des salaires; **trade-union rates,** le tarif syndical; **average r.,** taux moyen; **flat r.,** taux uniforme; **r. of interest, of discount,** taux d'intérêt, d'escompte; **market discount r.,** taux d'escompte hors banque; taux privé; **minimum lending r.,** *O:* **bank r.,** *U.S:* **prime r.,** taux d'escompte officiel; **rates for money on loan, money rates,** taux, loyer *m*, de l'argent; **Lombard r.,** taux des avances (sur nantissement); **rates of insurance,** taux, tarif, d'assurance; **low-r. insurance,** assurance *f* à tarif réduit; **r. of premium,** taux de la prime; *Adm:* **r. of income tax,** taux de l'impôt sur le revenu; (*b*) cours *m*; **r. of exchange,** cours, taux, de conversion (des monnaies); **the rates obtained at today's market,** les cours réalisés au marché d'aujourd'hui; **market r.,** cours du marché; **buying, selling, r.,** cours acheteur, vendeur; **normal r.,** cours fictif; *St.Exch:* **backwardation r.,** cours, taux, de déport; **carry-over, contango, r.,** cours, taux, de report; **demand, sight, r.,** cours, taux, à vue; **forward r.,** cours à terme; (*c*) prix *m*, tarif; **fixed r.,** tarif, prix, à forfait; **standard r.,** tarif uniforme; **special r.,** tarif spécial; **full r.,** plein tarif; **reduced, low, r.,** tarif réduit; **to give s.o. favourable rates,** accorder à qn des tarifs de faveur, des prix avantageux; **to sell sth. at a reasonable, fair, r.,** vendre qch. à un prix raisonnable; **hotel rates,** tarifs hôteliers; **commission rates,** tarif de courtage; *Journ:* **advertising, advertisement, rates,** tarif des annonces, de la publicité; *Post:* **postage, postal, rates,** tarifs postaux; **letter r.,** tarif (des) lettres; **first-class letter r.,** tarif lettres d'urgence; **newspaper r.,** tarif (des) périodiques; **printed-paper r.,** tarif (des) imprimés; **sample r.,** tarif (des) échantillons; **telegraph, telephone, rates,** tarif télégraphique, téléphonique; **inland rates,** tarif (du régime) intérieur; **night r.,** tarif de nuit; *Cust:* **preferential r.,** tarif préférentiel, de faveur; *Trans:* **flat mileage r.,** tarif kilométrique uniforme; **standard r. per mile,** base *f* kilométrique; **freight r.,** *Rail:* tarif (des) marchandises; *Nau:* (taux, cours, du) fret; **passenger r.,** tarif (des) passagers; *Rail:* **goods r.,** tarif (des) marchandises; **parcels r.,** tarif (des) messageries; **to fix the rates to be charged,** tarifer les prix; **r. fixing,** tarification des prix; **r. cutting,** forte réduction du tarif; (*d*) **r. of living,** train *m* de vie; pied sur lequel on vit; **to live at the r. of £10,000 a year,** vivre sur un pied de dix mille livres par an; **at that r.,** sur ce pied-là; à ce compte-là; de cette façon, manière; **I can't go on at that r.,** je ne peux pas continuer sur ce pied-là; **at any r.,** dans tous les cas, en tout cas, de toute façon; quoi qu'il en soit; **I did my duty at any r.,** toujours est-il que j'ai fait mon devoir. **4.** *Adm:* (*a*) taux (d'un impôt local); = centime *m* le franc; **the r. is 60 p. in the pound,** le taux est soixante pence par livre; (*b*) impôt local; contribution foncière; cotisation *f*; **to lay a r. on a building,** grever un immeuble; **to reduce the rates on a building,** dégrever un immeuble; **rent exclusive of rates,** loyer *m* non compris l'impôt mobilier; **rates assigned to an estate,** contributions affectées à une terre; **rates and taxes,** impôts et contributions; **county rates,** taxes régionales; = centimes départementaux; **borough rates,** taxes municipales; = centimes communaux; **this expenditure comes out of the rates,** cette dépense relève de la municipalité, de la commune; *A:* (*of pers.*) **to come on the rates,** avoir recours à l'Assistance publique; **r.-aided,** (foyer de marins, etc.) subventionné par la commune, par la municipalité; **r. collector,** percepteur *m* des impôts locaux, receveur municipal; **r. collection office,** recette (i) municipale, (ii) régionale. **5.** (*a*) *A:* classe *f*, rang *m*; (*b*) (*with num. a. prefixed, e.g.*) **fifth-r.,** de cinquième ordre; médiocre; *s.a.* FIRST-RATE, ETC. **6.** estimation *f*, évaluation *f*; **to value sth. at a low r.,** faire peu de cas de qch.

rate[2], *v.tr. & i.*
I. *v.tr.* **1.** (*a*) estimer, évaluer (qch.); fixer la valeur de (qch.); **to r. sth. high,** assigner une haute valeur à, faire grand cas de, qch.; **to r. sth. at its true value,** estimer qch. à sa valeur; **to r. a coin,** évaluer une pièce de monnaie; **he's rated (as) one of the best writers of today,** on le classe parmi les meilleurs auteurs d'aujourd'hui; **highly rated player,** joueur très coté; (*b*) considérer, regarder (comme); **to r. s.o. among one's friends,** mettre qn au nombre de ses amis; *F:* **to r. s.o.,** estimer qn. **2.** imposer, taxer (qn, qch.); tarifer (qch.); **to r. s.o., a property, at a certain sum,** taxer qn, un immeuble, à raison d'une certaine somme; **spirits are rated according to their alcoholic strength,** les spiritueux sont taxés, imposés, tarifés, selon leur teneur en alcool; **heavily rated building,** immeuble fortement grevé; *Ins:* **to r. s.o. up,** faire payer à qn une prime plus élevée. **3.** classer, classifier (une automobile, etc.); étalonner (une lampe, etc.); *Nau:* classer (un homme, un navire). **4.** régler, vérifier (un chronomètre). **5.** *esp. NAm:* (i) mériter, (ii) avoir droit à (un privilège, etc.).
II. *v.i.* **1.** (*a*) être classé **(as,** comme); (*b*) **machine that rates (at) four horsepower,** machine qui a une puissance nominale de quatre chevaux. **2.** *NAm:* **to r. with s.o.,** être estimé de qn.

rate[3], *v.tr. O:* tancer, semoncer, gourmander, morigéner (qn) **(for doing sth.,** d'avoir fait qch.); **to r. s.o. soundly,** tancer qn vertement; *F:* laver la tête à qn; flanquer un savon à qn.

rate[4]. **1.** *v.tr.* rouir (le lin, etc.). **2.** *v.i.* (*of hay, etc.*) pourrir.

rateability [reitə'biliti], *s.* capacité *f* d'être évalué.

rateable ['reitəbl], *a.* **1.** évaluable. **2.** imposable; **r. value,** valeur locative imposable (d'un immeuble); évaluation cadastrale (d'un terrain à bâtir).

rated ['reitid], *a.* **1.** *Tchn:* (*of characteristics, etc.*) indiqué par le constructeur; nominal, normal; de régime; *Veh:* **r. burden, carrying capacity,** charge normale (transportable); *Mec.E:* **r. load,** charge *f* de régime (d'un moteur, d'une machine); **r. power, pressure,** puissance, pression, nominale; *El:* **r. voltage,** tension nominale, de service, d'utilisation; *Av:* **r. altitude,** altitude *f* de rétablissement. **2.** (*with a. prefixed, e.g.*) **high-r.,** de forte puissance.

ratel ['reitel], *s. Z:* ratel *m*.

ratepayer ['reitpeiər], *s.* = contribuable *mf* à l'impôt local, foncier, à la contribution foncière.

-rater ['reitər], *s.* **1. first-r.,** as *m*; **second-r.,** médiocrité *f.* **2.** *Nau:* (*with number prefixed, e.g.*) **two-r., ten-r.,** yacht *m* de deux, dix, tonneaux.

rath [rɑ:θ], *s. Irish Ant:* place forte, enceinte fortifiée (située sur une colline).

rathe [reið], *a. A: & Lit:* (*of flower, etc.*) hâtif, précoce; **r.-ripe fruit,** fruit *m* précoce.

rather ['rɑ:ðər], *adv.* **1.** plutôt; **r. long than short,** plutôt long que court; **or r.,** ou plutôt, ou pour mieux dire; **last night or r. early this morning,** hier soir ou plutôt de bonne heure ce matin; **his occupation, or r. his profession,** son occupation, disons mieux, ou pour mieux dire, sa profession; **he recites r. than sings,** il récite plutôt qu'il ne chante; **the r. that . . .** d'autant plus que . . .. **2.** (*to some extent, slightly*) un peu; quelque peu; assez, plutôt, passablement; **r. better,** un peu mieux; **with r. a dazed look,** l'air quelque peu hébété; **r. pretty,** assez joli; **r. nice,** assez gentil; pas mal; **r. plain,** plutôt laid; **r. more,** un peu plus; **r. a lot of people,** pas mal de monde; **they have been on strike r. a lot,** ils ont fait grève assez souvent; **we numbered r. more than forty,** nous étions quarante et quelques; **to be r. out of sorts,** être un peu indisposé; **I r. think you know him,** je crois bien, j'ai idée, il me semble, que vous le connaissez; **I am r. inclined to agree with you,** je suis assez de votre avis; **I rather like it,** cela ne me déplaît pas; **he is r. touchy,** il est légèrement pointilleux. **3.** (*expressing preference*) plutôt (**than,** que); de préférence (**than,** à); **anything r. than that,** tout plutôt que, rien moins que, ça; **to choose one thing r. than another,** choisir une chose de préférence à une autre; **I'll take this r. than that,** je prendrai celui-ci de préférence à celui-là; **I would r. go,** j'aime, j'aimerais, mieux y aller; **I would r. not go,** j'aimerais autant ne pas y aller; **I would r. that you came tomorrow,** je préférerais que vous veniez demain; **I'd r. people didn't know about it,** je préfère qu'on n'en sache rien; **I would r. be loved than feared,** j'aime mieux être aimé qu'être craint; **I'd r. suffer than tell a lie,** plutôt souffrir que mentir; **I had, would, r. not, I'd r. not,** veuillez m'excuser; je n'y tiens pas; *F:* j'aime mieux pas; **I would sacrifice everything r. than that you should be disgraced,** je sacrifierais tout plutôt que de vous voir déshonoré. **4.** (*without doubt, assuredly*) (*a*) (*frequently* [rɑ:'θə:r]) **do you know him?—r.!** le connaissez-vous?—pour sûr! **r.!** je vous crois! bien sûr que oui! *P:* tu parles! (*b*) **r. not!** pas du tout! bien sûr que non!

rathite ['rɑ:θait], *s. Miner:* rathite *f.*

raticide ['rætisaid], *s.* raticide *m*, mort-aux-rats *f.*

ratification ['rætifikeiʃ(ə)n], *s. Jur: etc:* ratification *f*, homologation *f*; validation *f*; *Jur:* entérinement *m*; *Sp:* **r. of a record,** homologation d'un record; *Jur:* **act of r. and acknowledgement,** acte récognitif et confirmatif.

ratifier ['rætifaiər], *s.* personne *f* qui ratifie; ratificateur, -trice.

ratify ['rætifai], *v.tr. Jur: etc:* ratifier, sanctionner, valider, homologuer, *Jur:* entériner (des conclusions, une loi, un décret, etc.); **to r. a contract,** approuver un contrat; *Sp:* **to r. a record,** homologuer un record.

ratifying[1] ['rætifaiiŋ], *a.* (acte, etc.) ratificatif; (*of pers.*) ratificateur, -trice.

ratifying[2], *s.*, ratification *f.*

ratine [rə'ti:n], *s. Tex:* ratine *f.*

rating[1] ['reitiŋ], *s.* **1.** (*a*) estimation *f*, évaluation *f* (d'un pièce de monnaie, du caractère de qn, etc.); **engine r.,** calcul *m*, estimation, évaluation, de la puissance d'un moteur; (*b*) (i) tarification *f* (des transports, etc.), taxation (douanière, etc., d'une marchandise); (ii) répartition *f* des impôts locaux; (*c*) classement *m*, classification *f* (d'une auto, etc.); *Nau:* classement (d'un navire); étalonnage *m* (d'une lampe, etc.); (*d*) réglage *m* (d'un chronomètre). **2.** (*a*) évaluation (assignée à qch.); **he has a high r. for honesty,** on a une haute opinion de son honnêteté; **his r. with his colleagues isn't very high,** ses collègues ne le tiennent pas en haute estime; *Com:* **credit r.,** degré *m* de solvabilité; *NAm: Sch:* (*of candidate*) **to have the highest r. in an examination,** avoir les meilleures notes dans un examen; (*b*) *W.Tel: T.V:* (**popularity**) **r.,** indice *m* de popularité; taux *m*, cote *f* (d'écoute); *F:* (*of public figure, etc.*) **to have a high popularity r.,** jouir d'une grande popularité; (*c*) *Sp:* classe *f*, catégorie *f* (d'un athlète, yacht de course, etc.); *Box:* **featherweight r.,** série *f* poids-plume; (*d*) *Petr:* **octane r.,** indice (d')octane. **3.** (*a*) *Mec.E: El.E:* puissance nominale, régime (nominal) (d'un moteur, dynamo); **available r.,** puissance disponible; **maximum r.,** puissance maximale, maximum; **over r.,** surpuissance *f*; **r. performance,** rendement effectif; *Av:* **take-off r.,** puissance au décollage; *Aut: A:* **treasury r.,** puissance fiscale; (*b*) *Mch:* **boiler r.,** taux de vaporisation, débit prévu, d'une chaudière; (*c*) **ratings,** caractéristiques *f*, spécifications *f*; **nameplate ratings,** caractéristiques portées sur la plaque du constructeur; **r. plate,** plaque signalétique, du constructeur. **4.** *Navy:* (*a*) spécialité *f*, classe (d'un homme d'équipage, etc.); (*b*) **the ratings,** les matelots et gradés.

rating[2], *s. O:* semonce *f*, mercuriale *f*; verte réprimande; **to give s.o. a r.,** *F:* flanquer un savon à qn.

ratio, *pl.* **-os** ['reiʃiou, -ouz], *s.* **1.** raison *f*, rapport *m*, proportion *f*; **arithmetical r., geometrical r.,** raison arithmétique, géométrique; proportion arithmétique, géométrique; **harmonic r.,** proportion harmonique; **anharmonic, cross, r.,** rapport anharmonique; **common r.,** raison (de progression géométrique); **ultimate r.,** raison extrême; **in r. of one to three,** dans le rapport, la proportion, de un à trois; sous-triple; **in the same r.,** dans la même proportion (**as,** que); **in direct, inverse, r.,** en raison directe, inverse (**to,** de); directement, inversement, proportional (**to,** à); **the student-staff r. is twenty to one,** le rapport élèves-maître est de vingt pour un; **aspect r.,** (i) *Aer:* allongement *m* (d'une aile); **wing with an aspect r. of 10.75,** voilure à allongement 10.75; (ii) *T.V:* rapport hauteur-largeur de l'image; *Ph:* **mass r.,** rapport des masses, pondéral; **atomic r.,** rapport atomique; *Atom.Ph:* **breeding r.,** rapport de régénération; *Cmptr:* **deviation r.,** rapport de déviation; **one-to-zero r.,** rapport de discrimination (1 à 0); **break-make r.,** rapport d'impulsions; **selection r.,** rapport de sélection; **signal to noise r.,** rapport signal-bruit; *T.V:* **signal to image r.,** rapport signal-image; *Stat:* **correlation r.,** rapport de corrélation; *Mec.E:* **drive r.,** (rapport de) (dé)multiplication *f*; rapport d'entraînement; **reduction r.,** rapport de réduction; *I.C.E:* **carburettor mixture r.,** dosage *m* du carburateur; *El:* **voltage r.,** rapport de transformation des tensions; *Nau:* **balance r.,** rapport de compensation (du gouvernail). **2.** taux *m*; *I.C.E:* **compression r.,** taux de compression; compression *f* volumétrique; *Mec.E:* **feed drive r.,** taux d'avance; *Cmptr:* **error r.,** taux d'erreurs; **activity r.,** taux de mouvement (d'un fichier); **availability r.,** taux de disponibilité; *Rad:* **blip to scan r.,** taux de détection; *Com:* **mark-up r.,** taux de marque. **3.** coefficient *m*; *Fin: Book-k:* **cash r.,** coefficient de trésorerie; **r. of working expenses,** *U.S:* **operating r.,** coefficient d'exploitation; **price-earnings r.,** quotient *m* de capitalisation boursière par le dernier bénéfice annuel.

ratiocinate [ræti'ousineit], *v.i. Lit: & Hum:* raisonner, ratiociner.

ratiocination [rætiousi'neiʃ(ə)n], *s. Lit: & Hum:* raisonnement *m*, ratiocination *f.*

ratio-meter ['reiʃioumi:tər], *s. I.C.E:* indicateur *m* de pression (de réacteur).

ration[1] ['ræʃ(ə)n], *s. Mil: etc:* ration *f* (de pain, fourrage, etc.); *Mil:* **field r.,** ration de campagne; ration forte; **emergency rations,** vivres *m* de réserve; **iron rations,** (i) *Mil:* rations de combat; (ii) *F:* vivres de réserve; **to (go and) draw rations,** aller aux vivres; **rations went up after dark,** le ravitaillement se faisait à la nuit tombée; *F:* **decorations given out with the rations,** médailles décernées sans mérite; **short rations,** ration réduite; **to put on (short) rations,** rationner (une garnison, qn); mettre (qn) à la ration; **putting on rations,** rationnement *m*; **r. bread,** pain *m* de l'intendance, de troupe; *Adm:* **r. book,** carte *f* d'alimentation, de ravitaillement; **clothing r. book,** carte d'habillement; **r. book holder,** rationnaire *mf*; **goods off the r.,** marchandises vendues sans tickets, en vente libre.

ration[2], *v.tr.* **1.** (*a*) rationner (une garnison, un convalescent); mettre (qn) à la ration; (*b*) *Fig:* **to r. s.o. in food,** mesurer la nourriture à qn. **2. to r. (out) bread,** (i) rationner le pain; (ii) distribuer les rations de pain; *Fig:* **I have to r. my time,** je dois économiser mes loisirs.

rational ['ræʃənl], *a.* **1.** (*a*) raisonnable; doué de raison; **to be quite r.,** avoir toute sa tête; **r. mind,** esprit conséquent; (*b*) (*of explanation, etc.*) raisonné; conforme à la raison; **a r. French grammar,** grammaire raisonnée de la langue française; **r. belief,** croyance fondée sur la raison; croyance rationnelle; **r. tendencies (in religion),** tendances rationalistes; *F:* **r. footwear,** chaussures pratiques, rationnelles; *A:* **r. dress,** *s.pl.* **rationals,** culotte *f* (pour femme au lieu de jupe). **2.** *Ph: Mth: Astr:* (*of system, quantity, horizon*) rationnel. **3.** *s.* (*a*) **the r. and the irrational,** le rationnel et l'irrationnel; (*b*) *Mth:* quantité rationnelle.

rationale [ræʃə'nɑ:l(i)], *s.* **1.** raison *f* d'être. **2.** analyse raisonnée, exposé raisonné (d'un procédé).

rationalism ['ræʃ(ə)nəlizm], *s. Phil: Theol:* rationalisme *m.*

rationalist ['ræʃ(ə)nəlist], *a. & s.*, **rationalistic** [ræʃ(ə)nə'listik], *a.* rationaliste *mf.*

rationality [ræʃə'næliti], *s.* **1.** rationalité *f* (d'une croyance, etc.). **2.** faculté *f* de raisonner.

rationalization [ræʃ(ə)nəlai'zeiʃ(ə)n], *s.* (*a*) rationalisation *f* (d'une religion, industrie, etc.); organisation rationnelle (de l'industrie); (*b*) explication *f*, justification *f*, (de sa conduite, etc.) par de fausses raisons.

rationalize ['ræʃ(ə)nəlaiz], *v.tr.* **1.** (*a*) rationaliser (une religion, industrie, etc.); (*b*) **to r. one's conduct,** *v.i.* **to r.,** expliquer, excuser, sa conduite par de fausses raisons. **2.** *Mth:* **to r. an expression,** faire évanouir les quantités irrationnelles d'une expression.

rationalized ['ræʃ(ə)nəlaizd], *a. Elcs:* **r. unit system,** système d'unités (Giorgi) rationalisé.

rationally ['ræʃ(ə)nəli], *adv.* raisonnablement, rationnellement.

rationing ['ræʃəniŋ], *s.* rationnement *m.*

Ratisbon ['rætizbɔn], *Pr.n. Geog:* Ratisbonne *f.*

Ratitae [rə'taiti:], *s.pl. Orn:* ratites *m.*

ratite ['rætait], *a. & s. Orn:* **r. (bird),** ratite *m.*

ratlin(e) ['rætlin], **ratling** ['rætliŋ], *s. Nau:* enfléchure *f*; **r. stuff,** quarantenier *m.*

ratoon[1] [rə'tu:n], *s.* (i) rejeton *m*, (ii) **r. (crop),** récolte *f* de rejetons (de canne à sucre, de cotonnier, etc., après le recépage).

ratoon[2]. **1.** *v.i.* (*of sugar cane, etc.*) pousser des rejetons (après le recépage). **2.** *v.tr.* recéper (les cannes à sucre, etc.).

ratsbane ['rætsbein], *s.* **1.** *A:* = raticide *m*, mort-aux-rats *f.* **2.** *Bot: Dial:* cerfeuil *m.*

rat's tail ['rætsteil], *s.* **1.** mèche *f* (de cheveux maigre). **2.** *Vet:* queue-de-rat *f*, *pl.* queues-de-rat, arête *f* (à la jambe d'un cheval).

rat tail ['rætteil], *s.* **1.** *Ich:* macroure *m*, grenadier *m.* **2.** *Tls:* (lime *f*) queue-de-rat *f*, *pl.* queues-de-rat. **3.** *Vet:* (i) queue-de-rat (d'un cheval); (ii) cheval queue-de-rat. **4.** *attrib.* = RAT-TAILED.

rat-tailed ['rætteild], *a.* (lime, cheval) queue-de-rat, *pl.* queues-de-rat.

rat(t)an [rə'tæn], *s.* **1.** *Bot:* rotang *m.* **2.** *Com:* **r. (cane),** rotin *m*; jonc *m* d'Inde; souchet *m* d'Amérique; **r. (walking stick),** (canne *f* de) jonc; rotin.

rat(-tat)-tat ['ræt(ə)'tæt], *s. Onomat:* toc toc; pan pan; **to hear a r.-t. at the door,** entendre toc toc à la porte; entendre frapper à la porte.

ratteen [rə'ti:n], *s. Tex: A:* ratine *f.*

ratter ['rætər], *s.* **1.** (chien) ratier *m*; chat *m* qui prend des rats. **2.** (*pers.*) preneur *m* de rats. **3.** *P:* lâcheur *m*; traître *m.*

ratting ['rætiŋ], *s.* **1.** chasse *f* aux rats. **2. r. on a party, cause,** abandon *m* d'un parti, d'une cause; **r. on a duty,** manquement *m* à un devoir.

rattle[1] ['rætl], *s.* **1.** (*a*) hochet *m* (d'enfant); (*b*) crécelle *f* (d'alarme, etc.); (*c*) *pl. Rept:* **rattles,** sonnettes *fpl*; grelots *mpl*, cascabelle *f* (d'un crotale); (*d*) *Bot:* **yellow r., corn r.,** (rhinanthe *m*) crête-de-coq *f*; croquette *f*; rougette blanche; **red r.,** pédiculaire *f* des bois. **2.** *F:* (*pers.*) crécelle; moulin *m* à paroles. **3.** (*a*) bruit *m*, fracas *m* (de pierres, d'une voiture); bruit de ferraille, ferraillement *m* (d'une machine, d'une voiture); claquement *m* (d'une porte); cliquetis *m* (de chaînes, d'armes); tapotis *m* (d'une machine à écrire); trictrac *m* (de dés); crépitement *m* (d'une fusillade); grésillement *m* (de la grêle); broutage *m* (d'un outil de tour, etc.); crachement *m* (d'un haut-parleur); (*b*) *Med:* râle *m*; **death r.,** râle, râlement *m*, de la mort; (*c*) bavardage *m*, caquetage *m*; (*d*) tapage *m*, charivari *m*, bacchanal *m.*

rattle[2]. **1.** *v.i.* (*a*) faire entendre des bruits secs; (*of arms, etc.*) cliqueter; (*of car, machinery*) ferrailler; (*of rifle fire*) crépiter; (*of hail, rain*) crépiter, grésiller; (*of door, window*) trembler, branler; (*of articles in box*) ballotter; (*of wind on panes*) vibrer; **the crockery came rattling down,** la faïence est tombée avec fracas; **to make the windows r.,** faire trembler les vitres; **to r. at the door,** agiter la porte; *Veh: Aut:* **the body rattles,** la carrosserie fait du bruit; (*b*) (*of vehicle*) **to r. along, away, in, out,** rouler, partir, entrer, sortir, avec fracas, à toute vitesse; **the cart came rattling up to the door,** la charrette roula avec fracas jusqu'à la porte; (*c*) *F:* **to r. away, along,** bavarder, caqueter; **to r. on,** continuer à bavarder, parler tout du long de l'aune; *P:* en dégosier; **how she rattles on!** qu'elle a la langue bien pendue! (*d*) *Med:* râler. **2.** *v.tr.* (*a*) agiter (des chaînes, etc.) avec bruit; faire cliqueter (des clefs, des tasses, etc.); faire claquer (des castagnettes); faire sonner (son argent); **to r. the dice,** agiter les dés (dans le cornet); (*b*) consterner, bouleverser (qn); faire perdre tout son sang-froid à (qn); *Box:* ébranler (son adversaire); **somewhat rattled by what he was told,** assez fortement ébranlé par ce qu'il apprenait; **he never gets rattled,** il ne s'épate jamais; rien ne l'épate; il ne se laisse pas démonter; (*c*) faire (qch.) à toute vitesse; conduire (une charrette) à toute vitesse; *Nau:* **to r. up the anchor,** lever vivement l'ancre; (*d*) **to r. off a piece of work,** expédier un travail; **to r. off a poem,** réciter, débiter, rapidement (un poème, etc.); **to r. off one's prayers,** expédier ses prières; *F:* réciter ses prières à la six-quatre-deux; **to r. off a piece of music,** jouer au grand galop un morceau de musique.

rattle[3], *v.tr. Nau:* **to r. (down),** enflécher (les haubans).

rattle(-)box ['rætlbɔks], *s.* **1.** hochet *m* (en forme de boîte). **2.** *Bot: U.S:* (i) crotalaria *f*; (ii) silène enflé.

rattler ['rætlər], *s.* **1.** *Nau: etc:* **alarm rattlers,** klaxons *m* d'alarme. **2.** (*a*) guimbarde *f*, patache *f*; (*b*) *NAm:* train *m* de marchandises. **3.** *NAm:* = RATTLESNAKE. **4.** *F: O:* (*a*) coup dur; (*b*) cheval épatant; personne, chose, épatante.

rattlesnake ['rætlsneik], *s.* **1.** *Rept:* serpent *m* à sonnettes; crotale *m*; **horned r.,** serpent à sonnettes cornu; **prairie r.,** crotale des prairies; **pygmy r.,** serpent à sonnettes, crotale, pygmée; **timber r.,** crotale des bois; **Western diamond r.,** crotale diamantin de l'Ouest. **2.** *Bot: NAm:* **r. grass,** glycérie *f*.

rattletrap ['rætltræp], *s. F:* **1.** *Aut: etc:* vieille guimbarde, vieille bagnole; tapecul *m*, patache *f*. **2.** (*a*) babillard, -e; grand(e) bavard(e); (*b*) *P: O:* bouche *f*. **3. rattletraps,** bibelots *m*.

rattling[1] ['rætliŋ], *a.* **1.** bruyant, résonnant; crépitant; (voiture, etc.) qui roule avec fracas; **r. sabres,** sabres cliquetants. **2.** *F:* **at a r. pace,** au grand trot; **r. wind,** vent à écorner les bœufs. **3.** *F: O:* **r. good,** excellent, épatant; (dîner) rudement bon; (discours) tapé.

rattling[2], *s.* = RATTLE[1] 3.

rat(-)trap ['rættræp], *s.* **1.** piège *m* à rats; *Cy:* **r. pedals,** pédales *f* à scie(s), à dents. **2.** *NAm: P:* taudis *m*.

ratty ['ræti], *a.* **1.** (*a*) plein, infesté, de rats; (*b*) qui ressemble à un rat; **r. plait of hair,** natte de cheveux en queue de rat; (*c*) *NAm:* (i) de mauvaise qualité; moche; (ii) (appartement, etc.) mal soigné, délabré. **2.** *F: O:* fâché, en rogne, grincheux; grinchu; **he was really r.,** il était dans une de ces colères.

raucity ['rɔ:siti], *s.* raucité *f*.

raucous ['rɔ:kəs], *a.* **1.** rauque; **r. voice,** voix rauque, éraillée; *F:* voix de crécelle. **2.** *NAm:* **r. party,** réunion tapageuse, bruyante.

raucously ['rɔ:kəsli], *adv.* **1.** d'une voix rauque, éraillée. **2.** *NAm:* tapageusement.

raucousness ['rɔ:kəsnis], *s.* raucité *f* (de la voix).

raunchy ['rɔ:ntʃi], *a. U.S:* (*a*) de mauvaise qualité; moche; (*b*) (*of pers.*) (i) mal soigné; salaud; (ii) fort en gueule.

Rauracian [rɔ'reisiən], *a. Geol:* rauracien.

rauvite ['rɔ:vait], *s. Miner:* rauvite *f*.

rauwolfia [rɔ:'wɔlfiə], *s.* **1.** *Bot:* rauwolfia *f*. **2.** *Pharm:* réserpine *f*.

ravage[1] ['rævidʒ], *s.* ravage *m*; **the ravage(s) caused by the torrents,** les dévastations *f* des torrents; **the ravages of passion, of an epidemic,** le(s) ravage(s) des passions, d'une épidémie; **the ravages of time,** l'injure *f* des ans; *Lit:* l'outrage *m* des ans.

ravage[2]. **1.** *v.tr.* ravager, dévaster; **war had ravaged the whole country,** la guerre avait dévasté tout le pays; **ravaged face,** visage ravagé, meurtri. **2.** *v.i.* faire, causer, des ravages; **marauders ravaging for loot,** maraudeurs à la recherche du butin.

ravager ['rævidʒər], *s.* ravageur *m*, dévastateur *m*.

ravaging[1] ['rævidʒiŋ], *a.* ravageur; dévastateur, -trice.

ravaging[2], *s.* ravagement *m*.

rave[1] [reiv], *s.* (*usu. pl.*) **raves,** ridelles *f* (d'une charrette); **floating raves,** fausses ridelles; bers *m*.

rave[2], *s. F:* **1.** *Journ: etc:* éloge *m* enthousiaste; *attrib.* **r. review, notice,** critique *f*, revue *f*, dithyrambique. **2.** béguin *m*, toquade *f*.

rave[3], *v.i.* (*a*) *A:* (*of patient*) être en délire; avoir le délire; délirer; divaguer; *F:* battre la campagne; *F:* **you're raving!** vous divaguez! (*b*) (*in anger*) **to r. and storm,** jeter feu et flamme; tempêter; **to r. at, against, s.o.,** s'emporter, pester, contre qn; (*c*) (*of sea, wind*) être en furie; faire rage; (*d*) *F:* (*with enthusiasm*) **to r. about sth.,** être fou de qch.; s'extasier sur qch.; **it's nothing to r. about,** il n'y a pas de quoi crier (au) miracle.

rave(-)hook ['reivhuk], *s. Tls:* bec-de-corbin *m*, bec-de-corbeau *m*, *pl.* becs-de-corbin, -corbeau.

ravel[1] ['ræv(ə)l], *s.* **1.** emmêlement *m*, enchevêtrement *m* (de fils, etc.); **threads in a r.,** fils enchevêtrés, emmêlés. **2.** effilochure *f*.

ravel, *v.* **(ravelled) 1.** *v.tr.* (*a*) embrouiller, enchevêtrer, emmêler (un écheveau, les affaires, etc.); (*b*) **to r. (out),** défiler, défilocher, effiler, effilocher, éfaufiler (un tissu) (pour en faire de la charpie, etc.); (*c*) **to r. out,** débrouiller, démêler (des fils, une affaire). **2.** *v.i.* (*a*) (*of skein, etc.*) s'embrouiller, s'enchevêtrer; (*b*) **to r. (out),** s'effiler, s'effilocher.

ravelin ['rævlin], *s. A.Fort:* ravelin *m*, demi-lune *f*, *pl.* demi-lunes.

ravelled ['ræv(ə)ld], *a.* **1.** embrouillé, emmêlé, enchevêtré. **2.** effiloché.

ravelling ['ræv(ə)liŋ], *s.* **1.** effilochage *m*, défilage *m*. **2.** effilochure *f*, effilure *f*. **3.** *Civ.E:* érosion (de la chaussée causée par un défaut du liant).

raven[1] ['reiv(ə)n]. **1.** *s. Orn:* grand corbeau; *Fr.C:* corbeau. **2.** *a.* **r. (black),** noir comme un corbeau; *Lit:* **r. locks,** boucles d'un noir de jais, d'un noir d'ébène.

raven[2] ['ræv(ə)n]. *A: & Lit:* **1.** *v.i.* faire des ravages; vivre de rapine; (*of animal*) chercher sa proie; **to r. on sth.,** faire sa proie de qch.; se (re)paître de qch.; **to r. after sth.,** chercher à faire sa proie de qch.; **to r. for sth.,** être affamé de qch. **2.** *v.tr.* ravir, dévorer (la proie).

ravenala [rævi'neilə], *s. Bot:* ravenala *m*; arbre *m* du voyageur.

ravening[1] ['ræv(ə)niŋ], *a.* vorace, rapace; **r. wolves,** loups dévorants.

ravening[2], *s.* **1.** rapine *f*. **2.** rapacité *f*, voracité *f*.

Ravenna [rə'verə], *Pr.n. Geog:* Ravenne *f*.

ravenous ['ræv(ə)nəs], *a.* **1.** (*a*) *A:* rapace; (*b*) (animal) vorace. **2.** (*a*) **r. appetite,** appétit *m* vorace, féroce; **r. hunger,** faim dévorante; (*b*) affamé **(for,** de); *F:* **to be r.,** avoir une faim dévorante, une faim de loup, un appétit de cheval; *F:* mourir de faim.

ravenously ['ræv(ə)nəsli], *adv.* voracement; **to eat r.,** manger gloutonnement, goulûment.

ravenousness ['ræv(ə)nəsnis], *s.* **1.** voracité *f*. **2.** faim dévorante, de loup.

ravin ['rævin], *s. A: & Lit:* **1.** rapine *f*; **beast of r.,** bête *f* de proie. **2.** proie *f*.

ravine[1] [rə'vi:n], *s.* ravin *m*, ravine *f*.

ravine[2], *v.tr.* (*of torrent, etc.*) raviner (les terres).

raving[1] ['reiviŋ], *a.* **1.** (*a*) en délire; délirant; (*b*) furieux; fou, *f.* folle; **r. lunatic,** fou furieux. **2.** *F:* (succès) fou; (beauté) remarquable, extraordinaire.

raving[2], *s.* **1.** délire *m*, divagation *f*, frénésie *f*. **2. ravings,** paroles incohérentes; hallucinations nées du délire; **ravings of a madman,** divagations d'un fou.

ravioli [rævi'ouli], *s. Cu:* ravioli *mpl*.

ravish ['ræviʃ], *v.tr.* **1.** *O:* **1.** (*a*) ravir (qn, qch.); enlever (qn, qch.) de force; **ravished from our sight by his untimely death,** enlevé à nos yeux par une mort prématurée; (*b*) violer, forcer (une femme). **2.** ravir (d'admiration); transporter, enchanter (qn).

ravisher ['ræviʃər], *s. O:* **1.** (*a*) ravisseur *m*, voleur *m*; (*b*) ravisseur, violateur *m* (d'une femme). **2.** *F:* **what a r.!** quelle femme ravissante!

ravishing[1] ['ræviʃiŋ], *a.* **1.** *O:* **r. wolves,** loups dévorants, voraces, *A:* ravissants. **2.** *F:* (spectacle, etc.) ravissant, enchanteur; **r. woman,** femme ravissante; enchanteresse.

ravishing[2], **ravishment** ['ræviʃmənt], *s. O:* **1.** (*a*) enlèvement *m*, rapt *m*; (*b*) viol *m* (d'une femme). **2.** ravissement *m*; transports *mpl* (de joie, d'admiration).

ravishingly ['ræviʃiŋli], *adv.* d'une manière ravissante; **r. dressed,** habillée à ravir.

raw [rɔ:].

I. *a.* **1.** cru; **r. meat,** viande crue, saignante; (*for feeding lions, etc.*) carnage *m*; **r. apple,** pomme crue; **r. brick,** brique crue. **2.** (*a*) **r. material,** matière(s) première(s); matériaux bruts, non apprêtés; **r. skins,** peaux vertes; **r. silk,** soie *f* grège; **r. oil,** huile brute; **r. sugar,** sucre brut; **r. metal,** métal brut; **r. water,** eau brute, non traitée; *Brew:* **r. grain,** graines non maltées; *Cmptr:* **r. data,** données brutes, à traiter; (*b*) **r. colouring,** colori cru, agressif; couleurs crues, agressives; **r.(-flavoured) tea,** thé à goût âpre. **3.** sans expérience; inexpérimenté, novice, neuf; **a r. hand,** un novice; *F:* un bleu; **r. troops,** troupes non aguerries, inaguerries. **4.** à vif; **r. wound,** plaie vive, saignante; **r. flesh,** chair *f* à vif; **r. place,** écorchure *f*; endroit *m* à vif; **drink that makes one's throat r.,** boisson qui écorche le gosier; **my nerves are r.,** j'ai les nerfs à fleur de peau; **r. edge of the cloth,** bord coupé du tissu. **5. r. weather,** temps âpre, temps gris et froid.

II. *s.* (*a*) **to touch s.o. on the r.,** piquer, atteindre, toucher, qn au vif; toucher qn à un endroit sensible; (*b*) **in the r.,** (i) cru, brut; (ii) *F:* nu; **life in the r.,** la vie rude, primitive; *F:* **to bathe in the r.,** se baigner tout nu.

raw[2], *v.tr.* mettre à vif, écorcher (le dos d'un cheval, etc.).

rawboned ['rɔ:bound], *a.* maigre, décharné; (cheval) efflanqué.

rawhide ['rɔ:haid]. **1.** *s.* (*a*) cuir vert; cuir, peau *f*, en poil; (*b*) (i) fouet *m*, (ii) cordage *m*, en cuir vert. **2.** *a.* de, en, cuir vert.

rawly ['rɔ:li], *adv.* **the wind blew r.,** le vent soufflait aigrement, âprement.

rawness ['rɔ:nis], *s.* **1.** crudité *f* (des fruits, etc.). **2.** inexpérience *f* (d'une recrue, etc.). **3.** écorchure *f*; excoriation *f*. **4.** froid *m* humide; âpreté *f* (du temps).

ray[1] [rei], *s.* **1.** rayon *m*; (*a*) **r. of light,** rayon de lumière, lumineux; **red, orange, rays,** radiations rouges, orangées; *Phot:* **r. filter,** filtre *m*, écran *m*, orthochromatique; filtre coloré; **heat r.,** rayon calorifique; **cosmic rays,** rayons cosmiques, rayonnement *m* cosmique; *Elcs:* **cathode rays,** rayons cathodiques; **positive, canal, r.,** rayon positif, canal; *Rad.-A:* **alpha, beta, gamma, rays,** rayons, rayonnement, alpha, bêta, gamma; **hard, harsh, rays,** rayons durs; **soft rays,** rayons mous; **grenz, infraroentgen, rays,** rayons limites *m*, rayons ultra-mous; *Lit:* (*science fiction*) **death rays,** rayons de mort, qui tuent; (*b*) *Fig:* **a r. of hope,** un rayon, une lueur, d'espoir. **2.** *Opt:* visée *f*; **back r.,** visée inverse; **to take a r. on an object,** faire une visée sur un objet. **3.** *Nat.Hist:* rayon (d'une ombelle, nageoire, etc.); **starfish with five rays,** étoile *f* de mer à cinq branches; *Bot:* **medullary rays,** rayons médullaires; **r. flower,** fleur radiée; **r. florets,** fleurs extérieures, rayonnantes (d'une composée); *Bac:* **r. fungus,** actinomycès *m*. **4.** *Mth:* **half r.,** demi-droite *f*, *pl.* demi-droites.

ray[2], *v.* **to r. (forth, off, out),** (*a*) *v.tr.* darder, faire rayonner (la lumière); (*b*) *v.i.* rayonner; émettre des rayons (lumineux, etc.).

ray[3], *s. Ich:* (*a*) raie *f*; **bordered r.,** raie grise; **flowered r.,** raie fleurie; **painted r.,** raie mêlée; **smooth r.,** raie lisse; **spotted r.,** raie miroir; **undulate r.,** raie mosaïque; (*b*) **electric, torpedo, r.,** torpille *f*; **angel, shark, r.,** ange *m* de mer, angelot *m*; *F:* diable *m* de mer.

ray[4], *s. Mus:* **1. (fixed) r.,** ré *m*. **2.** (*movable r.*) la sous-tonique, la sous-médiante.

Rayah ['raiə], *s.* (*in Turkey*) raïa *m*.

rayed [reid], *a. Nat.Hist:* radié.

Rayleigh ['reili], *Pr.n. Ph:* **Rayleigh's equation, formula, etc.,** l'équation *f*, la formule, etc., de Rayleigh.

rayless ['reilis], *a.* **1.** (*a*) sans rayons (lumineux, actiniques, etc.); (*b*) sans lumière; obscur. **2.** *Bot:* (composée) sans fleurs rayonnantes.

raylet ['reilit], *s.* petit rayon, petite lueur (d'espoir, etc.).

rayon ['reiɔn], *s. Tex:* rayonne *f*.

rayonnant ['reiənənt], *a. Her: Arch:* (*of star, window tracery*) rayonnant.

raze [reiz], *v.tr.* **1.** (*a*) raser, démanteler (des fortifications, etc.); **to r. a building to the ground,** raser un édifice; abattre un édifice à ras de terre; **the city was razed to the ground,** la ville fut détruite de fond en comble; *Const:* **to r. a wall,** recéper un mur; (*b*) *Geol:* araser (un relief). **2.** *O: & Lit:* **to r. (out),** effacer, rayer, biffer (un mot, etc.); effacer (un souvenir) de la mémoire. **3.** *A:* érafler (la peau).

razee[1] [rei'zi:], *s. Nau: A:* vaisseau rasé.

razee[2], *v.tr. Nau: A:* raser (un vaisseau).

razing ['reiziŋ], *s.* **1.** (*a*) rasement *m* (d'une forteresse, etc.); (*b*) *Geol:* arasement *m* (d'un relief). **2.** *Tls:* **r. iron,** bec-de-corbin *m*, *pl.* becs-de-corbin.

razor ['reizər], *s.* **1.** rasoir *m*; **straight r.,** *F:* **cutthroat r.,** rasoir à manche; **hollow-ground r.,** rasoir évidé; **safety r.,** rasoir de sûreté, mécanique, américain; **electric r.,** rasoir électrique; **r. blade,** lame *f* de rasoir; **r. edge,** (i) fil *m*, tranchant *m*, de rasoir; (ii) arête *f* (de montagne) en lame de couteau; **to be on a r. edge, on the razor's edge,** se trouver dans une situation critique; être au bord de l'abîme; *W.Tel:* **r.-edge tuning,** accordage très poussé; **r. paste,** pâte *f* à rasoir; **r. stone,** pierre *f* à rasoir; **r. wipe,** essuie-rasoir *m*, *pl.* essuie-rasoir(s); frottoir *m* de barbier; *Phil:* **Occam's r.,** le rasoir d'Occam. **2. r. fish,** (i) *Ich:* rason *m*, razon *m*, rasoir; (ii) *Moll:* (*also* **r. clam, r. shell**) solen *m*, manche *m* de couteau.

razorback ['reizəbæk], *s.* **1.** dos tranchant (de cheval maigre, etc.). **2.** *attrib.* (*a*) *Z:* **r. (whale),** rorqual, -als, *m*; (*b*) *Z: NAm:* **r. (hog),** (espèce *f* maigre de) sanglier *m*; (*c*) **r. (hill),** colline *f* en dos d'âne.

razor-backed ['reizəbækt], *a.* (cheval, etc.) à dos tranchant; (colline) en dos d'âne.

razorbill ['reizəbil], *s.* petit pingouin, pingouin torda; *Fr.C:* gode *m*.

razz[1] [ræz], *s. P:* ridicule *f*; huées *fpl*; **to give s.o. the r.,** se moquer, se gausser, de qn.

razz[2], *v.tr. & i. P:* **to r. (at) s.o.,** se moquer, se gausser, de qn; narguer qn.

razzia ['ræziə], *s.* razzia *f*.

razzle(-dazzle) ['ræzl(dæzl)], *s. F:* **1.** bombe *f*, bamboche *f*, bordée *f*; **to go on the r.(-d.),** faire la noce, la nouba, la bringue; tirer une bordée. **2. r.-d.,** (*a*) tohu-bohu *m*; brouillamini *m*, pagaïe *f*; (*b*) tape-à-l'œil *m*, clinquant *m*; (*c*) *Sp: NAm:* jeu fait pour embrouiller l'équipe adverse.

razz(a)matazz ['ræz(ə)mətæz], *s. F:* **1.** = RAZZLE-DAZZLE. **2.** chose démodée, vieux jeu.

re[1] [rei], *s. Mus:* **1. (fixed re)** ré *m*. **2.** (*movable re*) la sous-tonique; la sous-médiante.

re² [riː]. **1.** *Lt. s. as prep.phr. Jur:* **(in) re Martin v. Thomas,** (en l')affaire Martin contre Thomas. **2.** *prep. Com:* **re your letter of June 10th,** relativement à, me référant à, au sujet de, votre lettre du 10 juin.

re- [riː], *pref.* **1.** re-, ré-, r-; **rebaptize,** rebaptiser; **reclothe,** rhabiller; **reinsurance,** réassurance. **2.** (*a*) (*before verb*) **to readjourn,** ajourner de nouveau; **to re-hear a case,** entendre à nouveau une cause; (*b*) (*before noun*) nouveau, -elle; **recolonization,** nouvelle colonisation.

reabsorb [riːəb'sɔːb], *v.tr.* réabsorber.

reabsorption [riːəb'sɔːpʃ(ə)n], *s.* réabsorption *f.*

reaccustom [riːə'kʌstəm], *v.tr.* réhabituer, rhabituer, réaccoutumer (**to,** à).

reach¹ [riːtʃ], *s.* **1.** (*a*) extension *f* (de la main); **to make a r. for sth.,** étendre la main pour qch.; (*b*) étendue *f*; portée *f* (du bras, etc.); *Box:* allonge *f*; **your r. is longer than mine,** votre bras s'étend plus loin que le mien; *Fenc:* **to have a long r.,** avoir beaucoup d'étendue; *Box:* **to have the longer r.,** être avantagé en allonge; **within s.o.'s r.,** à la portée de qn; **within r. of the hand,** à portée de la main; *F:* sous la main; **object placed well within r., within easy r., of s.o.,** objet placé bien à la portée de qn, à courte portée, à courte distance; **out of r.,** hors de portée; **out of, beyond, above, s.o.'s r.,** hors de la portée de qn; hors d'atteinte; **no help was within r.,** on était hors de portée de tout secours; **beyond the r. of (all) suspicion,** à l'abri de tout soupçon; **beyond the r. of envy,** au-dessus de la malveillance; **to put s.o. beyond the r., out of (the) r., of justice, of s.o.'s revenge,** soustraire qn aux recherches de la justice, à la vengeance de qn; **planets within the r. of an ordinary telescope,** planètes visibles à l'aide d'un téléscope ordinaire; **cars within the r. of small purses,** voitures à des prix abordables, à la portée des petites bourses; **posts within the r. of all,** emplois accessibles à tous; **the goal is within our r.,** nous touchons au but; (*c*) **hotel within easy r. of the station,** hôtel à proximité de la gare; **Versailles is within easy r. of Paris,** de Versailles on va facilement à Paris; (*d*) étendue *f* (de l'esprit); **beyond the r. of human intellect,** au-dessus de la portée de l'entendement humain; **it is beyond my r.,** cela me dépasse. **2.** (*a*) **r. of meadow,** étendue de prairies; **the far reaches of the valley,** les lointains *m* de la vallée; (*b*) **the higher reaches of the civil service,** les hauts échelons de l'administration. **3.** (*a*) partie droite (d'un fleuve) entre deux coudes; plan *m* d'eau; bief *m* (d'un canal); (*b*) *Nau:* bordée (courue avec le vent par le travers); **to make a r.,** courir une bordée. **4.** *Tex:* **r. of a drawing frame,** écartement *m* des rouleaux d'un banc d'étirage.

reach², *v.*

I. *v.tr.* **1. to r. out,** étendre; tendre, avancer (la main, etc.); **the tree reaches out its branches,** l'arbre étend ses branches. **2.** atteindre; **he could not r. his adversary,** il ne pouvait pas atteindre son adversaire; **can you r. the ceiling?** pouvez-vous toucher au plafond? **the law does not r. these cases,** la loi ne s'étend pas jusqu'à ces cas; **men who cannot be reached by reason,** hommes qu'on ne peut pas gagner par la raison; **the words reached his heart,** ces mots lui touchèrent le cœur. **3.** (*a*) arriver à, parvenir à; **we shall r. Paris in the evening,** nous serons à Paris, nous arriverons à Paris, dans la soirée; **to r. the summit of the mountain,** parvenir au sommet de la montagne; **windows reached by a flight of three steps,** fenêtres où l'on accède par trois marches; **to r. the end of one's journey,** arriver au bout de son voyage; **to have reached the end of life,** toucher au terme de la vie; **to r. old age,** arriver à la vieillesse; **to r. the age of sixty,** atteindre l'âge de soixante ans; **to r. perfection,** atteindre, toucher, à la perfection; **book that has reached its sixth edition,** livre qui a atteint sa sixième édition, qui en est à sa sixième édition; **to r. a high price,** atteindre un prix élevé; se vendre cher; **the sum total reaches a thousand francs,** le montant s'élève à mille francs; **production has reached an all time low,** la production est descendue à son plus bas; **the disease had reached the town,** la maladie avait gagné la ville; **your letter reached me today,** votre lettre m'est arrivée, m'est parvenue, aujourd'hui; **this letter never reached him,** cette lettre ne lui est jamais parvenue; **the sound reached my ears,** le son m'est venu aux oreilles, est arrivé jusqu'à mes oreilles; **these rumours reached me,** ces bruits vinrent jusqu'à moi; **all that has reached me about him,** tout ce que j'ai entendu dire de lui; (*b*) arriver à (une conclusion, etc.); **to r. an agreement,** aboutir à un accord; **no agreement was reached,** aucun accord n'est intervenu. **4.** (*a*) **to r. sth. to s.o.,** passer qch. à qn (en étendant le bras); **r. me (over) my gloves,** passez-moi mes gants; (*b*) **to r. sth. (down) from a shelf,** prendre qch. sur un rayon; **r. me (down) that plate,** descendez-moi cette assiette.

II. *v.tr. & i.* **to r. (to) sth.,** arriver, (*upwards*) s'élever, monter, (*downwards*) descendre, jusqu'à qch.; **to r. (up to) the skies,** s'élever jusqu'aux cieux, toucher aux cieux; **to r. (down to) the bottom,** atteindre le fond; descendre jusqu'au fond, jusqu'en bas; **curtains that do not r. the sill,** rideaux qui ne descendent pas jusqu'au rebord (de la fenêtre); **coat that reached (to) his heels,** habit qui lui descendait jusqu'aux talons; **boots reaching halfway up his legs,** bottes lui montant à mi-jambe; **she scarcely reaches up to your shoulder,** c'est à peine si elle vous vient à l'épaule; **to r. a height of six feet,** atteindre une hauteur de six pieds.

III. *v.i.* **1.** s'étendre; **territory that reaches from the sea to the hills,** territoire qui s'étend de la mer jusqu'aux collines; **as far as the eye could r.,** aussi loin que portait le regard; aussi loin que la vue, le regard, pouvait s'étendre; à perte de vue; **their voices reached across the lake,** leurs voix portaient jusqu'à l'autre côté du lac; **annals that r. back to ancient times,** annales qui remontent jusqu'aux temps anciens. **2. to r. out (with one's hand) for sth.,** tendre, avancer, la main pour prendre qch.; **to r. for a box on a shelf,** atteindre une boîte sur un rayon; **to r. across to give s.o. sth.,** se pencher, étendre le bras, pour donner qch. à qn; **he reached over to the table,** il étendit la main vers la table; **the mind reaches forward to an ideal,** l'âme tend vers un idéal, cherche à atteindre un idéal. **3.** *Nau: Y:* (*a*) courir une bordée; (*b*) **to r. ahead of a competitor,** prendre de l'avance sur un concurrent.

reach³, *v.i.* = RETCH².

reachable ['riːtʃəbl], *a.* accessible; à portée; **not r.,** hors de portée.

reacher in ['riːtʃər'in], *s. Tex:* passeur, -euse, de chaînes.

reach-me-down ['riːtʃmidaun], *a. & s.* **1. a r.-me-d. (suit),** un costume de confection, confectionné, tout fait; *F:* un décrochez-moi-ça; **to dress in r.-me-downs,** s'habiller au décrochez-moi-ça. **2. his elder brother's r.-me-downs,** les vêtements pour lesquels son frère aîné était devenu trop grand.

reacquire [riːə'kwaiər], *v.tr.* réacquérir; rentrer en possession de (qch.).

react [ri'ækt]. **1.** *v.i.* (*a*) réagir (**on,** sur; **to(wards),** à; **against,** contre); (*b*) *Fin:* (*of prices*) réactionner. **2.** *v.tr. Ch:* faire réagir (**sth. with sth.,** qch. avec qch.).

re-act ['riː'ækt], *v.tr. Th:* rejouer; jouer de nouveau (un rôle, une pièce).

reactance [ri'æktəns], *s. El:* réactance *f*; **leakage, stray, r.,** réactance de fuite, de dispersion; **r. coil,** (bobine *f* de) réactance; **r. relay,** télérelais *m* de réactance; **r. valve, tube,** tube *m* de réactance.

reactant [ri'æktənt], *s. Ch:* réactant *m.*

reacting [ri'æktiŋ], *a.* réagissant.

reaction [ri'ækʃ(ə)n], *s.* réaction *f.* **1.** (*a*) **chemical, nuclear, r.,** réaction chimique, nucléaire; **back r.,** réaction inverse, de recombinaison; **balanced, reversible, r.,** réaction réversible, équilibrée; **fission, fusion, r.,** réaction de fission, de fusion; **self-maintaining, -sustaining, (chain) r.,** réaction (en chaîne) auto-entretenue; **r. cycle,** cycle *m* de réaction; **r. kinetics,** cinétique *f* chimique; (*b*) *Mec: Mec.E:* **elastic r.,** force *f* élastique antagoniste; **r. of support,** réaction d'appui; **thrust r.,** réaction axiale; **r. propulsion,** propulsion par réaction; **r. engine, motor,** moteur *m* à réaction; réacteur *m*; **r. blades,** aubages *m* (de turbine) à réaction; *Hyd.E:* **r. wheel,** roue *f* à réaction, à tuyaux; tourniquet *m* hydraulique; (*c*) *El:* **anode r.,** réaction d'anode; **armature r.,** réaction d'induit; **r. coil,** bobine *f* de réaction; **r. coupling,** couplage réactif. **2.** (*a*) *Physiol: etc:* **auditory, tactile, visual, r.,** réaction auditive, tactile, visuelle; **cutaneous, skin, r.,** réaction cutanée; **degenerative r.,** réaction de dégénérescence; **Wassermann r.,** réaction de Wassermann; *Psy:* **r. formation,** formation réactionnelle; **r. agent,** réactif *m*; **r. type,** phénotype *m*; **r. time,** temps (mort) de réaction; (*b*) **r. against despotism,** réaction contre le despotisme; **what was his r. to the news?** quelle était sa réaction, comment a-t-il réagi, à cette nouvelle? *F:* **gut r.,** réaction dans son for intérieur. **3.** (*a*) **the reactions of a policy,** les contrecoups *m* d'une politique; (*b*) abattement *m* (à la suite de surexcitation); (*c*) *Fin:* **sharp r. of sterling on the foreign exchange market,** vive réaction du sterling sur le marché des changes; (*d*) *Pol:* **the (forces of) r.,** les forces *f* réactionnaires; le parti réactionnaire; (le parti de) la réaction.

reactionary [ri'ækʃən(ə)ri], **reactionist** [ri'ækʃənist], *a. & s. Pol:* réactionnaire (*mf*); antiprogressiste (*mf*); *a.* antiprogressif; **the reactionaries,** la réaction.

reactivate [ri'æktiveit], *v.tr.* **1.** *Ch: Elcs: Med:* réactiver (un catalyseur, un tube électronique, une maladie infectieuse, etc.). **2.** (*a*) *NAm:* (i) *Mil:* reconstituer, reformer, remettre sur pied (une unité); (ii) *Ind:* remettre en marche, en fonctionnement, en activité (une usine, etc.); (*b*) *Cmptr:* relancer (un programme).

reactivation [riækti'veiʃ(ə)n], *s.* **1.** *Ch: Elcs: Med:* réactivation *f* (d'un catalyseur, tube électronique, d'une maladie infectieuse, etc.). **2.** *Cmptr:* relance *f* (d'un programme).

reactivator [ri'æktiveitər], *s. Ch: Elcs: Med:* réactivateur *m.*

reactive [ri'æktiv], *a.* (*a*) *Ph: Ch: Atom.Ph:* réactif; *Mec:* **r. tenacity,** résistance *f* à l'écrasement; (*b*) *El:* réactif, déwatté; **r. circuit,** circuit réactif, de réaction; **r. component,** composante réactive, déwattée; **r. factor,** coefficient *m* de réactance; (*c*) *Physiol:* **r. movements,** mouvements réactionnels; *Psy:* **r. depression,** dépression réactionnelle.

reactivity [riæk'tiviti], *s. Ch: Atom.Ph: Mec:* réactivité *f*; *Mec:* pouvoir *m* de réaction; *Atom.Ph:* **residual, shut-down, r.,** réactivité résiduelle; **r. drift,** variation *f* de réactivité; **r. meter,** réactimètre *m*; *Med:* **natural, acquired r.,** réactivité naturelle, acquise.

reactor [ri'æktər], *s.* **1.** personne *f*, chose *f*, qui réagit (**to,** à). **2.** (*a*) *Ch: Ind:* réacteur *m* (tubulaire, etc.); (*b*) *Atom.Ph:* **nuclear r.,** réacteur nucléaire; pile *f* atomique; **experimental, industrial, r.,** réacteur expérimental. industriel; **marine (nuclear) r.,** réacteur (nucléaire) marin; **ship propulsion r.,** réacteur propulseur de navires; **breeder r.,** réacteur (auto)générateur, sur(ré)générateur; réacteur producteur de matière fissile; pile couveuse; **fission r.,** réacteur à fission; **power r.,** réacteur générateur d'énergie; **fast (neutron) r.,** réacteur rapide, à neutrons rapides; **thermal r.,** réacteur thermal, à neutrons thermiques; **circulating r.,** réacteur à combustible circulant; **plutonium r.,** réacteur au plutonium; **natural uranium r.,** réacteur à l'uranium naturel; **water-cooled r.,** réacteur refroidi à l'eau; **swimming pool type r.,** pile piscine; **r. engineering,** ingénierie *f* nucléaire; technologie *f* des piles; **r. waste,** déchets *mpl* de, du, réacteur; (*c*) *El:* bobine *f* de réactance; tamponneur *m.*

read¹ [riːd], *s.* **1.** (action *f* de lire) (*a*) **he was having a quiet r.,** il lisait tranquillement; **I'm going to have a good two hours' r.,** je vais passer deux bonnes heures à lire; (*b*) **to give s.o. a r. of one's book, of the paper,** laisser qn lire son livre, jeter un coup d'œil sur le journal. **2.** *Elcs: Cmptr:* lecture *f* (des sons, des données, par un dispositif automatique); **r. while writing,** lecture et écriture simultanées; **r.-after-write check,** contrôle *m* par lecture après écriture; **r.-write access,** consultation *f* et mise *f* à jour; **destructive, non destructive, r.,** lecture avec, sans, effacement; lecture destructive, non-destructive; **scatter r.,** lecture avec éclatement; **r. pulse,** impulsion *f* de lecture; **r. punch unit,** lecteur-perforateur *m*, *pl.* lecteurs-perforateurs; **r. roller,** cylindre *m* de lecture; **r. time,** temps *m* lecture, temps d'accès.

read², *v.* (*p.t. & p.p.* **read** [red])

I. *v.tr. & i.* lire. **1.** (*a*) **to r. a book, a newspaper,** lire un livre, un journal; **to teach s.o. to r.,** enseigner la lecture à qn; **to r. to oneself,** lire tout bas; lire des yeux; **to r. sth. (over) again,** relire qch.; **to r. sth. over and over (again),** lire et relire qch.; **on the ring one can r. these words,** sur l'anneau se lisent ces paroles; **to begin to r. a book,** commencer la lecture d'un livre; **I had just finished reading the letter,** je venais d'achever la lecture de la lettre; **have you anything to r.?** avez-vous de la lecture? **to r. through, over, a contract,** prendre lecture d'un contrat; *Adm:* **read [red] and approved,** lu et approuvé; **I r. it in a newspaper,** je l'ai lu, vu, dans un journal; **I have r. an account of it, I have r. of it,** j'en ai lu le récit; je l'ai lu quelque part; **I have r. of such a man,** j'ai lu une fois l'histoire d'un tel homme; **events that we r. of in history,** événements dont nous parle l'histoire; événements relatés dans l'histoire; (*b*) *Typ:* **to r. proofs,** corriger des épreuves; (*c*) **to r. up a subject,** étudier un sujet; se documenter sur un sujet; **he is reading for his examination,** il prépare, travaille, *F:* potasse, son examen; **to r. law, for the bar,** faire son droit; faire ses études de droit; suivre ses cours de droit. **2.** (*a*) **to r. sth. aloud,** lire qch. à haute voix, tout haut; **he reads well,** il lit bien; **to r. sth. out of, from, a book,** lire qch. dans un livre; donner lecture d'un passage pris dans un livre; **to r. a report (to the meeting),** donner lecture d'un rapport (à l'assemblée); **the bill was read for the first time,** lecture du projet a été faite pour la première fois; **after the will had been r.,** lecture faite du testament; **to take the minutes as r.,** approuver le procès-verbal sans lecture; **to r. to s.o.,** faire la lecture à qn; **the children were r. to every evening,** tous les soirs on faisait la lecture aux enfants; **she had been r. the story of Cinderella,** on lui avait lu l'histoire de Cendrillon; (*b*) *F:* **to r. s.o. a lecture,** faire une semonce à qn; sermonner, chapitrer, qn. **3. to r. s.o. to sleep,** endormir qn en lui faisant la lecture; **to r. oneself to sleep,** lire pour s'endormir. **4.** (*a*) lire (une langue étrangère, la musique); déchiffrer (la sténographie, les hiéroglyphes); **to r. (music) at sight,** lire à vue; (*b*) expliquer, interpréter (un songe, une énigme); deviner (le caractère de qn); **to r. the future,** lire dans l'avenir; **to r. s.o.'s hand,** lire dans la main de qn; **to r. the sky,** (i) (*of astrologer*) lire dans les astres; (ii) (*of meteorologist*) prévoir le temps; **to r. s.o.'s thoughts, s.o.'s heart,** lire dans la pensée, dans le cœur, de qn; **I can r. it in your eyes,** je le lis dans vos yeux; **his sincerity could be read in his eyes,** ses yeux respiraient la sincérité; **to r. s.o.'s mind clearly,** voir clair dans l'esprit de qn; **I can r. him like a book,** je le connais comme le fond de ma poche; je lis en lui comme dans un livre ouvert; **you are not to r. my silence as consent,** il ne faut pas interpréter mon silence comme un assentiment; **clause that may be read several ways,** article qui peut s'interpréter de plusieurs manières; **for this passage some commentators r. . . .,** au lieu de ce passage quelques commentateurs lisent. . ., donnent . . .; *Typ:* **(for) Lyons r. Lyon,** Lyons lisez Lyon; *Hum:* **he's frank, for frank r. rude,** il est franc, je précise, pour mieux dire, impoli; **to r. into a sentence what is not there,** mettre dans une phrase ce qui n'y est pas; **to r. between the lines,** lire entre les lignes; **I could r. jealousy between the lines,** entre les lignes je sentais transpirer la jalousie. **5.** lire (l'horloge, le thermomètre); relever (un compteur); faire, effectuer, la lecture sur (un instrument de précision); *Surv:* observer (un angle); *Cmptr:* (*of reading head*) **to r. a card,** faire la lecture d'une carte; *Cmptr:* **to r. backwards,** faire une lecture arrière; *Mil:* **to r. the battle,** observer le (déroulement du) combat. **6.** (*with passive force*) (*a*) **the script reads from right to left,** l'écriture se lit de droite à gauche; **the telegram read as follows,** le télégramme était libellé comme suit; (*b*) **the play reads better than it acts,** la pièce est meilleure à la lecture qu'à la scène; **the play doesn't r. well,** la pièce ne donne rien à la lecture; **it reads very well,** cela se suit bien; cela se laisse lire; **the book reads like a translation,** le livre fait l'effet d'une traduction; *F:* **do you r. me?** vous (me) comprenez? (*c*) **the clause reads both ways,** l'article peut s'interpréter dans les deux sens; (*d*) **the thermometer reads 30°,** le thermomètre marque, indique, trente degrés.

II. (*compound verbs*) **1. read back,** *v.tr.* (*a*) (*of stenographer*) **to r. back a letter to the person who has dictated it,** relire une lettre à celui qui l'a dictée; (*b*) **to r. back shorthand,** déchiffrer la sténographie; *Cmptr:* **to r. back a card,** traduire une carte (en clair).

2. read in, (*a*) *v.pr. Ecc:* **to r. oneself in,** faire la lecture, imposée par la loi, de certaines déclarations (en prenant possession de sa charge); (*b*) *v.tr. Cmptr:* mettre (des données) en mémoire; (*c*) *Tex:* lire (des cartons).

3. read off, *v.tr.* (*a*) lire (qch.) d'un trait, sans hésiter; lire (de la musique) à vue, à livre ouvert; (*b*) lire à haute voix (les noms sur une liste, etc.); (*c*) *v.tr. Tex:* lire (des cartons).

4. read out, *v.tr.* (*a*) lire (qch.) à haute voix; **to r. out the agenda,** donner lecture de l'ordre du jour; **to hear the will read out,** entendre lecture du testament; (*b*) *N.Am:* **to r. s.o. out of the party,** bannir qn du parti (en faisant l'annonce formelle); (*c*) *Cmptr:* **to r. data out (of storage),** extraire, sortir, des données de (la) mémoire.

read[3] [red], *a.* **1.** (*of speech, etc.*) lu. **2.** (*of pers.*) **well r.,** instruit, savant, lettré, érudit; qui a de la lecture, a beaucoup lu; très cultivé; **he is well r. in history,** il est versé dans, a une profonde connaissance de, il connaît bien, l'histoire; c'est un érudit en histoire; **fairly well r. in the humanities,** assez imbu de belles-lettres.

readable ['ri:dəbl], *a.* lisible; (i) (livre, etc.) qui se laisse lire; **is it r.?** est-ce intéressant à lire? (ii) **his handwriting is very r.,** son écriture est très lisible; **not r.,** illisible.

readdress [riə'dres], *v.tr.* mettre une nouvelle adresse sur, *F:* réaddresser (une lettre, etc.); changer l'adresse de (qch.); faire suivre (une lettre).

reader ['ri:dər], *s.* **1.** (*a*) celui qui lit; lecteur, -trice; **he's, she's, a great r.,** c'est un (grand) liseur, une (grande) liseuse; il, elle, lit beaucoup; **he's not much of a r.,** il n'aime guère la lecture; (*b*) **publisher's r.,** lecteur, -trice, de manuscrits; (*c*) *Typ:* **(proof) r.,** correcteur, -trice, d'épreuves. **2.** lecteur, -trice (à haute voix); *Ecc:* lecteur. **3.** *Sch:* (*a*) professeur *m* de faculté; (*b*) *Can:* assistant *m* de professeur de lycée. **4.** (*a*) *Mus:* **to be a good r. at sight,** être bon lecteur, bonne lectrice; (*b*) interprète *m* (de songes, etc.); (*c*) *Tex:* **r.-in, r.-off,** liseur, -euse, de dessins. **5.** (*device*) lecteur (de microfilm, etc.); *Cmptr:* **card, tape, r.,** lecteur de cartes (perforées), de bande perforée; **optical r.,** lecteur optique. **6.** *Sch:* (*a*) livre *m* de lecture; recueil *m* de morceaux choisis; **first r.,** premier livre de lecture; (*b*) livre, manuel *m* (de géographie, etc.).

readership ['ri:dəʃip], *s.* **1.** *Sch:* professorat *m* de faculté. **2. paper with a r. of two million,** journal avec deux millions de lecteurs; **an educated r.,** un public cultivé.

readily ['redili], *adv.* **1.** promptement; **the engine started r.,** le moteur est parti promptement, du premier coup; **to consent r.,** consentir avec empressement, volontiers, de bon cœur, sans se faire prier. **2.** aisément, facilement; **she is not r. moved to tears,** elle n'a pas les larmes faciles.

read-in ['ri:d'in], *s.* **1.** *Cmptr:* mise *f,* stockage *m,* en mémoire; mémorisation *f* (d'une donnée). **2.** *Tex:* lisage *m* (des cartons).

readiness ['redinis], *s.* **1.** (*a*) empressement *m,* alacrité *f* (à faire qch.); **r. to believe evil,** promptitude *f* à croire le mal; (*b*) bonne volonté. **2.** facilité *f,* vivacité *f* (d'esprit); **r. of speech,** facilité de parole; **r. of wit,** vivacité, promptitude, d'esprit; **r. of mind,** (i) ouverture *f* d'esprit; (ii) présence *f* d'esprit. **3. to be in r.,** être prêt **(for sth.,** pour qch.); **to have everything in r.,** avoir tout prêt; **have your revolver in r. to fire,** ayez votre revolver prêt à faire feu.

reading[1] ['ri:diŋ], *a.* qui lit; **the r. public,** le public qui lit, des lecteurs; le public liseur; le public ami des livres; **a r. man,** un (grand) liseur; *Sch: F:* un travailleur, un piocheur, un bûcheur; **he was neither a sporting man nor a r. man,** il n'aimait ni la chasse ni la lecture.

reading[2], *s.* **1.** (*a*) lecture *f;* **to be fond of r.,** aimer la lecture; **r. broadens the mind,** le commerce des livres élargit l'esprit; **book that makes good r., dull r.,** livre qui est intéressant à lire, d'une lecture ennuyeuse; **to have immense r.,** avoir énormément lu; **the r. matter of a newspaper,** la matière à lecture d'un journal; **r. book,** livre *m* de lecture; **r. glass,** loupe *f* (à lire); **r. lamp,** lampe *f* de table; lampe de travail, de bureau; **r. stand,** pupitre *m;* liseuse *f* (pour travail debout); **r. room,** (i) salle *f,* cabinet *m,* de lecture (d'une bibliothèque, etc.); (ii) *Typ:* salle de correction des épreuves; (*b*) lecture(s); **his r. has helped him to understand the problem,** ses lectures l'ont aidé à comprendre le problème; **I have brought you some r.,** je vous ai apporté de la lecture; **magazine that has too many pictures and not enough r.,** périodique qui a un excès d'illustrations et pas assez à lire; **r. list,** liste *f* de livres à lire; (*c*) **I'd like you to give it a r.,** j'aimerais que vous le lisiez; **on the first r.,** à première lecture; (*d*) lecture à haute voix; **r. of a will,** lecture, ouverture *f,* d'un testament; **second r.,** second énoncé; deuxième lecture; *Parl:* prise *f* en considération (d'un projet de loi); **bill rejected at the second r.,** projet repoussé en deuxième lecture; **poetry, play, readings,** lectures (publiques) de poésie, de pièces de théâtre; *A:* **penny readings,** lectures publiques d'œuvres célèbres (dont le prix d'entrée était d'un penny); (*e*) explication *f,* interprétation (d'une énigme, etc.); (*f*) *Mus:* lecture (de la musique); (*g*) *Tg:* **sound r.,** lecture au son. **2.** (*a*) (i) lecture (des renseignements fournis par un appareil de mesure); observation (faite sur un instrument de précision); relevé *m* (d'un compteur à gaz, etc.); **r. date,** date *f* de relevé (d'un compteur); **direct r. instrument,** instrument à lecture directe; (ii) *Elcs:* lecture (d'une carte perforée, bande magnétique, par un lecteur automatique); **reverse r.,** lecture arrière; **r. head,** tête *f* de lecture; lecteur (automatique); **r. rate,** vitesse *f* de lecture; *Cmptr:* **destructive, non-destructive, r.,** lecture destructive, non-destructive; lecture avec effacement, sans effacement; **r. station,** poste *m* de lecture; **r. track,** piste *f* de lecture; (*b*) indication, cote (fournie par un appareil de mesure); **barometer r., barometric r.,** hauteur *f,* lecture, barométrique; **depth r.,** cote de profondeur; **zero r.,** cote zéro, nulle; *W.Tel:* **dial readings,** réglages *m* (du poste); **table of dial readings,** tableau d'étalonnage; *Surv:* **rod r.,** cote sur la mire; **to take readings,** faire la lecture (des appareils de mesure, etc.); relever des cotes; *F:* faire des lectures; **to take monthly readings of the electricity (meter),** relever mensuellement le compteur, la consommation, d'électricité; *N.Am:* **to take readings of the importance of sth.,** prendre des renseignements sur l'importance de qch. **3.** (*a*) façon de lire; **I don't like his r.,** je n'aime pas la façon dont il lit; (*b*) interprétation *f* (d'un rôle, morceau de musique); **what is your r. of the facts?** comment interprétez-vous les faits? (*c*) leçon *f,* variante *f* (d'un texte); **true r.,** bonne leçon. **4.** (*compound nouns*) (*a*) **r. in** = READ-IN; (*b*) **r. out,** (i) lecture à haute voix; (ii) *Elcs: Cmptr:* = READ-OUT.

readjourn [ri:ə'dʒə:n]. **1.** *v.tr.* réajourner. **2.** *v.i.* s'ajourner à nouveau.

readjournment [ri:ə'dʒə:nmənt], *s.* réajournement *m.*

readjust [ri:ə'dʒʌst], *v.tr.* (*a*) rajuster, rectifier; régler à nouveau; remettre (un instrument) au point; **to r. one's dress, one's clothes,** se rajuster; (*b*) **to r. oneself, become readjusted,** *v.i.* **to r. to normal living,** se réadapter à la vie normale.

readjustment [ri:ə'dʒʌstmənt], *s.* (*a*) rajustement *m,* rectification *f;* nouveau réglage, remise *f* au point (d'un instrument); *Nau: etc:* régulation *f* (du compas); (*b*) *Med:* réadaptation.

readmission [ri:əd'miʃ(ə)n], *s.* (*a*) réadmission *f;* **free r.,** réadmission en franchise; **no r.,** on ne donne pas de billets de sortie; (*b*) réintégration *f* (d'un fonctionnaire).

readmit [ri:əd'mit], *v.tr.* (*a*) réadmettre (un spectateur sorti, un sociétaire exclu, etc.); (*b*) réintégrer (un fonctionnaire).

readmittance [ri:əd'mitəns], *s.* réadmission *f.*

readopt [ri:ə'dɔpt], *v.tr.* réadopter.

readoption [ri:ə'dɔpʃ(ə)n], *s.* réadoption *f.*

read-out ['ri:daut], *s.* **1.** *Elcs: etc:* (*a*) lecture *f* (des sons, données) (par un dispositif automatique); (*b*) *Cmptr:* extraction *f,* sortie *f,* restitution *f* (des informations mises en mémoire); **r.-o. and storage system,** système *m* de restitution et de mise en mémoire; **destructive, non-destructive, r.-o.,** lecture destructive, non-destructive; lecture avec, sans, effacement; **r.-o. pulse,** impulsion *f* de lecture. **2.** (*a*) *Cmptr:* informations extraites (de mémoire); (*b*) *Space:* informations transmises (par un satellite).

ready[1] ['redi], *a. adv. & s.*

I. *a.* **1.** (*a*) prêt; **are you r.?** êtes vous prêt? y êtes-vous? *Sp:* **(get) r.! (get) set! go!** à vos marques! prêts! partez! **to make, get, sth. r.,** préparer, apprêter, qch.; **get dinner r. for seven,** que le dîner soit prêt à sept heures; **dinner is r.,** le dîner est prêt; **to make a car r. (for driving, for the road),** mettre une voiture en état de marche; **car r. for driving,** voiture prête à conduire; **machine r. for assembly,** machine prête à être montée; **r. for use,** prêt à l'usage, à servir; *Publ:* **book now r., just r.,** livre sur le point de paraître, qui vient de paraître; (*at hotel*) **is my bill r.?** est-ce que vous avez établi ma note? **to make (oneself), to get, r.,** se préparer, s'apprêter, se disposer **(to do sth.,** à faire qch.); *F: O:* **r. to the last gaiter button,** prêt jusqu'au dernier bouton de guêtre; **r. for the fight,** prêt à combattre, au combat; **she was r. for her guests,** elle était prête à recevoir ses invités; **he's r. for you now,** il est prêt à vous recevoir; il vous attend; **he's r. for anything,** il est prêt à tout; **to be r. with sth.,** avoir, tenir, qch. tout prêt; **to be r. to do sth.,** être prêt à faire qch.; être en état de faire qch.; **we're r. to start,** nous sommes prêts à partir; **to be r. to face s.o.,** attendre qn de pied ferme; *Jur:* **case r. for hearing,** affaire en état; *Nau:* **all r.!** on est paré! **be r. to discharge the pilot,** soyez paré à débarquer le pilote; *Typ:* **to make r.,** mettre en train; **making r.,** mise *f* en train; *Tg:* **r. signal,** invitation *f* à transmettre; *U.S: Mil.Av:* **r. room,** salle dans laquelle les équipages reçoivent leur briefing; (*b*) (*of instrument, etc.*) **r. to hand,** sous la main, à portée de main; **there's a subject for a thesis r. to hand,** voilà un sujet de thèse tout trouvé; **r. money,** argent comptant, liquide; **to pay in r. money,** payer (au) comptant; **r. capital,** capital circulant. **2.** (*a*) prêt, disposé (à faire qch.); **if he is r. to lend you the money,** s'il est disposé à vous prêter l'argent; **he is a r. believer in miracles,** il croit volontiers aux miracles; **he is too r. to suspect,** il est trop vite disposé à soupçonner; **don't be too r. to believe him,** ne le croyez pas trop légèrement; (*b*) sur le point (de faire qch.); **r. to die of hunger,** sur le point de mourir de faim; **r. to swear with rage,** prêt à jurer de colère; **bud just r. to burst,** bourgeon tout près d'éclore, juste sur le point d'éclore. **3.** *O:* (*a*) **she is not very efficient, but she is r.,** elle n'est pas très capable, mais elle est pleine de bonne volonté; (*b*) complaisant; servile; **the r. ministers of vengeance,** les serviles instruments de la vengeance. **4.** prompt, facile; (*a*) **to have a r. wit,** avoir l'esprit prompt, présent; avoir l'esprit d'à-propos, l'esprit de repartie; **to be a r. speaker,** avoir la parole facile; **to have a r. tongue,** avoir la langue agile, bien pendue; **to have a r. pen,** avoir la plume facile; **r. understanding,** intelligence ouverte; **r. reply,** prompte repartie; **to be always r. with an answer,** avoir la réplique prompte; **he's very r. with his fists,** il est prompt à se battre; (*b*) **goods that meet with a r. sale,** marchandises de vente courante, qui partent bien, qui s'écoulent rapidement; **the story found r. acceptance,** l'histoire a été acceptée sans difficulté; **he gave a r. consent,** il a donné son consentement sans hésiter; **a r. subject for jokes,** un sujet de plaisanterie tout indiqué; **a r. source of revenue,** une source de revenu facile; *A:* **a r. way to do sth.,** un moyen facile, expéditif, de faire qch.; **the readiest way to get there,** le meilleur chemin pour y aller.

II. *adv.* **1. r. dressed,** tout habillé; **table r. laid,** table toute préparée. **2.** *F:* **the child who answers readiest,** l'enfant qui répond le plus promptement.

III. *s.* **1.** *Mil:* **to come to the r.,** apprêter l'arme; *Artil:* **guns at the r.,** pièces parées à faire feu. **2.** *P:* argent comptant; **to produce the r.,** mettre argent sur table; *P:* abouler la galette. **3.** *Typ:* mise *f* en train.

ready[2], *v.tr. esp. NAm:* apprêter, préparer (une chambre, etc.).

ready-cooked [redi'kukt], *a.* **r.-c. food,** aliments tout cuits; plats *m* à emporter.

readymade ['redimeid]. **1.** *a.* (article) tout fait; **r. clothes,** vêtements confectionnés, de confection; vêtements tout faits; confections *f*; le prêt-à-porter; **r. (clothes) shop,** maison *f* de confections; **r. phrases, excuses,** expressions, excuses, toutes faites. **2.** *s.* vêtement tout fait; complet tout fait; robe toute faite; confection; **r. clothier,** confectionneur *m*.

ready-witted [redi'witid], *a.* à l'esprit prompt, vif.

reaffirm [riːə'fəːm], *v.tr.* réaffirmer (qch.), affirmer de nouveau (qch.); **I r. what I said before,** j'en reviens à ce que j'ai déjà dit.

reaffirmation [riːæfə'meiʃ(ə)n], *s.* nouvelle affirmation; réaffirmation *f*.

reaffix [riːə'fiks], *v.tr.* réapposer (un sceau, etc.).

reaffixing [riːə'fiksiŋ], *s.* réapposition *f*.

reafforest [riːə'fɔrist], *v.tr.* reboiser (un terrain).

reafforestation [riːəfɔri'steiʃ(ə)n], *s.* reforestation *f*, reboisement *m*.

reagency [riː'eidʒənsi], *s. Ch:* **1.** pouvoir réactif. **2.** réaction *f*.

reagent [ri'eidʒənt], *s. Ch:* réactif *m*; **mercury r.,** réactif à base de mercure; **r. paper,** papier réactif.

reagin [ri'eidʒin], *s. Med:* réagine *f*.

re-aim [riː'eim]. **1.** *v.tr.* repointer (une arme) (**at,** sur). **2.** *v.ind.tr.* **to r.-a. at sth.,** viser de nouveau, repointer sur, qch.

re-aiming [riː'eimiŋ], *s.* repointage *m* (d'une arme à feu, etc.) (**at,** sur); nouvelle visée (**at,** sur).

real[1], *pl.* **-als, -ales** [rei'ɑːl, -ɑːlz, -ɑleiz], *s. Num:* réal *m*, *pl.* réaux.

real[2] ['riəl], *a.* & *adv.*

I. *a.* **1.** (*a*) vrai; **r. bottles and sham ones,** bouteilles vraies et bouteilles feintes; **a r. diamond,** un vrai diamant; **r. lace,** vraie dentelle; **r. silk,** soie naturelle; **r. flowers,** fleurs naturelles; **r. photograph,** photographie *f* véritable; **r. old nobility,** noblesse *f* de bon aloi; **a r. old salt,** un vrai loup de mer; **a r. friend,** un vrai, véritable, ami; **he's a r. man,** c'est vraiment un homme; **it's not a r. ironmonger's but you can get nails there,** ce n'est pas une quincaillerie sérieuse mais vous pouvez y acheter des clous; **it's the r. thing,** (i) c'est authentique; *F:* ce n'est pas du toc; (ii) c'est exactement ce qu'il nous faut; *F:* c'est au poil; *P:* **it's the r. Mackay** [mə'kai], **McCoy** [mə'kɔi], c'est du vrai de vrai; (*b*) véritable, réel; **the r. world,** le monde réel; **he is not the r. head of the business,** ce n'est pas le véritable chef; **you wouldn't find such a character in r. life,** vous ne trouveriez pas un caractère semblable dans la vie quotidienne, dans la réalité; **these things are r., and not fancies,** ce ne sont pas des chimères, ce sont des choses réelles; *s.* **the r. and the ideal,** le réel et l'idéal; **the r. value of things,** le véritable prix des choses; **as prices rise, r. incomes get smaller,** à mesure que les prix augmentent les revenus réels s'amenuisent; *Fin:* **r. value,** valeur effective; *Astr:* **r. movement,** mouvement *m* propre (d'un astre); *Theol:* **r. presence,** présence réelle (dans l'eucharistie); *Opt:* **r. image,** image réelle; *Mth:* **r. numbers,** nombres réels; (*c*) *Cmptr:* **r. time,** temps réel; **r.-time working, operation,** fonctionnement *m* en temps réel; **r.-time computer,** ordinateur exploité en temps réel; **r.-time processing,** traitement immédiat; **r.-time clock,** horloge *f* binaire. **2.** *Jur:* (*a*) **r. action,** action réelle; (*b*) **r. estate, property,** propriété immobilière; biens immobiliers, en immeubles; immeubles *mpl*; (*landed property only*) propriété foncière, biens fonciers; bien-fonds *mpl*; *NAm:* **r. estate agent, agency,** agent immobilier, agence immobilière.

II. *adv. NAm: F:* vraiment, très; **a r. fine day,** vraiment une belle journée; une très belle journée; **I was r. sorry,** ça me faisait vraiment de la peine; **that's r. nice of you,** c'est très gentil de votre part.

realgar [ri'ælgər], *s. Miner:* réalgar *m*.

realia [ri'eiliə], *s.pl. Phil:* realia *f*.

realign [riːə'lain], *v.tr.* **1.** *Town P:* aligner (un immeuble qui dépasse l'alignement de la rue). **2.** *Pol:* **to r. the parties,** regrouper les partis.

realignment [riːə'lainmənt], *s.* **1.** *Town P:* alignement *m*; **house scheduled for r.,** maison frappée d'alignement. **2.** *Pol:* regroupement *m* (des partis).

realism ['riəlizm], *s.* **1.** *Art: Lit: Phil:* réalisme *m*. **2. the harsh r. of his opinions,** le réalisme brutal de ses opinions.

realist ['riəlist], *a.* & *s.* **1.** *Art: Lit: Phil:* réaliste (*mf*). **2.** (*of opinions, etc.*) réaliste.

realistic [riə'listik], *a.* (*of pers., opinions, etc.*) réaliste; **r. style,** style plein de réalisme.

realistically [riə'listikli], *adv.* avec réalisme; **painted r.,** peint au naturel.

reality [ri'æliti], *s.* **1.** (*a*) la réalité; le réel; **to bring s.o. back to the world of r.,** ramener qn à la réalité, dans le vrai des choses; **in r. there was nothing to fear,** en réalité, dans le fait, il n'y avait rien à craindre; *Psy:* **r. principle,** principe *m* de réalité; (*b*) **the realities of everyday life,** les réalités de tous les jours; **we must stick to realities,** il faut s'en tenir aux réalités, dans le réel. **2.** vérité *f* (d'un tableau, etc.); **described with extraordinary r.,** décrit avec un réalisme extraordinaire.

realizable [riə'laizəbl], *a.* **1.** réalisable; (i) (projet, etc.) qui peut se faire; (ii) **assets that are hardly r.,** capital difficile à convertir en espèces, à réaliser. **2.** imaginable; dont on peut se rendre compte.

realization [riəlai'zeiʃ(ə)n], *s.* **1.** (*a*) réalisation *f* (d'un projet, etc.); (*b*) *Com: Fin:* conversion *f* en espèces; réalisation (d'un placement); mobilisation *f* (d'une indemnité); (*c*) *Jur:* conversion *f* (de biens meubles) en biens immeubles. **2.** conception nette (d'un fait, danger, etc.).

realize ['riəlaiz], *v.tr.* **1.** (*a*) réaliser (un projet, une espérance); **his hopes were realized,** ses espérances se réalisèrent; (*b*) *Com: Fin:* convertir (des biens) en espèces; réaliser (un placement); liquider (sa fortune); mobiliser (une indemnité); **these shares cannot be realized,** il n'y a pas de marché pour ces titres; (*c*) réaliser (des bénéfices); gagner (une fortune); (*d*) *Jur:* convertir (des biens meubles) en biens immeubles; (*e*) (*of goods*) **to r. a high price,** atteindre, rapporter, un haut prix. **2.** représenter (qch.) au naturel, avec réalisme. **3.** concevoir nettement, bien comprendre (qch.); s'apercevoir de (qch.); se rendre compte de (qch.); prendre conscience de (qch.); **we realized that he was blind,** nous nous aperçûmes qu'il était aveugle; **I realized it at the first glance,** je m'en suis rendu compte au premier coup d'œil; **I have realized my mistake,** je suis revenu de mon erreur; **I fully, quite, r. (the fact) that I may offend some people,** je ne dissimule pas, je ne méconnais pas, j'apprécie le fait, que je peux froisser quelques-uns; **the motor car was coming to be realized as a necessity,** on était en voie de se rendre compte que l'automobile était une nécessité.

realizer ['riəlaizər], *s.* réalisateur, -trice (d'un projet, de capitaux, etc.).

realizing ['riəlaiziŋ], *s.* = REALIZATION.

reallocate [riː'æləkeit], *v.tr.* réaffecter, *Jur:* réadjuger; **to r. funds to their original use,** réaffecter une subvention à sa destination première.

reallocation [riːælə'keiʃ(ə)n], *s.* réaffectation *f*; *Fin:* nouvelle répartition (d'actions); *Jur:* réadjudication *f*.

reallot [riːə'lɔt], *v.tr. Fin:* attribuer, répartir, (des actions) à nouveau.

reallotment [riːə'lɔtmənt], *s.* nouvelle répartition (d'actions, etc.); *Mil:* nouvelle affectation (d'une unité, etc.).

really ['riəli], *adv.* vraiment, réellement, à vrai dire; en effet; *F:* pour de vrai; **things that r. exist,** choses qui existent réellement; **it was r. my fault,** c'était vraiment, franchement, de ma faute; **that is r. a matter for the manager,** c'est là proprement l'affaire du gérant; **you r. must go to it,** il faut absolument que vous y alliez; **you are r. too kind,** vous êtes vraiment trop bon; **has he r. gone?** est-il parti pour de vrai? **is it r. true?** est-ce bien vrai? **r.?** vraiment? *F:* sans blague? **no r.!** pas possible! **did you find it?—not r.,** vous l'avez trouvé?—à vrai dire non, c'est-à-dire que non; **(well) r.!** ça alors! c'est le comble! **well r., that's a good one!** eh bien vrai, elle est bonne!

realm [relm], *s.* royaume *m*; **the Peers of the R.,** les pairs *m* du royaume; *Lit:* **the realms of heaven,** le royaume des cieux; **the realm(s) of fancy, possibility,** le domaine de l'imagination, du possible; **the r. of the dead,** l'empire *m* des morts.

realtor ['riəltər], *s. NAm:* agent immobilier.

realty ['riəlti], *s. Jur:* (*a*) objet immobilier; (*b*) *coll.* biens immobiliers; (biens) immeubles (*mpl*).

ream[1] [riːm], *s. Paperm:* rame *f* (de 20 mains = 480 feuilles); ramette *f* (de papier à lettres); **printer's r.,** rame de 516 feuilles; *F:* **he writes reams,** il écrit des pages et des pages.

ream[2], *v.tr.* **1.** *Mec.E:* (*a*) **to r. (out),** aléser, équarrir (un trou); aléser (un canon, cylindre, etc.); *Petr:* élargir (un trou de mine); **to r. to size,** aléser au diamètre voulu; (*b*) (*countersink*) fraiser, chanfreiner (un trou); (*c*) enlever (une inégalité) à l'alésoir; (*d*) sertir (une cartouche). **2.** *Nau:* élargir, patarasser (une couture) (avant de calfater). **3.** *NAm:* **to r. a lemon,** extraire le jus d'un citron sur un presse-citron.

reamer ['riːmər], *s.* **1.** (*pers.*) aléseur *m*. **2.** *Tls:* (*a*) **r. (bit),** alésoir *m*, aléseuse *f*, équarrissoir *m*; mèche *f* à entailles; louche *f*; queue-de-rat *f*, *pl.* queues-de-rat; **fluted r.,** alésoir cannelé; (*b*) **countersinking r.,** fraise *f*; (*c*) *Min:* **(drill) r.,** aléseur; (*d*) *NAm:* **lemon r.,** presse-citron *m inv*.

reaming ['riːmiŋ], *s.* **1.** (*a*) alésage *m*, équarrissage *m* (d'un trou); *Min:* élargissement *m* (d'un trou de sonde); *Metalw:* **r. machine,** aléseuse *f*; (*b*) (*countersinking*) fraisage *m*. **2.** *Nau:* travail *m* sur coque à la patarasse; **r. iron,** patarasse; coin *m* de calfat.

reanimate [riː'ænimeit], *v.tr.* ranimer, réanimer.

reanimation [riːæni'meiʃ(ə)n], *s.* **1.** *Biol:* réanimation *f*; anabiose *f*. **2.** retour *m* à la vie; reprise *f* (des affaires, etc.).

reanneal [riːə'niːl], *v.tr. Metalw:* recuire à nouveau.

reannex [riːæ'neks], *v.tr.* réannexer.

reannexation [riːænek'seiʃ(ə)n], *s.* réannexion *f*.

reap [riːp], *v.tr.* (*a*) moissonner (le blé, un champ); *v.i.* moissonner; faire la moisson; *B:* **whatsoever a man soweth that shall he also r.,** comme tu auras semé tu moissonneras; *Prov:* **we r. as we sow, we r. what we have sown,** on recueille ce qu'on a semé; on ne récolte que ce qu'on sème; on est puni par où l'on a péché; **he who sows the wind shall r. the whirlwind,** qui sème le vent récolte la tempête; (*b*) recueillir (le fruit de ses travaux); acquérir (de l'expérience, etc.); **I r. no benefit from it,** il ne m'en revient aucun avantage.

reaper ['riːpər], *s.* **1.** (*pers.*) moissonneur, -euse; coupeur *m* de blé; *Lit:* **the R.,** la Mort. **2.** (*machine*) moissonneuse *f*; **r.-binder,** moissonneuse-lieuse *f*, *pl.* moissonneuses-lieuses.

reaphook ['riːphuk], *s.* faucille *f*.

reaping ['riːpiŋ], *s.* moisson *f*; moissonnage *m*; fauchage *m*, fauchaison *f*; **r. hook,** faucille *f*; **r. machine,** moissonneuse *f*.

reappear [riːə'piər], *v.i.* réapparaître, reparaître; se représenter.

reappearance [riːə'piərəns], *s.* **1.** (*a*) réapparition *f*; **the r. of spring,** la renaissance du printemps; (*b*) *Th:* rentrée *f* (d'un acteur); (*c*) *Geol:* résurgence *f* (d'un cours d'eau souterrain). **2.** *Dy:* **white r.,** repousse *f* blanchâtre.

reapply [riːə'plai]. **1.** *v.tr.* réappliquer (de la peinture, etc.). **2.** *v.i.* s'adresser de nouveau (**to s.o.,** à qn).

reappoint [riːə'pɔint], *v.tr.* **1.** réintégrer (qn) dans ses fonctions. **2. to r. a representative to an assembly,** rétablir les fonctions de représentant auprès d'une assemblée.

reappointment [riːə'pɔintmənt], *s.* réintégration *f* (d'un fonctionnaire, etc.).

reapportion [riːə'pɔːʃ(ə)n], *v.tr.* redistribuer, répartir à nouveau.

reappraisal [riːə'preiz(ə)l], *s.* réévaluation *f*; **agonizing r.,** révision décharante.

rear[1] ['riər], *s.* & *a.*

I. *s.* **1.** *Mil:* (*a*) arrière *m*, derniers éléments (d'une formation); queue *f* (d'une colonne); arrières *mpl* (d'une grande unité); **to bring, close, up the r.,** fermer la marche (d'une unité); venir en queue (d'un cortège); *F:* **to fall to the r.,** quitter les rangs (pour se soulager); **to operate on the enemy's r.,** opérer sur ses arrières de l'ennemi; *F:* **to hang on to s.o.'s r.,** talonner qn; **in the r.,** en arrière, à l'arrière, en queue, sur les arrières; **to attack an army in the r.,** attaquer une armée sur ses arrières, prendre une armée à revers; **to take a position in the r.,** prendre une position à revers; **the r. (area(s)),** les zones *f* arrières; les arrières, derrières *m*; **to remove a casualty to the r.,** évacuer un blessé à l'arrière; **he was sent to the r.,** on l'a envoyé à l'arrière; (*b*) *P:* **the rear(s),** les latrines *f*, les cabinets *m*, les waters *m*. **2.** (*a*) arrière; derrière (d'une maison, etc.); **in the r. of the house,** derrière la maison; (*b*) dernier rang, queue (d'un cortège, etc.); **at the r. of the procession,** à la queue du cortège; **in the r. of the train,** en queue du train; **they saw it far in the r.,** ils le voyaient bien loin en arrière; (*c*) *F:* derrière, fesses *fpl*; **to give s.o. a kick in the r.,** flanquer un coup de pied au derrière de qn, enlever le ballon à qn.

II. *a.* (situé à l')arrière, (situé) en queue, de queue; **r. end,** (i) partie arrière, postérieure (de qch.); arrière-train *m*, *pl.* arrière-trains, train *m* arrière (d'un véhicule); (ii) *F:* derrière, fesses *fpl* (de qn); **r. entrance,** entrée *f* sur le(s) derrière(s) (d'un immeuble); entrée par derrière; **r. slope,** contre-pente *f, pl.* contre-pentes; *Opt:* **r. view,** *NAm:* **r. vision,** vue *f* arrière; **r.-vision mirror,** rétroviseur *m*; *Veh:* **r. lamp,** lanterne *f* arrière; **r. corner marker lamp,** feu *m* de gabarit; **r. lights,** feux arrières, *Aut:* feux rouges; **r. wheel,** roue *f* (d')arrière; *Aut:* **r. (-wheel) drive,** traction *f* arrière; **r.-drive car,** (voiture *f* à) traction arrière; voiture à roues arrières motrices; *Aut:* **r. window,** lunette *f* arrière; **r. portion of the train,** rame *f*, groupe *m*, de queue; *Phot:* **r. finder,** viseur postérieur; **r. shutter,** obturateur *m* arrière; *Cin: etc:* **r. projection,** projection *f* par transparence; *Mil:* **r. echelon,** échelon *m* arrière, dernier échelon; **r. element(s),** élément(s) *m(pl)* arrière, derniers éléments (d'une formation); **r. party,** élément, détachement *m*, de queue; **r. rank,** dernier rang; arrière-rang *m, pl.* arrière-rangs; **r.-rank man,** (i) homme *m* du dernier rang, (ii) serre-file *m, pl.* serre-files; *Av:* **r. gunner,** mitrailleur *m* arrière; *Navy:* **r. column,** colonne *f* de queue; **r. division,** arrière-garde *f* (d'une formation navale).

rear[2]. **1.** *v.tr.* (*a*) *A:* élever, construire (une cathédrale, etc.); ériger (une statue); (*b*) dresser, mettre debout (une échelle, un mât, etc.); arborer (un étendard); **to r. oneself up,** se dresser; **to r. one's head,** relever la tête. **2.** *v.tr.* élever (des animaux, des enfants); cultiver (des plantes). **3.** *v.i.* (*a*) (*of horse*) se cabrer, se dresser; (*b*) **high cliffs r. above the shore,** de hautes falaises se dressent au-dessus du rivage.

rear[3], *v.i. P:* se soulager.

rear-admiral [riə'rædmərəl], *s.m.* contre-amiral, *pl.* contre-amiraux.

rear-arch ['riərɑːtʃ], *s. Arch:* arc intérieur (d'une porte); arc en retrait.

rear-engined ['riərendʒind], *a.* avec le moteur à l'arrière, à moteur arrière; tout à l'arrière.

rearer ['riərər], *s.* **1.** éleveur, -euse (d'animaux). **2.** cheval *m* qui se cabre, qui a l'habitude de se cabrer.

rearguard ['riəgɑːd], *s. Mil:* arrière-garde *f, pl.* arrière-gardes; **r. action,** combat *m* en retraite, d'arrière-garde; action retardatrice.

rearhorse ['riəhɔːs], *s. Ent:* mante religieuse.

rearing ['riəriŋ], *s.* **1.** *A:* construction *f* (d'un édifice); érection *f* (d'une statue). **2.** élevage *m* (des animaux, etc.); **r. of children,** éducation *f* des enfants; façon *f* d'élever des enfants. **3.** cabrement *m*, acculement *m* (d'un cheval).

rearm [ri'ɑːm], *v.tr. & i.* réarmer.

rearmament [ri'ɑːməmənt], *s.* réarmement *m*; **moral r.,** réarmement moral.

rearmost ['riəmoust], *a.* dernier; de queue; *Navy:* (*in line ahead*) **r. ship,** serre-file *m, pl.* serre-files.

rear-mounted [riə'mauntid], *a.* (moteur, etc.) monté à l'arrière.

rearrange [riːə'rein(d)ʒ], *v.tr.* **1.** arranger de nouveau, réagencer (une chambre, les groupes dans une composition artistique, etc.); disposer, ranger, (des objets) dans un nouvel ordre; reclasser (des papiers); modifier (un système, tableau de service, etc.); remanier (un plan). **2.** remettre en ordre; rajuster (sa robe, etc.); **to r. one's hair,** remettre sa coiffure en ordre; (ré)arranger, rajuster, sa coiffure.

rearrangement [riːə'rein(d)ʒmənt], *s.* **1.** nouvel arrangement, réagencement *m* (d'une chambre, etc.); reclassement *m* (de papiers, etc.); modification *f* (d'un tableau de service, etc.); remaniement *m* (d'un plan, etc.); *Cmptr:* réorganisation *f*, remembrement *m* (d'un fichier); *Ch:* **molecular r.,** réarrangement moléculaire. **2.** remise *f* en ordre, rajustement *m* (de sa robe, coiffure, etc.).

rear-vault ['riːəvɔːlt], *s. Arch:* arrière-voussure *f, pl.* arrière-voussures.

rearward ['riəwəd]. **1.** *s.* arrière-garde *f*, derrières *mpl* (d'une armée); **in the r.,** à l'arrière, en arrière; (par) derrière; **in, to, r. of the column,** à l'arrière de la colonne. **2.** *a.* (*a*) situé à l'arrière; (*b*) (mouvement, regard) en arrière. **3.** *adv.* = REARWARDS.

rearwards ['riəwədz], *adv.* **1.** à l'arrière; (par) derrière. **2.** vers l'arrière.

reascend ['riːə'send], *v.tr. & i.* remonter; **to r. the throne,** remonter sur le trône.

reason[1] ['riːz(ə)n], *s.* **1.** raison *f*, cause *f*, motif *m*; **the r. for my absence,** la raison de mon absence; **there are reasons for that,** il y a des raisons pour cela, à cela; **there is a r. for his doing so,** il y a une raison à ce qu'il le fasse; **our reasons for hope,** nos raisons d'espérer; nos motifs d'espérance; **to give reasons for doing sth.,** (i) donner, fournir, des raisons pour avoir fait qch.; (ii) donner les raisons pour lesquelles qch. doit se faire; **to state one's reasons for a decision,** motiver une décision; **alleging as his r. that he had been wrongfully accused,** en alléguant comme motif, en motivant, qu'on l'avait accusé à tort; **he made my youth a r. for excluding me,** il argua de ma jeunesse pour m'exclure; *Jur:* **reasons adduced,** les attendus *m* (d'un jugement); *F: O:* **a woman's r.,** raison de femme; une raison qui n'en est pas une; **for reasons best known to myself,** pour des raisons de moi seul connues; **for reasons of State,** pour des raisons d'État; **for reasons of health,** pour raisons de santé; **for one r. or another,** pour une raison ou pour une autre; **for no other r. than that I forgot,** pour l'unique raison que j'ai oublié; **he will not come and for a very good r.,** il ne viendra pas et pour cause; **for more than one good r.,** à plus d'un titre; **for the same r. he's not to be trusted,** au même titre on ne peut pas se fier à lui; **for no r. at all,** sans motif, sans cause; **for the very r. that he had been asked not to do it,** précisément parce que, pour cela même qu'on l'avait prié de ne pas le faire; **the r. (for which, why) he came,** la raison pour laquelle il est venu; **I shall do it and for this r.,** je le ferai et voici pourquoi; **for which r. I intend to resign,** c'est pourquoi j'ai l'intention de donner ma démission; **the r. why,** le pourquoi; **tell me the r. why,** dites-m'en la raison; **what's the r. for it?** à quoi cela tient-il? **you have r. to be glad,** vous avez sujet de vous réjouir; **I have r. to believe that he's lying,** j'ai lieu de croire, je crois savoir, j'ai quelques raisons de croire, qu'il ment; **I have every r. to believe that he was in the plot,** j'ai toute raison, tout sujet, tout lieu, de croire qu'il a trempé dans le complot; **he complains and with (good) r.,** il a des raisons pour se plaindre; il se plaint et pour cause, et à bon droit; **to be proud, with good r., of one's success,** être fier à bon droit de son succès; **it's not without (good) r. that I detest him,** ce n'est pas pour rien que je le déteste; **the police have good r. to believe him guilty,** la police est bien fondée à le croire coupable; **I have good r. to complain,** j'ai de quoi me plaindre; **all the more r. for going, why I should go, there,** raison de plus pour y aller, pour que j'y aille; à plus forte raison dois-je y aller; **by r. of his infirmity,** à, pour, cause de, en raison de, son infirmité. **2.** raison; (*a*) faculté *f* de raisonner; **it is disputed whether dogs have r.,** on discute sur le point de savoir si les chiens sont doués de raison; **he lost his r.,** il a perdu la raison; (*b*) *Phil:* **principles of sufficient r.,** principes de raison suffisante. **3.** raison; bon sens; **there is r. in what you say,** il y a du bon sens dans ce que vous dites; **to hear, see, listen to r.,** entendre raison; **you can't make him listen to r., he will not listen to r.,** il n'en fait qu'à sa volonté; *F:* il n'entend ni à hue ni à dia; **to bring s.o. to r.,** faire entendre raison à qn; ramener, ranger, qn à la raison; **to try to bring s.o. to r.,** raisonner qn; **it stands to r. that the decision won't be popular,** il est évident, il va sans dire, que la décision ne sera pas populaire; **it stands to r.,** c'est évident, c'est tout naturel; cela va de soi; cela va sans dire; cela tombe sous le sens; **I cannot in r. do it,** je ne peux pas, raisonnablement, le faire; **as in r.,** comme de raison; **he will do everything in r.,** il est disposé à faire tout ce qui est raisonnable; **everything in r.,** il y a mesure à tout; **it cost me a sum out of all r.,** cela m'a coûté les yeux de la tête; **the price of fish is out of all r.,** le poisson est hors de prix.

reason[2]. **1.** *v.i.* **to r. from premises,** déduire des conclusions des prémisses; **to r. from past experience,** fonder ses raisons sur l'expérience du passé; **to r. in a circle,** revenir au point de départ; tourner dans un cercle (vicieux); **to r. on, about, a subject,** raisonner sur un sujet; **to r. with s.o.,** raisonner qn, avec qn; faire entendre raison à qn. **2.** *v.tr.* (*a*) **to r. out the answer to a problem,** déduire la solution d'un problème; **r. it out for yourself!** ce n'est pas si difficile que cela! (*b*) *O:* **to r. s.o. into obedience,** amener qn à l'obéissance (en le raisonnant); **to r. s.o. out of doing sth.,** dissuader qn de faire qch.; faire entendre raison à qn; **to r. s.o. out of his fear,** calmer la peur de qn (par de bonnes raisons).

reasonable ['riːz(ə)nəbl], *a.* raisonnable; (*a*) **r. man,** homme raisonnable, équitable; **(do) be r.,** tâchez d'être raisonnable; **it seems r. to me that he should do it,** je trouve naturel qu'il le fasse; **to offer a r. excuse,** alléguer valablement une excuse; **r. offer,** offre *f* acceptable, raisonnable; (*b*) **r. suspicions,** soupçons bien fondés; (*c*) modéré; **r. prices,** prix modérés, raisonnables, abordables; **r. in one's desires,** modéré dans ses désirs.

reasonableness ['riːzənəbəlnis], *s.* **1.** caractère *m* raisonnable; raison *f*; **there are times for r.,** la raison a ses heures. **2.** modération *f* (des prix, d'une demande). **3.** *Cmptr:* **r. check,** contrôle *m* de vraisemblance.

reasonably ['riːzənəbli], *adv.* raisonnablement; **to be r. fit,** être en assez bonne santé; **r. priced,** d'un prix raisonnable, abordable.

reasoned ['riːz(ə)nd], *a.* **1.** (*of analysis, exposition, etc.*) raisonné, accompagné de raisons; **r. refusal,** refus motivé. **2.** raisonnable; **r. diet,** régime logique, rationnel.

reasoner ['riːz(ə)nər], *s.* raisonneur, -euse; **he's a bad r.,** il raisonne mal.

reasoning[1] ['riːz(ə)niŋ], *a.* (*of creature, etc.*) doué de raison; **any r. man,** tout homme raisonnable, qui raisonne.

reasoning[2], *s.* **1.** raisonnement *m*; dialectique *f*; **to surpass s.o. in power of r.,** être meilleur dialecticien que qn; surpasser qn par la puissance du raisonnement; **there's no r. with him,** (i) il n'y a pas moyen de lui faire entendre raison; (ii) on ne peut pas raisonner avec lui. **2. the r. behind the decision,** les raisons *f* pour cette décision.

reasonless ['riːz(ə)nlis], *a.* **1.** sans raison, dénué de raison. **2.** sans raison, sans cause, sans motif.

reassemble [riːə'sembl]. **1.** *v.tr.* (*a*) rassembler; assembler de nouveau (les Chambres, etc.); (*b*) remonter, remettre en état (une machine); remboîter (un meuble, etc.); (*c*) *Cmptr:* réassembler (un programme). **2.** *v.i.* se rassembler; s'assembler de nouveau; **school reassembles tomorrow,** c'est demain la rentrée (des classes).

reassembling [riːə'sembliŋ], *s.* remontage *m* (d'une machine, d'un fusil, etc.); remboîtement *m* (d'un meuble).

reassembly [riːə'sembli], *s.* **1.** rentrée *f* (du Parlement). **2.** *Cmptr:* réassemblage *m* (d'un programme).

reassert [riːə'səːt], *v.tr.* affirmer (qch.) de nouveau; réaffirmer (une conviction, etc.).

reassertion [riːə'səːʃ(ə)n], *s.* réaffirmation *f*.

reassess [riːə'ses], *v.tr.* **1.** réimposer (un contribuable). **2.** réévaluer (les dommages, un immeuble, etc.).

reassessment [riːə'sesmənt], *s.* **1.** réimposition *f*. **2.** réévaluation *f*.

reassign [riːə'sain], *v.tr.* **1.** assigner (des terres, etc.) de nouveau; **to r. funds to their original use,** réaffecter une subvention à sa destination première. **2.** *Mil:* affecter (qn) de nouveau (**to a service,** à un service).

reassignment [riːə'sainmənt], *s.* **1.** nouvelle cession (d'une terre, etc.); **r. of funds to their original use,** réaffectation *f* d'une subvention à sa destination première. **2.** *Mil:* nouvelle affectation (de qn à un service).

reassume [riːə'sjuːm], *v.tr.* reprendre (un emploi, son calme habituel, etc.); réassumer (une responsabilité, etc.).

reassurance [ri(ː)ə'ʃuər(ə)ns], *s.* **1.** (*a*) action *f* de réassurer (qn); (*b*) **to be a r. to s.o.,** rassurer qn. **2.** *Ins:* réassurance *f*.

reassure [ri(ː)ə'ʃuər], *v.tr.* **1.** (*a*) rassurer (qn) (**on, about,** sur); **to r. s.o. of the truth of sth.,** rassurer qn sur la vérité de qch.; (*b*) rassurer, tranquilliser (qn); **to feel reassured,** se rassurer. **2.** *Ins:* réassurer.

reassuring [ri(ː)ə'ʃuəriŋ], *a.* (*of news, etc.*) rassurant.

reata [ri'ɑːtə], *s.* **1.** lasso *m*. **2.** corde *f* à piquet.

reate [riːt], *s. Bot:* renoncule flottante; grenouillette *f*.

reattach [riːə'tætʃ], *v.tr.* rattacher; refixer (des fils, etc.).

Réaumur ['reiəmjuər], *Pr.n. Ph:* **R. scale,** échelle *f* Réaumur.

reave [riːv], *v.* (*p.t. & p.p.* **reft** [reft]) *A: & Lit:* **1.** *v.i.* commettre des ravages; se livrer à la rapine; faire des razzias sur le bétail. **2.** *v.tr.* (*a*) ravager; razzier (le bétail); (*b*) enlever, ravir (**s.o. of sth.,** qch. à qn); arracher (**sth. from s.o.,** qch. à qn); **trees reft of their leaves,** arbres dépouillés de leurs feuilles; **the lands reft from the Crown,** les domaines arrachés à la Couronne.

reaver ['riːvər], *s. A: & Lit:* pillard *m*, brigand *m*; voleur *m* de bétail.

reaving ['riːviŋ], *s. A: & Lit:* rapine *f*.

reawaken [riːə'weik(ə)n]. **1.** *v.tr.* réveiller (un dormeur); **to r. an emotion in s.o.,** ranimer un sentiment chez qn. **2.** *v.i.* se réveiller de nouveau; se ranimer.

reback [riː'bæk], *v.tr.* rentoiler (une peinture); endosser à nouveau (un livre).

rebake [riː'beik], *v.tr. Cu: Cer:* recuire.

rebalance [riː'bæləns], *v.tr.* rééquilibrer (le budget, etc.).

rebale [riː'beil], *v.tr.* remettre (des marchandises, etc.) en balles, en ballots.

reballast [riː'bæləst], *v.tr.* ballaster à nouveau, recharger (une voie ferrée, une route).

reballasting [riː'bæləstiŋ], *s.* rechargement *m* (d'une route, etc.).

rebaptism [riː'bæptizm], *s.* rebaptisation *f*.

rebaptize [riːbæp'taiz], *v.tr.* rebaptiser.

rebarbative [ri'bɑːbətiv], *a.* rébarbatif; sinistre; rebutant; menaçant.

rebate[1] ['riːbeit], *s. Com: etc:* **1.** rabais *m*, remise *f*, escompte *m*, bonification *f*; (*on goods not up to sample*) réfaction *f*; **to allow a r. on an account,** faire une diminution sur un compte; *Adm:* **tax, rate, r.,** décharge *f* d'impôt. 2. ristourne *f*; remboursement *m*.

rebate[2] [ri'beit], *v.tr.* 1. *A:* (*a*) **to r. a blow,** amortir un coup, diminuer la force d'un coup; (*b*) émousser (une arme). 2. *NAm:* (*a*) faire un rabais, une diminution, de (tant d'argent); (*b*) donner un rabais, une remise, une bonification, à (qn).

rebate[3] ['ræbit], *s.* & *v.tr.* = RABBET[1,2].

rebbetzin, rebbitzin ['rebitzin], *s.f. Jew.Rel:* femme du rabbin.

Rebecca [ri'bekə], *Pr.n.f.* Rébecca.

rebec(k) ['ri:bek], *s. A.Mus:* rebec *m*.

rebed [ri:'bed], *v.tr. Mec.E:* **to r. a shaft,** refaire les portées d'un arbre; *Hort:* **to r. plants,** replanter des jeunes plants.

rebel[1] ['reb(ə)l]. 1. *s.* rebelle *mf*; révolté, -ée; insurgé, -ée. 2. *a.* **r. troops,** troupes insurgées, rebelles; **r. camp,** camp des rebelles.

rebel[2] [ri'bel], *v.i.* (**rebelled**) se rebeller; se révolter, se soulever (**against,** contre); **to r. against authority,** se rebeller contre l'autorité; récalcitrer; faire la mauvaise tête; **to r. against one's fate,** se révolter, se cabrer, contre son destin.

rebellion [ri'beliən], *s.* 1. rébellion *f*, révolte *f* (**against,** contre); soulèvement *m*; **district in open r.,** région en révolte ouverte. 2. *Jur: Scot:* contumace *f*.

rebellious [ri'beliəs], *a.* rebelle; (*a*) **r. act,** acte de rébellion; **r. troops,** troupes insubordonnées; **r. youth,** jeunesse insoumise; *Jur:* **r. assembly,** réunion *f* de plus de douze personnes en vue de commettre un acte illicite; *Fig:* **r. hair,** chevelure rebelle; (*b*) *Med:* (fièvre, ulcère) rebelle.

rebelliously [ri'beliəsli], *adv.* (se conduire) en rebelle; (répondre) d'un ton de défi.

rebelliousness [ri'beliəsnis], *s.* esprit *m* de rébellion; disposition *f* à la rébellion; insubordination *f*.

rebind [ri:'baind], *v.tr.* (*p.t.* & *p.p.* **rebound** [ri:'baund]) 1. relier (un livre) de nouveau, à neuf. 2. recercler (une roue).

rebinding [ri:'baindiŋ], *s.* 1. reliure *f* (d'un livre) à neuf. 2. recerclage *m* (d'une roue).

rebirth [ri:'bə:θ], *s.* renaissance *f* (d'une âme, nation, etc.); retour *m* à la vie.

rebite [ri:'bait], *v.tr. Engr:* raviver (une planche) à l'eau-forte.

rebiting [ri:'baitiŋ], *s. Engr:* remorsure *f*.

reblock [ri:'blɔk], *v.tr.* reformer (un chapeau); remettre (un chapeau) en forme.

reboil [ri:'bɔil]. 1. *v.i.* (*a*) rebouillir; (*b*) (*of wine, etc.*) entrer de nouveau en fermentation. 2. *v.tr.* faire rebouillir.

rebore[1] ['ri:bɔ:r], *s. Aut:* réalésage *m*.

rebore[2] [ri:'bɔ:r], *v.tr. Mec.E:* reforer (un trou, etc.); *Aut:* réaléser (un cylindre).

reborn [ri:'bɔ:n], *a.* né à nouveau; (espoir) renaissant; **to be r.,** renaître.

rebottle [ri:'bɔtl], *v.tr.* mettre (le vin) dans de nouvelles bouteilles.

rebottom [ri:'bɔtəm], *v.tr.* remettre un fond à (une boîte, etc.); remettre un siège à (une chaise); rempailler (une chaise paillée).

rebottoming [ri:'bɔtəmiŋ], *s.* remise *f* d'un fond (**of a box,** à une boîte); rempaillage *m* (d'une chaise paillée).

rebound[1] [ri'baund, 'ri:baund], *s.* 1. rebond *m*, rebondissement *m*; retour *m* brusque; détente *f* (d'un ressort); ricochet *m* (d'une balle); **to hit a ball on the r.,** frapper une balle au rebond; **hit by a bullet on the r.,** atteint par une balle au ricochet; *Fig:* **to take, catch, s.o. on the r.,** profiter du moment de détente de qn (après une émotion); **she married him on the r. after an unhappy love affair,** elle l'a épousé par contrecoup après une affaire de cœur malheureuse; *Fin: Com:* **sharp r. of the market,** reprise vigoureuse du marché; *Mec.E: etc:* **r. shock,** choc *m* de compression; **r. check, stop,** (i) butoir *m* de recul; (ii) amortisseur *m* de rebondissement. 2. *Sp:* (*basketball*) (i) ballon *m* qui fait rebond; (ii) prise *f* du ballon qui fait rebond.

rebound[2] [ri'baund], *v.i.* (*a*) (*of ball, etc.*) rebondir; **the trick he played rebounded on him,** le mauvais tour qu'il avait fait est retombé, a rejailli, sur lui; (*b*) (*of spring*) rebondir; se détendre; (*c*) se ressaisir; (*of pers.*) se ressaisir vivement (après un échec, etc.); *Fin: Com:* (*of market*) reprendre vivement.

rebounding[1] [ri'baundiŋ], *a.* rebondissant; bondissant.

rebounding[2], *s.* rebondissement *m*.

rebox [ri:'bɔks], *v.tr.* mettre (des chocolats, etc.) dans une nouvelle boîte; *Hort:* rencaisser (des orangers, etc.).

rebozo [ri'bouzou], *s.* longue écharpe (portée par les Mexicaines).

rebroadcast[1] [ri:'brɔ:dkɑ:st], *s. W.Tel:* retransmission *f*, rediffusion *f* (d'un programme).

rebroadcast[2], *v.tr. W.Tel:* retransmettre, rediffuser (un programme).

rebuff[1] [ri'bʌf], *s.* rebuffade *f*; **to meet with, suffer, a r.,** (i) (*of pers.*) essuyer un refus, un déboire, un échec; *F:* prendre la pilule; remporter une veste; (ii) (*of suggestion, etc.*) être repoussé.

rebuff[2], *v.tr.* repousser (qn, une proposition, etc.); rebuter, *F:* rebuffer, rembarrer (qn).

rebuild[1] [ri:'bild], *v.tr.* (*p.t.* & *p.p.* **rebuilt** [ri:'bilt]) rebâtir, reconstruire, refaire (un immeuble, de la maçonnerie, etc.); relever (des ruines, un mur); refaire (entièrement) (un appareil, etc.); refondre (un navire); **rebuilt typewriter,** machine à écrire entièrement refaite, remise à l'état de neuf; **idealists who want to r. the world,** idéalistes qui voudraient refaire le monde; *v.i.* **to r. after an earthquake,** faire la reconstruction après un tremblement de terre.

rebuild[2] ['ri:bild], *s. Arch:* reconstruction *f*, bâtiment reconstruit.

rebuilder [ri:'bildər], *s.* reconstructeur *m*.

rebuilding [ri:'bildiŋ], *s.* reconstruction *f*, réfection *f* (d'un édifice, de la maçonnerie, etc.); relèvement *m* (de ruines, etc.); réfection, remise *f* à neuf (d'un appareil, etc.); refonte *f* (d'un navire).

rebuke[1] [ri'bju:k], *s.* réprimande *f*, reproche *m*, blâme *m*.

rebuke[2], *v.tr.* (*a*) réprimander, reprendre, blâmer, gourmander (qn); **to r. s.o. for sth.,** reprocher qch. à qn; (*b*) **he rebuked their presumption,** il leur a reproché leur présomption.

rebuker [ri'bju:kər], *s.* réprimandeur, -euse.

rebuking [ri'bju:kiŋ], *a.* plein de reproches; (regard) sévère, de reproche.

rebukingly [ri'bju:kiŋli], *adv.* avec des reproches; d'un ton, air, de reproche; d'un ton sévère.

reburn [ri:'bə:n], *v.tr.* recuire (le ciment).

reburning [ri:'bə:niŋ], *s.* recuit *m* (du ciment).

reburnish [ri:'bə:niʃ], *v.tr.* repolir (le métal); brunir (l'or, etc.) à nouveau.

reburnishing [ri:'bə:niʃiŋ], *s.* repolissage *m*.

rebus ['ri:bəs], *s.* rébus *m*.

rebush [ri:'buʃ], *v.tr. Mec.E:* **to r. a bearing,** refaire les coussinets, les bagues, d'un palier; mettre des coussinets neufs, des bagues neuves, à un palier; regarnir un palier.

rebut [ri'bʌt], *v.tr.* (**rebutted**) 1. (*a*) réfuter (une accusation); démontrer la fausseté de (l'hypothèse, etc.); (*b*) *v.i. Jur:* dupliquer, riposter. 2. rebuter, repousser (qn).

rebutment [ri'bʌtmənt], **rebuttal** [ri'bʌt(ə)l], *s.* réfutation *f* (d'une accusation, etc.).

rebutter [ri'bʌtər], *s. Jur:* 1. duplique *f*. 2. réfutation *f*.

rebutton [ri:'bʌt(ə)n], *v.tr.* reboutonner.

rec [rek], *s. F: O:* (= **recreation ground**) terrain *m* de jeux, de sports.

recalcification [ri:kælsifi'keiʃ(ə)n], *s.* recalcification *f*.

recalcify [ri:'kælsifai], *v.tr.* recalcifier.

recalcitrance [ri'kælsitrəns], *s.* récalcitrance *f*; esprit *m* réfractaire.

recalcitrant [ri'kælsitrənt], *a.* (*of pers.*) récalcitrant, réfractaire; regimbeur, -euse; **subject r. to research,** sujet qui ne se prête pas aux recherches; *Med:* **r. disease,** maladie qui résiste aux traitements.

recalcitrate [ri'kælsitreit], *v.i.* récalcitrer, regimber (**at, against,** contre).

recalculate [ri:'kælkjuleit], *v.tr.* recalculer.

recalculation [ri:kælkju'leiʃ(ə)n], *s.* recalcul *m*.

recalesce [ri:kæ'les], *v.i.* (*of metal*) subir la récalescence.

recalescence [ri:kæ'les(ə)ns], *s. Metall: Ph:* récalescence *f*.

recall[1] [ri'kɔ:l], *s.* 1. (*a*) rappel *m* (de qn, de troupes, etc.); *Dipl:* **letters of r.,** lettres *f* de rappel; *Navy:* **general r. signal,** signal de rappel général; (*b*) *Can:* destitution *f* (d'un fonctionnaire) par une consultation populaire; (*c*) *Th:* **to give an actor a r.,** rappeler un acteur. 2. (*a*) évocation *f*, rappel (d'un souvenir); **total r.,** capacité *f* de se souvenir de tous les détails de quelque chose; (*b*) *Cmptr:* accès *m* (d'une mémoire). 3. rétractation *f*, révocation *f*; **decision past r.,** décision irrévocable; **it's past r.,** c'est irrémédiable; **lost beyond r.,** perdu irrévocablement.

recall[2] [ri'kɔ:l], *v.tr.* 1. (*a*) rappeler (un exilé, un ambassadeur, un acteur); **to r. s.o. to office, to life,** rappeler qn au pouvoir, à la vie; **to r. s.o. from his dreams,** tirer qn de ses rêves; rappeler qn à la réalité; **to r. s.o. to his duty,** rappeler, ramener, qn au devoir, à son devoir; **to r. s.o.'s attention to sth.,** appeler de nouveau l'attention de qn sur qch.; (*b*) demander le retour de (qch.). 2. (*a*) rappeler (qch. à qn); **everything here recalls my youth to me,** tout ici me retrace ma jeunesse; **legends that r. the past,** légendes remémoratrices, évocatrices, du passé, qui évoquent le passé; (*b*) **to r. sth. (to mind),** se rappeler qch., se souvenir de qch.; se retracer (un événement, etc.); **I don't r. his name,** je ne me souviens pas de son nom; **I don't r. you,** je ne vous remets pas; **I am beginning to r. his face,** son visage me revient; **how vividly I r. the scene!** avec quelle netteté je revois ce spectacle! 3. (*a*) rétracter (une promesse, etc.); retirer (sa parole); revenir sur (sa promesse, sa parole); (*b*) annuler (un jugement); révoquer (un décret, etc.).

recall[3] [ri:'kɔ:l], *v.tr.* **to r. the roll,** faire de nouveau l'appel des noms.

recallable [ri'kɔ:ləbl], *a.* 1. (réserviste, etc.) rappelable; qui peut être rappelé. 2. (souvenir) évocable; (événement) qu'il est possible de rappeler à la mémoire. 3. (édit, etc.) révocable; qui peut être rétracté; (jugement) annulable.

recaller [ri'kɔ:lər], *s.* remémorateur, -trice (du passé).

recalling [ri'kɔ:liŋ], *s.* 1. rappel *m* (d'un souvenir, d'un ambassadeur, etc.). 2. révocation *f* (d'une décision, etc.).

recant [ri'kænt]. 1. *v.tr.* rétracter, revenir sur (une opinion); abjurer (une erreur de doctrine, etc.), désavouer (une doctrine). 2. *v.i.* se rétracter.

recantation [ri:kæn'teiʃ(ə)n], **recanting**[1] [ri'kæntiŋ], *s.* rétractation *f*, abjuration *f* (**of,** de).

recanting[2], *a.* qui se rétracte.

recap[1] ['ri:kæp], *s. Aut: F:* pneu rechapé.

recap[2] [ri:'kæp], *v.tr.* (**recapped**) 1. recoiffer (une bouteille). 2. *Aut:* rechaper (un pneu).

recap[3] ['ri:kæp], *s. F:* récapitulation *f*; **let's do a r.,** faisons le point.

recap[4] ['ri:kæp], *v.tr. F:* = RECAPITULATE.

recapitalization [ri:kæpitəlai'zeiʃ(ə)n], *s. Fin:* changement *m* de la structure financière (d'une société).

recapitalize [ri:'kæpitəlaiz], *v.tr. Fin:* **to r. a company,** changer la structure financière d'une société.

recapitulate [ri:kə'pitjuleit], *v.tr.* récapituler, faire un résumé de (ce qu'on a dit, etc.); **to r. the evidence,** faire la récapitulation des témoignages; **let us r. the facts,** reprenons les faits; *v.i.* **let us r.,** faisons le point.

recapitulation [ri:kəpitju'leiʃ(ə)n], *s.* 1. récapitulation *f*; résumé *m*. 2. *Mus:* réexposition *f*.

recapitulator [ri:kə'pitjuleitər], *s.* récapitulateur, -trice.

recapping[1] [ri:'kæpiŋ], *s. Aut:* rechapage *m* (d'un pneu).

recapping[2], *s. F:* récapitulation *f*; résumé *m*.

recaption [ri:'kæpʃ(ə)n], *s. Jur:* reprise *f* (de biens).

recapture[1] [ri:'kæptjər], *s.* 1. reprise *f*. 2. *U.S:* saisie *f*, confiscation *f* (de superbénéfices).

recapture[2], *v.tr.* 1. (*a*) reprendre, recapturer, ratteindre, se remparer de (qn, qch.); **recaptured ship,** reprise *f*; (*b*) *U.S:* saisir, confisquer (des superbénéfices). 2. **to r. one's former enthusiasm,** retrouver son enthousiasme antérieur; **film that recaptures the spirit of the times,** film qui fait revivre l'esprit de l'époque.

recarbonization [ri:kɑ:bəni'zeiʃ(ə)n], **recarburization** [ri:kɑ:bjurai'zeiʃ(ə)n], *s. Ch: Metall:* recarburation *f*.

recarbonize [ri:'kɑ:bənaiz], **recarburize** [ri:'kɑ:bjuraiz], *v.tr. Ch: Metall:* recarburer (l'acier, etc.).

recase ['ri:'keis], *v.tr.* 1. rempaqueter (des marchandises) dans une nouvelle caisse. 2. recuveler (un puits). 3. *Bookb:* remboîter (un livre).

recasing [ri:'keisiŋ], *s.* 1. recuvelage *m* (d'un puits). 2. *Bookb:* remboîtage *m* (d'un livre).

recast[1] [ri:'kɑ:st], *s.* 1. *Metall:* refonte *f*. 2. nouveau calcul. 3. *Th:* nouvelle distribution des rôles.

recast[2], *v.tr.* (*p.t.* & *p.p.* **recast**) 1. *Metall:* refondre (une cloche, etc.); *Lit:* **to r. a poem, a sentence, a (literary) work,** refondre un poème; reconstruire, refaire, une phrase; remanier une œuvre littéraire; apporter des remaniements à un travail; *Journ:* **r. version of an article,** *F:* nouvelle mouture. 2. refaire le calcul de (ses dépenses, etc.); calculer de nouveau (qch.). 3. *Th:* (*a*) faire une nouvelle distribution des rôles de (la pièce); (*b*) donner un nouveau rôle à (un acteur).

recaster [ri:'kɑ:stər], *s.* remanieur, -euse (d'une œuvre littéraire etc.).

recasting [ri:'kɑ:stiŋ], *s.* = RECAST[1].

recce[1] ['reki], *s. F:* 1. *Mil:* reconnaissance *f*; reco *f*. 2. exploration *f*, investigation *f*.

recce[2], *v.i. F:* 1. *Mil:* faire une reconnaissance, une reco; aller en reconnaissance. 2. éclairer le terrain.

recede[1] [ri'si:d], *v.i.* 1. (*a*) (*of pers., thg*) s'éloigner, reculer; (*of tide, sea*) se retirer, baisser; **the mountains r. to the north,** les montagnes s'enfoncent au nord; (*from ship*) **the coast recedes,** les côtes s'enfuient; **as memories of the past r.,** à mesure que les souvenirs du passé s'effacent, diminuent; **his hair is receding,** ses tempes se dégarnissent; (*b*) **to r. a few paces,** reculer de quelques pas; *Mil:* **to r. from a position,** se retirer d'une position; accomplir un recul; (*c*) (*of sinew, tissue, etc.*)

se rétracter; (*d*) (*of forehead*) fuir. **2. to r. from an opinion, a promise,** abandonner une opinion; revenir sur une promesse; se dédire. **3.** décliner (en valeur); *St.Exch:* **oil shares receded three points,** les pétroles ont reculé, baissé, de trois points. **4.** *Art:* (*of background*) se renfoncer.

recede[2] [ri:'si:d], *v.tr.* recéder (**sth. to s.o.,** qch. à qn).

receding[1] [ri'si:diŋ], *a.* (*a*) qui s'éloigne, qui recule; **r. tide,** marée descendante; (*b*) **r. forehead,** front fuyant; **r. chin,** menton effacé.

receding[2], *s.* **1.** éloignement *m*, recul *m*; **r. of the gums from the teeth,** déchaussement *m* des dents. **2. r. from an opinion,** abandonnement *m* d'une opinion. **3.** *Art:* **r. of the background,** renfoncement *m*, fuite *f*, de l'arrière-plan.

receipt[1] [ri'si:t], *s.* **1.** *O:* & *NAm:* = RECIPE. **2.** (*a*) *Com: etc:* recette *f*; *pl.* **receipts,** recettes, rentrées *f*, encaissements *m*; **receipts and expenditure,** recettes et dépenses; **receipts and payments,** rentrées et sorties; (*b*) *A:* perception *f* (des impôts); *B:* **Matthew seated at the r. of custom,** Mathieu assis au lieu du péage; (*c*) réception *f*; *Com:* **I am in r. of your letter of March 4th,** j'ai bien reçu, je suis en possession de, votre lettre du 4 mars; **on r. of this letter, of your parcel,** au reçu de cette lettre; à la, dès, réception de votre envoi; **to pay on r.,** payer à (la) réception; **within ten days of r.,** dans les dix jours après réception; **to acknowledge r. of a letter,** accuser réception d'une lettre; *O:* **I am not yet in r. of a salary,** je ne reçois pas encore d'appointements; (*d*) *Cmptr:* réception (des données), entrée *f* (en stock). **3.** *Com: etc:* reçu *m* (**for goods, money,** de marchandises, d'argent); **r. for payment,** acquit *m* de paiement; **rent r.,** quittance *f* de loyer; **r. for a loan,** reconnaissance *f*; **formal r.,** quittance comptable; **custom house r.,** acquit de douane; billette *f*; **r. in full (discharge),** reçu, quittance, pour solde; quittance finale, libératoire; **r. for a dispatch,** accusé *m* de réception d'un envoi; **r. for a registered parcel,** récépissé *m* d'un envoi recommandé; **warehouse r.,** récépissé d'entrepôt; *Nau:* **ship's mate's, r.,** reçu, billet *m*, de bord; *Fin:* **application r. for shares,** récépissé de souscription à des actions; **send it with the r.,** envoyez-le avec la facture acquittée; **to give a r. for sth.,** donner acquit, quittance, décharge, de qch.; **r. book,** carnet *m* de quittances; (*formerly required in payment of duty*) **r. stamp,** timbre *m* de quittance; timbre-quittance *m*, *pl.* timbres-quittance.

receipt[2], *v.tr.* acquitter, quittancer, décharger (une facture); (*with rubber stamp*) apposer le tampon "acquitté" sur (une facture); **to r. a bill in the margin,** émarger une facture.

receipting [ri'si:tiŋ], *s.* mise *f* de "acquitté" (**of a bill,** sur une facture); (*in the margin*) émargement *m* (d'une facture).

receivability [risi:və'biliti], *s.* recevabilité *f*.

receivable [ri'si:vəbl], *a.* **1.** recevable, admissible. **2.** *Com:* **bills r.,** *s. NAm:* **receivables,** effets *m* à recevoir; **accounts r.,** dettes actives.

receive [ri'si:v], *v.tr.* **1.** (*a*) recevoir (un don, une nouvelle, une lettre); **on receiving your letter,** au reçu de votre lettre; **I have received your letter,** votre lettre m'est parvenue; **to r. money,** recevoir, toucher, de l'argent; **received the sum of £10,** reçu la somme de £10; (*on bill*) **received with thanks,** pour acquit; **I am expecting to r. payments,** j'attends des rentrées; **to r. a loan back,** rencaisser un prêt; **to r. one's salary,** toucher son traitement; **to r. s.o.'s confession,** recevoir la confession de qn; **to r. a petition,** accepter une pétition, une requête; *Ecc:* **to r. communion, absolution,** recevoir la communion, l'absolution; **finally the chassis receives the bodywork,** à la fin le châssis est pourvu de la carrosserie; *W.Tel: T.V:* **to r. a broadcast,** recevoir une émission; **to r. a station,** capter, accrocher, un poste; *Ten:* **to r. (the) service,** *v.i.* **to r.,** recevoir le service; (*b*) *Jur:* **to r. stolen goods,** receler des objets volés. **2.** recevoir, soutenir (un poids); **buttress which receives the weight of the roof,** arc-boutant qui supporte le poids du toit. **3.** recevoir, contenir (qch.); **bowl to r. the drips,** cuvette pour recevoir l'égoutture. **4.** (*a*) recevoir (des invités, le maire, etc.); accueillir (qn chez soi); **to r. s.o. with open arms,** accueillir qn à bras ouverts; **to be cordially received,** trouver un accueil chaleureux; **he was received with cheers,** on l'a reçu, l'a accueilli, avec des acclamations; **the proposal was well received,** la proposition reçut un accueil favorable; *v.i. O:* **she is not receiving today,** elle ne reçoit pas aujourd'hui; *Mil:* **to r. the reviewing officer,** présenter une troupe; (*b*) **to r. s.o. into the Church,** admettre qn dans l'Église. **5.** (*a*) recevoir (des salutations, des titres, etc.); **to r. sympathy,** recevoir des marques de sympathie; être l'objet de sympathie; (*b*) recevoir (un coup, etc.); **to r. a refusal,** essuyer, se voir opposer, un refus; **to r. thirty days,** être condamné à un mois de prison.

received [ri'si:vd], *a.* reçu, admis; **generally r. opinion,** opinion généralement reçue; opinion répandue; **r. pronunciation,** *NAm:* **r. standard,** la prononciation des gens cultivés.

receiver [ri'si:vər], *s.* **1.** (*a*) personne *f* qui reçoit (qch.); destinataire *mf* (d'une lettre); *Com:* réceptionnaire *mf* (d'un envoi); **givers and receivers,** ceux qui donnent et ceux qui reçoivent; (*b*) *NAm:* receveur *m* (des deniers publics); **receiver's office,** recette *f*; (*c*) *Jur:* **r. in bankruptcy, official r.,** administrateur *m* judiciaire (en matière de faillite); administrateur séquestre; liquidateur *m*; préposé *m* à la caisse des dépôts et consignations; (*in Fr.*) = syndic *m* de faillite; *Adm:* **r. of wreck,** syndic des naufrages; (*d*) **r. (of stolen goods),** receleur, -euse (d'objets volés); (*e*) *Ten:* relanceur, -euse. **2.** (*device*) (*a*) *Tp:* **(telephone, hand) r.,** récepteur *m*, écouteur *m*; *NAm:* **head r.,** casque *m* téléphonique; **r. hook,** crochet *m*, étrier *m* de suspension, de l'écouteur; **r. rest,** berceau *m* du récepteur; **to remove, lift, the r.,** décrocher (l'appareil, le récepteur); **to replace the r.,** raccrocher (l'appareil, le récepteur); (*b*) *Tg:* **telegraph r.,** récepteur télégraphique; **facsimile r.,** récepteur bélinographique; **r. printer,** téléimprimeur-récepteur *m*, *pl.* téléimprimeurs-récepteurs; (*c*) *W.Tel: etc:* **radio r.,** récepteur, poste *m*, radio; **television r.,** poste, récepteur, de télévision; téléviseur *m*; **radar r.,** récepteur radar; **plan position indicator r.,** récepteur panoramique; *Av:* **glide slope r.,** récepteur d'axe de descente; **marker beacon r.,** récepteur de radiobalise; (*d*) *Cmptr:* **data r.,** récepteur de données (d'un ordinateur). **3.** (*a*) récipient *m*, récepteur; *Ch:* récipient (de cornue); (*balloon flask*) ballon *m*; (*bell jar*) cloche *f*; (*bottle*) bouteille *f*; **air-pump r.,** récipient, cloche, de pompe pneumatique; **compressed air r.,** réservoir d'air comprimé; *Ch:* **florentine r.,** récipient florentin; matras *m*; *Ind:* **waste r.,** récipient à déchets; *Hyd.E:* **overflow r.,** collecteur *m*, récepteur, de trop-plein; *Cmptr:* **card r.,** récepteur, magasin *m* de réception, de cartes; (*b*) *Metall:* avant-creuset *m*, *pl.* avant-creusets (de cubilot).

receivership [ri'si:vəʃip], *s.* **1.** fonctions *fpl* de receveur; recette *f*. **2. official r.** = syndic *m* de faillite.

receiving[1] [ri'si:viŋ], *a.* récepteur, -trice; **r. agent, clerk,** réceptionnaire *mf*; **r. cashier,** (guichetier) encaisseur *m*; *Cmptr:* **r. field,** zone réceptrice; **r. terminal,** terminal récepteur; **r. tray,** récepteur *m* de papier (sur imprimante).

receiving[2], *s.* réception *f*. **1.** (*a*) **r. of goods,** réception de marchandises; **r. of money,** recette *f* d'argent; **r. certificate,** certificat *m* de réception; **r. office,** (i) *Post:* bureau *m* de réception, bureau réceptionnaire; (ii) *Rail:* bureau de(s) messageries; *Rail:* **r. station,** gare *f* de réception, réceptrice; *Navy:* **r. ship, hull,** caserne flottante; bâtiment-caserne *m*, *pl.* bâtiments-casernes; *F:* **to be at, on, the r. end (of the stick),** recevoir, encaisser, les coups; (*b*) **r. (of stolen goods),** recel *m* (d'objets volés); (*c*) **r. back,** rencaissage *m*, rencaissement *m* (d'un emprunt); (*d*) *Jur:* **r. order,** mandat *m* d'action; ordonnance *f* de mise sous séquestre. **2.** *Tg:* **r. by tape,** réception sur bande; *W.Tel:* **r. apparatus, set,** appareil *m* de réception; poste récepteur; radio-récepteur *m*; **r. loop,** cadre *m* de réception; **r. valve,** *NAm:* **r. tube,** tube *m* de réception; **r. end,** côté récepteur, côté réception; **r. level,** niveau *m* de réception; **r. station,** station réceptrice, poste récepteur.

recementation [ri:si'men'teiʃ(ə)n], *s. Ch: Metall:* recarburation *f*.

recency ['ri:s(ə)nsi], *s.* **1.** caractère récent, date récente (d'un événement, etc.). **2.** *Psy:* récence *f*; **law of r.,** effet *m* de récence.

recense [ri'sens], *v.tr.* faire la recension (d'un texte), réviser (un texte).

recension [ri'senʃ(ə)n], *s.* **1.** recension *f*, révision *f* (d'un texte). **2.** texte révisé.

recent ['ri:s(ə)nt], *a.* nouveau, -elle; frais, *f.* fraîche; **event of r. date,** événement de fraîche date, de date récente, contemporain; **r. news,** nouvelles récentes, fraîches; **it happened within r. memory,** la mémoire en est encore récente; **theirs was a r. acquaintance,** ils se connaissaient depuis peu; **all that is quite r.,** tout cela n'est que, ne date que, d'hier; *Geol:* **R. Quaternary,** quaternaire récent.

recently ['ri:s(ə)ntli], *adv.* récemment, nouvellement, tout dernièrement, dans ces derniers temps, naguère; **as r. as yesterday,** pas plus tard que d'hier; **until quite r.,** jusque dans ces derniers temps; **they are r. married,** ils sont mariés de fraîche date, depuis peu.

recentness ['ri:s(ə)ntnis], *s.* caractère récent, date récente (d'un événement, etc.).

receptacle [ri'septəkl], *s.* **1.** réceptacle *m*; **port which is the r. of all the scum of Europe,** port qui est le réceptacle de toute la racaille de l'Europe. **2.** récipient *m*; **r. to catch the drips,** récipient pour recueillir l'égouttage; *X-rays:* **film r.,** porte-film *m*, *pl.* porte-film(s); cassette *f*. **3.** *Bot:* réceptacle (d'une fleur, d'un champignon). **4.** *NAm: El:* prise de courant (femelle) (fixée à demeure).

receptaculum, *pl.* **-la** [ri:sep'tækjuləm, -lə], *s. Biol:* sac *m*; *Bot:* réceptacle *m*.

receptible [ri'septibl], *a.* capable de recevoir; récepteur, -trice.

reception [ri'sepʃ(ə)n], *s.* **1.** (*a*) réception *f* (d'un candidat à une académie, etc.); (*b*) (*at hotel*) **the r. desk, office,** la réception; *NAm:* **r. clerk,** réceptionniste *mf*, préposé, -ée, à la réception; **chief r. clerk,** chef *m* de réception; (*c*) **r. centre,** centre d'accueil (pour réfugiés, etc.); *Adm:* **r. stamp,** griffe *f* de réception; **r. order,** permis *m* de recevoir un aliéné (dans une maison de santé); permis d'internement. **2.** accueil *m*; **to give s.o. a kind, courteous, hearty, r.,** faire un accueil courtois, cordial, à qn; bien accueillir qn; recevoir qn aimablement; **to give s.o. an unfriendly r.,** faire mauvais accueil à qn; mal accueillir qn; **to give s.o. a warm r.,** (i) recevoir chaleureusement qn; faire à qn un accueil chaleureux; (ii) *Iron:* recevoir chaudement qn; recevoir qn avec une hostilité marquée; conspuer qn; **to meet with a hostile, favourable, r.,** recevoir, rencontrer, un accueil hostile, favorable; **the book, play, has had a favourable r.,** le livre, la pièce, a été accueilli(e) favorablement, a été bien reçu(e). **3.** réception (officielle, hebdomadaire, etc.); **we are going to a r.,** nous allons en soirée; **r. room,** (i) salle *f* de réception; salon *m*; (ii) pièce *f* (par opposition à chambre à coucher); **three r. rooms and five bedrooms,** trois pièces, trois salles, et cinq chambres à coucher. **4.** acceptation *f*, admission *f* (d'une théorie). **5.** *W.Tel:* réception; **autodyne r.,** réception autodyne, à réaction; **beat r.,** réception hétérodyne, par battement; **r. level,** niveau *m*, intensité *f*, de réception; **headphone r.,** réception au casque; **loudspeaker r., r. at loudspeaker strength,** réception en haut-parleur. **6.** *Psy:* **faculty of r.,** faculté *f* de recevoir les impressions; faculté d'assimilation; réceptivité *f*.

receptionist [ri'sepʃənist], *s.* préposé, -ée, à la réception, réceptionnaire *mf*, réceptionniste *mf* (d'un hôtel, d'un cabinet médical, d'un salon de beauté, etc.); **head r.,** chef *m* de (la) réception.

receptive [ri'septiv], *a.* (esprit, organe, etc.) réceptif; **r. medium, r. milieu,** milieu récepteur.

receptiveness [ri'septivnis], **receptivity** [ri:sep'tiviti], *s.* réceptivité *f*.

receptor [ri'septər], *s. Physiol: Tp: etc:* récepteur *m*; **r. (organ),** récepteur; *Hyd.E: etc:* **shower r.,** récepteur de douche.

recertification [ri:sə:tifi'keiʃ(ə)n], *s. Cmptr:* recertification *f*.

recertify [ri:'sərtifai], *v.tr. Cmptr:* recertifier.

recess[1] [ri'ses], *s.* **1.** (*a*) vacances *fpl* (des Chambres, tribunaux, etc.); intersession *f* (parlementaire); (*b*) *Sch: esp. NAm:* (l'heure *f* de la) récréation; (*c*) *NAm: Jur:* suspension *f* (d'audience). **2.** *Hist:* recez *m* (d'une Diète). **3.** *O:* recul *m* (des eaux, d'un glacier). **4.** (*a*) recoin *m*; **mountain recesses,** recoins, replis *m*, des montagnes; **in the innermost recesses of the soul,** dans les replis les plus secrets de l'âme; (*b*) enfoncement *m*; *Const:* rentrant *m* (de muraille); embrasure *f* (de porte, de fenêtre); niche *f* (de statue); alcôve *f* (de lit); évidement *m*, renfoncement *m*, encastrement *m*; **the wall forms a r. at this point,** le mur s'enfonce à cet endroit; **dining r.,** coin *m* (des) repas, coin salle à manger; **bookshelves in the recesses,** rayons de livres dans les retraits *m*; **r. under the staircase,** soupente *f* d'escalier; **statue placed, set, in a r.,** statue nichée dans une embrasure, placée dans une niche; *Arch:* **r. (tomb),** enfeu *m*; *Rail:* **safety r.,** niche d'évitement (dans un tunnel); *Mch:* **stuffing box r.,** niche de presse-étoupe; *Mec.E:* **spring r.,** logement *m* de ressort; *X-rays:* **film r.,** cassette *f*; (*c*) *Mec.E: etc:* alvéole *m*, évidement *m*, cavité *f*; trou *m* borgne (pour tête de vis); échancrure *f*, encoche *f* (dans une plaque, etc.); (*d*) *Anat:* cavité, sinus *m*, antre *m*.

recess[2]. **1.** *v.tr.* (*a*) évider; chambrer; pratiquer un enfoncement, une alcôve, dans (une muraille); (*b*) mettre (qch.) dans un enfoncement; encastrer (la tête d'une vis, etc.). **2.** *v.i. NAm:* (*of assembly*) (i) suspendre la séance; (ii) suspendre les séances.

recessed [ri'sest], *a.* **1.** (*a*) à enfoncement, à embrasure; creusé, évidé, échancré; (*b*) **r. pipe end,** embouchure *f* (de tuyau) à évidement annulaire. **2.** enfoncé; (lit) dans une alcôve, une niche; (devanture) en retrait; **r. arch,**

arc renfoncé; **r. (light) switch,** interrupteur encastré; *Mec.E: etc:* **r. head,** tête (de boulon, etc.) encastrée, noyée.

recessing [ri'sesiŋ], *s.* **1.** évidement *m* (d'un mur pour recevoir qch.); chambrage *m* (d'une plaque, etc.); **r. tool,** outil *m* à chambrer. **2.** encastrement *m* (de la tête d'une vis, etc.).

recession[1] [ri'seʃ(ə)n], *s.* **1.** recul *m*, retraite *f*; **r. of the sea from the coastline,** régression *f* de la mer. **2.** *Ecc:* sortie *f* du clergé. **3.** *Pol.Ec:* récession *f.*

recession[2], *s. Jur:* rétrocession *f* (des biens de qn).

recessional [ri'seʃən(ə)l]. **1.** *a. & s. Ecc:* **r. (hymn),** hymne chanté pendant que les officiants retournent à la sacristie; hymne de sortie du clergé. **2.** *a. Geog:* **r. moraine,** moraine *f* de récession, de retrait. **3.** *a.* **the r. activities of M.P.'s,** les activités des députés pendant les vacances.

recessive [ri'sesiv]. **1.** *a.* rétrograde; *Ling:* **r. accent,** accent remontant, régressif. **2.** *a. & s. Biol:* **r. (gene),** gène récessif; **r. (character),** caractère récessif, dominé; **r. (organism),** sujet récessif. **3.** *a. Pol.Ec:* récessif.

recessiveness [ri'sesivnis], *s. Biol:* récessivité *f.*

Rechabite ['rekəbait], *s.* **1.** *B.Hist:* Réc(h)abite *mf.* **2.** *s.* (*a*) abstinent, -ente; buveur, -euse, d'eau; (*b*) membre de *l'Independent Order of Rechabites* (société de secours mutuels dont les membres s'engagent à s'abstenir des boissons alcooliques).

recharge[1] [ri:'tʃɑ:dʒ]. **1.** *v.tr.* (*a*) recharger (un four, accumulateur, etc.); *F:* **to r. one's batteries,** rétablir ses forces; (*b*) accuser (qn) de nouveau. **2.** *v.tr. & i. Mil:* **to r. (the enemy),** charger (l'ennemi) de nouveau; faire une nouvelle charge.

recharge[2] ['ri:tʃɑ:dʒ], *s.* **1.** recharge *f*, rechargement *m* (d'un accumulateur, etc.); **to give a battery a r.,** recharger une batterie. **2.** objet *m* de remplacement, de rechange; recharge.

rechargeable [ri:'tʃɑ:dʒəbl], *a.* **1.** (appareil, etc.) qui peut être rechargé. **2.** (personne) susceptible d'être accusée de nouveau.

recharger [ri:'tʃɑ:dʒər], *s.* chargeur *m* (d'accumulateurs).

rechase [ri:'tʃeis], *v.tr.* raviver (un pas de vis, une ciselure).

rechasing [ri:'tʃeisiŋ], *s.* ravivage *m* (d'un pas de vis, etc.).

rechristen [ri:'kris(ə)n], *v.tr.* **1.** *Ecc:* rebaptiser (qn). **2.** *F:* donner un nouveau nom à, rebaptiser (une rue, etc.).

recidivism [ri'sidivizm], *s.* récidive *f*; rechute *f* dans le crime.

recidivist [ri'sidivist], *s.* récidiviste *mf.*

recipe ['resipi], *s.* **1.** *Cu: Pharm:* recette *f*; *Pharm:* formule *f*; *Med:* ordonnance *f.* **2.** *Fig:* recette; moyen *m* (de faire qch.); **r. for a happy life,** moyen de, recette pour, vivre heureux.

recipiency [ri'sipiənsi], *s.* réceptivité *f.*

recipient [ri'sipiənt]. **1.** *a.* réceptif; susceptible de recevoir; *Med: (blood transfusion)* **r. set,** appareil *m* de transfusion de sang. **2.** *s.* (*a*) personne *f* qui reçoit (un don, etc.); destinataire *mf* (d'une lettre); bénéficiaire *mf* (d'un chèque, effet); *Jur:* donataire *mf*; **r. of an allowance,** allocataire *mf*; *Med:* **r. of a transplant,** receveur, -euse, dans une transplantation d'organe; (*b*) *Ph:* récipient *m* (d'une machine pneumatique).

reciprocal [ri'siprəkl]. **1.** *a.* (*a*) *(of obligation, understanding, love, etc.)* réciproque, mutuel; **friendship must be r.,** l'amitié doit être mutuelle, réciproque, partagée, payée de retour; *Jur:* **r. contract,** contrat réciproque, bilatéral; (*b*) *Gram:* (pronom, verbe) réciproque; (*c*) *Log:* (concept, proposition, terme) réciproque, inverse; (*d*) *Mth:* (figure, polaire) réciproque; (fonction, nombre, raison) inverse; **r. matrix,** matrice réciproque, involutive; *Surv:* **r. bearing,** relèvement *m* inverse; (*e*) *Mec.E:* **r. gear,** engrenage *m* réciproque, à retour. **2.** *s.* (*a*) *Mth:* réciproque *f*, inverse *f* (d'une quantité); (*b*) *Log:* inverse, contrepartie *f.*

reciprocality [risiprə'kæliti], *s.* réciprocité *f.*

reciprocally [ri'siprək(ə)li], *adv.* **1.** réciproquement, mutuellement. **2.** *Mth:* inversement, réciproquement.

reciprocate [ri'siprəkeit]. **1.** *v.tr.* (*a*) échanger, se rendre mutuellement (des services, etc.); (*b*) répondre à, payer de retour (un sentiment); **to r. s.o.'s good wishes,** souhaiter la pareille à qn; **I r. your good wishes,** croyez bien que je fais pour vous tous les vœux que vous m'avez exprimés; **to r. s.o.'s kindness,** rendre l'amabilité de qn; (*c*) *Book-k:* **to r. an entry,** passer écriture conforme; passer une écriture en conformité; (*d*) *Mec.E:* donner un mouvement de va-et-vient à (un organe). **2.** *v.i.* (*a*) retourner le compliment; répondre au compliment; **he drank my health and I reciprocated,** il a bu à ma santé et je me suis empressé de boire à la sienne; (*b*) *Mec.E: (of piston, etc.)* avoir un mouvement alternatif, de va-et-vient.

reciprocating [ri'siprəkeitiŋ], *a. Mec.E:* (mouvement) alternatif; (machine) à mouvement alternatif, à mouvement de va-et-vient; **r. saw,** scie alternative; **r. engine,** moteur alternatif, à piston(s); **r. pump,** pompe alternative, à piston; **r. and rotating piston,** piston à mouvement louvoyant.

reciprocation [risiprə'keiʃ(ə)n], *s.* **1.** action *f* de payer de retour (un sentiment); retour *m* (d'un compliment). **2.** *Mec.E:* alternation *f* (de mouvement); va-et-vient *m inv.*

reciprocative [ri'siprəkeitiv, -kətiv], *a.* **1.** (sentiment, etc.) réciproque. **2.** *Mec.E:* (mouvement) alternatif, de va-et-vient.

reciprocator [ri'siprəkeitər], *s.* machine *f* à vapeur à double effet.

reciprocity [resi'prɔsiti], *s.* réciprocité *f*; **r. agreement, transactions,** convention *f*, transactions *f*, de réciprocité; *El:* **r. theorem,** théorème *m* de réciprocité (relatif à un réseau électrique).

recirculate [ri:'sə:kjuleit]. **1.** *v.i. Ind: Atom.Ph: (of fluid, water, etc.)* recirculer. **2.** *v.tr.* remettre (l'air circulé, etc.) en circulation, en circuit.

recirculating [ri:'sə:kjuleitiŋ], **recirculation** [ri:sə:kju'leiʃ(ə)n], *s. Ind: Atom.Ph:* recirculation *f*; remise *f* en circuit, en circulation.

recision [ri'siʒən], *s.* annulation *f.*

recital [ri'sait(ə)l], *s.* **1.** récit *m*, narration *f*, relation *f* (d'un incident, etc.); énumération *f* (des détails). **2.** récitation *f* (d'une poésie, etc.). **3.** (*a*) **music(al) r.,** récital *m*, *pl.* -als; audition *f*; **piano r.,** récital de piano; **Chopin r.,** récital de la musique de Chopin; **poetry r.,** récital poétique; **dance r.,** récital de danse; **to give a r.,** donner un récital; (*b*) *NAm:* concert *m* d'élèves. **4.** *Jur:* exposé *m* (des faits d'un contrat, etc.).

recitation [resi'teiʃ(ə)n], *s.* **1.** récitation *f* (de qch. appris par cœur); **to give a (poetry) r.,** réciter, dire, des vers. **2.** récitation, passage récité; **book of recitations,** livre *m* de récitations; recueil *m* de monologues. **3.** *NAm: Sch:* (*a*) épreuve orale; (*b*) leçon *f*; **r. room,** (salle *f* de) classe *f.*

recitative [resitə'ti:v], *s. Mus:* récitatif *m.*

recite [ri'sait]. **1.** *v.tr.* (*a*) réciter, déclamer (un poème); réciter (une leçon); (*b*) énumérer (des détails); (*c*) *Jur:* faire la relation de, exposer, citer (les faits). **2.** *v.i.* (*a*) réciter, dire, des vers: dire un monologue; **will you r. to us?** voulez-vous nous réciter quelque chose? (*b*) *NAm: Sch:* répondre à une épreuve orale.

reciter [ri'saitər], *s.* **1.** déclamateur *m*; diseur, -euse; narrateur, -trice; **the r. of the sonnet,** le diseur du sonnet; **she is a good r.,** elle dit bien; elle est bonne diseuse. **2.** livre *m* de récitations; recueil *m* de monologues.

reciting [ri'saitiŋ], *s.* **1.** récitation *f* (de qch. appris par cœur). **2.** énumération *f* (des détails, etc.).

reck [rek], *v.tr. & i. A: & Lit: (in interr. and neg. sentences only)* **to r. but little of sth.,** se soucier peu de qch.; faire peu de cas de qch.; **I r. not who he is, whether, if, he dies, that, though, he should die,** peu m'importe, me chaut, qui il est, s'il meurt, qu'il meure; **I r. not my life,** je fais peu de cas de ma vie; **what recks it me that she is penniless?** que m'importe qu'elle est sans le sou? **it recks little,** cela n'a pas d'importance.

reckless ['reklis], *a.* insouciant (**of,** de); téméraire; imprudent, irréfléchi; **he was r. of danger,** il se souciait peu du danger; c'était un casse-cou; **r. gambler,** homme aventureux au jeu; **r. demolition of ancient buildings,** démolition irréfléchie, insouciante, de bâtiments anciens; *Aut:* **r. driving,** conduite imprudente, téméraire; **r. driver,** conducteur imprudent; *F:* chauffard *m.*

recklessly ['reklisli], *adv.* témérairement, avec insouciance; sans réfléchir; imprudemment; à corps perdu; en casse-cou; **he spends r.,** il dépense sans compter.

recklessness ['reklisnis], *s.* insouciance *f* (**of,** de); imprudence *f*, témérité *f.*

Recklinghausen ['rekliŋhauzn], *Pr.n. Med:* **Recklinghausen's disease,** maladie *f* de Recklinghausen; neurofibromatose *f*; **Recklinghausen's disease of the bone,** maladie osseuse de Recklinghausen.

reckon ['rekən], *v.tr. & i.*

I. *v.tr.* (*a*) compter, calculer, faire le compte de, supputer (une somme, etc.); **the time is reckoned from midnight,** le temps est compté à partir de minuit; *v.i.* **reckoning from today,** à partir, à compter, d'aujourd'hui; **to r. sth. among, with, the assets,** compter, ranger, qch. parmi l'avoir; **to r. s.o. among the greatest writers,** mettre qn au rang, au nombre, des plus grands écrivains; **I r. him among my friends,** je le mets, le compte, au nombre de mes amis; **I do not r. him among my friends,** il n'est pas de mes amis; (*b*) compter, estimer, juger; **I r. he is forty,** je lui donne quarante ans; **I reckoned the explosion was ten miles away,** j'ai jugé que l'explosion était éloignée de dix milles; *F:* **I r. he will consent,** j'ai dans l'idée qu'il consentira; (*c*) **he is reckoned (as, to be) one of our best generals,** on le considère, regarde, comme un de nos meilleurs généraux.

II. *v.i.* **1.** compter, calculer; *O:* **to learn to r.,** apprendre le calcul, à calculer. **2. to r. on sth.,** compter sur qch.; **to r. with certainty on sth.,** tabler à coup sûr sur qch.; **I'm not reckoning on him,** je fais peu de fond sur lui; **they had not reckoned on finding me here,** ils ne comptaient guère me trouver ici; **I r. on his doing it,** je compte qu'il le fera. **3. to r. with s.o.,** faire rendre compte à qn; demander des comptes à qn; **to have to r. with s.o.,** avoir à compter avec qn; avoir affaire à qn; **a man to be reckoned with,** un homme avec qui il faut compter; **the bad climate has to be reckoned with,** il faut tenir compte du mauvais climat; **he had reckoned without his rivals,** il avait fait ses calculs sans tenir compte de ses rivaux; **to r. without one's host,** compter sans son hôte.

reckoner ['rek(ə)nər], *s.* **1.** *(pers.)* calculateur, -trice; compteur, -euse; chiffreur, -euse. **2.** *(thg)* barème *m* (d'intérêts, etc.); **ready r.,** barème (de comptes); (livre *m* de) comptes faits.

reckoning [rek(ə)niŋ], *s.* **1.** (*a*) compte *m*, comptage *m*, calcul *m*, supputation *f* (des intérêts, etc.); **to be out in one's r.,** s'être trompé dans son calcul; **you're a long way out in your r.,** vous êtes loin de compte; **day of r.,** (i) jour *m* de règlement; (ii) *Lit:* jour d'expiation; **we shall have a day of r.,** nous réglerons nos comptes un jour; **the hour of r.,** le quart d'heure de Rabelais; *Prov:* **short reckonings make long friends,** les bons comptes font les bons amis; (*b*) estimation *f*; **to the best of my r.,** autant que j'en puis juger; si je compte bien; **to take a r. of the situation,** dresser un bilan (de la situation); (*c*) *Nau:* **(dead) r.,** estime *f* (du point); point estimé, route *f* à l'estime; **to work out the ship's r.,** faire le point estimé; **by dead r.,** à l'estime; **latitude by dead r.,** latitude estimée; **to be ahead of one's r.,** être en avant de son estime. **2.** *(bill)* note *f*; *F: A:* **Dutch r.,** le coup de fusil; addition salée.

reclaim[1] [ri'kleim], *s.* **past r., beyond r.,** perdu à tout jamais; qui ne se corrigera jamais; qui ne s'amendera jamais.

reclaim[2]. **1.** *v.tr.* (*a*) réformer, corriger (qn); civiliser (des sauvages); **to r. s.o. to a sense of duty,** ramener qn au devoir; redonner à qn le sens du devoir; **to r. s.o. from vice,** tirer, faire sortir, qn du vice; **reclaimed prostitute,** fille repentie; **reclaimed drunkard,** ivrogne qui s'est ressaisi; (*b*) défricher (du terrain); gagner, prendre, (du terrain) sur l'eau; rendre (un terrain) cultivable; assécher (un marais); mettre (un marais) en valeur; **reclaimed land,** terrain reconquis (sur la nature); (*c*) *Ven:* apprivoiser (le faucon); (*d*) *Ind:* régénérer (le caoutchouc, les huiles de graissage, etc.); récupérer (un sous-produit); *Ind:* **reclaimed oil,** huile *f* de récupération. **2.** *v.i. A:* réclamer (**against,** contre).

re-claim [ri:'kleim], *v.tr. NAm:* demander le retour de, réclamer (qch.).

reclaimable [ri'kleiməbl], *a.* **1.** (personne) corrigible; que l'on peut ramener dans la bonne voie. **2.** (*a*) (terrain) défrichable, asséchable, qui peut être reconquis (sur la nature); (*b*) *Ind:* (sous-produit, etc.) récupérable.

reclaimer [ri'kleimər], *s.* **1.** *(pers.)* réformateur, -trice (de qn); (*b*) défricheur *m* (de terrain). **2.** *(thg) Ind:* épurateur *m*, récupérateur *m* (d'huile, etc.).

reclaiming [ri'kleimiŋ], *s.* = RECLAMATION **1.** (*a*), **2.**

reclamation [reklə'meiʃ(ə)n], *s.* **1.** (*a*) réforme *f*, correction *f* (de qn); (*b*) retour *m* au bien; amendement *m*; **after their r. from barbarism,** après qu'ils eurent été arrachés à la barbarie. **2.** défrichement *m*, dessèchement *m* (d'un terrain); assèchement *m*, mise *f* en valeur (des marais); régénération *f* (du sol, du caoutchouc, des huiles de graissage, etc.); récupération *f* (de sous-produits, etc.). **3.** *A:* réclamation *f.*

reclassification [ri:klæsifi'keiʃ(ə)n], *s.* reclassement *m* (des plantes, etc.); reclassification *f* (d'un document, secret, etc.); *Nau:* recotement *m* (d'un navire).

reclassify [ri:'klæsifai], *v.tr.* reclasser (des plantes, etc.); reclassifier (un document secret, etc.).

reclinate ['reklineit], *a.* incliné en arrière; *Bot:* (organe) récliné.

reclination [rekli'neiʃ(ə)n], *s.* **1.** inclinaison *f* en arrière. **2.** *Surg: A:* réclinaison *f* (d'une cataracte).

recline[1] [ri'klain]. **1.** *v.tr.* reposer, appuyer, coucher (sa tête sur qch.); **to r. one's body, one's limbs, on sth.,** se reposer sur qch. **2.** *v.i.* être couché, se reposer (**on,** sur); (*of head*) reposer, être appuyé (**on,** sur); **to r. on a couch,** être étendu, rester étendu, être à demi couché, sur un canapé.

recline[2], *s.* inclinaison *f* (d'un avion, etc.).

reclining [ri'klainiŋ], *s.* action de se coucher, se reposer (sur un canapé, etc.); **r. chair,** (i) chaise longue; (ii) fauteuil *m* de malade; chaise, voiture *f,* d'invalide; (*in aircraft, etc.*) **r. seat,** siège *m* (à dossier) inclinable.

reclose[1] [ri:'klouz]. **1.** *v.i.* (*of door, electric circuit, etc.*) se refermer; *El:* (*of circuit breaker*) se réenclencher. **2.** *v.tr.* refermer (une porte, un circuit électrique, etc.); *El:* réenclencher (un disjoncteur).

reclose[2], *s. El:* refermeture *f* (d'un circuit); réenclenchement *m* (d'un disjoncteur).

recloser [ri:'klouzər], *s. El:* dispositif *m* de réenclenchement.

reclosing [ri:'klouziŋ], **reclosure** ['ri:'klouʒər], *s. El:* refermeture *f* (d'un circuit); réenclenchement *m* (d'un disjoncteur); **r. circuit breaker,** disjoncteur à réenclenchement; **r. time,** durée *f* de réenclenchement.

reclothe [ri:'klouð], *v.tr.* **1.** rhabiller (qn); **to r. oneself,** remettre ses vêtements. **2.** fournir de nouveaux vêtements à (qn); remonter la garde-robe de (qn).

recluse [ri'klu:s]. **1.** *a.* (*a*) (*of pers.*) retiré du monde; reclus; (*b*) *A:* **a r. retreat,** une retraite loin du monde. **2.** *s.* reclus, -use; solitaire *mf*; monial *m,* -aux; anachorète *m*; **to live the life of a r.,** mener une vie recluse; vivre en reclus, en ermite.

reclusion [ri'klu:ʒ(ə)n], *s.* réclusion *f.*

reclusive [ri'klu:siv], *a.* (*of pers., life, etc.*) reclus.

recock [ri:'kɔk], *v.tr.* réarmer (un fusil).

recode [ri:'koud], *v.tr.* **1.** recoder, rechiffrer (un télégramme, etc.); mettre (qch.) en code, en chiffre. **2.** *Cmptr:* reprogrammer (une séquence, etc.); refaire la programmation de (qch.).

recognition [rekəg'niʃ(ə)n], *s.* reconnaissance *f.* **1.** (*a*) **fact which has obtained general r.,** fait qui a été reconnu de tous; (*of artist, etc.*) **to win r.,** s'imposer (à l'estime publique); *Dipl:* **r. of a foreign government,** reconnaissance d'un gouvernement étranger; (*b*) **in r. of his courage,** en reconnaissance de son courage. **2. he received no r.,** on ne lui accordait aucune considération. **3.** (*a*) **sign of r.,** signe *m* de reconnaissance; **he gave me a smile of r.,** il m'a donné un sourire pour me faire comprendre qu'il m'avait reconnu; **to alter sth. beyond r.,** changer qch. au point de le rendre méconnaissable, de le rendre impossible à identifier; **he has altered past r.,** il a tellement changé qu'il est devenu méconnaissable, qu'il n'est plus reconnaissable; *Mil: etc:* **r. signal,** signal *m* de reconnaissance, d'identification; *Av:* **r. light,** feu *m* d'identification; (*b*) *Cmptr:* **optical character r.,** reconnaissance optique de caractères; **pattern r.,** reconnaissance de formes. **4.** *Phil:* récognition *f.*

recognitive [ri'kɔgnitiv], **recognitory** [ri'kɔgnit(ə)ri], *a.* récognitif.

recognizable ['rekəgnaizəbl], *a.* reconnaissable; **he's so changed as to be not r.,** il est tellement changé qu'il n'est plus reconnaissable, qu'il est devenu méconnaissable; **the author is scarcely r. in his last novel,** on ne retrouve plus cet auteur dans son dernier roman; **gas r. by its smell,** gaz qui se reconnaît par son odeur.

recognizably [rekəg'naizəbli], *adv.* d'une manière reconnaissable; **they're r. foreign,** on les reconnaît comme étant étrangers.

recognizance [ri'kɔ(g)niz(ə)ns], *s. Jur:* **1.** caution personnelle; engagement *m* (par-devant le tribunal); **to enter into recognizances,** donner caution; s'engager à comparaître, à ne plus troubler l'ordre, etc. **2.** somme fournie à titre de cautionnement.

recognizant [ri'kɔ(g)niz(ə)nt], *a.* **to be r. of sth.,** reconnaître qch.

recognize ['rekəgnaiz], *v.tr.* reconnaître. **1.** (*a*) **to r. a government, s.o.'s rights,** reconnaître un gouvernement, les droits de qn; *Sp:* **to r. a record (officially),** homologuer un record; (*b*) **to r. s.o. as king,** reconnaître qn pour roi. **2. he knows he is wrong but won't r. it,** il sait qu'il a tort mais ne veut pas l'admettre, le reconnaître; **to refuse to r. one's signature,** refuser de reconnaître sa signature; nier sa signature; **to r. a natural child,** reconnaître (comme sien) un enfant naturel; **to r. a poor relation,** avouer un parent pauvre. **3.** (*a*) **to r. s.o. by his walk,** reconnaître qn à sa démarche; **they recognized each other at once as brothers-in-arms,** ils se reconnurent tout de suite frères d'armes; **I do not r. you,** je ne vous remets pas; (*b*) **he recognized me,** il m'a fait un signe de connaissance. **4.** connaître; **to r. the truth when one sees it,** reconnaître, connaître, la vérité lorsqu'on la voit; **to be the first to r. a fact,** être le premier à se rendre compte d'un fait, à saisir un fait. **5.** (*of chairman of a meeting, etc.*) **to r. a member,** donner la parole à un membre; **to be recognized,** avoir la parole.

recognized ['rekəgnaizd], *a.* reconnu, admis, accepté, reçu; (façon, etc.) classique; **the r. term,** le terme consacré; *Com:* **r. agent, merchant,** agent accrédité; commerçant patenté, attitré.

recoil[1] [ri'kɔil], *s.* **1.** (*a*) rebondissement *m,* détente *f* (d'un ressort, arc tendu, etc.); *Clockm:* **r. escapement,** échappement *m* à ancre; (*b*) contrecoup *m* (d'une explosion, d'un véhicule après collision, etc.); (*c*) recul *m* (d'une arme à feu); **non-r. gun,** canon *m* sans recul; **r. check, brake,** frein *m* (de recul); **r. guard,** écran *m* de protection; **r. reducer,** amortisseur *m* de recul; **r.-operated,** (mécanisme) actionné, mû, par le recul; fonctionnant par recul; **to take up, check, r.,** supprimer le recul; (*d*) *Atom.Ph:* **nuclear, radioactive, r.,** recul nucléaire, radioactif; **r. nucleus, particle,** noyau *m,* particule *f,* de recul; (*e*) *El:Elcs:* recul; démagnétisation; **r. curve,** courbe *f* de démagnétisation; **r. percentage,** pourcentage *m* de recul. **2.** (*of pers.*) (*a*) mouvement *m* de recul; reculade *f*; (*b*) répugnance *f* (**from,** pour); horreur *f* (**from,** de).

recoil[2], *v.i.* **1.** (*a*) (*of spring, bow*) se détendre; (*b*) (*of firearm*) reculer, repousser. **2.** (*of pers.*) reculer (**from,** devant); se révolter (**from,** contre); avoir horreur (**from,** de); **to r. from doing sth.,** reculer devant l'idée de faire qch.; se refuser à faire qch. **3.** (*of evil, etc.*) retomber (**on,** sur); se retourner (**on,** sur, contre); **the scandal will r. on me,** ce scandale retombera, rejaillira, sur moi. **4.** *Mil:* reculer, se replier (devant une attaque).

recoiling [ri'kɔiliŋ], *s.* **1.** recul *m.* **2.** répugnance *f* (**from,** pour); révolte *f* (**from,** contre); **r. from doing sth.,** répugnance *f* à faire qch.; refus *m* de faire qch.

recoilless [ri'kɔillis], *a.* (fusil, etc.) sans recul.

recoin [ri:'kɔin], *v.tr.* refrapper, refondre (la monnaie).

recoinage ['ri:'kɔinidʒ], *s.* refrappement *m,* refonte *f* (de la monnaie).

recollect[1] ['rekəlekt], *s. Rel.H:* récollet, -ette.

recollect[2] [rekə'lekt], *v.tr.* **1.** se rappeler (qch.); se souvenir de (qch.); (se) remettre (qch., qn); **I don't r. your name,** votre nom ne me revient pas; **I don't r. you,** je ne vous remets pas; **to r. having done sth.,** se rappeler avoir fait qch.; **as far as I r.,** autant qu'il m'en souvienne. **2.** *Lit:* **to r. oneself, one's thoughts,** se recueillir.

recollect[3] [ri:kə'lekt], *v.tr.* **1.** assembler, réunir, (des personnes, des choses) de nouveau; rallier (des troupes). **2.** *Lit:* rassembler (son courage); rappeler (ses esprits); **to r. oneself,** se ressaisir.

recollection [rekə'lekʃ(ə)n], *s.* **1.** souvenir *m,* mémoire *f*; **to bring, recall, sth. to s.o.'s r.,** rappeler qch. à la mémoire de qn; **recollections of a country parson,** souvenirs d'un curé de campagne; **I have some r. of it,** j'en ai quelque souvenir; **I have a vague r. of it,** j'en ai gardé un souvenir confus, un vague souvenir; **my first r. is of being taken to Bristol,** mon premier souvenir, c'est d'avoir été emmené à Bristol; **he has a very favourable r. of you,** il conserve, a conservé, de vous un excellent souvenir; **to the best of my r.,** autant que je m'en souviens; autant que je m'en souvienne; autant qu'il m'en souvient; autant qu'il m'en souvienne; **it has never occurred within my r.,** cela n'est jamais arrivé de mon temps. **2. r. (in God),** récollection *f*; recueillement *m* (de l'âme).

recollective [rekə'lektiv], *a.* qui peut se souvenir; plein de souvenirs; **r. memory,** mémoire rétentive; **after a r. silence he told the following story,** après un silence où il rappelait ses souvenirs, il raconta l'histoire suivante.

recolonization [ri:kɔlənai'zeiʃ(ə)n], *s. Biol: etc:* établissement *m* d'une nouvelle colonie (**of a habitat,** dans un habitat).

recolonize ['ri:'kɔlənaiz], *v.tr. Biol: etc:* établir une nouvelle colonie, rétablir une colonie, dans (une région, etc.).

recombinant [ri:'kɔmbinənt], *a. Biol:* (descendance, etc.) qui résulte de la recombinaison.

recombination [ri:kɔmbi'neiʃ(ə)n], *s. Biol: Ch:* recombinaison *f*; *Ch:* **r. coefficient,** coefficient *m* de recombinaison.

recombine [ri:kəm'bain]. **1.** *v.tr.* recombiner (des éléments). **2.** *v.i.* (*of elements*) se recombiner.

recombing [ri:'koumiŋ], *s. Tex:* deuxième peignage *m.*

recommence [ri:kə'mens], *v.tr. & i.* recommencer.

recommencement [ri:kə'mensmənt], *s.* recommencement *m.*

recommend [rekə'mend], *v.tr.* recommander. **1. to r. s.o. to do sth.,** recommander, conseiller, à qn de faire qch.; **I have been recommended (to come) to you,** on m'a adressé à vous; **my mother was recommended to try these pills,** ces pilules ont été recommandées à ma mère. **2.** (*a*) **to r. a candidate for a post,** recommander un candidat pour un emploi; **she has only her youth to r. her,** elle n'a que la jeunesse pour elle; **the hotel is to be recommended for its cooking,** l'hôtel se recommande par sa cuisine; **this book is not to be recommended,** ce livre est à déconseiller; **can you r. me a hairdresser?** pouvez-vous me recommander un coiffeur? **I can r. him as a driver,** je vous le recommande comme conducteur; (*b*) **the jury recommended the murderer to mercy,** les jurés ont signé le recours en grâce. **3. to r. sth. to the care of s.o., to s.o.'s care,** recommander qch. aux soins de qn; **to r. one's soul to God,** recommander son âme à Dieu.

recommendable [rekə'mendəbl], *a.* **1.** (ligne de conduite, etc.) recommandable, conseillable, à conseiller. **2.** (hôtel, etc.) à recommander.

recommendation [rekəmen'deiʃ(ə)n], *s.* recommandation *f.* **1. his youth is a r.,** sa jeunesse est une recommandation; **to write in r. of sth.,** écrire pour recommander qch.; **he carries his own r. with him,** il se recommande de lui-même; il porte son passeport sur lui; **I have come on the r. of one of your customers,** je viens sur la recommandation d'un de vos clients; **letter of r.,** lettre recommandative, de recommandation; *Fin:* **r. of dividend,** proposition *f* de dividende; *Jur:* **r. to mercy,** avis émis par le jury en faveur d'une commutation de peine. **2. the recommendations of a commission,** les avis rendus par une commission; **stockbroker's list of recommendations,** liste *f* de placements conseillés par un courtier.

recommission [ri:kə'miʃ(ə)n]. **1.** *v.tr.* (*a*) réarmer, armer de nouveau (un navire); (*b*) donner à (un officier) un nouveau commandement; réintégrer (un officier) dans les cadres. **2.** *v.i.* (*of ship*) réarmer; rentrer en armement.

recommit [ri:kə'mit], *v.tr.* **1.** renvoyer (un projet de loi) devant une commission. **2.** recommander de nouveau, confier de nouveau (**sth. to s.o.,** qch. à qn). **3. to r. s.o. to prison,** renvoyer, réintégrer, qn en prison. **4.** commettre de nouveau (un délit).

recommitment [ri:kə'mitmənt], **recommittal** [ri:kə'mit(ə)l], *s.* **1.** renvoi *m* (d'un projet de loi) devant une commission. **2.** renvoi (de qn) en prison; nouvel emprisonnement (de qn).

recompense[1] ['rekəmpens], *s.* **1.** récompense *f* (**for,** de); **sum granted as a r.,** *Jur:* somme *f* rémunératoire. **2.** dédommagement *m* (**for,** de); compensation *f* (**for,** de, pour); **as a r. for his trouble,** pour prix de sa peine. **3.** rétribution *f* (**for one's sins,** de, pour, ses péchés).

recompense[2], *v.tr.* **1.** récompenser (**s.o. for his kindness,** qn de sa bonté); **he was recompensed for the evil he had done,** il fut puni du mal qu'il avait fait. **2.** dédommager (**s.o. for sth.,** qn de qch.). **3.** compenser, réparer (un mal, un dommage). **4.** payer de retour (un service); répondre à (l'affection de qn).

recompilation [ri:kɔmpi'lei(ʃ)n], *s.* recompilation *f.*

recompile [ri:kəm'pail], *v.tr.* recompiler.

recompose [ri:kəm'pouz], *v.tr.* **1.** *Ch:* recomposer (une substance). **2.** rarranger (qch.). **3.** (*a*) calmer (qn) de nouveau; (*b*) **to r. oneself to sleep,** se disposer de nouveau à dormir.

recomposition [ri:kɔmpə'ziʃ(ə)n], *s. Ch:* recomposition *f.*

recompound [ri:kəm'paund], *v.tr. Ch:* recomposer.

recomputation [ri:kɔmpju'teiʃ(ə)n], *s.* recalcul *m*; réévaluation *f* (des stocks, etc.).

recompute [ri:kəm'pju:t], *v.tr.* recalculer; réévaluer (des stocks, etc.).

reconcilable ['rekənsailəbl], *a.* **1.** (*of statement, opinion*) conciliable, accordable (**with,** avec). **2.** (*of enemy, etc.*) qui peut être concilié.

reconcile ['rekənsail], *v.tr.* **1.** réconcilier (**s.o. with, to, s.o.,** qn avec qn); réconcilier, rajuster, raccommoder, remettre bien ensemble (deux personnes); **to become reconciled,** se réconcilier. **2.** *A:* se concilier, gagner (qn). **3.** *Ecc:* **to r. a heretic to the Church,** réconcilier un hérétique à l'Église. **4. to r. s.o. to sth.,** faire accepter qch. à, par, qn; faire se résigner qn à qch.; **to r. oneself to doing sth., to one's lot,** se résigner à faire qch., à son sort; **to r. oneself to one's work,** surmonter son aversion pour un travail. **5.** ajuster, arranger, mettre fin à (une querelle). **6.** concilier, faire accorder (des opinions, des faits); **to r. an opinion with, to, another,** concilier une opinion avec une autre; **evidence which cannot be reconciled with known facts,** témoignage *m* qui ne saurait être conciliable avec les faits connus; **to r. two points of view,** mettre d'accord deux points de vue; **you are trying to r. contraries,** vous essayez de concilier les contraires, de rendre compatibles les contraires; *Book-k:* **to r. one account with another,** faire accorder un compte avec un autre.

reconcilement [rekən'sailmənt], *s.* **1.** réconciliation *f,* rapprochement *m* (de deux personnes); **to establish a r. between enemies,** rétablir la concorde entre des ennemis. **2.** conciliation *f,* arrangement *m,* ajustement *m* (d'un différend). **3.** conciliation (d'opinions contraires).

reconciler ['rekənsailər], *s.* réconciliateur, -trice.

reconciliation [rekənsili'eiʃ(ə)n], *s.* **1.** = RECONCILEMENT. **2.** *Ecc:* réconciliation *f* (**with the Church,** à l'Église). **3.** *Book-k:* ajustement *m* (des écritures); **r. account,** compte collectif.

recondite ['rekəndait], *a.* (*of subject, knowledge*) abstrus, profond, mystérieux; (*of writer, style*) obscur.

reconditely ['rekəndaitli], *adv.* d'une manière abstruse; profondément, mystérieusement, obscurément.

reconditeness ['rekəndaitnis], *s.* caractère abstrus (d'une science); profondeur *f,* sens profond, sens caché (d'un écrit, etc.); obscurité *f* (de style).

recondition [ri:kən'diʃ(ə)n], *v.tr.* rénover, refaire; remettre (qch.) à neuf, en état; reconditionner (qch.); remettre (une route) en état de viabilité, (un taudis) en état habitable; *Cmptr:* réparer (une carte perforée); *Aut:* **reconditioned engine,** moteur révisé, reconditionné.

reconditioning ['ri:kən'diʃ(ə)niŋ], *s.* rénovation *f*; remise *f* à neuf, en état; réfection *f*; reconditionnement *m*; *Cmptr:* **r. shop,** atelier *m* de reconstruction, de réfection (de machines).

reconduct [ri:kən'dʌkt], *v.tr.* reconduire (qn).

reconduction ['ri:kən'dʌkʃ(ə)n], *s. Jur:* reconduction *f* (d'un bail, contrat).

reconfiguration ['ri:kənfigju'reiʃ(ə)n], *s. Cmptr:* nouvelle configuration, nouvelle composition.

reconfigure ['ri:kən'figər], *v.tr. Cmptr:* **to r. a computer,** modifier la configuration, composition, d'un ordinateur.

reconfirm [ri:kən'fə:m], *v.tr.* reconfirmer.

reconfirmation [ri:kɔnfə'meiʃ(ə)n], *s.* reconfirmation *f.*

reconnaissance [ri'kɔnis(ə)ns], *s. Mil: etc:* reconnaissance *f*; **close r.,** reconnaissance rapprochée, à courte distance; **distant, long-range, r.,** reconnaissance lointaine, à grande distance, en profondeur; **air, aerial, r.,** reconnaissance aérienne; **r. aircraft,** avion *m,* appareil *m,* de reconnaissance; **r. detachment, party,** détachement *m* de reconnaissance; **r. patrol,** patrouille *f* de reconnaissance; *Navy: Av:* **r. cruise,** croisière *f* de reconnaissance; *Surv:* **r. map, sketch, survey,** levé *m* de reconnaissance; *Av:* **r. strip,** bande photographique (réalisée au cours d'une reconnaissance photo); **to go, be sent, on r.,** aller, être envoyé, en reconnaissance; **to make a r.,** faire une reconnaissance; **to make a r. of a position,** faire une reconnaissance d'une position; reconnaître une position; *Fig:* **to make a r. before opening negotiations,** explorer, tâter, le terrain avant d'entamer des négociations.

reconnect ['ri:kə'nekt], *v.tr. El: etc:* réaccoupler; rebrancher (un câble, etc.).

reconnoitre[1] [rekə'nɔitər]. **1.** *v.tr. Mil: etc:* reconnaître (le terrain); **to r. the enemy,** faire une reconnaissance de l'ennemi; *Nau:* **to r. land,** chasser la terre. **2.** *v.i.* faire une reconnaissance; aller à la découverte; éclairer le terrain, la marche; *Surv:* faire des travaux de reconnaissance; **to r. as far as the enemy's fortifications,** pousser une reconnaissance jusqu'aux fortifications ennemies; **to r. with a view to negotiations,** explorer, tâter, le terrain en vue de négociations.

reconnoitre[2], *s.* reconnaissance *f.*

reconnoit(e)rer [rekə'nɔit(ə)rər], *s.* éclaireur *m.*

reconnoitring[1] [rekə'nɔitriŋ], *a.* (détachement *m,* etc.) en reconnaissance, d'exploration; **r. vessel,** éclaireur *m.*

reconnoitring[2], *s.* reconnaissance *f.*

reconquer [ri:'kɔŋkər], *v.tr.* reconquérir (**a country from the enemy,** un pays sur l'ennemi).

reconquest [ri:'kɔŋkwest], *s.* reconquête *f.*

reconsequent [ri:'kɔnsikwənt], *a. Geol:* (*of drainage*) reséquent.

reconsider [ri:kən'sidər], *v.tr.* **1.** reconsidérer, considérer de nouveau, envisager de nouveau, examiner à nouveau, repenser (une question); réviser, revoir (un jugement). **2.** revenir sur (une décision).

reconsideration [ri:kənsidə'reiʃ(ə)n], *s.* examen *m* à nouveau; reconsidération *f*; révision *f* (d'un jugement).

reconsolidate [ri:kən'sɔlideit], *v.tr.* reconsolider.

reconsolidation [ri:kənsɔli'deiʃ(ə)n], *s.* reconsolidation *f.*

reconstituent [ri:kən'stitjuənt], *a. & s. Med:* reconstituant (*m*).

reconstitute [ri:'kɔnstitju:t], *v.tr.* reconstituer (une société, un événement du passé, le lait concentré, etc.).

reconstitution [ri:kɔnsti'tju:ʃ(ə)n], *s.* reconstitution *f.*

reconstruct [ri:kən'strʌkt], *v.tr.* **1.** reconstruire, rebâtir (un édifice, etc.); refaire (une comédie); rebâtir (un roman, etc.); reconstituer (un fichier détruit, etc.). **2. to r. the facts, a crime,** reconstituer les faits, un crime. **3.** *Const:* **reconstructed stone,** pierre artificielle. **4.** *Surg:* restaurer (un membre, une fonction).

reconstruction ['ri:kən'strʌkʃ(ə)n], *s.* **1.** (*a*) reconstruction *f,* réfection *f*; reconstitution *f* (d'un fichier, etc.); refonte *f* (d'un système, etc.); *Fin:* reconstitution (d'une société); **economic and financial r.,** restauration économique et financière; **educational r.,** refonte de l'organisation de l'enseignement; (*b*) *U.S: Hist:* **the R.,** la reconstruction de l'Union (après la Guerre de Sécession). **2.** reconstitution (des faits, d'un crime, etc.). **3.** *Surg:* restauration *f* (d'un membre, d'une fonction); **occlusal r.,** restauration de l'occlusion (mandibulaire).

reconstructive [ri:kən'strʌktiv], *a. & s. Med:* reconstituant (*m*).

reconstructor [ri:kən'strʌktər], *s.* reconstructeur *m.*

reconvention [ri:kən'venʃ(ə)n], *s. Jur:* contre-accusation *f, pl.* contre-accusations; contre-plainte *f, pl.* contre-plaintes; action reconventionnelle; reconvention *f.*

reconversion [ri:kən'və:ʃ(ə)n], *s. Pol.Ec:* reconversion *f.*

reconvert ['ri:kən'və:t]. **1.** *v.tr.* reconvertir (des devises, etc.). **2.** *v.i.* se reconvertir.

reconvey [ri:kən'vei], *v.tr.* **1.** (*a*) transporter (qch.) de nouveau; (*b*) (*bring back*) reporter (qch.); ramener (qn). **2.** *Jur:* rétrocéder.

reconveyance [ri:kən'veiəns], *s.* **1.** nouveau transport. **2.** *Jur:* rétrocession *f.*

recopy [ri:'kɔpi], *v.tr.* recopier.

record[1] ['rekɔ:d], *s.* **1.** *Jur:* (*a*) enregistrement *m* (d'un fait); **matter of r.,** fait enregistré (qui peut être cité comme autorité); (*of judgment, fact*) **to be on r.,** être enregistré, être authentique; **to put a resolution on r.,** consigner une décision; **it is on r. that the room used to be haunted,** il est fait mention, il est rapporté, dans l'histoire qu'il y avait des revenants dans la chambre; **to go, put oneself, on r. as a pacifist,** se déclarer pacifiste; *NAm:* **to put oneself on r.,** s'assurer une place dans l'histoire; **to say sth. off the r.,** dire qch. en confidence; **off the r. I admit that I was wrong,** en secret, entre nous, j'avoue que j'avais tort; **to keep the r. straight I'll repeat what I said,** pour éviter des malentendus je vais répéter ce que j'ai dit; (*b*) **r. of a court,** feuille *f* d'audience; **to travel out of the r.,** statuer d'après un motif non articulé, sur une demande non formulée; (*c*) rôle *m* des minutes; **r. of evidence,** procès-verbal *m, pl.* procès-verbaux, de témoignage; (*d*) minute *f* (d'un acte, d'un jugement). **2.** (*a*) note *f,* mention *f*; **to make, keep, a r. of an observation,** faire une note d'une observation; inscrire une observation sur un registre; **to keep a r. of road accidents,** procéder au recensement des accidents de la circulation; **on the basis of such records it seems a dangerous occupation,** selon les éléments recensés il semble que c'est un métier dangereux; **I can find no r. of it,** je n'en trouve aucune mention; **for the r.,** *F:* **to keep the r. straight,** pour mémoire; *Com:* **to be shown only as a r.,** ne figurer que pour mémoire; *U.S: Mil:* **field r.,** journal de marche; (*b*) registre *m*; **r. of attendances,** registre de présence; **his r. of attendances is bad,** il ne figure presque jamais au registre de présence. **3. records:** (*a*) *Hist: etc:* archives *f,* registres, annales *f,* mémoires *m,* actes *m,* écritures *f*; *Com:* archives; **the earliest records extant,** les plus anciens documents qui nous soient parvenus; **the Public Records,** les Archives nationales; **Keeper of the Records,** archiviste *m,* greffier *m*; **official record(s) of a society,** bulletin officiel, organe officiel, d'une société; **r. office,** (i) *Jur:* greffe *m*; (ii) bureau *m* des archives; les Archives; **the regimental records,** l'historique *m* du régiment; (*b*) *Navy:* feuilles *f* de tir. **4.** monument *m,* document *m,* souvenir *m,* marque *f,* signe *m* (de qch.); inscription *f* (sur un monument, etc., pour perpétuer un événement, etc.). **5.** (*a*) carrière *f,* dossier *m,* antécédents *mpl* (de qn); **service r.,** état *m* de service; **he has a good r.,** ses états de service sont bons; **an employee's, an officer's, good r.,** les bonnes notes d'un employé, d'un officier; **his past r.,** (i) sa conduite passée; sa conduite dans le passé; (ii) (*of employee, etc.*) ses bonnes notes; **police r., criminal r. (of s.o.),** casier *m* judiciaire; **entered in the police r.,** inscrit au casier judiciaire; **to have, show, a clean r.,** avoir, présenter, un casier judiciaire intact, vierge; **to have a very bad r.,** avoir un dossier lourdement chargé; (*b*) **school r. card,** fiche *f* scolaire; curriculum vitae *m*; *Med:* **case r.,** fiche de patient, d'observation. **6.** *Sp: etc:* record *m*; **world r.,** record mondial; **to set up a r.,** établir un record; **to break, beat, the r.,** battre le record; **r.-breaking success,** succès qui bat tous les records; succès phénoménal; **two records fell,** deux records ont été battus; **to hold a r.,** détenir un record; **r. holder,** recordman *m, pl.* recordmen; recordwoman *f, pl.* recordwomen; détenteur *m* du record; **r. production,** production record, sans précédent; record *m*; **r. number of births,** nombre *m* record de naissances; **at a r. speed,** (i) à une vitesse record; (ii) à toute vitesse; **in r. time,** en, dans, un temps record; **in the r. time of four minutes,** dans un, le, temps record de quatre minutes. **7.** enregistrement *m*; (*a*) *Med:* **electrocardiograph r.,** tracé *m* d'un électrocardiographe; *Dent:* **wax r.,** enregistrement à la cire; **jaw relation r.,** enregistrement du rapport des maxillaires; (*b*) (**gramophone**) **r.,** (i) disque *m,* (ii) *A:* cylindre *m,* rouleau *m,* de phonographe; **the wax r.,** la cire; **mother r.,** matrice *f* de réserve; **music on records,** musique enregistrée; **to listen to records by famous musicians,** écouter des enregistrements par des musiciens célèbres; **r. cutter,** aiguille *f* à graver, style *m* (d'enregistrement phonographique); **r. collector, enthusiast,** discophile *mf*; **r. collecting,** discophilie *f*; **r. library,** discothèque *f,* phonothèque *f*; **r. club,** club *m* de disques; **r. changer,** changeur *m* de disques; **r. player,** tourne-disques *m inv*; (*c*) *Cin:* enregistrement *m* (du son); (*d*) *Cmptr:* **logical r.,** enregistrement, article *m,* logique; **physical r.,** enregistrement, article, physique; bloc *m*; **master r.,** enregistrement principal; **trailer r.,** enregistrement complémentaire; article fin, secondaire; **home r.,** enregistrement direct, article primaire; **r. head,** tête *f* d'enregistrement.

record[2] [ri'kɔ:d], *v.tr.* **1.** (*a*) enregistrer (un fait); consigner (qch.) par écrit; prendre acte de (qch.); minuter (un jugement, etc.); relever (la température, etc.); **the result is worth recording,** le résultat mérite d'être signalé; **he already has several convictions recorded against him,** son casier judiciaire est déjà très chargé; il a déjà plusieurs condamnations à son actif; il est déjà titulaire de plusieurs condamnations; (*b*) relater, narrer, rapporter; **Pepys records how thousands died from the plague,** Pepys raconte, rapporte, nous dit, que des milliers moururent de la peste; (*c*) **this stone records a famous battle,** cette pierre perpétue la mémoire d'une bataille célèbre; (*d*) (*of instrument*) enregistrer (des tremblements de terre, etc.); **the thermometer records ten degrees,** le thermomètre marque dix degrés; (*e*) *Adm:* recenser (des faits, etc.). **2.** enregistrer; **to r. a song,** enregistrer une chanson (sur disque); **to r. on tape,** enregistrer sur bande; *W.Tel:* **recorded programme,** programme enregistré; (*with passive force*) **instrument that does not r. well,** instrument qui ne se prête pas bien à l'enregistrement.

recordation [rekɔ:'deiʃ(ə)n], *s. esp. NAm:* enregistrement *m*; *U.S: Jur:* **r. of a document,** enregistrement, inscription *f,* d'un document sur le registre officiel.

recorder [ri'kɔ:dər], *s.* **1.** *Jur:* avocat nommé par la Couronne pour remplir certaines fonctions de juge. **2.** (*a*) celui, celle, qui consigne un fait par écrit; **he was a faithful r. of what he saw,** il transcrivait fidèlement ce qu'il voyait; (*b*) (i) archiviste *mf*; (ii) greffier *m*; (*c*) *Navy:* secrétaire *m* des feuilles de tir. **3.** artiste *mf* qui enregistre (sur disques, etc.). **4.** (*a*) (appareil) enregistreur (*m*); compteur *m*; **drum r.,** tambour enregistreur; tambour inscripteur; *Ind:* **time r.,** enregistreur de temps; *Hyd.E:* **flow r.,** enregistreur de débit; *Av:* **flight path r.,** enregistreur de trajectoire de vol; **instrumentation r.,** enregistreur magnétique d'instrumentation; *Atom.Ph:* **r. controller,** enregistreur-régulateur *m, pl.* enregistreurs-régulateurs; (*b*) **sound r.,** enregistreur sonore, du son; **cassette r.,** enregistreur à cassette; **stereo cassette r.,** Magnétophone *m* stéréo à cassettes; *Cin:* **sound-on-disc r.,** enregistreur sur disques. **5.** *Mus:* flûte *f* à bec.

recordership [ri'kɔ:dəʃip], *s.* **1.** (i) fonctions *fpl,* (ii) charge *f,* de *recorder.* **2.** charge (i) d'archiviste, (ii) de greffier.

recording [ri'kɔ:diŋ], *s.* **1.** enregistrement *m*; relation *f,* consignation *f,* par écrit; *Com:* notage *m* (d'une commande); *Tp:* inscription *f* (des demandes de communication); **r. operator,** annotateur, -trice, opérateur, -trice, d'enregistrement; **r. of accidents,** recensement *m* des accidents; **r. official,** agent chargé du recensement; **the r. angel,** l'ange *m* qui tient le registre des actes de chacun. **2.** (*a*) **sound r.,** enregistrement, prise *f,* du son; **sound-on-disc r.,** enregistrement sur disques; **r. on tape,** enregistrement sur bande magnétique; *Cin:* **variable density r.,** enregistrement à densité variable; **variable width r.,** enregistrement à densité constante; (*b*) **r. instrument, machine,** appareil enregistreur; **r. system,** système *m* d'enregistrement; mécanisme enregistreur; **r. channel, track,** voie *f* d'enregistrement; **r. tape,** ruban *m,* bande *f,* d'enregistrement; **r. blank,**

disque vierge; **r. room,** central *m* d'enregistrement; **r. pen,** stylet *m* enregistreur; **r. head,** tête enregistreuse (d'ordinateur, etc.); **r. barometer,** baromètre enregistreur; **r. tachometer,** tachymètre enregistreur; **r. altimeter,** altimètre enregistreur; **r. telegraph,** télégraphe imprimeur; téléimprimeur *m*; télétype *m*; *Cmptr:* **r. medium,** support *m* d'enregistrement (de données). **3.** enregistrement, chose enregistrée; **tape r.,** enregistrement sur bande magnétique; **to play a r.,** passer un enregistrement; *NAm:* **r. for a piano player,** rouleau perforé, bande perforée, pour piano mécanique.

recordist [ri'kɔ:dist], *s.* (*a*) opérateur, -trice, de magnétophone; (*b*) *W.Tel:* ingénieur *m* du son.

recork [ri:'kɔ:k], *v.tr.* reboucher (une bouteille).

recorking [ri:'kɔ:kiŋ], *s.* rebouchage *m*.

recount[1] [ri'kaunt], *v.tr.* raconter (**sth. to s.o.,** qch. à qn).

recount[2] ['ri:kaunt], *s.* **1.** recomptage *m*; nouvelle addition. **2.** nouveau dépouillement du scrutin (en cas de majorité très faible à une élection).

recount[3] [ri:'kaunt], *v.tr.* recompter; compter de nouveau (les votes, etc.).

recounting[1] [ri'kauntiŋ], *s.* racontage *m*.

recounting[2] [ri:'kauntiŋ], *s.* recomptage *m*.

recoup [ri'ku:p], *v.tr.* **1.** racquitter, dédommager (qn); **to r. s.o. (for) his losses,** dédommager, indemniser, qn de ses pertes; **to r. (oneself for) one's losses,** *v.i.* **to r.,** se rattraper de ses pertes; **to r. from s.o.,** se faire dédommager par qn; **to sell at a low price and r. oneself by large sales,** vendre à bas prix et se rattraper, se sauver, sur la quantité. **2.** *Jur:* défalquer, faire le décompte de (qch.).

recoupable [ri'ku:pəbl], *a.* (pertes, etc) dont on peut se rattraper.

recoupment [ri'ku:pmənt], *s.* **1.** dédommagement *m*. **2.** *Jur:* défalcation *f*, décompte *m*.

recourse [ri'kɔ:s], *s.* **1.** recours *m*; **to have r. to sth.,** avoir recours à qch., recourir à qch.; **to have r. to fraud,** avoir recours à la fraude; user de moyens frauduleux; **r. to arms is open to us,** la voie des armes nous est ouverte. **2.** (*a*) (*thg*) ressource *f*, expédient *m*; (*b*) (*pers.*) ressource. **3.** *Fin: Jur:* **to have r. to the endorser of a bill,** avoir recours contre l'endosseur d'un effet; **endorsement without r.,** endossement *m* à forfait; **to reserve right of r.,** se réserver le recours, un droit de recours.

recover[1] [ri'kʌvər], *v.tr. & i.* **1.** (*a*) recouvrer, retrouver (un objet perdu); retrouver (son appétit, sa voix); **I went to r. my umbrella,** je suis allé reprendre mon parapluie; **to r. a drowned man,** repêcher un noyé; *Ind:* **to r. by-products from coal,** recouvrer, récupérer, recueillir, capter, des sous-produits de la houille; *Mil:* **r. arms!** replacez l'arme! (*b*) **to r. one's breath, one's courage,** reprendre haleine, reprendre courage; **to r. one's senses, to r. one's reason,** reprendre ses sens, rentrer dans son bon sens; recouvrer sa raison; **to r. one's taste for sth.,** reprendre goût à qch.; **to r. consciousness,** reprendre ses esprits, ses sens; revenir à soi; **I am recovering my strength,** mes forces me reviennent. **2.** regagner (de l'argent perdu, l'affection de qn); recouvrer, regagner, rentrer en possession de (ses biens); rentrer dans (ses droits, ses débours); recouvrer, récupérer, faire rentrer (une créance); **to r. one's money,** récupérer son argent, rentrer en possession de son argent, rentrer dans ses fonds; **to r. money advanced,** rentrer dans ses avances; **to r. one's (fallen) fortunes,** se refaire une situation, une fortune; *Gaming:* **to r. one's losses,** se racquitter, *F:* se raccrocher; **to r. lost time,** rattraper le temps perdu; **to r. lost ground,** reprendre du terrain perdu; se rattraper; **he is recovering his credit,** son crédit se raffermit; **to r. a lost advantage,** reprendre le dessus; **having recovered his liberty he travelled,** rendu à la liberté il a voyagé; **to r. lost supporters,** rallier, ramener à soi, les renégats; **to r. sth. from s.o.,** reprendre qch. à qn; recouvrer qch. des mains de qn; **to r. (damages) from s.o.,** obtenir des dommages-intérêts de qn; se faire dédommager par qn; **after the war, France recovered Alsace,** après la guerre la France recouvra l'Alsace. **3.** *A:* **to r. an unconscious patient,** faire revenir à soi, ramener à la vie, un malade sans connaissance. **4. to r. (one's health),** guérir; se rétablir; revenir à la santé; **I am waiting until I have recovered,** j'attends le rétablissement de ma santé; **to r. from an illness,** se remettre, réchapper, guérir, d'une maladie; se rétablir; **his son, who is recovering from a severe illness,** son fils, convalescent d'une grave maladie; **the patient is recovering,** le malade reprend; **to be quite recovered,** être tout à fait remis, guéri, rétabli; **he has only just recovered,** il relève de maladie; **to r. from the effects of a war,** se remettre des effets d'une guerre; **to r. from one's astonishment, from a shock,** revenir, se remettre, de son étonnement, d'un choc; **the market is recovering,** le marché se ranime, reprend, est en reprise; **prices are recovering,** les prix se relèvent; les cours sont en reprise, se ressaisissent; **oils recovered five pence,** les pétroles se ranimèrent de cinq pence. **5. to r. (oneself),** se remettre, se ressaisir; **to r. one's balance,** recouvrer, reprendre, retrouver, son équilibre; *Av:* **to r. (from a dive, spin),** se rétablir (après un piqué, une vrille); faire une ressource. **6.** réparer (une erreur). **7.** (*a*) *Fenc:* **to r. (sword),** reprendre la garde; se remettre en grade (après la botte); (*b*) *Row:* **to r. (the oars),** ramener les avirons; revenir sur l'avant.

recover[2] [ri'kʌvər], *s.* **1.** *Fenc:* remise *f* en garde; retour *m* à la position de garde. **2.** *Row:* retour sur l'avant; dégagé *m*.

re(-)cover[3] ['ri:'kʌvər], *v.tr.* recouvrir; couvrir de nouveau; regarnir (des meubles); réentoiler (un matelas, etc.).

recoverable [ri'kʌvərəbl], *a.* **1.** (*of loss, etc.*) recouvrable, récupérable; (*of by-product, etc.*) récupérable; (*of mistake*) réparable. **2.** (*of patient*) guérissable.

re(-)covering [ri:'kʌvəriŋ], *s.* recouvrage *m* (d'un parapluie, etc.); réentoilage *m* (d'un matelas, etc.).

recovery [ri'kʌvəri], *s.* **1.** (*a*) recouvrement *m*, récupération *f* (d'un objet perdu); **losses beyond, past, r.,** pertes *f* irrécupérables, qu'il n'est plus possible de ravoir; *Navy:* **torpedo-r. vessel,** bâtiment *m* de ramassage des torpilles; *El:* **r. of a main no longer in use,** dépose *f* d'un câble hors service; *Aut:* **r. truck,** camion-grue *m*, *pl.* camions-grues; (*b*) récupération (de sous-produits, etc.); **heat r.,** récupération de la chaleur; *Atom.Ph:* **r. of waste uranium,** récupération, régénération *f*, des déchets d'uranium; **r. column,** colonne *f* de récupération. **2.** *Jur:* **r. of payment made by mistake,** répétition *f* d'indu; **action for r. of property,** (action *f* en) revendication *f*; réintégrande *f*; **r. of damages,** obtention *f* de dommages-intérêts. **3.** (*a*) *Med:* (i) rétablissement *m*, guérison *f* (de qn); **the patient is making a good r., is on the way to r.,** le malade est en bonne voie de guérison, est en bon train; **he has made a good r.,** il s'est bien refait; **he is past, beyond, r.,** il est dans un état désespéré; il a été condamné (par les médecins); **grief past r.,** douleur irrémédiable; (ii) **r. of consciousness, from a fainting fit,** retour *m* à la connaissance (après une syncope); (*b*) redressement *m* (économique, etc.); relèvement *m*, reprise *f* (des affaires); **trade r., industrial r.,** reprise, relance *f*, économique; **r. of prices, of international credit,** reprise des cours, du crédit international; **an obstacle to r.,** un obstacle à tout essai de redressement; *Hist:* **the r. on the Marne,** le redressement de la Marne; (*c*) *Sp:* (*from a losing position*) raccrochage *m*; **to make a brilliant r.,** se ressaisir, se raccrocher, brillamment; (*d*) *Ph:* rétablissement, récupération (d'un phénomène); **r. time,** *Atom.Ph:* délai *m* de rétablissement (de l'ionisation, etc.); *Elcs:* délai de récupération (de la sensibilité d'un appareil); *El:* **r. voltage,** tension *f* de rupture. **4.** (*a*) redressement (de qn qui a trébuché); (*b*) *Av:* redressement (après un piqué, etc.); ressource *f*. **5.** (*a*) *Fenc:* remise en garde; retour *m* à la position de garde; (*b*) *Row:* retour sur l'avant; dégagé *m*. **6.** redressement, rectification *f* (d'une erreur); *Cmptr:* **error r.,** reprise sur incident.

recreancy ['rekriənsi], *s.* **1.** lâcheté *f*. **2.** apostasie *f*.

recreant ['rekriənt]. *Lit:* **1.** *a.* (*a*) lâche; (*b*) infidèle. **2.** *s.* (*a*) lâche *m*; (*b*) renégat *m*, traître *m* apostat *m*.

re(-)create [ri:kri'eit], *v.tr.* recréer; créer (qch.) de nouveau; reconstituer (un fichier, etc.).

recreation[1] [rekri'eiʃ(ə)n], *s.* récréation *f*; (*a*) divertissement *m*, distraction *f*, délassement *m*; **a few moments of r.,** quelques moments de détente; **r. ground,** (i) terrain *m* de jeux; (ii) *Sch:* cour *f* de récréation; préau *m*; **r. room,** salle *f* de récréation, de jeux; (*b*) *Sch: Ecc:* **during the r.,** pendant la récréation.

recreation[2] [ri:kri'eiʃ(ə)n], *s.* nouvelle création; recréation *f*; reconstitution *f* (d'un fichier, etc.).

recreational [rekri'eiʃən(ə)l], *a.* relatif, destiné, à l'amusement, aux jeux, aux distractions, aux loisirs; **r. area,** aire réservée aux loisirs; terrain *m* de jeux.

recreationist [rekri'eiʃənist], *s. NAm:* fervent, -e, de jeux (surtout en plein air).

recreative[1] [rekri'eitiv], *a.* récréatif, divertissant.

recreative[2] [ri:kri'eitiv], *a.* qui recrée, de recréation.

recredit [ri:'kredit], *v.tr. Book-k:* extourner (une somme) au crédit.

recrement ['rekrimənt], *s. Physiol: etc:* récrément *m*.

recriminate [ri'krimineit], *v.i.* récriminer (**against s.o.,** contre qn).

recrimination [rikrimi'neiʃ(ə)n], *s.* récrimination *f*.

recriminative [ri'kriminətiv], **recriminatory** [rikrimi'neitəri], *a.* récriminatoire, récriminateur, -trice.

recross [ri:'krɔs], *v.tr.* **1.** retraverser; traverser de nouveau (une rue); repasser (une rivière); **the train recrosses the Thames,** le train passe une seconde fois sur la Tamise. **2.** recroiser (ses mains sur sa poitrine, etc.).

recrudesce [ri:kru:'des], *v.i.* (*of wound, sore, etc.*) s'enflammer de nouveau; (*of fever, etc.*) reprendre; (*of public disorders, etc.*) renaître, reprendre.

recrudescence [ri:kru:'des(ə)ns], *s.* recrudescence *f*; **r. of activity,** regain *m* d'activité; **the r. of civil disorder,** la recrudescence des troubles civils.

recrudescent [ri:kru:'des(ə)nt], *a.* recrudescent.

recruit[1] [ri'kru:t], *s. Mil:* (*a*) recrue *f*, conscrit *m*; **a raw r.,** une jeune recrue, *F:* un bleu; **to go through the r. stage,** faire ses classes; **to get recruits for a party among the middle classes,** faire des recrues pour un parti dans la bourgeoisie; (*b*) *U.S:* (i) soldat *m* de deuxième classe; simple soldat; (ii) matelot *m* de troisième classe.

recruit[2], *v.tr. & i.* **1.** (*a*) recruter (une armée, des troupes, des partisans); racoler (des partisans, *Hist:* des hommes pour l'armée, pour la marine); apporter des recrues à (une société, un parti); **cavalry officers were largely recruited from among the old nobility,** les officiers de cavalerie se recrutaient pour une bonne part dans la vieille noblesse; **to r. a party from the people,** recruter un parti parmi le peuple; **the new party was largely recruited from the middle classes,** le nouveau parti faisait de nombreuses recrues dans la bourgeoisie; (*b*) *A:* **to r. supplies,** se réapprovisionner. **2.** *O:* restaurer (la santé); remettre, remonter (qn); reprendre (des forces).

recruiter [ri'kru:tər], *s.* recruteur *m*.

recruiting [ri'kru:tiŋ], *s.* recrutement *m*; **r. agent,** agent *m* de recrutement; (agent) recruteur (*m*); *Mil:* **r. board,** conseil *m* de révision; **r. officer, sergeant,** officier recruteur; sergent recruteur; *Hist:* racoleur *m*; **r. station,** bureau *m* de recrutement; **the slums are a good r. ground for anarchists,** les taudis sont un bon terrain pour le recrutement des anarchistes.

recruitment [ri'kru:tmənt], *s.* **1.** recrutement *m* (de troupes, de partisans); racolage *m* (de partisans, *Hist:* d'hommes pour l'armée, la marine). **2.** réparation *f* (des forces); rétablissement *m* (de qn).

recrystallization [ri:kristəlai'zeiʃ(ə)n], *s.* recristallisation *f*.

recrystallize [ri:'kristəlaiz], *v.tr. & i.* recristalliser.

rectal ['rekt(ə)l], *a. Med: Anat:* rectal, -aux; du rectum; **r. injection,** lavement *m*.

rectally ['rektəli], *adv. Med:* (introduit) par l'anus, par le rectum.

rectangle ['rektæŋgl], *s.* rectangle *m*.

rectangled ['rektæŋgld], *a.* (prisme, etc.) rectangulaire.

rectangular [rek'tæŋgjulər], *a.* (*of figure*) rectangulaire, rectangle; (*of lines*) orthogonal, -aux; à angle droit; **r. coordinate,** coordonnée *f* rectangulaire; *Tp:* **r. wiring,** armement *m* en rectangle.

rectangularity [rektæŋgju'læriti], *s.* rectangularité *f*.

rectangularly [rek'tæŋgjuləli], *adv.* orthogonalement; à angle droit.

rectifiable ['rektifaiəbl], *a.* rectifiable.

rectification [rektifi'keiʃ(ə)n], *s.* **1.** (*a*) rectification *f*, redressement *m* (d'une erreur, etc.); (*b*) *Phot:* redressement des lignes déformées (lors du tirage à l'agrandisseur). **2.** *Dist:* rectification (de l'alcool, etc.). **3.** *Mth:* rectification (d'une courbe). **4.** *El:* redressement, rectification (du courant alternatif); **half-wave r.,** redressement par demi-alternances; **grid r.,** rectification par grille; **r. factor,** pourcentage *m*, taux *m*, de redressement; *Elcs:* **r. valve,** tube redresseur.

rectified ['rektifaid], *a.* **1.** (*of apparatus reading*) rectifié. **2.** (alcool) rectifié. **3.** *El:* (courant) redressé.

rectifier ['rektifaiər], *s.* **1.** (*pers.*) rectificateur, -trice. **2.** (*apparatus*) (*a*) *Dist:* rectificateur; **oil r.,** purificateur *m* d'huile; (*b*) *El: Elcs:* redresseur *m*, rectificateur (de courant); soupape *f* (électrique); **full-wave r.,** redresseur à deux alternances, à pleine onde; **half-wave r.,** redresseur à une alternance, à demi-onde; **mechanical r.,** redresseur mécanique; **crystal r.,** redresseur à cristal; **copper oxide r.,** redresseur à l'oxyde de cuivre; **selenium r.,** redresseur au sélénium; **barrier layer r.,** redresseur d'une couche d'arrêt; **dry (cell) r.,** redresseur sec, à semi-conducteurs; **electrolytic (cell) r.,** redresseur électrolytique; **mercury arc r.,** redresseur, soupape, à vapeur de mercure; **mercury pool r.,** redresseur à bain de mercure; **vacuum tube r.,** redresseur à lampe, à tube; **gaseous r.,** tube redresseur à gaz; **r. anode, cathode,** anode *f*, cathode *f*, de redresseur; **r. (vacuum) tube,** tube redresseur.

rectify ['rektifai], *v.tr.* **1.** (*a*) rectifier, corriger (un calcul, une erreur); réparer (un oubli, une erreur); **mistake that can be rectified,** erreur réparable; *Book-k:* **to r. an entry,** modifier, rectifier, une écriture; (*b*) *Dist:* rectifier, déflegmer (l'alcool). **2.** (*a*) *Mth:* rectifier (une courbe); (*b*) *El:* redresser (le courant alternatif).

rectifying[1] ['rektifaiiŋ], *a.* (*a*) (*of statement, etc.*) rectificatif; (*b*) *El: Elcs:* (système, etc.) redresseur; **r. valve,** *NAm:* **r. tube,** lampe, valve, redresseuse; tube redresseur; (*c*) *Opt:* **r. lens,** objectif *m* de redressement; (*d*) *Dist:* **r. column,** colonne *f* de déflegmation, à déflegmer.

rectifying[2], *s.* **1.** rectification *f* (d'une erreur, etc.); redressement *m* (d'une déformation, etc.). **2.** *Dist:* rectification, déflegmation *f* (de l'alcool).

rectilineal [rekti'liniəl], **rectilinear** [rekti'liniər], *a.* **1.** (*of movement, coordinate, geometrical figure, etc.*) rectiligne. **2.** *Phot:* **rapid rectilinear lens,** objectif *m* rectilinéaire; rectiligne; **wide-angle rectilinear lens,** rectiligne *m* grand angulaire. **3.** *T.V:* **r. scanning,** analyse *f* par lignes.

rectirostral [rekti'rɔstrəl], *a. Orn:* rectirostre.

rectiserial [rekti'siəriəl], *a.* rectisérié, en série droite.

rectitis [rek'taitis], *s. Med:* rectite *f.*

rectitude ['rektitju:d], *s.* **1.** rectitude *f* (d'une ligne droite). **2.** rectitude (de conduite); droiture *f* (de caractère).

rectitudinous [rekti'tju:dinəs], *a. Lit:* pharisaïque; **r. humbug,** tartufe *m.*

recto ['rektou], *s. Typ:* recto *m* (de la page).

rectocele ['rektousi:l], *s. Med:* rectocèle *f*; hernie *f* du rectum.

rectocolitis ['rektoukɔ'laitis], *s. Med:* recto-colite *f.*

rectometer [rek'tɔmitər], *s. Tex:* rectomètre *m.*

rectopexy ['rektoupeksi], *s. Surg:* rectopexie *f.*

rector ['rektər], *s.* **1.** (*a*) (*Church of Eng.*) ecclésiastique préposé à l'administration d'une paroisse et titulaire du bénéfice et de la dîme; **lay r.,** titulaire séculier d'un bénéfice (le préposé étant alors le *vicar*); (*b*) *U.S:* = curé *m.* **2.** (*a*) recteur *m* (d'une université); supérieur *m* (d'un collège de jésuites); **(Lord) R.,** représentant à l'administration élu par les étudiants d'une université écossaise; (*b*) *Scot:* directeur *m* (d'une école secondaire).

rectorate ['rektəreit], *s.* rectorat *m.*

rectorial [rek'tɔ:riəl], *a.* rectoral, -aux; de recteur; *a. & s. Sch:* **r. (election),** élection *f* du *rector* par les étudiants.

rectorship ['rektəʃip], *s.* rectorat *m.*

rectory ['rekt(ə)ri], *s. Ecc:* (*a*) bénéfice *m* du *rector*; rectorat *m*; (*b*) presbytère *m*, cure *f* (du *rector*).

rectoscope ['rektouskoup], *s. Med:* rectoscope *m.*

rectoscopy [rek'tɔskəpi], *s. Med:* rectoscopie *f.*

rectotomy [rek'tɔtəmi], *s.* rectotomie *f.*

recto-urethral [rektouju'ri:θrəl], *a. Anat:* recto-uréthral, -aux.

rectovaginal [rektouvæ'dʒainl], *a. Anat:* recto-vaginal, -aux.

rectovesical [rekou'vesik(ə)l], *a. Anat:* recto-vésical, -aux.

rectrix, *pl.* **-ices** ['rektriks, -isi:z], *s. Orn:* (penne) rectrice (*f*).

rectum, *pl.* **-ums, -a** ['rektəm, -əmz, -ə], *s. Anat:* rectum *m.*

rectus, *pl.* **-i** ['rektəs, -ai:], *s. Anat:* (muscle) droit (*m*).

recultivate [ri:'kʌltiveit], *v.tr.* remettre (des terres, un champ) en valeur, en culture.

recumbency [ri'kʌmbənsi], *s.* position couchée.

recumbent [ri'kʌmbənt], *a.* couché, étendu; *Sculp:* **r. effigy,** gisant *m*; *Geol:* **r. fold,** pli couché.

recuperate [ri'kju:pəreit]. **1.** *v.tr.* (*a*) remettre, rétablir, guérir (qn); (*b*) *Ind:* **to r. waste heat,** récupérer la chaleur perdue. **2.** *v.i.* se remettre, se rétablir, se refaire; reprendre des forces; guérir; **he had gone to the South of France to r.,** il était allé dans le Midi pour achever de se rétablir, *F:* pour récupérer (ses forces).

recuperation [rikju:pə'reiʃ(ə)n], *s.* **1.** (*of pers.*) rétablissement *m*, guérison *f.* **2.** *Ind:* récupération *f*, régénération *f* (de la chaleur, etc.).

recuperative [ri'kju:pərətiv], *a.* **1.** (pouvoir) de rétablissement. **2.** (remède) restauratif, réparateur, régénérateur. **3.** *Ind:* **r. air heater,** récupérateur *m.*

recuperator [ri'kju:pəreitər], *s.* **1.** *Ind:* récupérateur *m*, régénérateur *m* (de pertes d'énergie, etc.). **2.** *Artil:* récupérateur; **spring recuperators, oil recuperators,** récupérateurs à ressort, à huile; **r. spring,** ressort récupérateur.

recur [ri'kə:r], *v.i.* **(recurred) 1.** (*a*) revenir (**to a subject, etc.,** à, sur, un sujet, etc.); (*b*) **to r. to an expedient,** recourir à un expédient. **2.** (*a*) (*of idea, event, etc.*) **to r. to the memory,** revenir, se retracer, à la mémoire; (*b*) (*of question, event, etc.*) se reproduire, se renouveler; revenir, reparaître; (*of occasion*) se représenter; **festival that recurs every ten years,** fête qui revient tous les dix ans; (*c*) *Mth:* (*of figures*) se reproduire.

recurrence [ri'kʌrəns], *s.* **1.** (*a*) retour *m* (**to,** à); **there was no r. to this matter,** on n'est pas revenu sur ce sujet; (*b*) recours *m* (**to,** à). **2.** réapparition *f*, renouvellement *m*, retour, reproduction *f*; *Med:* récurrence *f* (d'une fièvre); récidive *f* (d'une maladie infectieuse); **the frequent r. of these attacks,** le retour fréquent de ces accès; **to be of frequent r.,** revenir fréquemment; *Pol.Ec: etc:* **r. equation,** équation fonctionnelle de récurrence; *Mth:* **r. formula,** formule *f* de récurrence; *Ph: etc:* **r. frequency,** périodicité *f.*

recurrent [ri'kʌrənt], *a.* **1.** récurrent; *Anat:* **r. artery,** artère récurrente; **r. nerve,** nerf récurrent; *Physiol:* **r. sensibility,** sensibilité récurrente; *Bot:* **r. veinlet,** veinule récurrente. **2.** (*a*) périodique; qui revient, se produit, périodiquement, par intervalles; cyclique; **r. event,** événement périodique; **r. expenses,** dépenses qui reviennent périodiquement; *Ph: etc:* **r. pulses,** impulsions périodiques; (*b*) récurrent; *Astr:* **r. novae,** novae récurrentes; *Med:* **r. fever,** fièvre récurrente, périodique; récurrente *f*; **r. cancer,** cancer récurrent, récidivant; **r. bronchial catarrh,** bronchite *f* chronique; *Mth:* **r. series,** série récurrente; *Ph: etc:* **r. state,** état récurrent; *El:* **r. network,** réseau récurrent.

recurring [ri'kə:riŋ], *a.* (*a*) périodique; qui revient; cyclique; (*b*) *Mth:* **r. series,** série récurrente; **r. decimal,** fraction décimale périodique.

recursion [ri'kə:ʃ(ə)n], *s. Log: etc:* récursion *f*, récurrence *f*; *Mth:* **r. formula,** formule *f* de récursion.

recursive [ri'kə:siv], *a. Log: etc:* récursif, récurrent; **r. definition,** définition récursive; *Cmptr:* **r. process,** processus récurrent.

recursivity [rikə'siviti], *s.* récursivité *f*, récurrence *f.*

recurvate [ri'kə:veit], *a. Nat.Hist:* recourbé.

recurvature [ri'kə:vətjər], *s. Nat.Hist:* recourbure *f.*

recurved [ri'kə:vd], *a.* (bec d'oiseau, etc.) recourbé, recurvé.

recurvirostral [rikə:vi'rɔstrəl], *a. Orn:* recurvirostre.

recusancy ['rekjuzənsi, ri'kju:zənsi], *s.* **1.** *Eng.Hist:* refus *m* (de la part des catholiques) d'assister à l'office dans une église anglicane. **2.** opposition *f* opiniâtre (à une autorité, un ordre).

recusant ['rekjuz(ə)nt, ri'kju:z(ə)nt]. **1.** *s. Eng.Hist:* catholique *mf* qui refusait d'assister à l'office dans une église anglicane; récusant, -ante. **2.** *a. & s.* dissident, -ente; réfractaire (*mf*) **(against,** contre).

recut [ri:'kʌt], *v.tr.* recouper; retailler (une lime); rafraîchir, aviver (une arête, etc.).

recutting [ri:'kʌtiŋ], *s.* retaillage *m.*

recycle [ri:'saikl], *v.tr.* (*a*) retraiter, recycler (des matières, eaux, usées); (*b*) remettre en circulation, réutiliser (une matière recyclée); (*c*) *Cmptr:* recycler (une programmation).

recycling [ri:'saikliŋ], *s.* (*a*) recyclage *m*, retraitement *m* (des matières, eaux, usées); (*b*) remise *f* en circulation, réutilisation *f* (d'une matière recyclée); (*c*) *Cmptr:* recyclage *m* (d'une programmation).

red [red], *a. & s.*

I. 1. *a.* **(redder, reddest)** (*a*) rouge; (*deep*) pourpre; **r. lips,** lèvres rouges, (*bright*) vermeilles; **r.(-rimmed) eyes,** yeux rouges, éraillés; **r. hands,** (i) mains rouges, *F:* mains de blanchisseuse; (ii) *Lit:* mains teintes de sang; *Lit:* **hands r. with the blood of martyrs,** mains trempées dans le sang des martyrs; *Lit:* **r. battle,** combat sanguinaire, sanglant; **r. vengeance,** vengeance sanguinaire, sanglante; **the r. hat,** le chapeau rouge (d'un cardinal); *Hist:* **the r. ribbon,** le ruban rouge (de l'Ordre du Bain); **to turn, go, r.,** (*of thg*) rougir; (*of pers.*) rougir, devenir rouge; (*of sky, etc.*) rougeoyer; **to go r. and pale by turns,** rougir et pâlir tour à tour; **to become r. with anger,** rougir de colère, se fâcher tout rouge; **to blush, flush, r.,** devenir (tout) rouge; **her cheeks burned redder and redder,** elle rougissait de plus en plus; *F:* **was my face r.!** ce que j'étais confus! *F:* **r. as a peony, tomato, turkey-cock, boiled lobster,** rouge comme une pivoine, un coq, une tomate; **it's like a r. rag to a bull,** c'est le rouge pour le taureau; **it's like a r. rag to him,** il voit rouge quand il entend dire cela; *Typ: etc:* **r. letters,** caractères *m* rouges; *Fig:* **we must mark that in r. letters,** il faut faire une croix à la cheminée; *Book-k:* **the r. side,** le débit, le doit; *U.S: F:* (*of account*) **to go into r. ink,** avoir une balance déficitaire; *Cu:* **r. meat,** (i) viande saignante; (ii) (viande de) bœuf *m*; *Geol:* **r. granite, marble,** granit *m*, marbre *m*, rose; *Geog:* **the R. Sea,** la mer Rouge; *Art:* **r. chalk,** sanguine *f*, rubrique *f*; **sketch in r. chalk,** (esquisse à la) sanguine; *Ecc:* **r. mass,** messe *f* rouge, du Saint-Esprit; *Astr:* **r. giant (star),** géante *f* rouge; **r. shift,** décalage *m* vers le rouge; *Aut:* **r. light,** feu *m* rouge; *Fig:* **to see the r. light,** se rendre compte du danger, sentir le danger; *F:* **r.-light, r.-lamp, district,** quartier mal famé, réservé; rue *f* des bordels; *Adm:* **r. box,** coffret recouvert de cuir rouge (qui contient des documents d'État); **r. tape,** (i) ruban rouge, bolduc *m* (rouge) (des documents officiels); (ii) *F:* routine administrative; fonctionnarisme *m*; bureaucratie *f*; paperasserie *f*; *F:* **you can't get away from r. tape,** tout est bureaucratisé; *Cmptr:* **r. tape operation,** opération *f* auxiliaire, de servitude, de service; *A:* **R. Book,** (almanach) nobiliaire *m*; annuaire *m* de la noblesse; **Chairman Mao's little R. Book,** le petit livre rouge de Mao-Tsé-Toung; *Miner:* **r. lead ore,** plomb *m* rouge; **r. lead,** minium *m*, mine anglaise; *Metall:* **r. heat,** chaude *f*, chaleur *f*, rouge; **dark r. heat,** chaude sombre; **to raise iron to r. heat,** porter le feu au rouge; *Med:* **r. gum,** strophulus *m*, feux *mpl* des dents; *Vet:* **r. water,** hématurie *f*, *F:* pissement *m* du sang; *Ich:* **r. hind,** mérou *m* rouge; *Bot:* **r. bine,** houblon *m* rouge; *NAm: Bot:* **r. root,** sanguinaire *f*; (*b*) (*of hair*) roux; **r. beard,** barbe rousse; **r.-bearded,** à la barbe rousse; **R. Max,** Max le Rouquin; (*c*) *Pol:* (i) rouge; de l'extrême gauche; (ii) *Can:* libéral; **r. government,** gouvernement *m* des Gauches; **the r. flag,** le drapeau rouge; (*song*) **the R. Flag,** l'Internationale *f*; **R. China,** la Chine communiste; *F:* **a r. shirt,** un anarchiste, *F:* **the r. peril,** l'anarchisme *m.* **2.** (*a*) *a. & s.* (*in Fr. a. inv.*) **cherry r.,** rouge cerise; **fiery r.,** rouge feu; **yellowish r.,** rouge orangé; **Indian r.,** ocre rouge; *Art:* **Titian r.,** blond vénitien; (*b*) *s. Dy: etc:* **Venetian r., English r.,** colcotar *m*, rouge anglais; **Indian r.,** ocre *f* rouge.

II. *s.* **1.** (*a*) rouge *m*; **dressed in r.,** habillé de, en, rouge; **the r. and white of her complexion,** son teint de lis et de rose; *F: A:* **the r., white and blue,** la marine anglaise; *F:* **to see r.,** se fâcher tout rouge; (*b*) *Med:* **r. blindness,** anérythropsie *f*; **to be r. blind,** être atteint d'anérythropsie; **r.-green blindness,** protanopie *f*; (*c*) *F:* **to be in the r.,** (i) (*of pers.*) avoir un compte débiteur; (ii) (*of account*) avoir une balance déficitaire; **at last I'm out of the r.,** j'ai enfin un compte en crédit. **2.** *Pol:* (*pers.*) rouge *mf.* **3.** *Games:* **the r.,** (i) (*roulette*) la rouge; (ii) *Bill:* la bille rouge.

redact [ri'dækt], *v.tr. Lit:* **1.** rédiger, dresser (un document, etc.). **2.** mettre au point (un article, etc.).

redaction [ri'dækʃ(ə)n], *s. Lit:* **1.** rédaction *f* (d'un document, etc.). **2.** mise *f* au point (d'un article).

redactor [ri'dæktər], *s.* rédacteur *m.*

redan [ri'dæn], *s. Fort:* redan *m.*

redbird ['redbə:d], *s. U.S: Orn:* (*a*) tangara *m* rouge; (*b*) cardinal *m*, -aux, d'Amérique.

red-blooded ['red'blʌdid], *a.* (*of pers.*) vigoureux, robuste.

redbreast ['redbrest], *s. Orn:* **(robin) r.,** (i) rouge-gorge *m*, *pl.* rouges-gorges; *F:* frileux *m*, frileuse *f*; (ii) *NAm:* grive *f* migratoire.

red-breasted ['red'brestid], *a. Orn:* à gorge rouge.

redbrick ['redbrik], *a. F:* **r. universities,** universités *f* de province modernes (par opposition à Oxford et Cambridge).

redbuck ['redbʌk], *s. Z:* impala *m*; gazelle *f* à pieds noirs.

redcap ['redkæp], *s. F:* (*a*) *Mil:* soldat *m* de la police militaire; *pl.* (*as a unit*) **the Redcaps** = la prévôté; (*b*) *NAm:* porteur *m* (dans une gare).

redcoat ['redkout], *s. Hist:* soldat anglais; **the redcoats,** *F:* les habits *m* rouges.

redd[1] [red], *v.tr. Scot: & NAm:* **to r. (up),** ranger (une pièce), mettre de l'ordre dans (la maison).

redd[2], *s. Pisc:* (*a*) (*spawning ground*) frayère *f*; (*b*) (*spawn*) frai *m.*

redden ['red(ə)n]. **1.** *v.tr.* rendre (qch.) rouge; rougir (qch.). **2.** *v.i.* devenir rouge; (*of sky*) rougir, rougeoyer; (*of hair, leaves, etc.*) roussir; (*of pers.*) rougir.

reddening ['red(ə)niŋ], *a.* rougissant, rougeoyant.

redding ['rediŋ], *s.* = REDDLE[1].

reddingite ['rediŋait], *s. Miner:* reddingite *f.*

reddish ['rediʃ], *a.* (*a*) (lumière, couleur) rougeâtre; (*b*) **r. hair,** cheveux *m* roussâtres.

reddle[1] ['red(ə)l], *s.* ocre *f* rouge, craie *f* rouge; rubrique *f.*

reddle[2], *v.tr.* frotter (qch.) d'ocre rouge, de rubrique; marquer (qch.) à l'ocre rouge; **to r. the (tiled) floor,** passer les dalles à l'ocre rouge.

rede[1] [ri:d], *s. A: Dial:* **1.** conseil *m.* **2.** interprétation *f*, explication *f.*

rede[2], *v.tr. A: Dial:* **1.** conseiller (qn); **to r. s.o. to do sth.,** conseiller à qn de faire qch. **2.** interpréter, expliquer (qch.); déchiffrer (une énigme).

redeal[1] [ri:'di:l], *s. Cards:* redonne *f.*

redeal[2], *v.tr. & i.* (*p.p. & p.t.* **redealt** [ri:'delt]) *Cards:* **to r. (the cards),** redistribuer les cartes; redonner.

redecorate [ri:'dekəreit], *v.tr.* peindre et tapisser (un appartement) à nouveau.

redeem [ri'di:m], *v.tr.* **1.** (*a*) racheter, dégager (une propriété, un nantissement, etc.); **to r. one's watch (from pawn),** retirer, dégager, sa montre; **to r. one's honour,** dégager son honneur; (*b*) rembourser (une obligation, annuité, etc.); **to r. a debt,** amortir une dette, se libérer d'une dette; **to r. a bill,** honorer une traite; **to r. a mortgage,** (i) (*of mortgagor*) éteindre, (ii) (*of purchaser of mortgaged property*) purger, une hypothèque; **to r. a promise,** tenir, accomplir, sa promesse; (*c*) obtenir, se procurer, le remboursement de (ses obligations remboursables, etc.); encaisser (un bon de caisse, etc.). **2.** (*a*) libérer, racheter (un esclave, un prisonnier); *Theol:* (*of Christ*) racheter (le genre humain); **redeemed from vice,** arraché au vice; (*b*) **his good points r. his faults,** ses qualités rachètent, compensent, ses défauts; **to r. oneself,** se racheter; **book redeemed from grossness by its sincerity,** livre qui rachète ses crudités par sa franchise. **3.** (*a*) *B:* **redeeming the time because the days are evil,** rachetant le temps car les jours sont mauvais; (*b*) **to r. the time,** réparer le temps perdu.

redeemability [ridi:mə'biliti], *s. Fin:* remboursabilité *f* (d'une obligation, etc.).

redeemable [ri'di:məbl], *a.* **1.** *Fin:* (*of stock, etc.*) rachetable, remboursable, amortissable. **2.** (faute, etc.) rachetable.

redeemer [ri'di:mər], *s.* **1.** rédempteur, -trice; *Theol:* **the R.,** le Rédempteur. **2.** racheteur, -euse (d'un esclave, *Fin:* d'une obligation, etc.).

redeeming[1] [ri'di:miŋ], *a.* **1.** rédempteur, -trice. **2.** compensatoire; qui rachète, qui fait compensation; **r. feature,** qualité *f* qui rachète les défauts, les fautes; **ugliness without one r. feature,** laideur que rien ne rachète, laideur désolante.

redeeming[2], *s.* (*a*) rachat *m*, dégagement *m* (d'un objet mis en gage, d'une propriété hypothéquée); (*b*) remboursement *m*, amortissement *m* (d'une obligation); **r. of a mortgage,** (i) (*by mortgagor*) extinction *f*, (ii) (*by purchaser of mortgaged property*) purge *f*, d'une hypothèque.

redefine [ri:di'fain], *v.tr.* donner une nouvelle définition de (qch.).

redeliver [ri:di'livər], *v.tr.* **1.** livrer de nouveau (un paquet à son destinataire, etc.); *Post:* présenter de nouveau (un pli recommandé, etc.). **2.** répéter (un avertissement, etc.); prononcer de nouveau (un discours).

redelivery [ri:di'livəri], *s.* nouvelle livraison (d'un paquet, etc.); *Post:* nouvelle présentation (d'un pli recommandé, etc.); **r. of ship to owners,** remise *f* d'un vaisseau aux armateurs.

redemise[1] [ri:di'maiz], *s. Jur:* rétrocession *f*.

redemise[2], *v.tr. Jur:* rétrocéder (un bien à qn).

redemption [ri'dem(p)ʃ(ə)n], *s.* **1.** (*a*) *Fin:* remboursement *m*, amortissement *m* (d'une obligation); rachat *m*, *Jur:* rédemption *f* (d'un emprunt, d'une concession); **accelerated r., r. before due date,** remboursement anticipé; **r. fund,** caisse *f* d'amortissement; **r. loan,** emprunt d'amortissement; **r. premium,** prime *f* de remboursement; **r. table,** plan *m* d'amortissement (d'une dette, etc.); **r. value,** valeur *f* de rachat, de remboursement; **terms of r.,** (i) condition *f* de rachat, de remboursement; (ii) plan d'amortissement; (*b*) **r. of a pledge, of a security,** dégagement *m*, retrait *m*, d'un gage, d'un nantissement; **r. of a mortgage,** (i) (*by mortgagor*) extinction *f*, (ii) (*by purchaser of mortgaged property*) purge *f*, d'une hypothèque; (*c*) *Jur:* **sale with power, option, of r.,** vente *f* avec faculté de rachat; vente à réméré; **covenant of r.,** pacte *m* de rachat. **2.** rachat, délivrance *f* (d'un esclave, etc.); *Theol:* rédemption *f* (du genre humain); **in the 500th year of our r.,** en l'an de grâce 500; **this setback proved his r.,** ce revers de fortune fut son salut. **3.** rachat (d'un crime, etc.); **the r. of sins,** la rédemption des péchés; **crime without, past, r.,** crime irréparable; **monument spoilt beyond (all hope of) r.,** monument qui a été abîmé irrémédiablement, irréparablement. **4. to join a society by r.,** acheter son entrée dans une société.

Redemptionist [ri'dem(p)ʃənist], *s.m. Ecc:* trinitaire, mathurin.

redemptive [ri'dem(p)tiv], *a.* rédempteur, -trice.

Redemptorist [ri'demptərist], *s. Ecc:* rédemptoriste *m*.

redeploy [ri:di'plɔi], *v.tr.* **1.** *Adm: Ind:* réorganiser (un service); redistribuer, procéder à une nouvelle répartition, implantation, de (la main-d'œuvre, etc.). **2.** *Mil:* redéployer (des unités, armes, etc.).

redeployment [ri:di'plɔimənt], *s.* **1.** *Adm: Ind:* réorganisation *f* (d'un service); nouvelle répartition, nouvelle implantation, redistribution *f*, reconversion *f* (de la main-d'œuvre, du matériel). **2.** *Mil:* redéploiement *m*, réimplantation *f* (des unités, du matériel, etc.).

redescribe ['ri:dis'kraib], *v.tr. Nat.Hist:* donner une nouvelle description à (une espèce, etc.).

redescription ['ri:dis'kripʃ(ə)n], *s. Nat: Hist:* nouvelle description (d'une espèce, etc.).

redesign ['ri:di'zain], *v.tr.* redessiner, modifier complètement (une machine, etc.); refondre (un texte, etc.).

redevelop [ri:di'veləp], *v.tr.* **1.** mettre (un bas quartier, etc.) en valeur. **2.** *Phot:* développer de nouveau (un cliché).

redevelopment [ri:di'veləpmənt], *s.* **1.** mise *f* en valeur (d'un bas quartier, etc.). **2.** *Phot:* nouveau développement.

redeye ['redai], *s.* **1.** *Ich:* rotengle *m*; gardon *m* rouge. **2.** *usu.* **red eye,** *NAm: P:* whisky *m*, alcool *m*, de mauvaise qualité.

red-eyed ['red'aid], *a.* **1.** aux yeux rouges. **2.** aux yeux éraillés.

red-faced ['red'feist], *a.* **1.** rougeaud, rubicond, sanguin; **a big r.-f. fellow,** un gros rougeaud. **2. r.-f. with anger, embarrassment,** rougissant de colère, de gêne.

redfish ['redfiʃ], *s.* **1.** (*a*) saumon *m* mâle à l'époque du frai; (*b*) *Com:* saumon. **2.** *Ich:* (*a*) rouget grondin; (*b*) *U.S:* sébaste *m*.

red-haired ['red'hɛəd], *a.* qui a les cheveux roux; roux, *f.* rousse; *F:* rouquin.

red-handed ['red'hændid], *a.* qui a les mains rouges de sang; *Fig:* **to be caught, taken, r.-h.,** être pris en flagrant délit, sur le fait, *F:* sur le tas, la main dans le sac.

redhead ['redhed], *s.* **1.** *F:* roussot, -ote; roux, *f.* rousse; rouquin, -ine. **2.** *Orn:* fuligule *f* d'Amérique; *Fr.C:* morillon *m* à tête rouge.

red-headed [red'hedid], *a.* **1.** = RED-HAIRED. **2.** *Orn: Z:* à tête rouge.

redhibition [redhi'biʃ(ə)n], *s. Jur:* rédhibition *f*.

redhibitory [red'hibitəri], *a. Jur:* rédhibitoire.

red-hot [red'hɔt], *a.* **1.** rouge, chauffé au rouge, porté au rouge, rougi au feu, d'un rouge ardent; **to make sth. r.-h.,** porter qch. au rouge. **2.** *F:* (*preceding noun*) (*a*) **r.-h. revolutionary,** ardent révolutionnaire; révolutionnaire à tous crins; **r.-h. enthusiasm,** enthousiasme chauffé à blanc; *NAm: P:* **r.-h. mamma,** petite amie pétillante; (*b*) **r.-h. news,** nouvelle dernière heure, toute chaude.

redia, *pl.* **-æ** ['ri:diə, -ii:], *s. Ann:* rédie *f*.

redial [ri:'daiəl], *v.tr.* (**redialled**) refaire (un numéro) (sur un cadran d'appel).

rediffusion [ri:di'fju:ʒ(ə)n], *s. W.Tel:* radiodiffusion relayée.

redingote ['rediŋgout], *s. Cost:* redingote *f* (de femme, *A:* d'homme).

redingtonite ['rediŋtənait], *s. Miner:* rédingtonite *f*.

redintegrate [re'dintigreit], *v.tr. A:* (*a*) rétablir (qch.) dans son intégrité; (*b*) **to r. s.o. in his possessions,** réintégrer qn dans ses possessions.

redintegration [redinti'greiʃ(ə)n], *s.* **1.** rétablissement intégral; *Psy:* rédintégration *f*; *Cryst:* **r. of crystals,** rédintégration des cristaux. **2.** réintégration *f* (de qn dans ses biens, etc.).

redirect [ri:d(a)i'rekt], *v.tr.* **1.** *Post:* réacheminer, réexpédier, faire suivre (une lettre, etc.). **2.** donner un nouvel itinéraire, une nouvelle route, à (un avion, etc.); **to be redirected,** recevoir une nouvelle route, un nouvel itinéraire.

redirection [ri:d(a)i'rekʃ(ə)n], *s.* **1.** *Post:* réacheminement *m*, réexpédition *f* (d'une lettre, etc.). **2.** affectation *f*, attribution *f*, d'un nouvel itinéraire, d'une nouvelle route (**of an aircraft, etc.,** à un avion, etc.); détournement *m* (d'un avion, etc.) sur un nouvel itinéraire.

rediscount[1] [ri:'diskaunt], *s. Com:* **1.** réescompte *m*. **2.** *F:* papier réescompté.

rediscount[2] [ri:dis'kaunt], *v.tr. Com:* réescompter.

rediscountable [ri:dis'kauntəbl], *a. Com:* réescomptable.

rediscounter [ri:dis'kauntər], *s. Com:* réescompteur *m*.

rediscounting [ri:dis'kauntiŋ], *s. Com:* réescompte *m*.

rediscover [ri:dis'kʌvər], *v.tr.* redécouvrir; retrouver.

rediscovery [ri:dis'kʌvəri], *s.* redécouverte *f*.

redissolve [ri:di'zɔlv], *v.tr.* redissoudre.

redistil [ri:dis'til], *v.tr.* (**redistilled**) *Dist:* redistiller; rectifier, cohober.

redistillation [ri:disti'leiʃ(ə)n], **redistilling** [ri:dis'tiliŋ], *s. Dist:* redistillation *f*; rectification *f*, cohobation *f*.

redistribute ['ri:dis'tribju:t], *v.tr.* (*a*) redistribuer; (*b*) répartir de nouveau (des circonscriptions électorales, etc.).

redistribution ['ri:distri'bju:ʃ(ə)n], *s.* (*a*) redistribution *f*; nouvelle distribution; (*b*) nouvelle répartition (de sièges parlementaires, etc.).

redivide ['ri:di'vaid]. **1.** *v.tr.* rediviser. **2.** *v.i.* se rediviser.

redivision [ri:di'viʒən], *s.* nouvelle division.

red-leg(s) ['redlegz], *s.* **1.** *Orn:* (*a*) chevalier *m* gambette; (*b*) maubèche *f* violette; (*c*) perdrix *f* rouge. **2.** *Bot:* persicaire *f*.

red-legged [red'legd], *a. Orn: Z:* aux pattes, pieds, rouges.

red-letter ['redletər], *a.* écrit, imprimé, en caractères rouges; *F:* **r.-l. day,** (i) *Ecc:* jour férié, de fête; (ii) jour mémorable; jour pour lequel on fera, a fait, une croix à la cheminée; **his return was a r.-l. day for the country,** son retour fit époque dans le pays.

redly ['redli], *adv.* (briller, etc.) avec un éclat rouge.

redneck ['rednek], *s. NAm: P:* **1.** paysan *m*; *F:* cul-terreux *m*, *pl.* culs-terreux. **2.** pauvre blanc, petit blanc.

redness ['rednis], *s.* **1.** rougeur *f*, couleur *f* rouge. **2.** rousseur *f* (des cheveux, etc.).

red-nosed ['red'nouzd], *a.* qui a le nez rouge; au nez rouge.

redo [ri:'du:], *v.tr.* **1.** refaire (une tâche, etc.). **2.** peindre et tapisser (un appartement) à nouveau.

redolence ['redələns], *s.* (i) odeur *f* suave; parfum *m*; (ii) odeur forte.

redolent ['redələnt], *a.* odorant; (i) parfumé; (ii) qui a une odeur forte (**of,** de); **r. of spring,** qui exhale une odeur de printemps; qui exhale, sent, fleure comme, le printemps; **town r. of times past,** ville qui respire l'ancien temps; **to be r. of the soil,** sentir le cru; **sauce r. of garlic,** sauce (i) qui fleure l'ail, (ii) qui pue l'ail.

redouble[1] ['ri:'dʌbl], *s. Cards:* surcontre *m*.

redouble[2] [ri:'dʌbl]. **1.** *v.tr.* (*a*) redoubler (ses cris, ses instances, etc.); **to r. one's efforts,** redoubler d'efforts, de zèle; (*b*) replier (une étoffe, etc.); plier en quatre; (*c*) *Cards:* **to r. spades,** surcontrer pique. **2.** *v.i.* (*a*) redoubler; **the rain redoubled,** la pluie redoubla; (*b*) *Cards:* surcontrer.

redoubled [ri:'dʌb(ə)ld], *a.* (*a*) redoublé; **r. blows,** coups redoublés; **with r. enthusiasm, anger,** avec un redoublement d'enthousiasme, de zèle; (*b*) **r. folds,** doubles plis.

redoubling [ri:'dʌbliŋ], *s.* redoublement *m* (de joie, d'enthousiasme, etc.).

redoubt [ri'daut], *s. Fort:* redoute *f*, réduit *m*.

redoubtable [ri'dautəbl], *a.* redoutable, formidable.

redoubted [ri'dautid], *a. A:* redouté.

redound [ri'daund], *v.i.* **1.** contribuer (**to,** à); **this will r. to your credit,** votre réputation y gagnera; **to r. to s.o.'s advantage,** contribuer à l'avantage de qn; tourner à l'avantage de qn; **it redounds to your honour,** c'est tout à votre honneur. **2.** résulter; rejaillir (**to,** sur).

redowa ['redəvə], *s. Danc: Mus: A:* redowa *f*.

redox ['redɔks], *a. & s. Ch:* redox (*m*); **r. reaction,** réaction *f* redox, d'oxydo-réduction; système *m* redox.

redpoll ['redpoul], *s.* **1.** *Orn:* sizerin flammé; **Arctic,** *NAm:* **hoary, r.,** sizerin blanchâtre; **greater r.,** sizerin du Groënland; **lesser r.,** sizerin cabaret; **mealy r.,** sizerin boréal. **2.** *Husb:* **redpolls,** race *f* de bœufs roux sans cornes.

redraft[1] [ri:'drɑ:ft], *s.* **1.** nouvelle rédaction (d'un document, etc.). **2.** *Com:* retraite *f*, traite *f* par contre.

redraft[2], *v.tr.* rédiger (un document) de nouveau.

redraw [ri:'drɔ:], *v.* (**redrew** [-'dru:]; **redrawn**) **1.** *v.i. Com:* faire retraite (**on s.o.,** sur qn). **2.** *v.tr.* (*a*) rédiger à nouveau, refaire (un document); (*b*) redessiner, refaire (un croquis); **to r. a line,** tirer de nouveau une ligne, tirer une nouvelle ligne; (*c*) **to r. lots,** retirer au sort; (*d*) *Metall:* réétirer (les métaux).

redrawing [ri:'drɔ:iŋ], *s.* **1.** nouvelle rédaction (d'un document). **2.** nouveau dessin (d'un plan, etc.). **3. r. of lots,** nouveau tirage au sort. **4.** *Metall:* réétirage *m*; **reverse r.,** réétirage inverse.

redress[1] [ri'dres], *s.* redressement *m*, réparation *f* (d'un tort); réforme *f* (d'un abus); soulagement *m* (d'un mal); **to seek r. at the hands of s.o.,** demander réparation, demander justice, à qn; *Jur:* **legal r.,** réparation légale; **injury beyond r., past r.,** *A:* **without r.,** tort irréparable, sans remède.

redress[2] [ri'dres], *v.tr.* **1.** rétablir (l'équilibre). **2.** redresser, réparer (un tort); redresser (un grief); corriger, réformer (un abus); soulager, porter remède à (une détresse); *Prov:* **a fault confessed is half redressed,** péché avoué est à demi pardonné.

redress[3] [ri:'dres], *v.tr.* **1.** rhabiller (qn); *Th:* **to r. a play,** changer les costumes d'une pièce; costumer une pièce à nouveau. **2.** *Tchn:* réapprêter (des peaux, etc.); *Const:* ravaler (le parement d'un mur).

redressable [ri'dresəbl], *a.* (tort) redressable, réparable; (faute) corrigible.

redresser [ri'dresər], *s.* redresseur, -euse, réparateur, -trice (de torts).

redressing[1] [ri'dresiŋ], *s.* **1.** rétablissement *m* (de l'équilibre). **2.** redressement *m*, réparation *f* (d'un tort); soulagement *m* (d'une détresse).

redressing[2] [ri:'dresiŋ], *s.* **1.** rhabillement *m* (de qn). **2.**

Tchn: nouvel apprêt (des peaux, etc.); *Const:* ravalement *m* (d'un mur).
red-roofed ['red'ru:ft], *a.* (maison, etc.) à toit rouge.
redruthite ['redruθait], *s. Miner:* chalcosite*f*, chalcosine *f.*
redshank ['redʃæŋk], *s. Orn:* chevalier *m* gambette; **spotted, dusky, r.,** chevalier arlequin.
red-short ['red'ʃɔ:t], *a. Metall:* (fer) cassant à chaud; (fer) rouverin, métis, de couleur.
redskin ['redskin], *s. Ethn:* Peau-Rouge *m, pl.* Peaux-Rouges.
redstart ['redstɑ:t], *s. Orn:* (*a*) rouge-queue *m, pl.* rouges-queues, à front blanc; **black r.,** rouge-queue noir; **Moussier's r.,** rouge-queue de Moussier; (*b*) **American r.,** fauvette flamboyante.
red-tailed ['redteild], *a.* à queue rouge; *Orn:* **r.-t. quelea,** mange-mil *inv* africain.
redtop ['redtɔp], *s. NAm: Bot:* agrostide *f.*
reduce [ri'dju:s], *v.tr.* **1.** (*a*) réduire, rapetisser (un dessin, etc.); amincir, amenuiser, amaigrir, affaiblir, alléger (une planche, etc.); (*in length*) raccourcir; **to r. one's weight,** se débarrasser de sa graisse; **exercise reduces fat people,** l'exercice dégraisse les obèses; *v.i.* **do you want to r.?** voulez-vous maigrir? *Cu:* **to r. a sauce, a syrup,** (faire) réduire une sauce, un sirop; *Med:* **to r. a swelling,** résoudre une tumeur; (*b*) réduire, abaisser (la température); réduire, (ra)baisser, diminuer (le prix, etc.); **reduced to £10 from £15,** réduction: £10 au lieu de £15; en vente à £10 au lieu de £15; **to r. taxes,** alléger les impôts; apporter des modérations à des impôts; **to r. the rates on a house,** dégrever un immeuble; **to r. expenses,** diminuer la dépense; *F:* rogner les dépenses; faire des économies; **to r. a claim,** réduire, *F:* amputer, une demande; **to r. speed,** réduire la vitesse; diminuer de vitesse; diminuer sa vitesse; ralentir la marche; *Ind:* **to r. the output,** ralentir la production; mettre une entreprise, une usine, en veilleuse; *El:* **to r. the voltage,** abaisser la tension; *Mec:* **to r. the friction,** adoucir le frottement; *Mec.E:* **to r. the gear ratio,** démultiplier les vitesses; (*c*) atténuer (un contraste); *Phot:* affaiblir, atténuer, baisser (un cliché dur, un film); (*d*) (*of illness*) affaiblir, amaigrir (qn). **2.** (*a*) **to r. sth. to ashes, to dust,** réduire qch. en cendres, en poussière; mettre qch. en poussière; **clothes reduced to rags,** vêtements à l'état de guenilles; **passions reduced to memories,** passions à l'état de souvenirs; (*b*) **to r. a fraction to lower terms,** réduire une fraction; **to r. a fraction to its lowest, simplest, terms,** simplifier une fraction; ramener une fraction à sa plus simple expression; **to r. kilos to grammes, fractions to the same denominator,** réduire des kilos en grammes, des fractions au même dénominateur; **to r. everything to a single principle,** tout ramener à un seul principe. **3.** (*a*) soumettre, réduire (**s.o. to obedience,** qn à l'obéissance); **to r. s.o. to silence,** faire taire qn; (*b*) *Mil:* réduire (une ville révoltée). **4.** réduire, amener (**s.o. to despair,** qn au désespoir); **he was reduced to begging, to beggary,** il en était réduit, arrivé, venu, à demander l'aumône; il en était réduit à la mendicité; **to r. s.o. to poverty,** mettre qn dans la misère. **5.** (*a*) abaisser (**s.o. to a lower rank,** qn à une situation inférieure); **to r. s.o. to the level of beasts,** ravaler qn au niveau des bêtes; (*b*) *Mil:* réduire (un homme) à un grade inférieur; rétrograder (un sous-officier); **to r. an N.C.O. to the ranks,** dégrader un sous-officier; faire rentrer un sous-officier dans les rangs; casser un sous-officier (de son grade). **6.** *Ch:* réduire, désoxyder (un oxyde); *Metall:* réduire (un minerai). **7.** *Med:* réduire (une fracture); remettre (une épaule démise).
reduced [ri'dju:st], *a.* **1.** réduit; (*a*) **r. scale,** échelle réduite; **much r. capital,** capital fortement ébréché; *Navy:* **ship with a r. crew,** bâtiment *m* en disponibilité armée; (*b*) *Com:* **r. price,** prix réduit, diminué; **at (greatly) r. prices,** au (grand) rabais; en solde; **ticket at r. rate,** billet à tarif réduit; **r. assessment on property,** dégrèvement *m*; (*c*) (*of pers.*) affaibli, amaigri (par la maladie); (*d*) *Adm: A:* (officier) en demi-solde. **2.** appauvri; **in r. circumstances,** dans l'indigence, dans la gêne.
reducer [ri'dju:sər], *s.* **1.** (*a*) *Mec.E: El; etc:* réducteur *m* (d'engrenage, de vitesse, *Mch:* de course, *El:* de tension); *Av: etc:* **noise r.,** réducteur de bruit; (*b*) (manchon) réducteur (pour tuyauterie). **2.** *Ch:* (agent) réducteur. **3.** *Phot:* (af)faiblisseur *m* (de cliché dur); **Farmer's r.,** affaiblisseur de Farmer. **4.** *Med:* (*a*) **fever r.,** antifébrile *m*; (*b*) **fracture r.,** réducteur.
reducibility [ridju:si'biliti], *s.* réductibilité *f.*
reducible [ri'dju:sibl], *a.* (*of amount, fraction, fracture, etc.*) réductible (**to,** à).
reducing[1] [ri'dju:siŋ], *a.* **1.** (*a*) réducteur, -trice; réduisant; *Ch:* **r. agent,** (agent) réducteur (*m*); **r. flame,** flamme réductrice; *Mec.E:* **r. coupling,** manchon réducteur, de réduction; **r. gear** = *reduction gear q.v. under* REDUCTION 3; *Mch:* **r. valve,** valve *f* de réduction; détendeur *m*; réducteur de pression; *Ch:* **r. gas,** gaz réducteur; *Metall:* **r. oven,** four *m* de réduction; *El:* **r. transformer,** transformateur abaisseur; *Av: etc:* **noise r. device,** dispositif réducteur de bruit; (*b*) *Phot:* (bain, etc.) affaiblisseur; **r. agent,** agent d'affaiblissement; (af)faiblisseur *m.* **2.** *Med:* (*a*) (cataplasme, etc.) résolutif; (*b*) (régime, etc.) amaigrissant.
reducing[2], *s.* = REDUCTION *except* **2.** (*b*).
reductase [ri'dʌkteis], *s. Ch:* réductase *f.*
reductio ad absurdum [ri'dʌkʃiouædəb'sə:dəm]. *Lt.phr.* réduction *f* à l'absurde; **r. ad a. reasoning,** raisonnement *m* par l'absurde.
reduction [ri'dʌkʃ(ə)n], *s.* **1.** (*a*) réduction *f* (d'échelle, d'un dessin, etc.); rapetissement *m*; (*in thickness*) amenuisement *m*, amaigrissement *m*, amincissement *m*; (*in length*) raccourcissement *m*; *Metalw:* (*by rolling*) laminage *m*; (*by hammering*) rétreinte *f* (d'une plaque); *Draw:* **r. compasses,** compas *m sg.* de réduction; *Phot:* **r. printing,** tirage *m* par réduction; *Metalw:* **r. roll(er),** cylindre lamineur; **cold r.,** laminage à froid; (*b*) **the r. in her figure,** l'amincissement, l'amaigrissement, de sa taille. **2.** (*a*) diminution *f*, réduction (numérique, etc.); baisse *f*, diminution (de température, *El:* de tension, etc.); **r. of prices, salaries,** réduction, diminution, baisse, des prix, salaires; modération *f* des prix; *Adm:* **r. of charges, duties,** *Rail:* **of carriage,** détaxe *f*; **r. of taxes, taxation,** allégement *m*, modération *f*, des impôts; dégrèvement *m* d'impôts; **r. of an indent,** amputation *f*, retranchement *m*, d'une demande (de fonds, etc.); **r. of excessive expenses,** dégonflement *m* de dépenses excessives; **staff r.,** réduction, compression *f*, du personnel; *Jur:* **r. of sentence,** réduction, remise partielle, relaxation, de peine; *Biol:* **r. division,** mitose réductionnelle; (*b*) *Com:* rabais *m*, remise *f*; **to make a r. on an article,** faire un rabais, une remise, sur un article. **3.** *Mec.E:* réduction (d'engrenage), démultiplication *f*; **r. ratio,** rapport *m* de démultiplication; **r. gear, unit,** (engrenage) démultiplicateur (*m*), réducteur (*m*); **r. gear assembly,** ensemble réducteur, train réducteur; **planetary r. gear,** réducteur à satellites; **worm r. gear,** réducteur à vis sans fin. **4. r. to ashes, to powder,** réduction en cendres, en poudre; **r. of things to order,** rétablissement *m* de l'ordre; *Surv:* **r. to the horizontal,** réduction à l'horizontale; *Mth:* **r. of an equation to its simplest terms,** réduction d'une équation à sa plus simple expression; *Cmptr:* **data r.,** condensation *f*, réduction, de données. **5.** *Ch:* réduction, désoxydation *f* (d'un oxyde); *Metall:* réduction (du minerai); **r. crucible,** creuset *m* de réduction; **r. furnace,** four *m* de réduction. **6.** *Mil:* (*a*) réduction (d'une place forte, etc.); (*b*) **r. in rank, to the next rank,** rétrogradation; **r. to the ranks,** cassation *f.* **7.** *Med:* (*a*) réduction (d'une fracture); **open r.,** réduction sanglante; (*b*) résolution *f* (d'une tumeur). **8.** *Phot:* affaiblissement *m*, atténuation *f* (d'un cliché dur).
reductive [ri'dʌktiv], *a.* réductif, réducteur, -trice.
redunca [ri'dʌŋkə], *s. Z:* redunca *f.*
redundance [ri'dʌndəns], *s.* = REDUNDANCY 1, 2.
redundancy [ri'dʌndənsi], *s.* **1.** *Lit:* redondance *f*; pléonasme *m*, tautologie *f*; **speech full of redundancies,** discours plein de redondances. **2.** surabondance *f*; profusion *f.* **3.** surplus *m*, excédent *m*; *Ind: etc:* surnombre *m*; **r. payment,** indemnité *f* de licenciement (de personnel en surnombre). **4.** *Cmptr:* redondance; **r. check,** contrôle *m* par redondance.
redundant [ri'dʌndənt], *a.* **1.** *Lit:* (mot) redondant, pléonastique, tautologique, parasite; qui fait double emploi (avec un autre). **2.** surabondant, superflu, excessif; **speech without a r. word,** discours sans un mot superflu, sans un mot de trop. **3.** *Ind: etc:* **r. staff,** personnel *m* en surnombre; **to be made r.,** être (déclaré en surnombre et) licencié; (*as a result of automation*) être en chômage technologique. **4.** *Cmptr:* (caractère) redondant, de complément, de garnissage; **r. check,** contrôle *m* par redondance.
redundantly [ri'dʌndəntli], *adv.* **1.** avec redondance. **2.** surabondamment.
reduplicate[1] [ri:'dju:plikət], *a.* **1.** *Gram: Mus: etc:* redoublé. **2.** *Bot:* (*of leaves*) rédupliqué; (*of aestivation*) réduplicatif.
reduplicate[2] [ri:'dju:plikeit], *v.tr.* redoubler, répéter; *Ling:* **reduplicating particle,** particule réduplicative.
reduplicated [ri:dju:plikeitid], *a. Gram:* (verbe, etc.) réduplicatif; **r. perfect,** parfait redoublé.
reduplication [ri:dju:pli'keiʃ(ə)n], *s.* **1.** redoublement *m*, répétition *f.* **2.** *Gram:* redoublement, réduplication *f.*
reduplicative [ri:'dju:plikətiv], *a. Bot:* (*of leaves*) rédupliqué; (*of aestivation*) réduplicatif.
Reduviidae [ridju:'vaiidi:], *s.pl. Ent:* réduviidés *m.*
reduvius [ri'dju:viəs], *s. Ent:* réduve *m.*
redweed ['redwi:d], *s. Bot:* **1.** phytolaque *m*; raisin *m* d'Amérique; épinard *m* de Virginie. **2.** coquelicot *m.*
redwing ['redwiŋ], *s. Orn:* (*a*) (grive *f*) mauvis (*m*); (*b*) *NAm:* **r. (blackbird),** carouge *m* à épaulettes rouges, *Fr.Can:* à épaulettes.
redwood ['redwud], *s.* **1.** *Bot:* sequoia toujours vert; sequoia à feuilles d'if. **2.** *Com:* (*a*) (*timber*) redwood *m*; (*b*) *Dy:* (bois *m* de) brésil (*m*).
redye ['ri:'dai], *v.tr.* (faire) reteindre (ses cheveux, une robe); *Tchn:* ramender, biser (une étoffe).
reebok ['ri:bɔk], *s. Z:* pélée *f*, antilope-chevreuil *f, pl.* antilopes-chevreuils.
re-echo [ri:'ekou]. **1.** *v.tr.* répéter, renvoyer (un son). **2.** *v.i.* retentir, résonner.
reed[1] [ri:d], *s.* **1.** (*a*) *Bot:* roseau *m*; phragmite *m*; jonc *m* (à balais); **bur r.,** ruban *m* d'eau; **r. mace,** massette *f*; canne *f* de jonc; quenouille *f*; *F:* **broken r.,** (i) (*pers.*) fumiste *m*; (ii) chose sur laquelle on ne peut compter; **to lean on a (broken) r.,** s'appuyer sur un roseau; (*b*) *Orn:* **r. warbler, wren, babbler, bird,** (rousserolle *f*) effarvatte *f*; rousserolle, fauvette *f*, des roseaux; **r. bunting, sparrow,** bruant *m* des roseaux; **r. pheasant,** mésange *f* à moustache; (*c*) *coll. O:* chaume *m*, glui *m* (à couvrir les toits). **2.** *Poet:* (*a*) flèche *f*; (*b*) chalumeau *m*, pipeau *m.* **3.** (*a*) *Mus:* anche *f* (de hautbois, de clarinette, etc.); **free r.,** anche libre; **beating, striking, r.,** anche battante; **r. organ,** harmonium *m*; (*of organ*) **r. stop,** jeu *m* d'anches; (*b*) (*in orchestra*) **the reeds,** les instruments *m* à anche; (*c*) *Nau:* **r. horn,** corne *f*, trompe *f*, à anche; (*d*) *Elcs:* **(dry) r. (relay),** relais sec à anche; **r. frequency meter,** fréquencemètre *m* à lame vibrante. **4.** *Tex:* peigne *m* (de métier à tisser); ros *m*, rot *m*; **r.-marked material,** tissu à chaîne irrégulière. **5.** *pl. Arch:* roseaux, rudentures *f*; *Join:* baguettes *f.* **6.** *Physiol:* caillette *f* (d'un ruminant).
reed[2], *v.tr.* **1.** *O:* couvrir (un toit) de chaume. **2.** *Mus:* mettre une anche à (un instrument). **3.** *Tex:* piquer (les fils de la trame) en peigne. **4.** *Arch:* orner (qch.) de roseaux, de rudentures, de cannelures rudentées; *Join:* orner (un meuble) de baguettes.
reedbed ['ri:dbed], *s.* roselière *f.*
reedbuck ['ri:dbʌk], *s. Z:* cervicapre *m*; antilope *f* des roseaux.
reeded ['ri:did], *a.* **1.** = REEDY. **2.** *O:* (toit) couvert de chaume. **3.** *Mus:* (instrument) à anche. **4.** agrémenté (i) *Arch:* de roseaux, de cannelures rudentées, (ii) *Join:* de baguettes.
reedfish ['ri:dfiʃ], *s. Ich:* poisson-roseau *m.*
reeding ['ri:diŋ], *s.* **1.** (*a*) *O:* recouvrement *m* (d'un toit) en chaume; (*b*) *Tex:* piquage *m* en peigne. **2.** *coll. Arch:* roseaux *mpl*; rudentures *fpl*; *Join:* baguettes *fpl*; *Tls:* **r. plane,** doucine *f* (à baguettes).
re-edit [ri:'edit], *v.tr.* rééditer (d'anciens ouvrages); donner une nouvelle édition critique (d'un texte); publier (qch.) avec de nouvelles annotations.
re-editing [ri:'editiŋ], *s.* réédition *f.*
reedling ['ri:dliŋ], *s. Orn:* mésange *f* à moustache.
re-educate [ri:'edjukeit], *v.tr.* (*a*) rééduquer, réadapter (qn); (*b*) *Med:* rééduquer (un paralysé, etc.).
re-education [ri:edju'keiʃ(ə)n], *s.* (*a*) rééducation *f*, réadaptation *f*; (*b*) *Med:* rééducation (d'un paralysé, etc.).
reedy ['ri:di], *a.* **1.** (*a*) abondant en roseaux; plein de, couvert de, roseaux; (*b*) *Poet:* (pipeau, lit, etc.) de roseaux. **2.** (*a*) **r. voice,** voix flûtée; voix ténue; (*b*) **the r. oboe,** le hautbois nasillard. **3.** (*of pers.*) grêle, mince (comme un roseau).
reef[1] [ri:f], *s. Nau:* ris *m*; **to take in a r.,** (i) prendre un ris; (ii) *Fig:* agir avec prudence; veiller au grain; **to shake out a r.,** larguer un ris; **r. knot,** nœud plat, nœud droit; **r. point, line,** garcette *f* de ris; hanet *m*, passeresse *f*; **r. tackle,** palanquin *m*; **r. band,** bande *f* de ris; **r. cringle,** patte *f* de ris; **r. earing,** raban *m* de ris; **rolling r.,** voile *f* à rouleau *m.*
reef[2], *v.tr. Nau:* **1. to r. a sail,** prendre un, des, ris à une voile; **to r. the sails,** prendre les ris; **to full r. the topsails,** prendre le bas ris; mettre les huniers au bas ris. **2.** (*a*) rentrer (le beaupré, le mât de hune); (*b*) (*of paddle wheel*) **to r. the paddles,** rentrer, raccourcir, les aubes.
reef[3], *s.* **1.** (*a*) récif *m*, banc *m*, chaussée *f*; **coral r.,** récif de corail; récif corallien; caye *f*; **fringing r.,** récif frangeant; **submerged r.,** récif sous-marin; écueil *m*, brisant *m*; (*b*) *Fig:* écueil, piège *m.* **2.** *Min:* filon *m*, veine *f*; roche *f* de fond.
reefed [ri:ft], *a.* (voile) à ris; **double-r.,** avec deux ris.
reefer[1] ['ri:fər], *s. Nau:* **1.** (*pers.*) (*a*) cargueur *m*; (*b*) midship(man) *m.* **2.** veste croisée en tissu épais;

vareuse *f*.

reefer[2], *s. F:* cigarette *f* de marihuana.

reefer[3], *s. U.S: F:* frigo *m*.

reefing ['ri:fiŋ], *s.* prise *f* de ris; **r. jacket** = REEFER[1] 2.

reek[1] [ri:k], *s.* **1.** *(a)* odeur forte, âcre, infecte; puanteur *f*; **r. of tobacco,** odeur âcre du tabac; relent *m* de tabac; *(b)* atmosphère nauséabonde, fétide. **2.** *Lit: & Scot: (a)* fumée *f*; *(b)* vapeur *f*, exhalaison *f*; *(on windowpane, etc.)* buée *f*.

reek[2], *v.i.* **1.** sentir mauvais; exhaler une mauvaise odeur, une odeur nauséabonde; **to r. of garlic,** empester l'ail; dégager une odeur d'ail; **his breath reeked of whisky,** il puait le whisky à pleine bouche; **this room reeks of tobacco,** ça empeste le tabac ici; cette salle sent le tabac à plein nez; *(of street, etc.)* **to r. of crime,** exhaler, suer, le crime. **2.** *Lit:* exhaler des vapeurs; fumer; **hands still reeking with blood,** mains encore fumantes de sang. **3.** *Scot: (of something burning, of chimney)* fumer.

Reekie (Auld) [ɔ:ld 'ri:ki], *Pr.n. Scot: F:* = Édimbourg.

reeking ['ri:kiŋ], *a.* **1.** empestant, puant. **2.** *Scot:* fumant.

reeky ['ri:ki], *a.* **1.** qui exhale des vapeurs. **2.** (nuage) de fumée. **3.** *(a)* enfumé, fumeux; *(b)* noirci de fumée.

reel[1] [ri:l], *s.* **1.** *Tex: etc:* dévidoir *m*, bobine *f*, tournette *f*; touret *m* (pour câbles, cordages); moulinet *m* (pour fils métalliques); *Ropem:* caret *m* (de corderie); **(silk) r.,** tracanoir *m*; **r. holder, stand,** porte-bobines *m inv.* **2.** *Fish:* moulinet (de canne à pêche); *Nau:* **log r.,** tour *m*, touret, de loch; *F:* **(straight) off the r.,** de suite, (tout) d'une traite, d'affilée; sans interruption, sans s'arrêter. **3.** *Needlew:* bobine (de coton, de soie); *Typ: etc:* bobine (de papier); **paper in reels,** papier continu; **r.-fed machine,** machine à marge en bobine; *Cin:* **film r.,** (i) bobine; (ii) bande *f*, rouleau *m*, de film; **upper r., top r.,** bobine dérouleuse, débitrice; **lower r., take-up r.,** bobine enrouleuse, réceptrice; *Rec:* **r. to r. tape recorder,** *F:* **r.-to-r.,** magnétophone *m* (à bobines); *Cmptr:* **file r.,** bobine émettrice, débitrice; **machine r.,** bobine réceptrice. **4.** *Paperm:* **entering r.,** rouleau d'entrée; **delivery r.,** rouleau de sortie, **5.** *Mill:* **bolting r.,** blutoire *m*. **6.** *W.Tel:* **aerial, antenna, r.,** rouet *m* d'antenne; *Av:* **r. antenna,** antenne pendante.

reel[2], *v.tr.* *(a) Tex: etc:* dévider, bobiner (le fil, etc.); tracaner (de la soie); **to r. off cocoon silk,** dévider la soie des cocons; *F:* **to r. off verses, a list,** débiter avec facilité, réciter d'un trait, des vers, une liste; *(b) Nau:* **to r. in, up, the log line,** remonter la ligne de loch; **to r. in a fish,** remonter un poisson.

reel[3], *s. Lit: (a)* titubation *f*; démarche chancelante; *(b)* tumulte *m* (des passions, etc.).

reel[4], *v.i.* **1.** tournoyer; **to make s.o.'s senses r.,** donner le vertige à qn; **my head is reeling,** la tête me tourne; **his mind, brain, reeled at the thought,** cette pensée lui donnait le vertige. **2.** *(a) (of pers.)* chanceler, tituber; *(of building)* s'ébranler; **to r. to and fro like a drunken man,** marcher en titubant, vaciller en marchant, aller en zigzag, comme un homme ivre; **he reeled out, back,** il est sorti, il a reculé, en chancelant; **to go reeling down the street,** descendre la rue en titubant; faire des embardées dans la rue; **the front rank reeled under the shock,** le premier rang plia sous le choc; **the ship reeled under the force of the wave,** le navire s'ébranla, s'abattit, sous le coup de la vague; *(b)* **the whole room was reeling,** toute la salle tournoyait autour de moi.

reel[5], *s.* *(a)* danse écossaise à quatre ou à huit (d'un mouvement très vif); branle écossais; **Virginia r.,** contredanse *f*; *(b) Mus:* contredanse.

reel[6], *v.i.* danser le *reel*.

re-elect [ri:i'lekt], *v.tr.* réélire.

re-election [ri:i'lekʃ(ə)n], *s.* réélection *f*.

reeler ['ri:lər], *s. Tex:* dévideur, -euse; bobineur, -euse; **silk r.,** (i) *(pers.)* tireur, -euse, de soie; (ii) *(machine)* tracanoir *m*.

re-eligible [ri:'elidʒibl], *a.* rééligible.

reeling[1] ['ri:liŋ], *s. Tex: etc:* dévidage *m*, bobinage *m*; tracanage *m* (de la soie); **r. machine,** (i) machine *f* à dévider; bobineuse *f*, bobinoir *m*; (ii) *(for silk)* tracanoir *m*.

reeling[2], *a.* *(a)* tournoyant; (tête) qui tourne; *(b)* (personne) qui chancelle, qui titube; **r. gait,** démarche chancelante, titubante.

reeling[3], *s.* = REEL[3].

re-embark [ri:im'bɑ:k]. **1.** *v.tr.* rembarquer. **2.** *v.i.* (se) rembarquer.

re-embarkation [ri:embɑ:'keiʃ(ə)n], *s.* rembarquement *m* (de personnes, de marchandises).

re-emerge [ri:i'mə:dʒ], *v.i.* ressortir, reparaître (à la surface de l'eau); **this problem has re-emerged,** ce problème vient de se reposer.

re-employ [ri:im'plɔi], *v.tr.* reprendre (qn); remployer, réemployer (qch.).

re-employment [ri:im'plɔimənt], *s.* réemploi *m* (de qn, qch.); *Fin:* remploi *m* (de fonds).

re-enact [ri:i'nækt], *v.tr.* **1.** remettre en vigueur, rétablir (une loi). **2.** reconstituer, reproduire (une scène).

re-enactment [ri:i'næktmənt], *s.* **1.** remise *f* en vigueur, rétablissement *m* (d'une loi). **2.** reconstitution *f*, reproduction *f* (d'un crime, etc.).

re-enforce [ri:in'fɔ:s], *v.tr. U.S:* = REINFORCE[2].

re-enforcement [ri:in'fɔ:smənt], *s. U.S:* = REINFORCEMENT.

re-engage [ri:in'geidʒ]. **1.** *v.tr.* *(a)* rengager (des troupes); rengager, réintégrer (des employés); reprendre (un domestique); *(b) Mec.E:* rengrener (une roue dentée, etc.); *Aut:* **to re-e. the clutch,** rembrayer. **2.** *v.i.* se rengager.

re-engagement [ri:in'geidʒmənt], *s.* rengagement *m*.

re-enlist [ri:in'list]. *Mil:* **1.** *v.tr.* rengager (des troupes). **2.** *v.i.* se rengager.

re-enlistment [ri:in'listmənt], *s. Mil:* *(a)* rengagement *m*; *(b) esp. U.S: (pers.)* rengagé, -ée.

re-enter [ri:'entər]. **1.** *v.i.* *(a)* rentrer; *Th:* **re-e. Macbeth,** Macbeth rentre; *(of spacecraft)* **to re-e. (into) the atmosphere,** rentrer dans l'atmosphère; *(b) Mus: (of instrument)* faire une rentrée, faire sa rentrée; *(c)* **to re-e. for an examination,** se présenter de nouveau à un examen; s'inscrire de nouveau pour un examen. **2.** *v.tr.* *(a)* rentrer dans (un endroit); **he never re-entered that house,** il ne rentra jamais dans cette maison; il n'a jamais remis les pieds dans cette maison; *(b)* réinscrire, inscrire de nouveau (**an item in an account,** un article sur un compte); *(c) Cmptr:* réintroduire (des informations); refrapper (des informations sur un clavier); relancer (un sous-programme); *(d) Engr:* revenir sur (un trait) avec le burin.

re-entrance [ri:'entrəns], *s.* = RE-ENTRY 1.

re-entrant [ri:'entrənt]. **1.** *a.* *(of angle, curve)* rentrant; *El:* **re-e. winding,** bobinage *m*, enroulement *m*, fermé; *Elcs:* **re-e. oscillator,** oscillateur *m* à cavités résonnantes en série. **2.** *s.* *(a) Fort:* rentrant *m*; *(b) Geol:* indentation *f*.

re-entry [ri:'entri], *s.* **1.** rentrée *f*; *Mus:* **re-e. of an instrument,** rentrée d'un instrument; *(in fugue)* **re-e. of the subject,** reprise *f* du sujet; *Cards:* **card of re-e.,** carte maîtresse. **2.** réinscription *f*. **3.** *(of spacecraft)* rentrée (dans l'atmosphère); **re-e. window,** corridor *m* d'entrée; **re-e. control system,** dispositif de contrôle de rentrée. **4.** *Cmptr:* réintroduction *f* (d'informations); retour *m* (d'un sous-programme); **re-e. document,** document aller-retour; **re-e. point,** point de retour (d'un sous-programme).

re-equip [ri:i'kwip], *v.tr.* rééquiper.

re-equipment [ri:i'kwipmənt], *s.* rééquipement *m*.

re-erect [ri:i'rekt], *v.tr.* **1.** reconstruire; remonter (une machine). **2.** dresser de nouveau (un mât, etc.).

re-erection [ri:i'rekʃ(ə)n], *s.* **1.** reconstruction *f*; remontage *m* (d'un appareil). **2.** remise *f* en place (d'un mât, d'un poteau).

re-establish [ri:is'tæbliʃ], *v.tr.* rétablir; **to re-e. s.o. in his possessions,** réintégrer qn dans ses biens; **to re-e. s.o. in public esteem,** réhabiliter qn dans l'opinion; **to re-e. the king's authority,** restaurer l'autorité du roi; **to re-e. a company's credit,** raffermir le crédit d'une maison; *Mil:* **to re-e. the line,** redresser la ligne; **to re-e. oneself,** se rétablir.

re-establishment [ri:is'tæbliʃmənt], *s.* rétablissement *m*; relèvement *m* (d'une fortune, etc.); réintégration *f* **(in,** dans); *Mil:* redressement *m* (de la ligne).

reeve[1] [ri:v], *s.* **1.** *Hist:* premier magistrat (d'une ville, d'une région). **2.** *A:* bailli *m*, intendant *m*. **3.** *Can:* président *m* (d'un conseil municipal), *Fr.C:* préfet *m*.

reeve[2], *s. Orn:* chevalier combattant femelle.

reeve[3], *v.tr.* (*p.t.* **rove** [rouv], **reeved;** *p.p.* **reeved, rove,** *A:* **roven** ['rouvn]) *Nau:* **1. to r. a rope,** passer un cordage **(through a block,** dans une poulie); **to r. a tackle,** passer les garants d'un palan; **to r. a rope to, around, a yard,** capeler un cordage sur une vergue, autour d'une vergue. **2.** *(of ship)* **to r. the shoals,** se frayer un chemin à travers les bas-fonds.

reeving ['ri:viŋ], *s. Nau:* passage *m* (d'un cordage); mouflage *m*.

re-examination [ri:igzæmi'neiʃ(ə)n], *s.* **1.** nouvel examen. **2.** *Jur:* nouvel interrogatoire (du témoin par la partie qui l'a fait citer) après l'interrogatoire contradictoire.

re-examine [ri:ig'zæmin], *v.tr.* **1.** *(a)* examiner (qn, qch.) de nouveau; *(b)* réviser (des lois, etc.). **2.** *Jur:* interroger de nouveau (un témoin que l'on a fait citer) après l'interrogatoire contradictoire.

re-exchange [ri:iks'tʃeindʒ], *s.* **1.** nouvel échange. **2.** *Com:* *(a)* rechange *m* (d'une lettre de change); *(b)* retraite *f*.

re-export[1] [ri:'ekspɔ:t], *s.* réexportation *f*; **re-e. trade,** commerce *m* intermédiaire.

re-export[2] [ri:eks'pɔ:t], *v.tr.* réexporter.

re-exportation [ri:ekspɔ:'teiʃ(ə)n], *s.* réexportation *f*.

ref [ref], *s. Sp: F:* arbitre *m*.

reface [ri:'feis], *v.tr.* **1.** revêtir de nouveau, réparer, remaçonner (un mur). **2.** *Mec.E: etc:* refaire les faces, les portées; *I.C.E:* **to r. the valves,** rectifier le siège des soupapes (à la fraise, etc.).

refan [ri:'fæn], *v.tr. Cmptr:* aérer à nouveau (des cartes).

refashion [ri:'fæʃ(ə)n], *v.tr.* refaçonner.

refashioning [ri:'fæʃəniŋ], *s.* refaçon *f*.

refasten [ri:'fɑ:sn], *v.tr.* rattacher; ragrafer.

refection [ri'fekʃ(ə)n], *s.* **1.** rafraîchissement *m*; réparation *f* de forces par la nourriture. **2.** *A:* repas léger; réfection *f*, collation *f*.

refectorian [ri:fek'tɔ:riən], *s. Ecc:* réfectorier, -ière.

refectory [ri'fekt(ə)ri], *s.* réfectoire *m*.

refer [ri'fə:r], *v.* **(referred) 1.** *v.tr.* *(a)* rapporter, rattacher (un fait à une cause, un événement à une date); faire remonter (un événement à une date); attribuer, imputer (qch. à une cause); rapporter (un animal, une plante, à une famille); *Med:* **referred pain,** irradiation *f*; *(b)* **to r. a matter to s.o.,** se, s'en, référer à qn d'une question; *Jur:* référer à qn d'une question; **to r. a request to s.o.,** soumettre une demande à qn; **to r. a question to s.o.'s decision, to s.o.'s judgment,** remettre une question, s'en rapporter, s'en remettre, à la décision de qn; s'en référer à qn, à l'avis de qn; **to r. a matter to a tribunal,** soumettre une affaire à un tribunal; renvoyer une affaire devant un tribunal; **let us r. the dispute to Socrates!** rapportons-nous-en dans cette discussion à Socrate! *(of bank)* **to r. a cheque to drawer,** refuser d'honorer un chèque (faute de provision); **referred to drawer,** voir le tireur; *A:* **I r. myself to your generosity, to your decision,** je m'en remets à votre générosité, à votre décision; *(c)* **to r. s.o. to s.o.,** renvoyer, adresser, qn à qn; **to r. a reader to a work,** renvoyer un lecteur à un ouvrage; *(in book)* **the reader is referred to . . .,** se reporter à . . .; **I referred him to a specialist,** je l'ai renvoyé à un spécialiste; **I have been referred to you,** on m'a recommandé de m'adresser à vous; **if they come I shall r. them to you,** s'ils viennent je vous les renverrai; *(d) Sch: etc:* ajourner, refuser (un candidat). **2.** *v.i.* *(a)* **to r. (back) to an authority,** s'en rapporter à, se reporter à, se référer à, une autorité; consulter une autorité; **I shall have to r. to the board,** il faudra que je consulte le conseil de direction; **to r. to a work,** faire référence à un ouvrage; **to r. to a document,** se reporter à un document; **to r. to a document as proof,** invoquer un document; **for my proof I r. to the passage quoted,** pour la preuve je m'en rapporte au passage cité; **he referred to his watch for the exact time,** il a consulté sa montre pour savoir l'heure exacte; *Com:* **referring to . . .,** nous référant à . . .; **referring to your letter,** comme suite à votre lettre; *(b) (of statement, etc.)* **to r. to sth.,** se rapporter, avoir rapport, avoir trait, à qch.; **this remark refers to you,** cette remarque est à votre adresse; *(c) (of pers.)* faire allusion à (qn); viser (qn); **I r. to you,** c'est de vous que je parle; **I am not referring to you,** je ne veux pas parler de vous; **who are you referring to?** de qui parlez-vous? à qui s'applique cette remarque? *(d) (of pers.)* **to r. to a fact,** faire mention d'un fait; signaler un fait; **the States referred to in this article,** les États visés dans l'article; **referred to as . . .,** désigné sous le nom de . . .; **he never refers to it,** il n'en parle jamais; **we won't r. to it again,** n'en reparlons plus.

referable [ri'fə:rəbl], *a.* *(a)* qu'on peut rapporter, attribuer **(to,** à); qui relève (de qch.); *(b)* **pottery r. to the bronze age,** poteries que l'on peut faire remonter à l'âge de bronze.

referee[1] [refə'ri:], *s.* **1.** *(a) Sp:* arbitre *m*; *(b) Jur:* arbitre (rapporteur); arbitre expert; compromissaire *m*; *(deciding between arbitrators)* tiers arbitre; **board of referees,** commission arbitrale; **Official R.,** juge rapporteur. **2.** personne à qui on peut s'en rapporter pour avoir des références sur qn.

referee[2], *v.i. & tr.* **(refereed)** *Sp: etc:* remplir les fonctions d'arbitre; **to r. (at) a match,** arbitrer un match; **will you r. (the match)?** voulez-vous être arbitre?

reference ['ref(ə)rəns], *s.* **1.** *(a)* renvoi *m* (d'une affaire) devant arbitre; renvoi, référence *f* (d'une question à une autorité, etc.); **he acted without r. to me,** il a agi sans me consulter; *(b)* compétence *f*, pouvoirs *mpl* (d'un tribunal); **terms of r. of a commission, order of r.,** délimitation *f* des pouvoirs d'une commission; mandat *m*, attributions *fpl*, d'une commission; **it is outside the r. of the commission,** c'est hors de la compétence, hors des attributions, de la commission; **under these terms of r.,** aux termes des instructions données. **2.** attribution *f*, rattachement *m* (d'un fait à une cause). **3.** (*a*) **r. to the samples submitted will prove that . . .,** si vous vous reportez aux échantillons soumis vous constaterez que . . .; **with r. to my letter of the 20th March,** me référant à, comme suite à, ma lettre du 20 mars; *Mth:* **to determine the position of a point by r. to two axes,** déterminer la position d'un point en le rapportant à deux axes; **r. system, frame,** référentiel *m*; **r. instrument,** appareil étalon; *El:* **r. circuit,** circuit de référence; *Phot:* **r. plate,** plaque *f* témoin; **r. solution,** solution *f* témoin; *Surv: etc:* **r. mark,** (trait *m*) repère *m*; **r. point,** coordonnée *f*; *Nau:* **r. position,** point *m*, position *f*, de référence; *Ind:* **r. gauge,** calibre *m* étalon; *Atom.Ph:* **r. source,** source (radioactive) de référence; *Cmptr:* **r. tape,** bande étalon, bande maîtresse; **r. table,** barème *m*; consultation *f* (**to a book,** d'un livre); **r. book, work, work of r.,** livre, ouvrage, de référence; ouvrage à consulter. **4.** rapport *m*; **to have r. to sth.,** avoir rapport, avoir trait, se rapporter, à qch.; **success seems to have very little r. to merit,** le succès semble avoir très peu de rapport avec le mérite; **in r., with r., to your letter,** en ce qui concerne votre lettre; relativement à votre lettre . . .; **without r. to . . .,** (i) sans égard pour, indépendamment de . . .; (ii) sans tenir compte de . . .. **5.** allusion *f* (**to,** à), mention *f* (**to,** de); **to make r. to a fact,** faire mention d'un fait, signaler un fait; **(a) r. was made to this conversation,** on a fait mention de, on a fait allusion à, on a parlé de, cette conversation; **this is another matter to which r. must be made,** c'est une autre affaire dont il convient de parler; **if any r. is made to me,** si on parle de moi. **6.** renvoi, référence (dans un livre); indication *f*, renseignement *m* (sur un plan); **to put down references on a map,** renseigner une carte; mettre des cotes, des indications, sur une carte; **r. point,** (i) point de repère; (ii) (*on map*) point coté; **r. square,** carreau-module *m*, *pl.* carreaux-modules; *Adm: Com:* (*at head of letter*) **r. AB,** rappeler dans la réponse AB; référence AB; *Typ:* **r. (mark),** renvoi; **footnote r.,** appel de note; **r. letter,** lettrine *f*. **7.** (*a*) renseignements *mpl*; références *fpl* (d'employé, etc.); **to give a r. (about s.o.),** fournir des renseignements sur qn; *Com: etc:* **to take up s.o.'s references,** prendre des renseignements sur qn; **to have good references,** avoir de bonnes références, de bonnes recommandations; (*b*) personne à qui on peut s'en rapporter pour avoir des références sur qn; *Jur:* répondant *m*; **who are your references?** quelles sont les personnes que vous pouvez donner en référence? **to give s.o. as a r.,** se recommander de qn; **you may use my name as (a) r.,** vous pouvez vous réclamer de moi; vous pouvez donner mon nom comme référence.

referendary [refə'rend(ə)ri], *a. & s.* référendaire (*m*); *Fr.Hist:* **Great R.,** Grand Référendaire (du Sénat impérial).

referendum [refə'rendəm], *s. Pol:* referendum *m*, référendum *m*; plébiscite *m*; *Sw.Fr:* votation *f* populaire.

referential [refə'renʃ(ə)l], *a.* qui renvoie à qch.; référant à qch.

referring [ri'fə:riŋ], *s.* (*a*) référence *f* (de qch. à une autorité); attribution *f*, rattachement *m* (d'un fait à une cause); (*b*) renvoi *m* (d'une affaire devant un tribunal, etc.); (*c*) *Sch: etc:* ajournement *m*, refus *m* (d'un candidat).

refill[1] ['ri:fil], *s.* objet *m* de remplacement, de rechange; recharge *f*, cartouche *f* (de stylo, de briquet); recharge (pour un tube de rouge à lèvres, etc.); mine *f* de rechange (pour porte-mine); feuilles *fpl* de rechange (pour carnet à feuilles mobiles), etc.

refill[2] [ri:'fil]. **1.** *v.tr.* remplir (qch.) (à nouveau); regarnir (un rayon, etc., *Mec.E:* des coussinets); **to r. the tanks with water,** regarnir les réservoirs d'eau; **to r. an oxygen cylinder,** recharger une bouteille d'oxygène; *Sm.a:* **to r. (a magazine),** réapprovisionner; **I refilled his glass,** j'ai rempli son verre; (*of bottle*) **not to be refilled,** ne pas réutiliser. **2.** *v.i.* se remplir à nouveau.

refilling [ri:'filiŋ], *s.* (nouveau) remplissage; rechargement *m*; recharge *f* (d'une bouteille d'oxygène); *Mec.E:* regarnissage *m* (des coussinets); *Sm.a:* **r. (of magazine),** réapprovisionnement *m*; *Mil:* **r. point,** centre de ravitaillement.

refine [ri'fain]. **1.** *v.tr.* (*a*) raffiner, affiner (les métaux); purger (l'or); raffiner (le sucre); raffiner, épurer (le pétrole); **to r. cast iron,** raffiner la fonte; **to r. pig iron,** blanchir la fonte en gueuses; (*b*) raffiner (les plaisirs, les goûts, la langue); épurer, purifier (les mœurs). **2.** *v.i.* (*a*) (*of metals, sugar, etc.*) s'affiner, se raffiner, s'épurer; (*b*) (*of taste, manners*) se raffiner; (*of morals*) s'épurer, se purifier; (*c*) (*of pers.*) renchérir (**on,** sur); *Lit:* **to r. on a question,** subtiliser sur une question.

refined [ri'faind], *a.* **1.** (or) fin, affiné; (pétrole) raffiné, épuré. **2.** (goût, homme) raffiné; (goût) délicat; (homme) distingué, cultivé.

refinement [ri'fainmənt], *s.* **1.** affinage *m* (des métaux); raffinage *m* (du sucre); raffinage, épuration *f* (des huiles). **2.** raffinement *m* (du goût, de qn); pureté *f* (des mœurs); **a person of r.,** un(e) raffiné(e); un(e) délicat(e); **to acquire r.,** se raffiner; **lack of r.,** vulgarité *f*. **3.** (*a*) raffinement, subtilité *f* (de la pensée); **r. of cruelty,** raffinement de cruauté; **without going into refinements,** sans entrer dans des subtilités; (*b*) **machine with all the latest refinements,** machine avec les perfectionnements les plus récents.

refiner [ri'fainər], *s.* raffineur, -euse (de pétrole, de sucre); affineur, -euse (de métaux).

refinery [ri'fainəri], *s. Ind:* raffinerie *f*, affinerie *f*; usine *f* de raffinage, d'affinage; **iron r.,** finerie *f*, mazerie *f*.

refining [ri'fainiŋ], *s.* **1.** affinage *m*, raffinage *m*, affinement *m* (des métaux); affinage, finage *m* (de la fonte); blanchiment *m* (de la fonte brute); raffinage (du sucre); raffinage, épuration *f* (des huiles); *Ind:* **r. furnace,** four *m* d'affinage, à affiner; *Metall:* finerie *f*, mazerie *f*; **r. works,** affinerie *f*; **r. point of a metal,** point de transformation d'un métal. **2.** raffinement *m* (des goûts); épuration *f* (des mœurs).

refit[1] ['ri:fit], *s.* **1.** *Nau:* (*a*) carénage *m*, radoub *m*, réparation *f*; (*b*) réarmement *m*, refonte *f* (d'un navire). **2.** rajustement *m*; réaménagement *m*, regarnissement *m* (d'une usine, etc.); remontage *m* (d'une arme à feu, d'une machine).

refit[2] [ri:'fit], *v.tr.* (**refitted**) remettre en état de service. **1.** *Nau:* (i) caréner, radouber, réparer; (ii) réarmer, refondre (un navire); *v.i.* (*of ship*) (i) réparer ses avaries; être au carénage; (ii) réarmer. **2.** rajuster (une machine, etc.); **to r. bearings,** remplacer des coussinets; **to r. valves,** roder des soupapes. **3.** réaménager, regarnir, remonter (une usine, etc.).

refitting [ri:'fitiŋ], *s.* = REFIT[1].

reflate [ri:'fleit], *v.tr. Pol.Ec:* ranimer, relancer (l'économie, etc.).

reflation [ri:'fleiʃ(ə)n], *s. Pol.Ec:* reflation *f*, expansion *f*, ranimation *f*; nouvelle inflation fiduciaire.

reflect [ri'flekt]. **1.** *v.tr.* (*a*) (*of surface*) réfléchir (la lumière, le son, une image); renvoyer (la chaleur, la lumière); refléter (la lumière, la couleur); répéter (une image); **to be reflected,** se réfléchir; **trees reflected in the water,** arbres qui se reflètent dans l'eau; **language always reflects the outlook of its generation,** la langue est toujours le reflet de l'esprit de chaque génération; **what I said in no way reflected what I was feeling,** mes paroles ne reflétaient nullement mes sentiments; **his words r. his thoughts,** ses paroles traduisent ses pensées; *Ph: etc:* **reflected light, wave,** lumière, onde, réfléchie; *Atom.Ph:* **reflected reactor,** pile, réacteur, à réflecteur; (*b*) **action that reflects credit on s.o.,** action qui fait honneur à qn; **to r. discredit on s.o.,** nuire à la réputation de qn; déshonorer, diffamer (qn); (*of behaviour*) **to be reflected on s.o. (else),** rejaillir, se refléter, sur qn. **2.** *v.i.* (*a*) **to r. on sth.,** réfléchir à, sur, qch.; méditer sur qch.; **to r. that . . .,** penser, se dire, que . . .; **to r. how, why, whether . . .,** se demander comment, pourquoi, si . . .; (*b*) **to r. on s.o.,** faire des réflexions à qn; adresser une critique, un reproche, à qn; critiquer, blâmer, qn; **to r. on s.o.'s honesty,** porter atteinte à, élever des doutes sur, l'honnêteté de qn; (*c*) (*of action, etc.*) **to r. (badly) on s.o.,** faire du tort à qn; nuire à (la réputation de) qn.

reflectance [ri'flektəns], *s.* (*a*) *Opt:* réflectance *f*, pouvoir réflecteur (d'une surface); (*b*) *Ph:* coefficient *m*, facteur *m*, de réflexion.

reflecting[1] [ri'flektiŋ], *a.* (miroir, etc.) réflecteur, catoptrique; **r. capacity, power,** pouvoir de réflexion; **r. material,** matière réfléchissante, de réflexion; **r. surface,** surface réfléchissante; *Phot:* **r. viewfinder,** viseur obscur, à chambre noire; *Elcs:* **r. electrode,** électrode *f* de réflexion.

reflecting[2], *s.* réfléchissement *m*, réflexion *f*, renvoi *m* (de la lumière).

reflection [ri'flekʃ(ə)n], *s.* **1.** (*a*) réflexion *f*, réfléchissement *m* (de la lumière, d'un son, d'une image); réverbération *f* (de la lumière); *Atom.Ph:* réflexion (d'un faisceau de neutrons, etc.); **(study of) r.,** catoptrique *f*; **r. meter,** réflectomètre *m*; *Elcs:* **r. electrode,** électrode *f* de réflexion; (*b*) **point of r. of a curve,** point de rebroussement d'une courbe. **2.** reflet *m*, image (réfléchie); **the r. of the trees on, in, the water,** le reflet des arbres dans l'eau; **to see one's r. in a mirror,** voir son image dans un miroir; **his fame is but a pale r. of that of his father,** sa réputation n'est qu'un pâle reflet de celle de son père. **3.** (*a*) blâme *m*, critique *f* (**on,** de); **to cast reflections on s.o.,** critiquer, blâmer, qn; faire des réflexions à qn; (*b*) **this is a r. on your character,** c'est une atteinte à votre intégrité. **4.** (*a*) réflexion, discernement *m*; (*b*) **on r.,** en y réfléchissant; (toute) réflexion faite; à la réflexion; tout bien réfléchi; **to do sth. without due r., without sufficient r.,** faire qch. sans avoir suffisamment réfléchi; faire qch. à l'étourdie; **danger that gives cause for r.,** danger qui donne à réfléchir. **5. reflections,** réflexions, pensées *f*, maximes *f*; **reflections on history,** considérations *f* sur l'histoire.

reflective [ri'flektiv], *a.* **1.** (*of surface*) qui réfléchit; réflecteur (*no f.*); réfléchissant, réflectif; **r. power,** pouvoir réfléchissant, réflecteur, de réflexion; réflectance *f*; **r. galvanometer,** galvanomètre à miroir; *Cmptr:* **r. foil, strip,** marque réfléchissante (de bande). **2.** (*a*) (homme, esprit) réfléchi; (*b*) (facultés) de réflexion. **3.** *Gram:* réfléchi.

reflectively [ri'flektivli], *adv.* **1.** avec réflexion; d'un air réfléchi. **2.** indirectement; par ricochet.

reflectiveness [ri'flektivnis], *s.* caractère réfléchi (de qn).

reflectivity [ri:flek'tiviti], *s. Ph: etc:* (i) réflectivité *f*; (ii) réflectance *f*.

reflectometer [ri:flek'tɔmitər], *s. Opt:* réflectomètre *m*.

reflector [ri'flektər], *s.* (*a*) appareil *m* à surface réfléchissante; *Phot: Ac: Atom.Ph: etc:* réflecteur *m*; *Elcs: W.Tel:* **aerial r.,** réflecteur d'antenne; *El:* **hole r.,** réflecteur à charbon passant; **corner r.,** (i) dièdre *m* d'aérien; (ii) *Rad:* réflecteur métallique; *Cy: etc:* **(red) r.,** cataphote *m*, catadioptre *m*; (*b*) *Opt:* réflecteur; télescope *m* (à réflexion, à miroir).

reflex[1] ['ri:fleks], *s.* **1.** reflet *m*. **2.** (*a*) *Physiol:* réflexe *m*; **knee r.,** réflexe rotulien; **Achilles' r.,** réflexe achilléen; **plantar r.,** réflexe plantaire; **to have good reflexes,** avoir du réflexe, des réflexes; avoir une bonne réflectivité; (*b*) *Ent:* **bleeding reflexes,** auto-hémorrhée *f*.

reflex[2], *a.* **1.** *Physiol:* (acte) réflexe; **r. arc,** arc *m* réflexe. **2.** (*of influence, etc.*) indirect. **3.** (*of thoughts, etc.*) introspectif. **4.** (*of light, etc.*) réfléchi, reflété; *Mth:* **r. angle,** angle rentrant. **5.** *Bot:* réfléchi. **6.** *Phot:* **r. (camera),** (appareil *m*) reflex *m*; **single lens, twin lens, r.,** reflex à un objectif, à deux objectifs. **7.** *W.Tel:* **r. set,** poste monté en reflex; *Elcs:* **r. amplification,** amplification réflexe; **r. circuit,** circuit reflex; *Ac:* **bass r.,** baffle *m* réflexe, écran *m* réflexe; bass-reflex *m*. **8.** *Typ: etc:* **r. copying,** copie réflexe; **r. paper,** papier réflexe.

reflexed [ri'flekst], *a. Bot:* réfléchi, recourbé.

reflexibility [rifleksi'biliti], *s. Ph:* réflexibilité *f*.

reflexible [ri'fleksibl], *a. Ph:* (rayon) réflexible.

reflexion [ri'flekʃ(ə)n], *s.* = REFLECTION.

reflexive [ri'fleksiv], *a. & s.* (*a*) *Gram:* **r. (verb),** verbe réfléchi; **r. (pronoun),** pronom (personnel) réfléchi; (*b*) *Phil: etc:* réflexif; *Mth:* **r. relation,** relation réflexive.

reflexively [ri'fleksivli], *adv. Gram:* au sens réfléchi.

reflexogenic [rifleksou'dʒenik], *a. Physiol:* réflexogène.

reflexologic [rifleksə'lɔdʒik], *a. Psy: Med:* réflexologique.

reflexologist [ri:flek'sɔlədʒist], *s. Psy: Med:* réflexologiste *mf*.

reflexology [ri:flek'sɔlədʒi], *s. Psy: Med:* réflexologie *f*.

refloat [ri:'flout], *v.tr.* **1.** renflouer, afflouer, relever, (re)mettre à flot, déséchouer (un navire échoué). **2.** *Fin:* (*a*) émettre de nouveau (un emprunt); (*b*) renflouer (une entreprise, une société).

refloating [ri:'floutiŋ], *s.* **1.** *Nau:* renflouement *m*, afflouage *m*, mise *f* à flot, déséchouage *m*. **2.** *Fin:* (*a*) nouvelle émission (d'un emprunt); (*b*) renflouement *m* (d'une société, etc.).

reflorescence [ri:flɔ:'res(ə)ns], *s.* refleurissement *m*.

refluence ['refluəns], *s.* refluement *m*, reflux *m*.

refluent ['refluənt], *a.* qui reflue.

reflux ['ri:flʌks], *s.* **1.** reflux *m*; refluement *m*; **r. valve,** soupape *f* de reflux; *Ch:* **r. condenser,** condenseur *m* à reflux. **2.** (*tide*) jusant *m*.

refold [ri:'fould], *v.tr.* replier, replisser.

reforest [ri:'fɔrist], *v.tr.* reboiser (un terrain).

reforestation [ri:fɔris'teiʃ(ə)n], *s.* reboisement (d'un terrain).

reform[1] [ri'fɔ:m], *s.* (*a*) réforme *f* (d'un abus, du calendrier, etc.); *A:* **r. school,** centre *m* d'éducation surveillée; *Hist:* **R. Bill, Act,** Bill *m*, Acte *m*, de réforme; (*b*) retour *m* (de qn) à la vertu.

reform[2]. **1.** *v.tr.* (*a*) réformer (une institution, un abus); améliorer (un système, etc.); **to r. an administration,** apporter des réformes à une administration; **Reformed Church,** Église réformée; (*b*) corriger (qn); ramener (qn) au bien; **to r. oneself,** se corriger; (*c*) *U.S: Jur:* corriger (un document). **2.** *v.i.* se corriger.

re(-)form [ri:'fɔ:m]. **1.** *v.tr.* reformer (un bataillon, etc.). **2.** *v.i.* (*of troops*) se reformer.

reformable [ri'fɔ:məbl], *a.* réformable, corrigible.

reformation [refə'meiʃ(ə)n], *s.* **1.** réforme *f*; *Rel.H:* **the R.,** la Réforme, la Réformation. **2.** retour *m* (de qn) à la vertu; changement *m* de conduite.

re(-)formation [ri:fɔ:'meiʃ(ə)n], *s.* nouvelle formation (de troupes, etc.).

reformational [refə'meiʃənəl], *a. Rel.H:* de la Réforme, de la Réformation.

reformative [ri'fɔ:mətiv], *a.* (mesures, etc.) de réforme.

reformatory [ri'fɔ:mət(ə)ri]. **1.** *a.* (mesures, etc.) de réforme. **2.** *s.* (*a*) *Hist:* école *f* de réforme; maison *f* de correction; (*b*) *NAm:* centre *m* d'éducation surveillée.

reformer [ri'fɔ:mər], *s.* **1.** réformateur, -trice; réformiste *mf.* **2.** *Rel.H:* réformateur.

reforming[1] [ri'fɔ:miŋ], *a.* réformateur, -trice.

reforming[2], *s.* **1.** réforme *f* (d'un abus, etc.). **2.** *Petr: etc:* reformage *m*, reforming *m* (de l'essence, etc.).

reformism [ri'fɔ:mizm], *s. Pol:* réformisme *m.*

reformist [ri'fɔ:mist]. **1.** *a. & s. Pol: etc:* réformateur, -trice; réformiste (*mf*). **2.** *Rel.H:* (*a*) *a.* réformateur; réformiste; (*b*) *s.* réformateur; partisan, -ane, de la Réforme.

refract [ri'frækt], *v.tr. Ph:* réfracter, faire dévier (un rayon lumineux); **to be refracted,** se réfracter.

refracting [ri'fræktiŋ], *a. Ph:* réfringent, réfractif, réfractant, réfracteur, -trice; **double r.,** à double réfraction, biréfringent; **r. angle,** angle réfringent (d'un prisme); **r. (optical) system,** dispositif *m* (optique) à réfraction.

refraction [ri'frækʃ(ə)n], *s. Ph: Opt: Atom.Ph:* réfraction *f*; **double r.,** double réfraction, biréfringence *f*; **angle of r.,** angle *m* de réfraction.

refractive [ri'fræktiv], *a.* réfractif, réfringent; **r. index,** indice *m* de réfraction; **r. power,** pouvoir réfractif, pouvoir réfringent; réfringence *f*; **r. (optical) system,** dispositif *m* (optique) à réfraction; **doubly r.,** biréfringent.

refractivity [ri:fræk'tiviti], *s.* réfringence *f.*

refractometer [ri:fræk'tɔmitər], *s.* réfractomètre *m*; **immersion, dipping, r.,** réfractomètre à immersion; **parallax r.,** réfractomètre à parallaxe.

refractometry [ri:fræk'tɔmitri], *s.* réfractométrie *f.*

refractor [ri'fræktər], *s. Opt:* **1.** (*a*) milieu réfringent; (*b*) dispositif réfringent, réfractif; lentille *f*, loupe *f*. **2.** réfracteur *m*; lunette *f* (d'approche); longue-vue *f*, *pl.* longues-vues.

refractoriness [ri'frækt(ə)rinis], *s.* **1.** indocilité *f*, insoumission *f*, récalcitrance *f*. **2.** (*a*) *Ch: Miner: etc:* nature *f* réfractaire; réfractérité *f*; (*b*) *Med:* (i) opiniâtreté *f* (d'une toux, etc.); (ii) immunité *f* (contre une maladie).

refractory[1] [ri'frækt(ə)ri], *a.* **1.** (*of pers.*) réfractaire, indocile, rebelle, récalcitrant, insoumis, indiscipliné. **2.** *Ch: Miner:* réfractaire, apyre; **r. ores,** minerais *m* rebelles. **3.** *Med:* (*a*) (fièvre, etc.) opiniâtre; (*b*) (personne, animal) réfractaire; (*c*) **r. period, phase,** période réfractaire.

refractory[2], *s.* réfractaire *m*; *Ch: Metalw:* **basic r.,** réfractaire basique.

refrain[1] [ri'frein], *s. Pros: Mus:* refrain *m.*

refrain[2]. **1.** *v.i.* se retenir, s'abstenir (**from,** de); **to r. from doing sth.,** s'abstenir de faire qch.; **she couldn't r. from crying,** elle avait peine à retenir ses larmes, à se retenir de pleurer; **to r. from useless words,** se garder de paroles inutiles; **he couldn't r. from smiling,** il n'a pu s'empêcher de sourire; **he can't r. from mentioning it,** il ne peut se passer d'en parler; **we have refrained from entering into further detail,** nous nous sommes interdit d'entrer dans d'autres détails. **2.** *v.tr. A:* refréner, retenir, contenir (ses passions); mettre un frein à (ses passions, etc.).

reframe [ri:'freim], *v.tr.* **1.** encadrer de nouveau (un tableau); mettre un nouveau cadre à (un tableau). **2.** façonner (qch.) à nouveau, refaire (qch.). **3.** remanier (une phrase, etc.).

refrangibility [rifrændʒi'biliti], *s. Ph: Opt:* réfrangibilité *f.*

refrangible [ri'frændʒibl], *a. Ph: Opt:* réfrangible.

refresh [ri'freʃ]. **1.** *v.tr.* (*a*) (*of food, drink*) rafraîchir, remonter (qn); (*of rest, amusement*) reposer, délasser, récréer, réconforter (qn); **to r. the eye, the mind,** reposer l'œil, l'esprit; **to r. oneself,** se restaurer; se rafraîchir; **I feel refreshed after my meal,** le repas m'a remis, m'a ravivé; **to awake refreshed,** s'éveiller bien reposé; *Lit:* **to r. the inner man,** se refaire, se restaurer; (*b*) rafraîchir (la mémoire); **to r. one's memory,** se dérouiller la mémoire; **to r. one's memory of, about, sth.,** se mettre qch. en mémoire; renouveler le souvenir de qch.; (*c*) ranimer (un feu éteint); (*d*) (*of rain, etc.*) rafraîchir (l'air). **2.** *v.i.* (*a*) se rafraîchir, se reposer; (*b*) se restaurer.

refresher [ri'freʃər], *s.* **1.** personne *f*, chose *f*, qui rafraîchit. **2.** *F:* (*food, drink*) rafraîchissement(s) *m*(*pl*). **3.** rafraîchissement (de la mémoire); **r. course,** (i) cours *m* d'entretien, de perfectionnement; (ii) recyclage *m*. **4.** *Jur:* honoraires supplémentaires (payés à l'avocat en cas de prolongation de l'affaire).

refreshing [ri'freʃiŋ], *a.* rafraîchissant; réparateur, -trice; délassant, qui repose; **r. sleep,** sommeil reposant, réparateur; **r. cup of tea,** tasse de thé ravigotante; **r. innocence,** aimable innocence; **it was quite r. to hear him,** cela faisait du bien de l'entendre.

refreshingly [ri'freʃiŋli], *adv.* d'une manière qui vous fait du bien, qui repose, qui fait plaisir.

refreshment [ri'freʃmənt], *s.* **1.** (*a*) rafraîchissement *m*, délassement *m*, repos *m*; (*b*) **to have some r.,** manger, boire, qch.; se désaltérer; se rafraîchir; **to order some r.,** commander à manger, à boire; *Rail: A:* **r. room,** buffet *m* (de gare); **r. Sunday,** le quatrième dimanche de carême. **2.** **refreshments,** rafraîchissements, sandwichs, boissons, etc. (servis à un buffet, à une soirée, etc.).

refrigerant [ri'fridʒərənt]. **1.** *a. & s. Med:* réfrigérant (*m*). **2.** *s. Ind:* (*freezing agent*) (mélange) réfrigérant; mélange frigorifique; substance réfrigérante.

refrigerate [ri'fridʒəreit]. **1.** *v.tr. Ind:* réfrigérer, frigorifier, refroidir; **refrigerated meat,** viande frigorifiée; *F:* congelé *m*; **refrigerated lorry,** camion frigorifique, réfrigéré; **refrigerated ship, car,** (navire *m*, wagon *m*) frigorifique *m*. **2.** *v.i.* (se) refroidir; se réfrigérer.

refrigerating[1] [ri'fridʒəreitiŋ], *a.* (*of temperature, etc.*) réfrigérant, frigorifique.

refrigerating[2], *s.* réfrigération *f*, frigorification *f*; refroidissement *m*; **the r. industry,** l'industrie *f* du froid; **r. plant,** installation *f*, matériel *m*, frigorifique; **r. equipment, system,** système, dispositif, de refroidissement; **r. machine,** machine *f* frigorifique; appareil réfrigérateur; glacière *f*; **r. engineer,** (ingénieur *m*) frigoriste *m.*

refrigeration [rifridʒə'reiʃ(ə)n], *s.* réfrigération *f*; frigorification *f* (de la viande); **the r. industry,** l'industrie *f* du froid; **industrial r.,** froid industriel.

refrigerative [ri'fridʒərətiv], *a. Med:* réfrigérant, réfrigératif.

refrigerator [ri'fridʒəreitər], *s.* (*a*) réfrigérateur *m*, *F:* glacière *f*; (*b*) *Ind:* machine *f* frigorifique; appareil réfrigérateur; congélateur *m*; (*c*) chambre *f* frigorifique; étuve froide; **r. van,** camion réfrigéré; *Rail:* **r. van,** *NAm:* **car,** (wagon *m*) frigorifique *m.*

refrigeratory [ri'fridʒərət(ə)ri]. **1.** *s.* réfrigérant *m* (d'alambic). **2.** *a.* réfrigérant, frigorifique.

refringency [ri'frindʒənsi], *s. Ph:* réfringence *f* (d'un cristal, etc.).

refringent [ri'frindʒənt], *a. Ph:* réfringent.

refuel [ri:'fjuəl], *v.* (**refuelled**) **1.** *v.tr.* ravitailler, réapprovisionner (un navire, un avion). **2.** *v.i.* (*a*) *Nau: etc:* mazouter; se ravitailler, se réapprovisionner (en combustible); *Av:* se ravitailler (en carburant); **to r. in flight,** se ravitailler en vol; (*b*) *Atom.Ph:* recharger (la pile, le réacteur, en combustible); changer le combustible.

refuelling [ri:'fjuəliŋ], *s.* (*a*) *Av: Nau: Veh:* (i) ravitaillement *m*, réapprovisionnement *m*, en combustible, en carburant; (ii) *Aut: Av:* le plein, le remplissage (du réservoir); *Av:* **r. airfield,** aérodrome *m* de ravitaillement; **r. boom,** perche *f* de ravitaillement en vol; **r. wagon,** camion-citerne *m*, *pl.* camions-citernes (d'aérodrome); **r. point,** (i) *Aut: Av:* poste *m*, station *f*, de ravitaillement (en carburant); (ii) *Av: Ball:* prise de ravitaillement en combustible, en carburant (sur un avion, etc.); **r. station,** poste de ravitaillement; (*b*) *Atom.Ph:* recharge *f* (de la pile, du réacteur, en combustible); changement *m* de combustible.

refuge[1] ['refju:dʒ], *s.* **1.** (*a*) refuge *m*, abri *m* (**from,** contre); **place of r.,** lieu *m* de refuge, d'asile; **haven, harbour, of r.,** port *m* de refuge, de salut; *A:* **(house of) r.,** (maison *f* de) refuge; hospice *m*; *B:* **city of r.,** ville de refuge; **to seek r.,** chercher refuge; **to take r.,** se réfugier (dans une église, chez qn, etc.); **to take r. in lying, behind a pretext,** se réfugier dans les mensonges; se retrancher derrière un prétexte; (*b*) (*pers.*) refuge; **God is my r.,** Dieu est mon recours, mon refuge. **2.** (*a*) lieu de refuge, d'asile; *A:* **night r.,** asile *m* de nuit; (*b*) (*in road*) refuge.

refuge[2]. *A:* **1.** *v.tr.* donner un asile, un refuge, à (qn). **2.** *v.i.* se réfugier.

refugee [refju:'dʒi:], *s.* réfugié, -ée.

refulgence [ri'fʌldʒəns], *s.* splendeur *f*, éclat *m.*

refulgent [ri'fʌldʒənt], *a.* resplendissant, éclatant; **r. smile,** sourire qui illumine le visage.

refund[1] ['ri(:)fʌnd], *s.* (*a*) *Com: etc:* remboursement *m*; **to obtain a r. of the money deposited,** se faire rembourser le cautionnement versé; (*b*) *Adm:* ristourne *f*; (*c*) *Jur:* restitution *f* d'indu.

refund[2] [ri(:)'fʌnd], *v.tr.* **1.** (*a*) rembourser (de l'argent, un paiement) (**to s.o.,** à qn); **to r. the cost of postage,** rembourser les frais de port; **to have money refunded,** rencaisser de l'argent; (*b*) ristourner (un paiement en trop); restituer (de l'argent); (*c*) *v.i. Jur:* faire restitution d'indu. **2.** **to r. s.o.,** rembourser qn.

re(-)fund [ri(:)'fʌnd], *v.tr.* fonder de nouveau (une dette).

refundable [ri(:)'fʌndəbl], *a.* remboursable (**over 25 years,** sur 25 ans).

refunding [ri(:)'fʌndiŋ], *s.* remboursement *m*; **r. loan,** emprunt *m* de remboursement.

refundment [ri(:)'fʌndmənt], *s.* remboursement *m.*

refurbish [ri:'fə:biʃ], *v.tr.* remettre à neuf, rénover.

refurbishment [ri:'fə:biʃmənt], *s.* remise *f* à neuf.

refurnish [ri:'fə:niʃ], *v.tr.* **1.** remeubler, regarnir, meubler de neuf (un appartement); remonter (un ménage). **2.** fournir, pourvoir, de nouveau.

refusable [ri'fju:zəbl], *a.* refusable.

refusal [ri'fju:z(ə)l], *s.* **1.** (*a*) refus *m*; **r. to stop,** refus de s'arrêter; **his r. of the job,** son refus d'accepter le poste; **r. to obey an order,** refus d'obéissance à un ordre; **to give a flat r.,** refuser (tout) net; **I will take no r.,** je n'admets pas de refus; (*b*) *Com:* **r. of goods,** refus de marchandises; (*c*) *Jur:* **r. of justice,** déni *m* de justice; (*d*) *Equit:* refus, dérobade *f*. **2.** droit *m* de refuser; droit de préemption; **to have the r. of sth.,** (i) avoir le droit d'accepter ou de refuser qch.; (ii) n'avoir qu'à dire le mot pour avoir qch.; **to have (the) first r. of sth.,** avoir la première offre de qch.; **he has not had, has not been given, the r. of it,** ce n'est pas à son refus. **3.** *Civ.E:* **to drive a pile to r.,** battre, enfoncer, un pieu (jusqu')à refus (de mouton); **pile driven to r.,** pieu qui refuse (le mouton).

refuse[1] ['refju:s]. **1.** *s.* rebut *m*, déchets *mpl*, détritus *m*, ordures *fpl*; épluchures *fpl* (de légumes, etc.); *Tex:* coron *m* (de laine); **household r.,** ordures ménagères; **town r.,** ordures de ville; résidus urbains; **garden r.,** balayures *fpl*, détritus, de jardin; **r. bin,** boîte à ordures (ménagères); poubelle *f*; **r. dump,** voirie *f*, dépotoir *m*; **r. collection,** service *m* de voirie. **2.** *a.* de rebut; *Const:* **r. material,** détritus de matériaux; *For:* **r. wood,** bois de déchet; *Ind:* **r. water,** eaux-vannes *fpl.*

refuse[2] [ri'fju:z], *v.*

I. *v.tr.* **1.** refuser (une offre, un don, qn comme mari); **that is not to be refused,** cela n'est pas de refus; **to r. a hundred pounds for a picture,** refuser cent livres d'un tableau. **2.** (*a*) rejeter, repousser (une requête); **to r. s.o. sth.,** refuser qch. à qn; (*of pers.*) **to r. obedience,** refuser obéissance; (*of pers., limbs*) **to r. to obey,** refuser d'obéir; **to r. s.o. admittance,** refuser (de laisser entrer) qn; **to be refused sth.,** essuyer un refus; **he was refused a hearing,** on refusa de l'entendre; **I don't see how we can r. them,** je ne vois pas comment on peut le leur refuser; **I have never been refused,** on ne m'a jamais rien refusé; **she refused to be seen home,** elle a refusé qu'on la raccompagne; elle a refusé l'offre qu'on lui a faite de la reconduire; (*b*) **to r. to do sth.,** refuser de faire qch.; se refuser, résister, à faire qch.; **when he refused to do it,** sur son refus de le faire; **to r. to admit that s.o. has any talent,** refuser tout talent à qn; *v.i.* **I asked him to come but he refused,** je l'ai prié de venir mais il a refusé. **3.** *Mil:* **to r. a wing,** refuser l'aile; **refused wing,** aile refusée. **4.** **horse that refuses the fences,** cheval qui refuse, qui se dérobe (devant les obstacles).

II. *v.i.* **1.** *Cards:* ne pas fournir (la couleur). **2.** (*of horse*) **to r. at a fence,** refuser, se dérober, devant un obstacle. **3.** (*of foundation pile, bolt, etc.*) refuser.

re-fuse [ri:'fju:z], *v.tr.* refondre.

refuser [ri'fju:zər], *s.* **1.** refuseur, -euse; refusant, -ante. **2.** *Equit:* cheval *m* qui refuse.

re-fusion [ri:'fju:ʒ(ə)n], *s.* refonte *f.*

refutable ['refjutəbl, ri'fju:təbl], *a.* réfutable.

refutal [ri'fju:tl], **refutation** [refju:'teiʃ(ə)n], *s.* réfutation *f* (d'un argument, etc.).

refute [ri'fju:t], *v.tr.* **1.** réfuter (une opinion, un argument, qn); **to r. a statement,** démontrer la fausseté d'une déclaration.

refuter [ri'fju:tər], *s.* réfutateur, -trice.

reg [reg], *s. Geog:* reg *m* (du Sahara).

regain[1] [ri'gein], *s.* = REGAINMENT.

regain[2], *v.tr.* **1.** regagner, recouvrer, récupérer (de l'argent perdu); regagner (la confiance de qn); **to r. possession of sth.,** rentrer en possession, reprendre possession, de qch.; **to r. consciousness,** reprendre connaissance, revenir à soi; **to r. one's freedom,** reconquérir, recouvrer, la liberté; **to r. lost ground,** regagner du terrain; **to r. one's footing,** reprendre pied; **to r. one's balance,** reprendre l'équilibre; **to r. strength,** reprendre des forces; se remonter; **the town was regaining its normal appearance,** la ville retrouvait, reprenait, son aspect normal. **2.** regagner (un endroit).

regainable [ri'geinəbl], *a.* recouvrable, regagnable.

regainment [ri'geinmənt], *s.* récupération *f* (d'une perte); rentrée *f* en possession (d'un bien, etc.).

regal ['ri:g(ə)l], *a.* royal, -aux; (*a*) qui appartient au roi, à la reine; **the r. power,** l'autorité royale; (*b*) digne d'un roi, d'une reine; **r. splendour,** magnificence royale; faste royal; **r. bearing,** prestance royale.

regale[1] [ri'geil]. **1.** *v.tr.* (*of pers.*) régaler (qn); **to r. s.o. with a story, a meal,** régaler qn d'une anecdote, d'un repas; **to r. oneself with sth.,** se régaler de qch.; *Lit:* **flowers to r. our eyes,** des fleurs pour réjouir nos yeux. **2.** *v.i.* se régaler (**with, on,** de).

regale[2] [ri'geili], *s. Fr.Hist:* régale *f.*

regalia[1] [ri'geiliə], *s.pl.* **1.** (*a*) insignes royaux; joyaux *m* de la Couronne; **the Coronation r.,** les honneurs *m*; (*b*) insignes (de franc-maçon, etc.); **the mayor came first in all his r.,** le maire venait en premier avec tous les insignes de son office. **2.** droits régaliens.

regalia[2], *s.* (cigare *m*) régalia *m.*

regalian [ri'geiliən], *a.* régalien.

regaling [ri'geiliŋ], *s.* régalade *f.*

regality [ri'gæliti], *s.* **1.** royauté *f,* souveraineté *f.* **2.** **regalities,** droits régaliens.

regally ['ri:gəli], *adv.* royalement.

regard[1] [ri'gɑ:d], *s.* **1.** *A: & Lit:* regard *m*; **to turn one's r. on s.o.,** tourner ses regards sur qn. **2.** égard *m,* point *m* (de vue); **in this r.,** à cet égard, de ce point de vue; **in my r.,** à mon égard; **with r. to . . .,** quant à . . .; concernant . . .; pour, en, ce qui concerne . . .; à l'égard de . . .; pour ce qui est de . . .; **in r. to, of . . .,** en ce qui concerne . . .; **neutrality of a gas in r. to a metal,** neutralité d'un gaz vis-à-vis d'un métal. **3.** égard (**to, for,** à, pour); attention *f* (**to, for,** à); considération *f* (**to, for,** pour); souci *m* (**to, for,** de); **without r. to morality or public opinion,** sans souci de la morale ni de l'opinion publique; **without r. to race or colour,** sans distinction de race ni de couleur; **sentence translated without r. to the context,** phrase traduite sans égard au contexte; **the next object of r. is . . .,** ce qui ensuite doit entrer en considération, c'est . . .; **to pay r. to . . .,** avoir égard à . . .; **to pay no r. to . . .,** ne faire aucune attention à . . .; **to have no r. for human life,** faire peu de cas de la vie humaine; **having r. to . . .,** si l'on tient compte de . . .; en raison de . . .; eu égard à . . .. **4.** (*a*) égard, respect *m,* estime *f,* déférence *f*; **to have great r. for s.o.,** avoir beaucoup d'estime pour qn; estimer beaucoup qn; **to hold s.o. in great r.,** tenir qn en haute estime; **to show r. for s.o.,** témoigner de l'estime, des égards, pour qn; traiter qn avec respect; se montrer plein de déférence pour qn; **to have a high r. for s.o.'s judgment,** avoir beaucoup de considération pour le jugement de qn; **out of r. for s.o.,** par égard, par respect, par déférence, pour qn; (*b*) *Corr:* (**please give**) **my kindest regards to your brother, to the family,** (présentez) mon meilleur souvenir, mes sincères amitiés, à votre frère, à toute la famille.

regard[2], *v.tr.* **1.** *A: & Lit:* regarder (**s.o., sth., fixedly,** qn, qch., fixement). **2.** faire attention, prendre garde, à (qn, qch.); **to r. s.o.'s advice,** tenir compte des conseils de qn. **3.** *A:* **to r. neither God nor man,** ne craindre ni Dieu ni homme; **I r. him so much that . . .,** j'ai tant de considération pour lui que . . .. **4.** (*a*) **to r. sth. as a crime,** regarder, considérer, qch. comme un crime; **to r. s.o. as a national hero,** considérer qn comme un héros national; **to r. oneself as a hero,** se regarder comme un héros; **please r. our communications as confidential,** veuillez bien considérer ces renseignements comme confidentiels; (*b*) **to r. sth. with horror,** regarder qch. avec horreur; **to r. sth., s.o., with suspicion,** avoir des soupçons au sujet de qch., sur qn. **5.** (*of thg*) regarder, concerner; **as regards . . .,** pour ce qui regarde . . .; en ce qui concerne . . .; pour ce qui est de . . .; quant à . . .; **she is very strict as regards discipline,** elle est très sévère sur le chapitre de la discipline.

regardant [ri'gɑ:d(ə)nt], *a. Her:* regardant.

regardful [ri'gɑ:dful], *a. O:* **1.** soigneux (**of,** de); attentif (**of,** à); qui prend garde (**of,** à). **2.** plein d'égards (**of s.o.,** pour, envers, qn).

regarding [ri'gɑ:diŋ], *prep.* à l'égard de; à l'endroit de; concernant; quant à; **r. your enquiry,** en ce qui concerne votre demande; **what are his intentions r. you?** quelles sont ses intentions à votre égard? **I have learnt nothing new r. this matter,** je n'ai rien appris de nouveau relativement à cette affaire; **your letter r. your brother,** votre lettre concernant votre frère; **considerations r. peace,** considérations qui regardent la paix, qui ont rapport à la paix; **questions r. France,** questions relatives à la France.

regardless [ri'gɑ:dlis], (*a*) *a.* peu soigneux (**of,** de); inattentif, indifférent (**of,** à); **r. of the future,** insouciant de l'avenir; sans se préoccuper de l'avenir; **r. of expense,** sans regarder à la dépense; (*b*) *adv.* **to do sth. r. of the consequences,** faire qch. sans se soucier, sans faire aucun cas, des conséquences; *F:* **press on r.!** allez-y quand même! continuons quand même! *F:* **got up r.,** tiré à quatre épingles; sur son trente-et-un.

regardlessly [ri'gɑ:dlisli], *adv.* avec insouciance, avec indifférence.

regardlessness [ri'gɑ:dlisnis], *s.* insouciance *f* (**of,** de); indifférence *f* (**of,** pour, à).

regatta [ri'gætə], *s.* régate(s) *f(pl)*; **rowing r.,** régate à l'aviron; **sailing r.,** régate à la voile.

regelate ['ri:dʒileit], *v.i.* (*of thawing snow*) (se) regeler; (*of pieces of ice*) se souder.

regelation [ri:dʒi'leiʃ(ə)n], *s.* regel *m,* regélation *f.*

regency ['ri:dʒənsi], *s.* régence *f*; *Eng.Hist:* **the R.,** la Régence (de Georges IV, 1810–20); **R. armchair,** fauteuil régence; **R. stripes,** étoffe *f* à rayures.

regenerate[1] [ri'dʒenərət], *a.* régénéré.

regenerate[2] [ri'dʒenəreit]. **1.** *v.tr.* régénérer; (*a*) *Ch:* régénérer (une substance, etc.); restituer (à une substance, etc.) ses qualités premières; **regenerated liquor,** solvant régénéré; *Atom.Ph:* **to r. plutonium,** régénérer du plutonium; **regenerated fuel,** combustible régénéré; *Metall:* **to r. burnt steel,** régénérer l'acier brûlé; (*b*) *Physiol:* reconstituer, reproduire (un organe détruit, etc.); (*c*) *Cmptr:* régénérer, recréer (un fichier, une mémoire); (*d*) *Rel:* régénérer, faire renaître (spirituellement). **2.** *v.i.* (*a*) (*of lobster's claw, etc.*) se régénérer; (*of tail, etc.*) repousser.

regenerating [ri'dʒenəreitiŋ], *a.* **1.** régénérateur, -trice; régénératif. **2.** *Tchn:* **r. chamber,** chambre *f* de récupération; *El:* **r. braking,** freinage *m* par récupération.

regeneration [ridʒenə'reiʃ(ə)n], *s.* **1.** régénération *f*; (*a*) *Ch: etc:* régénération (d'une substance, etc.); épuration *f* (des huiles de graissage, etc.); *Atom.Ph:* régénération (de neutrons, etc.); *Metall:* régénération (de l'acier brûlé); (*b*) *Physiol:* reconstitution (naturelle); régénération (d'un organe détruit, etc.); (*c*) *Cmptr:* régénération, recréation *f* (d'une mémoire, etc.); (*d*) *Rel:* régénération (spirituelle). **2.** *Elcs: W.Tel:* réaction (positive) (d'un amplificateur, d'un récepteur).

regenerative [ri'dʒenərətiv], *a.* **1.** (*a*) régénératif; *Log: etc:* **r. process,** processus régénératif; (*b*) régénérateur, -trice; *El:* **r. cell,** élément, pile, à régénération; *Ind:* **r. furnace,** four à régénérateur, à régénération; four à récupérateur, à récupération; *Atom.Ph:* **r. reactor,** pile régénératrice, réacteur régénérateur; *Cmptr:* **r. storage, store,** mémoire à régénération. **2.** (*a*) *Elcs:* **r. amplifier,** amplificateur à réaction; **r. circuit,** montage à réaction; **r. coupling,** couplage par réaction; *W.Tel:* **r. receiver,** récepteur à réaction; (*b*) *Mec.E:* **r. braking,** freinage par rétroaction, freinage rétroactif; **r. control,** commande (de vitesse) par rétroaction.

regenerator [ri'dʒenəreitər], *s.* **1.** (*pers.*) régénérateur, -trice. **2.** *Ind:* (*apparatus*) régénérateur *m,* récupérateur *m*; *Elcs:* **pulse r.,** régénérateur d'impulsions.

regent ['ri:dʒənt]. **1.** *a. & s.* (*a*) *Hist:* régent, -ente; (*b*) **prince r.,** prince régent. **2.** *s. NAm: Sch:* régent (du conseil d'administration d'une université, etc.).

regerminate [ri:'dʒə:mineit], *v.i.* germer de nouveau.

reggae ['regei], *s. Mus:* reggae *m.*

regicidal [redʒi'said(ə)l], *a.* régicide.

regicide[1] ['redʒisaid], *s.* (*pers.*) régicide *mf.*

regicide[2], *s.* (crime *m* de) régicide *m.*

regild [ri:'gild], *v.tr.* (*p.t.* **regilded;** *p.p.* **regilded,** *occ.* **regilt** [ri:'gilt]) redorer.

Regillus [re'dʒiləs], *Pr.n. A.Geog:* **Lake R.,** le lac Régille.

regime, régime [rei'ʒi:m], *s.* **1.** régime *m*; forme *f* de gouvernement, d'administration; **the old r.,** l'ancien régime; **to establish a new industrial r.,** établir un nouveau régime industriel. **2.** (*a*) *Hyd.E:* régime (d'un cours d'eau); (*b*) **temperature r.,** régime thermique. **3.** *Bot:* régime (de dattes, etc.).

regimen ['redʒimen], *s. Med: Gram:* régime *m.*

regiment[1] ['redʒimənt], *s.* **1.** (*a*) *Mil:* régiment *m*; **r. of the regular army,** régiment actif; (*b*) **regiments of people,** des régiments, des légions *f,* une armée, de gens. **2.** *A:* régime *m,* gouvernement *m*; **the r. of women,** le gouvernement par les femmes.

regiment[2], *v.tr.* **1.** recruter (des hommes). **2.** réglementer, organiser (des ouvriers, des industries, etc.).

regimental [redʒi'ment(ə)l]. **1.** *a.* régimentaire, de régiment, de corps de troupe; **r. badge, flag,** insigne, drapeau, du régiment; **r. band,** musique du régiment, fanfare du bataillon; **r. number,** numéro matricule; **r. headquarters,** état-major, poste de commandement, du régiment; **r. depot,** dépôt régimentaire, du régiment; dépôt de corps de troupe; **r. defence area,** sous-secteur *m, pl.* sous-secteurs; **r. workshop,** atelier de, du, corps; **r. supply train,** train régimentaire; **r. officer,** officier de (corps de) troupe; *U.S:* **r. executive,** commandant en second du régiment; *U.S:* **r. combat team,** groupement tactique. **2.** *s.pl.* regimentals, uniforme *m* (militaire), tenue *f* militaire; **in full regimentals,** en grande tenue.

regimentally [redʒi'mentəli], *adv.* par régiment.

regimentation [redʒimen'teiʃ(ə)n], *s.* **1.** recrutement *m* (d'hommes). **2.** *Adm:* réglementation *f* (de l'industrie, etc.); planning industriel; réglementarisme *m.*

Regina [ri'dʒainə], *Pr.n.f.* la reine régnante; *Jur:* **R. v. Thomas,** la Reine en cause avec Thomas.

Reginald ['redʒinəld], *Pr.n.m.* Renaud.

region ['ri:dʒən], *s.* **1.** région *f*; (*a*) *Geog:* **a desert, a mountainous, r.,** une région désertique, montagneuse; **the arctic regions,** les régions, les terres *f,* arctiques; (*b*) *Mil: U.S:* régions militaires; **air defense r.,** région de défence antiaérienne; (*c*) *Anat:* **the cervical, the lumbar, r.,** la région cervicale, lombaire; *Dent:* **denture-bearing r.,** surface *f,* zone *f,* de sustentation de la prothèse; (*d*) **this will cost in the r. of £500,** cela coûtera dans les £500, quelque chose comme £500. **2.** *Lit: etc:* **the lower, the nether, regions,** les enfers *m*; le royaume des morts, des ombres; l'empire *m* des morts; **the upper regions,** les espaces *m,* les régions, celestes. **3.** *A: & Lit:* **of a high, low, r.,** d'un rang élevé, de rang inférieur.

regional ['ri:dʒən(ə)l], *a.* (*a*) régional, -aux; local, -aux; **r. dialect,** dialecte régional; (*b*) régionaliste; **r. writer,** (écrivain *m*) régionaliste *mf*; (*c*) *Med:* **r. enteritis,** entérite localisée.

regionalism ['ri:dʒənəlizm], *s.* régionalisme *m.*

regionalist ['ri:dʒənəlist], *s.* régionaliste *mf.*

regionalistic [ri:dʒənə'listik], *a.* régionaliste.

regionalization [ri:dʒənəlai'zeiʃ(ə)n], *s.* régionalisation *f.*

regionalize ['ri:dʒənəlaiz], *v.tr.* régionaliser.

regisseur [reiʒi'sə:r], *s. Th: etc:* régisseur *m,* metteur *m* en scène.

register[1] ['redʒistər], *s.* **1.** (*a*) registre *m*; journal, -aux *m*; *Adm: etc:* sommier *m*; *Mil:* **arms r.,** contrôle général des armes; *Cust:* **r. of goods in bond,** sommier d'entrepôt; *Nau:* **ship's r.,** livre *m* de bord; **there are ten million people on the registers,** il y a dix millions d'immatriculés; **to enter an item in a r.,** rapporter, inscrire, noter, mettre, un article sur, dans, un registre; **r. of debenture holders,** registre, livre, des obligataires; **r. of members, of shareholders,** registre, livre, des actionnaires; *Sch:* **to take the r.,** faire l'appel; (*b*) registre (public); **public registers,** actes publics; **the registers of births, marriages and deaths** = les registres de l'état civil; **r. office,** bureau de l'état civil; **to be married at a r. office,** se marier civilement = se marier à la mairie; **police registers,** listes *f* de contrôle de la police; *Nau:* **r. (of seamen),** matricule générale; *U.S:* **Army R.,** Annuaire *m* militaire; **r. of voters, parliamentary r.,** liste électorale; liste de vote, des votants; **commercial r.,** registre de commerce (tenu par un commerçant); *Adm:* **trade r.,** registre du commerce; **cadastral, land, r.,** registre du cadastre; *Scot:* **R. House,** les Archives *f* (à Édimbourg); (*c*) *Nau: Adm:* lettre *f* de mer (d'un navire); acte *m* de nationalité; (*of Fr. ship*) acte de francisation. **2.** quantité marquée (par un pluviomètre, etc.); température marquée (par un thermomètre). **3.** (*a*) *Mus:* registre (d'un instrument, de la voix); étendue *f* (de la voix); **upper, lower, r. of the clarinet,** clairon *m*; chalumeau *m*; (*of organ*) **(stop) r.,** registre; (*b*) registre (du langage, d'une œuvre littéraire, etc.). **4.** (*a*) registre (d'un fourneau); tablier *m,* trappe *f,* rideau *m* (d'une cheminée); (*b*) *NAm:* bouche *f* de chaleur. **5.** compteur *m* (kilométrique, etc.). **6.** (*a*) correspondance exacte (entre parties rapportées, entre trous et goujons, etc.); (*b*) *Typ:* registre; **in r.,** en registre; **out of r.,** mal en registre; (*c*) *Phot:* coïncidence *f* du verre dépoli et de la plaque sensible; repérage *m.* **7.** *Cmptr:* registre; **check r.,** registre de contrôle; **index, modifier, r.,** registre d'index; **instruction, programme, r.,** registre d'instruction; **memory, storage, r.,** registre (de) mémoire; **shift(ing) r.,** registre à décalage; **standby r.,** registre de stockage; **base r.,** registre de base; **(sequence) control r.,** compteur *m* d'instruction. **8.** (*a*) compteur (numérique); (*b*) *Atom.Ph:* numérateur *m*; système *m* numérique de comptage; **r. unit,** élément numérateur.

register[2]. **1.** *v.tr.* (*a*) enregistrer, inscrire, immatriculer, enrôler; **to r. a name, a fact,** inscrire, enregistrer, consigner, un nom, un fait; **to r. a car, a security,** immatriculer une voiture, une valeur; **to r. a company,** faire enregistrer une société; **to r. a birth,** déclarer une naissance; **to r. a trademark,** déposer une marque de fabrique; **to r. (oneself) with the police,** se faire inscrire à la police (pour permis de séjour, etc.); **to r. (oneself on**

the voting list), se faire inscrire sur la liste électorale; *Jur:* **to r. a divorce,** transcrire un divorce; (*b*) **to r. luggage,** enregistrer des bagages; **to r. a letter,** recommander une lettre; (valeur déclarée) charger une lettre; (*c*) (*of thermometer, etc.*) marquer (tant de degrés); (*d*) faire coïncider exactement (des pièces rapportées, trous et goujons, etc.); *Typ:* pointer (les feuilles); *Phot: Typ: Engr:* repérer (les impressions); **carefully registered colour prints,** gravures en couleurs tirées au repérage; (*e*) *Artil:* **to r. the fire,** relever les éléments du tir, repérer le tir; (*f*) manifester, enregistrer (une émotion); **his face registered disappointment,** son visage a témoigné, a reflété, de la déception. **2.** *v.i.* (*a*) (*of parts, of holes and pins, etc.*) coïncider exactement; *Typ:* (*of impression*) être en registre; coïncider; **proof that registers well,** épreuve qui repère bien; (*b*) s'inscrire sur le registre (d'un hôtel, etc.); (*c*) **his name didn't r. with me,** son nom ne me disait rien; *F:* **it didn't r. (with her),** elle n'a rien pigé; (*d*) *Mil:* régler (le tir); (*e*) *War Adm:* **to r. with a tradesman,** s'inscrire chez un commerçant.

registered ['redʒistəd], *a.* (*a*) enregistré, inscrit, immatriculé; **(State) r. nurse,** infirmière diplômée (d'État); *Com:* **r. pattern,** modèle déposé; (*b*) *Fin:* **r. bond, debenture,** obligation nominative; **r. stock,** effets nominatifs; **r. securities,** titres nominatifs; **dividend of 6% on r. securities,** dividende de 6% au nominatif; **r. value,** valeur enregistrée, constatée; **conversion into r. shares,** mise au nominatif; (*c*) *Post:* **r. letter, parcel,** (i) lettre recommandée, colis recommandé; (envoi *m* en) recommandé *m*; (ii) lettre chargée (valeur déclarée), colis avec valeur déclarée; **r. post,** recommandés *mpl.*

registering[1] ['redʒist(ə)riŋ], *a. Tchn:* enregistreur, -euse.

registering[2], *s.* **1.** enregistrement *m*, inscription *f*, immatriculation *f*; *Jur:* **r. of a divorce,** transcription *f* d'un divorce. **2.** *Typ: Engr:* repérage *m*; *Phot:* cadrage *m*, mise *f* en page; *Typ:* pointage *m*. **3.** *Tchn:* engoujonnage *m*.

registrable ['redʒistrəbl], *a.* enregistrable.

registrant ['redʒistrənt], *s.* inscrivant, -ante.

registrar ['redʒistrɑːr, redʒis'trɑːr], *s.* teneur *m* des registres. **1.** *Jur:* greffier *m*; *Adm:* **r. of mortgages,** conservateur *m* des hypothèques; **companies r.,** directeur *m* du registre des sociétés; *Fin:* **r. of transfers,** agent *m* comptable des transferts. **2.** officier *m* de l'état civil; **registrar's office** = bureau de l'état civil; **the R. General,** le Conservateur des actes de l'état civil; **the R. General's Office,** les Archives *f* de l'état civil; **to inform the r. of a death,** informer l'état civil d'un décès. **3.** *Sch:* secrétaire *mf* et archiviste *mf* (d'une université, etc.). **4.** *Med:* (*a*) secrétaire *mf*; (*b*) interne *mf.*

registrarship ['redʒistrɑːʃip], *s.* charge *f* de greffier, d'archiviste, d'officier de l'état civil, etc.

registrary ['redʒistrəri], *s. Sch:* (*at Cambridge*) secrétaire *mf* et archiviste *mf.*

registrate ['redʒistreit], *v.i. Mus:* registrer.

registration [redʒis'treiʃ(ə)n], *s.* **1.** (*a*) enregistrement *m*, inscription *f*; immatriculation *f* (d'un véhicule); acte *m* de nationalité, *Fr:* de francisation (d'un navire); **land r.,** cadastration *f*, cadastrage *m*; **r. of mortgages,** inscription hypothécaire, des hypothèques; **r. of a trademark,** dépôt *m* d'une marque de fabrique; **r. of luggage,** enregistrement des bagages; **r. of a letter,** recommandation *f* d'une lettre; **r. fee,** (i) *Post:* taxe de recommandation; (ii) *Adm:* droit d'inscription; **r. certificate,** matricule *f*; **r. number,** (i) *Aut:* numéro *m* d'immatriculation; numéro minéralogique; (ii) *Adm:* (numéro) matricule *m*; **car with the r. number SPF 34R,** voiture immatriculée SPF 34R; (*of car*) **r. document** = carte grise; *Fin:* **r. and transfer fees,** droit d'inscription et de transfert; (*b*) *Artil:* réglage *m* (du tir); repérage *m*, relevé *m* des éléments du tir; (*c*) *Adm:* tenue *f* du registre, des registres. **2.** (*a*) *Typ: Engr: etc:* repérage *m*; *Phot:* cadrage *m*, mise *f* en page; (*b*) *Cmptr:* alignement *m*, cadrage *m* (des perforations, du papier); **r. gauge,** dispositif de cadrage; **off r.,** décadrage *m*; (*c*) *Mus:* registration *f.*

registry ['redʒistri], *s.* **1.** (*a*) enregistrement *m*; *Com:* **r. books,** livres d'ordre, de statistique; *Nau:* **certificate of r.,** lettre *f* de mer; certificat *m* d'inscription, d'immatriculation; acte *m* de nationalité; (*of Fr. ship*) acte de francisation; **port of r.,** port d'armement; port d'attache; (*b*) *U.S:* recommandation *f*, chargement *m* (d'une lettre); **r. fee,** taxe *f* de recommandation. **2.** *Fin: Adm:* bureau *m* d'enregistrement; greffe *m*. **3. r. (office),** (i) bureau de l'état civil; (ii) *A:* bureau, agence, de placement; **to be married at a r. office,** se marier civilement, = (*in Fr.*) se marier à la mairie; **r. office wedding,** mariage civil. **4.** *A:* registre *m*, livre *m*, journal, -aux *m*.

Regius ['riːdʒiəs], *a. Sch:* **R. professor,** professeur d'université (dont la chaire a été créée par Henri VIII ou créée postérieurement avec les mêmes prérogatives).

reglet ['reglit], *s. Arch:* réglet *m*; *Typ:* filet *m*, réglette *f.*

regnal ['regnəl], *a.* du règne, des règnes; **r. day,** anniversaire *m* de l'avènement au trône; **r. year,** année du règne comptée à partir de l'avènement.

regnant ['regnənt], *a.* (*of prince, opinion, etc.*) régnant; **r. passion,** passion dominante; **this belief was r. in his day,** de son temps cette croyance était très répandue.

regolith ['regəliθ], *s. Geol:* manteau superficiel de débris.

regorge [riː'gɔːdʒ]. **1.** *v.tr.* (*a*) vomir; (*b*) avaler de nouveau; ravaler. **2.** *v.i.* (*of river, etc.*) regorger, refluer.

regosol ['regəsɔl], *s. Geol:* régosol *m*.

regrade [riː'greid], *v.tr.* reclasser.

regrading [riː'greidiŋ], *s.* reclassement *m* (des fonctionnaires, etc.).

regrate[1] [ri'greit], *v.tr. Hist:* **1.** accaparer (des marchandises) pour les revendre à fort profit. **2.** revendre au détail; *v.i.* regratter.

regrate[2], *v.tr. Stonew:* regratter (un mur, etc.).

regrater [ri'greitər], *s. Hist:* **1.** accapareur, -euse. **2.** regrattier, -ière; revendeur, -euse.

regress[1] ['riːgres], *s.* **1.** retour *m* en arrière; rétrogression *f*, régression *f*. **2.** rentrée *f* (**into,** dans). **3.** déclin *m*; **progress and r.,** progrès et régression. **4.** *Ecc: Jur:* regrès *m*. **5.** *Rh:* régression, réversion *f.*

regress[2] [ri'gres], *v.i.* **1.** (*a*) retourner en arrière; (*b*) *Astr:* (*of planet*) rétrograder. **2.** (*a*) rétrograder; décliner; régresser; (*b*) *Psy:* rétrograder.

regression [ri'greʃ(ə)n], *s.* **1.** = REGRESS[1] 1. **2.** *Biol: Psy: etc:* régression *f*. **3.** *Mth:* rebroussement *m* (d'une courbe); **r. coefficient,** coefficient *m* de régression; **r. curve, line,** courbe, droite, de régression.

regressive [ri'gresiv], *a.* régressif.

regressively [ri'gresivli], *adv.* régressivement.

regressiveness [ri'gresivnis], *s. Biol: etc:* caractère régressif.

regret[1] [ri'gret], *s.* regret *m* (**of, for,** de); **r. for the loss of sth., at being refused sth.,** regret de la perte de qch., de se voir refuser qch.; **to feel r.,** éprouver, avoir, du regret; **to have no regrets,** n'avoir aucun regret, ne rien regretter; **he expressed his r. that. . .,** il a exprimé son regret que + *sub.*; **to express r. at not being able to do sth.,** exprimer le regret de ne pouvoir faire qch.; **to hear with r. of sth., that . . .,** apprendre qch. avec regret; apprendre avec regret que + *ind.*; **I state the fact with r.,** je le dis à regret; **to refuse with much r., with many regrets,** refuser avec beaucoup de regret, avec bien des regrets; **(much) to my r.,** à regret, à mon (grand) regret; *Fin:* (*to applicant for shares*) **letter of r.,** lettre d'avis de retour de souscription.

regret[2], *v.tr.* **(regretted)** regretter (qn, qch.); **to r. one's ignorance,** se lamenter de son ignorance; **to r. doing, having done, sth.,** regretter d'avoir fait qch.; **to r. not having done sth.,** regretter de ne pas avoir fait qch.; **I r. to have to leave you,** je regrette d'avoir à vous quitter; **I r. to have to say it,** je regrette d'avoir à le dire; il m'en coûte de le dire; **you won't r. following my advice,** vous ne regretterez pas d'avoir suivi mon conseil; **I r. that I cannot come on Monday,** je regrette de ne pas pouvoir venir lundi; **I r. to (have to) inform you that. . .,** j'ai le regret de vous annoncer que. . .; **we deeply r. to have to inform you of the death of your father,** nous avons la douleur, le regret, de vous annoncer la mort de votre père; **I r. to have to tell you that I'm leaving,** je suis au regret de vous annoncer que je vais partir; **he bitterly regretted having spoken,** il s'est mordu la langue d'avoir parlé; **we r. very much to hear . . .,** nous sommes désolés d'apprendre. . .; **I r. that he has gone so soon,** je regrette qu'il soit parti si tôt; **it is to be regretted that . . .,** il est à regretter, il est regrettable, que + *sub.*; **it's all the more to be regretted as, since . . .,** c'est d'autant plus regrettable que + *ind.*; **he died regretted by all, by the people,** il mourut regretté de tous, par le peuple; *Lit:* **regretted of all men,** regretté de tous.

regretful [ri'gretful], *a.* **1.** (*of pers.*) plein de regrets. **2.** (sentiment) de regret.

regretfully [ri'gretfuli], *adv.* avec regret, à regret.

regrettable [ri'gretəbl], *a.* (erreur, etc.) regrettable, à regretter; **r. situation,** contretemps fâcheux; **it is regrettable that . . .,** il est regrettable que + *sub.*; il est à regretter que + *sub.*

regrettably [ri'gretəbli], *adv.* regrettablement; **there was a r. small attendance,** il est à regretter que les assistants aient été si peu nombreux.

regretting [ri'gretiŋ], *s.* regrets *mpl.*

regrind [riː'graind], *v.tr.* (*p.t. & p.p.* **reground** [riː'graund]) **1.** rebroyer, remoudre (du blé, du café). **2.** (*a*) rémoudre, réaffûter (un outil); **tool that can easily be reground,** outil réaffûtable; (*b*) roder (une soupape).

regrinding [ri'graindiŋ], *s.* **1.** rebroyage *m*, remoulage *m* (du blé, etc.). **2.** (*a*) réaffûtage *m* (d'un outil); (*b*) rodage *m* (d'une soupape).

regroup [riː'gruːp]. **1.** *v.tr.* reclasser; regrouper. **2.** *v.i.* se regrouper.

regrouping [riː'gruːpiŋ], *s.* regroupement *m*.

regrowth [riː'grouθ], *s.* croissance nouvelle; *For:* repeuplement *m*.

regulable ['regjuləbl], *a.* réglable.

regular ['regjulər], *a. & s.*

I. *a.* **1.** (*a*) régulier; **r. polygon,** polygone régulier; **r. features,** traits réguliers; (*b*) régulier, exact; **r. pulse,** pouls régulier; **r. footsteps,** pas réguliers, mesurés; *Equit:* **r. step,** pas écouté; **as r. as clockwork,** exact comme une horloge; réglé comme du papier à musique; **r. service, income,** service, revenu, régulier; **r. salary,** traitement fixe; **my r. time for going to bed,** l'heure habituelle à laquelle je me couche; **he comes at r. hours,** il vient à des heures régulières, réglées; **to do sth. as a r. thing,** faire qch. régulièrement; **r. attendance,** assiduité *f*; **a r. visitor to the house,** un des familiers de la maison; *Rail:* **the r. travellers,** les abonnés *m*; **r. reader,** lecteur, -trice, fidèle; **r. customer,** bon client, bonne cliente; habitué, -ée; (*at restaurant*) **our r. waiter,** notre garçon habituel; **r. staff,** employés permanents; **r. agent,** agent attitré; **r. judge,** juge titulaire; **he took the class in the absence of the r. lecturer,** il a donné le cours en l'absence du titulaire. **2.** régulier, réglé, rangé; **a r. life,** une vie régulière, uniforme, réglée; **to keep r. hours,** avoir un emploi de temps précis; **man of r. habits,** homme ordonné, qui a des habitudes régulières; homme rangé dans ses habitudes. **3.** (*a*) régulier, dans les règles; réglementaire; **procedure that is not r.,** procédé qui n'est pas régulier; **in the r. manner,** réglementairement; (*b*) ordinaire, normal, -aux; **r. price,** prix ordinaire, prix de règle; **the r. stock consists of . . .,** la provision ordinaire consiste en . . .; *Ind:* **r. model,** modèle courant; type courant; (*c*) *Gram:* (verbe, etc.) régulier; (*d*) (cuisinier, médecin) de profession; (médecin, etc.) diplômé; (*e*) *Ecc:* (clergé) régulier; (*f*) *Mil:* **r. troops,** troupes régulières. **4.** *F:* (*intensive*) vrai, véritable; **a r. hero,** un vrai héros; **r. rascal,** vrai roublard; **r. set-to,** bataille en règle; **it's a r. swindle!** c'est une vraie attrape! *NAm:* **he's a r. guy, fellow,** c'est un bon type; c'est le type qu'il faut. **5.** *adv. P:* = REGULARLY; **it happens r.,** ça arrive tous les jours; **he was r. angry!** il était fâché, je ne vous dis que ça!

II. *s.* **1.** *Ecc:* régulier *m*; religieux *m*; (*b*) *Mil:* soldat *m* de l'armée permanente; militaire *m* de carrière; **regulars,** troupes régulières; réguliers. **2.** *F:* bon client; habitué; familier.

regularity [regju'læriti], *s.* régularité *f.*

regularization [regjulərai'zeiʃ(ə)n], *s.* régularisation *f.*

regularize ['regjuləraiz], *v.tr.* régulariser (un document, une situation, etc.).

regularly ['regjuləli], *adv.* **1.** régulièrement, d'une façon réglée; **to happen as r. as clockwork,** arriver comme mars en carême; **student attending lectures r.,** étudiant assidu aux cours. **2.** régulièrement, dans les règles.

regulate ['regjuleit], *v.tr.* **1.** régler, régulariser (la marche d'une machine); ajuster (la tension d'un ressort, etc.); *El:* **regulated voltage,** tension stabilisée; *Elcs:* **regulated frequency,** fréquence asservie; **to r. a watch,** régler une montre; **to r. the flow of a river,** régulariser un cours d'eau. **2.** régler, diriger (les affaires); réglementer (les affaires, les personnes); compasser (ses actions, etc.); fixer les règles pour (une procédure, etc.); **to r. one's expenditure,** régler, calculer ses dépenses; **to r. one's life by s.o.,** se régler sur qn; **to be regulated by s.o., by sth.,** régler sur qn, sur qch.

regulating[1] ['regjuleitiŋ], *a.* régulateur, -trice; de réglage; **self r.,** à réglage automatique.

regulating[2], *s.* = REGULATION 1.

regulation [regju'leiʃ(ə)n], *s.* **1.** (*a*) réglage *m* (d'un appareil, etc.); régulation *f* (des compas); **r. nut, screw,** écrou, vis, de réglage; *El:* **voltage r.,** régulation de la tension; **r. relay,** relais de régulation; (*b*) règlement *m*, réglementation *f* (des affaires, etc.); **to bring (sth.) under r.,** réglementer (qch.). **2.** règlement, arrêté *m*, ordonnance *f*, prescription *f*; **regulations,** règlement(s), réglementation, prescriptions, dispositions *f*; **contrary to, against, the regulations,** contraire aux prescriptions, au règlement; **to act in accordance with the regulations,** agir régulièrement; **it's not in accordance with the regulations,** ce n'est pas réglementaire; **provisional regulations,** règlement provisoire; **official regulations,** prescriptions légales; **army regulations,** règlements militaires; **customs regulations,** règlements de la douane; **hospital regulations,** régime *m* des hôpitaux; **safety regulations,** prescriptions relatives à la sûreté; **traffic, road, regulations,** police *f* du roulage, de la circulation; **to contravene police regulations,** contrevenir aux règlements de police; *Mil:* **r. revolver,** revolver d'ordonnance; **r. uniform,** tenue *f* réglementaire; *Nau:* **r. lights,** feux réglementaires.

regulative ['regjuleitiv], *a.* régulateur, -trice.

regulator ['regjuleitər], *s.* **1.** (*pers.*) régulateur, -trice; régleur, -euse. **2.** (*device*) *Clockm: El: Mec.E: etc:* régulateur *m*; modérateur *m* (de moteur); **self-acting r.,** autorégulateur *m*; **r. lever,** registre *m* (de prise de vapeur); **flow r.,** régulateur de débit; *El:* **voltage r.,** (i) graduateur *m*, (ii) régulateur, de tension; **automatic voltage r.,** régulateur automatique de tension; **constant voltage r.,** stabilisateur *m* de tension; **induction r.,** survolteur *m* d'induction; **frequency r.,** régulateur de fréquence; **field, slip, r.,** rhéostat *m* d'excitation; *Elcs:* **r. tube,** tube régulateur; *Cmptr:* **pilot wire r.,** régulateur à fil pilote; *Av:* **differential pressure r.,** contrôleur *m* de pression différentielle; (*of oxygen cylinder*) **feed r.,** doseur *m* d'oxygène; (mano-)détendeur *m*; *Hyd.E:* **canal r.,** prise *f* d'eau; **feed water r.,** régulateur d'eau d'alimentation; *Metall:* **blast r.,** registre de vent.

regulatory ['regjulət(ə)ri], *a.* **1.** régulateur, -trice. **2.** sujet à des règlements.

Regulidae [reg'ju:lidi:], *s.pl. Orn:* régulidés *m.*

reguline ['regjulain]. *Ch:* **1.** *a. A:* régulin. **2.** *s.* régulin *m.*

Regulus[1] ['regjuləs], *Pr.n.m. Rom.Hist: Astr:* Régulus.

regulus[2], *pl.* **-i** ['regjuləs, -ai], *s.* **1.** *A:* petit roi; roitelet *m.* **2.** *Orn:* roitelet (à tête rouge). **3.** *Ch: A:* régule *m*; **r. of antimony,** régule d'antimoine. **4.** *Metall:* (*a*) culot *m*; (*b*) matte blanche de cuivre.

regur ['regə:r], *s. Geol:* régur *m.*

regurgitate [ri:'gə:dʒiteit]. **1.** *v.tr.* régurgiter, vomir, rendre (sa nourriture). **2.** *v.i.* (*of liquids, etc.*) refluer, regorger.

regurgitation [ri:gə:dʒi'teiʃ(ə)n], *s.* régurgitation *f.*

rehabilitate [ri:(h)ə'biliteit], *v.tr.* **1.** (*a*) réhabiliter (qn); rétablir (qn) dans ses droits, etc.; **to r. s.o. in public opinion,** réhabiliter, rétablir, qn dans l'opinion; (*b*) réhabiliter (la mémoire, la réputation, de qn); redonner sa valeur à (qch.); remettre en honneur, en pratique (une coutume, etc.); remettre en usage (un vieux mot, une vieille expression). **2.** (*a*) rééduquer (les handicapés, les inadaptés, etc.); désintoxiquer et réadapter (un alcoolique, un drogué); réadapter (un convalescent); (*b*) reclasser (des chômeurs); réintégrer, réinsérer, dans la vie civile (des démobilisés). **3.** (*a*) réorganiser (un parti politique, etc.); assainir (des finances); assainir, réorganiser (les finances publiques); (*b*) remettre (qch.) en état; reconstituer, refaire (qch.); rénover (un vieux quartier, etc.); réhabiliter (un taudis).

rehabilitating [ri:(h)ə'biliteitiŋ], *a. Jur:* (*of order, etc.*) réhabilitant, réhabilitoire, réhabilitatoire.

rehabilitation [ri:(h)əbili'teiʃ(ə)n], *s.* **1.** réhabilitation *f* (d'un condamné, d'une réputation); réadaptation *f*, rééducation *f* (physique) (d'un convalescent); désintoxication *f* et réadaptation (des alcooliques, des drogués); rééducation, redressement *m* (des jeunes délinquents); reclassement *m*, réadaptation fonctionnelle (d'un fonctionnaire, etc.); **r. of the disabled,** rééducation des handicapés; **r. centre,** centre de rééducation professionnelle; **r. of ex-servicemen,** réintégration *f*, réinsertion *f*, des démobilisés dans la vie civile; réadaptation des démobilisés à la vie civile; **r. of occupied territories,** reconstruction *f* des pays occupés. **2.** assainissement *m* (des finances); **r. plan,** plan *m* (i) de réorganisation, (ii) d'assainissement (des finances).

rehandle [ri:'hændl], *v.tr.* traiter à nouveau (un sujet, une question); remanier (un ouvrage).

rehash[1] ['ri:hæʃ], *s. F:* réchauffé *m*, resucée *f*, (nouvelle) mouture (d'un livre, etc.); **it's just a r.,** ce n'est que du réchauffé.

rehash[2] [ri:'hæʃ], *v.tr. F:* remanier (un vieux conte, etc., sans changement important); ressasser (de vieux arguments, etc.).

rehear [ri:'hiər], *v.tr.* (*p.t. & p.p.* **reheard** [ri:'hə:d]) *Jur: etc:* entendre (une cause, etc.) de nouveau.

rehearing [ri:'hiəriŋ], *s. Jur: etc:* nouvelle audition.

rehearsal [ri'hə:s(ə)l], *s.* **1.** *A: & Lit:* récit détaillé, relation *f* (des aventures, des malheurs, de qn); **r. of old grievances,** énumération *f* d'anciens griefs. **2.** *Th:* répétition *f*; **dress r.,** répétition en costume; **the dress r.,** la (répétition) générale; l'avant-première *f*, *pl.* avant-premières; **to have a dress r.,** répéter en costume; **play in, under, r.,** pièce en répétition.

rehearse [ri'hə:s], *v.tr.* **1.** *A: & Lit:* raconter tout au long; énumérer (des faits, des griefs); repasser (une liste); réciter, dire (des prières). **2.** *Th:* (*a*) répéter (une pièce, etc.); faire la répétition (d'un ballet, etc.); (*b*) faire répéter (qn); (*c*) *v.i.* (*of pers.*) répéter.

rehearsing [ri'hə:siŋ], *s.* étude *f* (d'une pièce de théâtre); les répétitions *f.*

reheat[1] ['ri:hi:t], *s. Av:* postcombustion *f*; **r. fuel control system,** dispositif de régulation de postcombustion; **r. actuation, control,** commande de postcombustion; **r. nozzle,** canal *m* de postcombustion; **r. process,** réchauffage *m.*

reheat[2] [ri:'hi:t], *v.tr.* (*a*) réchauffer; (*b*) *Metall:* recuire, récrouir.

reheater [ri:'hi:tər], *s.* (*a*) *Mch:* réchauffeur *m*; (*b*) *Av:* dispositif *m* de postcombustion, de réchauffage.

reheating [ri:'hi:tiŋ], *s.* (*a*) réchauffage *m*, réchauffement *m*; *Mch:* **r. furnace,** four de réchauffage; (*b*) *Metall:* recuisson *f*, revenu *m.*

re-heel [ri:'hi:l], *v.tr.* remettre des talons à (des chaussures); *O:* refaire un talon à (une chaussette).

Rehoboam [ri:ə'bouəm]. **1.** *Pr.n.m. B.Hist:* Roboam. **2.** *s.* bouteille *f* de (vin de) champagne d'une contenance de 8 litres environ.

re-hoop [ri:'hu:p], *v.tr.* recercler (un fût).

re-hooping [ri:'hu:piŋ], *s.* recerclage *m* (d'un fût).

rehouse [ri:'hauz], *v.tr.* reloger (qn).

rehousing [ri:'hauziŋ], *s.* relogement *m.*

reification [ri:ifi'keiʃ(ə)n], *s. Phil:* réification *f.*

reify ['ri:ifai], *v.tr. Phil:* réifier, concrétiser, matérialiser (une abstraction).

reign[1] [rein], *s.* **1.** règne *m* (d'un roi, de la vérité, etc.); **in, under, the r. of. . .,** sous le règne de. . . . **2.** *A: & Lit:* royaume *m*, domaine *m.*

reign[2], *v.i.* régner (**over,** sur); **to r. supreme,** régner en maître; **silence reigns in the camp,** le silence règne dans le camp; *Lit:* **she reigns in my heart,** elle règne dans mon cœur.

reigning ['reiniŋ], *a.* régnant; **she was the r. beauty of her day,** elle fut la beauté suprême de son époque.

reignite [ri:'ig'nait], *v.tr.* rallumer.

reignition [ri:ig'niʃ(ə)n], *s.* nouvel allumage.

reillume [ri:i'lju:m], *v.tr. Lit:* éclairer de nouveau.

reimbursable [ri:im'bə:səbl], *a.* remboursable (**over 25 years,** sur 25 ans).

reimburse [ri:im'bə:s], *v.tr.* **1.** rembourser (de l'argent). **2. to r. s.o. (for) sth.,** rembourser qn de qch.; désintéresser qn; **to be reimbursed,** rentrer dans ses débours; se rembourser.

reimbursement [ri:im'bə:smənt], *s.* remboursement *m.*

reimbush [ri:im'buʃ], *v.tr. Ven:* rembucher.

reimbushment [ri:im'buʃmənt], *s. Ven:* rembuchement *m.*

reimplant [ri:im'plɑ:nt], *v.tr. Surg: etc:* réimplanter.

reimplantation [ri:implɑ:n'teiʃ(ə)n], *s. Surg: Dent:* réimplantation *f.*

reimport[1] [ri:'impɔ:t], *s.* réimportation *f.*

reimport[2] [ri:im'pɔ:t], *v.tr.* réimporter.

reimportation [ri:impɔ:'teiʃ(ə)n], *s.* réimportation *f.*

reimporting [ri:im'pɔ:tiŋ], *s.* réimportation *f.*

reimpose [ri:im'pouz], *v.tr.* **1.** réimposer (une taxe, etc.). **2.** *Typ:* réimposer (une feuille); remanier (les pages).

reimposing [ri:im'pouziŋ], *s.* = REIMPOSITION.

reimposition [ri:impə'ziʃ(ə)n], *s.* réimposition *f* ((i) d'une taxe, (ii) *Typ:* d'une feuille).

reimpression [ri:im'preʃ(ə)n], *s. Typ: Publ:* réimpression *f.*

rein[1] [rein], *s.* rêne *f* (de cheval monté); guide *f* (de cheval de voiture); **bearing, check, r.,** fausses rênes, rêne d'enrênement; **r. ring,** anneau *m* porte-rêne, *pl.* anneaux porte-rêne; **to put the r. on a horse,** serrer la bride à un cheval; **to hold the reins,** tenir les rênes, tenir la bride; *Veh:* tenir les guides; **to assume, hold, the reins of government,** prendre, tenir, les rênes du gouvernement; **with a loose, slack, r., with reins slack,** (i) (chevaucher) à bout de rênes; (ii) (mener qn) mollement; **to loosen, slacken, the reins,** lâcher les rênes, la rêne, la bride; laisser flotter les rênes; **to give a horse free r., the reins,** lâcher les rênes, la bride, à un cheval; donner (libre) carrière à un cheval; **to give s.o. a free r.,** lâcher la gourmette à qn; laisser à qn la bride sur le cou; lâcher la bride à qn; **to give r., the reins, to one's anger,** lâcher la bride à sa colère; **to give free r. to one's imagination,** donner libre cours, donner carrière, à son imagination; **to draw r.,** serrer la bride; s'arrêter; **if you don't draw r. a bit you'll go bankrupt,** si vous n'y allez pas plus doucement vous allez vous ruiner; **to keep a tight r. on, over, s.o.,** tenir la bride serrée, tenir la bride haute, à qn; **to drop the reins,** abandonner (les rênes); *Com: etc:* **to take over the reins,** se mettre en selle.

rein[2], *v.tr.* **to r. in a horse,** serrer la bride, les rênes, à un cheval; ramener, retenir, un cheval; *v.i.* **to r. in,** ramener son cheval au pas; **to r. s.o. in,** retenir qn; ramener qn sous la discipline; **to r. up a horse,** arrêter un cheval; **to r. back a horse,** (faire) reculer un cheval.

reincarnate[1] [ri:in'kɑ:n(e)it], *a.* réincarné.

reincarnate[2] [ri:in'kɑ:neit], *v.tr.* réincarner; **to be reincarnated,** se réincarner.

reincarnation [ri:inkɑ:'neiʃ(ə)n], *s.* réincarnation *f.*

reincorporate [ri:in'kɔ:pəreit], *v.tr.* réincorporer.

reindeer ['reindiər], *s.* (*usu. inv. in pl.*) *Z:* renne *m*; **a herd of r.,** un troupeau de rennes; **buck r.,** renne mâle; **doe r.,** renne femelle; *Geog:* **R. Lake,** lac *m* du Caribou; *Moss:* **r. moss, lichen,** cladonie *f.*

reinette [rei'net], *s. Hort:* **r. du Canada,** reinette *f* du Canada.

reinflate [ri:in'fleit], *v.tr.* regonfler (un ballon, etc.).

reinflation [ri:in'fleiʃ(ə)n], *s.* regonflement *m.*

reinforce[1] [ri:in'fɔ:s], *s. Artil:* renfort *m* (du canon).

reinforce[2], *v.tr.* **1.** (*a*) renforcer (une armée, une équipe, un orchestre); (*b*) affermir (la santé de qn, etc.); renforcer (un argument); appuyer (une demande); **to r. a sound,** renforcer un son. **2.** renforcer (un mur, un barrage, etc.); consolider (un échafaudage, des fondations); armer (une poutre, le béton); arc-bouter (une voûte, etc.); haubaner (un mât, etc.); **to r. a beam,** renforcer une poutre; **reinforced concrete,** béton armé; *Tex:* **reinforced fabric,** tissu renforcé, armé; **reinforced glass,** verre armé; *Metalw: etc:* **reinforced seam,** joint surépaissé.

reinforcement [ri:in'fɔ:smənt], *s.* **1.** (*a*) *Mil:* renforcement *m* (d'une unité, etc.); (*b*) *Const: etc:* renforcement, renforçage *m* (d'un barrage, etc.); armature *f*, ferraillage *m* (du béton). **2.** (*a*) *Mil:* (*usu. pl.*) renfort *m*; **to await reinforcements, a r. of 1000 men,** attendre un renfort, des renforts; attendre un renfort de 1000 hommes; (*b*) *Const: etc:* renforcement; **iron r.,** armature en fer; (*c*) (*office stationery*) œillet *m.*

reinforcing[1] [ri:in'fɔ:siŋ], *a.* (i) de renfort; (ii) d'armature; **r. troops,** troupes de renfort; *Mch:* **r. plate,** contre-plaque *f*, *pl.* contre-plaques, plaque *f* de renfort; *Tchn:* **r. collar,** collerette *f* de renforcement.

reinforcing[2], *s.* = REINFORCEMENT 1.

reingratiate [ri:in'greiʃieit], *v.tr.* faire rentrer en grâce (qn) (**with,** auprès de); **to r. oneself with s.o.,** rentrer en grâce auprès de qn.

reinhabit [ri:in'hæbit], *v.tr.* habiter de nouveau (une maison, un endroit).

reinless ['reinlis], *a.* **1.** (cheval) sans rênes, sans brides. **2.** (*of passion, etc.*) sans frein; sans retenue; débridé; effréné.

reins [reinz], *s.pl.* **1.** *Anat: A:* reins *m.* **2.** *Arch:* reins (d'une voûte).

reinsert [ri:in'sə:t], *v.tr.* (*a*) réinsérer (une annonce, etc.); (*b*) remettre (une pièce) en place.

reinsertion [ri:in'sə:ʃ(ə)n], *s.* (*a*) insertion *f* à nouveau; réinsertion *f* (d'une annonce, etc.); (*b*) remise *f* en place (d'une pièce, etc.).

reinstall [ri:in'stɔ:l], *v.tr.* réinstaller.

reinstate [ri:in'steit], *v.tr.* **1.** réintégrer (qn) (dans ses fonctions); rétablir (un fonctionnaire, etc.); rétablir (la santé de qn); **to r. s.o. in his possessions,** réintégrer qn dans ses possessions. **2.** remettre, rétablir, remplacer (qch.).

reinstatement [ri:in'steitmənt], *s.* **1.** réintégration *f* (de qn dans ses fonctions). **2.** rétablissement *m* (de qch.).

reinsurance [ri:in'ʃju:r(ə)ns], *s. Ins:* réassurance *f*; contre-assurance *f*, *pl.* contre-assurances; **r. policy,** police *f* de réassurance.

reinsure [ri:in'ʃjuər], *v.tr. Ins:* réassurer.

reinsurer [ri:in'ʃju:rər], *s. Ins:* réassureur *m.*

reintegrate [ri:'intigreit], *v.tr.* **1.** (*a*) rétablir (qch.) dans son intégrité; intégrer (qn, qch.) de nouveau (dans qch.); (*b*) *A:* **to r. s.o. in his possessions,** réintégrer qn dans ses possessions. **2.** *Mth:* réintégrer (une quantité).

reintegration [ri:inti'greiʃ(ə)n], *s.* **1.** réintégration *f* (de qn dans une société, etc.); rétablissement intégral. **2.** *Mth:* réintégration.

reinter [ri:in'tər], *v.tr.* (**reinterred**) renterrer.

reinterment [ri:in'tə:mənt], *s.* renterrement *m.*

reinterpret [ri:in'tə:prit], *v.tr.* réinterpréter.

reinterrogate [ri:in'terəgeit], *v.tr.* réinterroger; interroger de nouveau (le témoin, etc.).

reintroduce [ri:intrə'dju:s], *v.tr.* **1.** réintroduire (un sujet de conversation, etc.). **2.** représenter (qn); présenter (qn) de nouveau.

reintroducing [ri:intrə'dju:siŋ], *s.* = REINTRODUCTION.

reintroduction [ri:intrə'dʌkʃ(ə)n], *s.* **1.** réintroduction *f* (d'un sujet de conversation); **r. of goods into the country,** réimportation *f* de marchandises. **2.** nouvelle présentation (de qn à qn).

reinvest [ri:in'vest], *v.tr.* **1.** réinvestir (qn), revêtir (qn, qch.) (**with,** de). **2.** *Mil:* investir de nouveau (une ville, etc.). **3.** *Fin:* replacer (des fonds); trouver un nouveau placement pour (des fonds).

reinvestigate [ri:in'vestigeit], *v.tr.* examiner de nouveau

(une question); faire une nouvelle enquête sur (un crime, etc.).
reinvestment [ri:in'vestmənt], *s.* **1.** *Mil:* nouvel investissement (d'une ville, etc.). **2.** *Fin:* nouveau placement.
reinvigorate [ri:in'vigəreit], *v.tr.* rendre la vigueur, redonner de la vigueur, à (qn); revigorer, remonter, ranimer, *F:* retremper, ravigoter, requinquer (qn).
reinvigoration [ri:invigə'reiʃ(ə)n], *s.* revigorisation *f.*
reinvite [ri:in'vait], *v.tr.* réinviter.
reissue[1] [ri:'isju:], *s.* **1.** *(a) Fin:* nouvelle émission (de billets de banque, etc.); *(b) Cmptr:* réémission *f* (d'une instruction). **2.** *Publ:* réédition *f*; nouvelle édition, nouveau tirage.
reissue[2], *v.tr.* **1.** *(a) Fin:* émettre de nouveau (des actions, etc.); *(b) Cmptr:* réémettre (une instruction). **2.** *Publ:* rééditer (un livre); donner une nouvelle édition, un nouveau tirage (d'un livre).
reitbok ['ri:tbɔk], *s. Z:* rietbok *m*, cervicapre *m.*
reiter ['raitər], *s. Hist:* reître *m.*
reiterate [ri:'itəreit], *v.tr.* réitérer, répéter.
reiteration [ri:itə'reiʃ(ə)n], *s.* **1.** réitération *f*, répétition *f.* **2.** *Typ: A:* retiration *f.*
reiterative [ri:'itərətiv], *a.* réitératif.
Reithrodontomys [raiθrou'dɔntəmis], *s. Z:* reithrodontomys *m.*
reive [ri:v], *v.*, **reiver** ['ri:vər], *s. esp. Scot:* = REAVE, REAVER.
reject[1] ['ri:dʒekt], *s.* **1.** *(a)* (pièce *f* de) rebut *m*; **export r.,** article (de rebut) non destiné à l'exportation; *(b) Cmptr:* **r. bin, pocket, stacker,** case *f* rebut; **r. tape,** bande *f* erreurs. **2.** personne refusée; recrue reconnue impropre pour le service; réformé *m.*
reject[2] [ri'dʒekt], *v.tr.* *(a)* rejeter, repousser (une offre, une proposition); repousser (une mesure); rejeter (un projet de loi); réprouver (une doctrine); éconduire (un soupirant); **the stomach rejects indigestible food,** l'estomac rend, rejette, les aliments indigestes; **to r. the authenticity of a fact,** nier l'authenticité d'un fait; *B:* **rejected of God and of men,** renié de Dieu et des hommes; *(b)* refuser (des marchandises, un manuscrit, un candidat, etc.); *(of recruit)* **rejected on account of shortsightedness,** réformé pour myopie; *Ind:* **to r. a casting,** mettre une pièce au rebut; **rejected casting,** pièce à écarter; *(c) Surg:* rejeter (un greffon).
rejectable [ri'dʒektəbl], *a.* rejetable; à rejeter, à refuser.
rejectamenta [ridʒektə'mentə], *s.pl.* **1.** rebuts *m.* **2.** épaves rejetées par la mer. **3.** déjections *f.*
rejecter [ri'dʒektər], *s.* = REJECTOR.
rejection [ri'dʒekʃ(ə)n], *s.* **1.** *(a)* rejet *m* (d'un projet de loi, d'une proposition, etc.); refus *m* (d'une offre, etc.); *Publ:* **r. slip,** note *f* refusant un manuscrit; *(b)* réjection *f* (de la nourriture); régurgitation *f*; *(c)* **(graft) r.,** rejet (du greffon); *(d) W.Tel: etc:* **band r.,** rejet de bande; **r. band,** bande *f* au-dessus de la fréquence de coupure; bande de réjection, d'élimination; *T.V:* **sound r.,** réjection de la porteuse de son. **2.** *(a) Ind: etc:* **rejections,** pièces *f* de rebut; rebuts; *(b) Hort: etc:* rejettement *m*; *(c) Physiol:* **rejections,** déjections *f.*
rejector [ri'dʒektər], *s.* **1.** personne *f* qui rejette, qui repousse (une offre, etc.). **2.** *W.Tel:* **r. (circuit),** filtre (éliminateur).
rejigger [ri:'dʒigər], *v.tr. U.S:* réorganiser, remanier.
rejoice [ri'dʒɔis]. **1.** *v.tr. O: & Lit:* réjouir (qn); **I am rejoiced at it, by it,** je m'en réjouis; j'en suis enchanté, ravi; **I am rejoiced to hear it,** je me réjouis, je suis heureux, de l'entendre; *impers.* **it rejoices my heart to hear him,** cela me réjouit le cœur de l'entendre. **2.** *v.i.* *(a)* se réjouir; *F:* jubiler; **to r. at, over, sth.,** se réjouir de qch.; **he rejoices in the misfortune of others,** il se réjouit du malheur d'autrui; **to go on one's way rejoicing,** poursuivre son chemin plein de joie; **to r. to do sth.,** se réjouir de faire qch.; *Prov:* **it's a poor heart that never rejoices,** ce n'est pas tous les jours fête; *(b)* **to r. in sth.,** jouir de qch.; posséder qch.; **he rejoiced in the name of Bacon,** il portait le nom, il s'honorait du nom, de Bacon.
rejoicement [ri'dʒɔismənt], *s. O:* réjouissance *f.*
rejoicer [ri'dʒɔisər], *s.* **1.** celui qui se réjouit **(at,** de). **2.** fêtard, -arde.
rejoicing[1] [ri'dʒɔisiŋ], *a.* **1.** *O: (of news, etc.)* réjouissant. **2.** joyeux, jubilant; plein de joie; en joie.
rejoicing[2], *s.* **1.** réjouissance *f*, allégresse *f*; *F:* jubilation *f*; **ships dressed in token of r.,** navires pavoisés en signe de réjouissance; **it was an occasion for general r.,** ce fut la grande liesse. **2. the rejoicings,** les réjouissances; la fête.
rejoicingly [ri'dʒɔisiŋli], *adv.* avec joie; avec jubilation.
rejoin[1] [ri'dʒɔin], *v.i.* **1.** répliquer, répondre. **2.** *Jur: A:* dupliquer.
rejoin[2] [ri:'dʒɔin]. **1.** *v.tr.* *(a)* rejoindre, réunir **(sth. to, with, sth.,** qch. à qch.); remettre, rebouter (un membre cassé); *(b)* rejoindre, retrouver (qn, une compagnie, son régiment); *Mil: etc:* **the men rejoined their unit,** les hommes ont rallié leur unité; **to r. one's ship,** rallier le bord. **2.** *v.i. (of roads, lines, etc.)* se réunir, se rejoindre.
rejoinder [ri'dʒɔindər], *s.* **1.** réplique *f*, repartie *f*; **sharp r.,** riposte *f.* **2.** *Jur: A:* **defendant's r.,** duplique *f.*
rejoining [ri:'dʒɔiniŋ], *s.* réunion *f* (de qch. à qch.).
rejoint [ri:'dʒɔint], *v.tr.* **1.** *Carp: etc:* refaire un joint à (qch.). **2.** *Const:* rejointoyer (un mur, etc.).
rejointing [ri:'dʒɔintiŋ], *s. Const:* rejointoiement *m.*
rejuvenate [ri'dʒu:vineit]. **1.** *v.tr.* rajeunir (qn). **2.** *v.i.* rajeunir; redevenir jeune.
rejuvenation [ridʒu:vi'neiʃ(ə)n], *s.* **1.** *(a)* rajeunissement *m*; *(b) Med: etc:* régénération *f*; *(c) Hort: Geol:* rajeunissement. **2.** cure *f* de rajeunissement.
rejuvenesce [ridʒu:vi'nes], *esp. Biol:* **1.** *v.i. (of cells)* rajeunir; se revivifier. **2.** *v.tr.* rajeunir (des cellules).
rejuvenescence [ridʒu:vi'nes(ə)ns], *s. Biol:* rajeunissement *m*, revivification *f*, réjuvénescence *f.*
rejuvenescent [ridʒu:vi'nes(ə)nt], *a.* **1.** rajeunissant. **2.** en train de rajeunir.
rekey [ri:'ki:], *v.tr. Cmptr:* recomposer (sur un clavier); réintroduire (dans un ordinateur, etc.).
rekiln [ri:'kiln], *v.tr. Cer:* recuire.
rekindle [ri:'kindl]. **1.** *v.tr.* rallumer, renflammer (le feu, etc.); ranimer (l'espoir); réchauffer (le zèle de qn). **2.** *v.i.* se rallumer; *Lit:* **his love rekindled,** son amour se réveilla; son cœur se renflamma.
relapse[1] [ri'læps], *s.* **1. r. into sin, into vice,** rechute *f* dans le péché, dans le vice; **r. into crime,** récidive *f.* **2.** *Med:* rechute, récidive; **to have a r.,** faire, avoir, une rechute; rechuter.
relapse[2], *s. Theol:* relaps, -e.
relapse[3], *v.i.* **1. to r. into vice, into heresy,** retomber dans le vice, dans l'hérésie; **to r. into crime,** retomber dans le crime; récidiver; *Theol:* **relapsed heretic,** relaps, -e. **2.** *Med: (of patient)* rechuter; faire, avoir, une rechute.
relapser [ri'læpsər], *s. Theol:* relaps, -e.
relapsing [ri'læpsiŋ], *s.* rechute *f.*
relate [ri'leit]. **1.** *v.tr.* raconter, conter, narrer (une histoire, etc.); rapporter, *Jur:* relater (des faits); **to r. one's adventures,** faire le récit de ses aventures; **the historian who relates these facts,** l'historien narrateur de ces faits; **to r. sth. again,** renarrer qch.; **strange to r.!** chose étrange! chose étonnante à dire! **2.** *(a) v.tr. Nat.Hist: etc:* rapporter, rattacher (une espèce à une famille, etc.); apparenter (deux espèces); établir un rapport entre (deux faits, etc.); **we cannot r. this species to, with, any other,** nous ne pouvons apparenter cette espèce à aucune autre; *(b) v.i.* se rapporter, avoir rapport, avoir trait **(to,** à); **passage that relates to another,** passage qui se rapporte à un autre; **agreement relating to . . .,** convention ayant trait à . . .; **the charge relates to serious acts,** cette inculpation vise des faits graves; **the invention relates to . . .,** l'invention porte sur . . .; **he finds it difficult to r., he can't r. (to others),** il lui est difficile d'entrer en rapport avec les autres.
related [ri'leitid], *a.* **1.** *(a)* ayant rapport **(to,** à); **industries r. to shipbuilding,** industries connexes de la construction navale, qui se rattachent à la construction navale; **questions r. to a subject,** questions relatives à un sujet; *(b)* **r. ideas,** idées connexes; *Ch:* **r. elements,** éléments apparentés; *Mus:* **r. keys,** tons relatifs; *Nat.Hist:* **closely r. species,** espèces voisines. **2.** *(of pers.)* *(a)* apparenté **(to,** à); parent **(to,** de); *(by marriage)* allié **(to,** à); **he's r. to us,** il est notre parent; **they are r. (to each other),** ils sont parents entre eux; **we're r. by marriage,** nous sommes parents par alliance; **we're only r. on my mother's side,** nous ne sommes parents que par ma mère; **they are closely, nearly, r.,** ils sont proches parents; ils sont étroitement apparentés; *(by marriage)* ils sont alliés de près; **he is closely r. to me,** nous sommes proches parents; **they are very distantly r.,** il sont parents à un degré très éloigné; ils sont cousins à la mode de Bretagne; *(b) Gram:* **wrongly r. participle,** participe isolé, indépendant, sans soutien.
relatedness [ri'leitidnis], *s.* parenté *f* (de personnes); connexité *f* (d'idées, etc.).
relater [ri'leitər], *s.* raconteur, -euse; narrateur, -trice.
relating [ri'leitiŋ], *a.* **r. to . . .,** relatif à . . .; qui se rapporte à . . .; concernant . . .; *Adm: Jur:* afférent à . . .; **questions r. to a subject,** questions relatives à un sujet; **information r. to a matter,** renseignements afférents à une affaire; informations au sujet d'une affaire; **agreement r. to . . .,** convention ayant trait à . . ., afférente à . . ..
relation [ri'leiʃ(ə)n], *s.* **1.** relation *f*, récit *m* (d'événements, etc.); *Jur: (of public prosecutor)* **to act at the r. of s.o.,** agir à la suite d'une dénonciation. **2.** *(a)* relation, rapport *m*; **r. between cause and effect,** relation entre la cause et l'effet; **in r. to . . .,** relativement à . . .; par rapport à . . .; **the sun is motionless in r. to us,** le soleil est immobile quant à nous; **to bear a r. to . . .,** avoir rapport à . . .; **to bear no r. to . . ., to be out of all r. to . . .,** n'avoir aucun rapport avec . . .; **that has no r. to the present situation,** cela n'a rien à faire, rien à voir, avec la situation actuelle; *(b)* **human relations,** les relations humaines; **our relations with Holland,** nos relations avec la Hollande; **to have (business) relations with s.o.,** être en relations (d'affaires) avec qn; avoir, entretenir, des relations, des rapports (de commerce), avec qn; **public relations officer,** chef du service des relations avec le public, des relations publiques; *Pej:* **to have relations with crooks,** avoir des accointances *f* avec des escrocs; **suspected of relations with the enemy,** soupçonné d'accointance avec l'ennemi; **to enter into relations with s.o.,** (i) entrer, se mettre, en rapport, en relations, avec qn; entamer des relations avec qn; (ii) *Pej:* s'accointer avec qn, de qn; **to avoid all relations with strangers,** éviter tout contact avec les étrangers; **to break off all relations with s.o.,** rompre toutes relations, cesser tout rapport, ses relations, avec qn; **strained relations between two countries,** relations tendues entre deux pays; **patient-doctor relations,** rapports patient-médecin; **unlawful sexual relations,** rapports sexuels illicites. **3.** parent, -ente; **close, near, r.,** proche parent; **r. by marriage,** allié, -ée; **r. on the mother's side,** parent maternel; cognat *m*; **distant r.,** parent éloigné; **parents and relations,** ascendants directs et collatéraux; **what r. is he to you?** quelle est sa parenté avec vous? **is he any r. to you?** est-il de vos parents? **he's no r. to me, he's no r. of mine,** il n'est pas de mes parents; **he has no relations,** il n'a pas de famille; il est sans famille; **I have relations in Montreal,** j'ai de la famille à Montréal; **to treat s.o., sth., like a poor r.,** traiter qn, qch., en parent pauvre.
relational [ri'leiʃənəl], *a.* **1.** uni par des rapports étroits **(to,** avec); **r. words,** mots apparentés, connexes; **our r. duties to God and man,** nos devoirs envers Dieu et envers les hommes. **2.** *(a) Gram:* (mot) relatif; *(b) Phil:* relationnel; *(c) Cmptr:* **r. operator,** opérateur de relation.
relationless [ri'leiʃənlis], *a.* **1.** sans parents. **2.** sans relations.
relationship [ri'leiʃənʃip], *s.* **1.** *(a)* rapport *m*, connexité *f* (entre deux choses); *Anat:* **occlusal r.,** rapport occlusal; *Phil:* **the principle of r.,** le principe de connexité; **to bring two services into close r.,** établir des relations étroites entre deux services; *(b) (of pers.)* **to be in r. with s.o.,** avoir des relations avec qn; être en rapport, en commerce, avec qn; **patient-doctor r.,** rapports patient-médecin, entre le patient et le médecin. **2.** parenté *f*; *(by marriage)* parenté par alliance; **family r.,** lien *m* de parenté; **blood r.,** (degré *m* de) consanguinité *f*; proximité *f* de sang; parenté; **close, near, r.,** proximité de parenté.
relative ['relətiv]. **1.** *a.* *(a)* relatif, qui se rapporte **(to,** à); **negotiations r. to an alliance,** négociations relatives à une alliance, visant une alliance; *(b) (of movement, level, terms, etc.)* relatif; **r. silence,** silence relatif; **the r. advantages of two methods,** les avantages relatifs, respectifs, de deux méthodes; **they live in r. luxury,** ils vivent dans un luxe relatif; **luxury is r. to one's standard of living,** ce que nous appelons luxe dépend de notre niveau de vie; **everything is r.,** tout est relatif; *Ph: etc:* **r. humidity, pressure,** humidité, pression, relative; **the force is r. to the length of the lever,** la force exercée dépend de la longueur du levier; *Anat:* **r. positions of two organs,** relations *f* de deux organes; *Mil:* **r. rank,** assimilation *f* (d'un non-combattant, etc.); grade auquel un non-combattant est assimilé; **r. rank, captain,** assimilé au grade de capitaine; *(c) Gram:* **r. pronoun,** *s.* **r.,** (pronom) relatif *m*; **r. clause,** proposition relative; *Mus:* **r. keys,** tons relatifs; **r. major and minor,** modes relatifs; *Cmptr:* **r. address,** adresse relative; **r. code,** code relatif. **2.** *adv. F:* **I am writing r. to my health, to the rent,** je vous écris au sujet de ma santé, du loyer. **3.** *s.* *(a)* = RELATION 3; *(b) Phil:* **the r.,** le relatif.
relatively ['relətivli], *adv.* *(a)* relativement **(to,** à); par rapport (à); **that is only r. true,** cela n'est vrai que relativement; *(b)* **she is r. happy,** somme toute elle est assez heureuse.
relativeness ['relətivnis], *s.* relativité *f*; caractère relatif.
relativism ['relətivizm], *s. Phil:* relativisme *m.*
relativist ['relətivist], *s. Phil:* relativiste *mf.*
relativistic [relətі'vistik], *a.* relativiste.
relativity [relə'tiviti], *s.* relativité *f*; **theory of r.,** théorie de la relativité; **special (theory of) r., restricted (theory of) r.,** (théorie de la) relativité restreinte; **general r.,**

relativité généralisée; **laws of r.,** mécanique *f* relativiste.

relator [ri'leitər], *s.* (*a*) = RELATER; (*b*) *Jur:* dénonciateur, -trice.

relax [ri'læks]. **1.** *v.tr.* (*a*) relâcher (les muscles, l'attention, la discipline); décontracter, relaxer (les muscles); détendre, délasser (l'esprit); détendre, débander (un arc); **to r. one's efforts,** se relâcher dans ses efforts; **to r. one's hold, a blockade,** desserrer son étreinte, un blocus; **to r. one's features,** se dérider; **she relaxed her tone of severity,** son ton s'est adouci; **I read to r. my mind,** je lis pour me délasser l'esprit; (*b*) *Med:* **relaxed throat,** pharyngite subaiguë; (*c*) (*of climate*) épuiser, débiliter; (*d*) mitiger (une loi, une peine). **2.** *v.i.* (*a*) (*of muscles, etc.*) se relâcher, se détendre, se débander; **his face relaxed into a smile,** son visage s'est détendu dans un sourire; **if the cold relaxes,** si le froid diminue; (*b*) (*of pers.*) se détendre, se délasser, se décontracter, se relaxer; **to r. for an hour,** se détendre pendant une heure; prendre une heure de délassement; **to r. in one's efforts,** se relâcher dans ses efforts.

relaxant [ri'læks(ə)nt], *a. & s.* relâchant (*m*); décontractant (*m*); **muscle r.,** relaxant *m* musculaire, myorésolutif *m*.

relaxation [ri:læk'seiʃ(ə)n], *s.* **1.** (*a*) relâchement *m* (des muscles, des nerfs, de la discipline); décontraction *f*, détente *f*, relaxation *f* (des muscles); détente, délassement *m* (de l'esprit); (*b*) mitigation *f* (d'une loi, d'une peine). **2.** relâche *m & f*, délassement, repos *m*, détente; relaxation; récréation *f*; **to take some r.,** prendre un peu de relâche; se donner relâche; se délasser; **r. after the day's work,** détente après le travail de la journée; **this work is a r. for my mind,** ce travail me délasse, me détend, l'esprit, me donne un peu de répit; **these little jobs come as r.,** ces petits travaux me permettent de me détendre; **as a r., I . . .,** pour me délasser, je . . .; **he finds r. in reading,** il se délasse à lire; **fishing is his only r.,** la pêche est son seul délassement. **3.** *Ph:* relaxation; *Atom.Ph:* **r. length,** longueur de relaxation; **r. method,** méthode de relaxation; **r. time,** temps de relaxation; *El:* **r. oscillation,** oscillation de relaxation; **r. oscillator,** oscillateur à relaxation; *Elcs:* **r. scanning,** balayage de relaxation.

relaxin [ri'læksin], *s. Physiol:* relaxine *f*.

relaxing[1] [ri'læksiŋ], *a.* qui détend; (climat) épuisant, débilitant; *Med:* (médicament) relâchant.

relaxing[2], *s.* = RELAXATION 1.

relay[1] ['ri:lei], *s.* **1.** relais *m* (d'hommes, de chevaux); relève *f* (d'ouvriers); **to work in relays,** se relayer; *Sp:* **r. (race),** course *f* de relais; *A:* **r. horse,** cheval de relais. **2.** (*a*) *El: Elcs:* relais; contacteur-disjoncteur *m*, *pl.* contacteurs-disjoncteurs; **current r.,** relais d'intensité; **voltage r.,** relais de tension; **frequency r.,** relais de fréquence; **overload, overvoltage, r.,** relais à maxima, relais de surtension; **underload, undervoltage, r.,** relais à minima, relais de soustension; **underfrequency r.,** relais à seuil de fréquences; **phase sequence r.,** relais d'ordre de phase; **differential r.,** relais différentiel; **time delay(ed), time (lag), r.,** relais retardé, temporisé; relais à action différée, à retardement; **polarized, biased, r.,** relais polarisé; **electric, electronic, r.,** relais électrique, électronique; **(electro)magnetic r.,** relais (électro)-magnétique; **two step r.,** relais à deux seuils, à double effet, à action échelonnée; **switching r.,** relais de commutation; **equalizing r.,** relais d'équilibrage; **sensing r.,** relais détecteur; **protective r.,** relais de protection, relais protecteur; **selective r.,** relais de sélection, relais sélecteur; **cut-off r.,** relais de coupure; **load relief, load shedding, r.,** relais de délestage; **alarm r.,** relais avertisseur, relais de contrôle; **pilot r.,** relais pilote, relais de contrôle; **r. contact,** contact de relais; **r. magnet,** aimant de relais; **r. coil,** bobine de relais; (*b*) *Mec.E:* servomoteur *m*; relais-moteur *m*, *pl.* relais-moteurs; moteur asservi; (*c*) *Mec.E: I.C.E:* **starting r.,** relais de démarrage, de mise en marche, de mise en route; **regulating r.,** relais de réglage; **reverse pitch, reversing, r.,** relais de réversion; **throttle r.,** relais de commande des gaz; **belt housing r.,** relais de carter de volant; **transfer unit r.,** relais de boîte (de vitesses) auxiliaire; **transmission by r.,** transmission par relais; **r. valve,** tiroir-relais *m*, *pl.* tiroirs-relais. **3.** (*a*) *Tg:* retransmetteur *m*; (*b*) *Tp:* **(telephone) r.,** relais (téléphonique); **calling,** *NAm:* **ringing, r.,** relais d'appel, de sonnerie; **holding r.,** relais d'occupation; **clearing r.,** relais de fin de conversation; **metering,** *NAm:* **counting, r.,** relais compteur (d'impulsions); **relief r.,** relais de délestage; **automatic r. system,** *NAm:* **all-r. system,** système automatique tout à relais; (*c*) *W.Tel: T.V: etc:* retransmission *f*; radiodiffusion relayée; **connection for simultaneous r.,** position en simultané; **(automatic) tape r.,** retransmission, relais, (automatique) par bande perforée; **r. (station),** (station *f*, émetteur *m*) relais; station de répéteurs; répéteur *m*, réémetteur *m*; **r. broadcasting station,** relais de radiodiffusion; **r. broadcast,** émission *f* relais; **radio r.,** câble hertzien; **radio r. station,** station de câbles hertziens; **radio r. system,** réseau de câbles hertziens; faisceau hertzien; **r. reception,** réception *f* relais; **r. transmitter,** émetteur de station relais; **distance r.,** télérelais *m*; **impedance r.,** télérelais d'impédance; **reactance r.,** télérelais de réactance; **light r.,** relais photoélectrique; **microwave r.,** relais hertzien; **r. radar,** retransmission de la réception radar; (*d*) *Cmptr:* **r. computer, calculator,** calculatrice à relais; **r. centre,** centre de commutation.

relay[2] [ri(:)'lei], *v.tr.* (*p.t. & p.p.* **relayed** [ri(:)'leid]) *El: Tp: W.Tel: etc:* **1.** relayer (un message téléphonique, etc.); réémettre, retransmettre, relayer (une émission de radio, de télévision, etc.); transmettre (un message) par relais; retransmettre (un message). **2.** *Tg:* munir (une ligne) de relais.

re-lay ['ri:'lei], *v.tr.* (*p.t. & p.p.* **re-laid** [-'leid]) **1.** poser (un tapis, etc.) de nouveau, à nouveau; remettre (le couvert). **2.** reposer (une voie ferrée, etc.); remanier (une canalisation). **3.** *Nau:* remettre en batterie, repointer (un canon); **re-laid rope,** cordage morfondu.

relaying [ri(:)'leiiŋ], *s. Tg:* translation *f* (d'une dépêche); *W.Tel: T.V:* retransmission *f* (d'une émission).

re-laying [ri:'leiiŋ], *s.* nouvelle pose (de tuyaux, de câbles, etc.); repose *f*, réfection *f* (d'une voie ferrée, etc.); remaniement *m* (d'une canalisation). **2.** repointage *m* (d'une arme à feu).

relearn [ri:'lə:n], *v.tr.* rapprendre, réapprendre.

releasable [ri'li:səbl], *a.* **1.** (dispositif) qui peut se déclencher; *Tchn:* libérable. **2.** *Av:* (réservoir) à essence, etc.) largable. **2.** *Journ:* (informations) qu'on peut communiquer (au public); *Cin:* (film) qui peut être distribué.

release[1] [ri'li:s], *s.* **1.** (*a*) (*of pers.*) délivrance *f*, libération *f* (**from care,** du souci); décharge *f*, libération (**from an obligation,** d'une obligation); *Mil:* mise *f* en disponibilité; *Adm:* démobilisation *f*; **I granted him a r. from this debt, from the fine,** je lui ai fait la remise de cette dette, de l'amende; (*b*) élargissement *m*, (re)mise *f* en liberté, libération, *Jur:* relaxe *f* (d'un prisonnier); **order of r.,** (ordre *m* de) levée *f* d'écrou; **to order s.o.'s r.,** prendre des mesures d'élargissement à l'égard de qn; **r. (of prisoner) on licence,** libération conditionnelle (d'un prisonnier); **r. on bail,** mise en liberté provisoire (sous caution); **day r.,** jour de permission accordé aux employés d'une maison pour se perfectionner; (*c*) lâcher *m*, lancer *m* (de pigeons); (*d*) *Cust:* **r. of wine from bond,** congé *m* pour le transport des vins; **r. of goods against payment,** libération de marchandises; (*e*) (i) sortie *f*, mise en vente (d'une nouvelle voiture, etc.); (ii) *Journ:* autorisation *f* de publier (un article); (iii) *Journ:* **press r.,** communiqué *m* de presse; (iv) *Adm:* envoi *m*, diffusion *f* (d'un document); (v) *Cin:* distribution *f*, mise en circulation, sortie (d'un film); **film on general r.,** film qui passe dans plusieurs cinémas, qui passe à la région; (vi) *coll. Cin:* ensemble *m* des copies à distribuer. **2.** (*a*) *Ch: etc:* mise en liberté, libération, dégagement *m* (d'un gaz, etc.); émission *f* (de gaz asphyxiant, etc.); *Mch:* émission, échappement *m* (de la vapeur, etc.); relâchement *m* (de pression); **r. valve,** (i) soupape de sûreté; (ii) robinet *m* (d'une bouteille à gaz, etc.); *I.C.E:* **oil pressure r.,** reniflard *m*; (*b*) *Av:* largage *m* (d'une bombe, d'un parachute, etc.); **bomb r. (mechanism),** dispositif, système, de largage des bombes; **emergency r.,** largage d'urgence; **r. altitude,** altitude de largage; **brake parachute r.,** déclenchement *m*, sortie, du parachute de freinage; (*c*) *Mec.E: etc:* mise en marche, démarrage *m* (d'un appareil); décompression *f*, libération (d'un ressort); déclenchement, déclenche *f*, déclic *m*, desserrage *m*, déblocage *m*, dégagement *m*, libération (d'une pièce de mécanisme); *Mch.Tls:* débrayage *m*; **r. by cam,** débrayage par excentrique; **delayed action r.,** déclenchement différé; **full r.,** point mort (des freins); **brakes in r. position,** freins au repos; **ratchet r.,** relâchement par cliquet; **pawl r.,** déclencheur *m* de cliquet; **r. gear, device,** déclenche, déclencheur, déclic, débloqueur *m*; dispositif, mécanisme, de déclenchement, de débrayage, de déblocage; **r. button, knob,** bouton de déclenchement, de démarrage; démarreur *m*; *Phot:* **(shutter) r.,** (i) déclenchement (de l'obturateur); (ii) déclencheur; **bulb, pneumatic, r.,** (i) déclenchement à la poire, pneumatique; (ii) déclencheur à poire; **trigger r.,** (i) déclenchement, (ii) déclencheur, au doigt; *Typewr:* **carriage r. (lever),** levier, touche, de dégagement du chariot; (*d*) *El:* (i) déclenchement (d'un disjoncteur, etc.); décollage *m*, déblocage (d'éléments en contact); **non-volt r.,** déclenchement à tension nulle; **r. voltage,** tension de décollage; **r. time,** durée de réenclenchement; *Elcs:* **squelch r.,** déblocage d'un éliminateur de bruits de fond; *Tp:* **r. signal,** signal de fin de communication; (ii) disjoncteur, interrupteur *m*; (*e*) *Ph: etc:* **r. of energy,** libération de l'énergie; **Wigner r.,** libération d'énergie Wigner; *Atom.Ph:* **r. counter,** compteur à déclenchement; (*f*) *Cmptr:* libération (de la mémoire, etc.). **3.** *Com:* acquit *m*, quittance *f*, reçu *m*. **4.** *Jur:* cession *f*, transfert *m*, abandon *m* (de terres).

release[2], *v.tr.* **1.** (*a*) décharger, acquitter, libérer (qn d'une obligation); libérer (un débiteur); *Mil:* mettre (qch.) en disponibilité; **to r. a nun from her vows,** relever une religieuse de ses vœux; **to r. s.o. from his promise,** délier, relever, qn de sa promesse; rendre sa parole à qn; tenir qn quitte de sa promesse; **to r. s.o. from bondage,** délivrer qn de la captivité; (*b*) libérer, élargir, relâcher, relaxer (un prisonnier); **released on bail,** remis en liberté sous caution; **to r. a bird,** relâcher un oiseau; donner libre essor à un oiseau; (*c*) lâcher (des pigeons voyageurs); *Mil:* **to r. poison gas,** lâcher des gaz asphyxiants; (*d*) (i) sortir, mettre en vente (une nouvelle voiture, etc.); (ii) permettre la publication (d'un article); rendre public, divulguer (une nouvelle); envoyer, diffuser (un document écrit); (iii) *Cin:* distribuer (un film); mettre (un film) en circulation; (*e*) *Fin:* débloquer (des fonds); (*f*) **she tried to r. her hand,** elle a essayé de dégager sa main. **2.** (*a*) *Ch: etc:* dégager, laisser échapper (un gaz); émettre (de la fumée, etc.); **hydrogen is released at the cathode,** l'hydrogène est libéré, se dégage, à la cathode; (*b*) *Av:* lâcher, larguer (une bombe); lancer (un parachute); larguer (un réservoir à essence, etc.); (*c*) lâcher (son emprise, etc.); lâcher, détendre, faire jouer (un ressort); décliquer (un doigt d'encliquetage); déclencher, décoller (un organe); **to r. one's hold,** (i) desserrer son étreinte; (ii) lâcher prise; **to r. one's hold of sth.,** lâcher qch.; **to r. the brake,** desserrer, ôter, débloquer, dégager, le frein; **to r. the clutch,** débrayer; **to r. the monkey of a pile driver,** décliquer le mouton d'une sonnette; **to r. the trigger of a gun,** faire jouer la gâchette d'un fusil; *Phot:* **to r. the shutter,** déclencher l'obturateur; (*d*) *Cmptr:* libérer (la mémoire, etc.). **3.** *Jur:* (*a*) **to r. a debt, a tax,** remettre une dette, un impôt; faire (à qn) la remise d'une dette, d'un impôt; (*b*) abandonner, renoncer à (un droit, une créance); (*c*) céder, transférer (une terre).

releasee [rili:'si:], *s. Jur:* renonciataire *mf*, cessionnaire *mf*, abandonnataire *mf*.

releaser [ri'li:sər], *s.* **1.** (*device*) déclencheur *m*, démarreur *m*. **2.** *Cin:* (*pers.*) distributeur *m*, loueur *m* (de films).

releasor [ri'li:sər], *s. Jur:* renonciateur, -trice (**of a right,** à un droit); cédant, -ante (**of an estate,** d'une terre).

relegable ['religəbl], *a.* **1.** qu'on peut reléguer (**to,** à). **2.** qu'on peut (i) remettre, (ii) renvoyer (**to,** à).

relegate ['religeit], *v.tr.* **1.** reléguer (un tableau au grenier, un fonctionnaire aux colonies, etc.); bannir, exiler (qn); **girl relegated to a convent,** jeune fille séquestrée, mise en séquestre, dans un couvent; **to r. s.o. to the end of the table,** renvoyer qn au bout de la table; *Fb:* **to r. a team (to the next division),** reléguer une équipe à la division inférieure (de la Ligue); **to r. sth. to the past, to fable,** reléguer qch. dans le passé, parmi les fables. **2.** (*a*) **to r. a matter to s.o.,** (i) remettre une question à la décision de qn; (ii) confier, remettre, une affaire à qn; (*b*) renvoyer (qn à une autorité, etc.).

relegation [reli'geiʃ(ə)n], *s.* **1.** (*a*) *Jur:* relégation *f*, bannissement *m*, exil *m*; (*b*) *Fb:* renvoi *m* d'une équipe à la division inférieure (de la Ligue); (*c*) mise *f* à l'écart (d'un objet inutile, etc.). **2.** renvoi (d'une affaire à qn).

relent [ri'lent], *v.i.* s'adoucir, se radoucir; se laisser attendrir; se laisser fléchir; revenir sur une décision (sévère); **he would not r. (towards me),** il ne s'est pas laissé attendrir; il m'a tenu rigueur.

relentingly [ri'lentiŋli], *adv.* avec une certaine indulgence; avec moins de rigueur *f*.

relentless [ri'lentlis], *a.* (*a*) implacable, impitoyable, inflexible, intransigeant; (*b*) **r. persecution,** persécution sans rémission; **to be r. in doing sth.,** mettre de l'acharnement, s'acharner, à faire qch.

relentlessly [ri'lentlisli], *adv.* (*a*) implacablement, impitoyablement, inflexiblement; (*b*) sans rémission.

relentlessness [ri'lentlisnis], *s.* inflexibilité *f*, implacabilité *f*, intransigeance *f*; **r. in revenge,** acharnement *m* à la vengeance.

relet [ri:'let], *v.tr.* (i) relouer (une maison, etc.); (ii) renouveler le bail (d'une maison, etc.).

reletting [ri:'letiŋ], *s.* relocation *f*.

relevance ['reləvəns], **relevancy** ['reləvənsi], *s.* pertinence *f*, à-propos *m*; applicabilité *f* (**to,** à); convenance *f*; rapport *m* (**to,** avec).

relevant ['reləvənt], *a.* qui a rapport (**to,** à); applicable, pertinent (**to,** à); à propos (**to,** de); **r. facts,** faits pertinents, significatifs; **detail r. to the event,** détail qui touche à l'événement; détail pertinent; **the r. documents,** les documents qui se rapportent à l'affaire; *Jur:* les pièces justificatives; **all r. information,** tous renseignements utiles.
relevantly ['reləvəntli], *adv.* pertinemment.
relevel [ri:'levl], *v.tr.* (**relevelled**) reniveler.
relevelling [ri:'levliŋ], *s.* renivellement *m.*
reliability [rilaiə'biliti], *s.* sûreté *f*; honnêteté *f*, véracité *f* (de qn); sûreté (de la mémoire); crédibilité *f* (d'une rumeur); sûreté de fonctionnement, sécurité *f* du fonctionnement, régularité *f* de marche, fiabilité *f* (d'une machine); *Aut:* **r. test,** épreuve *f* de régularité; épreuve, course, d'endurance.
reliable [ri'laiəbl], *a.* sûr; (homme) sérieux, digne de confiance, de foi; (homme) de toute confiance, sur lequel on peut compter, auquel on peut se fier; (ami) solide, *Fr.C:* fiable; (caractère) d'une bonne trempe; (renseignement) sûr, qu'on peut croire; (machine) fiable, qui offre toute garantie; (machine) d'un fonctionnement sûr, de tout repos; **r. tool,** bon outil; **r. firm,** maison de confiance; **r. guarantee,** garantie solide; **r. list,** liste à laquelle on peut se fier; **to have sth. from a r. source,** tenir qch. de bonne source, de bonne part; *Jur:* **r. evidence, witness,** témoignage, témoin, sans reproche.
reliableness [ri'laiəblnis], *s.* = RELIABILITY.
reliably [ri'laiəbli], *adv.* sûrement; d'une manière digne de foi, de confiance.
reliance [ri'laiəns], *s.* **1.** confiance *f*; **to place r. in, on, s.o.,** mettre sa confiance dans qn; avoir (de la) confiance en, dans, qn; se fier à qn; compter sur qn; **I put little r. in him,** je ne me repose pas beaucoup sur lui; je fais peu de fond sur lui; **there is no r. to be placed on his word,** on ne peut pas se fier à sa parole; **self r.,** indépendance *f*; confiance en soi. **2.** personne, chose, en laquelle on met confiance; soutien *m*, appui *m.*
reliant [ri'laiənt], *a.* **to be r. on . . .,** (i) avoir confiance en, dans . . .; compter sur . . .; (ii) dépendre de (qn pour vivre); **self-r.,** indépendant; qui a confiance en soi.
relic ['relik], *s.* **1.** *Ecc:* relique *f.* **2.** *pl.* restes *m*; (*a*) dépouille mortelle; (*b*) **relics of the past,** vestiges *m* du passé; survivance *f* des temps passés.
relict ['relikt], *s.* **1.** *Jur:* veuve *f* (**of,** de). **2.** *Nat.Hist:* relique *f*, relicte *f.*
relief[1] [ri'li:f], *s.* **1.** (*a*) soulagement *m* (d'une douleur, etc.); allégement *m* (d'une détresse, etc.); **to bring r. to s.o.,** apporter du soulagement à qn; **to feel some r.,** éprouver un certain soulagement; **to heave a sigh of r.,** pousser un soupir de soulagement; **that's, what, a r.!** ouf! on respire! **it's a r. to talk about one's problems,** on soulage ses maux à les raconter; **it was somewhat of a r. to me when . . .,** j'ai été légèrement soulagé quand . . .; **to find r. in work,** trouver un dérivatif dans le travail; (*b*) **black dress without r.,** robe noire sans agrément; **blank wall without r.,** mur d'une nudité monotone; **a comic scene follows by way of r.,** une scène comique suit pour détendre les esprits; **it was a r. to the eye,** cela reposait la vue; (*c*) décharge *f*; **r. of pressure,** réduction *f* de pression; *Mch:* décompression *f*; *Mch:* **r. cock,** décompresseur *m*; **r. valve,** soupape *f* de sûreté, de décompression; clapet *m* de décharge; *I.C.E:* clapet d'excès de pression; **r. from taxation,** dégrèvement *m*; **tax r.,** allégement fiscal, des impôts. **2.** secours *m*, assistance *f*, aide *f*; (*a*) **to go to s.o.'s r.,** aller, se porter, au secours de qn, à l'aide de qn; **r. fund,** caisse de secours (en cas de sinistre, etc.); **r. train,** (i) train de secours; (ii) (train) supplémentaire *m*; **r. engine,** locomotive de secours; (*b*) *Adm: A:* **(poor) r.,** secours, aide, aux pauvres; assistance publique; **out(door) r.,** secours à domicile; **r. credits,** crédits de secours. **3.** (*a*) *Mil:* délivrance *f*, dégagement *m* (d'une ville, d'une place forte); **they went to the r. of the town,** ils sont allés au secours de la ville; **r. troops,** (troupes de) secours; (*b*) *Mil: etc:* relève *f* (d'une garde, etc.); *Nau:* relève du quart; **r. man,** (sentinelle *f* de) relève; **r. party, draft of reliefs,** (détachement de) relève; **r. worker,** travailleur suppléant. **4.** *Jur:* réparation *f* (d'un grief); redressement *m* (d'un tort); **he could get no r.,** il n'a pu obtenir justice. **5.** *Mec.E:* dégagement, dépouille *f* (d'un foret, d'une fraise); (*of tool*) **angle of r.,** angle de dépouille, d'incidence.
relief[2], *s.* **1.** *Art:* relief *m*; modelé *m*; **high r., low r.,** haut-relief, bas-relief; *Sculp:* **half r.,** demi-bosse *f*; **in r.,** en relief; (ouvrage) relevé en bosse; **to stand out in r.,** ressortir, saillir; se détacher, se découper (**against,** sur); s'accuser (**against,** contre); **to bring, throw, sth. into r.,** relever qch.; faire ressortir qch.; mettre qch. en relief; donner du relief à qch.; **to bring sth. out in strong r., in bold r.,** faire vivement ressortir qch.; **detail that is not in sufficient r.,** détail qui n'a pas assez de saillie; **to give r. to one's style,** donner du relief à son style; **r. map, model,** carte, plan, en relief. **2.** (*a*) *Geog:* relief (terrestre); (*b*) *Fort:* relief, élévation *f* (des remparts, etc.); (*c*) *Typ:* **r. printing,** typographie *f.*
relievable [ri'li:vəbl], *a.* **1.** (douleur) qu'on peut soulager; (mal) remédiable. **2.** *Mil:* (place forte) secourable.
relieve [ri'li:v], *v.tr.* **1.** (*a*) soulager, alléger (la misère, les souffrances, de qn); **I'm very relieved to hear it,** c'est un grand soulagement pour moi de l'apprendre; **to r. s.o.'s mind,** tranquilliser l'esprit de qn; **to r. one's feelings,** se décharger le cœur; se soulager; **to r. oneself, to r. nature,** faire ses besoins; se soulager; (*b*) **black dress relieved by, with, white lace,** robe noire agrémentée de dentelle blanche; **to r. the severity of one's mourning,** égayer son deuil; **his lecture was relieved by wit,** sa conférence était relevée par des traits d'esprit; **there was nothing to r. the gloom of the play,** il n'y avait rien pour racheter la mélancolie de la pièce; **to r. the tedium of the journey,** tromper l'ennui du voyage; **to r. the monotony we went for a walk,** pour nous changer les idées nous sommes allés nous promener; (*c*) soulager, décharger (une soupape, etc.); réduire (la pression); **to r. the strain on a beam,** soulager une poutre; **to r. congestion,** (i) faciliter la circulation (aux heures d'affluence, etc.); (ii) *Med:* décongestionner (les poumons, etc.). **2.** secourir, aider, assister (qn); venir en aide à (qn); subvenir aux besoins de (qn). **3. to r. s.o. of sth.,** soulager, délester, alléger, qn (d'un fardeau); débarrasser qn (de son manteau, etc.); délivrer, tirer, ôter, qn (d'un doute, etc.); dégager, délier, relever, affranchir, qn (d'une obligation); relever, destituer, qn (de ses fonctions); **to be relieved of a tax,** être allégé d'un impôt; **relieved of all anxiety,** hors d'inquiétude; allégé de tout souci; **it relieves me of all responsibility,** cela me dégage de toute responsabilité; **to r. s.o. of the necessity of working,** dispenser qn de travailler; *F:* **to r. s.o. of his wallet,** soulager qn de son portefeuille. **4.** (*a*) *Mil:* délivrer, dégager, secourir (une ville, une place forte); (*b*) relever, relayer (qn); *Mil:* **to r. the guard,** relever la garde; *Nau:* **to r. the watch,** relever, remplacer, au quart; changer le quart; faire la relève. **5.** *Mec.E:* dépouiller, dégager (un foret, un taraud). **6.** *Art: Sculp: etc:* relever, mettre en relief, donner du relief à (un motif); faire ressortir (une couleur, etc.); détacher (le sujet sur le fond); **relieved against a dark background,** qui ressort, qui se découpe, qui se détache, qui tranche, sur un fond noir.
reliever [ri'li:vər], *s.* **1.** (*a*) personne *f* qui soulage, qui secourt; secoureur *m*; (*b*) *Scot: Ecc.Hist:* **Relievers,** secoureurs. **2.** dispositif *m* de soulagement, d'allégement.
relieving[1] [ri'li:viŋ], *a.* **1.** (*a*) *Mil:* (armée) de secours; (*b*) (équipe, etc.) de relève; *Mil:* **r. troops,** (troupes de) relève *f.* **2.** *Nau:* **r. tackle,** palans *mpl* de retenue du gouvernail; palans de barre; attrape *f.* **3.** *Arch:* **r. arch,** arc de décharge; voûte de décharge; *Civ.E: etc:* arche de soutènement.
relieving[2], *s.* **1.** (*a*) soulagement *m*, allégement *m* (d'une douleur, etc.); (*b*) *Med:* soulagement (du ventre). **2.** (*a*) *Mil:* délivrance *f*, dégagement *m* (d'une ville, etc.); (*b*) relève *f*, relèvement *m* (d'une sentinelle, etc.).
relievo [ri'li:vou], *s.* *Art:* relief *m*; **alto r.,** haut-relief *m*; **basso r.,** bas-relief *m*; **in r.,** en relief.
relight[1] ['ri:lait], *s.* *Av:* réallumage *m* (d'un turboréacteur).
relight[2] [ri:'lait]. **1.** *v.tr.* rallumer; *Av:* réallumer (un turboréacteur). **2.** *v.i.* se rallumer.
relighting [ri:'laitiŋ], *s.* rallumage *m.*
religion [ri'lidʒən], *s.* religion *f*; culte *m*; *Adm:* confession *f*; **freedom of r.,** liberté *f* du culte; **established r.,** religion d'État; **to enter into r.,** entrer en religion; **her name in r. is Sister Anne,** elle s'appelle en religion sœur Anne; *F:* **to get r.,** se convertir; **to take to r.,** tomber, se jeter, dans la dévotion; **to make a r. of (doing) sth.,** se faire une religion de (faire) qch.; **what r. are you?** quelle religion pratiquez-vous? *Hist:* **the wars of r.,** les guerres de religion.
religionism [ri'lidʒənizm], *s.* (i) dévotion *f*; (ii) bigoterie *f.*
religionist [ri'lidʒənist], *s.* (i) dévot, -ote; (ii) bigot, -ote.
religiosity [rilidʒi'ɔsiti], *s.* bigoterie *f.*
religious [ri'lidʒəs]. **1.** *a.* (*a*) religieux, pieux, dévot; **he is very r.,** il est très pieux; **to lead a r. life,** vivre religieusement; (*b*) (ordre) religieux; **r. life,** vie religieuse, de religion; **r. book,** livre de piété, de dévotion; **r. exercises,** exercices spirituels; **r. habit,** habit monastique, de religieux; **r. minorities,** minorités de religion; **to be r.,** avoir de la religion; **r. persuasion,** confession *f*; **r. fanaticism,** fanatisme religieux; **r. persecution,** persécution religieuse; **r. wars,** guerres de religion; *Art:* **r. subject,** sujet de sainteté; (*c*) (soin, silence) religieux, scrupuleux; **r. exactitude,** exactitude scrupuleuse. **2.** *s.* (*inv. in pl.*) *Ecc:* religieux, -euse; **the r. of the Sacred Heart,** les dames *f* du Sacré-Cœur.
religiously [ri'lidʒəsli], *adv.* **1.** (*a*) religieusement, pieusement; (*b*) religieusement, scrupuleusement; **she r. polished the furniture even when the family was away,** elle polissait religieusement tous les meubles même quand la famille était absente. **2.** au point de vue religieux.
religiousness [ri'lidʒəsnis], *s.* (*a*) piété *f*, dévotion *f*; caractère religieux, pieux; (*b*) scrupulosité *f* (**in doing sth.,** à faire qch.).
reline [ri:'lain], *v.tr.* **1.** remettre une doublure à (un manteau, etc.); rentoiler (un tableau, etc.). **2.** (*a*) regarnir (un frein, un coussinet, etc.); revêtir à nouveau (un fourneau, un puits de mine); (*b*) *Mec.E: I.C.E:* rechemiser (un cylindre, etc.).
relining [ri:'lainiŋ], *s.* **1.** (*a*) remplacement *m* de la doublure (d'un manteau, etc.); rentoilage *m* (d'un tableau, etc.); (*b*) regarnissage *m* (de freins, etc.); rechemisage *m* (de cylindres). **2.** nouveau revêtement (intérieur).
relinquish [ri'liŋkwiʃ], *v.tr.* **1.** abandonner (une habitude, tout espoir); renoncer à (un projet, un droit); se dessaisir de (ses biens); *Jur:* délaisser (un droit, une succession); répudier (une succession); **to r. one's place, one's appointment,** abandonner, céder, sa place; résigner ses fonctions. **2.** lâcher prise de (qch.); lâcher (qch.).
relinquishing, relinquishment [ri'liŋkwiʃiŋ, -mənt], *s.* abandon *m*, abandonnement *m* (de ses biens, etc.); renonciation *f* (**of a right,** à un droit); dessaisissement *m* (d'une propriété, etc.); **r. of one's property,** dépouillement *m* volontaire de ses biens; *Jur:* **r. of a succession,** répudiation *f* d'une succession.
reliquary ['relikwəri], *s.* reliquaire *m*; **arched r.,** absidiole *f.*
reliquiae [ri'likwii:], *s.pl.* restes *m* (fossiles, etc.).
relish[1] ['reliʃ], *s.* **1.** (*a*) goût *m*, saveur *f* (d'un mets, etc.); **to give r. to a dish,** assaisonner un mets; **food has no r. when one is ill,** on ne trouve plus de goût à sa nourriture quand on est malade; **the r. of novelty,** l'attrait *m* de la nouveauté; **danger gives r. to an adventure,** le danger donne du relief, du piquant, à une aventure; (*b*) sauce piquante (à base de tomates, etc.); condiment *m* (de légumes, etc., au vinaigre); assaisonnement *m*; (*c*) *Cu:* soupçon *m*, pointe *f* (de piment, etc.); (*d*) *Cu:* petit hors-d'œuvre *inv*; amuse-gueule *m, pl.* amuse-gueules. **2. to eat sth. with r.,** manger qch. de bon appétit; savourer qch. avec délectation; **he used to tell the story with great r.,** il se délectait à raconter cette histoire; *O:* **to have a r. for sth.,** avoir du goût pour qch.; avoir un penchant à, pour (qch.); **he has little r. for games,** il prend, trouve, peu de plaisir aux jeux.
relish[2]. **1.** *v.tr.* (*a*) donner du goût à (un mets); relever le goût de (qch.); (*b*) (*of pers.*) goûter, savourer (un mets); trouver goût à (qch.); trouver bon (qch.); **he relished this simple family life,** il goûtait beaucoup cette simple vie de famille; **to r. doing sth.,** trouver du plaisir à faire qch.; **we didn't r. the idea,** l'idée *f* ne nous souriait pas; **I don't r. the prospect,** je ne goûte pas beaucoup cette perspective. **2.** *v.i.* *O:* **to r. of sth.,** avoir un léger goût de qch.; sentir (l'ail, etc.).
relive [ri:'liv], *v.tr.* revivre (sa vie, le passé).
reload [ri:'loud], *v.tr.* recharger (un navire, une arme à feu, etc.).
reloading [ri:'loudiŋ], *s.* rechargement *m*; *Nau:* **r. charges,** frais *m* de transbordement.
relocatable [ri:lou'keitəbl], *a.* *Cmptr:* réadressable, translatable, relogeable; en forme relative.
relocate [ri:lou'keit], *v.tr.* *Cmptr:* translater, reloger (un programme).
relocation [ri:lou'keiʃ(ə)n], *s.* replacement *m* (de personnel); *Cmptr:* réadressage *m*, translation *f*; **r. dictionary,** liste *f* d'adresses relogeables.
reluctance [ri'lʌktəns], *s.* **1.** répugnance *f* (**to do sth.,** à faire qch.); **to show (some) r. to do sth.,** montrer quelque répugnance à faire qch.; se montrer peu disposé, peu empressé, à faire qch.; montrer peu d'empressement à faire qch.; hésiter, résister, à faire qch.; **he showed no r. to . . .,** il ne s'est pas fait tirer l'oreille pour . . .; **to do sth. with r.,** faire qch. à regret, à contrecœur, à son corps défendant. **2.** *El:* réluctance *f*; résistance *f* magnétique; **specific r.,** résistivité *f* spécifique.
reluctant [ri'lʌktənt], *a.* **1.** qui résiste; qui agit à contrecœur; **to be r. to do sth.,** être peu disposé à faire qch.; hésiter à faire qch.; **however r. he was to write,**

quelque répugnance qu'il eût à écrire; **I feel r. to . . .,** j'éprouve de la répugnance à . . .; je répugne à . . .; il me répugne de . . .; **he seems r. to take up the matter,** il semble se désintéresser de l'affaire. **2.** (voyage) fait à contrecœur; (consentement) accordé à contrecœur.

reluctantly [ri'lʌktəntli], *adv.* avec répugnance; à contrecœur; à regret; de mauvais cœur; de mauvaise grâce; à son corps défendant; **I say it r.,** il m'en coûte de le dire; cela me coûte à dire; **he paid up, consented, very r.,** il s'est fait tirer l'oreille pour payer, pour consentir; **he accepted r.,** il a accepté de mauvaise grâce, en renâclant.

reluctivity [ri'lʌktiviti], *s.* reluctivité *f.*

rely [ri'lai], *v.i.* **to r. (up)on s.o., sth.,** compter sur, faire fond sur, qn, qch.; avoir confiance en qn; se reposer, s'appuyer, sur qn; se fier à qn; **I r. on him,** je compte sur lui; **I'm relying on it,** j'y compte (bien); **he's not to be relied on,** on ne peut pas compter sur lui; **I want a man I can r. on,** il me faut un homme de confiance; **I r. on you to help me,** je compte sur vous pour m'aider; **to r. on s.o. for sth.,** s'en remettre à qn de qch.; **to r. on s.o. to take charge of affairs,** se reposer sur qn du soin d'une affaire; **to r. on s.o.'s evidence,** s'en rapporter au, faire fond sur le, témoignage de qn; **this statement is not to be relied on,** ce rapport est sujet à caution; **we can't r. on the weather,** le temps n'est pas sûr; **you may r. upon it that I'll come, you may r. upon my coming,** vous pouvez compter que je viendrai; **I was relying on getting there by midnight,** je comptais arriver avant minuit; *Prov:* **r. on yourself only,** ne t'attends qu'à toi seul.

rem [rem], *s. Med: Meas:* rem *m.*

remagnetize [ri:'mægnitaiz], *v.tr.* réaimanter.

remain[1] [ri'mein], *s. A:* reste *m.*

remain[2], *v.i.* **1.** rester; **nothing remains of the meal,** il ne reste rien du repas; **the memory remained in my mind,** le souvenir m'en est resté dans l'esprit; **the few pleasures that r. to us,** les quelques plaisirs qui nous restent; **this objection remains,** cette objection subsiste; **there are four remaining,** il en reste quatre; **the fact remains that . . .,** il n'en est pas moins vrai que . . .; toujours est-il que . . .; tant (il) y a que . . .; **much yet remains to be done,** il reste encore beaucoup à faire; **worse things r. to be told,** mais il y a pis encore à raconter; **nothing remains (for me) but to . . .,** il ne (me) reste plus qu'à . . .; **it (only) remains for me to . . .,** il (ne) me reste (qu'à) (vous remercier, etc.); je n'ai plus qu'à (me retirer, etc.); **it remains to be seen whether . . .,** reste à savoir si . . .; **that remains to be seen,** c'est ce que nous verrons. **2.** demeurer, rester; *(a)* **to r. at home,** rester à la maison; se tenir chez soi; **to r. seated,** rester, demeurer, assis; **the police remained on the spot,** la police est demeurée sur les lieux; **to r. behind,** rester; ne pas partir; **the victory remained with the Greeks,** la victoire resta aux mains des Grecs; *(b)* **let it r. as it is,** laissez-le comme cela; **beauty remains but changes,** la beauté persiste mais évolue. **3.** *(a)* **one thing remains certain,** une chose reste certaine; **I r. convinced that . . .,** je demeure convaincu que . . .; **to r. faithful to s.o.,** rester fidèle à qn; **the weather remains fine,** le temps se maintient au beau; *(b) Corr:* **I r., Sir, yours truly,** veuillez agréer, Monsieur, l'expression de mes sentiments distingués.

remainder[1] [ri'meindər], *s.* **1.** *(a)* reste *m*, restant *m*, reliquat *m* (de fortune, etc.); **the r. of his life,** le reste de sa vie; *(b) Mth:* reste; **division with no r.,** division sans reste; *(in working out)* **3 r. 2,** 3, reste 2. **2.** *(a) coll.* **the r.,** les autres *mf*; **the r. sat down,** les autres se sont assis; *(b) Publ:* **remainders, r. line,** fin(s) *f* de série(s); bouillons *mpl* (d'exemplaires invendus); solde *m* d'édition; **r. sale,** solde d'édition; **to sell off the remainders,** liquider (les invendus); **r. buyer,** soldeur, -euse. **3.** *Jur:* substitution *f* (des biens); réversion *f*; **the estate is left to A with r. to B,** la succession passe à A avec réversion sur B.

remainder[2], *v.tr. Publ:* solder (une édition).

remainderman, *pl.* **-men** [ri'meindəmən], *s. Jur:* (i) héritier appelé, substitué; (ii) bénéficiaire *m* d'une réversion.

remaining [ri'meiniŋ], *a.* **the r. travellers,** le reste des voyageurs; les autres voyageurs; **our only r. hope,** le seul espoir qui nous reste; **to make the most of one's r. time,** jouir de son reste.

remains [ri'meinz], *s.pl.* *(a)* restes *m* (d'un repas, etc.); débris *m*, ruines *f* (d'un édifice); vestiges *m* (d'un ancien temple, etc.); **Roman r.,** des restes de la civilisation romaine; *(b)* œuvres *f* posthumes (d'un auteur); *(c)* **mortal r.,** restes mortels; dépouille mortelle; **to discover human r.,** découvrir des ossements *m.*

remake[1] ['ri:meik], *s. Cin: etc:* nouvelle version; nouvelle réalisation; réédition *f*; réenregistrement *m*; remake *m*; *F:* **it's a r.,** c'est du réchauffé.

remake[2] [ri:'meik], *v.tr.* (*p.t. & p.p.* **remade** [ri:'meid]) refaire; modifier; rebattre (un matelas).

remaking [ri:'meikiŋ], *s.* réfection *f.*

reman [ri:'mæn], *v.tr.* **(remanned) 1.** réarmer (un vaisseau); recharger, réarmer (un fusil). **2.** redonner du courage (à qn).

remand[1] [ri'ma:nd], *s. Jur:* renvoi *m* (d'un prévenu) à une autre audience; **detention under r.,** détention préventive; **to be on r.,** être renvoyé à une autre audience; **r. centre, home,** maison *f* de détention provisoire (pour mineurs renvoyés à une autre audience); centre *m* d'éducation surveillée.

remand[2], *v.tr. Jur:* renvoyer (un prévenu) à une autre audience; **he was remanded for a week,** sa cause a été remise à huitaine; **to r. a prisoner in custody,** renvoyer (à huitaine) la comparution de l'inculpé, avec détention provisoire; **person remanded in custody,** préventionnaire *mf*; **to r. a prisoner on bail,** mettre un inculpé en liberté sous caution.

remanence ['remənəns], *s. Magn:* rémanence *f.*

remanent ['remənənt], *a.* **1.** qui reste; de reste. **2.** *El: Magn:* rémanent, résiduel.

remark[1] [ri'ma:k], *s.* **1.** remarque *f*, attention *f*; **things worthy of r.,** choses dignes d'attention, dignes d'être remarquées. **2.** remarque, observation *f*, commentaire *m*; **to make, pass, let fall, a r.,** faire une remarque, une observation, une réflexion; **to let sth. pass without r.,** laisser passer qch. sans commentaire, sans faire d'observations; **did you make a r.?** avez-vous dit quelque chose? **to venture, hazard, a r.,** se permettre un mot; hasarder une observation; **this r. went home,** cette parole a porté; cette parole l'a piqué; **after some preliminary remarks,** après quelques avant-propos *m*; **your complimentary remarks,** les compliments *m* que vous avez bien voulu m'adresser; **to make remarks about s.o., to pass remarks on s.o.,** faire des observations sur qn; faire des commentaires sur qn; battre qn en brèche; **to make scathing remarks about s.o.,** tenir des propos moqueurs sur qn; **no remarks, please!** point, pas, d'observations, s'il vous plaît!

remark[2]. **1.** *v.tr.* *(a)* remarquer, observer (qn, qch., que . . .); noter (qch., que . . .); **it may be remarked that . . .,** constatons que . . .; *(b)* faire la remarque (que . . .); faire remarquer, faire observer (à qn que . . .); **she remarked that it was getting late,** elle déclara qu'il se faisait tard; **'I thought you had gone,' he remarked,** 'je croyais que vous étiez parti,' dit-il, déclara-t-il, remarqua-t-il. **2.** *v.i.* faire une remarque, faire des remarques **(on,** sur); **I remarked on it to my neighbour,** j'en ai fait l'observation à mon voisin; **you remember that I remarked on it,** vous vous souvenez que j'en ai fait la remarque.

remarkable [ri'ma:kəbl], *a.* remarquable; frappant; (mérite, etc.) singulier; (courage) signalé; **a man r. for his courage,** un homme remarquable par son courage; **one of the most r. men of our time,** un des hommes les plus remarquables de notre temps; **his playing is r. only for its flawless technique,** son jeu ne vaut que par sa technique impeccable; **our family has never been r.,** notre famille n'a jamais marqué.

remarkableness [ri'ma:kəbəlnis], *s.* ce qu'il y a de remarquable, de frappant **(of,** dans).

remarkably [ri'ma:kəbli], *adv.* remarquablement; **r. ugly person,** personne remarquable par sa laideur.

remarriage [ri:'mæridʒ], *s.* remariage *m*; nouveau mariage.

remarry [ri:'mæri]. **1.** *v.tr.* *(a)* épouser de nouveau (qn dont on est divorcé); se remarier avec (qn); *(b) (of registrar, etc.)* remarier (des divorcés). **2.** *v.i.* se remarier; contracter un nouveau mariage.

Rembrandtesque [rembræn'tesk], *a. Art:* rembranesque.

remediable [ri'mi:diəbl], *a.* réparable; remédiable.

remedial [ri'mi:diəl], *a.* réparateur, -trice; (traitement, etc.) curatif; *Med:* **r. exercises,** gymnastique corrective.

remedy[1] ['remidi], *s.* **1.** remède *m*; **r. for, against, a disease,** remède pour, contre, une maladie; **old wives' r.,** remède de bonne femme; **quack r.,** remède de charlatan; **heroic r., kill or cure r.,** remède héroïque; **it's past, beyond, r.,** c'est sans remède, c'est irrémédiable; **a r. for poverty,** un correctif à la pauvreté; **work is the best r. for boredom,** le travail est le meilleur remède contre l'ennui. **2.** *Jur:* réparation *f*; dédommagement *m*; **to have no r. at law,** n'avoir aucun recours contre qn. **3.** *Num:* **r. (of the Mint),** remède (d'aloi); (marge *f* de) tolérance *f.*

remedy[2], *v.tr.* remédier, (ap)porter remède, à (qch.); **it cannot be remedied,** on ne saurait y remédier; c'est sans remède.

remelt [ri:'melt], *v.tr.* refondre (un métal, etc.).

remelting [ri:'meltiŋ], *s.* refonte *f* (d'un métal, etc.).

remember [ri'membər], *v.tr.* **1.** *(a)* se souvenir de (qn, qch.); se rappeler, se remémorer (qch.); avoir mémoire de (qch.); retenir, ne pas oublier (une leçon, etc.); **I r. that . . .,** je me souviens, je me rappelle, que . . .; *Lit:* il me souvient que . . .; **few people r. that they were once young,** peu de gens se souviennent (d')avoir été jeunes; **now I r. that I left it at home,** il me revient à l'idée, en idée, que je l'ai laissé à la maison; *B:* **r. that thou art but dust,** souviens-toi que tu n'es que poussière; **r. what you told me,** rappelez-vous ce que vous m'avez dit; **to r. having promised sth.,** se rappeler (d')avoir promis qch.; **I r. seeing it,** je me souviens, il me souvient, de l'avoir vu; **I r. Anne saying that . . .,** je me souviens qu'Anne a dit que . . .; **I r. Mr Martin coming to see me,** je me souviens que M. Martin est venu me voir; **I r. his going,** je me rappelle son départ; **I don't r. your telling me, that you told me,** je ne me rappelle pas que vous me l'ayez dit; **to be able to r. things that happened a long time ago,** se souvenir de loin; **if I r. rightly,** si je m'en souviens bien; si j'ai bonne mémoire; **as far as I r.,** autant qu'il m'en souvient, autant qu'il m'en souvienne; **as far back as I can r.,** du plus loin qu'il m'en souvienne; **I can't r. his name for the moment,** son nom m'échappe pour l'instant; **don't you r. me?** (est-ce que) vous ne me remettez pas? **it will be something to r. you by,** ce sera un souvenir de vous; **do you r. about his bankruptcy?** vous souvenez-vous de sa faillite? *(b)* faire attention à (qch.); **one cannot r. everything,** on ne peut pas songer à tout; **I'll r. to do it,** je n'oublierai pas de le faire; je penserai à le faire; **r. not to turn right,** rappelez-vous qu'il ne faut pas tourner à droite; **that's worth remembering,** cela est à noter; *Lit:* **be it remembered (that),** n'oublions pas (que); ne l'oublions pas; **r. that he's only ten years old,** n'oubliez pas, tenez compte du fait, qu'il n'a que dix ans; *(c)* **he remembered me in his will,** il ne m'a pas oublié dans son testament; **r. me in your prayers,** ne m'oubliez pas dans vos prières; **r. the waiter!** n'oubliez pas le garçon! *(d)* **to r. oneself,** se ressaisir. **2. r. me (kindly) to them,** rappelez-moi à leur bon souvenir; faites-leur mes amitiés; dites-leur bien des choses de ma part; **r. me to Mrs Thomas,** mes compliments à Mme Thomas; **he asks to be remembered to you,** il me prie de le rappeler à votre bon souvenir. **3.** *A:* **I remembered me that . . .,** je me rappelais que . . .; il me souvenait que . . .; **they remembered them of it,** ils se le rappelèrent.

remembrance [ri'membrəns], *s.* **1.** souvenir *m*, mémoire *f*; **to have sth. in r.,** avoir qch. à la mémoire; **to the best of my r.,** autant qu'il m'en souvienne; autant que je puisse m'en souvenir; **to have no r. of sth.,** n'avoir aucun souvenir de qch.; **to call sth. to r.,** se rappeler qch.; se remémorer qch.; **to put s.o. in r. of sth.,** rappeler qch. à qn; **in r. of s.o., of sth.,** en souvenir, en mémoire, de qn, de qch.; **annual festival of r.,** fête commémorative; **R. Sunday,** dimanche le plus proche du 11 novembre (commémorant ceux qui ont été tués pendant les deux guerres mondiales); *A:* **R. Day,** l'anniversaire *m* de l'Armistice (de 1918). **2.** *pl. O:* **give my kind remembrances to him,** rappelez-moi à son souvenir.

remembrancer [ri'membrənsər], *s.* **1.** *A:* *(a)* souvenir *m*, mémento *m*; *(b)* carnet *m* (de notes); agenda *m*. **2.** *Adm:* *(a) Scot:* **King's, Queen's, and Lord Treasurer's R.,** fonctionnaire *m* qui perçoit les dettes dues au souverain; *(b) Hist:* **City R.,** représentant *m* du Conseil de la Cité de Londres devant les commissions parlementaires.

remetal [ri:'met(ə)l], *v.tr.* **(remetalled) 1.** *Civ.E:* recharger (une route). **2.** *Mec.E:* regarnir (un coussinet).

remex, *pl.* **-iges** ['ri:meks, 'remidʒi:z], *s. Orn:* rémige *f*; **the remiges,** les (plumes *f*) rémiges.

remigial [ri'midʒiəl], *a. Orn:* (plume) rémige.

Remigius [ri'midʒəs], *Pr.n.m.* (Saint) Remi, Remy.

remilitarization [ri:militərai'zeiʃ(ə)n], *s.* remilitarisation *f.*

remilitarize [ri:'militəraiz], *v.tr.* remilitariser.

remill [ri:'mil], *v.tr.* **1.** remoudre (du blé, etc.). **2.** *Tex:* fouler à nouveau (un tissu). **3.** *Mec.E:* fraiser à nouveau (un engrenage, etc.).

remilling [ri:'miliŋ], *s.* **1.** remoulage *m* (des céréales). **2.** *Tex:* nouveau foulage (d'un tissu).

remind [ri'maind], *v.tr.* **to r. s.o. of sth.,** rappeler, remémorer, qch. à qn; remettre qch. en mémoire à qn; faire souvenir qn de qch.; faire penser qn à qch.; **I was reminded of my promise,** on m'a fait souvenir de ma promesse; **that reminds me of . . .,** cela me rappelle . . .; **that reminds me!** à propos! **he reminds me of my brother,** il me fait penser à mon frère; il me rappelle mon frère; **she reminds me of a sparrow,** elle me fait l'effet d'un moineau; **to r. s.o. to do sth.,** rappeler à qn qu'il doit faire qch.; **r. me to write to him,** faites-moi penser à lui écrire; **she has reminded me that we're going there tonight,** elle me rappelle que nous y allons ce soir; **passengers are reminded that . . .,** il est rappelé à messieurs les voyageurs que . . ..

reminder [ri'maindər], *s.* (*a*) mémento *m*; **as a r.,** pour mémoire; **mentioned as a r.,** mentionné par mémoire; **as a r. that. . .,** pour rappeler que. . .; **this will be a r. to me,** cela me rafraîchira la mémoire; (*b*) **(letter of) r.,** lettre envoyée à titre d'avertissement; *Com:* lettre de rappel; **send me a r.,** envoyez-moi un mot pour me le faire rappeler; **I'll send him a r.,** je vais lui rafraîchir la mémoire; (*c*) *Com:* **r. of account due, of due date,** rappel *m* de compte, d'échéance.

reminisce [remi'nis], *v.i. F:* raconter ses souvenirs; remonter dans le passé.

reminiscence [remi'nisəns], *s.* **1.** réminiscence *f*; souvenir *m*; *Phil:* **Platonic r.,** la réminiscence platonicienne. **2. to write one's reminiscences,** écrire ses souvenirs.

reminiscent [remi'nisənt], *a.* **1.** qui se souvient; remémorateur, -trice; **a previous life of which we may be r.,** une vie antérieure dont nous avons peut-être conservé un vague souvenir. **2. r. of s.o., of sth.,** qui rappelle, évoque, qn, qch.; qui fait penser à qn, à qch.

reminiscently [remi'nisəntli], *adv.* de l'air de celui qui se souvient; **he smiled r.,** il a souri à ce souvenir.

remint [ri:'mint], *v.tr.* refondre (la monnaie).

remiss [ri'mis], *a.* **1.** négligent, insouciant; inexact à remplir ses devoirs; sans soin; **to be r. in doing sth.,** être négligent à faire qch. **2.** *A:* mou, *f.* molle; faible; peu zélé.

remissible [ri'misibl], *a.* (péché, etc.) rémissible.

remission [ri'miʃ(ə)n], *s.* **1.** *Theol:* **r. of sins,** pardon *m*, rémission *f*, remise *f*, des péchés; **to grant s.o. r. of his sins,** absoudre qn de ses péchés. **2.** remise (d'une peine, d'une dette, etc.); **r. of a tax,** remise d'un impôt; détaxe *f*; **r. (of examination fees, taxes, etc.),** exonération *f*; *Jur:* **with r. of sentence,** avec sursis. **3.** (*a*) relâchement *m*, adoucissement *m* (du froid, etc.); (*b*) *Med:* rémission, rémittence *f* (d'une fièvre, etc.).

remissly [ri'misli], *adv.* négligemment; sans soin; inexactement.

remissness [ri'misnis], *s.* négligence *f*, insouciance *f*; inexactitude *f* à remplir ses devoirs.

remissory [ri'misəri], *a. Jur:* rémissorial, -aux.

remit [ri'mit], *v.* **(remitted)**

I. *v.tr.* **1.** (*a*) remettre, pardonner, absoudre (les péchés); (*b*) remettre (une dette, une peine); faire remise de (qch.); **to r. a candidate's examination fees,** exonérer un candidat. **2.** relâcher (son zèle, ses efforts). **3.** (*a*) remettre, soumettre (une question à une autorité); (*b*) *Jur:* renvoyer (un procès à un autre tribunal); (*c*) remettre, différer (une affaire). **4.** *A:* remettre, rétablir (dans un certain état). **5.** *Com:* **to r. a sum to s.o.,** envoyer, remettre, une somme à qn; faire remise, faire envoi, d'une somme à qn; **kindly r. by cheque,** prière de nous couvrir par chèque; *Jur:* **they remitted the sum awarded against them,** ils ont versé la somme à laquelle ils avaient été condamnés.

II. *v.i.* **1.** (*of zeal, etc.*) se relâcher. **2.** diminuer d'intensité; (*of pain*) se calmer; s'apaiser; (*of storm*) se calmer, tomber.

remittal [ri'mit(ə)l], *s.* **1.** (*a*) rémission *f* **(of a sin,** d'un péché); (*b*) remise *f* **(of a penalty, of a debt,** d'une peine, d'une dette). **2.** *Jur:* renvoi *m* (d'un procès à un autre tribunal).

remittance [ri'mitəns], *s. Com:* remise *f* (d'argent); envoi *m* de fonds; **to send s.o. a r.,** faire une remise de fonds, un versement, à qn; *O:* **r. man,** émigrant vivant des mensualités que sa famille lui verse.

remittee [rimi'ti:], *s.* destinataire *mf* (d'un envoi de fonds).

remittence, remittency [ri'mitəns, -ənsi], *s. Med:* rémittence *f.*

remittent [ri'mitənt], *a. Med:* (*of fever, etc.*) rémittent.

remitter[1] [ri'mitər], *s. Com:* remettant, -ante; envoyeur, -euse (de fonds).

remitter[2], *s. Jur:* renvoi *m* **(to another court,** à, devant, un autre tribunal).

remitting [ri'mitiŋ], *a.* **1.** (*of bank, etc.*) remetteur, -euse. **2.** *Med:* (*of fever*) rémittent.

remnant ['remnənt], *s.* **1.** (*a*) reste *m*, restant *m*; ce qui reste; **the remnant(s) of a great army, of a large property,** le restant, les restes, d'une grande armée, d'une grande propriété; **only a r. survived,** les survivants *m* n'étaient plus qu'une petite bande; **the remnants of a great forest,** tout ce qui reste d'une grande forêt; (*b*) **I found a few remnants of food,** j'ai trouvé quelques restes, quelques bribes *f*, de nourriture. **2.** vestige *m* (d'un usage, d'une croyance, etc.). **3.** *Com:* coupon *m* (de tissu); **remnants,** soldes *m*; fins *f* de série.

remodel [ri:'mɔd(ə)l], *v.tr.* **(remodelled)** remodeler (une statue); refondre (un texte, etc.); remanier (un ouvrage); réorganiser (une armée, etc.); transformer (une machine).

remodeller [ri:'mɔd(ə)lər], *s.* remanieur, -euse.

remodelling [ri:'mɔd(ə)liŋ], *s.* nouveau modelage; remaniement *m*, refonte *f* (d'un ouvrage, etc.); réorganisation *f* (d'une usine, etc.); transformation *f* (d'une machine).

remonstrance [ri'mɔnstrəns], *s.* **1.** remontrance *f*; protestation *f*. **2.** *Hist:* remontrance.

remonstrant [ri'mɔnstrənt]. **1.** *a.* (*a*) (ton, air) de remontrance, de protestation; (personne) qui proteste; (*b*) *Ecc.Hist:* de remontrant, des remontrants. **2.** *s.* (*a*) remontreur, -euse; protestataire *mf*; (*b*) *Ecc.Hist:* remontrant *m.*

remonstrate ['remənstreit]. **1.** *v.i.* **to r. with s.o. (up)on sth.,** faire des remontrances, des reproches, à qn au sujet de qch.; réprimander, sermonner, qn au sujet de qch.; **he had remonstrated gently with her,** il l'avait reprise avec douceur; **to r. against sth.,** protester contre qch. **2.** *v.tr.* **to r. that. . .,** protester que. . .; faire remarquer que. . ..

remonstrating ['remənstreitiŋ], *a.* = REMONSTRANT 1 (*a*).

remonstratingly ['remənstreitiŋli], *adv.* d'un ton de remontrance, d'un ton de protestation; en protestant.

remonstrative [ri'mɔnstrətiv], *a.* (ton, lettre) de remontrance, de protestation.

remonstrator ['remənstreitər], *s.* remontreur, -euse; protestataire *mf.*

remontant [ri'mɔntənt], *a.* & *s. Hort:* (rosier, etc.) remontant.

remora ['remərə], *s.* **1.** *Ich:* rémora *m.* **2.** *A:* rémora, obstacle *m.*

remorse [ri'mɔ:s], *s.* **1.** remords *m* **(at,** de; **for,** pour); **to feel r.,** éprouver, avoir, du, des, remords, du repentir **(at having done sth.,** d'avoir fait qch.); **a feeling, a twinge, of r.,** un remords; **to be smitten with r.,** être pris de remords. **2. without r.,** sans (aucune) componction; sans pitié.

remorseful [ri'mɔ:sful], *a.* plein de remords; repentant.

remorsefully [ri'mɔ:sfuli], *adv.* avec remords.

remorseless [ri'mɔ:slis], *a.* **1.** sans remords. **2.** sans pitié; impitoyable; sans (aucune) componction.

remorselessly [ri'mɔ:slisli], *adv.* **1.** sans remords. **2.** sans pitié; impitoyablement.

remote [ri'mout], *a.* **1.** (*far apart*) éloigné, écarté; **sciences r. from each other,** sciences qui n'ont rien en commun. **2.** (*far off*) lointain; éloigné, écarté; reculé; **the house lies r. from the road,** la maison est située loin de la route; **considerations r. from the subject,** considérations éloignées du sujet; **r. country,** pays lointain, éloigné; **r. place,** endroit éloigné, écarté, isolé, reculé, retiré; **in the remotest part of Asia,** au fond de l'Asie; **at a r. period,** à une époque reculée, éloignée; **r. ages,** temps éloignés, reculés; **r. antiquity,** la haute antiquité; **r. ancestors,** ancêtres éloignés; **r. causes,** causes lointaines, éloignées. **3.** faible, léger, vague; **a r. resemblance,** une vague ressemblance; une ressemblance légère; **a r. idea of. . .,** une légère idée de. . .; **I haven't the remotest idea of what he meant,** je n'ai pas la moindre idée de ce qu'il voulait dire; **if by any r. chance he is still alive,** si par impossible il est encore vivant; **without the remotest chance of succeeding,** sans la moindre chance de réussir; **r. prospect,** éventualité peu probable.

remotely [ri'moutli], *adv.* **1.** loin; au loin; dans le lointain; **r. distant,** à une distance éloignée. **2.** de loin; **we are r. related,** nous sommes parents de loin. **3.** vaguement, faiblement; **it's only r. connected with the subject,** cela n'a qu'un faible rapport avec le sujet.

remoteness [ri'moutnis], *s.* **1.** (*a*) éloignement *m* (d'un village, etc.); (*b*) éloignement (d'un événement, etc.); époque reculée. **2.** (*a*) degré éloigné (de parenté); (*b*) faible degré (de ressemblance, etc.); **the r. of this prospect,** le peu de probabilité de cette éventualité.

remould[1] ['ri:mould], *s. Aut:* pneu rechapé.

remould[2] [ri:'mould], *v.tr. Tchn: etc:* remouler; mouler de nouveau; rechaper (un pneu).

remoulding [ri:'mouldiŋ], *s.* remoulage *m*; nouveau moulage; rechapage *m* (d'un pneu).

remount[1] ['ri:maunt], *s. Mil:* **1.** remonte *f*; **r. depot,** établissement *m*, dépôt *m*, de remonte; **r. officer,** officier de remonte. **2.** cheval *m* de remonte; **army remounts,** chevaux de troupe; **to provide remounts for a cavalry regiment,** remonter un régiment de cavalerie; (*of officer*) **to buy remounts,** aller à la, en, remonte.

remount[2] [ri:'maunt]. **1.** *v.tr.* (*a*) **to r. (one's horse),** remonter à cheval, sur son cheval; se remettre en selle; (*b*) *Mil:* remonter (un officier, un régiment de cavalerie); (*c*) rentoiler (un tableau). **2.** *v.i. O:* remonter (à une époque éloignée).

remounting [ri:'mauntiŋ], *s.* **1.** *Mil:* remonte *f* (de cavalerie). **2.** rentoilage *m* (d'un tableau).

removability [rimu:və'biliti], *s.* amovibilité *f* (d'un organe, d'un fonctionnaire, etc.).

removable [ri'mu:vəbl], *a.* **1.** détachable; (porte) mobile; (foyer) amovible; (table, machine) démontable; **r. by hand,** démontable à la main. **2.** transportable; qui peut être enlevé, déplacé. **3.** (*a*) (mal) extirpable; (*b*) (fonctionnaire) amovible, révocable.

removal [ri'mu:v(ə)l], *s.* **1.** (*a*) enlèvement *m* (d'une tache, etc.); suppression *f* (d'un mal, d'un abus); *Surg:* ablation *f* (d'une tumeur, etc.); *Ecc:* **r. of interdict,** mainlevée *f* d'interdit; (*b*) révocation *f* (d'un fonctionnaire); destitution *f* (d'un officier); (*c*) *F:* assassinat *m*, meurtre *m* (de qn). **2.** déplacement *m* (d'une épave, d'une usine, etc.); transport *m* (d'un colis, etc.); dépose *f* (de pavés, de rails); *For: etc:* transport, débardement *m* (du bois, de la pierre). **3.** (*a*) action *f* d'enlever (qch.); démontage *m* (d'un pneu, etc.); levée *f* (de scellés); *Med:* levée (d'un pansement, d'un appareil); **to order the r. of the body,** ordonner la levée du cadavre; (*b*) soustraction *f* (d'un document, etc.). **4.** déménagement *m*; changement *m* de domicile; **r. into a house,** emménagement *m*; **r. expenses,** frais de déplacement; **r. van,** camion de déménagement; **r. man,** déménageur *m.*

remove[1] [ri'mu:v], *s.* **1.** *Cu: A:* relevé *m.* **2.** *Sch: A:* (*a*) passage *m* à une classe supérieure; **examinations for the r.,** examens de passage; (*b*) classe *f* intermédiaire. **3.** (*a*) distance *f*; **at a certain r.,** à une certaine distance; (*b*) **it is but one r. from. . .,** cela est tout près de. . .; cela confine à. . ..

remove[2], *v.tr.* **1.** (*a*) enlever, effacer, ôter, faire disparaître, faire partir (une tache); enlever (les traces de qch.); écarter, lever (un obstacle); résoudre (une objection); (en)lever (un doute); chasser, dissiper (une appréhension); supprimer, faire cesser (un abus); ôter, dissiper (une douleur); supprimer, aplanir, lever (une difficulté); *Surg:* enlever, retrancher (une tumeur, etc.); opérer l'ablation (d'une tumeur); **to r. one's makeup,** se démaquiller; **to r. s.o.'s name from a list,** rayer qn d'une liste; **to r. a doubt from s.o.'s mind,** éclaircir qn d'un doute; **to r. the scale from a boiler,** désincruster, détartrer, une chaudière; **to r. the burr from a casting,** ébarber une pièce moulée; **to r. the water from a mixture,** séparer l'eau d'un mélange; (*b*) révoquer (un fonctionnaire); destituer, casser (un officier); (*c*) (= *steal*) soustraire (qch.); (*d*) *F:* (faire) assassiner, supprimer (qn). **2.** (*a*) déplacer (une machine, une épave, etc.); transporter, transférer (des colis, etc.); déménager (sa bibliothèque, etc.); *For: etc:* débarder (le bois coupé, la pierre d'une carrière); **his bed was removed to the sitting room, was removed downstairs,** on a transporté son lit dans le salon; on a descendu son lit au rez-de-chaussée; **to have one's furniture removed,** faire emporter ses meubles; **to r. oneself and all one's belongings,** faire place nette; *v.i. O:* **to r.,** déménager; se déplacer; changer de résidence; **to r. into the country,** aller habiter à la campagne; (*b*) éloigner (qch., qn); **his feeling was not far removed from love,** son sentiment n'était pas très éloigné de l'amour; **he's only one step removed from a swindler,** c'est un escroc ou peu s'en faut; (*c*) **first cousin once removed,** cousin(e) issu(e) de germain; parent(e) au cinquième degré; oncle, tante, neveu, nièce, à la mode de Bretagne; **cousin twice removed,** cousin issu de (fils) germain; (*d*) enlever, retirer (son chapeau); enlever (des assiettes, etc.); démonter (un pneu); déposer (des pavés, etc.); *Med:* enlever (un pansement); lever (un appareil); (*e*) déplacer (un fonctionnaire, etc.); (*f*) lever (une sentinelle); **you may r. the prisoner,** vous pouvez (r)emmener, faire sortir, le prévenu; **to r. a pupil from school,** retirer un élève de l'école; *Poet:* **death has removed him from our midst,** la mort nous l'a enlevé. **3.** *Cu: A:* (*of course*) **to be removed by sth.,** être suivi de qch.

remover [ri'mu:vər], *s.* **1.** (*pers.*) déménageur *m.* **2. varnish r.,** décapant *m* pour vernis; *Toil:* **superfluous hair r.,** crème *f* (d)épilatoire; dépilatoire *m*; **(nail varnish) r.,** dissolvant *m* (pour ongles); **makeup r.,** démaquillant *m.*

removing [ri'mu:viŋ], *s.* = REMOVAL; *Toil:* **r. cream,** crème *f* à démaquiller.

remunerate [ri'mju:nəreit], *v.tr.* **1.** rémunérer **(s.o. for his services,** qn de ses services). **2.** rémunérer, rétribuer (un service).

remuneration [rimjuːnə'reiʃ(ə)n], *s.* rémunération *f* **for,** de), rétribution *f*; **in r. for . . .,** en rémunération de . . ..

remunerative [ri'mjuːnərətiv], *a.* **1.** (travail, prix) rémunérateur, -trice. **2.** *Jur:* (legs, etc.) rémunératoire.

remunerativeness [ri'mjuːnərətivnis], *s.* caractère rémunérateur (d'une entreprise, etc.).

remuneratory [ri'mjuːnərətri], *a.* = REMUNERATIVE 2.

Remus ['riːməs], *Pr.n.m. Rom.Hist:* Rémus.

Renaissance [ri'neis(ə)ns], *s.* (*a*) *Art: Lit: etc:* Renaissance *f*; **R. style,** style (de la) Renaissance; (*b*) **r.,** renaissance.

renal ['riːn(ə)l], *a. Anat:* rénal, -aux; des reins.

rename [riː'neim], *v.tr.* débaptiser (qn, une rue); **the street has been renamed,** la rue a changé de nom.

renardite [ri'nɑːdait], *s. Miner:* renardite *f.*

renascence [ri'næsəns], *s.* **1.** retour *m* à la vie; renouveau *m.* **2.** renaissance *f.*

renascent [ri'næsənt], *a.* renaissant.

rend [rend], *v.* (*p.t. & p.p.* **rent** [rent]) **1.** *v.tr.* (*a*) *Lit:* déchirer (qch.); **to r. sth. asunder, apart,** déchirer, fendre, qch. en deux; **province rent from the empire,** province arrachée à l'empire; **to r. sth. in two,** déchirer qch. en deux; **to r. one's hair,** arracher ses cheveux; s'arracher les cheveux; **a cry rent the air,** un cri fendit l'air; **to r. the air with shouts,** déchirer l'air de ses cris; **to r. s.o.'s heart,** fendre, déchirer, le cœur à qn; **anarchy will r. the country,** l'anarchie déchirera le pays; **to turn and r. s.o.,** (i) *B:* se tourner et déchirer qn; (ii) tomber, fondre, sur qn; (*b*) *Tchn:* **to r. laths,** fendre le bois en lattes. **2.** *v.i. Lit:* se déchirer, se fendre.

render ['rendər], *v.tr.* rendre. **1.** (*a*) (*give in return*) **to r. good for evil,** rendre le bien pour le mal; (*b*) **to r. thanks to s.o.,** remercier qn; faire des remerciements à qn; **to r. thanks to God,** rendre grâce à Dieu. **2.** *Lit:* (*give up, surrender*) rendre (une forteresse, etc.); *B:* **r. unto Caesar the things that are Caesar's!** rendez à César ce qui appartient à César! **the grave will r. up its dead,** la tombe rendra ses morts. **3. to r. homage, a service, to s.o.,** rendre hommage, un service, à qn; **to r. help to s.o.,** prêter secours à qn; **to r. a tribute,** fournir un tribut. **4.** (*a*) rendre (un compte, une raison); **to r. an account of sth.,** rendre compte de qch.; **to r. a verdict,** rendre un verdict; (*b*) *Com:* **to r. an account to s.o.,** remettre un compte à qn; **as per account rendered, to account rendered,** suivant notre compte; suivant compte remis; suivant relevé remis. **5.** rendre (les traits de qn); interpréter (un morceau de musique, une œuvre dramatique); rendre, traduire (une phrase); **to r. a French expression into English,** rendre, traduire, une expression française en anglais. **6.** rendre, faire devenir; **his wealth renders him important, an important person,** sa fortune le rend important, fait de lui une personne importante. **7.** (*a*) *Cu:* **to r. (down) fat,** fondre de la graisse; (*b*) clarifier (l'huile). **8.** *Const:* **to r. a wall with cement,** enduire un mur de ciment; cimenter, gobeter, un mur. **9.** *Nau:* mettre (un palan) en force.

renderer ['rendərər], *s. Ind:* fondeur *m* (de suif, etc.).

rendering ['rendəriŋ], *s.* **1.** reddition *f* (d'un compte, *Lit:* d'une forteresse). **2.** rendu *m* (d'une expression, des traits de qn); interprétation *f* (d'un morceau de musique, etc.); traduction *f* (d'une phrase); **her r. of Chopin is very good,** elle rend très bien Chopin. **3.** fonte *f*, extraction *f* (de la graisse); clarification *f* (de l'huile). **4.** gobetage *m*; **cement r.,** enduit *m* de ciment.

renderset[1] ['rendəset], *s. Const:* crépi *m* et enduit *m.*

renderset[2], *v.tr.* (*p.t. & p.p.* **renderset;** *pr.p.* **rendersetting**) crépir et enduire (un mur).

rendezvous[1] ['rɔndivuː, *pl.* -vuːz], *s.* rendez-vous *m*; *Mil: etc:* **r. position, point** *m* de ralliement.

rendezvous[2], *v.* (*p.t. & p.p.* **rendezvoused** [-vuːd]; *pr.p.* **rendezvousing** [-vuːiŋ]. **1.** *v.i.* se rencontrer, se réunir. **2.** *v.tr.* réunir.

rending ['rendiŋ], *s. Lit:* déchirement *m*, arrachement *m*, fendage *m.*

rendition [ren'diʃ(ə)n], *s.* **1.** *Lit:* reddition *f* (d'une forteresse). **2.** (*a*) traduction *f* (d'une phrase); (*b*) interprétation *f* (d'un rôle, d'un morceau de musique, etc.).

rendzina [ren'dʒiːnə], *s. Geol:* rendzine *f.*

renegade[1] ['renigeid], *s.* renégat, -ate; **r. Christian,** chrétien apostasié.

renegade[2], *v.i.* apostasier; **to r. from one's party, one's religion,** renier son parti, sa religion.

renege, renegue [ri'niː(ː)g]. **1.** *v.i.* (*a*) *Cards:* faire une fausse renonce; renoncer à faux; (*b*) manquer à sa promesse (**on doing sth.,** de faire qch.). **2.** *v.tr.* (re)nier, renoncer à (qch.).

renew [ri'njuː], *v.tr.* (*a*) renouveler; **to be renewed,** se renouveler; **to r. a lease,** renouveler un bail; **to r. one's subscription, s.o.'s subscription,** se réabonner, réabonner qn (**to,** à); *Com:* **to r. a bill,** prolonger une lettre de change; (*of bill, etc.*) **unless renewed,** à moins de renouvellement; *Jur:* **to r. a title,** rénover un titre; *Gaming:* **to r. the bank,** arroser la banque; (*b*) renouer (une conversation, une correspondance); **to r. an attempt,** revenir à la charge; **to r. one's acquaintance with s.o.,** renouer, renouveler, refaire, connaissance avec qn; **to r. one's friendship with s.o.,** renouer (amitié) avec qn; **to r. the combat,** rengager le combat; **renewed outbreak of a fire,** recrudescence *f* d'un incendie; **to r. a tradition,** renouer une tradition; **to r. a promise,** renouveler une promesse; **to act with renewed zeal, to eat with renewed appetite,** renouveler de zèle, d'appétit; **to r. one's attention,** redoubler d'attention; **renewed activity,** activité redoublée; **renewed hopes,** nouvelles espérances; (*c*) remplacer (un organe de machine, etc.); renouveler (ses vêtements, l'air d'une chambre, etc.); **to r. one's staff,** renouveler son personnel.

renewable [ri'njuːəbl], *a.* renouvelable.

renewal [ri'njuːəl], *s.* **1.** (*a*) renouvellement *m* (d'un traité, etc.); **r. of a vow,** *Jur:* **of a title,** rénovation *f* d'un vœu, d'un titre; **r. of subscription,** réabonnement *m* (**to,** à); *Com:* **r. of a bill,** atermoiement *m*, prolongation *f*, d'une lettre de change; **r. bill,** retraite *f*; **r. of a lease,** renouvellement d'un bail; *Jur:* **r. of lease by tacit agreement,** tacite reconduction *f*; (*b*) **r. of acquaintance,** renouvellement, renouement *m*, des relations; **a r. of affection,** un revenez-y de tendresse; **r. of activity, of negotiations,** reprise *f*, regain *m*, d'activité, de négociations. **2.** remplacement *m* (d'un organe de machine, etc.).

renewing [ri'njuːiŋ], *s.* = RENEWAL.

reniform ['renifɔːm], *a. Nat.Hist: etc:* réniforme.

renin ['riːnin], *s. Bio-Ch:* rénine *f.*

renitency ['renitənsi, ri'naitənsi], *s. Med: A:* rénitence *f* (d'une tumeur, etc.).

renitent ['renitənt, ri'naitənt], *a. Med: A:* rénitent.

rennet[1] ['renit], *s.* présure *f*, caillette *f*; (*plant*) caille-lait *m inv*; **r. (stomach),** caillette.

rennet[2], *s. Hort:* reinette *f*, rainette *f.*

renounce[1] [ri'nauns], *s. Cards:* renonce *f.*

renounce[2]. **1.** *v.tr.* (*a*) renoncer à, abandonner (une prétention, un droit, une possession); répudier (une succession); **she renounces him,** elle renonce à lui; **to r. one's property,** se dévêtir de son bien; **to r. the world,** renoncer au monde; (*b*) (i) renoncer à, (un projet, une idée); (ii) dénoncer, abjurer (une convention); répudier, dénoncer (un traité); renier, désavouer (un ami); **to r. one's principles, one's party,** renier ses principes, son parti; **to r. one's faith,** renoncer à sa foi; apostasier; **to r. one's country,** abjurer sa patrie. **2.** *v.i.* (*a*) *Cards:* (i) renoncer; (ii) *A:* renoncer à faux; faire une fausse renonce; (*b*) *Jur:* répudier une succession, la nationalité française, etc.

renouncement [ri'naunsmənt], *s.* renoncement *m* (**of,** à); **r. of one's property,** dépouillement *m* volontaire de ses biens; *Jur:* **r. of a succession,** répudiation *f* d'une succession.

renouncer [ri'naunsər], *s.* **1.** *Jur:* renonciateur, -trice; renonçant, -ante. **2.** *Cards:* renonçant, -ante.

renouncing [ri'naunsiŋ], *s.* = RENOUNCEMENT.

renovate ['renəveit], *v.tr.* **1.** renouveler (l'air, l'eau). **2.** remettre à neuf (un vêtement); rénover (une maison, etc.); restaurer (un tableau); *Phot:* rafraîchir (un bain). **3.** *A:* restaurer (qn). **4.** *O:* relever (le moral, l'âme, de qn); *Lit:* régénérer, rénover (un art, les mœurs).

renovating ['renəveitiŋ], *a.* rénovateur, -trice.

renovation [renə'veiʃ(ə)n], *s.* rénovation *f*, renouvellement *m*; remise *f* à neuf (d'un vêtement); *Theol:* **r. of the soul,** renouvellement, régénération *f*, de l'âme.

renovator ['renəveitər], *s.* rénovateur, -trice.

renown [ri'naun], *s.* renommée *f*, renom *m*, célébrité *f*; **man of great, high, r.,** homme de grand renom; **to win r.,** se faire un grand nom.

renowned [ri'naund], *a.* renommé (**for,** pour); célèbre (**for,** par); fameux, illustre; en renom (**for,** pour).

rensselaerite ['ren(t)sələrait], *s. Miner:* rensselaerite *f.*

rent[1] [rent], *s.* **1.** déchirure *f*, accroc *m* (à un vêtement); déchirure (dans les nuages). **2.** fissure *f*, fente *f*, bâillement *m*, cassure *f* (de terrain). **3.** rupture *f*, schisme *m* (dans une société, dans un parti).

rent[2], *s.* **1.** loyer *m*; (prix *m* de) location *f*, prix locatif (d'une maison, etc.); fermage *m*, affermage *m* (d'une ferme); **high r.,** gros loyer, loyer élevé; **low r.,** petit loyer; **to owe three months' r.,** devoir trois mois de loyer; **quarter's r.,** terme *m*; **r. day,** jour du terme; **r.-free house, house free of r.,** maison exempte de loyer; **they live there r. free,** ils y habitent sans payer de loyer; **r. collector,** receveur *m* de loyers; **r. roll,** montant des loyers (d'une maison de rapport, etc.); **r. roll of an estate,** état des fermages d'une propriété; *Jur:* (*on landed property*) **rent(s) charge,** servitude *f* de rente à faire à un tiers. **2.** *A:* rente *f.*

rent[3]. **1.** *v.tr.* (*a*) (*let*) louer (une maison); affermer (une terre); (*b*) (*hire*) louer, prendre en location (une maison, un poste de télévision, etc.); affermer, prendre en location (une terre); **to r. a flat to, from, s.o.,** louer un appartement à qn; **to r. a house from the tenant,** sous-louer une maison. **2.** *v.i.* (*of house, etc.*) se louer, être loué; (*of land, etc.*) être affermé.

rentable ['rentəbl], *a.* (*of house, etc.*) qu'on peut louer; qui peut se louer; (*of land, etc.*) affermable.

rental ['rent(ə)l], *s.* **1.** (*a*) loyer *m*, location *f*, valeur locative (d'un immeuble); montant *m* du loyer; **yearly r.,** redevance annuelle; (*b*) revenu *m* provenant des loyers, état *m* des loyers. **2.** (*a*) (prix *m* de) location (d'une télévision, etc.); (*b*) *NAm:* maison *f*, appartement *m*, etc., qu'on loue; **r. library,** bibliothèque de prêt; (*c*) *Tp:* **fixed r.,** redevance d'abonnement.

renter ['rentər], *s.* **1.** locataire *mf* (d'un immeuble, etc.); fermier *m* (d'une terre). **2.** (*a*) loueur, -euse (de voitures, etc.); (*b*) *Cin:* distributeur, -trice (de films).

renting ['rentiŋ], *s.* location *f*, louage *m* (d'une maison, etc.); affermage *m* (d'une terre).

renumber [riː'nʌmbər], *v.tr.* renuméroter.

renumbering [riː'nʌmbəriŋ], *s.* renumérotage *m.*

renunciation [rinʌnsi'eiʃ(ə)n], *s.* **1.** renoncement *m*, renonciation *f* (**of sth.,** à qch.); abandon *m*, délaissement *m* (d'un droit); *Jur:* **r. of property,** désappropriation *f*; **r. of a succession,** répudiation *f* d'une, renonciation à une, succession. **2.** répudiation, désaveu *m*, reniement *m* (**of,** de); **r. on oath,** abjuration *f* (**of,** de).

renunciatory [ri'nʌnsiət(ə)ri], *a.* **1.** de renoncement; de renonciation. **2.** de désaveu; de reniement.

reoccupation [riːɔkju'peiʃ(ə)n], *s.* réoccupation *f* (d'un territoire, etc.).

reoccupy [riː'ɔkjupai], *v.tr.* réoccuper (un territoire, etc.).

reoccupying [riː'ɔkjupaiiŋ], *s.* réoccupation *f* (d'un territoire, etc.).

reopen [riː'oup(ə)n]. **1.** *v.tr.* (*a*) rouvrir (un livre, un compte, une blessure, un théâtre); *Metalw:* **to r. a (brazed, welded) seam,** dessouder une soudure; *Fig:* **to r. an old wound,** raviver une plaie; (*b*) reprendre, recommencer (les hostilités); recommencer (le feu); renouveler (une querelle, un procès); **the question cannot be reopened,** il n'y a pas à y revenir; *Jur:* **to r. a case of bankruptcy,** rapporter une faillite. **2.** *v.i.* (*a*) (*of wound*) se rouvrir; (*b*) (*of theatre*) rouvrir; (*of school, law court*) rentrer; **the shops, the schools, will r. on Monday,** la réouverture des magasins, la rentrée des classes, aura lieu lundi.

reopening [riː'oup(ə)niŋ], *s.* **1.** réouverture *f* (d'un théâtre, d'un magasin). **2.** rentrée *f* (des classes, des tribunaux, des Chambres).

reordain [riːɔː'dein], *v.tr.* réordonner (un ecclésiastique).

reorder[1] [riː'ɔːdər], *s. Com:* commande renouvelée; réapprovisionnement *m*; **r. level, point,** seuil *m* de réapprovisionnement.

reorder[2], *v.tr.* renouveler la commande de (qch.); faire une nouvelle commande de (marchandises, etc.); faire une commande de réapprovisionnement; commander à nouveau.

reorder[3], *v.tr.* remettre de l'ordre à, dans (qch.); reclasser (des informations, etc.).

reordination [riːɔːdi'neiʃ(ə)n], *s.* réordination *f* (d'un ecclésiastique).

reorganization [riːɔːgənai'zeiʃ(ə)n], *s.* réorganisation *f*; assainissement *m* (des finances); réforme *f* (de l'enseignement, etc.).

reorganize [riː'ɔːgənaiz]. **1.** *v.tr.* réorganiser; assainir (des finances). **2.** *v.i.* (*of company, etc.*) se réorganiser.

reorganizer [riː'ɔːgənaizər], *s.* réorganisateur, -trice.

reorganizing [riː'ɔːgənaiziŋ], *s.* = REORGANIZATION.

reorient(ate) [riː'ɔːriənt(eit)], *v.tr. & pr.* (se) réorienter.

reorientation [riːɔːriən'teiʃ(ə)n], *s.* réorientation *f.*

rep[1] [rep], *s. Tex:* reps *m*; **woollen r.,** reps de laine.

rep[2], (= *representative*) représentant *m*, voyageur *m* de commerce.

rep[3], *s. F: O:* vaurien *m*, voyou *m.*

rep[4], *s. F:* (= *repertory*) *Th:* **to be, play, in r.,** être acteur, -trice, dans un théâtre municipal.

rep[5], *s. U.S: F:* réputation *f.*

rep[6], *s. Atom.Ph:* rep *m.*

repack [riː'pæk], *v.tr.* **1.** rempaqueter, remballer, rencaisser (des marchandises). **2.** *Mch:* regarnir (un presse-étoupe, un piston); remplacer la garniture (d'un piston, d'une pompe); **to r. a joint,** refaire un joint.

repacking [riː'pækiŋ], *s.* **1.** rempaquetage *m*, remballage *m*, rencaissage *m* (de marchandises). **2.** *Mch:* regarnissage *m* (d'un piston).

repaint[1] [ˈri:peint], *s. Golf: F:* balle *f* de seconde main.
repaint[2] [ri:ˈpeint], *v.tr.* repeindre.
repair[1] [riˈpɛər], *s. A:* fréquentation *f* (**to a place,** d'un endroit); recours *m* (**to s.o.,** à qn); **to have r. to a place,** fréquenter un endroit; **place of great, of little, r.,** endroit très fréquenté, peu fréquenté; **place of safe r.,** abri sûr.
repair[2], *v.i. A:* **to r. to a place,** aller, se rendre, à un endroit; **to r. to s.o.,** avoir recours à qn.
repair[3], *s.* **1.** réparation *f* (d'un bâtiment, d'une machine, d'une route); rétablissement *m* (d'un bâtiment); remise *f* en état (d'une machine); réfection *f* (d'un mur); renfaîtage *m* (d'un toit); raccommodage *m* (d'un vêtement, d'un meuble); *Nau:* radoub *m* (d'une coque); **minor, slight, r.,** *Av:* **line r.,** petite, légère, menue, réparation; **major repairs,** grosses réparations; réparations importantes; **temporary r.,** réparation provisoire; **running r.,** réparation courante; **road repairs,** réfection des routes; *Aut:* **road(side) repairs,** dépannage *m*; **emergency repairs,** réparations de fortune; *Nau:* **damage r.,** réparation d'avarie; **to put into port for repairs,** relâcher pour faire des réparations; **to undergo repairs, to be under r.,** subir des réparations; être en réparation, en voie de réfection; **ship under r.,** navire en radoub; **r. ship,** bateau de réparations; navire-atelier *m, pl.* navires-ateliers; **to carry out repairs,** (faire) effectuer des réparations; **beyond r.,** hors d'état d'être réparé; **ruined beyond r.,** ruiné irréparablement, irrémédiablement; **r. shop,** atelier *m* de réparations; magasin où l'on fait les réparations; **r. mechanic,** mécanicien réparateur; **r. kit,** outillage *m*, trousse *f*, de réparation; *Mil:* **r. base, depot,** base, dépôt, de réparation; **r. van,** camion *m* atelier, atelier de réparation mobile; *Rail:* **r. truck,** voiture-atelier *f, pl.* voitures-ateliers. **2. to be in (good) r.,** être en bon état; être bien entretenu; **to be in bad r., to be out of r.,** être en mauvais état; être mal entretenu; avoir besoin de réparations; **to keep a road, a building, in (good) r.,** entretenir une route; tenir une route en bon état; entretenir un immeuble (en réparation); **the house is in urgent need of r.,** la maison a besoin d'être réparée; des réparations s'imposent (pour l'immeuble).
repair[4], *v.tr.* **1.** réparer, réfectionner (un bâtiment, une machine, une route); remettre en état (une machine); rhabiller (une montre); dépanner (une voiture); refaire, repiquer (un chemin); renfaîter (un toit); raccommoder (un vêtement); réparer, ressemeler (des chaussures); radouber (un filet, *Nau:* une coque). **2.** *A:* réparer, corriger (une faute); réparer (un tort); se rattraper de (ses pertes); réparer (une défaite). **3.** *A:* rétablir (sa santé).
repairable [riˈpɛərəbl], *a.* réparable, arrangeable.
repairer [riˈpɛərər], *s.* réparateur, -trice; répareur, -euse; raccommodeur, -euse; rajusteur, -euse; rhabilleur, -euse.
repairing [riˈpɛəriŋ], *s.* réparation *f*, repiquage *m*, raccommodage *m*, remise *f* en état, remaniage *m*, reprise *f*, rhabillage *m*, rhabillement *m*; **(full) r. lease,** bail qui engage le locataire à maintenir les locaux dans l'état où il les a reçus.
repairman, *pl.* **-men** [riˈpɛəmən], *s.m. U.S:* réparateur; dépanneur; électricien, plombier, menuisier, etc.
repaper [ri:ˈpeipər], *v.tr.* retapisser (une pièce).
reparable [ˈrepərəbl], *a.* (machine, faute, tort) réparable.
reparation [repəˈreiʃ(ə)n], *s.* **1.** *O:* réparation *f* (d'un bâtiment, d'une machine). **2.** réparation (d'un tort); **war reparations,** réparations de guerre; *Hist:* **the Reparations Commission,** la Commission des Réparations; **in r. of . . .,** en réparation de . . .; **to make r. (for an injury, etc.),** réparer (un tort, etc.).
reparative [ˈrep(ə)rətiv, riˈpærətiv], *a.* réparateur, -trice; réparatoire.
repartee [repɑ:ˈti:], *s.* repartie *f*; **to be good, quick, at r.,** avoir la repartie prompte, facile; avoir l'esprit de repartie; avoir de la repartie; avoir des reparties, des répliques, spirituelles.
repartition [ri:pɑ:ˈtiʃ(ə)n, repɑ:-], *s.* **1.** répartition *f* (des biens, des impôts); **the r. of land and water on the surface of the globe,** la répartition des eaux et des terres à la surface du globe. **2.** nouveau partage.
repass [ri:ˈpɑ:s]. **1.** *v.tr.* (*a*) *O:* repasser, retraverser (la mer, un fleuve); (*b*) passer de nouveau devant (la maison, etc.); (*c*) voter de nouveau (une loi). **2.** *v.i. O:* repasser, passer de nouveau (**in front of,** devant; **through,** à travers).
repast [riˈpɑ:st], *s. Lit:* repas *m*.
repatriate[1] [ri:ˈpætrieit], *v.tr.* rapatrier.
repatriate[2] [ri:ˈpætriət], *s.* rapatrié, -ée.
repatriation [ri:pætriˈeiʃ(ə)n], *s.* rapatriement *m*.
repave [ri:ˈpeiv], *v.tr.* repaver (une rue, etc.).
repaving [ri:ˈpeiviŋ], *s.* repavage *m* (d'une rue, etc.).
repay [ri(:)ˈpei], *v.tr.* (*p.t. & p.p.* **repaid** [ri(:)ˈpeid]) **1.** rendre (de l'argent, une visite); rendre, payer de retour (un service); rembourser, rendre (un prêt); **to r. good for evil, to r. evil with, by, good,** rendre le bien pour le mal; **to r. an injury,** se venger d'un tort; **to r. s.o.'s kindness,** récompenser qn de sa bonté; payer de retour la bonté de qn; *B:* **vengeance is mine, I will r., saith the Lord,** c'est moi qui ferai justice, moi qui rétribuerai, dit le Seigneur. **2.** (i) rembourser (qn); (ii) récompenser (qn) (**for,** de); **to r. s.o. in full,** s'acquitter envers qn; **to r. s.o. for his kindness,** récompenser qn de sa bonté; revaloir à qn sa bonté; **to r. s.o. with ingratitude,** payer qn d'ingratitude; **how can I r. you?** comment pourrai-je m'acquitter envers vous? **3. book that repays reading,** livre qui mérite, qui vaut la peine, d'être lu; **the effort will r. itself,** l'effort aura sa récompense; cela vaut la peine de faire un effort.
repayable [ri:ˈpeiəbl], *a.* remboursable (**over 25 years,** sur 25 ans).
repayment [ri:ˈpeimənt], *s.* **1.** remboursement *m* (d'une somme); **bond due for r.,** obligation amortie. **2.** récompense *f* (d'un service).
repeal[1] [riˈpi:l], *s.* abrogation *f* (d'une loi); révocation *f* (d'un décret); annulation *f* (d'une sentence).
repeal[2], *v.tr.* rapporter, abroger, annuler (une loi), révoquer, annuler (un ordre).
repealable [riˈpi:ləbl], *a.* révocable; abrogeable; rappelable.
repealer [riˈpi:lər], *s.* **1.** auteur *m* de l'ordre de révocation (d'un décret, etc.). **2.** *Hist:* partisan, -ane, de l'abrogation de l'Acte d'union entre la Grande-Bretagne et l'Irlande.
repeat[1] [riˈpi:t], *s.* **1.** (*of item in programme*) bis *m*. **2.** *Mus:* reprise *f*; **r. (mark),** (barre *f* de) reprise; renvoi *m*. **3.** répétition *f* (d'un motif décoratif); compartiment *m* (d'un ornement, etc.); *Tex:* rapport *m* (d'un dessin). **4.** émission *f* qui a déjà passé (à la télévision, à la radio). **5.** *Tg:* **r. signal,** invitation à répéter. **6.** *Com:* **r. (order),** commande renouvelée.
repeat[2]. **1.** *v.tr.* (*a*) répéter (une question); réitérer (un ordre); **repeated requests,** demandes réitérées; **it can't be repeated too often,** on ne saurait trop le répéter, le redire; **story not fit to be repeated,** histoire peu convenable; (*after a line of a song, etc.*) **r.,** bis; **to have sth. repeated,** faire répéter qch.; *Tg:* **to r. back a telegram,** collationner, répéter, un télégramme; **to have a telegram repeated,** faire collationner un télégramme; (*b*) *Pej:* rapporter (un méfait, etc.); **he repeats everything you tell him,** c'est un rapporteur; **to r. a secret,** répéter un secret; (*c*) répéter (une action, un dessin); recommencer (une tentative); renouveler (ses efforts); redoubler (une dose); *Sch:* (re)doubler (une classe); *Com:* renouveler (une commande); **I hope it won't be repeated,** j'espère que cela ne se répétera pas; **the next day the complaints were repeated,** le lendemain les plaintes se sont renouvelées; **to r. oneself,** se répéter; **history repeats itself,** l'histoire se répète; **to avoid repeating oneself,** éviter les redites; **he's always repeating himself,** il est très rabâcheur; *Com:* (*of special offer*) **cannot be repeated,** sans suite; (*d*) *O:* **to r. one's lessons,** réciter ses leçons; (*e*) **to r. a programme,** rediffuser une émission (de télévision, de radio). **2.** *v.i.* (*a*) (*of watch, alarm clock, rifle*) être à répétition; (*b*) *Mth:* (*of figures*) se répéter; (*c*) (*of food*) revenir, donner des renvois; **it's repeating on me,** j'ai des renvois; (*d*) *U.S:* voter deux fois dans une élection.
repeatable [riˈpi:təbl], *a.* qu'on peut répéter, recommencer.
repeatedly [riˈpi:tidli], *adv.* à plusieurs reprises, à maintes reprises; (maintes et) maintes fois; à coups répétés; à tout bout de champ.
repeater [riˈpi:tər], *s.* **1.** (*a*) *O:* celui, celle, qui répète (qch.); rediseur, -euse; (*b*) *U.S:* personne *f* qui vote deux fois dans une élection. **2.** (*a*) **r. (watch),** montre *f* à répétition, à sonnerie; **r. clock,** horloge à répétition; **r. (alarm clock),** réveille-matin *m inv* à répétition; (*b*) fusil *m* répétition; (*c*) *Navy:* répétiteur *m* (des signaux); *Nau:* **r. compass,** compas répétiteur; *Nau: Av: etc:* **heading r.,** répétiteur de cap; (*d*) *Elcs: etc:* répéteur *m*, réémetteur *m*; **pulse, line, r.,** répéteur d'impulsions, de ligne; **cable r.,** répéteur de câble; **r. station,** station de répéteurs; réémetteur; **telephone r.,** relais (amplificateur) téléphonique; *Tg:* **impulse r.,** translateur *m* d'impulsions. **3.** *Mth:* fraction *f* périodique.
repeating[1] [riˈpi:tiŋ], *a.* **1.** (fusil, réveille-matin) à répétition; (montre) à répétition, à sonnerie; *Clockm:* **r. spring,** tout-ou-rien *m inv.* **2.** *Nau: Surv:* (cercle) répétiteur; *Surv:* **r. theodolite,** théodolite répétiteur, réitérateur. **3.** *Navy:* **r. ship,** répétiteur *m* (des signaux). **4.** *Mth:* **r. decimal,** fraction périodique.
repeating[2], *s.* (*a*) répétition *f* (d'un mot, etc.); *Tg:* collationnement *m* (d'un télégramme); **his language won't bear r.,** les mots qu'il emploie ne sont pas à répéter; **your joke will bear r.,** votre plaisanterie mérite le bis, ne perdrait rien de son sel à être répétée; (*b*) répétition (d'une action); (*c*) *O:* récitation *f* (des leçons).
repêchage [ˈrepəʃɑ:ʒ], *s. Sp:* course *f*, épreuve *f*, de repêchage *m*.
repel [riˈpel], *v.tr.* (**repelled**) **1.** repousser (un assaillant, une attaque, une offre, un argument). **2.** repousser, rebuter, dégoûter (qn); répugner à (qn); inspirer de la répulsion à (qn); **to be repelled by s.o.,** éprouver de la répulsion pour qn.
repellent[1] [riˈpelənt], *a.* **1.** (*a*) répulsif; *Ph:* **r. force,** force répulsive; (*b*) imperméable. **2.** repoussant, répulsif, répugnant, antipathique; **r. features,** traits répulsifs; **r. food,** nourriture repoussante; **he has a r. manner,** il a l'abord antipathique, peu sympathique; **to be r. to s.o.,** repousser qn.
repellent[2], *s.* **1.** ce qui repousse, détruit. **2.** (*a*) **(insect) r.,** produit *m* anti-moustiques, etc.; (*b*) **(water) r.,** tissu *m*, surface *f*, imperméable.
repelling [riˈpeliŋ], *a.* répulsif.
repent[1] [ˈri:pənt], *a. Bot: Z:* (*of stalk, shoot, insect, etc.*) rampant.
repent[2] [riˈpent]. **1.** *v.i.* se repentir (**of,** de); **he repents of it,** il le regrette; il s'en mord les doigts, les pouces; **to make s.o. r.,** faire repentir qn; **to allow s.o. to r.,** laisser repentir qn; laisser qn se repentir. **2.** *v.tr.* se repentir de, regretter (qch.); **to r. having done sth.,** se repentir, avoir du repentir, d'avoir fait qch.; **he has bitterly repented it,** il s'en est repenti amèrement. **3.** *A:* (*a*) *v.pr.* **to r. oneself of sth.,** se repentir de qch.; (*b*) *v.impers.* **it repents me of. . .,** je me repens de. . .; **it repents me that I spoke ill of him,** je me repens d'avoir dit du mal de lui.
repentance [riˈpentəns], *s.* repentir *m*; **to show r.,** venir à résipiscence; *Lit:* **stool of r.,** sellette *f*.
repentant [riˈpentənt], *a.* **1.** repentant, repenti. **2.** (soupir) de repentir.
repenter [riˈpentər], *s.* repentant, -ante; repenti, -ie.
repenting[1] [riˈpentiŋ], *a.* = REPENTANT.
repenting[2], *s.* = REPENTANCE.
repentingly [riˈpentiŋli], *adv.* avec repentir; d'un ton de repentir.
repeople [ri:ˈpi:pl], *v.tr.* repeupler (un pays).
repeopling [ri:ˈpi:pliŋ], *s.* repeuplement *m* (d'un pays).
repercussion [ri:pəˈkʌʃ(ə)n], *s.* (*a*) répercussion *f* (d'une explosion, d'un choc, d'un son, etc.); **shock that causes repercussions throughout the system,** choc qui retentit dans tout l'organisme; (*b*) répercussion, contrecoup *m*, retentissement *m*, choc en retour (d'un événement, d'une décision, etc.); **the effects of fatigue have repercussions on the morale,** les effets de la fatigue se répercutent sur le moral.
repercussive [ri:pəˈkʌsiv], *a.* répercussif.
repertoire [ˈrepətwɑ:r], *s. Th:* répertoire *m*.
repertory [ˈrepət(ə)ri], *s.* **1.** répertoire *m* (de renseignements, etc.). **2.** *Th:* répertoire; **r. company,** troupe à demeure (dans une ville).
repetend [ˈrepitend], *s.* **1.** *Mth:* période *f* (d'une fraction périodique); **single r.,** période d'un seul chiffre. **2.** refrain *m*.
répétiteur [repetiˈtə:r], *s. Th:* (*of opera singer, etc.*) maître *m* de musique.
repetition [repiˈtiʃ(ə)n], *s.* **1.** (*a*) répétition *f* (d'un mot, etc.); *Mus:* reprise *f*; *Tg:* collation *f*, collationnement *m* (d'un télégramme); **r.-paid telegram,** télégramme collationné; *Cmptr:* **r. instruction,** instruction de répétition; **the subject lent itself to endless r.,** le sujet se prêtait à mille redites; (*b*) *Sch: O:* récitation *f*. **2.** répétition, réitération *f* (d'une action); recommencement *m* (d'une tentative); renouvellement *m* (d'un effort). **3.** répétition, réplique *f*; double *m* (d'une œuvre d'art, etc.).
repetitious [repiˈtiʃəs], *a.* (*of book, speech, work, etc.*) plein de répétitions.
repetitive [riˈpetitiv], *a.* (*a*) (*of pers.*) rabâcheur; (*b*) (*of book, speech, work, etc.*) plein de répétitions.
repetitiveness [riˈpetitivnis], *s.* qualité *f*, caractère *m*, de ce qui se répète.
rephrase [ri:ˈfreiz], *v.tr.* formuler à nouveau, reformuler (une question, etc.).
repine [riˈpain], *v.i.* être mécontent, se plaindre, se chagriner (**at, against,** de); murmurer (**at, against,** contre); exhaler des plaintes.
repiner [riˈpainər], *s.* mécontent, -ente; grognon, -onne.
repining[1] [riˈpainiŋ], *a.* **1.** disposé à se plaindre; mécontent. **2.** (ton) de mécontentement; (ton) dolent, plaintif; **r. mood,** humeur chagrine.
repining[2], *s.* mécontentement *m*, plaintes *fpl*, murmures *mpl*.
repiningly [riˈpainiŋli], *adv.* en murmurant, en se

plaignant.

repique[1] [riː'piːk], *s. Cards:* (*at piquet*) repic *m.*

repique[2]. *Cards:* **1.** *v.i.* faire (un) repic. **2.** *v.tr.* faire repic (l'adversaire).

replace [ri'pleis], *v.tr.* **1.** replacer (qch.); remettre (qch.) en place; remonter, refixer (une pièce); *Tp:* **to r. the receiver,** raccrocher le récepteur. **2.** remplacer (qn, qch.); **to r. a gas cooker by an electric one,** remplacer une cuisinière à gaz par une cuisinière électrique; **it will be easy to r. this plate,** cette assiette peut se remplacer facilement; **to be replaced by . . .,** être remplacé par . . .; **I shall ask to be replaced,** je demanderai à me faire remplacer; **oil has largely replaced coal,** le mazout s'est substitué au charbon; **nothing can r. a mother's care,** la sollicitude maternelle ne se supplée pas; **the living r. the dead,** les vivants succèdent aux morts.

replaceable [ri'pleisəbl], *a.* remplaçable.

replacement [ri'pleismənt], *s.* **1.** remise *f* en place; remontage *m* (d'un pneu, etc.). **2.** (*a*) remplacement *m*, substitution *f*; (*b*) *Ind:* pièce *f* de rechange; (*c*) (*pers.*) remplaçant, -ante.

replacing [ri'pleisiŋ], *s.* = REPLACEMENT 1, 2 (*a*).

replant [riː'plɑːnt], *v.tr.* replanter.

replantation [riːplɑːn'teiʃ(ə)n], *s.* replantage *m*, replantation *f.*

replanting [riː'plɑːntiŋ], *s.* replantage *m*, replantation *f.*

replaster [riː'plɑːstər], *v.tr.* replâtrer, recrépir (un mur).

replastering [riː'plɑːst(ə)riŋ], *s.* replâtrage *m.*

replate [riː'pleit], *v.tr.* **1.** replaquer (une feuille de cuivre). **2. to r. sth. with gold, silver, nickel, tin,** redorer, réargenter, renickeler, rétamer, qch.

replating [riː'pleitiŋ], *s.* **1.** replacage *m.* **2.** redorure *f*, réargenture *f*, renickelage *m*, rétamage *m.*

replay[1] ['riːplei], *s. Sp:* second match (après match nul); *T.V:* **action r.,** répétition *f* (d'une séquence).

replay[2] [riː'plei], *v.tr.* rejouer (un match).

replenish [riː'pleniʃ], *v.tr.* remplir (de nouveau) (**with,** de); **to r. one's supplies,** se réapprovisionner (**with,** de); **to r. a ship's stores,** compléter les vivres d'un navire; **to r. with water, with petrol,** faire le plein; se ravitailler en eau, en essence; *Phot:* **to r. a bath,** ajouter du révélateur à un bain; *Lit:* **she kept his glass replenished,** elle veillait à ce que son verre fût toujours plein.

replenisher [ri'pleniʃər], *s. Phot:* révélateur (ajouté à un bain).

replenishing [ri'pleniʃiŋ], *s.* (*a*) = REPLENISHMENT; (*b*) *Phot:* addition *f* de révélateur (à un bain).

replenishment [ri'pleniʃmənt], *s.* remplissage *m*; **r. of supplies,** réapprovisionnement *m*; **r. of ammunition,** ravitaillement *m* en munitions.

replete [ri'pliːt], *a.* rempli, plein, gorgé (**with,** de).

repletion [ri'pliːʃ(ə)n], *s.* réplétion *f*, satiété *f*; **to eat to r.,** manger jusqu'à satiété; **to drink to r.,** boire à sa soif.

repletive [ri'pliːtiv], *a. Med:* réplétif.

replevin [ri'plevin], *s. Jur:* mainlevée *f* de saisie; **to grant r.,** donner mainlevée (de saisie).

replevy [ri'plevi], *v.tr. Jur:* **1.** admettre (qn) à fournir caution. **2.** obtenir la mainlevée d'une saisie de (cheptel, meubles).

replica ['replikə], *s.* (*a*) reproduction *f*, copie *f*, double *m*, fac-similé *m* (d'un document, etc.); (*b*) *Art:* réplique *f*, double (d'une œuvre d'art); **to make an exact r. of sth.,** copier qch. trait pour trait.

replicate[1] ['replikət]. **1.** *a. Bot:* replicatif, replié. **2.** *s. Mus:* réplique *f.*

replicate[2] ['replikeit], *v.tr.* **1.** exécuter une réplique (d'une œuvre d'art). **2.** replier.

replication [repli'keiʃ(ə)n], *s.* **1.** (*a*) réponse *f*, repartie *f*, riposte *f*; (*b*) *Jur:* réplique *f.* **2.** répercussion *f*, retentissement *m.* **3.** (*a*) réplique, copie *f*, fac-similé *m*; (*b*) reproduction *f* en plusieurs exemplaires.

replier [ri'plaiər], *s.* personne *f* qui répond, qui réplique.

reply[1] [ri'plai], *s.* **1.** réponse *f*; **to make a r. to s.o.,** faire, donner, une réponse à qn; répondre à qn; **to make some r.,** répondre qch.; **I made no r.,** je n'ai rien répondu; **what have you to say in r.?** qu'avez-vous à répondre? **to drop s.o. a line in r.,** envoyer un mot de réponse à qn; **in r. to your letter,** en réponse à votre lettre; *Post:* **r. card,** carte-réponse *f*, *pl.* cartes-réponse(s); **(international) r. coupon,** coupon-réponse (international), *pl.* coupons-réponse; (*of telegram, envelope*) **r. paid,** réponse payée. **2.** *Jur:* (*a*) réplique *f*; (*b*) dernière affirmation du demandeur.

reply[2], *v.i.* & *tr.* (**replied**) répondre, répliquer (**to,** à); *Jur:* répliquer; **to r. smartly, wittily,** repartir; **what did he r.?** qu'a-t-il répondu? **'yes, madam,' he replied,** 'oui, madame,' a-t-il répondu, reprit-il; *Mil:* **to r. to the enemy's fire,** répondre au feu de l'ennemi.

repoint [riː'pɔint], *v.tr. Const:* rejointoyer (un mur).

repointing [riː'pɔintiŋ], *s. Const:* rejointoiement *m* (d'un mur).

repone [ri'poun], *v.tr. Jur: Scot:* **1.** rétablir (**s.o. to, in, an office,** qn dans une charge). **2.** réhabiliter (qn).

repopulate [riː'pɔpjuleit], *v.tr.* repeupler (un pays).

repopulation [riːpɔpju'leiʃ(ə)n], *s.* repeuplement *m* (d'un pays).

report[1] [ri'pɔːt], *s.* **1.** (*a*) rapport *m* (**on,** sur); compte rendu (**of proceedings, of a speech,** d'une cérémonie, d'un discours); procès-verbal *m*, *pl.* procès-verbaux (des débats d'une assemblée); exposé *m*, récit *m* (d'une affaire); **to make, draw up, a r. on sth.,** faire, rédiger, un rapport sur qch.; **to render, furnish, present, a r. to s.o. on sth.,** présenter, soumettre, un rapport à qn sur qch.; **to send in a r.,** envoyer un rapport; **joint r.,** rapport collectif; **progress r.,** rapport périodique; rapport d'avancement (des travaux); **company's (background) r.,** rapport sur la situation générale de la société; **annual r. (of a company),** rapport de gestion (d'une société); **chairman's, president's, r.,** rapport moral; **treasurer's r.,** rapport financier; *Com: Ind:* **audit(ors') r.,** rapport des commissaires (aux comptes); *St.Exch:* **stock market r.,** bulletin *m* des cours de la bourse; **r. by Mr Martin,** rapport rédigé par M. Martin; **policeman's r. (against s.o.),** procès-verbal; *Pol:* **the bill has reached the r. stage,** le rapport a été présenté; *Sch:* **end of term r.,** bulletin (trimestriel); carnet *m* (de notes); livret *m* (scolaire); notes trimestrielles; **examiner's r.,** notes des examinateurs; *Mil:* **sick r.,** rôle *m* des malades; *Jur:* **r. of inquiry, of investigation, of survey,** rapport d'enquête; **law reports,** (i) *Jur:* recueil *m* d'arrêts et de décisions judiciaires; recueil de jurisprudence; (ii) *Journ:* gazette *f*, chronique *f*, des tribunaux; nouvelles *f* judiciaires; *Nau:* **captain's (sworn) r.,** rapport du capitaine; *Nau: etc:* **damage r.,** rapport d'avarie(s); *Av:* **failure r.,** rapport d'incident; **to draw up a r. on an accident,** dresser procès-verbal d'un accident; **to present a r. on a plan,** rapporter sur un projet; **favourable r.,** bons renseignements; **false r.,** faux rapport; **we have received two reports on this firm,** nous avons reçu deux bulletins de renseignements sur cette maison; (*b*) **weather r.,** bulletin météorologique. **2.** (i) bruit *m* (qui court, qui se répand); rumeur *f*; (ii) nouvelle *f*; **groundless, unfounded, r.,** bruit qui ne repose sur rien; **newspaper r.,** reportage *m*; **to confirm a r.,** confirmer une nouvelle; **as r. will have it,** à ce qu'on prétend. **3.** *O: & Lit:* réputation *f*, renom *m*, renommée *f*; **man of good r.,** homme de bonne réputation; **of evil r.,** de mauvaise réputation; mal famé; **he held his course through good and evil r.,** il a poursuivi son but et a laissé dire. **4.** (*a*) détonation *f* (d'une arme à feu); coup *m* de fusil, de canon; (*b*) bruit d'explosion; détonation.

report[2].

I. *v.tr.* **1.** (*a*) rapporter, relater (un fait); rendre compte de (qch.); **to r. a speech, a meeting,** faire le compte rendu d'un discours, d'une séance; **to r. s.o.'s words,** rapporter les paroles de qn; **our Paris branch reports a marked improvement in business,** notre succursale à Paris nous annonce une amélioration sensible dans les affaires; **to r. progress to s.o.,** tenir qn au courant de la marche d'une affaire; exposer l'état de l'affaire (à qn); *Parl:* **to r. progress,** faire un rapport de l'état de la question; **to r. to s.o.,** envoyer, faire, un rapport à qn; **to r. to a superior,** rendre compte à un supérieur; *Parl:* **to r. a bill (to the House),** rapporter un projet de loi; *Jur:* **to r. to the court,** en référer au tribunal; (*b*) *Journ:* faire le reportage de (qch.); **to r. (for a newspaper),** faire des reportages; (*c*) rapporter, raconter, dire (qch.); **he is reported to be dead,** on le dit mort; on rapporte qu'il est mort; **it is reported that . . .,** le bruit court, on dit, que . . .; **he is reported as saying that . . .,** il aurait dit que . . .. **2.** (*a*) **to r. an accident to the police,** signaler un accident à la police; **to r. s.o. to the police,** dénoncer qn à la police; **to r. s.o. to a superior,** signaler qn à un supérieur; *Adm: Mil: etc:* **to r. s.o. sick, missing,** porter qn malade, absent; **to r. (oneself) sick,** se (faire) porter malade; **nothing to r.,** (i) rien à signaler; (ii) (*on report sheet, etc.*) néant; *Cust:* **to r. a vessel,** déclarer un navire; faire la déclaration d'entrée; (*b*) **to r. (oneself) (to s.o.),** se présenter à, devant (un supérieur) (en rentrant); *Mil:* **to r. to one's unit, to headquarters,** rallier son unité, son quartier général; se faire porter rentrant; **to r. to the company commander (as a defaulter),** être porté au rapport du commandant de compagnie; *Nau:* **to r. to the port authorities,** arraisonner avec les autorités du port; *Com:* **please r. to our branch in Paris,** veuillez vous rendre à notre succursale de Paris.

II. *v. ind.tr.* **to r. on sth.,** faire un rapport sur qch.; rendre compte de qch.; **to r. on a plan,** rapporter sur un projet; *Ven:* **to r. on the outcome of the beating,** faire son rapport; **he reports well of the scheme,** son rapport sur ce projet est favorable.

reportage [repɔː'tɑːʒ], *s. Journ: etc:* (*a*) reportage *m*; (*b*) article *m* (de journal).

reportedly [ri'pɔːtidli], *adv. Journ:* **the President has r. said that . . .,** le président aurait dit que . . ..

reporter [ri'pɔːtər], *s.* **1.** auteur *m* d'un rapport, d'un compte rendu; rapporteur *m* (d'une conférence). **2.** (*a*) journaliste *mf*, reporter *m*; (*b*) sténographe *mf* (parlementaire, etc.); **reporters' gallery,** tribune *f* des journalistes.

reporting [ri'pɔːtiŋ], *s.* reportage *m*; comptes rendus; *Journ:* **r. staff,** service *m* des informations.

reposal [ri'pouz(ə)l], *s. A: & Lit:* **r. of trust, of confidence, in s.o.,** confiance *f* en qn.

repose[1] [ri'pouz], *v.tr. Lit:* **to r. one's trust, one's confidence, one's hope, in s.o.,** mettre sa confiance, son espoir, en qn; se reposer sur qn.

repose[2], *s.* **1.** repos *m*; (*a*) **to seek r.,** chercher du repos; **to take r.,** se donner, prendre, du repos; **to work without r.,** travailler sans se reposer, sans repos, sans arrêt; (*b*) sommeil *m*; *Lit: or F:* **goodnight and sweet r.!** bonne nuit et dormez bien! *Ecc:* **r. of the Virgin,** mort *f* de la Vierge; (*c*) calme *m*, tranquillité *f*, sérénité *f* (d'esprit); **to disturb s.o.'s r.,** troubler le repos, la tranquillité, de qn; **features in r.,** traits au repos; **picture that lacks r.,** tableau qui manque de repos. **2.** *Civ.E:* **angle of r.,** angle naturel de repos, angle de talus.

repose[3]. **1.** *O: v.tr.* (*a*) reposer (qn, sa tête sur un oreiller); (*b*) **to r. oneself,** se reposer. **2.** *v.i.* (*a*) *O:* se reposer; (i) se délasser; (ii) dormir; (*b*) reposer (**on,** sur); **organization that reposes on the loyalty of its members,** organisation qui repose sur la loyauté de ses membres; (*c*) *Lit:* reposer (dans la mort).

reposeful [ri'pouzful], *a.* reposé, reposant; calme.

reposition [riːpə'ziʃ(ə)n], *v.tr.* changer la position de (qch.); remettre (qch.) en place; mettre (qch.) à la bonne place.

repository [ri'pɔzit(ə)ri], *s.* **1.** dépôt *m*, entrepôt *m*, magasin *m* (de marchandises, etc.); **furniture r.,** garde-meuble *m*, *pl.* garde-meuble(s). **2.** caveau *m* (de sépulture). **3.** répertoire *m* (de renseignements, etc.); **he is a r. of curious information,** c'est une mine de renseignements curieux. **4.** (*pers.*) *O: & Lit:* dépositaire *mf* (d'un secret, etc.); confident, -ente; **to make s.o. the r. of one's sorrows,** confier ses peines à qn.

repossess [riːpə'zes], *v.tr.* **1.** rentrer en possession de (qch.). **2.** *A: & Lit:* (*a*) **to r. s.o. of sth.,** remettre qn en possession de qch.; (*b*) **to r. oneself of sth.,** reprendre possession de qch.

repossession [riːpə'zeʃ(ə)n], *s.* rentrée *f* en possession (**of,** de).

repot [riː'pɔt], *v.tr.* rempoter (une plante).

repotting [riː'pɔtiŋ], *s.* rempotage *m* (d'une plante).

repoussé [rə'puːsei], *a.* & *s. Metalw:* repoussé (*m*); **r. work,** repoussage *m*; travail *m* de repoussé; **piece of plate in r. work,** pièce en argent martelé.

repp [rep], *s. Tex:* reps *m.*

reprehend [repri'hend], *v.tr.* **1.** reprendre, blâmer, réprimander (qn). **2.** *O:* **to r. s.o.'s conduct,** trouver répréhensible la conduite de qn; **to r. s.o.'s choice,** condamner le choix fait par qn.

reprehensible [repri'hensibl], *a.* répréhensible, blâmable, condamnable.

reprehensibleness [repri'hensib(ə)lnis], *s.* caractère *m* répréhensible (d'une action).

reprehensibly [repri'hensibli], *adv.* répréhensiblement; de façon répréhensible, blâmable.

reprehension [repri'henʃ(ə)n], *s.* réprimande *f*, blâme *m*, répréhension *f.*

reprehensive [repri'hensiv], *a.* répréhensif.

represent [repri'zent], *v.tr.* **1.** (*a*) représenter (qch. à l'esprit); **this picture represents a mill,** ce tableau représente un moulin; (*b*) *Th:* représenter (une pièce, une scène, un personnage); jouer (un personnage); (*c*) **the flag represents the nation,** le drapeau symbolise la nation; **this angel represents peace,** cet ange figure la paix. **2.** faire remarquer, signaler, représenter (**sth. to s.o.,** qch. à qn); **I will r. to him the dangers he is running,** je vais lui mettre sous, devant, les yeux les dangers qu'il court. **3.** (*a*) représenter (**s.o., sth., to be . . ., as . . .,** qn, qch., comme . . .); **he represents himself as a model of virtue,** il se donne pour un modèle de vertu; **exactly as represented,** exactement conforme à la description; (*b*) *O:* prétendre, dire. **4.** représenter (qn, une maison de commerce, une circonscription électorale); **the nation is represented by the House of Commons,** la nation est représentée par la Chambre des Communes.

representable [repri'zentəbl], *a.* représentable.

representation [reprizen'teiʃ(ə)n], *s.* **1.** (*a*) représentation *f* (de qch. à l'esprit); (*b*) *Th:* représentation (d'une pièce); interprétation *f* (d'un rôle); (*c*) *Cmptr:* **analogue, discrete, r.,** représentation analogue, discrète. **2.** (*a*) représentation (d'un roi par ses ambassadeurs, etc.); *Pol:* **proportional r.,** représentation proportionnelle; *Jur:* **to inherit by right of r.,** venir par représentation à une succession; (*b*) *coll.* les représentants *m.* **3.** (*a*) représentation, reproduction *f*; **this is a fair r. of their point of view,** cela représente bien leur point de vue; **there are many different representations of the Platonic doctrine,** la doctrine de Platon a été présentée de bien des façons; (*b*) **to make false representations to s.o.,** déguiser la vérité à qn. **4.** (*a*) (i) représentation; remontrance courtoise; protestation courtoise; (ii) exposé *m* des faits; **to make representations to s.o.,** faire des représentations à qn; **to consent to do sth. on the representations of s.o.,** consentir à faire qch. sur les instances *f* de qn; (*b*) *Dipl:* démarche *f*; **joint r.,** démarche collective; **to make representations,** faire une démarche.

representative [repri'zentətiv].
I. *a.* **1.** (*a*) *Phil:* (*of faculty, etc.*) représentatif; (*b*) **allegorical figure r. of the fertility of the soil,** figure allégorique qui représente, qui symbolise, la fertilité du sol. **2.** (*a*) **r. government,** gouvernement représentatif, par députés; *Jur:* **r. heir,** représentant, -ante; (*b*) **government that is r. of the will of the people,** gouvernement qui représente bien la volonté du peuple; (*c*) typique; *Com:* **r. sample,** échantillon type.
II. *s.* **1.** (*a*) représentant, -ante; délégué, -ée; **to send, appoint, a r. to a conference,** se faire représenter à une conférence; *Dipl:* **r. of the Holy See,** représentant du Saint-Siège; (*b*) **last r. of an illustrious race,** dernier descendant d'une race illustre. **2.** *Com: etc:* **district r.,** représentant régional; **foreign r.,** représentant à l'étranger; **sole representatives of a firm,** seuls représentants, seuls agents, d'une maison. **3.** *Pol:* député *m*; *U.S:* **the House of Representatives,** la Chambre des Représentants.

representativeness [repri'zentətivnis], *s.* représentativité *f* (d'un échantillon, etc.).

repress [ri'pres], *v.tr.* **1.** réprimer (des séditieux, une sédition). **2.** réprimer, retenir, contenir, rentrer, concentrer (ses désirs, ses passions); retenir, comprimer (ses larmes); *Psy:* refouler (ses sentiments); **repressed person,** personne renfermée; **to r. a sneeze,** étouffer un éternuement.

re(-)press [ri:'pres], *v.tr.* (*a*) presser de nouveau; **to r. a record,** remettre un disque sous presse; (*b*) *Cer:* represser.

repressible [ri'presibl], *a.* répressible, réprimable.

re(-)pressing [ri:'presiŋ], *s. Cer:* repressage *m.*

repression [ri'preʃ(ə)n], *s.* **1.** répression *f* (d'une sédition, de ses passions). **2.** *Psy:* **unconscious r.,** refoulement *m*; **conscious r.,** répression.

repressive [ri'presiv], *a.* répressif, réprimant; **r. measures,** mesures de répression.

repressor [ri'presər], *s. Biol:* répresseur *m.*

reprieve[1] [ri'pri:v], *s.* **1.** *Jur:* (*a*) *A:* sursis *m*; surséance *f*; (*b*) commutation *f* de la peine capitale; (*c*) lettre(s) *f*(*pl*) de grâce. **2.** répit *m*, délai *m.*

reprieve[2], *v.tr.* **1.** *Jur:* (*a*) *A:* accorder un sursis à (un condamné); surseoir à l'exécution (d'un condamné); (*b*) accorder à (un condamné) une commutation de la peine capitale; **they have been reprieved,** ils ont vu leur peine commuée. **2.** donner du répit à (un débiteur, etc.); accorder un délai à (qn).

reprimand[1] ['reprimɑ:nd], *s.* (*a*) réprimande *f*; (*b*) *Adm:* & *Jur:* blâme *m*; **to incur a r.,** s'attirer un blâme.

reprimand[2], *v.tr.* (*a*) réprimander; faire un réprimande, des observations, à (qn); **to r. s.o. severely,** réprimander qn sévèrement; **to be reprimanded by s.o. for having done sth.,** être réprimandé par qn pour avoir fait qch.; (*b*) *Adm:* & *Jur:* blâmer publiquement (qn).

reprimander ['reprimɑ:ndər], *s.* réprimandeur, -euse.

reprime [ri:'praim], *v.tr.* amorcer à nouveau (une pompe, etc.).

repriming [ri:'praimiŋ], *s.* réamorçage *m* (d'une pompe, etc.).

reprint[1] ['ri:print], *s.* réimpression *f*; nouveau tirage; **separate r. (of magazine article),** tirage à part; **r. edition,** (i) nouveau tirage; (ii) édition populaire.

reprint[2] [ri:'print], *v.tr.* réimprimer; faire un nouveau tirage (d'un livre); reproduire (un article, etc.); **this book is being reprinted,** on procède à la réimpression de ce livre, ce livre est en réimpression.

reprisal [ri'praiz(ə)l], *s.* représailles *fpl*; **as r. for sth.,** en représailles pour, de, qch.; **to make reprisal(s),** exercer des représailles; user de représailles; **to do sth. by way of r.,** agir par représailles.

reprise [ri'pri:z], *s. Mus:* (*a*) reprise *f*; (*b*) seconde exécution (d'une chanson, etc.).

reprises [ri'praiziz], *s.pl. Jur:* déductions *fpl* à faire sur un revenu foncier; **revenue above, beyond, r.,** revenu foncier net.

reproach[1] [ri'proutʃ], *s.* **1.** (*a*) motif *m* de honte, d'opprobre; **to be a r. to. . .,** être la honte, l'opprobre *m*, de . . .; (*b*) honte, opprobre; *B:* **God hath taken away my r.,** Dieu a ôté mon opprobre; **things that have brought r. upon him,** choses qui ont jeté l'opprobre, le discrédit, sur lui. **2.** reproche *m*, blâme *m*, censure *f*; **to abstain from r.,** s'abstenir de tout reproche, de faire aucun reproche; **to incur reproaches,** s'attirer des reproches; **she heaped reproaches on him,** elle l'a accablé de reproches; **beyond, above, r.,** irréprochable; irrépréhensible; **not beyond r.,** qui n'est pas à l'abri du reproche; **look of r.,** regard de reproche; regard réprobateur; **term of r.,** (i) expression de reproche; (ii) terme injurieux. **3.** *Ecc:* (*R.C. liturgy*) **Reproaches,** impropères *mpl.*

reproach[2], *v.tr.* **1.** faire, adresser, des reproches à (qn) (**about,** au sujet de); blâmer (qn); **to r. oneself,** se faire des reproches; **to r. s.o. with sth.,** reprocher qch. à qn; **to r. s.o. for, with, doing sth., for having done sth.,** reprocher à qn d'avoir fait qch.; **I have nothing to r. myself with,** je n'ai rien à me reprocher; **that is the last thing that one can r. him with,** c'est là son moindre défaut; **I didn't r. him in the slightest,** je ne lui ai pas fait le moindre reproche; **without meaning to r. you, I must point out that . . .,** sans reproche, je vous ferai observer que . . .. **2.** blâmer (l'ignorance de qn, etc.). **3.** être la honte, l'opprobre, de (qn, qch.).

reproachable [ri'proutʃəbl], *a.* reprochable; digne de reproche.

reproachful [ri'proutʃful], *a.* réprobateur, -trice; plein de reproche(s); **r. glance,** regard réprobateur, improbateur, improbatif; **r. tone,** ton de reproche.

reproachfully [ri'proutʃfuli], *adv.* avec reproche; d'un air, d'un ton, de reproche.

reprobate[1] ['reprəbeit], *a.* & *s.* **1.** *Ecc:* réprouvé, -ée. **2.** réprouvé; vaurien *m.*

reprobate[2], *v.tr.* (*a*) réprouver (un crime); blâmer, critiquer (qn); (*b*) *Theol:* (*of God*) condamner aux peines éternelles; réprouver.

reprobating ['reprəbeitiŋ], *a.* réprobateur, -trice.

reprobation [reprə'beiʃ(ə)n], *s.* réprobation *f.*

reprobatory [reprə'beitəri], *a.* réprobateur, -trice.

reprocess [ri:'prouses], *v.tr. Ind: etc:* recycler; *Atom.Ph:* **reprocessed fuel,** combustible régénéré.

reprocessing [ri:'prousesiŋ], *s. Ind: etc:* recyclage *m*; *Atom.Ph:* **fuel r.,** régénération *f* du combustible.

reproduce [ri:prə'dju:s]. **1.** *v.tr.* (*a*) reproduire (un tableau, un son, etc.); copier (un texte, etc.); **art which attempts to r. nature,** l'art qui veut reproduire la nature; **the features are well reproduced,** les traits sont bien rendus; (*b*) multiplier (par génération); (*c*) *Nat.Hist:* reproduire, régénérer (une queue, une pince, etc.). **2.** *v.i.* (*a*) se reproduire, se multiplier; proliférer; (*b*) **this print will r. well,** cette estampe se prêtera à la reproduction.

reproducer [ri:prə'dju:sər], *s.* **1.** (*pers.*) reproducteur, -trice (des œuvres d'autrui, etc.). **2.** (*device*) *Elcs: Rec:* reproducteur; **tape r.,** reproducteur de bande; *Cmptr:* **(card) r.,** reproductrice (de cartes).

reproducibility [ri:prədju:si'biliti], *s.* reproductibilité *f.*

reproducible [ri:prə'dju:sibl], *a.* reproductible.

reproducing[1] [ri:prə'dju:siŋ], *a.* reproducteur, -trice.

reproducing[2], *s.* reproduction *f.*

reproduction [ri:prə'dʌkʃ(ə)n], *s.* **1.** (*a*) *Biol: etc:* reproduction *f*; **(a)sexual r.,** reproduction (a)sexuée; **crude, net, r. rate,** taux brut, net, de reproduction; (*b*) reproduction (d'un tableau, d'un document, etc.); **exact r. of colour,** rendu exact des couleurs; **picture of which thousands of reproductions have been made,** tableau reproduit à des milliers d'exemplaires; *Publ:* **(all) r. and translation rights reserved for all countries,** tous droits de reproduction et de traduction réservés pour tous pays; (*c*) *Cmptr:* **r. code,** code de reproduction. **2.** reproduction, répétition *f*; copie *f*, imitation *f.*

reproductive [ri:prə'dʌktiv], *a.* reproducteur, -trice; **the r. organs,** les organes de la reproduction; les organes reproducteurs.

reproductiveness [ri:prə'dʌktivnis], *s.* reproductivité *f*, fertilité *f.*

reprographic [ri:prou'græfik], *a. Typ:* reprographique.

reprography [ri'prɔgrəfi], *s. Typ:* reprographie *f.*

reproof[1] [ri'pru:f], *s.* **1.** reproche *m*, blâme *m*, réprobation *f*; **word, look, of r.,** mot, regard, de reproche; **he spoke in r. of their cruelty,** il a réprouvé leur cruauté. **2.** réprimande *f*; **to administer a sharp r. to s.o.,** réprimander qn sévèrement.

reproof[2] [ri:'pru:f], *v.tr.* réimperméabiliser (un manteau, etc.).

reproofing [ri:'pru:fiŋ], *s.* réimperméabilisation *f* (d'un manteau, etc.).

reprove [ri'pru:v], *v.tr.* (*a*) reprendre, réprimander, blâmer, censurer (qn); **to r. s.o. for his faults,** reprendre qn de ses fautes; (*b*) condamner, réprouver (une action).

reprover [ri'pru:vər], *s.* réprobateur, -trice; censeur *m.*

reproving [ri'pru:viŋ], *a.* réprobateur, -trice; (ton) de reproche, de blâme.

reprovingly [ri'pru:viŋli], *adv.* d'un ton, d'un air, de reproche; en termes réprobateurs; **to look r. at s.o.,** regarder qn d'un air mécontent, sévère.

reprovision [ri:prə'viʒ(ə)n]. **1.** *v.tr.* réapprovisionner, ravitailler. **2.** *v.i.* se réapprovisionner, se ravitailler.

reps [reps], *s. Tex:* reps *m.*

reptant ['reptənt], *a. Nat.Hist:* rampant; reptatoire, reptile.

reptatorial [reptə'tɔ:riəl], **reptatory** ['reptət(ə)ri], *a. Nat.Hist:* reptatoire.

reptile ['reptail]. **1.** *s.* (*a*) reptile *m*; (*b*) *F:* (*pers.*) reptile; cafard *m.* **2.** *a.* reptile, rampant.

Reptilia [rep'tiliə], *s.pl.* reptiles *m.*

reptilian [rep'tiliən]. **1.** *a.* reptilien, reptile. **2.** *s.* reptile *m.*

republic [ri'pʌblik], *s.* république *f*; *Lit:* **the r. of letters,** la république des lettres.

republican [ri'pʌblikən], *a.* & *s.* républicain, -aine.

republicanism [ri'pʌblikənizm], *s.* républicanisme *m.*

republicanize [ri'pʌblikənaiz], *v.tr.* ériger (un état) en république.

republication [ri:pʌbli'keiʃ(ə)n], *s.* **1.** nouvelle édition, réédition *f* (d'un livre). **2.** (*a*) *Jur:* renouvellement *m* (d'un testament antérieur); (*b*) nouvelle publication (d'une loi, d'un décret).

republish [ri:'pʌbliʃ], *v.tr.* **1.** rééditer (un livre); publier de nouveau; donner une nouvelle édition (d'un ouvrage). **2.** (*a*) *Jur:* renouveler (un testament antérieur); (*b*) republier (une loi, un décret).

repudiate [ri'pju:dieit], *v.tr.* **1.** répudier (une épouse). **2.** répudier, désavouer, renier (un ami, une opinion); repousser (une accusation); nier (une dette); *Com: Jur:* refuser d'honorer (un contrat); **to r. the authorship of a book,** désavouer la paternité d'un livre; (*of government*) **to r. (its debts),** répudier ses engagements.

repudiation [ripju:di'eiʃ(ə)n], *s.* **1.** répudiation *f* (d'une épouse). **2.** (*a*) répudiation, désaveu *m* (de qn, d'une opinion); reniement *m* (d'une dette); (*b*) répudiation de ses engagements (par le gouvernement).

repudiator [ri'pju:dieitər], *s.* renieur, -euse (d'une dette); celui qui répudie, désavoue, renie (une opinion, etc.).

repugnance [ri'pʌgnəns], *s.* **1.** incompatibilité *f*, contrariété *f* (**of, between, ideas, etc.,** des idées, etc.); **r. of an action with, to, one's sense of duty,** incompatibilité d'une action avec la conception du devoir. **2.** répugnance *f*, antipathie *f* (**to, against,** pour); **to feel r. to sth., to doing sth.,** éprouver de la répugnance pour qch.; répugner à une action, à faire qch.; avoir de la répugnance pour qch., à faire qch.

repugnant [ri'pʌgnənt], *a.* **1.** incompatible (**to, with,** avec); contraire (**to, with,** à). **2.** répugnant (**to,** à); **to be r. to s.o.,** répugner à qn; **it is r. to me to . . .,** il me répugne de . . ..

repulse[1] [ri'pʌls], *s. O:* **1.** échec *m*; défaite *f* (de l'ennemi); **to meet with, suffer, a r.,** essuyer un échec. **2.** rebuffade *f*, refus *m*; **to meet with a r.,** essuyer un refus.

repulse[2], *v.tr.* **1.** repousser, refouler (un assaut, un ennemi). **2.** repousser (les avances de qn, une demande); refuser, rebuter, renvoyer (qn).

repulsion [ri'pʌlʃ(ə)n], *s.* **1.** *Ph:* répulsion *f.* **2.** répulsion, aversion *f*, répugnance *f*; **to feel r. for s.o.,** éprouver de la répulsion pour qn.

repulsive [ri'pʌlsiv], *a.* **1.** *Ph:* répulsif. **2.** (*of thg*) répulsif, repoussant, rebutant; **to look r.,** offrir un aspect repoussant. **3.** (*of pers.*) (*a*) *A:* qui repousse les avances; froid, distant; à l'abord difficile; (*b*) répugnant.

repulsively [ri'pʌlsivli], *adv.* **r. ugly,** d'une laideur repoussante.

repulsiveness [ri'pʌlsivnis], *s.* **1.** *Ph:* force répulsive. **2.** caractère repoussant, aspect répugnant.

repurchase[1] [ri:'pə:tʃəs], *s.* rachat *m*, *Jur:* réméré *m*; **with option of r.,** avec faculté de rachat, de réméré; **sale with privilege of r.,** vente à réméré.

repurchase[2], *v.tr.* racheter; **sale subject to right of vendor to r.,** vente à réméré.

reputable ['repjutəbl], *a.* **1.** (*of pers.*) honorable, estimé, estimable, de bonne réputation; réputé. **2.** (emploi) honorable.

reputably ['repjutəbli], *adv.* honorablement.

reputation [repju(:)'teiʃ(ə)n], *s.* réputation *f*, renom *m*;

to acquire, make, a r. (for oneself), se faire une réputation, un grand nom; **to have a r. for courage,** avoir une réputation de courage; **to have the r. of being, of doing, sth.,** avoir la réputation d'être, de faire, qch.; **to have the r. of being a skilful doctor,** avoir la réputation de médecin habile; **his r. as a surgeon,** sa réputation de chirurgien; **to know s.o. only by r.,** ne connaître qn que de réputation; **good r.,** bon renom, réputation; **to have a good, high, r.,** jouir d'une excellente réputation, d'une grande considération; **to have a bad r.,** (i) (*of pers.*) avoir une mauvaise réputation; (ii) (*of street, restaurant, etc.*) avoir une mauvaise réputation; être mal famé; **to get a bad r.,** se faire une mauvaise réputation; **to ruin s.o.'s r.,** perdre qn de réputation; *O:* **persons of r.,** personnes honorables.

repute[1] [ri'pju:t], *s.* réputation *f*, renom *m*, renommée *f*; **to know s.o. by r.,** connaître qn de réputation; *O:* **to be held in high r.,** (i) avoir une haute réputation; (ii) être bien noté; **he is in bad r.,** il a une mauvaise réputation; **doctor of r.,** médecin réputé, en grand renom; **family of good r.,** famille honorablement connue; **of no r.,** sans réputation; **place of ill r.,** endroit mal famé, de mauvaise réputation; **house of ill r.,** (i) maison de mauvaise réputation; maison louche, borgne; (ii) maison de passe.

repute[2], *v.tr.* (*usu. passive*) **to be reputed wealthy,** avoir la réputation d'être riche; **he is reputed to be a good doctor,** il a la réputation d'être, il passe pour (être), il est censé être, un bon médecin; **he is reputed to know everything about this science,** il est réputé ne rien ignorer de cette science; *Jur:* **reputed father,** père putatif.

reputedly [ri'pju:tidli], *adv.* (*a*) censément; suivant l'opinion commune; **he is r. the best heart specialist,** il passe pour le meilleur cardiologue; (*b*) *Jur:* putativement.

requeening [ri:'kwi:niŋ], *s. Ap:* remérage *m.*

request[1] [ri'kwest], *s.* **1.** (*a*) demande *f*, prière *f*, requête *f*; *Jur:* requête, sommation *f*; **r. for money, funds,** demande d'argent, de crédits; **at the r. of s.o.,** à la demande, sur la demande, à la requête, à la prière, de qn; **to do sth. at s.o.'s r.,** faire qch. sur la demande de qn; **at his r.,** sur sa demande; **at the urgent r. of . . .,** sur, à, la demande pressante de . . .; sur les instances pressantes de . . .; **samples sent on r.,** échantillons sur demande; **to make a r.,** faire, formuler, une demande; **to grant a r.,** accorder, satisfaire, faire droit à, une demande; **to be open to requests,** être accessible aux prières; *O:* **to make r. for sth.,** demander, solliciter, qch.; **by (popular) r.,** à la demande générale; **r. (bus) stop,** arrêt facultatif; *W.Tel:* **r. programme, show,** programme des auditeurs; **I've sent in a r. for some Mozart,** j'ai demandé du Mozart; (*b*) *Navy:* réclamation *f*; **r. book,** cahier de réclamations. **2.** recherche *f*, vogue *f*, demande; **to be in r.,** être recherché; être en vogue, avoir la vogue; **he is very much in r.,** on se le dispute.

request[2], *v.tr.* **1. to r. sth. of s.o.,** demander qch. à qn; solliciter qch. de qn. **2. to r. s.o. to do sth.,** demander à qn de faire qch.; prier qn de faire qch.; inviter qn à faire qch.; **to act when requested,** agir sur demande; **the public is requested to keep off the grass,** prière (au public) de ne pas marcher sur le gazon; *Com:* **as requested,** conformément à vos instructions, suite à votre demande. **3. to r. (permission) to do sth.,** demander à faire qch.

requicken [ri:'kwik(ə)n]. *A:* **1.** *v.tr.* ranimer, raviver. **2.** *v.i.* se ranimer, se raviver.

requiem ['rekwiəm], *s.* **1.** *Ecc:* **r. (mass),** (messe *f* de) requiem *m*; messe des morts; *Mus:* requiem. **2.** chant *m* funèbre.

require [ri'kwaiər], *v.tr.* **1. to r. sth. of s.o.,** demander, réclamer, qch. à qn; exiger qch. de qn; **what do you r. of me?** qu'exigez-vous de moi? *Lit:* que prétendez-vous de moi? **to r. s.o. to do sth.,** demander à qn de faire qch.; exiger de qn qu'il fasse qch.; **he required that I should appear,** il a exigé que je me présente; **the court requires you to attend,** la cour requiert que vous comparaissiez; **he had done all that was required by law,** il s'était conformé à toutes les exigences de la loi. **2.** exiger, demander, requérir, réclamer; **his wound requires very little care,** sa blessure réclame très peu de soins; **work that requires great precision,** travail qui nécessite une grande précision; **ore that requires special treatment,** minerai qui comporte des traitements particuliers; **this dress requires 3m. of material,** cette robe emploie 3m de tissu; **this plant requires plenty of water,** il faut beaucoup d'eau à cette plante; **have you everything you r.?** avez-vous tout ce qu'il vous faut? **it would r. a whole army to take the fort,** il faudrait une armée pour prendre la forteresse; **it required all his strength to hold them back,** il fallait toute sa force pour les retenir; **I shall do whatever is required,** je ferai tout ce qu'il faudra; je ferai le nécessaire; **if required,** s'il le faut; si besoin est; si c'est nécessaire; éventuellement; **when required,** au besoin; **as may be required, as circumstances may r.,** selon l'exigence du cas; selon les nécessités; **to cut sth. to the required length,** couper qch. à la longueur voulue; **in the required time,** dans le délai prescrit; en temps voulu; **to have the money required,** avoir l'argent nécessaire; **the qualifications required for this job,** les qualités requises pour ce poste; **this book is required reading,** on est obligé de lire ce livre; ce livre est prescrit; *Gram:* **verb that requires the preposition** *of* **before the noun,** verbe qui veut la préposition *of* devant le nom.

requirement [ri'kwaiəmənt], *s.* **1.** demande *f*, réclamation *f*. **2.** exigence *f*, nécessité *f*, besoin *m*; **to meet s.o.'s requirements,** répondre aux désirs de qn; satisfaire les exigences, aux exigences, de qn; **to make one's requirements known,** faire connaître ses besoins; **requirements for doing sth.,** moyens demandés, exigés, nécessaires, requis, pour faire qch. **3.** *usu.pl.* condition(s) requise(s); qualité voulue; **dimensional requirements of a machine,** spécifications dimensionnelles d'une machine.

requisite ['rekwizit]. **1.** *a.* requis (**to,** pour); nécessaire (**to,** à); indispensable (**to,** pour); exigé, voulu; **they lack the r. capital,** il leur manque le capital nécessaire. **2.** *s.* (*a*) condition requise (**for,** pour); (*b*) chose *f* nécessaire; **toilet requisites,** articles *m*, accessoires *m*, de toilette; **office requisites,** fournitures *f* de bureau; **travelling requisites,** articles de voyage.

requisiteness ['rekwizitnis], *s.* nécessité *f*, indispensabilité *f*.

requisition[1] [rekwi'ziʃ(ə)n], *s.* **1.** demande *f*; **on a r. by ten members,** sur la demande de dix membres; **repairs executed under the r. of the town council,** réparations exécutées sur la demande du conseil municipal; *Com: etc:* **r. for materials, for supplies,** demande de matériaux; commande *f* pour fournitures; **r. number,** numéro de référence. **2.** (*a*) *Mil:* réquisition *f*; **to levy requisitions on a village,** imposer des réquisitions à un village; **to put sth. in r., to call sth. into r.,** mettre qch. en réquisition; *A.Mil:* **horse registered for r.,** cheval de réquisition; (*b*) **to put sth. in r., to call sth. into r.,** mettre qch. à contribution; **his services were in constant r.,** on avait constamment recours à ses services; **the machine was in constant r.,** on se servait de la machine tout le temps.

requisition[2], *v.tr.* **1.** réquisitionner (des vivres, etc.); *A: & Mil:* mettre (des chevaux, etc.) en réquisition; **to r. s.o.'s services,** recourir, avoir recours, aux services de qn; **liable to be requisitioned,** requérable. **2.** faire des réquisitions dans (une ville).

requisitioning [rekwi'ziʃəniŋ], *s.* (mise *f* en) réquisition *f*.

requital [ri'kwait(ə)l], *s.* **1.** récompense *f*, retour *m*; **in r. of, for, sth.,** en récompense, en retour, de qch.; **the r. for laziness,** les sanctions *f* de la paresse. **2.** revanche *f*, représailles *fpl*, vengeance *f*; **in r. for this act of perfidy,** pour punir cette perfidie.

requite [ri'kwait], *v.tr.* **1.** récompenser, payer de retour (un service); revaloir (un tort); se venger (d'une injure); venger (une injure); **to r. s.o.'s love,** répondre à l'amour de qn; aimer qn en retour; **requited love,** amour partagé; **to r. evil with good,** rendre le bien pour le mal. **2.** *Lit:* **to r. s.o. for a service, for his perfidy,** récompenser qn d'un service, de sa perfidie; **he requites me with ingratitude,** il me paie d'ingratitude; **he will r. you,** il vous rendra la pareille.

rerail [ri:'reil], *v.tr.* remettre (une locomotive) sur les rails.

rerailer [ri:'reilər], *s. Rail:* (*machine*) enrailleur *m.*

rerailing [ri:'reiliŋ], *s.* remise *f* (d'une locomotive) sur (les) rails.

reread [ri:'ri:d], *v.tr.* relire.

rereading [ri:'ri:diŋ], *s.* relecture *f*; seconde lecture, lecture à nouveau.

rerebrace ['riəbreis], *s. Arm:* (canon *m* d')arrière-bras *m inv.*

rerecord [ri:ri'kɔ:d], *v.tr. Cin: T.V: Rec: etc:* réenregistrer.

rerecording [ri:ri'kɔ:diŋ], *s. Cin: T.V: Rec: etc:* réenregistrement *m*; repiquage *m* (d'un disque).

reredos ['riədɔs], *s. Ecc:* retable *m.*

re(-)route [ri:'ru:t], *v.tr.* dérouter (un navire, etc.).

re(-)routing [ri:'ru:tiŋ], *s.* déroutement *m*, déviation *f*, détournement *m* (d'un avion, etc.).

rerun[1] ['ri:rʌn], *s.* reprise *f* (d'un film, d'une course, etc.).

rerun[2] [ri:'rʌn], *v.tr.* (*p.t.* **reran** [ri:'ræn]; *p.p.* **rerun**; *pr.p.* **rerunning**) repasser (un film); refaire (une course).

res [reis, ri:z], *s. Jur:* chose *f*; **r. judicata,** chose jugée.

resale [ri:'seil], *s.* revente *f*; **r. value,** valeur à la revente; **to have a better r. value,** se revendre mieux.

resampling [ri:'sɑ:mpliŋ], *s. Petr: Min:* échantillonnage répété.

resaw [ri:'sɔ:], *v.tr.* rescier (des madriers).

resazurin [re'zæʒərin], *s. Ch:* résazurine *f*.

rescind [ri'sind], *v.tr.* rescinder (un acte); annuler (un vote, une décision); abroger (une loi); casser (un jugement); annuler, résoudre, résilier (un contrat); rétracter (un arrêt).

rescindable [ri'sindəbl], *a.* annulable, résiliable.

rescinding[1] [ri'sindiŋ], *a.* (clause, etc.) abrogatoire.

rescinding[2], *s.* = RESCISSION.

rescission [ri'siʒ(ə)n], *s.* rescision *f*, abrogation *f* (d'un acte); annulation *f*, résolution *f*, résiliation *f*, résiliement *m* (d'un contrat).

rescissory [ri'sisəri], *a. Jur:* (acte) rescisoire, rescindant.

rescore [ri:'skɔ:r], *v.tr. Mus:* réorchestrer (un opéra, etc.).

rescript ['ri:skript], *s.* **1.** *Ecc: etc:* rescrit *m.* **2.** (*a*) (nouvelle) transcription; (*b*) palimpseste *m.*

rescue[1] ['reskju:], *s.* **1.** délivrance *f*; (*from shipwreck, fire, etc.*) sauvetage *m*; **to come, go, to s.o.'s r., to the r.,** venir, aller, au secours de qn; porter, prêter (du) secours à qn; **r. apparatus, equipment,** appareil(s) de sauvetage; **r. party,** équipe de sauvetage, sauveteurs; caravane de secours; **r. work,** travaux de sauvetage; **air-sea r.,** sauvetage aérien en mer; sauvetage aéromaritime; **mountain r.,** secours en montagne; *Cards:* **r. bid,** enchère faite pour tirer son partenaire d'un mauvais pas. **2.** *Jur:* (*a*) délivrance illégale (d'un prisonnier); (*b*) *A:* reprise *f* par force (de biens).

rescue[2], *v.tr.* **1.** sauver, délivrer, secourir; porter, prêter, (du) secours à (qn); **to r. s.o. from danger,** arracher qn à un danger; **to r. s.o. from death,** arracher qn à la mort; **to r. s.o. from drowning,** sauver qn qui se noie; effectuer le sauvetage d'un noyé; **the rescued (men),** les rescapés; *Lit:* **to r. s.o. from poverty,** tirer qn de la misère; **to r. a name from oblivion,** sauver un nom de l'oubli. **2.** *Jur:* (*a*) arracher (un prisonnier) aux mains de la justice; délivrer (un prisonnier) par force; délivrer, dégager, (un prisonnier) des mains de la police; (*b*) *A:* reprendre de force (ses biens); recouvrer de force (les biens de qn).

rescuer ['reskjuər], *s.* **1.** libérateur, -trice. **2.** (*from fire, etc.*) secouriste *mf*; sauveteur *m.*

rescuing ['reskjuiŋ], *s.* sauvetage *m.*

reseal [ri:'si:l], *v.tr.* resceller (un acte); refermer (une enveloppe, etc.).

research[1] [ri'sə:tʃ], *s.* recherche *f* (**after, for,** de); **scientific, medical, r.,** recherche(s) scientifique(s), médicale(s); enquête *f* scientifique; **industrial r.,** recherche appliquée; **experimental r.,** recherche expérimentale; **to do, be engaged in, r. (on, into, sth.),** faire des recherches, des investigations, sur qch.; *Sch: F:* **to do r.** = préparer son doctorat, etc.; **r. work,** recherches, investigations; travaux de recherche; **r. worker, assistant,** (i) chercheur, -euse (de laboratoire); (ii) documentaliste *mf*; **scientific r. worker, r. scientist,** maître de recherche; **to be a r. worker,** faire de la recherche; **field r.,** prospection *f* sur le terrain; **market r.,** analyse *f* des marchés, étude de marché; **marketing r.,** recherche commerciale; *Ind:* **r. centre, department,** centre, service, de recherche; bureau d'études; **r. and development,** recherche et mise au point; **r. and development department,** atelier, services, d'études; *Cmptr:* **operations, operational, r.,** recherche opérationnelle; **chaining r.,** recherche par chaînage.

research[2], *v.i. & tr.* faire des recherches (scientifiques, etc.) (sur qch.).

re-search [ri:'sə:tʃ], *v.tr.* chercher de nouveau (dans un endroit); refouiller (ses poches); *Jur:* faire une nouvelle perquisition dans (une maison); *Cust:* revisiter (un navire).

researcher [ri'sə:tʃər], *s.* chercheur, -euse (scientifique, etc.); investigateur, -trice.

reseat [ri:'si:t], *v.tr.* **1.** rasseoir (qn), remettre (qn) sur son siège; faire rasseoir (qn); **to r. oneself,** se rasseoir. **2.** remettre un fond à (un pantalon, une chaise); rempailler (une chaise paillée); regarnir (un théâtre, etc.) de sièges. **3.** *I.C.E: etc:* **to r. a valve,** repasser, roder, fraiser, le siège d'une soupape.

réseau ['reizou], *s.* **1.** réseau *m* (de dentelle). **2.** *Astr:* réseau (de carrés de repère).

resect [ri'sekt], *v.tr. Surg:* réséquer (un os, etc.).

resectable [ri'sektəbl], *a. Surg:* résécable.

resection [ri'sekʃ(ə)n], *s. Surg:* résection *f* (d'un organe, etc.).

resectoscope [ri'sektəskoup], *s. Surg:* résecteur *m.*

reseda. 1. ['residə, 'rez-, ri'si:də], *s. Bot:* réséda *m.* **2.**

['residə, 'rez-], *a.* & *s.* (vert) réséda *inv.*
Resedaceae [resi'deisiː], *s.pl. Bot:* résédacées *f.*
reseed [riː'siːd]. *Bot:* **1.** *v.tr.* ressemer. **2.** *v.i.* & *pr.* se ressemer.
resell [riː'sel], *v.tr.* (*p.t.* & *p.p.* **resold** [riː'sould]) revendre.
resemblance [ri'zembləns], *s.* ressemblance *f* (**to,** à, avec; **between,** entre); **vague, faint, r.,** vague, légère, ressemblance; ressemblance lointaine; **strong r.,** grande ressemblance; **to bear a r. to s.o., sth.,** ressembler à qn, qch.; *Lit: Cin: etc:* **any r. to any person living or dead is purely accidental,** toute ressemblance avec des personnages réels ne peut être que fortuite.
resemble [ri'zembl], *v.tr.* **1.** ressembler à, approcher de (qn, qch.); **to r. one another,** se ressembler. **2.** *A:* comparer (**to,** à).
resent [ri'zent], *v.tr.* **1.** être offensé, froissé, de (qch.); avoir pris (qch.) en mauvaise part; être irrité de (qch.); **you r. my being here,** ma présence vous déplaît. **2.** s'offenser, se froisser, se fâcher, de (qch.); **I should r. a refusal,** vous me désobligeriez en refusant; un refus me blesserait.
resentful [ri'zentful], *a.* **1.** plein de ressentiment; rancunier. **2.** froissé, irrité (**of,** de).
resentfully [ri'zentfuli], *adv.* avec ressentiment; d'un ton, d'un air, rancunier.
resentfulness [ri'zentfulnis], *s.* ressentiment *m.*
resentment [ri'zentmənt], *s.* ressentiment *m*; rancœur *f,* rancune *f*; **to feel r. against s.o. on account of sth., for having done sth.,** faire grief à qn de qch.; garder rancune à qn, avoir de la rancune contre qn, avoir de la rancœur pour, contre, qn, d'avoir fait qch.; **his r. of his mother's attitude,** le ressentiment qu'il éprouvait de l'attitude de sa mère; *Lit:* **to cherish a secret r. against s.o.,** ressentir un dépit secret contre qn.
resequent [ri'siːkwənt], *a. Geol:* reséquent.
reserpine [ri'səːpin, -'zəː-], *s. Pharm:* réserpine *f.*
reservation [rezə'veiʃ(ə)n], *s.* **1.** (*a*) réservation *f* (de places, etc.); (*b*) *esp. NAm:* place retenue. **2.** réserve *f,* restriction *f*; **to enter a r. in respect of a contract,** apporter une réserve à un contrat; **without r.,** sans réserve; sans arrière-pensée; **not without r., with some r.,** non sans réserves, avec quelques réserves; **with reservations,** sous bénéfice d'inventaire; **with this r.,** à cette restriction près; sous le bénéfice de cette observation; **to make reservations,** faire des réserves; **with the r. of. . .,** à la réserve de . . .. **3.** *Ecc:* (*a*) réserve, réservat *m,* réservation (d'un bénéfice) (par le pape); (*b*) **the R. (of the Sacrament),** la sainte Réserve. **4.** *Jur:* réservation (d'un droit); **power of r.,** droit de réservation. **5.** (*a*) *Aut:* **central r.,** terreplein central; (*b*) *NAm:* terrain réservé; **Indian r.,** réserve indienne.
reserve¹ [ri'zəːv], *s.* **1.** (*a*) réserve *f* (d'argent, d'énergie); *Fin:* **bank reserves,** réserves bancaires; **cash reserves,** réserve de caisse; **r. for bad debts,** réserve, provision *f,* prévision *f,* pour créances douteuses; **hidden, secret, r.,** réserve latente, occulte; **r. fund,** fonds de réserve, de prévision, de prévoyance; **stocks forming the reserves necessary to maintain production,** stocks qui constituent le volant nécessaire à la production; **to allocate, appropriate, a sum to the contigency r.,** affecter une somme à la réserve de prévoyance; **to draw on the reserves,** puiser dans les réserves; (*of ammunition, money*) **to use up one's last reserves,** brûler ses dernières cartouches; *Games:* **to take a domino from the r.,** prendre un domino dans le talon, dans la réserve; **to have great reserves of energy, strength,** avoir beaucoup d'énergie, de force, en réserve; *Mch: etc:* **r. power, energy,** réserve de puissance, d'énergie; **r. machine,** machine de réserve, de secours; *Ph: N.Arch:* **r. buoyancy,** réserve de flottabilité; *Min:* **known reserves,** réserves prouvées; (*b*) **to have, keep, sth. in r.,** tenir qch. en réserve; *Mil:* **horse in r.,** (i) cheval de rechange; (ii) haut-le-pied *m inv.* **2.** (*a*) *Mil: etc:* **the reserves,** (i) les réserves; (ii) les réservistes *m*; **the r. (of the regular army),** la réserve (de l'armée active); **r. officer,** officier de réserve; **r. officers' training battalion,** bataillon d'élèves officiers de réserve; **in local r.,** en réserve d'unité; **to put a ship in r. (with maintenance party),** mettre un navire en réserve; (*b*) *Sp:* remplaçant, -ante. **3.** (*a*) terrain réservé; *For: Ven:* réserve; **nature r.,** réserve naturelle; (*b*) *Aut:* **centre r.,** terreplein central. **4.** (*a*) réserve, restriction *f*; **without r.,** sans réserve; sans restriction; **to make reserves,** faire des réserves; **with these reserves,** sous ces réserves; **to publish sth. with all (proper) r.,** publier qch. sous toutes réserves; *Bank:* **under r.,** sauf bonne fin; (*b*) (*at sale*) **r. price,** prix minimum; mise *f* à prix. **5.** (*in behaviour*) réserve, discrétion *f,* retenue *f*; **to maintain a wise r.,** observer une sage, prudente, réserve; **when he breaks through his r.,** quand il sort de sa réserve.
reserve², *v.tr.* réserver (**sth. for s.o., for another occasion,** qch. pour, à, qn, pour une autre occasion); mettre (qch.) en réserve; mettre (qch.) de côté; **to r. a seat for s.o.,** réserver, retenir, une place à qn; **reserved seat,** place réservée, louée; **to r. oneself a right,** se réserver un droit; **to r. the right to do sth.,** se réserver le droit de faire qch.; **I agree but I r. the right to reconsider my decision,** je consens, sauf à revenir sur ma décision; *Ecc:* **the Blessed Sacrament is reserved in this chapel,** le Saint-Sacrement se trouve dans cette chapelle; *Publ:* **all rights reserved,** tous droits (de reproduction, etc.) réservés; *War Adm:* (*1939–45*) **to be in a reserved occupation,** être affecté spécial, avoir une affectation spéciale.
re-serve [riː'səːv], *v.tr.* resservir (un plat); *Jur:* notifier une seconde fois (une citation).
reserved [ri'zəːvd], *a.* **1.** (*of pers.*) réservé, renfermé, discret, modeste, concentré; peu communicatif; **to be r. with s.o.,** être réservé, se tenir sur la réserve, avec qn. **2.** *Ecc:* **r. sin,** cas réservé.
reservedly [ri'zəːvidli], *adv.* avec réserve.
reservedness [ri'zəːvidnis], *s.* réserve *f,* retenue *f,* discrétion *f* (avec qn).
reserving [ri'zəːviŋ], *s.* réserve *f,* réservation *f.*
reservist [ri'zəːvist], *s. Mil: etc:* réserviste *m.*
reservoir ['rezəvwɑːr], *s.* **1.** *Hyd.E:* réservoir *m*; bassin *m* de retenue; retenue *f,* décharge *f* (d'un cours d'eau). **2.** (*a*) *Lit:* **a great r. of facts,** un grand réservoir, une réserve inépuisable, de faits; (*b*) *Mec.E:* **oil r.,** réservoir à huile; **air r.,** réservoir d'air (comprimé); *Aut: etc:* **brake fluid r.,** réservoir à liquide pour freins; (*c*) *Anat:* réservoir (de la bile, etc.).
reset¹ [ri'set], *s. Jur: Scot:* recel *m* (d'objets volés).
reset², *v.tr.* (**resetted**) *Jur: Scot:* receler (des objets volés).
reset³ [riː'set], *v.tr.* (*p.t.* & *p.p.* **reset;** *pr.p.* **resetting**) **1.** remettre (qch.) en place; replacer (qch.); remonter (des pierres précieuses, etc.); enfoncer de nouveau (un pieu, etc.); replanter (des rosiers, etc.); **to r. the table,** remettre le couvert; **to r. a sail,** rétablir une voile. **2. to r. an instrument to zero,** remettre un instrument à zéro; **to r. one's watch,** remettre sa montre à l'heure; *I.C.E:* **to r. the timing gear,** recaler l'engrenage de distribution; **to r. a spring,** retendre, rebander, un ressort. **3.** *Surg:* **to r. a (dislocated) limb,** remettre, remboîter, un membre (luxé); **to r. a (broken) bone,** remettre à nouveau un os (fracturé). **4.** raffûter, réaffûter (un outil). **5.** *Typ:* recomposer (un texte).
resetter [ri'setər], *s. Jur: Scot:* receleur, -euse (d'objets volés).
resetting¹ [ri'setiŋ], *s.* = RESET¹.
resetting² [riː'setiŋ], *s.* **1.** (*a*) remise *f* en place (de qch.); (*b*) remontage *m* (de pierres précieuses, etc.). **2.** *Surg:* remboîtement *m* (d'un membre luxé). **3.** raffûtage *m,* réaffûtage *m* (d'un outil). **4.** *Typ:* recomposition *f* (d'un texte).
resettle [riː'setl]. **1.** *v.tr.* (*a*) remettre (**sth. in its place,** qch. à sa place); rétablir (**s.o. in a country,** qn dans un pays); réinstaller (qn); **to r. oneself,** se rasseoir; se remettre sur son siège; se réinstaller; (*b*) coloniser de nouveau (un pays); (*c*) recaser (qn). **2.** *v.i.* (*a*) se fixer de nouveau (**in a place,** dans un endroit); se réinstaller; (*b*) (*of wine, etc., after transport*) se reposer.
resettlement [riː'set(ə)lmənt], *s.* transfert *m* de population; recasement *m* (de qn).
reshape [riː'ʃeip], *v.tr.* reformer, refaçonner; remanier (une œuvre littéraire, etc.).
reshaping [riː'ʃeipiŋ], *s.* remaniement *m,* remaniage *m* (de qch.).
resharpen [riː'ʃɑːp(ə)n], *v.tr.* raffûter, réaffûter (un outil); retailler (une lime, un crayon).
resharpening [riː'ʃɑːp(ə)niŋ], *s.* raffûtage *m,* réaffûtage *m* (d'un outil); retaillage *m* (d'une lime, etc.).
reship [riː'ʃip], *v.tr.* **1.** rembarquer, réembarquer, réexpédier (des marchandises). **2.** remonter (un gouvernail, une hélice).
reshipment [riː'ʃipmənt], *s.* rembarquement *m,* réexpédition *f* (de marchandises).
reshoe [riː'ʃuː], *v.tr.* referrer (un cheval, etc.).
reshoeing [riː'ʃuːiŋ], *s.* (nouveau) ferrage (d'un cheval, etc.).
reshuffle¹ [riː'ʃʌfl], *s.* (*a*) *Cards:* nouveau battement (des cartes); (*b*) *Pol:* **Cabinet r.,** remaniement ministériel.
reshuffle², *v.tr.* (*a*) rebattre, remêler (les cartes); (*b*) remanier (un personnel, etc.).
reshuffling [riː'ʃʌfliŋ], *s.* = RESHUFFLE¹.
reside [ri'zaid], *v.i.* **1.** (*of pers.*) résider (**at, in,** à, dans). **2.** (*of quality*) résider (**in s.o., sth.,** dans qn, qch.); **sovereign power resides in the people,** la souveraineté réside dans le peuple, appartient au peuple.
residence ['rezidəns], *s.* **1.** résidence *f,* demeure *f,* séjour *m*; **to have one's r. in. . ., at. . .,** résider à . . ., dans . . .; **during my r. abroad,** pendant mon séjour à l'étranger; **to take up (one's) r. in London,** établir sa demeure, son domicile, prendre domicile, à Londres; **to take up r. in a country,** se fixer, s'établir, dans un pays; **r. permit,** permis de séjour; **to change one's r.,** changer de domicile, de résidence; **place of r.,** lieu de résidence; domicile personnel, réel; **official of whom r. is required,** fonctionnaire pour qui la résidence est obligatoire; fonctionnaire tenu à la résidence; **to be in r.,** être en résidence; *Ecc:* **canon in r.,** chanoine en résidence; *Sch:* **r. of undergraduates,** internat *m* des étudiants; **the students are not yet in r.,** les étudiants ne sont pas encore rentrés. **2.** demeure, maison *f,* habitation *f*; **desirable r. for sale,** belle propriété à vendre; **secondary r. (in the country),** résidence secondaire (à la campagne); **grace and favour r.,** résidence concédée à titre gracieux, par faveur spéciale, par le souverain; *Navy:* **r. of the port admiral,** amirauté *f*; *NAm:* **r. section,** quartier résidentiel.
residency ['rezidənsi], *s.* **1.** *Hist:* (*a*) résidence (administrative) (d'un protectorat); (*b*) résidence (officielle) (du résident). **2.** résidence officielle (d'un haut fonctionnaire). **3.** *U.S: Med:* internat *m.*
resident ['rezidənt]. **1.** *a.* (*a*) résidant, qui réside; **to be r. in a place,** résider dans un endroit; **the canons were not r.,** les chanoines ne résidaient pas; **the r. population,** la population fixe; *Orn:* **r. birds,** oiseaux non migrateurs; oiseaux à demeure; (*b*) **r. teacher,** professeur à demeure; professeur résident; (*c*) **difficulties r. in the situation,** difficultés qui résident dans la situation. **2.** *s.* (*a*) habitant, -ante (d'un pays, d'une rue, etc.); pensionnaire *mf* (dans un hôtel, etc.); **residents' parking zone,** zone à stationnement réservé aux riverains; **residents' parking bay, place,** emplacement réservé aux riverains; **resident's parking permit,** permis de stationnement; *P.N:* **r. permit holders only,** stationnement interdit sauf aux riverains; (*b*) *Adm:* (*pers. living in a foreign country*) résident, -ente; (*c*) *Hist:* (ministre) résident; **the resident's wife,** la résidente; **R. General in Tunisia,** Résident général en Tunisie; (*d*) *U.S: Med:* interne *mf.*
residential [rezi'denʃ(ə)l], *a.* **1.** résidentiel; **r. area, district,** quartier résidentiel. **2. r. course (of study),** cours *m* à temps complet; **r. qualification,** (i) quotité d'imposition nécessaire pour être électeur; cens électoral; (ii) droit de vote en tant que propriétaire ou locataire.
residentiary [rezi'denʃəri]. **1.** *a.* résidant, qui réside. **2.** *s.* & *a. Ecc:* **(canon) r.,** chanoine résidant, obligé à la résidence.
residentship ['rezidəntʃip], *s. Hist:* résidence *f.*
residual [ri'zidjuəl]. **1.** *a.* (*a*) *Ph: etc:* résiduel, résiduaire; **r. magnetism,** magnétisme rémanent, résiduel; rémanence *f*; *El:* **r. charge,** charge résiduelle; **r. current,** courant résiduel; *Geol:* **r. clay,** argile résiduelle; (*b*) (*of objection, mistake, etc.*) qui reste; restant. **2.** *s.* (*a*) *Ch: etc:* résidu *m*; (*b*) *Mth: O:* reste *m* (d'une soustraction, etc.).
residuary [ri'zidjuəri], *a.* **1.** *Ch: etc:* résiduaire, résiduel. **2.** qui reste; restant; du reste; *Jur:* **r. legatee, devisee,** légataire à titre universel.
residue ['rezidjuː], *s.* **1.** *Ch: Ind: etc:* résidu *m*; reliquat *m*; *Petr:* **still r.,** résidus de distillation; *Cmptr:* **r. check,** contrôle sur reste. **2.** reste(s) *m(pl)* (d'une armée, etc.). **3.** *Jur:* reliquat (d'une succession); actif net après paiement de toutes les charges. **4.** *Mth: O:* résidu (d'une division).
residuum, *pl.* **-a** [ri'zidjuəm, -ə], *s. Ch: etc:* résidu *m*; reste *m.*
resign [ri'zain], *v.tr.* **1.** (*a*) résigner (une fonction); se démettre de; démissionner; donner sa démission; résigner ses fonctions, sa charge; *A:* abdiquer (la couronne); *Mil:* **to r. one's commission,** donner sa démission; **resigning officer,** (officier) démissionnaire *mf*; **to r. from the cabinet,** démissionner du gouvernement; **to r. as president of. . .,** démissionner de la présidence de . . .; *Parl:* **r.! r.!** démission! démission! (*b*) abandonner (un droit, tout espoir); *O:* renoncer à (la vie); abandonner, renoncer à (une tâche); (*c*) **to r. sth. to s.o.,** abandonner, céder, qch. à qn; faire l'abandon de qch. à qn. **2.** (*a*) **to r. oneself to s.o., sth.,** se livrer à qn, qch.; **to r. oneself to sleep,** s'abandonner au sommeil; (*b*) **to r. oneself, to be resigned, to one's fate, to doing sth.,** se résigner, être résigné, à son sort, à faire qch.; en prendre son parti.
re-sign [riː'sain], *v.tr.* signer (qch.) de nouveau, à nouveau; resigner (qch.).
resignatary [ri'zignət(ə)ri], *s.* résignataire *m.*
resignation [rezig'neiʃ(ə)n], *s.* **1.** (*a*) démission *f*; **to give (in), send in, tender, one's r.,** donner sa démission,

démissionner; (*b*) *Ecc:* résignation *f* (d'un bénéfice); (*c*) abandon *m* (d'un droit, etc.); *A:* abdication *f* (de la couronne, etc.). **2.** résignation (**to,** à); soumission *f*; **to accept one's fate with r.,** se résigner à son sort.

resignedly [ri'zainidli], *adv.* avec résignation; d'un air, d'un ton, de résignation; d'un air, d'un ton, résigné.

resile [ri'zail], *v.i.* **1.** (*a*) *A:* reculer vivement; (*b*) **to r. from a contract,** résilier un contrat; **to r. from a statement,** se dédire; se rétracter. **2.** (*of elastic body*) reprendre sa forme.

resilience, resiliency [ri'ziliəns(i)], *s.* **1.** (*a*) *Mec:* résilience *f*; résistance vive; résistance au choc; (*b*) (*of pers.*) élasticité *f* de caractère, de tempérament; **to have r.,** avoir du ressort; (*c*) (*of muscles, etc.*) élasticité. **2.** (*of ball*) rebond *m*.

resilient [ri'ziliənt], *a.* rebondissant, élastique, résilient; (*of pers.*) **to be r.,** avoir du ressort; **children are more r. than adults,** les enfants ont plus de ressort que les adultes; les enfants se remettent, se relèvent, plus vite que les adultes.

resilver [riː'silvər], *v.tr.* réargenter (un plat); rétamer (un miroir).

resilvering [riː'silv(ə)riŋ], *s.* nouvelle argenture (d'un plat); rétamage *m* (d'un miroir).

resin[1] ['rezin], *s.* **1.** résine *f*; **r. duct, canal,** (i) *Arb:* canal résinifère; (ii) *Bot:* résinocyste *m*; **natural r.,** résine végétale; **polyvinyl r.,** résine polyvinylique; **photosensitive r.,** résine photosensible; **thermo-setting r.,** résine thermodurcissable; **A-stage r.,** résol *m*; **B-stage r.,** résitol *m*; **C-stage r.,** résite *f*; *Ch:* **r. acid,** acide résinique; **r. industry,** industrie résinière; résinerie *f*; **r. factory,** résinerie; *For:* **to tap trees for r.,** résiner, gemmer, des arbres; **r. tapping,** résinage *m*, gemmage *m*; **r. tapper,** résinier, -ière; (ouvrier) gemmeur *m*; **to dip firewood in r.,** résiner des bûchettes. **2.** (*also* **rosin**) colophane *f*, brai sec, poix sèche.

resin[2], *v.tr.* résiner (des bûchettes, etc.).

resinaceous [rezi'neiʃəs], *a.* résineux.

resinate ['rezinət], *s. Ch:* résinate *m*.

resinic [re'zinik], *a. Ch:* résinique.

resiniferous [rezi'nifərəs], *a.* (arbre, etc.) résinifère.

resinifiable [rezini'faiəbl], *a.* résinifiable.

resinification [rezinifi'keiʃ(ə)n], *s.* résinification *f* (de l'huile, etc.).

resiniform [re'zinifɔːm], *a.* résiniforme.

resinify [re'zinifai]. **1.** *v.tr.* résinifier. **2.** *v.i.* (*of oil, etc.*) se résinifier.

resinite ['rezinait], *s. Miner:* résinite *m*.

resinoid ['rezinɔid], *a. & s.* résinoïde (*m*).

resinosis [rezi'nousis], *s. For:* écoulement exagéré de la résine.

resinous ['rezinəs], *a.* résineux; **to become r.,** se résinifier.

resist[1] [ri'zist], *s. Engr: Dy: etc:* réserve *f*.

resist[2], *v.tr.* **1.** (*a*) résister à (une attaque, la chaleur, une tentation); **to r. infection,** être résistant à l'infection; **a temptation too strong to be resisted,** une tentation trop forte pour que l'on pût y résister; (*b*) **I couldn't r. telling him,** je n'ai pas pu m'empêcher, me retenir, m'abstenir, de le lui dire; **he can't r. a joke,** il ne laisse jamais passer l'occasion de dire une plaisanterie; **I can't r. chocolates,** je ne peux pas résister aux chocolats; j'ai un faible pour les chocolats. **2.** (*a*) résister à, s'opposer à (un projet, etc.); refuser d'obéir à (un ordre); s'opposer à (une influence); **to r. authority,** résister à l'autorité; *Jur:* **to r. the authority of the Court,** faire rébellion à la justice; **to r. the police in the discharge of their duty,** faire rébellion aux agents dans l'exercice de leurs fonctions; **to r. arrest,** résister à l'arrestation; **it's best not to r.,** mieux vaut ne pas offrir de résistance, ne pas résister; (*b*) repousser (une suggestion, etc.); **to r. the evidence,** se refuser à l'évidence.

resistance [ri'zistəns], *s.* **1.** (*a*) résistance *f*; **to offer r.,** résister (à la police, à la loi, etc.); **to offer, make, a weak, a strong, r.,** offrir, opposer, une faible, une forte, résistance; **to offer no r.,** n'offrir, n'opposer, aucune résistance; ne pas résister; **she made no r.,** elle s'est laissé faire, emmener; **to meet with no r.,** ne rencontrer aucune résistance; **passive r.,** résistance passive; *Lit:* **weary of r.,** de guerre lasse; (*b*) *Pol: etc:* **r. (movement),** résistance; (*c*) **r. to disease, to contagion,** résistance à la maladie, à la contagion; **dermal r.,** résistance de la peau. **2.** (*a*) *Ph: etc:* résistance; **air r.,** résistance à l'air; **water r.,** résistance hydrodynamique; **frictional r.,** résistance de frottement; *Av:* **head r.,** résistance à l'avancement; **frictional, skin, r.,** résistance due au frottement; **deadhead, parasite, r.,** résistance nuisible; *Nau:* **towrope r.,** résistance de carène, à l'avancement; **lateral r.,** résistance à la dérive; **wake r.,** résistance de remous; **wave r.,** résistance due aux vagues; *Aut: etc:* **skid r.,** résistance au dérapage; *Metall:* **high r. steel,** acier à haute résistance; **steel has a greater r. than iron,** l'acier est plus résistant que le fer; *Fig:* **line of least r.,** ligne de moindre résistance; **to take the line of least r.,** aller au plus facile; suivre la loi du moindre effort; (*b*) *El:* résistance (électrique); **magnetic r.,** résistance magnétique; reluctance *f*; **specific r.,** résistivité *f*; **input r.,** résistance d'entrée; **earth r.,** résistance de terre; **primary, secondary, r.,** résistance du primaire, du secondaire; **contact r.,** résistance de contact; **damper r.,** résistance d'amortissement; **leakage r.,** résistance de fuite; **r. coupling,** couplage par résistance; couplage résistant; **r.-capacitance coupling,** couplage par résistance-capacité; **r. coil,** bobine, boudin, de résistance; **r. component,** composant à résistance; **r. box,** boîte de résistances; *Mch: etc:* **r. furnace,** four à résistance; **charge r. furnace,** four à charge constituant; **r. welding,** soudure électrique par résistance; **r. thermometer,** thermomètre à résistance; (*c*) *El: O:* (*device*) résistance; (*d*) *Tex:* **crease r.,** infroissabilité *f*.

resistant, resistent [ri'zistənt], *a.* résistant.

resister [ri'zistər], *s.* personne *f* qui résiste, qui oppose de la résistance; résistant, -ante; **passive r.,** partisan, -ane, de la résistance passive.

resistible [ri'zistibl], *a.* résistible.

resisting[1] [ri'zistiŋ], *a.* résistant; de résistance.

resisting[2], *s.* résistance *f*.

resistive [ri'zistiv], *a.* résistant; qui résiste; susceptible de résistance; *El:* **r. coupling,** couplage par résistance; couplage résistant.

resistivity [rizis'tiviti], *s. El:* résistivité *f*.

resistless [ri'zistlis], *a. A:* **1.** irrésistible. **2.** sans défense; incapable de résister. **3.** qui se laisse faire.

resistor [ri'zistər], *s. El: Elcs:* résistance *f*; **ballast r.,** résistance d'équilibrage, de régularisation (de courant); **bias r.,** résistance de polarisation (de grille); **bleeder r.,** résistance régulatrice de tension; **carbon r.,** résistance au carbone; **composition r.,** résistance agglomérée; **dropping r.,** résistance de chute; **fixed r.,** résistance de valeur fixe; **flexible r.,** cordon chauffant, cordon résistant; **grid (leak) r.,** résistance du circuit de la grille, résistance de fuite de la grille; **heating r.,** résistance de chauffage; **load r.,** résistance de charge; **series r.,** résistance en série; **sliding contact r.,** résistance à curseur; **variable r.,** résistance variable; rhéostat *m*; **wire(d), wire-wound, r.,** résistance bobinée; **r. colour code,** code des couleurs des résistances; **to burn out a r.,** griller une résistance.

resit[1] ['riːsit], *s. Sch: F:* examen *m* que l'on passe de nouveau.

resit[2] [riː'sit], *v.tr.* (*p.t. & p.p.* **resat** [riː'sæt]; *pr.p.* **resitting**) *Sch:* passer de nouveau (un examen).

resite ['rezait], *s. Ch:* résite *f*.

resitol ['rezitɔl], *s. Ch:* résitol *m*.

resize [riː'saiz], *v.tr. Ind:* remettre (une pièce, etc.) à la cote.

resnatron ['reznætrɔn], *s. Elcs:* resnatron *m*.

resojet ['riːzoudʒet], *s.* **r. (engine),** pulsoréacteur *m*.

resolder [riː'souldər], *v.tr.* ressouder.

resol(e) ['rezɔl, -oul], *s. Ch:* résol *m*.

resole [riː'soul], *v.tr.* ressemeler (des chaussures); remettre une semelle à (une chaussure).

resoling [riː'souliŋ], *s.* ressemelage *m* (de chaussures).

resoluble[1] [ri'zɔljubl], *a.* (problème, etc.) résoluble.

resoluble[2] [riː'sɔljubl], *a.* susceptible d'être redissous.

resolute ['rezəl(j)uːt], *a.* résolu, déterminé; **r. tone,** ton résolu; ton ferme; ton de résolution; **r. man,** homme de résolution; **to be r. for, against, sth.,** avoir résolu de (être décidé à, faire, ne pas faire, qch.

resolutely ['rezəl(j)uːtli], *adv.* résolument, avec détermination; **to come forward r.,** s'avancer avec résolution, hardiment; **to wait r. for s.o., sth.,** attendre qn, qch., de pied ferme.

resoluteness ['rezəl(j)uːtnis], *s.* résolution *f*, fermeté *f*.

resolution [rezə'l(j)uːʃ(ə)n], *s.* **1.** (*a*) *Ch: Med: Mus: etc:* résolution *f* (d'un composé, d'une tumeur, d'une dissonance, etc.); *T.V:* définition *f* (d'une image); **r. of water into steam,** résolution de l'eau en vapeur; *Pros:* **r. of a long syllable,** résolution d'une (syllabe) longue; *Mec:* **r. of forces,** décomposition *f* des forces; *Ph: Opt:* **r. of an instrument,** (pouvoir de) résolution, pouvoir résolvant, pouvoir séparateur, d'un instrument; *Phot:* **high r. photograph,** photographie à haute résolution; *Atom.Ph:* **r. (time),** (temps de) résolution; **r. time correction,** correction de temps de résolution; *Cmptr:* **logical r.,** résolution d'opérations logiques; **r. error,** erreur de résolution; (*b*) résolution (d'une difficulté, d'un problème, etc.). **2.** résolution, délibération *f* (d'une assemblée); proposition *f*, vœu *m*; ordre *m* du jour; **to put a r. to the meeting,** soumettre, proposer, une résolution; **to pass, carry, adopt, a r.,** adopter, prendre, une résolution, une décision, une délibération; **to reject a r.,** rejeter une proposition; **the committee passed a r. in favour of. . .,** le comité a adopté des vœux demandant que . . .. **3.** résolution, détermination *f*; **good resolutions,** bonnes résolutions; **to make a r.,** prendre une résolution; **to make a r. to do sth.,** prendre la résolution de, se résoudre à, faire vœu de, faire qch. **4.** résolution, fermeté *f*, décision *f*; **man of r.,** homme de résolution, homme résolu; **lack of r.,** manque de caractère; caractère irrésolu.

resolutive [rezə'l(j)uːtiv], *a.* **1.** *Med:* résolutif. **2.** *Jur:* (condition, etc.) résolutoire (d'un contrat).

resolutory [rezə'l(j)uːt(ə)ri], *a. Jur:* (condition) résolutoire (d'un contrat).

resolvable [ri'zɔlvəbl], *a.* (problème, etc.) résoluble; *Astr:* **r. nebula,** nébuleuse résoluble.

resolve[1] [ri'zɔlv], *s.* **1.** résolution *f*, détermination *f*; **to keep one's r.,** tenir sa résolution. **2.** *Lit:* résolution, fermeté *f*; **deeds of high r.,** nobles élans *m*. **3.** *NAm:* résolution, délibération *f* (d'une assemblée); proposition *f*, vœu *m*; ordre *m* du jour.

resolve[2].

I. *v.tr.* **1.** (*a*) résoudre (qch. en ses éléments); **water resolves itself into vapour,** l'eau se résout, se transforme, en vapeur; **the fog resolved itself into rain,** le brouillard s'est résolu en pluie; *Mec:* **to r. forces,** décomposer des forces; *Mus:* **to r. a discord,** résoudre une dissonance; **the sounds resolved themselves into a melody,** les sons ont pris la forme d'une mélodie; (*b*) **the House resolved itself into a committee,** la Chambre s'est constituée en commission; (*c*) *Opt: Phot:* **resolving power of a lens,** pouvoir séparateur, résolvant, de résolution, d'un objectif; *Atom.Ph:* **resolving time,** temps de résolution. **2.** résoudre (un problème, une difficulté); dissiper (un doute). **3.** (*a*) (*of committee, etc.*) résoudre, décider, adopter la résolution (de faire qch.); (*b*) (*of individual*) se résoudre à, prendre la résolution de (faire qch.); **to be resolved to do sth.,** être résolu, décidé, à faire qch. **4.** *A:* **to r. s.o. to do sth., on doing sth.,** résoudre, décider, déterminer, qn à faire qch.

II. *v.i.* **1.** se résoudre (en ses éléments); *Med:* (*of tumour*) se résoudre; se résorber. **2.** (*of pers.*) se résoudre (**on sth.,** à qch.); résoudre (**on sth.,** qch., de faire qch.); se résoudre, se décider, se déterminer (**to do sth.,** à faire qch.); prendre la résolution, le parti (de faire qch.).

resolvedly [ri'zɔlvidli], *adv.* résolument.

resolvent [ri'zɔlvənt], *a. & s. Med:* résolutif (*m*).

resolver [ri'zɔlvər], *s. Cmptr:* séparateur *m*.

resonance ['rez(ə)nəns], *s.* (*a*) *Mus:* résonance *f* (d'un instrument); vibration *f* (de la voix); (*b*) *Elcs: etc:* résonance; **r. level,** niveau de résonance; **r. curve,** courbe de résonance; **r. radiation,** radiation de résonance; **r. heating,** chauffage par résonance; *Atom.Ph:* **nuclear r.,** résonance atomique; **r. neutron,** neutron de résonance.

resonant ['rezən(ə)nt], *a.* (*a*) (*of sound, room, etc.*) résonnant; **r. voice,** voix résonnante, sonore; (*b*) *Elcs: etc:* **r. circuit,** circuit résonnant; **r. frequency,** fréquence de résonance; **r. aerial,** antenne syntonisée; **r. line,** ligne résonnante; **r. mode,** mode résonnant; **r. rise of a signal,** accroissement d'oscillation du signal.

resonate ['rezəneit], *v.i.* résonner, retentir (**with,** de).

resonator ['rezəneitər], *s. Elcs: etc:* résonateur *m*; **cavity r.,** résonateur à cavité, cavité résonnante; **input, output, r.,** résonateur d'entrée, de sortie; **r. grid,** grille de résonateur.

resorb [ri'sɔːb], *v.tr.* (*a*) réabsorber (qch.); (*b*) *Med:* résorber (une tumeur, etc.).

resorcin [ri'zɔːsin], *s. Ch:* résorcine *f*; *Dy:* **r. brown,** brun de résorcine.

resorcinol [ri'zɔːsinəl], *s. Ch:* résorcinol *m*.

resorption [ri'sɔːpʃ(ə)n], *s.* (*a*) réabsorption *f* (de qch.); (*b*) *Med:* résorption *f* (d'une tumeur, etc.).

resort[1] [ri'zɔːt], *s.* **1.** (*a*) ressource *f*; **to be the only r.,** être la seule chose à laquelle on puisse recourir; être la seule ressource; (*b*) recours *m*; **without r. to compulsion,** sans recourir à la force; sans avoir recours à la force; **in the last r., as a last r.,** en fin de compte; en dernière ressource; en dernier recours; en désespoir de cause; *Jur:* **in the last r.,** en dernier ressort. **2.** *A:* fréquentation *f*, affluence *f*, concours *m* (de personnes); **place of great r.,** lieu très fréquenté. **3.** (*a*) *O:* lieu de séjour, de rendez-vous; **famous r.,** séjour réputé; (*b*) **health r.,** station climatique, thermale; **seaside r.,** station balnéaire; plage *f*; **holiday r.,** (centre *m* de) villégiature *f*; **summer r.,** station estivale, d'été; **winter r.,** station d'hiver; **ski r.,** station de ski; station de sports d'hiver.

resort[2], *v.i.* **1.** avoir recours, recourir (**to,** à); user (**to,** de); **to r. to every kind of trick in order to do sth.,** user de tous les artifices pour faire qch.; **to r. to violence,** avoir recours à la violence; faire emploi de la violence; **to r. to lying,** recourir au mensonge. 2. (*a*) **to r. to s.o. (for help),** avoir recours, faire appel, recourir, s'adresser, à qn; (*b*) *O:* **to r. to a place,** (i) (*in numbers*) se rendre, affluer, dans un endroit; (ii) (*singly*) fréquenter, hanter, un lieu.

re-sort [ri:'sɔ:t], *v.tr.* reclasser (des documents, etc.); faire un nouveau triage de (la marchandise, etc.).

resorufin [rezou'ru:fin], *s. Ch:* résorufine *f.*

resound [ri'zaund]. 1. *v.i.* (*a*) (*of place*) résonner, retentir (**with cries,** de cris); (*b*) (*of voice, instrument*) résonner; (*c*) (*of fame, event*) avoir du retentissement (**through the world,** dans le monde). 2. *v.tr. A: & Lit:* (*a*) célébrer, chanter (les louanges de . . .); (*b*) faire résonner, faire retentir, répéter, renvoyer (des sons).

resounding [ri'zaundiŋ], *a.* résonnant, retentissant; (rire) sonore; (*of voice*) tonitruant, tonnant; **r. success,** succès bruyant.

resoundingly [ri'zaundiŋli], *adv.* d'une manière retentissante; bruyamment; avec fracas.

resource [ri'sɔ:s, -'zɔ:s], *s.* 1. (*a*) ressource *f*; **person of r.,** personne de ressource(s); **man of no r.,** homme incapable de se débrouiller; (*b*) ressource, expédient *m*; **deception was his only r.,** il ne pouvait s'en tirer qu'à l'aide d'une supercherie. 2. *pl.* (*a*) ressources (**in,** en); **to be at the end of one's resources,** être au bout de ses ressources, à bout de ressources; être à sa dernière ressource; **to draw upon one's own resources (to do sth.),** faire qch. par ses propres moyens; **to be left to, to be thrown upon, one's own resources,** n'avoir plus à compter que sur soi-même; être abandonné à ses propres moyens; être livré à soi-même; **he was left to his own resources,** il a dû se débrouiller tout seul; (*b*) *NAm: Fin:* actif disponible, liquide. 3. *O:* récréation *f*, distraction *f*, délassement *m*; **cards are our only r.,** notre seul moyen de distraction c'est de jouer aux cartes.

resourceful [ri'sɔ:sful, -'zɔ:s-], *a.* habile; ingénieux; **a r. man,** un homme de ressources.

resourcefully [ri'sɔ:sfuli, -'zɔ:s-], *adv.* habilement.

resourcefulness [ri'sɔ:sfulnis, -'zɔ:s-], *s.* ressource *f.*

resourceless [ri'sɔ:slis, -'zɔ:s-], *a.* 1. sans ressources. 2. qui manque de ressource; qui ne sait pas se débrouiller.

resourcelessness [ri'sɔ:slisnis, -zɔ:s-], *s.* manque *m* de ressource, de sens pratique.

resow [ri:'sou], *v.tr.* (**resowed** [ri:'soud]; **resown** [ri:'soun]) ressemer (un champ, le blé).

respect[1] [ri'spekt], *s.* 1. (*a*) *esp. Com:* (*reference*) rapport *m*, égard *m*; **to have r. to sth.,** avoir rapport à qch.; **with r. to . . .,** en ce qui concerne . . .; concernant . . .; quant à . . .; **there are difficulties with r. to the wording,** la rédaction offre des difficultés; *Gram:* **accusative of r.,** accusatif de relation, de point de vue; (*b*) rapport, égard, point *m* de vue; **in many respects,** à bien des égards, à plus d'un point de vue; **in some, in certain, respects,** sous quelques rapports; à certains égards; de certains côtés; **in all respects, in every r.,** sous tous les rapports; de tous points; à tous les points de vue; à tous (les) égards; **in one r.,** sous un rapport; **in this r.,** à cet égard, sous ce rapport; **the first differs from the others in this r., that . . .,** le premier diffère des autres en ceci, que . . .; **in no r.,** sous aucun rapport; à aucun égard; **in other respects,** sous d'autres rapports; à d'autres égards. 2. égard; **to have, pay, r. to sth.,** avoir égard à, tenir compte de, qch.; **without r. of persons,** sans acceptation de personnes. 3. (*a*) respect *m* (**for the truth,** pour la vérité); respect, déférence *f*, considération *f* (**for s.o.,** pour, envers, qn); **to have r. for s.o.,** avoir, témoigner, du respect à, envers, pour, qn, à l'égard de qn; **to have the greatest r., a healthy r., for s.o.,** avoir le plus grand respect pour qn; **he shows little r. for his parents,** il ne se montre guère respectueux envers ses parents; **r. for others,** le respect des autres, d'autrui; **he can command r.,** il sait se faire respecter; **to have lost, forfeited, all r.,** être perdu d'estime; **to fill s.o. with r.,** en imposer à qn; inspirer le respect à qn; **out of r. for . . .,** par respect, par égard, par considération, pour . . .; **with all due r. (to you),** sauf votre respect, sauf le respect que je vous dois; (soit dit) sans vouloir vous offenser, vous contredire; **to say with all due r. that. . .,** dire en termes respectueux que . . .; **a man with any r. for himself can only decline,** un homme qui se respecte ne saurait que refuser; (*b*) **r. for the law,** respect de la loi; **to enforce r. for a decree,** faire observer un décret. 4. *pl.* respects, hommages *m*, devoirs *m*; **to pay one's respects to s.o.,** rendre ses respects, ses devoirs, présenter ses hommages, à qn; *O:* **please give my respects to your daughter,** veuillez bien présenter mes respects à mademoiselle votre fille.

respect[2], *v.tr.* 1. respecter, honorer (qn); avoir, témoigner, du respect à, envers, pour (qn), à l'égard de (qn); **this man is universally respected,** cet homme est respecté de tous. 2. respecter, avoir égard à (qch.); (*a*) **he's a man who respects nothing,** c'est un homme qui ne respecte rien; **he respected my wish to be alone,** il a respecté mon désir, a eu égard à mon désir, d'être seul; **to r. s.o.'s opinion,** respecter l'opinion de qn; (*b*) **to r. the law,** avoir le respect des lois; **to r. a clause in a contract,** respecter une clause dans un contrat; (*c*) **I r. myself too much to do that,** je me respecte trop pour faire cela. 3. *A:* avoir rapport, avoir trait, à (qch.); se rapporter à (qch.); concerner (qch.); **as respects . . .,** pour ce qui est de . . .; quant à . . ..

respectability [rispektə'biliti], *s.* 1. (*a*) respectabilité *f*, honorabilité *f*; (*b*) *pl.* convenances *f*, bienséances *f*. 2. *A:* personne *f* honorable; **the respectabilities of the town,** les notabilités *f* de la ville.

respectable [ri'spektəbl], *a.* 1. respectable, digne de respect. 2. (*a*) respectable, honorable, convenable, honnête, comme il faut; **r. family,** famille honnête; **r. clothes,** vêtements convenables; **he always looks r.,** il est toujours habillé comme il faut; **hardly r.,** peu honorable; (*b*) **she is of a r. age,** elle est d'un âge canonique. 3. (*a*) *O:* respectable, passable; **a r. number of people,** un bon nombre de gens; **r. painter,** assez bon peintre; **r. weather,** assez beau temps, temps passable; (*b*) **a r. sum (of money),** une somme respectable, rondelette.

respectably [ri'spektəbli], *adv.* 1. respectablement, honorablement, convenablement, honnêtement, comme il faut. 2. *O:* pas mal, passablement.

respecter [ri'spektər], *s.* **to be no r. of the law,** ne pas respecter les lois; ne tenir aucun compte des lois; **to be no r. of persons,** ne faire acception de personnes; *Lit:* **death is no r. of persons,** la mort n'épargne personne.

respectful [ri'spektful], *a.* respectueux (**to,** envers, pour); **r. silence,** silence respectueux; **to stand at a r. distance,** se tenir à distance respectueuse; **to keep s.o. at a r. distance,** tenir qn en respect; **r. of the law,** respectueux des lois.

respectfully [ri'spektfuli], *adv.* respectueusement, avec respect; *Corr: O:* **(I remain) yours r.,** veuillez agréer l'expression de mes sentiments respectueux.

respectfulness [ri'spektfulnis], *s.* respect *m*; caractère respectueux.

respecting [ri'spektiŋ], *prep. A:* relativement à; quant à; par, ayant, rapport à; à l'égard de; en ce qui concerne, concernant; touchant; **questions r. a matter,** questions relatives à un sujet; questions touchant un sujet.

respective [ri'spektiv], *a.* respectif; **our r. homes,** nos demeures respectives.

respectively [ri'spektivli], *adv.* respectivement.

respirable ['respirəbl], *a.* 1. (gaz, etc.) respirable. 2. *A:* capable de respirer.

respiration [respi'reiʃ(ə)n], *s.* respiration *f*; **artificial r.,** respiration artificielle.

respirator ['respireitər], *s.* respirateur *m*; masque *m* respiratoire; *Mil:* masque à gaz.

respiratory [ri'spaiərət(ə)ri, ri'spirit(ə)ri, 'respireit(ə)ri], *a.* (organe, etc.) respiratoire; **r. system,** appareil, système, respiratoire; **r. disease,** maladie de l'appareil respiratoire.

respire [ri'spaiər], *v.tr. & i.* respirer.

respite[1] ['respait], *s.* 1. *Jur:* sursis *m*, délai *m*; **to get a r.,** obtenir un délai; *Com:* **to grant a r. for payment,** différer un paiement. 2. répit *m*, relâche *m & f*; **to have no r. from pain,** souffrir sans répit; **his toothache gives him no r.,** son mal de dents ne lui donne pas de trêve; **to work without r.,** travailler sans relâche.

respite[2], *v.tr.* 1. accorder un sursis à (un prévenu); surseoir à l'exécution (d'un condamné); remettre, différer, surseoir à (un jugement). 2. apporter du soulagement à (qn, une douleur).

resplendence, resplendency [ri'splendəns(i)], *s.* splendeur *f*, resplendissement *m*, éclat *m* (d'un astre, d'une cérémonie).

resplendent [ri'splendənt], *a.* resplendissant, éblouissant.

resplendently [ri'splendəntli], *adv.* avec splendeur; avec éclat; splendidement.

respond[1] [ri'spɔnd], *s.* 1. *Ecc:* répons *m*. 2. *Arch:* colonne engagée (soutenant une arête de voûte).

respond[2], *v.i.* 1. (*a*) répondre, faire une réponse; **to r. to a toast,** répondre à un toast; (*b*) *Ecc:* réciter, répéter, chanter, les répons. 2. (*a*) répondre, être sensible (à l'affection, à la bonté); se prêter (à une proposition); **to fail to r. to s.o.'s advances,** ne pas répondre aux avances de qn; **to r. to music,** apprécier la musique; (*of aircraft*) **to r. to the controls,** obéir aux commandes; **this car responds well,** cette voiture a de bonnes réactions; cette voiture est nerveuse; (*b*) (*of nerves, etc.*) réagir (**to,** contre). 3. *Jur: U.S:* être responsable; **to r. in damages,** être tenu des dommages.

respondent [ri'spɔndənt]. 1. *a.* (*a*) répondant; qui répond, donne la réponse; (*b*) qui répond, qui est sensible (**to an influence,** à une influence); qui réagit (**to a stimulus,** à un stimulus). 2. *s.* (*a*) *Sch: A:* répondant *m* (qui soutient la thèse); (*b*) *Jur:* (i) (*esp. in divorce case*) défendeur, -eresse; (ii) (*in appeal case*) intimé, -ée.

responder [ri'spɔndər], *s.* (*a*) *Telecom:* répondeur *m*; **active r., r. beacon,** répondeur actif; **passive r.,** répondeur passif; (*b*) *Av: etc:* **r. beacon,** balise répondeuse.

response [ri'spɔns], *s.* 1. (*a*) réponse *f*, réplique *f*; **he made no r.,** il n'a fait aucune réponse; (*b*) *Ecc:* répons *m*; **to make the responses at mass,** répondre la messe. 2. (*a*) réponse (à un sentiment, à un appel); **his r. to affection,** la façon dont il répondait à l'affection; **the appeal met with a generous r.,** on a répondu largement à l'appel; **the Anglo-French treaty met with a warm r.,** on a fait un accueil chaleureux au traité franco-anglais; **there was no r. to his appeal,** son appel est resté sans réponse; (*b*) *Physiol:* réponse, réaction *f*; **motor r.,** réponse, réaction, motrice; **native r.,** réponse instinctive, naturelle; **reflex r.,** réponse réflexe; *Med:* **biological r.,** réaction biologique; **defensive r.,** réaction de défense; (*c*) *Ph: Elcs:* **frequency r.,** réponse de, en, fréquence; **frequency r. characteristic,** caractéristique de réponse aux fréquences; **frequency, amplitude, r.,** réponse en fréquence, en amplitude; **bass r.,** réponse en basse fréquence; **thermal r.,** réponse thermique; **r. time,** temps de réponse; **r. curve,** courbe de réponse.

responsibility [rispɔnsi'biliti], *s.* (*a*) responsabilité *f*; **sense of r.,** sens des responsabilités; **to assume, accept, a r.,** accepter une responsabilité; **to accept personal r. for sth.,** engager sa responsabilité personnelle en ce qui concerne qch.; **to take the r. of sth., to accept r. for sth.,** prendre la responsabilité de qch.; prendre qch. sous sa responsabilité; **without r. on our part,** sans engagement ni responsabilité de notre part; **to do sth. on one's own r.,** faire qch. sous sa (propre) responsabilité, de son (propre) chef; **the r. rests with, devolves on, the tenant to make sure . . .,** la responsabilité incombe au locataire de s'assurer . . .; **it is the translator's r. to . . .,** c'est au traducteur qu'il incombe de . . .; **the r. that is laid on me, that falls on me,** la responsabilité qui m'est imposée, qui m'est impartie; (*b*) responsabilité (d'une faute); culpabilité *f*; **to refuse to accept any r. for the accident,** décliner toute responsabilité au sujet de l'accident; (*c*) **his new responsibilities give him no time for leisure,** ses nouvelles fonctions, attributions, ne lui laissent pas de loisirs.

responsible [ri'spɔnsibl], *a.* 1. (*a*) chargé (d'un devoir, etc.); **person r. for doing sth.,** personne à qui il incombe de faire qch.; **I am r. for the upkeep of the house,** j'ai la responsabilité de l'entretien de la maison; **I will be r. for his safety,** je me porte garant qu'il ne lui sera fait aucun mal; **r. before public opinion,** responsable vis-à-vis de l'opinion publique; **r. to s.o.,** responsable devant qn, envers qn; **the commission is r. to the government,** la commission relève du gouvernement; **the minister is r. to Parliament,** le ministre est responsable aux Chambres, devant, envers, les Chambres, vis-à-vis des Chambres; **to be r. to s.o. for sth.,** avoir à rendre compte à qn de qch.; être comptable à qn de qch.; **to be r. for s.o., for sth.,** répondre de qn, de qch.; **he is not r. for his actions,** il n'est pas maître de ses actes; (*b*) responsable (d'un accident, etc.); **to hold s.o. r. (for sth.),** tenir qn (pour) responsable (de qch.); *Jur:* **to be r. for s.o.'s actions,** être solidaire des actes de qn. 2. (*a*) capable, compétent, digne de confiance, sur qui on peut compter; **a r. man,** un homme sérieux; (*b*) **r. job,** poste qui entraîne des responsabilités; responsabilité.

responsion [ri'spɔnʃ(ə)n], *s.* 1. *A: & Lit:* réponse *f*. 2. *Sch:* **responsions,** examen *m* préliminaire d'admissibilité au grade de B.A. (à l'Université d'Oxford).

responsive [ri'spɔnsiv], *a.* 1. (*a*) impressionnable; facile à émouvoir; sensible (**to,** à); **to be r. to sth.,** répondre, être sensible, à qch.; (*b*) (*of engine, etc.*) nerveux; *Elcs: etc:* (détecteur) sensible. 2. *Ecc:* (liturgie) qui use de répons.

responsively [ri'spɔnsivli], *adv.* avec sympathie; en partageant les sentiments de celui avec lequel on se trouve; *Lit:* **she glanced at him and he smiled r.,** elle lui lança un coup d'œil auquel il répondit par un sourire.

responsiveness [ri'spɔnsivnis], *s.* 1. émotion *f* sympathique; sensibilité *f*; façon *f* dont on répond (**to sth.,** à qch.). 2. nervosité *f* (d'un moteur, etc.).

responsory [ri'spɔnsəri], *s. Ecc:* répons *m*.

respray[1] ['ri:sprei], *s.* peinture *f* (de qch.) au pistolet; **my car needs a r.,** ma voiture a besoin d'être repeinte.

respray[2] [ri:'sprei], *v.tr.* repeindre (qch.) au pistolet; **I've had my car resprayed,** j'ai fait repeindre ma voiture.

ressaut [re'sɔ:t], *s. Arch:* ressaut *m*.

rest[1] [rest], *s.* **1.** (*a*) repos *m*; **to have a good night's r.,** passer une bonne nuit; **I couldn't get any r.,** (i) je ne pouvais pas me reposer; (ii) *O:* je n'ai pas fermé l'œil (de la nuit); **at r.,** au, en, repos; *Lit:* **to be at r. with one's fathers,** reposer parmi ses pères; **to be laid to r.,** être enterré; **to set a question at r.,** régler, résoudre, décider, vider, une question; **to set s.o.'s mind, s.o.'s fears, at r.,** calmer, tranquilliser, l'esprit de qn; dissiper les craintes, les inquiétudes, de qn; **set your mind at r.!** ne vous inquiétez pas! tranquillisez-vous! (*b*) **to have, take, a r.,** se donner, prendre, du repos; se reposer; *Mil:* faire une, la, pause; **to take a r. from work,** se reposer de son travail; **to stop for a r.,** s'arrêter pour se reposer; **to give s.o. a r. from sth.,** permettre à qn de se reposer de qch.; **to give a machine, a horse, a r.,** laisser reposer une machine, un cheval; **a day of r., a day's r., a r. day,** un jour de repos; **the day of r.,** le jour du Seigneur; le repos dominical; (*c*) (*of moving body*) **to come to r.,** s'arrêter, s'immobiliser; *Ph:* **r. mass,** masse *f* au repos; *Atom.Ph:* **r. energy,** énergie *f* au repos. **2.** (*a*) *Mus:* pause, silence *m*; **semibreve r.,** pause; **breve r., double r.,** demi-bâton *m, pl.* demi-bâtons; **minim r.,** demi-pause *f, pl.* demi-pauses; **crotchet r.,** soupir *m*; **quaver r.,** demi-soupir *m, pl.* demi-soupirs; **semiquaver r.,** quart *m* de soupir; **bar's r.,** pause (indiquant le silence d'une mesure entière); (*b*) (*in elocution, verse*) repos. **3.** (*a*) *A:* abri *m* (pour marins, pour chauffeurs de taxi, etc.); foyer *m* (pour matelots); (*b*) **r. centre,** centre d'accueil; **r. home,** maison *f* de repos (pour convalescents, personnes âgées); (*in factory, etc.*) **r. room,** (i) salon *m* de repos; (ii) toilettes *fpl*; **r. cure,** cure de repos; *A:* **r. house,** hôtellerie *f*; *Mil:* **r. camp,** cantonnement de repos. **4.** (*a*) (*of chair*) **elbow r., arm r.,** accoudoir *m*, accotoir *m*; (*b*) *Bill:* chevalet *m*; *Mil:* **aiming r., rifle r.,** chevalet de pointage; **telescope r.,** affût *m* de télescope; *Tp:* **receiver r.,** étrier *m* du récepteur; *Dom.Ec:* **knife r.,** porte-couteau *m, pl.* porte-couteaux; **ashtray with cigarette r.,** cendrier *m* avec support pour cigarette; (*c*) *Mec.E:* (*on lathe*) support *m* d'outil; appui *m*.

rest[2], *v.*

I. *v.i.* **1.** (*a*) se reposer, avoir du repos, de la tranquillité; **to work without resting,** travailler sans se reposer; **he didn't r. until his request was granted,** il a continué sans répit jusqu'à ce qu'on lui eût accordé sa demande; **he will not r. until he has finished the job,** il ne relâchera pas ses efforts avant d'avoir terminé le travail; **he could not r. under this accusation,** cette accusation lui enlevait toute tranquillité; **to r. in the Lord,** se confier, mettre sa confiance, en l'Éternel; s'en remettre à Dieu; **may they r. in peace!** qu'ils reposent en paix! **the waves never r.,** les vagues ne sont jamais tranquilles; (*b*) se reposer, prendre du repos; **you need to r. (up),** il vous faut le repos complet; **to r. from one's work,** se reposer de son travail; **to feel rested,** se sentir (bien) reposé, rafraîchi; *A: & Lit:* **let us r. here awhile,** reposons-nous ici quelques instants; *Th: F:* (*of actor*) **to be resting,** se trouver sans engagement; chômer; *Agr:* **the land was often allowed to r.,** on laissait souvent la terre se reposer; (*c*) **there, so, the matter rests,** l'affaire en reste là, en est là; **the matter will not r. there,** l'affaire n'en demeurera pas là, n'en restera pas là; **I won't let it r. at that,** cela ne se passera pas ainsi; **let it r.!** n'en parlons plus! c'en est assez! *NAm: Jur:* **the defense, the prosecution, rests** = plaise au tribunal adopter mes conclusions. **2.** (*a*) se poser, être posé, s'appuyer, être appuyé; **his hand resting on the table,** sa main posée, appuyée, sur la table; **to let one's eyes r. on sth.,** (re)poser ses regards sur qch.; **beam that rests on a wall,** poutre qui s'appuie, qui prend appui, qui porte, sur un mur, qui bute contre un mur; **a heavy responsibility rests upon them,** une lourde responsabilité pèse sur eux; (*b*) **trade rests upon credit,** le commerce repose sur le crédit; **his fame rests on his novels,** sa gloire repose sur ses romans.

II. *v.tr.* **1.** (*a*) reposer, faire reposer (qn); **to r. a player for tomorrow's game,** laisser reposer un membre de l'équipe pour le match de demain; **to r. one's men,** faire, laisser, reposer ses hommes; rafraîchir ses hommes; **colour that rests the eyes,** couleur qui repose l'œil; **(God) r. his soul!** Dieu donne le repos à son âme! (*b*) appuyer (ses coudes sur la table); poser, déposer (un fardeau par terre); **to r. one's head on a cushion,** reposer la tête sur un coussin; **to shoot with the rifle rested,** tirer avec le fusil appuyé; **to r. an opinion on proof,** appuyer, fonder, une opinion sur des preuves. **2.** *esp. NAm: Jur:* **to r. the case,** conclure son plaidoyer.

rest[3], *s.* **1.** reste *m*, restant *m* (de la journée, d'une somme d'argent, etc.); **he did the r.,** il a fait le reste; **I'll do the r. of the washing up,** je ferai ce qui reste de la vaisselle; **(as) for the r.,** quant au reste, pour le reste, d'ailleurs; **and all the r. of it,** et tout le reste; et tout ce qui s'ensuit; et patati et patata; *P:* **and the r.!** et encore! tu parles! **2.** (*with pl. const.*) **the r.,** les autres *mf*; **the r. of us,** nous autres; les autres d'entre nous; **among the r.,** parmi les autres; entre autres. **3.** *Fin:* fonds *m* de réserve; réserve *f*. **4.** *Com: A:* arrêté *m* (de compte).

rest[4], *v.i.* **1.** (*a*) *A:* rester, demeurer; **the affair rests a mystery,** l'affaire demeure mystérieuse; (*b*) **r. assured that. . .,** soyez assuré que. . . . **2. it rests with you (to do sth.),** il dépend de vous, il ne tient qu'à vous, il vous incombe (de faire qch.); **it rests with him alone to. . .,** il appartient à lui seul de. . .; **it rests with us to see the matter through,** c'est à nous de mener l'affaire à bien; **it does not r. with me to. . .,** il est en dehors de mes pouvoirs de. . .; **his fate rests with you,** sa destinée dépend de vous; **the victory rests with us,** la victoire nous demeure; **the responsibility rests with the author,** la responsabilité incombe à l'auteur.

rest[5], *s. Arm:* (*for couched lance*) arrêt *m* (de lance); faucre *m*; **lance in r.,** lance en arrêt.

restaff [riː'stɑːf], *v.tr.* engager un nouveau personnel pour (un hôtel, etc.).

restage [riː'steidʒ], *v.tr. Th:* remonter (une pièce); remettre (une pièce) en scène.

restart [riː'stɑːt]. **1.** *v.tr.* (*a*) recommencer, reprendre (un travail); (*b*) (re)mettre (une machine) en marche; relancer (un moteur, etc.); (*c*) *Ven:* relancer (un cerf). **2.** *v.i.* (*a*) (*of work, war, etc.*) recommencer, reprendre; (*b*) (*of machine, etc.*) se remettre en marche.

restarting [riː'stɑːtiŋ], *s.* **1.** reprise *f* (d'un travail, d'un jeu). **2.** remise *f* en marche (d'une machine); relancement *m* (d'un moteur). **3.** *Ven:* relancement (d'un cerf, etc.).

restate [riː'steit], *v.tr.* exposer de nouveau (une théorie, un point de vue); énoncer de nouveau (un problème); spécifier de nouveau (des conditions); **the question needs to be restated,** la question a besoin d'être mise au point.

restaurant ['rest(ə)rɔ̃, -rɔ(ː)nt], *s.* restaurant *m*; *Rail:* **r. car,** wagon-restaurant *m, pl.* wagons-restaurants.

restaurateur [restərə'təːr], *s.* restaurateur *m*.

restbalk ['restbɔːk], *s. Agr:* billon *m*.

restful ['restful], *a.* qui repose, reposant; paisible, tranquille; **r. spot,** endroit reposant; **r. to the eyes,** qui repose les yeux, reposant pour la vue.

restfully ['restfuli], *adv.* paisiblement, tranquillement.

restfulness ['restfulnis], *s.* tranquillité *f*.

restharrow ['resthærou], *s. Bot:* bugrane *f*; arrête-bœuf *m inv*.

restiform ['restifɔːm], *a. Anat:* (corps) restiforme.

resting ['restiŋ], *s.* repos *m*; **r. place,** (lieu *m* de) repos; gîte *m*, abri *m*; **last r. place,** dernière demeure; lieu de sépulture.

Restio ['restiou], *s. Bot:* restio *m*.

Restionaceae [restiou'neisiiː], *s.pl. Bot:* restiacées *f*.

restitch [riː'stitʃ], *v.tr. Needlew:* repiquer (qch.).

restitute ['restitju(ː)t], *v.tr.* **1.** = RESTORE. **2.** restituer (de l'argent, etc.).

restitution [resti'tjuːʃ(ə)n], *s.* **1.** restitution *f*; **to make r. of sth.,** restituer qch.; *Jur:* **r. of conjugal rights,** réintégration *f* du domicile conjugal. **2.** (*a*) *Theol:* **the r. of all things,** le rétablissement final; (*b*) *Ph:* **r. of an elastic body,** retour *m* d'un corps élastique à sa forme primitive; *Mec:* **coefficient of r.,** coefficient de restitution; (*c*) *Cmptr:* **isochronous r.,** restitution isochrone.

restitutory [resti'tjuːtəri], *a.* restitutoire.

restive ['restiv], *a.* **1.** (*of horse*) rétif, vicieux; (*of pers.*) rétif, indocile, difficile, récalcitrant. **2.** nerveux, agité; à cran.

restively ['restivli], *adv.* **1.** (*of horse*) d'une manière rétive. **2.** (*of pers.*) nerveusement; d'une manière agitée.

restiveness ['restivnis], *s.* **1.** humeur rétive; nature vicieuse (d'un cheval). **2.** neverosité *f*, agitation *f*, énervement *m*.

restless ['restlis], *a.* **1.** *O:* sans repos. **2.** (*a*) agité; **r. hands, feet,** mains, pieds, qui ne peuvent pas rester tranquilles; **to be r. in one's sleep,** avoir le sommeil agité, troublé; **I've had a r. night,** j'ai passé une nuit agitée; (*b*) (enfant) agité, turbulent, remuant. **3.** nerveux, agité; **r. mind,** esprit agité; **r. eye,** regard inquiet; **the audience was getting r.,** l'auditoire s'impatientait; **for some time the crowd had been r.,** depuis quelque temps la foule s'agitait.

restlessly ['restlisli], *adv.* **1.** (*a*) avec agitation, avec inquiétude; **to turn sth. over r. in one's mind,** tourner et retourner qch. dans son esprit; (*b*) avec turbulence. **2.** nerveusement, fiévreusement; **to turn over r. in bed,** se retourner fiévreusement dans son lit.

restlessness ['restlisnis], *s.* **1.** (*a*) inquiétude *f*, agitation *f*; (*b*) turbulence *f*; mouvement incessant (de la mer, etc.). **2.** nervosité *f*; état fiévreux (des esprits); effervescence *f* (de la foule).

restock [riː'stɔk], *v.tr.* **1.** (*a*) repeupler (un étang, une garenne); rempoissonner (un étang); (*b*) *For:* reboiser (un terrain). **2.** *Com:* remonter, r(é)assortir, regarnir (un magasin); réapprovisionner (**with food,** en comestibles, en denrées).

restocking [riː'stɔkiŋ], *s.* **1.** (*a*) repeuplement *m*; rempoissonnement *m* (d'un étang); (*b*) reboisement *m* (d'un terrain). **2.** *Com:* r(é)assortiment *m* (d'un magasin, etc.); réapprovisionnement *m* (**with,** en).

restorable [ri'stɔːrəbl], *a.* **1.** qui peut être restitué, rendu. **2.** (monument, etc.) qui peut être restauré.

restoration [restə'reiʃ(ə)n], *s.* **1.** restitution *f* (de biens); remise *f* (d'objets trouvés); *Jur:* **r. of goods taken in distraint,** mainlevée *f* de saisie. **2.** restauration *f* (d'un monument historique, d'un bâtiment endommagé, d'un meuble, des mœurs, etc.); restitution *f* (d'un texte, d'un édifice détruit); rétablissement *m* (d'un texte, de l'ordre, de la paix, des communications, etc.); réfection *f* (d'un bâtiment); reconstitution *f* (d'un monument, etc.); rénovation *f* (d'un bâtiment, des mœurs, etc.). **3.** (*a*) réintégration *f* (d'un fonctionnaire); **r. to favour,** rentrée *f* en faveur; (*b*) rétablissement (de la santé); (*c*) relèvement *m* (d'une fortune). **4.** (*a*) restauration (d'une dynastie); (*b*) rétablissement sur le trône; *Hist:* **the R.,** la Restauration.

restorative [ri'stɔːrətiv], *a. & s.* **1.** *Med:* (*a*) fortifiant (*m*); reconstituant (*m*); (*b*) cordial (*m*), -aux; réconfortant (*m*). **2.** (*of sleep, etc.*) réparateur, -trice.

restore [ri'stɔːr], *v.tr.* **1.** restituer, rendre (qch.); **to r. sth. to s.o.,** rendre qch. à qn; *Jur:* ressaisir qn de qch.; **to r. his fortune, his property, to s.o.,** remettre qn en possession de sa fortune; remettre qn dans ses biens. **2.** (*a*) restaurer, reconstituer (un monument, etc.); réparer (un tableau); rénover (un meuble); **to r. one's reputation,** se refaire une réputation; (*b*) reconstituer, restituer, rétablir (un texte); reconstituer (un édifice endommagé, etc.). **3.** (*a*) **to r. sth. to its place, to its former condition,** remettre qch. en place, en état; **to r. a statue to its pedestal,** remettre une statue sur son piédestal; (*b*) rétablir, réintégrer (qn dans ses droits, dans ses fonctions, etc.); **to r. a dynasty,** restaurer une dynastie; **to r. the king (to the throne),** remettre, rétablir, le roi sur le trône; (*c*) **to r. s.o. to health,** rétablir la santé de qn; réparer les forces de qn; rendre la santé à qn; remettre qn (sur pied); **to be restored to health,** être revenu à la santé; être bien rétabli; **to r. s.o. to life,** ramener, rappeler, qn à la vie; **to feel (oneself) restored to life,** se sentir revivre; **to be restored to happiness,** renaître au bonheur; *Ecc:* **r. Thou them that be penitent,** rétablis ceux qui se repentent. **4.** (*a*) rétablir (la liberté, la discipline, la confiance, l'ordre); faire renaître (le calme, la confiance); restaurer (la paix, les mœurs, la discipline); **order is being restored,** l'ordre se rétablit; (*b*) **to r. s.o.'s strength,** redonner des forces à qn; réparer les forces de qn; **to r. the circulation,** réactiver la circulation.

restorer [ri'stɔːrər], *s.* **1.** (*a*) restaurateur, -trice (d'un tableau, d'une église); réparateur, -trice, rénovateur, -trice; (*b*) rétablisseur *m*, restituteur *m* (d'un texte). **2.** *Toil:* **hair r.,** régénérateur *m* des cheveux; *O:* **health r.,** fortifiant *m*.

restrain [ri'strein], *v.tr.* **1.** retenir, empêcher (qn) (**from,** de). **2.** détenir (qn); tenir (qn) emprisonné. **3.** contenir, refréner (ses passions); contenir, réprimer, comprimer, refouler (sa colère); retenir (sa curiosité); tenir (sa langue); contenir, comprimer, refouler, retenir (ses larmes); **to r. oneself,** se contraindre; **in restrained terms,** en termes mesurés; **restrained style,** style tempéré, sobre; **to r. s.o.'s activities,** mettre un frein, servir de frein, aux activités de qn; entraver les activités de qn; mettre obstacle à l'activité de qn.

restrainable [ri'streinəbl], *a.* qui peut être retenu, contenu, réprimé.

restrainedly [ri'streinidli], *adv.* avec retenue; avec contrainte, en termes modérés.

restrainer [ri'streinər], *s.* **1.** personne *f*, chose *f*, qui retient, contient, réprime. **2.** *Phot:* retardateur *m*, modérateur *m* (du révélateur).

restraining[1] [ri'streiniŋ], *a.* qui retient; restrictif; **r. force,** force compulsive; *Phot:* **r. bath,** bain ralentisseur.

restraining[2], *s.* **1.** restriction *f*, contrainte *f*; *Vet:* **r. apparatus,** appareil de contention. **2.** répression *f* (de ses passions, d'un abus). **3.** détention *f* (de qn).

restraint [ri'streint], *s.* **1.** (*a*) contrainte *f*, restriction *f*, entrave *f*, frein *m*, empêchement *m*; **to put a r. on s.o.,** contraindre qn; tenir qn dans la contrainte; **to put a r. on s.o.'s activity,** mettre frein à, entraver, l'activité de qn; **to break through every r., to break loose from all r.,** se donner libre cours; **to be under no r.,** avoir ses coudées franches; **wage r.,** limitation *f* des salaires; **r. of trade,** atteinte *f* à la liberté du commerce; **without r.,** sans contrainte, à sa guise; (*b*) contrainte; réserve *f,* gêne *f;* **to put a r. on oneself,** se contenir, se contraindre; **lack of r.,** abandon *m;* manque *m* de réserve; **to speak without r.,** parler avec liberté, en toute liberté; **to throw aside all r.,** ne garder aucune mesure; (*c*) sobriété *f* (de style, etc.); mesure *f.* **2.** contrainte par corps; interdiction *f* (d'un aliéné); emprisonnement *m;* séquestration *f;* contention *f;* **to keep s.o. under r.,** tenir qn emprisonné; **to put a lunatic under r.,** interner un aliéné; **lunatic under r.,** aliéné interdit; **to put s.o. under illegal r.,** séquestrer qn; *Jur: A:* **arrests and restraints of princes,** arrêts et contraintes de princes.

restrict [ri'strikt], *v.tr.* restreindre; réduire (les libertés publiques, etc.); resserrer (ses besoins); **to r. a word to a particular sense,** restreindre un mot à un sens particulier; **in a restricted sense,** dans un sens restreint; **his power was restricted within narrow limits,** son pouvoir était étroitement limité; **there is still a restricted membership,** le nombre d'adhérents reste restreint; **I am restricted to advising,** il ne m'est permis que de donner des conseils; **to r. oneself to . . .,** se limiter à . . .; **he is restricted to one glass of wine a day,** on ne lui permet qu'un verre de vin par jour; **to r. the consumption of alcohol,** restreindre la consommation de l'alcool; **restricted diet,** régime sévère; **restricted horizon,** horizon borné, rétréci; *Aut:* **to r. a road,** limiter la vitesse de la circulation sur une route; **restricted area,** (i) *Aut:* zone de limitation de vitesse, à vitesse limitée; (ii) *Adm: Mil: etc:* zone interdite; *Adm: etc:* **restricted document,** document secret; *Com:* **restricted market,** débouchés réduits; **restricted credit,** crédit restreint.

restriction [ri'strikʃ(ə)n], *s.* restriction *f;* (*a*) **r. of expenditure,** réduction *f* des dépenses; (*b*) *Aut:* **r. of speed,** limitation *f* de vitesse; (*c*) **to place, set, restrictions on sth.,** apporter des restrictions à qch.; (*d*) **mental r.,** restriction mentale.

restrictive [ri'striktiv], *a.* restrictif.

restrictively [ri'striktivli], *adv.* d'une façon restrictive; avec des restrictions.

restrictor [ri'striktər], *s. Mec.E: etc:* **three-way r.,** té *m* de réduction.

restring [riː'striŋ], *v.tr. p.t. & p.p.* **restrung** [riː'strʌŋ]. **1.** enfiler de nouveau (des perles). **2.** remonter (un violon); recorder (une raquette).

restringing [riː'striŋiŋ], *s.* **1.** enfilement *m* (de perles, etc.). **2.** remontage *m* (d'un violon); recordage *m* (d'une raquette).

restuff [riː'stʌf], *v.tr.* rembourrer de nouveau (un coussin, etc.).

result[1] [ri'zʌlt], *s.* **1.** résultat *m* (**of,** de); aboutissement *m* (des efforts de qn); **that's the r. of his education,** cela tient à son éducation; **the r. is that . . .,** il en résulte que . . ., cela fait que . . .; **the r. of which will be that . . .,** ce qui aura pour effet de . . .; **what will be the r. of it?** que va-t-il en sortir? qu'en résultera-t-il? qu'est-ce que cela aura pour conséquence? **to get, obtain, a r.,** avoir, obtenir, un résultat; **to yield results,** donner des résultats; **to have a favourable r.,** (i) bien aboutir; (ii) avoir, donner, de bons résultats; **to reach a favourable r.,** aboutir, arriver, à un résultat favorable; **as a r. of . . .,** par suite de . . .; **without r.,** sans résultat; **we shall have no results without advertising,** on n'arrivera jamais à rien sans publicité; *Com:* **trading results,** résultats de l'exercice, de l'exploitation; **results,** résultats (d'un examen, d'une compétition, etc.); **to give out the results (of a competition, etc.),** donner le classement; *Space:* **observed r.,** résultat d'observation. **2.** *Mth:* résultat.

result[2], *v.i.* **1.** résulter, provenir, découler (**from,** de); **it results from this that . . .,** il s'ensuit que . . .; **little will r. from all this,** il ne sortira pas grand-chose de tout cela; **consequences resulting from . . .,** conséquences découlant de . . .; **damage resulting from an accident,** dommage consécutif à un accident. **2.** aboutir (**in failure, in a discovery,** à un échec, à, dans, une découverte); **to r. in . . .,** avoir pour résultat de . . .; **it resulted in nothing,** il n'en est, a, rien résulté; cela n'a mené à rien; **it resulted in a large profit,** cela a donné de gros bénéfices; **this will r. in unpleasantness,** cela entraînera des désagréments; cela va vous amener des ennuis; **these revelations resulted in the fall of the government,** ces révélations ont eu pour résultat la chute du ministère. **3.** *Jur:* faire retour, revenir (**to s.o.,** à qn); **resulting trust,** trust par déduction qui (sous certaines conditions) revient à celui qui l'a créé.

resultant [ri'zʌltənt], *a. & s.* résultant; **because of the r. increase in price,** par l'élévation du prix que (cette opération, etc.) entraîne; **the r. economic benefits,** les avantages économiques qui en résultent; *Mec:* **r. (force),** (force) résultante *f;* **to find the r. of three forces,** composer trois forces.

resultative [ri'zʌltətiv], *a. Ling:* résultatif.

resultful [ri'zʌltful], *a.* plein de bons résultats; fructueux.

resultless [ri'zʌltlis], *a.* sans résultat.

resumable [ri'zjuːməbl], *a. Jur: etc:* recouvrable.

resume [ri'zjuːm], *v.tr.* **1.** reprendre, regagner (sa vigueur, etc.); **to r. one's seat,** reprendre sa place; se rasseoir. **2. to r. a territory,** rentrer en possession, reprendre possession, d'un territoire. **3.** (*a*) reprendre (une conversation, sa route, ses habitudes, des négociations); renouer (des relations); continuer, poursuivre (un discours); **to r. work,** se remettre au travail, à travailler; **to r. operations,** reprendre les travaux; **to r. one's duties,** reprendre son service, ses fonctions; rentrer en fonctions; **then he resumed his reading,** puis il s'est remis à lire, à sa lecture; **to r. correspondence with s.o.,** rentrer en correspondance avec qn; **she resumed her maiden name,** elle a repris son nom de jeune fille; **if hostilities should be resumed,** si les hostilités reprenaient; (*b*) **the House resumed yesterday,** (i) la rentrée des Chambres a eu lieu hier; (ii) les débats ont repris hier; (*c*) **'this was a great mistake', he resumed,** «c'était une grosse erreur», continua-t-il, reprit-il. **4.** reprendre (une histoire); récapituler (les faits).

résumé ['rizju(ː)mei], *s.* résumé *m,* abrégé *m.*

resummon [riː'sʌmən], *v.tr. A:* **1.** réassigner; citer (qn) de nouveau. **2.** reconvoquer (une assemblée).

resummons [riː'sʌmənz], *s. A:* **1.** réassignation *f,* nouvelle citation (de qn). **2.** reconvocation *f* (d'une assemblée).

resumption [ri'zʌmpʃ(ə)n], *s.* reprise *f* (de négociations, etc.); *Jur:* **r. of residence,** réintégration *f* de domicile.

resupinate [ri'suːpinət], *a. Bot:* résupiné.

resupination [riːsuːpi'neiʃ(ə)n], *s. Bot:* résupination *f.*

resupply [riːsə'plai], *v.tr.* réapprovisionner (**with,** de).

resurface [riː'səːfis]. **1.** *v.tr.* **to r. a road,** refaire le revêtement d'une route. **2.** *v.i. Nau:* refaire surface.

resurgence [ri'səːdʒ(ə)ns], *s.* (*a*) *Lit:* résurrection *f* (d'un peuple, d'une idée, etc.); *Pol.Ec:* reprise *f,* renouveau *m;* (*b*) *Geol:* résurgence *f* (d'un cours d'eau souterrain).

resurgent [ri'səːdʒ(ə)nt], *a.* (*a*) *Lit:* qui ressuscite; (*b*) *Geol:* résurgent.

resurrect [rezə'rekt]. **1.** *v.tr.* ressusciter, faire revivre (qn, *F:* une coutume, etc.); *A:* exhumer, déterrer (un corps). **2.** *v.i. A:* ressusciter.

resurrection [rezə'rekʃ(ə)n], *s.* **1.** (*a*) résurrection *f* (des morts); *Theol:* **the r. body,** le corps après la résurrection; (*b*) **the R.,** la résurrection de Jésus-Christ. **2.** *A:* exhumation *f,* déterrement *m,* de cadavres (aux fins de dissection); *A:* **r. man,** déterreur *m* de cadavres. **3.** *F:* résurrection, reprise *f* (d'une coutume, etc.); réchauffement *m* (d'un plat). **4.** *Bot:* **r. plant, fern,** (i) rose *f* de Jéricho; (ii) fleur *f* de Candie.

resurrectional [rezə'rekʃənl], *a.* résurrectionnel.

resurrectionist [rezə'rekʃənist], *s.* **1.** résurrection(n)iste *mf* (de théories démodées, etc.). **2.** *A:* déterreur *m* de cadavres (aux fins de dissection).

resurvey[1] [riː'səːvei], *s.* **1.** (*a*) révision *f;* nouvel examen; (*b*) contre-expertise *f* (d'un navire, d'un manuscrit, etc.). **2.** *Surv:* réarpentage *m;* nouvel arpentage; nouveau levé (topographique).

resurvey[2] [riːsə'vei], *v.tr.* **1.** (*a*) examiner de nouveau; revoir (un immeuble, la situation, etc.); (*b*) faire la contre-expertise (d'un navire, d'un manuscrit, etc.). **2.** *Surv:* réarpenter, arpenter de nouveau (un terrain); **to r. a district, a mine,** faire un nouveau levé d'une région, d'une mine.

resuscitate [ri'sʌsiteit]. **1.** *v.tr.* ressusciter, faire revivre (qn, qch.); rappeler (qn) à la vie. **2.** *v.i. O:* ressusciter; revenir à la vie.

resuscitation [risʌsi'teiʃ(ə)n], *s.* ressuscitation *f,* réanimation *f,* ranimation *f* (d'un asphyxié, etc.).

resuscitator [ri'sʌsiteitər], *s.* appareil *m* de réanimation.

ret [ret] (**retted**) **1.** *v.tr.* rouir (le lin, etc.). **2.** *v.i.* (*of hay, etc.*) pourrir.

retable [ri'teibl], *s. Ecc:* retable *m.*

retail[1] ['riːteil], *s. Com:* détail *m;* vente *f* au détail; **to sell (goods)** (*NAm:* **at**) **r.,** vendre (des marchandises) au détail; **wholesale and r. business,** commerce en gros et au détail; **r. trade,** commerce de détail; **r. dealer,** marchand, -ande, au détail; (marchand, -ande) détaillant, -ante; **r. price,** prix de détail; **r. price index,** indice des prix de détail.

retail[2] ['riːteil, riː'teil]. **1.** *v.tr.* (*a*) détailler, vendre au détail (des marchandises); (*b*) *F:* répéter, colporter (des nouvelles, une calomnie). **2.** *v.i.* (*of goods*) se vendre au détail, se détailler (**at, for, a certain price,** à un tel prix).

retailer ['riːteilər, riː'teilər], *s.* **1.** (commerçant, -ante) détaillant, -ante; marchand, -ande, au détail. **2.** *F:* colporteur, -euse, de nouvelles.

retain [ri'tein], *v.tr.* **1.** retenir, maintenir (qch. dans une position); **dam to r. the water,** barrage pour retenir, contenir, les eaux; **retaining dam,** barrage de retenue; *Hyd.E:* **retaining valve,** retour d'eau; *Const:* **retaining wall,** mur de soutènement, de revêtement, de retenue, d'appui. **2.** (*a*) *O:* engager, retenir (un domestique, etc.); prendre (qn) à son service; **to r. s.o.'s services,** retenir les services de qn; (*b*) **to r. a barrister, a counsel,** retenir un avocat (à l'avance); choisir un avocat; **retaining fee,** honoraires versés à un avocat pour s'assurer son concours éventuel; provision *f;* avance *f,* acompte *m.* **3.** conserver, garder (un bien, etc.); conserver (une coutume, une qualité, la chaleur, etc.); **to r. all one's faculties,** conserver toutes ses facultés; **to r. the power to . . .,** se réserver le droit de . . .; **to r. hold of sth.,** ne pas lâcher (prise de) qch.; ne pas abandonner qch. **4.** garder (qch.) en mémoire; retenir (qch.) dans son souvenir; garder le souvenir de (qch.); **to r. a clear memory of sth.,** conserver un souvenir net de qch.

retainer [ri'teinər], *s.* **1.** dispositif *m* de retenue; *Mec.E:* **r. ring,** bague d'arrêt, de retenue; **valve r.,** coiffe *f* de clapet. **2.** (*a*) *Hist:* (*pers.*) serviteur *m,* suivant *m;* **a lord's retainers,** la suite, le train, les gens *m,* d'un noble; (*b*) **an old (family) r.,** un vieux domestique. **3.** *Jur:* (*a*) (droit *m* de) rétention *f* (de qch.); (*b*) mandat donné à un avocat; (*c*) **(general) r.,** honoraires versés à un avocat pour s'assurer son concours éventuel; provision *f;* avance *f,* acompte *m.*

retake[1] ['riːteik], *s. Cin: T.V:* reprise *f* (d'une prise de vues).

retake[2] [riː'teik], *v.tr.* (*p.t.* **retook** [riː'tuk]; *p.p.* **retaken** [riː'teik(ə)n]) **1.** reprendre (une place forte, etc.); rattraper (un prisonnier qui s'est sauvé, etc.); **to r. a town from the enemy,** reprendre une ville à, sur, l'ennemi. **2.** *Cin: T.V:* retourner (un plan).

retaliate [ri'tælieit]. **1.** *v.tr.* (*a*) exercer des représailles, user de représailles, pour (un tort); payer de retour (une insulte, etc.); (*b*) **to r. an accusation upon s.o.,** retourner une accusation contre qn. **2.** *v.i.* **to r. (on s.o.),** rendre la pareille (à qn); user de représailles (envers qn); appliquer (à qn) la loi du talion.

retaliation [ritæli'eiʃ(ə)n], *s.* revanche *f,* représailles *fpl;* *Jur:* rétorsion *f;* **to inflict, to exercise, r.,** user de représailles; exercer des représailles; *Jur:* user de rétorsion; **to indulge in verbal r.,** se renvoyer des injures; **in r., by way of r.,** en revanche; par mesure de représailles; **the law of r.,** la loi du talion.

retaliatory [ri'tæliət(ə)ri], *a.* de représailles; **r. measures,** représailles *f;* *Jur:* mesures de rétorsion.

retard[1] [ri'tɑːd], *s.* retard *m.*

retard[2]. **1.** *v.tr.* (*a*) retarder (qch.); *I.C.E:* **to r. the ignition,** réduire l'avance; retarder l'allumage; *Mec:* **retarded acceleration,** accélération négative, retardatrice; *Const:* **retarded hemihydrate plaster,** (plâtre *m* de) semi-hydrate *m;* *Elcs:* **retarding field oscillator,** oscillateur à champs de freinage, à grille positive; (*b*) retarder (qn); **mentally retarded person,** personne attardée, arriérée; attardé, -ée. **2.** *v.i. A:* (*of pers.*) tarder; (*of thg*) retarder.

retardant [ri'tɑːdənt], *a. & s.* (produit) qui ralentit la vitesse de propagation (du feu, etc.); **flame r. (paint),** (peinture *f*) ignifuge *m;* **rust r. (coating),** (peinture) antirouille *m.*

retardate [ri'tɑːdeit], *s. NAm:* personne attardée, arriérée; attardé, -ée; (élève *mf*) retardé, -ée.

retardation [riːtɑː'deiʃ(ə)n], *s.* **1.** (*a*) retard *m;* (*b*) *Mus:* ralentissement *m* (de la mesure); (*c*) *Mus:* retard (harmonique). **2.** (*a*) *Mec: Ph:* retardation *f;* accélération négative, retardatrice, vitesse retardée; (*b*) *Mec: Ph:* freinage *m;* (*c*) *El:* **r. coil,** bobine d'arrêt. **3.** retard (des marées). **4.** *Psy:* arriération *f.*

retardative, retardatory [ri'tɑːdətiv, -'tɑːdət(ə)ri], *a.* retardateur, -trice.

retarder [ri'tɑːdər], *s.* **1.** *O:* celui, celle, qui retarde (qch.). **2.** (*a*) *Const:* retardateur *m* (de la prise); (*b*) *Rubberm:* retardateur; (*c*) *Rail:* retardateur; ralentisseur *m* (de vitesse).

retardment [ri'tɑːdmənt], *s.* **1.** *O:* retard *m;* retardement *m.* **2.** *Psy:* arriération *f.*

retch[1] [retʃ, riːtʃ], *s.* effort *m* pour vomir; haut-le-cœur *m inv.*

retch[2], *v.i.* faire des efforts pour vomir; avoir des haut-le-cœur.

retching ['retʃiŋ, 'riː-], *s.* efforts *mpl* pour vomir; des haut-le-cœur *m;* *Med:* vomiturition *f.*

retell [riː'tel], *v.tr.* (*p.t. & p.p.* **retold** [riː'tould]) (*a*) redire, répéter; (*b*) raconter de nouveau (une histoire).

retemper [riː'tempər], *v.tr.* **1.** *Metalw:* retremper (de l'acier, etc.). **2.** détremper, redélayer (du béton, etc.).

retempering [riːˈtempəriŋ], *s.* **1.** *Metalw:* retrempe *f* (de l'acier, etc.). **2.** regâchage *m*, redélayage *m* (du béton, etc.).

retention [riˈtenʃ(ə)n], *s.* **1.** *Med:* rétention *f* (d'urine, etc.). **2.** fixation *f*; *Med:* contention (d'une luxation). **3.** conservation *f* (d'un usage, etc.); maintien *m* (d'une autorité). **4.** *Psy:* mémorisation *f*, mémoire *f*.

retentive [riˈtentiv], *a.* **1.** (*a*) (*of memory*) tenace, fidèle, sûr; (*b*) **to be r. of sth.,** retenir, garder, conserver, qch.; **r. soil,** sol qui retient l'eau. **2.** *Anat:* (muscle) rétenteur. **3.** *Med:* (bandage, appareil) contentif.

retentiveness [riˈtentivnis], *s.* **1.** pouvoir *m*, faculté *f*, de retenir, de garder (qch.); **r. of memory,** fidélité *f*, sûreté *f*, ténacité *f*, de mémoire. **2.** *Psy:* rétentivité *f*. **3.** *Magn:* = RETENTIVITY.

retentivity [riːtenˈtiviti], *s.* *Magn:* rémanence *f*, persistance *f*, coercitivité *f*, force coercitive (d'un aimant).

retentor [riˈtentər], *s.* *Anat:* muscle rétenteur.

retest [ˈriːtest], *s.* *Ind: etc:* contre-essai *m*, *pl.* contre-essais.

retexture [riːˈtekstjər], *v.tr.* *Tex:* redonner sa forme à (un tissu, un vêtement).

retexturing [riːˈtekstjəriŋ], *s.* *Tex:* remise *f* en forme (d'un tissu, d'un vêtement).

rethread [riːˈθred], *v.tr.* **1.** renfiler (une aiguille, des perles, etc.). **2.** rénover les filets (d'une vis, d'un écrou).

retiarius [riːtiˈɛəriəs, riːʃi-, reti-], *s.* *Rom.Ant:* rétiaire *m*.

retiary [ˈriːʃiəri], *s.* *Arach:* orbitèle *m*; araignée *f* orbitélaire.

reticence [ˈretis(ə)ns], *s.* **1.** réticence *f*; **without any r.,** sans aucune réserve. **2.** caractère peu communicatif; réserve; taciturnité *f*.

reticent [ˈretis(ə)nt], *a.* peu communicatif; taciturne; réservé, discret, -ète; **to be very r. about, on, sth.,** faire (grand) mystère de qch.

reticently [ˈretis(ə)ntli], *adv.* avec réticence; avec réserve.

reticle [ˈretikl], *s.* réticule *m* (d'un instrument d'optique).

reticular [riˈtikjulər], *a.* réticulaire; en réseau; *Anat:* **r. formation (of the brain),** substance réticulaire grise; *Arch:* **r. (masonry) work,** appareil réticulé.

reticulate[1] [riˈtikjulət], *a.* réticulé; rétiforme.

reticulate[2] [riˈtikjuleit]. **1.** *v.tr.* couvrir (une surface) d'un réseau; diviser (une surface) en réseau; *Arch:* **reticulated (masonry) work,** appareil réticulé; *Geol: etc:* **reticulated structure,** structure maillée. **2.** *v.i.* former un réseau; se couvrir de mailles.

reticulation [ritikjuˈleiʃ(ə)n], *s.* réticulation *f*; forme réticulée; disposition *f* en forme de réseau; structure maillée; *Phot:* réticulation (de la gélatine).

reticule [ˈretikjuːl], *s.* **1.** *A:* (*handbag*) réticule *m*. **2.** réticule (d'un instrument d'optique).

reticulin [riˈtikjulin], *s.* *Physiol:* réticuline *f*.

reticulitis [ritikjuˈlaitis], *s.* *Vet:* réticulite *f*.

reticulocyte [riˈtikjulousait], *s.* *Biol:* réticulocyte *m*.

reticuloendothelial [ritikjulouendouˈθiːliəl], *a.* *Anat:* (système) réticulo-endothélial, -aux.

reticuloendotheliosis [ritikjulouendouθiːliˈousis], *s.* *Med:* réticulo-endothéliose *f*.

reticulosarcoma [ritikjulousɑːˈkoumə], *s.* *Med:* réticulo-sarcome *m*, *pl.* réticulo-sarcomes; réticulo-sarcomatose *f*, *pl.* réticulo-sarcomatoses.

reticulosis [ritikjuˈlousis], *s.* *Med:* réticulose *f*.

reticulum, *pl.* **-a** [riˈtikjuləm, -ə], *s.* **1.** *Z:* réticulum *m*, réseau *m*, bonnet *m* (d'un ruminant). **2.** *Anat: Biol:* réticulum, réseau; tissu réticulé.

retiform [ˈriːtifɔːm, ˈreti-], *a.* rétiforme.

retile [riːˈtail], *v.tr.* **1.** renouveler les tuiles (d'un toit). **2.** recarreler (une pièce, etc.).

retiling [riːˈtailiŋ], *s.* **1.** rénovation *f* (d'un toit). **2.** recarrelage *m* (d'une pièce, etc.).

retimber [riːˈtimbər], *v.tr.* reboiser (une région, etc.).

retime [riːˈtaim], *v.tr.* **1.** *I.C.E: etc:* régler à nouveau (l'allumage, l'arbre à cames). **2.** refaire une nouvel horaire.

retiming [riːˈtaimiŋ], *s.* *I.C.E: etc:* nouveau réglage (de l'allumage, etc.).

retina, *pl.* **-as, -ae** [ˈretinə, -əz, -iː], *s.* *Anat:* rétine *f* (de l'œil); *Med:* **detached r.,** rétine décollée.

retinaculum, *pl.* **-a** [retiˈnækjuləm, -ə], *s.* *Bot: Ent:* rétinacle *m*.

retinal [ˈretin(ə)l], *a.* rétinien; de la rétine.

retinalite [riˈtinəlait], *s.* *Miner:* rétinalite *f*.

retinasphalt(um) [retinˈæsfælt, -ˈfæltəm], *s.* *Miner:* rétinasphalte *m*.

retinene [ˈretiniːn], *s.* *Bio-Ch:* rétinal *m*, rétinène *m*.

retinite [ˈretinait], *s.* *Miner:* rétinite *f*.

retinitis [retiˈnaitis], *s.* *Med:* rétinite *f*.

retinopathy [retiˈnɔpəθi], *s.* *Med:* rétinopathie *f*.

retinoscopy [retiˈnɔskəpi], *s.* *Opt:* rétinoscopie *f*.

retinue [ˈretinjuː], *s.* suite *f* (d'un prince, etc.).

retinula, *pl.* **-ae** [reˈtinjulə, -liː], *s.* *Ent: etc:* rétinule *f*; **r. cells,** retinules, cellules rétiniennes.

retirade [retiˈrɑːd], *s.* *A.Fort:* retirade *f*.

retiral [riˈtaiər(ə)l], *s.* *A:* **1.** retraite *f* (d'un fonctionnaire, etc.). **2.** démission *f*.

retire[1] [riˈtaiər], *s.* *Mil: A:* **to sound the r.,** sonner la retraite.

retire[2], *v.*

I. *v.i.* **1.** (*a*) se retirer (**to a place,** dans un endroit); **to r. from the world,** se retirer du monde; **to r. into oneself,** rentrer en soi-même, se replier sur soi-même; se recueillir; (*b*) **to r. from the room,** quitter la pièce; *O:* **the ladies retired,** les dames se sont retirées, sont passées au salon; **to r. (to bed, for the night),** (aller) se coucher. **2.** se démettre (de ses fonctions); démissionner; **to r. (from business),** se retirer des affaires; **to r. (on a pension),** prendre sa retraite; **to r. at one's own request,** être mis à la retraite sur sa demande; **to have retired,** être en, à la, retraite; avoir pris sa retraite. **3.** (*a*) *Mil: etc:* reculer; se replier; battre en retraite; **to r. from the field,** se retirer de la lutte, du combat; (*b*) *Sp: etc:* **to r. from the field, from the race,** se retirer de la partie, du match; abandonner; (*c*) *Fenc:* **to r. while parrying,** rompre la mesure.

II. *v.tr.* **1.** mettre (qn) à la retraite. **2.** *Mil:* replier (les troupes); ramener (les troupes) en arrière. **3.** *Fin:* retirer, rembourser (un effet); retirer (une monnaie) de la circulation.

retired [riˈtaiəd], *a.* **1.** (*a*) (*of life, etc.*) retiré; **to live a r. life,** vivre dans la retraite; vivre retiré; mener une vie retirée; (*b*) (endroit, etc.) retiré, écarté, isolé, peu fréquenté. **2.** (*a*) (négociant, etc.) retiré des affaires; (officier, fonctionnaire) retraité, en retraite; **he's a r. teacher,** c'est un ancien professeur, un professeur en retraite; (*b*) *Mil:* **r. pay,** retraite des cadres; **on the r. list,** en retraite; retraité; **to put, place, s.o. on the r. list,** mettre qn à la retraite.

retirement [riˈtaiəmənt], *s.* **1.** (*a*) *Adm: Mil: etc:* retraite *f*; **optional r.,** retraite sur demande; **compulsory r.,** retraite d'office; **r. on account of age,** retraite par limite d'âge; **r. pension,** (pension *f* de) retraite; retraite de vieillesse; (*b*) **to live in r.,** vivre retiré du monde. **2.** (*a*) *Mil:* retraite, repli *m*, recul *m* (des troupes); (*b*) *Sp: Games:* abandon *m* (de la partie, du match) (par un des concurrents). **3.** *Fin:* retrait *m*, remboursement *m* (d'un effet); retrait (de monnaies). **4.** *A:* retraite, refuge *m*.

retiring[1] [riˈtai(ə)riŋ], *a.* **1.** (*of pers.*) renfermé, réservé; farouche, timide; **he is of a r. disposition,** il cherche toujours à s'effacer. **2.** (président, administrateur) sortant. **3.** *Mil: etc:* (avant-poste) qui se replie; *Navy:* **in r. order,** en ordre de retraite.

retiring[2], *s.* **1.** action *f* de se retirer d'un endroit. **2.** (*a*) mise *f* en, à la, retraite (d'un officier, etc.); **r. age,** âge de la retraite; (*b*) **r. from business,** cessation *f* de commerce.

retiringly [riˈtai(ə)riŋli], *adv.* modestement; en s'effaçant.

retool [riːˈtuːl], *v.tr.* **1.** rééquiper (une usine, etc.) (en outils). **2.** *NAm:* réorganiser (qch.).

retooling [riːˈtuːliŋ], *s.* **1.** rééquipement *m* (en outils) (d'une usine, etc.). **2.** *NAm:* réorganisation *f*.

retort[1] [riˈtɔːt], *s.* réplique *f* (**to,** à); riposte *f*; **to make an insolent r.,** répliquer par une insolence.

retort[2]. **1.** *v.tr.* (*a*) renvoyer, rendre, retourner (une injure); payer (une moquerie) de retour; **to r. a charge on s.o.,** relancer une accusation à qn; **to r. an argument against s.o.,** rétorquer un argument contre qn; (*b*) répliquer, riposter; (*c*) *Nat.Hist: etc:* **retorted,** (i) recourbé, tordu; (ii) retourné. **2.** *v.i.* **to r. (on s.o.),** riposter.

retort[3], *s.* *Ch: Ind:* cornue *f*; vase clos; **gas r.,** cornue à gaz.

retort[4], *v.tr.* *Ind:* distiller (du mercure, etc.) en vase clos.

retortion [riˈtɔːʃ(ə)n], *s.* **1.** renversement *m*, repliement *m*. **2.** *Jur:* rétorsion *f*, représailles *fpl*.

retouch[1] [ˈriːtʌtʃ], *s.* retouche *f* (**to a picture, etc.,** à un tableau, etc.).

retouch[2] [riːˈtʌtʃ], *v.tr.* retoucher (un travail, une photographie, etc.); faire des retouches à (un travail).

retoucher [riːˈtʌtʃər], *s.* *Art: Phot:* (*pers.*) retoucheur, -euse.

retouching [riːˈtʌtʃiŋ], *s.* *Phot:* retouche *f*; **r. desk,** pupitre à retouche(s); lecteur *m*; **r. varnish,** (vernis *m*) mattolin *m*; **r. instrument,** retouchoir *m*.

retrace[1] [riˈtreis], *v.tr.* **1.** remonter à l'origine de (qch.). **2.** reconstituer, retracer (le passé); se remémorer (le passé). **3.** **to r. one's steps,** revenir sur ses pas; rebrousser chemin.

retrace[2] [riːˈtreis], *v.tr.* (*a*) retracer (un dessin, etc.); (*b*) décalquer (un dessin, etc.) à nouveau.

retract [riˈtrækt]. **1.** *v.tr.* (*a*) rétracter; tirer (qch.) en arrière; *Surg:* écarter (les lèvres d'une plaie, etc.); **the snail retracts its horns,** l'escargot rétracte, rentre, ses cornes; **the cat retracts its claws,** le chat rentre ses griffes; *Av:* **to r. the undercarriage,** escamoter, rentrer, le train d'atterrissage; *Ling:* **to r. a vowel,** prononcer une voyelle avec la langue ramenée en arrière; **retracted vowel,** voyelle postérieure; (*b*) rétracter (ce qu'on a dit); reprendre, revenir sur (sa parole, etc.); désavouer, rétracter (une opinion, etc.); *v.i.* **to r.,** se rétracter; se dédire; *Jur:* **to r. a decree,** rétracter un arrêt. **2.** *v.i.* se rétracter; se contracter; (*of cat's claws, etc.*) rentrer.

retractable [riˈtræktəbl], *a.* **1.** (*a*) *Nat.Hist:* rétractile; (*b*) (*of handle, etc.*) escamotable; **r. ballpoint (pen),** stylo (à) bille à cartouche rétractable; *Av:* **r. undercarriage,** train d'atterrissage rentrant, escamotable, relevable. **2.** (*of comment, etc.*) rétractable; qui peut être désavoué, rétracté.

retractation [riːtrækˈteiʃ(ə)n], *s.* **1.** rétractation *f* (de sa parole); désaveu *m*, reniement *m* (d'une opinion). **2.** rétractation; palinodie *f*.

retractile [riˈtræktail], *a.* *Nat.Hist:* (organe, etc.) rétractile.

retractility [ritrækˈtiliti], *s.* *Nat.Hist:* rétractilité *f* (d'un organe, etc.).

retracting [riˈtræktiŋ], *a.* = RETRACTABLE 1.

retraction [riˈtrækʃ(ə)n], *s.* **1.** action *f* de rétracter (les cornes, etc.), de rentrer (les griffes, etc.); *Med:* rétraction *f*, contraction *f* (d'un organe, d'un muscle); *Ling:* **r. of the tongue,** recul *m* de la langue. **2.** = RETRACTATION 1.

retractive [riˈtræktiv], *a.* rétractif.

retractor [riˈtræktər], *s.* **1.** *Anat:* (muscle) releveur *m*. **2.** *Surg:* rétracteur *m*, écarteur *m*; releveur (de paupière).

retrain [riːˈtrein], *v.tr.* (*a*) *Med:* rééduquer (un muscle); (*b*) recycler (qn).

retraining [riːˈtreiniŋ], *s.* (*a*) *Med:* rééducation *f* (d'un muscle); (*b*) recyclage *m* (de qn).

retral [ˈriːtrəl], *a.* **1.** (*of part*) postérieur. **2.** (*of movement*) en arrière, vers l'arrière.

retranslate [riːtrɑːnsˈleit], *v.tr.* retraduire.

retranslation [riːtrɑːnsˈleiʃ(ə)n], *s.* **1.** nouvelle traduction. **2.** *Sch: O:* **r. exercise,** thème d'imitation.

retransmission [riːtrɑːnsˈmiʃ(ə)n], *s.* réexpédition *f* (d'un télégramme, etc.); *W.Tel: T.V:* retransmission *f* (d'une émission, etc.).

retransmit [riːtrɑːnsˈmit], *v.tr.* (**retransmitted**) réexpédier (un télégramme); *W.Tel: T.V:* retransmettre (une émission).

retransmitter [riːtrɑːnsˈmitər], *s.* *Elcs: Tg: etc:* retransmetteur *m*.

retraxit [riˈtræksit], *s.* *Jur:* désistement *m* (d'action).

retread[1] [riːˈtred], *v.tr.* (*p.t.* **retrod** [riːˈtrɔd]; *p.p.* **retrodden** [riːˈtrɔdn]) *O: & Lit:* fouler de nouveau (le sol).

retread[2] [riːˈtred], *v.tr.* (*p.t. & p.p.* **retreaded**) *Aut:* rechaper, retailler (un pneu).

retread[3] [ˈriːtred], *s.* *Aut:* pneu rechapé, retaillé.

retreading [riːˈtrediŋ], *s.* *Aut:* rechapage *m*, resculpturage *m* (d'un pneu).

retreat[1] [riˈtriːt], *s.* **1.** *Mil:* (*a*) retraite *f*; **to sound, beat, the r.,** sonner, battre, la retraite; **to beat a r.,** battre en retraite; **to cut off an army's r.,** couper la retraite à une armée; *Fig:* **to make good one's r.,** s'échapper, s'évader; (*b*) *Hist:* (*evening call*) retraite. **2.** (*a*) retrait *m*, recul *m* (des eaux, etc.); recul (d'un glacier); **r. of the sea,** régression marine; (*b*) *Ecc:* retraite; **to go into r. for a week,** faire une retraite de huit jours; *A:* **r. (house),** maison *f* de retraite. **3.** (*a*) abri *m*, asile *m*; retraite; (*b*) repaire *m*, nid *m* (de brigands, etc.).

retreat[2]. **1.** *v.i.* (*a*) se retirer, s'éloigner (**to a place,** vers un endroit); **to r. into a corner,** se rencogner; (*b*) *Box: etc:* rompre; *Mil:* battre en retraite; (*c*) (*of glacier*) reculer; (*d*) *A:* **retreating chin, forehead,** menton, front, fuyant. **2.** *v.tr.* *Chess:* ramener (une pièce en danger).

retreatant [riˈtriːtənt], *s.* *Ecc:* retraitant, -ante.

retree [riˈtriː], *s.* *Paperm:* **r. (paper),** papier *m* de rebut.

retrench [riˈtren(t)ʃ]. **1.** *v.tr.* (*a*) restreindre, réformer (ses dépenses); (*b*) diminuer, réduire (les privilèges, etc., de qn); faire des coupures dans (une œuvre littéraire); supprimer, retrancher (un passage dans un livre, etc.); (*c*) *A.Fort:* retrancher (une position). **2.** *v.i.* restreindre ses dépenses, faire des économies.

retrenchment [riˈtren(t)ʃmənt], *s.* **1.** réduction *f*, compression *f* (des dépenses); **policy of r.,** politique d'économies, de redressement. **2.** suppression *f*, retranchement *m* (d'un passage littéraire, etc.). **3.** *Mil:* *O:* retranchement.

retrial [riːˈtrai(ə)l], *s.* *Jur:* nouveau procès.

retribution [retriˈbjuːʃ(ə)n], *s.* **1.** châtiment *m*; jugement *m*; vengeance *f*; **the Day of R.,** le jour du jugement; l'heure du châtiment; **just r. of, for, a crime,** juste

récompense *f* d'un crime; **failure is a r. for laziness,** l'échec est la sanction de la paresse. **2.** *O:* récompense (d'un service).
retributive [ri'tribjutiv], *a.* **1.** vengeur, *f.* vengeresse; qui châtie; **r. punishment,** punition justicière. **2.** *O:* de récompense.
retributor [ri'tribjutər], *s.* vengeur, *f.* vengeresse.
retributory [ri'tribjut(ə)ri], *a.* = RETRIBUTIVE.
retrievable [ri'tri:vəbl], *a.* **1.** (somme) recouvrable. **2.** (perte, erreur) réparable. **3.** *Cmptr:* (instruction) accessible.
retrieval [ri'tri:v(ə)l], *s.* **1.** recouvrement *m* (de biens). **2.** rétablissement *m*, relèvement *m* (de sa fortune); rétablissement (de sa réputation). **3.** *(a)* réparation *f* (d'une perte, d'une erreur); *(b)* **beyond r., past r.,** (erreur, etc.) irréparable; **lost beyond r.,** perdu irréparablement. **4.** *Cmptr:* extraction *f*, recherche *f*, prise *f* en charge (d'une instruction); **information r.,** recherche documentaire, recherche d'information(s); **information r. system,** système de recherche documentaire.
retrieve[1] [ri'tri:v], *s. A:* = RETRIEVAL 3 *(b)*.
retrieve[2], *v.tr.* **1.** *(a) Ven:* (*of dog*) rapporter (le gibier); *Ten:* **to r. (a ball),** renvoyer une balle difficile; *(b)* recouvrer (des biens); retrouver (un objet perdu, sa liberté); **I went to r. my umbrella,** je suis allé reprendre mon parapluie; *(c) A:* ressusciter (des souvenirs); se rappeler (qch.); se souvenir de (qch.). **2.** *(a)* relever, rétablir (**s.o.'s fortunes,** la fortune de qn); **to r. one's honour, to r. oneself,** racheter son honneur; rétablir sa réputation; se réhabiliter; se racheter; *(b)* **to r. s.o. from ruin, from certain death,** arracher qn à la ruine, à une mort certaine; sauver qn d'une mort certaine. **3.** réparer (une perte, une erreur, etc.); remédier à (une situation); *Gaming: etc:* **to r. one's losses,** se racquitter, se refaire. **4.** *Cmptr:* retrouver, extraire, récupérer (une instruction).
retriever [ri'tri:vər], *s.* **1.** *Ven:* (chien *m*) retriever *m*; **a good r.,** un chien qui rapporte bien. **2.** *Breed:* retriever; **golden r.,** retriever golden, doré; **flat-coated r.,** retriever à poil plat; **curly-coated r.,** retriever à poil bouclé.
retrieving [ri'tri:viŋ], *a. Ven:* (chien) qui rapporte, retriever.
retrim [ri:'trim], *v.tr.* **(retrimmed)** regarnir, réarranger (qch.).
retro- ['retrou, 'retrə], *pref.* rétro-.
retroact [retrou'ækt], *v.i.* **1.** *O:* réagir (**against,** contre). **2.** (*of legislation*) rétroagir; avoir un effet rétroactif.
retroaction [retrou'ækʃ(ə)n], *s.* **1.** *O:* réaction *f*; contrecoup *m*. **2.** rétroaction *f* (d'une loi, etc.).
retroactive [retrou'æktiv], *a.* rétroactif.
retroactively [retrou'æktivli], *adv.* rétroactivement.
retroactivity [retrouæk'tiviti], *s.* rétroactivité *f*.
retrocede[1] [retrou'si:d], *v.i.* rétrograder, reculer.
retrocede[2], *v.tr.* rétrocéder, recéder, rendre (un territoire, etc.); *Jur:* rétrocéder (un droit).
retrocession[1] [retrou'seʃ(ə)n], *s.* **1.** rétrogradation *f*, recul *m*. **2.** *Med:* rétrocession *f* (d'une éruption, etc.).
retrocession[2], *s. Jur:* rétrocession *f* (d'un droit, etc.).
retrochoir ['retroukwaiər], *s. Ecc.Arch:* arrière-chœur *m*, *pl.* arrière-chœurs.
retrodeviation [retroudi:vi'eiʃ(ə)n], *s. Med:* rétrodéviation *f*.
retroflex(ed) ['retroufleks(t)], *a. Nat.Hist: etc:* rétrofléchi.
retroflexion [retrou'flekʃ(ə)n], *s. Med:* rétroflexion *f* (de l'utérus).
retrogradation [retrougrə'deiʃ(ə)n], *s.* **1.** *Astr:* rétrogradation *f*. **2.** *A:* retour *m* en arrière (dans un raisonnement, etc.). **3.** *(a) A:* décadence *f*, dégénérescence *f*; *(b) Nat.Hist: etc:* régression *f*.
retrograde[1] ['retrəgreid]. **1.** *a.* *(a)* rétrograde; **r. movement,** mouvement rétrograde (d'une constellation, etc.); mouvement en arrière, à reculons; **this is a r. step,** cela fait un pas en arrière; *(b)* décadent; *(c) O:* **in r. order,** en ordre inverse. **2.** *s.* *(a)* dégénéré, -ée.
retrograde[2], *v.i.* **1.** rétrograder; revenir, retourner, en arrière; reculer. **2.** *Astr:* (*of planet*) rétrograder. **3.** rétrograder, dégénérer.
retrogress [retrə'gres], *v.i.* = RETROGRADE[2] 1, 3.
retrogression [retrə'greʃ(ə)n], *s.* **1.** rétrogradation *f*, régression *f*, recul *m*. **2.** *Med:* rétrocession *f* (d'une éruption). **3.** *Astr:* rétrogradation.
retrogressive [retrə'gresiv], *a.* **1.** rétrogressif, régressif; rétrograde; *Geol:* **r. erosion,** érosion régressive. **2.** *Biol:* régressif; dégénérescent.
retroperitoneal [retrouperitə'ni:əl], *a. Anat:* rétropéritonéal, -aux.
retroposition [retroupə'ziʃ(ə)n], *s. Anat:* rétroposition *f*.
retropubic [retrou'pju:bik], *a. Anat:* rétropubien.
retropulsion [retrou'pʌlʃ(ə)n], *s. Med:* rétropulsion *f*.
retrorocket ['retrourɔkit], *s. Space:* rétrofusée *f*.
retrorse [ri'trɔ:s], *a. Nat.Hist:* recourbé, retourné.
retrospect[1] ['retrəspekt], *s.* **1.** renvoi *m* (à une autorité, etc.). **2.** coup d'œil rétrospectif; examen rétrospectif; vue rétrospective; **when I consider these events in r.,** quand je jette un coup d'œil rétrospectif sur ces événements.
retrospect[2], *v.i. A: & Lit:* **to r. on one's past life,** revoir en esprit sa vie passée; **to r. to an earlier period,** se reporter à une période plus ancienne.
retrospection [retrə'spekʃ(ə)n], *s.* rétrospection *f*; examen rétrospectif (des événements, etc.).
retrospective [retrə'spektiv], *a.* **1.** (examen) rétrospectif. **2.** (loi) avec effet rétrospectif; **r. effect of a statute,** rétroactivité *f* d'un statut. **3.** (vue) vers l'arrière; *Art:* **r. (exhibition),** rétrospective *f*.
retrospectively [retrə'spektivli], *adv.* **1.** rétrospectivement. **2.** rétroactivement.
retrosternal [retrou'stə:nl], *a. Anat:* rétrosternal, -aux.
retrovaccination [retrouvæksi'neiʃ(ə)n], *s. Med:* rétrovaccination *f*.
retroverse ['retrouvə:s], **retroverted** [retrou'və:tid], *a.* rétroversé.
retroversion [retrou'və:ʃ(ə)n], *s. Med:* rétroversion *f*, renversement *m* (de l'utérus, etc.).
retry [ri:'trai], *v.tr. Jur:* juger (un accusé, un procès) à nouveau.
retsina [ret'si:nə], *s.* (vin) résiné *m*.
retter ['retər], *s. Tex:* rouisseur *m*.
rettery ['retəri], *s. Tex:* rouissoir *m*, routoir *m*.
retting ['retiŋ], *s.* **1.** roui *m*, rouissage *m* (du lin, etc.); **r. ground, pit,** rouissoir *m*, routoir *m*. **2.** pourriture *f* (du foin).
retube [ri:'tju:b], *v.tr. Mch:* retuber (une chaudière).
returf [ri:'tə:f], *v.tr.* regazonner.
return[1] [ri'tə:n], *s.* **1.** *(a)* retour *m*; recrudescence *f* (d'une maladie); **the r. of the swallows,** le retour des hirondelles; **on my r.,** dès, à, mon retour; **on my r. home I wrote to him,** de retour à la maison, chez moi, je lui ai écrit; **on his r. to France,** à sa rentrée en France; **by r. (of post),** par retour (du courrier); **to wish s.o. many happy returns of the day,** souhaiter à qn (i) un heureux anniversaire, (ii) une bonne fête; **many happy returns (of the day)!** meilleurs vœux pour votre anniversaire! **there was a r. to public order,** l'ordre s'est rétabli; **r. journey,** (voyage de) retour; *Rail: etc:* **r. (ticket),** billet *m* de retour; aller *m* (et) retour; **r. (half of ticket),** coupon *m* de retour; **first class r. to Dover,** aller et retour en première pour Douvres; **empty, loaded, r.,** retour à vide, en charge; *Av:* **r. to base,** retour à la base, au terrain; **r. to station,** retour en vol; **r. to ramp,** retour à l'aire de stationnement; *Nau: etc:* **point of no r.,** point de non-retour; *Nau:* **r. to port,** rentrée *f* au port; **r. cargo, freight,** cargaison, chargement, fret, de retour; *(b)* **r. stroke,** (i) course de retour, course rétrograde (d'un piston); (ii) choc en retour; **r. oil flow,** retour d'huile; **r. block,** poulie coupée; **r. angle,** retour d'angle; (*in pipe*) **r. bend,** coude double; coude en U; *Av:* **hydraulic r. system,** circuit de retour hydraulique; *(c) Arch:* retour (d'un mur); **r. wall,** mur en retour; *(d) El:* circuit *m* de retour; **r. current,** courant de retour; contre-courant *m*; **r. voltage,** tension de retour; **r. conductor,** conducteur de retour; **r. shock,** choc en retour, contrecoup *m*. **2.** *Com:* *(a)* **returns,** recettes *f*; rentrées (provenant des ventes); **quick returns,** un prompt débit; une vente rapide; **gross returns,** recettes brutes; *(b)* revenu *m*, gain *m*, profit *m*; rendement *m*; rémunération *f*; **to bring (in) a fair r.,** rapporter un bénéfice raisonnable; **gross r.,** rendement brut; *Pol.Ec:* **law of diminishing returns,** loi du rendement non proportionnel. **3.** *(a)* renvoi *m*, retour, réexpédition *f* (de marchandises avariées, etc.); *Com:* **r. (of bill to drawer),** contre-passation *f*, contre-passement *m*; **on sale or r.,** (marchandises) vendues avec faculté de retour, en dépôt (avec reprise des invendus), sous, à, condition; *Publ:* (exemplaire) d'office; **to deliver goods on sale or r.,** livrer des marchandises en dépôt temporaire; *Post:* **r. address,** adresse de l'expéditeur; *(b)* restitution *f* (d'un objet volé, etc.); ristourne *f* (d'une somme payée en trop); remise *f* (d'un objet à sa place); rentrée (d'un livre); *Com: Fin:* **r. of a capital sum,** remboursement *m* d'un capital; **r. commission,** commission allouée en retour; *(c)* échange *m*; **to give sth. in r. for sth.,** donner qch. en échange de qch.; **in r. for which . . .,** moyennant quoi . . .; **he was given a receipt in r. for his money,** on lui a donné un reçu en retour de son argent; **if you will do sth. in r.,** si vous voulez bien faire qch. en retour; *(d) Com:* **returns,** rendus *m*; (*of books, newspapers*) invendus *m*, *F:* bouillons *m*; *(e)* **returns,** (i) *A:* déchets *m* de tabac; (ii) tabac blond. **4.** *(a)* renvoi, répercussion *f* (d'un son); *Tp:* retour (du cadran); *Av:* *Radar:* **ground r.,** écho *m* de sol; **r. of a control lever,** rappel *m*, recul *m*, d'un levier de commande; *Typew:* **carriage r.,** retour, rappel, de chariot; **r.-to-neutral mechanism,** dispositif de rappel à la position neutre; **r. spring,** ressort de rappel; **r. pulley,** poulie de renvoi; **r. rope,** câble de renvoi; **r. to reference, to zero,** retour à zéro (dans un appareil de mesure, etc.); *Cmptr:* **r. code,** code de retour; *(b) Mch.Tls:* retour (d'un outil); **idle r.,** retour à vide, à blanc; **quick r.,** retour rapide; **r. speed,** vitesse de retour; *(c) Ten: etc:* renvoi (de la balle); riposte *f*. **5.** *(a)* récompense *f*; **I should like to make some r. for your services,** je voudrais bien vous récompenser de vos services; **that's a poor r. for his kindness,** c'est mal répondre à sa gentillesse; **in r. for this service . . .,** en récompense, en retour, de ce service . . .; **you must expect the same treatment in r.,** il faut vous attendre à la pareille; *(b) Mil: etc:* **r. salute,** contre-salut *m*; *Sp:* **r. match, game,** match retour; revanche *f*; *Fenc:* **r. (thrust),** riposte *f*. **6.** *(a)* rapport officiel; état *m*, exposé *m*; compte rendu; relevé *m*, relèvement *m*; statistique *f*; *Adm:* recensement *m* (de la population, etc.); **nil r.,** état néant; **the official returns,** les relevés officiels; **r. of expenses,** état de frais, de dépenses; **sales returns,** statistique (des ventes); **bank r.,** situation *f* de la banque; **the weekly bank r.,** le bilan hebdomadaire; **quarterly r.,** rapport trimestriel; **trade returns,** statistique de commerce; *(b)* **income tax r.,** déclaration *f* de revenu. **7.** *Pol:* élection *f* (d'un député); **to announce the returns of the election,** annoncer les résultats du scrutin.
return[2], *v.*
I. *v.i.* **1.** (*come back*) revenir; (*go back*) retourner; **I was returning from a journey,** je rentrais de voyage; **to r. (to one's) home,** (i) rentrer (chez soi); (ii) regagner sa patrie; **I'll see you as soon as I r., the moment I r.,** je vous verrai dès, à, mon retour; **when he returned to France, to Paris,** lorsqu'il est rentré en France, à Paris; **he has gone, never to r.,** (i) il est parti pour ne plus revenir; il est parti sans espoir de retour; (ii) *Lit:* il est mort; il est parti à tout jamais; **to r. the way one came,** retourner par le chemin qu'on a pris pour venir; **they have returned,** ils sont de retour; **to be about to r., to be on the point of returning,** être sur son retour; **he is returning from Paris on the 10th,** il revient de Paris le dix; **to r. from the dead,** ressusciter d'entre les morts; **her colour returned,** elle a repris des couleurs; **the wires r. over pulleys,** les fils sont renvoyés (sur leur parcours) par des poulies; **property that returns to its owner,** biens qui reviennent, qui font retour, à leur propriétaire; *Nau:* **to r. to port,** rentrer au port. **2.** **to r. to a task,** reprendre une tâche; **I shall r. to this subject later,** je reviendrai plus tard à ce sujet; je reprendrai plus tard ce sujet; **to r. to one's old habits,** retomber dans ses vieilles habitudes. **3.** retourner, revenir (à un état antérieur); *B:* **unto dust shalt thou r.,** tu retourneras en poussière.
II. *v.tr.* **1.** *(a)* rendre (un livre emprunté, un dépôt, etc.); restituer (un objet volé, etc.); renvoyer (un cadeau, etc.); rembourser (un emprunt); **to r. property to its rightful owner,** restituer un bien à son propriétaire légitime; **territories returned to France,** territoires qui ont fait retour à la France; *Com:* **to r. an amount paid in excess,** ristourner une somme payée en trop; **to r. an article,** faire un rendu; **returned article,** (i) rendu; (ii) laissé *m* pour compte; *Fin:* **to r. a bill to drawer,** contre-passer un effet; **to r. a commission,** rétrocéder une commission; *Post:* **returned letter,** lettre renvoyée à l'expéditeur; *(b)* **to r. a book to its place,** remettre un livre à sa place; **fish must be returned to the water,** les poissons doivent être remis dans l'eau; **to r. one's sword to the scabbard,** remettre son épée (au fourreau); *A.Mil:* **to r. swords,** remettre l'épée, le sabre. **2.** renvoyer (la lumière, un son); renvoyer, rejeter (une balle, etc.); *Ten:* **to r. the service, a stroke,** relancer la balle; **spring to r. the valve to its seat,** ressort pour ramener, rappeler, la soupape sur son siège; *Typew:* **to r. the carriage,** rappeler le chariot. **3.** *(a)* rendre (une visite, un compliment); rendre (un coup); renvoyer (une accusation); *Mil:* **to r. fire,** riposter (au feu adverse); **to r. s.o.'s greeting,** rendre un salut à qn; répondre au salut de qn; **to r. like for like,** rendre la pareille; **to r. good for evil,** rendre le bien pour le mal; **to r. s.o.'s love,** répondre à l'amour de qn; payer de retour l'amour de qn; aimer qn en retour; *Cards:* **to r. clubs,** rejouer du trèfle (après son partenaire); *(b)* répondre, répliquer; donner comme réponse; **to r. a denial,** opposer une dénégation. **4.** *Com: Fin:* rapporter, donner (un bénéfice); **investment that returns good interest,** placement qui rapporte de gros intérêts; placement avantageux. **5.** *(a)* déclarer, rapporter; rendre compte de (qch.); **men returned unfit for duty,**

hommes déclarés incapables de reprendre leur service; **to r. one's income at £4,000,** faire une déclaration de £4,000 de revenu; **the liabilities are returned at £10,000,** le passif est estimé, évalué, à £10,000; (*b*) *Jur:* **the prisoner was returned guilty,** l'accusé a été déclaré coupable; (*c*) *Sp:* **returned time,** temps contrôlé, temps officiel. **6.** *Parl:* (*a*) **to r. the result of the poll,** faire son rapport sur les résultats du scrutin; (*b*) élire (un député); **returning officer,** directeur, -trice, du scrutin; **deputy returning officer,** scrutateur *m*; **returning borough,** ville qui a le droit d'envoyer un représentant au Parlement.

returnable [ri'tə:nəbl], *a.* **1.** *Jur:* (mandat) de renvoi. **2.** qui peut être rendu, renvoyé; restituable; **r. goods,** marchandises de retour; **r. bottle,** bouteille consignée; **empties are not r.,** on ne reprend pas les bouteilles. **3.** *Pol:* (candidat) éligible.

returnee [ritə:'ni:], *s. Pol:* émigré, -ée, réfugié, -ée, qui se rapatrie.

returning [ri'tə:niŋ], *s.* **1.** retour *m*; rentrée *f* (d'un émigrant, etc.). **2.** (*a*) retour (d'un objet prêté); restitution *f* (d'un objet volé); (*b*) renvoi *m* (de marchandises, etc.). **3.** *Parl:* élection *f* (d'un député).

retuse [ri'tju:s], *a. Bot:* (*of leaf*) rétus.

retzian ['retsiən], *s. Miner:* retziane *f.*

reub [ru:b], *s. NAm: F:* = REUBEN 2.

Reuben ['ru:bin]. **1.** *Pr.n.m. B.Hist:* Ruben. **2.** *s.m. NAm: F:* paysan *m*, rustaud *m*; **R. town,** patelin *m*, bled *m*.

reunification [ri:ju:nifi'keiʃ(ə)n], *s. Pol:* réunification *f.*

reunify [ri:'ju:nifai], *v.tr. Pol:* réunifier.

reunion [ri:'ju:niən], *s.* **1.** *O:* réunion *f* (des lèvres d'une plaie, d'une famille en désaccord, etc.). **2.** réunion, assemblée *f.*

Reunion, *Pr.n. Geog:* La Réunion.

reunionist [ri:'ju:niənist], *s. Ecc:* partisan(e) de la réunion de l'Église anglicane et de l'Église catholique.

reunite [ri:ju'nait]. **1.** *v.tr.* (*a*) unir de nouveau; réunir (des fragments, etc.); (*b*) réunir, rassembler (ses partisans, etc.); réconcilier (une famille, etc.); **since they became reunited,** depuis leur réconciliation; depuis leur rapprochement. **2.** *v.i.* se réunir; (*a*) se réconcilier; (*b*) (*of edges of wound, etc.*) se ressouder.

reusable [ri:'ju:zəbl], *a.* remployable.

reuse[1] [ri:'ju:s], *s.* réutilisation *f*; remploi *m.*

reuse[2] [ri:'ju:z], *v.tr.* remployer.

reussinite [ri:'ju:sinait], *s. Miner:* réussinite *f.*

rev[1] [rev], *s. Aut: F:* (*abbr. of* **revolution) four thousand revs a minute,** quatre mille tours *m* à la minute; **to keep the revs up,** ne pas laisser ralentir le moteur.

rev[2], *v.* **(revved)** *Aut: F:* **1.** *v.tr.* **to r. up the engine,** emballer, faire emballer, le moteur. **2.** *v.i.* **the engine began to r. up,** le moteur s'est emballé.

revaccinate [ri:'væksineit], *v.tr.* revacciner.

revaccination [ri:væksi'neiʃ(ə)n], *s.* revaccination *f.*

revalidation [ri:væli'deiʃ(ə)n], *s.* revalidation *f.*

revalorization [ri:vælərai'zeiʃ(ə)n], *s. Fin:* revalorisation *f* (du franc, etc.).

revalorize [ri:'væləraiz], *v.tr. Fin:* revaloriser (le franc, etc.).

revaluation [ri:vælju'eiʃ(ə)n], *s.* réévaluation *f*; réestimation *f*; *Fin:* revalorisation *f* (du franc, etc.).

revalue [ri:'vælju:], *v.tr.* réestimer; réévaluer (une propriété, etc.); *Fin:* revaloriser (le franc, etc.).

revamp [ri:'væmp], *v.tr.* **1. to r. a shoe,** remplacer l'empeigne d'une chaussure. **2.** réparer. **3.** modifier, améliorer.

revanchist [rə'vɑ̃ʃist], *s. Pol:* revanchard, -arde.

revarnish [ri:'vɑ:niʃ], *v.tr.* revernir (un meuble).

reveal[1] [ri'vi:l], *v.tr.* **1.** (*a*) révéler, découvrir (son jeu); faire connaître (un fait); **to r. one's soul to s.o.,** ouvrir son cœur à qn; **to r. one's identity,** se faire connaître; (*b*) laisser voir; **his conduct reveals great intelligence,** sa conduite accuse, fait preuve de, décèle, une grande intelligence; **in his letters he reveals himself as full of kindness,** ses lettres nous le montrent plein de bonté; (*c*) révéler, découvrir (un objet caché); déceler (un objet caché); dévoiler (un mystère); faire voir, mettre à jour (qch.); **the truth will be revealed some day,** la vérité se découvrira un jour. **2.** *Theol:* révéler; **revealed religion,** la religion révélée; la révélation divine.

reveal[2], *s. Arch:* jouée *f*; tableau *m* (de pied-droit); *Const:* **door with plain plaster r.,** porte cueillie en plâtre.

revealable [ri'vi:ləbl], *a.* que l'on peut révéler, dévoiler; qu'il est permis de faire connaître.

revealer [ri'vi:lər], *s.* révélateur, -trice.

revealing[1] [ri'vi:liŋ], *a.* révélateur, -trice; **r. dress,** robe décolletée, qui ne cache rien.

revealing[2], *s.* révélation *f.*

reveille [ri'veli, ri'væli], *s. Mil:* le réveil; la diane.

revel[1] ['rev(ə)l], *s. often pl.* (*a*) divertissement(s) *m(pl)*; réjouissances *fpl*; ébats *mpl. Hist:* **Master of the revels (of the King),** intendant *m* des menus plaisirs du roi; (*b*) bacchanale *f*, orgie *f*, *A: & Lit:* **r. rout,** (i) troupe tumultueuse; (ii) orgie, bacchanale.

revel[2], *v.* **(revelled; revelling) 1.** *v.i.* (*a*) se réjouir, se divertir, s'amuser; (*b*) festoyer; *F:* faire la noce; (*c*) **to r. in sth., in doing sth.,** se délecter à qch., à faire qch.; se complaire dans qch., à qch., à faire qch.; s'enivrer de qch., à faire qch.; faire ses délices de qch.; **to r. in one's freedom,** se réjouir de sa liberté; **to r. in words,** s'enivrer de mots. **2.** *v.tr.* **to r. away the time,** passer tout son temps à s'amuser.

revelation [revə'leiʃ(ə)n], *s.* **1.** révélation *f*; **it was a r. to me,** cela a été une révélation pour moi; **what a r.!** quelle surprise! **2.** *B:* **the R., (the Book of) Revelations,** l'Apocalypse *f*; les Révélations de saint Jean.

revelationist [revə'leiʃ(ə)nist], *s.* **1. the R.,** l'auteur *m* de l'Apocalypse. **2.** celui qui accepte la révélation divine.

revelatory [revə'leitəri], *a.* révélatoire.

reveller ['rev(ə)lər], *s.* (*a*) joyeux convive; (*b*) viveur, -euse, noceur, -euse, bambocheur, -euse.

revelling ['rev(ə)liŋ], **revelry** ['revəlri], *s.* (*a*) divertissements *mpl*, réjouissances *fpl*, ébats *mpl*; (*b*) bacchanale *f*, orgie *f.*

revendication [rivendi'keiʃ(ə)n], *s.* revendication *f.*

revenge[1] [ri'vendʒ], *s.* **1.** vengeance *f*; **to take r. on s.o. for sth.,** se venger de qch. sur qn; **to have one's r.,** se venger **(by doing sth.,** à faire qch.); **in r.,** pour se venger **(for,** de); **out of r.,** par vengeance; **my r. will keep,** il ne perdra rien pour attendre; **thirsting for r.,** altéré de vengeance; **he was still harbouring thoughts of r.,** il avait toujours la vengeance dans le cœur. **2.** (*esp. in games*) revanche *f*; contre-partie *f*; **when will you give us our r.?** quand nous donnerez-vous notre revanche?

revenge[2], *v.tr.* **1. to r. oneself, to be revenged,** se venger **(on s.o.,** sur qn); tirer vengeance, prendre vengeance **(on s.o.,** de qn); exercer sa vengeance **(on s.o.,** sur qn); **to r. oneself (on s.o.) for sth.,** se venger de qch. (sur qn); **to r. oneself on s.o. for an insult,** se venger de qn pour une injure; se venger d'une injure sur qn. **2.** venger (une injure) **(on, upon, s.o.,** sur qn). **3.** venger (qn).

revengeful [ri'vendʒful], *a.* **1.** vindicatif; porté à la vengeance. **2.** qui punit; vengeur, -eresse.

revengefully [ri'vendʒfuli], *adv.* vindicativement; par vengeance.

revengefulness [ri'vendʒfulnis], *s.* caractère vindicatif; esprit *m* de vengeance.

revenger [ri'vendʒər], *s.* vengeur, -eresse **(of,** de).

revenue ['revənju:], *s.* **1.** revenu *m*, rentes *fpl*; rapport *m* **(from an estate,** d'une terre). **2. the Public R.,** (i) le revenu de l'État; le Trésor public; (ii) *Adm:* le fisc; **the r. authorities,** les agents *m* du fisc; **r. cutter,** cotre *m*, canot *m*, de la douane; **r. office,** (bureau *m* de) perception *f*; recette *f.*

reverberant [ri'və:bərənt], *a.* (*of light, sound*) réverbérant.

reverberate [ri'və:bəreit]. **1.** *v.tr.* (*a*) renvoyer, répercuter, réfléchir (le son); (*b*) réverbérer, réfléchir (la lumière, la chaleur); **to be reverberated,** réverbérer. **2.** *v.i.* (*a*) (*of sound*) retentir, résonner, se réfléchir; (*b*) (*of light, heat*) réverbérer.

reverberating [ri'və:bəreitiŋ], *a.* **1.** résonnant; réverbérant. **2.** *Tchn:* = REVERBERATORY.

reverberation [rivə:bə'reiʃ(ə)n], *s.* (*a*) renvoi *m*, réfléchissement *m*, répercussion *f* (d'un son); (*b*) réverbération *f* (de la lumière, de la chaleur).

reverberative [ri'və:bəreitiv], *a.* réverbérant.

reverberator [ri'və:bəreitər], *s.* réflecteur *m* (de la chaleur, de la lumière); réverbère *m.*

reverberatory [ri'və:bərətəri], *a. & s. Metall:* **r. furnace, r.,** four *m* à réverbère.

revere [ri'viər], *v.tr.* révérer, vénérer.

reverence[1] ['rev(ə)r(ə)ns], *s.* **1.** (*a*) respect religieux; vénération *f*; **filial r.,** piété filiale; **to hold s.o. in r., to feel r. for s.o., regard s.o. with r.,** révérer qn; éprouver du respect, de la vénération, pour qn; **held in r. by all,** révéré de tous; **to pay r. to s.o.,** rendre hommage à qn; (*b*) *A:* **to make a r. to s.o.,** s'incliner devant qn; faire une révérence à qn. **2.** *A: & P:* **saving your r.,** sauf révérence; révérence parler. **3.** (*esp. in Ireland*) **your R., his R.,** monsieur l'abbé; **yes, your R.,** oui, mon révérend.

reverence[2], *v.tr.* révérer.

reverend ['rev(ə)r(ə)nd], *a.* **1.** vénérable; *A:* révérend. **2.** *Ecc:* (*a*) **the r. gentleman,** le révérend abbé, père, ou pasteur; (*b*) (*as title*) **the Rev. Father Martin,** le révérend père Martin; **the Rev. Ch. Thomas,** (i) le révérend Ch. Thomas; (ii) monsieur l'abbé Ch. Thomas; **the R. Mother Superior,** la révérende mère supérieure; (*of dean*) **Very R.,** très révérend; (*of bishop*) **Right R.,** très révérend; **the Right Rev. Bishop of. . .,** Monseigneur l'évêque de. . .; (*of archbishop*) **Most R.,** révérendissime; *s. F:* **a crowd of reverends,** une foule de prêtres.

reverent ['rev(ə)r(ə)nt], *a.* respectueux; plein de vénération.

reverential [revə'renʃ(ə)l], *a.* (respect) révérenciel; (crainte) révérencielle.

reverentially [revə'renʃ(ə)li], *adv.* avec respect; avec une crainte révérencielle.

reverently ['rev(ə)rəntli], *adv.* avec respect, avec vénération.

reverer [ri'viərər], *s.* vénérateur, -trice **(of,** de).

reverie ['revəri], *s.* rêverie *f*; **in a r.,** rêveur, -euse.

revers [ri'viər, *pl.* ri'viəz], *s.pl. Cost:* revers *mpl* (d'une veste, etc.).

reversal [ri'və:s(ə)l], *s.* **1.** *Jur:* réforme *f*, annulation *f* (d'un jugement). **2.** (*a*) renversement *m* (*Opt:* d'une image, *Log:* d'une proposition, etc.); inversion *f*, changement *m*; **r. of opinion,** revirement *m* d'opinion; *Ph:* **r. of polarity,** renversement de polarité; *El:* **r. of current,** inversion du courant; *Mec.E:* **r. of motion,** renversement de marche; **r. of stroke,** changement de course; (*b*) *Phot:* **r. film,** film inversible; (*c*) *Typ:* **offset r. process,** procédé *m* d'inversion. **3.** *Book-k:* contre-passement *m*; annulation (d'une écriture).

reverse[1] [ri'və:s], *a.* inverse, contraire, opposé **(to,** à); **in the r. order,** en ordre inverse; **in the r. direction,** dans la direction opposée; **r. side,** revers *m*, envers (d'une médaille), dos *m* (d'un tableau); **r. gradient,** contre-pente *f*; **r. current,** (i) contre-courant *m*; *Nau:* revolin *m*; (ii) *El:* courant *m* inverse; *Tp:* **r. charge call,** communication *f*, conversation *f*, percevable à l'arrivée, à la charge du destinataire, avec P.C.V.; *Cin:* **r. shot,** contrechamp *m*; *Book-k:* **r. entry,** écriture *f* inverse; *Typ:* **r. indention,** composition *f* en sommaire; *Geol:* **r. fault,** faille *f* inverse; *Mch:* **r. steam,** contre-vapeur *f*; **r. stroke,** contre-course *f* (du piston, etc.); *Mec: etc,* **r. motion, action,** marche *f* arrière; **r. gear,** inversion *f* de marche; **r. pitch,** pas *m* inverse; **r. thrust,** inversion de la poussée; *Mil:* **r. flank,** flanc extérieur (dans un mouvement de conversion); *Artil:* **r. fire,** tir *m* de revers.

reverse[2], *s.* **1.** (*a*) inverse *m*, contraire *m*, opposé *m*; **to be quite the r., the very r., of s.o.,** être tout le contraire, tout l'opposé, de qn; **he is sometimes pleasant, but generally the r.,** il est quelquefois aimable mais en général le contraire; (*b*) *Mil:* **to take a position in r.,** prendre une position à revers; (*c*) *Aut:* **to go into r.,** mettre en marche arrière; *A:* **r. pedal,** pédale *f* de marche arrière; (*d*) *Typew:* **automatic ribbon-r.,** retour *m* automatique du ruban; **ribbon-r. key,** levier *m* d'inversion de marche du ruban. **2.** (*a*) revers *m* (d'une médaille, d'une monnaie); (*b*) verso *m* (d'un feuillet). **3.** (*defeat*) revers; **r. of fortune,** revers de fortune; **to suffer a r.,** essuyer un revers, une défaite. **4.** *Fenc:* (coup *m* de) revers.

reverse[3], *v.tr.* **1.** renverser; *Mil:* **to r. arms,** renverser les fusils; *Opt:* **to r. an inverted image,** redresser une image invertie. **2.** (*a*) retourner (un habit, un tableau); (*b*) renverser (un mouvement); intervertir, renverser (l'ordre de qch.); changer complètement; **to r. a process,** avoir recours à une méthode inverse; **then the process is reversed,** ensuite c'est l'inverse *m* qui se produit; *Tp:* **to r. the charge(s),** demander une communication percevable à l'arrivée, avec P.C.V.; **to r. a policy,** prendre le contre-pied d'une politique; *Pol: etc:* **to r. one's opinions, one's policy,** faire volte-face; faire la pirouette; **now their roles are reversed,** maintenant les rôles sont intervertis; *El:* **to r. the wires,** intervertir les fils; *Fb:* **to r. the result,** inverser le résultat (dans la contre-partie); *Book-k:* **to r. an entry,** contre-passer, annuler, une écriture; (*c*) **to r. the engine,** *abs.* **to r.,** (i) renverser la marche de la machine; (ii) *Rail:* faire machine (en) arrière; *Nau: Rail:* marcher en arrière; *Aut:* **to r. (one's car),** faire marche arrière; **to r. (the car) out of the garage,** sortir du garage en marche arrière; *El:* **to r. the current,** inverser, invertir, le sens du courant; renverser le courant; *Mch:* **to r. steam,** renverser la vapeur. **3.** *Jur:* révoquer (une sentence); réformer (un jugement). **4.** *v.i. Danc:* valser de gauche à droite; renverser.

reversed [ri'və:st], *a.* **1.** renversé; *Her:* renversé, versé; *Arch:* **r. arch,** voûte renversée; *Mil:* **with r. arms,** les armes renversées. **2.** inverse, contraire, opposé; *Arch:* **r. moulding, r. curve,** contre-profil *m* (d'une cimaise); *Aut: etc:* **r. curvature,** double courbure *f* (d'un longeron, etc.); *El:* **r. current,** renverse *f* de courant; *Mch:* **r. steam,** contre-vapeur *f*; *Mec:* **r. velocity,** vitesse inversée; *Geol:* **r. fault,** faille *f* inverse; **r. fold,** pli renversé; *Tp:* **will you accept a r.-charge call?** accepterez-vous une communication (demandée) avec

P.C.V.?

reversely [ri'və:sli], *adv.* inversement, contrairement.

reverser [ri'və:rsər], *s. El:* inverseur *m* de courant; *Av:* **thrust r.,** inverseur de poussée.

reversibility [rivə:sə'biliti], *s.* réversibilité *f.*

reversible [ri'və:səbl], *a.* **1.** renversable. **2.** (tissu) sans envers, à envers réversible, à deux endroits; (tissu, vêtement) réversible, à double face. **3.** (*a*) (procédé *m,* etc.) réversible; **r. fan,** ventilateur *m* réversible; **r. gear,** engrenage *m* réciproque; **r. motion,** mouvement *m* réciproque; **r. (pitch) propeller,** hélice *f* à pas réversible; *Ch:* **r. reaction,** réaction *f* réversible; (*b*) *Rail:* **r. rail,** rail *m* à double champignon. **4.** *Phot:* (film *m,* émulsion *f*) inversible. **5.** (*of decree, judgment, sentence*) révocable, réformable.

reversing [ri'və:siŋ], *s.* **1.** renversement *m.* **2.** (*a*) inversion *f;* changement complet; *Book-k:* **r. of entry,** contre-passation *f,* contre-passement *m,* d'une écriture; (*b*) *Mch: Aut: etc:* changement de marche; inversion de marche; marche *f* (en) arrière; **r. light,** phare *m* de recul; *Nau:* **r. of the propeller,** acculée *f* de l'hélice; *Mec.E:* **r. lever,** renvoi *m,* levier *m* d'inversion de marche; *Mch:* **r. link,** coulisse *f* de changement de marche; **r. rod,** barre *f* de relevage; *El:* **r. key,** levier inverseur; **r. switch,** inverseur *m* de marche.

reversion [ri'və:ʃ(ə)n], *s.* **1.** *Jur:* (*a*) retour *m* (d'un bien); réversion *f;* (*b*) substitution *f;* (*c*) **right of r.,** réversion; droit *m* de retour (d'une donation); **to come into a r.,** entrer en possession d'un bien (i) par réversion, (ii) par substitution; **annuity in r. on the death of the holder,** rente *f* réversible après la mort du titulaire; **estate in r.,** bien grevé (i) d'une réversion, de droit de retour, (ii) de substitution. **2.** survivance *f* (d'une place, d'un bénéfice). **3.** retour (à un état antérieur); *Biol:* **r. to type,** réversion (au type primitif); *Med:* **r. to virulence,** retour à la virulence.

reversionary [ri'və:ʃən(ə)ri], *a.* **1.** (droit *m*) de réversion; **r. annuity,** annuité *f* réversible; rente viagère avec réversion; **to have a r. interest in an estate,** être détenteur du droit de réversion ou de substitution d'un domaine. **2.** atavique; **r. degeneration,** dégénérescence *f* atavique.

reversioner [ri'və:ʃənər], *s.* détenteur *m* d'un droit de réversion ou de substitution.

reversive [ri'və:siv], *a.* réversif.

revert[1] [ri'və:rt, 'ri:vərt], *s.* converti, -ie, qui revient à sa foi primitive.

revert[2] [ri'və:t]. **1.** *v.i.* (*a*) *Jur:* (*of office, property*) revenir, retourner (**to,** à); (*of estate*) **to r. to an ascendant,** faire retour à un ascendant; (*b*) retourner, revenir (**to a wild state,** à l'état sauvage); *Biol:* **to r. to type,** revenir au type primitif; **we are reverting to travel by rail,** on revient au chemin de fer; (*c*) revenir (**to a subject,** à un sujet); **to r. to our subject,** pour en revenir à la question, à notre sujet; **we shall r. to this matter,** nous reviendrons sur cette question; **we won't r. to the past,** ne retournons pas sur le passé. **2.** *v.tr. A:* **to r. one's eyes,** regarder derrière soi; **to r. one's steps,** revenir sur ses pas.

revertibility [rivə:rti'biliti], *s. Jur:* réversibilité *f.*

revertible [ri'və:rtibl], *a. Jur:* réversible (**to,** à, sur) (par droit de retour ou de substitution).

revet [ri'vet], *v.tr.* (**revetted**) *Const: Fort:* revêtir; garnir (un talus, etc.) d'un revêtement; *Ind:* merlonner.

revetment [ri'vetmənt], *s. Const: Fort:* revêtement *m;* **r. wall,** mur *m* de revêtement, de chemise; épaulement *m;* *Ind:* merlon *m;* merlonnage *m;* murette *f* de retenue.

revictual [ri:'vit(ə)l], *v.* (**revictualled**) **1.** *v.tr.* ravitailler, réapprovisionner. **2.** *v.i.* se ravitailler.

revictualling [ri:'vitəliŋ], **revictualment** [ri'vit(ə)lmənt], *s.* ravitaillement *m,* réapprovisionnement *m.*

review[1] [ri'vju:], *s.* **1.** (*a*) *Jur:* révision *f* (d'un procès); (*b*) **to keep a question under r.,** suivre une question de très près. **2.** *Mil:* revue *f;* **to hold a r.,** passer une revue; **to pass troops, one's sins, in r.,** passer en revue des troupes, ses péchés. **3.** examen *m,* revue (du passé, etc.); **a r. of the year,** recensement *m* des événements de l'année. **4.** critique *f,* compte rendu, examen critique (d'un livre); **r. copy,** exemplaire fourni au critique; exemplaire de service de presse. **5.** *Publ:* revue (périodique).

review[2], *v.tr.* **1.** revoir, réviser (un procès, etc.). **2.** revoir, examiner (des événements passés); passer (des faits, etc.) en revue. **3. to r. the troops, the fleet,** passer les troupes, la flotte, en revue; faire la revue, passer la revue, des troupes, de la flotte; (*of troops*) **to be reviewed,** passer en revue. **4. to r. a book,** faire la critique, le compte rendu, d'un livre.

reviewable [ri'vju:əbl], *a.* **1.** *Jur:* révisable. **2.** qui supporte l'examen.

reviewer [ri'vju:ər], *s.* critique *m.*

reviewing [ri'vju:iŋ], *s.* **1.** révision *f,* examen *m.* **2.** *Mil:* revue *f.* **3.** critique *f.*

revile [ri'vail]. **1.** *v.tr.* injurier (qn); dire, débiter, des injures à (qn); insulter (qn). **2.** *v.i.* se répandre en injures; **to r. against s.o.,** invectiver (contre) qn.

revilement [ri'vailmənt], *s.* **1.** injures *fpl.* **2.** discours injurieux.

reviler [ri'vailər], *s.* contempteur, -trice; dénigreur *m.*

reviling[1] [ri'vailiŋ], *a.* injurieux.

reviling[2], *s.* injures *fpl.*

revisable [ri'vaizəbl], *a. Jur:* révisable; (jugement, etc.) sujet à révision.

revisal [ri'vaiz(ə)l], *s.* révision *f.*

revise[1] [ri'va:iz], *s. Typ:* épreuve *f* de révision; seconde *f;* **second r., final r.,** troisième épreuve; tierce *f.*

revise[2], *v.tr.* **1.** (*a*) revoir, relire, réviser (un texte); corriger, réviser (des épreuves); (*b*) *Sch:* repasser, revoir, réviser (une leçon); **to be revised,** à revoir; *v.i.* **to r.,** réviser, faire des révisions. **2.** (*a*) réviser (les lois, la constitution); (*b*) **to r. a decision,** revenir sur une décision; remettre en question une décision.

revised [ri'vaizd], *a.* revu, révisé, corrigé; **the R. Version,** la traduction de la Bible de 1884.

reviser [ri'vaizər], *s.* réviseur *m;* correcteur, -trice (des épreuves).

revising [ri'vaiziŋ], *s.* révision *f.*

revision [ri'viʒ(ə)n], *s.* révision *f; Sch:* **r. notes (in chemistry),** mémento *m* (de chimie); **for r.,** à revoir.

revisional [ri'viʒənl], **revisionary** [ri'viʒən(ə)ri], *a.* révisionnel; de révision.

revisionism [ri'viʒənizm], *s. Pol:* révisionnisme *m.*

revisionist [ri'viʒənist], *a. & s. Pol:* révisionniste (*mf*).

revisit [ri:'vizit], *v.tr.* visiter de nouveau; revisiter; revoir, revenir voir (sa maison natale, etc.).

revisor [ri'vaizər], *s.* = REVISER.

revisory [ri'vaizəri], *a.* de révision; révisionniste.

revisualize [ri:'viʒjuəlaiz], *v.tr.* se représenter de nouveau (un événement passé).

revitalize [ri:'vaitəlaiz], *v.tr.* ranimer, revigorer.

revivable [ri'vaivəbl], *a.* que l'on peut ressusciter, ranimer, ou renouveler.

revival [ri'vaiv(ə)l], *s.* **1.** renaissance *f,* renouvellement *m* (des arts, de l'industrie); réapparition *f* (d'un usage); reprise *f,* relèvement *m* (des affaires); reprise (d'une pièce de théâtre); remise en vigueur (d'une loi); réveil *m,* renouvellement (de la nature); **the r. of trade,** la reprise des affaires; *Hist:* **the r. of learning,** la renaissance des lettres; la Renaissance. **2.** (*a*) retour *m* à la vie; retour des forces; (*b*) reprise des sens. **3.** *Rel:* réveil; **religious r.,** renouveau religieux; retour à la religion (par les masses); revival *m, pl.* revivals; **r. meetings,** réunions *f* dans le but de ranimer la foi (dans une ville, etc.).

revivalist [ri'vaivəlist], *s. Rel:* revivaliste *mf.*

revive [ri'vaiv]. **1.** *v.i.* (*a*) (*of pers.*) ressusciter, revenir à la vie; reprendre connaissance; reprendre ses sens; (*b*) (*of feelings*) se ranimer; se réveiller; renaître; **his spirits revived,** son courage s'est ranimé; **his hopes revived,** il a recommencé à espérer; **to feel one's hopes reviving,** renaître à l'espérance; sentir renaître l'espoir; (*c*) (*of custom, etc.*) se renouveler; reprendre; (*of fashion*) rentrer en vogue; (*of arts*) renaître; (*of business, commerce*) reprendre, se relever; (*of nature*) se réveiller; **industry is reviving,** l'industrie *f* commence à revivre; l'industrie reprend; **credit is reviving,** le crédit se rétablit; (*d*) *Ch:* (*of metal*) se revivifier. **2.** *v.tr.* (*a*) faire revivre (qn); rappeler (qn) à la vie; ressusciter (qn); faire reprendre connaissance à (qn); **that will r. you,** voilà qui vous remontera, qui vous remettra d'aplomb; (*b*) ranimer, faire revivre, faire renaître, renouveler (les espérances); réveiller, ranimer (un désir); rallumer (la colère de qn); raviver (la douleur, l'intérêt); ranimer, réparer (les forces de qn); rappeler, réveiller (un souvenir); renouveler (un usage); ressusciter (un parti politique); remettre en vogue (une mode); remettre en vigueur (une loi); **to r. the arts,** revivifier les arts; faire refleurir les arts; **to r. old connections,** renouer d'anciennes relations; **to r. an old charge,** reproduire une accusation; **to r. the conversation,** ranimer, relever, la conversation; **to r. trade,** ranimer, revivifier, le commerce, les affaires; **to r. s.o.'s drooping spirits,** remonter les esprits abattus de qn; **to r. s.o.'s courage,** remonter le courage de qn; **to r. s.o.'s memory of sth.,** rafraîchir à qn la mémoire de qch.; (*c*) ressusciter (un périodique); réchauffer (une histoire); *Th:* remonter, reprendre (une pièce); (*d*) retaper (un chapeau, un habit); rafraîchir (la peinture, etc.); rendre son lustre à (un métal, un bijou, etc.); **to r. leather,** redonner de la souplesse au cuir; (*e*) *Ch: A:* revivifier (le mercure).

reviver [ri'vaivər], *s.* **1.** celui qui fait revivre, qui ranime, qui renouvelle, qui remet en vogue; ressusciteur *m.* **2.** *F:* (*drink, etc.*) remontant *m;* coup *m* de cognac, de whisky. **3.** encaustique *f* (pour meubles, etc.).

revivification [rivivifi'keiʃ(ə)n], *s.* **1.** revivification *f.* **2.** *Ch: A:* réduction *f.*

revivify [ri'vivifai], *v.tr.* revivifier.

reviving[1] [ri'vaiviŋ], *a.* **1.** (*of strength, hope*) renaissant. **2.** (*of drink, etc.*) remontant.

reviving[2], *s.* **1.** renouvellement *m* (d'un usage, d'une douleur, etc.); remise *f* en vogue (d'une mode); remise en vigueur (d'une loi). **2.** *Th:* reprise *f* (d'une pièce). **3.** rafraîchissement *m* (d'une couleur).

revocability [revəkə'biliti], *s.* révocabilité *f.*

revocable ['revəkəbl], *a.* (*of pers., order, etc.*) révocable; **r. post,** emploi *m* amovible.

revocation [revə'keiʃ(ə)n], *s.* révocation *f* (d'un décret, d'une donation, *A:* d'un fonctionnaire); abrogation *f* (d'un décret); annulation *f.*

revocatory ['revəkətəri], *a.* révocatoire.

revoke[1] [ri'vouk], *s. Cards:* fausse renonce.

revoke[2]. **1.** *v.tr.* (*a*) révoquer (un ordre); révoquer, rapporter (un décret); annuler, contremander, rappeler (un ordre); retirer (son consentement); rétracter (une promesse); *Mil: etc:* **to r. an order,** lever une consigne; (*b*) **to r. a driving licence,** retirer un permis de conduire. **2.** *v.i. Cards:* renoncer à faux; faire une fausse renonce.

revolt[1] [ri'voult], *s.* révolte *f;* **to rise in r.,** se soulever, se révolter (**against,** contre); **to be in r.,** être en sédition, en révolte; **to rouse, stir up, the people to r.,** soulever le peuple.

revolt[2]. **1.** *v.i.* (*a*) se révolter, s'insurger, se soulever, se rebeller (**from, against,** contre); **to induce subjects to r. against their king,** insurger, soulever, des sujets contre leur roi; (*b*) se révolter (**at, against, sth.,** contre qch.); **common sense revolts at, against, such a supposition,** le bon sens se révolte contre une telle supposition. **2.** *v.tr.* (*of action, etc.*) révolter, indigner, dégoûter (qn).

revolted [ri'voultid], *a.* révolté, en révolte.

revolting [ri'voultiŋ], *a.* **1.** (*of action, conduct*) révoltant. **2. the r. troops,** les troupes insurgées, en révolte.

revoltingly [ri'voultiŋli], *adv.* d'une façon révoltante indigne, dégoûtante.

revolute ['revəlu:t], *a. Bot:* révoluté.

revolution [revə'lu:ʃ(ə)n], *s.* **1.** *Astr:* révolution *f* (d'une planète, etc.). **2.** (*a*) rotation *f* (autour d'un axe); (*b*) tour *m,* révolution (d'une roue); volée *f* (des ailes d'un moulin); *Av: Nau:* tour d'hélice; **the engine runs at two thousand revolutions a minute,** la machine fait deux mille tours à la minute; **maximum revolutions,** régime *m* maximum; *Aut: etc:* **r. counter,** indicateur *m* de tours, compte-tours *m inv.* **3.** (*a*) *Pol: etc:* révolution; *Hist:* **the French R.,** la Révolution française; **cultural r.,** révolution culturelle; (*b*) **industrial r.,** révolution industrielle; (*c*) **this new process has brought about a complete r. of the industry,** ce nouveau procédé a complètement transformé l'industrie; **a r. in outlook,** un changement intégral d'orientation.

revolutionary [revə'lu:ʃən(ə)ri]. **1.** *a. & s.* (*a*) révolutionnaire (*mf*); (*b*) **r. invention,** invention *f* qui fait révolution. **2.** *a.* giratoire.

revolutionism [revə'lu:ʃənizm], *s.* révolutionnarisme *m.*

revolutionist [revə'lu:ʃənist], *s.* partisan, -ane, de la révolution; révolutionnaire *mf.*

revolutionize [revə'lu:ʃənaiz], *v.tr.* révolutionner (un pays, la langue, une industrie).

revolve [ri'vɔlv]. **1.** *v.tr.* (*a*) (i) retourner, repasser, rouler (**a problem in one's mind,** un problème dans son esprit); (ii) ruminer (une pensée, etc.); (*b*) faire tourner (les roues, etc.). **2.** *v.i.* (*a*) (*of wheel, etc.*) tourner; **to r. on a spindle,** pivoter, tourner, sur un axe; **the whole household revolves round the baby,** toute la maisonnée tourne autour du bébé; (*b*) **the earth revolves round the sun,** la terre tourne, fait sa révolution, gravite, autour du soleil; (*c*) **the seasons, years, r.,** les saisons, les années, font leur révolution, reviennent.

revolver [ri'vɔlvər], *s.* revolver *m;* **six-chambered r.,** revolver à six coups.

revolving [ri'vɔlviŋ], *a.* **1.** (*a*) (mois *m,* années *f*) qui font leur révolution, qui reviennent; (*b*) *Bank:* **r. credit,** accréditif *m* automatiquement renouvelable. **2.** (corps *m,* planète *f*) en rotation, qui tourne, qui accomplit sa révolution. **3.** *Tchn:* tournant, pivotant, rotatif; à rotation; **r. chair,** fauteuil pivotant, tournant; (*with screw*) fauteuil à vis; **r. furnace,** four tournant; **r. bookcase,** bibliothèque tournante; **r. light,** feu tournant, feu à éclats (d'un phare, etc.); *Cer:* **r. table,** girelle *f* (d'une roue de potier); *Mec.E:* **r. tool holder,** porte-outil(s) *m inv* revolver; **r. crane,** grue *f* à pivot.

revue [ri'vju:], *s. Th:* revue *f;* **short r.,** revuette *f.*

revuist [ri'vju:ist], *s. Th:* revuiste *mf.*

revulsion [ri'vʌlʃ(ə)n], *s.* **1.** (*a*) revirement *m* (de sentiments, etc.); **r. of public feeling in favour of s.o.,** révolution *f* de l'opinion, retour *m* d'opinion, en faveur de qn; **r. from s.o., from a fashion,** réaction *f* contre qn, contre une mode; (*b*) répugnance *f*; écœurement *m*. **2.** *Med:* révulsion *f*.

revulsive [ri'vʌlsiv], *a.* & *s. Med:* révulsif (*m*).

reward[1] [ri'wɔ:d], *s.* **1.** récompense *f*; **a hundred pounds r.,** cent livres *f* de récompense; **to offer a r. for a stolen object,** offrir une récompense pour la restitution d'un objet volé; **to offer a r. for s.o.,** mettre à prix la tête de qn; **as a r. for. . .,** en récompense de. . ., pour prix de . . .; **hanging was the r. of desertion,** la désertion s'expiait sur l'échafaud; **to get a fair r. for, from, one's labour,** tirer de son travail une récompense légitime; *Prov:* **no r. without toil,** nul pain sans peine. **2.** *Publ: A:* livre *m* de prix; livre d'étrennes.

reward[2], *v.tr.* récompenser, rémunérer (**s.o. for sth.,** qn de qch.); **that's how he rewards me for my loyalty,** voilà comment il reconnaît mon dévouement; **to r. s.o. with sth.,** donner qch. en récompense à qn.

rewardable [ri'wɔ:dəbl], *a.* digne de récompense.

rewarder [ri'wɔ:dər], *s.* rémunérateur, -trice.

rewarding [ri'wɔ:diŋ], *a.* (*a*) rémunérateur, -trice; (*b*) **a r. book,** un livre qui vaut (la peine) d'être lu.

rewash [ri:'wɔʃ], *v.tr.* relaver.

reweld [ri:'weld], *v.tr. Metalw:* ressouder.

rewind[1] ['ri:waind], *s.* r(é)embobinage *m*.

rewind[2] [ri:'waind], *v.tr.* (**rewound** [ri:'waund]) **1.** (*a*) rebobiner (la soie, un induit); (*b*) *Cin: Typew: etc:* r(é)embobiner (le film, le ruban). **2.** remonter (une horloge, une montre).

rewinder [ri:'waindər], *s. Cin: etc:* réembobineuse *f*.

rewinding [ri:'waindiŋ], *s.* **1.** (*a*) rebobinage *m*; (*b*) *Typew: Cin: etc:* r(é)embobinage *m*. **2.** remontage *m* (d'une horloge).

rewire [ri:'waiər], *v.tr.* **to r. a house,** remettre à neuf, réaménager, la canalisation électrique d'une maison.

reword [ri:'wə:d], *v.tr.* recomposer, rédiger à nouveau (un paragraphe, etc.).

rewrite[1] ['ri:rait], *s. F:* remaniage *m* (d'un livre, etc.); **r. man,** remanieur *m*.

rewrite[2] [ri:'rait], *v.tr.* (**rewrote** [ri:'rout]; **rewritten** [ri:'rit(ə)n]) récrire, réécrire; remanier (un article, etc.).

rewriter [ri:'raitər], *s.* remanieur, -euse.

Rex [reks]. **1.** *Pr.n.m. Jur:* **R. v. Thomas,** le Roi en cause avec Thomas. **2.** *a. Bot:* **begonia r.,** bégonia *m* rex. **3.** *s. Z:* lapin *m* rex.

Reykjavik ['rekjəvik], *Pr.n. Geog:* Reikiavik *m*.

Reynard ['renɑ:d, 'rei-], *Pr.n.m. Lit:* **R. (the Fox),** maître Renard; compère le renard.

Reynold ['renəld], *Pr.n.m.* Renaud.

rhabditis [ræb'daitis], *s. Ann:* rhabdite *m*, rhabditis *m*.

Rhabdocoelida [ræbdou'si:lidə], *s.pl. Ann:* rhabdocèles *m*.

rhabdolith ['ræbdouliθ], *s. Prot:* rhabdolite *m*.

rhabdom(e) ['ræbdɔm, -doum], *s. Ent:* rhabdome *m*.

rhabdomancer ['ræbdəmænsər], *s.* r(h)abdomancien, -ienne, r(h)abdomant, -ante.

rhabdomancy ['ræbdəmænsi], *s.* r(h)abdomancie *f*, divination *f* à la baguette.

rhabdomyoma [ræbdoumai'oumə], *s. Med:* rhabdomyome *m*.

rhabdophane ['ræbdoufein], **rhabdophanite** [ræb'dɔfənait], *s. Miner:* rhabdophane *f*.

rhabdopleura [ræbdou'pluərə], *s. Z:* rhabdopleura *m*.

Rhacophoridae [rækou'fɔridi:], *s.pl. Amph:* rhacophoridés *m*.

Rhacophorus [ræ'kɔfərəs], *s. Amph:* rhacophore *m*.

Rhadamanthine [rædə'mænθain]; *a. Gr.Myth:* (jugement *m*) de Rhadamante; **R. judge,** juge *m* inflexible.

Rhadamanthus [rædə'mænθəs], *Pr.n.m. Gr.Myth:* Rhadamante.

Rhaetia ['ri:ʃə], *Pr.n. A.Geog:* la Rhétie.

Rhaetian ['ri:ʃən]. **1.** (*a*) *a. Geog:* rhétique; **the R. Alps,** les Alpes rhétiques; (*b*) *a.* & *s. A.Geog:* Rhétien, -ienne. **2.** *s. Ling:* rhétique *m*.

Rhaetic ['ri:tik], *a. Geol:* rhétien; **R. formation,** *s.* **R.,** rhétien *m*.

Rhaeto-Romanic [ri:tourou'mænik], *a.* & *s. Ling:* rhéto-roman (*m*).

Rhagionidae [rædʒi'ɔnidi:], *s.pl. Ent:* rhagionidés *m*.

rhagite ['rægait], *s. Miner:* rhagite *f*.

rhagium ['rægiəm], *s. Ent:* rhagie *f*.

Rhagoletis [rægou'li:tis], *s. Ent:* rhagoletis *m*.

Rhamnaceae [ræm'neisii:], *s.pl. Bot:* rhamnacées *f*.

rhamnaceous [ræm'neiʃəs], *a. Bot:* rhamnacé.

rhamnitol ['ræmnitɔl], *s. Ch:* rhamnite *m*, rhamnitol *m*.

rhamnose ['ræmnous], *s. Ch:* rhamnose *m*.

rhamnoside ['ræmnousaid], *s. Ch:* rhamnoside *m*.

rhamnus ['ræmnəs], *s. Bot:* rhamnus *m*.

Rhamphastidae [ræm'fæstidi:], *s.pl. Orn:* rhamphastidés *m*.

rhamphorhynchid [ræmfou'riŋkid], *s. Paleont:* rhamphorhynque *m*.

rhamphotheca [ræmfou'θi:kə], *s. Orn:* rhamphothèque *f*.

Rhaphidioptera [ræfidi'ɔptərə], *s.pl. Ent:* rhaphidioptères *m*.

rhapsode ['ræpsoud], *s. Gr.Ant:* rhapsode *m*.

rhapsodic(al) [ræp'sɔdik(l)], *a.* rhapsodique; de rhapsodie.

rhapsodist [r'æpsədist], *s.* **1.** (*a*) rhapsode *m*; (*b*) déclamateur, -trice de vers. **2.** rhapsodiste *m*, enthousiaste *mf*.

rhapsodize ['ræpsədaiz], *v.i.* **to r. over sth.,** entonner les louanges de qch.; s'extasier sur qch.

rhapsody ['ræpsədi], *s.* **1.** *Lit: Mus:* rhapsodie *f*. **2.** transports *mpl*; dithyrambe *m*.

rhatany ['rætəni], *s. Bot:* ratanhia *m*.

rhe [ri:], *s. Ph:* rhé *m*.

Rhea ['ri:ə]. **1.** *Pr.n.f. Myth:* Rhée, Rhéa. **2.** *s. Orn:* rhée *f*, nandou *m*; autruche *f* d'Amérique.

rhebok ['ri:bɔk] = REEBOK.

Rheidae ['ri:idi:], *s.pl. Orn:* rhéidés *m*, les nandous *m*.

Rheims [ri:mz], *Pr.n. Geog:* Reims *m*.

Rhemish ['ri:miʃ], *a.* de Reims; Rémois; **the R. Bible, Testament,** la version anglaise du Nouveau Testament publiée à Reims en 1582.

rhenic ['ri:nik], *a. Ch:* rhénique.

Rhenish ['reniʃ, ri:niʃ], *a. Geog:* rhénan; du Rhin; **R. wine,** vin *m* du Rhin.

rhenium ['ri:niəm], *s. Ch:* rhénium *m*.

rheobase ['ri:oubeis], *s. Ph:* rhéobase *f*.

rheograph ['ri:ougræf], *s. El:* rhéographe *m*.

rheolaveur [ri:ou'lævər], *s. Min:* rhéolaveur *m*.

rheology [ri'ɔlədʒi], *s. Ph:* rhéologie *f*.

rheometer [ri'ɔmitər], *s.* **1.** *El: A:* rhéomètre *m*, galvanomètre *m*. **2.** *Hyd.E:* rhéomètre.

rheophil(e) ['ri:oufil, -fail], **rheophilous** [ri'ɔfiləs], *a. Z:* rhéophile.

rheophore ['ri:oufɔ:r], *s. El:* rhéophore *m*.

rheoscope ['ri:ouskoup], *s. El:* rhéographe *m*.

rheoscopic [ri:ou'skɔpik], *a. El:* rhéoscopique.

rheostat ['ri:oustæt], *s. El:* rhéostat *m*; résistance *f* réglable, à curseur; **field r.,** rhéostat, résistance, de champ; **carbon r.,** rhéostat à compression de charbon; **load r.,** rhéostat de charge, d'absorption; **motor-controlled r.,** rhéostat à commande par servomoteur; **potentiometer r.,** rhéostat potentiométrique, en pont; **shunt r., speed regulating r.,** rhéostat de réglage de vitesse; **slide-wire, slider, r.,** rhéostat à curseur; *Veh: etc:* **starting r.,** rhéostat, résistance, de démarrage.

rheostatic [ri:ou'stætik], *a. El:* rhéostatique; **r. starter,** rhéostat *m* de démarrage; *Rail:* **r. braking,** freinage *m* rhéostatique.

rheostriction [ri:ou'strikʃ(ə)n], *s. Elcs:* rhéostriction *f*.

rheotactic [ri:ou'tæktik], *a. Biol:* rhéotaxique.

rheotaxis [ri:ou'tæksis], *s. Biol:* rhéotaxie *f*.

rheotome ['ri:outoum], *s. Med:* rhéotome *m*.

rheotropism [ri:ou'trɔpizm], *s. Biol:* rhéotropisme *m*.

rhesus ['ri:səs], *s.* **1.** *Z:* **r. (monkey),** (macaque *m*) rhésus *m*. **2.** *Physiol:* **R. factor,** facteur *m* Rhésus.

Rhetic ['ri:tik], *a.* & *s.* = RHAETIC.

rhetor ['ri:tɔ:r], *s. Gr.* & *Rom.Ant:* rhéteur *m*. **2.** *Pej:* rhéteur; parleur *m*; phraseur *m*.

rhetoric ['retərik], *s.* **1.** rhétorique *f*, éloquence *f*. **2.** *Pej:* rhétorique, emphase *f*; discours creux.

rhetorical [ri'tɔrik(ə)l], *a.* (*a*) (terme, etc.) de rhétorique; **r. question,** question pour la forme; (*b*) *Pej:* (style, etc.) emphatique, ampoulé.

rhetorically [ri'tɔrik(ə)li], *adv.* **1.** (*a*) suivant les règles de la rhétorique; en rhétoricien; (*b*) (poser une question) pour la forme. **2.** avec emphase; en rhéteur.

rhetorician [retə'riʃ(ə)n], *s.* **1.** (*a*) rhétoricien *m*; (*b*) *Pej:* rhéteur *m*. **2.** *Gr.* & *Rom.Ant:* rhéteur.

rheum[1] [ru:m], *s. A:* **1.** flux muqueux; salive *f*; pituite *f*; (*in the eyes*) chassie *f*. **2.** rhume *m*, catarrhe *m*. **3.** *pl.* **rheums,** rhumatismes *m*.

rheum[2] ['ri:əm], *s. Bot:* rheum *m.inv*.

rheumatic [ru(:)'mætik], *a. Med:* (*of pain, etc.*) rhumatismal, -aux; **r. person, r. patient,** *s.* **r.,** rhumatisant, -ante; **r. fever,** rhumatisme articulaire aigu; fièvre rhumatismale; **r. climate,** climat *m* à rhumatismes; **r. walk,** allure *f* de rhumatisant.

rheumatically [ru(:)'mætik(ə)li], *adv.* **r. affected,** souffrant de rhumatisme; **to walk r.,** avoir une allure de rhumatisant.

rheumaticky [ru(:)'mætiki], *a. F:* rhumatisant, rhumatisé; **to feel r.,** se sentir tout perclus (de rhumatismes).

rheumatics [ru(:)'mætiks], *s.pl. F:* rhumatisme *m*; **to be crippled with the r.,** être perclus de rhumatismes.

rheumatism ['ru(:)mətizm], *s.* rhumatisme *m*; **r. in the joints,** rhumatisme articulaire; **muscular r.,** myodynie *f*; **nodose r., osseous r.,** rhumatisme noueux, déformant; **to suffer from r.,** être sujet au rhumatisme; avoir des rhumatismes.

rheumatoid ['ru(:)mətɔid], *a.* rhumatoïde; **r. arthritis,** rhumatisme *m* articulaire.

rheumatologist [ru(:)mə'tɔlədʒist], *s. Med:* rhumatologue *f*.

rheumatology [ru(:)mə'tɔlədʒi], *s. Med:* rhumatologie *f*.

rheumy ['ru:mi], *a.* qui laisse couler un flux muqueux; **r. eyes,** yeux chassieux; **r.-eyed,** (aux yeux) chassieux.

Rhexia ['reksiə], *s. Bot:* rhexia *m*.

rhexis ['reksis], *s. Med:* rupture *f* d'un vaisseau sanguin.

rhinal ['rain(ə)l], *a.* nasal; du nez; (miroir) de rhinologie.

Rhinanthoideae [rainænθɔ'idii:], *s.pl. Bot:* rhinanthées *f*.

rhinanthus [rai'nænθəs], *s. Bot:* rhinanthe *m*.

rhinarium [rai'nɛəriəm], *s. Z: Ent:* rhinarium *m*.

Rhine (the) [ðə'rain], *Pr.n.m. Geog:* le Rhin; **the Upper, the Lower, R.,** le Haut, le Bas, Rhin; **R. wines,** vins *m* du Rhin.

Rhinegrave ['raingre:iv], *s.m.*, **Rhinegravine** ['raingreivi:n], *s.m. Hist:* Rhingrave.

Rhineland (the) [ðə'rainlənd], *Pr.n. Geog:* les pays rhénans; la Rhénanie.

Rhinelander ['rainlændər], *s.* Rhénan, -ane.

rhinencephalon [rainen'sefəlɔn], *s. Anat:* rhinencéphale *m*.

rhinencephalus [rainen'sefələs], *s. Ter:* rhinencéphale *m*, rhinocéphale *m*.

rhinestone ['rainstoun], *s. Lap:* **1.** caillou *m* du Rhin (en cristal de roche). **2.** faux diamant; strass *m*.

rhinitis [ri'naitis], *s. Med:* rhinite *f*; **chronic r.,** coryza *m* chronique.

rhino[1] ['rainou], *s. P: A:* argent *m*, *P:* pèze *m*, galette *f*.

rhino[2], *s. Z: F:* rhinocéros *m*.

Rhinobatidae [rainou'bætidi:], *s.pl. Ich:* rhinobatidés *m*.

rhinobatos [rai'nɔbætɔs], *s. Ich:* rhinobatos *m*.

rhinocephalus [rainou'sefələs], *s. Ter:* rhinencéphale *m*, rhinocéphale *m*.

rhinoceros [rai'nɔsərəs], *s.* **1.** *Z:* rhinocéros *m*; *F:* **she has a hide like a r.,** elle a une peau d'éléphant. **2.** *Ent:* **r. beetle,** rhinocéros.

Rhinocerotidae [rainɔsə'rɔtidi:], *s.pl. Z:* rhinocérotidés *m*.

rhinolalia [rainou'leiliə], *s. Med:* rhinolalie *f*.

rhinolaryngitis [rainoulærin'dʒaitis], *s. Med:* rhinolaryngite *f*.

rhinology [rai'nɔlədʒi], *s. Med:* rhinologie *f*.

Rhinolophidae [rainou'lɔfidi:], *s.pl. Z:* rhinolophidés *m*.

rhinoncus [rai'nɔŋkəs], *s. Ent:* rhinoncus *m*.

rhinonecrosis [rainoune'krousis], *s. Med:* rhinonécrose *f*.

rhino-pharyngeal [rainoufæ'rindʒiəl], *a. Med:* rhinopharyngien.

rhinopharynx [rainou'færiŋks], *s. Anat:* rhino-pharynx *m*.

rhinophonia [rainou'founiə], *s. Med:* rhinophonie *f*.

rhinophore ['rainoufɔ:r], *s. Moll:* rhinophore *m*.

rhinophyma [rainou'faimə], *s. Med:* rhinophyma *m*.

rhinoplastic [rainou'plæstik], *a. Surg:* rhinoplastique.

rhinoplasty ['rainouplæsti], *s. Surg:* rhinoplastie *f*.

rhinoptera [rai'nɔptərə], *s. Ich:* rhinoptera *f*.

rhinorrhagia [rainou'reidiʒə], *s. Med:* rhinorragie *f*.

rhinorrhœa [rainou'roə], *s. Med:* rhinorrhée *f*.

rhinosalpingitis [rainousælpin'dʒaitis], *s. Med:* rhinosalpingite *f*.

rhinoscleroma, *pl.* **-ata** [rainouskle'roumə, -ətə], *s. Med:* rhinosclérome *m*.

rhinoscope ['rainouskoup], *s. Surg:* speculum *m* nasi.

rhinoscopy [rai'nɔskəpi], *s. Surg:* rhinoscopie *f*.

rhinosimus [rainou'saiməs], *s. Ent:* rhinosime *m*.

rhinotheca, *pl.* **-ae** [rai'nɔθikə, -i:], *s. Orn:* rhinothèque *f*.

rhinotomy [rai'nɔtəmi], *s. Surg:* rhinotomie *f*.

Rhipidoglossa [ripidou'glɔsə], *s.pl. Moll:* rhipidoglosses *m*.

Rhipiphoridae [ripi'fɔridi:], *s.pl. Ent:* rhipiphoridés *m*.

Rhipiptera [ri'piptərə], *s.pl. Ent:* rhipiptères *m*.

rhizina [ri'zainə], **rhizine** ['raizi:n], *s. Moss:* rhizine *m*.

rhizo- ['rəizou, 'raizə, rai'zou, rai'zɔ], *comb.fm.* rhizo-.

rhizobium [rai'zoubiəm], *s. Bac:* rhizobium *m*.

rhizobius [rai'zoubiəs], *s. Ent:* rhizobius *m*.

rhizocarp ['raizoukɑ:p], *s. Bot:* rhizocarpée *f*.

Rhizocarpiae [raizou'kɑ:pii:], *s.pl.* rhizocarpes *f*.

rhizocarpian [raizou'kɑ:piən], **rhizocarpic** [raizou'kɑ:pik], **rhizocarpous** [raizou'kɑ:pəs], *a. Bot:* rhinzocarpé, rhizocarpique; rhizocarpien, -ienne.

Rhizocephala [raizou'sefələ], *s.pl. Crust:*

rhizocéphales *m.*
rhizocephalan [raizou'sefələn], *s. Crust:* rhizocéphale *m.*
rhizocephalous [raizou'sefələs], *a. Crust:* rhizocéphale.
rhizocrinus [raizou'krainəs], *s. Z:* rhizocrinus *m.*
Rhizoctonia [raizɔk'tounia], *s. Fung:* rhizoctonie *f*, rhizoctone *m.*
Rhizoflagellata [raizouflædʒi'leitə], *s.pl. Prot:* rhizoflagellés *m.*
rhizoflagellate [raizou'flædʒileit], *a. & s. Prot:* rhizoflagellé (*m*).
rhizogenetic [raizoudʒə'netik], **rhizogenic** [raizou'dʒenik], **rhizogenous** [rai'zɔdʒənəs], *a. Bot:* rhizogène.
rhizoglyphous [raizou'glifəs], *s. Ent:* rhizoglyphe *m.*
rhizoid ['raizɔid], *s. Bot:* rhizoïde *f.*
Rhizomastigina [raizoumæ'stidʒinə], *s.pl. Prot:* rhizomastigines *f.*
rhizomatic [raizou'mætik], **rhizomatous** [rai'zoumətəs], *a. Bot:* rhizomateux.
rhizome ['raizoum], *s. Bot:* rhizome *m.*
rhizomelic [raizou'melik], *a. Anat:* rhizomélique.
rhizomorph ['raizoumɔ:f], *s. Fung:* rhizomorphe *m.*
rhizomorphous [raizou'mɔ:fəs], *a.* rhizomorphe.
rhizomucor [raizou'mju:kɔ:r], *s. Med:* rhizomucor *m.*
rhizomyidae [raizou'maiidi:], *s.pl. Z:* rhizomyidés *m.*
rhizomys [rai'zoumis], *s. Z:* rhizomys *m.*
rhizopertha [raizou'pə:θə], *s. Ent:* rhizoperthe *m.*
rhizophagous [rai'zɔfəgəs], *a. Z: Ent:* rhizophage, radicivore.
Rhizophora [rai'zɔfərə], *s. Bot:* rhizophora *m*, rhizophore *m.*
Rhizophoraceae [raizoufɔ'reisii:], *s.pl. Bot:* rhizophoracées *f.*
rhizoplast ['raizouplæst], *s. Bot:* rhizoplaste *m.*
rhizopod ['raizoupɔd], *s. Prot:* rhizopode *m.*
Rhizopoda [rai'zɔpədə], *s.pl. Prot:* rhizopodes *m.*
rhizopodous [rai'zɔpədəs], *a. Prot:* rhizopode.
rhizopus ['raizoupəs], *s. Fung:* rhizopus *m.*
rhizosphere ['raizousfi:ər], *s. Bot:* rhizosphère *f.*
Rhizostomata [raizou'stoumətə], **Rhizostomae** [raizou'stoumi:], *s.pl. Coel:* rhizostomidés *m.*
rhizostome ['raizoustoum], *s. Coel:* rhizostome *m.*
rhizotaxis [raizou'tæksis], *s. Bot:* rhizotaxie *f.*
rhizotomy [rai'zɔtəmi], *s. Surg:* rhizotomie *f.*
rho [rou], *s. Gr.Alph:* rhô *m.*
rhodamin(e) ['roudəmi(:)n], *s. Ch:* rhodamine *f.*
rhodanthe [rou'dænθi], *s. Bot:* rhodante *m.*
Rhode Island Red ['roudailənd'red], *s. Husb:* coq *m*, poule *f*, de la race de Rhode Island.
rhodeose ['roudious], *s. Ch:* rhodéose *m.*
Rhodes[1] [roudz], *Pr.n. Geog:* **1.** (l'île *f* de) Rhodes *f.* **2.** **the Inner, the Outer, R.,** les Rhodes intérieures, extérieures (de la Suisse).
Rhodes[2], *Pr.n. Hist:* Rhodes: *Sch:* **R. scholar,** boursier *m* de la fondation Cecil Rhodes.
Rhodesia [rou'di:siə, -ziə], *Pr.n. Geog:* Rhodésie *f.*
Rhodesian [rou'di:siən, -ziən]. **1.** *a.* rhodésien; de Rhodésie; *Paleont:* **R. man,** l'homme de Rhodésie. **2.** *s.* Rhodésien, -ienne.
Rhodeus ['roudiəs], *s. Ich:* rhodeus *m.*
Rhodian ['roudiən]. *Geog:* (*a*) *a.* rhodién; (*b*) *s.* Rhodien, -ienne.
rhodic ['roudik], *a. Ch:* rhodique.
rhodinol ['roudinɔl], *s. Ch:* rhodinol *m.*
rhodite ['roudait], *s. Miner:* rhodite *f.*
rhodium[1] ['roudiəm], *s. Ch:* rhodium *m*; **to plate with r.,** rhodier.
rhodium[2], *s. Bot:* **r. (wood),** bois *m* de rose; bois de Rhodes; **oil of r.,** essence *f* de bois de rose.
rhodizionic [roudizai'ɔnik], *a. Ch:* (acide) rhodizionique.
rhodizite ['roudizait], *s. Miner:* rhodizite *f.*
rhodizonic [roudi'zɔnik], *a. Ch:* (acide) rhodizonique.
rhodochrosite [roudou'krousait], *s. Miner:* rhodochrosite *f*, manganspath *m.*
rhododendron, *pl.* **-ons, -a** [roudə'dendrən, -ənz, -ə], *s. Bot:* rhododendron *m*; **rusty-leaved r.,** rosagine *f.*
Rhodoid ['roudɔid], *s. R.t.m.* Rhodoïde *m.*
rhodolite ['roudəlait], *s. Miner:* rhodolite *f.*
rhodonite ['rɔdənait], *s. Miner:* rhodonite *f*; rubinspath *m.*
Rhodophyceae [roudou'faisii:], *s.pl. Algae:* rhodophycées *f.*
rhodopsin [rou'dɔpsin], *s. Bio-Ch:* rhodopsine *f.*
rhodospermous [roudou'spə:məs], *a. Bot:* rhodosperme.
rhodotypos [roudou'tipɔs], *s. Bot:* rhodotypos *m.*
Rhodymenia [roudi'mi:niə], *s. Algae:* rhodyménie *f*, rhodyménia *m.*
Rhoeadales [riə'deili:z], *s.pl. Bot:* rhœadales *f.*
rhomb [rɔm(b)], *s.* **1.** *Geom:* losange *m*; rhombe *m.* **2.** *Cryst:* rhomboèdre *m.*
rhombencephalon [rɔmben'sefəlɔn], *s. Anat:* rhombencéphale *m*, arrière-cerveau *m*, *pl.* arrière-cerveaux.
rhombic ['rɔmbik], *a.* rhombique, rhombe.
rhombiform ['rɔmbifɔ:m], *a. Cryst:* rhombiforme.
rhombohedral [rɔmbou'hi:drəl, -'hedrəl], *a. Cryst:* rhomboédrique.
rhombohedron, *pl.* **-a** [rɔmbou'hi:drən, -'hedrən, -ə], *s. Cryst:* rhomboèdre *m.*
rhomboid ['rɔmbɔid], *a. & s. Mth:* rhomboïde (*m*); *Anat:* **r. (muscle),** (muscle *m*) rhomboïde.
rhomboidal [rɔm'bɔid(ə)l], *a.* rhomboïdal, -aux; (muscle *m*) rhomboïde.
rhomboideus [rɔm'bɔidiəs], *s. Anat:* (muscle *m*) rhomboïde.
rhombus, *pl.* **-uses, -i** ['rɔmbəs, -əsiz, -ai], *s.* **1.** *Mth:* rhombus *m*, rhombe *m.* **2.** *Ich:* rhombe.
rhonchal ['rɔŋk(ə)l], *a. Med:* **r. breathing,** respiration râlante.
rhonchus, *pl.* **-i** ['rɔŋkəs, -ai], *s. Med:* rhonchus *m*; râle ronflant.
Rhone (the) [roun (ðə)], *Pr.n. Geog:* le Rhône; **the R. valley,** la vallée du Rhône; la vallée rhodanienne; **R. (valley) wines,** côtes *m* du Rhône.
rhopalium, *pl.* **-ia** [rou'peiliəm, -iə], *s. Coel:* rhopalie *f.*
Rhopalocera [roupə'lɔsərə], *s.pl. Ent:* rhopalocères *m.*
rhopaloceral, rhopalocerous [roupə'lɔsərəl, -əs], *a. Ent:* rhopalocère.
rhotacism ['routəsizm], *s. Ling:* rhotacisme *m.*
rhubarb ['ru:bɑ:b], *s.* **1.** *Bot: Pharm:* rhubarbe *f*; **Chinese r.,** rhubarbe de Chine; **Russian r.,** rhubarbe de Moscovie; **Turkey r.,** rhubarbe de Turquie; **Batavian r.,** rhubarbe batave; **East Indian r.,** rhubarbe des Indes; *Bot: Cu:* **common, garden, r.,** rhubarbe rhapontic. **2.** *Bot:* **prickly r.,** gunnère *f.*
rhumb [rʌm(b)], *s. Nau:* r(h)umb *m*; **r. line, A: r.,** (i) ligne *f* de rumb; (*on chart*) loxodromie *f*; (ii) rumb *m* de vent.
rhumbatron ['rʌmbətrɔn], *s. Elcs:* rhumbatron *m.*
rhus [rʌs], *s. Bot:* rhus *m.*
rhyacophil [rai'ækɔfil], *s. Ent:* rhyacophile *m.*
Rhyacophilidae [raiækɔ'filidi:], *s.pl. Ent:* rhyacophiles *m.*
rhyme[1] [raim], *s.* **1.** *Pros:* rime *f*; **masculine rhymes, feminine rhymes,** rimes masculines, féminines; **rhymes in couplets,** rimes plates, suivies; **alternate rhymes,** rimes croisées, alternées; **enclosing rhymes,** rimes embrassées; **rich r., perfect r.,** rime riche; **double r.,** rime double; rime léonine; **eye, sight, printer's, r.,** rime pour l'œil; **to look for a r. to a word,** chercher une rime à un mot; **without r. or reason,** sans rime ni raison; à tort et à travers; **there's neither r. nor reason about it,** cela ne rime à rien; cela n'a ni rime ni raison. **2.** *usu.pl.* vers (rimés); poésie *f*; **in r.,** en vers; **to put sth. into r.,** mettre qch. en vers.
rhyme[2]. **1.** *v.i.* (*a*) rimer; rimailler; faire des vers; (*b*) se servir de la rime; (*c*) (*of words*) rimer (**with,** avec); **to r. on paper,** rimer aux, pour les, yeux. **2.** *v.tr.* (*a*) faire rimer (des vers, des mots); **to r. a word with another,** faire rimer un mot avec un autre; (*b*) mettre en vers (un récit, ses pensées); (*c*) **to r. a sonnet,** écrire un sonnet.
rhymed [raimd], *a.* rimé; en vers (rimés).
rhyming[1] ['raimiŋ], *a. Pros:* rimé.
rhyming[2], *s.* **1.** recherche *f* de la rime; **r. dictionary,** dictionnaire *m* de rimes. **2.** *F:* versification *f.*
rhymeless ['raimlis], *a.* sans rime.
rhymer ['raimər], *s.* rimeur *m*; versificateur *m.*
rhymester ['raimstər], *s. Pej:* rimailleur *m*; poét(r)aillon *m.*
rhynchites [riŋ'kaiti:z], *s. Ent:* rhynchite *m.*
Rhynchobdellida [riŋkoub'delidə], *s.pl. Z:* rhynchobdellidés *m.*
Rhynchocephalia [riŋkouse'feiliə], *s.pl. Rept:* rhynchocéphales *m.*
rhynchocyon [riŋkou'saiɔn], *s. Z:* rhynchocyon *m.*
Rhynchonella [riŋkou'nelə], *s. Paleont:* rhynchonelle *f.*
Rhynchophora [riŋ'kɔfərə], *s.pl. Ent:* rhynchophores *m.*
rhynchophoran [riŋ'kɔfərən], *s.* rhynchophore *m.*
Rhynchospora [riŋkou'spɔ:rə], *s.pl. Bot:* rhynchospores *m.*
Rhynchota [riŋ'koutə], *s.pl.* rhynchotes *m.*
rhynia ['rainiə], *s. Bot: Paleont:* rhynia *f.*
rhyolite ['raioulait], *s. Miner:* rhyolit(h)e *f*, liparite *f.*
rhyparographer [ripə'rɔgrəfər], *s. Art:* rhyparographe *m.*
rhyparography [ripə'rɔgrəfi], *s. Art:* rhyparographie *f.*
rhyssa ['risə], *s. Ent:* rhysse *f.*
rhythm ['riðm], *s.* rythme *m*, cadence *f*; **to give r. to one's sentences,** cadencer ses phrases; **r. of work,** cadence de travail; *Mus:* **r. section,** section *f* rythmique (d'un orchestre de jazz, etc.).
rhythmic(al) ['riðmik(l)], *a.* rythmique, cadencé; **r. tread,** marche scandée.
rhythmically ['riðmik(ə)li], *adv.* avec rythme; avec cadence; *Mus:* en scandant bien la mesure.
rhytina [ri'ti:nə, -tainə], *s. Z:* rhytine *f* de Steller.
ria ['ri:ə], *s. Geog:* ria *f*; **r. coast,** côte *f* à rias.
rib[1] [rib], *s.* **1.** (*a*) *Anat:* côte *f*; **r. cage,** cage *f* thoracique; **true ribs, sternal ribs,** vraies côtes; **false ribs, short ribs, asternal ribs,** fausses côtes; côtes flottantes, asternales; *Cu:* **r. of beef,** côte de bœuf; **wing r.,** côte d'aloyau; **spare ribs,** côtes (découvertes) de porc; *F:* **you can see his ribs, his ribs stick out,** on lui voit, on lui compterait, les côtes; *A:* **to smite s.o. under the fifth r.,** tuer, poignarder, qn; (*b*) *A: & Lit:* épouse *f*, femme *f*; (allusion à la création d'Ève.) **2.** (*a*) *Nat.Hist:* nervure *f* (d'une feuille, d'une aile d'insecte); projecture *f* (d'une feuille); strie *f* (d'une coquille); (*b*) nervure (d'une voûte, d'une pièce venue de fonte); arête *f* (d'une baïonnette, d'une lame); *Bookb:* nervure; *Av:* ailette *f*; nervure; *Arch:* ogive *f*; **transverse r.,** doubleau *m*; **ridge r.,** lierne *f*; **intersecting ribs,** croisée *f* d'ogives; **wall r.,** (arc *m*) formeret *m*; **ribs of the treads of a comb escalator,** tasseaux *m* des marches d'un escalator à peignes; *I.C.E:* **ribs of a piston,** nervures d'un piston; **cooling ribs,** ailettes (de radiateur, de piston, etc.); *Nau:* **ribs of the parrel,** bigots *m* de racage; **ribs of the windlass,** taquets *m* du guindeau; *Mec.E:* **guide r.,** nervure-guide *f*, *pl.* nervures-guides; (*c*) (i) *Agr:* billon *m*; (ii) **the ribs left on the sand,** les rides laissées sur le sable (de la plage); (*d*) arête (d'une chaîne de montagnes); (*e*) *Min:* planche *f* (de charbon); pillier *m* de sûreté; (*f*) *Knit: Tex:* côte; (*g*) (*of melon, etc.*) côte. **3.** (*a*) support *m*, étançon *m*, entretoise *f*, ferme *f* (d'un échafaudage, etc.); baleine *f* (de parapluie); brin *m* (d'éventail); armature *f* (d'un foyer); *Av:* nervure, travée *f* (d'une aile); (*b*) *N.Arch:* membre *m*, membrure *f*; (*c*) *Typ:* coulisse *f* (d'une presse); (*d*) *Gym:* **r. stalls, ribs,** échelle suédoise, espalier *m.* **4.** éclisse *f* (de violon).
rib[2], *v.tr.* (**ribbed**) **1.** garnir (qch.) de côtes, de nervures; nervurer, renforcer (un carter, etc.); munir d'ailettes (un radiateur, etc.); rider (le métal, etc.); baleiner (un parapluie). **2.** *F:* taquiner (qn). **3.** labourer à demi (un champ); labourer (un champ) en billons.
ribald ['r(a)ibəld]. **1.** *a.* licencieux, obscène, impudique, paillard; **r. song,** chanson paillarde, grivoise; **r. joke,** paillardise *f*; **r. laughter,** rire gras. **2.** *s.* (*a*) *A: & Lit:* ribaud, -aude; paillard, -arde; (*b*) homme grossier, éhonté, aux propos orduriers.
ribaldry ['r(a)ibəldri], *s.* paillardises *fpl*; langage licencieux; obscénités *fpl*; grivoiserie *f.*
riband ['ribənd], *s.* ruban *m.*
ribband ['ribənd], *s.* **1.** (*a*) *Av: N.Arch:* lisse *f*, listeau *m*, fleuriau *m*; (*b*) *Mil.E:* guindage *m* (d'un pont de bateaux). **2.** ruban *m.*
ribbed [ribd], *a.* **1.** (coquillage) strié; (verre) à côtes, cannelé; (plafond *m*, radiateur *m*, etc.) à nervures; (sable) ridé; (édifice, etc.) ossaturé (**with,** de); *Arch:* **r. vault,** voûte *f* d'ogives, à nervures; *Const:* **r. frame,** bâti *m* à nervures; *Ind:* **r. plate,** fer *m* à nervure(s), à côte(s); **r. pipe,** tuyau *m* à ailettes; **r. housing,** carter nervuré. **2.** (bas, velours) à côtes, côtelé; *Crochet:* **r. stitch,** point *m* à côtes. **3.** *Bot:* (*of leaf*) à nervures, nervuré, nervifolié.
ribbing ['ribiŋ], *s.* **1.** *Ind: Mec.E:* nervurage *m.* **2.** *coll.* côtes *fpl* (d'un bas, etc.); nervures *fpl* (d'une feuille). **3.** *F:* taquinage *m.*
ribbon ['ribən], *s.* **1.** (*a*) ruban *m*; **to tie up one's hair with a r.,** attacher ses cheveux avec un ruban; *Typew:* **(inking) r.,** ruban (encreur); **r. factory,** fabrique *f* de rubans; rubanerie *f*; **r. industry, trade,** rubanerie; industrie rubanière; **r. maker, manufacturer,** rubanier, -ière; *Irish Hist:* **the R. Society,** la société secrète catholique fomentatrice de troubles agrariens (au début du XIXe siècle); (*b*) *Ich:* **r. fish,** (i) cépole *m*, fouet *m*; (ii) régalec *m*; (iii) gros-argentin *m*, trachyptère *m*; *Bot:* **r. grass,** phalaris *m*; roseau panaché; *Ann:* **r. worm,** némerte *f.* **2.** (*a*) ruban (d'une décoration); cordon *m* (d'un ordre); **blue r.,** ruban bleu; (*b*) *Navy:* **cap r.,** ruban légendé (du béret). **3.** *Equit: A: F:* **ribbons,** guides *f*; **to handle, hold, the ribbons,** tenir les guides; conduire. **4.** (*a*) ruban (de magnésium); (*b*) **steel r.,** ruban d'acier; feuillard *m*; (*c*) **r. brake,** frein *m* à ruban; **r. saw,** scie *f* à ruban, sans fin. **5.** bande *f*, ruban (de terre, de route, etc.); lambeau *m* (de ciel); **a long r. of white road,** un long ruban de route blanche; **r. development,** extension urbaine en bordure de route; *Miner:* **r. agate,** agate rubanée. **6.** *pl.* lambeaux; **to tear sth. to ribbons,** mettre qch. en lambeaux; déchiqueter qch.; **flag reduced to ribbons,** drapeau réduit en lanières.

ribboned ['ribənd], *a.* **1.** orné, garni, de rubans; enrubanné. **2.** *Nat.Hist: etc:* rubané, rubanaire.
ribes ['raibi:z], *s. Bot:* ribes *m*, groseillier *m.*
ribgrass ['ribgrɑ:s], *s. Bot:* plantain lancéolé; herbe *f* aux cinq coutures.
riboflavin(e) [raibou'fleivi(:)n], *s. Ch:* riboflavine *f*, rivoflavine *f*, lactoflavine *f.*
ribonic [rai'bɔnik], *a. Ch:* (acide) ribonique.
ribonuclease [raibou'nju:kleis], *s. Ch:* ribonucléase *f.*
ribonucleic [raibounju'kli:ik], *a. Ch:* (acide) ribonucléique.
ribonucleoprotein [raibounju:kliou'prouti:n], *s. Ch:* ribonucléoprotéide *m.*
ribose ['raibous], *s. Ch:* ribose *m.*
ribwort ['ribwə:t], *s. Bot:* = RIBGRASS.
riccia ['ritʃiə], *s. Moss:* riccie *f.*
ricciocarpus [ritʃiou'kɑ:pəs], *s. Bot:* ricciocarpus *m.*
rice [rais], *s.* **1.** *(a) Bot:* riz *m*; **r. straw,** paille *f* de riz; **r. grower,** riziculteur *m*; **r. growing,** riziculture *f*, culture *f* du riz; **r.-growing country,** pays rizier; **r. plantation, r. swamp,** rizière *f*; *(b)* **long grain, short grain, r.,** riz à grains longs, courts; **rough r.,** riz non décortiqué; paddy *m*; **husked r.,** riz décortiqué; **r. mill,** rizerie *f*; *(pers.)* **r. polisher,** rizier *m* glacier; **milled r., whitened r.,** riz blanc; **polished r., bright r.,** riz glacé; **ground r.,** farine *f* de riz; *Cu:* **r. pudding,** riz au lait; **r. shape, r. mould,** gâteau *m* de riz; *Cer:* **r.-grain decoration,** décoration *f* en grain de riz; **r.-stone glass,** verre *m* de riz, d'albâtre; **r. water,** eau *f* de riz; *Med:* **r.-water evacuations,** selles *f* riziformes; **r. paper,** papier *m* de riz; papier de Chine; *(c) Orn:* **r. bird,** (i) agripenne *m*; (ii) oiseau *m* de riz; *Z:* **r. rat,** rice-rat *m*, *pl.* rice-rats, oryzomys *m.* **2.** *Bot:* **Canadian (wild) r., Indian r.,** zizanie *f*; riz du Canada.
rice², *v.tr. Cu: U.S:* passer (des légumes) au presse-purée.
ricer ['raisər], *s. Cu: U.S:* presse-purée *m. inv.*
ricercar(e) [ri:tʃɛə'kɑ:r, -'kɑ:re], *s. Mus:* ricercare *m.*
rich [ritʃ], *a.* **1.** (personne, société) riche; **r. people,** *s.* **the r.,** les riches *m*; **r. man, woman,** richard, -arde; **extremely r.,** richissime; **as r. as Croesus,** *A:* **as a Jew,** riche comme Crésus; **r. and poor,** les riches et les pauvres; **the new, newly, r.,** les nouveaux riches; les parvenus *m*; **to grow r.,** s'enrichir; **this invention made him r.,** cette invention l'a enrichi. **2.** *(of country)* riche; *(of soil)* riche, fertile; **r. pastures,** gras pâturages; **r. vegetation,** végétation *f* riche; **r. concrete, r. limestone,** béton, calcaire, gras; **r. clay,** argile grasse; **r. language,** langue *f* riche; **r. in . . .,** riche en . . ., abondant en . . .; **book r. in information,** livre *m* riche de faits; **museum r. in paintings,** musée *m* riche en tableaux; **r. in hope,** riche d'espérances. **3.** (toilette *f*) magnifique; (meubles) de luxe, luxueux; (festin) somptueux. **4.** *(a)* **r. dish,** (i) plat grass; (ii) plat composé d'ingrédients de choix; (iii) plat de haut goût; plat fortement relevé; **I can't eat r. food,** je ne digère pas les plats gras; **r. cake,** gâteau où il entre beaucoup de beurre et d'œufs; **r. wine,** vin généreux, corsé, qui a du corps; *(b) I.C.E:* **r. mixture,** mélange *m* riche; carburation *f* riche. **5. r. colour,** couleur chaude; **the r. green of the tropics,** le vert intense des tropiques; **r. voice,** voix étoffée, ample, pleine; **r. smell,** parfum très fort; **r. style,** style riche, abondant. **6.** *F:* *(of incident, situation)* très divertissant; absurde, impayable, épatant.
Richard ['ritʃəd], *Pr.n.m.* Richard; *Lit:* **poor R.,** le Bonhomme Richard; *Jur:* **R. Roe, R. Miles** = M. Dubois.
richardia [ri'tʃɑ:diə], *s. Bot:* richardia *m*, richardie *f.*
richardsonia [ritʃəd'souniə], *s. Bot:* richardsonia *m.*
richellite [ri'ʃelait], *s. Miner:* richellite *f.*
riches ['ritʃiz], *s.pl.* richesse(s) *f(pl)*; **to amass great r.,** amasser de grandes richesses; **he had great r.,** il était très riche.
richly ['ritʃli], *adv.* **1.** richement, avec opulence; somptueusement, magnifiquement. **2.** *(a)* richement, abondamment, amplement, grandement; *(b)* entièrement; **he r. deserves it,** il l'a bien mérité.
richness ['ritʃnis], *s.* **1.** richesse *f*, abondance *f.* **2.** richesse (du sol); fertilité *f.* **3.** somptuosité *f*, magnificence *f*, luxe *m.* **4.** *(a)* richesse en principes nutritifs (d'un aliment); générosité *f* (du vin); *(b) I.C.E:* **r. of the mixture,** richesse du mélange. **5.** ampleur *f* (de la voix); richesse, coloris *m* (du style); **r. of colour,** chaleur *f* des tons.
ricinoleate [risi'noulieit], *s. Ch:* ricinoléate *m.*
ricinoleic [risinou'li:ik], *a. Ch:* (acide) ricinoléique.
ricinolein [risi'nouliin], *s. Ch:* ricinoléine *f.*
Ricinulei [risi'nju:lii:], *s.pl. Arach:* ricinuléides *m.*
ricinus ['risinəs], *s. Bot:* ricin *m.*
rick¹ [rik], *s.* meule *f* (de foin); **r. cloth,** bâche *f* de meule; **r. stand,** support *m*, tréteau *m*, de meule.
rick², *v.tr.* mettre (le foin) en meule(s); ameulonner (le foin).
rick³,⁴, *s. & v.tr.* = WRICK¹,².
rickardite ['rikɑ:dait], *s. Miner:* rickardite *f.*
ricker ['rikər], *s. Nau:* étance volante.
ricketiness ['rikitinis], *s.* manque *m* de solidité, état boiteux, disloquement *m*, état branlant (d'un meuble, etc.).
rickets ['rikits], *s.pl. Med:* **1.** rachitisme *m*, rachitis *m*, nouure *f*; **to have r.,** être rachitique; *F:* être noué. **2.** *(sg. in combination)* **ricket-producing,** qui engendre le rachitisme.
rickettsia [ri'ketsiə], *s. Med: Biol:* rickettsie *f.*
rickettsiosis [riketsi'ousis], *s. Med:* rickettsiose *f.*
rickety ['rikiti], *a.* **1.** *Med:* rachitique, *F:* noué; **to become r.,** devenir rachitique; se nouer. **2.** *F:* *(a)* **r. legs,** jambes chancelantes; *(b)* (esprit) boiteux, qui manque d'assiette; **r. ideas,** idées mal assises. **3.** (escalier) branlant, délabré; (pont) branlant; (fauteuil) bancal, (meubles) bancaux; **r. table,** table boiteuse, branlante, mal affermie sur ses pieds; **r. old car,** vieille voiture disloquée; **to be in a r. state,** ne tenir ni à fer ni à clou.
rickshaw ['rikʃɔ:], *s.* pousse-pousse *m inv*; **r. man,** pousse-pousse.
rickyard ['rikjɑ:d], *s.* cour *f* de ferme; pailler *m.*
ricochet¹ ['rikəʃei, *occ.* -ʃet], *s. Artil:* ricochet *m*; **r. fire, firing,** feu *m* par ricochet; tir *m* ricochet.
ricochet², *v.* (**ricochetted** ['rikəʃeid, -ʃetid], **ricochetting** ['rikəʃeiiŋ, -ʃetiŋ]) **1.** *v.i. (of projectile)* ricocher. **2.** *v.tr. Artil:* ricocher (une face d'ouvrage); battre (un ouvrage) à ricochets.
rictus ['riktəs], *s.* rictus *m.*
rid [rid], *v.tr.* (*p.t.* **ridded, rid;** *p.p.* **rid;** *pr.p.* **ridding**) débarrasser, délivrer (**s.o. of sth.,** qn de qch.); débarrasser (**a place of sth.,** un endroit de qch.); **to r. a country of bandits,** purger un pays de bandits; **to r. s.o. of his enemies,** délivrer qn de ses ennemis; **he was r. of a troublesome rival,** il était délivré d'un rival incommode; **to r. one's estate of debt,** purger ses terres de dettes; **to get r. of sth., to r. oneself of sth.,** se débarrasser, se défaire, de qch.; **to r. oneself of an idea,** s'ôter une idée de la tête; **to r. oneself of an obligation,** se libérer d'une obligation; **I've got r. of my car,** j'ai bazardé ma voiture; *Com:* **it is hard to get r. of these articles,** ces articles sont d'écoulement difficile; **to get r. of old stock,** écouler de la vieille marchandise; *Cards:* **to get r. of a card,** se défausser d'une carte; **to get r. of one's clubs,** se défausser à trèfle; *Mth:* **to get r. of x, y,** éliminer x, y; **to get r. of s.o.,** (i) se débarrasser de qn; *F:* se dépêtrer de qn; *(politely)* éconduire qn; renvoyer (un domestique); *F:* balayer, débarquer (un ministre, etc.); (ii) faire disparaître qn; supprimer qn; se défaire (d'un ennemi, d'un rival); **when she comes to see one, there's no getting r. of her,** quand elle vient en visite elle prend racine chez les gens.
ridable ['raidəbl], *a.* = RIDEABLE.
riddance ['rid(ə)ns], *s.* *(a)* débarras *m*; **good r.!** bon débarras! *(b)* délivrance *f* (**from,** de).
riddel ['rid(ə)l], *s. Ecc:* rideau *m* (d'autel).
ridden ['rid(ə)n], *a.* *(with noun prefixed)* *(of locality)* **gangster-r.,** infesté de gangsters; **cliché-r. language,** langage plein de clichés.
riddle¹ ['ridl], *s.* énigme *f*, devinette *f*; **to ask s.o. a r.,** proposer une énigme à qn; **to know the answer to the r.,** connaître le mot de l'énigme; **to speak in riddles,** parler par énigmes, par rébus.
riddle², *v. A: & Lit:* **1.** *v.i.* parler énigmatiquement; parler par énigmes. **2.** *v.tr.* **to r. (out) a dream, etc.,** résoudre l'énigme d'un rêve, etc.
riddle³, *s.* *(a)* crible *m*, claie *f*; **hand r.,** crible à main; *(if fine)* tamis *m* à main; *A:* **to turn the r. and shears,** faire tourner le sas; *O:* **to make a r. of s.o.,** cribler qn de balles; *(b) Ind:* *(machine)* cribleuse *f.*
riddle⁴, *v.tr.* **1.** cribler (le grain, etc.); passer (qch.) au crible; passer (du minerai) à la claie; *O:* **to r. evidence,** passer les témoignages au tamis. **2. to r. s.o. with bullets,** cribler qn de balles; **riddled with bullets,** en écumoire, comme une écumoire; **ship riddled with shots,** navire criblé de coups; **riddled with corruption,** criblé de corruption; **to r. s.o.'s arguments,** battre en brèche les arguments de qn.
riddler ['ridlər], *s.* cribleur, -euse.
riddling¹ ['ridliŋ], *a. A:* **1.** énigmatique. **2.** qui parle par énigmes.
riddling², *s.* **1.** criblage *m.* **2.** *pl.* refus *m* du crible; matières refusées par le crible; criblures *fpl.*
ride¹ [raid], *s.* **1.** *(a)* course *f*, promenade *f*, trajet *m* (à cheval, à bicyclette); **to go for a r., to take a r.,** aller se promener à cheval; faire une promenade à cheval; **to give s.o. a r.,** faire monter qn; faire faire une promenade à cheval à qn; **to give a child a r. on one's back,** porter un enfant sur son dos; **death r.,** chevauchée *f* à la mort (d'un escadron); *Turf:* **jockey who has had three rides during the day,** jockey qui a eu trois montes dans la journée; **horse that is a difficult r.,** cheval difficile à gouverner; *(b)* promenade, voyage *m* (en voiture, etc.); **to go for a r. in a car, for a car r.,** aller se promener en voiture; **the children had a r. on the camel,** les enfants ont fait un tour à dos de chameau; **r. on a roundabout,** tour de chevaux de bois; **it's a 20p. r. on the bus,** c'est un trajet de 20p, il y en a pour 20p, en autobus; **it's a quarter of an hour's r. on a bicycle,** il y en a pour un quart d'heure à bicyclette; **to steal a r. (on a lorry, on a train),** s'accrocher derrière un camion; voyager sans billet; **to take s.o. for a r.,** (i) emmener qn faire une promenade (à cheval, en voiture); (ii) *F:* enlever qn (pour l'assassiner, pour lui faire son affaire); (iii) *F:* faire marcher qn, duper qn, mener qn en bateau; **he's been taken for a r.,** on l'a eu. **2.** *(in forest)* allée cavalière; piste *f*; avenue *f*; laie *f*; **major r.,** laie sommière; **minor r., cross r.,** layon *m.*
ride², *v.* (*p.t.* **rode** [roud]; *p.p.* **ridden** ['rid(ə)n], *Nau:* **rode**)
I. *v.i.* **1.** *(a)* chevaucher; aller, se promener, monter, être monté, à cheval; être à cheval; **to r. astride,** monter à califourchon; **to r. side-saddle,** monter en amazone; **can you r.?** montez-vous à cheval? **he can't r.,** il ne sait pas monter à cheval; **I rode in my youth,** j'ai monté à cheval dans ma jeunesse; **he, she, rides well,** il, elle, monte bien (à cheval); il est bon cavalier; elle est bonne cavalière; **he rides easy,** il ne fatigue pas à cheval; *F:* **Hitler rides again!** cet homme est un second Hitler! *(b)* **to r. on an ass,** être, monter, à âne; aller à dos d'âne; **to r. on an elephant,** voyager, aller, à dos d'éléphant; **to r. on a stick,** être à cheval sur un bâton; **to r. on s.o.'s shoulders, on s.o.'s back,** être monté, être à cheval, sur les épaules, sur le dos, de qn; *(of child)* **to r. on s.o.'s knee,** être à califourchon, à cheval, sur le genou de qn; **witches r. by night,** les sorcières chevauchent la nuit; *(c)* *(on horseback, on a bicycle, etc.)* **to r. to a place,** se rendre à un endroit (à cheval, à bicyclette, etc.); **to r. along, by,** passer, **to r. away, off,** partir, s'éloigner, **to r. back,** retourner, revenir, **to r. in, up,** entrer, arriver, **to r. out,** sortir, **to r. on,** continuer sa route (à cheval, etc.); **he rode over to see us,** il est venu nous voir à cheval; **to r. up, down (in a lift),** monter, descendre (en ascenseur); *(d)* **to r. 50 kilometres,** aller, faire 50 kilomètres (à cheval, en voiture, etc.); **did he walk or r.?** est-ce qu'il est venu à pied ou à cheval? **he rode all the way,** il a fait tout le trajet à cheval, en autobus, etc.; *A:* *(of two pers.)* **to r. and tie,** monter (à cheval) tour à tour (en attachant le cheval et continuant à pied pendant que son compagnon le rattrape); **he rode straight at us,** il a lancé son cheval contre nous; **to r. at a good pace, at full speed,** aller bon train, à toute vitesse; **to r. like mad,** chevaucher à une allure folle; galoper à tombeau ouvert. **2.** *(a)* *Equit: Turf:* **he rides 76 kilos,** il pèse 76 kilos en selle; *(b)* *(with passive force)* *(of horse)* **to r. quietly, gracefully,** être une monture douce, gracieuse; *(c)* *(with passive force)* *(of ground)* **to r. well,** être favorable à l'équitation; **to r. soft, hard,** offrir un parcours doux, dur. **3.** aller, se promener, en voiture; aller, venir, être, en autobus; **the Queen was riding in the state coach,** la Reine passait dans le carosse royal; *(with passive force)* **this car rides very smoothly,** cette voiture est bien suspendue. **4.** *(a)* **the ship was riding over the waves,** le navire flottait, voguait, était porté, sur les eaux; **the ship rode into port,** le navire est entré dans le port; **the moon was riding high in the heavens,** la lune était haute dans le ciel, voguait haut dans le ciel; *(b)* *Nau:* *(of ship)* **to r. at anchor,** être mouillé; être au mouillage, à l'ancre; se balancer sur ses ancres; **we were riding by the starboard anchor,** nous étions sur l'ancre de tribord; **to r. hard,** fatiguer, tanguer, au mouillage; fatiguer l'ancre; **to r. easy,** ne pas fatiguer (au mouillage); ne pas fatiguer l'ancre; **to r. to the tide, to the wind,** être évité à la marée, au vent. **5.** *(a)* *Typ:* *Surg:* *(of type, of ends of fractured bone, etc.)* chevaucher; *(b)* *Nau: etc:* *(of rope)* être pris; travailler; *(c)* *(of skirt, etc.)* **to r. (up),** remonter.
II. *v.tr.* **1.** *(a)* **to r. a race,** courir une course; *(b)* traverser (le pays) à cheval; parcourir (les rues) à cheval. **2.** *(a)* **to r. a horse,** monter un cheval; être monté sur un cheval; *Turf:* **Comet ridden by Martin,** Comet monté par Martin; **to r. an ass, an elephant,** être monté à dos d'âne, d'éléphant; *F:* **to r. s.o.,** persécuter qn; **to r. a bicycle,** aller à, en, bicyclette; être monté sur une bicyclette; **witches r. broomsticks,** les sorcières chevauchent sur des manches à balai; **he was knocked down while riding a bicycle,** il a été renversé en circulant à bicyclette; **the motor cycle was ridden by . . .,** la motocyclette était conduite par . . .; **for sale: bicycle, never (been) ridden,** à vendre; bicyclette qui n'a jamais roulé; *(b)* **to r. one's horse at a fence,** diriger son

cheval sur une barrière; **to r. a horse to death,** crever, éreinter, un cheval; **to r. an idea to death,** être féru d'une idée; **he rides this theory to death,** cette théorie est son cheval de bataille; (*c*) opprimer, dominer; (*of nightmare*) oppresser (qn); (*esp. in the passive*) **ridden by fear,** sous le coup de la peur; dominé, hanté, par la peur; **ridden by prejudice,** dominé, gouverné, par les préjugés. **3. the ship rides the waves,** le navire vogue sur les flots; **to r. the storm, the whirlwind,** soutenir le choc de la tempête, le déchainement de l'indignation publique, etc. **4.** (*of horse, etc.*) monter (la femelle). **5.** *U.S:* (*of elevator, elevator boy*) **to r. s.o. up, down,** faire monter, faire descendre, qn.

III. (*compound verbs*) **1. ride down,** *v.tr.* (*a*) écraser, piétiner, renverser (qn); charger (la foule); (*b*) dépasser (qn) à cheval; (*c*) *Ven:* forcer (un cerf).

2. ride off, *v.tr.* (*at polo*) bousculer (un adversaire).

3. ride out, *v.tr.* **to r. out the storm,** (i) *Nau:* étaler la tempête; (ii) surmonter la crise.

4. ride over, *v.tr.* **to r. over s.o.,** passer sur le corps à qn; **to r. roughshod over s.o.,** malmener qn; traiter qn cavalièrement, sans ménagement.

rideable ['raidəbl], *a.* (cheval, etc.) que l'on peut monter; **there was nothing r. left in the camp,** dans le camp il ne restait plus une seule bête qui pût servir de monture.

ridel ['rid(ə)l], *s. Ecc:* rideau *m* d'autel.

rider ['raidər], *s.* **1.** cavalier, -ière; (*in circus*) écuyer, -ère; (*on cycle*) cycliste *mf*; (*on motorcycle*) motocycliste *mf*; *Mil:* **dispatch r.,** agent *m* de transmission; *Turf:* **gentleman r.,** amateur *m* qui monte en course; gentleman rider *m*; **to be a good r.,** monter bien à cheval; être bon cavalier, bonne cavalière. **2.** *N.Arch:* **riders,** porques *f.* **3.** *Geol: Min:* nerf *m* (de roche). **4.** (*a*) ajouté *m*, annexe *f*, papillon *m* (d'un document); avenant *m* (d'un verdict); clause additionnelle (d'un projet de loi); correctif *m* (à une formule); *Com:* allonge *f* (d'un effet de commerce); (*b*) *Mth:* exercice *m* d'application (d'un théorème). **5.** cavalier (d'une balance de précision).

riderless ['raidərləs], *a.* sans cavalier; (motocyclette) sans conducteur; *Rac:* **r. horse,** cheval *m* sauvage.

ridge[1] [ridʒ], *s.* **1.** (*a*) arête *f*, crête *f*, (d'une chaine de montagnes); **Vimy r.,** la crête de Vimy; **windcut r.,** arête vive; **anticlinal r.,** crête anticlinale; (*b*) faîte *m*, faîtage *m*, crête (d'un comble); *Arch:* **r. turret,** tour *f* à cheval; *Const:* **r. course,** les approches *f*; **r. bar, r. board,** longeron *m*, longrine *f*, de faîtage; **under r. board,** sous-faîte *m*, *pl.* sous-faîtes; **r. piece, r. tree,** faîtage *m*, faîte *m*; panne faîtière; lien *m*, poutre *f*, de faîte; longrine *f* de faîtage; **r. pole,** (i) *Const:* poutre *f* de faîte, (panne) faîtière *f*; faîtage; (ii) fune *f* (de tente); **r. roof,** toit *m* à deux égouts; toit en dos d'âne; **r. rope,** filière *f* (de tente, *Nau:* de beaupré); fune *f*; **r. tile,** (tuile) faîtière; enfaîteau *m*; **r. tiling,** enfaîtement *m*, faîtage; (*c*) **r. of the back,** épine dorsale; raie *f* du dos; **r. of the nose,** arête du nez; (*d*) *Nau:* banc *m* (de rochers, de récifs); (*e*) *Meteor:* **r. of high pressure,** dorsale *f* barométrique. **2.** chaîne *f*, rangée *f* (de coteaux); **secondary r.,** contrefort *m*; **lower r.,** arrière-chaîne *f*, *pl.* arrière-chaînes. **3.** *Agr:* billon *m*, butte *f*; **r. plough,** buttoir *m*, butteur *m*; (*for banking up foot of trees*) rechausseuse *f*. **4.** *Hort:* couche *f* (de fumier); meule *f*. **5.** arête, trace saillante, strie *f* (sur une surface); ride *f* (sur le sable).

ridge[2]. **1.** *v.tr.* (*a*) *Const:* **to r. a roof,** enfaîter un comble; couronner le faîte d'un comble; (*b*) *Agr: Hort:* disposer (le terrain) en sillons, en billons; (*c*) *Hort:* **to r. (out),** butter (des plantes); mettre (des concombres, etc.) dans un châssis de couche; (*d*) sillonner, canneler, strier (une surface); (*of tide, etc.*) rider (le sable). **2.** *v.i.* (*a*) (*of sea*) former des crêtes; (*b*) (*of rock, etc.*) se couvrir de stries; (*of sand*) se rider.

ridged [ridʒd], *a.* **1.** sillonné d'arêtes, de stries; strié; ridé. **2.** en dos d'âne.

ridgel ['ridʒel], *s.* = RIG[5].

ridger ['ridʒər], *s. Agr:* buttoir *m*; rechausseuse *f*, buttoir *m*; butteur *m*; (*for banking up foot of trees*) rechausseuse *f*.

ridging ['ridʒiŋ], *s.* **1.** *Const:* enfaîtement *m* (d'un comble); **r. tile,** faîtière *f*; enfaîteau *m*. **2.** *Hort:* buttage *m*; mise *f* en couche; **r. plough,** buttoir *m*, butteur *m*.

ridicule[1] ['ridikju:l], *s.* **1.** moquerie *f*, raillerie *f*, risée *f*, dérision *f*; **to sustain r.,** subir des railleries; **to hold s.o., sth., up to r., to turn s.o., sth., into r.,** se moquer de qn, de qch.; tourner qn, qch., en ridicule, en dérision; ridiculiser qn, qch.; **to give cause for r., to be open to r., to invite r.,** prêter à rire; **to lay oneself open to r.,** s'exposer au ridicule; **to be an object of r.,** *F:* être en butte au ridicule. **2.** *A:* **ridicules of our time,** les ridicules de notre époque.

ridicule[2], *v.tr.* se moquer de, railler, ridiculiser (qn, qch.); tourner (qn, qch.) en ridicule, en dérision.

ridiculous [ri'dikjuləs], *a.* ridicule; **it is perfectly r.,** c'est d'un ridicule achevé; **what a r. excuse!** plaisante excuse! **to make s.o., sth., r.,** rendre qn, qch., ridicule; ridiculiser qn, qch.; **to make oneself r.,** se rendre ridicule, se faire moquer de soi; prêter à rire; **the r. side of the situation,** le ridicule de la situation; **to laugh at s.o.'s r. ways,** se moquer des ridicules de qn; **it's quite r. people making such a fuss,** il est parfaitement ridicule que l'on en fasse une si grosse affaire; *s.* **from the sublime to the r.,** du sublime au ridicule.

ridiculously [ri'dikjuləsli], *adv.* ridiculement; (se conduire) d'une façon ridicule.

ridiculousness [ri'dikjuləsnis], *s.* ridicule *m*.

riding[1] ['raidiŋ], *a.* **1.** (*a*) monté (à cheval, en voiture); qui va à cheval; à cheval; (*b*) **smooth-, hard-r. car,** voiture bien, mal, suspendue. **2.** *Nau:* mouillé; à l'ancre; **the r. anchor,** l'ancre *f* qui porte. **3.** *Nau:* **r. cable,** chaîne *f* qui travaille.

riding[2], *s.* **1.** équitation *f*; exercice *m* à cheval; **to go in for r.,** monter à cheval, faire du cheval; **obstacle r.,** monte *f* à l'obstacle; **clever r. (of jockey),** monte adroite, intelligente; **r. costume,** habit *m* de cavalier; **r. habit,** amazone *f*; **r. boots,** bottes *f* à l'écuyère; **r. breeches,** culotte *f* de cheval; **r. gloves, gauntlets,** gants *m* de buffle; **r. whip,** stick *m*; cravache *f*; *A:* **r. hood,** capuchon *m*; pèlerine *f*; **Little Red R. Hood,** le petit Chaperon rouge; **r. mule,** mulet *m* de selle; **r. school,** école *f* d' équitation; manège *m*; académie *f* (d'équitation); **open-air r.-school,** manège découvert; **r. instructor, instructress,** professeur *m* d'équitation; maître *m* de manège; *Mil:* **r. master,** écuyer instructeur; officier instructeur de cavalerie. **2.** *Aut:* **smooth r. (of a car),** suspension douce. **3.** *Nau:* mouillage *m*; **r. sail,** voile *f* de cape. **4.** chevauchement *m* (i) des fragments d'un os fracturé, (ii) des tuiles d'un faîte. **5.** allée cavalière.

riding[3], *s. Adm:* **1.** *Hist:* **the East, West, North Riding,** les divisions est, ouest, nord, du comté d'York. **2.** (*in Canada*) circonscription électorale.

riebeckite ['ri:bekait], *s. Miner:* riebeckite *f*.

Riedel ['ri:dəl], *Pr.n. Med:* **R.'s disease,** maladie *f* de Riedel.

riegel ['ri:gəl], *s. Geog:* verrou *m* glaciaire.

Riehl ['ri:əl], *Pr.n. Med:* **R.'s melanosis,** mélanose *f* de Riehl.

riel ['ri:əl], *s. Num:* riel *m*.

Riesling ['ri:sliŋ], *s. Vit:* riesling *m*.

rifacimento [rifætʃi'mentou], *s. Lit:* refonte *f*, remaniement *m* (d'une œuvre littéraire).

rife [raif], *a.* **1. to be r.,** (*of disease, etc.*) régner, sévir; (*of rumour*) courir, courir les rues; **distress is r.,** on voit la misère partout; la misère sévit partout; **ailments that are r. during the summer,** maladies *f* qui courent pendant l'été; *A:* **to grow r., wax r.,** augmenter, redoubler; sévir de plus belle. **2.** *A:* abondant, nombreux; **to be r. with sth.,** abonder en qch.

Rif(f) [rif], *Pr.n. Geog:* **the R.,** le Rif.

Riffian ['rifiən]. *Geog:* **1.** *a.* rifain. **2.** *s.* Rifain, -aine.

riffle[1] [rifl], *s.* **1.** *Min:* (*gold*) rif(f)le *m*. **2.** *esp. U.S:* rides *fpl* (sur l'eau).

riffle[2]. **1.** *v.tr.* (*a*) troubler (la surface de l'eau); (*b*) battre (les cartes). **2.** *v.i.* **to r. through a pile of papers,** feuilleter un amas de documents.

riffler ['riflər], *s. Tls:* rifloir *m* (de sculpteur); lime *f* à archet; (lime) feuille-de-sauge *f*.

riff-raff ['rifræf], *s. coll.* canaille *f*, racaille *f*, gueusaille *f*; **all the r.-r.,** tout le bas peuple; tout le rebut de la société.

rifle[1] ['raifl], *v.tr.* **1.** piller (un endroit); (fouiller et) vider (les poches de qn); dévaliser, détrousser (qn); **to r. a tomb,** violer, spolier, un tombeau; **they rifled my pockets,** *F:* on m'a nettoyé; **to r. a cupboard (of its contents),** vider une armoire de son contenu. **2.** *Lit:* **the bees r. the honey from the flowers,** les abeilles butinent les fleurs.

rifle[2], *s.* **1.** *A:* rayure *f* (d'arme à feu). **2.** (*a*) fusil (rayé); carabine *f* (de chasse); **antitank r.,** fusil antichar; **automatic, semiautomatic, r.,** fusil automatique, semiautomatique; **gallery r.,** (i) carabine de stand; (ii) *Mil:* fusil de tir réduit; **grenade r.,** fusil lance-grenades; **magazine r.,** fusil à chargeur, à magasin, à répétition; **quick-firing r.,** fusil à tir rapide; **r. club,** société de tir; **r. competition,** concours de tir (au fusil); **r. firing,** fusillade *f*, feu *m* d'armes portatives; **r. oil,** graisse d'armes; **r. pit,** tranchée individuelle, trou de tirailleur; **r. practice,** (exercice de) tir au fusil; **r. rack,** râtelier d'armes; **r. range,** (i) portée de, du, fusil; (ii) champ, stand, de tir (au fusil); **r. rest,** appui de tir; **r. rod,** baguette de fusil, de nettoyage; *Mil:* **r. salute,** le (mouvement de) présentez armes; **r. shooting,** tir au fusil; **r. shot,** (i) coup de fusil; (ii) tireur *m* (au fusil); **within r. shot,** à portée de fusil; **he was a good r. shot,** c'était un bon tireur, *F:* un bon fusil; **r. sling,** bretelle de fusil; **r. slung,** le fusil, *Mil:* l'arme, à la bretelle; **r. slung crosswise,** le fusil, *Mil:* l'arme, en bandoulière; (*b*) *Mil:* **rifles,** fantassins (armés de fusils); fusiliers *m*; **a force of 500 rifles,** une troupe, un contingent, de 500 fantassins; **r. company,** compagnie de fusiliers voltigeurs; **r. section,** équipe, escouade, de fusiliers voltigeurs; **R. Corps,** corps des fusiliers, des chasseurs à pied; **r. green,** vert foncé *inv* (de l'uniforme du Rifle Corps).

rifle[3], *v.tr.* **1.** rayer (l'âme d'une arme à feu); **to r. to the left, to the right,** rayer à gauche, à droite. **2. to r. s.o.,** (i) tirer sur qn; (ii) abattre qn d'un coup de fusil; (iii) fusiller (un espion, etc.); *Fb: Golf: etc:* **to r. a shot,** envoyer la balle comme un coup de fusil.

riflebird ['raiflbə:d], *s. Orn:* ptiloris *m*.

rifleman, *pl.* **-men** ['raiflmən], *s.m.* **1.** *Mil:* (*a*) fantassin (armé du fusil); fusilier; (*b*) chasseur à pied; (*c*) tirailleur. **2.** *Orn:* ptiloris.

rifling[1] ['raifliŋ], *s.* pillage *m*.

rifling[2], *s.* **1.** rayage *m* (de l'âme d'une arme à feu); **r. bench,** banc de rayage; **r. machine,** machine à rayer; **r. rod,** tringle à rayer. **2.** *coll.* rayure(s) *f(pl)* (d'une arme à feu); **left-hand, right-hand, r.,** rayure(s) à gauche, à droite; *Artil:* **r. band,** ceinture de, à, forcement (d'un obus).

rift [rift], *s.* (*a*) fente *f*; déchirure *f*; fissure *f* (dans la terre, dans une roche, etc.); crevasse *f*; (*in schist*) délit *m*; *Geol:* **r. valley,** rift *m*; fossé *m* (tectonique); (*b*) *A: & Lit:* fêlure *f*; **a r. in the lute,** une fêlure dans le cristal de leur amitié; (*c*) **a r. in the smoke, in the fog,** une éclaircie dans la fumée, dans la brume.

rifted ['riftid], *a.* **1.** (*of wood, etc.*) crevassé, fissuré, fendu. **2.** (*of clouds, etc.*) percé d'une éclaircie, d'éclaircies.

rig[1] [rig], *s.* **1.** *Nau:* gréement *m* (d'un navire); gréement, capelage *m* (d'un mât); voilure *f*; **jury r.,** gréement de fortune. **2.** *F:* **r.(-out),** (i) toilette *f*, tenue *f*; (ii) *Pej:* accoutrement *m*; **to be in full r.,** être en grande tenue, en grand uniforme; **in full evening r.,** en grande tenue de soirée; **working r.,** tenue de corvée; **to get a new r.-out,** s'habiller de neuf. **3.** *Mec.E:* (*a*) équipement *m*, installation *f*, accessoires *mpl*; (*b*) mécanisme *m* de manœuvre; (*c*) *Min:* **oil(-drilling) r.,** (i) (*on land*) appareil *m* de forage pétrolier, derrick *m*; (ii) (*at sea*) plateforme (marine) de forage pétrolier, de forage sous-marin; derrick flottant. **4.** *Veh: U.S:* équipage *m*; voiture *f*; **(tractor-trailer) r.,** = semi-remorque *f*.

rig[2], *v.tr.* (**rigged**) *Nau:* gréer, équiper (un navire); gréer, capeler, garnir (un mât); garnir, armer, équiper (le cabestan); **to r. a derrick,** gréer un mât de charge; **to r. in,** rentrer (le beaupré, etc.); **to r. out,** pousser dehors (le beaupré, etc.); **to r. out the studding-sail boom,** sailler le bout-dehors; **to r. up,** monter, installer, fixer (un appareil, etc.); mâter (un mât de charge, etc.); *F:* **to r. s.o. out, up,** attifer, accoutrer, qn; *F:* **to r. sth. up,** faire une installation de fortune.

rig[3], *s.* **1.** *A:* farce *f*; mauvais tour. **2.** (*a*) *A:* coup monté; tripotage *m*; (*b*) *St.Exch:* (i) hausse *f*, (ii) baisse *f*, factice; coup de bourse.

rig[4], *v.tr.* **1.** *Fin: St.Exch:* **to r. the market,** agir sur le marché; travailler le marché; provoquer (i) une hausse, (ii) une baisse, factice; **to r. the wheat market,** tripoter sur les blés; *Pol:* **to r. an election,** truquer une élection. **2.** *Cards:* apprêter, truquer (les cartes).

rig[5], *s. Husb: etc:* cheval *m*, taureau *m*, bélier *m*, monorchide, à demi châtré.

rigadoon [rigə'du:n], *s. Danc: Mus: A:* rigodon *m*.

rigged [rigd], *a. Nau:* (*with adv. or noun prefixed, e.g.*) **well r.,** bien gréé; **cutter-r. boat,** canot voilé en cotre; **schooner-r. ship, yacht,** navire gréé en goélette; yacht *m* avec une voilure de goélette.

rigger[1] ['rigər], *s.* **1.** (*pers.*) (*a*) *Nau:* gréeur *m*, mâteur *m*; (*on board*) gabier *m*; (*b*) *Av:* monteur-régleur *m*, *pl.* monteurs-régleurs. **2.** *Mec.E:* poulie *f* à courroie; poulie de transmission; poulie de commande. **3.** *Nau:* **square r.,** navire gréé en carré.

rigger[2], *s. St.Exch:* agioteur *m*.

rigging[1] ['rigiŋ], *s.* **1.** (*a*) *Nau:* gréage *m* (d'un navire); **r. loft,** (i) (*in dockyard*) (atelier *m* de) garniture *f*; (ii) *Th:* cintre *m*, dessus *mpl* (de la scène); (*b*) *Mec.E:* équipage *m*, montage *m* (d'une machine). **2.** (*a*) *Nau:* gréement *m*, agrès *mpl*, garniture *f* (d'un navire); capelage *m* (d'un mât); **main r.,** haubans *mpl* de grand mât; **lower r.,** basse carène; **standing r.,** manœuvres dormantes, gréement dormant; **running r.,** manœuvres courantes, gréement courant; **to send up the r.,** capeler le gréement; (*b*) *Av:* gréement, haubanage *m*, câblage *m*; *Aer:* **r. line,** suspente *f*; (*c*) *Mec.E:* mécanisme *m* de manœuvre; tringlage *m*; timonerie *f*.

rigging[2], *s. St.Exch:* agiotage *m*.

right[1] [rait], *a., s. & adv.*

I. *a.* **1.** *Mth:* (*a*) *A:* **r. line,** ligne droite; (*b*) **r. angle,** angle droit; angle à l'équerre; **at r. angles to . . ., with . . .,** à angle droit avec . . .; perpendiculaire à . . .; **to meet at r. angles,** se croiser à angle droit, en retour d'équerre, orthogonalement; **r. angled,** rectangle, rectangulaire; à angle droit; **r.-angled triangle,** triangle *m* rectangle; **r.-angled bend,** coude *m* d'équerre; **r. cone, cylinder, prism,** cône, cylindre, prisme, droit; *Nau:* **r. sailing,** route droit sur un des quatre points cardinaux. **2.** (*morally good*) bon; juste; honnête; droit; équitable; **to know what is r. and wrong,** savoir ce qui est bien et ce qui est mal; **to be r. thinking, r. minded,** être bien pensant; avoir l'esprit droit; **more than is r.,** plus que de raison; **it's only r.,** ce n'est que justice; **it's only r. to tell you that . . .,** il n'est que justice de vous dire que . . .; **it is (only) r. that you should know,** il est juste que vous le sachiez; **it is r. that he should be grateful to you,** il est bien juste qu'il vous soit reconnaissant; **would it be r. for me to, should I be r. to, accept?** ferais-je bien d'accepter? **I thought it r. to go,** j'ai cru devoir y aller; j'ai jugé bon, à propos, d'y aller; **to take the r. view of things,** voir juste; **to do the r. thing,** (i) se conduire honnêtement, honorablement; (ii) faire ce qu'il fallait faire; **I know you'll do the r. thing by me,** je sais bien que vous me traiterez honorablement, comme il faut. **3.** (*a*) correct, juste, exact; **the r. use of a word,** l'emploi correct d'un mot; **to give the r. answer,** répondre juste; donner la réponse correcte; **my accounts aren't r.,** j'ai fait une erreur dans mes comptes, mes calculs; **he got all his sums right,** il n'a pas fait une seule erreur de calcul; **to put a mistake r.,** redresser, corriger, réparer, rectifier, une erreur; **the r. time,** (i) l'heure juste; (ii) le bon moment; **what's the r. time?** quelle heure est-il (exactement)? quelle est l'heure juste? **my watch is r.,** ma montre est à l'heure; **this clock is never r.,** cette pendule n'est jamais à l'heure, ne marche jamais bien; **to put one's watch r.,** régler sa montre; **it's r. to the nearest millimetre,** c'est exact à un millimètre (de) près; (*b*) (*of pers.*) **to be r.,** avoir raison; **you're quite r.!** vous avez bien raison! vous ne vous trompez pas! rien de plus juste! **I consider he's r.,** je lui donne raison; **are you r. in refusing?** avez-vous raison de refuser? est-ce que votre refus est justifié? (*c*) **the r. word,** le mot propre, juste; le mot qu'il faut; **the r. side of the material,** l'endroit *m*, le dessus, du tissu; **r. side, r. way, up,** à l'endroit, dans le bon sens; **it is not the r. width,** ce n'est pas de la largeur voulue, la largeur qu'il faut; **have you the r. amount?** avez-vous (i) votre compte? (ii) la monnaie exacte? **is this the r. house?** est-ce bien la maison? **these aren't the r. tools,** ce ne sont pas là les outils qu'il me, nous, faut; **to know the r. people,** (i) avoir des relations; (ii) avoir d'utiles relations; **the r. train,** le bon train, le train qu'il faut; **am I r. for Paris?** suis-je bien (i) dans le train de Paris, (ii) sur la route de Paris? **we're on the r. road,** nous sommes dans le bon chemin, dans la bonne voie; **to put s.o. r.,** (i) mettre qn sur la voie; (ii) détromper, désabuser, qn; dire à qn qu'il s'est trompé; **I must get this matter r.,** il me faut me renseigner sur cette question; **to show s.o. that one is r.,** se justifier auprès de qn; **I put myself r. with the authorities,** je me suis mis en règle avec les autorités; (*d*) (*most appropriate*) **in the r. place,** (i) bien placé; dans un endroit convenable; (ii) à sa place; **that's its r. place,** voilà sa vraie place; **the r. man in the r. place,** l'homme qu'il faut pour la tâche; l'homme de la situation; *P:* **she comes out in all the r. places,** elle est bien roulée, carrossée; elle a des rondeurs bien placées; **you came at the r. moment, the r. time,** vous êtes venu au bon moment, bien à propos; **to wait for the r. moment,** attendre le moment opportun; **to do sth. the r. way,** s'y bien prendre pour faire qch.; **there's only one r. way of doing it,** il n'y a qu'une façon de le faire qui soit la bonne; **the r. thing to do,** ce qu'il faut faire; ce qu'il y a de mieux à faire; **I've found the r. thing,** j'ai trouvé ce qu'il me faut; **he always says the r. thing,** il a le don de l'à-propos; il dit toujours ce qu'il faut; **are these the r. sort of apples for cooking?** ces pommes-là sont-elles bonnes à cuire? *F:* **he's one of the r. sort,** c'est un bon type; *P: O:* **she's found Mr. R.,** elle a trouvé le fiancé qui lui convient, un mari à son goût; **that's r.!** parfaitement! c'est ça! voilà qui est bien! c'est juste! **r. (you are)!** *F:* **r. oh!** bon! entendu! bien sûr! d'accord! *F:* **r.?** d'acc.? (*e*) **it's a fault on the r. side,** c'est pécher du bon côté; **he's on the r. side of forty,** il n'a pas encore quarante ans; **to get on the r. side of s.o.,** s'insinuer dans les bonnes grâces de qn; **to be on the r. side,** être bien placé; être du bon côté. **4.** (*in good condition*) (*a*) **to be in one's r. mind,** avoir toute sa raison; être en possession de tous ses sens, toutes ses facultés; **he's not in his r. mind,** *F:* **isn't r. in the head,** il n'a pas toute sa tête; *F:* il est un peu détraqué, toqué; **I'm not feeling quite r.,** je ne suis pas d'aplomb; *F:* je ne suis pas dans mon assiette; **as r. as rain,** *O:* **as a trivet,** en parfait état; en parfaite santé; **good nursing will put him r.,** les bons soins le remettront, **that'll put you r.,** voilà qui vous remontera, qui vous remettra d'aplomb; **to put things r.,** rétablir les choses; tout mettre en règle, en ordre; arranger une affaire; **things will come r., it will turn out (all) r. (in the long run),** les choses s'arrangeront; tout ira bien; (*b*) **everything's all r.,** tout est, va, très bien; **I'm sure it will be all r.,** cela ne fera pas de difficulté que je sache; vous n'avez pas à vous inquiéter là-dessus; **it's all r.,** (i) tout va bien; ne vous inquiétez pas; (ii) (*to pers. apologizing*) je vous en prie! **all r.!** bien! entendu! **are you all r.?** (i) est-ce que vous allez bien? (ii) vous ne vous êtes pas blessé? (iii) *Iron:* tu ne te sens pas bien? tu te sens bien, oui? **I'm perfectly all r.,** (i) je vais très bien, je me porte à merveille; (ii) je n'ai besoin de rien; **I'm all r. again now,** je suis tout à fait remis maintenant; **I've made everything all r. for my family,** j'ai pris des arrangements en faveur de ma famille; j'ai tout arrangé pour ma famille; **he'll be all r. for the rest of his life,** il est tranquille pour le reste de ses jours; **it's all r. for** ***you*** **to laugh!** permis à vous de rire! vous avez beau rire! **he's all r.,** *U.S: F:* **he's a r. guy,** c'est un bon type; *P:* **that's a bit of all r.!** voilà qui est épatant! ça fait mon beurre! *P:* **she's a bit of all r.!** voilà une jolie pépée, un beau petit lot! **5.** (*genuine*) (*a*) **r. whale,** baleine franche; **r. cognac,** cognac *m* d'origine; (*b*) *F:* **a r.,** *esp. U.S:* **r.-down, swindle,** une vraie escroquerie. **6.** (*a*) (côté, etc.) droit; **on the r. side,** à droite, sur la droite; **r. hand,** main droite; **on my r. hand,** sur ma droite; **he's my r. hand,** il est mon bras droit; **r. shot,** (i) coup *m* de fusil à droite; (ii) coup du canon droit; **a r.-and-left shot,** *s.* **a r. and left,** un (coup) double; un doublé; **r. wing,** (i) *Mil: Fb: etc:* aile droite; (ii) *Pol:* la droite; *Pol:* **r.-wing policy,** politique conservatrice, de droite; *Fb:* **r. winger,** ailier droit; (*b*) **r. screw,** vis *f* à droite; **r.-and-left screw,** vis à pas contraires; vis à filet à droite et à gauche.

II. *s.* **1.** le droit; la justice; le bien; **the fundamental principles of r.,** les principes fondamentaux du droit; **might and r.,** la force et le droit; **r. and wrong,** le bien et le mal; le juste et l'injuste; **to be in the r.,** avoir raison; être dans son droit; **to declare s.o. to be in the r.,** donner raison à qn; donner gain de cause à qn. **2.** (*a*) droit, titre *m*; privilège *m*; **divine r.,** droit divin; **to have a r., the r., to sth.,** avoir droit à qch.; **r. of inspection,** droit de regard; *Jur:* **rights granted by contract,** droits contractuels; **r. of common,** droit d'usage, de pâture; **r. to grass, to litter,** droit à l'herbe, à la litière; **r. holder,** usager *m* (d'un droit); **r. of way,** (i) *Jur:* servitude *f*, droit, jouissance *f*, de passage; (ii) *Aut:* priorité *f* de passage; (iii) *NAm:* la voie ferrée; *Fin:* **application rights,** droit(s), privilège, de souscription; **with r. of transfer,** avec faculté de transfert; **to have a, the r. to do sth.,** avoir le droit de faire qch.; être en droit de faire qch.; **I have the r. to ask for an explanation,** j'ai le droit de vous demander une explication; j'ai droit à une explication; **he has no r. to complain,** il n'a pas le droit de se plaindre; **what r. have you to do that?** de quel droit, à quel titre, faites-vous cela? *Jur:* **to have the r. to prosecute,** avoir qualité de poursuivre; **petitioner declared to have no r. of action,** demandeur nonrecevable dans son action; **r. to vote,** droit de vote; **r. of succession,** droit de succession, d'héritage; **by what r.?** de quel droit? à quel titre? **by r. of conquest,** par droit de conquête; **it belongs to him by r.,** cela lui appartient de droit; **to possess sth. in one's own r.,** posséder qch. de son chef; avoir qch. en propre; **in r. of one's wife,** du chef de sa femme; **she is a peeress in her own r.,** elle détient le titre de pairesse personnellement; elle est pairesse de son propre chef; (*b*) **the rights of man, human rights,** les droits de l'homme; *Hist:* **the Bill of Rights,** la Déclaration des droits des citoyens (1689); **to be within one's rights,** être dans son droit; **by rights,** en toute justice; **by rights he ought to have been president,** en toute justice c'est lui qui aurait dû être président; **by rights he ought to have been here by now,** selon mes, toutes les, prévisions il aurait dû être déjà arrivé; **to assert, stand on, one's rights,** soutenir ses droits; *P:* **I stand on my rights!** j'ai des droits, hein? **3.** (*a*) **to put, set, sth. to rights,** arranger qch.; mettre qch. en ordre, en règle; réparer qch.; **to put, set, things to rights,** réparer le désordre; tout mettre en ordre; (*b*) **to know the rights of the case,** savoir, connaître, les tenants et aboutissants de l'affaire; savoir qui a tort et qui a raison. **4.** (*a*) droite *f*; côté droit; **on the r.,** à droite; **on your r.,** à votre droite; **your neighbour on the r.,** votre voisin de droite; **to keep to the r.,** tenir la droite; **the first turning on the r.,** le premier tournant à droite; la première à droite; **from r. and left,** de droite et de gauche; (*b*) *Pol:* **the r.,** la droite; les conservateurs *m*; (*c*) *Box:* coup *m* du droit; (*d*) (i) coup de fusil à droite; coup de canon droit.

III. *adv.* **1.** (*a*) (*straight*) **go r. on,** continuez tout droit; **I'm going r. home,** je rentre tout droit, directement, chez moi; **he went r. at him,** il est allé droit vers lui; (*b*) **to do sth. r. away, r. off,** faire qch. (i) sur-le-champ, immédiatement, tout de suite, (ii) du premier coup, du premier bond, d'emblée; **I'm going r. away, r. now,** j'y vais tout de suite, de ce pas; *O:* **r. away!** (i) *Rail: etc:* en route! (ii) *Av:* enlevez (les cales)! **I'll be r. back,** je reviens tout de suite. **2.** (*a*) (*completely*) **to sink r. to the bottom,** couler droit au fond; **a wall r. round the house,** un mur tout autour de la maison; **he turned r. round,** il a fait un tour complet; **he took the door r. off its hinges,** il a fait sauter la porte de ses gonds; **the prisoner got r. away,** le prisonnier s'est évadé sans qu'on ait pu le rattraper; (*b*) (*exactly*) **r. at the top,** tout en haut; **r. at the other end,** tout à l'autre bout; **r. in the middle,** au beau milieu; en plein milieu; **r. in the middle of the harvest,** en pleine moisson; **to go r. through the middle of the town,** passer en plein centre de la ville; **shot r. through the heart,** frappé en plein cœur; **he threw it r. in my face,** il me l'a jeté en pleine figure; **r. against the wall,** tout contre le mur; **the wind was r. behind us,** nous avions le vent juste dans le dos; **breakers r. ahead!** des brisants droit devant, droit debout! *F:* **I'll be waiting r. here,** j'attendrai ici même; *F:* **r. on!** parfait! au poil! **3.** (*to the full*) **I know r. well that . . .,** je sais fort bien que . . .; *F: O:* **I was r. glad to hear it,** j'ai été fort heureux de l'apprendre; *Ecc:* **r. reverend,** très révérend; révérendissime. **4.** (*a*) (*justly*) **you did r. to wait,** vous avez bien fait d'attendre; **to act r.,** agir bien; (*b*) (répondre, etc.) correctement; (deviner) juste; **if I remember r.,** si je me souviens bien; **things are going r.,** tout va bien; **nothing goes r. with me,** rien ne me réussit; tout se tourne contre moi; **I got your letter all r.,** j'ai bien reçu votre lettre; **I got back all r.,** je suis arrivé à bon port; *F:* **and r. he did it,** et il l'a fait, bien sûr! **I'm sixty r. enough,** il est bien vrai que j'ai soixante ans; **he's to blame r. enough,** c'est bien de sa faute (à lui); **it's a hot summer r. enough,** pour un été chaud c'est un été chaud. **5.** à droite; **turn r.,** tournez à droite; **he looked neither r. nor left,** il n'a regardé ni à droite ni à gauche; **to hit out r. and left,** frapper de droite et de gauche; **he owes money r. and left,** il doit de l'argent de tous les côtés; *F:* **he cheated us r., left and centre,** il nous a eus jusqu'à la gauche; *Danc:* **r. and left,** chaîne anglaise; *Mil: etc:* **eyes r.!** tête à droite! **r. dress!** à droite, alignement! **r. turn!** *A:* **r. face!** à droite! par le flanc droit! *s.* **a r. turn, a r. face,** un à-droite; **r. about turn!** demi-tour à droite! *s.* **a r. about (turn),** un demi-tour à droite; une volte-face; *F: A:* **to send s.o. to the r. about,** envoyer promener qn.

right[2], *v.tr.* **1.** (*a*) redresser (un canot, une voiture, etc.); remettre (une voiture) sur ses roues; relever (un canot); (*of boat*) **to r. (itself),** se redresser, se relever; (*b*) *Nau:* redresser, mettre droite (la barre); remettre (la barre) à zéro. **2.** (*a*) redresser, réparer (un tort); (*b*) rendre justice à (qn); **your wrongs will be righted,** on vous fera justice. **3.** corriger, rectifier (une erreur).

righteous ['raitʃəs], *a.* **1.** droit, juste; vertueux; *s.* **the r.,** les bons; les justes. **2.** juste, justifié; **r. anger,** juste colère *f*.

righteously ['raitʃəsli], *adv.* justement; avec droiture; vertueusement.

righteousness ['raitʃəsnis], *s.* droiture *f*, vertu *f*; rectitude *f*; *Theol:* **the r. of Christ,** les mérites *m* du Christ.

rightful ['raitful], *a.* **1.** légitime, véritable; en droit; **r. heir,** héritier *m* légitime. **2.** (*of claim, etc.*) légitime, juste; justifié. **3.** (héritage, etc.) auquel on a droit; **to have one's r. share of sth.,** avoir sa bonne part de qch.

rightfully ['raitfuli], *adv.* légitimement; à juste titre; **I claimed what was r. mine,** j'ai réclamé mon dû.

right-hand ['raithænd], *a.* **1.** (gant, etc.) de la main droite; (*b*) **the r.-h. corner of the page,** le coin à droite de la page; **the r.-h. drawer,** le tiroir de droite; **on the r.-h. side,** à droite; **r.-h. man,** (i) *Mil:* homme de droite; (ii) bras droit (de qn); homme de confiance; **r.-h. side of an equation,** second membre d'une équation. **2. r.-h. screw, lock,** vis *f*, serrure *f*, à droite; *Av:* **r.-h. propeller,** hélice *f* à pas à droite.

right-handed [rait'hændid], *a.* **1.** (*of pers.*) droitier. **2.** *Box:* **r.-h. blow,** coup *m* du droit. **3.** (*a*) = RIGHT-HAND 2; (*b*) (outil) pour la main droite; (*c*) **r.-h. crystal,** cristal droit. **4.** *adv.* (*a*) (*in hunting*) **to turn r.-h.,** tourner à droite; (*b*) **to play tennis r.-h.,** jouer au tennis de la main droite.

right-handedness [rait'hændidnis], *s.* dextralité *f*.

right-hander [rait'hændər], *s.* **1.** (*pers.*) droitier, -ière. **2.**

Box: coup *m* du droit.
righting ['raitiŋ], *s.* **1.** redressement *m* (d'un canot, etc.); **r. force,** effort *m* de redressement. **2.** redressement, réparation *f* (d'un tort).
rightist ['raitist], *a. & s. Pol:* droitiste (*mf*); *a.* de droite.
rightly ['raitli], *adv.* **1. to act r.,** bien agir; agir sagement, avec sagesse; agir comme il convient; **to judge r.,** bien juger. **2.** (expliquer qch., etc.) correctement; **to see r.,** voir juste; **r. called, named, the Good,** nommé, appelé, à juste titre le Bon; **r. speaking,** à bien prendre les choses; pour parler juste; **r. or wrongly,** à tort ou à raison; **I cannot r. say,** je ne saurais dire au juste; **we r. judge people by the company they keep,** nous jugeons les gens à juste titre, à bon droit, d'après ceux qu'ils fréquentent.
rightness ['raitnis], *s.* (*a*) justesse *f* (d'une décision); (*b*) justesse, exactitude *f* (d'une réponse, d'un calcul).
righto [rai'tou], *int. F:* entendu! d'accord!
rightyho [raiti'ou], *int. P:* = RIGHTO.
rigid ['ridʒid], *a.* **1.** rigide, raide; **r. body,** corps *m* rigide; corps solide; **r. member,** organe *m* fixe (d'une machine, etc.); *A:* **r. airship,** *s.* **r.,** dirigeable *m* rigide; *F:* **I was completely r. with fright,** j'étais figé de terreur; **r. expression,** traits *m* rigides; **the r. etiquette of the court,** l'étiquette rigide de la cour. **2.** sévère, strict; **r. principles,** principes *m* sévères; **r. virtue,** vertu *f* inflexible, rigide.
rigidify [ri'dʒidifai], *v.tr.* rigidifier.
rigidity [ri'dʒiditi], *s.* **1.** rigidité *f*, raideur *f*; résistance *f*; *Med:* **cadaveric r.,** rigidité cadavérique. **2.** sévérité *f*; intransigeance *f*.
rigidly ['ridʒidli], *adv.* **1.** rigidement; raidement; d'un air intransigeant; **sitting r. on the chair,** assis raide sur la chaise. **2.** sévèrement, strictement.
rigmarole ['rigməroul], *s. F:* galimatias *m*; litanie *f*; discours incohérent, incompréhensible.
rigor ['raigɔːr, 'ri-], *s. Med:* **1.** frissons *m* (symptomatiques). **2. r. mortis,** rigidité *f* cadavérique; **cataleptic r.,** rigidité cataleptique.
rigorism ['rigərizm], *s.* rigorisme *m*, austérité *f*; *Theol:* rigorisme.
rigorist ['rigərist], *a. & s. Theol: etc:* rigoriste (*mf*).
rigorous ['rigərəs], *a.* rigoureux; **r. measures,** mesures *f* de rigueur.
rigorously ['rigərəsli], *adv.* rigoureusement; avec rigueur; en toute rigueur; (obéir) à la lettre.
rigour ['rigər], *s.* **1.** (*a*) rigueur *f*, sévérité *f*; dureté *f*; **the r. of the law,** la rigueur de la loi; (*b*) **the rigours of prison life,** les rigueurs de la vie de prison. **2.** rigueur, âpreté *f* (du temps). **3.** exactitude *f*, précision *f*, rigueur (d'une preuve, d'un calcul). **4.** raideur *f*, austérité *f* (d'une doctrine, etc.).
rig-out ['rigaut], *s. see* RIG[1] 2.
rile [rail], *v.tr. F:* agacer, exaspérer, irriter, énerver, chiffonner (qn); échauffer, remuer, émouvoir, la bile à (qn); **it riled him, he was riled about it,** il en rageait.
rill[1] [ril], *s.* (*a*) ruisselet *m*; petit ruisseau; *Geog:* **r. mark,** trace *f* de ruissellement; (*b*) *Dial:* rigole *f*.
rill[2]. **1.** *v.i.* ruisseler (doucement). **2.** *v.tr.* laisser des traces de ruissellement sur (les roches, etc.).
rille [ril], *s. Astr:* rainure *f* (sur la face de la lune).
rim[1] [rim], *s.* **1.** (*a*) jante *f*, pourtour *m*, bourrelet *m* (de roue); couronne *f*, jante (de poulie, de roue d'engrenage); limbe *m* (de volant); *Aut:* **well-base r.,** jante à base creuse; **straight-sided r.,** jante à tringles; **detachable r.,** jante amovible; **r. base,** plat *m* de jante; fond *m* de jante; **r. bead, r. clinch (of the tyre),** talon *m* d'accrochage (du pneu); (*b*) cercle *m* (d'un tamis). **2.** bord *m* (d'un vase, etc.); cordon *m*, cordonnet *m*, carnèle *f*, listeau *m* (d'une pièce de monnaie); rebord *m* (d'une cartouche, etc.); limbe (du soleil); rebord, ourlet *m* (de l'oreille); **spectacle rims,** monture *f* de lunettes.
rim[2], *v.tr.* **(rimmed) 1.** janter (une roue). **2.** border, entourer, cercler.
rimaye [ri:mei], *s. Geog:* rimaye *f*.
rime[1] [raim], *s.* givre *m*; gelée blanche; *For:* **r. break,** bris *m* de givre (dans un arbre).
rime[2,3], *s. & v.*, **rimer** ['raimər], *s.* = RHYME[1,2], RHYMER.
rimless ['rimlis], *a.* (lunettes) sans monture.
Rimmon ['rimən], *Pr.n.m. B:* Rimmon; **to bow down, worship, in the house of R.,** transiger avec sa conscience; faire comme les autres.
rimose [rai'mous], **rimous** ['raiməs], *a. Nat.Hist:* rimeux.
rimstone ['rimstoun], *s. Geol:* **r. bar,** barre *f* de travertin.
rind [raind], *s.* **1.** écorce *f* (mince), peau *f* (d'arbre, de plante). **2.** peau, pelure *f* (de légume, de fruit); pelure, croûte *f* (de fromage); couenne *f* (de lard). **3.** *Geol: Min:* couche supérieure en roche tendre.
rinderpest ['rindəpest], *s. Vet:* peste bovine.
ring[1] [riŋ], *s.* **1.** (*a*) anneau *m*; (*jewelled*) bague *f*; **wedding r.,** anneau nuptial, de mariage; alliance *f*; **engagement r.,** bague de fiançailles; **diamond r.,** bague de diamants; **eternity r.** = alliance de diamants; **signet r.,** chevalière *f*; **episcopal r., pastoral r.,** anneau épiscopal, pastoral; **to wear a r. (on one's finger),** porter une bague au doigt; **r. finger,** annulaire *m*; **r. stand, case,** baguier *m*; (*b*) **nose r.,** (i) anneau porté au nez; (ii) anneau nasal; nasière *f* (de taureau, etc.); **arm r.,** bracelet *m*; (*c*) (*for marking birds*) bague. **2.** (*a*) anneau, bague, rond *m*, rondelle *f* (de métal, etc.); ansette *f* (d'une médaille); rondelle (de bâton de ski); maille *f* (d'une cotte de mailles); **curtain r.,** anneau de rideau; **napkin r.,** rond de serviette; **umbrella r.,** rondelle de parapluie; **split r., key r.,** anneau brisé, bague fendue; **r. door-knocker,** boucle *f* de porte; *Nau:* **mooring r.,** boucle d'amarrage; organeau *m*; **anchor r.,** cigale *f* de l'ancre; organeau; *Gym:* **the rings,** les anneaux; *Sp:* **r. tilting, tilting at the r.,** jeu *m* de bagues; *Equit:* **bit r., bridle r.,** anneau porte-rêne; *Games:* **r. puzzle,** baguenaudier *m*; *Tchn:* **r. and staple,** anneau à happe; **r. bolt,** (i) anneau à fiche; piton *m* à boucle; (ii) boucle, bague, d'amarrage; **r. gauge,** calibre *m* à bague; bague-jauge *f*, *pl.* bagues-jauges; **r. spanner,** clef fermée, clef à œil; **r. magnet,** aimant *m* annulaire, circulaire; **r. splice,** épissure *f* à œillet; *Fish:* **r. net,** épuisette *f*; *Tex:* **r. frame, r. spinner,** métier *m* à anneaux; **r. spinning,** filage *m* à anneaux; (*b*) *Mec.E:* anneau, bague, frette *f*; virole *f*; **adjusting r.,** bague de réglage; **centring r.,** bague de centrage; **clamping r., set r.,** bague de serrage, de blocage, de calage; **coupling r.,** bague, virole, de raccordement; **deflecting r.,** anneau déflecteur; **distance r., spacer r.,** anneau d'écartement; (anneau) entretoise *f*; **expansion r.,** anneau de dilatation; **friction r.,** bague, rondelle, de frottement; **gimbal r.,** anneau à Cardan; cadre *m* de suspension à la Cardan; **knurled r.,** bague moletée; **locating r.,** anneau de fixation; **lock r., retainer r., retaining r.,** bague d'arrêt, de blocage; anneau de retenue; *Mch:* **lubricating r., oil r.,** anneau, bague, de graissage; anneau graisseur; bague à huile (de palier); **nave r. (of wheel),** frette de moyeu; **obturating r., obturator r.,** anneau obturateur; **O r.,** joint *m* torique; **safety r.,** anneau de sûreté; **screw-on r., threaded r.,** bague filetée; **seal(ing) r., r. seal,** bague, rondelle, d'étanchéité; **slinger r.,** anneau distributeur, bague distributrice; bague de projection (d'un liquide); **slip r.,** bague coulissante; **snap r.,** anneau, bague, à ressort; **split r.,** anneau fendu, bague fendue; demi-anneau *m*, *pl.* demi-anneaux; **stop r.,** bague d'arrêt; **swivel r.,** anneau pivotant, anneau à émerillon; **thrust (collar) r.,** bague (de) butée, bague de poussée; *Opt:* **focussing r.,** anneau, bague, de mise au point, de focalisation, de concentration; (*c*) *El:* **carbon r.,** bague en charbon; **collecting r., collector r.,** bague, lame *f*, collectrice; anneau collecteur (de dynamo); **Gramme r.,** anneau de Gramme; **guard r.,** anneau de garde (d'un électromètre, d'un microphone de téléphone); **r. armature,** induit *m* à, en, anneau; **r. coil,** bobinage toroïdal; **r. dynamo,** dynamo *f* à anneau; **r. modulator,** modulateur *m* en anneau; **r. motor,** moteur *m* à bagues; **r. transformer,** transformateur toroïdal; **r. winding,** enroulement *m* à, en, anneau; **r. connection,** montage *m* en boucle; (*d*) *Mch: I.C.E:* **(piston) r.,** segment *m* (de piston); **packing r.,** garniture *f*; **r. piston,** piston *m* à segments; **compression r., sealing r.,** segment d'étanchéité (de culasse); **(oil) scraper r.,** segment racleur; **split r.,** segment fendu; **double-slot, double-vent, r.,** segment à double fente; **lap-joint, step-cut, r.,** segment à coupure à redan, segment coupé à recouvrement; **oblique-slotted r., diagonal-joint r.,** segment à biseau, à joint à sifflet; (*e*) *Mch:* couronne *f*; **(clutch) r.,** couronne (d'embrayage); **annular r.,** couronne annulaire; **ball r.,** couronne de billes, bague à billes; **roller r.,** couronne à galets; **(turbine) r.,** couronne (de turbine); **blade r.,** couronne d'ailettes, d'aubes; **guide r.,** couronne directrice, couronne fixe; **r. gear,** couronne dentée; denture *f* annulaire; **r. nut,** écrou *m* à couronne. **3.** *Ch:* chaîne fermée; noyau *m*; **benzene r.,** noyau benzénique. **4.** (*a*) anneau (d'une planète); auréole *f*, halo *m* (autour du soleil, de la lune); aréole *f* (autour de la lune); cerne *m*, cernure *f* (autour des yeux); cerne, bleu *m*, marbrures *fpl* (autour d'une contusion, etc.); rond (de fumée); **he has rings round his eyes,** il a les yeux cernés, battus; **eyes with dark rings round them,** yeux cerclés de bistre; **a good stain-remover leaves no rings,** un bon détachant ne laisse pas d'auréole; *Astr:* **Saturn's rings,** les anneaux de Saturne; **mock sun r.,** faux halo; *Ph:* **coloured rings,** anneaux colorés; **Newton's rings, Nobili's rings,** anneaux de Newton, de Nobili; *Meteor:* **Bishop's rings,** anneaux de Bishop; (*of pers.*) **to run in rings,** courir en rond; *F:* **to make, run, rings round s.o.,** courir beaucoup plus vite que qn; surpasser qn; l'emporter sur qn; battre qn à plate(s) couture(s); (*b*) (*of tree*) anneau, cercle, annuel; couche annuelle; (*c*) *Orn:* collier *m* (d'un pigeon, etc.); **r.-necked,** à collier; **r. ouzel,** merle *m* à collier, à plastron; **r. dove,** pigeon ramier; palombe *f*; *Rept:* **r. snake,** couleuvre *f* à collier; serpent *m* d'eau; (*d*) incision annulaire (faite à un arbre). **5.** cercle *m* (d'arbres, de personnes, etc.); **sitting in a r.,** assis en rond, en cercle; **to dance in a r.,** danser en rond. **6.** (*a*) groupe *m*, bande *f*, petit cercle, (petite) coterie (de personnes); (*b*) *Com:* syndicat *m*; cartel *m*; **price r.,** coalition *f* de vendeurs; (*c*) **spy r.,** réseau *m* d'espionnage; (*d*) *St.Exch:* **the R.,** le Parquet; le marché officiel, en bourse. **7.** (*a*) arène *f*, piste *f* (de cirque, etc.); (*b*) **the r.,** le cirque. **8.** *Box: Wr:* (*a*) cercle formé par les spectateurs autour des boxeurs, des lutteurs; *Fig:* (*in dispute, etc.*) **to keep, hold, the r.,** laisser le champ libre aux adversaires; ne permettre aucune intervention au préjudice de l'une des parties; (*b*) enceinte *f*, ring *m*; (*c*) *F:* **the r.,** le pugilisme et les fervents de la boxe. **9.** *Turf:* **the R.,** (i) l'enceinte (du pesage); le pesage; (ii) les bookmakers *m*; **the silver r.,** l'enceinte des bookmakers qui acceptent les petits paris. **10.** *Mus:* **the R.,** la Tétralogie (de Wagner).
ring[2].
I. *v.i.* (*a*) (*of hawk*) monter en spirale; (*b*) (*of stag, fox*) courir en rond; décrire des cercles.
II. *v.tr.* **1.** (*a*) baguer (un oiseau); (*b*) boucler, anneler (un porc, un taureau); mettre un anneau au nez (d'une bête); (*c*) *Tchn:* baguer, fretter (un pieu, etc.); baguer (un tuyau). **2.** (*a*) **to r. (s.o., sth.) round, about, in,** encercler, entourer, cerner (qn, qch.); faire cercle autour de (qn, qch.); (*b*) *Ven:* rabattre, cerner (le gros gibier); battre (le terrain). **3.** *Arb:* baguer, cerner (un arbre, une branche); circoncire (un arbre fruitier). **4.** couper (des pommes, des oignons) en rondelles.
ring[3], *s.* **1.** son (clair, métallique); sonnerie *f* (de cloches); tintement *m* (de cloches, de pièces de monnaie); timbre *m*, intonation *f* (de la voix); *Tchn:* **r. of a coin,** son, voix, d'une pièce de monnaie; **it has a hollow r.,** cela sonne creux; **the r. of truth,** l'accent *m* de la vérité. **2.** (*a*) coup *m* de sonnette, de timbre; **there's a r. at the door,** on sonne (à la porte); **I recognize his r.,** je reconnais son coup de sonnette, sa manière de sonner; (*b*) *Tp:* appel *m* téléphonique; coup de téléphone; **I'll give you a r.,** je vous téléphonerai; je vous donnerai, passerai, un coup de téléphone, de fil. **3.** *Ecc:* jeu *m* de cloches; **r. of six bells,** jeu de six cloches.
ring[4], *v.* **(rang** [ræŋ], *A:* **rung** [rʌŋ]; **rung)**
I. *v.i. & tr.* **1.** *v.i.* (*a*) (*of bell*) sonner, tinter; **the bells are ringing,** les cloches *f* sonnent; on sonne les cloches; **to set the bells ringing,** mettre les cloches en branle; **the bells are ringing for church** = les cloches sonnent la messe; **the bell is ringing for dinner,** on sonne pour le dîner; **the bell rings in the kitchen,** le timbre, la sonnette, répond dans la cuisine; (*b*) (*of coin*) **to r. true, false,** sonner clair, sonner faux; **his answer did not r. true,** sa réponse n'a pas sonné franc, a sonné faux; **that rings true,** cela a l'accent de la vérité; (*c*) résonner, retentir **(with,** de); **the air rang with their cries,** l'air résonnait de leurs cris; (*d*) **his words still r. in my ears,** ses paroles sonnent encore à mes oreilles; **my ears are ringing,** mes oreilles tintent, bourdonnent. **2.** *v.tr.* (*a*) (faire) sonner (une cloche); **to r. the (door) bell, to r. (at the door),** sonner à la porte; **r. the bell!** sonnez! *v.ind.tr.* **to r. for the maid,** sonner la bonne; **to r. for some coffee,** sonner pour demander du café; **to r. for the lift,** appeler l'ascenseur; **to r. for mass, for service,** sonner la messe, l'office; **to r. the alarm,** sonner le tocsin; (*b*) faire sonner (une pièce de monnaie); (*c*) *O:* **to r. the bell,** (i) (*at fair*) faire sonner la sonnette de la tête de Turc; (ii) *F:* réussir le coup; décrocher le grand succès; (*d*) *F:* **does that r. a bell?** est-ce que cela vous rappelle, dit, quelque chose? **3.** *v.tr. Tp:* **I'll r. you,** je vous téléphonerai; je vous donnerai un coup de téléphone, de fil; **I'll r. you back, again, tomorrow,** je vous rappellerai demain.
II. (*compound verbs*) **1. ring down,** *v.tr. Th:* **to r. down the curtain,** sonner pour la chute du rideau.
2. ring in, *v.tr.* carillonner la venue de (qn); **to r. in the New Year,** célébrer la nouvelle année par une volée de cloches, par un carillon.
3. ring off, *v.i.* (*a*) *Tp:* **to r. off,** raccrocher (l'appareil); couper la communication; **don't r. off!** ne coupez pas! (*b*) *v.tr. Nau:* **r. off the engines,** terminer pour la machine.
4. ring out. (*a*) *v.tr.* **to r. out the Old Year,** sonner, carillonner, la fin de l'année; (*b*) *v.i.* sonner; retentir; **the bells were ringing out,** les cloches sonnaient à toute volée; **a shot rang out,** un coup de fusil a retenti.

5. **ring up,** *v.tr.* (*a*) *Th:* **to r. up the curtain,** sonner pour faire lever le rideau; (*in Fr.*) frapper les trois coups; (*b*) *Tp:* **to r. s.o. up,** donner un coup de téléphone, de fil, à qn; appeler qn au téléphone; téléphoner à qn; (*c*) enregistrer (une somme) (sur une caisse enregistreuse).

ringbark ['riŋbɑːk], *v.tr. Arb:* baguer, cerner (un arbre, une branche); circoncire (un arbre fruitier).

ringbarking ['riŋbɑːkiŋ], *s. Arb:* annélation *f.*

ringbone ['riŋboun], *s. Vet:* forme *f* (sur le paturon).

ringcraft ['riŋkrɑːft], *s.* le pugilisme; la boxe; **an expert in r., a master of r.,** un pugiliste de premier ordre.

ringed [riŋd], *a.* **1.** (doigt) bagué. **2.** (*a*) (*of planet*) entouré d'un anneau; (*b*) **black-r. eyes,** yeux cernés de noir, de bistre; (*c*) **broad-r., fine-r., tree,** arbre *m* à couches épaisses, minces; (*d*) (oiseau) à collier; (animal) annelé, qui a des anneaux; *Orn:* **r. plover,** pluvier *m* à collier.

ringent ['rindʒənt], *a. Bot:* (corolle) ringente.

ringer ['riŋər], *s.* **1.** (*a*) sonneur *m*; carillonneur *m*; (*b*) *Tp:* machine *f* d'appel; **r. station,** sonnerie *f* d'appel. **2.** (*a*) *esp. U.S: F:* **to be a dead r. for s.o.,** être le portrait vivant de qn; être qn tout craché; (*b*) *Turf: F:* cheval substitué pour un autre. **3.** *Austr: F:* (excellent) tondeur *m* (de moutons).

ringhals ['riŋhæls], *s. Rept:* sépédon *m.*

ringing[1] ['riŋiŋ], *s.* **1.** (*a*) baguage *m* (d'un oiseau); bouclement *m* (d'un taureau, etc.); (*b*) *Tchn:* baguage (d'un tube, etc.). **2.** *Arb:* baguage, cernement *m* (d'un arbre); incision *f* annulaire; **r. knife, r. shears,** bagueur *m*; coupe sève *m inv.*

ringing[2], *a.* **1.** (*of bell*) qui tinte, qui résonne. **2.** sonore, retentissant; **in r. tones,** d'une voix vibrante; **clear r. laugh,** rire *m* qui sonne clair.

ringing[3], *s.* **1.** (*a*) son *m*, sonnerie *f*, tintement *m* (de cloches); bruit *m* de sonnette; (*b*) *Tp:* appel *m*, sonnerie; **delayed r.,** sonnerie à retardement; **keyless r.,** appel automatique; **r. current,** courant *m* d'appel; **r. changeover switch,** commutateur *m* de sonnerie. **2.** (*a*) tintement (dans les oreilles); (*b*) retentissement *m.* **3.** *Civ. E:* **r. engine,** sonnette *f* à tiraude (pour pilotis).

ringlead ['riŋliːd], *v.tr.* organiser (une manifestation) (contre qn, qch.).

ringleader ['riŋliːdər], *s.* **1.** meneur, -euse. **2.** chef *m* de bande, d'émeute; agitateur, -trice; organisateur, -trice, de troubles.

ringlet ['riŋlit], *s.* **1.** petit anneau. **2.** boucle *f* (de cheveux); anneau *m*; anglaise *f*; **to wear one's hair in ringlets,** porter les cheveux en boucles; porter des anglaises. **3.** *Ent:* érébia *m*, satyre *m.*

ringman, *pl.* **-men** ['riŋmən], *s.m. Turf:* bookmaker; *F:* book.

ringmaster ['riŋmɑːstər], *s.* maître *m* de manège (d'un cirque); chef *m* de piste.

ringneck ['riŋnek], *s. Orn:* oiseau *m* à collier.

ringnecked ['riŋnekt], *a. Orn:* **r. plover,** pluvier *m* à collier; *NAm:* **r. pheasant,** faisan *m* de chasse, *Fr.C:* faisan à collier.

ringstraked ['riŋstreikt], *a. Nat.Hist:* annelé.

ringtail ['riŋteil], *s.* **1.** (*a*) *Orn:* soubuse *f*; (*b*) *Z:* **r. (monkey),** capucin *m.* **2.** *Nau:* bonnette *f* de tapecul, de sous-gui, de brigantine.

ringtailed ['riŋteild], *a.* à queue zébrée; **r. lemur,** lémur(e) *m* catta; **r. monkey,** capucin *m*; **r. cat,** chat à queue annelée.

ringwall ['riŋwɔːl], *s.* **1.** mur *m* de clôture; clôture *f.* **2.** parois intérieures (d'un four).

ringworm ['riŋwəːm], *s. Med:* teigne tonsurante, tondante, annulaire; herpès tonsurant; **crusted r., honeycomb r.,** teigne faveuse.

rink [riŋk], *s.* **1. (skating) r., (ice) r.,** patinoire *f*; **roller-skating r.,** salle *f* de patinage à roulettes; *F:* skating *m.* **2. (curling) r.,** terrain délimité sur la glace pour chaque équipe du jeu de *curling.* **3.** équipe *f* (aux jeux de *curling*, de boules, de palet).

rinse[1] [rins], *s.* (*a*) rinçage *m*; **to give a bottle a r.,** rincer une bouteille; (*b*) *Hairdr:* **colour r.,** rinçage; (*c*) *P: O:* **to have a r.,** se rincer le gosier, la dalle; boire quelque chose.

rinse[2], *v.tr.* **1.** (*a*) **to r. (out) a bottle,** rincer une bouteille; **to r. one's mouth,** se rincer la bouche; *F:* **to r. one's dinner down with a glass of beer,** arroser son dîner d'un verre de bière; (*b*) **to r. one's hands,** se rincer les mains. **2.** rincer (le linge); **to r. the dirt, out,** faire disparaître des impuretés au cours des rinçages.

rinser ['rinsər], *s.* **1.** (*pers.*) rinceur, -euse. **2.** (*machine*) rinceuse *f.*

rinsing ['rinsiŋ], *s.* **1.** rinçage *m*; **r. bowl,** rinçoir *m.* **2. rinsings,** rinçure(s) *f*(*pl*).

Riodinidae [raiou'dinidiː], *s.pl. Ent:* riodinides *m*, érycinides *m.*

riot[1] ['raiət], *s.* **1.** émeute *f*; rassemblement tumultueux; attroupement séditieux; attentat *m* contre l'ordre public; **there'll be riots,** il y aura des troubles *m*, des émeutes, des bagarres *f*; **to call out the r. squad** = appeler police secours; **the R. Act,** la loi contre des attroupements; **to read the R. Act,** (i) faire les trois sommations légales; (ii) *F:* semoncer, tancer, qn d'importance. **2.** (*a*) *A:* dérèglement *m*, désordre *m* (de mœurs); débordement *m* (de vice etc.); (*b*) orgie *f* (de couleurs, de fleurs, etc.). **3.** (*a*) **to run r.,** (*of pers., fancy, etc.*) se déchaîner, ne plus connaître de frein; (*of plants*) pulluler; croître en abondance; (*b*) **the play was a r.,** la pièce a fait fureur; (*c*) *F:* **it's, he's, a r.,** c'est rigolo; c'est un rigolo.

riot[2], *v.* **(rioted) 1.** *v.i.* (*a*) provoquer une émeute; causer une bagarre; s'ameuter; faire une manifestation violente; (*b*) faire du vacarme; (*c*) *A:* mener une vie déréglée, désordonnée. **2.** *v.tr. A:* **to r. away one's time, one's money,** gâcher, gaspiller, son temps, son argent, en orgies.

rioter ['raiətər], *s.* émeutier, -ière; séditieux, -ieuse.

rioting[1] ['raiətiŋ], *a.* qui fait émeute; **r. mob,** bande *f* d'émeutiers.

rioting[2], *s.* émeutes *fpl*; troubles *mpl*; bagarres *fpl*; manifestations violentes.

riotous ['raiətəs], *a.* **1.** (*of assembly, etc.*) séditieux; tumultueux, turbulent. **2.** (*a*) (*of pers.*) tapageur, -euse, bruyant; **r. students,** étudiants qui font des manifestations violentes; (*b*) *A:* (*of pers., habits*) déréglé, dissipé, dissolu.

riotously ['raiətəsli], *adv.* **1.** séditieusement; tumultueusement. **2.** d'une manière désordonnée; en grand désordre.

riotousness ['raiətəsnis], *s.* **1.** turbulence *f* (de la foule, etc.). **2.** *A:* dérèglement *m.*

rip[1] [rip], *s.* déchirure *f*; ouverture *f* en long; fente *f*; (*caused by horns or tusks of animal*) décousure *f.*

rip[2], *v.* **(ripped) 1.** *v.tr.* (*a*) **to r. (up),** fendre; déchirer; **to r. open,** ouvrir (un paquet) en le déchirant; éventrer (un sac, une enveloppe); **to r. up, open,** éventrer (qn); mettre les tripes à l'air (à qn); découdre (un vêtement, le ventre); **the boar ripped him up, open,** le sanglier l'a décousu; **to r. a tyre,** éventrer un pneu; (*b*) **to r. (up),** refendre (le bois, l'ardoise); scier de long; (*c*) *Const:* **to r. a roof,** enlever les tuiles d'un comble; découvrir un toit; (*d*) **to r. sth. off, away,** arracher, déchirer, qch.; *F: O:* **to r. s.o. off,** voler, rouler, qn; **to r. out the lining of a coat,** arracher la doublure d'un habit; **to r. a page out of a book,** déchirer une page d'un livre. **2.** *v.i.* (*a*) se déchirer, se fendre; **to r. along the seams,** se découdre; (*b*) *F:* **to r. into s.o.,** attaquer qn; **to r. (along),** aller, avancer, à toute vitesse, à fond de train; (*of pers.*) **let him r.!** laissez-le faire à sa guise! (*of car, etc.*) **let her r.!** mettez tous les gaz! laissez-la filer! (*c*) *F: O:* **to let r.,** faire une noce à tout casser.

rip[3], *s.* **1.** (*horse*) vieille rosse. **2.** (*a*) *O:* mauvais garnement; bambocheur, -euse; *A:* **an old r.,** un vieux marcheur; un vieux paillard; (*b*) *A:* gaillard (déluré); **he's a bit of a r.,** c'est un gaillard.

rip[4], *s.* **1.** clapotis *m* (du courant); bouillonnement *m* (des eaux d'un fleuve). **2.** étendue *f* d'eau agitée (dans un fleuve, etc.); **r. tide,** courant de retour.

riparian [rai'pɛəriən]. **1.** *a.* & *s.* riverain, -aine. **2.** *a. Nat.Hist:* ripicole.

ripcord ['ripkɔːd], *s.* (*a*) corde *f* de déchirure (d'un ballon); (*b*) corde d'ouverture, cordelette *f* de déclenchement (d'un parachute).

ripe [raip], *a.* **1.** (*a*) mûr; **r. wheat, corn,** blé mûr; **r. fruit,** fruits mûrs; **r. cheese,** fromage (bien) fait, bien à point; **r. timber,** bois (de forêt) mûr, exploitable; **r. abscess,** abcès mûr; **r. beauty,** beauté *f* dans sa maturité, en pleine fleur; *O:* **r. lips,** lèvres *f* vermeilles; **to grow r.,** mûrir; (*b*) **r. judgement,** jugement mûr; **a r. old age,** un bel âge; **people of riper years,** personnes d'un âge mûr; *O:* **r. scholar,** savant accompli; **r. experience,** expérience mûrie. **2. the plan is r. for execution,** le projet est mûr, est prêt à être exécuté; **time is r. for speaking the truth,** le temps est venu où on devrait dire la vérité; **opportunity r. to be seized,** occasion à saisir immédiatement; **r. for mischief,** prêt à faire le mal.

ripely ['raipli], *adv.* (*a*) mûrement; (*b*) avec un jugement mûr; avec maturité.

ripen ['raip(ə)n]. **1.** *v.tr.* (faire) mûrir; affiner (le vin, le fromage). **2.** *v.i.* (*a*) (*of fruit*) mûrir; tourner; (*under glass*) joûtir; (*of abscess*) mûrir; (*of plan, etc.*) mûrir; venir à maturité; **this cheese will never r.,** ce fromage ne viendra jamais à point, ne sera jamais fait; (*b*) **to r. into manhood,** atteindre l'âge d'homme.

ripeness ['raipnis], *s.* maturité *f*; état mûr.

ripening[1] ['raip(ə)niŋ], *a.* **1.** (*of sun*) qui fait mûrir; (*of season*) favorable à la maturité. **2.** mûrissant, qui mûrit; (blé) jaunissant.

ripening[2], *s.* maturation *f*; mûrissage *m*, mûrissement *m*; jaunissement *m* (du blé); véraison *f* (du raisin); affinage *m* (du fromage, du vin); mise *f* à point (d'un projet, etc.); (*for fruit*) **r. depot,** mûrisserie *f.*

ripienist [ripi'einist], *s. Mus:* ripiéniste *mf.*

ripieno [ripi'einou], *a.* & *s. Mus:* ripieno (*m*); **r. cornet,** piston *m* ripieno.

riposte[1] [ri'pɔst], *s. Box: Fenc: etc:* riposte *f.*

riposte[2], *v.i. Box: Fenc: etc:* riposter.

ripper ['ripər], *s.* **1.** *Tls:* (*a*) scie *f* à refendre; arpon *m*; (*b*) fendoir *m* (pour ardoises); (*c*) (*chisel*) burin *m* à défoncer; (*d*) *Civ. E:* défonceuse *f.* **2.** *Hist:* **Jack the R.,** Jack l'Éventreur. **3.** *F: A:* type épatant; chose épatante.

ripping[1] ['ripiŋ], *a. F: O:* épatant, fameux, formidable.

ripping[2], *s.* **1.** (*a*) déchirement *m*; **a r. sound,** un bruit de quelque chose qui se déchire, qui se fend; *Aer:* **r. panel,** panneau *m* de déchirure (d'un ballon); (*b*) *Tls:* **r. iron,** bec-de-corbin *m*, *pl.* becs-de-corbin. **2.** sciage *m* en long; refente *f* (du bois).

rippingly ['ripiŋli], *adv. F: O:* épatamment; d'une façon épatante.

ripple[1] [ripl], *s. Tex:* drège *f*; égreneuse *f* (pour le lin); égrugeoir *m.*

ripple[2], *v.tr. Tex:* dréger, égrener, égruger (le lin).

ripple[3], *s.* **1.** (*a*) ride *f* (sur l'eau); ondulation *f*; *Nau:* **cross r.,** revolin *m* de lame; ressac *m*; *Geog:* **sand r., r. mark,** ride de sable; sillon ondulé; ripple-mark *m*, *pl.* ripple-marks; **wind r.,** ride éolienne; (*b*) (*in hair*) ondulation; (*c*) *Tex:* **r. cloth,** ondulé *m* de laine; **r. silk,** cloqué *m* de soie. **2.** (*a*) gazouillement *m* (d'un ruisseau); léger clapotis (de l'eau); (*b*) murmure(s) *m*(*pl*) (de conversation); **a r. of laughter,** une vague de rires. **3.** *Ph:* série *f* d'ondes.

ripple[4]. **1.** *v.i.* (*a*) (*of sea, lake*) se rider; (*b*) (*of corn, hair*) onduler, ondoyer; (*c*) **the river rippled on,** la rivière coulait en ondoyant; (*d*) (*of stream*) murmurer, gazouiller; (*of tide*) clapoter; (*of laughter*) perler; partir en vagues. **2.** *v.tr.* (*of wind, etc.*) rider (l'eau, le sable).

rippled ['ripld], *a.* ridé; ondulé.

rippler ['riplər], *s. Tex:* = RIPPLE[1].

rippling[1] ['ripliŋ], *s. Tex:* égrenage *m*, égrugeage *m* (du lin); **r. comb** = RIPPLE[1].

rippling[2], *a.* (ruisseau) murmurant, gazouillant; **r. laughter,** rires perlés.

rippling[3], *s.* gazouillement *m*, clapotis *m* (de l'eau).

ripply ['ripli], *a.* (*of water, sand*) couvert de rides.

riprap[1] ['ripræp], *s.* **1.** *A:* pétarade *f* (de feux d'artifice, etc.). **2.** *Civ.E: Hyd.E:* enrochement *m* (d'un fond boueux, etc.).

riprap[2], *v.tr.* **(riprapped)** *Civ.E: Hyd.E:* enrocher.

riprapping ['ripræpiŋ], *s. Civ.E: Hyd.E:* enrochement *m.*

rip(-)roaring ['riprɔːriŋ], *a. F:* (*a*) tumultueux; pétaradant; (*b*) **a r. success,** une réussite du tonnerre; un succès fulgurant, de tous les diables.

ripsaw ['ripsɔː], *s. Tls:* scie *f* à refendre.

ripsnorter ['ripsnɔːtər], *s. F:* (*a*) type extraordinaire, bruyant, tapageur; (*b*) chose *f* extraordinaire; **a r. of a storm,** une tempête de tous les diables.

ripsnorting ['ripsnɔːtiŋ], *a. F:* tumultueux; tapageur, -euse.

riptide ['riptaid], *s.* raz *m* de courant.

Ripuarian [ripju(ː)'ɛəriən], *a.* & *s. Hist:* **the R. Franks, the Ripuarians,** les Francs *m* ripuaires, les Ripuaires *m*; **the R. code of law,** la loi ripuaire.

rise[1] [raiz], *s.* **1.** (*a*) *Lit:* **r. of day,** l'aube *f*; *Th:* **r. of the curtain,** lever *m* du rideau; (*b*) *Ven:* **to shoot a bird on the r.,** tirer un oiseau au cul levé; (*c*) *Fish:* (*of fish*) montée *f*; **to be on the r.,** moucheronner; monter à la mouche; **I haven't had a r. all day,** ça n'a pas mordu, je n'ai pas eu une touche, de toute la journée; *F:* **to take, get, a r. out of s.o.,** (i) berner qn; mystifier qn; faire marcher qn; se payer la tête, la figure, de qn; (ii) faire monter qn; mettre qn en colère; **you can't get a r. out of him,** (i) on ne la lui fait pas; (ii) il ne perd jamais son sang-froid; rien ne le démonte. **2.** (*a*) montée, côte *f* (de route); rampe *f*; **r. in the ground,** exhaussement *m* du terrain; (*sharp*) ressaut *m* de terrain; *Mth:* **r. of a curve,** pente *f* d'une courbe; (*b*) éminence *f*, élévation *f*; **church standing on a r.,** église située sur une hauteur; (*c*) *Oc:* seuil (sous-marin). **3.** (*a*) *Arch: Civ.E:* flèche *f*, hauteur sous clef (d'un arc, d'une voûte); rampant *m* (d'une voûte); (*b*) **r. of step,** (i) hauteur de marche; (ii) = RISER 2 (*a*); (*c*) *Metalw:* volée *f* (du marteau); (*d*) *Geol:* inclinaison *f* (d'une couche); (*e*) *N.Arch:* relevé *m*, relèvement *m*, acculement *m* (d'une varangue). **4.** *Min:* montage *m*, remontage *m*, remonte *f*, remontée *f* (des travaux). **5.** (*a*) crue *f* (des eaux); flot *m*, flux *m* (de la marée); hausse *f* (du baromètre); élévation *f*, relèvement (de température); augmentation *f*, accroissement *m* (de pression); **r. of the tide,** montée de l'eau; **r. and fall of the sea,** flot et jusant *m*, flux et reflux *m*, de la mer; **perceptible r. in temperature,** relèvement sensible de la température; **sudden r. of temperature,** saut *m* de température; *El:* **pressure r.,** surtension *f*; augmentation de tension; à-coup *m* de tension; (*b*) augmentation, élévation, hausse (de prix); augmentation (de salaire); renchérissement *m* (des denrées); **the r. in the price of wheat,** la hausse du prix du blé, le renchérissement du blé; **r. in value of a possession,** appréciation *f* d'un bien; plus-value *f*; **r. in the bank rate,** relèvement du taux de l'escompte; **food prices are on the r.,** le prix des denrées, le coût de la vie, est en hausse; **his fortunes are on the r.,** ses affaires reprennent; ses actions *f* (re)montent; *St.Exch:* **to speculate on, operate for, a r.,** jouer à la hausse; **to ask (one's employer) for a r.,** demander une augmentation; (*c*) *Mus:* **r. of half a tone,** hausse d'un demi-ton. **6.** avancement *m*; élévation (en rang); **r. to power,** montée au pouvoir; **the r. of Napoleon,** l'essor *m* de Napoléon; **r. and fall of an empire,** grandeur *f* et décadence *f* d'un empire. **7.** source *f*, naissance *f*, origine *f*; **to give r. to sth.,** faire naître, engendrer, produire, occasionner, qch.; donner lieu, donner naissance, à qch.; **privilege that gives r. to abuses,** privilège *m* qui prête, qui donne lieu, aux abus; **bacteria that give r. to fermentation,** bactéries *f* qui provoquent la fermentation; **to give r. to difficulties,** faire surgir des difficultés; entraîner, susciter, des difficultés; **to give r. to comment(s), to dissatisfaction,** provoquer des commentaires, le mécontentement; **it would give r. to misunderstandings,** cela donnerait lieu à des malentendus.

rise[2], *v.* (**rose** [rouz]; **risen** ['riz(ə)n])

I. *v.i.* **1.** (*a*) **to r. (to one's feet),** se lever; se mettre debout; (*after kneeling, after a fall*) se relever; se remettre debout; **he fell never to r. again,** il tomba pour ne plus (jamais) se relever; **to r. from one's seat,** se lever (de son siège); **to r. from table,** se lever de table; *Th: O:* **to r. at an actor,** (se lever pour) saluer un acteur d'acclamations; (*of horse*) **to r. on its hind legs,** se dresser; se cabrer; (*b*) *Pol:* **the House rose at five o'clock,** la Chambre a levé la séance à cinq heures; **Parliament will r. next week,** le Parlement va s'ajourner, entrera en vacances, la semaine prochaine; (*c*) **to r. early, late,** se lever tôt, tard; *F:* **r. and shine!** debout les morts! (*d*) **to r. (again) from the dead,** ressusciter des morts, d'entre les morts; **Christ is risen,** le Christ est ressuscité; **he looks as if he had risen from the grave,** il a l'air d'un déterré, il a une mine de déterré; **town rising from its ashes,** ville qui renaît de ses cendres. **2. to r. (in revolt),** se soulever, se révolter (**against,** contre); **the whole country had risen,** tout le pays était en révolte; **to r. in arms,** prendre les armes; **to r. in protest against sth.,** se soulever, se révolter, contre qch. **3.** (*a*) (*of sun, star*) se lever; (*of smoke, mist, balloon*), monter, s'élever; **I saw the sun r.,** j'ai vu lever le soleil; (*b*) **to r. off the ground,** quitter le sol; **to r. in the stirrups, the saddle,** faire du trot enlevé; *O:* trotter à l'anglaise; **to r. to the surface,** monter à la surface; **a drowning man rises three times,** une personne qui se noie remonte trois fois à la surface; (*c*) (*of fish*) **to r. to the bait,** monter à la mouche; moucheronner; mordre; *F:* (*of pers.*) **to r. to it,** se laisser provoquer; riposter à une provocation; **he didn't r. to it,** il a laissé passer l'occasion; (*d*) *Ven:* (*of game*) se lever, partir, s'envoler; (*e*) **a murmur rose from the crowd,** une rumeur s'est dégagée de la foule. **4.** (*a*) (*of ground, road, etc.*) monter, s'élever; (*of ground*) se relever; **the building is rising gradually,** l'édifice s'élève peu à peu; **the dough won't r.,** la pâte ne lève pas, ne bouffe pas; **the tide is rising,** la marée monte; **the sea is rising,** (i) la mer monte; (ii) la mer devient grosse, s'agite; *Nau:* la mer se creuse; **the river has risen,** le fleuve est en crue; **the barometer is rising,** le baromètre monte, remonte, est à la hausse; **the thermometer rose to more than 35°,** le thermomètre a dépassé 35°; **to r. and fall,** monter et retomber, monter et s'abaisser, s'élever et s'abaisser; **the boat rose and fell on the water,** le bateau se balançait sur l'eau; *Nau:* (*of ship*) **to r. with the sea,** s'élever à la lame; (*b*) **trees rising a hundred feet above the plain,** arbres *m* qui s'élèvent à cent pieds au-dessus de la plaine; **a building rose up out of the fog,** un bâtiment se dressait dans le brouillard; **steeples r. on all sides,** partout les clochers pointent; (*c*) **a picture rose in my mind,** une image s'est présentée à mon esprit; **a building rose to view,** un bâtiment se présenta à la vue; *Nau:* **a ship's mast was rising on the horizon,** un mât de navire sortait de l'eau, s'élevait à l'horizon; (*d*) (*of wind*) (i) se lever; (ii) croître, forcer; **her colour rose,** ses joues s'empourpraient; **his hopes are beginning to r.,** ses espérances commencent à croître; l'espérance lui vient; **his spirits are rising,** son moral remonte; **his voice rose,** sa voix s'élevait; sa voix devenait plus aiguë; son ton montait; **his voice rose above the noise of the crowd,** sa voix se faisait entendre au-dessus du bruit de la foule; (*e*) (*of prices*) monter, hausser; **prices are rising,** les prix sont à la hausse, sont en hausse; **prices have risen considerably,** les prix ont subi une forte hausse; **everything has risen (in price),** tout a augmenté de prix, tout renchérit; **sugar rose to five francs a kilo,** le prix du sucre s'éleva, le sucre a monté, est monté, à cinq francs le kilo. **5.** (*a*) **to r. above vanity,** être au-dessus de la vanité; **to r. above events,** se montrer supérieur aux événements; (*b*) **the horse rose at the fence,** le cheval s'enleva pour franchir l'obstacle; **to r. to the occasion,** s'élever à la hauteur des circonstances; se montrer à la hauteur de la situation; *F:* **I can't rise to it,** (i) je ne me sens pas d'humeur à le faire; (ii) je n'ai pas la force de le faire; (iii) je n'ai pas les moyens de le faire. **6. to r. in the world, in life,** faire son chemin; parvenir; **to r. to wealth,** devenir riche; **to r. to the rank of colonel,** monter au grade de colonel; **to r. in s.o.'s esteem,** monter, croître, dans l'estime de qn; **to r. purely by merit,** réussir par son seul mérite; **he rose from nothing,** il est parti de rien. **7.** (*of river*) prendre sa source (**at,** à; **in,** dans); **the quarrel rose from a misapprehension,** la querelle a eu son origine dans un malentendu, provient d'un malentendu, est née d'un malentendu. **8.** (*used adjectivally*) **high r. flats,** (appartements construits en) gratte-ciel.

II. *v.tr.* (*a*) *Ven:* **to r. a bird,** lever, faire lever, faire partir (un faisan, une perdrix); (*b*) *Fish:* **I couldn't r. a fish,** le poisson n'a pas mordu; je n'ai pas eu une touche (de la journée).

riser ['raizər], *s.* **1.** (*pers.*) **early r.,** personne matinale; **to be an early r.,** être matinal; (avoir l'habitude de) se lever de bonne heure, de bon matin, de grand matin. **2.** (*a*) *Const:* (ais *m* de) contremarche *f*; (*b*) *Bootm:* gorge *f* (du talon). **3.** (*a*) *Petr:* colonne montante; *Ind: Plumb:* canalisation ascendante; tuyau *m* de montée; colonne ascendante, montante; (*b*) *Metall:* (i) (trou *m* d')évent *m*; (ii) masselotte *f*.

risibility [rizi'biliti], *s. O:* **1.** risibilité *f*; faculté *f* de rire; disposition *f* à rire; **this excited our r., our risibilities,** cela nous a fait rire. **2. outbursts of r.,** éclats *m* de rire. **3.** risibilité; ridicule *m* (d'une situation, etc.); caractère *m* dérisoire (d'une offre, etc.).

risible ['rizibl], *a.* **1.** (*a*) *A:* rieur, -euse; disposé au rire; (*b*) (faculté, etc.) du rire. **2.** risible, ridicule; **a r. offer,** une offre dérisoire.

rising[1] ['raiziŋ], *a.* **1.** (*a*) (soleil) levant; (brume) qui s'élève; (*b*) **r. trot,** trot enlevé; (*c*) *Her:* **a falcon r.,** à un faucon essorant. **2.** (*a*) (route) qui monte; (baromètre, température) en hausse; **r. ground,** élévation *f* du terrain; éminence *f*; **r. tide,** marée montante; *Rail:* **r. gradient,** rampe *f*; *Hyd:* **r. water,** eau ascendante; *Const:* **r. damp,** humidité *f* qui monte du sol; (*b*) *Arch:* **r. arch,** voûte rampante; (*c*) **r. main,** (i) *Plumb:* conduite montante; (ii) *Min:* colonne *f* d'exhaure; (*d*) *Mec.E: Ind:* **r. table,** table *f* à hauteur variable; (*e*) *N.Arch:* **r. floor timbers,** varangues acculées; **r. wood,** contre-quille *f*, *pl.* contre-quilles; **r. line,** ligne *f* des façons; (*f*) *Phot:* **r. front,** objectif *m* à décentration *f*, à décentrement *m*, en hauteur. **3.** (*a*) (vent) qui se lève; (colère) qui croît, qui monte; (colère) croissante; **r. colour,** rougeur croissante; **r. importance,** importance croissante; (*b*) **r. price,** prix croissant, en hausse; **r. market,** marché orienté à la hausse; **to speculate on a r. market,** jouer à la hausse. **4. r. man,** homme *m* d'avenir, qui fait son chemin; **r. genius,** génie *m* à son orient. **5. the r. generation,** la génération montante, qui monte; la nouvelle, la jeune, génération. **6.** (*used adverbially*) **horse r. five,** cheval prenant cinq ans; **he's r. sixty,** il va sur (ses) soixante ans.

rising[2], *s.* **1.** (*a*) lever *m* (du rideau); (*b*) levée *f*, clôture *f* (d'une assemblée); **upon the r. of the House,** quand la Chambre se leva; **upon the r. of Parliament,** quand le Parlement entra en vacances; (*c*) **I don't like early r.,** je n'aime pas à me lever tôt; (*d*) **r. again, r. from the dead,** résurrection *f*. **2.** (*a*) ameutement *m*, insurrection *f*, révolte *f*, soulèvement *m*; (*b*) *O:* **r. of the stomach,** soulèvement de cœur. **3.** (*a*) lever, ascension *f* (d'un astre); (*b*) *Ven:* envol *m* (de gibier). **4.** (*a*) crue *f* (des eaux); ascension, poussée *f*, montée *f* (de la sève); **r. and falling,** mouvement *m* de hausse et de baisse, de montée et de descente; (*b*) *Nau:* **r. of the floor timbers,** acculement *m*, relevé *m*, des varangues. **5.** élévation *f*, avancement *m* (en rang).

risk[1] [risk], *s.* (*a*) risque *m*, péril *m*, aléa *m*, hasard *m*; **the risks of an undertaking,** les aléas d'une entreprise; **this business is full of risks,** ce genre d'affaires comporte beaucoup de risques; **the risks of war,** les hasards de la guerre; **there is a r. of his catching cold,** il risque de s'enrhumer; **there is a r. of his being robbed,** il court le risque d'être volé; **there is a certain r. in waiting,** il y a du risque à attendre; **to run, incur, a r.,** courir un risque; **to run the r. of losing everything,** courir le risque, risquer, de tout perdre; **to take risks,** courir des risques; **don't take too many risks,** prenez garde de trop vous exposer, de trop vous aventurer, de courir trop de risques; **it isn't worth the r.,** cela ne vaut pas le coup; **I'm not taking any risks,** je ne veux rien risquer; **with no r. of. . .,** sans risque de. . .; **without any r. to peace,** sans aucun danger pour la paix; **at the r. of his life,** au risque, au péril, de sa vie; **at one's own r.,** à ses risques et périls; **at the r. of displeasing him,** au risque de lui déplaire; **at the r. of a collision,** de manière à faire craindre une collision; **calculated r.,** risque calculé, bien pesé; *Surg:* **poor r. case,** malade chez qui une opération comporte un réel danger vital; (*b*) *Ins:* risque; **r. subscribed,** risque assuré; **theft r.,** risque de vol; **fire r.,** risque d'incendie; **war risks,** risques de guerre; **risks and perils at sea,** risques et périls de la mer; péril de mer; fortune *f* de mer; **maritime r., sea r.,** risque maritime, risque de mer; **craft r.,** risque d'allèges; **port r.,** risque de port; **hull port r.,** risque de port sur corps; **comprehensive, all risks, policy,** police *f* tous risques; **third-party r.,** risque du recours du tiers; **tenant's third-party r.,** risque locatif; (*pers., thg*) **a good, bad, r.,** un bon, mauvais, risque; **to underwrite a r.,** souscrire, partager, un risque.

risk[2], *v.tr.* risquer; (*a*) aventurer, hasarder (qch.); **to r. one's skin,** risquer sa peau; payer de sa personne; **to r. everything on one throw,** jouer, risquer, le tout pour le tout; jouer son va-tout; (*b*) **we must r. a battle,** il faut risquer le combat; **I wouldn't r. a crossing in such weather,** je ne me risquerais pas à tenter la traversée par un temps pareil; **I'll r. it,** je vais risquer le coup; risquons le coup; (*c*) **to r. defeat,** courir les chances d'une défaite; **to r. a sprained ankle, to r. breaking one's leg,** risquer, courir le risque, de se donner une entorse, de se casser la jambe; **I can't r. getting a puncture in the middle of the night,** je ne peux courir le risque, les chances, d'une crevaison au milieu de la nuit.

riskily ['riskili], *adv.* d'une manière hasardeuse, chanceuse; hasardeusement; aléatoirement.

riskiness ['riskinis], *s.* nature hasardeuse, aléatoire (d'une entreprise, etc.).

risky ['riski], *a.* **1.** hasardeux, chanceux, aléatoire. **2.** (*of story, etc.*) risqué, osé, scabreux; **to tell r. stories,** conter des gaillardises.

risotto [ri'zɔtou], *s. Cu:* risotto *m*.

risqué ['ri(:)skei], *a.* risqué, osé.

Riss [ris]. *Geol:* (*a*) *s.* riss *m*; (*b*) *a.* rissien.

Rissian ['risiən], *a. Geol:* rissien.

rissoa [ri'souə], *s. Moll:* rissoa *f*.

Rissoidae [ri'souidi:], *s.pl. Moll:* rissoïdés *m*.

rissole ['risoul], *s. Cu:* croquette *f*.

ritardando [ritɑ:'dændou], *adv. & s. Mus:* ritardando (*m*).

rite [rait], *s.* rite *m*, cérémonie *f*; **the Roman r.,** le rite romain; le rite de l'Église romaine; **Congregation of (Sacred) Rites,** Congrégation *f* des Rites; **to practise a r.,** pratiquer un rite; **to die fortified with the rites of the Church,** mourir muni des sacrements de l'Église; **funeral rites, burial rites,** rites funèbres; **the rites of freemasonry,** les rites de la franc-maçonnerie; **with all the customary rites and ceremonies,** dans les formes; **the rites of hospitality,** les rites de l'hospitalité.

ritornello [ritɔ:'nelou], *s. Mus:* ritournelle *f*.

rittingerite ['ritiŋdʒərait], *s. Miner:* rittingérite *f*.

ritual ['ritjuəl]. **1.** *a.* rituel; selon le rite, selon les rites. **2.** *s.* (*a*) rites, cérémonies *fpl*, cérémonial *m*; (*b*) (*book*) rituel *m*; (*c*) *Parl: etc:* rituel; (*d*) **she makes a r. of her household duties,** elle fait son ménage selon des rites immuables, dont elle ne déroge pas.

rituale [ritju'ɑ:li], *s. R.C.Ch:* rituale *m*.

ritualism ['ritjuəlizm], *s. Ecc:* ritualisme *m*, cérémonialisme *m*.

ritualist ['ritjuəlist], *a. & s.* ritualiste (*mf*).

ritualistic [ritjuə'listik], *a.* ritualiste.

ritually ['ritjuəli], *adv.* selon les rites; rituellement.

ritzy ['ritsi], *a. F:* (*a*) tape-à-l'œil, voyant, clinquant; (*b*) ultra-chic *inv.*

rival[1] ['raiv(ə)l], *a. & s.* (*a*) rival, -ale, *pl.* -aux, -ales; concurrent, -ente; (*b*) **as a harpist she has no r.,** comme harpiste elle n'a pas d'égal.

rival[2], *v.* (**rivalled**) **1.** *v.tr.* (*a*) rivaliser avec (qn, qch.); *occ.* rivaliser (qn); (*b*) **English church architecture rivals any in the world,** l'architecture ecclésiastique de l'Angleterre peut rivaliser avec celle de n'importe quel autre pays. **2.** *v.i.* rivaliser (**with,** avec).

rivalize ['raivəlaiz], *v.i.* rivaliser (**with,** avec).

rivalry ['raivəlri], *s.* (*a*) rivalité *f*; **political r.,** rivalité politique; **in r. with s.o.,** en concurrence avec qn; en rivalité avec qn; (*b*) émulation *f*.

rive [raiv], *v.* (**rived** [raivd]; **riven** ['riv(ə)n]) **1.** *v.tr.* (*a*) fendre (le bois, la roche, etc.); **trees riven by lightning,** arbres éclatés par la foudre; *Lit:* **riven heart,** cœur déchiré; (*b*) *A:* & *Lit:* **to r. sth. from s.o., from sth.,** arracher qch. à qn, de qch.; **to r. sth. off, away,** arracher qch. **2.** *v.i.* se fendre; éclater.

river[1] ['rivər], *s.* **1.** (*a*) cours *m* d'eau; (*entering sea*) fleuve *m*; (*tributary*) rivière *f*; **short coastal r.,** fleuve côtier; **the r. Thames,** la Tamise; **on the r. bank,** au bord de la rivière; **down r.,** en aval; **up r.,** en amont; **to cross the r. (of death),** trépasser, mourir; *Lit:* passer l'Achéron; *esp. U.S: P:* **up the r.,** en prison, en taule; **to send s.o. up the r.,** emprisonner qn, mettre qn en taule; *F:* **to sell s.o. down the r.,** trahir, vendre, qn; (*b*) **r. port,** port fluvial; **r. bar,** barre *f* de rivière; **r. wall,** bajoyer *m*; **r. pearl,** perle *f* (de moule) d'eau douce; *Myth:* **r. god,** fleuve; *Med:* **r. blindness,** onchocercose *f*; *Z:* **r. hog,** potamochère *m*. **2.** coulée *f* (de lave, etc.); flot *m*, fleuve (de sang); *Typ:* **r.** (*of white running down the page*) rue *f*, lézarde *f*. **3.** *Lap:* **diamond of the finest r.,** diamant *m* de la plus belle eau.

river[2] ['raivər], *s.* (*pers.*) fendeur *m* (de bois, de pierre).

river-borne ['rivəbɔ:n], *a.* (*of goods*) transporté par (voie d')eau.

riverine ['rivərain], *a.* riverain.

riverside ['rivəsaid], *s.* bord *m* de l'eau; rive *f*; **r. inn,** auberge située au bord de la rivière; **r. properties,** propriétés riveraines.

rivet[1] ['rivit], *s.* (*a*) rivet *m*; **binding r.,** rivet de montage; **brazier-head, oval-head, plug-head, r.,** rivet à tête en goutte de suif; **button-head, raised-head, r.,** rivet à tête bombée; **cheese-head, cylindrical-head, r.,** rivet à tête cylindrique; **clamp r.,** rivet de fixation; **cone-head, steeple-head, r.,** rivet à tête conique; **flat-head r.,** rivet à tête plate; **flush(-head) r.,** rivet à tête affleurée, à tête noyée, à tête perdue; **hollow r.,** rivet creux, rivet forcé; **pan-head r.,** rivet à tête tronconique; **round-head, cup-head, snap-head, r.,** rivet à tête ronde, à tête hémisphérique; **slotted r.,** rivet bifurqué; **snap(ped) r.,** rivet à tête bouterollée; **solid r.,** rivet plein; **split r.,** rivet fendu; **straight-neck, straight-shank, r.,** rivet à fût droit; **swell-neck, tapered-neck, r.,** rivet à fût renflé; **tubular r.,** rivet tubulaire; **to lay, drive, a r.,** poser un rivet; **to drive out a r.,** enlever un rivet; **to drive out the rivets,** dériveter; **r. head,** tête *f* de rivet; **r. hole,** trou *m* de rivet; **r. joint,** assemblage *m* à rivets; **r. plate, washer,** contre-rivure *f*; rosette *f*; **r. point,** rivure *f*; **r. shank,** fût *m*, tige *f*, de rivet; *Tls: etc:* **r. buster,** coupe-rivet *m*, *pl.* coupe-rivets; **r. gun,** pistolet *m* à river; rivoir *m* pneumatique; **r. hearth, r.-heating furnace,** forge *f*, fourneau *m*, à chauffer les rivets; **r. peen, r. punch, r. set, r. snap,** bouterolle *f*; chasse-rivet(s) *m inv*; **r. pliers, r. tongs,** pinces *f*, tenailles *f*, à rivets; (*pers.*) **r. driver,** riveur *m*; frappeur *m*; **r. heater,** chauffeur *m* de rivets; **r. holder,** teneur *m* de tas; appuyeur *m*; **r. passer,** passeur *m* de rivets; (*b*) (*for china*) attache *f*.

rivet[2], *v.tr.* (**rivet(t)ed**) (*a*) river (un clou, etc.); **to r. over the head of a bolt,** aplatir, bouteroller, la tête d'un boulon; (*b*) clouer (deux plaques de tôle, etc.); *Bootm:* **to r. on the sole,** clouer la semelle; (*c*) assembler avec des rivets; river; riveter; **to gun r.,** riveter au pistolet; **to r. cold, hot,** riveter à froid, à chaud; **to single-shot, multi-shot, r.,** riveter au monofrappe, au multifrappe; **rivet(t)ed together,** assemblés à rivets; **rivet(t)ed joint,** rivure *f*; (*d*) **his eyes were riveted on the speaker,** il avait les yeux fixés sur l'orateur; **I stood riveted to the spot,** je restais cloué sur place.

riveter ['rivitər], *s.* **1.** (*pers.*) riveur *m*, frappeur *m*. **2.** (*machine*) riveuse *f*, riveteuse *f*, rivoir *m*; machine *f*, presse *f*, à river; **hydraulic, pneumatic, r.,** riveteuse hydraulique, pneumatique; **percussion r.,** riveuse, riveteuse, à martelage.

rivetless ['rivitlis], *a.* sans rivets.

rivet(t)ing ['rivitiŋ], *s.* (*a*) *Metalw:* rivetage *m*; rivure *f*; **single, double, triple, quadruple, r.,** rivetage, rivure, sur un rang; rivetage double, triple, quadruple; **butt r.,** (i) rivetage à couvre-joints, à franc-bord; (ii) rivetage des abouts; **chain r.,** rivetage en chaîne; rivure parallèle; **hand r.,** rivetage à la main; **machine r.,** rivetage à la machine; rivetage mécanique; **r. machine,** machine *f* à river, riv(et)euse *f*; **hammer r.,** rivetage au marteau; **r. hammer,** rivoir *m*, matoir *m*; marteau *m* à river; marteau-riveur *m*, *pl.* marteaux-riveurs; **hydraulic r., pneumatic r.,** rivetage hydraulique, pneumatique; **cold r., hot r.,** rivure à froid, à chaud; **close r.,** rivure étanche; **flat r.,** rivure plate; **flush r.,** rivure à fleur; **cross r., staggered r.,** rivetage en quinconce; **battered-head r.,** rivure écrasée; **snapped-head r.,** rivure bouterollée; **r. lug,** cosse *f* à river; **r. press,** presse *f* à river; **r. die, r. punch, r. set,** bouterolle *f*; chasse-rivet(s) *m inv*; **r. ram, r. tool,** rivoir *m*; **r. tongs,** pinces, tenailles, à river; (*b*) *Bootm:* clouage *m*, clouure *f* (des semelles).

Riviera (the) [əərivi'ɛərə], *Pr.n. Geog:* **the (French) R.,** la Côte d'Azur; **the Italian R.,** la Riviera (italienne); **the Cornish R.,** la côte sud de la Cornouailles.

rivière [ri'vjɛər], *s.* rivière *f* de diamants.

rivina [ri'vainə], *s. Bot:* rivina *m*.

rivularia [rivju'lɛəriə], *s. Algae:* rivularia *m*, rivulaire *f*.

Rivulariaceae [rivjulɛəri'eisii:], *s.pl. Algae:* rivulariacées *f*.

rivulet ['rivjulit], *s.* ruisseau *m*; petit cours d'eau.

rix-dollar ['riksdɔlər], *s. Num: A:* rixdale *f*.

riziform ['rizifɔ:m], *a.* riziforme.

roach[1] [routʃ], *s. Ich:* gardon *m*; *F: A:* **to be as sound as a r.,** se porter à merveille; *A:* être sain, frais, comme un gardon.

roach[2], *v.tr. U.S:* couper en brosse (la crinière d'un cheval).

roach[3], *s. Nau:* échancrure *f* (du bas d'une voile).

roach[4], *s. NAm: Ent: F:* blatte *f*.

road[1] [roud], *s.* **1.** route *f*; chemin *m*; voie *f*; (*a*) **metalled, unmetalled, r.,** route empierrée, non empierrée; **r. metal,** matériaux *mpl* d'empierrement (pour routes); cailloutis *m*; **r. metalling,** cailloutage *m*; **paved r.,** chaussée (pavée); route pavée; **tarred r.,** route goudronnée; **macadam(ized) r.,** route macadamisée; **sealed r.,** route à revêtement étanche; **single-track, double-track, r.,** route à voie unique, à deux voies; **three-lane r.,** route à trois voies, à triple courant; **embanked r.,** route en remblai; **sunken r.,** chemin creux; route encaissée; **overhanging r.,** route en encorbellement; **r. making,** construction *f*, confection *f* de routes; **r. under repair,** route en réparation; **r. works, r. repairs,** travaux *mpl* de voirie; réfection *f* des chaussées; **r. surveyor,** agent voyer; **r. builder,** constructeur *m* de routes; **r. roller,** rouleau compresseur; *P.N: Aut:* **r. works (ahead),** travaux; *P.N:* **no r. markings,** marquages routiers interrompus; **major r., main r., first class r., A. r.** = route nationale; route de grande communication; grande route; **secondary r., B. r.** = route secondaire, route départementale; **through r.,** traverse *f*, route, directe; *P.N:* **no through r.,** voie sans issue; **busy r., r. with heavy traffic,** route à grande circulation; **local r., minor r.,** chemin vicinal; route d'intérêt local; **ring r., orbital r.,** route de ceinture; boulevard *m* périphérique; **toll r.,** route de péage; **approach r.,** route d'accès; **service r., accommodation r.,** *NAm:* **frontage r.,** chemin, voie, de desserte; chemin de terre, d'exploitation; passage *m* de service; **pack r.,** chemin muletier; **strategic, military r.,** route stratégique, militaire; *Mil:* **axial r.,** (route) pénétrante *f*; **supervised r.,** route à circulation réglementée; **reserved r., dispatch r.,** route gardée; **supply r.,** route, axe *m*, de ravitaillement; **abandoned r.,** route désaffectée; **r. unsuitable for motor vehicles,** route impraticable (aux automobiles); **r. conditions,** état *m* des routes; **r. transport,** transports routiers; **r. accidents,** accidents *m* de la circulation; **r. users,** usagers *m* de la route; **r. sense,** sens *m* de la route; **r. map,** carte routière; *Aut:* **r. fund licence** = vignette *f*; *Sp:* **r. race,** course *f* sur route; **r. racer,** bicyclette *f* de course sur route; vélo *m* de route; *Ind:* **r. run, r. test,** essai(s) *m(pl)* (d'une voiture) sur route; **rolling r.,** banc *m* d'essai à rouleaux; **rolling r. test,** essai(s) statique(s) sur banc à rouleaux; (*b*) rue *f*; **Church r.,** rue de l'Église; **they live in the same road as you,** ils habitent la même rue que vous; **this r. leads to the station,** ce chemin mène à la gare; *Adm:* **adopted r.,** route, rue, entretenue par la municipalité; **unadopted r.** = chemin privé; (*c*) **the r. to London,** la route de Londres; **to take the r. for London,** prendre la route de Londres; se mettre en route pour Londres; **the r. from London to Edinburgh,** la route de Londres à Édimbourg; **to take to the r.,** (i) *A:* se faire voleur de grand chemin; (ii) se faire clochard; **to be on the r.,** (i) être en route, en chemin, en voyage; (ii) *Com:* être représentant; (iii) *Com:* (*of representative*) être en tournée; **to be on the right r.,** être dans la bonne voie; **the r. to success,** le chemin, la voie, du succès; **to be on the r. to success, to fortune,** être en (bonne) voie de réussir, en train de faire fortune; **to be on the r. to recovery,** être en voie de guérison; (*d*) voie, chemin; **it's your r.,** vous avez la priorité; *Rail:* **to whistle for the r.,** demander la voie; siffler au disque; **to give (s.o.) the r.,** donner la voie à (un train); *P:* **get out of my r.!** ouste! (*e*) tablier *m* (d'un pont); **r. bearer,** poutrelle *f* (de pont de bateaux). **2.** chaussée *f*; **in the r.,** sur la chaussée; **to step into the r.,** s'engager sur la chaussée; quitter le trottoir; **car that holds the r. well,** voiture qui tient bien la route; *F:* **to hog the r.,** conduire au milieu de la chaussée; brûler le pavé. **3.** *Min:* galerie *f*, voie *f*; **air r.,** voie d'aérage. **4.** *Nau:* **road(s),** rade *f*; **outer r.,** rade extérieure; avant-port *m*; **in the roads,** en rade; **to leave the roads,** dérader; **roads well sheltered from the north,** bonne rade du nord. **5.** *NAm:* chemin de fer; voie ferrée; **running r.,** voie principale; **to run on the wrong r.,** circuler à contre-voie.

road[2], *v.tr. Ven:* (*of dog*) **to r. (up) the game,** suivre le gibier (ailé) à la piste; suivre la piste du gibier.

roadbed ['roudbed], *s. Civ.E:* (*a*) assiette *f*, encaissement *m* (de la route); plate-forme *f*, *pl.* plates-formes; (*b*) *Rail:* superstructure *f* (de la voie); terre-plein *m*, *pl.* terre-pleins.

roadblock ['roudblɔk], *s.* barrage routier, de route.

roadbook ['roudbuk], *s.* itinéraire *m*; guide routier.

roadhog ['roudhɔg], *s. F:* écraseur *m*, chauffard *m*.

roadholding ['roudhouldiŋ], *s.* (*of car, etc.*) tenue *f* de route.

roadhouse ['roudhaus], *s.* hôtellerie *f* en bord de route.

roadmaker ['roudmeikər], *s.* (*a*) constructeur *m* de routes; (*b*) travailleur *m* de la voirie.

roadman, *pl.* **-men, roadmender** ['roudmən, -mendər], *s.* cantonnier *m*; travailleur *m* de la voirie.

roadmaster ['roudmɑ:stər], *s.m. Rail:* brigadier-poseur, *pl.* brigadiers-poseurs.

roadrailer ['roudreilər], *s. Rail:* wagon *m* rail-route.

roadrunner ['roudrʌnər], *s. Orn:* coucou *m* terrestre de Californie, coureur *m* de routes.

roadside ['roudsaid], *s.* bord *m*, bas-côté *m*, côté *m*, de la route, de la chaussée; *Civ.E:* accotement *m*; **r. inn,** auberge, café, situé(e) au bord de la route; **r. flowers,** fleurs *f* des chemins; *Aut:* **r. repairs,** réparations *f* de fortune; dépannage *m*.

roadstead ['roudsted], *s. Nau:* rade *f*; **open r.,** rade foraine, ouverte; **sheltered r., closed r.,** rade-abri *f*, *pl.* rades-abris; rade fermée, abritée; **outer r.,** grande rade; **to leave the r.,** dérader.

roadster ['roudstər], *s.* **1.** cheval *m*, -aux, de fatigue. **2.** (*a*) (bicyclette *f*) routière *f*; (*b*) *Aut: O:* torpédo *m*.

roadway ['roudwei], *s.* **1.** chaussée *f*. **2.** (*a*) passage *m* carrossable; (*b*) voie *f*, tablier *m*, plancher *m*, aire *f* (de pont); (*c*) voie (de mine).

roadworthiness ['roudwə:ðinis], *s.* (*of vehicle*) aptitude *f* à rouler.

roadworthy ['roudwə:ði], *a.* (*of vehicle*) en état de rouler; en état de marche.

roam[1] [roum], *s. O:* petite promenade; flânerie *f*.

roam[2]. **1.** *v.i.* errer, rôder; **to r. about,** (i) battre du pays; (ii) se promener de-ci de-là; **to r. about the world,** courir le monde; vadrouiller de par le monde; *F:* rouler sa bosse. **2.** *v.tr.* errer par, parcourir (les rues, etc.); **to r. the seas,** sillonner les mers.

roamer ['roumər], *s.* vagabond, -onde; nomade *mf*; *F:* roule-ta-bosse *m inv*.

roaming[1] ['roumiŋ], *a.* errant, vagabond.

roaming[2], *s.* course errante; course à l'aventure.

roan[1] [roun]. **1.** *a.* rouan. **2.** *s.* (cheval) rouan *m*; vache rouanne; **red r.,** (cheval) aubère *m*.

roan[2], *s. Bookb:* basane *f*.

roar[1] [rɔ:r], *s.* **1.** (*a*) (*of pers.*) hurlement *m*; rugissement *m*, vocifération *f*; grands cris; **roars of laughter,** grands éclats de rire; **to set the table, the company, in a r.,** faire rire aux éclats la table, toute la société; (*of remark, etc.*) déclencher un fou rire; (*b*) rugissement (du lion); mugissement *m* (du taureau). **2.** grondement *m* (de canon, de tonnerre, d'une foule); mugissement (de la mer); clameurs *fpl* (du vent, de la tempête); ronflement *m*, brondissement *m* (d'un fourneau); **the waves were breaking with a r.,** les lames se brisaient avec fracas.

roar[2]. **1.** *v.i.* (*a*) (*of pers.*) hurler, rugir, vociférer; beugler; **to r. with pain,** hurler de douleur; **to r. with anger,** rugir de colère; **to r. with laughter,** éclater de rire; (*b*) (*of lion*) rugir; (*of bull*) mugir; (*of camel*) blatérer; (*c*) (*of thunder, storm*) gronder; (*of cannon*) tonner; (*of sea*) mugir; (*of fire*) ronfler; (*of stove*) brondir; **a car roared by,** une voiture a passé en ronflant; (*d*) *Vet:* (*of horse*) corner. **2.** *v.tr.* (*a*) **to r. (out) an order,** hurler, vociférer, un ordre; (*b*) **to r. s.o. down,** réduire qn au silence par des hurlements; (*c*) **to r. oneself hoarse,** s'enrouer, se casser la voix, à force de hurler.

roarer ['rɔ:rər], *s.* **1.** braillard *m*. **2.** *Vet:* (cheval) cornard *m*, corneur *m*, souffleur *m*. **3.** *Petr:* puits jaillissant.

roaring[1] ['rɔ:riŋ], *a.* **1.** (*a*) (homme) hurlant; (lion) rugissant; (taureau) mugissant; (*b*) (tonnerre) grondant; (feu) ronflant; (vent) mugissant; **a r. fire,** (i) une belle flambée; (ii) un feu d'enfer; **the r. forties,** les parages océaniques situés entre les 40e et 50e degrés de latitude; (c) *Vet:* **r. horse** = ROARER 2. 2. *F:* (a) **to do a r. trade,** faire un gros commerce; faire des affaires superbes, des affaires d'or; **r. success,** succès fou; *O:* **to have a (rip) r. time,** s'amuser follement; (b) *Scot:* **the r. game,** le curling.

roaring[2], *s.* 1. = ROAR[1]. 2. *Vet:* cornage *m.*

roast[1] [roust], *s.* 1. *Cu:* rôti *m*; **a r. of veal,** un rôti de veau; **pot r.,** rôti *m* à la cocotte; *F: O:* **he rules the r.,** il a la haute main; c'est lui le maître; il fait la loi chez lui. 2. **to give sth. a good r.,** bien rôtir qch. 3. *Metall:* **r. of ore,** fournée *f* de minerai (soumis au grillage).

roast[2], *v.* 1. *v.tr.* (a) rôtir, faire rôtir (la viande); cuire (la viande) au four; rôtir (des marrons); **to pot r. (a joint),** faire rôtir à la cocotte; **fire fit to r. an ox,** feu à rôtir un bœuf; **to r. oneself (in front of the fire),** se rôtir, se griller, devant le feu; (b) *Ind:* griller, calciner, fritter (le minerai); ressuer (le minerai de plomb, d'argent); (c) torréfier, griller, brûler (le café); (d) *A:* railler, blaguer, berner (qn). 2. *v.i.* (a) (*of meat, etc.*) rôtir; (b) *F:* **I was roasting in the sun,** je grillais au soleil.

roast[3], *a.* **r. meat,** viande rôtie; **r. pork,** porc rôti; rôti *m* de porc; **r. beef,** rôti de bœuf; rosbif *m*; **r. potatoes,** pommes de terre rôties (au four); *Bot: F:* **r. beef plant,** iris *m* fétide; iris-gigot *m.*

roaster ['roustər], *s.* 1. (*pers.*) rôtisseur, -euse. 2. (a) *Dom.Ec:* rôtissoire *f*; (b) *Metall:* four *m* à griller; four de grillage (de minerai); (c) brûloir *m*, torréfacteur *m* (à café). 3. animal *m*, volaille *f*, à rôtir. 4. *F: O:* journée *f* torride.

roasting[1] ['roustiŋ], *a.* (feu, etc.) brûlant; torréfiant.

roasting[2], *s.* 1. rôtissage *m*, cuisson *f* (de la viande); **r. meat,** viande *f* à rôtir; **r. jack,** tournebroche *m.* 2. *Metall:* **(ore) r.,** grillage *m*, calcination *f*, frittage *m*, fritte *f* (du minerai); ressuage *m* (du minerai de plomb, d'argent); **ore r. chamber, spot,** chambre *f*, aire *f*, de grillage du minerai. 3. torréfaction *f* (du café). 4. *F:* (a) *A:* raillerie *f*; (b) éreintage *m* (d'un auteur); (c) *O:* semonce *f*, réprimande *f*; *F:* savon *m*; **to give s.o. a r.,** (i) blaguer qn sans pitié; (ii) éreinter qn; (iii) flanquer un savon à qn.

rob [rɔb], *v.tr.* **(robbed)** voler, détrousser (qn); dévaliser (qn); piller (un verger); **to r. s.o. of sth.,** (i) voler, dérober, ravir, qch. à qn; (ii) escroquer qch. à qn; **to r. a tree of its fruit,** dépouiller un arbre; **to r. the till,** voler la caisse; **he has been robbed of his money,** on lui a volé, a dérobé, son argent; **he would r. a church,** il en prendrait sur l'autel; **to r. Peter to pay Paul,** décoiffer saint Pierre pour coiffer saint Paul; déshabiller, découvrir, saint Pierre pour habiller, couvrir, saint Paul; faire un trou pour en boucher un autre; *Min:* **to r. a mine,** écrémer une mine; *Sp:* **he was robbed of victory at the last moment,** au dernier moment on lui arracha la victoire.

robands ['roubəndz], *s.pl. Nau:* rabans *m* d'envergure, d'empointure, de faix; envergures *f.*

robber ['rɔbər], *s.* (a) voleur, -euse; (b) *A:* brigand *m*; **r. chief,** chef *m* de brigands; (c) *Crust:* **r. crab,** crabe *m* des cocotiers, crabe voleur; *Ent:* **r. fly,** asilidé *m*, asile *m.*

robbery ['rɔbəri], *s.* vol (qualifié); **armed r., r. under arms,** vol à main armée; **r. with violence,** vol avec violences, avec agression; *A:* **highway r.,** vol de grand chemin; brigandage *m*; **to commit highway r.,** voler sur les grands chemins; *F:* **it's highway r., sheer daylight r.!** c'est le coup de fusil! c'est de l'escroquerie pure et simple! c'est du vol manifeste!

robe[1] [roub], *s.* 1. (a) robe longue; **(baby's) christening r.,** robe de baptême; (b) *NAm:* (i) robe de chambre; (ii) sortie *f* de bain; (c) robe (d'office, de cérémonie); *Hist:* **the short r.,** la robe courte (des militaires); **the long r.,** la robe longue (des gens de droit et du clergé); **gentlemen of the r., the R.,** les gens *m* de robe; la robe; *Pej:* les robins *m*; **magistrate in his robes,** magistrat *m* en robe; **the Queen's Coronation robes,** les robes et insignes du sacre de la reine; **Master of the Robes,** grand maître de la garde-robe (du roi); **Mistress of the Robes,** dame d'honneur chargée de la garde-robe (de la reine). 2. *NAm:* **(buffalo) r.,** peau de buffle (employée comme couverture); **lap r.,** couverture *f* de voyage.

robe[2]. 1. *v.tr.* revêtir (qn) d'une robe d'office, de cérémonie. 2. *v.i.* revêtir sa robe, sa toge, etc.

Robert ['rɔbət]. 1. *Pr.n.m.* Robert; *Bot:* **herb R.,** herbe *f* à Robert; géranium robertin. 2. *F: A:* **a R.,** un agent de police.

Robin ['rɔbin]. 1. *Pr.n.m.* (*dim.*) Robert, Bob; **R. Goodfellow,** lutin *m* domestique; **R. Hood,** Robin des Bois. 2. *s.* (a) *Orn:* rouge-gorge *m*, *pl.* rouges-gorges; **American r.,** merle migrateur; *Fr.C:* merle américain; **Pekin r.,** leiothrix *f* jaune, rossignol *m* du Japon; **magpie r.,** dyal *m*; (b) *Bot:* **ragged R.,** lychnide *f* des prés; fleur *f* de coucou; *F:* **R. run (in) the hedge,** lierre *m* terrestre; **robin's eye,** herbe *f* à Robert, à l'esquinancie; géranium robertin; (c) *see* ROUND ROBIN.

robing ['roubiŋ], *s.* revêtissement *m* des robes de cérémonie, etc.; **r. room,** vestiaire *m* (d'un juge, etc.).

robinia [rou'biniə], *s. Bot:* robinier *m.*

roble ['roubl], *s. Bot:* roble *m*; (*timber*) pellin *m.*

robot ['roubɔt], *s.* (a) robot *m*; automate *m*; (b) **r. bomb,** bombe volante; (c) (*in S. Africa*) feux *m* de circulation.

robotization [roubɔtai'zeiʃ(ə)n], *s.* robotisation *f.*

robotize ['roubɔtaiz], *v.tr.* robotiser.

robur ['roubər], *s. Bot:* **r. (oak),** (chêne *m*) rouvre *m.*

roburite ['roubərait], *s. Exp:* roburite *f.*

robust [rou'bʌst], *a.* 1. (*of pers., faith, etc.*) robuste, vigoureux, solide; **r. appetite,** appétit *m* robuste; rude appétit; **he's not very r.,** il est d'une santé délicate. 2. (a) (*of machinery*) solide; (b) (*of wine*) qui a du corps; corsé.

robustious [rou'bʌstjəs], *a. F:* 1. *A:* robuste, vigoureux, solide. 2. violent, bruyant; **r. style,** style rude, énergique, robuste. 3. **r. climate,** climat *m* rude.

robustly [rou'bʌstli], *adv.* robustement, vigoureusement.

robustness [rou'bʌstnis], *s.* (a) nature *f* robuste; robustesse *f*; vigueur *f*; (b) bonne santé.

roc [rɔk], *s. Myth:* rock *m.*

rocaille [rɔ'kai], *s.* rocaille *f.*

rocambole ['rɔkæmboul], *s. Bot:* rocambole *f*; échalote *f* d'Espagne.

roccellic [rɔ'tʃelik], *a. Ch:* (acide) roccellique.

roccelline ['rɔtʃelain], *s. Ch:* roccelline *f.*

rochet ['rɔtʃit], *s. Ecc.Cost:* rochet *m*; surplis *m* à manches étroites.

rock[1] [rɔk], *s.* 1. (a) rocher *m*; roc *m*; **built on r.,** bâti sur le roc; **cut in(to) the r.,** creusé dans le roc; **r. island,** rocher isolé; **r. face,** paroi *f*; *Mount:* varappe *f*; **r. climber,** varappeur *m*; **r. climbing,** varappe; **r. basin,** bassin rocheux; **r. cavity,** cavité rocheuse; **r. glacier, r. stream,** glacier *m*, coulée *f*, de pierres; **r. cone,** cône rocheux; **r. dust,** pulvérin rocheux, schisteux; **r. flour,** dépôt finement trituré (des deltas pro-glaciaires); **r. bottom,** (i) fond rocheux; (ii) *F:* le fin fond; le comble; **r.-bottom price,** prix le plus bas; **prices have reached r. bottom,** les prix sont au plus bas; *Geol:* **r. step,** ressaut *m*; *Miner:* **r. crystal,** cristal *m* de roche; quartz hyalin; **r. alum,** alun *m* de roche; **r. cork,** liège *m* de montagne; liège fossile; *O:* **r. leather,** cuir *m* de montagne; **r. salt,** sel *m* gemme; *Bot:* **r. rose,** ciste *m*; hélianthème *m*; **r. maple,** érable dur; **r. melon,** cantaloup *m*; *Orn:* **r. bunting,** bruant fou; **r. dove, r. pigeon,** pigeon *m* biset; **r. hopper,** gorfou *m*, manchot sauteur; **r. pipit,** pipit maritime, obscur; **r. ptarmigan,** lagopède alpin; perdrix *f* de neige; *Z:* **r. whistler,** marmotte *f* des Alpes; *Tch:* **r. sucker,** lamproie *f* de mer; *Com:* **r. salmon,** squale *m*, cagnot *m*; *Prehist:* **r. shelter,** abri *m* sous roche; *Art:* **r. drawings,** dessins *m* rupestres; *Tls:* **r. drill, r. bit,** perforatrice *f* (de rocher); foreuse *f*, sonde *f*, sondeuse *f*, bosseyeuse *f*; rock-bit *m*, *pl.* rock-bits; (b) *Geol:* roche *f*; **basic rocks,** roches basiques; **igneous, sedimentary, metamorphic, rocks,** roches ignées, sédimentaires, métamorphiques; **endogenous, exogenous, rocks,** roches endogènes, exogènes; **volcanic, basaltic, rocks,** roches volcaniques, basaltiques; **crystalline rocks,** roches cristallines; (*in Bahamas, etc.*) **beach rocks,** dalles de grès (soudées par un ciment naturel); **honeycomb r.,** roche (à structure) alvéolaire; **mother r., parent r.,** roche mère; **(oil) source r.,** roche mère (de pétrole); **reservoir, container, carrier, r.,** roche-réservoir *f*, roche-magasin *f*, *pl.* roches-réservoirs, -magasins; *Min:* **country r., wall, r.,** roche encaissante. 2. (a) **a r.,** (i) un rocher, une roche; (ii) *NAm:* (*also*) une pierre; un moellon; **as firm as a r.,** ferme comme un roc; *Hist:* **the Tarpeian R.,** la Roche tarpéienne; *Geog:* **the R. of Gibraltar,** *F:* **the R.,** le Rocher de Gibraltar; *O:* **R. English,** l'anglais *m* de Gibraltar; *Nau:* **to run on, strike, the rocks,** se jeter sur des roches; donner sur les écueils; **to see rocks ahead,** (i) *Nau:* voir des rochers devant; (ii) *Fig:* voir surgir des obstacles, des difficultés; *F:* **to be on the rocks,** (i) (*of pers.*) être sans le sou, fauché, à sec, dans la dèche; (ii) (*of marriage*) être en échec, à vau-l'eau; *NAm:* **to throw rocks at s.o.,** jeter des pierres à qn; **whisky on the rocks,** whisky *m* aux glaçons, *Fr.C:* sur glace; *Cu:* **r. cake,** petit gâteau (à surface irrégulière, qui ressemble à un rocher); (b) *Ecc:* **the r. of our salvation,** le rocher de notre salut; **the R. of Ages,** Jésus-Christ; (c) *esp. U.S: P:* **rocks,** diamants *m*, cailloux *m.* 3. *Comest:* bâton(s) *m(pl)* de sucrerie.

rock[2], *s.* 1. bercement *m*; balancement *m*; **give baby a r.,** remue un peu le berceau (du bébé). 2. *Mus: Danc:* rock *m*; **r. 'n roll,** rock-and-roll *m.*

rock[3], *v.tr. & i.* (a) bercer, balancer, remuer; *Tchn:* dodiner (un blutoir, etc.); *Mec.E:* basculer (un levier, etc.); **to r. a child,** bercer un enfant; **to r. a child on one's knees,** balancer un enfant sur ses genoux; **to r. a cradle,** remuer, balancer, un berceau; **to r. a child to sleep,** endormir un enfant en le berçant; **ship rocked by the waves,** navire ballotté, balancé, par les flots; **we were rocked gently by the waves,** nous étions bercés par les flots; **to r. (backwards and forwards) in one's chair,** se balancer sur sa chaise, sur son fauteuil à bascule; **the house was rocked by, rocked with the shock of, the earthquake,** le tremblement de terre a secoué, a ébranlé, la maison; la maison oscillait, tremblait, sous le choc (du tremblement de terre); *Min:* (*gold*) **to r. the ore,** travailler le minerai au berceau; *Phot:* **to r. a plate,** balancer une plaque (dans le révélateur); (b) *F:* secouer, ébranler, alarmer (qn); **that'll r. him,** voilà qui va le surprendre, le secouer; **to r. the boat,** secouer la barque; faire du grabuge; (c) danser le rock.

rock[4], *s. A:* quenouille *f.*

rockbird ['rɔkbə:d], *s. Orn:* 1. macareux *m*, mormon *m.* 2. rupicole *m*, coq *m* de roche.

rockbound ['rɔkbaund], *a.* entouré de rochers; **r. coast,** côte hérissée de rochers.

rocker ['rɔkər], *s.* 1. (*pers.*) *A:* remueur, -euse (de l'enfant au berceau). 2. bascule *f* (de berceau, de fauteuil à bascule, etc.); *F:* **to be off one's r.,** avoir l'esprit dérangé; être un peu fou, timbré, loufoque. 3. (a) *Min:* (*gold*) berceau *m*; sas *m* mobile; (b) branloire *f* (d'un soufflet de forge); (c) *Phot:* balance-cuvette *m*, *pl.* balance-cuvettes; (d) (*skating*) (i) rocker *m*; (ii) patin *m* à lame recourbée; (e) *esp. NAm: F:* fauteuil *m* à bascule. 4. (a) *I.C.E:* culbuteur *m*; **r.-actuated engine,** moteur *m* à culbuteur; **r. adjuster, r. adjusting screw,** vis *f* de réglage de culbuteur; **r. box,** commande *f* de, du, culbuteur; **r. shaft,** axe *m* de culbuteur; **r. arm, lever,** (i) *I.C.E:* (doigt *m* de) culbuteur; (ii) *Mec.E:* basculeur *m*; **exhaust r. arm,** culbuteur d'échappement; **intake r. arm,** culbuteur d'admission; *Mch:* **r. shaft,** arbre *m* de renversement de marche; *Civ.E:* **r. bar,** bielle *f* (de pont métallique); (b) *El:* **(brush) r.,** armature *f* porte-balais; joug *m*, balancier *m*, du porte-balais.

rockery ['rɔkəri], *s.* rochers artificiels; jardin *m* de rocaille.

rocket[1] ['rɔkit], *s. Bot:* 1. **(garden, Roman) r.,** roquette *f.* 2. **(dame's) r.,** julienne *f* des dames. 3. **London r.,** vélaret *m.* 4. **blue r.,** (i) aconit *m* napel; tue-chien *m inv*; (ii) pied-d'alouette *m*, *pl.* pieds-d'alouette. 5. **corn r.,** roquette des champs.

rocket[2], *s.* 1. (a) *Pyr:* fusée *f*; **spinning r.,** tournante *f*; **r. signal, signal r.,** fusée de signalisation; fusée-signal *f*, *pl.* fusées-signaux; **r. signalling,** signalisation *f* par fusées; **tracer r.,** fusée traçante; **r. case,** gobelet *m*; **r. gun,** (i) *Pyr:* lance-fusée(s) *m*; (ii) *Nau:* lance-amarre *m*; **to fire, shoot, a r.,** lancer, tirer, une fusée; (b) *F:* **he's just had a r. from the old man,** il vient de se faire engueuler par (i) son père, son vieux, (ii) le patron. 2. (a) *Space: etc:* fusée; **first-stage r.,** fusée mère; **one-stage r.,** fusée à un étage, fusée monoétage; **two-stage r.,** fusée à deux étages; **chemical r.,** fusée chimique; **electric r.,** fusée (à propulsion) électrique; **ion(-drive) r.,** fusée (à propulsion) ionique; **liquid-propellant r.,** fusée à liquides, à propergol liquide; **photon(-drive) r., plasma(-drive) r.,** fusée à photons, à plasma; **solid-propellant r.,** fusée à poudre, à propergol solide; **(thermodynamic) nuclear r.,** fusée (à propulsion) nucléaire; **carrier r., propulsive r.,** fusée porteuse, propulsive; **r. propulsion,** propulsion *f* par fusée(s); **man r., personal r.,** fusée individuelle; **meteorological r.,** fusée météorologique; **sounding r., probe r.,** fusée sonde; **r. motor,** moteur *m* fusée; groupe *m* fusée; *Av:* **steering r.,** fusée de guidage; **r.-propelled aircraft,** avion propulsé par fusées; **r.-assisted takeoff,** décollage *m* avec fusée(s) d'appoint; **to launch a r.,** lancer une fusée; **r. launcher,** (i) appareil *m*, rampe *f*, de lancement de fusées; lance-fusée(s) *m*; (ii) *Mil:* lance-roquettes *m*; **r. base,** base *f* de lancement de fusées; (b) *Ball:* roquette *f*; **(aircraft) r. pod,** nacelle *f* porte-roquettes, lance-roquettes; **r.(-firing) aircraft,** avion (armé, équipé, de) lance-roquettes.

rocket[3], *v.i.* (a) (*of horse*) se lancer comme un éclair; (*of rider, etc.*) **to r. into s.o.,** fondre comme un éclair sur qn; caramboler contre qn; (*of rider*) **to r. off,** vider les arçons; (b) (*of partridge, aircraft*) monter en chandelle; (c) (*of prices*) monter en flèche.

rocketer ['rɔkitər], *s. F:* gibier (ailé) qui monte en chandelle.

rocketry ['rɔkitri], *s.* 1. l'étude *f*, la technologie, la technique, des fusées. 2. l'arsenal *m* des (projectiles-) fusées.

rockfall ['rɔkfɔ:l], *s.* éboulement *m.*

rock-fill ['rɔkfil], *a. Hyd.E: etc:* (barrage) en enrochement(s); **dumped r.-f. dam,** barrage en enrochement en vrac.

rockfish ['rɔkfiʃ], *s. Ich:* (*a*) poisson *m* de roche; (*b*) goujon *m* de mer; (*c*) labre *m.*

rockhead ['rɔkhed], *s. F:* idiot, -ote; bas-de-plafond *m*; andouille *f.*

Rockies (the) [ðə'rɔkiz], *Pr.n.pl. Geog:* les (Montagnes) Rocheuses.

rockiness ['rɔkinis], *s.* nature rocheuse, rocailleuse.

rocking[1] ['rɔkiŋ], *a.* **1.** oscillant; à bascule; **r. motion,** (i) *Mec: etc:* mouvement *m* de bascule; (ii) *Civ.E:* mouvement de ballant (d'un pont); (iii) *Rail:* mouvement de lacet (d'un wagon); (iv) *Aut:* louvoiement *m*, lacet *m* (d'une voiture). **2.** branlant.

rocking[2], *s.* **1.** balancement *m*, bercement *m*; oscillation *f*; *Mec.E:* basculage *m*; *Rail: etc:* mouvement *m* de lacet; **r. chair,** fauteuil *m* à bascule; berceuse *f*; **r. horse,** cheval *m* à bascule; *Geol:* **r. stone,** rocher branlant; pierre branlante; (*skating*) **r. turn,** rocker *m*; *Mch:* **r. valve,** distributeur oscillant, tournant. **2.** tremblement *m*, secousses *fpl*; branlement *m*. **3.** *Tchn:* dodinage *m* (d'un blutoir, etc.).

rockling ['rɔkliŋ], *s. Ich:* motelle *f*; loche *f* de mer.

rock-ribbed ['rɔkribd], *a. U.S: F:* (*of pers.*) inébranlable.

rockslide ['rɔkslaid], *s.* (*a*) avalanche *f* de rochers; (*b*) traînée *f* d'éboulis.

rockweed ['rɔkwi:d], *s. Algae:* fucus *m.*

rockwork ['rɔkwə:k], *s.* **1.** rocaille *f*; rochers artificiels. **2.** *Min:* travaux *mpl* en roche.

rocky[1] ['rɔki], *a.* **1.** rocailleux; rocheux, plein de rochers. **2.** de roc, de roche; rocheux; **r. soil,** terrain *m* de roche; **r. bottom,** fond *m* de roche; *Geog:* **the R. Mountains,** les Montagnes Rocheuses.

rocky[2], *a. F:* (*a*) chancelant, instable, branlant; **this table's a bit r.,** cette table n'est pas très stable; **his business is in a r. condition,** ses affaires vont mal; (*b*) **I feel a bit r.,** la tête me tourne; je ne suis pas dans mon assiette.

rococo [rə'koukou], *a. & s.* **1.** *Art: etc:* rococo (*m*). **2.** *F: O:* (*of pers., character, etc.*) vieux jeu; baroque.

rod [rɔd], *s.* **1.** baguette *f*, canne *f*. **2.** verge *f*; **to be beaten with rods,** être battu de verges; **to make, pickle, a r. for one's own back,** se préparer des ennuis; cueillir des verges pour se faire fouetter; **to have a r. in pickle for s.o.,** garder à qn un chien de sa chienne; avoir une dent contre qn; la garder bonne à qn; *Prov:* **spare the r. and spoil the child,** qui aime bien châtie bien. **3.** verge (d'huissier, de bedeau); **to rule s.o. with a r. of iron,** mener qn à la baguette; gouverner qn avec une main de fer; tyranniser qn. **4.** (*a*) (**fishing**) **r.,** canne à pêche; gaule *f*; **casting r.,** canne à lancer; **fly r.,** canne à mouche, à fouetter; **r. and line,** ligne *f* de pêche; **to fish with r. and line,** pêcher à la ligne; **r. fishing,** pêche *f* à la ligne; (*b*) pêcheur *m* à la ligne. **5.** *Meas:* perche *f* (= approx. 5 m). **6.** (*a*) tringle *f*; **curtain r.,** tringle de rideau; **stair r.,** tringle d'escalier; (*b*) **iron r.,** barre *f* de fer; **r. iron,** fer en verges; *Const:* (*in reinforced concrete*) **compression, tension, r.,** barre de compression, de tension; **copper r.,** barre de cuivre; *El:* **discharging r.,** excitateur *m* (pour condensateur, etc.); **carbon, zinc, r.,** crayon *m* de charbon, de zinc (de pile); **ferrite r.,** bâtonnet *m* de ferrite; *Atom.Ph:* **fuel r.,** barreau *m* de combustible; (*c*) *Mec.E: etc:* tige *f*; **threaded r.,** tige filetée, à vis; **control r.,** tringle de manœuvre; *Mch:* bielle *f* de commande; *Atom.Ph:* barre de réglage; **pump r.,** tige de pompe; *Ph:* **pendulum r.,** verge *f* de pendule; *Min:* **boring, drill, r.,** tige de sonde, de forage; *Aut:* **brake r.,** tige, tirant *m*, de frein; (**steering**) **cross r.,** barre d'accouplement; **driving r., main (connecting) r.,** bielle motrice, principale, maîtresse; **eccentric r.,** barre excentrique; tige du tiroir; *Av:* **fork r.,** biellette *f* double; *Mec.E:* (**system, series, of**) **rods,** tringlerie *f*; *Civ.E:* **auxiliary rods of a framework,** éléments *m* auxiliaires d'un système articulé; *NAm:* **to ride the rods,** voyager (comme passager clandestin) au-dessous d'un fourgon de chemin de fer; (*d*) *NAm: P:* revolver *m*, basset *m*. **7.** *Anat: etc:* (*a*) **retinal rods,** bâtonnets rétiniens; **r. and cone layer,** couche *f* des cônes et des bâtonnets; **r. pigment,** pourpre rétinien; **r. bacterium,** bâtonnet; (*b*) **condyle r.,** tige condylienne; (*c*) *Dent:* **enamel rods,** prismes *m* d'émail. **8.** *P:* verge; membre viril; pénis *m*. **9.** *Surv:* mire *f*; **graduated r.,** jalon gradué; **self-reading, speaking, r.,** mire parlante.

rodding ['rɔdiŋ], *s. Com:* (**iron**) **r.,** fer *m* en verges.

rode [roud], *v.i. Ven:* (*of wild fowl*) voler vers la terre au crépuscule; (*of woodcock*) sortir au crépuscule.

rodent ['roudənt]. **1.** *a.* (animal, ulcère, souci) rongeur. **2.** *s. Z:* rongeur *m*; *Adm:* **r. officer,** fonctionnaire chargé de la dératisation.

Rodentia [rou'dentiə], *s.pl. Z:* rongeurs *m.*

rodenticidal [roudenti'saidl], *a.* rodonticide.

rodenticide [rou'dentisaid], *s.* rodonticide *m.*

rodeo ['roudiou, rou'deiou], *s.* **1.** rodéo *m*. **2.** *F:* **motor cycle r.,** concours *m* de motocyclisme.

Roderick ['rɔd(ə)rik], **Rod(e)rigo** [rɔ'dri:gou], *Pr.n.m.* Rodrigue, Roderic.

Rodinal ['rɔdin(ə)l], *s. R.t.m: Phot:* Rodinal *m*; révélateur *m* au paramidophénol.

rodlike, rod-shaped ['rɔdlaik, -ʃeipt], *a.* (*a*) en forme de barre; (*b*) en forme de baguette, de bâton, de bâtonnet; *Nat. Hist:* bacilliforme; *Anat:* **r. cell,** bâtonnet *m.*

rod(s)man, *pl.* **-men** ['rɔd(z)mən], *s.m.* **1.** *Surv:* porte-mire, *pl.* porte-mires. **2.** *A:* pêcheur à la ligne. **3.** *NAm: P:* **rodman,** voleur armé; bandit.

rodomontade[1] [rɔdəmɔn'teid], *s. A: Lit:* rodomontade *f.*

rodomontade[2], *v.i. A: Lit:* faire le rodomont; faire des rodomontades; fanfaronner.

roe[1] [rou], *s. Z:* **r. (deer),** chevreuil *m*; **yearling r. deer,** brocard *m*; **r. calf,** faon *m* (de chevreuil); **r. (doe),** chevrette *f.*

roe[2], *s.* (*a*) (**hard**) **r.,** œufs *mpl* (de poisson); *Com:* **salted cod's r.,** rogue *f*; **r. corn,** œuf (de hareng, saumon, etc.); *Geol:* **r. stone,** oolithe *m or f*; (*b*) **soft r.,** laite *f*, laitance *f.*

roeblingite ['roubliŋait], *s. Miner:* rœblingite *f.*

roebuck ['roubʌk], *s.* chevreuil *m* (mâle).

roed [roud], *a.* (hareng) rogué; **hard-r.,** œuvé; **soft-r.,** laité.

roemeria [rou'meriə], *s. Bot:* rœmérie *f.*

roemerite ['roumərait], *s. Miner:* rœmérite *f*, römérite *f.*

Roentgen, Röntgen ['rə:ntjən, -gən]. **1.** *Pr.n.* Rœntgen, Röntgen; **R. rays,** rayons *m* Röntgen. **2.** *s. Rad.-A:* **roentgen, röntgen,** rœntgen *m*, röntgen *m.*

roentgenotherapy, röntgenotherapy ['rə:ntjənou'θerəpi, -gən-], *s. Med:* rœntgenthérapie *f.*

rogation [rə'geiʃ(ə)n], *s.* **1.** (*a*) *Ecc:* (*usu. pl.*) rogations *fpl*; **R. days,** Rogations; **R. Week,** la semaine des Rogations; **R. Sunday,** le dimanche avant l'Ascension; (*b*) *Bot:* **r. flower,** polygale commun; laitier *m*, herbe *f* au lait. **2.** *Rom. Hist:* rogation.

rogatory ['rɔgətəri], *a. Jur:* rogatoire; *U.S:* **r. commission, letter r.,** commission *f* rogatoire; **through a r. commission,** rogatoirement.

Roger[1] ['rɔdʒər], *Pr.n.m.* **1.** Roger; *Nau: F: A:* **the Jolly R.,** le pavillon noir (des pirates); *Danc: A:* (**Sir**) **R. de Coverley,** (variété de) contredanse *f*. **2.** *Med:* **Roger's disease,** maladie *f* de Roger; communication *f* interventriculaire. **3.** *int.* **R.!** (i) *W.Tel:* = reçu et compris! (ii) d'accord!

roger[2]. *P:* **1.** *v.i.* coïter. **2.** *v.tr.* coïter avec (une femme).

rognon ['rɔnjən], *s. Geol:* rognon *m.*

rogue[1] [roug], *s.* **1.** escroc *m*, filou *m*; fourbe *mf*; pendard, -arde; **rogues' gallery,** musée *m* de portraits, d'effigies, de criminels; *F:* trombinoscope *m*; *F:* **they looked a real rogues' gallery,** ils avaient tous une mine patibulaire; *Mil:* **rogues' march,** sonnerie *f*, air *m* de fifre, qui accompagne l'expulsion d'un mauvais soldat. **2.** malin, -igne; espiègle *mf*; farceur, -euse; **she's a little r.,** c'est une petite coquine, une petite friponne. **3.** *Jur: A:* vagabond *m*. **4.** (*a*) **r. (elephant), r., (buffalo),** éléphant *m*, buffle *m*, solitaire, rogue; solitaire *m*; (*b*) *Hort:* plant (i) peu vigoureux, (ii) qui ne répond pas à la variété semée; (*c*) *Rac:* cheval (i) vicieux, (ii) paresseux, (iii) qui refuse.

rogue[2]. **1.** *v.i. O:* faire l'escroc. **2.** *v.tr. Hort:* **to r. (out) a seed bed,** éliminer les plants mal venus, indésirables, d'un semis.

roguery ['rougəri], **roguishness** ['rougiʃnis], *s.* **1.** coquinerie *f*, friponnerie *f*, fourberie *f*; **a piece of r.,** une coquinerie, friponnerie, fourberie. **2.** malice *f*, espièglerie *f*, friponnerie (d'enfant).

roguish ['rougiʃ], *a.* **1.** (tour, etc.) de filou, d'escroc; (air) coquin, fripon, polisson. **2.** (enfant, etc.) malin, espiègle; **r. eyes,** yeux espiègles, fripons.

roguishly ['rougiʃli], *adv.* **1.** en escroc, en filou. **2.** avec espièglerie; malicieusement; d'un air fripon.

rohu ['rouhu:], *s. Ich:* rohu *m.*

roil [rɔil]. **1.** *v.tr. A:* troubler (l'eau, etc.). **2.** *v.tr. F: O:* embêter, faire endêver (qn). **3.** *v.i. NAm:* (*of stream, etc.*) tourbillonner.

roinek ['rɔinek], *s.* = ROOINEK.

roister ['rɔistər], *v.i.* faire du tapage, du chahut; faire la fête.

roisterer ['rɔistərər], *s.* tapageur, -euse; fêtard, -arde, cascadeur, -euse.

roistering[1] ['rɔistəriŋ], *a.* tapageur; bruyant; chahuteur; bambocheur.

roistering[2], *s.* tapage *m*; chahut *m*; noce *f*, fête *f*, bombe *f.*

Roland ['roulənd], *Pr.n.m.* Roland; *Fig:* **to give s.o. a R. for an Oliver,** rendre à qn la monnaie de sa pièce; **a R. for an Oliver,** un prêté rendu.

rolandic [rə'lændik], *a. Anat:* (région, etc.) rolandique; **r. fissure,** scissure *f* de Rolando.

rôle [roul], *s. Th: & Fig:* rôle *m*; **his r. is to advise the minister on finance,** il a pour rôle de renseigner le ministre sur les finances; **to play an important r. in sth.,** jouer un rôle important dans qch.

roll[1] [roul], *s.* **1.** (*a*) rouleau *m* (de papier, de musique, de tissu, etc.); pièce *f* (de tissu); *Cin:* rouleau, galette *f* (de film pour prise de vues); *Phot: Paperm: etc:* bobine *f* (de film, de papier, etc.); *Tex:* **r. of carded wool,** loquette *f*; *attrib. Dressm: Tail:* **r. collar,** col roulé; *Cost:* **r. neck sweater,** chandail *m* à col roulé; *Furn:* **r. top,** rideau *m* (de bureau américain); **r. shutter,** rideau (de classeur, etc.); (*b*) *Arch:* volute *f* (de chapiteau ionique); (*c*) *Cu:* **boiled jam r.,** pudding bouilli farci de confiture (en forme de bûche); **Swiss r.** = bûche *f*; biscuit roulé; *Bak:* (**bread**) **r.,** petit pain; **bridge r.,** petit pain mollet; **ham r.** = sandwich *m* au jambon; (*d*) coquille *f* (de beurre); (*e*) *NAm:* liasse *f* (de billets de banque). **2.** *Adm: etc:* rôle *m*, contrôle *m*, liste *f*; **nominal r.,** état nominatif; contrôle nominatif; **r. call,** appel (nominal); *Mil: Nau:* **to put, enter, a man on the rolls,** porter un homme sur les contrôles; **to be on the rolls,** être porté sur les contrôles; **his name is on the r.,** son nom se trouve sur la liste; **on the rolls of fame,** dans les annales de la gloire; **a long r. of heroes,** une longue liste de héros; **to call the r.,** faire l'appel; **the r. of honour,** la liste de ceux qui sont morts pour la patrie; **to strike s.o. off the rolls,** *Jur:* rayer qn du tableau, du barreau; *Mil: etc:* rayer qn des états; *Jur:* **to strike an action off the r.,** biffer un procès. **3.** canon *m*, bâton *m* (de soufre); bâton (de cannelle); rouleau, carotte *f*, torquette *f*, boudin *m*, rôle *m* (de tabac); **r. tobacco,** tabac roulé; *F:* **he has rolls of fat,** il a des bourrelets *m* de graisse. **4.** *Arch:* **r. (moulding),** moulure *f* à rouleau. **5.** (*roller*) (*a*) rouleau, cylindre *m* (de laminoir, etc.); *Tex:* rouleau, ensouple *f* (d'un métier); *Metalw:* **roughing(-down) r.,** cylindre dégrossisseur, ébaucheur; **bottom, lower, r.,** cylindre du dessous, femelle; **top, upper, r.,** cylindre du dessus, mâle; *Paperm:* **beater r.,** cylindre porte-lames, cylindre travailleur; *Cmptr:* **print r.,** rouleau, cylindre, d'impression; (*b*) *Metalw:* **rolls,** train *m* (de laminoir); **two-, three-high rolls,** train duo, trio; **roughing rolls,** train ébaucheur, dégrossisseur; gros train; **crushing rolls,** moulin *m*, broyeur *m*, à cylindres. **6.** *Tls: Bookb:* roulette *f*. **7.** *Aut:* **r. bar,** arceau *m* de sécurité.

roll[2], *s.* **1.** (*a*) *Nau: Av:* roulis *m*; **angle of r.,** angle *m* de roulis; **r. axis,** axe *m* de roulis; *Av:* **r. and yaw axes,** trièdre *m* de référence; *Nau:* **downward r.,** roulis sous le vent; **weather r.,** rappel *m* de roulis, rappel au vent; **to walk with a r.,** se balancer, se dandiner, en marchant; avoir une démarche chaloupée; (*b*) *Av:* gauchissement *m* (des ailerons); **r. control,** commande *f* de gauchissement; (*c*) **the r. of the sea,** la houle; (*d*) *Lit:* **the r. of the ages,** le déroulement des époques. **2.** (*a*) roulement *m* (d'une balle, etc.); (*b*) (*of horse, etc.*) **to have a r. on the ground,** se rouler par terre; (*c*) *Av:* vol *m* en tonneau; **eight point hesitation r.,** tonneau *m* à facettes en huit points; **flick r.,** tonneau rapide; **slow r.,** tonneau lent; **falling leaf r.,** descente *f* en feuille morte; (*d*) *Sp:* (i) (*high jump*) **western r.,** rouleau costal; **to do a r.,** suater en rouleau; (ii) (*canoeing*) esquimautage *m*. **3.** roulage *m*, roulement *m* (d'un véhicule); *Av:* **landing r.,** longueur *f* de roulement à l'atterrissage. **4.** roulement (de tambour, de tonnerre); **r. on the side drum,** batterie *f.*

roll[3], *v.*

I. *v.tr.* **1.** (*a*) rouler (un tonneau, une bille, etc.); *NAm: F:* **to r. the dice, the bones,** jeter les dés; (*b*) **to r. one's eyes,** rouler les yeux; (*c*) **to r. string into a ball,** rouler de la ficelle en pelote, peloter de la ficelle; **to r. a snowball,** faire une boule de neige. **2. to r. one's r's,** rouler, faire sonner, faire ronfler, les r; grasseyer. **3.** (*a*) rouler, passer au rouleau (le gazon); cylindrer (une route, la couche d'empierrement); (*b*) laminer (les métaux); travailler (les métaux) au laminoir; planer (l'or); *Leath:* calandrer (les peaux); (*c*) *Cu:* **to r. (out) pastry,** étendre la pâte au rouleau; abaisser, biller, la pâte; **to r. and fold,** feuilleter (la pâte); (*d*) (*with passive force*) **steel that rolls well,** acier qui se lamine facilement. **4.** (*a*) **to r. (up) paper,** rouler, enrouler, du papier; **to r. a flag round its staff,** enrouler un drapeau autour de sa hampe; **to r. (up) one's cloak,** faire un rouleau de son manteau; *Cu:* **loin of mutton boned and rolled,** carré de mouton roulé; **to r. cigarettes,** rouler des cigarettes; **the hedgehog is rolling itself into a ball,** le hérisson se roule en boule; (*b*) **chauffeur and gardener rolled into one,** chauffeur et jardinier en une seule personne. **5.** *NAm:*

P: **to r. a drunk,** pratiquer le vol au poivrier sur un ivrogne.

II. *v.i.* rouler. **1.** (*a*) **the barrel started rolling,** le tonneau se mit à rouler; **the ball rolled under the table,** la balle a roulé sous la table; *Fig:* **some heads will r. in the government,** quelques ministres vont être limogés; (*of pers.*) **to r. downhill,** faire une roulade; **to r. downstairs,** rouler, débouler, du haut en bas de l'escalier; (*b*) *Av:* voler en tonneau. **2.** *v.i.* & *pr.* **to r. (oneself) from side to side,** se retourner, se rouler, de côté et d'autre; **to r. in the mud,** se rouler dans la boue; **the mule tried to r.,** la mule a essayé de se retourner sur le dos, de se rouler par terre; *F:* **to be rolling in money, to be rolling (in it),** rouler sur l'or (et sur l'argent); nager dans l'opulence; remuer, ramasser, l'argent à la pelle; être riche à crever. **3. the river was rolling over the stones,** la rivière roulait, coulait, sur les pierres; **the planets r. on their courses,** les planètes accomplissent leurs révolutions; **I could hear the sea rolling,** j'entendais déferler la mer. **4.** (*of thunder*) gronder, rouler; (*of organ, voice*) rendre un son grave et prolongé; **to hear the drums rolling,** entendre le roulement des tambours. **5.** (*of ship, aircraft*) rouler; avoir du roulis; avoir un mouvement de roulis; **to r. heavily,** rouler bas; donner de forts roulis; **to r. (in one's walk),** se dandiner, se balancer, en marchant; marcher avec un roulis prononcé.

III. (*compound verbs*) **1. roll about.** (*a*) *v.tr.* rouler (qch.) çà et là; (*b*) *v.i.* rouler çà et là.

2. roll along. (*a*) *v.tr.* rouler (qch.) le long de la route, etc.; (*b*) *v.i.* (i) rouler; (*of car*) avancer (en roulant); **to r. along in one's car,** rouler dans sa voiture; (ii) *F:* arriver, se ramener; **r. along about three o'clock,** venez vers les trois heures.

3. roll away. (*a*) *v.tr.* éloigner, faire rouler (qch.); (*b*) *v.i.* s'éloigner (en roulant); **the mist is rolling away,** la brume se retire; le vent emporte la brume.

4. roll back. (*a*) *v.tr.* (i) rouler (qch.) en arrière; **to r. back a stone,** faire rouler une pierre en arrière; *Mil:* **to r. back the enemy,** faire reculer l'ennemi; (ii) *NAm:* (*of government*) **to r. back prices,** baisser les prix; (iii) *Cmptr:* **to r. back the processing,** faire une reprise du traitement; (*b*) *v.i.* (i) rouler en arrière; reculer (en roulant); (*of car*) reculer en dérive; (ii) (*of eyes*) chavirer.

5. roll by, *v.i.* passer (en roulant); (*of time*) s'écouler.

6. roll down. (*a*) *v.tr.* rouler (qch.) de haut en bas; descendre (qch.) (en le roulant); (*b*) *v.i.* **to r. down a slope,** rouler sur une pente; **to r. down the hill,** débouler sur la pente; **the tears rolled down his cheeks,** les larmes coulaient sur ses joues.

7. roll in. (*a*) *v.tr.* (i) faire entrer (qch.); (ii) (*at hockey*) remettre (la balle) en jeu; (*b*) *v.i.* (i) entrer en roulant; (*of dray, etc.*) entrer lourdement, avec un fracas des roues; (ii) **to watch the waves r. in,** regarder les vagues déferler sur le rivage; (iii) *Com: F:* **orders are rolling in,** les commandes affluent; (iv) *F:* **he rolled in at midnight,** il a rappliqué à minuit; (v) *F:* **it's time to r. in,** il est l'heure de se coucher, se pagnoter.

8. roll of. (*a*) *v.i.* tomber (en roulant); **excuses rolled off his tongue,** il débitait des excuses; (*b*) *v.tr.* (i) sortir (qch.) (en le roulant); (ii) *Typ: etc:* **to r. off 20,000 copies,** imprimer 20,000 exemplaires.

9. roll on. (*a*) *v.i.* continuer de rouler; (*of time*) s'écouler; **the river rolled on towards the ocean,** le fleuve coulait vers la mer; *F:* **r. on the holidays!** vivement, vite, les vacances! (*b*) *v.tr.* (i) étendre (de la peinture, etc.) avec le rouleau; (ii) passer (un vêtement) en le faisant rouler sur le corps.

10. roll out. (*a*) *v.tr.* (i) faire sortir (qch.) en le roulant; rouler (qch.) dehors; *F:* **to r. out the red carpet for s.o.,** recevoir qn avec la croix et la bannière, avec tous les égards possibles; (ii) **to r. out verse,** débiter des vers sur un ton rythmé, d'une voix ronflante; faire ronfler des vers; (iii) faire disparaître (des inégalités) au rouleau; (iv) *Cu:* étendre (la pâte); (*b*) *v.i.* (i) (*of pers.*) sortir (d'un café, etc.) en roulant, en se dandinant, en titubant; (ii) (*of ball, etc.*) rouler dehors; *F:* (*of pers.*) **to r. out (of bed),** se dépagnoter.

11. roll over. (*a*) *v.tr.* (i) **to r. sth. over,** retourner qch.; (ii) **to r. s.o. over,** culbuter qn; (*b*) *v.i.* (i) se retourner (en roulant); (ii) **to r. over on the ground,** rouler sur le sol; **to r. over (and over),** rouler sur soi-même (plusieurs fois); (iii) (*of car, etc.*) faire capote.

12. roll up. (*a*) *v.tr.* (i) rouler, enrouler (une carte, de la musique, etc.); relever, retrousser (ses manches); (ii) **to r. up the enemy's flank,** rabattre le flanc de l'ennemi; se rabattre sur le flanc de l'ennemi; (iii) envelopper (qch.); **to r. oneself up in a blanket,** s'enrouler dans une couverture; (*b*) *v.i.* (i) (*of smoke, etc.*) s'élever en volutes; (ii) (*of blind, etc.*) s'enrouler; (*of kitten, etc.*) **to r. up into a ball,** se mettre, se rouler, en boule; ramasser son corps en boule; (iii) (*of dying insect*) se tordre, se crisper; *F:* (*of guests, etc.*) arriver, se ramener; s'abouler; **r. up about three o'clock,** venez vers les trois heures.

rollaway ['roulәwei], *s. NAm:* lit pliant monté sur roulettes.

rollback ['roulbæk], *s.* **1.** *NAm:* (*a*) baisse *f* de prix (par action gouvernementale); (*b*) **the r. of the enemy forces,** le repoussement, la retraite, des armées ennemies. **2.** *Cmptr:* **r. routine,** programme *m* de reprise.

roll-ball ['roulbɔ:l], *s. Av:* roulé-boulé *m*; **r.-b. technique,** technique *f* du roulé-boulé.

Rolle [rɔl], *Pr.n. Mth:* **Rolle's theorem,** théorème *m* de Rolle.

rolled [rould], *a.* **1.** (papier) en rouleau; (paquet) roulé; **r. (up) leaf,** feuille enroulée; *Mil: A:* **r. greatcoat,** manteau *m* en cor de chasse; capote roulée et portée en bandoulière. **2.** *Metalw:* laminé; venu de, au, laminage; **r. iron,** (fer) laminé; fer cylindré. **3. r. gold,** doublé *m*, plané *m*; **r.-gold watch,** montre en plaqué or, en doublé. **4.** (gazon) passé au rouleau, roulé.

roller ['roulәr], *s.* **1.** (*a*) rouleau *m* (de pâtissier, etc.); **paint r.,** rouleau à peinture; (*b*) rouleau, cylindre *m*; *Typew:* **impression r.,** rouleau, cylindre, porte-papier; *Typ:* **damping r.,** rouleau mouilleur; **ink-feed r.,** rouleau preneur; **inking r., colour r.,** rouleau encreur, rouleau toucheur; **rider r.,** rouleau chargeur; **r. mark(ing),** coup *m* de rouleau; *Bookb:* **r. backer,** rouleau; *Mec.E: Ind:* **feed r.,** cylindre, rouleau, entraîneur, d'entraînement, d'amenage; **return r.,** rouleau de renvoi; *Metalw:* **drawing r.,** cylindre, rouleau, étireur; **rollers,** laminoir *m*; **plate rollers,** laminoir à tôle; (*c*) **(road) r.,** rouleau (compresseur); cylindre compresseur, de compression; *Agr:* **heavy, weighted, r.,** plombeur *m*; **toothed r.,** rouleau à dents; hérisson *m*, croskill *m*; **Cambridge r.,** rouleau squelette; *Hort:* **garden r.,** rouleau de jardin, à, pour, gazon; *Civ.E:* **sheep's foot r.,** rouleau à pieds de mouton; **vibrating r.,** rouleau compresseur vibrateur; (*d*) *Paperm: Tex:* calandre *f*; *Tex:* **r. beam,** porte-cylindre *m inv*; (*e*) galet *m*, rouleau; *Furn:* roulette *f* (de fauteuil, etc.); *Mec.E:* **cam r.,** galet, grain *m*, de came; *I.C.E:* **tappet r.,** galet de poussoir; **contact r.,** galet de contact; **striking r.,** galet d'entraînement; came *f*, doigt *m* (de la croix de Malte); **flanged r.,** galet à boudin, à joue; **single-flanged r.,** galet à une joue, à un seul boudin; **double-flanged r.,** galet à deux joues, à double boudin; **centre-flanged r.,** galet à boudin central; **tension r.,** galet de tension, tendeur; **bearing r.,** rouleau de roulement; **support(ing) r.,** galet, rouleau, de support; galet-support *m, pl.* galets-support(s); **r. pin,** axe *m*, goujon *m*, de galet, de rouleau; **r. shaft,** arbre *m* porte-galet; **r. ring,** couronne *f* de galets; **r. retainer,** cage *f* à galets; **r. path, track,** chemin *m*, piste *f*, de roulement; **r. bearing,** (i) *Mec.E:* coussinet *m* à rouleaux; palier *m* à rouleaux; roulement *m* à rouleaux; (ii) *Civ.E:* chariot *m* de dilatation (de pont métallique); **twin r. bearing,** roulement à rouleaux jumelés; **thrust r. bearing,** butée *f* à rouleaux; **r. chain,** chaîne *f* à galets; (*f*) (*for moving heavy objects*) cylindre rouleur; rouleau transporteur; **transport by rollers,** transport *m* par, sur, rouleaux; **r. conveyor,** transporteur *m* à rouleaux; (*g*) tourniquet *m*, tambour *m* (de cabestan); *Ropem:* virolet *m* (de corderie); (*h*) cylindre denté (de boîte à musique). **2.** (*a*) enrouleur *m*, rouleau (de store, carte géographique, etc.); **spring (-actuated) blind r.,** enrouleur automatique de store; **r. blind,** store *m* sur rouleau; **r. map,** carte *f* (géographique) sur rouleau; (*b*) *Hairdr:* bigoudi *m*, rouleau. **3.** *Med:* **r. (bandage),** bande roulée. **4.** *Nau:* lame *f* de houle; **blind r.,** vague *f* de fond. **5.** *Orn:* (*a*) pigeon culbutant; (pigeon) rouleur *m*; (*b*) rollier *m* d'Europe; (*c*) geai bleu. **6.** *Rept:* serpent *m* corail, rouleau. **7.** (*pers.*) cylindreur *m*; *Min:* rouleur *m*; *Metalw:* lamineur *m*.

roller(-)coaster ['roulә'koustәr], *s. NAm:* montagnes *f* russes.

rollick[1] ['rɔlik], *s.* **1.** gaieté exubérante. **2.** ébats *mpl*, folâtrerie *f*. **3.** bordée *f*, bamboche *f*, noce *f*.

rollick[2], *v.i.* folâtrer; faire la fête, la noce, la bombe; rigoler.

rollicker ['rɔlikәr], *s.* noceur *m*, vadrouilleur *m*, tapageur *m*.

rollicking[1] ['rɔlikiŋ], *a.* joyeux; jovial, -aux, d'une gaieté exubérante; rigoleur, -euse; **to lead a r. life,** mener une vie de patachon, de bâton de chaise; **the r. side of life,** le côté tapageur de la vie; **r. laughter,** rires bruyants.

rollicking[2], *s.* folâtrerie *f*; rigolades *fpl*; vie *f* de bohème.

roll-in ['roul'in], *s. Sp:* (*hockey*) touche *f*.

rolling[1] ['rouliŋ], *a.* **1.** roulant, qui roule; **r. bridge,** pont roulant; *Prov:* **a r. stone gathers no moss,** pierre qui roule n'amasse pas mousse; *Fig:* **he's a r. stone,** (i) il a roulé sa bosse partout; *F:* c'est un roule-ta-bosse, roule-ta-bille, *inv*; (ii) il ne s'applique à rien. **2. the r. years,** les années qui s'écoulent. **3.** (brouillard) qui avance; (fumée) qui s'élève en volutes. **4.** (*a*) (bateau) qui roule, a du roulis; (*b*) (*of pers.*) **to have a r. gait, walk,** se balancer, se dandiner, en marchant; (*c*) *Ind:* **r. furnace,** four oscillant. **5.** (*a*) **r. sea,** mer grosse, houleuse; mer démontée; (*b*) **r. country,** pays ondulant, ondulé, accidenté; région *f* à ondulations; **the r. nature of the ground,** les ondulations *f* du terrain. **6.** *Nau:* **r. hitch,** amarrage *m* à fouet.

rolling[2], *s.* **1.** roulement *m* (d'une bille, etc.); *Mec:* **r. friction,** frottement *m* de roulement; *Mec.E:* **r. arc,** arc *m* de roulement (d'un engrenage); **r. circle,** cercle primitif. **2.** (*a*) roulades *fpl* (dans la poussière, etc.); (*b*) rotation *f* (du corps); (*c*) *Sp:* (*canoeing*) esquimautage *m*; (*d*) *F:* **dice r.,** jeu *m* de dés. **3.** (*a*) *Ind: etc:* cylindrage *m*; *Metalw:* laminage *m*, travail *m* au laminoir; **r. press,** presse *f* à cylindres; (*for glazing*) **r. machine,** glaceur *m*; *Metalw:* **cold r.,** laminage, cylindrage, à froid; écrouissage *m*; **hot r.,** laminage à chaud; **r. mill,** (i) usine *f* de laminage; laminerie *f*; (ii) laminoir *m*; (*b*) cylindrage (d'une pelouse, chaussée, etc.); (*c*) *Cu:* **r. pin,** rouleau *m* (à pâtisserie). **4.** roulis *m* (d'un navire, avion, véhicule); *Nau:* **r. chocks,** quilles *f* de roulis; **r. tank,** caisse *f* à roulis. **5.** *Nau:* **r. gear,** rouleau *m* (du gui). **6.** roulement *m* (du tambour, tonnerre). **7.** *NAm: P:* vol *m* au poivrier (d'un ivrogne). **8. r. stock,** (i) *Rail:* matériel roulant; (ii) parc *m* (d'une entreprise de transports).

Rollinia [rɔ'liniә], *s. Bot:* rollinia *m*.

rollmops ['roulmɔps], *s. Cu:* rollmops *m*.

Rollo ['rɔlou], *Pr.n.m. Hist:* Rollon.

roll-on ['roulɔn], *s.* **1.** *Cost:* gaine *f* (élastique). **2.** *Toil:* flacon *m* à bille. **3.** *attrib.* **r.-on roll-off ferryboat,** (bâtiment *m*, navire *m*) roulier *m*.

roll-out ['roulaut], *s. Ind:* sortie *f* d'usine (d'un avion, etc.).

roll-up ['roulʌp], *a.* **r.-up map,** carte *f* à enrouler.

roloway ['rɔlәwei], *s. Z:* roloway *m*, cercopithèque *m* diane.

roly-poly ['rouli'pouli], *s.* **1.** *Cu:* pudding bouilli farci de confiture (en forme de bûche). **2.** *F:* **r.-p. (child, puppy),** boulot, -otte; grassouillet, -ette.

Rom, *pl.* **Roma** [rɔm, 'rɔmә], *s.m.* romanichel.

Romagna (the) [ðәrou'mɑ:njә], *Pr.n. Geog:* la Romagne.

Romagnese ['roumәnji:z]. *Geog:* **1.** *a.* romagnol. **2.** *s.* Romagnol, -ole.

Romagnol ['roumәnjɔl], *s. Geog:* Romagnol, -ole.

Romaic [rou'meiik]. **1.** *a.* romaïque. **2.** *s. Ling:* le romaïque.

Roman ['roumәn]. **1.** *a.* romain; (*a*) **the R. legions,** les légions romaines, de Rome; **R. numerals,** chiffres romains; **R. law,** le droit romain; **R. architecture,** architecture romaine; l'ordre *m* composite; **R. nose,** nez busqué, aquilin; **R. cement,** ciment romain; **R. alum,** alun *m* de Rome; **R. balance, beam, steelyard,** balance romaine; romaine *f*; *Med:* **R. fever,** paludisme *m*; (*b*) **the Holy R. Empire,** le Saint-Empire romain (germanique); *Ecc:* **the R. rite,** le rite romain; **R. Catholic,** catholique (*mf*); **R. Catholicism,** catholicisme *m*; (*c*) *Typ:* **r. (type),** (caractère) romain. **2.** *s.* Romain, -aine; *B:* **(the Epistle to the) Romans,** l'épître *f* aux Romains.

romance[1] [rә'mæns], *s.* **1.** *Ling:* **Romance,** le roman; la langue romane; **R. languages,** langues romanes, néo-latines; **student of R. languages,** romaniste *m*. **2.** (*a*) *Lit:* roman *m* de chevalerie, d'aventures, etc.; **hero of r.,** (i) héros de roman; (ii) *F:* homme chevaleresque; **the age of r.,** les temps chevaleresques; (*b*) histoire *f* romanesque; conte bleu; fable *f*, roman; aventure *f* romanesque; **historical r.,** roman de cape et d'épée; **it's quite a r.,** c'est tout un roman; cela tient du roman; **r. writer,** romancier, -ière, qui donne dans le romanesque; (*c*) **r. between two young people,** idylle *f* entre deux jeunes gens; (*d*) **we took it for a r., but it was true,** nous l'avons pris pour un conte, mais c'était vrai; (*e*) **love of r.,** amour du romanesque; **the r. of the sea,** la poésie de la mer. **3.** *Mus:* romance *f*.

romance[2], *v.i.* exagérer; lâcher la bride à son imagination; inventer à plaisir; **you're romancing!** vous blaguez!

romancer [rә'mænsәr], *s.* **1.** romancier, -ière ((i) de l'ancien temps, (ii) qui donne dans le romanesque). **2.** *F:* auteur *m* d'un récit de pure imagination ((i) brodeur, -euse; (ii) menteur, -euse).

Romanche [rou'mænʃ], *a.* & *s. Ling:* romanche (*m*).

romancing [rә'mænsiŋ], *s.* (*a*) exagération *f*; (*b*) pure invention.

romanesque [roumən'esk], *a.* & *s. Arch: etc:* roman (*m*).

Romania [rou'meiniə], *Pr.n. Geog:* Roumanie *f.*

Romanian [rou'meiniən]. **1.** *Geog:* (*a*) *a.* roumain; (*b*) *s.* Roumain, -aine. **2.** *s. Ling:* roumain *m.*

Romanic [rə'mænik]. **1.** *a.* & *s. Ling:* (le) roman. **2.** *a.* romain; (qui dérive) des Romains.

Romanism ['roumənizm], *s.* **1.** *Hist:* influence *f*, étude *f*, de Rome, des Romains. **2.** *Ecc:* romanisme *m*, catholicisme *m.*

Romanist ['roumənist]. **1.** *s.* romaniste *mf* (qui s'intéresse à la Rome antique, au droit romain, aux langues romanes). **2.** *a.* & *s. Ecc: usu. Pej:* romaniste (*mf*), catholique (*mf*).

Romanity [rou'mæniti], *s. Hist:* romanité *f.*

Romanization [roumənai'zeiʃ(ə)n], *s.* **1.** *Hist:* romanisation *f* (d'un peuple, etc.). **2.** *Ecc:* conversion *f* au catholicisme. **3.** *Typ:* **romanization,** transcription *f* en caractères romains.

Romanize ['roumənaiz]. **1.** *v.tr.* (*a*) romaniser (un peuple vaincu, etc.); (*b*) convertir (un pays, etc.) au catholicisme; (*c*) *Typ:* transcrire (un texte) en caractères romains. **2.** *v.i. Ecc:* (se) romaniser; embrasser la foi de l'Église romaine; donner dans le catholicisme.

Romanizer ['roumənaizər], *s. Ecc: usu. Pej:* romanisant, -ante.

Romanizing[1] ['roumənaiziŋ], *a. Ecc:* romanisant.

Romanizing[2], *s.* = ROMANIZATION.

Romano-Buddhist [rou'mɑ:nou'budist], *a.* (art) gréco-bouddhique.

Romano-Gallican [rou'mɑ:nou'gælikən], *a. Ecc:* romano-gallican.

romantic [rə'mæntik]. **1.** *a.* (*a*) romanesque; qui tient du roman; qui a le goût du roman; **r. story,** histoire *f* romanesque; **r. adventure,** aventure *f* romanesque; **r. name,** nom romanesque, de roman; **r. young woman,** jeune fille romanesque, exaltée; (*b*) **r. landscape,** paysage *m* romantique; **r. site,** site *m* pittoresque; (*c*) *Art: Lit: Mus:* romantique; **the r. school,** l'école *f* romantique. **2.** *s.* (*a*) *Art: Lit: Mus:* romantique *mf*; (*b*) **romantics,** idées romanesques, exaltées.

romantically [rə'mæntik(ə)li], *adv.* **1.** romanesquement; pittoresquement. **2.** romantiquement, en romantique.

romanticism [rə'mæntisizm], *s.* **1.** idées *f* romanesques. **2.** *Art: Lit: Mus:* romantisme *m.*

romanticist [rə'mæntisist], *s. Art: Lit: Mus:* romantique *mf.*

romanticize [rə'mæntisaiz]. **1.** *v.tr.* romancer (une idée, un incident, etc.); faire tout un roman de (qch.). **2.** *v.i.* donner dans le romanesque.

Romany ['rɔməni]. **1.** *s.* (*a*) romanichel, -elle; bohémien, -ienne; (*b*) *coll.* les romani *m*, les bohémiens; (*c*) *Ling:* le romanichel; la langue tzigane. **2.** *a.* (vie, etc.) de romanichel.

romaunt [rə'mɔ:nt], *s. Lit:* roman *m*; **the R. of the Rose,** le Roman de la Rose.

Romberg ['rɔmbə:g], *Pr.n. Med:* **Romberg's sign,** signe *m* de Romberg.

rombowline [rʌm'boulin], *s. Nau:* larderasse *f*; filin *m* et toile *f* usagés.

Rome [roum], *Pr.n. Geog: Hist:* **1.** Rome *f*; *Prov:* **R. was not built in a day** = Paris n'a pas été fait, bâti, en un jour; l'arbre ne tombe pas du premier coup; **when in R. you must do as the Romans do,** à Rome il faut vivre comme à Rome; il faut hurler avec les loups; **all roads lead to R.,** tous les chemins mènent à Rome. **2.** *Ecc:* **(the Church of) R.,** l'Église romaine; le catholicisme; **converts to R.,** convertis à l'Église romaine, au catholicisme.

romeite ['roumiait], *s. Miner:* roméine *f*, roméite *f.*

Romish ['roumiʃ], *a. Ecc: Pej:* catholique; **R. tendencies,** tendances romanisantes.

romp[1] [rɔmp], *s.* **1.** (*a*) *O:* jeune fille garçonnière; gamine *f*; (*b*) enfant turbulent(e). **2.** gambades *fpl*; ébats *mpl*; jeu turbulent; **to have a r. in the hay,** prendre ses ébats dans les foins. **3.** *Rac: etc:* **to win in a r.,** arriver dans un fauteuil.

romp[2], *v.i.* **1.** s'ébattre (bruyamment); faire le diable. **2.** *Rac: etc:* **to r. away with a race,** gagner une course haut la main; **to r. in, home,** arriver premier en se promenant; arriver dans un fauteuil; **to r. past s.o.,** dépasser qn sans effort; **to r. through an examination,** passer un examen sans le moindre effort; **to r. through a piece of work,** expédier un travail (i) sans difficulté, (ii) à la va-irte.

romper ['rɔmpər], *s.* **r. suit, rompers,** barboteuse *f* (d'enfant).

romping ['rɔmpiŋ], *s.* ébats *mpl*; turbulence *f.*

rondache [rɔn'dæʃ], *s.* (*a*) *Arm:* rondache *f*; bouclier *m* circulaire; (*b*) (*soldier*) rondachier *m.*

rondacher [rɔn'dæʃər], *s. Mil: A:* rondachier *m.*

rondeau ['rɔndou], *s. Lit:* rondeau *m.*

rondel ['rɔnd(ə)l], *s. Lit:* rondel *m.*

Rondeletia [rɔndi'li:ʃjə], *s. Bot:* rondeletia *m.*

rondellier [rɔn'deliər], *s. Mil: A:* rondachier *m.*

rondo ['rɔndou], *s. Mus:* (*a*) (*piece of music*) rondeau *m*; (*b*) (*movement of symphony, etc.*) rondo *m.*

rondure ['rɔndjuər], *s. A:* rondeur *f.*

Roneo[1] ['rouniou], *R.t.m:* **1.** (*machine*) (*also* **Roneograph**) Ronéo *f.* **2.** (*copy reproduced*) Ronéo *m.*

Roneo[2], *v.tr.* **(Roneoed, Roneo'd)** *R.t.m:* ronéotyper, *F:* ronéoter.

Röntgen ['rə:ntjən -gən], *see* ROENTGEN.

roo [ru:], *s. Austr: F:* kangourou *m.*

rood [ru:d], *s.* **1.** *Ecc:* (*a*) *A:* **the Holy R.,** la sainte Croix; l'Arbre *m* de la Croix; (*b*) crucifix *m* (au centre du jubé); **r. arch,** arche *f* du jubé; **r. beam,** poutre *f* du jubé; **r. cloth,** voile *m* du crucifix (déployé pendant le carême); **r. loft,** (galerie *f* du) jubé; **r. screen,** jubé. **2.** *Meas: A: & Dial:* rood *m*; quart *m* d'arpent.

roof[1] [ru:f], *s.* **1.** toit *m*; (*a*) comble *m*, toiture *f*; **thatched r.,** toit, couverture *f* de, en, chaume; **tiled r.,** toit, couverture, en, de, tuiles; **flat r.,** toit en terrasse, en plate-forme; **pitched r.,** toit penché; **single pitch r.,** toit, comble, à une seule pente, à un versant; **pent, lean-to, r.,** comble en appentis, toit à un égout; **shell r.,** toit en voûte; *Rail:* (*over platform*) **(umbrella) r.,** marquise *f*; **r. frame,** charpente *f* de comble; **r. timbering,** les combles; **to build a room in the r. space,** aménager les combles en pièce habitable; **r. light,** lucarne *f*; **leaded r. light,** nochère *f*; **r. membrane,** (i) membrane *f* de toiture; (ii) complexe *m* d'étanchéité; **r. garden,** jardin *m* sur un toit en terrasse; *F:* **to lift, raise, the r.,** (i) applaudir à tout casser; (ii) faire du vacarme; **when he heard this he hit, went through, the r.,** quand il a entendu cela il est sorti de ses gonds; **then the r. fell in,** c'était la débâcle; (*b*) **to be without a r. over one's head,** se trouver sans logement; **they live under the same r.,** ils habitent sous le même toit; **workshops and offices under the same r.,** ateliers et bureaux dans le même bâtiment; **family still under the paternal r.,** famille encore sous le toit paternel; **while they were under his r.,** pendant qu'ils étaient chez lui. **2.** (*a*) voûte *f* (de tunnel, caverne, etc.); **the r. of heaven,** la voûte des cieux; (*b*) *Anat:* **r. of the mouth,** (voûte du) palais, voûte palatine; *F:* **mustard that takes the r. off your mouth,** moutarde qui vous emporte la bouche. **3.** *Aut:* toit, pavillon *m*, capotage *m*; **sliding, sunshine, r.,** toit ouvrant; **soft r.,** pavillon flexible; **r. light,** plafonnier *m.* **4.** *Min:* ciel *m*, plafond *m*, toit, faite *m*, banc *m* de ciel (d'une mine). **5.** *Mch:* ciel (de foyer); *Metall:* dôme *m* (d'un four à réverbère). **6.** *Ecc:* ciel (d'autel). **7.** *Av:* plafond (opérationnel, etc.).

roof[2], *v.tr.* **1.** (*a*) *Const:* couvrir (une maison, etc.); **house roofed with tiles,** maison couverte de, en, tuiles; (*b*) **to r. a hen run (in, over),** recouvrir le parcours d'un poulailler d'un toit. **2.** abriter, loger (qn).

roofage ['ru:fidʒ], *s.* = ROOFING 2.

-roofed [ru:ft], *a.* (*with adj. or noun prefixed*) **red-roofed,** à toit, toiture, rouge; **thatch-r.,** à toit de chaume.

roofer ['ru:fər], *s.* **1.** *Const:* couvreur *m* (de maisons). **2.** *F: A:* lettre de remerciement (écrite à un hôte).

roofing ['ru:fiŋ], *s.* **1.** pose *f* de la toiture; **r. strip,** volige *f*; latte *f* volige. **2.** (*a*) **r. (materials),** (matériaux *m* de) couverture *f* pour toitures; (*b*) toiture, couverture, garniture *f* de comble; **slate r.,** toiture d'ardoises.

roofless ['ru:flis], *a.* **1.** sans toit, sans toiture; à ciel ouvert. **2.** (*of pers.*) sans abri, sans asile. **3.** *Cards:* (*poker*) sans maximum de relance.

roofscape ['ru:fskeip], *s. Art:* paysage *m* de toits.

rooftop ['ru:ftɔp], *s.* toit *m.*

rooftree ['ru:ftri:], *s.* **1.** charpente *f* de toiture; poutre *f* de faîte; faîtage *m.* **2.** *Lit: A:* toit *m*; demeure *f*; **my humble r.,** mon humble toit.

rooinek ['rouinek], *s.* (*in S. Africa*) **1.** *Hist: Pej:* soldat anglais. **2.** nouveau venu, nouveau débarqué (dont la nuque rougit au soleil).

rook[1] [ruk], *s.* **1.** *Orn:* corbeau *m* freux; freux *m*; *F:* corbeau; *Sm.a:* **r. rifle,** carabine *f* de chasse de petit calibre. **2.** *F: O:* filou *m*, escroc *m*; *P:* (*at cards, etc.*) grec *m.*

rook[2], *v.tr. F:* refaire, rouler, escroquer, filouter, (qn) au jeu; (*of shopkeeper, etc.*) écorcher (qn); **to r. s.o. of his money,** filouter son argent à qn.

rook[3], *s. Chess:* tour *f*; *Her:* **chess r.,** roc *m* (d'échiquier).

rook[4], *v.i. Chess: A:* roquer.

rookery ['rukəri], *s.* **1.** colonie *f* de freux; corbeautière *f.* **2. seal r.,** colonie de phoques; **penguin r.,** colonie de manchots; rookerie *f*; **auk r.,** pingouinière *f*; **gull r.,** roche *f* aux mouettes. **2.** *F: A:* quartier *m* de taudis misérables; **r. district,** bas quartier; **r. of prostitutes,** quartier de filles.

rookie, rooky ['ruki], *s. P:* **1.** *Mil:* recrue *f*, bleu *m.* **2.** *Sp:* (i) novice *m*; (ii) nouveau membre (d'une équipe).

rooking ['rukiŋ], *s. F:* **1.** (*at gambling*) escroquerie *f.* **2.** (*overcharging*) écorchage *m*; coup *m* de fusil; **to get a r.,** se faire écorcher.

rooklet ['ruklit], *s. Orn:* jeune freux *m.*

room[1] [ru:m, rum], *s.* **1.** (*a*) place *f*, espace *m*; **to take up a great deal of r.,** occuper beaucoup de place; être très encombrant; **there is plenty of r.,** il y a amplement de la place; ce n'est pas la place qui manque; **there is no r.,** il n'y a pas de place; **you have plenty of r. here,** vous êtes au large ici; **there is still r. in the case,** il y a encore de la place, du vide, dans la valise; **I have no r. to write more,** la place me manque pour vous en écrire davantage; **to be cramped for r.,** être à l'étroit; **there is no r. to turn (in),** il n'y a pas de place pour se retourner; **to give oneself r. to move,** se donner de l'air; **to give oneself plenty of r. to jump,** prendre du champ pour sauter; **we have no r. for a piano,** nous n'avons pas de place pour mettre un piano; **to make r. for a piece of furniture,** faire de la place pour un meuble; **to make r. for s.o.,** faire place à qn; laisser le champ libre à qn; **to make r. for s.o. to pass,** faire de la place, s'écarter, se ranger, pour laisser passer qn; **to make r. for s.o. on the staff,** faire une place pour qn parmi le personnel; **we have no r. for incompetents,** les incapables n'ont pas de place ici; (*b*) *F:* **I'd rather have his r. than his company,** je me consolerais facilement de son absence; *O:* **in r. of s.o., in s.o.'s r.,** au lieu de qn, à la place de qn. **2.** lieu *m*; **there's r. for uneasiness,** il y a lieu d'être inquiet **(at,** de); **there's no r. to suppose that he's not in the plot,** il n'y a pas lieu de supposer qu'il n'est pas dans le complot; **there's r. for discussion on that point,** il y a là matière à controverse; **no r. for dispute, for fear,** aucun sujet de désaccord, de crainte; **that leaves no r. for doubt,** cela ne laisse place à aucun doute; le doute n'est plus permis; **there is no r. for hesitation,** il n'y a pas à hésiter; l'hésitation n'est pas possible, n'est pas permise; **there is (plenty of) r. for improvement,** cela laisse (beaucoup) à désirer; on peut faire mieux encore. **3.** (*a*) (*in house, etc.*) pièce *f*; (*public room*) salle *f*; **(bed)r.,** chambre *f* (à coucher); **double r.,** chambre à deux personnes, à grand lit; **double-bedded r., r. with twin beds,** chambre à deux lits; **single r.,** chambre à une personne; **spare r.,** chambre d'ami; **dining r.,** salle à manger; **(reception) r., sitting r.,** salon *m*; *F:* **the smallest r. in the house,** les cabinets *m*; le petit coin, endroit; **private r.,** (*in restaurant*) cabinet particulier; (*in hotel*) salon réservé; (*in hotel*) **public rooms,** salles; (*in house*) **reception rooms,** appartements *m* de réception; salon et salle à manger; **r. temperature,** température ambiante, de la pièce; (*of wine*) **serve at r. temperature,** servir chambré; (*at hotel*) **r. service,** repas servis dans les chambres; *Tp:* **r. service, please!** service des repas, s'il vous plaît! **r. and board,** pension *f* et chambre; **r. to r. telephone,** téléphone intérieur, d'appartement; *NAm:* **r. clerk,** employé(e) à la réception; (*b*) **the whole r. burst out laughing,** tout le monde éclata de rire; (*c*) **(furnished) rooms to let,** chambres garnies à louer; *F:* **to have a r. to let,** *NAm:* **to rent,** avoir une case vide, une araignée au plafond; **(set of) rooms,** appartement, logement *m*; **to live in rooms,** vivre en garni; **I have rooms in town,** j'ai un appartement en ville; **come to my rooms and talk it over,** venez chez moi pour en parler. **4.** (*a*) *Ind: etc:* salle, hall *m* (des chaudières, etc.); (*b*) *Nau:* **store r.,** soute *f*; **torpedo r.,** magasin *m* des torpilles. **5.** *Min:* taille *f.* **6. salt r.,** compartiment *m* de marais salant.

room[2], *v.* **1.** *v.i.* (*a*) vivre en garni; (*b*) partager un logement **(with s.o.,** avec qn); **to r. together,** vivre ensemble dans le même logement. **2.** *v.tr.* loger (qn); donner à coucher à (qn); fournir une chambre à (qn).

-roomed [ru(:)md], *a.* (*with num. or adj. prefixed*) **three-r., four-r. flat,** appartement *m* de trois, quatre, pièces.

roomer ['ru:mər], *s. NAm:* locataire *mf* qui prend ses repas dehors; **I was a r. at the time,** à cette époque je vivais en garni.

roomette [ru'met], *s. NAm:* (*a*) *Rail:* compartiment *m* de wagon-lit; (*b*) petite chambre.

roomful ['ru(:)mful], *s.* salle pleine, pleine salle, chambrée *f* **(of,** de).

roomily ['ru:mili], *adv.* (être logé) spacieusement, à l'aise.

roominess ['ru:minis], *s.* ample espace *m*, dimensions spacieuses (d'une maison, etc.); dimensions généreuses (d'une cabine, etc.).

rooming ['ru:miŋ], *s.* vie *f* en garni; *NAm:* **r. house,** maison *f* de rapport; maison, immeuble *m*, dont les pièces sont louées en garni; immeuble à studios.

roommate ['ru(:)m'meit], *s.* compagnon *m*, compagne *f*, de chambre.

roomy ['ru:mi], *a.* spacieux; où l'on a de la place; (vêtement) ample, d'amples proportions; **layout that makes the cabin more r.,** agencement qui donne plus de place, d'espace, dans la cabine.

roost[1] [ru:st], *s.* **1.** (*a*) juchoir *m*, perchoir *m*; **to go to r.,** (i) (*of hens*) se jucher; (ii) *F:* (*of pers.*) aller se coucher; aller au pieu; **hen gone to r.,** poule juchée; **to be at r.,** (i) (*of bird*) être perché, juché; (ii) (*of pers.*) être couché; **to come off the r.,** déjucher; *F:* **to rule the r.,** avoir la haute main, être le maître, faire la loi, chez soi; (*of crime, mistake, etc.*) **to come home to r.,** retourner sur son auteur; (*b*) *F:* (i) logement *m*, niche *f*, gîte *m*; (ii) nid *m*, retraite *f* (de brigands, etc.). **2.** (*birds roosting*) perchée *f*.

roost[2]. **1.** *v.i.* (*of hens*) se percher (pour la nuit), se jucher; *F: O:* **where do you r.?** où logez-vous, perchez-vous? **2.** *v.tr. F: O:* donner à coucher à (qn); héberger (qn) pour la nuit.

roost[3], *s.* raz *m* de courant (au large des Orcades et des îles Shetland).

rooster ['ru:stər], *s.* **1.** coq *m*. **2.** *P: esp. NAm:* (i) crâneur *m*, fanfaron *m*; (ii) vaniteux *m*.

roosting ['ru:stiŋ], *a.* (*of hens*) perché, juché.

root[1] [ru:t], *s.* **1.** *Bot:* (*a*) racine *f*; griffe *f*, patte *f* (d'anémone, d'asperge, etc.); **clinging r.,** crampon *m*; **aerial r.,** racine aérienne, racine-asperge *f*, *pl.* racines-asperges; **adventitious r.,** racine adventive; **tap r.,** racine pivotante; **r. cap,** coiffe *f* de racine, pilorhize *f*; **r. hair,** poil *m* radiculaire; **the r. hairs,** le chevelu; *Arb:* **r. swelling,** empattement *m*, patte *f* (de la racine); **r. pruning,** suppressions *fpl* de racines; **r. beer,** boisson faite de racines de plantes comestibles; **to pull up a plant by the roots,** déraciner une plante; arracher une plante par les racines; **to cut a tree off at the roots,** couper un arbre à blanc estoc; **to take r., strike r.,** jeter, pousser, des racines; prendre racine; prendre pied; **the tree has taken firm r., has taken r. again,** l'arbre a bien pris, a repris; **people who have no roots,** des gens sans racines; *B:* **the axe is laid unto the r. of the trees,** la cognée est déjà mise à la racine des arbres; **to strike at the r. of an evil,** atteindre, couper, un mal dans sa racine; aller à la source du mal; **to destroy abuses, a race, r. and branch,** extirper des abus, une race; **a r. and branch revision,** une révision complète, à fond; (*b*) **edible roots,** racines alimentaires; *Agr:* **r. crops,** (cultures *f* de) racines alimentaires; **r. cleaner,** décrotteur *m*; **r. cutter, r. slicer,** coupe-racines *m inv.* **2.** *B:* **r. of Jesse,** racine de Jessé. **3.** racine (d'une dent, d'un ongle); **r. of a hair,** racine d'un cheveu, bulbe pileux; **roots of a mountain,** racines d'une montagne; *Mec.E:* **r. of a cog,** racine, pied *m*, d'une dent d'engrenage; **r. circle,** cercle *m* de pied, de racine, de fond de creux (d'un engrenage); **r. line,** ligne *f* de racine, droite *f* d'évidement (d'un engrenage); *Av:* **wing r.,** emplanture *f* de l'aile; *Dent:* **r. post,** pivot *m*, tenon *m*, radiculaire. **4.** source *f*, souche *f*, fondement *m*; **laziness lies at the r. of his troubles,** la paresse est la cause première de ses maux; **money is the r. of all evil,** l'argent est la source de tous les maux; **to get to the r. of things,** aller au fond des choses; **this action strikes at the r. of all government,** par cet acte le gouvernement est frappé dans son principe même; **custom having its root(s) in the natural instincts of man,** coutume qui prend sa source dans les instincts naturels de l'homme, qui part des instincts naturels de l'homme; **r. ideas,** idées maîtresses; idées fondamentales; **r. fallacy,** erreur foncière; **r. cause,** cause première. **5.** *Mth:* racine (d'une équation, d'un nombre); **square, cube, r.,** racine carrée, cubique; **twice r. seven,** deux fois la racine carrée de sept; **r. sign,** (signe) radical *m*, -aux; *El:* **r.-mean-square value, voltage,** valeur *f*, tension *f*, efficace. **6.** *Ling:* racine (d'un mot); **r. word,** mot racine, mot souche; **r. syllable,** syllabe radicale. **7.** *Mus:* **r. (note),** base *f*, son fondamental, basse fondamentale (d'un accord).

root[2], *v.*

I. *v.tr. & i.* **1.** *v.tr.* (*a*) enraciner (des plantes); **to remain rooted to the spot, ground,** rester cloué, figé, sur place; **vices that become deeply rooted,** vices qui jettent de profondes racines, qui s'enracinent profondément; (*b*) *P: O:* **to r. s.o.,** enlever le ballon à qn; donner à qn un coup de pied quelque part. **2.** *v.i.* (*of plants*) s'enraciner, prendre racine.

II. (*compound verbs*) **1. root in,** *v.tr. Hyd.E:* empatter, planter, enter (les aubes d'une roue).

2. root out, up, *v.tr.* déraciner, arracher (une plante); déraciner, exterminer (un abus).

root[3]. **1.** *v.i.* (*a*) (*of swine, etc.*) fouiller avec le groin; fouger; nasiller; (*b*) *F:* (*of pers.*) **to r. among, in, papers,** fouiller dans des paperasses; (*c*) *esp. NAm: F:* **to r. for one's team,** encourager son équipe (de ses applaudissements, etc.); **to r. for a candidate,** appuyer un candidat (aux élections); prôner un candidat. **2.** *v.tr.* (*of boar, etc.*) fouiller (la terre); *F:* **to r. sth. out, up,** trouver qch. (en fouillant); dénicher qch.

rootage ['ru:tidʒ], *s. Bot:* racinage *m*.

root-eating ['ru:ti:tiŋ], *a. Nat.Hist:* radicivore.

rooted ['ru:tid], *a.* **1.** (*a*) enraciné; **shallow-r. tree,** arbre à enracinement superficiel; (*b*) **r. cutting,** bouture qui a des racines. **2.** (préjugé, etc.) enraciné, invétéré.

rootedly ['ru:tidli], *adv.* profondément.

rootedness ['ru:tidnis], *s.* enracinement *m* (d'une opinion, etc.).

rooter[1] ['ru:tər], *s.* **1.** (*pers.*) **r. out, up,** déracineur, -euse, extirpateur, -trice. **2.** *Agr:* dessoucheur *m*. **3.** *Civ.E:* (machine) défonceuse *f*.

rooter[2], *s. NAm: F:* (*a*) applaudisseur *m* frénétique; (*b*) fana(tique) *mf* (d'une équipe, etc.).

roothold ['ru:thould], *s.* endroit *m* où une plante peut prendre racine; **to get a r. on a rock,** prendre racine sur une roche.

rooting ['ru:tiŋ], *s.* **1.** enracinement *m*. **2.** (*a*) *Hyd.E:* **rooting in,** empattement *m* (des aubes d'une roue); (*b*) **rooting out, up,** déracinement *m*; extirpation *f*, extermination *f*, éradication *f*.

rootle ['ru:tl], *v.tr. & i.* = ROOT[3].

rootless ['ru:tlis], *a.* (*of plant*) sans racines; *s.* (*pers.*) **the r.,** les gens sans racines.

rootlet ['ru:tlit], *s.* petite racine; radicelle *f*; radicule *f*.

rootstalk ['ru:tstɔ:k], *s. Bot:* rhizome *m*.

rootstock ['ru:tstɔk], *s.* **1.** *Bot:* rhizome *m*, souche *f* (d'iris, etc.). **2.** *Fig:* souche, origine *f*.

rooty ['ru:ti], *a.* (terrain, etc.) plein de racines.

ropable ['roupəbl], *a. Austr: & N.Z: P:* (*of pers.*) furieux; mis hors de ses gonds.

rope[1] [roup], *s.* **1.** (*a*) corde *f*, cordage *m*, fil retors; *Nau:* filin *m*; (*small*) passeresse *f*; **hemp(en) r.,** cordage en chanvre; **tarred r.,** cordage goudronné; filin noir; **white, untarred, r.,** filin blanc; franc-filin *m*, *pl.* francs-filins; **plain-laid r.,** cordage simple; **fibre-clad r.,** filin mixte; **three-stranded, four-stranded, r.,** filin en trois, en quatre; **steel r.,** filin d'acier; **wire r.,** câble *m* métallique; *F:* **it's money for old r.,** c'est donné (pour une bouchée de pain); **r. yarn,** (i) fil *m* de caret; (ii) *U.S: F:* bagatelle *f*; **r. ladder,** échelle *f* de corde; **r. house, r. yard,** corderie *f*; **r. maker, manufacturer,** cordier *m*; **r. making,** corderie; (*b*) **(piece of) r.,** corde; **bell r.,** (i) cordon *m* de sonnette; (ii) corde d'une cloche; *Mount:* **(climbing) r.,** corde (d'assurance, d'attache); **to put on the r.,** s'encorder; **to come down on a doubled r.,** faire une descente en rappel; **(climbers on the) r.,** (alpinistes en) cordée *f*; **first on the r.,** premier *m* de cordée; *Nau:* **bolt, awning, r.,** ralingue *f*; **jaw r.,** bâtard *m* de racage; **running ropes,** manœuvres courantes; **rope's end,** (i) bout *m* de manœuvre; (ii) *Hist:* garcette *f*; **to give a ship's boy the rope's end,** passer un mousse à la garcette; **to know the ropes,** (i) (*of sailor*) connaître ses manœuvres; (ii) *F:* connaître son affaire, le terrain; savoir comment s'y prendre; être au courant; savoir nager; connaître la combine, les tenants, les aboutissants; **to show s.o. the ropes,** (i) mettre qn au courant; (ii) dresser, former, qn; **to give s.o. (plenty of) r.,** laisser à qn pleine liberté d'action, lâcher la bride à qn; **give him enough r. and he'll hang himself,** laissez-le faire et il va s'enferrer tout seul; **to come to the end of one's r.,** (i) se trouver arrêté dans la carrière du crime; (ii) être au bout de son rouleau; *P:* **to be on the high r.,** être pendu; danser en l'air, sur rien; **crime worthy of the r.,** crime pendable, qui mérite la corde; (*c*) *Box: Rac: etc:* **the ropes,** les cordes, *F:* les ficelles; *Fig:* **to be up against the ropes,** être aux abois; avoir le dos au mur; (*d*) (*also* **tightrope**) corde tendue, raide; (*e*) *Mec.E: etc:* **r. drive,** commande *f* par câble; **r. brake,** frein *m* à corde; (*f*) *Arch:* **r. moulding,** torsade *f*; (*in basket making*) **r. border,** torche *f* d'osier. **2.** *P:* (*a*) tabac fort, perlot *m*, trèfle *m*; (*b*) (i) marijuana *f*, chanvre *m*, pot *m*; (ii) cigarette *f* de marijuana, stick *m*. **3.** glane *f*, chapelet *m* (d'oignons); rangée *f*, grand collier (de perles). **4.** (*in beer, etc.*) graisse *f*.

rope[2], *v.*

I. *v.tr.* **1.** corder (un paquet). **2.** (*a*) attacher avec une corde; **to r. s.o. to a tree,** lier qn à un arbre; **to r. (on, down) the load on a truck,** lier la charge d'un camion; **to r. climbers (together),** encorder des alpinistes; **climbers roped together,** alpinistes en cordée; (*b*) *NAm:* prendre (un animal) au lasso. **3.** *Nau:* ralinguer (une voile). **4.** *Rac:* tirer (un cheval) (pour l'empêcher de gagner); *v.i.* **jockey accused of roping,** jockey accusé d'avoir tiré son cheval.

II. *v.i.* **1.** (*of beer, etc.*) devenir graisseux; (*when poured*) filer. **2.** *Mount:* (*of climbers*) s'encorder.

III. (*compound verbs*) **1. rope down,** *v.i. Mount:* faire une descente en rappel.

2. rope in, *v.tr.* (*a*) (*also* **rope round**) entourer (un terrain) de cordes; (*b*) *F:* **to r. s.o. in,** (i) entraîner qn dans un projet; s'assurer le concours de qn; associer qn à une entreprise; (ii) prendre (un filou) dans une rafle.

3. rope off, *v.tr.* réserver (une partie de la salle, etc.) au moyen d'une corde tendue.

ropeable ['roupəbl], *a.* = ROPABLE.

rope-bands ['roupbændz], *s.pl. Nau:* = ROBANDS.

ropedancer ['roupdænsər], *s.* danseur, -euse, de corde; funambule *mf*; équilibriste *mf*.

ropedancing ['roupdænsiŋ], *s.* funambulie *f*; danse *f* sur la corde.

ropery ['roupəri], *s.* corderie *f*.

rope's-end [roups'end], *v.tr. Nau: Hist:* passer (un mousse, etc.) à la garcette.

rope-soled ['roupsould], *a.* (espadrilles, etc.) à semelles de corde.

ropewalk ['roupwɔ:k], *s.* corderie *f*.

ropewalker, -walking ['roupwɔ:kər, -wɔ:kiŋ], *s.* = ROPEDANCER, -DANCING.

ropeway ['roupwei], *s.* câble (pour transport) aérien; voie *f* à câble aérien; transporteur *m* par câbles.

rop(e)y ['roupi], *a.* **1.** visqueux; (*of beer, etc.*) graisseux; (*when poured*) filant, qui file; **r. wine,** vin gras, graisseux; (*of wine*) **to become r.,** tourner à la graisse; graisser, bouter. **2.** *P:* (*usu.* **ropey**) (*of goods*) de mauvaise qualité; toc, tocard, de camelote; (*of excuse, etc.*) de mauvaise foi. **3.** *Geol:* **r. lava,** lave cordée.

ropiness ['roupinis], *s.* **1.** viscosité *f*; (*in beer, wine*) graisse *f*, pousse *f*. **2.** *P:* mauvaise qualité (d'une marchandise, etc.).

roping ['roupiŋ], *s.* **1.** (*a*) cordage *m* (d'un ballot); (*b*) liage *m* (de la charge d'un camion, etc.); (*c*) *NAm:* prise *f* (d'une bête) au lasso. **2.** *coll.* cordages *mpl*. **3.** *Mount:* **r. (up),** encordement *m*.

roque [rouk], *s. NAm: Games:* roque *m*.

roquelaure ['rɔkəlɔ:r], *s. A.Cost:* roquelaure *f*.

roquet[1] ['roukei, -ki], *s.* (*croquet*) touche *f* (de la balle d'un adversaire avec la sienne).

roquet[2], *v.tr. & i.* (**roqueted** ['roukeid, -kid]) (*croquet*) toucher (une autre balle avec la sienne).

roquet-croquet ['roukei'kroukei, -ki], *v.tr.* (**roquet-croqueted** [-'kroukeid, -kid]) (*croquet*) roquer (deux balles).

roqueting ['roukeiiŋ, -kiiŋ], *s.* (*croquet*) touche *f*.

rorqual ['rɔ:kwəl], *s. Z:* rorqual, -als *m*; balénoptère *m*; **lesser r.,** petit rorqual.

Rorschach ['rɔ:ʃæk], *Pr.n. Psy:* **R. test,** test *m* de Rorschach.

rort [rɔ:t], *s. Austr: P:* coup monté; (vilain) tour.

rorty ['rɔ:ti], *a. P:* **1.** (*of pers.*) allumé, émoustillé. **2. to have a r. time,** faire la noce.

Rosa ['rouzə], *Pr.n.f.* Rose, Rosa.

rosace ['rouzeis], *s. Arch:* rosace *f*.

Rosaceae [rou'zeisii:], *s.pl. Bot:* rosacées *f*.

rosaceous [rou'zeiʃəs], *a.* (*a*) rosacé; *Bot:* **r. flower,** fleur rosacée; (*b*) (*of colour*) rosâtre.

Rosales [rou'zeili:z], *s.pl. Bot:* rosales *f*.

rosalia[1] [rou'zeiliə], *s. Mus:* rosalie *f*.

rosalia[2], *s. Ent:* rosalie *f*.

Rosalind ['rɔzəlind], *Pr.n.f.* Rosalinde.

Rosamond ['rɔzəmənd], *Pr.n.f.* Rosemonde.

rosaniline [rou'zænilain], *s. Ch:* rosaniline *f*.

rosarian [rou'zɛəriən], *s.* rosiériste *mf*.

rosarium [rou'zɛəriəm], *s. Hort:* roseraie *f*, rosarium *m*.

rosary ['rouzəri], *s.* **1.** rosaire *m*; **lesser r.,** chapelet *m*; **to go through the r.,** dire le rosaire; **Buddhist r.,** chapelet bouddhique; *Bot:* **r. pea,** arbus *m* à chapelet, liane *f* réglisse. **2.** *Hort:* roseraie *f*.

Roscian ['rɔʃiən], *a. Rom.Th:* de Roscius; (jeu, etc.) digne de Roscius.

Roscoe, rosco(e) ['rɔskou], *s. NAm: P:* revolver *m*, pétard *m*.

roscoelite ['rɔskoulait], *s. Miner:* roscoélite *f*.

rose[1] [rouz], *s.* **1.** *Bot:* (*a*) rose *f*; **wild r., briar r.,** rose sauvage, de cochon, de chien; églantine *f*; **monthly, Indian, China, r.,** rose des quatre saisons, de tous les mois; **r. bowl,** coupe *f* à fleurs; **r. leaf,** feuille *f*, pétale *m*, de rose; *Fig: O:* **a crumpled r. leaf,** une petite contrariété (en amour); une anicroche; **r. honey,** miel *m* rosat; **r. vinegar,** vinaigre *m* rosat; *Ent:* **r. beetle, chafer,** cétoine dorée, hanneton vert; *Fig:* **bed of roses,** lit *m* de roses; **life is not a bed of roses, not all roses, not roses all the way,** tout n'est pas rose dans la vie; **her life wasn't a bed of roses,** elle n'avait pas la vie bien rose; *Lit:* **path strewn with roses,** chemin fleuri; *Prov:* **no r. without a thorn, every r. has its thorn,** pas de rose sans épine; chaque médaille a son revers; il n'y a pas de viande sans os; *Fig: O:* **she was a r. when she was**

young, elle était une beauté dans sa jeunesse; **she has lost her roses,** elle a perdu son teint de roses; **under the r.,** en cachette, en confidence; *Her:* **heraldic r.,** rose héraldique; *Hist:* **the Wars of the Roses,** la guerre des Deux-Roses; (*b*) **r. (bush, tree),** rosier *m*; **wild r.,** rosier sauvage, églantier *m*; *Hort:* **bush r.,** rosier buisson, nain; **standard r. (tree),** *NAm:* **tree r.,** rosier sur tige; **r. bed,** parterre *m* de rosiers; massif *m*, corbeille *f*, de rosiers; **r. garden,** roseraie *f*; **r. grower,** rosiériste *mf*; **r. gall,** bédégar *m*, éponge *f* d'églantier, galle *f* du rosier; (*c*) **r. of Jericho,** jérose *f* hygromètre; rose de Jéricho; **r. of May,** narcisse *m* des poètes, œillet *m* de Pâques; **r. of Sharon,** (i) herbe *f* de Saint-Jean; millepertuis *m*; (ii) *B:* rose de Saron; **Alpine r.,** (i) laurier-rose *m*, *pl.* lauriers-rose(s), des Alpes; rosage *m*, rosagine *f*; (ii) edelweiss *m*; **r. apple,** pomme *f* de rose, jambose *f*; **r. apple (tree),** jambosier *m*; **r. laurel,** laurier-rose *m*, *pl.* lauriers-rose(s). **2.** (*colour*) (couleur *f* de) rose *m*; **dark, light, r. material,** tissu (d'un) rose foncé, clair; **r. red,** (i) *a.* vermeil; (ii) *s.* vermillon *m*; **r. pink,** (i) *a.* (couleur de) rose *m*; rosé, incarnat; (ii) *s.* (*colour*) rose *m*; (*ink, chalk*) rosette *f*. **3.** (*a*) (*on hat, shoe, etc.*) rosette; (*b*) *Ven:* fraise *f* (d'andouiller). **4.** pomme *f*, aspersoir *m* (d'arrosoir); crépine *f*, aspirant *m*, lanterne *f*, grenouillère *f* (de pompe); *Mch:* reniflard *m*. **5.** *El:* (*a*) **(ceiling) r.,** rosace *f* de plafond; (*b*) **connecting r.,** rosace de canalisation. **6. r. burner,** brûleur *m* à couronne (de réchaud à gaz, etc.). **7. r. pattern, ornamentation, work,** rosaces; **r. punch,** roset(t)ier *m*; **r. engine,** machine *f*, tour *m*, à guillocher; **r. engine ornamentation,** guillochage *m*; **r. engine tool,** guilloche *f*. **8.** *Tls:* **r. (countersink) bit,** fraise *f* champignon; fraise taillée, à roder; *Carp:* **r. nail,** clou *m* à tête de diamant. **9.** *Med:* **r. rash,** roséole *f*; *F:* **the r.,** l'érésipèle *m*, l'érysipèle *m*. **10. compass card r.,** rose des vents. **11.** *Arch:* **r. window,** rosace, rose. **12.** *Lap:* **r.(-cut) diamond,** diamant (taillé) en rose. **13.** *Mus:* rose (de luth, etc.). **14.** *Metall:* **r. copper,** (cuivre *m* de) rosette.

rose[2], *v.tr.* roser, rosir; teindre, teinter, en rose.

Rose[3], *Pr.n. Med:* **Rose's position,** position *f* de Rose.

rosé ['rouzei], *s.* vin rosé.

roseate ['rouziət], *a. Lit:* couleur de rose *inv*; rose, rosé; **to take a r. view of things,** voir les choses en rose, avec optimisme.

rosebay ['rouzbei], *s. Bot:* (i) laurier-rose *m*, *pl.* lauriers-rose(s); (ii) laurier *m* des marais; (iii) **r. (willow-herb),** *NAm:* **r. willow,** laurier (de) Saint-Antoine, épilobe *m* à épi(s).

rosebud ['rouzbʌd], *s.* **1.** bouton *m* de rose; **r. mouth,** bouche *f* de cerise. **2.** *O:* jeune fille séduisante.

rose-coloured ['rouzkʌləd], *a.* rose, rosé; couleur de rose *inv*; **to see things through r.-c. spectacles,** voir tout en rose, en beau, couleur de rose; *Orn:* **r.-c. starling, pastor,** (martin *m*) roselin *m*.

rosed [rouzd], *a.* **1.** (*a*) rose, rosé; (*b*) couvert, orné, de roses. **2.** (arrosoir) à pomme.

rosefinch ['rouzfinʃ], *s. Orn:* roselin *m* rose.

rosefish ['rouzfiʃ], *s. Ich:* sébaste *m*, cherre *m*.

rose-like ['rouzlaik], *a.* rosacé.

roselite ['rouzəlait], *s. Miner:* rosélite *f*.

rosella [rou'zelə], *s. Orn:* **crimson r.,** perruche *f* de Pennant; **eastern r.,** perruche omnicolore; **western r.,** perruche de Stanley.

rosellinia [rɔse'liniə], *s. Fung:* rosellinia *f*.

rosemary ['rouzməri], *s. Bot:* romarin *m*, encensier *m*.

Rosenbach ['rouznbæk], *Pr.n. Med:* **Rosenbach's syndrome,** syndrome *m* de Rosenbach.

rosenbuschite ['rouzənbuʃait], *s. Miner:* rosenbuschite *m*.

Rosenkavalier ['rouzənkævəliər], *Pr.n. Mus:* le Chevalier de la Rose.

Rosenmüller ['rouzənmylər], *Pr.n. Anat:* **Rosenmüller's fossa, organ,** fosse *f*, organe *m*, de Rosenmüller.

rose noble ['rouz'noubl], *s. Num: A:* noble *m* à la rose.

roseocobaltic ['rouzioukou'bɔ:ltik], *a. Ch:* roséocobaltique.

roseola [rou'zi:ələ], *s. Med:* roséole *f*.

roseroot ['rouzru:t], *s. Bot:* rhodiola *m*.

rosery ['rouzəri], *s.* roseraie *f*.

rose-scented ['rouzsentid], *a.* parfumé à la rose, au parfum de rose.

rosetangle ['rouztæŋgl], *s. Algae:* céramium *m*.

Rosetta [rə'zetə], *Pr.n. Geog:* Rosette *f*; *Archeol:* **the R. Stone,** la pierre de Rosette.

rosette [rə'zet], *s.* **1.** (*a*) chou *m*, -oux (de ruban); cocarde *f*; rosette *f* (de la Légion d'honneur, etc.); (*b*) *Bot:* rosette (de feuilles); (*c*) *Sculp: Arch:* rosette. **2. r. burner,** brûleur *m* à couronne. **3.** *Metall:* **r. copper,** (cuivre *m* de) rosette. **4.** *Arb:* **r. (disease),** rosette. **5.** rosace *f* (de tête de clou, etc.); *El:* **ceiling r.,** rosace de plafond.

rosewater ['rouzwɔ:tər], *s.* eau *f* de rose.

rosewood ['rouzwud], *s.* **1.** *Com:* bois *m* de rose; **Brazilian r.,** bois de violette, palissandre *m*; **East Indian r.,** trac *m*; **African r.,** bois de santal rouge **2.** *Bot:* **Jamaica r.,** baumier *m* de la Jamaïque. **3. r. oil,** essence *f* de bois de roses.

Rosicrucian [rouzi'kru:ʃən]. **1.** *s.* rose-croix *m inv.* **2.** *a.* de la rose-croix, des rose-croix.

rosin[1] ['rɔzin], *s.* colophane *f*.

rosin[2], *v.tr. Mus:* frotter (l'archet) de colophane; colophaner (l'archet).

Rosinante [rɔzi'nænti]. **1.** *Pr.n. Lit:* Rossinante. **2.** *s. O:* cheval *m* étique; rossinante *f*.

rosinate ['rɔzineit], *s. Ch:* résinate *m*.

rosiness ['rouzinis], *s.* couleur *f* rose; incarnat *m*; roseur *f*; **the r. of her cheeks,** les roses *f* de ses joues.

rosiny ['rɔzini], *a.* résineux.

Rosminian [rɔs'miniən], *a. & s. Rel:* rosminien, -ienne.

rosolic [rɔ'zɔlik], *a. Ch:* rosolique.

rosolio [rɔ'zouliou], *s.* (*cordial*) rossolis *m*.

rossite ['rɔsait], *s. Miner:* rossite *f*.

rosso antico ['rɔsouæn'ti:kou], *s. Geol:* rouge *m* antique.

rostellar [rɔ'stelər], *a. Nat.Hist:* (*a*) en forme de rostelle; (*b*) rostellé.

rostellate [rɔ'steleit], *a. Bot:* rostellé.

rostellum [rɔ'steləm], *s. Nat.Hist:* rostelle *f*; *Bot:* rostellum *m* (d'une orchidée).

roster ['rɔstər], *s. Mil: etc:* (*a*) **(duty) r.,** tableau *m*, contrôle *m*, de service; **by r.,** à tour de rôle; (*b*) liste *f*, rôle *m*, feuille *f*; *Nau:* liste d'embarquement; *Adm:* **promotion r., advancement r.,** tableau d'avancement.

rostral ['rɔstrəl], *a.* rostral, -aux; *Rom.Hist:* **r. column, crown,** colonne, couronne, rostrale.

rostrate ['rɔstreit], *a. Nat.Hist:* rostré.

rostrated [rɔ'streitid], *a. Rom.Ant:* (*of column, etc.*) rostral, -aux.

rostriferous [rɔ'strifərəs], *a.* rostrifère.

rostriform ['rɔstrifɔ:m], *a. Nat.Hist:* rostriforme.

rostrum, *pl.* **-a, -ums** ['rɔstrəm, -ə, -əmz], *s.* **1.** (*a*) *Rom.Ant:* **the Rostra,** les rostres *m*; (*b*) estrade *f*, tribune *f*; *Sp:* podium *m*; (*at auction*) **to take the r.,** monter sur l'estrade; prendre le marteau (du commissaire-priseur). **2.** (*a*) *Rom.Ant:* rostre *m* (d'une galère); (*b*) *Nat.Hist:* rostre, bec *m*.

rosulate ['rɔzjuleit], *a. Bot:* en forme de rosette.

rosy ['rouzi], *a.* de rose, rose, rosé, vermeil; **r. cheeks,** joues vermeilles; **her r. complexion, cheeks,** les roses *f* de son teint; son teint de rose; ses joues vermeilles; (*of sky, etc.*) **to become, turn, r.,** prendre une teinte rose; se roser; rosir; *Fig:* **to paint everything in r. colours,** peindre tout en beau, en rose; **a r. prospect,** une perspective souriante, attrayante; *Orn:* **r. bill,** canard *m* peposaca.

rosy-fingered ['rouzi'fiŋgəd], *a. Lit:* (l'Aurore *f*) aux doigts de rose.

rot[1] [rɔt], *s.* **1.** pourriture *f*, putréfaction *f*, carie *f*; *Agr: Hort:* rot *m*; (*of lettuce, etc.*) morve *f*; **to cut the r. out of a timber,** enlever la pourriture d'une poutre; *Hort:* **brown r.,** rouille *f* des feuilles; rosée *f* de farine; faux oïdium; mildiou *m*, mildew *m*; (*of fruit*) moniliose *f*. **2.** *Vet:* (*of sheep, etc.*) **liver r., the r.,** distomatose *f*; pourriture; cachexie aqueuse; bouteille *f*. **3.** *F:* bêtises *fpl*; **that's (a lot of) r.!** tout ça c'est des racontars, des sottises, *P:* des bobards, des foutaises! **to talk (utter) r.,** dire des imbécillités; **his speech was complete r.,** son discours a été nul; il nous a débité des niaiseries, des sottises; **what r.!** quelle idiotie! quelle imbécillité! *P:* quelle foutaise! **4.** (*in sport, war, etc.*) démoralisation *f*; **the r. set in,** le moral (des joueurs, des combattants) a flanché; **to stop the r.,** parer à la panique, démoralisation; enrayer la crise.

rot[2], *v.* **(rotted) 1.** *v.i.* (*a*) (se) pourrir; se décomposer, se putréfier; se carier; **they let him r. in prison,** on le laissait pourrir dans un cachot; (*of bough, etc.*) **to r. off, away,** tomber en pourriture; (*b*) *F:* dire des bêtises; **he's only rotting,** il n'est pas sérieux; il est en train de blaguer. **2.** *v.tr.* pourrir, faire pourrir, décomposer, putréfier, carier; **oil rots rubber,** l'huile désagrège le caoutchouc. **3.** *F: O:* railler, blaguer (qn).

rota ['routə], *s.* **1.** *R.C.Ch:* **the R. (Romana),** la Rote. **2.** liste *f* de roulement; liste, tableau *m*, contrôle *m*, de service; **members preside according to a r.,** les membres exercent la présidence à tour de rôle. **3.** *A.Mus:* rot(t)e *f*, canon *m*.

rotameter ['routəmi:tər], *s.* compteur *m* de fluide, débitmètre *m*.

Rotarian [rə'teəriən], *s.* rotarien *m*.

rotary ['routəri], *a.* **1.** rotatif, rotatoire; (*a*) **r. motion,** mouvement rotatif, circulaire, de rotation; **r. traffic,** circulation *f* giratoire; *a. & s. NAm:* **r. (intersection),** rond-point *m*, *pl.* ronds-points, croisement *m*, à circulation giratoire; *Ph:* **r. polarization,** polarisation *f* rotatoire; (*b*) tournant; **r. knob,** bouton tournant; *Cin:* **r. shutter,** obturateur rotatif; *El:* **r. switch,** commutateur rotatif; **r. crane,** grue pivotante; *Min:* **r. rig, drill,** rotary *m*; *Typ:* **r. machine, printing press,** (machine) rotative (*f*); *F:* roto *f*; **r. printer,** rotativiste *m*; *Av:* **r. engine,** moteur rotatif; **r.-wing aviation,** giraviation *f*; **r.-wing aircraft,** giravion *m*; *Ind:* **r. drier,** essoreuse *f* centrifuge; *Mch:* **r. furnace,** four rotatif, rotatoire, tournant; **r. valve engine,** machine à tiroirs rotatifs, à plateaux tournants; (*c*) (système, etc.) rotatif, de rotation. **2. R. Club,** Rotary Club *m*.

rotate[1] [rə'teit]. **1.** *v.i.* (*a*) tourner; (*of pivot*) basculer, pivoter; (*b*) (*of pers.*) remplir ses fonctions à tour de rôle; rouler. **2.** *v.tr.* (*a*) tourner; faire tourner; faire basculer (un creuset, etc.); **to r. a wheel by hand,** faire tourner une roue à la main; **to r. a telescope through an angle of 90°,** faire faire une rotation de 90° à une lunette; (*b*) remplir (des fonctions) à tour de rôle; (*c*) *Agr:* alterner, varier (les cultures); **to r. the crops on poor soil,** assoler une terre peu fertile.

rotate[2] ['routeit], *a.* rotiforme; *Bot:* (*of corolla*) rotacé.

rotating[1] [rə'teitiŋ], *a.* **1.** tournant, rotatif, à rotation; **r. body,** corps *m* en rotation; **r. radio beacon,** phare tournant; *El:* **r. field,** champ tournant; *Aer:* (*of propeller*) **opposite-r.,** contrarotatif. **2.** *Agr:* **r. crops,** cultures alternantes.

rotating[2], *s.* rotation *f*; **r. moment,** moment *m* de rotation.

rotation [rə'teiʃ(ə)n], *s.* **1.** (*a*) (mouvement *m* de) rotation *f*; **axis of r.,** axe *m* de rotation; **clockwise, anticlockwise, r.,** rotation à droite, à gauche; (*b*) basculage *m* (d'un creuset, etc.). **2.** (*a*) succession *f* tour à tour; rotation, roulement *m*; *Ind:* **r. roll,** (tableau *m* de) roulement; **by, in, r.,** par roulement, à tour de rôle; **the chair is taken in r.,** on occupe le fauteuil présidentiel à tour de rôle; (*b*) *Agr:* **r. of crops, r. cropping,** rotation des cultures; assolement *m*; **three-course, four-course, r.,** assolement triennal, quadriennal; *Husb:* **r. crossing,** croisement rotatif. **3.** rotation, tour *m*; **rotations per minute,** tours-minute *mpl*.

rotational [rə'teiʃənl], *a.* (mouvement, etc.) rotatif, de rotation; **r. inertia,** inertie *f* de rotation.

rotative ['routətiv, rou'teitiv], *a.* **1.** (*a*) rotatif, tournant; (*b*) (*of force, etc.*) rotateur, -trice. **2.** (*a*) (service, etc.) qui se fait par roulement; (*b*) *Agr:* (culture) en assolement.

rotator [rou'teitər], *s.* **1.** *Anat:* (muscle) rotateur (*m*). **2.** appareil rotateur; *Nau:* hélice *f* (de loch). **3.** *Nat.Hist:* *O:* rotifère *m*.

rotatory [rou'teitəri], *a.* rotatoire, de rotation; *Ph:* **r. power,** pouvoir *m* rotatoire (d'un cristal, etc.).

rotch(e) [rɔtʃ], *s. Orn:* mergule *m*.

rote[1] [rout], *s.* (*used only in* **by r.**) **to say, learn, sth. by r.,** dire, apprendre, qch. mécaniquement, par cœur, comme un perroquet; **to know sth. by r.,** savoir qch. par cœur; **to do sth. by r.,** faire qch. par routine.

rote[2], *s. A.Mus:* rot(t)e *f*.

rotenone ['routənoun], *s. Ch: Ind:* roténone *f*.

rotgut ['rɔtgʌt], *s. F:* (*spirits*) tord-boyau *m*; casse-gueule *m*, casse-pattes *m*, casse-poitrine *m*, riquiqui *m*, bistouille *f*; (*beer*) bibine *f*; (*wine*) piquette *f*.

rothoffite ['rɔθəfait], *s. Miner:* rothoffite *f*.

rothole ['rɔthoul], *s. Can:* endroit *m* où la glace est pourrie.

rotifer ['routifər], *s. Nat.Hist:* rotifère *m*.

Rotifera [rou'tifərə], *s.pl. Nat.Hist:* rotifères *m*.

rotiform ['routifɔ:m], *a.* rotiforme.

rotogravure ['routougrəvjuər], *s.* (*process, print*) rotogravure *f*.

rotor ['routər], *s.* (*a*) *Mec.E:* rotor *m* (de turbine, compresseur, etc.); **air-cleaner r.,** centrifugeur *m* d'un épurateur d'air; (*b*) *El:* rotor, enduit *m*; *I.C.E:* balai rotatif (du distributeur); **r. current, circuit,** courant *m*, circuit *m*, rotorique; (*c*) **helicopter r.,** rotor, sustentateur rotatif, d'un hélicoptère; **tail r.,** rotor de queue; **r. tip velocity,** vitesse circonférentielle du rotor; **flexible-r., rigid-r., aircraft,** appareil *m* à rotor flexible, rigide.

rotorcraft ['routəkrɑ:ft], *s.* giravion *m*.

rototill ['routoutil], *v.tr.* cultiver (la terre) avec un rotavator.

rotproof ['rɔtpru:f], *a.* à l'épreuve de la pourriture; (bois, etc.) imputrescible; (étoffe) qui résiste à l'humidité, à la chaleur.

rotted ['rɔtid], *a.* **1.** pourri, carié; *Agr:* **r. manure,** fumier décomposé. **2.** *Vet:* atteint de (la) distomatose; mangé de douves.

rotten ['rɔt(ə)n], *a.* **1.** pourri, putréfié, carié; **r. egg,** œuf pourri, gâté; **r. fruit,** fruits gâtés; **to smell r.,** sentir le pourri; *F:* **he's r. to the core,** il est pourri de vices; il est corrompu jusqu'à la moelle des os; **r. with prejudices,** pourri de préjugés; **r. society,** société galeuse. **2.** *F:* de mauvaise qualité; lamentable; moche; **r. weather,** temps de chien; **r. job,** sale besogne *f*; **he played a r. game,** (i) il a joué abominablement; (ii) il a fait un sale tour; **I'm feeling r.,** je me sens mal fichu, je me sens patraque; **r. luck!** quelle guigne! pas de veine! **3.** *Vet:* (mouton) au foie douvé.

rottenly ['rɔtənli], *adv. F:* (se conduire, etc.) très mal, d'une façon pitoyable, abominablement.

rottenness ['rɔtənnis], *s.* **1.** état *m* de pourriture, de décomposition. **2.** *F:* **the r. of the weather, of his acting,** le sale temps; son jeu pitoyable.

rottenstone[1] ['rɔtənstoun], *s. Geol:* tripoli anglais; terre pourrie d'Angleterre; potée *f* de montagne.

rottenstone[2], *v.tr.* polir avec du tripoli; tripolir.

rotter ['rɔtər], *s. F:* **1.** sale type *m*, sale moineau *m*; pignouf *m.* **2.** *O:* raté *m*; propre *m* à rien; bon *m* à rien.

rotting[1] ['rɔtiŋ], *a.* qui pourrit, se carie; en pourriture.

rotting[2], *s.* **1.** pourriture *f*, putréfaction *f*, carie *f*; *Paperm:* pourrissage *m*; **subject to r.,** putrescible; **proof against r.,** (i) imputrescible; (ii) (tissu) qui résiste à l'humidité, au soleil. **2.** *F:* blague *f*, bêtises *fpl.*

rotula ['rɔtjulə], *s. Anat:* rotule *f.*

rotulian [rɔ'tju:liən], *a. Anat:* rotulien.

rotund [rə'tʌnd], *a.* **1.** rond, arrondi; **his r. figure,** ses formes arrondies. **2.** (discours) emphatique, grandiloquent; (style) ampoulé.

rotunda [rə'tʌndə], *s. Arch:* rotonde *f.*

rotundate [rə'tʌndeit], *a. Bot:* arrondi.

rotundity [rə'tʌnditi], *s.* **1.** *(a)* rondeur *f*, rotondité *f* (d'une courbe, etc.); *(b)* rotondité (de qn); embonpoint *m.* **2.** rondeur, grandiloquence *f* (de style).

rouble ['ru:bl], *s. Num:* rouble *m.*

roucou ['ru:ku:], *s.* **1.** *Dy:* ro(u)cou *m.* **2.** *Bot:* **r. (tree),** ro(u)couyer *m.*

roué ['ru:ei], *s.* vieux débauché; *F:* vieux marcheur.

rouge[1] [ru:ʒ], *s.* **1.** *(a)* *Toil:* rouge *m*; *(b)* **jeweller's r.,** rouge à polir; rouge d'Angleterre, de Prusse. **2.** *Cards:* **r. et noir,** ['ru:ʒei'nwɑ:r], trente et quarante *m.*

rouge[2], *v.tr. & i.* **to r. (one's cheeks),** se mettre du rouge aux joues; se farder.

rough[1] [rʌf], *a., adv. & s.*

I. *a.* **1.** *(a)* *(to the touch)* rude, rugueux, raboteux; *(of surface, skin)* rêche, rugueux, rude; *(of paper)* rugueux, inégal, -aux; *(of cloth)* rêche, gros, grossier; **r. hands,** mains calleuses; **r. tongue,** langue rugueuse; **r. edges,** tranches non ébarbées, non rognées (d'un livre); **r. linen, leather,** grosse toile, gros cuir; **r.-grained,** à gros grain, à grain grossier; **r. thread,** fil bourru; **r. side (of a skin, of leather),** côté *m* chair; grain *m*; **r. side of a tennis racket,** envers *m*; côté des nœuds; *Ten:* **r. or smooth?** corde ou nœud? *F:* **to give s.o. the r. edge of one's tongue,** laver la tête à qn; passer un savon à qn; *(b)* *(uneven)* *(of road)* raboteux; *(of coast, outline, etc.)* accidenté; *(of ground)* inégal, raboteux; accidenté, bosselé; *(c)* *(undressed, unrefined, etc.)* brut; **in the r. state,** à l'état brut; *Metalw:* **r. stamping,** pièce brute d'estampage; **r.-forged,** brut de forge; **r.-stamped,** brut d'estampage; **to r.-bore, to r.-drill, a casting,** percer un trou dans une pièce; *Mec.E:* **to r.-bore,** aléser d'ébauche; aléser à brut; **r. boring,** alésage *m* d'ébauche; ébauche *f* à la fraise; **to r.-grind,** dégrossir, blanchir (un outil) à la meule; émoudre (un outil); **r. grinding,** dégrossissage *m* à la meule; **to r.-turn,** ébaucher (au tour); dégrossir; **r. turning,** ébauchage *m*; *Const:* **to r.-coat,** ravaler (une façade); **r. coating,** ravalement *m*; *Ven:* **to go r. shooting,** chasser devant soi; *(d)* *F:* **to feel r.,** se sentir patraque; ne pas être dans son assiette. **2.** *(violent)* grossier; brutal, -aux; brusque, rude, dur; *(of treatment)* mauvais, dur, brutal; *(of wind)* violent; **r. sea,** mer agitée, mauvaise, forte, grosse, houleuse; **to have a r. crossing, passage,** faire une mauvaise traversée; avoir une grosse mer pour la traversée; *F:* **he's had a r. passage, a r. deal, a r. ride, a r. time of it,** il en a bavé; il a mangé de la vache enragée; **r. handling,** *F:* **r. stuff,** brutalités *fpl*; **the rough(er) element (of the population),** la canaille, les voyous *m*; **to be r. with s.o.,** brutaliser, rudoyer, qn; *F:* **it was r. on him,** c'était dur pour lui; **that's r.!** c'est vache! c'est dur à avaler! **r. and ready,** (i) exécuté grossièrement; fait à la hâte; (ii) *(of pers.)* cavalier, sans façon; **r. and ready methods,** méthodes grossières et expéditives; procédés au petit bonheur; **to do sth. in a r. and ready manner,** faire qch. à vue de nez; **done in a r. and ready fashion,** taillé à coups de hache, de serpe; **r. and ready installation,** installation de fortune; **r. and tumble,** mêlée *f*, bousculade *f*; corps-à-corps *m inv*; **r. and tumble fight, game,** combat, jeu, où l'on n'observe pas de règles; **r. and tumble life,** vie mouvementée. **3.** *(of manners)* grossier, fruste; *(of speech)* bourru, rude; *(of style)* fruste; *F:* **r. customer,** sale type, mauvais coucheur; *F:* **to give s.o. a r. time,** traiter qn avec sévérité; être vache avec qn; **r. welcome,** accueil rude (mais sincère); accueil bourru; **r. accommodation,** logement rudimentaire; *Dom.Ec:* **r. work,** le gros ouvrage, *F:* le plus gros; **r. justice,** justice sommaire; **he'd had a r. upbringing,** il avait été élevé à la va-comme-je-te-pousse. **4.** approximatif; **r. sketch,** (i) ébauche *f*, esquisse *f*, pochade *f*, griffonnage *m*; (ii) plan *m* en croquis; croquis *m* de projet; premier jet; aperçu *m*; **r. translation,** traduction approximative; **r. draft,** *Sch:* **r. work,** brouillon *m*; **r. calculation,** calcul grossier, approximatif; **r. average,** moyenne approximative; **r. guess,** approximation *f*; **at a r. guess,** par aperçu, par approximation; approximativement; **r. estimate,** évaluation en gros; estimation approximative, devis approximatif; **at a r. guess, estimate, it's worth . . .,** cela vaut approximativement . . .; à vue d'œil, cela vaut. . . ; *Lap:* **r. cutting,** brutage *m*, ébrutage *m* (d'un diamant); *Metalw:* **r. facing,** dressage d'ébauche. **5.** *(a)* *(of voice)* rude, rauque, âpre; *(b)* *Gr.Gram:* **r. breathing,** esprit rude; *(c)* *(of wine)* gros, grossier, âpre, rude.

II. *adv.* *(a)* rudement, grossièrement; **to play r.,** jouer brutalement; *(b)* *F:* **to sleep r.,** coucher sur la dure.

III. *s.* **1.** *(a)* terrain accidenté; *(b)* *Golf:* **to be in the r.,** être dans l'herbe longue. **2.** crampon *m* (d'un fer à cheval); crampon à glace. **3.** (le) côté désagréable des choses; **to take the r. with the smooth,** prendre le bien avec le mal; à la guerre comme à la guerre. **4.** *(pers.)* vaurien *m*, voyou *m*, canaille *f*, bandit *m.* **5.** *(a)* état brut; **wood in the r.,** bois (à l'état) brut; bois en grume; *(b)* ébauche *f* (d'un tableau, etc.); **statue in the r.,** statue brute; ébauche d'une statue.

rough[2], *v.tr.* **1. to r. (up) the hair,** ébouriffer (les cheveux); faire hérisser (le poil). **2.** *(a)* *Farr:* ferrer (un cheval) à glace; (faire) acièrer (un cheval); acièrer les fers (d'un cheval); *(b)* dépolir (le verre); *(c)* *Const:* piquer, bretter, bretteler (un mur, etc.). **3.** *F:* *(a)* **to r. it,** (i) vivre à la dure; (ii) en voir de dures; manger de la vache enragée; **you'll have to r. it at the start,** vous aurez la vie dure pour commencer; **we've, you've, got to r. it,** à la guerre comme à la guerre; *(b)* **to r. s.o. up,** rudoyer, malmener, maltraiter, rosser, cogner, qn. **4. to r. (down),** dégrossir (une lentille, etc.); *Sculp:* **to r. in a block of marble,** ébaucher un bloc de marbre; **to r. out,** ébaucher (un plan), dégrossir (une pièce, une statue), concevoir (un projet) dans ses grandes lignes.

roughage ['rʌfidʒ], *s. Physiol:* ballast *m*; matières *fpl* inassimilables, non digestibles (de la nourriture).

roughcast[1] ['rʌfkɑ:st], *s.* **1.** *Const:* crépi *m*, gobetis *m*, ravalement *m*, hourdage *m*, hourdis *m.* **2.** ébauche *f* (d'un plan, etc.).

roughcast[2], *v.tr.* *(p.t. & p.p.* **roughcast)** **1.** *Const:* crépir, hourder, gobeter, encroûter, hérisser, hérissonner (un mur, etc.); ravaler (une façade). **2.** ébaucher (un plan, etc.).

roughcaster ['rʌfkɑ:stər], *s. Const:* ravaleur *m.*

roughcasting ['rʌfkɑ:stiŋ], *s.* **1.** crépissage *m*, hourdage *m* (d'un mur, etc.); ravalement *m* (d'une façade). **2.** ébauchage *m* (d'un plan, etc.).

rough-coated ['rʌfkoutid], *a.* (cheval) hérissé, à long poil; (chien) à poil dur.

roughdry ['rʌfdrai], *v.tr.* faire sécher (le linge, etc.) sans repasser.

roughen ['rʌf(ə)n]. **1.** *v.tr.* *(a)* rendre rude, rugueux, âpre; *(b)* *Stonew:* boucharder (la pierre). **2.** *v.i.* *(a)* devenir rude, rugueux, âpre; **her hands had roughened,** ses mains étaient devenues calleuses; *(b)* *(of the sea)* grossir; devenir houleuse.

rougher ['rʌfər], *s.* *(pers.)* **1.** *Metalw:* ébaucheur *m.* **2.** *Art:* **r. out,** praticien *m* (qui ébauche une statue).

rough-footed [rʌf'futid], *a. Orn:* (pigeon, etc.) pattu.

rough(-)handle [rʌf'hændl], *v.tr.* malmener (qn).

roughhew [rʌf'hju:], *v.tr.* *(p.t.* **roughhewed;** *p.p.* **roughhewn)** ébaucher, dégrossir (une statue, etc.); dégrossir, bûcher (du bois d'œuvre); **roughhewn plan,** projet ébauché.

roughhouse[1] ['rʌfhaus], *s. F:* barouf(le) *m*, boucan *m.*

roughhouse[2]. *F:* **1.** *v.i.* chahuter. **2.** *v.tr.* **to r. s.o.,** malmener, maltraiter, qn.

roughing ['rʌfiŋ], *s.* **1. r. (down, out),** dégrossissage *m*, dégrossissement *m*; ébauchage *m*; **r. tool,** ciseau *m* à dégrossir; ébauchoir *m*; *Metalw:* **r. cut,** passe *f* de dégrossissage (au tour); coupe *f* d'ébauche; **r. mill,** train, équipage, dégrossisseur; fraise à dégrossir; **r. roller, cylinder,** cylindre dégrossisseur, cylindre ébaucheur; **r. roll,** dégrossisseur *m.* **2.** *Const:* crépissage *m*, ravalement *m* (d'un mur); **r.-in coat (of plaster),** gobetis *m.* **3.** *Farr:* ferrage *m* à glace.

roughish ['rʌfiʃ], *a.* **1.** un peu rude, rugueux. **2.** (mer) assez houleuse. **3.** (individu) un peu fruste, mal dégrossi.

roughleg ['rʌfleg], *s. Orn:* buse pattue; **ferruginous r.,** buse rouilleuse.

rough-legged ['rʌfleg(i)d], *a.* **1.** *Orn:* (pigeon) pattu. **2.** (chien, etc.) à poil long sur les pattes.

roughly ['rʌfli], *adv.* **1.** rudement, brutalement, brusquement, âprement; **to treat s.o. r.,** maltraiter, malmener, rudoyer, qn; **the wind blew r.,** le vent était violent; **you're going about it rather r.,** vous y allez un peu fort. **2.** grossièrement; **r. painted, bound,** peint, relié, grossièrement; **r. made,** taillé à la serpe, à coups de serpe; **r. made table,** table grossièrement façonnée; **to sketch sth. r.,** faire un croquis sommaire de qch. **3.** approximativement; à peu près; en gros; dans ses lignes générales; **r. speaking,** en général; généralement parlant; **to estimate sth. r.,** estimer qch. à peu près, en gros, approximativement; **we are steering r. north,** notre cap est aux environs du nord.

roughneck ['rʌfnek], *s. F:* **1.** vaurien *m*, voyou *m*, canaille *f*, bandit *m.* **2.** *Petr:* manœuvre *m* de sonde, foreur *m.*

roughness ['rʌfnis], *s.* **1.** *(a)* rudesse *f*, aspérité *f*, rugosité *f*; *(b)* rugosité, inégalité *f* (du sol, du chemin); mauvais état (du chemin); anfractuosités *fpl* (d'un rocher, d'une côte). **2.** *(a)* grossièreté *f*, brusquerie *f*, sans-façon *m*; manières bourrues; *(b)* agitation *f*, état agité (de la mer). **3.** aspérité, âpreté *f*, rudesse (de la voix); qualité *f* fruste (du style).

roughometer [rʌ'fɔmitər], *s. Civ.E: etc:* rugosimètre *m.*

roughrider ['rʌfraidər], *s.* **1.** dresseur *m*, dompteur *m*, de chevaux. **2.** *Mil:* cavalier *m* appartenant à un corps irrégulier.

roughshod ['rʌfʃɔd], *a.* *(a)* (cheval) ferré à glace; acièré; *(b)* **to ride r. over s.o.,** fouler qn aux pieds; traiter qn cavalièrement, brutalement, sans ménagement, avec rudesse, avec insolence.

rough-spoken [rʌf'spouk(ə)n], *a.* *(a)* bourru; *(b)* au langage grossier.

roughstone ['rʌfstoun], *s. Const:* pierre bourrue.

roulade [ru:'lɑ:d], *s.* **1.** *Mus:* roulade *f.* **2.** *NAm: Cu:* paupiette *f* (de viande).

rouleau, *pl.* **-eaux, -eaus** [ru:'lou, -ouz], *s.* rouleau *m* (de pièces de monnaie).

roulette [ru:'let], *s.* **1.** *Gaming:* roulette *f*; **Russian r.,** roulette russe. **2.** *Mth:* roulette; (courbe *f*) trochoïde *f.* **3.** *Tls:* roulette, molette *f* (de graveur, etc.); molette (à perforer).

Roumania [ru(:)'meiniə], *Pr.n. Geog:* Roumanie *f.*

Roumanian [ru(:)'meiniən]. **1.** *a. Geog:* roumain. **2.** *s.* *(a)* *Geog:* Roumain, -aine; *(b)* *Ling:* roumain *m.*

Roumelia [ru:'mi:liə], *Pr.n. A.Geog:* **(Eastern) R.,** Roumélie (Orientale).

Roumelian [ru:'mi:liən]. *A.Geog:* *(a)* *a.* rouméliote; *(b)* *s.* Rouméliote *mf.*

round[1] [raund], *a. & s.*

I. *a.* **1.** rond, circulaire; **r. hole,** trou rond; *Lit:* **the R. Table,** la Table ronde; *Pol: Ind: etc:* **r. table conference,** table ronde; **r. tower,** tour ronde; **to make sth. r.,** arrondir qch.; **to become r.,** s'arrondir; **eyes r. with astonishment,** yeux arrondis par l'étonnement; **to listen in r.-eyed amazement,** écouter les yeux ronds; **to stare r.-eyed,** ouvrir de grands yeux étonnés; **r. face, cheeks,** visage rond, joues rondes; **r. shoulders,** épaules voûtées; dos rond, voûté; **r.-shouldered, r.-backed,** aux épaules voûtées, au dos voûté, bombé; **to be r.-shouldered,** avoir le dos rond, voûté, bombé; être voûté; **r. hand,** (écriture) ronde *f*; écriture grosse; **written in r. hand,** écrit en ronde; *Ling:* **r. vowel,** voyelle prononcée en arrondissant les lèvres; *Com:* **r. bars (of iron),** ronds *m*, rondins *m*; **r. timber,** bois non équarri; *Tls:* **r. file,** lime ronde; **r. nut,** écrou cylindrique; *Bot:* **r.-leaved,** rotundifolié, à feuilles rondes. **2.** *(a)* **r. dance,** danse en rond; ronde; **r. voyage,** voyage circulaire; **r. trip,** aller *m* et retour; **r. robin,** (i) pétition revêtue de signatures en rond, en cercle; (ii) *NAm: Sp:* poule *f*; *(b)* *Nau:* **r. turn,** tour mort (de cordage). **3.** *(a)* **r. dozen,** bonne douzaine; **r. figure, number,** chiffre, nombre, rond; **in r. figures,** en chiffres ronds; **r. sum,** compte rond; *(b)* **good r. sum,** somme rondelette; **that's a good r. sum,** cela fait une assez belle somme. **4.** *A:* **to be r. with s.o.,** parler à qn franchement, rondement, sans façons.

II. *s.* **1.** *(a)* cercle *m*, rond *m*; **cylinder out of r.,** cylindre ovalisé; *(b)* *Art:* **sculpture in the r.,** ronde(-)bosse *f*; **figures (modelled) in the r.,** figures de, en, ronde(-)bosse; **to draw from the r.,** dessiner d'après la bosse; **the description is true in the r.,** la description est juste dans son ensemble; *(c)* **theatre in the r.,** théâtre en rond. **2.** *(a)* barreau *m*, échelon *m* (d'une échelle, etc.); *(b)* *Arch:* rond (de moulure); *(c)* *Com:* **rounds (of iron),**

ronds, rondins *m*; (*d*) *Cu:* **r. of beef,** gîte *m* à la noix; **r. (of bread),** tranche *f* (de pain); **r. of toast,** tranche de pain grillé; **r. of sandwiches,** sandwich de pain de mie (coupé en deux, en quatre); *F:* **a r. of cheese,** un sandwich au fromage. **3.** (*a*) *Lit:* **the yearly r. of the earth,** la révolution annuelle de la terre; (*b*) **the daily r.,** la routine de tous les jours; le train-train quotidien; **one continual r. of pleasure,** une succession perpétuelle de plaisirs. **4.** (*a*) tour *m*; **to have a r. of golf,** faire une tournée de golf; *Knit:* **r. of stitches,** tour de mailles; **the story went the r. (of the village, etc.),** l'histoire a passé de bouche en bouche, a fait le tour (du village, etc.); **rumour that is going the rounds,** bruit qui court; (*b*) tournée *f*; **the postman's r.,** la tournée du facteur; **the inspector is on his r.,** l'inspecteur est en tournée; **to make, do, one's rounds, to go on one's rounds,** faire sa tournée; **to do a hospital r.,** (i) faire sa visite à l'hôpital; (ii) faire une clinique; **to make a r. of visits,** faire une tournée, une série, de visites; (*c*) *Mil:* ronde (d'inspection); (*of officer*) **to go the rounds,** faire sa, la, ronde. **5.** (*a*) *Box:* round *m*, reprise *f*; (*b*) *Ten:* tour, série (d'un tournoi); **to have a bye to the third r.,** être exempt jusqu'au troisième tour; (*c*) *Sp:* manche *f* (d'une compétition); (*d*) *Equit:* **clear r.,** sans-faute *m inv.* **6.** (*a*) **to stand a r. of drinks,** payer une tournée (générale); **to serve a r. of drinks,** donner à boire à tout le monde; **to serve a r. of rum,** verser du rhum à la ronde; (*b*) *Cards:* tour; levée *f*; (*c*) *Mil:* **r. of ten shots,** salve *f* de dix coups; **r. of applause,** salve d'applaudissements; **r. after r. of cheers,** des cascades *f* d'acclamations; (*d*) *Mil:* **r. (of ammunition),** cartouche *f*; (*of company*) **to fire a r.,** tirer un coup (chacun). **7.** *Mus:* canon *m*; fugue *f* (pour voix égales); *Danc:* ronde.

round[2], *adv. & prep.*

I. *adv.* **1.** (*a*) **to go r. (in a circle),** tourner (en rond); décrire un cercle, des cercles; *Fig:* **to go r. in circles,** tourner en rond; **the earth goes r.,** la terre tourne sur elle-même; **the wheels go r.,** les roues tournent; **my head's going r.,** la tête me tourne; **there's a rumour going r. that . . .,** le bruit court, circule, que . . .; **to turn r. and r.,** tournoyer; **to run, fly, r. and r.,** courir, voler, en rond, en cercles; **to turn, look, r.,** se retourner; **turn your chair r.,** tournez votre chaise! **let's go into town and have a look r., and look r.,** allons visiter la ville; (*b*) **all the year r.,** (pendant) toute l'année; **this brings us r. to winter,** cela nous ramène à l'hiver; **winter came r.,** l'hiver est revenu, est arrivé; (*c*) **to bring s.o. r. (after fainting),** remettre, ranimer, qn; **to come r. (after fainting),** revenir à soi; se remettre; **to come r. to s.o.'s opinion,** se ranger à l'opinion de qn; **we soon won him r.,** nous l'avons vite gagné à notre cause; (*d*) **it's the other way r.,** c'est (tout) le contraire. **2.** (*a*) autour; **garden with a wall right r., all r.,** jardin avec un mur tout autour; **to be 3 metres r.,** avoir 3 mètres de tour; **the town walls are 4 km r.,** les murs de la ville ont 4 km de pourtour, de circuit; **her waist is only 60 cm r.,** elle n'a que 60 cm de tour de taille; **to show s.o. r.,** faire faire à qn le tour de la maison, du jardin, etc.; **taking it, taken, all r.,** dans l'ensemble; en général; (*b*) **the villages r. about,** les villages à l'entour. **3.** **to hand r., pass r., the cakes,** faire passer, faire circuler, les gâteaux; **to pass the bottle r., to hand r. the bottle,** (faire) passer la bouteille à la ronde; **tea was served, handed, r.,** on a servi le thé à tout le monde; **there's not enough to go r.,** il n'y en a pas assez pour tout le monde; **will the meat go r.?** est-ce qu'il y aura assez de viande? **to pay for drinks all r.,** payer une tournée (générale). **4.** (*a*) **don't come across, come r., go r.,** ne traversez pas, faites le tour! **it's a long way r.,** cela fait un grand détour; **to take the longest way r.,** prendre par le plus long, prendre le chemin le plus long; (*b*) **to order the car r.,** demander qu'on amène la voiture; **to ask s.o. r. for the evening,** inviter qn à venir passer la soirée; **he brought his friend r. (with him),** il a amené son ami (avec lui); **if you are r. this way next week,** si vous passez par ici la semaine prochaine.

II. *prep.* **1.** (*a*) (*position*) autour de; **to wear a scarf r. one's neck,** porter un foulard au cou, autour du cou; **to take hold of s.o. r. the waist,** saisir qn à bras-le-corps; **sitting r. the table,** assis autour de la table; **there was a crowd r. the church,** il y avait une foule autour de l'église; **newspaper with a wrapper r. it,** journal avec une bande autour; **he's 95 cm r. the chest,** il a un tour de poitrine de 95 cm; il a 95 cm de tour de poitrine; **shells were exploding r. (about) him,** des obus éclataient autour de lui; **it'll be somewhere r. a hundred pounds,** cela fera dans les cent livres; **r. (about) midday,** vers midi; (*b*) (*motion*) **to travel r. the world,** faire le tour du monde; **to row, sail, swim, r. the island,** faire le tour de l'île à la rame, à la voile, à la nage; **to take, show, s.o. r. the garden,** faire faire à qn le tour du jardin; **to go r. the museum,** visiter le musée; **come and look r. the house,** venez voir la maison! **to look r. the room,** jeter un coup d'œil autour de la pièce; **the earth moves r. the sun,** la terre tourne autour du soleil; **to go r. (and r.) sth.,** tourner autour de qch.; faire et refaire le tour de qch.; (*of birds*) **to fly r. (and r.) sth.,** tournoyer autour de qch. **2.** **to go r. an obstacle,** contourner un obstacle; **to sail r. a cape,** doubler, franchir, un cap; **to go r. the corner,** (*of pers.*) tourner le coin; (*of vehicle*) prendre le virage; **the grocer r. the corner,** l'épicier du coin; *F:* **to be, go, r. the bend,** être, devenir, fou, louftingue.

round[3], *v.*

I. *v.tr. & i.* **1.** *v.tr.* (*a*) arrondir (qch.); rendre (qch.) rond; *Danc:* **to r. one's arm,** arrondir le bras; *Ling:* **to r. a vowel,** arrondir une voyelle; *Tchn:* **to r. the bottom of a cauldron,** gironner un chaudron; (*b*) *Nau:* garnir (un cordage); fourrer (un espar); (*c*) contourner (un obstacle); *Nau:* doubler, franchir, arrondir (un cap); contourner (une île); *Aut:* prendre (un virage). **2.** *v.i.* (*a*) s'arrondir; devenir rond; (*b*) **to r. on one's heel,** faire demi-tour; *F:* **to r. on s.o.,** (i) dénoncer, vendre, qn; (ii) tomber sur qn; s'en prendre inopinément à qn; **when I tried to intervene, they both rounded on me,** quand j'ai voulu m'interposer, ils se sont retournés tous les deux contre moi.

II. (*compound verbs*) **1.** (*a*) **round down,** *v.tr.* (arrondir (une somme) (au chiffre inférieur); (*b*) *Nau:* affaler (un palan).

2. **round in,** *v.tr. Nau:* rentrer vivement (un cordage).

3. **round off,** *v.tr.* arrondir (un angle, sa fortune); **to r. off one's land,** arrondir son champ; **to r. off one's sentences,** arrondir ses phrases; **to r. off one's speech with a neat compliment,** achever son discours avec un compliment bien tourné; **to r. off the negotiations,** achever les négociations.

4. **round out,** *v.i.* (*of aircraft*) se redresser.

5. **round to,** *v.i. Nau:* lofer (un voilier).

6. **round up,** *v.tr.* (*a*) rassembler (du bétail); cerner, rabattre (des bêtes); rafler (des filous); faire une rafle de (filous); *F:* cueillir (une bande); (*b*) arrondir (une somme) (au chiffre supérieur).

roundabout ['raundəbaut], *s. & a.*

I. *s.* **1.** *A:* (*a*) détour *m*; chemin détourné; (*b*) circonlocution *f*; (*c*) enclos *m*, clôture *f*, circulaire. **2.** (*a*) (manège *m* de) chevaux *mpl* de bois; carrousel *m*; *F:* **what you lose on the swings you gain on the roundabouts,** à tout prendre on ne gagne ni ne perd; l'un dans l'autre, je n'y perds rien; (*b*) *Aut:* rond-point *m*, *pl.* ronds-points; *Adm:* carrefour *m* à giration, à sens giratoire.

II. *a.* **1.** (chemin) détourné, indirect; **to take a r. way,** faire un détour, un crochet; *F:* prendre le chemin des écoliers; **that was a r. way of. . .,** c'était une manière détournée de. . .; **to hear of sth. in a r. way,** apprendre qch. par la bande, indirectement; **to lead up to a question in a r. way,** aborder de biais une question; **r. phrase,** circonlocution *f*. **2.** *A:* rebondi, grassouillet, boulot.

rounded ['raundid], *a.* arrondi; **r. cheeks,** joues rebondies; **r. limbs,** membres arrondis, rondelets; **r. bank,** talus curviligne; *Arch:* **r. moulding,** rond *m* (de moulure); *Nau:* **r. stern,** arrière en cul-de-poule; arrière rond.

roundel ['raund(ə)l], *s.* **1.** (*a*) *Her:* tourteau *m*; (*b*) *A:* plateau *m* en bois; (*c*) *Jewel: etc:* rondeau *m*; (*d*) *Arch:* œil-de-bœuf *m*, *pl.* œils-de-bœuf; (*e*) *Av:* cocarde *f*. **2.** *A:* (*a*) *Poet:* rondeau; (*b*) *Mus: Danc:* ronde *f*. **3.** *Arm:* rondache *f*.

roundelay ['raundilei], *s. A:* (*a*) chanson *f* à refrain; rondeau *m*; (*b*) chant *m* d'oiseau; (*c*) *Danc:* ronde *f*.

rounder ['raundər], *s.* **1.** *Games:* (*a*) **rounders,** balle *f* au camp, thèque *f*; (*b*) tour complet accompli sans arrêt (par un joueur). **2.** *Tls:* arrondisseur *m*. **3.** *U.S: F:* flâneur *m*; fainéant *m*.

Roundhead ['raundhed], *s. Hist:* Tête ronde (adhérent de Cromwell).

roundheaded [raund'hedid], *a.* à tête ronde.

roundhouse ['raundhaus], *s.* **1.** *Nau: A:* (*a*) rouf *m*; (*b*) toilettes *fpl* de l'avant; poulaine *f*; (*c*) chambre *f* du conseil. **2.** *NAm: Rail:* rotonde *f*. **3.** *Hist:* corps *m* de garde; salle *f* de police.

rounding ['raundiŋ], *s.* **1.** (*a*) **r. (off),** arrondissement *m* (d'un domaine, d'une phrase); *Tchn:* arrondissage *m*; *Bookb:* endossure *f*, endossage *m* (d'un livre); *Com: etc:* **r. off, up, down, of a sum,** arrondissement d'une somme; *Tls:* **r. adze,** (h)erminette *f* à gouge; (*b*) *Nau:* (i) garniture *f*, (ii) garni *m* (d'une manœuvre); fourrure *f* (d'un espar). **2.** *N.Arch:* bouge *m* (du pont, des baux).

roundly ['raundli], *adv. O:* **1.** rondement, vivement. **2.** (parler) rondement, franchement, carrément.

roundness ['raundnis], *s.* **1.** (*a*) rondeur *f*; rotondité *f* (d'un globe, etc.); arrondi *m* (du menton, etc.); (*b*) rotondité, bosse *f*, protubérance *f* (sur une surface). **2.** (*a*) rondeur (de style); (*b*) *A:* rondeur, franchise *f* (de paroles); (*c*) sonorité *f*, rondeur, ampleur *f* (de la voix).

roundnosed ['raundnouzd], *a.* **1.** au nez arrondi, camus. **2.** *Tls:* **r. chisel,** dégorgeoir *m*.

roundoff ['raundɔf], *s. Gym:* rondade *f*.

roundsman, *pl.* **-men** ['raundzmən], *s.m.* **1.** *Com:* livreur. **2.** *U.S:* agent de police chargé de fonctions de surveillance; brigadier.

roundtop ['raundtɔp], *s. Nau:* hune *f*.

roundup ['raundʌp], *s.* **1.** (*a*) rassemblement *m* (du bétail, etc.); grande battue (à cheval); (*b*) rafle *f* (de filous); arrestations *fpl* en masse. **2.** *N.Arch:* bouge vertical (du pont, des barrots, etc.).

roundworm ['raundwə:m], *s. Ann:* ascaride *m* lombricoïde.

roup[1] [raup], *s. Scot:* vente (publique) aux enchères; criée *f*.

roup[2] [raup], *v.tr. Scot:* **1.** mettre (qch.) aux enchères; vendre (un mobilier, etc.) à la criée. **2.** vendre les biens de (qn); exécuter (qn).

roup[3] [ru:p], *s.* diphtérie *f* aviaire, des volailles.

roupy ['ru:pi], *a.* (*of fowl*) atteint de la diphtérie.

rouse[1] [rauz], *s. Mil: A:* réveil *m*.

rouse[2], *v.*

I. *v.tr.* **1.** (*a*) *Ven:* (faire) lever, faire partir, lancer (le gibier); (*b*) **to r. s.o. (from sleep),** éveiller, réveiller, qn; arracher qn au sommeil; **to r. s.o. from his reflections,** arracher qn à ses réflexions; *Fig:* **to r. the sleeping lion,** réveiller le chat qui dort; **to r. the camp,** donner l'alerte au camp; **to r. s.o. up, to r. s.o. from listlessness,** faire sortir qn de son apathie; secouer l'indifférence, l'énergie, de qn; secouer (les puces à) qn; aiguillonner qn; **I tried to r. him,** j'ai voulu le faire sortir de sa torpeur; **to r. oneself,** se secouer; se défiger; sortir de son apathie; **to r. s.o. to action,** inciter qn à agir; **to r. the people,** remuer, activer, le peuple; (*c*) mettre (qn) en colère; irriter (qn); **he is terrible when roused,** il est terrible quand il est monté; (*d*) *Brew:* agiter (le moût, etc.). **2.** soulever (l'indignation, etc.); susciter (l'admiration, etc.); *Lit:* **to r. the passions,** éveiller les passions. **3.** *Nau:* **to r. in a cable, a rope,** haler, embraquer, une chaîne, un cordage; **r. together!** halez ensemble! **to r. out the night watch,** faire le branlebas du soir, réveiller le quart de nuit.

II. *v.i. O:* **to r. (up),** (i) se réveiller; (ii) se secouer; sortir de sa torpeur.

rouse[3], *s. A:* **1.** rasade *f* (de vin, etc.). **2.** bacchanale *f*; b(e)uverie *f*.

rouse[4], *v.tr.* saler (les harengs).

rouseabout ['rauzəbaut], *s. Austr: F:* homme *m* à tout faire, manœuvre *m*.

rouser ['rauzər], *s.* **1.** *A: & Lit:* (*a*) (*pers.*) (i) excitateur, -trice; (ii) éveilleur *m*; (*b*) stimulant *m*. **2.** *Brew:* agitateur *m* mécanique. **3.** *F:* (*a*) qch. de sensationnel, de saisissant; (*b*) gros mensonge; craque *f*, bobard *m*.

rousing ['rauziŋ], *a.* **1.** qui éveille, qui réveille, qui excite; **r. cheers,** applaudissements chaleureux; **r. speech,** discours entraînant, enlevant, vibrant; **r. chorus,** refrain entraînant. **2.** (*a*) *F:* sensationnel, formidable; **r. lie,** gros mensonge, craque *f*, bobard *m*; (*b*) **r. fire,** belle flambée; feu ronflant.

roussette [ru:'set], *s.* **1.** *Ich:* roussette *f*. **2.** *Z:* (chauve-souris *f*) roussette.

roust [raust]. *F:* **1.** *v.tr.* (*a*) *U.S:* **to r. s.o. (out, up),** réveiller qn, tirer qn de son lit; (*b*) **to r. s.o. out,** flanquer qn à la porte, balancer qn. **2.** *v.i. Austr:* tempêter, fulminer.

roustabout ['raustəbaut], *s. F:* **1.** (*a*) *NAm:* débardeur *m*; (*b*) *Petr:* contremaître *m* de production. **2.** *Austr:* homme *m* à tout faire; manœuvre *m*.

rout[1] [raut], *s.* **1.** *O:* bande *f* (de fêtards). **2.** *Jur:* attroupement *m* (de trois personnes au moins, dans une intention délictueuse). **3.** *A:* raout *m*; réception (mondaine); soirée *f*.

rout[2], *s. Mil:* déroute *f*; débandade *f*; **to put troops to r.,** mettre des troupes en déroute; **to break into a r.,** se débander.

rout[3], *v.tr.* **1.** *Mil:* mettre (une armée) en déroute; disperser, défaire, enfoncer (une armée); **to r. the enemy,** mettre l'ennemi en fuite. **2.** *Carp:* détourer (une pièce); **to r. out,** (i) dénicher (qn, qch.); tirer (qn) de son lit, etc.; faire sortir, faire déguerpir (qn); (ii) *Carp:* évider (une rainure); rainurer (une planche); toupiller (une moulure); (iii) *Engr: Typ:* échopper (du métal, etc.).

rout[4], *v.tr. & i.* = ROOT[3].

route[1] [ru:t], *s.* **1.** itinéraire *m*; route *f*, voie *f*; chemin *m*; *Mount:* course *f*; **to map out a r.,** tracer un itinéraire; **by the usual r.,** par la route habituelle; **commercial,**

trade, r., route commerciale; **shipping r.,** route de navigation; **sea r.,** route de mer, route maritime; *Av:* **air r.,** voie aérienne, route aérienne, aéroroute *f*; **overland r.,** route terrestre; **bus r.,** (i) ligne *f* d'autobus; (ii) itinéraire, parcours *m*, d'un autobus; **explorer r.,** itinéraire d'exploration; **compass r.,** route au compas; **reserved r.,** itinéraire réservé; **r. of a procession,** parcours d'un défilé; *Com:* **r. to be followed by a consignment of goods,** acheminement *m* d'un colis; *Mount:* **to find the r.,** faire la trace; *Aut: P.N:* **all routes,** toutes directions; **r. map,** (i) levé *m* d'itinéraire; (ii) carte routière; **r. chart,** carte de la route à suivre. **2.** *Mil:* (*often* [raut]) (*a*) **r. of withdrawal,** itinéraire de repli; **column of r.,** colonne de route; **r. march,** marche *f* d'entraînement (au pas de route); marche militaire; (*b*) *A:* ordres *mpl* de marche. **3.** *NAm:* tournée *f* (du facteur, etc.).

route², *v.tr.* router, acheminer (un colis, etc.).

routeman, *pl.* **-men** ['ru:tmən], *s.m. NAm:* livreur.

router ['rautər], *s. Tls:* couteau *m* (d'une mèche à trois pointes); **r. (plane),** guimbarde *f*.

routine [ru:'ti:n], *s.* **1.** routine *f*; **to do sth. as a matter of r.,** faire qch. d'office; **the daily r.,** la routine de tous les jours; le train-train journalier, quotidien; **office r.,** travail courant du bureau; **it's just r.,** c'est une simple formalité; **r. visit,** visite habituelle; **r. examination,** examen de routine, examen systématique; **r. work,** travail de routine, travail routinier, courant; affaires courantes; **r. enquiries,** constatations d'usage; **r. patrol,** ronde *f*; *Av:* **r. flight,** mission de routine. **2.** *Mil: etc:* tableau *m* de service. **3.** *Th:* enchaînement *m* (de pas de danse); numéro *m* (d'un comique, etc.). **4.** *Cmptr:* programme *m*, sous-programme *m*, *pl.* sous-programmes.

routing¹ ['rautiŋ], *s. Carp:* détourage *m* (d'une pièce); **r. (out),** (i) *Carp:* évidage *m* (d'une rainure), toupillage *m* (d'une moulure); (ii) *Engr: Typ:* échoppage *m* (du métal, etc.); **r. machine,** machine à échopper.

routing² ['ru:tiŋ], *s.* routage *m*, acheminement *m* (d'un colis, etc.); *Com:* **r. slip,** fiche de transmission *f*; *Mil:* (*often* ['rautiŋ]) **r. of reinforcements, of circuits,** acheminement des renforts, des circuits.

routinist [ru:'ti:nist], *s.* routinier, -ière.

roux [ru:], *s. Cu:* roux *m*.

rove¹ [rouv], *s.* (*a*) *O:* **to be on the r.,** rôder, vagabonder; (*b*) *Ent:* **r. beetle,** staphylin *m*.

rove². **1.** *v.i.* (*a*) rôder; vagabonder, errer; **his eyes roved from one to the other,** ses yeux erraient de l'un à l'autre; *Lit:* **his mind roved back to his youth,** sa pensée vagabonde revint sur sa jeunesse; (*b*) *Fish: A:* pêcher au vif, à la cuiller. **2.** *v.tr.* parcourir (la campagne, un pays); (*of pirate, etc.*) **to r. the seas,** écumer les mers.

rove³, *s. Metalw:* rosette *f*; rondelle *f*; contre-rivure *f*, *pl.* contre-rivures.

rove⁴, *s. Tex:* mèche *f*; boudin *m*.

rove⁵, *v.tr. Tex:* **to r. the slivers,** faire la mèche; boudiner.

rover¹ ['rouvər], *s.* **1.** (*a*) rôdeur, -euse; vagabond, -onde; (*b*) *Scout:* routier *m*. **2.** (*archery*) but *m* à une portée fixée à volonté; **to shoot at rovers,** viser un but choisi à volonté. **3.** (*croquet*) (*a*) **r. (ball),** (balle *f*) corsaire *m*; (*b*) (*pers.*) corsaire.

rover², *s. Nau: Hist:* forban *m*, corsaire *m*, pirate *m*; écumeur *m* (de mer).

rover³, *s. Tex:* **1.** banc *m* à broches; boudineuse *f*. **2.** (*pers.*) boudineur, -euse.

roving¹ ['rouviŋ], *a.* vagabond, nomade; *Lit:* **r. thoughts,** pensées vagabondes; *F:* **to have a r. eye,** avoir l'œil égrillard, coquin; **r. ambassador, reporter,** ambassadeur, journaliste, itinérant.

roving², *s.* vagabondage *m*; **r. instincts,** instincts nomades; **r. life,** vie errante, nomade; **to be of a r. disposition,** être de caractère aventureux.

roving³, *s. Tex:* **1.** boudinage *m*; **r. frame,** banc *m* à broches, boudineuse *f*. **2.** (*a*) mèche *f*, bobine *f*, de préparation; (*b*) *coll.* mèches; boudins *mpl*.

row¹ [rou], *s.* **1.** (*a*) rang *m*, rangée *f*; ligne *f*; file *f*; alignement *m*; alignée *f*; **r. of trees,** rangée d'arbres; **r. of cars,** file de voitures; **r. of figures,** (i) (*horizontal*) ligne, (ii) (*vertical*) colonne *f*, de chiffres; **r. of pearls,** rang de perles; **r. of medals,** brochette *f* de décorations; **r. of lights,** rampe *f* (de lumières); **r. of bricks,** assise *f* de briques; **r. of knitting, of crochet,** rang, tour *m*, de tricot, de crochet; **in a r.,** en rang, en ligne; **to put things in a r.,** mettre des objets en rang; aligner des objets; **all in a r.,** tous sur un rang; **in rows,** par rangs; **in two rows,** sur deux rangs; *F:* **two Sundays in a r.,** deux dimanches de suite; (*b*) *Agr: Hort:* ligne, rayon *m*; **in rows,** en lignes, en rayons; **r. of onions, of lettuces,** rang, rayon, d'oignons, de laitues. **2.** (*a*) rang (de chaises, etc.); **in the front, third, r.,** au premier, au troisième, rang; *Th:* **front r. of the stalls,** premier rang des fauteuils d'orchestre; (*b*) **r. of houses,** ligne, rangée, de maisons; (*c*) (*in street names, etc.*) rue *f*. **3.** *Typew:* rang. **4.** *Cmptr:* ligne (de carte perforée, de matrice); colonne (de bande perforée); **check r.,** rangée de contrôle; **r. binary,** perforation *f* en binaire par ligne.

row² [rou], *s.* **1.** promenade *f* en barque, en canot; partie *f* de canotage; **to go for a r.,** faire une promenade, se promener, en canot; canoter; faire du canotage; faire de l'aviron. **2.** **it was a long r.,** il a fallu ramer longtemps.

row³ [rou]. **1.** *v.i.* (*a*) ramer; *Nau:* nager, voguer; **to r. hard,** faire force de rames; **to r. in a race,** ramer dans une course; prendre part à une course d'aviron; **to r. across the river,** traverser la rivière en canot; **to r. round the island,** faire le tour de l'île à la rame; **to r. towards the source of the river,** remonter vers la source de la rivière; **to r. down the river,** descendre la rivière; (*with cogn. acc.*) **to r. a fast stroke,** ramer vite; **to r. a race,** faire une course d'aviron; **to r. stroke,** être chef de nage; donner la nage; (*b*) canoter; faire du canotage; (*c*) (*of oarsman*) **to be rowed out,** être à bout de forces. **2.** *v.tr.* (*a*) faire aller (un bateau) à la rame; conduire (un bateau) à l'aviron; (*b*) conduire (qn) dans une embarcation à rames; **to r. s.o. across the river,** transporter qn (en canot) sur l'autre rive; (*c*) lutter de vitesse avec (qn).

row⁴ [rau], *s.* **1.** chahut *m*, tapage *m*, vacarme *m*; charivari *m*; *F:* ramdam *m*; **to make, kick up, a r.,** (i) faire du chahut; chahuter; faire du fracas, du tapage, *F:* du boucan, du chambard, du barouf(le), du bastringue; (ii) *F:* rouspéter, grogner; *F:* **a, the, hell of a r.,** un bruit de tous les diables; un barouf, un raffut, du diable; **what's all the r. about?** qu'est-ce qu'il y a? qu'est-ce qui se passe? **2.** bagarre *f*, rixe *f*, dispute *f*; scène *f*; chamaillerie *f*; attrapade *f*, attrapage *m*; **family r.,** querelle *f* de famille; **to have a r. with s.o.,** se quereller, se disputer, *F:* se chamailler, avec qn; **to get mixed up in a r.,** être mêlé à une dispute; **there'll be a r.!** il va y avoir du grabuge, de la casse! **3.** *F:* réprimande *f*, semonce *f*; savon *m*; **to get into a r.,** se faire attraper; se faire laver la tête; **there'll be a r.!** vous allez vous faire attraper!

row⁵ [rau]. *F:* **1.** *v.tr. A:* (i) attraper, semoncer (qn); (ii) faire une scène à (qn). **2.** *v.i.* se quereller (**with s.o.,** avec qn); s'attraper, s'engueuler; **he's always rowing with his girl friend,** il se dispute toujours avec son amie.

rowan ['rauən, 'rou-], *s. Bot:* **1.** **r. (tree),** sorbier *m* (domestique); cormier *m*; sorbier commun, des oiseaux, des oiseleurs. **2.** **r. (berry),** sorbe *f*; corme *f*.

rowboat ['roubout], *s. esp. NAm:* bateau *m*, canot *m*, à rames; canot à aviron.

rowdiness ['raudinis], *s.* turbulence *f*; tapage *m*; chahut *m*, désordres *mpl*.

rowdy ['raudi]. **1.** *a.* tapageur, chahuteur; **to be r.,** chahuter. **2.** *s.* (*a*) chahuteur, -euse; (*b*) voyou *m*.

rowdyism ['raudiizm], *s.* tapage *m*; chahut *m*.

rowel¹ ['rauəl], *s.* **1.** molette *f* (d'éperon). **2.** *Vet:* **(draining) r.,** séton anglais; séton à, en, rouelle.

rowel², *v.tr.* **(rowelled)** **1.** éperonner (un cheval). **2.** *Vet:* appliquer un séton à (un animal).

rower ['rouər], *s.* rameur, -euse; canotier, canoteur *m*; *Nau:* nageur, canotier.

rowing ['rouiŋ], *s.* conduite *f* (d'un bateau) à l'aviron; *Nau:* nage *f*; *Sp:* aviron *m*, canotage *m*; **to go r.,** canoter; faire du canotage; faire une promenade, se promener, en canot; faire de l'aviron; **r. boat,** bateau, canot, à rames; canot à aviron; **r. barge,** barque à rames; **r. exercise, drill,** (i) canotage; (ii) *Nau:* exercice de nage; **r. match,** course à la rame; course d'aviron; **r. club,** cercle d'aviron; *Gym:* **r. machine,** machine à ramer.

rowing² ['rauiŋ], *s. F:* **1.** attrapade *f*, semonce *f*; réprimande *f*. **2.** querelle *f*, dispute *f*.

rowlandite ['rouləndait], *s. Miner:* rowlandite *f*.

rowlocks ['rɔləks], *s.pl.* tolets *m*, dames *f*, toletières *f*; **swivel r.,** tolets à fourche; systèmes *m* (d'un bateau).

Roxburghe ['rɔksbərə], *s. Bookb:* **R. (binding),** reliure *f* amateur sans coins, dos sans ornement, tranche supérieure dorée, gouttière et pied non rognés.

royal ['rɔiəl]. **1.** *a.* (*a*) royal, -aux; du roi, de la reine; **His, Her, R. Highness,** son Altesse royale; **the r. household,** la maison du roi, de la reine; **the r. family,** la famille royale; **with r. consent,** avec le consentement du roi, de la reine; **r. charter,** acte du souverain; charte royale; **the r. we,** le pluriel de majesté; **r. blue,** bleu *inv* (de) roi, (de) France; **r. tennis,** (jeu *m* de) paume *f*; (*b*) royal, princier; magnifique; **r. bearing,** attitude digne d'un roi; *O:* **to be in r. spirits,** être en verve; *O:* **to have a (right) r. time,** s'amuser follement, royalement; (*c*) *Bot:* **r. fern,** osmonde royale; *Fung:* **r. agaric,** royal *m*; (*d*) *Ap:* **r. jelly,** gelée royale; (*e*) *Nau:* **r. (sail),** cacatois *m*; **r. mast, r. yard,** (mât *m*, vergue *f*, de) cacatois; (*f*) *Paperm:* **r. (paper)** = grand raisin; **long r., super r.** = (papier) jésus *m*; (*g*) *Cards:* **r. flush,** quinte royale. **2.** *s.* (*a*) cerf *m* à douze andouillers; (*b*) **the Royals,** (i) *Mil:* le Royal Écossais; (ii) *Navy:* la Royale; (*c*) *F:* membre *m* de la famille royale.

royalism ['rɔiəlizm], *s.* royalisme *m*.

royalist ['rɔiəlist], *a. & s.* royaliste (*mf*).

royally ['rɔiəli], *adv.* royalement; en roi, en reine.

royalty ['rɔiəlti], *s.* **1.** royauté *f*. **2.** (*a*) *O:* **Royalties,** (i) personnages royaux; (ii) membres *m* de la famille royale; (*b*) *coll.* **hotel patronized by r.,** hôtel fréquenté par les personnages royaux. **3.** (*a*) *Hist: For: etc:* droit régalien; (*b*) **royalties,** (i) redevance (due à un inventeur, au détenteur de la propriété littéraire ou artistique d'une œuvre); (ii) *Publ:* droits *m* d'auteur; **r. of 10% on the published price,** droit de 10% sur le prix fort; (*c*) **royalties,** (i) *Min:* redevance tréfoncière; (ii) *Petr:* royalties *f*.

Royston ['rɔistən], *Pr.n. Orn:* **R. crow,** corneille mantelée, cendrée.

rozzer ['rɔzər], *s. P:* agent *m* de police; flic *m*.

rsi ['riʃi], *s. Rel:* rishi *m inv*.

rub¹ [rʌb], *s.* **1.** frottement *m*; friction *f*; **to give sth. a r. (up),** (i) donner un coup de torchon, de brosse, à qch.; (ii) frotter, astiquer (des cuivres, etc.); **to give s.o. a r. down,** faire une friction à qn; frictionner qn; **to give a horse a r. down,** panser, étriller, brosser, bouchonner, un cheval; *Med:* **pleural r.,** frottement pleural. **2.** (*a*) (*bowls*) inégalité *f* (du terrain); *Fig:* **there's the r.!** c'est là la difficulté! voilà le hic! *Lit:* c'est là que gît le lièvre; **to come to the r.,** arriver au moment difficile; (*b*) *Golf:* **r. of, on, the green,** risque *m* de jeu.

rub², *v.tr. & i.* **(rubbed)** **1.** *v.tr.* (*a*) frotter; **to r. one's leg with liniment,** se frotter, se frictionner, la jambe avec de l'embrocation; **to r. one's hand against, on, over, sth.,** frotter sa main sur qch.; **to r. ears of corn in one's hands,** froisser des épis dans les mains; **to r. one's hands (together),** se frotter les mains; **to r. one's eyes,** frotter ses yeux; se frotter les yeux; **to r. two stones together,** frotter deux pierres l'une contre l'autre; **to r. noses with s.o.,** saluer qn d'un frottement de nez à nez; *F:* **he rubs shoulders with all the actors,** il coudoie, côtoie, tous les acteurs; il s'associe, fraye, avec tous les acteurs; *F: O:* **to r. up one's knowledge of a subject,** se remettre au courant d'un sujet; **to r. up one's Greek,** dérouiller son grec; **to r. s.o. (up) the wrong way,** prendre qn à rebrousse-poil; contrarier, énerver, irriter, fâcher, qn; échauffer la bile, les oreilles, à qn; **what's rubbed you up the wrong way?** quelle mouche vous pique? (*b*) **to r. sth. dry,** sécher qch. en le frottant; **to r. one's hands sore,** se faire mal aux mains à force de les frotter; (*c*) **to r. a horse down,** panser, étriller, brosser, bouchonner, un cheval; **to r. s.o., oneself, down,** frictionner qn, se frictionner (après un bain, etc.); **to r. down a block of marble, a wall, paintwork,** adoucir un marbre, regratter un mur, poncer de la peinture; **to r. sth. (down) to a powder,** réduire qch. en poudre; triturer qch.; *Phot:* **to r. down a negative,** user un cliché; *Nau:* **to r. down the seams of a sail,** frotter les coutures d'une voile; **to r. sth. off, away, out,** enlever qch. par le frottement; **to r. the nap off materials,** user du tissu jusqu'à la corde; **to r. one's skin off,** s'écorcher légèrement; **to r. the skin off one's knees,** s'érafler les genoux; **to r. sth. in,** faire pénétrer qch. par des frictions, en frottant; *F:* **don't r. it in!** n'insistez pas davantage (sur ma gaffe, etc.)! ne remuez pas le fer dans la plaie! c'en est assez, quand même! **to r. oil into one's skin,** se faire une friction d'huile; *Cu:* **to r. the butter into the flour,** mélanger (avec les doigts) le beurre et la farine; **to r. out a word,** effacer, gommer, un mot; **to r. sth. through a sieve,** passer qch. au tamis; **to r. sth. over a surface,** enduire une surface de qch.; *F: O:* **to r. s.o. out,** liquider, descendre, qn; (*d*) **to r. a brass, an inscription,** prendre un frottis d'un cuivre, d'une inscription. **2.** *v.i.* (*a*) frotter (**against,** contre); (*of pers.*) **to r. (up) against s.o., sth.,** se frotter contre qn, qch.; **the wheel is rubbing against the brake,** la roue frotte contre le frein; **something's rubbing,** il y a quelque chose qui frotte; **these shoes r.,** ces chaussures me font mal; **this colour rubs off easily,** cette couleur s'enlève facilement; *F:* **it rubs off on them,** cela déteint sur eux; *F:* **to r. along,** se débrouiller, se tirer d'affaire; **we manage to r. along,** on vit tant bien que mal; **we r. along very well,** nous nous accordons très bien.

rub³, *s. Cards:* rob(re) *m*.

rub-a-dub ['rʌbədʌb], *s.* rataplan *m*, rantanplan *m* (d'un tambour).

rubato, *pl.* **-os, -i** [ru:'bɑ:tou, -ouz, -i:], *a. & s. Mus:* **(tempo) r.,** tempo *m* rubato.

rubber[1] ['rʌbər], *s.* **1.** (*a*) frottoir *m*; **blackboard r.,** effaceur *m*; (*b*) *Tls:* carreau *m*; *Nau:* outil *m* du voilier. **2.** (*pers.*) (*a*) frotteur, -euse; (*b*) *O:* masseur, -euse (de hammam). **3.** (*a*) caoutchouc *m*; gomme *f* élastique; **crêpe r.,** crêpe *m* de latex; **hard r.,** caoutchouc durci; vulcanite *f*; ébonite *f*; **foam, sponge, r.,** caoutchouc mousse; **synthetic r.,** caoutchouc synthétique; **r. ball,** balle en caoutchouc; balle élastique; **r. band,** (i) élastique *m*; (ii) courroie *f* en caoutchouc; *El:* **r. (-covered) cable,** câble à revêtement en caoutchouc, sous (gaine de) caoutchouc; **r.-cored golf ball,** balle à noyau de caoutchouc; **r. dinghy,** canot pneumatique; **r. hose, gloves,** tuyau *m*, gants *m*, en caoutchouc; **r. overshoes,** *NAm:* **rubbers,** caoutchoucs; **r. boots,** bottes de caoutchouc; *F:* **r. cheque,** chèque sans provision; *St.Exch:* **r. shares,** *F:* **rubbers,** caoutchoucs; *Adm: etc:* **r. stamp,** (i) (α) timbre *m* (de, en) caoutchouc; tampon *m*; (β) légende *f*, vignette *f*, du tampon de caoutchouc; (γ) *Com:* griffe *f*, cachet *m*, timbre (d'une maison); (ii) *F:* (*pers.*) béni-oui-oui *m inv*; rond-de-cuir *m*, *pl.* ronds-de-cuir; **r. stamp parliament,** parlement ratificateur; **to r.-stamp sth.,** apposer un cachet sur qch., estampiller qch.; *F:* **to r.-stamp a decision,** approuver une décision sans discussion; entériner une décision; (*b*) **r. (eraser),** gomme (à effacer); (*c*) *Bot:* **r. tree,** arbre *m* à gomme; **r.-bearing tree,** arbre caoutchoutifère; **r. plant,** caoutchouc, caoutchoutier *m*; **Japanese r. plant,** crassule *f*; (*d*) *F:* rondelle *f* de caoutchouc (d'une pompe); (*e*) *Hyg: P:* préservatif *m*; capote anglaise; **r. goods,** préservatifs. **4.** *Const:* brique poreuse; brique tendre.

rubber[2]. **1.** *v.tr.* *O:* = RUBBERIZE. **2.** *v.i.* = RUBBERNECK[2].

rubber[3], *s. Cards:* rob(re) *m*; **to play a r.,** faire un robre; **the r. (game),** la belle.

rubberize ['rʌbəraiz], *v.tr.* caoutchouter; imprégner, enduire (un tissu, etc.) de caoutchouc; **rubberized material,** tissu caoutchouté.

rubberneck[1] ['rʌbənek], *s. F:* (*a*) badaud, -aude; flâneur, -euse; curieux, -euse; (*b*) touriste *mf*.

rubberneck[2], *v.i. F:* (*a*) badauder, faire le badaud; flâner; (*b*) excursionner; visiter (des monuments, etc.).

rubbery ['rʌbəri], *a.* (*a*) caoutchouteux; (*b*) coriace.

rubbing ['rʌbiŋ], *s.* **1.** (*a*) frottage *m* (de qch. avec qch.); *Med: etc:* friction *f*; **r. surface,** frottoir *m* (d'une boîte d'allumettes, etc.); **r. down,** (i) pansage *m*, étrillage *m*, bouchonnement *m*, bouchonnage *m* (d'un cheval); (ii) adoucissage *m* (d'une surface); regrattage *m* (d'un mur); ponçage *m* (de la peinture); *Phot:* **(local) r. down,** usure (locale) (d'un cliché); *Cu:* **r.-in method,** façon de mélanger le beurre et la farine du bout des doigts; *N.Arch:* **r. strake,** bourrelet *m* de défense; ceinture *f* (d'une embarcation); liston *m*, listeau *m*; (*b*) frottement *m* (d'un organe de machine, etc.); *Nau:* ripage *m* (d'un câble). **2.** calque *m* par frottement; frottis *m*; **to take a r. of an inscription,** prendre un frottis d'une inscription; poncer une inscription; calquer une inscription par frottement.

rubbish ['rʌbiʃ], *s.* **1.** (*a*) ordures *fpl*; immondices *fpl*, détritus *mpl*; (*of buildings*) décombres *mpl*; déblai *m*; *Ind: etc:* rebuts *mpl*; déchets *mpl*; **r. bin,** boîte *f* à ordures, à déchets; poubelle *f*; (*indoors*) seau *m* à ordures, à déchets; (*in building*) **r. chute, shoot,** vide-ordures *m inv*; **r. dump,** dépotoir *m*; dépôt *m* d'ordures; décharge publique; **r. heap,** (i) tas *m* d'ordures; amas *m* de décombres; (ii) dépotoir; (*b*) fatras *m*; choses *fpl* sans valeur; **old r.,** vieilleries *fpl*; *F:* **good riddance to bad r.,** un bon débarras; (*c*) camelote *f*; **never buy r.,** achetez toujours de la bonne qualité. **2.** bêtises *fpl*, sottises *fpl*; niaiseries *fpl*; **to talk r.,** débiter des absurdités *f*; dire des bêtises, des niaiseries, des sottises; raconter des histoires; radoter; **(what) r.! what a load of (old) r.!** quelle fichaise! quelle blague!

rubbishy ['rʌbiʃi], *a.* **1.** (endroit) plein de décombres. **2.** sans valeur; (marchandises) (i) de rebut; (ii) de mauvaise qualité; **that's all r. (stuff),** tout ça c'est de la camelote; *F:* **a r. film,** un navet.

rubble ['rʌbl], *s. Const:* **1.** (*a*) **r. (stone),** moellon (brut); *Civ.E:* (*for roads*) brocaille *f*; **mortar r.,** plâtras *m*; **to fill up the empty spaces with r.,** bloquer les vides; **r. masonry,** maçonnerie *f* de moellons; maçonnerie brute, sans assises; maçonnerie en pierres de carrière; **r. wall,** mur sans assises; **r. worker,** terrasseur *m*; (*b*) *Geol:* moellon; **rock r.,** moellon de roche. **2. r. (work),** moellon(n)age *m*; blocage *m*; blocaille *f*; maçonnerie brute en blocage, en moellons; limo(u)sinage *m*, hourdage *m*; **polygonal r.,** appareil polygonal; **spalled r.,** appareil en moellons smillés. **3.** (*after demolition, etc.*) décombres *mpl*, déblai *m*.

rube [ru:b], *s. NAm: F:* paysan *m*, rustaud *m*; culterreux, *pl.* culs-terreux.

rubefacient [ru:bi'feiʃ(ə)nt], *a. & s. Med:* rubéfiant (*m*).

rubefaction [ru:bi'fækʃ(ə)n], *s. Med:* rubéfaction *f*.

rubefy ['ru:bifai], *v.tr. Med:* rubéfier.

rubella [ru:'belə], *s. Med:* rubéole *f*.

rubellite ['ru:bəlait], *s. Miner:* rubellite *f*; apyrite *f*.

ruberythric [ru:bə'riθrik], *a. Ch:* **r. acid,** acide *m* rubérythrique.

rubescent [ru:'bes(ə)nt], *a.* rubescent.

Rubia ['ru:biə], *s. Bot:* rubia *m*.

Rubiaceae [ru:bi'eisii:], *s.pl. Bot:* rubiacées *f*.

rubiaceous [ru:bi'eiʃəs], *a. Bot:* rubiacé.

Rubiales [ru:bi'eili:z], *s.pl. Bot:* rubiales *f*.

rubicelle ['ru:bisel], *s. Miner: Lap:* rubasse *f*, rubace *f*, rubicelle *f*, rubacelle *f*.

Rubicon ['ru:bikən]. **1.** *Pr.n. Geog:* Rubicon *m*; *Fig:* **to cross the R.,** franchir le Rubicon; sauter le pas. **2.** *s. Cards:* rubicon.

rubicund ['ru:bikənd], *a.* rubicond; rougeaud.

rubidium [ru:'bidiəm], *s. Ch:* rubidium *m*.

rubify ['ru:bifai], *v.tr. Med:* rubéfier.

rubiginous [ru:'bidʒinəs], *a.* rubigineux; couleur de rouille *inv*.

rubious ['ru:biəs], *a. A: & Lit:* couleur de rubis.

ruble ['ru:bl], *s. Num:* rouble *m*.

rubric ['ru:brik], *s. Ecc: Typ: etc:* rubrique *f*.

rubrical ['ru:brik(ə)l], *a.* des rubriques; contenu dans les rubriques.

rubricate ['ru:brikeit], *v.tr.* rubriquer; traiter en rouge (une initiale, etc.).

rubrician [ru:'briʃ(ə)n], *s. Ecc:* rubriciste *m*, rubricaire *m*.

rubstone ['rʌbstoun], *s.* pierre *f* à aiguiser, à affûter.

Rubus ['ru:bəs], *s. Bot:* rubus *m*.

ruby ['ru:bi], *s.* **1.** *Miner: Lap:* (*a*) rubis *m*; **true r., Oriental r.,** rubis oriental; **spinel r.,** (rubis) spinelle *m*; **balas r.,** rubis balais; **Bohemian r.,** rubis de Bohême, de Hongrie; **r. mine,** mine *f* de rubis; **r.(-studded) bracelet,** bracelet (garni) de rubis; *B:* **her price is far above rubies,** elle a bien plus de prix que les perles; (*b*) **r. copper (ore),** cuprite *f*; **r. silver (ore),** (i) pyrargyrite *f*, argyrythrose *f*; (ii) proustite *f*; (*c*) *Ph:* **r. laser,** laser *m* à rubis. **2.** *A:* rubis, bouton *m* (sur le nez, etc.). **3.** *Typ: A:* corps *m* 5½. **4.** *a. & s.* (*a*) **r. (red),** rouge (*m*), *Lit:* rubis *inv*; **r. port,** porto *m* rouge; **r. lips,** lèvres vermeilles; lèvres carmin; *F:* **r. red nose,** nez vineux; *Z:* **r. spaniel,** ruby *m*, *pl.* rubies; ruby-spaniel *m*, *pl.* ruby-spaniels; *Glass:* **r. (glass),** verre *m* rubis; (*b*) **r. wedding,** noces *fpl* de vermeil. **5.** (*a*) *Orn:* rubis-émeraude *m inv*; **r.-and-topaz hummingbird,** rubis-topaze *m inv*; **r.-throated hummingbird,** petit rubis de la Caroline; (*b*) *Ent:* **r.-tailed wasp, fly,** chrysis *f*, guêpe dorée.

rubytail ['ru:biteil], *s. Ent:* chrysis *f*; guêpe dorée.

rubythroat ['ru:biθrout], *s. Orn:* (i) petit rubis de la Caroline; (ii) calliope sibérienne.

ruche[1] [ru:ʃ], *s. Needlew:* ruche *f*.

ruche[2], *v.tr. Needlew:* rucher (du tissu).

ruched [ru:ʃt], *a. Needlew:* à ruches; garni de ruches.

ruching ['ru:ʃiŋ], *s. Needlew:* ruche *f*, ruché *m*.

ruck[1] [rʌk], *s.* **1.** (*a*) *Rac:* peloton *m* (des coureurs); (*b*) *Rugby Fb:* mêlée ouverte. **2. the (common) r.,** le commun (du peuple); **to get out of the r.,** sortir du rang, de l'ornière.

ruck[2], *s.* (*in cloth*) faux pli, froissement *m*; ride *f*; (*in garment*) godet *m*.

ruck[3], *v.* (*a*) **to r. (up),** (i) *v.tr.* froisser, friper, chiffonner, plisser (des vêtements, etc.); (ii) *v.i.* (*of sheet, etc.*) se froisser, se plisser; (*of garment*) goder; (*b*) *v.i. Rugby Fb:* former une mêlée ouverte.

ruckle[1] ['rʌkl], *s.* = RUCK[2].

ruckle[2], *v.tr. & i.* = RUCK[3].

ruckle[3], *s. Scot:* râle *m*, râlement *m*.

ruckle[4], *v.i. Scot:* râler.

rucksack ['rʌksæk, 'ruk-], *s.* sac *m* à dos; sac d'alpiniste, de campeur; rucksack *m*.

ruckus ['rʌkəs], *s. F: O:* (*a*) chahut *m*, vacarme *m*, boucan *m*; (*b*) dispute *f*, bagarre *f*.

ruction ['rʌkʃ(ə)n], *s. F:* bagarre *f*, dispute *f*; **there'll be ructions,** il va y avoir du grabuge, de la casse.

rudbeckia [rʌd'bekiə], *s. Bot:* rudbeckia *f*, rudbeckie *f*.

rudd [rʌd], *s. Ich:* rotengle *m*, rotangle *m*; gardon *m* rouge.

rudder ['rʌdər], *s.* **1.** *Nau:* gouvernail *m*; **balanced r.,** gouvernail compensé, à double safran; **underhung r.,** gouvernail suspendu; *N.Arch:* **r. case, trunk,** louve *f*, jaumière *f*; manchon *m* du gouvernail. **2.** *Av:* gouverne *f*, gouvernail, de direction; **rudders,** empennage *m*; **rudder(s) and ailerons,** gouvernes; **r. bar,** palonnier *m* (du gouvernail de direction); **r. horn balance,** guignol *m* de gouverne de direction; **r. deflection,** braquage *m* direction. **3.** queue *f* (d'orientation) (d'un moulin à vent, etc.).

rudderhead ['rʌdəhed], *s. Nau:* tête *f* du gouvernail.

rudderless ['rʌdəlis], *a.* (navire) sans gouvernail, à la dérive.

rudderport ['rʌdəpɔ:t], *s. N.Arch:* jaumière *f*.

rudderpost ['rʌdəpoust], *s. N.Arch:* étambot *m* arrière.

ruddiness ['rʌdinis], *s.* teint coloré.

ruddle[1] ['rʌdl], *s.* ocre *f* rouge, craie *f* rouge; arcanne *f*.

ruddle[2], *v.tr.* frotter (qch.) d'ocre rouge; marquer (qch.) à l'ocre rouge.

ruddock ['rʌdək], *s. Orn:* rouge-gorge *m*, *pl.* rouges-gorges.

ruddy[1] ['rʌdi]. **1.** *a.* (*a*) (teint) coloré, haut en couleur; **r. cheeks,** joues rouges, hâlées; (*b*) rouge, rougeâtre; **r. glow of a fire,** lueur rouge, rougeoyante, d'un feu; (*c*) (animal, oiseau) roux, *f.* rousse; (*d*) *P:* **you r. fool!** espèce d'imbécile! **2.** *adv. P:* **it's r. cold,** il fait bigrement froid.

ruddy[2], *v.tr.* rendre rouge.

rude [ru:d], *a.* **1.** (*a*) primitif, rude; grossier; non civilisé, barbare; **r. style,** style fruste; **r. voice,** voix sans raffinement; (*b*) (outil, etc.) grossier; rudimentaire; **r. methods,** méthodes grossières; **r. beginnings,** commencements informes; **r. verses,** vers faits sans art; **r. drawing,** dessin primitif, sans art; (*c*) **r. ore,** minerai brut. **2.** violent, brusque; rude; **r. passions,** passions violentes; **r. shock,** choc violent; rude secousse. **3. r. health,** santé robuste. **4.** (*of pers.*) impoli, grossier; mal élevé; impertinent, insolent; **to be r. to s.o.,** être impoli avec qn; répondre grossièrement; dire des grossièretés *f* à qn; **he was most r.,** il a été on ne peut plus grossier; **r. remark,** indiscrétion *f*; **would it be r. to enquire . . .?** peut-on demander sans indiscrétion . . .? (*b*) (*of thg*) scabreux, licencieux, osé, obscène; **r. drawing,** dessin *m* obscène.

rudely ['ru:dli], *adv.* **1.** primitivement, rudement; grossièrement; **r. fashioned,** fabriqué sans art. **2.** violemment; brusquement; rudement; **r. awakened,** brusquement éveillé; éveillé en sursaut. **3.** (parler, etc.) impoliment, grossièrement.

rudeness ['ru:dnis], *s.* **1.** (*a*) caractère primitif (des coutumes, etc.); manque *m* d'art; manque de civilisation (d'un peuple); barbarie *f* (de style, etc.); (*b*) violence *f*, rudesse *f* (des passions, etc.). **2.** (*of pers.*) impolitesse *f*, grossièreté *f*; impertinence *f*, insolence *f*.

ruderal ['ru:dərəl], *a. Bot:* rudéral, -aux.

rudiment ['ru:dimənt], *s.* **1.** *Biol:* rudiment *m* (d'une queue, etc.). **2.** *pl.* rudiments, éléments *m*, premières notions (de grammaire, etc.).

rudimentary, rudimental [ru:di'ment(ə)ri, -'ment(ə)l], *a.* (organe, etc.) rudimentaire.

Rudista [ru:'distə], *s.pl. Paleont:* rudistes *m*.

Rudolph ['ru:dɔlf], *Pr.n.m.* Rodolphe.

rudolphine [ru:'dɔlfin], *a. Astr:* **R. tables,** tables rodolphines.

rue[1] [ru:], *s. A:* **1.** repentir *m*, regret *m*. **2.** compassion *f*.

rue[2], *v.tr.* regretter amèrement (une action); se repentir de (qch.); éprouver des remords de (qch.); s'en mordre les doigts; **I have come to r. it,** j'en suis au repentir; **to r. the day when . . .,** regretter le jour où . . .; **to have cause to r. sth.,** pâtir de qch.

rue[3], *s. Bot:* rue *f*.

rueful ['ru:ful], *a.* triste, lugubre; pitoyable.

ruefully ['ru:fuli], *adv.* tristement, lugubrement.

ruefulness ['ru:fulnis], *s.* tristesse *f*; air *m* triste, lugubre; ton *m* triste, lugubre.

ruelle [ru'el], *s.* **1.** *A:* ruelle *f* (de lit). **2.** *Fr.Hist:* ruelle.

ruellia [ru:'eliə], *s. Bot:* ruellia *m*.

ruff[1] [rʌf], *s.* **1.** *Cost:* fraise *f*, collerette *f*. **2.** *Z: Orn:* collier *m*, cravate *f*. **3.** *Orn:* pigeon *m* à cravate.

ruff[2], *s. Orn:* (chevalier) combattant *m*.

ruff[3], *s. Ich:* grémille *f*; perche goujonnière.

ruff[4], *s. Cards:* coupe *f* (avec un atout).

ruff[5], *v.tr. Cards:* couper (avec un atout).

ruff[6], *s. A:* = RUFFLE[4].

ruffed [rʌft], *a.* **1.** *A:* (*of pers.*) portant une fraise. **2.** *Nat.Hist:* (animal, oiseau) à collier.

ruffian ['rʌfiən], *s.* (*a*) bandit *m*, brute *f*; (*b*) *F:* **young ruffians,** petits polissons, chenapans, *m*.

ruffianly ['rʌfiənli], *a. A:* (homme) brutal; (conduite) de bandit, de brute, de brigand.

ruffle[1] ['rʌfl], *s.* **1.** (*a*) *A:* trouble *m*, agitation *f*; (*b*) *O:* contrariété *f*, ennui *m*; (*c*) rides *fpl* (sur l'eau). **2.** (*a*) *Cost:* (*at wrist*) manchette *f* (en dentelle); ruche *f*; (*at breast*) jabot plissé; (*at neck*) fraise *f*; (*b*) *Nat.Hist:* collier *m*; cravate *f* (d'un oiseau, etc.). **3.** fraise (de porc, etc.).

ruffle[2]. **1.** *v.tr.* (*a*) **to r. s.o.'s hair,** ébouriffer les cheveux de qn; décoiffer, dépeigner, qn; **hair ruffled by the breeze,** cheveux agités par la brise; (*of bird*) **to r. (up) its feathers,** hérisser ses plumes; **to r. the surface of the water,** troubler, crisper, rider, la surface de l'eau; **to r.**

s.o., s.o.'s feelings, *F:* **s.o.'s feathers,** (i) froisser, (ii) irriter, énerver, contrarier, (iii) troubler, qn; (*b*) rucher (des manchettes, etc.); plisser (un jabot, etc.). **2.** *v.i.* (*of hair*) s'ébouriffer; (*of feathers*) se hérisser; (*of sea*) s'agiter, se rider.

ruffle[3], *s. A:* dispute *f*, querelle *f*, bagarre *f*.

ruffle[4], *s. Mus:* ra *m* (sur le tambour).

ruffled ['rʌf(ə)ld], *a.* (*a*) (*of dress, etc.*) (*at wrist*) à manchettes; (*at breast*) à jabot; (*at neck*) à fraise; (*b*) *Nat.Hist:* à collier, à cravate; (*c*) (*of pers.*) froissé, énervé.

ruffler ['rʌflər], *s.* (*device*) fronceur *m* (de machine à coudre).

ruficaudate [ru:fi'kɔ:deit], *a. Nat.Hist:* ruficaude.

ruficornate [ru:fi'kɔ:neit], *a. Nat.Hist:* ruficorne.

Rufinus [ru:'fainəs], *Pr.n.m.* Rufin.

rufous ['ru:fəs], *a. Nat.Hist:* roux, *f.* rousse; rougeâtre.

rug [rʌg], *s.* **1.** couverture *f*; **travelling r.,** couverture de voyage; plaid *m*. **2.** (petit) tapis, carpette *f*; *NAm:* tapis; **bedside r.,** descente *f* de lit; *NAm:* **scatter, throw, r.,** carpette.

Rugbeian [rʌg'bi:ən], *s.m.* (ancien) élève du collège de Rugby.

rugby ['rʌgbi], *s.* **r. (football),** rugby *m*; **R. Union,** rugby à quinze; **R. League,** rugby à treize; **r. player,** rugbyman, *pl.* rugbymen.

rugged ['rʌgid], *a.* **1.** (*of ground*) raboteux, accidenté, inégal, -aux, bosselé; (*of road, path*) raboteux, dur; (*of bark, etc.*) rugueux; **r. outlines,** profil anguleux; anfractuosités *fpl*. **2. r. features,** traits rudes, irréguliers; visage taillé à coups de serpe. **3.** *O:* (*of pers., character*) bourru, rude; (*of style*) fruste, raboteux; **r. kindness,** tendresse bourrue; **r. life,** vie rude, mouvementée, dure. **4.** vigoureux, robuste.

ruggedness ['rʌgidnis], *s.* **1.** nature raboteuse, aspérité *f*, rugosité *f* (d'une surface, etc.); anfractuosités *fpl* (d'un rocher, etc.); *Sculp:* **the r. of the execution,** le rocheux du travail. **2.** *O:* rudesse *f* (de qn).

rugger ['rʌgər], *s. F:* rugby *m*.

rugose ['ru:gous], **rugous** ['ru:gəs], *a. Nat.Hist:* rugueux.

rugosity [ru:'gɔsiti], *s.* rugosité *f*.

ruin[1] ['ruin], *s.* **1.** ruine *f*; renversement *m*, effondrement *m* (d'un état, d'une fortune, etc.); **to fall, lie, in ruin(s),** tomber, être, en ruine; **to go to r.,** se délabrer; tomber en ruine; **to bring s.o. to r.,** ruiner, perdre, qn; **to bring about the r. of s.o., of sth.,** achever la ruine de qn, de qch.; *Fin:* **this failure means r. for us,** cette faillite nous perd; **he's on the road to r.,** il va, court, à la ruine. **2.** (*often pl.*) ruine(s); décombres *mpl*; **their castle is an old r.,** leur château est une vieille ruine; **the building is a r.,** l'édifice est en ruines; **ramparts (fallen) in ruins,** remparts dégradés; *O:* **to lay a town in r.,** mettre une ville en ruine; détruire une ville de fond en comble. **3. to be, prove, the r. of s.o.,** ruiner, perdre, qn; **pride will be his r.,** son orgueil le perdra; **it will be the r. of him,** ce sera sa ruine; **gambling has led to, was, his r.,** le jeu a fait son malheur; *F:* **mother's r.,** gin *m*; pousse-au-crime *m inv*.

ruin[2], *v.tr.* ruiner. **1.** (*a*) abîmer (la récolte, une robe, etc.); (*b*) **to r. one's life, one's prospects,** gâcher sa vie, son avenir; **to r. one's eyes,** user la vue, les yeux; s'esquinter les yeux; **to r. one's health,** ruiner sa santé; se ruiner la santé; **to r. s.o.'s reputation,** perdre qn de réputation; ruiner la réputation de qn; (*c*) **ruined castle,** château en ruines, ruiné. **2. her extravagance ruined him,** ses folles dépenses l'ont ruiné; **to r. oneself gambling, to be ruined by gambling,** se ruiner au jeu; **he is utterly ruined,** il est complètement ruiné.

ruination [ru:i'neiʃ(ə)n], *s.* ruine *f*, perte *f*; **it will be the r. of him,** ce sera sa ruine; **to be the r. of s.o.,** faire la ruine de qn.

ruiniform ['ru:inifɔ:m], *a. Geol:* ruiniforme.

ruinous ['ru:inəs], *a.* **1.** (tombé) en ruines; délabré. **2.** ruineux; **r. expense,** dépenses ruineuses; (*of undertaking*) **to prove r. to s.o.,** être la ruine de qn.

ruinously ['ru:inəsli], *adv.* ruineusement; **r. expensive,** ruineux.

rule[1] [ru:l], *s.* **1.** règle *f*; (*a*) **to lay, set, sth. down as a r.,** établir qch. en règle générale; arrêter une disposition générale; **to serve as a r. to s.o.,** servir de règle à qn; **as a (general) r.,** en règle générale; en général; en principe; à l'ordinaire; d'ordinaire; **as is the r.,** comme c'est la règle; **this is the exception rather than the r.,** c'est exceptionnel plutôt que de règle; **the exception proves the r.,** sans règle il n'y aurait pas d'exceptions; **to do things by r., to act according to r.,** agir dans les règles, suivant les règles; **r. of thumb,** méthode *f*, procédé *m*, empirique; *Mth: O:* **r. of three,** règle de trois; **chain r.,** règle conjointe; (*b*) **we make it a r. to go and see him,** il est de règle de lui rendre visite; **he makes it a r. to go to bed early,** il se fait une règle, une loi, de se coucher de bonne heure; **rules of conduct,** règles, normes *f*, de conduite; *Ecc:* **r. of an order,** règle d'un ordre; (*c*) **rules and regulations,** statuts *m* et règlements *m*; **hospital rules,** régime *m* des hôpitaux; *Ind:* **work(ing) to r.,** grève *f* de zèle; **to work to r.,** faire la grève de zèle; **the rules of the game,** les règles, les lois, du jeu; **to observe, play according to, the rules (of the game),** jouer selon les règles; entrer dans les règles du jeu; **it's against the rules,** c'est contre les règles; ce n'est pas réglementaire; **the r. of the road,** (i) *Aut:* le code de la route; les règlements de la circulation; (ii) *Nau:* les règles de route; règlements pour prévenir les abordages; *Av:* **visual flight rules,** règles de vol à vue; **instrument flight rules,** règles de vol aux instruments; vol sans visibilité. **2.** (*a*) empire *m*, autorité *f*, administration *f*, domination *f*; **under the r. of a tyrant,** sous l'empire d'un tyran; **under his r.,** sous son administration; **under British r.,** sous l'autorité britannique; **the Netherlands had come under Spanish r.,** les Pays-Bas étaient tombés au pouvoir de l'Espagne; **majority r.,** règle majoritaire; **mob r.,** voyoucratie *f*; (*b*) *Hist:* **the Rules,** zone *f* aux alentours des prisons pour dettes, où certains prisonniers pouvaient habiter sous caution; **prisoners on r.,** prisonniers admis à prendre un garni dans la zone. **3.** *Jur:* décision *f*, arrêt *m*, ordonnance *f*; **r. of court,** décision du tribunal; règlement judiciaire. **4.** (*a*) *Carp: Mec.E:* règle (graduée); **(metre) r.,** mètre *m*; **pocket r.,** règle, mètre, de poche; **folding r.,** mètre pliant; **drawing r.,** règle à dessin, à dessiner; **r. joint,** articulation *f*, noix *f* (d'une règle de poche); (*b*) *Surv:* **sight r.,** règle à éclimètre, règle de visée; **sighting r.,** alidade *f*. **5.** *Typ:* (*a*) **(brass) r.,** filet *m*; **thin, thick, r.,** filet maigre, gras; **French r., swell r.,** filet anglais; **r. box,** encadrement *m* en filets; (*b*) **em r.,** tiret *m*, moins *m*; **en r.,** tiret sur demi-cadratin; (*c*) filet à composer.

rule[2], *v.*

I. *v.tr.* **1.** gouverner (un état); gouverner, commander (un peuple); **to r. (over) a nation,** régner sur une nation; **to r. the waves,** tenir la mer; être maître, maîtresse, des mers; **to r. one's passions,** contenir, maîtriser, commander à, ses passions; **to be ruled by s.o.,** subir la loi de qn; être sous la coupe de qn; **to allow oneself to be ruled by s.o.,** se laisser mener, diriger, guider, par qn. **2.** (*a*) *Jur: etc:* décider, statuer; **to r. sth. out of order,** déclarer que qch. n'est pas en règle; **to r. that . . .,** décider, déterminer, que . . .; **ruled case,** affaire jugée; (*b*) **that's a possibility that can't be ruled out,** c'est une possibilité qui s'impose à l'attention, que l'on ne saurait écarter, éliminer. **3.** régler, rayer (du papier); **to r. a line,** tirer une ligne avec une règle; tracer une ligne à la règle; **to r. off a paragraph,** tirer une ligne au-dessous d'un paragraphe; *Com:* **to r. off an account,** clore, arrêter, régler, un compte.

II. *v.i.* **prices are ruling high,** les prix restent élevés; les prix se maintiennent; **the prices ruling at the moment,** les prix qui se pratiquent en ce moment.

ruler ['ru:lər], *s.* **1.** souverain, -aine (**of, over,** de); celui, celle, qui gouverne. **2.** règle *f*, mètre *m*; **folding r.,** mètre pliant. **3.** *Tchn:* (*pers.*) régleur *m* (de papier, etc.).

ruling[1] ['ru:liŋ], *a.* **1.** souverain, dominant, dirigeant; **the r. classes,** les classes dirigeantes; **r. passion,** passion dominante. **2. r. price,** cours actuel; cours, prix *m*, du jour.

ruling[2], *s.* **1.** gouvernement *m*; action *f* de gouverner, de diriger. **2.** ordonnance *f*, décision *f* (d'un juge, etc.) (sur un point de droit); jurisprudence *f*; **to give a r. in favour of s.o.,** rendre, prononcer, une décision en faveur de qn; décider en faveur de qn; **to make a r. by summary process,** statuer sommairement. **3.** réglage *m*, réglure *f* (d'une feuille de papier); **close r.,** réglure serrée; **r. pen,** tire-ligne *m*, *pl.* tire-lignes; *Phot.Engr:* **r. of the screen,** linéature *f* de la trame.

rum[1] [rʌm], *s.* **1.** *Dist:* rhum *m*. **2.** *NAm: F:* boisson *f* alcoolique; **r. hole,** bar *m*. **3.** *Moss:* **r. sucker,** polytric commun.

rum[2], *a.* **(rummer)** *F:* drôle, bizarre; louche; **a r. 'un,** un drôle d'individu, de type, de corps, de numéro.

Rumania [ru(:)'meiniə], *Pr.n. Geog:* Roumanie *f*.

Rumanian [ru(:)'meiniən]. **1.** *a. Geog:* roumain. **2.** *s.* (*a*) *Geog:* Roumain, -aine; (*b*) *Ling:* roumain *m*.

rumba ['rʌmbə], *s. Danc: Mus:* rumba *f*.

rumble[1] ['rʌmbl], *s.* **1.** bruit sourd; grondement *m* (du tonnerre, etc.); roulement *m* (d'une charrette, etc.); gargouillement *m*, gargouillis *m* (des intestins); borborygmes *mpl*; *Aut:* résonance *f* (de la carrosserie). **2.** *A:* (*in carriage*) siège *m* de derrière; (*in car*) spider *m*. **3.** *Metall:* tonneau *m* à dessabler. **4.** *NAm: F:* rixe *f*, bagarre *f* (entre bandes de jeunes voyous).

rumble[2], *v.i.* (*of thunder, etc.*) gronder (sourdement), rouler; (*of stomach*) gargouiller; **a cart rumbled along the street,** une charrette a passé bruyamment, avec bruit, dans la rue.

rumble[3], *v.tr. F:* flairer, se douter de, subodorer (qch.); voir venir (qn, qch.); **I soon rumbled him,** j'ai bien vite deviné son jeu.

rumbling ['rʌmbliŋ], *s.* (*a*) **r. (sound),** grondement *m* (de tonnerre, etc.); roulement *m* (d'une charrette, etc.); **stomach rumblings,** gargouillement *m*, gargouillis *m* (des intestins); borborygmes *m*; (*b*) *Metall:* **r. mill,** tonneau *m* à dessabler.

rumbowline [rʌm'boulin], *s. Nau:* larderasse *f*; filin *m* et toile *f* usagés.

rumbustious [rʌm'bʌstʃəs, -iəs], *a. F:* turbulent; tapageur, chahuteur, -trice.

Rumelia [ru:'mi:liə], *Pr.n. A.Geog:* **(Eastern) R.,** Roumélie (Orientale).

Rumelian [ru:'mi:liən]. *A.Geog:* (*a*) *a.* rouméliote; (*b*) *s.* Rouméliote *mf*.

rumen, *pl.* **rumens, rumina** ['ru:mən, -ənz, -inə], *s. Z:* rumen *m*, panse *f* (d'un ruminant).

ruminant ['ru:minənt]. **1.** *a.* & *s. Z:* ruminant (*m*). **2.** *a.* (*of pers.*) méditatif.

Ruminantia [ru:mi'nænʃiə], *s.pl. Z:* ruminants *m*.

ruminate[1] ['ru:mineit]. **1.** *v.i.* (*of animal*) ruminer. **2.** *v.i.* & *tr.* ruminer, méditer; **to r. (on, over, about) a plan,** ruminer, remâcher, un projet.

ruminate[2] ['ru:minət], *a. Bot:* ruminé.

ruminating[1] ['ru:mineitiŋ], *a.* (*of animal*) ruminant.

ruminating[2], *s.* = RUMINATION.

rumination [ru:mi'neiʃ(ə)n], *s.* **1.** *Z:* rumination *f*. **2.** (*of pers.*) rumination, méditation *f*.

ruminative ['ru:minətiv], *a.* méditatif.

ruminatively ['ru:minətivli], *adv.* en ruminant; en méditant; (parler) d'un ton méditatif.

rumly ['rʌmli], *adv. F: O:* d'une manière drôle, bizarre, curieuse.

rummage[1] ['rʌmidʒ], *s.* **1.** *Nau: A:* changement *m* d'arrimage. **2.** (*a*) recherches *fpl*, fouille *f* (dans de vieux documents, etc.); (*b*) *Cust:* visite *f* de douane (à bord). **3.** vieilleries *fpl*; objets divers; choses *fpl* de rebut; **r. sale,** (i) déballage *m*, braderie *f*; (ii) vente *f* de charité, de bienfaisance.

rummage[2]. **1.** *v.tr.* (*a*) fouiller, farfouiller (une armoire, ses poches; dans une armoire, dans ses poches); **to r. sth. out, up,** trouver qch. à force de recherches; dénicher qch.; (*b*) *Cust:* visiter (un navire). **2.** *v.i.* **to r. in one's pockets,** fouiller dans ses poches; **to r. everywhere,** fouiller partout; **to r. for sth.,** fouiller pour trouver qch.; **to r. about among old papers,** fouiller, fourrager, fourgonner, dans de vieux documents.

rummaging ['rʌmidʒiŋ], *s.* recherches *fpl*; farfouillement *m*.

rummer ['rʌmər], *s.* grand verre à boire.

rummy[1] ['rʌmi], *a. F: O:* bizarre, drôle.

rummy[2], *s. Cards:* **(gin) r.,** rami *m*.

rumour[1] ['ru:mər], *s.* **1.** rumeur *f*, bruit *m* (qui court); on-dit *m inv*; **r. has it, there's a r. going round, that . . .,** le bruit court, circule, que . . .; **vague rumours,** de vagues rumeurs. **2.** *A:* & *Lit:* **the r. of the sea, of the wind,** la rumeur des flots, du vent.

rumour[2], *v.tr.* (*a*) *O:* répandre, ébruiter (une nouvelle, etc.); (*b*) **it is rumoured that . . .,** le bruit court que . . .; on raconte que . . .; **he is rumoured to be . . .,** le bruit court, on dit, qu'il est . . ..

rump [rʌmp], *s.* **1.** croupe *f* (d'un quadrupède); croupion *m* (d'un oiseau); *F:* croupe, croupion, postérieur *m* (d'une personne); *Cu:* culotte *f*, cimier *m* (de bœuf); **r. steak,** romsteck *m*, rumsteck *m*. **2.** *F:* restes *mpl*, restant *m* (d'un parti politique, etc.); *Hist:* **the R. (Parliament),** le Parlement Croupion.

rumple ['rʌmpl], *v.tr.* chiffonner, friper, froisser (une robe, etc.); ébouriffer (les cheveux); **to r. s.o.'s hair,** dépeigner, décoiffer, écheveler, qn.

rumpus ['rʌmpəs], *s. F:* (i) chahut *m*, vacarme *m*, boucan *m*; (ii) dispute *f*, bagarre *f*; **to kick up, make, a r.,** (i) faire un chahut à tout casser; faire du boucan; (ii) se bagarrer; **to have a r. with s.o.,** avoir une prise de bec avec qn; s'engueuler; *esp. NAm:* **r. room,** salle de jeux.

rumrunner ['rʌmrʌnər], *s. NAm: F:* contrebandier *m* (de l'alcool).

rumrunning ['rʌmrʌniŋ], *s. NAm: F:* contrebande *f* (de l'alcool).

run[1] [rʌn], *s.* **1.** (*a*) **to start off at a r.,** partir au pas de course; **he came up at a r.,** il est arrivé en courant; **he came at me with a r.,** il s'est précipité sur moi; **to break into a r.,** se mettre à courir; prendre le pas de course; **she's always on the r.,** elle est tout le temps à courir; **to keep the enemy on the r.,** harceler l'ennemi; **we've got them on the r.,** ils nous fuient; nous les avons mis en déroute; **criminal on the r.,** malfaiteur recherché par la police; **to make a r. for it,** s'enfuir, se sauver; **to have ten minutes' r. before breakfast,** courir pendant dix minutes avant le petit déjeuner; *O:* **prices have come down with a r.,** les prix ont dégringolé; *Nau:* **to lower the yards at the r.,** amener les vergues en pagaïe; (*b*) course *f*; **to have a long r.,** faire une longue course (à pied, à cheval); courir longtemps; **the horse had already had a long r.,** le cheval avait déjà fait, fourni, une longue course; **to have a r. for one's money,** en avoir pour son argent; **to give s.o. a (good) r. for his money,** (i) en donner à qn pour son argent; (ii) donner du fil à retordre à qn; (*c*) élan *m*; **to make a r. at s.o.,** s'élancer sur qn; **he took a short r. and cleared the gate,** après un court élan il a franchi la barrière; (*d*) *Cr: etc:* course (faite par le batteur); **to make ten runs,** marquer dix points; (*e*) (i) remonte *f*, montaison *f* (du saumon, etc.); (ii) remonte, banc *m* (de saumons, etc.); (*f*) *Bill: Golf:* **to get plenty of r. on the ball,** faire courir la bille, la balle; donner de l'effet en dessus. **2.** (*a*) promenade *f*; **to go for a r. (in the car),** faire une promenade (en voiture); **preliminary r.,** sortie *f* préliminaire (d'une voiture, d'un navire, etc.); **trial r.,** (i) course d'essai (d'une voiture, d'une locomotive); voyage d'essai (d'un navire); (ii) *Aut:* essai (que l'on fait faire à un client); (*b*) trajet *m*; parcours *m*; **a r. of 50 kilometres,** un parcours de 50 kilomètres; **our town is two hours' r. from London,** notre ville est à deux heures (de chemin de fer, de voiture) de Londres; **it's a quick r. as far as Cardiff,** jusqu'à Cardiff le trajet est rapide, on peut rouler vite; **it's an easy day's r.,** on fait le trajet facilement dans la journée; *Nau:* **contract for the r.,** maréage *m*; **we had a good r.,** la traversée a été bonne; **the ship reached port after a six weeks' r.,** le navire est arrivé au port après un voyage de six semaines; **the ship has been taken off its usual r.,** on a assigné le navire à un autre parcours; (*c*) *Av:* roulement *m* (au décollage, à l'atterrissage); (*d*) marche *f* (d'une machine); **trial r. of a new plant, of an engine,** marche d'essai du matériel neuf, d'une machine; **r. of a blast furnace, of a stamping mill,** campagne *f* d'un haut fourneau, d'un bocard; *Typ:* **r. of ten thousand (copies),** tirage *m* à dix mille. **3.** (*a*) *Min:* **r. of a lode,** direction *f*, cours *m*, d'un filon; (*b*) *N.Arch:* formes *fpl* arrière, coulée *f* arrière, échappée *f*, façons *fpl* de l'arrière (d'un navire); **stern r.,** évidement *m*; **ship with a clean r.,** navire à l'arrière évidé; (*c*) **r. of sea, of tide,** courant *m* de marée; (*d*) cours, marche, suite *f* (des événements); rythme *m*, cadence *f* (des vers); **the ordinary r. of things,** la routine de tous les jours; **the r. of the market was against us,** les tendances du marché nous étaient défavorables, étaient contre nous; **we had a good r. of cards,** les cartes nous ont été favorables. **4.** (*a*) **a r. of bad luck,** une suite de malheurs; **we had a r. of good luck last week,** la semaine dernière la chance nous a souri; **a r. of bad weather,** une période de mauvais temps; *Cards:* **r. of three,** séquence *f* de trois; *Th:* **this play has already had a r. of 200 nights,** cette pièce a déjà eu 200 représentations; **to have a long r.,** (i) (*of fashion*) rester longtemps en vogue; (ii) (*of play*) tenir longtemps l'affiche; *Cin:* **first r.,** présentation *f*, première *f* (d'un film); **he had a long r. in office,** il est resté longtemps dans ses fonctions, en selle; **in the long r.,** à la longue; en fin de compte; au bout du compte; **it will pay in the long r.,** cela rapportera à la longue, avec le temps; (*b*) *Tchn:* **r. of pipes,** suite, ligne *f*, de tuyaux; **total r. of a pipeline,** parcours global d'un pipe-line; (*c*) *Gaming:* **r. on the red,** série *f* à la rouge; *Bill:* **r. of cannons,** série de carambolages. **5.** descente *f* (sur une banque); ruée *f* (sur des valeurs en bourse); **a r. on oils,** une ruée sur les pétroles; **a r. on the banks,** un retrait massif de dépôts bancaires; *Com:* **there was a great r. on that (particular) line,** ces marchandises étaient d'écoulement facile; tout le monde demandait cet article; **there's a great r. on this novel,** on demande beaucoup ce roman. **6.** (*a*) généralité *f*, commun *m* (des hommes, etc.); **the ordinary r. of mankind,** le commun des mortels; **they are different from our ordinary r. of customers,** ils sont différents de nos clients habituels; (*b*) (i) *Min:* **r. of the mine, mine r., r.-of-mine coal,** tout-venant *m*; (ii) **it's just r. of the mill,** *O:* **r. of the mine,** c'est un article courant; c'est ce qu'il y a de plus ordinaire, de plus courant. **7.** libre accès *m*; **to give s.o. the r. of one's library,** mettre sa bibliothèque à la disposition de qn; **to have the r., free r., of the house,** avoir libre accès, être libre d'aller partout, dans la maison. **8.** (*a*) galerie *f* (de la taupe); *Ven:* coulée (d'un lapin, etc.); **sheep r.,** pâturage *m* de moutons; bergerie *f*; **hen r., chicken r.,** parcours de poulailler; **pigeon r.,** volière *f*; (*b*) **ski r.,** descente *f* à ski; **toboggan r.,** piste *f* de toboggan; (*c*) *Rail:* **level r.,** palier *m*. **9.** maille *f* qui file (dans un bas, etc.). **10.** *Mus:* roulade *f*, tirade *f*, trait *m*.

run², *v.* (*p.t.* **ran** [ræn]; *p.p.* **run**; *pr.p.* **running**)

I. *v.i.* **1.** (*a*) courir; **to r. as fast as one can, at top speed,** courir à toutes jambes; **to r. like a hare,** *F:* **like anything, like blazes, like mad, like hell, like the devil,** courir comme un dératé, comme un lièvre; **he runs like a deer,** c'est un cerf à la course; **he set off running,** il s'est mis à courir; **to r. towards s.o., to r. up to s.o.,** courir à, vers, qn; courir trouver qn; **to come running towards s.o.,** accourir vers qn; **he ran to the station,** il a couru à, vers, la gare; **to r. to meet s.o.,** courir au-devant de qn; **to r. to help s.o.,** courir, voler, au secours de qn; **to r. past s.o.,** (i) (*also* **r. by**) passer devant qn, à côté de qn (en courant); (ii) dépasser qn; **to r. to meet one's troubles,** aller au-devant des ennuis; **to r. upstairs, up the stairs,** monter l'escalier en courant, à toute hâte; **to r. up, down, the street,** monter, descendre, la rue en courant; **don't r. about like that,** ne courez pas çà et là de cette façon! **I'll just r. across, round, over, to the grocer's,** je vais faire un saut chez l'épicier; **to r. after s.o.,** courir après qn; (*of man*) **to r. after women,** courir le jupon; **to r. into, out of, the room,** entrer dans, sortir de, la pièce en courant; **to r. into, (up) against, sth.,** se heurter contre qch.; **to r. into, across, up against, s.o.,** rencontrer qn par hasard; tomber sur qn; **r. along!** allez-vous-en! filez! **r. for it!** sauve qui peut! **to r. back,** retourner, revenir, en courant; (*b*) (*with cogn. acc.*) **to r. a race,** courir, disputer, une course; **the Derby was r. in a snowstorm,** le Derby a été couru dans une tempête de neige; (*c*) **to r. a kilometre,** courir, faire, un kilomètre; *Ven:* **to r. a scent,** suivre une piste; **to r. (about) the streets,** courir les rues; **to r. an errand, a message,** faire une course; **to r. the rapids,** franchir les rapides; **to r. the blockade,** forcer le blocus. **2.** fuir, s'enfuir, se sauver; **to r. from s.o.,** se sauver (pour échapper à qn); **to r. from a place,** s'enfuir d'un endroit; **we must r. for it!** sauvons-nous! **3.** **to r. in a race,** courir, disputer, une épreuve, une course; **to r. second,** arriver second; **the cup will be r. for tomorrow,** la coupe se courra demain; **this horse ran well,** ce cheval a fourni une belle carrière; **to r. for Parliament,** se présenter à la députation; **to r. for office,** se porter candidat. **4.** (*of salmon, etc.*) remonter les rivières; faire la montaison. **5.** *Nau:* courir, filer, faire route; **to r. so many knots,** filer tant de nœuds; **to r. before the wind,** courir vent arrière; fuir devant le vent; **to r. free,** courir largue; **to r. before the sea,** fuir devant la lame; fuir arrière à la lame; gouverner l'arrière à la lame; avoir la mer de l'arrière; **we had to r. before it,** il a fallu fuir; **we had to r. into Falmouth,** nous avons dû nous réfugier dans le port de Falmouth; **to r. on the rocks,** donner sur les roches. **6.** (*a*) aller, marcher; **sledges r. on snow,** les traîneaux vont, glissent, sur la neige; **the table runs on wheels,** la table peut se rouler; **car that runs well,** voiture qui roule bien; **trains running to Paris,** trains à destination de Paris; **to r. past a signal,** brûler un signal; (*b*) circuler; **the traffic runs day and night,** les voitures circulent jour et nuit; **trains running between London and the coast,** trains qui font le service, le trajet, le parcours, entre Londres et la côte; **a bus runs between Waterloo and Aldwych,** un autobus fait la navette entre (la gare de) Waterloo et Aldwych; **the trains are not running,** les trains ne fonctionnent plus, ont cessé de circuler; **this train is not running today,** ce train est supprimé aujourd'hui; **boats that r. daily,** bateaux qui font la traversée tous les jours; **the buses stop running at midnight,** après minuit il n'y a plus d'autobus. **7.** (*a*) **a murmur ran through the crowd,** un murmure a parcouru la foule; **a cheer ran down the line,** des acclamations ont éclaté tout le long de la ligne; **the idea keeps running through my mind,** cette idée ne me sort pas de l'esprit, me revient continuellement à l'esprit; **that song keeps running through my head,** cette chanson me trotte dans la tête; **it runs in the family, in the blood,** cela tient de la famille, est dans le sang; (*b*) **the conversation ran something like this,** la conversation suivait à peu près ces lignes; **his mind kept running on the problem,** il roulait ce problème dans sa tête; **his life runs very smoothly,** sa vie s'écoule paisiblement; **things must r. their course,** il faut que les choses suivent leur cours; *Pros:* **these verses do not r. smoothly,** ces vers ne coulent pas; *Com:* **the bill has 15 days to r.,** l'effet a 15 jours à courir; **the lease has only a year to r.,** le bail n'a plus qu'un an à courir; *Th:* **the play has r. for 200 nights,** la pièce a eu 200 représentations; **the play has been running for a year,** la pièce tient l'affiche depuis un an; (*c*) (*of amount, number*) **to r. to . . .,** monter, s'élever, à . . .; **the increase in business may r. to tens of thousands (of pounds),** l'augmentation du chiffre d'affaires pourra bien être de l'ordre de dizaines de milliers de livres; **the interval sometimes runs to half an hour,** l'entr'acte pousse parfois à la demi-heure; **this paper runs to 32 pages,** ce journal est publié sur 32 pages; (*d*) **I can't, my money won't, r. to a car,** je n'ai pas assez d'argent pour (i) acheter, (ii) avoir, entretenir, une voiture; **I can't r. to that,** cela est au-dessus de mes moyens. **8.** (*of engine, etc.*) fonctionner, marcher; (*of wheel, spindle, etc.*) tourner; **the engine's running,** le moteur marche, tourne, est en marche; **machine that runs well,** machine qui fonctionne, qui roule, bien; **the engine is running smoothly,** le moteur tourne rond; **to r. at a high speed,** tourner à grande vitesse, marcher à une allure (très) rapide; **this machine runs off the mains,** cet appareil se branche sur le secteur; **mandrel running in bearings,** mandrin tournant dans des coussinets; **rope that runs in a pulley,** corde renvoyée par une poulie, qui passe dans une poulie; **the drawer doesn't r. easily,** le tiroir ne joue pas bien. **9.** (*a*) (*of colour in fabric*) déteindre; (*of ink on paper*) s'étendre; (*of dye*) s'étendre, couler (au lavage); **colour that runs in the wash,** couleur qui déteint au lavage; *Typ:* **ink that won't r.,** encre qui ne s'étend pas; (*b*) (*of stocking, etc.*) filer, se démailler. **10.** (*a*) (*of liquid, sand, etc.*) couler; **the river runs smoothly,** la rivière coule tranquillement, a un cours tranquille; **the river runs into a lake,** la rivière débouche, se jette, dans un lac; **the tide is running strong,** le courant de marée est fort; **there was a heavy sea running,** la mer était grosse; il y avait grosse mer; **the wine ran (all) over the table,** le vin s'est répandu sur la table; **I felt the blood running to my head,** j'ai senti le sang me monter à la tête; **the rivers ran blood,** les rivières coulaient rouge, étaient teintes de sang; **wait until the water runs hot,** attendez l'arrivée de l'eau chaude; **his funds are running low,** ses fonds baissent; **our stores are running low,** nos provisions s'épuisent, tirent à leur fin; (*b*) **the floor was running with water,** le parquet ruisselait; il y avait de l'eau répandue sur le plancher; **the streets ran with wine,** le vin coulait dans les rues; **his nose was running,** il avait le nez qui coulait; (*of horse*) **to r. at the nose,** jeter sa gourme; **her eyes were running,** ses yeux pleuraient; **running sore,** plaie qui suppure; **my pen's running,** mon stylo bave, coule; *Metall:* **casting that has r.,** pièce qui a coulé; *Artil:* (*of gun*) **to r. at the muzzle,** s'égueuler; (*c*) **the ice cream is beginning to r.,** la glace commence à fondre; **money runs through his fingers like water (through a sieve),** l'argent lui fond entre les mains; c'est un panier percé. **11.** (*a*) s'étendre; **the road runs alongside the river,** la route suit, longe, la rivière; **there is a passage running through the house,** un couloir traverse la maison; **to r. north and south,** être orienté du nord au sud; **chain of mountains that runs from north to south,** chaîne de montagnes qui court du nord au sud; **the coast runs north and south,** la côte gît nord et sud; **the line runs from . . . to . . .,** la ligne s'étend depuis . . . jusqu'à . . .; **the road runs quite close to the village,** la route passe tout près du village; (*b*) **how does the first line r.?** quelles sont les paroles du premier vers? **to r. to extremes,** pousser les choses à l'extrême; **he runs to sentimentality,** il tombe dans la sentimentalité; (*of plant*) **to r. to seed,** monter en graine; (*of pers.*) **to r. to fat,** prendre de l'embonpoint; grossir; (*c*) **prices are running high,** les prix sont élevés en général; les prix sont plutôt élevés.

II. *v.tr.* **1.** (*a*) chasser, courre (le renard, etc.); **to r. a fox to earth,** chasser un renard jusqu'à son terrier; (*b*) **to r. s.o. hard, close,** presser qn; serrer qn de près; **to be hard r.,** (i) être serré de près; (ii) être gêné, embarrassé, à bout de ressources; **to r. s.o. (clean) off his legs,** faire courir qn jusqu'à ce qu'il tombe de fatigue, jusqu'à ce qu'il ne tienne plus debout; **you'll r. me off my legs,** à ce train-là vous me romprez les jambes. **2.** (*a*) mettre (un cheval) au galop; (*b*) mettre (du bétail) au vert. **3.** (*a*) **to r. the car into the garage,** rentrer la voiture dans le garage; garer la voiture; **to r. s.o. (in, up) to town, back home,** conduire qn en ville, reconduire qn chez lui; **to r. logs,** flotter des bois; **to r. a boat ashore,** atterrir une embarcation; **to r. a ship on a rock,** donner sur les écueils; **to r. one's head against the door,** se heurter la tête contre la porte; (*b*) **to r. trains between X and Y,** établir un service de trains entre X et Y; **an express train is run between X and Y,** il y a un train direct entre X et Y; **sleeping cars are r. on Fridays and Saturdays,** il y a un service de wagons-lits le vendredi et le samedi; **they are running an extra train today,** il y aura aujourd'hui un train supplémentaire; (*c*) introduire (de l'alcool) en contrebande; **to r. arms,** faire la contrebande des armes. **4.** (*a*) faire fonctionner, faire travailler (une machine); **I can't afford to r. a car,** je n'ai pas les moyens d'entretenir une voiture; **they r. two cars,** ils ont deux voitures; *Av:* (*for checking*) **to r. the engines,** faire le point fixe; (*b*) *Com:* **to r. a cheap line,** vendre un article à bon marché, en réclame. **5.** (*a*) diriger (une affaire); tenir (un magasin, un hôtel); exploiter (une ferme, etc.); diriger (un théâtre); éditer, gérer (un journal, une revue); **to r. s.o.'s house,** tenir le ménage de qn; **it's his secretary who runs the business,** c'est sa secrétaire qui dirige l'affaire; (*b*) **to r. a (high) temperature,** faire de la température; avoir (de) la fièvre. **6.** *Turf:* **to r. a horse,** faire courir un cheval; engager un cheval dans une course; *Pol: etc:* **to r. a candidate,** (i) mettre en avant un candidat; (ii) appuyer un candidat. **7.** (faire) passer; **to r. a sword through s.o.,** passer à qn une épée à travers le corps; transpercer qn d'un coup d'épée; **to r. pipes through a wall,** faire passer des tuyaux à travers un mur; (*croquet*) **to r. a hoop,** passer un arceau d'un seul coup; **to r. a thorn, a needle, into one's finger,** s'enfoncer une épine, une aiguille, dans le doigt; **to r. one's fingers over sth.,** promener, faire glisser, ses doigts sur qch.; **he ran his finger down the list,** il a parcouru la liste en la suivant du doigt; **to r. one's fingers over the strings of a harp,** faire frémir les cordes d'une harpe; **he ran his hand through his hair,** il a passé sa main dans ses cheveux; **to r. one's pen through a word,** rayer, biffer, un mot; **I'll r. the sheets through the (washing) machine,** je vais passer les draps à la machine (à laver); *Typ:* **to r. type round a block,** habiller une gravure; *Cmptr:* **to r. a programme,** passer un programme. **8. to r. molten metal into a mould,** couler, jeter, du métal en fusion dans un moule. **9.** *St.Exch:* **to r. stock against one's client,** se porter contrepartiste de son donneur d'ordres; faire la contrepartie. **10.** tracer (une ligne). **11.** *Needlew:* coudre (un tissu) au point devant, au point glissé, au point coulé.

III. (*compound verbs*) **1. run away,** *v.i.* (*a*) (*of pers.*) s'enfuir, se sauver; s'échapper; **they ran away and hid in the bushes,** ils ont couru se cacher dans les buissons; **to r. away from school,** se sauver de l'école; **to r. away from the facts,** se refuser à l'évidence des faits; (*b*) (*of horse*) s'emballer, s'emporter; prendre le mors aux dents; **the horse ran away with him,** le cheval l'a emporté au galop; (*c*) **to r. away with s.o.,** enlever qn; **to r. away with sth.,** emporter, enlever, qch.; **to r. away with the idea that . . .,** se mettre dans la tête que . . ., s'imaginer que . . .; **his imagination runs away with him,** son imagination prend la galopade; **that runs away with a lot of money,** cela mange beaucoup d'argent.

2. run down. (*a*) *v.i.* (*of spring*) se détendre; (*of clockwork*) se décharger; (*of clock*) s'arrêter (faute d'être remontée); (*of accumulator*) se décharger à plat; (*of dynamo*) se désamorcer; **the clock is running down, is r. down,** la pendule a besoin d'être remontée; (*b*) *v.tr.* (i) **to r. down a ship,** (α) (aborder et) couler un navire; couler bas un navire; couler à fond un navire; (β) laisser porter sur un navire; *F:* **to r. s.o. down,** heurter, renverser, qn; (*of motorist, etc.*) écraser qn; (ii) *Ven:* forcer, mettre aux abois (un cerf); (iii) rabaisser, ravaler, dénigrer, déprécier, décrier, diffamer, éreinter (qn); médire de (qn); (iv) **to r. down the boilers,** vider les chaudières; (v) diminuer (les effectifs, etc.); laisser épuiser (les stocks).

3. run in. (*a*) *v.i.* (i) *Box:* combattre de près, entrer en corps-à-corps; *Rugby Fb:* aller à l'essai; (ii) *Nau:* **to r. in to a bay,** donner dans une baie; (*b*) *v.tr.* (i) *F:* **to r. s.o. in,** arrêter qn; **to be, get, r. in,** se faire ramasser; (ii) *Nau: A:* rentrer (le beaupré, un canon); (iii) *I.C.E:* roder (un moteur); **running in,** en rodage.

4. run into. (*a*) *v.i.* (i) **to r. into debt,** faire des dettes; s'endetter; (ii) **to r. into sth.,** entrer en collision avec (une voiture, un arbre, etc.); (*of vehicle*) heurter, accrocher, enfoncer, entrer dans (un autre, etc.); (*of train*) rencontrer, tamponner (un autre); (*of ship*) aborder (un autre); (*of pers.*) **to r. into s.o.,** (α) se heurter contre qn; bousculer qn; (β) rencontrer qn par hasard; se trouver nez à nez avec qn; **to r. into difficulties,** rencontrer, buter contre, des difficultés; **his income runs into tens of thousands,** son revenu s'élève à des dizaines de milliers de livres; **takings r. into five figures,** la recette atteint les cinq chiffres; **book that has r. into five editions,** livre dont on a publié cinq éditions; (*b*) *v.tr.* (i) **to r. one's car into a wall,** rentrer dans un mur avec sa voiture; aller s'emboutir contre un mur; (ii) **that will r. me into considerable expense,** cela me coûtera cher, m'entraînera des frais considérables.

5. run off. (*a*) *v.i.* (i) fuir, s'enfuir, se sauver; **to r. off with the cash,** filer avec l'argent; (ii) (*of liquid*) s'écouler; (*b*) *v.tr.* (i) **to r. off an article,** écrire, rédiger, un article rapidement; *Typ:* **machine that runs off** *x* **copies a minute,** machine qui imprime *x* feuilles par minute; (ii) faire écouler (un liquide); *Metall:* couler (le métal); **to r. off the water from a boiler,** vider l'eau d'une chaudière; (iii) *Sp:* **to r. off a heat,** courir une éliminatoire.

6. run on. (*a*) *v.i.* (i) (*of verse*) enjamber; *Typ:* (*of words*) se rejoindre; être liés; (*of text*) suivre sans alinéa; (*of chapter*) suivre sur la même page; (*as instruction*) **r. on,** alinéa à supprimer; faire suivre; (ii) **how she runs on!** ce qu'elle débite! ce qu'elle a la langue bien pendue! (*b*) *v.tr. Typ:* **to r. on the matter,** faire suivre sans alinéa.

7. run out. (*a*) *v.i.* (i) **the tide is running out,** la mer se retire; (ii) (*of lease*) expirer; **we're running out of time, time is running out,** il nous reste peu de temps; *Lit:* **the sands are running out,** la dernière heure approche, a sonné; **to r. out of provisions,** épuiser ses provisions; être à court, à bout, de provisions; **I've r. out of cigarettes,** je n'ai plus de cigarettes; **we ran out of petrol,** nous avons eu une panne d'essence; (iii) (*of rope*) filer, se dérouler; (iv) *Equit:* refuser; (v) *F:* **to r. out on s.o.,** abandonner qn, laisser tomber qn; (*b*) *v.tr. & ind.tr.* (i) **to r. out a race,** terminer une course; (ii) *Cr:* mettre (un batteur) hors jeu pendant sa course; (iii) (laisser) filer (une corde); élonger (une amarre); (iv) *Nau:* pousser dehors, (une passerelle, *A:* le beaupré, un canon).

8. run over, *v.i.* (*a*) parcourir (un document); *Mus:* **to r. one's fingers over the keys,** passer les doigts sur les touches (du piano); (*b*) *Aut:* écraser (qn); **the car ran over his legs,** la voiture lui a passé sur les jambes; (*c*) (*of vessel or contents*) déborder; regorger; (*of liquid*) se répandre.

9. run through. (*a*) *v.i.* (i) parcourir (un document); feuilleter (un livre); **he ran through his pockets but couldn't find it,** il a fouillé dans ses poches mais il ne l'a pas trouvé; (ii) **to r. through a fortune,** gaspiller, dissiper, dévorer, manger, une fortune; *Th:* **to r. through one's part,** répéter son rôle; (*b*) *v.tr. A:* **to r. s.o. through (and through),** percer qn d'outre en outre, de part en part; transpercer, enfiler, qn; **he ran him through,** il lui passa son épée au travers du corps.

10. run up. (*a*) *v.i.* (i) **to r. up against s.o.,** (α) rencontrer qn par hasard; (β) être, entrer, en conflit avec qn; **to r. up against difficulties,** buter contre, se heurter à, des difficultés; (ii) (*of fish*) remonter la rivière; (*b*) *v.tr.* (i) laisser grossir (un compte); laisser accumuler (des dettes); (ii) (*at auction*) **to r. up the bidding,** pousser les enchères; (iii) **to r. up a flag,** hisser un drapeau, un pavillon; (iv) confectionner (une robe) (à la hâte); coudre (une couture, etc.).

run[3], *a.* **1.** (*a*) **r. butter,** beurre fondu pour conserve; **r. honey,** miel extrait des rayons; (*b*) *Metall:* **r. steel,** acier coulé. **2.** *Min:* **r. coal,** houille grasse.

runabout ['rʌnəbaut], *s.* **1.** (*a*) *A:* vagabond, -onde; (*b*) *Austr:* **runabouts,** bêtes *f* paissant en liberté. **2.** (*a*) *Aut:* petite voiture; deuxième voiture (pour faire des courses en ville, etc.); (*b*) *Nau:* petit canot à moteur; runabout *m.*

runagate ['rʌnəgeit], *s. A: & Dial:* **1.** vagabond, -onde. **2.** fuyard, -arde; fugitif, -ive.

runaway ['rʌnəwei]. **1.** *a. & s.* (*a*) fuyard, -arde; fugitif, -ive; **r. (prisoner),** prisonnier fugitif; **r. (slave),** esclave fugitif; (*b*) **r. (horse),** cheval emballé, échappé; (*c*) **r. lorry, train,** camion, train, fou; *Rail:* **r. track,** wagon parti à la dérive; **r. switch,** aiguille *f* de déraillement. **2.** *a.* (*a*) (mariage) à la suite d'un enlèvement, par enlèvement; **to make a r. match with s.o.,** enlever une jeune fille pour l'épouser; (*of the girl*) se laisser enlever pour être épousée; (*b*) **r. ring, knock,** coup de sonnette tiré, coup frappé, à une porte par plaisanterie et après lequel on se sauve; (*c*) **r. win,** victoire remportée haut la main. **3.** *a. Mec.E:* **r. governor,** sûreté *f* contre l'emballement.

runback ['rʌnbæk], *s. Sp: etc:* recul *m.*

runcinate ['rʌnsineit], *a. Bot:* ronciné.

run down[1] [rʌn'daun], *a.* **1.** (*of clock*) au bas; (*of accumulator*) à plat, épuisé, déchargé. **2.** *F:* (*of pers.*) **to be, feel, r. d.,** être, se sentir, épuisé, affaibli, fatigué; **I was completely r. d.,** j'étais complètement à plat.

rundown[2] ['rʌndaun], *s.* (*a*) recensement minutieux; (*b*) diminution *f* des effectifs.

rune [ru:n], *s.* **1.** rune *f.* **2.** *A:* (*a*) charme *m*, incantation *f*; (*b*) poésie *f* (nordique).

rung [rʌŋ], *s.* **1.** échelon *m*, barreau *m*, roulon *m*, barre *f* (de) traverse *f* (d'une échelle); bâton *m* (d'une chaise). **2.** *Mec.E:* fuseau *m* (de lanterne).

runged [rʌŋd], *a.* à échelons.

rungless ['rʌŋlis], *a.* sans échelons, sans traverses.

runic ['ru:nik], *a.* (*of letters, verse*) runique.

runiform ['ru:nifɔ:m], *a.* runiforme.

run-in ['rʌnin]. **1.** *a.* inséré. **2.** *s.* querelle *f*, rixe *f.*

runlet[1] ['rʌnlit], *s. A:* barillet *m.*

runlet[2], *s.* ruisseau *m*; filet *m* d'eau.

runnable ['rʌnəbl], *a. Ven:* **r. stag,** cerf courable.

runnel ['rʌn(ə)l], *s.* **1.** (*a*) ruisseau *m*; filet *m* d'eau; (*b*) ruisseau (de rue); caniveau *m.* **2.** *Agr:* échau *m*, -aux.

runner ['rʌn(ə)r], *s.* **1.** (*a*) (*pers., horse, etc.*) coureur, -euse; *Turf:* **five runners,** cinq partants *m*; **non r.,** non partant; (*b*) messager *m*, courrier *m*; *esp. U.S:* **bank r.,** garçon *m* de recette; encaisseur *m*; (*c*) racoleur *m*; *Fin:* démarcheur *m*; (*d*) *Hist:* **(Bow-Street) R.,** sergent *m* (de police); (*e*) contrebandier *m*; **(blockade) r.,** forceur *m* de blocus; (*f*) *U.S:* mécanicien *m* (conducteur de locomotive); (*g*) *Mil:* agent *m* de transmission; (*h*) *St.Exch:* **r. of stock,** contrepartiste *m* (de son donneur d'ordres). **2.** *Orn:* **Indian r. (duck),** coureur indien; **road r.,** coucou *m* terrestre de Californie; coureur de routes. **3.** *Hort:* (*a*) coulant *m*, stolon *m*, stolone *f*, filet *m*, marcotte *f*, traînée *f* (de fraisier, etc.); (*b*) **scarlet r. bean,** haricot *m* d'Espagne; haricot à rames, à filets. **4.** maille partie, maille lâchée (d'un tricot, etc.). **5.** (meule) courante *f*; surmeule *f* (de moulin); **edge r.,** broyeur *m* à meules verticales. **6.** patin *m* (de traîneau); lame *f* (de patin). **7.** (*a*) *Nau:* chaîne *f* de charge; itague *f*; **r. and tackle,** palan *m* sur itague; bastague *f*, bastaque *f*; (*b*) anneau *m* mobile; (*c*) tendeur *m* (de cordon de tente). **8.** (*a*) (*sliding ring*) coulant *m* (de bourse, etc.); *Harn:* panurge *m*; (*b*) curseur *m*; *El:* **r. resistance,** résistance *f* à curseur. **9.** (*a*) chariot *m* de roulement; chariot roulant; trolley *m*; (*b*) galet *m* (de roulement); (*c*) roue *f* parasite, intermédiaire; (*d*) roue mobile, couronne *f* mobile (d'une turbine, d'une pompe centrifuge); (*e*) coulisseau *m* (de lit, de tiroir). **10.** (*a*) poulie *f* fixe; (*b*) poulie-guide *f*, *pl.* poulies-guides; galet-guide *m*, *pl.* galets-guides (de courroie). **11.** *Metall:* (*a*) trou *m*, jet *m*, de coulée; chenal *m*, -aux, de coulée; (*b*) jet, masselotte *f.* **12.** têtière *f* (de canapé); (*of carpet*) chemin (d'escalier, de couloir); **(table) r.,** jeté *m* (de table). **13. r.-up,** (i) *Sp: etc:* (bon) second; (ii) (*at auction sale*) compère chargé de pousser les enchères.

running[1] ['rʌniŋ], *a.* **1.** (*a*) (*of pers.*) courant; (*b*) *Fb:* **r. kick,** coup de pied donné en courant; *Sp:* **r. jump,** saut *m* avec élan; *P:* **go and take a r. jump at yourself!** va te faire foutre! **r. fight,** (i) *Mil:* escarmouche *f* de route; (ii) *Navy:* combat *m* en chasse, en retraite; **to keep up a r. fight,** (i) se battre en retraite; (ii) *Navy:* soutenir, appuyer, la chasse; *Cin: Phot:* **r. shot,** prise *f* de vues en mouvement. **2. r. water,** eau courante; eau vive; (*in hotel*) **room with r. water,** chambre *f* avec eau courante; **r. spring,** source vive; **r. stream,** ruisseau coulant; *Med:* **r. cold,** fort rhume de cerveau; **r. sore,** plaie *f* qui suppure; plaie en suppuration. **3.** (*a*) (style) coulant; (*b*) **r. hand,** écriture cursive; (écriture) coulée *f*; expédiée *f.* **4.** (*a*) continu; **r. pattern,** dessin continu; **r. accompaniment,** accompagnement soutenu; *Mil:* **r. fire,** feu roulant; *Typ:* **r. title, r. headline,** titre courant (d'un volume); (*b*) **r. account,** compte courant; **r. expenses,** dépenses courantes; (*c*) *A:* **r. board,** (i) *Aut:* marchepied *m*; (ii) *Rail:* tablier *m.* **5.** (*a*) **r. block,** poulie *f* mobile; moufle *f* mobile; (*b*) *Nau:* **r. rigging, r. gear,** manœuvres courantes; **r. bowline,** laguis *m.* **6.** *Needlew:* **r. stitch,** point devant, point droit, point coulé, point glissé.

running[2], *s.* **1.** course(s) *f*(*pl*); **r. match,** course *f* à pied; lutte *f* à la course; **r. track,** piste *f*; **to make, take up, the r.,** mener la course; **to be in the r.,** avoir des chances d'arriver; **he's out of the r., not in the r.,** il n'a aucune chance (d'être nommé, d'arriver); il ne compte plus; **blockade r.,** forcement *m* de blocus; **r. in,** (i) coulage *m* (du métal en fusion, etc.); (ii) rodage *m* (d'un moteur). **2.** (*a*) marche *f*, fonctionnement *m* (d'une machine, etc.); roulement *m* (d'une voiture); marche, circulation *f*, roulement (de trains); **smooth r.,** allure régulière; **in r. order,** en bon état (de marche); prêt au service; (*of car, etc.*) **r. costs,** frais *mpl* d'entretien; (*b*) *Rail:* (*of company*) **to have r. rights over another line,** avoir libre parcours sur un autre réseau; (*c*) direction *f* (d'un hôtel, etc.); exploitation *f* (des chemins de fer, etc.); (*d*) **r. down,** (i) déchargement *m* (d'un accu, etc.); désamorçage *m* (d'une dynamo); (ii) dépréciation *f*, ravalement *m*, éreintement *m* (de qn); (*e*) introduction *f* (de l'alcool, etc.) en contrebande. **3.** (*a*) écoulement *m* (des eaux); ruissellement *m* (de l'eau, etc.); *Med:* écoulement, suppuration *f*; (*b*) coulage *m* (du liquide d'un tonneau). **4.** *Needlew:* point devant, point droit, point coulé, point glissé. **5.** *Dist:* **runnings,** têtes *f*; **last runnings,** queues *f.*

runny ['rʌni], *a. F:* (*a*) *Cu: etc:* (trop) liquide; **r. honey,** miel liquide; (*b*) **r. nose,** nez qui coule.

runoff ['rʌnɔf], *s.* **1.** *Hyd.E:* écoulement *m*; *Geog:* ruissellement *m.* **2.** *Sp:* (course) finale *f*; *U.S:* **r. match,** match *m* de barrage; *Pol: U.S:* **r. election,** scrutin *m* de ballottage.

runologist [ru:'nɔlədʒist], *s.* runologue *mf.*

runology [ru:'nɔlədʒi], *s.* l'étude *f* des runes.

run-on [ˈrʌnɔn], *a. & s. Typ:* (matière *f*) qui suit sans alinéa.

runt [rʌnt], *s.* **1.** (*a*) bœuf *m*, vache *f*, de race petite; (*b*) petit dernier (d'une portée de porcs). **2.** (*a*) (cheval) ragot *m*; (*b*) mauvais cheval; rosse *f*. **3.** pigeon romain. **4.** rustre *m*. **5.** *F:* (*a*) nain *m*, nabot *m*; (*b*) avorton. **6.** trognon *m* (de chou).

run-through [ˈrʌnθruː], *s.* **1.** *Bill:* coulé *m*. **2.** *Fb:* percée *f*. **3.** (*a*) lecture *f* rapide; (*b*) *Th:* répétition *f* rapide.

runty [ˈrʌnti], *a. F:* rabougri, riquiqui.

run-up [ˈrʌnʌp], *s.* **1.** (*a*) *Golf:* coup roulé d'approche; (*b*) *Fb:* percée *f*. **2.** *Fish:* montaison *f* (du saumon). **3.** *Av:* **the pilot was making his r.-u. to the target,** le pilote fonçait sur l'objectif.

runway [ˈrʌnwei], *s.* **1.** *Ven:* coulée *f* (du cerf). **2.** (*a*) *Mec.E: etc:* chemin *m* de roulement; **elevated r.,** estacade *f*; **crane r.,** pont roulant; (*b*) piste *f*, voie *f*, de roulement (d'une poulie); (*c*) monorail aérien, transporteur; chemin de fer suspendu; voie suspendue; **overhead r.,** transporteur aérien; (*d*) glissière *f* (de fenêtre). **3.** *Av:* piste *f* d'envol; **r. localizer,** radiophare *m* d'alignement de piste.

rupee [ruːpiː], *s. Num:* roupie *f*.

Rupert [ˈruːpət], *Pr.n.m.* Rupert; *Ph:* **Prince Rupert's drop, ball, tear,** larme *f* batavique; bombe-chandelle *f*, *pl.* bombes-chandelles.

rupestral, rupestrine [ruːˈpestrəl, -train], *a.* rupestre.

rupia [ˈruːpiə], *s. Med:* rupia *m*.

rupicolous [ruːˈpikələs], *a. Nat.Hist:* rupicole.

ruppia [ˈrʌpiə], *s. Bot:* ruppia *m*, ruppie *f*, ruppelle *f*.

rupture[1] [ˈrʌptjər], *s.* **1.** (*a*) rupture *f* (de négociations, etc.); rupture, séparation *f*, brouille *f* (entre amis, entre époux); (*b*) *El:* **r. of the arc,** rupture, désamorçage *m*, de l'arc. **2.** *Med:* (*a*) éclatement *m*, rupture (d'une veine, etc.); (*b*) hernie *f*.

rupture[2]. **1.** *v.tr.* (*a*) *O:* rompre (des relations, etc.); (*b*) **to r. a ligament, a blood vessel** se rompre un tendon, un vaisseau sanguin; claquer un tendon. **2.** *v.i.* (*of membrane, etc.*) se rompre.

ruptured [ˈrʌptjəd], *a.* **1.** rompu. **2.** *Med:* (intestin) hernié; (*of pers.*) **to be r.,** avoir une hernie, être hernieux.

rupturewort [ˈrʌptjəwəːt], *s. Bot:* herniaire *f*, herniole *f*; herbe *f* aux hernies; **smooth r., glabrous r.,** herniaire glabre; turquette *f*.

rupturing [ˈrʌptjəriŋ], *s.* rupture *f*.

rural [ˈruərəl], *a.* rural, -aux; rustique, champêtre; des champs, de (la) campagne; **r. occupations,** travaux *m* des champs; **r. sports,** jeux *m* champêtres; *Ecc:* **r. dean,** doyen rural.

ruralize [ˈruərəlaiz]. **1.** *v.tr.* rendre rural; rendre rustique; donner un aspect rustique, campagnard, à (une localité, etc.). **2.** *v.i. O:* habiter la campagne.

rurally [ˈruərəli], *adv.* (situé) à la campagne.

ruridecanal [ruəriˈdekən(ə)l], *a. Ecc:* qui appartient à un doyen rural; qui relève du doyen rural.

ruse [ruːz], *s.* ruse *f*, stratagème *m*, subterfuge *m*; piège *m*.

rush[1] [rʌʃ], *s.* **1.** *Bot:* (*a*) jonc *m*; **hard r.,** jonc glauque; **r. bed, plantation of rushes,** jonchaie *f*; (*b*) **flowering r.,** butome *m* à ombelles; jonc fleuri; **sweet r.,** jonc odorant; roseau *m* aromatique; lis *m* des marais. **2.** jonc, paille *f* (pour fonds de chaises); **r.-bottomed chair,** chaise paillée, à fond de paille; **r. mat,** natte *f* de jonc; paillasson *m*.

rush[2], *v.tr.* **1.** joncer, pailler (une chaise). **2.** *A:* joncher (un plancher) de joncs.

rush[3], *s.* **1.** (*a*) course précipitée; mouvement *m* rapide; **a r. through Europe,** un tour rapide en Europe; **to make a r. at s.o.,** s'élancer, se jeter, se précipiter, sur qn; *Hist:* **the r. for the Channel ports,** la course à la Manche (1914); (*b*) **general r.,** ruée générale; bousculade *f*; **gold r.,** ruée vers l'or; **the r. for the coast,** la ruée vers, sur, la côte; **there was a r. for safety,** ce fut une ruée pour se mettre à l'abri; **there was a r. to the doors,** on s'est bousculé pour gagner les portes; on s'est précipité vers les portes; **there was a r. for the papers,** on s'arrachait les journaux; **the r. hours,** les heures d'affluence, de pointe; **a r. period,** (i) une poussée (d'affaires, etc.); (ii) (*at shop*) le moment d'affluence (de la clientèle); (*c*) *Rugby Fb:* charge *f* à fond. **2.** hâte *f*, empressement *m*; **we had a r. to get the job done,** il a fallu nous hâter pour achever le travail; **life is too much of a r. in London,** la vie à Londres est trop enfiévrée; **the r. of modern life,** la vie fiévreuse d'aujourd'hui; **r. order,** commande urgente; **r. work,** (i) travail de première urgence; (ii) travail fait à la va-vite, à la galopée. **3. a r. of air,** un coup d'air, une chasse d'air; **a r. of cold air,** une bouffée d'air glacé; **r. of water,** coup d'eau; **r. of steam,** jet *m* de vapeur; **r. of blood to the head,** un coup de sang; un afflux, une affluence, de sang; *El:* **r. of current,** accélération *f* brusque de courant; soubresaut *m* de courant; à-coup *m* de courant; *F:* **it came on me with a r.,** c'était un coup de fouet. **4.** *Cin:* **rushes,** épreuves *f*.

rush[4], *v.i. & tr.*

I. *v.i.* **1.** (*a*) se précipiter; se jeter, se lancer, s'élancer; **to r. about,** courir çà et là; **to r. into a room,** entrer précipitamment; faire irruption dans une pièce; **to r. in where angels fear to tread,** y aller avec audace sans se rendre compte du danger, sans se soucier des précautions à prendre; **to r. into a business deal,** se jeter étourdiment dans une affaire; **to r. into danger,** courir au danger tête baissée; **to r. to conclusions,** conclure trop hâtivement, à la légère; (*b*) **to r. out,** sortir précipitamment; **to r. (across) to the window,** se précipiter à la fenêtre; **to r. down,** descendre impétueusement, précipitamment; **he came rushing down the stairs,** il a dégringlé l'escalier; **stream that rushes down the mountain side,** ruisseau *m* qui dévale de la montagne; **to r. up,** (i) monter à la hâte; (ii) accourir; **to r. upstairs,** monter l'escalier à la hâte; **to r. back,** revenir en toute hâte, en vitesse; revenir brusquement; **he rushed back to his friends,** il s'est précipité pour retrouver, rejoindre, ses amis; **to r. to a place,** gagner un endroit à toute vitesse; se rendre précipitamment quelque part; **to r. through France,** traverser la France à la galopade, à la galope; **to r. through one's prayers,** expédier ses prières; **to r. past s.o.,** (i) dépasser qn, (ii) croiser qn, au galop, à toute vitesse; (*c*) **to r. at, on, s.o.,** se ruer, se jeter, sur qn; fondre sur qn; **to r. at the enemy,** courir sus à l'ennemi; (*d*) **to r. for the goldfields, for gold,** se ruer vers, sur, l'or. **2. the wind was rushing through the tunnel,** le vent s'engouffrait dans le tunnel; **the blood rushed to his cheeks, to his head,** le sang lui est monté au visage, à la tête.

II. *v.tr.* **1.** (*a*) pousser, entraîner, violemment; **to r. s.o. out of the room,** chasser qn brusquement de la pièce; **he was rushed to hospital,** on l'a transporté d'urgence à l'hôpital; **to r. s.o. into an undertaking,** entraîner qn dans une entreprise sans lui donner le temps de réfléchir; **to r. a country into war,** précipiter un pays dans la guerre; **he rushed me through lunch,** il m'a fait déjeuner au galop; **I don't want to r. you,** je ne voudrais pas vous bousculer; prenez votre temps; **don't r. me,** laissez-moi le temps de souffler; **he refuses to be rushed,** il refuse de se laisser mener trop vite; **to r. a bill through (the House),** faire passer un projet de loi à la hâte; *Th:* **to r. the ending,** brusquer le dénouement; (*b*) *Mil:* **to r. up reinforcements,** amener, envoyer, des renforts à toute hâte; (*c*) *F: O:* **to r. s.o. for sth.,** faire payer à qn un prix exorbitant pour qch.; estamper qn; **he rushed me ten pounds for it,** il me l'a fait payer dix livres; **he rushed me for a fiver,** il m'a fait cracher cinq livres. **2.** *Ind: etc:* dépêcher (un travail); expédier (un travail) à toute vitesse; exécuter (une commande) d'urgence; **r. it,** c'est urgent; **you needn't r. it,** ce n'est pas pressé. **3.** (*a*) **horse that rushes his fences,** cheval qui se précipite sur l'obstacle avec trop d'impétuosité; cheval qui fonce sur l'obstacle; *F:* **don't r. your fences!** regardez-y bien! réfléchissez donc! (*b*) **the audience rushed the platform,** le public a envahi l'estrade; *Mil:* **to r. a position,** (i) prendre d'assaut une position; (ii) bondir à l'assaut d'une position; **to r. a trench,** surprendre une tranchée; s'emparer d'une tranchée par surprise.

rushed [rʌʃt], *a.* **1.** débordé de travail. **2.** (travail) fait à la va-vite, bâclé.

rusher [ˈrʌʃər], *s. F:* **he's a terrible r.,** il est toujours pressé, il ne veut jamais prendre son temps.

rushing[1] [ˈrʌʃiŋ], *a.* (vent, fleuve) impétueux; *B:* **a r. mighty wind,** un vent qui souffle avec véhémence.

rushing[2], *s.* course précipitée; mouvement impétueux; précipitation *f*.

rushlight [ˈrʌʃlait], *s.* chandelle *f* à mèche de jonc.

rushy [ˈrʌʃi], *a.* (terrain, etc.) couvert de joncs.

rusk [ˈrʌsk], *s. Comest:* = biscotte *f*.

russet [ˈrʌsit]. **1.** *s.* (*a*) *Tex: A:* drap *m* de bure de couleur brunâtre, grisâtre; (*b*) *Hort:* reinette grise, rainette grise. **2.** *a. & s.* (couleur *f*) roussâtre; roux, *f.* rousse; feuille-morte (*m*) *inv.* **r. pear,** rousselet *m*. **3.** *a. A:* simple; rustique.

Russia [ˈrʌʃə]. **1.** *Pr.n. Geog:* Russie *f*; **White R.,** Russie blanche, Biélorussie *f*. **2.** *s.* **R. leather, R. calf, r.,** cuir *m* de Russie.

Russian [ˈrʌʃən]. **1.** *s.* (*a*) Russe *mf*; **Little R.,** Petit(e) Russe; Ruthène *mf*; **White R.,** (i) Russe Blanc; Biélorusse *mf*; (ii) *Hist:* Russe tsariste; (*b*) *Ling:* russe *m*. **2.** *a.* russe; de Russie; **R. leather,** cuir *m* de Russie; *Cost: A:* **R. boots,** bottes *f* de cuir pour dames; *Z:* **R. wolfhound,** lévrier *m* russe.

Russianization [rʌʃənaiˈzeiʃ(ə)n], *s.* russification *f*.

Russianize [ˈrʌʃənaiz], *v.tr.* russifier.

Russianizing [ˈrʌʃənaiziŋ], *s.* russification *f*.

Russophil(e) [ˈrʌsouf(a)il], *a. & s.* russophile (*mf*).

Russophobe [ˈrʌsoufoub], *a. & s.* russophobe (*mf*).

russula [ˈrʌsjulə], *s. Fung:* russule *f*; **r. cyanoxantha,** russule cyanoxante, charbonnière; **r. fellea, geranium-scented r.,** russule amère; **greenish r.,** russule verdoyante.

rust[1] [rʌst], *s.* **1.** rouille *f*; **to cover sth. with r.,** (en)rouiller qch.; **to get covered with r.,** se couvrir de rouille; se rouiller; **to rub the r. off,** enlever la rouille; dérouiller (qch.); **r. preventive, r. preventer,** antirouille *m inv*; **r.-preventing,** antirouille; **r.-resistant, r.-free,** inoxydable; antirouille; **r.-(coloured), r.-red,** rouilleux; roux, *f.* rousse; roussâtre. **2.** (*a*) *Agr:* rouille; **black r.,** charbon *m* des céréales; nielle *f*; (*b*) *Ent:* **carrot r. fly,** psile *f*; *Arach:* **r. mite,** phytopte *m*.

rust[2]. **1.** *v.i.* se rouiller; s'oxyder; **the nut has rusted on to the screw, the screw has rusted into the nut,** l'écrou s'est rouillé avec la vis; (*of leak*) **to r. up,** s'obstruer par la rouille; *Lit:* **better to wear out than r. away,** mieux vaut se tuer de travail que de croupir dans l'oisiveté. **2.** *v.tr.* rouiller (le fer, etc.); **idleness rusts the mind,** l'oisiveté *f* rouille l'esprit.

rustic [ˈrʌstik]. **1.** *a.* rustique; champêtre; paysan; **r. manners, r. ways,** mœurs *f* rustiques, manières paysannes; paysannerie *f*; *Const:* **r. work,** ouvrage *m* rustique; **r. seat,** banc *m* rustique; *Pal:* **r. lettering,** écriture *f* rustique. **2.** *s.* (*a*) paysan, -anne; campagnard, -arde; (*b*) rustaud, -aude; rustre *m*.

rustically [ˈrʌstikəli], *adv.* rustiquement.

rusticate [ˈrʌstikeit]. **1.** *v.i.* se retirer à la campagne; habiter la campagne; **he's retired and is rusticating in Somerset,** il a pris sa retraite et il plante ses choux dans le Somerset. **2.** *v.tr.* (*a*) rendre rustique; (*b*) *Arch:* rustiquer (un mur, etc.); (*c*) *Sch:* renvoyer, exclure, temporairement (un(e) étudiant(e)).

rustication [rʌstiˈkeiʃ(ə)n], *s.* **1.** vie *f* à la campagne. **2.** *Arch:* ouvrage *m* rustique. **3.** *Sch:* renvoi *m* temporaire (d'un(e) étudiant(e)).

rusticity [rʌsˈtisiti], *s.* rusticité *f*.

rustily [ˈrʌstili], *adv.* **the door moved r. on its hinges,** la porte grinçait sur ses gonds rouillés.

rustiness [ˈrʌstinis], *s.* rouillure *f*; rouille *f*; **I'm ashamed of the r. of my French,** j'ai honte d'avoir oublié le français comme ça.

rusting [ˈrʌstiŋ], *s.* rouillement *m*, rouillage *m*; oxydation *f* (du fer).

rustle[1] [ˈrʌsl], *s.* bruissement *m*, frémissement *m*, friselis *m* (des feuilles); frou-frou *m* (de la soie, d'une robe); froissement *m* (de papiers).

rustle[2]. **1.** *v.i.* (*a*) (*of leaves, paper*) produire un bruissement; (*of leaves*) bruire, frémir; (*of garment*) faire frou-frou; froufrouter; **I heard a deer r. through the bracken,** j'ai entendu un cerf froisser les fougères; (*b*) *esp. NAm: F:* se dépêcher; s'y mettre énergiquement. **2.** *v.tr.* faire bruire, faire frémir (les feuilles, etc.); faire froufrouter (la soie); froisser (le papier). **3.** *v.tr.* (*a*) rassembler, ramener (le bétail); cueillir (du bois); (*b*) voler (du bétail, etc.); (*c*) **to r. up support,** rassembler des partisans; **she can always r. up a good meal,** elle peut toujours confectionner un bon repas.

rustler [ˈrʌslər], *s.* **1.** *F:* voleur, -euse (de bétail). **2.** *NAm:* homme expéditif; remueur *m* d'affaires.

rustless [ˈrʌstlis], *a.* **1.** sans rouille. **2.** inoxydable, inrouillable; antirouille *inv*.

rustling[1] [ˈrʌsliŋ], *a.* bruissant; (jupon, etc.) froufroutant; **r. leaves,** feuilles frémissantes; **r. silk,** soie chuchotante.

rustling[2], *s.* **1.** (*a*) = RUSTLE[1]; (*b*) *Med:* bruit *m* de frôlement. **2.** *F:* vol *m* de bétail.

rustproof[1] [ˈrʌstpruːf], *a.* antirouille *inv*.

rustproof[2], *v.tr.* protéger (qch.) contre la rouille.

rustre [ˈrʌstər], *s. Her:* ruste *f*, rustre *f*.

rustred [ˈrʌstəd], *a. Her:* rustré.

rusty[1] [ˈrʌsti], *a.* **1.** (*a*) rouillé; **r. knife,** couteau rouillé; **to get r.,** se rouiller; **at sixty your joints begin to get r.,** à soixante ans les articulations commencent à se rouiller, perdent de leur souplesse; **my French is getting r.,** mon français se rouille, est rouillé; (*b*) (*of voice*) enroué, rauque, éraillé. **2.** couleur de rouille; rouilleux; **r. black coat,** manteau *m* d'un noir rouilleux. **3.** *Agr:* (blé) rouillé.

rusty[2], *a. O:* (cheval) rétif, quinteux; *F:* (*of pers.*) **to turn r., to cut up r.,** se rebiffer; regimber, rechigner; **don't get r.,** ne vous fâchez pas.

rut[1] [rʌt], *s.* **1.** ornière *f*; *Fig:* **to get into a r.,** s'encroûter; s'enliser dans la routine; **to get out of the r.,** sortir de l'ornière, de la routine. **2.** *Mec.E:* grippure *f* (d'un palier, etc.).

rut[2], *v.* (rutted) **1.** *v.tr.* sillonner (un chemin) d'ornières. **2.** *v.i. Mec.E:* (*of bearing, etc.*) gripper.

rut[3], *s.* (*of stag, etc.*) rut *m*.

rut⁴, *v.i.* (**rutted**) (*of stag, etc.*) être en rut.
rutabaga [ru:tə'bɑ:gə], *s.* rutabaga *m.*
Rutaceae [ru'teisii:], *s.pl. Bot:* rutacées *f.*
rutaceous [ru'teiʃəs], *a. Bot:* rutacé.
ruth [ru:θ], *s. A:* pitié *f*; compassion *f.*
Ruthene [ru(:)'θi:n], *a. & s.* = RUTHENIAN 1.
Ruthenia [ru:'θi:niə], *Pr.n. Hist:* Ruthénie *f.*
Ruthenian [ru:'θi:niən]. **1.** *Hist:* (*a*) *a.* ruthène; (*b*) *s.* Ruthène *mf.* **2.** *s. Ling: A:* ruthène *m.*
ruthenic [ru(:)'θi:nik], *a. Ch:* ruthénique.
ruthenium [ru(:)'θi:niəm], *s. Ch:* ruthénium *m.*
rutherford ['rʌðəfəd], *s. Atom.Ph:* rutherford *m.*
rutherfordine, rutherfordite [rʌðə'fɔ:dain, -dait], *s. Miner:* rutherfordite *f.*
ruthless ['ru:θlis], *a.* impitoyable; sans pitié, sans merci; (*of act, etc.*) brutal, -aux; **to be r. in claiming one's money,** être sans pitié à réclamer son argent.
ruthlessly ['ru:θlisli], *adv.* impitoyablement; sans pitié, sans merci; **to be r. plain-spoken,** dire la vérité brutale.
ruthlessness ['ru:θlisnis], *s.* nature *f* impitoyable; cruauté *f.*
rutilant ['ru:tilənt], *a. Lit:* rutilant.
rutilated ['ru:tileitid], *a. Miner:* **r. quartz,** flèches *fpl* d'amour.
rutile ['ru:til], *s. Miner:* rutile *m*; schorl *m* rouge; flèches *fpl* d'amour.
rutilism ['ru:tilizm], *s. Physiol:* rutilisme *m.*
rutin ['ru:tin], *s. Bio-Ch:* rutine *f,* rut(in)oside *m.*
rutting ['rʌtiŋ], *s.* (*of stag, etc.*) rut *m*; **r. season,** saison *f* du rut.
rutty ['rʌti], *a.* **1.** (chemin) coupé d'ornières. **2.** *Mec.E:* (palier) strié de grippures.
rye [rai], *s.* **1.** (*a*) seigle *m*; **to harvest the r.,** faire les seigles; **r. bread,** pain *m* de seigle; (*b*) **r. grass,** ivraie *f* vivace; fausse ivraie; faux seigle; ray-grass *m*; **perennial r. grass,** ray-grass anglais. **2.** *NAm:* whisky *m* (à base de seigle); **mine's a r.!** je prendrai un whisky.
ryepeck ['raipek], *s.* pieu *m* d'amarrage (dans une rivière); perche *f,* gaffe *f* (d'amarrage).
ryot ['raiət], *s.* (*in India*) ryot *m,* paysan *m.*

S

S, s [es], *s.* **1.** (la lettre) S, s *m*; esse *f*; *Tp:* **S for Sammy,** S comme Suzanne; *Typ:* **long s,** s allongé; *Hist:* **collar of s's,** emblème *m* de la maison de Lancastre. **2.** (courbe *f* en) S; esse; **S(-shaped) hook,** crochet en S; S de suspension; **S wrench,** clef cintrée en S; **S curve,** courbure double; *Aut:* **S bend,** virage *m* en S; *Const: etc:* **S-shaped wall anchor,** fer *m* en S. **3.** *A:* (*abbr. for Lt.* **solidus**) shilling *m.*

's [s, z]. **1.** *A:* (*euphemistic abbr. of* **God's** *in oaths*) **'sblood!** sangdieul **'sdeathl** mordieu! morbleu! **2.** (*shortened form of*) (*a*) **is: it's raining,** il pleut; **he's coming,** il vient; **what's the matter? whatever's the matter?** qu'est-ce qu'il y a (donc)? (*b*) **has: he's found a knife,** il a trouvé un couteau; **what's he doing?** qu'est-ce qu'il fait? (*c*) **us: let's go!** partons! **shall we go out?—come on, let's!** est-ce qu'on sort?—c'est une bonne idée! pourquoi pas? **let's see!** (i) montrez-nous! (ii) *F:* laissez-moi voir! (iii) voyons! **3.** (*genitive case*) (*for pl. nouns and some polysyllabic sing. nouns ending in s,* **s'**) (*a*) (*possessive*) **the pupil's books,** les livres de l'élève; **the pupils' books,** les livres des élèves; **the King of England's daughter,** la fille du roi d'Angleterre; **my father-in-law's house,** la maison de mon beau-père; **my friend's brother's wife,** la femme du frère de mon ami; **a friend of my brother's,** un ami de mon frère; **at my aunt's,** chez ma tante; **when I left the doctor's,** en partant de chez le docteur; **at the grocer's,** chez l'épicier; **the grocer's will be shut,** l'épicerie sera fermée; **a baker's and post office combined,** une boulangerie bureau de poste; **St. Paul's (cathedral, school),** la cathédrale, le collège, de Saint Paul; **we go to St Joseph's,** nous allons (à la messe) à l'église Saint-Joseph; **St Thomas's Street,** la rue Saint Thomas; **Achilles' heel,** le talon d'Achille; **Charles's Wain,** le Grand Chariot, la Grande Ourse; **for goodness' sake,** pour l'amour de Dieu; (*b*) (*objective*) **Caesar's accusers,** les accusateurs de César; (*c*) (*classifying*) **to sit in the chairman's seat,** occuper le fauteuil présidentiel; **the artist's temperament,** un tempérament d'artiste; **we found a lark's nest,** nous avons trouvé un nid d'alouette; **a fireman's uniform,** un uniforme de (sapeur) pompier; **ladies' and children's wear,** articles *m* pour dames et enfants; (*d*) (*genitive of nouns of measure*) **give me a pound's worth,** donnez-m'en pour une livre; **an hour's delay,** une heure de retard; **in an hour's time,** dans une heure; **in a minute or so's time,** au bout d'une ou deux minutes; **a moment's hesitation,** un moment d'hésitation. **4. the Thomas's,** les Thomas, la famille Thomas; **a series of o's,** une série d'o; **to mind one's P's and Q's,** se surveiller; faire bien attention.

Saar [sɑːr], *Pr.n. Geog:* **the S.,** la Sarre; **in the S.,** en Sarre; **the S. Basin,** le bassin de la Sarre; **the industries of the S.,** les industries sarroises.

Saarburg ['sɑːbəːg], *Pr.n. Geog:* Sarrebourg.

Saarlander ['sɑːlændər], *s. Geog:* Sarrois, -oise.

sabadilla [sæbə'dilə], *s. Bot:* sabadille *f,* céradille *f,* cébadille *f.*

Sabaean [sæ'biən]. **1.** *Hist:* (*a*) *a.* sabéen; (*b*) *s.* Sabéen, -éenne. **2.** *Ling:* sabéen *m.*

Sabaism ['seibeiizm], *s. Rel.H:* sabéisme *m,* sabaïsme *m.*

Sabaoth ['sæbeiɔθ], *s. B:* Sabaoth; **Lord (God) of S.,** Jehovah Sabaoth; le Seigneur des armées.

Sabbatarian [sæbə'tɛəriən], *s.* **1.** observateur, -trice (i) du sabbat, (ii) du dimanche. **2.** *Rel.H:* sabbataire *mf.*

Sabbatarianism [sæbə'tɛəriənizm], *s. Rel:* sabbatisme *m.*

sabbath ['sæbəθ], *s.* **1.** (*a*) **s. (day),** (jour du) sabbat *m* (des Juifs); **s. school,** école *f* du samedi pour l'instruction religieuse; **s. day's journey,** (i) chemin *m* du sabbat; (ii) *Fig:* voyage facile; *F:* **it's a s. day's journey from here to the station,** il y a un bon bout de chemin d'ici à la gare; (*b*) dimanche *m* (des chrétiens); **s. day observance,** observation *f* du dimanche; (*c*) *B:* **remember the s. day to keep it holy,** souviens-toi du sabbat pour le sanctifier; **to keep, break, the s.,** observer, violer, (i) le sabbat, (ii) le dimanche. **2. witches' s.,** sabbat.

sabbatia [sæ'beiʃiə], *s. Bot:* sabbatia *m.*

sabbatical [sə'bætikl], *a. Jew.Rel:* sabbatique; **s. year,** année *f* sabbatique; *Sch: etc:* **s. year, term,** *s.* **sabbatical,** année, trimestre *m,* de congé (accordé(e) à un professeur, etc., pour faire des recherches, etc.).

sabbatine ['sæbətain], *a. Rel.H:* **s. (bull),** bulle sabbatine.

sabbatize ['sæbətaiz]. **1.** *v.i.* sabbatiser; observer (i) le sabbat, (ii) le dimanche. **2.** *v.tr.* **to s. the Lord's Day,** observer le jour du Seigneur.

sabbaton ['sæbətɔn], *s. A.Arm:* (sorte de) soleret *m.*

Sabean [sæ'biːən], *a. & s.* = SABAEAN.

sabella [sæ'belə], *s. Ann:* sabelle *f.*

sabellaria [sæbe'lɛəriə], *s. Ann:* sabellaria *m.*

Sabellariidae [sæbelə'raiidiː], *s.pl. Ann:* sabellariens *m.*

Sabellian [sæ'beliən]. **1.** *Rom.Hist:* (*a*) *a.* sabellien, sabellique; (*b*) *s.* Sabellien, -ienne. **2.** *Rel.H:* *a. & s.* sabellien, -ienne.

sabellid [sæ'belid], *s. Ann:* sabellien *m.*

Sabellidae [sæ'belidiː], *s.pl. Ann:* sabelliens *m.*

sabia ['seibiə], *s. Bot:* sabia *m.*

sabicu ['sæbikuː], *s. Bot:* sabicu *m.*

Sabina [sæ'bainə, -biːmə], *Pr.n.f.* Sabine.

Sabine ['sæbain]. *A.Hist:* (*a*) *a.* sabin; (*b*) *s.* Sabin, -ine; **the rape of the Sabines,** l'enlèvement *m* des Sabines.

sabir [sæ'biər], *s. Ling:* sabir *m.*

sable[1] ['seibl], *s.* **1.** *Z:* (martre *f*) zibeline *f.* **2. s. (fur),** zibeline; **s. coat,** manteau *m* de zibeline. **3.** *Art:* **s. (brush),** pinceau *m* en poil de martre.

sable[2]. **1.** *Her:* (*a*) *s.* sable *m;* (*b*) *a.* (écusson, etc.) de sable. **2.** *a. & s.* (*a*) *A: & Lit:* noir (*m*); (vêtements *m*) de deuil; **all in (rueful) sables clad,** tout de noir vêtu; (*b*) *a.* *Z:* **s. antelope,** égocère *m,* hippotrague *m,* antilope noire.

sabot ['sæbou], *s.* **1.** *Cost:* sabot *m.* **2.** sabot (de pieu, de projectile, etc.).

sabotage[1] ['sæbətɑːʒ], *s.* sabotage *m.*

sabotage[2], *v.tr.* saboter.

saboteur [sæbə'təːr], *s.* saboteur, -euse.

sabre ['seibər], *s.* **1.** *Mil:* sabre *m;* **s. cut,** (i) coup *m* de sabre; (ii) (*scar*) balafre *f;* **to rattle one's s.,** traîner, faire sonner, son sabre; *A:* **s. rattling,** rodomontades *fpl;* menaces *fpl* de guerre. **2.** *Glassm:* sabre.

sabrebill ['seibəbil], *s. Orn:* xiphorhynche *m.*

sabretache ['seibətæʃ], *s. A.Mil:* sabretache *f.*

sabretooth ['seibətuːθ], *s. Paleont:* (*also* **sabre-toothed lion, tiger**) machérode *m.*

sabrewing ['seibəwiŋ], *s. Orn:* campyloptère *m.*

sabulous ['sæbjuləs], *a.* **1.** sablonneux. **2.** *Med:* (*of urine, etc.*) graveleux.

saburra [sæ'bʌrə], *s. A.Med:* saburre *f.*

saburral [sæ'bʌrəl], *a. A.Med:* saburral, -aux.

sac [sæk], *s. Nat.Hist:* sac *m;* **embryo s.,** sac embryonnaire; **yolk s.,** membrane vitelline; *Moll:* **ink s.,** poche *f* du noir; *Orn:* **air s.,** sac aérien.

saccate ['sækeit], *a. Nat.Hist:* en forme de poche, de sac: sacciforme.

saccharase ['sækəreis], *s. Physiol:* saccharase *f.*

saccharate ['sækəreit], *s. Ch:* saccharate *m.*

saccharic [sə'kærik], *a. Ch:* (acide *m*) saccharique.

saccharide ['sækəraid], *s. Ch:* saccharide *m.*

sacchariferous [sækə'rifərəs], *a.* (plante, etc.) sacchariféré.

saccharifiable ['sækərifaiəbl], *a. Ch:* saccharifiable.

saccharification [sækərifi'keiʃ(ə)n], *s. Ch:* saccharification *f;* **s. of starch,** amylolyse *f.*

saccharify [sə'kærifai], *v.tr. Ch:* saccharifier.

saccharifying [sə'kærifaiiŋ], *a.* saccharifiant.

saccharimeter [sækə'rimitər], *s. Ch: Ind:* saccharimètre *m.*

saccharimetry [sækə'rimitri], *s. Ch:* saccharimétrie *f.*

saccharin ['sækərin], *s. Ch: etc:* saccharine *f.*

saccharine ['sækəriːn], *a. Ch:* saccharin; *F: O:* (sourire, etc.) sucré.

saccharization [sækərai'zeiʃ(ə)n], *s.* saccharification *f;* **s. of starch,** amylolyse *f.*

saccharoid ['sækərɔid], *a. Geol: etc:* saccharoïde.

saccharometer [sækə'rɔmitər], *s.* sacchomètre *m;* *Brew:* saccharimètre *m,* glucomètre; pèse-moût *m inv;* *Med:* diabétomètre *m.*

Saccharomyces [sækərou'maisiːz], *s. Fung:* saccharomyces *m,* saccharomycète *m.*

saccharomycete [sækərou'maisiːt], *s. Fung:* saccharomycète *m.*

saccharose ['sækərous], *s. Ch:* saccharose *m or f.*

sacciform ['sæksifɔːm], *a. Bot: etc:* sacciforme; en forme de poche, de sac.

saccophore ['sækoufɔːr], *s. Z:* saccophore *m;* rat *m* à bourse.

saccorhiza [sækou'raizə], *s. Algae:* laminaire bulbeuse.

saccular ['sækjulər], *a.* sacciforme.

saccule ['sækjuːl], *s. Anat:* saccule *m.*

sacculina [sækju'lainə], *s. Crust:* sacculine *f.*

sacerdotal [sæsə'dout(ə)l], *a.* sacerdotal, -aux.

sacerdotalism [sæsə'doutəlizm], *s.* sacerdotalisme *m.*

sachem ['seitʃəm], *s.* **1.** sachem *m.* **2.** *U.S: F:* chef *m* (d'un parti politique).

sachet ['sæʃei], *s.* sachet *m.*

sack[1] [sæk], *s.* **1.** (*a*) (grand) sac; **s. of coal, of flour,** sac de charbon, de farine; **s. of oats,** poche *f* d'avoine; **s. hoist, lift,** monte-sac *m inv;* **s. and bag trade,** sacherie *f;* *Sp:* **s. race,** course *f* en sacs; (*b*) *F:* **to hit the s.,** se coucher, se pieuter; (*c*) *Cost:* (i) *O:* manteau non ajusté, à lignes verticales; paletot *m,* pardessus *m,* sac; (ii) *A:* traîne *f* (retombant des épaules) d'une robe de cérémonie; (*d*) *Ent:* **s. moth,** mimallonide *m;* **s. bearer,** larve *f* de mimallonide. **2.** *F:* **to give s.o. the s.,** congédier, sa(c)quer, balancer, qn; mettre, flanquer, qn à la porte; **to get the s.,** être congédié, sa(c)qué.

sack[2], *v.tr.* **1.** ensacher, mettre en sac (du charbon, etc.).

2. *F:* congédier, sa(c)quer, qn; mettre, flanquer, qn à la porte.

sack[3], *s. Mil: etc:* sac *m*, pillage *m* (d'une ville, etc.).

sack[4], *v.tr. Mil: etc:* saccager, piller, mettre à sac, au pillage (une ville, etc.).

sack[5], *s. A:* **(Canary) s.,** vin *m* des Canaries; **sherry s.,** vin de Xérès.

sackbut ['sækbʌt], *s. Mus: A:* **1.** saquebute *f.* **2.** *Gr.Ant:* sambuque *f.*

sackcloth ['sækklɔθ], *s.* **1.** *Tex:* toile *f* à sacs; grosse toile; serpillière *f*; toile d'emballage. **2.** *B: etc:* sac *m*; bure *f* (au sens figuré); **s. and ashes,** le sac et la cendre; **to do penance in s. and ashes,** faire pénitence avec le sac et la cendre, sous le sac et la cendre.

sackful ['sækful], *s.* sachée *f*, plein sac (de farine, etc.); **whole sackfuls of money,** des sacs tout pleins d'argent.

sacking[1] ['sækiŋ], *s.* **1.** mise *f* en sac (du charbon, etc.). **2.** *F:* congédiement *m* (d'un employé). **3.** = SACKCLOTH 1.

sacking[2], *s. Mil: etc:* saccage *m*, (mise *f* à) sac *m* (d'une ville, etc.).

sacral[1] ['seikrəl, 'sæk-], *a. Anat:* sacré; du sacrum.

sacral[2], *a.* rituel; sacral, -als.

sacralization [seikrəlai'zeiʃ(ə)n, sæk-], *s. Surg:* sacralisation *f.*

sacralize ['seikrəlaiz, -'sæk-], *v.tr. Surg:* sacraliser.

sacrament ['sækrəmənt], *s.* **1.** *Ecc:* sacrement *m*; **the (Most) Holy S., the Blessed S., the S. of the altar,** le saint Sacrement (de l'autel); le saint sacrifice; le Très Saint Sacrement; **the s. of baptism,** le sacrement du baptême; **to receive, partake of, the s.,** s'approcher des sacrements; communier; *F:* recevoir le bon Dieu; **to give the last sacraments to a dying person,** administrer les derniers sacrements à un mourant. **2.** *A:* serment *m*; **to take the s. to do sth.,** faire vœu solennel d'accomplir qch.

sacramental [sækrə'mentəl]. **1.** *a.* (*a*) sacramentel; *F:* **to pronounce the s. words,** prononcer les paroles sacramentelles; (*b*) **s. obligation,** obligation *f* sous serment; vœu *m*. **2.** *s.pl. Ecc:* **the sacramentals,** les sacramentaux *m.*

sacramentally [sækrə'mentəli], *adv.* sacramentellement, sacramentalement.

sacramentarian [sækrəmen'tɛəriən], *s. Rel.H:* sacramentaire *m* (calviniste ou zwinglien).

sacramentary [sækrə'mentəri], *s.* **1.** *Ecc: A:* (*book*) sacramentaire *m.* **2.** *Rel.H:* = SACRAMENTARIAN.

sacrarium, *pl.* **-ia** [sæ'krɛəriəm, -iə], *s.* **1.** *Rom.Ant:* sacrarium *m.* **2.** *Ecc:* (*a*) sanctuaire *m* (d'une église); (*b*) *R.C.Ch:* piscine *f.*

sacred ['seikrid], *a.* **1.** (*a*) sacré; **s. place,** lieu sacré; *Rom.Hist:* **the S. Way,** la Voie sacrée; *Z:* **s. baboon,** hamadryas *m*, tartarin *m*; *Ich:* **s. fish,** oxyrhynque *m*; mormyre *m* à trompe; (*b*) **tree, animal, s. to . . .,** arbre, animal, consacré à . . ., dédié à . . .; **s. to the memory of . . .,** consacré à la mémoire de . . . . **2.** (*a*) *Ecc:* sacré, saint; **s. history,** l'Histoire sainte; **s. books,** (i) livres *m* d'Église; (ii) livres saints; **s. and profane,** sacré et profane; **Convent of the S. Heart,** couvent *m* du Sacré-Cœur; **the s. orders,** les ordres majeurs; (*b*) **s. music, s. procession,** musique religieuse, procession religieuse. **3.** (*of promise, right, etc.*) sacré, inviolable; **s. duty,** devoir sacré; **s. interests,** intérêts *m* intangibles; **His S. Majesty,** la personne sacrée du Souverain; **to hold a promise s.,** considérer une promesse comme sacrée; **to these urchins nothing is s.,** pour ces gamins rien n'est sacré; **nothing was s. to him,** il ne respectait rien; **nothing was s. from him,** rien n'était à l'abri de ses outrages.

sacredly ['seikridli], *adv.* religieusement; (*a*) pieusement; (*b*) inviolablement.

sacredness ['seikridnis], *s.* **1.** caractère sacré (d'un lieu, etc.). **2.** inviolabilité *f* (d'un serment, etc.).

sacrifice[1] ['sækrifais], *s.* **1.** (*a*) sacrifice *m*, immolation *f* (d'une victime); **to offer (up) sth. as a s.,** offrir qch. en sacrifice **(to,** à); **to win a battle at a great s. of life,** remporter la victoire au prix de grands sacrifices; (*b*) victime; offrande *f.* **2.** *Theol:* sacrifice (du Christ); **the S. of the Mass, the eucharistic S.,** le saint sacrifice, le sacrifice de la messe; **to offer a s. of praise (and thanksgiving) to God,** faire, offrir, à Dieu un sacrifice de louanges. **3.** (*a*) sacrifice, abnégation *f* (de qch.); renoncement *m* (à qch.); **to make sacrifices to obtain one's end,** faire de grands sacrifices pour arriver à ses fins; **his parents made every s. to educate him,** ses parents ont fait de grands sacrifices, *F:* se sont saignés aux quatre veines, pour lui faire faire ses études; **he succeeded at the s. of his health,** il a réussi en sacrifiant sa santé; **the last s.,** le sacrifice de sa vie; (*b*) *Com:* mévente *f*; vente *f* à perte; **to sell sth. at a s.,** sacrifier, mévendre, qch.; vendre qch. à perte, à toute offre acceptable; **s. prices,** prix *m* au-dessous des prix coûtants.

sacrifice[2], *v.tr.* **1.** sacrifier, immoler, offrir en sacrifice. (une victime); *v.i.* **to s. to idols,** sacrifier aux idoles; offrir des sacrifices aux idoles. **2.** (*a*) sacrifier, renoncer à (qch.); faire abnégation de (ses intérêts, etc.); **to s. oneself,** se sacrifier **(for,** pour); **to s. everything in the interests of one's family,** immoler tout aux intérêts de sa famille; **to s. one's friends to one's ambition,** sacrifier ses amis à son ambition; (*b*) *Com:* sacrifier, mévendre, vendre à perte (des marchandises).

sacrificer ['sækrifaisər], *s.* sacrificateur, -trice; immolateur *m.*

sacrificial [sækri'fiʃ(ə)l], *a.* **1.** sacrificatoire. **2.** *Com:* (vente *f*) à perte; (prix *m*) au-dessous des prix coûtants.

sacrificing ['sækrifaisiŋ]. **1.** *a.* (prêtre) sacrificateur. **2.** *s.* sacrifice *m.*

sacrilege ['sækrilidʒ], *s.* sacrilège *m*; **it would be s. to build the motorway through here,** ce serait un sacrilège que de faire passer l'autoroute par ici.

sacrilegious [sækri'lidʒəs], *a.* sacrilège; **s. person,** sacrilège *mf.*

sacrilegiously [sækri'lidʒəsli], *adv.* d'une manière sacrilège.

sacring ['seikriŋ], *s. Ecc: A:* **1.** consécration *f* (du pain et du vin); **s. bell,** sonnette *f* de l'élévation. **2.** sacre *m* (d'un roi, d'un évêque).

sacrist ['seikrist], **sacristan** ['sækristən], *s. Ecc:* sacristain *m.*

sacristine ['sækristi:n], *s.f. Ecc:* sacristine.

sacristy ['sækristi], *s. Ecc:* sacristie *f.*

sacro- ['seikrou, 'sækrou], *comb.fm. Anat:* sacro-.

sacrococcygeal [seikroukɔk'sidʒiəl], *a. Anat:* sacro-coccygien.

sacrofemoral [seikrou'femərəl], *a. Anat:* sacro-fémoral.

sacroiliac [seikrou'iliæk], *a.* & *s.* (articulation) sacro-iliaque (*f*).

sacrolumbal ['seikrou'lʌmb(ə)l], *a. Anat:* sacro-lombaire.

sacrolumbalis [seikroulʌm'bælis], *s. Anat:* (muscle) sacro-lombaire (*m*).

sacrosanct ['sækrousæŋkt], *a.* (*usu. iron.*) sacro-saint, *pl.* sacro-saint(e)s; intangible.

sacrosciatic [seikrousai'ætik], *a. Anat:* **s. ligament,** (ligament) sacro-sciatique (*m*).

sacrospinal [seikrou'spainəl], *a. Anat:* sacro-épineux.

sacrospinalis [seikrouspai'nælis], *s. Anat:* muscle sacro-épineux.

sacrovertebral [seikrou'və:tibrəl], *a. Anat:* **s. joint,** (articulation) sacro-vertébrale (*f*).

sacrum ['seikrəm, 'sæk-], *s. Anat:* sacrum *m.*

sad [sæd], *a.* **(sadder, saddest) 1.** (*a*) triste, malheureux; **to become s.,** s'assombrir, s'attrister; **to look s.,** avoir l'air triste, malheureux, affligé, mélancolique; **to make s.o. s.,** attrister, chagriner, affliger, qn; **we were very s. to hear of our friend's death,** nous étions désolés d'apprendre la mort de notre ami; **to be s. at heart,** avoir le cœur gros, serré; *O:* **in s. earnest,** bien sérieusement; **a sadder and a wiser man,** un homme (i) instruit par le malheur, (ii) désillusionné; (*b*) (*of news, etc.*) affligeant, désolant, fâcheux; (*of loss, etc.*) cruel; (*of place, etc.*) morne, lugubre; **a s. state of poverty,** une misère à faire pitié; **he came to a s. end,** il a eu, fait, une triste fin. **2.** déplorable; *O:* **a s. mistake,** une erreur déplorable, une fâcheuse erreur; **to make s. work of . . .,** s'acquitter peu brillamment de . . . . **3.** *Cu:* (*of cake, etc.*) pâteux, lourd, mal levé.

sadden ['sæd(ə)n]. **1.** (*a*) *v.tr.* attrister, chagriner, affliger (qn); (*b*) *v.i.* s'affliger, s'attrister. **2.** *v.tr. Dy:* ternir (la couleur).

saddening ['sæd(ə)niŋ], *a.* attristant, affligeant.

saddle[1] ['sædl], *s.* **1.** (*a*) selle *f* (de cheval); sellette *f* (de cheval de trait); **hunting s.,** selle anglaise; *Mil:* **service s.,** selle d'armes; *A:* **hussar s., light cavalry s.,** selle de cavalerie légère; **dragoon s., heavy cavalry s.,** selle allemande; **s. horse,** cheval *m* de selle; monture *f*; **cross s.,** selle d'homme; **side s.,** selle de dame (qui monte en amazone); **to ride side s.,** monter en amazone; **s. bow,** pontet *m*, arçon *m*; **s. sore,** plaie causée par la selle; **to be s. sore,** avoir les fesses meurtries par la selle; *Vet:* **s. gall,** écorchure *f* sous la selle; foulure *f*; mal *m* de rognon; **s. room,** sellerie *f*; **s.-shaped,** ensellé; en forme de selle; **to rise in the s.,** (i) se dresser sur ses étriers; (ii) faire du trot enlevé; **to leap into the s.,** sauter en selle; **in the s.,** (i) en selle, monté; (ii) en plein exercice (de ses fonctions); en selle; **to get into the s. again,** (i) (*after a fall*) remonter; se remettre en selle; (ii) (*after illness, etc.*) reprendre son travail, se remettre en selle; (*b*) selle (de bicyclette). **2.** *Geog:* col *m* (de montagne). **3.** *Cu:* selle (de mouton, de chevreuil); râble *m* (de lièvre). **4.** *Tchn:* (*a*) gâche *f*; (*b*) support *m* (d'un cric, etc.); sabot *m*, balancier *m* (d'une poutre verticale); *I.C.E:* selle, assiette *f* (de cylindre); *Mec.E:* sellette (de machine à aléser); chariot *m*, traînard *m* (d'un tour); **to block the s.,** verrouiller le chariot sur la coulisse; **s. boiler,** chaudière horizontale; (*c*) *Av:* **nose gear s.,** support de train avant. **5.** (*a*) *Z:* manteau *m*, mantelure *f* (de chien); (*b*) **s. hackle, s. feather,** plume *f* de dos (d'un coq domestique); (*c*) *Moll:* **s. oyster, s. shell,** anomie *f.*

saddle[2], *v.tr.* (*a*) seller (un cheval); embâter (une bête de somme); (*b*) *F:* **to s. s.o. with sth.,** charger, encombrer, qn de qch.; mettre qch. sur le dos de qn; **I'm fed up with being saddled with other people's troubles, mistakes,** j'en ai assez d'endosser les soucis des autres, de me faire imputer les bévues des autres; **she's saddled with five children,** elle a cinq enfants sur les bras, sur le dos.

saddleback ['sædlbæk], *s.* (*a*) *Arch:* (toit *m* en) bâtière *f*; toit en dos d'âne; (*b*) (*of hill*) ensellement *m*; (*c*) *Geol:* pli anticlinal; (*d*) *Orn:* (i) corneille mantelée, cendrée; religieuse *f*; jacobine *f*; (ii) *N.Z:* créadion *m*; (*e*) cochon noir avec une ceinture blanche; (*f*) mâle adulte du phoque stellé.

saddlebacked ['sædlbækt], *a.* (*a*) *Arch:* (toit) en bâtière, en dos d'âne; **s. coping,** bahut *m* (d'un parapet); (*b*) (colline, etc.) en dos d'âne; (*c*) (cheval) ensellé; (*d*) **s. crow,** corneille mantelée, cendrée; **s. gull,** mouette (i) marine, (ii) brune.

saddlebag ['sædlbæg], *s.* **1.** *Equit: Cy: etc:* sacoche *f* (de selle). **2.** *Furn: A:* moquette *f.*

saddlebar ['sædlba:r], *s.* **1.** *Harn:* bande *f* d'arçon. **2.** *Cy:* tige *f* de selle. **3.** barlotière *f* (de vitrail).

saddlebill ['sædlbil], *s. Orn:* jabiru *m* d'Afrique.

saddlecloth ['sædlklɔθ], *s.* housse *f* de cheval; couverture *f*, tapis *m*, de selle.

saddler ['sædlər], *s.* **1.** sellier *m*; bourrelier *m.* **2.** *U.S:* cheval *m* de selle.

saddlery ['sædləri], *s.* **1.** (*trade*) sellerie *f*, bourrellerie *f.* **2.** (*room*) sellerie. **3.** sellerie, harnachement *m* de selle.

saddletree ['sædltri:], *s.* **1.** *Harn:* bois *m* de selle. **2.** *Bot: U.S:* tulipier *m.*

saddling ['sædliŋ], *s.* sellage *m* (d'un cheval); embâtage *m* (d'une bête de somme).

Sadducean [sædju'si:ən], *a.* saducéen.

Sadducee ['sædjusi:], *s.* Saducéen, -éenne.

Sadduceeism ['sædjusiizm], *s.* saducéisme *m.*

sadiron ['sædaiən], *s. Dom.Ec: O:* fer *m* à repasser.

sadism ['seidizm], *s.* sadisme *m.*

sadist ['seidist], *s.* sadique *mf.*

sadistic [sə'distik], *a.* sadique.

sadistically [sə'distik(ə)li], *adv.* avec sadisme.

sadly ['sædli], *adv.* **1.** tristement; **to look s. at sth.,** regarder qch. tristement, d'un air triste. **2.** déplorablement; **he's s. lacking in intelligence,** il manque vraiment d'intelligence. **3.** très; beaucoup; **you're s. mistaken,** vous vous trompez étrangement.

sadness ['sædnis], *s.* tristesse *f*, mélancolie *f*; *Bot:* **tree of s.,** arbre *m* triste.

sadomasochism [seidou'mæsəkizm], *s. Psy:* sadomasochisme *m.*

sadomasochist [seidou'mæsəkist], *s. Psy:* sadomasochiste *mf.*

sadomasochistic [seidoumæsə'kistik], *a. Psy:* sadomasochiste.

saeter ['seitər], *s.* pâturage *m* d'été (en Norvège).

safari[1] [sə'fa:ri], *s.* safari *m*; **on s.,** en safari; **s. park,** réserve *f* d'animaux sauvages.

safari[2], *v.i.* aller en safari.

safe [seif], *s.* **1.** coffre-fort *m*, *pl.* coffres-forts; *Bank:* **night, deposit, s.,** coffret *m* de nuit; *Nau:* **the money s.,** la caisse du bord; **s. deposit,** dépôt *m* en coffre-fort; **s.-deposit company,** service *m* de coffres-forts. **2.** *Dom.Ec:* **(meat) s.,** garde-manger *m inv.* **3.** *Sm.a.* **rifle (set) at s.,** carabine *f* au cran de sûreté. **4.** *U.S:* condom *m.*

safe[2], *a.* **1.** (*a*) en sûreté, à l'abri; **s. from sth.,** à l'abri de, en sûreté contre, qch.; **now we can feel s.,** nous voilà à l'abri, hors de danger; **at last we are s.,** enfin nous voilà saufs, nous voilà sauvés; **is it s. for David to play on the beach alone?** est-ce qu'on peut laisser David jouer tout seul sur la plage? **the money is s. in your hands,** l'argent est en sûreté entre vos mains; **to be s. from recognition,** ne pas risquer d'être reconnu; (*b*) (sain et) sauf; **s. and sound, s. in life and limb,** sain et sauf; **s. arrival,** arrivée sain(s) et sauf(s); **we got s. into port,** nous sommes arrivés à bon port; **a s. passage,** une heureuse traversée; **to see s.o. s. home,** reconduire qn chez lui; **to come s. home again,** rentrer sans accident; revenir à bon port; **with a s. conscience,** en toute sûreté de conscience; la conscience tranquille; **his honour is s.,** son honneur est à couvert, est sauf. **2.** (*a*) (*of place, thg*) sans danger, sûr; **s. retreat,** asile assuré, sûr; **to put s.o., sth., in a s. place,** mettre qn, qch., en lieu sûr, en sûreté; **the matter is in s. hands,** l'affaire est en mains sûres; **s. road,** route sûre; **s. beach,** plage sûre; **s. beach for children,** plage où les enfants sont en sécurité, sont hors de danger; **s. roadstead,** rade sûre; **s. anchorage,** bon mouillage; mouillage sain; **at a s. distance,** à distance respectueuse; **district in which it is not s. to go out at night,** quartier qui n'est pas sûr la nuit; *Med:* **s. dose,** dose inoffensive; (*b*) (*of building, bridge, etc.*) solide; (*c*) **not s.,** dangereux; **these toys aren't s.,** ces jouets sont dangereux; **is it s. to leave him alone?** est-ce qu'il n'y a pas de danger à le laisser seul? *Tchn:* **s. load,** charge *f* admissible; charge de sécurité; *El:* **s. operating voltage,** tension *f* de régime; *Tls:* **s. edge of a file,** côté *m* lisse, champ *m* lisse, d'une lime; **s.-edge file,** lime à champs lisses; *Phot:* **s. light,** (i) éclairage *m* inactinique; (ii) écran *m* inactinique; (*d*) **to be on the s. side,** tenir le bon bout; être du bon côté; être à couvert; **in order to be on the s. side,** pour plus de sûreté, pour être plus sûr; **the safest course would be to . . .,** le plus sûr serait de . . .; **to play a s. game,** avoir un jeu sûr, serré; **s. investment,** placement sûr, de tout repos, de père de famille; **it's as s. as the Bank of England, as s. as houses,** c'est de l'or en barres; **horse which is a s. winner, which is s. to win,** cheval qui est sûr, certain, de gagner; **it is s. to say that . . .,** on peut dire à coup sûr que . . .. **3.** (*of critic, politician, etc.*) prudent, circonspect. **4.** *adv.* **to play (it) s.,** ne rien risquer; jouer serré.

safebreaker, safecracker ['seifbreikər, -'krækər], *s.* perceur *m* de coffres-forts.

safe-conduct [seif'kɔndʌkt], *s.* sauf-conduit *m*, *pl.* sauf-conduits.

safeguard¹ ['seifgɑ:d], *s.* **1.** *A:* (*a*) sauvegarde *f*, sauf-conduit *m*, *pl.* sauf-conduits; (*b*) (sauve)garde *f*, escorte *f*. **2.** sauvegarde, garantie *f* (**against,** contre); **to obtain safeguards,** s'entourer de garanties. **3.** *Rail:* chasse-pierres *m inv*, garde *f* (d'une locomotive).

safeguard², *v.tr.* sauvegarder, protéger (les intérêts, les droits, de qn); mettre (ses intérêts) à couvert; **to be safeguarded against sth.,** avoir des sauvegardes contre qch.; être à l'abri de qch.; **to s. an industry,** sauvegarder, protéger, une industrie.

safeguarder ['seifgɑ:dər], *s.* protecteur, -trice.

safeguarding ['seifgɑ:diŋ], *s.* sauvegarde *f*; protection *f*.

safe(-)keeping [seif'ki:piŋ], *s.* bonne garde; **to be in s.,** être sous bonne garde, en sûreté.

safely ['seifli], *adv.* **1.** sans accident, sans dommage; **to arrive s.,** arriver sain et sauf, sans accident; (*of ship, etc.*) arriver à bon port; **the parcel arrived s.,** le paquet est arrivé sans dommage; **to see s.o. s. home,** reconduire qn chez lui; **to come home s.,** rentrer sans encombre, sans accident; **to put sth. s. away,** mettre qch. en lieu sûr, en sûreté. **2.** sûrement, sans danger, sans risque; **money s. invested,** argent bien placé; **I can s. say that . . .,** je puis dire à coup sûr, sans crainte, sans contredit, que . . .

safeness ['seifnis], *s.* **1. a feeling of s.,** un sentiment de sécurité *f*, de sûreté *f*. **2.** solidité *f* (d'un pont). **3.** sûreté (d'une affaire, d'un placement, etc.).

safety ['seifti], *s.* sûreté *f*, sécurité *f* (de qch., de qn); salut *m* (de qn); **to endanger the s. of the workmen,** compromettre la sécurité des ouvriers; **to seek s. in flight,** chercher son salut dans la fuite; **for safety's sake,** pour plus de sûreté; **to climb up a tree for s.,** grimper dans un arbre pour se mettre en sûreté; **in a place of s.,** en lieu sûr; en lieu de sûreté; **to be in s.,** être à l'abri, hors de danger; **to travel in s.,** voyager en sûreté; **road s.,** prévention routière; **to swim to s.,** parvenir en lieu sûr (à la nage); **to be able to do sth. with s.,** pouvoir faire qch. en toute sécurité; **s. first!** prudence est mère de sûreté! la sécurité d'abord! soyez prudents! **s.-first policy,** politique de prudence; **to play for s.,** (i) jouer au plus sûr; (ii) louvoyer, tendre les voiles du côté où vient le vent; **public s.,** la sécurité publique; *Hist:* **Committee of Public S.,** Comité *m* de salut public; *Sm.a:* **to put one's rifle at s.,** mettre son fusil au cran de sûreté; **s. bolt,** arrêt *m* de sûreté; **s. device,** dispositif *m* de sécurité, de protection; (*of pitshaft cage*) parachute *m* (de mine); *Min:* **s. lamp,** lampe de sûreté; **s. measures,** mesures de sécurité; **s. vault,** chambre blindée (d'une banque, etc.); *Paperm:* **s. cheque paper,** papier de sûreté; **s. hook,** crochet de sûreté; mousqueton *m*; **s. lock,** serrure de sûreté; *Aut: etc:* serrure à condamnation; *Ind:* **s. factor,** facteur, coefficient, de sécurité; (*on lift*) **s. clutch, s. brake,** parachute; **s. guard,** appareil protecteur; **s. fuse,** (i) *Min:* mèche *f* de sûreté; cordon *m* Bickford; (ii) *El:* (plomb) fusible *m* de sûreté; coupe-circuit *m inv* de sécurité; *El:* **s. gap,** parafoudre *m*; *Arch:* **s. arch,** arc *m* de décharge; *For:* **s. belt,** essartement *m* de protection (contre le feu); *Cin: A:* **s. film,** film ininflammable; *Ch:* **s. bottle,** flacon de garde; **s. net,** filet *m*; **s. pin,** épingle *f* de nourrice, de sûreté; épingle double; *Artil:* **fuse s. pin,** goupille *f* de sûreté; *Aut: etc:* **s. glass,** verre *m* de sécurité; glace *f* sécurit (*R.t.m.*), **s. belt,** ceinture *f* de sécurité; **s. chain,** (i) (*of door*) chaîne *f* de sûreté, de porte; (ii) (*of bracelet, etc.*) chaînette *f* de sûreté; **s. valve,** (i) *Mch:* soupape *f* de sûreté; (ii) *Fig:* soupape; *Med:* **s. test,** essai *m* d'innocuité.

saffian ['sæfiən], *s. Leath:* (variété de) maroquin *m*.

safflorite ['sæflərait], *s. Miner:* safflorite *f*.

safflower ['sæflauər], *s. Bot:* carthame *m*; kentrophylle *m*; safran bâtard; *Dy: Pharm:* safranum *m*; **s. oil,** huile *f* de carthame.

saffron ['sæfrən], *s.* **1.** (*a*) *Cu: Pharm:* safran *m*; **to colour a cake with s.,** safraner un gâteau; **s. oil,** essence *f* de safran; *Ch: Dy:* **s. yellow,** safranine *f*; (*b*) *Bot:* **s. (crocus),** safran; **bastard s., s. thistle,** safran bâtard, carthame *m*; **wild s., meadow s.,** colchique *m* d'automne; safran des prés; *F:* tue-chien *m inv*; mort *f* aux chiens; veillotte *f*, veilleuse *f*; **s. plantation,** safranière *f*. **2.** *a.* & *s.* (*colour*) safran *inv*; jaune safran *inv*. **3.** *Orn:* **s. finch,** bouton-d'or *m* ordinaire.

saffronwood ['sæfrənwud], *s.* (bois *m* d')éléodendron *m*.

safranin(e) ['sæfrəni(:)n], *s. Ch: Dy:* safranine *f*.

safrol(e) ['sæfrɔl], *s. Ch:* safrol(e) *m*.

sag¹ [sæg], *s.* **1.** (*a*) affaissement *m*, fléchissement *m* (du sol, d'un toit, etc.); (*b*) *Com:* baisse *f* (des valeurs, etc.); (*c*) *Nau:* dérive *f* (vers le côté sous le vent). **2.** flèche *f*, ventre *m* (d'une ligne, d'un cordage, etc.); contre-arc *m*.

sag², *v.i.* (**sagged**) **1.** (*a*) (*of platform, roof, pavement, etc.*) s'affaisser, fléchir, donner, ployer, plier, arquer (sous un poids, etc.); **roof that sags,** toit *m* qui courbe; (*b*) (*of bridge, gate, door, etc.*) pencher d'un côté, s'incliner; gauchir; (*c*) (*of cheeks, breasts, hem of garment, etc.*) pendre; (*d*) (*of cable, etc.*) se relâcher, se détendre; (*of curtain, beam, rope, line, etc.*) fléchir au milieu; faire ventre; faire guirlande; faire flèche; cintrer; (*of trolley-line, etc.*) faire la chaînette (entre les supports); *Nau:* (*of ship*) avoir du contre-arc; (*of yard*) avoir de l'arc. **2.** *Com:* (*of prices*) baisser, fléchir, se détendre; **prices are sagging,** les prix fléchissent, mollissent. **3.** *Nau:* **to s. to leeward,** tomber sous le vent; être dépalé.

saga ['sɑ:gə], *s. Lit:* saga *f*; **s. (novel),** roman-cycle *m*, roman-fleuve *m*, *pl.* romans-cycles, -fleuves; roman *m* cyclique.

sagacious [sə'geiʃəs], *a.* (*of pers., mind*) sagace, avisé; perspicace; entendu; (*of dog, etc.*) intelligent, rusé; (*of action, remark*) plein de sagesse.

sagaciously [sə'geiʃəsli], *adv.* sagacement; avec sagacité; avec entendement.

sagaciousness, sagacity [sə'geiʃəsnis, -'gæsiti], *s.* sagacité *f*, perspicacité *f*; intelligence *f* (d'un animal); sagesse *f* (d'une remarque, etc.).

sagamore ['sægəmɔər], *s.* = SACHEM 1.

sagartia [sæ'gɑ:tiə], *s. Coel:* sagartia *f*, sagartie *f*.

sagathy ['sægəθi], *s. Tex: A:* sayette *f*.

sage¹ [seidʒ]. **1.** *a. Lit:* (*of pers., conduct, etc.*) sage, prudent, judicieux, discret, -ète. **2.** *s.* philosophe *m*, sage *m*; **the Seven Sages,** les sept Sages.

sage², *s.* **1.** *Bot: Cu:* sauge *f*; **bitter s., wood s.,** sauge amère; sauge des bois; **meadow s.,** sauge des prés; sauge sauvage; **s. cheese,** fromage persillé à la sauge; **s. tea,** infusion *f* de sauge; *a.* & *s.* **s. green,** vert cendré *inv*. **2.** (*a*) *Orn:* **s. thrasher,** moqueur *m* des armoises; **s. sparrow,** pinson *m* de Bell; **s. chippy,** pinson *m* de Brewer; **s. grouse, cock,** tétras *m* centrocerque; (*b*) *Z:* **s. hare, rabbit,** lièvre *m* des artémisiées.

sagebrush ['seidʒbrʌʃ], *s.* **1.** *Bot:* armoise *f* d'Amérique. **2.** (*a*) *Orn:* **s. chippy,** pinson *m* de Brewer; (*b*) *Z:* **s. rabbit,** lièvre *m* des artémisiées.

sagely ['seidʒli], *adv. Lit:* sagement, prudemment; judicieusement.

sageness ['seidʒnis], *s. Lit:* sagesse *f*, prudence *f*; discrétion *f*.

sagenite ['sædʒinait], *s. Miner:* sagénite *f*.

saggar ['sægər], *s.* **1.** *Cer:* casette *f*. **2.** *Metall:* caisse *f*, boîte *f*, de cémentation.

sagging¹ ['sægiŋ], *a.* **1.** (*a*) (*of roof, pavement, etc.*) affaissé, fléchi, ployé; (*b*) (*of gate, etc.*) incliné; penché d'un côté; déjeté; (*c*) (*of cheek, breast, hem of garment, etc.*) flasque, tombant, pendant; (*d*) (*of line, beam, etc.*) courbe, fléchi au milieu; (*of rope, etc.*) lâche; *Nau:* (*of ship*) contre-arqué; (*e*) *Com: Fin:* (*of prices, etc.*) qui se détendent; (*of market*) creux; en baisse. **2.** *Nau:* (*of ship*) dépalé, tombé sous le vent.

sagging², *s.* **1.** (*a*) affaissement *m*, fléchissement *m* (d'un toit, du sol, etc.); (*b*) inclinaison *f* (d'une porte, d'un pont, etc.); tombée *f* (d'une porte, d'une barrière); gauchissement *m* (d'un châssis, etc.); (*c*) flèche *f* (d'une ligne, d'un cordage, etc.); *Nau:* (i) contre-arc *m*; (ii) arc *m* (d'une vergue); **s. strain,** effort *m* du contre-arc; (*d*) *Com:* baisse *f*, fléchissement, affaissement (des prix); **s. of the market, s. of the franc,** défaillance *f* du marché, du franc. **2.** *Nau:* = SAG¹ 1 (*c*).

sagina [sæ'dʒainə], *s. Bot:* sagine *f*.

sagitta ['sædʒitə]. **1.** *Pr.n. Astr:* la Flèche. **2.** *s. Mth:* flèche (d'un arc de cercle).

sagittal ['sædʒit(ə)l], *a. Anat:* sagittal, -aux; **s. crest,** crête sagittale; **s. suture,** suture sagittale.

sagittaria [sædʒi'tɛəriə], *s. Bot:* sagittaire *f*.

Sagittariidae [sædʒitə'raiidi:], *s.pl. Orn:* sagittaridés *m*, les serpentaires *m*.

sagittarius [sædʒi'tɛəriəs]. **1.** *s. Rom.Ant: Her:* sagittaire *m*. **2.** *Pr.n. Astr:* le Sagittaire.

sagittary ['sædʒitəri], *s. Rom.Ant: Myth:* sagittaire *m*.

sagittate ['sædʒiteit], *a. Bot: etc:* sagitté; **s.-leaved,** sagittifolié.

sago ['seigou], *s.* (*a*) *Bot:* **s. palm,** sagoutier *m*; (*b*) *Cu:* sagou *m*; **s. pudding,** sagou au lait.

sagoin [sæ'gɔin], *s. Z:* sagouin *m*, ouistiti *m*.

sagum, *pl.* **-a** ['seigəm, -ə], *s. Rom.Ant:* saie *f*, sagum *m*.

Saguntine [sæ'gʌntain]. *Geog:* (*a*) *a.* sagontin; (*b*) *s.* Sagontin, -ine.

Sagunto [sæ'gʌntou]. *Pr.n. Geog:* Sagonte.

Saguntum [sæ'gʌntəm]. *Pr.n. A.Hist: Archeol:* Sagonte.

Sahara [sə'hɑ:rə]. *Pr.n. Geog:* **the S. (Desert),** le Sahara.

Saharan, Saharian, Saharic [sə'hɑ:r(i)ən, -'hɑ:rik], *a. Geog:* saharien.

Sahel [sə'hi:l]. *Pr.n. Geog:* **the S.,** le Sahel; **the Algerian S.,** le Sahel algérien.

Sahelian [sə'hi:liən]. *Geog:* (*a*) *a.* sahélien; (*b*) *s.* Sahélien, -ienne.

sahib ['sɑ:ib], *s.m.* sahib.

Sahidic [sə'hidik], *a.* & *s. Ling:* saïdique (*m*), sahidique (*m*).

saiga ['saigə], *s. Z:* **s. (antelope),** saïga *m*.

Saigon [sai'gɔn]. *Pr.n. Geog:* Saïgon *m*.

sail¹ [seil], *s.* **1.** *Nau:* (*a*) voile *f*; **set of sails,** jeu *m* de voiles; **after sails,** voiles de l'arrière; **head sails,** voiles de l'avant; **light sails, upper sails,** voiles hautes; **lower sails,** voiles basses; basses voiles; **square s.,** voile carrée; **to hoist, lower, a s.,** hisser, amener, une voile; **to take in a s.,** ramasser, serrer, rentrer, une voile; **to brail up a s.,** carguer une voile; *Fig:* **to haul in one's sails,** (i) rabattre de ses prétentions; en rabattre; (ii) réduire ses dépenses, son train de maison; (*b*) *coll.* voile(s), voilure *f*, toile *f*; **to make s.,** faire (de la) voile, de la toile; **to make more s.,** augmenter de voile, de toile; augmenter la voilure; alarguer; **to reduce s. for a squall,** saluer un grain; parer au grain; (*of ship*) **under s.,** sous voile(s); à la voile; **under full s.,** toutes voiles dehors; à pleines voiles; **to get under s.,** mettre à la voile; faire voile; appareiller; **to keep under easy s.,** faire peu de toile; (*c*) *attrib.* **s. loft, room,** voilerie *f*; **s. locker,** soute *f* à voiles; **s. cover,** étui *m* de voile; **s. needle,** aiguille *f* à voiles; carrelet *m*; (*d*) (*ship*) **s. ho!** voilier en vue! **a fleet of twenty s.,** une flotte de vingt voiles, de vingt voiliers; *A:* **twenty s. of the line,** vingt vaisseaux de ligne; (*e*) *F: A:* **sails,** le maître voilier. **2.** (*a*) aile *f*, volant *m*, toile (de moulin); **s. arm,** châssis *m*, bras *m* (d'un moulin à vent); **s. axle,** arbre moteur (d'un moulin à vent); (*b*) *Nau:* **wind s.,** manche *f* à vent, à air (en toile); (*c*) *Ich:* nageoire dorsale (du pèlerin); (*d*) *Moll:* lamelle *f* (d'un tentacule de nautile); **s. arm,** tentacule (du nautile).

sail², *s.* **1.** sortie *f* à la voile; promenade *f* en voilier, en bateau à voiles. **2. it will be a three hours' s.,** la traversée prendra trois heures sous voile.

sail³. **1.** *v.i.* (*a*) (*of sailing ship*) aller à la voile; faire voile; (*of any ship*) naviguer; faire route; **to s. up the coast,** remonter la côte; **to s. round a cape,** contourner un promontoire; **to s. into harbour,** entrer, donner, dans le port; **to s. at ten knots,** filer dix nœuds; (*b*) partir; prendre la mer; **ship about to s. for Bordeaux,** navire en partance pour Bordeaux; **the ship sails, we s., at ten o'clock,** le bateau part à dix heures; (*c*) *F:* **to s. into a room,** entrer majestueusement dans une pièce; **to s. into s.o.,** (i) heurter qn; (ii) tomber sur, attaquer, qn. **2.** *v.tr.* & *i.* (*a*) **to s. (on, over) the seas,** parcourir les mers; naviguer (sur) les mers; (*b*) planer (dans l'air, etc.); *Aer:* voler; (*of bird, etc.*) **to s. through the sky,** planer dans le ciel; **there were clouds sailing by,** des nuages voguaient dans le ciel; **to s. through a piece of work,** expédier un travail (i) en moins de deux, (ii) sans la moindre difficulté **3.** *v.tr.* (*a*) manœuvrer (un voilier); naviguer (un navire); (*b*) **to s. a toy boat on a pond,** faire naviguer un petit bateau sur un bassin.

sailboat ['seilbout], *s. NAm:* voilier *m*; bateau *m* à voiles.

sailcloth ['seilklɔθ], *s. Tex:* toile *f* à voile(s); canevas *m*.

-sailed ['seild], *a.* **white-s.,** à voiles blanches; **full-s.,** à pleines voiles.

sailer ['seilər], *s.* **1.** (*sailing ship*) voilier *m*; **good, bad, s.,** bon, mauvais, voilier. **2.** (*any ship*) marcheur *m*; **fast, slow, s.,** bon, mauvais, marcheur.
sailfish ['seilfiʃ], *s. Ich:* (*a*) pèlerin *m*; (*b*) voilier *m*.
sailing ['seiliŋ], *s.* **1.** (*a*) navigation *f*; **orthodromic, great circle, s.,** navigation orthodromique; navigation par, sur, l'arc de grand cercle; **rhumbline, loxodromic, plane, s.,** navigation loxodromique, plane; **it's (all) plane, plain, s.,** cela va tout seul; (*b*) *Sp:* nautisme *m*; (*c*) navigation à voile; **s. ship,** voilier *m*; **s. boat,** canot *m* à voiles; **s. barge,** chaland *m* à voiles; gabare *f*; **s. craft,** bateaux *mpl* à voiles; **s. master,** maître *m*, capitaine *m*, en yacht; (*d*) marche *f*, allure *f* (d'un voilier, d'un navire); **fast s.,** bonne marche; **s. before the wind,** allure du vent arrière; **to change the point of s.,** changer d'allure; **order of s.,** ordre *m* de marche; **s. qualities,** points *m*, allures, qualités *f*, nautiques (d'un navire); **s. line,** ligne *f* de flottaison lège (d'un navire). **2.** départ *m*, appareillage *m*; **port, time, of s.,** port *m*, heure *f*, de départ; **(list of) sailings,** (liste *f* de) départs; bâtiments *mpl* en partance.
sailmaker ['seilmeikər], *s.* (*pers.*) voilier *m*.
sailmaking ['seilmeikiŋ], *s.* voilerie *f*.
sailor ['seilər], *s.* (*a*) marin *m* (officier ou matelot); **sailors' home,** foyer *m* du marin; (*b*) **to be a good s.,** avoir le pied marin; **to be a bad s.,** être sujet au mal de mer; (*c*) *Cost: A:* **s. suit,** costume marin (d'enfant); **s. hat,** (i) canotier *m* (pour femmes); (ii) Jean-Bart *m* en paille (de petit garçon).
sailoring ['seiləriŋ], *s. O:* matelotage *m*; **to go s.,** se faire matelot.
sailplane ['seilplein], *s. Av: O:* planeur *m*.
sailplaning ['seilpleiniŋ], *s.* vol *m* à voile.
saimiri [sai'miəri:], *s. Z:* saïmiri *m*.
sain [sein], *v.tr. A: & Lit:* **1.** bénir (d'un signe de croix); **to s. oneself,** se signer. **2.** guérir (qn).
sainfoin ['seinfɔin], *s. Bot: Agr:* sainfoin *m*.
saint [seint], *s.* **1.** (*a*) saint, -e; **saint's day,** fête *f* de saint; fête patronale; **All Saints' (Day),** la Toussaint; **calendar of saints,** calendrier *m* ecclésiastique; *F:* **to try the patience of a s.,** lasser la patience d'un saint; **he's a little plaster s.,** c'est un petit saint de bois; *Rel:* **Latter-day Saints,** les Saints du dernier jour; (*b*) [sənt], *with Pr.n.* (*abbr. usu.* **St.** *thus written here or* **S.**) **St. George,** Saint Georges; **St. George's Day,** la Saint-Georges; *Geog:* **St. George's Channel,** le canal de Saint-Georges; *Orn:* **St. George's duck,** tadorne *mf* de Belon; **St. Cecilia,** Sainte Cécile; **St. Angelo,** Saint Ange; **the castle of St. Angelo,** le fort Saint-Ange; **St. Bernard,** (i) Saint Bernard; (ii) (chien *m*) saint-bernard *inv*; *Geog:* **St. Helena,** Sainte-Hélène *f*; **St. John,** Saint Jean; **St. John the Baptist,** Saint Jean-Baptiste; **the feast of St. John, St. John's Day, St. John's Eve,** la Saint-Jean; *Bot:* **St. John's bread,** caroubier *m*; **St. John's wort,** mille(-) pertuis *m inv*; herbe *f* de Saint-Jean; *Geog:* **St. John (river),** le Saint-Jean; **St. Lawrence,** le (fleuve) Saint-Laurent; **St. Lawrence Seaway,** voie *f* maritime du Saint-Laurent; **St. Lucia,** Sainte-Lucie *f*; **St. Petersburg,** (i) *A:* Saint-Pétersbourg *m*; (ii) *U.S:* Saint Petersburg; *ellip.* **St. Peter's,** (la cathédrale, l'église) Saint-Pierre; (*with loss of possessive sign*) **St. Albans, St. Andrews,** (la ville de) Saint-Albans, Saint-Andrews. **2. the Communion of Saints,** la Communion des Saints; *O:* **to be with the Saints,** être dans l'autre monde.
sainted ['seintid], *a. O:* **1.** (*of pers.*) saint, canonisé; (*of place*) saint, consacré, sacré; *F:* **my s. aunt!** mon Dieu! **2.** (*of pers.*) saint, vertueux, pieux.
sainthood ['seinthud], *s.* sainteté *f*.
saintliness ['seintlinis], *s.* sainteté *f*.
saintly ['seintli], *a.* (*of life, action, etc.*) (de) saint; *Iron:* **to put on a s. air,** prendre un air de petit saint.
Sais [seis]. *Pr.n. A.Geog:* Saïs *f*.
Saite ['seiait]. **1.** *a. A.Hist:* (dynastie, période) saïte. **2.** *s.* habitant, -ante, de Saïs.
Saitic [sei'itik], *a. A.Geog:* saïte; de Saïs.
sajou [sə'dʒu:], *s. Z:* sajou *m*.
sake [seik], *s.* **1. to do sth. for the s. of s.o., for s.o.'s s.,** faire qch. dans l'intérêt de qn, par égard pour qn, en considération de qn, à cause de qn; **I forgive you for her s.,** je vous pardonne à cause d'elle, par égard pour elle; **self-denial for the s. of others,** abnégation dans l'intérêt d'autrui; **do it for the s. of your family,** faites-le pour (l'amour de) votre famille; **do it for my s.,** faites-le pour moi, pour me faire plaisir; **for God's s., for goodness(') s.,** pour l'amour de Dieu; **for the s. of the cause,** pour le besoin de la cause; **for the s. of example,** pour l'exemple; **word brought in for the s. of the rhyme,** mot employé pour la rime; **for old times' s., for old sake's s.,** en souvenir du passé; **for old acquaintance(') s.,** en souvenir de notre vieille amitié; **for conscience(') s.,** par acquit de conscience; **for economy's s.,** par économie; **to talk for talking's s., for the s. of talking,** parler pour le plaisir de parler; **to worry for the s. of worrying,** se tourmenter à plaisir; **art for art's s.,** l'art pour l'art. **2.** *U.S: F:* **sakes alive! sakes!** grand Dieu! par exemple!
saké ['sɑ:ki], *s. Dist:* saké *m*, saki *m*.
saker ['seikər], *s.* **1.** *Orn:* faucon *m* sacre. **2.** *A.Arms:* sacre *m*.
sakeret ['seikərit], *s. Orn:* sacret *m*.
saki ['sɑ:ki], *s. Z:* saki *m*; **hairy s.,** saki moine.
sal [sæl], *s.* (*a*) *A.Ch:* sel *m*; (*b*) **s. ammoniac,** sel ammoniac; **s. volatile,** (solution *f* de) sels volatils anglais.
salaam[1] [sə'lɑ:m], *s. F:* salamalec *m*; grand salut; *Corr:* **salaams to all the family,** meilleurs vœux à toute la famille.
salaam[2], *v.tr. & i.* faire des salamalecs, un grand salut (à qn).
salacetol [sə'læsitɔl], *s. Ch:* salacétol *m*.
salacious [sə'leiʃəs], *a.* (*of pers., story, etc.*) salace, lubrique, ordurier.
salaciousness [sə'leiʃəsnis], **salacity** [sə'læsiti], *s.* salacité *f*, lubricité *f*.
salad ['sæləd], *s.* salade *f*; **to mix the s.,** tourner, fatiguer, remuer, touiller, la salade; **green s.,** salade (verte); **mixed s.,** salade panachée; **Russian s.,** salade russe; **lobster s.,** salade de homard; **fruit s.,** (i) macédoine *f*, salade, de fruits; (ii) *Mil: F:* brochette *f* de décorations; **s. basket,** panier *m* à salade; **s. bowl,** saladier *m*; **s. dressing,** (i) vinaigrette *f*; (ii) sauce *f* genre mayonnaise; **s. oil,** huile *f* comestible, de table; *F:* **s. days,** années *f* de jeunesse, d'inexpérience.
salade ['sæləd, sə'lɑ:d], *s. Arm:* salade *f*.
Salamanca [sælə'mæŋkə]. *Pr.n. Geog:* Salamanque *f*.
salamander ['sæləmændər], *s.* **1.** *Amph:* salamandre *f*; **alpine s., black s.,** salamandre alpestre, salamandre noire; **dwarf s.,** salamandre naine; **giant s.,** salamandre géante d'Asie, du Japon; **giant American s.,** salamandre géante américaine; **(North American) grotto s.,** salamandre des grottes (nord-américaine); **red s.,** salamandre rouge; **redbacked s.,** plethodon *m*; **(European) spotted s.,** salamandre tachetée; **(American) tiger s.,** salamandre tigrée, salamandre-tigre *f*; **water s.,** triton *m*. **2.** *Her:* **s. (in flames),** salamandre; patience *f*. **3.** (*a*) *Cu:* couvercle *m* à braiser; four *m* de campagne; (*b*) *O:* **s. stove,** salamandre. **4.** tisonnier ardent; allumoir *m*. **5.** *Metall:* carcas *m*, loup *m*, cochon *m*.
Salamandridae [sælə'mændridi:], *s.pl. Amph:* salamandridés *m*.
salamandrine [sælə'mændrin], *a.* de salamandre.
salami [sə'lɑ:mi], *s. Comest:* salami *m*.
Salamis ['sæləmis]. *Pr.n. A.Geog:* Salamine *f*.
salangane ['sæləŋgein], *s. Orn:* salangane *f*.
salariat [sæ'lɛəriət], *s. coll. Pol.Ec: Ind:* = cadres *mpl*.
salaried ['sælərid], *a. Ind: Com:* **1.** (personnel) aux appointements; **s. staff** = cadres *mpl*; **lower s. staff,** cadres moyens; **higher s. staff,** cadres supérieurs; **high-s. official,** fonctionnaire bien rétribué, à forts appointements. **2.** (*of post*) rétribué.
salary ['sæləri], *s.* traitement *m*, appointements *mpl*; **s. of a member of Parliament, M.P.'s s.,** indemnité *f* parlementaire; **to draw one's s.,** toucher ses appointements; **to draw a fixed s.,** toucher un traitement fixe; **my s. has been raised,** mes appointements ont été augmentés; *F:* j'ai été augmenté.
salda ['sældə], *s. Ent:* salde *m*.
Saldidae ['sældidi:], *s.pl. Ent:* saldidés *m*.
sale [seil], *s.* **1.** vente *f*; (*a*) débit *m*, mise *f* en vente (de marchandises); **cash s.,** vente au comptant; **credit s.,** vente à crédit; **s. value,** valeur marchande; valeur vénale; **ready s.,** vente facile; écoulement *m* rapide; **to find a quick s. for sth.,** trouver un placement rapide pour qch.; **goods for which there is a sure s.,** marchandises de placement sûr, qui ont un grand débit; **article for which there is no s.,** article qui n'a pas de marché; **house for s.,** maison à vendre; **business for s.,** fonds *m* à céder; **to exhibit sth. for s.,** mettre qch. en vente; exposer qch. à l'étalage; **to put sth. up for s.,** offrir, mettre, qch. en vente; **these things are not for s.,** ces choses-là ne sont pas à vendre; **not for general s., not for s. to the general public,** hors commerce; **on s.,** en vente; **s. by private treaty, contract, agreement,** vente à l'amiable, de gré à gré; **s. by sealed tender,** vente par soumission cachetée; **s. with option of repurchase,** vente à réméré, avec faculté de rachat; *St.Exch:* **s. for the account,** vente à terme; **s. contract,** contrat *m* de vente; *St.Exch:* bordereau *m* de vente; **bill of s.,** acte de vente; **subject to a bill of s.,** hypothéqué; *Ind:* **sales area,** point *m* de vente; **sales department,** service commercial, service ventes; **sales room,** (i) magasin *m* de vente(s); (ii) salle *f* de vente (aux enchères); **there is sales resistance to these lines,** ces marchandises sont d'une vente difficile; **sales talk,** boniment *m*; **sales book,** livre *m* de(s) vente(s); journal *m* des débits; facturier *m*; (*b*) **s. by auction, auction s., s. to the highest bidder,** vente à l'enchère, aux enchères; criée *f*; vente à la criée; (*at auction*) **day's s.,** vacation *f*; **s. ring,** cercle *m* d'acheteurs; *Jur:* **compulsory s.,** adjudication forcée; **s. by order of the court,** vente judiciaire; (*c*) **to attend a s.,** assister à une vente; **s. of work,** vente de charité; **bring and buy s.,** vente (de charité) où l'on apporte qch. à vendre et en principe achète qch. **2.** *Com:* **(clearance) s.,** soldes *mpl*; **(bargain) s.,** vente (de) réclame, au rabais; **closing-down s.,** soldes avant départ; liquidation *f* du stock avant départ; **the sales are on,** c'est le moment des soldes; **to go round the sales,** courir les soldes; **to buy goods at the sales,** acheter des soldes; **s. goods,** soldes; **s. price,** prix *m* de solde.
saleability [seilə'biliti], *s. Com:* qualité marchande (d'un article); facilité *f* d'écoulement.
saleable ['seiləbl], *a.* (*of goods, etc.*) vendable, marchand; de vente facile, courante; **readily s.,** qui se vend bien.
saleableness ['seiləbəlnis], *s. Com:* qualité marchande (d'un article); facilité *f* d'écoulement.
Salem ['seiləm]. *Pr.n.* (*a*) *B:* Salem; (*b*) *Geog:* (*U.S.*) Salem; (*c*) (i) Salem (nom d'un temple protestant); (ii) *s. A:* temple.
salep ['sælep], *s. Cu:* salep *m*.
saleratus [sælə'reitəs], *s. Cu: U.S:* bicarbonate *m* de soude.
Salernitan [sə'lə:nit(ə)n]. *Geog:* (*a*) *a.* salernitain; de Salerne; (*b*) *s.* Salernitain, -aine.
Salerno [sə'lə:nou]. *Pr.n. Geog:* Salerne *f*.
saleroom ['seilru:m], *s.* salle *f* de(s) vente(s).
salesclerk ['seilzklə:k], *s. NAm:* vendeur, -euse.
salesgirl ['seilzgə:l], *s.f.* vendeuse.
Salesian [sə'li:ʒən], *s. R.C.Ch:* salésien *m*, prêtre *m* de Saint François de Sales.
saleslady ['seilzleidi], *s.f. O:* vendeuse.
salesman, *pl.* **-men** ['seilzmən], *s.m. Com:* **1.** vendeur; employé à la vente; **he's a born s.,** il a le commerce dans le sang. **2.** représentant de commerce; courtier.
salesmanship ['seilzmənʃip], *s.* l'art *m* de vendre.
salespeople ['seilzpi:pl], *s.pl. Com:* vendeurs *m*.
saleswoman, *pl.* **-women** ['seilzwumən, -wimin], *s.f.* vendeuse.
salet ['sælit], *s. A.Arm:* salade *f*.
Salian[1] ['seiliən], *a. & s. Rom.Ant:* salien, -ienne.
Salian[2]. *Hist:* **1.** *s.* Salien, -ienne. **2.** *a.* salien, salique; **S. Franks,** Francs saliens; **S. kingdom,** royaume *m* salique.
saliant ['seiliənt], *a. Her:* (cheval) cabré, effaré; (*of unicorn, goat, etc.*) saillant.
Salic ['sælik], *a. Hist:* **S. law,** loi *f* salique.
Salicaceae [sæli'keisii:], *s.pl. Bot:* salicacées *f*.
salicet ['sæliset], *s. Mus:* salicional *m* (d'orgue).
salicin ['sælisin], *s. Ch:* salicine *f*.
salicional [sə'liʃən(ə)l], *s. Mus:* salicional *m* (d'orgue).
salicyl ['sælisil], *s. Ch:* salicyle *m*; **s. alcohol,** alcool *m* salicylique, saligénine *f*.
salicylaldehyde [sælisil'ældihaid], *s. Ch:* aldéhyde *m* salicylique.
salicylate[1] [sə'lisileit], *s. Ch:* salicylate *m*; **sodium s.,** salicylate de sodium; **methyl s.,** salicylate de méthyle; **phenyl s.,** salicylate de phényle; salol *m*.
salicylate[2], *v.tr.* salicyler (la bière, etc.).
salicylic [sæli'silik], *a. Ch:* (acide *m*) salicylique; **s. aldehyde,** aldéhyde *m* salicylique.
salience, saliency ['seiliəns(i)], *s.* projection *f*; (*a*) nature saillante, caractère saillant (d'une configuration, etc.); (*b*) angle saillant; saillant *m*, saillie *f*.
salient ['seiliənt], *a.* **1.** (*a*) *A: & Lit:* (*of animal*) bondissant; (*of spring, water*) jaillissant; (*b*) *Her:* **ram s.,** bélier saillant; **horse s.,** cheval cabré, effaré. **2.** (*a*) (*of angle, etc.*) saillant; en saillie; **s. eyes,** yeux saillants; *El:* **s. pole,** pôle saillant (de dynamo); (*b*) *s. Fort:* saillant *m*; *Hist:* **the S.,** le saillant d'Ypres (1914–18). **3.** (trait) saillant, frappant; **s. features of an agreement,** traits saillants, caractéristiques *f*, d'une convention.
saliferous [sæ'lifərəs], *a. Geol:* (*of rock*) salifère, salicole; **s. system,** système saliférien.
salifiable [sæli'faiəbl], *a. Ch:* salifiable.
salification [sælifi'keiʃ(ə)n], *s.* salification *f*.
saligenin [sæ'lidʒənin], *s. Ch:* saligénine *f*, alcool *m* salicylique.
saligot ['sæligɔt], *s. Bot:* saligot *m*, macre *f*, châtaigne *f* d'eau.
Salii ['seiliai], *s.pl. Rom.Ant:* Saliens *m*.
salimeter [sæ'limitər], *s.* salinomètre *m*.

salina [sæ'lainə], *s.* marais salant; salin *m*; saline *f*.
saline ['seilain]. **1.** *a.* (*a*) (*of spring, water, taste, etc.*) salin, salé; **s. marshes,** marais salants; **s. lake,** lac salé; (*b*) *Med: Pharm:* (purgatif) salin; (*c*) **normal s. solution,** solution *f* physiologique. **2.** *s. Med:* (*a*) purgatif salin; sel purgatif; (*b*) sérum *m* physiologique. **3.** *s.* = SALINA.
salinity [sə'liniti], *s.* salinité *f*, salure *f* (de l'eau de mer, etc.).
salinometer [sæli'nɔmitər], *s.* salinomètre *m*.
salite ['sælait], *s. Miner:* salite *f*.
saliva [sə'laivə], *s.* salive *f*.
salival [sə'laiv(ə)l], **salivary** [sə'laivəri], *a.* (*of glands, etc.*) salivaire.
salivate ['sæliveit]. **1.** *v.i.* saliver. **2.** *v.tr.* faire saliver (qn).
salivation [sæli'veiʃ(ə)n], *s.* salivation *f*.
sallenders ['sæləndəz], *s.pl. Vet:* crevasses *f* du pli du jarret (chez le cheval); malandres *f*.
sallet ['sælit], *s. A.Arm:* salade *f*.
salley ['sæli], *s. Bot: Dial:* saule *m*; marsault *m*; *Lit:* **down by the s. gardens,** près de la saulaie.
sallow[1] ['sælou], *s. Bot:* saule *m*; **goat s.,** (saule) marsaux *m*, marsault *m*, marceau *m*; **s. thorn,** argousier *m*, hippophaé *m*.
sallow[2], *a.* (teint *m*) jaune, jaunâtre, olivâtre; *occ.* (teint) plombé, brouillé.
sallow[3], *v.tr.* jaunir, brouiller (le teint); **face sallowed by long residence in the tropics,** visage jauni, décoloré, par un long séjour sous les tropiques.
sallowness ['sælounis], *s.* ton *m* jaunâtre (du teint).
Sallust ['sæləst]. *Pr.n.m. Lt.Lit:* Salluste.
sally[1] ['sæli], *s.* **1.** *Mil:* sortie *f* (des assiégés). **2.** (*a*) excursion *f*, sortie; (*b*) escapade *f*, fredaine *f*. **3.** (*a*) saillie *f*, sursaut *m*, élan *m* (d'activité, d'émotion, etc.); (*b*) **s. (of wit),** saillie (d'esprit); boutade *f*; pointe *f* d'esprit; trait *m* d'esprit.
sally[2], *v.i.* **1.** *Mil:* **to s. (out),** faire une sortie. **2.** *O:* **to s. forth, out,** (i) sortir; se mettre en route; partir en promenade; (ii) (*of liquid*) jaillir; (*of blood*) gicler.
sally[3], *s.* **1.** branle *m* (d'une cloche); mise *f* en branle. **2.** garniture *f* de corde (qu'empoigne le sonneur de cloches); **s. hole,** trou *m* de corde (dans la voûte du clocher).
Sally[4]. *Pr.n.f.* (*dim.*) Sarah; *Cu:* **S. Lunn,** (sorte de) petit pain au lait (qui se mange rôti et beurré).
sally[5], *s. Bot: Dial:* = SALLEY.
sallyport ['sælipɔ:t], *s. Fort:* (*a*) poterne *f* de sortie, de secours (d'une place forte, etc.); porte *f* de sortie; (*b*) poterne.
salmagundi [sælmə'gʌndi], *s. Cu:* salmigondis *m*.
Salmanasar [sælmə'neizər]. *Pr.n.m. A.Hist:* Salmanasar.
salmi ['sælmi], *s. Cu:* salmis *m* (de perdrix, etc.).
salmin(e) ['sælmi(:)n], *s. Bio-Ch:* salmine *f*.
salmon ['sæmən]. **1.** *s.* (*usu. inv. in pl.*) *Ich:* (*a*) saumon *m*; **young s.,** saumoneau *m*; **river full of s.,** rivière pleine de saumons; **s. breeding,** salmoniculture *f*; **s. gaff,** saumier *m*; **s. ladder, s. leap, s. pass,** échelle *f* à poissons, à saumon(s); (*b*) **s. trout,** truite saumonée, truite de mer; **quinnat s., Chinook s., king s., black s.,** quinnat *m*; **sockeye s.,** saumon américain, *Fr.C:* saumon sockeye; *Can:* **landlocked s.,** saumon d'eau douce, *Fr.C:* ouananiche *f*. **2.** *a. & s.* (*colour*) saumon *inv*; **s. pink ribbons,** rubans saumon; **s. dress,** robe saumon.
Salmonella [sælmə'nelə], *s. Bac:* salmonella *f inv*, salmonelle *f*.
salmonellosis [sælmənə'lousis], *s. Med: Vet:* salmonellose *f*.
salmonid ['sæ(l)mənid], *s. Ich:* salmonidé *m*, salmoné *m*.
Salmonidae [sæ(l)'mɔnidi:], *s.pl. Ich:* salmonidés *m*.
salol ['sælɔl], *s. Ch: Pharm:* salol *m*; salicylate de phényle.
Salome [sə'loumi], *Pr.n.f. B.Hist:* Salomé.
salometer [sæ'lɔmitər], *s.* salinomètre *m*.
Salomonian, Salomonic [sælə'mouniən, -'mɔnik], *a.* salomonien; du roi Salomon.
salon ['sælɔ̃], *s.* **1.** (*a*) salon *m*; (*b*) *A:* réception *f* (de notabilités). **2.** (*a*) salon d'exposition (d'une modiste, etc.); (*b*) *Art:* **the S.,** le Salon; (*c*) **beauty s.,** institut *m* de beauté.
Salonika [sə'lɔnikə]. *Pr.n. Geog:* Salonique *f*.
saloon [sə'lu:n], *s.* **1.** (*a*) salle *f*, salon *m*; **billiard s.,** salle de billard; **hairdressing s.,** salon de coiffure; **dancing s.,** dancing *m*; **s. rifle,** carabine *f* de salon; (*b*) *NAm:* café *m*; bar *m*; débit *m* de boissons; **s. keeper,** cabaretier *m*, cafetier *m*; (*c*) **s. bar** = bar *m*. **2.** *Nau:* salon (de paquebot); la cabine; **s. passenger,** voyageur, -euse, de première classe; **s. deck,** pont *m* de première classe. **3.** (*a*) *Rail:* **s. (coach, carriage),** wagon-salon *m*, *pl.* wagons-salons; voiture-salon *f*, *pl.* voitures-salons; (*b*) *Aut:* **s. (car),** conduite intérieure; **two-door s.,** coach *m*; **four-door s.,** berline *f*; **seven-seater s.,** familiale *f*.
Salopian [sə'loupiən], *a. & s.* **1.** (originaire, habitant, -ante) (i) du Shropshire, (ii) de la ville de Shrewsbury. **2.** *Sch:* (i) élève, (ii) ancien élève, du collège de Shrewsbury.
salpa, *pl.* **-as, -ae** ['sælpə, -əz, -i:], *s. Nat.Hist:* salpe *f*, salpa *f*.
Salpidae ['sælpidi:], *s.pl. Nat.Hist:* salpidés *m*.
salpiglossis [sælpi'glɔsis], *s. Bot:* salpiglossis *m*.
salpingectomy [sælpin'dʒektəmi], *s. Surg:* salpingectomie *f*.
salpingian [sæl'pindʒiən], *a. Anat:* salpingien.
salpingitis [sælpin'dʒaitis], *s. Med:* salpingite *f*.
salpingography [sælpiŋ'gɔgrəfi], *s. Med:* salpingographie *f*.
salpingo-ovaritis [sælpiŋgououvə'raitis], *s. Med:* salpingo-ovarite *f*.
salpingostomy [sælpiŋ'gɔstəmi], *s. Surg:* salpingostomie *f*.
salpingotomy [sælpiŋ'gɔtəmi], *s. Surg:* salpingotomie *f*.
salpinx ['sælpiŋks], *s.* **1.** *Gr.Ant:* salpinx *m*. **2.** *Anat:* (*a*) trompe *f* d'Eustache; (*b*) trompe de Fallope.
salse [sæls], *s. Geol:* salse *f*.
salsify ['sælsifi], *s. Bot:* salsifis *m*; **black s.,** salsifis noir; salsifis d'Espagne; scorsonère *f*.
salsola [sæl'soulə], *s. Bot:* salsola *m*.
salt[1] [sɔlt], *s. & a.*
I. *s.* **1.** (*a*) *Cu:* sel (commun); *Ch:* chlorure *m* de sodium; **cake of s.,** salignon *m*; **rock s., fossil s.,** sel gemme; halite *f*; **sea s., bay s.,** sel marin; sel de mer; sel gris; **s. marsh,** marais salant; saline *f*; salin *m*; salanque *f*; **s. pan,** (i) marais salant; (ii) vase *m* de saunage; mords *m*; **s. meadow,** pré salé; **s. mine,** mine *f* de sel; **s. pit,** saline *f*; mine *f* de sel; **s. spring,** source *f* saumâtre, saline; **s. lake,** lac salé; *Geog:* **the Great S. Lake,** le Grand Lac Salé; *U.S: F:* (*of politician*) **to row up S. River,** tomber dans l'oubli; *Ind: Oc:* **s. gauge,** halomètre *m*; **kitchen s.,** sel marin, selde cuisine; gros sel; **table s.,** sel de table; sel blanc; **the s. industries,** les industries *f* salicoles; *Lit:* **to eat s. with s.o.,** partager le pain et le sel avec qn; **to eat s.o.'s s.,** (i) recevoir l'hospitalité de qn; (ii) être à la charge de qn; *A:* **to be true to one's s.,** servir fidèlement ses chefs; se montrer loyal; *Hist:* **s. tax,** la gabelle; **to take s. with sth.,** prendre du sel avec qch.; **I eat my salad just with s.,** je mange ma salade à la croque au sel; **to take a story with a grain, a pinch, of s.,** croire à une histoire avec certaines restrictions, avec quelques réserves, non sans réserves; en prendre et en laisser; ne pas prendre une histoire à la lettre; prendre l'histoire avec un grain de sel; **that is what he says, but it must be taken with a grain of s.,** voilà ce qu'il dit, mais il faut faire la part de l'exagération; **he's not worth his s.,** il ne vaut pas le pain qu'il mange, l'eau qu'il boit; il ne gagne pas sa nourriture; *F: O:* (*to child*) **put a pinch of s. on his tail,** mets-lui un grain de sel sur la queue; **you're not made of s.!** vous n'avez pas peur d'une averse? *B:* **ye are the s. of the earth,** vous êtes le sel de la terre; **he is of the s. of the earth,** c'est un homme comme il y en a peu; *A:* **conversation full of s.,** conversation pleine de sel, de piquant; **attic s.,** sel attique; (*b*) *A:* = SALTCELLAR; **to sit (at table) above, below, the s.,** être assis au haut bout, au bas bout, de la table; (*c*) *A:* marais salant; (*d*) **salts,** poussée *f* du large (à l'embouchure d'un fleuve); (*e*) *F:* **old s.,** loup *m* de mer; vieux matelot; vieux bourlingueur des mers. **2.** (*a*) *Ch:* sel; **acid s.,** sursel *m*; **basic s.,** sous-sel *m*; **metal(lic) s.,** sel métallique; **double s.,** sel double; **tin s.,** sel d'étain; chlorure stanneux; **silver s.,** sel d'argent; *Com:* **spirit(s) of salts,** esprit *m* de sel; acide *m* chlorhydrique; (*b*) *Pharm: etc:* **salt(s) of lemon,** (i) mélange de sel d'oseille et de potasse (employé pour enlever les taches); (ii) sel d'oseille; **bath salts,** sels de bain; (*c*) *Cer:* **s. glaze,** demi-émaillage *m*; vernissage *m* par salage; **s.-glazed earthenware,** grès salé.
II. *a.* salé. **1.** (*a*) **s. water,** eau salée; eau saline; eau de mer; **s. provisions, s. butter,** vivres salés, beurre salé; **s. beef,** *Nau: P:* **horse,** bœuf *m* de conserve; *Lit:* **to weep s. tears,** pleurer amèrement; pleurer à chaudes larmes; **s. wit,** esprit salé; *F: O:* **s. stories,** histoires salées, corsées, grivoises; (*b*) (*of food*) **too s.,** trop salé. **2.** **s. plant,** plante marine, salicole; plante qui croît dans les marais salants; *U.S:* **s. grass, s. hay,** herbe *f*, foin *m*, des prés salés. **3.** (*of concretion, etc.*) salin; (*of rocks, ground*) salifère, saliférien.
salt[2], *v.tr.* **1.** (*a*) **to s. (down) meat, butter,** saler de la viande, du beurre; **to s. down, away (money, etc.),** économiser, mettre en lieu sûr (de l'argent, etc.); (*b*) saupoudrer (qch.) de sel; faire dégorger (des escargots); (*c*) saler (un mets); assaisonner (un mets, etc.) de sel; (*d*) jeter du sel sur (la neige). **2.** *Vet:* immuniser (un cheval). **3.** (*a*) *Phot:* saler (le papier); (*b*) *Soapm:* **to s. out (soap),** relarguer (le savon). **4.** (*a*) *Com: F: O:* cuisiner, truquer (des livres de compte, etc.); (*b*) *F: O:* **to s. the bill,** saler l'addition; (*c*) *Min:* **to s. a mine,** saler une mine (d'or, etc.); tapisser le front d'une mine.
saltant ['sæltənt], *a. Her:* (bouc, écureuil) sautant, saillant.
saltarello [sæltə'relou], *s. Danc: Mus:* saltarelle *f*.
saltation [sæl'teiʃ(ə)n], *s.* **1.** *Rom.Ant:* saltation *f*, danse *f*. **2.** *Biol:* mutation *f* **3.** *Geog:* saltation.
saltatorial [sæltə'tɔ:riəl], **saltatory** ['sæltətəri], *a.* **1.** *Nat.Hist:* saltatoire; **the methods of nature are s.,** la nature procède par sauts. **2.** *Med:* **s. spasm,** chorée *f* saltatoire.
saltbox ['sɔltbɔks], *s.* boîte *f* à sel; salière *f* (de cuisine).
saltcat ['sɔltkæt], *s. Husb:* salègre *m* (pour pigeons, etc.).
saltcellar ['sɔltselər], *s.* **1.** salière *f* (de table). **2.** *F:* salière (derrière la clavicule).
salted ['sɔltid], *a.* **1.** (*of meat, butter, etc.*) salé. **2.** (*a*) (*of horse, etc.*) immunisé; (*b*) *F: O:* (*of campaigner, etc.*) aguerri, endurci; **an old s. veteran,** un vieux dur à cuire. **3.** *Phot:* (*of paper*) salé.
salter ['sɔltər], *s.* **1.** (*a*) saunier *m*; fabricant, -ante, de sel; (*b*) salinier, -ière; saunier; ouvrier, -ière, dans une fabrique de sel. **2.** *O:* marchand, -ande, de salaisons, de conserves, etc.; épicier *m* droguiste. **3.** saleur, -euse (de poissons, etc.).
saltern ['sɔltə:n], *s.* **1.** fabrique *f* de sel. **2.** marais salant.
salt-free ['sɔltfri:], *a.* (régime) sans sel.
salticid ['sæltisid], *s. Arach:* saltique *m*, salticidé *m*.
Salticidae [sæl'tisidi:], *s.pl. Arach:* salticidés *m*.
saltigrade ['sæltigreid], *a. & s. Arach:* **s. (spider),** saltigrade *m*.
saltiness ['sɔltinis], *s.* salure *f*, salinité *f*.
salting ['sɔltiŋ], *s.* **1.** salaison *f*, salage *m* (de la viande, etc.); **s. tub,** saloir *m*. **2.** *Vet:* immunisation *f* (des chevaux). **3.** *Phot:* salage, salaison (des papiers). **4.** *Soapm:* relargage *m*. **5.** *O:* truquage *m* (des comptes, d'une mine d'or). **6.** **saltings,** prés salés.
saltire ['sæltaiər], *s. Her:* sautoir *m*; **s. couped,** flanchis *m*, flanquis *m*; **a s. or,** au sautoir d'or; **three saltires or,** à trois flanchis d'or; **in s.,** en sautoir; **parti per s.,** écartelé en sautoir.
saltireways, -wise ['sæltaiəweiz, -waiz], *adv.* en sautoir.
saltish ['sɔltiʃ], *a.* légèrement salé; saumâtre; qui a un goût de sel.
saltless ['sɔltlis], *a.* (régime, etc.) sans sel; (*of food, poem, speech, etc.*) fade, insipide.
saltmill ['sɔltmil], *s.* égrugeoir *m* de table.
saltness ['sɔltnis], *s.* salure *f*, salinité *f* (de l'eau de mer, etc.).
saltorel ['sæltərel], *s. Her:* flanchis *m*, flanquis *m*.
saltpetre [sɔlt'pi:tər], *s.* salpêtre *m*; nitrate *m* de potassium; **Chile s., cubic s.,** nitre *m* du Chilli; cubique, nitrate de soude; caliche *m*; **s. works, bed,** nitrière *f*; **s. worker,** salpêtrier *m*; **to treat with s.,** salpêtrer (la terre, etc.); **s. rot,** salpêtre (sur les murs); *Pyr: etc:* **s. paper,** papier *m* d'amorce.
saltshaker ['sɔltʃeikər], *s.* salière *f* saupoudroir.
saltspoon ['sɔltspu:n], *s.* cuiller *f* à sel; pelle *f* à sel.
saltwater ['sɔltwɔ:tər], *a.* **s. fish,** poisson *m* de mer; **s. ditch,** fossé *m* d'eau salée; *Med:* **s. treatment,** thalassothérapie *f*; *Geog:* **s. pool,** lagon *m*; **s. lake,** lagune *f*.
saltweed ['sɔltwi:d], *s. Bot: NAm:* (espèce d')arroche *f*.
saltworks ['sɔltwə:ks], *s.* (*a*) saunerie *f*, saline *f*; (*b*) raffinerie *f* de sel.
saltwort ['sɔltwə:t], *s. Bot:* **1.** soude *f*; **prickly s.,** kali *m*. **2.** **black s.,** glaux *m*. **3.** salicorne *f*.
salty ['sɔlti], *a.* **1.** **s. deposit,** grumeaux *mpl* de sel. **2.** (*of taste, sauce, etc.*) salé, saumâtre. **3.** *F:* (*of anecdote, book*) (i) piquant; (ii) salé, corsé.
salubrious [sə'lu:briəs], *a.* salubre, sain.
salubriously [sə'lu:briəsli], *adv.* salubrement.
salubrity [sə'lu:briti], *s.* salubrité *f*.
saluki [sə'lu:ki], *s. Z:* sloughi *m*; lévrier arabe, persan.
Salut ['sælju:t], *s. R.C.Ch:* (*evening service*) salut *m*.
salutary ['sæljut(ə)ri], *a.* salutaire (**to,** à).
salutation [sælju'teiʃ(ə)n], *s.* salutation *f*; *Ecc:* **the Angelic S.,** la Salutation angélique, l'Ave Maria.
salutatory [sælju:'teit(ə)ri], *a.* **1.** (formule *f*) de salutation. **2.** *Sch: U.S:* **s. oration,** allocution *f* de bienvenue.
salute[1] [sə'lu:t], *s.* (*a*) salut *m*, salutation *f*; *Fenc:* **s. with foils,** salut des armes; *A: & Lit:* **chaste s.,** chaste baiser *m*; (*b*) *Mil: Navy:* salut; **to give a s.,** faire, exécuter, un salut; **to return, acknowledge, a s.,** rendre un salut; **return s., answering s.,** contre-salut *m*; **to exchange salutes,** échanger le salut; **to be entitled to a s.,** avoir droit à un salut; **to stand at (the) s.,** garder l'attitude du salut; **s. with the sword,** salut de l'épée; **s. of the**

colour(s), salut au drapeau; **to beat a s., to beat the general s.,** battre aux champs; (*at a march past*) **to take the s.,** passer les troupes en revue; (*c*) *Mil: Navy:* **s. with the guns,** salut du canon; salve *f*; **to fire a s.,** tirer une salve; **to fire a s. of ten guns,** saluer de dix coups; exécuter une salve (de salut) de dix canons, de dix coups de canon; **to fire a s. in honour of s.o.,** tirer le canon à qn, en l'honneur de qn; **to return a s. gun for gun,** rendre un salut coup pour coup.

salute[2]. **1.** *v.tr.* (*a*) **to s. s.o. emperor,** saluer qn empereur; (*b*) **to s. s.o. with a smile, a kiss, a word,** accueillir, saluer, qn par un sourire, un baiser, un mot; saluer qn d'un sourire, d'un mot. **2.** *v.tr. & i. Mil:* faire un salut, faire le salut militaire; **to s. (s.o.) with the hand, with the sword,** saluer (qn) de la main, de l'épée, du sabre; **to s. with twenty guns,** saluer de vingt coups; *Fenc:* **to s. with the foils,** saluer des armes. **3.** *v.tr. O:* (*of sound*) **to s. the ear,** frapper l'oreille.

saluting [sə'lu:tiŋ], *s. Mil:* salut *m*; **s. of the colours,** salut au drapeau, aux couleurs; **s. point,** emplacement *m* où se trouve le personnage, les autorités, recevant le salut des troupes qui défilent; **s. fire,** salve *f* d'honneur.

salvable ['sælvəbl], *a.* **1.** *Ins:* qui peut être sauvé; susceptible de sauvetage. **2.** *Theol:* que l'on peut sauver; (âme *f*) en état de salut.

Salvadoraceae [sælvədo'reisii:], *s.pl. Bot:* salvadoracées *f*.

Salvador(i)an, -ean [sælvə'dɔ:r(i)ən]. *Geog:* **1.** *a.* salvadorien. **2.** *s.* Salvadorien, -ienne.

salvage[1] ['sælvidʒ], *s.* **1.** indemnité *f*, droit *m*, prime *f*, de sauvetage; (*paid to salvage tug*) indemnité de remorquage. **2.** sauvetage *m* (d'un navire, etc.); assistance *f* maritime; **s. company,** corps *m*, société *f*, de sauvetage (de marchandises); **s. agreement,** contrat *m* de sauvetage; **s. dues,** droits de sauvetage; *Nau:* **s. plant,** appareils *mpl* de renflouage; **s. tug,** remorqueur *m* de sauvetage; **s. vessel,** (i) navire *m* de relevage; (ii) *Navy:* dock *m* de sauvetage (pour sous-marins); bateau sauveteur. **3.** objets sauvés (d'un naufrage, d'un incendie). **4.** récupération *f* (de matières pour l'industrie).

salvage[2], *v.tr.* **1.** (*a*) *Nau: etc:* sauveter, sauver, relever, renflouer (un navire, etc.); effectuer le sauvetage (d'un navire, etc.); sauver, récupérer (des objets dans un incendie, etc.); (*b*) récupérer (une voiture, etc.); *F:* rattraper (une mayonnaise, etc.); **salvaged goods,** matériel sauvé, récupéré. **2.** *Mil: U.S: P:* chiper, chaparder (qch.).

salvageable ['sælvidʒəbl], *a.* récupérable.

salvager ['sælvidʒər], *s. Ins:* sauveteur *m* (de marchandises).

salvaging ['sælvidʒiŋ], *s.* sauvetage *m*; récupération *f*.

salvation [sæl'veiʃ(ə)n], *s.* salut *m*; (*a*) **to work out one's own s.,** travailler à son (propre) salut; faire son salut; **to find s.,** faire son salut; **to seek s. in sth.,** chercher son salut dans qch.; **without that there is no hope of s.,** hors de là, point de salut; **S. Army,** Armée *f* du Salut; (*b*) **Joan of Arc was the s. of France,** Jeanne d'Arc fut le salut de la France; **you've been my s.,** vous m'avez sauvé.

salvationist [sæl'veiʃ(ə)nist], *s.* salutiste *mf*.

Salvatorian [sælvə'tɔ:riən], *s.m. R.C.Ch:* Salvatorien.

salve[1] [sælv, sɑ:v], *s. Pharm:* onguent *m*, baume *m*, pommade *f* (pour les lèvres, etc.); baume, apaisement *m* (pour les sentiments, etc.).

salve[2], *v.tr.* adoucir, apaiser, calmer (les sentiments, l'amour-propre, etc., de qn); **to do sth. to s. one's conscience,** faire qch. par acquit de conscience.

salve[3] [sælv], *v.tr.* = SALVAGE[2] 1(*a*).

salve[4] ['sælvi], *s. R.C.Ch:* salvé *m*.

salver ['sælvər], *s.* plateau *m* (d'argent, etc.).

salvia ['sælviə], *s. Hort:* (espèce *f* de) sauge *f* (cultivée pour l'ornement).

Salviniaceae [sælvini'eisii:], *s.pl. Bot:* salviniacées *f*.

salvo[1], *pl.* **-oes** ['sælvou(z)], *s. A:* **1.** (*a*) réservation *f*, réserve *f* (de ses droits, etc.); **with an express s. of all my rights,** réservation faite de tous mes droits; (*b*) *F:* restriction mentale; subterfuge *m*, échappatoire *f*, faux-fuyant *m*, *pl.* faux-fuyants. **2.** moyen *m* pour sauver (la réputation de qn, etc.), pour apaiser (la conscience, etc.).

salvo[2], *s. Mil: Navy:* salve *f*; **to fire a s.,** (i) *Artil:* tirer, lancer, une salve; (ii) *Sm.a:* tirer une rafale, une salve; **fire by salvoes,** tir *m*, feu *m*, par salves, par rafales; *F:* **s. of applause,** salve d'applaudissements.

salvor ['sælvər], *s. Nau:* sauveteur *m*.

Salzburg ['sæltsbə:g]. *Pr.n. Geog:* Salzbourg *m*.

Sam [sæm]. *Pr.n.m.* (*dim.*) Samuel; *F:* **Uncle S.,** l'oncle Sam; les États-Unis; les Américains; *A:* **upon my S.,** parole d'honneur; *Mil: A:* **S. Browne (belt),** ceinturon *m* et baudrier *m* (d'officier); *F:* bricole *f*.

samara ['sæmərə], *s. Bot:* samare *f* (de l'orme, etc.).

Samaria [sə'mɛəriə], *Pr.n. Geog:* Samarie *f*; *B:* **the woman of S.,** la Samaritaine.

Samaritan [sə'mærit(ə)n]. **1.** *a.* samaritain; *Jew.Rel:* **S. version,** texte samaritain du Pentateuque. **2.** *s.* Samaritain, -aine; *B:* **the good S.,** le bon Samaritain; **to be a good s.,** être secourable, charitable.

Samaritanism [sə'mæritənizm], *s.* **1.** doctrine des Samaritains, samaritanisme *m*. **2.** caractère secourable, charitable.

samarium [sə'mɛəriəm], *s. Ch:* samarium *m*.

samarskite ['sæmɑ:skait], *s. Miner:* samarskite *f*.

samba ['sæmbə], *s. Danc:* samba *f*.

sambar ['sæmbər], *s. Z:* sambar *m*; (cerf *m*) rusa *m*.

sambo ['sæmbou], *s.* **1.** *Ethn:* zambo *m*. **2.** *Pej:* moricaud *m*.

sambuca [sæm'bju:kə], *s. A.Mus: Rom.Ant:* sambuque *f*.

sambur ['sæmbər], *s. Z:* sambar *m*; (cerf *m*) rusa *m*.

same [seim]. **1.** *a. & pron.* (*a*) (le, la) même, (les) mêmes; **to repeat the s. words,** répéter les mêmes mots; **put it back in the s. place,** remettez-le à la place où vous l'avez trouvé; **at the s. time that this was happening,** au moment même où cela se passait; **he's the s. age as me,** il est du même âge que moi; **his name is the s. as mine,** son nom est le même que le mien; il a le même nom que moi; **I found her just the s. as before,** je l'ai retrouvée la même qu'autrefois; **they were sold the s. day that they came in,** ils ont été vendus le jour même de leur arrivée; **a lady in the s. carriage as me,** une dame dans le même compartiment que moi; **all seated at the s. table,** tous assis à une même table; **to live in the s. house,** habiter la même maison; **the barrels are exactly the s. height, the s. width, the s. depth,** les fûts sont juste de la même hauteur, de la même largeur, de la même profondeur; **of the s. kind,** semblable, similaire; **in the s. way,** de même, de la même façon; **we are going the s. way,** nous allons dans la même direction; **be sure you all tell the s. story, be sure that you all say the s.,** assurez-vous bien que vous allez raconter tous la même histoire; **a Happy New Year to you!—the s. to you!** je vous souhaite une bonne année!—à vous de même, à vous pareillement; **I should have done the s.,** j'aurais fait de même; j'aurais agi de la même façon; **the very s. thing, one and the s. thing,** une seule et même chose; tout à fait la même chose; (*of letters*) **from the s. to the s.,** du même au même; **at the s. time,** (i) en même temps; (ii) à la fois; **to settle several matters at (one and) the s. time,** arranger plusieurs affaires du même coup; **it's the s. everywhere,** il en est ainsi partout; il en est de même partout; **it is no longer the s. thing,** ce n'est plus la même chose; **it, all that, amounts, comes, to the s. thing,** tout cela revient au même; *F:* tout cela c'est du pareil au même; **it's all the s., it's just the s.,** c'est tout un; *F:* c'est tout comme; **it's all the s. to me,** cela ne me fait rien; ça m'est égal; **if it's all the s. to you,** si cela ne vous fait rien; si ça vous est égal; **it's the s. with me, with him,** il en va de même pour moi, pour lui; **you still look the s.,** vous n'avez pas changé; **she was always the s. to me,** (i) à mes yeux elle a toujours été la même; (ii) elle a toujours été la même, elle n'a jamais changé, envers moi; **it's much the s.,** c'est à peu près la même chose; **he's much about the s.,** il va à peu près de même; **the s. old daily round,** le train-train quotidien; (*b*) (*he, she, it, etc.*) **the s.,** celui-là, celle-là; *pl.* ceux-là, celles-là; (*nom.*) il, elle; lui, *pl.* eux; *B:* **he that shall endure to the end, the s. shall be saved,** qui aura persévéré jusques à la fin, celui-là sera sauvé; **that s. man is now a millionaire,** lui-même, ce même homme, est à présent millionnaire; *Com:* **coat lined with the s.,** manteau doublé du même; *F:* **the s. again?** encore un (verre de whisky, etc.)? **the s. again!** remettez ça! *P:* **s. here!** et moi aussi! et moi de même! **2.** *adv.* de même; **to think, feel, act, the s.,** penser, sentir, agir, de même; *F:* **we like good things the same as you,** nous aimons les bonnes choses tout comme vous-même; **all the s.,** malgré tout; quand même; tout de même; **it is very good of you all the s.,** c'est très gentil de votre part tout de même; **all the s. it has cost us a lot,** n'empêche que cela nous a coûté cher; **come along, all the s.!** venez toujours! **the word exists, but all the s. it is very rarely used,** le mot existe mais il est quand même peu usité; **I feel anxious all the s.,** cela ne laisse pas (que) de m'inquiéter; **when I am away things go on just the s.,** quand je suis absent tout marche comme d'habitude, comme à l'ordinaire.

samel ['sæm(ə)l], *a. Cer:* (brique, tuile) mal cuite.

sameness ['seimnis], *s.* **1.** (*a*) identité *f* (**with,** avec); (*b*) ressemblance *f* (**with,** à). **2.** monotonie *f*, uniformité *f* (d'un paysage, de la vie, etc.).

Samian ['seimiən]. (*a*) *a. Geog:* samien; *Archeol:* **S. ware,** poteries arétines, d'Arezzo; (*b*) *s. Geog:* Samien, -ienne.

samiresite [sæ'miərisait], *s. Miner:* samirésite *f*, bétafite *f*.

samisen ['sæmisen], *s. Mus:* shamisen *m*; san-heen *m inv*.

samite ['sæmait], *s. Tex: A:* samit *m*; brocart lamé.

samlet ['sæmlit], *s. Ich:* saumoneau *m*.

Sammy ['sæmi]. **1.** *Pr.n.m.* (*dim.*) Samuel. **2.** *s. F:* (*a*) *O:* **simple S.,** nigaud *m*; (*b*) *Hist:* (1914–18) soldat américain.

Samnite ['sæmnait], *s. Rom.Hist:* Samnite *mf*.

Samoan [sə'mouən]. *Geog:* (*a*) *a.* samoan, de Samoa; (*b*) *s.* Samoan, -ane.

Samosata [sæmou'sɑ:tə], *Pr.n. A. Geog:* Samosate.

Samosatenian [sæmousə'ti:niən], *s. Rel.H:* samosat(én)ien, -ienne.

Samothrace ['sæmouθreis], *Pr.n.* (l'île de) Samorthrace *f*.

Samothracian [sæmou'θreisiən]. *Geog:* (*a*) *a.* samothracien; (*b*) *s.* Samothracien, -ienne.

samovar ['sæməvɑ:r], *s.* samovar *m*.

Samoyed ['sæmɔied], **Samoyede** ['sæmɔii:d]. **1.** *Ethn:* (*a*) *a.* samoyède; (*b*) *s.* Samoyède *mf*. **2.** *Z:* chien *m* samoyède.

Samoyedic [sæmɔi'edik], *a.* samoyède.

samp [sæmp], *s. U.S:* gruau *m* de maïs.

sampan ['sæmpæn], *s. Nau:* sampan(g) *m*.

samphire ['sæmfaiər], *s. Bot:* **1.** bacile *m* maritime; fenouil marin, de mer; perce-pierre *f*, *pl.* perce-pierres; passe-pierre *m*, *pl.* passe-pierre(s); casse-pierre(s) *m inv*; c(h)riste-marine *f*, *pl.* c(h)ristes-marines. **2.** salicorne *f*.

sample[1] ['sɑ:mpl], *s. Com: etc:* échantillon *m* (de tissu, de blé, de vin, etc.); prise *f*, prélèvement *m* (de gaz, de minerai, de sang, etc.); témoin *m* (de câble, etc.); essai *m* (de vin); **up to s.,** pareil, conforme, à l'échantillon; **to be up to s.,** répondre à l'échantillon; **picked s.,** échantillon choisi; **representative s.,** échantillon type; **reference s.,** contre-échantillon *m*; **true, fair, s.,** échantillon représentatif; **s. survey,** enquête *f* par sondage; **to take a s. (test),** opérer un sondage; **to send sth. as a s.,** envoyer qch. à titre d'échantillon; **to keep a stock of samples, a s. stock,** tenir un dépôt d'échantillons; **to buy sth. from s.,** acheter qch. d'après l'échantillon, sur montre; **to give a s. of one's knowledge,** donner un échantillon, un exemple, de son érudition; **s. book, card,** collection *f*, carte *f*, d'échantillons; **s. box of sth.,** boîte *f* échantillon de qch.; *Hort:* **s. plot, s. area,** parcelle *f* d'essai; *For:* **s. tree,** arbre *m* type.

sample[2], *v.tr.* (*a*) *Com:* prendre, prélever, des échantillons d'(un tissu, etc.); échantillonner; goûter à, déguster (un vin); lotir (du minerai); (*b*) goûter (un mets, etc.); essayer (un nouveau restaurant, etc.); **it was the first time I had sampled camp life,** c'était ma première expérience des camps.

sampler[1] ['sɑ:mplər], *s.* **1.** *Needlew:* modèle *m* de broderie (sur canevas). **2.** *For:* arbre type (laissé debout dans une coupe).

sampler[2], *s.* **1.** (*pers.*) échantillonneur, -euse. **2.** (**grain**) **s.,** sonde *f*.

sampling ['sɑ:mpliŋ], *s.* prise *f* d'échantillons; échantillonnage *m*; lotissage *m* (d'un minerai); gustation *f* (d'un mets, etc.); *Com: Ind:* **random s.,** prélèvement *m* d'échantillons au hasard; **s. tube,** tâte-vin *m inv*.

Samson ['sæms(ə)n]. *Pr.n.m.* (*a*) *B.Hist:* Samson; **a real S.,** un vrai Hercule; (*b*) *Nau:* **S. post,** épontille *f* à manche; étance *f* à coches.

samurai ['sæmurai], *s. inv.* sam(o)uraï *m*.

san [sæn], *s. Sch: F:* infirmerie *f*.

sanative ['sænətiv], *a.* (*a*) curatif; guérisseur, -euse; (*b*) salutaire.

sanatorium, *pl.* **-iums, -ia** [sænə'tɔ:riəm, -iəmz, -iə], *s.* **1.** sanatorium *m*, *pl.* sanatoriums, *occ.* sanatoria. **2.** *Sch:* infirmerie *f*.

sanatory ['sænətəri], *a. Lit:* curatif; guérisseur, -euse.

sanbenito [sænbə'ni:tou], *s. Rel.H:* san-benito *m*, *pl.* san-benitos.

Sancho ['sæntʃou]. *Pr.n.m. Hist:* **S. the Great,** Sanche le Grand: *Lit:* **S. Panza,** Sancho Pança.

sanctification [sæŋ(k)tifi'keiʃ(ə)n], *s.* sanctification *f*.

sanctified ['sæŋ(k)tifaid], *a.* (*a*) (*of pers.*) sanctifié, saint; (*of thg*) consacré; (*b*) **s. air,** air confit (en dévotion); air papelard.

sanctifier ['sæŋ(k)tifaiər], *s. Theol:* sanctificateur, -trice; **the S.,** le Sanctificateur.

sanctify ['sæŋ(k)tifai], *v.tr.* **1.** sanctifier (qn, qch.); consacrer (un jour, un terrain, etc.). **2. custom sanctified by time,** coutume consacrée par le temps.

sanctifying[1] ['sæŋ(k)tifaiiŋ], *a.* sanctifiant; sanctificateur, -trice.

sanctifying[2], *s.* sanctification *f*.

sanctimonious [sæŋ(k)ti'mouniəs], *a.* (*of pers., voice, manner, etc.*) papelard, cafard, cagot, béat; **his s. air,**

son air confit (en dévotion); son air de ne pas y toucher.

sanctimoniously [sæŋ(k)ti'mouniəsli], *adv.* d'une manière papelarde, cafarde; béatement; d'un air de petit saint.

sanctimoniousness [sæŋ(k)ti'mouniəsnis], **sanctimony** ['sæŋ(k)timəni], *s.* papelardise *f*, cafarderie *f*, cagoterie *f*.

sanction[1] ['sæŋ(k)ʃ(ə)n], *s.* **1.** *Jur:* **vindicatory s., punitive s.,** sanction pénale; **remuneratory s.,** sanction rémunératoire; *Pol:* **to impose sanctions on a country,** prendre des sanctions contre un pays. **2.** sanction, autorisation *f*, consentement *m*, approbation *f*; **without s.o.'s s.,** sans le consentement de qn; **with the s. of the author,** avec l'autorisation de l'auteur; **s. of custom,** sanction de l'usage; **s. by usage,** consécration *f* par l'usage. **3.** *Hist:* sanction, ordonnance *f*, décret *m*; **the Pragmatic S.,** la Pragmatique sanction.

sanction[2], *v.tr.* **1.** *Jur:* sanctionner; attacher des sanctions (pénales) à (une loi, etc.). **2.** *(a) Jur:* ratifier (une loi, etc.); *(b)* sanctionner, approuver, autoriser (qch.); encourager (une action); **it is custom that sanctions an error,** c'est l'habitude qui consacre une erreur; **sanctioned by usage,** sanctionné, consacré, par l'usage.

sanctionist ['sæŋ(k)ʃənist], *a. & s.* sanctionniste (*mf*).

sanctionize ['sæŋ(k)ʃənaiz], *v.i. Pol:* employer des sanctions pénales (contre un pays, etc.).

sanctity ['sæŋ(k)titi], *s.* **1.** sainteté *f* (d'une personne, d'une vie, etc.). **2.** caractère sacré (d'un terrain, d'un serment, etc.); inviolabilité *f* (de la vie privée, etc.); **to violate the s. of the oath,** forfaire à la religion du serment.

sanctorale [sæŋ(k)tə'reili:], *s. Ecc:* sanctoral *m*.

sanctuary ['sæŋ(k)tj(u)əri], *s.* **1.** *(a)* sanctuaire *m*, temple *m*, église *f*; *(b)* (*sacrarium*) sanctuaire, Saint *m* des Saints; *Lit:* **the s. of the heart,** le sanctuaire du cœur. **2.** *Ecc: Jur:* asile (sacré); refuge *m*; **right of s.,** droit *m* d'asile; immunité *f*; **to take s.,** chercher asile; **to violate, break, s.,** violer un asile. **3.** *(a)* refuge (d'oiseaux); **wild life s.,** réserve *f* zoologique; *(b) Ven:* période *f* d'interdiction.

sanctum ['sæŋ(k)təm], *s.* **1.** sanctuaire *m*, sacrarium *m*; **the s. sanctorum,** le Saint des Saints. **2.** sanctuaire; cabinet privé.

sanctus ['sæŋ(k)təs], *s. Ecc: Mus:* sanctus *m*.

sand[1] [sænd], *s.* *(a)* sable *m*; **aeolian s., windborne s.,** sable éolien; **loamy s.,** sable gras, argileux; **bituminous s.,** sable bitumineux; *Const: etc:* **sharp s.,** sable liant, mordant; **scouring s., welding s., fine s.,** sablon *m*; *Metall:* **foundry s., fire s., moulding s.,** sable de moulage; **dry s.,** sable recuit, étuvé; **green s.,** sable vert, humide, glauconieux; **parting s.,** sable sec, à saupoudrer; **to scour with s.,** sablonner; **choked with s.,** ensablé; **anchor buried in s.,** ancre ensablée; **to build on s.,** bâtir sur le sable; **s. castle,** château fort en sable (construit par les enfants sur la plage); **s. dune,** dune *f*; **s. drift,** sable mouvant; congère *f* de sable; *Meteor:* **s. cloud,** tourbillon *m* de sable; **s. spout,** trombe *f* de sable; **s. bed,** (i) *Geol:* couche *f* de sable; (ii) *Metall:* moule ouvert en sable; **s. belt,** (i) *Geol:* zone *f* de sable; (ii) *Metalw: etc:* courroie *f* à poncer; *Metalw:* **s. casting,** (i) moulage *m*, coulée *f*, au sable; (ii) pièce fondue en sable; *Metall:* **s. floor,** chantier *m* de moulage en sable; **s. mould,** moule *m* de sable; **s. moulding,** moulage en sable; **s. hole,** trou *m* de sable (dans une pièce venue de fonte); *Ind: etc:* **s. sprayer,** sablière *f*; **s. pump,** pompe *f* à sable; **s. pipe,** tuyau sableur; tuyau d'amenée du sable; **s. yacht,** aéroplage *f*; *(b)* **on the sand(s),** (i) sur la plage; (ii) sur un banc de sable; *(c)* **in number as the sands on the sea shore,** aussi nombreux que les grains de sable de la mer; *(d) Med:* **urinary s.,** sable, gravier *m*; *(e) Vet:* **s. crack,** seime *f*; *(f) Ich:* **s. eel, s. la(u)nce,** lançon *m*, ammodyte *f*; anguille *f* platbec, de sable; **lesser s. eel,** équille *f*; **Mediterranean s. eel,** circelle; **s. pride,** petite lamproie; **s. flea,** (i) *Ent:* puce pénétrante, chique *f*; (ii) *Crust:* (*also* **s. hopper**) talitre *m*, puce de mer; **s. fly,** (i) *Ent:* phlébotome *m*, simuliidé *m*, simulie *f*; (ii) *Fish:* mouche *f* jaune à deux ailes; *Med:* **s.-fly fever,** fièvre *f* de phlébotome, de trois jours, d'été; *Ann:* **s. mason,** lanice *m*, maçon *m* des sables; *Echin:* **s. star,** ophiure *f*; *(g) Orn:* **s. lark,** pluvier *m* à collier; **s. martin,** hirondelle *f* de rivage; cotyle *f*; *F:* mottereau *m*; *(h) Bot:* **s. reed,** ammophile *f*, roseau *m* des sables; *(i) NAm: F:* **to have plenty of s.,** avoir du courage, du cran.

sand[2], *v.tr.* **1.** sabler (une allée, etc.); **to s. the floor,** répandre du sable sur le plancher. **2.** *(a)* (*of alluvium*) **to s. (up),** ensabler (l'embouchure d'un fleuve, etc.); *(b) v.i.* (*of river mouth, etc.*) **to s. up,** s'ensabler. **3.** additionner de sable (le sucre, etc.); mettre du sable dans (le sucre). **4.** sabler, sablonner; nettoyer (qch.) avec du sable; *Metalw:* **to s. down a plate,** poncer, sabler, une tôle.

sandal[1] ['sænd(ə)l], *s.* sandale *f*.

sandal[2], *s. Bot:* **s. (tree),** santal *m*.

sandalwood ['sænd(ə)lwud], *s. Bot:* (bois *m* de) santal *m*; *(a)* **s. proper, white s.,** santal blanc; santal citrin; **s. oil,** essence *f* de santal citrin; *(b)* **yellow s.,** santal citrin de Cochinchine; *(c)* **red s.,** santal rouge (des Indes); *(d)* **false s.,** ximénie *f*.

sandarac ['sændəræk], *s.* **1.** *Miner:* réalgar *m*; *A:* sandaraque *f*. **2.** **(gum) s.,** sandaraque; gomme *f* de genévrier; vernis sec; *Bot:* **s. (tree),** callitris *m*; thuya *m* de Barbarie.

sandbag[1] ['sæn(d)bæg], *s.* *(a) Fort: etc:* sac *m* à terre; *Aer: Nau:* sac de lest; *(b) F:* assommoir *m*; boudin *m*; *(c)* coussin *m* (de graveur, de ciseleur); *(d)* bourrelet *m* (de porte, fenêtre, etc.); boudin.

sandbag[2], *v.tr.* **(sandbagged)** *(a)* protéger (un bâtiment, etc.) avec des sacs de terre, de sable; *(b)* mettre des bourrelets à (une fenêtre, une porte); *(c)* assommer (qn) (d'un coup de boudin sur la nuque); *F:* sabler (qn).

sandbank ['sændbæŋk], *s.* banc *m* de sable; sommail *m*; (*in river*) javeau *m*, allaise *f*.

sandbar ['sændbɑ:r], *s.* somme *f*; ensablement *m* (à l'embouchure d'un fleuve); banc *m* de sable.

sandbath ['sændbɑ:θ], *s. Ch: etc:* bain *m* de sable.

sandblast[1] ['sændblɑ:st], *s. Glassm: Metalw: etc:* jet *m* de sable; (*machine*) sableuse *f*; **s. sharpening,** affûtage *m* (de limes) par projection de sable.

sandblast[2], *v.tr.* passer (une surface) au jet de sable; décaper (une surface); sabler (une surface).

sandblaster ['sændblɑ:stər], *s.* **1.** (*pers.*) sableur *m*. **2.** sableuse *f*, machine *f* à sabler.

sandblasting ['sændblɑ:stiŋ], *s.* décapage *m*, décapement *m*, au (jet de) sable; *Glassm:* projection *f* de sable; *Metalw:* affûtage *m* (de limes) par projection de sable; sablage *m* (d'une surface).

sandbox ['sændbɔks], *s.* **1.** *A:* sablier *m* (pour répandre le sable sur l'écriture). **2.** *Metall:* caisse *f* à sable; *Golf:* boîte *f* à sable; *Rail:* sablière *f*, jette-sable *m inv* (de locomotive). **3.** *Bot:* **s. tree,** sablier.

sandboy ['sændbɔi], *s.m.* **as jolly, as happy, as a s.,** gai comme un pinson.

sanded ['sændid], *a.* **1.** *(a)* (*of path, floor, etc.*) sablé; *(b) Const:* (*of wood*) paré de sable (pour prendre l'apparence de la pierre). **2.** (*of sugar, flour, etc.*) sableux; additionné de sable.

sander ['sændər], *s. Tls:* ponceuse *f*; **orbital s.,** ponceuse vibrante.

sanderling ['sændəliŋ], *s. Orn:* bécasseau *m* sanderling, sanderling *m* des sables, *Fr.C:* sanderling.

sanders ['sændəz], *s. Bot:* *(a) A:* (bois *m* de) santal *m*; *(b)* **(red) s.,** santal rouge (des Indes).

sandglass ['sændglɑ:s], *s.* sablier *m*.

sandgrouse ['sændgraus], *s. inv. Orn:* ganga *m*; **black-bellied s.,** ganga unibande; **pintailed s.,** ganga cata; **spotted s.,** ganga du Sénégal; **Pallas's s.,** syrrhapte paradoxal, poule *f* des steppes.

sandhi ['sændi:], *s. Ling:* sandhi *m*.

sandhill ['sændhil], *s.* dune *f*.

sandhog ['sændhɔg], *s.* ouvrier *m* travaillant dans l'air comprimé.

sandiness ['sændinis], *s.* qualité sablonneuse (du sol, etc.).

sanding ['sændiŋ], *s.* **1.** sablage *m* (d'une allée, etc.). **2.** **s. (up),** ensablement *m* (d'un port, etc.). **3.** sablage, sablonnage *m*; nettoyage *m* au sable. **4.** ponçage *m*.

sandiver ['sændivər], *s. Glassm:* suin(t) *m* (du verre).

sandman, *pl.* **-men** ['sændmæn], *s.m. A:* sablonnier; sablier; *F:* (*to children*) **the s. has come,** le marchand de sable passe.

sandnatter ['sændnætər], *s. Rept:* ammodyte *f*.

sandpaper[1] ['sændpeipər], *s.* papier sablé, verré, émerisé; papier de verre.

sandpaper[2], *v.tr.* frotter (qch.) au papier de verre; poncer, doucir, dresser, (une surface) au papier de verre.

sandpapering ['sændpeip(ə)riŋ], *s.* ponçage *m*.

sandpiper ['sændpaipər], *s. Orn:* bécasseau *m*; chevalier *m*; **common s.,** chevalier guignette; **green s.,** chevalier cul-blanc; **grey-rumped s.,** chevalier à pieds courts; **marsh s.,** chevalier stagnatile; **solitary s.,** chevalier solitaire; **wood s.,** chevalier sylvain; **Baird's s.,** bécasseau de Baird; **broad-billed s.,** bécasseau falcinelle; **semi-palmated s.,** bécasseau semi-palmé; **Terek s.,** bargette *f* de Terek; **spoonbill s.,** eurynorhynche *m*; **upland s., Bartram's s.,** bartramie *f* à longue queue, *Fr.C:* maubèche *f* des champs; **Aleutian s.,** bécasseau aléoutien; **buff-breasted s.,** bécasseau rousset, *Fr.C:* bécasseau roussâtre; **least s.,** bécasseau minuscule; **pectoral s.,** bécasseau tacheté, à poitrine cendrée; **purple s.,** bécasseau maritime, violet; *NAm:* **red-backed s.,** bécasseau variable, *Fr.C:* bécasseau à dos roux; **Siberian pectoral s.,** *NAm:* **sharp-tailed s.,** bécasseau à queue pointue, *Fr.C:* bécasseau à queue fine; **spotted s.,** chevalier grivelé, *Fr.C:* maubèche *f* branle-queue; **stilt s.,** bécasseau à échasses; **wester s.,** bécasseau du nord-ouest; **white-rumped s., Bonaparte's s.,** bécasseau de Bonaparte, *Fr.C:* bécasseau à croupion blanc.

sandpit ['sændpit], *s.* sablière *f*, sablonnière *f*, arénière *f*; carrière *f* à sable.

sandshoes ['sændʃu:z], *s.pl. O:* = espadrilles *f*.

sandsoap ['sændsoup], *s.* savon minéral.

sandspit ['sændspit], *s.* cordon sablonneux; langue *f* de sable.

sandstone ['sændstoun], *s. Geol: etc:* grès *m*, molasse *f*; roche *f* psammitique; **red. s.,** grès rouge; **Old Red S.,** vieux grès rouge; **bunter s., New Red S.,** grès bigarré; **hard s.,** grignard *m*, grisart *m*; **shelly s.,** grès falun; **s. grit,** grès grossier; **s. quarry,** carrière *f* de grès; grésière *f*, gréserie *f*; **s. formation,** formation gréseuse; **s. wheel,** meule *f* en grès.

sandstorm ['sændstɔ:m], *s.* simoun *m*; tempête *f*, pluie *f*, de sable.

sandwich[1] ['sænwidʒ], *s.* **1.** *(a)* sandwich *m*, *pl.* sandwichs, sandwiches; **ham sandwiches,** sandwichs au jambon; **open s.,** canapé *m*, tranche de pain garnie; *(b) Sch:* **s. course,** cours intercalaire; *Tchn:* **s. material,** matériau *m* composite, sandwich; *(c)* **s. man,** homme-sandwich, *pl.* hommes-sandwiches; **s. board,** panneau *m*, placard *m*, de publicité (que porte l'homme-sandwich). **2.** *Geog:* **the S. Islands,** les îles *f* Sandwich.

sandwich[2], *v.tr.* serrer, intercaler (**between,** entre); **to be sandwiched between two people,** être (pris) en sandwich entre deux personnes.

sandworm ['sændwə:m], *s. Ann:* arénicole *f* des pêcheurs.

sandwort ['sændwə:t], *s. Bot:* arénaire *f*; sabline *f*.

Sandy[1] ['sændi]. *F:* **1.** *Pr.n.m. Scot:* (*dim. of Alexander*) Alexandre. **2.** *s.* (i) *O:* Écossais *m*; (ii) rouquin *m*.

sandy[2], *a.* **1.** (*of earth, etc.*) sableux, sablonneux, arénacé, arénifère; (*of path, etc.*) sablé; **s. stretches of coast,** longues grèves de sable; *Nau:* **s. bottom,** fond *m* de sable. **2.** (*of hair, etc.*) roux pâle *inv*; blond roux *inv*; **s.-haired,** aux cheveux d'un blond roux.

sane [sein], *a.* (*of pers.*) sain d'esprit; sensé; (*of views, speech, etc.*) raisonnable; sensé; **to be s.,** avoir toute sa raison; **s. mind,** esprit bien équilibré.

sanely ['seinli], *adv.* raisonnablement; sensément.

san fairy (ann) [sænfeəri(æn)], *phr. F: A:* (1914–18 *war*) ça ne fait rien.

San Franciscan [sænfrən'siskən], *a. & s.* (habitant, -ante) de San Francisco.

sangfroid [sɑ̃:(ŋ)frwɑ:], *s.* sang-froid *m*.

sangrail, sangreal (the) [ðəsæŋ'greil], *s. Lit:* le Saint-Graal, le Saint-Gréal.

sanguinaria [sæŋgwi'nɛəriə], *s. Bot:* sanguinaire *f*.

sanguinariness ['sæŋgwinərinis], *s.* caractère *m* sanguinaire (d'un combat, etc.).

sanguinary ['sæŋgwinəri], *a.* *(a)* sanguinaire; (bataille) sanguinaire, sanglante; *(b) P:* (*euphemism for* BLOODY) sacré.

sanguine ['sæŋgwin]. **1.** *a.* *(a)* (*of complexion, etc.*) d'un rouge sanguin; rubicond; *(b)* (*of temperament*) sanguin; *(c)* (*of pers., disposition, etc.*) confiant, optimiste; **to be of a s. disposition,** être porté à l'optimisme; **to be, feel, s. about the future,** avoir confiance en l'avenir; être plein d'espoir, d'espérance, pour l'avenir; **it surpassed our most s. expectations,** cela a dépassé toutes nos espérances. **2.** *s. Art:* sanguine *f* (crayon ou dessin).

sanguinely ['sæŋgwinli], *adv.* avec confiance; avec espoir; avec optimisme.

sanguineness ['sæŋgwinnis], *s.* confiance *f*; espoir *m*; optimisme *m*.

sanguineous [sæŋ'gwiniəs], *a.* **1.** *Med:* (crachat, etc.) sanguin, de sang. **2.** *Bot: etc:* d'un rouge sanguin; couleur de sang. **3.** (*of pers.*), (*constitution*) sanguin, pléthorique.

sanguinivorous [sæŋgwi'nivərəs], *a. Nat.Hist:* sanguinivore.

sanguinolent [sæŋ'gwinələnt], *a. Med: etc:* sanguinolent; teint de sang; **s. sputum,** crachat sanguinolent.

Sanhedrim, Sanhedrin [sæn'(h)i:drim, 'sænidrim, -in], *s. Jew.Hist:* Sanhédrin *m*.

sanicle ['sænikl], *s. Bot:* sanicle *f*, sanicule *f*; **wood s.,** sanicle d'Europe; **Yorkshire s.,** grassette *f*; **American s.,** heuchera *m*, heuchère *f*.

sanidine ['sænidi:n], *s. Miner:* sanidine *f*.

sanies ['seinii:z], *s. Med:* sanie *f*.

sanify ['sænifai], *v.tr. O:* améliorer les conditions hygiéniques (d'un endroit); assainir (un endroit).

sanious ['seiniəs], *a. Med:* sanieux.
sanitarian [sæni'tɛəriən], *a. & s. A:* hygiéniste (*mf*).
sanitarium [sæni'tɛəriəm], *s. NAm:* = SANATORIUM.
sanitary ['sænit(ə)ri], *a.* hygiénique, sanitaire; **s. control, inspection,** surveillance *f* hygiénique; **s. inspector,** inspecteur *m* de la salubrité publique; *Mil: etc:* **s. cordon,** cordon *m* sanitaire; *Plumb:* **s. ware,** matériel *m* sanitaire, le sanitaire; **s. engineer,** technicien *m* en équipement sanitaire; **s. engineering,** (i) technique *f* sanitaire; (ii) constructions *fpl* et matériel sanitaires; *Nau:* **s. water,** eau sanitaire; **s. pump,** pompe sanitaire.
sanitation [sæni'teiʃ(ə)n], *s.* système *m* sanitaire; hygiène publique.
sanity ['sæniti], *s.* **1.** santé *f* d'esprit; jugement sain. **2.** modération *f*; bon sens.
San Marino [sænmæ'ri:nou]. *Pr.n. Geog:* (la république de) Saint-Marin.
sans [sænz], *prep. Lit: A:* sans; **s. teeth, s. eyes,** sans dents, sans yeux.
sanserif [sæn'serif], *s. Typ:* caractères *mpl* sans obit et sans empattement.
sansevieria [sænsə'viəriə], *s. Bot:* sansevière *f*.
Sanskrit ['sænskrit], *a. & s. Ling:* sanscrit (*m*), sanskrit (*m*).
Sanskritist ['sænskritist], *s.* sanscritiste *m*, sanskritiste *m*.
Santa (Claus) ['sæntə(klɔ:z)]. *Pr.n.m.* le Père Noël.
Santa Cruz [sæntə'kru:z]. *Pr.n. Geog:* **S. C. Island,** l'île *f* Sainte-Croix.
santal[1] ['sænt(ə)l], *s.* = SANDALWOOD.
Santal[2]. *Ethn:* (*a*) *a.* santal, -als; (*b*) *s.* Santal, -ale.
Santali [sæn'tɑ:li], *s. Ling:* santal *m*.
Santo Domingo [sæntoudo'miŋgou]. *Pr.n. Geog:* Saint-Domingue *m*; la République Dominicaine.
santolina [sæntou'li:nə], *s. Bot:* santoline *f*; aurone *f* femelle.
santon ['sæntɔn], *s.* santon *m* ((i) ascète musulman; (ii) figurine provençale autour de la crèche de Noël).
santonic [sæn'tonik], *a. Ch:* (acide) santonique.
santonica [sæn'tɔnikə], *s.* **1.** *Bot:* santonine *f*. **2.** *Pharm:* semen-contra *m*.
santonin ['sæntənin], *s. Ch:* santonine *f*.
sap[1] [sæp], *s.* **1.** (*a*) *Bot:* sève *f*; **cellular s.,** suc *m* cellulaire; **s. green,** vert *m* de sève; (*b*) *NAm:* **s. house,** sucrerie *f* (où l'on fait le sucre d'érable); (*c*) *Fig:* vigueur *f*, sève. **2.** = SAPWOOD. **3.** *F:* niais, -aise; andouille *f*; **don't be such a s.!** ne sois pas si bête!
sap[2], *s. Mil: etc:* sape *f*; **direct double s.,** sape debout; **zigzag s.,** sape en zigzag; **underground s.,** sape en galeries de mine; **s. work,** sapement *m*; (*in trench*) travail *m* en sape; **s. roller,** gabion farci, roulant; **to drive a s.,** exécuter, pousser, une sape.
sap[3], *v.* **(sapped) 1.** *v.tr. & i. Mil: Civ.E:* saper, miner (des fondations, etc.); saper (une muraille, etc.); approcher (d'un endroit) à la sape; **to s. forward,** pousser des approches. **2.** *v.tr.* saper, miner (les fondements d'une doctrine, etc.); **fever has sapped his strength,** la fièvre l'a miné.
sapajou ['sæpədʒu:], *s. Z:* sapajou *m*, sajou *m*.
sapanwood ['sæpænwud], *s. Bot: Dy:* (bois *m* de) sap(p)an *m*; brésillet *m* des Indes; césalpinie *f* sappan.
sapele [sæ'pi:li], *s.* **s. (mahogany),** sapelli *m*, sapelly *m*.
saphead[1] ['sæphed], *s. F:* niais, -aise; andouille *f*.
saphead[2], *s. Mil:* tête *f* de sape.
saphina [sæ'fi:nə], *s. Ant:* saphène *f*; **long s., internal s.,** grande saphène; **short s., posterior s.,** petite saphène.
sapid ['sæpid], *a. Lit:* **1.** (*of food, etc.*) sapide, savoureux. **2.** (*of conversation, etc.*) intéressant.
sapidity [sæ'piditi], *s. Lit:* sapidité *f*.
sapience ['seipiəns], *s. A: & Lit:* (*a*) sagesse *f*, *A:* sapience *f*; (*b*) *Pej:* pédanterie *f*, pédantisme *m*.
sapient ['seipiənt], *a. A: & Lit:* (*a*) sage, savant; (*b*) *Pej:* pédant.
sapiential [sæpi'enʃəl], *a. B:* **the s. books,** les livres sapientiaux.
Sapindaceae [sæpin'deisii:], *s.pl. Bot:* sapindacées *f*.
sapindaceous [sæpin'deiʃəs], *a. Bot:* sapindé, sapindacé.
sapless ['sæplis], *a.* (*of plant, wood*) sans sève; desséché; (*of soil*) stérile; (*of pers., character*) sans vigueur; mou; (*of saying, idea*) insipide, fade.
sapling ['sæpliŋ], *s.* **1.** jeune arbre *m*; plant *m*, plançon *m*, baliveau *m*; *For:* **saplings,** boisage *m*; **to plant saplings on a piece of ground,** mettre un terrain en boisement; *For:* **s. wood,** gaulis *m*. **2.** (*a*) jeune homme *m*; adolescent *m*; (*b*) levron *m*, jeune lévrier *m*.
sapodilla [sæpə'dilə], *s. Bot:* **1. s. (plum),** sapotille *f*. **2. s. (tree),** sapotillier *m*.
sapogenin [sæ'pɔdʒinin], *s. Ch:* sapogénine *f*.
saponaceous [sæpɔ'neiʃəs], *a.* **1.** saponacé, savonneux. **2.** *A:* (*of pers., manner*) mielleux; onctueux; flagorneur.
saponaria [sæpɔ'nɛəriə], *s. Bot:* saponaire *f*.
saponary [sæpɔ'nɛəri], *s. Bot:* saponaire officinale.
saponifiable [sæpɔni'faiəbl], *a.* saponifiable.
saponification [sæpɔnifi'keiʃ(ə)n], *s.* saponification *f*.
saponifier [sæ'pɔnifaiər], *s.* saponifiant *m*.
saponify [sæ'pɔnifai]. **1.** *v.tr.* saponifier (de la graisse, etc.). **2.** *v.i.* se saponifier.
saponin ['sæpənin], *s. Ch:* saponine *f*.
sapor ['seipɔər], *s. Lit:* saveur *f*.
sapota [sə'poutə], *s. Bot:* (*fruit*) sapotille *f*; (*tree*) sapotillier *m*.
Sapotaceae [sæpou'teisii:], *s.pl. Bot:* sapotacées *f*.
sapotoxin [sæpou'tɔksin], *s. Ch:* sapotoxine *f*.
sappan(wood) ['sæpæn(wud)], *s. Bot:* (bois *m* de) sap(p)an *m*; césalpinie *f* sappan.
sapper ['sæpər], *s. Mil:* sapeur *m*; mineur *m*; **engineer s.,** sapeur du génie; *A:* **regimental s., infantry s.,** sapeur du régiment; *A:* **s. cyclist,** sapeur-cycliste *m*, *pl.* sapeurs-cyclistes; *F:* **the sappers,** le génie.
sapphic ['sæfik]. **1.** *a.* (*a*) *Pros:* **s. stanza,** strophe *f* saphique; (*b*) saphique, lesbien; **s. vice,** saphisme *m*. **2.** *s.pl. Pros:* **sapphics,** vers *m* saphiques.
Sapphira [sæ'faiərə]. *Pr.n.f. B.Hist:* Saphire.
sapphire ['sæfaiər], *s.* **1.** *Miner: Lap:* saphir *m*; **indigo-blue s.,** saphir mâle; **white s., water s.,** saphir blanc, saphir d'eau; **s. ring,** bague *f* de saphirs; *Miner:* **s. quartz,** saphir faux. **2.** *Orn:* saphir. **3.** *a. & s.* (couleur de) saphir *inv.* **4.** *Rec:* saphir.
sapphirine[1] ['sæfirain], *s. Miner:* saphirine *f*.
sapphirine[2], *a.* saphirin; *Ich:* **s. gurnard,** trigle *m* hirondelle.
Sapphism ['sæfizm], *s.* saphisme *m*, tribadisme *m*.
Sappho ['sæfou], *Pr.n.f. Gr.Lit:* Sapho.
sappiness ['sæpinis], *s.* **1.** abondance *f* de sève; teneur *f* en sève (du bois). **2.** *F:* stupidité *f*, bêtise *f*.
sapping ['sæpiŋ], *s. Mil: etc:* sapement *m*, sape *f* (d'une muraille, *Fig:* d'une croyance); travail *m* en sape.
sappy ['sæpi], *a.* **1.** (*a*) (*of tree, Fig: of youth, etc.*) plein de sève; (*b*) (*of timber*) vert. **2.** *F:* bête, stupide.
sapraemia [sæ'pri:miə], *s. Med:* saprémie *f*.
saprobe ['sæproub], **saprobiont** [sæ'proubiɔnt], *s.* saprobionte *m*.
saprobic [sæ'proubik], *a. Bot:* saprophytique.
saprogenic [sæprou'dʒenik], **saprogenous** [sæ'prɔdʒinəs], *a. Med:* saprogène.
saprolegnia [sæprou'legniə], *s. Fung:* saprolégnie *f*.
Saprolegniales [sæproulegni'eili:z], *s.pl. Fung:* saprolégniales *f*.
sapropel ['sæproupel], *s. Geog:* sapropel *f*, sapropèle *f*.
sapropelic [sæprou'pelik, -pi:lik], *s.* sapropélique.
saprophagous [sæ'prɔfəgəs], *a. Ent: etc:* saprophage.
saprophyte ['sæproufait], *s. Nat.Hist:* saprophyte *m*.
saprophytic [sæprou'fitik], *a. Bot:* saprophytique.
saprozoic [sæprou'zouik], *a. Prot:* saprozoïte.
saprozoon [sæprou'zouɔn], *s. Prot:* saprozoïte *m*.
sapsucker ['sæpsʌkər], *s. Orn:* pic *m*; **Williamson's s.,** pic de Williamson; **yellow-bellied s.,** pic maculé.
sapucaia [sæpu'kaia], *s. Bot:* **s. (tree),** sapucaia *m*; **s. nut,** marmite *f* de singe.
sapwood ['sæpwud], *s.* (bois *m* d')aubier *m*; *Carp:* aubour *m*; **false s.,** faux aubier; **s. rot,** pourriture *f* de l'aubier.
sar [sɑ:r], *s. Ich:* sargue *m*.
saraband ['særəbænd], *s. Danc: Mus:* sarabande *f*.
Saracen ['særəs(ə)n]. **1.** *Hist:* (*a*) *a.* sarrasin; (*b*) *s.* Sarrasin, -ine; *Her:* **Saracen's head,** tête de Maure. **2.** *a. Agr:* **S. corn,** (blé *m*) sarrasin *m*; blé noir.
Saracenic [særə'senik], *a.* sarracénique; sarrasin.
Saragossa [særə'gɔsə], *Pr.n. Geog:* Saragosse *f*.
Sarah ['sɛərə], *Pr.n.f.* Sara(h).
Saratoga [særə'tougə], *Pr.n. A:* **S. trunk,** malle bombée.
sarbacane ['sɑ:bəkein], *s.* sarbacane *f*.
sarcasm ['sɑ:kæzm], *s.* **1.** raillerie *f*, ironie *f*; esprit *m* sarcastique; sarcasme *m*. **2. (piece of) s.,** sarcasme.
sarcastic [sɑ:'kæstik], *a.* sarcastique; mordant; **s. remark,** sarcasme *m*.
sarcastically [sɑ:kæstik(ə)li], *adv.* d'une manière sarcastique; avec sarcasme; ironiquement.
sarcelle [sɑ:'sel], *s. Orn:* sarcelle *f*.
sarcellé, sarcelly ['sɑ:səlei, -li:], *a. Her:* **cross s.,** croix recercelée.
sarcenet ['sɑ:snet], *s. Tex:* = SARSENET.
sarcina, *pl.* **-as, -ae** ['sɑ:sinə, -əz, -i:], *s. Bac:* sarcine *f*.
sarco- ['sɑ:kou, sɑ:'kɔ], *comb.fm.* sarco-.
sarcoblast ['sɑ:koublæst], *s. Nat.Hist:* sarcoblaste *m*.
sarcocarp ['sɑ:koukɑ:p], *s. Bot:* sarcocarpe *m*.
sarcocele ['sɑ:kousi:l], *s. Med:* sarcocèle *m or f*.
sarcocolla [sɑ:kou'kɔlə], *s.* **1.** *Bot:* sarcocollier *m*. **2.** *A: Pharm: Com:* sarcocolle *f*.
sarcocyst ['sɑ:kousist], *s.* sarcocyste *m*.
sarcode ['sɑ:koud], *s. Biol:* sarcode *m*.
sarcoderm ['sɑ:koudə:m], *s. Bot:* sarcoderme *m*.
sarcoid ['sɑ:kɔid], *a. & s. Med:* sarcoïde (*f*).
sarcolactic [sɑ:kou'læktik], *a. Ch:* (acide) sarcolactique, paralactique.
sarcolemma [sɑ:kou'lemə], *s. Anat:* sarcolemme *m*, myolemme *m*.
sarcolite ['sɑ:koulait], *s. Miner:* sarcolite *f*.
sarcology [sɑ:'kɔlədʒi], *s.* sarcologie *f*.
sarcoma [sɑ:'koumə], *s. Med:* sarcome *m*.
sarcomatosis [sɑ:koumə'tousis], *s. Med:* sarcomatose *f*.
sarcomatous [sɑ:'kɔmətəs, -koum-], *a.* sarcomateux.
sarcomere ['sɑ:koumiər], *s. Anat:* sarcomère *m*.
sarcophaga [sɑ:'kɔfəgə], **sarcophagid** [sɑ:'kɔfəgid, -dʒid], *s. Ent:* sarcophage *f*.
sarcophagus, *pl.* **-phagi** [sɑ:'kɔfəgəs, -fədʒai], *s.* sarcophage *m*.
sarcophagy [sɑ:'kɔfədʒi], *s.* sarcophagie *f*.
sarcophile ['sɑ:koufail], *s. Z:* sarcophile *m*.
sarcoplasm ['sɑ:kouplæzm], **sarcoplasma** [sɑ:kou'plæzmə], *s. Anat:* sarcoplasme *m*.
sarcoplasmic, -plastic [sɑ:kou'plæzmik, -'plæstik], *a. Anat:* sarcoplastique.
sarcoptes [sɑ:'kɔpti:z], *s. Arach:* sarcopte *m*.
sarcoptid [sɑ:'kɔptid], *s. Arach:* sarcopte *m*; sarcoptidé *m*.
Sarcoptidae [sɑ:'kɔptidi:], *s.pl. Arach:* sarcoptidés *m*.
Sarcoramphus [sɑ:kou'ræmfəs], *s. Orn:* sarcoramphe *m*.
sarcosin(e) ['sɑ:kousi(:)n], *s. Ch:* sarcosine *f*.
sarcosis [sɑ:'kousis], *s. Physiol:* sarcose *f*.
sarcosoma [sɑ:kou'soumə], **sarcosome** ['sɑ:kousoum], *s.* sarcosome *m*.
Sarcosporidia [sɑ:kouspɔ'ridiə], *s.pl. Prot:* sarcosporidies *f*.
sarcosporidiosis [sɑ:kouspɔridi'ousis], *s. Vet: Med:* sarcosporidiose *f*.
sard [sɑ:d], *s. Miner:* sardoine *f*.
Sardanapalian [sɑ:dənə'peiliən], *a.* (luxe *m*, etc.) sardanapalesque.
Sardanapalus [sɑ:də'næpələs]. *Pr.n.m. A.Hist:* Sardanapale.
Sardica ['sɑ:dikə]. *Pr.n. A.Geog:* Sardique *f*.
sardine [sɑ:'di:n], *s. Ich:* sardine *f*; **tinned, canned, sardines,** sardines (conservées) à l'huile; **s. fisher, s. curer,** sardinier, -ière; **s. boat, s. net,** sardinier *m*.
Sardinia [sɑ:'diniə]. *Pr.n. Geog:* Sardaigne *f*.
Sardinian [sɑ:'diniən]. **1.** *Geog:* (*a*) *a.* sarde, (*b*) *s.* Sarde *mf*. **2.** *s. Ling:* sarde *m*.
Sardis ['sɑ:dis], *Pr.n. A.Geog:* Sardes *f*.
sardonic [sɑ:'dɔnik], *a.* (*a*) *Med:* (rire) sardonien; (*b*) (expression *f*, rire) sardonique.
sardonically [sɑ:'dɔnik(ə)li], *adv.* d'une manière sardonique; sardoniquement.
sardonyx ['sɑ:dəniks], *s. Miner:* agate *f* onyx; sardonyx *m*, sardoine *f*.
sargasso, *pl.* **-os, -oes** [sɑ:'gæsou, -ouz], *s. Algae:* sargasse *f*; *Geog:* **the S. Sea,** la mer des Sargasses.
sarge [sɑ:dʒ], *s. F: Mil: Av:* sergent *m*; **O.K. s.!** bien, chef!
sargo, sargus ['sɑ:gou, -gəs], *s. Ich:* sargue *m*; sparaillon *m*.
sari ['sɑ:ri], *s. Cost:* sari *m*.
sarigue [sæ'ri:g], *s. Z:* sarigue *m,f.* la sarigue.
sarissa, *pl.* **-ae** [sə'risə], *s. Gr.Hist:* sarisse *f*.
sark[1] [sɑ:k], *s. Scot:* (*a*) chemise *f*; (*b*) chemise de nuit.
Sark[2]. *Pr.n. Geog:* Sercq *m*.
sarkinite ['sɑ:kinait], *s. Miner:* sarkinite *f*.
sarky ['sɑ:ki], *a. F: O:* sarcastique, mordant.
Sarmatia [sɑ:'meiʃə]. *Pr.n. A.Geog:* Sarmatie *f*.
Sarmatian [sɑ:'meiʃ(ə)n]. *A.Geog:* **1.** *s.* Sarmate *mf.* **2.** *a.* sarmatique, sarmate.
Sarmatic [sɑ:'mætik], *a. A.Geog:* sarmatique, sarmate.
sarmentose, sarmentous [sɑ:'mentous, -təs], *a. Bot:* sarmenteux.
sarong [sə'rɔŋ], *s. Cost:* sarong *m*.
Sarpedon [sɑ:'pi:dɔn]. *Pr.n.m. Gr.Lit:* Sarpédon.
sarracenia [særə'si:niə], *s. Bot:* sarracénie *f*.
Sarraceniaceae [særəseni'eisii:], *s.pl. Bot:* sarracéniacées *f*.
Sarraceniales [særəseni'eili:z], *s.pl. Bot:* sarracéniales *f*.
sarrusophone [sæ'rʌsəfoun, -'ru:z-], *s. Mus:* sarrussophone *m*.
sarsaparilla [sɑ:səpə'rilə], *s. Bot: Pharm:* salsepareille *f*.
sarsen ['sɑ:s(ə)n], *s.* **1.** *Prehist:* **s. (boulder, stone),** monolithe *m*; monolithe tumulaire (des plaines du Wiltshire). **2.** *Geol:* **s. stone,** grès mamelonné.
sarsenet ['sɑ:snet], *s. Tex:* taffetas léger; florence *m*, armoisin *m*; **s. ribbon,** ruban *m* de taffetas.

sartorial [sɑː'tɔːriəl], *a.* de tailleur; *Hum:* **s. artist,** artiste tailleur.
sartorially [sɑː'tɔːriəli], *adv.* **s. impeccable,** à la mise, d'une élégance, impeccable.
sartorite ['sɑːtərait], *s. Miner:* sartorite *f.*
sartorius [sɑː'tɔːriəs], *s. Anat:* sartorius *m*; muscle couturier.
Sarum ['sɛərəm]. *Pr.n. Ecc:* (évêché *m* de) Salisbury *m*; **S. use,** liturgie particulière à l'évêché de Salisbury (avant la Réformation).
sash[1] [sæʃ], *s. Cost:* (*a*) écharpe *f*, ceinture *f* (d'étoffe) (portée par les officiers); (*b*) ceinture (de dame, d'enfant); large ceinture à nœud bouffant.
sash[2], *s. Const:* châssis *m* mobile, cadre *m* (d'une fenêtre à guillotine, d'une glace à coulisse); **French s.,** châssis à fiches; **inner s., double s.,** contre-fenêtre *f*, contre-châssis *m*; **s. window,** fenêtre *f* à guillotine, à coulisse.
sashcord ['sæʃkɔːd], *s.* corde *f* (d'une fenêtre à guillotine).
sasin ['sæsin], *s. Z:* antilope *f* cervicapre (de l'Inde); cervicapre *m.*
sasine ['seisin], *s. Jur: Scot:* saisine *f.*
sass[1] [sæs], *s. U.S: P:* culot *m*, toupet *m.*
sass[2], *v.tr. U.S: P:* se payer la tête de (qn); faire l'insolent avec (qn).
sassaby [sæ'seibi], *s. Z:* (espèce *f* de) damalisque *m.*
sassafras ['sæsəfræs], *s. Bot:* sassafras *m*; **dwarf s., swamp s.,** arbre *m* du castor; *Ch:* **s. oil,** essence *f* de sassafras; **Tasmanian s. oil,** essence d'athérosperme.
Sassanian [sæ'seiniən], **Sassanid** ['sæsənid]. *A.Hist:* (*a*) *a.* (art, etc.) sassanide; (*b*) *s.* Sassanide *m.*
Sassenach ['sæsənæk], *s. Scot:* Anglais, -aise.
sassolin(e), sassolite ['sæsouli(ː)n, -lait], *s. Miner:* sassoline *f*; acide borique hydraté naturel.
sasswood, sassywood ['sæs(i)wud], *s. Bot:* mançone *m*, tali *m*, teli *m.*
sassy ['sæsi], *a. U.S: P:* effronté, qui a du culot.
Satan ['seit(ə)n]. *Pr.n.m.* Satan; **it's like S. reproving sin,** les morveux veulent moucher les autres.
satanic [sə'tænik], *a.* satanique, diabolique; **His S. Majesty,** le diable.
satanically [sə'tænik(ə)li], *adv.* sataniquement, diaboliquement.
satanism ['seitənizm], *s.* satanisme *m.*
satanist ['seitənist], *s.* démonolâtre *mf*; sataniste *mf*; *a.* (culte, etc.) de Satan.
satchel ['sætʃ(ə)l], *s.* sacoche *f*; *Sch:* cartable *m.*
sate [seit], *v.tr.* **1.** assouvir (sa faim, ses passions, etc.); rassasier, satisfaire (qn, la faim); **to s. one's thirst for blood,** s'abreuver de sang; **sated lion,** lion repu. **2.** = SATIATE 1.
sateen [sə'tiːn], *s. Tex:* satinette *f*; satin *m* de coton.
satellite ['sætəlait], *s.* (*a*) *Astr: etc:* satellite *m*; **artificial s.,** satellite artificiel; **manned s.,** satellite habité; **unmanned s.,** satellite non habité; **stationary, synchronous, s.,** satellite stationnaire, synchrone; **earth-orbiting, moon-orbiting, s.,** satellite terrestre, lunaire; **data-gathering s.,** satellite de renseignement, de collecte de données; **earth-resources, resource-census, s.,** satellite de détection, satellite recenseur, des ressources naturelles; satellite de prospection; **geodetic, geophysical, s.,** satellite géodésique, géophysique; **navigation(al) s.,** satellite de navigation; **(tele)communications s.,** satellite de télécommunications; **meteorological, weather, s.,** satellite météorologique; **to launch a s. into orbit,** lancer un satellite en orbite; (*b*) **s. (state),** (état *m*) satellite; **s. town,** ville *f*, agglomération *f*, satellite; (*c*) *Biol:* trabant *m*, satellite.
satellitism ['sætəlaitizm], *s.* satellitisme *m.*
satiate ['seiʃieit], *v.tr.* **1.** rassasier (qn) jusqu'au dégoût (**with,** de); blaser (**with,** de). **2.** *occ.* = SATE 1.
satiated ['seiʃieitid], *a.* soûl, rassasié (de manger, etc.); gorgé, rassasié, blasé (de plaisirs, etc.).
satiating ['seiʃieitiŋ], *a.* rassasiant, affadissant.
satiation [seiʃi'eiʃ(ə)n], *s.* **1.** rassasiement *m.* **2.** satiété *f.*
satiety [sə'taiəti], *s.* satiété *f*; **to eat to s.,** manger jusqu'à plus faim; **to indulge in a pleasure to (the point of) s.,** goûter un plaisir jusqu'à satiété; se blaser d'un plaisir.
satin[1] ['sætin], *s.* **1.** *Tex:* satin *m*; **s. cloth,** drap *m* de satin; **s. weave,** armure *f* satin; **s. ribbon,** ruban satiné; ruban (de) satin; **s. dress,** robe *f* de, en, satin; **Denmark s.,** satin pour souliers de dames. **2.** *Bot:* **s. flower,** (i) (*also* **s. pod, white s.**), lunaire *f*; médaille *f* (de Judas); monnaie *f* du pape; (ii) stellaire *f.* **3.** (*a*) *Ind: Com:* **s. finish,** apprêt satiné (du papier, etc.); *Paperm:* **s. paper,** papier satiné; papier (à lettres) brillant; **s. white,** blanc satin (pour papiers chargés); *Miner:* **s. spar, s. stone,** spath satiné; (*b*) *Art: etc:* **s. of the skin,** satiné *m* de la peau; (*c*) *Needlew:* **(raised) s. stitch,** plumetis *m*; **s. stitch embroidery,** broderie *f* au passé.
satin[2], *v.tr.* satiner (le papier, etc.).
satiner ['sætinər], *s.* satineur, -euse (du drap, du papier, etc.).
satinette [sæti'net], *s.* **1.** *Tex:* (*a*) (*silk*) satinade *f*; (*b*) (*cotton*) satinette *f.* **2.** *Orn:* pigeon *m* satinette.
sating ['seitiŋ], *s.* assouvissement *m* (de la faim, des passions).
satining ['sætiniŋ], *s.* satinage *m*; **s. machine,** satineuse *f.*
satinwood ['sætinwud], *s.* (bois) satiné *m*; bois de satin.
satiny ['sætini], *a.* satiné.
satire ['sætaiər], *s.* **1.** *Lit:* satire *f* (**on,** contre). **2.** satire, sarcasme *m.*
satiric(al) [sə'tirik(l)], *a.* **1.** satirique. **2. satirical,** sarcastique, ironique.
satirically [sə'tirik(ə)li], *adv.* satiriquement; ironiquement; d'un ton moqueur.
satirist ['sætirist], *s.* **1.** (auteur, écrivain) satirique *m.* **2.** esprit mordant, malicieux.
satirize ['sætiraiz], *v.tr.* satiriser; faire la satire de (qch.).
satisfaction [sætis'fækʃ(ə)n], *s.* **1.** (*a*) acquittement *m*, paiement *m*, liquidation *f* (d'une dette); désintéressement *m* (d'un créancier); accomplissement *m* (d'une condition); exécution *f* (d'une promesse); *Jur:* **to enter s.,** enregistrer l'acquittement d'une obligation pécuniaire; (*b*) **s. for an offence,** réparation *f*, expiation *f*, d'une offense; **to demand s. for an insult,** demander raison d'un affront; exiger réparation par les armes; *A:* **to give s.o. s. (by a duel),** faire raison à qn, faire réparation à qn (par les armes); **to refuse s.o. s.,** refuser de satisfaire qn; **to obtain s. from s.o.,** tirer raison de qn; **to give s. for sth.,** rendre raison de qch.; **to make full, ample, s. to s.o.,** dédommager qn amplement, entièrement; **in s. of a wrong,** en dédommagement d'un tort; (*c*) assouvissement *m* (de la faim, d'une passion). **2.** (*a*) satisfaction *f*, contentement *m* (**at, with,** de); **to give s.o. s.,** donner du contentement à qn; satisfaire, contenter, qn; **to give s.o. cause for s.,** donner sujet de satisfaction à qn; **to have the s. of doing sth.,** avoir la satisfaction de faire qch.; **to express s.,** exprimer sa satisfaction; **I note with s. that. . .,** je suis heureux de noter que . . .; **to look at sth. with s.,** regarder qch. complaisamment, avec plaisir; **to his (entire) s.,** à sa grande satisfaction; **the work will be done to your s.,** le travail sera fait de manière à vous satisfaire; **to prove sth. to s.o.'s s.,** convaincre qn de qch.; (*b*) **it is a s. for me, it gives me great s., to know that . . .,** je suis heureux d'apprendre que . . .
satisfactorily [sætis'fækt(ə)rili], *adv.* d'une manière satisfaisante; de façon satisfaisante; **business is going on s.,** les affaires marchent à souhait.
satisfactoriness [sætis'fækt(ə)rinis], *s.* caractère satisfaisant (d'un travail, etc.).
satisfactory [sætis'fækt(ə)ri], *a.* **1.** satisfaisant; **s. reason,** raison satisfaisante; **s. pupil,** élève qui donne satisfaction; **the result is not very s.,** le résultat laisse à désirer; **the result is completely s.,** le résultat ne laisse rien à désirer; **to bring negotiations to a s. conclusion,** mener à bien des négociations; **to give a s. account of one's movements,** justifier de ses mouvements. **2.** *Theol:* satisfactoire, expiatoire.
satisfiable [sætis'faiəbl], *a.* que l'on peut satisfaire, contenter.
satisfied ['sætisfaid], *a.* (client, etc.) content, satisfait.
satisfy ['sætisfai], *v.tr.* **1.** (*a*) payer, liquider (une dette); s'acquitter (d'une dette, d'une obligation); exécuter (une promesse); faire droit à (une réclamation); remplir (une condition); désintéresser (ses créanciers); *Mth:* **to s. an equation,** satisfaire à une équation; **I am not satisfied with mere words,** je ne me paie pas de mots, de phrases; (*b*) satisfaire (qn); faire réparation à, satisfaire à (l'honneur); **(in order) to s. one's conscience,** pour l'acquit de sa conscience, par acquit de conscience. **2.** (*a*) satisfaire, contenter (qn); donner sujet de satisfaction à (qn); **to be satisfied with sth.,** (i) être content, satisfait, de qch.; (ii) se contenter de qch.; **I have every reason to be satisfied with the result,** j'ai tout lieu de me féliciter du résultat; *Sch:* **to s. the examiners,** être reçu à un examen; (*b*) satisfaire, assouvir, donner satisfaction à (un désir, un appétit, etc.); **in order to s. your curiosity,** pour satisfaire votre curiosité; **to s. all requirements,** satisfaire, suffire à, tous les besoins; *v.i.* **food that satisfies,** nourriture qui satisfait. **3.** convaincre, assurer, satisfaire (qn); éclaircir (un doute, etc.); **I am satisfied that he was telling the truth,** je suis sûr, convaincu, qu'il disait la vérité; **in order to s. you on this point,** pour vous satisfaire, pour éclaircir vos doutes, à cet égard; **I have satisfied myself that he (really) did it,** je me suis assuré qu'il l'a fait; **I am not wholly satisfied with the explanation,** j'ai du mal à accepter cette explication.
satisfying ['sætisfaiiŋ]. *a.* **1.** satisfaisant; qui contente; (*of food*) nourrissant; **s. meal,** repas satisfaisant; **s. job,** travail qui donne de la satisfaction. **2.** (argument, etc.) convaincant.
satisfyingly ['sætisfaiiŋli], *adv.* de façon satisfaisante.
satrap ['sætræp], *s. A.Hist:* satrape *m.*
satrapy ['sætrəpi], *s. A.Hist:* satrapie *f.*
Satsuma [sæt'suːmə]. **1.** *Pr.n. Geog:* Sats(o)uma *m*; *Cer:* **S. ware,** faïence *f* de Sats(o)uma; sats(o)uma; sa *m.* **2.** *s.* **s. (orange),** satsuma *f.*
saturable ['sætjərəbl], *a.* saturable.
saturate[1] ['sætjəreit], *v.tr.* **1.** imprégner, saturer, tremper, imbiber (**with,** de); **to become saturated with sth.,** s'imprégner de qch. **2.** *Ch: Ph:* saturer (une solution, etc.).
saturate[2], *a. Ch: Ph:* saturé.
saturated ['sætjəreitid], *a.* **1.** (terrain, vêtement, etc.) trempé. **2.** *Ch: Ph:* (*of solution, compound, etc.*) saturé; (*of vapour*) saturant. **3.** (*of colour*) riche; non combiné avec le blanc; intense.
saturation [sætjə'reiʃ(ə)n], *s.* **1.** imprégnation *f*; trempage *m.* **2.** *Ch: Ph:* saturation *f*; **magnetic s.,** saturation magnétique; **to dissolve a salt to s.,** dissoudre un sel jusqu'à saturation, jusqu'à refus; **s. point,** point *m* de saturation; *El:* **s. voltage,** tension *f* de saturation (d'une cellule photo-électrique, etc.); *Com:* **the market has reached s. point,** le marché est saturé; *Mil:* **s. bombing,** bombardement *m* en masse.
Saturday ['sætədi], *s.* samedi *m*; **he's coming on S.,** il viendra samedi; **he comes on Saturdays,** il vient le samedi; **he comes every S.,** il vient tous les samedis; **Holy S.,** le samedi saint.
Saturn ['sætən]. **1.** *Pr.n. Astr: Myth:* Saturne *m.* **2.** *s. A.Ch:* saturne; plomb *m.*
Saturnalia [sætə'neiliə], *s.pl. Rom.Ant:* saturnales *f.*
saturnalian [sætə'neiliən], *a.* des saturnales.
Saturnian [sæ'təːniən], *a.* **1.** *Astr: Myth:* saturnien; de Saturne; **the S. age,** l'âge *m* d'or. **2.** *A.Pros:* **S. verse,** vers saturniens.
saturnic [sæ'təːnik], *a. Med:* saturnin; atteint de saturnisme.
saturniid [sætə'naiid], *a.* & *s. Ent:* (papillon) saturnide (*m*); saturniidé *m.*
Saturniidae [sætə'naiidiː], *s.pl. Ent:* saturnides *m*, saturniidés *m.*
saturnine ['sætənain], *a.* **1.** (*of pers.*) taciturne, sombre; **to be of a s. disposition,** avoir du sombre dans l'âme. **2.** (*a*) saturnin; de plomb; **s. poisoning,** intoxication *f* par le plomb; saturnisme *m*; (*b*) *Med:* **s. symptoms,** symptômes *m* de saturnisme.
saturnism ['sætənizm], *s. Med:* saturnisme *m*; intoxication *f* par le plomb.
satyr ['sætər], *s.* **1.** *Myth:* satyre *m*; **she s.,** satyresse *f*; **dance of satyrs,** danse *f* satyrique. **2.** *Ent:* **s. (butterfly),** satyre.
satyriasis [sæti'raiəsis], *s. Med:* **1.** satyriasis *m.* **2.** priapisme *m.*
satyric [sə'tirik], *a. Gr.Lit:* satyrique; **s. drama,** drame *m* satyrique; satyre *f.*
satyrid ['sætirid], *s. Ent:* satyride *m*, satyridé *m.*
Satyridae [sæ'tiridiː], *s.pl. Ent:* satyrides *m*, satyridés *m.*
satyrion [sæ'tiriən], *s. Bot:* satyrion *m*; orchis *m* bouc.
satyrism ['sætirizm], *s.* satyrisme *m.*
sauce[1] [sɔːs], *s.* **1.** (*a*) *Cu:* sauce *f*; **tomato s.,** sauce tomate; **white s.,** sauce béchamel; **shrimp s.,** beurre *m* de crevettes; **caper s.,** sauce aux câpres; **s. cook,** saucier *m*; (*b*) assaisonnement *m*; condiment *m*; *A: & Lit:* **the s. of danger,** le sel du danger; **to add (a) s. to sth.,** relever le goût de qch.; *Prov:* **what's s. for the goose is s. for the gander,** ce qui est bon pour l'un l'est aussi pour l'autre; (*c*) *NAm:* accompagnement *m* de légumes verts, de salade, de fruits, etc. **2.** (*tobacco ind., gilding*) sauce. **3.** *F:* impertinence *f*, insolence *f*; culot *m*; toupet *m*; **none of your s.!** pas d'impertinence! **what s.! you've got a s.!** quel toupet! quel culot! **4.** *Bot:* **s. alone,** alliaire *f*; **s. alone oil,** essence *f* d'alliaire. **5.** *U.S: P:* boisson *f* alcoolique.
sauce[2], *v.tr.* **1.** *A:* assaisonner (un mets). **2.** *A: & Lit:* donner de l'agrément, du piquant, à (une nouvelle, etc.). **3.** *F:* dire des impertinences à (qn); manquer de respect à (qn).
sauceboat ['sɔːsbout], *s.* saucière *f.*
saucebox ['sɔːsbɔks], *s. F:* effronté, -ée; impertinent, -ente.
saucepan ['sɔːspən], *s.* casserole *f*; poêlon *m*; **double s.,** bain-marie *m*, *pl.* bains-marie; **to cook in a double s.,** faire cuire au bain-marie; **a s. of hot water,** une casserole (pleine) d'eau chaude.
saucepanful ['sɔːspənful], *s.* casserolée *f.*
saucer ['sɔːsər], *s.* (*a*) soucoupe *f*; **s. of milk,** soucoupe de lait; *F:* **flying s.,** soucoupe volante; *F:* **with eyes like**

saucers, aux yeux en soucoupe, en boule de loto; (*b*) *Art:* (*for mixing water colours*) godet *m* à couleur.

saucerful ['sɔ:səful], *s.* (pleine) soucoupe (**of,** de).

saucily ['sɔ:sili], *adv.* (*a*) impertinemment; d'un ton effronté; (*b*) d'un air gamin; d'un air mutin; (*c*) *O:* (chapeau porté) coquettement, crânement, avec chic.

sauciness ['sɔ:sinis], *s. F:* (*a*) impertinence *f*; toupet *m*; culot *m*; (*b*) gaminerie *f*; (*c*) *O:* élégance *f*; chic *m*.

saucy ['sɔ:si], *a. F:* (*a*) impertinent, effronté; culotté; *A:* **s. baggage,** petite effrontée; (*b*) fripon, gamin; **s. smile,** sourire mutin, aguichant; (*c*) *O:* **s. little hat,** petit chapeau coquet, chic; (*d*) (*of book, etc.*) osé, risqué.

Saudi ['saudi]. (*a*) *a.* séoudite, saoudite; **S. Arabia,** Arabie *f* séoudite, saoudite; (*b*) *a. & s.* **S. (Arabian),** Arabe *mf* séoudite, saoudite.

sauerkraut ['sauəkraut], *s. Cu:* choucroute *f*.

sauger ['sɔ:gər], *s. Ich:* sandre *f*.

Saul [sɔ:l]. *Pr.n.m. B.Hist:* Saül; **is S. also among the prophets?** (i) *B:* Saül aussi est-il entre les prophètes? (ii) où la vérité va-t-elle se nicher?

sauna ['saunə, 'sɔ:-], *s.* sauna *m*.

saunter[1] ['sɔ:ntər], *s.* **1.** promenade faite à loisir; flânerie *f*. **2. to come along at a s.,** arriver, s'amener, tout doucement.

saunter[2], *v.i.* **to s. (along),** flâner; marcher nonchalamment; se balader; déambuler; **to s. along, down, the street,** descendre doucement la rue; descendre la rue en flânant.

saunterer ['sɔ:ntərər], *s.* flâneur, -euse; baladeur, -euse.

sauntering ['sɔ:nt(ə)riŋ], *s.* flânerie *f*; badauderie *f*, badaudage *m*.

Sauria ['sɔ:riə], *s.pl. Rept:* sauriens *m*.

saurian ['sɔ:riən], *a. & s. Rept:* saurien (*m*).

sauriasis, sauriosis [sɔ:ri'eisis, -'ousis], *s. Med:* sauriasis *m*.

Saurischia [sɔ:'riskiə], *s.pl. Paleont:* saurischiens *m*, sauripelviens *m*.

sauroid ['sɔ:rɔid], *a. & s. Ich:* sauroïde (*m*).

Sauropoda [sɔ:'rɔpədə], *s.pl. Paleont:* sauropodes *m*.

sauropsid [sɔ:'rɔpsid], *s. Z:* sauropsidé *m*.

Sauropsida [sɔ:'rɔpsidə], *s.pl. Z:* sauropsidés *m*.

Sauropterygia [sɔ:rɔptə'ridʒiə], *s.pl. Paleont:* sauroptérygiens *m*.

sauropterygian [sɔ:rɔptə'ridʒiən], *s. Paleont:* sauroptérygien *m*.

Sauruaceae [sɔ:ru:'reisii:], *s.pl. Bot:* saururacées *f*.

Saururae [sɔ:'ru:ri:], *s.pl. Orn: Paleont:* saururés *m*.

saury ['sɔ:ri], *s. Ich:* scombrésoce *m*.

sausage ['sɔsidʒ], *s.* **1.** (*a*) *Cu:* (*fresh, usu. eaten hot*) saucisse *f*; *esp. U.S:* **blood s.,** boudin (noir); **s. skin,** peau *f* à saucisses; boyau *m*; **s. roll** = friand *m*; (*b*) (*preserved, hard, dry*) saucisson *m*; (*c*) *P:* **not a s.,** nib de nib. **2.** (*a*) *Min: etc:* boudin (d'explosif); (*b*) *Mil: F:* **s. (balloon),** ballon *m* d'observation; *F:* saucisse; (*c*) *F:* **s. dog,** teckel *m*. **3.** *Bot:* **s. tree,** arbre *m* à saucisses, kigelia *m*.

sausagemeat ['sɔsidʒmi:t], *s.* chair *f* à saucisse.

saussurite ['sɔ:sərait, 'sousjurait], *s. Miner:* saussurite *f*; jade *m* de Saussure; jade tenace.

saussuritization [sɔ:suriti'zeiʃ(ə)n], *s.* saussuritisation *f*.

sauté[1] ['souti], *a. & s. Cu:* sauté (*m*); **s. potatoes,** pommes (de terre) sautées.

sauté[2], *v.tr. Cu:* (faire) sauter (des pommes de terre).

savable ['seivəbl], *a.* **1.** que l'on peut sauver; dont l'âme peut être sauvée. **2.** récupérable.

savage[1] ['sævidʒ]. **1.** *a.* (*a*) (*of race, custom, etc.*) sauvage, barbare; non civilisé; *Her:* **s. man,** sauvage *m*; (*b*) (animal, coup) féroce; (coup) brutal, -aux; (visage) farouche; (*c*) *F:* (*of pers.*) furieux; en rage, en colère; **to make a s. attack on s.o.,** s'attaquer férocement à qn. **2.** *s.* sauvage *mf*.

savage[2], *v.tr.* (*a*) (*of animal, esp. of horse*) attaquer, mordre (qn, les autres bêtes); (*b*) *F:* (*of pers.*) attaquer (qn) du bec et des ongles.

savagely ['sævidʒli], *adv.* sauvagement, férocement; furieusement.

savageness ['sævidʒnis], **savagery** ['sævidʒ(ə)ri], *s.* **1.** sauvagerie *f*, barbarie *f* (d'une race, d'une coutume, etc.); **to live in s.,** vivre à l'état sauvage. **2.** férocité *f* (d'un animal, d'un coup); brutalité *f* (d'un coup).

savanna(h) [sə'vænə], *s. Geog:* savane *f*; **s. park,** savane-parc *f*.

savant ['savɑ̃, 'sævənt], *s.* savant, -ante.

savarin ['sævərin], *s. Cu:* savarin *m*.

savate [sæ'væt], *s. Box:* savate *f*, chausson *m*.

save[1] [seiv], *s.* **1.** *F: Dial:* économie *f*; **a great s. in heating,** une grande économie de chauffage. **2.** *Fb:* arrêt *m* (du ballon) (par le gardien); **to make a s.,** parer à l'attaque.

save[2], *v.tr.* **1.** (*a*) sauver (qn, une bête); **to s. s.o.'s life,** sauver la vie à, de, qn; **the doctors could not s. him,** les médecins étaient incapables de le sauver; **he has saved several lives at sea,** il a fait plusieurs sauvetages en mer; **he was saved from the wreck,** il a réchappé du naufrage; **to s. oneself by grabbing a rope,** se raccrocher, se reprendre, à un cordage; **to s. s.o. from death,** arracher qn à la mort; **to s. s.o. from drowning,** sauver qn qui se noie; tirer qn de l'eau; **to s. s.o. from s.o.'s anger,** préserver qn de la colère de qn; **to s. s.o. from a danger,** sauver qn d'un danger; dérober qn à un danger; **to s. s.o. from falling,** empêcher qn de tomber; **I went with him to s. him from promising impossibilities,** je l'ai accompagné pour veiller à ce qu'il ne promit rien d'impossible; **to s. s.o. from bad companions,** arracher qn à de mauvaises fréquentations; *Fb: etc:* (*of goalkeeper*) **to s. a goal,** arrêter le ballon; *Sp:* **to s. the game,** éviter la défaite; (*b*) *Theol:* **to s. one's soul,** sauver son âme; **whoso loveth God shall be saved,** quiconque aime Dieu fera son salut; **as I hope to be saved,** sur ma part de paradis; (*c*) sauver, protéger, sauvegarder (son honneur, etc.); **to s. the situation,** se montrer à la hauteur des circonstances; faire le nécessaire (pour parer à la catastrophe, etc.); **to s. appearances,** sauver, sauvegarder, les apparences; sauver les dehors; **to s. expense,** éviter des dépenses; **(God) s. me from my friends!** Dieu me protège contre mes amis! **God save the King, the Queen!** Dieu sauve le Roi, la Reine! *A:* **s. us!** Dieu nous garde! **2.** (*a*) mettre (qch.) de côté; **to s. the crusts for the chickens,** mettre de côté les croûtons pour les donner aux poules; **to s. silver paper for the hospitals,** garder le papier d'argent pour les hôpitaux; **s. a dance for me,** réservez-moi une danse; (*b*) économiser, épargner, mettre de côté (de l'argent); **I have money saved,** j'ai de l'argent de côté; **to s. every penny one can,** mettre sou sur sou; regarder à chaque sou; **to s. little by little,** économiser sou par sou; **he does not know how to s. money,** l'argent lui brûle la poche, lui fond entre les mains; **to s. on sth.,** économiser sur qch.; *v.i.* **to s. (up),** économiser pour l'avenir; faire des économies; épargner son argent; thésauriser; **to s. for one's old age,** amasser pour sa vieillesse; *Prov:* **a penny saved is a penny gained, is a penny earned,** qui épargne gagne; il n'y a pas de petites économies; les petites économies font les bonnes maisons. **3.** ménager (ses vêtements, etc.); économiser (le travail, etc.); éviter (une dépense, de la peine, etc.); **to s. time,** gagner du temps; faire une économie de temps; **to s. space,** ménager de l'espace; **we shall s. two pages,** on gagnera deux pages; **you'll s. money by it,** vous y gagnerez (de l'argent); **in this way you s. twenty per cent,** vous faites ainsi une économie de vingt pour cent; *Ind:* **to s. labour,** économiser la main-d'œuvre; **I am saving my strength,** je me ménage; je ménage mes forces; **I might as well have saved my breath, my pains,** j'avais beau parler; j'ai perdu ma peine; **to s. oneself for sth.,** se réserver pour qch. **4.** (*a*) **to s. s.o. sth.,** éviter, épargner, qch. à qn; **this has saved him a great deal of expense, of trouble,** cela lui a évité beaucoup de dépense, beaucoup de peine; **we have saved (ourselves) a kilometre by going this way,** nous avons gagné un kilomètre en prenant par ici; **they would be saved all this work,** cela leur épargnerait tout ce travail; **to s. s.o. the trouble of doing sth.,** épargner à qn la peine de faire qch.; (*b*) **to s. s.o. from sth., from doing sth.,** épargner qch. à qn; épargner à qn la peine de faire qch.; **we try to s. the wounded from being jolted.** nous tâchons d'épargner, d'éviter, les secousses aux blessés. **5.** *A:* attraper, ne pas manquer (la poste, le train, etc.).

save[3]. **1.** *prep. A: & Lit:* (*a*) sauf, excepté, hormis; à l'exception de; exception faite de; **he lost all his family s. one son,** il a perdu toute sa famille sauf un fils; **all, s. the doctor,** tous, à l'exception du docteur; **all is lost s. honour,** tout est perdu fors l'honneur; **s. on this point we are agreed,** à cela près, à ce détail près, nous sommes d'accord; **s. as otherwise provided in the articles,** sauf dispositions contraires des statuts; **to be happy, what is required s. to desire nothing?** pour être heureux, que faut-il sinon ne rien désirer? (*b*) **s. for a grazed arm he is unhurt,** il est indemne sauf une écorchure au bras; **he would be happy s. for one thing,** il serait heureux si ce n'était une chose. **2.** *conj.* (*a*) *A: & Lit:* **s. he be dead, he will return,** à moins qu'il ne soit mort, il reviendra; (*b*) *conj.phr.* **s. that. . .,** hormis que . . ., sauf que . . ., sinon que . . ., excepté que . . .; **I know nothing s. that she loves you,** je ne sais rien hors, hormis, qu'elle vous aime.

save-all ['seivɔ:l], *s.* **1.** *Mch:* appareil économiseur. **2.** *A:* binet *m*; brûle-bout(s) *m inv*; brûle-tout *m inv* (de bougeoir). **3.** *Nau: F:* petite voile supplémentaire établie au-dessous d'une autre voile.

saveloy ['sævəlɔi], *s. Comest:* cervelas *m*.

saver ['seivər], *s.* **1.** (*a*) sauveur *m*, libérateur, -trice (de sa patrie, etc.); (*b*) sauveteur *m* (de vie, de biens). **2.** appareil économiseur; **s. of time, of labour,** économiseur *m* de temps, de travail. **3.** épargnant, -ante.

savin(e) ['sævin], *s.* **1.** *Bot:* **s. (tree),** (genévrier *m*) sabine *f*; savinier *m*. **2.** *Pharm:* sabine.

saving[1] ['seiviŋ], *a., prep. & conj.*

I. *a.* **1.** (*a*) qui sauve; qui protège; (conseil, etc.) salutaire; (*b*) (qualité, etc.) qui rachète des défauts. **2.** (*a*) (*of pers.*) économe, ménager (**of,** de); parcimonieux; (*b*) (*of system, etc.*) économique. **3. s. clause,** clause *f* de sauvegarde; clause restrictive; réservation *f*.

II. *prep. & conj. A:* **1.** *prep. & conj.* = SAVE[3]. **2.** *prep.* sauf; sans blesser; sans porter atteinte à; **s. your presence,** sauf votre respect.

saving[2], *s.* **1.** (*a*) délivrance *f*; salut *m* (de qn, des âmes, des vies); **this was the s. of him,** cela a été son salut; (*b*) sauvetage *m*; (*c*) protection *f* (de qn, qch.). **2.** (*a*) économie *f*, épargne *f*; **labour s.,** (i) économie de travail; (ii) *Ind: etc:* économie de main-d'œuvre; **s. in handling costs,** économie dans le coût de la manutention; (*b*) **savings,** économies; *Pol.Ec:* dépôts *m* d'épargne; **to live on one's savings,** vivre de ses épargnes; **to draw on one's savings,** prendre sur ses économies; faire appel à ses économies; **(National) Savings Bank** = Caisse (Nationale) d'Épargne; **(National) savings certificate** = bon *m* d'épargne.

saviour ['seivjər], *s.* sauveur *m*; *Theol:* **Our S.,** Notre Sauveur.

savoir-faire [sævwɑ:'fɛər], *s.* adresse *f*; savoir-faire *m*.

savoir-vivre [sævwɑ:'vi:vrə], *s.* savoir-vivre *m*.

Savonarola [sævənə'roulə]. *Pr.n.m. Hist:* Savonarole.

savory ['seivəri], *s. Bot: Cu:* sarriette *f*; **summer s.,** sarriette des jardins; **winter s.,** sarriette des montagnes; **s. oil,** essence *f* de sarriette.

savour[1] ['seivər], *s.* **1.** saveur *f*, goût *m*, arôme *m* (d'un mets, etc.); *Lit:* **I find no s. left in life,** pour moi la vie n'a plus ni goût ni saveur. **2.** trace *f*, soupçon *m*, pointe *f* (d'ail, d'hérésie); **to have a s. of fanaticism,** sentir le fanatisme.

savour[2]. **1.** *v.tr. A:* (*of pers.*) savourer (un mets, etc.). **2.** *v.i.* (*of thg*) **to s. of sth.,** sentir qch.; tenir de qch.; **love that savours of jealousy,** amour *m* qui tient de la jalousie; **doctrine that savours of heresy,** doctrine *f* qui sent le fagot.

savourless ['seivəlis], *a.* fade, insipide; sans saveur.

savoury ['seivəri]. **1.** *a.* (*a*) (goût, mets) savoureux, appétissant; succulent; **to make a dish s.,** donner du goût à un mets; relever un plat; *F:* **he looked even less s. than the majority of tramps,** il avait l'air encore plus répugnant que la plupart des chemineaux; (*b*) (mets) piquant ou salé; **s. herbs,** plantes assaisonnantes, aromatiques; **s. omelette,** omelette *f* aux fines herbes, etc. **2.** *s.* entremets non sucré (de fin de repas).

Savoy [sə'vɔi]. **1.** *Pr.n.* (*a*) *Geog:* Savoie *f*; (*b*) **the House of S.,** la Maison de Savoie. **2.** *s.* (*a*) **s. (cabbage)** chou, *pl.* choux, frisé de Milan; (*b*) **s. biscuit,** biscuit *m* à la cuillère.

Savoyard [sə'vɔiɑ:d, 'sæv-]. *Geog:* (*a*) *a.* savoyard, savoisien; (*b*) *s.* Savoyard, -arde; Savoisien, -ienne.

savvy[1] ['sævi], *s. P:* jugeotte *f*.

savvy[2], *v.tr. P:* savoir; comprendre, piger; **savvy?** compris? tu piges?

saw[1] [sɔ:], *s.*

1. *Tls:* scie *f*; (*a*) **carpenter's s.,** scie de charpentier; **marble s.,** scie à marbre; **metal s.,** scie à métaux; **quarryman's s.,** scie de carrier; **stone s.,** scie à pierre; **stone-cutter's s.,** scie de tailleur de pierre(s); **veneer s.,** scie de placage, à plaquer; **wood s.,** scie à bois; **bookbinder's s.,** grecque *f*; **carborundum s.,** disque *m* au carborundum; **diamond s.,** disque diamanté; (*b*) **alternating, reciprocal, s.,** scie alternative; *Surg:* **amputating s.,** scie à amputation; **back s., carcass s.,** scie à dos; **band s., belt s., ribbon s.,** scie à ruban, scie à lame sans fin; **bow s., turning s.,** scie à chantourner (à main); **buck s.,** scie à bûches; **chain s.,** scie articulée, scie à chaîne; tronçonneuse *f*; **circular s.,** *U.S:* **buzz s. (for wood, for metal),** scie circulaire (à bois, à métaux); **cold s.,** scie à froid; **cross-cut(ting) s.,** scie de travers, tronçonneuse; **endless s.,** scie sans fin; **felling s., lumberman's two-handed s.,** scie passe-partout; **frame s.,** scie à cadre, à châssis; **gang s.,** scie à plusieurs lames, scie multiple; **hand s.,** scie à main; **small hand s.,** scie égoïne; **hot s.,** scie à chaud; **jig s., scroll s.,** scie à chantourner (mécanique); **keyhole s., compass s.,** scie à guichet; **long s., pit s.,** scie de long; **machine s., power s.,** scie mécanique; **pad s.,** scie à guichet démontable, scie à manche; **rip s., split s.,** scie à refendre; **tenon s.,** scie à tenon; (*c*) **s. blade,** lame *f*, feuille *f*, de scie; **s. cut, s. kerf,** trait *m* de scie; **s. frame,** châssis *m*, monture *f*, affût, *m*, arçon *m*, de scie; porte-scie *m inv*; **s. guard,**

protecteur *m*, chapeau *m*, de scie; **s. guide,** guide-lame *m inv* (de scie); **s. pad,** manche *m* porte-scie; **s. tooth,** dent *f* de scie; **s.-tooth roof,** toit *m* en dent de scie; (toit en) shed *m*; *W.Tel:* **s.-tooth wave,** onde *f* en dent de scie; **s.-toothed,** en dent de scie; (toit) en shed; **s. file,** lime *f* à affûter les scies; tiers-point *m*, *pl.* tiers-points; **s. set, s. swage, s. wrench, s. wrest,** tourne-à-gauche *m inv*; *Bookb:* **s. cutting,** grecquage *m*; *Mch.Tls:* **s. arbor, s. mandrel, s. spindle,** arbre *m* porte-scie; **s. bench,** machine *f* à scier, scierie *f*; **circular-s. bench,** scierie circulaire; **s. carriage,** chariot *m* porte-scie; **s. doctor,** machine à découper les creux (des dents de scies); **s. grinder, s.-sharpening machine,** machine à affûter les lames de scies; **s. timber,** (i) bois *m* de sciage; (ii) bois à ouvrer. **2.** *(a) Ich:* harpon *m* à bords dentelés (de scie de mer); *(b) Ent:* tarière *f* (de mouche à scie).

saw², *v.tr.* (*p.t.* **sawed;** *p.p.* **sawn; sawed) 1.** scier (le bois, etc.); sciotter (la pierre, le marbre); **to s. up wood,** débiter du bois; **sawn timber,** (bois de) sciage *m*; **to s. through timber,** tronçonner le bois; scier le bois en travers; **to s. off a piece of wood,** scier (et détacher) un morceau de bois; **to s. off the end of a plank,** araser une planche; **to s. off the waste,** enlever l'excédent à la scie; **sawed-off shotgun,** carabine *f* à canon tronçonné; **to s. out a piece (of wood),** découper, chantourner, un morceau (de bois); (*with passive force*) **wood that saws well,** bois qui se scie bien; *F:* **to s. the air,** battre l'air (avec ses bras); **to s. on the fiddle,** racler du, le, violon; *U.S: F:* **to s. wood,** vaquer à ses affaires; *Equit:* **to s. a horse's mouth,** scier du bridon. **2.** *Bookb:* **to s.(-cut),** grecquer (les feuilles).

saw³, *s.* adage *m*; proverbe *m*; maxime *f*; dicton *m*; aphorisme *m*.

sawbill ['sɔːbil], *s. Orn:* merganser *m*.

sawbones ['sɔːbounz], *s. F:* chirurgien *m*, carabin *m*.

sawbuck ['sɔːbʌk], *s. NAm:* **1.** = SAWHORSE. **2.** *F:* billet *m* de dix dollars.

sawdust¹ ['sɔːdʌst], *s.* sciure *f* (de bois); bran *m* de scie; *F:* **to knock the s. out of s.o.,** bourrer qn à coups de poing; rosser qn; rentrer dedans à qn.

sawdust², *v.tr.* répandre de la sciure sur (le plancher, etc.).

sawfish ['sɔːfiʃ], *s. Ich:* (poisson *m*) scie (*f*).

sawfly ['sɔːflai], *s. Ent:* tenthrède *f*; lophyre *m*; mouche *f* à scie; **stem s.,** cèphe *m*; **turnip s.,** athalia *f*; **rose s.,** (i) cladie *m*; (ii) hylotome *m* (des rosiers); **willow s.,** hylotome (des saules).

sawhorse ['sɔːhɔːs], *s. Mec.E:* chevalet *m* de sciage, de scieur; chèvre *f*; bidet *m*.

sawing ['sɔːiŋ], *s.* **1.** sciage *m* (du bois); **s. (up),** débitage *m* (du bois). **2.** *Bookb:* grécage *m*.

sawlog ['sɔːlɔg], *s.* bille *f*.

sawmill ['sɔːmil], *s.* scierie *f*.

sawpit ['sɔːpit], *s.* fosse *f* de scieur de long; **s. frame, horse,** baudet *m*.

saw(-)wort ['sɔːwəːt], *s. Bot:* serrette *f*, sarrette *f*; serratule *f*.

sawyer ['sɔːjər], *s.* **1.** scieur *m* (de long). **2.** arbre immergé dans le courant d'un fleuve (et dangereux pour la navigation). **3.** *U.S: Ent:* longicorne *m* (dont les larves attaquent le bois mort).

sax¹ [sæks], *s. Tls:* hache *f* d'ouvrage (de couvreur); asseau *m*, assette *f*.

sax², *s. Mus: F:* saxo(phone) *m*; **alto s.,** saxophone alto.

saxatile ['sæksətail], *a. Nat.Hist:* saxatile.

saxe [sæks], *a. & s.* **s. blue,** bleu *m* de Saxe; **s. blue dress,** robe bleu de Saxe.

saxhorn ['sækshɔːn], *s. Mus:* saxhorn *m*.

saxicava, *pl.* **-ae** [sæk'sikəvə, -iː], *s. Moll:* saxicave *f*.

saxicavous [sæk'sikəvəs], *a. Moll:* saxicave.

Saxicolinae [sæksikou'lainiː], *s.pl. Orn:* saxicoles *m*.

saxicoline, saxicolous [sæk'sikoulain, -ləs], *a. Nat.Hist:* saxicole.

Saxifragaceae [sæksifrə'geisiiː], *s.pl. Bot:* saxifrag(ac)ées *f*.

saxifrage ['sæksifreidʒ], *s. Bot:* **1.** saxifrage *f*; **yellow s.,** saxifrage d'automne; **white meadow s.,** saxifrage granulée; casse-pierre(s) *m inv*, perce-pierre *f*, *pl.* perce-pierres; christemarine *f*; **rue-leaved s.,** saxifrage tridactyle, à trois doigts; **mossy s.,** saxifrage mousseuse; saxifrage hypnoïde; gazon *m* mousse; **wood s.,** saxifrage cunéiforme. **2. golden s.,** saxifrage dorée; **burnet s.,** pied-de-chèvre *m*, *pl.* pieds-de-chèvre; **meadow s.,** séséli *m*.

saxist ['sæksist], *s. Mus:* saxophoniste *mf*; **alto s.,** joueur, -euse, du saxophone alto.

Saxon ['sæks(ə)n]. **1.** *(a) a. Geog: etc:* saxon; saxonique; **S. architecture,** architecture anglaise préromane; *(b) s.* Saxon, -onne. **2.** *s. Ling:* saxon *m*.

Saxonian [sæk'souniən], *a. & s. Geol:* saxonien (*m*).

Saxony ['sæksəni]. *Pr.n. Geog:* Saxe *f*.

saxophone ['sæksəfoun], *s. Mus:* saxophone *m*.

saxophonist [sæk'sɔfənist], *s. Mus:* saxophoniste *mf*; joueur, -euse, de saxophone.

saxotromba [sæksou'trɔmbə], *s. Mus:* saxotromba *m*.

saxtuba [sæks'tjuːbə], *s. Mus:* tuba *m*.

say¹ [sei], *s.* dire *m*, parole *f*, mot *m*; **to have one's s.,** dire ce qu'on a à dire; dire son mot; dire ce que l'on a sur le cœur; **now I can have my s.,** maintenant (c'est) à moi la parole; **let me have my s.,** laissez-moi parler; laissez-moi dire un mot; **I have no s. in the matter,** je n'ai pas voix au chapitre.

say², *v.tr.* (*p.t.* **said** [sed]; *p.p.* **said;** *3rd sg. pr. ind.* **says** [sez], *A:* **sayeth** ['seiəθ], **saith** [seθ]) dire. **1.** *(a)* (*utter*) **to s. a word,** dire un mot; **you have only to s. the word,** vous n'avez qu'à le dire, qu'à donner l'ordre; **to ask s.o. to s. a few words,** prier qn de prendre la parole; **to s. good morning to s.o.,** dire bonjour à qn; **she said nothing,** elle n'a rien dit; **who shall I s. called, rang?** c'est de la part de qui? **to s. sth. again,** répéter, redire, qch.; (*in defiance*) **just s. that again!** répétez un peu pour voir! **I'm not saying,** je ne dis rien; **I can't, couldn't, s.,** je ne sais pas; je n'en sais rien; **it goes without saying that. . .,** il va de soi, cela va sans dire, que . . .; **that goes without saying,** cela va sans dire; *F:* cela ne fait pas un pli; **there's no saying . . .,** (il est) impossible de dire, on ne sait pas (quand . . ., etc.); **there's no saying what will happen,** on ne peut pas dire ce qui arrivera; **it isn't said,** cela ne se dit pas; **what do you s.?** que dites-vous? qu'est-ce que vous dites? **what d'you s. to that?** qu'en dites-vous, pensez-vous? **what did you s.?** (i) qu'avez-vous dit? (ii) pardon? **that's just what I was about to s.,** c'est justement ce que j'allais dire; **he never hears what is said to him,** il n'entend jamais ce qu'on lui dit; **I don't care what you s.,** vous avez beau dire; **whatever he may s.,** quoi qu'il en ait; quoi qu'il dise, malgré ce qu'il dit; **to s. yes, no,** dire (que) oui, (que) non; **to s. yes one moment and no the next,** changer souvent d'avis; **I offered you a drink and you said no,** je vous ai offert à boire et vous avez refusé; *F:* **I wouldn't s. no to a glass of beer,** je boirais bien, volontiers, un verre de bière; un verre de bière ne serait pas de refus; **what do you s. to a drink?** si on prenait un verre? **what do you s. to a game of bridge?** si on faisait un bridge? ça vous dit-il, vous dirait-il, de faire une partie de bridge? **he goes to the club—so he says!** il va au cercle—à l'en croire! *B:* **thus saith the Lord,** ainsi dit l'Éternel; ainsi parle le Seigneur; **"I accept," he said,** "j'accepte," dit-il; *P:* **"not on your life!" says I,** "absolument pas," "pas du tout," que je dis; **says you!** que tu dis! **says who?** chiche? *(b)* (*express orally or otherwise*) **he said that you were here,** il a dit que vous étiez ici; **all *that* can be said in a couple of words,** tout ça tient en deux mots; **s. it with flowers!** dites-le avec des fleurs! **as I said in my letter,** comme je vous l'ai dit dans ma lettre; **the Bible says, it says in the Bible, that. . .,** comme on lit dans la Bible . . .; **the text of the treaty says . . .,** le texte du traité porte ces mots . . .; **the church clock says ten,** le cadran de l'église marque dix heures; **let it be said,** soit dit en passant; **what did you s. your job was?** qu'est-ce que vous faites déjà? **you don't mean to s. he's 86,** vous n'allez pas me dire qu'il a 86 ans; **I mean to s.!** tout de même! quand même! *F:* **though I s. it who, that, shouldn't,** bien que ce ne soit pas à moi de le dire; **as they s., as people s.,** comme on dit; **so to s.,** pour ainsi dire; **as one might s.,** comme qui dirait; **one might as well s. . . .,** autant dire . . .; **one may well s. so,** c'est bien le cas de le dire; **or perhaps I should s. . . .,** ou pour mieux dire . . .; **I must s. . . .,** j'avoue . . ., je dois dire . . ., il faut avouer . . .; franchement . . .; **this news surprises me, I must s.,** cette nouvelle me surprend, je l'avoue; **I *will* s. this about you that . . .,** je vous rends ce témoignage que . . .; **that is to s. . . .,** c'est-à-dire . . .; (à) savoir . . .; **three books at £5, that's to s. £15,** trois livres à £5, soit £15; **his language was coarse, not to s. blasphemous,** son langage était grossier, même, voire, pour ne pas dire, blasphématoire; **have you said anything about it to him?** lui en avez-vous parlé? **I don't want anything to be said about it,** je ne veux pas qu'on en dise rien; je ne veux pas que cela s'ébruite; **I remember something was said about it,** je me souviens qu'on en a parlé; **the less said the better, least said soonest mended,** moins nous parlerons, mieux cela vaudra; **s. no more!** n'en dites pas davantage! **to s. nothing of that,** sans parler de cela; **he knows no English, to s. nothing of French,** il ne sait pas l'anglais, sans parler du français; **that painting says nothing to me,** ce tableau ne me dit rien; **he doesn't s. much,** il parle peu; il est peu communicatif; **he has very little to s. for himself; he never has anything to s. for himself,** (i) il est peu communicatif; (ii) il ne sait pas se faire valoir; **he has plenty to s. for himself,** (i) *F:* il a la langue bien pendue; (ii) il sait se faire valoir, se mettre en avant; **what have you to s. for yourself?** (i) quelles sont vos nouvelles? (ii) eh bien, expliquez-vous! **we had nothing to s. to each other,** nous n'avions rien à nous dire; **there is something to be said on both sides,** il y a du pour et du contre; **this much can be said at present, that. . .,** on peut affirmer dès maintenant que . . .; **there is much to be said for beginning now,** il y a de bonnes raisons pour s'y mettre dès maintenant; **there is much to be said for this invention,** cette invention se recommande à plusieurs points de vue; **I can't s. much for his progress in maths,** en math il reste plutôt faible; **that doesn't s. much for his intelligence,** cela ne dénote pas beaucoup d'intelligence; **don't s. he didn't cheat!** avec ça qu'il n'a pas triché! *F:* **you don't s. (so)!** c'est pas vrai! allons donc! pas possible! vraiment? ça alors! ça par exemple! **you can s. that again! you've said it!** vous l'avez dit! bien vrai! *(c)* (*report*) **they s. that . . ., it is said that. . .,** on dit que . . .; on prétend que . . .; **it is said,** on le dit, le prétend; **I've heard it said that . . .,** j'ai entendu dire que . . .; **that is what people are saying,** voilà ce qu'on raconte; **I don't care what people may s.,** je me moque du qu'en-dira-t-on; **he is said to have a large fortune,** on lui donne, on lui attribue, une grande fortune; **he is said to be rich,** on le dit riche; on dit qu'il est riche; **this tree is said to be 200 years old,** on dit que cet arbre a 200 ans; **nobody can be said to have understood him,** on ne peut pas affirmer que personne l'ait jamais compris; **a ship is said to list when it leans over to one side,** on dit qu'un navire gîte lorsqu'il penche sur le côté; *(d)* (*hold an opinion*) **anyone would s. that he was asleep,** on dirait qu'il dort; **I should s. she is intelligent,** autant que j'en puis juger elle est intelligente; **I should s. not,** je ne crois pas; je crois que non; **it is difficult to s. (when, where, which, etc.),** il est difficile de dire, on ne saurait préciser, on ne sait pas (quand, où, quel, etc.); **and so s. all of us,** et nous pensons tous de même; c'est ce que nous disons tous; **didn't I s. that he would come!** je le disais bien qu'il viendrait! **didn't I s. so!** quand je vous le disais! je vous l'avais bien dit! *(e)* **it was you who said I was to do it,** c'est vous qui m'avez dit de le faire, qui me l'avez dit; *(f)* **(let us, shall we, shall I) s.,** disons; **come and have lunch one of these days, s. Sunday,** venez déjeuner un de ces jours, disons dimanche, par exemple dimanche; **if I had, s., £10,000 a year,** si j'avais, mettons £10,000 par an; **three times round the track, s. 4 km,** trois tours de piste, soit 4 km; **99 pence, s. a pound,** 99 pence, autant dire une livre; **well, s. it were true, what then?** eh bien, mettons que ce soit vrai, même si c'était vrai, quand même ça serait vrai, alors quoi? *(g)* (*exclamatory*) **I s.,** *NAm:* **s.!** dites donc! **s., I've got an idea,** écoutez donc, j'ai une idée; *NAm:* **s., can you . . .?** pardon, monsieur, pourriez-vous . . .? (*expressing surprise*) **I s.!** pas possible! fichtre! **I'll s.! I should s. so!** vous avez raison! et comment donc! **I should s. not!** jamais de la vie! **2.** dire, réciter (une prière, etc.); faire (ses prières); **to s. mass,** dire la messe; **to s. grace,** dire le bénédicité.

saying ['seiiŋ], *s. (a)* dit *m* (de qn); **historical s.,** mot *m* historique; *(b)* **(popular) s.,** adage *m*, proverbe *m*, maxime *f*, dicton *m*, aphorisme *m*; **as the s. goes,** comme dit le proverbe; comme on dit; selon le dicton.

say-so ['seisou], *s. F:* **1. on his s.-so,** selon ce qu'il dit, sur sa parole. **2. to have the s.-so,** avoir voix au chapitre.

say(y)id ['seijid], *s.* sidi *m*.

sbirro, *pl.* **sbirri** ['sbirou, 'sbiriː], *s.* sbire *m*.

'sblood [zblʌd], *int. A:* morbleu!

scab¹ [skæb], *s.* **1.** *(a) Vet:* gale *f*, bouquet *m*; *(b) Hort:* (*of plants*) gale; *F:* rogne *f*. **2.** *(a)* (*on wound*) croûte *f*, escarre *f*; *(b) Metall:* (i) dartre *f*; (ii) peau *f* de crapaud (de moulage). **3.** *P:* (*pers.*) *(a) Ind:* renard *m*, jaune *m*; *(b)* canaille *f*; sale type *m*; vilain coco; salaud *m*; saligaud *m*.

scab², *v.i.* **(scabbed) 1.** (*of wound*) **to s. (over),** former une croûte; se cicatriser. **2.** *Metall:* dartrer. **3.** *P:* supplanter les grévistes; trahir ses camarades.

scabbard ['skæbəd], *s.* fourreau *m* (d'une épée); gaine *f* (d'un poignard, etc.); **to throw away the s.,** jurer la guerre à outrance; s'en remettre au sort des armes; *Sm.a:* **s. catch,** pontet *m* (de fusil, etc.); *Ich:* **s. fish,** lépidope *m*; jarretière *f*.

scabbed [skæbd], *a.* = SCABBY 2.

scabbiness ['skæbinis], *s.* **1.** état galeux (d'un animal). **2.** *(a)* état croûteux (d'une blessure, etc.); *(b) Metall:* état dartreux (d'un moulage). **3.** *P: O:* mesquinerie *f*; pingrerie *f*.

scabbing ['skæbiŋ], *s.* formation *f* (i) *Med:* d'une croûte, (ii) *Metall:* d'une dartre.

scabble ['skæbl], *v.tr.* dégrossir, smiller (la pierre de carrière); **scabbled stone,** moellon smillé.
scabbling ['skæbliŋ], *s.* smillage *m,* esmillage *m.*
scabby ['skæbi], *a.* **1.** *Vet:* (*of sheep, etc.*) galeux; **s. mouth,** ecthyma contagieux. **2.** (*a*) (*of sore, etc.*) croûteux, scabieux; (*b*) (*of metal casting*) dartreux. **3.** *P: O:* (*a*) (*of pers., thg*) mesquin, sordide, méprisable; (*b*) (*of pers.*) ladre, pingre.
scabetic [skə'betik], *a.* = SCABIETIC.
scabies ['skeib(i)i:z], *s. Med:* gale *f.*
scabietic [skeibi'i:tik], *a. Med:* galeux; scabieux.
scabiosa [skeibi'ousə], *s. Bot:* scabieuse *f,* scabiosa *m;* knautia *m.*
scabious ['skeibiəs]. **1.** *a.* = SCABBY 1, 2. **2.** *s. Bot:* scabieuse *f;* **purple s., sweet s.,** scabieuse fleur de veuve; veuve *f;* fleur *f* des veuves; **blue s., devil's bit s.,** scabieuse tronquée; scabieuse succise; succise *f;* mors *m* du diable; herbe *f* de Saint Joseph; **field s., meadow s.,** scabieuse des champs; **small s.,** scabieuse colombaire.
scabrous ['skeibrəs], *a.* **1.** (*of surface, etc.*) rugueux, raboteux; *Bot:* **s. leaved,** scabrifolié. **2.** (*of topic, tale, etc.*) scabreux, risqué; licencieux, indécent.
scabrousness ['skeibrəsnis], *s.* **1.** scabrosité *f,* rugosité *f* (d'une surface). **2.** scabreux *m,* caractère scabreux, caractère risqué, indécence *f* (d'un récit, etc.).
scabwort ['skæbwə:t], *s. Bot:* aunée *f* hélène.
scacchite ['skækait], *s. Miner:* scacchite *f.*
scad [skæd], *s. Ich:* carangue *f,* saurel *m,* chinchard *m;* maquereau bâtard.
scads [skædz], *s.pl. NAm: F:* grande quantité (de qch.); **there's s. of it,** il y en a des tas.
scaffold[1] ['skæf(ə)ld], *s.* **1.** *A:* (*a*) échafaud *m,* estrade *f* (pour représentations); (*b*) tribunes *fpl* (pour spectateurs). **2.** échafaud (pour exécutions); **to go to, to mount, the s.,** monter à, sur, l'échafaud; **to perish, die, on the s.,** mourir sur l'échafaud; **to bring s.o. to the s.,** faire tomber la tête de qn. **3.** *Const:* = SCAFFOLDING 1. **4.** *Metall:* engorgement *m* (d'un haut fourneau).
scaffold[2]. **1.** *v.tr. Const:* dresser un échafaudage contre (une maison, etc.), autour (d'une maison, etc.). **2.** *v.i. Metall:* (*of furnace*) s'engorger.
scaffolder ['skæf(ə)ldər], *s. Const:* ouvrier *m* qui dresse des échafaudages.
scaffolding ['skæf(ə)ldiŋ], *s.* **1.** *Const:* échafaudage *m;* **fixed s.,** sapine *f;* **s. pole,** écoperche *f,* perche *f* d'échafaudage; **horizontal s. pole,** tendière *f.* **2.** *Metall:* = SCAFFOLD[1] 4.
scagliola [skæl'joulə], *s. Const:* scagliola *f.*
scala ['skeilə], *s. Moll:* scalaire *f,* scale *f.*
scalar ['skeilər], *a. & s. Mth:* scalaire (*m*); **s. quantity,** grandeur scalaire; *El:* **s. field,** champ scalaire.
scalare [skə'lɑ:ri, -rei], *s. Ich:* scalaire *f,* ange noir du Brésil.
scalariform [skə'lærifɔ:m], *a. Nat.Hist:* scalariforme; *Bot:* **s. vessels,** vaisseaux scalariformes; *Algae:* **s. conjunction,** conjugaison scalariforme.
Scalariidae [skælə'raiidi:], *s.pl. Moll:* scalariidés *m.*
scalawag ['skæləwæg], *s.* = SCALLYWAG.
scald[1] [skɔ:ld], *s.* **1.** échaudure *f* (sur la main, etc.). **2.** *Hort:* (*disease of apples*) scald *m.*
scald[2], *v.tr.* **1.** échauder, ébouillanter (la main, etc.); **to s. one's foot,** s'échauder, s'ébouillanter, le pied; **to be scalded to death,** mourir de ses brûlures (après l'explosion d'une chaudière, etc.). **2.** (*a*) échauder, peler (un porc, etc.); blanchir (un chou, etc.); échauder, ébouillanter (des fruits, etc., pour les perler); (*b*) faire chauffer (le lait, etc.) juste au-dessous du point d'ébullition; **scalded cream,** crème échaudée; (*c*) **to s. (out) a vessel,** échauder, ébouillanter, un récipient.
scald[3], *s.* **scaldic** ['skɔ:ldik], *a.* = SKALD, SKALDIC.
Scaldesian [skɔl'di:ziən], *a. & s. Geol:* (étage) scaldisien *m.*
scaldfish ['skɔ:ldfiʃ], *s. Ich:* fausse limande.
scaldhead ['skɔ:ldhed], *s. Med:* teigne faveuse.
scalding[1] ['skɔ:ldiŋ], *a.* (*of liquid*) **s. (hot),** brûlant, tout bouillant; *Lit:* **s. tears,** larmes brûlantes.
scalding[2], *s.* **1.** échaudage *m,* ébouillantage *m;* (*in slaughterhouse*) **s. room,** échaudoir *m;* **s. tub,** échaudoir. **2.** *Cu:* (*a*) blanchiment *m* (de la viande, etc.); ébouillantage (de légumes, etc.); (*b*) cuisson *f* (du lait, etc.) juste au-dessous du point d'ébullition.
scale[1] [skeil], *s.* **1.** (*a*) (*on fish, reptile, bud, etc.*) écaille *f;* *Med:* (*on skin*) écaille, squame *f;* *Lit:* **the scales fell from his eyes,** les écailles lui tombèrent des yeux; ses yeux furent dessillés; (*b*) *Ent:* **San José s.,** pou *m* de San José; **s. insect, s. louse,** coccidé *m,* cochenille *f;* **s. blight,** maladie des plantes produite par la cochenille; *Ann:* **s. worm,** polynoé *f;* *Bot:* **bird's nest s. fern,** doradille *f* nid d'oiseau; (*c*) **s. armour,** armure *f* à écrevisse, à écailles; **s. work,** ornementation *f* en forme d'écailles; imbrication *f.* **2.** *Metalw:* (*a*) barbure *f* (de pièce coulée); balèvre *f,* dartre *f;* (*b*) *coll.* **scale(s),** écailles de fer, battitures *fpl,* pailles *fpl,* paillettes *fpl;* **mill s., roll s.,** scories *fpl* de laminoir; **hammer scale(s), forge scale(s),** scorie de forge; martelures *fpl;* paille de fer; havresac *m.* **3.** incrustation *f,* dépôt *m;* tartre *m* (des dents); teigne *f* (des vieux arbres); *Metall:* calamine *f;* (*on copper, iron, etc.*) oxyde *m;* **embedded s.,** épaisseur *m* d'oxydation; **boiler s.,** tartre, entartrage *m,* incrustation; dépôt calcaire; calcin *m,* crasse *f;* **s. preventive, preventer, remover,** tartrifuge *m,* désincrustant *m,* anticalcaire *m.* **4.** (*a*) **the scales of a lancet, of a razor,** la châsse d'une lancette, d'un rasoir; (*b*) *Mil:* **(shoulder) s.,** contre-épaulette *f, pl.* contre-épaulettes.
scale[2], *v.* **1.** *v.tr.* (*a*) écailler; (*by scalding*) limoner (un poisson, etc.); (*b*) détartrer, nettoyer, ruginer (les dents); piquer, désencroûter, décrasser, désincruster, détartrer, écailler (une chaudière, un tube); flamber (un canon); exfolier (un arbre, un os, etc.); **to s. a sheet of iron,** décaper une tôle; (*c*) *Austr: F:* rouler (qn); (*d*) entartrer, incruster (une chaudière, etc.). **2.** *v.i.* (*a*) **to s. (off),** écailler; (*of skin*) se desquamer; (*of bark, bone, etc.*) s'exfolier; (*of colour*) s'effeuiller; (*of wall, ceiling, etc.*) se déplâtrer; (*b*) (*of boiler, etc.*) s'entartrer, s'incruster.
scale[3], *s.* (*a*) **s. (pan),** plateau *m,* plat *m* (de balance); (*deep*) bassin *m;* **to throw sth. into the s.,** jeter qch. dans la balance; mettre qch. en balance; **to tip, turn, the scale(s) at 100 kilos,** peser un peu plus de 100 kilos; **to turn the scale(s) (in favour of sth.),** emporter, faire pencher, la balance (en faveur de qch.); (*of jockey*) **to ride, to go, to s.,** passer au pesage; (*b*) **scales,** *O:* **pair of scales,** balance; (*for gold*) trébuchet *m;* **platform scales,** bascule *f;* (*with steelyard*) balance romaine; **household, kitchen, shop, scales,** balance ordinaire, à plateaux; **letter scales,** pèse-lettres *m inv;* **bathroom scales,** pèse-personne *m, pl.* pèse-personnes; **baby scales,** pèse-bébé *m, pl.* pèse-bébés; **to hold the scales even,** tenir la balance égale; juger avec impartialité; (*c*) *Astr:* **the Scales,** la Balance.
scale[4]. **1.** *v.tr. A:* peser (qch.). **2.** *v.i.* **to s. six kilos,** peser, avoir un poids de, six kilos; *Turf:* **to s. in,** passer au pesage.
scale[5], *s.* **1.** *A:* (*a*) échelle *f;* (*b*) escalier *m.* **2.** (*a*) échelle (de thermomètre, de baromètre, etc.); graduation(s) *f* (d'un thermomètre, d'un système numérique, etc.); série *f,* suite *f* (de nombres, etc.); *Mth:* **logarithmic s.,** échelle logarithmique; **decimal s.,** échelle décimale; *Meteor:* **visibility s.,** échelle de visibilité; (*of winds*) **Beaufort s.,** échelle de Beaufort; **sea s.,** notation *f* de la mer; *Ind:* **standard s. (of machine part sizes, etc.),** échelle des calibres; *Rail: etc:* **tonnage s.,** échelle de jauge; **s. of salaries,** échelle, barème *m,* des traitements; **s. of prices, of charges,** échelle, gamme *f,* des prix; **sliding s.,** échelle mobile (des salaires, des prix); **sliding-s. tariff,** tarif dégressif; **s. of values,** échelle des valeurs; **the social s.,** l'échelle sociale; **at the top of the s.,** en haut, au sommet, de l'échelle; (*b*) cadran gradué; (*c*) règle (divisée); **linear s.,** échelle linéaire; (*d*) échelle (d'une carte, d'un graphique, etc.); (*of graph, etc.*) **vertical, horizontal, s.,** échelle verticale, horizontale; **map on a s. of one centimetre to a metre, of one in a hundred,** carte au centième; **small-s., large-s., map,** carte à petite, à grande, échelle; **to draw sth. to scale,** dessiner qch. à l'échelle; **s. drawing,** dessin *m* à l'échelle; **s. model,** maquette *f,* modèle réduit; **not to s.,** les proportions ne sont pas respectées; **on a reduced s.,** à échelle réduite; en petit; en miniature; **to do things on a large s.,** faire les choses sur une grande échelle; **on a national, nationwide, s.,** à l'échelle nationale; **small-s. firm,** petite entreprise; **this plan cannot be carried out on such a small s.,** ce projet est irréalisable à une si petite échelle; **small-s. war,** guerre en miniature; **on a greater, wider, s.,** sur une plus grande échelle; dans de plus vastes proportions; **on an extraordinarily large s.,** qui sort des proportions ordinaires; **the s. of the disaster,** l'étendue *f* de la calamité, du sinistre; (*e*) *Mus:* gamme; **major, minor, s.,** gamme majeure, mineure; **chromatic s.,** gamme, échelle, chromatique; **to sing up the s.,** monter la gamme; **to practise scales,** faire des gammes; (*f*) **s. of colours, of tones,** échelle, gamme, de couleurs, de nuances.
scale[6], *v.tr.* **1.** (*a*) escalader (un mur, une forteresse, etc.); faire l'ascension (d'une montagne); (*b*) *Austr: F:* (monter dans un train, etc. et) resquiller (sa place). **2.** tracer (une carte) à l'échelle; établir (un dessin) à l'échelle; **to s. down,** établir (un dessin) à une échelle réduite; **to s. up, down, prices, etc.,** augmenter, réduire, des prix, etc., selon une échelle mobile; **to s. down production,** ralentir la production.
scaleboard ['skeilbɔ:d], *s. A:* lame *f* mince (de bois).
scaled [skeild], *a.* **1.** écailleux, squameux. **2.** écaillé.
scalene ['skeili:n], *a. Mth:, Anat:* (triangle, muscle) scalène.
scalenohedral [skeilinou'hi:drəl], *a. Cryst:* scalénoèdre.
scalenohedron [skeilinou'hi:drən], *s. Cryst:* scalénoèdre *m.*
scalenus [skei'li:nəs], *s. Anat:* **s. (muscle),** scalène *m.*
scaler[1] ['skeilər], *s.* **1.** (*a*) écailleur, -euse (de poissons); (*b*) *Mch:* piqueur *m,* nettoyeur *m,* batteur *m* (de chaudières). **2.** *Tls:* (*a*) écailleur *m* (de poissons); (*b*) *Mch:* (*for boilers*) détartreur *m;* (*c*) *Dent:* rugine *f;* **tooth s.,** détartreur.
scaler[2], *s. Austr: F:* resquilleur, -euse (d'une place dans un train, etc.).
scaliness ['skeilinis], *s.* écailles *fpl* (d'un poisson, etc.); squamosité *f* (de la peau, etc.).
scaling[1] ['skeiliŋ], *s.* **1.** (*a*) écaillage *m* (d'un poisson, etc.); (*b*) détartrage *m* (des dents); piquage *m,* décrassage *m,* décrassement *m,* désincrustation *f,* détartrage (d'une chaudière, des tubes); décapage *m,* décapement *m* (des feuilles de fer); flambage *m* (d'un canon); *Mch:* **s. tools,** outils détartreurs; **s. brush,** brosse à tubes; **boiler s. device,** désincrusteur *m.* **2.** *Mch:* formation *f* du tartre; entartrage *m,* incrustation *f* (d'une chaudière).
scaling[2], *s.* **1.** escalade *f;* *Mil: A:* **s. ladder,** échelle *f* d'escalade, de siège. **2.** (*a*) graduation *f* (des prix, des salaires, etc.); **s. up, down,** augmentation *f,* réduction *f,* à l'échelle; (*b*) dessin *m* (d'une carte) à l'échelle; tracé *m* à l'échelle.
scallion ['skæljən], *s. Bot:* ciboule *f,* échalote *f.*
scallop[1] ['skɔləp], *s.* **1.** (*a*) *Moll:* **s. (shell),** peigne *m,* coquille *f* Saint-Jacques; pecten *m;* (*b*) *Cu:* coquille Saint-Jacques; (*c*) **fish served in s. shells,** coquilles de poisson; (*d*) *Cu:* escalope *f* (de veau, etc.); (*e*) **(potato) scallops,** beignets *m* de pommes de terre. **2.** *Needlew: etc:* feston *m,* dent *f,* dentelure *f,* découpure *f.*
scallop[2], *v.tr.* **1.** *Cu:* faire cuire (du poisson, etc.) en coquille(s); **scalloped oysters,** huîtres gratinées en coquilles. **2.** *Needlew:* festonner; découper, denteler; **scalloped handkerchief,** mouchoir échancré; **scalloped design,** dessin dentelé; *Arch:* **scalloped moulding,** moulure en écailles.
scallywag ['skæliwæg], *s. F:* **1.** propre à rien *m;* bon-à-rien *m, pl.* bons-à-rien; vaurien, -ienne; mauvais garnement. **2.** *U.S:* bœuf efflanqué, rabougri; bête mal venue.
scalops ['skeilɔps], **scalopus** ['skæləpəs], *s. Z:* scalope *m.*
scalp[1] [skælp], *s.* **1.** (*a*) *Anat:* épicrâne *m;* (*b*) *Anat:* cuir chevelu (de la tête). **2.** *NAm:* scalp(e) *m;* **s. dance,** danse du scalpe; **to be out for scalps,** (i) partir en guerre; (ii) *F:* chercher qui démolir, qui éreinter.
scalp[2], *v.tr.* **1.** (*a*) (*of NAm: Indians*) scalper (un ennemi); (*b*) *F: O:* (*of critic*) éreinter (un auteur, un livre); (*c*) *Surg:* ruginer (un os). **2.** *esp. NAm:* (*a*) revendre (des billets de théâtre, etc.) à profit; (*b*) *St.Exch:* boursicoter.
scalpel ['skælp(ə)l], *s. Surg:* scalpel *m.*
scalper ['skælpər], *s. NAm:* **1.** chasseur *m* de têtes. **2.** *F:* trafiquer *m* (de billets, d'actions cotées); boursicoteur *m.*
scalping ['skælpiŋ], *s.* **1.** scalp(e) *m;* *Surg:* **s. iron,** rugine *f.* **2.** *NAm:* (*a*) trafic *m* (sur les billets de théâtre, etc.); (*b*) *St.Exch:* boursicotage *m.*
scalpriform ['skælprifɔ:m], *a. Z:* (dent de rongeur) en forme de ciseau.
scaly ['skeili], *a.* **1.** (*a*) (*of fish, skin, etc.*) écailleux, squameux; *Med:* **s. eruption,** éruption écailleuse; (*b*) (*of slate, etc.*) écailleux; (*of metal*) paillé, lamelleux, lamellé; (*of boiler*) tartreux. **2.** *P: A:* (*a*) mesquin, ladre, pingre; (*b*) médiocre, minable.
Scamander [skæ'mændər]. *Pr.n. A.Geog:* Scamandre *m.*
scammony ['skæməni], *s. Bot: Pharm:* scammonée *f.*
scamp[1] [skæmp], *s.* (*a*) vaurien, -ienne; mauvais sujet; garnement *m;* fripouille *f;* (*b*) *F:* **my s. of a nephew,** mon garnement, mon galopin, de neveu; (*of child*) **young, little, s.,** petit galopin, petit polisson, petit coquin.
scamp[2], *v.tr. F:* bâcler, torcher, torchonner, saboter, bousiller (un travail); faire (un travail) à la vapeur, au galop; **scamped work,** travail fait à la diable, à la va-vite.
scamper[1] ['skæmpər], *s.* (*a*) course *f* folâtre, allègre; (*b*) course rapide; **after a s. through Europe,** après un tour rapide en Europe; après avoir visité l'Europe au galop.
scamper[2], *v.i.* (*a*) courir allègrement, d'une manière folâtre; (*b*) **to s. away, off,** détaler, décamper; s'enfuir, se sauver, à toutes jambes; *F:* prendre ses jambes à son

cou; (*c*) **to s. through France,** traverser la France à la galopade, au galop; **to s. through a book,** parcourir un livre à la hâte.

scamper[3], *s. F:* bâcleur, -euse (de travail); bousilleur, -euse.

scampering ['skæmpəriŋ], *s.* = SCAMPER[1].

scampi ['skæmpi], *s.pl. Cu:* (plat *m* de) langoustines *f.*

scamping ['skæmpiŋ], *s.* bâclage *m*, sabotage *m*, bousillage *m* (d'un travail); *Ind:* action de faire des heures supplémentaires en dépit de ses collègues.

scan[1] [skæn], *s.* **1.** regard scrutateur. **2.** *El:* **s. axis,** axe radioélectrique; **s. frequency,** fréquence de balayage; **horizontal, vertical, s.,** balayage horizontal, vertical; **radar s.,** balayage radar.

scan[2], *v.tr.* **(scanned) 1.** *Pros:* (*a*) scander, mesurer (des vers); (*b*) (*with passive force*) (*of verse*) se scander (facilement, mal, etc.); **this line won't s.,** le vers est faux. **2.** (*a*) examiner, scruter; sonder du regard; **to s. the horizon,** examiner attentivement, sonder, scruter, l'horizon; **to s. the crowd,** promener un regard, ses regards, sur la foule; **to s. s.o.'s face,** scruter le visage de qn; **he scanned the audience,** ses yeux fouillaient la salle; (*b*) jeter un coup d'œil sur (qch.); **to s. a book,** feuilleter, parcourir, un livre; **to s. the newspaper,** jeter un coup d'œil sur le journal; parcourir rapidement le journal; (*c*) *Rad: Elcs: etc:* balayer, explorer (l'image à transmettre, la piste sonore).

scandal ['skænd(ə)l], *s.* **1.** scandale *m*; honte *f*; affaire scabreuse; **it's a s.,** c'est un scandale; **it's a s. that such a thing should be possible,** il est scandaleux, honteux, qu'une telle chose soit possible; **it's a s. that he should have been acquitted,** c'est une honte qu'il ait été acquitté; **to create a s.,** faire un scandale; causer du scandale; faire un éclat. **2.** médisance *f*; potins *mpl*, cancans *mpl*, commérages *mpl*; **to talk s.,** faire des commérages. **3.** *Jur:* (*a*) allégations diffamatoires, injurieuses; (*b*) atteinte *f* à la dignité du tribunal; manque *m* de respect.

scandalize[1] ['skændəlaiz], *v.tr.* **1.** médire (de qn), calomnier (qn). **2.** scandaliser, choquer, offusquer (qn).

scandalize[2], *v.tr. Y:* **to s. the mainsail,** arriser le pic.

scandalmonger ['skænd(ə)lmʌŋgər], *s.* cancanier, -ière; clabaudeur, -euse; médisant, -ante; colporteur, -euse, d'histoires scandaleuses; mauvaise langue.

scandalmongering ['skænd(ə)lmʌŋgəriŋ], *s.* médisance *f*; potins *mpl*, cancans *mpl*, commérages *mpl.*

scandalous ['skændələs], *a.* **1.** (*a*) (*of conduct, event, etc.*) scandaleux, infâme, odieux, honteux; (*of price, etc.*) **it's s.!** c'est scandaleux! c'est épouvantable! (*b*) *A:* **s. tongues,** mauvaises langues. **2.** *Jur:* (*of statement, writing*) diffamatoire, calomnieux.

scandalously ['skændələsli], *adv.* scandaleusement, d'une manière scandaleuse.

scandalousness ['skændələsnis], *s.* caractère scandaleux, infâme, odieux, honteux (d'une action, d'un spectacle, etc.); indignité *f*, infamie *f* (de la conduite de qn, etc.).

scandent ['skændənt], *a. Bot:* grimpant.

Scandinavia [skændi'neiviə]. *Pr.n. Geog:* Scandinavie *f.*

Scandinavian [skændi'neiviən]. **1.** *a.* scandinave. **2.** *s.* (*a*) Scandinave *mf*; (*b*) *Ling:* scandinave *m.*

Scandinavianism [skændi'neiviənizm], *s.* scandinavisme *m.*

scandium ['skændiəm], *s. Ch:* scandium *m.*

scandix ['skændiks], *s. Bot:* scandix *m.*

scanner ['skænər], *s.* **1.** scrutateur, -trice; sondeur, -euse (de la pensée de qn, etc.). **2.** *Pros:* personne *f* qui scande (des vers). **3.** (*a*) **radar s.,** déchiffreur *m* de radar, explorateur *m* radar, balayeur *m* radar, organe de balayage radar; antenne *f* (de) radar; (*b*) *Cmptr:* **visual, optical, s.,** lecteur *m*, liseur *m*, optique.

scanning[1] ['skæniŋ], *a.* scrutateur, -trice.

scanning[2], *s.* **1.** scansion *f* (de vers). **2.** (*a*) examen minutieux; (*b*) *T.V: etc:* balayage *m*, exploration *f* (de l'image à transmettre, de la piste sonore); *El:* captation *f*; **radar s.,** exploration, balayage, radar; **s. apparatus,** appareil explorateur; **s. cell,** cellule exploratrice; **s. coil,** aimant de cadrage *m*; (*c*) *Cmptr:* analyse *f*, scrutation *f*; **visual, optical, s.,** lecture *f* optique; **mark s.,** lecture optique de marques.

scansion ['skænʃ(ə)n], *s. Pros:* scansion *f.*

scansorial [skæn'sɔ:riəl], *a. & s. Orn:* grimpeur (*m*).

scant[1] [skænt], *a.* **1.** *A: & Lit:* rare, insuffisant, peu abondant, limité; **s. vegetation,** végétation pauvre; **to live on a s. income,** vivre pauvrement; **s. weight,** poids bien juste; poids faible; **to show s.o. s. hospitality,** se montrer peu hospitalier envers qn; **to be s. of, in, sth.,** avoir peu de qch.; **s. of breath,** (i) hors d'haleine; essoufflé; (ii) poussif. **2.** *A: Nau:* (vent) pointu.

scant[2]. **1.** *v.i. A: Nau:* (*of wind*) refuser. **2.** *v.tr. A:* **to s. s.o. of sth.,** mesurer qch. à qn avec parcimonie.

scanties ['skæntiz], *s.pl. Cost: F:* minislip *m*, petite culotte.

scantily ['skæntili], *adv.* insuffisamment; peu abondamment; **s. dressed,** (i) vêtu à la légère; à peine vêtu; (ii) mal protégé contre le froid.

scantiness ['skæntinis], *s.* insuffisance *f*, rareté *f* (de provisions, etc.); pauvreté *f* (de la végétation); étroitesse *f* (d'un vêtement); faiblesse *f*, insuffisance (de poids).

scantling ['skæntliŋ], *s.* **1.** *A:* petite quantité (de qch.). **2.** *Const:* (*a*) menu bois de sciage; volige *f*; (*b*) bois équarri; bois d'équarrissage; volige, madrier *m*; *N.Arch:* échantillon *m*; échantillonnage *m.* **3.** échantillon, équarrissage *m.*

scantly ['skæntli], *adv.* = SCANTILY.

scants [skænts], *s.pl. Cost: F:* minislip *m*; petite culotte.

scanty ['skænti], *a.* (*of quantity, supply, etc.*) insuffisant, à peine suffisant; rare; peu abondant; limité; (*of garment, etc.*) étriqué; **s. hair,** cheveux rares; **s. meal,** maigre repas; repas sommaire, succinct.

scape[1] [skeip], *s.* **1.** *Arch:* escape *f*, fût *m* (d'une colonne). **2.** (*a*) *Bot:* hampe *f*, scape *m*; (*b*) *Orn:* tuyau *m* (de plume); (*c*) *Ent:* scape (de l'antenne).

scape[2], *s.* **1.** *A: & Lit:* fuite *f*, évasion *f.* **2.** échappement *m*; *Clockm:* **s. wheel,** roue *f* de rencontre.

scape[3], *v.tr. A:* **to s. hanging,** échapper à la potence.

scapegoat ['skeipgout], *s.* bouc *m* émissaire; souffre-douleur *m inv.*

scapegrace ['skeipgreis], *s. O:* **1.** vaurien, -ienne; garnement *m*; mauvais sujet; **my s. of a nephew,** mon polisson de neveu. **2.** petit garnement; enfant incorrigible, insupportable.

scapement ['skeipmənt], *s. Clockm:* échappement *m.*

Scaphandridae [skæ'fændridi:], *s.pl. Moll:* scaphandridés *m.*

Scaphirhynchidae [skæfi'riŋkidi:], *s.pl. Ich:* scaphirhynques *m.*

scaphocephalic [skæfouse'fælik], **scaphocephalous** [skæfou'sefələs], *a. Anthr:* scaphocéphale.

scaphocephalism, scaphocephaly [skæfou'selfəlizm, -'sefəli], *s. Anthr:* scaphocéphalie *f.*

scaphoid ['skæfɔid], *a. & s.* scaphoïde (*m*).

Scaphopoda [skæ'fɔpədə], *s.pl. Moll:* scaphopodes *m.*

scapiform ['skeipifɔ:m], *a. Bot:* scapiforme.

scapigerous [skei'pidʒərəs], *a. Bot:* scapigère.

scapolite ['skæpəlait], *s. Miner:* scapolite *f.*

scapula, *pl.* **-ae** ['skæpjulə, -i:], *s. Anat:* scapula *f*, omoplate *f.*

scapulalgia [skæpju'lældʒiə], *s. Med:* scapulalgie *f.*

scapular ['skæpjulər]. **1.** *a. Nat.Hist:* scapulaire; *Anat:* **s. arch,** ceinture *f* scapulaire; ceinture thoracique; *Surg:* **s. bandage,** *s.* **s.,** scapulaire *m*; *Orn:* **s. feathers,** *s.* **scapulars,** rémiges *f* scapulaires. **2.** *s. Ecc:* = SCAPULARY.

scapulary ['skæpjuləri], *s. Ecc:* scapulaire *m.*

scapulectomy [skæpju'lektəmi], *s. Surg:* scapulectomie *f.*

scapulo-humeral [skæpjulou'hju:mərəl], *a. Anat:* scapulo-humeral, -aux.

scar[1] [skɑ:r], *s.* **1.** cicatrice *f*, couture *f*; (*on face*) balafre *f*; **s. faced,** balafré; *Med:* **s. tissue,** tissu cicatriciel; *Fig:* **this bitter disappointment left a permanent s.,** cette cruelle déception l'a marqué pour la vie. **2.** *Bot:* cicatrice, hile *m.*

scar[2], *v.* **(scarred) 1.** *v.tr.* (*a*) laisser une cicatrice sur (la chair); marquer (le visage, etc.) d'une cicatrice; balafrer (le visage); **to be scarred,** porter des cicatrices; **district heavily scarred by the war,** pays dévasté par la guerre; (*b*) **to s. up,** cicatriser (une plaie). **2.** *v.i.* (*of wound*) **to s. (over),** se cicatriser.

scar[3], *s.* (*in mountain range, etc.*) rocher escarpé, muraille *f.*

scar[4], *s. Ich:* **s. (fish),** scare *m*; perroquet *m* de mer.

scarab ['skærəb], *s.* **1.** *Ent:* **s. (beetle),** scarabée *m*, *esp.* scarabée sacré. **2.** *Egyptian Ant: Lap:* scarabée.

scarabaeid [skærə'bi:id], *s. Ent:* scarabéidé *m.*

Scarabaeidae [skærə'bi:idi:], *s.pl. Ent:* scarabéidés *m.*

scarabaeus [skærə'bi:əs], *s.* **1.** *Ent:* scarabée sacré. **2.** *Egyptian Ant:* scarabée.

scaraboid ['skærəbɔid]. **1.** *a. Ent:* scarabéoïde. **2.** *a. & s. Ant:* scaraboïde (*m*).

Scaramouch ['skærəmautʃ, -mu:ʃ]. *Pr.n.m. A.Th:* Scaramouche.

scarce [skɛəs]. **1.** *a.* (*a*) (*of commodities*) rare, peu abondant; **vegetables were s. last winter,** l'hiver dernier les légumes étaient rares, il y avait très peu de légumes; **good engravers are growing s.,** les bons graveurs se font rares; **because of the economic crisis money has become s.,** par suite de la crise économique l'argent s'est raréfié; *F:* **to make oneself s.,** s'éclipser, s'esquiver, décamper; (*b*) *A:* (*of pers.*) **to be s. of food, of money,** être à court de vivres, d'argent. **2.** *adv. A: & Lit:* = SCARCELY.

scarcely ['skɛəsli], *adv.* **1.** à peine; guère; presque pas; **I have s. any left,** il ne m'en reste presque plus; **she could s. speak,** c'est à peine si elle pouvait parler; à peine pouvait-elle parler; **he thinks of s. anything else,** il ne pense guère à autre chose; **you'll s. believe it,** vous aurez de la peine, du mal, à le croire; **I s. know,** je ne sais trop; **I s. know what to say,** je ne sais trop que dire, comment répondre; **s. ever,** presque jamais; **he had s. come in when the telephone rang,** à peine était-il rentré que le téléphone a sonné. **2.** (*expressing incredulity*) sûrement pas! **he can s. have said that,** il n'a sûrement pas dit cela; **s.!** j'en doute!

scarcen ['skɛəsən], *v.* **1.** *v.i.* devenir rare, peu abondant; se raréfier. **2.** *v.tr.* raréfier (qch.).

scarceness ['skɛəsnis], *s.* = SCARCITY.

scarcity ['skɛəsiti], *s.* rareté *f*; manque *m*, pénurie *f*, disette *f* (de qch.); **the s. of rain has ruined the wheat harvest,** la sécheresse a ruiné la récolte de blé; **s. of labour,** manque, disette, de main d'œuvre; **there is a s. of provisions,** les provisions *f* font défaut, manquent; **in view of the s. of money,** vu la crise d'argent.

scare[1] [skɛər], *s.* panique *f*, alarme *f*; **to cause, create, a s.,** semer l'alarme, la panique; *F:* **you gave me an awful s.,** vous m'avez fait rudement peur; *Journ:* **s. headline,** manchette sensationnelle.

scare[2], *v.* **1.** *v.tr.* effrayer, effarer, alarmer, apeurer; faire peur à (qn); épouvanter (qn); **to s. the game away,** effaroucher le gibier; **he was scared out of the attempt,** la peur lui fit abandonner la tentative. **2.** *v.i.* s'effrayer, s'alarmer; **I don't s. easily,** je ne m'effraie pas facilement, pour rien.

scarecrow ['skɛəkrou], *s. Agr:* épouvantail *m*, mannequin *m*; *F:* (*of pers.*) (i) épouvantail; (ii) grand escogriffe; **she's an awful s.,** (i) c'est un remède contre, à, l'amour; (ii) elle est terriblement fagotée; **to be dressed like a s.,** être mis à faire peur; être fagoté comme l'as de pique.

scared ['skɛəd], *a.* apeuré, épeuré; **s. look,** regard effaré, épeuré; air épouvanté; **to be s. to death, out of one's wits,** avoir une peur bleue; avoir la peur au ventre; **he was s. stiff of women,** il avait une peur bleue des femmes, de la femme.

scaredness ['skɛədnis], *s.* effarement *m*; épouvante *f.*

scaredy-cat ['skɛədikæt], *s. F:* personne *f* timide; peureux, -euse.

scarehead ['skɛəhed], *s. U.S: Journ:* manchette sensationnelle.

scaremonger ['skɛəmʌŋgər], *s.* alarmiste *mf*; semeur, -euse, de panique.

scaremongering ['skɛəmʌŋgəriŋ], *s.* (colportage *m* de) nouvelles *f* alarmistes, fausses alarmes; **she adores s.,** elle adore semer la panique, nous tenir en alarme.

scarf[1], *pl.* **scarfs, scarves** [skɑ:f(s), skɑ:vz], *s.* écharpe *f*; cache-col *m*, *pl.* cache-col(s); cache-nez *m inv*; (*in silk*) foulard *m*; cravate *f*; **s. ring,** coulant *m* d'écharpe, de cravate.

scarf[2], *s.* **1. s. (joint),** assemblage *m* à mi-bois, à écart, joint biseauté, en bec de flûte; enture *f*, empatture *f*; **plain s.,** écart *m* simple; **bird's mouth s.,** écart double; **box s.,** écart à mi-bois; **hook s.,** écart à croc; **skew s.,** écart à sifflet. **2.** *Metalw:* chanfrein *m* de soudure.

scarf[3], *v.tr.* **1.** *Carp: N.Arch:* enter, écarver, assembler à mi-bois (deux planches, etc.). **2.** *Metalw:* amorcer (deux bouts à souder, etc.).

scarf[4], *s.* (*in whaling*) taillade *f*, entaille *f* (dans le corps de la baleine).

scarf[5], *v.tr.* taillader (le lard de la baleine); découper, dépecer (la baleine).

scarface ['skɑ:feis], *s.* balafré *m*; **Henri de Guise, known as S.,** Henri de Guise (dit) le Balafré.

scarfed [skɑ:ft], *a. Carp:* (*of boards, etc.*) assemblés à mi-bois, à enture, à écart, en mouchoir.

scarfer ['skɑ:fər], *s. Metalw:* mateur *m.*

scarfing ['skɑ:fiŋ], *s.* **1.** *Carp:* assemblage *m* à mi-bois, à enture, à écart. **2.** *Metalw:* amorçage *m.* **3.** = SCARF[2].

scarfpin ['skɑ:fpin], *s.* épingle *f* de cravate.

scarfskin ['skɑ:fskin], *s. Anat:* épiderme *m*, cuticule *f.*

scarfweld(ing) ['skɑ:fweld(iŋ)], *s. Metalw:* soudure *f* à chanfrein, à recouvrement, par amorces.

scarfwelded ['skɑ:fweldid], *a.* soudé en écharpe.

scarid ['skærid], *s. Ich:* scaride *m*, scaridé *m.*

Scaridae ['skæridi:], *s.pl. Ich:* scaridés *m*, scarides *m.*

scarification [skærifi'keiʃ(ə)n], *s. Surg: Agr:* scarification *f.*

scarificator ['skærifikeitər], *s. Surg:* scarificateur *m.*

scarifier ['skærifaiər], *s.* **1.** *Surg:* = SCARIFICATOR. **2.** *Civ.E:* **road s.,** piocheuse scarificatrice. **3.** *Agr:* scarificateur *m*, extirpateur *m*; déchaumeur *m*, déchaumeuse *f*; écroûteuse *f.*

scarify ['skærifai], *v.tr.* **1.** scarifier (la peau, le sol); écroûter, ameublir (le sol). **2.** *F:* éreinter (un auteur, etc.).

scarifying[1] ['skærifaiiŋ], *a.* (reproche, etc.) qui touche au vif, sanglant.

scarifying[2], *s.* **1.** *Agr:* écroûtage *m*, scarifiage *m*. **2.** *F:* éreintement *m* (d'un auteur, d'un ouvrage).

scariose, scarious ['skεərious, -iəs], *a. Bot:* scarieux.

scarlatina [skɑ:lə'ti:nə], *s. Med:* scarlatine *f*; **s. patient,** scarlatineux, -euse.

scarlatiniform, scarlatinoid [skɑ:lə'ti:nifɔ:m, -'ti:nɔid], *a. Med:* scarlatiniforme.

scarlet ['skɑ:lət], *a. & s.* écarlate (*f*); *Dy:* **s. grains,** graines *f* d'écarlate (du chêne kermès); **s. dress,** robe *f* coquelicot; **to blush, flush, go, s.,** devenir cramoisi, rouge comme une pivoine; comme un homard; **he flushed s.,** son visage s'empourpra; *Bot:* **s. pimpernel,** mouron *m* rouge; **s. runner,** haricot *m* d'Espagne; *Med:* **s. fever,** scarlatine *f*; *R.C.Ch:* **to don the s.,** endosser l'écarlate; revêtir la pourpre cardinalice; **s. hat,** chapeau *m* de cardinal; *F: A:* **to wear the King's s.,** porter l'uniforme; être soldat; *A:* **a s. woman,** une prostituée; **the s. woman,** (i) *B:* la femme vêtue d'écarlate; (ii) *Hist: F:* (*also* **the s. whore**), l'Église catholique romaine.

scarp[1] [skɑ:p], *s.* **1.** *Fort:* escarpe *f*. **2.** escarpement *m* (d'une colline); versant abrupt (d'une montagne).

scarp[2], *v.tr. Fort: etc:* escarper (un fossé, etc.).

scarp[3], *s. Her:* écharpe *f*.

scarped [skɑ:pt], *a.* escarpé; (versant) abrupt, à pic.

scarper ['skɑ:pər], *v.i. P:* tirer, déguerpir.

scarred [skɑ:d], *a.* (*of face, etc.*) couturé (de cicatrices); portant des cicatrices; balafré; **war-s. country,** pays dévasté par la guerre.

scarus ['skεərəs], *s. Ich:* scare *m*; perroquet *m* de mer.

scary ['skεəri], *a. U.S: F:* **1.** effroyable, redoutable. **2.** (*of pers.*) timide, peureux.

scat [skæt], *int. F:* filez! fichez le camp! allez ouste! décampez!

scathe[1] [skeið], *s. A: & Lit:* dommage *m*, blessure *f*; **without s.,** indemne; sain et sauf.

scathe[2], *v.tr. A: & Lit:* **1.** nuire, causer du dommage, à (qch.); (*of lightning*) foudroyer (un arbre), ravager (une campagne). **2.** cingler (qn) de sa satire.

scatheless ['skeiðlis], *a. A: & Lit:* sans dommage, sans blessure; sain et sauf; indemne.

scathing ['skeiðiŋ], *a.* (*of remark, sarcasm, etc.*) acerbe, moqueur, mordant, cinglant, caustique; **s. retort,** réplique cassante, cinglante; réplique à l'emporte-pièce; **s. irony,** ironie mordante; **he can be very s.,** il sait être très cinglant; **to write a s. criticism of a play,** soumettre une pièce à une critique sanglante, virulente.

scathingly ['skeiðiŋli], *adv.* d'une manière acerbe, caustique, mordante; d'un ton cassant, cinglant.

scatological [skætə'lɔdʒik(ə)l], *a.* (littérature) scatologique; **s. tastes, s. literature,** scatologie *f*.

scatology [skə'tɔlədʒi], *s.* **1.** (*a*) étude *f* des corprolit(h)es; (*b*) *Med:* étude des fèces. **2.** scatologie *f*.

scatophage ['skætoufeidʒ], *s. Ent:* scatophage *m*.

scatophagous [skə'tɔfəgəs], *a. Ent: etc:* scatophage, merdivore.

scatophagy [skæ'tɔfədʒi], *s.* scatophagie *f*.

scatopsid [skæ'tɔpsid], *s. Ent:* scatopse *m*.

Scatopsidae [skæ'tɔpsidi:], *s.pl. Ent:* scatopsidés *m*.

scatter[1] ['skætər], *s.* (*a*) (*of shot, etc.*) éparpillement *m*; dispersion *f*; **s. rugs, cushions,** petits tapis, coussins, placés çà et là dans une pièce; **s. mats,** dessous *m* de verres; (*b*) *W.Tel:* **forward s. radio link,** câble hertzien transhorizon; **forward s. relay,** relais transhorizon.

scatter[2]. **1.** *v.tr.* (*a*) disperser, mettre en fuite (une armée, etc.); dissiper (des nuages, etc.); égailler, faire envoler (des oiseaux); *Games:* **to s. the opponent's bowls,** bouler; (*b*) éparpiller (des feuilles, des papiers, etc.); semer (des graines) à la volée; disséminer (des graines); répandre (du gravier); *Ph:* (*of surface*) diffuser, répandre (la lumière); **scattered light,** lumière diffuse; **path scattered with leaves,** chemin jonché de feuilles; **scattered over the floor,** éparpillés sur le plancher; **scattered all over the street,** éparpillés par toute la rue; **the houses lie scattered in the valley,** les maisons s'éparpillent dans la vallée; **houses scattered around a village,** maisons éparses autour d'un village; **thinly scattered population,** population clairsemée; (*of gun*) **to s. (the shot),** écarter le plomb. **2.** *v.i.* (*of crowd, etc.*) se disperser; (*of birds, etc.*) s'égailler; (*of army*) se débander; (*of clouds, etc.*) se dissiper; (*of shot*) s'éparpiller, s'écarter.

scatterbrain ['skætəbrein], *s. F:* étourdi, -ie; écervelé, -ée; évaporé, -ée; **what a s.!** quelle tête d'oiseau!

scatterbrained ['skætəbreind], *a. F:* étourdi, écervelé, évaporé; **to be s.,** avoir une tête de linotte.

scattering ['skætəriŋ], *s.* **1.** dispersion *f* (d'une armée, etc.); éparpillement *m* (de feuilles, etc.); diffusion *f* (de la lumière). **2.** petit nombre; petite quantité; **he only has a s. of followers,** ses adhérents sont peu nombreux.

scattily ['skætili], *adv. F:* étourdiment.

scattiness ['skætinis], *s. F:* étourderie, inconséquence *f*.

scatty ['skæti], *a. F:* (*a*) étourdi, écervelé; (*b*) farfelu, toqué.

scaup [skɔ:p], *s. Orn:* **s. (duck),** fuligule *f* milouinan, canard *m* milouinan; **lesser s. duck,** petite fuligule, *Fr.Can:* petit morillon.

scavenge ['skævindʒ]. **1.** *v.tr.* (*a*) *A:* ébouer, balayer (les rues, etc.); (*b*) *Artil:* écouvillonner (un fusil); (*c*) *I.C.E:* **to s. the burnt gases,** balayer, refouler, expulser, les gaz brûlés. **2.** *v.i.* (*of pers., animal*) fouiller dans les ordures.

scavenger ['skævindʒər], *s.* **1.** (*a*) *A:* boueur *m*; balayeur *m* des rues; **sewer s.,** égoutier *m*; (*b*) (*pers., animal*) fouilleur, -euse, d'ordures. **2.** *Ent: Z:* insecte *m*, animal *m*, nécrophage, scatophage, coprophage; **s. beetle,** nécrophore *m*; scarabée *m* nécrophage; **s. crab,** crabe *m* nécrophage.

scavenging ['skævindʒiŋ], *s.* **1.** (*a*) *A:* ébouage *m*, balayage *m* (des rues); enlèvement *m* des ordures; (*b*) **s. seems to be this dog's main occupation,** ce chien est toujours à fouiller dans les poubelles. **2.** *Artil:* écouvillonnage *m* à l'air (d'un fusil). **3.** *I.C.E: etc:* évacuation *f*, balayage, refoulement *m* (des gaz brûlés, de la vapeur, etc.); *Mch:* **s. valve,** soupape de balayage.

scelidosaur ['selidousɔ:r], *s. Paleont:* scelidosaurus *m*.

Scelidosaurus [selidou'sɔ:rəs], *s. Paleont:* scelidosaurus *m*.

scelidotherium [selidou'θiəriəm], *s. Paleont:* scelidotherium *m*.

Scelionidae [seli'ɔnidi:], *s.pl. Ent:* scélionides *m*.

scenario [si'nɑ:riou], *s. Th:* scénario *m*; canevas *m* (d'une pièce); **s. writer,** scénariste *mf*.

scend[1] [send], *s. Nau:* encombrement vertical.

scend[2], *v.i. Nau:* (*of ship*) plonger dans le creux de la lame; tanguer fortement.

scene [si:n], *s.* **1.** *Th: A:* scène *f*; *F:* **to appear on the s.,** entrer en scène; **to quit the s.,** mourir. **2.** (*a*) *Th:* (*place of action of a play*) scène; **s. change, change of s.,** changement de décor; **the s. is set in London,** l'action *f* se passe à Londres; (*b*) théâtre *m*, lieu *m* (d'un événement); **the political s.,** la scène politique; **the s. of operations,** le théâtre des opérations; (*in narrative*) **the s. changes,** l'action change de lieu; **a change of s. would do him good,** un changement d'air lui ferait du bien; **it is a s. of strife,** c'est le théâtre d'une lutte continuelle; **the scenes of his early exploits,** les lieux de ses premiers exploits; **the s. of the crime,** le(s) lieu(x) du crime; *F:* **it's not my s.,** ce n'est pas mon genre. **3.** (*a*) *Th:* (*subdivision of a play*) scène; **act three, s. two,** deuxième scène du troisième acte; (*b*) scène, incident *m*, spectacle *m*; **it was a painful s.,** c'était une scène pénible. **4.** (*a*) *Th:* **(set) s.,** décor *m*; **scenes painted by . . .,** décors par . . .; **s. dock,** remise *f* à décors; **s. painter,** peintre *m* de décors; **behind the scenes,** (i) dans les coulisses, derrière la toile; (ii) *F:* dans les coulisses, dans la coulisse; **to know what's going on behind the scenes,** savoir ce qui se passe dans la coulisse; connaître, voir, le dessous des cartes; **behind the scenes in politics,** les coulisses de la politique; (*b*) vue *f*, paysage *m*; **the s. from the window,** la vue de la fenêtre. **5.** *F:* **to make a s.,** faire une scène; faire de l'esclandre; **now don't make a s.!** allons, calmez-vous! ne fais pas une scène!

scenedesmus [si:ni'dezməs], *s. Algae:* scénédesmus *m*.

scenery ['si:nəri], *s.* **1.** (*a*) *Th:* décors *mpl*; (mise *f* en) scène *f*; (*b*) *F:* **you need a change of s.,** il vous faut du changement. **2.** paysage *m*; vue *f*.

sceneshifter ['si:nʃiftər], *s. Th:* machiniste *m*.

sceneshifting ['si:nʃiftiŋ], *s. Th:* changement *m* de décors.

scenic ['si:nik], *a.* **1.** (*a*) (*of performance, etc.*) scénique; théâtral, -aux; *Cin: O:* **s. film,** film spectaculaire d'après nature; film à grands tableaux d'après nature; (*b*) (*of emotion, effect*) théâtral; exagéré. **2.** *O:* (*at fair*) **s. railway,** montagnes *fpl* russes. **3.** *Art:* (tableau) qui représente un incident.

scenographer [si:'nɔgrəfər], *s.* scénographe *mf*.

scenographic(al) [si:nə'græfik(əl)], *a.* scénographique; **s. scale,** échelle perspective.

scenography [si:'nɔgrəfi], *s.* **1.** scénographie *f*. **2.** *A:* dessin *m* en perspective.

Scenopinidae [si:nou'pinidi:], *s.pl. Ent:* scénopinidés *m*.

scent[1] [sent], *s.* **1.** (*a*) parfum *m*, senteur *f*; odeur *f* agréable (des fleurs, etc.); odeur (d'un cigare); (*b*) **bottle of s.,** flacon de parfum; **s. spray,** vaporisateur *m*; *O:* **s. bag,** sachet à parfums; **she uses too much s.,** elle se parfume trop. **2.** (*a*) *Ven:* fumet *m*, vent *m*, assentement *m* (de la bête); **s. bag,** drag *m*; *Nat.Hist:* **s. marking,** urination par laquelle un animal marque son territoire; **s. gland, organ,** glande à sécrétion odoriférante; **s. bag,** poche à sécrétion odoriférante (du porte-musc, etc.); *Ent:* **s. scale,** androconie *f*; (*b*) *Ven:* piste *f*, voie *f*, trace *f*; **the hound was following the s. of a hare,** le chien suivait la piste d'un lièvre; (*of pack*) **to get on the s., to pick up the s.,** empaumer la voie; assentir la voie; **the dogs are on the s.,** les chiens ont rencontré; *F:* **to be on the right s.,** être sur la piste; **to lose the s., to be thrown off the s.,** perdre la trace; être, venir, à bout de voie; **to pick up the s. again,** retrouver la trace; **to put the dogs on the s.,** mettre les chiens sur la voie; **to throw the dogs off the s., to put the dogs on the wrong s.,** dépister les chiens; mettre les chiens en défaut; donner le change aux chiens; *F:* **to put s.o. on a false s.,** aiguiller qn sur une fausse piste; donner le change à qn; **to throw people off the s.,** dérouter les soupçons; **to throw the police off the s.,** dérouter la police; **to get s. of sth.,** avoir vent de qch. **3.** odorat *m*, flair *m* (d'un chien); **dog that has no s.,** chien qui n'a pas de nez.

scent[2], *v.tr.* **1.** (*of hounds, etc.*) **to s. (out) game,** flairer, sentir, éventer, halener, le gibier; **keen-scented dog,** chien au nez fin. **2.** (*a*) (*of flower, etc.*) parfumer, embaumer (l'air, etc); **scented plant,** plante odorante, odoriférante; (*b*) **to s. sth. with sth.,** parfumer, imprégner, qch. de qch.; **scented soap,** savon parfumé.

scentless ['sentlis], *a.* **1.** (fleur, etc.) inodore, sans odeur. **2.** *Ven:* (terrain, etc.) qui ne révèle pas le fumet, sans fumet.

scepsis ['skepsis], *s. Phil:* scepticisme *m*.

sceptic ['skeptik], *s.* sceptique *mf*.

sceptical ['skeptik(ə)l], *a.* sceptique.

sceptically ['skeptik(ə)li], *adv.* sceptiquement; avec scepticisme; d'un air, d'un ton, sceptique, incrédule.

scepticism ['skeptisizm], *s.* scepticisme *m*.

sceptre ['septər], *s.* sceptre *m*; **to hold, wield, the s.,** tenir le sceptre.

sceuophylax [skju:'ɔfilæks], *s. Ecc:* scévophylax *m*.

schadenfreude ['ʃɑ:dənfrɔidə], *s.* joie maligne (qu'on éprouve en face du malheur d'autrui).

Schaffhausen ['ʃæfhauz(ə)n], *Pr.n. Geog:* Schaffhouse.

schapping ['ʃæpiŋ], *s. Tex:* schappage *m*.

schapska ['ʃæpskə], *s. A.Mil.Cost:* (s)chapska *m*.

schedule[1] ['ʃedju:l, *NAm:* 'skedju:l], *s.* **1.** (*a*) *Jur:* annexe *f* (à une loi, aux statuts d'une société, etc.); (*b*) bordereau *m*; note explicative. **2.** (*a*) *Com: Ind:* nomenclature *f* (des pièces, etc.); inventaire *m* (des machines, etc.); barème *m* (des prix); **s. of charges,** liste officielle des taux; tarif *m*; (*b*) *Adm:* cédule *f* (d'impôts); (*c*) *Jur:* (*in bankruptcy*) bilan *m* (de l'actif et du passif). **3.** (*a*) plan *m* (d'exécution d'un travail, etc.); **work s.,** planning *m*; **s. work,** travail de régime; **to be on s.,** se poursuivre suivant le planning; **to be behind s.,** être en retard sur les prévisions; **to be ahead of s.,** être en avance sur l'horaire prévu, sur les délais prévus; **everything went off according to s.,** tout a marché selon les prévisions; **tight, detailed, s.,** horaire (strictement) minuté; **his day is run on a tight s.,** sa journée est soigneusement minutée; **I work to a very tight s.,** mon temps est très minuté; (*b*) *Rail: etc:* horaire; indicateur *m*; **on, up to, s.,** (train) à l'heure; **to arrive on s.,** arriver à l'heure indiquée.

schedule[2], *v.tr.* **1.** (*a*) *Jur:* ajouter (un article) comme annexe (à une loi, etc.); (*b*) ajouter (une note) en bordereau. **2.** inscrire (un article, etc.) sur une liste, sur l'inventaire; **scheduled prices,** prix selon le tarif; **scheduled taxes,** impôts cédulaires; **scheduled disease,** maladie dont la déclaration aux autorités est obligatoire. **3.** (*a*) dresser un plan, un programme, de (qch.); arrêter (le programme); **the mayor is scheduled to make a speech,** le maire doit prononcer un discours; (*b*) inscrire (un train) à l'horaire; **the train is scheduled to arrive at noon,** selon l'indicateur le train arrive à midi; **to arrive at the scheduled time,** arriver à l'heure indiquée; **scheduled services,** services réguliers. **4. to s. as an ancient monument, as a place of historic interest,** classer (comme) monument historique.

scheduling ['ʃedju(:)liŋ, *NAm:* 'skedju(:)liŋ], *s. Ind:* établissement *m* d'un programme de marche.

scheelite ['ʃi:lait], *s. Miner:* scheelite *f*.

schefferite ['ʃefərait], *s. Miner:* schefférite *f*.

Scheldt [skelt, ʃelt]. *Pr.n. Geog:* Escaut *m*.

scheltopusik [ʃeltou'p(j)u:zik], *s. Rept:* scheltopusik *m*.

schema, *pl.* **-ata** ['ski:mə, -ətə], *s.* **1.** schéma *m*, diagramme *m*. **2.** *Rh:* figure *f* de mots. **3.** *Phil:* schème *m*. **4.** *Psy:* **body s.,** schéma corporel.

schematic [ski'mætik]. **1.** *a.* schématique. **2.** *s.* plan *m* schématique.

schematically [ski'mætik(ə)li], *adv.* schématiquement.
schematism ['ski:mətizm], *s. Phil: etc:* schématisme *m.*
schematization [ski:mətai'zeiʃ(ə)n], *s.* schématisation *f.*
schematize ['ski:mətaiz], *v.tr.* **1.** schématiser; représenter (qch.) par un diagramme. **2.** *Phil:* schématiser (les catégories).
scheme[1] [ski:m], *s.* **1.** (*a*) arrangement *m*, combinaison *f*; **the s. of things,** l'ordre *m* de la nature; **colour s.,** combinaison de(s) couleurs; coloris *m*; **it's a good colour s.,** les couleurs sont bien agencées; **rhyme s.,** disposition *f* des rimes; (*b*) *Jur:* **s. of composition (between debtor and creditors),** concordat préventif (à la faillite); (*c*) système *m*; **s. of marking (of examination papers),** barème *m* des notes. **2.** résumé *m*, exposé *m* (d'un sujet d'étude); plan *m* (d'un ouvrage littéraire). **3.** (*a*) plan, projet *m*; **s. for a canal,** étude *f* d'un canal; *Mil: etc:* **tactical s.,** thème *m* tactique; (*b*) *Pej:* machination *f*, intrigue *f*, complot *m*, cabale *f*; **to lay a s.,** ourdir, tramer, une machination; **the best laid schemes,** les combinaisons les mieux étudiées; **to lay a s. to do sth.,** combiner de faire qch.; **to thwart s.o.'s schemes,** ruiner les desseins *m* de qn; contrecarrer les projets de qn. **4.** *Arch:* **s. arch,** arc surbaissé.
scheme[2]. **1.** *v.i.* intriguer, ruser, comploter; **to s. to do sth.,** combiner de faire qch.; intriguer pour faire qch. **2.** *v.tr. O:* machiner, combiner (une conspiration, etc.).
schemer ['ski:mər], *s.* **1.** faiseur, -euse, de projets, de plans; homme, femme, à projets. **2.** *Pej:* intrigant, -ante; comploteur *m*; tripoteur, -euse; **he was a s. all his life,** il a comploté toute sa vie; *F:* **he's a clever s.,** il sait nager.
scheming[1] ['ski:miŋ], *a.* intrigant, tripoteur.
scheming[2], *s.* **1.** plans *mpl*, projets *mpl.* **2.** *Pej:* machinations *fpl*, intrigues *fpl*; menées *fpl* (d'un parti politique); combinaisons *fpl*, *F:* combines *fpl.*
schemozzle [ʃi'mɔzl], *s. F:* = SHEMOZZLE.
scherzando [skɛət'sændou]. *Mus:* **1.** *s.* scherzo *m.* **2.** *adv.* scherzando.
scherzo ['skɛətsou], *s. Mus:* scherzo *m.*
Scheveningen ['skeivəniŋən]. *Pr.n. Geog:* Schéveningue.
schiedam ['ski:dæm], *s.* schiedam *m*, genièvre *m.*
schilling ['ʃiliŋ], *s. Num:* schilling (autrichien).
schipperke ['ʃipəki, 'ski-], *s.* (chien, chienne) schipperke *mf.*
schism ['s(k)izm], *s.* schisme *m.*
schismatic [s(k)iz'mætik], *a. & s.* schismatique (*mf*).
schismatical [s(k)iz'mætik(ə)l], *a.* schismatique.
schist [ʃist], *s. Miner:* schiste *m*; **mica s.,** micaschiste *m*, schiste micacé.
schistoid ['ʃistɔid], *a. Miner:* schistoïde.
schistose, schistous ['ʃistous, -təs], *a. Miner:* schisteux.
schistosity [ʃis'tɔsiti], *s. Geol:* schistosité *f.*
schistosoma [ʃistou'soumə], **schistosome** ['ʃistousoum], *s. Ann:* schistosome *m.*
schistosomiasis [ʃistousou'maiəsis], *s. Med:* schistosomiase *f.*
Schizaeaceae [skizi'eisii:], *s.pl. Bot:* schizaeacées *f*, schizéacées *f.*
schizanthus [sk(a)i'zænθəs], *s. Bot:* schizanthe *m.*
schizo ['skitsou], *a. & s. F:* schizophrène (*mf*).
schizocarp ['skizouka:p], *s. Bot:* fruit *m* schizocarpique.
schizocarpic, schizocarpous [skizou'ka:pik, -pəs], *a. Bot:* schizocarpique.
schizocoele ['skizousi:l], *s.* schizocœle *m.*
schizogamy [ski'zɔgəmi], *s. Biol:* schizogamie *f.*
schizogenesis [skizou'dʒenisis], *s. Biol:* schizogénèse *f.*
schizogonic [skizou'gɔnik], **schizogonous** [ski'zɔgənəs], *a. Prot:* schizogonique.
schizogony [ski'zɔgəni], *s. Prot:* schizogonie *f.*
schizoid ['skitsɔid], *a. & s. Psy:* schizoïde (*mf*).
schizoidism ['skitsɔidizm], *s. Psy:* schizoïdie *f.*
schizolite ['skizoulait], *s. Miner:* schizolite *f.*
schizolysigenous [skizoulai'sidʒinəs], *a. Bot:* schizolysigène.
schizomycete [skizou'maisi:t], *s. Bac:* schizomycète *m.*
schizont ['sk(a)izɔnt], *s. Prot:* schizonte *m.*
schizophasia [skitsou'feiz'iə], *s. Psy:* schizophasie *f.*
schizophrene ['skitsoufri:n], *s. Psy:* schizophrène *mf*, schizophrénique *mf.*
schizophrenia [skitsou'fri:niə], *s. Psy:* schizophrénie *f.*
schizophrenic [skitsou'fri:nik], *a. & s. Psy:* schizophrène (*mf*), schizophrénique (*mf*).
Schizophyceae [skizou'faisii:], *s.pl. Bot:* schizophycées *f.*
Schizophyta [ski'zɔfətə], *s.pl. Bac: Algae:* schizophytes *m.*
schizophyte ['skizoufait], *s. Bac: Algae:* schizophyte *m.*
schizopod ['skizoupɔd], *s. Crust:* schizopode *m.*
schizostely [ski'zɔsteli], *s. Bot:* schizostélie *f.*
schizothyme ['skitsouθaim], *s. Psy:* schizothyme *mf.*
schizothymia [skitsou'θaimiə], *s. Psy:* schizothymie *f.*
schizothymic [skitsou'θaimik], **schizothymous** [skitsou'θaiməs], *a. Psy:* schizothymique, schizothyme; **a s. personality,** un, une, schizothyme.
schlieren ['ʃliərən], *s. Av:* **s. photography technique,** méthode *f* des stries.
Schmalkaldic ['ʃma:lkældik], *a. Hist:* **the S. League,** la ligue de Smalkalde.
schmal(t)z [ʃmɔ:(:)lts], *s. F:* **1.** (*a*) musique très sentimentale; (*b*) sensiblerie *f*, sentimentalité doucereuse. **2.** *U.S: Cu:* graisse de volaille fondue.
schmal(t)zy ['ʃmɔ(:)ltsi], *a. F:* doucereusement sentimental; à l'eau de rose.
schnauzer ['ʃnautsər], *s.* (*dog*) schnauzer *m.*
schnozzle ['ʃnɔzl], *s. P:* nez *m*, pif *m.*
scholar ['skɔlər], *s.* **1.** (*a*) *A:* élève *mf*, écolier, -ière (d'une école primaire); (*b*) *A:* élève, disciple *m* (of, de); (*c*) personne *f* qui apprend; **to be an apt s.,** apprendre facilement. **2.** savant, -ante; lettré, -ée; érudit, -ite; intellectuel, -elle; *esp.* humaniste *m*; **a great s.,** un homme d'un grand savoir; **a fine s.,** un fin lettré; **Latin s.,** latiniste *mf*; **Greek s.,** helléniste *mf*; **Hebrew s.,** hébraïste *mf*, hébraïsant, -ante; **Chinese s.,** sinologue *mf*; **English s.,** angliciste *mf*; **French s.,** spécialiste *mf* du français; **German s.,** germaniste *mf*; **he's a good German s.,** il sait l'allemand à fond; **he's no s.,** son éducation laisse à désirer; ce n'est pas un lettré. **3.** *Sch:* boursier, -ière.
scholarly ['skɔləli], *a.* savant, érudit; **a very s. man,** un homme d'un grand savoir.
scholarship ['skɔləʃip], *s.* **1.** savoir *m*, science *f*; érudition *f*; **he's an historian of great s.,** c'est un érudit en histoire. **2.** *Sch:* bourse *f* (d'études); **open s.,** bourse accessible à tous; **travel(ling) s.,** bourse de voyage; **to win, gain, a s.,** obtenir une bourse.
scholastic [skə'læstik]. **1.** *a.* (*a*) (philosophie, théologie) scolastique; (*b*) (*of schools, etc.*) scolaire; scolastique; **s. agency,** agence de placement pour professeurs; (*c*) (*of manner, speech, etc.*) pédant. **2.** *s. Phil: Theol:* scolastique *m.*
scholasticism [skə'læstisizm], *s. Phil:* la scolastique; le scolasticisme.
scholiast ['skouliæst], *s. Lit:* sc(h)oliaste *m.*
scholium, *pl.* **-ia** ['skouliəm, -iə], *s.* **1.** *Lit:* sc(h)olie *f.* **2.** *Mth:* sc(h)olie *m.*
school[1] [sku:l], *s.* **1.** (*a*) école *f*; **nursery s.,** école maternelle, *F:* maternelle *f*; **infant s.,** école pour enfants de 5 à 7 ans; **primary s.,** *A:* **elementary s.,** école primaire; école communale; *A:* **board s.** = école primaire communale; *A:* **S. Board** = conseil de l'enseignement primaire; *A:* **central s.** = école primaire supérieure; **secondary s.,** (i) établissement d'enseignement secondaire; (ii) *A:* = lycée *m*, collège *m*; **secondary modern s.** = collège d'enseignement général; **comprehensive s.** = centre *m* d'études secondaires; **grammar s., high s.** = lycée; *A:* **direct grant (grammar) s.** = collège d'enseignement privé subventionné par l'État; **independent s., private s.** = école, collège, libre; **public s.,** (i) collège privé (de niveau supérieur) (avec internat); (ii) *U.S:* = **state s.; state s.,** école d'État, établissement national; **denominational s.,** école confessionnelle; **approved s.,** centre d'éducation surveillée; **Sunday s.,** école du dimanche; **what s. were you at?** où avez-vous fait vos études? **to keep, run, a s.,** tenir (une) école; **s. hall,** salle de réunion, des fêtes; **s. furniture, equipment,** matériel scolaire; **s. book,** livre de classe; livre scolaire; **s. bus,** (auto)car scolaire; "transport d'enfants," "transport scolaire"; **s. bus service,** service de ramassage des écoliers; (*b*) (les élèves d'une) école; **the s. was assembled,** on avait réuni tous, toutes, les élèves; **the whole s. knew it,** tous, toutes, les élèves le savaient; toute l'école le savait; **the upper s.,** les grandes classes; **the middle, lower, s.,** les classes moyennes; les petites classes. **2.** (*schooling*) **to go to s.,** aller en classe; **to be at s.,** être en classe; **we were at s. together,** nous avons été en classe ensemble; **when I was at s.,** quand j'allais en classe; **to come out of s.,** sortir de classe; **s. begins at nine,** les classes commencent à neuf heures; **I arrived ten minutes before s.,** je suis arrivé dix minutes avant la classe; **there will be no s. today,** il n'y aura pas classe aujourd'hui; *F:* **you'd better go back to s. again,** il faut vous remettre sur les bancs; **s. attendance,** scolarisation *f*; **compulsory s. attendance,** scolarité *f* obligatoire; **s. leavers,** jeunes gens qui ont terminé leurs études secondaires; **s. leaving age,** âge de fin de scolarité; **to raise the s. leaving age,** prolonger la scolarité; (**of**) **s. age,** (d')âge scolaire; **s. year, life,** année, vie, scolaire; **s. fees,** frais scolaires, frais de scolarité; **s. report,** livret scolaire; bulletin (trimestriel); *NAm:* **to teach s.,** être dans l'enseignement. **3.** école, académie *f*, institut *m* (d'enseignement technique, industriel, etc.); **art s., s. of art,** école des beaux-arts; **s. of mines,** école des mines; **regimental s.,** école régimentaire; **s. of dancing,** académie, école, de danse; **s. of music,** académie de musique; conservatoire *m*; **language s.,** école de langues; **fencing s.,** académie, salle *f*, d'escrime; **driving s., s. of motoring,** auto-école *f,pl.* auto-écoles; école de conduite; *Equit: U.S:* **high s.,** haute école; **night s.,** cours *mpl* du soir; *A:* **continuation s.,** (i) cours d'adultes; cours complémentaire; (ii) école du soir; **summer s.,** cours de vacances. **4.** *pl. Hist: of Phil:* **the Schools,** l'École; la philosophie scolastique (du moyen âge). **5.** (*in universities*) (*a*) faculté *f*; **the Arts S.,** la Faculté des lettres; (*b*) **schools,** (i) salle d'examen; (ii) (*at Oxford*) examen *m* (pour le B.A.); **to sit for one's schools,** se présenter à l'examen. **6.** (*a*) *Art: Lit: Phil:* école; *Art:* **the Flemish s., the Italian s.,** l'école flammande; l'école italienne; *Phil:* **the Platonic s.,** l'école de Platon; (*b*) **s. of thought,** école (de pensée, d'opinions); *F:* **one of the old s.,** un homme de la vieille école; (*c*) disciples *mpl* (d'un maître); **he founded no s.,** il n'a pas laissé de disciples; il n'a pas fait école; (*d*) *F:* personnes réunies pour jouer de l'argent. **7.** *Mus:* livre *m* d'instruction; méthode *f* (de violon, etc.).
school[2], *v.tr.* **1.** (*a*) envoyer (un enfant) à l'école; (*b*) instruire (qn); faire l'éducation de (qn). **2.** former (un enfant, un cheval, l'esprit de qn, etc.); discipliner (sa voix, son geste, etc.); **to s. s.o. to do sth.,** entraîner, dresser, qn à faire qch.; *Lit:* **to s. oneself to patience,** s'astreindre à la patience; apprendre à patienter; **to s. s.o. in a part,** apprendre son rôle à qn.
school[3], *s.* banc voyageur (de poissons); bande *f* (de marsouins).
schoolboy ['sku:lbɔi], *s.m.* écolier; élève; **when I was a s.,** lorsque j'étais, j'allais, en classe; **to behave like a s.,** se conduire comme un gamin, comme un écolier; **s. slang,** argot scolaire; argot des écoles; **s. howler,** bévue d'écolier.
schoolchild, *pl.* **-children** ['sku:ltʃaild, -tʃildrən], *s.* (i) écolier, -ière; (ii) *Adm:* enfant *mf* d'âge scolaire.
schoolday ['sku:ldei], *s.* **1** jour *m* de classe. **2. schooldays,** vie *f* scolaire; années *f* de classe, d'école; **in my schooldays,** au temps où, quand, j'allais en classe.
schoolfellow ['sku:lfelou], *s.* camarade *mf* de classe.
schoolgirl ['sku:lgə:l], *s.f.* écolière; élève; **to behave like a s.,** se comporter comme une petite gamine; **s. complexion,** teint de jeune fille.
schoolhouse ['sku:lhaus], *s.* **1.** (bâtiment *m*, maison *f*, d')école *f.* **2.** maison du directeur, de la directrice (faisant corps avec l'école).
schooling ['sku:liŋ], *s.* instruction *f*, éducation *f*; **he has had no s.,** il n'a pas reçu d'instruction; **he paid for his nephew's s.,** il a subvenu aux frais d'études de son neveu.
schoolma'am, schoolmarm ['sku:lma:m], *s.f. F:* (*a*) *esp. U.S:* maîtresse d'école; institutrice; (*b*) **she's a real s.,** (i) c'est une pédante; (ii) c'est une vraie prude.
schoolman, *pl.* **-men** ['sku:lmən], *s.m.* **1.** *Hist. of Phil:* scolastique; **the Schoolmen,** l'École *f.* **2.** *NAm:* professeur.
schoolmaster ['sku:lma:stər], *s.m.* (*in primary school*) instituteur; maître (d'école); (*in secondary school*) professeur.
schoolmate ['sku:lmeit], *s.* camarade *mf* de classe.
schoolmistress ['sku:lmistris], *s.f.* (*in primary school*) institutrice; maîtresse (d'école); (*in secondary school*) professeur *m.*
schoolroom ['sku:lru:m], *s.* (*in school*) (salle *f* de) classe *f*; *A:* (*in private house*) salle d'étude.
schoolteacher ['sku:lti:tʃər], *s.* (*in primary school*) instituteur, -trice; maître *m*, maîtresse *f* (d'école); (*in secondary school*) professeur *m.*
schooltime ['sku:ltaim], *s.* **1.** heures *fpl* de classe; **in s.,** pendant les heures de classe; pendant la classe; pendant les classes. **2.** vie *f* scolaire; années *fpl* de classe, d'école.
schooner[1] ['sku:nər], *s.* **1.** *Nau:* schooner *m*; goélette *f*; **fore-and-aft s.,** goélette franche; **three-mast(ed) s.,** trois-mâts *m* goélette, latin; **s. brig,** brick-goélette *m*; **s. yacht,** yacht gréé en goélette; **s.-rigged,** gréé en goélette. **2.** *U.S:* (**prairie**) **s.,** chariot *m* (des premiers colons).

schooner[2], *s.* (*a*) grande flûte, grand verre (à bière); (*b*) grand verre à vin de Xérès.

Schoop ['ʃu:p], *Pr.n. Metall:* **S. process,** schoopage *m.*

schorl(ite) ['ʃɔ:l(ait)], *s. Miner:* tourmaline noire, schorl *m.*

schorlaceous [ʃɔ:'leiʃəs], **schorlous** [ʃɔ:ləs], *a. Miner:* schorlacé.

schorlomite ['ʃɔæloumait], *s. Miner:* schorlomite *f.*

schottische [ʃɔ:ti:ʃ], *s. Danc: Mus:* scotti(s)ch *f.*

schreibersite ['ʃraibəsait], *s. Miner:* schreibersite *f.*

schreinering ['ʃrainəriŋ], *s. Tex:* similisage *m* (des cotonnades).

Schubertian [ʃu:'bə:tiən], *a. Mus:* schubertien.

schungite ['ʃʌŋgait], *s. Miner:* schungite *f.*

schuss[1] [ʃu:s], *s. Ski:* schuss *m.*

schuss[2], *v.i. Ski:* descendre schuss.

Schwei(t)ser ['ʃwaitsər], *Pr.n. Ch:* **Schwei(t)zer's reagent,** liqueur *f* Schweitzer.

sciaena [sai'i:nə], *s. Ich:* sciène *f.*

Sciaenidae [sai'i:nidi:], *s.pl. Ich:* sciénidés *m.*

sciaen(o)id [sai'i:n(ɔ)id], *a. & s. Ich:* sciénidé (*m*).

scialytic [saiə'litik], *a.* scialytique; **s. light,** lampe scialytique.

sciapod ['saiəpɔd], *s. Myth:* sciapode *mf.*

sciara ['saiərə], *s. Ent:* sciara *f.*

sciascopy [sai'æskəpi], *s. Med:* skiascopie *f*; pupilloscopie *f.*

sciatic [sai'ætik], *a. Anat:* sciatique; **the s. (nerve),** le nerf sciatique.

sciatica [sai'ætikə], *s. Med:* sciatique *f.*

science ['saiəns], *s.* **1.** *A:* science *f*, savoir *m*; **the seven liberal sciences,** les sept sciences libérales. **2.** science; **the exact sciences,** les sciences exactes; **pure s.,** science pure, abstraite; **applied s.,** sciences appliquées; **physical s.,** les sciences physiques; **natural s.,** sciences naturelles; **social s.,** sciences sociales; *F: A:* **the dismal s.,** l'économie politique; **the s. of chemistry,** la (science de la) chimie; **to study s.,** étudier les sciences; *Sch:* **s. master, mistress,** professeur *m* de sciences; **s. knows no frontiers,** la science n'a pas de patrie; **to raise betting to a s.,** ériger le pari en étude scientifique; **s. fiction,** science-fiction *f*; littérature *f* d'anticipation; **s.-fiction novel,** roman *m* d'anticipation.

scienter [sai'entər]. *Jur:* (*a*) *adv.* à bon escient; (*b*) *s.* **to prove a s.,** prouver qu'un acte a été commis ou permis à bon escient.

scientific [saiən'tifik], *a.* scientifique; **s. research,** recherches scientifiques; **s. instruments,** instruments de précision; *Sch: etc:* **he's not very s.,** il est peu doué pour les sciences; **s. cruelty,** cruauté étudiée; **s. game,** jeu qui est une véritable science; **s. boxer,** boxeur qui possède la science du combat.

scientifically [saiən'tifik(ə)li], *adv.* scientifiquement.

scientist ['saiəntist], *s.* **1.** scientifique *mf*; homme *m* de science; savant, -ante. **2.** (*adept of scientism*) scientiste *mf*; **Christian S.,** scientiste chrétien(ne).

scientism ['saiəntizm], *s.* scientisme *m.*

scientistic [saiən'tistik], *a.* scientiste.

scientologist [saiən'tɔlədʒist], *s.* scientologiste *mf.*

scientology [saiən'tɔlədʒi], *s.* scientologie *f.*

sci-fi ['saifai], *s. F:* science-fiction *f.*

scilicet ['sailiset], *adv.* à savoir; c'est-à-dire.

scilla ['silə], *s. Bot:* scille *f.*

Scillonian [si'louniən], *a. & s.* (originaire *mf*, habitant, -ante) des Sorlingues.

Scilly ['sili], *Pr.n. Geog:* **the S. Isles,** les Sorlingues *f.*

scimitar ['simitər], *s.* cimeterre *m.*

Scincidae ['skinsidi:], *s.pl. Rept:* scincidés *m*, les scinques *m.*

scintigram ['sintigræm], *s.* scinti(llo)gramme *m.*

scintigraphy [sin'tigrəfi], *s.* scinti(llo)graphie *f.*

scintilla [sin'tilə], *s. Lit:* soupçon *m*, parcelle *f*, fragment *m*; **a mere s. of evidence,** un simple soupçon de preuve; un indice infime; **not a s. of truth,** pas un atome de vérité.

scintillant ['sintilənt], *a.* scintillant, étincelant.

scintillate ['sintileit], *v.i.* scintiller, étinceler; **scintillating with wit,** qui scintille, qui pétille, d'esprit.

scintillating ['sintileitiŋ], *a.* scintillant, étincelant; **s. wit,** esprit scintillant, pétillant.

scintillation [sinti'leiʃ(ə)n], *s.* scintillation *f*, scintillement *m* (des étoiles, de l'esprit, etc.); *Ph:* **s. counter,** compteur à scintillations, scintillateur *m*; **s. meter,** scintillomètre *m*; **s. spectometer,** spectomètre *m* à scintillations.

scintillator ['sintileitər], *s. Atom.Ph:* scintillateur *m*; **liquid, organic, s.,** scintillateur liquide, organique.

scintillometer [sinti'lɔmitər], *s. Ph: etc:* scintillomètre *m.*

scion ['saiən], *s.* **1.** *Hort:* (*a*) scion *m*, ente *f*, greffon *m*; (*b*) *A:* rejeton *m*, pousse *f*; surgeon *m*. **2.** descendant *m*, rejeton, héritier *m* (d'une race noble, etc.); **s. of a noble house,** rejeton d'une famille noble.

sciophyte ['saioufait], *s. Bot:* plante *f* sciaphile.

scioptic [sai'ɔptik], *a.* scioptique.

Scipio ['s(k)ipiou], *Pr.n.m. Rom.Hist:* Scipion; **the Scipios,** les Scipions.

scirrhoid ['sirɔid], *a. Med:* squirreux.

scirrhosity [si'rɔsiti], *s. Med:* squirrosité *f.*

scirrhous ['sirəs], *a. Med:* squirreux; **s. cancer,** cancer *m* en cuirasse.

scirrhus ['sirəs], *s. Med:* squirre *m.*

scissel ['sisəl], *s. Num:* cisaille *f*; rognures *fpl* (de flans).

scissile ['sisail], *a. Miner:* scissile, fissile.

scission ['siʃ(ə)n], *s.* **1.** cisaillement *m*, cisaillage *m*. **2.** scission *f*, division *f* (dans un parti, etc.).

scissiparity [sisi'pæriti], *s.* scissiparité *f.*

scissiparous [si'sipərəs], *a.* scissipare.

scissor[1] ['sizər], *s.* **1.** (*a*) **(pair of) scissors,** ciseaux *mpl*; **cutting-out scissors,** ciseaux de couturière; **buttonhole scissors,** ciseaux à boutonnières; **nail scissors,** ciseaux à ongles; **cuticle scissors,** ciseaux de manucure, à envies; **short-bladed scissors,** ciseaux à lames courtes; *Journ: etc:* **to work with scissors and paste,** travailler à coups de ciseaux; *El:* **scissors arc lamp,** lampe à charbons à angle obtus; *Rail:* **scissors crossing,** traversée *f* bretelle; **s. grinder,** rémouleur *m* de ciseaux; (*b*) *Gym: Wr: etc:* **scissors,** ciseaux; *Wr:* **body scissors,** ciseaux au corps; **head, leg, scissors,** ciseaux de tête, de jambe; **flying scissors,** ciseaux de volée; *Rugby Fb:* **scissors (movement),** le ciseau; **s. jump,** saut en hauteur avec élan; *Ski:* **scissors stop,** arrêt *m* en ciseaux; *Swim:* **scissors kick,** les ciseaux. **2.** *Const:* **(hoisting) scissors,** louve *f* à pinces. **3.** (*a*) *Orn:* **s. bill,** rhyncops *m*; bec-en-ciseaux *m*, *pl.* becs-en-ciseaux; coupeur *m* d'eau; (*b*) *Z:* **s. tooth,** dent carnassière.

scissor[2], *v.tr.* (dé)couper (qch.) avec des ciseaux; cisailler (qch.).

scissurellid [si'sju:rəlid], *s. Moll:* scissurelle *f.*

Scissurellidae [sisju'relidi:], *s.pl. Moll:* scissurellidés *m.*

Scitamineae [sitə'minii:], *s.pl. Bot:* scitaminées *f.*

scitamineous [sitə'miniəs], *a. Bot:* scitaminé.

sciurid [sai'(j)uərid], *s. Z:* sciuridé *m.*

Sciuridae [sai'(j)uəridi:], *s.pl. Z:* sciuridés *m.*

sciurine ['sai(j)urain], *a. Z:* de l'écureuil; des sciuridés.

sciuromorph [sai'(j)uərəmɔ:f], *s. Z:* sciuromorphe *m.*

Sciuromorpha [sai(j)urə'mɔ:fə], *s.pl. Z:* sciuromorphes *m.*

sclera ['skliərə], *s. Anat:* sclérotique *f*; cornée *f* opaque; blanc *m* de l'œil.

scleral ['skliər(ə)l], *a. Anat:* scléral, -aux.

sclerectasia [skliərek'teiziə], *s. Med:* sclérectasie *f.*

sclerectomy [skliə'rektəmi], *s. Surg:* sclérectomie *f.*

sclerema [skliə'ri:mə], *s. Med:* sclérème *m*; **s. neonatorum,** sclérème des nouveau-nés.

sclerenchyma [skliə'reŋkimə], **sclerenchyme** [skliə'reŋkaim], *s. Nat.Hist:* sclérenchyme *m.*

scleriasis [skliə'raiəsis], *s. Med:* sclériase *f.*

sclerification [skliərifi'keiʃ(ə)n], *s.* sclérification *f.*

sclerified ['skliərifaid], *a. Nat.Hist:* sclérifié, durci.

sclerify ['skliərifai], *v.tr. Bot:* faire subir une sclérification.

sclerite ['skliərait], *s. Nat.Hist:* sclérite *f.*

scleritis [skliə'raitis], *s. Med:* sclérite *f*, sclérotite *f.*

sclerobase ['skliəroubeis], *s. Z:* sclérobase *f.*

scleroblast ['skliəroublɑ:st], *s. Spong:* scléroblaste *m.*

sclerochoroiditis [skliəroukɔ:rɔi'daitis], *s. Med:* sclérochoroïdite *f.*

scleroconjunctivitis [skliəroukənjʌŋ(k)ti'vaitis], *s. Med:* scléroconjonctivite *f.*

sclerodactylia [skliəroudæk'tiliə], **sclerodactyly** [skliərou'dæktili], *s. Med:* sclérodactylie *f.*

scleroderm ['skliəroudə:m], *s.* **1.** *Ich:* scléroderme *m*. **2.** *Coel:* sclérenchyme *m* (d'un madrépore).

scleroderma [skliərou'də:mə], *s.* **1.** *Med:* sclérodermie *f*. **2.** *Fung:* scléroderma *m.*

sclerodermatous [skliərou'də:mətəs], *a.* **1.** *Z:* sclérodermé. **2.** *Med:* scléreux.

sclerodermia [skliərou'də:miə], *s. Med:* sclérodermie *f.*

sclerogenic [skliərou'dʒenik], *a. Med:* sclérogène.

sclerokeratitis [skliəroukerə'taitis], *s. Med:* sclérokératite *f.*

scleroma, *pl.* **-mas, -mata** [skliə'roumə(z), -mətə], *s. Med:* rhinosclérome *m*; scleriase *f.*

sclerometer [skliə'rɔmitər], *s. Mec: Cryst:* scléromètre *m.*

sclerophthalmia [skliərɔf'θælmiə], *s. Med:* sclérophtalmie *f.*

sclerophyll ['skliərəfil], *a. & s. Bot:* sclérophylle (*m*).

sclerophyllous [skliərou'filəs], *a. Bot:* sclérophylle.

scleroprotein [skliərou'prouti:n], *s. Bio-Ch:* scléroprotéine *f.*

scleroscope ['skliərəskoup], *s. Mec:* scléroscope *m*; **s. hardness,** dureté *f* au scléroscope.

sclerose ['skliərous, -rouz], *v.tr. & i. Med:* (se) scléroser.

sclerosed ['skliəroust], *a. Med:* scléreux, sclérosé.

sclerosis, *pl.* **-oses** [skliə'rousis, -ousi:z], *s. Med:* sclérose *f*; **multiple, disseminated, insular, s.,** sclérose en plaques.

sclerostome ['skliəroustoum], *s. Ann:* sclérostome *m.*

sclerote ['skliərout], *s. Fung:* sclérote *m.*

sclerotic [skliə'rɔtik]. **1.** *a.* (*a*) scléreux, sclérosé; (*b*) *Anat:* sclérotical. **2.** *s. Anat:* sclérotique *f.*

sclerotin ['skliəroutin], *s. Bio-Ch:* sclérotine *f.*

sclerotinia [skliərou'tiniə], *s. Fung:* sclérotinia *m.*

sclerotitis [skliərou'taitis], *s. Med:* sclérotite *f.*

sclerotium [skliə'rouʃ(i)əm], *s. Fung:* **1.** sclérote *m*. **2.** sclérotium *m.*

sclerotized ['skliəroutaizd], *a. Ent:* sclérifié.

sclerotomy [skliə'rɔtəmi], *s. Med:* sclérotomie *f*; scléroticotomie *f.*

sclerous ['skliərəs], *a. Med: etc:* (tissu) scléreux.

scobicular [skə'bikjulər], **scobiform** ['skəbifɔ:m], *a. Nat.Hist:* scobiculé, scobiforme.

scobinate ['skəbineit], *a. Nat.Hist:* scobiné.

scobs [skɔbz], *s.pl.* **1.** sciure *f*; copeaux *mpl*; limaille *f*. **2.** scorie *f*, scories.

scoff[1] [skɔf], *s.* **1.** sarcasme *m*, moquerie *f*, raillerie *f*. **2.** *A:* (*pers.*) objet *m* de risée; **to be the s. of s.o.,** être en butte aux sarcasmes de qn; **to be the s. of the town,** être la risée de la ville.

scoff[2], *v.i.* se moquer; **to s. at s.o.,** railler, bafouer, qn; se moquer, se gausser, de qn; **to be scoffed at,** recueillir des railleries; *Lit:* **to s. at dangers,** mépriser les dangers.

scoff[3], *s. P:* nourriture *f*; boustifaille *f*, bouffe *f.*

scoff[4], *v.tr. P:* manger, bouffer, boulotter, bâfrer (de la nourriture).

scoffer ['skɔfər], *s.* moqueur, -euse; railleur, -euse.

scoffing[1] ['skɔfiŋ], *a.* moqueur, -euse; railleur, -euse.

scoffing[2], *s.* moquerie *f*, raillerie *f.*

scoffingly ['skɔfiŋli], *adv.* en dérision, en raillant, par moquerie.

scofflaw ['skɔflɔ:], *s. U.S:* violateur, -trice, de la loi.

scoke [skouk], *s. U.S: Bot:* phytolaque *m.*

scold[1] [skould]. **1.** *s.f.* (femme) querelleuse; mégère; grondeuse, bougonne, ronchon, ronchonneuse. **2.** *occ. s.m.* grondeur, bougon, ronchon, ronchonneur.

scold[2]. **1.** *v.i.* gronder, grogner, crier, criailler, ronchonner **(at s.o.,** contre qn). **2.** *v.tr.* gronder, réprimander, tancer, morigéner, attraper (qn).

scolding[1] ['skouldiŋ], *a.* (*of woman, tone, etc.*) grondeur, -euse; bougon, -onne; ronchonneur, -euse.

scolding[2], *s.* **1.** gronderie *f*, réprimande *f*, semonce *f*; **to give s.o. a good s.,** morigéner qn; laver la tête à qn. **2.** **constant s.,** des criailleries *f* sans fin.

scolecite[1] ['skɔlisait], *s. Miner:* scolécite *f*, scolésite *f.*

scolecite[2], *s. Fung:* scolécite *m.*

scolecospore [skou'li:kouspɔ:r], *s. Bot: Fung:* scolécospore *f.*

scolex ['skouleks], *pl.* **-eces** [skou'li:si:z], *also* **-ices** ['skoulisi:z], *s. Med: Ann:* scolex *m* (du ténia).

scolia ['skouliə], *s. Ent:* scolie *f.*

scoliid ['skouliid], *s. Ent:* scoliidé *m.*

Scoliidae [skɔ'laiidi:], *s.pl. Ent:* scoliidés *m.*

scoliosis [skɔli'ousis], *s. Med:* scoliose *f.*

scoliotic [skɔli'ɔtik], *a. Med:* scoliotique.

scollop[1,2] ['skɔləp], *s. & v.* = SCALLOP[1,2].

scolopaceous [skɔlou'peiʃ(ə)s], *a. Orn:* qui appartient aux scolopacidés.

Scolopacidae [skɔlou'pæsidi:], *s.pl. Orn:* scolopacidés *m.*

scolopacine [skɔlou'peisi:n, -ain]. *Orn:* **1.** *a.* = SCOLOPACEOUS. **2.** *s.* scolopacidé *m.*

scolopendra [skɔlou'pendrə], *s. Myr:* scolopendre *f.*

Scolopendridae [skɔlou'pendridi:], *s.pl. Myr:* scolopendridés *m.*

scolopendrium [skɔlou'pendriəm], *s. Bot:* scolopendre *f.*

scolopidium, *pl.* **-ia** [skɔlou'pidiəm, -iə], *s. Ent:* scolopidie *f.*

scolytid [skɔ'litid], *s. Ent:* scolytidé *m.*

Scolytidae [skɔ'litidi:], *s.pl. Ent:* scolytidés *m.*

scolytus ['skɔlitəs], *s. Ent:* scolyte *m.*

scomber ['skɔmbər], *s. Ich:* scombre *m*, maquereau *m.*

Scombresocidae [skɔmbrə'sɔsidi:], *s.pl. Ich:* scombresocidés *m.*

scombresox ['skɔmbrəsɔks], *s. Ich:* scombrésoce *m.*

Scombridae ['skɔmbridi:], *s.pl. Ich:* scombridés *m.*

scombroid ['skɔmbrɔid]. *Ich:* **1.** *a.* & *s.* scombre (*m*). **2.** *s.* scombridé *m.*
sconce[1] [skɔns], *s.* **1.** bougeoir *m.* **2.** applique *f*; candélabre fixé au mur; **piano s.,** flambeau *m* de piano. **3.** bobèche *f* (d'un chandelier, d'un bougeoir).
sconce[2], *s.* **1.** *Fort:* fort détaché; blockhaus *m,* fortin *m.* **2.** *A:* coin *m* du feu (d'une grande cheminée).
sconce[3], *s.* (*at some universities*) amende (d'une tournée de bière) (infligée par des condisciples).
sconce[4], *v.tr.* (*at some universities*) mettre (un étudiant) à l'amende; lui faire payer une tournée (à titre d'amende).
sconce[5], *s. P: A:* **1.** tête *f*; caboche *f.* **2.** jugeote *f,* bon sens.
scone [skɔn, skoun], *s.* **1.** petit pain au lait (souvent aux raisins secs) (cuit au four ou sur une plaque de fer); *Austr: F:* **s. hot,** de premier ordre, épatant. **2.** *Austr: F:* tête *f,* caboche *f.*
scoop[1] [sku:p], *s.* **1.** (*a*) *Nau:* épuisette *f,* écope *f*; (*b*) pelle *f* à main; **grocer's s.,** main *f*; *Husb:* **manure s.,** louche *f*; (*c*) *Surg:* curette *f*; (*d*) **aural s.,** cure-oreille *m, pl.* cure-oreilles. **2.** (*a*) *Civ.E:* cuiller *f,* godet *m* (de drague); *Hyd.E:* **noria s.,** godet; **s. wheel,** tympan *m*; *Fish:* **s. net,** drague *f*; (*b*) *I.C.E:* cuiller de graissage; plongeur *m,* cuiller d'huile (de tête de bielle); mentonnet lubrificateur; *Rail:* cuiller (de locomotive pour ramasser l'eau). **3.** **(coal) s.,** seau *m* à charbon (coupé en biseau).
scoop[2], *s.* **1.** creux *m,* concavité *f,* excavation *f.* **2.** (*a*) coup *m* de pelle; **at one s.,** d'un seul coup (de pelle); (*b*) *F:* coup de chance; **to make a s.,** réussir un coup; (*c*) *Journ: F:* nouvelle sensationnelle (que l'on est le premier à publier); scoop *m*; (*d*) *Dressm:* **s. neck,** décolleté (arrondi). **3.** *Mus: F:* port *m* de voix.
scoop[3], *v.tr.* **1.** **to s. (out),** écoper (l'eau) (d'un bateau); excaver (la terre); évider (du bois, etc.); vider (une tomate, etc.); *Engr: Typ: etc:* **to s. out a line,** échopper un trait; **to s. up,** (i) ramasser (du charbon, de la farine, etc.) avec la pelle; (ii) épuiser, écoper (l'eau, etc.). **2.** *F:* (*a*) réussir un beau coup; **to s. in £100 a day,** ramasser £100 par jour; (*b*) *Journ:* **to s. the other papers,** publier (une nouvelle, etc.) avant les autres journaux; faire un scoop.
scooper ['sku:pər], *s.* (*a*) outil *m* à évider; gouge *f*; (*b*) *Engr: etc:* échoppe *f* (à évider).
scoot[1] [sku:t], *s. F:* fuite précipitée; **to do a s.,** filer; s'enfuir; prendre ses jambes à son cou.
scoot[2], *v.i. F:* **to s. (off, away),** détaler, filer, déguerpir, se débiner; prendre ses jambes à son cou.
scooter ['sku:tər], *s.* **1.** *NAm:* bateau *m* à voiles et à patins (pour navigation sur la glace). **2.** (*a*) (*for child*) trottinette *f,* patinette *f*; (*b*) **(motor) s.,** scooter *m.*
scooterist ['sku:tərist], *s.* scootériste *mf.*
scopa ['skoupə], *s. Ent:* scopule *f,* scopula *f*; brosse *f* (de patte d'abeille).
scopate ['skoupeit], *a. Ent:* (patte) à brosse.
scope [skoup], *s.* **1.** (*a*) portée *f,* étendue *f,* rayon *m* (d'une action, du savoir de qn, etc.); domaine *m,* étendue (d'une science, etc.); **within the s. of an amateur,** à la portée d'un amateur; **it's beyond, outside, my s.,** cela n'est pas de, ne rentre pas dans, ma compétence; **s. of an undertaking,** portée, envergure *f,* d'une entreprise; **to extend the s. of one's activities,** élargir le champ de son activité; **it does not come within the s. of this work,** cela ne rentre pas dans le plan de cet ouvrage; cela est au delà des limites de cette étude; **word that is not within the s. of a child's vocabulary,** mot qui ne fait pas partie du vocabulaire d'un enfant; (*b*) espace *m,* place *f* (pour les mouvements de qn, etc.); **he hasn't enough s.,** il n'a pas assez de champ d'action; **this job will give me more s. to work independently,** cet emploi me donnera davantage de liberté, de latitude, d'agir indépendamment, selon mes propres idées; **to give full, free, s. to (s.o., one's imagination, etc.),** donner libre carrière à, laisser le champ libre à (qn, son imagination, etc.); *F:* **and that will give you plenty of s.!** comme ça tu ne seras pas gêné! comme ça tu auras le champ libre! **2.** *Nau:* **(riding) s.,** touée *f* (de l'amarre de mouillage).
scopelid ['skɔpəlid], *s. Ich:* scopèle *m,* scopélide *m.*
Scopelidae [skɔ'pelidi:], *s.pl. Ich:* scopélidés *m.*
Scopidae ['skɔpidi:], *s.pl. Orn:* scopidés *m,* les ombrettes *f.*
scopiform ['skoupifɔ:m], *a. Z:* fasciculaire.
scopolamine [skɔ'pɔləmi:n], *s. Pharm:* scopolamine *f.*
scops [skɔps], *s. Orn:* **s. (owl),** petit duc, scops *m.*
scopula, *pl.* **-ae** ['skɔpjulə, -i:], *s. Ent:* scopule *f,* scopula *f*; brosse *f* (de patte d'abeille).
scorbutic [skɔ:'bju:tik], *a.* & *s. Med:* scorbutique (*mf*).
scorbutus [skɔ:'bju:təs], *s. Med:* scorbut *m.*
scorch[1] [skɔ:tʃ], *s.* **1.** roussissement *m*; brûlure superficielle. **2.** *Aut: etc: F: O:* course *f* à toute vitesse, à une allure dangereuse.
scorch[2]. **1.** *v.tr.* (*of sun, fire, etc.*) roussir, brûler légèrement (le linge, etc.); (*of sun*) rôtir, flétrir, dessécher (l'herbe, etc.); (*of frost*) griller (les bourgeons, etc.); **scorched earth policy,** tactique *f,* politique *f,* de la terre brûlée. **2.** *v.i.* (*of material, etc.*) roussir; brûler légèrement, à la surface. **3.** *v.i. Aut: etc: F: O:* **to s. (along),** brûler le pavé; filer à toute vitesse; aller un train d'enfer.
scorcher ['skɔ:tʃər], *s. F:* **1.** (*a*) journée *f* torride; (*b*) *O:* riposte, remarque, cinglante. **2.** *Aut: etc: A:* chauffard *m*; cycliste *mf* casse-cou. **3.** *A:* **it's, she's, a s.,** c'est épatant; elle est épatante.
scorching[1] ['skɔ:tʃiŋ]. **1.** *a.* (*of sun, wind, etc.*) brûlant, ardent; **s. heat,** chaleur *f* torride; **s. criticism,** critique *f* caustique. **2.** *adv. F:* **it's s. hot here,** on rôtit ici.
scorching[2], *s.* **1.** roussissement *m* (du linge, etc.); dessèchement *m* (de l'herbe, etc.). **2.** *Aut: etc: F: O:* allure excessive, de chauffard.
scorchingly ['skɔ:tʃiŋli], *adv.* **it's s. hot,** il fait une chaleur torride; on rôtit (ici).
score[1] [skɔ:r], *s.* **1.** (*on skin, etc.*) éraflure *f,* couture *f,* entaille *f*; (*on rock, etc.*) strie *f*; (*on leather, etc.*) incision *f*; (*on cylinder, etc.*) rayure *f*; **scores in a bearing,** grippures *f* d'un palier. **2.** (*a*) trait *m* (de repère); repère *m*; (*b*) gorge *f,* (en)goujure *f* (de poulie). **3.** (*a*) (en)coche *f*; (*b*) (i) *O:* (*at a pub, etc.*) ardoise *f*; **to pay one's s.,** régler son compte; (ii) **to pay off old scores,** régler de vieilles dettes, de vieux comptes; vider d'anciens griefs. **4.** (*a*) *Sp: Games:* marque *f,* score *m*; **what's the s.?** quel est le score? quelle est la marque? où en est le jeu? **to make a good s.,** faire un bon nombre de points; (*at shooting range*) faire un bon carton; **to open the s.,** ouvrir la marque; *Fb: etc:* marquer le premier but; *Cards:* (*bridge*) **s. below the line,** marque; **to keep the s.,** marquer, compter, les points; *Cards:* tenir la marque; (*b*) *F:* (i) réponse bien envoyée; (ii) aubaine *f,* coup *m* de fortune; **to make a s.,** toucher son adversaire (au vif); (*c*) *F:* **to know the s.,** être au courant. **5.** *Mus:* partition *f*; **full s., open s.,** partition d'orchestre; **vocal s.,** partition de chant; **short s.,** partition réduite; **piano and vocal s.,** partition pour piano et chant; **in s.,** contenant toutes les parties. **6.** (*a*) (*pl.* **score**) vingt; une vingtaine; **a s. of people,** une vingtaine de gens; **five s.,** cent; une centaine; **half a s.,** une dizaine; *F:* **you can find them by the s.,** on les ramasse à la pelle; (*b*) *F:* **scores,** un grand nombre; **scores of times,** beaucoup, des tas, de fois; **scores of people,** une masse, une foule, de gens. **7.** point *m,* compte *m,* question *f,* sujet *m*; **don't worry on that s.,** n'ayez aucune crainte à cet égard, sur ce chapitre, sur ce point; soyez tranquille là-dessus; **on the s. of . . .,** à titre de . . .; **on more scores than one, on more than one s.,** à plus d'un titre; **on the s. of ill health,** pour raison de santé; **on what s.?** à quel titre? pour quelle raison? sous quel rapport?
score[2], *v.tr.* **1.** (*a*) érafler, couturer (qch.); inciser (le cuir); strier (un rocher, etc.); rayer (un cylindre, la terre, le papier, etc.); **face scored with lines,** visage creusé, haché, de rides (profondes); **mountainside scored by torrents,** flanc de montagne sillonné par les torrents; **to s. a metal plate for surfacing,** gratteler une plaque de métal; *Engr:* **to s. the plate with the graver,** buriner la planche; (*b*) faire un trait de plume au-dessous de (qch.); **to s. a passage in a book,** souligner un passage dans un livre; (*c*) *NAm: F:* tancer (qn) d'importance; laver la tête à (qn). **2.** (*a*) entailler, (en)cocher (une latte de bois, etc.); **to s. a tally,** faire des coches à une taille; (*b*) *F: O:* **to s. up the drinks,** inscrire les consommations à l'ardoise; **to score (up) a debt,** porter une dette en compte; **to s. (up) a debt against, to, s.o.,** enregistrer, inscrire, une dette au passif de qn; **he'll s. up that remark against you,** il vous fera payer cette observation. **3.** *v.tr.* & *i. Sp: Games:* (*a*) compter, marquer, les points; (*b*) faire, marquer (trente points, etc.); **to fail to s.,** ne marquer aucun point, aucun but; *Fb: etc:* **to s. a goal,** marquer, enregistrer, un but; **neither side scored,** aucun but n'a été enregistré; *Rugby Fb:* **to s. a try,** marquer un essai; *Cr:* **to s. 50, a century,** marquer 50 points; faire une centaine; (*c*) réussir; **to s. a success,** remporter, enregistrer, un succès; **that's where he scores,** c'est par là qu'il l'emporte; voilà où il est avantagé; *F:* **to s. (points) off s.o.,** river son clou à qn; **to s. at s.o.'s expense,** se faire mousser au détriment de qn. **4.** *Mus:* (*a*) noter (un air); (*b*) orchestrer (une composition); **scored for piano, violin and flute,** arrangé pour piano, violon et flûte. **5.** *v.i. P:* obtenir de la drogue.
scoreboard ['skɔ:bɔ:d], *s.* **1.** *A:* (*in public house*) ardoise *f.* **2.** *Games:* tableau *m* (où on indique où en est le match).
scorecard ['skɔ:kɑ:d], *s. Games:* carte *f,* fiche *f,* de score; *Golf:* carte du parcours; (*at shooting range*) carton *m.*
scored [skɔ:d], *a.* **1.** (*a*) (*of skin, etc.*) éraflé, couturé; (*of rock, etc.*) strié; (*of cylindre, etc.*) rayé; (*of gun barrel*) affouillé; (*b*) **s. pulley,** poulie *f* à gorge. **2.** (*a*) (*of words*) biffé, rayé; (*b*) souligné.
scorekeeper ['skɔ:ki:pər], *s. Games:* marqueur, -euse (des points).
scorer ['skɔ:rər], *s. Games:* **1.** marqueur, -euse (des points). **2.** celui, celle, qui marque des points; marqueur, -euse, de but.
scoria, *pl.* **-iae** ['skɔ:riə, -ii:], *s.* **1.** *Metall: etc:* scorie *f,* mâchefer *m,* crasse *f.* **2.** **volcanic scoriae,** scories volcaniques.
scoriaceous [skɔri'eiʃ(ə)s], *a. Metall: etc:* scoriacé.
scorification [skɔrifi'keiʃ(ə)n], *s. Metall: etc:* scorification *f.*
scorify ['skɔrifai]. **1.** *v.tr.* scorifier. **2.** *v.i.* se scorifier.
scoring ['skɔ:riŋ], *s.* **1.** éraflement *m* (de la peau, etc.); striation *f* (d'un rocher); rayage *m,* grippage *m* (d'un cylindre, etc.); affouillement *m* (d'un canon). **2.** (*a*) entaillage *m,* encochage *m* (d'un bâton, etc.); (*b*) **s. (up),** (i) *O:* inscription *f* à l'ardoise (des consommations); (ii) inscription, enregistrement *m* (d'une dette). **3.** *Games:* marque *f* (des points); **to open the s.,** ouvrir la marque; **at half time the s. hadn't started,** la mi-temps est survenue sur un score encore vierge; *Bill:* **s. board,** tableau *m,* boulier *m*; *Mil: etc:* **s. book,** carnet *m* de tir. **4.** *Mus:* (*a*) notation *f* (d'un air); (*b*) orchestration *f* (d'une composition), arrangement *m* (pour divers instruments); (*c*) *Cin:* sonorisation *f* (d'un film).
scorn[1] [skɔ:n], *s.* (*a*) dédain *m,* mépris *m*; **to pour s. on an idea,** rejeter une proposition d'un ton de mépris; *O:* & *Lit:* **to think s. of s.o., sth.,** dédaigner, mépriser, qn, qch.; (*b*) *O:* & *Lit:* objet *m* de mépris.
scorn[2], *v.tr.* **1.** dédaigner, mépriser, ne faire aucun cas de (qn, qch.); **he scorned my advice,** il a méprisé mes conseils; il a rejeté mes conseils avec un air de mépris, de dédain. **2.** **to s. to do sth.,** trouver indigne de soi, dédaigner, de faire qch.
scorner ['skɔ:nər], *s.* contempteur, -trice **(of,** de); railleur, -euse.
scornful ['skɔ:nful], *a.* (*of pers., smile, etc.*) dédaigneux, méprisant; **to be s. of s.o., sth.,** dédaigner, mépriser, qn, qch.; traiter qn, qch., avec mépris; **s. attitude,** air *m* de mépris; *s. Lit:* **to sit in the seat of the s.,** se moquer de la religion, des choses sacrées.
scornfully ['skɔ:nfuli], *adv.* dédaigneusement, avec mépris.
scornfulness ['skɔ:nfulnis], *s.* dédain *m,* mépris *m*; attitude dédaigneuse, méprisante; air, ton, dédaigneux.
scorodite ['skɔrədait], *s. Miner:* scorodite *f.*
Scorpaenidae [skɔ:'pi:nidi:], *s.pl. Ich:* scorpénidés *m.*
scorper ['skɔ:pər], *s.* **1.** *Engr: etc:* échoppe *f,* onglette *f.* **2.** (*for wood*) gouge *f.*
Scorpio ['skɔ:piou], *Pr.n. Astr:* le Scorpion.
scorpioid ['skɔ:piɔid]. **1.** *s. Arach:* scorpion *m,* scorpionidé *m.* **2.** *a. Bot:* scorpioïde; **s. cyme,** cyme *f* scorpioïde.
scorpion ['skɔ:piən], *s.* **1.** *Arach:* scorpion *m*; **book s., false s.,** pseudoscorpion *m,* faux scorpion, scorpion des livres; **whip s., s. spider,** pédipalpe *m.* **2.** *Astr:* **the S.,** le Scorpion; **the Scorpion's heart,** le Cœur du Scorpion; Antarès *m.* **3.** *Bot:* **s. broom, s. thorn,** épine fleurie; **s. grass,** myosotis *m*; oreille *f* de souris; **scorpion's tail,** scorpiurus *m*; chenillette *f*; *Ent:* **s. fly,** panorpe *f*; scorpion volant; mouche *f* scorpion; **water s., s. bug,** scorpion d'eau, scorpion aquatique; népidé *m*; *Ich:* **s. fish,** scorpène *f,* scorpion *m* de mer; diable *m* de mer; rascasse *f*; **sea s.,** cottidé *m*; *Paleont:* **giant sea s.,** euryptéride *m,* euryptéridé *m*; *Moll:* **s. shell,** lambis *m,* ptérocère *m.* **4.** *A.Mil:* scorpion. **5.** *P:* habitant, -ante, de Gibraltar.
Scorpionida [skɔ:pi'ɔnidə], *s.pl. Arach:* scorpionidés *m,* scorpionides *m.*
scorpiurus [skɔ:pi'juərəs], *s. Bot:* scorpiurus *m,* chenillette *f.*
scorzonera [skɔ:tsə'nɛərə], *s. Bot: Cu:* scorsonère *f,* scorzonère *f*; salsifis noir.
Scot[1] [skɔt], *s.* **1.** Écossais, -aise. **2.** *Hist:* **the Scots,** les Scots *m.*
scot[2], *s.* **1.** *A:* écot *m*; **to pay one's s.,** payer son écot. **2.** *Hist:* **s. and lot,** taxes communales. **3.** (*a*) **to get off s. free,** s'en tirer indemne, sain et sauf; demeurer indemne; **he didn't get off s. free,** il y a laissé des plumes, il a perdu des plumes; (*b*) **to get sth. s. free,** recevoir qch. gratis, sans frais.

scotch[1] [skɔtʃ], *s.* cale *f*; taquet *m* d'arrêt, sabot *m* d'arrêt (placé sous une roue).

scotch[2], *v.tr.* caler, accoter (une roue, etc.).

scotch[3], *s.* **1.** entaille *f*; trait *m* (au couteau, etc.). **2.** *Games:* ligne *f* de limite (au jeu de marelle).

scotch[4], *v.tr.* mettre (qn, une bête) hors d'état de nuire, hors de combat; mettre le frein à, mettre fin à (un projet, etc.).

Scotch[5]. **1.** (*not used of persons in Scotland*) (*a*) *a.* écossais; d'Écosse; **S. terrier,** scottish-terrier *m*; **S. pine, fir,** pin *m* d'Écosse; **S. mist,** bruine *f*, crachin *m*; **S. thistle,** acanthe *f* sauvage; (*b*) *F:* **the S.,** les Écossais. **2.** *s.* (*a*) *Ling:* l'anglais *m* d'Écosse; (*b*) *F:* whisky écossais, scotch *m*; **a (glass of) S.,** un whisky, un scotch. **3.** *a. R.t.m:* **S. tape,** Scotch *m.*

scotching ['skɔtʃiŋ], *s.* calage *m* (d'une roue, etc.).

Scotchman, *pl.* **-men** ['skɔtʃmən], *s.* **1.** (*not used in Scotland*) Écossais *m.* **2.** *Nau:* défense *f* de gréement, de pont.

Scotchwoman, *pl.* **-women** ['skɔtʃwumən, -wimin], *s.f.* (*not used in Scotland*) Écossaise.

scoter ['skoutər], *s. Orn:* macreuse *f*; **common s.,** *NAm:* **American s., black s.,** macreuse noire, *Fr.C:* macreuse à bec jaune; **surf s.,** macreuse à lunettes, canard *m* marchand, *Fr.C:* macreuse à front blanc; **velvet s.,** *NAm:* **white-winged s.,** macreuse brune, double macreuse, *Fr.C:* macreuse à ailes blanches.

scotia[1] ['skouʃə], *s. Arch:* scotie *f*, nacelle *f.*

Scotia[2]. *Pr.n. A.Geog:* Scotie *f*; *Lit:* Écosse *f.*

Scotic ['skɔtik], *a. Hist:* des Scots, de la Scotie.

Scoticism ['skɔtisizm], *s.* = SCOTTICISM.

Scotism ['skoutizm], *s. Phil:* scotisme *m.*

Scotist ['skoutist], *a.* & *s. Phil:* scotiste (*mf*); de Duns Scot.

Scotland ['skɔtlənd]. *Pr.n.* **1.** *Geog:* l'Écosse *f.* **2.** **S. Yard** = la Sûreté.

scotodinia [skoutou'diniə], *s. Med:* scotodinie *f.*

scotoma, *pl.* **-mas, -mata** [skɔ'toumə(z), -mətə], *s. Med:* scotome *m*; **scintillating s.,** scotome scintillant.

scotopic [skɔ'tɔpik], *a.* scotopique.

Scots [skɔts], (*esp. in Scotland, in reference to nationality*) **1.** *a.* écossais; **S. law,** droit écossais; **the S. Guards,** la Garde écossaise; les Écossais; **S. pine,** pin *m* d'Écosse; *Hist:* **pound S.,** livre écossaise. **2.** *s.* **to talk S.,** parler l'anglais d'Écosse.

Scotsman, *pl.* **-men** ['skɔtsmən], *s.m.* Écossais; *Rail: Hist:* **the Flying S.,** le rapide de Londres à Édimbourg.

Scotswoman, *pl.* **-women** ['skɔtswumən, -wimin], *s.f.* Écossaise.

Scott [skɔt], *int.* **Great S.!** Grand Dieu!

Scotticism ['skɔtisizm], *s.* mot écossais; idiotisme écossais; tournure (de phrase) écossaise.

Scottie ['skɔti], *s. F:* (*a*) *O:* Écossais *m*; (*b*) scottish-terrier *m.*

Scottish ['skɔtiʃ], *a.* (*a*) écossais; **S. history, S. literature,** l'histoire, la littérature, écossaise; **S. accent,** accent écossais; **the S. Border,** les marches *f* d'Écosse; **the S. chiefs,** les chefs écossais; *Ling:* **S. Gaelic,** le gaélique d'Écosse; (*b*) **the London S.,** (i) régiment, (ii) équipe *f* de rugby, recrutée parmi les Écossais résidant à Londres.

scoundrel ['skaundrəl], *s.* chenapan *m*, coquin *m*, scélérat *m*, canaille *f*, vaurien *m*, gredin *m*, fripouille *f*; **that s. of a lawyer!** ce gredin d'homme de loi!

scoundrelly ['skaundrəli], *a.* scélérat, vil, canaille; **a s. trick,** un vilain tour.

scour[1] ['skauər], *s.* **1.** (*a*) nettoyage *m*, (r)écurage *m* (de qch.); **to give a saucepan a good s.,** récurer à fond une casserole; (*b*) *Hyd.E:* (i) chasse *f* (d'un réservoir de chasse, etc.); (ii) force érosive, force d'affouillement (d'un cours d'eau). **2.** *Tex:* dégraissant *m.* **3.** *Vet:* (*also U.S:* **scours**) diarrhée *f.*

scour[2], *v.tr.* **1.** (*a*) nettoyer, lessiver, frotter (le plancher, etc.); astiquer (les cuivres, etc.); **to s. (out) a saucepan,** nettoyer, récurer, une casserole; **to s. clothes,** lessiver le linge (de corps); **to s. corn,** nettoyer le grain; *U.S:* **to s. up metal work,** fourbir, astiquer, la serrurerie, les cuivres; (*b*) *Tex:* dessuinter, dégraisser, échauder, dégorger (la laine); **scoured wool,** laine lavée à chaud; (*c*) *Leath:* balayer (le cuir); (*d*) *Metalw:* décaper, dérocher (une surface métallique). **2.** (*a*) curer, chasser (un port, etc.); donner une chasse d'eau à (un égout, etc.); **to s. a ditch,** nettoyer un fossé à grande eau; (*b*) (*of river*) affouiller, dégrader (les rives); (*c*) purger (un malade, les intestins, etc.); **food liable to s. sheep,** aliments *m* susceptibles de donner la diarrhée aux moutons; *Fish:* **to s. the worms,** débourber les vers (de terre); faire dégorger les vers.

scour[3]. **1.** *v.i.* **to s. (about),** battre la campagne; courir partout; **to s. after s.o.,** courir à la poursuite de qn. **2.** *v.tr.* parcourir, battre (la campagne); (*of pirates*) balayer, écumer (la mer); **to s. a wood,** fouiller un bois; **to s. the country for s.o.,** battre la campagne à la recherche de qn.

scourer[1] ['skauərər], *s.* **1.** (*pers.*) (*a*) nettoyeur, -euse; (r)écureur, -euse; (*b*) dégraisseur, -euse (de laine, etc.); balayeur *m* (de cuir); (*c*) décapeur *m* (de métal); (*d*) cureur *m* (de fossés, de puits, etc.). **2.** *Dom.Ec:* **(pot) s.,** cure-casseroles *m inv*; éponge *f* métallique, en nylon, etc. **3.** *Agr:* épointeuse *f.*

scourer[2], *s. A:* & *Lit:* **s. of the seas,** écumeur *m* de mer.

scourge[1] [skə:dʒ], *s.* **1.** *A:* & *Lit:* fouet *m*; *Ecc:* (*for self-flagellation*) discipline *f.* **2.** fléau *m*; (*a*) **Attila, the S. of God,** Attila, le Fléau de Dieu; (*b*) **war is the greatest s.,** la guerre est le pire des fléaux; *Med: F: A:* **the white s.,** la tuberculose.

scourge[2], *v.tr.* **1.** *A:* & *Lit:* fouetter, flageller (qn); *Ecc:* **to s. oneself,** se donner la discipline; *B:* **when they had scourged Jesus,** après avoir fait fouetter Jésus. **2.** affliger, opprimer, châtier (un peuple, etc.); être un fléau pour (la population). **3.** *Scot:* (*of crop*) épuiser (la terre).

scourger ['skə:dʒər], *s. A:* & *Lit:* flagellateur *m*, fouetteur *m.*

scouring ['skauriŋ], *s.* **1.** (*a*) nettoyage *m*, récurage *m*, frottage *m*; nettoiement *m* (du grain); (*b*) *Tex:* dessuintage *m*, dégraissage *m*, dégorgement *m*, échaudage *m* (de la laine); (*c*) *Leath:* balayage *m* (du cuir); (*d*) *Metalw:* décapage *m*, dérochage *m*; (*e*) **s. machine,** (i) machine *f* à nettoyer; (ii) *Leath:* balayeuse *f* mécanique; (iii) *Metalw: etc:* décapeuse *f*, machine à décaper; *Hyd.E:* **s. sluice,** écluse *f* de chasse; (*f*) *Bot:* **s. rush,** prêle *f.* **2.** (*a*) curage *m* (d'un port, etc.); nettoyage à grande eau (d'un fossé); (*b*) affouillement *m*, dégradation *f* (des rives d'un fleuve par les eaux); (*c*) purgation *f* (des intestins). **3.** **scourings,** impuretés enlevées du grain par le nettoyage.

scouse[1] [skaus], *s. Nau: F:* ratatouille *f*, ragoût *m.*

Scouse[2]. *F:* **1.** *a.* & *s.* (habitant, -ante) de Liverpool. **2.** *s. Ling:* l'anglais *m* de Liverpool.

scout[1] [skaut], *s.* **1.** (*a*) *Mil:* éclaireur *m*, avant-coureur *m*; **ground s.,** éclaireur de position; (*b*) **(boy) s.,** (*Catholic*) scout *m*; (*non Catholic*) éclaireur *m*; *U.S:* **(girl) s.,** guide *f*, éclaireuse *f*; **Chief s.,** chef-scout, *pl.* chefs-scouts; chef éclaireur; (*c*) *Aut:* dépanneur *m* (employé par les associations automobiles); (*d*) recruteur *m* (de talent); (*e*) *NAm: F:* **a good s.,** un bon type. **2.** (*a*) *Navy:* **s. (ship),** vedette *f*; (croiseur-) éclaireur *m*, *pl.* (croiseurs-)éclaireurs; **submarine s.,** (i) patrouilleur *m* contre sous-marins; (ii) *Aer: A:* dirigeable *m* de reconnaissance; (*b*) *Av:* avion *m* de reconnaissance; patrouilleur; (*c*) **s. car,** (i) *Mil: etc:* voiture *f* de reconnaissance; (ii) *Can:* véhicule *m* à chenilles (utilisé dans les régions marécageuses). **3.** *Mil: etc:* reconnaissance *f*; **to be, go, on the s.,** être, aller, en reconnaissance.

scout[2], *v.i.* (*a*) *Mil:* aller en reconnaissance; éclairer le terrain, la marche; aller à la découverte; **to s. in front of the advance,** éclairer l'avance; (*b*) **the campers were scouting for firewood,** les campeurs cherchaient du bois pour le feu; (*c*) *Cin: Sp: etc:* **to s. for talent,** se mettre à la recherche de futures vedettes.

scout[3], *s. Orn: F:* (*a*) petit pingouin; (*b*) guillemot *m*; (*c*) macareux *m.*

scout[4], *s. Sch:* garçon *m* de service (à Oxford, Yale, Harvard); domestique attaché(e) au service des étudiant(e)s.

scout[5], *v.tr.* repousser (une proposition, etc.) avec mépris, avec dédain.

scouter ['skautər], *s. Scout:* chef *m* de troupe.

scouting ['skautiŋ], *s.* **1.** (*a*) *Mil: etc:* reconnaissance *f*, éclairage *m*; **s. party,** reconnaissance; (*b*) *Av:* **s. aircraft,** avion éclaireur; **to go off s.,** partir en éclaireur, en reconnaissance. **2.** *Scout:* scoutisme *m.*

scoutmaster ['skautmɑ:stər], *s. Scout:* chef *m* de troupe.

scow [skau], *s. Nau:* (*a*) chaland *m*, gabare *f*, chatte *f*; **mud s.,** chaland à vase; ac(c)on *m*; (*b*) **(ferry) s.,** toue *f.*

scowl[1] [skaul], *s.* air maussade, menaçant, renfrogné; froncement *m* de(s) sourcils; **to look at s.o. with a s.,** menacer qn du regard; regarder qn de travers, d'un air menaçant, renfrogné.

scowl[2], *v.i.* **1.** (*of pers.*) se renfrogner; prendre un air maussade; froncer les sourcils; **to s. at s.o.,** menacer qn du regard; regarder qn de travers, en fronçant les sourcils, d'un air menaçant, renfrogné. **2.** *Lit:* (*of sky, etc.*) s'assombrir, s'obscurcir; (*of cliff, etc.*) menacer.

scowling ['skauliŋ], *a.* maussade, renfrogné, menaçant.

scowlingly ['skauliŋli], *adv.* d'un air maussade, renfrogné, menaçant; en fronçant les sourcils.

scrabble ['skræbl], *v.i.* **1.** (*a*) **to s. about,** gratter (çà et là); jouer des pieds et des mains; **to s. for sth.,** jouer des pieds et des mains pour attraper qch.; (*b*) chercher à quatre pattes (pour retrouver qch.). **2.** *occ.* = SCRIBBLE.

scrag[1] [skræg], *s.* **1.** (*a*) personne décharnée, maigre; bête efflanquée, au long cou décharné; (*b*) *F:* cou (décharné); **the s. of the neck,** la nuque. **2.** *Cu:* **s. (end) of mutton,** bout saigneux, collet *m*, de mouton.

scrag[2], *v.tr.* **(scragged)** *F:* **1.** pendre, garrotter (qn); tordre le cou à (qn). **2.** *Rugby Fb:* saisir (un adversaire) autour du cou. **3.** *Sch:* cravater (qn) et le bourrer de coups.

scrag[3], *s.* **1.** tronçon *m*, souche *f* (d'un arbre); chicot *m.* **2.** excroissance *f*; chicot (de branche); éperon *m* (de roche). **3.** terrain rocailleux.

scragginess[1] ['skræginis], *s.* (*of pers., neck, etc.*) décharnement *m*, maigreur *f.*

scragginess[2], *s.* rugosité *f*, anfractuosité *f* (d'un rocher, etc.); état noueux (d'une branche, etc.); rabougrissement *m* (d'un arbre).

scraggy[1] ['skrægi], *a.* (*of pers., limbs, etc.*) décharné, maigre; qui n'a que la peau et les os.

scraggy[2], *a.* (*of rock, etc.*) rugueux, anfractueux, raboteux; (*of branch, etc.*) noueux; (*of tree*) rabougri.

scram[1] [skræm], *v.i.* **(scrammed)** *F:* filer, décamper; se débiner; ficher le camp; **s.!** (allez) ouste! fiche le camp!

scram[2], *s. Atom.Ph:* arrêt *m* brusque, automatique.

scramble[1] ['skræmbl], *s.* **1.** marche *f*, ascension *f*, difficile; escalade *f* à quatre pattes; *Sp:* **(motorcycle) s.,** moto-cross *m.* **2.** (*a*) mêlée *f*, lutte *f*; **it was a s. to get there,** on se disputait pour y arriver; **the s. for, after, wealth,** la lutte pour l'argent; (*b*) *Av: F:* décollage immédiat (en cas d'alerte, etc.). **3.** brouillage *m* (i) *W.Tel: Elcs:* par altération systématique de la modulation; (ii) *Tp:* par inversion du spectre de fréquence; (iii) d'un texte codé.

scramble[2]. **1.** *v.i.* (*a*) monter, descendre, entrer, sortir, etc., à quatre pattes; jouer des pieds et des mains; **to s. up a hill,** grimper une colline à quatre pattes; **to s. through a hedge,** jouer des pieds et des mains pour traverser une haie; **to s. through one's work,** faire son travail en hâte, à la va-vite, à la six-quatre-deux; (*b*) **to s. for sth.,** se battre, se bousculer, pour avoir qch.; se battre à qui aura qch.; se disputer qch.; **to s. into one's clothes,** enfiler ses vêtements n'importe comment; (*c*) *Av: F:* décoller rapidement (en cas d'alerte, etc.); (*d*) *Sp:* faire du moto-cross. **2.** *v.tr.* (*a*) brouiller (des œufs); **scrambled egg,** (i) œuf brouillé; (ii) *Mil: F:* galon doré (sur la casquette d'un officier); (*b*) *Tp: Elcs: etc:* brouiller (un message, un texte codé).

scrambler ['skræmblər], *s.* (*a*) *Tp: W.Tel: Elcs:* (circuit) brouilleur *m*; système *m* de brouillage d'une émission; (*b*) (*for cipher*) brouilleur.

scrambling ['skræmbliŋ], *s.* = SCRAMBLE[1].

scran [skræn], *s.* (*a*) *Dial: F:* bouts *mpl* de pain; restes *mpl*; **bad s. to you!** que le diable vous emporte! (*b*) **s. bag,** (i) *Nau:* caisson *m* des objets trouvés; (ii) *Mil:* musette *f.*

scrannel ['skrænəl], *a. A:* (*of sound*) faible, ténu, aigre, nasillard.

scrap[1] [skræp], *s.* **1.** (*a*) petit morceau; bout *m*, brin *m*, chiffon *m* (de papier); fragment *m* (de porcelaine, etc.); parcelle *f* (de terrain, etc.); bout (de ruban); bribe *f* (de pain, etc.); **tea without a s. of sugar,** thé sans une parcelle de sucre; **not a s. of evidence,** pas une parcelle de preuve; **a little s. of a man,** un petit bout d'homme; **to catch scraps of a conversation,** saisir des bouts, des bribes, de conversation; **to pick up scraps of knowledge,** ramasser des bribes de connaissances; **s. of comfort,** fiche *f* de consolation; **that won't help you a s., do you a s. of good,** vous n'en tirerez pas le moindre avantage; **s. paper,** (papier *m*) brouillon *m*; *Hist:* **the s. of paper,** le chiffon de papier; (*b*) découpure *f* (pour album); coupure *f* (de journal). **2.** (*a*) **scraps (left over),** restes *m*, reliefs *m* (d'un repas); débris *mpl* (d'une volaille, etc.); déchets *m* (de papeterie, d'usine, etc.); **a few scraps of food,** quelques rogatons *m*; **to eat up the scraps,** manger des restes; **scraps of cloth,** chippes *f*, bouts, bribes, de tissu; **scraps of fur,** retailles *fpl*; (*b*) *coll.* (*from buildings*) démolitions *fpl*; (*from crushed slag*) **s. (metal),** bocage *m*; **(foundry) s.,** résidus *m* métalliques; riblons *mpl*; caffûts *mpl*; vieilles fontes; **s. iron, s. steel,** ferraille *f*; mitraille *f* de fer; fer *m* de masse; débris *mpl* de fer; déchet *m*; **mill s.,** déchets de fabrication; **s. merchant,** marchand *m* de ferraille; ferrailleur, -euse; récupérateur *m* (de ferrailles); **to sell**

(sth.) for s., vendre (qch.) à la casse.

scrap², *v.tr.* **(scrapped) 1.** mettre (qch.) au rebut; mettre hors service (une machine, etc.); envoyer, mettre, (un navire, etc.) à la ferraille, à la casse; *Ind:* **to s. plant,** réformer le matériel. **2.** mettre au rancart (une théorie, un projet).

scrap³, *s. F:* (*a*) querelle *f*, rixe *f*; batterie *f*; bagarre *f*; (*b*) *Box:* match *m*; **to have a s.,** (i) se battre; (ii) se quereller; (*c*) *Mil:* engagement *m*, échauffourée *f*.

scrap⁴, *v.i.* **(scrapped)** *F:* se quereller, se battre, se bagarrer.

scrapbook ['skræpbuk], *s.* album *m* (de découpures, etc.).

scrape¹ [skreip], *s.* **1.** (*a*) coup *m* de grattoir, de racloir; *F: O:* **a s. of the pen,** (i) un trait de plume; (ii) quelques mots griffonnés; **to give a carrot a s.,** gratter une carotte; **to give one's shoes a s.,** racler la semelle de ses chaussures; (*b*) *F: O:* révérence *f* gauche, courbette *f* (avec glissade); (*c*) *F:* mince couche *f* (de beurre, de confitures, etc.); (*d*) coup d'archet raclé (sur le violon); (*e*) grincement *m* (d'un violon, etc.); (*f*) *F:* **to give oneself a s.,** se raser (rapidement); se racler. **2.** *F:* mauvaise affaire, embarras *m*, mauvais pas; **to get into a s.,** se mettre dans un mauvais pas, dans le pétrin, dans l'embarras; s'attirer des ennuis; **to get out of a s.,** se tirer d'affaire, d'embarras; **to get s.o. into a s.,** attirer des ennuis, des désagréments, du désagrément, à qn; **to get s.o. out of a s.,** dépêtrer qn; **we're in a nice s.!** nous voilà propres! nous voilà dans de beaux draps!

scrape², *v.*

I. *v.tr.* **1.** érafler, écorcher (la peau, une surface polie, etc.); **to s. one's shins, one's elbow,** s'érafler les tibias, le coude; *Nau:* **hawser that scrapes the gunwale,** aussière qui rifle sur le plat-bord; (*of ship*) **to s. the bottom,** sillonner le fond; talonner; *Golf:* **to s. the ball,** racler la balle. **2.** (*a*) (*clean*) racler, gratter (qch.); regratter, ravaler (un mur); décaper (un métal); *Cu:* gratter (des carottes, etc.); *Tan:* racler, dépiler, drayer, écharner (une peau); *Surg:* ruginer (un os); **to s. down (a surface),** enlever des rugosités au grattoir; racler (re)gratter (une surface); **to s. off the paint,** racler, enlever, la peinture; **to s. one's shoes,** racler la semelle de ses chaussures; s'essuyer les pieds; **to s. one's plate,** gratter le fond de son assiette; nettoyer son assiette; *F:* **to s. one's chin,** se raser (rapidement); se racler; *Nau:* **to s. a ship's bottom,** nettoyer la carène d'un navire; *Fig:* **to s. the barrel,** racler les fonds de tiroir; (*b*) (*smooth*) riper (une sculpture, etc.); racler, raturer (le parchemin); *Engr:* boësser (une plaque); *Civ.E:* **to s. a bank,** décaper un accotement; (*c*) **with her hair scraped back,** aux cheveux tirés. **3.** faire grincer (qch.); **to s. the bow across the fiddle,** faire grincer l'archet sur le violon; *F:* **to s. the fiddle,** *v.i.* **to s. (on the fiddle),** racler, gratter, du violon; **to s. one's feet along the floor,** frotter, traîner, les pieds sur le plancher. **4.** (*laboriously*) (*a*) **to s. (an) acquaintance with s.o.,** trouver moyen de lier connaissance avec qn, d'entrer en relations avec qn; (*b*) **to s. (together, up) a sum of money,** amasser petit à petit, peu à peu, sou par sou, une somme d'argent; *A:* **s.-penny,** avare *mf*; liardeur, -euse; grippe-sou *m, pl.* grippe-sous.

II. *v.i.* **1.** (*a*) gratter; **branches that s. against the shutters,** branches *f* qui frottent les volets; **my hand scraped along the wall,** ma main frottait le mur, s'est éraflée contre le mur; (*b*) (*of wheel, pen, violin, etc.*) grincer. **2.** (*a*) **to s. against, along, the wall,** raser le mur; passer tout près du mur; *F:* **to s. along,** vivoter, s'en tirer péniblement, à peine joindre les deux bouts; **to s. through,** passer tout juste par une ouverture, etc.; *F:* être reçu tout juste (à un examen); (*b*) *F:* **to s. clear of prison,** échapper tout juste à la prison; friser la prison; **to s. into a team,** arriver tout juste à se faire accepter dans une équipe; **to s. home,** atteindre son but, parvenir à ses fins, avec difficulté; gagner tout juste la partie.

scrape-down ['skreipdaun], *s. F:* raclage *m*, nettoyage *m* (d'une surface).

scraper ['skreipər], *s.* **1.** (*pers.*) (*a*) gratteur *m*, racleur *m*; (*b*) *F:* racleur (de violon); violoneur *m*. **2.** (*thg*) (*a*) (*for scratching up or away*) racloir *m*, gratte *f*, grattoir *m*, rognoir *m*, racle *f*, raclette *f*; décapeuse *f*; *Hort:* ratissoire *f*; *Nau:* gratte, (*blunt*) râteau *m*; **mason's s., painter's s.,** gratte; *Civ.E:* **road s.,** écorcheuse *f*, piocheuse *f* (de routes); **(drag) s.,** scraper *m*; **(brickmaker's) s.,** ratissette *f*; *Aut: etc:* **ice s.,** grattoir (pour pare-brise, etc.); (*b*) (*for smoothing*) *Leath: Bookb:* paroir *m*; *Leath: Carp:* alumelle *f*; *Sculp:* ripe *f*; **zinc-worker's s.,** ébarboir *m*, grattoir; **triangular s.,** ébardoir *m*; *Surg:* **bone s.,** rugine *f*; (*c*) (*cleaner*) curette *f*; grappin *m*, raclette *f* (de ramoneur); *Min:* curette (pour trou de mine); **street s.,** rabot *m* (d'ébouage); **pipe s.,** nettoie-pipes *m inv*; *Mch:* **tube s.,** nettoie-tubes *m inv*; **door s., boot s., shoe s.,** décrottoir *m*; gratte-pieds *m inv*; *Med:* **tongue s.,** racloire *f*; gratte-langue *m inv*.

scraperboard ['skreipəbɔːd], *s. Art:* carte *f* grattage.

scrapheap ['skræphiːp], *s.* tas *m* de ferraille; **to throw sth. on the s.,** mettre qch. à la ferraille, au rebut.

scraping¹ ['skreipiŋ], *a.* qui gratte, qui racle.

scraping², *s.* **1.** éraflement *m* (d'un doigt, etc.); ripage *m* (d'une aussière). **2.** (*a*) raclage *m*, grattage *m* (de qch.); regrattement *m*, ravalement *m* (d'un mur); décapage *m*, décapement *m* (d'un métal); décrottage *m* (des souliers, etc.); *Cu:* grattage, ratissage *m* (des navets, etc.); *Tan:* dépilage *m*, drayage *m* (d'une peau); **s. tool,** racloir *m*; **s. iron,** drayoire *f*; *Leath:* **s. knife,** dague *f*; (*b*) ripage (d'une sculpture); raturage *m* (du parchemin); *Civ.E:* décapage (d'un accotement). **3.** grincement *m* (d'une plume, d'une scie, d'un violon, etc.); grattement *m*; **a s. of chairs,** un bruit de chaises (qu'on traîne); **we heard a s. noise at the door,** nous avons entendu un grattement à la porte. **4. bowing and s.,** salamalecs *mpl*; courbettes *fpl*. **5. scrapings,** raclures *f* (de bois); grattures *f* (de métal); raclures, grattures, ratissures *f* (de pommes de terre, etc.); bribes *f*, restes *m*, fragments *m* (de nourriture); **pan scrapings,** raclons *m*; **leather scrapings,** bourrier *m*; écharnures *f* de cuir.

scrapman, *pl.* **-men** ['skræpmən], *s. esp. U.S:* marchand *m* de ferraille; ferrailleur *m*.

scrapper ['skræpər], *s. F:* pugiliste *m*; batailleur *m*.

scrappily ['skræpili], *adv.* de façon décousue; par bribes, par fragments; **to be s. educated,** avoir des bribes d'instruction.

scrapping¹ ['skræpiŋ], *s.* **1.** mise *f* au rebut; destruction *f*; mise hors service (d'un navire, etc.); réforme *f* (du matériel). **2.** mise au rancart (d'une théorie, etc.).

scrapping², *s.* (*a*) lutte *f*, combat *m*; bagarres *fpl*; jeu *m* de mains; (*b*) pugilat *m*.

scrapple ['skræpl], *s. NAm: Cu:* croquettes *fpl* de viande et de maïs.

scrappy¹ ['skræpi], *a.* **1.** (*of collection, etc.*) hétérogène, hétéroclite; (*of speech, style, etc.*) décousu. **2. s. education,** éducation *f* qui présente beaucoup de lacunes; **s. knowledge,** bribes *fpl* de connaissances; **s. piece of work,** travail bâclé, fait à moitié, sans soin, à la va-vite. **3. s. meal,** (i) maigre repas; (ii) repas composé de restes.

scrappy², *a. NAm: F:* batailleur.

scratch¹ [skrætʃ], *s.* **1.** (*a*) coup *m* d'ongle, de griffe, de patte; (*b*) égratignure *f*, éraflure *f*, éraillure *f* (sur la peau); griffure *f*; **to go through the war without a s.,** sortir de la guerre indemne, sans une égratignure; **to get off with a s. or two,** échapper avec des blessures insignifiantes, avec quelques égratignures; (*c*) rayure *f*, frottis *m*, (sur une surface polie); striation *f* (sur un rocher, etc.); égratignure (sur un film, etc.); (*d*) *NAm:* **s. pad,** bloc-notes *m*, *pl.* blocs-notes; **s. paper,** brouillon *m*; (*e*) *Vet:* **scratches,** crevasses *f* du paturon. **2.** (*a*) grattement *m* (de la peau); **to give one's head a s.,** se gratter la tête; (*b*) grincement *m* (d'une plume); frottement *m* (d'une allumette); (*c*) *Tp:* **line scratches,** bruits *m* de ligne. **3.** *Sp:* (*a*) **s. (line),** scratch *m*; ligne *f* de départ (d'une course); **s. race,** course scratch; **to start (at) s.,** partir scratch; *F:* **to start from s.,** partir de zéro; **to start from s. again,** repartir à zéro; **to come up to s.,** (i) se mettre en ligne; (ii) *F:* se montrer à la hauteur (de l'occasion); s'exécuter; **to bring s.o. up to s.,** (i) amener qn à se décider, à s'exécuter; (ii) chauffer qn (pour un examen); **to keep s.o. up to s.,** serrer les côtes à qn; **he's not up to s.,** il ne fait pas le poids; **when it comes to the s.,** quand on en vient au fait; (*b*) **s. (player),** scratch *m*; joueur, -euse, classé(e) à zéro (dans un tournoi).

scratch², *v.*

I. *v.tr.* **1.** (*a*) (*of cat, etc.*) égratigner, griffer (qn); donner un coup, des coups, de griffe à (qn); (*b*) (*of thorn, etc.*) écorcher, érafler, érailler (la peau); **to s. oneself,** s'égratigner; **to s. one's hands,** s'égratigner les mains; (*c*) rayer (le verre, etc.); strier (la roche, etc.); **stone scratched with letters,** pierre gravée de lettres; *Cin:* **scratched film,** film rayé, égratigné; (*d*) **to s. s.o.'s eyes out,** arracher les yeux à qn. **2.** (*a*) gratter (le métal, la peau qui démange); frotter (une allumette); **to s. one's head,** se gratter la tête; **to be always scratching (oneself),** être toujours à se gratter; **you s. my back and I'll s. yours,** passez-moi la casse (ou la rhubarbe), et je vous passerai le séné; (*b*) **to s. the surface,** (i) gratter la surface; (ii) manquer de profondeur; ne pas aller au fond (de la question, etc.); effleurer (le problème, etc.). **3.** (*of bird, animal*) gratter (le sol); **to s. a hole,** creuser un trou avec les griffes; **to s. up a bone,** déterrer un os (en grattant); **to s. together, s. up, a few pounds,** ramasser quelques livres; **to s. a living,** joindre péniblement les deux bouts. **4. to s. out a word,** rayer, biffer, raturer (un mot); (*with penknife*) gratter, effacer; **to s. s.o. off, from, a list,** rayer, biffer, qn d'une liste; *Turf:* **to s. a horse,** (i) déclarer forfait pour un cheval; (ii) (*of stewards*) scratcher un cheval; *Sp:* (*of organizers*) **to s. a match,** décommander un match. **5.** griffonner, écrire (quelques mots); **to s. (off) a few lines,** griffonner quelques lignes.

II. *v.i.* **1.** (*a*) **cat that scratches,** chat qui griffe; (*b*) (*of pers., animal*) se gratter; (*of bird, animal*) gratter (dans la terre, etc.); **to s. about, around, for evidence,** dénicher des preuves; **to s. at the door,** gratter à la porte. **2.** (*of pen, etc.*) grincer, gratter. **3.** *Sp:* (*of entrant*) déclarer forfait.

scratch³, *a.* (repas, etc.) improvisé, sommaire; **a s. collection,** une collection hétérogène; un ramas (de bibelots, etc.); *Sp:* **s. team,** équipe improvisée.

Scratch⁴, *Pr.n. A:* **Old S.,** le Diable.

scratchboard ['skrætʃbɔːd], *s. Engr: etc:* papier *m* procédé.

scratchbrush¹ ['skrætʃbrʌʃ], *s. Tls: Metalw:* gratte-boësse *f*, gratte-bosse *f*, *pl.* gratte-boësses, -bosses.

scratchbrush², *v.tr. Metalw:* gratte-boësser, gratte-bosser (un article en argent, etc.); gratter (le métal) à la brosse.

scratchbrushing ['skrætʃbrʌʃiŋ], *s.* grattage *m* à la brosse.

scratchcard ['skrætʃkɑːd], *s.* = SCRATCHBOARD.

scratcher ['skrætʃər], *s.* **1.** (*pers.*) gratteur, -euse; chat, etc., qui griffe. **2.** *Tls:* grattoir *m*, gratteau *m*.

scratching ['skrætʃiŋ], *s.* **1.** (*a*) coups *mpl* d'ongle, de griffe, de patte; (*b*) écorchement *m*, éraflement *m* (de la peau); (*c*) rayage *m*, striation *f* (d'une surface); (*d*) **s. ground,** partie *f* d'une basse-cour où la volaille s'ébroue dans la poussière; **s. post,** poteau contre lequel le bétail peut se gratter. **2.** grattement *m* (de la tête, etc.). **3.** rayage, radiation *f* (d'un nom sur une liste, *Sp:* d'un concurrent). **4.** grattement *m*; grincement *m* (d'une plume); frottement *m* (d'une allumette); bruit *m* de surface, bruit de fond (d'un disque).

scratchproof ['skrætʃpruːf], *a.* inrayable.

scratchweed ['skrætʃwiːd], *s. Bot: F:* grat(t)eron *m*.

scratchwork ['skrætʃwəːk], *s. Art:* sgraffite *m*; graffite *m*; graffiti *mpl*; fresque *f* à la manière égratignée.

scratchy ['skrætʃi], *a.* **1.** (*a*) (*of drawing*) au trait maigre, peu assuré; (*b*) **s. writing,** pattes *fpl* d'araignée; pattes de mouche; (*c*) *Mus: etc:* **s. performance,** exécution inégale, qui manque d'ensemble. **2.** (*a*) (*of pen, etc.*) (i) qui gratte; (ii) qui grince (sur le papier); grinçant; (*b*) (*of stuff*) rugueux, grossier; qui gratte la peau. **3.** *Vet:* **s. feet,** crevasses *fpl* du paturon.

scrawl¹ [skrɔːl], *s.* (*a*) griffonnage *m*, gribouillage *m*, barbouillage *m*; *F:* grimoire *m*; pattes *fpl* de mouche; écriture *f* de chat; **his writing is a s.,** il écrit comme un chat; (*b*) petit mot écrit à la hâte.

scrawl², *v.tr. & i.* griffonner, gribouiller (une lettre, etc.); écrire comme un chat; **to s. (all) over a piece of paper,** barbouiller une feuille de papier.

scrawling ['skrɔːliŋ], *s.* gribouillage *m*, griffonnage *m*.

scrawly ['skrɔːli], *a.* **s. writing,** pattes *fpl* d'araignée, pattes de mouche.

scrawny ['skrɔːni], *a. F:* maigre, décharné.

scray [skrei], *s. Orn: F:* sterne *m*; hirondelle *f* de mer.

scream¹ [skriːm], *s.* **1.** (*a*) cri perçant; **s. of anguish,** cri d'angoisse; **to give a s.,** pousser un cri aigu, un cri de terreur; **screams of pain,** cris, hurlements *m*, de douleur; (*b*) **screams of laughter,** de grands éclats de rire. **2.** *F: O:* chose amusante, grotesque; **it was a perfect s.,** c'était à se tordre, à mourir de rire; c'était désopilant, rigolo; **he's a s.,** il est tordant, désopilant.

scream². **1.** *v.i.* (*a*) pousser un cri perçant, un cri aigu; pousser des cris; crier; **to s. (out) with pain, for help,** crier, hurler, de douleur; crier au secours; *F:* **give it me or I'll s.,** je veux ça ou je pleure; (*b*) **to s. (with laughter),** rire à gorge déployée; rire aux éclats; **he made us s. with laughter,** il nous a bien fait rire; il nous a fait tordre; (*c*) (*of animal, bird*) crier, pousser des cris aigus; (*of eagle*) trompeter, glatir; (*of peacock*) brailler; (*of jay*) cajoler; (*of rabbit, hare*) couiner; (*of locomotive, etc.*) siffler; (*d*) **colours that s. (at, with, each other),** couleurs qui jurent ensemble; (*e*) *P:* vendre ses complices; vendre la mèche. **2.** *v.tr.* **to s. oneself hoarse,** s'enrouer à (force de) crier; **baby**

has screamed himself black in the face, le petit a crié jusqu'à en avoir le visage tout congestionné.

screamer ['skri:mər], *s.* **1.** crieur, -euse; brailleur, -euse. **2.** *Orn:* kamichi *m.* **3.** *F: O:* (*a*) histoire tordante, désopilante; **he's a s.,** il est tordant, impayable; (*b*) = STUNNER. **4.** *F:* (*a*) point *m* d'exclamation; (*b*) *NAm: Journ:* titre flamboyant, en gros caractères.

screaming[1] ['skri:miŋ], *a.* **1.** (*a*) (*of pers.*) criard, brailleur; (*of locomotive*) sifflant; (*of sound*) perçant; (*b*) **s. colours,** (i) couleurs voyantes, criardes; (ii) couleurs qui jurent (ensemble). **2.** *F: O:* (*of farce, etc.*) tordant; marrant; **the play's a s. farce,** la pièce est un fou rire, est à mourir de rire.

screaming[2], *s.* (*a*) cris *mpl* (de terreur, etc.); hurlements *mpl*; (*b*) *Orn:* **the s. of the swifts,** les cris perçants des martinets; (*c*) sifflement *m* (de locomotive).

screamingly ['skri:miŋli], *adv. F: O:* **s. funny,** tordant, marrant; **it was s. funny,** c'était à se tordre (de rire).

scree [skri:], *s. Geol:* éboulis *m* (sur une pente de montagne); (*in the Alps*) clapier *m.*

screech[1] [skri:tʃ], *s.* (*a*) cri perçant; cri aigu; cri rauque; (*b*) crissement *m* (de pneus, etc.); (*c*) *Orn:* **s. owl,** effraie *f.*

screech[2], *v.i.* (*a*) (*of pers., parrot, etc.*) pousser des cris perçants, aigus, rauques; *F:* (*of singer*) chanter d'une voix aiguë; chanter comme une chouette, un perroquet, un goéland; (*b*) (*of tyres*) crisser.

screeching ['skri:tʃiŋ], *s.* (*a*) cris perçants, aigus; (*b*) crissement *m* (de pneus, etc.).

screed [skri:d], *s.* **1.** *Const:* **(floating) s.,** cueillie *f*; guide *m* (pour plâtrage). **2.** (*a*) harangue *f*, jérémiade *f*; longue tartine; (*b*) longue liste (de réclamations, etc.); (*c*) longue lettre.

screen[1] [skri:n], *s.* **1.** (*a*) *Furn:* écran *m*: (*against draught*) paravent *m*; **folding s.,** paravent pliant, à panneaux mobiles; **fire s.,** écran de cheminée; *A:* **banner s.,** écran à bannière; (*b*) cloison *f*; grille *f* (en fer forgé, etc.); *Ecc.Arch:* **choir s.,** grille de chœur; **rood s.,** jubé *m*; *Metalw:* **s. bar(s),** fer(s) à barreaux de grille; (*c*) *Nau:* **canvas s.,** toile *f* abri, rideau *m* en toile; **(bridge, ladder, hatchway) s.,** toile *f* (de protection) de passerelle, d'échelle, de panneau; (*d*) *Meteor:* **thermometer s.,** abri *m* pour thermomètres; *Petr:* **mud s.,** abri, armoire *f*, à boues; (*e*) rideau (protecteur); **s. of trees,** rideau d'arbres; **under s. of night,** sous le couvert, à la faveur, de la nuit; **to act as a s. for a criminal,** couvrir un criminel; *Mil:* **cavalry s.,** rideau de cavalerie; **fire s.,** rideau de feu (d'armes automatiques); *Artil:* tir *m* de barrage; *Navy:* **smoke s.,** nuage artificiel; rideau de fumée; **anti-submarine, A/S, s.,** écran de protection contre sous-marins; (*f*) *Ind: etc:* **protective s., safety s.,** écran de protection, de sécurité; **fire s.,** écran ignifuge; **heat s.,** écran thermique; *Atom.Ph:* **lead s., concrete s.,** écran de plomb, de béton; *Av:* **blast s.,** déflecteur *m* de souffle; (*g*) *Mil: etc:* **(camouflage) s.,** écran (de camouflage); masque *m*; **decoy s.,** écran trompe-l'œil, écran piège; **dumb s.,** faux écran; **moving s.,** écran mobile; **road s.,** masque de route; *Nau:* **navigation light s.,** écran de feux de navigation, de route; **flash s.,** écran cache-lueurs. **2.** *Cin: etc:* écran (de projection); *coll.* **the s.,** le cinéma, l'écran; **panoramic s.,** écran panoramique; **wide s.,** écran panoramique géant; **glass-pearl s.,** écran perlé; **sound s.,** écran trans-sonore; **television s.,** écran de télévision; *F:* **the small s.,** la télé, le petit écran; **to put a play on the s.,** mettre, présenter, une pièce à l'écran; **s. rights,** droits *m* d'adaptation à l'écran; **s. test,** bande *f*, bout *m*, d'essai; *T.V:* **monitor s.,** écran de contrôle; **radar s.,** écran (de, du), radar; *Rad:* **display s.,** (i) écran lumineux; (ii) écran de veille; *X Rays:* **fluoroscopic s.,** écran radioscopique. **3.** *El: Elcs:* écran (de tube cathodique, etc.); **electric, magnetic, s.,** écran électrique, magnétique; **cathode s.,** écran cathodique; **dark-trace s.,** écran luminescent; **Faraday s.,** écran électrostatique, écran de Faraday; **s. room,** cage *f* de Faraday; **s. room test,** essai *m* en cage (de Faraday) (du matériel électrique, électronique); **fluorescent s.,** écran fluorescent; **intensifying s.,** écran renforçateur; **s. current,** courant *m* d'écran; **s. grid,** grille-écran *f*, *pl.* grilles-écrans; **s. grid current, s. voltage,** courant *m*, tension *f*, de grille-écran. **4.** (*a*) *Phot: Opt:* (*for camera*) filtre *m*; *F:* écran; (*for dark room work*) écran; (*for colour photography*) réseau *m* mosaïque polychrome; **colour s.,** filtre coloré; **compensating s.,** filtre compensateur, correcteur; **orthochromatic s.,** filtre orthochromatique; **bayonet s.,** filtre à baïonnette; **slip-on, push-on, s.,** filtre à friction; **screw-in s.,** filtre vissant, à vis; (*b*) *Phot: Engr:* trame *f*; **circular, lenticular, s.,** trame circulaire, lenticulaire; **coarse, fine, s.,** grosse trame, trame fine; **cross-lined, square-ruled, s.,** trame quadrillée; **half-tone s.,** trame de similigravure; **one-way, ruled, s.,** trame lignée; **s. angle,** angle *m* de trame; **s. aperture, s. distance,** ouverture *f*, écart *m*, de trame; **s. carrier,** porte-trame *m*, *pl.* porte-trame(s); **to take a negative through a ruled s.,** tramer un cliché; **s. negative,** cliché tramé; **s. work,** (travail) tramé *m.* **5.** (*a*) *Civ.E: Min: etc:* crible *m*, tamis *m*, claie *f*, grille (à cribler), sas *m*; **gravel s.,** crible à gravier; **sand s.,** crible, claie, à (sasser le) sable; **ore s.,** grille à (cribler le) minerai; **jigging, vibrating, s.,** crible à secousses, tamis oscillant; **revolving s.,** crible rotatif, trommel *m*; **the screens,** le hangar de criblage; *Paperm:* **chip s.,** classeur *m*, trieur *m*, de copeaux; *Atom.Ph:* **s. and sump,** tamis et cuve *f* d'écoulement; **s. classifier,** classeur à tamis; **s. analysis,** analyse *f* granulométrique; granulométrie *f*; (*b*) *Mec.E: etc:* tamis filtrant, filtre, crépine *f*; **oil s.,** filtre à huile; *Petr: etc:* **s. pipe,** tube *m* filtre; (*c*) *NAm:* grille de ventilation (dans une porte, etc.). **6.** *Dent:* **oral s.,** bâillon labial, vestibulaire.

screen[2], *v.tr.* **1.** (*a*) cacher (qch.) derrière un écran, un paravent; (*b*) **to s. sth. from view,** cacher, masquer, dérober, qch. aux regards, à la vue; **the sun was screened by the clouds,** le soleil était voilé par les nuages; **to s. oneself behind sth.,** se cacher derrière qch.; (*c*) *Mil:* **to s. the enemy advance,** jalonner l'avance de l'ennemi. **2.** (*a*) abriter, protéger (qn, qch.); mettre (qn, qch.) à l'abri, à couvert; **screened from the wind,** protégé contre le vent; *Mil:* **to s. a battery from fire,** protéger une batterie contre les coups adverses, contre le feu adverse; (*b*) **light armoured elements screened our advancing forces,** des éléments blindés légers couvraient la progression de nos troupes; **to s. a criminal,** couvrir (les agissements d')un criminel; (*c*) *El: Elcs:* blinder (un câble, une antenne, etc.); *W.Tel:* **to s. a valve,** blinder une lampe. **3.** *Cin: etc:* (*a*) projeter, passer (un film); *T.V:* **this programme will be screened tomorrow,** cette émission passera à l'écran, à la télévision, demain; cette émission aura lieu demain; (*b*) mettre, porter, (une pièce, un roman) à l'écran. **4.** *Phot:* **to s. a lens,** munir l'objectif d'un filtre correcteur. **5.** (*a*) *Civ.E: Min: etc:* cribler, passer au crible (du gravier, du charbon, du minerai, etc.); passer (du sable, etc.) au tamis, au crible, à la claie; tamiser, sasser (de la farine, du sable, etc.); cribler, sasser, nettoyer (le grain); (*b*) (i) trier, sélectionner (du personnel); filtrer (des immigrants, etc.); examiner et interroger (un suspect, etc.); *Med:* soumettre (qn) à une visite de dépistage, à un contrôle sanitaire; (ii) filtrer, passer au crible (des nouvelles, etc.).

screened [skri:nd], *a.* **1.** (*a*) caché, dissimulé, dérobé, voilé (aux regards, à la vue); (*b*) abrité, à l'abri, protégé; *Meteor:* **s. temperature,** température *f* sous abri; *Mil:* **s. battery,** batterie défilée; (*c*) *El: Elcs:* (*of aerial, cable, condenser, etc.*) blindé; *W.Tel:* **s. valve,** lampe blindée; **s. grid valve,** valve *f* à grille blindée, à grille-écran; *I.C.E:* **s. ignition system,** dispositif d'allumage blindé. **2.** (*a*) *Civ.E: Min: etc:* (gravier, minerai, etc.) criblé, passé au crible; (sable, etc.) tamisé, sassé; (grain) criblé, sassé, nettoyé; (*b*) (*of pers.*) contrôlé, trié, examiné (et interrogé); filtré; (*of news, etc.*) filtré, passé au crible.

screener ['skri:nər], *s. Ind: etc:* cribleur, -euse; tamiseur, -euse.

screening ['skri:niŋ], *s.* **1.** (*a*) mise *f* (de qch.) derrière un écran, un paravent; mise à l'abri; dissimulation *f* aux regards; (*b*) *Mil: etc:* **s. forces,** forces *f* de rideau, de couverture; **s. of the enemy advance by covering troops,** jalonnement *m* de l'avance ennemie par des éléments de couverture; (*c*) *Elcs: W.Tel:* **s. effect,** effet *m* d'écran; **s. constant, number,** constante *f* d'effet d'écran; **s. factor,** facteur *m* de réduction (du flux électronique) (dû à l'effet d'écran). **2.** *El: Elcs:* blindage *m* (d'un câble, d'une antenne, d'un condensateur, etc.). **3.** (*a*) *Civ.E: Min: etc:* criblage *m*, passage *m* au crible (du gravier, etc.); passage (du sable, etc.) au tamis, au crible, à la claie; tamisage *m*, sassement *m* (de la farine, du sable, etc.); sassement, nettoyage *m* (du grain); filtrage *m* (des huiles de graissage, etc.); **s. machine,** crible *m* mécanique, trieur *m*; **s. plant, shed,** installation *f*, hangar *m*, de criblage; **screenings,** criblure *f* (résultant du sassement du grain); déchets *mpl* de criblage, refus *m* de crible; (*b*) triage *m* sélection *f* (du personnel); filtrage (des immigrants, etc.); interrogatoire *m* de dépistage (d'un suspect); triage, dépistage *m* (des contagieux); filtrage (des nouvelles, etc.); examen sélectif (de demandes d'emploi, etc.).

screenplay ['skri:nplei], *s. Cin:* scénario *m.*

screenwriter ['skri:nraitər], *s.* dialoguiste *mf.*

screever ['skri:vər], *s.* barbouilleur *m* de trottoir.

screw[1] [skru:], *s.* **1.** vis *f*; (*a*) **brass s.,** vis en laiton; **wooden s.,** vis en bois; **right-handed, left-handed, s.,** vis à droite, à gauche; **male s., external s.,** vis mâle, pleine; **female s., internal s., companion s.,** (i) vis femelle, intérieure, creuse; (ii) écrou *m*; **cap s.,** vis à tête; **captive s.,** vis imperdable; **cheese-headed s.,** *U.S:* **fillister-headed s.,** vis à tête cylindrique; **countersunk(-head) s.,** vis à tête fraisée, à tête noyée, à tête perdue; **crossheaded s.,** *R.t.m:* **Phillips (head) s.,** vis (à tête) cruciforme; **differential s.,** vis différentielle, à pas différentiel; **single-threaded, double-threaded, s.,** vis à filet simple, à double filet; **flange s.,** vis à embase; **flathead(ed) s.,** vis à tête plate; **flush s.,** vis noyée; **grub s., headless s.,** vis sans tête; **hexagon-head s.,** vis (à) six pans, à tête à six pans; **hourglass s., Hindley's s.,** vis globique, globoïdale; **interrupted s.,** vis à filets, à secteurs, interrompus; **knurled s.,** vis (à tête) moletée, bouton moleté; **lag s.,** vis à bois à tête carrée, tire-fond *m inv*; **machine s.,** vis mécanique; **milled-edge s., thumb s.,** vis à molette, à tête moletée; **oval-head(ed) s.,** vis à tête bombée; **round-head(ed) s.,** vis à tête ronde; **slotted-head s.,** vis à tête fendue; **socket-head s.,** vis à tête à douille, à tête creuse; **square-head(ed) s.,** vis à tête carrée; **square-thread(ed) s.,** vis à filet carré; **(self-)tapping s.,** vis autotaraudeuse, vis Parker; **taper s.,** vis conique; **wing s., butterfly s., thumb s.,** vis à oreilles, à ailettes; (écrou *m*) papillon *m*; **worm s., endless s., perpetual s.,** vis sans fin; **s. head,** tête de vis; **s. pitch,** pas *m* de vis; **s. thread,** filet *m* de vis; **s. threading,** filetage *m* de vis; **to tighten a s. (hard),** serrer une vis (à bloc); *Fig:* **to tighten the s.,** serrer la vis (à qn); (*b*) **wood s.,** vis à bois; **metal s.,** vis à métaux; **concrete s.,** vis à, de, scellement; *Mec.E: etc:* **adjusting s.,** (i) vis de réglage; (ii) (*of alidade*) vis de rappel; **binding s.,** (i) vis de serrage, de pression; (ii) *El:* serre-fil *m*, *pl.* serre-fils; **bleeder s.,** vis de purge, de purgeur; vis-purgeur *f*, *pl.* vis-purgeurs; **clamp(ing) s., fastening s., lock(ing) s.,** vis de blocage, de serrage, de fixation; **connecting s.,** vis d'assemblage, d'accouplement; **fine-adjustment s.,** vis de fin réglage, de fin calage; **hold-down s., anchor s.,** vis de fixation, de retenue; **levelling s., foot s.,** vis calante, de calage; **locating s.,** vis de centrage, de montage, de positionnement; **micrometer s.,** vis micrométrique; **pressing s., pressure s.,** vis de pression; **set s.,** (i) vis d'arrêt, de fixation, de pression; (ii) vis de pointeau; **stop s., thrust s.,** vis de butée, d'arrêt; vis-butoir *f*, *pl.* vis-butoirs; **tangent s.,** (i) vis tangente (sans fin); (ii) vis micrométrique; **tangent s., and sector,** vis (sans fin) et secteur; **tightening s.,** vis de serrage, de fixation; *Mch.Tls: etc:* **elevating s.,** vis de levage (de la console); **feed s., lathe s.,** vis d'entraînement; (*of lathe, screw cutter*) **lead(ing) s., guide s.,** vis-mère *f*, *pl.* vis-mères; **bench s.,** vis presse *f*, étau *m*, d'établi; *Artil:* **breech s.,** vis de culasse; **breech-mechanism s.,** vis de mécanisme de culasse; **elevating (tangent) s.,** vis de pointage en hauteur; **horizontal aiming s.,** vis de pointage en direction; *El:* **contact s.,** vis de contact; **terminal s.,** vis-borne *f*, *pl.* vis-bornes; borne filetée; (*c*) **s. eye, s. ring,** vis à œil, piton *m* (à vis), laceret *m*; **s. hook,** crochet *m* à vis, piton (à vis); **s. pile,** pieu *m*, pilot *m*, à vis; **s. shoe,** sabot *m* à vis (de pieu à vis); **s. bolt,** boulon *m* à vis, à écrou; **s. cap, s. top,** couvercle vissant, à vis (d'un bocal, d'un pot); bouchon vissant, à vis (d'une bouteille); gobelet vissant (d'une bouteille isolante); **s.-topped bottle,** bouteille à bouchon vissant; **s.-topped jar,** bocal, pot, à couvercle vissant; *El:* **s. base, s. cap,** culot *m* à vis, culot Edison; **s. contact,** contact *m* à vis; **s. socket,** douille *f* à vis, douille Edison; *Mec.E: etc:* **s. bushing,** (i) fourrure filetée; (ii) vis-grain *m*, *pl.* vis-grains; **s. collar,** bague *f* à vis; **s. coupling,** manchon *m*, union *f*, à vis; **s. gear,** (i) engrenage hélicoïdal; (ii) appareil(lage) *m*, outillage *m*, de vissage; **s. locking,** freinage *m* de la visserie; **s.-locking device,** dispositif *m* de freinage de vis, arrêt *m* de sûreté (de vis); **s. micrometer,** micromètre *m* à vis; **s. plug,** bouchon fileté, tampon *m* à vis; **s. wheel,** roue *f* à dents hélicoïdales (engrenant sur une vis sans fin); *Tls:* **s. auger,** tarière *f* à vis, double spire *f* en hélice; tarière rubanée; (tarière) torse *f*; perçoir *m* en spirale; **s. caliper,** palmer *m*; **s. chuck,** mandrin *m* (de tour) à vis, à queue-de-cochon; **s. clamp,** (i) presse *f* à main; (ii) serre-joint *m inv*; **s. frame,** serre-joint (de menuisier); **s. jack,** cric *m* à vis, vérin *m* à vis, vérin de calage; *Carp:* viole *f*; **s. plate,** filière *f* monobloc; **s. press, s. punch,** (i) presse à vis; (ii) balancier *m* (à frapper la monnaie); **s. spanner, s. wrench,** clef anglaise, clef à vis, à molette; **s. tap,** taraud; **s. cutter,**

(i) (*pers.*) fileteur, -euse; tourneur -euse, de vis; (ii) *Mch.Tls:* tour *m* à fileter, taraudeuse *f*; **s. cutting,** filetage *m*, taraudage *m*, décolletage *m*; **s.-cutting industry,** visserie *f*; **s.-cutting lathe, s.-cutting machine,** tour, machine *f*, à fileter, à tarauder, à décolleter; taraudeuse, décolleteuse *f*; (*d*) *Ind:* **s. conveyor,** vis de transport, vis transporteuse; transporteur *m*, transporteuse *f*, à vis; *Hyd.E:* **Archimedes, Archimedean, s.,** vis d'Archimède; (*e*) **loose s.,** (i) écrou desserré; (ii) (*loosely fitting*) écrou gai; *F:* **to have a s. loose,** être toqué, déboulonné; avoir une araignée au plafond; (*f*) *A:* **the screws,** les poucettes *f*; *F:* **to put the screws on s.o., to tighten the s.,** serrer la vis à qn; forcer la main à qn; *F: O:* **to have the screws,** souffrir de rhumatismes; (*g*) *F:* rossignol *m*, carouble *f* (de cambrioleur). **2.** *Av: Nau:* **s. (propeller),** hélice *f* (d'avion, de bateau); **helicopter s.,** rotor *m* d'hélicoptère; **twin s.,** hélice double; **two-, three-, four-, bladed s.,** hélice à deux, trois, quatre, pales, ailes; *Nau:* **tunnel s.,** hélice sous voûte; **to disconnect the s.,** désembrayer l'hélice. **3.** (*a*) coup *m* de tournevis; tour *m* de vis; **give it another s.,** serrez-le encore un peu; (*b*) *Bill: Ten: etc:* effet *m*; **to put a s. on the ball,** (i) *Bill:* faire de l'effet (de côté); (ii) *Ten: etc:* donner de l'effet à la balle; couper la balle; *Austr: P:* **take a s. at that!** regarde-moi ça! visse-moi ça! (*c*) cornet *m*, papillote *f* (de tabac, etc.); **s. of paper,** cornet, morceau chiffonné, de papier; (*d*) *F: O:* avare *m*, pingre *m*, ladre *m*; **an old s.,** un vieux ladre; (*e*) *P:* gardien *m* de prison, gaffe *m*; **bent s.,** gaffe véreux; (*f*) *V:* coït *m*. **4.** *F:* mauvais cheval, rosse *f*, carcan *m*. **5.** *F:* salaire *m*, paye *f*; **to get a good s.,** être bien payé. **6.** (*a*) *Bot:* **s. pine,** pandanus *m*, *F:* baquois *m*, vaquois *m*; (*b*) *Moll:* **s. shell,** turritelle *f*, térèbre *f*.

screw², *v.*

I. *v.tr.* **1.** (*a*) visser (qch.); **to s. sth. (on) to sth.,** visser qch. à, sur, qch.; *F:* **his head's screwed on the right way,** il a la tête solide, la tête sur les épaules; **to s. sth. into sth.,** visser qch. dans qch.; (*with passive force*) **the nozzle screws on to the end of the hose,** la lance se visse au bout du tuyau; **the knobs s. into the drawer,** les boutons se vissent sur le tiroir; (*b*) **to s. sth. (down),** fixer, assujettir, qch. avec des vis; **to s. down a coffin,** visser un cercueil; **to s. two pieces of wood together,** visser deux morceaux de bois ensemble; **screwed together,** assemblé(s) à vis; **to s. off,** dévisser (un écrou, un couvercle); (*with passive force*) **the end screws off for cleaning,** le bout se dévisse pour faciliter le nettoyage. **2.** (*a*) **to s. (up),** visser; serrer (un écrou); (res)serrer (un tourniquet, les chevilles d'un violon, etc.); **to s. sth. (up) tight,** visser qch. à bloc; **screwed home,** vissé à fond; **to s. up a piece of paper,** tortiller du papier; **to s. sth. up in a piece of paper,** entortiller qch. dans un morceau de papier; **to s. up one's eyes,** plisser les yeux; **face screwed up with pain,** visage crispé par la douleur; **to s. up one's courage,** prendre son courage à deux mains; **to s. oneself up to do sth.,** se forcer à faire qch.; *P:* **to s. up a piece of work,** gâcher, bousiller, un travail; (*b*) **to s. s.o.'s neck,** tordre le cou à qn; **to s. one's head round to see sth.,** se tordre, *F:* se dévisser, la tête pour voir qch.; (*c*) **to s. money from, out of, s.o.,** extorquer de l'argent à qn; **to s. a promise out of s.o.,** arracher une promesse à qn; (*d*) *Bill:* donner de l'effet à (une bille); *Ten: etc:* couper (une balle); (*e*) *P:* cambrioler, caroubler (une maison); (*f*) *V:* **to s. a girl,** s'envoyer, culbuter, une fille. **3.** *Tchn:* **to s. (cut),** fileter (une vis, un boulon); tarauder (un tuyau, etc.).

II. *v.i.* **1.** (*of tap, etc.*) tourner (à gauche, à droite). **2.** *Bill:* (*of ball*) rebondir de travers; dévier; **to s. back,** (i) (*of player*) faire de l'effet rétrograde, de l'effet à revenir; faire un rétro; (ii) (*of ball*) revenir en arrière. **3.** *F: A:* être parcimonieux; liarder.

screwback ['skru:bæk], *s. Bill:* effet *m* rétrograde, à revenir; rétro *m*; **to bring off a s.,** combiner un effet de recul; réussir un rétro.

screwball ['skru:bɔ:l], *a.* & *s. esp. U.S: F:* loufoque (*mf*).

screwdriver ['skrudraivər], *s.* (*a*) tournevis *m*; **ratchet s.,** tournevis à rochet; **crossheaded s.,** *R.t.m:* **Phillips s.,** tournevis cruciforme; (*b*) *F:* **Birmingham s.,** marteau *m*.

screwed [skru:d], *a.* **1.** (boulon) fileté, à vis; (manchon) taraudé; **s. rod,** tige *f* à vis. **2.** *F:* ivre, éméché, rétamé. **3.** *U.S: F:* fichu.

screwing ['skru:iŋ], *s.* **1.** serrage *m* (d'un écrou); **s. (up, down, on),** vissage *m*; **s. off,** dévissage *m*. **2.** *Tchn:* filetage *m*, taraudage *m* (d'un écrou, etc.); **s. die,** filière *f*. **3.** *Bill: etc:* effet *m*. **4.** *P:* cambriolage *m*.

screwnail ['skru:neil], *s.* vis *f* à bois.

screw-on ['skru:ɔn], *a.* **s.-on earrings,** boucles d'oreilles vissées, à vis; **s.-on lens,** objectif *m* détachable, mobile.

screwy ['skru:i], *a. F:* (*a*) fou, cinglé, dingue, loufoque; (*b*) ivre, rétamé.

scribble¹ ['skribl], *s.* **1.** griffonnage *m*, gribouillage *m*. **2.** *F: O:* petit billet; **send me a s.,** envoyez-moi un petit mot, deux mots. **3.** écriture *f* illisible; pattes *fpl* de mouche.

scribble², *v.* (*a*) *v.tr.* griffonner, gribouiller (quelques mots à qn, une note dans son carnet, etc.); (*b*) *v.i.* (i) barbouiller du papier; noircir du papier; mettre du noir sur du blanc; (ii) faire du journalisme; écrivailler; (iii) **he scribbles dreadfully,** il a une écriture affreuse.

scribble³, *v.tr. Tex:* écharper, drousser, scribler (la laine).

scribbler¹ ['skriblər], *s.* **1.** griffonneur, -euse; *F:* gribouilleur, -euse; barbouilleur, -euse (de papier). **2.** *F:* écrivassier, -ière; écrivailleur, -euse; gratte-papier *m inv*, gâte-papier *m inv*; gâteur, -euse, de papier; noircisseur *m* de papier.

scribbler², *s. Tex:* **1.** drousseur, -euse (de laine); cardeur, -euse, en gros. **2.** machine *f* à carder.

scribbling¹ ['skribliŋ], *s.* griffonnage *m*, gribouillage *m*; barbouillage *m* de papier; **s. paper,** (papier *m* à) brouillon *m*; **s. block, pad,** bloc *m* mémento.

scribbling², *s. Tex:* écharpage *m*, droussage *m*, scriblage *m*; cardage *m* en gros; **s. machine,** briseuse *f*; grosse carde.

scribe¹ [skraib], *s. Hist:* (*pers.*) scribe *m*.

scribe², *s. Tls:* **s. (awl),** pointe *f* à tracer, de traçage; aiguille *f* à tracer; style *m* de repérage; tracelet *m*; tire-ligne *m*, *pl.* tire-lignes.

scribe³, *v.tr.* **1.** *Carp: Const:* tracer, trusquiner (une ligne); **scribing block,** trusquin *m* à équerre; **scribing compass,** rouanne *f*. **2.** *Mec.E: etc:* repérer, pointer (le centre, etc.).

scrim [skrim], *s. Tex:* canevas léger.

scrimmage¹ ['skrimidʒ], *s.* **1.** mêlée *f*; escarmouche *f*, bagarre *f*, bousculade *f*. **2.** *U.S: Fb:* mêlée; **loose s., tight s.,** mêlée ouverte, fermée.

scrimmage². **1.** *v.i.* (*a*) lutter; se quereller; se bousculer; (*b*) s'empresser, s'activer. **2.** *v.tr. U.S: Fb:* mettre (le ballon) en mêlée.

scrimp¹ [skrimp], *a.* = SKIMPY.

scrimp², *v.tr.* & *i.* = SKIMP.

scrimpy ['skrimpi], *a.* = SKIMPY.

scrimshank ['skrimʃæŋk], *v.i. Mil: P:* tirer au flanc; fricoter, cagner, cagnarder.

scrimshanker ['skrimʃæŋkər], *s. Mil: P:* tireur *m* au flanc; tire-au-flanc *m inv*; fricoteur *m*, cagnard *m*.

scrimshanking ['skrimʃæŋkiŋ], *s. Mil: P:* cagnardise *f*; tirage *m* au flanc.

scrimshaw ['skrimʃɔ:], *s. coll. Nau: O:* petits objets de fantaisie (fabriqués au cours des voyages).

scrip¹ [skrip], *s. A:* besace *f*; panetière *f* (de pèlerin, etc.).

scrip², *s. Fin:* **1.** (*a*) **s. (certificate),** certificat *m* d'actions provisoire; (*b*) *coll.* valeurs *fpl*, titres *mpl*, actions *fpl*; **registered s.,** titres nominatifs; (*c*) **s. (issue),** titres attribués à un actionnaire (au lieu de dividende, etc.). **2.** *U.S:* coupures (émises en cas de crise).

scripholder ['skriphouldər], *s. Fin:* détenteur, -trice, de titres.

script [skript], *s.* **1.** (*a*) manuscrit *m*; (*b*) *Sch:* copie *f* (d'examen); (*c*) *Jur:* (document) original *m*, -aux; (*d*) *Cin:* scénario *m*; **shooting s.,** scénario découpé; découpage *m*; *Cin: T.V:* **s. girl,** script-girl *f*, *pl.* script-girls. **2.** (*a*) (*as opposed to print*) écriture *f*; **Gothic s.,** écriture gothique; (*b*) *Typ:* **s. (type),** cursive *f*; (*c*) **s. (writing),** (écriture en) script *m*.

scriptorium, *pl.* **-ia, -iums** [skrip'tɔ:riəm, -iə, -iəmz], *s.* écriture *f* (de monastère); salle *f* de travail, de rédaction (d'un dictionnaire, etc.).

scriptural ['skriptjərəl], *a.* scriptural, -aux; biblique; des saintes Écritures.

scripture ['skriptjər], *s.* (*a*) **Holy S., the Scriptures,** l'Écriture sainte, les (saintes) Écritures; **S. history,** l'histoire sainte; **quotation from the Scriptures,** citation tirée de la Bible, de l'Écriture; (*b*) *Sch:* **s. (lesson),** histoire sainte.

scriptwriter ['skriptraitər], *s. Cin: etc:* scénariste *mf*.

scrivello [skri'velou], *s.* (*ivory trade*) escarbeille *f*.

scrivener ['skrivnər], *s. A:* **1.** (*a*) scribe *m*, copiste *m*; écrivain public; (*b*) notaire *m*, *A:* tabellion *m*; (*c*) changeur *m*, prêteur *m* (d'argent); courtier *m* de change. **2.** *F: Pej:* plumitif *m*; secrétaire *m*; gratte-papier *m inv*.

scrivenery ['skrivnəri], *s. A:* métier *m* de scribe, de copiste.

scrobe [skroub], *s. Ent:* scrobe *m*.

scrobicular, scrobiculate [skrou'bikjulər, -leit], *a. Nat.Hist:* scrobiculé.

scrobicularia [skroubikju'lɛəriə], *s. Moll:* scrobiculaire *f*.

scrofula ['skrɔfjulə], *s. Med:* scrofule *f*; écrouelles *fpl*; **s. case,** scrofuleux, -euse.

scrofularoot ['skrɔfjuləru:t], *s. Bot:* érythrone *m*.

scrofulism ['skrɔfjulizm], *s. Med:* scrofulisme *m*.

scrofulous ['skrɔfjuləs], *a. Med:* scrofuleux.

scroll¹ [skroul], *s.* **1.** rouleau *m* (de parchemin, de papier); **the Dead Sea scrolls,** les manuscrits *m* de la Mer morte. **2.** (*a*) *Art: etc:* banderole *f* à inscription; phylactère *m*; fil(l)atière *f*; (*b*) *Her:* listel *m*, liston *m*, listeau *m*. **3.** (*a*) *Arch: etc:* spirale *f*, enroulement *m*; volute *f* (de chapiteau ionique); aileron *m* (de portail, etc.); **Vitruvian s.,** postes *fpl*; (*b*) (*in writing*) enjolivement *m*, enjolivure *f*, arabesque *f*; (*c*) *Engr: etc:* cartouche *m* (encadrant un titre); (*d*) crosse *f*, volute (de violon); (*e*) *Mec.E:* **s. gear, s. wheel,** engrenage *m* à spirale; *Tls:* **s. saw,** scie *f* à chantourner, à découper; sauteuse *f*.

scroll². **1.** *v.tr.* (*a*) mettre (du papier) en rouleau; (*b*) enjoliver (son écriture); orner (un titre, etc.) d'arabesques, de volutes. **2.** *v.i.* (*of paper*) se mettre en rouleau.

scrolled [skrould], *a. Arch: etc:* voluté.

scrollwork ['skroulwə:k], *s. Arch:* ornementation *f* en volute; enroulements *mpl*.

scroop¹ [skru:p], *s.* grincement *m* (de porte, de verrou); frou-frou *m* aigre (de la soie).

scroop², *v.i.* (*of door, belt*) grincer; (*of silk*) froufrouter.

scrophularia [skrɔfju'lɛəriə], *s. Bot:* scrofulaire *f*, scrophulaire *f*.

Scrophulariaceae [skrɔfjulɛəri'eisii:], *s.pl. Bot:* scrophulariacées *f*, scrofulariacées *f*.

scrotal ['skroutəl], *a. Anat:* scrotal, -aux.

scrotiform ['skroutifɔ:m], *a. Bot:* scrotiforme.

scrotocele ['skroutousi:l], *s. Med:* scrotocèle *f*.

scrotum, *pl.* **-ta, -tums** ['skroutəm, -tə, -təmz], *s. Anat:* scrotum *m*; bourses *f* (testiculaires).

scrounge¹ [skraundʒ], *s. F:* **1.** (*a*) **to be on the s.,** être à la recherche de choses à chiper; grappiller; (*b*) **to have a s. round for sth.,** aller à la recherche de qch. **2.** = SCROUNGER.

scrounge². *F:* **1.** *v.tr.* (*a*) (*steal*) chiper, agrafer, chaparder, barboter (qch.); **they've scrounged my tobacco,** on m'a chipé, chauffé, mon tabac; (*b*) (*sponge*) écornifler (un dîner, du tabac); (*c*) **they were scrounging fuel in the ruins,** ils récupéraient du combustible dans les ruines. **2.** *v.i.* (*a*) **to s. round for sth.,** aller à la recherche de qch.; (*b*) **to s. on s.o.,** vivre aux crochets de qn.

scrounger ['skraundʒər], *s. F:* (*a*) chipeur, -euse; chapardeur, -euse; (*b*) écornifleur, -euse.

scrounging ['skraundʒiŋ], *s. F:* (*a*) chipage *m*, chapardage *m*, barbotage *m*, grappillage *m*; (*b*) écornifflerie *f*, écorniflage *m*; (*c*) récupération *f*.

scrub¹ [skrʌb].

I. *s.* **1.** (*a*) arbuste rabougri; (*b*) broussailles *fpl*; brousse *f*; garrigue *f*; **to wander through the s.,** broussailler; *U.S:* **s. pine,** pin *m* de Virginie. **2.** (*a*) brosse *f* à soies courtes; brosse usée; **deck s.,** lave-pont *m*, *pl.* lave-ponts; (*b*) barbe *f* de trois jours; (*c*) petite moustache hérissée. **3.** (*a*) *Husb:* **scrubs,** race bovine de petite taille; (*b*) *esp. U.S: F:* personne rabougrie, d'apparence insignifiante; pauvre diable *m*.

II. *a.* **1.** (*of vegetation*) rabougri. **2.** *esp. U.S:* (*of pers., animal*) misérable, malingre, chétif, rabougri.

scrub², *s.* **1.** friction *f* (à la brosse); nettoyage *m*; **to give the table a good s.,** bien laver la table avec une brosse; frotter la table à la brosse; **the saucepan wants a s.,** la casserole a besoin d'un récurage, d'être récurée; **I was giving the floor a s.,** j'étais en train de savonner le plancher; *Nau:* **s. broom,** goret *m*; *U.S:* **s. brush,** brosse dure, de chiendent, de cuisine. **2.** *F:* femme *f* de corvée, souffre-douleur *m inv*. **3.** *U.S:* (*a*) joueur *m* qui n'est pas membre de l'équipe régulière; **s. team,** équipe de deuxième ordre; (*b*) partie *f* de baseball entre équipes réduites.

scrub³, *v.tr.* (**scrubbed**) **1.** (*a*) récurer (une casserole); laver, frotter, nettoyer, (le plancher) avec une brosse, à la brosse; *v.i.* **to s. away at the floor,** nettoyer vigoureusement le plancher; (*of surgeon*) **to s. up,** se brosser les mains, etc. (avant d'opérer); (*b*) *Nau:* (i) goreter, (ii) briquer (le pont, etc.). **2.** *Ch:* laver, épurer (un gaz). **3.** (*a*) *Rec:* démagnétiser (une bande); (*b*) *F:* annuler (qch.); passer l'éponge sur (qch.).

scrubbable ['skrʌbəbl], *a.* lavable, nettoyable.

scrubber ['skrʌbər], *s.* **1.** (*pers.*) laveur, -euse (à la brosse). **2.** (*a*) **paint s.,** brosse *f* à peinture; **pan s.,** lavette *f* métallique; (*b*) *Ch:* épurateur *m*; flacon laveur; *Gasm:* épurateur, scrubber *m*; **air s.,**

épurateur d'air; filtre *m* à air.

scrubbing ['skrʌbiŋ], *s.* **1.** (*a*) récurage *m*; nettoyage *m*, lavage *m*, avec une brosse dure; **s. brush,** brosse dure, de chiendent, de cuisine; (*b*) *Nau:* (i) goretage *m*; (ii) briquetage *m*. **2.** *Ch:* lavage, épuration *f* (d'un gaz). **3.** = SCRUB² 1.

scrubby ['skrʌbi], *a.* **1.** (*a*) (arbre, animal, etc.) rabougri; (*b*) (terrain) broussailleux, couvert de broussailles. **2.** (*of chin*) mal rasé; (*of moustache*) hérissé; **s. beard,** barbe *f* de trois jours. **3.** *F:* (*of pers.*) insignifiant; minable, de piètre apparence; **a s. lot,** un tas de minables.

scrubland ['skrʌblænd], *s.* terrain broussailleux; brousse *f*.

scrubwoman, *pl.* **-women** ['skrʌbwumən, -wimin], *s.f. U.S:* femme de ménage.

scruff [skrʌf], *s.* nuque *f*; peau *f* de la nuque; **to take an animal by the s. of the, its, neck,** saisir un animal par la peau du cou; **to hold s.o. by the scruff of the, his, neck,** tenir qn par la peau du cou; tenir qn au collet.

scruffy ['skrʌfi], *a. F:* mal soigné; mal fichu; **s. hotel,** hôtel *m* minable.

scrum [skrʌm], *s.* (*a*) *Rugby Fb:* mêlée *f*; **s. half,** demi *m* de mêlée; **s. cap,** protège-oreilles *m inv*; serre-tête *m inv*; (*b*) *F:* mêlée, bousculade *f*.

scrummage ['skrʌmidʒ], *s.* = SCRUM.

scrump [skrʌmp], *v.i. F:* voler des pommes.

scrumptious ['skrʌm(p)ʃəs], *a. F:* (*of food, etc.*) délicieux, épatant, fameux.

scrumpy ['skrʌmpi], *s. Dial:* cidre nouveau.

scrunch¹ [skrʌn(t)ʃ], *s.* **1.** coup *m* de dents. **2.** bruit *m* de broiement; craquement *m*, grincement *m*.

scrunch². **1.** *v.tr.* (*a*) croquer (qch. avec les dents); broyer, écraser (qch.); (*b*) **to s. up a piece of paper,** plisser, tortiller, un bout de papier. **2.** *v.i.* craquer, grincer, crisser; **the snow scrunched under our feet,** la neige crissait sous nos pieds.

scrunchy ['skrʌn(t)ʃi], *a.* (biscuit, etc.) croquant.

scruple¹ ['skru:pl], *s.* **1.** *Pharm.Meas:* scrupule *m* (de 20 grains). **2.** *A:* grain *m*, très petite quantité (de qch.); quantité minime.

scruple², *s.* scrupule *m* (de conscience); **a man of no scruples,** un homme peu scrupuleux, sans scrupules; **to have scruples about sth., about doing sth.,** avoir, éprouver, des scrupules au sujet de qch.; se faire (un cas de) conscience, se faire (un) scrupule, de faire qch.; **to have no scruples, to make no s., about doing sth.,** n'avoir aucun scrupule à faire qch.; ne pas se gêner pour, ne pas hésiter à, faire qch.; **he is not troubled by any scruples,** il ne s'embarrasse d'aucun scrupule.

scruple³, *v.i.* **to s. to do sth.,** avoir des scrupules à faire qch.; se faire (un) scrupule, se faire (un cas de) conscience, de faire qch.; **he doesn't s. to go there,** il n'hésite pas à, il ne se gêne pas pour, y aller; **he didn't s. to say so,** il n'a pas craint de le dire.

scrupulosity [skru:pju'lɔsiti], *s.* = SCRUPULOUSNESS.

scrupulous ['skru:pjuləs], *a.* **1.** (*of pers., conscience, etc.*) scrupuleux (**about, over,** sur); **to be s. in doing sth.,** être scrupuleux à faire qch.; **he is not too s., not over-s.,** il est peu scrupuleux, peu délicat; il a la conscience large. **2.** (*of care, work*) scrupuleux, exact, méticuleux, minutieux; **with s. care,** avec un soin minutieux, religieux.

scrupulously ['skru:pjuləsli], *adv.* **1.** scrupuleusement, consciencieusement. **2.** méticuleusement, minutieusement; **s. careful,** méticuleux; **s. exact,** exact jusqu'au scrupule.

scrupulousness ['skru:pjuləsnis], *s.* **1.** scrupulosité *f* (**in doing sth.,** à faire qch.). **2.** esprit scrupuleux.

scrutator [skru:'teitər], *s.* scrutateur, -trice; investigateur, -trice.

scrutineer [skru:ti'niər], *s.* scrutateur, -trice (des votes, du scrutin).

scrutinize ['skru:tinaiz], *v.tr.* (*a*) scruter, sonder (qch.); examiner (qch.) minutieusement; **to s. s.o.'s face,** scruter le visage de qn (d'un regard pénétrant); dévisager qn; **to s. a proposal,** examiner à fond une proposition; (*b*) **to s. votes,** vérifier, pointer, des suffrages (en cas de contestation d'une élection); **to s. an electoral list,** pointer une liste électorale.

scrutinizer ['skru:tinaizər], *s.* scrutateur, -trice; investigateur, -trice.

scrutinizing¹ ['skru:tinaiziŋ], *a.* scrutateur, -trice; investigateur, -trice; inquisiteur *m*; **s. look,** regard pénétrant, scrutateur.

scrutinizing², *s.* (*a*) examen minutieux (de qch.); (*b*) *Pol:* vérification *f*, pointage *m* (des suffrages) (en cas d'élection contestée).

scrutiny ['skru:tini], *s.* (*a*) examen minutieux; investigation ou recherche minutieuse; **his record does not bear s.,** son passé ne supporte pas un examen rigoureux; **after a careful s.,** après un examen attentif; (*b*) *Pol:* vérification *f* (des bulletins de vote) (en cas de contestation); **s. of an electoral list,** pointage *m* d'une liste électorale; **to demand a s.,** contester la validité d'une élection.

scry [skrai], *v.i.* pratiquer la divination par le cristal.

scryer ['skraiər], *s.* voyant, -ante (qui pratique la divination par le cristal); cristallomancien, -ienne.

scuba ['skju:bə], *s.* (*abbr. for* s(elf)-c(ontained) u(nderwater) b(reathing) a(pparatus)) scaphandre *m* autonome; **s. diving,** plongée sous-marine autonome.

scud¹ [skʌd], *s.* **1.** course précipitée, rapide; fuite *f*. **2.** (*a*) (*of clouds*) diablotins *mpl*; (*b*) rafale *f*; (*c*) embrun (chassé par le vent).

scud², *v.i.* (**scudded**) **1.** (*of pers., animal, etc.*) courir droit et vite; filer comme le vent; **to s. away, off,** s'enfuir, filer, détaler; **the clouds were scudding across the sky,** les nuages galopaient à travers le ciel. **2.** *Nau:* fuir devant le temps; **to s. before the wind, to s. along,** fuir vent arrière; avoir (le) vent sous vergue; être vent sous vergue; cingler.

scuff [skʌf]. **1.** *v.tr.* (*a*) effleurer; (*b*) frotter, racler, user (avec les pieds); (*c*) **to s. away the tread of the tyre,** user la bande de roulement; (*d*) érafler (le cuir, etc.); (*with passive force*) (*of leather*) s'érafler; (*e*) **to s. up the snow, the dust,** soulever la neige, la poussière, faire voler la neige, la poussière (en traînant le pas). **2.** *v.i.* traîner les pieds.

scuffed [skʌft], *a.* (*of shoe, etc.*) éraflé.

scuffle¹ ['skʌfl], *s.* mêlée *f*, rixe *f*, échauffourée *f*, bousculade *f*; bagarre *f*.

scuffle², *v.i.* **1.** se battre, se bousculer; se bagarrer. **2. to s. through a job,** accomplir une tâche tant bien que mal, à la hâte. **3.** (*a*) traîner les pieds; (*b*) manifester en raclant le plancher.

scuffle³, *s. Hort:* **s. (hoe),** ratissoire *f* à pousser.

scuffle⁴, *v.tr.* sarcler (avec une ratissoire à pousser).

sculduddery, sculduggery [skʌl'dʌdəri, -'dʌgəri], *s.* = SKULDUGGERY.

scull¹ [skʌl], *s.* **1.** *Row:* (*a*) aviron *m* de couple; (*b*) aviron, rame *f*. **2.** godille *f*.

scull². **1.** *v.i.* (*a*) ramer, nager, en couple, à couple; (*b*) godiller; (*c*) ramer. **2.** *v.tr.* **to s. a boat,** faire avancer un bateau (i) à couple, (ii) à la godille, (iii) à la rame.

sculler ['skʌlər], *s.* **1.** (*a*) rameur *m* de couple; (*b*) godilleur *m*. **2.** (*boat*) **double s.,** outrigger *m* à deux rameurs de couple; double-scull *m*, *pl.* doubles-sculls.

scullery ['skʌləri], *s.* (*a*) arrière-cuisine *f*, *pl.* arrière-cuisines; souillarde *f*; (*b*) **s. maid,** laveuse *f* de vaisselle.

sculling ['skʌliŋ], *s. Row:* **1.** nage *f* à couple. **2.** nage à la godille.

scullion ['skʌljən], *s. A:* marmiton *m*; laveur *m* de vaisselle.

sculp(t) [skʌlp(t)]. (*a*) *v.tr.* sculpter (une statue); (*b*) *v.i.* faire de la sculpture.

sculpin ['skʌlpin], *s.* **1.** *Ich:* callionyme *m*. **2.** *A:* homme *m* de rien; bête *f* sans valeur.

sculptor ['skʌlptər], *s.* sculpteur *m*; **animal s.,** animalier *m*.

sculptress ['skʌlptris], *s.f.* femme sculpteur.

sculptural ['skʌlptjərəl], *a.* sculptural, -aux. **1. the s. arts,** les arts sculpturaux. **2. s. beauty,** beauté sculpturale, plastique.

sculpturally ['skʌlptjərəli], *adv.* **1.** conformément aux règles de la sculpture. **2. s. beautiful,** plastiquement belle.

sculpture¹ ['skʌlptjər], *s.* sculpture *f* (l'art ou l'œuvre); **ancient sculptures,** des marbres *m* antiques.

sculpture², *v.tr.* **1.** sculpter (une statue, la pierre, etc.); *v.i.* faire de la sculpture; **to s. a statue out of stone, in stone,** sculpter une statue dans la pierre. **2.** orner (un fronton, etc.) de sculptures, de bas-reliefs. **3. rocks sculptured by erosion,** rochers sculptés par l'érosion.

sculpturesque [skʌlptjə'resk], *a.* sculptural, -aux; (beauté) plastique.

scum¹ [skʌm], *s.* **1.** (*a*) écume *f*, mousse *f*; (*on wine*) chapeau *m*; **to take the s. off,** écumer (le pot, etc.); (*b*) *Metall:* scories *fpl*, crasse(s) *f*(*pl*), chiasse *f*; *Typ:* graissage non-adhérent. **2. the s. of society,** le rebut de la société; **s. of the earth!** excrément de la terre!

scum², *v.* (**scummed**) **1.** *v.tr.* écumer (le bouillon, etc.). **2.** *v.i.* écumer; se couvrir d'écume.

scumble¹ ['skʌmbl], *s. Art:* glacis *m*; frottis *m*, frotté *m*.

scumble², *v.tr. Art:* **1.** glacer, frotter (le ciel, le fond); **background scumbled with blue,** fond frotté de bleu. **2.** fondre, blaireauter (un ciel, etc.); *Draw:* estomper (une ligne, etc.).

scumcock ['skʌmkɔk], *s. Mch:* robinet *m* d'extraction à la surface; robinet de purge.

scummer ['skʌmər], *s.* (*utensil*) écumoire *f*.

scumming ['skʌmiŋ], *s.* **1.** écumage *m*; *Metall:* **s. hole,** chio *m* de décrassage. **2. scummings,** scories *f*, crasses *f*.

scummy ['skʌmi], *a.* **1.** écumeux; couvert d'écume; *Metall:* recouvert de crasse, de scories. **2.** *F:* méprisable, minable, sans valeur.

scuncheon ['skʌnʃ(ə)n], *s. Arch: Join:* écoinçon *m* (de chambranle de fenêtre, etc.).

scunner¹ ['skʌnər], *s.* dégoût *m*; **to take a s. at, against, sth.,** prendre qch. en dégoût.

scunner². **1.** *v.i.* **to s. at sth.,** prendre qch. en dégoût; se révolter à l'idée de faire qch. **2.** *v.tr.* dégoûter, révolter (qn).

scupper¹ ['skʌpər], *s. Nau:* dalot *m* (de pont); **s. hose,** manche *f* de dalot; **s. leather,** maugère *f*; placard *m* de dalot; **s. nail,** clou *m* à maugère, à pompe; **s. pipe, shoot,** tuyau *m* de dalot.

scupper², *v.tr. F:* (*a*) surprendre et massacrer (des troupes, l'équipage, etc.); **he was scuppered in 1915,** il a reçu son compte en 1915; (*b*) couler à fond (un navire, un projet, etc.); saborder (un navire).

scurf [skə:f], *s.* pellicules *fpl* (du cuir chevelu); farine *f* (d'une dartre); (*on old trees*) teigne *f*; (*in boiler*) incrustation *f*, tartre *m*.

scurfer ['skə:fər], *s.m.* nettoyeur, piqueur, de chaudières.

scurfiness ['skə:finis], *s.* état pelliculeux (de la tête, etc.); état farineux (de la peau).

scurfy ['skə:fi], *a.* (*a*) (*of head, etc.*) pelliculeux; (*b*) **s. affection of the skin,** dartre *f*.

scurrility [skʌ'riliti], *s.* **1.** goujaterie *f*; grossièreté *f*, obscénité *f* (de langage, etc.); bassesse *f* (d'une personne, d'une action). **2. to indulge in scurrilities,** prononcer, publier, des goujateries, des grossièretés, sur le compte de qn.

scurrilous ['skʌriləs], *a.* (*of language, etc.*) grossier, injurieux, ordurier; (*of pers.*) ignoble, vil; **s. accusation,** accusation outrageante; **to make a s. attack on s.o.,** s'attaquer bassement à qn; se répandre en injures contre qn.

scurrilously ['skʌriləsli], *adv.* grossièrement, injurieusement, ignoblement.

scurrilousness ['skʌriləsnis], *s.* = SCURRILITY.

scurry¹ ['skʌri], *s.* **1.** galopade *f*; débandade *f*; **a general s. towards the door,** une bousculade vers la porte. **2.** course *f* de vitesse pour poneys. **3.** tourbillon *m* (de neige, de poussière, d'oiseaux en vol).

scurry², *v.i.* aller, courir, à pas précipités; se hâter; **to s. off, away,** détaler, décamper; **to s. through one's work,** expédier son travail.

scurvied ['skə:vid], *a. Med:* scorbutique.

scurvily ['skə:vili], *adv. A:* bassement, avec bassesse; indignement.

scurvy¹ ['skə:vi], *s.* **1.** *Med:* scorbut *m*. **2.** *Bot:* **s. grass,** cochléaria *m*; *F:* herbe *f* aux cuillers.

scurvy², *a. A:* (*of conduct, pers.*) bas, vil, vilain, indigne; **s. action,** turpitude *f*; **s. fellow,** goujat *m*, plat personnage; **s. trick,** rosserie *f*, vilain tour, goujaterie *f*; **to play s.o. a s. trick,** faire une crasse, une chinoiserie, à qn.

scut [skʌt], *s.* **1.** couette *f* (de lièvre, de lapin, etc.). **2.** *P: A:* mufle *m*, rosse *f*; sale type *m*.

scutage ['skju:tidʒ], *s. Hist:* écuage *m*.

scutal ['skju:təl], *a.* **1.** *Nat.Hist:* (*a*) du scutum; (*b*) en forme d'écusson, d'écaille. **2.** *Her:* de l'écu; **extra-s.,** (devise, etc.) en dehors de l'écu.

scutate ['skju:teit], *a.* **1.** *Nat.Hist:* pourvu d'un scutum; écailleux; *Ich:* écussonné. **2.** *Bot:* scutiforme.

scutch¹ [skʌtʃ], *s. Tex:* **1.** = SCUTCHER 1. **2.** déchets *mpl* de teillage.

scutch², *v.tr. Tex:* écanguer, teiller, écoucher, espader (le chanvre, le lin).

scutch³, *s. Bot:* **s. (grass),** chiendent *m*.

scutcheon ['skʌtʃ(ə)n], *s.* **1.** *Her:* écu *m*, écusson *m*. **2.** *Hort:* **s. graft,** greffe *f* en écusson.

scutcher ['skʌtʃər], *s. Tex:* **1.** *Tls:* écang *m*, écangue *f*, écouche *f*, brisoir *m*, teilleuse *f*, espade *f*. **2.** (*pers.*) écangueur, -euse; teilleur, -euse.

scutching ['skʌtʃiŋ], *s. Tex:* écangage *m*, teillage *m*, espadage *m*; **s. machine,** teilleuse *f*, briseuse *f*.

scute [skju:t], *s. Nat.Hist:* scutum *m*.

scutellar [skju:'telər], *a. Ent: etc:* scutellaire.

scutellaria [skju:te'lɛəriə], *s. Bot:* scutellaire *f*.

scutellate ['skju:tileit], *a.* **1.** *Bot:* scutelliforme. **2.** (*or* **scutellated**) *Nat.Hist:* pourvu d'une scutelle; couvert de scutelles.

scutellation [skju:ti'leiʃ(ə)n], *s. Nat.Hist:* scutellation *f*.

scutellerid [skju:'telərid], *s. Ent:* scutellère *f*, scutelléridé *m*.

Scutelleridae [skju:te'leridi:], *s.pl. Ent:* scutelléridés *m*.

scutelliform [skju:'telifɔ:m], *a. Bot:* scutelliforme.
scutellum, *pl.* **-la** [skju:'teləm, -lə], *s. Nat.Hist:* scutelle *f*; *Bot:* scutellum *m* (d'une graminée).
Scutibranchia [skju:ti'bræŋkiə], **Scutibranchiata** [skju:tibræŋki'eitə], *s.pl. Moll:* scutibranches *m.*
scutifoliate [skju:ti'foulieit], *a. Bot:* scutifolié.
scutiform ['skju:tifɔ:m], *a.* scutiforme.
scutiger ['skju:tidʒər], **scutigera** [skju:'tidʒərə], *s. Myr:* scutigère *f.*
Scutigeridae [skju:ti'dʒeridi:], *s.pl. Myr:* scutigéridés *m.*
scutter[1,2] ['skʌtər], *s. & v.i. Dial:* = SCAMPER[1,2].
scuttle[1] ['skʌtl], *s.* **1.** seau *m* à charbon. **2.** *Husb: etc:* corbeille *f.*
scuttle[2], *s.* **1.** *Nau:* (*a*) écoutillon *m*; descente *f*; (*b*) hublot *m*; lentille *f* (de cabine); **air s.,** hublot d'aération; ventouse *f.* **2.** *Aut: A:* bouclier *m* avant; auvent *m.* **3.** *U.S:* trappe *f* (de toit, de plancher).
scuttle[3], *v.tr. Nau:* saborder (un navire); **to s. one's ship,** s'envoyer par le fond.
scuttle[4], *s.* fuite *f*; course précipitée; débandade *f*; **to do a s.,** filer.
scuttle[5], *v.i.* (*a*) courir à pas précipités; **to s. (off, away),** déguerpir, filer, détaler; (*of rabbit, etc.*) débouler; (*b*) *Pol: F:* abandonner une politique; renoncer à une ligne de conduite; se retirer; **if we s. out of Northern Ireland,** si nous nous lavons les mains de l'Irlande du Nord.
scuttlebutt ['skʌtlbʌt], *s.* **1.** *Nau:* charnier *m* (d'eau douce). **2.** *esp. U.S:* racontars *mpl*; commérages *mpl*; **he started a round of s. to the effect that . . .,** il a fait courir le bruit que . . ..
scuttler ['skʌtlər], *s.* assureur frauduleux qui saborde son navire.
scuttling ['skʌtliŋ], *s. Nau:* sabordement *m.*
scutum, *pl.* **-a** ['skju:təm, -ə], *s. Rom.Ant: Nat.Hist:* scutum *m.*
scybala ['sibələ], *s.pl. Med:* scybales *f.*
Scydmaenidae [sid'mi:nidi:], *s.pl. Ent:* scydménidés *m.*
Scyliorhinidae [siliou'rinidi:], *s.pl. Ich:* scyliorhinidés *m.*
Scylla ['silə]. *Pr.n. Myth:* Scylla *m*; **to fall from S. into Charybdis,** tomber de Charybde en Scylla.
scyllaea [si'li:ə], *s. Moll:* scyllée *f*, scylle *f.*
Scyllaeidae [si'li:idi:], *s.pl. Moll:* scylléidés *m.*
scyllarian [si'lɛəriən], *s. Crust:* scyllare *m.*
Scyllaridae [si'læridi:], *s.pl. Crust:* scyllaridés *m.*
scyllarus [si'lɛərəs], *s. Crust:* scyllare *m.*
Scylliorhinidae [siliou'rinidi:], *s.pl. Ich:* scyliorhinidés *m.*
scyphate ['saifeit], *a.* scyphiforme.
scyphistoma [sai'fistəmə], *s. Coel:* scyphistome *m.*
Scyphomedusae [saifoume'dju:si:], *s.pl. Coel:* scyphoméduses *f.*
scyphomedusan [saifoume'djuzən], *s. Coel:* scyphoméduse *f.*
scyphopolyp [saifou'pɔlip], *s. Coel:* scyphistome *m.*
Scyphozoa [saifou'zouə], *s.pl. Coel:* scyphozoaires *m.*
scyphulus ['saifjuləs], *s. Nat.Hist:* scyphule *m.*
scyphus, *pl.* **-i** ['saifəs, -ai], *s.* **1.** *Gr.Ant:* coupe *f.* **2.** *Bot:* couronne *f* en entonnoir; scyphule *m* (de lichen).
scytale ['sitəli], *s.* **1.** *Gr.Ant:* scytale *f.* **2.** *Rept:* scytale *m.*
scythe[1] [saið], *s. Agr:* faux *f*; **short-handled s.,** dail *m*, daille *f*; **s. stone,** pierre *f* à aiguiser (les faux); dalle *f*, dail *m*, daille *f.*
scythe[2], *v.tr.* faucher (le blé, etc.).
scythed [saiðd], *a. A.Mil:* (chariot) armé de faux, à faux.
Scythia ['siðiə]. *Pr.n. A.Geog:* Scythie *f.*
Scythian ['siðiən]. **1.** *A.Geog:* (*a*) *a.* scythique, scythe; (*b*) *s.* Scythe *mf.* **2.** *s. Ling:* scythe *m.*
Scythic ['siðik], *a.* scythique, scythe.
scytodepsic [saitou'depsik], *a. Leath:* scytodepsique.
'sdeath [zdeθ], *int. A:* mordieu! morbleu!
sea [si:], *s.* **1.** mer *f*; (*a*) **at the bottom of the s.,** au fond de la mer; **s. bottom, s. floor,** fond sous-marin; fond de mer; **s. level,** niveau (moyen) de la mer; **pressure corrected to s. level,** pression (barométrique) ramenée au niveau de la mer; **an arm of the s.,** un bras de mer; **on land and s., by land and s.,** sur terre et sur mer; **by the s.,** au bord de la mer; **by s.,** par (voie de) mer; **beyond, over, the sea(s),** outre-mer; au delà des mers; par delà les mers; **from beyond the s.,** d'outre-mer; **to be mistress of the sea(s),** régner sur les flots; **to smell of the s.,** sentir la mer, la marine; (*of pers.*) **to put to s.,** s'embarquer; **to go to s.,** se faire marin; **to serve at s.,** servir sur mer; **s. voyage,** voyage *m* par mer, en mer; traversée *f*; **s. air,** air marin, de la mer; **s. breeze, wind,** brise *f*, vent *m*, de mer, du large; **room with a s. view,** chambre avec vue sur la mer; **s. bathing,** bains *mpl* de mer; **s. battle,** bataille navale; **s. green,** vert *m* de mer; vert d'eau; **s.-green eyes,** yeux glauques; *Jur:* **s. carrier,** transporteur *m* par mer; **s. damage,** fortune *f* de mer; *Nau:* **s. chest,** coffre *m* de marin, de bord; *Lit:* **s. fever,** l'appel *m* de la mer; *A:* **s. coal.** houille *f*, charbon *m*, de terre; (*b*) **the open s., the high seas,** le large, la haute mer, la grande mer, la pleine mer, la mer libre; **on the high seas, out at s.,** en haute mer, en pleine mer, au grand large; (*of ship*) **to put (out) to s.,** prendre la mer, le large; **to put out to s. again,** reprendre la mer; (*in heavy weather*) **to keep the s.,** tenir la mer; **to stand out to s.,** se tenir au large; **to stand out, go out, to s.,** porter au large; gagner le large, prendre le large; mettre le cap sur le large; **head on to s.,** le cap au large; **ship at s.,** navire en mer; **the ship had been at s. for three weeks,** le navire tenait la mer depuis trois semaines; *F:* **to be all at s.,** être tout dérouté, désorienté, désemparé; patauger; perdre le nord; être aux champs; n'y être pas du tout; n'y voir que du bleu; ne savoir sur quel pied danser; y perdre son latin; **I am completely at s.,** je ne m'y reconnais plus; *Nau:* **to have plenty of s. room,** (i) avoir de l'évitée; (ii) avoir une belle dérive, de la chasse, de l'eau à courir; *F:* (*of pers.*) **s. legs,** le pied marin; **to find, get, one's s. legs,** s'amariner; **he hasn't found his s. legs,** il n'a pas encore le pied marin; (*c*) *Geog:* **inland s., enclosed s.,** mer intérieure; *A:* **the four seas,** les mers qui entourent la Grande-Bretagne; **the seven seas,** toutes les mers du monde; (*d*) **S. Lord,** lord *m* de l'Amirauté; **s. captain,** capitaine *m* (i) de la marine marchande, (ii) au long cours; *Scout:* **s. scout,** scout marin; *Hist:* **s. king,** chef *m* de pirates scandinaves; *A:* **s. rover,** corsaire *m*, pirate *m*, flibustier *m*; écumeur *m* de mer; *Myth:* **s. god,** dieu marin, de la mer; triton *m*; **s. goddess,** déesse marine, de la mer; **s. nymph,** néréïde *f*, océanide *f*; nymphe marine, de la mer; (*of graceful swimmer*) **she's a real s. nymph,** c'est une véritable ondine; (*e*) **s. fish,** poisson *m* de mer; **s. fishery, fishing,** pêche *f* maritime; *Ich:* **s. bream,** (i) pagel *m*; (ii) dorade bilunée; castagnole *f*; **black s. bream,** brème *f* de mer, canthère *m*; **s. tench,** brème de mer; (*of the Mediterranean*) molle *f*; **s. dace,** *F:* **s. wolf,** bar(s) *m*; loup *m* de mer; **s. perch,** serran *m*, *F:* loup de mer; **s. pike,** brochet *m* de mer; orphie *f*; **s. trout,** truite *f* de mer; **s. angel,** ange *m* de mer; angelot *m*; moine *m*; **s. ape,** renard *m*; **s. barrow,** oreiller *m* de mer; **s. bat,** (i) chauve-souris *f* de mer; (ii) mante *f*, manta *f*, grand diable de mer; **s. cock,** coq *m* de mer; **s. clown,** bouffon *m* des mers, antennaire *m*; **s. devil,** diable de mer; raie pêcheresse; lophie pêcheuse; baudroie *f*; poisson-grenouille *m*, *pl.* poissons-grenouilles; crapaud pêcheur, crapaud de mer; **s. fox,** renard (marin); **s. hen,** cycloptère *m*, lump *m*; **s. needle,** aiguille *f* de mer; orphie *f*; **s. owl,** lompe *m*, lump; *F:* porte-écuelles *m inv*; **s. porcupine,** (i) diodon *m*, poisson porc-épic; (ii) (= *sea urchin*) *Echin:* oursin *m*; **s. raven,** hémitriptère *m*; **s. robin,** malarmat *m*; **s. snail,** liparis *m*; **s. toad,** raie pêcheuse; diable de mer; *U.S:* callionyme *m*; (*f*) *Orn:* **s. eagle,** pygargue *m*, orfraie *f*; *F:* grand aigle des mers; **bald s. eagle, white-headed s. eagle,** pygargue leucocéphale; **white-tailed,** *U.S:* **gray, s. eagle,** pygargue à queue blanche; **Pallas's s. eagle,** pygargue de Pallas; **s. lark,** alouette *f* de mer; petite maubèche; pluvier *m* à collier; tourne-pierre *m*, *pl.* tourne-pierres; **s. swallow,** hirondelle *f* de mer; sterne *m*, goélette *f*; **s. hawk,** = SKUA; **s. parrot,** macareux *m*, mormon *m*; *F:* **s. pie,** huîtrier *m* pie; pie *f* de mer; (*g*) *Z:* **s. bear,** otarie *f*, ours marin, de mer; **s. calf,** phoque commun; veau marin; **s. cow,** vache marine (lamantin, dugong, morse, hippopotame); **s. elephant,** macrorhine *m*; *F:* éléphant *m* de mer; phoque *m* à trompe; **s. goose,** oie-de-mer *f*, dauphin *m*; *F:* **s. hog,** marsouin *m*; cochon *m* de mer; **s. otter,** loutre *f* de mer; loutre marine; enhydre *m*; **s. pig,** marsouin *m*; pourceau *m* de mer; cochon *m* de mer; dauphin *m*; dugong *m*; vache marine; *Rept:* **s. snake,** hydrophis *m*, serpent marin; pélamide *f*; **s. serpent,** (i) serpent *m* de mer; (ii) (*also* **s. monster**) monstre marin; **s. tortoise,** tortue *f* de mer; *F:* **s. lawyer,** (i) requin (féroce); (ii) (*pers.*) rouspéteur *m*, chicaneur *m*; *Ann: F:* **s. mouse,** hérisson *m* de mer; aphrodite *f*; **s. bread,** (i) *Spong:* halicondrie *f*; (ii) (*also* **s. biscuit**) biscuit *m* de mer, *F:* cassant *m*; (*h*) *Crust:* **s. acorn,** balane *m*, gland *m* de mer, turban *m* rouge; **s. louse,** cymothoé *m*, calige *m*; *F:* cloporte *m* de mer; pou *m* de mer, *pl.* poux de mer; limule *m* polyphème; crabe *m* des Moluques; **s. spider,** araignée *f* de mer; **common s. slater,** ligie *f*, lygie *f*; pou de mer; *Moll:* **s. arrow,** calmar *m* flèche; **s. ear,** ormeau *m*; oreille *f* de mer; ormet *m*, ormier *m*; **s. hare,** aplysie *f*, téthys *f*, *F:* lièvre marin; **s. lemon,** doris *f*; **s. mat,** flustre *f*; *F:* **s. screw,** turritelle *f*, térèbre *f*; **s. silkworm,** pinne *f*, *F:* jambonneau *m*; **s. silk,** byssus *m* des pinnes; **s. grapes,** œufs *m* de seiche; *F:* raisins *m* de mer; *Coel:* **s. anemone,** actinie *f*; *F:* anémone *f* de mer; ortie *f* de mer; **s. belt, s. hanger,** ceste *m*; ceinture *f* de Vénus; **s. fan,** gorgone *f* éventail; **s. nettle,** méduse *f*; **s. pear,** bolténie *f*; **s. pen,** penne *f* de mer, plume *f* de mer; **s. squirt,** ascidie *f*; outre *f* de mer; *F:* **edible s. squirt,** *Dial: S. of Fr.* violet *m*, vioulet *m*; figue *f* de mer; **s. basket, s. spider,** euryale *m*; *Echin:* **s. chestnut, s. egg,** échinoïde *m*, oursin *m*; châtaigne *f* de mer; hérisson de mer; **s. cucumber,** (i) concombre *m* de mer; (ii) trépang *m*, bêche-de-mer *f*; **s. hedgehog,** (i) oursin *m*; (ii) *Ich:* poisson *m* globe; **s. lily,** crinoïde *m*; lis *m* à bras; lis de mer; **s. slug,** (i) concombre de mer; trépang; bêche-de-mer; (ii) *Moll:* nudibranche *m*; **s. urchin,** oursin *m*; hérisson, châtaigne, de mer; **edible s. urchin,** oursin violet; (*i*) *Bot:* **s. aster, s. starwort,** aster *m*; **s. bells,** chou *m* de mer, *pl.* choux de mer; **s. bent, s. reed,** roseau *m* des sables; **s. daffodil,** pancratier *m* maritime; scille blanche; **s. fennel,** fenouil marin, de mer; bacile *m*; criste-marine *f*; **s. grass,** salicorne herbacée; ruppie *f* (maritime); zostère *f* maritime; *F:* baugue *f*, bauque *f*; **s. heath,** frankénie *f*; **s. milkwort, s. trifoly,** glaux *m*; **s. onion,** scille *f* maritime; **s. rocket,** roquette *f* maritime; caquillier *m*; *Algae:* **s. belt, girdle,** baudrier *m* de Neptune; laminaire digitée; **s. lace,** chorda *m*; **s. lettuce,** laitue *f* de mer, ulve *f*; **s. thong,** courroies *fpl* de mer; **s. palm,** (i) palmier *m* de mer, lessonia *m*; (ii) postelsia *m*; **s. tangle,** laminaire digitée; *Surg:* **s. tangle tent,** tente de laminaire; *Algae:* **s. whipcord,** lacet *m* de mer; *F:* boyau *m*; **s. wrack, s. oak,** fucus *m*, varech *m*; balayures *fpl* de la mer. **2.** (*a*) (*state of the sea*) **heavy s., strong s.,** grosse mer; mer grosse, houleuse; **choppy s.,** clapotis *m*; **quarter s.,** mer de la hanche; **there's a s., a heavy s.,** il y a de la mer; **long s.,** mer longue; **short s.,** mer courte, hachée; **in anything of a s.,** pour peu qu'il y ait de la mer; (*b*) lame *f*, houle *f*; **to run before the s.,** gouverner l'arrière à la lame; avoir la mer de l'arrière: fuir devant la lame; **to keep head to s.,** se tenir debout à la lame; **head s.,** mer debout; mer contraire; **beam s.,** mer de travers; (*c*) coup *m* de mer; paquet *m* de mer; (grosse) vague; **green s.,** eau verte; **to ship a (green) s.,** embarquer une lame, un coup de mer, un paquet de mer; **to take a green s.,** capeler une lame; **to ship, be struck by, a (heavy) s.,** recevoir une lame; essuyer un coup de mer. **3.** océan *m*, infinité *f*, multitude *f*; **a s. of faces,** un océan de visages; **a s. of blood,** une mer de sang; *Lit:* **a s. of troubles,** une multitude de soucis.
seabird ['si:bə:d], *s.* oiseau *m* de mer.
seaboard ['si:bɔ:d], *s.* littoral *m*, -aux; bord *m* de la mer; rivage *m* (de la mer); **the Atlantic s.,** le littoral atlantique; **s. provinces,** provinces avoisinant la mer.
seaboots ['si:bu:ts], *s.pl.* bottes *f* de marin, de mer.
seaborne ['si:bɔ:n], *a.* (*of trade*) maritime; (*of goods*) transporté par mer.
seacoast ['si:koust], *s.* littoral *m*, -aux; côte *f* (de la mer).
seadog ['si:dɔg], *s.* **1.** (*a*) *Z: F: O:* phoque *m*, veau marin; (*b*) *Her:* chien *m* de mer. **2.** *F:* **an old s.,** un vieux marin; un vieux loup de mer. **3.** *Nau:* lueur *f* à l'horizon (pronostic de mauvais temps).
seafarer ['si:fɛərər], *s.* homme *m* de mer; marin *m.*
seafaring[1] ['si:fɛəriŋ], *a.* (gens, etc.) de mer, qui naviguent; **s. man,** marin *m.*
seafaring[2], *s.* voyages *mpl* par mer.
seaflower ['si:flauər], *s. Coel:* actinie *f*, anémone *f* de mer.
seafood ['si:fu:d], *s. coll.* fruits *mpl* de mer; *Comest:* **s. platter,** salade *f* de fruits de mer.
seafowl ['si:faul], *s.inv.* oiseau(x) *m(pl)* de mer.
seafront ['si:frʌnt], *s.* **1.** partie *f* d'une ville qui fait face à la mer; **house on the s.,** maison qui donne sur la mer. **2.** digue *f*, esplanade *f*; front *m* de mer; **to walk on, along, the s.,** se promener sur la digue.
seagirt ['si:gə:t], *a. Lit:* entouré, ceint, par la mer; **a s. island,** une île ceinturée par les flots.
seagoing ['si:gouiŋ], *a.* (navire, etc.) de mer, affecté à la navigation maritime; **s. trade,** commerce *m* maritime; **s. personnel,** personnel navigant.
seagull ['si:gʌl], *s. Orn:* mouette *f*, goéland *m.*
sea-island ['si:ailənd], *a. Tex:* **s.-i. cotton,** coton *m* à longue soie; *Bot:* **s.-i. myrtle,** baccharis *m.*
seakale ['si:keil], *s. Bot:* crambe *m*, crambé *m* (maritime); chou marin.
seal[1] [si:l], *s.* **1.** (*a*) *Z:* phoque *m*; *F:* veau marin; **bearded s.,** phoque barbu; **crabeater, crab-eating, s.,** phoque crabier; **elephant s.,** mirounga *m*, éléphant *m*

de mer; phoque à trompe; macrorhine *m*; **grey s.,** phoque gris; **hooded s.,** phoque à capuchon; capucin *m*; **monk s.,** phoque moine; **mottled s.,** phoque marbré; **eared s.,** otarie *f*, otariidé *m*; lion *m* de mer; **fur s.,** otarie à fourrure; ours marin; (*b*) **s. oil,** huile *f* de phoque; **s. fisher,** chasseur *m*, pêcheur *m*, de phoques; **s. fishery,** (i) pêche *f* des phoques; (ii) pêcherie *f* de phoques. **2.** *Com:* **coney s.,** fourrure *f* genre loutre; colombia *f*; **electric s.,** colombia électrique; **Hudson s.,** fourrure genre loutre. **3.** *Leath:* (peau *f* de) phoque.

seal[2], *v.i.* chasser, pêcher, le phoque.

seal[3], *s.* **1.** (*a*) (*on deed, etc.*) sceau *m*; (*on letter*) cachet *m*; **to break the s. of a letter,** rompre le cachet d'une lettre; *Jur:* **given under my hand and s.,** signé et scellé par moi; **contract under s.,** convention scellée; **under the s. of silence, of secrecy,** sous le sceau du silence, du secret; **to put one's s. to a document,** marquer un document de son sceau; **to set one's s. to sth.,** autoriser, confirmer, qch.; donner son approbation à qch.; *Lit:* **death had already set its s. on his face,** la mort avait déjà mis son empreinte sur son visage; **to set the s. on s.o.'s reputation,** mettre le sceau à la réputation de qn; **s. of distinction,** cachet de distinction; **book that bears the s. of genius,** livre qui porte le sceau, le cachet, du génie; *Lit: A:* **s. of love,** (i) baiser *m*; (ii) enfant *m*; (*b*) cachet (de bouteille de vin, etc.); *Jur:* (*affixed to property, etc.*) **official s.,** scellé *m*; **to affix, remove, the seals,** apposer, lever, les scellés; **under s.,** sous scellés; *Com: etc:* **lead s.,** (i) plomb *m* (pour sceller une caisse, etc.); (ii) capsule *f* (de bouteille de vin); **custom house s.,** plomb de la douane. **2.** (*instrument*) sceau, cachet; *Adm:* **the Great S.,** le grand sceau (employé pour les actes publics); (*of Lord Chancellor or Secretary of State*) **to return the seals,** se démettre; démissionner. **3.** *Tchn:* (*a*) dispositif *m* d'étanchéité; joint *m* étanche; rondelle *f* étanche; tampon *m*, fermeture *f*, clôture *f*; **hermetic s., vacuum s.,** joint hermétique; (*b*) (liquide) obturateur *m* (d'un siphon, etc.).

seal[4], *v.tr.* **1.** (*a*) sceller (un acte, etc.); cacheter (une lettre); **sealed tender,** soumission cachetée; **his fate is sealed,** son sort est décidé, réglé; c'en est fait de lui; (*b*) cacheter (une bouteille de porto, etc.); *Cust:* (faire) plomber (des marchandises, etc.); *Jur:* apposer les scellés sur (une porte, un meuble, etc.); (*c*) *Mil: etc:* **to s. a design,** adopter définitivement un modèle; **sealed pattern equipment,** équipement réglementaire, d'ordonnance. **2.** (*a*) **to s. (up),** fermer; **to s. (up) a letter,** fermer une lettre; **the frontier has been sealed,** la frontière est fermée; **the area was sealed off,** le quartier a été isolé, cerné, par la police, entouré d'un cordon de police; (*b*) rendre (qch.) étanche, étancher (qch.); **to s. up the windows,** fermer hermétiquement les fenêtres; **to s. a mineshaft, a pipe,** obturer, boucher, un puits de mine, un tuyau; *Civ.E:* **sealed road,** route *f* à revêtement étanche; (*c*) **to s. s.o.'s lips,** mettre un cachet, un cadenas, sur la bouche de qn; **my lips are sealed,** il m'est défendu de parler; (*d*) assurer l'étanchéité (d'un joint, etc.); (*e*) *Cu:* saisir (de la viande). **3.** sceller, fixer (un crampon dans un mur, etc.).

sealer[1] ['si:lər], *s.* **1.** (*ship*) phoquier *m*. **2.** (*pers.*) chasseur *m*, pêcheur *m*, de phoques.

sealer[2], *s.* **1.** (*a*) scelleur *m* (d'un document); (*b*) *Adm:* vérificateur *m* des poids et mesures. **2.** *Tls:* pince *f* à plomber, à sceller; *Mch: etc:* sertisseuse *f*.

sealery ['si:ləri], *s.* (*a*) pêcherie *f* de phoques; (*b*) colonie *f*, rookerie *f*, de phoques.

sealine ['si:lain], *s.* **1.** (*at sea*) horizon *m*; ligne *f* d'horizon. **2.** *Petr:* conduite marine; sea-line *m*, *pl.* sea-lines.

sealing[1] ['si:liŋ], *s.* chasse *f* au phoque; pêche *f* des phoques; **s. fleet,** flotte phoquière.

sealing[2], *s.* **1.** (*a*) scellage *m* (d'un acte, etc.); cachetage *m* (d'une lettre, etc.); **s. wax,** cire *f* à cacheter; **stick of s. wax,** bâton *m* de cire à cacheter; (*b*) *Cust:* plombage *m* (des marchandises, etc.). **2. s. (up),** fermeture *f* (de qch.); obturation *f* (d'un puits de mine, d'un tuyau). **3.** scellement *m*, fixage *m* (d'un crampon dans un mur, etc.). **4. s. compound,** (i) lut *m*, mastic *m*, compound *m* de fermeture (pour joints); *Aut:* antifuite *m inv* (de radiateur); (ii) vernis *m* hermétique.

sealion ['si:laiən], *s. Z:* otarie *f*; lion marin; **Steller's s.,** eumétopias *m*, otarie de Steller.

sealskin ['si:lskin], *s.* **1.** (peau *f* de) phoque *m*; **black s.,** phoque noir. **2.** *Com:* (fourrure *f* en) loutre *f*; (peau de) loutre.

seam[1] [si:m], *s.* **1.** (*a*) *Needlew:* couture *f*; **flat s.,** couture rabattue, plate; **round(ed) s.,** couture rabattue ronde; **French s.,** couture double; couture anglaise; **overcast s., dressmaking s.,** surjet *m*; **outside-stitched s.,** couture piquée; **welted s.,** couture en baguette; **openwork s.,** couture de raccord ajourée; *Tail:* **s. presser,** carreau *m*; (*b*) (*in metal pipe, between boards, etc.*) couture, joint *m*; **brazed s.,** brasure *f*; **welded s., soldered s.,** joint soudé; soudure *f*; **s. welding,** soudage *m* à molettes; (*c*) *Metalw: Plumb:* **welted s.,** agrafage *m*, agrafe *f*; (*d*) *N.Arch:* **ship's seams,** coutures d'un navire; **lapped s.,** couture à clin; (*e*) *F:* **room, hall, bursting at the seams,** salle pleine à crouler, à craquer. **2.** (*a*) (*on face, etc.*) (i) cicatrice *f*, couture, balafre *f*; (ii) ride *f*; (*b*) (*in wood, rock, etc.*) fissure *f*, gerçure *f*; (*c*) *Metall:* couture (d'une pièce venue de fonte); (*d*) *Metall:* veine *f*, paille *f* (dans le métal). **3.** (*a*) *Geol:* ligne *f* de séparation (des couches); (*b*) *Min: etc:* couche *f*, gisement *m*, gîte *m*, veine; **flat s.,** plateure *f*; **edge s.,** dressant *m*.

seam[2], *v.tr.* **1.** (*a*) *Needlew:* faire une couture à (un vêtement, etc.); **to s. up a garment,** assembler un vêtement; (*b*) *Metalw: Plumb:* agrafer (des tôles, etc.). **2.** couturer; marquer (un visage, etc.) de cicatrices, (un rocher, etc.) de fissures; **face seamed with scars,** visage couturé de cicatrices.

seaman, *pl.* **-men** ['si:mən], *s.m.* **1.** marin, matelot; *Navy:* matelot de la marine nationale; **the seamen of a ship,** l'équipage *m* d'un navire; **ordinary s.,** matelot de troisième classe, de pont; novice (au commerce); **able (-bodied) s.,** gabier breveté; matelot de deuxième classe; **leading s.,** matelot (breveté) de première classe; quartier-maître, *pl.* quartier(s)-maîtres; **s. gunner,** canonnier *m*. **2.** (*a*) manœuvrier; (*b*) navigateur; **a good s.,** un bon manœuvrier, un bon navigateur; **the Romans were no seamen,** les Romains étaient peu marins, n'entendaient rien aux choses de la mer.

seamanlike ['si:mənlaik]. **1.** *a.* de marin, d'un bon marin. **2.** *adv.* en bon marin.

seamanship ['si:mənʃip], *s.* manœuvre *f* et matelotage *m*; la manœuvre; expertise *f* du marin.

seamark ['si:mɑ:k], *s. Nau:* (*a*) amer *m*; (*b*) balise *f*.

seamew ['si:mju:], *s. Orn:* = SEAGULL.

seaming ['si:miŋ], *s.* **1.** (*a*) couture *f*; *Nau:* **s. needle,** aiguille *f* à voiles; (*b*) *Metalw:* agrafage *m* (de tôles). **2.** *coll.* coutures; *Furn:* **s. lace,** galon *m* (pour masquer les coutures).

seamless ['si:mlis], *a.* **1.** (bas *m*, tapis *m*, etc.) sans couture. **2.** *Metalw:* (*of tube, etc.*) sans soudure.

seamstress ['semstris], *s.f.* ouvrière couturière.

seamy ['si:mi], *a.* **the s. side of life,** l'envers *m*, les dessous *m*, de la vie; le revers de la médaille; **to know the s. side of life, of things,** connaître la vie sous toutes ses coutures; **the s. side of politics,** le vilain côté, les dessous, de la politique.

seance ['seiɑ:ns], *s.* séance *f* de spiritisme.

seapiece ['si:pi:s], *s. Art:* marine *f*.

seaplane ['si:plein], *s. Av:* hydravion *m*; **s. base,** station hydroaérienne; hydrobase *f*.

seaport ['si:pɔ:t], *s.* port *m* maritime, de mer.

sear[1] [siər], *s. Sm.a:* gâchette *f* (d'un fusil); **s. spring,** ressort *m* de gâchette; petit ressort.

sear[2], *v.tr.* **1.** (*of heat, frost*) flétrir, dessécher (les feuilles, le grain, etc.); faner (les feuilles). **2.** (*a*) cautériser (une blessure, etc.); *Vet:* appliquer les feux à (une bête); *Lit:* endurcir (la conscience, etc.); dessécher (le cœur); (*b*) marquer au fer rouge.

sear[3], *a.* = SERE.

search[1] [sə:tʃ], *s.* **1.** (*a*) recherche(s) *f*(*pl*); **to make a s.,** (i) faire des recherches; (ii) (*in property transactions*) faire une enquête de commodo et incommodo; **to make a s. for s.o.,** (re)chercher qn; **the s. for, after, sth.,** la recherche de qch.; **in (the course of) my s. I found . . .,** au cours de mes recherches j'ai trouvé . . .; **in s. of sth.,** à la recherche de qch.; **to be in s. of sth.,** être en quête de qch.; chercher qch.; être à la recherche de qch.; **s. party,** expédition *f* de secours; (*b*) *Magn:* **s. coil,** bobine *f* d'essai, d'exploration; *Cmptr:* **binary s., dichotomizing s.,** recherche dichotomique; **s. cycle,** cycle *m* de recherche; **s. key,** critère *m* de recherche. **2.** (*a*) *Cust:* visite *f*; **right of s.,** droit *m* de visite; (*at sea*) droit de recherche; (*b*) *Jur:* perquisition *f* (à domicile); **s. warrant,** mandat *m*, ordre *m*, de perquisition; (*c*) fouille *f* (dans un tiroir, etc.).

search[2]. **1.** *v.tr.* inspecter (un endroit); chercher dans (un endroit, une boite, un livre); fouiller dans (un tiroir, une bibliothèque); fouiller (un suspect, les poches de qn); scruter, sonder (un visage); **we searched the whole town for him,** nous avons parcouru toute la ville à sa recherche; *Cust:* **to s. a ship, s.o.'s suitcase,** visiter un navire, la valise de qn; *Jur:* **to s. a house,** faire une perquisition, une visite domiciliaire; perquisitionner dans une maison; *Surg:* **to s. a wound,** sonder une plaie; *Lit:* **to s. men's hearts,** scruter, sonder, les cœurs; **to s. one's own heart,** rentrer en soi-même; **to s. one's memory,** scruter sa mémoire; *F:* **s. me!** je n'ai pas la moindre idée! **2.** *v.i.* faire des recherches; **to s. for new remedies,** chercher des remèdes nouveaux; **to s. after truth,** rechercher la vérité; **to s. for s.o., sth.,** (re)chercher qn, qch.; **to s. through the dictionary for a word,** scruter tout le dictionnaire pour trouver un mot.

searcher ['sə:tʃər], *s.* **1.** (*a*) (re)chercheur, -euse; **s. of men's hearts,** scrutateur, -trice, des cœurs; (*b*) *Cust:* douanier *m*; visiteur, -euse; (*c*) *Jur:* perquisiteur *m*, perquisitionneur *m*. **2.** *Surg:* sonde *f*.

searching[1] ['sə:tʃiŋ], *a.* **1.** (examen) minutieux, attentif, rigoureux; (regard) pénétrant, scrutateur; (vent) pénétrant; **s. study,** étude pénétrante; **to give s.o. a s. look,** scruter qn du regard; **s. inquiry,** enquête approfondie; **s. questions,** questions qui vont au fond des choses; **to put s.o. through a s. examination,** (i) interroger, (ii) *Med:* examiner, minutieusement qn. **2.** (*of pers.*) chercheur, -euse; fureteur, -euse; quêteur, -euse.

searching[2], *s.* **1.** inspection *f* (d'un endroit, etc.); fouille *f* (d'un suspect, etc.); *Cust:* visite *f*; *Jur:* perquisition *f*. **2.** recherche *f* (**for,** de); **thorough s.,** enquête approfondie.

searchingly ['sə:tʃiŋli], *adv.* (examiner) minutieusement; (regarder qn, etc.) d'un œil scrutateur, pénétrant.

searchlight ['sə:tʃlait], *s.* (*a*) projecteur *m*; (*of aircraft*) **signal s.,** projecteur (de signalisation) du bord; *Mil:* **s. battery, unit,** batterie *f*, unité *f*, de projecteurs; (*b*) (*beam*) projection *f*; **to turn a s. on sth.,** donner un coup de projecteur sur qch.

seared ['siəd], *a.* **1.** (*of leaf*) flétri, fané. **2.** *Lit:* (*of conscience*) endurci, insensible.

searing ['siəriŋ], *s.* flétrissement *m*; cautérisation *f*; **s. iron,** fer *m* à cautériser; cautère actuel.

seascape ['si:skeip], *s.* **1.** panorama marin; vue *f* sur la mer. **2.** *Art:* marine *f*.

seascapist ['si:skeipist], *s. Art:* mariniste *mf*.

seashell ['si:ʃel], *s.* coquille *f* de mer; coquillage *m*.

seashore ['si:ʃɔ:r], *s.* (*a*) rivage *m*; bord *m* de la mer; côte *f*, littoral *m*; (*b*) plage *f*.

seasick ['si:sik], *a.* **to be s.,** avoir le mal de mer.

seasickness ['si:siknis], *s.* mal *m* de mer; *Med:* naupathie *f*.

seaside ['si:said], *s.* bord *m* de la mer; **house at the s.,** maison *f* au bord de la mer; **s. resort,** plage *f*; station *f* balnéaire.

season[1] ['si:zn], *s.* **1.** saison *f*; (*a*) **the four seasons,** les quatre saisons; **the dry s.,** la saison sèche; la belle saison; **the rainy s.,** la saison des pluies; **the s. of Lent, the Lenten s.,** le carême; **late s.,** arrière-saison *f*; (*b*) époque *f*; **very early in the s.,** très tôt en saison; **hunting s.,** saison de la chasse; *Ven:* **close s., open s.,** chasse (ou pêche) fermée, ouverte; **the close s. for partridge(s), for salmon, extends from . . . to . . .,** la chasse aux perdrix, la pêche au saumon, est fermée de . . . à . . .; (*in tourist industry, etc.*) **the slack s., the off s.,** la morte-saison; **the tourist s., the holiday s.,** la saison touristique, des vacances; la haute saison; (*of oysters, etc.*) **to be in, out of, s.,** être de saison, hors de saison; **strawberries are in s.,** c'est la saison des fraises; les fraises sont maintenant de saison; (*of animal*) **in s.,** en rut; en chaleur; (*c*) *O:* **the (London) s.,** la saison (où la haute société se trouve à Londres); **the s. is at its height,** la saison bat son plein. **2.** période *f*, temps *m*; **to last for a s.,** durer pendant quelque temps; **at that s.,** en ce temps-là; **in due s.,** en temps voulu, en temps et saison; **word in s.,** mot dit à propos; **remark out of s.,** remarque déplacée; **in s. and out of s.,** à tout propos et hors de propos; à tout propos et sans propos; à tout bout de champ; *Cin:* **this film will be shown for a short s.,** ce film sera projeté pendant une courte période; **a short s. of French films,** un petit festival de films français. **3. s. ticket,** *F:* **s.,** carte *f* d'abonnement; **to take a s. ticket,** prendre un abonnement; **s. ticket holder,** abonné, -ée.

season[2]. **1.** *v.tr.* (*a*) assaisonner, apprêter, accommoder, relever (un mets); (*b*) dessécher, (faire) sécher, étuver, conditionner (le bois); abreuver, aviner (un tonneau); mûrir, laisser se faire (le vin); (*c*) acclimater, endurcir (qn); aguerrir (un soldat); amariner (un matelot); (*d*) tempérer, modérer (la justice, etc.); **justice seasoned with mercy,** justice tempérée de miséricorde. **2.** *v.i.* (*of wood*) se sécher; (*of wine, etc.*) mûrir, se faire.

seasonable ['si:znəbl], *a.* **1.** (*of weather, etc.*) de (la) saison; **s. weather,** un temps de saison. **2.** (*of help, advice*) opportun, à propos.

seasonably ['si:znəbli], *adv.* opportunément, à propos;

en temps voulu, opportun; en temps utile.

seasonal ['siːzən(ə)l], *a.* (changements, etc.) des saisons; (commerce) saisonnier, qui dépend de la saison; **s. disease,** maladie saisonnière; **s. worker,** (ouvrier) saisonnier *m*; **s. unemployment,** chômage saisonnier.

seasoned ['siːzənd], *a.* **1.** (*of dish*) assaisonné; **highly s. dish,** plat relevé, épicé; *O:* **highly s. anecdote,** anecdote relevée, épicée. **2.** (*a*) (*of wood, cigar, etc.*) sec, *f.* sèche; (*of wine*) mûr, fait; **well s. timber,** bois bien sec; (*b*) (*of pers.*) acclimaté, endurci; (soldat) aguerri; (matelot) amariné.

seasoning ['siːzəniŋ], *s.* **1.** (*a*) *Cu:* assaisonnement *m*, apprêt *m* (d'un mets); (*b*) dessiccation *f*, dessèchement *m*, séchage *m* (du bois, etc.); abreuvage *m*, avinage *m* (d'un tonneau); maturation *f* (du vin, etc.); **kiln s.,** étuvage *m* (du bois); (*c*) acclimatement *m*, endurcissement *m* (de qn); aguerrissement *m* (des troupes, etc.); amarinage *m* (d'un matelot); (*d*) modération *f* (de la justice, etc.). **2.** *Cu:* assaisonnement, condiment *m*.

seat[1] [siːt], *s.* **1.** (*a*) siège *m*; banc *m*; chaise *f*; banquette *f* (d'autobus, de train, etc.); gradin *m* (d'amphithéâtre); selle *f* (de bicyclette); lunette *f* (de W.C.); **adjustable s.,** siège réglable; *Av:* **ejection, ejector, s.,** *F:* **hot s.,** siège éjectable; *U.S: F:* **the hot s.,** la chaise électrique; **to be in the hot s.,** être dans une situation embarrassante; être sur la sellette; *Aut: etc:* **front s., back s.,** siège avant, arrière; **folding s.,** siège pliant; *Aut: Th: etc:* **flap s., bracket s., folding s.,** strapontin *m*; **(caulker's) s.,** selle, sellette *f*; (*b*) **to take a s.,** s'asseoir; **to keep one's s.,** rester assis; (*c*) *Trans: Th: etc:* place *f*; **keep a s. for me,** gardez une place pour moi; **I can't find a s.,** je ne trouve pas de place assise; **to book a s.,** retenir, réserver, une place; **to take one's s.,** prendre place; *Rail:* **take your seats!** en voiture! (*d*) *Parl: etc:* siège; **to have a s. in the House,** être député; **to have a s. on the Council,** être conseiller (municipal); **to lose one's s.,** ne pas être réélu. **2.** (*a*) siège, fond *m* (d'une chaise); **upholstered s.,** coussin *m*; (*b*) *F:* (*of pers.*) derrière *m*; fesses *fpl*; **he came down (heavily) on his s.,** il est tombé sur le derrière; (*c*) fond *m* (de pantalon); **to wear out the s. of one's trousers,** user le fond de son pantalon. **3.** (*a*) théâtre *m* (de la guerre, etc.); siège, centre *m* (du gouvernement, d'une industrie); chef-lieu *m* (judiciaire); centre (intellectuel); foyer *m* (de science, d'une maladie, etc.); *Med:* **the s. of the trouble,** le siège du mal; (*b*) **country s., s. in the country,** château *m*; manoir *m*. **4.** *Equit:* assiette *f*; **to have a good s.,** avoir de l'assiette, de la tenue; bien se tenir en selle, à cheval; **to have a poor s.,** ne pas avoir de tenue; se tenir mal (à cheval); **to keep one's s.,** conserver l'assiette; **to lose one's s.,** être désarçonné. **5.** *Tchn:* siège (d'une soupape); chaise (d'un coussinet); embase *f*, assiette, surface *f* d'appui, surface de contact (d'une machine, etc.); alvéole *m or f* (d'un diamant); **s. of a slide valve,** glace *f* d'un tiroir; *I.C.E:* **cylinder s.,** selle, assiette (de cylindre); **needle-valve s.,** siège du pointeau (du carburateur).

seat[2], *v.* **1.** *v.tr.* (faire) asseoir (un enfant, etc.); asseoir, établir (un roi sur le trône, etc.); **I found him seated on the table,** je l'ai trouvé assis sur la table. **2.** *v.tr.* (*a*) placer (qn); trouver place pour (qn); **to s. the guests,** disposer, placer, les invités; **as soon as everyone is seated,** dès que tout le monde aura trouvé sa place; (*b*) **bus to s. thirty,** autobus à trente places (assises); **hall that can s. five hundred (people),** salle où peuvent s'asseoir cinq cents personnes; **this table seats twelve,** on tient douze à cette table. **3.** *v.tr.* (*a*) (re)mettre le siège à (une chaise); recanner, rempailler, rembourrer à nouveau (une chaise); (*b*) remettre un fond à (une culotte). **4.** *v.tr.* fournir (une salle, etc.) de chaises; *Nau:* banquer (une embarcation); **hall seated to hold a thousand,** salle avec places assises pour mille personnes; **part of the cathedral is seated with pews,** une partie de la cathédrale est garnie de bancs. **5.** *v.tr.* (*a*) asseoir, poser (une machine, etc.); *Mec.E: etc:* faire reposer, faire porter, caler, (une pièce) sur son siège; *El:* **to s. the brushes,** ajuster, caler, les balais; *I.C.E:* **to s. a valve,** assurer, ajuster, l'assise d'une soupape; (*b*) (*with passive force*) (*of part*) **to s. on . . .,** porter, reposer, sur . . .; **this valve seats badly,** cette soupape ne porte pas, ne repose pas, ne bute pas, exactement sur son siège. **6.** *v.tr.* **the trouble, the pain, is seated in . . .,** le mal, la douleur, a son siège dans . . .. **7.** *v.i.* (*of skirt, etc.*) faire des poches.

seatbelt ['siːtbelt], *s. Aut: Av:* ceinture *f* (de sécurité); *Aut:* **inertia reel s.,** ceinture à enrouleur (automatique); **rear s.,** ceinture à l'arrière; **fasten your seatbelts,** attachez vos ceintures.

seated ['siːtid], *a.* **1.** assis. **2.** (*with adv. prefixed*) **deep (-)s.,** profond; enraciné; fermement établi; (*of conviction*) intime; (*of trousers*) **double s.,** à double fond.

seater ['siːtər], *s.* (*with num. a. prefixed*) *Aut:* **two s., four s.,** voiture à deux, à quatre, places; *Av:* **single s., two s., three s., four s.,** monoplace *m*, biplace *m*, triplace *m*, quadriplace *m*.

seating ['siːtiŋ], *s.* **1.** (*a*) allocation *f* des sièges, des places; **the s. of the guests was a delicate matter,** la disposition des invités était une affaire délicate; (*b*) places assises (**for a hundred people,** pour cent personnes); bancs *mpl* et sièges *mpl* (dans une église, une salle, etc.); **additional s.,** chaises *f*, sièges, supplémentaires; **s. accommodation, capacity,** nombre *m* de places (assises) (dans une église, etc.). **2.** matériaux *mpl* pour sièges de chaises. **3.** *Tchn:* portage *m*; ber *m*, berceau *m* (de chaudière); siège (de soupape); embase *f*, lit *m* de pose, piètement *m* (d'une machine); assiette *f*, logement *m*, point *m* d'attache (d'un organe de machine); alvéole *m or f* (d'un diamant, *Artil:* d'une ailette d'obus); *I.C.E:* **needle-valve s.,** siège du pointeau (du carburateur); *N.Arch:* **engine s.,** carlingage *m*. **4.** montage *m*, ajustage *m* (d'une pièce, d'une soupape, etc.).

seawall ['siːwɔːl], *s.* digue *f*; endiguement *m*, chaussée *f*.

seaward ['siːwəd]. **1.** *adv.* (*also* **seawards**) vers la mer, le large; du côté du large. **2.** *a.* (*of tide, etc.*) qui se dirige vers le large; qui porte au large; **s. breeze,** brise *f* du large. **3.** *s.* **to s.,** du côté du large; vers le large.

seawater ['siːwɔːtər], *s.* eau *f* de mer.

seaway ['siːwei], *s. Nau:* **1.** route *f*, sillage *m* (d'un navire). **2.** mer dure; levée *f* (de la mer); **ship that behaves well in a s.,** navire qui tient bien la mer. **3. the St. Lawrence S.,** la voie maritime du Saint-Laurent.

seaweed ['siːwiːd], *s.* (*a*) *Bot:* algue *f*, goémon *m*; (*b*) *Agr:* varech *m*.

seawife, *pl.* **-wives** ['siːwaif, -waivz], *s. Ich:* vieille *f*.

seaworthiness ['siːwəːðinis], *s.* bon état de navigabilité; valeur *f* nautique, aptitude *f* à tenir la mer (d'un navire).

seaworthy ['siːwəːði], *a.* (*of ship*) en (bon) état de navigabilité; qui tient la mer.

sebaceous [si'beiʃəs], *a.* (*of gland, etc.*) sébacé; **s. cyst,** kyste sébacé.

sebacic [si'bæsik], *a. Ch:* sébacique.

Sebastian [si'bæstiən], *Pr.n.m.* Sébastien.

sebesten [si'bestən], *s.* (*a*) **s. (plum),** sébeste *m*; (*b*) **s. (tree),** sébestier *m*.

sebiferous, sebific [se'bifərəs, -'bifik], *a. Anat: Bot:* sébifère.

sebk(h)a ['sebkə], *s. Geog:* sebk(h)a *f*, sebkra *f*.

seborrh(o)ea [sebou'riə], *s. Med:* séborrhée *f*.

seborrh(o)eic [sebou'riːik], *a. Med:* séborrhéique.

sebum ['siːbəm], *s. Physiol:* sébum *m*.

sec[1] [sek], *s. F:* **half a s.! just a s.!** un instant! un moment! une seconde!

sec[2], *s. Mth:* sécante *f*.

sec[3], *a. F:* secondaire; *Sch: O:* **sec. mod.** = collège *m* d'enseignement secondaire.

secale [se'keili], *s. Bot:* sécale *m*.

secam ['sekæm], *s. T.V:* secam *m*.

secant ['sekənt, 'siː-]. *Mth:* **1.** *a.* (*of line, surface*) sécant. **2.** *s.* sécante *f* (d'un arc, d'un angle).

secateurs ['sekətə(ː)z, sekə'tiːəz], *s.pl. Tls: Hort:* sécateur *m*.

secede [si'siːd], *v.i.* faire scission, faire sécession (**from,** de); **to s. from a party,** se séparer d'un parti.

seceder [si'siːdər], *s. Pol: etc:* séparatiste *mf*; sécessionniste *mf*; scissionnaire *mf*; *Rel:* dissident, -ente.

seceding [si'siːdiŋ], *a.* sécessionniste, scissionnaire; dissident.

secession [si'seʃ(ə)n], *s.* sécession *f*; scission *f*; *Rel:* dissidence *f*; **the s. of the Church of England,** la scission de l'Église d'Angleterre; *U.S: Hist:* **the War of S.,** la Guerre de Sécession.

secessionism [si'seʃənizm], *s.* sécessionnisme *m*.

secessionist [si'seʃənist], *a. & s.* (*a*) scissionniste (*mf*); (*b*) *U.S: Hist:* sécessionniste (*mf*).

seclude [si'kluːd], *v.tr.* **1.** tenir (qn, qch.) retiré, éloigné, écarté (**from,** de); **to s. oneself,** se reclure; se retirer du monde; vivre dans la solitude, dans l'isolement; **to s. sth. from public view,** dérober qch. à la curiosité du public. **2.** interner (des pigeons voyageurs).

secluded [si'kluːdid], *a.* (endroit) écarté, retiré; **s. life,** vie retirée, cloîtrée, solitaire; **to live a s. life, to live s.,** se reclure; se retirer du monde; vivre dans la solitude.

seclusion [si'kluːʒ(ə)n], *s.* **1.** solitude *f*, retraite *f*, isolement *m*; **in s.,** retiré du monde; **to live in s.,** vivre retiré; vivre dans la retraite, dans l'isolement. **2.** internement *m* (de pigeons voyageurs).

second[1] ['sekənd], *s.* **1.** (*a*) seconde *f* (de temps); *Clockm:* **second(s) hand,** aiguille *f* de secondes, aiguille trotteuse; **centre second(s) hand,** grande aiguille trotteuse; **split seconds hand,** trotteuse *f* double (de chronomètre compteur); **timed to a split s.,** chronométré à une fraction de seconde près; **in a split s.,** en moins d'une seconde; en un rien de temps; **we'll be there in twenty minutes to the s.,** nous y serons dans vingt minutes montre en main; **punctual to a s.,** ponctuel à la seconde; **wait a s.!** attendez une seconde, un instant! **I'll be back in a s.,** je reviens dans un moment, dans un instant. **2.** *Mth: Astr:* seconde (de degré).

second[2], *a. & s.*

I. *a.* **1.** second; deuxième; (*a*) **the s. (day) of the month,** le deuxième (jour) du mois; **the s. of March,** le deux mars; **twenty-s., thirty-s.,** vingt-deuxième, trente-deuxième; **ninety-s.,** quatre-vingt-douzième; **to live on the s. floor,** habiter (i) au deuxième, au second, étage, (ii) *NAm:* au premier; **Charles the S.,** Charles Deux; **in the s. place,** deuxièmement, en second lieu; **every s. day,** tous les deux jours; **s. marriage,** secondes noces; **to marry for the s. time,** se marier en secondes noces; (*at meal*) **to take a s. helping,** reprendre; **to get one's s. wind,** (i) reprendre haleine; (ii) se remettre; reprendre ses activités; **production slackened, then got its s. wind,** la production, après avoir ralenti, a repris l'essor; *Sch:* **s. form** = classe de cinquième; *Aut:* **s. gear,** deuxième vitesse *f*; *s.* **to start in s.,** démarrer en deuxième; *Gram:* **s. person,** seconde, deuxième, personne; **s. conjugation,** seconde, deuxième, conjugaison; (*b*) **the s. city in Europe,** la deuxième ville de l'Europe; **the s. largest city in the world,** la deuxième ville du monde (en importance); la plus grande ville du monde sauf une; **to be s. to s.o. (in seniority, etc.),** venir après qn; **to take s. place,** passer second; **he is s. to none in intelligence,** pour l'intelligence il ne le cède à personne; **we are in a position s. to none,** nul n'est mieux placé que nous; **to be s. in command,** commander en second; *Mus:* **the s. violins,** les seconds violons; *Sp:* **the s. team,** la deuxième équipe; (*c*) **s. best,** deuxième; **my s.-best umbrella,** mon deuxième parapluie, mon parapluie de tous les jours; *s.* **it's only a s. best,** ce n'est qu'un pis-aller; **to come off s. best,** être battu; passer second; céder à qn; **s. class,** de seconde classe; de second ordre; *Rail:* **to travel s. class,** voyager en deuxième, en seconde; *Post:* **s.-class mail** = tarif normal; *F:* **s.-class citizen,** citoyen, -enne, de seconde zone; **s. rate,** médiocre, inférieur; de qualité inférieure; **s.-rate artist,** artiste de second ordre; **he's a s.-rater,** c'est une médiocrité. **2.** second; autre; nouveau; **a s. Attila,** un nouvel, un second, Attila; **s. nature,** seconde nature; **s. childhood,** deuxième enfance; **s. sight,** clairvoyance *f*, seconde vue; *O:* **at s. hand,** de deuxième main; d'occasion.

II. *s.* **1.** (le) second, (la) seconde; (le, la) deuxième; **you're the s. to ask me that,** vous êtes la deuxième personne à me demander cela; *Sp: etc:* **to come in a good s.,** arriver bon second; **s. in command,** (i) *Mil:* commandant *m* en second; (ii) *Nau:* commandant, officier *m*, en second; le second; *Sch:* **to get a s.** = être reçu à la licence avec mention assez bien; *F:* (*at meal*) **anyone for seconds?** qui est-ce qui va reprendre? **2.** *Mus:* (*a*) **major, minor, s.,** seconde majeure, mineure; (*b*) (*in concerted music*) deuxième partie *f*. **3. seconds,** (i) *Com:* articles *m* de deuxième qualité; (ii) *Mill:* griot *m*. **4.** (*a*) (*in duel*) témoin *m*; (*b*) *Box:* second; soigneur *m*.

second[3], *v.tr.* **1.** ['sekənd]. (*a*) seconder (qn); appuyer, soutenir (des troupes, etc.); **to be seconded by s.o.,** être secondé de, par, qn; (*b*) (*in debate, etc.*) **to s. a motion,** appuyer une proposition. **2.** [si'kɔnd] mettre (un officier) en disponibilité, hors cadre (pour fonctions spéciales, civiles, etc.); (*esp. in passive*) **to be seconded,** être mis hors cadre; **seconded personnel,** personnel détaché, en détachement; **to be seconded for service with . . .,** être mis à la disposition de . . .; être détaché auprès de . . .; **seconded from the regular army,** prélevé sur, détaché de, l'armée régulière.

secondary ['sekənd(ə)ri], *a. & s.*

I. *a.* **1.** secondaire; (*of evidence*) indirect; **s. meaning of a word,** sens dérivé d'un mot; *Gr.Gram:* **s. tenses,** temps seconds; *Sch:* **s. education,** enseignement *m* secondaire, du second degré; *Astr:* **s. planet,** *s.* **s.,** planète *f* secondaire; satellite *m*; *Opt:* **s. image,** image *f* secondaire; *El:* **s. battery,** pile *f* secondaire; batterie *f* d'accumulateurs; **s. current,** courant induit; courant secondaire; **s. cell,** élément *m* d'accumulateur; **s. wiring,** *s.* **s.,** (enroulement *m*) secondaire *m* (d'un transformateur); *Geol:* **s. era,** ère *f* secondaire; *Phil:*

Theol: **s. causes,** causes secondes. **2.** (rôle, etc.) peu important, accessoire; **a very s. matter,** une question de très peu d'importance; **of s. importance,** d'importance secondaire; **s. road** = route secondaire, départementale; *Ling:* **s. stress,** accent *m* secondaire. **II.** *s.* **1.** *Ecc:* membre *m* secondaire du chapitre. **2.** *Orn:* rémige *f* secondaire. **3.** *Ent:* aile antérieure. **4.** *Geol:* ère *f* secondaire. **5.** *Med:* **secondaries,** accidents *m* secondaires (de la syphilis).

seconde [sə'gɔnd], *s. Fenc:* seconde *f.*

seconder ['sekəndər], *s.* (*a*) **to be the s. of a proposal,** appuyer une proposition; (*b*) **proposer and s. of a candidate,** parrain *m* et deuxième parrain d'un candidat.

secondhand [sekənd'hænd]. **1.** *adv.* de seconde main; d'occasion; **to hear news s.,** recevoir des nouvelles de seconde main, d'un tiers. **2.** *a.* (nouvelle, etc.) de seconde main; (marchandises) d'occasion, de revente; **s. car,** voiture usagée, d'occasion; **s. copy,** exemplaire *m* d'occasion; **s. dealer,** revendeur, -euse; (*in books*) bouquiniste *m*; **s. bookshop,** librairie *f* d'occasion; **s. clothes shop,** friperie *f*; **s. market,** marché *m* de revente.

secondly ['sekəndli], *adv.* deuxièmement; en second, en deuxième, lieu; secundo.

secondment [si'kɔndmənt], *s.* détachement *m.*

secrecy ['si:krisi], *s.* **1.** discrétion *f*; **to rely on s.o.'s s.,** compter sur la discrétion de qn; **under pledge of s.,** sous le secret; **to bind s.o. to s.,** faire jurer le silence à qn. **2. in s.,** en secret; **there's no s. about it,** on n'en fait pas mystère *m*; *Jur:* **s. of correspondence,** secret des lettres.

secret ['si:krit]. **1.** *a.* (*a*) secret, -ète; caché; **to keep sth. s.,** tenir, garder, qch. secret; garder le secret au sujet de qch.; cacher, celer, taire, qch.; **the news must be kept s.,** cette nouvelle doit rester secrète; **to be in s. communication with the enemy,** pratiquer des intelligences avec l'ennemi; **s. meeting, s. assembly,** conciliabule *m*; **s. agent,** (i) agent secret; (ii) affidé(e); *F:* **the s. service,** les agents secrets du gouvernement; espionnage *m* et contre-espionnage *m*; **s. service funds,** les fonds secrets; **s. partner,** (associé *m*) commanditaire *m*; bailleur *m* de fonds; **s. door,** porte cachée, dérobée; **s. spring,** ressort secret, caché; **desk with a s. compartment,** bureau *m* à secret; *Lit:* **the s. places of the heart,** les plis *m* et les replis *m* du cœur; (*b*) *O:* (*of pers.*) discret; peu communicatif; **s. as the grave,** muet comme la tombe; (*c*) (*of place*) secret, caché, retiré. **2.** *s.* (*a*) secret *m*; **to keep, betray, tell, a s.,** garder, trahir, révéler, un secret; **he can't keep a s.,** il ne peut pas garder le secret; **to tell each other secrets,** se faire des confidences; **we have no secrets from each other,** nous n'avons aucun secret l'un pour l'autre; **I make no s. of it,** je n'en fais pas mystère; je ne m'en cache pas; **to entrust s.o. with a s.,** confier un secret à qn; faire une confidence à qn; **to let s.o. into the s.,** mettre qn dans le secret, dans le complot; **to be in the s.,** être dans le secret; être du secret; **an open s.,** le secret de tout le monde; le secret de Polichinelle; **as a great s.,** (dire qch.) en confidence, en grand secret; **the s. of his success,** le secret de son succès; **the secrets of nature,** les mystères *m* de la nature; (*b*) **in s.,** en secret; (*c*) *R.C.Ch:* secrète (prononcée tout bas avant la préface).

secretaire [sekri'tεər], *s. Furn:* secrétaire *m.*

secretarial [sekri'tεəriəl], *a.* (travail, etc.) de secrétaire; **to do a s. course,** suivre un cours de dactylographie.

secretariat [sekri'tεəriət], *s.* secrétariat *m.*

secretary ['sekrit(ə)ri], *s.* **1.** (*a*) secrétaire *mf*; **private s.,** secrétaire particulier, -ière; **his s. is Miss Martin,** sa secrétaire est Mlle Martin; **honorary s.,** secrétaire honoraire; **Minister's principal private s.** = chef *m* de cabinet; **company s., executive s.,** secrétaire de direction; **doctor's, dentist's, s.,** secrétaire médicale; (*b*) **S. of State,** ministre *m* (à portefeuille), secrétaire d'État; **Foreign S.,** *U.S:* **S. of State** = ministre des Affaires étrangères; **S. General (to the United Nations),** secrétaire général (des Nations Unies); (*c*) *Dipl:* **(1st, 2nd, 3rd) s.,** = secrétaire d'ambassade. **2.** *Typ:* cursive *f.* **3.** *Orn:* **s. (bird),** serpentaire *m*, secrétaire *m.*

secretaryship ['sekrit(ə)riʃip], *s.* (*a*) secrétariat *m*; fonction *f* de secrétaire; (*b*) **during his Foreign S.,** pendant qu'il était ministre des Affaires étrangères.

secrete[1] [si'kri:t], *v.tr. Physiol:* (*of gland, etc.*) sécréter.

secrete[2], *v.tr.* soustraire (qch.) à la vue; cacher (qn, qch.); *Jur:* receler (des objets volés).

secretin [si'kri:tin], *s. Physiol:* sécrétine *f.*

secretion[1] [si'kri:ʃ(ə)n], *s. Physiol:* sécrétion *f.*

secretion[2], *s. Jur:* recel *m*, recèlement *m* (d'objets volés).

secretive[1] ['si:krətiv, si'kri:tiv], *a.* (*of pers.*) réservé, dissimulé.

secretive[1] [si'kri:tiv], *a. Physiol:* = SECRETORY 1.

secretiveness [si'kri:tivnis], *s.* (*of pers.*) réserve *f.*

secretly ['si:kritli], *adv.* secrètement, clandestinement; en secret; en cachette; à la dérobée; à porte close; sous cape.

secretory [si'kri:təri]. *Physiol:* **1.** *a.* (*of duct, etc.*) sécréteur, -euse, -trice; (phénomène *m*) sécrétoire. **2.** *s.* organe sécréteur.

sect [sekt], *s.* secte *f.*

sectarian [sek'tεəriən]. **1.** *a.* (esprit, culte) sectaire; **s. bias,** parti pris confessionnel; **s. quarrels,** querelles partisanes. **2.** *s.* sectaire *mf.*

sectarianism [sek'tεəriənizm], *s.* sectarisme *m*; esprit *m* sectaire.

sectile ['sektail], *a.* sécable.

section[1] ['sekʃ(ə)n], *s.* **1.** sectionnement *m*, section *f*, coupage *m*, division *f* (de qch.); *Surg:* **s. of a nerve,** section d'un nerf. **2.** (*a*) tranche *f*, lamelle *f*; **thin s.,** mince lame *f*, lamelle; **microscopic s.,** mince lame, plaque *f*, lamelle (d'une substance pour examen au microscope); (*in lottery, etc.*) **first, second, s.,** première, deuxième, tranche; (*b*) *Mth:* section; **conic sections,** sections coniques; **plane s.,** section plane; **square s.,** section carrée; (*c*) *Arch: Const: etc:* coupe *f*, profil *m*, section; **s. drawing,** dessin *m* en coupe; **shown in s.,** représente en coupe; **horizontal s.,** coupe, section, horizontale; **longitudinal s.,** coupe, section, longitudinale; profil longitudinal; **standard s.,** profil normal; **oblique s.,** coupe, section, oblique; **traverse s.,** coupe, profil, en travers; section transversale; **half s.,** demi-coupe *f*, *pl.* demi-coupes; **vertical s.,** (i) *Draw:* coupe, section, verticale; profil vertical; (ii) *Arch:* sciographie *f*; **drawing in vertical s.,** dessin sciographique, en coupe verticale; *N.Arch:* **inner s.,** section sur membrure; **outer s.,** section hors bordé; **midship s.,** coupe au maître; (*d*) *Metalw: Civ.E: etc:* profilé *m* (en métal); **iron, steel, sections,** profilés en fer, en acier; **horseshoe s.,** fer cavalier; **T s.,** fer à, en, T; **U s., channel s.,** profilé, section, en U; *Aut:* **rolled s. chassis,** châssis *m* en métal profilé; **s. mill,** laminoir *m* à profilés; *Av:* **aerofoil s.,** profil aérodynamique; **airfoil s., wing s.,** profil d'aile, section de l'aile; **maximum cross s.,** maître-couple *m*, *pl.* maîtres-couples; *Aedcs:* **laminar flow s.,** profil laminaire. **3.** (*a*) section, portion *f* (de qch.); partie *f*, division *f* (d'une structure, etc.); tronçon *m* (de tube, de voie ferrée, etc.); section, tronçon (de circuit, de ligne, électrique, etc.); compartiment *m* (d'un tiroir, etc.); *Com:* rayon *m* (d'un magasin); *Rail: U.S:* compartiment (d'un wagon-lit); *esp. U.S:* **business s. (of a town),** quartier commercial (d'une ville); *Cmptr:* **input, output, s.,** zone *f* d'entrée, de sortie (des données); **sections of an orange,** loges *f*, tranches, d'une orange; *Rail:* **block s.,** section de block; **blocked, clear, s.,** section bloquée, débloquée; **s. crew, gang,** équipe *f* d'entretien (des voies d'une section); **s. foreman,** chef *m* de section; **s. hand,** agent *m* de la voie; *Av:* **nose s.,** section avant, nez *m* (de l'appareil); **wing s.,** élément *m* d'aile (pour le montage de la voilure); (*of wing*) **centre s.,** plan central; **inner, outer, s.,** aile médiane, extrême; **wing-tip s.,** saumon *m* d'aile; (*b*) élément (constitutif, préfabriqué); **bookcase (built) in sections,** bibliothèque formée d'éléments; **greenhouse sold in sections,** serre vendue en éléments préfabriqués; (*c*) *Bookb:* cahier *m*; (*d*) *Ap:* cadre *m* (dans une ruche); (*e*) (i) *Hist:* (*esp. U.S: Austr:*) concession *f* (de terrains); (ii) *U.S:* lotissement *m* (d'un mille carré); (*f*) division *f* (d'un document, etc.); article *m* (d'une loi, etc.); *Typ:* section, paragraphe *m*, alinéa *m*; **s. mark** (§), paragraphe; **s. four of the act,** l'article quatre de la loi; (*g*) *Journ:* rubrique *f*; **sports s.,** rubrique sport; (*h*) *St.Exch:* rubrique, compartiment; **s. of the list,** rubrique de la cote; **mining, oil, s.,** compartiment minier, pétrolier; (*i*) *Mus:* (*in orchestra*) groupe *m* (de cuivres, etc.); (*j*) **all sections of the population,** toutes les couches de la population, toutes les catégories sociales; **members are divided into sections according to their interests,** les membres sont groupés selon leurs intérêts; (*k*) *Mil:* (i) section (d'un état-major, d'un service); **personnel s.,** section du personnel; **supply and evacuation s.,** section ravitaillements et évacuations; *Artil:* **range s.,** personnel d'observation; (ii) (*fighting unit*) groupe de combat (d'une section d'infanterie); équipe *f* (de fusiliers, de grenadiers); escouade *f*; *A.Artil:* section (d'une batterie); *U.S:* section (d'une compagnie d'artillerie, etc.); **armoured-car s.,** groupe d'automitrailleuses; **antitank s.,** groupe d'engins antichars; **machine-gun s.,** groupe de mitrailleuses; **rifle s.,** groupe, équipe, de fusiliers voltigeurs; **s. commander, leader,** chef de groupe, d'équipe, *U.S:* chef de section.

section[2], *v.tr.* couper, diviser (qch.) en sections; diviser (une région) par sections; sectionner (un pays, etc.).

sectional ['sekʃən(ə)l], *a.* **1.** appartenant à une classe, à un parti; **s. jealousies,** jalousies *f* de classe, de parti. **2.** (dessin, etc.) en coupe, en profil; **s. area, surface,** surface *f* de section; **s. iron,** fers profilés; profilés *mpl* en fer. **3.** (*a*) sectionnel; en sections; **s. bookcase,** bibliothèque démontable, par éléments, formée d'éléments; **s. boiler,** chaudière sectionnelle, à petits éléments; (*b*) *O:* (papier) quadrillé.

sectionalism ['sekʃənəlizm], *s. U.S:* régionalisme *m*; esprit *m* de clocher.

sectionalize ['sekʃənəlaiz], *v.tr.* sectionner (une région, etc.).

sectionalizing ['sekʃənəlaiziŋ], *s.* sectionnement *m.*

sectionally ['sekʃən(ə)li], *adv.* par sections; par éléments.

sector ['sektər], *s.* **1.** (*a*) *Mth: Astr:* secteur *m*; **s. of a circle,** secteur circulaire; **spherical s.,** secteur sphérique; (*b*) *Mil: Adm:* secteur; *Adm:* **public, private, s.,** secteur public, privé; **provided by the public s.,** dont les autorités publiques se chargent; **to cut public s. housing,** réduire la construction de nouvelles H.L.M.; **the public s. borrowing requirement for next year is likely to be in the region of** x **million,** l'augmentation de la dette publique pendant l'année prochaine pourra bien être de l'ordre de x millions; *Mil:* **s. of defence,** secteur de défense; *Rad:* **surveillance s.,** secteur de surveillance. **2.** (*a*) *Mec.E:* secteur, couronne *f*; **toothed s., s. gear,** secteur denté, couronne dentée; **tooth, notch, of a s.,** cran *m* d'un secteur; **s. and gate,** secteur à grille; *Artil:* **elevation s.,** secteur de pointage en hauteur; **threaded s. (of breech block),** secteur fileté (de culasse); (*b*) *Cin:* secteur (de l'obturateur). **3.** *Mth:* compas *m* de proportion.

sectorial [sek'tɔ:riəl], *a.* sectoriel.

secular ['sekjulər], *a.* **1.** (*a*) *Ecc:* **s. priest, s. s.,** (prêtre) séculier *m*; (*b*) (*of history, art, etc.*) séculier, laïque, civil; (enseignement *m*) laïque; **s. life,** vie séculière, mondaine; **s. music,** musique *f* profane; **the s. arm,** le bras séculier; la justice temporelle. **2.** (*a*) (fête *f*, etc.) séculaire; *Rom.Ant:* **s. games,** jeux *m* séculaires; **s. hymn,** chant *m* séculaire; *Myth:* **the s. bird,** le phénix; (*b*) (*of tree, etc.*) séculaire; très ancien; (*of custom, etc.*) de longue date, séculaire; (*c*) *Astr:* **s. variation,** variation *f* séculaire; *Pol.Ec:* **s. trend of prices,** mouvement *m* (i) séculaire, (ii) périodique, des prix; (*d*) *Lit:* **s. fame,** renommée *f* durable.

secularism ['sekjulərizm], *s.* **1.** *Phil:* sécularisme *m*; matérialisme *m.* **2.** laïcisme *m*; politique *f* en faveur de la laïcité des écoles.

secularist ['sekjulərist]. **1.** *a.* (philosophe, philosophie) matérialiste. **2.** *s.* partisan, -ane (i) du sécularisme, du matérialisme; (ii) de la laïcité des écoles.

secularity [sekju'læriti], *s.* **1.** sécularité *f* (du clergé); laïcité *f* (de l'enseignement). **2.** *Astr: etc:* caractère *m* séculaire (d'une variation, etc.).

secularization [sekjulərai'zeiʃ(ə)n], *s.* sécularisation *f* (de biens ecclésiastiques, etc.); désaffectation *f* (d'une église); laïcisation *f* (d'une école, etc.).

secularize ['sekjuləraiz], *v.tr.* séculariser (un domaine, etc.); laïciser (une école, etc.); **secularized church,** église désaffectée.

secund [si'kʌnd], *a. Bot:* second; unilatéral, -aux.

secundine ['sekəndi:n, -ain], *s.* **1.** *Obst:* **secundines,** secondines *f*; arrière-faix *m inv.* **2.** *Bot:* secondine.

secundiparous [sekən'dipərəs], *a.* secondipare.

secundly [si'kʌndli], *adv. Bot:* unilatéralement; dans une disposition seconde.

secundus [se'kʌndəs], *a. Sch: O:* **Long s.,** Long cadet.

securable [si'kjuərəbl], *a.* (*a*) procurable, trouvable; (propriété, etc.) que l'on peut acquérir; (*b*) que l'on peut garantir; (*c*) que l'on peut (i) immobiliser; (ii) bien fermer.

secure[1] [si'kjuər], *a.* **1.** (*a*) (*free from anxiety*) sûr; **s. future,** avenir assuré; **s. investment,** placement sûr, de tout repos; (*b*) **to feel s. of victory,** être assuré, certain, de la victoire. **2.** (*a*) (*safe*) en sûreté; à l'abri; sauf; **now we can feel s.,** nous voilà à l'abri, hors de danger; **to make a country s.,** assurer un pays; **a s. retreat,** un asile assuré, sûr; **s. from, against, attack,** à l'abri de toute attaque; protégé contre les attaques; **s. from intrusion,** à l'abri des importuns; (*b*) **the prisoner is s.,** le prisonnier est en lieu sûr. **3.** (*of door, plank, etc.*) fixé, assujetti; (*of foundations*) solide; (*of foothold, grasp*) ferme, sûr; **to make a plank s.,** assujettir une planche; **to make sure that the car door is s.,** s'assurer que la portière est bien fermée; **to make the boat s.,** bien amarrer le canot.

secure[2], *v.tr.* **1.** (*a*) mettre (qn, qch.) en sûreté, à l'abri (du danger); **to s. a crop,** rentrer une récolte; **to s. s.o. from sth.,** garantir qn de qch.; prémunir qn contre qch.; **to s. troops from surprise,** mettre des troupes à l'abri de toute surprise; **to s. oneself against interruptions,** se garantir des dérangements; **to s. a town (with a wall),** fortifier une ville (au moyen d'une muraille); **to s. a pass,** garder un défilé; (*b*) mettre (un prisonnier) en lieu sûr, en lieu de sûreté; (*c*) *Mil:* **to s. arms,** mettre l'arme sous le bras gauche. **2.** (*a*) immobiliser; assurer, assujettir (qch. qui a du jeu); fixer (un volet qui bat, etc.); retenir (qch. à sa place); accorer (un tonneau, etc.); amarrer (un canon); arrimer (une cargaison); **to s. a stop screw,** bloquer une vis d'arrêt; **to secure the door,** verrouiller la porte; *Nau:* **to s. the boats, the anchor, all moveable articles,** saisir les canots, l'ancre, tous les objets mobiles; (*b*) *Surg:* **to s. an artery,** ligaturer une artère. **3.** *Jur: Com:* nantir (un prêteur) (par une hypothèque, d'un titre, etc.); **secured by pledges,** nanti de gages; **to s. a debt by mortgage,** garantir une créance par une hypothèque; hypothéquer une créance; **mortgage secured on property,** hypothèque assise sur des biens, qui frappe des biens. **4.** (*a*) assurer; **to s. a retreat,** s'assurer, se ménager, une retraite; **to s. s.o.'s liberty,** obtenir, assurer, la liberté de qn; (*b*) obtenir, acquérir; se procurer (qch.); **he secured a good seat,** il s'est assuré une bonne place; **to s. nomination as president,** obtenir d'être nommé président; se faire nommer président; **to s. acceptance of sth.,** faire accepter qch.; **to s. one's object,** atteindre son but; **to s. s.o.'s services,** s'assurer de l'aide de qn, des services de qn; **to s. an actor for a part,** engager, retenir, un acteur pour un rôle; (*c*) **to s. sth. for s.o.,** procurer qch. à qn. **5.** *Hort:* **to s. a bud,** épincer les bourgeons situés à côté du bourgeon qu'on veut laisser fleurir.

secured [si'kjuəd], *a.* **1.** (avenir, etc.) sûr, assuré. **2.** *Jur:* (emprunt) garanti, gagé; (créancier) garanti, nanti.

securely [si'kjuəli], *adv.* **1.** (*a*) sûrement; avec sécurité; sans danger; (*b*) avec confiance. **2.** fermement, solidement; **to establish oneself s. in a position,** s'établir solidement dans une position.

securiform [si'kjuərifɔːm], *a. Nat.Hist:* sécuriforme.

security [si'kjuəriti], *s.* **1.** (*a*) sécurité *f*, sûreté *f*; **to do sth. in s.,** faire qch. en toute sécurité; **to live in s.,** vivre en sûreté, en sécurité; **collective s.,** sécurité collective; **s. device,** dispositif *m* de sûreté; *Adm:* **social s.,** sécurité sociale; *Adm: Mil: etc:* **s. clearance,** certificat *m* d'habilitation (à un degré de secret); **clearance of s.o. for s.,** (i) attribution *f* à qn d'un certificat d'habilitation; (ii) procédure *f* en vue de l'attribution à qn d'un certificat d'habilitation; **he's a s. risk,** il constitue un danger, un risque, pour la sécurité; *Mil:* **field s.,** sûreté en campagne; (*b*) confiance *f*; **you may count on him with s.,** vous pouvez compter sur lui en toute confiance; (*c*) **s. of judgment,** certitude *f* de jugement; (*d*) stabilité *f*; solidité *f* (d'une fermeture, etc.); (*e*) *Adm:* organes *m* de renseignements et de sécurité. **2.** (moyen *m* de) sécurité; sauvegarde *f*. **3.** *Com: Jur:* (*a*) caution *f*, cautionnement *m*; gage *m*, garantie *f*; (*collateral*) nantissement *m*; **s. for a debt,** garantie d'une créance; **sufficient s.,** caution bonne et solvable; **additional s.,** nantissement, contre-caution *f*; **to give a s.,** verser une caution; **to give sth. as (a) s.,** donner qch. en gage, en cautionnement; **to pay in a sum as a s.,** verser une provision, des provisions; verser une somme par provision; **to lodge a s.,** effectuer un cautionnement; **to lodge stock as additional s.,** déposer des titres en nantissement; **as s. for the sum,** en couverture de la somme; **to lend money on s.,** prêter de l'argent sur nantissement, sur gage, avec de bonnes sûretés; **to lend money without s.,** prêter de l'argent à découvert; **account opened without s.,** compte ouvert sans garantie; *Jur:* **s. for costs,** (i) (*given by plaintiff*) caution judiciaire; caution judicatum solvi; (ii) (*before appeal*) (frais) préjudiciaux *m*; **personal s.,** garantie mobilière; **offer of s. for an individual,** acte *m* de soumission; (*b*) (*pers.*) donneur, -euse, de caution; caution; garant, -ante; accréditeur *m*; *Jur:* répondant *m*; **to stand, become, security for s.o.,** se porter caution, se porter garant, se porter fort, pour qn; donner une garantie pour qn; **to stand security for a signature, for a debt,** avaliser une signature; assurer une créance; (*c*) *Fin:* **securities,** (i) titres *m*, valeurs *f*, fonds *mpl*; (ii) portefeuille *m* titres; *F:* portefeuille; **government, gilt-edged, public, securities,** fonds d'État; fonds publics, effets publics; **outstanding securities,** titres en circulation, non amortis; **registered securites,** titres nominatifs; **transferable securities,** valeurs mobilières; **securities department,** service *m* des titres (d'une banque); **the s. market,** le marché des valeurs; la Bourse.

sedan[1] [si'dæn], *s.* **1.** *A:* **s. (chair),** chaise *f* à porteurs. **2.** *Aut: NAm:* voiture *f* à conduite intérieure; **four-door s.,** berline *f*.

Sedan[2], *Pr.n. Geog:* Sedan; *Hist:* **S. brought about the fall of the Second Empire,** la bataille et capitulation de Sedan entraîna l'effondrement du Second Empire; *Tex:* **S. cloth,** sedan *m*.

sedate[1] [si'deit], *a.* **1.** (*of pers.*) posé, reposé; (maintien) composé, calme; (esprit) rassis. **2.** *A:* (*of furniture, etc.*) sobre; discret, -ète.

sedate[2], *v.tr. Med:* donner un sédatif à (qn); **he's been sedated,** on lui a fait prendre un sédatif.

sedately [si'deitli], *adv.* posément, calmement; d'une manière composée; **to walk s.,** s'avancer à pas posés.

sedateness [si'deitnis], *s.* manière posée; maintien *m* calme.

sedation [si'deiʃ(ə)n], *s. Med:* sédation *f*.

sedative ['sedətiv], *a.* & *s. Med:* sédatif (*m*); calmant (*m*).

se defendendo ['siːdiːfen'dendou], *Lt.adv.phr. Jur:* en cas de légitime défense.

Sedentaria [seden'tɛəriə], *s.pl. Ann:* sédentaires *f*.

sedentarily ['sedənt(ə)rili], *adv.* sédentairement.

sedentariness ['sedənt(ə)rinis], *s.* vie *f* sédentaire; habitudes *f* sédentaires; sédentarité *f*.

sedentary ['sedənt(ə)ri], *a.* **1.** (*a*) (*of posture*) assis; (*b*) (emploi, etc.) sédentaire; **s. life,** vie *f* sédentaire. **2.** (*a*) (*of troops*) sédentaire; (*b*) *Nat.Hist:* (oiseau, araignée, polychète) sédentaire; (mollusque) privé de locomotion; (*c*) (tribu) sédentaire. **3.** *s.* sédentaire *mf*.

sederunt [se'diərənt], *s. Jur: Scot:* séance *f*; audience *f* (du tribunal).

sedge [sedʒ], *s.* **1.** *Bot:* (*a*) carex *m*; laîche *f*; **sweet s.,** souchet long; souchet odorant; (*b*) joncs *mpl*, roseaux *mpl*. **2. s. (fly),** *Ent:* phrygane *f*; *Fish:* sedge (fly) *m*. **3.** *Orn:* **s. warbler,** phragmite *m* des joncs, rousserolle *f* des phragmites.

sedile, *pl.* **sedilia** [se'daili, -'diliə], *s. Ecc:* siège *m* du clergé (auprès de l'autel).

sediment[1] ['sedimənt], *s.* sédiment *m*, dépôt *m*; boue *f* (d'un accu, d'un encrier, etc.); lie *f* (du vin); *Ch:* résidu *m*; **s. in a boiler,** vidange(s) *f*(*pl*) d'une chaudière; **wine that forms a s.,** vin *m* qui dépose; *Med:* **urinary s.,** sédiment urinaire; boue urinaire; *Geol:* **deposition of s.,** atterrissement *m*, alluvionnement *m*.

sediment[2]. **1.** *v.tr.* déposer (de la boue, etc.). **2.** *v.i.* (*a*) déposer; (*b*) se déposer; se sédimenter.

sedimental [sedi'ment(ə)l], *a.* (dépôt *m*) sédimentaire.

sedimentary [sedi'ment(ə)ri]. *Geol:* **1.** *s.* **stratum,** couche *f* sédimentaire; **s. mantle, cover,** couverture *f*, manteau *m*, sédimentaire; **s. rock,** roche *f* sédimentaire. **2.** *s.* terrain *m* de sédiment.

sedimentate ['sedimenteit], *v.tr.* **to s. sewage,** traiter les eaux d'égout pour les faire déposer.

sedimentation [sedimen'teiʃ(ə)n], *s.* sédimentation *f*.

sedimentological [sedimentə'lɔdʒikl], *a.* sédimentologique.

sedimentologist [sedimen'tɔlədʒist], *s.* sédimentologiste *mf*.

sedimentology [sedimen'tɔlədʒi], *s.* sédimentologie *f*.

sedition [si'diʃ(ə)n], *s.* sédition *f*; **to talk s.,** tenir des propos séditieux.

seditionary [si'diʃən(ə)ri], *a.* & *s.* séditieux, -euse.

seditionist [si'diʃənist], *s.* séditieux, -euse.

seditious [si'diʃəs], *a.* séditieux; **s. assemblies,** attroupements séditieux.

seditiously [si'diʃəsli], *adv.* séditieusement; **to speak s.,** tenir des propos séditieux.

seduce [si'djuːs], *v.tr.* **1.** séduire, corrompre (qn); *Lit:* **to s. s.o. from the path of duty,** détourner qn de son devoir. **2. to s. a woman,** séduire une femme; mettre à mal une femme; abuser d'une femme.

seducer [si'djuːsər], *s.* **1.** séducteur, -trice; corrupteur, -trice. **2.** (*a*) séducteur (d'une femme); (*b*) *F:* tombeur *m*, croqueur *m*, de filles.

seducible [si'djuːsibl], *a.* séductible.

seduction [si'dʌkʃ(ə)n], *s.* **1.** (*a*) séduction *f*, corruption *f* (de qn); **she tried to exert her powers of s. upon her jailers,** elle tenta de séduire ses geôliers; (*b*) séduction (d'une femme). **2.** attrait *m*, charme *m*, séduction (de qch.); allèchement *m* (de la volupté, etc.).

seductive [si'dʌktiv], *a.* **1.** séduisant, attrayant; **s. offer,** offre séduisante, alléchante; **s. smile,** sourire aguichant. **2.** (discours, etc.) suborneur.

seductively [si'dʌktivli], *adv.* d'une manière séduisante, attrayante.

seductiveness [si'dʌktivnis], *s.* caractère séduisant, attrayant (d'une offre, etc.); attraits *mpl*, charmes *mpl* (d'une femme); séduction *f* (du style, du regard).

sedulity [se'djuːliti], *s.* = SEDULOUSNESS.

sedulous ['sedjuləs], *a.* (travailleur, etc.) assidu, appliqué; (soin) assidu; **to pay s.o. s. attention,** faire l'empressé auprès de qn; **to be s. in doing sth.,** être diligent, empressé, à faire qch.; s'empresser à faire qch.

sedulously ['sedjuləsli], *adv.* assidûment; diligemment; avec empressement.

sedulousness ['sedjuləsnis], *s.* assiduité *f*, application *f*; diligence *f*, empressement *m* (**in doing sth.,** à faire qch.).

sedum ['siːdəm], *s. Bot:* orpin *m*.

see[1] [siː], *v.* (**saw** [sɔː]; **seen** [siːn])

I. *v.tr.* **1.** voir; (*a*) **I saw it with my own eyes,** je l'ai vu de mes (propres) yeux; **I saw him again yesterday,** je l'ai revu hier; **the cathedral can be seen from a long way off,** la cathédrale se voit, est visible, de loin; **to s. the sights of the town,** visiter les monuments de la ville; **once you have seen it you will never forget it,** quiconque l'a vu ne saurait l'oublier; *F:* **once seen never forgotten,** c'est d'une laideur, d'un grotesque, inoubliable; **there is nothing to s., to be seen,** il n'y a rien à voir; **there was not a house to be seen,** il n'y avait pas une seule maison de visible; **nothing could be seen of him,** il restait invisible; on ne le voyait nulle part; **to s. s.o. in the distance,** apercevoir qn dans le lointain; **the moment I saw him,** dès que je l'ai aperçu, vu; **I could hardly s. the outline,** c'est à peine si je distinguais les contours; **s. what a mess you've made!** regardez-moi ce fouillis, ce désordre, ce gâchis! **s. page 50,** voir, voyez, page 50; se reporter à la page 50; **s. above,** se reporter plus haut; **s. (on) the back,** voir au verso; **he likes to be seen,** il aime à se faire voir; **I'm not fit to be seen,** je ne suis guère présentable; **she seems to s. everything,** elle semble tout voir; *F:* elle n'a pas les yeux dans sa poche; *F:* **to s. things,** avoir des hallucinations, des visions; (*b*) **those who can s.,** ceux qui voient; **as far as the eye can s.,** aussi loin qu'on peut voir; à perte de vue; **it happened in the street, where everyone could s.,** cela se passait dans la rue, en pleine rue, sous les regards de tout le monde; **it was too dark to s. clearly,** il faisait trop noir pour bien voir; **you can't s. anything here,** on ne voit rien ici; **I can't s. to read here,** je n'y vois pas assez clair pour lire; **cats can s. in the dark,** les chats y voient clair la nuit; (*c*) **to s. s.o. do, doing, sth.,** voir qn faire qch.; **I was sorry to s. them leave their home,** j'étais désolé de les voir quitter leur maison; **I saw him taking, take, the apples,** je l'ai vu prendre les pommes; je l'ai vu qui prenait les pommes; **I saw him fall,** je l'ai vu tomber; **to s. s.o. coming,** voir venir qn; **he was seen walking down the street,** on l'a vu qui descendait la rue; **I can't s. myself undertaking this,** je ne me vois pas dans ce rôle; **I saw it done,** je l'ai vu faire; **a house I should like to s. rebuilt,** une maison que j'aimerais voir reconstruire; *F:* **I'll s. you damned, in hell, first!** *O:* **I'll s. you further first!** va-t-en au diable! va te faire pendre! pour qui me prends-tu? (*d*) **to s. s.o. home,** reconduire qn, accompagner qn, jusque chez lui; **I'll s. you to the door,** je vais vous accompagner jusqu'à la porte; **I saw him to the station,** je l'ai accompagné jusqu'à la gare; **I'll s. you part of the way,** je ferai un bout de chemin avec vous; (*e*) **he has seen a great deal of the world,** (i) il a beaucoup voyagé; (ii) il a une vaste expérience du monde; il connaît bien la vie; **this house has seen many different owners,** cette maison a changé de propriétaire beaucoup de fois; *Mil:* **the first time he saw action,** quand il a reçu le baptême du feu; *F:* **he'll never s. forty again,** il a quarante ans sonnés. **2.** (*a*) comprendre, saisir (une pensée, etc.); reconnaître (ses erreurs, etc.); **they cannot s. the truth,** la vérité leur échappe; **that's easy to s.,** cela se comprend facilement; **I don't s. the point,** je ne saisis pas la nuance; **I quite s. the difficulties,** je n'ignore pas les difficultés; **he can't s. a joke,** il n'entend pas la plaisanterie; **as far as I can s., from what I s.,** à ce que je vois; autant que j'en puis juger; **I s. what you're driving, getting, at,** je vois où vous voulez en venir; **I don't s. the advantage of that,** je n'en vois pas l'avantage; **I don't s. throwing away £100,** je ne vois pas pourquoi je gaspillerais une centaine de livres; **I can't s. that he is to blame,** je ne puis pas admettre que c'est sa faute; **I s.!** je comprends! **(d'you) s.?** vous comprenez? vous y êtes? **you s., it was like this,** voilà ce qui est arrivé, vous comprenez, vous voyez; **you s., I never liked them,** c'est que je ne les ai jamais aimés; (*b*) observer, remarquer (qch.); s'apercevoir de (qch.); **I see that it's time to go,** je vois, j'aperçois, qu'il est temps de partir; **I see that you've changed your mind,** je vois que vous avez changé d'avis; **we could s. that he was blind,** nous pouvions voir qu'il était aveugle; **s. for yourself,**

voyez pour vous-même; **you can s. for yourself!** vous pouvez le constater! **s. what courage can do!** ce que c'est que le courage! **one can s. the real meaning when . . .,** le sens véritable apparaît lorsque . . .; **I can s. no fault in him,** je ne lui connais pas de défaut; **to refuse to s. any good in s.o.,** refuser toute qualité à qn; **if he had the courage I should like to s. in him,** s'il avait le courage que je lui voudrais; **to s. oneself in one's children,** se reconnaître dans ses enfants; **I don't know what you can s. in her,** je ne sais pas pourquoi vous l'admirez; **we have seen how he goes about things,** nous avons remarqué la façon dont il agit; **it remains to be seen whether . . .,** reste à savoir si . . .; **it remains to be seen, wait and s., we shall s.,** qui vivra verra; nous verrons bien; c'est ce que nous verrons; (*c*) voir, juger, apprécier (qch. d'une certaine manière); **to s. everything in an unfavourable light,** voir tout en noir; **to s. things in a wrong light,** juger de travers; **I s. things differently now,** aujourd'hui je vois les choses autrement; **this is how I s. it,** voici comme j'envisage la chose; **if you s. fit to do it,** si vous jugez convenable, bon, à propos, de le faire; **I can't s. my way clear to do it,** je ne vois pas comment m'y prendre pour le faire. **3.** examiner (qch.); regarder (qch.) avec attention; **let me s. that letter again,** repassez-moi cette lettre (pour que je la relise); **let us s. where we are, what we have done,** voyons où nous en sommes; **I'll s. what I can do,** je vais voir ce que je pourrai faire; **s. if, whether, this hat suits you,** voyez si ce chapeau vous va; **is the door locked?—I'll go and s.,** est-ce que la porte est fermée à clef?—je vais y aller voir; je vais m'en assurer; **let's s. (it)!** faites voir! **let me s.!** (i) faites voir! (ii) attendez un moment! *F:* **s. here!** écoutez donc! dites donc! tenez! voyons! **4. to s. (to it) that everything is in order,** s'assurer que tout est en ordre; **you'll s. that he has everything he needs,** vous veillerez à ce qu'il ait tout ce qu'il lui faut, à ce qu'il ne manque de rien; **I shall s. (to it) that he comes,** je me charge de le faire venir; **I shall s. that he comes on time,** je vais m'assurer qu'il arrive à temps; **I had seen to it that everything was provided,** j'avais pourvu à ce que rien ne manquât; je m'étais assuré qu'il y avait tout ce qu'il fallait; **s. that you don't miss the train!** faites attention de ne pas manquer le train! **5.** (*a*) fréquenter, avoir des rapports avec, voir (qn); **he sees a great deal of the Longs,** il fréquente beaucoup les Long; il est souvent chez les Long; **I've seen a great deal of Mr Martin,** j'ai eu de nombreuses occasions de voir M. Martin; j'ai vu M. Martin bien souvent; **we s. less of him in winter,** nous le voyons moins l'hiver; **we don't s. much of each other,** nous ne nous voyons pas souvent; **when shall I s. you again?** quand est-ce que je vais vous revoir? *F:* **s. you soon! (I'll) be seeing you!** à bientôt! **(I'll) s. you Thursday!** à jeudi! (*b*) **to go to, and, s. s.o.,** aller voir qn; faire une visite à qn; **I called but I couldn't s. him,** j'ai passé chez lui mais je n'ai pas pu le voir, mais il n'était pas là; **I couldn't manage to s. the general,** je ne suis pas arrivé jusqu'au général; **I'd like to s. you on business,** je voudrais vous parler d'affaires; **to s. a doctor,** consulter un médecin; (*c*) *F:* **I shall have to s. him,** il faut que je m'approche de lui (pour lui graisser la patte); (*d*) recevoir (un visiteur); **I can't s. him today,** je ne peux pas le recevoir aujourd'hui; **he doesn't s. anybody,** il ne voit, en reçoit, personne.

II. (*compound verbs*) **1. see about,** *v. ind. tr.* s'occuper de, se charger de (qch.); **I'll s. about it,** (i) je m'en occuperai, je m'en charge; (ii) j'y réfléchirai; je verrai; **I'd better s. about (doing) the washing up,** je ferai bien de faire la vaisselle; il me faut bien faire la vaisselle.

2. see in, *v.tr.* faire entrer (qn); **to s. the new year in,** faire le réveillon du nouvel an.

3. see into, *v.ind.tr.* (*a*) **to s. into the future,** voir, pénétrer, dans l'avenir; **to try to s. into s.o.'s mind,** essayer de pénétrer dans l'esprit de qn; (*b*) examiner (une affaire, etc.).

4. see off, *v.tr.* (*a*) **to s. s.o. off at the station, at the airport,** accompagner qn jusqu'à la gare, jusqu'à l'aéroport (pour lui dire au revoir); (*b*) **to s. s.o. off (the premises),** s'assurer du départ de qn; se débarrasser de qn; (*to dog*) **s. him off!** chasse-le! fais-le partir!

5. see out, *v.tr.* (*a*) (i) accompagner (qn) jusqu'à la porte; (ii) s'assurer de la sortie de (qn); (*b*) voir la fin de (qch.); assister à (un spectacle, etc.) jusqu'au bout; mener (une entreprise, etc.) à bonne fin; (*c*) survivre à (qn); **he'll s. us all out!** il nous enterrera tous; **he won't s. the night out,** il ne vivra pas jusqu'au matin; *F:* **this suit will s. me out,** ce complet me durera jusqu'à la fin de ma vie.

6. see over, see round, *v.ind.tr.* visiter, voir (une maison, etc.).

7. see through. (*a*) *v.i.* (i) voir à travers (qch.); *B:* **now we s. through a glass, darkly,** nous voyons présentement confusément et comme dans un miroir; (ii) pénétrer les intentions de (qn); pénétrer, percer à jour (un mystère); **I'm beginning to s. through it,** je commence à y voir clair; (*b*) *v.tr.* assister à (un spectacle, etc.) (jusqu'au bout); mener (une affaire) à bonne fin, jusqu'au bout; **I'll s. it through,** je vais tenir jusqu'au bout.

8. see to, *v.ind.tr.* s'occuper de (qn, qch.); **to s. to the children,** s'occuper, prendre soin, des enfants; **I'll s. to the washing up,** je ferai la vaisselle; **I'll s. to it,** je vais m'en occuper; je m'en charge; **to s. to everything,** avoir l'œil à tout; s'occuper de tout; **it must be seen to,** il faut que quelqu'un s'en charge, s'en occupe.

see[2], *s. Ecc:* siège épiscopal; (*of bishop*) évêché *m*; (*of archbishop*) archevêché *m*; métropole *f*; **the Holy S., the Apostolic S.,** le Saint-Siège; le siège apostolique.

seeable ['si:əbl], *a.* visible.

seed[1] [si:d], *s.* **1.** (*a*) *Bot:* graine *f*, grain *m* , pépin *m* (d'une fruit); **a mustard s.,** un grain de moutarde; **s. leaf, lobe,** cotylédon *m*; feuille germinale; **s. coat,** tégument *m*; **s. vessel,** péricarpe *m*; **s. fern,** fougère *f* à ovules, ptéridospermée *f*; *For:* **s. bearer, s. tree,** (arbre *m*) porte-graine *m inv*; *Orn:* **s. eaters,** granivores *m*; *Ind:* **s. cotton,** coton brut (avant l'égrenage); (*b*) *Agr: Hort:* **seed(s),** semence *f*; graine(s); **to sow, plant, seeds,** faire la semence; semer des graines; **lawn s.,** graine pour gazon; **to keep onions for s.,** réserver des oignons pour la graine; **flowers grown from s.,** fleurs qui proviennent de semis *m*; **this plant can be grown from s. or from cuttings,** on peut cultiver cette plante en semant des graines ou en en faisant des boutures; **to go, run, to s.,** (i) (*of plant*) monter en graine; (ii) (*of land*) s'affricher; (iii) (*of pers.*) se laisser aller; s'avachir; **s. corn,** grain de semence; **s. potatoes,** pommes *f* de terre à semence; **s. bed,** couche *f* de semis; germoir *m*; *For:* semis, pépinière *f*; **s. box, tray, pan,** boîte *f*, terrine *f*, à semis; **s. hole,** poquet *m*; **s. kiln,** four *m* à sécher; sécherie *f*; **s. drill, lip,** semoir *m*; **the s. trade,** la graineterie, la grèneterie; **s. merchant,** grainier, -ière (-fleuriste); grainetier, -ière; grènetier, -ière; **s. merchant's, s. shop,** graineterie *f*, grèneterie *f*; (*c*) *Anat:* (*in joints*) **s. bodies,** grains d'orge; *Med:* **s. lymph,** lymphe *f* d'ensemencement; (*d*) **the seeds of discord,** les semences, les germes *m*, de discorde; **to sow (the) seeds of discord,** semer la discorde; (*e*) frai *m* (d'huître); **s. oysters,** naissain *m*; (*f*) **s. pearls,** semence de perles; **s. diamonds,** semence de diamants; (*g*) *Ten:* tête *f* de série. **2.** (*a*) = SEMEN; (*b*) *B: Lit:* descendance *f*, lignée *f*; **those of his s.,** ceux de sa lignée; **the s. of Abraham,** la semence d'Abraham; **I will raise up thy s. after thee,** je ferai lever ta postérité après toi.

seed[2], **1.** *v.i.* (*of plant*) (*a*) monter en graine; porter semence; (*b*) (*of cereals*) grener; venir à graine; (*c*) s'égrener. **2.** *v.tr.* (*a*) ensemencer, semer (un champ. etc.); (*b*) enlever la graine (d'un fruit); égruger (des raisins, etc.); *Tex:* égrener (le lin); (*c*) *Ten:* **to s. the players,** trier les joueurs (de façon que les plus forts ne se rencontrent pas dès le commencement du tounoi); **seeded players,** têtes *f* de série.

seedcake ['si:dkeik], *s.* gâteau parfumé au carvi.

seed-eater, seed-finch ['si:di:tər, -fin(t)ʃ], *s. Orn:* sporophile *m*.

seeder ['si:dər], *s.* **1.** *Agr:* semoir *m*. **2.** poisson *m* qui fraye.

seediness ['si:dinis], *s. F:* **1.** état râpé, minable, misérable; tenue *f* minable. **2.** état de malaise; manque *m* d'énergie.

seeding ['si:diŋ], *s.* **1.** grenaison *f* (des céréales). **2.** ensemencement *m* (d'un champ, etc.); les semailles *f*; **s. machine,** semoir *m* (mécanique); **s. plough,** charrue-semoir *f*, *pl.* charrues-semoirs. **3.** épépinage *m* (des melons, etc.); égrugeage *m* (des raisins); *Tex:* égrenage *m* (du lin).

seedless ['si:dlis], *a.* (*a*) *Bot:* asperme; (*b*) (fruit) sans pépins.

seedling ['si:dliŋ], *s. Hort:* (jeune) plant *m*; élève *f*; *Arb:* jeune brin *m*; sauvageon *m*; **self-sown seedlings,** semis naturel; **s. plants,** plants non repiqués; **s. forest,** futaie *f*.

seedsman, *pl.* **-men** ['si:dzmən], *s.m.* grainier(-fleuriste); grainetier, grènetier.

seedsnipe ['si:dsnaip], *s. Orn:* thinocore *m*, attagis *m*.

seedtime ['si:dtaim], *s.* (époque *f* des) semailles *fpl*; la semaison.

seedy ['si:di], *a.* **1.** (*of plant*) plein de graines; (épi) grenu. **2.** *F:* (*a*) (*of pers.*) d'aspect minable, miteux; (*b*) (vêtement) râpé, usé, fatigué, miteux, minable; (*c*) (*of hotel, street, etc.*) moche. **3.** *F:* (*of pers.*) souffrant, mal en train, patraque; **to feel s.,** ne pas être dans son assiette.

seeing[1] ['si:iŋ]. **1.** *a.* voyant; qui voit; **s.-eye dog,** chien *m* d'aveugle. **2.** *conj.* **s. (that) . . .,** vu que . . .; puisque . . .; étant donné que . . .; **s. (that) you're there,** puisque vous êtes là; **s. that he refuses there is nothing more to be done,** puisqu'il refuse, dès qu'il refuse, du moment qu'il refuse, il n'y a plus rien à faire.

seeing[2], *s.* vue *f*; vision *f*; **s. is believing,** voir c'est croire; **within s. distance,** à portée de la vue.

seek [si:k], *v.tr.* (*p.t. & p.p.* **sought** [sɔ:t]) *mainly O: & Lit:* **1.** (*a*) chercher (un objet perdu); rechercher, quêter, tâcher d'obtenir (l'amitié de qn, de l'avancement, etc.); **to s. s.o. (out),** chercher (et trouver) qn; **to s. employment,** chercher un emploi; être en quête d'un emploi; **to s. shelter,** chercher un abri; se réfugier (sous qch.); **they sought each other's company,** ils se recherchaient; **to s. death,** chercher à se faire tuer; **to s. s.o.'s life,** en vouloir à la vie de qn; **to s. s.o.'s approval,** quêter l'approbation de qn; **to s. s.o.'s help,** rechercher, demander, l'aide de qn; *B:* **s. and ye shall find,** cherchez et vous trouverez; (*with passive force*) **the reason is not far to s.,** la raison est plutôt claire; (*b*) (*of dog*) **to s. game,** quêter. **2.** (*a*) **to s. sth. from, of, s.o.,** demander qch. à qn; **to s. advice,** demander conseil; **to s. satisfaction from s.o.,** demander satisfaction à qn; (*b*) **to s. to do sth.,** essayer de, chercher à, s'efforcer de, faire qch.; (*c*) *v.ind.tr.* **to s. for, after, sth.,** (re)chercher, poursuivre, qch.; **to be much sought after,** être très recherché, très couru.

seeker ['si:kər], *s.* chercheur, -euse; **a s. after truth,** un chercheur de vérité; **gold s.,** chercheur d'or; **pleasure seekers,** gens *m* en quête de plaisirs.

seeking ['si:kiŋ], *s.* recherche *f*, quête *f* (de qch.); poursuite *f* (de la gloire, etc.); recherche (des faveurs); **the quarrel was not, was none, of my s.,** ce n'est pas moi qui ai cherché querelle.

seel [si:l], *v.tr.* (*a*) (*in falconry*) ciller (les paupières du faucon); (*b*) *A:* aveugler, tromper, duper (qn).

seem [si:m], *v.i.* sembler, paraître. **1.** (*a*) **to s. tired,** paraître fatigué; avoir l'air fatigué; **he seems old to me,** il me paraît vieux à moi; **he seems to be honest,** il semble être honnête; **how does it s. to you?** que vous en semble? qu'en pensez-vous? **it seems like a dream,** on dirait un rêve; on croirait rêver; **there seems to be some difficulty,** il semble (i) qu'il y a quelque difficulté, (ii) qu'il y ait quelque difficulté; (*b*) **I s. to remember that . . .,** il me semble me souvenir que . . .; **I s. to have heard his name,** il me semble avoir entendu son nom; **I seemed to be floating on a cloud,** j'avais l'impression que je flottais sur un nuage; **I s. to love you more and more,** il me semble que je t'aime de plus en plus; **I s. to have been putting my foot in it,** (i) j'ai l'impression que je viens de commettre une gaffe; (ii) il paraît que j'ai commis une gaffe; *F:* **I don't s. to fancy it,** je ne sais pas pourquoi, mais ça ne me dit rien. **2.** *impers.* **it seems (that) . . ., it would s. that . . .,** il paraît, il semble, que . . .; **it seems that she writes poetry, she writes poetry it seems,** il paraît qu'elle fait des vers; **it seems funny to go away without saying goodbye,** il me semble étrange de partir sans dire adieu; **it seems to me that you are right,** il me semble que vous avez raison; à mon avis, selon moi, vous avez raison; **it seemed to me (that) I was dreaming,** il me semblait, on aurait dit, que je rêvais; **it seemed as though, as if . . .,** il semblait que + *sub.*; on aurait dit que + *ind.*; **it seemed as if he didn't understand,** on aurait dit qu'il ne comprenait pas; il avait l'air de ne pas comprendre; **it seems so, it would s. so, so it seems,** à ce qu'il paraît; il y a apparence; **it seems not, it wouldn't s. so,** il paraît que non.

seeming ['si:miŋ], *a.* apparent; soi-disant *inv*; **with s. kindness,** avec une apparence de bonté.

seemingly ['si:miŋli], *adv.* apparemment; en apparence; **he was s. content,** il paraissait être satisfait, être content de son sort; **s. he's telling the truth,** il y a grande apparence qu'il dit vrai.

seemliness ['si:mlinis], *s. O:* **1.** décorum *m*; bienséance *f*, convenance(s) *f(pl)*; décence *f*, honnêteté *f*. **2.** aspect *m* agréable; beauté *f*.

seemly ['si:mli], *a.* **1.** *O:* convenable, bienséant, décent; **it is not s. that I should go alone, for me to go alone,** il n'est pas convenable que j'aille toute seule; **it is not s. to praise oneself,** il n'est pas honnête de se louer soi-même. **2.** *A:* agréable à voir; de belle stature.

seep [si:p], *v.i.* (*a*) suinter; s'infiltrer; **the water was seeping through the earth, through the tunnel,** l'eau filtrait à travers la terre, à travers le tunnel; (*b*) *F:* **information was seeping out,** des renseignements

filtraient.
seepage ['si:pidʒ], *s.* **1.** suintement *m*; infiltration *f*. **2.** fuite *f*, déperdition *f* (par infiltration); cheminement *m*; *F:* fuite (des renseignements, etc.).
seeping ['si:piŋ], *s.* suintement *m*; (in)filtration *f*; **there was a s. out of information,** des renseignements filtraient.
seer ['si(:)ər], *s. Lit:* prophète *m*.
seersucker ['si(:)əsʌkər], *s. Tex:* coton gaufré, crépon *m* de coton.
seesaw[1] ['si:sɔ:]. **1.** *s.* bascule *f*, balançoire *f*, branloire *f*; tape-cul *m*, *pl.* tape-culs; **to play at s.,** jouer à la bascule. **2.** *a.* **s. motion,** (i) mouvement *m* basculaire; mouvement de bascule; (ii) mouvement de va-et-vient; va-et-vient *m inv*.
seesaw[2], *v.i.* **1.** jouer à la bascule. **2.** (*of machine-part, etc.*) basculer; osciller; se balancer; *F:* (*of pers.*) **to s. between two opinions,** balancer entre deux opinions; être tantôt d'une opinion tantôt de l'autre.
seethe [si:ð], *v.* **1.** *A:* (*a*) *v.tr.* faire bouillir (de l'eau, etc.); *B:* **to s. a kid in its mother's milk,** cuire le chevreau dans le lait de sa mère; (*b*) *v.i.* (*of liquid*) bouillir. **2.** *v.i.* (*a*) (*of liquid*) bouillonner; s'agiter; (*b*) (*of crowd, etc.*) s'agiter, grouiller, foisonner; **the street is seething with people,** la foule grouille dans la rue; la rue grouille de monde; **country seething with discontent, with excitement, etc.,** pays *m* en fermentation, en effervescence; **the people were seething with excitement,** tous les esprits étaient surexcités; **to be seething with anger,** être en proie à une vive irritation; bouillir de colère.
seething[1] ['si:ðiŋ], *a.* bouillonnant, agité; grouillant, foisonnant; **the s. waters,** les eaux tourmentées; **a s. mass of worms,** une masse grouillante, foisonnante, de vers.
seething[2], *s.* bouillonnement *m*; agitation *f*; grouillement *m*, foisonnement *m*.
see-through ['si:θru:], *a. Cost:* (*of blouse, etc.*) (de tissu) transparent.
segar [si'gɑ:r], *s. Com: A:* cigare *m*.
Seger ['zeigər, 'sei-]. *Pr.n. Cer:* **S. cone,** cône *m* de Seger, cône pyrométrique.
Segesta [se'dʒestə]. *Pr.n. A.Geog:* Ségeste.
segment[1] ['segmənt], *s.* **1.** (*a*) *Mth:* segment *m* (d'une sphère, etc.); **s. of a circle,** segment de cercle; **spherical s.,** segment sphérique; (*b*) *Mth:* **s. of a line,** segment linéaire; (*c*) quartier *m*, loge *f*, tranche *f* (d'une orange); (*d*) *El:* **commutator s.,** segment, lame *f*, touche *f*, du commutateur; (*e*) *Mec.E:* **s. gear,** secteur denté; secteur crénelé; **s. rack,** crémaillère *f* du secteur denté; **s. wheel,** roue *f* à segments dentés. **2.** *Ann:* segment, anneau *m*, métamère *m*, somite *m* (d'un ver).
segment[2] [seg'ment]. **1.** *v.tr.* couper, partager, (qch.) en segments; segmenter. **2.** *v.i. Biol:* se partager en segments; se segmenter.
segmental [seg'ment(ə)l], *a.* segmentaire; *Arch:* **s. arch,** (i) arc surbaissé, voûte surbaissée; arche surbaissée (d'un pont); (ii) (*pointed*) ogive surbaissée.
segmentary ['segmənt(ə)ri], *a. Mth: Nat.Hist:* segmentaire.
segmentation [segmen'teiʃ(ə)n], *s. Biol:* segmentation *f*; **s. cavity,** nucléole *m* (d'une cellule).
segmented [seg'mentid], *a.* **1.** segmentaire; formé de segments; **s. mirror,** miroir *m* à facettes. **2.** *Biol:* divisé par segmentation.
segmentina [segmen'tainə], *s. Moll:* segmentina *m*.
Segovia [se'gouviə], *Pr.n. Geog:* Ségovie *f*.
Segovian [se'gouviən]. **1.** *a.* ségovain, ségovien. **2.** *s.* Ségovain, -aine; Ségovien, -ienne.
segregate[1] ['segrigeit]. **1.** *v.tr.* isoler, mettre à part (qch.); mettre de côté (qch.); séparer (deux espèces, etc.) l'un(e) de l'autre; ségréger (des races); **to s. the sexes,** séparer les deux sexes. **2.** *v.i.* (*a*) se diviser; se désunir (**from,** de); (*b*) se grouper à part (**from,** de).
segregate[2]. **1.** *a. Nat.Hist:* (*of species, etc.*) solitaire, séparé. **2.** *s. Bot:* espèce séparée.
segregation [segri'geiʃ(ə)n], *s.* ségrégation *f*; séparation *f*, isolement *m*; **to oppose the policy of s.,** s'opposer au ségrégationnisme.
segregationist [segri'geiʃənist], *a.* & *s. Pol:* ségrégationniste (*mf*); **s. demonstrators,** manifestants ségrégationnistes.
segregative ['segrigeitiv], *a.* ségrégatif.
seguidilla [segi'di:ljə], *s. Danc: Mus:* séguedille *f*, séguidille *f*.
sei [sei], *s. Z:* **s. (whale),** rorqual *m* de Rudolphi.
seiche [seiʃ], *s. Geog:* seiche *f*; variation *f* de niveau (d'un lac); oscillation du niveau (de l'eau).
Seidlitz ['sedlits]. *Pr.n. Geog:* Sedlitz *m*; *Pharm: O:* **S. powder,** sel *m* de Sedlitz.
seigneur [sein'jə:r], *s.m.* seigneur (de Sercq).
seigneurial [sein'jə:riəl], *a. Hist:* seigneurial, -aux.
seigneury ['seinjəri], *s. Hist:* seigneurie *f*.
seigniorage ['seinjəridʒ], *s. Hist:* seigneuriage *m*.
seignorial [sein'jɔ:riəl], *a. Hist:* seigneurial, -aux.
seine[1] [sein], *s. Fish:* seine *f*, senne *f*.
seine[2], *v.tr.* pêcher (des maquereaux, etc.) à la seine; seiner (des maquereaux, etc.).
seiner ['seinər], *s. Fish:* (*a*) pêcheur *m* à la seine; (*b*) (*boat*) senneur *m*.
seise [si:z], *v.tr. Jur:* **to s. s.o. of, with, an estate,** mettre qn en possession d'un bien, d'un héritage; **to be, stand, seised of a property,** posséder une propriété de droit; *A:* **parliament will be seised of these facts in due course,** ces faits seront portés à la connaissance du Parlement en temps utile.
seisin ['si:zin], *s. Jur:* saisine *f*, ensaisinement *m*; **to give s.,** ensaisiner.
seism [saizm], *s. Geol:* séisme *m*; tremblement *m* de terre.
seismal ['saizməl], *a. Geol:* s(é)ismal, -aux.
seismic ['saizmik], *a. Geol:* (secousse *f*, etc.) s(é)ismique; **s. observation point,** emplacement *m* du géophone.
seismicity [saiz'misiti], *s. Geol:* s(é)ismicité *f*.
seismogram ['saizməgræm], *s.* s(é)ismogramme *m*.
seismograph ['saizməgræf], *s. Geol:* s(é)ismographe *m*.
seismographer [saiz'mɔgrəfər], *s.* s(é)ismologiste *mf*, s(é)ismologue *mf*.
seismographic(al) [saizmə'græfik(l)], *a.* s(é)ismographique.
seismography [saiz'mɔgrəfi], *s. Geol:* s(é)ismographie *f*.
seismological [saizmə'lɔdʒik(ə)l], *a. Geol:* s(é)ismologique.
seismologist [saiz'mɔlədʒist], *s. Geol:* s(é)ismologiste *mf*, s(é)ismologue *mf*.
seismology [saiz'mɔlədʒi], *s. Geol:* s(é)ismologie *f*.
seismometer [saiz'mɔmitər], *s. Geol:* s(é)ismomètre *m*.
seismonastic [saizmə'næstik], *a. Bot:* séismonastique.
seismonasty ['saizmənæsti], *s. Bot:* séismonastie *f*, thigmonastie *f*.
Seisonacea, Seisonidea [saisou'neisiə, -'nidiə], *s.pl. Nat.Hist:* seisonides *m*.
seizable ['si:zəbl], *a.* (*of goods, etc.*) saisissable.
seize[1] [si:z], *s. Mec.E: Aut:* **s. (up),** grippure *f*.
seize[2], *v.*
I. *v.tr.* **1.** *Jur:* = SEISE. **2.** (*a*) *Jur:* confisquer, arrêter, saisir (qch.); opérer la saisie de (qch.); **to s. goods (in transit),** faire arrêt sur des marchandises; **the goods were seized,** les marchandises ont été confisquées; **three nationalist papers were seized,** on a saisi trois journaux nationalistes; (*b*) **to s. s.o.,** arrêter qn; appréhender qn (au corps). **3.** saisir; (*a*) se saisir, s'emparer, de qch.; **to s. a fortress,** prendre une forteresse; **to s. an enemy ship,** capturer un navire ennemi; **they seized all they could,** ils se sont saisis de, ils ont fait main basse sur, tout ce qu'ils ont pu; (*b*) **to s. (hold of) s.o., sth.,** saisir, empoigner, s'emparer de, mettre la main sur, gripper, agripper, qn, qch.; attraper (une balle); saisir (une idée); **to s. s.o. by the throat,** prendre qn à la gorge; **to s. s.o. by the collar,** empoigner qn par le collet; saisir, prendre, qn au collet; colleter qn; **she seized him by the arm,** elle lui a empoigné le bras; (*of birds, etc.*) **to s. insects,** happer des insectes; *Ven:* (*of hound*) **to s. a boar by the ears,** coiffer un sanglier; (*c*) **to be seized with fright,** être saisi, frappé, d'effroi; **to be seized with apoplexy,** être frappé d'apoplexie; avoir une attaque d'apoplexie; **he was seized with a fit of rage,** il fut pris d'un accès de colère; il lui prit un accès de colère; **to be seized with a desire to do sth.,** être pris du désir de faire qch.; **to s. the opportunity of doing sth.,** saisir, empoigner, l'occasion de faire qch.; **to s. the meaning of sth.,** prendre, saisir, le sens de qch.; se rendre compte du sens de qch.; (*d*) *v.ind.tr.* **they seized on the newcomer,** ils ont happé, accaparé, le nouvel arrivant; **to s. on a pretext for leaving,** saisir un prétexte, se saisir d'un prétexte, pour partir. **4.** *Nau:* amarrer, faire un amarrage à, aiguilleter (deux cordages, etc.).
II. *v.i. Mec.E:* (*of part*) gripper, coincer; se coller; **to s. up,** (se) caler; **the bearings have seized (up),** les coussinets ont grippé, se sont bloqués; **the brake is seizing,** le frein prend, mord, brutalement; le frein se coince.
seizin ['si:zin], *s. Jur:* saisine *f*.
seizing ['si:ziŋ], *s.* **1.** (*a*) saisie *f* (d'une propriété, de marchandises, etc.); prise *f* (d'une forteresse, etc.); capture *f* (d'un navire ennemi, etc.); (*b*) empoignement *m* (de qn, de qch.). **2.** *Nau:* (*a*) amarrage *m*, aiguilletage *m*; (*b*) amarrage, aiguillette *f*, bridure *f*; **temporary s.,** genope *f*; **throat s.,** amarrage en étrive; **flat s.,** amarrage à plat; **racking s.,** amarrage en portugaise; **round s.,** amarrage plat avec bridure; **cross s.,** amarrage croisé. **3.** *Mec.E: etc:* grippage *m*, grippement *m*, coincement *m*, calage *m* (d'un piston, etc.); grippage (d'une soupape); blocage *m* (d'un organe); **s. up,** grippure *f*.
seizure ['si:ʒər], *s.* **1.** (*a*) *Jur:* appréhension *f* au corps (**of s.o.,** de qn); mainmise *f* (**of s.o.,** sur qn); (*b*) *Jur:* saisie *f* (de marchandises); **s. of real estate,** saisie immobilière; **s. of crops,** saisie-brandon *f*, *pl.* saisies-brandons; **s. under a prior claim,** saisie-revendication *f*, *pl.* saisies-revendications; (*c*) prise *f* (d'une ville, etc.); capture *f* (d'un navire ennemi, etc.); mainmise (sur une province, etc.). **2.** *Med:* **(apoplectic) s.,** attaque *f* d'apoplexie; **fulminating s.,** apoplexie foudroyante; **to have a s.,** tomber en apoplexie; être frappé d'apoplexie. **3.** *Mec.E:* grippure *f*, calage *m*; arrêt *m* de fonctionnement.
sejant ['si:dʒənt], *a. Her:* assis, séant; accroupi.
Sejanus [se'dʒeinəs]. *Pr.n.m. Rom.Hist:* Séjan.
sejugous ['si:dʒugəs], *a. Bot:* sexjugué.
selachian [si'leikiən], *a.* & *s. Ich:* sélacien (*m*).
Selachii [si'leikiai], *s.pl. Ich:* sélaciens *m*.
Selaginaceae [selædʒi'neisii:], *s.pl. Bot:* sélaginacées *f*.
selaginella [selædʒi'nelə], *s. Bot:* sélaginelle *f*.
Selaginellales [selædʒine'leili:z], *s.pl.* sélaginelles *f*.
seldom ['seldəm], *adv.* rarement; peu souvent; **I s. see him now,** je ne le vois plus que rarement; je ne le vois plus guère; **he s. if ever, s. or never, goes out,** il sort rarement, pour ne pas dire jamais; **he is s. seen,** on le voit rarement; il est rare qu'on le voie; **such things are s. seen now,** de telles choses se font rares.
select[1] [si'lekt], *a.* **1.** choisi; *Parl:* **s. committee,** commission *f* d'enquête. **2.** de (premier) choix; choisi; d'élite; *F:* select, sélect; **s. club,** club très fermé, select; **s. audience,** public choisi; **s. society,** le monde select; *s.* **the s.,** l'élite *f*; **to be a s. party,** être en petit comité.
select[2], *v.tr.* choisir (des objets); trier (des minerais, etc.); sélectionner (des joueurs, une équipe); **to s. from . . .,** choisir parmi . . .; **to s. a specimen at random,** prélever un spécimen au hasard; (*of secret agents, etc.*) **very carefully selected,** trié sur le volet.
selected [si'lektid], *a.* (*a*) choisi; *Lit:* **s. passages,** morceaux choisis; *Fin:* **s. investments,** placements sélectionnés; (*b*) *Com:* de choix.
selecting[1] [si'lektiŋ], *a.* sélecteur, -trice.
selecting[2], *s.* choix *m*, tri *m*; prélèvement *m*; *Tp:* **s. switch,** sélecteur *m*.
selection [si'lekʃ(ə)n], *s.* **1.** choix *m*, sélection *f*; *Biol:* **natural s.,** sélection naturelle; *Tp:* **step by step s.,** sélection pas à pas; *For:* **s. felling,** jardinage *m*; *Sp:* **s. match, race,** critérium *m*, critère *m*; match *m* de sélection. **2.** **a good s. of wines,** un bon choix de vins; **to make a s.,** faire un choix; **selections from Byron,** (recueil de) morceaux choisis de Byron; *Mus:* **selections from Chopin,** sélection empruntée à Chopin; **s. from** *Faust*, fantaisie *f* sur *Faust*; *Turf:* **our selections,** nos pronostics *m*.
selective [si'lektiv], *a. W.Tel: etc:* sélectif; sélecteur, -trice; *Phot:* **s. filter,** écran sélecteur, de sélection; *Biol:* **s. breeding,** élevage *m* à base de sélection; *Psy:* **s. affinities,** affinités électives; (*of pers.*) **to be s.,** savoir choisir, choisir avec discernement.
selectively [si'lektivli], *adv.* sélectivement.
selectivity [selek'tiviti], *s.* sélectivité *f*.
selectman, *pl.* **-men** [si'lektmən], *s.m. U.S:* = conseiller municipal.
selectness [si'lektnis], *s.* excellence *f*, supériorité *f*, qualité choisie (de marchandises, etc.); caractère choisi, fermé (d'un club, etc.).
selector [si'lektər], *s.* **1.** (*a*) celui, celle, qui choisit, qui sélectionne; *Sp:* sélectionneur, -euse (de l'équipe nationale, etc.); (*b*) *Agr:* **seed s.,** sélectionneur, -euse. **2.** (*a*) *Aut:* (*automatic gearbox*) **s. lever,** levier *m* de sélection; (*b*) *W.Tel:* **s. of audible frequencies,** sélecteur *m* de fréquences audibles; (*c*) *Tp:* **plug s.,** sélecteur à fiche; (*d*) *El:* **s. switch,** combinateur *m*; (*e*) *Rec:* tête chercheuse.
selenate ['selineit], *s. Ch:* séléniate *m*.
Selene [se'li:ni], *Pr.n.f. Gr.Myth:* Selênê, Séléné.
selenian [si'li:niən], *a. Astr:* sélénien, sélénique.
seleniate [si'li:nieit], *s. Ch:* séléniate *m*.
selenic[1] [si'lenik, -'li:nik], *a. Astr:* sélénique, sélénien.
selenic[2], *a. Ch:* (acide *m*) sélénique.
Selenicereus [seli:ni'siriəs], *s. Bot:* selenicereus *m*.
selenide ['selinaid], *s. Ch:* séléniure *m*.
seleniferous [seli'nifərəs], *a. Miner:* sélénifère.
selenious [si'li:niəs], *a. Ch:* sélénié; (acide) sélénieux.

Selenipedium [sili:ni'pi:diəm], *s. Bot:* selenipedium *m.*
selenite[1] ['selinait], *s. Ch:* sélénite *f.*
Selenite[2] [si'li:nait], *s.* Sélénien, -ienne; Sélénite *mf*; habitant, -ante, de la lune.
selenitic [seli'nitik], *a. Ch:* séléniteux.
selenium [si'li:niəm], *s. Ch:* sélénium *m*; **s. cell,** cellule *f* au sélénium.
selenocentric [sili:nou'sentrik], *a. Astr:* sélénocentrique.
selenocyanic [sili:nousai'ænik], *a. Ch:* (acide *m*) sélénocyanique.
selenodesy [selin'ɔdesi], *s. Astr:* sélénodésie *f.*
selenodont [si'li:noudɔnt], *a. & s. Z:* (mammifère *m*) sélénodonte *m.*
selenographer [seli'nɔgrəfər], *s. Astr:* sélénographe *mf.*
selenographic(al) [sili:nou'græfik(əl)], *a.* sélénographique.
selenography [seli'nɔgrəfi], *s.* sélénographie *f.*
selenolite [si'li:noulait], *s. Miner:* sélénolite *f.*
selenologist [seli'nɔlədʒist], *s. Astr:* sélénologue *mf.*
selenology [seli'nɔlədʒi], *s. Astr:* sélénologie *f.*
selenous [si'li:nəs, 'selinəs], *a. Ch:* sélénié; sélénieux.
Seleucia [si'l(j)u:siə]. *Pr.n. A.Geog:* Séleucie *f.*
Seleucid, *pl.* **-ids, -idae** [si'l(j)u:sid, -idz, -idi:], *a. & s. A.Hist:* Séleucide (*m*).
self, *pl.* **-selves** [self, selvz]. **1.** *s.* (*a*) le moi; la personnalité; la personne; **s. is the only person we know,** le moi est la seule personne que nous connaissons; **s. is his god,** il se fait un dieu de lui-même; **the higher s., the lower s.,** la partie supérieure, inférieure, de notre être; **one's better s.,** le meilleur côté de notre nature; **a second s.,** un autre lui-même; **he's my second, my other, s.,** c'est un autre moi-même; c'est mon alter ego; **he's quite his old s. again,** (i) il est complètement rétabli; (ii) il est tout à fait comme auparavant; **Martin became his silent s. again,** Martin rentra dans la taciturnité qui lui était propre; *F:* **he considers nothing but his own precious s., it's nothing but s. with him,** il ne considère rien que sa chère petite personne; *O:* **your own dear s.,** votre, ta, chère personne; **all by one's very s.,** absolument tout seul; *Com:* **your good selves,** vous-mêmes; vous; (*b*) *Hort:* fleur *f* de couleur uniforme. **2.** *pron.* (*a*) *Com:* (*on cheques*) **pay s., selves,** payez à moi-même, à nous-mêmes; *P:* **on behalf of s. and partners,** de la part de mes associés et de moi-même; (*b*) *for compound pronouns* MYSELF, HIMSELF, ITSELF, *etc., see these words.* **3.** *a.* **wooden tool with s. handle,** outil *m* de bois avec manche de même; **velvet hat with s. trimming,** chapeau de velours garni de même; **s. silver Persian cat,** chat argenté unit; **s. carnation,** œillet *m* de couleur uniforme; **s. whisky,** whisky pur, non mélangé; **s. colour,** couleur *f* (i) uniforme, (ii) naturelle.
self- [self], *comb.fm.* automatique; auto-; de soi-même. NOTE: *in the following* **self-** *compounds, the phonetics of the second word only has been given.*
self-abandonment [-ə'bændənm(ə)nt], *s.* abnégation *f*; renoncement *m* de soi-même.
self-abasement [-ə'beism(ə)nt], *s.* humiliation *f* de soi-même; *Theol:* anéantissement *m.*
self-absorbed [-əb'sɔ:bd], *a.* égoïste.
self-abuse [-ə'bju:s], *s.* onanisme *m.*
self-accusation [-ækju'zeiʃ(ə)n], *s.* auto-accusation *f.*
self-acting [-'æktiŋ], *a. Mec.E: etc:* (appareil *m*, etc.) automatique, automoteur, -trice, à mise en marche automatique; **s.-a. regulator,** autorégulateur *m*; *Rail:* **s.-a. points,** aiguille *f* à contrepoids; *Tex:* **s.-a. mule,** self-acting *m.*
self-addressed [-ə'drest], *a.* (enveloppe) adressée à soi-même.
self-adhesive [-əd'hi:ziv], *a.* autocollant.
self-adjusting [-ə'dʒʌstiŋ], *a. Tchn:* à autoréglage.
self-admiration [-ædmə'reiʃ(ə)n], *s.* admiration *f* de soi-même.
self-advertisement [-əd'və:tizmənt], *s.* mise *f* en avant de sa personne; réclame intéressée; *F:* battage *m.*
self-apparent [-ə'pærənt], *a.* évident; de toute évidence.
self-approbation, -approval [-æprə'beiʃ(ə)n, -ə'pru:v(ə)l], *s.* suffisance *f.*
self-approving [-ə'pru:viŋ], *a.* (sourire, etc.) suffisant.
self-assertion [-ə'sə:ʃ(ə)n], *s.* autorité *f*; caractère impérieux; affirmation *f* de soi-même, de sa volonté; sentiment *m*, affirmation, de sa propre importance; outrecuidance *f.*
self-assertive [-ə'sə:tiv], *a.* autoritaire; impérieux; dominateur, -trice; assuré, tranchant, cassant, affirmatif; outrecuidant.
self-assurance [-ə'ʃuər(ə)ns], *s.* confiance *f* en soi; assurance *f*; aplomb *m*; sûreté *f* de soi(-même).
self-assured [-ə'ʃu:əd], *a.* = SELF-CONFIDENT.
self-awareness [-ə'wɛənis], *s.* conscience *f* de soi-même.
selfcentred [-'sentəd], *a.* égocentrique.
self-centring [-'sentriŋ], *a. Mec.E:* (mandrin *m*, etc.) à serrage concentrique, à centrage automatique; autocentreur.
self-checking [-'tʃekiŋ], *a.* contrôlé automatiquement; à contrôle automatique.
self-closing [-'klouziŋ], *a.* (porte) battante.
self-cocker [-'kɔkər], *s.* revolver *m* à armement automatique.
self-cocking [-'kɔkiŋ], *a.* à armement automatique.
self-collected [-kə'lektid], *a.* (*of pers.*) calme; serein; plein de sang-froid.
self-coloured [-'kʌləd], *a.* concolore; *Tex:* (tissu) uni.
self-command [-kə'mɑ:nd], *s.* maîtrise *f* de soi; sang-froid *m*; empire *m* sur soi-même.
self-communion [-kə'mju:niən], *s.* recueillement *m.*
self-complacence, -complacency [-kəm'pleisəns(i)], *s.* satisfaction *f* (de soi-même); fatuité *f.*
self-complacent [-kəm'pleis(ə)nt], *a.* satisfait, content, de soi.
self-conceit [-kən'si:t], *s.* suffisance *f*, vanité *f*; infatuation *f* (de soi); (*of a man*) fatuité *f*; présomption *f*, amour-propre *m*; **he is full of, is eaten up with, s.-c.,** c'est un vaniteux; il est infatué de lui-même; il est pétri d'amour-propre; il est pourri d'orgueil.
self-conceited [-kən'si:tid], *a.* suffisant, vaniteux, présomptueux, avantageux; infatué de soi-même.
self-confessed [-kən'fest], *a.* qui s'accuse soi-même; qui reconnaît sa culpabilité; (maoïste, etc.) avéré.
self-confidence [-'kɔnfid(ə)ns], *s.* (*a*) confiance *f* en soi; assurance *f*; sûreté de soi; aplomb *m*; **he's full of s.-c.,** il ne doute de rien; **to have no s.-c., to lack s.-c.,** se défier de soi-même; (*b*) présomption *f.*
self-confident [-'kɔnfid(ə)nt], *a.* (*a*) sûr de soi; plein d'assurance; (*b*) présomptueux.
self-confidently [-'kɔnfid(ə)ntli], *adv.* (*a*) avec assurance; (*b*) présomptueusement.
selfconscious [-'kɔnʃəs], *a.* **1.** *Phil:* conscient. **2.** (*a*) (*of pers.*) embarrassé, gêné; intimidé; **to make s.o. s.,** intimider qn; **s. smile,** sourire contraint; **in a s. manner,** d'un air emprunté; (*b*) poseur; (style, etc.) affecté.
selfconsciousness [-'kɔnʃəsnis], *s.* **1.** *Phil:* conscience *f.* **2.** (*a*) contrainte *f*, embarras *m*, gêne *f*; (*b*) pose *f*, affectation *f.*
self-constituted [-'kɔnstitjutid], *a.* (*of committee, etc.*) qui s'est formé, constitué, de sa propre initiative; **s.-c. authority,** autorité usurpée.
self-contained [-kən'teind], *a.* **1.** (*of pers.*) réservé, circonspect, concentré; peu communicatif. **2.** (appareil, etc.) indépendant, complet par lui-même; autonome; **s.-c. industries,** industries qui se suffisent à elles-mêmes; **s.-c. flat,** appartement indépendant, avec entrée particulière; *Mil:* **s.-c. unit,** fraction constituée.
self-content(ment) [-kən'tent(mənt)], *s.* contentement *m* de soi.
self-contented [-kən'tentid], *a.* content de soi.
self-contradictory [-kɔntrə'dikt(ə)ri], *a.* en contradiction avec soi-même; qui se contredit.
self-control [-kən'troul], *s.* sang-froid *m*; empire *m* sur soi-même; possession *f* de soi-même; maîtrise personnelle; maîtrise de soi; **to exercise s.-c.,** faire un effort sur soi-même; **to have no s.-c.,** ne savoir pas se maîtriser; **to lose one's s.-c.,** perdre tout empire sur soi-même; ne plus se maîtriser; **to regain one's s.-c.,** se ressaisir.
self-convicted [-kən'viktid], *a.* condamné, *Jur:* convaincu, par ses propres actes, par ses propres paroles.
self-criticism [-'kritisizm], *s.* autocritique *f.*
self-deceit, -deception [-di'si:t, -di'sepʃ(ə)n], *s.* illusion *f*; déception *f* de soi-même.
self-defeating [-di'fi:tiŋ], *a.* autodestructeur, -trice.
self-defence [-di'fens], *s.* défense personnelle; autodéfense *f*; *Jur:* légitime défense; **the (noble) art of s.-d.,** (i) le noble art; la boxe; (ii) *A:* l'escrime *f*; **to kill s.o. in s.-d.,** tuer qn en légitime défense; **to be able to plead s.-d.,** être en état de légitime défense; **weapon carried for s.-d.,** porte-respect *m inv.*
self-denial [-di'naiəl], *s.* (*a*) abnégation *f* de soi; renoncement(s) *m(pl)*; privations *fpl*; (*b*) frugalité *f.*
self-denying [-di'naiiŋ], *a.* (*a*) qui fait abnégation de soi; qui renonce à soi; qui s'impose des privations; (*b*) frugal, -aux.
self-depreciation [-dipri:si'eiʃ(ə)n], *s.* modestie exagérée.
self-destruction [-dis'trʌkʃ(ə)n], *s.* autodestruction *f*; suicide *m.*
self-determination [-ditə:mi'neiʃ(ə)n], *s. Pol:* autodétermination *f.*
self-discipline [-'disiplin], *s.* discipline *f* (que l'on s'impose); maîtrise *f* de soi.
self-drive [-'draiv], *s.* **s.-d. cars for hire,** location *f* de voitures sans chauffeur.
selfeducated [-'edjukeitid], *a.* autodidacte.
self-effacing [-i'feisiŋ], *a.* qui aime à s'effacer.
self-elected [-i'lektid], *a.* élu, nommé, par soi-même.
self-energized, -energizing [-'enədʒaizd, -dʒaiziŋ], *a. Aut:* (frein *m*, etc.) auto-serreur, servo-moteur.
self-esteem [-i'sti:m], *s.* estime *f*, respect *m*, de soi; amour-propre *m.*
self-evident [-'evid(ə)nt], *a.* évident en soi; qui saute aux yeux, qui est clair comme le jour; **it's s.-e.,** les choses parlent d'elles-mêmes; **s.-e. truth,** vérité *f* de (monsieur de) La Police.
self-examination [-igzæmi'neiʃ(ə)n], *s.* examen *m* de conscience.
self-excitation, -excitement [-eksi'teiʃ(ə)n, -ik'saitm(ə)nt], *s. El:* autoexcitation *f.*
self-exciting [-ik'saitiŋ], *a. El:* autoexcitateur, -trice; **s.-e. dynamo,** dynamo *f* à autoexcitation.
self-explanatory [-ik'splænət(ə)ri], *a.* qui s'explique de soi-même.
self-expression [-ik'spreʃ(ə)n], *s.* libre expression *f.*
self-faced [-'feist], *a.* (moellon) brut, non taillé.
self-feeder [-'fi:dər], *s. Husb:* appareil *m* d'alimentation automatique.
self-feeding [-'fi:diŋ], *a.* **1.** *Mec.E: etc:* à alimentation automatique, continue. **2.** **s.-f. reamer,** alésoir *m* à bout fileté pour l'amorçage.
self-fertilization [-fə:tilai'zeiʃ(ə)n], *s. Nat.Hist:* autofécondation *f*; *Bot:* fécondation directe.
self-fertilizing [-'fə:tilaiziŋ], *a. Nat.Hist:* autofertile; *Bot:* à fécondation directe.
self-fluxing [-'flʌksiŋ], *a. Metalw:* (soudure) autofondante, décapante.
self-governing [-'gʌvəniŋ], *a.* autonome.
self-government [-'gʌvənm(ə)nt], *s.* autonomie *f.*
self-hardening [-'hɑ:dniŋ], *a. Metall:* (acier) autotrempant.
self-heal [-'hi:l], *s. Bot:* brunelle *f*; prunelle commune.
self-help [-'help], *s.* efforts personnels; **s.-h. manuals,** manuels *m* aide-toi toi-même.
self-humiliation [-hjumili'eiʃ(ə)n], *s.* abaissement *m* de soi; *Theol:* anéantissement *m.*
self-ignition [-ig'niʃ(ə)n], *s. I.C.E:* allumage spontané; inflammation spontanée; auto-allumage *m.*
self-importance [-im'pɔ:təns], *s.* suffisance *f*, présomption *f*; **eaten up with s.-i.,** pourri d'orgueil; infatué de soi-même.
self-important [-im'pɔ:tənt], *a.* suffisant, présomptueux, vaniteux.
selfimposed [-im'pouzd], *a.* (tâche, etc.) dont on a pris de soi-même la responsabilité.
self-improvement [-im'pru:vm(ə)nt], *s.* éducation personnelle.
self-induced [-in'dju:st], *a. Med:* (symptôme, etc.) provoqué par soi-même.
self-inductance [-in'dʌkt(ə)ns], *s. El:* **1.** = SELF-INDUCTION. **2.** coefficient *m* de self-induction; (self-) inductance *f.*
self-induction [-in'dʌkʃ(ə)n], *s. El:* induction *f* propre; self-induction *f*; auto-induction *f*; auto-inductance *f*; **s.-i. on opening, on closure,** self-induction d'ouverture, de fermeture; **coefficient of s.-i.,** inductance *f*; **s.-i. circuit,** circuit *m* à self(-induction); **s.-i. coil,** bobine *f* de self: bobine d'auto-inductance; *F:* self *f*; **s.-i. current,** extra-courant *m.*
self-inductive [-in'dʌktiv], *a. El:* selfique.
self-indulgence [-in'dʌldʒ(ə)ns], *s.* sybaritisme *m*; satisfaction *f* égoïste de ses appétits; habitude *f* de s'écouter, de ne rien se refuser.
self-indulgent [-in'dʌldʒ(ə)nt], *a.* sybarite; qui se dorlote; qui ne se refuse rien.
self-inflicted [-in'fliktid], *a.* (*of penance, etc.*) que l'on s'inflige à soi-même; **s.-i. wound,** mutilation *f* volontaire.
selfing ['selfiŋ], *s. Bot:* fécondation, pollinisation, directe.
self-instruction [-in'strʌkʃ(ə)n], *s.* étude personnelle, sans maître.
self-interest [-'int(ə)rest], *s.* intérêt (personnel); **to act from s.-i.,** agir dans un but intéressé.
self-interested [-'int(ə)restid], *a.* (*of pers., motive*) intéressé; **for s.-i. motives,** (faire qch.) par intérêt.
selfish ['selfiʃ], *a.* égoïste, intéressé; **to act from a s. motive,** agir par calcul, dans un but intéressé.
selfishly ['selfiʃli], *adv.* égoïstement, d'une manière intéressée; **to act s.,** agir en égoïste.
selfishness ['selfiʃnis], *s.* égoïsme *m*; **he did it out of s.,** il l'a fait par intérêt.
self-justification [-dʒʌstifi'keiʃ(ə)n], *s.* justification *f*

de sa propre conduite; autojustification *f*; apologie *f*.
self-knowledge [-'nɔlidʒ], *s.* connaissance *f* de soi.
selfless ['selflis], *a.* désintéressé; altruiste.
selflessness ['selflisnis], *s.* désintéressement *m*; altruisme *m*.
self-locking [-'lɔkiŋ], *a.* **1.** *Mec.E:* à blocage automatique; auto-bloqueur; **s.-l. nut,** écrou *m* indesserrable. **2.** à verrouillage, fermeture, automatique.
self-love [-'lʌv], *s.* **1.** égoïsme *m*; amour *m* de soi. **2.** *Psy:* narcissisme *m*.
self-lubricating [-'lu:brikeitiŋ], *a. Mec.E:* (palier) (auto)graisseur.
self-lubrication [-lu:bri'keiʃ(ə)n], *s.* autograissage *m*.
selfmade ['selfmeid], *a.* (homme) qui est (le) fils de ses œuvres, qui est l'architecte, l'artisan, l'ouvrier, de sa fortune, qui est parti de rien, qui est arrivé par lui-même.
self-mastery [-'mɑ:st(ə)ri], *s.* maîtrise personnelle; empire *m* sur soi-même.
self-mutilation [-mjuti'leiʃ(ə)n], *s.* mutilation *f* volontaire.
self-nursing [-'nə:siŋ], *s.* allaitement naturel (d'un enfant par sa mère).
self-opinionated [-ə'piniəneitid], *a.* opiniâtre, entêté; qui ne démord pas de ses opinions; suffisant.
self-pity [-'piti], *s.* attendrissement *m* sur soi-même; **he's full of s.-p.,** il s'apitoie trop sur son sort.
self-pollination [-pɔli'neiʃ(ə)n], *s. Bot:* autopollinisation *f*; pollinisation directe.
self portrait [-'pɔ:treit], *s.* (*a*) portrait *m* de l'artiste par lui-même; auto-portrait *m*; (*b*) portrait de l'auteur (dans une autobiographie, etc.).
self-possessed [-pə'zest], *a.* calme; maître de soi; qui a beaucoup d'aplomb, de sang-froid; qui a un grand flegme, qui est d'un grand flegme; qui a de l'empire sur soi-même; **to remain entirely s.-p.,** rester entièrement maître de soi; garder tout son sang-froid.
self-possession [-pə'zeʃ(ə)n], *s.* aplomb *m*, sang-froid *m*, flegme *m*, empire *m* sur soi-même; **to lose one's s.-p.,** perdre son aplomb; **to regain one's s.-p.,** se remettre; se ressaisir; reprendre son sang-froid.
self-preservation [-prezə'veiʃ(ə)n], *s.* conservation *f* (de soi-même); **the instinct of s.-p.,** l'instinct *m* de (la) conservation, de sa propre conservation.
self-propelled, -propelling [-prə'peld, -'peliŋ], *a.* (*of vehicle*) automoteur, -trice; automobile; autopropulsé; à autopropulsion.
self-propulsion [-prə'pʌlʃ(ə)n], *s.* autopropulsion *f*.
self-protection [-prə'tekʃ(ə)n], *s.* autoprotection *f*.
self-punishment [-'pʌniʃmənt], *s. Psy:* autopunition *f*.
selfraising ['selfreiziŋ], *a. Cu:* **s. flour,** farine préparée contenant de la levure chimique.
self-recording, -registering [-ri'kɔ:diŋ, -'redʒistriŋ], *a.* (*of apparatus*) enregistreur, -euse.
self-regarding [-ri'gɑ:diŋ], *a.* (personne) qui ne considère que soi-même; **from s.-r. motives,** (faire qch.) par intérêt.
self-regulating [-'regjuleitiŋ], *a. Mec.E:* autorégulateur, -trice; à autoréglage; à autorégulation.
self-reliance [-ri'laiəns], *s.* indépendance *f*; confiance *f* en soi.
self-reliant [-ri'laiənt], *a.* indépendant; qui a confiance en soi.
self-renunciation [-rinʌnsi'eiʃ(ə)n], *s.* abnégation totale de soi.
self-reproach [-ri'prou(t)ʃ], *s.* reproches *mpl* que l'on se fait à soi-même; remords *m*.
self-respect [-ri'spekt], *s.* respect *m* de soi; amour-propre *m*, fierté *f*; **to lose all s.-r.,** tomber dans la dégradation; perdre toute dignité.
self-respecting [-ri'spektiŋ], *a.* qui se respecte, qui a de l'amour-propre; **no s.-r. man could do anything but refuse,** un homme qui se respecte ne saurait que refuser.
self-restrained [-ris'treind], *a.* retenu; qui a de l'empire sur soi-même; qui sait se contenir.
self-restraint [-ris'treint], *s.* retenue *f*; modération *f*; empire *m* sur soi; **to exercise s.-r.,** se contenir; se retenir.
selfrighteous [-'raitjəs], *a.* pharisaïque.
selfrighteousness [-'raitjəsnis], *s.* pharisaïsme *m*.
self-righting [-'raitiŋ], *a.* (*of lifeboat, etc.*) à redressement automatique; inchavirable.
self-sacrifice [-'sækrifais], *s.* abnégation *f* (de soi); immolation *f* du moi; **he had his education by the s.-s. of his parents,** ses parents ont fait de grands sacrifices pour lui faire faire ses études.
selfsame ['selfseim], *a.* identique; absolument le même.
self-satisfaction [-sætis'fækʃ(ə)n], *s.* contentement *m* de soi; fatuité *f*, suffisance *f*.
self-satisfied [-'sætisfaid], *a.* content de soi; suffisant.
self-sealing [-'si:liŋ], *a. Tchn:* (dispositif) à obturation automatique.
self-seeding[1] [-'si:diŋ], *s. Bot:* semaison *f*; dispersion naturelle des graines.
self-seeding[2], *a. Bot:* à dispersion naturelle.
self-seeking[1] [-'si:kiŋ], *a.* égoïste; **from s.-s. motives,** (agir) dans un but intéressé.
self-seeking[2], *s.* égoïsme *m*.
self-service [-'sə:vis], *s. Com:* libre-service *m*; **s.-s. store,** magasin libre-service; *F:* self-service *m*.
self-starter [-'stɑ:tər], *s.* **1.** *Aut:* démarreur *m*. **2.** *Typew:* ajuste-tabulateur *m inv*.
self-sterile [-'sterail], *a. Bot:* autostérile.
self-sterility [-ste'riliti], *s. Bot:* autostérilité *f*.
selfstyled ['selfstaild], *a.* soi-disant *inv*, prétendu.
self-sufficiency [-sə'fiʃənsi], *s.* **1.** indépendance *f*; *Pol.Ec:* **national s.-s.,** autarcie *f*. **2.** vanité *f*, suffisance *f*.
self-sufficient [-sə'fiʃənt], *a.* **1.** (*of pers., thg*) indépendant; autosuffisant. **2.** (*of pers.*) suffisant.
self-suggestion [-sə'dʒestjən], *s.* autosuggestion *f*.
self-supporting [-sə'pɔ:tiŋ], *a.* indépendant; (*of pers.*) qui suffit à ses besoins; (*of business*) qui fait, couvre, ses frais.
self-surrender [-sə'rendər], *s.* abandon *m* (de soi-même) (**to,** à); abdication *f* de sa volonté.
self-tapping [-'tæpiŋ], *a.* **s.-t. screw,** vis *f* à métaux, vis Parker.
self-taught [-'tɔ:t], *a.* **1.** (*of pers.*) autodidacte. **2.** (*of knowledge*) que l'on a appris tout seul.
self-timing [-'taimiŋ], *a. Phot:* (obturateur) comportant réglage automatique de temps de pose.
selfwill [-'wil], *s.* obstination *f*, entêtement *m*, opiniâtreté *f*.
selfwilled [-'wild], *a.* opiniâtre, obstiné, volontaire.
self-winding [-'waindiŋ], *a.* (pendule *f*) à remontage automatique.
seligmannite ['seligmənait], *s. Miner:* seligmannite *f*.
Selim ['selim], *Pr.n. Hist:* Sélim; **S. the Grim,** Sélim le Cruel.
Seljuk, Seljukian [se'lju:k(iən)], *Pr.n. Hist:* Seldjoukide *m*, Seldjoucide *m*.
sell[1] [sel], *s. F:* **1.** vente *f*; **hard s.,** vente au sabot; **soft s.,** vente facile, à publicité discrète. **2.** déception *f*; attrape *f*; blague *f*; **what a s.!** quelle déception! ça, c'est une sale blague!
sell[2], *v.* (*p.t. & p.p.* **sold** [sould])
I. *v.tr.* **1.** (*a*) vendre (qch.); vendre, placer (des marchandises); **to s. sth. back to s.o.,** revendre qch. à qn; **to s. goods easily,** écouler, placer, facilement des marchandises; **difficult to s.,** de vente, d'écoulement, difficile; **to s. sth. by auction,** vendre qch. à la criée, aux enchères; **to s. sth. for cash,** vendre qch. au comptant; **to s. sth. on credit,** vendre qch. à terme, à crédit; **to s. sth. at a loss,** vendre qch. à perte; mévendre qch.; **to sell sth. dear, cheap,** vendre qch. cher, (à) bon marché; **he sold it to me for £10,** il me l'a vendu (pour) £10; **I'm selling it on commission,** je l'ai en placement; *St.Exch:* **to s. short, to s. a bear,** vendre à découvert; *Mil: A:* **to s. one's commission,** vendre son brevet; *F:* **I couldn't s. my father the idea,** je n'ai pas pu faire accepter l'idée à mon père; **to be sold on an idea,** être entiché d'une idée; (*b*) (*with passive force*) **goods that s. well,** marchandises d'écoulement facile, qui se vendent bien, qui se placent facilement; **certain to s.,** d'un débit assuré; **this book sells well,** ce livre est de bonne vente, se vend bien; **what are plums selling at?** combien valent, à combien se vendent, les prunes? **land to s., to be sold,** terrain *m* à vendre. **2.** (*a*) vendre, trahir (un secret, son pays, etc.); **to s. one's conscience,** trafiquer de sa conscience; (*b*) *F:* **to s. oneself,** se faire accepter, se faire valoir; (*c*) *F:* duper, tromper, refaire (qn); **you've been sold!** on vous a refait! **sold again!** attrapé!
II. (*compound verbs*) **1. sell off,** *v.tr.* solder, écouler à bas prix (des marchandises); se défaire de (ses marchandises); liquider (son stock, etc.); *F:* bazarder (ses effets).
2. sell out, (*a*) *v.tr.* (i) *Fin:* réaliser (tout un portefeuille d'actions); *St.Exch:* **to s. out against a client,** exécuter un client; (ii) *Com:* vendre tout son stock de (qch.); se défaire de (ses marchandises); **the edition is sold out,** l'édition est épuisée; **I'm sold out,** j'ai tout vendu; **we're sold out of eggs,** nous n'avons plus d'œufs; (*b*) *v.tr.* dénoncer, vendre, trahir (qn); *v.ind.tr.* **to s. out on an ideal,** trahir un idéal; (*c*) *v.i. Mil: A:* vendre son brevet.
3. sell up, *v.tr.* vendre, faire saisir (un failli); *Jur:* discuter (un débiteur) en ses biens; **he went bankrupt and was sold up,** il a fait faillite et tout ce qu'il possédait a été vendu.
sellaite ['seləait], *s. Miner:* sellaïte *f*.
seller ['selər], *s.* **1.** (*pers.*) (*a*) vendeur, -euse; **s. of shares,** réalisateur *m* de titres; *St.Exch:* **seller's option,** prime *f* vendeur, pour livrer; **seller's market,** marché *m* à la hausse; (*b*) marchand, -ande; débitant, -ante (**of,** de). **2.** (*of thg*) **good s.,** article de bonne vente, d'écoulement facile, qui se vend facilement; **bad s.,** article de mauvaise vente, d'écoulement difficile. **3.** *Turf:* course *f* à réclamer.
selling ['seliŋ], *s.* vente *f*, écoulement *m*, placement *m* (de marchandises, etc.); **s. price,** prix de vente; prix marchand, fort; **(conventional) s. weight,** poids vénal; **s. point,** (i) point *m* de vente; (ii) avantage spécial (d'un produit) susceptible d'intéresser un client; **cheapness is not a s. point but quality is,** ce n'est pas le prix qui compte mais la qualité; le client éventuel s'occupe de la qualité et non pas du prix; *Turf:* **s. race, plate,** course *f*, prix, à réclamer; **s. off, out,** liquidation *f* (des stocks); *Fin:* (re)vente *f*, réalisation *f* (de titres, etc.); *Mil: A:* **s. out,** vente de son brevet.
Sellotape ['selouteip], *s. R.t.m:* ruban adhésif cellulosique.
sellout ['selaut], *s. F:* **1.** trahison *f*. **2. this play's a s.,** cette pièce a fait salle comble. **3.** *Com:* **this line has been a s.,** cet article s'est vendu à merveille (et il ne nous en reste plus).
selvage, selvedge ['selvidʒ], *s.* **1.** *Tex:* lisière *f*; cordeau *m* (de lainages épais); **cloth with a good s.,** drap bien coiffé; **end s.,** entre-bande *f* (d'une pièce d'étoffe); **s. tape,** cache-couture *m*; extra-fort *m*. **2.** *Geol:* salbande *f*. **3.** rebord *m*, têtière *f* (de serrure).
semainier [sə'meinie], *s. Furn:* semainier *m*.
semanteme [si'mænti:m], *s. Ling:* sémantème *m*.
semantic [si'mæntik], *a. Ling:* sémantique.
semantician [simæn'tiʃ(ə)n], **semanticist** [si'mæntisist], *s.* sémanticien, -ienne; sémantiste *mf*.
semantics [si'mæntiks], *s.pl. Ling:* sémantique *f*.
semaphore[1] ['seməfɔ:r], *s.* sémaphore *m*; *Rail: etc:* **s. signal,** signal *m* à bras.
semaphore[2], *v.tr.* transmettre (une communication) par sémaphore.
semaphorist ['seməfɔ:rist], *s.* sémaphoriste *m*.
semasiological [simeisiou'lɔdʒikl], *a. Ling:* sémantique.
semasiology [simeisi'ɔlədʒi], *s. Ling:* sémasiologie *f*, sémantique *f*.
semblance ['sembləns], *s.* apparence *f*, semblant *m*; simulacre *m*; **a (mere) s. of friendship,** un semblant d'amitié; une pure, une fausse, apparence d'amitié; **without the s. of an excuse,** sans le moindre semblant d'excuse.
semé ['semei], *s. Bookb:* semé *m*.
semé(e) ['semei], *a. Her:* **s. of, with, fleurs-de-lis,** semé de fleurs de lis.
semeiological [si:maiə'lɔdʒikl], *a. Med:* sémiologique.
semeiologist [si:mai'ɔlədʒist], *s. Med:* sémiologue *mf*.
semeiology [si:mai'ɔlədʒi], *s. Med:* sémiologie *f*.
semeiotic [si:mai'outik], *a. Med:* sémiotique.
semeiotician [si:maiou'tiʃ(ə)n], *s. Med:* sémioticien, -ienne.
semeiotics [si:mai'outiks], *s.pl. Med:* sémiotique *f*.
Semele ['semili], *Pr.n.f. Myth:* Sémélé.
sememe ['semi:m], *s. Ling:* sémème *m*.
semen ['si:men], *s. Physiol:* sperme *m*, semence *f*.
semester [si'mestər], *s. NAm:* semestre *m* (scolaire).
semi ['semi], *s. F:* maison jumelée.
semi- ['semi], *pref.* semi-; demi-.
NOTE: *for the* semi- *compounds, phonetics have been given only for the second part of the word, unless the main stress falls on* semi-.
semiamplexicaul [æm'pleksikɔ:l], *a. Bot:* semi-amplexicaul.
semiannual ['ænju:əl], *a.* semi-annuel; semestriel.
semiannually ['ænjuəli], *adv.* semestriellement; deux fois par an.
semi-arid ['ærid], *a.* semi-aride.
semi-armour-piercing ['ɑ:məpiəsiŋ], *a. Mil:* semi-perforant; **s.-a.-p. projectile,** projectile *m* de semi-rupture; **s.-a.-p. effect,** semi-rupture *f*.
semi-automatic [ɔ:tə'mætik], *a.* (mécanisme) semi-automatique.
semi-ballistic [bə'listik], *a.* semi-balistique.
semibreve ['semibri:v], *s. Mus:* ronde *f*.
semicarbazone ['kɑ:bəzoun], *s. Ch:* semicarbazone *f*.
semi-centenary [sen'ti:nəri], *s.* cinquantenaire *m*.
semi-centennial [sen'teniəl], *a.* qui revient tous les cinquante ans.
semi-centrifugal [sentri'fju:gəl], *a.* semi-centrifuge.
semi-chorus ['kɔ:rəs], *s.* moitié *f* du chœur.

semicircle ['semisə:kl], *s.* **1.** demicercle *m, pl.* demicercles. **2.** *Surv:* graphomètre *m.*
semicircular ['sə:kjulər], *a.* demi-circulaire, semicirculaire; en demi-cercle; **s. protractor,** rapporteur *m* demi-cercle.
semicolon ['koulən], *s.* point-virgule *m, pl.* points-virgules.
semi-column ['kɔ:ləm], *s. Arch:* demi-colonne *f, pl.* demi-colonnes.
semiconductivity [kəndʌk'tiviti], *s. El:* semi-conductivité *f.*
semiconductor [kən'dʌktər], *s. El:* semi-conducteur *m*; **extrinsic, intrinsic, s.,** semi-conducteur extrinsèque, intrinsèque; **intermetallic s.,** semi-conducteur intermétallique.
semiconscious ['kɔnʃəs], *a.* à demi conscient; qui est en train de perdre, de reprendre, connaissance.
semiconsonant ['kɔnsənənt], *s.* semi-consonne *f, pl.* semi-consonnes.
semiconsonantal [kɔnsə'nɔntl], *a.* semi-consonantique.
semi-convergent [kən'və:dʒənt], *a. Mth:* (série) semi-convergente.
semicrystalline ['kristəlain], *a. Geol:* semi-cristallin.
semi-cubical ['kju:bikl], *a. Mth:* semi-cubique.
semicylinder ['silindər], *s.* demi-cylindre *m, pl.* demi-cylindres.
semicylindrical [si'lindrikl], *a.* demi-cylindrique; hémicylindrique.
semi-darkness ['dɑ:knis], *s.* pénombre *f*; demi-obscurité *f*; demi-jour *m.*
semidemisemiquaver ['semidemisemikweivər], *s. Mus:* quadruple croche *f.*
semi-deployed [di'plɔid], *a. Mil:* semi-déployé.
semi-deponent [di'pounənt], *a. & s.* (verbe) semi-déponent.
semi-detached [di'tætʃt], *a.* (maison) jumelée, jumelle, double.
semidin(e) ['semid(a)in], *s. Ch:* semidine *f.*
semi-double ['dʌbl], *a. Bot: etc:* semi-double.
semi-duplex ['dju:pleks], *a.* semi-duplex.
semi-elliptic [e'liptik], *a.* semi-elliptique; **s.-e. spring,** ressort *m* semi-elliptique, à demi-pincette.
semifinal ['fain(ə)l]. *Sp:* **1.** *a.* demi-final, -als. **2.** *s.* demi-finale *f, pl.* demi-finales.
semifinalist ['fainəlist], *s. Sp:* joueur, -euse, de la demi-finale.
semi-fitting ['fitiŋ], *a.* (*of dress, etc.*) mi-cintré.
semi-floret ['flɔ:ret], *s. Bot:* demi-fleuron *m, pl.* demi-fleurons.
semifloscular, semiflosculose, semiflosculous ['flɔskjulər, -lous, -ləs], *a. Bot:* semi-flosculeux.
semifluid ['flu:id]. **1.** *a.* semi-fluide, semi-liquide, à demi fluide. **2.** *s.* semi-fluide *m, pl.* semi-fluides.
semi-invalid ['invəlid], *s.* maladif, -ive.
semi-literate ['litərət], *a.* semi-illettré.
semi-logarithmic [lɔgə'riθmik], *a. Mth:* semi-logarithmique.
semilunar ['lu:nər], *a. Anat: etc:* (os, cartilage, etc.) semi-lunaire.
semi-manufactured [mænju'fæktjəd], *a.* mi-ouvré.
semi-manufactures [mænju'fæktjəz], *s.pl.* demi-produits *m.*
semi-mat(t) ['mæt], *a.* (papier) semi-mat.
semimembranosus [membrei'nousəs], *s. Anat:* (muscle *m*) demi-membraneux *m.*
semi-metal ['metl], *s. Ch:* demi-métal *m, pl.* demi-métaux.
semi-metallic [mi'tælik], *a. Ch:* demi-métallique.
semi-military ['milit(ə)ri], *a.* paramilitaire.
seminal ['si:min(ə)l, 'sem-], *a. Physiol: Bot:* séminal, -aux; **s. fluid,** sperme *m*, liquide séminal; **in the s. state,** à l'état latent; embryonnaire; **s. work,** œuvre féconde, qui a eu une forte influence.
seminar ['seminɑ:r], *s. Sch:* (*a*) séminaire *m*; (*b*) *U.S:* cycle *m* d'études.
seminarist ['seminərist], *s. R.C.Ch:* séminariste *m.*
seminary ['seminəri], *s.* **1.** *R.C.Ch:* (*a*) séminaire *m*; (*b*) *Hist:* **the seminaries,** *a.* **the s. priests,** le clergé séculier (d'Angleterre). **2.** *A:* **(young ladies') s.,** pensionnat *m* de jeunes filles.
seminase ['semineis], *s. Bio-Ch:* seminase *f.*
semination [semi'neiʃ(ə)n], *s. Bot:* sémination *f.*
seminiferous [semi'nifərəs], *a. Bot: Anat:* séminifère.
Seminoles ['seminoulz], *s.pl. Ethn:* Séminoles *m.*
seminoma [semi'noumə], *s. Med:* séminome *m.*
semi-nomadic [nou'mædik], *a.* semi-nomade.
semi-nomadism ['noumədizm], *s.* semi-nomadisme *m.*
semi-nude ['nju:d], *a.* à moitié nu, à demi nu.
semi-nymph ['nimf], *s. Ent:* semi-nymphe *f, pl.* semi-nymphes.
semi-obscurity [ɔb'skjuəriti], *s.* pénombre *m.*
semi-occasionally [ə'keiʒən(ə)li], *adv. F:* de temps en temps; à de rares intervalles; assez rarement.
semi-official [ə'fiʃ(ə)l], *a.* semi-officiel; officieux.
semi-officially [ə'fiʃəli], *adv.* d'une manière semi-officielle, officieusement.
semiology [si:mai'ɔlədʒi], *s. Med:* sémiologie *f.*
semi-opal ['oup(ə)l], *s.* semi-opale *f*, demi-opale *f, pl.* semi-, demi-opales.
semi-opaque [ou'peik], *a.* demi-opaque.
semiotic [simai:'outik], *a. Med:* sémiotique.
semiotician [si:mai:ou'tiʃ(ə)n], *s. Med:* sémioticien, -ienne.
semiotics [si:mai:'outiks], *s.pl. Med:* sémiotique *f.*
semi-palmate(d) ['pa:lmeit, pɑ:l'meitid], *a. Orn:* semi-palmé.
Semi-Pelagianism [pe'leidʒiənizm], *s. Rel.H:* semi-pélagianisme *m.*
semipermeable ['pə:miəbl], *a.* semi-perméable.
semi-polar ['poulər], *a. Ch:* semi-polaire.
semi-portable ['pɔ:təbl], *a.* (chaudière, etc.) mi-fixe.
semi-portal ['pɔ:t(ə)l], *a.* **s.-p. bridge crane,** semi-portique *m.*
semi-precious ['preʃəs], *a. Lap:* semi-précieux; fin.
semi-profile ['proufail], *a.* (portrait) de trois quarts.
semiquaver ['semikweivər], *s. Mus:* double croche *f.*
semi-rigid ['ridʒid], *a.* semi-rigide.
semi-selfpropelled [selfprə'peld], *a.* semi-autopropulsé.
semi-selfpropulsion [selfprə'pʌlʃ(ə)n], *s.* semi-autopropulsion *f.*
semishingled ['ʃiŋg(ə)ld], *a. A.Hairdr:* (cheveux) taillés à la boule.
semi-silvered ['silvə:d], *a. Opt:* semi-argenté.
semiskilled ['skild], *a.* semi-qualifié.
semi-solid ['sɔlid], *a. Ch: etc:* semi-solide.
semi-sparkling ['spɑ:kliŋ], *a.* (vin) pétillant.
semisteel ['sti:l], *s. Metall:* fonte aciérée.
Semite ['semait], *s. Ethn:* Sémite *mf.*
Semitic [si'mitik], *a. Ethn:* sémitique.
Semitism ['semitizm], *s.* sémitisme *m.*
semitone ['semitoun], *s. Mus:* demi-ton *m*, semi-ton *m.*
semitonic ['tɔnik], *a. Mus:* (intervalle) d'un demi-ton; **s. scale,** gamme *f* chromatique.
semitrailer ['treilər], *s. Veh:* semi-remorque *f, pl.* semi-remorques.
semi-transparency [træn'spærənsi], *s.* demi-transparence *f*, semi-transparence *f.*
semi-transparent [træn'spærənt], *a.* demi-transparent, semi-transparent; à demi transparent; translucide.
semitropical ['trɔpikl], *a.* subtropical, -aux.
semitubular ['tju:bjulər], *a.* semi-tubulaire.
semivowel ['vauəl], *s.* semi-voyelle *f, pl.* semi-voyelles.
semolina [semə'li:nə], *s.* semoule *f*; **s. pudding,** semoule au lait.
sempervivum [sempə'vaivəm], *s. Bot:* sempervivum *m inv*, joubarbe *f.*
sempiternal [sempi'tə:nəl], *a. Lit:* sempiternel, éternel.
sempiternally [sempi'tə:nəli], *adv. Lit:* sempiternellement, éternellement.
Sempronia [sem'prouniə], *Pr.n.f. Rom.Hist:* Sempronie.
sempstress ['sem(p)stris], *s.* = SEAMSTRESS.
senaite ['senait], *s. Miner:* senaïte *f.*
senarmontite [senɑ:'mɔntait], *s. Miner:* sénarmontite *f.*
senary ['si:nəri], *a. Mth: etc:* sénaire.
senate ['senət], *s.* (*a*) *Pol:* sénat *m*; **s. house,** sénat; (*b*) *Sch:* conseil *m* de l'université.
senator ['senətər], *s.* **1.** *Pol:* sénateur *m.* **2.** *Jur: Scot:* **s. of the College of Justice,** juge *m.*
senatorial [senə'tɔ:riəl], *a.* sénatorial, -aux; sénatorien.
senatorian [senə'tɔ:riən], *a.* sénatorien.
senatorship ['senətəʃip], *s.* office *m*, dignité *f*, de sénateur.
send[1] [send], *v.* (*p.t. & p.p.* **sent** [sent])
I. *v.tr.* **1.** (*a*) envoyer (qn); **to s. a child to school,** envoyer un enfant à l'école; **to send s.o. as ambassador to London,** envoyer qn en ambassade à Londres; nommer qn ambassadeur à Londres; **to s. s.o. with a message to s.o.,** envoyer qn avec un mot pour qn; **to s. s.o. on an errand,** envoyer qn faire une commission; **to s. s.o. for sth.,** envoyer qn chercher qch., à la recherche de qch.; **I'll s. him for her,** je l'enverrai la chercher; **to s. a member to parliament,** envoyer, déléguer, un député à la Chambre; **to be sent into the world,** être mis au monde; **to s. s.o. away,** renvoyer, congédier (qn); **to s. s.o. back,** renvoyer qn; **s. him along!** envoyez-le me voir; dites-lui de venir me voir; (*b*) envoyer, faire parvenir (qch.); expédier (une lettre, etc.); remettre (de l'argent, etc.); **to s. word to s.o.,** envoyer un mot à qn; faire savoir qch. à qn; **to s. one's love to s.o.,** envoyer, (faire) faire, ses amitiés à qn; **to s. clothes to the laundry,** donner du linge à blanchir; **to send sth. every month,** faire un envoi tous les mois; **to s. goods elsewhere,** déplacer des marchandises; (*of bulky purchase, etc.*) **I'll have to have it sent,** il faut qu'on me le livre; **all the fish is sent to London,** tout le poisson est acheminé sur Londres; **I've sent back the umbrella,** j'ai renvoyé, rendu, le parapluie; **I'll s. my sister round for it,** ma sœur viendra le chercher; *F:* **to s. round the hat,** faire la quête. **2.** (*drive, compel*) **force that sends sth. in a certain direction,** force qui fait marcher, qui pousse, qch. dans une certaine direction; **it sent a shiver down my spine,** cela m'a fait passer un frisson dans le dos; **your question has sent me to the dictionary,** votre question m'a fait chercher dans le dictionnaire; **the blow sent him sprawling,** le coup l'a renversé, l'a envoyé rouler; **the blow sent the child crying to his mother,** ainsi frappé, l'enfant a couru pleurer dans les bras de sa mère. **3.** *A:* accorder, envoyer (qch.); **God s. that I may arrive in time,** Dieu veuille que j'arrive à temps; puissé-je arriver à temps; **s. him, her, victorious,** que Dieu lui donne, lui accorde, la victoire; **what fortune sends us,** ce que la fortune nous envoie. **4.** *v.ind.tr.* **to s. for s.o., sth.,** envoyer chercher qn, qch.; **we sent for a barrel of beer,** nous avons fait venir un tonneau de bière; **s. to my house for it,** envoyez quelqu'un le prendre chez moi; **to s. for de Gaulle,** faire appel à de Gaulle; **we sent for the doctor,** (i) nous avons appelé, envoyé chercher, (ii) nous avons fait venir, le médecin. **5.** (*a*) **you'll s. me mad,** vous allez me rendre fou; (*b*) *F:* **she, it, sends me,** elle, cela, me transporte; (*c*) *F:* (*of drugs*) faire voyager (qn).
II. (*compound verbs*) **1. send down,** *v.tr.* (*a*) faire descendre (qch.); (*b*) renvoyer, expulser (un étudiant de l'université); (*c*) *F:* envoyer (qn) en prison; faire coffrer (qn); (*d*) *Nau:* dépasser (un mât); dégréer (une vergue).
2. send in, *v.tr.* (*a*) faire (r)entrer (qn); (faire) servir (le dîner); **to s. in one's name,** se faire annoncer; (*b*) livrer, rendre (un compte); **he has sent in his bill,** il nous a envoyé sa note; **applications should be sent in before May 10th,** les demandes devront être remises avant le 10 mai; **to s. in one's resignation,** envoyer, donner, sa démission; (*c*) *Cr:* envoyer (un batteur) au guichet.
3. send off, *v.tr.* (*a*) expédier (une lettre, etc.); (*b*) **to s. s.o. off,** accompagner qn à l'aéroport, à la gare (pour lui dire au revoir); (*c*) *Sp:* renvoyer, expulser (un joueur) du terrain.
4. send on, *v.tr.* (*a*) faire suivre (une lettre); (*b*) transmettre (un ordre).
5. send out, *v.tr.* (*a*) envoyer (qn) dehors; faire sortir (qn); mettre (un élève) à la porte; (*b*) lancer, expédier (des prospectus); (*c*) jeter, vomir (des nuages de fumée, etc.); émettre (des signaux, de la chaleur, etc.); (*d*) (*of plant*) **to s. out leaves,** pousser des feuilles.
6. send up, *v.tr.* (*a*) faire monter (qn, qch.); **to s. up a balloon,** mettre un ballon en ascension; **to s. up a rocket,** lancer une fusée; *Parl:* **to s. up a bill (to the upper House),** présenter un projet de loi à la Chambre supérieure; (*b*) *Nau:* passer, guinder (un mât); (*c*) faire monter (les prix, la température, etc.); (*d*) *F:* se moquer de, parodier (qn, qch.); *Th:* prendre (une pièce, son rôle) à la rigolade; (*e*) *F:* mettre (qn) en prison; coffrer (qn).
send[2], *s. Nau:* encombrement vertical.
send[3], *v.i.* **(sended)** *Nau:* (*of ship*) plonger dans le creux de la lame; tanguer fortement.
sender ['sendər], *s.* **1.** (*pers.*) envoyeur, -euse; expéditeur, -trice (des marchandises); expéditionnaire *mf* (des marchandises). **2.** *Tg: Tp:* (*device*) manipulateur *m*, transmetteur *m*; **Morse s.,** clef *f* Morse.
clef *f* Morse.
send-off ['sendɔf], *s. F:* (*a*) fête *f* d'adieu; démonstration *f* d'amitié (au départ de qn); **to give s.o. a good s.-o.,** assister en nombre au départ de qn (pour lui souhaiter bon voyage); (*b*) inauguration réussie; **the press has given the book a good s.-o.,** le livre a eu beaucoup d'excellentes critiques dans les journaux; (*c*) enterrement *m.*
send-up ['sendʌp], *s. F:* satire *f*, parodie *f.*
senebiera [senə'biərə], *s. Bot:* sénebière *f*, senebiérie *f.*
Seneca ['senikə], *Pr.n.m. Lt.Lit:* Sénèque.
senecio [se'nekiou], *s. Bot:* seneçon *m.*
senega ['senigə], *s.* **1.** *Bot:* polygala *m* de Virginie. **2.** *Pharm:* **s. (root),** (racine *f* du) polygala de Virginie.
Senegal [seni'gɔ:l], *Pr.n. Geog:* (République *f* du) Sénégal.
Senegalese [senigə'li:z]. *Geog:* (*a*) *a.* sénégalais; (*b*) *s.* Sénégalais, -aise.

Senegambia [seni'gæmbiə], *Pr.n. Geog: Hist:* Sénégambie *f.*

senescence [si'nes(ə)ns], *s.* sénescence *f.*

senescent [si'nes(ə)nt], *a.* sénescent.

seneschal ['seniʃ(ə)l], *s. Hist:* sénéchal, -aux *m.*

seneschalsy ['seniʃ(ə)lsi], *s. Hist:* sénéchaussée *f.*

senile ['si:nail], *a.* sénile; **s. gangrene,** gangrène *f* sénile; **s. decay,** dégénérescence *f* sénile; sénilité *f*; **s. dementia, s. deterioration, s. psychosis,** démence *f* sénile; **he's eighty but not at all s.,** malgré ses quatre-vingts ans il n'est pas du tout sénile.

senility [se'niliti], *s.* sénilité *f,* caducité *f*; vieillesse avancée; démence *f* sénile.

senior ['si:njər]. **1.** *a.* (*a*) aîné, doyen; **Long s.,** Long aîné; **Bernard Long s.,** Bernard Long père; **he's two years s. to me,** il est mon aîné de deux ans; (*b*) (le plus) ancien, (la plus) ancienne; le plus élevé, la plus élevée (en grade); supérieur, -eure; **s. in rank,** de grade supérieur; **to be s. to s.o.,** être l'ancien, le doyen, de qn; **he is four years s. to me,** il est mon ancien de quatre ans; **the s. Service,** la marine; **the s. boys, girls, of a school,** les grands, grandes (élèves); **s. citizens,** retraité(e)s; personnes âgées; **illnesses that s. citizens are liable to,** maladies *f* propres au troisième âge; **s. clerk,** (i) *Adm:* premier commis, commis principal; chef de bureau; (ii) (*in lawyer's office*) premier clerc; **s. partner,** associé principal; **the s. officer,** le doyen des officiers; **my s. officer,** mon officier supérieur; **a s. command,** un commandement supérieur; *Sch:* **s. master, mistress,** professeur *m* en premier; **s. French master, mistress,** premier professeur de français; *Fin:* **s. shares,** actions *f* de capital, de priorité. **2.** *s.* (*a*) aîné, -ée; doyen, -enne (d'âge); **she is his s. by three years,** elle est son aînée de trois ans; (*b*) (le plus) ancien, (la plus) ancienne; le plus élevé, la plus élevée (en grade); supérieur, -eure; doyen, -enne; **to be s.o.'s s.,** être l'ancien, le doyen, de qn; **he is my s. by two years,** il est mon ancien de deux ans; (*of pupils*) **the seniors,** les grand(e)s; (*c*) *Sch: U.S:* étudiant(e) de quatrième (et dernière) année.

seniority [si:ni'ɔriti], *s.* **1.** priorité *f* d'âge; supériorité *f* d'âge; doyenneté *f*; **he is chairman by s.,** il est président d'âge. **2.** ancienneté *f* (de grade); **to be promoted by s.,** avancer (de grade), être promu, à l'ancienneté; **right of s.,** droit *m* d'ancienneté.

senna ['senə], *s. Bot: Pharm:* séné *m*; **s. tea,** infusion *f* de séné; tisane *f* de séné; **s. pods,** follicules *m* de séné.

sennet[1] ['senit], *s. Th: A:* fanfare *f* (pour annoncer une entrée solennelle des acteurs).

sennet[2], *s. Ich:* spet *m.*

sennight ['senait], *s. A:* semaine *f*; huit jours *m*; **this day s.,** aujourd'hui en huit.

sennit ['senit], *s. Nau:* tresse *f* (de chanvre, de paille).

Senonian [se'nouniən], *a. & s. Geol:* sénonien (*m*).

sensation [sen'seiʃ(ə)n], *s.* **1.** sensation *f*; sentiment *m,* impression *f* (de malaise, de bien-être, etc.); **I had the s. of falling,** j'avais l'impression que je tombais; *Psy:* **articular s.,** sens *m* articulaire; **after s.,** image consécutrice. **2.** sensation; effet sensationnel; (*of event, etc.*) **to create, make, cause, a s.,** faire sensation; **all out to cause a s.,** à l'affût du sensationnel; **book that made a s.,** livre qui a fait sensation, du bruit, scandale.

sensational [sen'seiʃən(ə)l], *a.* **1.** *Phil:* qui dépend des sens. **2.** sensationnel, à sensation; **s. event,** incident, événement, sensationnel; *Journ:* **yesterday Versailles was the scene of a s. affair,** un drame s'est déroulé hier à Versailles; **s. piece of news,** nouvelle sensationnelle, à sensation; **s. novel,** roman *m* à sensation, à gros effets.

sensationalism [sen'seiʃənəlizm], *s.* **1.** recherche *f* du sensationnel. **2.** *Phil:* sensualisme *m,* sensationnisme *m.*

sensationalist [sen'seiʃənəlist], *s.* **1.** colporteur *m* de nouvelles à sensation; dramatiseur, -euse. **2.** auteur *m* de romans à sensation; auteur à effets corsés. **3.** *Phil:* sensualiste *mf,* sensationniste *mf.*

sensationalize [sen'seiʃənəlaiz], *v.tr.* exagérer (un incident, etc.).

sensationally [sen'seiʃənəli], *adv.* d'une manière sensationnelle.

sensationism [sen'seiʃənizm], *s. Phil:* sensationnisme *m,* sensualisme *m.*

sensationist [sen'seiʃənist], *s.* **1.** celui, celle, qui recherche le sensationnel. **2.** *Phil:* sensationniste *mf,* sensualiste *mf.*

sense[1] [sens], *s.* **1.** (*a*) sens *m*; **the five senses,** les cinq sens; **the sixth s.,** le sixième sens; l'instinct *m*; l'intuition *f*; **to have a keen s. of smell, of hearing,** avoir l'odorat fin, l'ouïe fine; **to be in possession of all one's senses,** jouir de toutes ses facultés; **pleasures of the senses,** plaisirs sensuels, des sens; **to excite the senses,** éveiller les sens; (*b*) les sens; **s. organs,** organes *m* des sens; **s. data,** percepta *mpl*; **s. impression,** sensation *f.* **2.** (*a*) **to be in one's senses,** être sain d'esprit; **are you out of your senses?** avez-vous perdu l'esprit? avez-vous votre raison? vous perdez la raison! **you've taken leave of your senses,** vous avez perdu le sens commun; **any man in his senses,** tout homme jouissant de son bon sens, qui est dans son bon sens; **you're out of your senses!** tu déménages! **to come to one's senses (again),** rentrer dans son bon sens; revenir à la raison; **to bring s.o. to his senses,** ramener qn à la raison; dégriser qn; **to frighten s.o. out of his senses,** effrayer qn jusqu'à lui faire perdre la raison; (*b*) **to lose one's senses,** perdre connaissance; **to come to one's senses,** (i) revenir à soi; reprendre ses sens; (ii) sortir d'un rêve; reprendre le sentiment de la réalité des faits. **3.** (*a*) sensation *f,* sens; **a s. of pleasure, of warmth,** une sensation de plaisir, de chaleur; **inward s.,** sens interne; **to have a s. of having done something wrong,** avoir le sentiment d'avoir mal agi; **to labour under a s. of injustice,** nourrir un sentiment d'injustice; (*b*) sentiment, conscience *f*; **s. of colour, of beauty,** sentiment des couleurs, de la beauté; **to have a s. of time,** avoir le sentiment de l'heure; **to lose all s. of reality,** perdre la notion de la réalité; **he has no stage s.,** il n'a pas le sentiment de la scène; il manque d'instinct dramatique; **to have a high s. of duty,** avoir un haut sentiment de ses devoirs; **keen, delicate, s. of humour,** sentiment très vif, très fin, de l'humour; **to lose one's s. of justice,** perdre le sens de la justice; **to have a high s. of one's own importance,** avoir une haute opinion de soi-même, un vif sentiment de sa propre importance; (*c*) **to take the s. of the meeting,** prendre l'opinion, le sentiment, de l'assemblée; consulter l'assemblée (sur une question). **4.** bon sens; jugement *m*; **common s., good s.,** sens commun; bon sens; jugement sain; **he's got plenty of good s.,** il ne manque pas de sens (commun); c'est un homme intelligent; **to show good s.,** faire preuve de bon sens; **sound common s.,** le gros bon sens; **to talk s.,** parler raison; **there's no s. in that, that doesn't make s.,** cela n'a pas de sens; cela ne rime à rien; **what's the s. of talking like that?** à quoi bon, à quoi cela rime-t-il, de parler comme cela? **he's a man of s.,** c'est un homme de bon sens, un homme intelligent; **to have the (good) s. to do sth.,** avoir l'intelligence de faire qch.; **he ought to have had, to have shown, more s.,** il aurait dû faire preuve de plus de jugement. **5.** sens, signification *f* (d'un mot); **these words don't make s.,** ces mots n'ont pas de sens, sont incompréhensibles; **to make s. out of nonsense,** attacher un sens à l'inintelligible; **I can't make s. of it,** je n'arrive pas à le comprendre; **in the literal s.,** au sens propre; **in the full s. of the word,** dans toute la force, l'acception, du terme; **in the ordinary s. of the word,** au sens ordinaire du mot; **figurative s.,** sens figuré, acception figurée; **to interpret sth. in the good, the bad, s.,** prendre qch. en bonne, en mauvaise, part; **to take a word in the wrong s.,** prendre un mot à contre-sens; **he is an artist in more senses than one, in all senses of the word, in every s. of the word,** c'est un artiste dans tout l'acception du terme; **in a s.,** d'une certaine façon; dans un (certain) sens; d'un certain point de vue; **in the s. that. . .,** en ce sens que. . .; *Gram:* **s. agreement,** syllepse *f.* **6.** (*a*) *Ph: etc:* direction *f,* sens; **s. of emission,** direction d'émission (des radiations); **s. of rotation,** sens de rotation; (*b*) (*in direction finding*) **s. finding, research,** lever *m* du doute; **s. finder,** indicateur *m* du lever du doute. **7.** *Cmptr:* lecture *f* (par exploration); **s. line, winding,** fil *m* de lecture; **s. signal,** signal *m* de sortie de lecture.

sense[2], *v.tr.* **1.** sentir (qch.) intuitivement; pressentir (qch.); avoir le sens de (qch.). **2.** comprendre, saisir (qch.). **3.** *Phil:* percevoir (qch.) par le sens. **4.** *Elcs: etc:* (*a*) (i) explorer, palper, sonder; (ii) (*of satellite, etc.*) détecter, capter (un corps céleste); (*b*) *Cmptr:* (i) explorer; lire (par exploration); (ii) tester (un indicateur).

senseless ['senslis], *a.* **1.** (*of pers.*) sans connaissance, inanimé; **to fall s.,** tomber sans connaissance; **knocked s.,** assommé, privé de connaissance (par un choc). **2.** (*of pers., thg, conduct, etc.*) qui n'a pas le sens commun; insensé, stupide, déraisonnable; dénué de sens, de raison; **a s. remark,** une bêtise; **at the end of this s. journey,** à la fin de ce stupide voyage. **3.** dépourvu des facultés des sens; insensible.

senselessly ['senslisli], *adv.* insensément, déraisonnablement, stupidement, sottement.

senselessness ['senslisnis], *s.* **1.** manque *m* de bon sens; stupidité *f.* **2.** insensibilité *f.*

sensibility [sensi'biliti], *s.* **1.** sensibilité *f* (d'un organe, etc.); **s. to an influence,** sensibilité à une influence. **2.** (*emotional*) sensibilité, émotivité *f*; **mawkish s.,** sensiblerie *f*; **to ruffle s.o.'s sensibilities,** faire outrage aux susceptibilités *f* de qn.

sensible ['sensəbl], *a.* **1.** (*a*) sensible, perceptible; qui peut être saisi par les sens; (*b*) **s. horizon,** horizon apparent, visible; **s. heat,** sensible. **2.** (*of quantity, difference, etc.*) sensible, appréciable; assez considérable; **s. rise in temperature,** hausse *f* appréciable de la température. **3.** *A: & Lit:* (*aware*) (*of pers.*) conscient (**of,** de); **to be s. of one's danger,** se rendre compte du danger; **he became s. of a confused noise,** il eut conscience d'un bruit confus; **I am very s. of my defects,** je me rends parfaitement compte de mes défauts; **to be s. of the fact that. . .,** apprécier le fait que. . .; **s. of an honour,** sensible à un honneur; **s. of the enormity of his crime. . .,** se rendant compte de l'énormité du crime qu'il avait commis. . .; **to be s. of s.o.'s kindness,** être sensible à l'amabilité, aux amabilités, de qn. **4.** sensé, raisonnable, judicieux; **s. person,** personne sensée, pleine de bon sens; **s. people,** les gens sensés; les esprits sages; **s. choice,** choix judicieux; **be s.,** soyez raisonnable; **the s. donkey stood perfectly still,** l'âne a sagement gardé l'immobilité; **s. clothes,** vêtements commodes, pratiques; **s. shoes,** chaussures rationnelles.

sensibleness ['sensibəlnis], *s.* bon sens; jugement (sain); intelligence *f*; raison *f.*

sensibly ['sensibli], *adv.* **1.** sensiblement, perceptiblement, d'une manière appréciable. **2.** sensément, raisonnablement, judicieusement; avec bon sens; **to be s. dressed,** porter des vêtements pratiques.

sensillum, *pl.* **-a** [sen'siləm, -ə], *s. Ent:* **(campaniform) s.,** sensille *f* (campaniforme).

sensing ['sensiŋ], *s.* **1.** *Elcs: etc:* (i) exploration *f*; (ii) détection *f*; (iii) analyse *f*; **s. component member,** organe *m* sensible; **remote s.,** télédétection *f*; **s. technology,** technique *f* de la détection; **s. relay,** relais détecteur; **s. device, unit,** organe détecteur; explorateur *m,* palpeur *m,* sonde *f*; (*in satellite, etc.*) détecteur *m,* capteur *m* (de corps céleste). **2.** *Cmptr:* lecture *f* (par exploration); **mark s.,** lecture *f* de marques; **s. station,** poste *m* de lecture.

sensitive ['sensitiv], *a.* **1.** *occ.* sensible, sensitif; (qui a la faculté) des sens; *Bot:* **s. plant,** sensitive *f,* mimeuse *f,* mimosa *m or f,* herbe vivante. **2.** (*a*) (*of skin, tooth*) sensible, sensitif; **horse with a s. mouth,** cheval à la bouche chatouilleuse, sensible; **s. to sth.,** sensible à qch.; **s. to moisture,** sensible à l'humidité; (*of pers.*) **to be s. to cold,** être frileux, -euse; **plant s. to frost,** plante délicate; (*b*) (*of pers.*) susceptible; impressionnable; **don't be so s.,** ne soyez pas si susceptible; **s. on questions of honour,** sensible, chatouilleux, sur l'honneur; **public opinion is very s. about this,** l'opinion publique est toujours inquiète, est ombrageuse, à ce sujet; (*c*) **s. scales,** balance *f* sensible; *Com: Fin:* **s. market,** marché instable, prompt à réagir; *Phot:* **s. plate,** plaque impressionnable, sensible à la lumière; **s. paper,** papier sensible, sensibilisé. **3.** *s.* personne *f* sensible aux influences psychiques, qui a le pouvoir médiumnique; sujet *m* sensible.

sensitively ['sensitivli], *adv.* sensiblement; d'une manière sensible, sensitive; (écrire, etc.) avec sensibilité.

sensitiveness ['sensitivnis], **sensitivity** [sensi'tiviti], *s.* **1.** sensibilité *f,* sensitivité *f*; faculté *f* de sentir (d'une plante, etc.); promptitude *f* à réagir. **2.** (*a*) sensibilité (de caractère); susceptibilité *f*; (*b*) sensibilité (d'une machine, d'une cellule photo-électrique); **lack of s.,** insensibilité *f*; *Phot:* **s. of an emulsion,** impressionnabilité *f,* rapidité *f,* d'une émulsion; **initial s.,** sensibilité initiale, seuil *m* (d'une émulsion).

sensitizable [sensi'taizəbl], *a. Phot:* (papier) sensibilisable.

sensitization [sensitai'zeiʃ(ə)n], *s. Med: Phot:* sensibilisation *f.*

sensitize ['sensitaiz], *v.tr.* sensibiliser, rendre sensible.

sensitized ['sensitaizd], *a. Phot:* (papier) sensible, impressionnable.

sensitizer ['sensitaizər], *s. Phot:* sensibilisateur *m.*

sensitizing ['sensitaiziŋ], *s.* (*a*) *Phot:* sensibilisation *f*; **s. bath,** bain *m* à sensibiliser; sensibilisateur *m*; (*b*) **their aim is the s. of public opinion,** leur but est la sensibilisation de l'opinion (à un problème).

sensitometer [sensi'tɔmitər], *s. Phot:* sensitomètre *m.*

sensitometric [sensitou'metrik], *a. Phot:* sensitométrique.

sensitometry [sensi'tɔmitri], *s. Phot:* sensitométrie *f.*

sensor ['sensər], *s. Elcs: etc:* **1.** (*a*) détecteur *m*; *Av:* **error s.,** détecteur d'erreur(s); *Mec.E:* **leak s.,** détecteur de fuite(s); (*b*) *Space:* (*in satellite, etc.*) détecteur, capteur *m*; **nuclear test detection s.,** détecteur d'explosions expérimentales nucléaires; **star s.,** capteur stellaire;

star Canopus s., capteur de Canope; **sun s.**, capteur solaire; (*c*) sonde *f*, jauge *f*; **s. unit**, bloc *m* de sonde; **temperature s.**, sonde thermométrique; *Space:* (*in rocket*) **depletion s., level s.**, jauge, canne *f*, de niveau (pour vérifier le niveau des ergols); (*d*) *Elcs: Ph:* analyseur *m*; **discrete Doppler s.**, analyseur Doppler. **2.** *Cmptr:* dispositif *m* de lecture; lecteur *m*.

sensorial [sen'sɔːriəl], *a.* sensoriel; **s. power**, énergie sensorielle, vitale.

sensorimetric [sensɔːri'metrik], *a. Psy:* sensorimétrique.

sensorimetry [sensɔː'rimitri], *s. Psy:* sensorimétrie *f*.

sensorimotor [sensəri'moutər], *a.* (*a*) *Anat:* (nerf) sensitivo-moteur; (*b*) *Psy:* sensorimoteur, -trice.

sensorium, *pl.* **-ia** *or* **-iums** [sen'sɔːriəm, -iə, -iəmz], *s.* sensorium *m*.

sensory ['sensəri], *a.* sensoriel; **s. organs**, organes des sens; **s. nerve**, nerf sensoriel; **s. cell**, cellule sensorielle.

sensual ['sensjuəl], *a.* **1.** sensuel; (instinct) animal; **the average s. man**, l'homme moyen sensuel; **s. pleasures**, plaisirs *m* des sens. **2.** sensuel, voluptueux; libidineux.

sensualism ['sensjuəlizm], *s.* **1.** *Phil:* sensualisme *m*. **2.** sensualité *f*.

sensualist ['sensjuəlist], *s.* **1.** *Phil:* sensualiste *mf*. **2.** sensualiste; voluptueux, -euse.

sensuality [sensju'æliti], *s.* sensualité *f*.

sensualize ['sensjuəlaiz], *v.tr.* sensualiser; animaliser.

sensually ['sensjuəli], *adv.* avec sensualité; sensuellement.

sensuous ['sensjuəs], *a.* **1.** (*of pleasure, life, etc.*) sybaritique, voluptueux; (*of charm, etc.*) capiteux. **2.** qui provient des sens; matérialiste.

sensuously ['sensjuəsli], *adv.* d'une manière sybaritique; avec volupté.

sensuousness ['sensjuəsnis], *s.* sybaritisme *m*; volupté *f*.

sentence[1] ['sentəns], *s.* **1.** *Jur:* (*a*) jugement *m* (en matière pénale ou ecclésiastique, et en matières de l'Amirauté); sentence *f*, condamnation *f*; **life s.**, condamnation à vie; **s. of death, death s.**, arrêt *m*, sentence, de mort; condamnation à mort; **under s. of death**, condamné à mort; **to pass (a) s.**, prononcer une condamnation, une sentence; **to pass s. of three months' imprisonment on s.o.**, condamner qn à trois mois de prison; **to give rise to a s. under criminal law**, entraîner une condamnation au pénal; (*b*) peine *f*; **commutation of s.**, commutation *f* de peine; **while he was serving his s.**, pendant la durée de sa peine; pendant qu'il purgeait sa peine; **given a suspended (prison) s. of one year**, condamné à un an de prison avec sursis. **2.** *Gram:* phrase *f*; **well constructed s.**, phrase bien coupée, bien arrondie, bien construite. **3.** *A:* (*a*) opinion *f*; (*b*) sentence, adage *m*, maxime *f*.

sentence[2], *v.tr. Jur:* condamner (qn); prononcer une condamnation, une sentence, contre (qn); **to s. s.o. to a month's imprisonment, to death**, condamner qn à un mois de prison, à mort.

sententious [sen'tenʃəs], *a.* (*of pers., speech, etc.*) sentencieux; (*of pers.*) qui ne parle que par sentences.

sententiously [sen'tenʃəsli], *adv.* sentencieusement; **to talk s.**, ne parler que par sentences; parler d'un ton d'oracle.

sententiousness [sen'tenʃəsnis], *s.* (i) caractère, (ii) ton, sentencieux.

sentient ['senʃənt], *a.* (*of being, etc.*) sentant, sensible; **s. experience**, ce que l'on apprend par les sens.

sentiment ['sentimənt], *s.* **1.** (*a*) *A: & Lit:* sentiment *m*, mouvement *m* de l'âme; **s. of pity**, sentiment de pitié; **noble sentiments**, sentiments nobles; **to indulge in high-flown s.**, se permettre de grands sentiments; **have you ever shown any s. towards her?** lui avez-vous jamais témoigné les moindres sentiments? (*b*) sentiment, opinion *f*, avis *m*; **these are my sentiments**, voilà mon sentiment, mon opinion; voilà comme je pense. **2.** *Art:* sentiment, connaissance *f* sympathique (du sujet, etc.). **3.** sentimentalité *f*; (*mawkish*) sensiblerie *f*; **one cannot mix s. and business**, on ne fait pas de sentiment en affaires.

sentimental [senti'ment(ə)l], *a.* (*a*) sentimental, -aux; **s. value**, valeur sentimentale; (*b*) **s. novel**, roman sentimental, d'une sensiblerie romanesque; **s. comedy**, la comédie larmoyante (du 18e. siècle); **don't be so s.!** pas tant de sentiment!

sentimentalism [senti'mentəlizm], *s.* sentimentalisme *m*; sensiblerie *f*.

sentimentalist [senti'mentəlist], *s.* personne sentimentale; **he's, she's, a s.**, c'est un(e) sentimental(e).

sentimentality [sentimen'tæliti], *s.* sentimentalité *f*; sensiblerie *f*.

sentimentalize [senti'mentəlaiz]. **1.** *v.i.* faire du sentiment, de la sensiblerie; sentimentaliser. **2.** *v.tr.* apporter du sentiment, de la sensiblerie, dans (une œuvre, etc.).

sentimentally [senti'mentəli], *adv.* sentimentalement; avec sensiblerie.

sentinel ['sentin(ə)l], *s.* (*a*) factionnaire *m*; sentinelle *f*; **to stand s.**, monter la garde; être de garde, de faction; *Lit:* **to stand s. over s.o., sth.**, veiller sur qn, sur qch.; (*b*) *Crust:* **s. crab**, podophthalme *m* vigil.

sentry ['sentri], *s. Mil:* (i) (*guard*) factionnaire *m*, sentinelle *f*; (ii) (*in the field*) guetteur *m*, sentinelle; **s. over the arms**, sentinelle devant les armes; **advanced, outlying, s.**, guetteur avancé, sentinelle avancée; **double s.**, guetteur, sentinelle, double; **gas s.**, éclaireur *m*; **on s.**, en, de, faction; en sentinelle; (de service) de guet; **s. beat**, (i) parcours *m*, cent pas *m*, d'une sentinelle; (ii) secteur *m* de surveillance (d'un guetteur); **s. box**, guérite *f*; **sentry's orders**, consignes *f* d'une sentinelle, d'un guetteur; **s. post**, emplacement *m*, poste *m*, d'une sentinelle, d'un guetteur; **to be on s. (duty), to do s. duty, to stand s.**, être en sentinelle, en faction, de faction; monter la garde, la faction; être (de service) de guet; *Fig:* faire la sentinelle; **to come off s.**, quitter la garde, la faction; sortir de faction; quitter le (service de) guet; **to go on s.**, entrer en faction; prendre la faction, la garde; prendre le (service de) guet; **to post a s.**, placer une sentinelle, un guetteur; poser un factionnaire; **to put s.o. on s.**, mettre qn en faction, en sentinelle; mettre qn de garde; **to relieve a s.**, relever un factionnaire, une sentinelle, un guetteur; **sentries will be found by B company**, la deuxième compagnie fournira les sentinelles, les guetteurs; **to force a s.**, forcer la consigne.

Senussi (the) [ðəsi'njuːsi], *s.pl.* (*in N. Africa*) le Senous(s)i.

sepal ['sep(ə)l], *s. Bot:* sépale *m*.

sepalled ['sepəld], *a. Bot:* calicé.

sepaloid ['sepəlɔid], *a. Bot:* sépaloïde.

sepalous ['sepələs], *a. Bot:* sépalaire.

separability [sepərə'biliti], *s.* séparabilité *f*.

separable ['sep(ə)rəbl], *a.* séparable.

separate[1] ['sep(ə)rət]. **1.** *a.* (*a*) (*of parts, etc.*) séparé, détaché (**from**, de); (*b*) (*of existence, interests, etc.*) distinct; indépendant; (*of room, entrance, etc.*) particulier; **entered in a s. column**, inscrit dans une colonne particulière; (*of married couple*) **to sleep in s. rooms**, faire chambre à part; **to sleep in s. beds**, dormir dans des lits jumeaux; *Jur:* **(married woman's) s. estate**, biens réservés (de la femme mariée); *Can:* **s. school** = école libre. **2.** *s.* (*a*) *Typ: U.S:* tirage *m* à part; (*b*) *Com:* **separates**, rayon *m* des dépareillés *m*.

separate[2] ['sepəreit]. **1.** *v.tr.* (*a*) séparer, désunir, détacher, décoller (**from**, de); déprendre (deux objets collés ensemble); départir (les métaux); dédoubler (un brin de fil, etc.); **to s. two boxers**, séparer deux boxeurs; **to s. truth from error**, dégager la vérité de l'erreur; **these words cannot be separated from their context**, on ne devrait pas séparer ces mots de leur contexte, considérer ces mots sans tenir compte de leur contexte; **to s. milk**, écrémer, centrifuger, le lait; *Hort:* **to s. a layer**, sevrer une marcotte; (*b*) désunir (les membres d'une famille, etc.); détacher (qn de sa famille, etc.); **he is separated from his wife**, il est séparé de sa femme; **to s. a pair of pigeons**, déparier un couple de pigeons; (*c*) **the Channel separates England from France**, la Manche sépare la France et l'Angleterre; **the gulf that separates him from his colleagues**, l'abîme (qui s'ouvre) entre lui et ses collègues. **2.** *v.i.* (*a*) (*of thg*) se séparer, se détacher, se décoller, se désunir (**from**, de); *Ch:* **to s. out**, se séparer (par précipitation); (*b*) (*of pers.*) **when we separated for the night**, quand nous nous sommes quittés pour la nuit; **to s. from s.o.**, se séparer de, rompre avec, qn; (*c*) (*of man and wife*) se séparer de corps et de biens; **my wife and I have decided to s.**, ma femme et moi avons décidé de nous séparer.

separately ['sep(ə)rətli], *adv.* séparément.

separation [sepə'reiʃ(ə)n], *s.* **1.** (*a*) séparation *f*; écrémage *m* (du lait); *Min:* classement *m* (du minerai); **wet s. of ore**, triage *m* du minerai par voie humide; *Ind:* **magnetic s.**, déferrage *m*; *Petr:* **dry s.**, séparation à sec; *Mch:* **baffle s.**, séparation (de l'eau de la vapeur) par heurtement, par choc; *Ph:* **momentum s.**, séparation par fractionnement; *Atom.Ph:* **isotope s.**, séparation isotopique, des isotopes; (*b*) **s. of the bark from the tree**, séparation de l'écorce de l'arbre; (*c*) séparation (d'avec qn); *Mil:* **s. allowance**, allocation faite à la femme (d'un soldat); (*d*) *Jur:* **judicial s., s. from bed and board**, séparation judiciaire, séparation de corps (et de biens); **de facto s.**, séparation amiable, de fait; **s. order**, jugement *m* de séparation. **2.** écart *m*, distance *f*; *Opt:* **s. of the lenses, of the nodal points**, écart, écartement *m*, des lentilles, des points nodaux; **lenses with fixed s.**, lentilles à écartement invariable.

separatism ['sepərətizm], *s.* séparatisme *m*.

separatist ['sepərətist], *s.* séparatiste *mf*.

separative ['sepərətiv], *a.* séparatif; séparateur, -trice.

separator ['sepəreitər], *s.* (*a*) (*device*) séparateur *m*; *Gasm:* colonne *f* d'épuration; **centrifugal s.**, séparateur centrifuge; **oil s.**, séparateur d'huile; **cream s.**, (i) écrémeuse *f*; (ii) centrifugeur *m*; *Min:* **ore s.**, classeur *m*, trieur *m* (de minerai); *Ind:* **magnetic s.**, séparateur magnétique; **electromagnetic s.**, électrotrieuse *f*; *Mch:* **baffle s.**, séparateur à chicanes; *Atom.Ph:* **isotope s.**, séparateur d'isotopes; (*b*) *Cmptr:* (i) séparateur, caractère *m* de séparation; (ii) déliasseuse *f*; **record, unit, s.**, séparateur d'enregistrements, d'unités; **s. card**, carte *f* intercalaire.

separatrix ['sepərətriks], *s. Typ:* ligne *f*, trait *m*, de séparation entre les corrections (en marge d'une épreuve).

sepia ['siːpiə], *s.* **1.** *Moll:* sépia *f*, seiche *f*. **2.** *Art: etc:* sépia; **s. (drawing)**, (dessin *m* à la) sépia; **s. paper**, papier *m* bistre; *Phot:* **s. toning**, virage *m* sépia.

sepiola [siːpi'oulə], *s. Moll:* sépiole *f*, petite seiche.

Sepiolidae [siːpi'oulidiː], *s.pl. Moll:* sépiolidés *m*.

sepiolite ['siːpioulait], *s. Miner:* sépiolite *f*.

sepoy ['siːpɔi], *s. Mil:* cipaye *m*.

seps [seps], *s. Rept:* seps *m*.

sepsis ['sepsis], *s. Med:* (*a*) putréfaction *f*, putrescence *f*; (*b*) septicémie *f*; infection *f* septicémique.

septal ['sept(ə)l], *a. Nat.Hist:* septal, -aux; du septum, des septums.

septangular [sep'tæŋgjulər], *a. Mth:* heptagonal, -aux.

septarium, *pl.* **-ia** [sep'tɛəriəm, -iə], *s. Geol:* nodule *m* de calcaire argileux.

septate ['septeit], *a.* (*a*) *Anat:* (organe) à septum; (*b*) *Bot:* (spore) cloisonnée; (*c*) *Coel:* (polypier) à septes.

September [sep'tembər], *s.* septembre *m*; **in S.**, au mois de septembre, en septembre; **(on) the first, the seventh, of S.**, le premier, le sept, septembre; *Fr.Hist:* **the S. massacres**, les septembrisades *f*.

Septembrist [sep'tembrist], **Septembrizer** [sep'tembrizər], *s. Fr. Hist:* septembriseur *m*.

septemvir, *pl.* **-viri** ['septemviər, -'viər(a)i], *s. Rom. Hist:* septemvir *m*.

septemvirate [sep'temviəreit], *s. Hist:* septemvirat *m*.

septenary [sep'tiːnəri], *a. & s.* septénaire (*m*).

septennate [sep'teneit], *s.* septennat *m*.

septennial [sep'teniəl], *a.* septennal, -aux.

septennially [sep'teniəli], *adv.* tous les sept ans.

septennium [sep'teniəm], *s.* septennat *m*.

septentrional [sep'tentriənəl], *a.* septentrional, -aux; du nord.

septet(te) [sep'tet], *s. Mus:* septuor *m*.

septic ['septik], *a.* (*a*) *Med:* septique; **s. poisoning**, septicémie *f*; *F:* **to go s.**, s'infecter; *Hyg:* **s. tank**, fosse *f* septique; (*b*) moche, infect; **how perfectly s.!** que c'est moche, infect! **he's perfectly s.!** il est vraiment impossible, au-dessous de tout!

septic(a)emia [septi'siːmiə], *s. Med:* septicémie *f*; **bacillary s.**, bacillémie *f*; **haemorrhagic s.**, septicémie hémorragique.

septic(a)emic [septi'siːmik], *a. Med:* septicémique.

septicidal [septi'said(ə)l], *a. Bot:* (déhiscence) septicide.

septicity [sep'tisiti], *s. Med:* septicité *f*.

septicopy(a)emia [septikoupai'iːmiə], *s. Med:* septicopyoémie *f*.

septiferous [sep'tifərəs], *a. Nat.Hist:* septifère.

septiform ['septifɔːm], *a. Nat.Hist:* septiforme.

septillion [sep'tiliən], *s.* **1.** septillion *m* (10^{42}). **2.** *U.S:* quatrillion *m* (10^{24}).

septime ['septiːm], *s. Fenc:* septime *f*.

Septimus ['septiməs]. *Pr.n.m.* Septime.

septivalent [septi'veilənt], *a. Ch:* septivalent, heptavalent.

septuagenarian [septjuədʒe'nɛəriən], *s. & a.* septuagénaire (*mf*).

Septuagesima [septjuə'dʒesimə], *s. Ecc:* **S. (Sunday)**, (le dimanche de) la Septuagésime.

Septuagint ['septjuədʒint], *s.* version *f* (de la Bible) des Septante; la Septante.

septum, *pl.* **-a** ['septəm, -ə], *s.* (*a*) *Anat:* septum *m* (du nez, etc.); (*b*) *Bot:* cloison *f* (d'une spore); (*c*) *Coel:* septe *m* (d'un polypier).

septuor ['septjuɔːr], *s. Mus:* septuor *m*.

septuple ['septjupl], *a. & s.* septuple (*m*).

sepulchral [si'pʌlkr(ə)l], *a.* sépulcral, -aux; **s. vault**, caveau *m*; **s. stone**, pierre *f* tumulaire; **s. voice**, voix sépulcrale, caverneuse.

sepulchre ['sep(ə)lkər], *s.* sépulcre *m*, tombeau *m*; **the Holy S.**, le Saint Sépulcre.

sepulture ['sepəltjər], *s.* **1.** sépulture *f*; mise *f* au tombeau; inhumation *f*. **2.** *A:* (*a*) (lieu *m* de) sépulture (des rois, etc.); (*b*) tombeau *m*.

sequacious [si'kweiʃəs], *a. Lit:* **1.** qui manque

d'originalité; (imitateur) servile. **2.** (*a*) qui a l'esprit de suite; (*b*) (*of argument, etc.*) cohérent.

sequel ['si:kw(ə)l], *s.* suite *f* (d'un roman, etc.); **in the s. to this story,** dans la suite de cette histoire; **as a s. to these events,** comme suite à ces événements; **action that had an unfortunate s.,** acte qui a entraîné des suites malheureuses, qui a eu des conséquences malheureuses.

sequelae [si'kwi:li:], *s.pl. Med:* séquelles *f* (d'une maladie, d'un accident, etc.); *Obst:* suite *f* de couches.

sequence[1] ['si:kwəns], *s.* **1.** (*a*) succession *f*; ordre naturel; **in s.,** en série; en succession; **in historical s.,** par ordre historique; **logical s.,** enchaînement *m* logique; (*b*) suite *f*, série *f*, chaîne *f* (d'événements, etc.); (*c*) *Cin:* (i) séquence *f* (de liaison); (ii) scène *f* (de film); *T.V:* **s. of interlace,** séquence d'entrelacement; *El:* **phase s.,** séquence d'appel; *Cmptr:* **control s.,** séquence (d'exécution) des instructions; **calling s.,** séquence d'appel; **random-number s.,** séquence de nombres aléatoires; **collating, collation, s.,** séquence d'interclassement; **s. chart,** diagramme *m* de fonctionnement; **s. access storage,** mémoire *f* à accès séquentiel; **s. check(ing),** contrôle *m* de séquence; **to s. check,** contrôler la séquence; **s. number,** numéro *m* d'ordre; **s. numbering,** immatriculation *f*; (*d*) *Mus:* **s. of chords,** (i) marche *f* des accords; (ii) séquence; (*e*) *Gram:* **s. of tenses,** concordance *f* des temps; (*f*) *Cards:* séquence. **2.** *Ecc:* séquence, prose (chantée avant l'Évangile).

sequence[2], *v.tr.* ordonner, mettre en séquence, classer.

sequencing ['si:kwənsiŋ], *s.* classement *m*; mise *f* en séquence; *Cmptr:* **s. by merging,** rangement *m* par interclassement.

sequent ['si:kwənt], *a. Lit:* (*a*) (*of effect, etc.*) conséquent, qui s'ensuit, résultant; (*b*) (*of event, etc.*) consécutif (à).

sequential [si'kwenʃ(ə)l], *a.* (*a*) séquentiel; consécutif; *Cmptr:* **s. computer,** calculateur séquentiel; **s. control,** exécution *f* des instructions en séquence; (*b*) (*of teaching, history, etc.*) continu.

sequentially [si'kwenʃəli], *adv.* séquentiellement; *Cmptr:* **s. numbered,** à numérotage séquentiel; **s. ordered, organized, file,** fichier séquentiel.

sequester [si'kwestər]. **1.** *v.p. Lit:* **to s. oneself (from the world),** se retirer (du monde). **2.** *v.tr.* (*a*) confisquer, s'approprier (qch.); (*b*) *Jur:* séquestrer (les biens d'un débiteur, un bien en litige); mettre (un bien) en, sous, séquestre; (*c*) *Ch:* complexer.

sequestered [si'kwestəd], *a.* **1.** *Lit:* (*of life*) retiré, isolé; (*of place*) retiré, perdu; peu fréquenté; **to lead a s. life,** vivre loin du monde. **2.** *Jur:* (*of property*) en, sous, séquestre.

sequestering [si'kwest(ə)riŋ], *a. Ch:* (agent) chélateur, complexant.

sequestrate [si'kwestreit], *v.tr. Jur:* séquestrer (les biens du débiteur, etc.); mettre (un bien) en, sous, séquestre; **three nationalist papers were sequestrated,** on a saisi trois journaux nationalistes.

sequestration [sikwes'treiʃ(ə)n], *s.* **1.** *Lit:* retraite *f*; éloignement *m* du monde; séquestration *f*. **2.** (*a*) confiscation *f*; appropriation *f*; (*b*) *Jur:* séquestration; mise *f* en, sous, séquestre; **writ of s.,** séquestre *m* (judiciaire).

sequestrator ['sikwestreitər], *s. Jur:* (*pers.*) séquestre *m*.

sequestrectomy [sikwes'trektəmi], *s. Surg:* séquestrectomie *f*.

sequestrotomy [sikwes'trɔtəmi], *s. Surg:* séquestrotomie *f*.

sequestrum, *pl.* **-a** [si'kwestrəm, -ə], *s. Med:* séquestre *m* (d'os nécrosé).

sequin ['si:kwin], *s.* sequin *m*.

sequoia [si'kwɔiə], *s. Bot:* sequoia *m*, wellingtonia *m*; **giant s.,** sequoia géant.

serac ['seræk], *s. Geol:* sérac *m* (de glacier).

seraglio [se'rɑ:liou], *s.* sérail, -ails *m*; harem *m*.

serapeum [serə'pi:əm], *s. Archeol:* sérapéum *m*.

seraph, *pl.* **seraphs, seraphim** ['serəf, əfs, -əfim], *s.* séraphin *m*.

seraphic [se'ræfik], *a.* séraphique; *Ecc.Hist:* **the S. Doctor,** le docteur séraphique (saint Bonaventure).

seraphically [se'ræfik(ə)li], *adv.* d'une manière, d'un air, séraphique.

Serb [sə:b], *s.* Serbe *mf*.

Serbia ['sə:biə]. *Pr.n. Geog:* Serbie *f*.

Serbian ['sə:biən]. **1.** *a. Geog: Ethn:* serbe. **2.** *s. Ling:* serbe *m*.

Serbo-Croat [sə:bou'krouət]. **1.** *Geog:* (*a*) *a.* serbo-croate; (*b*) *s.* Serbo-croate *mf*. **2.** *s. Ling:* serbo-croate *m*.

Serbo-Croatian [sə:boukrou'eiʃən], *a. Geog:* serbo-croate.

sere ['siər], *a. Lit:* (*of leaf, etc.*) flétri, desséché, fané.

serenade[1] [serə'neid], *s.* sérénade *f*.

serenade[2], *v.tr.* donner une sérénade à (qn).

serenader [serə'neidər], *s.* donneur *m*, joueur *m*, de sérénades.

serenata [serə'nɑ:tə], *s. Mus:* sérénade *f*.

serendipity [seren'dipiti], *s.* découverte heureuse et inattendue; don *m* de faire des trouvailles.

serene [si'ri:n], *a.* **1.** (*of sky, sea, pers., etc.*) serein, calme, tranquille, paisible; (*of sky*) clair; **her face wore a s. look,** son visage exprimait le calme; *F: O:* **all s.!** (i) ça y est! c'est bien! (ii) pas de pet! pas de paix! **2.** (*title*) sérénissime; **His S. Highness,** son Altesse sérénissime.

serenely [si'ri:nli], *adv.* tranquillement; avec calme, avec sérénité; d'un visage serein.

sereneness [si'ri:nnis], *s.* sérénité *f*, calme *m*, tranquillité *f*.

serenity [si'reniti], *s.* **1.** sérénité *f*, calme *m*, tranquillité *f*. **2.** (*title*) sérénité.

serf [sə:f], *s.* serf, *f.* serve.

serfage ['sə:fidʒ], **serfdom** ['sə:fdəm], *s.* servage *m*.

serge [sə:dʒ], *s. Tex:* serge *f*; **cotton s.,** sergé *m*; **silk s.,** serge de soie; **s. coat,** manteau *m* en serge.

sergeant ['sɑ:dʒ(ə)nt], *s.* **1.** *A:* **s. of the watch,** sergent *m* de nuit. **2. S. at Arms,** (i) *A:* huissier *m* d'armes; (ii) commandant *m* militaire du Parlement. **3.** (*a*) (*infantry, air force*) sergent; (*artillery, armoured corps, cavalry*) maréchal *m* des logis; (*in all arms*) sous-officier *m*, *pl.* sous-officiers; (*W.R.A.C. & W.R.A.F.*) cinquième catégorie; **mess s.,** sous-officier d'ordinaire; **platoon s.,** sous-officier adjoint (au chef de section); **quartermaster s.,** *U.S:* **staff s.,** sergent fourrier, sergent comptable; maréchal des logis fourrier, maréchal des logis comptable; **senior quartermaster s.,** *U.S:* **first s.,** sergent major, maréchal des logis major; **staff s.,** *Mil.Av:* **flight s.,** *U.S:* **master s.,** sergent-chef *m*, *pl.* sergents-chefs; maréchal des logis chef; (*W.R.A.F.*) quatrième catégorie; **supply s.,** sous-officier d'approvisionnement; (*b*) **police s.,** brigadier *m*.

sergeant-major [sɑ:dʒ(ə)nt'meidʒər], *s. Mil: A:* adjudant *m*; (*W.R.A.C.*) quatrième catégorie *f*; **company s.-m.,** adjudant de compagnie; (*W.R.A.C.*) deuxième catégorie; **regimental s.-m.,** adjudant-chef *m*, *pl.* adjudants-chefs; (*W.R.A.C.*) première catégorie.

sergette [sə:'dʒet], *s. Tex:* sergette *f*.

Sergius ['sə:dʒiəs]. *Pr.n.m.* Serge.

serial ['siəriəl]. **1.** *a.* qui appartient à la série; *Mus:* sériel; **s. number,** numéro *m* de série; numéro d'ordre; *Ind: etc:* numéro matricule (d'un moteur, etc.). **2.** (*a*) *a.* en série; formant série; **s. story,** roman-feuilleton *m*, *pl.* romans-feuilletons; **s. writer,** feuilletoniste *mf*; **s. rights,** droit *m* de reproduction dans les journaux et périodiques; droit de reproduction en feuilleton; (*b*) *s.* roman-feuilleton; *W.Tel:* radioroman *m*; *T.V:* téléroman *m*; **they began screening a new s. yesterday,** on a commencé hier la diffusion d'un nouveau feuilleton.

serialism ['siəriəlizm], *s. Mus:* sérialisme *m*.

serialize ['siəriəlaiz], *v.tr.* **1.** (*a*) arranger (des résultats, etc.) en série; (*b*) fabriquer (un article) en série. **2.** *Journ:* publier, *T.V:* diffuser (un roman, etc.) en feuilleton.

serially ['siəriəli], *adv.* **1.** en, par, série. **2.** *Journ: etc:* en feuilleton.

seriate[1] ['siərieit], *v.tr.* sérier (des questions, des résultats, etc.).

seriate[2], **seriated** ['siərieitid], *a.* sérié, disposé par séries, en série.

seriatim [siəri'eitim], *adv. Lit:* successivement, au fur et à mesure; par rang d'ordre; **to examine the questions s.,** examiner successivement les questions.

seriation [siəri'eiʃ(ə)n], *s.* sériation *f*.

sericeous [si'riʃiəs], *a. Nat.Hist:* soyeux.

sericicultural [serisi'kʌltjər(ə)l], *a.* séricicole.

sericiculture ['serisikʌltjər], *s.* sériciculture *f*.

sericiculturist [serisi'kʌltjərist], *s.* sériciculteur *m*.

sericin ['serisin], *s. Ser:* séricine *f*.

sericite ['serisait], *s. Miner:* séricite *f*.

sericitic [seri'sitik], *a. Geol:* séricíteux.

sericitization [serisaiti'zeiʃ(ə)n], *s. Geol:* séricitisation *f*.

sericultural [seri'kʌltjər(ə)l], *a.* séricicole.

sericulture ['serikʌltjər], *s.* sériciculture *f*.

sericulturist [seri'kʌltjərist], *s.* sériciculteur *m*.

seriema [seri'emə], *s. Orn:* cariama *m*.

series ['siəri:z], *s.* **1.** série *f*, suite *f* (de malheurs, etc.); série (de couleurs, de questions, d'articles, etc.); échelle *f*, gamme *f* (de couleurs, etc.); *Publ:* collection *f*; *W.Tel: etc:* série, cycle *m*; *Geol:* série; *Mth:* **infinite s.,** série, suite, infinie; **convergent s.,** série convergente; **Fourier s.,** série de Fourier; *Ch:* **s. of reactions,** réactions *f* caténaires; **a s. of unfortunate events,** une suite d'événements malheureux; *Ch:* **homologous s.,** série homologue. **2.** *adv.phr.* **in s.,** en série, en succession; **reservoirs arranged in s.,** réservoirs *m* en chapelet; *El:* **connection in s., s. connection,** montage *m* en série; embrochage *m*; **to connect in s.,** monter, brancher, en série; **to connect cells in s.,** grouper des éléments en série, en tension, en cascade; **s.-parallel connection,** montage en série-parallèle, en série mixte; **s.-wound dynamo,** dynamo excitée en série, en tension; **s. winding,** enroulement *m* en série; **battery in s.,** batterie *f* en cascade.

serif ['serif], *s. Typ:* (*at top of letter*) obit *m*; (*at foot of letter*) empattement *m*.

serigraphy ['serigræfi], *s.* sérigraphie *f*.

serin ['serin], *s. Orn:* serin *m* cini.

serine ['seri:n], *s. Bio-Ch:* sérine *f*.

seringa [sə'riŋgə], *s. Bot:* **1.** seringa(t) *m*. **2.** hévée *f*, siphonie *f*.

serinuria [seri'nju:riə], *s. Med:* sérinurie *f*.

seriocomic [siəriou'kɔmik], *a.* (*of actor, song, etc.*) moitié sérieux moitié comique; (*of poem*) héroï-comique.

seriola [sə'raioulə], *s. Ich:* sériole *f*.

serious ['siəriəs], *a.* **1.** sérieux, grave; **s. illness,** maladie sérieuse; **s. wound,** blessure *f* grave, grave blessure; **s. mistake,** grosse faute; **s. damage,** dommages *m* sensibles; **things are becoming s.,** cela prend un aspect sérieux; l'affaire se corse. **2.** (*a*) **s. artist,** artiste sérieux; **s. promise,** promesse sérieuse, sincère; (*b*) (*of pers.*) réfléchi, sérieux; **I have never given the subject s. thought,** je n'y ai jamais pensé sérieusement; **s. mood,** humeur sérieuse; **he is never s. about anything,** il ne traite jamais rien au sérieux; **I'm s.,** je ne plaisante pas.

seriously ['siəriəsli], *adv.* sérieusement. **1. s. ill,** gravement malade; **s. wounded,** gravement, grièvement, blessé; *Mil:* **the s. wounded,** les grands blessés. **2. to take sth. (too) s.,** prendre qch. (trop) au sérieux; **to take oneself s.,** se prendre au sérieux; **don't take it so s.,** ne prenez pas cela au tragique; **are you saying that s.?** parlez-vous sérieusement? **listen to me s.,** écoutez-moi sérieusement, posément; **but s., what will you do?** plaisanterie à part, qu'allez-vous faire?

serious-minded [siəriəs'maindid], *a.* (*of pers.*) réfléchi, sérieux; **s.-m. people,** les esprits sérieux.

seriousness ['siəriəsnis], *s.* **1.** gravité *f* (d'une situation, d'une maladie, etc.). **2.** sérieux *m* (de maintien, etc.). **3. in all s.,** sérieusement. **4. written in a style not in keeping with the s. of the subject,** écrit dans un style au-dessous de la dignité du sujet.

seriph ['serif], *s.* = SERIF.

serjeant ['sɑ:dʒ(ə)nt], *s.* **1.** *A:* **s. of the watch,** sergent *m* de nuit. **2.** (*a*) *A:* **s. at law,** avocat *m* (d'un ordre supérieur du barreau); (*b*) **Common S.,** magistrat *m* de la corporation de Londres (adjoint au *Recorder*); (*c*) **S. at Arms,** (i) *A:* huissier *m* d'armes; (ii) commandant *m* militaire du Parlement.

sermon ['sə:mən], *s.* **1.** *Ecc:* sermon *m*; homilie *f*; (*Protestant Ch:*) prêche *m*; **collection of sermons,** sermonnaire *m*; **writer of sermons, s. writer,** sermonnaire; *B:* **the S. on the Mount,** le Sermon sur la montagne; **to preach a Passion s., a course of Lenten sermons,** prêcher une passion, un carême. **2.** *F:* sermon, sermonnade *f*, semonce *f*.

sermonize ['sə:mənaiz]. **1.** *v.i. Pej:* sermonner, prêcher. **2.** *v.tr. F:* sermonner, semoncer, chapitrer (qn); faire la leçon, la morale, à (qn).

sermonizer ['sə:mənaizər], *s. F: Pej:* sermonneur, -euse.

sermonizing ['sə:mənaiziŋ], *s. Pej:* **1.** prêcherie *f*; **no s.!** pas de sermons! **2.** moralisation *f*, remontrances *fpl*.

serodiagnosis [siəroudaiəg'nousis], *s. Med:* sérodiagnostic *m*.

serology [siə'rɔlədʒi], *s. Med:* sérologie *f*.

sero-reaction [siərouri'ækʃ(ə)n], *s. Med:* séro-réaction *f*, *pl.* séro-reactions.

serosa [si'rousə], *s. Anat:* (membrane) séreuse *f*.

serosity [si'rɔsiti], *s.* sérosité *f*.

serotherapeutic [siərouθerə'pju:tik], *a. Med:* sérothérapique.

serotherapy [siərou'θerəpi], *s. Med:* sérothérapie *f*.

serotine ['serətain], *s. Z:* (grande) sérotine.

serotinous [se'rɔtinəs], *a. Bot:* à floraison tardive.

serotonin [serou'tounin], *s. Ch:* sérotonine *f*.

serous ['siərəs], *a. Anat:* (*of* fluide, etc.) séreux; **s. membrane,** (membrane) séreuse *f*.

serovaccination [siərouvæksi'neiʃ(ə)n], *s. Med:* sérovaccination *f*.

serow [sə'rou], *s. Z:* capricorne *m*.

Serpens ['sə:penz], *Pr.n. Astr:* le Serpent.

serpent ['sə:p(ə)nt], *s.* **1.** (*a*) *Rept:* serpent *m*; **young s.,** serpenteau *m*; **s. lizard,** seps *m*; *F: A:* **the (old) S.,** le Serpent; le démon; **the wisdom of the s.,** la prudence du serpent; (*b*) *Pyr:* serpenteau; (*c*) *Orn:* **s. eater,** serpentaire *m*; secrétaire *m*; (*d*) **s. grass,** renouée *f* vivipare; (*e*) *Paleont:* **serpent's tongue,** glossopètre *m*; dent *f* fossile de requin. **2.** *Mus: A:* serpent. **3.** *Astr:* **the S.,** le Serpent.

serpentaria [sə:pən'tɛəriə], **serpentary** ['sə:pənt(ə)ri], *s. Bot:* (aristoloche) serpentaire *f.*

Serpentarius [sə:pən'tɛəriəs], *Pr.n. Astr:* le Serpentaire.

serpentiform [sə:'pentifɔ:m], *a.* serpentiforme; serpentueux.

serpentine[1] ['sə:pəntain], *s. Miner:* serpentine *f*; marbre serpentin; ophite *m*, ophiolite *f.*

serpentine[2], *a. Lit:* serpentin; (ruisseau, sentier) sinueux, tortueux, serpentant; **s. windings,** sinuosités *f*; **s. wisdom,** la prudence du serpent.

serpentinization [sə:pentainai'zeiʃ(ə)n], *s. Geol:* serpentinisation *f.*

serpentinoid, serpentinous ['sə:pəntainɔid, -əs], *a. Geol:* serpentineux.

serpierite ['sə:piərait], *s. Miner:* serpiérite *f.*

serpiginous [sə:'pidʒinəs], *a. Med:* serpigineux.

serpigo [sə:'paigou], *s. Med:* serpigo *m*; croûte serpigineuse.

serpula, *pl.* **-ae** ['sə:pjulə, -i:], *s. Ann:* serpule *f.*

serra, *pl.* **-ae** ['serə, -i:], *s. Anat:* engrenure *f* (du crâne); *Bot:* **serrae of a leaf,** dents *fpl*, dentelure *f*, d'une feuille.

serradella, serradilla [serə'delə, -'dilə], *s. Bot:* serradelle *f.*

serranid [se'rænid], *a. & s.* serranide (*m*); *s.* serranidé *m.*

Serranidae [se'rænidi:], *s.pl. Ich:* serranides *m*, serranidés *m.*

serrasalmo, serrasalmus [serə'sælmou, -məs], *s. Ich:* serrasalme *m.*

serrate ['sereit], *a. Nat.Hist:* denté en scie; en dents de scie; dentelé; *Bot:* **s.-leaved,** serratifolié; *Num:* **s. coins,** monnaie *f* serrate.

serrated [se'reitid], *a. Nat.Hist:* denté en scie; *Anat:* **s. suture,** engrenure *f* (du crâne); **s. edge,** denture *f*; **deeply s. leaf,** feuille *f* à bords fortement dentés; **knife with a s. edge,** couteau *m* à scie.

serration [se'reiʃ(ə)n], **serrature** ['serətjər], *s. Nat.Hist: etc:* dentelure *f*; denture *f*; *Anat:* engrenure *f* (du crâne).

serratus [se'reitəs], *s. Anat:* muscle dentelé.

serrefile ['seəfail]. *A.Mil:* **1.** *s.* (*a*) serre-file *m*; (*b*) *coll.* les serre-files; **s. officers,** officiers *m* en serre-file. **2.** *adv.* **to march s.,** marcher en serre-file.

serricorn ['seriko:n], *a. & s. Ent:* serricorne (*m*).

Serricornia [seri'kɔ:niə], *s.pl. Ent:* serricornes *m.*

serried ['serid], *a. Lit:* serré; **in s. ranks,** en rangs serrés, en rangs pressés.

serriform ['serifɔ:m], *a. Nat.Hist:* serriforme; denté en scie.

serrula ['serulə], *s. Nat.Hist:* serrule *f.*

serrulate(d) ['seruleit(id)], *a. Nat.Hist:* serrulé, denticulé.

serrulation [seru'leiʃ(ə)n], *s.* dentelure fine.

sertularia [sə:tju'lɛəriə], *s. Coel:* sertulaire *f.*

Sertulariidae [sə:tjulæ'raiidi:], *s.pl. Coel:* sertularidés *m*, sertulariidés *m.*

sertulum, *pl.* **-la** ['sə:tjuləm, -lə], *s. Bot:* sertule *m.*

serum, *pl.* **-ums, -a** ['siərəm, -əmz, -ə], *s. Physiol:* sérum *m*; **blood s.,** sérum sanguin, du sang; **s. albumin,** sérum-albumine *f*; **s. globulin,** sérum-globuline *f*; **chylous s.,** sérum chyleux; *Med: Vet:* **s. therapy,** sérothérapie *f*; **antitoxin s.,** sérum antitoxique; **protective s.,** immunisant *m*; **s. accident,** accident sérique; **s. rash,** exanthème *m* sérique; **s. sickness,** maladie *f* du sérum; réaction *f* sérique; *Med:* **truth s.,** sérum de vérité.

serval ['sə:v(ə)l], *s. Z:* serval *m*, -als.

servant ['sə:v(ə)nt], *s.* **1.** (*a*) **(domestic) s.,** domestique *mf*; servante *f*, bonne *f*; *Lit:* serviteur *m*; **general s.,** bonne à tout faire; **to keep a s.,** avoir une domestique; **a large staff of servants,** une nombreuse domesticité; **school servants,** agents *m* (des lycées); *Mil:* **officer's s.,** ordonnance *m or f*; (*b*) serviteur, servante (de Dieu, etc.); (*c*) *Corr. esp. Dipl:* **your most humble and obedient s.,** votre très humble et très obéissant serviteur. **2.** (*a*) employé, -ée; **public servants,** employés d'un service public; **civil s.,** fonctionnaire *m* (de l'État); **to become a civil s.,** entrer dans l'administration; *Jur:* **servants and agents,** préposés *m*; (*b*) *Mec.E:* **s. apparatus,** appareil commandé.

serve[1] [sə:v], *s. Ten: F:* service *m*; **it's your s.!** à vous de servir!

serve[2], *v.tr. & i.* **1.** (*a*) (*of pers.*) servir (un maître, une cause, etc.); **to s. God, one's country,** servir Dieu, sa patrie; **to have served one's country well,** bien mériter de la patrie; **to be served by s.o.,** disposer des services de qn; être servi par qn; **if I can do anything to s. you,** si je puis vous être utile en, à, quelque chose; **to s. one's own interests,** servir ses propres intérêts; *Artil: A:* **to s. a gun,** servir, exécuter, une pièce; (*b*) *v.i.* **to s. in the army,** servir dans l'armée; **he had served under La Fayette,** il avait servi, marché, sous La Fayette; il avait fait la guerre avec La Fayette; **to s. with s.o.,** faire la guerre avec qn; **to have served ten years,** avoir dix ans de service(s); *Jur:* **to s. on the jury,** être du jury; (*c*) *v.tr.* **to s. one's apprenticeship,** faire son apprentissage; **to have served one's time,** (i) avoir fait son temps de service; (ii) sortir d'apprentissage; **to s. one's sentence,** *F:* **to s. one's time,** subir, purger, sa peine; **he served a sentence of five years' imprisonment,** il a fait cinq ans de prison. **2.** (*a*) *v.tr. & i.* (*of thg*) être utile à (qn); suffire à (qn); **to s. the purpose,** remplir le but, faire l'affaire; **tool that serves several purposes,** outil *m* qui sert à plusieurs usages; outil à plusieurs fins; **what has he done that serves any useful purpose?** qu'a-t-il fait d'utile? **the desks s. as tables,** les pupitres servent de tables, tiennent lieu de tables; **to s. as a pretext, as an example,** servir de prétexte, d'exemple; **a few words served to persuade him,** il suffit de quelques mots pour le persuader; *A:* **it will s. you nothing to . . .,** cela ne vous servira à rien de . . .; (*b*) **if my memory serves me right,** si j'ai bonne mémoire; (*c*) *A. & Lit:* **when occasion serves,** lorsque l'occasion est favorable. **3.** *v.tr.* desservir; **priest who serves two villages,** prêtre qui dessert deux villages; **this town is not served by a railway any more,** cette ville n'a plus de chemin de fer. **4.** (*a*) (*in shop*) **to s. s.o. with a pound of butter,** servir une livre de beurre à qn; **are you being served?** est-ce qu'on s'occupe de vous? (*b*) *v.tr.* **tradesman who has served us for ten years,** marchand qui nous sert, qui fournit chez nous, depuis dix ans; (*c*) *v.i.* **to s. in a shop,** être vendeur, -euse. **5.** (*a*) *v.tr. & i. Ecc:* **to s. (at) (mass),** servir la messe; (*b*) *v.i.* **to s. (at table),** servir à table; *v.tr.* **to s. s.o. with soup, with vegetables,** servir du potage, des légumes, à qn; **to s. (up) a dish,** servir un mets; mettre un mets sur la table; **dinner is served, madam,** le dîner est servi, c'est servi, madame; *O:* madame est servie; **s. hot,** servir, servez, chaud; **served with tomato sauce,** accommodé à la sauce tomate. **6.** *v.tr. & i. Ten:* **to s. (the ball),** servir (la balle); **to s. an easy ball to s.o.,** servir une balle facile à qn; **to s. an ace,** servir une balle impossible à rendre. **7.** *v.tr. Jur:* **to s. a writ, a summons, on s.o., to s. s.o. with a writ, a summons,** délivrer, signifier, notifier, une assignation, une citation, à qn. **8.** *v.tr.* traiter (qn) (bien, mal); **he served me very badly,** il a très mal agi envers moi; **to s. s.o. a dirty trick,** jouer un vilain tour à qn; **it serves you right!** vous n'avez que ce que vous méritez! vous l'avez bien gagné! ça vous apprendra! c'est bien fait! vous ne l'avez pas volé! **9.** *v.tr.* (*of stallion*) servir, saillir, couvrir, monter, étalonner (la jument). **10.** *v.tr. Nau:* fourrer, surlier, garnir (un cordage).

server ['sə:vər], *s.* **1.** (*a*) (*at table*) serveur, -euse; (*b*) *Ten:* serveur, -euse; servant *m*; (*c*) *Ecc:* (*at mass*) acolyte *m*, répondant *m*, servant. **2.** (*a*) plateau *m* (de service); (*b*) **salad, fish, servers,** service *m* à salade, à poisson; (*c*) *U.S:* = service (à café, à thé).

Servetus [sə:'vi:təs], *Pr.n.m. Rel.H:* Michel Servet.

service[1] ['sə:vis], *s.* service *m.* **1.** (*a*) **in the s. of God, of one's country,** au service de Dieu, de son pays, sa patrie; **to die in the King's, Queen's, s.,** mourir au service du roi, de la reine; **I am (entirely) at your s.,** je suis à votre (entière) disposition; (*motto*) **service,** servir! **ten years' s.,** dix années de service; **promotion according to length of s.,** avancement selon l'ancienneté *f*; (*b*) *Mil: etc:* **military s., national s.,** *U.S:* **selective s.,** service militaire, national; **when I was doing my military s.,** quand j'étais au régiment; **active s.,** (i) service actif; (ii) service en campagne, services de guerre; **on active s.,** (i) en activité de service; (ii) en campagne; (iii) *Post:* franchise *f* militaire; **killed on active s.,** tué en service commandé; **general s., combatant s.,** service armé; **limited s., non-combatant s.,** service auxiliaire; **fit, unfit, for s.,** apte, inapte, au service; **unfit for active s.,** inapte à faire campagne; **staff s.,** service d'état-major; **on detached s.,** en mission; (*of aircraft, etc.*) **in operational s.,** en service opérationnel; *Navy:* **s. afloat,** service à bord, à la mer; **s. ashore,** service à terre; **harbour s.,** service au port; *attrib.* **s. ammunition,** munitions réelles, de guerre; **s. dress,** tenue *f* de campagne; (*c*) **domestic s.,** service domestique; **to be in s.,** être en service; **to go into s.,** entrer en service; se placer comme domestique; (*d*) (*in hotel, etc.*) service; **ten per cent s. charge,** service dix pour cent; **s. lift, hoist,** monte-plats *m inv*; **s. hatch,** guichet *m*; **s. flat,** appartement *m* avec service compris (et repas à volonté); **rent plus s. charge,** loyer plus charges; (*e*) *Adm: Ind: etc:* **contract s.,** service contractuel; **s. agreement,** contrat *m* de service; **24-hour s.,** service permanent, de 24 heures sur 24; (*f*) **to bring, put, (a machine, a vehicle) into s.,** mettre (un appareil, un véhicule) en service; **to put a ship into s.,** (i) mettre un navire en service, inaugurer un navire; (ii) mettre un navire en armement; **s. life,** durée *f* de vie, longévité *f* (d'un matériel); durée, potentiel *m*, d'utilisation; **my car has seen long s.,** ma voiture a beaucoup roulé, m'a servi longtemps; **this pen has given me good s.,** ce stylo m'a bien servi; (*g*) *Av:* **s. ceiling,** plafond *m* pratique (d'un appareil); *Mch:* **s. horse power,** puissance normale; *Mch: El:* **s. test,** essai *m* en charge; *Veh:* **s. speed,** vitesse commerciale; **s. weight,** poids *m* en ordre de marche. **2.** (*a*) **to do s.o. a s.,** rendre (un) service à qn; **exchange of friendly services,** échange de bons procédés; **to make use of s.o.'s services,** user de l'intermédiaire de qn; accepter l'aide de qn; **his services to education,** les services qu'il a rendus à l'enseignement; **services rendered,** services rendus; **in consideration of your services,** en rémunération de vos services, de vos démarches; **they offered us their services for cleaning our premises,** ils nous ont offert leurs services pour le nettoyage de nos locaux; *Pol. Ec:* **goods and services,** biens et services; (*b*) utilité *f*; **to be of some s.,** être de quelque utilité; servir à quelque chose; **to be of s. to s.o.,** être utile à qn; **can I be of any s. to you?** puis-je vous être utile, vous aider en aucune manière? **3.** (*a*) **the civil s.,** l'administration *f*, la fonction publique; **to be in the civil s.,** être fonctionnaire, être dans l'administration; *Hist:* **the Indian Civil S.,** le service d'administration de l'Inde anglaise; **the Foreign, Diplomatic, S.,** le service diplomatique, la diplomatie, *F:* la carrière; *F:* **the Secret S.** = le Deuxième Bureau; (*b*) *Mil: etc:* **the s.,** (i) l'armée *f*; (ii) la marine; (iii) l'armée de l'air; **a s.,** un service (administratif, logistique, etc.); **the (armed) services,** les forces armées; l'armée, la marine et l'armée de l'air; **the Senior S.,** la Marine; **to be discharged from the s.,** être congédié du service; **which branch of the services were you in?** vous avez servi dans quelle arme? **Joint Services Staff College** = École *f* d'État-major interarmes; *attrib.* **s. uniform,** uniforme *m* militaire, réglementaire; **s. rifle,** fusil *m* réglementaire, de l'armée; **s. vehicle,** véhicule *m* militaire, de l'armée; *Navy:* **s. boat,** canot *m* réglementaire; **s. families,** les familles *f* de militaires; **s. personnel,** personnel *m* militaire; **to use s. labour,** utiliser, avoir recours à, la main-d'œuvre militaire. **4.** (*a*) **public services,** services publics; **postal, telephone, services,** services postaux, téléphoniques; **social services,** services sociaux; **medical, dental, services,** services médicaux, dentaires; (*b*) *Trans:* service (aérien, ferroviaire, etc.); **bus s.,** service d'autobus, de cars; *Austr: N.Z:* **s. bus, car,** autocar *m*; **there is a good train s. between here and London,** il y a un bon service de trains entre ici et Londres; **we have a good bus, train, s.,** notre ville est bien desservie par les autobus, par le chemin de fer; notre ville a de bonnes relations ferroviaires; **goods, freight, s.,** service de marchandises; **passenger s.,** service de voyageurs; (*c*) distribution *f* (d'eau, de gaz, d'électricité); **water-supply s.,** fourniture *f* d'eau; *El:* **s. cable, conductor,** colonne montante (de réseau); **s. lead, pipe,** branchement *m* d'abonné; **s. voltage,** tension *f* de service; *El: Tp: W.Tel: etc:* **s. area,** zone *f* de desserte; région desservie; *NAm:* **s. centre,** ville commerciale (qui dessert toute une région). **5.** (*a*) (i) entretien *m*; (ii) dépannage *m* (d'un appareil ménager, etc.); **my car needs a complete s.,** ma voiture a besoin d'une révision générale; *Aut:* **s. station,** station-service *f*, *pl.* stations-service; **s. area,** *NAm:* **s. centre,** aire *f* de services (au bord d'une autoroute); *P.N:* **services, 10 km,** essence, 10 km; **after-sales s.,** service après vente; **s. engineer,** technicien *m* d'entretien; **s. equipment,** appareillage *m*, matériel *m*, d'entretien; **s. manual, handbook,** manuel *m* d'entretien; (*b*) *Artil: etc:* service (de la pièce). **6.** *Ecc:* office *m*; culte *m*; **morning, evening, s.,** office du matin, du soir; **the communion s.,** la sainte communion; **open-air s.,** *Mil:* **drumhead s.,** office en plein air; **to attend s.,** assister à l'office, au culte. **7.** *Jur:* délivrance *f*, signification *f* (d'un acte, d'une assignation); **request for s.,** demande *f* en vue de la signification des actes; **personal s.,** signification à personne; **substituted s.,** signification à un représentant de la personne assignée. **8.** *Breed:* service (par l'étalon, etc.). **9. tea, dinner, s.,** service à thé; service de table. **10.** *Ten:* service; **to have a good s.,** avoir un bon service; **s. line,** ligne *f* de fond; **s. court,** rectangle *m* de service; **side or s.?** service ou côté? **to win one's s.,** faire un service gagnant. **11.** *Nau:* fourrure *f* (d'un cordage).

service[2], *v.tr.* faire la révision (d'une voiture); entretenir, faire l'entretien (d'un appareil ménager, d'un poste de télévision, etc.).

service[3], *s. Bot:* **s. (tree),** sorbier *m*, cormier *m*; **wild s.**

tree, alisier *m* des bois; (alisier) aigrelier *m*; **s. apple, s. berry,** corme *f*, sorbe *f*; **s.-apple cider,** cormé *m*.

serviceability [sə:visə'biliti], *s.* (*of thg*) (*a*) état satisfaisant (du point de vue fonctionnement); solidité *f*; facilité *f* d'entretien; disponibilité *f* technique (d'un matériel); (*b*) utilité *f*.

serviceable ['sə:visəbl], *a.* **1.** *A:* (*of pers.*) serviable. **2.** (*of thg*) (*a*) en état de fonctionner; utilisable; (navire, etc.) bon pour le service; (*b*) utile; de bon usage; avantageux; **s. clothes,** vêtements pratiques, de bon service; (*c*) pratique, commode.

serviceableness ['sə:visəblnis], *s.* **1.** *A:* (*of pers.*) serviabilité *f*. **2.** (*of thg*) = SERVICEABILITY.

serviceman, *pl.* **-men** ['sə:vismən, -men], *s.m.* **1.** soldat; mobilisé; *Hist:* **national s.,** soldat (qui fait son service militaire), appelé, militaire du contingent; **ex-s.,** ancien mobilisé; ancien combattant; **disabled ex-s.,** mutilé de guerre. **2.** *NAm:* technicien d'entretien; dépanneur.

servicewoman, *pl.* **-women** ['sə:viswumən, -wimin], *s.f.* soldate, femme-soldat, *pl.* femmes-soldats.

servicing ['sə:visiŋ], *s.* (*a*) entretien *m*; maintenance *f*; *Aut:* révision *f*; *Av:* entretien (courant) en piste; **periodic, routine, s.,** entretien courant (périodique); *Av:* **s. platform,** plate-forme *f* d'entretien, plate-forme d'accès (pour l'entretien des appareils); (*b*) *Mil: Av:* **cross s.,** prestation(s) mutuelle(s) de service(s).

servient ['sə:viənt], *a. Jur:* **s. tenement, s. land,** fonds servant.

serviette [sə:vi'et], *s.* serviette *f* de table.

servile ['sə:vail], *a.* **1.** (*of race, condition, etc.*) servile; d'esclave; (métier *m*) servile, de domestique, d'esclave; **s. yoke,** joug asservissant; *Ecc:* **s. work,** œuvres *f* serviles; *Rom.Hist:* **the s. wars,** les guerres *f* serviles; *Ling: Gram:* **s. words,** mots *m* outils; **s. letters,** lettres *f* serviles (de l'hébreu). **2. s. imitation,** imitation *f* servile. **3.** (*of pers.*) servile; trop complaisant; bas, *f.* basse; abject, vil.

servilely ['sə:vailli], *adv.* **1.** servilement; avec servilité; bassement. **2.** (traduire, etc.) servilement, trop exactement.

servilism ['sə:vilizm], *s. Pol: etc:* servilisme *m*.

servility [sə:'viliti], *s.* **1.** *A:* = SERVITUDE 1. **2.** servilité *f*, exactitude trop étroite (d'une copie, etc.). **3.** (*of pers.*) servilité; abjection *f*, bassesse *f*.

serving[1] ['sə:viŋ], *a.* (soldat) au service.

serving[2], *s.* **1.** service *m* (d'un maître); *A:* **s. man, woman,** domestique *mf*; serviteur *m*. **2.** (*a*) service (du dîner, etc.); *Ten:* service (d'une balle); (*b*) portion *f* (d'un mets). **3.** *Jur:* signification *f*, notification *f* (d'une citation). **4.** *Breed:* (*of stallion*) service, saillie *f*. **5.** *Nau:* (*a*) fourrage *m*, garniture *f* (d'un cordage); **s. mallet,** maillet *m* à fourrer; mailloche *f*; **s. board,** minahouet *m*; (*b*) revêtement *m*, enveloppe *f* (d'un câble, etc.); surliure *f*.

servitor ['sə:vitər], *s.* **1.** *A: & Lit:* serviteur *m*. **2.** *Hist: Sch:* (*Oxford University*) boursier *m* (qui à l'origine remplissait les fonctions de domestique).

servitude ['sə:vitju:d], *s.* **1.** servitude *f*, esclavage *m*, asservissement *m*, domesticisme *m* (d'un peuple, etc.). **2.** *Jur:* **penal s.,** travaux forcés; prison *f* cellulaire; **penal s. for life,** travaux forcés à perpétuité; **a term of penal s.,** travaux forcés à temps, à terme. **3.** *Jur:* servitude (réelle ou personnelle); *esp. Scot:* **praedial s.,** servitude prédiale; **apparent s.,** servitude apparente.

servo ['sə:vou], *s.* **1.** servomoteur *m*. **2. s. (system),** servomécanisme *m*; *Cmptr:* **s. multiplier,** multiplicateur *m* à servomécanisme. **3.** servocommande *f*; **s. input, output,** excitation *f*, réponse *f*, d'une servocommande; **operated by hydraulic servos,** attaqué, mû, par servocommandes hydrauliques.

servobrake ['sə:voubreik], *s. Aut:* servofrein *m*.

servocontrol [sə:voukən'troul], *s. Av: etc:* servocommande *f*.

servomechanism [sə:vou'mekənizm], *s.* servomécanisme *m*.

servomotor [sə:vou'moutər], *s. Mch:* servomoteur *m*.

sesame ['sesəmi], *s.* **1.** *Bot:* sésame *m*; till *m*, teel *m*; **s. oil,** huile *f* de sésame. **2.** (*magic formula*) **open s.!** sésame, ouvre-toi! **money is an open s.,** l'argent est un bon passe-partout, un véritable sésame, ouvre bien des portes.

Sesameae [se'seimii:], *s.pl. Bot:* sésamées *f*.

sesamia [se'seimiə], *s. Ent:* sésamie *f*.

sesamoid ['sesəmɔid], *a. & s. Anat:* **s. (bone),** (os) sésamoïde *m*; **s. ligament,** ligament sésamoïdien.

sesamoiditis [sesəmɔi'daitis], *s. Vet:* sésamoïdite *f*.

sesban ['sesbæn], *s. Bot:* sesbania *f*, sesbanie *f*.

seseli ['sesili], *s. Bot:* séséli *m*.

sesqui- ['seskwi], *pref. Ch: etc:* sesqui-.

sesquialter [seskwi'æltər], *a. Mth:* sesquialtère.

sesquialtera [seskwi'æltərə], *s. Mus:* (jeu *m* de) fourniture *f* (d'un orgue); sesquialtère *m or f*.

sesquibasic [seskwi'beisik], *a. Ch:* sesquibasique.

sesquicarbonate [seskwi'kɑ:bəneit], *s. Ch:* sesquicarbonate *m*.

sesquifluoride [seskwi'fluəraid], *s. Ch:* sesquifluorure *m*.

sesquiiodide [seskwi'aiədaid], *s. Ch:* sesquiiodure *m*.

sesquioxide [seskwi'ɔksaid], *s. Ch:* sesquioxyde *m*.

sesquipedalian [seskwipi'deiliən]. **1.** *a. & s.* (mot *m*) sesquipédale; *F:* (vocable) long d'une aune, long d'une toise. **2.** *a.* (style) ampoulé; (*of pers.*) pédant, prétentieux.

sesquiquadrate [seskwi'kwɔdreit], *s. Astr:* sesquiquadrat *m*.

sesquisalt [seskwi'sɔlt], *s.* sesquisel *m*.

sesquisulphide [seskwi'sʌlfaid], *s. Ch:* sesquisulfure *m*.

sesquiterpene [seskwi'tə:pi:n], *s. Ch:* sesquiterpène *m*.

sesquitertia [seskwi'tə:ʃiə], *s. Mus:* quarte *f* juste.

sessile ['sesail], *a.* (*of leaf, horn, tumour, etc.*) sessile; *Bot:* **s.-leaved,** à feuilles sessiles; sessilifolié; **s.-flowered,** sessiliflore.

Sessiliventres [sesili'ventri:z], *s.pl. Ent:* sessiliventres *m*.

session ['seʃ(ə)n], *s.* **1.** *A:* tenue *f* (d'une assemblée, des assises, etc.). **2.** (*a*) *Pol: etc:* session *f*; séance *f*; **sessions of a commission,** réunions *f* d'une commission; **to have a long s.,** faire une longue séance; **at the opening of the s.,** à audience ouvrante; *Parl:* **to go into secret s.,** se former en comité secret; *F:* **to have a s. on, about, sth.,** discuter le coup; (*b*) *St.Exch:* séance; bourse *f*. **3.** (*a*) temps pendant lequel un corps délibérant est assemblé; session; *Parl:* **the autumn s.,** la session d'automne; **the House is now in s.,** la Chambre siège actuellement; (*b*) *Sch: U.S:* trimestre *m* scolaire, universitaire; (*c*) *U.S: & Scot:* année *f* universitaire. **4.** *Jur:* (*a*) *A:* **petty sessions** = tribunal *m* d'instance; **quarter sessions,** assises trimestrielles; (*b*) *Scot:* **the Court of S.,** la haute cour; la cour suprême. **5.** *Scot:* **(kirk) s.,** tribunal ecclésiastique.

sesterce ['sestə:s], **sestertius,** *pl.* **-ii** [ses'tə:ʃiəs, -iai], *s. Rom.Ant:* sesterce *m*.

sestet(te) [ses'tet], *s.* **1.** *Mus:* sextuor *m*. **2.** *Pros:* les six dernières lignes d'un sonnet; les deux tercets.

sestina [ses'ti:nə], *s. Pros:* sextine *f*.

seston ['sestɔn], *s. Biol:* seston *m*.

set[1] [set], *s.* **1.** ensemble *m*; (*a*) jeu *m* (d'outils, de pièces de rechange, de brosses, de boîtes, de cendriers, de dominos, d'aiguilles, etc.); équipage *m*, assortiment *m*, attirail *m* (d'outils); série *f* (de poids, de casseroles, de conférences, *Nau:* de pavillons); groupe (moteur); batterie *f*, groupe (de turbines); train *m* (d'engrenages, de roues); batterie (d'ustensiles de cuisine); suite *f* (d'estampes); collection complète (des œuvres de qn); corps *m*, ensemble (de doctrines); convoi *m*, rame *f* (de wagons); service *m* (de porcelaine); parure *f* (de lingerie, de boutons de chemise, de pierres précieuses); *Mth:* **theory of sets,** théorie *f* des ensembles; **s. of golf clubs,** jeu de crosses; **s. of bells,** sonnerie *f* (d'église, etc.); **s. of spanners,** série, jeu, de clefs; **s. of anastigmats,** trousse *f* anastigmatique; **s. of pulleys,** garniture *f* de poulies; **s. of springs,** paquet *m*, faisceau *m*, de ressorts; *Rail:* **s. of points,** groupe de changements de voie; **s. of (carpenter's, etc.) boring and piercing tools,** vrillerie *f*; **s. of fire irons,** garniture de foyer; *A:* **mantel(piece) s.,** garniture de cheminée; **writing s.,** garniture de bureau; **toilet s.,** *O:* **dressing-table s.,** garniture de toilette; **s. of cigarette cards,** série, collection *f*, d'images de paquets de cigarettes; **construction s.,** jeu de construction; *Mus:* *A:* **s. of instruments,** pupitre *m* (de violes, etc.); **in sets,** (outils, etc.) en jeux complets; *El:* **generating s.,** groupe électrogène; **converter s.,** groupe convertisseur; **chairs, the s. of six, £200,** chaises, £200 les six; **to dance a s. of lancers,** danser les lanciers; (*b*) **radio, television, s.,** poste *m* de radio, de télévision; **transistor s.,** poste à transistors; **battery s.,** poste à piles; **(all) mains s.,** poste (sur le) secteur; **frequency-modulation s.,** poste à modulation de fréquence; **transmitting s.,** poste émetteur; **receiving s.,** poste récepteur; **transmitter-receiver s.,** poste émetteur-récepteur; *A:* **crystal s.,** poste à galène; *Cin:* **sound s.,** bloc *m* sonore; (*c*) *Cmptr:* (i) jeu, ensemble (de caractères, d'instructions, etc.); (ii) liasse *f* (de papier sur imprimante, etc.); (iii) positionnement *m*, mise *f* à 1; **s. of wire brushes,** brosse *f* (de lecture); **calling s.,** poste appelant; **user's s.,** poste d'utilisateur; (*d*) *Ten:* manche *f*, set *m*; **to win the first s.,** gagner le premier set; **s. point,** point qui, s'il est gagné, décidera du set; (*e*) groupe, catégorie *f* (de personnes); **a fine s. of officers,** un magnifique groupe d'officiers; **s. of thieves,** bande *f* de voleurs; **literary, political, s.,** coterie *f* littéraire, politique; **the smart s.,** le monde élégant; **the racing s.,** le monde des courses; **I'm not in, don't belong to, their s.,** je ne suis pas de leur monde; je n'appartiens pas à leur milieu; **we're not in the same s.,** nous ne fréquentons pas les mêmes milieux; *F:* **what a s.!** quelle engeance! **2.** (*a*) *Poet:* **at s. of sun,** au coucher du soleil; **at s. of day,** au déclin du jour; (*b*) couvée *f* (d'œufs); (*c*) *Ven:* arrêt *m* (d'un chien); **to be at dead s.,** être en arrêt; **to make a dead s.,** tomber en arrêt; faire un bel arrêt (**at,** devant); *F:* **to make a dead s. at s.o.,** (i) attaquer furieusement qn; (ii) (*of woman*) se jeter à la tête d'un homme. **3.** (*a*) conformation *f*, direction générale (d'une chaîne de montagnes, etc.); attitude *f*, posture *f* (du corps); assiette *f* (d'une poutre); tournure *f*, coupe *f* (d'un vêtement); disposition *f* des plis (d'une draperie); **s. of the features,** modelé *m* des traits; physionomie *f*; **I knew him by the s. of his head, of his hat,** je l'ai reconnu à son port de tête, à sa manière de porter son chapeau; **s. of the legs of a horse,** aplomb *m* des membres d'un cheval; *Tls:* **s. of a (machine) tool,** angle *m* d'attaque d'un outil; **s. of the saw teeth, of a saw,** voie *f*, chasse *f*, d'une scie; *Nau:* **s. of the sails,** (i) orientation *f* des voiles; (ii) façon *f* dont les voiles sont établies; (*b*) direction *f* (du courant, de la marée); *Nau:* lit *m* (du vent); courant *m*, tendances *fpl* (de l'opinion publique); (*c*) *Mec.E:* déviation *f*; déformation *f* (d'une pièce); flèche *f*, bande *f*, bandé *m* (d'un ressort); **permanent s.,** déformation permanente, allongement rémanant; **to give a s. to a plate,** déformer une plaque; **to take a s.,** se déformer, se fausser; (*d*) *Veh:* **s. of the axles, axle s.,** carrossage *m*, chasse *f*, devers *m*, des essieux; **s. of the axle pin,** carrossage de la fusée; (*e*) *Typ:* approche *f*; (*f*) *Hairdr:* (i) mise *f* en plis; **to have a shampoo and s.,** se faire faire un shampooing et une mise en plis; (ii) *F:* lotion *f* de mise en plis; (*g*) *Austr: N.Z: F:* **to have a s. against s.o.,** en avoir contre qn. **4.** (*a*) *Hort:* plant *m* à repiquer; plançon *m*; bouture *f*; (*b*) *Hort:* fruit noué; (*c*) *Civ.E:* **(paving) s., square s., stone s.,** pavé *m* d'échantillon; (*d*) *Min:* châssis *m*, cadre *m* (de galerie); (*e*) *Th:* décor *m*; mise en scène; **box s.,** décor de trois fermes et plafond; **rehearsed on the s.,** répétition *f* sur le plateau. **5.** *Tls:* (*a*) **saw s.,** tourne-à-gauche *m inv*; (*b*) **nail s.,** chasse-clou(s) *m inv*; chasse-pointe(s) *m inv*; (*c*) *Metalw:* **rivet s.,** chasse-rivet(s) *m inv*; **cup s.,** bouterolle *f*; (*d*) *Metalw:* ciseau *m* à arête plate; tranche *f*; **cold s., hot s.,** tranche à froid, à chaud. **6.** *Const:* enduit *m*; dernière couche (appliquée à une paroi, etc.). **7. badger's s.,** terrier *m* de blaireau.

set[2], *v.* (*p.t. & p.p.* **set**; *pr.p.* **setting**)

I. *v.tr.* **1.** (*a*) asseoir, placer (qn sur le trône, dans une place d'honneur); *Lit:* **to s. sth. above rubies,** priser qch. plus que des rubis; (*b*) **to s. a hen, eggs,** mettre une poule, des œufs, à couver; mettre une poule au nid. **2.** (*a*) mettre, poser (qch. sur, contre, qch., devant qch., qn); **to s. one's glass (down) on the table,** poser son verre sur la table; **to s. a dish on the table, in front of,** *O:* **before, s.o.,** servir un plat (à qn); **to s. sth. back in its place,** remettre, replacer, reposer, qch. à sa place; **to s. a plan before the council,** soumettre, proposer, un projet au conseil; **to s. one's name, hand, seal, to a document,** apposer sa signature, son sceau, à un acte, en bas d'un document; **to s. money by, aside, apart,** mettre de l'argent de côté, en réserve; faire des économies; (*b*) **to s. s.o. on his feet again,** remettre qn sur pied; **to s. a man on guard at the corner of a wood,** poster, aposter, un homme au coin d'un bois; **boundary stone s. between two fields,** borne plantée entre deux champs; (*c*) **to s. one's affections on s.o.,** fixer ses affections sur qn; **to s. one's heart on sth., avoir qch. au cœur; vouloir absolument (faire, avoir) qch.; (*d*) **the house is set in the heart of the woods,** la maison est située au milieu des bois. **3. to s. the table,** mettre le couvert, la table; **to s. the table for two,** mettre deux couverts. **4.** (*a*) **to s. a melody half a tone higher, lower,** hausser, baisser, un air d'un demi-ton; (*b*) **to set words, a poem, to music,** mettre des paroles en musique; **to set new words to an old tune,** ajuster un air ancien sur des paroles nouvelles; **to s. *Othello* to music,** écrire une partition sur *Othello*. **5.** (*a*) **to s. a stake in the ground,** enfoncer, planter, un pieu dans la terre; (*b*) **to s. seeds, a plant,** planter des graines; mettre une plante en terre. **6.** (*a*) **to s. a watch, the clock (right),** régler une montre, la pendule; mettre une montre, la pendule, à l'heure; **to s. one's watch by the town clock,** prendre l'heure à l'horloge de la ville; **to s. one's watch by the time signal,** régler sa montre sur le signal horaire; **to s. the alarm (clock) for, at, five o'clock,** mettre le réveille-matin sur cinq heures; *Aut:* **to s. the speedometer to zero,** ramener le compteur à zéro; *Navy:* **to s. a torpedo,** régler une torpille; **to s. the controls,** régler, repérer, les commandes; (*b*) *Mch: etc:* régler, caler; *I.C.E:* **to s. the**

camshaft, régler l'arbre à cames; **to s. the spark gap,** calibrer l'écartement des pointes (de la bougie); *El:* **to s. the brushes,** ajuster, caler, les balais; *Phot:* **to s. the shutter,** caler l'obturateur; (*c*) **to s. the iron of a plane,** régler, ajuster, le fer d'un rabot; **to s. (the teeth of) a saw,** donner de la voie à une scie; **to s. a file,** redresser une lime; (*d*) **to s. one's hat straight,** ajuster son chapeau; *Hairdr:* **to have one's hair set,** se faire faire une mise en plis. **7.** (*a*) **to s. a butterfly,** monter un papillon (en spécimen); (*b*) *Th:* **to s. a scene,** monter un décor; **the second act is set in a street,** le second acte se passe dans une rue; (*c*) **to s. a gem, diamonds,** monter, sertir, enchâsser, chatonner, une pierre; mettre des diamants en œuvre; **ring set with rubies,** bague ornée de rubis; **set with diamonds,** orné, incrusté, de diamants; **plain-set stone,** pierre à monture simple; (*d*) *Mec.E:* **to s. a shaft in its bearings,** loger un arbre dans les paliers; *Metall:* **to s. a core,** mettre en place un noyau (de moule); *Metalw:* **to s. a rivet,** poser un rivet; (*e*) *Nau:* **to s. a sail,** déployer, établir, une voile; mettre une voile au vent; mettre dehors une voile; **to s. the sails,** déferler les voiles; **(with) all sails set,** toutes voiles dehors; portant tout dessus; **to have her topsails set,** avoir ses huniers haut; **the sails are well set,** les voiles sont bien tendues. **8.** (*a*) **to s. a snare,** dresser, tendre, un piège; **to s. snares,** colleter; **to s. a trap for s.o.,** tendre un piège à qn; (*b*) **to s. a wolf trap, a (camera) shutter,** armer un piège à loups, un obturateur. **9. to s. (the edge of) a razor,** affiler, repasser, un rasoir; **to s. a chisel,** aiguiser, affûter, un ciseau; **to s. a tool on the oilstone,** doucir un outil; **to s. a saw,** affûter une scie. **10.** *Typ:* **to s. type,** composer; **to s. a page,** composer une page. **11. to s. a day, a date,** fixer, désigner, arrêter, une date, un jour; **to s. the pitch of an organ,** fixer le diapason d'un orgue; **to s. limits to sth.,** assigner des limites à qch. **12. to s. the fashion,** fixer, mener, la mode; donner le ton, la note; **to s. a fashion,** lancer une mode; faire école; *Row:* **to s. the stroke,** régler l'allure; donner la cadence; conduire l'équipe; *Nau:* **to s. the course,** tracer la route; **the course was set to the west,** la route fut fixée à l'ouest. **13.** *Surg:* **to s. a bone, a limb,** remettre un os, un membre; **to s. a fracture,** réduire une fracture; **to s. a dislocation,** réduire, remboîter, une luxation. **14. to s. one's teeth,** serrer les dents; **to s. one's jaws in an effort to control oneself,** contracter les mâchoires dans un effort de volonté; **lips firmly set,** lèvres fortement serrées. **15.** (*a*) *Const:* **to s. a wall,** appliquer un enduit, la dernière couche, sur une muraille; (*b*) *Tan:* étirer (les peaux). **16.** (*a*) **to s. s.o. on his way,** (i) mettre qn dans le bon chemin; (ii) accompagner qn un bout de chemin; **to s. s.o. on the wrong track,** aiguiller qn sur une fausse piste; **to s. the police on the tracks of a thief,** mettre la police aux trousses d'un voleur; **to s. a dog on s.o., at s.o., at an animal,** lâcher un chien contre qn; lancer un chien après qn, un lièvre, etc.; (*b*) conduire (un bachot) à la gaffe; pousser au fond; *Ven:* **to s. to the fowl,** s'approcher du gibier (dans un bachot). **17.** (*a*) **to s. s.o. to do sth.,** mettre qn à faire qch.; **to s. oneself to do sth.,** se mettre à faire qch.; s'appliquer à faire qch.; **to s. a man to work,** mettre un homme au travail; (*b*) **that set me thinking,** cela m'a fait réfléchir, m'a donné à réfléchir; **to s. the dog barking,** faire aboyer le chien; provoquer les aboiements du chien; **the smoke set her coughing,** la fumée l'a fait tousser; **to s. s.o. laughing,** faire rire qn; faire partir qn d'un éclat de rire; **to s. the company laughing,** provoquer, déchaîner, les rires; **to s. people talking,** (i) déclencher la conversation; (ii) provoquer des commentaires; **to s. a rumour going,** faire courir, donner cours à, un bruit; (*c*) **to s. sth. going,** mettre qch. en train; **to s. machinery going,** mettre un mécanisme en marche. **18. to s. a good example,** donner un bon exemple; **to s. oneself a task,** s'imposer, entreprendre, une tâche; **to s. (s.o.) a question,** poser une question (à qn); **to s. s.o. a problem,** donner un problème à résoudre à qn; poser un problème à qn; *Sch:* **to s. an essay,** donner un sujet de dissertation (à une classe); **to s. a book,** mettre un livre au programme (d'études); **to s. an exam(ination) paper,** choisir les questions d'une épreuve écrite.

II. *v.i.* **1.** (*a*) (*of sun, moon*) se coucher; **we saw the sun set(ting),** nous avons vu le coucher du soleil; (*b*) *Lit:* (*of fame, etc.*) s'éteindre, pâlir; **his star is setting,** son étoile pâlit, est à son déclin; **his star has set, is set,** son étoile a pâli. **2.** (*a*) atteindre son plein développement; (*of character*) se former, s'affermir; (*of foundations*) se tasser, prendre son assiette; (*b*) (*of dress*) (bien, mal) prendre la taille; **to s. badly,** faire des faux plis; **this sleeve doesn't s. well,** la manche ne tombe pas bien; *Nau:* (*of a sail*) **to s. well, badly,** bien, mal, établir. **3.** (*a*) (*of the face, eyes*) s'immobiliser; devenir fixe(s); (*of the features*) se figer; (*b*) (*of broken bone*) se ressouder, se nouer; (*c*) (*of blossom, fruit*) se former, (se) nouer; (*d*) (*of tree*) reprendre racine; (*e*) *Ost:* (*of spawn*) se fixer (sur qch.). **4.** (*a*) (*of white of egg, blood*) se coaguler; (*of blood*) se figer, se concréter; (*of milk*) (se) cailler; (*of jelly*) prendre; (*b*) (*of cement*) faire prise; prendre, durcir. **5.** *Ven:* (*of dog*) (i) arrêter; (ii) tomber en arrêt. **6.** *Danc:* **to s. (to partners),** balancer; faire chassé-croisé; **to s. to the right,** balancer à droite. **7.** (*of current, etc.*) **to s. southwards,** porter au sud; **a current that sets through the straits,** un courant qui balaie le détroit; **if the wind sets from the south,** si le vent souffle, se met à souffler, du sud; **the tide sets to the west,** la marée porte à l'ouest; **the tide is setting in, out,** la marée commence à monter, à descendre, à se retirer; *Lit:* **the tide has set in his favour,** ses actions remontent. **8. to s. to work,** se mettre au travail, à l'œuvre.

III. (*compound verbs*) **1. set about,** *v.i.* (*a*) **to s. about a piece of work,** se mettre à, entreprendre, un travail; s'emmancher un travail; **to s. about doing sth.,** se mettre à faire qch.; se mettre en devoir de faire qch.; **it's time to s. about it,** il est temps de s'y mettre; **I don't know how to s. about it,** je ne sais pas comment m'y prendre, par où commencer; (*b*) *F:* **to s. about s.o.,** attaquer qn, tomber sur qn.

2. set against, *v.tr.* (*a*) **to s. s.o. against s.o.,** prévenir, indisposer, animer, irriter, exciter, acharner, qn contre qn; monter (la tête à) qn contre qn; **he has s. everyone against him,** il s'est mis tout le monde à dos; **he's trying to s. you against me,** il cherche à me nuire auprès de vous; (*b*) **to s. oneself, one's face, against sth.,** s'opposer résolument à qch.; (*c*) opposer (qch. à qch.); contre-balancer (qch. par qch.); *Com:* **set against your invoice,** à valoir sur votre facture.

3. set apart, *v.tr.* isoler (qn); **a feeling of being s. apart,** un sentiment d'isolement; **they s. themselves apart,** ils faisaient bande à part; **there's something about their conversation that sets it apart,** leur conversation a une qualité à part.

4. set aside, *v.tr.* (*a*) rejeter; laisser (qch.) de côté; (*b*) écarter (une proposition, etc.); ne tenir aucun compte (d'un ordre); **to s. aside one's personal feelings,** mettre de côté, faire abnégation de, tout sentiment personnel; (*c*) *Jur:* casser, infirmer (un jugement, etc.); rejeter (une réclamation); annuler (un testament).

5. set back. (*a*) *v.tr.* (i) *Const: etc:* renfoncer (une façade); **house s. back (from the road),** maison en retrait (de la route); **to s. back one's shoulders,** effacer les épaules; (*of horse*) **to s. back its ears,** coucher les oreilles; **ears set back,** oreilles collées contre la tête; (ii) *Aut:* **to s. back the trip recorder to zero,** remettre le compteur de trajet à zéro; (iii) **this will s. him back,** cela retardera sa guérison; *F:* **it s. me back £5000,** ça m'a coûté £5000; (*b*) *v.i. Rail:* faire marche arrière.

6. set down, *v.tr.* (*a*) (i) **the train stops to s. down passengers only,** le train ne s'arrête que pour déposer, laisser descendre, des voyageurs; (ii) *A:* **to s. s.o. down,** remettre qn à sa place; rembarrer qn; (*b*) **to s. sth. down in writing,** coucher qch. par écrit; **condition s. down in the contract,** condition énoncée dans le contrat.

7. set forth, *v.i. A:* se mettre en route, en voyage; partir.

8. set in. (*a*) *v.i.* commencer; **winter is setting in,** l'hiver *m* commence; **before winter sets in,** avant le début, la venue, de l'hiver; **night was setting in,** la nuit se faisait; **a reaction is setting in,** une réaction se dessine, s'annonce; **the cold (weather) has set in again,** le froid redonne, a repris; **rain is setting in; it is setting in for a wet day,** le temps se met à la pluie; (*b*) *v.tr.* encastrer, entabler (une pierre, une poutre); emboîter (une mortaise, etc.); poser (une vitre); *Dressm:* monter (une manche, des fronces).

9. set off. (*a*) *v.tr.* (i) **to s. off a debt,** compenser une dette; **to s. off a gain against a loss,** opposer un gain à une perte; compenser une perte par un gain; (ii) faire ressortir, faire valoir, rehausser, relever (les charmes de qn, une couleur); donner du relief à (la beauté, etc.); mettre (qch.) en relief, en valeur; servir de lustre (au talent de qn, etc.); *Paint:* **to s. off one colour with another,** réchampir une couleur avec une autre; **her dress sets off her figure,** sa robe fait valoir, dégage, sa taille; (iii) rapporter (un angle); (iv) faire partir (une fusée, etc.); **to s. off fireworks,** tirer un feu d'artifice; **this answer s. them off laughing,** cette réponse a déclenché les rires; **this answer s. him off on a long disquisition,** cette réponse l'a lancé dans une longue disquisition; (*b*) *v.i.* (i) se mettre en route, en chemin; partir; **to s. off on a journey,** se mettre en voyage; **to s. off again,** repartir; se remettre en route; **to s. off running,** partir en courant; prendre sa course; (ii) *Typ:* (*of wet ink*) maculer, décharger.

10. set out. (*a*) *v.tr.* (i) *O:* équiper (qn); (ii) arranger, disposer; **to s. out one's ideas clearly,** exposer clairement ses idées; **his work is well set out,** son travail est bien présenté; **to s. out one's wares,** étaler, disposer, ses marchandises; (iii) *Mth: Surv: etc:* **to s. out a curve,** faire le tracé d'une courbe; tracer une courbe (d'abaque, par des points donnés); (iv) *Typ:* espacer (les caractères, les mots); (v) *Const:* **to s. a stone out,** poser une pierre en délit; (*b*) *v.i.* (i) se mettre en route, en chemin; partir (en voyage); **just as he was setting out,** au moment de son départ; **to s. out for France,** prendre le chemin de la France; partir pour la France; **to s. out for school,** partir pour l'école; **to s. out again,** repartir; **to s. out for home again,** reprendre le chemin de la maison; **to s. out against an enemy,** se mettre en campagne contre un ennemi; **to s. out in pursuit, in search, of s.o.,** se mettre à la poursuite, à la recherche, de qn; (ii) **I didn't s. out to attack the government,** je n'avais aucune intention d'attaquer le gouvernement.

11. set to, *v.i.* (*a*) se mettre (résolument) au travail, à l'œuvre; (*b*) *F:* (*of two pers.*) avoir une prise de bec; en venir aux coups.

12. set up. (*a*) *v.tr.* (i) dresser (un mât, une statue, *Artil:* une batterie, *Typ:* une lettre tombée); élever, ériger (une statue); élever (une barrière, une potence); planter (un drapeau); monter (un échafaud); installer (une batterie); monter, ajuster (une machine, une pile); armer (un appareil); **to s. up a dictatorship,** établir une dictature; se faire dictateur; *Surv:* **to s. up a theodolite,** mettre un théodolite en station; **to s. up milestones along a road,** borner une route; **to s. sth. up again,** relever qch.; (ii) *Typ:* **to s. up a MS.,** composer un MS; (iii) *Nau:* rider (les haubans); (iv) exalter, élever (qn); (v) *U.S:* arranger (un déjeuner, etc.); tramer (un complot); agencer (qch.); (vi) *P:* **I've been s. up good and proper,** on m'a monté le coup; on m'a bien eu; (vii) établir (une agence, une école, un record); créer, organiser, instituer, constituer (un comité, un tribunal); organiser (une ambulance); créer, fonder (une maison de commerce); monter (un magasin); **to s. up house,** s'installer dans une maison; **to s. up one's abode somewhere,** établir son domicile, s'établir, quelque part; *A:* **to s. up a carriage,** s'acheter une voiture; (viii) occasionner, causer; **food that sets up an irritation,** aliment *m* qui occasionne de l'irritation; (ix) **to s. s.o. up in business, as a grocer,** établir qn, lancer qn, dans un commerce, dans l'épicerie; (x) *Jur:* **to s. up a counterclaim,** intenter une demande reconventionnelle; (xi) **to s. up a shout,** pousser une clameur; **to s. up a howl,** se mettre à hurler; (xii) donner, rendre, de la vigueur à (qn); rétablir, développer, le physique de (qn); **a fortnight in the country will s. you up,** une quinzaine à la campagne va vous remettre d'aplomb, vous ragaillardir, vous fortifier; **the country air has set him up again,** l'air de la campagne l'a remis; (xiii) *F:* **s. them up again,** encore une tournée; (*b*) *v.i.* (i) **to s. up in business, as a chemist,** s'établir dans le commerce; s'établir pharmacien(ne); **he has s. up for himself,** il s'est établi à son (propre) compte; (ii) *P:* **to s. up with s.o.,** se coller avec qn; (iii) se poser (en savant, en critique, etc.); **I don't s. up to be better than you,** je n'ai pas la prétention, je ne présume pas, de vous être supérieur; (iv) (*of bullet*) faire champignon.

13. set upon, *v.i.* **to be s. upon by s.o.,** être attaqué par qn.

set[3], *a.* **1.** (*a*) **s. face,** visage immobile, composé, compassé, aux traits rigides; **s. gaze,** regard *m* fixe; **s. smile,** sourire figé; (*b*) *Mec.E: etc:* **s. pin,** goupille *f* de calage; **s. nut,** contre-écrou *m*; **s. bolt,** (i) prisonnier *m*; (ii) goujon *m* (de fixation); **s. hammer,** chasse (carrée); paroir *m*; *P: O:* **to have s.o. s.,** tenir qn à la gorge; (*c*) (ressort) bandé, tendu; *Sp:* **(get) s.!** en position! attention! *F:* **to be all s.,** être prêt(s) à commencer; (*d*) **s. grease,** graisse consistante; **hard s.,** ferme, figé; (ciment) bien pris; (*e*) **the fruit is s.,** le fruit est formé, noué; (*f*) **well s. person,** personne à la taille cambrée; (*g*) *Sp:* **to be s.,** (*of runner*) avoir repris son souffle, être bien en train; (*of batsman*) être bien dans son assiette, bien à son jeu. **2.** (*a*) **s. price,** prix *m* fixe; **s. time,** heure fixée, prescrite; **to dine at a s. hour,** dîner à heure fixe; **at s. hours,** à des heures réglées; **s. purpose,** ferme intention *f*; **s. ideas,** idées arrêtées; *Ind:* **s. work,** répétition *f* en série; (*b*) **s. phrase,** cliché *m*; expression consacrée; locution figée; **s. phrases,** expressions toutes faites; **s. forms,** les formes prescrites; **s. form of prayer,** prière *f* liturgique; **s. dinner,** (i) *O:* dîner *m* dans les formes; dîner de cérémonie; dîner prié; (ii) (dîner de) table *f* d'hôte; dîner à prix fixe; **s. speech,** discours composé à l'avance, étudié, préparé, apprêté; (*c*) **s. piece,** (i) *Cu:* pièce montée; (ii) *Pyr:* pièce montée, pièce d'artifice; (iii) *Th:* ferme *f*; *Th:* **s. scene,** décor (monté); *Rugby Fb:* **s. scrum,** mêlée ordonnée par l'arbitre; (*d*) **s. task,** tâche assignée; *Sch:* **s. subject,** sujet imposé aux candidats; **s. books,** les auteurs *m* du programme. **3. to be s. on sth.,** être résolu, déterminé, à qch.; s'obstiner à qch.; tenir beaucoup à ce que qch. se fasse; **to be (dead) s. on doing sth.,** être résolu, déterminé, opiniâtre, buté, à faire qch.; avoir à cœur de faire qch.; **to be dead s. against s.o.,** s'acharner après, contre, sur, qn.

seta, *pl.* **-ae** ['si:tə, -i:], *s. Nat.Hist:* poil *m* raide; soie *f*; cerque *m*; sétule *f*.

setaceous [si'teiʃəs], *a. Nat.Hist:* sétacé.

setaria [si'tɛəriə], *s. Bot:* sétaire *f*.

setback ['setbæk], *s.* **1.** (*a*) recul *m* (dans les affaires, etc.); *Fin: St.Exch:* tassement *m*, repli *m*; **his business has had a s., he's had a s. in his business,** ses affaires ont reculé; (*b*) rechute *f* (dans une maladie); **to have a s.,** rechuter; (*c*) déconvenue *f*, déception *f*; échec *m*; revers *m* de fortune; **to encounter a great many setbacks,** essuyer bien des traverses. **2. s. device,** dispositif *m* de remise à zéro (du compteur, etc.). **3.** *Arch:* décrochement *m*.

setbowl ['setboul], *s. NAm:* lavabo *m*.

setdown ['setdaun], *s.* **1.** *A:* (longueur *f* de la) course (en taxi). **2.** (*a*) humiliation *f*, rebuffade *f*; (*b*) *F:* verte semonce; **to give s.o. a s.,** laver la tête à qn.

setiferous, setigerous [si'tifərəs, -'tidʒərəs], *a.* sétifère, sétigère.

setiform ['si:tifɔ:m], *a.* sétiforme; en forme de soie.

set-in[1] ['setin], *a.* (*a*) encastré; (*b*) *Dressm:* **s.-in sleeve,** manche rapportée.

set-in[2], *s.* (*a*) insertion *f*; (*b*) commencement *m*, venue *f* (de l'hiver, des pluies, etc.).

setness ['setnis], *s.* **1.** formalité *f* (de style); compassement *m* (de conduite). **2.** fixité *f* (du regard); rigidité *f* (des traits); fermeté *f* (d'intention); **s. of purpose,** détermination *f*. **3.** opiniâtreté *f*.

set-off ['setɔf], *s.* **1.** contraste *m*; **s.-o. to beauty,** (i) ornement *m* de la beauté; (ii) repoussoir *m* à la beauté; **as a s.-o.,** par contraste. **2.** (*a*) compensation *f* (d'une dette); *Book-k:* écriture *f* inverse; **as a s.-o. against (sth.),** en compensation de (qch.); comme dédommagement de (qch.); en contrepartie de, à (qch.); (*b*) *Jur:* (*counterclaim*) reconvention *f*; demande reconventionnelle. **3.** (*a*) *Arch:* saillie *f*, ressaut *m*; (*b*) *Civ.E:* berme *f*. **4.** *Typ:* maculage *m*.

seton ['si:tən], *s. Vet: Surg:* séton *m* (à mèche).

setophaga [se'tɔfəgə], *s. Orn:* sétophage *m*.

setose ['si:tous], *a. Nat.Hist:* séteux.

set(-)out ['setaut], *s.* **1.** début *m*, commencement *m*; **at the first s.-o.,** au début, au premier abord; **I've been against the scheme from the s.-o.,** j'ai déconseillé ce projet dès, depuis, le commencement. **2.** étalage *m* (de marchandises, de nourriture). **3.** *O:* (*a*) équipage *m* (de chevaux et voiture, etc.); (*b*) *F:* accoutrement *m* (ridicule); (*c*) équipement *m*, trousseau *m*.

set square ['setskwɛər], *s.* équerre *f* (à dessin).

sett [set], *s.* **1.** *Civ.E:* **(paving) s., square s., stone s.,** pavé *m* d'échantillon. **2.** terrier *m* de blaireau.

settee [se'ti:], *s. Furn:* canapé *m*; causeuse *f*; **back-to-back s.,** boudeuse *f*; **bed s., s. bed,** lit-canapé *m*, *pl.* lits-canapés.

setter ['setər], *s.* **1.** (*pers.*) (*a*) poseur, -euse; metteur *m* en œuvre (d'un instrument scientifique, etc.); *Const:* **stone s.,** poseur de pierres de taille; **boiler-tube s.,** ajusteur *m* de tubes de chaudière; (*b*) *Typ:* **type s.,** compositeur, -trice; **machine s.,** opérateur, -trice; (*c*) *Th:* **stage s.,** chef *m* machiniste; (*d*) monteur *m*, sertisseur *m*, metteur en œuvre (de diamants, etc.); (*e*) affûteur *m* (de scies); (*f*) tendeur *m* (de pièges); **snare s.,** colleteur *m*; (*g*) poseur, -euse (de questions, de devinettes, etc.); **to be the s. of an exam(ination) paper,** choisir les questions d'une épreuve; (*h*) *Artil:* **sight s.,** servant *m* de hausse; (*i*) *Const:* **s. out,** *pl.* **setters out,** appareilleur *m*. **2.** (*a*) (*dog*) setter *m*; **Irish s.,** setter irlandais; **English s.,** setter anglais, Laverack; **Gordon s.,** setter noir et feu, Gordon; (*b*) *F: A:* (*pers.*) mouchard *m*. **3.** *Tls:* **nut s.,** serre-écrou *m inv*.

setterwort ['setəwə:t], *s. Bot:* ellébore *m* fétide.

setting[1] ['setiŋ], *a.* **1.** (soleil) couchant; (astre) baissant, couchant; (astre, gloire) sur son déclin. **2.** (fruit *m*) en formation, en train de (se) nouer. **3. slow-s. cement, quick-s. cement,** ciment *m* à prise lente, à prise rapide.

setting[2], *s.* **1.** (*a*) mise *f*, pose *f* (de qch.); apposition *f* (d'un sceau); (*b*) disposition *f*, arrangement *m*; **s. to music,** mise en musique; (*c*) enfoncement *m* (d'un pieu); plantation *f* (de graines, etc.); (*d*) réglage *m*; mise à l'heure (d'une horloge); ajustage *m*; *Mec.E: etc:* calage *m* (d'un tiroir, d'une soupape, *Phot:* de l'obturateur); **s. to zero,** remise *f* à zéro (d'un compteur); (*e*) montage *m* (d'un spécimen); *Ent:* **s. board,** planche *f* à épingler; (*f*) montage, sertissage *m*, mettage *m* (d'une pierre); mise en place, installation *f* (d'une chaudière, etc.); établissement *m* (d'une voile); dressage *m* (d'un piège); armement *m* (d'un piège, d'un obturateur); mise en voie (des dents d'une scie); mise en plis (des cheveux); *Hairdr:* **s. lotion,** lotion *f* pour mise en plis; (*g*) aiguisage *m*, affûtage *m*, affilage *m*, doucissage *m* (d'un outil); (*h*) pose *f* (d'un rivet); (*i*) *Typ:* **s. (up),** composition *f*; **page s.,** mise en page; **s. rule,** filet *m* à composer; **s. stick,** composteur *m*; (*j*) fixation *f*, désignation *f* (d'une date, etc.); (*k*) réduction *f* (d'une fracture, etc.); remboîtement *m* (d'une luxation); clissage *m* (d'un membre fracturé); coaptation *f* (des os); (*l*) imposition *f* (d'une tâche); (*m*) *Sch:* groupement *m* (des élèves dans une classe selon leurs aptitudes). **2.** (*a*) coucher *m* (du soleil, etc.); (*b*) tassement *m* (de fondations, etc.); (*c*) recollement *m* (d'un os brisé); (*d*) nouure *f*, formation *f* (du fruit); (*e*) affermissement *m*; prise *f* (du ciment); coagulation *f* (de l'albumine). **3.** (*a*) cadre *m*, encadrement *m* (d'un récit, d'une fête, etc.); *Th:* mise en scène; (*b*) monture *f*, serte *f* (d'un diamant); logement *m* (d'une chaudière, d'une cornue); **to tighten up the s. of a diamond,** serrer le feuilletis d'un diamant; (*c*) *Anat:* **tail s.,** attache *f* de la queue; (*d*) *Mus:* (i) ton *m* (d'un morceau); (ii) **s. for violin,** arrangement pour violon; (*e*) *Dom.Ec:* **place s.,** couvert *m*. **4.** (*a*) **s. apart, aside,** mise à part; **s. aside,** (i) rejet *m* (d'une demande); (ii) *Jur:* annulation *f*, cassation *f*; (*b*) **s. off,** (i) départ *m*; (ii) *Typ:* maculage *m*; **s. out,** (i) départ; (ii) *Const:* pose *f* en délit; (*c*) *Mec.E:* **s. over,** désaxage *m*, excentration *f*; (*d*) **s. up,** (i) montage *m*, dressage *m*, ajustage *m*; érection *f*, installation *f*; appareillage *m*; (ii) instauration *f*; établissement *m*, création *f*, fondation *f*; implantation *f* (d'une nouvelle industrie, etc.); **s. up of a new régime,** établissement, instauration, d'un nouveau régime; (iii) *Gym:* **s. up exercises,** exercices *m* d'assouplissement, pour développement physique.

settle[1] [setl], *s.* banc *m* à dossier.

settle[2], *v.*

I. *v.tr.* **1.** (*a*) établir, installer (qn, un peuple, etc.) (dans un pays); (*b*) coloniser, peupler (un pays); (*c*) rendre stable; **a good thunderstorm would s. the weather,** il nous faut un bon orage pour que le temps se remette; (*d*) mettre bien en place; **to s. one's feet in the stirrups,** assurer ses pieds dans les étriers; *Artil:* **to s. a gun,** asseoir une pièce. **2.** (*a*) **to s. an invalid (down) for the night,** arranger un malade pour la nuit; (*b*) **to s. one's children,** établir ses enfants; **to s. one's daughter,** marier, caser, sa fille; (*c*) **to s. one's affairs,** mettre ordre à ses affaires (avant de mourir, de partir en voyage, etc.). **3.** (*a*) clarifier, laisser rasseoir, reposer (un liquide); (*b*) **to s. s.o.'s doubts,** dissiper les doutes de qn. **4.** *Nau:* (*a*) **to s. a sail,** abaisser une voile; (*b*) **to s. the land,** noyer la terre. **5.** concerter (son visage, etc.); rasseoir (son esprit); apaiser, calmer (qn, les nerfs, etc.); **give me something to s. my stomach,** donnez-moi quelque chose pour me remettre l'estomac. **6.** fixer, déterminer (un jour, un endroit, etc.); **the terms were settled,** on convint des conditions; **your appointment is as good as settled,** votre nomination est quasiment une affaire faite; **it's as good as settled,** l'affaire est dans le sac; **everything is settled, it's settled, the matter is settled,** c'est une affaire faite, tout est d'accord; **that's settled then,** alors c'est dit; tenez donc cela pour dit; c'est convenu; **to s. to do sth.,** décider de faire qch. **7.** (*a*) résoudre, décider, statuer sur (une question); trancher, aplanir, arranger (un différend); vider, (r)ajuster (une querelle); arranger, liquider (une affaire); **to s. a question once and for all,** trancher une question, décider d'une question, une fois pour toutes; **to s. the succession,** décider la succession à la couronne; **questions not yet settled,** questions en suspens; **that settles it!** (i) voilà qui tranche la question! voilà qui décide tout! voilà qui est net! (ii) cela me décide! **s. it among yourselves, any way you like,** arrangez cela entre vous; arrangez cela comme vous voudrez; arrangez-vous; **to s. a matter amicably,** régler une question à l'amiable; *Jur:* **to s. a lawsuit amicably,** arranger un procès; **to s. out of court,** transiger avant jugement; **settled between the parties,** arrangé à l'amiable; (*of arbitrator*) **to s. a case,** arbitrer une affaire; (*b*) conclure, terminer (une affaire); régler, solder, balancer (un compte); payer (une dette, une amende, un compte); **to s. one's bills, to s. up,** payer ses comptes; **I'll s. (the bill) for everybody,** c'est moi qui payerai (la note); *F:* **that'll s. his account!** voilà qui réglera son compte! *F:* **that settled him,** *P:* **his hash,** (i) ça lui a réglé son compte; (ii) ça lui a rabattu le caquet; *F:* **and now I'll s. with you!** maintenant à nous deux! **8. to s. an annuity on s.o.,** constituer, assigner, une annuité à qn; asseoir une annuité sur qn; **to s. all one's property on one's wife,** mettre tous ses biens sur la tête de sa femme.

II. *v.i.* **1.** (*a*) **to s. (down),** élire domicile, s'établir, se fixer (dans un lieu); **to s. somewhere else,** se fixer ailleurs; se transplanter; (*b*) **to s. (down) in an armchair,** s'installer dans un fauteuil; **she had settled (herself) in a corner,** elle s'était installée, pelotée, dans un coin; **to s. (down) to sleep,** se disposer à dormir; (*c*) (*of bird, insect, etc.*) se percher, se poser (sur un arbre, etc.); (*d*) **the snow is settling,** la neige prend, ne fond pas; (*e*) **the wind is settling in the north,** le vent s'établit dans le nord; le vent souffle ferme du nord; (*f*) **to s. (down) to work, to do sth.,** se mettre sérieusement au travail, à faire qch.; **he can't s. (down) to anything,** il ne se décide pas à choisir une occupation. **2.** (*of liquid*) se clarifier, déposer, prendre son rassis, se rasseoir, se reposer; (*of sediment*) se déposer, se précipiter; **to let (sth.) s.,** laisser déposer (un précipité); laisser rasseoir (le vin); laisser reposer (une solution). **3.** (*a*) (i) (*of ground, pillar, gun, etc.*) prendre son assiette, s'asseoir, se tasser; (*of ground*) se seller; (ii) (*of pillar, foundation, etc.*) se déniveler, s'affaisser, farder; prendre coup, faire coup; **things are settling into shape, are settling down,** (i) les choses commencent à prendre tournure; (ii) l'ordre se rétablit; (*b*) (*of ship*) **to s. (down),** couler, (s')enfoncer, s'immerger. **4.** (*of passion, excitement*) s'apaiser, se calmer; **the weather is settling,** le temps se calme. **5. to s. for sth.,** convenir, décider, d'accepter qch.; **I settled for £100,** j'ai décidé d'accepter £100; **as there's no meat I'll s. for fish,** comme il n'y a pas de viande, je prends du poisson.

III. (*compound verbs*) **1. settle down,** *v.i.* (*s.a.* SETTLE II, *v.i.*) (*a*) **to s. down to a meal,** se mettre à table; **to s. down (round the fire) for the evening,** s'installer (autour du feu) pour (y passer) la soirée; **to s. down to a job,** attaquer, se mettre à, un travail, une tâche; (*b*) (i) (*of pers.*) se ranger, devenir sérieux, s'assagir; **to s. down (for life),** se marier; se caser; **she has no desire to s. down,** elle n'a aucune envie de se fixer; **marriage has made him s. down,** le mariage l'a rangé; **he's beginning to s. down at school,** il commence à s'habituer à l'école; (ii) (*of thg*) reprendre le train de la vie ordinaire; **as soon as the market settles down,** aussitôt que le marché reprend son train (ordinaire).

2. settle in, *v.i.* s'installer, s'établir (dans une nouvelle maison, etc.).

settled ['set(ə)ld], *a.* **1.** (*a*) (*of state*) invariable, sûr; (*of idea, habit*) fixe, enraciné; **s. intention,** intention bien arrêtée; **s. policy,** politique continue; **s. weather,** temps fait, fixe, sûr; beau *m* fixe; *Nau:* temps établi; **s. rain,** pluie persistante; *Nau:* **s. wind,** brise établie; **s. peace,** paix *f* durable; **man of s. convictions,** homme *m* aux convictions arrêtées; **I am a man of s. habits,** je suis un homme d'habitude; (*b*) (*of pers., character*) rassis, réfléchi; (*of bearing, etc.*) tranquille, calme; (*c*) (*of pers.*) rangé; *esp.* marié. **2.** (*a*) (*of affair, question, etc.*) arrangé, décidé; (*b*) (*of bill, etc.*) réglé, soldé. **3.** (*of pers.*) domicilié, établi; (*of thg*) bien assis; (*of government, etc.*) établi. **4.** (*of ground, etc.*) tassé, sellé, compact. **5.** (*of estate, etc.*) constitué (**on s.o.,** à qn). **6.** (*of country*) colonisé.

settlement ['set(ə)lmənt], *s.* **1.** (*a*) établissement *m* (d'un peuple dans un pays, etc.); installation *f* (de qn dans une maison, etc.); (*b*) colonisation *f*, peuplement *m* (d'un pays); **land awaiting s.,** terres non encore concédées; (*c*) **the s. of Europe after the War,** la restauration de l'Europe après la Guerre; (*d*) *esp. U.S:* installation (d'un pasteur). **2.** (*a*) tassement *m*, affaissement *m* (des terres); (*b*) *Artil:* assise *f* (d'une pièce); (*c*) clarification *f* (d'un liquide). **3.** (*a*) règlement *m* (d'une affaire, d'un litige); arrangement *m*, solution *f* (d'un différend, etc.); résolution *f*, décision *f* (d'une question); détermination *f* (d'une date, etc.); conclusion *f* (d'un traité, etc.); (*b*) *Com:* règlement, paiement *m*, apurement *m* (d'un compte); **s. of account,** arrêté *m* de compte; **in (full) s.,** pour règlement de tout compte; **cheque in s. of your account,** chèque *m* pour balancer votre compte; (*c*) *St. Exch:* liquidation *f*; **the s.,** le terme; **dealings for s.,** négociations *f* à terme; **s. day,** jour *m* de (la) liquidation, du règlement; **yearly s.,** liquidation de fin d'anée; (*d*) accord *m* (entre deux puissances, etc.); **to make a s. with s.o.,** faire un accord, entrer en accommodement, en venir à un accommodement, avec qn; **they have reached a s.,** ils sont arrivés à un accord amical; *Com:* **legal s.,** (*between merchant and creditors*), concordat *m* (après faillite); *Jur:* **s. arrived at by the parties inter se, s. before judgment,** transaction *f* (avant jugement); (*e*) *Jur:* **s. of an annuity,** constitution *f* de rente (**on,** en faveur de); **(deed of) s.,** acte *m* de disposition; contrat *m* de constitution; **family s.,** pacte *m* de famille; **marriage s.,** (i) contrat de mariage; (ii) (*in favour of daughter*) dot *f*; (*in favour of wife*) douaire *m*; (**marriage**) **s. in trust** = régime dotal; (*f*) *Hist:* **Act of S.,** Acte de Succession (au trône). **4.** *Jur:* domicile légal; (*of pauper*) domicile de secours. **5.** (*a*) colonie *f* (de peuplement); **colonial s.,** établissement colonial; **penal s.,** colonie pénitentiaire, de déportation; (*b*) *O:* œuvre social (dans les quartiers pauvres d'une grande ville). **6.** *U.S:* (*a*) petit village; (*b*) *A:* baraquements *mpl* des esclaves.

settler ['setlər], *s.* **1.** colon *m*, immigrant, -ante (dans un pays nouvellement découvert). **2.** *F:* coup décisif; argument décisif; **that was a s.!** ça lui a réglé son compte! **3.** *Metall:* settler *m*; cuve *f* de lavage. **4.** *Austr: Orn: F:* **settler's clock,** martin-pêcheur *m* (d'Australie).

settling ['setliŋ], *s.* **1.** = SETTLEMENT 1. **2.** (*a*) apaisement *m* (d'une agitation, des nerfs, etc.); (*b*) clarification *f* (d'un liquide); *Winem:* **s. vat,** cuve *f* de débourbage (du champagne, etc.); (*c*) précipitation *f*, dépôt *m* (du sédiment); *Dy: etc:* **s. vat, tub,** reposoir *m*; *Ind:* **s. tank,** bassin *m* de colmatage; (*d*) tassement *m*; affaissement *m* (du terrain); dénivellement *m* (d'un pilier, des fondements, etc.); *Civ.E:* **amount of s.,** flèche *f* d'abaissement; **s. crack,** lézarde *f* de tassement; (*e*) *Artil:* assise *f* (d'une pièce); (*f*) **settlings,** dépôt, sédiment *m*. **3.** = SETTLEMENT 3 (*a*). **4.** (*a*) conclusion *f*, terminaison *f* (d'une affaire); **s.** (**up**), règlement *m*, apurement *m* (d'un compte); (*b*) *St. Exch:* liquidation *f*; **s. day,** jour *m* de (la) liquidation, du règlement. **5. s.** (**down, in**), installation *f* (dans une nouvelle maison, etc.).

settlor ['setlər], *s. Jur:* disposant, -ante, constituteur, -trice (d'une annuité, etc.).

set-to ['settu:], *s. F:* (*a*) assaut *m* (de boxe); (*b*) lutte *f*, combat *m*, bagarre *f*; **a real, regular, s.-to,** une bataille en règle; (*c*) prise *f* de bec.

setula ['si:tjulə], *s. Bot:* sétule *f*.

set-up ['setʌp], *s. F:* **1.** organisation *f*; **it's an odd s.-up,** c'est une drôle de boîte, d'affaire. **2.** installation *f*; **you've got a nice s.-up here,** vous êtes bien installé ici. **3.** (*a*) machination *f*, coup monté; (*b*) *esp. U.S:* match *m* de boxe dont le résultat a été arrangé d'avance.

setwall ['setwɔ:l], *s. Bot:* nard *m* de montagne.

seven [sev(ə)n]. **1.** *num.a. & s.* (*a*) sept (*m*); **two sevens are fourteen,** deux fois sept font quatorze; **s.-strand(ed) rope,** septain *m*; **s.-league(d) boots,** bottes *f* de sept lieues (du Petit Poucet); *A:* **s.-day case of razors,** semainier *m*; *Cards:* **s. of hearts,** le sept de cœur; *Hist:* **the S. Years' War,** la Guerre de sept ans; **the S. Sleepers (of Ephesus),** les Sept Dormants *m*; (*b*) *Z:* **s. sleeper,** loir gris; *Ich:* **s.-grill(ed) shark,** heptanche *m*, perlon *m*. **2.** *s. Aut: A:* **an Austin s.,** une sept chevaux (Austin).

sevenfold ['sev(ə)nfould]. **1.** *a.* septuple. **2.** *adv.* sept fois autant; **to increase s.,** septupler; **to return a kindness s.,** rendre un bienfait au septuple.

seventeen [sev(ə)n'ti:n], *num.a. & s.* dix-sept (*m*); **she's s.,** elle a dix-sept ans; *O:* **to be sweet s.,** être dans la fleur de ses dix-sept printemps.

seventeenth [sev(ə)n'ti:nθ]. **1.** *num.a. & s.* dix-septième (*mf*); **Louis the S.,** Louis dix-sept; (**on**) **the s. of May,** le dix-sept mai. **2.** *s.* (*fractional*) dix-septième *m*.

seventeenthly [sev(ə)n'ti:nθli], *adv.* dix-septièmement.

seventh ['sevənθ]. **1.** *num.a. & s.* septième (*mf*); **in the s. place,** septièmement; en septième lieu; septimo; **to be in the s. heaven (of delight),** être aux anges, au septième ciel, dans l'enchantement; ne pas toucher à terre; **Edward the S.,** Édouard Sept; **the s. of May,** le sept mai; **the s. day,** samedi *m*; *Rel:* **S.-day Adventist,** adventiste *mf* du septième jour; sabbataire *mf*. **2.** *s.* (*a*) (*fractional*) septième *m*; (*b*) *Mus:* septième *f*; (note *f*) sensible *f*.

seventhly ['sevənθli], *adv.* septièmement; en septième lieu; septimo.

seventieth ['sevəntiiθ]. **1.** *num.a. & s.* soixante-dixième (*mf*); *Belg: Sw. Fr: Fr.C:* septantième (*mf*). **2.** *s.* (*fractional*) soixante-dixième *m*.

seventy ['sevənti], *num.a. & s.* soixante-dix (*m*); *Belg: Sw. Fr: Fr.C:* septante (*mf*); **s.-one, s.-nine,** soixante et onze, soixante-dix-neuf; **s.-five,** (i) soixante-quinze; (ii) *Artil: A:* (pièce *f* de) soixante-quinze *m*; **to be in one's seventies,** être septuagénaire; **in the seventies of the last century,** dans les années soixante-dix du siècle dernier; entre 1870 et 1880; *B:* **to forgive s.o. until s. times seven,** pardonner qn jusqu'à septante fois sept.

sever ['sevər]. **1.** *v.tr.* (*a*) désunir, disjoindre (les parties d'un tout); rompre (l'amitié, une liaison, etc.); **to s. a beam,** sectionner une poutre; **to s. one's connections with s.o.,** se désassocier de qn, d'avec qn; cesser toutes relations avec qn; (*b*) **to s. sth. from sth.,** séparer qch. de qch. **2.** *v.i.* (*a*) (*of pers.*) se séparer (**from,** de); (*b*) (*of rope, etc.*) (se) rompre; casser en deux; (*c*) *Jur:* (*of co-defendants*) adopter des défenses différentes.

severable ['sevərəbl], *a.* séparable (**from,** de).

several ['sev(ə)r(ə)l], *a.* **1.** (*a*) *O:* séparé; différent; **on three s. occasions,** à trois occasions (différentes); **the s. members of the committee,** les divers membres du comité; (*b*) *Jur:* (bien) individuel, divis; (responsabilité) individuelle; **the members of this community have no s. estates,** les membres de cette communauté ne possèdent pas de biens en particulier; **joint and s. bond,** obligation solidaire; **joint and s. liability,** responsabilité (conjointe et) solidaire; (*c*) respectif; **our s. rights,** nos droits respectifs; *Lit:* **each went his s. way, they went their s. ways,** ils s'en allèrent, chacun de son côté, chacun de leur côté. **2.** (*a*) plusieurs; divers; quelques; **I've been there s. times,** j'y suis allé plusieurs fois; **the works of s. artists,** les œuvres de divers artistes; **he and s. others,** lui et plusieurs autres; (*b*) (*with noun function*) **I have s.,** j'en ai plusieurs; **s. of us, of them,** plusieurs d'entre nous, d'entre eux; **s. of the team are absent,** plusieurs de l'équipe manquent; **s. of our party heard it,** plusieurs membres de notre groupe l'ont entendu.

severalfold ['sev(ə)rəlfould]. **1.** *a.* multiple. **2.** *adv.* **it will increase s.,** il fera plus que doubler.

severally ['sev(ə)rəli], *adv.* séparément, individuellement, isolément; *Jur:* **s. liable,** responsables isolément, individuellement; **jointly and s.,** conjointement et solidairement; par divis et indivis.

severalty ['sev(ə)rəlti], *s. Jur:* propriété individuelle, non solidaire; divis *m*; **land held in s.,** bien tenu individuellement, sans solidarité, par divis.

severance ['sevər(ə)ns], *s.* **1.** séparation *f*, désunion *f*, disjonction *f* (**from,** de); rupture *f* (des relations, etc.); **s. of communications,** interruption complète de communication; *Ind: etc:* **s. pay,** compensation *f* pour perte d'emploi. **2.** *Jur:* disjonction (de deux ou plusieurs causes).

severe [si'viər], *a.* **1.** (*of pers.*) sévère, strict, rigoureux (**with,** envers); **s. expression,** regard *m* sévère; **to take s. measures,** prendre des mesures de rigueur; **s. sentence,** sentence rigoureuse; **unduly s. regulations,** règlements draconiens; **a s. reprimand,** une verte réprimande; **to be very s. with one's children,** être très sévère envers ses enfants. **2.** (*a*) (temps) rigoureux; (hiver, climat) rigoureux, rude, dur; **the cold was s.,** le froid sévissait; (*b*) **s. blow,** coup *m* rude; **s. trial,** rude épreuve *f*; **s. loss,** grosse perte, forte perte; **s. pain,** douleur violente, cruelle; vive douleur; **s. cold,** gros rhume; **s. illness, wound,** maladie *f* grave; grave blessure *f*; **s. bombardment,** bombardement *m* intense; **there had been s. fighting in the northern sector,** la lutte avait été particulièrement violente dans le secteur nord; **to be in s. distress,** être dans une grande misère, dans une grande gêne. **3.** (style, etc.) sévère, austère, sans agréments; **s. beauty,** beauté *f* sévère.

severely [si'viəli], *adv.* **1.** sévèrement, strictement; avec sévérité; **to deal s. with an abuse,** sévir contre un abus; **to look at s.o. s.,** lancer à qn un regard sévère, faire les gros yeux à qn; **to leave sth. s. alone,** ne pas toucher à qch.; laisser qch. entièrement de côté; se bien garder de toucher à qch.; **I was left s. alone,** personne ne m'a accordé la moindre attention. **2.** grièvement, gravement (malade, blessé, etc.); **he has suffered s.,** il a beaucoup souffert; **s. tried,** durement éprouvé, rudement éprouvé. **3.** sévèrement, austèrement (bâti, écrit, etc.); **s. plain,** d'une simplicité sévère.

Severinus [sevə'rainəs]. *Pr.n.m. Ecc.Hist:* Séverin.

severity [si'veriti], *s.* **1.** sévérité *f*, dureté *f*, rigueur *f* (de qn, d'une punition, etc.). **2.** (*a*) rigueur, inclémence *f* (du temps, du climat, etc.); rudesse *f* (du temps); (*b*) gravité *f* (d'une maladie, d'une perte, etc.); violence *f* (d'une douleur); (*c*) rigueur, caractère rigoureux (d'un examen, etc.); difficulté *f* (d'une épreuve). **3.** sévérité, austérité *f*, simplicité *f* (de style, etc.).

Severus ['sevərəs, si'viərəs]. *Pr.n.m. Rom.Hist:* Sévère; **Septimus S.,** Septime Sévère.

severy ['sevəri], *s. Arch:* pan *m* de voûte.

Seville ['sevil]. *Pr.n. Geog:* Séville *f*; **S. orange,** orange amère.

Sevill(i)an [se'vil(i)ən]. *Geog:* (*a*) *a.* sévillan; (*b*) *s.* Sévillan, -ane.

Sèvres [seivr]. *Pr.n.* (*a*) *Geog:* Sèvres; (*b*) **S. porcelain,** porcelaine *f* de Sèvres; **a set of old S.,** un service de vieux sèvres.

sew [sou], *v.tr. & i.* (*p.t.* **sewed** [soud]; *p.p.* **sewn** [soun], *occ.* **sewed**) **1.** coudre (un vêtement, etc.); (*with awl*) piquer; *Bookb:* brocher, coudre (les feuilles d'un livre); **to s. on a button,** (re)coudre, attacher, un bouton. **2.** (*a*) *F:* **it's all sewn up,** tout est fixé, arrangé; (*b*) *F:* (i) **to s. s.o. up,** éreinter, épuiser, qn; **to be sewed up,** être éreinté, vanné, fourbu; (ii) *O:* **sewed up,** soûl comme une grive, comme un Polonais; **to get s.o. sewed up,** soûler, enivrer, qn.

sewage ['s(j)u:idʒ], *s.* eau(x) *f*(*pl*) d'égout(s); effluent *m*; **s. system,** système *m* du tout à l'égout; **s. farm,** champs *mpl* d'épandage; *Agr:* **s. (water),** eaux-vannes *fpl*.

sewellel [sə'weləl], *s. Z:* castor *m* de montagne nord-américain.

sewer[1] ['souər], *s.* couseur, -euse; *Bookb:* brocheur, -euse.

sewer[2] ['s(j)u:ər], *s. Civ.E:* égout *m*; **public s.,** égout municipal; **main s.,** égout collecteur; **s. grating,** grille *f* de regard d'égout; **s. gases,** miasme égoutier; **s.** (**of vice, etc.**) cloaque *m* (de vice, etc.).

sewerage ['s(j)u:əridʒ], *s.* **1.** système *m* d'égouts. **2.** *F:* = SEWAGE.

sewerman, *pl.* **-men** ['s(j)u:əmən], *s.m.* égoutier.

sewin ['sju(:)in], *s. Ich:* grosse truite du pays de Galles.

sewing ['souiŋ], *s.* **1.** couture *f*; *Bookb:* brochage *m*; **plain s.,** couture simple; **s. circle, s. bee,** cercle *m* de couture; **s. needle,** aiguille *f* à coudre; **s. cotton, thread,** fil *m* à coudre; **s. machine,** machine *f* à coudre; **s. outfit,** nécessaire *m* de couture; *A:* **s. maid,** couturière *f*; lingère *f*; **s. woman,** couturière à domicile; *Bookb:* **s. press,** cousoir *m*; *Bootm:* **s. awl,** carrelet *m* de cordonnier. **2.** ouvrage *m* (à l'aiguille).

sewn [soun], *a.* cousu; **hand s., machine s.,** cousu (à la) main, à la machine.

sex[1] [seks], *s.* sexe *m*; (*a*) *Biol:* **s. determination,** détermination *f* du sexe; **s. linked,** lié au chromosome sexuel; *Psy:* **the s. urge,** le désir sexuel; **s. obsessed,** souffrant d'obsession sexuelle; *Med:* atteint d'aphrodisie; aphrodisiaque; **s. organs,** organes sexuels, génitaux; le sexe; **the s. act,** l'acte sexuel; rapports sexuels; *F:* **to have s. with s.o.,** faire l'amour avec qn; **s. appeal,** attrait sexuel, sex-appeal *m*; **s. kitten,** fille provocante, sexy, allumée; pin-up particulièrement aguichante; (*b*) *O:* **the fair s.,** le beau sexe; **the sterner s.,** les hommes; le sexe fort.

sex[2], *v.tr.* **1.** déterminer le sexe de (qn, un animal); *Husb:* **sexed chicks,** poussins sexés. **2.** *F:* **to s. up (a novel, etc.),** introduire du sexe (dans un roman, etc.).

sexagenarian [seksədʒi'nɛəriən], *a. & s.* sexagénaire (*mf*).

sexagenary [sek'sædʒinəri, seksə'dʒi:nəri], *a. & s.* **1.** *Mth:* = SEXAGESIMAL. **2.** = SEXAGENARIAN.

Sexagesima [seksə'dʒesimə], *s. Ecc:* **S.** (**Sunday**), (le dimanche de) la Sexagésime.

sexagesimal [seksə'dʒesim(ə)l]. *Mth:* **1.** *a.* sexagésimal, -aux; astronomique. **2.** *s.* fraction sexagésimale, astronomique.

sexangular [seks'æŋgjulər], *a.* hexagonal, -aux; hexagone.

sexdigital, sexdigitate [seks'didʒit(ə)l, -teit], *a.* (*of hand, foot*) sexdigital, -aux; (*of pers.*) sexdigitaire.

sexdigitism [seks'didʒitizm], *s.* sexdigitisme *m*.

sexdigitist [seks'didʒitist], *s.* sexdigitaire *mf*.

sexed [sekst], *a.* **1.** *Nat.Hist:* sexué. **2.** *Psy:* **highly s.,** à tendances sexuelles très prononcées; **over s.,** hypersexué; **under s.,** frigide, froid. **3.** *P:* **s. up,** excité, allumé, chaud; **to get a woman s. up,** chauffer une femme.

sexennial [sek'seniəl], *a.* sexennal, -aux.

sexer ['seksər], *s. Husb:* celui, celle, qui détermine le sexe d'un poussin.

sexiferous [sek'sifərəs], *a. Bot:* sexifère.

sexifid ['seksifid], *a. Bot:* sexfide.

sexiness ['seksinis], *s.* charme, caractère, provocant; airs provocants; tendances sexuelles prononcées.

sexless ['sekslis], *a.* (*a*) asexué; *Bot:* **s. flower,** fleur *f* neutre; (*b*) *F:* froid, frigide.

sexological [seksə'lɔdʒikl], *a.* sexologique.

sexologist [sek'sɔlədʒist], *s.* sexologue *mf*.

sexology [sek'sɔlədʒi], *s.* sexologie *f*.

sexpot ['sekspɔt], *s.f. F:* femme très sexy; allumeuse.

sext [sekst], *s. Ecc:* sexte *f*.

sextain ['sekstein], *s. Pros:* sizain *m*, sixain *m*.

Sextans ['sekstænz], *Pr.n. Astr:* le Sextant.

sextant ['sekstənt], *s. Mth: Nau:* sextant *m*.

sextet [seks'tet], *s.* **1.** *Mus:* sextuor *m*; (*jazz*) sextette *f*. **2.** *NAm: Sp:* équipe *f* de hockey (sur glace).

sextile ['sekstail], *a. Astrol:* (aspect, etc.) sextil.

sextillion [seks'tiliən], *s.* **1.** sextillion *m* (10^{36}). **2.** *U.S:* mille trillions (10^{21}).

sexto, *pl.* **-os** ['sekstou, -ouz], *adv. & s. Typ:* in-six (*m*).

sextodecimo [sekstou'desimou], *s. Typ:* in-seize *m inv.*

sextolet ['sekstoulet], *s. Mus:* sixain *m*, sextolet *m*.

sexton ['sekst(ə)n], *s.* **1.** *Ecc:* sacristain *m* et sonneur *m* de cloches (et fossoyeur *m*). **2.** *Ent:* **s. (beetle),**

nécrophore *m*; *F:* fossoyeur, enfouisseur *m*, ensevelisseur *m*.
sextuple[1] ['sekstjupl], *a.* & *s.* sextuple (*m*).
sextuple[2], *v.tr.* sextupler.
sextuplet ['sekstjuplet], *s.* **1.** *Mus:* sextolet *m*, sixain *m*. **2.** (*child*) sextuplé, -ée.
sextuplicate [seks'tjuplikeit], *s. Typw: etc:* **in s.,** en sextuple.
sexual ['seksjuəl], *a.* sexuel; **s. intercourse,** rapports sexuels; **the s. organs,** les organes sexuels; **to rouse the s. instincts,** éveiller les sens; *Bot:* **the s. system, method,** la classification linnéenne.
sexuality [seksju'æliti], *s.* **1.** sexualité *f.* **2.** tendances sexuelles prononcées.
sexualize ['seksjuəlaiz], *v.tr.* attribuer un sexe à (des objets inanimés, etc.); sexualiser.
sexually ['seksjuəli], *adv.* **1.** d'une manière sexuelle. **2.** quant au sexe.
sexupara, *pl.* **-rae** [seks'jupərə, -ri:], **sexupare** ['seksjupɛər], *s. Ent:* insecte *m* sexupare.
sexuparous [seks'jupərəs], *a. Ent:* sexupare.
sexvalent [seks'veilənt], *a. Ch:* hexavalent.
sexy ['seksi], *a. F:* qui excite les instincts sexuels; (*of pers.*) sensuel, sexy; (sexuellement) provocant; chaud; capiteux, affriolant; **a s. little piece,** une petite femme croustillante.
seybertite ['saibə:tait], *s. Miner:* seybertite *f.*
Seychelles [sei'ʃelz], *Pr.n. Geog:* Seychelles.
seymouria [si:'mɔ:riə], *s. Paleont:* seymouria *m*.
Seymouriamorpha [si:mɔ:riə'mɔ:fə], *s.pl. Paleont:* seymouriamorphes *m*.
sez you [sez'ju:], *int. P:* (= *says you*) tu parles! et ta sœur!
sfumato [sfu:'mɑ:tou], *s. Art:* sfumato *m*.
sgraffito, *pl.* **-ti** [sgræ'fi:tou, -ti:], *s. Art:* sgraffite *m*.
sh [ʃ], *int.* chut!
shabbily ['ʃæbili], *adv.* **1.** pauvrement, piètrement (meublé, vêtu, etc.); **s. dressed,** miteux, râpé. **2.** (*a*) (se conduire) mesquinement, petitement, vilainement; (*b*) *O:* chichement; d'une manière avare.
shabbiness ['ʃæbinis], *s.* **1.** état râpé, usé, élimé (d'un vêtement, etc.); état défraîchi, piètre état (d'un chapeau, d'un meuble, etc.); apparence pauvre, *F:* miteuse (de qn). **2.** (*a*) mesquinerie *f*, petitesse *f* (de conduite, etc.); (*b*) mesquinerie (d'un cadeau); (*c*) *O:* parcimonie *f.*
shabby ['ʃæbi], *a.* **1.** (vêtement, etc.) râpé, usé, élimé, fripé, fatigué; (mobilier, etc.) pauvre, minable; **s. hat,** chapeau délabré, miteux; **s. clothes,** vêtements minables, miteux, râpés; **s. room,** pièce minable, tristement meublée; **s. armchair,** fauteuil usé, minable; **s. house,** maison délabrée, minable; maison de pauvre, de piètre, apparence; (*of pers.*) **to look s.,** avoir l'air minable, miteux; **to be s. genteel,** cacher la misère sous des apparences de dignité; s'efforcer de sauver les apparences; (*of material*) **to become s.,** se délustrer, s'élimer. **2.** (*a*) (*of pers., conduct*) mesquin, vilain, petit; peu honorable; **s. trick,** mesquinerie *f*, petitesse *f*; **s. excuse,** prétexte mesquin, peu convaincant; (*b*) *O:* chiche; parcimonieux.
shabrack, shabraque ['ʃæbræk], *s. A.Mil.Harn:* chabraque *f*, schabraque *f.*
shack[1] [ʃæk], (i) graine tombée (qui se trouve dans les champs après la moisson); (ii) (*in woods*) glands tombés; (*of pigs, etc.*) **to be, run, go, at s.,** être en pâture dans le chaume.
shack[2], *s.* cabane *f*, hutte *f*; bicoque *f.*
shack[3], *v.i. P:* **to s. up (with s.o.),** cohabiter, se coller (avec qn).
shack[4], *s. Fish: U.S:* **1.** appât ramassé au cours du voyage. **2.** poisson commun.
shack[5], *v.tr. Games:* (*baseball*) pourchasser, retrouver (la balle).
shack[6], *v.i. U.S: F:* **to s. along,** déambuler.
shackle[1] ['ʃækl], *s.* **1. shackles,** fers *m* (d'un prisonnier, etc.); **the shackles of convention,** les entraves *f* des conventions sociales; **the shackles of rhyme,** la contrainte de la rime. **2.** (*a*) maillon *m* de liaison, manille *f* d'assemblage (d'une chaîne); menotte *f* (de palonnier); anse *f*, branche *f* (d'un cadenas); bélière *f* (d'un couteau); cigale *f* (d'une ancre); *Rail:* étrier *m* d'attelage; **closed s.,** manille fermée, en forme de D; *Nau:* **joggle s.,** manille d'affourche, d'affourchage; **joiner s.,** manille d'assemblage, de jonction; **rocking s.,** manille de corps mort; *Veh:* **spring shackles,** jumelles *f*; huit *m* de ressort; brides *f* de ressort; **s. bolt,** cheville *f* d'assemblage; *Rail:* **s. bar,** bielle *f* d'attelage; (*b*) *Nau.Meas:* **s. of cable,** maillon de chaîne (= 30 mètres). **3.** *Tg:* **s. (insulator),** isolateur *m* d'angle, d'arrêt.
shackle[2], *v.tr.* **1.** mettre les fers à, entraver (un prisonnier, etc.); **shackled by conventions,** entravé par les conventions. **2.** (*a*) maniller, mailler (une chaîne, etc.); étalinguer (une ancre); *Rail:* **to s. a coach on to a train,** accoupler une voiture à un train; (*b*) monter (un ressort) à jumelles. **3.** *Tg:* passer (un fil) sur un isolateur d'angle.
shacktown ['ʃæktaun], *s. NAm: F:* bidonville *f.*
shad [ʃæd], *s. Ich:* alose *f*; **s. net, seine,** alosier *m*.
shadberry ['ʃædberi], *s. Bot:* **1.** amélanche *f.* **2.** amélanchier *m*.
shadblow ['ʃædblou], *s. Bot:* **s. (serviceberry),** amélanchier *m*.
shadbush ['ʃædbuʃ], *s. Bot:* amélanchier *m*.
shaddock ['ʃædɔk], *s. Bot:* pamplemousse *f*; **s. (tree),** shaddock *m*.
shade[1] [ʃeid], *s.* **1.** (*a*) ombre *f*; **in the s. of a tree,** à l'ombre d'un arbre; **temperature in the s.,** température *f* à l'ombre; **to keep in the s.,** (i) rester à l'ombre; (ii) rester dans l'obscurité; **to put s.o. in, to throw s.o. into, the s.,** éclipser qn; faire ombre à qn; **her beauty threw all other women into the s.,** sa beauté effaçait toutes les autres femmes; **a s. of annoyance on his face,** une ombre de contrariété sur son visage; **the shades of night,** les ombres, les voiles *m*, de la nuit; les ténèbres *f*; **the Shades,** (i) *Lit:* les Enfers; (ii) *F: A:* le bar (d'un hôtel); (iii) *F: A:* débit *m* de boissons (surtout pour la vente du vin); (*b*) *Art:* ombre (dans un tableau); (*c*) *For:* **s. bearer, s. tree,** essence *f* d'ombre. **2.** (*a*) nuance *f* (de couleur, de signification, d'opinion, etc.); teinte *f*; **different shades of blue,** différentes nuances de bleu; **obtainable in any s.,** procurable dans n'importe quel ton, dans n'importe quelle nuance; **newspapers of every s., of all shades, of opinion,** journaux *m* de toutes nuances; **there is a s. of meaning,** il y a une nuance; (*b*) nuance; petit peu; tantinet *m*; **ribbon a s. too blue,** ruban un rien trop bleu; **a s. longer,** un tant soit peu, un tantinet, plus long; **he is a s. better,** il va un tout petit peu mieux; il y a un léger mieux; **a s. of regret,** une nuance de regret; **a s. of disapproval in his voice,** un rien, un soupçon, de désapprobation dans sa voix. **3.** (*a*) pâle reflet *m*, ombre (de qch.); **not a s. of doubt,** pas le moindre doute; (*b*) *O:* ombre, fantôme *m* (d'un mort); *A:* **shades of Demosthenes! shades of Julius Cæsar!** par Démosthène! par Jules César! **4.** (*a*) **lamp s.,** abat-jour *m inv*; *Opt:* **lens s., ray s.,** pare-soleil *m inv* (d'un télescope); œillère *f* (d'une lunette de visée, etc.); (*of sextant, etc.*) **coloured s.,** verre coloré; (*b*) *NAm:* store *m* (de fenêtre); (*c*) *Nau:* tente *f*; **s. deck,** pont *m* tente; (*d*) (*for clocks, etc.*) globe *m*.
shade[2], *v.*
I. *v.tr.* **1.** (*a*) ombrager (qch.); couvrir (qch.) d'ombre; **trees that s. the house,** arbres *m* qui ombragent la maison, qui donnent de l'ombre à la maison; **to s. (sth.) from the sun,** abriter (qch.) du soleil; *Hort:* ombrer (une serre); **to s. one's eyes with one's hand,** se faire un abat-jour de sa main; mettre la main en abat-jour (sur les yeux); **to s. a light,** (i) voiler, atténuer, une lumière; (ii) masquer une lumière; **to s. a lamp,** mettre un abat-jour à une lampe; (*b*) obscurcir, assombrir (le visage, etc.). **2.** *Art:* ombrer, mettre des ombres à (un dessin). **3.** (*a*) nuancer (un tissu, etc.); **to s. away, s. off, colours,** dégrader des couleurs; **to s. off a charcoal drawing,** estomper un fusain; (*b*) *Com: NAm:* **to s. prices,** établir des prix dégressifs; **prices shaded for quantities,** tarif dégressif pour le gros.
II. *v.i.* **blue that shades (off) into green,** bleu qui se fond en vert; **these categories shade into one another,** ces catégories se confondent.
shaded ['ʃeidid], *a.* **1.** (*a*) (chemin, etc.) ombragé, à l'ombre; (*b*) (lampe *f*, etc.) à abat-jour. **2.** (*a*) *Art:* (dessin) ombré; (*b*) *Mapm: etc:* hachuré. **3.** (*of embroidery, feathers, etc.*) nuancé; **s.-silver cat,** chat argenté nuancé.
shadeless ['ʃeidlis], *a.* (*a*) sans ombre; (*b*) qui ne donne pas d'ombre.
shade-loving ['ʃeidlʌviŋ], *a. Bot:* sciaphile.
shadflower ['ʃædflauər], *s. Bot:* amélanchier *m*.
shadily ['ʃeidili], *adv. F:* d'une manière louche.
shadiness ['ʃeidinis], *s.* **1.** ombre *f*, ombrage *m* (d'un sentier, etc.). **2.** *F:* aspect *m* louche (d'une affaire, etc.); manque *m* d'honnêteté, réputation suspecte (de qn).
shading ['ʃeidiŋ], *s.* **1.** projection *f* d'une ombre (sur qch.); protection *f* (de qch.) contre la lumière; *Hort:* **s. mat,** claie *f*, paillasson *m*, à ombrer. **2.** (*a*) *Art:* dessin *m* des ombres; *Mapm:* **hill s.,** modelé *m*; (*b*) ombres (d'un dessin). **3.** (*a*) nuancement *m* (de couleurs); **s. (away, off),** dégradation *f* (d'une couleur); estompage *m*; dégradé *m*; **s.-off tints,** teintes dégradées; (*b*) *T.V:* tache *f.*
shadoof [ʃæ'du:f], *s.* shadouf *m*, chadouf *m*.
shadow[1] ['ʃædou], *s.* ombre *f.* **1.** (*a*) obscurité *f*; **in the s.,** à, dans, l'ombre; dans l'obscurité; **the shadows of evening,** la nuit qui vient; l'ombre qui se fait; **the s. of death,** les ombres de la mort; **under the s. of a terrible accusation,** sous le coup d'une accusation terrible; **to be under the s. of misfortune,** être sous l'emprise du malheur; (*b*) noir *m* (d'un tableau, d'une photographie); **deep shadows,** (i) les accents *m* (d'un tableau); (ii) les grands noirs (d'un cliché); *X-Rays:* **a s. on the right lung,** un voile au poumon droit; **to have (dark) shadows round, under, one's eyes,** avoir les yeux cernés; avoir des cernes *m* aux yeux; *Toil:* **eye s.,** fard *m* à paupières; (*c*) *F:* **five o'clock s.,** la barbe du soir, le foin de la journée. **2.** (*a*) **to cast a s.,** projeter une ombre; faire ombre; **pillars that cast long shadows,** piliers qui allongent de grandes ombres; **this cast a s. over the festivities,** cela a jeté un voile de tristesse, une ombre, sur la fête; la fête s'en est trouvée assombrie; **coming events cast their shadows,** les événements à venir se font pressentir; **to catch at shadows, to run after a s.,** courir après une ombre; *B:* **under the s. of Thy wings,** sous l'ombre de tes ailes; **town nestling in the s. of a mountain,** ville nichée à l'ombre d'une montagne; **to be afraid of one's own s.,** avoir peur de son ombre; **to quarrel with one's own s.,** se faire du mauvais sang à propos de rien; se faire du tort; **may your s. never grow less!** tous mes vœux pour votre prospérité! **not the s. of a doubt,** pas l'ombre d'un doute; (*b*) *Box:* **s. boxing,** assaut *m* d'entraînement contre un adversaire fictif. **3.** (*a*) *Rom.Ant:* ombre (amenée par un convive); (*b*) compagnon, *f.* compagne, inséparable (de qn); (*c*) ombre (d'un mort); **to wear oneself to a s.,** (i) se manger les sangs; (ii) s'épuiser (de travail); **he's worn to a s., he's a mere s. of his former self,** il n'est plus qu'une ombre, que l'ombre de lui-même; (*d*) agent *m* de la police secrète; filateur, -trice. **4.** *Pol:* **s. government,** gouvernement *m* fantôme; contre-gouvernement *m*; **s. cabinet,** cabinet *m* fantôme.
shadow[2], *v.tr.* **1.** (*a*) ombrager (qch.); couvrir (qch.) de son ombre; (*b*) *Tex:* chiner (un tissu). **2.** filer, *F:* pister (qn); **to s. a suspect,** prendre un suspect en filature; **shadowed by the police,** filé, pisté, par la police.
shadower ['ʃædouər], *s.* filateur, -trice (d'un suspect, etc.).
shadowgraph ['ʃædougræf], *s.* **1.** silhouette *f*; ombre faite avec les mains; ombre chinoise. **2.** *Med: A:* radiographie *f*; radiogramme *m*.
shadowing ['ʃædouiŋ], *s.* filature *f*, pistage *m* (d'une personne suspecte).
shadowless ['ʃædoulis], *a.* sans ombre.
shadowy ['ʃædoui], *a.* **1.** (chemin, etc.) ombragé, ombreux; (couloir, etc.) peu éclairé, sombre, ténébreux. **2.** (songe, etc.) chimérique; (projet) indécis, vague; (contour) vague, indistinct; **a s. form emerged from the fog,** une silhouette vague se dessinait dans le brouillard.
Shadrach ['ʃeidræk]. **1.** *Pr.n.m. B.Hist:* Shadrac. **2.** *s. Metall:* loup *m*, cochon *m*; carcas *m*.
shady ['ʃeidi], *a.* **1.** (*a*) qui donne de l'ombre; ombreux; (*b*) ombragé; couvert d'ombre; ombreux; **s. drive,** allée couverte; *F:* **to be on the s. side of forty,** avoir dépassé la quarantaine. **2.** *F:* (*of transaction, etc.*) louche, équivoque; (*of pers.*) louche, d'une probité douteuse; **he's a s. looking customer,** il a l'air bien louche; **s. financier,** financier véreux; **s. business,** (i) commerce *m* interlope, qui se fait en fraude; (ii) affaire véreuse; **there's something s. going on,** il y a du louche dans cette affaire; **the s. side of politics,** les dessous *m* de la politique.
shaft[1] [ʃɑ:ft], *s.* **1.** (*a*) hampe *f*, bois *m* (d'une lance, etc.); (*b*) manche *m* (de club de golf, d'un outil à long manche). **2.** (*a*) flèche *f*, trait *m*; (*b*) *A:* javelot *m*, javeline *f*; **the shafts of satire, of ridicule,** les flèches, les traits, les dards *m*, de la satire, du ridicule; **the shafts of Cupid,** les traits de l'Amour.**3.** rayon *m* (de lumière); éclair *m* (de foudre); sillon *m* (d'un éclair). **4.** (*a*) tige *f* (de plume d'oiseau, de candélabre, etc.); *Anat:* corps (du tibia, etc.); *Row:* collet *m* (d'aviron); (*b*) *Arch:* fût *m*, escape *f*, vif *m* (d'une colonne); *Const: Ind:* souche *f* (de cheminée d'usine); *Metall:* cuve *f* (de haut fourneau); **s. furnace,** four *m* à cuve; (*c*) *Av:* corps *m* (de réacteur); **single-s. engine,** réacteur *m* à un corps; **two-s. engine,** réacteur à deux corps, à double corps; **three-s., triple-s., engine,** réacteur à trois corps, à triple corps; **triple-s. fan engine,** réacteur à double corps et à double flux. **5.** (*a*) *Mec.E:* arbre *m*; (*stationary*) axe *m*; **cranked s.,** arbre coudé; arbre à manivelle, à vilebrequin; **cross s.,** arbre transversal; **eccentric s.,** arbre excentrique; **flanged s.,** arbre à collerette; **flexible s.,** arbre flexible, souple; transmission *f* flexible, souple; **grooved s., splined s.,** arbre cannelé, à cannelures; **heavy s.,** gros arbre; **hollow s.,** arbre creux; **horizontal**

s., lying s., arbre horizontal; **loose s.,** arbre fou; **overhead s.,** arbre suspendu; **rocking s.,** arbre oscillant; **sliding s.,** arbre coulissant; **telescopic s.,** arbre télescopique; **through s.,** arbre traversant; **vertical s., upright s.,** arbre vertical; **worm s.,** arbre à vis sans fin; **actuating s., control s.,** arbre de commande; **adaptor s.,** arbre de montage; *Aut:* **clutch s.,** arbre primaire; **connecting s.,** arbre de liaison; **coupling s.,** arbre d'accouplement; **drive s., driving s., engine s., power s.,** arbre moteur, arbre d'entraînement, arbre menant, arbre de couche; **driven s.,** arbre commandé, conduit, mené; arbre récepteur; *Aut:* arbre secondaire; **gear s.,** arbre porte-pignon; **main s., first-motion s.,** arbre principal, arbre d'entraînement; **intermediate s., secondary s., second-motion s.,** arbre intermédiaire, secondaire; *Av: N.Arch:* **propeller s.,** arbre porte-hélice, arbre d'hélice; *Mch:* **reverse s., reversing s.,** arbre de renversement de marche, arbre de relevage; **roller s.,** arbre porte-galet; **thrust s.,** arbre de butée; **timing s.,** arbre de distribution; **torque s.,** arbre, barre *f*, de torsion; **transmission s.,** arbre de transmission, de renvoi; **turbine s.,** arbre de turbine; **s. alignment,** alignement *m* des arbres; **s. bearing, s. carrier,** palier *m* d'arbre, palier de transmission; **s. collar, s. neck,** collier *m* d'arbre; **s. coupling,** accouplement *m* d'arbres; manchon *m* d'accouplement, manchon d'assemblage, d'arbres; **s. drive,** prise *f* de mouvement de l'arbre d'entraînement; **s. gear,** pignon *m* d'arbre de renvoi; **s. horsepower,** puissance *f* sur l'arbre, puissance au frein; **s. key,** clavette *f*, cale *f*, d'arbre; **s. strut,** support *m* d'arbre; *N.Arch:* **s. tunnel, s. trunk, s. alley,** tunnel *m* d'arbre(s); (*b*) *Min: Petr:* **drilling s.,** corps *m* de sonde. **6.** *Veh:* brancard *m*, limon *m*; **pair of shafts,** limonière; **s. tip,** mouflette *f*; **s. pin,** attel(l)oire *f*; **s. bar,** empannon *m*; épar(t) *m*; **s. horse,** cheval *m* de brancard; limonier *m*. **7.** *Tex:* (*set of heddles*) lame *f*.

shaft[2], *s.* **1.** (*a*) *Min:* puits *m*; **air s., ventilation s.,** puits d'aérage, conduit *m* d'air, cheminée *f* d'appel; **blind s., internal s.,** puits intérieur, bure *f*; **central s., main s.,** puits central, principal; **discovery s., prospecting s., trial s.,** puits d'essai, d'exploration, de prospection, de recherche; **drain s.,** puits de drainage; **force s.,** avant-puits *m inv*; **hoisting s.,** puits d'extraction; **metal-lined s., ironclad s.,** puits blindé; **pumping s., water s.,** puits d'épuisement, d'exhaure; **return s.,** puits de sortie d'air; **s. lined with concrete,** puits bétonné; **s. lining,** revêtement *m* de puits; **sump s.,** puits collecteur; puits d'épuisement, d'exhaure; **timbered s.,** puits boisé; **twin shafts,** puits jumeaux; **winding s., working s.,** puits d'extraction, d'exploitation, de travail; **to sink a s.,** foncer, creuser, un puits; **s. sinking,** fonçage *m*, foncement *m*, creusage *m*, creusement *m*, d'un puits; (*b*) *Archeol:* **s. grave, tomb,** puits de sépulture. **2.** cage *f* (d'un ascenseur).

shafted ['ʃɑːftid], *a.* **1.** (outil, etc.) à long manche; (lance, etc.) à hampe; **steel-s. golf club,** club *m* de golf à manche d'acier. **2.** *Arch:* (*of archway, etc.*) à fûts; posé sur des fûts.

shafting ['ʃɑːftiŋ], *s.* **1.** *Mec.E:* **(line of) s.,** ligne *f* d'arbres; (arbres *mpl* de) transmission *f*; les arbres; **the shop s.,** la transmission de l'atelier; **main s.,** transmission principale; **counter s.,** transmission secondaire; **flexible s.,** transmission flexible. **2.** *Arch:* fûts *mpl*; escapes *fpl*.

shag[1] [ʃæg], *s.* **1.** (*a*) *A:* poil rude, touffu, emmêlé; (*b*) broussaille *f*. **2.** *Tex: A:* peluche *f*; **long-pile s.,** peluche long-poil. **3.** tabac fort (coupé fin).

shag[2], *s. Orn:* cormoran huppé, cormoran largup.

shag[3], *v.* (**shagged**) *P:* **1.** *v.tr.* coïter. **2.** *v.i.* **to s. (off),** partir, décamper.

shagbark ['ʃægbɑːk], *s. Bot:* **s. (hickory),** noyer blanc d'Amérique.

shagged [ʃægd], *a. P:* **s. (out),** éreinté, brisé, fourbu, claqué, crevé, vanné.

shagginess ['ʃæginis], *s.* rudesse *f*, longueur *f* de poil (d'un poney, etc.); état mal peigné, état ébouriffé (des cheveux); **the s. of his beard,** sa barbe hirsute.

shaggy ['ʃægi], *a.* **1.** poilu; (poney, etc.) à longs poils, à poils rudes; (cheveux) ébouriffés; (barbe) hirsute, touffue; (sourcils *mpl*) en broussailles; (terrain) couvert de broussailles; (arbre) touffu; *Tex:* (drap) peluché, pelucheux, poilu, à long poil; **s. dog story** = histoire farfelue, de fous. **2.** *Bot:* (*of leaf, stem, etc.*) poilu, velu.

shagreen[1] [ʃæ'griːn], *s.* **1.** *Leath:* (peau *f* de) chagrin *m*; cuir chagriné; galuchat *m*. **2.** peau de requin (servant de lissoir).

shagreen[2], *v.tr.* chagriner (le cuir); **shagreened leather,** peau chagrinée; cuir galuchatisé.

shah [ʃɑː], *s.* shah *m* (de Perse).

shake[1] [ʃeik], *s.* **1.** (*a*) secousse *f*; **to give sth. a good s.,** bien secouer, bien agiter, qch.; **to give oneself a s.,** se secouer; **to give a carpet a good s.,** bien secouer un tapis; **a s. of the head,** un hochement de tête; **to answer with a s. of the head,** répondre d'un mouvement de tête; **with a s. of the hand,** d'une poignée, d'un serrement, de main; **he's had a s.,** sa santé a eu une secousse; **in a s., in a brace of shakes, in two shakes of a lamb's tail,** en un rien de temps; en moins de rien; **half a s.!** un moment! une seconde! *F:* **to give s.o. a fair s.,** agir loyalement envers qn; être régulier avec qn; **I didn't get a fair s.,** on ne m'a pas traité comme il faut; *P:* **to put the s. on s.o.,** faire casquer, cracher, qn; (*b*) tremblement *m* (de la main, etc.); *U.S: N.Z:* tremblement de terre; *F:* **to be all of a s.,** trembler dans tous ses membres; **to have the shakes,** (i) avoir la tremblade, la tremblote; (ii) avoir la frousse; (iii) avoir le délirium tremens; (*c*) *Mus:* trille *m*; (*d*) **with a s. in his voice,** d'une voix tremblotante, mal assurée. **2.** *Comest:* **egg s., milk s.,** lait *m* de poule. **3.** (*in wood*) gerçure *f*, crevasse *f*; **ring s., cup s.,** roulure *f*; **star s., heart s.,** cadran(n)ure *f*, maille *f*. **4.** (*a*) *Coop:* = SHOOK[1]; (*b*) *Const:* bardeau *m* (de fente). **5.** *F:* **to be no great shakes,** être médiocre; ne pas être, ne pas valoir, grand-chose; ne pas valoir cher; **he's no great shakes,** (i) il ne vaut pas cher; il ne casse rien; (ii) *Sp:* il n'est pas de première force.

shake[2], *v.* (*p.t.* **shook** [ʃuk]; *p.p.* **shaken** ['ʃeik(ə)n])

I. *v.tr.* **1.** secouer (qn, qch.); agiter (un liquide, un dé, etc.); **s. the bottle,** agiter le flacon; **goods shaken in transit,** marchandises ballottées pendant le transport; **to s. one's head,** (i) secouer, hocher, la tête; (ii) (*in dissent*) faire non de la tête; faire signe que non; **to s. one's fist at s.o.,** menacer qn du poing; **to s. one's finger at s.o.,** réprimander qn avec un mouvement du doigt; **to s. s.o. by the hand, to s. hands with s.o.,** serrer la main à, de, qn; donner une poignée de main à qn; **they shook hands on it, over the bargain,** ils se sont touché dans la main; *F:* ils ont topé; *F:* **s.!** (i) félicitations! (ii) (*to seal bargain*) touchez là! tope (là)! **to s. oneself free (from sth.),** se dégager (de qch.) d'une secousse; **to s. oneself free of s.o.,** se dégager des mains de qn; **I had to s. him to make him wake up,** j'ai dû le secouer pour le réveiller; *Nau:* **to s. a sail,** faire ralinguer une voile. **2.** ébranler, secouer, faire chanceler (un bâtiment, etc.); ébranler (une opinion, etc.); **to s. the table,** ébranler, faire vaciller, la table; **to s. s.o.'s faith,** ébranler la foi de qn; **that has shaken my faith in him,** cela m'a fait douter de sa bonne foi; **threats cannot s. my purpose,** les menaces ne sauraient m'ébranler; **event that shook the country,** événement *m* qui a profondément troublé le pays, qui a bouleversé le pays; **he was very much shaken by his illness,** il a été bien secoué par sa maladie; **he was badly shaken by the accident,** il a été très bouleversé par l'accident; **his credit has been badly shaken,** son crédit a reçu une rude secousse; *F:* **that'll s. him!** cela le fera tiquer! **voice shaking with, shaken by, emotion,** voix émue. **3.** *Mus:* triller (un passage). **4.** *Coop:* mettre (une barrique) en botte. **5.** *Austr: P:* voler, cambrioler (qn).

II. *v.i.* **1.** trembler; (*of building, etc.*) chanceler, branler; (*of door, window*) branler; (*of voice*) trembloter, chevroter; **to make the bridge s.,** faire trembler le pont; **his hand was shaking,** la main lui tremblait; **to s. with fright, with rage,** trembler, frémir, de crainte, de colère; **to s. all over,** trembler de tout son corps, de tous ses membres; *F:* **to s. in one's shoes,** trembler dans sa peau; grelotter de peur; être dans des transes; **his voice was shaking,** sa voix tremblait. **2.** *Mus:* faire des trilles. **3.** *Nau:* (*of sail*) ralinguer; être en ralingue; faséyer, faséier; (*of mast*) fouetter; **to keep the sails shaking,** tenir les voiles en ralingue; **don't let her s.!** défiez du vent! **4.** (*of wood*) se gercer.

III. (*compound verbs*) **1. shake down.** (*a*) *v.tr.* (i) secouer, hocher (des fruits); faire tomber (des fruits) en secouant l'arbre; *NAm: P:* **to s. s.o. down for ten dollars,** faire cracher dix dollars à qn; faire casquer qn de dix dollars; (ii) tasser (du thé dans une boîte) en le secouant; (*b*) *v.i.* (i) trouver un logement, un lit, improvisé; s'installer; **to s. down for the night,** se coucher, s'installer pour la nuit; (ii) **to s. down (to a routine, in a job),** s'habituer (à une routine, à un travail); s'y habituer; **the team is shaking down,** l'équipe *f* se forme.

2. shake off, *v.tr.* (*a*) **to s. the dust off sth.,** secouer la poussière de qch.; **to s. off the dust from one's feet,** secouer la poussière de ses pieds, de ses souliers (en quittant un endroit dont on n'a pas eu lieu de se louer); **to s. s.o. off,** se dégager des mains de qn; **he shook off his attacker,** d'une secousse violente il s'est dégagé de son assaillant; **to s. off the yoke,** secouer le joug; s'affranchir du joug; **to s. off one's prejudices,** revenir de ses préjugés; se défaire de ses préjugés; **to s. off a cold,** venir à bout d'un rhume; (*b*) *F:* se débarrasser, se défaire, se décramponner, se dépêtrer, de (qn); semer (un importun, *Sp:* un concurrent); **I can't s. him off,** il ne me lâche pas d'un cran; il est poissant; c'est une chenille.

3. shake out, *v.tr.* (*a*) secouer; faire sortir (la poussière, etc.); vider (un sac) en le secouant; (*b*) déferler (une voile, un drapeau); *Nau:* **to s. out a reef,** larguer un ris.

4. shake up, *v.tr.* (*a*) secouer, brasser (un oreiller, etc.); (*b*) *F:* éveiller, secouer, stimuler (qn); secouer l'indifférence, l'inertie, de (qn).

shakedown ['ʃeikdaun], *s.* (*a*) *F:* lit improvisé, sommaire; lit de fortune (installé par terre); (*b*) *NAm: F:* chantage *m*; demande *f* d'argent; exaction *f*, extorsion *f*; *Av: etc:* **s. flight,** vol *m* d'essai; **s. cruise,** croisière *f* d'essai.

shaken ['ʃeikn], *a.* (*a*) (*of pers., foundation, etc.*) secoué, ébranlé; **to feel s. after a fall,** se ressentir d'une chute; (*b*) *Coop:* (*of cask*) mis en botte; (*c*) (*of timber*) gercé, roulé, cadrané.

shake-out ['ʃeikaut], *s. St.Exch: F:* déconfiture *f* des boursicoteurs.

shaker ['ʃeikər], *s.* (*a*) secoueur, -euse; (*b*) *Rel.H:* Trembleur, -euse; Shaker *m*; (*c*) (appareil *m*) secoueur; **salad s.,** panier *m* à salade; **cocktail s.,** shaker *m*.

Shakespearian [ʃeiks'piəriən], *a.* shakespearien; de Shakespeare.

shake-up ['ʃeikʌp], *s. F:* **1.** remaniement *m* (du personnel). **2.** commotion *f*, bouleversement *m*.

shakily ['ʃeikili], *adv.* peu solidement; faiblement; d'une manière branlante; (marcher) à pas chancelants; (écrire) d'une main tremblante; (parler) d'une voix chevrotante.

shakiness ['ʃeikinis], *s.* manque *m* de stabilité, de fermeté, de solidité (d'un bâtiment, d'une chaise, etc.); faiblesse *f* (de qn, de la santé, des connaissances); tremblement *m* (de la main); chevrotement *m* (de la voix); instabilité *f* (du crédit, d'une position, etc.).

shaking[1] ['ʃeikiŋ], *a.* tremblant, branlant; **s. voice,** voix tremblotante, chevrotante; *Med: A:* **s. palsy,** paralysie agitante, maladie *f* de Parkinson.

shaking[2], *s.* (*a*) secouage *m*, secouement *m* (de qch.); ballottage *m*, ballottement *m* (de marchandises pendant le transport, etc.); remuage *m* (d'un tamis, etc.); **s. of the head,** (i) hochement *m* de tête; (ii) (*in dissent*) signe *m* de dénégation, de refus; **to give s.o., sth., a good s.,** bien secouer (un tapis, un enfant, etc.); **car that will give us a s. (up),** voiture qui nous donnera une secouée; **we got a good s. (up),** nous avons été pas mal cahotés; *Ind:* **s. shoot,** couloir *m* à secousses; (*b*) ébranlement *m* (d'une maison, etc.); tremblement *m* (du sol, des vitres, etc.); branlement *m*, trépidation *f* (d'une machine, etc.); tremblotement *m* (de la voix); (*c*) *Coop:* mise *f* en botte (d'une barrique).

shako ['ʃækou], *s. Mil.Cost:* shako *m*.

shaky ['ʃeiki], *a.* **1.** (bâtiment, meuble, etc.) branlant, peu solide; (toit) hasardeux; (pont) tremblant; (santé) faible, chancelante; (position) mal affermie; **s. hand,** main tremblante, vacillante; **s. writing,** écriture tremblée; **s. voice,** (i) voix mal assurée, tremblotante, chevrotante; (ii) voix altérée par l'émotion; **to be s. on one's legs,** *F:* **on one's pins,** avoir les jambes branlantes; *F:* ne pas tenir sur ses quilles; être mal assuré sur ses quilles; **I feel very s.,** (i) je suis tout tremblant; (ii) je ne me sens pas bien solide; je me sens mal assuré sur mes jambes; (iii) je suis tout patraque; je ne suis pas dans mon assiette; **s. business, s. undertaking,** entreprise périclitante; **his position, his credit, is s.,** ses affaires vont mal; il branle dans le manche; **his case is very s.,** son cas est véreux; **his English is s.,** il est faible en anglais; il parle, écrit, mal l'anglais; il n'est pas sûr de lui en anglais. **2.** (arbre) crevassé; (bois) gerçuré, gercé; **to become s.,** se gercer.

shale [ʃeil], *s.* schiste (argileux, ardoisier); argile schisteuse; **alum shales,** schistes alunifères; **oil s.,** schiste bitumineux; **s. oil,** huile *f* de schiste.

shall [*stressed* ʃæl, *unstressed* ʃ(ə)l], *modal aux. v.* (*pr.* **shall, shalt** [*stressed* ʃælt, *unstressed* ʃ(ə)lt], **shall;** *p.t. & condit.* **should** [*stressed* ʃud, *unstressed* ʃ(ə)d], **shouldst** [ʃudst]: *no other parts;* **shall not** *and* **should not** *are often contracted into* **shan't** [ʃɑːnt], **shouldn't** ['ʃudnt]).

I. 1. *with full meaning, denotes duty or a command.* (*a*) (*in general precepts*) (*second and third pers.*) **thou shalt not kill,** tu ne tueras point; **ships s. carry three lights,** les navires sont tenus de porter trois feux; **these rules s. be followed by . . .,** le présent règlement devra être suivi par . . .; **everything is as it should be,** tout va très bien; **which is as it should be,** ce qui n'est que justice; (*b*) (*in particular cases*) (*second and third pers.*) **he s. do it if I order it,** il devra le faire si je l'ordonne; **he s. not die!** il ne faut pas qu'il meure! **he shall not do it,** je défends qu'il le fasse; **he says he won't do it—he s.!** il dit qu'il ne le fera pas—je l'ordonne! **he says he will do it—he s. not!** *F:* **he shan't!** il dit qu'il le fera—je le défends! **they say they won't pay, but they shall,** ils disent qu'ils ne payeront pas, mais on les y forcera; **you** *shall* **do it!** vous le ferez, je le veux! je veux que vous le fassiez! (*c*) (*advice, remonstrance, etc.*) (*all three persons*) **you, we, should go,** il convient que vous y alliez, que nous y allions; **you should do it at once,** vous devriez le faire tout de suite; **d'you think I should?** vraiment? **you should have come earlier,** vous auriez dû arriver plus tôt; **you, he, she, they, should not have gone,** il ne fallait pas y aller; **it was an accident that should have been foreseen,** c'était un accident à prévoir; **you should see it,** il faut voir cela; **you should have seen him!** il fallait le voir! si vous l'aviez vu! **you should feel the heat in there!** il fait un chaud là-dedans! **this inquiry should be reopened,** c'est une question à reprendre; **you should not speak so loudly,** vous ne devriez pas parler si haut; **you shouldn't laugh at him,** vous avez tort de vous moquer de lui; (*d*) (*pure expression of opinion*) **he, we, should have arrived by this time,** il devrait être arrivé, nous devrions être arrivés, à l'heure qu'il est; **that should suit you!** voilà qui fera sans doute votre affaire! **this weather should be ideal for anglers,** ce temps doit être ce que les pêcheurs peuvent désirer de mieux; **I should think so!** je crois bien! *Iron:* **I should worry!** (i) ce n'est pas mon affaire! (ii) ne te tracasse pas pour ça! **2.** (*in deference to another*) **s. I open the window?** voulez-vous que j'ouvre la fenêtre? **I'll call the children, s. I?** je vais appeler les enfants, hein? **let's go in, s. we?** rentrons, voulez-vous? **throw it away!—s. I (really)?** jette ça!—faut-il vraiment? **he asked me if he should open the window,** il m'a demandé si je voulais qu'il ouvre la fenêtre, s'il fallait ouvrir la fenêtre; **s. he come?** voulez-vous qu'il vienne? **s. we play a game of whist?** (i) (*as we usually do*) faisons-nous une partie de whist? (ii) (*sudden inspiration*) si nous faisions une partie de whist! **what s. I, we, do?** que faire? **what should I have said?** qu'est-ce que j'aurais dû dire? **3.** (*with weakened force, exclamatory, in rhetorical questions*) (*a*) **why should you suspect me?** pourquoi me soupçonner (, moi)? **how should I not be happy?** comment ne serais-je pas heureux? **whom should I meet but Martin!** voilà que je rencontre Martin! ne voilà-t-il pas que je rencontre Martin! **when I arrived at my office, who should be sitting there but Louise!** lorsque je suis arrivé à mon bureau, devinez qui j'y ai trouvé installée: Louise! **who s. describe their surprise?** comment décrire leur surprise! (*b*) (*in subordinate clauses*) **whatever sum s. be received from him s. be shared between us,** quelle que soit la somme à recevoir de lui, nous la partagerons; toute somme à recevoir de lui sera partagée entre nous; **he ordered that they should be released,** il ordonna qu'on les relâchât; **she insisted that he should wear his hair short,** elle exigeait qu'il porte les cheveux courts; **it's odd that we should meet again in the same place,** il est curieux que nous nous rencontrions de nouveau dans le même endroit; **he deserves that we should do sth. for him,** il mérite que nous fassions qch. pour lui; **I was watching for the moment when his work should be finished,** je guettais le moment où il aurait achevé son travail; **they recommend that classes should be smaller,** ils proposent de réduire le nombre des élèves dans les classes; **the important thing is to ensure that those who teach should be qualified,** l'important, c'est d'obtenir que tous ceux qui enseignent aient les titres nécessaires; (*c*) (*in 'if' clauses*) **if he should come, should he come, (you will) let me know,** si par hasard il vient, s'il vient, faites-le-moi savoir, vous me le ferez savoir; **if he should come they would let you know,** s'il venait on vous le ferait savoir; **should I be free I shall come,** si je suis libre je viendrai; **should it prove correct that . . .,** au cas où il serait exact que . . .; **should the occasion arise, should it (so) happen,** le cas échéant; **in case he should not be there,** au cas, en cas, où il n'y soit pas, dans le cas où il n'y serait pas.

II. (*used as an auxiliary verb forming the future tenses*) **1.** (*still expressing something of the speaker's will, assurance, promise, menace, etc. So used in the 2nd and 3rd persons. For the 1st pers. see* WILL[3]) **and the Lord shall guide thee continually,** et l'Éternel te conduira continuellement; *B:* **he that soweth iniquity shall reap vanity,** celui qui sème la perversité moissonnera le tourment; **you shan't have any!** tu n'en auras pas! **you shall pay for this!** vous me le payerez! **he said you should pay for this,** il a dit que vous le lui payeriez; **they shall see what I'm made of,** on verra de quel bois je me chauffe; **"you shall hear from me before long," he shouted,** "je vous promets que vous aurez de mes nouvelles sous peu!" cria-t-il; **go to bed at once; Louise shall bring you up some hot whisky,** couchez-vous tout de suite; je vais dire à Louise de vous apporter un grog. **2.** (*simple future*) (*a*) (*used in the 1st pers. For the 2nd and 3rd pers. see* WILL[3]) (i) **tomorrow I s. go and he will arrive,** demain, moi je partirai et lui arrivera; **we shall hope to see you again,** nous espérons avoir l'occasion de vous revoir; **my holiday was over; the next day I should be far away,** mon congé était fini; le lendemain je serais bien loin; **will you be there?—I shall,** y serez-vous?—oui (, j'y serai); **no, I s. not; no, I shan't,** non (, je n'y serai pas); **he had promised that I should be there,** il avait promis que je serais là; (ii) (*immediate future*) **I shall explain the situation to you and you will listen,** je vais vous expliquer la situation et vous allez m'écouter; (*b*) (*used in the second pers. in interrogation*) **s. you come tomorrow?** vous viendrez demain? (*Cp.* **will you come tomorrow?** voulez-vous venir demain?). **3.** (*in the main clause of conditional sentences*) **if he comes I shall speak to him,** s'il vient je lui parlerai; **we should come if we were invited,** nous viendrions si on nous invitait; **we would have consented if you had asked,** nous aurions consenti si vous nous l'aviez demandé; **had you written to me I should have answered you,** si vous m'aviez écrit je vous aurais répondu; **I shouldn't (do it) if I were you,** (i) à votre place je n'en ferais rien; (ii) je ne vous le conseille pas. **4.** (*in softened affirmation*) **I should like a drink,** je prendrais bien quelque chose; **I should think you are right,** j'ai idée que vous avez raison; **I should have thought that you would have known better,** j'aurais pensé que vous auriez été plus avisé; **I shouldn't be surprised (if . . .),** cela ne me surprendrait pas (que + *pr. sub.*); **we shall probably be right in saying that . . .,** il est probable que nous ne nous tromperons pas de beaucoup si nous affirmons que . . ..

shalloon [ʃəˈluːn], *s. Tex: A:* chalon *m*; **milled s.,** cadis ras, foulé.

shallop [ˈʃæləp], *s. Nau: A:* chaloupe *f*, péniche *f*, pinasse *f*.

shallot [ʃəˈlɔt], *s.* échalote *f*.

shallow[1] [ˈʃælou]. **1.** *a.* (*a*) (*of water, stream, etc.*) peu profond; (*of dish, etc.*) plat; *Nau:* **s. water,** hauts fonds; eau *f* maigre; maigre eau; **to be in s. water,** se trouver dans les petits fonds; **s. draught,** faible tirant *m* (d'un navire); (*b*) (*of soil*) peu profond; superficiel; **s.-rooted,** (arbre) à enracinement superficiel; **s. steps,** des marches basses; (*c*) (*of pers., etc.*) superficiel, frivole, qui manque de fond; **s. friendship,** amitié *f* de surface; **s. mind,** esprit superficiel; **s. knowledge,** connaissances superficielles. **2.** *s.* (*in sea, river, etc.*) (*often in pl.*) bas-fond *m, pl.* bas-fonds; haut-fond *m, pl.* hauts-fonds; plateau *m*; maigres *mpl*.

shallow[2]. **1.** *v.tr.* rendre (un lac, etc.) moins profond. **2.** *v.i.* (*of river, etc.*) devenir moins profond.

shallowness [ˈʃælounis], *s.* (*a*) (le) peu de profondeur (de l'eau, d'un plat, etc.); (*b*) caractère superficiel; superficialité *f*, frivolité *f*, manque *m* de fond (de qn, de l'esprit); futilité *f* (de la conversation, etc.).

Shalmaneser [ʃælməˈniːzər]. *Pr.n.m. A.Hist:* Salmanasar.

shaly [ˈʃeili], *a.* schisteux.

sham[1] [ʃæm]. **1.** *a.* faux; truqué; (*of illness, etc.*) simulé, feint; (*of jewel, etc.*) factice; *F:* en toc; **s. piety,** piété apparente; **s. title,** titre vain; titre d'emprunt; **s. peace,** paix fourrée; **a s. colonel,** un faux colonel; **s. republic,** simulacre *m* de république; *Mil:* **s. fight, s battle,** combat simulé, fictif, simulacre de combat; petite guerre; *Fin:* **s. dividend,** dividende fictif; *Jur:* **s. plea,** moyens *mpl* dilatoires. **2** *s.* (*a*) feinte *f*, trompe-l'œil *m inv*, *P:* chiqué *m*; **that's all s.,** tout ça c'est de la frime; **his life was one long s.,** sa vie n'a été qu'une longue comédie; **bill which is only a s.,** projet *m* de loi qui n'est qu'un trompe-l'œil; **he is all s.,** tout en lui est artificiel; (*b*) *A:* **sheet s.,** faux retour de drap (de lit); (*c*) **he's a s.,** c'est un imposteur.

sham[2], *v.tr.* (**shammed**) feindre, simuler; **to s. sickness,** feindre, simuler, contrefaire, une maladie; faire semblant d'être malade; faire le malade; *Mil: P:* maquiller; **to s. sleep,** faire semblant de dormir; feindre de dormir; **to s. modesty,** (i) faire le, la, modeste; (ii) (*of woman*) faire la vertueuse; *P:* la faire à la vertu; **to s. enthusiasm,** faire de l'enthousiasme à froid; **he's only shamming,** c'est une comédie qu'il nous joue; tout ça c'est de la frime; il fait semblant; **he shammed dead,** il fit le mort.

shama [ˈʃɑːmə], *s. Orn:* shama *m*.

shaman [ˈʃɑːmən], *s. Rel:* chaman *m*.

shamanism [ˈʃɑːmənizm], *s. Rel:* chamanisme *m*.

shamanist [ˈʃɑːmənist], *s. Rel:* chamaniste *mf*.

shamateur [ˈʃæmətəːr], *s. Sp: F:* amateur marron.

shamateurism [ˈʃæmətə(ː)rizm], *s. Sp: F:* amateurisme marron.

shamble[1] [ˈʃæmbl], *s.* démarche traînante, dégingandée.

shamble[2], *v.i.* **to s. (along),** aller à pas traînants; s'avancer en traînant le pas; **to s. in, out,** entrer, sortir, à pas traînants, en traînant les pieds; **to s. up to s.o.,** approcher qn d'un pas traînant.

shambles [ˈʃæmblz], *s.pl.* (*usu. with sg. const.*) (*a*) abattoir *m*, égorgeoir *m*; (*b*) scène *f* de carnage, de boucherie; (*c*) *F:* désordre *m*, gâchis *m*; **the room was an absolute s.,** la pièce était dans un désordre épouvantable; **what a s.!** quelle pagaille!

shambling [ˈʃæmbliŋ], *a.* (*of gait, etc.*) traînant; dégingandé; (*of pers.*) à pas traînants; dégingandé.

shambolic [ʃæmˈbɔlik], *a. F:* chaotique; en pagaille.

shame[1] [ʃeim], *s.* (*a*) honte *f*; **overwhelmed with s.,** écrasé de honte; **to put s.o. to s.,** (i) confondre qn; (ii) faire honte à qn, faire rougir qn; (iii) l'emporter sur qn; **to cover s.o. with s.,** couvrir qn de honte; **to my s. I must confess that . . .,** à ma honte je dois avouer que . . .; **to cry s.,** crier au scandale; **to cry s. on s.o.,** crier tollé, haro, sur qn; se récrier contre qn; **s. (up)on you!** honte à vous! **all the more s. to you!** c'est d'autant plus honteux à vous! **for s.!** quelle honte! vous n'avez pas honte! **to blush for, with, s.,** (i) rougir de honte; (ii) rougir de pudeur; **without s.,** immodeste, éhonté; **to be past s., lost to all (sense of) s.,** avoir perdu toute honte, toute pudeur, tout sentiment de honte; *Lit:* avoir toute honte bue; *O:* **I would think s. to . . .,** j'aurais honte de . . .; **you ought to think s. of yourself!** vous devriez avoir honte! (*b*) **it would be a s. to act in this way,** il serait honteux, abominable, d'agir ainsi; **it's a s. to laugh at him,** ce n'est pas bien de se moquer de lui; **it's a (great) s.!** c'est honteux! **it's a sin and a s.!** c'est une indignité! (*c*) **what a s.!** quel dommage! quelle pitié!

shame[2], *v.tr.* faire honte à, mortifier, humilier (qn); couvrir (qn) de honte; **to s. s.o. into doing sth.,** agir sur l'amour-propre de qn pour lui faire faire qch.; **to be shamed into doing sth.,** faire qch. par amour-propre.

shamefaced [ˈʃeimfeist], *a.* **1.** (à l'air) honteux; embarrassé, penaud, confus, décontenancé; **in a s. manner,** d'un air honteux. **2.** *Lit:* timide; pudique; modeste.

shamefacedly [ʃeimˈfeisidli], *adv.* **1.** d'une manière embarrassée, honteuse; d'un air penaud. **2.** *Lit:* timidement; pudiquement, modestement.

shamefacedness [ʃeimˈfeisidnis], *s.* **1.** fausse honte; mauvaise honte; embarras *m*. **2.** *Lit:* timidité *f* pudique; modestie *f*.

shameful [ˈʃeimful], *a.* **1.** honteux, abominable, scandaleux, infâme, indigne. **2.** *A:* = SHAMEFACED.

shamefully [ˈʃeimf(u)li], *adv.* **1.** honteusement, abominablement, scandaleusement; d'une manière indigne. **2.** *A:* = SHAMEFACEDLY.

shamefulness [ˈʃeimf(u)lnis], *s.* **1.** honte *f*, infamie *f*, indignité *f*. **2.** *A:* = SHAMEFACEDNESS.

shameless [ˈʃeimlis], *a.* **1.** (*a*) (*of pers., conduct*) éhonté, effronté, impudent, cynique; sans honte; (*b*) (*of pers.*) sans pudeur; sans vergogne; dévergondé; (*of woman*) impudique; (*c*) (conduite, posture) impudique. **2.** (*of action*) honteux, scandaleux, abominable, indigne.

shamelessly [ˈʃeimlisli], *adv.* effrontément; d'une manière éhontée; sans pudeur, sans vergogne; **to lie s.,** mentir impudemment, cyniquement.

shamelessness [ˈʃeimlisnis], *s.* **1.** (*a*) impudeur *f*; (*b*) impudicité *f*. **2.** effronterie *f*, impudence *f*; absence *f* de tout sentiment de honte.

shaming[1] [ˈʃeimiŋ], *a.* mortifiant, humiliant.

shaming[2], *s.* mortification *f*, humiliation *f* (de qn).

shammer [ˈʃæmər], *s.* simulateur, -trice; imposteur *m*.

shammy (leather) [ˈʃæmi(ˈleðər)], *s.* peau *f* de chamois.

shampoo[1] [ʃæmˈpuː], *s.* **1.** (*action*) shampooing *m*; **to give s.o. a s.,** donner, faire, un shampooing à qn; **dry s.,** friction *f*; **to give s.o. a dry s.,** frictionner la tête à qn; **s. and set,** shampooing et mise en plis. **2.** (*product*) shampooing; **liquid s.,** shampooing liquide; **dry s.,** shampooing sec; **s. powder, s. in powder form,** shampooing en poudre; **carpet s.,** shampooing pour tapis.

shampoo[2], *v.tr.* **to s. one's hair,** se laver la tête se donner un shampooing; **to s. s.o., s.o.'s hair,** donner, faire, un shampooing à qn.

shampooer [ʃæmˈpuːər], *s.* **1.** *Hairdr:* (*pers.*) shampouineur, shampouineuse *f*. **2.** (*machine*) **(carpet) s.,** shampouineur *m*.

shampooing [ʃæmˈpuːiŋ], *s.* shampooing *m*; (*for carpets*) **s. machine,** shampouineur *m*.

shamrock [ˈʃæmrɔk], *s. Bot:* trèfle *m* d'Irlande; petit trèfle jaune; (*of Irishman*) **to wear the s. on St Patrick's day,** porter le trèfle à la St-Patrice.

shandrydan [ˈʃændridæn], *s.* **1.** carriole irlandaise. **2.** *F:*

(*a*) *A:* berlingot *m*; (*b*) patache *f*, bagnole *f*, guimbarde *f*.

shandy ['ʃændi], **shandygaff** ['ʃændigæf], *s.* (i) mélange *m* de bière et de *ginger beer*; (ii) panaché *m*.

Shanghai[1] [ʃaŋ'hai]. **1.** *Pr.n. Geog:* Shangaï *m*, Changhaï *m*. **2.** *s. Austr:* fronde *f*; lance-pierre *m, pl.* lance-pierres.

shanghai[2], *v.tr. Nau: F:* **1.** (*a*) **to s. a man,** enivrer ou 'endormir' un homme pour l'embarquer sur un navire à court d'équipage; shanghaier; (*b*) forcer (**s.o. into doing sth.,** qn à faire qch.). **2.** *Austr:* tirer sur (une bête, un homme) avec un lance-pierre.

Shanghainese [ʃæŋhai'ni:z], *a. & s.* (habitant, originaire) de Changhaï.

shank[1] [ʃæŋk], *s.* **1.** (*a*) **shanks,** jambes *f*, *F:* quilles *f*; *F:* **to go, come, ride, on Shanks' mare, pony,** prendre le train onze; prendre la voiture des cordeliers, des capucins; (*b*) (i) **s. (bone),** tibia *m*; (ii) *Farr:* canon *m* (du membre antérieur); (iii) métatarse *m* (d'oiseau); (*c*) *Cu:* jarret *m* (de bœuf); manche *m* (de gigot de mouton); (*d*) jambe (d'un bas). **2.** (*a*) branche *f*, bras *m* (de ciseaux); (*b*) tige *f* (de plante, de clef, de rivet, etc.); *Bot:* pédoncule *m*; fût *m* (d'une colonne); manche *m* (d'un aviron); branche (de clef, de rivet, etc.); hampe *f* (d'hameçon); tuyau *m* (de pipe à tabac); soie *f* (de ciseau, d'alêne, de couteau de table, etc.); *Typ:* corps *m*, tige (de lettre); **anchor s.,** (i) *Nau:* verge *f* (d'ancre); (ii) *Her:* stangue *f* (d'ancre); *Nau:* **s. painter,** serre-bosse *m, pl.* serre-bosses; (*c*) queue *f* (d'un bouton); (*d*) *Bootm:* cambrillon *m*.

shank[2], *v.tr.* **1.** munir (un ciseau, etc.) d'une soie, (un bouton) d'une queue. **2.** *Golf:* talonner (la balle). **3.** *P: A:* **to s. it,** faire le trajet à pied; prendre le train onze. **4.** *v.i. Hort:* (*of plant*) **to s. (off),** pourrir par la tige.

shanked [ʃæŋkt], *a.* **1.** à tige, à branche; (*of knife, tool*) à soie; (*of button*) à queue. **2.** (*with adj. prefixed, e.g.*) **short-s.,** (homme) aux jambes courtes; (clef) à courte tige.

shankless ['ʃæŋklis], *a.* sans tige.

shanny ['ʃæni], *s. Ich:* blennie *f*.

Shansi [ʃæ'si:]. *Pr.n. Geog:* Chan-Si *m*.

shan't [ʃa:nt] SEE SHALL.

Shantung [ʃæ'tʌŋ]. **1.** *Pr.n. Geog:* Chantoung *m*. **2.** *Tex:* shant(o)ung *m*.

shanty[1] [ʃænti], *s.* hutte *f*, cabane *f*, baraquement *m*, baraque *f*, bicoque *f*, masure *f*; **s. town,** bidonville *m*.

shanty[2], *s.* chanson *f* de bord.

shape[1] [ʃeip], *s.* **1.** (*a*) forme *f*, configuration *f* (de la terre, etc.); façon *f*, coupe *f* (d'un habit, etc.); **what s. is his hat?** de quelle forme est son chapeau? **liquids take the s. of their containers,** les liquides se conforment aux récipients, épousent la forme des récipients, qui les contiennent; **in s. he resembled a barrel,** par la forme il ressemblait à une barrique; **trees of all shapes,** des arbres de toutes les formes; **my hat was knocked out of s.,** mon chapeau a été déformé; **to get out of s., to lose (its) s.,** se déformer; (*of shoes, etc.*) s'avachir; **timber cut exactly to s.,** pièce *f* allant à la demande; **hat out of s.,** chapeau déformé; *Journ:* etc: **to put,** *F:* **get, knock, an article into s.,** mettre un article au point; **to keep in s.,** garder sa forme; **the plan is in quite good s.,** le projet est en bonne voie; (*of boxer, etc.*) **to be in good, first-class, poor, s.,** être en bonne forme, en petite forme; (*b*) taille *f*, tournure *f*; **of elegant s.,** de taille élégante; aux contours gracieux; (*c*) forme indistincte; apparition *f*; **two shapes loomed up in the darkness,** deux formes se dessinèrent, surgirent, dans l'obscurité. **2. to give s. to a plan,** faire prendre corps à un projet; **to take s.,** prendre forme; prendre tournure; **our plans are taking s.,** nos projets se dessinent; **the rumours assumed a more definite s.,** les bruits prirent plus de consistance. **3.** forme, sorte *f*, espèce *f*; **no communication in any s. or form,** aucune communication de n'importe quelle sorte; **something in the s. of. . .,** une espèce, une sorte, de . . .; **invitation in the s. of a command,** invitation *f* en forme d'ordre. **4.** (*a*) *Cu:* (i) (*for jellies, etc.*) moule *m*; (ii) **rice s.,** gâteau *m* de riz; **chocolate s.,** crème au chocolat; (*b*) (i) forme (pour chapeau); (ii) carcasse *f* (de chapeau). **5.** (*of iron, etc.*) profil *m*, profilé *m*.

shape[2]. **1.** *v.tr.* (*a*) façonner, modeler (de l'argile, etc.); tailler (un bloc de pierre, etc.); toupiller (le bois); profiler (une moulure, etc.); gabarier (une plaque de blindage); emboutir (une chaudière, etc.); *Cer:* contourner (un vase, etc.); (*on potter's wheel*) tournasser; (*with a jig*) calibrer; **to s. sth. out of sth.,** façonner qch. avec qch.; tailler qch. dans qch.; **to s. sth. like sth.,** donner à qch. la forme de qch.; **to s. the clay into an urn,** donner à l'argile la forme d'une urne; **to s. a coat to the figure,** ajuster un manteau à la taille; **to s. s.o.'s character,** pétrir le caractère de qn; **to s. the destiny of man,** diriger, régler, modeler, la destinée de l'homme; **to s. one's life according to an end in view, to certain principles,** régler sa vie d'après un but à atteindre; conformer sa vie à certains principes; (*b*) former, inventer (un plan); **I had no time to s. my answer,** je n'ai pas eu le temps de méditer ma réponse; (*c*) *Lit:* **to s. one's course,** diriger ses pas, se diriger (**towards,** vers); faire route (**for,** sur); *Nau:* **to s. a course,** faire, donner, une route; tracer une route (sur la carte); **to s. the course of public opinion,** imprimer une direction à l'opinion. **2.** *v.i.* (*a*) se développer; **to s. (up) well,** promettre; **the affair is shaping (up) well,** l'affaire prend bonne tournure, prend couleur; **let's see how he shapes (up) in his new job,** voyons comment il va se tirer de son nouvel emploi; **things are shaping badly,** l'affaire prend une mauvaise tournure, un fâcheux aspect; l'affaire tourne mal; **as things are shaping,** d'après la tournure que prennent les événements; **he's shaping (up) well at, in, Latin,** il mord au latin; **the crops are shaping (up) well,** la récolte s'annonce bien; la montre des blés est belle; (*b*) **to s. up to s.o.,** avancer sur qn en posture de combat.

shaped [ʃeipt], *a.* **1.** façonné, taillé; *Metalw:* **s. piece,** pièce profilée, emboutie. **2. well s., badly s.,** bien, mal, formé; bien, mal, venu; **strangely s.,** d'une forme bizarre; **egg-s.,** en forme d'œuf; **heart-s., wedge-s.,** en forme de cœur, de coin; **her face was delicately s.,** elle avait le tour du visage délicat; elle avait le visage finement ciselé; **badly s. saddle,** selle (de cheval) mal façonnée, qui n'a pas de tenue.

shapeless ['ʃeiplis], *a.* informe; difforme; qui manque de galbe; **s. legs,** jambes toutes d'une venue.

shapelessness ['ʃeiplisnis], *s.* **1.** manque *m* de forme; manque de galbe, d'élégance. **2.** difformité *f*.

shapeliness ['ʃeiplinis], *s.* beauté *f* de forme; belles proportions; galbe *m*.

shapely ['ʃeipli], *a.* (*of pers., foot, etc.*) bien fait; **a s. leg,** une belle jambe; *F:* une jambe faite au tour; (*of pers.*) **to be s.,** être bien fait de sa personne; *F:* avoir du galbe; être bien tourné.

shaper ['ʃeipər], *s.* **1.** (*pers.*) façonneur, -euse; *Metalw:* emboutisseur *m*; estampeur, -euse; *Woodw:* toupilleur *m*; moulurier *m* à la machine; *Mec.E:* limeur *m*; *Cer:* calibreur *m*; **the s. of our destinies,** celui qui dirige notre destin; **the s. of the plan,** l'auteur *m* du projet. **2.** (*a*) étau-limeur *m*, *pl.* étaux-limeurs; limeuse *f*; (*b*) machine *f* à façonner, à fraiser; fraise *f*; toupie *f*; (*c*) *Metalw:* emboutissoir *m*. **3.** *Dom.Ec:* **butter s.,** frise-beurre *m inv*.

shaping ['ʃeipiŋ], *s.* **1.** façonnement *m*, façonnage *m* (d'un bloc de pierre); gabariage *m* (d'une plaque de blindage); emboutissage *m* (d'une chaudière); contournement *m* (d'un vase, etc.); **s. machine, s. vice,** = SHAPER 2; **s. of character,** développement *m*, formation *f*, du caractère. **2.** invention *f*, formation, conception *f* (d'un projet); mise *f* au point.

shard[1] [ʃa:d], *s.* tesson *m* (de poterie); **to break into shards,** se briser (en fragments).

shard[2], *s. Ent:* élytre *m* (de coléoptère).

share[1] [ʃεər], *s. Agr:* soc *m* (de charrue); **s. beam,** âge *m*, flèche *f* (de charrue).

share[2], *s.* **1.** (*a*) part *f*, portion *f*; **in equal shares,** par portions égales; **to fall to s.o.'s s., to the s. of s.o.,** tomber, échoir, en partage à qn; **to have a s. in. . .,** avoir part à . . .; **the lion's s.,** la part du lion; **s. in profits,** participation *f* aux bénéfices; tantième *m* (des bénéfices); **to give s.o. a s. in the profits,** mettre qn de part; **to claim a s. in sth.,** prétendre part à qch.; *Jur:* **to claim one's proportionate s.,** réclamer son contingent; **to go shares,** partager (**with,** avec); faire part à plusieurs; **they had always gone shares,** ils avaient toujours partagé leurs possessions; **to go half shares with s.o.,** mettre qn de part à demi; **shares!** partageons! **to come in for a s. of sth.,** avoir sa part de qch.; (*b*) **(fair) s.,** portion juste; lot *m*; *Jur:* **legal s.,** réserve légale (d'une succession); **to have one's fair s.,** être bien loti; **to come in for one's full s. of sth.,** avoir sa bonne part de qch.; **I've had my s. of worries,** j'ai eu ma bonne part, mon lot, de soucis; **to want more than one's s.,** vouloir plus que sa part, *F:* tirer à soi la couverture; **to have more than one's s. of wit,** avoir de l'esprit plus que sa dose; **he has more than his s. of illness,** il est malade plus souvent qu'à son tour; **to each his due s.,** à chacun ce qui lui revient; (*c*) *Agr:* **s. cropping,** métayage *m*; **s. cropper,** métayer, -ère. **2.** contribution *f*, écot *m*, cotisation *f*, quote-part *f*, *pl.* quotes-parts; **I gave ten francs as my s.,** j'ai donné dix francs pour ma contribution; **to pay one's s.,** payer sa (quote-)part; **everyone will pay his own s.,** chacun paiera son écot; **to go shares with s.o. in the expense of a taxi,** se cotiser pour prendre un taxi; partager avec qn les frais d'un taxi; **to take a s. in the conversation,** contribuer (pour sa part) à la conversation; **to take a personal s. in the work,** payer de sa personne; **to take, bear, one's s. of the burden,** prendre, avoir, sa part du fardeau; **he doesn't do his s.,** il n'y met pas du sien; **you had a s. in this,** (i) vous y êtes pour quelque chose; (ii) vous y avez mis du vôtre; **to have a s. in an undertaking,** avoir un intérêt, être intéressé, dans une entreprise; **initial s.,** apport *m*; **s. of capital introduced by a partner,** apport, mise *f*, d'un associé. **3.** *Fin:* (*in a company, etc.*) action *f*, titre *m*, valeur *f*; **registered s., personal s.,** action nominative; **fully paid(-up) s.,** action (entièrement) libérée; **partly paid(-up) s.,** action non libérée; titre mixte; **s. on which one third has been paid,** action libérée du tiers; **ordinary s.,** action ordinaire; **deferred s.,** action différée; **transferable s.,** action au porteur; **qualification s.,** action statutaire; action de garantie; **partnership s.,** part d'association; **founder's s.,** part bénéficiaire; part de fondateur; **dividend s.,** action de jouissance; action de bénéficiaire; **to hold shares,** posséder, détenir, des actions; être actionnaire; **s. certificate,** titre *m* d'action(s), de titre(s); certificat provisoire; *St.Exch:* **s. pushing,** marronnage *m*; **s. pusher,** courtier marron; placeur *m*, placier *m*, de valeurs douteuses.

share[3]. **1.** *v.tr.* (*a*) partager; **he would s. his last penny,** il partagerait son dernier sou; **to s. sth. with s.o.,** partager qch. avec qn; (*b*) avoir part à (qch.); **to s. an office with s.o.,** partager un bureau avec qn; **to s. s.o.'s opinion,** partager l'avis de qn; **I s. all his secrets,** il me met dans tous ses secrets; **to s. and s. alike,** partager entre tous également. **2.** *v.tr. & ind.tr.* **to s. (in) sth.,** prendre part à, avoir part à, participer à, s'associer à, qch.; **to s. in the profits,** participer, avoir part, aux bénéfices; **to s. (in) s.o.'s grief,** partager la douleur de qn; **he shares (in) my troubles as well as my pleasures,** il participe à mes peines comme à mes plaisirs; **I want you to s. in my happiness,** je veux vous associer à mon bonheur; **to s. (out) the loot,** partager, distribuer, répartir, le butin; **to s. out the work,** répartir, distribuer, le travail.

shareholder ['ʃεəhouldər], *s. Fin:* actionnaire *mf*, sociétaire *mf* (d'une société anonyme); **registered s.,** porteur *m* d'actions nominatives.

shareholding[1] ['ʃεəhouldiŋ], *a. Fin:* **the s. public,** le public détenteur de titres, d'actions; les actionnaires *m*.

shareholding[2], *s.* **1.** possession *f* d'actions, de titres; **employee s.,** actionnariat ouvrier. **2. shareholdings,** actions *f*.

share-out ['ʃεəraut], *s.* partage *m*; distribution *f*; répartition *f*.

sharer ['ʃεərər], *s.* partageant, -eante; participant, -ante; **sharers in a distribution,** participants à une répartition; *Jur:* **s. in an estate,** portionnaire *mf*.

sharing ['ʃεəriŋ], *s.* **1.** partage *m* (du butin, de ses biens, etc.). **2.** participation *f*, partage; **profit s.,** participation aux bénéfices; **time s.,** partage de temps; temps partagé; utilisation collective (d'un ordinateur).

shark [ʃa:k], *s.* **1.** (*a*) *Ich:* requin *m*; **blue s.,** requin bleu; **sand s.,** odontaspis *m*, requin de sable; **common sand s.,** peau-bleu *m*, *pl.* peaux-bleus; **bramble s.,** requin bouclé; **white s.,** requin blanc, requin carcharadonte; **mackerel s.,** requin marsouin; chien-dauphin, *pl.* chiens-dauphins; lamie *f* long-nez; **hammer-head(ed) s.,** marteau *m*, maillet *m*, demoiselle *f*; **spine s.,** humantin *m*; chien *m* de mer; **cat s.,** scyliorhinidé *m*; **basking s.,** pèlerin *m*; **s. oil,** huile *f* de foie de requin; (*b*) *Ent:* **s. moth,** cucullie *f*. **2.** *F:* escroc *m*; requin; usurier *m*; accapareur, -euse; (*esp. of lawyer*) brigandeau *m*; **financial sharks,** les requins de la finance. **3.** *N Am: F:* **As** *m*; type calé; **to be a s. at maths,** être très fort, calé, en math.

sharkskin ['ʃa:kskin], *s.* peau *f* de requin, de chagrin; galuchat *m*.

Sharon ['ʃεərən]. *Pr.n. Geog:* **the Plain of S.,** la plaine de S(h)aron; **rose of S.,** rose de Saron.

sharp[1] [ʃa:p], *a., s. & adv.*

I. *a.* **1.** (*a*) (*of knife, edge*) tranchant, aiguisé, affilé; (*of spear, tooth, point*) aigu, pointu; **s. edge of a sword,** tranchant *m* d'un sabre; (*b*) (*of features, etc.*) anguleux, tiré, accentué; (*of chin, peak, etc.*) pointu; (*of angle*) saillant, aigu; (*of curve*) prononcé, à petit rayon; (*of ascent*) raide, escarpé; (*of descent*) rapide, raide; **s. roof,** toit pointu, en pointe; **s. turn,** tournant *m* brusque; **s. rise, drop, in prices,** forte hausse, baisse, des prix; *N.Arch:* **s. bottom,** carène fine; (*c*) (*of outline, Phot: of image*) net, *f.* nette; *W.Tel:* **s. tuning,** accord serré; (*d*) **s. contrast,** contraste marqué. **2.** (*a*) (*of sight*) perçant; (*of hearing*) fin, subtil; (*of glance, wit*) pénétrant; (*of pers.*) **s. (witted),** fin, éveillé, intelligent, dégourdi; **a s. mind,** un esprit délié; **a s. child,** un enfant vif, intelligent; **he's as s. as a needle,** il est fin comme l'ambre, malin comme un singe; plus fin que lui n'est pas bête; **he was s. enough to answer diplomatically,** il a eu l'adresse de faire une réponse diplomatique; (*b*) (*of pers., etc.*) rusé, malin, retors; peu scrupuleux; **s. practice(s),** procédés indélicats, peu honnêtes; **to be too s. for s.o.,** être trop malin pour qn; **he was too s. for you,** il vous a roulé. **3.** (*a*) (combat) vif, acharné; **it was a s. engagement,** l'affaire a été chaude; (*b*) (orage) violent; **s. shower,** forte averse; **s. frost,** forte gelée; **s. attack of fever,** fort accès de fièvre; **s. appetite,** vif appétit; (*c*) (hiver) rigoureux; (air, vent) vif, perçant; (froid) pénétrant, piquant; **s. pain,** douleur cuisante; vive douleur; **it's a bit s. this morning,** il fait frisquet ce matin; (*d*) rapide; (trot) vif; **to take a s. walk,** faire une promenade à vive allure, d'un pas rapide; **that was s. work!** cela n'a pas pris longtemps! (*e*) **in a s. voice,** d'une voix coupante, cinglante; **to make a s. retort,** (i) répondre d'une voix cassante; (ii) faire une réplique cinglante; **in a s. tone,** d'un ton âpre, acerbe, cassant; **s. reproof,** verte réprimande; **s. tongue,** langue acérée, caustique; **don't be so s. with me!** ne me parlez pas de ce ton cassant! ne me reprenez pas comme ça! **4.** (*of taste, sauce*) piquant; (*of apple, etc.*) aigre, acide; (*of wine*) vert. **5.** (*a*) (*of sound*) pénétrant, perçant, aigu, aigre; **a s. whistle,** un coup de sifflet perçant; (*b*) *Mus:* (fa, etc.) dièse; (*of singer, violinist, etc.*) **you're s.!** vous chantez, jouez, faux (en haussant le ton); (*c*) *Ling:* **s. consonant,** consonne forte.

II. *s.* **1.** *Mus:* dièse *m*; **double s.,** double dièse. **2.** *Ling:* consonne forte. **3. sharps,** (i) *Mill:* issues *fpl* de blé; recoupe *f*; (ii) aiguilles longues et fines. **4.** (*a*) = SHARPER; (*b*) *NAm: F:* expert, -erte; connaisseur *m*.

III. *adv.* **1. s. cut outline,** profil nettement découpé; *N.Arch:* **s. built ship,** navire *m* à formes fines; **s. pointed pencil,** crayon taillé fin; **s. edged,** (i) (*of knife, etc.*) tranchant, affilé; (ii) (*of roof, etc.*) à arête vive; aux arêtes vives; **s. edged orifice,** orifice percé en mince paroi. **2.** (*a*) (s'arrêter) brusquement, subitement, court; (*b*) (tourner) brusquement; **turn s. right,** prenez à angle droit. **3.** ponctuellement, exactement; **at four o'clock s.,** à quatre heures sonnantes, précises, *F:* tapantes. **4.** *F:* **look s.!** vite! dépêchez-vous! remuez-vous! **5.** *Nau:* **to brace the yards s. (up),** orienter à bloc; brasser en pointe. **6.** *Mus:* **to sing s.,** chanter faux (en haussant le ton).

sharp², *v.* **1.** *v.tr. & i. A:* duper (qn); filouter (qch. à qn); tricher (au jeu, etc.). **2.** *v.tr. NAm: Mus:* diéser (une note).

sharpen ['ʃɑːp(ə)n], *v.*

I. *v.tr.* **1.** (*a*) affiler, affûter, aiguiser, repasser (un couteau, un outil, etc.); passer (un couteau, un sabre) à la meule; **to s. with a file,** affûter à la lime; **razor that needs sharpening,** rasoir *m* qui a perdu son fil; (*b*) tailler en pointe, appointer, aiguiser (un bâton, etc.); **to s. a pencil,** tailler un crayon; (*of cat, etc.*) **to s. its claws,** faire ses griffes; (*c*) rendre (un angle) plus saillant; aviver (une arête); (*d*) accentuer (un trait, un contraste). **2. to s. s.o.'s wits,** éveiller l'esprit de qn; *F:* dégourdir qn; **the danger had sharpened his wits,** le danger lui avait éveillé l'esprit. **3.** (*a*) aviver, aggraver (la douleur, l'animosité); aviver, exciter (une passion, un désir); **a cocktail sharpens the appetite,** un cocktail aiguise, ouvre, l'appétit; (*b*) rendre plus sévère (une loi, le caractère de qn, etc.); **to s. one's voice,** donner de l'acerbité à sa voix; prendre un ton plus acerbe, plus cassant, plus âpre. **4.** *Cu:* relever, donner du piquant à, (une sauce). **5.** *Nau:* orienter à bloc, brasser en pointe (les vergues). **6.** *Mus:* diéser (une note).

II. *v.i.* **1.** (*of faculties, etc.*) s'aiguiser. **2.** (*of the voice*) devenir plus acerbe, plus âpre. **3.** (*of sound*) devenir plus pénétrant, plus perçant, plus aigu.

sharpener ['ʃɑːp(ə)nər], *s.* **1.** (*pers.*) affûteur, -euse; aiguiseur *m*; affileur *m*; repasseur, -euse (à la meule). **2.** machine *f* à affûter; affûteuse *f*; aiguisoir *m*; **knife s.,** affiloir *m* (pour couteaux); **pencil s.,** taille-crayon *m*, *pl.* taille-crayons.

sharpening ['ʃɑːp(ə)niŋ], *s.* **1.** (*a*) affilage *m*, affûtage *m*, aiguisage *m*, repassage *m* (d'un outil, etc.); (*b*) accentuation *f* (d'un contraste). **2.** affinage *m* (de l'intelligence). **3.** aggravation *f* (d'une douleur, etc.). **4.** relèvement *m* (d'une sauce). **5.** *Nau:* orientation *f* à bloc; brassage *m* en pointe. **6.** *Mus:* haussement *m* (d'une note) d'un demi-ton.

sharper ['ʃɑːpər], *s.* (*a*) escroc *m*; aigrefin *m*; chevalier *m* d'industrie; (*b*) *Cards:* tricheur, -euse.

sharp-eyed ['ʃɑːpaid], *a.* aux yeux perçants; à la vue perçante.

sharp-faced ['ʃɑːpfeist], *a.* **1.** (personne) à visage en lame de couteau. **2.** (outil, etc.) à vive arête.

sharp-featured [ʃɑːp'fiːtʃəd], *a.* (*a*) aux traits tirés, amaigris; (*b*) à visage en lame de couteau.

sharping ['ʃɑːpiŋ], *s. O:* escroquerie *f*; tricherie *f*.

sharply ['ʃɑːpli], *adv.* **1.** (*a*) (*of pencil, etc.*) **s. pointed,** à pointe fine, taillé fin; (*b*) (dessiné, qui se détache) nettement; **s. divided into two classes,** partagé nettement en deux classes; **to bring sth. s. home,** mettre qch. en relief d'une façon saisissante. **2.** raidement, brusquement; **the road dips s.,** la route plonge brusquement; **it climbs s.,** la montée est raide; **he turned s.,** il a tourné brusquement, court. **3.** (*a*) (marcher) vivement, à vive allure, d'un pas rapide; (geler) fort; (frapper qn) raide; (*b*) (regarder, écouter) attentivement; **he looked s. at her,** il l'a regardée d'un œil pénétrant; (*c*) (réprimander) sévèrement; **to speak s. to s.o.,** adresser qn brusquement, d'une voix cassante; **to treat s.o. s.,** rudoyer qn; **to answer s.,** répondre d'un ton brusque, acerbe. **4.** (sonner) sec, avec un bruit sec.

sharpness ['ʃɑːpnis], *s.* **1.** (*a*) acuité *f*, finesse *f* (du tranchant d'un couteau, etc.); acuité, acutesse *f* (d'une pointe, etc.); (*b*) aiguité *f* (d'un angle); *Nau:* finesse (des formes d'un navire); (*c*) *Aut: etc:* **s. of the turn,** raccourci *m* du virage; (*d*) netteté *f* (des contours, d'une image photographique); *W.Tel:* finesse (de l'accord); (*e*) caractère marqué (d'un contraste). **2.** (*a*) finesse (de l'esprit, de l'ouïe); **s. of sight,** acuité de la vue; acuité visuelle; (*b*) intelligence *f* (d'un enfant). **3.** (*a*) acuité (de la douleur, etc.); (*b*) **there's a s. in the air,** il fait frisquet; (*c*) sévérité *f*, acerbité *f*, âpreté *f* (du ton, d'une réprimande); brusquerie *f* (du ton); acerbité, aigreur *f* (d'humeur); aspérité *f* (du caractère, de la voix). **4.** (goût) piquant *m* (d'une sauce); acidité *f*, aigreur (d'une pomme, etc.). **5.** acuité, qualité pénétrante, qualité perçante (d'un son).

sharp(-)set ['ʃɑːpset], *a.* **1.** *O:* **to be s.,** être en grand appétit; avoir l'estomac creux; se sentir un creux dans l'estomac; **to be s. on sth.,** avoir un vif désir de qch. **2.** (*of tool*) bien aiguisé; affilé.

sharpshod ['ʃɑːpʃɔd], *a.* (cheval) ferré à glace.

sharpshooter ['ʃɑːpʃuːtər], *s. Mil:* tirailleur *m*; tireur *m* d'élite.

sharp-sighted [ʃɑːp'saitid], *a.* **1.** à la vue perçante. **2.** perspicace.

sharp-tailed ['ʃɑːpteild], *a. Orn:* **s.-t. grouse,** tétras *m* à longue queue, *Fr.C:* gelinotte *f* à queue fine; *NAm:* **s.-t. sandpiper,** bécasseau *m* à queue pointue, *Fr.C:* bécasseau à queue fine; **s.-t. sparrow, s.-t. finch,** *Fr.C:* pinson *m* à queue aiguë.

sharp-tongued [ʃɑːp'tʌŋd], *a.* qui a la langue acérée, caustique.

sharp-toothed [ʃɑːp'tuːθt], *a.* aux dents aiguës.

shatter ['ʃætər]. **1.** *v.tr.* (*a*) fracasser; briser en éclats; mettre en pièces; **the glass was shattered,** le verre a volé en éclats; **his right arm was shattered,** il a eu le bras droit fracassé; **the explosion shattered the house,** l'explosion a fait crouler la maison; (*b*) briser, renverser (des espérances); (*c*) détraquer, délabrer (la santé); ébranler, détraquer (les nerfs); *F:* **I was absolutely shattered!** j'étais complètement bouleversé(e)! **2.** *v.i.* se briser (en éclats); se fracasser.

shattered ['ʃætəd], *a.* **1.** (*of glass, etc.*) brisé, fracassé, en éclats; (*of building*) écroulé; **s. hopes,** espérances brisées. **2. s. health,** santé détraquée, délabrée; **s. nerves,** nerfs fortement ébranlés; **s. in mind and body,** détraqué au physique et au moral.

shattering¹ ['ʃæt(ə)riŋ], *a.* **1.** (coup) écrasant; **s. news,** des nouvelles renversantes. **2.** *Exp:* **s. charge,** charge brisante.

shattering², *s.* **1.** brisement *m*, éclatement *m* (d'une glace, etc.); *Exp:* **s. properties,** brisance *f*. **2.** ruine *f*, délabrement *m* (de la santé, etc.); ébranlement *m* (des nerfs); renversement *m* (des espérances).

shave¹ [ʃeiv], *s. Tls:* plane *f*, racloir *m*; **s. hook,** ébardoir *m*, grattoir *m* (triangulaire); racloir en forme de cœur.

shave², *s.* **1.** rasage *m*; **to have a s.,** (i) se raser; (ii) *O:* se faire raser; **to give s.o. a s.,** raser qn; **this razor gives you a really close s.,** avec ce rasoir vous pouvez vraiment vous raser de près; **haircut or s., sir?** les cheveux ou la barbe, monsieur? **2.** coup affleurant, à fleur de peau; *F:* **that was a close s.!** vous l'avez échappé belle! il était moins cinq! **3.** *Cu:* **shaves,** copeaux *m* (de chocolat).

shave³, *v.tr.* **1.** (*a*) raser; faire la barbe à (qn); **to s. s.o.'s head,** raser la tête à qn; **to s. off one's moustache,** se raser la moustache; (*b*) *v.pr. & i.* **to s. (oneself),** se raser, se faire la barbe. **2.** (*a*) doler, planer (le bois, les peaux); *Metalw:* soumettre (un engrenage, etc.) au shaving; **to s. off a slice of sth.,** couper une mince tranche de qch.; (*b*) *F:* **to s. the budget estimates,** rogner les prévisions budgétaires. **3.** friser, raser, effleurer (qch.). **4.** *P: A:* tondre, plumer (qn).

shavegrass ['ʃeivgrɑːs], *s. Bot:* prêle *f*; *F:* queue-de-cheval *f*.

shaveling ['ʃeivliŋ], *s.* (*a*) *usu. Pej: A:* tonsuré *m*, clerc *m*; (*b*) *F:* (tout) jeune homme.

shaven ['ʃeiv(ə)n], *a.* **1.** (*of monk*) tonsuré; (*of head, chin*) rasé; **clean s.,** (homme) sans barbe ni moustache; (visage) glabre. **2.** (*of wood, surface*) plané.

shaver ['ʃeivər], *s.* **1.** (*a*) raseur *m*, barbier *m*; (*b*) *F:* **young s.,** gosse *m*, gamin *m*, moutard *m*. **2. electric s.,** rasoir *m* électrique.

shavetail ['ʃeivteil], *s. U.S: F: Pej:* sous-lieutenant *m*.

Shavian ['ʃeiviən]. **1.** *a.* inspiré des doctrines de G. B. Shaw; **S. humour,** humour *m* à la G. B. Shaw. **2.** *s.* disciple *mf* de G. B. Shaw.

shaving ['ʃeiviŋ], *s.* **1.** (*a*) rasage *m*; **s. is compulsory in the army,** les soldats sont tenus de se raser; **s. brush,** blaireau *m*; pinceau *m* à barbe; savonnette *f*; **s. cream,** crème *f* à raser; **s. mirror,** miroir *m* à barbe; **s. soap, s. stick,** savon *m* à barbe; bâton *m* de savon pour la barbe; (*b*) dolage *m*, planage *m* (du bois, des peaux); *Metalw:* shaving *m*, rasage; *Carp:* **s. horse,** banc *m* d'âne. **2.** copeau *m*, planure *f* (de bois, de métal); rognure *f* (de métal); lèchette *f* (de pain); **shavings,** copeaux, raboture(s) *f*; (*of metal*) rognures; (*for scrubbing floors*) **iron shavings,** paille *f* de fer.

shaw¹ [ʃɔː], *s. Scot:* fane *f* (de pommes de terre, de navets).

shaw², *s. A: & Lit:* taillis *m*, fourré *m*.

shawl [ʃɔːl], *s.* châle *m*; fichu *m*; **head s.,** frileuse *f*.

shawm [ʃɔːm], *s. Mus: A:* chalumeau *m*.

shay [ʃei], *s. Veh: A: & Dial:* chaise *f*, cabriolet *m*.

she [ʃi, ʃiː], *pers. pron. nom. f.* **1.** (*a*) (*of pers., female animal*) elle; **s. was running,** elle courait; **s. didn't see me,** elle ne m'a pas vu; **what's s. doing?** qu'est-ce qu'elle fait? **here s. comes!** la voici (qui vient)! **the tigress had heard and s. sprang,** la tigresse avait entendu et elle s'élança; (*of cow*) **she's a good milker,** elle donne beaucoup de lait; (*b*) (*of thing personified as female*) (i) (*of a motor vehicle, Lit: the moon, nature, a nation, etc.*) elle; **she's still running in,** elle est toujours en rodage; (ii) (*of a ship*) il; **s. sails at ten o'clock,** il part à dix heures; **she's a fine ship,** c'est un beau navire. **2.** (*stressed*) (*a*) elle; **s. and I,** elle et moi; **I guessed that** *she* **was the mother,** j'ai deviné que c'était elle la mère; *she* **knows nothing about it,** elle n'en sait rien, elle; (*now usu. considered pedantic*) **it is s.,** c'est elle; **if I were s.,** si j'étais à sa place; (*b*) (*antecedent to a rel. pron.*) *A.Lit:* **s. whom you saw,** celle que vous avez vue; **s. of whom you speak,** celle dont vous parlez. **3.** (*as substantive*) (*a*) *F:* femelle; **it's a s.,** (*of baby*) c'est une (petite) fille; (*of animal*) c'est une femelle; **that's a fine dog—it's a s.,** voilà un beau chien—c'est une chienne; *Lit:* **the not impossible s.,** la femme qu'on pourrait aimer; (*b*) *attrib.* **s. ass,** ânesse *f*; **s. bear,** ours *m* femelle; ourse *f*; **s. cat,** chatte *f*; **s. devil,** diablesse *f*; **s. elephant,** éléphant *m* femelle; éléphante *f*; **s. goat,** chèvre *f*; *F:* bique *f*; **s. monkey,** singe *m* femelle; guenon *f*; (*c*) *Bot: Austr:* **s. oak,** casuarine *f*, filao *m*. **4.** *Austr: N.Z: F:* **she'll be right!** ça ira! tout ira bien! ça marche maintenant!

shea ['ʃiə], *s. Bot:* **s., s. tree, s. butter tree,** karité *m*, butyrospermum *m*; arbre *m* à beurre; bassia butyracée; **s. butter, s. nut oil,** beurre *m* de karité, de Galam.

sheading ['ʃiːdiŋ], *s.* subdivision administrative de l'île de Man.

sheaf¹, *pl.* **-ves** [ʃiːf, -vz], *s.* **1.** (*a*) gerbe *f* (de blé, etc.); **loose s.,** javelle *f*; (*machine*) **s. binder,** lieuse *f*; (*b*) **s. of flowers,** gerbe de fleurs. **2.** faisceau *m*, botte *f* (de verges, de piquets, etc.); liasse *f* (de papiers); **I had a whole s. of letters this morning,** j'ai reçu toute une botte de lettres ce matin. **3.** *Ball:* **s. of fire,** faisceau de trajectoires; gerbe de tir.

sheaf², *v.tr.* = SHEAVE².

shear¹ [ʃiər], *s.* **1.** (*a*) **(pair of) shears,** cisaille(s) *f(pl)*; (grands) ciseaux; **hand shears,** cisaille à main; **lever shears,** cisaille à levier; **garden shears,** cisaille à haie; *Arb:* **ringing shears,** bagueur *m*; coupe-sève *m inv*; *Mec.E:* **guillotine, crocodile, alligator, shears,** cisaille, cisailleuse *f* à guillotine; *Metalw:* **block shears, tinman's shears,** hachard *m*; **rotary shears,** cisailles circulaires; **scroll shears,** cisaille à chantourner; **bevelling shears,** cisailles chanfreineuses; **mechanical shears, power shears,** cisailleuse mécanique; *Dressm: etc:* **pinking shears,** ciseaux à denteler; *Lit:* **the shears of Atropos,** les ciseaux de la Parque; (*b*) **shears,** tondeuse *f* (à moutons); *Austr:* **off the shears,** (mouton) fraîchement tondu. **2.** *Mec.E: Const: etc:* **shears, s. legs,** bigue *f*; grue *f* de chargement.

shear², *s.* **1.** tonte *f* (de laine); *Dial:* **s. hog,** agneau *m* entre la première et la seconde tonte. **2.** (*a*) cisaillement *m* (de métaux); (*b*) *Mec:* (effort *m* de) cisaillement; (*c*) *Geol:* **wind s.,** cisaillement du vent; **s. zone,** zone *f* de cisaillement; **s. structure,** structure cisaillée.

shear[3], *v.* (*p.t.* **sheared,** *esp. Austr:* **shore** [ʃɔːər]; *p.p.* **shorn** [ʃɔːn], **sheared,** *Austr:* **shore**) **1.** *v.tr.* (*a*) **to s. (off),** couper (une branche, etc.); **to s. through sth.,** trancher qch.; (*b*) *Metalw:* cisailler (une tôle, etc.); (*c*) *Tex:* ciseler (le velours). **2.** *v.tr.* (*a*) tondre (un mouton, etc.); *Austr:* **I sheared about ten thousand this year,** cette année j'avais à tondre, j'ai fait tondre, à peu près dix mille moutons; *Tex:* **to fine-s. cloth,** affiner le drap; **to be shorn of sth.,** être dépouillé, privé, de qch.; (*b*) (*with passive force*) (*of sheep*) **to s. a good fleece,** produire une belle toison. **3.** *v.tr. Mec:* cisailler (qch.). **4.** *v.i. Mec:* (*of material*) céder sous le cisaillement; se cisailler.

shear[4], *s. Mec.E:* **shears of a lathe,** glissières *f*, coulisses *f*, flasques *m*, d'un tour.

shearbill ['ʃiəbil], *s. Orn:* rhyncops *m*; bec-en-ciseau *m*, *pl.* becs-en-ciseaux.

shearer ['ʃiərər], *s.* **1.** (*pers.*) (*a*) tondeur, -euse (de moutons); (*b*) *Metalw:* cisailleur *m*. **2.** (*machine*) (*a*) *Metalw:* cisailleuse *f*; (*b*) tondeuse *f* (pour moutons).

shearing ['ʃiəriŋ], *s.* **1.** (*a*) taille *f* (d'une haie, etc.); cisaillement *m*, cisaillage *m* (d'une tôle, etc.); tonte *f*, tondaison *f* (des moutons); tondage *m*, tonture *f* (du drap); *Tex:* (**fine**) **s.,** affinage *m* (du drap); (*b*) *Mec:* cisaillement; **s. stress,** effort *m* de cisaillement; (*c*) *Geol:* cisaillement; (*d*) **s. machine** = SHEARER 2. **2. shearings,** tontes (de laine); tontisse *f*, tonture (du drap).

shearling ['ʃiəliŋ], *s. Husb:* agneau, mouton, qui a été tondu une fois; mouton d'un an.

shearman, *pl.* **-men** ['ʃiəmən], *s.m. Metalw:* cisailleur.

sheartail ['ʃiəteil], *s. Orn:* **s. (hummingbird),** oiseau-mouche *m* enicure.

shearwater ['ʃiəwɔːtər], *s. Orn:* puffin *m*; **Audubon's s.,** puffin obscur; **Cory's s.,** puffin cendré; **great s.,** *NAm:* **greater s.,** puffin majeur, *Fr.C:* grand puffin; **little s.,** *NAm:* **allied s.,** petit puffin, *Fr.C:* puffin obscur; **Manx s.,** puffin des Anglais, *Fr.C:* puffin manx; **pink-footed s.,** puffin à pattes roses; **short-tailed s.,** *NAm:* **slender-billed s.,** puffin à bec grêle, *Fr.C:* puffin à bec mince; **sooty s.,** puffin fuligineux.

sheatfish ['ʃiːtfiʃ], *s. Ich:* silure *m*.

sheath[1], *s.* [ʃiːθ], *s.* (*pl.* [ʃiːðz] *or* [ʃiːθs]) **1.** (*a*) manchon protecteur; douille protectrice, fourreau *m* (d'épée, de parapluie, etc.); couverture *f* (de parapluie); étui *m* (de ciseaux, etc.); gaine *f* (de couteau); *El:* cuirasse *f* (d'un câble); (**whetstone**) **s.,** coffin *m* (d'un aiguisoir); *Const:* **s. dress,** fourreau; *Atom.Ph:* **fuel cladding s.,** gaine de combustible; **electron s.,** gaine d'électrons; **ion s.,** gaine d'ions; (*b*) *Anat:* enveloppe *f* (d'un organe); fourreau (du cheval, du taureau, etc.); gaine (de muscle, d'artère, etc.); *Bot:* gaine; enveloppement *m* (d'une graine); *Ent:* **wing s.,** élytre *m*, étui; **s.-winged,** coléoptère; (*c*) (**contraceptive**) **s.,** préservatif *m*, condom *m*; (*d*) *El:* **induction s.,** écran inductif. **2.** *Phot:* (**plate**) **s.,** châssis (négatif). **3.** *Civ.E:* remblai *m* de pierres sèches (pour empêcher le débordement d'une rivière).

sheath[2], *v.tr.* = SHEATHE 3.

sheathbill ['ʃiːθbil], *s. Orn:* chionis *m*, bec-en-fourreau *m*.

sheathe [ʃiːð], *v.tr.* **1.** (re)mettre au fourreau, rengainer (une épée, etc.); engainer (un couteau, etc.); *Lit:* **to s. the sword,** cesser les hostilités; faire la paix. **2.** *Nat.Hist:* envelopper (qch.) dans une gaine; **the leaves s. the stem,** les feuilles engainent la tige. **3.** (*a*) revêtir, recouvrir, doubler (un toit, un navire, etc.) (**with,** de, en); *Min:* cuveler (un puits de mine); *N.Arch:* **to s. a ship's bottom,** souffler la carène d'un navire; (*b*) *El:* armer (un câble). **4.** *Phot:* mettre (une plaque) dans le châssis.

sheathed [ʃiːðd], *a.* **1.** (poignard, etc.) engainé; (sabre) au fourreau. **2.** revêtu d'une enveloppe; *Bot:* (*of stalk, etc.*) entouré d'une gaine; *Anat: etc:* vaginé. **3.** (*a*) revêtu, doublé (de métal, en métal, etc.); *N.Arch:* **sheathed ship,** vaisseau doublé; (*with wood*) vaisseau soufflé; (*b*) *El: etc:* **s. cable,** câble *m* sous gaine; câble armé.

sheathing[1] ['ʃiːðiŋ], *a. Bot:* **s. leaves,** feuilles entourantes, engainantes.

sheathing[2], *s.* **1.** (*a*) mise *f* au fourreau (d'une épée); mise dans sa gaine (d'un couteau, etc.); (*b*) armement *m* (d'un câble). **2.** (*a*) revêtement *m* (de, en, métal); *N.Arch:* doublage *m*; **wooden s.,** soufflage *m*; **s. felt,** ploc *m*; (*b*) *Mec.E: etc:* enveloppe *f*, garniture *f*; chemise *f* (d'un cylindre, etc.); (*c*) armure *f*, armature *f*, cuirasse *f*, gaine *f* (d'un câble); (*d*) *Min:* cuvelage *m* (d'un puits). **3.** *Civ.E:* = SHEATH[1] 3.

sheathknife ['ʃiːθnaif], *s.* couteau *m* à gaine.

sheave[1] [ʃiːv], *s.* **1.** réa *m*, rouet *m* (de poulie); *Nau:* **dead s., dumb s.,** engoujure *f* (d'un mât); **s. hole,** (i) mortaise *f*; (ii) *Nau:* clan *m*, chaumard *m* (de poulie). **2.** *Mec.E: Mch:* (**eccentric**) **s.,** plateau *m*, disque *m*, corps *m*, d'excentrique. **3.** cache-entrée *m inv* (de trou de serrure).

sheave[2], *v.tr.* gerber, engerber, enjaveler (le blé, etc.); mettre en bottes (des osiers, etc.).

sheave[3], *v.i. Row:* **1.** scier, culer. **2.** ramer face en avant.

Sheba ['ʃiːbə], *Pr.n. A.Geog:* Saba *f*; **the Queen of S.,** la reine de Saba.

shebang [ʃi'bæŋ], *s. esp. NAm: P:* **1.** *O:* hutte *f*, cabane *f*. **2. the whole s.,** tout le bataclan; **I'm sick of the whole s.,** j'en ai plein le dos.

shebeen [ʃi'biːn], *s. Dial:* (*Irish*) débit de boissons clandestin.

shed[1] [ʃed], *s. Tex:* foule *f*, encroix *m*, pas *m*, envergeure *f* (de la chaîne).

shed[2], *s.* **1.** (*a*) hangar *m*; **lean-to s.,** appentis *m*; **open s.,** auvent *m*; **building s.,** *Const:* atelier *m* de construction; *N.Arch:* cale couverte; **machine s.,** hangar des machines; *Rail:* **engine s.,** remise *f* de locomotives; garage *m*, dépôt *m*, des machines; *Tex:* **weaving s.,** atelier de tissage; (*b*) *Nau: etc:* **the storing sheds,** les magasins *m*; (*c*) baraque *f*; baraquement *m*; (*d*) *Const:* **s. roof,** toit *m* en appentis; (toit en) shed *m*; comble *m* en dents de scie. **2.** *Tg:* cloche *f* (d'isolateur).

shed[3], *v.tr.* (*p.t. & p.p.* **shed;** *pr.p.* **shedding**). **1.** (*a*) perdre (ses dents, ses feuilles, etc.); (*of animal*) jeter (sa peau, ses cornes, etc.); (*of crab, etc.*) dépouiller (sa carapace); (*of plant, flower*) **to shed its leaves, its petals,** s'effeuiller; (*b*) *O:* se défaire de (qn); semer (un importun); (*c*) *El:* **to s. the load,** délester; *O:* **to s. one's clothes,** se dévêtir; se dépouiller de ses vêtements; (*d*) **to s. one's husband in the divorce court,** se divorcer de son mari. **2.** répandre, verser (des larmes, le sang); (r)épandre (de la lumière); déverser (de l'eau); **to s. one's blood for one's country,** verser son sang pour la patrie; **the lamp was shedding a soft light,** la lampe versait une douce lumière; **to s. light on sth.,** éclairer une affaire. **3.** *Tex:* **to s. the warp,** former la foule, l'encroix, le pas.

shedder ['ʃedər], *s.* (*a*) *Ich:* saumon *m* femelle après la fraieson; (*b*) *Crust:* crabe *m* qui vient de jeter sa carapace.

shedding ['ʃediŋ], *s.* **1.** (*a*) perte *f*, chute *f* (des feuilles, des dents, etc.); (*b*) *El:* **load s.,** délestage *m*. **2.** effusion *f* (de sang, etc.). **3.** *Tex:* formation *f* de la foule, de l'encroix, du pas.

sheen [ʃiːn], *s.* luisant *m*, luminosité *f*; lustre *m*, reflet *m* (de la soie, etc.); brillant *m*, chatoiement *m* (d'un tissu, d'un bijou, etc.); miroitement *m* (d'une pièce d'eau, etc.); luisance *f* (des cheveux); **hair with a s. like gold,** cheveux *mpl* à reflets d'or; **plumage with a blue s.,** plumage glacé d'azur; **the sun threw a s. over the sea,** le soleil faisait reluire la mer; **to take the s. off sth.,** délustrer qch.

sheeny ['ʃiːni], *s. P: Pej:* youpin, -ine; youtre *mf*, ioutre *mf*.

sheep [ʃiːp], *s. inv. in pl.* **1.** (*a*) mouton *m*; **black s.,** brebis noire; **the black s. (of the family, etc.),** la brebis galeuse; **lost s., stray s.,** brebis perdue, égarée; **to feel like a lost s.,** se sentir dépaysé; **they follow one another like s., they're just a lot of s.,** ils suivent le mouvement; ce sont les moutons de Panurge; **to separate the s. from the goats, the s. and the goats,** séparer les brebis d'avec les boucs; (*b*) **s. farmer,** *N.Z: F:* **s. cocky,** éleveur *m* de moutons; **s. farming,** élevage *m* de moutons; **s. pen,** parc *m* à moutons; bercail *m*; **s. run, s. walk,** pâturage *m* (pour moutons); **s. shearer,** (i) (*pers.*) tondeur, -euse (de moutons); (ii) tondeuse *f* mécanique; **s. shearing,** tonte *f*, tondaison *f*; **s.-shearing machine,** tondeuse mécanique; **s. shears,** tondeuse; forces *fpl*; *Ent: Vet:* **s. bot,** œstre *m* du mouton; **s. tick,** mélophage *m*; pou *m* de mouton; *Vet:* **s. pox,** variole ovine, des moutons; clavelée *f*, claveau *m*; rougeole *f* des moutons; **inoculation against s. pox,** clavelisation *f*; **s. wash, s. dip,** bain *m* parasiticide (pour moutons); (*c*) *Z:* **maned s.,** arui *m*; (*d*) *Bot:* **sheep's bit,** fausse scabieuse; **sheep's fescue,** fétuque ovine; *F:* coquioule *f*. **2.** *Bookb:* basane *f*.

sheepcote ['ʃiːpkout], *s. A:* bergerie *f*.

sheepdog ['ʃiːpdɔg], *s.* chien *m* de berger; chien à moutons; berger *m*; **Old English s.,** berger anglais sans queue; bobtail *m*.

sheepfold ['ʃiːpfould], *s.* parc *m* à moutons; bercail *m*.

sheepish ['ʃiːpiʃ], *a.* **1.** penaud; interdit, décontenancé; **to look s.,** rester penaud; rester tout sot. **2.** timide; embarrassé, gauche.

sheepishly ['ʃiːpiʃli], *adv.* **1.** d'un air penaud; d'un air interdit, décontenancé. **2.** d'un air embarrassé, timide.

sheepishness ['ʃiːpiʃnis], *s.* **1.** timidité *f*; fausse honte; gaucherie *f* (dans le monde). **2.** air penaud.

sheeplike ['ʃiːplaik], *a.* **they're completely s.,** ils suivent le mouvement; ce sont les moutons de Panurge.

sheepman, *pl.* **-men** ['ʃiːpmən], *s.m. U.S:* éleveur de moutons.

sheepshank ['ʃiːpʃæŋk], *s. Nau:* (nœud *m* de, en) jambe *f* de chien.

sheepskin ['ʃiːpskin], *s.* **1.** peau *f* de mouton; **s. rug,** tapis *m* en peau de mouton. **2.** *Leath: Bookb:* basane *f*. **3.** parchemin *m*; *esp. U.S:* diplôme *m* (sur parchemin).

sheer[1] [ʃiər], *s. Nau:* embardée *f*; **to give her a slight s. to starboard,** faire embarder légèrement sur tribord.

sheer[2], *v.i. Nau:* **1.** embarder; faire une embardée. **2. to s. off,** (i) larguer les amarres (pour laisser passer un autre navire à quai); alarguer; prendre le large; (ii) *F:* (*of pers.*) partir, prendre le large; *F:* **s. off!** débarrasse le plancher! **to s. off from a ship,** passer à bonne distance d'un navire; déborder d'un navire; **to s. off a point,** décoller d'un quart.

sheer[3], *s. N.Arch:* tonture *f*, relèvement *m*; **to build with a s.,** tonturer (un navire); **s. line,** tonture *f* (du pont); **s. strake,** carreau *m*; vibor(d) *m*; **s. rail,** liston *m*, listeau *m*, listel *m*; **s. pole,** quenouillette *f* de cap-de-mouton; **s. draught, s. drawing, s. plan,** élévation *f*; projection longitudinale; plan diamétral; *Nau:* **s. hulk,** ponton *m* à mâture, ponton-mâture *m*, *pl.* pontons-mâture; mâture flottante; machine *f* à mâter; **leg of a sheers,** hanche *f*, anche *f*, bras *m*, d'une bigue.

sheer[4]. **1.** *a.* (*a*) pur, véritable, vrai, franc, *f.* franche; **it's s. robbery,** c'est un véritable vol; **a s. impossibility,** une impossibilité absolue; **it's s. madness,** c'est de la folie pure (et simple); c'est de la pure folie; **a s. waste of time,** une simple perte de temps; **out of s. malice, kindness,** par pure méchanceté, par pure bonté; **it was s. stupidity,** c'était franchement stupide; **by s. accident,** par pur accident; **to do sth. by s. strength of arm,** faire qch. à la seule force du poignet; **to grow rich by s. hard work,** faire une fortune entièrement par son travail; **in s. desperation she wrote to him,** en désespoir de cause elle lui écrivit; (*b*) perpendiculaire; (rocher, chemin, etc.) à pic, abrupt, escarpé; **s. coast,** côte *f* accore; (*c*) *Tex:* (*of linen, etc.*) léger, fin, transparent, diaphane; **s. silk stockings,** bas de soie extra-fins. **2.** *adv.* (*a*) tout à fait; complètement; **the tree was torn s. out by the roots,** l'arbre fut bel et bien déraciné; (*b*) (tomber, etc.) perpendiculairement, à pic, à plomb; **hill that descends s. to the town,** colline qui descend abruptement à la ville.

sheer[5], *v.i. A:* (*of rock, etc.*) (i) se dresser, (ii) descendre, perpendiculairement, à pic, à plomb.

sheering ['ʃiəriŋ], *s. Nau:* embardées *fpl*.

sheerlegs ['ʃiəlegz], *s.pl. Mec.E: Const: etc:* bigue *f*; grue *f* de chargement.

sheerly ['ʃiəli], *adv.* **1.** purement, véritablement; absolument, complètement. **2.** abruptement, à pic.

sheet[1] [ʃiːt], *s.* **1.** (*a*) drap *m* (de lit); *F:* **to get between the sheets,** se mettre au lit, dans les bâches; se pieuter; (*b*) *Hist:* (**penitential**) **white s.,** linge blanc des pénitents; (*c*) *A: & Lit:* voile *f*. **2.** (*a*) feuille *f*, feuillet *m* (de papier); **loose s., fly s.,** feuille volante; **books in sheets,** livres *m* en feuilles, en blanc; *Com:* **order s.,** bulletin *m* de commande; bordereau *m* de commission; **sale s.,** bordereau de vente; *Ind:* **time, work, job, s.,** feuille de présence; *Mil:* **daily duty s.,** état *m* de service; (*b*) *F: O:* journal *m*, -aux; feuille; **to figure in the society sheets,** défrayer la chronique mondaine. **3.** (*a*) feuille (de verre, de plomb, etc.); feuille, tôle *f*, lame *f*, plaque *f* (de métal); **heavy-gauge s.,** tôle forte; **copper sheets,** tôle de cuivre; **s. copper,** cuivre *m* en tôles, en feuilles, en lames, en planches; **s. iron,** (fer *m* en) tôle *f*; fer en feuilles; **formed s. iron,** tôle emboutie; **s.-iron pipe,** tuyau *m* en tôle; **s. lead** [led], plomb laminé; plomb en feuilles; **s. mill,** laminoir *m* à tôles; tôlerie *f*; **s. glass,** verre *m* à vitres; **s. rubber,** feuille anglaise; *Cu:* **baking s.,** plafond *m* (de four); (*b*) *Civ.E: Min:* **s. piles,** palplanches *f*. **4.** (*a*) nappe *f* (d'eau, d'écume, de feu, etc.); couche *f*, nappe (de neige); **s. of ice,** (i) couche de glace (sur un objet); (ii) nappe de glace (sur l'eau, sur la terre); (*b*) **s. lightning,** éclairs *mpl* diffus; éclairs en nappe(s).

sheet[2], *v.tr.* **1.** couvrir, garnir, (qch.) d'un drap, d'une bâche; **to s. over a waggon,** bâcher un wagon. **2. the town was sheeted over with snow,** la ville était enveloppée, recouverte, de neige. **3.** *Min:* **to s. a gallery,** blinder, limander, une galerie.

sheet[3], *s. Nau:* écoute *f*; **single, double, s. bend,** nœud *m* d'écoute simple, double; *F:* **to be three sheets in the wind,** être aux trois quarts ivre.

sheet[4], *v.tr. Nau:* border (une voile); **to s. home,** border à bloc, à joindre.

sheet[5], *s.* **s. (anchor),** ancre *f* de veille; **s. cable,** chaîne *f* de veille; *Fig:* **our s. anchor,** notre ancre de salut, notre (dernière) planche de salut.

sheeted ['ʃi:tid], *a.* enveloppé d'un drap; drapé; **s. corpse,** cadavre enveloppé d'un linceul, enseveli.

sheeting ['ʃi:tiŋ], *s.* **1.** *Tex:* toile *f* pour draps; **waterproof s.,** drap *m* d'hôpital. **2.** *Civ.E: Min:* blindage *m*; *Min:* limande *f* (d'une galerie); **s. pile,** palplanche *f*; *Const:* **s. plank,** tavaillon *m* (de comble). **3.** *coll.* tôlerie *f*; tôles *fpl.* **4.** *Nau:* braie *f* (du gouvernail, de la pompe).

sheetpiling ['ʃi:tpailiŋ], *s. Civ.E:* palée *f*; *Hyd.E:* encrèchement *m.*

sheik(h) [ʃeik, ʃi:k], *s.m.* **1.** cheik, s(c)heik. **2.** (*usu.* [ʃi:k]) *P: A:* beau garçon; charmeur; tombeur (de femmes).

sheila ['ʃi:lə], *s.f. Austr: N.Z:* jeune femme, gonzesse.

shekel ['ʃek(ə)l], *s.* **1.** *A.Meas: & Num:* sicle *m*; **the s. of the sanctuary,** le sicle royal du sanctuaire. **2.** *F:* **shekels,** argent *m*, galette *f.*

sheld-duck, shelduck ['ʃel(d)dʌk], *s. Orn:* tadorne *m* de Belon; **ruddy s.,** tadorne casarca (roux).

sheldrake ['ʃeldreik], *s. Orn:* **1.** tadorne *m.* **2.** *U.S:* harle *m.*

shelf, *pl.* **shelves** [ʃelf, ʃelvz], *s.* **1.** (*a*) tablette *f* (de rayonnage); planche *f* (d'armoire); rayon *m* (d'armoire, de bibliothèque); étagère *f* (de buffet, etc.); plateau *m* (de four, etc.); **sliding s.,** tirette *f* (de classeur); **wall s.,** rayon le long du mur; **set of shelves,** étagère; **s. space,** rayonnage *m*; **s. rail,** galerie *f*; *Aut:* **window s.,** plage *f* arrière; (*b*) (*pers.*) (*in supermarket, etc.*) **s. filler,** réassortisseur, -euse; (*of goods*) **to stay on the shelves,** être de vente difficile; *F:* **to put s.o., sth., on the s.,** remiser qn, qch.; **to be on the s.,** être au rancart; être laissé pour compte; **she's on the s.,** elle est en passe de devenir vieille fille; elle a coiffé sainte Catherine. **2.** *N.Arch:* **s. (piece),** bauquière *f*; gouttière renversée. **3.** (*a*) rebord *m*, corniche *f*, saillie *f* (d'un rocher, d'un précipice, etc.); (*b*) *Civ.E:* ressaut *m* (d'une voie); (*c*) *Geog: Oc:* terrasse *f*; plate-forme *f*; replat *m*; seuil *m*; banc *m* (de roche, de sable); **continental s.,** plate-forme continentale; plateau continental; **insular s.,** socle (continental); (*left exposed at low tide*) **dry s.,** sèche *f*; **s. edge,** flexure continentale; **s. sea,** mer bordière; (*of glacier in sea*) **s. ice,** plate-forme flottante; (*d*) *Geol: Min:* roche *f* de fond.

shelfback ['ʃelfbæk], *s. U.S: Bookb:* dos *m* (du livre).

shell[1] [ʃel], *s.* **1.** (*a*) coquille *f* (de mollusque, d'escargot); carapace *f* (de homard, de tortue); écaille *f* (d'huître, de moule, de tortue); **(empty) shells,** coquillages *mpl*; *Lit:* **Triton's s.,** la conque de Triton; **to come out of one's s.,** sortir de sa chrysalide, de sa coquille; révéler ses qualités; surprendre tout le monde par ses qualités de causeur; **to retire into one's s.,** rentrer, se renfermer, dans sa coquolle, dans sa coquille, dans son cocon; *a. & s.* **s. pink,** rose pâle (*m*) *inv*; *Agr:* **s. marl,** falun *m*; **s. marl pit,** falunière *f*; *Archeol:* **s. heap, s. mound, s. midden,** kjœkken-mœdding *m*; (*b*) coquille (d'œuf, de noix); coque (d'œuf plein); écale *f* (de noix); gousse *f*, cosse *f* (de pois, etc.); *Ent:* enveloppe *f* (de nymphe); **s. of cocoa beans,** coque, pelure *f*, de cacao; (*c*) **electron(ic) s.,** couche *f*, cortège *m*, électronique; (*d*) forme *f* vide; simple apparence *f*; **his knowledge is a mere s.,** son savoir est tout en surface. **2.** (*a*) **s. of butter,** coquille de beurre; (*b*) *Sm.a:* coquille (d'une épée); (*c*) *Arm:* timbre *m* (de casque); (*d*) *Tls:* cuiller *f* (de tarière, etc.); **s. bit,** mèche-cuiller *f*, *pl.* mèches-cuillers. **3.** (*a*) *Mch:* paroi *f*, corps *m*, coque (de chaudière); **double-s. boiler,** chaudière *f* à double paroi; **subsidiary s.,** (tube *m*) bouilleur *m*; (*b*) caisse *f*, chape *f* (de poulie); boisseau *m* (de robinet); caisse (de tambour); (*c*) enveloppe extérieure; *Metall:* manteau *m* (de moule); *Aut:* calandre *f*, coquille (de radiateur); (*d*) **s. of a penknife,** platines *fpl* d'un canif. **4.** carcasse *f*, squelette *m*, coque (de navire, etc.); carcasse, cage *f* (d'un édifice); **after the fire only the s. was left,** après l'incendie il ne restait (de la maison) que la carcasse; *N.Arch:* **s. plating,** tôle *f* de bordé. **5.** grandes lignes (d'un projet). **6.** (*a*) écorce *f* (de la terre); (*b*) *Typ:* (*of electrotype*) **(copper) s.,** coquille. **7.** (*a*) cercueil *m* provisoire; (*b*) **lead(en) s.,** doublure *f* en plomb (pour cercueil); caisse *f* de plomb. **8.** *Row:* canot *m* de course. **9.** (*a*) *Artil:* obus *m*; projectile creux; projectile d'éclatement; **time s.,** obus à fusée à temps, obus fusant; **capped s.,** obus à coiffe, à ogive; **false-cap s.,** obus à fausse ogive; **long-shouldered s.,** obus à ogive effilée; **solid-headed s.,** obus à ogive pleine; **taper-based s.,** obus à culot tronconique; **thick-walled s.,** obus de semi-rupture; **armour-piercing s.,** obus de rupture; **atomic s.,** obus atomique; **gas s., chemical s.,** obus à gaz, obus chimique, obus toxique; **high-explosive s.,** obus explosif; **fragmentation s.,** obus à fragmentation; **percussion s.,** obus percutant; **shrapnel s.,** obus à mitraille; **illuminating s., star s., light s.,** obus éclairant; **incendiary s.,** obus incendiaire; **smoke s.,** obus fumigène; **tracer s.,** obus traceur; **rocket-propelled s.,** obus-fusée *m*, *pl.* obus-fusées; **blank s.,** obus à blanc; **blind s., dud s.,** obus non explosé; **blind-loaded s.,** obus inerte; **dummy s.,** faux obus; **live s.,** obus armé; **service s., live s.,** obus réel, obus de combat; **loaded s.,** obus chargé; **practice s.,** obus d'exercice; **spent s.,** obus mort; **body of the s.,** corps *m* de l'obus; **s. base,** culot *m* d'obus; **to clear (sth.) of shells,** désobuser (le terrain, etc.); **s. clearance,** désobusage *m*; **s. hole,** trou *m* d'obus; cratère *m*; entonnoir *m*; (*b*) *Pyr:* bombe (flamboyante, etc.). **10.** *Sch: A:* classe *f* intermédiaire.

shell[2], *v.*

I. *v.tr.* **1.** (*a*) écaler, décortiquer (des noix, etc.); écosser, égrener (des pois, etc.); écailler (des huîtres, des moules); éplucher (des crevettes); **to s. green walnuts,** cerner des noix; (*b*) (*with passive force*) **nuts, peas, that s. easily,** noix *f* qui se laissent écaler, pois *m* qui se laissent écosser. **2.** *A: & Lit:* couvrir (qch.) d'une carapace. **3.** *Mil:* bombarder, obuser (les positions ennemies, etc.).

II. (*compound verb*) **shell out,** *v.tr. & i. F:* **to s. out (one's money),** payer la note; débourser; casquer, éclairer; **to be shelling out all the time, always shelling out,** avoir toujours l'argent à la main.

shellac[1] [ʃe'læk], *s.* (*a*) laque *f* en écailles, gomme-laque *f*; *Ch:* shellac *m*; **bleached s.,** gomme-laque blanche; (*b*) *Aut: etc:* **gasket s.,** ciment *m* pour joints.

shellac[2], *v.tr.* (**shellacked**) **1.** traiter à la gomme-laque. **2.** *U.S: P:* **to be shellacked,** être verni, soûl; avoir sa cuite. **3.** *U.S: P:* (*a*) battre, rosser (qn); passer (qn) à tabac; tabasser (qn); (*b*) *Sp:* battre (qn) à plate(s) couture(s); vaincre, écraser (qn).

shellacking [ʃe'lækiŋ], *s.* **1. to give sth. a s.,** traiter qch. à la gomme-laque. **2.** *U.S: P:* (*a*) rossée *f*; (*b*) *Sp:* défaite *f*, raclée *f.*

shellback ['ʃelbæk], *s.* **1.** *Rept:* tortue *f* aquatique. **2.** *Nau: F:* vieux marsouin; vieux loup de mer.

shellbark ['ʃelbɑ:k], *s. Bot:* **s. (hickory),** hickory *m*; noyer blanc.

shelled [ʃeld], *a.* **1.** (*a*) *Moll: Rept: etc:* à coquille, à écaille, à carapace; testacé; *Bot:* à coquille, à écale, à gousse, à cosse; (*b*) (explosif *m*) en obus. **2.** (*of nuts, etc.*) écalé; (*of peas, etc.*) écossé, égrené; *N.Am:* **s. corn,** maïs égrené.

sheller ['ʃelər], *s.* (*a*) (*pers.*) écosseur, -euse (de pois, etc.); écailleur, -euse (d'huîtres); (*b*) (*machine*) écosseuse *f* (pour pois, haricots, etc.); égreneuse *f* (pour maïs, etc.).

shellfire ['ʃelfaiər], *s.* tir *m* à obus; **to be under s.,** subir un bombardement.

shellfish ['ʃelfiʃ], *s.* **1.** (*a*) mollusque *m* (comestible); testacé *m*; coquillage *m*; (*b*) crustacé *m.* **2.** *coll.* mollusques et crustacés; *Cu:* fruits *mpl* de mer; **bird that feeds on s.,** oiseau qui se nourrit de coquillages.

shellflower ['ʃelflauər], *s. Bot:* chélone *f*; moluque odorante.

shelling ['ʃeliŋ], *s.* **1.** égrenage *m* (de pois, etc.); décorticage *m* (d'amandes, etc.); épluchage *m* (de crevettes); écaillage *m* (d'huîtres); **s. machine,** écosseuse *f.* **2.** *Mil:* bombardement *m.* **3.** *F:* **s. out,** déboursement *m.*

shellproof ['ʃelpru:f], *a.* blindé; à l'épreuve des obus.

shell-shaped ['ʃelʃeipt], *a.* conchiforme.

shellshock ['ʃelʃɔk], *s. Med:* psychose *f* traumatique; syndrome commotionnel; **he was suffering from s.,** il était atteint de syndrome commotionnel.

shellshocked ['ʃelʃɔkt], *a. Med:* (invalide) commotionné.

shellwork ['ʃelwə:k], *s.* (décoration *f* en) coquillages *mpl.*

shelly ['ʃeli], *a.* **1.** (terrain) coquilleux. **2.** *Geol:* (calcaire, etc.) coquillier; **s. bed,** coquillart *m.*

Shelta ['ʃeltə], *s. Ling:* patois *m* des Romanichels d'Irlande.

shelter[1] ['ʃeltər], *s.* **1.** (*a*) lieu *m* de refuge; abri *m* (contre la pluie, à un arrêt d'autobus, etc.); asile *m*, refuge *m* (pour indigents, etc.); abrivent *m* (pour sentinelles, etc.); *Prehist:* **rock s.,** abri sous roche; (*b*) *Mil:* **air raid s.,** abri contre les attaques aériennes, abri de défense passive; **armoured s.,** abri blindé; **cave s.,** abri-caverne *m*, *pl.* abris-cavernes; **cut-and-cover s.,** abri à fouille ouverte; **bullet-proof, shell-proof, bomb-proof, splinter-proof, gas-proof, s.,** abri à l'épreuve des balles, des obus, des bombes, des éclats de projectiles, des gaz; **unit s., crew s.,** abri collectif; **marker's s.,** abri de champ de tir, abri de marqueur. **2.** (*a*) **under s.,** à l'abri, à couvert; (*of tree, etc.*) **to give, afford, s.,** offrir un abri; **to take s. under sth., from sth.,** s'abriter, se mettre à l'abri, sous qch., de, contre, qch.; **he took s. in silence,** il s'est retranché dans le silence; **to seek s. under a tree,** chercher l'abri d'un arbre; **to find s.,** trouver un abri; trouver asile; **to give s. to s.o.,** abriter qn; offrir un asile, un refuge, à qn; retirer qn chez soi; (*b*) *Biol:* **s. association,** faux parasitisme; **s. parasite,** faux parasite; **s. belt,** *For:* rideau protecteur; *Agr: etc:* brise-vent *m inv*; *Mil:* **s. tent,** tente-abri *f*, *pl.* tentes-abris; **s. trench,** tranchée-abri *f*, *pl.* tranchées-abris; trou *m* de tirailleur; *Nau:* **s. deck,** pont-promenade abrité, *pl.* ponts-promenades.

shelter[2]. **1.** *v.tr.* (*a*) abriter; **to s. s.o., sth., from the rain,** abriter qn, qch., de, contre, la pluie; préserver qn, qch., contre la pluie; garantir qn, qch., de la pluie; **trees that s. a house from the wind,** arbres qui défendent une maison du vent, qui protègent la maison contre le vent; (*b*) donner asile à, recueillir (un malheureux, etc.); gîter (un voyageur). **2.** *v.i.* s'abriter, se mettre à l'abri, à couvert (**from,** contre); **to s. under a tree, from the wind,** s'abriter sous un arbre; s'abriter du vent, contre le vent; **to s. from the rain,** se mettre à couvert (de la pluie).

sheltered ['ʃeltəd], *a.* abrité (**against, from,** contre); *Pol.Ec:* **s. industry,** industrie garantie contre la concurrence étrangère; **s. workshop,** atelier *m* pour les handicapés qui ont besoin de conditions spéciales.

sheltering ['ʃelt(ə)riŋ], *a.* protecteur, -trice.

shelterless ['ʃeltəlis], *a.* sans abri, sans refuge, sans asile.

sheltie, shelty ['ʃelti], *s. Scot:* (i) poney *m*, (ii) chien *m* de berger, de Shetland.

shelve [ʃelv], *v.* **1.** *v.tr.* munir, garnir, (une bibliothèque, etc.) de rayons; rayonner (une bibliothèque, etc.). **2.** *v.tr.* mettre (des livres, etc.) sur un rayon, sur les rayons. **3.** *v.tr. F:* (i) classer (une question, etc.); (ii) accrocher, ajourner, laisser dormir, enterrer (une question, etc.); mettre (un projet) en veilleuse; mettre (qn) au rancart, sur une voie de garage; remiser (qn); **my request has been shelved,** ma demande est restée, dort, dans les cartons. **4.** *v.i.* (*of surface*) aller en pente, en talus; **the shore shelves down to the sea,** le rivage s'incline vers la mer.

shelving[1] ['ʃelviŋ], *s.* **1.** (*a*) aménagement *m* des rayons (d'une bibliothèque, etc.); arrangement *m* (des livres, etc.) sur les rayons; (*b*) *F:* (i) classement *m*, (ii) enterrement *m*, ajournement *m* (d'une question, etc.); mise *f* au rancart (de qn). **2.** (ensemble *m* de) rayons *mpl*; rayonnage *m*; **adjustable s.,** rayons mobiles; **steel s.,** rayonnage en acier.

shelving[2], *a.* (*of shore, surface*) en pente; incliné.

Shem [ʃem], *Pr.n.m. B.Hist:* Sem.

shemmy ['ʃemi], *s. Gaming: F:* chemin *m* de fer.

shemozzle[1] [ʃi'mɔzl], *s. F:* **1.** (*a*) boucan *m*, chahut *m*; (*b*) querelle *f*, prise *f* de bec; rixe *f.* **2.** embrouillement *m.*

shemozzle[2], *v.i. F:* décamper, filer.

shenanigan [ʃi'nænigən], *s. esp. N.Am: F:* (*a*) mystification *f*, fumisterie *f*; (*b*) escapade *f*, fugue *f*; (*c*) entourloupette *f.*

shepherd[1] ['ʃepəd], *s.m.* (*a*) berger, pâtre; **s. boy,** petit pâtre; **shepherd's plaid, check,** plaid *m* en damier; (*b*) *Ecc:* **the Good S.,** le bon Pasteur; *B:* **the Lord is my S.,** l'Éternel *m* est mon berger; *Hist:* **the S. Kings,** les rois bergers; *Astr: Dial:* **the Shepherd's Lamp,** l'Étoile *f* du Berger; *Z: U.S:* **German s.,** berger allemand; **s. dog,** chien *m* de berger; (*c*) *Bot:* **shepherd's club,** molène *f*; bouillon-blanc *m*; **shepherd's knot,** tormentille *f*; **shepherd's purse,** capselle *f*; bourse-à-berger *f*; bourse-à-pasteur *f*; tabouret *m*, mallette *f*; **shepherd's rod, staff,** cardère poilue; verge *f* à pasteur.

shepherd[2], *v.tr.* **1.** (*a*) surveiller, garder, soigner (les moutons); (*b*) (*of priest, etc.*) soigner, guider (ses ouailles). **2.** conduire, piloter (des touristes, des élèves, etc.).

shepherdess ['ʃepədes], *s.f.* bergère.

sherardize ['ʃerədaiz], *v.tr. Metall:* shérardiser (le fer, l'acier).

sherardizing ['ʃerədaiziŋ], *s.* shérardisation *f*; galvanisation *f* au gris de zinc.

sherbert ['ʃə:bət], *s.* **1.** sorbet *m* (du Levant, etc.). **2. s. (powder),** limonade sèche (pour préparer une boisson gazeuse). **3.** (*water ice*) sorbet.

sherd [ʃə:d], *s.* tesson *m* (de poterie).

sherif [ʃe'ri:f], *s.* chérif *m* (titre arabe).

sherifate ['ʃerifeit], *s.* chérifat *m.*

sheriff ['ʃerif], *s.* **1.** *Adm:* shérif(f) *m* (représentant de la Couronne dans un comté). **2.** *Jur: Scot:* premier président (d'un comté); **s. substitute** = juge *m* de première instance. **3.** *U.S:* chef de la police (d'un comté); shérif; **deputy s.,** citoyen assermenté faisant fonction d'agent de police.

Sherpa ['ʃə:pə], *s. Ethn:* sherpa *mf.*

sherry ['ʃeri], *s.* vin *m* de Xérès; xérès *m*; **s. glass** = verre *m* à madère; **s. cobbler,** boisson frappée, composée de xérès, de citron et de sucre.

Shetland ['ʃetlənd]. **1.** *Pr.n. Geog:* **the S. Islands, the Shetlands,** les îles *f* Shetland; **S. pony,** poney shetlandais, de Shetland. **2.** *s. Tex:* shetland *m.*

Shetlander [ˈʃetləndər], *s. Geog:* Shetlandais, -aise.

Shetlandic [ʃetˈlændik], *a. Geog:* shetlandais.

shew[1,2] [ʃou], *s. & v. A: & Lit:* = SHOW[1,2].

shewbread [ˈʃoubred], *s. Jew.Rel:* pain *m* de proposition.

Shiah [ˈʃi(:)ə], *a. & s. Rel:* **S. (Moslem),** musulman (de la secte) chiite.

shibboleth [ˈʃibəleθ], *s. (a) B.Hist:* s(c)hibboleth *m*; *(b)* mot *m* d'ordre (d'un parti, etc.); **outworn shibboleths,** doctrines vieux-jeu, désuètes.

shick(ed) [ʃik(t)], *a. esp. Austr: P:* ivre, soûl.

shicker [ˈʃikər], *v.tr. & i. Austr: P:* boire; **to get shickered,** s'enivrer, se soûler.

shield[1] [ʃi:ld], *s.* **1.** *(a) Arm:* bouclier *m*; **s. bearer,** écuyer *m*; **body s.,** pavois *m*; *B:* **the Lord, our s. and buckler,** l'Éternel, notre sauvegarde *f*, notre bouclier; *(b) Her:* écu *m*, écusson *m*; *(c) Geol:* bouclier; **the Laurentian s.,** le bouclier canadien. **2.** *Tchn:* tôle protectrice; bouclier; écran protecteur; contre-porte *f* (de foyer); *Mil:* pare-balles *m inv*, pare-éclats *m inv*; *Artil:* bouclier, masque *m* (d'un canon); **apron s.,** bouclier articulé; **mud s.,** (i) *Aut:* cuvette *f* de protection (du moteur); (ii) *Min:* abri *m*, armoire *f*, à boues; *Aut:* **sun s.,** pare-soleil *m inv*; *Av:* (*of instrument panel*) **glare s.,** auvent *m* d'éclairage; *Space:* **ablative s.,** bouclier thermique; **heat s.,** (i) protection *f* thermique; (ii) *Cin:* contre-platine *f* de refroidissement; *Ind:* **hand s.,** garde-main *m*, *pl.* garde-main(s); protège-main *m inv*; **face s.,** masque protecteur; (*baseball*) **body s.,** plastron *m*. **3.** (*in spray painting*) masque, cache *m*. **4.** *(a) Hort:* **s. bud,** écusson *m*; **to graft a s. bud on a fruit tree,** écussonner un arbre fruitier; **s. grafting,** écussonnage *m*; greffe *f* en écusson; *(b) Bot:* **water s.,** cabomba *m*; **s. fern,** aspidie *f*; *Echin:* **s. urchin,** clypéastre *m*. **5.** *U.S:* plaque *f*, médaille *f*, de policier.

shield[2], *v.tr.* **1.** protéger (**from, against,** contre); couvrir (qn) de sa protection; **to s. s.o. from criticism,** soustraire qn à la censure; mettre qn à l'abri de la censure; **to s. s.o. from punishment,** faire échapper qn à la punition; **to s. s.o. from danger,** protéger qn contre le danger; **to s. s.o. with one's (own) body,** faire un bouclier de son corps à qn. **2.** *(a)* **to s. a machine from the heat,** mettre une machine à l'abri de la chaleur; **to s. one's eyes,** se protéger les yeux; *(b)* (*in spray painting*) masquer (les surfaces); *(c) El: W.Tel:* blinder (un transformateur, une valve, etc.).

shielding [ˈʃi:ldiŋ], *s.* **1.** protection *f* (**against, from,** contre). **2.** *(a)* (*in spray painting*) masquage *m*; *(b) Mil: etc:* blindage *m*.

shield-shaped [ˈʃi:ldʃeipt], *a. Nat.Hist:* clypéiforme, scutiforme, pelté.

shieling [ˈʃi:liŋ], *s. Scot:* **1.** pâturage *m*. **2.** abri *m* (pour moutons, chasseurs, etc.).

shift[1] [ʃift], *s.* **1.** *(a)* changement *m* (de position, etc.); renverse *f* (de la marée, du courant); décalage *m* (des joints d'un mur, etc.); **to make a s.,** changer de place; se déplacer; **s. of the wind,** saute *f*, renversement *m* du vent; changement de vent; *Typew:* **s. key,** touche *f* des majuscules, de manœuvre; **s. lock,** dispositif *m* de blocage; **s.-lock (key),** touche *f* de blocage; fixe-majuscules *m inv*; *NAm: Aut:* **(gear) s.,** changement de vitesse; *Atom.Ph:* **isotope s.,** déplacement isotopique; *Mus:* (*of piano*) **s. of the hammers,** déplacement *m* des marteaux; *Nau:* **s. of stowage,** désarrimage *m*; *Metalw:* **die s.,** faux rapport (en forgeage); *Ling:* **consonant s.,** mutation *f* consonantique; **s. in meaning,** glissement *m* de sens; *(b) Mus:* (*in violin playing*), (i) démanchement *m*, démanché *m*, mutation; (ii) position *f*; *(c) Astr:* **red s.,** décalage *m* vers le rouge; *(d) Cmptr:* décalage, glissement; **s. register,** registre à décalage, à glissement; **circular s.,** décalage circulaire; **ring s.,** rotation *f*, permutation *f*, circulaire. **2.** *Ind: etc: (a)* équipe *f*, poste *m*, brigade *f*, relais *m* (d'ouvriers); *Min:* coupe *f*; **day s., night s.,** équipe de jour, de nuit; **to work in shifts,** travailler par équipes; se relayer; *(b)* journée *f* de travail; **an eight-hour s.,** une période de relève de huit heures; **to work eight-hour shifts,** se relayer toutes les huit heures; faire les trois huits; **I'm on first s.,** je suis du premier huit; **night s.,** *F:* **graveyard s.,** service *f* de nuit (de police, pompiers, etc.); to **be on night s., the graveyard s.,** être de nuit. **3.** *Cost: (a) A:* chemise *f* (de femme); **to take s.o. in her s.,** épouser qn sans dot; *(b)* robe *f* fourreau. **4.** *(a)* expédient *m*, ressource *f*; **to be at one's last s.,** être aux abois, à sa dernière ressource; **to make s.,** s'arranger; se débrouiller; **I can make s. with it,** je m'arrangerai avec ça; ça ira, quand même; **we'll have to make s. without it,** il va falloir s'en passer; *(b)* échappatoire *f*; faux-fuyant *m*, *pl.* faux-fuyants; biaisement *m*; **shifts and excuses,** des échappatoires et des excuses. **5.** *F:* **to get a s. on,** se dépêcher; se magner.

shift[2], *v.*

I. *v.tr. (a)* changer (qch.) de place; remuer, bouger, déplacer (qch.); **he shifted his chair,** il a changé sa chaise de place; **to s. furniture,** remuer, déplacer, les meubles; **I can't s. it,** je ne peux pas le bouger; **to s. the cargo,** déplacer la cargaison; **to s. the responsibility onto s.o.,** rejeter, reverser, la responsabilité sur (le dos de) qn; *(b)* changer; **the river shifts its course every year,** chaque année la rivière change de cours; *Th:* **to s. the scenery,** changer le décor; *F:* **to s. one's quarters,** changer de résidence; *El:* **to s. the brush,** décaler le balai; *Rail:* **to s. all the trains one hour forward, back,** décaler les trains d'une heure; *(c) Nau:* **to s. a sail,** changer une voile; *(d) NAm: Aut:* **to s. (the gears),** changer de vitesse; **to s. up,** passer à une vitesse supérieure; *(e) v.i.* (*in violin playing*) démancher; *(f) v.tr. & i. Cmptr:* décaler; faire un décalage; **to s. in, out,** introduire, éliminer, par décalage.

II. *v.i.* **1.** *(a)* changer de place; remuer, bouger, se déplacer; **he's always shifting about, around,** il se déplace tout le temps; *Nau:* (*of cargo*) se désarrimer; **part of the load has shifted,** une partie du chargement s'est déplacée; *(b)* changer; *Th:* **the scene shifts,** la scène change; **the wind has shifted (round),** le vent a tourné, sauté, viré; **the wind shifts to the west,** le vent hale l'ouest. **2.** *F: (a)* **to s. (for oneself),** se débrouiller; trouver des expédients, se tirer d'affaire; se suffire; **he can s. for himself,** (i) il est débrouillard; (ii) qu'il se débrouille! *(b) O:* équivoquer, finasser, biaiser.

shifter [ˈʃiftər], *s.* **1.** (*pers.*) *Th:* **scene s.,** machiniste *m*. **2.** (*device*) levier *m* de déplacement.

shiftily [ˈʃiftili], *adv.* peu franchement; en tergiversant.

shift-in [ʃiftˈin], *a. Cmptr:* (caractère) de code normal.

shiftiness [ˈʃiftinis], *s.* sournoiserie *f*; astuce *f*; manque *m* de franchise; fausseté *f*.

shifting[1] [ˈʃiftiŋ], *a.* **1.** qui se déplace; **s. sand,** banc changeant; sables mouvants; *Mus:* **s. keyboard,** clavier *m* mobile (d'un piano). **2.** *(a)* (*of relationship, scene, etc.*) changeant; (*of wind, etc.*) inégal, -aux; *(b) F:* (*of pers. etc.*) = SHIFTY.

shifting[2], *s.* **1.** *(a)* déplacement *m* (de qch. par qn); *Th:* **scene s.,** changement *m* des décors; *Nau:* **s. of the cargo,** changement de l'arrimage; *Mec.E:* **s. of the belt,** changement, débrayage *m*, passe *f*, de la courroie; *Rail:* **s. track,** dérailleur *m*; *(b) Mus:* (*in violin playing*) mutation *f*, démanchement; *(c) NAm: Aut:* **(gear) s.,** changement de vitesse; **s. up,** montée *f* de vitesse. **2.** changement (de place, de direction, etc.); mouvement *m*, déplacement (de qch.); (*of cargo*) désarrimage *m*; *Cmptr:* décalage *m*; *El:* **s. of the brushes,** décalage des balais; *Aut:* **s. of the sliding gears,** coulissement *m* des baladeurs; *Ling:* **consonant s.,** mutation *f* consonantique.

shiftless [ˈʃiftlis], *a.* (*of pers.*) **1.** paresseux, mou, *f.* molle; sans énergie. **2.** peu débrouillard; godiche; qui manque d'initiative, de ressource; (*of action*) inefficace, futile.

shiftlessly [ˈʃiftlisli], *adv.* d'une manière inefficace, futile; sans initiative.

shiftlessness [ˈʃiftlisnis], *s.* **1.** paresse *f*; manque *m* d'énergie. **2.** manque de ressource, d'initiative; inefficacité *f*; futilité *f* (d'une action).

shift-out [ʃiftˈaut], *a. Cmptr:* (caractère) de code spécial.

shiftwork [ˈʃiftwə:k], *s. Ind:* travail *m* par équipes.

shifty [ˈʃifti], *a.* (individu) roublard, retors; (regard) faux, sournois, peu franc; **s. behaviour,** conduite ambiguë; **s. eyes,** yeux fuyants.

Shiite [ˈʃi:ait], *a. & s.* = SHIAH.

shikra [ˈʃikrə], *s. Orn:* épervier *m* shikra.

shiksa [ˈʃiksə], *s.f. P: Pej:* fille non-juive; goyette *f*.

shill [ʃil], *s. esp. NAm: P: (a)* baron *m*; complice *mf* d'un camelot qui attire les clients par achats simulés; *(b)* compère *m* (d'un escroc, d'un joueur professionnel); (*of gaming house*) **half the players there are shills,** la moitié des joueurs sont (des employés) de la maison.

shillelagh [ʃiˈleilə], *s.* gourdin irlandais.

shilling [ˈʃiliŋ], *s. A.Num:* shilling *m*; **to cut s.o. off with a s.,** déshériter qn; *A:* **to take the King's, the Queen's, s.,** s'engager; **a s. book,** un livre d'un shilling.

shillyshally[1] [ˈʃiliʃæli]. *F:* **1.** *a.* barguigneur, -euse; (*of policy, etc.*) vacillant, irrésolu, hésitant. **2.** *s.* barguignage *m*, lanternerie *f*, tergiversation *f*, vacillation *f*, chipotage *m*, irrésolution *f*, hésitations *fpl*, atermoiements *mpl*.

shillyshally[2], *v.i. F:* barguigner, lanterner, tergiverser; tourner autour du pot; chipoter; vaciller; hésiter (à faire qch.).

shillyshallyer [ˈʃiliʃæliər], *s. F:* barguigneur, -euse; lanternier *m*; chipotier, -ière.

shillyshallying [ˈʃiliʃæliiŋ], *a. & s.* = SHILLYSHALLY[1].

Shiloh [ˈʃailou], *Pr.n. (a) B.Geog:* Silo; *(b) U.S: Geog: Hist:* Shiloh.

shim[1] [ʃim], *s. (a) Mec.E: etc:* cale *f* de support (de rail, de moteur, etc.); pièce *f* d'épaisseur; **adjusting s.,** cale de réglage; *(b) Atom.Ph:* **s. rod,** barre *f* de compensation.

shim[2], *v.tr.* (**shimmed**) caler (un rail de chemin de fer, etc.).

shimmer[1] [ˈʃimər], *s.* lueur *f*; faible miroitement *m*, chatoiement *m*; **s. of jewellery,** ruissellement *m* de pierreries; **the s. of the moon on the lake,** les reflets *m* de la lune sur le lac; **the sun cast a s. over the sea,** le soleil faisait miroiter la mer.

shimmer[2], *v.i.* miroiter, luire, chatoyer.

shimmering [ˈʃiməriŋ], *a.* miroitant, luisant, trémulant; **s. colours,** teintes changeantes, chatoyantes.

shimmy[1] [ˈʃimi], *s.* **1.** *A: & U.S: F:* chemise *f* (de femme). **2.** *Danc: A:* shimmy *m*. **3.** flottement *m* des roues avant; shimmy.

shimmy[2], *v.i.* osciller.

shin[1] [ʃin], *s.* **1.** *(a) Anat:* (i) le devant du tibia, de la jambe; (ii) canon *m* (du cheval); **to give s.o. a kick on the shin(s),** donner un coup de pied à qn dans, sur, le tibia; *Sp:* **s. guard, s. pad,** jambière *f*; protège-tibias *m inv*; *(b) Cu:* jarret *m* (de veau, de bœuf). **2.** *Rail:* éclisse *f*.

shin[2], *v.* (**shinned**) *F:* **1.** *v.i. (a)* **to s. up a tree,** grimper à un arbre (à la force des bras et des jambes); **to s. down,** dégringoler; descendre rapidement; *(b) U.S: O:* **to s. it, to s. off,** déguerpir. **2.** *v.tr. O:* donner un coup, des coups, de pied à (qn) dans, sur, le tibia.

shinbone [ˈʃinboun], *s. Anat:* tibia *m*.

shindig [ˈʃindig], *s. esp. NAm: F: (a)* réunion bruyante, boum *m*, pince-fesses *m inv*; *(b)* fête (publique ou privée); réunion. **2.** = SHINDY **1.**

shindy [ˈʃindi], *s. F:* **1.** *(a)* tapage *m*, chahut *m*, boucan *m*, vacarme *m*; **to kick up a s.,** chahuter; faire du chahut, du tapage, du boucan; faire du train; faire un train, un bruit, de tous les diables; faire le diable à quatre; casser les vitres; faire les cent (dix-neuf) coups, les quatre cents coups; *(b)* **to kick up a s. (about sth.),** élever des protestations énergiques (contre qch.); faire de l'esclandre. **2.** *U.S:* = SHINDIG **1.**

shine[1] [ʃain], *s.* **1.** éclat *m*, lumière *f*; **rain or s.,** par tous les temps, par n'importe quel temps; qu'il pleuve ou qu'il fasse beau. **2.** (*on shoes, etc.*) brillant *m*; (*on textiles, etc.*) luisant; **to give the brass a s.,** astiquer les cuivres; **to take the s. off sth.,** défraîchir, délustrer, qch.; *F:* **to take the s. out of s.o.,** éclipser, surpasser, qn. **3.** *F:* = SHINDY **1. 4.** *U.S: F:* **shines,** tours *m*, ruses *f*, farces *f*. **5.** *U.S: F:* **to take a s. to s.o.,** s'éprendre, s'enticher, de qn.

shine[2], *v.i.* (**shone** [ʃɔn]; **shone**) **1.** (*of sun, etc.*) briller; (*of polished article*) (re)luire; **a cat's eyes s. in the dark,** les yeux du chat brillent dans l'obscurité; **the moon is shining,** il fait clair de lune; **the sun is shining,** il fait du soleil; le soleil brille, donne; **his face was shining with joy,** la joie rayonnait sur son visage; sa figure rayonnait de joie; *F:* **he doesn't s. in conversation,** il ne brille pas dans la conversation. **2. to s. on,** éclairer, illuminer (qch.); **the sun shines on the door,** le soleil donne sur la porte; **the sun shone hot on our heads,** le soleil nous tapait sur la tête; **the full moon was shining on the road,** la lune en son plein illuminait la route; **the moonlight shone into the room,** la lune éclairait la pièce. **3.** *v.tr.* (**shined; shined**) *esp. NAm:* polir, cirer (les chaussures, etc.); astiquer (les cuivres, etc.). **4.** *v.ind.tr. NAm: P:* **to s. up to s.o.,** chercher à lier avec qn; faire de la lèche auprès de qn.

shiner [ˈʃainər], *s. F:* **1.** *A:* jaunet *m*, pièce *f* d'or, d'argent; **shiners,** argent *m*, pognon *m*, braise *f*. **2.** (*pers.*) *(a)* **(shoe) s.,** cireur, -euse (de chaussures); *(b)* polisseur, -euse. **3.** *Paperm:* **shiners,** points clairs, brillants (dans le papier).

shingle[1] [ˈʃiŋgl], *s.* **1.** *Const:* bardeau *m*, aissante *f*, aisseau *m*, essente *f*, échandole *f*, tavaillon *m*; **steel s.,** bardeau en acier. **2.** *NAm:* plaque *f* (de cuivre) (de médecin, d'avocat, etc.); **to hang out one's s.,** ouvrir un cabinet, une étude. **3.** *Hairdr: A:* coupe *f* à la garçonne.

shingle[2], *v.tr.* **1.** *Const:* couvrir (un toit) de bardeaux; essenter (un toit). **2.** *A:* **to s. s.o., s.o.'s hair,** couper les cheveux de qn à la garçonne; **to s. one's hair,** se faire couper les cheveux à la garçonne.

shingle[3], *s.* galets *mpl*; (gros) cailloux *mpl*; **s. beach,** plage *f* de galets.

shingle[4], *v.tr. Metall:* cingler (le fer); faire ressuer (la loupe).

shingleback [ˈʃiŋglbæk], *s. Rept:* **Australian s.,** lézard *m* pomme-de-pin.

shingled [ˈʃiŋgld], *a.* **1.** (toit) essenté, couvert de bardeaux. **2.** *A:* (cheveux) coupés à la garçonne.

shingler[1] ['ʃiŋglər], *s.* **1.** *Const:* couvreur *m* en bardeaux. **2.** *A:* coiffeur, -euse, spécialiste de la coupe à la garçonne.

shingler[2], *s. Metall:* **1.** (*pers.*) cingleur *m*. **2.** machine *f* à cingler; cingleur, cingleuse *f*.

shingles ['ʃiŋglz], *s. Med:* zona *m*.

shingling ['ʃiŋgliŋ], *s. Metall:* cinglage *m*, ressuage *m* (de la loupe); **s. machine,** machine à cingler; **s. rollers,** cingleur (rotatif); laminoir cingleur.

shingly ['ʃiŋgli], *a.* couvert de galets; caillouteux; **s. beach,** plage *f* de galets.

shininess ['ʃaininis], *s.* luisance *f*; (*due to wear*) lustrage *m*.

shining ['ʃainiŋ], *a.* brillant, (re)luisant; **s. example of sth.,** exemple brillant, insigne, de qch.

shinny[1] ['ʃini], *v.i. NAm: F:* **to s. up a tree,** grimper à un arbre.

shinny[2], *s. NAm: F:* hockey *m* (sur glace).

Shintoism ['ʃintouizm], *s.* shintoïsme *m*, shintô *m*.

Shintoist ['ʃintouist], *s.* shintoïste *mf*.

shinty ['ʃinti], *s.* (*esp. Irish*) (jeu qui ressemble au) hockey.

shiny ['ʃaini], *a.* (*a*) brillant, luisant; **my nose is s.,** j'ai le nez trop luisant; **s. cheeks,** joues vernissées; (*b*) **clothes made s. by long wear,** vêtements lustrés par l'usage; vêtements râpés, élimés; **chairs s. with use,** chaises polies par l'usage.

ship[1] [ʃip], *s.* **1.** (*a*) navire *m*; **sailing s.,** voilier *m*, navire à voiles; **s. rigged,** gréé en trois-mâts carré; **fully rigged s., s.-rigged vessel,** trois-mâts carré; **four-masted s.,** quatre-mâts carré; **three-island s.,** navire à trois superstructures; **gas-turbine s.,** navire à turbine à gaz; **nuclear-powered s.,** navire à propulsion nucléaire; **seagoing s.,** navire de mer; **sister s., twin s.,** navire frère, jumeau; **passenger s.,** paquebot *m*; **merchant s.,** navire marchand, de commerce; cargo *m*; **container s.,** navire porte-containers, à manutention verticale; **vehicle cargo s., drive-on, drive-off s.,** navire porte-véhicules, à manutention horizontale; **trailer s.,** navire porte-remorques; de ligne cuirassé; **refrigerator s.,** navire frigorifique; **depot s., supply s.,** (navire) ravitailleur *m*; **weather s.,** navire météo(rolegique); **training s.,** vaisseau-école *m, pl.* vaisseaux-écoles; *Hist:* **long s., Viking s.,** drakkar *m*, drake *m*; **convict s.,** bagne flottant; *Navy:* **capital s.,** bâtiment grosse unité, capital-ship *m*; **radar picket s.,** bâtiment piquet radar; **landing s.,** bâtiment de débarquement; **logistic s., maintenance s., support s.,** navire de soutien logistique; *Hist:* **s. of the line,** vaisseau *m* de ligne; **to lay down a s.,** mettre un navire en chantier, sur cale; **to launch a s.,** lancer un navire; **to fit out, equip, a s.,** armer un navire; **to lay up a s.,** désarmer un navire; *Hist:* **s. money,** impôt *m* pour la construction des vaisseaux de guerre; **the ship's company,** l'équipage *f*; les hommes du bord; **ship's carpenter,** matelot charpentier; charpentier *m* du bord; **ship's boy,** mousse *m*; *A:* **s. fever,** typhus *m*; **s. to shore communications,** communications *f* entre les navires et la côte; **s. to shore telephone,** téléphone *m* bâtiment-terre; (*b*) *Fig:* **the s. of State,** le char de l'État; **the s. of the desert,** le chameau; **when my s. comes home,** dès que j'aurai fait fortune, quand mes galions seront arrivés. **2.** *F:* avion *m*.

ship[2], *v.* (**shipped**)

I. *v.tr.* **1.** embarquer (une cargaison, etc.); enrôler, embarquer (l'équipage). **2.** (*a*) *Com:* (i) mettre (des marchandises) à bord; (ii) envoyer, expédier (des marchandises, etc., par voie de mer, *esp. NAm:* par chemin de fer, par la poste, etc.); **to s. coal to France,** expédier du charbon en France; (*b*) (*with passive force*) **fruit that ships badly,** fruits qui supportent mal le transport, qui ne se prêtent pas au transport. **3.** (*of ship*) **to s. water,** embarquer de l'eau; **to s. a sea,** embarquer une lame, un coup de mer, un paquet de mer; **we're shipping water,** la mer embarque. **4.** *Nau:* (*a*) monter, mettre en place l'hélice, le gouvernail, etc.); (*b*) **to s. oars,** (i) armer les avirons; (ii) rentrer, border, les avirons.

II. *v.i.* (*a*) (*of passenger*) s'embarquer; (*b*) (*of sailor*) armer sur un navire; **to s. as cook,** embarquer comme cuisinier.

III. (*compound verb*) **ship out,** *v.i. P:* s'enfuir, décamper.

shipboard ['ʃipbɔːd], *s.* bord *m* (de navire); **on s.,** à bord.

shipbreaker ['ʃipbreikər], *s.* démolisseur *m* de navires.

shipbreaking ['ʃipbreikiŋ], *s.* démolition *f* de navires.

shipbroker ['ʃipbroukər], *s.* courtier *m* maritime.

shipbrokerage ['ʃipbroukəridʒ], *s.* courtage *m* maritime.

shipbuilder ['ʃipbildər], *s.* constructeur *m* de navires.

shipbuilding ['ʃipbildiŋ], *s.* construction navale; architecture navale.

shipload ['ʃiploud], *s.* chargement *m*; cargaison *f*; fret *m*.

shipmaster ['ʃipmɑːstər], *s.m.* capitaine, patron (d'un navire marchand).

shipmate ['ʃipmeit], *s.* compagnon *m* de bord; camarade *m* de bord; **we were shipmates in the X,** nous avons servi ensemble dans le X.

shipment ['ʃipmənt], *s.* **1.** (*a*) embarquement *m*, mise *f* à bord (de marchandises, etc.); (*b*) expédition *f*, envoi *m* (de marchandises) par mer; **overseas s.,** envoi outre-mer. **2.** (*goods shipped*) chargement *m*.

shipowner ['ʃipounər], *s.* propriétaire *m* de navire; armateur *m*; *Jur:* l'armateur (ou son représentant).

shippen, shippon ['ʃipən], *s. Dial:* étable *f*.

shipper ['ʃipər], *s.* (*a*) chargeur *m*, expéditeur *m* (de marchandises par mer); (*b*) affréteur *m*.

shipping ['ʃipiŋ], *s.* **1.** (*a*) embarquement *m*, mise *f* à bord (d'une cargaison, etc.); enrôlement *m*, embarquement (d'un équipage); **s. port,** port d'embarquement; **s. charges,** frais *mpl* de mise à bord; **s. bill,** connaissement *m*; **s. agent,** agent *m* maritime; (*for goods*) expéditeur *m*; commissionnaire chargeur; **s. office,** (i) (*for sailors*) l'Inscription *f* maritime; (ii) agence *f* maritime; bureau *m* de réception des marchandises; *Vet:* **s. fever, s. pneumonia,** septicémie *f* hémorragique; (*b*) expédition *f*, envoi *m* (de marchandises par voie de mer, *esp. NAm:* par chemin de fer, etc.); **s. advice,** avis *m* d'expédition; (*c*) montage *m*, mise en place (de l'hélice, du gouvernail, etc.). **2.** *coll.* navires *mpl* (d'un pays, d'un port); marine marchande; **idle s.,** tonnage désarmé; **s. intelligence,** nouvelles *f* maritimes; **movement of s.,** mouvement *m* maritime; mouvements des navires. **3.** navigation *f*; **dangerous to, for, s.,** dangereux pour la navigation; **s. routes,** routes *f* de navigation.

shipshape ['ʃipʃeip]. **1.** *a.* bien tenu, bien arrangé; (qui a l'air) marin; en bon ordre; fin prêt; **everything's s.,** tout est à sa place; **things are beginning to get s.,** on commence à s'organiser, à tout mettre en ordre. **2.** *adv.* en marin; comme à bord; comme il faut.

shipway ['ʃipwei], *s.* **1.** *N.Arch:* couettes dormantes, de lancement. **2.** canal *m* maritime, de navigation.

shipworm ['ʃipwəːm], *s. Moll:* taret *m*; ver *m* de mer.

shipwreck[1] ['ʃiprek], *s.* naufrage *m*; (*of ship*) **to suffer s.,** faire naufrage; **the s. of one's fortune,** le naufrage, la ruine, de sa fortune; **to make s. of one's life,** manquer sa vie.

shipwreck[2], *v.tr.* (*usu. in passive*) **to be shipwrecked,** faire naufrage.

shipwrecked ['ʃiprekt], *a.* naufragé.

shipwright ['ʃiprait], *s.* (*a*) (i) constructeur *m*, (ii) réparateur *m* (de navires, de bateaux); (*b*) charpentier *m* du bord.

shipyard ['ʃipjɑːd], *s.* atelier *m*, chantier *m*, de constructions navales; chantier maritime; chantier naval.

shiralee [ʃi'rɑːliː], *s. Austr: F:* baluchon *m* (de clochard).

Shiraz ['ʃiəræz], *Pr.n. Geog:* Chiraz *m*.

shire ['ʃaiər], *s.* comté *m*; **the shires,** les comtés centraux (de l'Angleterre); **s. horse,** (type de) cheval anglais de gros trait; *Can:* **s. town,** chef-lieu *m* de comté.

shirk[1] [ʃəːk], *s.* = SHIRKER.

shirk[2], *v.tr. & i.* manquer à, se soustraire à, se dérober à (une obligation, etc.); renâcler à, devant (une besogne); esquiver (un devoir); négliger son devoir; *Mil:* (i) tirer au flanc; fricoter; (ii) s'embusquer; **to s. school,** sécher l'école; **to s. the question,** esquiver, éluder, la question.

shirker ['ʃəːkər], *s.* renâcleur *m*; personne *f* qui manque à ses obligations, qui néglige son devoir; *Mil:* (i) tireur *m* au flanc; (ii) embusqué *m*; **to be no s.,** être franc du collier.

shirking ['ʃəːkiŋ], *s.* manquement *m* à son devoir, à ses obligations.

shirr[1] [ʃəːr], *s.* **1.** *Tex:* (*a*) tissu, ruban, caoutchouté; (*b*) fil en caoutchouc (tissé dans le tissu). **2.** *Dressm:* bouillonné *m*.

shirr[2], *v.tr. Dress:* bouillonner, froncer.

shirred [ʃəːd], *a.* **1.** *Tex:* (ruban, etc.) caoutchouté. **2.** *Dressm:* bouillonné. **3.** *Cu:* **s. eggs,** œufs (i) à la crème, (ii) au beurre (cuits au four).

shirt [ʃəːt], *s.* (*a*) chemise *f* (d'homme); **soft s.,** chemise molle, souple; **stiff s., dress s.,** chemise empesée (de soirée); **sports s.,** chemise sport; (*with short sleeves*) chemisette *f*; **sweat s.,** polo *m*; *F:* (*pers.*) **stuffed s., boiled s.,** pédant *m*; prétentieux *m*; crâneur *m*; **clean s.,** chemise propre, blanche, fraîche, **to change one's s., to put on a clean s.,** changer de chemise; **to be in one's s. sleeves,** être en bras, en manches, de chemise; **s. collar,** col *m* de chemise; **s. with collar attached,** chemise au col tenant; **s. button,** bouton *m* de chemise; **s. front,** plastron *m*, devant *m*, de chemise; **I've spilt it down my s. front,** j'en ai arrosé ma chemise; *F:* **I haven't a s. to my back, to my name,** je n'ai rien à me mettre sur le dos; **he'd give the very s. off his back,** il donnerait jusqu'à sa chemise; *Turf: F:* **to put one's s. on a horse,** parier tout ce qu'on possède sur un cheval; jouer le tout pour le tout; *F:* **to lose one's s.,** (i) tout perdre, être lessivé; (ii) *U.S:* s'emporter, prendre la chèvre; *F:* **keep your s. on!** ne vous emballez pas! calmez-vous! ne vous énervez pas! (*b*) *Arm:* **s. of mail,** chemise de mailles; (*c*) *Hist:* **Red Shirts, Black Shirts, Brown Shirts,** Chemises rouges, noires, brunes; (*d*) **s. (blouse, waist),** chemisier *m* (de femme).

shirting ['ʃəːtiŋ], *s. Tex:* toile *f* pour chemises; shirting *m*; *Cin:* **s. screen,** écran *m* de toile.

shirtless ['ʃəːtlis], *a.* sans chemise; sans même une chemise à se mettre sur le dos.

shirtmaker ['ʃəːtmeik(ə)r], *s.* chemisier, -ière.

shirtwaister [ʃəːtweistər], *s. Cost:* robe *f* chemisier.

shirty ['ʃəːti], *a. F:* irritable; en rogne; **to get s.,** se fâcher, s'emporter.

shish kebab ['ʃiʃkibæb], *s. Cu:* chiche-kebab *m, pl.* chiche-kebabs.

shit[1] [ʃit], *s. V:* **1.** merde *f*; **the s. house,** les chiottes *f*. **2.** (*pers.*) (*a*) salaud *m*, merdeux *m*; (*b*) avorton *m*. **3.** *int.* merde!

shit[2], *v.i. V:* chier.

shittim ['ʃitim], *s. B:* **s. (wood),** bois *m* d'acacia; bois de setim.

shiv [ʃiv], *s. P:* (*a*) couteau *m*; (*b*) rasoir *m*.

Shiva ['ʃiːvə], *Pr.n.,* **Shivaism** ['ʃiːvəizm], *s.* = SIVA, SIVAISM.

shivaree [ʃivə'riː], *s. NAm:* (*a*) réunion (bruyante) pour fêter un mariage; (*b*) sérénade (bruyante, dérisoire) faite à des nouveaux mariés.

shive[1] [ʃaiv], *s.* bouchon *m* (de bocal); bonde *f* (de tonneau).

shive[2], *s.* chènevotte *f*.

shive[3], *v.tr. P:* taillader (qn); marquer (qn) avec un couteau, un rasoir.

shiver[1] ['ʃivər], *s.* **1.** éclat *m*, fragment *m*; **to break, burst, into shivers,** se briser, voler, en éclats; **to break sth. to shivers,** briser qch. en éclats. **2.** pierre schisteuse.

shiver[2]. **1.** *v.tr.* fracasser (qch.); briser (qch.) en éclats, en morceaux; étonner (le silex, etc.). **2.** *v.i.* se fracasser; voler en éclats; se briser en morceaux; *Nau:* (*of mast*) se briser.

shiver[3], *s.* frisson *m*; **it sent cold shivers down my back,** cela m'a donné un frisson, m'a donné froid dans le dos; *F:* **to have the shivers,** avoir la tremblote; **it gives me the shivers to think of it,** ça me fait trembler, frémir, ça me donne le frisson, quand j'y pense.

shiver[4]. **1.** *v.i.* **to s. with cold,** frissonner, grelotter, trembler, de froid; **to s. with fear,** trembler, trembloter, frissonner de peur; **to s. like a leaf, a jelly,** trembler comme une feuille. **2.** *Nau:* (*a*) *v.i.* (*of sail*) faseyer, faséier, barbeyer, ralinguer; **to keep the sails shivering,** tenir les voiles en ralingue; (*b*) *v.tr.* faire faseyer, faire ralinguer (les voiles); déventer (les voiles).

shivering[1] ['ʃiv(ə)riŋ], *a.* tremblant, tremblotant, grelottant, frissonnant.

shivering[2], *s.* tremblement *m*, frissonnement *m*; **the s. of the wind,** la frisure du vent; **to have a s. fit,** être pris de frissons.

shivery ['ʃivəri], *a.* **1.** = SHIVERING[1]. **2. to feel s.,** avoir des frissons; se sentir fiévreux; **it gives you a s. feeling,** cela donne le frisson.

shoal[1] [ʃoul]. **1.** *a.* **s. water,** eau peu profonde; *Nau:* **to be in s. water,** raguer le fond. **2.** *s.* haut-fond *m, pl.* hauts-fonds; bas-fond *m, pl.* bas-fonds; banc *m*; (*in fairway*) sommail *m*.

shoal[2], *v.i. Nau:* (*of water, coast*) diminuer de profondeur, de fond; **the water shoals,** le fond diminue.

shoal[3], *s.* banc voyageur (de poissons); bande *f* (de marsouins); *F:* foule *f*, multitude *f* (de personnes); grande quantité, tas *m* (de lettres, etc.); **we had shoals of letters,** nous avons reçu un tas, une avalanche, de lettres.

shoal[4], *v.i.* (*of fish*) se réunir en bancs; aller, voyager, par bancs; (*of porpoises*) se réunir en bande.

shoaling ['ʃouliŋ], *s. Nau:* diminution *f* de fond; atterrage *m*; **good s.,** fond *m* diminuant régulièrement.

shoat [ʃout], *s. Husb:* goret *m*.

shock[1] [ʃɔk], *s. Agr:* moyette *f*, meulette *f*, meulon *m*.

shock[2], *v.tr. Agr:* **to s. (up),** moyetter (les gerbes); mettre (les gerbes) en meulettes, en moyettes, en meulons.

shock[3], *s.* **s. of hair,** tignasse *f*.

shock[4], *s.* **1.** (*a*) choc *m*, heurt *m*; impact *m* (d'une collision, etc.); secousse *f*, à-coup *m, pl.* à-coups; **to stand the s.,** résister au choc; *Mec.E: etc:* **rebound s.,** choc de compression; **s. absorption,** amortissement *m* (des chocs); *Aut: etc:* **s. absorber,** amortisseur *m* (de chocs); (*b*) *Geol:* séisme *m*; **distant s.,** téléséisme *m*; **slight**

(earthquake) **shocks were felt,** on a senti de petites secousses sismiques; (*c*) **s. wave,** onde *f* de choc; **acoustic s.,** choc acoustique; (*d*) *Mil: Fenc:* rencontre *f,* choc, assaut *m*; *Mil:* **s. tactics, action,** tactique *f,* action *f,* de choc; **s. troops,** troupes *f* d'assaut, de choc; force *f* de choc. **2.** (*a*) coup *m,* choc (porté par une mauvaise nouvelle, etc.); **his marriage was a great s. to her,** son mariage a été pour elle un rude coup, un coup de massue; **the news gave me a terrible s.,** cette nouvelle m'a commotionné; **it gave me a dreadful s., such a s.,** cela m'a porté un coup terrible; cela m'a tourné le sang; **the s. killed him, he died of the s.,** il est mort de saisissement; **it gave me a s. to see the change in him,** j'ai été frappé de le voir tellement changé; **be prepared for a s.,** attendez-vous à encaisser un choc, à une drôle de surprise; **to recover from a s.,** se remettre d'une secousse; **when I had recovered from the s.,** après mon premier étourdissement; **the market has not yet recovered from the s. of the budget,** le marché n'est pas encore rétabli du coup du budget; (*b*) *Med:* choc; traumatisme *m*; **(mental) s.,** commotion (mentale); **post-operative s.,** choc postopératoire; (*c*) **electric s.,** choc, commotion *f,* électrique; **to get an electric s.,** (i) être électrisé; (ii) être électrocuté; **he had received a severe electric s.,** une décharge électrique l'avait commotionné; (*d*) *Med:* **s. therapy,** thérapeutique *f* du choc; **electric s. treatment,** traitement *m* par électrochocs.

shock[5], *v.tr.* **1.** (*a*) choquer, scandaliser, effaroucher (qn); **book that shocked the public,** livre *m* qui a fait scandale; **easily shocked,** pudibond, choquable; **he's not easily shocked,** il est peu choquable; **he's easily shocked,** il s'offusque, se scandalise, d'un rien; **to be shocked at, by, sth.,** être choqué de, scandalisé par, qch.; (*b*) bouleverser (qn); frapper (qn) d'indignation, d'horreur; **a spectacle that shocked me,** un spectacle qui m'a révolté; **I was shocked to hear that. . .,** j'ai été bouleversé, atterré, choqué, d'apprendre que. . .; cela m'a apporté un coup d'apprendre que. . .; (*c*) **to s. the ear,** blesser l'oreille. **2.** (*a*) donner une secousse, un choc, électrique à (qn); (*b*) *Med:* **to be shocked,** être commotionné; souffrir de choc (traumatique).

shockable ['ʃɔkəbl], *a.* **he's easily s., not easily s.,** il est choquable, peu choquable; il s'offusque, ne s'offusque pas, d'un rien.

shocked [ʃɔkt], *a.* (*a*) (*of pers., voice, face, etc.*) choqué, scandalisé; (*b*) bouleversé; sous le coup d'une secousse pénible; atterré.

shocker ['ʃɔkər], *s. F:* **1.** (*a*) chose affreuse; **that hat's a s.,** ce chapeau est affreux; (*b*) **he really is a s.!** il est vraiment impossible, au-dessous de tout! **2.** *Publ: O:* roman *m* à gros effets, sensationnel; roman noir. **3. that was a real s.,** ç'a été une surprise pénible, un rude coup.

shockhead ['ʃɔkhed], *s.* tête ébouriffée; cheveux *mpl* en broussaille.

shockheaded ['ʃɔkhedid], *a.* à la tête ébouriffée; **S. Peter,** Pierre l'Ébouriffé.

shocking ['ʃɔkiŋ], *a.* **1.** (*of spectacle, behaviour, etc.*) (i) choquant; (ii) révoltant, affreux; **s. news,** nouvelle atterrante, bouleversante; **s. omissions,** omissions choquantes; **s. behaviour,** conduite *f* indigne; **it is s. to see. . .,** il est abominable, révoltant, de voir. . .; **how s.!** quelle horreur! **2.** *F:* (*of weather, etc.*) abominable, exécrable, très mauvais; **his writing is s.,** il a une écriture abominable; il écrit affreusement mal; **s. pain,** douleur *f* atroce. **3.** *adv. P:* **he carried on something s.!** il nous a fait une scène abominable!

shockingly ['ʃɔkiŋli], *adv.* **1.** abominablement, affreusement; **he writes s. (badly),** il écrit affreusement mal; **he plays s.,** il joue abominablement. **2.** excessivement, extrêmement; **s. dear, difficult,** excessivement cher, difficile; **s. late,** terriblement en retard; **s. bad taste,** du dernier mauvais goût.

shockproof ['ʃɔkpru:f], *a.* **1.** (*of scientific instrument, etc.*) antichoc *inv*; à l'épreuve des secousses; protégé contre les chocs. **2.** (*of pers.*) (*a*) inébranlable; (*b*) *F:* peu choquable.

shod [ʃɔd]. *See* SHOE[2].

shoddiness ['ʃɔdinis], *s.* mauvaise qualité (d'un tissu, etc.).

shoddy[1] ['ʃɔdi], *s.* **1.** *Tex:* drap *m* de laine d'effilochage, de renaissance; laine *f* de renaissance; tissu *m* de renaissance. **2.** (marchandises *fpl* de) camelote *f*; pacotille *f.* **3.** *Agr:* azotine *f.*

shoddy[2], *a.* **1.** *Tex:* (*of cloth*) d'effilochage, de renaissance. **2.** (marchandises, etc.) de camelote, de pacotille; **s. goods,** de la camelote.

shoe[1] [ʃu:], *s.* **1.** (*a*) chaussure *f,* soulier *m*; **a pair of shoes,** une paire de chaussures, de souliers; **leather, suede, shoes,** chaussures de cuir, de daim; **walking shoes,** chaussures, souliers, de marche; **lace-up shoes,** richelieus *m*; **high-heeled shoes,** chaussures à talons hauts; **evening shoes,** sandales *f* du soir; **gym shoes,** sandales, chaussons *m*; **ballet shoes,** chaussons (de danse); **s. polish,** cirage *m*; **s. cream,** crème *f* pour chaussures; **s. tree,** forme *f,* tendeur *m,* embauchoir *m* (pour chaussures); **s. rack,** porte-chaussures *m inv*; *U.S:* **s. parlor,** salon *m* de cirage de chaussures; **to put on, take off, one's shoes,** se chausser, se déchausser; mettre, enlever, ses chaussures; **I buy my shoes at Raoul's,** je me chausse chez Raoul; **the (boot and) s. industry,** (l'industrie de) la chaussure; (*b*) **to put the s. on the right foot,** s'en prendre à celui qui le mérite; **to step into s.o.'s shoes,** prendre la place de qn; succéder à qn; **he's not fit to step into your shoes,** il n'est pas de calibre à vous remplacer; **I shouldn't like to be in his shoes,** je ne voudrais pas être à sa place; **to be waiting for dead men's shoes,** attendre la mort de qn (pour le remplacer); **that's another, a very different, pair of shoes,** ça c'est une autre paire de manches; (*c*) *Bot:* **shoes and stockings,** lotier *m*; corne *f* du diable. **2.** fer *m* (de cheval); **to cast, throw, a s.,** perdre un fer; se déferrer; **my horse has a s. loose,** mon cheval a un fer qui lâche; *Vet:* **s. boil,** capelet *m,* campane *f.* **3.** *Tchn:* sabot *m,* lardoire *f* (d'un pieu, etc.); dauphin *m* (de tuyau d'écoulement); sabot, dé *m,* soc *m* (de lance); sabot, mâchoire *f,* patin *m* (de frein); patin (de traineau); bourrelet *m* de renforcement (d'un fourreau pour fusil, etc.); patin, savate *f,* semelle *f* (de crosse de piston); sabot, balai *m,* patin, frotteur *m* (de prise de courant de tramway); *Artil:* semelle (d'un affût); *Nau:* savate, semelle (d'ancre, de bigue); sole *f* (de gouvernail); *Sm.a:* **anti-recoil s.,** sabot anti-recul; *Aut:* **Denver s.,** bobinette *f*; *Veh:* **s. brake,** frein *m* à sabots.

shoe[2], *v.tr.* (*p.t.* **shod** [ʃɔd]; *p.p.* **shod;** *pr.p.* **shoeing**) **1.** chausser (qn); **to be well shod,** être bien chaussé. **2.** (*p.t. & p.p. also* **shoed**) ferrer; mettre un fer à (un cheval); **to cold s.,** ferrer à froid. **3.** garnir d'une ferrure, d'une semelle, d'un patin, etc.; saboter, armer (un pieu, un poteau, etc.); bander, embattre (une roue); **iron-shod stick,** bâton ferré. **4.** *Nau:* brider (l'ancre).

shoebill ['ʃu:bil], *s. Orn:* balæniceps *m,* baléniceps *m,* bec-en-sabot *m, pl.* becs-en-sabot.

shoeblack ['ʃu:blæk], *s.* cireur *m* (de chaussures).

shoebox ['ʃu:bɔks], *s.* boîte *f* à chaussures, à souliers.

shoebrush ['ʃu:brʌʃ], *s.* brosse *f* à chaussures, à souliers.

shoeflower ['ʃu:flauər], *s. Bot:* ketmie *f* rose de Chine.

shoehorn ['ʃu:hɔ:n], *s.* chausse-pied *m, pl.* chausse-pieds.

shoeing ['ʃu:iŋ], *s.* **1.** ferrage *m,* ferrure *f* (d'un cheval); **s. smith,** maréchal-ferrant *m, pl.* maréchaux-ferrants. **2.** pose *f* d'une ferrure, d'un patin, etc.; mise *f* d'un sabot (à un pieu, etc.); embattage *m,* ferrage (d'une roue).

shoelace ['ʃu:leis], *s.* lacet *m* (de soulier); cordon *m* de soulier; **he's not fit to tie your shoelaces,** il n'est pas digne de vous déchausser.

shoeleather ['ʃu:leðər], *s.* cuir *m* pour chaussures; cuir de molleterie; **he's as good a man as ever trod s.,** il n'y a pas de meilleur homme au monde; **you might as well save your s.,** c'est inutile que vous y alliez; autant vous épargner le trajet.

shoemaker ['ʃu:meikər], *s.* **1.** fabricant *m* de chaussures; chausseur *m.* **2.** cordonnier *m*; *Prov:* **the shoemaker's wife is always the worst shod,** les cordonniers sont les plus mal chaussés.

shoemaking ['ʃu:meikiŋ], *s.* fabrication *f* de chaussures; **the s. industry,** (l'industrie de) la chaussure.

shoemender ['ʃu:mendər], *s.* cordonnier *m.*

shoeshine ['ʃu:ʃain], *s. NAm:* **1.** (*action*) cirage *m* de chaussures. **2.** aspect luisant (de chaussures fraîchement cirées). **3.** cireur *m* de chaussures.

shoestrap ['ʃu:stræp], *s.* barrette *f* de soulier.

shoestring ['ʃu:striŋ], *s.* (*a*) lacet *m* de chaussure; *F:* **on a s.,** à peu de frais; **to set up (in) business on a s.,** s'établir avec de minces capitaux; **they're doing it on a s.,** ils tirent sur la corde; (*b*) **s. fungus,** tête-de-méduse *f.*

shogun ['ʃougu:n], *s. Hist:* shogoun *m.*

shoo[1] [ʃu:], *int.* (*a*) (*to chickens*) ch-ch! (*b*) (*to children, etc.*) allez! filez!

shoo[2], *v.tr.* **to s. (away, off) the chickens,** chasser, faire enfuir, les poules; *F:* **the police shooed everybody away,** la police a chassé tout le monde.

shoo-in ['ʃu:in], *s. NAm: F:* **1.** cheval, etc., qui va censément arriver dans un fauteuil. **2.** match, etc., censé facile à gagner.

shook[1] [ʃuk], *s. Coop:* futaille *f* en botte; botte *f* (de douves profilées et chanfreinées).

shook[2], *v.tr. Coop:* mettre (une futaille) en botte.

shoot[1] [ʃu:t], *s.* **1.** *Bot:* pousse *f* (d'une plante); rejet *m,* rejeton *m,* scion *m*; *Vit:* sarment *m,* pampre *m*; **to cut the shoots off a vine,** assarmenter une vigne; **young, tender, shoot,** tendrille *f,* tendron *m.* **2.** (*in river*) rapide *m*; étranglement *m.* **3.** (*a*) *Ind: etc:* couloir *m*; plan incliné; conduit (incliné); glissière *f*; **shaking s.,** conduit oscillant; **rubbish s.,** conduit, manche *f,* à ordures; **wooden s.,** coulisse *f*; **parcel s.,** coulisseau *m*; *Nau:* **cargo s.,** glissière de chargement; (*for escaping from fire, etc.*) **canvas s.,** sac *m* de sauvetage; **coal s.,** couloir, manche, à charbon; *Min:* **ore s.,** cheminée *f,* couloir, à minerai; (*b*) **(rubbish) s.,** dépôt *m* d'immondices; décharge publique; (*c*) *Hyd.E:* **overflow s.,** déversoir *m* (de bassin, etc.). **4. s. of ore,** coulée *f* de minerai. **5.** élancement *m* (de douleur). **6.** *Tex:* duite *f.* **7.** (*a*) (i) partie *f* de chasse; (ii) gibier (tué); (*b*) *Mil: etc:* **to carry out a s.,** effectuer un tir; (*c*) concours *m* de tir; *Sp:* **s. off,** (i) épreuve (de tir) éliminatoire; (ii) (*for a prize*) épreuve finale. **8.** chasse gardée. **9.** *F:* **the whole (bang) s.,** tout le bataclan, tout le tremblement, tout le bazar.

shoot[2], *v.* (*p.t. & p.p.* **shot** [ʃɔt])

I. *v.i.* **1.** se précipiter; se lancer; s'élancer; (*of star*) filer; **the dog shot past us,** le chien nous a dépassés comme un éclair, comme une flèche; **he shot into the room,** il est entré dans la pièce en éclair, en trombe; **children s. across streets without looking,** les enfants se précipitent pour traverser la rue sans faire attention; **to s. down a slope,** glisser à toute vitesse sur une pente; **to s. up a hill,** monter une colline à grande vitesse; **to s. through sth.,** traverser qch. rapidement, à toute vitesse; **to s. ahead, forward,** foncer, s'élancer, à toute allure; devancer les autres (concurrents); (*of ship*) courir de l'avant; **to s. ahead of s.o.,** (dé)passer qn à toute allure, comme un trait, comme un éclair. **2.** (*of pain*) lanciner, élancer; **I've got pains shooting through my shoulder,** j'ai des élancements dans l'épaule. **3.** (*of tree, bud, etc.*) pousser, bourgeonner; (*of plant*) germer.

II. *v.tr. & i.* **1.** *v.tr.* franchir (un rapide); passer rapidement sous (un pont); *Aut:* **to s. the (traffic) lights,** griller, brûler, le feu rouge; *F:* **to s. the moon,** déménager à la cloche de bois; mettre la clef sous la porte; faire un trou à la lune. **2.** *v.tr.* (*a*) précipiter, lancer (qch.); pousser vivement (un verrou); **we were shot out of the car,** nous avons été éjectés de la voiture, précipités hors de la voiture; **we shot the dirty dishes into the sink,** nous avons entassé bien vite la vaisselle sale dans l'évier; (*b*) verser, décharger, déposer, culbuter (des décombres, le minerai, etc.); **to s. coal into the cellar,** déverser, décharger, du charbon dans la cave; *P:* **to s. the cat,** vomir; dégobiller; mettre cœur sur le carreau; piquer, écorcher, un renard; renarder; (*c*) *Fish:* jeter (un filet); **to s. the lines,** élonger les lignes; *F:* **to s. a line,** (i) exagérer son importance; (ii) baratiner; (iii) monter un bobard. **3.** *v.tr.* darder, faire jaillir (des rayons, etc.). **4.** *v.tr. & i.* (*a*) décocher (une flèche); lancer, tirer (un projectile, une balle, etc.); **to s. a glance at s.o.,** lancer, décocher, un regard à qn; darder un regard sur qn; (*b*) décharger (un fusil, etc.); **don't s.!** ne tirez pas! **to s. straight,** bien viser; **to s. well,** bien tirer; **gun that shoots well,** fusil qui tire bien; **to s. wide of the mark,** (i) viser à côté du but; mal viser; (ii) être loin de la vérité; se tromper du tout au tout; **to s. at s.o., at sth.,** tirer, faire feu, sur qn, sur qch.; **to s. at s.o. with a revolver,** tirer sur qn avec un revolver; **I nearly shot at him,** j'ai failli lui tirer dessus; **to be shot at,** essuyer un coup de feu; *F:* **his secretary's there to be shot at,** son, sa, secrétaire est payé(e) pour encaisser; (*c*) atteindre, blesser (qn) d'un coup de feu; **to s. s.o. in the leg,** blesser qn d'un coup de feu à la jambe; **he was shot through the leg,** il a eu la jambe traversée, transpercée, d'une balle, par une balle; **to be shot in the arm,** être atteint (d'un coup de feu) au bras; **he had an arm shot away,** il a eu un bras emporté; *F: O:* **I'll be shot if. . .,** le diable m'emporte si. . .; (*d*) tuer (qn) d'un coup de feu; fusiller (un espion); **to s. s.o. dead,** *U.S:* **to death,** tuer qn net, raide; **to s. s.o. through the head,** tuer qn d'une balle dans la tête; **to s. oneself through the head,** se tirer une balle dans la tête; se brûler la cervelle; *Mil:* **to be (court-martialled and) shot,** être passé par les armes; **to s. a deserter,** passer un déserteur par les armes; (*e*) chasser (le gibier); **to s. sparrows,** tirer aux moineaux; **to s. a partridge,** tirer une perdrix; **to s. over an estate,** chasser dans un domaine; **I don't s.,** je ne suis pas chasseur; (*f*) **to s. a match,** concourir, participer, à un concours de tir. **5.** *v.tr. & i. Cin:* tourner (un film); filmer; *F:* **s.!** (i) allez-y! (ii) allons, accouche! **6.** *Games:* (*a*) *v.tr. & i.* **to s. a marble,** caler une bille; *Fb: etc:* **to s. (the ball),** shooter; (*b*) *v.tr.* **to s. a goal,** marquer un but; (*c*) *Golf:* **to s. a 64,** faire le parcours en 64 coups. **7.** *v.tr. Carp:* dresser, dégauchir, recaler (le champ d'une planche, etc.); équarrir (une planche) à la varlope.

III. (*compound verbs*) **1. shoot down,** *v.tr.* (*a*) abattre (qn) à coups de fusil, d'un coup de fusil; (*b*) abattre, descendre (un avion).

2. shoot off. (*a*) *v.i.* (i) partir comme un trait, comme un éclair, comme une flèche; (ii) *Sp:* passer par une épreuve (de tir éliminatoire); (*for prize*) participer à l'épreuve finale; (*b*) *v.tr.* (i) emporter (qch.) par une balle, par un obus; **he had a foot shot off,** il a eu un pied emporté, fauché, par un obus; (ii) *P:* **to s. one's mouth off,** (*α*) bavarder (indiscrètement); parler à tort et à travers; être atteint de diarrhée verbale; (*β*) révéler un secret; vendre la mèche.

3. shoot out. (*a*) *v.i.* sortir comme un trait; (*of light, water*) jaillir; **the sun shot out,** le soleil s'est montré tout à coup; **to s. out of a side street,** déboucher brusquement d'une rue latérale; **the flames were shooting out of the window,** les flammes jaillissaient de la fenêtre; (*b*) *v.tr.* (i) lancer (des étincelles, etc.); **the snake shot out its tongue,** le serpent a dardé sa langue; **the snails shot out their horns,** les escargots ont sorti leurs cornes; (ii) *F:* **to s. it out,** avoir un règlement de comptes.

4. shoot up. (*a*) *v.i.* (i) (*of flame, etc.*) jaillir; (*of ball, aircraft, etc.*) **to s. up (like a rocket),** monter en chandelle; (ii) (*of prices*) augmenter rapidement; monter en flèche; (iii) (*of plant*) pousser rapidement; (*of child*) grandir rapidement; s'élancer; **she has shot up into a young woman,** elle est tout d'un coup devenue (une) jeune femme; (*b*) *v.tr. F:* terroriser (une ville, etc.) (en tirant des coups de feu).

shooter ['ʃu:tər], *s.* **1.** (*a*) *esp. U.S:* chasseur, -euse; tireur, -euse; (*b*) *Games:* marqueur *m* de but; (*c*) *F:* **line s.,** vantard, -arde; baratineur *m.* **2.** *P:* arme *f* à feu; revolver *m.* **3.** *Cr: F:* balle *f* rapide qui rase le sol (au rebond).

shooting[1] ['ʃu:tiŋ], *a.* **1.** qui s'élance; (*of water, flame*) jaillissant; **s. star,** (i) étoile filante; (ii) *Bot:* gyroselle *f*; **s. pains,** douleurs lancinantes, fulgurantes. **2.** *F:* **s. war,** guerre chaude.

shooting[2], *s.* **1.** franchissement *m* (d'un rapide); course *f* rapide (sous un pont, etc.). **2.** (*a*) déchargement *m* (de décombres, etc.); *Fish:* jet *m* (d'un filet); (*b*) jaillissement *m* (de rayons, etc.). **3.** (*a*) décochement *m* (d'une flèche); coups *mpl* de revolver, etc., coups de feu; (*b*) tir *m* (avec une arme à feu); **s. range, ground,** (i) champ *m* de tir; stand *m* d'infanterie; (ii) polygone *m* d'artillerie; **s. match, competition,** concours *m* de tir; *F:* **the whole s. match,** tout le bataclan; **s. gallery,** tir; stand; casse-pipes *m inv*; (*c*) coup de feu (porté à qn); fusillade *f* (d'un espion, etc.); meurtre *m* (de qn) (avec une arme à feu); (*d*) la chasse (à tir); **pigeon s.,** tir aux pigeons; **clay pigeon s.,** ball-trap *m*; **the s. season,** la saison de la chasse; **pheasant s. begins on October 1st.,** la chasse aux faisans ouvre le 1er octobre; **s. rights,** droits *m* de chasse; **s. party,** partie *f* de chasse; **s. box,** pavillon *m* de chasse; **s. jacket,** veston *m* de chasse; **s. stick,** (i) canne-siège *f, pl.* cannes-sièges; (ii) *Typ:* décognoir *m*; *Aut:* **s. brake,** break *m* de chasse, canadienne *f*; (*e*) *F:* **bug s.,** recherche *f,* élimination *f,* d'erreurs. **4.** *Cin:* tournage *m* (d'un film); **s. script,** (i) *Cin: T.V:* découpage *m*; (ii) *T.V:* scénario définitif. **5.** *Carp:* dressement *m* (du champ d'une planche); **s. block, board,** planche à dresser; **s. plane,** varlope *f* à équarrir.

shoot-out ['ʃu:taut], *s. F:* échange *m* de coups de feu; règlement *m* de comptes.

shop[1] [ʃɔp], *s.* **1.** (*a*) magasin *m*; (*small*) boutique *f*; **grocer's s.,** épicerie *f*; **baker's s.,** boulangerie *f*; **shoe s.,** magasin de chaussures; **pet s.** = oisellerie *f, Fr.C:* animalerie *f*; **duty-free s.,** boutique hors taxes; **mobile s.,** camionnette-boutique *f, pl.* camionnettes-boutiques; **back s.,** arrière-boutique *f, pl.* arrière-boutiques; *O:* **s.!** il y a quelqu'un (pour servir)? **to go from s. to s.,** courir les magasins; **to set up s.,** ouvrir un magasin; s'établir comme commerçant, -ante; **to keep (a) s.,** tenir un magasin; **to shut up s.,** fermer boutique; suspendre ses activités; prendre sa retraite; *Sp:* fermer le jeu; (*of children*) **to play at (keeping) s.,** jouer à la marchande; *F:* **you've come to the right s.,** vous tombez bien; **you've come to the wrong s.,** vous tombez mal; vous vous trompez de porte; il y a erreur d'aiguillage; *F:* **all over the s.,** en, dans la, confusion; en désordre; **he leaves his things all over the s.,** il laisse promener ses affaires dans tous les coins; **s. front,** devanture *f* de magasin; **s. window,** vitrine *f*; devanture (de magasin); étalage *m*; **in the s. window,** dans la vitrine, en vitrine, en étalage; **s. assistant,** vendeur, -euse (de magasin); employé(e) de magasin; (*b*) (*as name*) maison *f*; **the Pen S.,** la Maison du Porte-Plume. **2.** *Ind: etc:* atelier *m*; **assembly s.,** atelier de montage, d'assemblage; **fitting s.,** atelier d'ajustage; **pattern s.,** atelier de modelage; **erecting s.,** halle *f* de montage; **s. erecting,** montage *m* à blanc (d'un pont, d'une machine); **machine s.,** (i) atelier de construction mécanique, de construction, de réparation, de machines; (ii) atelier d'usinage; (iii) atelier des machines; **repair s.,** atelier de réparations; **carpenter's s.,** atelier de menuiserie; **to go through the shops,** suivre un cours d'apprentissage; **s. foreman,** chef *m* d'atelier; **closed s.,** entreprise qui n'admet que du personnel appartenant à un certain syndicat; **open s.,** entreprise qui admet du personnel non syndiqué; *Cmptr:* **punch card s.,** atelier mécanographique. **3.** (*a*) *F:* bureau *m,* maison, où on travaille; la boîte; **to talk s.,** parler métier, parler affaires; (*b*) *Th: F:* **to be out of a s.,** se trouver sans engagement; (*c*) *Mil: F: A:* **the S.,** l'école *f* d'artillerie et de génie de Woolwich. **4.** *St.Exch:* introducteurs *mpl*; **s. shares,** actions *f* à introduction. **5.** *P:* prison *f,* boîte, taule *f.*

shop[2], *v.* **(shopped) 1.** *v.i.* **to s., to go shopping,** (aller) faire ses courses, des achats; (*for food*) aller faire son marché; aller aux provisions; *Fr.C:* magasiner; **I spent the whole morning shopping,** j'ai passé toute la matinée à courir les magasins, à faire mes achats, mon marché; **to s. around,** chercher des occasions. **2.** *v.tr. esp. U.S:* envoyer (une locomotive, etc.) à un atelier de réparations. **3.** *v.tr. P:* (*a*) (faire) coffrer (qn); mettre (qn) en prison, en boîte; (*b*) dénoncer, trahir, moucharder (qn).

shop(-)board ['ʃɔpbɔ:d], *s. A:* comptoir *m*; **tailor's s.,** établi *m* de tailleur.

shopfitter ['ʃɔpfitər], *s.* installateur *m,* agenceur *m,* de magasins.

shopgirl ['ʃɔpgə:l], *s.f. often Pej:* vendeuse, employée, de magasin.

shophar ['ʃoufa:r], *s. Jew.Rel:* schofar *m.*

shopkeeper ['ʃɔpki:pər], *s.* commerçant, -ante; boutiquier, -ière; **a nation of shopkeepers,** une nation de boutiquiers.

shopkeeping ['ʃɔpki:piŋ], *s.* le (petit) commerce.

shoplifter ['ʃɔpliftər], *s.* voleur, -euse, à l'étalage, à la détourne; voleur de grands magasins.

shoplifting ['ʃɔpliftiŋ], *s.* vol *m* à l'étalage, à la détourne.

shopman, *pl.* **-men** ['ʃɔpmən], *s.m.* **1.** *O:* (*a*) vendeur; employé de magasin; (*b*) commerçant. **2.** *U.S:* mécanicien (dans un atelier de réparations).

shopper ['ʃɔpər], *s.* acheteur, -euse.

shopping ['ʃɔpiŋ], *s.* achats *mpl*; courses *fpl*; **to do one's s.,** faire ses courses; (*for food*) faire son marché, aller aux provisions; **window s.,** lèche-vitrine(s) *m*; **s. street,** rue commerçante; **s. centre,** quartier commerçant; centre commercial; **s. precinct,** *Can:* **s. plaza,** centre commercial (fermé à la circulation automobile); **s. bag, basket,** sac *m,* panier *m,* à provisions.

shopsoiled, shopworn ['ʃɔpsɔild, -wɔ:n], *a.* (article) défraîchi, qui a fait l'étalage.

shopwalker ['ʃɔpwɔ:kər], *s.* (*a*) chef *m* de rayon; (*b*) inspecteur, -trice, surveillant, -ante (de magasin).

shoran ['ʃɔ:ræn], *s. Rad:* shoran *m.*

shore[1] [ʃɔ:ər], *s.* (*a*) rivage *m,* littoral *m,* côte *f*; bord *m* (de la mer); bord, rive *f* (d'un lac, d'un fleuve); (= *beach*) plage *f*; **on the s.,** sur le rivage; au bord de la mer; **house on the s.,** maison près du rivage; (*b*) *Nau:* **the s.,** la terre; **on s.,** à terre; **to go on s.,** se rendre à terre; mettre pied à terre; débarquer; **off s.,** au large; **in shore,** près de la côte; **to run a boat in s.,** pousser un bateau au rivage; **clear s.,** côte saine; (*of ship*) **to keep close to the s., to hug the s.,** côtoyer; **s. clothes,** habits portés à terre; frusques *f* d'escale; *Navy: etc:* **s. boat,** (i) (*for officers*) canot-major *m*; (ii) (*for ratings, etc.*) canot *m* de service, des permissionnaires; (*c*) **s. fauna,** faune littorale; *Crust:* **s. crab,** crabe commun; carcin enragé; **s. skipper,** talitre *m,* puce *f* de mer; (*d*) *Lit:* **distant shores,** de lointains rivages; des plages lointaines; **to return to one's native shore(s),** rentrer dans son pays natal.

shore[2], *v.tr.* (*a*) débarquer (des marchandises, etc.); (*b*) *A: & Lit:* **shored by three seas,** borné par trois mers.

shore[3], *s. Const: etc:* étai *m,* étançon *m,* appui *m*; contre-boutant *m*; *Min:* butte *f,* chandelle *f*; *N.Arch:* accore *m*; clef *f* d'accorage; béquille *f*; épontille *f*; (*of wall*) **racking s.,** contre-fiche *f.*

shore[4], *v.tr.* **to s. (up),** étayer, étançonner, enchevaler (une maison, etc.); reprendre (un édifice) en sous-œuvre; buter, contre-bouter, arc-bouter, chevaler, appuyer, mettre un appui à (un mur); étrésillonner (une tranchée, etc.); *Min:* chandeller (le toit d'une galerie); *N.Arch:* épontiller, accorer, béquiller (un navire).

shorea ['ʃouriə], *s. Bot:* shorea *m.*

shoreless ['ʃɔ:lis], *a. Lit:* (mer, océan) sans bornes.

shoreline ['ʃɔ:lain], *s.* rivage *m*; bord *m* de mer; *Geol:* **abandoned s.,** rivage fossile.

shoreward(s) ['ʃɔ:wəd(z)], *adv.* vers la terre.

shoring ['ʃɔ:riŋ], *s.* **1. s. (up),** étayement *m,* étayage *m,* étançonnement *m,* enchevalement *m* (d'un mur, etc.); *N.Arch:* accorage *m,* épontillage *m* (d'un navire). **2.** *coll.* chevalement *m.*

shorn [ʃɔ:n], *a.* **1.** *A: & Lit:* (*of head*) rasé; (moine) tonsuré; (champ) tondu. **2.** (mouton) tondu.

short[1] [ʃɔ:t], *a., s. & adv.*

I. *a.* **1.** (*in space*) court; (*a*) **to go by the shortest road, to go the shortest way,** prendre par le plus court, au plus court; prendre la route la plus directe; **a s. way off,** à peu de distance; **a s. distance from the station,** à une petite distance de la gare; **at s. range,** à courte portée; **s. steps,** petits pas; **to walk with s. quick steps,** trotter dru et menu; **to take shorter steps,** raccourcir le pas; **to tie up a dog on a s. leash,** attacher un chien de court; **a s. man,** un homme de petite taille; un petit homme; **to be s. in the arm, in the leg,** avoir les bras courts, les jambes courtes; **your coat is s. in the arms,** votre manteau est trop court des manches; *Cr:* **s. leg,** position à gauche du joueur qui est au guichet; **hair cut s.,** cheveux coupés court; **s. beard,** barbiche court taillée; *Rail:* **s. length of rail,** coupon *m*; *Nau:* **s. sea,** mer courte; (*b*) *Turf:* **s. price,** faible cote *f*; (*c*) *A.Arms:* **s. sword,** sabre-briquet *m, pl.* sabres-briquets. **2.** court, bref; (*a*) de peu de durée; **at s. intervals,** à de courts intervalles; **of s. duration,** de peu de durée; **days are getting shorter,** les jours (se) raccourcissent, (se) rapetissent; **for a s. time,** pour peu de temps; passagèrement; **in a s. time,** sous peu; bientôt; **a s. time ago,** il y a peu de temps; **a s. sleep,** un petit somme; **s. life,** courte vie; **he believes in a s. life and a merry one,** il la fait courte et bonne; il a pour principe: "courte et bonne"; **s. and sweet,** court et bon; **to have a s. memory,** avoir la mémoire courte, fugitive; être court de mémoire; *Ling:* **s. vowel,** voyelle brève; *Pros:* **s. syllable,** syllabe brève; *Fin:* **s. bills, bills at s. date,** billets *m,* traites *f,* à courte échéance; papier court; **deposit, loan, at s. notice,** dépôt *m,* prêt *m,* à court terme; *Jur:* **s. cause,** (i) affaire *f* à plaider sommairement; affaire dont les débats ne prennent pas plus de dix minutes; (ii) (en Cour de Chancellerie) affaire à plaider par observation; **s. witness list,** liste spéciale d'affaires à plaider sommairement; **to make s. work of (sth.),** expédier (qch.); faire justice de (qch.); avoir bon marché de (qch.); ne faire qu'une bouchée de (qch.); trancher (un problème, une difficulté); **to make s. work of it,** ne pas y aller par quatre chemins; mener rondement les choses; **he made s. work of his mass,** il eut bientôt expédié sa messe; (*b*) **s. story,** nouvelle *f,* conte *m*; **s. history of France,** précis *m* d'histoire de France; **Harrap's Shorter French and English Dictionary,** Édition abrégée du Dictionnaire Harrap français-anglais; **the shorter catechism,** le petit catéchisme; **s. list,** liste choisie (d'aspirants à un poste, etc.); **in s.,** bref; en un mot; enfin; en résumé; en somme; en définitive; **in s., she loves you,** elle vous aime, quoi! **he is called Bob for s.,** on l'appelle Bob pour abréger, par abréviation; **Bill is s. for William,** Bill est un diminutif de William; **a s. drink, something s.,** un whisky, un apéritif, etc. (plutôt qu'une bière); *F:* du court; (*c*) (pouls *m*) rapide; (haleine) courte; (*d*) (style) concis, serré; (*e*) (*of reply, tone, etc.*) brusque; sec, *f.* sèche; tranchant, abrupt; **to be s. of speech,** parler abruptement; parler sec; **to be s. with s.o.,** être sec, cassant, avec qn; trancher net avec qn; rebuter qn; **he was very s. with me,** il s'est montré très brusque; **s. temper,** caractère brusque, vif. **3.** (*a*) (*of weight, measure, etc.*) insuffisant; **to give s. weight,** ne pas donner le poids; vendre à faux poids; tricher sur le poids; **he never gives s. weight,** il fait toujours bon poids; **the weight is fifty grammes s.,** il manque cinquante grammes au poids; **there are three collars s.,** trois faux-cols font défaut; il me manque trois faux-cols; **it is two francs s.,** il s'en faut de deux francs; **ten pounds s.,** dix livres de manque, de moins; **I am twenty francs s.,** il me manque vingt francs; **the cashier is two pounds s.,** le caissier a une erreur de deux livres en moins; **water in s. supply,** approvisionnement d'eau réduit; *Com:* **s. delivery,** livraison partielle; **to prevent s. delivery,** éviter des manquants dans la marchandise; *Ind:* **to be on s. time,** être en chômage partiel; **little, not far, s. of it,** peu s'en faut; **he is not far s. of thirty,** il n'a guère moins de trente ans; **it is little s. of folly,** c'est presque de la folie; cela tient de la folie; **it was nothing s. of a masterpiece,** ce n'était rien moins qu'un chef-d'œuvre; **the receipts fall s. of expectations by five million,** les recettes sont inférieures de cinq millions à la somme prévue; **nothing s. of violence would compel him,** la violence seule le contraindrait; **everything s. of murder,** tout si ce n'est le meurtre; (*b*) (*of pers.*) **to be s. of sth.,** être à court de qch.; être dépourvu de qch.; **s. of petrol,** à bout d'essence; **to be s. of work,** chômer de besogne; **to be s. of staff,** manquer de, être à court de, main-d'œuvre; **I'm s. of money,** je suis à court d'argent; je manque d'argent; *Cards:* **to be s. of, in, spades,** avoir une renonce à pique; **to go s. of sth.,** se priver de qch.; **I went s. to lend you the sum,** je me suis gêné pour vous prêter cette somme; **to run s. of sth.,** venir à bout de (ses provisions, etc.); **we are running s. of provisions, our provisions are running s.,** les vivres *m* commencent à manquer, à s'épuiser; **we ran s. of butter,** le beurre vint à manquer; (*c*) *St.Exch:* (contrat, vente, vendeur) à découvert. **4.** (*a*) *Cu:* **s. pastry,** pâte brisée; (*b*) (*of metal, clay*) aigre, cassant; *Cer:* **s. paste,** pâte courte. **II.** *s.* **1.** (*a*) **the long and the s. of it,** le fin mot de l'affaire; **he knows the long and the s. of it,** il connaît l'affaire à fond; (*b*) *Cost:* **shorts,** (i) short *m*; (ii) *NAm:* caleçon *m*. **2.** (*a*) *Pros:* (syllabe) brève *f*; (*b*) *Ling:* voyelle brève; (*c*) *Artil:* coup court. **3.** *Com:* **s. in the cash,** déficit *m* dans l'encaisse. **4.** *St.Exch:* (*a*) vente *f* à découvert; **to raid the shorts,** (pour)chasser le découvert; *see also* COVER[2] 8; (*b*) (*pers.*) baissier *m*. **5.** *Mill:* **shorts,** remoulage *m*. **6.** *El: F:* court-circuit *m, pl.* courts-circuits. **7.** *Cin:* court métrage. **III.** *adv.* **1.** brusquement; court; **to stop s., to pull up s.,** s'arrêter (tout) court, net; *F:* s'arrêter pile; **to stop s. in the middle of a speech,** rester court dans un discours; **to turn s. (round),** tourner court; faire volte-face; **to take s.o. up s., to cut s.o. s.,** couper la parole à qn; **to be taken s.,** (i) être pris de court; être pris au dépourvu; (ii) *F:* être pris d'un besoin pressant, de colique. **2. the arrow fell s.,** la flèche est tombée court; **to fall s. of the mark,** ne pas atteindre le but; **to fall, come, s. of sth.,** être, rester, au-dessous de qch.; (*of pers.*) ne pas arriver, ne pas être, à la hauteur de qch.; **to fall s. of one's duty,** manquer à son devoir; **to fall s. of what is required,** pécher par défaut; **his success fell s. of my expectations,** son succès a été au-dessous de mon attente, n'a pas répondu à mon attente; **it falls far s. of it,** il s'en faut de beaucoup; **the work falls s. of genius,** ce travail n'atteint pas au génie; **to fall s. of perfection,** ne pas réaliser entièrement la perfection; **s. of murder he would do anything,** il est capable de tout sauf de tuer; **s. of a miracle we are ruined,** à moins d'un miracle nous sommes perdus; **s. of burning it,** à moins de le brûler; **to stop s. of crime,** s'arrêter au seuil du crime; **his friendship stops s. of his purse,** son amitié ne va pas jusqu'à sa bourse. **3.** *St.Exch:* (*a*) (vendre) à découvert; (*b*) (emprunter) à courte échéance.

short[2], *v.i. El: F:* = SHORT-CIRCUIT.

shortage ['ʃɔːtidʒ], *s.* **1.** (*a*) insuffisance *f*, manque *m* (de poids, etc.); **s. of staff,** pénurie *f*, manque, de personnel; **s. in the cash,** tare *f* de caisse; **to make up, make good, the s.,** combler le déficit; (*b*) *Com:* **shortages,** manquants *m*. **2.** crise *f*, disette *f*; **food s.,** disette; **s. of teachers,** crise du recrutement des professeurs; **the paper s.,** la crise du papier.

short-billed [ʃɔːt'bild], *a. Orn:* brévirostre, curtirostre.

shortbread, shortcake ['ʃɔːtbred, -keik], *s. Cu:* = sablé *m*; **strawberry shortcake,** sablé (fourré) aux fraises.

shortchange[1] ['ʃɔːt(t)ʃeindʒ], *a. F:* **s. artist,** escroc *m*, filou *m*.

shortchange[2], *v.tr. F:* (*a*) voler (qn) (en lui rendant la monnaie); tricher (qn) sur la monnaie; (*b*) rouler (qn).

short circuit [ʃɔːt'səːkit], *s. El:* court-circuit *m, pl.* courts-circuits.

short-circuit. 1. *v.tr.* (*a*) *El:* court-circuiter; mettre (une résistance) en court-circuit; (*b*) *Fig:* court-circuiter (qn). **2.** *v.i. El:* (*of current*) se mettre en court-circuit.

short-circuiter [ʃɔːt'səːkitər], *s. Elcs:* court-circuiteur *m, pl.* court-circuiteurs.

short-circuiting [ʃɔːt'səːkitiŋ], *s. El:* court-circuitage *m*; **s.-c. device,** court-circuiteur *m*.

shortcoming ['ʃɔːtkʌmiŋ], *s.* **1.** *usu. pl.* **shortcomings,** défauts *m*, imperfections *f*; points *m* faibles (chez qn). **2.** manque *m*, déficit *m*, insuffisance *f*.

short-dated [ʃɔːt'deitid], *a. Fin:* (billet) à courte échéance; (papier) court.

shorten ['ʃɔːt(ə)n]. **1.** *v.tr.* (*a*) raccourcir, rapetisser, faire une diminution à (une jupe, etc.); abréger (un texte, une tâche, *Pros:* une syllabe, etc.); **Albert is often shortened to Bert,** le diminutif d'Albert est Bert; *Mil: etc:* **to s. step,** raccourcir le pas; *Artil:* **to s. the range,** raccourcir le tir; *Row:* **to s. the stroke,** mollir; (*b*) *Nau:* **to s. sail, to s. her down,** diminuer la voilure; diminuer de voile, de toile; (*c*) *Nau:* **to s. in,** embraquer de la chaîne, de la touée; embraquer le mou (d'une amarre); (*d*) *A:* **baby not yet shortened,** petit enfant encore en vêtements longs. **2.** *v.i.* (*of days, etc.*) (se) raccourcir, (se) rapetisser; décroître, diminuer. **3.** *v.tr. Cu:* **to s. pastry,** travailler la pâte avec une matière grasse.

shortening ['ʃɔːt(ə)niŋ], *s.* **1.** raccourcissement *m*, rapetissement *m*, abrègement *m*; décroissance *f* (des jours); *Fin:* **s. of credit,** amoindrissement *m* de crédit. **2.** *Cu:* matière grasse (pour faire de la pâte).

shortfall ['ʃɔːtfɔːl], *s.* déficit *m*, manque *m*.

short-focus [ʃɔːt'foukəs], *a. Opt:* (objectif) de courte distance focale.

shorthair ['ʃɔːtheər], *s.* chat à poil court.

shorthaired ['ʃɔːtheəd], *a.* (homme) à cheveux courts; (chat) à poil court.

shorthand ['ʃɔːthænd], *s.* sténographie *f*; **s. writing,** écriture *f* sténographique; **typed s.,** sténotypie *f*; sténo *f* mécanique; **to take a speech down in s.,** sténographier un discours; **take this down in s.,** prenez ceci en sténo; **s. symbols,** caractères *m* sténographiques; (*pers.*) **s. typist,** sténodactylographe *mf*; *F:* sténodactylo *mf*; (*machine*) **s. typewriter,** sténotype *f*; **s. writer, s. reporter,** sténographe *mf*; *Jur:* **s. writer's notes,** notes *f* sténographiques d'audience.

shorthanded [ʃɔːt'hændid], *a.* à court de personnel, de main-d'œuvre, d'ouvriers; **to be s.,** manquer de personnel.

short(-)haul ['ʃɔːthɔːl], *a. Av:* **s.-h. craft,** engin *m*, avion *m*, à décollage court.

short-headed [ʃɔːt'hedid], *a. Anthr:* brachycéphale.

shorthorn ['ʃɔːthɔːn], *s.* (*a*) race bovine shorthorn: (*b*) shorthorn *m*.

shorthorned ['ʃɔːthɔːnd], *a. Z:* brévicorne; à cornes courtes.

shortia ['ʃɔːtiə], *s. Bot:* shortia *m*.

shortie ['ʃɔːti], *s. Cost: F:* chemise de nuit (etc.) courte.

shortish ['ʃɔːtiʃ], *a.* assez, plutôt, court; (*of pers.*) courtaud.

short-jointed [ʃɔːt'dʒɔintid], *a.* (cheval) court-jointé.

short-legged [ʃɔːt'leg(i)d], *a.* à jambes courtes; *Nat.Hist:* brévipède.

shortlist ['ʃɔːtlist], *v.tr.* **to s. a candidate, an applicant,** retenir une candidature, une demande.

short-lived [ʃɔːt'livd], *a.* (*of pers., animal*) qui ne vit que peu de temps, qui a la vie courte; qui meurt jeune, avant son temps; (*of joy, triumph, etc.*) bref, éphémère, de courte durée; **s.-l. success,** des succès sans lendemain.

shortly ['ʃɔːtli], *adv.* **1.** (raconter qch., etc.) brièvement, en termes brefs, en peu de mots. **2.** (répondre, etc.) brusquement, sèchement. **3.** bientôt, prochainement; sous peu, avant peu; **s. after(wards),** peu (de temps) après; bientôt après; à peu de temps de là; **s. before four o'clock,** juste avant quatre heures; **he will be leaving s. for Africa,** il va bientôt partir pour l'Afrique.

shortness ['ʃɔːtnis], *s.* **1.** (*a*) peu *m* de longueur (de bras, d'une jupe, etc.); (*b*) brièveté *f*, courte durée, peu de durée (de la vie, etc.); **s. of memory,** manque *m* de mémoire, peu de mémoire; *Pros:* **s. of a vowel,** brévité *f* d'une voyelle; (*c*) brusquerie *f* (d'humeur). **2.** manque, insuffisance *f* (de vivres, d'argent, etc.). **3.** friabilité *f*; aigreur *f* (du métal).

short-range [ʃɔːt'reindʒ], *a.* (tir, missile, etc.) à courte portée; (tir) réduit; *Meteor:* **s.-r. forecast,** prévision *f* sur période courte.

shortsighted [ʃɔːt'saitid], *a.* **1.** myope; à la vue courte; à la vue basse; **I am getting s.,** ma vue baisse. **2.** imprévoyant; peu clairvoyant; peu perspicace; **s. politics,** politique *f* de myope.

shortsightedness [ʃɔːt'saitidnis], *s.* **1.** myopie *f*. **2.** imprévoyance *f*; manque *m* de perspicacité, de prescience, de clairvoyance.

short-staffed [ʃɔːt'stɑːft], *a.* **to be s.-s.,** manquer de personnel, de main-d'œuvre.

short-stemmed [ʃɔːt'stemd], *a. Bot:* brévicaule.

short-styled [ʃɔːt'staild], *a. Bot:* (fleur) brévistyle.

short-tail ['ʃɔːtteil], *s. Orn:* brève *f*, grive *f* superbe.

short-tailed ['ʃɔːtteild], *a. Nat.Hist:* brévicaude.

short-tempered [ʃɔːt'tempəd], *a.* vif; d'un caractère emporté; à l'humeur vive.

short-term ['ʃɔːttəːm], *a.* **1.** (détenu) qui subit un emprisonnement de courte durée. **2.** *Fin:* (placement, etc.) à court terme; **s.-t. indebtedness,** argent emprunté à courte échéance.

short-time ['ʃɔːttaim], *a.* **1.** (contrat, etc.) à court terme. **2. s.-t. worker, working,** chômeur, chômage, partiel.

short-waisted [ʃɔːt'weistid], *a.* (*of pers.*) court de poitrine; qui a le buste court; (*of dress, etc.*) à taille haute.

short-weight ['ʃɔːtweit], *v.i. F:* estamper sur le poids de qch.

short-winded [ʃɔːt'windid], *a.* anhéleux, poussif; à l'haleine courte; *F:* asthmatique; (cheval) qui a du vent; **to be s.-w.,** respirer court; manquer de souffle.

shortwing ['ʃɔːtwiŋ], *s. Orn:* brachyptère *m*.

shorty ['ʃɔːti], *s. F:* homme, femme, de petite taille.

shot[1] [ʃɔt], *a.* **1.** (poisson) qui a déposé ses œufs. **2.** (lièvre, etc.) atteint, tué, d'un coup de feu; *O:* **to fall like a s. rabbit,** tomber raide. **3.** *Tex: etc:* (*a*) changeant, à reflets changeants; chatoyant, chatoyé; (velours) glacé; **s. silk,** taffetas changeant; soie chatoyante; soie gorge-de-pigeon; caméléon *m* de soie; **with s. effects,** aux reflets chatoyants; *T.V:* **s.-silk effect,** moirure *f*; (*b*) **beard s. with grey,** barbe parsemée de gris.

shot[2], *s.* **1.** (*a*) *Artil:* (i) *A:* boulet(s) *m(pl)*; **round s.,** boulet(s) rond(s); **solid s.,** boulet(s) plein(s); **spent s.,** boulet mort; **to fire hot s.,** tirer à boulets rouges; *Fig:* **as long as I have a s. in the locker,** tant que j'aurai un sou vaillant, tant que je ne serai pas à bout de ressources; **I've still got a s. in the locker,** il me reste encore de quoi voir venir, il me reste encore quelques ressources, une ressource; **without a s. in the locker,** sans un sou, sans ressources, à bout de ressources; (ii) *coll.* projectiles *mpl*; **concussion s., racking s.,** projectiles à concussion; **chilled s.,** obus fondus en coquille; (*b*) *Sm.a:* (*coll. sg. preferred to pl.*) (i) *A:* balle *f*; **wasted s.,** balle perdue; (ii) *Ven:* plomb *m*; **small s.,** menu plomb, petit plomb; **sporting s.,** plomb de chasse; dragée *f*, grenaille *f*; **bird s., dust s.,** cendrée *f*, menuisaille *f*; **to take a (flying) s. at a bird,** tirer un oiseau (au vol); *F:* **to be off like a s.,** partir comme un trait, comme une flèche; **he was off like a s.,** il est parti raide comme balle; crac! le voilà parti! **he accepted like a s.,** il a accepté d'emblée, sans hésitation; il a sauté sur la proposition; (*c*) *Metall:* grenaille *f*; **chilled s.,** grenaille d'acier trempé; **lead s.,** grenaille de plomb; **s. peened,** grenaillé (au marteau); **s. peening,** grenaillage *m* (au marteau); *Min:* **s. boring, drilling,** forage *m*, sondage *m*, à la grenaille d'acier; *Elcs:* **s. effect,** effet *m* de grenaille, de grêle (provoqué par une lampe dans un amplificateur); (*d*) *Sp:* poids *m*; **to put the s.,** lancer le poids; (*e*) *Bot:* **Indian s.,** canna *m*, balisier *m*, safran *m*, marron. **2.** (*a*) coup *m* (de feu); **cannon s., gun s.,** coup de canon; **pistol s.,** coup de pistolet; **aimed s.,** coup ajusté, coup pointé; **enfilade s.,** coup d'enfilade; **fouling s.,** coup de décrassement; **spent s.,** coup amorti; *Navy:* **warning s.,** coup de semonce; **series, set, of shots,** série *f*, succession *f*, de coups de feu; **to fire a s.,** tirer un coup de feu; **to fire s. by s.,** tirer coup par coup; **single s.,** tir *m* coup par coup; **without firing a s.,** sans tirer un (seul) coup de feu, de fusil; sans brûler une (seule) cartouche; sans coup férir; **to receive a s. wound,** recevoir un coup de feu, une blessure par arme à feu; *Artil:* **ranging s., setting s., sighting s.,** coup de réglage; **long s., over s.,** coup long; **s. that falls short,** coup court; **trial s., proof s.,** coup d'essai (de portée); *Fig:* **that's a s. at you,** ça, c'est une pierre dans votre jardin, c'est vous qui êtes visé; **parting s.,** remarque *f*, réplique *f*, qu'on lance en partant; *Ball:* **s. group,** rectangle *m* de dispersion (des coups d'une arme à feu); **horizontal, vertical, s. group,** rectangle de dispersion horizontal, vertical; (*b*) (*pers.*) tireur, -euse; *Ven:* chasseur *m*; **he's a good s.,** il est bon tireur, bon chasseur; **he's one of our best shots,** c'est un de nos meilleurs fusils; (*c*) *F:* **a big s.,** un type important, un gros manitou, *P:* une grosse légume. **3.** coup; (*a*) *Games:* **it's your s.,** à vous de jouer; **good s.!** bien joué! **to practise a new s.,** s'exercer à un nouveau coup; *Ten: etc:* **a beautiful s.,** une belle balle; **drop s.,** amortie *f*; **passing s.,** passing-shot *m*; **(match) winning s.,** balle de match; *Fig:* **I'll have a s. at it,** je vais essayer, tenter le coup; **it's worth having a s. at,** cela vaut le coup; **it came off (at the) first s.,** cela a réussi au premier coup; **he made a s. at the answer,** il a répondu au petit bonheur; **he made a good s. at it,** (i) il est arrivé fort près du but; (ii) il s'est très bien acquitté; **to make a bad s.,** (i) rater son coup; (ii) deviner faux; **to make a long s.,** (i) viser de loin; (ii) (*also* **a s. in the dark**) deviner au hasard; (iii) prendre un (gros) risque; **not by a long s.,** il s'en faut de beaucoup; (*b*) *Fb: etc:* **s. (at the goal),** shot *m*, shoot *m*; (*c*) *Fish:* (i) coup de filet; (*d*) *Phot:* photo *f*; *Cin:* (i) prise *f* de vue; (ii) section *f* de film; (iii) plan *m*; **high angle s.,** plongée *f*; **low angle s.,** contre-plongée *f*, *pl.* contre-plongées; **pan s.,** panoramique *f*; **dolly s., follow s.,** travelling *m* en poursuite; **close s.,** plan rapproché; **medium s.,** plan moyen; **close medium s.,** plan américain, italien; **long s., distance s., master s.,** plan d'ensemble; **stock shots,** séquences *f* de réserve; (*e*) *Med: F:* piqûre *f*; *P:* (*drugs*) piquouse *f*; **s. in the arm,** (i) piqûre au bras; (ii) remontant *m*, stimulant *m*, coup de fouet; **to give a s. in the arm to a flagging scheme,** donner un coup d'accélérateur, de fouet, à un projet languissant; (*f*) petit verre, goutte *f* (d'eau de vie, etc.). **4.** *Min:* (*a*) pétard *m*, mine *f*; **s. hole,** trou *m*, chambre *f* de mine; (*b*) coup de mine; **to fire a s.,** tirer un coup de mine; allumer une mine; (*c*) *Ent:* **s.-hole borer,** scolyte *m*. **5.** *Tex:* (*a*) chasse *f*; (*b*) duite *f*.

shot[3], *v.tr.* **(shotted) 1.** charger (une arme à feu). **2.** plomber (une ligne de pêche, etc.). **3.** (*a*) grenailler (le métal); (*b*) *v.i.* (*of metal*) se grenailler.

shot[4], *s.* écot *m*; **to pay one's s.,** payer son écot.

shotblast ['ʃɔtblɑːst], *v.tr. Tchn:* grenailler, décaper au jet d'abrasif.

shotblasting ['ʃɔtblɑ:stiŋ], *s. Tchn:* grenaillage *m*, décapage *m* au jet d'abrasif.

shotgun ['ʃɔtgʌn], *s.* fusil *m* de chasse; *F:* **s. wedding,** mariage forcé.

shott [ʃɔt], *s. Geog:* chott *m*.

shotted ['ʃɔtid], *a.* (*of fishing line, etc.*) plombé.

shotten ['ʃɔt(ə)n], *a.* (*old p.p. of* SHOOT[2]) *Fish:* **s. herring,** hareng guais, hareng gai.

shotting ['ʃɔtiŋ], *s.* grenaillage *m* (d'une pièce métallique).

shoulder[1] ['ʃouldər], *s.* **1.** (*a*) épaule *f*; **s. blade,** (i) *Anat:* omoplate *f*; (ii) paleron *m* (de cheval, etc.); **s. joint,** joint *m*, articulation *f*, de l'épaule; **to have one s. higher than the other,** avoir une épaule plus haute que l'autre; avoir la taille déviée, déjetée; **round shoulders,** dos rond, voûté; *Med:* **frozen s.,** périarthrite scapulohumérale; *Vet:* **s. strain,** écart *m* (d'épaule); (*of horse*) **s.-pegged,** chevillé, aux épaules chevillées; **he's got broad shoulders,** (i) il est large d'épaules, il est d'une forte carrure; (ii) *Fig:* il a bon dos; *Tail:* **line of s.,** ligne des épaules; **this coat is too narrow across the shoulders,** ce manteau est trop étroit de carrure; ce manteau est étriqué, ne dégage pas assez les épaules; **off(-)the(-)s. dress,** robe (décolletée) dégageant les épaules; **slung across, over, the s.,** en bandoulière; **s. piece,** (i) pièce *f* (d'un vêtement) qui couvre les épaules; (ii) *Artil:* crosse *f* (de canon à tir rapide); (iii) *Arm:* épaulière *f*; **s. bag,** sac *m* en, à, bandoulière; **s. belt,** baudrier *m*; **s. strap,** (i) bretelle *f*, bandoulière *f*, brassière *f* (d'un sac, etc.); (ii) (*on women's clothes*) épaulette *f*, patte *f* d'épaules; (*on women's underwear*) bretelle; *Mil: etc:* **s. strap,** *U.S:* **s. loop,** *U.S: Navy:* **s. mark, s. board,** patte d'épaule; attente *f*, épaulette; **s. flash,** écusson *m*; **s. braid,** fourragère *f*; **s. knot,** aiguillette *f*; *Av:* **s. harness,** bretelles; **to bring the gun to the s.,** épauler le fusil; **to hit out straight from the s.,** frapper directement, en plein; **to tell s.o. sth. straight from the s.,** dire qch. carrément, brutalement, à qn; **I let him have it straight from the s.,** je ne le lui ai pas envoyé dire; **to square one's shoulders,** raidir sa volonté; **to have a good head on one's shoulders,** avoir la tête sur les épaules; avoir de la tête, du bon sens; *Prov:* **you can't put an old head on young shoulders,** il ne faut pas chercher la sagesse d'un vieillard chez un jeune homme; **to stand head and shoulders above the rest,** dépasser les autres d'une tête; **s. high,** à la hauteur des épaules; **to carry s.o. s. high,** porter qn en triomphe; (*of dog*) **75 cm high at the s.,** 75 cm au garrot; **s. to s.,** côte à côte; épaule contre épaule; **to stand s. to s.,** se soutenir les uns les autres; **to lay the blame on s.o.'s shoulders,** rejeter la faute sur qn; **to put one's s. to the wheel,** (i) pousser à la roue; se mettre à l'œuvre (avec énergie); (ii) faire un effort; (*b*) *Cu:* épaule, palette *f* (de mouton, etc.); *Nau:* **s. of mutton sail,** (voile à) houari *m*; (*c*) épaulement *m* (de colline, etc.); contrefort *m* (de montagne); ressaut *m* (de terrain); **(hard) s.,** bas-côté *m* (d'une route); accotement (stabilisé); (*d*) *Gym:* **s. stand,** appui renversé sur les épaules. **2.** (*a*) **s. (piece),** (i) collet *m* (de raquette, de bouteille); (ii) *Leath:* collet (d'une peau); (iii) *Sm.a:* busc *m* (de la crosse); (iv) *Typ:* épaule (d'une lettre); (*b*) *Typ:* **s. note,** manchette *f*; (*c*) *Tchn: etc:* épaulement, arasement *m*; arrêtoir *m* (de tenon, etc.); embase *f* (de boulon, de ciseau, etc.); bourrelet *m* (de tuyau, etc.); talon *m* (de lame d'épée, etc.); épaulement (de pneu); *Nau:* épaulette (de mât); *Rail:* contrefort (de coussinet); *Artil:* ressaut (d'un projectile); *Sm.a:* **recoil s.,** tenon *m* de recul; (*d*) *Carp:* **s. cut,** arasement (de tenon).

shoulder[2], *v.tr.* **1.** pousser (qn, qch.) avec l'épaule, de l'épaule; **to s. one's way through the crowd,** se frayer un chemin, un passage, à travers la foule en poussant avec les épaules, à coups d'épaules; **to s. s.o. out of the way, aside,** écarter, repousser, qn d'un coup d'épaule. **2.** mettre, charger, (qch.) sur l'épaule; **to s. one's gun,** mettre son fusil sur l'épaule; **to s. a burden,** se charger d'un fardeau; **to s. the responsibility,** endosser, assumer, la responsabilité. **3.** *Mil:* **to s. arms,** se mettre au port d'armes; **s. arms!** portez armes! **4.** *Carp: etc:* épauler (une poutre, etc.); **shouldered chisel,** ciseau à embase.

shouldering [ʃould(ə)riŋ], *s.* **1.** bousculement *m*. **2.** épaulement *m* (d'un essieu, d'un tenon, etc.).

shout[1] [ʃaut], *s.* **1.** (*a*) cri *m* (de joie, de douleur, etc.); **shouts of laughter,** éclats *m* de rire; **give me a s. when you're ready,** fais signe quand tu es prêt; *F:* **give me a s. at eight,** veux-tu (i) m'appeler, (ii) me réveiller, à 8 heures; (*b*) clameur *f*; acclamation *f*; **they greeted him with shouts of 'long live the King',** ils l'ont accueilli aux cris de 'vive le Roi'. **2.** *F:* tournée *f* (de boissons); **it's my s.,** c'est ma tournée; c'est moi qui paie la tournée.

shout[2]. **1.** *v.i.* (*a*) **to s. (out),** crier; s'écrier; pousser un cri, des cris, une clameur; **to s. at the top of one's voice,** crier à tue-tête; **to s. for s.o.,** appeler qn de toutes ses forces, à grands cris; **to s. for help,** crier, appeler, au secours; **to s. at s.o.,** crier contre, après, qn; **to s. like mad,** s'égosiller; crier comme un sourd; *v.pr.* **to s. oneself hoarse,** s'enrouer à force de crier; (*b*) *Austr: N.Z: F:* payer une tournée (de boissons). **2.** *v.tr.* (*a*) crier (qch.); vociférer (des injures, etc.); **to s. abuse at s.o.,** crier des injures à qn; **to s. approbation,** exprimer son approbation par des cris, par des clameurs; **to s. (out) an order,** crier une commande; **he shouted out her name,** il a crié son nom; **to s. to s.o. to do sth.,** crier à qn de faire qch.; (*b*) **the speaker was shouted down,** l'orateur a été hué; (*c*) *Austr: N.Z: F:* **to s. s.o. a drink,** payer à boire à qn.

shouter ['ʃautər], *s.* crieur, -euse; acclamateur, -trice.

shouting ['ʃautiŋ], *s.* cris *mpl*, acclamations *fpl*, clameur *f*; **it's all over bar the s.,** c'est dans le sac, les applaudissements suivront.

shove[1] [ʃʌv], *s.* (*a*) *F:* coup *m* (d'épaule, etc.); poussée *f*; impulsion *f*; **to give sth. a s.,** pousser qch.; donner une poussée à qch.; (*b*) *Fish:* **s. net,** tr(o)uble *f*, caudrette *f*; crevettier *m*, crevettière *f*.

shove[2], *F:* **1.** *v.tr.* pousser (qn, un objet); **to s. off (a boat),** pousser (une embarcation) au large; déborder (une embarcation d'un navire); **don't s. (me),** ne (me) poussez pas; **to s. s.o. around,** (i) bousculer, ballotter, qn; (ii) faire marcher qn; **to s. (one's way) through the crowd,** se frayer un chemin à travers la foule; **to s. s.o., sth., along, forward,** pousser qn, qch., en avant; faire avancer qn, qch.; **to s. one's way to the front, to s. oneself forward,** se pousser (dans le monde); **to s. by, past, s.o.,** passer près de qn en le bousculant; **to s. s.o., sth., aside, away,** écarter qn, qch., d'une poussée; repousser, éloigner, qn, qch.; **he shoved the whole affair on to me,** il m'a mis toute l'affaire sur les bras; **to s. sth. into a drawer,** fourrer qch. dans un tiroir; **s. it in the box,** jette-le dans la boîte. **2.** *v.i.* (*a*) *F:* **to s. along, on,** avancer (laborieusement); se frayer un chemin; aller de l'avant; (*b*) *F:* **to s. off,** partir; décamper; se mettre en route; **I'm shoving off home,** je file, je m'en vais, chez moi; *P:* **s. off!** fiche(-moi) le camp!

shove[3], *s. Tex:* chènevotte *f* (du chanvre).

shove-halfpenny, -ha'penny ['ʃʌvheipni], *s.* = (jeu *m* de) galet *m*.

shovel[1] ['ʃʌv(ə)l], *s.* (*a*) pelle *f*; **(manure) s.,** louche *f*; **(smith's) s.,** palette *f*; **coal s.,** pelle à charbon, à feu; *Civ.E: etc:* **power s.,** pelle mécanique; pelleteur *m*, pelleteuse *f*; **steam s.,** pelle à vapeur; (*b*) *A:* **s. hat,** chapeau d'ecclésiastique, chapeau romain; (*c*) **s.-nosed,** au nez, au museau, au bec, en spatule.

shovel[2], *v.tr.* **(shovelled)** pell(et)er (le charbon, etc.); prendre, jeter, (le charbon, etc.) à la pelle; **to s. out,** (re)jeter (qch.) à la pelle; **to s. away (the snow, etc.),** déblayer (la neige, etc.); enlever (la neige, etc.) à la pelle; **to s. up,** ramasser, entasser, (le grain, etc.) à la pelle; *F:* **to s. (up) one's food, to s. food into one's mouth,** manger gloutonnement; bâfrer sa mangeaille; **to s. it down,** se goinfrer, se gaver.

shovelboard ['ʃʌv(ə)lbɔ:d], *s. A:* = (jeu *m* de) galet *m*.

shovelfish ['ʃʌv(ə)lfiʃ], *s. Ich:* spatule *f*.

shovelful ['ʃʌv(ə)lful], *s.* pelletée *f*, pellée *f*, pellerée *f* (de sable, etc.).

shovel(l)er ['ʃʌv(ə)lər], *s.* **1.** (*pers.*) pelleteur *m*. **2.** *Orn:* (canard *m*) souchet *m*.

shovelling ['ʃʌv(ə)liŋ], *s.* (*a*) **s. (up),** pell(et)age *m*; ramassage *m* à la pelle; **s. away,** déblaiement *m* (de la neige, etc.); (*b*) *Nau:* paléage *m* (du grain, etc.).

shoving ['ʃʌviŋ], *s.* (*a*) **s. (forward, out),** poussée *f* (en avant, au dehors); **s. back,** repoussement *m*; (*b*) *Nau:* **s. off,** poussée au large.

show[1] [ʃou], *s.* **1.** mise *f* en vue; étalage *m*, exposition *f* (de qch.); **s. of hands,** vote *m* à main(s) levée(s); **to vote by s. of hands,** voter à mains levées; **to be on s.,** être exposé; **the s. pupil of the class,** l'élève vedette; **s. house, s. flat,** maison, appartement, témoin, type; *Com:* **s. card,** (i) pancarte *f*; (ii) étiquette *f* (de vitrine, etc.); affiche *f* à chevalet; (iii) carte *f* d'échantillons; **s. window,** vitrine *f*, devanture *f* (de magasin); étalage; *Mus:* **s. pipes,** montre *f* d'orgue; *Tex:* **s. end of a web,** chef *m* d'une pièce de drap. **2.** (*a*) exposition (de marchandises, d'horticulture, etc.); exhibition *f* (de bêtes sauvages, etc.); concours *m*, comice *m* (agricole, etc.); **motor s.,** salon *m* de l'automobile; **boat s.,** salon de plaisance; **air s.,** salon de l'aviation; **fashion s.,** présentation *f* de collections; **dog s.,** exposition canine; **s. breeder, s. breeding,** éleveur, -euse, élevage *m*, de bêtes, d'oiseaux, etc., à concours; **s. animal,** bête à concours; *Equit:* **s. jumping,** jumping *m*; **s. jumping competition,** concours hippique; épreuves *fpl* d'obstacles; **s. jumper,** cheval *m* d'obstacle, de concours; jumper *m*; (*b*) spectacle *m*; (*at a fair*) **travelling s.,** spectacle forain; **the Lord Mayor's S.,** la procession solennelle du Lord-Maire de Londres (à travers les rues de la Cité); **outside s.,** parade *f* de saltimbanques (d'un spectacle forain); *F:* **to make a s. of oneself,** se donner en spectacle; se rendre ridicule; (*c*) spectacle, concert *m*; émission *f* (de radio, de télévision); **to go to a s.,** aller au spectacle; **to stop the s.,** être applaudi avec enthousiasme par les spectateurs; **to steal the s.,** capter l'attention, magnétiser l'assemblée; (r)emporter la vedette; **film s.,** séance *f* de cinéma; *W.Tel: T.V:* **talk, chat, s.,** interview-variétés *m, pl.* interviews-variétés; **one-man s.,** solo *m*; **s. business,** industrie *f*, monde *m*, du spectacle; **to be in s. business,** appartenir au monde des spectacles; **s. bill,** affiche (de spectacle); **s. girl,** girl *f*; (*d*) étalage; **wonderful s. of flowers,** étalage merveilleux de fleurs; **to put up a good s.,** se bien acquitter; *F:* **good s.!** très bien! mes compliments! bravo! (c'est) au poil! **our furniture makes a poor s.,** notre mobilier fait triste figure; **it was a poor, bad, s.!** c'était plutôt manqué! (*e*) *F:* occasion *f*, chance *f*; **to give s.o. a (fair) s.,** laisser franc jeu à qn. **3.** (*a*) (i) apparence *f*; (ii) semblant *m*, simulacre *m*; **s. of generosity,** affectation *f* de générosité; **to make a s. of resistance, of repentance,** faire un semblant de résistance; avoir un semblant de repentir; **to make a s. of being angry,** faire semblant, faire mine, d'être fâché; **to make a great s. of friendship,** faire de grandes démonstrations d'amitié; (*b*) parade *f*, ostentation *f*, étalage, apparat *m*, affichage *m*; **with all the s. of a state ceremony,** avec tout l'apparat d'une cérémonie d'État; **to be fond of s.,** aimer l'éclat, la parade; **to make a s. of learning,** faire parade d'érudition; **to make a s. of one's wealth, of one's knowledge,** faire étalage de ses richesses, de ses connaissances; déployer ses richesses; afficher ses connaissances; **to do sth. for s.,** faire qch. pour les apparences, pour la montre, pour la parade, pour la galerie, pour faire de l'effet; **to do things with less s.,** faire les choses avec moins d'apparat. **4.** *F:* affaire *f*; **to run the s.,** être à la tête de l'affaire; diriger l'affaire; tenir la queue de la poêle; **I run the s.,** c'est moi qui fais marcher l'affaire. **5.** (*a*) *Obst:* eaux *fpl* de l'amnios; (*b*) *Physiol:* début *m* de règles. **6.** *Min:* indice *m* (de pétrole, etc.).

show[2], *v.* (*p.t.* **showed** [ʃoud]; *p.p.* **shown** [ʃoun]; *Lit:* (*as conscious archaism*) *pr.* **shew** [ʃou], *p.p.* **shewn** [ʃoun]) **I.** *v.tr.* **1.** montrer; (*a*) faire voir, laisser voir, exposer, exhiber (qch.); **to s. sth. to s.o., to s. s.o. sth.,** montrer, faire voir, qch. à qn; **just s. me your work,** faites voir un peu votre ouvrage; **tree that is beginning to s. its fruit,** arbre qui commence à faire voir ses fruits; **to s. the colours,** déployer le pavillon; montrer son pavillon; **what can I s. you, madam?** qu'est-ce que vous désirez, madame? madame désire (quelque chose)? **to s. one's wares,** déployer, étaler, ses marchandises; **to s. goods in the window,** exposer des marchandises à la devanture; **he got a prize for the dog he showed,** il a reçu un prix pour le chien qu'il a exposé; **picture shown at the Academy,** tableau exposé au Salon de Londres; **to s. a picture, a film (on the screen),** projeter une image, un film (sur l'écran); **we're going to s. some films this evening,** nous allons passer des films ce soir; **cinema now showing** *Catherine of Russia*, cinéma qui passe, qui présente, *Catherine de Russie*; *T.V:* **this programme will be shown tomorrow,** cette émission passera sur l'écran demain; **to s. one's ticket, one's passport,** montrer, exhiber, son billet; présenter son passeport; **to s. one's cards, one's hand,** (i) jouer cartes sur table; (ii) découvrir son jeu; *Cards:* **to s. down,** mettre cartes sur table; étaler son jeu; *Nau:* **to s. a light,** (i) porter, (ii) démasquer, un feu; **to have sth. to s. for one's money,** en avoir pour son argent; **to s. one's legs,** exposer ses jambes; **to s. one's face somewhere,** se montrer, montrer son nez, le bout de son nez, quelque part; **he never shows his face at the window,** il ne met jamais le nez à la fenêtre; **he won't s. his face here again,** il ne se montrera plus ici; **colour that doesn't s. the dirt,** couleur qui n'est pas salissante; **to s. oneself,** se montrer, se faire voir; (*for inspection, etc.*) se présenter, s'exhiber; (*at a reception, etc.*) faire acte de présence; (*of thg*) **to s. itself,** devenir visible, se montrer, se manifester, se révéler; **their impatience showed itself in noisy interruptions,** leur impatience se manifestait par de bruyantes interruptions; (*b*) représenter, figurer (qch. par la peinture, par le discours, etc.); **the picture shows three figures,** le tableau représente trois personnes; **machine shown in section,** machine figurée en coupe; (*c*) indiquer; **place shown on a map,** lieu indiqué sur une carte; **as shown in the illustration,** comme l'indique l'illustration; (*of watch,* *thermometer, etc.*) **to s. the time, the temperature,** indiquer, marquer, l'heure, la température; **the thermometer shows a rise in temperature,** le thermomètre accuse une élévation de température; **the indicator shows a speed of . . .,** l'indicateur accuse une vitesse de . . .; **to s. a profit,** faire ressortir un bénéfice; **the balance sheet shows a loss,** le bilan fait ressortir, se traduit par, une perte; **the accounts s. a net profit of . . .,** les comptes se soldent par un bénéfice net de . . .; **to s. great improvement,** montrer, accuser, une grande amélioration. **2.** (*a*) **to s. s.o. the way,** indiquer, montrer, tracer, le chemin à qn; **to s. the way,** poser, planter, des jalons (dans une science, etc.); **they have shown the way to their successors,** ils ont jalonné la route à ceux qui suivront; **to s. s.o. where he is to stand, sit,** montrer à qn où il devra se tenir, s'asseoir; (*b*) conduire (qn) (pour lui montrer le chemin, etc.); **to s. s.o. to his room,** conduire qn à sa chambre; **to s. s.o. to his seat,** placer qn; **to s. s.o. round the town,** faire visiter, faire voir, la ville à qn; promener qn par la ville; **let me s. you round,** laissez-moi vous guider, vous piloter; **we were shown over the house,** on nous a fait visiter la maison; **to s. s.o. into a room,** introduire, faire entrer, qn dans une pièce; **to s. s.o. up(stairs), down(stairs),** faire monter, faire descendre, qn; **to s. s.o. in,** faire entrer qn; **to s. s.o. out,** reconduire qn; accompagner qn jusqu'à la porte. **3.** (*a*) montrer (des qualités); manifester (ses sentiments, etc.); témoigner (sa reconnaissance, l'étonnement, etc.); marquer, laisser voir, laisser paraître (ses sentiments); **to s. intelligence, courage,** faire preuve d'intelligence, de courage; **to s. unexpected daring,** déployer une audace inattendue; **to s. an interest in s.o.,** témoigner de l'intérêt à qn; **to s. contempt for s.o.,** témoigner du dédain à qn; **to s. one's contempt for s.o.,** laisser paraître son dédain pour qn; **to s. zeal in doing sth.,** il a apporté du zèle à faire qch.; faire preuve de zèle; **to s. a taste for sth.,** témoigner d'un goût pour qch.; **his face showed his delight,** son visage annonçait sa joie; **he has more knowledge than he cares to s.,** il a plus de connaissances qu'il n'en laisse paraître; **choice that shows s.o.'s taste,** choix qui déclare, qui accuse, les goûts de qn; **he showed no sign of having heard anything,** il n'a manifesté en aucune façon avoir rien entendu; **he shows his age,** il accuse, il fait (bien), son âge; **to s. one's true character,** se démasquer; **to s. oneself (to be) a coward,** se montrer lâche; **he showed himself a first-rate leader,** il s'est révélé excellent chef; **he's shown himself to be a practical man,** il s'est montré homme pratique; **time will s.,** qui vivra verra; (*b*) révéler, montrer, accuser, faire ressortir (qch.); **his round shoulders s. his age,** son dos voûté accuse, révèle, son âge; **garment that shows the figure,** vêtement qui dessine la taille; (*c*) prouver, démontrer (que le triangle ABC est égal au triangle DEF, etc.); **to s. s.o. to be a rogue,** prouver la coquinerie de qn; **a mere glance will s. that . . .,** il suffit d'un coup d'œil pour se rendre compte que . . .; **it, which, only, all, goes to s. that . . .,** ce qui prouve que . . .; *F:* **I'll s. you!** je vous apprendrai! **to s. cause, reason,** exposer ses raisons; offrir des raisons valables; *Jur:* **to s. one's right,** faire apparoir de son bon droit. **II.** *v.i.* se montrer, (ap)paraître, transparaître, se voir; se laisser voir; **the buds are beginning to s.,** les bourgeons commencent à se montrer, à paraître; **your slip's showing,** votre jupon dépasse; **his veins s. under the skin,** ses veines apparaissent, transparaissent, sous la peau; **that stain will never s.,** cette tache ne se verra aucunement; **it shows in your face,** cela se voit, se lit, sur votre visage; **to s. to advantage,** faire bonne figure; *F:* **to s. willing,** faire preuve de bonne volonté. **III.** (*compound verbs*) **1. show off.** (*a*) *v.tr.* (i) faire valoir, mettre en valeur (qch.); **setting that shows off a stone,** monture qui fait valoir, qui rehausse, un bijou; **coat that shows off the figure well,** manteau qui marque, dessine, bien la taille; (ii) faire parade, montre, étalage, spectacle, de (qch.); mettre (des marchandises) en évidence; **he likes to s. off his strength,** il aime à faire parade de sa force; **to s. off one's daughter,** faire briller sa fille; mettre sa fille en avant; (*b*) *v.i.* parader, poser; se pavaner; aimer, chercher, à épater; se donner des airs; s'étaler, s'afficher; faire de l'épate; **to s. off in front of s.o.,** chercher à épater qn; **stop showing off!** cessez de faire l'important, de vous donner des airs! **2. show up.** (*a*) *v.tr.* (i) faire connaître (qn); démasquer, dénoncer (un imposteur, etc.); dévoiler (une imposture); révéler (un défaut, etc.); **to s. up s.o.'s faults,** mettre en évidence les défauts de qn; (ii) attirer l'attention sur (qn); **he's been shown up,** le voilà grillé; (*b*) *v.i.* (i) se dessiner, se détacher, ressortir (sur un fond); se silhouetter (à, sur, l'horizon); *Sp: etc:* **to s. up well, badly,** se bien, mal, acquitter; (ii) *F:* se présenter, être présent; faire acte de présence; **they'll s. up at twelve,** ils s'amèneront à midi.

showbiz ['ʃoubiz], *s. F:* industrie *f*, monde *m*, du spectacle.

showboard ['ʃoubɔ:d], *s.* planche *f* à affiche; écriteau *m* d'annonces.

showboat ['ʃoubout], *s. U.S: A:* bateau-théâtre *m, pl.* bateaux-théâtres (sur le Mississipi).

showbread ['ʃoubred], *s. Jew.Rel:* pain *m* de proposition.

showcase ['ʃoukeis], *s. Com:* vitrine *f*, montre *f*.

showdown ['ʃoudaun], *s.* **1.** *Cards:* étalement *m* de son jeu (sur la table). **2.** (*a*) révélation *f*, mise *f* au point, à jour, de ses projets, de ses capacités, de ses exploits, etc.; **to call for a s.,** sommer qn de mettre cartes sur table; (*b*) *F:* confrontation *f*, déballage *m*; **he forced him to a s.,** il l'a forcé à montrer ses cartes, à abattre son jeu, à découvrir son jeu; **if it comes to a s.,** s'il faut en venir au fait.

shower[1] ['ʃouər], *s.* exposant, -ante (à une exposition, etc.); exhibiteur, -trice; exposeur *m*, montreur, -euse.

shower[2] ['ʃauər], *s.* **1.** (*a*) averse *f*; giboulée *f*; grain *m*; **(heavy) s.,** ondée *f*; (*b*) **s. of blows, of stones,** volée *f*, grêle *f*, pluie *f*, de coups; volée de pierres; **s. of sparks,** gerbe *f* d'étincelles; **s. of insults,** avalanche *f* d'injures. **2.** *Toil:* douche *f*; **hot and cold s.,** douche écossaise; **to have, to take, a s.,** prendre une douche, se doucher; **s. unit,** bloc-douche *m, pl.* blocs-douches; **s. cabinet,** cabine de douche; **s. attachment,** douchette *f*; *O:* **s. bath,** bain-douche *m, pl.* bains-douches. **3.** (*a*) *Astr:* essaim *m* (de météores); (*b*) *Ph:* **(cosmic ray) s.,** gerbe cascade. **4.** *NAm: F:* réception *f* où chacun apporte un cadeau (de noce, etc.). **5.** *F:* **what a s.!** quelle bande, quel tas, de crétins!

shower[3] ['ʃauər]. **1.** *v.tr.* (*a*) verser; faire tomber (de l'eau, etc.) par ondées; (*b*) **to s. blows on s.o.,** faire pleuvoir des coups sur qn; **to s. invitations on s.o., to s. s.o. with invitations,** accabler qn d'invitations; **to s. gifts, honours, on s.o.,** combler qn de cadeaux, d'honneurs; **to s. money on s.o.,** arroser qn (d'une pluie d'or); **questions were showered on him,** on l'a assailli de questions. **2.** *v.i.* (*a*) pleuvoir; (*of rain*) tomber par ondées; **congratulations showered (down) on her,** les félicitations pleuvaient sur elle; on l'accablait de félicitations; (*b*) *Toil:* prendre une douche, se doucher.

showerproof ['ʃauəpru:f], *a. Tex:* imperméabilisé.

showery ['ʃauəri], *a.* (temps, jour) de giboulées, à ondées; (temps) pluvieux; **it's s. (weather),** il pleut par ondées; le temps est à l'averse.

showground ['ʃougraund], *s.* (*a*) champ *m* de foire, de comice agricole; (*b*) terrain *m* de concours hippique, etc.

showily ['ʃouili], *adv.* (habillé, etc.) d'une façon prétentieuse, voyante, criarde; avec ostentation; (meublé) avec un luxe criard, tapageur.

showiness ['ʃouinis], *s.* prétention *f*, clinquant *m*, faste *m*; luxe criard, tapageur; ostentation *f*; (*of colours*) caractère voyant.

showing ['ʃouiŋ], *s.* **1.** exposition *f*, mise *f* en vue, représentation *f* (de qch.); **on this s.,** si l'on envisage ainsi les faits; **on your own s.,** à ce que vous dites, vous faites, vous-même; *Cin:* **first s.,** en première vision. **2.** manifestation *f*, témoignage *m* (de ses sentiments, etc.). **3.** démonstration *f*, preuve *f* (d'un fait).

showman, *pl.* **-men** ['ʃoumən], *s.m.* (*a*) directeur, metteur en scène (d'un spectacle); (*at a fair*) forain; (*b*) montreur de curiosités (à une foire, etc.).

showmanship ['ʃoumənʃip], *s.* art *m* de la mise en scène.

show-off ['ʃouɔf], *s.* **1.** exposition *f*, manifestation *f* (de qch.). **2.** *F:* (*pers.*) poseur, -euse; m'as-tu-vu *m inv*; comédien, -ienne.

showpiece ['ʃoupi:s], *s.* article *m* d'exposition, de vitrine; objet *m*, monument *m*, etc., de grand intérêt.

showplace ['ʃoupleis], *s.* endroit *m* pittoresque; monument *m*, d'intérêt architectural, touristique.

showring ['ʃouriŋ], *s.* arène *f* (i) d'exposition, (ii) de vente (de chevaux, etc.), (iii) de concours hippique, etc.

showroom ['ʃouru:m], *s.* salle *f*, salon *m*, magasin *m*, d'exposition (d'une maison de commerce); salle de démonstration (de voitures, etc.).

showstopper ['ʃoustɔpər], *s. F:* acteur, -trice, chanteur, -euse, numéro *m*, etc., applaudi(e) avec enthousiasme par les spectateurs.

showy ['ʃoui], *a.* (*of appearance, dress, decoration, etc.*) prétentieux, voyant; tapageur; tape-à-l'œil *inv*; qui a de l'éclat; **s. hat,** chapeau criard; **s. patriotism,** patriotisme *m* de parade.

shrapnel ['ʃræpn(ə)l], *s. Artil:* **1.** shrapnel *m*; obus *m* à balles, à mitraille; **base burster s.,** shrapnel à charge arrière; **central burster s.,** shrapnel à charge centrale; **front burster s.,** shrapnel à charge avant; **s. bullet,** balle *f* de shrapnel; **s. firing,** tir *m* (d'obus) à balles, à mitraille. **2.** éclats *mpl* d'obus.

shred[1] [ʃred], *s.* filament *m*, fil *m*, brin *m*; lambeau *m*, fragment *m* (de tissu, etc.); petit morceau (de viande, etc.); **to cut sth. into shreds,** couper qch. en petites languettes; **to tear sth. (in)to shreds,** déchiqueter, lacérer, qch.; mettre qch. en lambeaux; **to tear s.o.'s reputation, s.o., to shreds,** déchirer qn à belles dents; démolir qn; **her dress was all in shreds,** sa robe était tout en lambeaux; **meat cooked to shreds,** viande en charpie, en marmelade; **there isn't a s. of evidence,** il n'y a pas la moindre preuve; **not a s. of truth,** pas un grain de vérité.

shred[2], *v.tr.* **(shredded)** couper (qch.) par bandes, par petits morceaux en long, par languettes; déchirer (qch.) en lambeaux; déchiqueter, lacérer (du tissu, etc.); défibrer (la canne à sucre); *Cu:* râper (des légumes); *Paperm:* délisser, effilocher (des chiffons).

shredder ['ʃredər], *s.* **1.** (*pers.*) défibreur, -euse; *Paperm:* délisseur, -euse. **2.** (*device*) (*a*) *Dom.Ec:* **vegetable s.,** coupe-légumes *m inv*; râpe *f* à légumes; *Sug.-R:* **cane s.,** défibreur *m*; (*b*) (*for papers, etc.*) effilocheuse *f*.

shredding ['ʃrediŋ], *s.* déchiquetage *m* (du tissu, etc.); défibrage *m* (de la canne à sucre); *Cu:* râpage *m* (de légumes); *Paperm:* délissage *m*, effilochage *m* (de chiffons).

shrew[1] [ʃru:], *s. Z:* musaraigne *f*; **water s.,** musaraigne aquatique, souris *f* d'eau; **common s.,** musette *f*; **elephant s.,** macroscélide *m*, rat *m* à trompe; **African elephant s.,** rat à trompe africain; **forest elephant s.,** pétrodrome *m*; **Etruscan s.,** pachyure *f* étrusque; **otter s.,** potamogale *m*; **dusky s.,** musaraigne obscure; **Chinese s. hedgehog,** gymnure chinois; **the shrews,** les soricidés *m*; **the tree shrews,** les tupaïdés *m*, les tupaiidés *m*.

shrew[2], *s.f.* femme criarde, querelleuse, acariâtre; mégère, chipie, harpie; pie-grièche, *pl.* pies-grièches; teigne.

shrewd [ʃru:d], *a.* **1.** (*of pers., etc.*) sagace, perspicace, fin, clairvoyant; qui a du flair, du nez; qui a le nez fin, creux; **s. businessman,** homme d'affaires d'une grande acuité; **s. reasoning,** raisonnement judicieux; **s. wit,** esprit fin, subtil; **he's a s. man,** c'est une fine mouche; **s. answer,** réponse adroite. **2.** *A: & Lit:* (*a*) (*of cold, weather, etc.*) sévère, âpre; (*b*) **s. blow,** coup bien placé; **s. thrust,** critique qui porte juste; trait acéré. **3.** (*intensive*) **I've got a s. idea that . . .,** je suis porté à croire, il est fort probable, que . . .; **to make a s. guess,** avoir de fortes raisons pour deviner.

shrewdly ['ʃru:dli], *adv.* sagacement, finement; avec finesse; avec perspicacité.

shrewdness ['ʃru:dnis], *s.* sagacité *f*, perspicacité *f*; pénétration *f* d'esprit; clairvoyance *f*, acuité *f*, finesse *f*.

shrewish ['ʃru:iʃ], *a.* (femme) acariâtre, querelleuse, grondeuse, criarde.

shrewishly ['ʃru:iʃli], *adv.* d'une façon acariâtre, querelleuse, grondeuse; en mégère.

shrewishness ['ʃru:iʃnis], *s.* humeur acariâtre, querelleuse.

shrewmouse, *pl.* **-mice** ['ʃru:maus, -mais], *s. Z:* = SHREW[1].

shriek[1] ['ʃri:k], *s.* **1.** cri déchirant; cri perçant (d'une personne, d'un animal); **s. of anguish,** cri d'angoisse; **shrieks of laughter,** grands éclats de rire; **the s. of a railway engine,** le cri strident, le sifflement, d'une locomotive; **to give a s.,** pousser un cri (perçant). **2.** *F:* point *m* d'exclamation.

shriek[2]. **1.** *v.i.* pousser un cri aigu, des cris aigus; hurler; (*of railway engine*) siffler, déchirer l'air; **to s. at the top of one's voice,** crier à tue-tête; pousser des cris d'orfraie; **to s. (out) with pain,** crier de douleur; **to s. with horror,** pousser un cri d'horreur; **to s. with laughter,** rire aux éclats; s'esclaffer, pouffer (de rire); **colours that s. at one another,** couleurs qui hurlent (ensemble). **2.** *v.tr.* **to s. (out) a warning,** avertir qn d'un cri; pousser un cri d'avertissement.

shrieking[1] ['ʃri:kiŋ], *a.* qui pousse des cris aigus, éperdus; (locomotive) sifflant, qui déchire l'air; **s. colours,** couleurs criardes, qui hurlent (ensemble).

shrieking[2], *s.* cris stridents; sifflement *m* (d'une locomotive); **the s. of the wind, of the storm,** les clameurs aiguës du vent, de la tempête.

shrieval ['ʃri:v(ə)l], *a. Adm:* qui a rapport au shérif; **s. functions,** fonctions de shérif.

shrievalty ['ʃri:v(ə)lti], *s. Adm:* **1.** fonctions *fpl* de shérif. **2.** (*a*) juridiction *f* du shérif; (*b*) période *f* d'exercice des fonctions de shérif.

shrift [ʃrift], *s. A:* confession *f* et absolution *f*; **short s.,** délai accordé à un condamné avant son exécution pour se confesser; *Fig:* **to give s.o. short s.,** expédier vite qn; **he got short s.,** il a été renvoyé avec perte et fracas.

shrike [ʃraik], *s. Orn:* pie-grièche *f, pl.* pies-grièches; **red-backed s.,** pie-grièche écorcheuse; **lesser grey s.,** pie-grièche à poitrine rose; **great grey,** *NAm:* **northern, northwestern, s.,** pie-grièche grise, *Fr.C:* pie-grièche boréale; **woodchat s.,** pie-grièche rousse; **masked s.,** pie-grièche masquée; **loggerhead s.,** pie-grièche migratrice; **fiscal s.,** pie-grièche fiscale; **Isabelline s.,** pie-grièche isabelle; **helmet s.,** bagadais *m*; **swallow s.,** langrayen *m*; **cuckoo s.,** échenilleur *m*; **ant s.,** batara *m*, thamnophile *m*.

shriketit ['ʃraiktit], *s. Orn:* falconelle *f*.

shrill[1] [ʃril], *a.* (*of voice, sound, etc.*) à note aiguë; aigu, strident, criard, aigre, glapissant, perçant; **to utter s. cries,** pousser des cris aigus; **in a s. voice,** d'une voix perçante, élevée, pointue; **the s. blast of a bugle,** la note aiguë d'un clairon; **s. whistle,** coup de sifflet strident.

shrill[2]. *A: & Lit:* **1.** *v.i.* pousser, avoir, un son aigu, strident; **a whistle shrilled,** un coup de sifflet déchira l'air. **2.** *v.tr.* (*a*) **to s. (out) a song,** chanter une chanson d'une voix aiguë; (*b*) **to s. out abuse,** lancer des injures d'une voix criarde.

shrillness ['ʃrilnis], *s.* acuité *f*, stridence *f* (de la voix, d'un son, etc.).

shrilly ['ʃrili], *adv.* d'un ton aigu, criard; avec un son aigu, strident.

shrimp[1] [ʃrimp], *s.* (*a*) *Crust:* crevette (grise); **brine s.,** artémia *f*; **opossum s.,** mysidacé *m*; **skeleton s.,** caprelle *f*; **s. boat,** crevettier *m*; *Comest:* **s. paste,** beurre *m* de crevettes; (*b*) *F:* (*pers.*) nabot, -ote, puce *f*; gringalet *m*, avorton *m*.

shrimp[2], *v.i.* **to go shrimping, to s.,** pêcher la crevette, faire la pêche à la crevette.

shrimper ['ʃrimpər], *s.* **1.** pêcheur, -euse, de crevettes. **2.** (*boat*) crevettier *m*.

shrimpfish ['ʃrimpfiʃ], *s. Ich:* poisson *m* rasoir.

shrine[1] [ʃrain], *s.* **1.** châsse *f*, reliquaire *m*. **2.** tombeau *m*, mausolée *m*, de saint(e). **3.** chapelle *f*, autel *m*, consacré(e) à un(e) saint(e).

shrine[2], *v.tr. A: & Lit:* enchâsser (une sainte relique, une image) **(in,** dans).

shrink[1] [ʃriŋk], *s.* **1.** *O:* mouvement *m* de recul, d'aversion (de qn). **2.** rétrécissement *m* (d'un tissu); retrait *m* (du bois, etc.). **3.** *F:* psychiatre *mf*, psychanalyste *mf*.

shrink[2], *v.* (**shrank** [ʃræŋk]; **shrunk** [ʃrʌŋk], *as adj.* **shrunken** ['ʃrʌŋk(ə)n]) **1.** *v.i.* (*a*) se contracter; se resserrer; (se) rétrécir; rapetisser; (*of wood, etc.*) jouer, travailler; (*of material, etc.*) rétrécir, raccourcir; *Tex:* rentrer; **his gums are shrinking,** ses dents se déchaussent; **he is beginning to s. (with age),** il commence à se tasser; **shrunk(en) with age,** tassé par l'âge; **to s. in the wash, in washing,** rétrécir au lavage; **metals that s. when cooling,** métaux qui se contractent en refroidissant; **my income has shrunk,** mon revenu s'est amoindri, a diminué; **her whole body seemed to s. (away),** son corps entier semblait se rapetisser; **shrunken breasts,** seins flétris, fanés; *Anthr:* **shrunken heads,** têtes réduites; (*b*) reculer; se retirer, se dérober; **to s. away,** s'éloigner timidement; **he shrank back,** il a eu un mouvement de recul; **to s. (back) from sth.,** reculer devant, se dérober à, qch.; **to s. (away) with, (back) in, horror,** reculer d'horreur; **to s. from doing sth.,** reculer, répugner, hésiter, à faire qch.; craindre de faire qch.; **his mind shrank from painful memories,** son esprit se dérobait aux souvenirs pénibles; (*c*) **to s. into oneself,** devenir réservé, renfermé; rentrer en soi-même; (*d*) se faire tout petit (par timidité, etc.). **2.** *v.tr.* contracter (du métal); (faire) rétrécir (un tissu); **fully shrunk material,** tissu irrétrécissable; **to s. on a (cartwheel) tyre,** embattre (à chaud) un bandage; fretter une roue; **to s. on a crank,** emmancher une manivelle à chaud; **to s. on a collar,** caler une frette à chaud, à retrait; **shrunk-on fit,** calage *m* à retrait.

shrinkable ['ʃriŋkəbl], *a.* rétrécissable.

shrinkage ['ʃriŋkidʒ], *s.* contraction *f*, retrait *m* (du métal); retrait (du bois); rétrécissement *m*, *Tex:* rentrée *f* (du tissu); *Cin:* retrait, contraction (du film); *Metall:* **s. hole,** retassure *f* (dans un lingot d'acier); **s. crack,** (i) *Metall:* tapure *f* (dans du métal coulé); (ii) *Geol:* gerçure (due au soleil); fente *f*, cassure *f*, de retrait.

shrinker ['ʃriŋkər], *s.* **head s.,** (i) *Anthr:* réducteur *m* de têtes; (ii) *F:* psychiatre *mf*, psychanalyste *mf*.

shrinking ['ʃriŋkiŋ], *s.* = SHRINKAGE; **s. (away, up),** rétrécissement *m*, rapetissement *m*. **2. s. (away, back) from sth.,** reculement *m* devant qch.; répugnance *f* à une action. **3.** *Tchn:* **s. on,** emmanchement *m* à chaud; calage *m*, serrage *m*, à chaud, à retrait; embattage *m* (d'un bandage de roue).

shrive ['ʃraiv], *v.* (*p.t.* **shrove** ['ʃrouv]; *p.p.* **shriven** ['ʃriv(ə)n]) *A:* **1.** *v.tr.* confesser, absoudre (un pénitent); donner l'absolution à (un pénitent). **2.** *v.pr.* **to s. oneself,** se confesser; **to die shriven,** mourir confès, confesse.

shrivel ['ʃriv(ə)l], *v.* (**shrivelled**) **1.** *v.tr.* **to s. (up),** rider, ratatiner, recroqueviller, dessécher (la peau, une pomme, etc.); (*of sun*) brûler, hâler (les plantes); **the fire has shrivelled up the leather,** le feu a racorni, recroquevillé, le cuir; **the old man's shrivelled face,** le visage parcheminé, ratatiné, ridé, du vieillard. **2.** *v.i.* **to s. (up),** se rider, se ratatiner, se dessécher; se parcheminer, se recroqueviller; se racornir.

shrivelling ['ʃrivəliŋ], *s.* **s. (up),** dessèchement *m* (de la peau, d'une pomme, etc.); racornissement *m* (du cuir, etc.).

shriving ['ʃraiviŋ], *s. A:* confession *f* et absolution *f* (de qn).

shroff [ʃrɔf], *s.* sarraf *m*, changeur égyptien.

shroud[1] [ʃraud], *s.* **1.** linceul *m*, suaire *m*; **to wrap a corpse in a s.,** ensevelir un cadavre; **in a s. of mystery,** enveloppé de mystère; *Lit:* **under a s. of darkness,** sous les voiles *m* de la nuit; à l'abri *m* de la nuit. **2.** *Mec.E: etc:* (*a*) bouclier *m*, blindage *m*; (*b*) joue *f* (de pignon); *Mch:* bandage *m* (de roue à aubes); *Tls:* **inner s.,** virole intérieure; **outer s.,** virole extérieure; (*c*) *I.C.E:* **impeller s. (plate),** plaque *f* d'étanchéité du compresseur. **3.** *Aer:* (*a*) carénage *m*; (*b*) cloche *f*, frette *f*; **jet pipe s.,** virole de cône arrière; **shrouded blade,** aube *f* caisson; (*in turbine engine*) aube renforcée.

shroud[2], *s.* (*a*) *Nau:* hauban *m*; **s.-laid rope,** cordage commis en quatre; (*b*) (*of parachute*) **s. (lines),** suspentes *fpl*.

shroud[3], *v.tr.* **1.** (*a*) ensevelir (un cadavre); envelopper (un cadavre) d'un linceul, d'un suaire; (*b*) envelopper, voiler (qch.) **(in, de)**; *Lit:* **to s. sth. from the vulgar gaze,** cacher, dérober, qch. aux regards vulgaires; **shrouded in mist,** enveloppé de brume; **shrouded in gloom,** (i) (*of place*) enténébré; (ii) (*of pers.*) endeuillé, plongé dans la tristesse; ténébreux; **crime shrouded in mystery,** crime enveloppé de mystère. **2.** *Tchn:* emboîter (un engrenage); *W.Tel:* blinder (un transformateur).

shrouding ['ʃraudiŋ], *s.* **1.** (*a*) ensevelissement *m* (d'un cadavre) dans le suaire; (*b*) enveloppement *m* (de qch.). **2.** *Tchn:* emboîtement *m* (d'un engrenage); *W.Tel:* blindage *m* (d'un transformateur); *Hyd.E:* bandage *m* (d'une roue à aubes).

Shrove [ʃrouv], *s.* **S. Tuesday,** (le) mardi gras; **S. Monday,** le lundi gras; **S. Sunday,** (le dimanche de) la Quinquagésime.

Shrovetide ['ʃrouvtaid], *s. Ecc:* les jours gras.

shrub[1] [ʃrʌb], *s. Bot:* arbrisseau *m*, arbuste *m*; *For:* **undesirable s.,** mort-bois *m, pl.* morts-bois.

shrub[2], *s.* **1.** boisson composée de jus de fruit, de sucre et d'alcool. **2. raspberry s.,** boisson composée de jus de framboise, de vinaigre et de sucre.

shrubbery ['ʃrʌbəri], *s.* bosquet *m*; plantation *f* d'arbustes, d'arbrisseaux; massif *m* d'arbustes.

shrubby ['ʃrʌbi], *a.* **1.** qui ressemble à un arbuste, à un arbrisseau; frutescent; **s. tree,** arbrisseau. **2.** (*a*) (*of plantation, undergrowth, etc.*) arbustif; (*b*) couvert d'arbustes.

shrug[1] [ʃrʌg], *s.* **s. (of the shoulders),** haussement *m* d'épaules; **s. of resignation,** geste *m* de résignation.

shrug[2], *v.tr.* (**shrugged**) **to s. (one's, the, shoulders),** hausser les épaules; avoir un haussement d'épaules; **to s. sth. off,** laisser de côté, oublier momentanément, qch.; *F:* **to s. off one's jacket,** tomber la veste.

shrunken ['ʃrʌŋk(ə)n], *a.* contracté; (*of material*) rétréci; (*of features, etc.*) ratatiné; *Anthr:* **s. heads,** têtes réduites.

shuck[1] [ʃʌk]. *NAm:* **1.** *s.* cosse *f*, gousse *f* (de petits pois, etc.); spathe *f* (de maïs); brou *m* (de noix); écale *f* (de noix, de châtaigne); bogue *f* (de châtaigne); coquille *f* (d'huître, de palourde). **2.** *F:* (*a*) *int.* **shucks!** mince (alors)! flûte (alors)! allons donc! (*b*) *s.pl.* **it's not worth shucks!** ça ne vaut pas chipette!

shuck[2], *v.tr. NAm:* écosser (des petits pois, etc.); écaler (des noix); éplucher (du maïs); décortiquer (des amandes, etc.); écailler (des huîtres); *F:* **to s. off one's jacket,** tomber la veste.

shucking ['ʃʌkiŋ], *s. NAm:* décorticage *m* (d'amandes, etc.); épluchage *m* (de maïs).

shudder[1] ['ʃʌdər], *s.* frisson *m*, frémissement *m*, frissonnement *m*; **a s. passed over him,** il a été pris d'un frisson; *F:* **it gives me the shudders,** j'en ai le frisson.

shudder[2], *v.i.* (*a*) **to s. with cold, with horror,** frissonner de froid, d'horreur; frémir d'horreur; **I s. to think of it, at the thought of it,** j'ai le frisson rien que d'y penser; (*b*) (*of ship*) vibrer.

shuddering ['ʃʌdəriŋ], *s.* frisson *m*, frémissement *m*, frissonnement *m*.

shuffle[1] [ʃʌfl], *s.* **1.** (*a*) mouvement traînant des pieds; marche traînante, pas traînants; **to walk with a s.,** traîner les pieds (en marchant); (*b*) *Danc:* frottement *m* de pieds; **soft shoe s.,** danse de music-hall (exécutée en chaussons); **double s.,** (i) (sorte *f* de) sabotière *f*; (ii) pas *m* caractéristique de la sabotière. **2.** battement *m*, mélange *m* (des cartes); **to give the cards a s.,** battre, mêler. *F:* touiller, brasser, les cartes; **it's your s.,** c'est à vous de battre les cartes. **3.** (*a*) atermoiement *m*, tergiversations *fpl*, entortillage *m*; louvoiement *m*; (*b*) faux-fuyant *m, pl.* faux-fuyants; équivoque *f*; **to do a double s.,** chercher des faux-fuyants. **4.** *F:* **cabinet s.,** changement *m* de ministres.

shuffle[2]. **1.** *v.tr. & i.* **to s. (one's feet),** traîner les pieds; **to s. (along),** traîner les savates, avancer lentement avec un frottement de pieds, en traînant les pieds, en traînant le pas; frotter les pieds en marchant; traîner la jambe, les jambes; **to s. in, out,** entrer, sortir, en traînant les pieds, à pas traînants; **to s. off,** s'en aller en traînant le pas. **2.** *v.tr.* (*a*) (entre)mêler, (em)brouiller, confondre, jeter pêle-mêle (des papiers, etc.); (*b*) *Cards:* battre, mêler, brouiller, brasser (les cartes); (*c*) **to s. the dominoes,** brasser les dominos; (*d*) **to s. off a responsibility,** se débarrasser d'une responsabilité; **to s. off responsibility onto, upon, s.o.,** rejeter la responsabilité sur qn; **to s. one's clothes on, off,** passer, ôter, ses vêtements à la hâte; *Lit:* **to s. off this mortal coil,** dépouiller ce corps mortel. **3.** *v.i.* atermoyer, louvoyer, biaiser, tortiller; équivoquer, tergiverser; se dérober.

shuffleboard ['ʃʌflbɔːd], *s. A:* = (jeu *m* de) galet *m*.

shuffler ['ʃʌflər], *s. F:* personne *f* qui use de faux-fuyants, de détours, d'équivoques.

shuffling[1] ['ʃʌfliŋ], *a.* **1.** (*of pers.*) qui traîne les pieds; (*of gait*) traînant. **2.** *F:* (*of conduct, speech*) équivoque, évasif; **s. politician,** politicien fuyant, évasif.

shuffling[2], *s.* = SHUFFLE[1].

Shulamite ['ʃuːləmait]. *Pr.n.f.* **the S.,** la Sulamite.

shun[1] [ʃʌn], *v.tr.* (**shunned**) fuir, éviter (qn, qch.); **to s. society,** se cacher, se dérober, au monde; fuir le monde; **to s. everybody,** s'éloigner de tout le monde.

'shun[2], *int. Mil: etc: F:* (= *attention!*) garde à vous!

Shunammite ['ʃuːnəmait], *s. A.Geog:* Sunamite *mf*.

shunt[1] [ʃʌnt], *s.* **1.** *Rail:* garage *m*, manœuvre *f*, changement *m* de voie (d'un train); **s. line,** voie *f* de garage, d'évitement; **limit of s. (signal),** (signal de) limite de manœuvre. **2.** *El:* shunt *m*, dérivation *f*; **ground s.,** shunt de masse; **to put in s.,** mettre en dérivation, en shunt; shunter; **condenser with a s. resistance,** condensateur shunté (par une résistance); **s. circuit,** circuit dérivé, en dérivation; circuit shunt; **s. dynamo, s.(-wound) motor,** dynamo, moteur, en dérivation; **s. box,** boîte de résistance shunt; **s. winding,** enroulement *m*, excitation *f*, en shunt, en dérivation; **s. field,** champ de dérivation; **s. field rheostat,** résistance shunt; *Telecomm:* **s. field relay,** relais à champ en shunt; *Elcs:* **galvanometer s.,** galvanomètre shunté; **s. feed,** alimentation *f* parallèle; **s. resistor,** résistance de dérivation, en parallèle. **3.** *Surg:* shunt.

shunt[2], *v.* **1.** *Rail:* (*a*) *v.tr.* garer, manœuvrer (un train, des wagons); **to s. a train onto a branch line, onto a siding,** aiguiller, dériver, un train sur un embranchement, sur une voie de garage; (*of wagon*) **s. with care,** défense de tamponner; *F:* **to s. s.o., sth.,** mettre qn, qch., au rancart; **to s. a scheme,** ajourner un projet; **to s. the conversation onto something else,** détourner la conversation sur autre chose; (*b*) *v.i.* (*of train*) se garer. **2.** *v.tr. El:* shunter, dériver (un circuit, etc.) monter (un condensateur) en dérivation; bifurquer (un courant).

shunter ['ʃʌntər], *s.* **1.** *Rail:* (*pers.*) agent *m*, homme *m*, de manœuvre(s). **2.** *El:* dérivateur *m*. **3.** *Fin:* arbitragiste *m* (entre bourses du même pays).

shunting ['ʃʌntiŋ], *s.* **1.** (*a*) *Rail:* garage *m*, manœuvre *f*; changement *m* de voie; aiguillage *m*; **s. operations,** manœuvres de triage *m*; **s. engine,** locomotive *f*, machine *f*, de manœuvre; locotracteur *m*; **s. track,** voie de manœuvre; **s. loop,** voie de dédoublement; **s. yard,** gare de manœuvres; **s. limit (signal),** (signal de) limite de manœuvre; (*b*) *F:* ajournement *m* (d'un projet); mise *f* au rancart (de qn, de qch.). **2.** *El:* dérivation *f*, shuntage *m*. **3.** *Fin:* arbitrage *m* de place à place (entre deux bourses du même pays).

shush [ʃʌʃ]. **1.** *v.tr.* faire taire (qn). **2.** (*a*) *v.i.* demander le silence; (*b*) *int.* [ʃ] chut!

shut [ʃʌt], *v.* (*p.t. & p.p.* **shut;** *pr.p.* **shutting**)

I. *v.tr. & i.* **1.** *v.tr.* (*a*) fermer (une porte, un magasin, une boîte, un livre, etc.); **to s. the door on s.o., in s.o.'s face,** fermer la porte au nez de qn; refuser de recevoir qn; **to find the door s.,** trouver la porte fermée, trouver porte close; se trouver en face d'une porte fermée; **s. the door, please,** fermez la porte, s'il vous plaît; (*on transfer books of banks, etc.*) **s. for dividend,** clôture *f* pour dividende; **to s. one's eyes,** fermer les yeux; **to s. one's ears to sth.,** rester sourd à qch.; **to s. one's mouth,**

(i) fermer la bouche; (ii) *F:* se taire, fermer son bec; *F:* **to keep one's mouth s.,** avoir la bouche cousue; **to s. s.o.'s mouth (for him),** faire taire qn; clore, clouer, le bec à qn; *P:* **s. your mouth!** ferme ton bec! la ferme! ta gueule! *P:* **to be s. of s.o.,** être débarrassé de qn; (*b*) **to s. one's finger, one's dress, in the door,** se pincer le doigt, laisser prendre sa robe, dans la porte; **they s. him in the cellar,** ils l'ont enfermé dans la cave; **we're s. in by hills,** nous sommes entourés de collines; *Petr:* **s.-in pressure,** pression statique (dans un puits); **s.-in well,** puits fermé. **2.** *v.i.* (*of door, lid, etc.*) (se) fermer; **the door won't s.,** la porte ne ferme pas; **the door s. to,** la porte s'est fermée (toute seule); **the park shuts at four o'clock,** le parc ferme à quatre heures.

II. (*compound verbs*) **1. shut down.** (*a*) *v.tr. Ind:* fermer (une usine, etc.); *Tchn:* couper (la vapeur); *Av:* arrêter (le moteur); (*b*) *v.i.* (*of factory, etc.*) (i) chômer; (ii) fermer ses portes.

2. shut off, *v.tr.* (*a*) couper, interrompre, intercepter (la vapeur); fermer (l'eau); *Rail:* (*of steam engine*) **to s. off steam,** mettre le registre au point mort; *Aut:* **to s. off the engine,** couper, arrêter, le moteur; *Mus:* (*organ*) **to s. off the pedal coupler,** ôter la tirasse; (*b*) séparer, isoler (**from,** de); **to be s. off from society,** être exclu du monde.

3. shut out, *v.tr.* (*a*) exclure (qn, l'air, la lumière, une éventualité, etc.); intercepter (la lumière); **to s. s.o. out, to s. out the light,** empêcher qn, la lumière, d'entrer; **the trees s. out the view,** les arbres bouchent la vue; **to s. s.o. out (from sth.),** exclure qn (de qch.); (*b*) **to s. s.o. out (of doors),** fermer la porte à qn; ne pas admettre qn; **s. the dog out!** mets le chien dehors!

4. shut up. (*a*) *v.tr.* (i) enfermer (qn, qch.); **to s. oneself up,** se renfermer, se calfeutrer, se claquemurer; rester claustré chez soi; (ii) **to s. s.o. up (in prison),** emprisonner qn; (iii) fermer (une porte, une maison); **to s. up shop,** fermer la boutique; *F:* **we'll have to s. up shop for a bit,** il va falloir suspendre nos activités pendant quelque temps; (iv) condamner (une porte, une pièce); obstruer (un orifice, etc.); (v) *F:* réduire (qn) au silence, rembarrer (qn); couper le sifflet, clouer le bec, à (qn); (vi) *Metalw:* encoller (les amorces d'une soudure, etc.); (*b*) *v.i. F:* se taire, ne plus dire mot; ne plus souffler mot; **s. up!** taisez-vous! *P:* la ferme! ta gueule! fiche(z)-moi la paix! la barbe! **they shouted to him to s. up,** on lui a crié de se taire, de la fermer.

shutdown ['ʃʌtdaun], *s. Ind:* (i) fermeture *f*, (ii) chômage *m* (d'une usine).

shute [ʃu:t], *s. Tex:* trame *f*.

shut-eye ['ʃʌtai], *s. F:* somme *m*, roupillon *m*; **to have a bit of s.-e.,** faire un (petit) somme; faire, piquer, un roupillon.

shut-in ['ʃʌtin], *s. NAm:* malade, vieillard, etc., confiné chez soi, dans un hôpital.

shut-off ['ʃʌtɔf], *s.* (*a*) *Hyd.E:* bonde *f* (d'un étang); pale *f*, vanne *f* (d'un réservoir); (*b*) robinet *m*; soupape *f*.

shut-out ['ʃʌtaut], *s.* **1.** *Ind:* lock-out *m inv.* **2.** *Cards:* **s.-o. bid,** ouverture préventive.

shutter[1] ['ʃʌtər], *s.* **1.** volet *m*; **inside shutters,** volets intérieurs; **outside shutters,** contrevents *m*, volets; **slatted shutters,** persiennes *f*; **folding shutters,** volets pliants, volets brisés; **padded s.,** sourdière *f*; (*for shop front*) **revolving, rolling, s.,** volet, roulant, à rouleau; rideau ondulé; **sectional steel s.,** volet, rideau, tablier *m*, de fer (de devanture); **to open, close, the shutters,** ouvrir, fermer, les volets; **to pull the s. up, down,** lever, baisser, le volet (roulant); **to take down the shutters,** enlever les volets (d'un magasin); ouvrir le magasin; **to put up the shutters,** mettre les volets (d'un magasin); fermer la, les, devanture(s); fermer le magasin, la boutique; **we'll have to put up the shutters,** il n'y a plus, nous n'avons plus, qu'à fermer boutique; **s. of a confessional,** guichet *m* d'un confessional; *Cin:* **fire s.,** volet à guillotine (d'une cabine de projection); *Aut: Av:* **radiator s.,** volet, persienne, de radiateur; **thermostatic s.,** volet thermique, thermo-régulateur; *I.C.E:* **air s.,** obturateur *m* d'air, étrangleur *m*; **air s. lever,** commande *f* d'étrangleur; *Tp:* **exchange s.,** volet de standard téléphonique; **drop indicator s.,** volet d'indicateur d'appel. **2.** (*a*) *Phot:* obturateur; **diaphragm s.,** obturateur au diaphragme; **iris-diaphragm s.,** obturateur à diaphragme iris; **drop s.,** obturateur à guillotine; **focal plane s.,** obturateur de plaque, focal; **roller blind s.,** obturateur à rideau; **rotary s.,** obturateur rotatif; **delayed action s.,** obturateur à action différée; **programmed, programme type, s.,** obturateur programmé; **everset s.,** obturateur toujours armé; **s. release,** déclencheur *m* d'obturateur; **to set, release, the s.,** armer, déclencher, l'obturateur; **s. setting,** (i) *Phot:* armement *m*, (ii) *Cin:* calage *m*, de l'obturateur; *Cin:* **two-bladed, three-bladed, s.,** obturateur à deux, à trois, pales; (*b*) *Phot:* **s. of a dark slide, of a plate holder,** volet, rideau, de châssis; (*c*) *Mec.E:* **valve s.,** obturateur de vanne; **s. valve,** vanne *f* à obturateur, robinet *m* à guillotine; **s. vane,** aubage *m* obturateur (de turbine); (*d*) *Atom.Ph:* **neutron s.,** obturateur à neutrons; **cadmium s.,** obturateur au cadmium; **gravity-operated s.,** obturateur actionné par gravité; **rotating s.,** obturateur rotatif. **3.** (*a*) *Metall:* écluse *f*; (*b*) *Hyd.E:* haussette *f*, hausse *f* (de vanne); **s. weir,** vanne à hausses; (*c*) *N.Arch:* tape *f* de dame; (*d*) **ventilator s.,** vanne de ventilateur. **4.** *Mus:* (*organ*) **(Venetian) shutters,** jalousies *f* (de la caisse d'expression). **5.** *Civ.E:* banche *f*.

shutter[2], *v.tr.* mettre les volets à (une fenêtre, une maison); fermer les volets d('une maison, etc.); fermer la devanture d('un magasin); **shuttered window, house,** fenêtre, maison, aux volets fermés, clos.

shuttering ['ʃʌtəriŋ], *s.* **1.** mise *f* des volets. **2.** *coll.* (*a*) volets *mpl*; persiennage *m*; (*b*) *Const:* coffrage *m* (du béton).

shutting ['ʃʌtiŋ], *s.* fermeture *f* (d'une porte, d'une boîte, etc.); **s. down of a factory,** (i) fermeture, (ii) chômage *m*, d'une usine; **s. off,** interruption *f*, interception *f* (de la vapeur); fermeture (de l'eau); **s. out,** exclusion *f* (de qn, de l'air).

shuttle[1] ['ʃʌtl], *s.* **1.** *Tex: Needlew: etc:* navette *f*; **s. winder,** dévidoir *m* (de machine à coudre). **2.** (*a*) *Trans:* navette; **s. service,** service *m* de navettes; navette; **frequent s. service between station and town,** navettes fréquentes entre la gare et la ville; *Rail:* **s. train,** (train *m* qui fait la) navette; **line over which a s. service is run,** ligne exploitée en navette; **s. working,** exploitation, service, en navette; *Space:* **space s.,** navette spatiale; (*b*) *Mec.E:* **s. (movement),** (mouvement *m* de) va-et-vient *m inv*; (mouvement de) navette; mouvement alternatif; **s. valve,** clapet *m* navette, soupape *f* navette, soupape va-et-vient; *El:* **s. type magneto,** magnéto *f* à volet tournant; **s.-wound armature,** induit *m* en double T; induit Siemens; *Av:* **s. bombing,** bombardement par va-et-vient; *Cmptr:* **s. printer,** imprimante *f* à navette.

shuttle[2], *v.tr.* & *i.* faire la navette, le va-et-vient; aller et venir; *Cmptr:* **to s. data in and out,** introduire et extraire alternativement des informations.

shuttle[3], *s. Hyd.E:* vanne *f*; **s. plate,** tablier *m* de vanne.

shuttlecock ['ʃʌtlkɔk], *s. Games:* volant *m*.

shuttling ['ʃʌtliŋ], *s.* va-et-vient *m*, navette *f*.

shy[1] [ʃai], *s.* écart *m*, faux bond (d'un cheval).

shy[2], *v.i.* (**shied; shying**) (*of horse*) avoir, faire, un écart; faire, marquer, un haut-le-corps; se dérober, se rejeter; broncher; (*of horse, pers.*) **to s. at sth.,** prendre ombrage de qch.; *Fig:* (*of pers.*) tiquer sur qch.

shy[3], *a.* (**shyer, shyest;** *occ.* **shier, shiest**) **1.** (*of bird, child, etc.*) sauvage, farouche, timide; (*of horse, etc.*) peureux, ombrageux; (*of pers.*) timide, modeste, réservé; **to make s.o. s.,** intimider qn; **s.(-looking) boy,** garçon (d'aspect) timide; **to be s. of people,** être gêné, mal à l'aise, parmi les gens; **he's not s. with women,** il est assez hardi avec les femmes; **to fight s. of sth.,** se défier, se méfier, de qch.; **to fight s. of a job,** éviter une besogne; renâcler à une besogne; **he fights s. of me,** il cherche à m'éviter; **to be s. of doing sth.,** hésiter à faire qch.; **they are s. of speaking,** ils ne s'enhardissent pas à parler; **don't be s. of telling me,** ne vous gênez pas pour me le dire; **don't pretend to be s.,** ne faites pas le, la, timide; **the fish are s.,** les poissons ne mordent pas. **2.** *F: O:* **to be s. of money,** être à court d'argent, manquer d'argent; **I'm a fiver s.,** (i) je suis en perte de cinq livres; (ii) il me manque cinq livres. **3.** *Nau:* (vent) pointu.

shy[4], *s. F:* **1.** jet *m*, lancement *m* (d'une pierre, etc.); (*at fairs*) **5p a s.,** 5p le coup; **three shies for 15p.,** trois coups pour 15p; **to take a s. at a bird,** lancer une pierre à un oiseau; viser un oiseau avec une pierre. **2.** *O:* essai *m*, tentative *f* (pour atteindre qch.); **to have a s. at doing sth.,** essayer de faire qch.; s'essayer à faire qch.

shy[5], *v.* (**shield; shying**) *F:* **1.** *v.i.* lancer, jeter, balancer, qch. (**at,** à). **2.** *v.tr.* **to s. a stone at s.o.,** lancer une pierre à qn.

shyer ['ʃaiər], *s.* cheval ombrageux; cheval peureux.

shying ['ʃaiiŋ], *s.* écart *m*, faux bond (d'un cheval).

Shylock ['ʃailɔk], *s.* créancier *m* impitoyable; usurier *m*; **he's a real S.,** il est âpre à réclamer son argent.

shyly ['ʃaili], *adv.* timidement, modestement; avec embarras.

shyness ['ʃainis], *s.* timidité *f*, réserve *f*, modestie *f* (de qn); sauvagerie *f* (d'un animal, de qn); **to lose one's s.,** s'enhardir; secouer sa timidité.

shyster ['ʃaistər], *s. esp. NAm: F:* (*a*) avocassier *m*; procédurier, -ière, chicaneur, -euse; (*b*) homme *m* d'affaires véreux, marron, (à l'esprit) retors.

si [si:], *s. Mus:* **1.** (*in the fixed do system*) si *m*. **2.** (*in the movable do system*) la sensible.

sial ['saiəl], *s. Geol:* sial *m*.

siala- ['saiələ], *pref. Med:* siala-.

sialagogic [saiələ'gɔdʒik], *a. Med:* sialagène, sialagogue.

sialagogue ['saiələgɔg], *s. Med:* sialagogue *m*.

sialic [sai'ælik], *a. Bio-Ch:* **s. acid,** acide sialique.

sialid(an) ['saiəlid, sai'ælidən], *s. Ent:* sialis *m*.

Sialidae [sai'ælidi:], *s.pl. Ent:* sialidés *m*.

Sialis ['saiəlis], *s. Ent:* sialis *m*.

sialo- [saiələ], *pref. Med:* sialo-.

sialodochitis [saiəloudɔ'kaitis], *s. Med:* sialodochite *f*.

sialography [saiə'lɔgrəfi], *s. Med:* sialographie *f*.

sialorrhoea [saiələ'riə], *s. Med:* sialorrhée *f*, sialisme *m*.

Siam [sai'æm], *Pr.n.* Siam *m*; **Upper, Lower, S.,** le haut, le bas, Siam; **the Gulf of S.,** le golfe de Siam.

siamang ['saiəmæŋ, 'si:-], *s. Z:* (gibbon) siamang *m*.

Siamese [saiə'mi:z]. **1.** *a.* (*a*) *Geog:* siamois; **S. twins,** (i) frères siamois, sœurs siamoises; (ii) (ami(e)s, compagnons *m*, compagnes *f*) inséparables *mf*; **S. cat,** *s.* **S.,** (chat) siamois *m*; **seal point S.,** siamois brun phoque; **blue point S.,** siamois bleu (point); **chocolate point S.,** siamois chocolat au lait; **red point S.,** siamois à masque orange; *Ich:* **S. fighting fish,** combattant siamois; (*b*) *Tchn:* jumelé; **s. connection, joint,** *s.* **s.,** tubulaire *f* en Y. **2.** *s.* (*a*) *Geog:* Siamois, -oise; (*b*) *Ling:* siamois.

sib [sib]. *A:* & *Scot:* **1.** *a.* apparenté (**to,** à); parent (**to,** de). **2.** *s.* parent, -ente.

Siberia [sai'biəriə], *Pr.n. Geog:* Sibérie *f*.

Siberian [sai'biəriən]. *Geog:* (*a*) *a.* sibérien; **S. husky, dog,** chien *m* de Sibérie; (*b*) *s.* Sibérien, -ienne.

siberite ['saibərait], *s. Miner:* sibérite *f*.

sibilant ['sibilənt]. **1.** *a.* sifflant; *Med:* sibilant; **s. râle,** râle sibilant; sibilance *f*. **2.** *s. Ling:* (lettre, consonne) sifflante *f*.

sibilate ['sibileit], *v.tr.* prononcer (une lettre, etc.) en sifflant, en chuintant.

sibilation [sibi'leiʃ(ə)n], *s.* sifflement *m*; sibilation *f*, chuintement *m*.

sibling ['sibliŋ], *s.* l'un(e) de deux, de plusieurs, enfants qui ont (i) les mêmes parents, (ii) le même père ou la même mère.

sibyl ['sibil], **1.** *s.* sibylle *f*. **2.** *Pr.n.f.* Sibylle.

sibylline ['sibilain], *a.* sibyllin; **the s. books,** les livres sibyllins; **s. leaves,** feuilles de la sibylle.

sic[1] [sik]. *Lt.adv.* sic, ainsi.

sic[2], *v.tr.* (*p.t.* & *p.p.* **sicced;** *pr.p.* **siccing**) *NAm: O:* = SICK[3].

Sicambri [si'kæmbrai], *s.m.pl. A.Hist:* Sicambres.

siccative ['sikətiv], *a.* & *s.* siccatif (*m*).

sice[1] [sais], *s. A:* (*on dice*) six *m*; **to throw s. cinque,** amener six et cinq.

sice[2], *s. A:* (*esp. in India*) (i) palefrenier *m*; (ii) domestique monté.

Sicilian [si'siliən]. *Geog:* (*a*) *a.* sicilien; *Hist:* **the S. Vespers,** les Vêpres siciliennes; (*b*) *s.* Sicilien, -ienne.

siciliana, -ano [sisili'ɑ:nə, -'ɑ:nou], *s. Danc: Mus:* sicilienne *f*.

Sicily ['sisili], *Pr.n. Geog:* Sicile *f*; *Hist:* **Kingdom of the Two Sicilies,** Royaume *m* des Deux-Siciles.

sick[1] [sik], *a.* **1.** malade; *Hist:* **the S. Man (of Europe),** la Turquie; **the s.,** les malades; *Mil: etc:* **to report s.,** se faire porter malade; *Mil: etc:* **s. list,** rôle *m*, état *m*, des malades; **to be on the s. list,** (i) être malade; (ii) *Mil: etc:* être porté malade; (iii) *Nau:* être sur les cadres; *Mil: etc:* **s. call, parade,** visite *f* des malades; **the doctor's s. calls,** les visites du médecin; **s. leave,** congé *m* (i) de maladie, (ii) *Mil: etc:* de réforme; **s. pay,** allocation *f* de maladie; **s. benefit,** prestations en cas de maladie (pourvues par une assurance sociale, etc.); assurance *f* maladie; **s. bay,** infirmerie *f*; *Navy:* **s. bay, s. berth,** poste des malades; **s. berth attendant,** infirmier, -ière; **s. bed,** lit de malade, de douleur; **s. nurse,** garde-malade *mf*, *pl.* gardes-malades; *F:* **s. humour,** humour noir; **s. joke,** plaisanterie macabre; *A:* **to be s. of a fever,** être malade d'une fièvre; avoir la fièvre; *A:* **s. unto death, dying,** malade à mourir. **2. to be s.,** vomir, rendre; **to feel s.,** avoir mal au cœur; avoir des nausées, avoir l'estomac barbouillé, avoir des haut-le-cœur; **s. feeling,** malaise *m*; **s. headache,** migraine *f*; **he was as s. as a cat, a dog,** il a été malade comme un chien; *F:* **it makes me s.,** cela me donne la nausée, cela m'écœure, cela me donne envie de vomir, c'est à vomir; *F:* **it makes me s. just to think of it,** cela me donne mal au cœur, cela me donne la nausée, cela me soulève le cœur, rien que d'y penser; *F:* **s.-making,** écœurant; *P:* **you make me s.!** tu m'écœures! *NAm:* **to be s. at, to, in, on, one's stomach,** avoir mal au cœur. **3.** *Lit:* **to be s. at heart,** être abattu; avoir le cœur navré; être écœuré, dégoûté; *F:* **he was very s. at, about, failing his exam,** son échec l'a tout retourné; **he did look s.!** il en faisait une tête! **to grow s.**

of sth., se dégoûter de qch.; prendre qch. en dégoût; **to be s. of sth.,** être las, dégoûté, de qch.; **I'm s. (to death) of hearing that it's my fault,** j'en ai assez d'entendre dire que c'est de ma faute; **I'm s. and tired of the whole business, I'm s. to death of it,** j'en ai assez, j'en ai plein le dos; j'en ai par-dessus la tête; j'en ai marre, j'en ai ras le bol; **I'm s. (and tired) of hearing (about) it,** j'en ai les oreilles rebattues; **I'm s. and tired of telling you,** je me tue à vous le dire. **4.** *Nau:* qui a besoin d'une réfection, de réparations; **paint-s. ship,** navire qui a besoin d'être repeint.

sick², *v.tr. F:* **to s. sth. up,** vomir, dégobiller, qch.

sick³, *v.tr. O:* **1.** (*of dog*) s'élancer sur (qn); attaquer (qn); **s.! s.!** pille! pille! **2. to s. the dog on s.o.,** lancer, lâcher, le chien contre qn.

sicken ['sik(ə)n]. **1.** *v.i.* (*a*) *O:* tomber malade (**of, with,** de); (*of plants*) languir, s'étioler, dépérir; (*b*) **to be sickening for an illness,** *F:* **for sth.,** couver une maladie, qch.; (*c*) **to s. at the sight of sth., to see sth.,** être écœuré de voir qch., à la vue de qch.; **to s. of sth.,** se lasser, se dégoûter, de qch. **2.** *v.tr.* (*a*) rendre (qn) malade; donner mal au cœur à (qn); soulever le cœur de, à (qn); **his breath sickened me,** son haleine m'a donné mal au cœur, m'a donné la nausée; *F:* **his business methods s. me,** ses procédés me révoltent, me soulèvent le cœur; (*b*) **to s. s.o. of sth.,** dégoûter, écœurer, qn de qch.; **to s. s.o. of doing sth.,** décourager qn de faire qch.

sickener ['sik(ə)nər], *s. F: O:* déception *f*; aventure écœurante. **2.** spectacle écœurant.

sickening ['sik(ə)niŋ], *a.* à vous soulever le cœur; écœurant, dégoûtant; **s. smell,** odeur nauséabonde; **s. fear,** peur qui serre le cœur; **s. spectacle,** spectacle écœurant, révoltant; *F:* **how perfectly s.!** c'est vraiment écœurant! c'est à vous donner la nausée!

sickeningly ['sik(ə)niŋli], *adv.* de façon à vous soulever le cœur, à vous écœurer.

sickish ['sikiʃ], *a.* **to feel s.,** (i) ressentir, éprouver, un léger malaise, du malaise; (ii) avoir une légère nausée.

sickl(a)emia [sik(ə)'li:miə], *s. Med:* sicklémie *f*.

sickle ['sikl], *s.* (*a*) *Agr:* faucille *f*; *Pol:* **the hammer and s.,** la faucille et le marteau; (*b*) *Med:* **s. cell,** drépanocyte *m*; (*c*) *Nat.Hist:* **s.-shaped,** falciforme, falculaire; **s. (feather),** faucille, plume arquée (de la queue du coq).

sicklebill ['siklbil], *s. Orn:* (*a*) courlis *m*, courlieu *m*; (*b*) (*Madagascar*) falculie *f*; (*c*) (*New Guinea*) **short-tailed s.,** drépanornis *m*; **long-tailed s.,** épimaque *m*; (*d*) (*Hawaii*) hémignathe *m*; (*e*) oiseau-mouche huppé, *pl.* oiseaux-mouches.

sickliness ['siklinis], *s.* **1.** état maladif, mauvaise santé (de qn); étiolement *m* (des plantes). **2.** pâleur *f* (de teint); teinte blafarde (du ciel, etc.). **3.** caractère écœurant, nauséabond (d'une odeur, etc.); fadeur *f* (d'un goût, d'un sentiment); *F:* sentimentalité outrée (d'un roman, etc.).

sickly ['sikli], *a.* **1.** (*a*) (*of child, etc.*) maladif, souffreteux, malingre; (*of plant*) débile, malade, étiolé, veule; (*b*) (*of colour, light*) faible, pâle; (*of complexion*) pâle, terreux; **s. pallor,** pâleur maladive; **a s. winter sun,** un soleil d'hiver blafard; **a s. white,** un blanc terreux; (*c*) **s. smile,** sourire pâle, veule, contraint. **2.** (*of climate*) malsain, insalubre. **3.** (*a*) (*of taste, etc.*) fade; (*of smell*) écœurant, nauséabond; **s. sweet,** douceâtre; (*b*) (*of sentiment*) qui écœure, qui dégoûte; *F:* (*of tone of voice, tune, etc.*) sentimental, -aux; gnangnan *inv.*

sickness ['siknis], *s.* **1.** maladie *f*; **sleeping s.,** maladie du sommeil; **is there any s. on board?** avez-vous des malades à bord? **s. benefit,** prestations en cas de maladie (pourvues par une assurance sociale, etc.); assurance *f* maladie; **to draw s. benefit,** bénéficier de l'assurance maladie. **2.** (*a*) mal *m*; malaise *m*; **mountain s.,** mal des montagnes; **motion s.,** mal des transports; mal de cœur; nausées *fpl*; (**bouts of**) **s.,** vomissement(s) *m*(*pl*); **morning s.,** nausées matinales (se produisant au début de la grossesse).

sickroom ['sikru:m], *s.* chambre *f* de malade, des malades.

sicula, *pl.* **-ae** ['sikjulə, -i:], *s. Paleont:* sicula *f*.

Siculi ['sikjuli:], *s.pl. A.Geog:* Sicules *m*.

Sicyon ['siʃiən, 'sis-]. *Pr.n. A.Geog:* Sicyone *f*.

Sicyonian [siʃi'ouniən, sis-]. *A.Geog:* (*a*) *a.* sicyonien; (*b*) *s.* Sicyonien, -ienne.

sida ['saidə], *s. Bot:* sida *m*.

sidalcea [sai'dælsiə], *s. Bot:* sidalcea *m*.

side¹ [said], *s.* **1.** (*a*) côté *m*, flanc *m*; **to be lying on one's s.,** être couché sur le côté; **right, left, s.,** côté droit, gauche; **the arrow pierced his s.,** la flèche lui perça le flanc; (*of animal*) **to lash its sides,** se battre les flancs; **by the s. of s.o.,** à côté de qn; **by my s., at my s.,** à côté de moi; à mes côtés; **s. by s. (with s.o.),** l'un à côté de l'autre; côté à côté (avec qn); à côté de (qn); (*of ships*) bord à bord; **we were s. by s.,** nous étions à côté l'un de l'autre; **to collide s. on with sth., to have a s.-on collision with sth.,** se heurter de côté contre qch.; *F:* **to split, burst, one's sides (with laughing),** se tenir les côtes, se tordre (de rire); crever de rire; **s.-splitting,** désopilant, tordant, marrant, crevant; (*b*) **s. of beef,** demi-carcasse *f* de bœuf; **s. of bacon,** flèche de lard. **2.** côté (d'une maison, d'une boîte, d'un triangle); pan *m* (d'un objet taillé, d'un comble); rein *m*, pied-droit *m*, *pl.* pieds-droits, piédroit *m* (d'une voûte); aisselle *f* (de la voûte d'un four); flanc, versant *m* (d'une montagne); paroi *f* (d'un fossé, d'un vase, d'une tranchée); flanc (d'un vase); lisière *f* (d'une forêt); *Tchn:* flasque *m* (d'un tour, d'un treuil); **s. of a ship,** bande *f*, bord *m*, bordé *m*, côté, flanc, muraille *f*, d'un navire; **in, close to, the ship's s.,** en abord; **weather s.,** côté du vent; **lee s.,** bord sous le vent; *N.Arch;* **(deck)house s.,** paroi longitudinale, latérale (de rouf); **long s. (of a roof),** long-pan *m*, *pl.* longs-pans; **s. of an equation,** membre *m* d'une équation; **sides of spectacles,** branches *f* de lunettes; **a square metre is a square whose s. is one metre,** un mètre carré est un carré d'un mètre de côté; *Geol:* **s. of a fault,** lèvre *f* d'une faille. **3.** (*surface*) (*a*) côté; *Rec:* face *f* (d'un disque); **the right s. (of sth.),** le bon côté (de qch.); le bon, beau, côté, l'endroit *m* (d'un tissu); **the wrong s. (of sth.),** le mauvais côté (de qch.); l'envers *m* (d'un tissu); **the under s., upper s., of sth.,** le dessous, le dessus, de qch.; (*of garment*) **right s. out,** à l'endroit; **wrong s. out,** à l'envers; **printed on one s. only,** imprimé d'un seul côté; **the address is on the other s.,** l'adresse est ci-contre; **the dark s. of the moon,** la face cachée de la lune; *Leath:* **hair s. of the skin,** fleur *f* de la peau; *Bookb:* **cloth sides, paper sides, of a book,** plats *m* toile, plats papier, d'un livre; **front s.,** plat supérieur; **off s.,** plat inférieur; (*b*) **the good, the bad, s. of the business,** le bon, le mauvais, côté de l'affaire; **the other s. of the picture,** le revers de la médaille; **the bright s. of things,** le bon côté, l'aspect *m* favorable, des choses; l'envers du décor; **to look on the bright s. (of things),** voir les choses du bon côté, prendre les choses par le bon côté; voir tout en beau; **he always looks on the gloomy s. of things,** il voit tout en noir; **the comical s. of a situation,** l'élément *m* comique d'une situation; **to be, to get, on the right s. of s.o.,** être, se mettre, dans les petits papiers de qn; **to get on the wrong s. of s.o.,** prendre qn à rebrousse-poil; **to hear, look at, both sides (of a question),** considérer les deux aspects d'une question; entendre, envisager, le pour et le contre; **much might be said on both sides,** les deux points de vue sont soutenables, sont également valables; **there are two sides to every question,** qui n'entend qu'une partie n'entend rien; qui n'entend qu'une cloche n'entend qu'un son; **he can see only one s. of the question,** il ne considère qu'un aspect de la question; il est simpliste; **there are many sides to his character,** son caractère est très complexe; **his good s.,** ses bons côtés; **sit on my good s.,** mettez-vous du côté où j'entends mieux; **the educational s. of the cinema,** le côté culturel du cinéma; **his speech was a bit on the long s.,** son discours était plutôt long; **his trousers are on the short s.,** son pantalon est plutôt court; **the weather's on the cool s.,** il fait plutôt froid. **4.** (*a*) **on this s.,** de ce côté(-ci); **on that s.,** de ce côté-là; par(-)delà; **on this s. of sth.,** de ce côté(-ci), en deçà, de qch.; **(on) this s. of Christmas,** avant Noël; **on that s. of sth.,** de ce côté-là, au delà, de qch.; par delà qch.; **on the other s. (of sth.),** de l'autre côté (de qch.); **with a dog on either s.,** flanqué de deux chiens; **they were sitting on either s. of the fire,** ils étaient assis au coin du feu, chacun de leur côté; **on both sides,** des deux côtés, de part et d'autre; **on all sides, on every s.,** de tous (les) côtés; partout; **on the left hand, right hand, s.,** à (main) gauche, à (main) droite; **on the south s.,** du côté sud; **to be on the right s. of forty,** avoir moins de quarante ans; **to be on the wrong s. of forty,** avoir quarante ans sonnés; **to wear one's hat on one s.,** porter son chapeau de côté; **the tower leans on, to, one s.,** la tour penche d'un côté; **to put sth. on, to, one s.,** mettre, laisser, qch. de côté; mettre qch. à l'écart; **to take s.o. on, to, one s.,** prendre qn à part, en particulier; **to stand on, to, one s.,** se tenir à l'écart, à part; **to move to one s.,** se ranger, s'écarter, s'effacer; **from all sides, from every s.,** de tous (les) côtés, de toutes parts; **from s. to s.,** d'un côté à l'autre, de-ci de-là; **he zigzagged from s. to s. of the street, from one s. of the street to the other,** il zigzaguait d'un côté à l'autre de la rue; (*on packing cases, etc.*) **this s. up,** haut; *Th:* **right s., left s. (of the stage),** côté cour, côté jardin (de la scène); *Ten:* **the choice of s. or service,** le choix du service ou du côté; (*b*) *Bill:* **running s.,** effet *m* en tête, en avant; **check s.,** effet contraire, rétrograde; **to put on s.,** prendre, faire, de l'effet (de côté); (*c*) *F:* **to put on s.,** se donner des airs; prendre des airs; poser; se faire valoir; plastronner; crâner; **he puts on s.,** il est poseur; (*d*) **to do a bit of gardening on the s.,** faire un peu de jardinage (pour qn) dans ses heures libres; *F:* **to make sth., a bit, on the s.,** se faire des petits à-côtés; **profits on the s.,** de la gratte; *P:* **to have a bit on the s.,** avoir une petite amie; prendre un petit à-côté. **5.** (*a*) parti *m*; **to be on the right s.,** être du bon parti; **to vote for a s.,** voter pour un parti; **he doesn't know which s. to take,** il ne sait pas de quel bord se ranger; **to take sides,** se ranger d'un côté; sortir de la neutralité; **to take sides with s.o., to take the s. of s.o.,** se ranger avec qn, du côté de qn; **he's on our s.,** il est avec nous, de notre parti, de notre côté; **to change sides,** changer de camp, virer de bord; *Pol: etc:* faire volte-face; **you have the law on your s.,** vous avez la loi pour vous; **time's on our s.,** le temps travaille pour nous; **mistakes were made on both sides,** des erreurs ont été commises de part et d'autre; *Jur:* **the other s.,** la partie adverse; **to hear counsel on both sides,** entendre les avocats des deux parties; (*b*) *Games:* équipe *f*, camp *m*; **to be on the same s.,** être du même camp; **to pick sides,** tirer les camps; *Rugby Fb:* **no s.,** fin *f* de partie; **to let the s. down,** trahir, décevoir, ses amis, etc.; (*c*) (*lineage*) côté; **well connected on his mother's s.,** de haute parenté par sa mère, du côté maternel, du côté de sa mère; bien apparenté du côté de sa mère; **it was the father's s. that inherited,** c'est la ligne paternelle qui a hérité. **6.** *attrib.* latéral, -aux; de côté; **s. entry, entrance,** entrée de côté; entrée latérale; **s. door,** porte latérale ((i) porte de dégagement; (ii) porte de service, petite porte); **s. street,** rue latérale, transversale; contre-allée *f*, *pl.* contre-allées; **s. road,** chemin latéral; route secondaire; **s. view,** vue de profil, de côté; **s. view of the hotel,** l'hôtel vu de côté; **s. glance,** (i) regard en coin, de côté; coup d'œil oblique; (ii) brève allusion; **with a s. glance at her,** en la regardant de côté, du coin de l'œil; **s. face,** profil *m*; **s. issue,** question d'importance, d'intérêt, secondaire; **the s. issues of a question,** les à-côtés d'une question; **s. effect,** effet, résultat *m*, réaction *f*, secondaire (d'un médicament, etc.); **s. effects,** répercussions *f*; *O:* **s. dish,** entremets *m*, hors-d'œuvre *m inv*; **s. salad,** salade *f* (pour accompagner un bifteck, etc.); **s. drum,** tambour *m*; **(long) s. drum,** caisse roulante; **shallow s. drum,** caisse plate; **high-pitched s. drum,** caisse claire; **s. pocket,** poche de côté; **s. comb,** petit peigne (porté de côté); **s. table,** petite table; desserte *f*; *NAm:* **s. chair,** chaise *f* (de salle à manger, etc.); *Ecc.Arch:* **s. chapel,** chapelle latérale; **s. altar,** autel latéral, subordonné; **s. aisle,** (i) *Ecc.Arch:* nef latérale; bas-côté *m*, *pl.* bas-côtés; (ii) *Th: etc:* passage latéral, de côté; *Th:* **s. box,** loge de côté; *Th: Cin:* **s. lighting,** éclairage latéral, de côté; **s. step,** (i) *Box: Mil: Danc:* pas de côté; (ii) *Veh:* marchepied *m* de côté; *Veh:* **s. frame,** longeron *m* (de caisse); (*in a bus, etc.*) **s. seat,** siège, banquette, de côté; *O:* **s. lamps,** lanternes *f*, feux *m*, de côté; **s. rail,** (i) *Rail:* contre-rail *m*, *pl.* contre-rails; (ii) rambarde *f* (de navire); garde-fou *m* (de pont), *pl.* garde-fous; *Nau:* **s. rope,** tire-veille *f inv*; **s. bunkers,** soutes latérales; *A:* **s. wheel steamer, s. wheeler,** vapeur *m* à roues; **s. wind,** vent de côté; *F:* **to hear of sth. by a s. wind,** apprendre qch. par ricochet, indirectement, de source indirecte; *Gym:* **s. horse,** cheval d'arçons; *Harn:* **s. leather, pad,** garde-flanc(s) *m inv*; *Ch:* **s. chain,** chaîne latérale (d'atomes); **s. tool,** outil, ciseau, de côté; **lathe s. tool,** outil à dresser; *A:* **s. whiskers,** favoris *m*, pattes *f* (de lapin, de lièvre).

side². **1.** *v.i.* **to s. with s.o.,** se ranger du côté de qn; se ranger sous les drapeaux, sous la bannière, de qn; prendre le parti de qn; prendre fait et cause pour qn; faire cause commune avec qn; **to s. with the strongest party,** se ranger du côté du plus fort; **to s. against s.o.,** prendre parti contre qn, se tourner contre qn. **2.** *v.tr.* **to s. rough timber,** débiter le bois brut; **sided timber,** bois dégrossi.

side³, *v.tr. Dial:* **to s. the table, the dishes,** débarrasser, desservir, la table.

sidebar ['saidba:r], *s. Harn:* aube *f* (de selle).

sideboard ['saidbɔ:d], *s.* **1.** *Furn:* buffet *m*; desserte *f*. **2.** *N.Arch:* planche *f* à roulis. **3.** *F:* **sideboards,** favoris *m*; pattes *f* (de lapin, de lièvre).

sideburns ['saidbə:nz], *s.pl. F:* = SIDEBOARD 3.

sidecar ['saidka:r], *s.* **1.** *A:* carriole irlandaise à deux roues. **2.** side-car *m*, *pl.* side-cars, sidecar *m* (de motocyclette). **3.** *esp. NAm:* cocktail composé de cointreau, de cognac et de jus de citron.

sidekick ['saidkik], *s. F:* associé, -ée, sous-fifre *m*, *pl.* sous-fifres; camarade *mf*; copain, copine.

sidelight ['saidlait], *s.* **1.** *Phot: etc:* lumière *f* oblique, qui vient de côté; *Fig:* **to throw a s. on a subject,** (i) éclairer fortuitement un sujet; (ii) donner un aperçu indirect sur un sujet; **sidelights on history,** la petite histoire; les à-côtés *m* de l'histoire. **2.** *Const:* fenêtre latérale. **3.** *(a) A:* lanterne latérale (d'une voiture, etc.); *(b)* **sidelights,** (i) *Aut:* feux *m* de position; (ii) *Nau: etc:* feux de côté.

sideline ['saidlain], *s.* *(a)* ligne latérale; *Fb: etc:* ligne de touche; **to be on the sidelines,** ne pas participer à un jeu, etc.; ne pas se mêler à une affaire; *(b)* occupation *f* secondaire; violon *m* d'Ingres; *(c) Com:* article *m* à côté.

sideling ['saidliŋ]. *A:* **1.** *a.* (mouvement, marche) oblique, de côté. **2.** *adv.* obliquement; de côté.

sidelong ['saidlɔŋ]. **1.** *adv.* (se mouvoir) obliquement, de côté; **to look s. at s.o.,** regarder qn de côté, du coin de l'œil; faire des yeux en coulisse à qn; lorgner qn (du coin de l'œil). **2.** *a.* (regard) oblique, de côté, en coulisse; **to give s.o. a s. glance,** regarder qn de côté, du coin de l'œil.

sidenote ['saidnout], *s.* note *f* en marge; note marginale; *(on document)* apostille *f.*

sidepiece ['saidpi:s], *s.* **1.** brancard *m* (d'une voiture); montant *m* (d'une échelle, d'une galerie de mine, etc.). **2. cap with sidepieces,** bonnet à oreillons *m.*

sideral ['sidərəl], *a.* **1.** = SIDEREAL. **2.** *Astrol: A:* (influence, etc.) funeste (provenant des astres).

siderazot(e) [sidə'ræzout], *s. Miner:* sidérazote *f.*

sidereal [sai'diəriəl], *a. Astr: (of day, year, etc.)* sidéral, -aux; **s. time,** heure *f* astronomique, temps sidéral; **Greenwich s. time,** temps sidéral de Greenwich; **local s. time,** temps sidéral local.

siderite ['saidərait], *s. (a)* sidérite *f*; *(b) Miner:* sidérose *f*, fer *m* spathique.

sideritic [sidə'ritik], *a. Miner:* sidérique.

sideritis [sidə'raitis], *s. Bot:* sideritis *m*; *F:* thé *m* de campagne.

siderocyte ['sidərousait], *s. Med:* sidérocyte *m.*

siderography [sidə'rɔgrəfi], *s.* sidérographie *f.*

siderolite ['sidəroulait], *s. Miner:* sidérolithe *f.*

sideromelane [sidərou'melein], *s. Miner:* sidéromélane *f.*

sideronatrite [sidərou'neitrait], *s. Miner:* sidéronatrite *f.*

siderosis [sidə'rousis], *s. Med:* sidérose *f*, sidérosis *f.*

siderostat ['sidəroustæt], *s. Astr:* sidérostat *m.*

siderotil ['sidəroutil], *s. Miner:* sidérotyle *m.*

siderous ['sidərəs], *a. Miner:* sidéré.

sideroxylon [sidərɔk'sailɔn], *s. Bot:* sideroxylon *m.*

sideshow ['saidʃou], *s.* **1.** spectacle, jeu, forain (à une foire, etc.). **2.** *F:* affaire *f*, bataille *f*, etc., d'importance secondaire.

sideslip[1] ['saidslip], *s.* **1.** *Aut: Cy: Ski:* dérapage *m.* **2.** *Av:* glissade *f* (sur l'aile); **s. indicator,** indicateur de glissement latéral. **3.** *A:* enfant *mf* illégitime.

sideslip[2], *v.i.* **1.** *Aut: Cy: Ski:* déraper. **2.** *Av:* glisser sur l'aile.

sideslipping ['saidslipiŋ], *s.* **1.** *Aut: Cy: Ski:* dérapage *m.* **2.** *Av:* glissement *m* (sur l'aile).

sidesman, *pl.* **-men** ['saidzmən], *s.m. Ecc:* = marguillier adjoint.

sidestep ['saidstep]. **1.** *v.i.* faire un pas de côté; *Box: etc:* esquiver. **2.** *v.tr. F:* éviter (une question).

sidestick ['saidstik], *s. Typ:* biseau *m* (pour serrer la forme).

sidestroke ['saidstrouk], *s. Swim:* nage *f* sur le côté, à la marinière.

sidetrack[1] ['saidtræk], *s. Rail:* voie *f* de garage; voie secondaire; *(to factory, etc.)* voie de débord; *Fig:* **to get on a s.,** s'écarter du sujet.

sidetrack[2], *v.* **1.** *v.tr.* *(a)* garer (un train); aiguiller (un train) sur une voie de garage; *(b) Fig:* (i) détourner l'attention de (qn); (ii) remettre à plus tard (un projet, etc.); **to be sidetracked by sth.,** se détourner sur qch. **2.** *v.i. (of train)* se garer; *Fig:* **then he sidetracked into politics,** puis il a délaissé sa profession pour entrer dans la politique.

sidetracking ['saidtrækiŋ], *s.* garage *m* (d'un train); aiguillage *m* (d'un train) sur une voie de garage.

sidewalk ['saidwɔ:k], *s. esp. NAm:* trottoir *m.*

sidewall ['saidwɔ:l], *s.* **1.** *Min:* paroi latérale (de galerie). **2.** *Hyd.E:* bajoyer *m* (d'écluse). **3.** *Aut: Cy:* flanc *m* (d'un pneu).

sideward ['saidwəd]. **1.** *a.* (mouvement) de côté; latéral, -aux. **2.** *adv.* = SIDEWARDS.

sidewards ['saidwədz], *adv.* (regarder, etc.) de côté.

sideways, *O:* **sidewise** ['saidweiz, -waiz]. **1.** *adv.* de côté; latéralement; **to jump s.,** faire un saut de côté; **to walk s.,** marcher en crabe; **to turn s.,** se tourner de côté; **to stand s.,** s'effacer; **the tower leans s.,** la tour penche d'un côté. **2.** *a.* latéral, -aux; de côté; **s. motion,** mouvement latéral; **s. position of the body,** effacement *m* du corps.

sidewinder ['saidwaindər], *s. Rept: U.S:* serpent à sonnettes cornu.

siding ['saidiŋ], *s. Rail:* *(a)* voie *f* de garage, d'évitement; **shunting s.,** voie de triage; *(b)* **(private) s.,** embranchement *m*; voie de raccordement (d'usine, etc.); **loading, goods, s.,** voie de chargement.

sidle ['saidl], *v.i.* **to s. along, in, out,** s'avancer, entrer, sortir, timidement, de côté, de guingois; **sidling along the wall,** longeant le mur, se coulant le long du mur (pour ne pas être vu); **to s. up to s.o.,** se couler auprès de qn, vers qn.

Sidon ['said(ə)n], *Pr.n. A.Geog:* Sidon.

Sidonian [sai'douniən]. *A.Geog:* *(a) a.* sidonien; *(b) s.* Sidonien, -ienne.

siege[1] [si:dʒ], *s.* **1.** *Mil:* siège *m*; **regular s.,** siège en règle, en forme; **to lay s. to a town,** assiéger une ville; mettre le siège devant une ville; faire le siège d'une ville; **to raise the s.,** lever le siège; **to declare a state of s. (in a town),** déclarer l'état de siège (dans une ville); *Mil: Hist:* **s. artillery, s. gun,** artillerie *f*, pièce *f*, de siège. **2.** *Glassm:* banc *m* (d'un fourneau de fusion).

siege[2], *v.tr. A:* assiéger, mettre le siège devant (une ville); faire le siège (d'une ville).

siegenite ['si:gənait, 'zi:g-], *s. Miner:* siegénite *f.*

siemens ['si:mənz], *s. El.Meas:* siemens *m.*

Siena [si'enə], *Pr.n. Geog:* Sienne *f.*

Sienese [siə'ni:z]. *Geog:* *(a) a.* siennois; *(b) s.* Siennois, -oise.

sienna [si'enə], *s.* **1.** terre *f* de Sienne; **raw, burnt, s.,** terre de Sienne naturelle, brûlée. **2.** *a. (colour)* **s. (brown),** terre de Sienne *inv.*

sierra [si'erə], *s. Geog:* sierra *f.*

Sierra Leone [sierəli'oun(i)], *Pr.n. Geog:* Sierra Leone *m.*

Sierra Leonean [sierəli'ouniən], *a. & s. Geog:* (originaire *mf*, habitant, -ante) de Sierra Leone.

siesta [si'estə], *s.* sieste *f*; **to take a s.,** faire la sieste.

sieve[1] [siv], *s.* **1.** *(with coarse mesh)* crible *m*; *(with fine mesh)* tamis *m*; *(for grain)* van *m*; sas *m*; *Min: Civ.E:* **drum s.,** crible à tambour rotatif; **fixed, movable, s.,** crible à grille fixe, mobile; **wire gauze s.,** tamis de gaze métallique; **to pass sth. through a s.,** tamiser qch.; passer qch. au tamis, au crible; **s. frame,** cerce *f* de tamis; *F:* **he's got a head like a s.,** il a une mémoire de lièvre; sa mémoire est une passoire; *Lit:* **to draw water with a s.,** remplir le tonneau des Danaïdes. **2.** *F: O:* jaseur, -euse; bavard, -arde. **3.** *Bot:* **s. tube,** crible.

sieve[2], *v.tr.* = SIFT 1.

sifaka, sifac [si'fa:kə, 'si:fæk], *s. Z:* propithèque *m*; lémurien *m* malgache.

sift [sift]. **1.** *v.tr.* *(a)* passer (qch.) au tamis, au crible, au sas; passer (qch.) par l'étamine; tamiser, bluter (la farine); escarbiller (des cendres); vanner (le blé); cribler (du sable, etc.); **sifted plaster,** plâtre au sas; **to s. sugar over a cake,** saupoudrer un gâteau de sucre; **to s. out pebbles from sand,** séparer au tamis les cailloux du sable; *(b)* examiner minutieusement, passer par l'étamine (des preuves); approfondir, éplucher (une question); **to s. (out) the facts,** passer les faits au crible. **2.** *v.i. (of dust, etc.)* filtrer **(through,** à travers); *(of light)* filtrer, se tamiser, être tamisé (à travers, par).

sifter ['siftər], *s.* **1.** *(pers.)* tamiseur, -euse; cribleur, -euse; sasseur, -euse. **2.** *(a) (sieve)* tamis *m*, crible *m*; sas *m*; *(b)* appareil *m* à cribler; cribleuse *f*; tamiseuse *f*; *Mill:* sasseur *m.* **3.** saupoudroir *m* (à sucre).

sifting ['siftiŋ], *s.* **1.** *(a)* tamisage *m*, criblage *m*, sassement *m*, blutage *m* (de qch.); *(b)* examen minutieux (des preuves, etc.); démêlement *m* (du vrai et du faux). **2. siftings,** criblure(s) *f(pl).*

sigh[1] [sai], *s.* soupir *m*; **heavy, deep, long(-drawn), s.,** gros, profond, long, soupir; **to breathe, give, a s.,** pousser, laisser échapper, un soupir; soupirer; **he breathed, heaved, a s. of relief,** il a poussé un soupir de soulagement; **to give a long s.,** pousser un long soupir; soupirer longuement; **with a s.,** en soupirant; **the Bridge of Sighs,** le Pont des Soupirs.

sigh[2]. **1.** *v.i.* *(a)* soupirer; pousser, laisser échapper, un soupir; **to s. with relief,** pousser un soupir de soulagement; *Lit:* **the wind is sighing in the trees,** le vent soupire, frémit, dans les arbres; *(b) O:* **to s. for, after, sth.,** soupirer pour, après, qch.; désirer ardemment qch.; **to s. for home,** avoir la nostalgie du foyer; **to s. for lost friends,** regretter des amis perdus; **to s. over a mistake,** déplorer une erreur. **2.** *v.tr. Lit:* **to s. out, forth, a prayer,** prononcer une prière en soupirant, parmi des soupirs.

sighing[1] ['saiiŋ], *a.* qui soupire; soupirant.

sighing[2], *s.* soupirs *mpl*; **s. of the wind,** soupir, plainte *f*, du vent.

sight[1] [sait], *s.* **1.** *(faculty of vision)* vue *f*; *(a)* **to have good s., bad s.,** avoir la vue bonne, mauvaise; **to have long s.,** avoir la vue longue; être presbyte; être hypermétrope; **short s.,** myopie *f*; **to have short s.,** avoir la vue basse, courte; être myope; **s. testing,** examen de la vue; **to lose one's s.,** perdre la vue; devenir aveugle; **he lost his s. in the war,** il est aveugle de guerre; *(b)* **to catch s., get a s., of s.o., sth.,** apercevoir, aviser, entrevoir, qn, qch.; **to lose s. of s.o.,** perdre qn de vue; **I didn't lose s. of him,** je ne l'ai pas perdu de vue; (i) je l'ai suivi des yeux; (ii) je suis resté en relations avec lui; **we've lost s. of him lately,** voilà assez longtemps que nous ne l'avons vu, que nous sommes sans nouvelles de lui; *Nau:* **to lose s. of land,** perdre terre; **to lose s. of the fact that . . .,** perdre de vue que . . .; **I can't bear the s. of him, I hate the very s. of him,** je ne peux pas le sentir; je ne peux pas le voir; **he stopped at the s. of the picture,** il s'est arrêté en voyant le tableau; **to translate at s.,** traduire à première vue, à livre ouvert; **to shoot s.o. at s.,** faire feu, tirer, sur qn à première vue; *Mus:* **to play at s.,** jouer à vue, déchiffrer; **to s. read,** (i) lire à vue; (ii) *Mus:* déchiffrer; **s. reading,** (i) lecture *f* à vue; (ii) déchiffrement *m* (de la musique); *Com: Fin:* **bill payable at s.,** effet *m* payable à vue; **bill, draft, at s.,** *NAm:* **s. draft,** effet, papier, traite, à vue; **the currency of the bill of exchange is three months after s.,** l'échéance de la lettre de change est de trois mois de vue; *St.Exch:* **s. quotation,** cotation *f* à vue; **at first s.,** à première vue; du, au, premier coup d'œil; à, dès, l'abord; au premier abord; **to fall in love at first s.,** tomber amoureux à première vue **(with,** de); **it was a case of love at first s.,** c'était le coup de foudre; **I loved her at first s.,** je l'ai aimée du premier coup; **to know s.o. by s.,** connaître qn de vue; *NAm:* **on sale s. unseen,** à vendre tel quel, sur description, sans inspection; *Cust:* **s. entry,** déclaration *f* provisoire; *Tchn:* **s. check, control,** contrôle à vue, contrôle visuel; mirage *m*; **to s.-check,** contrôler visuellement, mirer; **s. gauge,** niveau *m* à vue; **s. feed,** débit *m* visible; **s.-feed lubricator, oilcup,** graisseur à débit visible; **s.-feed needle valve,** pointeau de débit visible; **s.(-feed) glass,** verre de débit visible; *(c) (way of looking)* **to find favour in s.o.'s s.,** trouver grâce devant qn; **guilty in the s. of the law,** coupable aux yeux de la loi. **2.** *(range of vision)* **to come into s.,** (ap)paraître; **to be within s.,** être à portée de la vue; être en vue; **to be (with)in s. of land, of Dieppe,** être en vue de (la) terre, de Dieppe; **land in s.!** terre! **ship reported in s.,** navire signalé en vue; **there is nothing in s.,** il n'y a rien en vue; **my goal is in s.,** j'approche de mon but; je touche au but; **I just caught s. of him in the crowd,** je l'ai entrevu dans la foule; **keep him in s.,** ne le perdez pas de vue; **to come within s. of the town,** arriver en vue de la ville; **out of s.,** caché aux regards; **to vanish out of s.,** disparaître; **the land disappeared from s., was lost to s.,** la terre s'est perdue de vue; **he was soon out of s.,** nous l'avons bientôt perdu de vue; **to put sth. out of s.,** mettre qch. hors de vue; faire disparaître qch.; éloigner, cacher, qch.; **to keep out of s.,** se tenir hors de vue; se cacher, se dérober; **he didn't let her out of his s.,** il ne la perdait pas de vue; il ne la quittait pas d'une semelle; **out of my s.!** hors de ma vue! hors d'ici! *Prov:* **out of s., out of mind,** loin des yeux, loin du cœur. **3.** *Opt:* *(a)* visée *f* (avec un instrument d'optique, une arme à feu, etc.); *Surv:* coup *m* de lunette; **back s.,** visée arrière, coup arrière; **fore s.,** visée avant, coup avant; **angle of s.,** angle *m* de visée, de site; **line of s.,** (i) ligne *f* de visée (d'un instrument d'optique); (ii) ligne de mire, de tir (d'une arme à feu); **to take a s. on sth.,** viser, mirer, qch.; faire un coup de lunette; *(b)* appareil *m* de visée, de pointage (d'un instrument, d'une arme à feu); viseur *m*; œilleton *m* (de viseur); lumière *f* (de sextant); voyant *m* (de mire de nivellement); *Opt:* **rear s.,** viseur arrière; pinnule *f* arrière; *Artil:* **quadrant s.,** appareil de pointage à secteur; **s. (vane),** pinnule *f* (d'alidade, etc.); **alidade, compass, with sights,** alidade *f*, boussole *f*, à pinnules; **cross-hair s.,** pinnule à fils; *Artil: Sm.a:* **(back) s., (rear) s.,** hausse *f*; cran *m* de mire; **rear-s. guard,** protège-hausse *m*, *pl.* protège-hausses; **(fore) s., (front) s.,** (i) guidon *m*; bouton *m* de mire; (ii) *Artil:* fronteau *m* de mire, guidon de tir; **aperture s., peep s.,** hausse à œilleton; **circular front s.,** guidon annulaire; **extension s.,** hausse à rallonge; **fine s., full s.,** guidon fin, guidon plein; **leaf s., flap s.,** hausse à charnière, à clapet, à curseur; **illuminated s., night s.,** guidon lumineux; **lensatic s., telescopic s.,** hausse optique, télescopique; hausse à lunette; **radial s., central s.,** hausse médiane; **rod s.,** hausse à tige; **side s.,** hausse latérale; **step s.,** hausse à gradins; **s. gradations,** graduations *f* de la hausse, échelle *f* de hausse; **s. leaf,** planche(tte) *f* de hausse; **s. notch,** cran *m* de hausse; **open-notch s.,** hausse à cran ouvert; **s. slide,** curseur *m* de hausse; **s. with slide,** hausse à curseur; **to adjust sights,** prendre, régler, la hausse; **to lay on a target with open s.,** tirer à vue sur un objectif; **to set the s. at 1,000 metres,** mettre la hausse à 1.000 mètres; **to lower one's sights,** viser moins haut, baisser ses prétentions. **4. s. (hole),** (i) *Opt:* lumière *f* (de pinnule, etc.); (ii) regard *m*, fenêtrelle *f* (de visite, d'inspection, d'égout, etc.); *I.C.E:* **(glass) s. of the drip feed,** viseur de compte-gouttes. **5.** (*a*) spectacle *m*; **sad s.,** spectacle navrant; **it's a s. to see,** cela vaut la peine d'être vu; **it's a magnificent s.,** c'est un spectacle, un coup d'œil, superbe; **it was a s. for sore eyes,** (i) c'était réjouissant à voir; c'était un spectacle qui réjouissait les yeux; (ii) ç'a été une agréable surprise; (*b*) *F:* **his face was a s.,** si vous aviez vu son visage! **to make a s. of oneself,** se rendre ridicule; *esp.* se fagoter, s'affubler; **what a s. you are! you do look a s.!** comme vous voilà fait! comme vous voilà affublé, arrangé, accoutré, ajusté! de quoi avez-vous l'air! (*c*) chose digne d'être vue; **the sights,** (i) les sites *m* pittoresques; (ii) les monuments *m*, les curiosités *f* (de la ville, etc.). **6.** *P:* **a s. of. . .,** énormément de. . .; **there was a s. of people,** il y avait énormément de monde; **it cost me a s. of trouble, of money,** ça m'a coûté énormément de peine, un argent fou; **he's a damn s. too clever for you,** il est de beaucoup plus fort que vous; il vous dégotte.

sight[2], *v.tr.* **1.** (*a*) apercevoir, aviser (qn, qch.); *Nau:* **to s. land,** reconnaître la terre; relever la terre; avoir connaissance de terre; atterrir; **to s. a ship,** apercevoir un navire; venir en vue d'un bâtiment; (*b*) *Com:* **to s. a bill,** voir un effet. **2.** viser, observer (un astre, etc.). **3.** pointer (un fusil); **to s. the mark,** mirer le but; **to s. at 1,000 metres,** mettre la hausse à 1.000 mètres. **4.** munir (une arme à feu) d'une hausse; ajuster un appareil de visée à (un instrument).

sighted ['saitid], *a.* **1.** qui voit; **the s.,** les voyants *m*. **2.** (*with adj. prefixed*) **weak-s.,** à la vue faible; **long-s.,** presbyte; hypermétrope; à la vue longue, à longue vue; **to be long-s.,** avoir la vue longue; **far-s.,** prescient, prudent; sagace, prévoyant; **short-s.,** myope. **3.** *Opt:* (instrument, viseur) à pinnule(s); **s. alidade, level,** alidade *f*, niveau *m*, à pinnules.

sighter ['saitər], *s.* **1.** *Phot: etc:* aiguille *f* de mire (de viseur). **2.** *Mil: etc:* coup *m* de réglage; (*in rifle competition*) balle *f* d'essai.

sighting ['saitiŋ], *s.* **1.** vue *f*; *Ven:* **several sightings of teal have been reported,** on a vu des sarcelles à plusieurs reprises. **2.** visée *f* (avec un instrument d'optique, avec une arme à feu); pointage *m* (d'une arme à feu, etc.); **long-range s.,** visée à longue portée; **s. in the dark,** visée dans l'obscurité; *Artil:* **bore s.,** visée dans l'âme, par le canon; **line of s.,** ligne *f* de visée, de pointage, de mire; **plane of s.,** plan *m* de pointage; **s. apparatus, s. gear, s. instrument,** appareil *m*, instrument *m*, de visée, de pointage; **s. angle,** angle *m* de visée; **s. axis,** axe *m* de visée, de pointage; *Mil: etc:* **s. blister, s. hood,** coupole *f* de visée (d'une tourelle); **s. chart,** table *f* de visée; **s. equipment,** les appareils, les instruments, de visée, de pointage; **s. slit, s. aperture,** lumière *f*, voyant *m* (d'un instrument à pinnule); **s. slot,** fente *f* de visée; **s. system,** dispositif *m*, système *m*, de visée, de pointage; **s. telescope,** lunette *f* de visée, de pointage; **s. tube, s. piece,** viseur *m* (d'alidade, etc.); **s. unit,** (i) viseur; (ii) *Artil: etc:* appareil, dispositif, de pointage; **s. vane,** mire *f*, pinnule *f*; **s. shot,** (i) *Artil:* coup *m* de réglage; (ii) (*in rifle competition*) balle *f* d'essai. **3.** *Com:* visa *m* (d'une lettre de change).

sightless ['saitlis], *a.* aveugle; privé de la vue; **s. eyes,** yeux éteints.

sightlessness ['saitlisnis], *s.* cécité *f*.

sightly ['saitli], *a.* agréable à voir; séduisant; de physique agréable; avenant.

sight(-)see ['saitsi:], *v.i.* visiter des sites pittoresques, les curiosités (d'une ville).

sightseeing ['saitsi:iŋ], *s.* tourisme *m*; **we spent the day s.,** nous avons passé la journée à visiter le pays, les monuments.

sightseer ['saitsi:ər], *s.* touriste *mf*; excursionniste *mf*.

sightworthy ['saitwə:ði], *a.* *O:* qui vaut la peine d'être vu; (chose) à voir.

sigil ['sidʒil], *s.* sceau *m*, cachet *m*.

Sigillaria [sidʒi'lɛəriə], *s. Paleont:* sigillaire *f*, sigillaria *f*.

sigillate(d) ['sidʒileit(id)], *a. Bot: Cer: etc:* sigillé.

sigillation [sidʒi'leiʃ(ə)n], *s.* sigillation *f*.

sigillographer [sidʒi'lɔgrəfər], *s.* sigillographe *m*.

sigillographical [sidʒilou'græfikl], *a.* sigillographique.

sigillography [sidʒi'lɔgrəfi], *s.* sigillographie *f*.

Sigismund ['sigismənd]. *Pr.n.m.* Sigismond.

siglum, *pl.* **sigla** ['sigləm, -lə], *s. Pal:* sigle *m*.

sigma ['sigmə], *s. Gr.Alph:* sigma *m*.

sigmatic [sig'mætik], *a. Gr.Gram:* (aoriste, futur) sigmatique.

sigmatism ['sigmətizm], *s. Ling:* sigmatisme *m*.

sigmodon ['sigmədɔn], *s. Z:* sigmodonte *m*.

sigmoid ['sigmɔid], *a. Anat:* (cavité, etc.) sigmoïde; (*of the colon*) **s. flexure,** anse *f* sigmoïde; *Med:* **tumour of the s. flexure,** tumeur sigmoïdienne.

sigmoidectomy [sigmɔi'dektəmi], *s. Surg:* sigmoïdectomie *f*.

sigmoiditis [sigmɔi'daitis], *s. Med:* sigmoïdite *f*.

sigmoidostomy [sigmɔi'dɔstəmi], *s. Surg:* sigmoïdostomie *f*.

sign[1] [sain], *s.* **1.** signe *m*; (*a*) **to make a s., signs, to s.o.,** faire (un) signe, des signes, à qn; **s. of the cross,** signe de la croix; **to make the s. of the cross,** se signer; **to make an affirmative s., a negative s.,** faire signe que oui, que non; **s. language,** (langage *m*) mimique *f*; **s. languages,** les langages par signes; (*b*) **s. of recognition,** signe de reconnaissance; *Mil:* **the s. and the countersign,** le mot d'ordre et le mot de ralliement; (*c*) *Tg:* **call s.,** indicatif *m* d'appel; (*d*) **s. manual,** signature *f*, *esp.* la signature du souverain; **under the king's s. manual,** signé de la main du roi; revêtu de la signature du roi. **2.** (*a*) indice *m*, indication *f*; **sure s.,** indice certain; **it's a good, bad, s.,** c'est bon, mauvais, signe; **s. of rain,** signe, marque *f*, de pluie; **a sudden fall of the barometer is a s. of storm,** une chute barométrique est une indication, une annonce, d'orage; **s. of the times,** marque, signe, des temps; **s. of bad breeding,** preuve *f*, marque, de mauvaise éducation; **as a s. of. . .,** en signe de. . .; **he gave no s. of having heard anything,** il n'a manifesté en aucune façon avoir rien entendu; **there's no s. of his coming,** rien n'annonce sa venue; *R.C.Ch:* **sensible s.,** signe sensible; (*b*) trace *f*; **no s. of. . .,** nulle, aucune, trace de. . .; **there is little s. of progress,** les progrès se font attendre; **there are signs that the flower beds have been trampled on,** il apparaît, on voit, que quelqu'un a marché dans les parterres; **the room showed signs of having been recently occupied,** la pièce révélait une occupation récente; **to show no s. of life,** ne donner aucun signe de vie, ne pas donner signe de vie; **there are no signs of it,** il n'en reste aucune trace; **there was no s. of him,** (i) on ne l'a pas aperçu; (ii) il restait invisible; *Theol:* **outward and visible s.,** signe extérieur et visible (de la grâce, etc.). **3.** (*a*) (*of pub, inn, etc.*) enseigne *f*; **at the s. of the Golden Lion,** à l'enseigne du Lion d'Or; **s. writer, painter,** peintre en lettres; peintre d'enseignes; (*b*) **(shop) s.,** enseigne, écriteau *m*; **electric, illuminated, s.,** enseigne, réclame, lumineuse; **neon s.,** enseigne, réclame, au néon; **flashing s.,** réclame à éclipse; (*c*) **(road) signs,** signalisation *f* des routes; signalisation routière; **road s.,** panneau indicateur, plaque indicatrice (de route); signal *m* de route; signal routier; **international (system of) road signs,** signalisation routière internationale; **direction, traffic, s.,** panneau de signalisation (routière); **advance warning s.,** panneau de présignalisation; (*d*) *W.Tel: etc:* **studio warning s.,** indicateur *m* d'occupation; (*e*) **s. of the zodiac,** signe du zodiaque; **lucky s.,** signe de chance. **4.** (*a*) *Mth: Mus: etc:* symbole *m*; **positive s., plus s.,** signe positif; (signe) plus *m*; **negative s., minus s.,** signe négatif; (signe) moins *m*; **algebraical s.,** signe algébrique; **astronomical signs,** signes astronomiques; (*b*) *Cmptr:* **s. digit,** chiffre de signe; **s. bit,** bit de signe; *Elcs:* **s. reversing, s. changing, amplifier,** amplificateur inverseur de signe. **5.** *Ling:* **s. process,** impression *f* sémantique.

sign[2], *v.*

I. *v.tr.* **1.** (*a*) *A:* signer (qn, qch.); marquer (qn, qch.) d'un signe; (*b*) signer (son nom, un document, un chèque, etc.); viser (un compte); **the letter was signed by the president,** la lettre portait la signature du président; **to s. a bill,** accepter une traite; **to s. a contract,** signer, passer, un contrat; *Jur:* **signed, sealed and delivered in presence of. . .,** fait et signé en présence de. . .; **s. here,** signez là! **to s. for s.o.,** signer pour qn; *Com:* **to s. for goods,** signer à l'arrivée; **he signs himself Victor,** il signe Victor; **to s. sth. away, over, to s.o.,** céder qch. par écrit (à qn); **to s. away one's birthright,** renoncer (par écrit) à son droit d'aînesse. **2.** *O:* **to s. assent,** faire signe que oui; **to s. (to, for) s.o. to do sth.,** faire signe à qn de faire qch.

II. (*compound verbs*) **1. sign off,** *v.i.* (*a*) (*of workers in factories, etc.*) signer le registre (en quittant le travail); se pointer au départ; (*b*) *W.Tel:* terminer l'émission (en jouant l'indicatif).

2. sign on. (*a*) *v.tr.* embaucher (un ouvrier); engager (un matelot, etc.); (*b*) *v.i.* (i) (*of workers*) s'embaucher; (*of soldier, etc.*) s'engager, signer l'engagement; (ii) (*of workers in factories, etc.*) signer le registre (en arrivant au travail); se pointer à l'arrivée; (iii) *W.Tel:* commencer l'émission (en jouant l'indicatif); (iv) *F:* s'inscrire au chômage.

3. sign up. (*a*) *v.i.* s'inscrire à (un cours, etc.); (*of soldier, etc.*) s'engager, signer l'engagement; (*b*) *v.tr. Sp: Th: etc:* donner un contrat à, engager (qn).

signal[1] ['sign(ə)l], *s.* **1.** (*sign*) signal, -aux *m*; signe *m*; **warning s.,** signal avertisseur, d'avertissement, d'alerte, de mise en garde; **alarm s.,** signal d'alarme, d'alerte; **all clear s.,** signal de fin d'alerte (aérienne); **answering s.,** signal d'aperçu; **code s., conventional s.,** signal conventionnel; **counter-s.,** contre-signal, -aux *m*; **storm s.,** signal de mauvais temps, d'avis de tempête; **time s.,** signal horaire; **acoustic, sound, s.,** signal acoustique, sonore, phonique; *Tp:* **calling s.,** *U.S:* **line s.,** indicatif *m* d'appel; **cleardown s., clearing s.,** signal de début, de fin, de communication; **line disengaged,** *U.S:* **free line, s.,** signal de ligne libre; **line engaged,** *U.S:* **busy, s.,** signal de ligne occupée; signal *pas libre*; **s. communications,** télécommunications *fpl*, transmissions *fpl*; **s. communications by orbiting relay,** télécommunications par satellite relais; *Mil:* **main line of s. communications,** axe *m* des transmissions; *Av:* **identification, authentification, recognition, s.,** signal d'identification; **dropping s.,** signal de largage; **bomb-release s.,** signal de largage des bombes; **s. area,** aire *f* à signaux; **to give, make, send, a s.,** faire, envoyer, un signal; **to receive a s.,** recevoir un signal; **to catch a s.,** capter un signal (à l'improviste); **he gave a s. for silence,** il a fait signe de faire silence, de se taire; **the pilot gave the s. to remove the chocks,** le pilote a fait signe d'enlever les cales (de l'avion); **to give the starting s., the s. for departure,** donner le signal de, du, départ; *Mil:* **to give the s. to open fire,** donner le signal de l'ouverture du feu. **2.** (*a*) **visible, visual, s.,** signal visible, visuel, optique; **traffic signals,** feux *m* de circulation; *NAm:* **s. red,** vermillon chinois; **light s.,** signal lumineux; **intermittent (light) s.,** (signal) clignotant *m*; clignoteur *m*; *Nau:* **flashing s.,** signal à éclats, par scott; **s. light,** (i) *Nau:* fanal, -aux *m*; (ii) (lampe) témoin *m*; **lamp s.,** signal (i) *Mil:* par lampe, par projecteur, (ii) *Nau: Rail: etc:* par fanal, par fanaux; **s. lamp,** (i) lampe *f*, projecteur *m*, de signalisation; (ii) (lampe) témoin; voyant (lumineux); lampe indicatrice; **arm s., hand s.,** signal à bras; **semaphore s.,** signal sémaphorique, *Navy:* à bras; **s. arm,** bras *m* de signal (d'un sémaphore); **flag s.,** signal (i) *Mil:* par fanion(s), (ii) *Nau:* à pavillon, (iii) *Rail:* par drapeau; **s. flag,** (i) *Mil:* fanion *m* de signalisation; (ii) *Nau:* pavillon *m* signaux; (iii) *Rail:* drapeau *m* (de signalisation); **Morse signals,** signaux Morse; **panel s.,** signal par panneau(x); **fog s.,** signal de brouillard, de brume; **firework s., pyrotechnic s.,** signal par artifices, signal pyrotechnique; **s. firework,** artifice *m* de signalisation; bengale *m*; **s. flare,** (i) fusée éclairante; (ii) bengale; **s. rocket,** fusée de signalisation; fusée-signal *f*, *pl.* fusées-signaux; **s. cartridge,** cartouche *f* de signalisation; (*b*) *Nau:* **harbour signals, port signals,** signaux de port; **(harbour) traffic signals,** signaux de mouvements de port; **entering, leaving, signals,** signaux d'entrée, de sortie (de port); **quarantine s.,** signal sanitaire; **submarine, underwater, s.,** signal sous-marin; **tide signals,** signaux de marée; **s. letters,** numéro *m* (d'un navire); **s. book,** livre *m*, code *m*, des signaux; **s. locker,** armoire *f*, caisson *m*, coffre *m*, à signaux; (*c*) *Rail:* **disc s.,** disque *m*; **distant s.,** signal à distance, signal avancé; **fixed s.,** signal fixe; **home s.,** signal rapproché; **square s.,** (signal) carré *m*; **block s.,** signal de cantonnement; **covering, protecting, s.,** signal de protection; **line-protecting s.,** signal de protection de la voie; **clear s., off s.,** signal de voie libre, signal effacé; **to throw a s. off,** ouvrir un signal; **stop s., on s.,** signal d'arrêt immédiat, signal de voie fermée, signal fermé; **to put, set, a s. on,** fermer un signal; **slacken speed s.,** signal de ralentissement; **s. aspect,** visibilité *f* des signaux; **s. box, cabin,** poste *m*, cabine *f*, d'aiguillage; **s. tower,** poste de signaux; **s. wire,** fil *m* de transmission (de signaux). **3.** *Elcs: etc:* (*a*) *W.Tel:* **call s.,** indicatif *m* d'appel; **input s.,** signal d'entrée; **feedback s.,** signal de ré(tro)action; **output s.,** signal de sortie, signal émis; **parasitic, interfering, s.,** signal parasite; **repeated s.,** signal de répétition; **s. component,** composante *f* de signal; **multi-component s.,** signal complexe; **single-component s.,** signal à composante unique; **s. frequency,** fréquence *f* de signal; **s. shifter,** oscillateur *m* à fréquence variable; **s. grid,** grille *f* de contrôle (de tube électronique); **s./noise, s.-to-noise, ratio,** rapport *m* signal/bruit; **s. strength,** intensité *f* de réception; **s. voltage,** tension *f* (efficace) de signal; **s. wave,** onde *f* de trafic, de travail; **station s.,** indicatif de poste, de station; (*b*) *T.V:* **blanking s.,** signal de suppression; **camera s., picture s., video s.,** signal d'image, de vision, de caméra; signal vidéo; **grey s.,** signal de gris; **s. plate,** plaque atténuatrice; **s.-to-image ratio,** rapport signal/image; (*c*) *Comptr:* **enabling s.,** signal de validation; **inhibiting s.,** signal d'interdiction; **sense s.,** signal de (sortie) lecture; **s. regeneration,** régénération *f* de signal; **s. reshaping,** remise *f* en forme de, du, signal.

4. (*a*) *Mil:* **The Royal Corps of Signals,** *F:* **Signals,** *U.S:* **the Signal Corps,** le Corps des Transmissions, les Transmissions; **s. centre,** centre *m* des transmissions; **s. connection,** raccordement *m* des transmissions; **s. equipment,** matériel *m* de(s) transmissions; **s. office,** bureau *m* des transmissions; **s. officer,** officier *m* des transmissions; **chief s. officer,** commandant *m* des transmissions; **s. operating instructions,** ordre *m* pour les transmissions, ordre particulier des transmissions; **s. plan,** plan *m* des liaisons, des transmissions; **s. unit,** unité *f* des transmissions; (*b*) *Navy:* **yeoman of signals,** maître-timonier *m, pl.* maîtres-timoniers; **chief yeoman of signals,** chef *m* de timonerie; **s. boy,** mousse *m* de timonerie.

signal[2], *v.* (**signalled**) **1.** *v.i.* donner un signal, faire des signaux (**to,** à); signaler; **I signalled to him (to stop),** je lui ai fait signe (de s'arrêter); *Aut:* **to s. before stopping,** prévenir, avertir, avant de s'arrêter. **2.** *v.tr.* (*a*) signaler (un train, un navire); (*b*) transmettre (un ordre); *Aut:* **to s. that one is turning,** signaler un changement de direction; (*c*) *Rail:* **track signalled for two-way working,** voie banalisée.

signal[3], *a.* (service) signalé, insigne; (succès) éclatant, remarquable; (récompense, faveur) insigne; (échec) notoire.

signalization [signəlai'zeiʃ(ə)n], *s.* signalisation *f*; balisage *m*.

signalize ['signəlaiz], *v.tr.* **1.** signaler, marquer (une victoire, un succès). **2.** baliser (une route, etc.).

signaller ['signələr], *s.* signaleur *m*.

signalling ['signəliŋ], *s.* (*a*) signalisation *f*; avertissement *m*; transmission *f* de signaux; *Nau:* timonerie *f*; **automatic s.,** signalisation automatique; **visual s.,** (i) signalisation optique; télégraphie optique; (ii) *Nau:* timonerie *f*; **arm s.,** signalisation à bras; **hand s.,** (i) *Nau: etc:* signaux *mpl* à bras; (ii) *Rail:* pilotage *m*; **flag s.,** (i) *Mil:* signalisation par fanions; (ii) *Nau:* signaux par pavillons; (iii) *Rail:* signalisation par drapeau; **s. flag,** (i) fanion *m* de signalisation; (ii) pavillon *m* pour signaux; (iii) drapeau *m* (de signalisation); **lamp s.,** signalisation par lampe(s), par projecteur(s); **s. lamp, lantern,** lanterne-signal *f, pl.* lanternes-signaux; fanal, -aux *m* à signaux; lanterne *f* à signaux; **s. by fireworks, by rockets,** signalisation, signaux, par artifices, par fusées; **s. pistol, cartridge,** pistolet *m*, cartouche *f*, de signalisation; *T.V:* **cue s.,** signalisation d'ordres; **panel s.,** signalisation par panneaux; **s. panel,** panneau *m* de signalisation; **s. device,** dispositif *m* de signalisation, signalisateur *m*; **s. distance,** distance *f* de signalisation; **within s. distance,** à portée de signalisation, des signaux; (**diver's**) **s. line,** corde *f* de communication (de scaphandrier); *Elcs:* **s. generator,** générateur *m* de signaux; *Tp:* **s. faults, s. troubles,** dérangement *m* d'appel; *Tg:* **s. key,** manipulateur *m*; (*b*) balisage *m* (d'une route, etc.); (*c*) signaux.

signally ['signəli], *adv.* remarquablement; d'une façon éclatante, signalée; avec éclat; d'une façon notoire.

signalman, *pl.* **-men** ['signəlmən], *s.m.* signaleur; sémaphoriste; *Navy:* timonier; *Rail:* bloqueur.

signation [sig'neiʃ(ə)n], *s.* signation *f*.

signatory ['signət(ə)ri], *a. & s.* signataire (*mf*); **s. to an agreement,** signataire d'un contrat; **the signatories to a treaty,** les (co)signataires (*mf*) d'un traité; **governments signatories to a convention,** gouvernements signataires d'une convention.

signature ['signətjər], *s.* **1.** signature *f*; *Adm:* visa *m*; **stamped s.,** griffe *f*; **facsimile s.,** signature autographiée; **to put one's s. to a letter,** apposer sa signature à une lettre; **his s. was on the letter,** la lettre portait sa signature; **to submit a decree to the president for s.,** présenter un décret à la signature du président; *Com: etc:* **for s.,** pour signature; **joint s.,** signature collective; **the s. of the firm,** la signature sociale; *W.Tel:* *T.V:* **s. tune,** indicatif (musical) (d'une émission). **2.** *Pharm:* *A:* mode *f* d'administration. **3.** *Typ:* (*a*) signature (d'un cahier); (*b*) **we are sending you the first four signatures,** nous vous envoyons les quatre premiers cahiers, les cahiers A à D. **4.** *Mus:* **key s.,** armature *f*, armure *f* (de la clef).

signboard ['sainbɔ:d], *s.* **1.** enseigne *f* (d'auberge, etc.). **2.** (*notice board*) écriteau indicateur.

signer ['sainər], *s.* signataire *mf*; *Hist:* *U.S:* **the Signers,** les signataires de la Déclaration d'Indépendance (1776).

signet ['signit], *s.* **1.** sceau *m*, cachet *m*; **s. ring,** (i) (*used for sealing*) anneau *m* sigillaire, à cachet; (ii) (bague *f*) chevalière *f*. **2.** *Scot:* **writer to the s.** = avoué *m*.

significance [sig'nifikəns], *s.* **1.** signification *f* (d'un mot, d'un geste, etc.); **what is the s. of this ceremony?** que signifie cette cérémonie? **look of deep s.,** regard très significatif; *Pol.Ec:* **s. test,** test de signification; **level of s.,** seuil de signification (des données). **2.** importance *f*, conséquence *f*, portée *f*; **incident of no real s.,** incident sans importance, sans portée; **event of great s.,** événement de la plus haute importance.

significans [sig'nifikænz], *s.* *Ling:* signifiant *m*.

significant [sig'nifikənt], *a.* **1.** (mot, geste, regard, sourire) significatif; **features s. of weakness,** traits qui accusent la faiblesse; **nothing is more s. of a man's character than what he finds laughable,** il n'y a pas de meilleur indice du tempérament d'un homme que ce qu'il trouve risible. **2.** *Mth:* **s. figure,** chiffre significatif. **3.** (événement, etc.) important, d'importance, de grande portée. **4.** *Theol:* **s. signs of grace,** signes signifiants de la grâce.

significantly [sig'nifikəntli], *adv.* (*a*) (regarder, etc.) d'une manière significative; **he smiled s.,** il a souri d'un air entendu; il a eu un sourire significatif; (*b*) **s. cheaper,** sensiblement moins cher.

signification [signifi'keiʃ(ə)n], *s.* signification *f*, sens *m* (d'un mot, d'une phrase, etc.); *Ling:* signifié *m*.

significative [sig'nifikətiv], *a.* significatif (**of,** de).

significatum, *pl.* **-a** [signifi'kɑ:təm, -'kɑ:tə], *s.* *Ling:* signifié *m*.

signify ['signifai]. **1.** *v.tr.* signifier; (*a*) être (le) signe de (qch.); **a broad forehead signifies intelligence,** un front large est (un) signe d'intelligence, indique l'intelligence; (*b*) (*of word, etc.*) signifier, vouloir dire; (*c*) déclarer, faire connaître (ses intentions, sa volonté, etc.); **to s. one's consent,** signifier son consentement. **2.** *v.i.* importer; **it doesn't s.,** cela ne fait rien; cela n'a aucune importance; cela n'importe guère; **what does it s.?** qu'importe?

signing ['sainiŋ], *s.* signature *f* (d'un document); passation *f* (d'un acte); acceptation *f* (d'une traite); **s. fee,** jeton *m* de signature (d'un directeur de société); *Publ:* *Lit:* **s. party,** séance de signature.

signpost[1] ['sainpoust], *s.* (*a*) poteau *m*, panneau *m*, de signalisation; poteau indicateur; signal *m* de route; (*b*) *Fig:* indication *f*; **the new scheme is a s. to the future,** ce nouveau projet montre le chemin de l'avenir.

signpost[2], *v.tr.* marquer (une route) de poteaux indicateurs, signaliser (une route); **well, badly, signposted road,** route dont la signalisation est bonne, défectueuse.

signposting ['sainpoustiŋ], *s.* signalisation routière, des routes.

Sikh [si:k], *a. & s.* *Rel:* sikh, -e.

silage ['sailidʒ], *s.* *Agr:* fourrage ensilé.

silane ['silein], *s.* *Ch:* silane *m*.

silcrete ['silkri:t], *s.* *Geol:* croûte siliceuse.

silence[1] ['sailəns], *s.* silence *m*; (*a*) **dead, unbroken, s.,** silence absolu; **a breathless s.,** un silence ému, anxieux; **deathlike s.,** silence de mort; **there was a sudden s.,** il s'est fait un silence subit; **to keep s.,** garder le silence; se taire; **to break (the) s.,** rompre le silence; **to call for s.,** réclamer le silence; **to maintain a stubborn s.,** se renfermer dans le mutisme; garder obstinément le silence; **to reduce s.o. to s.,** réduire qn au silence; faire taire qn; imposer silence à qn; **to suffer in s.,** souffrir en silence; **they heard me out in frozen s.,** ils m'ont écouté jusqu'au bout dans un silence glacial; **s.!** (du) silence! taisez-vous! (*notice in library, etc.*) défense *f* de parler; les conversations sont interdites; *Prov:* **s. is golden,** le silence est d'or; **s. gives consent,** qui ne dit mot consent; qui se tait consent; (*b*) **the s. of the law on this point,** le silence de la loi à ce sujet; **to write to s.o. after five years' s.,** écrire à qn après un silence de cinq ans; **to pass over sth. in s.,** passer qch. sous silence; (*c*) **the s. of the night, of the grave,** le silence de la nuit, du tombeau; (*d*) *Aer:* **cone of s.,** cône de silence.

silence[2], *v.tr.* (*a*) réduire (qn) au silence; imposer silence à (qn); faire taire (un adversaire, sa conscience); confondre (un menteur, etc.); étouffer (les plaintes); faire cesser, éteindre, faire taire (le feu de l'ennemi); **to s. criticism,** fermer, clouer, la bouche à la critique; (*b*) **to s. a noise,** amortir, étouffer, un bruit; *I.C.E:* **to s. the exhaust,** assourdir, étouffer, l'échappement.

silencer ['sailənsər], *s.* *Sm.a: etc:* amortisseur *m* de son, de bruit; (dispositif *m*) silencieux *m*; *I.C.E:* silencieux; pot *m* d'échappement.

silencing ['sailənsiŋ], *s.* (*a*) *Sm.a: etc:* amortissement *m* du son; (*b*) réduction *f* du bruit (d'un moteur).

silene [sai'li:ni], *s.* *Bot:* silène *m*.

silent ['sailənt], *a.* **1.** silencieux; (*a*) **to keep s.,** (i) observer le silence; (ii) garder le silence, se taire (**about,** sur); demeurer silencieux; se tenir coi, coite; **he knows when to keep s.,** il sait se taire; **to remain s.,** rester muet; **to become s.,** se taire; **be s.!** taisez-vous! **s. as the grave,** muet comme la tombe; *Ecc:* **s. orders,** ordres (religieux) qui gardent le silence; **member of a s. order,** silentiaire *m*, silenciaire *m*; **s. majority,** majorité silencieuse; **s. propaganda,** propagande faite sans bruit; **s. sorrow,** douleur muette; (*in prisons*) **s. system,** régime *m* cellulaire; (*b*) **a s. man,** un homme silencieux, taciturne, peu loquace, peu communicatif; (*c*) *Com:* **s. partner,** (associé *m*) commanditaire *m*; bailleur *m* de fonds. **2.** (*a*) silencieux, insonore; **s. footsteps,** des pas silencieux; **s. running of an engine,** allure silencieuse d'un moteur; **s. mesh gearbox,** boîte de vitesses à engrènements silencieux; (*b*) *Ling:* **s. letter,** lettre muette; **the k is s.,** le k ne se prononce pas, le k est muet.

silentiary [sai'lenʃiəri], *s.* *Hist:* *Ecc:* silenciaire *m*, silentiaire *m*.

silently ['sailəntli], *adv.* silencieusement, en silence, sans bruit.

Silenus [sai'li:nəs], *Pr.n.m.* (*a*) *Gr.Myth:* Silène; (*b*) *Z:* **S. ape,** silène *m*.

Silesia [sai'li:ziə]. **1.** *Pr.n.* *Geog:* Silésie *f*. **2.** *s.* *Tex:* silésienne *f*.

Silesian [sai'li:ziən]. *Geog:* (*a*) *a.* silésien; (*b*) *s.* Silésien, -ienne.

silex ['saileks], *s.* *Miner:* silex *m*.

silhouette[1] [silu(:)'et], *s.* (*a*) silhouette *f*; **to see s.o. in s.,** voir qn en silhouette; *Mil:* **s. (target),** silhouette; (*b*) ombre chinoise.

silhouette[2], *v.tr.* silhouetter, projeter en silhouette; **to be silhouetted against a light background,** se silhouetter, se détacher (en silhouette), sur un fond clair.

silhouettist [silu(:)'etist], *s.* faiseur, -euse, de silhouettes.

silica ['silikə], *s.* *Ch:* silice *f*.

silicate[1] ['silikət], *s.* *Ch:* silicate *m*; **aluminium s.,** silicate d'aluminium; **to treat (a road, etc.) with s.,** silicat(is)er (une route, etc.).

silicate[2] ['silikeit], *v.tr.* silicat(is)er (une route, etc.).

silicating ['silikeitiŋ], *s.* silicatisation *f*, silicatage *m* (d'une route, etc.).

siliceous [si'liʃəs], *a.* *Ch:* siliceux; *Geol:* **s. springs,** sources boueuses.

silicic [si'lisik], *a.* *Ch:* (acide) silicique.

silicicolous [sili'sikələs], *a.* *Bot:* silicicole.

silicide ['silisaid], *s.* *Ch:* siliciure *m*.

siliciferous [sili'sifərəs], *a.* silicifère.

silicification [silisifi'keiʃ(ə)n], *s.* **1.** *Miner:* silicification *f* (des roches). **2.** *Ind:* silicatisation *f*, silicatage *m* (du bois).

silicify [si'lisifai]. **1.** *v.tr.* (*a*) (*of natural agency*) silicifier (le bois, la pierre); (*b*) *Ind:* silicatiser (le bois, etc.); imprégner (le bois) de silicate. **2.** *v.i.* se silicifier.

silicious [si'liʃəs], *a.* = SILICEOUS.

silicle ['silikl], *s.* *Bot:* silicule *f*.

silico- ['silikou], *pref.* silico-.

silicocalcareous [silikoukæl'kɛəriəs], *a.* silicocalcaire.

silicochloroform [silikou'klɔrəfɔ:m], *s.* silicochloroforme *m*.

Silicoflagellata [silikouflædʒə'leitə], *s.pl.* *Prot:* silicoflagellés *m*.

silicofluoride [silikou'flu:əraid], *s.* *Ch:* fluosilicate *m*.

silicomanganese [silikoumæŋgə'ni:z], *s.* *Metall:* silicomanganèse *m*.

silicon ['silikən], *s.* *Ch:* silicium *m*; **combined with s.,** silicié; **s. hydride,** hydrogène silicié; **s. dioxide,** dioxyde de silicium; silice *f*; **s. carbide,** carbure de silicium; carborundum *m*; *Metall:* **s. bronze,** bronze siliceux; bronze au silicium.

silicone ['silikoun], *s.* *Ch:* silicone *f*.

silicosis [sili'kousis], *s.* *Med:* silicose *f*; chalicose *f*, chalicosis *m*.

silicotic [sili'kɔtik], *a. & s.* *Med:* silicotique (*mf*).

silicotitanate [silikou'taitəneit], *s.* *Ch:* silicotitanate *m*.

silicotungstate [silikou'tʌŋsteit], *s.* *Ch:* silicotungstate *m*.

silicula [si'likjulə], *s.* *Bot:* silicule *f*.

siliculose [si'likjulous], *a.* *Bot:* siliculeux.

siliqua, *pl.* **-quae** ['silikwə, -kwi:], *s.* *Bot:* & *Rom.Ant:* *Num:* silique *f*.

silique [si'li:k], *s.* *Bot:* silique *f*.

siliquiform [si'likwifɔ:m], *a.* *Bot:* siliquiforme.

siliquose, siliquous ['silikwous, -kwəs], *a.* *Bot:* siliqueux.

Silistria [si'listriə]. *Pr.n.* *Geog:* Silistria *f*, Silistrie *f*.

silk [silk], *s.* **1.** soie *f*; (*a*) **raw s.,** soie grège, brute, crue, écrue; **thrown s.,** soie moulinée, ouvrée; soie torse; organsin *m*; **spooled s.,** soie bobinée; **s. waste, waste s.,** bourre *f* de soie; (fils de) schappe *m or f*; capiton *m*; strasse *f*; déchets *mpl* de soie; **s. yarn,** fil *m* de soie; **sewing, knitting, s.,** soie à coudre, à tricoter; **s. stockings,** bas de, en, soie; **a black s. dress,** une robe de soie noire; **the s. industry,** l'industrie soyère, séricicole, de la soie; **s. culture,** sériciculture; *f*; **s. trade, factory,** soierie *f*; **s. mill,** filature *f* de soie; **s.-growing country,** pays séricicole; **s. throwing,** organsinage *m*, moulinage *m*, ouvraison *f*; **s. thrower, throwster,** organsineur, euse, moulineur, -euse, moulinier, -ière; **s. breeder, grower,** sériciculteur *m*; éducateur, -trice, de vers à soie; **s. weaver,** tisseur *m* de soie; tisserand *m* en soie; **s. merchant,** marchand, -ande, de soieries; **s. reel, winder,** tour *m*, dévidoir *m*, de cocons; *Ent:* **s.(-producing) gland, insect,** glande, insecte, séricigène; *Hist:* **the S. road,** la route de la soie; (*b*) *Tex:* **wild s.,** soie sauvage; **vegetable s.,** soie végétale; **oiled s.,** taffetas *m* imperméable; **figured s.,** lampas *m*; **shot s.,** taffetas changeant; soie chatoyante; soie gorge-de-pigeon; étoffe *f* caméléon; **s. fabric(s), silk(s),** soierie; **s. finish,** similisage *m*; **to s.-finish,** similiser; **s.-finished cotton,** coton similisé, simili *m*; **s. screen,** écran *m*, trame *f*, de soie; **s. screen printing, process,** sérigraphie *f*; **s. paper,** papier *m* de soie. **2.** (*a*) *Turf:* **silks,** casaque *f* (de jockey); (*b*) *Jur:* **to take s.,** être nommé conseiller du roi, de la reine (*Fr.C:*); (*c*) *Jur: F:* (i) conseiller du roi, de la reine; (ii) *coll.* les conseillers du roi, de la reine. **3.** (*a*) *Bot:* **s. cotton,** kapok *m*, capoc *m*; **s. cotton tree,** bombax *m*, fromager *m*; **s. grass,** (i) karata(s) *m*; (ii) pit(t)e *f*, pita *f*; **s. tree,** julibrissin *m*; **s. vine,** periploca *m*; (*b*) *Bot: NAm:* **(corn) s.,** style (soyeux) (de la fleur femelle du maïs); (*c*) *Husb:* **s. fowl,** soyeuse *f*.

silken [ˈsilk(ə)n], *a.* **1.** *A:* (*a*) de, en, soie; (*b*) vêtu de soie. **2.** *Lit:* soyeux; **s. curls,** boucles de soie. **3.** *Lit:* (*of voice, words*) doucereux, mielleux.

silkiness [ˈsilkinis], *s.* **1.** nature soyeuse (d'un tissu). **2.** (*a*) moelleux *m* (de la voix, des paroles); (*b*) *Pej:* ton doucereux, mielleux.

silkweed [ˈsilkwiːd], *s. Bot: U.S:* asclepias *m*; plante à soie; apocyn *m* à ouate soyeuse; soyeuse *f*; coton *m* sauvage.

silkworm [ˈsilkwəːm], *s.* ver *m* à soie; **s. moth,** bombyx *m* (mori, du mûrier); **s. breeder,** sériciculteur *m*; éducateur, -trice, de vers à soie; magnanier, -ière; **s. breeding,** sériciculture *f*; éducation des vers à soie; magnanerie *f*; **s. nursery, farm,** coconnière *f*, magnanerie; **s. rot,** muscardine *f*.

silky [ˈsilki]. **1.** *a.* (*a*) soyeux; **s. lustre,** éclat soyeux; (*b*) **s. voice,** voix moelleuse; (*c*) *Pej:* doucereux, mielleux. **2.** *s.* (*breed of fowl*) soyeuse *f*.

sill [sil], *s.* **1.** (*a*) *Const: etc:* sole *f*, semelle *f*, sablière basse (de cadre); seuil *m* (de dormant de porte); **staircase s.,** patin *m* d'escalier; (*b*) *Rail: Veh:* longrine *f*, longeron *m* (de wagon, de caisse); brancard *m* (de caisse). **2.** (*a*) (*of window*) rebord *m*, appui *m*, tablette *f*, de fenêtre; (*b*) *N.Arch:* radier *m* (de bassin); **port s.,** seuil *m*, seuillet *m* (de sabord). **3.** (*a*) seuil, traverse *f* (d'une porte); (*b*) *Min:* sole, semelle (d'une galerie); (*c*) *Hyd.E:* heurtoir *m*, buse *m*, seuil, radier *m* (de bassin, d'écluse); **main s.,** racinal *m*; **look s.,** seuil, radier, d'écluse; busc *m*. **4.** (*a*) *Geol:* filon-couche *m*, *pl.* filons-couches; (*b*) *Miner:* lentille *f* de roche; (*c*) *Oc:* seuil.

sillabub [ˈsiləbʌb], *s. Cu:* entremets sucré semblable au sabayon.

sillily [ˈsilili], *adv.* sottement, niaisement, bêtement.

silliness [ˈsilinis], *s.* sottise *f*, bêtise *f*, niaiserie *f*.

silly [ˈsili]. **1.** *a.* (*a*) (*of pers.*) sot, *f.* sotte; stupide, bête, idiot; **don't be so s.!** ne sois pas si bête, si stupide! ne fais pas le sot, la sotte! **you s. child!** petit(e) idiot(e)! petit(e) imbécile! **(you) s. fool, ass!** imbécile! idiot(e)! **he's very s.,** il est d'une bêtise extrême; **it would make me look s.,** j'aurais l'air bien bête, stupide, ridicule; **she looks very s. in that hat,** ce chapeau lui donne un air ridicule; (*b*) **s. question,** question bête, stupide; **s. answer,** réponse stupide, ridicule, saugrenue; **that was a s. thing to do!** ça, ce, n'était pas très intelligent! **to say sth. s.,** dire une bêtise; (*to child*) **don't do anything s.,** ne fais pas de bêtises; *Journ: F:* **the s. season,** l'époque des vacances (dépourvue de nouvelles sérieuses); (*c*) **to knock s.o. s.,** (i) étourdir, assommer, qn; (ii) démonter qn; casser bras et jambes à qn; **the blow knocked me s.,** (i) le coup m'en a fait voir trente-six chandelles; (ii) le coup m'a fait perdre connaissance. **2.** *s. F:* sot, sotte; idiot, -ote; niais, -aise.

sillybilly [ˈsiliˈbili], *s. F:* (*to child*) idiot, -ote, imbécile *mf*.

silo[1] [ˈsailou], *s.* (*a*) *Agr:* silo *m*; **s. filler,** ensileuse *f*; (*b*) *Ball:* **launching s.,** puits *m*, silo, (de lancement).

silo[2], *v.tr.* ensiler, mettre en silo (du fourrage, etc.).

Siloam [saiˈlouəm]. *Pr.n. B: Geog:* **the pool of S.,** la piscine de Siloé.

siloxane [siˈlɔksein], *s. Ch:* siloxane *m*.

silpha [ˈsilfə], *s. Ent:* silphe *m*, bouclier *m*.

Silphidae [ˈsilfidi], *s.pl. Ent:* silphidés *m*.

silphium [ˈsilfiəm], *s. Bot:* silphium *m*.

silt[1] [silt], *s.* dépôt (vaseux), vase *f*, limon *m* (dans un chenal, etc.); (apports *mpl* de) boue *f*; *Geol:* apports de ruissellement; lais *m*, relais *m*; **deposition of s.,** colmatage *m*; envasement *m*.

silt[2], *v.* **to s. (up). 1.** *v.tr.* envaser, ensabler (un port, un canal). **2.** *v.i.* (*of harbour, etc.*) s'envaser, s'ensabler; se combler.

siltation [silˈteiʃ(ə)n], *s.* envasement *m*, colmatage *m* (d'un canal, etc.).

silting [ˈsiltiŋ], *s.* (*a*) *Min: Petr:* embouage *m* (d'une galerie, etc.); (*b*) **s. (up),** envasement *m*, ensablement *m*, colmatage *m* (d'un port, etc.).

Silures [siˈljuːriːz]. *Pr.n.pl. Hist:* Silures *m*.

Silurian [siˈljuːriən]. **1.** *a. Hist: Geol:* silurien. **2.** *s.* (*a*) *Hist:* Silurien, -ienne; (*b*) *Geol:* silurien *m*.

silurid [siˈljuːrid], *s. Ich:* silure *m*.

Siluridae [siˈljuːridiː], *s.pl. Ich:* siluridés *m*.

silurus, *pl.* **-i** [siˈljuːrəs, -ai], *s. Ich:* silure *m*.

silva [ˈsilvə], *s.* **1.** flore *f* sylvestre; forêts *fpl* (d'une région). **2.** (*in S. America*) selvas *fpl*.

silvan [ˈsilvən]. **1.** *s.* (*a*) *Myth:* sylvain *m*; (*b*) homme, oiseau, animal, etc., sylvain. **2.** *a.* (*a*) sylvestre; (*b*) (oiseau, etc.) sylvain; (*c*) (plante) sylvatique, sylvestre.

Silvanus [silˈveinəs]. *Pr.n.m. Rom.Myth:* Sylvain, Silvain.

silver[1] [ˈsilvər], *s.* **1.** argent *m*; **bar s.,** argent en barre(s); **coin, standard, s.,** argent au titre; **oxidized s.,** argent oxydé; **fulminating s.,** argent fulminant; **imitation s.,** similargent *m*; **nickel,** *O:* **German, s.,** maillechort *m*; argent blanc, d'Allemagne; argentan *m*, argenton *m*; **black s., brittle s. ore,** stéphanite *f*; *Med:* **s. poisoning,** argyrie *f*; argyrisme *m*. **2.** *attrib.* (*a*) d'argent, en argent; **s. medal,** médaille *f* d'argent; *Sp: F:* **he won the s.,** il a remporté la médaille d'argent; **s. inkstand,** encrier en argent; **s. spoon,** cuillère *f* d'argent; **he was born with a s. spoon in his mouth,** il est né coiffé; **s. plate,** (i) (*layer of silver*) argenture *f*, argentage *m*; (ii) (*tableware*) argenterie *f*; argent orfévré; vaisselle *f* d'argent; plaqué *m* (argent), doublé *m* (argent); (iii) plat d'argent; **to s.-plate sth.,** argenter qch.; **s.-plated metal,** métal argenté; **s.-plated watch,** montre en plaqué, en doublé; **s.-plated tableware,** doublé (argent); **s. plating,** argenture *f*, argentage *m*; **s. plater,** argenteur *m*; **s. gilt,** vermeil *m*; **s. gilt dishes,** plats en vermeil; **s. foil, leaf,** argent battu; feuille *f* d'argent (battu); argent en feuille; **s. paper,** (i) *A:* papier de soie blanc; (papier) serpente *f*; (ii) papier d'étain; papier argenté, d'argent; (iii) *Phot:* papier aux sels d'argent; **s. band,** orchestre composé uniquement d'instruments de cuivre argenté à embouchure; **s.-headed pin, walking stick,** épingle à tête d'argent, canne à pomme d'argent; *Miner:* **s. glance,** argyrose *f*, argentite *f*; **s.-bearing,** argentifère; *Ch:* **s. solution,** solution argentique; **s. bromide, halide, nitrate,** bromure *m*, halogénure *m*, nitrate *m*, d'argent; **s. salt,** sel d'argent; *Phot:* **s. image,** image argentique; **s. bath,** bain d'argent; **s. print,** épreuve (positive) sur papier aux sels d'argent; **s. printing,** tirage *m* sur papier aux sels d'argent; *Metalw:* **s. solder,** brasure *f* à l'argent; (*b*) argenté; **s. hair,** cheveux argentés; **s.-haired, s.-headed,** aux cheveux argentés; *Lit:* **the s. dawn,** l'aube argentine; **the moon cast a s. shimmer on the waves,** la lune argentait les flots; **s. grey,** gris argenté *inv*; **the s. streak,** la Manche; **s. thaw,** verglas *m*; *Lit:* (*of voice, etc.*) **s.-toned,** argentin; **s.-tongued,** éloquent; à la langue dorée; **s. wedding,** noces *fpl* d'argent; *Cin:* **s. screen,** (i) écran argenté; (ii) l'écran, le cinéma; **S. Stick,** officier supérieur des *Life Guards* de service au palais du roi, de la reine; *Hist: Lit:* **the s. age,** l'âge d'argent; **s. Latin,** latin littéraire du Ier siècle apr. J.-C.; *Bot:* **s. bell (tree),** halesia *m*, halésie *f*; *Fung:* **s. leaf (disease), s. blight,** stéréon *m* pourpre; *Z:* **s. fox,** renard argenté. **3. s. (money),** argent monnayé; **s. coin,** (i) pièce *f* d'argent; (ii) *coll.* (pièces d')argent; **a pound in s.,** une livre en argent, en pièces d'argent, en monnaie d'argent. **4.** argenterie; argent orfévré; vaisselle d'argent; plaqué (argent), doublé (argent).

silver[2]. **1.** *v.tr.* (*a*) argenter (des couverts, etc.); (*b*) étamer (un miroir); (*c*) *Lit:* (*of moon, etc.*) argenter (les flots, etc.); **grief had silvered his hair,** le chagrin lui avait argenté, blanchi, les cheveux. **2.** *v.i.* (*of hair, etc.*) s'argenter, blanchir.

silverbeak [ˈsilvəbiːk], *s. Orn:* rhamphocèle *m*.

silverbill [ˈsilvəbil], *s. Orn:* bec-d'argent *m*, *pl.* becs-d'argent.

silverer [ˈsilvərər], *s.* (*a*) argenteur *m*, plaqueur *m* (de métal); (*b*) étameur *m* (de miroirs).

silver(-)eye [ˈsilvəai], *s. Orn:* zostérops *m*, oiseau *m* à lunettes.

silverfish [ˈsilvəfiʃ], *s.* **1.** *Ich:* argentine *f*. **2.** *Ent:* lépisme *m*; poisson *m* d'argent.

silvering [ˈsilvəriŋ], *s.* **1.** (*action*) (*a*) argenture *f*, argentage *m*, argentation *f* (d'un métal); (*b*) étamage *m* (d'un miroir). **2.** (*layer*) (*a*) (*on metal*) argenture *f*; (*b*) (*on mirror*) tain *m*.

silverite [ˈsilvərait], *s. Pol.Ec: U.S:* argentiste *m*.

silvern [ˈsilvəːn], *a.* (*a*) *A:* & *Lit:* = SILVERY; (*b*) *Prov:* **speech is s., silence is golden,** la parole est d'argent mais le silence est d'or; il est bon de parler et meilleur de se taire.

silverpoint [ˈsilvəpoint], *s. Art:* **(sketch in) s.,** gravure *f* à la pointe d'argent.

silverside [ˈsilvəsaid], *s.* **1.** *Cu:* gîte *f* à la noix. **2.** *Ich:* athérine *f*.

silverskin [ˈsilvəskin], *s. Comest:* petit oignon blanc confit au vinaigre.

silversmith [ˈsilvəsmiθ], *s.* orfèvre *m*; **silversmith's trade,** orfèvrerie *f*.

silverware [ˈsilvəwɛər], *s.* argenterie *f* (de table).

silverweed [ˈsilvəwiːd], *s. Bot:* potentille ansérine; argentine *f*.

silverwork [ˈsilvəwəːk], *s.* orfèvrerie *f*.

silvery [ˈsilvəri], *a.* (*a*) (nuage, flot) argenté; (écailles, etc.) d'argent; (*b*) (rire, timbre) argentin.

Silvester [silˈvestər]. *Pr.n.m.* Sylvestre.

silvicolous [silˈvikələs], *a. Biol:* sylvicole.

silviculture [ˈsilvikʌltʃər], *s.* sylviculture *f*.

simar(o)uba [siməˈruːbə], *s. Bot:* simar(o)uba *m*; *Pharm:* **s. bark,** écorce de simar(o)uba.

Simar(o)ubaceae [siməruːˈbeisiiː], *s.pl. Bot:* simar(o)ubacées *f*.

Simeon [ˈsimiən]. *Pr.n.m.* Siméon; **S. Stylites,** Siméon Stylite.

simian [ˈsimiən]. **1.** *a.* simiesque, simien. **2.** *s. Z:* anthropoïde *m*; **the simians,** les simiens *m*.

Simiidae [siˈmaiidiː], *s.pl. Z:* simiidés *m*, simiens *m*.

similar [ˈsimilər]. **1.** *a.* (*a*) semblable, pareil, ressemblant, analogue, assimilable **(to,** à); similaire; du même ordre; du même genre; **your case is s. to mine,** votre cas est semblable au mien; **to hold s. views to s.o.,** partager les idées de qn; (*b*) *Mth:* **s. triangles,** triangles semblables. **2.** *s.* (*a*) *A:* semblable *m*, chose *f* semblable; pareil *m*, pareille *f* **(of,** de); (*b*) *Med:* **law of similars,** loi de similitude *f*.

similarity [simiˈlæriti], *s.* ressemblance *f*, similitude *f*, similarité *f*; *Mth:* similitude (de triangles); **s. of character,** affinité *f*; **to establish points of s.,** établir un rapprochement.

similarly [ˈsimiləli], *adv.* pareillement, de façon semblable; semblablement.

simile [ˈsimili], *s.* comparaison *f*, image *f*, similitude *f*.

similitude [siˈmilitju(ː)d], *s.* **1.** ressemblance *f*, similitude *f*. **2.** (*a*) *A:* comparaison *f*, image *f*; similitude; (*b*) allégorie *f*.

similize [ˈsimilaiz], *v.tr.* comparer.

simmer[1] [ˈsimər], *s. Cu: O:* **to keep sth. at a s., on the s.,** (faire) mijoter qch.

simmer[2]. **1.** *v.i.* (*a*) (*of liquid*) frémir, mitonner; (*of food in pot*) mijoter, bouillotter; cuire à petits bouillons; cuire à petit feu, à feu doux; **let the soup s. for a few minutes,** laisser mijoter la soupe pendant quelques minutes; (*b*) (*of revolt, etc.*) fermenter; être près d'éclater; **ideas were simmering in his mind,** des idées mijotaient dans sa tête; **he was simmering with rage,** la colère montait en lui; il était prêt à éclater de colère; (*of pers.*) **to s. down,** s'apaiser peu à peu; reprendre son sang-froid; se calmer. **2.** *v.tr.* (faire) mijoter (un ragoût, etc.).

simmering[1] [ˈsiməriŋ], *a.* (liquide) qui frémit; (ragoût, etc.) qui mijote, qui bouillotte.

simmering[2], *s.* **1.** frémissement *m* (d'un liquide); cuisson *f* à petits bouillons, à petit feu, à feu doux (d'un ragoût, etc.). **2.** ferment *m* (de révolte, etc.).

simnel [ˈsimn(ə)l], *s.* **s. (cake),** gâteau *m* de Pâques, de la mi-carême.

Simois [ˈsimouis]. *Pr.n. A.Geog:* le (fleuve) Simoïs.

Simon [ˈsaimən]. *Pr.n.m.* Simon; **S. Magus,** Simon le Magicien; **simple S.,** niais *m*, nigaud *m*, nicodème *m*; **(the real) S.(-)Pure,** la véritable personne; l'objet *m* authentique.

simoniac [saiˈmouniæk], *a.* & *s. Ecc:* simoniaque (*m*).

simoniacal [saiməˈnaiək(ə)l], *a. Ecc:* simoniaque.

simoniacally [saiməˈnaiək(ə)li], *adv.* en simoniaque.

Simonides [saiˈmɔnidiːz]. *Pr.n.m. Gr.Lit:* Simonide.

simonist [ˈsaimənist], *s. Ecc:* simoniaque *m*.

simony [ˈs(a)iməni], *s. Ecc:* simonie *f*.

simoom, simoon [siˈmuːm, -ˈmuːn], *s.* simoon *m*, simoun *m*.

simp [simp], *s. NAm: F:* nigaud, -aude; niais, -aise; bêta, -tasse.

simper[1] [ˈsimpər], *s.* sourire affecté, minaudier.

simper[2], *v.i.* minauder, mignarder; grimacer; sourire avec affectation; faire des mines, des grimaces; faire la bouche en cœur.

simperer [ˈsimpərər], *s.* minaudier, -ière.

simpering[1] [ˈsimpəriŋ], *a.* minaudier, mignard, affecté; **s. ways,** minauderies *f*, affectation *f*.

simpering[2], *s.* minauderie *f*, grimaces *fpl.*

simperingly ['simpəriŋli], *adv.* en minaudant.

simple ['simpl]. **1.** *a.* (*a*) simple, naturel (de caractère); sans affectation; **s. people, folk,** gens simples; **to have s. tastes,** avoir des goûts simples; **the s. life,** la vie simple; **she gave us a very s. meal,** elle nous a servi un repas très simple; (*b*) simple, naïf, crédule, innocent; **s. hearted,** simple, ingénu, candide; **s.-minded,** simple (d'esprit); naïf, candide; **s.-mindedness,** simplicité *f* (d'esprit, de caractère); naïveté *f*, candeur *f*; **she's a s. soul,** elle est candide, naïve; **I'm not so s. as to believe that,** je ne suis pas assez simple, assez innocent, pour croire cela; je n'ai pas la naïveté de croire cela; *P:* **don't be so bloody s.!** ne fais pas l'idiot! (*c*) **s. method,** méthode simple, élémentaire; **the problem is very s.,** le problème est très simple; **to become s., simpler,** se simplifier; (*d*) *Bot:* **plant with s. leaves,** plante simplicifoliée, à feuilles simples; *Med:* **s. fracture,** fracture simple; *Opt: Phot:* **s. lens,** lentille, objectif, simple; *Com:* **s. interest,** intérêts simples; *Gram:* **s. sentence,** proposition indépendante; (*e*) *Jur:* **s. contract,** convention verbale, tacite; obligation chirographaire; **s. contract creditor,** créditeur chirographaire; **his s. word is enough,** sa simple parole suffit; (*f*) **that's the plain and s. truth,** c'est la vérité pure et simple. **2.** *s.* (*a*) *Bot: A:* **simples,** simples *m*, herbes médicinales; (*b*) *Tex:* semple *m* (de métier à tisser).

simpleness ['simpəlnis], *s.* (*a*) candeur *f*, simplicité *f*, naïveté *f* (d'un enfant, etc.); (*b*) bêtise *f*, sottise *f*, niaiserie *f*, naïveté.

simpleton ['simpəltən], *s.* nigaud, -aude; niais, -aise; naïf, -ïve; bêta, -tasse; jobard *m*; gobeur, -euse; nouille *f*.

simplex ['simpleks], *s. Cmptr: Telecom:* simplex *m*; **s. circuit,** communication *f* simplex.

Simplicidentata [simplisiden'teitə], *s.pl. Z:* simplicidentés *m*.

simpliciter [sim'plisitər], *adv. Jur: Scot:* universellement, absolument; sans limite; **to resign s.,** démissionner sans faire valoir aucun droit (à la retraite, etc.).

simplicity [sim'plisiti], *s.* **1.** (*a*) candeur *f*, simplicité *f*, ingénuité *f*, naïveté *f* (d'un enfant, etc.); **look of s.,** air bonhomme, bon enfant; **to speak with s.,** parler simplement, sans apprêt; (*b*) bêtise *f*, sottise *f*, naïveté. **2.** (*a*) simplicité (d'un problème, etc.); **it's s. itself,** c'est simple comme bonjour; c'est bête comme chou; (*b*) absence *f* de recherche, simplicité (dans la tenue).

simplification [simplifi'keiʃ(ə)n], *s.* simplification *f*.

simplifier ['simplifaiər], *s.* simplificateur, -trice.

simplify ['simplifai], *v.tr.* simplifier (un raisonnement, un calcul, etc.); **to s. a process,** apporter des simplifications à un procédé; **to become simplified,** se simplifier.

simplifying[1] ['simplifaiiŋ], *a.* (*of method, etc.*) simplificateur, -trice.

simplifying[2], *s.* simplification *f*.

simplism ['simplizm], *s.* simplisme *m*.

simplistic [sim'plistik], *a.* simpliste.

simply ['simpli], *adv.* **1.** (parler, agir) simplement; **s. dressed,** vêtu sans recherche, avec simplicité; vêtu simplement. **2.** (*a*) absolument; **you look s. lovely!** vous êtes absolument parfaite! **I s. won't do it,** je refuse absolument de le faire; **you s. must,** il le faut absolument; **I was s. amazed by it,** j'en étais tout à fait abasourdi; **the weather's s. ghastly,** il fait un temps de chien; (*b*) uniquement; tout simplement; **purely and s.,** purement et simplement; **he did it s. to test you,** il l'a fait uniquement pour vous éprouver; **it's s. a matter of time,** c'est une simple question de temps; **I was s. telling him . . .,** je lui disais tout bonnement . . .; **to believe s.o. s. on his word,** croire qn sur sa simple parole.

simulacrum, *pl.* **-a** [simju'lækrəm, -ə], *s.* simulacre *m*, semblant *m*.

simulate ['simjuleit], *v.tr.* simuler, feindre (une maladie, etc.); affecter (de l'enthousiasme, etc.); imiter l'apparence de (qn, qch.); prendre l'aspect de (qn, qch.); se faire passer pour (qn); **simulated pearl,** perle artificielle; **simulated debt,** dette simulée; *Ling:* **word simulating another word,** mot mal formé par fausse analogie avec un autre mot.

simulation [simju'leiʃ(ə)n], *s.* (*a*) simulation *f*, feinte *f*; (*b*) *Av:* **flight s.,** simulation de vol; **s. experience,** expérience acquise sur simulateur; *Cmptr:* **real time s.,** simulation en temps réel; *Atom.Ph: etc:* **analogue, digital, s.,** simulation analogique, numérique.

simulator ['simjuleitər], *s.* (*a*) simulateur, -trice; (*b*) *Tchn:* simulateur; *Av:* **flight s.,** simulateur de vol; *Atom.Ph: etc:* **analogue, digital, s.,** simulateur analogique, numérique.

simulcast ['siməlkɑ:st], *s. W.Tel: T.V:* transmission simultanée.

simuliid [si'mju:liid], *s. Ent:* simulie *f*.

Simuliidae [simju'laiidi:], *s.pl. Ent:* simuliidés *m*.

Simulium [si'mju:liəm], *s. Ent:* simulie *f*.

simultaneity [siməltə'ni:iti], **simultaneousness** [sim(ə)l'teiniəsnis], *s.* simultanéité *f*.

simultaneous [siməl'teiniəs], *a.* (*a*) simultané; *Mth:* **s. equations,** équations simultanées; **s. translation,** traduction simultanée; *W.Tel:* **connection for s. relay,** position en simultané; **s. access,** accès simultané; (*b*) **s. with . . .,** qui a lieu en même temps que . . .; (*c*) *Mil: etc:* **s. movement,** mouvement d'ensemble.

simultaneously [siməl'teiniəsli], *adv.* (*a*) simultanément; (*b*) en même temps (**with,** que).

sin[1] [sin], *s.* (*a*) péché *m*; **original s.,** péché originel; **deadly, mortal, s.,** péché mortel, capital; **the seven deadly sins,** les sept péchés capitaux; **s. against the Holy Ghost,** péché contre le Saint-Esprit; **the forgiveness of sins,** le pardon des offenses *f*; *B.Hist:* **s. offering,** sacrifice *m* expiatoire; **to live in s.,** vivre maritalement en dehors du mariage; *F:* vivre dans le collage; **living in s.,** unis dans le péché; **to die in s.,** mourir dans le péché; **I have committed no s.,** je n'ai point commis, fait, de péché; *F:* **for my sins, I was appointed . . .,** pour mes péchés j'ai été nommé . . .; *F:* **like s.,** furieusement, violemment; **it was raining like s.,** il pleuvait à seaux; (*b*) *O:* offense (contre les convenances, l'art, le bon goût); *F:* **it's a s. to touch up these pictures,** c'est un meurtre (que) de retoucher ces tableaux; **it's a s. to stay indoors today,** c'est un crime de rester à la maison aujourd'hui.

sin[2], *v.i.* (**sinned**) (*a*) pécher; commettre un péché, des péchés; **to s. against heaven,** pécher contre le ciel; **to s. against the light,** pécher consciemment; **liable to s.,** peccable; (*b*) *O:* **to s. against propriety,** blesser les convenances; manquer aux convenances; (*c*) (*of pers.*) **more sinned against than sinning,** plus à plaindre qu'à blâmer.

Sinai ['sainiai]. *Pr.n. Geog:* Sinaï *m*; **the S. Peninsula,** la presqu'île de Sinaï; **Mount S.,** le mont Sinaï.

Sinaitic [sainei'itik], *a. Geog:* sinaïtique.

Sinanthropus [si'nænθrəpəs], *s. Anthr:* sinanthrope *m*, homme *m* de pékin.

sinapic [si'næpik], *a. Ch:* (acide) sinapique.

sinapine ['sinəpain], *s. Ch:* sinapine *f*.

sinapism ['sinəpizm], *s. Med:* sinapisme *m*.

Sinbad ['sinbæd]. *Pr.n.m. Lit:* **S. the sailor,** Sinbad le marin.

since [sins]. **1.** *adv.* depuis; (*a*) **I've not seen him s.,** je ne l'ai pas revu depuis; **I saw him on Sunday but not s.,** je l'ai vu dimanche mais pas depuis; **he's been in perfect health ever s.,** depuis (lors), sa santé a été parfaite; (*b*) *O:* (*ago*) **many years s.,** il y a bien des années; **long s.,** (i) depuis longtemps; (ii) il y a longtemps; **that was long s.,** il y a longtemps de cela; **not long s.,** il n'y a pas très longtemps; **how long s.?** depuis combien? **how long is it s.?** il y a combien de cela? **2.** *prep.* depuis; **s. his death,** depuis sa mort; **s. early June,** dès les premiers jours de juin; **he's been there s. 5 o'clock,** il est là depuis cinq heures; **I've been here (ever) s. lunch,** je suis là depuis le déjeuner; **I haven't been out s. yesterday, s. Tuesday,** je ne suis pas sorti depuis hier, depuis mardi; **I haven't seen him s. Christmas,** je ne l'ai pas vu depuis Noël; **he's been up s. dawn,** il est debout depuis l'aube; **s. the day I first saw her I've been in love with her,** je l'aime depuis le jour où je l'ai vue pour la première fois; **s. the time of Dickens,** depuis Dickens; **s. the time I came to live in London,** depuis que j'habite Londres; **s. then, s. that time,** depuis ce temps-là, depuis lors; **s. that moment,** à partir de ce moment; à compter de ce moment; **s. when?** depuis quand? *F:* **s. when do you come into a room without knocking?** depuis quand est-il permis d'entrer sans frapper? **s. seeing you,** depuis que je vous ai vu. **3.** *conj.* (*a*) depuis que; que; **s. I've been here,** depuis que je suis ici; **we haven't seen him s. he got married,** nous ne l'avons pas vu depuis qu'il s'est marié, depuis son mariage; **it's a week s. he arrived,** il y a huit jours qu'il est arrivé; ça fait une semaine qu'il est là; **s. I've known him,** depuis que je le connais; depuis le temps que je le connais; **it's a long time s. I saw her,** il y a longtemps que je ne l'ai vue; je ne l'ai pas vue depuis longtemps; **it's a long time s. I first met her,** notre première rencontre date de longtemps; **he hasn't spoken to me s. we left Dover,** il ne m'a pas parlé depuis Douvres; **(ever) s. I lived in London,** depuis que j'habite Londres; (*b*) puisque; **I'll do it s. I must,** je le ferai puisqu'il le faut; **s. you refuse,** puisque, dès lors que, du moment que, vous refusez; **you didn't hear then, s. you said nothing,** vous n'aviez donc pas entendu, que vous ne disiez rien; *Lit:* **a more dangerous, s. unknown, foe,** un ennemi plus dangereux puisqu'inconnu.

sincere [sin'siər], *a.* (*a*) sincère; franc, *f.* franche; **he is completely s.,** il est de bonne foi; (*b*) (sentiment) sincère.

sincerely [sin'siəli], *adv.* sincèrement; en conscience; *Corr:* **yours s.,** veuillez agréer, Monsieur, etc., l'expression de mes sentiments distingués, les meilleurs.

sincerity [sin'seriti], *s.* sincérité *f*; bonne foi; **in all s.,** de la meilleure foi du monde; la main sur la conscience; **speaking in all s. . . .,** en toute sincérité . . .; **to speak with a show of s.,** parler avec un air de vérité.

sincipital [sin'sipit(ə)l], *a. Anat:* sincipital, -aux.

sinciput ['sinsipʌt], *s. Anat:* sinciput *m*.

Sind [sind]. *Pr.n. Geog:* Sind(h) *m*.

sindon ['sindən], *s.* **the s. (of Christ),** le sindon, le saint Suaire.

sine [sain], *s. Mth:* sinus *m* (d'un angle); **s. compass,** compas, boussole, des sinus; **s. curve, wave,** onde sinusoïdale; sinusoïde *f*; *Elcs:* **s.-cosine potentiometer,** potentiomètre à variations sinusoïdales.

sinecure ['sainikjuər], *s.* sinécure *f*, prébende *f*.

sinecurism ['sainikju:rizm], *s.* sinécurisme *m*.

sinecurist ['sainikju:rist], *s.* sinécuriste *mf*.

sine die ['saini'daii:, 'sinei'diei], *adv.phr.* sine die; indéfiniment.

sine qua non [sainikwei'nɔn, si:neikwɑ:'noun], *adv.phr. & s.* sine qua non; condition *f* indispensable; (condition) indispensable.

sinew ['sinju:], *s.* **1.** (*a*) *Anat:* tendon *m*; *Cu:* (*in meat*) croquant *m*, tirant *m*; (*b*) *Fig:* **a man of s.,** un homme musclé; un homme fort. **2. sinews,** nerf *m*, force *f*, vigueur *f*; **the sinews of war,** le nerf de la guerre; **the sinews of an undertaking,** l'armature financière d'une entreprise.

sinewless ['sinju:lis], *a.* **1.** *Anat:* sans tendon(s). **2.** *Fig:* sans force; sans vigueur; mou, *f.* molle.

sinewy ['sinju(:)i], *a.* **1.** (*of meat*) tendineux. **2.** (bras, etc.) musclé, nerveux, vigoureux.

sinfonia [sin'founiə], *s. Mus:* symphonie *f*.

sinfonietta [sinfouni'etə], *s. Mus:* sinfonietta *f*.

sinful ['sinful], *a.* **s. person,** pécheur, *f.* pécheresse; **s. pleasure,** plaisir coupable; **it is s. to . . .,** c'est un péché de . . .; il est criminel de . . .; **s. world,** monde de pécheurs; **s. waste,** gaspillage scandaleux.

sinfully ['sinfuli], *adv.* d'une façon coupable; en pécheur.

sinfulness ['sinfulnis], *s.* **1.** caractère criminel (d'un acte); culpabilité *f*. **2.** le péché.

sing[1] [siŋ], *s. NAm:* réunion *f* de chant.

sing[2], *v.* (**sang** [sæŋ]; **sung** [sʌŋ]) **1.** *v.tr. & i.* (*a*) chanter (un air, une chanson); **to s. sth. to the tune of . . .,** chanter qch. sur l'air de . . .; **to s. up,** chanter plus fort, de bon, de grand, cœur; **s. up, boys!** allons, les gars, qu'on vous entende! **s. to me, for me!** chante pour moi! **s. me a song!** chante-moi une chanson! **to s. to the guitar,** accompagner son chant, s'accompagner, sur la guitare; chanter avec un accompagnement de guitare; **to s. in tune,** chanter juste; **to s. out of tune,** chanter faux; détonner; *F:* **to s. small,** (i) déchanter; rabattre de ses prétentions; (ii) filer doux; **to s. another, a different, tune,** changer de ton; se conduire d'une façon différente; **to s. s.o. to sleep,** endormir qn en chantant; chanter pour endormir qn; **to s. in the New Year,** chanter l'an neuf; **to s. out the Old Year,** célébrer (par des chants) la fin de l'année; **to s. out an order,** crier un ordre; *Ecc:* **to s. mass,** chanter la messe; (*b*) **to s. s.o.'s praises,** chanter les louanges de qn; **to s. (of) s.o.'s exploits,** chanter, célébrer, les exploits de qn; *Lit:* **I s. of arms and the man,** je chante l'homme et les armes. **2.** *v.i.* (*a*) (*of the wind, etc.*) siffler; (*of the ears*) tinter, bourdonner; **the kettle is singing,** la bouilloire chante; (*b*) *F:* informer contre (qn); moucharder; (*c*) *F:* **s. out if you need me,** appelez si vous avez besoin de moi.

singable ['siŋəbl], *a.* chantable.

Singalese [siŋ(g)ə'li:z], *a. & s. Geog:* = SINHALESE.

Singapore [siŋə'pɔ:r], *Pr.n. Geog:* Singapour *m*.

singe[1] [sindʒ], *s.* **1.** légère brûlure; roussissement *m*, roussissure *f* (sur le linge, etc.). **2.** *A.Hairdr:* brûlage *m* (des cheveux).

singe[2], *v.tr.* **1.** brûler (qch.) légèrement; roussir (du linge, etc.); **to s. one's wings,** se brûler à la chandelle. **2.** (*a*) passer (qch.) à la flamme; flamber (une volaille, un cochon); *Hort:* couliner (des arbres fruitiers); *Tex:* **to s. (off) cloth,** griller l'étoffe; (*b*) *A.Hairdr:* flamber (les cheveux); **to have one's hair singed,** se faire brûler les cheveux; **to s. s.o.'s hair,** faire un brûlage à qn.

singeing ['sindʒiŋ], *s.* passage *m* à la flamme; brûlage *m* (de qch.); flambage *m* (d'une volaille, d'un cochon, etc.); roussissement *m*, roussissure *f* (du linge, etc.); *Tex:* grillage *m* (d'un tissu); *Hort:* coulinage *m* (des arbres fruitiers).

singer ['siŋər], *s.* **1.** chanteur, *f.* chanteuse, (*operatic,* *etc.*) cantatrice; *Ecc:* chantre *m*; **ballad s.,** (i) chanteur de romances, de ballades; (ii) *A:* chanteur des rues. **2.** *Lit:* (*poet*) chantre.

Singhalese [siŋgə'li:z, siŋ(h)ə-], *a. & s. Geog:* = SINHALESE.

singing[1] ['siŋiŋ], *a.* chanteur, -euse; qui chante; **s. bird,** oiseau chanteur; **s. saw,** scie musicale; *W.Tel:* **s. arc,** arc chantant.

singing[2], *s.* **1.** chant *m* (de qn, d'un oiseau, etc.); **church s.,** chants *mpl* d'église; **to learn s.,** apprendre le chant; **s. lesson, master, mistress,** leçon, maître, maîtresse, de chant; *Ecc.Arch:* **s. gallery, loft,** tribune *f.* **2.** sifflement *m,* (d'une flèche, du vent, etc.); **s. in the ears,** bourdonnement *m,* tintement *m,* d'oreilles.

single[1] ['siŋgl], *s.* **1.** *Ten: etc:* (partie *f*) simple *m*; single *m*; **to play a s.,** jouer un simple; **men's singles, women's singles,** simple messieurs, simple dames. **2.** (*a*) *Cr:* course *f* unique; (*baseball*) coup *m* de base; (*b*) disque *m* 45 tours (à deux chansons); (*c*) billet *m* simple; aller *m* (simple); (*d*) billet (de banque) d'une livre, *NAm:* d'un dollar; (*e*) *U.S:* maison *f,* appartement *m,* pour une seule personne, pour une seule famille.

single[2], *a.* **1.** (*a*) seul, unique; **a s. example will not suffice, no s. example will suffice,** il ne suffit pas d'un seul exemple; **mind occupied with a s. idea,** esprit occupé d'une seule idée; **not a s. person survived,** pas un seul n'en a réchappé; **not a s. one,** pas un seul; pas un; **I hadn't a s. cartridge,** je n'avais pas une (seule) cartouche; **(one) s. case,** (un) cas unique; **I haven't seen a s. soul,** je n'ai pas vu âme qui vive; **don't say a s. word,** ne dites pas un seul mot, un traître mot; **he hasn't (got) a s. penny,** il n'a pas le premier sou; *Pol:* **ballot, voting, for a s. member,** scrutin uninominal, votation uninominale; *Ins: etc:* **s. premium,** prime unique; *Fin:* **a s. loan,** un seul et même emprunt; **s. sum,** somme payée en une fois; *Cr:* **s. wicket,** guichet unique; **s.-track railway, s. line,** chemin de fer, ligne, à voie unique, à une voie; *Aut:* **s.-line traffic only,** circulation à sens unique (alterné); **to do sth. s. handed,** faire qch. seul, sans aide, tout seul; **he manages the factory s. handed,** il dirige l'usine seul; **I did it s. handed,** je l'ai fait tout seul, à moi seul; **to attack a tiger s. handed,** attaquer seul un tigre; **to fight ten men s. handed,** se battre tout seul contre dix hommes; **to sail s. handed,** naviguer seul; **s.-handed fishing rod,** canne à pêche qui se manie d'une main; **s.-breasted jacket,** veston droit; *Aut: etc:* **s.-cylinder engine,** moteur monocylindrique; *Typ:* **s.-cylinder machine,** machine en blanc; **s. acting, s.-action, machine, engine,** machine, moteur, à simple effet; **s.-valve machine,** machine monovalve; **s.-engined aircraft,** (avion *m*) monomoteur *m*; **s.-screw ship,** navire à une hélice; **s.-wheeled vehicle,** véhicule monoroue; **s.-banked rowing boat,** canot armé en pointe; **s.-banked oars,** avirons en pointe; **s.-deck bus, s.-decker (bus),** autobus *m* sans impériale; *El:* **s.-phase circuit, current,** circuit, courant, uniphasé, monophasé; **s.-phase traction current,** monophasé *m* de traction; **s.-pole switch,** interrupteur unipolaire; **s.-wire circuit,** circuit unifilaire; **s.-barrelled gun,** fusil *m* à un canon, à un coup; **s. loader,** fusil à un coup, sans magasin; **s.-cut file,** lime *f* à simple taille; *Mus:* **s.-stringed instrument,** instrument monocorde; *Bot: Anat:* **s. rooted,** uniradiculaire; *Equit: NAm:* **s. foot,** amble rompu; (*b*) individuel, particulier; **s. parts,** pièces détachées (d'une machine); **every s. day,** tous les jours (que Dieu fait). **2.** (*a*) **s. bed,** lit à une place, pour une personne; **s. bedroom,** chambre à un lit, pour une personne; *Nau:* **s. cabin,** cabine individuelle; **s. seater,** (i) (voiture *f*) monoplace *f*; (ii) (avion *m*) monoplace *m*; **s. eyeglass,** monocle *m*; **in s. rank,** sur un rang; *Nau:* **order in s. line,** ordre simple; **s. sculler,** canot *m* pour un seul rameur; as *m*; **to s.-scull,** (i) aller à la godille; godiller; (ii) ramer seul; **to s.-scull a boat,** (i) faire aller un canot à la godille; (ii) manier seul les deux avirons d'un canot; *Bot:* **s. flower,** fleur simple; (*b*) (*of pers.*) célibataire; non marié(e); **a s. man, woman,** un, une, célibataire; **he, she, is s.,** il est garçon, elle est demoiselle; il, elle, ne s'est pas marié(e); **he remained s.,** il est resté célibataire, garçon; **she remained s.,** elle est restée célibataire, demoiselle; *O:* **s. blessedness,** le bonheur du célibat. **3.** (*a*) sincère, honnête, simple; *B:* **the s. eye,** l'œil simple; **if thine eye be s.,** si ton œil est sain, net; **with a s. eye,** en ne visant qu'un but; avec une intention bien arrêtée; **s. eyed,** (i) sincère, honnête, probe; (ii) constant, invariable, entêté, obstiné; **s. minded,** (i) sincère, honnête, droit, loyal, -aux; (ii) entêté, obstiné; constant (dans la poursuite d'un but); invariable, immuable (dans ses convictions, etc.); **s. mindedness,** (i) sincérité *f,* loyauté *f*; (ii) unité *f* d'intention; entêtement *m,* obstination *f*; constance *f*; **s. mindedly,** (i) sincèrement, honnêtement, loyalement; (ii) d'une façon entêtée; avec constance; invariablement; **a s. heart,** un cœur sincère; **s. hearted,** sincère, honnête, droit, loyal; **s. heartedness,** sincérité; loyauté.

single[3], *v.tr. & ind.tr.* **1.** *Hort:* **to s. (out) seedlings,** éclaircir, séparer, des plants. **2. to s. out s.o., sth.,** (i) choisir qn, qch.; (ii) remarquer, distinguer, qn, qch.; (iii) monter qch. en épingle. **3.** *Nau:* **to s. (up) the ropes,** dédoubler les amarres.

singleness ['siŋgəlnis], *s.* **1.** sincérité *f,* honnêteté *f,* probité *f* (d'un motif, du cœur, de l'esprit). **2.** (*a*) unicité *f,* unification *f* (d'une idée, etc.); (*b*) **with s. of purpose,** avec un seul but en vue; avec constance. **3.** *O:* célibat *m.*

singlestick ['siŋg(ə)lstik], *s. Sp:* canne *f*; **to play at s.,** faire de (l'escrime à) la canne; **s. play,** canne.

singlet ['siŋglit], *s.* **1.** *Cost:* (*a*) maillot *m* de corps; gilet *m* (de coton, de flanelle); (*b*) *Sp:* maillot. **2.** *Atom.Ph:* singlet *m*; **charge s.,** singlet de charge.

singleton ['siŋg(ə)ltən], *s. Cards:* singleton *m.*

singly ['siŋgli], *adv.* **1.** séparément; un à un; **articles sold s.,** articles qui se vendent séparément, à la pièce; **to question the witnesses s.,** interroger les témoins individuellement, un à un; *Mth:* **if** *x* **and** *y* **are varied s. . . .,** si l'on fait varier *x* et *y* séparément . . .; *Adm: Mil:* **men travelling s.,** hommes voyageant isolément. **2.** *O:* seul, sans aide; **I can't do it s.,** je ne puis le faire (à moi) seul. **3.** *A:* **he was devoted s. to his art,** il se vouait uniquement à son art.

sing-sing ['siŋsiŋ], *s. Z:* (antilope *f*) sing-sing *m, pl.* sing-sings.

singsong[1] ['siŋsɔŋ], *s.* **1.** chant *m* monotone; ton chantant; psalmodie *f*; mélopée *f*; **s. accent,** accent chantant; **to recite sth. in a s. (manner),** psalmodier qch.; **in a s. voice,** d'un ton traînant. **2.** *F:* concert improvisé (entre amis).

singsong[2], *v.i.* psalmodier; parler d'une voix traînante.

singular ['siŋgjulər], *a.* **1.** (*a*) *A:* seul, unique; (*b*) *Gram:* **s. (number),** (nombre) singulier; *s.* **in the s.,** au singulier; (*c*) *Mth:* **s. points in a curve,** points singuliers d'une courbe. **2.** (*a*) rare, remarquable, surprenant; **s. courage,** courage rare, insigne; (*b*) singulier, bizarre.

singularity [siŋgju'læriti], *s.* singularité *f.* **1.** particularité *f.* **2.** bizarrerie *f.* **3.** exemple *m* unique, remarquable.

singularize ['siŋgjuləraiz], *v.tr.* singulariser.

singularly ['siŋgjuləli], *adv.* singulièrement; (*a*) remarquablement; **there was something s. honest about him,** il avait un air particulièrement honnête; il y avait en lui quelque chose de très honnête; (*b*) bizarrement.

Sinhalese [sin(h)ə'li:z]. *Geog:* **1.** *a.* cing(h)alais. **2.** *s.* Cing(h)alais, -aise; (*b*) *Ling:* cing(h)alais *m.*

sinicize ['sinisaiz], *v.tr.* siniser.

sinicization [sinisai'zeiʃ(ə)n], **sinification** [sinifi'keiʃ(ə)n], *s.* sinisation *f.*

sinister ['sinistər], *a.* **1.** (*a*) (influence, présage, événement) sinistre; **with a s. purpose,** dans un mauvais dessein; (*b*) **s. smile,** sourire sinistre; **s. air,** air menaçant, qui n'annonce rien de bon; **a man of s. appearance,** un homme de mauvaise mine. **2.** (*a*) *A:* senestre, sénestre, gauche; (*b*) *Her:* **the s. half of the shield,** le côté senestre, sénestre, de l'écu.

sinistral ['sinistrəl], *a. Conch: etc:* (enroulement) senestre, sénestre, sinistrorsum; **s. shell,** coquille senestre, sénestre.

sinistrally ['sinistrəli, si'nis-], *adv.* sinistrorsum.

sinistrogyrate, sinistrogyric [sinistrou'dʒaiəreit, -'dʒaiərik], *a.* (écriture) sinistrogyre.

sinistrorsal [sinis'trɔ:s(ə)l], *a. Conch: etc:* (enroulement) sinistrorsum.

sinistrorsally [sinis'trɔ:səli], *adv.* sinistrorsum, senestrorsum, sénestrorsum.

sinistrorse ['sinistrɔ:s], *a. Nat.Hist:* (tige, etc.) sinistrorse.

sinistrosis [sinis'trousis], *s. Med:* sinistrose *f.*

sink[1] [siŋk], *s.* **1.** (*a*) évier *m* (de cuisine); **s. unit,** bloc-évier *m, pl.* blocs-éviers; **s. tidy,** coin *m* d'évier; *A:* **(housemaid's) s.,** plombs *mpl*; **to pour (sth.) down the s.,** jeter (qch.) à l'égout; (*b*) lavabo *m*; (*c*) (i) *A:* égout *m,* cloaque *m,* bourbier *m,* puisard *m*; (ii) *Fig:* **s. (of iniquity),** cloaque, sentine *f* (de tous les vices); (*d*) *A:* **s. stone,** souillard *m.* **2.** *Geol: etc:* effondrement *m,* emposieu *m,* entonnoir *m*; bétoire *f,* aven *m,* doline *f.* **3.** *Th: A:* trappe *f* (de plateau).

sink[2], *v.* (*p.t.* **sank** [sæŋk]; *p.p.* **sunk** [sʌŋk], *A:* **sunken** ['sʌŋkən])

I. *v.i.* **1.** tomber au fond (des eaux); aller au fond; s'enfoncer dans les flots; (*of ship*) couler au fond; couler bas; sombrer, couler; (*of ship*) **to s. by the bow,** couler de l'avant; (*of pers.*) **to s. like a stone,** couler à pic; s'engloutir (dans les flots); **he was left to s. or swim,** il a été abandonné à la grâce de Dieu; **here goes! s. or swim!** allons-y! il faut risquer le tout pour le tout! il faut jouer notre va-tout! allons-y! advienne que pourra! au petit bonheur! *F:* **we're sunk,** nous sommes coulés, ruinés, perdus, fichus. **2.** (*a*) **to s. into the mud, the snow,** s'enfoncer, pénétrer, dans la boue, la neige; **to s. into quicksand,** s'enliser dans des sables mouvants; **we sank into it up to our knees,** nous y avons enfoncé jusqu'aux genoux; **the car sank into the mud,** la voiture s'est enlisée dans la boue; **the dye must be allowed to s. in,** il faut donner à la teinture le temps de pénétrer; (*of words*) **to s. into the memory, into the mind,** entrer dans la mémoire, dans l'esprit; se graver dans la mémoire; **his words are beginning to s. in,** ses paroles commencent à faire impression; **the lesson hasn't sunk in,** la leçon n'a pas été (i) apprise, (ii) (bien) comprise; (*b*) **to s. into vice, oblivion,** tomber dans le vice, dans l'oubli; **sunk in thought,** plongé dans ses pensées; **to s. deep(er) into crime,** s'enfoncer dans le crime; **to s. into a deep sleep,** s'endormir profondément. **3.** (*subside*) (*a*) **to s. (down),** s'affaisser; (*of wall, building, etc.*) s'affaisser, se tasser, farder; (*of supports, piers, etc.*) se déniveler; (*b*) (*of pers.*) **to s. (down) into an armchair,** se laisser tomber, s'affaisser, s'affaler, s'enfoncer, s'effondrer, dans un fauteuil; **he sank back in his chair,** il s'est renversé sur sa chaise; **to s. to the ground,** (se laisser) tomber à terre; **to s. under a burden,** s'abattre, succomber, sous un fardeau; **his legs sank under him,** ses jambes se sont pliées sous lui, ont défailli; **his heart sank at the news,** à cette nouvelle son cœur s'est serré; à cette nouvelle il a eu un serrement de cœur; **his spirits sank,** son courage s'est abattu. **4.** (*of ground, etc.*) descendre; aller en descendant; s'abaisser; **to s. out of sight,** disparaître; **the sun is sinking,** le soleil baisse. **5.** baisser (en valeur, en puissance); diminuer, s'affaiblir, décliner; **prices are sinking,** les cours baissent, sont en baisse; **the patient is sinking fast,** le malade baisse, décline, s'affaiblit, rapidement; **his voice sank to a whisper,** sa voix s'est réduite à un murmure; **he has sunk in my estimation,** il a baissé, diminué, dans mon estime.

II. *v.tr.* **1.** (*a*) couler, faire sombrer (un navire); envoyer (un navire) au fond; (*b*) mouiller (une mine); foncer (un puits). **2.** (faire) baisser (qch. à un niveau inférieur); enfoncer (un pieu, etc.); **stone sunk into the wall,** pierre encastrée dans le mur; **to s. one's teeth into sth.,** enfoncer ses dents dans qch.; *F:* **to s. a drink, a pint,** vider un pot; s'envoyer un demi; **sunk carving,** sculpture en creux; **sunk key,** clavette encastrée, noyée; **pin with sunk head,** cheville à tête perdue; *Phot:* (*of lens*) **sunk mount,** monture noyée; *El:* **sunk stud,** plot noyé; *Const:* **sunk stone,** pierre perdue. **3.** (*a*) creuser, foncer, forer (un puits); **to s. a bore hole,** opérer un sondage; (*b*) *Engr:* **to s. a die,** graver un coin en creux. **4.** supprimer (une objection, etc.); laisser de côté (son opinion, etc.); **to s. one's name, one's title,** renoncer à son nom, à son titre; **they sank their differences,** ils ont fait table rase de leurs différends. **5.** *Fin:* éteindre, amortir (une dette). **6.** (*a*) **to s. money in an annuity,** placer de l'argent en viager, à fonds perdu; (*b*) **to s. money in an undertaking,** enterrer, engloutir, de l'argent dans une entreprise. **7. to s. the ball,** (i) *Bill:* mettre la bille dans la blouse; (ii) *Golf:* envoyer la balle dans le trou.

sinkable ['siŋkəbl], *a.* (bateau, etc.) submersible.

sinkage ['siŋkidʒ], *s.* enfoncement *m,* enlisement *m* (des roues d'une voiture, etc.).

sinker ['siŋkər], *s.* **1.** (*pers.*) **well s.,** *Min:* **shaft s.,** avaleur *m*; fonceur *m* de puits; puisatier *m.* **2.** (*a*) *Navy:* crapaud *m* d'amarrage, de mouillage (d'une mine); (*b*) plomb *m* (d'une ligne de pêche); **sinkers of a net,** cliquettes *fpl,* lest *m,* d'un filet; (*c*) *NAm: F:* (i) mauvaise pièce (de monnaie); (ii) gâteau lourd; (iii) beignet soufflé; (*d*) *Tex:* platine *f.*

sinkhead ['siŋkhed], *s. Metall:* masselotte *f.*

sinkhole ['siŋkhoul], *s.* **1.** *O:* souillard *m* (de dallage, etc.). **2.** *Geol: etc:* effondrement *m*; emposieu *m,* entonnoir *m*; bétoire *f,* aven *m,* doline *f*; **s. pond, lake,** lavogne *f*; lac de doline.

sinking[1] ['siŋkiŋ], *a.* qui s'enfonce, qui s'affaisse; (mur, etc.) qui se tasse; **s. ship,** navire qui coule; navire en perdition; **with a s. heart,** le cœur défaillant; avec un serrement de cœur.

sinking[2], *s.* **1.** (*a*) enfoncement *m* (des pieds dans la boue, etc.); enlisement *m* (de qn dans une fondrière, etc.); engloutissement *m* (d'un navire); (*b*) action de couler (un navire); (*in war*) **the s. of a ship,** le torpillage d'un navire; *M.Ins:* **permanent s.,** submersion *f* sans possibilité de renflouement. **2.** affaissement *m,* abaissement *m* (du sol, etc.); tassement *m* (d'un édifice, etc.); serrement *m,* oppression *f* (du cœur); abattement *m* (des esprits); **that s. feeling,** ce sentiment de défaillance.

3. affaiblissement *m*, déclin *m* (des forces, etc.); abaissement (de la voix, etc.). 4. creusage *m*, creusement *m*, fonçage *m*, foncement *m*, forage *m* (d'un puits). 5. (*a*) amortissement *m*, extinction *f* (d'une dette); **s. fund,** fonds *m*, caisse *f*, d'amortissement; (*b*) placement *m* (d'une somme) à fonds perdu.

sinless ['sinlis], *a.* exempt de péché; sans péché; innocent, pur.

sinlessly ['sinlisli], *adv.* sans péché; purement.

sinlessness ['sinlisnis], *s.* innocence *f*, pureté *f*.

sinner ['sinər], *s.* (*a*) pécheur, *f.* pécheresse; *O:* **as I am a s.!** sur ma part du paradis! (*b*) *A:* mauvais sujet.

sinnet ['sinit], *s. Nau:* tresse *f* (de chanvre, de paille).

Sinn Fein [ʃin'fein], *s. Pol:* (*in Ireland*) Sinn fein *m*.

Sinn Feiner [ʃin'feinər], *s.* Sinn-feiner *m*; partisan, -ane, du Sinn fein.

sinning[1] ['siniŋ], *a.* fautif; qui pèche; qui a péché.

sinning[2], *s.* péché *m*.

Sino- ['sainou], *comb.fm.* sino-.

Sino-Japanese [sainoudʒæpə'ni:z]. *Geog:* 1. *a.* sino-japonais. 2. *s.* (*a*) Sino-Japonais, -aise; (*b*) *Ling:* sino-japonais *m*.

sinological [s(a)inou'lɔdʒik(ə)l], *a.* sinologique.

sinologist [s(a)i'nɔlədʒist], **sinologue** ['s(a)inəlɔg], *s.* sinologue *mf*.

sinology [s(a)i'nɔlədʒi], *s. Ling: etc:* sinologie *f*.

Sinope [si'noupi], *Pr.n. Geog:* Sinop *f*.

sinople ['sinəpl], *s.* 1. *Miner:* sinople *m*. 2. *Her:* sinople.

sinter[1] ['sintər], *s. Geol:* tuf *m*, tuf(f)eau *m*; travertin *m*; **calcareous s.,** tuf, travertin, calcaire; silex *m* molaire; **siliceous s.,** tuf siliceux; *Metall:* **s. slag,** sorne *f*.

sinter[2]. 1. *v.tr.* (*a*) agglomérer; *Metall:* fritter; (*b*) *El:* concrétionner (un filament). 2. *v.i.* s'agglomérer; se concrétionner.

sintering ['sintəriŋ], *s.* (*a*) agglomération *f*; *Metall:* frittage *m*; **s. oven, furnace,** four de frittage; (*b*) *El:* concrétion *f* (d'un filament).

sinuate ['sinjuət], *a. Bot:* sinué.

sinuosity [sinju'ɔsiti], *s.* (*a*) sinuosité *f*, anfractuosité *f*; (*b*) virage *m*, lacet *m* (d'une route, etc.).

sinuous ['sinjuəs], *a.* 1. sinueux, tortueux, ondoyant, onduleux, anfractueux; *Mil:* **s. line of trenches,** tranchées au tracé vermiculaire. 2. (*of pers.*) souple, agile.

sinus ['sainəs], *s. Anat:* sinus *m*, antre *m*; *Med:* fistule *f*; **s. tract,** trajet fistuleux; **frontal sinuses,** sinus frontaux; **maxillary s.,** sinus maxillaire; **s. of the aorta,** sinus du cœur.

sinusitis [sainə'saitis], *s. Med:* sinusite *f*.

sinusoid ['sainəsɔid], *s. Mth:* sinusoïde *f*; onde sinusoïdale.

sinusoidal [sainə'sɔid(ə)l], *a. Mth:* (*of function, etc.*) sinusoïdal, -aux.

Sion ['saiən]. *Pr.n. B.Geog:* Sion.

Siouan ['su:ən], *a. Ethn:* sioux *inv*.

Sioux [su:]. *Ethn:* 1. *a.* sioux *inv*. 2. *s.* (*a*) Sioux *mf*; (*b*) *Ling:* sioux *m*.

sip[1] [sip], *s.* petite gorgée; petit coup; goutte *f*; **to drink sth. in sips,** siroter, buvoter, qch.

sip[2], *v.tr.* (**sipped**) boire à petites gorgées, à petits coups; **to s. sth. (up),** siroter, buvoter, déguster, savourer, qch.

siphon[1] ['saif(ə)n], *s.* siphon *m*; (*a*) **plunging s.,** pipette *f* tâte-vin; sonde *f* à vin; **s. barometer,** baromètre à siphon; **s. gauge,** calibre *m* à siphon; *Hyd.E:* **regulation s.,** épanchoir *m* à siphon (d'un canal); *Tg:* **s. recorder,** siphon recorder; (*b*) **(soda water) s.,** siphon (d'eau de Seltz); (*c*) *Z:* siphon.

siphon[2]. 1. *v.tr.* siphonner (un liquide); *Fin:* **to s. off an excess,** éponger, résorber, un excédent (financier). 2. *v.i.* (*of water, etc.*) se transvaser; s'écouler (par un siphon).

siphonage ['saifənidʒ], *s.* siphonnement *m*; *Med:* siphon(n)age *m*.

siphonal ['saifən(ə)l], *a. Z:* (tube, etc.) siphonal, -aux; siphoïde.

Siphonales [saifə'neili:z], *s.pl. Algae:* siphonales *f*.

siphonanth ['saifənænθ], *s. Coel:* siphonanthe *m*.

Siphonaptera [saifə'næptərə], *s.pl. Ent:* siphonaptères *m*.

Siphonaria [saifə'nɛəriə], *s.pl. Moll:* siphonaires *m*.

Siphonariidae [saifɔnə'raiidi:], *s.pl. Moll:* siphonariidés *m*.

siphonet ['saifənet], *s. Ent:* cornicule *f* (du puceron).

siphonic [sai'fɔnik], *a.* siphonal, -aux, siphoïde.

siphoning ['saifəniŋ], *s.* siphonnement *m*.

Siphonocladales [saifənɔklə'deili:z], *s.pl. Algae:* siphonocladales *f*.

siphonogamous [saifə'nɔgəməs], *a. Bot:* siphonogame.

siphonogamy [saifə'nɔgəmi], *s. Bot:* siphonogamie *f*.

Siphonophora [saifə'nɔfərə], *s.pl. Coel:* siphonophores *m*.

siphonophore ['saifənoufɔ:r], *s. Coel:* siphonophore *m*.

siphonostele ['saifənousti:l], *s. Bot:* siphonostèle *f*.

Siphonostomata [saifənou'stoumətə], *s.pl. Crust: Moll:* siphonostomes *m*.

siphonostomatous [saifənou'stoumətəs], *a. Nat.Hist:* siphonostome.

siphonostome ['saifənoustoum], *s. Crust: Moll:* siphonostome *m*.

siphuncle ['saifʌŋkl], *s. Nat.Hist:* (*a*) siphon *m* (de coquille); (*b*) siphonule *m* (de puceron).

sippet ['sipit], *s. Cu:* croûton *m*.

Sipunculacea [saipʌŋkju'leisiə], *s.pl. Ann:* sipunculiens *m*.

sipunculid, -culoid [sai'pʌŋkjulid, -kjulɔid], *a. & s. Ann:* **s. (worm),** siponcle *m*.

Sipunculida, -culoidea [saipʌŋ'kju:lidə, -kju'lɔidiə], *s.pl. Ann:* sipunculidés *m*.

sir[1] [sə:r, sər], *s.* 1. (*a*) (*as form of address to a superior, esp. NAm: to an equal*) Monsieur *m*; **yes, s.,** (i) oui, monsieur; (ii) *Mil: etc:* (*to superior officer*) oui, mon capitaine, mon colonel, etc.; (*to equal or inferior*) oui, capitaine, monsieur; (iii) *Navy:* oui, commandant, amiral; **dinner is served, s.,** Monsieur est servi; *A:* **fair s.,** beau sire; (*b*) *Corr:* **(Dear) S.,** Monsieur; (*less formal*) Cher Monsieur; **Dear Sirs,** Messieurs; (*c*) *Sch: P:* **s. told me,** le maître me l'a dit. 2. sir (titre d'un *baronet* et d'un *knight* en Angleterre, et qui ne s'emploie jamais sans le prénom, ainsi; Sir Walter Scott, Sir Walter); *A:* **S. Knight,** sire chevalier.

sir[2], *v.tr.* (**sirred**) *F:* appeler qn Monsieur; **don't s. me,** ne m'appelez pas Monsieur; **he was sirring me all the time,** il me donnait du Monsieur gros comme le bras.

sirdar ['sə:da:r], *s. Mil:* sirdar *m*.

sire[1] [saiər], *s.* 1. (*a*) *A: & Lit:* père *m*, aïeul *m*; (*b*) *Breed:* père (en parlant des quadrupèdes); *esp.* étalon *m*; **pedigree sires,** reproducteurs *m* d'élite. 2. *A:* (*title of address to king or emperor*) sire *m*.

sire[2], *v.tr.* (*of stallion, etc.*) engendrer, procréer (un poulain, etc.); être le père (d'un poulain, etc.).

siren ['saiərən], *s.* 1. (*a*) *Myth:* sirène *f*; **s. song,** chant de sirène; (*b*) *O:* femme fatale; tentatrice *f*; sirène. 2. (*a*) *Ac:* sirène; (*b*) *Ind: Nau: etc:* sirène (d'usine, de navire, d'alarme); trompe *f* d'alarme; trompe (d'une voiture de pompiers); avertisseur *m* (à deux tons) (d'une voiture de police); **to sound, blow, the s.,** faire marcher, faire retentir, la sirène; *Cost: A:* **s. suit,** combinaison *f* à fermeture éclair. 3. *Amph:* sirène.

Sirenia [saiə'ri:niə], *s.pl. Z:* sirènes *f*, siréniens *m*.

sirenian [saiə'ri:niən], *s. Z:* sirénien *m*.

Sirenidae [saiə'renidi:], *s.pl. Amph:* sirénidés *m*.

sirex ['saiəreks], *s. Ent:* sirex *m*.

siriasis [si'raiəsis], *s. Med:* insolation *f*; coup *m* de soleil.

Siricidae [si'risidi:], *s.pl. Ent:* siricidés *m*.

Sirius ['siriəs], *Pr.n. Astr:* Sirius *m*.

sirloin ['sə:lɔin], *s. Cu:* aloyau *m* (de bœuf); faux-filet *m*.

sirocco [si'rɔkou], *s. Meteor:* siroc(c)o *m*.

sirrah ['sirə], *s. A:* 1. Monsieur *m*; **come, s. host, some ale!** allons, l'hôtelier, de la bière! 2. *Pej:* maraud! coquin!

sir(r)ee [sə(:)'ri:], *s. NAm: F:* monsieur; **yes, s.!** oui, oui, certainement! oui, bien sûr! mais oui! oui-da! **no, s.!** mais non! ah! ça non! sûrement non!

sirup ['sirəp], *s. NAm:* sirop *m*.

sirvente [siə'vɑ̃:(n)t], *s. Hist. of Lit:* (*a form of Provençal lay*) sirvente *m*.

sis [sis], *s.f. F:* (*sister*) sœurette; (petite) sœur.

sisal ['sais(ə)l], *s. Bot:* **s. (plant),** agave *f* d'Amérique; sisal *m*; **s. hemp, grass, fibre,** fibre *f* d'agave; chanvre *m* du Yucatan; (fibre de) sisal.

Sisera ['sisərə], *Pr.n.m. B.Hist:* Sisara.

siskin ['siskin], *s. Orn:* tarin *m* (des aulnes); **pine s.,** chardonneret *m* des pins.

sissy ['sisi], *s. F:* 1. = SIS. 2. *Pej:* (*a*) homme, garçon, efféminé; femmelette *f*; (*b*) enfant, etc., peureux; poule mouillée; mollasson, -onne.

sister ['sistər], *s.f.* 1. sœur; **own s., full s., s. german,** sœur de père et mère; sœur germaine; **the Thomas sisters,** les sœurs Thomas; **my dear little s.,** ma chère petite sœur; ma sœurette chérie; **s.-in-law,** belle-sœur; **sisters-in-law,** belles-sœurs; *Lit:* **the Fatal Sisters, the Sisters three, the three Sisters,** les Parques. 2. (*a*) *Ecc:* religieuse; sœur; **S. of Charity,** sœur, fille, de la Charité; sœur de Saint-Vincent-de-Paul; sœur hospitalière; **S. of Mercy,** sœur de la Charité; sœur hospitalière; **grey s.,** cordelière; **the Little Sisters of the Poor,** les petites Sœurs des pauvres; **S. Ursula,** la sœur Ursule; **come in, S.,** entrez, ma sœur; (*b*) (*in hospital*) **(ward) s.,** infirmière-major; **theatre s., X-ray s.,** infirmière-major qui fait le service de la salle d'opération, qui fait le service de radiographie. 3. *attrib.* (*a*) (*of a society*) **our s. members,** nos consœurs; **s. nations,** nations sœurs; **s. company,** compagnie sœur; société sœur; **s. ships,** (i) bâtiments identiques, similaires; bâtiments de même série; navires jumeaux; frères *m*; (ii) navires appartenant au même armateur, à la même compagnie; *Ins:* **s. ship clause,** clause prévoyant la collision avec un navire appartenant au même propriétaire; (*b*) *Nau:* **s. block,** baraquette *f*, navette *f*; poulie *f* vierge; *N.Arch:* **s. keelson,** contre-carlingue *f*, *pl.* contre-carlingues; (*c*) **s. hook,** croc *m* à ciseaux.

sisterhood ['sistəhud], *s.* communauté religieuse (de sœurs).

sisterlike ['sistəlaik], *a. & adv.* de sœur; en sœur.

sisterliness ['sistəlinis], *s.* affection *f*, sympathie *f*, de sœur.

sisterly ['sistəli], *a.* de sœur; **in a s. fashion,** en sœur; comme une sœur.

Sistine ['sisti:n, -tain], *a.* **the S. chapel,** la chapelle Sixtine.

sistrum ['sistrəm], *s. A.Mus:* sistre *m*.

sisymbrium [si'simbriəm], *s. Bot:* sisymbre *m*, sisymbrium *m*.

Sisyphean [sisi'fiən], *a. Myth:* (rocher, travail) de Sisyphe.

Sisyphus ['sisifəs]. *Pr.n.m. Myth:* Sisyphe.

sit[1] [sit], *s.* 1. *F:* **we had a long s. at the station,** nous avons dû attendre longtemps à la gare; **come and have a s. down,** venez vous asseoir; **s.-down meal,** repas servi à table; *Ind:* **s.-down strike,** grève *f* sur le tas; grève des bras croisés; **s.-in,** (grève avec) occupation *f* des locaux. 2. *A:* ajustement *m* (d'un vêtement); **he admired the perfect s. of her dress,** il admirait comme sa robe tombait bien.

sit[2], *v.* (*p.t. & p.p.* **sat** [sæt]; *pr.p.* **sitting**)

I. *v.i.* 1. (*a*) (*of pers.*) s'asseoir; être assis, rester assis (dans un fauteuil, par terre, etc.); se tenir (dans une pièce, etc.); **these chairs are not to be sat on,** ces chaises-là ne sont pas faites pour s'y asseoir; **we usually s. in the living room,** nous nous tenons d'ordinaire dans le salon; **would you rather s. here?** préférez-vous vous mettre ici? **where would you like me to s.? where shall I s.?** où dois-je me mettre, m'asseoir? **to s. round the fire,** faire cercle autour du feu; **s. by the fire,** mettez-vous auprès du feu; **to s. together,** s'asseoir l'un(e) à côté de l'autre, côte à côte; **s. (closer) together,** serrez-vous! **to s. still,** rester sans bouger; rester tranquille, immobile; **to s. with one's back to s.o.,** tourner le dos à qn; **he was sitting reading,** il était assis à lire, assis en train de lire; **we sat looking at each other,** nous restions (assis) à nous regarder; **to s. with s.o.,** tenir compagnie à qn; **to s. at home,** se tenir chez soi; rester inactif; **to s. at a desk,** s'asseoir à, derrière, un bureau; **to s. at (the) table,** s'asseoir, se mettre, à (la) table; s'attabler; **they were sitting at (the) table,** ils étaient (assis) à (la) table; ils étaient attablés; **we were sitting at lunch, at dinner,** nous étions en train de déjeuner, de dîner; **to s. over the brandy, over one's work,** rester attablé à savourer un cognac, à son travail; **to s. smoking a pipe,** rester (assis) à savourer une pipe; **to s. over a book,** s'absorber dans la lecture d'un livre; **he sits over his books,** il passe des heures penché sur ses livres; *Cards:* **to s. over, under, s.o.,** jouer après, avant, qn; être assis à gauche, à droite, de qn; *A:* **we s. under the Reverend Thomas,** nous faisons partie des ouailles du révérend Thomas; c'est le révérend Thomas qui est notre pasteur; *O:* **he had sat under Professor X,** il avait suivi les cours du professeur X; **to s. in state,** trôner; **he sat through the whole play without laughing,** il est resté jusqu'à la fin de la pièce sans rire; *F:* **to s. tight,** (i) ne pas bouger de sa place; ne pas se laisser ébranler; ne pas céder; (ii) avoir les pieds nickelés; *P:* **he does nothing but s. on his backside,** il ne bouge pas d'une semelle; *F:* **to s. on s.o.,** rabrouer qn; remettre qn à sa place; rabattre, rabaisser, le caquet à qn; moucher qn; asseoir qn; s'asseoir sur qn; **he's always sitting on** ***me***, c'est toujours à moi qu'il en a; *Equit:* **to s. close,** rester assis (en trottant); (*b*) **to s. for one's portrait,** poser pour son portrait; **to s. for, to, an artist,** poser chez un artiste; servir de modèle à un artiste; **who sat for this statue?** qui a posé pour cette statue? (*c*) **to s. on the committee, on the jury,** être du comité, du jury; **to s. in Parliament** = être député; **to s. for a constituency,** représenter une circonscription électorale. 2. (*of assemblies*) siéger; être en séance; tenir séance; **the assembly sitting at Versailles,** l'assemblée réunie à Versailles; **the assembly declared that it would s. until the conclusion of the business,** l'assemblée s'est déclarée en permanence; **the court is sitting,** la séance est ouverte; **the courts do not s. in August,** les tribunaux vaquent au mois d'août; **a committee is sitting on the question,** une commission discute, délibère sur, la question; *Jur:* (*of judge*) **to s. on a case,** juger une affaire; *F:* **to s. on a project,** laisser dormir un projet; ne pas s'occuper d'un projet. **3.** (*a*) (*of bird*) (se) percher (sur un arbre, etc.); être perché, branché; (*b*) (*of hen*) **to s. (on eggs),** couver (des œufs); (*c*) *Ven:* **to find a hare sitting,** trouver un lièvre au gîte; **to shoot a pheasant sitting,** tirer un faisan au perché; tirer un faisan branché, au sol, qui se rase. **4.** (*a*) *Lit:* (*of thg*) **joy sat on every countenance,** la joie régnait sur tous les visages; *A:* **how sits the wind?** (i) d'où vient le vent? (ii) *Fig:* où en est l'affaire? **his responsibilities s. heavy on him,** ses responsabilités pèsent sur lui, lui sont à charge; **sorrow sits lightly on him,** la douleur ne l'accable pas, ne lui pèse pas; *F:* **this food sits heavy on the stomach,** cette nourriture pèse sur l'estomac; (*b*) *O:* (*of garment*) tomber (bien, mal); aller; **to s. badly,** gongonner; être mal ajusté. **5.** *A:* (*of clothes, etc.*) seoir (on, à); **forwardness that sits ill on a young lady,** effronterie qui sied mal, qui messied, à une jeune fille.

II. *v.tr.* **1. to s. a horse well, badly,** se tenir bien, mal, à cheval; avoir une bonne, mauvaise, assiette; **he was taught to s. a horse,** il a appris à monter à cheval; **he was sitting an old horse,** il montait un vieux cheval; il était monté sur un vieux cheval. **2. to s. a child on the table,** asseoir un enfant sur la table; **to s. a hen (on eggs),** mettre une poule à couver. **3.** *A: & Lit:* **with an impudent air that sat him ill,** d'un air effronté qui lui seyait mal. **4. to s. an exam,** passer un examen.

III. (*compound verbs*) **1. sit back,** *v.i.* (*a*) **to s. back in one's chair,** se renverser dans sa chaise, son fauteuil; s'appuyer sur le dossier de sa chaise, son fauteuil; (*b*) *F:* se détendre, se reposer, se relaxer; **to s. back and let the others do the work,** regarder les autres travailler.

2. sit down. (*a*) *v.i.* (i) s'asseoir; prendre un siège; **please s. down,** asseyez-vous, s'il vous plaît, je vous en prie; veuillez vous asseoir; **to s. down again,** se rasseoir; (*at table*) se remettre à (la) table; **to s. down at (the) table, to a meal,** se mettre à table, s'attabler; **to s. down to a game of bridge,** s'installer pour faire une partie de bridge; **to s. down under an insult,** avaler, endurer, supporter, une insulte; *Equit:* **to s. down to a trot,** faire du trot assis; (ii) *Mil: A:* **to s. down before a town,** mettre le siège à une ville; (iii) *Av: F:* atterrir; (*b*) *v.tr.* **s. him down on the grass,** asseyez-le sur le gazon; *F:* **s. yourself down!** asseyez-vous donc! *Mil: A:* **to s. one's army down before a town,** asseoir le camp devant une ville.

3. sit in, *v.i.* (*a*) entrer dans une partie de cartes; (*b*) faire grève avec occupation des locaux; (*c*) **to s. in on a rehearsal, a meeting,** assister à une répétition, une réunion (sans y participer).

4. sit out. (*a*) *v.i.* s'asseoir dehors; être assis dehors; (*b*) *v.tr.* (i) ne pas prendre part à (un jeu, etc.); **to s. out a dance (with s.o.),** sauter une danse (en passant le temps avec son partenaire); **I didn't s. out a single dance,** je n'ai pas manqué une seule danse; (ii) **to s. a lecture out,** rester (patiemment) jusqu'à la fin d'une conférence; endurer un conférencier jusqu'au bout de sa conférence; **he sat it out,** il est resté jusqu'à la fin; (iii) **to s. s.o. out,** ne pas se lever avant le départ de qn; rester jusqu'après le départ de qn.

5. sit up. (*a*) *v.i.* (i) se tenir droit; se redresser (sur sa chaise); **s. up straight!** tiens-toi droit! *F:* **to make s.o. s. up,** étonner, épater, qn; **I sent him a letter to make him s. up,** je lui ai écrit très vertement; **I'll make you s. up!** vous aurez de mes nouvelles! (ii) **to s. up (in bed),** se dresser, se mettre, se lever, sur son séant; (*of convalescent*) **he's beginning to s. up and take notice, take nourishment,** il est en train de se remettre; (iii) (*of dog*) **to s. up (and beg),** faire le beau; (iv) **to s. up (late),** veiller tard; se coucher tard; **to s. up for s.o.,** (rester levé à) attendre qn; veiller en attendant le retour de qn; **my wife is sitting up for me,** ma femme veillera jusqu'à mon retour; **to s. up with someone who is ill,** garder, veiller, (au chevet d')un malade; (v) **to s. up to (the) table,** approcher sa chaise de la table; (*b*) *v.tr.* **to s. s.o. up,** soulever qn; asseoir qn sur son séant.

sitar [ˈsitɑːr], *s. Mus:* sitar *m.*

sitatunga [sitəˈtʌŋgə], *s. Z:* situtounga *m.*

site[1] [sait], *s.* **1.** emplacement *m*, situation *f* (d'un édifice, d'une ville, d'un camp, etc.); **(archaeological) s.,** site *m* (archéologique); **prehistoric s.,** site, gisement *m*, préhistorique; **picturesque s.,** site pittoresque; **caravan, camp(ing), s.,** (terrain *m* de) camping *m*; **launching s.,** aire *f* de lancement; **on-s. computer,** ordinateur installé chez l'utilisateur. **2. (building) s.,** (i) terrain à bâtir; (ii) chantier *m* (de construction); **on s.,** sur le chantier; sur place; **to dress the stones on the s.,** tailler les pierres sur le tas; **to be on s.,** être à pied d'œuvre; **to bring equipment on s.,** amener du matériel à pied d'œuvre; **bringing on s. (of equipment),** mise à pied d'œuvre (du matériel). **3.** *Artil: Surv: etc:* **(angle of) s.,** (angle de) site.

site[2], *v.tr.* placer, situer (un bâtiment, etc.); *Mil:* **to s. machine gun emplacements,** établir des emplacements *m* de mitrailleuse.

sitfast [ˈsitfɑːst], *s. Vet:* cor *m*, induration *f* (sur le dos d'un cheval).

sith [siθ]. *A: & Lit:* **1.** *conj.* (*a*) puisque; (*b*) depuis que. **2.** *adv. & prep.* depuis.

sit(i)ology [saiˈtɔlədʒi, si-, sitiˈɔlədʒi], *s.* sitiologie *f*, diététique *f*.

sitrep [ˈsitrep], *s. Mil: etc: F:* rapport *m*, compte rendu (de la situation actuelle).

sitta [ˈsitə], *s. Orn:* sittelle *f*.

sitter [ˈsitər], *s.* **1.** personne assise. **2.** personne qui pose (chez un artiste); (i) modèle *mf*; (ii) client, -ente. **3.** *F:* **s.(-in),** gardien, -ienne, d'enfants; (*professional*) garde-bébé *mf, pl.* gardes-bébés. **4.** (*a*) (poule) couveuse *f*; (*b*) *F: Ven:* **to fire at a s.,** tirer un animal au repos, un lièvre au gîte, un sanglier baugé, un oiseau au perché, branché, au sol; *Sp:* **to miss a s.,** rater un but tout fait; **it was a s. for me,** c'était chose facile; c'était un coup tout fait; *Cards:* **any call less than little slam was a s.,** tout appel au-dessous de petit schlem était imperdable.

sitting[1] [ˈsitiŋ], *a.* **1.** assis; *Art:* **s. figure,** figure assise. **2.** (*of tribunal, etc.*) séant; en séance; siégeant; qui siège; **s. magistrate,** juge en conseil; juge siégeant; **s. tenant,** locataire *mf* en possession des lieux; *Parl:* **our s. member,** le député qui nous représente actuellement, qui siège actuellement. **3.** (*a*) (animal) au repos; (lièvre) au gîte; (sanglier) baugé; (faisan) au perché, branché, au sol; (*b*) **s. hen,** poule en train de couver.

sitting[2], *s.* **1.** (*a*) posture assise; **s. still,** immobilité *f*; **s. and standing room,** (i) assez de places pour s'asseoir et se tenir debout; (ii) places assises et places debout; **s. up (late),** veille *f*; (*in house*) **s. room,** (i) salon *m*; (ii) salle *f* de séjour; *Fr.C:* vivoir *m*; (*b*) pose *f* (pour son portrait, etc.); **to paint a portrait in three sittings,** faire un portrait en trois séances *f*. **2.** (*a*) (*for meals*) **first, second, s.,** premier, deuxième, service; **to serve 500 people in, at, one s.,** servir 500 personnes à la fois; **to write two chapters at one s.,** écrire deux chapitres d'un trait, d'un (seul) jet, d'un coup, en une fois; (*b*) séance, réunion *f* (d'une commission, etc.); tenue *f* (d'une assemblée); **s. of a court,** audience *f*; **s. of a congress,** assises *fpl*; *Jur:* **private s. (of judges),** délibéré *m*; **the sittings,** les (quatre) sessions *f* de l'année judiciaire. **3.** *O:* siège réservé, place réservée (dans une église). **4.** *Husb:* (*a*) (*of hen*) couvaison *f*, incubation *f*; (*b*) couvée *f* (d'œufs).

situate[1] [ˈsitjueit], *v.tr.* **1.** situer (une maison, etc.); **house s. in St. Thomas' Street,** maison située dans la rue Saint-Thomas; *Jur:* maison sise rue Saint-Thomas. **2.** (*of pers.*) **this is how I'm situated,** voici ma position; voici la situation dans laquelle je me trouve; **situated as he is,** dans la position où il se trouve; **awkwardly, badly, situated,** dans une situation, une position, embarrassante.

situate[2], *a.* (*always follows noun*) (*of house, etc.*) situé, *Jur:* sis (dans un lieu).

situated [ˈsitjueitid], *a.* situé; **pleasantly s. house,** maison bien située.

situation [sitjuˈeiʃ(ə)n], *s.* **1.** situation *f*, emplacement *m* (d'un édifice); situation (d'une ville). **2.** situation (politique, etc.); **financial s.,** situation financière, de fortune; **overall economic s.,** conjoncture économique; **to explain the s.,** exposer la situation; **embarrassing, awkward, s.,** situation embarrassante; **to find oneself in an unfortunate s.,** se trouver dans une déplorable conjoncture; *F:* **what's, how's, the coffee s.?** il nous reste assez de café? combien nous reste-t-il de café? **3.** *Th:* situation (dramatique). **4.** emploi *m*, place *f*, position *f*; **to get a s.,** se placer; obtenir un emploi; (*in advertisements*) **situations vacant,** offres *fpl* d'emplois; situations vacantes; **situations wanted,** demandes *fpl* d'emplois.

sit-upon [ˈsitəpɔn], *s. F:* derrière *m*, postérieur *m.*

situtunga [sitəˈtʌŋgə], *s. Z:* situtounga *m.*

Siva [ˈsiːvə], *Pr.n.m. Hindu Rel:* Civa, Siva.

Sivaism [ˈsiːvəizm], *s. Hindu Rel:* çivaïsme *m*, sivaïsme *m.*

Sivaite [ˈsiːvəait], *s. Hindu Rel:* çivaïte *mf*, sivaïste *mf.*

six [siks]. **1.** *num. a. & s.* (*a*) six (*m*); **I have s.,** j'en ai six; **number s.,** (le) numéro six; **twenty-s.,** vingt-six; **s. fours, four sixes, are twenty-four,** six fois quatre, quatre fois six, font vingt-quatre; *A: F:* **two and s.,** deux shillings et six pence; **s. and a half,** six et demi; **at s. (o'clock),** à six heures; **at s. thirty,** à six heures et demie; **the s. thirty (train),** le (train de) (i) six heures trente, (ii) dix-huit heures trente; **the flight will arrive at s. (hours) thirty,** le vol arrivera à six heures trente; **to be s. (years old),** avoir six ans; **s. of my students,** six de, d'entre, mes étudiants; **coach and s.,** carrosse à six chevaux; *F:* **I take sixes, a s.** = (i) (*in shoes*) je chausse du 39; (ii) (*in gloves*) je gante du six; j'ai six de pointure; **packet of s. (packs of cards, etc.),** sizain *m*, sixain *m*; (*at dice*) **to throw sixes,** amener double-six; (*at dominoes, etc.*) **double s.,** double-six *m, pl.* doubles-six; *Cards:* **the s. of hearts,** le six de cœur; *F:* **it's s. of one and half a dozen of the other,** c'est blanc bonnet et bonnet blanc; l'un vaut l'autre; c'est kif-kif; c'est du kif; **we're all, everything's, at sixes and sevens,** tout est désorganisé, en désordre; tout est sens dessus dessous; tout est en pagaïe, pagaille, pagaye; c'est la pagaïe; (*of rowing crew, etc.*) **to be at sixes and sevens,** manquer d'ensemble; cafouiller; *F:* **to be s. feet under,** être enterré; (*b*) **s.-cylinder car,** une six cylindres; **s.-seater (car),** voiture *f* à six places; **s. day bicycle race,** les six jours *m*; *Pol:* **the S. Counties,** (les six comtés de la province d'Ulster qui constituent) l'Irlande *f* du Nord; *Hist:* **the S. Day War,** la guerre des Six jours; *Mus:* **s.-eight (time),** (mesure *f* à) six-huit *m*; **s.-four (time),** (mesure à) six-quatre *m.* **2.** *s.* (*a*) *Cr:* six points (marqués par le batteur); *F:* **to knock s.o. for s.,** étendre, démolir, qn; battre qn à plate(s) couture(s); donner une tabassée à qn; **he got up suddenly and knocked the table for s.,** il s'est levé tout d'un coup et a renversé la table; (*b*) *Scout:* sixaine *f* (de louveteaux, etc.).

sixain [ˈsiksein, ˈsiːzein], *s. Lit: Pros:* sizain *m*, sixain *m.*

sixer [ˈsiksər], *s.* **1.** *Cr: O:* six points (marqués par le batteur). **2.** *Scout:* chef *m* d'un groupe de six louveteaux, de six jeannettes.

six-fingered [ˈsiksˈfiŋgəd], *a.* (i) (*of hand*) sexdigital, -aux; (ii) (*of pers.*) sexdigitaire.

sixfold [ˈsiksfould]. **1.** *a.* sextuple. **2.** *adv.* six fois autant; au sextuple; **to increase s.,** sextupler; **he repaid me s.,** il me l'a rendu au sextuple.

six-foot [ˈsiksfut], *a.* de six pieds; *Rail:* **the s.-f. way,** l'entre-voie *f, pl.* entre-voies.

six-footer [ˈsiksˈfutər], *s. F:* homme (haut) de six pieds.

six-gun [ˈsiksgʌn], *s.* revolver *m*, pistolet *m*, à six coups.

six-master [siksˈmɑːstər], *s. Nau:* six-mâts *m inv.*

sixpence [ˈsikspəns], *s.* **1.** six pence. **2.** *A:* pièce *f* de six pence; **two and s.,** deux shillings et six pence.

sixpenn'orth [siksˈpenəθ], *s. F: O:* = SIXPENNYWORTH.

sixpenny [ˈsikspəni], *attrib.a.* (*a*) (bonbon, etc.) qui coûte, qui vaut, six pence; à, de, six pence; **s. stamp,** timbre de six pence; (*b*) *A:* **s. piece, bit,** pièce *f* de six pence; *s. F:* **a s.,** une publication à six pence, à bon marché.

sixpennyworth [siksˈpeniwəθ], *s. O:* **to buy s. of chocolate,** acheter pour six pence de chocolat.

sixscore [ˈsiksskɔːr], *s. A:* cent vingt.

six-shooter [siksˈʃuːtər], *s.* revolver *m*, pistolet *m*, à six coups.

six-sided [siksˈsaidid], *a.* qui a six côtés; hexagone.

sixte [sikst], *s. Fenc:* sixte *f*; **to parry in s.,** parer en sixte.

sixteen [ˈsiks(ˈ)tiːn], *num. a. & s.* seize (*m*); **she is s.,** elle a seize ans; **s. houses,** seize maisons; **to live at number s.,** demeurer au numéro seize.

sixteenmo [siksˈtiːnmou], *a. & s. Typ:* (format, volume) in-seize (*m*), in-16 (*m*).

sixteenth [ˈsiks(ˈ)tiːnθ]. **1.** *num. a. & s.* seizième (*mf*); **Louis the S.,** Louis Seize; **the s. house,** la seizième maison; **(on) the s. (of August),** le seize (août); **in the s. chapter of the book,** au chapitre seizième du livre; **in (the) s. place,** en seizième lieu, seizièmement; **the s. in his, her, class,** le, la, seizième de sa classe; *Mus: NAm:* **s. note,** double croche *f*. **2.** *s.* (*fraction*) seizième *m*; **three sixteenths,** trois seizièmes.

sixteenthly [siksˈtiːnθli], *adv.* seizièmement; en seizième lieu.

sixth [siksθ]. **1.** *num. a. & s.* sixième (*mf*); **Henry the S.,** Henri Six; **(on) the s. (of December),** le six (décembre); **the s. in his, her, class,** le, la, sixième de sa classe; **to live on the s. floor,** demeurer au sixième (étage); **in (the) s. place,** en sixième lieu; sixièmement; *Sch:* **the s. form** = les classes terminales; *F:* **the s.** = la terminale; **the upper s. (form)** = la (classe) terminale; **the lower s. (form)** = la (classe de) première; **s. former** = élève *mf* des classes terminales; élève de la (classe de) première. **2.** *s.* (*a*) (*fraction*) sixième *m*; **five sixths,** cinq sixièmes; (*b*) *Mus:* sixte (majeure, mineure); **chord of the s.,** accord *m* de sixte.

sixthly [ˈsiksθli], *adv.* sixièmement; en sixième lieu.

sixtieth [ˈsikstiəθ], *num. a. & s.* soixantième (*mf*).

sixtine [ˈsikstiːn], *a.* (*a*) *Ecc.Hist:* relatif aux papes appelés Sixte; (*b*) relatif à la chapelle Sixtine.

six-toed [ˈsiksˈtoud], *a.* (i) (*of foot*) sexdigital, -aux; (ii) (*of pers.*) sexdigitaire.

Sixtus [ˈsikstəs]. *Pr.n.m. Ecc.Hist:* Sixte; **S. the Fifth,** Sixte Quint.

sixty [ˈsiksti], *num. a. & s.* soixante (*m*); **s.-one,** soixante et un; **s.-third,** soixante-troisième; **about s. books,**

some s. books, s. books or so, une soixantaine de livres; **page s.,** page soixante; **he's not far off s., he's getting on for s., he's about s.,** il approche de la soixantaine; **he's in his sixties,** il a passé la soixantaine; **in the sixties (of our century),** pendant les années soixante (de notre siècle).

sixty-four [siksti'fɔ:r], *num. a. & s.* soixante-quatre (*m*); *F:* **the s.-f. (thousand) dollar question,** la question du gros lot, la question super-banco; la question vitale, cruciale.

sixty-fourmo [siksti'fɔ:mou], *a. & s. Typ:* (format, volume) in-soixante-quatre (*m*), in-64 (*m*).

sizable ['saizəbl], *a.* = SIZEABLE.

sizar ['saizər], *s. Sch: A:* étudiant boursier, étudiante boursière (à l'université de Cambridge et à Trinity College, Dublin).

size[1] [saiz], *s.* **1.** (*a*) grandeur *f*, dimension *f*, mesure *f*; étendue *f*; grosseur *f*, volume *m*; **scale of sizes,** échelle de grandeurs; **to take the s. of sth.,** mesurer qch.; **to reduce the s. of classes to 25,** réduire, ramener, l'effectif *m* des classes à 25; **hall of great, vast, s.,** salle de vastes proportions; **of no great s.,** d'assez peu d'étendue; assez petit; plutôt petit; **of ordinary s.,** de dimensions ordinaires; **of equal s., of the same s.,** *O:* **of a s.,** d'égale grandeur; de (la) même grandeur; de la même grosseur; de la même taille; **of different sizes,** de grandeur inégale; de toutes (les) grandeurs; **(in) all shapes and sizes,** (de) toutes (les) grandeurs; (de) toutes les grosseurs; **of some, a certain, s.,** assez grand, gros; plutôt grand, gros; **books arranged according to s.,** livres disposés par rang de taille; **to be the s. of. . .,** être aussi grand, aussi gros, que . . .; **piece of butter the s. of a walnut,** morceau de beurre gros comme une noix; **(about) the s. of an egg,** (à peu près) grand comme un œuf; **full s.,** (en) vraie grandeur; (en) grandeur naturelle; grandeur nature; **a town of that s.,** une ville de cette importance; **the insurance varies according to the s. of the car,** l'assurance varie selon l'importance de la voiture; *F:* **that's about the s. of it,** c'est à peu près cela; vous y êtes presque; **to cut s.o. down to s.,** rabaisser qn; rabattre le caquet à qn; (*b*) *Ind:* cote *f*, dimension; **standard s.,** cote d'origine; **standardized s.,** dimension uniformisée, standardisée; **nominal, normal, s.,** cote nominale, cote normale; **to finish a piece to s.,** usiner une pièce à la cote de finition; **to cut a piece to s.,** tailler une pièce à la dimension, à la cote; **cut to (the required) s.,** taillé aux cotes (requises), à la dimension; **pieces that are not the right s., not to s.,** pièces qui ne sont pas de mesure. **2.** (*a*) (*of pers., horse, etc.*) taille *f*; **a boy of his s.,** un garçon de sa taille; **a boy half his s., twice his s.,** un garçon deux fois moins grand, deux fois plus grand, que lui; (*b*) *Com:* numéro *m* (d'un article); taille (de vêtements); encolure *f* (de chemise); pointure *f* (de chaussures, de gants, de coiffures); **three sizes too big,** trop grand de trois numéros; **a s. larger, smaller,** une pointure au-dessus, au-dessous; **large, small, s.,** grand, petit, modèle; **hat s., head s., s. in hats,** tour *m* de tête; mesure de coiffure; **what s. do you take? what's your s.? what s. are you?** (*in dresses, etc.*) quelle est votre taille? *F:* quelle taille faites-vous? (*in shoes*) quelle pointure chaussez-vous? (*in gloves*) quelle est votre pointure de gants? (*in hats*) du combien coiffez-vous? **I take s. five (in) (shoes)** = je chausse du 38; **she takes s. seven (in) (gloves)** = elle gante du sept; **I've nothing in your s.,** je n'ai rien à votre taille, à votre pointure; **s. stick,** pied *m* à coulisse (d'un marchand de chaussures); **to try sth. for s.,** essayer qch. (pour voir si cela vous convient); (*c*) format *m*, (d'un livre, de papier, de plaques photographiques); (*d*) calibre *m* (d'un fusil, d'une cartouche, d'un obus); grosseur (du plomb de chasse).

size[2], *v.tr.* **1.** classer (des objets) par grosseur, par dimension, par ordre de dimensions; *Mil:* **to s. a company,** aligner une compagnie par rang de taille. **2.** *Ind: etc:* (*a*) (*to gauge*) calibrer (une pièce); (*b*) (*to finish to size*) mettre (un trou, une pièce) à la cote, à dimensions; usiner (une pièce) à la cote de finition; ajuster (une pièce); (*c*) égaliser (le plomb de chasse, les grains de poudre, etc.); (*d*) **to s. sth. up,** jauger, prendre les dimensions de, qch.; *F:* **to s. s.o. up,** évaluer, classer, j(a)uger, qn; mesurer qn des yeux; toiser qn.

size[3], *s.* **1.** *Tchn:* apprêt *m*; (*a*) colle *f*, encollage *m*; **animal s.,** colle animale; **vegetable s.,** colle végétale; **glue s.,** colle de peau, de Flandre; **builder's s.,** colle au baquet; *Paint:* **s. colour(ing), s. paint,** peinture *f* à la colle; (peinture en, à la) détrempe *f*; *Paperm:* **white s.,** lait *m* de colle; (*b*) *Tex:* empois *m*. **2.** *Med:* couenne *f* inflammatoire.

size[4], *v.tr.* apprêter, coller, encoller (le papier, etc.); maroufler (la toile); *Tex:* parer; **to s. the warp,** basser la chaîne.

sizeable ['saizəbl], *a.* d'une belle taille; assez grand, plutôt grand.

sized [saizd], *a.* **1.** classé par ordre de grandeur, de taille, de dimensions; *Const:* **s. slate,** ardoise d'échantillon. **2.** (*with adj. or adv. prefixed*) **fair s.,** assez grand; d'une belle dimension; d'une grandeur raisonnable; **large s.,** grand; de grande taille; de grandes dimensions; (livre, papier, etc.) de grand format; **medium s.,** de grandeur moyenne; de grosseur moyenne; de taille moyenne; **medium-s. factory,** usine de moyenne importance; **small s.,** de petite taille.

sizer ['saizər], *s.* **1.** *Min: etc:* (*pers.*) trieur, -euse. **2.** *Tls:* calibreur *m*. **3.** *Tex:* (*pers.*) encolleur, -euse.

sizing[1] ['saiziŋ], *s.* **1.** classement *m* par ordre de grandeur, de grosseur; *Mil:* alignement *m* par rang de taille; *Min:* **s. screen,** crible *m* classeur. **2.** *Ind: etc:* (*a*) calibrage *m* (de fruits, etc.); *Tls:* **s. gauge,** calibreur *m*; (*b*) mise *f* à la cote (d'une pièce); (*c*) vérification *f* de la cote, des dimensions (d'une pièce).

sizing[2], *s.* **1.** collage *m*, encollage *m* (du papier, etc.); apprêtage *m*, parage *m* (de la soie, du fil); apprêtage (d'une surface à peindre); *Tex:* **s. machine,** (en)colleuse *f*, pareuse *f*. **2.** colle *f*; *Paint:* apprêt *m*.

sizzle[1] ['sizl], *s.* grésillement *m* (d'une poêle, de saucisses, de la friture, etc.).

sizzle[2], *v.i.* (*of frying pan, sausages, etc.*) grésiller.

sizzling[1] ['sizliŋ]. **1.** *a.* (*of frying pan, sausages, etc.*) grésillant. **2.** *adv.* **s. hot,** tout chaud; qui sort de la friture; *F:* **s. hot day,** jour torride.

sizzling[2], *s.* = SIZZLE[1].

sjambok ['ʃæmbɔk], *s.* (*in S. Africa*) gros fouet en cuir de rhinocéros.

skald [skɔ:ld], *s. Lit.Hist:* scalde *m*.

skaldic ['skɔ:ldik], *a. Lit.Hist:* (poésie) scaldique.

skate[1] [skeit], *s. Ich:* raie *f*; pocheteau *m*; **flapper s.,** raie blanche.

skate[2], *s.* patin *m*; **ice s.,** patin à glace; **roller s.,** patin à roulettes; **s. sailing,** patinage *m* à (la) voile; *F:* **to get one's skates on,** se dépêcher, se grouiller.

skate[3], *v.i.* (*a*) patiner, faire du patin (sur glace); **to roller s.,** patiner sur roulettes; skatiner, faire du skating; *F:* **to s. round sth.,** tourner autour du pot; **to s. over sth.,** effleurer un sujet; (*b*) *NAm:* (*ice hockey*) jouer; **we're skating against Minnesota next Tuesday,** nous avons une rencontre avec l'équipe de Minnesota mardi prochain.

skate[4], *s. U.S: F:* **1.** (*a*) sale type *m*; vaurien *m*; mufle *m*; (*b*) individu *m*, type. **2.** (*horse*) rosse *f*.

skateboard[1] ['skeitbɔ:d], *s. Sp:* planche *f* à roulettes; *F:* skateboard *m*, skate *m*; *Fr.C: R.t.m:* rouli-roulant *m*.

skateboard[2], *v.i. Sp:* faire de la planche à roulettes, *F:* du skate, *Fr. C:* du rouli-roulant.

skateboarder ['skeitbɔ:dər], *s. Sp:* personne *f* qui fait de la planche à roulettes; *F:* skate(-)boarder *m*, skater *m*.

skater ['skeitər], *s.* patineur, -euse (sur glace); **roller s.,** patineur à roulettes.

skating ['skeitiŋ], *s.* patinage *m* (sur glace); **roller s.,** patinage à roulettes; skating *m*, skatinage *m*; **s. rink,** (i) patinoire *f*; piste *f* de patinage; (ii) (*for roller skating*) skating; **s. club,** cercle de patineurs.

skatol(e) ['skætoul], *s. Ch:* scatol *m*.

skean ['ski:n], *s.* (*a*) *Irish & Scot.Hist:* couteau-poignard *m*, *pl.* couteaux-poignards; (*b*) *Scot: Cost:* **s. dhu** [ski:n'du:], couteau-poignard qui se porte enfoncé dans la chaussette.

skedaddle[1] [ski'dædl], *s. F:* (i) fuite précipitée; (ii) fuite en débandade; débandade *f*.

skedaddle[2], *v.i. F:* (*a*) se sauver à toutes jambes; décamper, déguerpir; filer (en vitesse); s'esquiver; (*b*) se sauver, s'enfuir, à la débandade.

skedonk [ski'dɔŋk], *a. F:* (*in S. Africa*) (*of car*) vieux, délabré, cabossé.

skeet [ski:t], *s.* **1.** *A: Nau:* écope *f* (à long manche). **2.** *Sp:* **s. (shooting),** tir *m* au pigeon (d'argile); (genre de) ball-trap *m*.

skeeter[1] ['ski:tər], *s. NAm: F:* **1.** moustique *m*. **2.** *Sp:* bateau *m* à patins.

skeeter[2], *s.* tireur, -euse, au ball-trap.

skeg [skeg], *s. N.Arch:* talon *m* (de la quille).

skegger ['skegər], *s. Ich:* saumoneau *m*.

skein [skein, ski:n], *s.* **1.** (*a*) écheveau *m* (de soie, de laine); (*b*) *Fig:* **(tangled) s.,** écheveau, confusion *f*, embrouillamini *m*, dédale *m* (des affaires, de la politique). **2.** vol *m* (d'oies sauvages, etc.).

skeining ['skeiniŋ, 'ski:-], *s. Tex:* échevet(t)age *m*.

skeletal ['skelit(ə)l], *a.* squelettique; **s. soil,** sol squelettique.

skeletogenous [skeli'tɔdʒinəs], *a. Biol:* squelettogène.

skeletology [skeli'tɔlədʒi], *s.* squelettologie *f*.

skeleton[1] ['skelit(ə)n], *s.* **1.** squelette *m*, ossature *f* (d'homme, d'animal, de feuille, etc.); carcasse *f* (d'animal); *Fig:* **s. in the cupboard, in the closet,** secret honteux de la famille; **s. at the feast,** rabat-joie *m inv*, trouble-fête *m inv*; **he's a living s.,** c'est un vrai squelette; il n'a plus que la peau et les os; on lui compterait les côtes. **2.** (*a*) charpente *f*, carcasse, squelette, (cadre d')ossature (d'un bâtiment, d'un navire, etc.); châssis *m* (de montage); **s. pier,** digue à claire-voie; **s. case,** caisse à claire-voie; **s. shelf,** rayon à claire-voie; **s. key,** (clef à) crochet *m* (de serrurier); fausse clef; rossignol *m*; (*b*) monture *f*, carcasse (d'un parapluie); (*c*) canevas *m*, esquisse *f*, squelette, ébauche *f* (d'un roman, d'une théorie, etc.); **s. essay,** plan détaillé, canevas, de composition; *Surv:* **s. map,** canevas; carte muette; **s. tracing,** croquis-calque *m* (d'une frontière, etc.); **s. triangulation,** canevas; (*d*) **s. staff,** personnel réduit; **a s. staff of three is always on duty,** la permanence comprend trois employés; **s. organization,** organisation schématique, squelettique; **s. crew,** équipage réduit; *Mil:* **s. peace army,** armée-cadre *f*, *pl.* armées-cadres; **s. force,** formation cadres *mpl*; unité cadres; **s. drill,** exercice au cordeau; exercices de cadres.

skeleton[2], *v.tr. A: & Lit:* = SKELETONIZE 2.

skeletonize ['skelitənaiz], *v.tr.* **1.** squelettiser (une feuille, un oiseau). **2.** faire le canevas (d'un roman, d'une pièce de théâtre, etc.). **3.** réduire (son personnel) au strict nécessaire; réduire (un bataillon) à ses cadres.

skeletonizing ['skelitənaiziŋ], *s.* squelettisation *f* (d'une feuille, etc.).

skellum ['skeləm], *s. Scot:* vaurien *m*, chenapan *m*.

skelm [skelm], *s.* (*in S. Africa*) vaurien *m*.

skelp[1] [skelp], *s. Scot:* taloche *f*, gifle *f*, fessée *f*.

skelp[2], *v.tr. Scot:* donner une taloche, une gifle, une fessée, à (un enfant); talocher, gifler, fesser.

skelp[3], *s.* (*gun making*) maquette *f*.

skelping ['skelpiŋ], *s. Scot:* taloche *f*, gifle *f*, fessée *f*.

skene [ski:n], *s.* (*a*) *Irish & Scot.Hist:* couteau-poignard *m*, *pl.* couteaux-poignards; (*b*) *Scot: Cost:* **s. dhu** [ski:n'du:], couteau-poignard qui se porte enfoncé dans la chaussette.

skep [skep], *s.* **1.** panier *m*; (*for packing glass, etc.*) harasse *f*. **2.** *Ap:* ruche *f* en paille.

skeptic ['skeptik], *s. N.Am:* = SCEPTIC, *etc.*

skerrick ['skerik], *s. Austr:* **not a s.,** pas un morceau; **I haven't a s. of wool left,** il ne me reste pas un seul bout de laine.

skerry ['skeri], *s.* récif *m*; rocher isolé.

sketch[1] [sketʃ], *s.* **1.** (*a*) *Art: Lit:* croquis *m*, esquisse *f*; *Mus:* esquisse; **character s.,** portrait *m* littéraire; **first s.,** premier jet; **freehand s.,** dessin *m* à main levée; **pen and ink s., pencil s.,** dessin à la plume, au crayon; **coloured s.,** croquis en couleur; **to make a s. of sth.,** faire le croquis de qch.; croquer qch.; **s. block,** bloc à croquis; bloc de papier à dessin; **s. map,** croquis; plan sommaire (d'un terrain); (*b*) *Surv:* levé *m* (topographique); **compass s.,** levé à la boussole; **s. made from memory,** levé de mémoire; (*c*) *Arch: etc:* **dimensional s.,** croquis coté. **2.** (*a*) **s. of a plan,** exposé *m* d'un projet; (*b*) *Th: T.V:* sketch *m*, saynète *f*. **3.** *F:* personne, chose, (i) *O:* amusante, (ii) ridicule.

sketch[2], *v.tr.* **1.** esquisser, dessiner à grands traits, croquer (un paysage, etc.); faire un, le, croquis de (qch.); faire, dessiner, des croquis; **to s. in the details,** dessiner sommairement des détails; **to s. out a novel,** faire le canevas, l'esquisse, d'un roman. **2. to s. (out),** esquisser, tracer (un projet, etc.); donner un exposé (d'un projet, etc.).

sketchbook ['sketʃbuk], *s.* cahier *m*, album *m*, de croquis.

sketcher ['sketʃər], *s.* dessinateur, -trice, de croquis; artiste *mf* (peintre), aquarelliste *mf*, amateur.

sketchily ['sketʃili], *adv.* d'une manière imprécise, incomplète, vague; sans détails.

sketchiness ['sketʃinis], *s.* manque *m* de fini, de précision, de perfection, de détails.

sketching ['sketʃiŋ], *s.* action *f* de croquer, d'esquisser; dessin *m* rapide, à main levée; **s. block,** bloc à croquis; bloc de papier à dessin.

sketchy ['sketʃi], *a.* (ouvrage) qui manque de précision, de perfection; (dessin) qui manque de détails, (dessin) à grands traits; **s. features,** traits imprécis; **s. knowledge,** connaissances superficielles, sommaires; **s. notions,** idées plutôt vagues.

skew[1] [skju:], *s.* **1.** biais *m*, obliquité *f* (d'un pont, d'une arche, etc.); **the angle of s. of a bridge,** le biais, l'angle du biais, d'un pont; **on the s.,** de, en, biais; obliquement. **2.** *Mec.E:* (*of engagement dogs, etc.*) **skews,** rampe hélicoïdale.

skew[2]. **1.** *a. Arch: Mec: etc:* (pont, mur) biais; (section) oblique; **s. arch,** arche, voûte, biaise; arche, voûte, oblique; **s. (bevel) gear,** roue hyperbolique; **s. teeth,**

denture inclinée; **s.-eyed,** aux yeux louches; aux yeux qui louchent; **s. (turning) chisel,** biseau *m*; **s. carving chisel,** fermoir *m* néron, (à) nez rond; **s. nailing,** clouage en oblique; *Mth:* **s. (surface),** (surface) indéveloppable. **2.** *adv.* de, en, biais; de travers; obliquement; *F:* **s.-whiff** [skju:'(h)wif], de, en, biais; de travers, de traviole.

skew[3]. **1.** *v.i.* (*a*) biaiser, obliquer; (*b*) *O:* **to s. at s.o., at sth.,** regarder qn, qch., de côté, de travers. **2.** *v.tr.* (*a*) couper en sifflet, en biseau; (*b*) fausser, déjeter (des informations, etc.).

skewback ['skju:bæk], *s. Arch:* naissance *f* d'une voûte.

skewbald ['skju:bɔ:ld], *a.* (cheval) blanc à taches alezanes; (cheval) blanc et roux.

skewer[1] ['skju(:)ər], *s.* **1.** *Cu:* brochette *f*, broche *f*. **2.** *F:* (*a*) épée *f*; (*b*) baïonnette *f*.

skewer[2], *v.tr.* (*a*) *Cu:* brocheter, embrocher (de la viande, etc.); **skewered meat,** brochette(s) *f*(*pl*) (de viande); (*b*) *Mec.E: etc:* **skewered cut,** coupure en séton.

ski[1], *pl.* **ski, skis** [ski:(z)], *s.* (*a*) ski *m*; **to put on one's skis,** mettre, attacher, fixer, ses skis; **equipped with skis,** chaussé de skis; **he came down on skis,** il est descendu à, en, skis; **s. binding,** fixation(s) *f*(*pl*); **s. tip,** spatule *f*; **s. boots,** chaussures de ski; **s. stick,** *U.S:* **s. pole,** bâton de ski; **s. school,** école de ski; **s. lift, tow,** remonte-pente *m*, *pl.* remonte-pentes; téléski *m*; remontée *f* mécanique; **s. run, slope,** piste de ski; **s. jump,** (i) saut de ski; tremplin *m*; (ii) *Civ.E:* saut de ski; **s. jump(ing),** saut en, à, ski(s); (*b*) *Mil:* **s. troops,** éclaireurs skieurs.

ski[2], *v.i.* (*p.t. & p.p.* **skied**) skier; pratiquer le ski; faire du ski; aller à, en, skis; **to s. down the slope,** descendre la piste à, en, skis.

skiagram, skiagraph ['skaiəgræm, -græf], *s.* **1.** *Med: etc:* radiographie *f*; skiagramme *m*. **2.** *Arch: etc:* sciagraphie *f*, sciographie *f*.

skiagrapher [skai'ægrəfər], *s.* radiographe *m*, radiologue *m*.

skiagraphy [skai'ægrəfi], *s. Astr:* skiagraphie *f*, sciographie *f*.

skiascopy [skai'æskəpi], *s. Med: Opt:* skiascopie *f*, pupilloscopie *f*.

skiatron ['skaiətrɔn], *s. Elcs:* skiatron *m*.

skid[1] [skid], *s.* **1.** *Const: etc:* poutrelle *f* de rampe; *Artil: etc:* poutrelle. **2.** (*a*) *Veh:* sabot *m* d'enrayage; enrayure *f*, lugeon *m*; patin *m* d'arrêt; (*b*) *Nau:* (*for guns, etc.*) cabrion *m* d'arrêt; (*c*) *Com:* palette *f* sur patins; (*d*) *Av:* patin; **landing s.,** patin d'atterrissage; **tail s.,** béquille *f* (arrière); patin de queue; **wing s.,** protège-aile *m*, *pl.* protège-ailes; (*e*) *Nau:* défense *f* (de muraille); défense fixe en bois; (*f*) *Nau:* chantier *m* à rouleaux; semelle *f* de lancement; (*g*) *U.S:* **s. road,** (i) voie de glissement (pour le transport du bois); (ii) quartier d'une ville fréquenté par les forestiers; *NAm: F:* **s. row,** quartier mal famé; bas-fonds *mpl*; zone *f*; (*h*) **s.-mounted,** à glissière; monté sur glissières, sur patins. **3.** *Aut: etc:* (*a*) dérapage *m*; **dry s.,** dérapage à sec; **controlled s.,** dérapage contrôlé; (*b*) (*sideways*) embardée *f*; **half-turn s.,** tête-à-queue *m inv*; **full-turn s.,** tête-à-queue complet; (*c*) *F:* **s. lid,** casque de moto; (*d*) *F:* **to put the skids under s.o.,** (i) faire échouer qn; (ii) flanquer qn à la porte; **on the skids,** sur la pente savonneuse; en perte de vitesse.

skid[2], *v.* (**skidded**) **1.** *v.tr.* (*a*) ensaboter, enrayer (une roue); caler (une pièce d'artillerie, un fût, etc.); (*b*) mettre sur traîneau; (*c*) faire faire une embardée, un dérapage, à (une voiture). **2.** *v.i.* (*a*) *Aut: etc:* (*of tyre, wheel*) déraper, glisser, patiner, riper; **the car skidded across the road,** la voiture a dérapé, a chassé; **to s. right round,** faire (un) tête-à-queue; (*b*) *Av:* glisser sur l'aile.

skidding ['skidiŋ], *s.* **1.** ensabotement *m*, enrayage *m*. **2.** (*a*) dérapage *m* (d'un pneu, d'une voiture); patinage *m* (d'une roue); (*b*) *Av:* glissement *m* (sur l'aile).

skiddy ['skidi], *a. Aut:* (route, surface) glissante.

skidpan ['skidpæn], *s.* **1.** sabot *m* d'enrayage; enrayure *f*, lugeon *m*; patin *m* d'arrêt. **2.** *Aut:* piste savonnée.

skidway ['skidwei], *s. U.S:* voie *f* de glissement (pour le transport du bois, etc.).

skier ['ski:ər], *s.* skieur, -euse.

skiff [skif], *s.* **1.** *Nau:* (*a*) esquif *m*, embarcation *f*, yole *f*; (*b*) youyou *m* (de navire marchand). **2.** *Row:* skif(f) *m*.

skiffle ['skif(ə)l], *s. Mus:* skiffle *m*; **s. group,** skiffle-group *m inv*.

ski(-)ing ['ski:iŋ], *s.* ski *m*; **to go s.,** faire du ski; **good s. snow,** neige skiable; **slope fit for s.,** piste skiable; **cross country s.,** ski de fond; *Sw.Fr:* ski de randonnée.

skilful ['skilful], *a.* adroit, habile; **to be s. with one's hands,** être adroit des mains, de ses mains; **s. cook,** cuisinier achevé; **to be s. at, in, doing sth.,** être habile, adroit, à (faire) qch.

skilfully ['skilfuli], *adv.* habilement, adroitement; avec adresse, habileté, dextérité; d'une main habile.

skilfulness ['skilfulnis], *s.* habileté *f*, adresse *f*, dextérité *f*.

skill [skil], *s.* **1.** habileté *f*, adresse *f*, dextérité *f*; **technical s.,** habileté, aptitude *f*, technique; compétence *f* technique; **s. in doing sth.,** (i) talent *m*, habileté, pour faire qch.; (ii) art *m* de faire qch.; **to manage one's business with s.,** conduire ses affaires avec dextérité; **s. in the use of firearms,** dextérité à manier les armes à feu; **feat of s.,** tour d'adresse; **lack of s.,** maladresse *f*, inhabileté *f*. **2.** *NAm:* métier *m*; art *m* pratique.

skilled [skild], *a.* habile; **s. worker,** ouvrier, -ière, qualifié(e); (ouvrier) professionnel *m*; **s. labour,** main-d'œuvre spécialisée, qualifiée, professionnelle, expérimentée; **to be s. in an art, in business,** être fort en, versé dans, un art; se connaître en affaires; s'entendre aux affaires; **to be s. in doing sth.,** être habile, adroit, à faire qch.

skillet ['skilit], *s. Dom.Ec:* (*a*) *A:* poêlon *m*, casserole *f* (à long manche et à trois pieds); (*b*) *NAm:* poêle *f* (à frire).

skillion ['skiliən], *a. & s. Austr:* (toit *m*) en appentis *m*.

skilly ['skili], *s. Cu:* = lavasse *f*; bouillie *f*, soupe *f*, à la farine d'avoine.

skim[1] [skim], *s.* **1.** vol plané (d'un oiseau, d'un avion). **2.** **s. (milk),** lait écrémé; **s. (milk) cheese,** fromage maigre.

skim[2], *v.tr. & i.* (**skimmed**) **1.** écumer (le bouillon, etc.); écrémer (le lait, le verre en fusion, etc.); **to s. the fat off the soup,** dégraisser la soupe; **the cream has been skimmed off,** la crème a été prélevée; **skimmed milk,** lait écrémé; **to s. the cream off sth.,** prendre la meilleure partie de qch. **2.** effleurer, raser (une surface); **to s. over sth.,** glisser, passer à la hâte, sur qch.; **to s. (along, over) the ground,** voler au ras du sol; raser le sol; **the aircraft skimmed the ground,** l'avion a fait du rase-mottes, a volé en rase-mottes; l'avion est passé au ras du sol; **to s. (over) the water,** raser l'eau; voler à fleur d'eau; **to s. over, through, a novel,** parcourir rapidement, feuilleter, un roman; lire un roman du pouce; *Ten:* **ball that just skims the net,** balle à fleur de corde; balle qui frôle la corde, qui rase le filet.

skimmer ['skimər], *s.* **1.** (*a*) (*for soup, metals*) écumoire *f*; (*for milk*) écrémoir(e) *m*(*f*); écrémette *f*, écrémeuse *f*; écope *f*, escope *f*; (*for glass*) casse *f*, écrémeuse *f*; écrémoir(e); (*b*) (*pers.*) écrémeur, -euse, écumeur, -euse (du lait, etc.). **2.** *Orn:* rhynchops *m*; bec-en-ciseaux *m*, *pl.* becs-en-ciseaux. **3.** *Cr:* balle *f* qui rase le sol.

skimming ['skimiŋ], *s.* **1.** écumage *m*; écrémage *m*; *Metall:* décrassage *m*, décrassement *m*; **s. ladle,** écumoire *f*; **s. dish,** écope *f*, escope *f* (pour écrémer le lait). **2.** *usu. pl.* écume *f*; *Ind:* produits *mpl* d'écumage. **3.** *Av:* vol *m* en rase-mottes.

skimp [skimp]. **1.** *v.tr.* (*a*) *O:* **to s. s.o. in food,** mesurer la nourriture à qn; compter les morceaux à qn; (*b*) **to s. the food,** lésiner sur la nourriture; **to s. the material in making a dress,** lésiner sur le tissu d'une robe; être parcimonieux de tissu en faisant une robe; **skimped coat,** manteau étriqué; (*c*) *F:* **to s. one's work,** saboter, bâcler, son travail. **2.** *v.i.* lésiner sur tout; vivre avec parcimonie; économiser; regarder (à la dépense).

skimpily ['skimpili], *adv.* insuffisamment, parcimonieusement (meublé, etc.); **s. made dress,** robe étriquée.

skimpiness ['skimpinis], *s.* insuffisance *f*, manque *m*; aspect étriqué (d'un vêtement).

skimping[1] ['skimpiŋ], *a.* parcimonieux, économe, regardant.

skimping[2], *s.* **1.** épargne *f*, économie *f*; lésine(rie) *f*; parcimonie *f*; **s. is no saving,** autant dépense chiche que large. **2.** *F:* bâclage *m* (d'un travail).

skimpy ['skimpi], *a.* **1.** (*of pers.*) parcimonieux, économe, regardant. **2.** insuffisant; **s. skirt,** jupe étriquée, (bien) juste; **s. meal,** maigre repas.

skin[1] [skin], *s.* **1.** peau *f*; **outer s.,** épiderme *m*; **true, inner, s.,** derme *m*; **thin s.,** épiderme sensible; *Fig:* **to have a thin s.,** être susceptible; **to have a thick s.,** avoir la peau dure; **fair, soft, s.,** peau blanche, douce; (*of snake, etc.*) **to cast, throw, its s.,** faire peau neuve; se dépouiller; changer de peau; muer; **the boiling water had taken the s. off his foot,** l'eau bouillante lui avait dépouillé le pied; **he cannot change his s.,** il mourra dans sa peau; **next to one's s.,** à même, sur, la peau; **I always wear cotton next to my s.,** je porte toujours du coton sur la peau; **he wore this belt next to his s.,** il portait cette ceinture à même la peau; **to strip to the s.,** se mettre tout nu; se déshabiller; **wet to the s.,** mouillé jusqu'aux os; (*of wound, emotions*) **s. deep,** à fleur de peau; superficiel; peu profond; **beauty is but s. deep,** la beauté n'est qu'à fleur de peau; *Toil:* **s. care,** soins *mpl* de la peau; **s. cream,** crème *f* de beauté; **s. food,** crème nourrissante; *Med:* **s. graft(ing),** greffe cutanée; **s. test,** cuti-réaction *f*, *pl.* cuti-réactions; réaction cutanée; **tuberculin s. test,** cuti-réaction à la tuberculine; *F:* **s. hospital,** hôpital *m*, -aux, pour maladies de la peau; *F:* **s. flick,** film *m* porno(graphique); *F:* **he's nothing but, he's all, s. and bone,** il n'a que la peau et les os; il n'a que la peau sur les os; on lui compterait les côtes; ce n'est qu'un paquet, un sac, d'os; les os lui percent la peau; il est étique, décharné; **to come out of it with a whole s.,** s'en tirer sain et sauf, indemne; s'en tirer la vie sauve; **to fear for one's s.,** craindre pour sa peau; ménager sa peau; **to sell one's s. dearly,** vendre (bien) cher sa peau; **to jump out of one's s.,** ne pas tenir dans sa peau; **to escape by, with, the s. of one's teeth,** s'échapper de justesse; **to save one's (own) s.,** sauver sa peau; se tirer d'affaire; *F:* **to get under s.o.'s s.,** (i) ennuyer, barber, raser, qn; (ii) donner, taper, sur les nerfs de qn; échauffer les oreilles à qn; énerver qn; *F:* **I've got her under my s.,** je l'ai dans la peau; *P:* **(the) s. off your nose!** à la bonne vôtre! *F:* **it's no s. off my nose,** ce n'est pas mon affaire; ça ne me touche pas; ce ne sont pas mes oignons; cela m'est égal; *F:* **s. game,** escroquerie *f*, filouterie *f*. **2.** (*a*) dépouille *f*, peau (d'un animal); **skins,** peausserie(s) *f*(*pl*); **fur skins,** pelleterie(s) *f*(*pl*); **raw skins,** peaux vertes; **dropped skins,** peaux descendues; **sheared s.,** peau rasée; **unhaired s.,** peau en tripe; **rabbit s.,** peau de lapin; **s. dealer,** (i) marchand, -ande, de fourrures; pelletier, -ière; fourreur *m*; (ii) peaussier *m*; **s. dresser,** peaussier; pelletier; apprêteur *m* de fourrures; **s. dressing,** peausserie; **s. wool,** laine morte; pelade *f*; *Ent:* **s. moth,** teigne *f* des pelleteries; (*b*) *Sp:* **to s. dive,** faire de la plongée sous-marine autonome; **s. diving,** plongée sous-marine autonome; plongée libre; **s. diver,** plongeur, -euse, sous-marin(e) autonome; *Com:* **s. pack(ag)ing,** emballage moulant; *Const:* **s. coat,** dernière couche (de plâtre); (*c*) (*for wine, etc.*) outre *f*; (*d*) feuille *f* (de parchemin). **3.** (*a*) *Bot:* tunique *f* (d'une graine); pellicule *f* (d'un grain de café, etc.); (*b*) peau (de fruit, de saucisse); **banana s.,** peau, pelure *f*, de banane; **onion s.,** pelure, robe *f*, d'oignon; *Cu:* **potatoes (cooked) in their skins,** pommes de terre en robe de chambre. **4.** (*a*) *Nau:* chemise *f* (de voile); (*b*) *Nau:* bordé extérieur (d'un navire, d'un canot); enveloppe *f*, coque *f* (d'un navire); *Av:* revêtement *m* (du fuselage, de la coque); **stressed s.,** revêtement travaillant; **lower, upper, s. (of the wing),** intrados *m*, extrados *m*; *N.Arch: Av:* **s. friction, resistance,** frottement superficiel (d'un navire, d'un avion); frottement de l'eau, de l'air, sur la surface; *El:* **s. effect,** effet *m* pelliculaire; effet Kelvin; effet de peau. **5.** (*a*) peau, pellicule (sur le lait, etc.); crème (sur le lait); (*b*) *Metall:* croûte *f* (de la fonte).

skin[2], *v.* (**skinned**)

I. *v.tr.* **1.** (*a*) écorcher, dépouiller, *F:* dépiauter (un lapin, etc.); enlever, détacher, la peau d('un animal); **to s. alive,** écorcher vif; **to s. one's knees,** s'écorcher les genoux; *Gym: F:* **to s. the cat,** faire l'estrapade; *F:* **to s. s.o.,** dépouiller, écorcher, estamper, tondre, plumer, qn (au jeu); *F:* **to s. a flint,** tondre un œuf; (*b*) peler, éplucher (un fruit, etc.); (*c*) *Metall:* **to s. a casting,** décroûter une pièce coulée. **2.** (*a*) *N.Arch:* **to s. a ship,** revêtir un navire; (*b*) *Nau:* **to s. up a sail,** faire la chemise d'une voile.

II. *v.i.* **1.** (*a*) se dépouiller de sa peau; (*b*) perdre de l'épiderme; se desquamer. **2.** *Med:* (*of wound*) **to s. over,** se recouvrir de peau; se cicatriser. **3.** *NAm: F:* **to s. through a gap in the fence,** passer tout juste, se glisser, par un trou dans la clôture.

skinflint ['skinflint], *s. F:* avare *mf*, grigou *m*, *pl.* grigous; rapiat, *f.* rapiate; pingre *mf*; grippe-sou *m*, *pl.* grippe-sous.

skinful ['skinful], *s.* **1.** (pleine) outre (de vin, etc.). **2.** *P:* **he's had, got, a s.,** il est soûl; il a pris une (bonne) cuite; il a sa cuite; il a son compte; il est plein (comme une outre).

skinhead ['skinhed], *s. F:* (*a*) homme chauve, à la tête rasée; (*b*) *A:* jeune voyou *m* aux cheveux coupés ras.

skink [skiŋk], *s. Rept:* scinque *m*; **medicinal s.,** scinque des apothicaires, scinque du Sahara; poisson *m* de sable; **(Australian) blue-tongued s.,** scinque à langue bleue (d'Australie); **Southern European eyed s.,** chalcide européen.

skinless ['skinlis], *a.* sans peau; à peau mince.

skinned [skind], *a.* **1.** (*with adj. prefixed*) **dark, rough, s.,** à (la) peau brune, rêche; qui a la peau brune, rêche. **2.** avec la peau enlevée; (lapin) dépouillé; (fruit) épluché; (bois) écorcé.

skinner ['skinər], *s.* **1.** écorcheur *m* (de lapins, etc.). **2.** peaussier *m*, pelletier, -ière, apprêteur *m* de fourrures. **3.** (*a*) marchand, -ande, de fourrures; pelletier, fourreur *m*; (*b*) peaussier.

skinniness ['skininis], *s. F:* maigreur *f*, décharnement *m*.

skinning ['skiniŋ], *s.* **1.** (*a*) écorchement *m* (d'un lapin); (*b*) épluchement *m* (d'un fruit); (*c*) *Metall:* décroûtage *m* (d'une pièce coulée). **2.** *Med:* **s. over (of a wound),** cicatrisation *f* (d'une blessure). **3.** desquamation *f* (de la peau).

skinny ['skini], *a.* **1.** *F:* (*of pers.*) décharné; maigre; (poulet, etc.) qui n'a que la peau et les os; (cheval, etc.) efflanqué, étique; (*of child*) maigrelet, -ette; maigrichon, -onne; maigriot, -otte; **s. little man,** criquet *m.* **2.** membraneux. **3.** *F: O:* avare, rapiat.

skint [skint], *a. P:* **to be s.,** être sans le sou, fauché, raide (comme un passe-lacet), à fleur.

skintight ['skintait], *a.* (vêtement) collant.

skip[1] [skip], *s.* **1.** (petit) saut; gambade *f.* **2.** *Mus:* saut. **3.** *W.Tel:* trajet *m* de réflexion; **s. zone,** zone *f* de silence, zone morte; **s. distance,** étendue *f* de la zone de silence; distance *f* de saut. **4.** *Cmptr:* saut; tabulation (i) horizontale, (ii) verticale; **overflow s.,** saut au haut du feuillet suivant; **tape s.,** saut de bande; **s. instruction,** instruction de branchement, de saut. **4.** (*esp. at Trinity College, Dublin*) domestique *m.*

skip[2], *v.* (**skipped**) **1.** *v.i.* (*a*) (*of lambs, children*) sauter, sautiller, gambader; **to s. along, in, off, out,** avancer, entrer, s'en aller, sortir, en gambadant, en dansant, en sautant; (*b*) **to s.,** *NAm:* **to s. rope,** sauter à la corde; *NAm:* **s. rope,** corde à sauter; (*c*) **to s. from one subject to another, from subject to subject,** bondir, sauter, d'un sujet à un autre; papillonner, voleter, voltiger, de sujet en sujet; (*d*) *F:* **to s. (off),** filer; se sauver; décamper; *v.tr. F:* **to s. bail,** se dérober à la justice (alors qu'on jouit de la liberté provisoire). **2.** *v.tr. & i.* **to s. (over) a passage in a book,** omettre, sauter (par-dessus), passer, un passage d'un livre; **I skipped a whole chapter,** j'ai passé tout un chapitre; **to read without skipping,** lire sans rien sauter; **to s. a meal,** sauter un repas; la sauter; *Sch:* **to s. a form,** enjamber, sauter, une classe; *F:* **s. it!** (i) ça suffit! ça va comme ça! passons! laisse courir! (ii) file! décampe! **3.** *v.tr. Av:* **to s.-bomb,** bombarder en rase-mottes.

skip[3], *s. Const: Min: etc:* wagonnet *m,* benne *f,* herche *f,* tonne *f;* cuf(f)at *m,* godet *m,* caisse guidée; *Ind:* skip *m;* **self-dumping s.,** skip à déversement automatique; **tilting s.,** skip basculant.

skip[4], *s. Games:* (*a*) chef *m* d'équipe (aux jeux de boules et de *curling*); (*b*) *F:* = SKIPPER[2] 3.

skipjack ['skipdʒæk], *s.* **1.** *A:* jouet *m* d'enfant en forme d'animal sauteur (fabriqué avec la lunette d'une volaille). **2.** *Ich:* bonite *f* à ventre rayé. **3.** *Ent:* taupin *m;* marteau *m,* tape-tape *m inv.*

skipper[1] ['skipər], *s.* **1.** (*pers.*) sauteur, -euse. **2.** *Ent:* (*a*) ver *m* du fromage; (*b*) taupin *m;* marteau *m,* tape-tape *m inv;* (*c*) gerris *m,* araignée *f* d'eau; (*d*) hespéri(d)e *f,* pamphile *m,* échiquier *m.* **3.** *Ich:* (*a*) scombrésoce *m,* saurel *m;* (*b*) aiguille *f* de mer.

skipper[2], *s.* **1.** (*a*) *Nau: Av:* capitaine *m,* patron *m* (d'un navire); commandant *m* de bord (d'un avion); (*b*) *Nau: F:* **the s.,** le capiston. **2.** *Nau: F:* **skipper's daughters,** vagues *f* à crêtes d'écume; moutons *m.* **3.** *Games:* capitaine, chef *m* (d'une équipe sportive).

skipper[3], *v.tr. F:* être le commandant (d'un navire), le commandant à bord (d'un avion), le chef (d'une équipe sportive).

skipping ['skipiŋ], *s.* **1.** gambades *fpl,* sauts *mpl.* **2.** saut à la corde; **s. rope,** corde à sauter. **3.** omission *f* (de qch.); *Typew:* sautage *m* (d'un espace). **4.** *Cmptr:* **overflow s.,** saut au haut du feuillet suivant.

skips [skips], *s.pl. Paperm:* papiers *m* pour patrons, pour doublage de caisses.

skirl[1] [skərl], *s. Scot:* (*a*) cri aigu; (*b*) son aigu (de la cornemuse); **to set up a s.,** se mettre à jouer de la cornemuse.

skirl[2], *v.i. Scot:* **1.** crier. **2.** jouer (de la cornemuse) avec un son aigu.

skirmish[1] ['skə:miʃ], *s. Mil:* escarmouche *f,* échauffourée *f,* rencontre *f;* **s. drill,** exercice *m* de progression en ordre dispersé, en tirailleurs; **s. line,** ligne de tirailleurs; *Fig:* **s. of wit,** assaut *m* d'esprit; **verbal s.,** escarmouche verbale.

skirmish[2], *v.i. Mil: etc:* (*a*) combattre par escarmouches; (*b*) combattre en tirailleurs; tirailler (**with,** contre); (*c*) (*of pers.*) **to s. round,** fouiller, fureter.

skirmisher ['skə:miʃər], *s. Mil:* tirailleur *m.*

skirmishing ['skə:miʃiŋ], *s. Mil: etc:* escarmouches *fpl;* combats *mpl* de tirailleurs; **in s. order,** en tirailleurs.

skirret ['skirit], *s. Bot:* chervi(s) *m;* berle *f.*

skirt[1] [skə:t], *s.* **1.** *Cost:* (*a*) jupe *f* (de femme); **flared s.,** jupe évasée; jupe en forme, à godets; **divided s.,** jupe-culotte *f, pl.* jupes-culottes; **wrapover s.,** jupe portefeuille; **s. hand, maker,** jupier, -ière; **s. dance,** (i) danse de ballet, (ii) danse folklorique, dans laquelle les longues et amples jupes plissées sont maniées avec effet; (*b*) pan *m,* basque *f* (de pardessus, etc.); *A:* jupe (de redingote); (*c*) *P:* **(bit of) s.,** femme *f,* jeune fille *f,* poupée *f;* poule *f;* **she's a nice bit of s.,** c'est une jolie pépée; (*d*) (*of animal*) diaphragme *m,* flanc *m; Cu:* **s. of beef,** flanchet *m* de bœuf. **2.** (*a*) *Harn:* **(saddle) s.,** petit quartier (de la selle); (*b*) (*of hovercraft*) jupe; **segmented s.,** jupe segmentée; **s. retraction system, jack,** dispositif, vérin, de levage de la jupe. **3.** *I.C.E:* jupe (du piston). **4.** *A:* **skirts,** bord *m,* extrémité *f* (d'un village, etc.); lisière *f,* bordure *f,* orée *f* (d'un bois).

skirt[2], *v.tr. & i.* contourner (un village, une colline); (*of pers.*) longer, serrer (le mur, etc.); (*of ship*) côtoyer (le rivage); **to s. the coast,** échelonner la côte; **the path skirts (along, round) the wood,** le sentier côtoie, contourne, le bois.

skirting ['skə:tiŋ], *s.* **1.** (*a*) bord *m,* bordure *f;* (*b*) *Const:* **s. (board),** plinthe *f;* socle *m* de lambris. **2.** tissu *m* pour jupes.

skit[1] [skit], *s. Lit: Mus: Th:* pièce *f* satirique, charge *f,* fantaisie *f* burlesque; satire *f* (**on,** de); **to produce a s. on sth.,** mettre sur scène une satire de qch.

skit[2], *v.* (**skitted**) **1.** *v.tr.* parodier (un acteur); travestir (une chanson, etc.). **2.** *v.i.* faire des allusions satiriques (à qn).

skit[3], *s. F:* grand nombre, foule *f;* **there were skits of them,** il y en avait des tas.

skite[1] [skait], *s. Scot: Austr: F:* vantard, -arde.

skite[2], *v.i. Scot: Austr: F:* se vanter.

skitter ['skitər], *v.i.* **1.** courir vite. **2.** (*of waterfowl*) **to s. along the water,** effleurer l'eau (en l'éclaboussant); raser l'eau.

skittish ['skitiʃ], *a.* **1.** (*a*) (*of horse*) ombrageux, peureux, remuant; (*b*) (*of pers.*) capricieux, fantasque, inconstant. **2.** (femme) évaporée, folâtre, frivole, coquette.

skittishly ['skitiʃli], *adv.* **1.** d'un air, d'un ton, fantasque, espiègle. **2.** en faisant la coquette.

skittishness ['skitiʃnis], *s.* **1.** ombrage *m* (d'un cheval); inconstance *f,* caprice *f* (d'une personne). **2.** pétulance *f,* légèreté *f,* frivolité *f* (d'une femme).

skittle[1] ['skitl], *s.* **1.** **s. (pin),** quille *f.* **2.** (*a*) **(game of) skittles,** jeu *m* de quilles; **set of skittles,** quillier *m;* jeu de quilles; **to set up the skittles,** quiller; **to play (at) skittles,** jouer aux quilles; **s. alley,** (terrain *m* de) jeu de quilles; (*b*) *F:* partie d'échecs qui n'est pas jouée sérieusement.

skittle[2], *v.tr.* **1.** **to s. the pins,** abattre les quilles. **2.** *Cr:* **to s. the batsmen out,** mettre les batteurs hors jeu.

skive[1] [skaiv], *s. Lap:* polissoir *m* (de diamant, etc.).

skive[2], *v.tr. Leath: etc:* doler (les peaux); fendre (le caoutchouc) en feuilles minces.

skive[3]. *F:* **1.** *v.tr. O:* échapper à (un devoir, etc.). **2.** *v.i.* **to s. (off),** tirer au flanc, au cul; s'esquiver.

skiver[1] ['skaivər], *s.* **1.** *Leath:* (*a*) (*pers.*) doleur *m* (de peaux); (*b*) *Tls:* doloir *m;* (*machine*) doleuse *f.* **2.** *Bookb: etc:* parchemin *m* mince; peau fendue; mouton scié.

skiver[2], *s. F:* tire(-)au(-)flanc *m inv,* tire(-)au(-)cul *m inv.*

skiving ['skaiviŋ], *s. F:* tirage *m* au flanc, au cul.

skivvy ['skivi], *s. F:* **1.** *Pej: O:* domestique *f;* bon(n)iche *f;* bonne *f* à tout faire. **2.** *U.S:* (*a*) sous-vêtement *m* d'homme; (*b*) caleçon *m,* short *m* (en coton).

skrimshank ['skrimʃæŋk], *v.i. Mil: F:* tirer au flanc, au cul.

skrimshanker ['skrimʃæŋkər], *s.* tire(-)au(-)flanc *m inv,* tire(-)au(-)cul *m inv.*

skua ['skju(:)ə], *s. Orn:* labbe *m,* stercoraire *m,* mouette pillarde; **long-tailed s., Buffon's s.,** labbe longicaude, labbe à longue queue; **arctic, Richardson's s.,** labbe parasite; **pomarine s.,** labbe pomarin; **great s.,** *NAm:* **s.,** labbe cataracte, grand labbe.

skulduggery [skʌl'dʌgəri], *s.* **1.** *esp. Scot: A:* adultère *m;* fornication *f.* **2.** procédés *mpl* peu honnêtes; manigances *fpl,* tripotage *m.*

skulk[1] [skʌlk], *s.* **1.** (*a*) personne qui se cache, qui se tient cachée; personne furtive; (*b*) paresseux, -euse, fainéant, -ante; carotteur, -euse; carottier, -ière; feignant, -ante, faignant, -ante; tire(-)au(-)flanc *m inv,* tire(-)au(-)cul *m inv;* cagnard *m,* embusqué *m.* **2.** **s. (of foxes),** bande *f* de renards.

skulk[2], *v.i.* **1.** se cacher; se tenir caché. **2.** rôder furtivement; **to s. in, out,** entrer, sortir, furtivement, à la dérobée. **3.** paresser, fainéanter; avoir les pieds nickelés; échapper (au devoir); tirer au flanc, au cul; carotter; *Ven:* **skulking hound,** chien couard.

skulker ['skʌlkər], *s.* = SKULK[1] 1.

skulking ['skʌlkiŋ], *s.* paresse *f,* fainéantise *f.*

skull [skʌl], *s.* crâne *m;* boîte crânienne; **fracture of the s.,** fracture du crâne; **s. and crossbones,** tête *f* de mort et tibias; *Fig:* **he's got a thick s.,** il a le crâne, l'esprit, étroit; il a la tête dure.

skullcap ['skʌlkæp], *s.* **1.** calotte *f* (de prêtre, etc.). **2.** *Anat:* sinciput *m.* **3.** *Bot:* scutellaire *f.*

skunk [skʌŋk], *s.* **1.** *Z:* mouf(f)ette *f,* mofette *f;* putois *m* d'Amérique; **little spotted s.,** petite moufette; skung tacheté; **striped s.,** moufette commune, skung rayé; **hog-nosed s., white-backed s.,** conépate *m;* **Javanese s.,** télagon *m,* teledon *m,* blaireau puant. **2.** (*fur*) skunks *m,* sconce *m,* scons(e) *m,* skons *m,* skuns *m,* skongs *m,* scunce *m.* **3.** *F:* chameau *m,* mufle *m,* malotru *m,* rosse *f.*

skutterudite ['skʌtərədait], *s. Miner:* skutterudite *f.*

sky[1] [skai], *s.* **1.** ciel *m, pl.* cieux; *Art: Tchn:* ciels; **the skies were blue,** les cieux étaient bleus; **cloudy, overcast, s.,** ciel nuageux, couvert; **under the open s.,** au grand air; (dormir) à la belle étoile; à ciel ouvert; *Av: Hist:* **open skies,** principe de libre inspection des bases et établissements d'aviation militaire; *Art:* **Van Gogh's skies,** les ciels de Van Gogh; **s. blue,** bleu céleste; bleu (de) ciel; ciel; azur *m;* **s-blue dress,** robe bleu (de) ciel; **s. sign,** enseigne lumineuse (sur un bâtiment); *Th:* **s. pieces,** frises *f;* **the sky's the limit,** tout va! c'est sans bornes, c'est illimité; **to praise s.o. to the skies,** porter, mettre, qn aux nues; porter qn au pinacle; élever qn jusqu'au ciel; chanter les louanges de qn; couvrir qn d'applaudissements; **the bridge was blown s. high,** le pont a sauté jusqu'aux cieux; **prices are s. high,** les prix sont excessifs; (*of building, etc.*) **to stand sharp against the s.,** se découper nettement sur le ciel; *Prov:* **red s. at night (is the) shepherd's delight,** rouge le soir, espoir; *Aer: Sp:* **s. diving,** parachutisme *m* en chute libre; saut *m* en parachute avec ouverture retardée; **s. diver,** parachutiste *mf* qui pratique la chute libre; *F:* **s. pilot,** prêtre *m,* pasteur *m;* aumônier *m; W.Tel:* **s. wave,** onde ionosphérique; *Phot:* **s. filter,** écran de ciel; *Astr:* **s. map,** carte astronomique, céleste; carte du ciel. **2.** (*climate*) **the sunny skies of Italy,** le climat ensoleillé d'Italie; les ciels bleus d'Italie.

sky[2], *v.tr.* (**skied**) (*a*) *Cr: Ten: etc:* lancer (la balle) en chandelle; (*b*) *Row:* lever trop haut (la palette de l'aviron); (*c*) *Art:* jucher (un tableau); exposer (un tableau) au plafond.

Skye [skai], *Pr.n. Geog:* (l'île *f* de) Skye; **S. (terrier),** skye-terrier *m, pl.* skye-terriers, terrier *m* de l'île de Skye.

skyjack[1] ['skaidʒæk], *s. F:* piraterie aérienne; détournement *m* d'avion; saisie *f* d'un avion (par des terroristes, etc.).

skyjack[2], *v.tr. F:* pirater un avion; détourner un avion.

skyjacker ['skaidʒækər], *s. F:* pirate *m* de l'air.

skyjacking ['skaidʒækiŋ], *s. F:* = SKYJACK[1].

skylark[1] ['skailɑ:k], *s. Orn:* alouette *f* des champs.

skylark[2], *v.i. F:* rigoler, batifoler, plaisanter; faire des farces; faire du chahut, chahuter.

skylarker ['skailɑ:kər], *s. F:* batifoleur, -euse; farceur, -euse; plaisantin *m;* chahuteur, -euse.

skylarking ['skailɑ:kiŋ], *s. F:* rigolade *f;* farces *fpl;* chahut *m.*

skylight ['skailait], *s.* jour *m* (dans le toit, le plafond); (*a*) châssis vitré; (*in attic*) (lucarne) faîtière *f;* (*pivoted*) abattant *m;* (châssis, fenêtre *f,* lucarne, à) tabatière *f;* lucarne à charnière; (*in cellar*) soupirail, -aux; (*above stairs*) lanternon *m,* lanterneau *m;* (*b*) *Nau:* claire-voie *f, pl.* claires-voies; **s. grating,** caillebotis *m* de claire-voie.

skyline ['skailain], *s.* (ligne *f* d')horizon *m;* profil *m* de l'horizon; **the New York s.,** la ligne, le profil, que New York découpe sur le ciel.

skyman, *pl.* **skymen** ['skaimən], *s.m. F:* parachutiste.

skyrocket[1] ['skairɔkit], *s. Pyr:* fusée blanche, éclairante.

skyrocket[2], *v.i.* (*of prices, etc.*) monter en flèche.

skysail ['skaiseil], *s. Nau:* contre-cacatois *m inv.*

skyscape ['skaiskeip], *s.* (*a*) vue *f* du ciel; (*b*) *Art:* étude *f* de ciel; tableau *m* représentant des nuages, une partie du ciel.

skyscraper ['skaiskreipər], *s.* **1.** *Nau:* aile *f* de pigeon; (aile de) papillon *m.* **2.** gratte-ciel *m inv.*

skyward(s) ['skaiwəd(z)], *adv.* vers le ciel.

skyway ['skaiwei], *s.* **1.** *Av:* route aérienne; **the skyways of the world,** les voies aériennes mondiales. **2.** *NAm: Civ.E:* enjambement *m,* passage supérieur, saut-de-mouton *m, pl.* sauts-de-mouton; route surélevée.

sky(-)writing ['skairaitiŋ], *s. Av:* publicité aérienne.

slab[1] [slæb], *s.* **1.** (*a*) *Tchn:* plaque *f,* tranche *f,* dalle *f* (de marbre, etc.); table *f,* plaque (d'ardoise); dalle (de pierre, de verre laminé); carreau *m* (de fulmicoton, etc.); *Metall:* brame *f,* lopin *m* (de fer); *Pyr:* galette *f* (d'explosif); (*b*) (*of timber*) dosse *f;* (*c*) **s. of gingerbread,** pavé *m* de pain d'épice; **s. of cake,** (grosse) tranche de gâteau; **s. of fish,** darne *f,* dalle, de poisson; **s. of chocolate,** plaque, tablette *f,* de chocolat; *Com:* **s. rubber,** caoutchouc en plaques épaisses; (*d*) *U.S:* **s.-sided,** (i) (*of pers.*) grand et maigre; dégingandé; (ii) (*of animal*) efflanqué. **2.** *Typ:* marbre *m* (pour broyer les couleurs).

slab², *v.tr.* (**slabbed**) **1.** (*a*) **to s. marble,** trancher le marbre; (*b*) **to s. timber,** ôter, couper, les dosses du bois. **2.** daller (le sol); paver (le sol) de dalles.

slab³, *s. Nau: A:* mou *m*, battant *m* (d'une voile).

slabbing ['slæbiŋ], *s.* **1.** tranchage *m* (du marbre). **2.** dallage *m*, pavage *m*.

slabline ['slæblain], *s. Nau: A:* dégorgeoir *m* de voile; fausse cargue.

slabstone ['slæbstoun], *s.* dalle *f*, plaque *f* (de pierre).

slack¹ [slæk], *s.* (i) menu charbon; charbonnaille *f*; (ii) poussier *m*; **compressed s.,** briquettes *fpl*.

slack², *s.* **1.** (*a*) mou *m*, ballant *m*, étale *m* (d'un câble, d'une courroie); **to take up the s. in a cable,** mettre un câble au raide; *Nau: etc:* **to take in the s.,** prendre du lâche, embraquer le mou; (*b*) *Mec.E:* jeu *m* (nuisible); **to take up the s.,** rattraper le jeu. **2.** *Nau:* mer *f* étale; étale de la marée, du flot. **3.** ralentissement *m* d'activité (dans les affaires, etc.); morte-saison *f*. **4.** *Cost:* **slacks,** pantalon *m* (sport, de dame).

slack³, *a.* **1.** (*a*) (cordage) mou, lâche, flasque, ballant, détendu, mal tendu; (écrou) desserré, qui a du jeu; **s. side of a belt, of a transmission rope,** brin mou, brin conduit, d'une courroie, d'un câble de transmission; (*of rope*) **to be, hang, s.,** avoir du mou; (**acrobat's**) **s. rope,** corde *f* lâche; voltige *f*; **performer on the s. rope,** voltigeur, -euse; **to perform on the s. rope,** voltiger, faire de la voltige; (*b*) (main, prise) faible, sans force, qui étreint mal; *Fig:* **to have a s. hand, rein, on sth.,** gouverner qch. sans fermeté, mollement. **2.** (*a*) (*of pers.*) négligent, nonchalant, inexact, peu zélé; mou *f*. molle; *F:* flémard, flemmard; **to be s. about one's work,** se relâcher dans son travail; **to get, become, s.,** se relâcher, se laisser aller; **after doing so well you mustn't get s.,** après avoir si bien travaillé, il ne faut pas vous relâcher; **to be s. in, about, doing sth.,** être lent, paresseux, à faire qch.; *O:* **s. weather,** temps qui rend paresseux, temps mou; (*b*) *Nau:* **ship s. in stays,** navire lent (à virer de bord). **3.** (*a*) peu vif; faible; **trade is s.,** le commerce est stagnant; **business is s.,** les affaires vont mal, ne marchent pas; le marché est faible; **s. periods,** moments *m* de creux; **s. time,** (période d')accalmie *f*; **the s. season,** la morte-saison, la saison creuse; **s. sea, s. water,** mer étale; étale *m* de la marée, du flot; *Ind: Rail: etc:* **s. hours,** heures creuses, de faible trafic; *O:* **s. oven,** four modéré; (*b*) **to have a s. morning,** passer une matinée désœuvrée; **we're s. this afternoon,** nous ne sommes pas très occupés, nous sommes désœuvrés, cet après-midi. **4.** *adv.* (*a*) mollement; (*b*) imparfaitement; **s.-baked bread,** pain gras-cuit.

slack⁴. **1.** *v.tr.* (*a*) ralentir (l'allure, l'activité); (*b*) détendre, relâcher (un cordage); donner du mou à (une courroie, une voile); desserrer (un écrou); *Mch:* **to s. off the pressure,** relâcher la pression; *Nau:* **to s. the mooring ropes,** choquer les amarres; (*c*) **to s. lime,** éteindre, amortir, détremper, la chaux; **air-slacked lime,** chaux fusée, chaux éteinte à l'air. **2.** *v.i.* (*a*) (*of lime*) s'éteindre, s'amortir; (*b*) (*of train*) **to s. up,** ralentir; (*c*) *F:* (*of pers.*) **to s.** (**off**), se relâcher; paresser, mollir; avoir un poil dans la main; flemmarder, flemmer, fainéanter; avoir la flemme, tirer sa flemme; **your pupils are slacking,** vos élèves se relâchent.

slacken ['slæk(ə)n]. **1.** *v.tr.* (*a*) ralentir (le pas, ses efforts, son ardeur); **to s. speed,** diminuer de vitesse; ralentir (la marche); *Mus:* **to s. the time,** allonger, élargir, le tempo, la mesure; *Artil:* **to s. the rate of fire,** ralentir la cadence; *Nau:* **to s. a ship's way,** casser l'erre d'un navire; (*b*) détendre, relâcher, mollir (un cordage); détendre (les muscles); desserrer (un écrou); donner du mou à (un cordage, une voile); *Mec.E:* donner du jeu à (un organe); **to s. the reins,** lâcher la bride, les rênes; (*c*) affaiblir (l'opposition); adoucir (la sévérité). **2.** *v.i.* (*a*) (*of pers.*) **to s.** (**off, up**), se relâcher; devenir négligent, nonchalant; diminuer d'efforts; (*b*) (*of rope*) prendre du mou; (*c*) (*of speed*) ralentir; (*of energy, mind, etc.*) diminuer (de force, d'ardeur); **business is slackening,** les affaires deviennent stagnantes; **the storm slackened,** la tempête s'est calmée; (*d*) (*of the tide*) mollir; (*e*) (*of lime*) s'éteindre, s'amortir.

slackening ['slækniŋ], *s.* ralentissement *m* (de zèle); diminution *f* (de force, de zèle, de vitesse); amortissement *m* (de l'erre d'un navire); relâchement *m* (d'un cordage, d'ardeur, d'efforts); desserrage *m* (d'un écrou); avachissement *m* (d'un ressort); détente *f* (des muscles, etc.); **s. of speed,** ralentissement.

slacker ['slækər], *s. F:* paresseux, -euse; flémard, -arde; flemmard, -arde; tire(-)au(-)cul *m inv*, tire(-)au(-)flanc *m inv*.

slacking ['slækiŋ], *s.* **1.** ralentissement *m* (de l'allure, etc.). **2.** relâchement *m* (d'un cordage); desserrage *m* (d'un écrou). **3.** extinction *f* (de la chaux). **4.** *F:* manque *m* d'application au travail; paresse *f*, flemme *f*; **there is far too much s. in the summer term,** les élèves en prennent trop à leur aise pendant le trimestre d'été.

slackly ['slækli], *adv.* **1.** (agir) négligemment, nonchalamment, mollement; sans énergie, sans vigueur. **2.** (lier qch.) mollement, lâchement, sans fermeté.

slackness ['slæknis], *s.* **1.** (*a*) manque *m* d'énergie; négligence *f*, nonchalance *f*, incurie *f*, mollesse *f*; inexactitude *f* (à remplir ses devoirs); paresse *f*, fainéantise *f*; *F:* flemme *f*; (*b*) désœuvrement *m*; (*c*) relâchement *m* (de la discipline). **2.** détente *f* (des muscles, etc.); avachissement *m* (du corps); mou *m* (d'un cordage). **3.** *Com:* stagnation *f*, manque d'activité, marasme *m* (des affaires).

slade¹ [sleid], *s.* sep *m*, cep *m* (de charrue).

slade², *s. A: & Dial:* **1.** vallon *m*. **2.** clairière *f*.

slag¹ [slæg], *s.* **1.** *Metall:* scorie(s) *f(pl)* (de métal); crasse *f*, laitier(s) *m(pl)*, mâchefer *m* (de haut fourneau); **to rake out the s. from a furnace,** décrasser un fourneau; **basic s.,** scories de déphosphoration; **s. hole,** sortie *f* du laitier; trou *m* à laitier; **s. brick, cement,** brique, ciment, de laitier; **s. wool,** laine de laitier, de scorie; laine minérale; *Geol:* **volcanic s.,** scories volcaniques. **2.** *P:* mocheté *f*, vieille bique; remède *m* d'amour.

slag², *v.* (**slagged**) *Metall:* **1.** *v.tr.* scorifier. **2.** *v.i.* se scorifier; former des scories.

slagging ['slægiŋ], *s. Metall:* scorification *f*.

slaggy ['slægi], *a. Metall:* scoriacé; **s. cobalt,** cobalt oxydé noir; *Geol:* **s. lava,** laves scoriacées, scories volcaniques.

slagheap ['slæghi:p], *s.* crassier *m*.

slain [slein], *a. U.S: esp. Journ:* tué; **the mother of the s. child,** la mère de l'enfant tué.

slake [sleik]. **1.** *v.tr.* (*a*) **to s. one's thirst,** étancher, apaiser, éteindre, sa soif; se désaltérer; *Lit:* **to s. one's thirst for blood,** s'abreuver de sang; se désaltérer de sang; s'assouvir de carnage; (*b*) **to s. lime,** éteindre, amortir, détremper, la chaux; **slaked lime,** chaux éteinte. **2.** *v.i.* (*of lime*) s'éteindre, s'amortir.

slakeless ['sleiklis], *a. Lit:* (soif) inextinguible; (vengeance) insatiable.

slaking ['sleikiŋ], *s.* **1.** étanchement *m*, assouvissement *m* (de la soif). **2.** extinction *f* (de la chaux).

slalom ['slæləm], *s. Ski:* slalom *m*.

slam¹ [slæm]. **1.** *s.* claquement *m* (d'une porte, etc.); **the door closed with a s.,** la porte a claqué. **2.** *adv.* **s.** (**bang**) **in the middle of . . .,** en plein dans . . ..

slam², *v.* (**slammed**) **1.** *v.tr.* **to s. a door, a window** (**to**), claquer, faire claquer, une porte, une fenêtre; **to s. the door in s.o.'s face,** claquer, fermer, la porte au nez de qn; **to s. down the lid of a box,** fermer violemment une boîte; **she slammed the book** (**down**) **on the table,** elle a flanqué le livre sur la table. **2.** *v.i.* (*of door, etc.*) se fermer avec bruit; claquer.

slam³, *s.* (*a*) *Cards:* (*at bridge*) chelem *m*, schelem *m*, vole *f*; **grand s.,** grand chelem; **little, small, s.,** petit chelem; **to make a s.,** faire (le) chelem, la vole; (*b*) *Sp:* **the grand s.,** le grand chelem.

slam⁴, *v.i. Cards:* faire chelem.

slamming ['slæmiŋ], *s.* claquement *m* (d'une porte, etc.).

slander¹ ['slɑ:ndər], *s.* calomnie *f*; *Jur:* diffamation verbale; **s. and libel,** diffamation; **s. action,** procès *m* en diffamation.

slander², *v.tr.* calomnier, *Jur:* diffamer (qn).

slanderer ['slɑ:ndərər], *s.* calomniateur, -trice; *Jur:* diffamateur, -trice.

slandering ['slɑ:ndəriŋ], *s.* = SLANDER¹.

slanderous ['slɑ:ndərəs], *a.* (propos) calomnieux, calomniateur; *Jur:* diffamatoire.

slanderously ['slɑ:ndərəsli], *adv.* calomnieusement.

slang¹ [slæŋ], *s.* argot *m*; langue verte; jargon *m* (d'un groupe de personnes); expression populaire; **thieves' s.,** argot des voleurs; **underworld s.,** argot du milieu; **theatrical, stage, s.,** argot des coulisses; **students' s.,** argot des écoles, d'étudiants, estudiantin; **s. phrase, expression,** expression *f* argotique; argotisme *m*.

slang², *v.tr. F:* (*a*) critiquer, éreinter, injurier, engueuler, enguirlander (qn); (*b*) réprimander sévèrement (qn); laver la tête à, donner, passer, un savon à (qn).

slangily ['slæŋili], *adv.* (s'exprimer, etc.) en termes d'argot, en langue verte, en langage populaire.

slanginess ['slæŋinis], *s.* caractère *m* argotique (d'une conversation, du style).

slanging ['slæŋiŋ], *s. F:* (*a*) pluie *f* d'injures; **s. match,** prise *f* de bec, engueulade *f*; (*b*) verte réprimande.

slangy ['slæŋi], *a.* **1.** (*of pers.*) qui aime à s'exprimer en argot; qui est amateur de la langue verte; argotier. **2.** (style, langage) argotique; (terme) populaire, d'argot.

slant¹ [slɑ:nt], *s.* **1.** (*a*) pente *f*, inclinaison *f*; dénivellement *m*, dénivellation *f*; *Rail:* **vertical s.,** dévers *m* (du rail extérieur); (*b*) **s. of light,** rayon *m*, rai *m*, de lumière. **2.** (*a*) biais *m*, biseau *m*; **on the s., at a s.,** de biais, obliquement, en écharpe; **the car was hit on the, a, s.,** la voiture a été prise en écharpe, a été accrochée par le travers; (*b*) *Min:* diagonale *f*, thierne *f*. **3.** *F:* (*a*) point *m* de vue; **to get s.o.'s s. on a question,** saisir la manière dont qn envisage une affaire; **I got a new s. on the question,** j'ai obtenu une nouvelle opinion, un nouveau point de vue, sur la question; (*b*) **information with a s. on it,** informations tendancieuses, faussées.

slant², *a.* oblique; en écharpe; **s. eyes,** yeux bridés; **s. eyed,** aux yeux bridés; *Mth:* **s. height,** longueur *f* de l'arête (d'un cône); *Artil:* **s. fire,** tir *m* oblique; tir d'écharpe, en écharpe.

slant³. **1.** *v.i.* (*a*) être en pente; (s')incliner; (*b*) être oblique; **the morning sun slanted over the village,** le soleil du matin dardait ses rayons obliques sur le village. **2.** *v.tr.* (*a*) incliner (qch.); mettre (qch.) en pente; déverser (un mur); **the rain was slanted by the wind,** la pluie tombait obliquement sous la poussée du vent; (*b*) *F:* **to s. the facts,** fausser les faits; **slanted news,** informations tendancieuses; **to s. a magazine for women readers,** orienter une revue vers le goût féminin.

slanting ['slɑ:ntiŋ], *a.* (*a*) (toit) en pente, incliné; (*b*) (direction, coup de sonde) oblique; **s. rain,** pluie qui tombe en oblique; **s. handwriting,** écriture couchée, inclinée; (écriture) bâtarde *f*; *Typ:* **s. letters,** lettres couchées.

slantingly ['slɑ:ntiŋli], *adv.* obliquement; de, en, biais.

slantwise, slantways ['slɑ:ntwaiz, -weiz], *adv.* obliquement; en, de, biais; en écharpe; en sifflet; **to cut sth. s.,** couper qch. de biais, en sifflet.

slap¹ [slæp].

I. *s.* **1.** coup *m*, claque *f*, tape *f*; *F:* calotte *f*; **s. on the shoulder,** claque, tape, sur l'épaule; **s. in the face,** gifle *f*, soufflet *m*; *Fig:* **s. in the face, in the eye,** affront *m*, soufflet, camouflet *m*, nasarde *f*, rebuffade *f*; *Fig:* **s. on the back,** félicitations *fpl*; *P:* **s. and tickle,** partie de pelotage *m*. **2.** *I.C.E: Mch:* **piston s.,** claquement *m* des pistons.

II. *adv.* **the car went s. into the wall,** la voiture est entrée en plein dans le mur; *F:* **s. bang,** brusquement; de but en blanc; **they ran s.** (**bang**) **into each other,** ils se sont rentrés en plein dedans, ils ont foncé en plein l'un dans l'autre.

slap², *v.* (**slapped** [slæpt]) **1.** *v.tr.* (*a*) frapper (qn) avec la main (ouverte); donner, allonger, une claque, une tape, à (qn); donner une fessée à (un enfant, etc.); **to s. s.o.'s face, to s. s.o. on the face,** gifler, souffleter, qn; appliquer, allonger, une gifle à qn; **to s. s.o. on the back,** (i) donner à qn une claque, une tape, sur le dos; (ii) *Fig:* féliciter qn; **he slapped his forehead,** il s'est frappé le front; *F:* **to s. s.o. down,** flanquer un savon à qn; (re)mettre qn à sa place, rembarrer, rebuffer, qn; **he slapped the money** (**down**) **on the table,** il a jeté, flanqué, l'argent sur la table. (*b*) *Cer:* **to s. the clay,** travailler l'argile en la jetant fortement sur la table. **2.** *v.i. I.C.E: Mch:* (*of pistons, etc.*) claquer.

slapdash ['slæpdæʃ], *a. & adv.* sans soin(s); **s. work,** travail à la six-quatre-deux; travail bâclé; **s. worker,** sabreur *m* de besogne; **to do sth. s., in a s. manner,** faire qch. à la va-vite, à la six-quatre-deux, au petit bonheur; **to paint** (**sth.**) **in a s. manner,** strapasser, strapassonner (un tableau).

slap(-)happy [slæp'hæpi], *a. F:* **1.** (*a*) plein d'entrain, d'humeur joyeuse; (*b*) farfelu, insouciant; **he's s.,** il fait les choses au petit bonheur. **2.** (*of boxer, etc.*) ivre de coups.

slapjack ['slæpdʒæk], *s. Cu: U.S:* (genre de) crêpe *f*.

slapping ['slæpiŋ], *s.* **1.** (*a*) claques *fpl*, gifles *fpl*; (*b*) fessée *f*, fouettée *f*. **2.** *I.C.E: Mch:* claquement *m* (des pistons, etc.).

slapstick ['slæpstik], *s.* **1.** batte *f* d'Arlequin. **2. s.** (**comedy**), arlequinades *fpl*, comédie bouffonne, farce *f*.

slap-up ['slæpʌp], *a. F:* fameux, soigné, chic; **s. meal,** festin *m*, repas excellent, somptueux; **to give s.o. a s. lunch,** faire bien déjeuner qn.

slash¹ [slæʃ], *s.* **1.** estafilade *f*, entaille *f*, taillade *f*; (*on the face*) balafre *f*, estafilade. **2.** *A.Cost:* crevé *m*, taillade. **3.** (*a*) *Bot:* laciniure *f*, lacinie *f* (dans une feuille); (*b*) *For: Hort:* **s. hook,** fauchard *m*. **4.** *NAm: For:* (*a*) déchets *mpl* (d'abattage); débris (laissés par un orage, etc.); (*b*) clairière *f*, éclaircie *f*. **5.** *P:* **to have a s.,** uriner, jeter de la lance.

slash², *v.tr.* **1.** (*a*) taillader (la chair); balafrer, écharper, entailler (le visage); (*b*) cingler (un cheval, etc.) (d'un coup de fouet); (*c*) *v.i.* frapper à droite et à gauche, à tort et à travers; ferrailler, sabrer; **to cut and s.,** frapper d'estoc et de taille; (*d*) (*criticize*) éreinter, esquinter (un ouvrage littéraire, etc.); (*e*) réduire (les salaires, etc.); **all prices slashed,** tous prix réduits. **2.** (*a*) *A.Cost:* faire des crevés, des taillades, dans (un vêtement); **slashed doublet,** pourpoint à taillades; **slashed sleeve,** manche à crevés; (*b*) *Bot:* **slashed leaf,** feuille laciniée. **3.** faire claquer (un fouet). **4.** (*a*) *NAm: For:* abattre les arbres (d'une forêt, etc.); (*b*) *Mil:* **to s. the trees,** abattre les arbres (pour former un abattis).

slasher ['slæʃər], *s.* **1.** *F:* batailleur, -euse, ferrailleur *m.* **2.** *Lit: etc:* critique *m* acerbe. **3.** *For: Hort:* **double-edged s.,** fauchard *m.*

slashing[1] ['slæʃiŋ], *a.* **1.** (*of criticism, etc.*) mordant, cinglant, acerbe; **s. critic,** (critique) éreinteur *m*; **s. review,** revue cinglante. **2.** *F:* excellent, épatant, de premier ordre, du tonnerre.

slashing[2], *s.* **1.** taillades *fpl,* entailles *fpl*; coups *mpl* de sabre, de fouet. **2.** *A.Cost:* crevé *m.* **3.** *Lit: etc:* critique incisive, cinglante, acerbe. **4.** *NAm: For:* (*a*) clairière *f,* éclaircie *f*; (*b*) *pl.* déchets *m* (d'abattage).

slat[1] [slæt], *s.* **1.** lame *f,* lamelle *f,* planchette *f,* latte *f* (de jalousie, etc.); traverse *f* (de lit); **s. iron,** fer en lattes; *F:* **slats,** côtes *fpl.* **2.** *Av:* bec *m* d'attaque.

slat[2]. **1.** *v.tr.* garnir de lames. **2.** *v.i.* (*of sails, etc.*) fouetter, claquer, battre.

slate[1] [sleit], *s.* **1.** (*a*) *Geol:* ardoise *f*; schiste ardoisier; **s. colour(ed), s. grey,** ardoisé; (gris) ardoise *inv*; **s. blue,** (i) bleu ardoise *inv*; (ii) (*of marble, etc.*) bleu turquin *inv*; **s. worker, quarryman,** ardoisier *m,* perrier *m,* perrayeur *m*; **s. splitter,** répartonneur *m*; **s. quarry,** ardoisière *f*; carrière *f* d'ardoise; **s. industry,** ardoiserie *f*; *Miner:* **s. spar,** argentine *f*; spath schisteux; (*b*) *Const:* (feuille *f* d')ardoise; **s. hanging,** armement *m*; **s. nail,** clou à ardoises; *F:* **to have a s. loose,** être un peu toqué; avoir la tête fêlée. **2.** (**writing**) **s.,** ardoise (pour, à, écrire); **s. pencil,** crayon d'ardoise; *A:* **s. club,** petite société mutuelle de capitalisation, dans laquelle chaque membre verse une cotisation hebdomadaire; *F:* **on the s.,** sur la note, sur le compte; **to clean the s.,** (i) se débarrasser de, (ii) renoncer à, ses engagements; **to wipe the s. clean,** faire table rase (du passé); passer l'éponge sur le passé; **I have a clean s.,** (i) je n'ai pas de dettes; (ii) mon casier judiciaire est vierge. **3.** *NAm: Pol:* liste *f* provisoire des candidats.

slate[2], *v.tr.* **1.** *Const:* couvrir (un toit) d'ardoise, en ardoise; ardoiser (un toit); **slated roof,** toit en ardoise, d'ardoises. **2.** *NAm: Pol:* inscrire (un candidat) sur la liste; adopter (un candidat).

slate[3], *v.tr. F:* **1.** réprimander, vertement (qn); passer un savon à (qn). **2.** critiquer, éreinter, esquinter (un auteur, un livre, etc.); **to s. a play,** déshabiller une pièce.

slateman, *pl.* **-men** ['sleitmən], *s.* ardoisier *m,* perrier *m,* perrayeur *m.*

slater ['sleitər], *s.* **1.** (*pers.*) couvreur *m* (en ardoise); ardoisier *m.* **2.** *Crust:* cloporte *m*; **common sea s.,** ligie *f,* lygie *f.* **3.** *Leath:* queurse *f,* queurce *f,* cœurse *f,* cœurce *f.*

slateworks ['sleitwəːks], *s.pl.* (*often with sg. const.*) ardoiserie *f.*

slather[1] ['slæðər], *s. F:* **1.** *NAm:* grande quantité; **slathers of people,** flopée *f* de gens. **2.** *Austr: & N.Z:* **open s.,** liberté *f* d'action, libre carrière *f.*

slather[2], *v.tr. NAm: F:* (*a*) étaler (de la confiture, etc.) en couches épaisses; (*b*) gaspiller (de l'argent, etc.).

slating[1] ['sleitiŋ], *s.* **1.** recouvrement (d'un toit) d'ardoises. **2.** *Const:* couverture *f* en ardoise; ardoises *fpl.* **3.** *Leath:* queursage *m,* cœursage *m.*

slating[2], *s. F:* **1.** verte réprimande; semonce *f,* savon *m,* écopage *m.* **2.** *Lit: etc:* critique *f* acerbe; éreintement *m,* éreintage *m,* déshabillage *m.*

slatted ['slætid], *a.* (*of shutters, etc.*) à lames, à planchettes.

slattern ['slætə(ː)n], *s.f.* femme mal soignée, mal peignée; traîne-savate *inv*; souillon.

slatternliness ['slætənlinis], *s.* manque *m* d'ordre, de propreté.

slatternly ['slætənli], *a.* (*of woman*) mal soignée, mal peignée, qui traîne la savate; qui manque d'ordre, de propreté.

slaty ['sleiti], *a.* **1.** *Geol:* ardoisier, schisteux. **2.** (*of colour*) ardoisé.

slaughter[1] ['slɔːtər], *s.* **1.** abattage *m* (d'animaux de boucherie, etc.). **2.** tuerie *f,* carnage *m,* massacre *m,* boucherie *f* (de gens).

slaughter[2], *v.tr.* **1.** abattre (des animaux de boucherie, etc.); **the butcher slaughters once a week,** le boucher tue tous les huit jours. **2.** (*a*) tuer, égorger, massacrer (des gens); (*b*) *F:* **to s. an opponent,** battre un adversaire à plate(s) couture(s).

slaughterer ['slɔːtərər], *s.* **1.** tueur, -euse, massacreur, -euse, égorgeur, -euse (de gens). **2.** abatteur *m,* assommeur *m,* tueur (de bœufs, etc.); saigneur *m* (de porcs).

slaughterhouse ['slɔːtəhaus], *s.* abattoir *m.*

slaughtering ['slɔːtəriŋ], *s.* **1.** abattage *m* (d'animaux de boucherie, etc.). **2.** tuerie *f,* carnage *m,* massacre *m,* boucherie *f* (de gens).

slaughterman, *pl.* **-men** ['slɔːtəmən], *s.m.* abatteur, assommeur, tueur (de bœufs, etc.); saigneur (de porcs).

slaughterous ['slɔːtərəs], *a. Lit:* meurtrier.

Slav [slɑːv]. *Ethn:* (*a*) *a.* slave; (*b*) *s.* Slave *mf.*

slave[1] [sleiv], *s.* esclave *mf*; **to be s.o.'s s.,** être l'esclave de qn; **to be the s. of, a s. to, a passion,** être l'esclave d'une passion; vivre dans l'esclavage des passions; **s. of fashion,** esclave de la mode; **slaves of love,** captifs *m* de l'amour; **to be a s. to etiquette,** être asservi à l'étiquette; **to be a s. to duty,** ne connaître que son devoir; **to be a s. to one's work,** être esclave de son travail; **we soon become slaves to a habit,** une habitude devient vite une sujétion; **he was sold as a s.,** il fut vendu comme esclave; **s. trade, traffic,** traite *f* des noirs, des nègres; commerce *m,* trafic *m,* des esclaves; **white s. trade,** traite des blanches; **white s.,** (fille, femme) victime *f* de la traite des blanches; **s. trader, dealer,** marchand *m* d'esclaves; (**black**) **s. trader,** négrier *m*; **s. driver,** (i) *A:* surveillant *m* des esclaves; (ii) *F:* garde-chiourme *m, pl.* garde(s)-chiourme(s); **s. labour,** travail *m* d'esclave; *O:* **s. bangle,** bracelet d'esclave; *Hist:* **the s. states,** les états *m* esclavagistes (de l'Amérique du Nord); **the S. Coast,** la Côte des Esclaves; *Geog:* **the S. River,** la rivière des Esclaves; **the Great S. Lake,** le Grand lac des Esclaves; **the Lesser S. Lake,** le Petit lac des Esclaves; *Ent:* **s. ant,** esclave *f*; *Tchn:* **s. mechanism,** esclave *m* mécanique, servomécanisme *m,* robot *m*; *Elcs:* **s. circuit,** circuit asservi; *W.Tel:* **s. station,** station asservie.

slave[2], *v.i.* travailler comme un nègre; peiner, bûcher; **I slaved there for ten years,** je me suis crevé là-dedans pendant dix ans; **to s. away at (sth.),** s'échiner, s'éreinter, à (qch.); travailler d'arrache-pied à (qch.).

slaver[1] ['slævər], *s.* **1.** bave *f,* salive *f.* **2.** *Lit:* flatterie grossière; flagornerie *f.*

slaver[2] ['slævər], *v.i.* baver (**over,** sur).

slaver[3] ['sleivər], *s.* **1.** *Nau:* (bâtiment) négrier *m.* **2.** (*pers.*) marchand *m* d'esclaves; **black s.,** négrier *m*; **white s.,** courtier *m* de chair humaine.

slavering[1] ['slævəriŋ], *a.* baveur.

slavering[2], *s.* émission *f* de bave; sialorrhée *f.*

slavery[1] ['sleivəri], *s.* **1.** esclavage *m*; **abolition of s.,** abolition de l'esclavage; **to sell s.o. into s.,** vendre qn comme esclave; **to reduce a nation to s.,** asservir une nation; **to reduce s.o. to s.,** réduire qn en esclavage; **white s.,** traite *f* des blanches. **2.** asservissement *m* (**to a passion,** à une passion). **3.** *F:* travail tuant; **this work is sheer s.,** ce travail est un véritable esclavage. **4.** *Ent:* esclavagisme (des fourmis).

slavery[2] ['slævəri], *a.* **1.** baveux; souillé de bave. **2.** *Lit:* **s. compliments,** basse flatterie; flagornerie *f.*

Slavic ['slɑːvik], *a. & s. Ethn: Ling:* slave (*m*).

Slavi(ci)sm ['slɑːvi(si)zm], *s.* (pan)slavisme *m.*

slavish ['sleiviʃ], *a.* (soumission) d'esclave; (imitation) servile.

slavishly ['sleiviʃli], *adv.* (obéir) en esclave; (imiter) servilement.

slavishness ['sleiviʃnis], *s.* servilité *f.*

Slavist ['slɑːvist], *s.* slaviste *mf,* slavisant *m.*

Slavonia [slə'vouniə]. *Pr.n. Geog:* Slavonie *f.*

Slavonian [slə'vouniən]. *Geog:* (*a*) *a.* slavon; (*b*) *s.* Slavon, -onne.

Slavonic [slə'vɔnik]. **1.** *a. Ethn:* slave; **student of S. languages,** slavisant, -ante; **student of S. history, customs, etc.,** slaviste *mf.* **2.** *s. Ling:* slave *m*; **Church S., Old (Church) S.,** slavon *m,* vieux slave, slave ecclésiastique, esclavon *m.*

slaw [slɔː], *s. esp. NAm: Comest:* salade *f* de chou cru.

slay[1] [slei], *s. Tex:* ros *m,* rot *m.*

slay[2], *v.tr.* (**slew** [sluː]; **slain** [slein]) (*a*) *Lit:* tuer; mettre à mort; assassiner; **the slain,** les morts *m*; les massacrés *m*; (*b*) *esp. NAm: F:* **you're slaying me!** tu me fais rigoler! tu me fais tordre!

slayer ['sleiər], *s.* tueur, -euse; meurtrier, -ière, assassin *m* (**of,** de).

slaying ['sleiiŋ], *s.* tuerie *f,* boucherie *f*; massacre *m*; meurtre *m.*

sleaziness ['sliːzinis], *s.* **1.** *Tex:* manque *m* de consistance (d'un tissu). **2.** *F:* apparence *f* louche, aspect *m* sordide, répugnant (d'un endroit, etc.).

sleazy ['sliːzi], *a.* **1.** *Tex:* (tissu) mince, léger, sans consistance. **2.** *F:* (*a*) (quartier, etc.) louche, sordide, répugnant, dégueulasse, mal soigné; (*b*) (*of pers.*) dégueulasse.

sled[1,2] [sled], *s. & v. NAm:* = SLEDGE[1,2].

sledding ['slediŋ], *s. NAm:* promenade *f* en traîneau; *F:* **easy, smooth, s.,** travail *m* facile, qui va comme sur des roulettes; **tough, hard, s.,** travail pénible, tuant.

sledge[1] [sledʒ], *s.* traîneau *m*; (*in the Alps*) ramasse *f.*

sledge[2]. **1.** *v.i.* aller en traîneau; **to go sledging,** se promener en traîneau; faire une promenade en traîneau. **2.** *v.tr.* transporter (qch.) en traîneau.

sledge[3], *s.* = SLEDGEHAMMER.

sledgehammer ['sledʒhæmər], *s. Tls:* (*a*) marteau *m* de forgeron; marteau à deux mains, à frapper devant; frappe-devant *m inv*; (*b*) (*for stones*) masse *f,* massette *f,* têtu *m,* batterand *m,* batterant *m*; (*c*) **s. arguments,** arguments massue.

sleek[1] [sliːk], *a.* **1.** (*a*) lisse, luisant, poli; **s. hair,** cheveux lisses; **s. horse,** cheval d'un beau poil; (*of horse, etc.*) **s. coat,** robe polie; **s. wet otter,** loutre vernissée d'eau; (*b*) (*of pers.*) luisant de santé. **2.** (*of manner*) mielleux; doucereux; onctueux.

sleek[2], *v.tr.* lisser (les cheveux, le poil d'un animal, *Metall:* un moule).

sleeker ['sliːkər], *s. Metall:* lissoir *m.*

sleeking ['sliːkiŋ], *s. Metall:* lissage *m* (d'un moule).

sleekly ['sliːkli], *adv.* **1.** avec une apparence lisse, luisante. **2.** *Fig:* mielleusement; doucereusement; onctueusement.

sleekness ['sliːknis], *s.* **1.** luisant *m* (d'une peau, du satin, etc.). **2.** onctuosité *f* (de ton, de manières).

sleep[1] [sliːp], *s.* **1.** sommeil *m*; **short s.,** somme *m*; **deep, sound, s.,** sommeil profond; **dead, heavy, s.,** sommeil de plomb, de mort; **waking s.,** sommeil éveillé; **beauty s.,** sommeil avant minuit (considéré comme le plus réparateur); *Lit:* **the last s., the s. that knows no waking, the s. of death, of the tomb,** le sommeil de la mort, du trépas, de la tombe; le sommeil éternel; le repos éternel; le dernier sommeil; *Med:* **electric s.,** sommeil induit par traitement électrique; **to go, drop off, to s.,** s'endormir, s'assoupir; **to go, get, drop off, to s. again,** se rendormir; **he's gone to s.,** il dort; **to fall into a deep, sound, s.,** s'endormir d'un profond sommeil, profondément; **to put, send, lull, s.o. to s.,** endormir, assoupir, qn; **to sing a child to s.,** endormir un enfant en chantant; *Med:* **to put s.o. to s.,** endormir qn; *Vet: F:* **to put an animal to s.,** piquer un animal; **s.-inducing drug,** (médicament *m*) somnifère *m,* soporifique *m,* soporifère *m,* soporatif *m*; **to read oneself to s.,** lire pour s'endormir; **he was overcome with s.,** il a cédé, succombé, au sommeil; **he's ready to drop with s.,** il tombe, il meurt, de sommeil; il dort debout; **I'm losing s. over it,** j'en perds le sommeil; **to try to get some s.,** essayer d'avoir un peu de sommeil, de dormir un peu; **to come out of one's s.,** s'éveiller; **to rouse s.o. from his s.,** réveiller qn; arracher qn au sommeil; **to have one's s. out,** dormir son soûl; finir de dormir; finir son somme; **to have a good (night's) s.,** faire, dormir, un bon somme; bien dormir; **I didn't get a wink of s. all night,** je n'ai pas dormi, je n'ai pas fermé l'œil, de (toute) la nuit; j'ai passé une nuit blanche; **I didn't get much s.,** je n'ai pas très bien dormi; **in my s.,** pendant que je dors, que je dormais; **to walk in one's s.,** être somnambule; **to talk in one's s.,** rêver tout haut. **2. my foot's gone to s.,** j'ai des fourmis dans le pied; j'ai le pied endormi, engourdi.

sleep[2], *v.i. & tr.* (*p.t. & p.p.* **slept** [slept]) **1.** dormir; (*a*) **to s. like a log, like a top,** dormir à poings fermés; dormir comme un sabot, comme une souche, comme une marmotte, comme un loir; dormir d'un sommeil de plomb; **to s. well, badly,** bien, mal, dormir; **to s. soundly,** dormir profondément; dormir sur les deux oreilles; **to s. lightly,** avoir le sommeil léger; **to s. with one eye open,** dormir en gendarme; ne dormir que d'un œil, que sur une oreille; dormir les yeux ouverts; **to s. solidly, without waking, without a break,** ne faire qu'un somme; **to s. the night through,** dormir toute la nuit; **to s. through a noise,** ne pas être réveillé par un bruit; **I haven't slept a wink all night,** je n'ai pas dormi, je n'ai pas fermé l'œil, de (toute) la nuit; j'ai passé une nuit blanche; **to try to s.,** chercher le sommeil; **he can't s. for thinking about it,** il n'en dort pas; **to s. on a question,** *F:* **to s. on it,** consulter son chevet, *F:* son oreiller, son bonnet de nuit; **s. on it,** attendez à demain; la nuit porte conseil; (*b*) *Lit:* **to s. the sleep of the just,** dormir du sommeil du juste; (*c*) **to s. oneself sober** = cuver son vin. **2.** coucher; (*a*) **to s. at an hotel, at a neighbour's, in a barn,** coucher à un hôtel, chez un voisin, dans une grange; **to s. away from home,** découcher; **to s. rough,** coucher à la belle étoile, sur la dure; **I slept under a hedge,** j'ai passé la nuit sous une haie; **to s. in,** (i) être pensionnaire (dans son lieu de travail); (*of servant*) coucher à la maison; **to s. late, on,** *occ.* **in,** (i) faire la grasse matinée; (ii) ne pas se réveiller à l'heure; **the bed had not been slept in for months,** on n'avait pas dormi, couché, dans le lit depuis des mois; **the bed had not been slept in,** le lit n'avait pas été défait; **to s. out,** (i) découcher; (ii) (*of servant*) coucher à son domicile, venir en journée; (*b*) **to s. with s.o.,** coucher avec qn; **to**

s. together, coucher ensemble; *F:* **to s. around,** coucher avec n'importe qui. **3.** *Lit:* **to s. in the churchyard, with one's fathers, in the Lord,** reposer dans le cimetière, avec ses pères, en Dieu. **4.** (*of spinning top*) dormir. **5.** *v.tr.* (*a*) *F:* **house that sleeps ten people,** maison où dix personnes peuvent coucher; **this room sleeps four,** on peut coucher à quatre dans cette chambre; (*b*) **to s. off a headache,** faire passer un mal de tête en dormant; **to s. off a hangover,** *F:* **to s. it off** = cuver son vin; **to s. the day, the hours, away,** passer la journée, les heures, à dormir, en dormant.

sleeper ['sli:pər], *s.* **1.** (*a*) dormeur, -euse; **to be a light, a heavy, s.,** avoir le sommeil léger, profond; **the Seven Sleepers (of Ephesus),** les sept Dormants *m* (d'Éphèse); (*b*) *Com:* (associé *m*) commanditaire *m*; bailleur *m* de fonds. **2.** *Const: etc:* (*a*) poutre horizontale; sole *f*; lambourde *f* (de parquet, etc.); gîte *m* (de plancher, *Artil:* de plate-forme); **s. of staircase,** patin *m* d'escalier; (*b*) *Rail:* **(cross) s.,** traverse *f*; **longitudinal s.,** long(ue)rine (longitudinale); **long s.,** longrine transversale; **s. screw,** tirefond *m*, tire-fond *m inv*; **s. spacing,** travelage *m*. **3.** *Rail:* wagon-lit *m*, *pl.* wagons-lits. **4.** (*earring*) clou *m*. **5.** *NAm:* **sleeper(s),** pyjama *m* d'enfant.

sleepily ['sli:pili], *adv.* (répondre, etc.) d'un air endormi, somnolent.

sleepiness ['sli:pinis], *s.* **1.** envie *f* de dormir; assoupissement *m*, somnolence *f*, sommeil *m*. **2.** apathie *f*, indolence *f*, léthargie *f*, mollesse *f*. **3.** blétissement *m*, blétissure *f* (d'un fruit).

sleeping[1] ['sli:piŋ], *a.* **1.** dormant, endormi; *Prov:* **let s. dogs lie,** ne réveillez pas le chat qui dort. **2.** *Com:* **s. partner,** (associé *m*) commanditaire *m*; bailleur *m* de fonds.

sleeping[2], *s.* sommeil *m*; **s. pill, tablet,** (comprimé *m*) somnifère *m*; **s. draught,** (potion *f*) somnifère, soporifique *m*; **s. accommodation,** logement *m*; **the house has s. accommodation for ten,** c'est une maison où dix personnes peuvent coucher; **s. quarters,** chambres *fpl*; dortoir(s) *m*(*pl*); *Rail:* **s. car(riage),** wagon-lit *m*, *pl.* wagons-lits; **s. bag,** sac *m* de couchage; **s. suit,** pyjama *m* (d'enfant); combinaison *f* de nuit; *Med:* **s. sickness,** maladie *f* du sommeil; trypanosomiase africaine.

sleepless ['sli:plis], *a.* **1.** (*a*) sans sommeil; **s. night,** nuit sans sommeil, d'insomnie; nuit blanche; **to have a s. night,** passer une nuit blanche; (*b*) (*of pers.*) insomnieux. **2.** *Lit:* (*of mind*) sans cesse en éveil; (*of sea, etc.*) agité; **s. energy,** énergie inlassable.

sleeplessness ['sli:plisnis], *s.* insomnie *f*.

sleepwalker ['sli:pwɔ:kər], *s.* somnambule *mf*.

sleepwalking ['sli:pwɔ:kiŋ], *s.* somnambulisme *m*.

sleepy ['sli:pi], *a.* **1.** (*a*) somnolent; **to be, feel, s.,** avoir envie de dormir; avoir sommeil; **to get, grow, s.,** commencer à avoir sommeil; **to make s.o. s.,** assoupir qn; (*b*) **s. look,** air endormi; **s. little town,** petite ville inactive, endormie. **2.** (*a*) apathique, engourdi, indolent, léthargique; mou, *f.* molle; (*b*) *Med:* **s. sickness,** (i) encéphalite *f* léthargique, épidémique; (ii) maladie *f* du sommeil; trypanosomiase africaine. **3.** (*of fruit*) blet, *f.* blette.

sleepyhead ['sli:pihed], *s. F:* endormi, -ie; individu à moitié endormi.

sleet[1] [sli:t], *s.* **1.** neige à moitié fondue. **2.** *NAm:* (*a*) grésil *m*; (*b*) verglas *m*; givre limpide, transparent.

sleet[2], *v.impers.* **it's sleeting,** (i) il tombe de la neige fondue; la pluie tourne à la neige; (ii) *NAm:* il grêle, il grésille.

sleety ['sli:ti], *a.* **1.** (vent) chargé de pluie mêlée de neige. **2.** (temps, jour) de pluie et de neige, où il tombe de la neige fondue.

sleeve [sli:v], *s.* **1.** (*a*) manche *f*; **short s.,** manche courte, mancheron *m*; **long s.,** manche longue; **to remove the sleeve(s) from a dress,** démancher une robe; **s. hole,** emmanchure *f* (de robe, etc.); **s. button,** bouton *m* de manchette; **to put sth. up one's s.,** mettre qch. dans sa manche; *O:* **s. dog,** chien *m* de manchon; *F:* **to have a plan up one's s.,** avoir un expédient en réserve; avoir un expédient dans son sac à malice; **to have more than one trick up one's s.,** avoir plus d'un tour dans son sac; (*b*) *Moll:* **s. fish,** calmar *m*, encornet *m*. **2.** (*a*) *Mec.E:* chemise *f*, fourreau *m*, gaine *f* (souple); manchon *m*, douille *f*, bague *f* (d'assemblage); *Typ:* corps *m*, douille (d'une fiche); **abrasive s.,** manchon abrasif; **adjusting s.,** manchon de réglage; **coupling, connecting, s.,** manchon, douille, bague, d'accouplement, de raccord; **guide s.,** douille de guidage; **identification s.,** gaine repère (de câble, etc.); **insulating s.,** gaine isolante; **jointing s.,** manchon de raccordement; **loose s.,** manchon fou; **oil s.,** manchon de graissage; **screwed, threaded, s.,** manchon fileté, taraudé; **securing s.,** manchon de fixation; **s. nut,** manchon fileté, taraudé; **s. nut joint,** assemblage à manchon taraudé; *Mch.Tls:* **s.-type spindle,** broche type à fourreau; *I.C.E:* **s. valve,** chemise, fourreau, de distribution; chemise coulissante; chemise-tiroir *f*, *pl.* chemises-tiroirs; tiroir *m*; **s. valve engine,** moteur sans soupapes; moteur à fourreau, à chemise coulissante; **cylinder s. (of a sleeve valve engine),** chemise (intérieure) de cylindre (d'un moteur sans soupapes); *Aut:* **axle s.,** boîte *f* d'essieu; *Veh:* **axle tree s.,** couvre-essieu *m*, *pl.* couvre-essieux; (*b*) *Sm.a:* **cleaning rod s.,** porte-baguette *m inv*; (*c*) *Mil:* tromblon *m* (lance-grenades); (*d*) *Tls:* barillet *m* (de palmer); (*e*) *Rec:* pochette *f* (de disque). **3.** *Tchn:* **(air) s.,** manche (à air); **suction s.,** manche d'aspiration; *Aer: etc:* **deflation s.,** manche de dégonflage, de dégonflement; **inflation s.,** manche de gonflage, de gonflement; *MilAv:* **s. (target),** manche(-cible) *f*, *pl.* manches(-cibles); **towed s.,** manche(-cible) remorquée.

sleeveboard ['sli:vbɔ:d], *s.* jeannette *f*; pied *m* à manches, à repasser; planchette *f* à repasser (des manches); **(tailor's) s.,** passe-carreau *m*, *pl.* passe-carreaux; cifran *m*.

sleeved [sli:vd], *a.* (vêtement) à manches; **long-s., short-s., dress,** robe à manches longues, à manches courtes.

sleeveless ['sli:vlis], *a.* (robe, etc.) sans manches.

sleigh[1] [slei], *s.* traîneau *m*; **s. bell,** grelot *m*, clochette *f*; **s. dog,** chien de traîneau; **s. ride,** promenade en traîneau.

sleigh[2]. **1.** *v.i.* aller, voyager, se promener, en traîneau. **2.** *v.tr.* transporter (des marchandises, etc.) en traîneau.

sleigher ['sleiər], *s.* voyageur, -euse, promeneur, -euse, en traîneau.

sleighing ['sleiiŋ], *s.* **1.** promenades *fpl* en traîneau. **2.** transport *m* en traîneau.

sleight [slait], *s.* (*a*) *A:* habileté *f*, adresse *f*, dextérité *f*; (*b*) tromperie *f*, fourberie *f* habile, passe-passe *m inv*; **s. of hand,** prestidigitation *f*; escamotage *m*; tour de passe-passe.

slender ['slendər], *a.* **1.** mince, ténu; fusiforme; (*of figure*) svelte, fluet, gracile, effilé, élancé, délié; (*of fingers*) fuselé; **s. waist,** taille fine, fluette; **s. hands,** mains déliées; **s. thread,** fil délié; **this dress makes you look s.,** cette robe vous amincit; **to get, grow, become, more s.,** s'amincir. **2.** (*of intelligence, hope, etc.*) faible; (*of income, etc.*) modique, maigre, médiocre, modeste, exigu; **s. means,** ressources médiocres, exiguës; maigres ressources; **of s. means,** peu fortuné, pauvre.

slenderize ['slendəraiz], *v.tr. NAm:* amincir.

slenderly ['slendəli], *adv.* **1.** (*of pers.*) **s. built,** d'une taille svelte; fluet. **2.** maigrement, faiblement, modestement, modiquement.

slenderness ['slendənis], *s.* **1.** minceur *f*, ténuité *f*; sveltesse *f* (de qn, de la taille). **2.** maigreur *f*, modicité *f*, exiguïté *f* (d'une fortune, etc.); faiblesse *f* (des ressources).

sleuth[1] ['slu:θ], *s.* (*a*) limier *m*; (*b*) *F:* limier, détective *m*; **the sleuths,** les limiers de la police.

sleuth[2], *v.i. F:* faire le détective.

sleuthhound ['slu:θhaund], *s.* (*a*) limier *m*; (*b*) *F:* limier, détective *m*.

slew[1] [slu:], *s.* **1.** *Nau:* virage *m*; *Aut:* tête(-)à(-)queue *m inv.* **2.** *Elcs:* balayage *m* rapide; **s. rate,** vitesse *f* de balayage (rapide).

slew[2]. **1.** *v.tr.* **to s. sth. round,** faire pivoter qch. **2.** *v.i.* (*of crane, etc.*) **to s. (round),** pivoter, virer; (*of car*) faire un tête(-)à(-)queue; *Nau:* dévirer, trévirer; *Nau:* **to s. to starboard,** venir brusquement sur tribord; *Av:* **to s. round in taxying,** faire cheval de bois.

slew[3], *s. NAm:* flopée *f*, tas *m*; grand nombre, grande quantité.

slewed [slu:d], *a. P:* ivre, bourré, blindé.

slewing ['slu:iŋ], *s.* **1.** pivotement *m*, virage *m* (d'une grue, etc.). **2.** *Elcs:* = SLEW[1] 2.

sley [slei], *s. Tex:* ros *m*, rot *m*.

slice[1] [slais], *s.* **1.** (*a*) tranche *f* (de pain); côte *f*, tranche (de melon); darne *f* (de gros poisson); (*thin*) lèche *f*, lèchette *f* (de viande, etc.); **(round) s. of lemon,** rond *m*, rondelle *f*, rouelle *f*, de citron; **s. of bread and jam,** tartine *f* de confiture; **to cut bread in slices,** couper le pain en tranches; *Mil:* **divisional s.,** tranche divisionnaire; (*b*) **to take a large s. of the credit for sth.,** s'attribuer une large part du mérite de qch.; **a s. of life,** une tranche de vie. **2.** (*a*) *Dom.Ec:* **fish s.,** truelle *f* (à poisson); (*b*) *Tls: Ind: etc:* **s. bar,** lance *f* à feu, ringard *m* (de chaufferie); (*c*) *Paperm:* règle *f* d'épaisseur; régulateur *m* (dans la manufacture du papier couché); (*d*) *Typ:* (i) racloir *m*; (ii) planchette *f* (de galée à coulisse); **s. galley,** galée à coulisse. **3.** *Golf:* coup qui fait dévier la balle à droite; *Ten:* coup droit coupé; chop *m*.

slice[2], *v.tr.* **1.** **to s. (up),** couper, découper (qch.) en tranches; **to s. off a piece of chicken,** trancher, couper, détacher, un morceau de poulet; **to s. thinly,** émincer (la viande, etc.). **2.** *Lit:* fendre (l'air, les vagues, etc.). **3.** (*a*) *Ten:* couper (la balle); (*b*) *Golf:* faire dévier la balle à droite.

slicer ['slaisər], *s.* machine *f* à trancher (le pain, le jambon, etc.).

slicing ['slaisiŋ], *s.* coupe *f* en tranches.

slick[1] [slik], *a. F:* (*a*) habile, adroit; (*b*) bien rangé; en bon ordre; lisse; luisant; (*c*) malin, rusé; **a s. customer,** une fine mouche, un fin matois.

slick[2], *s.* **1.** *Tls:* **s. (chisel),** lissoir *m*. **2.** (*a*) nappe *f* d'huile; (*b*) plaque *f* de neige.

slick[3]. **1.** *v.tr.* (*a*) *Leath:* étirer, lisser (une peau); (*b*) **to s. one's hair down,** lisser ses cheveux. **2.** *U.S:* (*a*) *v.tr.* mettre (une chambre) en ordre; (*b*) *v.i.* **to s. up,** faire un bout de toilette; s'attifer; se pomponner.

slick[4], *s. Metall:* schlich *m*; minerai broyé.

slickenside(s) ['sliənsaid(z)], *s.*(*pl*) *Geol:* surface *f* de glissement; strie *f* de froissement; cuirasse filonienne.

slicker ['slikər], *s.* **1.** *Tls:* (*a*) *Leath:* étire *f*; (*b*) *Metall:* polissoir *m* de mouleur. **2.** *NAm:* imperméable *m*; manteau *m* en toile huilée; ciré *m*. **3.** *NAm: F:* (*a*) escroc adroit, combinard *m*, aigrefin *m*; (*b*) **(city) s.,** affranchi *m*, homme du milieu.

slickness ['sliknis], *s. F:* (*a*) habileté *f*, dextérité *f*, adresse *f*; ruse *f*; (*b*) ruse, astuces *fpl*.

slide[1] [slaid], *s.* **1.** (*a*) glissade *f*, glissement *m*; **to have a s.,** faire une glissade; *Av:* **tail s.,** glissade sur la queue; (*b*) éboulement *m*, glissement (de terrain); (*c*) *Mus:* (i) (*ornament*) coulé *m*; (ii) (*in violin playing, etc.*) glissade. **2.** (*a*) (*on snow or ice*) glissoire *f*, glissade; (*in playground*) toboggan *m*; (*b*) plan *m* de glissement; piste *f* en pente; *For:* **timber s.,** glissoir *m*; (*c*) *Av:* toboggan, rampe *f* (de secours); **escape s.,** toboggan d'évacuation; **dual escape s.,** rampe double d'évacuation; **inflatable escape s.,** toboggan pneumatique d'évacuation. **3.** (*a*) *Mec.E:* glissière *f*; guide *m*; coulisse *f*; coulant *m* (de cage de mine); **s. lathe,** tour *m* parallèle, à charioter; **s. bar,** coulisseau *m*; (i) glissière de crosse; (ii) guide de la tête de piston; (iii) coulisse, jumelle *f* (de tour); **s. bar bracket,** porte-glissière *m inv*; **s. face,** voie *f* à glissière; **s. guide,** glissière-guide *f*, *pl.* glissières-guides; guide (de pièce mécanique mobile); **s. guide groove,** rainure *f* de guidage; rainure-guide *f*, *pl.* rainures-guides; **s. guide rib,** nervure *f* de guidage; nervure-guide *f*, *pl.* nervures-guides; **s. rail,** rail *m* de glissement; glissière; **s. rest,** support *m* à chariot; (*of lathe*) chariot *m* porte-outil(s); support porte-outils, chariot de tour; **revolving s. rest,** chariot tournant; **self-acting s. rest,** chariot à marche automatique; **s. rod,** tige directrice; **s. shoe,** glissière; **s. fit,** ajustage glissant; *Mch.Tls:* **bed, tool, s.,** chariot porte-outil; **bottom s.,** chariot inférieur (de tour); **cutter s.,** chariot à couteaux (de raboteuse à bois); **turret s.,** chariot porte-tourelle (de tour); **cross s.,** coulisseau; chariot transversal (de tour, etc.); *Aut:* **seat s.,** glissière de siège; **window s.,** glissière, coulant, de glace; (*b*) *Artil:* **(recoil) slides,** glissières (de recul); (*of machine gun*) **belt feed, strip feed, s.,** glissière d'alimentation. **4.** (*a*) pièce *f* (d'une machine, etc.) qui glisse, qui coulisse; coulant (d'une bourse); curseur *m* (d'une règle, d'un compas, d'une hausse de fusil, etc.); coulisseau, réglette *f* (d'une règle à calcul); *Row:* glissière; **pull-out s. (of desk, etc.), writing s. (of desk),** tablette coulissante, tirette *f* (d'un bureau, etc.); **s. rule,** règle à calcul (logarithmique); règle à calculer; **circular s. rule,** cercle *m* à calculer; **s. rule dial,** cadran *m* à réticule de règle à calcul; **s. calliper,** calibre *m*, pied *m*, à coulisse; *esp. NAm:* **s. fastener,** fermeture éclair, à glissière; *Opt:* **draw s., focusing s.,** tube *m* de réglage, tube à tirage, coulant (d'un microscope, etc.); *El:* **s. contact,** curseur, frotteur *m*; **s. resistance, selector,** rhéostat *m*, sélecteur *m*, à curseur; **s. wire,** fil *m* à contact glissant; curseur; **s. wire bridge,** pont à fil; **s. wire potentiometer,** potentiomètre à contact glissant; **s. wire rheostat,** rhéostat à curseur; *El: Elcs:* **s. back,** baisse *f* de potentiel grille; **s. back voltmeter,** voltmètre à comparaison; (*b*) *Mch:* tiroir *m* (de distribution); **lead of s.,** avance *f* du tiroir; **shell s.,** tiroir en coquille; **scavenge s.,** tiroir de balayage; **starting s.,** tiroir de lancement; **s. box,** boîte de tiroir; **s. face,** glace *f* du tiroir; **s. rod,** tige de tiroir; **s. valve,** tiroir (de distribution); soupape *f*, valve *f*, vanne *f*, à tiroir; **balanced, equilibrated, s. valve,** tiroir compensé, équilibré; **cut-off s. valve,** tiroir de détente; **rocking s. valve,** tiroir oscillant; **s. valve case, chest,** boîte à tiroir; **s. valve distributor,** distributeur *m* à tiroir; **s. valve face,** barrette *f* de tiroir; **s. valve gear,** distribution *f* par tiroir; **s. valve ports,** orifices *m* du tiroir; **s. valve rod, spindle,** tige de tiroir; (*c*) *Mus:* coulisse (de trombone, etc.); **s. trombone, trumpet,** trombone, trompette, à coulisse; (*d*) *Mus:* **(tuning) s.,** pompe *f* d'accord (d'un instrument à vent); **s. head,**

pompe d'accord (d'une flûte, etc.). 5. (*a*) (*microscopy*) (**object**) **s.**, (plaque *f*, lame *f*) porte-objet *m*, *pl.* porte-objet(s); lamelle *f*; (*b*) *Phot:* (**colour**) **s.**, diapositive *f* (en couleur); *A:* **lantern s.**, diapositive de projection; vue *f* (de projection); projection (lumineuse); **lecture illustrated with slides,** conférence avec projections; **stereo s.**, plaque stéréoscopique; **s. carrier,** châssis *m* (passe-vues) (de projecteur). 6. *Phot:* **dark s.**, châssis porte-plaques; châssis négatif; **roller blind s.**, châssis à brisures; **book form s.**, châssis à charnière. 7. *Toil:* (**hair**) **s.**, barrette.

slide[2], *v.* (*p.t. & p.p.* **slid** [slid])

I. *v.i. & tr.* 1. *v.i.* (*a*) glisser, coulisser; **mechanism that slides between runners,** mécanisme qui glisse, coulisse, entre des guides; (*of part*) **to s. into mesh,** engrener par coulissement; (*b*) (*of pers.*) **to s.** (**on ice**), faire des glissades; **to s. down the banisters,** glisser le long de la rampe; **to s. down a rope,** se laisser couler, se laisser glisser le long d'une corde; *Nau:* s'affaler par un cordage; **to s. down a slope,** glisser sur une pente; (*c*) **he slid on the floor and fell heavily,** il a glissé sur le parquet et est tombé lourdement; **the dish slid off the table,** le plat a glissé de sur la table; (*d*) **to s. over a delicate subject,** glisser sur un sujet délicat; (*e*) **he slid behind the curtain,** il s'est glissé derrière le rideau; (*f*) **to let things, everything, s.,** laisser tout aller à la dérive, à vau-l'eau; se désintéresser de tout. 2. *v.tr.* (faire) glisser; (*a*) **to s. sth. into one's pocket,** glisser qch. dans sa poche; **he slid the drawer back (into place),** il a tout doucement fermé le tiroir; (*b*) *For:* **to s. timber,** faire glisser, lancer, du bois sur le glissoir.

II. (*compound verbs*) 1. **slide away, by,** *v.i. Lit:* (*of time*) s'écouler, couler, passer.

2. **slide down,** *v.i.* descendre en glissant; glisser jusqu'en bas.

3. **slide off,** *v.i. F:* décamper; filer.

4. **slide out,** *v.i. F:* se glisser dehors; s'éclipser discrètement; se défiler.

slider ['slaidər], *s.* 1. (*a*) (*pers.*) glisseur, -euse; (*b*) *Rept: U.S:* (variété de) tortue *f* aquatique. 2. curseur *m* (d'une bobine électrique, etc.); tirette *f* (de fermeture éclair). 3. (*a*) *Veh:* sassoire *f* (de l'avant-train); (*b*) *Nau:* chariot *m* de gouvernail.

slideway ['slaidwei], *s.* 1. *Mch:* coulisse *f* (de tiroir). 2. *For:* glissoir *m*.

sliding[1] ['slaidiŋ], *a.* glissant, coulissant, mobile; **s. door,** porte coulissante, glissante; porte à coulisse, à glissières; **s. window,** fenêtre, glace, à glissières, coulissante; **s. panel,** panneau coulissant, mobile; **s. sash,** châssis à coulisse, à glissières, à guillotine (de fenêtre); **s. seat,** (i) *Row:* banc à coulisses, à glissières; glissière *f*; (ii) *Aut:* siège réglable, mobile; **s. ring, runner,** coulant *m* (de bourse, etc.); **s. calliper, gauge,** calibre, équerre, pied, à coulisse; **s. leg (of tripod stand),** pied coulissant, branche coulissante (d'un trépied); **s. (leg) tripod,** trépied à branches coulissantes, trépied télescopique; *Opt:* **s. tube,** tube à tirage, coulant (d'un microscope, etc.); *Phot:* **s. front camera,** appareil à décentrement; *El:* **s. contact,** contact glissant; curseur *m*; **s. condenser,** condensateur à armatures mobiles; **s. switch,** commutateur à glissement; *Mec.E:* **s. parts,** organes mobiles; **s. joint,** joint glissant; **s. rod,** allonge *f*; **s. shaft,** arbre coulissant; **s. axle,** essieu mobile; **s. dog,** crabot baladeur; **s. gear,** engrenage mobile, train baladeur; **s. gear transmission,** transmission par train baladeur; *Mch.Tls:* **s. bed, bench,** banc coulissant; **s. bed lathe,** tour à banc coulissant; **s. headstock, puppet,** poupée mobile, poupée courante (de tour); **s. head milling machine,** fraiseuse à tête coulissante; **s. table milling machine,** fraiseuse à table coulissante; *Surv:* **s. staff, vane,** mire à coulisse, mire mobile; *Mth:* **s. vector,** vecteur glissant; glisseur *m*; *Ski:* **s. step,** pas glissé; *Pol.Ec: etc:* **s. scale,** échelle *f* mobile (des prix, etc.); **s. scale tariff,** tarif dégressif; **s. wage scale,** échelle mobile des salaires.

sliding[2], *s.* (*a*) glissement *m*; glissades *fpl*; (*b*) *Mec.E:* coulissement *m*, glissement (des organes mobiles, etc.); **s. path,** guidage *m*; (*c*) *Mch.Tls:* chariotage (longitudinal); **s. lathe,** tour à charioter; (*d*) *For:* glissage *m* (du bois); lancement *m* (du bois sur le glissoir).

slight[1] [slait], *a.* 1. (*thin*) mince, ténu; (*of figure*) frêle; peu musclé; menu, svelte, fluet; maigrelet, maigrichon, maigriot. 2. (*small*) (*of pain, mistake, etc.*) léger, petit; (*of intelligence, etc.*) faible; (*of profit, etc.*) maigre, petit; (*of occasion, etc.*) de peu d'importance; (*of damage*) peu considérable; (*of wound*) sans gravité; **a s. cold,** un petit rhume; *Mil:* **s. work,** ouvrage à faible profil; **to make a s. gesture,** faire un léger geste; esquisser un geste; **a s. accident,** un petit accident; **there are s. grounds for complaint,** il y a peu de raisons de se plaindre; **a s. improvement,** un léger mieux; **to a s. extent,** quelque peu; **not the slightest danger,** pas le moindre danger; **without the slightest difficulty,** sans aucune difficulté; **to take offence at the slightest thing,** se fâcher pour un rien; se piquer d'un rien; **on the slightest pretext,** sous un prétexte bien mince, quelconque; **I haven't the slightest idea,** je n'en ai pas la moindre idée; **not in the slightest,** pas du tout, pas le moins du monde; aucunement; **I didn't reproach him in the slightest,** je ne lui ai pas fait le moindre reproche.

slight[2], *s.* 1. *A:* mésestime *f* (**for,** de). 2. manque *m* de considération, d'égards; affront *m*; **to put a s. on s.o.,** faire peu de cas de qn; traiter qn sans considération; manquer d'égards pour, à, qn; négliger qn; faire un affront à qn.

slight[3], *v.tr.* 1. *A:* aplanir (qch.); *A.Mil:* raser (une ville, etc.). 2. (*a*) faire peu de cas de (qn); traiter (qn) sans considération; manquer d'égards pour, à (qn); négliger, dédaigner (qn); faire un affront, une impolitesse, à (qn); ravaler (qn); **to feel slighted,** éprouver un froissement, subir des affronts; (*b*) *O:* méconnaître (ses devoirs).

slighting ['slaitiŋ], *a.* (air) de mépris.

slightingly ['slaitiŋli], *adv.* avec peu de considération, d'égards; dédaigneusement.

slightly ['slaitli], *adv.* 1. **s. built,** (i) au corps frêle; (ii) à la taille mince, svelte. 2. légèrement, faiblement, peu; **s. better,** (il va) un petit peu mieux; **to be s. out of sorts,** être un tantinet indisposé; **I know him s.,** je le connais un peu; **we are s. disappointed,** nous sommes quelque peu déçus; **he looks s. foreign,** il a l'air un peu étranger.

slightness ['slaitnis], *s.* 1. minceur *f*, ténuité *f* (d'une pièce de bois, etc.); sveltesse *f*, minceur (du corps). 2. légèreté *f*, petitesse *f* (d'une faute, etc.); faiblesse *f* (de l'intelligence de qn, d'une différence, etc.); maigreur *f* (du profit, etc.); peu *m* d'importance, insignifiance *f* (des dégâts, etc.).

slily ['slaili], *adv.* 1. (*a*) *A:* avec finesse; adroitement; (*b*) sournoisement; cauteleusement. 2. malicieusement; d'une manière espiègle.

slim[1] [slim], *a.* (**slimmer; slimmest**) 1. (*a*) svelte, élancé, mince, gracile, fluet, menu; (*of fingers, etc.*) fuselé, menu; **s.-waisted,** à la taille svelte; (*b*) (*of chance, hope, etc.*) mince, léger; **on the slimmest evidence,** sur les preuves les moins concluantes. 2. *A:* rusé; malin, -igne; astucieux.

slim[2], *v.* (**slimmed**) 1. *v.tr.* amincir; **dress that slims you (down), that is slimming,** robe amincissante, qui vous amincit, qui vous maigrit. 2. *v.i.* **to be slimming,** maigrir; suivre un régime amaigrissant.

slime[1] [slaim], *s.* 1. limon *m*, vase *f*; (*used as a fertilizer*) wagage *m*; (*gold mining*) boue *f*, poussier *m*, de minerai; slime *m*; *Metall: Min:* **slimes,** schlamm(s) *m*(*pl*); **anode s.,** boue de l'anode; **s. pit,** bassin *m* de dépôt des boues, des schlamms; **stone covered with a green s.,** pierre couverte d'une boue verte et gluante. 2. (*a*) humeur visqueuse (qui couvre les poissons, etc.); bave *f* (de limace, etc.); (*b*) *Bac:* **s. bacteria,** myxobactériales *f*, synbactéries *f*. 3. *A:* bitume *m* (liquide); **s. pit,** puits de bitume.

slime[2], *v.tr.* couvrir de limon, de vase, de bave; **hull slimed with mud,** coque engluée de boue.

sliminess ['slaiminis], *s.* 1. état vaseux, boueux, gluant; viscosité *f*. 2. *F:* servilité *f*, obséquiosité *f*.

sliming ['slaimiŋ], *s. Bac:* croissance *f*, développement *m*, de myxobactériales.

slimly ['slimli], *adv.* 1. **s. built,** à la taille mince, svelte; gracile, fluet, menu. 2. *A:* (agir) avec ruse, avec astuce, astucieusement.

slimmer ['slimər], *s.* personne *f* qui suit un régime amaigrissant.

slimming ['slimiŋ], *s.* amincissement *m*; **to be on a s. diet,** suivre un régime amaigrissant; **s. course,** cure *f* d'amaigrissement.

slimness ['slimnis], *s.* 1. taille *f* mince; minceur *f*, sveltesse *f*, gracilité *f*; **she is losing her s.,** sa taille commence à s'empâter. 2. *A:* ruse *f*, astuce *f*.

slimy ['slaimi], *a.* 1. (*a*) limoneux, vaseux; **s. mud,** boue grasse; (*b*) (*of paste, etc.*) visqueux, gluant. 2. (*a*) couvert de vase, de limon; (pavé, etc.) glissant; (*b*) (*of fish*) couvert d'une sécrétion visqueuse, gluante; (*of slug, etc.*) couvert de bave. 3. *F:* (*of pers.*) servile, obséquieux; **s.-tongued,** doucereux, mielleux.

sling[1] [sliŋ], *s.* 1. fronde *f*; *Lit:* **the slings and arrows of outrageous fortune,** les traits *m* dont nous meurtrit l'outrageuse fortune. 2. (*a*) *Med:* écharpe *f*; **to have one's arm in a s.,** avoir, porter, le bras en écharpe; (*b*) bandoulière *f* (de harpe, etc.); bretelle *f*, courroie *f* (de bidon, etc.); bretelle (de fusil, de sac à dos, de civière, etc.); brassières *fpl* (de sac à dos); *Mil:* **slings and belts,** buffleterie(s) *f*(*pl*); **sword (belt) s.,** bélière *f*; **s. swivel,** battant *m* de crosse *f* (de fusil); **s. cart,** triqueballe *m*; *U.S:* **s. chair,** transatlantique *m*, *F:* transat *m*; (*c*) (*for hoisting sth.*) *Nau: etc:* élingue *f*; cravate *f*; (*for hoisting animals*) ventrière *f*; **yard s.,** cravate, estrope *f*, de hissage; **bag s.,** élingue à sacs; **platform s.,** plateau *m* à caissage; **boat slings,** pattes *f* d'embarcation; **chain s.,** élingue en chaîne; **net s.,** élingue en filet; filet *m* d'élingue, de chargement; **rope s.,** élingue en filin; **s. load,** palanquée *f*; élinguée *f*; **s. dog,** patte, griffe *f*, d'élingue; *Const:* (**rope**) **s.,** braye *f*, brayer *m* (de maçon); (*d*) (*for hoisting s.o.*) agui *m*, chaise *f* (pour charpentier, calfat, etc.); **rescue s.,** bridage *m* (de sauvetage); (*e*) *Nau:* suspente *f*; **yard s.,** *U.S:* **quarter s.,** suspente de vergue; **rudder s.,** suspente de gouvernail; **s. band,** collier de suspente; (*f*) *Farr: Vet:* travail *m* (pour chevaux), *pl.* travails.

sling[2], *v.tr.* (*p.t. & p.p.* **slung** [slʌŋ]) 1. lancer, jeter ((i) avec une fronde, (ii) *F:* avec la main); *F:* **to s. mud at s.o.,** couvrir qn de boue, de fange; traîner qn dans la boue, la fange; déblatérer contre, éclabousser, qn; **to s. s.o. out,** faire déguerpir qn, flanquer qn dehors; *P:* **to s. the lingo,** parler l'argot. 2. suspendre; **to s. a hammock,** suspendre, *Nau:* crocher, gréer, un hamac; **to s. sth. over one's shoulder,** jeter qch. sur l'épaule; passer la bandoulière de qch. sur son épaule; mettre qch. en bandoulière; **slung rifle,** fusil à la grenadière; **slung crosswise,** en bandoulière; *A:* **slung shot,** assommoir *m* (boulet attaché à une courroie); **to carry sth. slung round one's neck,** porter qch. autour du cou; *Mil:* **to s. arms,** mettre l'arme (i) à la bretelle, (ii) en bandoulière; **s. arms!** l'arme à la bretelle! 3. élinguer (un fardeau); **to s. up a load with a crane,** hisser, guinder, un fardeau avec une grue.

sling[3], *s.* boisson composée de gin, de rhum, d'eau-de-vie, etc., sucrée et parfumée; grog *m*.

slingback ['sliŋbæk], *a. & s.* (chaussure *f*) à talon découvert; sandale *f*.

slinger ['sliŋər], *s.* 1. (*pers.*) (*a*) *A.Mil:* frondeur *m*; (*b*) *F:* lanceur, -euse, jeteur, -euse (de pierres, etc.); (*c*) *Nau: etc:* élingueur *m*. 2. (*device*) *Tchn:* bague *f* d'étanchéité; **sand s.,** machine *f* à projeter du sable; *Av:* **s. ring,** anneau distributeur, bague distributrice (d'huile, etc.).

slinging ['sliŋiŋ], *s. Nau: etc:* élingage *m* (d'un fardeau).

slingshot ['sliŋʃɔt], *s. NAm:* fronde *f*.

slink[1] [sliŋk], *s.* 1. (*a*) allure furtive; (*b*) individu *m* à l'allure furtive; rôdeur *m*. 2. *Husb:* (*a*) veau, etc., né avant terme; (*b*) chair *f*, peau *f*, d'animal né avant terme.

slink[2], *v.* (*p.t. & p.p.* **slunk** [slʌŋk]) 1. *v.i.* **to s. off, away,** partir furtivement, en catimini; s'éclipser; **to s. in,** entrer furtivement. 2. *v.tr.* (*of animal*) **to s. its young,** mettre bas avant terme; **s. calf,** veau né avant terme.

slinking[1] ['sliŋkiŋ], *a.* (regard, etc.) furtif.

slinking[2], *s.* 1. **s. off, away,** départ furtif; **s. in,** entrée furtive. 2. (*of animal*) mise *f* bas avant terme.

slinkskin ['sliŋkskin], *s. Tan:* peau *f* d'animal né avant terme.

slinky ['sliŋki], *a. F:* (*a*) (*of figure*) svelte, mince; (*b*) (*of clothing*) collant, ajusté.

slip[1] [slip], *s.* 1. (*a*) glissade *f*, glissement *m*, faux pas; **it was only a s. of the hand,** sa main a glissé; *Engr:* **s. of the graver,** échappement *m* du burin; (*b*) **to give s.o. the s.,** se dérober à qn; fausser compagnie à qn; faire faux bond à qn; (*c*) faute *f*, erreur *f*, d'inattention; faute d'étourderie; mot *m* de travers; **to make a s.,** faire une étourderie, un lapsus; **s. of the pen,** petite erreur d'orthographe; **he made a s. of the tongue,** la langue lui a fourché; **it was a s. of the tongue,** ce n'est pas ça que j'ai voulu dire; (*d*) écart *m* (de conduite); peccadille *f*; (*e*) *Geol:* glissement *m*, effondrement *m*, éboulement *m* (de terrain); glissement (de l'une des deux lèvres d'une faille); **s. fault,** faille d'effondrement; *Cryst:* **s. band, line,** ligne de glissement; **s. face, plane,** face, plan, de glissement. 2. (*a*) glissement, patinage *m*; **s. noose,** nœud coulant; **s. stitch,** (i) *Knit:* maille glissée; (ii) *Needlew:* point perdu; *Nau: etc:* **s. hook,** croc *m* à échappement, d'étalingure; **s. rope,** amarre *f* en double; **s. knot,** nœud coulant; *Carp: etc:* languette rapportée; **s. tongue joint,** assemblage à languette rapportée; *Mec.E:* **belt s.,** patinage de la courroie; **s. fit,** ajustage doux; **s. bolt,** verrou à platine; *Aut:* **clutch s.,** patinage de l'embrayage; **s. clutch, connection,** embrayage par glissement, à friction; *El:* **s. of the rotor,** glissement du rotor; **s. ring,** bague collectrice (de dynamo, etc.); anneau collecteur de prise de courant; collecteur *m*; **s. ring brush,** balai de bague collectrice; **s. ring motor,** moteur à bagues collectrices; (*b*) *Av: Nau:* recul *m* (de l'hélice); **apparent, negative, true, s.,** recul apparent, négatif, effectif; **s. ratio,** coefficient de recul; (*c*) *Av:* **turn and s. indicator,** indicateur de glissement latéral; (*d*) déperdition *f*, perte *f* (d'eau dans une pompe, de gaz dans un compteur, etc.). **3.** laisse *f*, slip *m* (de chien de chasse). **4.** *Rail:* **s. carriage, coach,** voiture, rame, décrochée, à décrocher, en cours de route; **s. points, s. switch, slips,** traversée(s)-jonction(s) *f*(*pl*); **double, simple, s. points,** traversée-jonction double, simple. **5.** (*a*) *Cost:* **(foundation) s.,** combinaison *f* (de femme); fond *m* de robe; **half, waist, s.,** jupon *m*; **your slip's showing,** votre jupon dépasse; *F:* vous cherchez une belle-mère? *O:* **gym s.,** tunique *f* (d'écolière); *A:* **bathing slips,** slip de bain; (*b*) **(pillow) s.,** taie *f* d'oreiller. **6.** (*a*) cale *f* de chargement (d'un bac); (*b*) *N.Arch:* **building s.,** cale, chantier *m*, de construction; **ship on the slips,** navire sur cale(s), en chantier, en construction. **7.** *Bookb:* nerf *m*. **8.** *Th:* **the slips,** les coulisses *f*. **9.** *Cr:* (*a*) chasseur posté à droite du garde-guichet; (*b*) **the slips,** station *f* à droite du garde-guichet; **to cut the ball through the slips,** détourner la balle à droite du guichet.

slip[2], *v.* **(slipped** [slipt])

I. *v.i.* **1.** (*a*) glisser; (*of knot*) couler, courir; (*of earth, etc.*) s'ébouler; *Mec.E: etc:* (*of belt, etc.*) patiner, glisser; *El: etc:* (*of frequency, etc.*) se décaler; **his foot slipped,** son pied a glissé; le pied lui a manqué; **I slipped on a banana skin, in the mud,** j'ai glissé sur une peau de banane, dans la boue; **he slipped off his chair onto the ground,** il a glissé de sa chaise jusqu'à terre; *F:* **you're slipping,** tu perds les pédales; **to s. from s.o.'s hands, through s.o.'s fingers,** échapper des mains de qn; glisser entre les doigts de qn; **the knife slipped from his hands,** le couteau lui a glissé des mains; **it slipped through my fingers,** cela m'est échappé des doigts; (*b*) se glisser, se couler; **to s. into a room,** se glisser, se couler, dans une pièce; entrer à pas de loup dans la pièce; **he slipped off the table,** il s'est laissé glisser de sur la table; **to s. through the crowd,** se faufiler, se couler, dans la foule; **to s. into bed,** se couler, se glisser, entre les draps, dans son lit; **to s. into one's dressing gown,** passer, enfiler, sa robe de chambre; **to s. into bad habits,** se laisser aller à, prendre, de mauvaises habitudes; **error that has slipped into the text,** faute qui s'est glissée, qui a passé, dans le texte; (*c*) *F:* aller (vivement); **just s. round, across, over, down, to the post,** allez donc, faites un saut, courez, jusqu'au bureau de poste; **to s. across the fields,** passer, filer, à travers les champs; (*d*) (*of bolt*) **to s. home,** fermer à fond. **2.** (*a*) faire une (faute d')étourderie, une bévue; se fourvoyer, se tromper; (*b*) *A:* faire un écart de conduite. **3. to let s.,** lâcher (un lévrier, etc.); laisser échapper (une belle occasion, une observation, un secret); **to let one's pen s. from one's fingers,** laisser échapper son stylo; **he let s. one or two words,** il lui est échappé un ou deux mots.

II. *v.tr.* **1.** (*a*) se dégager de (qch.); (*of animal*) **to s. its chain, leash, lead,** se détacher; (*of horse*) **to s. the halter,** se délicoter; **the dog has slipped its collar,** le chien s'est dégagé de son collier; (*b*) **his name has slipped my mind, my memory,** son nom m'échappe, ne me revient pas; son nom m'est sorti de la mémoire; **to s. s.o.'s attention,** échapper à l'attention de qn. **2.** (*a*) *Ven:* lâcher, découper (les chiens); **to s. the hounds,** laisser courre; (*b*) *Nau:* **to s. a cable,** larguer, filer, une amarre par le bout; **to s. one's moorings,** filer le corps-mort; (*c*) *Rail:* décrocher (une voiture en cours de route); (*d*) (*of animal*) **to s. its young,** mettre bas avant terme; (*e*) *Cards:* **to s. the cut,** faire sauter la coupe. **3.** (*a*) couler, glisser (qch. dans la main à, de, qn, une lettre à la poste); **to s. the bolt (home),** pousser le verrou à fond; **he slipped the letter into his pocket,** il a glissé la lettre dans sa poche; **I slipped my arm round her waist,** je lui ai passé mon bras autour de la taille; (*b*) *Med:* **to s. a disc,** se faire une hernie discale; (*c*) *Knit:* **to s. one,** glisser une maille; (*d*) *F:* **to s. sth., one, over on s.o.,** donner le change à qn; mystifier, duper, qn. **4.** *Aut:* **to s. the clutch,** laisser patiner l'embrayage; débrayer à demi.

III. (*compound verbs*) **1. slip away,** *v.i.* (*a*) (*of pers.*) filer (à l'anglaise); s'esquiver, s'éclipser; partir en tapinois; se défiler; (*b*) (*of time*) s'écouler, couler, (se) passer, fuir; *Lit:* **youth is slipping away,** la jeunesse s'enfuit.

2. slip by, *v.i.* = SLIP AWAY (*b*).

3. slip down, *v.i.* (*a*) descendre en glissant; se couler en bas (de l'arbre, etc.); (*b*) (*of socks, etc.*) tomber; glisser.

4. slip in, *v.i.* entrer (en passant).

5. slip off. (*a*) *v.tr.* enlever, ôter, retirer (un vêtement); (*b*) *v.i.* (i) filer, s'esquiver, s'éclipser, se défiler; (ii) se détacher; tomber.

6. slip on, *v.tr.* enfiler, passer, mettre (un vêtement).

7. slip out, *v.i.* (*a*) s'échapper; **to let sth. s. out,** laisser échapper qch.; **the secret has slipped out,** le secret a transpiré; (*b*) sortir (à la dérobée); **I'm just slipping out for a few minutes,** je sors pour quelques moments.

8. slip up, *v.i.* (*a*) se tromper; faire une faute, une bourde; (*b*) échouer; faire fiasco.

slip[3], *s.* **1.** (*a*) (i) *Hort:* bouture *f*, plant *m*, plançon *m*, plantard *m*; (*for grafting*) scion *m*; (ii) *Lit:* (*pers.*) rejeton *m*; (*b*) *F:* **s. of a boy, of a girl,** garçon fluet, élancé, jeune fille fluette, élancée; **mere s. of a woman,** tout petit bout de femme; **fine s. of a girl,** beau brin de fille; (*c*) *Ich: Com: A:* petite sole. **2.** (*a*) bande étroite (de toile, de terre, etc.); **s. of paper,** bande, fiche *f*, bordereau *m*, bout *m*, de papier; **pay (advice) s.,** *esp. NAm:* **wage s.,** bulletin *m*, feuille *f*, fiche, de paie; *F: O:* **s. of a room, of a garden,** petite chambre étroite, petit jardin étroit; (*b*) *F:* billet *m*, bordereau; *Ins:* projet de police signé par les contractants; (*c*) *Typ:* **(proof) s.,** placard *m*; **to pull the matter in slips,** placarder des épreuves. **3.** *Th:* **slips,** couloir *m* du balcon.

slip[4], *v.tr. Hort:* bouturer (une plante).

slip[5], *s. Cer:* barbotine *f*, engobe *m*; **to paint, coat, with s.,** engober; **s. painting,** engobage *m*.

slipcase ['slipkeis], *s. esp. Publ:* étui *m*.

slipcover ['slipkʌvər], *s. Furn:* housse *f*; *esp. Publ:* étui *m*.

slipe [slaip], *s.* **s. (wool),** laine morte.

slipknot ['slipnɔt], *s.* **1.** nœud coulant. **2.** nœud de bec d'oiseau.

slip-on ['slipɔn], *s. F:* (*a*) **s.-ons,** *a.* **s.-on shoes,** mocassins *m*; (*b*) *NAm:* pull-over *m*, *pl.* pull-overs.

slipover ['slipouvər], *s.* pull-over *m*, *pl.* pull-overs (sans manches).

slippage ['slipidʒ], *s.* (*a*) *Mec.E: etc:* glissement *m*, patinage *m*; ripage *m*, ripement *m* (du câble sur le treuil, etc.); (*b*) *Cryst:* glissement (d'un cristal); (*c*) décalage *m* (entre opérations); *El:* **frequency s.,** décalage de fréquence.

slipper ['slipər], *s.* **1.** (*a*) **(bedroom) s.,** pantoufle *f*; **(ladies' backless) slippers,** mules *f*; **Turkish slippers,** babouches *f*; *O:* **s. bath,** sabotière *f*; (baignoire *f*) sabot *m*; (*b*) *Av:* **s. tank,** réservoir *m* auxiliaire (largable). **2.** (*a*) *Mec.E:* patin *m* (de frein); (*b*) *Mch:* **piston rod s.,** glissière *f* de bielle. **3.** *A:* bassin *m* (de lit). **4.** (*a*) *Prot:* **s. animalcule,** paramécie *f*; (*b*) *Moll:* **s. limpet, s. shell,** crépidula *f*.

slipperiness ['slipərinis], *s.* **1.** nature glissante, glissance *f* (d'une surface). **2.** caractère rusé; sournoiserie *f*, fourberie *f*.

slipperwort ['slipəwəːt], *s. Bot:* calcéolaire *f*.

slippery ['slipəri], *a.* **1.** (*of pavement, handrail, fish, etc.*) glissant; **it's s. (underfoot),** le pavé est gras, glissant; il y a du verglas; ça glisse. **2.** (*a*) instable, incertain; sur lequel on ne peut compter; **to be on a s. slope, on s. ground,** être sur un terrain glissant, une pente glissante; (*b*) (sujet) délicat, scabreux. **3.** fin, rusé, sournois, retors, matois; **he's as s. as an eel,** il glisse, échappe, comme une anguille; il glisse entre les doigts (comme une couleuvre, un poisson); **a s. customer,** une fine mouche; un fin matois.

slipping[1] ['slipiŋ], *a.* glissant, qui glisse; (courroie) qui patine.

slipping[2], *s.* **1.** glissement *m*; glissade *f* (sur une peau de banane, etc.); éboulement *m*, glissement (de terrain, etc.); patinage *m* (d'une courroie, etc.); ripage *m*, ripement *m* (de câble sur le treuil, etc.). **2.** (*a*) *Ven:* découple(r) *m* (des chiens); (*b*) *Rail:* décrochement *m* (d'une voiture en cours de route); (*c*) *Bootm:* **last s.,** déformage *m*.

slippy ['slipi], *a. F:* (*a*) glissant; (*b*) rapide; **to be, look, s.,** se dépêcher, s'activer, se (dé)grouiller; **look s.!** grouille-toi!

sliproad ['sliproud], *s.* bretelle *f* (de raccordement, d'accès); (i) entrée *f*, (ii) sortie *f* (d'une autoroute).

slipshod ['slipʃɔd], *a.* **1.** *A:* en savates. **2. s. person,** personne (i) mal soignée, (ii) négligente; **she looks s.,** elle a l'air débraillé; **s. work,** travail négligé, bâclé; **s. style,** style négligé, débraillé; **book written in a s. manner,** livre écrit sans soin.

slipshodness ['slipʃɔdnis], *s.* négligence *f*.

slipslop ['slipslɔp], *s. F:* **1.** (*a*) aliments *m* liquides; bouillons *mpl*; (*b*) lavasse *f*, rinçure *f*. **2.** écriture *f*, discours *m*, conversation *f*, d'une sensibilité outrée, déplacée; sensiblerie *f*.

slipstream ['slipstriːm], *s.* (*a*) sillage *m*, remous *mpl* (d'air, d'eau); (*b*) *Av:* souffle *m*, vent *m*, de l'hélice; **directional s.,** vent d'hélice de route; **inherent s.,** vent d'hélice automatique; **deflected s.,** aile, voilure, soufflée; écoulement défléchi; **deflected s. aircraft,** avion à aile, à voilure, soufflée; **aileron, wing, in the s.,** aileron, aile, dans le vent de l'hélice; aileron soufflé, aile soufflée.

slip(-)up ['slipʌp], *s.* **1.** gaffe *f*, bévue *f*. **2.** échec *m*, fiasco *m*; **should any s.(-)up occur,** s'il arrive quelque difficulté, quelque contretemps.

slipware ['slipwɛər], *s. Cer:* faïence engobée.

slipway ['slipwei], *s.* **1.** cale *f* (d'un bac, etc.). **2.** *N.Arch:* cale de construction, de lancement; slip *m*, cale (de halage, de carénage); slipway *m*; coi(t)te *f*, couette *f*, anguille *f*; longrine *f*, longuerine *f* (de lancement); coi(t)tes, couettes, mortes; chantier *m* de construction.

slit[1] [slit], *s.* (*a*) fente *f*; fissure *f*, rainure *f*; (*between curtains, etc.*) entrebâillement *m*, entrebâillure *f*; (*in wall, for shooting through, etc.*) taillade *f*; (*made by surgeon*) incision *f*; (*in openwork, etc.*) ajour *m*; **s. of a letterbox,** guichet *m* d'une boîte aux lettres; **the window was a mere s. in the wall,** la fenêtre n'était qu'une fente, qu'une brèche, dans le mur; **s. eyed,** (i) aux yeux bridés; (ii) aux yeux en amande; **s. eared,** à l'oreille fendue, aux oreilles fendues; *Carp: Mec.E: etc:* **s. and tongue junction,** assemblage à fourchette; (*b*) *Tail:* **s. pocket,** fente verticale donnant accès aux vêtements de dessous; fausse poche; (*c*) *Mil:* **s. trench,** tranchée étroite; trou *m* de tirailleur.

slit[2], *v.tr.* (*p.t. & p.p.* **slit**; *pr.p.* **slitting**) (*a*) fendre; **to s. s.o.'s throat,** couper la gorge à qn; égorger qn; **to s. open a sack,** éventrer un sac; **s. skirt,** jupe fendue; (*b*) *Surg:* faire une incision dans (la chair); **the blow s. his cheek,** le coup lui a déchiré la joue; (*c*) refendre (le cuir, le bois, etc.); **to s. metal,** découper des bandes de tôle.

slither[1] ['sliðər], *s.* glissement *m*, glissade *f*; reptation *f*.

slither[2]. **1.** *v.i.* (*a*) glisser; manquer de tomber; **to s. into a room,** s'insinuer dans une pièce; **to s. down a hill,** dégringoler une pente; (*b*) (*of snake, worm*) ramper. **2.** *v.tr. O:* traîner (les pieds, etc.).

slithering ['sliðəriŋ], *s.* = SLITHER[1].

slithery ['sliðəri], *a.* glissant.

slitter ['slitər], *s. Ind:* **1.** (*pers.*) fendeur *m*. **2.** (*a*) *Tls:* fendoir *m*; (*b*) *Metalw:* machine *f* à découper les bandes de tôle.

slitting ['slitiŋ], *s.* fendage *m*, fenderie *f*; *Tls:* **s. file,** lime à couteau; *Metalw:* **s. machine** = SLITTER 2(*b*); **s. mill,** fenderie *f*.

sliver[1] ['sl(a)ivər], *s.* **1.** (*a*) tranche (fine); *Fish:* morceau de poisson monté en appât; (*b*) éclat *m* (de bois, d'obus); *Carp:* garni *m*. **2.** *Tex:* ruban *m* (de lin cardé); mèche *f* de préparation.

sliver[2]. **1.** *v.tr.* (*a*) couper (qch.) en tranches (fines); (*b*) *Tex:* établir les rubans (de lin cardé). **2.** *v.i.* (*of wood, shell*) éclater; voler en éclats.

sloanea ['slouniə], *s. Bot:* quapalier *m*, sloanea *m*.

slob [slɔb], *s.* **1.** (*a*) (*esp. Irish*) vase *f*, limon *m*; (*b*) plage *f* de boue; **s. land,** terre d'alluvion; *esp. Can:* **s. (ice),** glace fondante. **2.** *F:* rustaud *m*, goujat *m*; **big fat s.,** gros lard.

slobber[1] ['slɔbər], *s. F:* **1.** (*a*) bave *f*, salive *f*; (*b*) sentimentalité larmoyante, excessive. **2.** boue *f*; limon *m*; neige à moitié fondue; bourbe *f*.

slobber[2]. *F:* **1.** *v.i.* (*a*) baver; (*b*) faire du sentimentalisme, larmoyer; **to s. (all) over s.o.,** (i) manger qn de caresses; (ii) témoigner une tendresse exagérée envers qn, s'attendrir sur qn. **2.** *v.tr.* (*a*) couvrir (qch.) de bave; (*b*) gâcher, bousiller (un travail).

slobberchops ['slɔbətʃɔps], *s. F:* = SLOBBERER.

slobberer ['slɔbərər], *s. F:* baveur, -euse.

slobbering ['slɔb(ə)riŋ], *a. F:* qui bave; baveux.

slobbery ['slɔb(ə)ri], *a. F:* **1.** (*a*) baveux; **s. kisses,** baisers mouillés; (*b*) sentimental, larmoyant. **2.** *esp. U.S:* (travail) négligé, fait sans soin.

sloe [slou], *s. Bot:* **1.** prunelle *f*; **s. gin** = (alcool *m* de) prunelle. **2. s. bush, tree,** prunellier *m*; épine noire.

slog[1] [slɔg], *s. F:* **1.** coup (violent). **2.** corvée *f*; turbin *m*, boulot *m*.

slog[2], *v.* **(slogged)** *F:* **1.** *v.tr.* (*a*) cogner, battre (qch., qn); rouer (qn) de coups; (*b*) *Cr:* **to s. the ball,** frapper fort sur la balle. **2.** *v.i.* (*a*) *Box:* cogner dur (au hasard); *Cr:* donner de grands coups de batte; (*b*) turbiner, trimer, boulonner; **to s. away at sth.,** travailler avec acharnement à qch.; bûcher; (*c*) **to s. on, along,** marcher d'un pas lourd, péniblement.

slogan ['slougən], *s.* **1.** *Hist:* cri *m* de guerre, de bataille (de clan écossais). **2.** (*a*) cri de guerre, de bataille; mot *m* d'ordre (d'un parti politique); (*b*) *Com:* devise *f*; slogan *m*; (*c*) (*accompanying postmark*) flamme *f* (d'oblitération postale).

slogger ['slɔgər], *s. F:* **1.** *Box: Cr:* cogneur *m* (qui frappe au hasard). **2.** travailleur acharné, abatteur *m* de besogne, de travail; bourreau *m* de travail; bûcheur *m*; turbineur *m*.

slogging ['slɔgiŋ], *s. F:* **1.** rossée *f*; volée *f* de coups. **2.** travail dur; corvée *f*, turbin *m*.

sloop [sluːp], *s.* **1.** *Nau:* sloop *m*; **s.-rigged ship,** navire gréé en sloop. **2.** *Navy:* aviso *m*.

sloot [sluːt], *s.* (*in S. Africa*) ravin *m*, ravine *f*.

slop[1] [slɔp], *s.* **1.** (*a*) *A:* fondrière *f*; (*b*) fange *f*, boue *f*, bourbe *f*. **2.** *pl.* (*a*) boissons renversées (sur la table, etc.); (*b*) (*tasteless drink*) rinçure *f*, lavasse *f*, bibine *f*; (*c*) *O:* aliments *m* liquides; bouillons *m*; (*d*) eaux ménagères; eaux sales; eaux grasses (de cuisine); **s. pail,** (i) seau à eaux sales, de ménage; (ii) seau de toilette, hygiénique; (*e*) fonds *m* de tasse; **s. basin,** vide-tasses *m inv.* **3.** *F:* sentimentalité excessive; sensiblerie *f*. **4.** *Cer:* barbotine *f*, engobe *m*.

slop[2], *v.* **(slopped) 1.** *v.tr.* renverser, répandre (un liquide); **to s. beer over the table,** répandre de la bière sur la table; **to s. paint on a door,** barbouiller une porte de peinture. **2.** *v.i.* (*a*) (*of liquids*) **to s. (over),** déborder; *F: O:* **to s. over s.o.,** témoigner une tendresse exagérée envers qn, s'attendrir sur qn; (*b*) **to s. about in the mud,** patauger, barboter, patouiller, dans la boue.

slop[3], *s.* **1.** blouse *f*; sarrau *m*. **2.** *pl.* (*a*) *A: & Dial:* large pantalon *m*; pantalon de marin; (*b*) effets *m*, frusques *f* (d'un matelot); sac *m* du marin; (*c*) vêtements *m* de confection; confections *f*; (*d*) *Nau:* **slops, s. room,** magasin *m* d'habillement.

slop[4], *s. P:* agent *m* de police, flic *m*.

slope[1] [sloup], *s.* **1.** (*a*) pente *f*, inclinaison *f*; **steep s.,** pente raide, rapide, forte; **gentle s.,** pente douce, faible; **downward, downhill, s.,** pente descendante; descente *f*; déclivité *f*; **upward, uphill, s.,** pente ascendante; montée *f*; **gradual s.,** pente graduelle; **vertical s.,** pente à pic; *Mil:* **with rifle at the s.,** l'arme sur l'épaule; *Surv: etc:* **angle of s.,** angle de pente; **change of s.,** rupture *f* de pente; **scale of slopes,** échelle des pentes; **correction for s.,** correction de pente; (*b*) *Av:* **s. (of glide path), glide s.,** pente radiogoniométrique; trajectoire *f*, axe *f*, de descente, d'atterrissage; **glide s. receiver,** récepteur de pente. **2.** (*a*) pente; talus *m*; (*in road, railway*) rampe *f*; (*in road*) côte *f*; *Ski:* piste *f*; **half way down, up, the s.,** à mi-pente; **mountain s.,** versant *m* de montagne; *Aut:* **to start off up a s.,** démarrer en rampe; *Oc:* **continental s.,** pente continentale; talus continental; (*b*) *Mil:* (*of parapet*) **superior s.,** plongée *f*.

slope[2]. **1.** *v.i.* (*a*) être en pente; incliner, pencher; **to s. down,** descendre; décliner; **to s. up,** monter; (*of writing*) **to s. forward, backward,** pencher à droite, à gauche; (*b*) aller en pente; aller en descendant; s'abaisser; **the garden slopes down to the river,** le jardin dévale, se prolonge en déclive, vers la rivière. **2.** *v.tr.* (*a*) couper (qch.) en pente; taluter (un remblai, etc.); déverser (un mur); (*b*) **to s. (out) the neck of a dress,** échancrer, évider, le col d'une robe; (*c*) *Nau:* **to s. the ports,** mettre les sabords en ardoise; *Mil:* **to s. arms,** mettre l'arme sur l'épaule; **s. arms!** arme sur l'épaule! **to s. swords,** reposer le sabre.

slope[3], *v.i. F:* **to s. off,** décamper, filer, se défiler, déguerpir.

sloper ['sloupər], *s. Civ.E:* taluteuse *f*.

sloping[1] ['sloupiŋ], *a.* (*a*) en pente; incliné; (jardin, etc.) en talus; (terrain) déclive; **s. approach of a bridge,** rampe *f* d'accès d'un pont; **s. shoulders,** épaules tombantes; *Nau:* **s. funnel,** cheminée dévoyée; *Typ:* **s. letters,** lettres couchées; **s. (hand)writing,** écriture couchée; *Hort:* **s. bed,** côtière *f*; (*b*) en biais.

sloping[2], *s.* (*a*) talutage *m* (d'un remblai, etc.); (*b*) **s. (out),** évidage *m* (d'un col de robe, etc.).

sloppiness ['slɔpinis], *s.* **1.** *A:* état détrempé (de la nourriture, etc.); état bourbeux, boueux (d'une rue, etc.). **2.** (*a*) (*of pers.*) mollesse *f*, avachissement *m*; **s. of mind,** manque *m* de netteté dans les idées, dans le raisonnement; (*b*) manque de soin (dans un travail); négligence *f* (de style); (*c*) ampleur *f*, largeur excessive (d'une robe mal coupée, etc.); (*d*) *F:* sentimentalité excessive.

sloppy ['slɔpi], *a.* **1.** (*a*) *A:* (chemin, etc.) détrempé, bourbeux, fangeux, plein de flaques; (*b*) (plancher) mouillé; (table) qui n'a pas été essuyée. **2.** (*a*) *F:* (*of pers.*) mou, *f.* molle; flasque; **she has become very s.,** elle s'est avachie; (*b*) *F:* (travail) fait sans soin, bousillé; (style) négligé, débraillé; (*c*) (vêtement) mal ajusté, trop large; *F:* **s. joe,** pull-over *m* très ample; (*d*) *F:* (roman, etc.) larmoyant; **s. sentimentality,** sensiblerie *f*.

slopseller ['slɔpselər], *s. A:* marchand, -ande, de confections; confectionneur, -euse.

slopshop ['slɔpʃɔp], *s. A:* **1.** magasin *m* de confections. **2.** friperie *f*, braderie *f*.

slopwork ['slɔpwə:k], *s. A:* **1.** *Tail:* confection *f*. **2.** travail bousillé; bousillage *m*.

slosh[1] [slɔʃ], *s.* **1.** (*a*) neige à demi fondue; (*b*) fange *f*, bourbe *f*. **2.** *P:* (*a*) (*drink*) lavasse *f*; (*b*) goutte *f*, soupçon *m* (de cognac, etc.). **3.** éclaboussement *m* (de l'eau); clapotage *m*, clapotement *m*, clapotis *m* (des vagues, etc.). **4.** *F:* (*a*) coup (violent), gnon *m*; (*b*) sensiblerie *f*; sentimentalité excessive.

slosh[2]. **1.** *v.i.* (*a*) (*of liquid*) **to s. (around),** jaillir en éclaboussures; clapoter; (*b*) (*of pers., animal*) **to s. about,** barboter, patouiller, patauger. **2.** *v.tr. F:* (*a*) **to s. paint on a wall,** flanquer de la peinture sur un mur; (*b*) flanquer un coup à (qn), tabasser (qn).

sloshed ['slɔʃt], *a. P:* ivre, soûl.

sloshing ['slɔʃiŋ], *s.* **1.** éclaboussement *m* (de l'eau); clapotage *m*, clapotement *m*, clapotis *m* (des vagues, etc.). **2.** *F:* rossée *f*, pile *f*.

sloshy ['slɔʃi], *a.* **1.** (*a*) détrempé par la neige; (*b*) boueux, bourbeux, fangeux. **2.** *F:* excessivement sentimental.

slot[1] [slɔt], *s.* **1.** (*a*) *Mec.E: etc:* entaille *f*, encoche *f*, rainure *f*, mortaise *f*, cannelure *f*; fente *f* (de la tête d'une vis, de l'aile d'un avion, d'une tirelire); **to cut slots,** mortaiser, buriner, des rainures; **bayonet s.,** encoche à baïonnette; **bevelled s.,** mortaise inclinée; **cotter s.,** logement *m* de la clavette; **s. hole,** trou *m*; entaille, encoche; **s.-drilling machine,** machine à rain(ur)er; rainureuse *f*; *Tls:* **s. file,** fendante *f*; *I.C.E:* **s. in the piston wall, in the sleeve,** lumière *f*; *El:* **slots between the commutator bars,** entre-lames *f* du collecteur; **s. winding,** enroulement (d'induit) à rainures; **to put a coin in the s.,** introduire une pièce de monnaie dans la fente (d'un distributeur, etc.); **s. machine,** (i) (*for chocolate, cigarettes, etc.*) distributeur (automatique); (ii) *esp. NAm:* machine, appareil, à sous; *F:* tire-sou *m*, *pl.* tire-sous; **s. meter,** compteur (à gaz) à paiement préalable; (*b*) *W.Tel: T.V: etc:* portion délimitée de l'horaire de diffusion; créneau *m* (horaire); **prime time s.,** créneau de pointe. **2.** *Th: A:* trap(p)illon *m* (dans le plateau).

slot[2], *v.* **(slotted) 1.** *v.tr. Mec.E: etc:* tailler un trou, une fente, une rainure, dans (qch.); entailler, encocher, rain(ur)er, mortaiser (qch.); **to s. sth. into sth.,** insérer, glisser, mettre, placer, qch. dans qch. **2.** *v.i.* s'introduire, glisser, se mettre (**into sth.,** dans qch.).

slot[3], *s. Ven:* foulées *fpl*, voies *fpl*, erres *fpl*, piste *f*, traces *fpl*, passées *fpl* (d'une bête).

slot[4], *v.tr. Ven:* suivre les foulées, la piste (d'une bête).

slot[5], *s. A: & Dial:* (*a*) verrou *m*; (*b*) barre *f* (de bois, de métal).

sloth [slouθ], *s.* **1.** paresse *f*, fainéantise *f*, oisiveté *f*; indolence *f*, assoupissement *m*. **2.** *Z:* (*a*) paresseux *m*; **three-toed s.,** paresseux à trois doigts; paresseux tridactyle; aï *m*, bradypus *m*, bradype *m*; **two-toed s.,** paresseux à deux doigts; cholèpe *m*; (*b*) **s. (monkey),** (i) nycticèbe *m*; loris lent; (ii) potto *m*; pérodicte *m*, pérodictus *m*; (*c*) **s. (bear),** ours jongleur; ours lippu, à longues lèvres; mélurse *m*, mélursus *m*.

slothful ['slouθful], *a.* paresseux, fainéant; indolent.

slothfully ['slouθfuli], *adv.* paresseusement; avec indolence.

slothfulness ['slouθfulnis], *s.* = SLOTH 1.

slothound ['slɔthaund], *s.* limier *m*.

slotted ['slɔtid], *a.* à fente(s); à encoche(s); à rainure(s); à mortaise(s); rainuré; **s. screw,** vis à filets interrompus; *El:* **s. armature,** induit à rainures; armature à encoches; *Av:* **s. wing,** aile à fente; *Dom.Ec:* **s. spoon,** cuillère à trous.

slotter ['slɔtər], *s.* **1.** *Ind:* opérateur, -trice, d'une mortaiseuse. **2.** *Mec.E:* mortaiseuse; étau mortaiseur.

slotting ['slɔtiŋ], *s.* entaillage *m*, encochement *m*, mortaisage *m*; *Mec.E:* **s. machine,** mortaiseuse *f*; étau mortaiseur; **die s. machine,** machine à dégorger; *Tls:* **s. file,** fendante *f*.

slouch[1] [slautʃ], *s.* **1.** démarche *f* mollasse; mollesse *f*, lourdeur *f*, d'allure; **to walk with a s.,** traîner le pas; **s. of the shoulders,** épaules arrondies. **2. s. hat,** (grand) chapeau mou, rabattu. **3.** *F:* (*a*) lourdaud *m*; (*b*) fainéant, -ante; bousilleur *m*; *esp. NAm:* **he's no s.,** il n'est pas empoté; **it's no s. (of a place),** ce n'est pas mal (comme endroit).

slouch[2], *v.i.* se laisser aller (en marchant); se tenir d'une façon négligée; manquer de tenue; avoir une allure lourde, vulgaire; **don't s.!** tenez-vous droit! **to s. about,** traîner le pas.

sloucher ['slautʃər], *s.* **1.** lourdaud *m*. **2.** fainéant, -ante.

slouching ['slautʃiŋ], *a.* (*a*) (*of pers.*) (i) qui a une allure molle, qui traîne le pas; (ii) aux épaules arrondies; (*b*) (allure) mollasse.

slough[1] [slau], *s.* (*a*) bourbier *m*, fondrière *f*; (*b*) terrain marécageux.

slough[2] [slʌf], *s.* **1.** (*of reptile, insect*) dépouille *f*, mue *f*; exuvie *f*; (*of snake*) **to cast its s.,** quitter sa peau, changer de peau; se dépouiller; jeter sa dépouille; muer. **2.** *Med:* escarre *f*, eschare *f*; croûte *f* (sur une plaie).

slough[3] [slʌf]. **1.** *v.i.* (*a*) (*of reptile, etc.*) se dépouiller; muer; (*b*) (*of scab, etc.*) **to s. off, away,** tomber; se détacher; (*c*) (*of wound*) se couvrir d'une escarre. **2.** *v.tr.* (*of reptile, insect*) **to s. its skin,** se dépouiller; jeter sa dépouille; muer; *Lit:* **to s. (off) a bad habit,** se dépouiller d'une mauvaise habitude.

slo(u)ghi ['slu:gi], *s.* (chien *m*) slo(u)ghi *m*, sloaghy *m*.

sloughing ['slʌfiŋ], *s.* **1.** mue *f* (d'un serpent, etc.); *Vet:* **s. of the hoof,** avalure *f* du sabot. **2.** *Med:* formation *f* d'une escarre; escarrification *f*, escharification *f*.

sloughy[1] ['slaui], *a.* (*a*) bourbeux, marécageux; (*b*) coupé de fondrières.

sloughy[2] ['slʌfi], *a. Med:* qui ressemble à une escarre; couvert d'une escarre.

Slovak ['slouvæk]. **1.** *a. Ethn:* slovaque. **2.** *s.* (*a*) *Ethn:* Slovaque *mf*; (*b*) *Ling:* slovaque *m*.

Slovakia [slou'vækiə], *Pr.n. Geog:* Slovaquie *f*.

sloven ['slʌv(ə)n], *s.* **1.** mal peigné, -ée, mal soigné, -ée; débraillé, -ée; maritorne *f*; souillon *f*. **2.** bousilleur, -euse; gâcheur, -euse, de besogne.

Slovene, Slovenian ['slouvi:n, -'vi:niən]. **1.** *a. Ethn:* slovène. **2.** *s.* (*a*) *Ethn:* Slovène *mf*; (*b*) *Ling:* slovène *m*.

Slovenia [slou'vi:niə], *Pr.n. Geog:* Slovénie *f*.

slovenliness ['slʌv(ə)nlinis], *s.* **1.** négligence *f* (de mise); mise négligée; laisser-aller *m inv*; débraillé *m* (de la tenue). **2.** négligence; manque *m* de soin; **the s. of his style,** son style débraillé.

slovenly ['slʌv(ə)nli], *a.* **1.** (*of pers.*) mal peigné, mal soigné, débraillé; **s. appearance,** tenue débraillée; **s. way of walking,** allure déhanchée. **2.** (*a*) (*of pers.*) négligent; qui manque de soin; sans soin; (*b*) (travail) négligé, bousillé; (style) débraillé; **done in a s. way,** fait sans soin.

slow[1] [slou], *a. & adv.*

I. *a.* **1.** (*a*) lent; **s. steps,** pas lents; **at a s. trot,** au trot ralenti; **s. speed,** petite vitesse; ralenti *m*; *Cin: etc:* **(in) s. motion,** (au) ralenti; **s.-motion film,** film tourné au ralenti; *Mch: Mec.E:* **s. running,** ralenti; **he was a s. speaker, s. of speech,** il parlait toujours lentement; il avait la parole lente; **to be s. over sth., doing sth.,** mettre longtemps à faire qch.; **it's s. work,** ça ne va pas vite; **to give s.o. the s. handclap,** applaudir qn avec ironie (par des battements de mains lents et rythmés); **to be s. and steady, s. and sure,** ne pas trop se presser; *Lit:* ménager sa monture; *Cu:* **to cook sth. in a s. oven,** faire cuire qch. à four doux; *Med:* **s. digestion,** digestion lente, paresseuse; **s. pulse,** pouls lent; **s. heart,** bradycardie *f*; ralentissement du rythme cardiaque; **s. poison,** poison lent; *Rail:* **s. train,** (train *m*) omnibus *m*; **s. line,** voie des trains omnibus; *Nau:* **ship s. in tacking,** navire lent; *Atom.Ph:* **s. reactor,** réacteur à neutrons lents; *Aut: etc:* **we've got a s. puncture,** il y a un pneu qui se dégonfle lentement; (*b*) (*of pers.*) **to be s. to start sth., in starting sth.,** tarder, être lent, être peu empressé, à commencer qch.; apporter du retard à commencer qch.; **to be s. to do sth.,** être lent, mettre de la lenteur, à faire qch.; **s. to act, to take action, s. in action,** lent à agir; *Lit:* **s. to anger,** lent à la colère, à s'emporter; (*c*) **s. (of intellect),** lent d'esprit, à l'esprit lourd; **s. child,** enfant attardé, arriéré; (*d*) (spectacle, etc.) ennuyeux, qui manque d'entrain; (ville, etc.) qui manque d'entrain; **business is s.,** les affaires ne vont pas; les affaires traînent; (*e*) *Games:* (terrain, billard, etc.) qui ne rend pas. **2.** (*of clock, watch*) en retard; **my watch is five minutes s.,** ma montre retarde de cinq minutes, a cinq minutes de retard; je retarde de cinq minutes; **your watch is s. by the town clock,** votre montre a du retard sur l'horloge de la ville.

II. *adv.* (*A:* = **slowly,** *still used in certain phrases*) (*a*) lentement; **to go s.,** (i) aller lentement; (ii) *Ind:* faire la grève perlée; (*of engine*) **to run s.,** tourner au ralenti; *P.N:* **s.!** ralentir! *Nau:* **s. ahead! astern!** en avant, en arrière, doucement! (*b*) **the clock is going s.,** la pendule retarde; (*c*) **s. moving, going,** (i) qui se meut lentement; lent; à marche lente; (ii) *Z:* tardigrade; **s. footed, paced,** (i) aux pas lents; (ii) *Z:* tardigrade; **s. spoken,** à la parole lente; **s. tempered,** lent à s'emporter, à la colère; **s. witted,** à l'esprit lourd, paresseux; d'esprit lent; **s. acting,** à action lente; **s.-acting spring,** ressort paresseux; **s.-running machine,** machine à faible vitesse, à régime lent; **s. burning,** (i) qui brûle lentement; à combustion lente; (ii) peu combustible; ininflammable; *Exp:* **s.-burning powder,** poudre lente; **s.-flowing stream,** ruisseau qui coule lentement.

slow[2]. **1.** *v.i.* (*a*) **to s. down, up,** ralentir (son allure, sa marche); ralentir le pas; diminuer de vitesse; *Aut:* (*of engine*) prendre le ralenti; **the train was slowing down,** le train ralentissait (sa marche, son allure); **to s. down at a bend,** ralentir au tournant; **the gunfire was slowing down,** le feu commençait à mollir; **I've slowed down, up, a bit,** (i) je travaille, marche etc., moins vite qu'autrefois; (ii) j'ai un peu ralenti mes efforts; (*b*) **to s. down, up (to a stop),** s'arrêter. **2.** *v.tr.* **to s. sth. down, up,** ralentir qch.; **this scene slows down the action,** cette scène ralentit l'action; *Artil:* **to s. down the fire,**

ralentir le feu; *Ind:* **to s. down production,** marcher au ralenti.

slowcoach ['sloukoutʃ], *s. F:* lambin, -ine; traînard, -arde; endormi, -ie.

slowdown ['sloudaun], *s.* (*a*) ralentissement *m* (des affaires, etc.); (*b*) grève perlée; travail *m* au ralenti.

slowing ['slouiŋ], *s.* **s. down,** ralentissement *m* (de l'allure, de la production, etc.); *Atom.Ph:* ralentissement (des neutrons); **s. down density,** densité de ralentissement (des neutrons).

slowly ['slouli], *adv.* lentement; avec lenteur; (écrire) lentement, à main posée; **engine running s.,** moteur au ralenti; **drive s.!** au pas! ralentir! **to cook sth. s.,** faire cuire qch. à feu doux, à four doux; (*of plant, etc.*) **to grow s.,** être long à pousser; *Com:* **goods which sell s.,** marchandises qui s'écoulent mal.

slowness ['slounis], *s.* **1.** (*a*) lenteur *f*; **s. to answer,** lenteur à répondre; (*b*) lourdeur *f*, lenteur (d'esprit); (*c*) manque *m* d'entrain (d'un spectacle, etc.). **2.** retard *m* (d'une pendule, etc.).

slowpoke ['sloupouk], *s. NAm: F:* = SLOWCOACH.

slow-worm ['slouwə:m], *s. Rept:* orvet *m* (fragile); serpent *m* de verre.

slub[1] [slʌb], *s. Tex:* **1.** bouton *m* floche; **s. yarn,** fil flammé. **2.** mèche *f* (de laine cardée).

slub[2], *v.tr.* (**slubbed**) *Tex:* boudiner (le fil).

slubber[1] ['slʌbər]. **1.** *v.tr. A: & Lit:* salir, barbouiller (qch.). **2.** *v.i. O:* **to s. over a job,** bâcler, saboter, une besogne.

slubber[2], *s. Tex:* **1.** (*pers.*) boudineur, -euse. **2.** (*machine*) boudineuse *f*.

slubbing ['slʌbiŋ], *s. Tex:* boudinage *m* (du fil); **s. machine,** boudineuse *f*; **s. frame,** banc à broches en gros.

sludge[1] [slʌdʒ], *s.* **1.** (*a*) vase *f*, fange *f*, bourbe *f*; neige à moitié fondue; (*b*) (**sewage**) **s.,** vidanges *fpl*; *Metalw: etc:* boue *f* d'émoulage; *Min:* schlamms *mpl*; *Metall:* **anode s.,** boue de l'anode; **activated s.,** boue activée; (*c*) *Mch:* boue; tartres boueux; **s. hole,** trou de sel; **s. cock,** robinet à boue; (*d*) *Mec.E:* cambouis *m*; résidu cambouisé. **2.** glaçons à moitié pris (sur la surface de la mer).

sludge[2], *v.tr. Min:* déschlammer.

sludgy ['slʌdʒi], *a.* **1.** (*a*) vaseux, fangeux, bourbeux; (*b*) *Ind:* boueux. **2.** (mer) pleine de glaçons, à moitié gelée.

slue [slu:], *v.tr. & i.* = SLEW[2].

slug[1] [slʌg], *s. Moll:* limace *f*; **small grey s.,** petite limace grise; loche *f*.

slug[2], *s.* **1.** (*a*) lingot *m*; (*b*) balle *f*, plomb *m* (d'une arme à feu); (*c*) *NAm:* jeton *m*, pièce fausse (pour distributeur automatique). **2.** *Typ:* (*a*) lingot; garniture *f*; (*b*) ligne-bloc *f* (de linotype), *pl.* lignes-blocs. **3.** *esp. NAm: F:* goutte *f*, coup *m* (d'eau-de-vie, etc.); **to have a s.,** boire un coup. **4.** *Mec.Meas:* unité *f* de masse du système pied-livre-seconde. **5.** *Atom.Ph:* cylindre *m* (de combustible nucléaire).

slug[3], *v.* (**slugged**) **1.** *v.tr.* (*a*) charger (une arme à feu) de balles, de plombs; (*b*) *NAm:* insérer une pièce fausse dans (un distributeur automatique). **2.** *v.i.* (*of bullet*) épouser les rayures du canon.

slug[4], *s. NAm: F:* coup violent, triquée *f*, taloche *f*.

slug[5]. *NAm: F:* **1.** *v.tr.* (*a*) battre, tabasser, cogner (qn); rouer (qn) de coups; **to s. it out,** se rentrer dedans; (*b*) (*in baseball*) **to s. the ball,** frapper fort sur la balle. **2.** *v.i.* (*a*) **to s.** (**away**), (continuer à) se battre, se tabasser; (*b*) turbiner, trimer, boulonner; travailler avec acharnement.

slug-abed ['slʌgəbed], *s. F: A:* paresseux, -euse (qui fait la grasse matinée).

sluggard ['slʌgəd], *a. & s.* paresseux, -euse; fainéant, -ante.

sluggish ['slʌgiʃ], *a.* **1.** paresseux, fainéant; léthargique; *F:* flémard, flemmard; (esprit) lourd, inerte, pesant, engourdi. **2. s. river,** rivière lente, paresseuse; **s. pulse,** pouls lent, paresseux; **s. liver,** foie paresseux, engorgé; **to have a s. liver,** souffrir d'une atonie du foie; **s. digestion,** digestion paresseuse, laborieuse; difficulté à digérer; **s. compass,** compas peu sensible; compas qui dort; *Aut:* **s. engine,** moteur mou, peu nerveux.

sluggishly ['slʌgiʃli], *adv.* **1.** paresseusement. **2.** (*of river, etc.*) **to flow s.,** couler lentement.

sluggishness ['slʌgiʃnis], *s.* **1.** (*a*) paresse *f*, fainéantise *f*; *F:* flemme *f*; (*b*) lourdeur *f*, pesanteur *f* (de l'esprit). **2.** lenteur *f* (d'une rivière, etc.); paresse (du foie, de l'intestin); engorgement *m*, atonie *f* (du foie); **s. of the compass,** défaut *m* de sensibilité du compas; *Aut:* **s. of the engine,** mollesse *f* du moteur.

sluice[1] [slu:s], *s.* **1.** *Hyd.E:* (*a*) écluse *f*; bonde *f*, pale *f* (d'étang); **open s.,** gueule-bée *f*, *pl.* gueules-bées; **to open the sluices of a reservoir,** lâcher les écluses d'un réservoir; débonder un réservoir; **s.** (**gate**), porte *f* d'écluse; vanne *f*; **system of s. gates,** vannage *m*; *Lit:* **the s. gates of heaven have opened,** les écluses, les vannes, du ciel sont ouvertes; **s.** (**valve**), vanne (de communication); robinet-vanne *m*, *pl.* robinets-vannes; vannelle *f*; *N.Arch:* **s. valve,** diaphragme *m*, vanne à glissière (dans une cloison étanche); (*b*) canal *m*, -aux, de décharge (du trop-plein d'un réservoir); (*c*) *Min:* débourbeur *m*; **s. box,** augette *f*; (*d*) **put it down the s.,** versez-le aux égouts. **2.** *F:* **to give sth. a s. down,** laver qch. à grande eau.

sluice[2]. **1.** *v.tr.* (*a*) *Hyd.E:* vanner (un cours d'eau); (*b*) **to s. out the water in a reservoir,** laisser échapper l'eau d'un réservoir (par les vannes); **to s. a pond,** lâcher les vannes d'un étang; débonder un étang; (*c*) lâcher les bassins de chasse dans (une rivière, un canal); (*d*) laver à grande eau; débourber (un égout); **to s. oneself down with cold water,** s'inonder d'eau fraîche; *Min:* **to s. the ore,** laver, débourber, le minerai. **2.** *v.i.* (*of water, etc.*) **to s. out,** couler à flots.

sluiceway ['slu:swei], *s.* canal *m*, -aux, à vannes.

sluicing ['slu:siŋ], *s.* **1.** *Hyd.E:* vannage *m* (d'un cours d'eau). **2.** vidange *f* (de l'eau d'un réservoir, etc.) par les écluses; **s. water,** éclusée *f*. **3.** lavage *m* à grande eau; débourbage *m* (d'un égout, du minerai). **4.** écoulement *m* à flots. **5.** *Min:* **ground s.,** exploitation *f* des alluvions par canaux.

sluit [slu:t], *s.* (*in S. Africa*) ravin *m*, ravine *f*.

slum[1] [slʌm], *s.* (*a*) rue *f*, impasse *f*, sordide; (*b*) bas quartier, quartier pouilleux, pauvre; (*c*) taudis *m*; **s. clearance** (**campaign**), suppression *f* des taudis, lutte *f* contre les taudis.

slum[2], *v.i.* (**slummed**) (*a*) *A:* **to go slumming,** faire des visites (i) de charité, (ii) de curiosité, dans les quartiers pauvres; (*b*) *F:* **to go slumming** (**with s.o.**), **to s. it,** s'abaisser à faire qch. (en compagnie de qn).

slum[3], *s. U.S: P:* ratatouille *f*.

slumber[1] ['slʌmbər], *s.* (*a*) *Lit:* sommeil *m* (paisible); assoupissement *m*; somme *m*; **to fall into a s.,** s'endormir, s'assoupir; **to disturb, break in upon, s.o.'s slumber(s),** troubler, interrompre, le sommeil de qn; (*b*) *Com:* **s. wear,** vêtements *mpl* de nuit; *O:* **s. suit,** pyjama *m* (de femme, d'enfant); **s. cap,** bonnet *m*, filet *m*, de nuit.

slumber[2], *v. Lit:* **1.** *v.i.* sommeiller; être assoupi; dormir (paisiblement). **2.** *v.tr.* **to s. away the golden hours,** passer à dormir des heures précieuses.

slumberer ['slʌmbərər], *s. Lit:* dormeur, -euse.

slumbering ['slʌmbəriŋ], *a. Lit:* qui dort; assoupi, endormi.

slumberous ['slʌmb(ə)rəs], *a. Lit:* somnolent, assoupi; **the s. waves,** la mer qui dort; **s. eyelids,** paupières lourdes de sommeil; **s. village,** village endormi, engourdi.

slumgullion [slʌm'gʌliən], *s. U.S:* **1.** *P:* (*a*) lavasse *f*; (*b*) ratatouille *f*. **2.** mélange *m* d'huile, de sang et d'eau qui inonde le pont pendant le dépècement des baleines. **3.** *P: A:* sale type *m*; vaurien *m*; mufle *m*.

slumming ['slʌmiŋ], *s. F:* **intellectual s.,** abaissement intellectuel.

slummy ['slʌmi], *a.* **s. district,** bas quartier; quartier pouilleux, de taudis; **s. street,** rue sordide.

slump[1] [slʌmp], *s. Com:* baisse soudaine, forte baisse, chute *f*, effondrement *m*, dégringolade *f* (des cours, etc.); crise *f*; **s. in trade,** marasme *m* des affaires; **s. in the wine trade,** mévente *f* des vins; **the s. in the book trade,** la crise du livre; **s. in the pound,** dégringolade de la livre; **theatre s.,** marasme dont souffrent les théâtres; **the s.,** la crise, la dépression, économique.

slump[2], *v.i.* **1.** (*a*) s'enfoncer (dans un bourbier, etc.); (*b*) tomber lourdement, comme une masse; s'affaisser; **to s. into a chair,** s'affaler dans un fauteuil. **2.** *Com: Ind: etc:* (*of prices, etc.*) baisser tout à coup; s'effondrer, dégringoler.

slump[3], *v.tr. Scot:* mettre (qch.) en bloc, en masse, en tas.

slumping ['slʌmpiŋ], *s.* baisse *f*, chute *f*, effondrement *m*, dégringolade *f* (des prix, etc.).

slunkskin ['slʌŋkskin], *s. Tan:* peau *f* d'animal mis bas avant terme.

slur[1] [slə:r], *s.* **1.** (*a*) insulte *f*, affront *m*; **to put, cast, a s. on s.o.,** infliger un affront à qn, traiter qn sans considération; (*b*) tache *f*; flétrissure *f*; souillure *f*; **to cast a s. on s.o.'s reputation,** ternir, flétrir, porter atteinte à, la réputation de qn; diffamer qn. **2.** *Typ:* macule *f*, maculage *m*, maculature *f*. **3.** *Mus:* (*a*) (*sign*) liaison *f*; (*b*) (*slurred passage*) coulé *m*. **4.** (*in speech*) mauvaise articulation.

slur[2], *v.tr.* (**slurred**) (*a*) *A:* calomnier, dénigrer (qn); porter atteinte à (la réputation de qn); (*b*) **to s. one's words** (**in speaking**), mal articuler ses mots; bredouiller; **to s.** (**over**) **a word,** bredouiller, escamoter, un mot; **to s.** (**over**) **a fact,** passer légèrement, glisser, sur un fait; **his speech was slurred,** il articulait mal, il bredouillait; ses paroles étaient indistinctes; (*c*) *Mus:* lier (deux notes); couler (un passage); **to s. two notes** (**on manuscript**), marquer deux notes d'une liaison; **slurred passage,** passage coulé, louré; **slurred notes,** notes liées coulant; (*d*) *Typ:* maculer, mâchurer (une page); *v.i.* (*of press*) friser, papilloter.

slurring ['slə:riŋ], *s.* **1.** *A:* calomnie *f*; dénigrement *m*. **2.** (*a*) **s. of one's words,** mauvaise articulation; bredouillage *m*; **s. over,** manque *m* de précision, de soin; **s. over of awkward facts,** escamotage *m* de faits embarrassants; (*b*) *Mus:* liaison *f*. **3.** *Typ:* maculage *m*, papillotage *m*, frisage *m* (d'une épreuve, etc.).

slurry ['slʌri], *s.* **1.** boue *f* (de rivière); *Metalw:* boue d'émoulage. **2.** *Const:* coulis *m*, lait *m* (de ciment); *Metall:* coulis de terre réfractaire; bouillie *f*.

slush[1] [slʌʃ], *s.* **1.** (*a*) neige à moitié fondue; **to tramp through the s.,** patauger dans la neige; (*b*) fange *f*, bourbe *f*; gâchis *m*. **2.** (*a*) *Mec.E:* graisse lubrifiante; (*b*) *Nau:* graisse de coq; (*c*) *Const:* crépi *m*. **3.** *F:* sensiblerie *f*. **4.** *F:* **s. fund,** fonds pour graisser la patte à certaines personnes; **s.** (**money**) **payments,** graissage *m* de patte.

slush[2]. **1.** *v.tr. F: O:* éclabousser, crotter (qn, sa voiture). **2.** *v.tr.* (*a*) *Nau: A:* **to s. down a mast,** graisser un mât; (*b*) *Const:* crépir (un mur); (*c*) laver (qch.) à grande eau. **3.** *v.i.* **to s. about,** patauger, barboter, patouiller (dans la neige, etc.).

slushing ['slʌʃiŋ], *s.* **1.** *Min:* embouage *m*; *Mec.E:* **s. oil,** huile antirouille. **2.** *F:* graissage *m* de patte.

slushy ['slʌʃi], *a.* (*a*) (i) détrempé par la neige; (ii) boueux, bourbeux, fangeux, patouilleux; (*b*) *F:* **s. sentimentality,** sentimentalité fadasse; **s. film, novel,** film, roman, sentimental.

slut [slʌt], *s.f.* **1.** salope; guenipe; sagouine; saligaude. **2.** (*a*) coureuse; *F:* catau; catin; (*b*) *F: A:* coquine.

sluttish ['slʌtiʃ], *a.* (*of woman*) malpropre, sale; mauvaise ménagère.

sluttishly ['slʌtiʃli], *adv.* malproprement, salement; en salope; **she does everything s.,** elle salope tout ce qu'elle fait.

sluttishness ['slʌtiʃnis], *s.* malpropreté *f*, saleté *f*; saloperie *f*.

Sluys [slɔis], *Pr.n. Geog:* l'Écluse *f*.

sly [slai], *a.* (**slyer, slyest**) **1.** (*a*) rusé, madré; (*b*) cauteleux, sournois; hypocrite; **s. dog,** (i) fin, gros, matois; madré *m*; (ii) retors *m*; **s. looking,** à la mine chafouine; (*c*) *s. F:* **to do sth. on the s.,** faire qch. furtivement, à la dérobée, en sourdine, en cachette, en tapinois, en catimini, sous cape. **2.** malin, -igne, malicieux, espiègle, futé.

slyboots ['slaibu:ts], *s. F:* **1.** (*a*) cachottier, -ière; sournois, -oise; (*b*) petit(e) rusé(e); petit(e) finaud(e), petit(e) futé(e). **2.** espiègle *mf*; petit malin, petite maligne; petit(e) coquin(e).

slyly ['slaili], *adv.* **1.** (*a*) avec finesse; adroitement; (*b*) sournoisement, cauteleusement. **2.** malicieusement; d'une manière espiègle.

slyness ['slainis], *s.* **1.** (*a*) finesse *f*; (*b*) sournoiserie *f*. **2.** malice *f*, espièglerie *f*.

slype [slaip], *s. Ecc.Arch:* corridor *m*.

smack[1] [smæk], *s. O:* léger goût; saveur *f*, soupçon *m* (de vanille, d'ail, etc.); soupçon, teinté *f* (de malice, de pédanterie, etc.).

smack[2], *v.i.* **to s. of sth.,** avoir un léger goût de qch., un arrière-goût de qch.; **to s. of the soil,** sentir le cru; **opinions that s. of heresy,** opinions *f* qui sentent, qui fleurent, l'hérésie.

smack[3], *s. & adv.*

I. *s.* **1.** claquement *m*, clic-clac *m* (d'un fouet, etc.); **with a s. of his tongue,** avec un claquement de langue; **I heard the s. of a whip, of a kiss,** j'ai entendu claquer un fouet, un baiser. **2.** claque *f*; **s. in the face,** (i) gifle *f*, calotte *f*; (ii) *F:* affront *m*, rebuffade *f*; **to give a child a s. on the bottom,** donner une fessée à un enfant; **I hit him a s. in the eye,** je lui ai collé mon poing sur l'œil; **he gave the ball a hard s.,** il frappa vigoureusement la balle; *F:* **to have a s. at s.o.,** donner un coup de patte à qn; **to get another s. at s.o.,** rechoper qn; **to have a s. at sth.,** essayer de faire qch.; **have a s. at it,** essayez un coup. **3.** *F:* gros baiser retentissant; grosse bise.

II. *adv.* **1. to go s.,** faire clic-clac; claquer; **s. went the whip,** le fouet claqua. **2. he fell s. on the floor,** il est tombé paf! **to bump s. into a tree,** donner en plein contre un arbre; **to hit s.o. s. on the nose,** flanquer un coup à qn en plein sur le nez; **s. in the middle,** en plein milieu; vlan!

smack[4]. **1.** *v.tr.* (*a*) faire claquer (un fouet, sa langue); **to s. one's tongue,** clap(p)er de la langue; **to s. one's lips,** faire claquer ses lèvres; *F:* se lécher les babines; (*b*) frapper, taper (avec le plat de la main); donner une claque à (qn); claquer (qn); **to s. s.o.'s face,** donner une gifle à qn; gifler qn; plaquer un soufflet à qn; **to s. s.o.'s bottom,** (i) claquer les fesses, le derrière, à qn; (ii) administrer une fessée à (un enfant); **he smacked back the ball,** il a relancé dur la balle. **2.** *v.i.* (*of whip*) claquer.

smack[5], *s. Nau:* **(fishing) s.,** bateau pêcheur; bateau de pêche.

smacker ['smækər], *s.* **1.** (*a*) *F:* gifle retentissante; (*b*) *F:* gros baiser, grosse bise; (*c*) *P:* **to rub smackers,** se sucer le caillou, la poire. **2.** *P:* (*a*) livre *f* sterling; (*b*) dollar *m.*

smacking[1] ['smækiŋ], *a.* **1.** (baiser) retentissant. **2.** *Nau:* **s. breeze,** vent frais; bonne brise.

smacking[2], *s.* **1.** claquement *m* (d'un fouet, etc.); clap(p)ement *m* (de la langue). **2.** fouettée *f*; fessée *f.*

Smalkaldic [smælkældik], *a. Hist:* **S. League,** ligue *f* de Smalkalde.

small [smɔ:l], *a., s. & adv.*

I. *a.* petit. **1.** (*a*) menu; **s. pebbles,** menus cailloux; **s. man,** petit homme; homme de petite taille; **s. child,** (i) enfant petit; (ii) enfant en bas âge; petit enfant; **to make sth. smaller,** rapetisser qch.; **of s. dimensions,** de petites, faibles, dimensions; de dimensions exiguës; **s. waist,** taille *f* mince; **s. stature,** petite taille; **dress that makes one look s.,** robe qui vous rapetisse; **to make oneself s.,** se faire tout petit; rentrer le cou entre, dans, les épaules; **s. territory,** territoire exigu; **a s. coffee,** une demi-tasse (de café); **a s. whisky,** une demi-mesure (de whisky); **s. dose,** faible dose; **sitting by a s. fire,** assis auprès d'un pauvre feu; **he's a s. eater,** il n'est pas gros mangeur; *Husb:* **s. stock,** (i) menu bétail; (ii) cheptel restreint; *Ven:* **s. game,** menu gibier; **s. shot,** menu plomb; **s. arms,** armes portatives; *A:* **s. sword,** épée *f* d'escrime; *Nau:* **of s. tonnage,** (navire) de faible tonnage; *Typ:* **s. letters,** minuscules *f*; **s. capitals, s. caps,** petites majuscules; **to print in s. type,** imprimer en petits caractères; *F:* (*in contract, etc.*) **the s. print,** les petits caractères, l'important *m* du bas de la page; (*b*) **in s. numbers,** en petit nombre; **the classes should be smaller,** les classes devraient être moins nombreuses; **the population is smaller than ours by a million,** la population est d'un million inférieure à la nôtre; **s. committee,** comité restreint; commission restreinte; **s. party,** (i) parti peu nombreux; (ii) réunion peu nombreuse; **we were a s. party,** nous étions peu nombreux; *s. A:* **a s. and early,** une petite réunion d'amis, d'intimes (qui ne se termine pas tard). **2.** (*a*) **s. wine,** vin léger; petit vin; **s. beer,** petite bière; (*b*) **s. voice,** (i) voix fluette; (ii) petite voix (que l'on entend à peine). **3. s. progress,** progrès *m* peu sensibles; légers progrès; peu de progrès; **s. resources,** faibles ressources *f*; **s. income,** revenu *m* modique; mince revenu; **s. harvest, s. crop,** maigre récolte *f*; **to leave school with a s. stock of knowledge,** quitter l'école avec un mince bagage; *Lit:* **to have s. Latin and less Greek,** savoir peu de latin et encore moins de grec; **not the smallest difference,** pas la moindre différence; **and s. blame to him,** et ce n'était nullement sa faute; **it's s. wonder that . . .,** ce n'est guère étonnant que + *sub.*; **to pay only s. attention to sth.,** n'accorder que peu d'attention à qch.; **it was no s. surprise to me,** à ma grande surprise; **of no s. consequence,** de très grande importance; **no s. commotion,** pas mal de tapage. **4.** (*a*) peu important; peu considérable; **it's only a s. matter,** ce n'est qu'une bagatelle; *F:* (*of s.o., sth.*) **to be s. beer, s. potatoes,** être insignifiant; **s. cards,** basses cartes; **s. change,** petite monnaie; **s. details,** menus détails; **the smallest details,** les moindres détails; **s. events,** petits incidents (de la vie); **a s. hotel,** un hôtel modeste; **s. sale,** vente peu importante; **the smaller industries,** la petite industrie; **s. shopkeeper,** petit commerçant; **s. landowner,** petit propriétaire; **in a s. way,** en petit; modestement; *Journ: F:* **s. ads,** petites annonces; (*b*) **the smallest possible number of people,** le moins de gens possible. **5.** mesquin, chétif; **s. mind,** petit esprit; **only a s. man could behave like that,** il n'y a qu'un petit esprit pour agir de la sorte; **I felt very s.,** je n'étais pas fier; je ne savais où me mettre; **to look s.,** avoir l'air penaud; **to make s.o. look s.,** humilier qn; ravaler qn; rabattre le caquet à qn.

II. *s.* **1. s. of the back,** creux *m,* chute *f,* des reins; **pains in the s. of the back,** douleurs *f* aux reins; **s. of the leg,** bas *m* de la jambe; *Sm.a:* **s. of the butt,** poignée *f* de la crosse. **2.** menu *m* du charbon; menus; charbonnaille *f.* **3. smalls,** (i) *A:* (*also* **s. clothes**), culotte (collante); pantalon collant; (ii) *F:* lingerie *f,* sous-vêtements *mpl*; **to wash one's smalls,** faire sa petite lessive; (iii) *Sch:* examen *m* préliminaire d'admissibilité (à l'Université d'Oxford).

III. *adv.* **1.** (hacher, etc.) menu, en petits morceaux. **2.** (écrire) menu, en petits caractères. **3.** *A:* **to talk s.,** parler bas.

smallage ['smɔ:lidʒ], *s. Bot:* ache *f.*

smallholder ['smɔ:lhouldər], *s. Agr:* petit cultivateur, exploitant.

smallholding ['smɔ:lhouldiŋ], *s. Agr:* petite propriété.

smallish ['smɔ:liʃ], *a.* assez, plutôt, petit.

small-minded [smɔ:l'maindid], *a.* à l'esprit mesquin, étroit; **a s.-m. man,** un petit esprit.

smallness ['smɔ:lnis], *s.* **1.** petitesse *f*; modicité *f* (de revenus); exiguïté *f,* faiblesse *f* (d'une somme). **2. the s. of his mind,** sa petitesse d'esprit, sa mesquinerie.

smallpox ['smɔ:lpɔks], *s. Med:* petite vérole; variole *f*; **discrete s.,** variole discrète; **confluent s.,** variole confluente; **s. lymph,** lymphe *f* variolique; **s. pustules,** pustules *f* varioliques; **s. patient,** varioleux, -euse.

small-scale ['smɔ:lskeil], *a.* **1. s.-s. model,** modèle réduit; **s.-s. map,** carte *f* à petite échelle. **2. s.-s. business,** entreprise peu importante, de peu d'étendue.

small-time ['smɔ:ltaim], *a. F:* insignifiant, médiocre; sans envergure; **s.-t. crook,** petit escroc.

small-timer ['smɔ:ltaimər], *s. F:* homme, femme, insignifiant(e); minus *m.*

small-toothed ['smɔ:ltu:θt], *a.* à petites dents; **s.-t. comb,** peigne fin; *Z:* **s.-t. palm civet,** civette *f* de Sumatra.

small-town ['smɔ:ltaun], *a. F:* provincial, de province.

small-towner [smɔ:l'taunər], *s. F:* provincial, -ale.

smalt [smɔ:lt], *s. Glassm:* smalt *m*; émail *m* de cobalt.

smaltine ['smɔ:ltain, -ti:n], **smaltite** ['smɔ:ltait], *s. Miner:* smaltine *f,* smaltite *f.*

smaragd ['smærægd], *s. A:* émeraude *f.*

smaragdine [smæ'rægdi:n, -dain], *a.* smaragdin.

smaragdite [smæ'rægdait], *s. Miner:* smaragdite *f.*

smarm [smɑ:m], *v. F:* **1.** *v.tr.* **to s. one's hair down,** s'aplatir les cheveux à la pommade. **2.** *v.tr. & i.* **to s. (up to, over) s.o., to s. s.o. all over,** flagorner qn.

smarmy ['smɑ:mi], *a. F: Pej:* patelin, mielleux, doucereux, flagorneur.

smart[1] [smɑ:t], *s.* douleur cuisante; cuisson *f* (d'une blessure); cinglure *f* (d'une lanière, d'une insulte); *A:* **s. money,** (i) *Mil: Navy:* pension *f* pour blessure; (ii) amende *f* pour résiliation de contrat; forfait *m.*

smart[2], *v.i.* (*a*) (*of wound, etc.*) cuire, brûler; picoter; **the smoke made my eyes s.,** la fumée me piquait, picotait, les yeux; **my eyes are smarting,** les yeux me cuisent, me brûlent, me picotent; (*b*) (*of pers.*) souffrir; **to s. under an injustice,** souffrir sous le coup d'une injustice; **to s. under, be smarting from, an insult,** être cinglé par une insulte; souffrir sous le coup d'une insulte; ressentir vivement une insulte; **he'll make you s. for it,** il vous le fera payer cher.

smart[3], *a.* **1.** (coup de fouet) cuisant, cinglant; (coup de marteau) sec; **s. box on the ear,** bonne gifle; **s. reprimand,** verte réprimande; **s. shower,** bonne averse. **2.** vif; prompt; alerte; **s. pace,** allure vive, leste; **s. walk,** promenade *f* à une allure vive; **s. attack,** vive attaque; *Mil:* **s. encounter,** affaire chaude; **s. piece of work,** travail fait vite et bien; **that's s. work!** vous vous y êtes allé(s) bien vite! vous allez vite en besogne! **s. in answering,** prompt, vif, à répondre; **to be s. at repartee,** être preste à la réplique; *adv.* **look s. (about it)!** dépêchez-vous! remuez-vous! **3.** (*a*) habile, adroit; à l'esprit éveillé; fin, affûté; dégourdi, débrouillard; **s. lad wanted,** on demande un jeune homme intelligent; **s. business man,** homme d'affaires habile; **s. answer,** réponse adroite; *F:* **he's a s. one,** c'est une fine mouche; **s. trick,** (i) truc ingénieux; (ii) bon tour; **s. piece of mechanism,** mécanisme ingénieux; *Turf:* **the s. money was on Destrier,** les gens éveillés ont parié sur Destrier; (*b*) *Pej:* malin, *f.* maligne; **to be too s. for s.o.,** être trop malin pour qn; **trying to be s., eh?** tu essaies de faire le malin, hein? **s. practice,** conduite peu scrupuleuse; escroquerie *f.* **4.** (*of dress, pers., etc.*) élégant, distingué, chic; coquet, pimpant; **s. dress,** (i) robe habillée; (ii) robe dernier cri, à la mode; **to make oneself s.,** se faire beau, belle; **you do look s.!** comme vous voilà beau! **she's smarter than her sister,** elle s'habille mieux que sa sœur; **s. society, the s. set,** le monde élégant; les gens chics; **he thinks it s. to do that,** il croit chic, à la mode, de faire ça.

smarten ['smɑ:t(ə)n]. **1.** *v.tr.* (*a*) **to s. sth. (up),** accélérer (la production, etc.); mettre de l'entrain, du nerf, dans (une société, etc.); animer (le dialogue d'une pièce, etc.); **to s. s.o. up,** dégourdir qn; (*b*) **to s. oneself up,** se faire beau; refaire sa toilette; **to s. up one's flat,** donner du chic à, refaire, son appartement; *F:* **to s. (oneself) up a bit,** se faire un brin de toilette. **2.** *v.i.* **to s. up,** (i) s'animer; (ii) (*of pers.*) se dégourdir; prendre du chic.

smarting[1] ['smɑ:tiŋ], *a.* (*of pain, eyes*) cuisant, brûlant.

smarting[2], *s.* douleur cuisante; (sensation *f* de) brûlure *f*; (*after shaving*) feu *m* du rasoir.

smartish ['smɑ:tiʃ], *a. F:* **to land s.o. a s. one,** flanquer à qn un coup assez rude.

smartly ['smɑ:tli], *adv.* **1.** promptement, vivement; sans mollesse; **to answer s.,** riposter du tac au tac; **to pull sth. s.,** tirer vivement qch.; **to pull s.o. up s.,** réprimander qn vertement; **to walk s.,** marcher d'une allure vive, lestement; **he turned s. round,** il s'est retourné brusquement; **s. executed,** fait vite et bien; **to start s.,** commencer promptement; **he drove s. away,** (i) il est parti au grand trot de son cheval; (ii) il a démarré vivement, bon train. **2.** habilement, adroitement. **3.** (s'habiller, etc.) élégamment.

smartness ['smɑ:tnis], *s.* **1.** (*a*) vivacité *f* (d'esprit); intelligence *f*; esprit débrouillard, débrouillardise *f*; (*b*) à-propos *m* (d'une réponse). **2.** habilité peu scrupuleuse; finesse *f,* matoiserie *f.* **3.** élégance *f,* coquetterie *f* (de toilette, etc.); chic *m.*

smartweed ['smɑ:twi:d], *s. Bot:* persicaire *f* âcre.

smarty ['smɑ:ti], *s. P:* **s. (pants),** cuistre *m,* je-sais-tout *m.*

smash[1] [smæʃ], *s., a. & adv.*

I. *s.* **1.** (*a*) coup dur, écrasant; *Wr:* **forearm s.,** manchette *f*; **he fell with a terrible s.,** il est tombé comme une masse; (*b*) *Ten:* coup écrasé; volée haute; smash *m.* **2.** (*a*) mise *f* en morceaux, en miettes; fracassement *m*; *A:* **to go to s.,** (i) se briser; être réduit en morceaux; (ii) (*of scheme, etc.*) faire fiasco; échouer; (iii) (*of pers.*) faire faillite; (*b*) désastre *m,* sinistre *m* (de chemin de fer); collision *f,* tamponnement *m* (de trains, de voitures); **there's been a s. on the line,** il y a eu un accident de chemin de fer. **3.** (*a*) débâcle *f*; faillite (commerciale); krach *m* (d'une banque); déconfiture *f* (à la Bourse); (*b*) déroute *f*; défaite complète. **4.** *U.S:* **(brandy) s.,** cognac *m* à la glace et à la menthe. **5.** *a. & s.* **s. (hit),** gros succès, succès fou.

II. *adv.* **1. to go s.,** (*of firm*) faire faillite, tomber en faillite; (*of bank*) sauter; **he lost all his money when the bank went s.,** il a perdu tout ce qu'il possédait dans le krach de la banque. **2. to run s. into sth.,** se heurter de front contre qch.; (*of car*) s'emboutir contre (un mur, etc.).

smash[2], *v.*

I. *v.tr.* **1.** (*a*) **to s. sth. on, against, sth.,** heurter, choquer, cogner, lancer, qch. contre qch. avec violence; **to s. one's head against the wall,** se casser la tête contre le mur; (*b*) *Ten:* écraser, tuer, massacrer, smasher (la balle). **2.** (*a*) **to s. sth. to pieces,** briser qch. en morceaux; fracasser qch.; mettre qch. en miettes; **to s. open a box,** éventrer une boîte (à coups de marteau, etc.); **to s. the door open,** enfoncer la porte; (*b*) détruire (qn, qch.); écraser, démolir, anéantir, annihiler (une armée, etc.); *Sp:* **to s. a record,** pulvériser un record; (*c*) ruiner (qn); faire faire faillite à (qn); faire échouer (un projet).

II. *v.i.* **1.** se heurter violemment (contre qch.); **the car smashed into the wall,** la voiture s'est écrasée contre le mur, est allée s'emboutir contre le mur. **2. to s. (in pieces),** éclater en morceaux, en pièces; se briser. **3.** *A:* (*of firm, etc.*) faire faillite.

III. (*compound verbs*) **1. smash in,** *v.tr.* enfoncer, défoncer (une boîte, etc.); enfoncer (une porte); *F:* **to s. s.o.'s face in,** casser la figure, *F:* la gueule, à qn.

2. smash up, *v.tr.* briser (qch.) en morceaux; fracasser (qch.); démolir (une voiture, etc.); *F:* **to s. s.o. up,** battre qn, rosser qn, tabasser qn, casser la gueule à qn.

smash-and-grab [smæʃnd'græb], *a.* **s.-a.-g. raid,** rafle *f* (de bijoux, etc.) après bris de devanture.

smasher ['smæʃər], *s.* **1.** briseur, -euse; écraseur, -euse. **2.** *F:* (*a*) coup écrasant, assommant; (*b*) critique mordante; réponse écrasante; (*c*) **to come a s.,** faire une violente culbute. **3.** *F:* **what a s.!** ce qu'elle est belle! **that's a s.!** que c'est épatant!

smashing[1] ['smæʃiŋ], *a.* (*a*) (coup) écrasant, assommant; *F:* **a s. victory,** une victoire fracassante; (*b*) *F:* formidable; **she's s.!** ce qu'elle est belle!

smashing[2], *s.* **1.** brisement *m,* écrasement *m.* **2.** destruction *f*; écrasement (d'une armée, etc.); défaite *f.*

smashup ['smæʃʌp], *s. F:* (*a*) destruction complète; *Aut: Rail: etc:* grave collision *f*; **there's been a s.,** il y a eu de la casse; (*b*) débâcle *f.*

smattering ['smæt(ə)riŋ], *s.* légère connaissance (d'une langue, etc.); **to have a s. of sth.,** savoir un peu, quelques bribes (d'anglais, etc.); avoir des notions de (chimie, etc.); **to acquire a s. of Greek,** acquérir quelques connaissances en grec.

smear[1] ['smiər], *s.* **1.** (*a*) tache *f,* macule *f,* souillure *f*; (*b*) **s. campaign,** campagne *f* de calomnies. **2.** (*for microscope slide*) frottis *m* (de sang, etc.).

smear[2], *v.tr.* **1.** (*a*) barbouiller, salir **(with,** de); **to s. s.o.'s reputation,** salir la réputation de qn; (*b*) enduire **(with,** de); **to s. one's face with cleansing cream,** enduire son visage de démaquillant; (*c*) torcher, bousiller (un plancher en terre battue). 2. maculer, barbouiller (une page écrite, etc.); **to s. a blot,** étaler une tache d'encre; (*of outline*) **to get smeared,** s'estomper. 3. **to s. one's opponents,** monter une campagne de calomnies contre ses adversaires.

smearing ['smiəriŋ], *s.* barbouillage *m.*

smeary ['smiəri], *a.* 1. taché, barbouillé; aux contours brouillés. 2. graisseux.

smectite ['smektait], *s.* smectite *f*; argile *f* smectique; terre *f* à foulon.

smegma ['smegmə], *s. Physiol: Vet:* smegma *m*; *Vet: F:* cambouis *m.*

smell[1] [smel], *s.* 1. **(sense of) s.,** odorat *m*; flair *m* (d'un chien); *Ven:* sentiment *m* (d'un chien de chasse); **to have a keen sense of s.,** avoir l'odorat fin. 2. (*a*) odeur *f*, senteur *f*, parfum *m* (des fleurs, etc.); **sweet s.,** odeur douce; **nasty, bad, s.,** mauvaise odeur; **there's a bad s. in my room,** cela sent mauvais dans ma chambre; **musty s.,** relent *m*; **stale s. of beer, of spirits,** relent de bière, d'alcool; **(pleasant) s. of cooking,** fumet *m* de cuisine; (*b*) mauvaise odeur. 3. **to take a s. at sth.,** flairer qch.; respirer (un flacon de sels, etc.).

smell[2], *v.* (*p.t. & p.p.* **smelt,** *occ.* **smelled)**

I. *v.tr. & i.* 1. *v.tr. & ind.tr.* (*a*) flairer (qch.); sentir (une fleur); respirer l'odeur (d'un bouquet); **the dog smelt my shoes,** le chien a flairé, a reniflé, mes chaussures; (*b*) avoir de l'odorat; odorer; **not all animals can s.,** tous les animaux n'odorent pas; **he can't s.,** il n'a pas d'odorat; il ne sent rien; (*c*) sentir l'odeur de (qch.); sentir, percevoir (une odeur); **I can s. something burning,** je sens quelque chose qui brûle; ça sent le brûlé; **the horses put on speed as they s. their stable,** les chevaux se pressent comme ils sentent l'écurie; (*d*) sentir, flairer, pressentir (le danger, etc.); (*e*) **the dog smelt his way to the kitchen, to his master's retreat,** le chien, guidé par son flair, est arrivé à la cuisine, à la retraite de son maître. 2. *v.i.* (*a*) (*of flower, etc.*) sentir; **to s. good, bad, strong(ly),** sentir bon, mauvais, fort; **they s. sweet,** elles sentent bon; **to s. of violets,** sentir, fleurer, la violette; **these flowers don't s.,** ces fleurs n'ont pas d'odeur; **to s. of vanilla,** odorer la vanille; **room that smells damp,** pièce qui sent l'humidité; (*b*) sentir (mauvais); avoir une forte odeur; **how it smells!** comme ça sent! quelle odeur! **his feet s.,** il sent des pieds; **his breath smells,** il sent de la bouche; il a une mauvaise haleine; il a l'haleine mauvaise.

II. (*compound verb*) **smell out,** *v.tr.* (*of dog*) flairer, dépister (le gibier); (*of pers.*) flairer, découvrir (un secret, etc.).

smeller ['smelər], *s. P: A:* nez *m.*

smelliness ['smelinis], *s. F:* mauvaise odeur; puanteur *f*, fétidité *f* (d'un taudis, etc.).

smelling[1] ['smeliŋ], *a.* odoriférant, odorant; **sweet s.,** qui sent bon; aux douces odeurs.

smelling[2], *s.* humage *m* (du parfum d'une fleur); *O:* **s. salts,** sels (volatils) anglais, sel de vinaigre; **s. bottle,** flacon *m* de sels.

smelly ['smeli], *a. F:* (*a*) malodorant, puant; (*b*) suspect, louche.

smelt[1] [smelt], *v. Metall:* 1. *v.tr.* (*a*) fondre (le minerai); (*b*) extraire (le métal) par fusion. 2. *v.i.* (se fondre); **ore that smelts readily,** minerai qui fond facilement.

smelt[2], *s. Ich:* éperlan *m.*

smelter[1] ['smeltər], *s.* 1. (*pers.*) (*a*) fondeur *m* (de minerai); (*b*) métallurgiste *m.* 2. (*a*) *F:* fonderie *f*; usine *f* métallurgique; (*b*) four *m* de fusion; **s. gases,** gaz *m* de(s) four(s) de fusion.

smelter[2], *s.* pêcheur *m* d'éperlans.

smeltery ['smeltəri], *s. Metall:* fonderie *f.*

smelting ['smeltiŋ], *s.* 1. (*a*) fonte *f*, fusion *f* (d'un minerai, d'un métal); **electric, electrothermic, s.,** fusion électrique, électrothermique; **copper s., lead s., tin s.,** fusion du cuivre, du plomb, de l'étain; **s. of gold ores,** fonte des minerais aurifères; smeltage *m*; **s. of iron ores,** fonte, affinage *m*, des minerais de fer; **s. furnace,** four *m* de fusion; **s. powder,** poudre *f* de fusion; **s. trial,** essai *m* de fusion; (*b*) extraction *f* (du métal) par fusion; **s. works,** fonderie *f*; **copper s. works,** fonderie de cuivre. 2. (*science, profession*) la métallurgie.

smew [smju:], *s. Orn:* 1. harle *m* piette. 2. *NAm:* harle couronné; *Fr.C:* bec-scie couronné.

smidgen ['smidʒin], *s. NAm: F:* petite quantité.

smilax ['smailæks], *s.* 1. *Bot:* smilax *m*, salepareille *f.* 2. *Hort:* asparagus *m* (asparagoïdes).

smile[1] [smail], *s.* sourire *m*; **scornful s.,** sourire de mépris; **pitying s.,** sourire de pitié; **wintry s.,** sourire de découragement; **this question raised, provoked, a general s.,** cette question a fait sourire tout le monde; **he greeted us with a s.,** il nous a accueilli en souriant, avec un sourire; **with a s. on his lips,** le sourire aux lèvres; **to give a faint s.,** sourire du bout des lèvres; esquisser un sourire; **to force a s.,** grimacer un sourire; avoir un sourire forcé, contraint; **to give s.o. a s.,** adresser un sourire à qn; **she gave her most gracious s.,** elle souriait de son plus gracieux sourire; **she was all smiles,** elle était toute souriante; son visage s'épanouissait en un large sourire; **face wreathed in smiles,** visage rayonnant.

smile[2], *v.i. & tr.*

I. *v.i.* sourire; **he smiled disdainfully,** il a fait un sourire dédaigneux; il a souri dédaigneusement; **she was smiling up at me,** elle levait vers moi un regard souriant; **to s. at s.o.,** sourire à qn; adresser un sourire à qn; **Fortune smiles on him,** la fortune lui sourit, lui rit, lui fait bon visage; **to s. at s.o.'s ineffectual, vain, efforts,** sourire des vains efforts de qn; (*of child*) **to s. in his sleep,** rire aux anges; **to keep smiling,** *Lit:* **to s. in the face of adversity,** garder le sourire; faire bonne mine à mauvais jeu; faire bonne contenance; **to come up smiling,** (i) *Box:* reprendre la lutte avec le sourire aux lèvres; (ii) sortir de tous ses embarras sans perdre sa bonne humeur; se montrer supérieur aux revers, aux déceptions; **he always comes up smiling,** il garde toujours le sourire.

II. *v.tr.* 1. *with cogn. acc.* **to s. a bitter smile,** sourire amèrement; avoir un sourire amer; **she smiled her most gracious smile,** elle souriait de son plus gracieux sourire. 2. (*a*) **to s. s.o.'s fears away,** écarter d'un sourire les craintes de qn; (*b*) **to s. a welcome to s.o.,** accueillir qn avec, par, un sourire; **to s. one's gratitude, one's satisfaction,** exprimer sa gratitude, son contentement, par un sourire.

smiling ['smailiŋ], *a.* souriant; **the s. countryside,** la riante campagne; **to look s.,** être tout souriant.

smilingly ['smailiŋli], *adv.* en souriant; avec un sourire.

sminthurid [smin'θju:rid], *s. Ent:* sminthure *m*, sminthuridé *m.*

Sminthuridae [smin'θju:ridi:], *s.pl. Ent:* sminthuridés *m.*

smirch[1] [smə:tʃ], *s.* tache *f*; salissure *f*, souillure *f*; **s. of grease,** tache de cambouis; noircissure *f*; **he came out of it without a s. on his character,** il en est sorti sans une tache à sa réputation.

smirch[2], *v.tr.* tacher; salir, souiller; **smirched reputation,** réputation souillée, salie.

smirk[1] [smə:k], *s.* sourire affecté, minaudier; minauderie *f*; **smirks and smiles,** simagrées *f* de politesse.

smirk[2], *v.i.* sourire d'un air affecté; minauder, mignarder; **to s. and smile,** faire des simagrées.

smirking[1] ['smə:kiŋ], *a.* affecté; minaudier.

smirking[2], *s.* minauderie(s) *f(pl)*; mignardise(s) *f(pl)*; simagrées *fpl.*

smite[1] [smait], *s. A: & Lit:* coup *m*; bruit *m* de coup.

smite[2], *v.tr.* **(smote** [smout]; **smitten** ['smitən]) frapper.
1. *A: & Lit:* **to s. one's thigh,** se frapper, se taper, la cuisse avec la main; **the report of a gun smote my ear,** une détonation me frappa l'oreille; **to s. the enemy,** frapper, battre, l'ennemi; **to s. s.o. down,** abattre qn; frapper qn à mort; *B:* **when I shall s. the land of Egypt,** quand je frapperai le pays d'Égypte; **my conscience smote me,** je fus frappé de remords; **my heart smote me,** j'eus un serrement de cœur; **to s. the lyre,** pincer de la lyre. 2. **to be smitten with blindness,** être frappé de cécité; devenir aveugle; **they were smitten with the plague,** ils sont tombés malades de la peste; **smitten with fear, with remorse,** sous le coup de l'effroi; pris de remords; **to be smitten with a desire to do sth.,** être pris de désir de faire qch.; **smitten with a mad ambition,** pris d'une folle ambition; **I was smitten with the beauty of the scene,** la beauté du paysage m'a fait une profonde impression; *F:* **to be smitten with a girl,** être épris, amouraché, d'une jeune fille. 3. *v.i. Lit:* (*a*) **his knees smote together,** ses genoux s'entrechoquaient; (*b*) **he smote upon the door with his sword,** il frappa sur la porte avec son épée; **a sound smote upon his ear,** un son lui frappa l'oreille; (*c*) **they smote off the heads of their enemies,** ils coupèrent les têtes de leurs ennemis.

smiter ['smaitər], *s. A: & Lit:* frappeur, -euse.

smith[1] [smiθ], *s.* 1. forgeron *m*; **shoeing s.,** maréchal ferrant. 2. *Amph:* **Brazilian s.,** (rainette *f*) forgeron du Brésil.

smith[2], *v.tr. & i.* 1. forger (le fer, une épée). 2. travailler comme forgeron, comme maréchal ferrant.

smithereens [smiðə'ri:nz], *s.pl. F:* morceaux *m*; miettes *f*; **the ship was blown to s.,** l'explosion a réduit le navire en miettes; **to smash, knock, sth. to s.,** briser, réduire, qch. en éclats, en mille morceaux, en miettes; mettre qch. en capilotade; atomiser qch.

smithery ['smiθəri], *s.* 1. travaux *mpl* de forge, de maréchalerie. 2. = SMITHY.

smithing ['smiθiŋ], *s.* = SMITHERY 1.

smithsonite ['smiθsənait], *s. Miner:* smithsonite *f.*

smithy ['smiði], *s.* forge *f*; **shoeing s.,** (atelier *m* de) maréchalerie *f.*

smock[1] [smɔk], *s.* 1. *A: & Dial:* chemise *f* (de femme). 2. blouse *f*, sarrau *m.* 3. **s. mill,** moulin *m* à toit tournant.

smock[2], *v.tr. Needlw:* orner (une robe, etc.) de smocks.

smocking ['smɔkiŋ], *s. Needlw:* (*a*) fronces *fpl* smock; smocks *mpl*; (*b*) nids *mpl* d'abeilles.

smog [smɔg], *s. F:* brouillard fumeux, smog *m.*

smokable ['smoukəbl]. 1. *a.* que l'on peut fumer; fumable; **quite a s. cigar,** cigare *m* qui se laisse fumer. 2. *s.pl. F: A:* **smokables,** tabac *m.*

smoke[1] [smouk], *s.* 1. (*a*) fumée *f*; (*of furnace, etc.*) **to emit s.,** fumer; dégager de la fumée; **s. black,** noir *m* de fumée; **s. bomb,** bombe *f* fumigène; **s. helmet,** casque *m* à fumée; casque pare-fumée; casque respiratoire; **s. signals,** signaux *m* de fumée; **s. brown, grey,** brun, gris, fumée (*inv*); *F:* (*of project, etc.*) **to end in, go up in, s.,** s'en aller en fumée; n'aboutir à rien; *A:* **to go like s.,** aller comme sur des roulettes; *F: O:* **the Big S.,** une grande ville, *esp.* Londres; **to go up to the (great) S.,** aller à Londres, à une grande ville; *Prov:* **there's no s. without fire,** il n'y a pas de fumée sans feu; **there's no fire without s.,** il y a une ombre à tout; il n'y a pas de parfait bonheur; (*b*) **s. bush, s. plant, s. tree,** arbre *m* à perruque; fustet *m*; coquecigrue *f.* 2. (*a*) **let's have a s.,** si on fumait une cigarette, une pipe, un cigare? **after dinner we had a quiet s.,** après le dîner nous avons fumé tranquillement; **s. room,** fumoir *m*; (*b*) *F: O:* cigare *m*, cigarette *f*; **pass round the smokes,** faites circuler les cigares, les cigarettes.

smoke[2]. 1. *v.i.* (*a*) (*emit smoke, vapour*) fumer; **the lamp is smoking,** la lampe fume, charbonne, file; **the horses' flanks were smoking,** les flancs des chevaux fumaient; les chevaux étaient tout fumants; (*b*) *F:* rougir; (*c*) *Austr: F:* **to s. (off),** filer, déguerpir. 2. *v.tr.* (*a*) (i) fumer (du jambon, des harengs, etc.); boucaner (la viande, le poisson); (ii) enfumer (une plante, les pucerons, etc.); (iii) **to s. out (a fox, etc.),** enfumer, faire déguerpir (un renard, etc.); (*b*) noircir de fumée, enfumer (le plafond, etc.); (*c*) *v.tr. & i.* fumer (du tabac); **do you s.?** fumez-vous? êtes-vous fumeur? **do you mind if I s.?** la fumée vous gêne-t-elle? (*with passive force*) **this pipe smokes well,** cette pipe se fume bien, est bonne; **to s. oneself sick,** se rendre malade à force de fumer; (*d*) *F: A:* **to s. s.o.,** (i) se moquer de qn; (ii) découvrir le pot aux roses.

smokebox ['smoukbɔks], *s. Mch:* boîte *f* à fumée.

smoked [smoukt], *a.* 1. (*a*) (jambon, etc.) fumé; (*b*) (plafond, etc.) enfumé; (*c*) **s. glass,** (i) verre fumé, noirci à la fumée; (ii) verre à teinte fumée. 2. *Cu:* qui a un goût de fumée.

smokehole ['smoukhoul], *s.* 1. trou *m* (dans une cabane, etc.) pour laisser échapper la fumée. 2. bouche *f* (de cheminée). 3. *Geol:* fumerolle *f* (de volcan).

smokehouse ['smoukhaus], *s.* fumoir *m* (pour harengs, de tannerie, etc.).

smokeless ['smouklis], *a.* (houille, poudre) sans fumée; **s. furnace,** foyer *m* fumivore; **s. combustion,** combustion exempte de fumée; **s. zone,** zone *f* où il est interdit de rejeter de la fumée.

smoke-o(h) ['smoukou], *s. Austr: F:* = pause-café *f.*

smokeproof[1] ['smoukpru:f], *a.* à l'épreuve de la fumée.

smokeproof[2], *v.tr.* rendre (qch.) à l'épreuve de la fumée.

smokeproof[3], *s. Engr:* fumé *m.*

smoker ['smoukər], *s.* 1. (*pers.*) (*a*) *Ind:* fumeur, -euse (de jambon, etc.); (*b*) fumeur, -euse (de tabac); **heavy s.,** grand fumeur; *Med:* **smoker's heart, smoker's throat,** maladie de cœur, de gorge, occasionnée par le tabagisme. 2. *F: Rail: etc:* compartiment *m* pour fumeurs. 3. *Ap:* enfumoir *m.*

smokescreen ['smoukskri:n], *s.* écran *m* de fumée; nuage artificiel, rideau *m* de fumée.

smokestack ['smoukstæk], *s. O:* 1. cheminée *f* (de locomotive, de bateau à vapeur). 2. cheminée d'usine, etc.

smokewood ['smoukwud], *s. Bot:* fustet *m.*

smokiness ['smoukinis], *s.* 1. condition fumeuse (de l'atmosphère, etc.); atmosphère enfumée (d'une ville, etc.). 2. goût *m* de fumée.

smoking[1] ['smoukiŋ], *a.* fumant, qui fume; **s. horses,** chevaux fumants (de sueur); **s. hot,** tout fumant.

smoking[2], *s.* 1. émission *f* de fumée. 2. fumage *m* (de jambon, etc.). 3. (*tobacco*) **no s. (allowed),** défense *f* de fumer; on ne fume pas ici; **do you mind my s.?** la fumée ne vous gêne pas? vous me permettez de fumer? *Rail: etc:* **s. compartment,** compartiment *m* pour fumeurs; **s. room,** fumoir *m*; *O:* **s. concert,** concert *m* où il est permis de fumer; **s. jacket,** veston *m* d'intérieur; **s. cap,** calotte grecque; bonnet grec.

smoky ['smouki], *a.* 1. (*a*) (*of atmosphere*) fumeux; fuligineux; (*of room*) plein de fumée; enfumé; **s. towns,**

villes enfumées; (*b*) *esp. U.S:* (horizon, etc.) brumeux. **2.** (*a*) (plafond, etc.) noirci par la fumée; (*b*) *Geol:* **s. quartz,** quartz enfumé. **3. s. lamp,** lampe fumeuse, qui fume, qui file; **s. fire,** feu *m* qui fume. **4.** (goût *m*) de fumée.

smolt [smoult], *s. Ich:* saumon *m* d'un à deux ans; saumon qui descend à la mer; smolt *m*, tacon *m*.

smooch [smu:tʃ], *v.i. P:* se bécoter; se peloter.

smooth[1] [smu:ð], *a.* **1.** (*a*) (surface *f*, pâte *f*) lisse; (chemin, etc.) uni, égal, sans aspérités; **to make s.,** lisser (ses cheveux), aplanir (une route, etc.); (*of road*) **to grow smoother,** s'aplanir; **s. as glass, as ice,** poli, uni, comme la glace, comme une glace; **s. paper,** papier *m* lisse; papier glacé; **s. forehead,** front *m* sans rides; **s. skin,** peau douce, satinée; **s. sea,** mer calme, unie, plate; (*of sea*) **as s. as a millpond,** calme, plate, comme un lac; (*b*) (tige, menton) glabre; (drap) à poil ras. **2.** (*a*) doux, *f.* douce; **s. running,** fonctionnement doux, régulier (d'une machine); roulement silencieux; **s. shave,** rasage *m* en douceur; (*b*) **s. wine,** vin moelleux; **s. style,** style uni, coulant, moelleux; (*c*) **s. temper,** humeur égale, facile; (*d*) doucereux, mielleux; **s. tongue,** langue doucereuse; *F:* **s. type, character,** (i) personne mielleuse; beau parleur; (ii) un malin; (*e*) *adv.* **s.-tempered,** au caractère égale, facile; **s.-spoken,** aux paroles doucereuses, mielleuses.

smooth[2], *s.* **1. to give one's hair a s. (down),** lisser ses cheveux; se lisser les cheveux. **2.** *Nau:* accalmie *f*, embellie *f*. **3.** (*a*) partie *f* lisse (de qch.); (*b*) terrain uni.

smooth[3], *v.tr.* **1.** (*a*) **to s. (down),** lisser (ses plumes, ses cheveux, etc.); **to s. s.o. down,** apaiser l'irritation de qn; (*b*) aplanir, unir, recaler, planer, blanchir (une planche); égaliser (le terrain); (*c*) défroisser (un vêtement); **to s. out a crease,** faire disparaître un faux pli; **to s. out material,** éclancher, écrancher, le drap; **to s. out, over, difficulties,** aplanir des difficultés; (*d*) **to s. one's brow,** dérider son front; se dérider; **to s. the way for s.o.,** aplanir la voie pour qn. **2. to s. off (an angle, etc.),** adoucir (un angle, etc.).

smoothbore ['smu:ðbɔər], *s.* canon *m* à âme lisse, fusil *m* à canon lisse.

smoothbored ['smu:ðbɔ:d], *a.* à âme, à canon, lisse.

smoother ['smu:ðər], *s.* **1.** (*pers.*) aplanisseur, -euse. **2.** *Tls:* lissoir *m*.

smoothgrind ['smu:ðgraind], *v.tr.* (*p.t. & p.p.* **-ground** [graund]) écacher (un outil).

smoothie ['smu:ði], *s. F:* = SMOOTHY.

smoothing ['smu:ðiŋ], *s.* lissage *m*; aplanissement *m*, aplanissage *m*, adoucissage *m* (du bois, etc.); égalisation *f* (du terrain); *Carp:* **s. plane,** rabot *m* à repasser; *Leath:* **s. stick,** formoir *m*; *Laund: O:* **s. iron,** fer *m* à repasser.

smoothly ['smu:ðli], *adv.* **1.** uniment; sans inégalités. **2.** (marcher, travailler) doucement; (*of machine*) **to work, go, s.,** marcher sans à-coups, sans secousses; **everything's going on s.,** tout va comme sur des roulettes; **things are not going s.,** cela ne marche pas comme il faut. **3.** (parler) mielleusement, d'un ton doucereux, flatteur.

smoothness ['smu:ðnis], *s.* **1.** (*a*) égalité *f* (d'une surface); douceur *f*, satiné *m* (de la peau); (*b*) calme *m* (de la mer, de tempérament). **2.** douceur (de la marche d'une machine, du trot d'un cheval); bon fonctionnement (d'une machine, d'une administration, etc.); *Lit:* **s. of style,** coulant *m* du style; *Mus:* **s. of execution,** égalité de jeu. **3.** (*of pers.*) douceur feinte; air doucereux.

smooth-running [smu:ð'rʌniŋ], *a.* (*of machinery, etc.*) à marche douce, régulière.

smoothy ['smu:ði], *s. F:* personne mielleuse, trop polie; chattemite *f*.

smother[1] ['smʌðər], *s.* **1.** (*a*) fumée épaisse, étouffante; (*b*) brouillard épais; (*c*) nuage épais de poussière; **s. of foam,** tourbillon *m* d'eau écumante. **2.** feu *m* qui couve.

smother[2]. **1.** *v.tr.* (*a*) étouffer (qn, le feu, ses sentiments); suffoquer (qn); éteindre, étouffer (un son); *F:* **to smother s.o. with kisses,** étouffer, accabler, manger, qn de caresses; **to s. a curse,** réprimer un juron; **to s. a cry,** retenir un cri; **to s. one's laughter,** pouffer dans son mouchoir; **to s. one's pride,** faire taire son orgueil; **to s. (up) a scandal,** cacher, couvrir, un scandale; (*b*) recouvrir; **strawberries smothered in, with, cream,** fraises enrobées de crème; **to s. sth. with ink,** barbouiller qch. d'encre; **to be smothered in furs,** être emmitouflé de fourrures; **smothered in dust,** enfariné de poussière. **2.** *v.i.* suffoquer.

smothered ['smʌðəd], *a.* (cri) sourd.

smothering ['smʌð(ə)riŋ], *s.* étouffement *m*; suffocation *f*.

smoulder[1] ['smouldər], *s.* **1.** fumée épaisse. **2.** feu *m* qui couve.

smoulder[2], *v.i.* (*a*) (*of coal, etc.*) brûler lentement, sans flamme; (*b*) (*of fire, rebellion, etc.*) couver (sous la cendre).

smouldering[1] ['smould(ə)riŋ], *a.* (*a*) (charbon, etc.) qui brûle sans fumée; (*b*) (feu, etc.) qui couve (sous la cendre).

smouldering[2], *s.* combustion lente.

smudge[1] [smʌdʒ], *s.* tache *f*; noircissure *f*; salissure *f*; bavure *f* de plume; **you've got a s. on your nose,** vous avez une tache (de suie, d'encre, etc.) sur le nez.

smudge[2], *v.tr.* salir, souiller, tacher (ses mains, etc.); barbouiller, maculer (son écriture); étaler (une tache); *Typ:* mâchurer (une épreuve).

smudge[3], *s. U.S:* **1.** fumée épaisse, étouffante. **2. s. (fire),** feu *m* fumigène (de déchets humides, etc.) allumé en plein air pour écarter les moustiques, etc.; *Hort:* **s. pot,** foyer *m* fumigène.

smudgy ['smʌdʒi], *a.* **1.** taché, souillé, sali; (*of writing*) barbouillé, maculé, boueux. **2.** (contour, etc.) estompé, noyé.

smug [smʌg], *a.* (*a*) (ton, air) suffisant, avantageux; satisfait de soi-même; **there's something s. about him, he has a s. look,** il a l'air suffisant; **s. optimism,** optimisme béat; (*b*) *A:* tiré à quatre épingles.

smuggle [smʌgl], *v.tr. & i.* (faire) passer (des marchandises, etc.) en contrebande, en fraude; **to s. sth. into, out of, a country,** entrer, sortir, qch. en contrebande; **to s. sth. into a room,** apporter qch. subrepticement, à la dérobée, furtivement, dans une pièce; **to s. sth. away, out,** emporter qch. subrepticement; faire disparaître qch.

smuggler ['smʌglər], *s.* contrebandier, -ière; fraudeur, -euse (à la douane).

smuggling ['smʌgliŋ], *s.* contrebande *f*; fraude *f* (aux droits de douane).

smugly ['smʌgli], *adv.* d'un air suffisant.

smugness ['smʌgnis], *s.* suffisance *f*.

smut[1] [smʌt], *s.* **1.** (*a*) parcelle *f* de suie; flocon *m* de suie; (*b*) tache *f* de suie, noiré *m* (**on the face,** au visage); (*c*) insecte *m* minuscule; petite bête. **2.** *coll.* saletés *fpl*, grivoiseries *fpl*, indécences *fpl*, ordures *fpl*; **to talk s.,** dire des malpropretés, des saletés, des ordures. **3.** (*a*) *Agr:* charbon *m*, suie *f*, brûlure *f*, nielle *f* (des céréales); **stinking s.,** carie *f*; (*b*) *Fung:* **s. fungi, smuts,** ustilaginales *fpl*.

smut[2], *v.* **(smutted) 1.** *v.tr.* noircir, salir (qch.); tacher (de suie). **2.** *v.i. Agr:* (*of cereals*) être atteint du charbon, de la nielle, de carie; (se) carier.

smutball ['smʌtbɔ:l], *s. Agr:* grain de blé moucheté.

smutch [smʌtʃ], *v.tr. A:* = SMUDGE[2].

smutted ['smʌtid], *a.* **1.** noirci, taché (de suie). **2.** *Agr:* (blé) charbonné, carié, atteint du charbon, de carie; maculé, moucheté, niellé.

smuttily ['smʌtili], *adv.* indécemment, grossièrement.

smuttiness ['smʌtinis], *s.* **1.** noirceur *f*, saleté *f*. **2.** obscénité *f*, grivoiserie *f*, grossièreté *f* (d'une remarque, etc.). **3.** *Agr:* état maculé, niellé, charbonné (du blé).

smutty ['smʌti], *a.* **1.** (*a*) noirci, noir; sali (de suie); **s. yellow,** jaune sale; *Typ:* **s. proof,** épreuve boueuse; (*b*) (*of conversation, etc.*) malpropre, ordurier, grossier, grivois; **s. joke,** plaisanterie grossière; **to tell s. stories,** en dire de vertes. **2.** (*a*) *Agr:* = SMUTTED 2; (*b*) (arbre) piqué, entamé (par la pourriture).

Smyrna ['smɔ:nə], *Pr.n. Geog:* Smyrne *f*.

snack[1] [snæk], *s.* **1.** *A:* part *f*, lot *m*, portion *f*; **to go snacks,** partager (qch. avec qn). **2.** léger repas; casse-croûte *m inv*; collation *f*; **to have a s.,** casser la croûte; prendre un casse-croûte; manger un morceau sur le pouce; **s. bar,** casse-croûte; *F:* snack(-bar).

snack[2], *v.i. esp. NAm: F:* casser la croûte; manger un morceau sur le pouce.

snaffle[1] ['snæfl], *s. Harn:* **s. (bit),** mors *m* de filet; **s. (bridle),** bridon *m*; **s. rein,** rêne *f* de filet.

snaffle[2], *v.tr.* **1.** conduire (un cheval) sur le bridon. **2.** *P:* voler, chiper (qch.).

snafu[1] [snæ'fu:], *a. P:* en (grand) désordre; chaotique; amoché; bousillé; foutu.

snafu[2], *v.tr. P:* mettre (qch.) en désordre; rendre (une situation) chaotique; bousiller (qch.).

snag[1] [snæg], *s.* **1.** (*a*) chicot *m* ((i) d'arbre, (ii) de dent); (*b*) chicot, souche *f*, au ras d'eau ou formant écueil; entrave *f* à la navigation fluviale; (*c*) écueil *m*, obstacle caché; pierre *f* d'achoppement; accroc *m*; *F:* os *m*; **to look for the s. in sth.,** chercher finesse à qch.; **to strike, hit, a s., to come across a s.,** se heurter à un obstacle, à une anicroche; avoir un pépin; **all sorts of little snags,** toutes sortes de petites difficultés, d'accrocs; **there's a s.,** il y a quelque chose qui ne marche pas; **there's, that's, the s.!** voilà le hic! **2.** (*a*) saillie *f*, dent *f*, protubérance *f*; (*b*) andouiller *m* (de bois de cerf). **3.** *Austr: P:* **snags,** saucisses *f*.

snag[2], *v.tr.* **(snagged) 1.** (*a*) (*of boat*) **to be snagged,** se heurter contre un chicot submergé; toucher un écueil; (*b*) *F:* faire un accroc à (sa robe, etc.). **2.** (*a*) mettre (une rivière, un chenal) en bon état de navigation; enlever les chicots et autres écueils; (*b*) *Agr: etc:* essoucher, défricher (un terrain). **3.** *U.S:* **to s. a casting,** ébarber une pièce de fonte.

snaggletooth ['snægltu:θ], *s.* dent saillante.

snaggletoothed ['snægltu:θt], *a.* aux dents saillantes.

snaggy ['snægi], *a.* **1.** (*a*) noueux, épineux; (*b*) (*of land*) hérissé de souches. **2.** (*of river, etc.*) semé d'obstacles submergés.

snail[1] [sneil], *s.* **1.** (*a*) escargot *m*; colimaçon *m*; limaçon *m*; **edible s.,** escargot comestible; **Roman s., Burgundy s.,** escargot de Bourgogne; **s. breeding,** héliciculture *f*; **s. breeder,** héliciculteur *m*; **at a snail's pace,** à pas de tortue; (*b*) **water s.,** (i) *Moll:* hélice *f* aquatique; (ii) *Hyd.E:* pompe spirale; (*c*) *Ich:* **sea s.,** liparis *m*. **2.** *Clockm:* **s. (wheel),** limaçon.

snail[2], *v.tr. Clockm:* tailler (un arbre) en limaçon.

snailery ['sneiləri], *s.* escargotière *f*; parc *m* à escargots.

snailfish ['sneilfiʃ], *s. Ich:* limace *f* de mer.

snake[1] [sneik], *s.* (*a*) *Rept:* serpent *m*; **common s., grass s., ringed s., water s.,** couleuvre *f* à collier, serpent d'eau; hydrophis *m*; **European smooth s.,** couleuvre lisse; **ribbon s.,** couleuvre jarretière; **egg-eating s.,** serpent mangeur d'œufs; **chicken s.,** serpent mangeur de poules; **rainbow s.,** serpent arc-en-ciel; **indigo s.,** serpent indigo; **leopard s.,** couleuvre léopard; **Indian rat s.,** serpent ratier; **corn s., red rat s.,** serpent des blés; **king s.,** serpent-roi *m*; **milk s.,** serpent de lait; **s. charmer,** charmeur, -euse, de serpents; *Fig:* **to cherish, nourish, a s. in one's bosom,** réchauffer un serpent dans son sein; **a s. in the grass,** (i) un danger caché; une anguille sous roche; (ii) un faux jeton, un individu louche; *F:* **to see snakes,** avoir le delirium tremens; **great snakes!** grand Dieu! (*b*) *Rept:* **hooded s.,** cobra (-capello) *m*, naja *m*; **spitting s.,** sépédon *m*; **flying s.,** chrysopélé *m*; **cat s.,** boïga *m*; *Amph:* **Congo s.,** amphiuma *m*, amphiume *m*; (*c*) *Ich:* **s. mackerel,** maquereau-serpent *m*, *pl.* maquereaux-serpents; (*d*) *Bot:* **snake's head (fritillary, lily),** fritillaire *f* méléagride, (fritillaire) damier *m*; (*e*) *Games:* **snakes and ladders,** jeu enfantin du genre du jeu de l'oie; (*f*) *U.S:* **s. fence,** clôture *f* en treillis, en lattes disposées en zig-zag.

snake[2]. **1.** *v.i.* (*a*) (*of road, smoke, etc.*) serpenter; (*of parachute*) se mettre en torche; *Aut:* **the trailer began to s.,** la remorque s'est mise à serpenter; (*b*) **to s. along,** ramper; *F:* **to s. off,** s'esquiver. **2.** *v.tr.* (*a*) *Nau:* serpenter (deux amarres); (*b*) faire serpenter (un câble, etc.); (*c*) *NAm:* traîner (des troncs d'arbre).

snakebird ['sneikbə:d], *s. Orn:* ahinga *m*, *F:* oiseau-serpent *m*, *pl.* oiseaux-serpents.

snakebite ['sneikbait], *s.* morsure *f* de serpent.

snakefish ['sneikfiʃ], *s. Ich:* **1. red s.,** cépole *m*, ruban *m*, fouet *m*. **2.** régalec *m*. **3.** synodonte *m*.

snakehead ['sneikhed], *s.* **1.** *Bot:* chélone *f*. **2.** *Ich:* **s. (millet),** tête-de-serpent *m*, ophicéphalidé *m*.

snakeheaded ['sneikhedid], *a.* à tête de serpent; **s. fish** = SNAKEHEAD 2.

snake(-)like ['sneiklaik], *a.* anguiforme, ophidien.

snake(-)ring ['sneikriŋ], *s. Fish: etc:* anneau spiral, serpentiforme.

snakeroot ['sneikru:t], *s. Bot:* serpentaire *f*; **Virginia(n) s.,** (i) serpentaire de Virginie, aristoloche *f* serpentaire; (ii) polygale *m* de Virginie; **button s., corn s.,** (i) liatris *m*; (ii) érynge *m*, eryngium *m*, panicaut *m*.

snakestone ['sneikstoun], *s.* **1.** pierre *f* à aiguiser (des carrières d'Écosse). **2.** *Paleont: F:* ammonite *f*.

snakeweed ['sneikwi:d], *s. Bot:* **1.** bistorte *f*; liane *f* à serpents. **2.** = SNAKEROOT.

snakewood ['sneikwud], *s.* **1.** *Bot:* (*a*) strychnos *m*; *F:* bois *m* de couleuvre; (*b*) ophioxylon *m*; bois de serpent; serpentine *f*; (*c*) piratinère *m* de Guyane. **2.** *Com:* bois satiné; bois de lettres.

snaking ['sneikiŋ], *s.* serpentage *m*; *Av:* oscillation *f* de lacet.

snaky ['sneiki], *a.* **1.** (*a*) couleuvrin; de serpent; **the Gorgon's s. hair,** la chevelure de la Gorgone, hérissée de serpents; (*b*) (langue, etc.) perfide, de vipère; (homme) perfide; (*c*) *Austr: F:* (i) irritable; (ii) fâché, irrité. **2.** (*of road, etc.*) serpentant, sinueux, tortueux. **3.** infesté de serpents.

snap[1] [snæp], *s., a. & adv.*

I. *s.* **1.** (*a*) coup *m* de dents; **to make a s. at sth., at s.o.,** tâcher de happer qch.; (*of dog*) essayer, faire mine, de mordre qn; (*b*) coup de ciseaux; (*c*) coup sec, claquement *m* (des dents, d'un fouet, etc.); bruit *m* d'un bouton pression qui se ferme; **to shut one's mouth with a s.,** fermer la bouche en faisant claquer ses dents; **the**

box shut with a s., la boîte s'est fermée en claquant, avec un coup sec; **with a s. of the fingers he left us,** il nous a quittés en faisant claquer ses doigts (en signe de défi); *A:* **I don't care a s.,** je m'en soucie comme d'une guigne. **2. to answer with a s.,** répondre d'un ton sec, mordant, cassant. **3.** cassure *f*, rupture soudaine; **there was a s.,** quelque chose a cassé. **4.** (*a*) *Th: O:* engagement *m* de courte durée; (*b*) **cold s.,** courte période de temps froid; froid soudain; coup de froid. **5.** *F:* énergie *f*, vivacité *f*, entrain *m*; **put some s. into it!** un peu d'énergie! **6.** *Cu:* biscuit croquant; croquet *m* au gingembre. **7.** (*a*) **s. (fastener),** (i) fermoir *m* (de livre, de valise, etc.); (ii) agrafe *f*, fermoir (de collier), cadenas *m* (de bracelet); (iii) bouton (fermoir) à pression, fermoir pression, bouton pression, *F:* pression *f*; **s. bolt,** verrou *m* à fermeture automatique, à ressort; **s. lock,** serrure *f* à ressort; housset *m*, houssette *f* (de malle, etc.); *El:* **s. contact,** contact *m* à languette; (*b*) **s. (hook),** (porte-)mousqueton *m* (de chaîne de montre, etc.); (*c*) **s. of a lock,** bouterolle *f* d'une serrure. **8.** *Tls: Metalw:* **(rivet) s., s. tool,** bouterolle, chasse-rivet(s) *m inv*, mandrin *m* d'abattage. **9.** *Phot:* = SNAPSHOT[1]. **10.** *Cards:* jeu enfantin où il faut reconnaître le premier deux cartes pareilles. **11.** *U.S: F:* **soft s.,** chose *f* facile; coup tout fait.

II. *a.* instantané, imprévu; **with s. action,** à détente brusque; **s. decision,** décision rapide; *Parl:* **s. division,** vote *m* de surprise; **s. firing,** tir *m* au jugé; **s. shot,** coup (de fusil) lâché sans viser.

III. *adv.* **to go s.,** faire crac; se casser net; **s. went my stick!** crac! voilà ma canne cassée, qui se casse!

snap[2], *v.* **(snapped** [snæpt])

I. *v.i.* **1.** (*a*) (*of dog, etc.*) **to s. at s.o., sth.,** chercher à mordre, à happer, à saisir, qn, qch.; donner un coup de dents à qn, à qch.; (*of dog*) **to s. at a hare,** bourrer un lièvre; (*of trigger, etc.*) **to s. back,** revenir brusquement; **to s. at an opportunity,** saisir vivement une occasion; sauter sur une belle occasion; (*b*) *F:* **to s. (out) at s.o.,** s'adresser à qn d'un ton sec, cassant; rembarrer qn. **2.** (*of teeth, whip, etc.*) claquer; faire un bruit sec; (*of fastener*) se fermer avec un bruit sec; (*of pistol*) (i) partir, *P:* péter; (ii) rater. **3.** (*of stick, rope, etc.*) **to s. (in two),** se casser net; se rompre avec un bruit sec.

II. *v.tr.* **1.** (*of dog, etc.*) saisir (qch.) d'un coup de dents; happer (qch.); **the dog snapped a chop from the table,** le chien a happé une côtelette sur la table. **2.** (*a*) faire claquer (un fouet, etc.); **to s. one's teeth (together),** (faire) claquer ses dents; **to s. one's fingers,** faire claquer ses doigts; **to s. one's fingers at s.o., in s.o.'s face,** narguer qn; faire la nique, la figue, à qn; (*b*) **to s. a spring,** déclencher un ressort; **to s. a pistol at s.o.,** tirer un coup de pistolet à qn; (*c*) *Phot: F:* **to s. s.o., sth.,** prendre un instantané de qn, de qch.; prendre qn, qch. **3.** casser, rompre (une canne, etc.); **snapped tendon,** tendon claqué; **to s. sth. in two,** casser qch. net. **4. to s. (out) words,** jeter des mots d'un ton cassant, bref; **to s. out an order,** donner un ordre d'un ton sec; **"no," he snapped,** "non," dit-il d'un ton sec, d'un ton brusque. **5.** (*a*) faire (qch.) brusquement; *Parl:* **to s. a division on a question,** mettre une question aux voix sans donner le temps de la discuter; (*b*) *v.tr. & i. F:* **to s. out of it,** se secouer. **6.** *Mec.E:* bouteroller (un rivet).

III. (*compound verbs*) **1. snap off.** (*a*) *v.tr.* (i) enlever (qch.) d'un coup de dents; *F:* **to s. s.o.'s head off,** rembarrer vivement qn; (ii) casser (le bout d'une canne, etc.); (*b*) *v.i.* se détacher brusquement, avec un bruit sec; se casser.

2. snap to, *v.i.* **the lid snapped to,** le couvercle s'est refermé avec un bruit sec (et en faisant jouer la serrure).

3. snap up, *v.tr.* saisir, happer (qch.); **the bird snapped up the fly,** l'oiseau a gobé, a happé, la mouche; **to s. up a bargain,** saisir une occasion; sauter sur une occasion; **goods that are quickly snapped up,** marchandises qui s'enlèvent vite, qu'on s'arrache; **the tickets are being snapped up like hot cakes,** les billets s'enlèvent comme des petits pains.

snapdragon ['snæpdrægən], *s.* **1.** *Bot:* muflier *m*, gueule-de-lion *f*, gueule-de-loup *f*, *pl.* gueules-de-lion, -de-loup. **2.** jeu *m* (de Noël) qui consiste à happer des raisins secs dans du cognac flambant et à les manger tout chauds.

snaphead ['snæphed], *s.* *Metalw:* **1.** rivure bouterollée, tête bouterollée (de rivet); **s. rivet,** rivet *m* à tête ronde, rivet bouterollé. **2.** *Tls:* bouterolle *f*; chasse-rivet(s) *m inv.*

snapper ['snæpər], *s.* **1.** (*a*) personne hargneuse; (*b*) **s. up (of unconsidered trifles),** ramasseur, -euse, de tout ce qui se trouve sous la main. **2.** (*a*) *Ich:* lutjanide *m*; (*b*) *Rept:* **alligator s.,** tortue *f* vorace alligator.

snappily ['snæpili], *adv.* **1.** (parler) d'un ton hargneux, irrité. **2. to do sth. s.,** se dépêcher de faire qch.

snapping[1] ['snæpiŋ], *a.* **1.** hargneux, revêche. **2.** (chien) hargneux, qui cherche à mordre.

snapping[2], *s.* **1.** claquement *m* (de dents). **2.** brusque rupture *f* (d'un bâton, d'une branche morte). **3.** déclenchement *m* (d'un ressort).

snappish ['snæpiʃ], *a.* = SNAPPY 1.

snappishness ['snæpiʃnis], *s.* mauvaise humeur; humeur hargneuse, ton hargneux; irritabilité *f*.

snappy ['snæpi], *a.* **1.** (*a*) irritable; (ton) hargneux; (*b*) (chien) hargneux. **2.** (style, etc.) vif, plein d'allant, plein de sève; **s. phrase, story,** locution pleine de sel; histoire bien bouclée. **3.** *Aut: O:* (moteur) nerveux; *F:* **make it s.!** dépêche-toi! grouille-toi! plus vite que ça!

snapshot[1] ['snæpʃɔt], *s.* **1.** *Phot: F:* instantané *m*. **2.** *Cmptr:* **s. programme,** programme *m* d'analyse sélective; **s. dump,** vidage dynamique sélectif, à la demande.

snapshot[2], *v.tr.* **(snapshotted)** *Phot: A:* prendre un instantané de (qn).

snare[1] ['snɛər], *s.* **1.** (*a*) *Ven:* lacet *m*, lacs *m*, filet *m*, collet *m*, panneau *m*, attrape *f*, attrapoire *f*; (*for moles, etc.*) arbalète *f*; **bird s.,** tenderie *f* aux oiseaux; **to lay, set, a s.,** dresser, tendre, un filet, un lacet; **to lay snares,** colleter; **to be caught in a s.,** être pris au lacet; (*b*) piège *f*; (*of pers.*) **to be caught in a, the, s., caught in one's own s.,** être pris à son propre piège, tomber dans le piège; être pris au piège, dans ses propres lacets; **it's a s. and a delusion,** c'est un miroir aux alouettes. **2.** *Surg:* **(nasal polypus) s.,** serre-nœud *m*, *pl.* serre-nœud(s). **3.** *Mus:* **s. drum,** tambour *m* à timbre; caisse claire; **snares of a drum,** timbre *m* d'un tambour.

snare[2], *v.tr.* (*a*) prendre (un oiseau) au filet; chasser, prendre, (un lapin) au collet, au lacet; attraper (un animal); (*b*) prendre (qn) au piège; attraper (qn).

snarer ['snɛərər], *s.* tendeur *m* de lacets; chasseur *m* au collet; colleteur *m*; piégeur *m*.

snark [snɑːk], *s.* *Lit:* chimère *f* (animal imaginaire créé par Lewis Carroll).

snarky ['snɑːki], *a.* *F:* désagréable, maussade.

snarl[1] [snɑːl], *s.* (*of dog, pers.*) grondement *m*, grognement *m*; (*of tiger*) feulement *m*; (*of lion, tiger, etc.*) rauquement *m*; **he answered with a s.,** il a répondu d'un ton hargneux.

snarl[2], *v.i.* **1.** (*of animal*) montrer les dents; grogner, gronder; (*of tiger*) feuler; (*of lion, tiger, etc.*) rauquer. **2.** (*of pers.*) **to s. at s.o.,** grogner, gronder, contre qn.

snarl[3], *s.* **1.** *Tex:* vrillage *m*, vrille *f*, boucle *f*. **2.** (*a*) enchevêtrement *m*, emmêlement *m*, entortillement *m*; (*b*) **(traffic) s. (up),** embarras *m* de voitures; embouteillage *m*.

snarl[4]. **1.** *v.i.* (*a*) *Tex:* (*of yarn*) vriller; (*b*) s'emmêler, s'enchevêtrer, se nouer. **2.** *v.tr.* (*a*) emmêler, enchevêtrer; (*b*) **to s. (up) the traffic,** provoquer des embouteillages; **the traffic was all snarled up,** il y avait un embouteillage.

snarl[5], *v.tr.* *Metalw:* travailler (une aiguière d'argent, etc.) au repoussé, au repoussoir.

snarler[1] ['snɑːlər], *s.* grondeur, -euse; grogneur, -euse; grognon *mf*.

snarler[2], *s.* *Metalw:* **1.** travailleur *m* au repoussé. **2.** *Tls:* repoussoir *m*.

snarling[1] ['snɑːliŋ], *a.* grondant, grognant; (*of pers., dog, etc.*) hargneux.

snarling[2], *s.* grondement *m*, grognement *m*.

snarling[3], *s.* *Metalw:* repoussé *m*, repoussage *m*; **s. iron,** repoussoir *m*.

snarly ['snɑːli], *a.* *F:* hargneux, grognon.

snatch[1] [snætʃ], *s.* **1.** (*a*) mouvement vif (pour saisir qch.); **to make a s. at sth.,** chercher à saisir, à attraper, qch.; étendre vivement la main pour saisir qch.; (*b*) *F:* kidnapping *m*, enlèvement *m* (de qn); **bank s.,** attaque *f*, atteinte *f* (en vol armé) sur une banque; hold-up *m* d'une banque; **s. and grab robbery,** vol *m* à l'esbrouffe; (*c*) *Sp:* (*weight-lifting*) arraché *m*. **2.** (*a*) courte période; **s. of sleep,** petit somme; **to sleep in, by, (short) snatches,** dormir par courts intervalles; **to work by snatches,** travailler à bâtons rompus, par échappées, par boutades, par accès, d'une façon décousue; *Mec.E:* **s. horse-power,** puissance maxima; (*b*) fragment *m*; **snatches of song,** fragments de chanson; **to overhear snatches of conversation,** surprendre des bouts *m*, des bribes *f*, de conversation; **they could hear snatches of the waltz,** la musique de la valse leur arrivait par bouffées.

snatch[2], *v.tr. & i.* **1.** saisir, empoigner (qch.); s'emparer brusquement, se saisir, de (qch.); agripper (qch.); (*of birds, etc.*) **to s. insects,** happer des insectes; **to s. at sth.,** tâcher de saisir qch.; faire un mouvement pour saisir qch.; **to s. sth. up,** ramasser vivement qch.; **he snatched (up) his revolver from, off, the table,** il a saisi son revolver sur la table; **to s. (at) an opportunity,** saisir une occasion; **to s. a meal,** manger un morceau sur le pouce; **to s. a bit of sleep,** faire un petit somme; **to s. a few hours' sleep,** dérober quelques heures de sommeil à son travail; *Sp:* **to s. a win,** gagner à l'arraché; **(weight-lifting) to s. a weight,** arracher un poids. **2. to s. sth. (away) from s.o.,** arracher, enlever, qch. à qn; **to s. sth. out of s.o.'s hands,** arracher qch. des mains de qn; *F:* **she had her handbag snatched,** on lui a volé son sac à main; **to s. a baby,** kidnapper un bébé.

snatcher ['snætʃər], *s.* **1.** voleur *m* à l'esbrouffe; esbrouffeur *m*. **2. (baby) s.,** kidnappeur, -euse. **3. baby s.,** celui, celle, qui épouse une femme, un homme, nettement plus jeune que lui, qu'elle.

snatchy ['snætʃi], *a.* irrégulier.

snazzy ['snæzi], *a.* *F:* chic, qui fait fureur.

sneak[1] [sniːk], *s.* **1.** pleutre *m*; pied plat, cuistre *m*; capon, -onne. **2.** *Sch: F:* cafard, -arde; mouchard *m*; rapporteur, -euse; capon, -onne. **3.** *F:* **s. thief,** chipeur, -euse; chapardeur, -euse. **4.** *Cr:* balle lancée à ras de sol; balle traîtresse. **5.** *F:* **sneaks** = SNEAKERS 2. **6.** *Cin: etc:* **s. preview,** banc *m* d'essai.

sneak[2]. **1.** *v.i.* (*a*) **to s. off, away,** partir furtivement, en catimini; s'éclipser; se défiler; **to s. in, out,** se glisser furtivement, se faufiler, dans un endroit, hors d'un endroit; entrer, sortir, à pas de loup; (*b*) *Sch: F:* moucharder, cafarder, caponner, rapporter; **to s. on s.o.,** moucharder, cafarder, qn. **2.** *v.tr.* (*a*) *P:* voler, chiper, subtiliser (qch.); (*b*) **to s. a glance at s.o.,** glisser un œil vers qn.

sneaker ['sniːkər], *s.* **1.** *Cr:* = SNEAK[1] 4. **2.** *NAm:* **sneakers,** chaussons *m*; espadrilles *f*; mocassins *m*.

sneaking ['sniːkiŋ], *a.* **1.** (*a*) furtif; **to have a s. liking for sth.,** avoir un penchant caché, inavoué, pour qch.; (*b*) sournois, dissimulé. **2.** rampant, servile.

sneakingly ['sniːkiŋli], *adv.* **1.** (*a*) furtivement, en cachette; secrètement, à la dérobée; (*b*) sournoisement; en dessous. **2.** servilement.

sneaky ['sniːki], *a.* *F:* = SNEAKING.

sneck[1] [snek], *s.* *Scot:* (*a*) loquet *m*, clenche *f*, clenchette *f* (d'une porte); (*b*) arrêt *m* de sûreté, birloir *m* (d'une fenêtre à guillotine).

sneck[2], *v.tr.* *Scot:* (*a*) **to s. the door,** fermer la porte (au loquet), tirer le loquet; (*b*) assujettir (la fenêtre à guillotine).

sneer[1] ['sniər], *s.* **1.** sourire *m* de mépris; rire moqueur; ricanement *m*. **2.** sarcasme *m*.

sneer[2], *v.i.* sourire, rire, d'un air moqueur; ricaner; **to s. at s.o.,** (i) se moquer, se gausser, de qn; parler de qn d'un ton méprisant; (ii) lancer des sarcasmes à qn; **to s. at riches,** dénigrer les richesses; se moquer des richesses.

sneerer ['sniərər], *s.* ricaneur, -euse; moqueur, -euse.

sneering[1] ['sniəriŋ], *a.* ricaneur, -euse; moqueur, -euse; sarcastique.

sneering[2], *s.* **1.** ricanerie *f*. **2.** sarcasmes *mpl*.

sneeringly ['sniəriŋli], *adv.* d'un air méprisant, sarcastique; en ricanant.

sneeze[1] [sniːz], *s.* éternuement *m*; **to stifle, strangle, a s.,** réprimer une envie d'éternuer.

sneeze[2], *v.i.* éternuer; *F:* **to s. one's head off,** éternuer à tout casser; **that's not to be sneezed at,** cela n'est pas à dédaigner; il ne faut pas cracher dessus.

sneezer ['sniːzər], *s.* éternueur, -euse.

sneezewort ['sniːzwəːt], *s.* *Bot:* achillée *f* sternutatoire; herbe *f* à éternuer; bouton *m* d'argent; ptarmique *f*.

sneezing ['sniːziŋ], *s.* éternuement *m*; *Med:* sternutation *f*; **s. powder,** poudre sternutative, sternutatoire, à éternuer.

snell [snel], *s.* *Fish:* empile *f*.

snick[1] [snik], *s.* **1.** entaille *f*, encoche *f*. **2.** coup *m* de ciseaux; entaille (dans l'étoffe). **3.** *Cr:* coup (de batte) léger qui fait dévier la balle.

snick[2], *v.tr.* **1.** entailler, encocher; faire une entaille dans (le drap, etc.). **2.** *Cr:* **to s. the ball,** couper légèrement la balle.

snick[3], *s.* *F:* petit bruit sec.

snicker[1] ['snikər], *s.* **1.** = SNIGGER[1]. **2.** (*of horse*) hennissement *m*.

snicker[2], *v.i.* **1.** = SNIGGER[2]. **2.** (*of horse*) hennir.

snickersnee [snikə'sniː], *s.* *A:* gros couteau.

snide [snaid]. *F:* **1.** *a.* (*a*) faux, *f.* fausse; factice; (*b*) **s. remarks,** remarques insidieuses. **2.** *s.* (*a*) fausse monnaie; (*b*) bijouterie *f* factice; toc *m*.

snider ['snaidər], *s.* *Mil: A:* fusil *m* Snider.

sniff[1] [snif], *s.* reniflement *m*; **to take a s. at sth.,** renifler qch.; **with a s. of disgust,** en reniflant d'un air dégoûté; **to get a s. of fresh air,** prendre un peu, une bouffée, d'air frais; **one s. of it is enough to kill one,** une seule bouffée suffit pour tuer un homme.

sniff[2], *v.tr. & i.* **1.** (*a*) renifler; être enchifrené; (*b*) **to s. at an idea,** renifler sur une idée; marquer du dédain, de la répugnance, pour une idée; *F:* **the offer is not to be**

sniffed at, l'offre n'est pas à dédaigner. 2. (*a*) flairer (un bon dîner, un danger, etc.); (*b*) **to s. (at) sth.,** flairer, renifler, qch.; **the dog sniffed (at) my hand,** le chien m'a flairé la main; (*c*) **to s. out a scandal,** déterrer un scandale. 3. humer, renifler (une prise de tabac, etc.); aspirer (la cocaïne); **to s. in the fresh air,** se remplir les poumons d'air frais; *Med:* **to s. up a solution,** aspirer une solution par le nez; **to be sniffed up the nostrils,** pour être aspiré par les narines.

sniffer ['snifər], *s.* (*a*) renifleur, -euse; (*b*) **drug-s. dog, explosives-s. dog,** chien détecteur, flaireur, de narcotiques, d'explosifs; **s. out of scandals,** déterreur *m* de scandales; (*c*) **cocaine s.,** celui, celle, qui aspire la cocaïne.

sniffing[1] ['snifiŋ], *a.* qui renifle; morveux, enchifrené.

sniffing[2], *s.* 1. reniflement *m, F:* reniflerie *f.* 2. aspiration *f.* 3. humage *m.*

sniffle[1] ['snifl], *s.* petit rhume (de cerveau).

sniffle[2], *v.i. F:* 1. être enchifrené; renifler. 2. pleurnicher.

sniffling[1] ['snifliŋ], *a.* 1. enchifrené; enrhumé du cerveau; morveux; (enfant) qui renifle. 2. pleurnicheur, -euse.

sniffling[2], *s.* 1. reniflement *m.* 2. pleurnicherie *f.*

sniffy ['snifi], *a. F:* 1. (*a*) dédaigneux; (*b*) de mauvaise humeur; **to be s. about sth.,** (i) prendre qch. en mauvaise part; (ii) regarder qch. avec mépris. 2. *O:* d'odeur suspecte; malodorant. 3. **s. cold,** rhume *m* de cerveau; **s. child,** enfant qui renifle.

snifter ['sniftər], *s.* 1. *F: O:* vent carabiné. 2. *F:* goutte *f,* petit verre (d'alcool). 3. *Mch:* **s. valve,** reniflard *m.*

snifting ['sniftiŋ], *s. Mch:* **s. hole,** narine *f* (de pompe); **s. valve,** reniflard *m.*

snigger[1] ['snigər], *s.* (*a*) rire intérieur, en dessous; petit rire sournois, contenu; léger ricanement; (*b*) petit rire grivois, rosse.

snigger[2], *v.i.* rire sous cape, en dedans; ricaner tout bas.

sniggerer ['snigərər], *s.* ricaneur, -euse.

sniggering ['snigəriŋ], *s.* rires *mpl* en dessous; petits rires cyniques, de dénigrement; ricanements contenus, grivois.

sniggle[1,2] ['snig(ə)l], *s. & v.i.* = SNIGGER[1,2].

sniggle[3]. 1. *v.i. Fish:* **to s. for eels,** pêcher l'anguille. 2. *F: O:* (*a*) *v.i.* se glisser, se faufiler (dans une pièce, etc.); (*b*) *v.tr.* introduire (qch.) furtivement **(into,** dans).

snip[1] [snip], *s.* 1. morceau coupé; bout *m,* petit morceau (de papier, de toile). 2. (*a*) petite entaille, petite encoche; (*b*) coup *m* de ciseaux. 3. *Tls:* **snips,** pince *f* à couper; cisaille *f* pour tôles. 4. *P: A:* tailleur *m.* 5. *F:* (*a*) certitude *f;* affaire certaine; *Turf:* gagnant sûr; (*b*) affaire avantageuse; occasion *f.*

snip[2], *v.tr.* **(snipped** [snipt]) couper (du papier, du tissu) avec des ciseaux, d'un coup de ciseaux; **to s. sth. off,** enlever, détacher (qch.) d'un coup de ciseaux.

snipe[1] [snaip], *s.* 1. *Orn:* (*pl.* **snipe)** (*a*) bécassine *f;* **to go s. shooting,** chasser la bécassine; **I got four s.,** j'ai tué quatre bécassines; **moor full of s.,** lande qui abonde en bécassines; (*b*) **common s.,** *NAm:* **Wilson's s.,** bécassine des marais, *Fr.C:* bécassine ordinaire; **jack s.,** *NAm:* **European jack s.,** bécassine sourde; **great s.,** bécassine double; **painted s.,** rhynchée *f,* bécassine peinte; **pintail s.,** bécassine à queue pointue; **red-breasted s.,** limnodrome gris, *Fr.C:* bécasseau *m* à long bec; **seed s.,** thinocore *f;* **summer s.,** charlot *m* de plage; alouette *f* de mer. 2. (*a*) *Ich:* **s. eel,** orphie *f;* bécassine de mer; (*b*) *Ent:* **s. fly,** leptis *m.* 3. *F:* **(gutter) s.,** gamin, -ine. 4. *U.S: F:* mégot *m* (de cigare, de cigarette).

snipe[2]. 1. *v.i.* chasser la bécassine. 2. *Mil: v.tr. & i.* **to s. (at) the enemy,** canarder l'ennemi; tirer à l'affût, en embuscade, sur l'ennemi; effectuer, pratiquer, un tir de précision, un tir à tuer, sur l'ennemi; **to be sniped at,** essuyer le feu des tireurs isolés, des tireurs à l'affût, en embuscade, des tireurs d'élite; **to be sniped,** être blessé, tué, *F:* descendu, par un tireur isolé, par un tireur à l'affût, en embuscade, par un tireur d'élite.

sniper ['snaipər], *s. Mil:* canardeur *m;* tireur d'élite embusqué; tireur isolé.

sniping ['snaipiŋ], *s.* 1. chasse *f* à la bécassine. 2. *Mil: etc:* tir *m* d'embuscade, à tuer. 3. *Pol:* bombardement *m* de questions.

snippet ['snipit], *s.* 1. bout *m,* morceau (coupé). 2. court extrait (d'un livre, etc.); **to dole sth. out in snippets,** n'en servir que des miettes, des fragments.

snipping ['snipiŋ], *s.* morceau coupé; petit coupon (de tissu).

snitch[1] [snitʃ], *s. P:* 1. nez *m,* pif *m;* **s. rag, cloth,** mouchoir *m,* tire-jus *m inv.* 2. mouchard *m;* **to turn s.,** vendre ses complices; moucharder.

snitch[2], *P:* (*a*) *v.i.* vendre la mèche; **to s. on s.o.,** dénoncer, moucharder, qn; (*b*) *v.tr.* voler, chaparder (qch.).

snitcher ['snitʃər], *s. P:* mouchard *m,* indicateur *m,* dénonciateur *m.*

snivel[1] ['sniv(ə)l], *s.* 1. morve *f,* roupie *f; F:* **to have the snivels,** avoir le nez qui coule, être enrhumé. 2. (*a*) reniflement larmoyant; (*b*) pleurnicherie *f.*

snivel[2], *v.i.* **(snivelled)** 1. avoir le nez qui coule; être morveux, enchifrené; renifler. 2. pleurnicher, larmoyer; y aller de sa larme.

sniveller ['sniv(ə)lər], *s.* pleurnicheur, -euse.

snivelling[1] ['sniv(ə)liŋ], *a.* 1. (nez *m*) qui coule; (*of pers.*) morveux, enchifrené; **s. cold,** rhume *m* de cerveau. 2. pleurnicheur, -euse; larmoyant.

snivelling[2], *s.* 1. reniflement *m.* 2. pleurnicherie *f,* pleurnichement *m.*

snob [snɔb], *s.* 1. *A:* cordonnier *m.* 2. (*a*) *A:* bourgeois *m,* philistin *m;* (*b*) poseur, -euse; snob *mf; F: Pej:* snobard, -arde; **he's, she's, a bit of a s.,** c'est un(e) snobinard(e).

snobbery ['snɔbəri], *s.* morgue *f,* pose *f;* affectation *f;* snobisme *m;* **inverted s.,** snobisme à rebours; **intellectual s.,** snobisme intellectuel.

snobbish ['snɔbiʃ], *a.* poseur, -euse; snob.

snobbishly ['snɔbiʃli], *adv.* en snob.

snobbishness ['snɔbiʃnis], *s.* = SNOBBERY.

snog [snɔg], *v.i. F:* (*of couple*) se caresser.

snogging ['snɔgiŋ], *s. F:* bécotement *m.*

snood ['snu:d], *s.* 1. *Fish:* (*a*) cordée *f,* pile *f;* (*b*) avançon *m.* 2. *Cost:* (*a*) *A:* bandeau *m,* serre-tête *m inv* (pour les cheveux) (porté par les jeunes filles); (*b*) *O:* filet *m* pour cheveux.

snook[1] [snu:k], *s. Ich:* brochet *m* de mer.

snook[2], *s. P:* pied *m* de nez; **to cock a s. at s.o.,** faire un pied de nez à qn; faire la nique à qn.

snooker[1] ['snu:kər], *s.* (sorte de) jeu *m* de billard.

snooker[2], *v.tr.* **to be snookered,** (i) *Bill:* se trouver dans l'impossibilité de frapper directement la bille; (ii) *F:* se trouver en mauvaise posture; être réduit à l'impuissance; *F:* **to s. s.o.,** mettre qn dans une impasse.

snoop[1] [snu:p], *v. F:* 1. *v.tr.* voler, subtiliser, chiper, chaparder (qch.). 2. *v.i.* **to s. (around),** fourrer le nez partout; fureter, fouiner; **to s. on s.o.,** fourrer son nez dans les affaires de qn.

snoop[2], *s.* = SNOOPER.

snooper ['snu:pər], *s. F:* 1. fureteur *m,* fouineur *m.* 2. inquisiteur *m;* inspecteur officiel.

snoopy ['snu:pi], *a. F:* curieux, fouineur, fureteur.

snoot [snu:t], *s. P:* (*a*) nez *m,* pif *m;* (*b*) *esp. NAm:* museau *m,* gueule *f.*

snootful ['snu:tful], *s. esp. NAm: P:* **to have a s.,** être ivre, soûl.

snootiness ['snu:tinis], *s. F:* morgue *f,* crânage *m,* pose *f.*

snooty ['snu:ti], *a. F:* arrogant, orgueilleux, dédaigneux, gommeux.

snooze[1] [snu:z], *s. F:* petit somme; **to have a s.,** faire un petit somme; faire la sieste.

snooze[2], *v.i. F:* sommeiller; faire un petit somme, un roupillon.

snore[1] [snɔ:r], *s.* ronflement *m* (d'un dormeur).

snore[2], *v.i.* ronfler; **to s. like a pig,** ronfler comme un orgue, comme une toupie; **to s. gently, faintly,** ronflot(t)er.

snorer ['snɔ:rər], *s.* ronfleur, -euse.

snoring[1] ['snɔ:riŋ], *a.* ronflant.

snoring[2], *s.* ronflement *m.*

snorkel ['snɔ:kl], *s.* (i) schnorchel *m,* schnorkel *m;* (ii) masque sous-marin.

snorkelling ['snɔ:k(ə)liŋ], *s.* plongée sous-marine.

snort[1] [snɔ:t], *s.* 1. reniflement *m;* ébrouement *m* (d'un cheval, etc.); ronflement *m* (d'une machine à vapeur). 2. (*a*) haut-le-corps *m inv* de dédain, de colère, d'impatience; reniflement de dégoût; **to give a s. of rage,** bouffer de rage; (*b*) **s. of laughter,** court éclat de rire. 3. *F:* goutte *f,* petit verre (d'alcool).

snort[2]. 1. *v.i.* (*a*) faire (entendre) un ronflement; renifler fortement; (*of horse*) s'ébrouer, renâcler; **to s. with rage,** bouffer de rage; **to s. with laughter,** rire par courts éclats; **to s. at sth.,** dédaigner qch.; (*b*) (*of engine*) ronfler; tousser. 2. *v.tr.* **to s. out an answer,** répondre brusquement; grogner une réponse.

snort[3], *s. F:* schnorchel *m,* schnorkel *m.*

snorter ['snɔ:tər], *s.* 1. (*a*) *A:* ronfleur *m;* (*b*) renâcleur *m.* 2. *F:* (*a*) chose épatante; (*b*) **he wrote me back a s.,** il m'a (r)envoyé une lettre carabinée; (*of problem*) **that's a real s.,** ça va nous donner du fil à retordre; (*c*) *Nau:* vent carabiné; (*d*) goutte *f,* petit verre (d'alcool, etc.).

snorting[1] ['snɔ:tiŋ], *a.* (cheval *m*) qui s'ébroue, renâcle.

snorting[2], *s.* ronflement *m;* reniflement *m;* ébrouement *m* (d'un cheval).

snot [snɔt], *s. P:* 1. morve *f;* **s. rag,** mouchoir *m,* tire-jus *m inv.* 2. *Pej:* (*pers.*) morveux, -euse.

snotty ['snɔti]. 1. *a.* (*a*) morveux; **s. children,** enfants *m* avec la morve, avec la chandelle, au nez; (*b*) sale, dégoûtant. 2. *s.* aspirant *m* de marine, midship *m.*

snout [snaut], *s.* 1. (*a*) museau *m;* mufle *m* (de taureau, etc.); groin *m* (de porc, de hérisson); boutoir *m* (de sanglier); museau (de brochet); (*b*) *F:* nez *m,* pif *m;* (*c*) *Bot:* **calf's s.,** tête *f* de mort; muflier *m;* (*d*) *Ent:* **s. butterfly,** libythéide *m;* **s. moth,** pyralididé *m;* (*e*) *Cu:* **to remove the snouts and stalks,** éplucher (les groseilles). 2. (*a*) *A:* bec *m* (de navire, d'un rocher, etc.); (*b*) bec, buse *f,* ajutage *m* (de tuyère, etc.); tuyère *f* (de haut fourneau).

snow[1] [snou], *s.* 1. (*a*) neige *f;* **we've had some s., there has been a fall of s.,** il a neigé; il est tombé de la neige; **a flurry of s.,** une rafale, une bourrasque, de neige; **driven s.,** neige vierge; **drifting, driving, s.,** neige qui forme des congères, *Fr.C:* poudrerie *f;* **the s. is drifting,** il fait des congères, *Fr.C:* il poudre; **s. cover,** enneigement *m;* tapis nival; **s. report,** bulletin *m* d'enneigement; **s. surveying,** relevé *m* d'enneigement, sondage *m* nivométrique; **s. gauge,** nivomètre *m;* **permanent, eternal, s.,** neiges permanentes, éternelles, perpétuelles; **the (permanent) s. line,** la ligne, la limite, des neiges (persistantes; permanentes); **s. bridge,** pont *m* de neige; **s. slips, slides,** glissements *m* de neige; **s. patch erosion,** érosion nivale; *Rail: etc:* **s. shield, s. shed,** (*on road*) **s. fence,** paraneige *m;* **s. train,** train *m* des skieurs; **s. tyres,** pneus *m* neige; **s. goggles,** lunettes *f* d'alpiniste; **s. blindness,** cécité *f,* ophtalmie *f,* des neiges; **to be s. (-)blind,** être atteint de la cécité des neiges; *U.S: Dial:* **many snows ago,** il y a bien des années; (*b*) *Orn:* **s. bunting,** bruant *m* des neiges; **s. goose,** oie *f* des neiges; **s. grouse,** ptarmigan *m;* lagopède alpin; **s. partridge,** lerwa *m;* **s. pheasant, s. cock,** tétraogalle *m;* *Z:* **s. leopard,** léopard *m* des neiges; once *f.* 2. (*a*) *Ind:* **carbonic acid, carbon dioxide, s.,** neige carbonique; *Med:* **carbon dioxide s. pencil,** cryocautère *m;* (*b*) *Cu:* **apple s.,** pommes meringuées; (*c*) *T.V: Rad:* neige (points blancs mobiles); (*d*) *P:* (i) cocaïne *f,* coco *f,* neige; (ii) *esp. U.S:* héroïne *f,* poudre *f.*

snow[2]. 1. *v.i. impers.* neiger; **it's snowing,** il neige, il tombe de la neige; *F:* **it's snowing down south,** votre jupon dépasse; vous cherchez une belle-mère? 2. *v.tr.* **to be snowed in, up,** être enneigé; être retenu, bloqué, pris, par la neige; être enseveli sous la neige; **snowed under with work,** submergé, débordé, écrasé, de besogne; **snowed under with invitations,** débordé d'invitations.

snow[3], *s. Nau: A:* senau *m.*

snowball[1] ['snoubɔ:l], *s.* 1. (*a*) boule *f,* pelote *f,* de neige; *P:* **he hasn't a snowball's chance in hell,** il n'a pas l'ombre d'une chance; (*b*) *Cu:* (entremets sucré) boule de neige. 2. *Bot:* **s. (tree, bush),** boule-de-neige *f, pl.* boules-de-neige; rose *f* de Gueldre. 3. *P:* = SNOWBIRD.

snowball[2]. 1. *v.tr. & i.* lancer des boules de neige (à qn); se battre à coups de boules de neige. 2. *v.i.* (*of story, debts, etc.*) faire boule de neige.

snowbank ['snoubæŋk], *s.* banc *m* de neige.

snowberry ['snouberi], *s. Bot:* (*a*) **(West Indian) s.,** chiocoque *m;* (*b*) symphorine *f* boule-de-neige.

snowbird ['snoubə:d], *s. P:* cocaïnomane *mf.*

snowblink ['snoubliŋk], *s.* reflet *m,* clarté *f,* des glaces (sur l'horizon).

snowblower ['snoublouər], *s.* souffleuse *f* (de neige).

snowboot ['snoubu:t], *s.* botte *f* de neige; après-ski *m inv.*

snowbound ['snoubaund], *a.* retenu, pris, bloqué, par la neige; enseveli sous la neige.

snowbush ['snoubuʃ], *s. Bot:* céanothe, céanote, velouté.

snowcapped, snowclad ['snoukæpt, -klæd], *a.* couvert, couronné, encapuchonné, de neige.

snowcat ['snoukæt], *s. F:* = SNOWMOBILE.

snowdrift ['snoudrift], *s.* congère *f;* amoncellement *m* de neige.

snowdrop ['snoudrɔp], *s. Bot:* 1. perce-neige *m inv.* 2. **s. tree,** (i) chionanthe *m,* chionanthus *m,* arbre *m* de neige; (ii) halesia *m,* halésie *f.*

snowed [snoud], *a. P:* drogué à la cocaïne, enneigé.

snowfall ['snoufɔ:l], *s.* chute *f* de neige.

snowfield ['snoufi:ld], *s.* champ *m* de neige.

snowflake ['snoufleik], *s.* 1. flocon *m* de neige. 2. *Bot:* nivéole *f.* 3. *Orn:* bruant *m* des neiges.

snowiness ['snouinis], *s.* nivosité *f.*

snowlike ['snoulaik], *a.* niviforme; nivéen.

snowman, *pl.* **-men** ['snoumæn, -men], *s.m.* (*a*) bonhomme de neige; (*b*) **the abominable s.,** l'abominable homme des neiges.

snowmobile ['snoumoubi:l], *s.* tracteur *m* automobile pour expéditions polaires, *Fr.C:* auto-neige *f,* motoneige *f.*

snowplough[1], *NAm:* **-plow** ['snouplau], *s.* 1. *Trans: Rail:* chasse-neige *m inv;* **rotary s.,** chasse-neige rotatif. 2. *Ski:* chasse-neige; **s. turn,** virage *m* (en) chasse-neige.

snowplough[2], *v.i. Ski:* freiner, virer, en chasse-neige.

snowscape ['snouskeip], *s. Art:* paysage *m* de neige.

snowshoe ['snouʃu:], *s.* raquette *f.*

snowshoer ['snouʃu:ər], *s.* raquetteur *m* (*Fr.C.*).

snowstorm ['snoustɔ:m], *s.* tempête *f,* tourbillon *m,* rafale *f,* de neige.

snowsuit ['snous(j)u:t], *s.* = ensemble *m* ski.

snow(-)white ['snou(h)wait]. **1.** *a.* (*a*) blanc comme (la) neige; d'un blanc, d'une blancheur, de neige; (*b*) *O: Lit:* pur, innocent. **2.** *Pr.n.f.* **S.W.,** Blanche-Neige.

snowy ['snoui], *a.* neigeux; de neige; (la saison) des neiges; **it's s. today,** il tombe, il va tomber, de la neige aujourd'hui; **s. (white) hair,** cheveux blancs (comme neige).

snub[1] [snʌb], *s.* **1.** mortification *f,* avanie *f,* rebuffade *f,* affront *m,* ravalement *m*; *F:* soufflet *m*; *F:* **he got a (real) good s.,** il a été mouché de belle façon. **2.** *Nau:* arrêt soudain (d'un câble avec lequel on prend un tour mort).

snub[2], *v.* (**snubbed**) **1.** *v.tr.* remettre (qn) à sa place; rabrouer, rebuffer, rembarrer (qn); faire un affront à (qn); **to be snubbed,** être remis à sa place. **2.** *v.tr. & i. Nau:* (*a*) arrêter (un cordage) en prenant un tour mort; transfiler (un cordage); filer, choquer, à la demande; **snubbing post,** bitte *f* de tournage; (*b*) briser l'erre (d'un navire).

snub[3], *a.* (nez) camard, camus, retroussé.

snubber ['snʌbər], *s.* **1.** (*pers.*) rabroueur, -euse; **he's a terrible s.,** il essaie de mettre tout le monde à sa place. **2.** *Elcs:* (*a*) verrou *m* électromagnétique; (*b*) (*of autopilot*) solénoïde *m* de blocage. **3.** *NAm: Aut: A:* amortisseur *m* à courroie.

snubby ['snʌbi], *a.* (nez) un peu retroussé, (légèrement) camus.

snub-nosed ['snʌbnouzd], *a.* au nez retroussé, camus.

snuff[1] [snʌf], *s.* **1.** = SNIFF[1]. **2.** (*a*) *Med: O:* poudre *f* à priser; (*b*) tabac *m* à priser; **to take s.,** priser; **a pinch of s.,** une prise; **s. taker,** priseur, -euse (de tabac); **s. mill,** moulin à tabac. **3.** prise (de tabac). **4.** *F: O:* **to be up to s.,** ne pas se moucher du pied; être dessalé, dégourdi; **he's not up to s.,** il n'est pas à la hauteur; **it's not up to s.,** ça ne vaut pas cher. **5.** *a.* **s. (coloured),** (couleur) tabac *inv*; cachou *inv.*

snuff[2]. **1.** *v.i. & tr.* = SNIFF[2]. **2.** *v.i.* priser (du tabac).

snuff[3], *s.* mouchure *f,* lumignon *m* (de chandelle).

snuff[4]. **1.** *v.tr.* **to s. (out),** moucher (une chandelle). **2.** *v.tr. & i. P:* **to s. it, to s. out,** mourir, lâcher la rampe, éteindre sa lampe.

snuffbox ['snʌfbɔks], *s.* tabatière *f.*

snuffer[1] ['snʌfər], *s.* priseur, -euse (de tabac).

snuffer[2], *s.* **1.** *Th: etc: A:* moucheur, -euse (de chandelles). **2.** *pl.* **(pair of) snuffers,** mouchettes *f*; **snuffer(s) tray,** porte-mouchettes *m inv.*

snuffle[1] ['snʌfl], *s.* **1.** (*a*) reniflement *m*; (*b*) **snuffles,** enchifrènement *m*; **to have the snuffles,** être enchifrené; être enrhumé du cerveau; avoir le nez bouché. **2.** ton nasillard.

snuffle[2], *v.i.* **1.** (*a*) renifler; **to s. at sth.,** flairer, sentir, qch.; (*b*) être enchifrené; avoir le nez bouché. **2.** nasiller.

snuffler ['snʌflər], *s.* **1.** renifleur, -euse. **2.** nasilleur, -euse.

snuffles ['snʌflz], *s.pl. F:* **to have the s.,** (i) renifler; (ii) être enchifrené; avoir le nez bouché.

snuffling[1] ['snʌfliŋ], *a.* **1.** qui renifle; enchifrené; morveux. **2.** nasillard.

snuffling[2], *s.* **1.** reniflement(s) *m(pl).* **2.** nasillement *m.*

snuffy[1] ['snʌfi], *a.* sali par le tabac (à priser).

snuffy[2], *a. F:* (*a*) irrité; (*b*) irritable; (*c*) dédaigneux, hautain.

snug[1] [snʌg], *a.* **1.** *Nau:* (navire) paré (à tout événement). **2.** (*of house, etc.*) confortable, où l'on est bien; (*of pers.*) bien abrité; bien au chaud; **s. little bed,** petit lit douillet; **it is very s. in here,** on est bien ici; **s. woollen vest,** gilet de laine bien chaud; *F:* **s. little job,** gentil petit emploi; emploi pépère; **s. little fortune,** fortune rondelette; **s. and cosy,** clos et coi; **to make oneself s.,** se mettre à son aise; se calfeutrer (dans sa chambre, etc.); **to make s.o. s. by the fire,** installer qn douillettement auprès du feu; **to make a horse s. for the night,** installer un cheval pour la nuit; **to lie s. in bed,** être bien au chaud dans son lit; être couché douillettement; *F:* **as s. as a bug in a rug,** tranquille comme Baptiste. **3. to lie s.,** rester coi; se tenir caché; **to lie s. in a hole,** être tapi dans un trou. **4.** *adv. F:* = SNUGLY. **5.** *s. O:* = SNUGGERY 2.

snug[2], *v.* (**snugged**) **1.** *v.i. A:* = SNUGGLE. **2.** *v.tr.* (*a*) mettre (tout) en ordre; (*b*) *Nau:* parer (un navire) à tout événement; **to s. a sail,** ferler une voile.

snug[3], *s. Mec.E:* dent *f,* ergot *m.*

snuggery ['snʌgəri], *s.* **1.** petite pièce intime (et bien calfeutrée); petit bureau. **2.** rendez-vous *m* des intimes (dans un café).

snuggle [snʌgl]. **1.** *v.i.* **to s. up to s.o.,** se pelotonner, se blottir, contre qn; se serrer (frileusement) contre qn; **to s. into s.o.'s arms,** se pelotonner entre les bras de qn; **to s. down in bed,** se blottir dans son lit; **village snuggling in the valley,** village niché dans la vallée. **2.** *v.tr.* **to s. a child close to one,** serrer un enfant dans ses bras; attirer un enfant tout contre soi.

snugly ['snʌgli], *adv.* confortablement, douillettement; (chaudement) à l'aise; **s. wrapped in her furs,** douillettement enveloppée dans ses fourrures; **garment that fits s.,** vêtement bien ajusté à la taille.

snugness ['snʌgnis], *s.* (*esp. of small room*) confort, bien-être (associé à la chaleur).

so [sou], *adv. & conj.*

I. *adv.* **1.** (*a*) si, tellement; **he's so kind,** il est tellement aimable, gentil; **she isn't so very old,** elle n'est pas tellement vieille; **the young and the not so young,** les jeunes et les moins jeunes; **it was so kind of you to . . .,** il était bien aimable, si gentil, de votre part de . . .; **I'm not so sure of that,** je n'en suis pas bien sûr; **it's so easy,** c'est si, tellement, facile; **so good a dinner,** un si bon dîner; **so serious a wound,** une blessure aussi grave; **it is so clear that. . .,** *Lit:* **so clear it is that. . .,** tant il est évident que . . .; **he's not so stupid as he looks,** il n'est pas aussi, si, stupide qu'il n'en a l'air; **he's not so clever as she is,** il est moins intelligent qu'elle; **he's not so well today,** il va moins bien aujourd'hui; **so bad as to be worthless,** si mauvais que cela ne vaut rien; **he wouldn't be so stupid as to do that,** il ne serait pas si bête que de faire cela; **would you be so kind as to give me a hand (with this)?** voudriez-vous avoir la gentillesse de me donner un coup de main? **in a place so remote as . . .,** dans un endroit aussi lointain, aussi éloigné, que . . .; **he is not so severe as that,** il n'est pas si sévère que cela; **who would be so mean as not to admire him?** quel est l'homme assez mesquin pour ne pas l'admirer? **the children were submitted to so severe a discipline that they rebelled,** les enfants étaient soumis à une telle discipline qu'ils se sont révoltés; **he is so rich that he doesn't know what he is worth,** il est riche au point d'ignorer sa fortune; **he is so ill that he cannot speak,** il est si gravement malade qu'il ne peut pas parler; **I shan't drive so fast that you won't be able to enjoy the scenery,** je ne conduirai pas si vite pour que vous ne puissiez pas admirer le paysage; **he's not so clever that he doesn't sometimes make mistakes,** il n'est pas si habile qu'il ne se trompe quelquefois; **so many mistakes have been made,** on s'est si souvent trompé; on a tant commis de fautes; **so much,** tellement, tant; **I loved him so (much),** je l'aimais tant; **we enjoyed ourselves so much,** nous nous sommes tellement, bien, amusés; **loving her so much, he could not blame her,** l'aimant à ce point, il ne pouvait pas la blâmer; **the answer so annoyed him, annoyed him so much, that . . .,** la réponse l'a fâché tellement que . . .; **God so loved the world,** Dieu a tant aimé le monde; **he so loved us that he even died for us,** il nous a aimés jusqu'à mourir pour nous; (*b*) **if it takes so many men so long to do so much work,** s'il faut à tant d'hommes tant de temps pour faire tant de travail; **so many articles a day,** tant d'articles par jour. **2.** (*a*) ainsi; de cette façon; de cette manière; comme cela; **stand just so,** tenez-vous ainsi, comme ça; **gently! just so, like that!** doucement! bien, comme ça! **so it was that he became a soldier,** c'est ainsi qu'il est devenu soldat; **while he was so occupied,** pendant qu'il était ainsi occupé; **why do you cry so?** pourquoi pleurez-vous ainsi? **as X is to Y, so Y is to Z,** comme X est à Y, Y est à Z; **so many men so many minds,** autant de têtes autant d'avis; **they're so many rogues,** ce sont des filous; **they came in sheepishly like so many schoolboys,** ils sont entrés timidement comme autant d'écoliers; **men are so constituted that . . .,** les hommes sont ainsi faits que . . .; **she so arranged things that. . .,** elle a fait en sorte que + *sub.*; **I have been so informed,** c'est ce que l'on m'a dit; voilà ce que j'ai compris; **it so happened that I was there,** le hasard a voulu que je fusse là; je m'y suis trouvé par hasard; **and so on, and so forth,** et ainsi du reste; et ainsi de suite; et le reste; **so to say, so to speak,** pour ainsi dire; comme qui dirait; **so saying,** à ces mots; *Lit:* **so Æneas,** ainsi parla, parlait, Énée; (*b*) **has the train gone?—I think so, believe so,** est-ce que le train est parti?—je crois, je pense, que oui; **he's clever!—you think so?** il est intelligent!—vous le croyez? **I suppose so, I expect so,** je le suppose; sans doute; il faut le croire; **I fancy so,** il me semble que oui; c'est ce qu'il me semble; **I hope so,** je l'espère bien; **I'm afraid so,** j'en ai bien peur; **I didn't say so,** moi, je n'ai pas dit cela; **is she really ill?—so it seems,** elle est donc vraiment malade?—à ce qu'il paraît; **so I told him,** c'est ce que je lui ai dit; **he goes to the club—so he says!** il va au cercle—qu'il dit! **I told you so!** je vous l'avais bien dit! quand je vous le disais! **I have no intention of doing so,** je n'ai aucune intention de le faire; **if you can do so,** si vous pouvez le faire; **if he had been less so,** s'il l'avait été moins; **so much so that. . .,** à tel point que . . .; tellement que . . .; **much more so,** bien plus encore; **that's so,** c'est bien vrai; parfaitement; effectivement; bien sûr; **and so it is,** eh bien oui, effectivement; **is that so?** vraiment? **it's, that's, not so,** il n'en est pas ainsi; **that being so,** puisqu'il en est ainsi; dans ces conditions; **so be it!** soit! qu'il en soit ainsi! (*c*) **if so,** s'il en est ainsi; **why so?** pourquoi cela? **how so?** comment cela? **perhaps so,** cela se peut; **quite so, just so,** parfaitement; vous l'avez dit; absolument; **and so to bed,** sur quoi je suis allé, je vais, me coucher; **a hundred pounds or so,** une centaine de livres; **a week or so,** une huitaine de jours; **in a month or so,** dans un mois ou deux; **in a minute or so,** dans une minute à peu près; (*d*) **a little girl** *so* **high,** une petite haute comme ça, pas plus haute que ça; (*e*) **he's right and so are you,** il a raison et vous aussi; **and so am I, are we,** et moi, et nous, aussi; **I thought you were French—and so I am,** je pensais que vous étiez Français—mais si (je le suis); **he thinks he can do it—so he can,** il pense qu'il peut le faire—mais oui, en effet, il le peut; (*f*) **you're late!—so I am!** vous êtes en retard!—c'est vrai! **you could come here first—so I could,** vous pourriez venir ici d'abord—c'est vrai! en effet, oui! **3.** *conj.phrs.* **so that, so as to:** (*a*) (*purpose*) **he stepped aside so that I could go first,** il s'est reculé pour me laisser passer; **speak so that you can be understood, so as to be understood,** parlez de sorte qu'on vous comprenne; **he stood up so as to, so that he could, see better,** il s'est levé afin de mieux voir; **I'll go and dress so as not to, so that I won't, keep you waiting,** je vais m'habiller pour ne pas vous faire attendre; **we hurried so as not to, so that we shouldn't, be late,** nous nous sommes dépêchés pour ne pas être en retard; (*b*) (*consequence*) **he tied me up so that I couldn't move,** il m'a ligoté de sorte, de façon, que je ne pouvais pas bouger; **he went out without an overcoat, so that he caught cold,** il est sorti sans pardessus, de sorte qu'il a attrapé un rhume. **4.** (*used adverbially & adjectivally*) **so so,** médiocre(ment), passable(ment); comme ci comme ça; **how are you?—so so,** comment vas-tu?—comme ci comme ça; **to feel so so,** ne pas être (entièrement) dans son assiette; **how's business going?—so so,** comment vont les affaires?—comme ci comme ça; doucement; **how's his work shaping?—so so,** il travaille bien?—comme ci comme ça; plutôt médiocrement; **it's so so,** c'est entre les deux; **the cooking is only so so,** la cuisine est médiocre, quelconque.

II. *conj.* **1.** donc, c'est pourquoi; **he has a bad temper, so be careful,** il a mauvais caractère, par conséquent faites attention; **the cost of living is high, so we must economize,** la vie est chère, donc nous devons, il nous faut, économiser; **we did not hear from him for a long time, so we thought that he was dead,** nous n'avions pas eu de nouvelles de lui depuis longtemps, si bien que nous le croyions mort; **he wasn't there, so I came back again,** il n'était pas là, donc je suis revenu; comme il n'était pas là je suis revenu. **2. so there you are!** vous voilà donc! **so that's what it is!** ah! c'est comme ça! **so you're not coming?** vous ne venez donc pas? **so now he is dead,** le voilà donc mort; **so I am reduced to . . .,** me voilà réduit à . . .. **3.** *A:* pourvu que, à condition que, si; **so (it) pleases your Majesty,** n'en déplaise à votre Majesté.

soak[1] [souk], *s.* **1.** trempe *f*; imbibition *f*; *O:* **to put (sth.) in s.,** (i) tremper, mettre à tremper, faire tremper (le linge sale); (ii) faire macérer (des cornichons, etc.); dessaler (la viande, le poisson). **2.** (*a*) *Tan: etc:* bain *m*; (*b*) **I intend to have a good s. (in the bath),** je vais prendre un bon bain. **3.** *P:* (*a*) ribote *f,* cuite *f*; (*b*) ivrogne *m,* soûlard *m.*

soak[2], *v.*

I. *v.tr. & i.* **1.** *v.tr.* (*a*) (*of liquid*) tremper, imbiber, détremper, imprégner; **the rain soaked me to the skin,** la pluie m'a trempé jusqu'aux os; (*b*) **to s. sth. in sth.,** tremper qch. dans qch.; imbiber qch. de qch.; **to s. leather in hot tallow,** imbiber, imprégner, le cuir de suif chaud; **to s. a sponge,** imbiber une éponge; **to s. a cask,** combuger une futaille; *Tan:* **to s. skins,** confire, détremper, reverdir, les peaux; **to s. oneself in the classics,** s'imprégner des classiques; (*c*) *F:* (i) *A:* rouer (qn) de coups; (ii) écorcher (un client); **to s. the rich,** faire payer les riches. **2.** *v.i.* (*a*) (*of thg in soak*) baigner, tremper (**in sth.,** dans qch.); (*b*) (*of liquid*) s'infiltrer, s'imbiber (**into sth.,** dans qch.); (*c*) *P:* boire comme une éponge; se saturer d'alcool; se soûler.

II. (*compound verbs*) 1. **soak away,** *v.i.* (*of water, etc.*) disparaître par infiltration.
2. **soak in.** (*a*) *v.i.* (*of plant*) s'emboire; (*of liquid*) pénétrer; (*b*) *v.tr.* **to s. in water,** s'imprégner d'eau, absorber de l'eau.
3. **soak through,** *v.i.* (*a*) s'infiltrer à travers (qch.); **the rain has soaked through my overcoat,** la pluie a percé mon pardessus; (*b*) pénétrer, s'infiltrer.
4. **soak up,** *v.tr.* absorber, boire, imbiber (un liquide); **to s. up water,** s'imprégner d'eau; absorber de l'eau.
soakage ['soukidʒ], *s.* 1. eau *f* d'infiltration, d'imbibition. 2. infiltration *f.*
soakaway ['soukəwei], *s. Civ.E:* puisard *m.*
soaked ['soukt], *a.* trempé; **s. to the skin, s. through,** trempé jusqu'aux os; mouillé comme un canard; **s. ground,** sol détrempé; **s. in paraffin wax,** imprégné, imbibé, de paraffine; **oil-s. rag,** linge imbibé d'huile.
soaker ['soukər], *s. F:* 1. buveur, -euse; ivrogne *m.* 2. pluie battante; déluge *m* de pluie.
soaking[1] ['soukiŋ], *a.* 1. trempé, mouillé. 2. **s. rain, downpour,** pluie battante.
soaking[2], *s.* trempage *m,* trempe *f,* baignage *m;* **a good s.,** un bon arrosage; **to get a s.,** se faire tremper; recevoir une saucée.
so-and-so ['soun(d)sou], *s. F:* (*a*) **Mr. So-and-so, Mrs. So-and-so,** Monsieur un tel, Un Tel, Untel; Madame une telle; Monsieur, Madame, Chose; (*b*) *Pej:* **the so-and-so played me a dirty trick,** cet individu m'a joué un vilain tour; **she's a crafty little so-and-so,** c'est une fine mouche; **the old so-and-so! what a so-and-so!** quel sale type!
soap[1] [soup], *s.* 1. (*a*) savon *m;* **Castile s.,** savon blanc; **shower s.,** *F:* **s. on a rope,** savonnette *f* sautoir; **toilet s.,** savon de toilette; **household s.** = savon de Marseille; **cake of s.,** pain *m* de savon; (*small*) savonnette; **shaving s.,** savon à barbe; **soft s.,** (i) savon noir, vert, mou; (ii) *F:* flatterie *f;* eau bénite; **saddle s., leather s.,** savon de selle; **pumice s.,** savon ponce; **sand s.,** savon minéral; **sugar s.,** (variété de) décapant *m* (pour peinture); **to wash with s.,** savonner (qch.); **the s. industry, trade,** l'industrie savonnière; **s. boiling, manufacturing,** savonnerie *f;* **s. boiler, manufacturer,** savonnier *m;* fabricant *m* de savon; **s. powder,** lessive *f* en poudre; (*b*) *W.Tel: T.V: F:* **s. opera,** feuilleton sentimental, à l'eau de rose; (*c*) *P:* **no s.,** rien à faire; je ne marche pas. 2. *Ind:* **aluminium, lead, etc., s.,** savon d'aluminium, de plomb, etc.; **glass s.,** savon des verriers; *Miner:* **mountain s., rock s.,** savon de montagne, savon blanc, savon minéral.
soap[2], *v.tr.* 1. savonner (le linge, etc.). 2. *F:* **to (soft-) s. s.o.,** flatter qn; coucher le poil à qn; passer la main dans le dos à qn; flagorner qn.
soapbark ['soupbɑːk], *s. Bot:* (*a*) bois *m* de Panama; (*b*) **s. (tree),** (i) quillaja savonneux; (ii) pithecolobium *m.*
soapberry ['soupberi], *s. Bot:* (*a*) pomme *f* de savon; cerise gommeuse; (*b*) **s. (tree),** savonnier *m;* rita *m.*
soapbox ['soupbɔks], *s.* caisse *f* à savon; *F:* **s. orator,** orateur *m* de carrefour; harangueur *m.*
soapdish ['soupdiʃ], *s.* plateau *m* à savon; porte-savon *m inv.*
soapfish ['soupfiʃ], *s. Ich:* poisson-savon *m.*
soapflakes ['soupfleiks], *s.pl.* savon *m* en paillettes.
soapiness ['soupinis], *s.* (*a*) caractère savonneux, nature savonneuse (de qch.); goût *m,* odeur *f,* de savon; (*b*) *F:* (*of pers.*) onctuosité *f.*
soapnut ['soupnʌt], *s. Bot:* noyau *m* de savonnier.
soaproot ['soupruːt], *s. Bot:* saponaire *f* d'Orient.
soapstone ['soupstoun], *s. Miner:* (*a*) stéatite *f,* talc *m;* pierre savonneuse, pierre de savon; pierre ollaire; craie *f* de Briançon; (*b*) saponite *f;* pierre de savon.
soapsuds ['soupsʌdz], *s.pl.* eau *f* de savon; lessive *f.*
soapwood ['soupwud], *s. Bot:* **s. (tree),** pithecolobium *m.*
soapworks ['soupwəːks], *s.pl.* (*usu. with sg. const.*) savonnerie *f.*
soapwort ['soupwəːt], *s. Bot:* saponaire *f; F:* herbe *f* à foulon.
soapy ['soupi], *a.* 1. (*a*) savonneux; qui sent le savon; **s. taste,** goût *m* de savon; (*b*) **s. potatoes,** pommes de terre cireuses; (*c*) *Nat.Hist:* saponacé. 2. *F:* (*of pers., voice*) doucereux, onctueux, mielleux, insinuant.
soar [sɔːr], *v.i. esp. Lit:* (*a*) prendre son essor; monter, s'élever (dans les airs); **to s. to the heights of fame,** s'élever jusqu'au faîte de la renommée; **rents have soared,** les loyers ont fait un bond; (*b*) planer (dans les airs); (*of the mind*) voler; **his ambitions s. high,** il plane dans les airs.
soaring[1] ['sɔəriŋ], *a.* 1. (*a*) (oiseau *m,* flèche *f*) qui monte, s'élève, dans les airs; **s. steeple,** clocher élancé; (*b*) **s. flight,** vol plané (d'un oiseau). 2. (*of prices, etc.*) qui vont en croissant; **because of s. prices,** en raison de la hausse des prix.
soaring[2], *s.* (*a*) essor *m;* (*b*) hausse *f,* élévation *f* (des prix); (*c*) vol plané (d'un oiseau).
sob[1] [sɔb], *s.* sanglot *m; F:* **s. story, s. stuff,** (i) littérature *f* d'une sentimentalité larmoyante; (ii) *Th:* drame larmoyant; (*of old lag, etc.*) **to tell s.o. a s. story,** raconter ses souffrances à qn; raconter une histoire pour apitoyer qn; **to put on a s. act,** pleurer des larmes *f* de crocodile; *Journ:* **s. sister,** journaliste (mâle ou femelle) spécialisé(e) dans le mélodrame.
sob[2], *v.* **(sobbed)** 1. *v.i.* sangloter; pousser des sanglots; **to s. into one's handkerchief,** sangloter dans son mouchoir. 2. *v.tr.* (*a*) **to s. (out) sth.,** dire qch. en sanglotant; sangloter (un aveu, des excuses); (*b*) **she was sobbing her heart out,** elle pleurait à chaudes larmes, à gros sanglots; (*c*) **she sobbed herself to sleep,** elle s'est endormie en sanglotant.
sobbing ['sɔbiŋ], *a.* **in a s. voice,** d'une voix sanglotante, pleine, brisée, de sanglots.
sobeit [sou'biːit], *conj. A:* pourvu que (+ *sub.*).
sober[1] ['soubər], *a.* 1. (*a*) sobre, modéré, tempéré, raisonnable; (*b*) calme, rassis, posé, tranquille, sérieux; **s. mind,** esprit rassis; **as s. as a judge,** sérieux comme un juge; **s. face,** visage *m* grave; **in s. earnest,** bien sérieusement; **s. opinion,** opinion réfléchie; (*c*) *O:* **to be in one's s. senses,** jouir de son bon sens; (*d*) **s. fact,** fait réel; **in s. fact,** en réalité; **s. truth,** la simple vérité; **s. estimate,** évaluation prudente; (*e*) **s. colours,** couleurs sobres, peu voyantes; **s. dress,** vêtement discret; robe discrète. 2. (*a*) qui n'est pas ivre; qui n'a pas bu; **he was anything but s.,** il était plutôt gris; on ne peut pas dire qu'il n'était pas pris de boisson; **he never goes to bed s.,** il ne se couche jamais sans être pris de boisson; **to sleep oneself s.,** cuver sa boisson, son vin; **when he's s. (again),** quand il sera dessoulé, dégrisé; (*b*) qui ne s'enivre jamais; tempérant.
sober[2]. 1. *v.tr.* (*a*) **to s. (down),** assagir, dégriser (un déréglé, etc.); **to s. (up),** désenivrer, dégriser, dessouler (un homme ivre); **this news sobered him,** cette nouvelle l'a dégrisé; (*b*) **to s. down a colour,** adoucir une couleur. 2. *v.i.* (*a*) (*of reckless pers., enthusiast*) **to s. down,** s'assagir, se dégriser; faire une fin; (*b*) **to s. (down),** reprendre son sang-froid; (*c*) (*of intoxicated pers.*) **to s. up,** se désenivrer; se dégriser; se dessouler.
soberly ['soubəli], *adv.* (*a*) sobrement, modérément; avec tempérance; sagement; (*b*) avec calme; tranquillement, sérieusement; (*c*) (vêtu) discrètement.
sober-minded [soubə'maindid], *a.* sérieux; sain d'esprit; de caractère sobre; pondéré, sage.
soberness ['soubənis], *s.* (*a*) sobriété *f,* modération *f,* tempérance *f;* **s. of speech,** sobriété de parole; (*b*) calme *m,* tranquillité *f,* sérieux *m.*
sobersides ['soubəsaidz], *s. F: O:* personne grave, rassise, pondérée.
sobriety [sou'braiəti], *s.* 1. = SOBERNESS. 2. (*of pers.*) état *m* sobre, de sobriété.
so-called [sou'kɔːld], *a.* (*a*) appelé ainsi; ainsi nommé; **Peter the Cruel, properly so-c.,** Pierre dit le Cruel, appelé ainsi à juste titre; (*b*) **the so-c. temperate zone,** la zone dite tempérée; **a so-c. doctor,** un soi-disant, un prétendu, docteur; un docteur marron; **so-c. improvements,** prétendus progrès; **so-c. coffee,** (i) ersatz *m* de café; (ii) café *m* imbuvable; *Sp:* **so-c. amateur,** amateur marron.
soc(c)age ['sɔkidʒ], *s. Hist:* socage *m.*
soccer ['sɔkər], *s. F:* football(-association) *m.*
sociability [souʃə'biliti], *s.* sociabilité *f.*
sociable ['souʃəbl]. 1. *a.* (*a*) sociable; (*of pers.*) **to become more s.,** s'apprivoiser; **merely to be s.,** (faire qch.) simplement pour ne pas être impoli; (*b*) *Z:* **s. animals,** (animaux) sociétaires *m; Orn:* **s. weaver(bird),** tisserin républicain; (*c*) *U.S:* **s. evening,** *s.* **sociable,** soirée amicale, passée dans l'intimité; réunion *f* des membres de l'église, du patronage. 2. *s.* (*a*) *Furn: A:* causeuse *f;* (*b*) *A.Veh:* sociable *m;* (*c*) *A:* tricycle *m* à deux places côte à côte.
sociableness ['souʃəbəlnis], *s.* sociabilité *f.*
sociably ['souʃəbli], *adv.* sociablement, amicalement; en bonne entente.
social ['souʃ(ə)l], *a.* 1. social, -aux; (*a*) **s. problems,** problèmes sociaux, d'ordre social; **s. sciences,** sciences humaines; **s. reformer,** réformateur, -trice, de la société; **the s. order,** l'ordre social; **s. work, s. service,** œuvres sociales; **the s. services,** les services sociaux, d'assistance sociale; **(medical) s. worker,** assistante sociale (d'un hôpital); *Adm:* **s. security,** sécurité sociale; (*b*) mondain; **to reach the top of the s. ladder,** atteindre le sommet de l'échelle sociale; **s. position,** rang *m* dans la société; **to have a busy s. life,** sortir beaucoup; *O:* **s. evening,** (i) soirée *f;* (ii) réception *f;* (iii) réunion *f,* veillée *f* (entre voisins); *s.* **(Church) s.,** soirée, réunion (entre membres d'une église); (*c*) *Pol:* **s. democracy,** social-démocratie *f;* **s. democrat,** social-démocrate *mf, pl.* social-démocrates. 2. *Nat.Hist:* social; qui vit en société; **the beaver is a s. animal,** les castors sont des animaux sociaux; **man is an essentially s. animal,** l'homme est essentiellement sociable. 3. *A.Hist:* **the Social Wars,** les Guerres entre Alliés; les Guerres Sociales.
socialism ['souʃəlizm], *s.* socialisme *m;* **State s.,** étatisme *m;* socialisme d'État; **Christian s.,** socialisme chrétien.
socialist ['souʃəlist], *a. & s.* socialiste (*mf*).
socialistic [souʃə'listik], *a. O:* socialiste.
socialite ['souʃəlait], *s. F:* membre *m* de la haute société; homme, femme, du monde; mondain, -aine.
sociality [souʃi'æliti], *s. Nat.Hist:* socialité *f.*
socialization [souʃəlai'zeiʃ(ə)n], *s. Pol.Ec: O:* socialisation *f* (de capitaux, d'industries).
socialize ['souʃəlaiz]. 1. *v.tr.* (*a*) rendre social; (*b*) *Pol.Ec: O:* socialiser, nationaliser (la propriété); *U.S:* **socialized medicine,** médecine *f* d'État. 2. *v.i. U.S:* **to s. with s.o.,** frayer avec qn; **he won't s.,** il n'accepte jamais une invitation.
socially ['souʃəli], *adv.* socialement.
society [sə'saiəti], *s.* 1. société *f;* (*a*) compagnie *f* (de qn); **to avoid the s. of one's colleagues,** éviter la société de ses collègues; **to be fond of s.,** aimer la compagnie; *A:* **to have no s. with s.o.,** ne pas entretenir de rapports avec qn; (*b*) la haute société, le (grand) monde; **fashionable s.,** le beau monde; **to go into, move in, s.,** aller dans le monde; **s. people,** gens *m* du monde; *Journ:* **s. news, column,** mondanités *f;* échos mondains; (*c*) **consumer s.,** société de consommation; **alternative s.,** société alternative. 2. société (de Jésus, de la Croix rouge, etc.); association *f;* **charitable s.,** œuvre *f* de bienfaisance, de charité. 3. *Geog:* **the S. Islands,** les îles *f,* l'archipel *m,* de la Société; les îles Tahiti, Taïti.
Socinian [sou'siniən], *a. & s. Rel.H:* socinien, -ienne.
Socinianism [sou'siniənizm], *s. Rel.H:* socinianisme *m.*
Socinus [sou'sainəs], *Pr.n.m. Rel.H:* Socin.
sociocentrism [sousiou'sentrizm], *s.* sociocentrisme *m.*
sociocracy [sousi'ɔkrəsi], *s.* sociocratie *f.*
sociocultural [sousiou'kʌltjər(ə)l], *a.* socio-culturel.
socioeconomic [sousiouiːkə'nɔmik], *a.* socio-économique.
sociogenesis [sousiou'dʒenəsis], *s.* sociogénèse *f.*
sociogenetic [sousioudʒe'netik], *a.* sociogénétique.
sociogeography [sousioudʒiː'ɔgrəfi], *s.* socio-géographie *f.*
sociogram ['sousiougræm], *s.* sociogramme *m.*
sociological [sousiou'lɔdʒik(ə)l], *a.* sociologique.
sociologist [sousi'ɔlədʒist], *s.* sociologiste *mf,* sociologue *mf.*
sociology [sousi'ɔlədʒi], *s.* sociologie *f.*
sociometrist [sousi'ɔmitrist], *s.* sociométriste *mf.*
sociometry [sousi'ɔmitri], *s.* sociométrie *f.*
sock[1] [sɔk], *s.* 1. chaussette *f;* **(ankle) socks, (short) socks,** socquettes *f,* mi-chaussettes *f; F:* **put, shove, a s. in it!** ferme-la! ta gueule! 2. semelle intérieure (d'une chaussure). 3. *A.Th:* brodequin *m,* socque *m;* **to put on the s.,** chausser le brodequin, jouer la comédie; *Lit:* **if Jonson's learned s. be on,** si on joue une comédie de Jonson.
sock[2], *s. P:* coup *m,* gnon *m,* baffe *f,* beigne *f;* (*in the eye*) pochon *m;* **to give s.o. a s. on the jaw,** flanquer une beigne à qn; *O:* **to give s.o. socks,** flanquer à qn une bonne raclée; battre qn à plate couture.
sock[3], *v.tr. & i. P:* 1. **to s. a brick at s.o.,** lancer un briqueton à qn. 2. **to s. (into) s.o.,** donner un gnon, flanquer une beigne, une bonne raclée, à qn.
sock[4], *s. Sch: F:* (*esp. at Eton*) bonbons *mpl,* gâteaux *mpl,* friandises *fpl;* provisions *fpl;* mangeaille *f.*
sock[5], *v.tr. & i. Sch: F:* manger; **to s. s.o.,** payer à qn de la mangeaille.
socket ['sɔkit], *s.* (*a*) *Anat: etc:* alvéole *m or f* (de dent, de diamant); cavité *f* articulaire, glène *f* (d'un os); **ball and s. joint,** emboîtement *m* réciproque; énarthrose *f;* **to wrench one's arm out of its s.,** se désarticuler, déboîter, luxer, le bras; **eye s.,** orbite *f* de l'œil; (*of horse*) salière *f;* **his eyes were starting from their sockets,** les yeux lui sortaient des orbites, de la tête; (*b*) botte *f,* soc *m* (d'une hampe de bannière, de drapeau, de lance); *Mec.E:* godet *m* (de pied de machine); bobèche *f* (de bougeoir); cuissard *m* (de jambe artificielle); *Furn:* **castor s.,** sabot *m; El:* **cable s.,** cosse *f* de câble; (*c*) crapaudine *f* (de gond de porte); *Nau:* crapaudine, saucier *m* (de mèche de cabestan); crapaudine (d'épontille); (*d*) emboîtement *m,* emplanture *f; Av:* emplanture, encastrement *m* (d'aile d'avion); *Nau:* emplanture, socle *m* (de mât); *Tg: Tp:* **pole s.,** socle de poteau; *Plumb:* **pipe s.,** emboîtement. manchon *m,* de tuyau; **s. pipe,** tuyau *m,* conduite *f,* à emboîtement; (*e*) douille *f;* **s. of a shovel,**

douille d'une pelle; **drill s.,** douille, manchon, de foret; *Mil:* **bayonet s.,** douille de baïonnette; *Carp:* **brace s., s. of a bit-stock,** baril *m* de vilebrequin; *Mec.E:* **clamping s.,** douille de blocage; **coupling s.,** douille de connexion; **crank s.,** douille de manivelle; **screw s.,** douille à vis, douille filetée; **s.-head screw,** vis *f* à tête à douille, à tête creuse; **s. spanner, s. wrench,** clef *f* à douille, à tube; clef tubulaire; **s. punch,** emporte-pièce *m inv*; découpoir *m*; **s. sleeve,** manchon *m* de douille; (*f*) *El:* **(lamp) s.,** douille, culot *m* (de lampe); **coupler s.,** douille de collecteur, de connecteur; **bayonet s.,** douille à baïonnette; **key s.,** douille, culot, à clé, à interrupteur; **screw s.,** douille, culot, à vis; douille, culot, Edison; **plug and s. point,** prise *f* de courant; **s. (connector),** prise (de courant) femelle; **wall s.,** prise de courant murale; *Rec: etc:* **microphone s.,** prise microphone; **headphones s.,** prise de casque; **s. antenna,** antenne-secteur *f, pl.* antennes-secteur; (*g*) support *m*; *El:* **s. adapter,** support adapteur; *Elcs: W.Tel:* **(tube) s.,** support de tube électronique, de tube à vide; **cushioned s.,** support antivibrateur; **wafer s.,** support plat; *Mch:* **fire-bar s.,** support de grille; *Mch-Tls:* **s. of rest,** support de chariot.

sockeye ['sɔkai], *s.* **s. (salmon),** saumon *m* rouge du Pacifique (*Salmo nerka*).

socle [sɔkl], *s. Arch:* socle *m*.

Socrates ['sɔkrətiːz], *Pr.n.m.* Socrate.

Socratic [sɔ'krætik], *a.* socratique; **S. irony,** ironie *f* socratique; **S. method,** méthode *f* socratique.

sod[1] [sɔd], *s.* **1.** gazon *m*; **under the s.,** enterré; sous (la) terre; **to put s.o. under the sod,** (i) enterrer qn; (ii) *P:* faire son affaire à qn, assassiner qn. **2. s. (of grass, of turf),** motte gazonnée; motte de gazon; **to cut, turn, the first s.,** donner le premier coup de bêche; **s. cutter,** tranche-gazon *m inv*. **3.** *Ent:* **s. web worms,** crambus *m*.

sod[2], *v.tr.* **(sodded) to s. over, up,** gazonner (un terrain).

sod[3], *s. P:* (*not in polite use*) (*a*) pédé *m*; (*b*) bougre *m*; **poor s.!** pauvre con! (*c*) **odds and sods,** petits bouts, bribes *f* et morceaux *m*; (*of pers.*) **a few odds and sods,** trois pelés et un tondu.

sod[4], *v. P:* (*not in polite use*) **1.** *v.tr.* **s. you!** va te faire foutre! **s. it!** merde, alors! **2.** *v.i.* **to s. off,** foutre le camp.

soda ['soudə], *s.* (*a*) *Ch: etc:* soude *f*; **caustic s.,** soude caustique; *Miner:* **native s.,** natron *m*; **s. ash,** cendre *f* de soude; alcali minéral; **s. salt,** sel *m* sodique; *Com:* **common s., washing s., s. crystals,** carbonate *m* de soude, cristaux *mpl* de soude; **bicarbonate of s., baking s.,** bicarbonate *m* de soude; **s. bread, s. cake,** pain *m*, gâteau *m*, qu'on fait lever au bicarbonate de soude; (*b*) **s. (water),** eau *f* de Seltz; soda *m*; **ice cream s.,** limonade *f*, etc., contenant une glace; **s. fountain,** bar *m* pour glaces et rafraîchissements (non alcooliques); *U.S: F:* **s. jerk(er),** serveur *m* dans un *soda fountain*.

sodalite ['soudəlait], *s. Miner:* sodalite *f*.

sodality [sou'dæliti], *s. Ecc:* sodalité *f*, congrégation *f*, confrérie *f*.

sodden[1] ['sɔd(ə)n], *a.* **1.** (*a*) (*of field*) (dé)trempé; (*b*) (*of bread, etc.*) mal cuit; pâteux; (*of vegetables, etc.*) qui a bouilli trop longtemps; imprégné d'eau; **s. with grease,** dégouttant de graisse. **2. s. with drink,** abruti par l'alcool, par la boisson.

sodden[2]. **1.** *v.tr.* (*a*) détremper (la terre, etc.); (*b*) abrutir (les facultés) par la boisson. **2.** *v.i.* s'imprégner d'humidité.

sodd(y)ite ['sɔd(i)ait], *s. Miner:* sodd(y)ite *f*.

sodic ['soudik], *a. Ch:* sodique.

sodium ['soudiəm], *s. Ch:* sodium *m*; **s. salt,** sel *m* sodique; **s. nitrate,** nitrate *m*, azotate *m*, de soude; **s. carbonate,** carbonate *m* de soude; **s. chloride,** chlorure *m* de sodium; **s. sulphate,** sulfate *m* de soude, de sodium; *Pharm:* **s. cacodylate,** cacodylate *m* de soude; *esp. U.S:* **barbital s.,** véronal *m* sodique.

sodoku ['sɔdəkju], *s. Med:* sodoku *m*.

Sodom ['sɔdəm]. *Pr.n. B.Geog:* Sodome *f*.

sodomite ['sɔdəmait], *s.* sodomite *m*, pédéraste *m*.

sodomize ['sɔdəmaiz], *v.i.* sodomiser.

sodomy ['sɔdəmi], *s.* sodomie *f*, pédérastie *f*.

soever [sou'evər]. *adv. Lit:* **in any way s.,** n'importe comment; **how great s. it may be,** quelque grand que ce soit.

sofa ['soufə], *s. Furn:* sofa *m*, canapé *m*; **s. bed,** lit-canapé *m, pl.* lits-canapés; canapé-lit *m, pl.* canapés-lits.

soffit ['sɔfit], *s. Arch:* soffite *m*, douelle *f*, intrados *m*; cintre *m*, coquille *f*; *Th: A:* **the soffits,** les frises *f*.

soft [sɔft], *a., s., adv. & int.*

I. *a.* **1.** mou, *f.* molle; tendre; (*a*) **as s. as butter, as wax,** mou comme le beurre, comme la cire; **s. mud,** boue inconsistante, liquide, grasse; **s. soil, ground,** terrain mou; **s. iron,** fer doux, fer tendre; **s. stone,** pierre tendre, grasse; **s. rock,** roche *f* tendre; **s. coal,** houille grasse; **s. pencil,** crayon *m* tendre; **s. cheese,** fromage mou; *Nau: F:* **s. tack,** pain *m*; *Cer:* **s. paste,** pâte *f* tendre; **s. porcelain,** porcelaine *f* tendre; (*b*) **s. to the touch,** mou, doux, au toucher; moelleux; **s. pillow,** oreiller mou, doux, douillet; **s. skin,** peau douce, veloutée; **s. hair,** cheveux souples, soyeux; **as s. as silk,** doux comme du satin; **s. hat,** chapeau mou; **s. leather,** cuir *m* souple; *Com:* **s. goods,** produits *m* textiles; tissus *m*; **s. furnishings,** tapis *m* et tissus d'ameublement; (*c*) (*of pers.*) (i) mou, qui manque de vigueur; (ii) doux, malléable; **s. muscles,** muscles mous, flasques; (*of horse*) **s. mouth,** bouche tendre, sensible; **to be s.-mouthed,** avoir la bouche tendre, sensible; ne pas avoir d'appui; **to become s.,** s'amollir; **you mustn't be so s. with them,** il faut les traiter plus sévèrement; (*d*) **s. X rays,** rayons mous; (*e*) *St.Exch:* **oils are s.,** les pétroles sont faibles. **2.** doux, *f.* douce; (*a*) **s. rain,** pluie douce; **s. wind,** vent doux; **s. weather,** temps mou; **s. day,** journée (i) tiède, (ii) humide, de pluie; **s. water,** eau douce, non calcaire; **s. colours,** couleurs douces, suaves; *Art:* **s. flesh tints,** chairs morbides; **s. light,** lumière douce, atténuée; **the light is growing softer,** la lumière s'atténue; **s. brown eyes,** yeux d'un brun doux; **s. outline,** contour mou, flou; *Phot:* **s. focus,** flou *m*; **s. focus lens,** objectif *m* anachromatique, pour le flou; **s. paper,** papier donnant doux, pour effets doux; **s. light,** source lumineuse produisant des ombres à contours flous; *Cin: Th:* **s. lighting,** éclairage donnant des ombres à contours flous; **s. voice, s. music,** voix douce, musique douce; **s. step,** pas feutré, ouaté; **s.-footed,** aux pas feutrés, ouatés; **to give a s. tap on the door,** frapper doucement à la porte; *Av: Space:* **s. landing,** atterrissage *m* en douceur; *Com:* **s. sell,** publicité *f* discrète; *B:* **a s. answer turneth away wrath,** une réponse douce apaise la fureur; **to have a s. tongue,** parler d'un ton mielleux; *Ling:* **s. consonant,** consonne douce; (*b*) **s. drinks,** boissons *f* non alcooliques; **s. drugs,** drogues douces; (*c*) **s. life,** vie douce; *F:* **a s. job,** un emploi pépère, un filon, un bon fromage, une planque; **to have a s. time (of it),** se la couler douce; (*d*) **s. words,** mots doux, tendres; **s. heart,** cœur *m* tendre; **to have a s. spot, a s. place in one's heart, for s.o.,** avoir un faible pour qn; *F:* **to be s. on s.o.,** être amoureux, épris, entiché, de qn. **3.** (*a*) *F:* stupide, bête; **he isn't as s. as he looks,** il n'est pas si bête qu'il n'en a l'air; **don't be s.!** ne fais pas l'imbécile! **he's gone s. in the head!** il a perdu la boule! (*b*) *s. P:* **you great s.!** espèce d'idiot! espèce d'andouille!

II. *adv. & int.* **1.** *adv.* (*a*) *Lit:* **but s.! who comes?** silence! qui est-ce qui arrive? (*b*) *F:* doucement; **to have it s.,** se la couler douce; *P:* **don't talk s.!** ne dis pas de bêtises, de sottises!

soft-boiled ['sɔftbɔild], *a.* (œuf) mollet.

softback, soft-cover ['sɔftbæk, -kʌvər], *s. esp. U.S:* livre *m* de poche.

soften ['sɔfn]. **1.** *v.tr.* (*a*) amollir, ramollir (la cire, etc.); (*b*) assouplir (le cuir); attendrir (les choux, etc.); détremper, adoucir (l'acier); *Tan:* **to s. skins,** détremper, reverdir, les peaux; (*c*) affaiblir, énerver; **troops softened by idleness,** troupes amollies par l'oisiveté; (*d*) adoucir (une couleur, sa voix, l'eau); assourdir, atténuer (une couleur, une lumière); radoucir (le ton, la colère de qn); *Phot:* atténuer (des contours); **to s. a painting,** donner du moelleux à un tableau; **curtains that s. the light,** rideaux qui tamisent la lumière; **to s. a contrast,** amoindrir, adoucir, atténuer, un contraste; *Veh:* **to s. the suspension,** adoucir la suspension; (*e*) attendrir, émouvoir (qn); **to s. s.o. (up),** amadouer qn; **to be softened at the sight of sth.,** s'attendrir à la vue de qch.; (*f*) soulager (la douleur). **2.** *v.i.* (*a*) s'amollir, se ramollir; (*b*) s'adoucir, se radoucir; **the weather is softening,** le temps s'adoucit; (*c*) s'attendrir.

softener ['sɔfnər], *s.* **1.** (*pers.*) *Tan:* reverdisseur *m* (de peaux). **2.** (*a*) substance amollissante; ramollissant *m*; ramollitif *m*; (*b*) **water s.,** adoucisseur *m* d'eau.

softening[1] ['sɔfniŋ], *a.* **1.** *Pharm: etc:* amollissant, adoucissant; (onguent) fondant. **2.** (ton, etc.) qui s'adoucit.

softening[2], *s.* (*a*) amollissement *m*, ramollissement *m*; **s. of the brain,** ramollissement du cerveau; cérébromalacie *f*; (*b*) assouplissement *m* (du cuir); (*c*) *Metalw:* détrempe *f*, adoucissage *m* (de l'acier); (*d*) adoucissement *m* (du caractère); (*e*) adoucissement (de l'eau); assourdissement *m* (de la lumière); *Phot: etc:* **s. of contrasts, of outlines,** atténuation *f* des contrastes, des contours; (*f*) attendrissement *m*.

soft-eyed [sɔft'aid], *a.* aux yeux doux.

soft grass ['sɔftgrɑːs], *s. Bot:* **(meadow) s.,** houlque laineuse.

softhead ['sɔfthed], *s. F:* sot, sotte; niais, -aise; andouille *f*.

softheaded [sɔft'hedid], *a. F:* bête, niais; faible d'esprit; **he's getting s.,** il perd la boule.

softhearted [sɔft'hɑːtid], *a.* au cœur tendre, compatissant, sensible; **to be s.,** être compatissant, avoir de la sensibilité; **he's too s.,** il a trop de cœur.

softheartedness [sɔft'hɑːtidnis], *s.* sensibilité *f*; bonté *f* de cœur; indulgence *f*.

softie ['sɔfti], *s. F:* = SOFTY.

soft-land [sɔft'lænd], *v.i. & tr. Av: Space:* (faire) atterrir (un avion, etc.) en douceur, sans heurts; **to s.-l. on the moon,** alunir sans heurts.

softly ['sɔftli], *adv.* **1.** (*a*) doucement; **to walk s.,** marcher sans bruit; ouater ses pas; (*b*) tendrement. **2.** mollement.

softness [sɔftnis], *s.* **1.** douceur *f* (de la peau, d'un tissu, du climat, etc.); tiédeur *f* (de l'air). **2.** (*a*) mollesse *f* (de caractère); manque *m* d'énergie, de caractère; (*b*) flou *m* (des contours); *Phot:* **chromatic s.,** flou chromatique. **3.** *F:* niaiserie *f*; simplicité *f*.

soft-nosed [sɔft'nouzd], *a.* **s.-n. bullet,** balle *f* déformable.

soft(-)pedal [sɔft'pedl]. **1.** *v.i. Mus:* appuyer sur, se servir de, la pédale douce (d'un piano). **2.** *v.i. & tr. F:* ralentir, y aller doucement, ne pas trop insister; atténuer, amoindrir (l'importance d'un incident); obscurcir (une affaire).

soft-sawder [sɔft'sɔːdər], *v.tr.* = SOFT-SOAP.

soft-shell(ed) [sɔft'ʃeld], *a.* **1.** à coquille molle; (œuf) hardé. **2.** (tortue, etc.) à carapace molle.

soft-skinned [sɔft'skind], *a.* **1.** (*a*) à (la) peau tendre, douce; (*b*) (*of pers.*) trop sensible. **2.** *Mil:* **s.-s. vehicles,** véhicules non blindés.

soft-soap [sɔft'soup], *v.tr. F:* flatter, passer la pommade à (qn).

soft-solder [sɔft'souldər], *v.tr.* souder à la soudure tendre, à l'étain.

soft-spoken [sɔft'spoukən], *a.* **1.** (*of pers.*) mielleux, doucereux; aux paroles mielleuses; au doux parler. **2.** (*of words*) mielleux, doucereux.

software ['sɔftwɛər], *s. Cmptr:* logiciel *m*; programmerie *f*; *F:* software *m*; **s. engineer,** ingénieur *m* en programmation; **s. package,** collection *f*, ensemble *m*, de programmes; **s. programmer,** programmeur *m* d'étude.

softwood ['sɔftwud], *s.* **1.** *Carp: etc:* bois *m* tendre. **2.** *For:* essences *f* conifères.

softy ['sɔfti], *s. F:* **1.** (*a*) **a s.,** un mou, une molle; un homme efféminé; (*b*) couard, -arde; (*c*) **to be a terrible s.,** être sentimental à l'excès, d'une sensiblerie excessive. **2.** = SOFTHEAD.

soggy ['sɔgi], *a.* **1.** détrempé; saturé d'eau. **2.** (*of bread*) pâteux; mal cuit; lourd. **3.** (*of heat, atmosphere*) lourd; saturé d'humidité.

soh [sou], *s. Mus:* **1.** (*fixed soh*) sol *m inv.* **2.** (*movable soh*) la dominante.

soigné ['swæŋjei], *a.* soigné, élégant.

soil[1] [sɔil], *s.* (*a*) sol *m*, terrain *m*, terroir *m*, terreau *m*, terre *f*; **to cultivate the s.,** cultiver la terre; **rich s.,** terroir fertile, gras; terre grasse; **artificial s.,** terres de rapport; **sandy s.,** sol sablonneux; **light s., loose s.,** terre meuble; **alluvial s.,** terrain d'alluvion(s); **vegetable s.,** terre végétale; terreau; **grown s.,** terre naturelle, vierge; **virgin s.,** terre vierge; **fossil s.,** paléosol *m*; (*b*) *Lit:* **one's native s.,** le pays natal, le sol natal; **son of the s.,** fils *m* de la terre; **to smack, be redolent, of the s.,** sentir le terroir, le cru; **attachment to, love of, the s.,** esprit terrien; **to be bound up in the s.,** être attaché à la terre, à son terroir; *Hist:* **bound to the s.,** attaché à la glèbe.

soil[2], *v.tr.* mettre (un cheval) au régime vert, au vert.

soil[3], *s.* **1.** souillure *f*, salissure *f*. **2.** (*a*) *A:* saleté *f*; (*b*) *Hyg: O:* **night s.,** vidanges *fpl*; gadoue *f*. **3.** *Ven:* (*a*) *A:* souille *f* (de sanglier); (*b*) (*of deer*) **to take s.,** battre l'eau; prendre l'eau.

soil[4]. **1.** *v.tr.* (*a*) souiller, salir; encrasser (ses habits); maculer (son linge); **it felt as if I had soiled my hand,** j'avais l'impression d'une souillure à la main; (*b*) (*with passive force*) **fabric apt to s., that soils easily,** tissu salissant, qui se salit, se tache, facilement. **2.** *v.i. Ven: A:* (i) (*of boar*) prendre souille, se vautrer dans la boue; (ii) (*of deer*) battre l'eau.

soiled [sɔild], *a.* souillé, sali, défraîchi; **s. linen, clothes, clothing,** linge *m* sale; **s. dress,** robe défraîchie.

soiling ['sɔiliŋ], *s. Husb:* mise *f* au vert; régime vert; **s. crop,** fourrage vert.

soirée ['swɑːrei], *s. A:* soirée *f*; réception *f*.

sojourn[1] ['sɔdʒ(ː)n], *s. A: & Lit:* **1.** séjour *m*. **2.** lieu *m* de séjour.

sojourn[2], *v.i. A: & Lit:* séjourner; **after sojourning in Paris,** après (avoir fait) un séjour à Paris.

sojourner ['sɔdʒənər], *s. A: & Lit:* **I was a s. in a strange land,** j'étais de passage dans un pays étranger.
soke [souk], *s. A: & Jur:* **1.** droit *m* de juridiction. **2.** juridiction *f*, ressort *m*.
sol¹ [sɔl], *s. Mus:* sol *m*.
sol², *s. Ph: Ch:* sol *m*.
sola¹ ['soulə], *s. Bot:* æschynomène *f*; sola *m*; *Cost:* **s. topee,** casque colonial en sola.
sola². **1.** *a.f. Th: O:* seule. **2.** *s. Com:* **s. of exchange,** seule *f* de change.
solace¹ ['sɔləs], *s. Lit:* consolation *f*, soulagement *m*; **to find s. in sth.,** trouver sa, une, consolation dans qch.; **she is my only s.,** elle est ma seule consolation, ma seule joie.
solace², *v.tr. Lit:* consoler (qn); soulager, adoucir (la douleur de qn); **I solaced myself with this thought,** j'ai trouvé une consolation dans cette pensée.
solacement ['sɔləsmənt], *s. Lit:* consolation *f*, soulagement *m*.
solan ['soulən], *s. Orn:* **s. (goose),** fou *m* (de Bassan).
Solanaceae [sɔlə'neisii:], *s.pl. Bot:* solanacées *f*; solanées *f*.
solanaceous [sɔlə'neiʃəs], *a. Bot:* solanacé; solané.
solar ['soulər], *a.* (système *m*, mythe *m*, etc.) solaire; **s. rays,** rayons *m* solaires; **s. flare,** éruption *f* solaire; **s. wind,** vent *m* solaire; **s. power,** énergie *f* solaire; houille *f* d'or; **s. furnace,** four *m* solaire; insolateur *m*; **s. battery,** pile *f* solaire; **s. tower,** tour *f* solaire; *Opt:* **s. eye-piece,** bonnette *f* à verre jaune (pour longue-vue); *Anat:* **s. plexus,** plexus *m* solaire.
solarium, *pl.* **-ia** [sou'lɛəriəm, -iə], *s.* **1.** *Med:* (*for sun baths*) solarium *m*. **2.** *Moll:* cadran *m*, solarium.
solarization [soulərai'zeiʃ(ə)n], *s. Phot:* solarisation *f* (d'un cliché).
solarize ['souləraiz]. **1.** *v.tr. Phot:* solariser; **solarized image,** image *f* de solarisation. **2.** *v.i.* se solariser.
Solasteridae [sɔlæs'teridi:], *s.pl. Echin:* solastéridés *m*.
solatium [sou'leiʃiəm], *s.* **1.** (somme donnée à titre de) compensation *f*. **2.** *Jur:* dommages-intérêts payés à titre de réparation morale (en sus des dommages-intérêts matériels).
soldanella [sɔldə'nelə], *s. Bot:* soldanelle *f*.
solder¹ ['sɔldər, 'souldər], *s.* soudure *f*; **fine, coarse, s.,** soudure grasse, maigre; **hard s., brazing s.,** soudure forte; brasure *f*; **soft s.,** soudure tendre; claire-étoffe *f*, claire-soudure *f*; **cored s.,** soudure enrobée; **brass s.,** soudure de cuivre, de laiton; **tin s.,** soudure d'étain; **spelter s.,** soudure à base de zinc.
solder², *v.tr. Metalw:* souder; **to hard-s.,** souder au cuivre, au laiton; braser; **to soft-s.,** souder à l'étain; **to dip s.,** souder au bain; **to copper-s.,** braser au cuivre.
solderer ['sɔldərər], *s.* soudeur, -euse.
soldering ['sɔldəriŋ], *s.* soudure *f*, soudage *m* (hétérogène); **hard s.,** soudure au cuivre, au laiton; brasage *m*, brasement *m*; brasure *f*; **soft s.,** soudure à l'étain; **lamp s., blowpipe s.,** soudure au chalumeau; **dip-s.,** soudure par immersion; **s. bit, s. iron,** soudoir *m*; **s. hammer,** soudoir à, en, marteau; **s. lamp,** fer à souder.
soldier¹ ['souldʒər], *s.* **1.** (*a*) soldat *m*; militaire *m*; **three soldiers and two civilians,** trois militaires et deux civils; **private s.,** simple soldat; (soldat de) deuxième classe *m*; **fellow s.,** camarade *m* (de régiment); frère *m* d'armes; **an old s.,** (i) un vieux soldat; (ii) un ancien soldat, un vétéran; *Pej:* un (vieux) soudard; (iii) *esp. U.S: F:* une bouteille vide, un cadavre; **s. of fortune,** soldat, officier *m*, de fortune; aventurier *m*; *A:* **s. of the line,** soldat d'infanterie de ligne, *F:* lignard *m*; *A:* **to go for a s.,** se faire soldat; **tin s.,** soldat de plomb; *Nau:* **soldier's wind,** vent *m* largue; vent de demoiselle; (*b*) tacticien *m*, stratégiste *m*; **great s. but poor politician,** grand capitaine mais piètre politicien; (*c*) *Nau: F:* (i) fainéant *m*; genou creux; tire-au-flanc *m inv*; (ii) marin *m* d'eau douce. **2.** (*a*) *Ent:* **s. (ant),** soldat des bois; **s. (beetle),** téléphore *m*; rhagonyque *f*; (*b*) *Crust:* **s. (crab),** soldat marin, bernard-l'ermite *m*; (*c*) *Bot:* **s. orchis,** orchis *m* militaire; (*d*) *Orn:* **s. bird,** sturnelle *f*. **3.** *Vet:* **red s.,** (i) rouget *m*; mal *m* rouge; (ii) porc atteint du rouget, du mal rouge. **4.** *Comest: F:* (*to dip in boiled egg*) mouillette *f*.
soldier², *v.i.* **1.** faire le métier de soldat; **to s. on,** (i) rester au service; (ii) *F:* continuer à se maintenir. **2.** *U.S: & Nau: F:* flémarder; tirer au flanc.
soldierfish ['souldʒəfiʃ], *s. Ich:* (*a*) holocentridé *m*, poisson-soldat *m*; (*b*) *Austr:* apogon *m*, poisson-cardinal *m*.
soldiering ['souldʒəriŋ], *s.* le métier, la carrière, militaire, des armes.
soldierlike, soldierly ['souldʒəlaik, -li], *a.* de soldat, digne d'un soldat; **s. bearing,** allure martiale, militaire.
soldiery ['souldʒəri], *s. O: coll.* soldats *mpl*, militaires *mpl*; **to call out the s.,** faire appel à la force armée, la troupe.
sole¹ [soul], *s.* **1.** plante *f* (du pied); (*of horse, etc.*) sole *f*. **2.** semelle *f* (de chaussure); **inner s.,** première *f*; **middle s.,** béquet *m*, becquet *m*; **s. leather,** cuir *m* pour semelles; (*light*) molleterie *f*; **shoe with a single s., a double s.,** chaussure à semelle simple, à double semelle. **3.** semelle (de rabot, de crosse de golf, etc.); plan *m* (d'un rabot); *N.Arch:* talon *m*, talonnière *f* (du gouvernail); *Min:* plancher *m*, semelle, sole (d'une galerie de mine); *Metall: Mch:* aire *f*, sole (d'un fourneau); *Const: etc:* plate-forme *f*, *pl.* plates-formes; semelle, patin *m* (d'une fondation); racinal *m*, -aux (d'une grue); **s. piece, s. plate,** semelle, patin, couchis *m* (d'une fondation); *Nau:* savate *f* (d'un étançon); *Mec.E:* plaque *f* de fondation, sole (d'une machine); *Veh:* **s. bar,** longeron *m*. **4.** *Agr:* cep *m*, sep *m* (d'une charrue).
sole², *v.tr.* (*a*) mettre une semelle à (une chaussure); (*b*) ressemeler (une chaussure).
sole³, *s. Ich:* sole *f*; **Dover s.,** (vraie) sole; **lemon s.,** plie *f* sole; limande *f* sole; **variegated s.,** sole perdrix, langue-de-chat *f*, *pl.* langues-de-chat.
sole⁴, *a.* **1.** seul, unique; **his s. reason,** son unique raison; **his father's s. support,** le seul soutien de son père; **with a small bed as s. furniture,** avec pour tout mobilier un petit lit; **the s. management,** l'entière direction; **s. right,** droit exclusif; **s. legatee,** légataire universel. **2.** *A:* solitaire, isolé.
solecism ['sɔlisizm], *s.* **1.** solécisme *m*; faute *f* de grammaire; locution vicieuse. **2.** solécisme (de conduite); faute contre le savoir-vivre.
solecistic [sɔli'sistik], *a.* **s. construction,** construction incorrecte; solécisme *m*.
solecize ['sɔlisaiz], *v.i.* faire un solécisme; *Lit:* soléciser.
Soleidae [sɔ'li:idi:], *s.pl. Ich:* soléidés *m*.
solely ['soulli], *adv.* seulement, uniquement; **s. responsible,** entièrement responsable; **to be s. entitled to do sth.,** avoir le droit exclusif de faire qch.; **I went there s. to see it,** j'y suis allé dans le seul but de le voir, uniquement pour le voir.
solemn ['sɔləm], *a.* **1.** (*of oath, etc.*) solennel; **s. silence,** silence solennel; **s. question,** question grave, qui donne à réfléchir; **s. fact,** réalité sérieuse; **s. duty,** devoir sacré; **s. warning,** avertissement donné avec la gravité que comportent les circonstances; **s. ceremony,** solennité *f*; **it is the s. truth,** je vous jure que c'est vrai; *Jur:* **s. agreement,** contrat solennel. **2.** (*of pers.*) grave, sérieux; **to put a s. face on it,** prendre un air solennel; **to keep a s. face,** composer son visage; maîtriser son envie de rire; **as s. as a judge,** sérieux comme un évêque; **to speak in a s. tone,** parler d'un ton solennel.
solemness ['sɔləmnis], *s.* = SOLEMNITY 1.
solemnity [sə'lemniti], *s.* **1.** (*a*) solennité *f*; **with all s.,** en toute solennité; (*b*) gravité *f*, sérieux *m* (de maintien). **2.** *Lit:* fête solennelle; solennité.
solemnization [sɔləmnai'zeiʃ(ə)n], *s.* solennisation *f*; célébration *f* (d'un mariage).
solemnize ['sɔləmnaiz], *v.tr.* **1.** solenniser (une fête); célébrer, bénir (un mariage). **2.** prêter de la solennité à (un lieu); rendre (une occasion) solennelle, grave.
solemnizing ['sɔləmnaiziŋ], *s.* = SOLEMNIZATION.
solemnly ['sɔləmli], *adv.* **1.** solennellement; **I s. and sincerely believe that . . .,** en mon âme et conscience je suis convaincu que . . .. **2.** gravement, sérieusement; **to speak s.,** parler avec solennité.
solen ['soulən], *s. Moll:* solen *m*; (manche *m* de) couteau *m*.
Solenidae [sɔ'lenidi:], *s.pl. Moll:* solénidés *m*.
solenodon [sɔ'lenoudɔn], *s. Z:* **Cuban s.,** solénodon *m*.
Solenoglypha [sɔle'nɔglifə], *s.pl. Rept:* solénoglyphes *m*.
solenoglyphic [sɔlenou'glifik], *a. Rept:* solénoglyphe.
solenoid ['sɔlənɔid], *s. El:* solénoïde *m*.
solenoidal [sɔlə'nɔidl], *a. El:* solénoïdal, -aux.
solenopsis [sɔli'nɔpsis], *s. Ent:* solénopsis *m*.
soleus ['souliəs], *s. Anat:* muscle *m* soléaire.
solfa¹ ['sɔlfɑ:], *s. Mus:* **1.** (*a*) solmisation *f*; (*b*) solfège *m*. **2. tonic s.,** système de solmisation dans lequel le do est mobile et représente toujours la tonique.
solfa², *v.tr. Mus:* solfier.
solfatara [sɔlfæ'tɑ:rə], *s. Geol:* solfatare *f*, soufrière *f*.
solfataric [sɔlfæ'tɑ:rik], *a. Geol:* solfatarien.
solfeggio, *pl.* **-ios, -gi** [sɔl'fedʒiou, -iouz, -dʒi:], *s. Mus:* solfège *m*.
solicit [sə'lisit]. (*a*) *v.tr. O: & Lit:* solliciter (qch. de qn); **to s. votes,** solliciter, briguer, des voix, des suffrages; (*b*) *v.tr. & i.* (*of prostitute*) raccrocher; racoler (sur la voie publique); faire le raccroc.
solicitation [səlisi'teiʃ(ə)n], *s.* **1.** *O: & Lit:* sollicitation *f*; **s. of votes,** brigue *f* de votes; **at s.o.'s s.,** sur les instances de qn. **2.** (*of prostitute*) raccrochage *m*, racolage *m* (sur la voie publique).
soliciting [sə'lisitiŋ], *s.* = SOLICITATION.
solicitor [sə'lisitər], *s.* **1.** (*a*) *Jur:* = notaire *m*; **S. General,** conseiller *m* juridique de la Couronne; (*b*) *Com: etc:* chef *m* du contentieux. **2.** *Com: U.S:* placier, -ière; *Pej:* racoleur *m*.
solicitous [sə'lisitəs], *a. esp. Lit:* soucieux, désireux (de qch.); préoccupé (de qch.); **s. attention to detail,** soin méticuleux des détails.
solicitously [sə'lisitəsli], *adv.* avec sollicitude; soucieusement; **to enquire s. whether . . .,** demander avec sollicitude si . . ..
solicitousness, solicitude [sə'lisitəsnis, -tju:d], *s.* sollicitude *f*, souci *m*, préoccupation *f*.
solid ['sɔlid]. **1.** *a.* solide; ferme; (*a*) **s. food,** (i) aliment *m* solide; (ii) *Med:* régime *m* solide; **s. flesh,** chair consistante; (*of fluid*) **to become s.,** se solidifier; (*b*) **to build on s. foundations,** bâtir sur le solide; **to dig down to s. ground,** creuser jusqu'au solide; **on s. ground,** sur un terrain ferme; **s. granite,** granit résistant; **cut in the s. rock,** taillé dans la pierre vive, à même la pierre; (*c*) **man of a s. build,** homme bien charpenté, bien découplé; **s. common sense,** solide bon sens; **s. thinker,** penseur solide; **s. character,** caractère *m* d'une bonne trempe; **to have s. reasons for believing sth.,** avoir des raisons solides pour croire qch.; **there's nothing s. about it,** cela manque de fond; *Jur:* **s. consideration,** motif sérieux; **s. defence,** défense *f* valable; (*d*) plein, massif; **s. contents,** volume plein, réel; **s. tyre,** pneu plein; **s. rubber cable,** câble en caoutchouc plein; **s. wall,** mur plein, sans ouvertures; **s. mahogany table,** table *f* en acajou massif, plein; *F:* **he's s. mahogany from the neck up,** il a une tête de bûche; **s. silver,** argent massif; *adv. Metall:* **to cast s.,** couler plein; **pond frozen s.,** étang gelé jusqu'au fond; **s. bank of clouds,** masse *f* uniforme de nuages; nuages épais; *Phot:* **s. printing,** tirage *m* en plein format, sans dégradateur ni cache; *Typ:* **s. page, s. composition,** page *f*, composition *f*, solide; *adv.* **matter set s.,** texte non interligné; *Mth:* **s. angle,** angle *m* solide; angle polyédrique; **s. measures,** mesures *f* de volume; **s. geometry,** géométrie *f* dans l'espace; **to sleep for nine s. hours,** *adv.* **to sleep for nine hours s.,** dormir neuf heures d'affilée, neuf bonnes heures; **three days' s. rain,** trois jours d'une pluie continue, ininterrompue; **s. vote,** vote *m* unanime; (*e*) en une seule pièce; **wheel s. with another,** roue *f* solidaire d'une autre; *adv.* **parts cast s.,** parties coulées monobloc, venues de fonte l'une avec l'autre. **2.** *s.* (*a*) solide *m*; *Mth:* **s. of revolution,** corps *m*, solide, de révolution; (*b*) **milk solids,** extrait *m* du lait; **non-fat solids,** solides non gras; **egg s.,** œufs granulés, en poudre, en paillettes.
solidago [sɔli'deigou], *s. Bot:* solidage *f*.
solidarism ['sɔlidərizm], *s.* solidarisme *m*.
solidarist ['sɔlidərist], *s.* solidariste *mf*.
solidaristic [sɔlidə'ristik], *a.* solidariste.
solidarity [sɔli'dæriti], *s.* solidarité *f*.
solid-drawn [sɔlid'drɔ:n], *a. Metalw:* (tube) étiré sans fente.
solid-forged [sɔlid'fɔ:dʒd], *a. Metall:* monobloc *inv*.
solidifiable [səlidi'faiəbl], *a.* (i) qui peut se solidifier; (ii) congelable.
solidification [səlidifi'keiʃ(ə)n], *s.* (i) solidification *f*; (ii) congélation *f* (de l'huile).
solidify [sə'lidifai]. **1.** *v.tr.* (*a*) solidifier; concréter (l'huile, le sang); (*b*) consolider. **2.** *v.i.* (*a*) se solidifier; (*b*) se prendre en masse; se figer; se congeler; se concréter; (*c*) se consolider.
solidifying [sə'lidifaiiŋ], *s.* = SOLIDIFICATION.
solidity [sə'liditi], *s.* **1.** solidité *f*. **2.** *Jur:* solidarité *f*.
solidly ['sɔlidli], *adv.* **1.** solidement; **s. held,** tenu fermement, solidement; **to build s.,** bâtir à chaux et à sable, à chaux et à ciment; **s. built man,** homme bien charpenté, bien découplé, bien bâti; **to work s.,** travailler sérieusement. **2. to vote s. for sth.,** voter qch. à l'unanimité, comme un seul homme; **a s. Conservative town,** une ville massivement conservatrice.
solidness ['sɔlidnis], *s.* **1.** solidité *f*. **2.** unanimité *f* (d'un vote).
solid-state [sɔlid'steit], *a. Elcs:* **s.-s. component,** composant transistorisé, semi-conducteur; **s.-s. computer,** ordinateur transistorisé.
solidungular, *a.,* **solidungulate,** *a. & s.* [sɔlid'ʌŋgjulər, -leit]. *Z:* solipède (*m*).
solidus, *pl.* **-i** ['sɔlidəs, -ai, -i:], *s.* **1.** *Rom.Num:* solidus *m*. **2.** *Typ:* barre transversale, oblique.
solifluction, solifluxion [sɔli'flʌkʃən], *s. Geol:* solifluction *f*.
solifluctional [sɔli'flʌkʃən(ə)l], *a. Geol:* solifluidal, -aux.
soliloquist, soliloquizer [sə'liləkwist, -kwaizər], *s.* monologueur *m* (qui se parle à lui-même).

soliloquize [sə'liləkwaiz], *v.i.* faire un soliloque, soliloquer; monologuer.
soliloquy [sə'liləkwi], *s.* soliloque *m*; monologue (intérieur).
soling ['souliŋ], *s. Bootm:* (*a*) mise *f* d'une semelle; (*b*) ressemelage *m*.
soliped, solipede ['sɔliped, -pi:d], *a. & s. Z:* solipède (*m*).
solipsism ['sɔlipsizm], *s.* solipsisme *m*.
solipsist ['sɔlipsist], *a. & s.* solipsiste (*mf*).
solitaire [sɔli'tɛər], *s.* **1.** *A:* solitaire *m*, anachorète *m*. **2.** **s. (diamond),** solitaire. **3.** *Games:* (*a*) solitaire; (*b*) *Cards:* (jeu *m* de) patience *f*. **4.** *Orn:* solitaire; **Townsend's s.,** solitaire de Townsend.
solitarily ['sɔlit(ə)rəli], *adv.* solitairement; tout seul.
solitariness ['sɔlit(ə)rinis], *s.* solitude *f*; sentiment *m* d'être seul.
solitary ['sɔlit(ə)ri]. **1.** *a.* (*a*) solitaire; seul, isolé; *Bot:* **s. flower,** fleur *f* solitaire; **not a s. person,** pas un seul; (*b*) *Lit:* (lieu) solitaire, retiré, isolé. **2.** *s. A:* solitaire *m*, anachorète *m*.
solitude ['sɔlitju:d], *s.* **1.** solitude *f*, isolement *m*; **to live in s.,** vivre dans la solitude. **2.** *Lit:* (*a*) lieu *m* solitaire; (*b*) lieu inhabité, dépeuplé; solitude; désert *m*.
sollar ['sɔlər], *s. Min:* palier *m*.
solleret [sɔlə'ret], *s. Arm:* soleret *m*.
solo ['soulou], *s.* **1.** *Mus:* solo *m*; **violin s.,** solo de violon; **to play s.,** jouer en solo; **s. violin,** violon *m* solo; soliste *mf*; **s. organ,** clavier *m* de récit. **2.** *Cards:* **s. (whist),** whist *m* de Gand; **to go s.,** jouer solo. **3.** *Av:* **s. flight,** vol *m* solo *inv*; **to make a s. flight, to fly s.,** voler seul; *F:* **when did you first go s.?** quand est-ce que tu as fait ton premier vol solo?
soloist ['soulouist], *s. Mus:* soliste *mf*.
Solomon ['sɔləmən], *Pr.n.* **1.** (*a*) Salomon *m*; (*b*) *Bot:* **Solomon's seal,** sceau *m* de Salomon; *F:* grenouillet *m*. **2.** *Geog:* **the S. Islands, the Solomons,** les îles *f* Salomon; **S. Islander,** Salomonien, -ienne.
Solothurn ['sɔləθə:n], *Pr.n. Geog:* Soleure.
solstice ['sɔlstis], *s. Astr:* solstice *m*; **summer s., winter s.,** solstice d'été, d'hiver.
solstitial [sɔl'stiʃ(ə)l], *a. Astr:* solsticial, -aux.
solubility [sɔlju'biliti], *s.* solubilité *f* (d'un sel, etc.).
solubilizer ['sɔljubilaizər], *s. Ch: etc:* solubilisant *m*.
soluble ['sɔljubl], *a.* **1.** soluble; *occ.* dissoluble; **s. in alcohol,** soluble dans l'alcool; **s. when heated,** soluble à chaud; **slightly s.,** peu, légèrement, soluble; **highly s.,** très, abondamment, soluble; **to make (sth.) s.,** solubiliser, rendre soluble (qch.). **2.** (problème *m*) soluble, résoluble, qui peut être résolu.
solunar [sɔ'lu:nər], *a.* solunaire.
solus ['souləs], *a.* (*f.* **sola**) *esp. Th:* seul, seule.
solute [sɔ'l(j)u:t]. **1.** *a.* dissous, en solution. **2.** *s.* corps dissous, en solution.
solution [sə'lu:ʃ(ə)n], *s.* solution *f*. **1.** (*a*) *Ch: etc:* solution, dissolution *f*; **salt in s.,** sel *m* en solution; (*b*) solution; liqueur *f*; **s. chemistry,** chimie *f* des solutions; **standard s.,** solution au titre; solution, liqueur, titrée; solution normale; **concentrated s., strong s., stock s.,** solution concentrée, forte; **diluted s., weak s.,** solution diluée, faible, étendue; **saturated, supersaturated, s.,** solution saturée, sursaturée; **solid s.,** solution solide; **liquid s.,** solution liquide; **brine s.,** solution de sel ordinaire; **pregnant s.,** solution mère; **buffer s.,** solution tampon; **alkaline s.,** solution, liqueur, alcaline; **copper sulphate s.,** solution de sulfate de cuivre; **litmus s.,** teinture *f* de tournesol; **electrolytic s.,** solution d'électrolyte; *El:* **battery s.,** électrolyte *m*; **rubber s.,** dissolution de caoutchouc; *Phot:* **fixing s.,** solution de fixage; *Biol:* **Ringer's s.,** liquide *m* de Ringer; *Cryst:* **s. plane,** direction *f* de solution; (*c*) *Engr: etc:* solution, bain *m*; **etching s.,** solution de morsure; **bleaching s.,** bain, solution, de blanchiment; **damping, fountain, s.,** solution, eau *f*, de mouillage; **resensitizing s.,** solution de décapage; **washout s.,** solution d'enlevage. **2.** (*a*) (*solving*) résolution *f*, solution (d'une difficulté, d'une équation); (*b*) (*answer*) solution; résultat *m* (d'un problème de mathématique); **alternative s.,** solution de rechange, de remplacement; **feasible s.,** solution acceptable, réalisable; *Mth:* **inapplicable, non-valid, s.,** solution étrangère; **there is no real s. to this,** ce cas ne comporte aucune solution; **the only s. is recourse to arms,** la seule solution est le recours aux armes. **3.** (*a*) **s. of continuity,** solution de continuité; (*b*) *Med: A:* solution (d'une maladie).
Solutrean, Solutrian [sə'lu:triən], *a. Prehist:* solutréen; de Solutré.
Solutreo-Magdalenian [sə'lu:trioumægdə'li:niən], *a. Prehist:* solutréo-magdalénien.
solvability [sɔlvə'biliti], *s.* **1.** *O:* solvabilité *f* (d'un commerçant, etc.). **2.** solubilité *f* (d'un sel, etc.). **3.** résolubilité *f* (d'un problème).
solvable ['sɔlvəbl], *a.* **1.** (sel) soluble. **2.** (problème) résoluble.
solvate ['sɔlveit], *s. Ch:* solvate *m*.
solvated [sɔl'veitid], *a. Ch:* (colloïde, etc.) solvatisé.
solvation [sɔl'veiʃ(ə)n], *s. Ch:* solvatisation *f* (d'un colloïde).
solve [sɔlv], *v.tr.* **1.** résoudre (un problème, une équation); **this question is not easily solved, has not yet been solved,** cette question n'est pas facile à résoudre, reste toujours en suspens; **measures taken with a view to solving the economic crisis,** mesures prises en vue de combattre la crise économique; **to s. a riddle,** trouver le mot de l'énigme. **2.** *A:* solder, liquider (une dette). **3.** *A:* dissoudre (un sel).
solvency ['sɔlvənsi], *s.* solvabilité *f*.
solvent ['sɔlvənt]. **1.** *a. Com: Jur:* solvable; **security given by a s. man,** caution bourgeoise. **2.** (*a*) *a.* dissolvant; (*b*) *s.* dissolvant *m*, solvant *m*; **rubber s.,** dissolvant du caoutchouc.
solver ['sɔlvər], *s.* celui, celle, qui trouve la solution (du problème, etc.).
soma ['soumə], *s. Biol: etc:* soma *m*.
Somali [sou'mɑ:li]. **1.** *Geog:* (*a*) *a.* somali; somalien; **the S. Coast,** la Côte des Somalis; (*b*) *s.* Somali, -ie; **the Somali,** les Somalis. **2.** *s. Ling:* somali *m*.
Somalia [sou'mɑ:liə], *Pr.n. Geog:* (République démocratique de) Somalie *f*.
Somaliland [sou'mɑ:lilænd], *Pr.n. Geog: Hist:* Somalie *f*; **British, Italian, S.,** Somalie britannique, italienne; **French S.,** Côte française des Somalis.
somatic [sou'mætik], *a. Biol:* somatique; **s. cell,** somatocyte *m*.
somatization [soumətai'zeiʃ(ə)n], *s. Psy:* somatisation *f*.
somato- ['soumətou, soumə'tɔ], *comb.fm. Biol:* somato-.
somatogenetic, somatogenic [soumətoudʒe'netik, -'dʒi:nik], *a.* somatogène.
somatognosis [soumətou'nousis], *s.* somatognosie *f*.
somatologic(al) [soumətou'lɔdʒik(l)], *a.* somatologique.
somatology [soumə'tɔlədʒi], *s.* somatologie *f*.
somatopleure [soumətou'plə:r], *s.* somatopleure *f*.
somatopsychic [soumətou'saikik], *a.* somatopsychique.
somatotropic [soumətou'trɔpik], *a.* somatotrope; **s. hormone,** somat(h)ormone *f*.
sombre ['sɔmbər], *a.* sombre; (*a*) **s. wood,** bois sombre, ténébreux; **s. colours,** couleurs sombres; (*b*) (*of pers., mood, etc.*) sombre, morne.
sombrely ['sɔmbəli], *adv.* sombrement; d'un air sombre, morne.
sombrero [sɔm'brɛərou], *s. Cost:* sombrero *m*.
some [sʌm], *a., pron. & adv.*
I. *a.* **1.** (*a*) **s. similar profession,** quelque (autre) profession analogue; **we must find s. solution,** il nous faut trouver quelque, une, solution; **s. sort of an excuse,** une excuse quelconque; **he'll come s. day,** il arrivera un de ces jours; **s. day this week,** dans le courant de la semaine; avant la fin de la semaine; **s. days he is better,** certains jours il va mieux; **s. place of your choice,** un endroit de votre choix; **s. places,** certains endroits; **there is s. difficulty about this,** cela présente certaines difficultés; **s. books are difficult to read,** il y a des livres qui sont difficiles à lire; certains livres sont difficiles à lire; **s. people say . . .,** il y en a qui disent . . .; (*b*) **(some . . . or other) s. book or other,** un livre quelconque; je ne sais quel livre; **s. writer or other,** un vague écrivain; **he consulted s. doctor or other,** il a consulté (i) je ne sais quel médecin, (ii) *Pej:* un médecin quelconque, qui ne vaut rien. **2.** de; **to drink s. water,** boire de l'eau; **I ate s. fruit,** j'ai mangé des fruits; **could you give me s. lunch?** pouvez-vous me donner à déjeuner? **he was waiting for s. friends,** il attendait des amis. **3.** (*certain quantity or number*) **I felt s. (slight) uneasiness,** je ressentais quelque inquiétude; **it needs s. degree of courage to do that,** il y a quelque courage à faire cela; cela demande du courage; **that would be s. help,** cela faciliterait un peu les choses; **in s. measure,** jusqu'à un certain point; **to s. degree,** quelque peu; **s. distance away,** à quelque distance; **s. days ago,** il y a quelques jours; **he stood for s. time without moving,** il restait pendant quelque temps sans bouger; **he has been waiting for s. time,** il attend depuis quelque temps; **after spending s. time in London,** après avoir séjourné quelque temps à Londres; **it will take s. time,** cela prendra pas mal de temps; **at s. length,** assez longuement. **4.** *F:* (*intensive*) **(that was) s. storm!** quelle tempête! **he's s. doctor!** (i) c'est un médecin à la hauteur, un grand médecin; (ii) comme médecin il est nul; **she's s. girl!** c'est une fille formidable! quelle jolie pépée! **he's s. lad, your friend!** quel numéro, ton ami! **that was s. meal!** ce que nous avons bien mangé! **(that was) s. speed!** quelle vitesse! **s. hope!** quelle illusion!
II. *pron.* **1.** *pl.* (*pers.*) certains; **s. or all of them,** tous ou certains d'entre eux; **s. believe that . . .,** il y en a qui croient que . . .; certains croient que . . .; **s. of them agree with us,** les uns, certains, sont de notre avis; **they went off, s. one way, s. another,** ils se sont dispersés, qui d'un côté, qui de l'autre; **s. of my friends,** certains de mes amis. **2.** (*thg*) **I have s.,** j'en ai; **give me s.,** donnez-m'en; **take s.!** (i) (*of it*) prenez-en! (ii) (*of them*) prenez-en quelques-uns! **I've s. more,** (i) j'en ai encore; (ii) j'en ai d'autres; **give me s. of that wine,** donnez-moi de ce vin; **s. of the time, s. of the afternoon,** une partie du temps, de l'après-midi; **s. of the paper is damaged,** une partie du papier est avariée; **I agree with s. of what you say,** je suis d'accord avec une partie de ce que vous dites; **s. of the most beautiful scenery in the world,** un des plus beaux paysages du monde; *F:* **he wants the lot and then s.,** il lui faut tout et le reste; **he's up to all the tricks and then s.,** il les sait toutes et une par-dessus.
III. *adv.* **1.** environ, quelque *inv*; **s. twenty, thirty, pounds,** une vingtaine, une trentaine, de livres; **s. five hundred people,** environ cinq cents personnes; quelque cinq cents personnes; **s. fifteen minutes,** un bon petit quart d'heure; **s. few minutes,** quelques minutes. **2.** *esp. NAm: F:* (*intensive*) considérablement; et comment! **to go it s.,** y aller en plein; **it annoyed him s.,** il en était pas mal fâché; **they were beaten s.,** ils ont été battus, et comment!
somebody ['sʌmbədi], *pron. & s.* quelqu'un. **1.** *pron.* **s. told me so,** quelqu'un, on, me l'a dit; **s. has left the gas on,** il y a quelqu'un qui a oublié de fermer le gaz; **somebody's knocking,** on frappe; **s. is missing,** il manque quelqu'un; **s. passing at the time,** un passant; **I want s. strong enough to . . .,** il me faut quelqu'un d'assez fort pour . . .; **she reminded him of s. he had seen before,** elle lui rappelait quelqu'un de déjà vu; **s. (or other) has told him . . .,** je ne sais qui lui a dit . . .; **Mr S. (or other),** Monsieur Chose; **s. else,** quelqu'un d'autre; un autre; **s. extra,** quelqu'un de plus. **2.** *pron. & s.* (*pl.* **somebodies** ['sʌmbədiz]) **he's (a) s.,** c'est un personnage; ce n'est pas le premier venu; **he thinks he's s.,** il se croit quelqu'un; il se croit sorti de la côte d'Adam; **they're somebodies in their own village,** ils sont quelqu'un dans leur village; ce sont des personnages dans leur village; **I might have become s.,** j'aurais pu devenir quelqu'un.
somehow ['sʌmhau], *adv.* **1.** de façon ou d'autre, d'une manière ou d'une autre; **we shall manage it s. (or other),** bien ou mal, tant bien que mal, nous y parviendrons; nous y arriverons sûrement d'une manière ou d'une autre. **2.** **I never liked him s.,** je ne sais pourquoi mais il ne m'a jamais été sympathique; **s. (or other) it's different,** il y a pourtant une différence.
someone ['sʌmwʌn], *pron.* = SOMEBODY 1.
someplace ['sʌmpleis], *adv. NAm: F:* = SOMEWHERE.
somersault[1] ['sʌməsɔ:lt], *s.* (i) *Gym:* saut périlleux; culbute *f*; (ii) (*accidental*) culbute; **to turn a s.,** faire (i) le saut périlleux, (ii) la culbute.
somersault[2], *v.i.* (i) *Gym:* faire le saut périlleux, des sauts périlleux; (ii) faire la culbute.
somerset[1,2] ['sʌməset], *s. & v.i. A:* = SOMERSAULT[1,2].
something ['sʌmθiŋ].
I. *s. or pron.* quelque chose *m*. **1.** (*a*) **say s.,** dites quelque chose; **s. or other,** quelque chose; une chose ou une autre; **s. (or other) always happens just as I'm leaving,** il arrive toujours quelque chose quand je suis sur mon départ; **s. went wrong,** quelque chose a cloché; **s. went wrong with his car,** il a eu une panne de voiture; **Jim s. (or other),** Jacques je ne sais plus quoi; **there's s. the matter with him,** il a quelque chose; **there's s. about him I don't like,** il y a en lui je ne sais quoi qui me déplaît; **s. tells me he'll come,** quelque chose me dit qu'il viendra; **s. to drink,** de quoi boire; quelque chose à boire; **to ask for s. to drink,** demander (quelque chose) à boire; **can I get you s.?** qu'est-ce que je puis vous offrir (à manger, à boire)? **let's have s. to eat,** mangeons quelque chose; **let's have a little s., a spot of s.,** si on prenait un petit verre; **to slip s.o. s.,** (i) glisser un pourboire à qn; (ii) graisser la patte à qn; **and s. besides,** et encore un peu; **give me s. to sit on,** donnez-moi un siège, une chaise; **s. to live for,** une raison de vivre; **to have s. to be annoyed about,** avoir de quoi se fâcher; **s. inexplicable,** quelque chose d'inexplicable; **s. new,** quelque chose de nouveau, de neuf; **I've s. else to do,** j'ai autre chose à faire; **there was s. suspicious about him,** il avait un je ne sais quoi de louche; **he's s. in a bank,** il travaille dans une banque; **he'll finish up as an admiral or s.,** il terminera sa carrière comme amiral ou quelque chose de ce genre; **if**

I don't pass my exam I'll have to go into a shop or s., si j'échoue à l'examen il faudra que je devienne vendeur de magasin ou quelque chose dans ce genre; **when he goes skiing he always breaks a leg or s.,** quand il fait du ski s'il ne se casse pas la jambe c'est toujours un autre accident pareil; **the four s. train,** le train de quatre heures et quelque chose; **in the year eleven hundred and s.,** en l'an onze cent et tant; *F:* **you s. fool!** sacré imbécile! (*b*) **an indefinable s.,** un je ne sais quoi d'indéfinissable; **he has that s. that implies a good education,** il a ce je ne sais quoi qui est la marque d'une bonne éducation. **2.** (*a*) **to speak with s. of a foreign accent,** parler avec un accent plus ou moins étranger; **there's s. of an improvement,** il y a une certaine amélioration; **he's s. of a miser,** il est un peu, quelque peu, tant soit peu, avare; **when he returned he found himself s. of a hero,** à son retour il s'est vu acclamer comme un héros; **now you see s. of what I have to put up with,** cela vous laisse entrevoir ce que j'ai à supporter; **he has seen s. of the world,** (i) il a voyagé; (ii) il a l'expérience du monde; **perhaps we shall see s. of you now,** peut-être que maintenant on vous verra un peu; (*b*) **his plan has s. in it, there's s. in his plan,** son projet mérite considération; **people began to think there must be s. in it,** on commença à croire que le bruit n'était pas sans fondement; **there's s. in what you say, there's s. in that,** il y a de la vérité dans ce que vous dites; **there's s. in him,** il a du fond; il a de l'étoffe; **he has s. to do with it,** il y est pour quelque chose; **well, that's s.!** bon, c'est toujours quelque chose! c'était déjà quelque chose! **now I'm going to show you s.! now you're going to see s.!** vous allez voir ce que vous allez voir! **there's s. to be going on with!** (i) voilà un petit acompte; (ii) (*when slapping a child*) ça t'apprendra! **he thinks himself s.,** il se croit quelqu'un, quelque chose; **that was quite s.!** c'était vraiment quelque chose!

II. *adv.* (*a*) quelque peu, tant soit peu; **he is s. less than just to me,** il ne me rend pas pleine justice; **animal s. like a guinea pig,** animal *m* qui ressemble à un cochon d'Inde; (*intensive*) **that's s.** ***like*** **a cigar!** voilà un vrai cigare! **all told we were s. over a hundred,** en tout nous étions un peu plus de cent; (*b*) *P:* (*intensive*) **he treated me s. shocking, s. awful,** il m'a traité d'une façon abominable.

sometime ['sʌmtaim], *adv.* **1.** *occ.* = SOMETIMES. **2.** (*a*) autrefois, jadis; **s. priest of this parish,** autrefois prêtre de cette paroisse; (*b*) *adj.* **Mr. Martin, my s. tutor,** M. Martin, autrefois mon professeur. **3.** (*often written in two words*) **s. (or other),** tôt ou tard; un jour ou l'autre; **s. before dawn,** avant l'aube; **s. last year,** au cours de l'année dernière; **s. in August,** pendant le mois d'août; **s. soon,** bientôt; un de ces quatre matins; un de ces jours; *F:* **see you s.!** à bientôt!

sometimes ['sʌmtaimz], *adv.* quelquefois, parfois; **he is s. late,** il arrive parfois en retard; **s. one, s. the other,** tantôt l'un, tantôt l'autre.

someway ['sʌmwei], *adv. F:* **s. (or other),** de façon ou d'autre.

somewhat ['sʌm(h)wɔt]. **1.** *adv.* quelque peu; un peu; tant soit peu; **it's s. difficult,** c'est assez difficile; **to be s. surprised,** être tant soit peu, passablement, étonné; **s. disappointed,** quelque peu déçu; légèrement déçu; **a s. complicated account,** un récit assez compliqué; **to arrive s. late,** arriver assez tard. **2.** *s.* **he was s. of a coward,** il était quelque peu poltron; **this was s. of a relief,** c'était en quelque sorte un soulagement; c'était un léger soulagement; **it is s. of a difficulty,** c'est assez difficile; **adventure that loses s. in the telling,** aventure qui perd de son sel quand on la raconte.

somewhen ['sʌm(h)wen], *adv. esp. Lit:* **somewhere, somehow, s.,** quelque part, de quelque façon, un jour ou l'autre.

somewhere ['sʌm(h)wɛər], *adv.* **1.** quelque part; **it's s. in the Bible,** cela se trouve quelque part dans la Bible; **it must come from s.,** cela doit bien venir de quelque part; **s. near us,** pas bien loin de chez nous; **s. in the world,** de par le monde; **s. in France,** quelque part en France; **s. else,** ailleurs; autre part; **s. or other,** je ne sais où; *F:* **I'll see him s. first!** qu'il aille au diable! **lost s. between London and Dover,** perdu entre Londres et Douvres; **he lives s. near Oxford,** il habite dans les environs d'Oxford. **2. he is s. around fifty,** il a environ, à peu près, cinquante ans; **s. before two (o'clock),** vers les deux heures; **s. between sunrise and sunset,** entre le lever et le coucher du soleil.

somite ['soumait], *s. Nat.Hist:* somite *m*, segment *m*, métamère *m*.

somnambulant [sɔm'næmbjulənt], *a.* & *s.* somnambule (*mf*).

somnambulism [sɔm'næmbjulizm], *s.* somnambulisme *m*, noctambulisme *m*; *O:* **artificial s.,** somnambulisme provoqué; hypnose provoquée.

somnambulist [sɔm'næmbjulist], *s.* somnambule *mf*, noctambule *mf*.

somnambulistic [sɔmnæmbju'listik], *a.* somnambule; somnambulique.

somniferous, somnific [sɔm'nifərəs, -'nifik], *a.* somnifère, soporifique, endormant.

somniloquist [sɔm'niləkwist], *s.* somniloque *mf*.

somniloquize [sɔm'niləkwaiz], *v.i.* parler en dormant.

somniloquy [sɔm'niləkwi], *s.* somniloquie *f*.

somnolence ['sɔmnələns], *s.* somnolence *f*, assoupissement *m*.

somnolent ['sɔmnələnt], *a.* somnolent, assoupi.

son [sʌn], *s.m.* fils; **how is your s.?** comment va votre fils? **the S. of God, of Man,** le fils de Dieu, de l'homme; **the sons of men,** les hommes; **s. of Belial,** fils de Bélial.

sonant ['sounənt]. *Ling:* **1.** *a.* sonore. **2.** *s.* consonne *f* sonore.

sonar ['souna:r], *s. Nau:* (*from Sound Navigation Ranging*) sonar *m*, radar *m* ultrasonique; **active, passive, s.,** sonar actif, passif; **airborne s.,** sonar aéroporté; **dipping s.,** sonar trempant; **towed s.,** sonar remorqué; **variable-depth s.,** sonar à immersion variable; **fire-control s.,** sonar de tir; **hull s.,** sonar de coque; **monitoring s.,** sonar d'écoute; **search s., surveillance s.,** sonar de veille; **tracking s.,** sonar d'attaque.

sonata [sə'na:tə], *s. Mus:* sonate *f*.

sonatina [sɔnə'ti:nə], *s. Mus:* sonatine *f*.

sondage [sɔn'da:ʒ], *s. Archeol: etc:* sondage *m* (du sol).

sone [soun], *s. Ac:* sone *m*.

song [sɔŋ], *s.* **1.** chant *m*; **to burst, break, into s.,** se mettre tout à coup à chanter; entonner un chant; **the s. of the birds,** le chant, le ramage, des oiseaux; **bird in s.,** oiseau *m* qui chante. **2.** (*a*) chanson *f*; **s. book,** recueil *m* de chansons; chansonnier *m*; **s. writer,** compositeur, -trice, de chansons; **s. without words,** romance sans paroles; **action s.,** chanson mimée; **marching s.,** chanson de route; *Nau:* **capstan s.,** chanson à virer; **hauling s.,** chanson à hisser; *F:* **to buy sth. for an old s., for a (mere) s.,** acheter qch. à vil prix, pour rien, pour une bagatelle, pour une bouchée de pain; **it went for a s.,** cela s'est vendu pour rien; *F:* **he made a great s. and dance about it,** il en faisait un tas d'histoires, un foin de tous les diables; **that's nothing to make a s. about,** (i) il n'y a pas de quoi se récrier, de quoi s'exclamer; (ii) cela ne vaut pas grand-chose; **that'll make him sing another s.,** ça lui fera changer de ton, chanter sur une autre note; (*b*) *Lit:* chant; **s. of victory,** chant de victoire; (*c*) *Ecc:* cantique *m*; **the S. of Songs, the S. of Solomon,** le Cantique des Cantiques.

songbird ['sɔŋbə:d], *s.* oiseau chanteur.

songless ['sɔŋlis], *a. Orn:* qui ne chante pas.

songster ['sɔŋstər], *s.m.* **1.** chanteur. **2.** poète, chantre. **3.** oiseau chanteur.

songstress ['sɔŋstris], *s.f.* chanteuse.

sonic ['sɔnik], *a. Ph:* acoustique, audible; **s. altimeter,** altimètre *m* acoustique; *Av:* **s. barrier, s. wall,** mur *m* du son; **s. boom,** bang *m* supersonique; *Nau:* **s. depth-finder,** sondeur *m* acoustique; *W.Tel:* **s. frequency,** fréquence *f* acoustique, fréquence audible.

sonically ['sɔnik(ə)li], *adv.* soniquement.

soniferous [sɔ'nifərəs], *a.* **1.** qui propage le son. **2.** sonore, résonnant.

son-in-law ['sʌninlɔ:], *s.m.* **1.** gendre, beau-fils, *pl.* beaux-fils. **2.** *A:* (= *stepson*) beau-fils.

sonnet ['sɔnit], *s. Pros:* sonnet *m*; **s. writer,** sonnettiste *mf*; auteur *m*, faiseur *m*, de sonnets; **s. sequence,** suite *f* de sonnets.

sonny ['sʌni], *s.m. F: O:* mon petit, mon fiston, mon petiot.

sonobuoy ['sɔnoubɔi], *s. Elcs:* bouée *f* sonore (de détection marine).

sonometer [sɔ'nɔmitər], *s. Ph:* sonomètre *m*.

sonorific [sɔnə'rifik], *a.* (corps) sonore, résonnant.

sonority [sɔ'nɔriti], *s.* sonorité *f*.

sonorous ['sɔnərəs], *a.* sonore; **s. voice,** voix sonore, timbrée; **s. titles,** titres ronflants.

sonorously ['sɔnərəsli], *adv.* d'un ton sonore.

sonorousness ['sɔnərəsnis], *s.* sonorité *f*.

soon [su:n], *adv.* **1.** (*a*) bientôt, tôt; **s. after,** bientôt après; peu après; **s. after four,** un peu après quatre heures; **you'll be better s.,** vous serez vite guéri, bientôt guéri; **it will s. be three years since I came to London,** voici bientôt trois ans que je suis à Londres; **he s. came home,** il ne tarda pas à rentrer; **he'll be here very s.,** il sera ici sous peu; **how s. may I expect you?** quand devrai-je vous attendre? **how s. can you be ready?** en combien de temps serez-vous prêt? **must you leave so s.?** vous faut-il partir si tôt? **too s.,** trop tôt; avant le temps; avant l'heure; **an hour too s.,** trop tôt d'une heure; (arriver, etc.) avec une heure d'avance; **it ended all too s.,** cela a fini bien trop vite; **I got out of the house none too s.,** je me suis sauvé de la maison juste à temps; (*b*) **as s. as, so s. as,** aussitôt que, dès que; **I'll see him as s. as he comes,** je le verrai aussitôt, dès, qu'il arrivera; je le verrai aussitôt, dès, son arrivée; **as s. as I arrived in London,** dès mon arrivée à Londres; **as s. as he was married he . . .,** aussitôt marié il . . .; **as s. as he saw them,** du moment qu'il les a vus; **as s. as possible,** le plus tôt possible; aussitôt que possible; dans le plus bref délai; *Com: etc:* incessamment; (*c*) **I would as s. die as live in poverty,** j'aimerais autant mourir que de vivre dans la misère; **I would just as s. stay,** j'aime autant rester; **I would just as s. stay here,** j'aimerais (tout) autant rester ici. **2. sooner:** (*a*) plus tôt; **the sooner you begin the sooner you will have finished,** plus tôt vous commencerez plus vite vous aurez fini; **the s. the better,** le plus tôt sera le mieux; **s. or later,** tôt ou tard; **no sooner said than done,** sitôt dit, sitôt fait; aussitôt dit, aussitôt fait; **no sooner had he finished than he was arrested,** à peine eut-il fini qu'il fut arrêté; (*b*) plutôt; **death sooner than slavery,** plutôt la mort que l'esclavage; **sooner than give in I would die,** je mourrais plutôt que de céder; **I would sooner die,** j'aimerais mieux mourir. **3.** *Journ: F:* **soonest,** (faire qch.) aussitôt que possible; **it will be next week at soonest, the soonest possible is next week,** ce sera la semaine prochaine au plus tôt; *Prov:* **least said soonest mended,** trop gratter cuit, trop parler nuit.

soot[1] [sut], *s.* **1.** suie *f*; **soft black s.,** noir *m* de fumée. **2.** *I.C.E: etc:* encrassement *m*, calamine *f*. **3.** *Med:* **s. cancer,** cancer *m* des ramoneurs.

soot[2], *v.tr.* **1.** tacher, enduire, couvrir, (qch.) de suie. **2.** fertiliser (la terre) avec la suie. **3.** *I.C.E:* **to s. up the plugs,** calaminer, encrasser, les bougies; *v.i.* (*of plug*) **to s. up,** s'encrasser.

sooth [su:θ], *s. A:* vérité *f*; **to speak, to say, s.,** dire la vérité; **s. to say,** à vrai dire; **in (good) s.,** en vérité; vraiment.

soothe [su:ð], *v.tr.* calmer, apaiser (la douleur); calmer (les nerfs); tranquilliser (l'esprit); apaiser (un bébé qui crie, etc.); flatter (qn, sa vanité); **to s. s.o.'s anger,** apaiser la colère de qn.

soothing ['su:ðiŋ], *a.* calmant, apaisant; **in a s. voice,** d'une voix calmante; *Med:* **s. remedy,** remède lenitif; **s. draught, s. ointment,** potion calmante, onguent calmant.

soothingly ['su:ðiŋli], *adv.* avec douceur; d'un ton, d'un air, doux, calmant.

soothsayer ['su:θseiər], *s.* **1.** *A:* & *Lit:* devin *m*, *f.* devineresse; prophète *m*, *f.* prophétesse. **2.** *Ent: F:* mante *f*, mantidé *m*.

soothsaying ['su:θseiiŋ], *s. A:* & *Lit:* prédiction *f*; divination *f*; pronostication *f*.

sootiness ['sutinis], *s.* (*a*) état fuligineux; noirceur *f*; (*b*) encrassement *m* (d'un moteur, etc.).

sooting ['sutiŋ], *s. I.C.E:* **s. (up),** encrassement *m* (des bougies, du moteur).

sooty ['suti], *a.* **1.** couvert de suie; noir de suie; **s. wall,** mur noir de suie. **2.** qui contient de la suie; fuligineux; **s. atmosphere,** atmosphère fuligineuse; **s. deposit,** (i) dépôt charbonneux, de suie; (ii) dépôt de calamine; *Orn:* **(light-mantled) s. albatross,** albatros fuligineux.

sop[1] [sɔp], *s.* **1.** morceau de pain, etc., trempé; *A:* soupe *f*; *O:* **s. in the pan,** tranche *f* de pain frite; **sops,** soupe au lait. **2.** (*a*) pot-de-vin *m*, *pl.* pots-de-vin; (*b*) don *m* propitiatoire; concession *f*; *Lit:* **to throw a s. to Cerberus,** jeter le gâteau à Cerbère.

sop[2], *v.tr.* **(sopped) 1.** tremper, faire tremper (le pain); **to s. one's bread in the gravy,** tremper son pain dans la sauce; saucer son pain. **2. to s. up a liquid,** éponger un liquide.

Sophia [sə'faiə], *Pr.n.f.* Sophie.

sophism ['sɔfizm], *s.* sophisme *m*; argument captieux.

sophist ['sɔfist], *s.* sophiste *mf*.

sophistic(al) [sə'fistik(l)], *a.* sophistique, sophiste; (argument) captieux.

sophistically [sə'fistik(ə)li], *adv.* sophistiquement.

sophisticate[1] [sə'fistikeit], *s.* personne sophistiquée.

sophisticate[2]. **1.** *v.tr. O:* (*a*) sophistiquer, falsifier, frelater (un vin, etc.); (*b*) sophistiquer (un sujet); falsifier (un document); pervertir, altérer (un texte). **2.** *v.i.* sophistiquer.

sophisticated [sə'fistikeitid], *a.* **1.** *O:* sophistiqué, falsifié; (*of text*) altéré; (*of wine*) frelaté. **2.** (*of pers.*) sophistiqué; aux goûts raffinés, intellectuels; (*of style*) recherché; (*of equipment, machinery*) (très) perfectionné, raffiné; complexe.

sophistication [səfisti'keiʃ(ə)n], *s.* **1.** *O:* sophistication *f*, falsification *f*. **2.** raisonnements sophistiques, captieux, fallacieux. **3.** (*a*) (*of pers.*) sophistication; goûts compliqués; intérêts intellectuels; (*b*) (*of style*) recherche *f*, raffinement *m*; (*c*) (*of machinery, etc.*) perfectionnement *m*.

sophistry ['sɔfistri], *s*. **1.** sophistique *f*; **use of s.,** sophistication *f*; **to indulge in s.,** sophistiquer. **2.** sophisme *m*.

Sophoclean [sɔfə'kliːən], *a*. sophocléen.

Sophocles ['sɔfəkliːz], *Pr.n.m. Gr.Lit:* Sophocle.

sophomore ['sɔfəmɔːr], *s. Sch: NAm:* étudiant, -ante, de seconde année.

sophomoric [sɔfə'mɔːrik], *a. NAm:* prétentieux, suffisant.

Sophonisba [sɔfə'nizbə], *Pr.n.f. Rom.Hist:* Sophonisbe.

sophora [sɔ'fɔːrə], *s. Bot:* sophore *m*, sophora *m*.

sopor ['soupɔːr], *s. Med:* sopor *m*.

soporiferous [sɔpə'rifərəs], *a*. = SOPORIFIC.

soporiferousness [sɔpə'rif(ə)rəsnis], *s*. **1.** qualités *f* soporifiques (d'un médicament). **2.** assoupissement *m*.

soporific [sɔpə'rifik], *a. & s.* somnifère (*m*), soporifère (*m*), soporifique (*m*), soporatif (*m*); **s. draught,** potion assoupissante; **s. reading,** lecture endormante.

soporous ['soupərəs], *a. Med:* (sommeil, etc.) soporeux.

soppiness ['sɔpinis], *s. F:* mollesse *f*; fadasserie *f*.

sopping [sɔpiŋ], *a*. trempé; **s. wet,** tout trempé; trempé comme une soupe; mouillé à tordre; (*of pers.*) trempé jusqu'aux os.

soppy ['sɔpi], *a*. **1.** (terrain, etc.) détrempé. **2.** *F:* (*a*) (*of pers.*) mou, *f*. molle; flasque; (*of sentiment*) fadasse; *Sch:* **to be s. on s.o.,** avoir un béguin pour qn; (*b*) stupide, bête; **don't be s.!** ne sois pas si bête! **(you) s. idiot!** gros bêta! **that was a s. thing to do!** quelle idiotie!

sopranino [sɔpræ'niːnou], *s. Mus:* sopranino *m*.

sopranist [sɔ'prɑːnist], *s. Mus:* **1.** sopraniste *mf*; soprano *mf*. **2.** sopraniste *m*, castrat *m*.

soprano, *pl.* **-os, -i** [sɔ'prɑːnou, -ouz, -iː], *s. Mus:* soprano *mf, pl.* soprani, sopranos; **s. voice,** voix *f* de soprano; **to sing the s. part,** chanter le dessus.

sora ['sɔːrə], *s. Orn:* marouette *f* de la Caroline, *Fr.C:* râle *m* de la Caroline.

sorb [sɔːb], *s. Bot:* **1. s. (apple),** (i) sorbe *f*; (ii) alise *f*. **2. s. (apple)(tree),** (i) sorbier *m*, cormier *m*; (ii) alisier *m*.

sorbet ['sɔːbet, -bei], *s. Cu:* sorbet *m*.

sorbic ['sɔːbik], *a. Ch:* (acide) sorbique.

sorbite[1] ['sɔːbait], *s. Metall:* sorbite *f*.

sorbite[2], **sorbitol** ['sɔːbitɔl], *s. Ch:* sorbite *f*, sorbitol *m*.

sorbose ['sɔːbous], *s. Ch:* sorbose *m*.

sorcerer ['sɔːs(ə)rər], *s.m.* sorcier; magicien.

sorceress ['sɔːs(ə)ris], *s.f.* sorcière; magicienne.

sorcery ['sɔːs(ə)ri], *s.* sorcellerie *f*.

sordes ['sɔːdiːz], *s.* (*with sg. or pl. const.*) **1.** crasse *f* (du corps). **2.** *Med:* (*in typhoid fever, etc.*) fuliginosités *fpl*.

sordid ['sɔːdid], *a*. **1.** sordide; (*a*) sale, crasseux; *Nat.Hist:* **s. yellow,** jaune sale *inv*; (*b*) bas, vil; (rue, etc.) sordide; *F:* **but it's so s.!** c'est tellement infect! **2.** *Med:* (*of suppuration, etc.*) infect, fétide.

sordidly ['sɔːdidli], *adv.* sordidement; (*a*) salement; (*b*) bassement.

sordidness ['sɔːdidnis], *s.* sordidité *f*; (*a*) saleté *f*; (*b*) bassesse *f*; (*c*) *A:* avarice *f* sordide; ladrerie *f*.

sordine ['sɔːdiːn], **sordino** [sɔː'diːnou], *s. Mus:* sourdine *f*.

sore [sɔːr], *a., adv. & s.*

I. *a*. **1.** (*a*) douloureux, endolori; **s. to the touch,** douloureux au toucher; **his foot is still s.,** son pied lui fait toujours mal; **to be s. all over,** être tout brisé, tout courbaturé; avoir mal partout; (*b*) enflammé; irrité; **s. eyes,** yeux enflammés; **s. throat,** mal *m* de gorge; **I've a s. throat, my throat's s.,** j'ai mal à la gorge; ma gorge me fait mal; (*c*) **to have a s. finger, a s. place on one's finger,** avoir une (petite) plaie, une écorchure, au doigt; **one always seems to knock oneself on a s. place, a s. spot,** on se cogne toujours où on a mal, sur l'endroit sensible; **it's a s. point, a s. subject, with him,** il est très sensible, très chatouilleux, sur ce point; voilà un sujet sur lequel il n'aime pas revenir; (*d*) *Vet:* **s. mouth,** ecthyma contagieux. **2.** (*of pers.*) (*a*) chagriné; **to be, feel, s. about sth.,** être chagriné, dépité, au sujet de qch.; **I was very s. at missing him,** ça m'a vraiment donné de la peine de ne pas le voir; *Lit:* **s. at heart,** désolé; (*b*) *NAm: F:* fâché; **to be, get, s.,** se fâcher. **3.** *Lit:* **in s. distress,** dans une grande détresse; **to be in s. need of sth.,** avoir grandement besoin de qch.; **s. trial,** cruelle épreuve; **s. temptation,** tentation *f* difficile à vaincre.

II. *adv. A: & Lit:* gravement; grièvement; **s. distressed,** dans une grande détresse.

III. *s*. **1.** (*a*) plaie *f*; écorchure *f*; **to (re)open an old s.,** raviver une ancienne plaie; rouvrir d'anciennes plaies; évoquer un souvenir pénible; (*b*) *O:* **(running) s.,** ulcère *m*; *A:* **Delhi s.,** bouton *m* d'Alep; ulcère d'Orient. **2.** *A:* chagrin *m*; douleur *f*.

soredium [sɔː'riːdiəm], *s. Moss:* sorédie *f*.

sorehead ['sɔːhed], *s. esp. NAm: F:* rancunier, -ière; type *m* froissable.

sorely ['sɔːli], *adv. Lit:* gravement; grandement; **s. wounded,** gravement, grièvement, blessé; **s. tried,** fort éprouvé; cruellement, durement, éprouvé; **s. distressed,** dans une grande détresse; très affligé; **s. needed,** dont on a grandement besoin; **s. pressed,** aux abois; **s. tempted,** soumis à une grande tentation.

soremuzzle ['sɔːmʌzl], *s. Vet:* ecthyma contagieux.

soreness ['sɔːnis], *s*. **1.** endolorissement *m*; douleur *f*. **2.** (*a*) chagrin *m*; peine *f*; (*b*) *esp. NAm: F:* rancune *f*; irritabilité *f*.

sorghum ['sɔːgəm], *s. Bot:* sorg(h)o *m*; **sweet s.** (*also* **sorgho**), sorg(h)o sucré, à sucre.

Soricidae [sɔ'risidiː], *s.pl. Z:* soricidés *m*; les musaraignes *f*.

Soricoidea [sɔri'kɔidiə], *s.pl. Z:* soricoïdes *m*.

sorites [sou'raitiːz], *s. Log:* sorite *m*.

soroptimist [sɔ'rɔptimist], *s.* membre *m* d'un cercle féminin professionnel.

sororate [sɔ'rɔːreit], *s. Anthr:* sororat *m*.

sorority [sə'rɔːriti], *s*. **1.** *A:* communauté religieuse. **2.** *NAm:* cercle féminin; cercle d'étudiantes.

sorosis [sɔ'rousis], *s. Bot:* sorose *f*.

sorrel[1] ['sɔrəl], *s. Bot:* oseille *f*; **wood s., sheep's s.,** oxalide blanche; petite oseille; oseille sauvage; **salts of s.,** sel *m* d'oseille.

sorrel[2]. **1.** *a*. (cheval) saure, alezan. **2.** *s*. alezan *m*; **chestnut s.,** alezan châtain.

Sorrento [sɔ'rentou], *Pr.n. Geog:* Sorrente.

sorrow[1] ['sɔrou], *s.* douleur *f*, chagrin *m*, tristesse *f*; **s. stricken, plunged in s.,** accablé de douleur; **to my s.,** à mon (grand) regret; **more in s. than in anger,** avec plus de compassion que de colère; **it was a great s. to me that he went away,** son départ m'a donné beaucoup de peine; *B:* **Man of Sorrows,** l'homme de douleur(s), le Christ.

sorrow[2], *v.i. esp. Lit:* s'affliger, être affligé, s'attrister, se chagriner (**over, at, about, sth.,** de qch.); **to s. over s.o.'s death,** pleurer la mort de qn; **to s. for, after, s.o., sth.,** pleurer qn, qch.

sorrowful ['sɔrəful], *a*. (*of pers.*) affligé, chagriné; triste; (*of news, etc.*) attristant, pénible; **s. look,** regard attristé, douloureux, mélancolique, désolé.

sorrowfully ['sɔrəf(u)li], *adv.* tristement; avec chagrin; d'un air affligé, attristé, désolé; d'un ton affligé, douloureux.

sorrowing ['sɔrouiŋ], *a*. affligé; attristé; plongé dans la douleur.

sorry ['sɔri], *a*. **1.** (*a*) fâché, chagriné, désolé; **to be s. about sth.,** être fâché, désolé, de qch.; **he is s. he did it, s. for having done it,** il est fâché, il se repent, de l'avoir fait; **to be s. not to have done sth.,** avoir du regret de ne pas avoir fait qch.; **I am s. he was punished,** je suis fâché qu'il ait été puni; **I was not s. to go to bed,** ce n'est pas à regret que je suis monté me coucher; **if you refuse you will be s. later on,** si vous refusez vous le regretterez plus tard; *F:* **you'll be s. for it,** il vous en cuira; **I'll make you s. (for this)!** vous me le paierez! **I'm (very) s. to hear that . . .,** je regrette (infiniment), je suis désolé, d'apprendre que . . .; j'apprends avec peine, avec chagrin, que . . .; **I'm s. to say that . . .,** je regrette d'avoir à vous dire que . . .; **I'm s. about that,** cela me fait de la peine; **I'm so s. to keep you waiting,** excusez-moi de vous faire attendre; **(I'm) s.!** pardon! excusez-moi! **he wrote to say he was s.,** il a écrit une lettre d'excuses; (*b*) **I'm s. for him,** (i) je le plains; il me fait pitié; (ii) *Iron:* le voilà dans de beaux draps! il va lui en cuire! **to look s. for oneself,** avoir l'air piteux; faire piteuse mine. **2.** *O:* mauvais; pauvre, misérable, piteux; **s. steed,** méchant cheval; *A:* pauvre haridelle *f*; **s. jest,** mauvaise plaisanterie; **to make a s. meal,** faire piteuse chère; **to be in a s. plight,** (i) être en mauvaise passe, dans une passe difficile; (ii) être mal en point; être dans un état piteux; **to cut a s. figure,** faire piteuse figure.

sort[1] [sɔːt], *s*. **1.** (*a*) sorte *f*, genre *m*, espèce *f*; classe *f*; **all sorts of men,** des hommes de toutes sortes; **all sorts and conditions of men,** toutes les conditions humaines; (toute) la race humaine; **what s. of a man is he?** comment est-il? **he's not a bad s., quite a decent s.,** il est plutôt sympathique; **she's a good s.,** elle est vraiment bonne, vraiment sympathique; elle est toujours prête à vous donner un coup de main; **his father was just that s.,** son père était de ce genre-là; **a strange s. of man,** un homme bizarre; **and other people of the same s.,** et autres gens semblables; **this,** *F:* **these, s. of people,** les gens de cette espèce; ces gens-là; **what s. of tree is it?** quelle sorte d'arbre est-ce? **what s. of car is it?** c'est une voiture de quelle marque? **books of different sorts,** des livres de plusieurs genres, de tous les genres; **what s. of day was it?** (i) quel temps faisait-il? (ii) vous avez passé une journée agréable? **why ask that s. of question,** *F:* **these s. of questions?** pourquoi poser des questions de ce genre? **I've heard all sorts of things about him,** j'en ai entendu de toutes les couleurs sur son compte; **that's the s. of thing I mean,** ça c'est à peu près ce que je veux dire; **I can't stand that s. of thing,** je ne peux pas souffrir tout ça, des choses comme ça; **something of the s., of that s.,** quelque chose de pareil, de semblable, dans ce genre-là; **nothing of the s.,** (i) rien de semblable, de la sorte; (ii) pas du tout! **I've a s. of idea, a s. of feeling, that . . .,** *F:* **I s. of feel that . . .,** j'ai une sorte d'idée, une sorte d'impression, que . . .; j'ai comme une idée que . . .; *F:* **I s. of expected it,** je m'en doutais presque; **the trees formed a s. of arch,** les arbres formaient comme une arche; **a s. of family likeness,** un vague air de famille; (*b*) *Pej:* **coffee of a s.,** un vague, soi-disant, café; un café quelconque; **a peace of sorts,** une paix telle quelle; **some s. of writer, a writer of sorts,** quelque vague écrivain; un écrivain quelconque; **to make some s. of excuse,** faire des excuses quelconques; **to make some s. of (a) reply,** répondre d'une façon quelconque, tant bien que mal; **a translation of a s.,** ce qui pouvait passer pour une traduction; (*c*) **to be out of sorts,** (i) être indisposé, mal en train; ne pas être dans son assiette; (ii) être de mauvaise humeur, *F:* mal fichu. **2.** *Lit:* manière *f*, façon *f*; **in some s.,** à un certain degré; jusqu'à un certain point. **3.** *Typ:* sorte; **sorts,** assortiment *m*; **missing s., short s.,** sorte manquante; **superfluous s.,** sorte surabondante. **4.** *Cmptr:* tri *m*; **block s.,** tri par grands groupes; **merging s.,** rangement *m* par interclassement; **s. routine,** (sous-)programme *m* de tri; **s. file,** fichier *m* de tri; **s. key,** indicatif *m*, clef *f*, critère *m*, de tri.

sort[2]. **1.** *v.tr.* (*a*) trier, faire le tri de (qch.); assortir; classer (des papiers, etc.); **to s. out,** éliminer (par tri); **they sorted themselves into groups,** ils se sont arrangés en groupes; **to s. rags,** trier des chiffons; **to s. timber,** triquer le bois; **to s. (over) ore,** trier le minerai; *Cards:* **to s. (out) one's cards, one's hand,** arranger ses couleurs; *Post:* **to s. the letters,** (i) trier, (ii) router, les lettres; *Tan:* **to s. skins,** lotir les peaux; *Typ:* **to s. out pie,** dépâtisser les caractères; (*b*) *Scot:* ranger, mettre en ordre (une pièce, des tiroirs, etc.); (*c*) *Scot:* **bring him to me, I'll s. him!** amenez-le-moi, je vais l'arranger, je vais lui régler son compte. **2.** *v.i. A: & Dial:* (*a*) **to s. with s.o.,** fréquenter qn; frayer avec qn; (*b*) **to s. with sth.,** s'accorder avec qch.

sorter ['sɔːtər], *s*. (*a*) (*pers.*) trieur, -euse; classeur, -euse; assortisseur, -euse; *Com: etc:* **sorter's number,** numéro *m* de classement; *Ind:* **waste s.,** repasseur, -euse, de déchets; *Post:* **(letter) s.,** trieur de lettres; (*b*) (*device*) trieur (de minerai, etc.); trieuse (de laine, *Cmptr:* de cartes, etc.); **s. reader,** trieuse-liseuse *f*, *pl.* trieuses-liseuses; trieuse-lectrice *f*, *pl.* trieuses-lectrices.

sortie ['sɔːtiː], *s. Mil: etc:* sortie *f*; *Av:* sortie, vol *m*.

sortilege ['sɔːtilidʒ], *s*. **1.** *A:* (*a*) divination *f* par le tirage au sort; (*b*) tirage au sort. **2.** maléfice *m* sortilège *m*.

sorting ['sɔːtiŋ], *s.* triage *m*, tri *m*; classement *m*, classification *f*; *Hort:* (*for seeds, etc.*) **s. board,** volet *m*; *Post:* **s. office,** bureau *m* de tri; *Cmptr:* **s. program(me),** programme *m* de tri.

sortition [sɔː'tiʃ(ə)n], *s. O:* tirage *m* au sort.

sorus ['sɔːrəs], *s. Bot:* sore *m* (de fougère).

sot[1] [sɔt], *s.* ivrogne *m*; soûlard, -arde; poivrot *m*; **he looks a s.,** il a une trogne d'ivrogne.

sot[2], *v.i.* (**sotted**) *O:* s'abrutir (dans l'ivresse).

soteriology [sɔtiəri'ɔlədʒi], *s. Theol:* sotériologie *f*.

sottish ['sɔtiʃ], *a*. abruti par l'alcool; (air, etc.) d'ivrogne.

sottishly ['sɔtiʃli], *adv.* en ivrogne.

sottishness ['sɔtiʃnis], *s.* abrutissement (occasionné par l'alcoolisme).

sotto voce [sɔtou'voutʃi], *adv.* (*a*) (parler, etc.) tout bas, à demi-voix; (*b*) *Mus:* sotto-voce; (chanter) à demi-voix; (jouer) à demi-jeu.

soubrette [suː'bret], *s. Th:* soubrette *f*.

Souchong ['suːʃɔŋ], *s. Com:* **S. (tea),** souchong *m*; thé noir.

souffle ['suːfl], *s. Med:* souffle *m*; **uterine s.,** souffle utérin, placentaire.

soufflé ['suːflei]. *Cu:* **1.** *a*. soufflé. **2.** *s*. soufflé *m*; **cheese s.,** soufflé au fromage; **s. dish,** moule *m* à soufflés.

sough[1] [sʌf], *s*. **1.** (*a*) marais *m*, marécage *m*; (*b*) mare *f*, flaque *f*. **2.** tranchée *f*, drain *m*, d'écoulement; *Min:* arrugie *f*.

sough[2] [sau, sʌf], *s. esp. Lit:* murmure *m*, susurration *f*, frémissement *m* (du vent, etc.).

sough[3] [sau, sʌf], *v.i. esp. Lit:* (*of wind, etc.*) murmurer, susurrer; **the wind soughs in the trees,** le vent frémit dans les arbres.

soul [soul], *s.* âme *f.* **1.** (*a*) **to throw oneself body and s., heart and s., into sth.,** se donner corps et âme à qch.; se jeter de tout son cœur dans (une entreprise, etc.); mettre toute son énergie à faire qch.; **with all my s.,** de tout mon cœur; de toute mon âme; **his whole s. revolted at the idea,** tout son être se révoltait à cette idée; **I couldn't (do it) to save my s.,** je ne le ferais pour rien au monde; *O:* **upon my s.!** sur mon âme! **he can't, daren't, call his s. his own,** il est entièrement dominé; **I can't call my s. my own these days,** en ce moment je n'ai pas un instant à moi; **to have a s. for music,** avoir la fibre de la musique; **he has a s. above money,** il est au-dessus des préoccupations d'argent; **to have no s.,** être terre à terre; *Ecc:* **to have cure of souls,** avoir charge d'âmes; (*b*) **he's the s. of discretion,** il est la discrétion même. **2. departed souls,** les âmes des trépassés; **souls in purgatory,** les âmes du purgatoire; les âmes en peine; **to pray for s.o.'s s.,** prier pour l'âme de qn; **God rest his s.!** que Dieu ait son âme! **All Souls' Day,** la Fête des Morts. **3.** (*a*) **population of two thousand souls,** population *f* de deux mille âmes; **ship lost with all souls,** navire perdu corps et biens; **without meeting a living s.,** sans rencontrer âme qui vive; **there wasn't a s. in the street,** il n'y avait pas un chat dans la rue; **who will believe it?—not a s.,** qui le croira?—pas un; (*b*) **he's a good s.,** c'est une bonne âme; **be a good s. and say nothing about it,** soyez assez gentil pour n'en pas dire mot; **poor s.!** pauvre créature! le, la, pauvre! **poor little s.!** pauvre petit(e)! **4. s. (music),** (sorte de) blues *m* (élaboré par les Noirs d'Amérique du Nord); *F:* soul *m*; *esp. U.S:* **s. brother, sister,** frère, sœur; **s. food,** nourriture traditionnelle des Noirs américains.

soul-destroying ['souldistrɔiŋ], *a.* (emploi, etc.) abrutissant, d'une monotonie mortelle.

soulful ['soulful], *a.* (*a*) plein d'âme; **a s. tone,** un ton qui trahit toute l'âme; **s. eyes,** yeux expressifs; **s. music,** musique *f* qui émeut l'âme; (*b*) sentimental, -aux.

soulfully ['soulfuli], *adv.* (*a*) (chanter) avec âme, avec expression; (*b*) sentimentalement.

soulless ['soullis], *a.* **1.** sans âme; inexpressif; terre à terre. **2.** (emploi) abrutissant.

soullessness ['soullisnis], *s.* manque *m* d'âme, d'élévation.

soulmate ['soulmeit], *s.* âme *f* sœur.

soul-searching ['soulsə:tʃiŋ]. **1.** *a.* (question, regard) qui sonde le(s) cœur(s). **2.** *s.* examen *m* de conscience; **there was a lot of s.-s. about it,** beaucoup de gens ont dû faire un examen de conscience là-dessus.

soul-stirring ['soulstə:riŋ], *a.* qui remue l'âme; émouvant.

sound[1] [saund], *s.* son *m*; (*a*) son; bruit *m*; **there was not a s. to be heard,** on n'entendait pas le moindre bruit; **the s. of a dog barking,** le bruit d'un chien qui aboie; **a queer s.,** un bruit étrange, insolite; **musical s.,** son musical; **vowel s.,** son vocalique; **hollow s.,** son creux; bruit sourd; **within (the) s. of. . .,** à portée du son de . . .; **the s. of a bell,** le son d'une cloche; *T.V: etc:* **to turn up, turn down, the s.,** augmenter, diminuer, le volume; **I don't like the s. of it,** cela ne me dit rien qui vaille; cela me paraît suspect, *F:* louche; **he's angry by the s. of it,** il est fâché, ça en a tout l'air, à ce qu'il paraît; (*b*) *Ph: Mus: etc:* son; **high-pitched, low-pitched, s.,** son aigu, grave; **s. absorber,** amortisseur *m* de bruit, de son; *Ph:* **s. wave,** onde *f* sonore; **s. pulse,** pulsation *f* sonore; **s. velocity,** vitesse *f* du son; **s. pressure,** pression *f* sonore; **s. vibration,** vibration *f* sonore; **s. level, s. intensity,** niveau *m*, intensité *f*, sonore; intensité acoustique; **s. analyser,** sonomètre *m*; **s. location,** (i) localisation *f*, repérage *m*, du son; (ii) repérage acoustique; **s. locator,** localisateur *m*, détecteur *m*, (i) du son, (ii) acoustique; **s. detection,** détection (i) des sons, (ii) acoustique; **s. detector,** (i) détecteur de son; *Geol:* géophone *m*; (ii) détecteur acoustique; *Mil: etc:* **s. ranging,** repérage par le son; télémétrie *f* acoustique; **s.-ranging radar,** radar *m* acoustique (de télémétrie); **s.-ranging signals,** signaux *m* phototélémétriques; *Av:* **s. barrier,** mur *m* du son; *Rec: Cin: T.V: etc:* **s. recording,** enregistrement *m* du son; **s. recorder,** enregistreur *m* du son; **s. reproduction,** reproduction *f* sonore, du son; *Cin:* lecture *f* du son; **s. reproducer,** reproducteur *m* de son(s); *Cin:* lecteur *m* de son; **s. pick-up,** prise *f* de son; **s.-on-disc recording,** enregistrement sur disques; *Cin:* **s. track,** bande *f*, piste *f*, sonore; **s. screen,** écran *m* transsonore; **s. effects,** effets *m* sonores; bruitage *m*; **to add the s. effects to a film,** sonoriser un film, *Elcs: etc:* **s. modulated,** modulé à fréquence acoustique; **s. head,** (i) *Elcs:* tête sonore; (ii) *Cin:* lecteur de son; *Mus:* **s. board,** (i) table *f* d'harmonie (de piano); (ii) tamis *m* (d'orgue); (iii) abat-voix *m inv* (de chaire, etc.); **s. box,** (i) caisse *f* de résonance (d'un instrument à cordes); (ii) diaphragme *m* (de phonographe); **s. bar,** barre *f* (de violon); **s. hole,** ouïe *f*, baie *f*, (de violon, de guitare); esse *f* (de violon); rose *f* (de guitare); **s. post,** âme *f* (d'un violon, etc.); **s. bow,** panse *f*, frappe *f* (d'une cloche); (*c*) *Ph:* (*branch of the science*) l'acoustique *f*.

sound[2], *v.*

I. *v.i.* **1.** sonner, résonner; retentir; **the trumpet was sounding,** la trompette sonnait; **there are notes on this piano that don't s.,** ce piano a des notes qui ne sonnent pas, qui ne parlent pas. **2.** (*a*) **to s. like a drum,** résonner comme un tambour; **it sounds hollow,** cela sonne creux, rend un son creux; **to s. harsh,** rendre un son dur; être dur à l'oreille; **it doesn't s. right,** cela sonne faux; **to s. well,** sonner bien (à l'oreille); (*b*) paraître, sembler; **name that sounds French,** nom qui a une consonance française; **that sounds odd!** voilà qui paraît étrange, bizarre! **how does it s. to you?** quelle impression est-ce que cela vous fait? **the noise sounded a long way off,** le bruit semblait venir de loin; **it sounds like Mozart,** on dirait du Mozart; **it sounded as if the roof was falling in,** on aurait dit que le toit s'écroulait; **it sounds like a dog barking,** on dirait un chien qui aboie; **he doesn't s. like a man to . . .,** d'après ce que vous dites il ne serait pas homme à . . .; **that doesn't s. very well coming from you,** ces paroles sont déplacées dans votre bouche; **it would s. very well in a speech,** cela ferait bon effet dans un discours; **it sounds like heresy,** cela a l'air d'une hérésie, sent l'hérésie; **it sounded like a promise,** cela pouvait passer pour une promesse, pouvait être interprété comme une promesse.

II. *v.tr.* **1.** (*a*) sonner (le tocsin, etc.); **to s. the trumpet,** sonner de la trompette; **to s. the horn,** sonner, donner, du cor; *Aut:* **to s. one's horn,** appuyer sur l'avertisseur; *Mil:* **to s. reveille, the retreat,** sonner le réveil, la retraite; *A:* **to s. to horse,** sonner le boute-selle; (*b*) *Lit:* **to s. s.o.'s praises,** chanter les louanges de qn. **2.** prononcer (une lettre); **the h is not sounded,** l'h ne se prononce pas, est muet. **3.** (*a*) *Med:* ausculter (qn, la poitrine); (*by percussion*) percuter (la poitrine); **he sounded my chest,** il m'a ausculté; (*b*) *Rail: etc:* vérifier (une roue) au marteau.

sound[3], *s. Med:* sonde *f*.

sound[4], *v.tr.* **1.** (*a*) *v.tr. & i. Nau:* sonder; prendre, trouver, le fond; (*b*) *v.tr. Med:* sonder (une plaie); (*c*) *v.tr.* pressentir, sonder (qn sur qch., à propos de qch.); tâter (qn à propos de qch.); **to s. public opinion,** sonder l'opinion. **2.** *v.i.* (*of whale*) faire la sonde; sonder, foncer; plonger au fond.

sound[5], *s.* **1.** (i) détroit *m*; goulet *m*; (ii) bras *m* de mer; *Geog:* **the S.,** le Sund. **2.** *Ich:* vessie *f* natatoire; vésicule aérienne.

sound[6], *a. & adv.*

I. *a.* **1.** (*a*) (*of pers., animal*) sain; **s. body,** corps sain; **s. constitution,** constitution *f* robuste; santé *f* solide, robuste; **man of s. constitution,** homme solide; **s. in body and mind,** sain de corps et d'esprit; **of s. mind,** sain d'esprit; *Jur:* **of s. disposing mind,** sain d'esprit (pour rédiger un testament); *Vet:* **s. horse,** cheval sans tare; **s. in wind and limb, s. and free from vice,** sain et net, au corps sain; *F:* (*of pers.*) **to be s. in wind and limb,** avoir bon pied bon œil; se porter comme le Pont-Neuf; avoir le coffre bon; **I'm as s. as a bell,** je suis en parfaite santé; (*b*) (*of thg*) en bon état; non endommagé; solide; **s. timber,** bois *m* sans tare; **s. fruit,** fruits sains; *Com:* **goods in s. condition and fit for acceptance,** marchandises bonnes et recevables; *Const:* **s. stone,** pierre franche; (*c*) *Agr:* **s. ground,** terrain *m* à bon sous-sol. **2.** sain, solide; (*a*) **s. financial position,** situation financière solide; **to be a s. man,** avoir du crédit sur la place; avoir une solide réputation financière; être solide; **s. statesman,** homme d'état solide, au jugement sain; **s. business,** entreprise saine, solide; *Ins:* **s. value,** valeur saine; **s. currency,** devise, monnaie, saine; (*b*) (argument) valide, irréfutable; (raisonnement) juste; **his arguments are s.,** ses arguments se tiennent; **s. deduction,** déduction saine, juste, légitime; **s. doctrines,** (i) doctrines saines; (ii) doctrines orthodoxes; **s. piece of advice,** bon conseil; **it isn't s. finance,** ce n'est pas de la finance sérieuse, de la bonne finance; *Jur:* **s. title,** titre *m* valable, valide, légal. **3. s. sleep,** sommeil profond; sommeil de plomb; **I'm a s. sleeper,** je dors bien; je dors à poings fermés; **to give s.o. a s. thrashing,** administrer une bonne correction à qn; *F:* rosser qn d'importance.

II. *adv.* **to be s. asleep,** être profondément endormi; dormir à poings fermés.

sounder[1] ['saundər], *s.* (*device*) (*a*) *Tg:* parleur *m*, sounder *m*; (*b*) *Tp:* ronfleur *m*.

sounder[2], *s. Nau:* sondeur *m*; **echo s.,** sondeur acoustique, sondeur à écho; écho-sondeur *m*, *pl.* écho-sondeurs; **supersonic echo s.,** écho-sondeur à ultrasons, écho-sondeur ultrasonore.

sounder[3], *s.* harde *f*, bande *f*, troupe *f* (de sangliers).

sounding[1] ['saundiŋ], *s.* **1.** résonnement *m*; retentissement *m* (d'un tambour, etc.); *Mil:* **the s. of the retreat,** le signal de la retraite; **s. board,** (i) abat-voix *m inv* (de chaire, etc.); (ii) table *f* d'harmonie (de piano); tamis *m* (d'orgue). **2.** *Med:* auscultation *f*; percussion *f*.

sounding[2], *s.* **1.** (*a*) *Nau:* sondage *m*, brassiage *m*; **echo s.,** sondage acoustique; **supersonic echo s.,** sondage aux ultra-sons; **s. line,** (ligne *f* de) sonde *f*; **s. lead** [led], (plomb *m* de) sonde; **s. machine,** sondeur *m*; **s. pipe,** tuyau *m* de sonde; **s. rod,** (i) (*for pump, well, ship's hold*) sonde; (ii) *Mec.E:* jauge *f* (à huile); (*b*) *Meteor:* sondage (atmosphérique); **upper air s.,** sondage (atmosphérique) en altitude; **bottomside, topside, s.,** sondage (ionosphérique) en contrebas, en contre-haut; **vertical s.,** sondage (ionosphérique) vertical; **s. balloon,** ballon *m* de sondage. **2.** *Nau:* **soundings,** les sondes; les fonds; **line of soundings,** ligne *f* des fonds; **to be in soundings,** être sur les sondes; **to keep in safe soundings,** se maintenir par des fonds suffisants; **to be out of soundings,** être hors des fonds; **to take soundings,** sonder; prendre le fond; **to call the soundings,** chanter le fond; **what are the soundings?** quel est le fond? **to strike, reach, soundings,** trouver le fond.

soundless[1] ['saundlis], *a.* muet; silencieux.

soundless[2], *a. esp. Lit:* (mer, etc.) insondable, sans fond.

soundly ['saundli], *adv.* **1.** sainement, avec un jugement sain; judicieusement; (raisonner) solidement. **2.** (*a*) **to sleep s.,** dormir profondément, à poings fermés, sur les deux oreilles; (*b*) **to thrash s.o. s.,** administrer une bonne correction à qn; *F:* rosser qn d'importance.

soundness ['saundnis], *s.* **1.** (*a*) état sain (de l'esprit, etc.); bon état (des poumons, etc.); (*b*) bon état, bonne condition (des marchandises, etc.). **2.** solidité *f* (d'une entreprise); solvabilité *f*. **3.** (*a*) solidité (d'un argument, etc.); sûreté *f*, rectitude *f*, justesse *f* (d'un jugement, etc.); **I have confidence in the s. of his judgement,** j'ai confiance en la sûreté de son jugement; (*b*) orthodoxie *f* (d'une doctrine).

soundproof[1] ['saundpru:f], *a.* (*of room, etc.*) insonorisé; insonore.

soundproof[2], *v.tr.* insonoriser (une pièce, etc.).

soundproofing ['saundpru:fiŋ], *s.* insonorisation *f*; isolement *m* acoustique, isolation *f* phonique.

soup[1] [su:p], *s.* **1.** (*a*) soupe *f*; potage *m*; **thick (cream) s.,** crème *f*; velouté *m*; **vegetable s.,** soupe aux légumes; **onion s.,** soupe à l'oignon; **s. plate,** assiette creuse, à soupe; **s. spoon,** cuillère *f* à soupe; **s. tureen,** soupière *f*; **s. ladle,** louche *f*; *F:* **to be in the s.,** être dans le pétrin, dans la panade; (*b*) *F:* brouillard (épais); *Av:* nuages impénétrables; (*c*) *Aut:* *F:* puissance *f* (d'un moteur), jus *m*. **2.** *P:* (*burglar's term*) nitroglycérine *f*, jus.

soup[2], *v.tr. F:* **to s. up,** (i) gonfler (un moteur); (ii) exagérer, épicer (une histoire, etc.); **a souped-up job,** une affaire survoltée.

soupçon ['su:psɔn], *s.* soupçon *m*.

souper ['su:pər], *s. F:* **pea s.,** brouillard épais, purée *f* de pois.

soupling ['su:pliŋ], *s. Tex:* assouplissage *m*.

soupy ['su:pi], *a. F:* (*a*) (*of weather*) très brumeux; (*b*) sentimental; larmoyant.

sour[1] ['sauər], *a. & s.*

I. *a.* **1.** (*a*) (fruit, etc.) aigre, acide, sur, vert; (*b*) (lait, pain, etc.) aigre, suri; (vin) suret, verjuté; **to turn s.,** tourner à l'aigre; surir; s'acidifier; (*of wine*) tourner au vinaigre; **to turn sth. s.** (faire) aigrir qch.; **to smell s.,** sentir l'aigre; **the plan went s. on him,** le projet (i) a perdu son charme, (ii) a mal tourné, pour lui; (*c*) (*of soil*) trop humide; froid et détrempé; (*d*) *Arb:* **s. sap,** nécrose hivernale. **2.** (*of pers.*) revêche; aigre (comme verjus); acerbe; (femme) acariâtre; **s. face,** mine sèche; visage *m* revêche; **s. remarks,** propos aigres-doux.

II. *s.* **1.** *Ind: Paperm:* eau acidulée. **2.** *esp. NAm:* boisson alcoolique relevée de citron; **whisky s.,** whisky au citron.

sour[2]. **1.** *v.i.* (*a*) surir; (s')aigrir; (*b*) **her temper has soured,** son caractère a aigri, s'est aigri. **2.** *v.tr.* (*a*) aigrir (le lait, etc., le caractère); **soured by poverty, by misfortune,** aigri par la misère, par le malheur; (*b*) **to s. s.o.'s life,** enfieller la vie de qn; (*c*) *Ind:* laver à l'eau acidulée; *Tex:* vitrioler (un tissu); (*d*) *Leath:* mettre en confit (les peaux).

source [sɔ:s], *s.* (*a*) source *f* (d'un fleuve, etc.); **the Rhone has its s. in the Alps,** le Rhône prend sa source dans les Alpes; (*b*) **to trace a tradition back to its s.,** remonter aux sources, à l'origine, d'une tradition; **contract vitiated at the s.,** contrat originellement vicié; **s. of infection,** foyer *m* d'infection; **s. of heat,** foyer de chaleur; **light s.,** source lumineuse; *Astr:* **radio s.,** radiosource *f*; **the s. of all our troubles,** la source de tous nos malheurs, de tous nos maux; **a s. of great grief to his family,** une source, une cause, de grands chagrins pour sa famille; *Prov:* **idleness is the s. of all evil,** l'oisiveté est la mère de tous les vices; **I have it from a good s.,** je le sais de bonne source, de bon lieu, de bonne part; **I have learnt from another s. that . . .,** j'ai appris par ailleurs que . . .; **information from an American s.,** informations *fpl* de source américaine; **s. materials,** matériaux *mpl* (d'un livre, etc.); *Hist:* **s. book,** recueil *m* de textes originaux.

sourdough ['sauədou], *s. NAm: F:* vétéran *m* (des placers d'Alaska).

soured ['sauəd], *a.* **1.** (*of food, etc.*) aigri, suri. **2.** (*of pers.*) aigri, revêche.

sourface ['sauəfeis], *s. F:* = SOURPUSS.

sourfaced ['sauəfeist], *a.* au visage morose, revêche.

souring ['sauəriŋ], *s.* **1.** aigrissement *m*; tourne *f* (du vin). **2.** (*a*) *Tex:* vitriolage *m*; (*b*) *Leath:* mise *f* en confit.

sourish ['sauəriʃ], *a.* aigrelet, suret.

sourly ['sauəli], *adv.* (répondre, etc.) aigrement, avec aigreur, d'un ton revêche, acerbe; (regarder qn, qch.) d'un air morose, renfrogné, revêche.

sourness ['sauənis], *s.* **1.** aigreur *f*, acidité *f* (d'un fruit, etc.); aigreur (du lait). **2.** aigreur (de qn); humeur *f* revêche.

sourpuss ['sauəpus], *s. F:* personne morose, revêche, renfrognée; rabat-joie *m inv*; trouble-fête *m inv*; chipie *f*.

soursop ['sauəsɔp], *s. Bot:* **1.** cachiman *m*, cachiment *m*, *F:* corossol hérissé. **2. s. (tree),** cachimentier *m*, *F:* corossolier *m*.

souse[1] [saus], *s.* **1.** *Cu:* (*a*) marinade *f* (de pieds de porc, d'oreilles, de museau, etc.); (*b*) saumure *f*, marinade. **2.** (*of pers.*) (*a*) immersion *f* (dans l'eau); plongeon *m*, bain *m*; (*b*) trempée *f*, saucée *f*; *A:* **to get a s.,** (i) tomber à l'eau; (ii) recevoir une forte averse; être trempé jusqu'aux os; (iii) être coiffé d'un seau d'eau. **3.** *P:* (*a*) soûlerie *f*; (*b*) ivrogne *mf*; soûlard, -arde.

souse[2]. **1.** *v.tr.* (*a*) *Cu:* faire mariner (le poisson, etc.); (*b*) plonger, immerger (**in,** dans); (*c*) tremper, noyer, asperger (**with water,** d'eau); (*d*) **to s. water over sth.,** répandre de l'eau sur qch., arroser qch. **2.** *v.i.* mariner.

souse[3], *v.i. A:* (*of hawk, etc.*) fondre, s'abattre (sur la proie).

soused [saust], *a.* **1.** *Cu:* mariné; **s. venison,** marinade *f* de chevreuil; **s. herrings,** harengs marinés. **2.** trempé, noyé. **3.** *P:* ivre, soûl.

sousing ['sausiŋ], *s.* **1.** *Cu:* marinage *m*. **2.** trempée *f*, saucée *f*.

souslik ['su:slik], *s. Z:* **spotted s.,** souslik *m*; **European s.,** spermophile *m*, écureuil terrestre européen.

sou'sou'east [sausau'i:st]. *See* SOUTH-SOUTH-EAST.

sou'sou'west [sausau'west]. *See* SOUTH-SOUTH-WEST.

soutane [su:'tɑ:n], *s. Ecc.Cost:* soutane *f*.

south[1] [sauθ]. **1.** *s.* (*a*) sud *m*, midi *m*; **true s.,** sud géographique; **magnetic s.,** sud magnétique; **house facing (the) s.,** maison (exposée) au sud, au midi; **wind blowing from the s.,** vent *m* qui vient, souffle, du sud; **on the s., to the s. (of sth.),** au sud (de qch.); du côté du sud; **bounded on the s. by sth.,** borné au sud par qch.; (*b*) le sud, le midi (d'un pays); **he lives somewhere in the s.,** il habite quelque part dans le sud (de Londres, de l'Angleterre, de l'Europe, etc.); **the S. of France,** le Midi (de la France); (*c*) *U.S: Hist:* **the S.,** les États *m* du sud (des États-Unis); les sudistes *m*. **2.** *adv.* (*a*) au sud; **to travel s.,** voyager vers le sud; **to lie s. of a place,** se trouver, être situé, au sud d'un endroit; (*of wind*) **to blow s.,** venir, souffler, du sud; *Nau:* **to sail due s.,** aller droit vers le sud; avoir le cap au sud; faire du sud; **s. by east,** sud-quart-sud-est; **s. by west,** sud-quart-sud-ouest; (*b*) **to go S.,** aller dans le sud, dans le midi; *U.S:* **down S.,** au sud des limites de la Pennsylvanie. **3.** *a.* (*a*) sud *inv*; (vent) du sud; (pays) du sud, méridional, -aux; austral, -als, -aux; (mur, fenêtre) qui fait face au sud; **s. side,** côté sud; **on the s. side (of sth.),** au sud (de qch.); du côté du sud; **s. latitude,** latitude sud; **the s. rooms,** les pièces exposées au sud, au midi; **the s. coast,** la côte sud; *Ecc.Arch:* **s. transept,** transept *m* sud; (*b*) **S. Africa,** l'Afrique australe; **the Republic of S. Africa,** la République sud-africaine; *Hist:* **the Union of S. Africa,** l'Union sud-africaine; **S. African,** (i) *a.* sud-africain; (ii) *s.* Sud-africain, -aine; **S. America,** Amérique *f* du Sud; **S. American,** (i) *a.* sud-américain; de l'Amérique du Sud; (ii) *s.* Sud-américain, -aine; Américain, -aine, du Sud; **S. Australia,** l'Australie méridionale; **S. Carolina,** la Caroline du Sud; **the S. Downs,** les Collines *f* du sud (de l'Angleterre) (de Beachy Head au Hampshire); **S. Korean,** (i) *a.* sud-coréen; (ii) *s.* Sud-coréen, -éenne; **the S. Pole,** le pôle sud; **the S. Sea,** le Pacifique sud; la Mer du Sud; **the S. Sea Islands,** les îles *f* du Pacifique; l'Archipel océanien; l'Océanie *f*; **S. Sea Islander,** indigène *mf* des îles du Pacifique; Océanien, -ienne; **S. Vietnam,** Sud-Vietnam; **S. Vietnamese,** (i) *a.* sud-vietnamien; (ii) *s.* Sud-vietnamien, -ienne.

south[2], *v.i.* **1.** *Astr:* (*of star*) passer le méridien. **2.** *Nau:* (*of ship*) courir vers le sud; faire route au sud.

southbound ['sauθbaund], *a.* (train, etc.) allant vers le sud; (autobus, etc.) en direction de la banlieue sud.

southcountryman, *pl.* **-men** [sauθ'kʌntrimən], *s.m.* habitant du sud.

southeast [sauθ'i:st]. **1.** *s.* sud-est *m*; *Nau:* suet *m*. **2.** *adv.* vers le sud-est; **s. by east,** sud-est-quart-est; **s. by south,** sud-est-quart-sud. **3.** *a.* du sud-est.

southeaster [sauθ'i:stər], *s.* vent *m* du sud-est.

southeasterly [sauθ'i:stəli]. **1.** *a.* (vent, etc.) du sud-est; (quartier, etc.) (du, au) sud-est; (direction) vers le sud-est. **2.** *adv.* vers le sud-est.

southeastern [sauθ'i:stən], *a.* (région, etc.) du sud-est.

southeastward [sauθ'i:stwəd]. **1.** *s.* sud-est *m*. **2.** *a.* au, du, sud-est. **3.** *adv.* vers le sud-est.

southeastwards [sauθ'i:stwədz], *adv.* vers le sud-est.

southerly ['sʌðəli]. **1.** *a.* (*a*) (i) (vent) du sud, qui vient du sud; (ii) (courant) qui se dirige vers le sud; (*b*) **s. point,** point situé au sud, vers le sud; (*of house*) **s. aspect, s. exposure,** exposition *f* au midi, au sud; *Nau:* **to steer a s. course,** faire route au sud; mettre le cap au sud. **2.** *adv.* (*a*) vers le sud; (*b*) **the wind blows s.,** le vent souffle du sud.

southern ['sʌðən], *a.* **1.** (du) sud; du midi; méridional, -aux; austral, -aux; **s. aspect,** aspect méridional; **the s. counties,** les comtés *m* du sud; **s. Italy,** l'Italie *f* du sud; **the countries of s. Europe,** les pays méridionaux; **the s. hemisphere,** l'hémisphère sud, austral; **S. Africa,** l'Afrique *f* du Sud; **the S. Alps,** les Alpes néozélandaises, du Sud; **S. Lights,** aurore australe; *Astr:* **the S. Cross,** la Croix du Sud. **2.** *U.S: Hist:* (armée, etc.) sudiste.

southerner ['sʌðənər], *s.* **1.** habitant, -ante, du sud; méridional, -ale. **2.** *U.S: Hist:* sudiste *mf*.

southernmost ['sʌðənmoust], *a.* (point, etc.) le plus au sud.

southernwood ['sʌðənwud], *s. Bot:* auron(n)e *f*; *F:* citronnelle *f*; garde-robe *f*.

southing ['sauθiŋ], *s.* **1.** *Astr:* passage *m* au méridien. **2.** *Nau:* chemin *m* sud.

southmost ['sauθmoust], *a.* (point, etc.) le plus au sud.

southpaw ['sauθpɔ:], *s.* gaucher, -ère; *Box:* fausse garde; gaucher.

southron ['sʌðrən], *a. & s. Scot:* Anglais, -aise.

south-south-east, *Nau:* **sou'sou'east** [sau(θ)sau(θ)'i:st]. **1.** *a. & s.* sud-sud-est (*m*). **2.** *adv.* (vers le) sud-sud-est.

south-south-west, *Nau:* **sou'sou'west** [sau(θ)sau(θ)'west]. **1.** *a. & s.* sud-sud-ouest (*m*); *Nau:* susuroît *m*. **2.** *adv.* (vers le) sud-sud-ouest.

southward ['sauθwəd]. **1.** *s.* sud *m*; **to the s.,** vers le sud. **2.** *a.* au, du, sud; du côté du sud. **3.** *adv.* **s. bound,** allant vers le sud.

southwards ['sauθwədz], *adv.* vers le sud.

southwest, *Nau:* **sou'west** [sau(θ)'west]. **1.** *s.* sud-ouest *m*; *Nau:* suroît *m*. **2.** *adv.* vers le sud-ouest; **s. by west,** sud-ouest-quart-ouest; **s. by south,** sud-ouest-quart-sud. **3.** *a.* du sud-ouest; **s. wind,** (vent *m* du) sud-ouest; *Hist:* **S. Africa,** le Sud-ouest africain.

southwester, *Nau:* **sou'wester** [sau(θ)'westər], *s.* **1.** (vent *m* du) sud-ouest *m*; le suroît. **2.** = SOU'WESTER 2.

southwesterly, *Nau:* **sou'westerly** [sau(θ)'westəli]. **1.** *a.* (vent, etc.) du sud-ouest; (quartier, etc.) sud-ouest; du, au, sud-ouest; (direction) vers le sud-ouest. **2.** *adv.* vers le sud-ouest.

southwestern [sauθ'westən], *a.* du sud-ouest.

southwestward [sauθ'westwəd]. **1.** *s.* sud-ouest *m*. **2.** *a.* au, du, sud-ouest. **3.** *adv.* vers le sud-ouest.

southwestwards [sauθ'westwədz], *adv.* vers le sud-ouest.

souvenir [su:və'niər], *s.* souvenir *m*.

sou'west [sau'west]. *See* SOUTH-WEST.

sou'wester [sau'westər], *s.* **1.** *Nau:* = SOUTHWESTER 1. **2.** *Cost:* suroît *m*, ciré *m*.

sou'westerly [sau'westəli]. *See* SOUTHWESTERLY.

sovereign ['sɔvrin]. **1.** *a.* souverain, suprême; **s. rights,** droits *m* de souveraineté; **the mind is s. master,** l'esprit est souverainement maître; **s. beauty,** beauté souveraine; **the s. good,** le souverain bien; **s. remedy,** remède souverain, infaillible; **to hold s.o. in s. contempt,** avoir un souverain mépris pour qn. **2.** *s.* (*a*) souverain, -aine; monarque *m*; (*b*) *Num: A:* souverain *m* (pièce d'or de la valeur d'une livre).

sovereignty ['sɔvrənti], *s.* souveraineté *f*.

soviet ['souviet]. **1.** *s.* soviet *m*; **Supreme S.,** soviet suprême. **2.** *a.* soviétique; **the Union of Socialist S. Republics, the S. Union,** l'Union *f* des Républiques socialistes soviétiques, l'Union soviétique.

sovietism ['souviətizm], *s.* soviétisme *m*.

sovietization [souvietai'zeiʃ(ə)n], *s.* soviétisation *f*.

sovkhoz ['sɔvkhɔz], *s. Pol.Ec:* sovkhoze *m*.

sow[1] [sou], *v.tr. & i.* (*p.t.* **sowed** [soud]; *p.p.* **sown** [soun], **sowed**) (*a*) semer (des graines, un champ); **to s. a field with wheat,** ensemencer un champ de blé; emblaver un champ; **to s. broadcast,** semer à la volée, à tout vent; **to s. in holes,** semer par poquets; **to s. in furrows,** semer en sillons; **to s. in rows, in drills,** semer en lignes; **to s. on stony ground,** semer en terre ingrate; **field sown with daisies,** champ semé, parsemé, de pâquerettes; **to s. discord, terror,** semer, répandre, la discorde, la terreur; **to s. the seed of discontent,** semer le mécontentement; (*with passive force*) **the seeds of revolution were sowing,** la révolution se préparait; (*b*) *Navy:* **to s. mines,** semer des mines.

sow[2] [sau], *s.* **1.** (*a*) *Z:* truie *f*; *F: O:* **to get the wrong s. by the ear,** être loin du compte; se fourvoyer; (*b*) laie *f* (sanglier femelle); (*c*) *Crust:* **s. (bug),** cloporte *m*, *F:* cochon *m* de Saint-Antoine; (*d*) *Bot:* **s. thistle,** laiteron *m*, *F:* lait *m* d'âne; **corn s. thistle,** laiteron des champs; **spiny s. thistle,** laiteron épineux. **2.** *Metall:* (*a*) gueuse *f* intermédiaire (de fer fondu); gueuse des mères; (*b*) **s. (channel),** mère-gueuse *f*, *pl.* mères-gueuses; rigole *f*; chenal, -aux *m*; (*c*) cochon *m*, loup *m*.

sowbelly ['saubeli], *s. esp. Mil: Nau: F:* porc salé.

sowbread ['saubred], *s. Bot:* cyclamen *m*, pain *m* de pourceau.

sower ['souər], *s.* **1.** (*pers.*) semeur, -euse. **2.** (*device*) semoir *m*.

sowing ['souiŋ], *s.* semailles *fpl*, semis *m*; ensemencement *m*; **s. time, season,** la semaison; la saison des semailles.

soy(a) ['sɔi(ə)], *s.* (*a*) **s. (bean),** soya *m*, soja *m*; (*b*) **s. sauce,** sauce piquante (de soya).

sozzled ['sɔzld], *a. P:* ivre, soûl, cuit.

spa [spɑ:], *s.* (*a*) source thermale; (*b*) station thermale, ville *f* d'eau.

space[1] [speis], *s.* **1.** espace *m*, intervalle *m* (de temps); **in the s. of a year,** dans l'espace d'un an; **after a short s. of time,** après un court intervalle; **for a short s. of time,** pendant quelque temps. **2.** (*a*) espace; **he sat staring into s.,** il était assis, le regard perdu dans le vide, dans l'espace; **the conquest of s.,** la conquête de l'espace; **outer s.,** espace extra-atmosphérique; **cosmic s.,** espace cosmique; **interstellar s.,** espace interstellaire, intersidéral; **interplanetary s.,** espace interplanétaire; **deep s.,** espace lointain; **s. vacuum,** vide spatial, interplanétaire; **s. flight,** vol, voyage, spatial; vol, voyage, interplanétaire; **manned, unmanned, s. flight,** vol d'un véhicule spatial habité, non habité; **s. travel,** voyages dans l'espace; astronautique *f*, spationautique *f*; **s. traveller,** voyageur, -euse, de l'espace; astronaute *mf*, cosmonaute *mf*, spationaute *mf*; **s. station,** (i) station spatiale (d'observation, de télécommunications, etc.); (ii) position *f* (d'un satellite, d'un astronef, etc.) dans l'espace; **s. vehicle,** véhicule spatial, astronef, spationef *m*; **s. rocket,** fusée spatiale, interplanétaire; **s. suit,** vêtement spatial, combinaison spatiale, scaphandre *m* (d'astronaute); **s. probe,** sonde spatiale; **s. medicine,** médecine spatiale; **s. meteorology,** météorologie spatiale; **s. warfare,** guerre spatiale; (*b*) *Mth: Ph:* **three-dimensional, four-dimensional, s.,** espace à trois, à quatre, dimensions; espace tridimensionnel, quadridimensionnel; **relativistic s.,** espace relativiste; **s.-time,** espace-temps *m*; **s.-time coordinates,** coordonnées *f* espace-temps; **s.-time curvature,** courbure *f* espace-temps; **s.-time continuum,** continuum *m* espace-temps; **s.-time structure,** structure *f* espace-temps; *Ph:* **acceleration s.,** espace d'accélération; **expansion s.,** espace d'expansion, espace libre; **phase s.,** espace de phase; **s. ray,** rayon indirect; **s. wave,** onde *f* ionosphérique, onde réfléchie; *Opt:* **image s.,** espace image; **object s.,** espace objet; *El: Elcs:* (*of klystron*) **buffer s.,** espace intermédiaire; **buncher s.,** espace de modulation; **catcher s.,** espace de captation; **drift s.,** espace de glissement; **reflection s.,** espace de réflexion; (*of vacuum tube*) **dark s.,** espace sombre; **anode, cathode, dark s.,** espace sombre anodique, cathodique; **Crookes, Faraday, dark s.,** espace sombre de Crookes, de Faraday; **s. charge,** charge *f* d'espace; **s. charge density,** densité de charge d'espace; **s. charge field,** champ de charge d'espace; **s. charge grid,** grille de champ; (*c*) espace; étendue *f*; place *f*; **open spaces,** espaces verts; étendues non bâties; **wide open spaces,** vastes paysages; **living s.,** espace vital; **enclosed s.,** espace clos; **hollow s.,** espace creux; **in a confined s.,** dans un espace restreint, resserré; **in the limited s. at our disposal,** dans l'espace limité, restreint, dont nous disposons; avec le peu de place dont nous disposons; **to take up a considerable amount of s.,** prendre, occuper, beaucoup de place; être encombrant; **there isn't enough s. for an extra cupboard,** il n'y a pas assez de place pour une autre armoire; **the trouble about this flat is lack of s.,** l'inconvénient de cet appartement c'est qu'il est trop petit; **the smallest possible s.,** le minimum de place; **to clear a s. on the table,** débarrasser la table; *F:* **s. saver,** gagne-place *m, pl.* gagne-places; **s.-saving,** qui permet de gagner de la place; (meuble, etc.) compact; *Nau:* **cargo s.,** espace en cale; **s. factor,** coefficient d'encombrement; *Psy:* **s. perception,** perception spatiale. **3.** *(a)* espace libre; espacement *m*, intervalle; *(in a quarry)* rue *f*; **s. between two things,** espace entre deux choses; écartement *m* de deux choses; *(between rails)* entre-rail *m, pl.* entre-rails; *(between teeth of cog wheel)* évidement *m*, creux *m*, vide *m*, entre dent *f*; *(between joists)* solin *m*; *(between lines of writing, etc.)* interligne *m*; entre-ligne *m*; **blank s.,** (endroit *m* en) blanc *m*; **s. reserved for official use,** case, partie, réservée à l'administration; **to write one's name in the s. indicated,** écrire son nom à l'emplacement indiqué, dans la case indiquée; **do not write in this s.,** laissez cet espace libre; *Typew:* **s. between letters,** intervalle; **s. bar,** barre *f* d'espacement; *(b) Anat:* **marrow s.,** espace, zone *f*, médullaire; **intercostal s.,** espace intercostal; **interdental s.,** espace, intervalle, interdentaire; *Dent:* **s. obtainer,** dispositif pour augmenter, pour ouvrir, l'espace dentaire; **s. maintainer, retainer,** dispositif de maintien d'espace interdentaire; **denture s.,** espace prothétique; *Med:* **s.-occupying tumour,** lésion intracrânienne expansive; *(c) Mus:* espace (entre deux lignes de la portée); *(d) Typ:* espace *f* (en métal); blanc; **thick s., middle s.,** espace fort, moyen; **s. lines,** interlignes; **s. rule,** filet *m* maigre.

space², *v.tr.* **1.** *(a)* **to s. (out),** espacer; disposer (des objets, etc.) de distance en distance; échelonner, diluer (des troupes, etc.); **the posts are spaced ten feet apart,** les poteaux sont plantés à dix pieds d'intervalle, se succèdent à des intervalles de dix pieds; **to s. out payments over ten years,** échelonner des versements sur dix ans; **to s. out one's visits,** espacer ses visites; **you should s. your words more evenly,** vous devriez espacer vos mots plus soigneusement; *Typ:* **to s. (out) the lines, the type,** espacer les lignes, les lettres; **to s. out the matter,** blanchir la composition; donner de l'air à la composition; *(b)* **to s. off,** diviser, subdiviser (une ligne); répartir (des trous). **2.** *(with passive force) Typ:* **letters that s. too much,** lettres qui chassent trop.

spacecraft [ˈspeiskrɑːft], *s.* véhicule spatial, engin spatial, astronef *m*, spationef *m*; **manned, unmanned, s.,** véhicule spatial habité, non habité.

spaced [speist], *a.* **1.** *(a)* espacé, écarté, séparé; **s. lathing,** lattage *m*, lattis *m*, espacé; *W.Tel:* **s. aerial, s. antenna,** antenne séparée, antenne étalée; **s. loop (of direction-finder),** cadre séparé (de radiogoniomètre); **s.-antenna, s.-loop, direction-finder,** radiogoniomètre *m* à antennes séparées (ou étalées), à cadres séparés; *(b) Cryst:* **closely-s. lattice,** réseau (cristallin) à faible pas. **2.** *Typ:* **close s., thick s.,** aux espaces fins, forts.

spaceless [ˈspeislis], *a.* sans bornes; illimité.

spaceman, *pl.* **-men** [ˈspeismæn, -men], *s.m.* **1.** *(a)* astronaute, cosmonaute, spationaute, voyageur de l'espace; *(b)* astronauticien. **2.** *(occ. in science fiction)* habitant de l'espace.

spacer [ˈspeisər], *s.* **1.** *Typ:* espace *f*. **2.** *Typew:* barre *f* d'espacement; **back s.,** rappel *m* de chariot; rappel arrière. **3.** *Mec.E:* pièce *f* d'écartement, écarteur *m*; rondelle *f* d'écartement, d'épaisseur; entretoise *f*; **close-tolerance s.,** entretoise calibrée; **stop s.,** entretoise butée.

spaceship [ˈspeisʃip], *s.* = SPACECRAFT.

spacewoman, *pl.* **-women** [ˈspeiswumən, -wimin], *s.f.* *(a)* femme cosmonaute; *(b)* astronauticienne.

spacing [ˈspeisiŋ], *s.* **1.** *(a)* espacement *m*, écartement *m* (des arbres, des poteaux télégraphiques, des rivets, etc.); *El:* **electrode s.,** écartement des électrodes; *N.Arch:* **frame s.,** écartement des membrures; maille *f*; *(b) Typ:* espacement (des lettres, des lignes); interlignage *m*; *Typew:* **typed in single, double, s.,** dactylographié, tapé, à simple, à double, interligne; *(c) Tg: W.Tel:* écart *m*, intervalle *m* (des impulsions); **s. interval,** intervalle de manipulation; **s. current,** courant *m* de repos; *(d) Mec.E:* **blade s.,** pas *m* des aubes (d'une turbine, etc.); **s. plate,** plaque *f* d'écartement; **s. ring,** bague *f* d'entretoise; *Atom.Ph: Cryst:* **lattice s.,** pas d'un réseau (atomique, cristallin). **2.** *(a) Anat:* **(tooth) s.,** écartement interdentaire; diastème *m*; **inter-canine s.,** diastème inter-canines; **inter-incisor s.,** diastème inter-incisif; *(b) Med:* intervalle d'apyrexie.

spacious [ˈspeiʃəs], *a.* **1.** *(a)* spacieux, vaste; *(b)* ample. **2.** *Lit:* **s. times, age,** époque *f* aux larges visées.

spaciousness [ˈspeiʃəsnis], *s.* **1.** vaste étendue *f*; spaciosité *f*; dimensions spacieuses (d'une maison, etc.). **2.** grandeur *f*, ampleur *f* (d'une époque).

spade¹ [speid], *s.* **1.** *Tls:* *(a)* bêche *f*; **(child's seaside) s.,** pelle *f*; **to call a s. a s.,** appeler les choses par leur nom; appeler un chat un chat; dire le mot et la chose; *(b) Hort: etc:* **s. (graft),** profondeur *f* de fer de bêche; *(c)* couteau *m* à dépecer (les baleines). **2.** *Artil:* **trail s.,** bêche de (la) crosse.

spade², *v.tr.* **1.** bêcher (la terre, etc.). **2.** dépecer (une baleine).

spade³, *s.* *(a) Cards:* pique *m*; **ace of spades,** as *m* de pique; **to play a s., to play spades,** jouer pique; *(b)* **s. guinea,** guinée frappée à l'époque de Georges IV (qui portait un écusson en forme de pique); *(c) Pej:* nègre *m*.

spadefish [ˈspeidfiʃ], *s. Ich:* *(a)* éphippe *m*; *(b)* spatule *f*.

spadeful [ˈspeidful], *s.* pleine bêche; pelletée *f*.

spadework [ˈspeidwəːk], *s.* **1.** travaux *mpl* à la bêche; le gros travail. **2.** *(a)* travaux de défrichement; *(b)* travaux d'approche, de sape. **3.** travaux préliminaires, déblaiement *m* du terrain (en vue d'une enquête, d'une recherche scientifique, etc.).

spadger [ˈspædʒər], *s. F:* moineau *m*, piaf *m*.

spadiceous [speiˈdiʃəs], *a. Bot:* **1.** spadicé. **2.** brunâtre.

Spadiciflorae [speidaisiˈflɔːriː], *s.pl. Bot:* spadiciflores *f*.

spadicifloral [speidaisiˈflɔːr(ə)l], *a. Bot:* spadiciflore.

spadille [spəˈdil], *s. Cards:* spadille *m*; as *m* de pique.

spadix, *pl.* **-dices** [ˈspeidiks, -disiːz], *s. Bot:* spadice *m*, massue *f*.

spado [ˈspeidou], *s.m. Jur:* impuissant, eunuque.

spaghetti [spəˈgeti], *s.* *(a) Cu:* spaghetti *mpl*; *(b) Elcs:* souplisseau *m*.

spahi [ˈspɑː(h)iː], *s. Mil:* spahi *m*.

Spain [spein], *Pr.n. Geog:* Espagne *f*.

Spalacidae [spæˈlæsidiː], *s.pl. Z:* spalacidés *m*.

spalax [ˈspælæks], *s. Z:* spalax *m*.

spall¹ [spɔːl], *s.* éclat *m* (de pierre); épaufrure *f*.

spall². **1.** *v.tr.* *(a) Min:* broyer (le minerai); *(b) Stonew: Const:* smiller, dégrossir (la pierre); *(c)* épaufrer (la pierre); diviser (la pierre) en éclats. **2.** *v.i.* s'écailler; éclater; *(of stone)* s'épaufrer, s'effriter.

spallation [spæˈleiʃ(ə)n], *s. Atom.Ph:* spallation *f*.

spalled [spɔːld], *a. Const:* (moellon) smillé; **s. rubble,** appareil *m* en moellons smillés.

spalling [ˈspɔːliŋ], *s.* **1.** *Min:* broyage *m*. **2.** *Stonew:* smillage *m*; **s. hammer,** smille *f*. **3.** effritement *m*, écaillage *m* (de la pierre, etc.).

spalpeen [spælˈpiːn], *s. (Irish)* *(a)* coquin *m*, fripon *m*; *(b)* voyou *m, pl.* voyous; *(c)* gamin *m*.

spalt [spɔːlt], *s. Metall:* spalt *m*.

span¹ [spæn], *s.* **1.** *(a)* (i) empan *m* (de la main); (ii) *A: Meas:* empan (9 inches, 229 mm); *(b) (of bird, aircraft)* **wing s.,** envergure *f*; **full arm s.,** envergure (des bras). **2.** *(a)* portée *f* (entre deux appuis); ouverture *f*, largeur *f* (d'une arche); écartement *m* (de deux piliers, etc.); volant *m* (d'un poutre); **s. between supports,** distance *f* entre supports; **arch with a s. of 80 metres,** arc *m* de 80 mètres de portée; *(b)* travée *f* (d'un pont, d'un comble); **single s. bridge,** pont *m* à travée unique, à une seule arche; *(c)* hangar *m*, serre *f*, avec toit à deux versants; **s. roof,** comble *m* à deux égouts, à deux versants, à double pente; *(d)* **s. wire,** (i) fil tendeur, hauban tendeur (entre deux poteaux, etc.); (ii) fil aérien; ligne suspendue; *(e) N.Arch:* **davit s.,** entremise *f* de bossoir; **s. shackle,** échaudis *m*. **3.** *(a)* petite étendue (de terre, etc.); *(b) O: Lit:* court espace de temps; **for a long s.,** longtemps; **our mortal s.,** notre séjour *m* terrestre. **4.** *Ent:* **s. worm,** (chenille) arpenteuse *f*.

span², *v.tr.* **(spanned) 1.** *(a)* mesurer (à l'empan, par empan); *(b)* encercler (le poignet) avec la main. **2.** *(a) (of bridge, etc.)* franchir, traverser, enjamber (une rivière, etc.); **three bridges s. the river,** trois ponts enjambent le fleuve; *Rail:* **gantry spanning four sets of rails,** portique *m* chevauchant quatre voies; *(b)* **his life spans nearly the whole century,** sa vie couvre, embrasse, presque tout le siècle.

span³, *s.* **1.** *(a) esp. N.Am:* paire *f*, couple *m* (de chevaux, de bœufs); *(b) (S. Africa)* attelage *m* (de bœufs). **2.** *Nau:* patte *f* d'oie; *Navy: A:* brague *f* (de canon).

span⁴, *v.tr.* **1.** *(esp. S. Africa)* *(a)* **to s. (in),** atteler (des chevaux, des bœufs); *(b)* **to s. out,** dételer. **2.** *Nau:* brider, saisir (une vergue, etc.).

spancel¹ [ˈspæns(ə)l], *s.* entrave *f* (pour vache, etc.).

spancel², *v.tr.* **(spancelled)** entraver (une vache, etc.).

spandrel [ˈspændr(ə)l], *s. Arch:* écoinçon *m*; tympan *m* (d'un arc, etc.); **s. wall,** mur *m* qui remplit le tympan.

spangle¹ [ˈspæŋgl], *s.* **1.** *Tex: etc:* paillette *f*, *(large)* paillon *m*; **gold spangles,** paillettes d'or. **2.** *Bot:* **oak s.,** galle *f* en grain de groseille (des feuilles du chêne).

spangle², *v.tr.* pailleter **(with,** de); parsemer de paillettes; **spangled with silver,** pailleté d'argent; *Lit:* **meadow spangled with flowers,** pré parsemé, émaillé, de fleurs.

spangling [ˈspæŋgliŋ], *s. Cost: etc:* pailletage *m*.

spangolite [ˈspæŋgoulait], *s. Miner:* spangolite *f*.

Spaniard [ˈspænjəd], *s.* Espagnol, -ole.

spaniel [ˈspænjəl], *s.* épagneul *m*; *Ven:* chien couchant; **(English) toy s., King Charles s.,** épagneul King Charles, épagneul nain anglais; **cocker s.,** épagneul cocker; **springer s.,** épagneul springer; **Brittany s.,** épagneul breton; **Irish water s.,** épagneul d'eau irlandais.

Spanish [ˈspæniʃ]. **1.** *a.* espagnol; **S. American,** hispano-américain; *Com:* **S. black, S. red,** noir *m*, rouge *m*, d'Espagne; *Bot:* **S. onion,** oignon *m* d'Espagne; **S. oyster plant, S. salsify,** scolymus *m* (comestible); **S. broom,** genêt *m* d'Espagne; *Tan:* **S. leather,** cuir *m* de Cordoue; *Hist:* **the S. Main,** (i) la Terre-ferme; (ii) la mer des Antilles; **the War of the S. Succession,** la Guerre de la Succession d'Espagne. **2.** *s. Ling:* espagnol *m*. **3.** *s.pl.* **the S.,** les Espagnols *m*.

spank¹ [spæŋk], *s.* claque *f* sur le derrière; fessée *f*.

spank². **1.** *v.tr.* fesser (un enfant); administrer une fessée, une fouettée, à (un enfant). **2.** *v.i. (of horse, etc.)* **to s. along,** aller bon train; filer à bonne allure.

spanker [ˈspæŋkər], *s.* **1.** *Nau:* brigantine *f*; **s. boom,** gui *m* de la brigantine; bôme *m*. **2.** *(a)* cheval *m* qui va bon train; *(b) F: O:* chose *f* de premier ordre, de premier rang.

spanking¹ [ˈspæŋkiŋ], *s.* fessée *f*.

spanking², *a.* **1.** *F: A:* de premier ordre; de premier rang; chic, épatant. **2.** **to go at a s. pace,** aller bon train; filer raide; brûler le terrain; *Nau:* **s. breeze,** belle brise, bonne brise.

spanner [ˈspænər], *s.* **1.** *Tls:* clef *f*; **s. for hexagonal nuts,** clef à six pans; **adjustable s.,** (i) *(or* **shifting s.)** clef anglaise; clef à molette; (ii) clef universelle; **bent s., elbowed s., skew s.,** clef coudée; **bolt s.,** serre-écrou *m inv*; **box s., socket s.,** clef à douille, à tire-fonds; **crocodile s.,** clef crocodile, clef à mâchoires dentées; **face s.,** clef à griffes sur le côté; **gap s.,** clef à fourche; **single-ended, double-ended, s.,** clef simple (à fourche), clef double (à fourches); **hook s.,** clef à ergot, à griffe; **rack s.,** clef à crémaillère; **ratchet s.,** clef à cliquet, à rochet; **ring s.,** clef fermée; *F:* **to throw a s. in the works,** mettre des bâtons dans les roues. **2.** *Civ.E:* entretoise *f*.

spanopn(o)ea [spænɔpˈniːə], *s. Med:* spanopnée *f*.

spar¹ [spɑːr], *s.* **1.** *(a)* perche *f*, poteau *m*; *(b)* chevron *m* (d'un comble). **2.** *Nau:* *(a)* espar(t) *m*; bout *m* de mât; mâtereau *m*; **spars lashed together,** drome *f*; **awning s.,** espar de tente; *(b)* **the spars,** la mâture. **3.** *Av:* **wing s.,** poutrelle *f*; bras *m* d'aile; caisson *m* de voilure; **fin s. box,** caisson de dérive.

spar², *s. Miner:* spath *m*; **brown s.,** spath brunissant; breunnérite *f*; **diamond s., adamantine s.,** spath adamantin; corindon *m*; **heavy s.,** spath pesant; barytine *f*; **pearl s.,** spath perlé; **satin s.,** sélénite fibreuse; **Greenland s.,** cryolit(h)e *f*.

spar³, *s.* **1.** combat *m* de coqs. **2.** *(a)* assaut de boxe amical; combat d'entraînement; *(b)* assaut de paroles; escarmouche *f*; *F:* prise *f* de bec.

spar⁴, *v.i.* **(sparred) 1.** *(of cocks)* se battre. **2.** *(of pers.)* **to s. with s.o.,** (i) faire un assaut de boxe amical avec qn; (ii) argumenter avec qn; s'escrimer contre qn.

spar⁵, *s. Ich:* spare *m*.

sparable [ˈspærəbl], *s. Bootm:* clou carré (sans tête); pointe *f*.

spar-deck [ˈspɑːdek], *s. N.Arch:* spardeck *m*.

spare¹ [ˈspeər], *a.* & *s.*

I. *a.* **1.** *(a)* frugal, -aux; **s. diet,** régime frugal; *(b) (of pers.)* sec, *f.* sèche; maigre, fluet; **s. figure,** corps sec; **he was tall and s.,** c'était un grand mince. **2.** plus qu'il n'en faut; de trop, de reste; disponible; **s. time,** (i) temps *m* disponible; (ii) moments perdus; loisirs *mpl*; **in my s. time,** à mes heures perdues; **s.-time activities,** les loisirs; *Sch: etc:* activités dirigées; **to take a s.-time job,** prendre un deuxième emploi en dehors de son travail régulier; **s. capital,** capital *m* disponible; fonds *m* disponibles; **s. room,** chambre *f* d'ami(s); **s. bed,** lit *m* à la disposition des amis; **we have a s. bed,** on peut vous offrir un lit (pour la nuit); **I have s. copies of these books,** j'ai ces livres en surnombre; **we have some s. rope,** nous avons de la corde de reste, en surplus. **3.** (pièces, accessoires, vêtements) de rechange, de remplacement; **s. parts,** pièces de réserve, de rechange; pièces détachées; *F:* **s.-part surgery,** chirurgie *f* de greffage; **to pack a s. dress,** mettre une robe de rechange dans sa valise; **have you a s. handkerchief?** as-tu un mouchoir à me prêter? **s. machine,** machine *f* de réserve, de remplacement; **s. hands,** ouvriers *m* supplémentaires; *Aut:* **s. wheel, s. can of petrol,** roue *f*, bidon *m* d'essence, de secours; **s. tyre,** (i) pneu de rechange; (ii) *F:* bourrelet *m* de graisse; *Artil: etc:* **s. number,** suppléant *m* (de servant de pièce, etc.); *Nau:* **s. anchor, s. bunker,** ancre *f*, soute *f*, de réserve. **4.** *P:* **to go s.,** être furieux, sortir de ses gonds.

II. *s.* **1. to take up the s. in a rope,** raidir un cordage; *Nau:* embraquer le mou. **2.** (*a*) **spares,** pièces de rechange; pièces détachées; réserves *f*; **I've lost my handkerchief; have you a s.?** j'ai perdu mon mouchoir; en as-tu un à me prêter? (*b*) (*pers.*) *Sp: etc: F:* suppléant, -ante.

spare[2], *v.tr.* **1.** épargner, ménager; **to s. one's strength,** ménager ses forces; **to s. no expense, not to s. expense,** ne pas regarder à la dépense; **to s. no pains,** ne pas ménager sa peine; ne pas marchander sa peine; **he spared no pains to please me,** il n'a rien épargné pour me contenter; il n'est pas de soins qu'il n'ait pris pour me faire plaisir. **2.** (*a*) se passer de (qch.); se priver de (qch.); **can you s. it?** pouvez-vous vous en passer? je ne vous en prive pas? **if you can s. this book, do lend it me,** si vous n'avez que faire de ce livre, prêtez-le-moi; **we can't s. him,** il nous est indispensable; **we can (easily) s. him,** nous pouvons nous passer de lui; nous n'avons pas besoin de lui; nous pouvons le libérer; **to have nothing to s.,** n'avoir que le strict nécessaire; être réduit à la portion congrue; **we have three to s.,** nous en avons trois de trop, de reste; **to have enough and to s. (of sth.),** avoir plus qu'il n'en faut (de qch.); avoir ce qu'il faut (de qch.) et au delà; en avoir de reste; **you have enough and to s.,** vous êtes plus qu'à l'aise; **there is room and to s.,** la place ne manque pas; il y a de la place à revendre; (*b*) **I cannot s. the time to finish it,** je n'ai pas le temps de le finir; le temps me fait défaut pour le finir; **every hour I can s.,** toutes les heures dont je peux disposer; **to have no time to s.,** (i) ne pas avoir de temps de libre; (ii) ne pas avoir de temps à perdre; n'avoir que juste le temps (pour attraper le train, etc.); **when I have time to s.,** quand j'ai du temps de trop, de reste; quand j'ai des loisirs; **to have five minutes to s.,** avoir cinq minutes à soi; **I have a minute to s.,** je peux disposer d'un instant; **you haven't a moment to s.,** vous avez tout juste le temps; **to catch a train with five minutes to s.,** prendre un train avec cinq minutes de battement; (*c*) **to s. s.o. sth.,** donner, céder, qch. à qn; **can you s. me a hundred francs?** pouvez-vous me prêter cent francs? **how much time can you s. me?** combien de temps pouvez-vous me consacrer? **can you s. me a few moments?** voulez-vous m'accorder quelques minutes? **3.** (*a*) faire grâce à (qn); **s. me!** grâce! épargnez-moi! **if he is spared,** s'il vit; **death spares no one,** la mort n'épargne, ne respecte, personne, ne fait grâce à personne; tout le monde doit mourir; **to s. an ancient monument,** respecter un monument historique; **he spares nobody,** il ne fait de quartier à personne; **to s. s.o.'s feelings,** ménager qn; épargner qn; **s. my blushes!** ne me faites pas rougir! **I'll s. you the rest,** je vous fais grâce du reste; (*b*) ménager (qn, son cheval); **he doesn't s. himself,** il ne se ménage pas; **to s. s.o. the trouble of doing sth.,** éviter à qn la peine de faire qch.

sparganium [spɑː'geiniəm], *s. Bot:* sparganier *m*.

sparid ['spærid], *s. Ich:* sparidé *m*.

Sparidae ['spæridiː], *s.pl. Ich:* sparidés *m*.

sparing ['spɛəriŋ], *a.* frugal, -aux; ménager, -ère; économe, épargnant, parcimonieux; **to be s. with the butter,** épargner, ménager, le beurre; **with a s. hand,** d'une main chiche, avare; *Lit:* **he is s. of praise, s. in his praise,** il est chiche, ménager, parcimonieux, avare, de louanges; il ne prodigue pas les éloges; **s. of words,** sobre de paroles.

sparingly ['spɛəriŋli], *adv.* **1.** frugalement; maigrement; **to eat s.,** manger sobrement, avec retenue; demeurer sur son appétit; **to use sth. s.,** ménager qch.; être ménager, -ère, de qch. **2.** d'une manière restreinte; modérément.

spark[1] [spɑːk], *s.* **1.** (*a*) étincelle *f*; (*from fire*) flammèche *f*; **short-lived s.,** bluette *f*; lueur fugitive; **to throw out sparks,** émettre, jeter, lancer, des étincelles; **the s. of life, the vital s.,** l'étincelle de la vie; **s. of wit,** étincelle, lueur, bluette, d'esprit; **he hasn't a s. of generosity in him,** il n'a pas la moindre parcelle, il n'a pas deux sous, de générosité; (*b*) *El: etc:* étincelle; **fat s.,** étincelle (bien) nourrie; **lean, stringy, s.,** étincelle médiocre; **condensed s.,** étincelle condensée; **branched s.,** étincelle ramifiée; **break s., induction s.,** étincelle de rupture; **breakdown s.,** étincelle disruptive; **s. discharge,** décharge disruptive; **jump s.,** étincelle éclatante; **s. frequency, rate,** fréquence *f* d'étincelles, d'éclatement, de récurrence; **s. lag,** retard *m* d'étincelle; **s. arrester,** déchargeur *m*, éclateur *m* (pare-étincelles); parafoudre *m*; *W.Tel:* **pilot s.,** étincelle auxiliaire; **quenched s.,** étincelle amortie, étouffée, éteinte; **s. quench,** éliminateur *m* d'étincelles; pare-étincelles *m inv*; **s. gap,** (i) *El:* distance explosive, d'éclatement; (ii) *I.C.E:* pont *m* d'allumage; (iii) *W.Tel:* éclateur; **quenched s. gap,** éclateur à étincelles amorties; **s. micrometer,** éclateur réglable; **s. condenser,** condensateur *m* antiparasite; **s. generator,** générateur *m* à étincelles; **s. transmitter,** émetteur *m* (télégraphique) à étincelles; **s. telegraphy,** télégraphie *f* à étincelles; *Atom.Ph:* **s. chamber,** chambre *f* à étincelles; **s. counter,** compteur *m* d'étincelles; *Rad:* **s. switch,** contracteur *m* à étincelles; **s. photography,** photographie *f* ultra-rapide par étincelles; stroboscopie *f* par étincelles; (*c*) *I.C.E:* **s. ignition,** allumage *m* par bougies; **jump-s. distributor,** distributeur *m* à étincelles sautantes; **to adjust, advance, retard, the s.,** régler, avancer, retarder, l'allumage; mettre de l'avance, réduire l'avance, à l'allumage; *NAm:* **s. plug,** bougie *f* (*s.a.* SPARKING); (*d*) *Metalw:* **s. machining, welding,** usinage *m*, soudage *m*, par étincelage; **s. guard,** pare-étincelles; (*e*) *Med:* **s. therapy,** étincelage *m*, fulguration *f*; (*f*) *Nau: Av: F:* **sparks,** le radio. **2. diamond sparks,** semence *f* de diamants.

spark[2]. **1.** *v.i.* (*a*) émettre des étincelles; (*of dynamo, etc.*) cracher; *El:* **sparking discharge,** décharge *f* par étincelle; (*b*) *A:* étinceler; (*c*) (*of current*) **to s. across the terminals,** jaillir entre les bornes. **2.** *v.tr.* (*a*) faire éclater, allumer, (qch.) avec une étincelle électrique; (*b*) **the current sparks the gap,** le courant produit une étincelle qui jaillit à travers l'intervalle; (*c*) *v.ind.tr.* **to s. off an idea,** provoquer une idée; **to s. off a revolution,** déclencher une révolution, mettre le feu aux poudres.

spark[3], *s.* **1.** *A:* élégant *m*, gandin *m*; beau cavalier; *A:* petit-maître *m*, *pl.* petits-maîtres. **2. gay s.,** gaillard *m*, joyeux compagnon, gai luron; noceur *m*.

spark[4], *v.i. O:* **to s. (it),** faire le galant.

sparkation [spɑː'keiʃ(ə)n], *s. Metalw:* étincelage *m*; **s. system,** usinage *m* par étincelage.

sparker ['spɑːkər], *s. Petr:* étinceleur *m*.

sparking ['spɑːkiŋ], *s. El:* **1.** (*a*) émission *f* d'étincelles; (*accidental*) débordement *m*, jaillissement *m*, d'étincelles; crachement *m*; **s. at the brushes,** crachement aux balais (d'une dynamo); **s. coil,** bobine *f* d'induction; (*b*) production *f* d'un arc (intempestif). **2.** allumage *m* par étincelle électrique; **advanced s., s. advance,** avance *f* à l'allumage; **s. plug** (*NAm:* **spark plug**) bougie *f* (d'allumage); **desiccant s. plug,** bougie déshydratante; **double-point s. plug,** bougie bipolaire; **screened, shielded, s. plug,** bougie blindée; **the s. plug's dead,** la bougie est grillée, ne donne plus.

sparkle[1] ['spɑːkl], *s.* **1.** étincelle *f*; brève lueur; bluette *f*; **not a s. of wit,** pas la moindre parcelle d'esprit. **2.** (*a*) étincellement *m*; éclat *m*, pétillement *m* (des yeux); feux *mpl* (d'un diamant); **there was a s. in his eyes,** ses yeux étincelaient; (*b*) **wine that has lost its s.,** vin *m* qui ne pétille plus. **3.** vivacité *f* d'esprit.

sparkle[2], *v.i.* **1.** (*a*) étinceler, scintiller; (*of jewel*) chatoyer, éclater, miroiter; (*of sea*) brasiller; **her eyes sparkled (with joy),** ses yeux étincelaient, pétillaient, brillaient (de joie); **the lights s. in the water,** les lumières *f* miroitent dans l'eau; **book sparkling with wit,** livre *m* qui pétille d'esprit; (*b*) (*of wine*) pétiller, mousser. **2.** (*of fire*) émettre des étincelles; pétiller.

sparkler ['spɑːklər], *s.* **1.** *Pyr:* allumette japonaise. **2.** *P:* **sparklers,** diamants *m*.

sparkless ['spɑːklis], *a. El:* **s. breaking,** interruption *f* sans étincelles; **s. running,** fonctionnement *m* sans crachements.

sparklet ['spɑːklit], *s.* **1.** petite étincelle; bluette *f*. **2.** sparklet *m* (à eau de seltz).

sparkling[1] ['spɑːkliŋ], *a.* **1.** (*a*) étincelant, brillant; (*of jewel*) miroitant; (*of sea*) brasillant; **s. effect,** effet étincelant, endiamanté; **s. wit,** vivacité *f* d'esprit; **s. conversation,** conversation brillante, pétillante d'esprit; (*b*) (vin) mousseux; (limonade) gazeuse; **semi-s. wine,** vin pétillant. **2.** (feu) qui émet des étincelles; pétillant; *Metalw:* **s. heat,** chaude suante.

sparkling[2], *s.* **1.** étincellement *m*; scintillement *m*, scintillation *f*. **2.** pétillement *m*.

sparklingly ['spɑːkliŋli], *adv.* **1.** d'une manière étincelante. **2.** vivement; avec vivacité.

sparkmeter ['spɑːkmiːtər], *s. El:* spinthéromètre *m*, spinthermètre *m*.

sparkover ['spɑːkouvər], *s. El:* décharge disruptive.

sparling ['spɑːliŋ], *s. Ich:* éperlan *m*.

sparoid ['spærɔid], *a. Ich:* sparoïde.

sparred [spɑːd], *a.* **1.** (clôture, etc.) en treillis. **2.** (navire) mâté.

sparrer ['spɑːrər], *s.* (*a*) boxeur *m* (qui fait des assauts de démonstration); (*b*) contradicteur *m*.

sparring ['spɑːriŋ], *s.* boxe amicale; boxe de démonstration; **s. match,** (i) assaut de boxe amical, de démonstration; (ii) match *m* de boxe; (iii) *F:* prise *f* de bec; **s. partner,** (i) partenaire *m* (d'un boxeur); sparring-partner *m*; (ii) *F:* adversaire, contradicteur amical.

sparrow ['spærou], *s. Orn:* (*a*) moineau *m*; **hen s.,** passière *f*; **house s.,** *NAm:* **English s.,** moineau domestique, franc; **rock s.,** moineau soulcie; **tree s.,** moineau friquet; (*b*) *NAm:* pinson *m* (*Fr.C.*); **Baird's s.,** pinson de Baird; **sage, Bell's, s.,** pinson de Bell; **Brewer's s.,** pinson de Brewer; **chipping s.,** pinson familier; **clay-coloured s.,** pinson des plaines; **field s.,** pinson des champs; **golden-crowned s.,** pinson à couronne dorée; **grasshopper s.,** pinson sauterelle; **Harris's s.,** pinson à face noire; **Henslow's s.,** pinson de Henslow; **Ipswich s.,** pinson d'Ipswich; **lark s.,** pinson à joues marron; **Leconte's s.,** pinson de Leconte; **Lincoln's s.,** pinson de Lincoln; **pinewoods s.,** pinson des pinières; **savannah s.,** pinson des prés; **sharp-tailed s.,** pinson à queue aiguë; **song s.,** pinson chanteur; **swamp s.,** pinson des marais; **tree s.,** pinson hudsonien; **vesper s.,** pinson vespéral; **white-crowned s.,** pinson à couronne blanche; **white-throated s.,** pinson à gorge blanche; (*c*) **hedge s.,** accenteur *m* mouchet; fauvette *f* d'hiver; (*d*) **fox s.,** bruant *m* renard; **white-throated s.,** bruant à col blanc; (*e*) **diamond s.,** diamant *m* à gouttelettes; pardalot *m*; (*f*) **Java s.,** calfat *m*, padda *m*, moineau *m* de Java, oiseau *m* de riz.

sparrowhawk ['spærouhɔːk], *s. Orn:* épervier *m* (d'Europe); **Levant s.,** épervier à pieds courts; **American s.,** faucon *m* des moineaux.

sparrow(-)wort ['spærouwəːt], *s. Bot:* passerine *f*.

sparse [spɑːs], *a.* (*of trees, population, etc.*) clairsemé, épars, éparpillé; peu dense; **s. hair,** cheveux rares, clairsemés; **s. vegetation,** végétation éparse.

sparsely ['spɑːsli], *adv.* peu abondamment; **s. populated,** qui a une population clairsemée; peu peuplé; **s. covered with trees,** aux arbres clairsemés; **s. scattered,** semés, éparpillés, çà et là.

sparseness ['spɑːsnis], *s.* faible densité *f* (de la population); manque *m* (de végétation).

sparsiflorous [spɑːsi'flɔːrəs], *a. Bot:* sparsiflore.

sparsifolious [spɑːsi'fouliəs], *a. Bot:* sparsifolié.

sparsile ['spɑːsail], *a. Astr:* sparsile.

Sparta ['spɑːtə], *Pr.n. Geog:* Sparte *f*.

spartacism ['spɑːtəsizm], *s. Pol.Hist:* spartakisme *m*.

spartacist ['spɑːtəsist], *a. & s. Pol.Hist:* spartakiste (*mf*).

Spartan ['spɑːtən]. **1.** *a.* (*a*) *Geog:* spartiate; (*b*) **to lead a s. life,** vivre en spartiate; mener une vie austère. **2.** *s.* (*a*) *Geog:* Spartiate *mf*; (*b*) spartiate, homme austère.

spartein ['spɑːtiːiːn], *s. Med:* spartéine *f*.

sparterie ['spɑːtəri], *s.* sparterie *f*.

spasm ['spæzm], *s.* **1.** *Med:* spasme *m*, angoisse *f*; **clonic spasms,** spasmes cloniques; convulsions *f* (cloniques); **tonic spasms,** spasmes toniques; **functional spasms,** spasmes fonctionnels. **2.** accès *m* (de toux, de jalousie); **spasms of grief,** affres *f* de chagrin; **in a s. of temper,** dans un accès, un mouvement, de colère; **to work in spasms,** travailler par accès, par à-coups, par boutades, à bâtons rompus.

spasmodic [spæz'mɔdik], *a.* **1.** (*a*) *Med:* (dyspnée) spasmodique; (toux) férine; (*b*) (saut, etc.) involontaire, convulsif. **2. s. work,** travail fait irrégulièrement, par saccades, par à-coups; **s. style,** style inégal.

spasmodically [spæz'mɔdik(ə)li], *adv.* **1.** (*a*) *Med:* spasmodiquement; (*b*) involontairement, convulsivement. **2.** irrégulièrement; inégalement; (travailler) par à-coups.

spasmolytic [spæzmou'litik], *a. Med:* spasmolytique.

spasmophilia [spæzmou'filiə], *s. Med:* spasmophilie *f*.

spastic ['spæstik]. **1.** *a.* (paraplégie, etc.) spasmodique. **2.** *s.* paraplégique *mf* (spasmodique).

spasticity [spæs'tisiti], *s. Med:* spasmodicité *f*.

spat[1] [spæt], *s.* frai *m*, naissain *m* (d'huîtres, de moules).

spat[2], *v.i.* **(spatted)** (*of oysters*) frayer.

spat[3], *s.* **1.** *Cost:* demi-guêtre *f*, *pl.* demi-guêtres; guêtre *f* de ville. **2.** *Av:* **wheel s.,** carénage *m* de roue.

spat[4], *s. NAm: F:* **1.** (*a*) querelle *f*, prise *f* de bec; (*b*) claque *f*, tape *f*. **2.** bruit sec, claquement *m* (d'une balle, etc.).

spat[5], *v.i.* **(spatted)** *NAm: F:* **1. to s. with s.o.,** se quereller, avoir une prise de bec, avec qn. **2.** claquer; faire clac.

Spatangida, Spatangina, Spatangoid(e)a [spæ'tændʒidə, -tæn'dʒainə, -tæn'gɔid(i)ə], *s.pl. Echin:* spatangides *m*, spatangoïdes *m*.

spatangoid [spæ'tæŋgɔid], *a. Echin:* spatangide.

spatangus [spæ'tæŋgəs], *s. Echin:* spatangue *m*.

spatchcock[1] ['spætʃkɔk], *s. Cu:* poulet *m*, poussin *m*, à la crapaudine.

spatchcock[2], *v.tr.* **1.** *Cu:* faire cuire (un poulet, un poussin) à la minute, à la crapaudine. **2.** *F: O:* faire une insertion dans (un rapport, etc.) (à la dernière minute).

spate [speit], *s.* crue *f*; **river in s.,** rivière *f* en crue; **a s. of letters,** une avalanche de lettres.

spathaceous [spæ'θeiʃəs], *a. Bot:* spathé, spathacé.

spathe [speið], *s. Bot:* spathe *f.*

spathella [spæ'θelə], *s. Bot:* spathelle *f.*

spathic ['spæθik], *a. Miner:* (fer, etc.) spathique.

spathiform ['spæθifɔ:m], *a. Miner:* spathiforme.

spathose [spæ'θous], *a.* **1.** *Miner:* spathique. **2.** *Bot:* spathé, spathiforme.

spatial ['speiʃ(ə)l], *a.* **1.** *Mth: Ph:* spatial, -aux; **s. co-ordinates,** coordonnées spatiales; **s. variables,** variables *f* d'espace; **s. interval,** intervalle *m* de variable d'espace; *Atom.Ph:* **s. distribution,** distribution spatiale; **s. resolving power,** pouvoir *m* de résolution spatiale; *Ch:* **s. isomerism,** stéréo-isomérie *f.* **2. s. existence,** existence *f* dans l'espace.

spatiality [speiʃi'æliti], *s.* spatialité *f.*

spatialization [speiʃəlai'zeiʃ(ə)n], *s.* spatialisation *f.*

spatially ['speiʃəli], *adv.* en ce qui concerne l'espace; dans l'espace.

spatio-temporal [speiʃiou'tempər(ə)l], *a.* spatio-temporel; *Mth:* (coordonnées) espace-temps.

spatter[1] ['spætər], *s.* éclaboussure *f*; *Ind:* projection *f* (de soudure).

spatter[2]. **1.** *v.tr.* **to s. s.o. with mud, to s. mud over s.o.,** éclabousser qn de boue. **2.** *v.i.* (*of liquid*) jaillir, gicler; **the rain spattering down on the pavement,** la pluie qui tombe en éclaboussant, qui gicle, sur le trottoir. **3.** *v.i.* = SPLUTTER[2] 2 (*a*).

spatterdash ['spætədæʃ], *s. A:* jambière *f*, houseau *m*, guêtre *f.*

spatterdock ['spætədɔk], *s. Bot:* nénuphar *m* (des étangs); lis *m* jaune.

spatterwork ['spætəwɔ:k], *s.* peinture *f* à la bruine.

spatula ['spætjulə], *s. Pharm: Surg: etc:* spatule *f*; *Dom.Ec:* spatule, gâche *f.*

spatular ['spætjulər], *a.* spatulé.

spatulate ['spætjuleit], *a. Nat.Hist:* spatulé; **s. fingers,** doigts *m* en spatule.

spatule ['spætju:l], *s. Orn:* œil *m* (de plume).

spatuliform [spæ'tju:lifɔ:m], *a. Nat.Hist:* spatuliforme.

spavin ['spævin], *s. Vet:* éparvin *m.*

spavined ['spævind], *a. Vet:* atteint d'éparvin; boiteux.

spawn[1] [spɔ:n], *s.* **1.** frai *m*; œufs *mpl* (de poisson, etc.); **frog's s.,** frai de grenouille. **2.** *F:* (*a*) progéniture *f*; rejeton *m*; (*b*) *A:* produit *m*, résultat *m*. **3. mushroom s.,** blanc *m* de champignon.

spawn[2]. **1.** *v.i.* (*a*) (*of fish, etc.*) frayer; (*b*) *F:* (*of pers.*) se multiplier; (*c*) **to s. from sth.,** naître de qch.; (*d*) **waters spawning with fish,** eaux *f* qui regorgent de poisson, où le poisson abonde. **2.** *v.tr.* (*a*) (*of fish, frog, etc.*) déposer (son frai, ses œufs); (*b*) *F:* engendrer, produire, donner naissance à (qch.).

spawner ['spɔ:nər], *s.* poisson *m* qui fraye.

spawning ['spɔ:niŋ], *s.* (le moment du) frai *m*; **s. time, season,** fraie *f*, fraieson *f*; (*of salmon*) entraison; **s. ground,** frayère *f.*

spay [spei], *v.tr. Vet:* châtrer (une femelle); **spayed ewe,** moutonne *f.*

spaying ['speiiŋ], *s. Vet:* castration *f* (d'une femelle).

speak [spi:k], *v.* (*p.t.* **spoke** [spouk], *A:* **spake** [speik]; *p.p.* **spoken** ['spouk(ə)n])

I. *v.i.* **1.** (*a*) parler; **man is an animal that speaks,** l'homme est un animal qui parle, qui a le don de la parole; **without speaking,** sans parler; sans rien dire; (*b*) **to s. to s.o.,** (i) parler à qn; adresser la parole à qn; s'adresser à qn; (ii) réprimander qn; **to s. to s.o. about sth.,** parler à qn de qch.; **I'll s. to him about it,** je lui en toucherai un mot; **to s. to s.o. again,** reparler à qn; **to s. to oneself,** se parler à soi-même; **to s. rudely to s.o.,** parler à qn d'une manière grossière; **is that the way she speaks to you?** elle le prend sur ce ton! **I know him to s. to,** nous nous disons bonjour; **they s. when they meet,** ils se parlent quand ils se rencontrent; **speaking for myself,** pour ma part; quant à moi; en ce qui me concerne; *F:* **s. for yourself!** parle pour toi! **honestly speaking,** franchement; **roughly speaking,** approximativement; **so to s.,** pour ainsi dire; **he is so to s. one of the family,** il est comme qui dirait de la famille; *Tp:* **who's speaking?** c'est de la part de qui? qui est à l'appareil? **Mr. Thomas?—yes, speaking,** M. Thomas?—lui-même; (*c*) **the facts s. for themselves,** ces faits n'ont pas besoin de commentaires, se passent de commentaires, parlent d'eux-mêmes; **this discovery speaks for itself,** cette découverte se recommande par elle-même; inutile d'insister sur, de souligner, l'importance de cette découverte; **that speaks well for his courage,** cela fait honneur à son courage; (*d*) (*of gun, organ, etc.*) parler; **suddenly the guns spoke,** tout à coup le canon parla, se fit entendre; *Mus:* **the cor anglais speaks a fifth lower than the oboe,** le cor anglais sonne une quinte plus bas que le hautbois; (*e*) *Ven:* (of dog) donner de la voix; (*f*) (*of deaf-mute, etc.*) **to s. by signs,** parler par gestes. **2.** faire un discours; prendre la parole; **he spoke on the subject of . . .,** il a parlé de . . .; il a traité de . . .; **Mr. X rose to s.,** M. X a demandé la parole; **to have the right to s.,** avoir le droit de se faire entendre; avoir droit à la parole.

II. *v.tr.* **1.** (*a*) dire (un mot, ses pensées); **to s. the truth,** dire la vérité; **when he spoke these words,** lorsqu'il prononça ces paroles; **not to s. a word,** ne pas dire, ne pas prononcer, un mot; **he has never spoken a word to me,** il ne m'a jamais adressé la parole; **he has never spoken a word to me about it,** il ne m'en a jamais touché un mot; **there had been hardly a word spoken between him and Louise,** Louise et lui avaient à peine échangé deux paroles; *B:* **that it might be fulfilled which was spoken by the prophet,** ainsi devait s'accomplir l'oracle du prophète; (*b*) **to s. one's mind,** dire sa pensée; dire sa façon de penser; dire ce qu'on pense; parler sans contrainte; parler à sentiments ouverts; avoir son franc parler; **let me s. my mind,** laissez-moi vous dire franchement ce que je pense; **to s. one's mind to s.o.,** parler franchement à qn; *F:* **to s. one's piece,** faire son petit discours; dire ce qu'on a à dire. **2.** indiquer, accuser (qch.); témoigner de (qch.); **eyes that s. affection,** yeux *m* qui témoignent de l'amitié. **3.** parler (une langue); **do you s. French?** parlez-vous français? **he speaks French fairly well,** il parle passablement le français; **English is spoken everywhere,** l'anglais se parle partout; *P.N:* **English spoken,** on parle anglais. **4.** (*a*) *A:* s'adresser à (qn); (*b*) *Nau:* parler à, héler, arraisonner (un navire); **date when a ship was last spoken,** date à laquelle un navire a été signalé la dernière fois.

III. (*compound verbs*) **1. speak for,** *v.i.* (*a*) **to s. for s.o.,** (i) parler, (ii) plaider, pour qn; (*b*) retenir, réserver (des places, etc.).

2. speak of, *v.i.* (*a*) parler de (qch.); **to s. of sth. again,** reparler de qch.; **speaking of . . .,** à propos de . . .; **she has hardly any voice to s. of,** elle n'a pour ainsi dire pas de voix; **it's nothing to s. of,** ce n'est rien; cela ne vaut pas la peine d'en parler; **to s. well, highly, of s.o., sth.,** dire du bien, beaucoup de bien, de qn; parler en bons termes, en termes très flatteurs, élogieux, de qn; vanter qch.; **he is well spoken of,** el a une bonne réputation; on en dit beaucoup de bien; **to s. ill of s.o.,** dire du mal de qn; parler en mauvais termes, mal parler, de qn; médire de qn; **to s. disparagingly of s.o.,** tenir des propos désobligeants pour qn; (*b*) être significatif de (qch.); **his pinched features spoke of privation,** ses traits hâves trahissaient les privations; **everything in the house speaks of good taste,** tout dans la maison indique un goût raffiné.

3. speak out, *v.i.* (*a*) parler fort, à haute voix; (*b*) parler franchement.

4. speak up, *v.i.* (*a*) parler plus fort; parler plus haut; (*b*) **to s. up for s.o.,** parler hautement pour qn; parler en faveur de qn.

speakeasy ['spi:ki:zi], *s. U.S: F: A:* débit, bar, clandestin.

speaker ['spi:kər], *s.* **1.** parleur, -euse; (*in dialogue*) interlocuteur, -trice; **the s. was his own son,** celui qui lui parlait, qui avait parlé, était son propre fils; **the first, last, s.,** celui qui a parlé le premier, le dernier; **I'm a plain s.,** j'appelle les choses par leur nom. **2.** (*in public*) orateur *m*; **to be a fluent, a good, an easy, s.,** avoir la parole facile, avoir le don de la parole; **to be the s. (of a deputation, etc.),** porter la parole. **3.** *Parl:* **the S.** = le Président (des Communes); **Mr. S.** = Monsieur le Président. **4.** haut-parleur *m*, *pl.* haut-parleurs.

speaking[1] ['spi:kiŋ], *a.* **1.** (*a*) (*of doll, etc.*) parlant; (*b*) (*of eyes, etc.*) expressif, éloquent; **a s. likeness,** un portrait parlant, vivant. **2.** (*with adj. or adv. prefixed, e.g.*) **slow-s.,** qui a la parole lente; **English-s.,** de langue anglaise, anglophone; **French-s.,** francophone.

speaking[2], *s.* **1.** (*a*) parler *m*, discours *m*, parole *f*; **plain s.,** franchise *f*, franc-parler *m*; **I'm on s. terms with him,** je le connais assez pour lui parler, pour lui dire bonjour (en passant); **I was already on s. terms with my neighbours,** j'en étais déjà à échanger quelques paroles avec mes voisins; **we're no longer on s. terms,** nous sommes brouillés; nous ne nous parlons plus; (*b*) **s. tube,** tube *m* acoustique, *Nau: etc:* porte-voix *m inv*; *Av:* aviophone *m*; *Mus:* **s. front,** montre parlante (d'un orgue). **2. public s.,** l'art *m* oratoire; *F:* **unaccustomed as I am to public s.,** n'ayant pas l'habitude de parler en public.

spear[1] ['spiər], *s.* **1.** lance *f*; *Ven:* épieu *m*; (*for throwing*) javelot *m*, javeline *f*; *A:* **the s. side (of the family),** l'ascendance *f* et la descendance mâle; le côté paternel. **2.** *Fish:* foène *f*, fouine *f*, trident *m*; **(underwater) s. fishing,** pêche, chasse (sous-marine) au harpon. **3.** *A:* pointe *f* de chevaux de frise. **4.** *A:* (homme armé d'une) lance. **5.** *Petr:* harpon à câble; **centre s.,** harpon.

spear[2], *v.tr.* (*a*) frapper, (trans)percer, tuer, (qn) d'un coup de lance, (une bête) d'un coup d'épieu; (*b*) prendre (un poisson) à la foène, à la fouine; foéner, harponner (un poisson); (*c*) piquer (une olive avec un bâtonnet, un morceau de viande avec une fourchette).

spear[3], *s.* brin *m* (d'herbe); jet *m*, tige *f* (d'osier).

spear[4], *s. Min:* tige *f*, gaule *f*, verge *f* (de pompe).

speargrass ['spiəgra:s], *s. Bot:* **1.** chiendent *m*. **2.** *U.S:* pâturin *m.*

spearhead[1] ['spiəhed], *s.* (*a*) fer *m*, pointe *f*, de lance; (*b*) *Mil:* pointe *f*; **to launch a s. against . . .,** pousser une pointe sur . . ..

spearhead[2], *v.tr.* (*a*) *Mil:* **airborne troops spearheaded the crossing of the river,** les troupes aéroportées ont forcé les premières le passage du fleuve; (*b*) **to s. a movement,** être à l'avant-garde d'un mouvement.

spearman, *pl.* **-men** ['spiəmən], *s.m. Hist:* homme armé d'une lance; lance *f.*

spearmint ['spiəmint], *s. Bot:* menthe verte; baume vert.

spearwort ['spiəwɔ:t], *s. Bot:* renoncule *f*, douve *f*; **great s.,** renoncule langue; grande douve; **lesser s.,** petite douve; renoncule flammule; flammette *f.*

spec [spek], *s. F:* = SPECULATION 2.

special ['speʃ(ə)l]. **1.** *a.* (*a*) spécial, -aux, particulier (**to,** à); *Journ:* **our s. correspondent,** notre envoyé spécial; **to make a s. study of French,** se spécialiser en français; **s. mission,** mission particulière; **s. feature, characteristic,** particularité *f*; **he thinks he's in a s. category,** il croit à une particularité d'essence de sa personne; **s. tool,** outil façonné exprès; *Com:* **s. price,** prix *m* de faveur; *Post: U.S:* **s. delivery,** envoi *m* par exprès; *Jur:* **s. case,** affaire *f* où les parties viennent devant le tribunal pour faire statuer sur un point de droit; *F:* **I'm a s. case,** je suis un cas d'espèce; (*b*) particulier; **to take s. care over sth.,** apporter des soins particuliers à qch., un soin extrême à qch.; **s. friend,** ami intime; **I've nothing s. to tell you,** je n'ai rien de particulier à vous dire; **for s. occasions,** pour les jours de fête; (*c*) *Com: Ind:* (article *m*) hors série; *Journ:* **s. events,** reportage *m* hors série; (*d*) *Cin: T.V: etc:* **s. effects,** trucages *m*. **2.** (*a*) *a.* & *s.* **s. (constable),** citoyen assermenté faisant fonction d'agent de police; (*b*) *s.* train spécial; (*c*) *s.* édition spéciale (d'un journal); (*d*) *s.* **today's s.,** plat *m* du jour.

specialism ['speʃəlizm], *s.* spécialisme *m*, spécialisation *f*; *esp. U.S: Sch:* (*of student*) **to choose sth. as one's s.,** faire sa spécialité de qch.; se spécialiser dans, en, qch.

specialist ['speʃəlist], *s.* spécialiste *mf*; **to become a s. in electronics, an electronics s.,** se spécialiser dans l'électronique; **to consult a s.,** consulter un spécialiste; *Med:* **heart s.,** cardiologue *mf.*

specialistic [speʃə'listik], *a.* (esprit, etc.) spécialiste.

speciality [speʃi'æliti], *s.* **1.** spécialité *f* (d'un magasin, etc.); objet spécial d'étude, de recherches (d'une fabrique, etc.); **to make a s. of sth.,** se faire une spécialité de qch.; **that's my s.,** ça c'est mon fort, c'est ma spécialité. **2.** qualité particulière; particularité *f*, caractéristique *f*. **3.** *Jur:* = SPECIALTY 1.

specialization [speʃəlai'zeiʃ(ə)n], *s.* (*a*) spécialisation *f*; (*b*) *Biol:* adaptation spéciale (d'un organe, d'une espèce).

specialize ['speʃəlaiz]. **1.** *v.tr.* (*a*) *A:* (*specify*) particulariser, spécialiser; (*b*) désigner, adapter, à un but spécial; **to s. one's studies,** se spécialiser dans un groupe d'études. **2.** *v.i.* (*a*) se spécialiser; **to s. in historical research,** se spécialiser dans les recherches historiques; *Com:* **to s. in secondhand cars,** se spécialiser dans la vente des voitures d'occasion; *Iron:* **she specializes in that sort of blunder,** elle est spécialiste de ce genre de gaffes; (*b*) *Biol:* se différencier.

specializing ['speʃəlaiziŋ], *s.* spécialisation *f.*

specially ['speʃəli], *adv.* spécialement, particulièrement; surtout; **I went there s. to see them,** j'y ai été spécialement pour les voir, dans le seul but de les voir; **be s. careful to . . .,** ayez surtout soin de . . .; **it's not s. good,** ce n'est pas particulièrement bon.

specialty ['speʃəlti], *s.* **1.** *Jur:* contrat formel sous seing privé. **2.** *esp. NAm:* = SPECIALITY 1.

speciation [spi:ʃi'eiʃ(ə)n], *s. Biol:* spéciation *f.*

specie ['spi:ʃi:], *s.* (*no pl.*) espèces monnayées; numéraire *m*; **to pay in s.,** payer en espèces; *Pol.Ec:* **s. point,** point *m* de l'or.

species ['spi:ʃi:z], *s. inv.* **1.** (*a*) *Nat.Hist:* espèce *f*; **the human s.,** l'espèce humaine; **the horse s.,** la race chevaline; **the origin of s.,** l'origine *f* des espèces; (*b*)

For: essence *f*. 2. espèce, sorte *f*, genre *m*; **weapons of various s., various s. of weapons,** armes *f* de différentes espèces. 3. *Theol:* **(Eucharistic) s.,** espèces.

specifiable [spesi'faiəbl], *a.* déterminable, distinguable; qu'on peut préciser, spécifier.

specific [spi'sifik]. 1. *a.* (*a*) spécifique; **s. cause, s. distinction,** cause *f*, distinction *f*, spécifique; *Ph:* **s. weight, s. gravity,** poids *m* spécifique; **mean s. weight,** densité moyenne; *El:* **s. resistance,** résistance *f* spécifique; **one of his s. beliefs,** une de ses croyances particulières; *Jur:* **in each s. case,** dans chaque cas d'espèce; **s. legatee,** légataire à titre particulier; **s. performance,** exécution intégrale d'un contrat (sans alternative de paiement de dommages-intérêts); *Nat.Hist:* **s. name,** nom *m* spécifique; **s. epithet,** désinence *f* spécifique; (*b*) (*of statement, etc.*) précis; (*of order, etc.*) explicite; **s. aim,** but déterminé. 2. *s.* (*a*) *Med:* spécifique *m* (**for,** contre); (*b*) *U.S: Ind:* **specifics,** description précise; caractéristiques *f*.

specifically [spi'sifik(ə)li], *adv.* 1. spécifiquement. 2. précisément; avec précision.

specification [spesifi'keiʃ(ə)n], *s.* 1. spécification *f* (des détails, etc.). 2. (*a*) description précise; devis descriptif; *Civ.E:* (*of work to be carried out*) descriptif *m*; **patent s., specifications of a patent,** mémoire descriptif d'une invention; description de brevet; *Mec.E:* **type specifications,** clauses *f* techniques; **specifications of a car,** caractéristiques *f* d'une voiture; **specifications of work to be done,** prescriptions *f* des travaux à exécuter; **specifications of a contract,** stipulations *f* d'un contrat; *Ind:* **acceptance s.,** prescription pour la réception; (*b*) *Const: Ind:* **specifications,** cahier *m* des charges; (*c*) *Jur:* **s. of charge,** chef *m* d'accusation.

specificity [spesi'fisiti], *s. Med:* spécificité *f* (d'un médicament, etc.).

specify ['spesifai], *v.tr.* spécifier, désigner, déterminer; préciser (des conditions, etc.); **it is specified in the agreement,** cela est spécifié dans le contrat; **specified load,** charge prévue, prescrite; **unless otherwise specified,** sauf indication contraire; **fittings not specified in the plans,** agencements dont le devis ne porte pas mention.

specifying ['spesifaiiŋ], *a.* spécificatif.

specimen ['spesimin], *s.* (*a*) spécimen *m* (botanique, etc.); **s. of Gothic architecture,** spécimen d'architecture gothique; **the finest specimens in his collection,** les plus belles pièces de sa collection; *Fish:* **s. fish,** poisson *m* digne de figurer dans un musée; *Ent:* **s. case,** insectier *m*; (*b*) spécimen, exemple *m*, échantillon *m*, exemplaire *m* (de qch.); **this is a s. of what I can do,** c'est un exemple, un échantillon, de ce que je suis capable de faire; **s. number of a publication,** numéro *m* spécimen d'une publication; **s. page,** page *f* spécimen; page type; *Publ:* **s. copy,** livre *m* à l'examen; *Med:* **to take a s. of s.o.'s blood, a blood s. from s.o.,** prélever une goutte de sang à qn; *F:* **a s.,** un échantillon d'urine; (*c*) *F:* (*of pers.*) **odd s.,** drôle *m* de type; **what a s.!** quel type!

speciosity [spi:ʃi'ɔsiti], *s.* = SPECIOUSNESS.

specious ['spi:ʃəs], *a.* (*of appearance*) spécieux, trompeur; (*of argument, etc.*) captieux, spécieux.

speciously ['spi:ʃəsli], *adv.* spécieusement, trompeusement.

speciousness ['spi:ʃəsnis], *s.* spéciosité *f*; apparence trompeuse.

speck[1] [spek], *s.* 1. petite tache; point *m*, goutte *f* (de couleur, d'encre); mouche *f*, moucheture *f*, tacheture *f*; *Med:* **floating specks (in front of the eyes),** mouches volantes. 2. (*a*) grain *m*, atome *m* (de poussière); grumeau *m* (de sel); **the ship was only a s. on the horizon,** le navire n'était qu'un point noir à l'horizon; *Paperm:* **specks,** poivres *m* (dans la feuille); points noirs; (*b*) brin *m* (de consolation, etc.); **not a s. of generosity,** pas un brin, pas pour deux sous, de générosité. 3. (*a*) défaut *m*; souillure *f*, tache (sur le caractère de qn); (*b*) tavelure *f* (sur un fruit).

speck[2], *v.tr.* tacheter, moucheter.

speck[3], *s. Dial:* (*U.S: & S. Africa*) 1. viande grasse; lard *m*. 2. graisse *f*, lard (de baleine, d'hippopotame).

specked [spekt], *a.* tacheté, moucheté; (fruit) tavelé.

speckle[1] ['spekl], *s.* petite tache; point *m* (de couleur); moucheture *f*, tacheture *f*; (*on bird's feathers*) **speckles,** madrures *f*, mailles *f*; tiqueture *f*.

speckle[2], *v.tr.* tacheter, moucheter; diaprer; (*of flowers*) émailler (les prés).

speckled ['spekld], *a.* tacheté, moucheté, tiqueté, truité; (*of plumage*) grivelé; (*of hen*) bariolé; **bird s. with white,** oiseau tacheté de gouttes blanches.

speckling ['spekliŋ], *s.* tacheture *f*, moucheture *f*.

specksioneer [spekʃə'niər], *s.m.* chef baleinier.

specs [speks], *s.pl. F:* lunettes *f*.

spectacle ['spektəkl], *s.* 1. spectacle *m*; **harrowing s.,** spectacle navrant; **it was a magnificent s.,** c'était un coup d'œil superbe; **to make a s. of oneself,** se donner en spectacle. 2. **spectacles,** (i) lunettes *f*; (ii) *Rail:* lunettes (d'une cabine de locomotive); **to put on one's spectacles,** mettre, chausser, ses lunettes; **s. case,** étui *m* à lunettes.

spectacled ['spektəkld], *a.* 1. qui porte des lunettes; portant lunettes; à lunettes. 2. *Z:* **s. bear,** ours *m* à lunettes; *Rept:* **s. cobra,** serpent *m* à lunettes; *Orn:* **s. warbler,** fauvette *f* à lunettes.

spectacular [spek'tækjulər]. 1. *a.* spectaculaire; **s. play,** pièce *f* à spectacle; pièce à décors; **s. rocks,** rochers impressionnants; **s. demonstration,** manifestation théâtrale; manifestation dans le but d'impressionner, d'épater, le public. 2. *a. & s. Cin:* **s. (film),** superproduction *f*.

spectator [spek'teitər], *s.* spectateur, -trice; assistant, -ante; **the spectators,** l'assistance *f*; **I had been a s. of the whole affair,** j'avais assisté à toute l'affaire.

spectral ['spektrəl], *a.* (*a*) *Ph: Ch:* **s. analysis,** analyse spectrale; **s. band,** bande spectrale, bande du spectre; **s. colours,** couleurs spectrales; **s. composition,** composition spectrale; **s. density,** densité spectrale; **s. filter,** filtre spectral; **s. line,** raie spectrale, raie du spectre; **s. range,** région spectrale; **s. reflectivity,** réflectance spectrale; **s. selectivity,** sélectivité spectrale; **s. sensitivity,** sensibilité spectrale; **s. source,** source spectrale; (*b*) spectral; fantomal, -aux, -als; fantomatique; *Z:* **s. bat, lemur = spectre bat, spectre lemur,** *q.v. under* SPECTRE.

spectre ['spektər], *s.* (*a*) spectre *m*, fantôme *m*, apparition *f*; *Meteor:* **Brocken s.,** spectre du Brocken; **the s. of war,** le spectre de la guerre; (*b*) *Z:* **s. bat,** vampire *m* spectre; **s. lemur,** tarsier *m* aux mains rousses; *Ent:* **s. insect,** phasmidé *m*; *Crust:* **s. shrimp,** caprelle *f*.

spectro- ['spektrou, spek'trɔ], *comb.fm.* spectro-.

spectro-analysis [spektrouə'nælisis], *s.* analyse spectrale.

spectrochemical [spektrou'kemikl], *a.* spectrochimique; **s. analysis,** analyse *f* spectrochimique.

spectrochemistry [spektrou'kemistri], *s.* spectrochimie *f*.

spectrocolorimetry [spektroukʌlə'rimitri], *s.* spectrocolorimétrie *f*.

spectrogram ['spektrougræm], *s. Ph: Opt:* spectrogramme *m*; **mass s.,** spectrogramme de masse; **(sound) s.,** spectrogramme acoustique.

spectrograph ['spektrougræf], *s. Ph:* spectrographe *m*; **diffraction s.,** spectrographe à diffraction; **electron s.,** spectrographe électronique; **lens s.,** spectrographe à lentilles; **magnetic s.,** spectrographe magnétique; **mass s.,** spectrographe de masse; **nuclear-resonance s.,** spectrographe à résonance nucléaire; **pulse s.,** spectrographe à impulsions; **quartz s.,** spectrographe à quartz; **velocity s.,** spectrographe de vitesse.

spectrographer [spek'trɔgrəfər], *s.* spectroscopiste *mf*.

spectrographic [spektrou'græfik], *a.* spectrographique.

spectrography [spek'trɔgrəfi], *s. Ph:* spectrographie *f*; **absorption s.,** spectrographie d'absorption; **mass s.,** spectrographie de masse; **emission s.,** spectrographie d'émission.

spectroheliogram [spektrou'hi:liougræm], *s. Astr:* spectrohéliogramme *m*.

spectroheliograph [spektrou'hi:liougræf], *s. Astr:* spectrohéliographe *m*.

spectrohelioscope [spektrou'hi:liouskoup], *s. Astr:* spectrohélioscope *m*.

spectrology [spek'trɔlədʒi], *s.* étude *f* des fantômes.

spectrometer [spek'trɔmitər], *s. Ph:* spectromètre *m*; **neutron s.,** spectromètre neutronique; **nuclear s.,** spectromètre nucléaire; **alpha-ray s.,** spectromètre (de rayons) alpha; **beta-ray s.,** spectromètre (de rayons) bêta; **gamma-ray s.,** spectromètre (de rayons) gamma; **X-ray s.,** spectromètre à rayons X; **radiation s.,** spectromètre de rayonnement; **optical s.,** spectromètre optique; **lens s.,** spectromètre à lentilles; **double-focusing s.,** spectromètre à double focalisation; **double-coincidence, single-coincidence, s.,** spectromètre à coïncidence double, de coïncidence simple; **crystal s.,** spectromètre à cristal; **magnetic s.,** spectromètre magnétique; **scintillation s.,** spectromètre à scintillation; **versatile s.,** spectromètre à usages variés; **mass s.,** spectromètre de masse.

spectrometric [spektrou'metrik], *a.* spectrométrique.

spectrometry [spek'trɔmitri], *s. Ph:* spectrométrie *f*; **neutron s.,** spectrométrie neutronique; **coincidence s.,** spectrométrie à, de, coïncidences; **single-channel, two-channel, coincidence s.,** spectrométrie de coïncidences à canal unique, à deux canaux; **mass s.,** spectrométrie de masse.

spectrophotography [spektroufə'tɔgrəfi], *s.* spectrophotographie *f*.

spectrophotometer [spektroufə'tɔmitər], *s.* spectrophotomètre *m*; **recording s.,** spectrophotomètre enregistreur.

spectrophotometry [spektroufə'tɔmitri], *s.* spectrophotométrie *f*; photométrie spectrale.

spectroradiometer [spektroureidi'ɔmitər], *s. Ph:* spectroradiomètre *m*.

spectroradiometry [spektroureidi'ɔmitri], *s. Ph:* spectroradiométrie *f*.

spectroscope ['spektrəskoup], *s. Ph:* spectroscope *m*; **direct-vision s.,** spectroscope à vision directe; **grating s.,** spectroscope à réseau; **prism s.,** spectroscope à prisme; **semicircular s.,** spectroscope semicirculaire.

spectroscopic(al) [spektrou'skɔpik(l)], *a. Ph:* spectroscopique; **s. analysis,** analyse spectroscopique, analyse spectrale; **s. notation,** notation spectroscopique; *Astr:* **s. parallax,** parallaxe *f* spectroscopique; *Ch: etc:* **s. test,** essai spectroscopique.

spectroscopist [spek'trɔskəpist], *s.* spectroscopiste *mf*.

spectroscopy [spek'trɔskəpi], *s. Ph:* spectroscopie *f*; **beta, gamma, s.,** spectroscopie bêta, gamma; **X-ray s.,** spectroscopie par rayons X; **microwave s.,** spectroscopie de micro-ondes; **electron s.,** spectroscopie électronique; **neutron s.,** spectroscopie neutronique; **nuclear s.,** spectroscopie nucléaire.

spectrum, *pl.* **-tra** ['spektrəm, -trə], *s. Ph: etc:* spectre *m*; **the colours of the s.,** les couleurs spectrales, du spectre; (*a*) **solar s.,** spectre solaire; **prismatic s.,** spectre prismatique; **band s.,** spectre de bandes; **s. band,** bande *f* du spectre; **absorption s.,** spectre d'absorption; **molecular s.,** spectre de molécules, moléculaire; **neutron s.,** spectre de neutrons, neutronique; **nuclear s.,** spectre du noyau, nucléaire; **ion s.,** spectre d'ions, ionique; **electron s.,** spectre électronique; **alpha-particle s.,** spectre (de particules) alpha; **beta-ray s.,** spectre (de rayons) bêta; **gamma-ray s.,** spectre (de rayons) gamma; **X-ray s.,** spectre de rayons X, spectre radiologique; **actinic s.,** spectre actinique; **radiation s.,** spectre de rayonnement; **microwave s.,** spectre de micro-ondes; **line s.,** spectre de raies; **arc s.,** spectre d'arc; **channelled, fluted, s.,** spectre cannelé; **continuous, discontinuous, s.,** spectre continu, discontinu; **diffraction s.,** spectre de diffraction; **diffuse s.,** spectre diffus; **fission s.,** spectre de fission; **emission s.,** spectre d'émission; **mass s.,** spectre de masse; **s. analysis,** analyse spectrale; **s. analyser,** appareil *m* d'analyse spectrale; analyseur *m* de spectre; **electronic direct-reading s. analyser,** spectrolecteur *m* électronique; **s. locus,** courbe *f* de spectre; (*b*) **magnetic s.,** spectre magnétique; **aerodynamic s.,** spectre aérodynamique; **hydrodynamic s.,** spectre hydrodynamique; (*c*) *Ch:* **antibacterial s.,** spectre antibactérien; (*d*) **a wide s. of political opinions,** toute une gamme d'opinions politiques.

specular ['spekjulər], *a.* 1. (minéral *m*) spéculaire; **s. iron ore,** fer *m* spéculaire; **s. pig(-iron),** fonte miroitante. 2. *Opt: Phot:* **s. density,** densité *f* par réflexion.

specularia [spekju'lɛəriə], *s. Bot:* spéculaire *f*.

speculate ['spekjuleit], *v.i.* 1. **to s. on, about, sth.,** (i) spéculer, méditer, sur qch.; (ii) faire des conjectures sur qch. 2. *Fin:* spéculer; **to s. on the Stock Exchange,** spéculer, jouer, à la Bourse; agioter; **to s. in rubber,** spéculer, jouer, sur le caoutchouc; **to s. for a fall,** jouer, miser, à la baisse.

speculating ['spekjuleitiŋ], *s.* spéculation *f*; *St.Exch:* **s. in contangoes,** jeu *m* sur les reports.

speculation [spekju'leiʃ(ə)n], *s.* 1. (*a*) spéculation *f*, méditation *f* (**on,** sur); contemplation *f* (**on,** de); (*b*) conjecture *f*; **to be the subject of much s.,** donner lieu à bien des conjectures; **it was pure s. on his part,** c'était (une) pure conjecture de sa part. 2. (*a*) *Fin:* spéculation; *St.Exch:* agio *m*; **to buy sth. on s.,** acheter qch.; (i) par spéculation, à titre de spéculation, pour faire une spéculation, (ii) (*F:* **on spec**) à tout hasard; (*b*) entreprise spéculative; *St.Exch:* coup *m* de Bourse; **to buy sth. as a s.,** acheter qch. en vue de l'avenir, à titre spéculatif, à titre de spéculation; **to make a good, a bad, s.,** faire une bonne, une mauvaise, affaire.

speculative ['spekjulətiv], *a.* 1. (*a*) spéculatif, contemplatif, méditatif; **s. philosophy,** philosophie inquisitive, spéculative; (*b*) conjectural, -aux; théorique; **these are merely s. assumptions,** ce sont là de pures hypothèses, de pures conjectures. 2. *Fin:* spéculatif; fait par spéculation; **s. tendencies,** penchant *m* à la spéculation; **s. purchases,** achats spéculatifs.

speculatively ['spekjulətivli], *adv.* 1. (*a*) spéculativement; (*b*) d'un air méditatif. 2. *Fin:* par spéculation.

speculator ['spekjuleitər], *s.* **1.** spéculatif, -ive; penseur *m.* **2.** spéculateur, -trice; *St.Exch:* joueur, -euse, à la Bourse; agioteur *m*; **small s.,** boursicotier, -ière; **land bought by speculators,** terrains achetés par des spéculateurs.

speculum, *pl.* **-ums, -a** ['spekjuləm, -əmz, -ə], *s.* **1.** *Med:* speculum *m*, spéculum *m*; **ear s.,** otoscope *m*; **anal s.,** anuscope *m.* **2.** miroir *m* (d'un télescope, etc.). **3.** (*a*) miroir (sur l'aile d'un oiseau); (*b*) *Ent:* ocelle *m.* **4. s. (metal),** métal *m* pour miroirs.

speech [spi:tʃ], *s.* **1.** (*a*) **(faculty of) s., to lose the power of s.,** perdre la parole; **if animals had the power of s.,** si les animaux pouvaient parler; **fear deprived him of s.,** la peur l'a rendu muet; (*b*) **(manner of) s.,** articulation *f*; élocution *f*; façon *f* de parler, de s'exprimer; **to be slow of s.,** parler lentement; avoir l'articulation lente; ne pas avoir la parole facile; **to have a ready flow of s.,** parler facilement; avoir de la faconde; **to be abrupt in one's s.,** parler d'une manière brusque; **to be slovenly in one's s.,** (i) articuler mal; (ii) parler sans faire attention à ce qu'on dit; **s. therapy,** traitement *m* orthophonique; orthophonie *f*; **s. therapist,** orthophoniste *mf.* **2.** paroles, propos *mpl*; *Lit:* **to have s. with s.o.,** parler à qn; s'entretenir avec qn; **without further s.,** sans plus rien dire. **3.** langue *f* (d'un peuple); parler *m* (d'une région, d'une classe sociale). **4.** discours *m*; allocution *f*; **to make a s.,** faire, prononcer, un discours; **s. making,** l'art *m* oratoire; discours; **s. maker,** orateur *m*; *often Pej:* faiseur, -euse, de discours; *Parl:* **the King's, Queen's S., the S. from the Throne,** le Discours du Trône, de la Couronne; *Sch:* **s. day** = distribution *f* des prix. **5.** *Gram:* **parts of s.,** parties *f* du discours; **direct, indirect, s.,** discours, style, direct, indirect; **figure of s.,** figure *f* de rhétorique. **6.** *Mus:* sonorité *f*, rapidité *f* d'attaque (d'un tuyau d'orgue).

speechifier ['spi:tʃifaiər], *s. F: Pej:* discoureur, -euse; faiseur, -euse, de discours; phraseur, -euse; péroreur, -euse.

speechify ['spi:tʃifai], *v.i. F: Pej:* discourir; pérorer; laïusser.

speechifying ['spi:tʃifaiiŋ], *s. F: Pej:* beaux discours; **after all the s.,** après tous les laïus.

speechless ['spi:tʃlis], *a.* **1.** incapable de parler; sans voix; aphone. **2.** interdit, interloqué, muet; **s. with surprise, with fright,** muet, interloqué, de surprise, d'épouvante; **emotion left him s.,** l'émotion lui a coupé la parole.

speechlessly ['spi:tʃlisli], *adv.* sans prononcer une parole, un mot; d'un air interdit.

speechlessness ['spi:tʃlisnis], *s.* **1.** mutisme *m*; **it reduced him to s.,** cela lui a coupé la parole. **2.** aphonie *f.*

speed¹ [spi:d], *s.* **1.** vitesse *f*; (*a*) vitesse, rapidité *f*; célérité *f*; *Lit:* **to make all s.,** faire diligence; se hâter; **with all possible s.,** aussi rapidement, aussi vite, que possible; **at top s., at full s.,** à toute vitesse; au plus vite; le plus rapidement possible; *F:* en quatrième vitesse; (*of runner*) à toutes jambes; (*of bird*) à tire d'aile; (*of horseman*) au grand galop, ventre à terre, à bride abattue, à franc étrier; **at the top of one's s.,** de toute sa vitesse, à fond de train; (*of motorist*) **to drive at top s.,** rouler à toute vitesse, à toute allure; **to take a bend, a corner, at s.,** prendre un virage à grande vitesse, *F:* sur les chapeaux de roues; (*b*) *Mch: Veh:* vitesse, régime *m*; **rated s.,** vitesse nominale, de régime; **synchronous s.,** vitesse synchrone; **maximum s.,** vitesse maximale, maximum; régime maximal, maximum; vitesse limite; **car with a maximum s. of 150 km an hour,** voiture avec un plafond de 150 km à l'heure; **cruising s.,** vitesse, régime, de croisière; vitesse économique; **average s.,** vitesse moyenne; **normal running s.,** vitesse de régime; **average s. including stops,** vitesse commerciale; **actual s.,** vitesse réelle; **adjustable s.,** vitesse réglable, variable; **peripheral s.,** vitesse circonférentielle, tangentielle, périphérique; **geared-down s.,** vitesse démultipliée; démultiplication *f*; **geared-up s.,** vitesse multipliée; multiplication *f*; **to gather, lose, s.,** prendre, perdre, de la vitesse; **to reduce the s.,** ralentir; *Mch:* **s. reducer,** réducteur *m* de vitesse; **to pick up s.,** (*of train, etc.*) prendre de la vitesse, gagner en vitesse; (*of car*) reprendre; *Aut:* **s. at the different gears,** rendement *m* des différentes vitesses; **s. test,** essai *m* à grande vitesse, de survitesse; **s. indicator,** indicateur *m* de vitesse; *Av:* badin *m*; *Av:* **vertical s. indicator,** variomètre *m*; *Mch:* **s. recorder,** enregistreur *m* de vitesse; **s. limit,** (i) *Mch:* vitesse maximale, maximum; régime maximal, maximum; (ii) *Aut:* limite *f* de vitesse autorisée; vitesse maximum autorisée; **to exceed the s. limit,** dépasser la vitesse autorisée; **exceeding the s. limit,** excès *m* de vitesse; **s. trap,** zone *f* de contrôle de vitesse; *F:* **s. cop,** motard *m*; *F:* **s. merchant,** chauffard *m*; fou *m* du volant; (*c*) *Nau:* **sea(-going) s., normal s.,** vitesse de route; **critical s.,** vitesse critique; (*of submarine*) **surface s.,** vitesse en surface; **submerged s.,** vitesse en plongée, en immersion; **full s. ahead! astern!** en avant, en arrière, toute! **half s. ahead!** en avant demi-vitesse! (*d*) *Av:* **ground s.,** vitesse (par rapport) au sol; **take-off s.,** vitesse de décollage; **climbing s.,** vitesse de montée; **flying s.,** vitesse de vol (en palier); **air s.,** vitesse par rapport à l'air; **equivalent, indicated, true, air s.,** vitesse équivalente, Badin, propre; **descent s.,** vitesse descensionnelle; **landing s.,** vitesse d'atterrissage; **touch-down s.,** vitesse d'impact; **s. course,** base étalonnée (pour calculer la vitesse des avions); (*e*) *Cmptr:* **calculating, computing, s.,** vitesse de calcul; **60 speed,** 60 mots par minute; *T.V:* **spot s.,** vitesse d'exploration; (*f*) *Phot:* rapidité *f* (d'une émulsion); rapidité, luminosité *f* (d'un objectif). **2.** *I.C.E:* (*gear*) vitesse; **three-s. gearbox,** boîte *f* à trois vitesses; *U.S:* **four-s. car,** voiture à quatre vitesses; *Mch:* **s. selector,** sélecteur *m*, variateur *m*, de vitesse. **3.** *A:* succès *m*, prospérité *f*; **to wish s.o. good s.,** souhaiter bonne chance à qn. **4.** *P:* amphétamine *f*, speed *m.* **5.** *esp. U.S: F:* **it's not my s.,** ce n'est pas mon genre; ça ne me plaît guère.

speed², *v.tr. & i.*

I. (*p.t. & p.p.* **sped**) **1.** *v.i.* (*a*) se hâter, se presser; aller vite; **to s. along,** foncer; **he sped down the street,** il a descendu la rue à toute vitesse; **to s. off,** partir à toute vitesse; **to s. from the mark,** prendre un bon départ; bien partir; **time was speeding by,** le temps filait; (*b*) *A:* prospérer; réussir. **2.** *v.tr.* (*a*) **to s. the parting guest,** (i) souhaiter bon voyage à un invité qui part; (ii) *F:* encourager, presser, un invité à partir plus vite; **to s. an arrow from the bow,** décocher une flèche; (*b*) *A:* **God s. you!** que Dieu vous aide, vous fasse prospérer! (*as conscious archaism*) **God s.!** = bon voyage!

II. (*p.t. & p.p.* **speeded**) **1.** *v.tr.* (*a*) régler la vitesse (d'une machine); (*b*) **to s. up the work,** activer, accélérer, le travail; **that will s. things up a bit!** comme ça nous irons plus vite! **to s. up the traffic,** accélérer la circulation. **2.** *v.i. Aut: etc:* (i) faire de la vitesse; (ii) dépasser la vitesse autorisée; **I was caught speeding,** j'ai eu une contravention (pour excès) de vitesse.

speedboat ['spi:dbout], *s.* canot *m* automobile; hors-bord *m inv.*

speeder ['spi:dər], *s. Aut: F:* chauffard *m*; fou *m* du volant.

speedily ['spi:dili], *adv.* vite, rapidement; promptement; en toute hâte.

speediness ['spi:dinis], *s.* rapidité *f*; célérité *f*; promptitude *f.*

speeding ['spi:diŋ], *s.* **1.** grande vitesse; *Aut: etc:* excès *m* de vitesse. **2.** réglage *m* de la vitesse (d'une machine). **3. s. up,** accélération *f* (d'un travail, etc.).

speedlamp, speedlight ['spi:dlæmp, -lait], *s. U.S: Phot:* lampe *f* éclair, flash *m* électronique.

speedometer [spi:'dɔmitər], *s.* (*a*) *Aut: etc:* indicateur *m* de vitesse; compteur *m* (de vitesse); **the s. showed 150,** le compteur marquait 150; (*b*) *Mch:* tachymètre *m.*

speedster ['spi:dstər], *s. esp. U.S: F:* chauffard *m*, fou *m* du volant.

speed(-)up ['spi:dʌp], *s.* accélération *f*; allure accélérée; **there will have to be a s. in production,** il va falloir accélérer la production.

speedway ['spi:dwei], *s.* **1.** *Rac:* piste *f* (d'autodrome); circuit *m* de vitesse. **2.** *NAm:* = autoroute *f.*

speedwell ['spi:dwel], *s. Bot:* véronique *f*; **common s.,** véronique mâle; thé *m* d'Europe; **germander s.,** véronique petit-chêne; **daisy-leaved s.,** véronique fausse-pâquerette; **ivy-leaved s.,** véronique à feuilles de lierre.

speedy ['spi:di], *a.* (*a*) rapide, prompt; **s. revenge,** prompte vengeance; **a s. decision,** une décision rapide; (*b*) *Sp:* (coureur, etc.) vite.

Speier ['spaiər], *Pr.n. Geog:* Spire.

speiss [spais], *s. Metall:* speiss *m.*

spel(a)ean [spe'li:ən], *a.* des cavernes; qui habite les cavernes.

spel(a)eological [spiliə'lɔdʒikl], *a.* spéléologique.

spel(a)eologist [spili'ɔlədʒist], *s.* spéléologue *mf.*

spel(a)eology [spili:'ɔlədʒi], *s.* spéléologie *f.*

spell¹ [spel], *s.* **1.** charme *m*, incantation *f*; formule *f* magique. **2.** charme, sort *m*, maléfice *m*; **to cast a s. over s.o., to put a s. on s.o., to lay s.o. under a s.,** jeter un sort à, sur, qn; ensorceler, envoûter, qn; **to break the s.,** rompre le charme; **music with a mysterious s.,** musique qui exerce un charme mystérieux; **under a spell,** sous un charme; ensorcelé, maléficié; **under the s. of s.o.'s beauty,** envoûté par la beauté de qn; **to be under the s. of s.o.'s personality,** subir l'ascendant de qn.

spell², *v.tr.* (*p.t. & p.p.* **spelt** *or* **spelled**) **1.** épeler; (*in writing*) orthographier (un mot); **he can't spell,** il ne sait pas l'orthographe; **if only you would learn to s. (correctly)!** si seulement vous appreniez l'orthographe! **to s. badly, incorrectly,** faire des fautes d'orthographe; **to s. out, s. over, sth.,** déchiffrer, lire, qch. péniblement; **do I have to s. it out for you?** faut-il que je te l'explique davantage, que je mette les points sur les i? **to s. a word backwards,** épeler, écrire, un mot à rebours; **spelt in full,** écrit en toutes lettres; **how is it spelt?** comment cela s'écrit-il? **2. what do these letters s.?** quel mot forment ces lettres? **3.** signifier; **an imprudence would s. disaster, would s. death, for you,** une imprudence vous précipiterait au désastre, à la mort; **that would s. disaster!** ce serait le désastre!

spell³, *s.* **1.** relais *m*, relève *f.* **2.** (*a*) tour *m* (de travail, etc.); **to do a s. of duty,** faire un tour de service; **to work by spells,** travailler à tour de rôle; se relayer; **to take spells at the pumps,** se relayer aux pompes; **three hours at a s.,** trois heures de suite, d'arrache-pied; trois heures tout d'un trait; (*b*) **to have another s. of prison,** retâter de la prison. **3.** (courte) période; temps *m*; (*a*) **to rest for a (short) s.,** se reposer pendant quelque temps; *Mil:* **s. of rest in billets,** période de repos; (*b*) **a long s. of cold weather,** une longue période, une longue passe, de froid; une série de jours froids; **during the cold s.,** pendant le coup de froid; **another cold s., a new s. of cold,** une reprise, une recrudescence, du froid; **we're in for a s. of wet weather,** le temps se met, va se mettre, à la pluie; (*c*) **to suffer from dizzy spells,** être sujet à des vertiges; (*d*) *Austr:* (période de) repos *m.*

spell⁴, *v.tr.* **1.** *NAm: F:* relayer, relever (qn) (dans son travail). **2.** *Austr:* laisser reposer (un cheval).

spellbinder ['spelbaindər], *s.* orateur entraînant (qui tient ses auditeurs sous le coup de son éloquence); envoûteur *m.*

spellbinding ['spelbaindiŋ], *a.* (*a*) incantatoire; (*b*) qui fascine.

spellbound ['spelbaund], *a.* (*a*) retenu par un charme; sous l'influence d'un charme; (*b*) charmé, fasciné, magnétisé; envoûté; **to listen s.,** écouter, figé sur place sous le charme de l'orateur.

speller ['spelər], *s.* **1. to be a good, a bad, s.,** être fort, faible, en orthographe; savoir, ne pas savoir, l'orthographe. **2.** syllabaire *m*, alphabet *m.*

spelling ['speliŋ], *s.* (*a*) épellation *f*; orthographe *f*; **literal s.,** orthographe d'usage; **his s. is weak,** il est faible en orthographe; **s. mistake,** faute *f* d'orthographe; **s. book,** syllabaire *m*, alphabet *m*; **s. bee,** concours (oral) d'orthographe; (*b*) **reformed s.,** néographie *f*; **s. reform,** réforme *f* orthographique; **another s. of the same word,** une autre orthographe du même mot.

spelt [spelt], *s. Agr:* épeautre *m or f.*

spelter ['speltər], *s. Com:* zinc *m*; *Metalw:* **s. solder,** zinc *m* à souder.

spelunker [spe'lʌŋkər], *s. NAm: F:* spéléologue *mf.*

spencer¹ ['spensər], *s. Cost:* spencer *m*; tricot *m.*

spencer², *s. Nau:* voile *f* goélette.

spend [spend], *v.tr.* (*p.t. & p.p.* **spent** [spent]) **1.** dépenser (de l'argent); consumer (une fortune); **to s. too much money,** faire trop de dépenses; trop dépenser d'argent; **to s. one's money on cigarettes,** dépenser son argent en cigarettes; **I prefer to s. my money on useful things,** je préfère dépenser mon argent à des choses utiles; **to s. five pounds on a knickknack,** mettre cinq livres à un bibelot; **her father has spent a great deal on her education,** son père a dépensé beaucoup pour son éducation; **to s. money on s.o.,** faire des dépenses pour qn; **he has spent all his fortune on her,** il a dissipé, a gaspillé, toute sa fortune pour elle; **I'm always spending,** j'ai toujours l'argent à la main; **he spends money like water,** l'argent lui fond entre les mains; **without spending a penny,** sans bourse délier, sans rien débourser; *F:* **to s. a penny,** aller faire une petite commission, aller faire pipi. **2. to s. time on sth., doing sth.,** consacrer, employer, du temps à (faire) qch.; **it's no use spending more than an hour on it,** c'est peine perdue d'y consacrer plus d'une heure. **3.** passer, employer (son temps); **to s. Sunday in the country,** passer le dimanche à la campagne; **how do you s. your free time?** qu'est-ce que vous faites pendant vos heures libres? **to s. one's time gardening,** passer son temps à jardiner. **4.** épuiser (ses forces); consumer (son énergie); **his anger will soon s. itself,** sa colère s'épuisera, passera, vite; **our ammunition was all spent,** nos munitions étaient épuisées; *Lit:* **the day was far spent,** le jour était écoulé; c'était tard dans la journée.

spending ['spendiŋ], *s.* dépense *f*; **s. capacity, power,** capacité *f*, pouvoir *m*, d'achat; **s. money,** argent *m* de poche; argent pour ses dépenses courantes.

spendthrift ['spendθrift], *s.* dépensier, -ière; gaspilleur, -euse; prodigue *mf*; dissipateur, -trice; **s. habits,** habitudes dépensières.

Spenserian [spen'siəriən], *a. Pros:* **S. stanza,** strophe spensérienne.

spent [spent], *a.* (*a*) épuisé (de fatigue); (*b*) **s. storm,** orage apaisé; **s. volcano,** volcan éteint; **s. bullet,** balle morte; **s. cartridge,** cartouche vide, brûlée; *Ch:* **s. acid,** acide épuisé; *Tex:* **s. bobbin,** bobine dévidée; *Mec.E:* **s. oil,** huile décomposée; *Paperm: etc:* **s. liquor,** lessive usée; (*c*) (poisson *m*) qui a lâché ses œufs; **s. herring,** hareng gai, vide.

Spergula ['spəːgjulə], *s. Bot:* spergule *f.*

Spergularia [spəgju'lɛəriə], *s. Bot:* spergulaire *f.*

sperm[1] [spəːm], *s.* (*a*) *Physiol:* sperme *m*; semence *f* (des mâles); (*b*) *Bot:* **s. nucleus,** anthérozoïde *m.*

sperm[2], *s.* **1.** *Z:* **s. (whale),** cachalot *m*; **s. whaler,** (i) (*pers.*) chasseur *m* de cachalots; (ii) (navire) cachalotier. **2.** = SPERMACETI.

spermaceti [spəːmə'seti], *s.* spermaceti *m*; blanc *m* de baleine; ambre blanc; **s. candle,** bougie diaphane; bougie de blanc de baleine; **s. oil,** huile de spermaceti.

spermaduct ['spəːmədʌkt], *s. Anat:* spermiducte *m.*

spermagone ['spəːməgoun], **spermagonium,** *pl.* **-ia** [spəːmə'gouniəm, -iə], *s. Bot:* spermogonie *f.*

Spermaphyta [spəː'mæfitə], *s.pl. Bot:* spermaphytes *fpl.*

spermary ['spəːməri], *s. Anat:* glande séminale.

spermatheca, *pl.* **-cae** [spəːmə'θiːkə, -siː], *s. Ent:* sperma(to)thèque *f.*

spermatic [spəː'mætik], *a. Anat:* (cordon, etc.) spermatique.

spermatid ['spəːmətid], *s. Biol:* spermatide *f.*

spermato- ['spəːmətou], *comb.fm.* spermato-.

spermatoblast ['spəːmətoublæst], *s. Biol:* spermatoblaste *m.*

spermatocele [spəː'mætousiːl], *s. Med:* spermatocèle *f.*

spermatocidal [spəːmətou'said(ə)l], *a.* spermaticide, spermicide.

spermatocyst [spəː'mætousist], *s. Bot:* spermatocyste *m.*

spermatocystitis [spəːmətousis'taitis], *s. Med:* spermatocystite *f.*

spermatocyte ['spəːmətousait], *s. Biol:* spermatocyte *f*; **primary, secondary, s.,** spermatocyte de premier, de deuxième, ordre.

spermatogenesis [spəːmətou'dʒenisis], *s. Biol:* spermatogénèse *f.*

spermatogonium, *pl.* **-ia** [spəːmətou'gouniəm, -iə], *s. Biol:* spermatogonie *f.*

spermatophore ['spəːmətoufɔːr], *s. Biol:* spermatophore *m.*

Spermatophyta [spəːmə'tɔfitə], *s.pl. Bot:* spermatophytes *fpl.*

spermatophyte ['spəːmətoufait], *s. Bot:* spermophore *m.*

spermatorrh(o)ea [spəːmətou'riə], *s. Med:* spermatorrhée *f.*

spermatozoid [spəːmətou'zouid], *s. Bot:* spermatozoïde *m*, anthérozoïde *m.*

spermatozoon, *pl.* **-oa** [spəːmətou'zouən, -ouə], *s. Biol:* spermatozoïde *m*; spermatule *m*; spermie *f*; zoosperme *m.*

spermicidal [spəːmi'said(ə)l], *a.* spermicide, spermaticide.

spermicide ['spəːmisaid], *s.* spermicide *m.*

spermiduct ['spəːmidʌkt], *s. Anat:* spermiducte *m.*

spermin(e) ['spəːmi(ː)n], *s. Bio-Ch:* spermine *f.*

spermiogenesis [spəːmiou'dʒenisis], *s. Biol:* spermiogénèse *f.*

spermoderm ['spəːmoudəːm], *s. Bot:* spermoderme *m.*

spermoduct ['spəːmoudʌkt], *s. Anat:* spermiducte *m.*

spermogone ['spəːmougoun], **spermogonium** *pl.* **-ia** [spəːmou'gouniəm, -iə], *s. Bot:* spermogonie *f.*

spermophile ['spəːmoufail], *s. Z:* spermophile *m*; écureuil terrestre européen.

spermophyte ['spəːmoufait], *s. Bot:* spermophore *m.*

spermophytic [spəːmou'fitik], *a. Bot:* spermophore.

spermotoxin [spəːmou'tɔksin], *s. Bio-Ch:* spermotoxine *f.*

sperrylite ['sperilait], *s. Miner:* sperrylite *f.*

spessartine, spessartite ['spesɑːtiːn, -tait], *s. Miner:* spessartine *f.*

spet [spet], *s. Ich:* spet *m.*

spew[1] [spjuː], *s. F:* vomissement *m*, vomissure *f*, vomi *m*; dégobillage *m*, dégobillis *m*, dégueulade *f*, dégueulis *m.*

spew[2], *v.tr. & i. F:* vomir; dégobiller, dégueuler; **to s. out,** rejeter (avec dégoût).

spewing ['spjuːiŋ], *s. F:* vomissement *m*; dégobillage *m.*

Sphacelaria [sfæsi'lɛəriə], *s. Algae:* sphacelaria *f.*

Sphacelariales [sfæsilɛəri'ɑːliːz], *s.pl. Algae:* sphacélariales *f.*

sphacelate[1] ['sfæsileit]. *Med:* **1.** *v.tr.* sphacéler, gangrener. **2.** *v.i.* se sphacéler, se gangrener.

sphacelate[2], *a. Med:* sphacelé.

sphacelation [sfæsi'leiʃ(ə)n], *s. Med:* sphacèle *m*; mortification *f.*

sphacelia [sfæ'siːliə], *s. Fung:* sphacélie *f.*

sphacelus ['sfæsiləs], *s. Med:* sphacèle *m*; gangrène sèche; nécrose *f.*

Sphacteria [sfæk'tiəriə], *Pr.n. A.Geog:* Sphactérie *f.*

Sphaeralcea [sfiərəl'siːə], *s. Bot:* sphæralcea *m.*

Sphaeriaceae [sfiəri'eisiiː], *s.pl. Fung:* sphaeriacées *f.*

Sphaeriidae [sfiə'raiidiː], *s.pl. Moll:* sphæriidés *m.*

sphaerite ['sfiːərait], *s. Miner:* sphærite *f.*

Sphaerium ['sfiəriəm], *s. Moll:* sphaerium *m.*

Sphaeroma [sfiə'roumə], *s. Crust:* sphérome *m.*

sphaerosiderite [sfiərou'sidərait], *s. Miner:* sphérosidérite *f.*

Sphagnaceae [sfæg'neisiiː], *spl. Moss:* sphagnacées *f.*

Sphagnales [sfæg'nɑːliːz], *s.pl. Moss:* sphagnales *f.*

sphagnum, *pl.* **-ia** ['sfægnəm, il], *s. Moss:* sphagnum *m*, sphaigne *f.*

sphalerite ['sfælərait], *s. Miner:* sphalérite *f*, blende *f.*

Sphecidae ['sfesidiː], *s.pl. Ent:* sphécidés *m.*

Sphegidae ['sfedʒidiː], *s.pl. Ent:* sphégidés *m.*

sphene [sfiːn], *s. Miner:* sphène *m.*

Spheniscidae [sfə'nisidiː], *s.pl. Orn:* sphéniscidés *m.*

Sphenisciformes [sfənisi'fɔːmiːz], *s.pl. Orn:* sphénisciformes *m.*

spheno- ['sfiːnou], *comb.fm.* sphéno-.

sphenobasilar [sfiːnou'bæzilər], **spenobasilic** [sfiːnoubə'zilik], *a. Anat:* sphéno-basilaire.

sphenodon ['sfiːnoudɔn], *s. Rept:* sphénodon *m*, hattéria *m*, hattérie *f.*

sphenoid ['sfiːnɔid], *a. & s. Anat:* sphénoïde (*m*).

sphenoidal [sfi(ː)'nɔidl], *a. Anat:* sphénoïdal, -aux, sphénoïdien; **s. fissure,** fente sphénoïdale; **s. sinus,** sinus sphénoïdal; **s. bone,** (os) sphénoïde *m.*

sphenoiditis [sfi(ː)nɔi'daitis], *s. Med:* sphénoïdite *f.*

sphenomaxillary [sfiːnoumæ'ksiləri], *a. Anat:* sphéno-maxillaire.

sphenopalatine [sfiːnou'pælətain], *a. Anat:* sphéno-palatin.

sphere [sfiər], *s.* **1.** *Astr: Mth: etc:* sphère *f*; **the celestial s.,** (i) la sphère céleste; (ii) *Lit:* les cieux, le ciel; *Astr:* **oblique, right, parallel, s.,** sphère oblique, droite, parallèle; (*round the sun*) **colour s.,** chromosphère *f.* **2.** (*a*) milieu *m*, sphère; *O:* **she belonged to another s.,** elle appartenait à un autre milieu; **to be out of one's s.,** être hors de sa sphère; se sentir dépaysé; (*b*) domaine *m*, sphère; **s. of action,** sphère d'action; **limited s.,** cadre restreint; **to extend one's s. of activity,** étendre, agrandir, élargir, sa sphère d'activité; agrandir le champ de son activité; *Com:* **your proposal lies outside the s. of our activities,** votre offre ne rentre pas dans le genre d'affaires de notre maison; **that does not come, that is not, within my s.,** cela ne rentre pas dans ma compétence; cela n'est pas de mon domaine, de mon ressort; cela est en dehors de mes pouvoirs; **in the political s.,** sur le plan politique; **s. of influence,** sphère, zone *f*, d'influence; sphère d'intérêts; **the French s. of influence in Africa,** la zone d'influence française en Afrique.

spherical ['sferik(ə)l], *a.* **1.** sphérique, en forme de sphère; *Mch:* **s. head rod,** bielle à rotule. **2. s. geometry,** géométrie sphérique; **s. angle, polygon,** angle, polygone, sphérique; *Opt:* **s. aberration,** aberration sphérique.

spherically ['sferik(ə)li], *adv.* sphériquement.

sphericity [sfe'risiti], *s.* sphéricité *f.*

spheroid ['sfiərɔid]. **1.** *s.* sphéroïde *m*; **prolate s.,** sphéroïde allongé; **oblate s.,** sphéroïde aplati. **2.** *a.* = SPHEROIDAL.

spheroidal [sfiə'rɔidl], *a.* sphéroïdal, -aux.

spheroidizing ['sfiərɔidaiziŋ], *s. Metalw:* sphéroïdisation *f*, globulation *f.*

spheromaniac [sfiərou'meiniæk], *s.* passionné, -ée, des jeux de balle, de boule; *esp.* passionné du jeu de boules.

spherometer [sfiə'rɔmitər], *s. Ph:* sphéromètre *m.*

spherular ['sferjulər], *a.* sphérulaire.

spherule ['sferjuːl], *s.* sphérule *f*; petite sphère.

spherulite ['sferjulait], *s. Geol:* sphérolithe *m.*

spherulitic [sferju'litik], *a. Geol:* (roche) sphérolithique.

Sphex [sfeks], *s. Ent:* sphex *m.*

sphincter ['sfiŋ(k)tər], *s. Anat:* sphincter *m*, orbiculaire *m.*

sphincteral ['sfiŋ(k)tər(ə)l], **sphincteric** [sfiŋ(k)'terik], *a. Anat:* spinctérien.

sphincterotomy [sfiŋ(k)tə'rɔtəmi], *s. Surg:* sphinctérotomie *f.*

Sphingidae ['sfindʒidiː], *s.pl. Ent:* sphingidés *m.*

sphinx, *pl.* **sphinges, sphinxes** [sfiŋks, 'sfindʒiːz, 'sfiŋksiz], *s.* **1.** *Myth:* sphinx *m*; **female s.,** sphinge *f.* **2.** *Z:* **s. (baboon),** papion *m.* **3.** *Ent:* sphinx; **the sphinxes,** les sphingidés *m*, les crépusculaires *m.*

sphragide ['sfrædʒaid], *s. Miner:* sphragide *f*, sphragidite *f.*

sphragistics [sfrə'dʒistiks], *s.pl.* sphragistique *f*, sigillographie *f.*

sphygmic ['sfigmik], *a. Med:* sphygmique.

sphygmo- ['sfigmou, sfig'mɔ], *comb.fm. Med:* sphygmo-.

sphygmogram ['sfigmougræm], *s. Med:* sphygmogramme *m.*

sphygmograph ['sfigmougræf], *s. Med:* sphygmographe *m.*

sphygmography [sfig'mɔgrəfi], *s. Med:* sphygmographie *f.*

sphygmomanometer [sfigmoumə'nɔmitər], *s. Med:* sphygmomanomètre *m*, tensi(o)mètre *m.*

sphygmometer [sfig'mɔmitər], *s. Med:* sphygmomètre *m*, pulsomètre *m.*

sphygmophone ['sfigməfoun], *s. Med:* sphygmophone *m.*

sphygmoscope ['sfigməskoup], *s. Med:* sphygmoscope *m.*

sphygmus ['sfigməs], *s. Physiol:* pouls *m*, pulsation *f*, battement *m.*

Sphyraena [sfai'riːnə], *s. Ich:* sphyraena *f*, sphyrène *f.*

Sphyraenidae [sfai'riːnidiː], *s.pl. Ich:* sphyrénidés *m.*

Sphyrna ['sfəːnə], *s. Ich:* sphyrna *m.*

Sphyrnidae ['sfəːnidiː], *s.pl. Ich:* sphyrnidés.

spic [spik], *s. U.S: P: Pej:* = SPI(C)K.

spica ['spaikə], *s.* **1.** *Bot:* épi *m*; *Astr:* **S. (of Virgo),** Épi de la Vierge. **2.** *Med:* **s. (bandage),** spica *m*, spic *m.*

spicate(d) ['spaikeit(id)], *a.* **1.** *Bot:* épié; en épi, à épi. **2.** spiciforme, apiciforme.

spice[1] [spais], *s.* **1.** épice *f*, aromate *m*; **mixed spice(s),** quatre épices; **s. box,** boîte aux épices; **s. cake,** gâteau aux quatre épices; *Orn:* **s. bird,** damier commun. **2.** *A:* teinte *f* (de fourberie); nuance *f* (d'hypocrisie); brin *m*, soupçon *m* (de jalousie); grain *m* (de malice). **3. to give s. to a story,** pimenter un récit; **book that lacks s.,** livre qui manque de sel; **the s. of life,** le sel, l'agrément *m*, le piquant, de la vie; **the s. of adventure,** le piment de l'aventure.

spice[2], *v.tr.* **1.** épicer (un gâteau, une boisson, etc.). **2.** épicer, pimenter, assaisonner, relever, agrémenter (un récit, etc.).

spicebush ['spaisbuʃ], *s. Bot: U.S:* benjoin odoriférant.

spiced [spaist], *a.* **1.** épicé; d'épices. **2.** aromatique, parfumé.

spicery ['spaisəri], *s.* **1.** *O:* épices *fpl.* **2.** *A:* office *f* (où étaient gardées les épices).

spiciferous [spai'sifərəs], *a. Orn:* spicifère; à aigrette en épi.

spiciform ['spaisifɔːm], *a. Bot:* spiciforme.

spicily ['spaisili], *adv.* d'une manière piquante; avec du piquant; lestement.

spiciness ['spaisinis], *s.* **1.** goût épicé. **2.** piquant *m*, sel *m* (d'un récit).

spi(c)k [spik], *s. U.S: P: Pej:* Hispano-Américain, -aine; *esp.* Mexicain, -aine.

spick and span ['spikən'spæn], *adj.phr.* reluisant de propreté; propre comme un sou nef; *F:* nickel; (*of pers.*) tiré à quatre épingles.

spicknel ['spiknəl], *s. Bot:* meum *m*; fenouil *m* des Alpes.

spicula, *pl.* **-ae** ['spaikjulə, -iː], *s.* = SPICULE.

spicular ['spaikjulər], *a. Miner: etc:* spiculaire, apiciforme.

spiculate(d) ['spaikjuleit(id)], *a. Bot:* spiculé.

spicule ['spaikju(ː)l], *s.* **1.** spicule *m* (d'éponge); épillet *m*, aiguillon *m* (de plante). **2.** (*a*) cristal *m* spiculaire, apiciforme, *pl.* cristaux; (*b*) esquille *f* (d'os). **3.** *Astr:* spicule.

spicy ['spaisi], *a.* **1.** épicé; assaisonné d'épices; (goût) relevé. **2.** aromatique, parfumé. **3.** *Lit: A:* (littoral, etc.) abondant en épices. **4.** (*of story, conversation, etc.*) (i) piquant, croustillant, croustilleux, assaisonné, relevé; (ii) salé, épicé, poivré; **s. tale,** histoire épicée, poivrée, corsée, grivoise, faisandée, salée, gaillarde, leste; **to tell s. stories,** en dire de vertes; dire, débiter, des gaudrioles. **5.** *F: A:* pimpant, chic.

spider ['spaidər], *s.* **1.** (*a*) *Arach:* araignée *f*; **web-spinning, web-making, s.,** araignée fileuse; **garden s.,** épeire *f* diadème; **house s.,** araignée domestique; tégénaire *f*; **geometric s.,** orbitèle *m*; **red s. (mite),** tétranyque *m*; *F:* tisserand *m*; **jumping s.,** saltique *f*, ménémère *m*; **bird-eating s.,** mygale *f*, aviculaire *m*; **bird s.,** t(h)éraphose *f*; **black widow s.,** veuve noire; **spider's web, s. web,** toile *f* d'araignée; **s. legged,** aux pattes longues et minces (comme une araignée); *Opt:*

etc: **s. lines, wires,** fils *m* d'araignée d'un réticule; fils réticulaires; réticule; (*b*) *Ent:* **s. ant,** mutille *f*; **s. wasp,** pompile *m*; *Crust:* **s. crab,** maïa *m*, maja *m*; araignée de mer; crabe triangulaire; *Orn:* **s. catcher, hunter,** tichodrome *m* des murailles; échelette *f*; grimpereau *m* des murailles; arachnothère *m*; *Z:* **s. monkey,** atèle *m*, arachnoïde *m*; singe-araignée *m, pl.* singes-araignées; **woolly s. monkey,** brachytèle *m*. **2.** *Nau:* (*outrigger*) potence *f*. **3.** (*a*) *Mec.E: etc:* croisillon *m*, brassure *f* (de roue); *El:* **s. armature,** induit *m* à croisillon(s); (*b*) *Metall:* (*of mould*) armature *f* (de châssis, de noyau); (*c*) **s. (wheel),** poulie *f* à chicanes; (*d*) *Aer: etc:* **s. (support),** araignée (du moteur). **4.** *A.Veh:* **s. (cart, phaeton),** spider *m*, araignée. **5.** *Ac:* spider *m* (d'un haut-parleur). **6.** *Min:* *F:* araignée. **7.** *Aut:* araignée, fixe-au-toit *m inv*. **8.** *U.S:* (*a*) *A:* poêle *f* à frire à trois pieds; (*b*) poêle à frire.

spiderflower ['spaidəflauər], *s. Bot:* tibouchina *m*.

spiderlike ['spaidəlaik], *a.* aranéen, aranéeux.

spiderman, *pl.* **-men** ['spaidəmæn, -men], *s.m.* ouvrier qui travaille au sommet des édifices; homme-mouche, *pl.* hommes-mouches.

spiderwort ['spaidəwəːt], *s. Bot:* **1.** (*a*) tradescantia *m*; éphémère *f* de Virginie; misère *f*; (*b*) commélyne *f*, commelina *f*, commelyna *f*. **2.** anthericum *m*, phalangium *m*.

spidery ['spaidəri], *a.* **1.** d'araignée; aranéen, aranéeux; qui ressemble à une araignée; **s. handwriting,** pattes *fpl* d'araignée. **2.** (grenier, etc.) infesté d'araignées.

spiegel(eisen) ['spiːg(ə)l(aiz(ə)n)], *s. Metall:* spiegel *m*; fonte *f* au manganèse, fonte spéculaire.

spiel[1] [ʃpiːl, spiːl], *s. F:* boniment *m*, baratin *m*.

spiel[2], *v. F:* **1.** *v.i.* avoir du bagou(t); baratiner, pérorer, (en) dégoiser; faire du baratin. **2.** *v.tr.* **to s. off a whole list of names,** débiter, dégoiser, toute une liste de noms.

spieler ['spiːlər], *s. F:* **1.** beau parleur; baratineur, -euse; bonimenteur *m*. **2.** *esp. Austr:* (*a*) tricheur, -euse, aux cartes; bonneteur *m*; (*b*) chevalier *m* d'industrie; escroc *m*.

spier ['spaiər], *s.* épieur, -euse (**on,** de).

spiff [spif], *s. U.S: Com: F:* prime (payée au vendeur).

spiffing ['spifiŋ], *a. F: O:* épatant.

spif(f)licate ['spiflikeit], *v.tr. F: O:* écraser, rosser, démolir (un adversaire); anéantir (l'ennemi).

spig [spig], *s. U.S: P: Pej:* = SPI(C)K.

spigelia [spai'dʒiːliə], *s. Bot:* spigélie *f*, spigelia *f*.

spignel ['spignəl], *s. Bot:* ménu *m*; fenouil *m* des Alpes.

spigot[1] ['spigət], *s.* **1.** fausset *m*, broche *f*, cannelle *f*, cannette *f* (de tonneau). **2.** (*a*) clef *f* (de robinet); (*b*) robinet *m*. **3.** (*a*) saillie *f*, ergot *m* (d'un tenon, d'un arbre de transmission, etc.); (*b*) **(pipe) s.,** bout *m* mâle (d'un tuyau); *Civ.E: etc:* **s. and socket joint,** *U.S:* **bell and s. joint,** joint, assemblage, à emboîtement, à emboîture. **4.** *Mec.E:* téton *m* de centrage.

spigot[2], *v.i.* s'encastrer (**into,** dans).

spigotty, spiggoty ['spigəti], *s. U.S: P: Pej:* = SPI(C)K.

spike[1] [spaik], *s.* **1.** pointe *f* (de fer); piquant *m* (de fil de fer barbelé, etc.); (*on railing, etc.*) lance *f*; **tent pole s.,** goujon *m* de mât; (*on woman's shoes*) **s. heel,** talon *m* aiguille. **2.** (*a*) **s. (nail),** clou *m* à large tête, à tête de diamant; broche *f*; clou barbelé; **s. drawer, extractor,** (pince *f* à) pied-de-biche *m*, pied-de-chèvre *m, pl.* pieds-de-biche, -de-chèvre; (*b*) *Civ.E:* clameau *m*, clampe *f*; (*c*) *Rail: etc:* crampon *m* (d'attache); chevillette *f*; **screw s.,** tire-fond *m inv*; (*d*) *Sp: F:* **spikes,** chaussures *fpl* à pointes; (*e*) *Artil:* clou (à enclouer). **3.** *Bot:* (*a*) épi *m*; hampe (florale); (*b*) **s. (lavender),** lavande mâle; grande lavande; spic *m*; (lavande) aspic *m*; **s. (lavender) oils,** huile, essence, de spic, d'aspic. **4.** *Ven:* dague *f* (d'un jeune cerf). **5.** *F: O:* Anglican, -ane, d'un ritualisme exagéré.

spike[2]. **1.** *v.tr.* (*a*) *Civ.E: etc:* clouer, cheviller; (*b*) armer (qch.) de pointes; **to s. a gate,** hérisser, barbeler, une grille de pointes; **spiked gate,** grille à pointes, garnie de pointes; *Sp:* **spiked shoes,** chaussures à pointes; *Bot:* **spiked flowers,** fleurs à épis, épiées; (*c*) *Artil: A:* enclouer (un canon); *Fig:* **to s. s.o.'s guns,** priver qn de ses moyens d'action; contrarier, contrecarrer, entraver, les projets de qn; **I spiked his guns for him,** je lui ai damé le pion; (*d*) *Sp:* percer le pied (d'un concurrent) (dans une course où l'on porte des chaussures à pointes); (*e*) corser (une boisson); **spiked drink,** boisson additionnée, relevée, d'alcool; (*f*) *NAm:* mettre fin à, faire avorter (une affaire); contrarier, contrecarrer, entraver (des projets); démentir, contredire (un bruit). **2.** *v.i.* (*of plants*) former des épis.

spikehorn ['spaikhɔːn], *s.* (*a*) dague *f* (d'un jeune cerf); (*b*) daguet *m*.

spikelet ['spaiklit], *s. Bot:* épillet *m*, spicule *m*.

spikenard ['spaiknaːd], *s.* **1.** *A.Toil:* nard (indien). **2.** *Bot:* **ploughman's s.,** conysa *m*, conyza *f*.

spiky ['spaiki], *a.* **1.** à pointe(s) aiguë(s); **s. hair,** cheveux hérissés. **2.** armé de pointes. **3.** *F: O:* (Anglican) qui affecte un ritualisme intransigeant.

spile[1] [spail], *s.* **1.** (*a*) cheville *f*, fausset *m*, broche *f* (d'un tonneau); (*b*) *Nau:* épite *f*, cheville. **2.** pilot *m*, pilotis *m*, pieu *m*.

spile[2], *v.tr.* (*a*) boucher (un trou) avec un fausset; (*b*) *U.S:* pratiquer un trou de fausset dans (un fût).

spiling ['spailiŋ], *s.* **1.** pilotage *m*. **2.** *coll.* pilots *mpl*, pilotis *m*, pieux *mpl*.

spilite ['spailait], *s. Miner:* spilite *f*.

spill[1] [spil], *s.* culbute *f*, chute *f* (de cheval, de voiture); **to have, take, a s.,** culbuter; (*from bicycle, horse*) *F:* ramasser une pelle, une bûche.

spill[2], *v.* (*p.t. & p.p.* **spilt, spilled** [spilt, spild])

I. *v.tr.* **1.** (*a*) répandre, renverser (un liquide, du sel); verser (du sang); **without spilling a drop,** sans laisser tomber une goutte; **a lot of ink has been spilt about this question,** on a fait couler beaucoup d'encre autour de cette question; (*b*) *U.S:* dire, débiter (des paroles). **2.** (*a*) désarçonner, démonter (un cavalier); verser (les occupants d'une voiture); **we were all spilled into the ditch,** nous avons tous été jetés dans le fossé; (*b*) *Nau:* étouffer, déventer (une voile).

II. *v.i.* (*of liquid*) se répandre; s'écouler.

spill[3], *s.* allumette *f* (de papier, de copeau); allume-feu *m inv*.

spillage ['spilidʒ], *s.* (*a*) action *f* de répandre un liquide; (*b*) quantité (de liquide) répandue.

spiller ['spilər], *s. Lit:* **s. of blood,** celui, celle, qui répand, qui a répandu, le sang.

spillikin ['spilikin], *s.* jonchet *m*; **to play (at) spillikins,** jouer aux jonchets.

spillover ['spilouvər], *s.* **1.** surplus *m*, déversement *m*, de population. **2.** *U.S:* = SPILLAGE.

spillway ['spilwei], *s. Hyd.E:* évacuateur *m* de crues; déversoir *m*.

spilth [spilθ], *s. A:* **1. s. of blood,** effusion *f* de sang. **2.** = SPILLAGE.

spin[1] [spin], *s.* **1.** (*a*) tournoiement *m*; mouvement *m* rotatoire; (mouvement de) rotation *f* (d'une balle, etc.); **s. of a top,** rotation d'une toupie; *Games:* **to put s. on a ball,** donner de l'effet à une balle; *Cr:* **s. bowler,** lanceur *m* qui donne de l'effet à la balle; *Dom.Ec:* **s. drier,** essoreuse *f* (centrifuge); **s. drying,** essorage *m*; *Mec:* **plane of s.,** plan de rotation; *Ball:* **s.-stabilized projectile,** projectile stabilisé sur sa trajectoire par rotation; (*b*) *Atom.Ph:* (*of particle*) spin *m*; **electron s.,** spin de l'électron, spin électronique; **integral, half-integral, s.,** spin entier, demi-entier; **isobaric s.,** spin isobarique; **nuclear s.,** spin du noyau, spin nucléaire; **zero s.,** spin zéro; **s. effect,** effet de spin; **s. momentum,** impulsion du spin; **s. orientation,** orientation du spin; **s. wave,** onde de spin; (*c*) *Av:* vrille *f*; **flat s.,** vrille à plat; tonneau *m*; **inverted s.,** vrille sur le dos; **outside s.,** vrille inversée; **steep s.,** vrille serrée; **to get, fall, into a s.,** se mettre en vrille; descendre, tomber, en vrille; **to recover from a s.,** faire une ressource après une vrille; *Fig:* **to be in a flat s.,** ne pas savoir où donner de la tête; être paniqué, affolé; (*d*) *Aut:* **clutch s.,** collage *m* de l'embrayage; (*e*) *Mth:* rotationnel *m* (d'un vecteur). **2.** tour *m*, promenade *f* (en voiture, etc.); **to go for a s.,** aller faire un tour, une promenade (en voiture, etc.); se balader en voiture. **3.** *Austr: F:* (i) coup *m* de chance; (ii) malchance *f*, tuile *f*.

spin[2], *v.* (*p.t. & p.p.* **spun** [spʌn]; *p.t. A:* **span** [spæn]; *pr.p.* **spinning**)

I. 1. *v.tr.* (*a*) filer (la laine, le coton, etc.); (*of spider*) **to s. its web,** filer sa toile; (*b*) **to s. a top,** lancer, fouetter, une toupie; **to s. a coin,** faire tourner en l'air une pièce de monnaie; jouer à pile ou face; *Fb: etc:* **to s. the coin,** tirer au sort; **to s. s.o. round,** faire tourner, faire pivoter, faire tournoyer, qn; *Dom.Ec:* **to s. dry,** (faire) essorer (du linge); (*c*) *Fish:* pêcher à la cuillère; **to s. the bait,** faire tourner la cuillère; *v.i.* **to s. for fish,** pêcher au lancer; (*d*) *Metalw:* emboutir, repousser (une feuille de métal) au tour; (*e*) *Metall: Glassm:* couler (du métal, du verre) par force centrifuge; centrifuger (du métal, du verre); (*f*) *Sch: F: O:* recaler (un candidat). **2.** *v.i.* (*a*) (*of top, etc.*) tourner; (*of suspended object*) tournoyer; (*of aircraft*) descendre, tomber, en vrille; (*of compass*) être affolé, s'affoler; **to s. round and round,** tournoyer, tourbillonner; **to s. like a top,** tourner, tournoyer, comme une toupie; **my head's spinning,** la tête me tourne; **to s. round,** (i) (*of car*) faire un tête-à-queue; (ii) (*of pers.*) (α) pivoter, virevolter; (β) se retourner vivement; faire un demi-tour; **the blow sent him spinning,** le coup l'a fait chanceler, l'a envoyé rouler; **to send s.o. spinning against the wall,** repousser violemment, envoyer dinguer, qn contre le mur; (*b*) *Veh:* (*of wheel*) patiner (sur place); glisser.

II. (*compound verb*) **spin out,** *v.tr.* délayer, traîner (un discours); faire durer, prolonger (une discussion); faire traîner (une affaire, un récit) en longueur; tirer (une affaire) en longueur; **just to s. out the time,** seulement pour faire passer le temps; **to s. out one's money,** *v.i.* **to make one's money s. out,** ménager son argent.

spina bifida [spainə'bifidə], *s. Med:* spina-bifida *m*, rachischisis *m*.

spinaceous [spi'neiʃəs], *a. Bot:* spinacié.

spinach ['spinidʒ, *esp. NAm:* -itʃ], *s. Bot:* épinard *m*; *Cu:* épinards *mpl*; **wild s.,** toute-bonne *f*; **mountain s.,** arroche *f* des jardins; bonne-dame *f*; **New Zealand s.,** tétragone étalée; **perpetual s., s. beet,** bette *f* à couper; **s. dock,** patience *f*; oseille *f* épinard.

spinage ['spinidʒ], *s. O:* = SPINACH.

spinal ['spain(ə)l], *a. Anat:* spinal, -aux; vertébral, -aux; **s. column,** colonne vertébrale; **s. canal,** canal vertébral; **s. disease,** maladie de la moelle épinière; **s. curvature,** déviation de la colonne vertébrale.

spindle[1] ['spindl], *s.* **1.** *Tex:* fuseau *m*; **s. side,** côté maternel (d'une famille); **s.-shaped,** fusiforme; fuselé; (*of pers.*) **s. shanked,** à jambes en fuseau; à jambes fuselées; *F:* aux mollets de coq. **2.** (*a*) *Mec.E: etc:* arbre *m*, axe *m*, mandrin *m*, broche *f*; (*of potter's wheel, etc.*) pivot *m*; (*of axle, shaft*) fusée *f*; **s. pin,** verge *f* (de girouette, etc.); **pump s.,** axe de pompe; **lathe s.,** arbre, broche, de tour; **tailstock s.,** arbre de contre-pointe; *Tls:* **drilling s.,** arbre porte-foret; *I.C.E: Mch:* **valve s.,** tige *f* de soupape; **s. valve,** soupape à guide; **throttle valve s.,** axe de papillon; *Mch:* **steam s.,** aiguille de réglage; *El.E:* **insulator s.,** tige d'isolateur; *Nau:* **s. of the capstan,** mèche *f* du cabestan; *Woodw:* **s. moulding machine,** toupie *f*, toupilleuse *f*; *U.S:* **s. file,** pique-notes *m inv*; (*b*) *Biol:* **(nucleus) s.,** fuseau achromatique, central (de cellule); (*c*) *Moll:* **s. (shell),** fuseau; (*d*) *Bot:* **s. (tree),** fusain *m*.

spindle[2]. **1.** *v.i.* s'élever en fuseau; (*of plants*) pousser en hauteur. **2.** *v.tr.* *Woodw:* façonner (qch.) à la toupie; toupiller (un longeron d'avion, etc.).

spindleberry ['spindlberi], *s. Bot:* baie *f* du fusain.

spindleshanks ['spindlʃæŋks], *s.pl.* **1.** jambes *f* en fuseau; *F:* mollets *m* de coq. **2.** (*with sg. const.*) type grand et maigre; manche *m* à balai.

spindly ['spindli], *a.* (*a*) (*of pers.*) maigrelet, maigrichon; (*of legs*) fuselé; (*b*) (*of furniture, etc.*) peu solide, peu robuste.

spindrift ['spindrift], *s.* embrun(s) *m*(*pl*.); poussière; poudrin *m*.

spine [spain], *s.* **1.** *Nat.Hist:* piquant *m*, épine *f* (d'une plante, d'un poisson, d'un hérisson, etc.); aiguillon *m* (d'une plante); radiole *f*, piquant (d'un oursin). **2.** *Anat:* épine dorsale; colonne vertébrale; échine *f*; **s. chiller,** histoire *f* à vous glacer le sang; roman *m*, film *m*, d'épouvante. **3.** *Bookb:* dos *m* (d'un livre). **4.** *Geog:* arête *f*.

spined [spaind], *a.* **1.** *Z:* vertébré. **2.** à épines; épineux; à piquants.

spinel [spi'nel, 'spin(ə)l], *s. Miner:* spinelle *m*, candite *f*; **ruby s., s. ruby,** rubis spinelle; **chromic s.,** picotite *f*; **iron s.,** pléonaste *m*.

spineless ['spainlis], *a.* **1.** sans épines, sans piquants. **2.** *Fig:* (*of pers.*) faible; mou, *f.* molle; veule; qui manque de caractère.

spinelessness ['spainlisnis], *s. Fig:* mollesse *f*; veulerie *f*; manque *m* de caractère.

spinescence [spai'nes(ə)ns], *s. Bot:* spinescence *f*.

spinescent [spai'nes(ə)nt], *a. Bot:* spinescent.

spinet [spi'net], *s. Mus:* épinette *f*.

spinetail ['spainteil], *s. Orn:* synallaxe *m*.

spiniferous [spai'nifərəs], *a. Nat.Hist:* spinifère, spinigère, épineux.

spinifex ['spainifeks], *s. Bot:* spinifex *m*, herbe *f* porc-épic.

spiniform ['spainifɔːm], *a. Nat.Hist:* spiniforme.

spinigerous [spai'nidʒərəs], *a. Nat.Hist:* spinigère.

spinnable ['spinəbl], *a.* (coton, etc.) filable.

spinnaker ['spinəkər], *s. Nau:* spinnaker *m*, spinacker *m*; voile *f* de fortune.

spinner ['spinər], *s.* **1.** *A:* araignée (fileuse). **2.** (*a*) *Tex:* fileur, -euse; filateur *m*; (*b*) *Metalw:* repousseur *m* (au tour); (*c*) **s. of tales, yarns,** débiteur, -euse, conteur, -euse, d'histoires. **3.** (*a*) machine *f* à filer; métier *m* à filer; (*b*) *Dom.Ec:* *F:* essoreuse *f* (centrifuge). **4.** *Nat.Hist:* filière *f* (de ver à soie, etc.). **5.** *Fish:* (*a*) cuillère *f*; (*b*) reproduction *f* d'éphémère à l'état imago; **red s.,** imago rousse. **6.** *Av:* casserole *f*, cône *m*, capot *m*, d'hélice. **7.** *Rad:* explorateur *m*; aérien rotatif, antenne rotative.

spinneret ['spinəret], *s.* **1.** *Nat.Hist:* filière *f* (de ver à soie, etc.). **2.** *Ind:* filière (de métier à filer la soie artificielle).

spinnery ['spinəri], *s.* filature *f.*

spinney ['spini], *s.* petit bois; bosquet *m,* breuil *m.*

spinning[1] ['spiniŋ], *a.* (*a*) tournant; *Tchn:* **non-s.,** antigiratoire; *Atom.Ph:* **s. electron,** électron tournant; (*b*) (*of suspended object*) tournoyant.

spinning[2], *s.* **1.** filage *m* (au rouet); *Ind:* filature *f*; **cotton s.,** filature, filage, du coton; **s. machine,** machine à filer; **s. wheel,** rouet *m*; **s. frame,** métier *m* à filer; *Tex:* **s. can,** pot de filature; **s. mill, factory,** filature; *Ent:* **s. gland,** filière *f* (de l'araignée, du ver à soie). **2.** (*a*) tournoiement *m*; rotation *f*; affolement *m* (de l'aiguille magnétique); *Av:* vrille *f*; **s. motion, movement,** mouvement rotatif, de rotation; **s. top,** toupie *f*; (*b*) patinage *m,* glissement *m* (des roues). **3.** pêche *f* à la cuillère, au lancer; **s. rod,** canne à lancer. **4.** (*a*) *Metalw:* repoussage *m* (au tour); **flame s.,** repoussage à la flamme; **s. lathe,** tour *m* à repousser; (*b*) *Metall: Glassm:* centrifugation *f.*

spinode ['spainoud], *s. Mth:* point *m* de rebroussement (d'une courbe).

spin(-)off ['spinɔf], *s.* (*a*) avantage *m,* bénéfice *m,* supplémentaire; (*b*) sous-produit *m, pl.* sous-produits; produit *m* secondaire, accessoire; (produit) dérivé *m*; (*c*) nouveau débouché, nouveau marché; débouché plus large.

spinose, spinous ['spainous, -nəs], *a.* épineux.

Spinozism [spi'nouzizm], *s. Phil:* spinosisme *m,* spinozisme *m.*

Spinozist [spi'nouzist], *s. Phil:* spinosiste *mf,* spinoziste *mf.*

Spinozistic [spinou'zistik], *a. Phil:* spinosiste, spinoziste.

spinster ['spinstər], *s.* **1.** (*a*) célibataire *f*; femme, fille, non mariée; (*b*) *Pej:* vieille fille. **2.** *Tex: A:* fileur, -euse.

spinsterhood ['spinstəhud], *s.* **1.** état *m* de fille; célibat *m.* **2.** *coll. A:* les vieilles filles.

spinthariscope [spin'θæriskoup], *s. Ph:* spinthariscope *m.*

spinule ['spainju:l], *s. Nat.Hist:* spinule *f.*

spinulose, spinulous ['spainjulous, -ləs], *a. Nat.Hist:* spinuleux.

spiny ['spaini], *a.* (*a*) *Nat.Hist:* épineux; couvert d'épines, de piquants; spinifère, spinigère; *Z:* **s. rat,** échimyidé *m*; rat épineux, à piquants; (*b*) **s. problem,** problème épineux.

spiracle ['spaiərəkl], *s.* **1.** (*a*) *A:* soupirail, -aux *m*; (*b*) évent *m* (de volcan). **2.** (*a*) évent (d'un cétacé); (*b*) *Ent:* stigmate *m.*

spiraea [spai'riə], *s. Bot:* spirée *f.*

spiral[1] ['spaiər(ə)l]. **1.** *s.* (*a*) spirale *f,* hélice *f,* hélicoïde *m*; **lefthand s.,** spirale à gauche; **in a s.,** en spirale; (*of rocket, etc.*) **to ascend in a s.,** vriller; *Rec:* **lead-out s.,** colimaçon *m*; (*b*) spire *f*; tour *m* (de spirale); (*c*) *Av:* **s. (climb, dive),** montée *f,* descente *f,* en spirale; (*d*) **vicious s.,** cycle infernal; **wage-price s., inflationary s.,** course *f,* spirale, des prix et des salaires. **2.** *a.* spiral, -aux; spiralé; hélicoïdal, -aux, hélicoïde; en spirale; vrillé; en hélice; (ressort) en boudin; (mouvement, etc.) spiroïde, spiroïdal, -aux; en colimaçon; *Nat.Hist:* cochléaire; **s. curl of smoke,** volute *f,* spirale, de fumée; **s. balance,** peson à hélice, à ressort; **s. wheel,** roue hélicoïdale; **s.-grained wood,** bois tors, à fibres torses; *Bookb:* **s. binding,** reliure spirale; **s.-bound notebook,** bloc-notes à reliure spirale; *El:* **s.-wound filament,** filament boudiné; *Mth:* **s. line,** hélice; *Mec.E:* **s. cutting,** taillage hélicoïdal; **s. gear(ing),** engrenage hélicoïdal; *Astr:* **s. nebula,** nébuleuse spirale; *Surg:* **s. bandage,** bandage en spirale.

spiral[2], *v.i.* **(spiralled)** former une spirale; tourner, monter, en spirale; (*of steam, smoke*) tire(-)bouchonner; *Av:* (*of aircraft*) **to s. up,** monter en spirale; vriller; **to s. down,** descendre en spirale.

spiralization [spaiərəlai'zeiʃ(ə)n], *s.* spiralisation *f.*

spirally ['spaiərəli], *adv.* en spirale, en hélice.

spiraloid ['spaiərəlɔid], *a.* spiraloïde.

spiran(e) ['spaiəræn, -rein], *s. Ch:* spiranne *m.*

spirant ['spaiər(ə)nt]. *Ling:* **1.** *a.* spirant; **s. consonant,** consonne soufflante. **2.** *s.* spirante *f.*

spirated ['spaiəreitid], *a.* spiralé; en spirale; en vrille.

spire[1] ['spaiər], *s.* **1.** *Arch:* aiguille *f,* flèche *f* (d'église). **2.** flèche (d'arbre); tige *f* (de graminée); *Moll:* **s. shell,** hydrobie *f,* hydrobia *f.*

spire[2], *v.i. Lit:* s'élever en flèche, en pointe.

spire[3], *s.* spire *f,* tour *m* (d'une hélice, etc.).

spireme ['spaiəri:m], *s. Biol:* spirème *m.*

spirifer ['spaiərifər], *s. Paleont:* spirifère *m,* spirifer *m.*

Spiriferidae [spaiəri'feridi:], *s.pl. Paleont:* spiriféridés *m.*

spiriform ['spaiərifɔ:m], *a.* spiriforme.

spirillar [spaiə'rilər], *a.* **1.** *Bac:* qui tient du spirille; en forme de spirille. **2.** (maladie) déterminée par un spirille.

spirillosis [spaiəri'lousis], *s. Med:* spirillose *f.*

spirillum [spaiə'riləm], *s. Bac:* spirille *m.*

spiring ['spaiəriŋ], *a. Lit:* qui s'élève en flèche.

spirit[1] ['spirit], *s.* **1.** esprit *m,* âme *f*; **body, soul and s.,** corps, âme et esprit; **I'll be with you in (the) s.,** mon esprit vous accompagnera; je serai avec vous de cœur; mes pensées *f* voleront vers vous; **peace to his s.,** la paix soit de son âme; *Lit:* **he was vexed in s.,** il avait l'esprit tourmenté; *B:* **the poor in s.,** les pauvres d'esprit. **2.** (*incorporeal being*) esprit; (*a*) **God is a s.,** Dieu est un pur esprit; **the Holy S.,** la Saint-Esprit; l'Esprit saint; **evil s.,** esprit malin, mauvais génie; **elfish s.,** esprit follet; *Lit:* **Socrates' familiar s.,** le démon, le génie, de Socrate; **to invoke the s. of liberty,** invoquer le génie de la Liberté; (*b*) **to raise a s.,** évoquer un esprit; **to believe in spirits,** croire aux esprits, aux revenants; **s. rapper,** médium *m* (spirite) (qui évoque des esprits frappeurs); **s. rapping,** communication avec des esprits frappeurs; typtologie *f*; **s. writing,** psychogramme *m.* **3.** (*pers.*) esprit; **one of the most ardent spirits of his time,** un des esprits les plus ardents de son époque; **the leading s.,** (i) l'âme, le chef (d'une enterprise); (ii) le meneur, la meneuse (d'une révolte); **a master s.,** un esprit puissant. **4.** esprit, disposition *f*; **the s. of wisdom,** l'esprit de la sagesse; **the s. of the age,** l'esprit du siècle; **the real s. of Spain,** le véritable génie de l'Espagne; **party s.,** esprit de parti; **to have, get, the party s.,** participer dans la gaieté de la réunion; **one should follow the s. of the law rather than the letter,** il faut s'attacher à l'esprit de la loi plutôt qu'à la lettre; **in a s. of mischief,** par espièglerie; **to enter into the s. of sth., the s. of the thing,** entrer dans l'esprit de qch.; entrer de bon cœur dans (la partie); s'adapter à qch.; se mettre en harmonie avec (le travail, etc.); *F:* **that's the s.!** à la bonne heure! **5.** (*a*) caractère *m,* cœur *m,* courage *m*; **man of unbending s.,** homme d'un caractère inflexible; **man of s.,** homme de caractère; homme courageux; **to show s.,** montrer du caractère, du courage; **show a little s.,** montrez un peu de courage; **to catch s.o.'s s.,** être enflammé par le courage de qn; (*b*) ardeur *f,* feu *m,* entrain *m,* fougue *f*; **to have s.,** avoir de l'allant; **he went on playing with s.,** il a continué de jouer avec entrain, avec brio; **to work with s.,** travailler avec courage; (*c*) **he's full of spirits,** il est très remuant, très diable; **animal spirits,** esprits animaux; **to be full of animal spirits,** être plein de vie, d'entrain, de verve; **good spirits,** gaieté *f*; bonne humeur; **to be in good spirits,** être gai, dispos; être de bonne humeur; **high spirits,** gaieté, entrain; **to be in high spirits,** être en train, en verve; être d'une gaieté folle; **poor, low, spirits,** abattement *m,* découragement *m*; **to be in low spirits,** être abattu, accablé; se sentir tout triste; avoir le moral à zéro; **to keep up one's spirits,** ne pas perdre courage; ne pas se décourager; ne pas se laisser abattre; **to put s.o. in (good) spirits,** mettre qn en train, de bonne humeur; égayer qn; **to raise, revive, s.o.'s spirits,** relever, remonter, le courage, le moral, de qn; faire reprendre courage à qn; **their spirits rose,** ils reprenaient courage, leur moral se relevait. **6.** (*a*) **spirits,** spiritueux *mpl*; alcools *mpl*; **wines and spirits,** vins et spiritueux; **wine and s. merchant,** négociant *m* en vins et spiritueux; **I don't drink any spirits apart from whisky,** je ne prends pas d'alcools, sauf le whisky; *Cu:* **clear spirits,** alcool blanc; (*b*) *Ch: etc:* **(volatile) s.,** esprit; **raw spirits,** esprit brut; **white s., petroleum s.,** white-spirit *m*; **methylated spirits,** alcool dénaturé, à brûler; **surgical s.** = alcool à 90°; **spirits of camphor,** alcool camphré; **s. lamp, stove,** lampe, réchaud, à alcool; *Th: etc:* **s. gum,** gomme arabique (pour coller de faux cheveux); **s. duplicator,** duplicateur à alcool; **s. thermometer,** thermomètre à alcool; *A:* **motor s.,** essence *f* (pour voitures); *Dy:* **s. blue,** bleu *m* à sel d'étain; *Orn:* **s. duck,** (i) garrot *m* albéole, *Fr.C:* petit garrot; (ii) garrot à œil d'or, canard *m* garrot, *Fr.C:* garrot commun; (*c*) *A.Ch:* **spirit(s) of turpentine,** essence de térébenthine; **spirit(s) of salt,** esprit-de-sel *m*; **spirit(s) of wine,** esprit-de-vin *m,* alcool vinique; (*d*) *Pharm:* alcoolat *m* (de menthe, etc.).

spirit[2], *v.tr.* **(spirited) to s. s.o. away, off,** faire disparaître qn, enlever qn, comme par enchantement; **if I were spirited away to some distant planet,** si je me trouvais transporté dans une planète aux confins de l'univers; **to s. sth. away, off,** subtiliser, escamoter, qch.

spirited ['spiritid], *a.* **1.** (*of pers.*) **(high)-s.,** vif, animé, ardent; plein de feu, de fougue, de verve, d'ardeur, de courage, de cœur; verveux; intrépide; (*of horse*) fougueux. **2.** (*of style, reply, etc.*) chaleureux, entraînant, plein de verve; **s. conversation,** conversation animée, pleine d'entrain; **s. discussion,** vive discussion, discussion verveuse; **s. speech,** discours fougueux, verveux; **s. attack,** attaque fougueuse; **s. music,** musique entraînante; **to give a s. performance,** jouer avec brio.

spiritedly ['spiritidli], *adv.* ardemment, chaleureusement, courageusement, fougueusement; avec feu, avec verve, avec entrain, avec fougue.

spiritedness ['spiritidnis], *s.* ardeur *f,* feu *m,* courage *m,* cœur *m,* entrain *m,* verve *f*; fougue *f* (d'un cheval).

spiritism ['spiritizm], *s.* = SPIRITUALISM 1.

spiritist ['spiritist], *s. & a.* = SPIRITUALIST 1.

spiritistic [spiri'tistik], *a.* (séance, etc.) spirite, spiritiste.

spiritless ['spiritlis], *a.* **1. s. body,** corps sans vie, inanimé. **2.** (style) sans vie, terne, monotone; qui manque de verve; (conversation, etc.) sans entrain, qui manque d'entrain. **3.** sans courage, sans énergie, sans caractère; lâche. **4.** abattu, triste, déprimé. **5.** sans force, sans vigueur, sans ardeur; mou, *f.* molle; faible.

spiritlessly ['spiritlisli], *adv.* **1.** sans vie. **2.** sans vigueur. **3.** sans courage; sans énergie. **4.** sans entrain; tristement. **5.** faiblement, mollement.

spiritlessness ['spiritlisnis], *s.* manque *m* de caractère, de courage, d'entrain, de verve; léthargie *f.*

spiritual ['spiritjuəl]. **1.** *a.* (*a*) spirituel; de l'esprit; **s. life,** vie spirituelle; **s. power,** pouvoir spirituel; le spirituel; **lords s.,** les évêques *m* et archevêques *m* (qui siègent à la Chambre des Lords); **s. court,** tribunal ecclésiastique; **s. father,** père spirituel, directeur spirituel; (*b*) **s. features,** traits purs, raffinés, intellectuels; (*c*) spirituel, immatériel. **2.** *s.* **negro s.,** (negro-)spiritual *m, pl.* (negro-)spirituals.

spiritualism ['spiritjuəlizm], *s.* **1.** *Psychics:* spiritisme *m.* **2.** *Phil:* spiritualisme *m.*

spiritualist ['spiritjuəlist], *s. & a.* **1.** *Psychics:* spirite (*mf*). **2.** *Phil:* spiritualiste (*mf*).

spiritualistic [spiritju(ə)'listik], *a.* **1.** *Psychics:* spirite, spiritiste. **2.** *Phil:* spiritualiste.

spirituality [spiritju'æliti], *s.* **1.** spiritualité *f* (de l'âme, etc.). **2.** *Hist:* **spiritualities,** biens *m* et bénéfices *m* ecclésiastiques.

spiritualization ['spiritjuəlai'zeiʃ(ə)n], *s.* spiritualisation *f.*

spiritualize ['spiritjuəlaiz], *v.tr.* spiritualiser.

spiritually ['spiritjuəli], *adv.* spirituellement, immatériellement.

spirituous ['spiritjuəs], *a.* spiritueux, alcoolique.

spirivalve ['spaiərivælv], *a. Moll:* spirivalve; en spirale; en hélice.

spirketting ['spə:kitiŋ], *s. N.Arch:* virure bretonne.

spirochaeta [spaiərou'ki:tə], **spirochaete** ['spaiərouki:t], *s. Bac:* spirochète *m.*

spirochaetosis [spaiərouki:'tousis], *s. Med:* spirochétose *f.*

Spirodela [spaiərou'di:lə], *s. Bot:* spirodela *m,* spirodèle *f.*

Spirographis [spaiə'rɔgrəfis], *s. Ann:* spirographe *m.*

spirogyra [spaiərou'dʒairə], *s. Algae:* spirogyre *m.*

spiroid ['spaiərɔid], **spiroidal** [spaiə'rɔidl], *a.* spiroïde, spiroïdal, -aux.

spirometer [spaiə'rɔmitər], *s. Med:* spiromètre *m,* pnéomètre *m.*

spirometric(al) [spaiərou'metrik(l)], *a. Physiol:* spirométrique.

spirometry [spaiə'rɔmitri], *s. Physiol:* spirométrie *f.*

Spirorbis [spaiə'rɔ:bis], *s. Ann:* spirorbe *m,* spirorbis *m.*

spiroscope ['spaiərouskoup], *s. Med:* spiroscope *m.*

spirt[1,2] [spə:t], *s. & v.* = SPURT[1,2].

spirula ['spaiərjulə], *s. Moll:* spirule *f.*

spit[1] [spit], *s.* **1.** *Cu:* broche *f*; **electric s.,** rôtissoire *f*; **s. rack,** hâtier *m.* **2.** *Geog:* langue *f* de sable; flèche (littorale); (*at confluence of two rivers*) bec *m*; **shingle s.,** cordon; levée *f* de galets; (*at mouth of river*) delta renversé.

spit[2], *v.tr.* **(spitted)** (*a*) embrocher, mettre à la broche (un rôti, etc.); (*b*) *Lit:* embrocher (qn).

spit[3], *s.* **1.** (*a*) crachat *m,* salive *f*; *F:* **he's the dead, the very, s., the s. and image, of his father,** c'est son père tout craché; *F:* **s. and polish,** astiquage *m,* fourbissage *m*; *NAm: F:* **s. curl,** accroche-cœur *m, pl.* accroche-cœurs; (*b*) crachement *m.* **2.** crachin *m* (de pluie).

spit[4], *v.* (*p.t. & p.p.* **spat** [spæt]; *pr.p.* **spitting**) **1.** *v.i.* (*a*) cracher; **to s. in s.o.'s face, in s.o.'s eye, to s. at s.o.,** cracher au visage à qn; (*b*) (*of cat*) cracher; félir; (*of pen*) cracher, crachoter; (*of fire*) crépiter, pétiller; (*of hot fat*) sauter, pétiller, grésiller; (*c*) crachiner; **it's spitting (with rain),** il crachine, il fait du crachin; il tombe quelques gouttes; (*d*) *El:* (*of collector, etc.*) cracher; (*e*) *Metall:* (*of silver, etc.*) rocher; (*f*) *I.C.E:* (*of engine*) **to s. back,** avoir des retours de flamme (au carburateur); **the engine's spitting,** le moteur a des retours. **2.** *v.tr.* cracher (de la salive, du sang, des injures); **to s. sth. out,** cracher qch.; recracher qch. (de mauvais); *F:* **s. it**

out! dis-le! accouche! vide ton sac!

spit[5], *s.* **1.** profondeur *f* de fer de bêche; **to dig the ground two spit(s) deep,** labourer la terre à deux fers de bêche. **2.** bêche pleine (de terre).

spital ['spitl], *s. A:* hôpital, -aux *m*; hospice *m*; asile *m* (des indigents).

spitball ['spitbɔ:l], *s. NAm:* (*a*) boulette *f* de papier mâché; (*b*) balle *f* de baseball dont un côté a été imprégné de salive (afin de lui imprimer une trajectoire courbe).

spite[1] [spait], *s.* **1.** (*a*) rancune *f*; (*b*) malveillance *f*; (*c*) pique *f*, dépit *m*; **from, out of, s.,** (i) par rancune; (ii) par dépit; par pique; (iii) par malveillance, par méchanceté *f*; par animosité *f*; **to have a s. against s.o.,** en vouloir à qn; garder rancune à qn; avoir de la rancune, avoir une dent, contre qn; *Jur: U.S:* **s. fence,** clôture élevée à seule fin d'ennuyer un voisin. **2.** *prep.phr.* **in s. of. . .,** en dépit de . . .; malgré . . .; **in s. of what he said,** en dépit de son dire; il a eu beau dire; **in s. of everything,** malgré tout; malgré cela; **in s. of his wealth,** malgré sa fortune; **I'll do it in s. of him,** je le ferai malgré lui; **in s. of myself,** malgré que j'en aie; **in s. of all I could say,** malgré tout ce que j'ai pu dire; **in s. of all you may say,** malgré que vous en ayez (à dire).

spite[2], *v.tr.* vexer, contrarier (qn); **he does it to s. me,** il le fait pour me tracasser, pour m'ennuyer.

spiteful ['spaitful], *a.* rancunier, vindicatif; méchant, malveillant; **s. tongue,** langue venimeuse; mauvaise langue; **s. remark,** observation méchante; rosserie *f*.

spitefully ['spaitfuli], *adv.* **1.** par dépit, par rancune; par méchanceté; **to answer s.,** répondre avec dépit. **2.** méchamment; d'un air, d'un ton, vindicatif.

spitefulness ['spaitfulnis], *s.* méchanceté *f*; rancœur *f*; malveillance *f*.

spitfire ['spitfaiər], *s.* rageur, -euse.

Spitsbergen ['spitsbə:gən], *Pr.n. Geog:* Spitzberg *m*, Spitsberg *m*.

spitter ['spitər], *s.* **1.** cracheur, -euse. **2.** *U.S:* = SPITBALL (*b*).

spitting ['spitiŋ], *s.* (*a*) crachement *m*; expectoration *f*; *P.N:* **no s.,** défense de cracher; (*b*) *Metall:* rochage *m* (de l'argent, etc.); (*c*) *I.C.E:* crachotement *m* (du moteur); **s. back,** retour *m* de flamme (au carburateur).

spittle ['spitl], *s.* salive *f*, crachat *m*; bave *f* (du crapaud).

spittoon [spi'tu:n], *s.* crachoir *m*.

spitz [spits], *s.* (*dog*) **giant s.,** grand loulou, grand laika; **German s.,** loulou moyen, spitz-allemand; **Finnish s.,** loulou finlandais; **dwarf s.,** spitz nain, loulou de Poméranie.

spiv [spiv], *s.* (*a*) profiteur *m*, trafiquant *m* du marché noir; chevalier *m* d'industrie; (*b*) parasite *m*.

splanchnic ['splæŋknik], *a. Anat:* splanchnique.

splanchnicectomy [splæŋkni'sektəmi], *s. Surg:* splanchnicectomie *f*.

splanchnicotomy [splæŋkni'kɔtəmi], *s. Surg:* splanchnicotomie *f*.

splanchnocoel(e) ['splæŋknousi:l], *s. Anat:* splanchnocèle *m*.

splanchnology [splæŋk'nɔlədʒi], *s. Anat:* splanchnologie *f*.

splanchnopleure ['splæŋknoupluər], *s. Anat:* splanchnopleure *f*.

splanchnoptosis [splæŋknoup'tousis], *s. Med:* splanchnoptose *f*.

splash[1] [splæʃ], *s.* **1.** éclaboussement *m*, projection *f* (de l'eau, du métal fondu); clapotement *m*, clapotage *m*, clapotis *m* (des vagues); **to fall into the water with a s.,** tomber dans l'eau en faisant floc, flac; *F:* **to make a (big) s.,** faire sensation; faire de l'épate; *Journ:* **s. headline,** grosse manchette; **s. back,** panneau protecteur (d'évier, etc.); **s. guard,** (i) *Veh: U.S: & A:* pare-boue *m inv*; garde-boue *m inv* (d'une voiture, etc.); (ii) *Ind:* rabat-(l')eau *m inv* (d'une meule); *Mec.E: etc:* pare-gouttes *m inv*; *Mch:* **s. lubrication, feed,** graissage par barbotage *m*; *Metalw:* **s. core,** plaque *f* anti-érosion. **2.** (*a*) éclaboussure *f* (de boue, d'encre, etc.); **splashes of rain,** grosses gouttes de pluie; **ship straddled with splashes,** navire encadré de gerbes *f* (d'eau); (*b*) tache *f* (de couleur, de lumière); **splashes of colour,** (i) bariolage *m*; (ii) tachetures *f* (sur la robe d'une bête); (*c*) *F:* **a whisky and s.,** un whisky soda; **just a s., please,** très peu, juste un soupçon, (d'eau, etc.), s'il vous plaît; (*d*) *Num:* barbille *f*; **s.-struck coin,** pièce avec barbilles; (*e*) **water s.,** gué (peu profond). **3.** *int.* floc! flac! ploc!

splash[2]. **1.** *v.tr.* (*a*) éclabousser (**s.o. with water,** qn d'eau); (*b*) **to s. water about,** faire jaillir, faire gicler, de l'eau; faire rejaillir des éclaboussures; **to s. water at one another,** se jeter de l'eau; **to s. water on, over, the floor, to s. the floor with water,** répandre de l'eau par terre; **to s. ink on sth.,** tacher qch. d'encre; **the wheels splashed up the mud,** les roues faisaient gicler la boue; *F:* **to s. one's money about, to s. out,** prodiguer son argent; dépenser sans compter; jeter son argent par les fenêtres; se prodiguer; **I've splashed out on a new hat,** je me suis payé, donné, le luxe d'acheter, je me suis offert, un nouveau chapeau; *Journ:* **to s. a piece of news,** mettre une nouvelle en manchette; (*c*) **to s. one's way across a field,** traverser un champ en pataugeant; (*d*) **to s. oneself,** s'éclabousser (d'eau, etc.); se tacher (de peinture, etc.); **to s. oneself, to s. one's face, with water,** s'asperger, s'asperger la figure, d'eau. **2.** *v.i.* (*a*) (*of liquid*) jaillir en éclaboussures; (*of waves*) clapoter; (*of tap*) cracher; **to s. up,** gicler; (*b*) (*of pers., animal*) barboter; patauger, patouiller; (*of space capsule*) **to s. down,** amerrir; **to s. into the water,** entrer, tomber, dans l'eau en faisant floc, en faisant rejaillir des éclaboussures; **the elephant splashed across the river,** l'éléphant a traversé la rivière avec un bruit d'eau éclaboussée, avec un grand bruit d'éclaboussures; **to s. about in the water,** barboter, s'agiter, dans l'eau; s'ébrouer; **the fish splashed at the end of the line,** le poisson se débattait au bout de la ligne.

splashboard ['splæʃbɔ:d], *s.* **1.** panneau protecteur (d'évier, etc.). **2.** *Ind:* rabat-(l')eau *m inv* (d'une meule). **3.** *Veh: A:* pare-boue *m inv*; garde-boue *m inv*; bavolet *m*.

splashdown ['splæʃdaun], *s.* amerrissage *m* (d'un engin spatial).

splasher ['splæʃər], *s.* = SPLASHBOARD[1,2,3].

splashing[1] ['splæʃiŋ], *a.* (eau, etc.) qui jaillit en éclaboussures; (vague) qui clapote.

splashing[2], *s.* = SPLASH[1] 1.

splash(-)proof ['splæʃpru:f], *a.* étanche aux, à l'abri des, projections d'eau, etc.

splashy ['splæʃi], *a.* (terrain) bourbeux, couvert de flaques d'eau.

splat[1] [splæt], *s. Furn:* panneau central (du dossier d'une chaise) (découpé en balustre).

splat[2], *int.* ploc!

splatter[1] ['splætər], *s.* éclaboussure *f*.

splatter[2]. **1.** *v.tr.* **to s. s.o. with mud, to s. mud over s.o.,** éclabousser qn de boue. **2.** *v.i.* (*of liquid*) jaillir, gicler.

splay[1] [splei], *s.* **1.** (*a*) *Arch:* ébrasement *m*; embrasure *f*; (*b*) (*bevelled edge*) chanfrein *m*, coupe *f* oblique. **2.** (*of bowl, cup, etc.*) évasement *m*; évasure *f*.

splay[2]. **1.** *v.tr.* (*a*) **to s. (out) one's hands,** étendre ses mains; (*b*) *Arch: etc:* **to s. the sides of a window,** ébraser, évaser, une fenêtre; **to s. an opening,** délarder une ouverture; **to s. out an embrasure,** pratiquer une embrasure; (*c*) *Carp:* couper (qch.) en biseau, en sifflet; chanfreiner (qch.). **2.** *v.i.* **to s. out,** s'évaser.

splay[3], *a.* (*a*) (*of knees, etc.*) tourné en dehors; (*b*) *Const:* **s. brick,** brique biaise, chanfreinée.

splayed [spleid], *a.* **1.** (*of opening*) ébrasé; évasé; *Arch:* **s. window,** abat-jour *m inv.* **2.** *Carp:* en sifflet; à sifflet; chanfreiné.

splayfoot ['spleifut], *s.* pied plat (tourné en dehors).

splayfooted [splei'futid], *a.* (*of pers.*) aux pieds plats tournés en dehors; **s. table,** table au(x) pied(s) épaté(s).

spleen[1] [spli:n], *s.* **1.** *Anat:* rate *f*. **2.** (*a*) *O: & Lit:* spleen *m*; humeur noire; **to have the s.,** avoir le spleen; avoir un accès d'humeur noire; **in a fit of s.,** dans un moment d'humeur noire; (*b*) mauvaise humeur; bile *f*; dépit *m*; **to vent one's s. (up)on s.o.,** décharger sa rate, sa bile, sur qn; tourner son dépit contre qn; décharger, épancher, son fiel sur qn; **to vent all one's s.,** jeter tout son venin.

spleen[2], *v.tr. A:* dérater (un chien, etc.).

spleenful ['spli:nful], *a. Lit:* **1.** splénétique, spleenétique; atrabilaire; hypocondriaque. **2.** de mauvaise humeur.

spleenwort ['spli:nwə:t], *s. Bot:* asplenium *m*; *F:* doradille *f*.

splenalgia [spli(:)'nældʒiə], *s. Med:* splénalgie *f*.

splenalgic [spli(:)'nældʒik], *s. Med:* splénalgique.

splendent ['splendənt], *a.* **1.** (*of mineral. insect, etc.*) luisant; (*of mineral*) brillant. **2.** *Lit:* (*of pers.*) éminent, illustre, célèbre, brillant.

splendid ['splendid], *a.* splendide; superbe; magnifique; **s. sight,** spectacle brillant, magnifique; **s. palace,** palais magnifique; **s. weather,** temps superbe, splendide, magnifique; **a s. friend,** un excellent ami; *F:* un ami épatant; **she's simply, just, s.!** elle est vraiment merveilleuse! **s. dinner,** dîner magnifique; **that's s.!** à la bonne heure! félicitations! *F:* chouette!

splendidly ['splendidli], *adv.* splendidement; magnifiquement; **the patient is doing s.,** le malade fait des progrès magnifiques; **I'm getting on s.,** ça marche comme sur des roulettes; **they get on s.,** ils s'accordent le mieux du monde.

splendiferous [splen'difərəs], *a. F: O:* magnifique, mirobolant.

splendour ['splendər], *s.* splendeur *f*; magnificence *f*, éclat *m*.

splenectomy [spli(:)'nektəmi], *s. Surg:* splénectomie *f*.

splenetic [spli'netik], *a.* **1.** *Med:* (maladie) splénétique. **2.** *Lit:* = SPLEENFUL.

splenic ['splenik], *a. Anat:* (artère, maladie) splénique; *Vet:* **s. fever,** (maladie *f* du) charbon.

splenitis [spli'naitis], *s. Med:* splénite *f*.

splenius, *pl.* **-ii** ['spli:niəs, -iai], *s. Anat:* splénius *m*.

splenization [spleni'zeiʃ(ə)n, spli:ni-], *s. Med:* splénification *f*, splénisation *f* (des poumons, etc.).

splenocele ['spli:nousi:l], *s. Med:* splénocèle *m*; hernie *f* de la rate.

splenocyte ['splenousait, 'spli:nou-], *s. Anat:* splénocyte *m*.

splenography [spli(:)'nɔgrəfi], *s. Med:* splénographie *f*.

splenoid ['spli:nɔid], *a. Med:* splénoïde.

splenomegaly [splenou'megəli, spli:nou-], *s. Med:* splénomégalie *f*.

splenopathy [sple'nɔpəθi, spli:-], *s. Med:* splénopathie *f*.

splenopneumonia [splenounju:'mouniə, spli:nou-], *s. Med:* spléno-pneumonie *f*.

splenotomy [spli(:)'nɔtəmi], *s. Surg:* splénotomie *f*.

splice[1] [splais], *s.* **1.** *Nau: etc:* (*in rope, etc.*) épissure *f*; *El: etc:* (*in wire cable*) ligature *f*; épissure; joint épissé; **s. box,** boîte de jonction (de câbles); *Nau:* **cut s.,** greffe *f*. **2.** (*a*) *Carp:* enture *f*; *Cr:* enture du manche (de la batte); *F:* **to sit on the s.,** jouer un jeu serré; ne pas prendre de risques; *Rail:* **s. piece,** éclisse *f*; (*b*) collage *m*, collure *f*, point *m* de collage (d'un film, etc.); *Cin:* **s. bump,** bruit *m* de collage, de collure; (*c*) (*in magnetic tape*) raccord *m*.

splice[2], *v.tr.* **1.** *Nau: etc:* épisser (un cordage, un câble); *El:* **spliced joint,** ligature *f*; épissure *f*; joint épissé; *Tex:* **nylon spliced,** renforcé nylon. **2.** (*a*) *Carp:* enter (deux pièces de bois); (*b*) (*with fishplate*) éclisser (des rails, etc.). **3.** *Cin: etc:* coller (un film); raccorder, faire un raccord à (une bande magnétique). **4.** *F:* **to get spliced,** se marier.

splicer ['splaisər], *s.* **1.** *Tls:* pince *f* à épisser. **2.** *Cin:* (*a*) (*pers.*) colleur, -euse; (*b*) presse *f* à coller; colleuse *f*.

splicing ['splaisiŋ], *s.* **1.** épissage *m* (de câbles). **2.** (*a*) *Carp:* enture *f* (de deux pièces de bois); (*b*) (*with fishplate*) éclissage *m* (de rails, etc.). **3.** *Cin: etc:* collage *m* (d'un film, d'une bande magnétique); raccordement *m* (d'une bande magnétique); **s. table,** table de montage (de films); **s. unit,** presse *f* à coller; colleuse *f*; **s. girl,** monteuse; **s. tape,** ruban de collage.

spline[1] [splain], *s. Mec.E: etc:* **1.** (*a*) languette *f* (pour fixation de la roue sur l'arbre); clavette *f* linguiforme; (*b*) saillie *f* (d'un arbre); ergot *m*. **2.** cannelure *f*, rainure *f*, nervure *f*; **dovetail s.,** cannelure en queue d'aronde; **two-s. hole,** trou à deux rainures.

spline[2], *v.tr. Mec.E: etc:* **1.** claveter. **2.** canneler, rainurer.

splined [splaind], *a.* **1.** claveté; à clavettes. **2.** (arbre) cannelé, à rainure(s).

splint[1] [splint], *s.* **1.** *Med:* attelle *f*, éclisse *f*; clisse *f*; (*cradle-shaped*) gouttière *f*; (*flat*) palette *f* à pansement; **to put a limb in splints,** éclisser, clisser, un membre. **2. s. (bone),** (i) *Farr:* os métacarpien (du cheval); (ii) *Anat:* péroné *m*. **3.** *Vet:* suros *m*. **4. s. (coal),** houille sèche à longue flamme; houille flambante. **5.** (*in S. Africa*) éclat *m* de diamant.

splint[2], *v.tr. Med:* éclisser, clisser, mettre une atelle à (un membre fracturé).

splinter[1] ['splintər], *s.* éclat *m* (de bois, d'obus, etc.); picot *m* (de bois); éclaboussure *f* (de métal); *Nau:* écli *m* (de bois); *Surg:* esquille *f* (d'os fracturé); **I've got a s. in my finger,** j'ai une écharde dans le doigt; *Veh:* **s. bar,** volée (à laquelle sont attachés les traits); *Pol:* **s. group,** groupe, mouvement, séparatiste.

splinter[2]. **1.** *v.tr.* (*a*) briser (qch.) en éclats; faire voler (qch.) en éclats; faire éclater (qch.); (*b*) craquer (un aviron, un mât, etc.). **2.** *v.i.* (*a*) voler en éclats; éclater; (*b*) craquer, éclater.

splintered ['splintəd], *a.* (bois, etc.) en éclats, éclaté, craqué; (os) en esquilles, esquilleux; **s. fragment,** éclat *m* (de bois); esquille *f* (d'os).

splintering ['splintəriŋ], *s.* éclatement *m*, craquement *m* (de bois, etc.).

splinterless ['splintəlis], *a.* **s. glass,** verre se brisant sans éclats; verre de sécurité.

splinterproof ['splintəpru:f], *a.* **1.** à l'épreuve des éclats, protégé contre les éclats (d'obus, de bombe, etc.); **s. shelter,** abri à l'épreuve des éclats d'obus; abri pare-éclats; **s. shield,** pare-éclats *m inv.* **2. s. glass,** verre se brisant sans éclats; verre de sécurité.

splintery ['splintəri], *a.* (bois) éclatable; (os) esquilleux; *Miner:* **s. fracture,** cassure esquilleuse.

splinting ['splintiŋ], *s. Med:* éclissage *m*, clissage *m* (d'un membre fracturé).

split[1] [split], *s.* **1.** fente *f* (dans un mur, etc.); fissure *f*, cassure *f*, crevasse *f* (dans une roche, etc.); déchirure *f* (dans une robe, une voile, etc.); gerçure *f*, fissure, crevasse (de la peau); *Metalw:* crique *f*. **2.** division *f*, séparation *f*; rupture *f*, scission *f* (dans un parti politique, etc.). **3.** (*a*) *Leath:* couche *f* de peau fendue; (*b*) *Basketm: etc:* lame *f* de gaulis; (*c*) *Tex:* dent *f* (de ros); (*d*) *F:* (i) demi(-bouteille) *f*, quart *m* de bouteille (d'eau de Vichy, etc.); (ii) demi-verre *m* (de liqueur). **4.** *Cu:* **Devonshire s.,** brioche fourrée à la crème; **banana s.,** banane *f* à la crème. **5. to do the splits,** faire le grand écart; *Wr:* **splits,** écartèlement *m*.

split[2], *v.* (*p.t. & p.p.* **split;** *pr.p.* **splitting**) **1.** *v.tr.* (*a*) fendre (du bois, etc.); (re)fendre (de l'ardoise); faire éclater (du bois, etc.); cliver (la roche, etc.); déliter (la pierre); **to s. an apple,** couper une pomme en deux; **to s. (down) slate into layers,** déliter de l'ardoise; *Leath:* **to s. a hide,** dédoubler une peau; *Atom.Ph:* **to s. the atom,** fissionner, désintégrer, diviser, l'atome; **to s. sth. off,** détacher, séparer, enlever, qch. (par clivage); **to s. off a splinter from a piece of wood,** enlever un éclat; (*b*) déchirer; **I've s. my skirt,** j'ai déchiré, fendu, ma jupe; **the wind has s. the sails,** le vent a déchiré les voiles; (*c*) diviser, partager (une somme, etc.) **(into equal shares,** en parts égales); **to s. the cost of sth.,** participer aux frais de qch.; **to s. an act (down) into scenes,** diviser un acte en scènes; **to s. sth. up,** fragmenter, diviser, séparer, fractionner, qch.; *Opt:* **to s. (up) light,** décomposer, disperser, la lumière; *Ch:* **to s. up a compound into its elements,** dédoubler un composé en ses éléments; *Mth:* **to s. up a fraction,** décomposer une fraction; *Artil:* **to s. up the fire,** disperser le tir; (*d*) *Pol:* **to s. a party (on a question),** diviser un parti (sur une question); provoquer une rupture dans le parti; désunir le parti; **to s. the vote,** partager les voix (dans un parti, par une candidature intempestive); **to s. one's vote,** *esp. U.S:* **to s. the ticket,** partager ses votes entre plusieurs candidats; panacher un bulletin de vote; *Fin:* **to s. shares,** partager, fractionner, scinder, des actions; *F:* **can you s. a pound (for me)?** pouvez-vous me donner la monnaie d'une livre? **I don't want to s. another fiver,** je ne veux pas (être obligé d')entamer un autre billet de £5; **to s. a bottle,** partager une bouteille (de vin). **2.** *v.i.* (*a*) (*of wood, etc.*) se fendre, se crevasser, éclater; (*of stone*) se déliter; se dédoubler; (*of rock*) se cliver; (*of the skin, etc.*) se gercer; **the ship s. in two,** le navire s'est cassé en deux; **to s. open,** se fendre largement; s'ouvrir; **to s. off,** se séparer, se détacher (par clivage); (*b*) (*of dress, sail, etc.*) se déchirer; (*of seam in dress, etc.*) craquer; se défaire; **his coat has s. at the seams,** les coutures de son manteau ont craqué, se sont défaites; (*c*) *F:* **my head's splitting,** j'ai un mal de tête fou; **you're making my head s.,** vous me fendez, me cassez, me rompez, la tête; (*d*) **the government s. on the Irish question,** la question d'Irlande a provoqué la scission du ministère; **to s. up,** se fractionner; *Ph:* (*of ions*) se dédoubler; **the party s. up into three groups,** le parti s'est séparé, s'est divisé, s'est scindé, en trois groupes; **Paul and Anne have s. up,** Paul et Anne se sont séparés, se sont quittés, ont rompu; (*e*) *F:* **to s. on s.o.,** dénoncer qn; vendre (un complice, un camarade); rapporter; cafarder, faire le cafard; (*f*) *F:* s'en aller, partir; se carapater; **let's s.!** allons! fichons le camp!

split[3], *a.* **1.** fendu; **s. peas,** pois cassés; **s. cane fishing rod,** canne à pêche en bambou refendu; **s. ends,** cheveux fourchus; *Mec.E:* **s. pulley, wheel,** poulie en plusieurs pièces; *Tls:* **s. key,** clef anglaise; *El:* **s. phase motor,** moteur à phase auxiliaire; *Elcs:* **s. anode magnetron,** magnétron à anode fendue; *Cin:* **s. reel,** bobine fractionnée; *Gram:* **to use a s. infinitive,** intercaler un adverbe entre **to** et le verbe (p.ex. **to utterly disbelieve, to deliberately ignore**); *Psy:* **s. personality, mind,** dédoublement *m* de personnalité; esprit dédoublé, schizophrène; *Games:* **s. shot, stroke,** coup *m* qui disperse les boules, les billes; (*at croquet*) coup roqué; *Fin:* **s. stocks,** stocks scindés; *Leath:* **s. hide,** peau sciée.

splitter ['splitər], *s.* **1.** fendeur, -euse (de bois, d'ardoise, etc.). **2.** *Phot:* (*device*) **beam s.,** diviseur *m* des rayons. **3.** *Leath:* machine *f* à refendre les peaux; fenderie *f*. **4.** *Hyd.E:* arête médiane (de roue de Pelton).

splitting[1] ['splitiŋ], *a.* qui (se) fend.

splitting[2], *s.* **1.** fendage *m* (de peaux, etc.); éclatement *m* (de bois, etc.); refendage *m* (de bois, d'ardoises, etc.); délitement *m*, délitage *m*, délitation *f* (de la pierre); *Pol:* panachage *m* (d'un bulletin de vote); *Atom.Ph:* **s. of the atom,** fission *f*, désintégration *f*, de l'atome; *Ind:* **s. mill,** fenderie *f*; **s. up,** fragmentation *f*, division *f*, fractionnement *m* (de qch.); *Ph:* dédoublement *m* (des ions). **2. s. (up),** division, partage *f*, morcellement *m* (d'une terre, etc.); séparation *f* (de deux personnes, etc.); scindement *m*, éclatement (d'un parti politique, etc.); *Mth:* **s. up into partial fractions,** décomposition *f* en fractions partielles.

splodge[1] [splɔdʒ], *s. F:* = SPLOTCH[1].

splodge[2], *F:* **1.** *v.tr.* = SPLOTCH[2]. **2.** *v.i.* **to s. through the mud,** patauger dans la boue.

splodgy ['splɔdʒi], *a. F:* taché; barbouillé; (tableau) peinturluré.

splosh[1] [splɔʃ]. *F: s.* **1.** (bruit *m* d')éclaboussement *m*; **he fell into the water with a s.,** il est tombé dans l'eau en faisant floc, flac. **2.** *int.* floc! flac! ploc!

splosh[2], *v.i. F:* (*a*) (*of liquid*) jaillir en éclaboussures; (*b*) (*of pers., animal*) barboter, patauger; patouiller; **to s. into the water,** entrer, tomber, dans l'eau en faisant floc; **to s. about in the water,** s'agiter, barboter, dans l'eau; s'ébrouer.

splotch[1] [splɔtʃ], *s. F:* tache *f* (de couleur, d'encre, etc.).

splotch[2], *v.tr. F:* tacher, barbouiller (**with,** de).

splotchy ['splɔtʃi], *a. F:* taché; barbouillé.

splurge[1] [splə:dʒ], *s. F:* **1.** esbrouffe *f*; épate *f*; démonstration bruyante. **2.** éclaboussement *m*; déluge *m* (d'eau).

splurge[2]. *F:* **1.** *v.i.* (*a*) faire de l'esbrouffe, de l'épate; faire des dépenses extravagantes; (*b*) lancer des éclaboussures; battre l'eau. **2.** *v.tr.* claquer son argent; jeter son argent par les fenêtres.

splutter[1] ['splʌtər], *s.* **1.** bredouillement *m*. **2.** crachement *m* (d'un stylo, *El:* d'un collecteur, etc.); bafouillage *m* (d'un moteur).

splutter[2]. **1.** *v.tr.* (*a*) éclabousser, répandre (du liquide); (*b*) **to s. (out) a threat,** proférer une menace en bredouillant; bredouiller une menace. **2.** *v.i.* (*a*) (*of pers.*) lancer de la salive (en parlant); envoyer des postillons; postillonner; *F:* crachoter, crachouiller; (*b*) (*of pers.*) bredouiller, bafouiller; (*c*) (*of pen*) cracher; *I.C.E:* (*of engine*) bafouiller; *El:* (*of collector, etc.*) cracher.

splutterer ['splʌtərər], *s.* **1.** lanceur, -euse, de salive, de postillons; crachoteur, -euse. **2.** bredouilleur, -euse.

spluttering ['splʌtəriŋ], *s.* (*a*) action *f* d'envoyer des postillons; (*b*) bredouillement *m*, bafouillage *m*; (*c*) crachement *m* (d'un stylo); *I.C.E:* bafouillage, crachotement *m* (du moteur); *El:* crachement, crépitement *m* (d'un arc).

Spode [spoud], *s. Cer:* porcelaine *f*, céramique *f* (de la fabrique de J. Spode).

spodiosite ['spoudiəsait], *s. Miner:* spodiosite *f*.

spodumene ['spɔdjumi:n], *s. Miner:* spodumène *m*, triphane *m*.

spoil[1] [spɔil], *s.* **1.** (*usu.pl.*) dépouilles *fpl*; butin *m*; **to claim one's share of the spoil(s),** demander sa part du gâteau; *U.S:* **spoils system,** octroi *m* des places aux adhérents du parti arrivé au pouvoir; *O:* **to make s. of s.o.'s house,** piller la maison de qn. **2.** *Min: etc:* **s. (earth),** déblai(s) *m(pl)*; décombres *mpl*; rejet *m*; **s. bank,** talus *m* de déblai; champbord *m*; cavalier *m* (sur les côtés d'une route); **s. heap,** halde *f* (de déblais); terri(l) *m*; crassier *m*. **3.** *Cards:* **s. five,** jeu de cartes dans lequel un joueur doit ramasser trois plis sur cinq.

spoil[2], *v.* (*p.t. & p.p.* **spoiled** *or* (*except in sense* 2) **spoilt** [spɔild, spɔilt]) **1.** *v.tr.* (*a*) gâter, abîmer, gâcher, endommager (qch.); avarier (des marchandises); altérer, gâter (la viande, le vin); **she spoilt her dress,** elle a abîmé, gâté, sa robe; **this book was spoilt by the rain,** ce livre a été abîmé par la pluie; **to get spoilt, spoiled,** s'abîmer; **to s. the set, the collection,** dépareiller le service, la collection; **to s. s.o.'s fun,** gâter, gâcher, le plaisir de qn; **don't s. the fun,** il ne faut pas empêcher de s'amuser; ne faites pas le rabat-joie; laissez faire; **to s. the beauty of sth., s.o.,** déparer qch.; détruire, nuire à, la beauté de qn; *F:* **it spoils her,** ça lui fait tort; *F: O:* **I'll s. his beauty for him,** je vais l'amocher; je vais lui abîmer le portrait; **to s. a sauce,** manquer, rater, une sauce; **to s. a joke,** enlever tout le sel d'une plaisanterie; **to s. s.o.'s appetite,** couper l'appétit, la faim, à qn; *Com:* **to s. the market,** gâcher le métier; *Pol:* **spoilt paper,** bulletin (de vote) nul; (*b*) gâter (un enfant); **her husband spoils her,** son mari la gâte. **2.** *v.tr. A: & Lit:* (*a*) dépouiller, spolier (**s.o. of sth.,** qn de qch.); frustrer (qn); **to s. the Egyptians,** (i) *B:* dépouiller les Égyptiens; (ii) *Fig:* piller, dépouiller, l'ennemi (héréditaire); (*b*) piller, saccager (une ville). **3.** *v.i.* (*of fruit, fish, etc.*) se gâter, s'abîmer; s'avarier, s'altérer; se détériorer; se tarer; se corrompre; **to be spoiling for a fight,** brûler du désir de se battre.

spoilage ['spɔilidʒ], *s.* (*a*) avarie *f*, pourriture *f*; (*b*) *Typ:* déchets *mpl* de tirage.

spoiler ['spɔilər], *s.* **1.** (*a*) destructeur, -trice; gâcheur, -euse; (*b*) *A: & Lit:* spoliateur, -trice; pillard, -arde. **2.** *Aut:* déflecteur *m* (aérodynamique); *Av:* volet hypersustentateur; spoiler *m*.

spoiling ['spɔiliŋ], *s.* **1.** (*a*) détérioration *f*; avarie *f*; (*b*) *A: & Lit:* spoliation *f*; pillage *m*. **2.** *Aut: Av:* emploi *m* de déflecteurs (aérodynamiques).

spoilsman, *pl.* **-men** ['spɔilzmən], *s.m. Pol: U.S:* homme attaché à un parti par des intérêts personnels (et qui après une élection exige sa part du butin).

spoilsport ['spɔilspɔ:t], *s. F:* trouble-fête *mf inv*, rabat-joie *mf inv*; gêneur, -euse; empêcheur, -euse, de danser en rond.

spoke[1] [spouk], *s.* **1.** (*a*) rayon *m*, rai(s) *m* (de roue); *Aut:* **the spokes of the steering wheel,** les rayons du volant; **single-s. steering wheel,** volant monobranche; *Tls:* **s. setter,** serre-rayons *m inv* (de bicyclette); (*b*) *Nau:* poignée *f*, manette *f* (de roue de gouvernail); (*c*) *Anat:* radius *m*. **2.** (*a*) échelon *m* (d'échelle); (*b*) bâton *m* (à enrayer); **to put a s. in s.o.'s wheel,** mettre des bâtons dans les roues de, à qn; contrarier les desseins de qn.

spoke[2], *v.tr.* **1.** enrayer (une roue); monter les rais, les rayons. **2.** retenir, bloquer (la roue) en barrant les rais.

spoken ['spoukn], *a.* **1. the s. word, language,** la parole. **2. to be well s. of,** avoir une bonne réputation. **3.** (*with adj. or adv. prefixed*) **a well-s. man,** (i) un homme à la parole courtoise; (ii) un homme qui parle bien; *A: & Lit:* **fair s.,** aux belles paroles.

spokeshave ['spoukʃeiv], *s. Tls: Carp:* vastringue *f*, wastringue *f*; rabot *m*; racloir *m*, racloire *f*.

spokesman, *pl.* **-men** ['spouksmən], *s.* **1.** porte-parole *m inv*, interprète *mf* (d'un parti, etc.); **to act as s. for s.o.,** être le porte-parole de, prendre la parole pour, au nom de, qn. **2.** *O:* orateur, -trice.

spokeswoman, *pl.* **-women** ['spoukswumən, -wimin], *s.f.* **1.** = SPOKESMAN 1. **2.** *O:* (femme) orateur *m*; oratrice *f*.

spokewise ['spoukwaiz], *adv.* radialement.

spoking ['spoukiŋ], *s.* enrayage *m*.

Spoleto [spɔ'li:tou, -'letou], *Pr.n. Geog:* Spolète.

spoliate ['spoulieit], *v.tr.* spolier, dépouiller; piller.

spoliation [spouli'eiʃ(ə)n], *s.* **1.** (*a*) spoliation *f*, dépouillement *m*; acte spoliateur; (*b*) pillage *m*. **2.** *Jur:* destruction *f*, altération *f* (de documents probants).

spoliative ['spouliətiv], *a. Med:* (traitement, etc.) spoliatif.

spoliator ['spoulieitər], *s.* **1.** spoliateur, -trice. **2.** pilleur *m*.

spoliatory ['spouli'eit(ə)ri], *a.* spoliateur, -trice.

spondaic [spɔn'deiik], *a. Pros:* spondaïque.

spondee ['spɔndi:], *s. Pros:* spondée *m*.

Spondias ['spɔndiæs], *s. Bot:* spondias *m*.

spondulicks, spondulix [spɔn'dju:liks], *s. F: O:* argent *m*; fric *m*, braise *f*, pognon *m*.

spondyl ['spɔndil], *s.* **1.** *Anat: A:* spondyle *m*, vertèbre *f*. **2.** *Moll:* spondyle.

spondylarthritis [spɔndila:'θraitis], *s. Med:* spondylarthrite *f*.

Spondylidae [spɔn'dilidi:], *s.pl. Moll:* spondylidés *m*.

spondylitis [spɔndi'laitis], *s. Med:* spondylite *f*; **rheumatoid, ankylosing, s.,** spondylarthrite ankylosante; **s. deformans,** spondylose *f* rhizomélique.

spondylolisthesis [spɔndiloulis'θi:sis], *s. Med:* spondylolisthésis *m*.

spondylosis [spɔndi'lousis], *s. Med:* spondylose *f*.

spondylus, *pl.* **-i** ['spɔndiləs, -ai], *s. Anat: Moll:* = SPONDYL.

sponge[1] [spʌn(d)ʒ], *s.* **1.** (*a*) éponge *f*; *Toil:* **s. bag,** trousse de toilette, de voyage; **s. holder, dish,** porte-éponge(s) *m*; **s. bath,** tub *m*, bassin *m*; *Tex:* **s. cloth,** tissu éponge; **to throw in the s.,** (i) *Box:* jeter l'éponge; abandonner; (ii) *Fig:* s'avouer vaincu; abandonner, quitter, la partie; *O:* **to pass the s. over an incident,** passer l'éponge sur un incident; **s. fisher,** pêcheur, -euse, d'éponges; *Spong:* **basket s.,** euplectelle *f*; **breadcrumb, crumb-of-bread, s.,** halichondrie *f*; *Crust:* **s. crab,** dromie *f*; *Bot:* **s. cucumber, gourd, vegetable s.,** éponge végétale, luffa *m*; **s. tree,** acacia *m* de Farnèse; (*b*) coup *m* d'éponge; **to give sth. a s.,** passer l'éponge sur, donner un coup d'éponge à, qch.; (*c*) *Artil: A:* écouvillon *m*; (*d*) *Surg:* tampon *m*. **2.** (*a*) *Cu:* (i) pâte *f* à pain; (ii) gâteau *m* mousseline; **s. biscuit** = madeleine *f*; **s. finger,** biscuit *m* à la cuillère; (*b*) *Metall:* **metallic s.,** éponge métallique; **s. iron,** fer spongieux. **3.** *F:* (*a*) gros buveur, ivrogne *m*, sac *m* à vin; (*b*) parasite *m*; écornifleur, -euse; pique-assiette *m inv*.

sponge[2]. **1.** *v.tr* (*a*) éponger (qch.); nettoyer (qch.) avec une éponge; passer l'éponge sur (qch.); laver (une voiture) à l'éponge; **to s. sth. up,** éponger, étancher, qch.; **to s. s.o. down,** doucher qn avec une éponge; **to s. down a horse,** éponger un cheval; **to s. off, out, a stain,** éponger une tache; enlever, effacer, une tache à l'éponge; passer l'éponge sur une tache; (*b*) *Med:*

lotionner (une plaie); (*c*) *Tex:* décatir, délustrer (un tissu); (*d*) *Artil: A:* **to s. out a gun,** écouvillonner une pièce à l'eau; (*e*) *F:* écornifler, grappiller (un repas, etc.); **to s. a drink,** se faire offrir un apéritif, etc. **2.** *v.i.* (*a*) pêcher les éponges; (*b*) *F:* écornifler; faire le parasite; écumer les marmites; **to s. on s.o.,** vivre aux crochets, aux dépens, de qn; gruger qn; **to s. on s.o. for cigarettes,** écornifler des cigarettes à qn.

spongelet ['spʌn(d)ʒlit], *s. Bot:* = SPONGIOLE.

sponger ['spʌn(d)ʒər], *s.* **1.** *Tex:* **(cloth) s.,** décatisseur, -euse. **2.** pêcheur, -euse, d'éponges. **3.** *F:* parasite *m*; écornifleur, -euse; pique-assiette *m inv.*

Spongiae ['spʌn(d)ʒii:], *s.pl. Coel:* spongiaires *m*, porifères *m*.

spongiform ['spʌn(d)ʒifɔ:m], *a.* spongiforme.

Spongilla [spʌn'(d)ʒilə], *s. Coel:* spongille *f*.

spongin ['spʌn(d)ʒin], *s. Bio-Ch:* spongine *f*.

sponginess ['spʌn(d)ʒinis], *s.* spongiosité *f*.

sponging[1] ['spʌn(d)ʒiŋ], *a. F:* (*of pers.*) parasite.

sponging[2], *s.* **1.** (*a*) nettoyage *m* à l'éponge; (*b*) *Med:* lavage *m* (d'une plaie) avec une lotion; (*c*) *Tex:* décatissage *m*, délustrage *m* (d'un tissu); (*d*) *Artil: A:* **s. out (of a gun),** écouvillonnage *m* à l'eau. **2.** pêche *f* des éponges. **3.** *F:* écorniflage *m*. **4.** *Hist:* **s. house,** prison *f* provisoire pour dettes.

spongioblast ['spʌn(d)ʒioublæst, 'spɔn-], *s. Biol:* spongioblaste *m*.

spongiole ['spʌn(d)ʒioul, 'spɔn-], *s. Bot:* spongiole *f* (de racine).

spongioplasm ['spʌn(d)ʒiouplæzm, 'spɔn-], *s. Biol:* spongioplasme *m*.

spongoid ['spɔŋgɔid], *a. Anat: Med:* (tissu, os, etc.) spongoïde.

Spongospora [spɔŋ'gɔspərə], *s. Fung:* spongospora *m*.

spongy ['spʌn(d)ʒi], *a.* spongieux; *Anat:* (tissu) caverneux; *Metall:* (fer, etc.) spongieux; *Ch:* **s. platinum,** noir *m* de platine.

sponsion ['spɔnʃ(ə)n], *s. Jur:* garantie (personnelle), caution *f* **(on behalf of,** en faveur de).

sponson ['spɔns(ə)n], *s.* **1.** *N.Arch:* encorbellement *m*. **2.** *Av:* **stabilizing s.,** nageoire *f*.

sponsor[1] ['spɔnsər], *s.* **1.** *Jur:* garant *m*, répondant *m* **(for s.o.,** de qn); caution *f*. **2.** (*a*) (*at baptism*) parrain *m*, marraine *f*; **to stand s. to a child,** tenir un enfant sur les fonts (baptismaux); (*b*) (*introducing new member to club, etc.*) parrain; (*c*) *W.Tel: T.V:* **to be s. to a programme,** offrir un programme; subventionner un programme (de ses fonds personnels).

sponsor[2], *v.tr.* **1.** être le garant de, répondre pour, se porter caution pour (qn); parrainer (qn). **2.** *W.Tel: T.V:* **to s. a programme,** offrir un programme; subventionner un programme (de ses fonds personnels).

sponsorship ['spɔnsəʃip], *s.* (*a*) *Jur:* garantie *f*, caution *f*; (*b*) parrainage *m*; **joint s.,** co(m)paternité *f*.

spontaneity [spɔntə'ni:iti, -'nei-], *s.* spontanéité *f*.

spontaneous [spɔn'teiniəs], *a.* spontané, primesautier; (i) (mouvement) automatique; (ii) (acte, aveu) volontaire; *Th:* **his acting is s.,** il a un jeu rond, aisé, naturel.

spontaneously [spɔn'teiniəsli], *adv.* spontanément; (i) automatiquement; (ii) volontairement; de son propre mouvement, de sa propre volonté; de bonne volonté; *Th:* **to act s.,** jouer avec rondeur, avec naturel.

spontaneousness [spɔn'teiniəsnis], *s.* spontanéité *f*.

spontoon [spɔn'tu:n], *s. A.Arms:* esponton *m*, demi-pique *f*.

spoof[1] [spu:f], *s. F:* attrape *f*; duperie *f*; mystification *f*; bluff *m*; blague *f*; **s. sale,** vente *f* pour la frime.

spoof[2], *v.tr. F:* mystifier, attraper, duper, charrier (qn); faire marcher (qn); **you've been spoofed,** on vous a eu.

spoofer ['spu:fər], *s. F:* mystificateur *m*; pince-sans-rire *m inv*; charrieur, -euse; blagueur, -euse.

spook[1] [spu:k], *s. F:* spectre *m*, fantôme *m*, revenant *m*, apparition *f*.

spook[2], *v.tr. F:* (*a*) (*of ghost*) hanter (qn, un endroit); (*b*) *N Am:* effrayer (un animal, qn).

spooky ['spu:ki], *a. F:* (histoire, etc.) de spectres, de revenants; (endroit) hanté.

spool[1] [spu:l], *s.* **1.** (*a*) *Tex:* bobine *f*, can(n)ette *f*, fusette *f*; espo(u)lin *m*, époulin *m*; dévidoir *m*; (*large*) roquetin *m*; **silk s.,** roquetin, rochet *m*, roquet *m*; **s. of a sewing machine,** can(n)ette; (*b*) *esp. U.S:* **s. of thread,** bobine de coton (à coudre). **2.** *Fish:* tambour *m* (de moulinet). **3.** (*a*) *El:* (corps *m* de) bobine; (*b*) *Phot: Cin:* bobine (de film); rouleau *m*; *Cin:* **supply s.,** bobine débitrice; **take-up s.,** bobine enrouleuse; **uncoiling, unwinding, s.,** bobine de déroulement; **s. box,** carter *m* (pour bobines); (*c*) *Typew:* **(ribbon) s.,** bobine du ruban.

spool[2], *v.tr. Tex: etc:* bobiner; enrouler, dévider, (r)envider (du fil, etc.); **to s. off,** débobiner, dévider, dérouler.

spooling ['spu:liŋ], *s.* bobinage *m*; dévidage *m*; (r)envidage *m*; **s. off,** débobinage *m*; dévidage *m*, déroulement *m*; **s. machine,** bobineuse *f*, bobinoir *m*.

spoon[1] [spu:n], *s.* **1.** cuillère *f*, cuiller *f*; **coffee s.,** cuillère à café, à moka; petite cuillère; **dessert s.,** cuillère à dessert, à entremets; **soup s.,** cuillère à soupe; **basting s.,** (petite) louche; **wooden s.,** (i) cuillère à ragoût, à sauce; cuillère anglaise; mouvet *m*, mouvette *f*; *Fr.C:* micoine *f*; (ii) *Hist:* (*at Cambridge*) (cuillère en bois donnée à) un candidat reçu le dernier (à l'examen de mathématiques); **to take, get, the wooden s.,** arriver bon dernier; être classé le dernier; **he has to be fed with a s.,** il faut lui faire avaler les aliments à la cuillère; **s. meat,** aliment *m* liquide; *Nat.Hist:* **s.-shaped,** (feuille, etc.) cochléaire, en cuilleron; *F:* **greasy s.,** gargote *f*; bistro(t) *m* de qualité inférieure. **2.** (*a*) *Fish:* **s. (bait), trolling s.,** cuillère; **s. net,** épuisette *f*; (*b*) *Tls:* **s. drill,** cuillère; **s. gouge,** gouge *f* à nez rond, à cuillère; **s. auger,** tarière creuse à bout rond, tarière à cuillère; (*c*) *Metall: etc:* **flux assay s.,** éprouvette *f*; **(moulder's) s. tool,** spatule *f*; (*d*) *Golf:* crosse *f* de bois numéro 3; spoon *m*; (*e*) aviron *m* à lame incurvée. **3.** *F: A:* **to be spoons on s.o.,** avoir le béguin pour qn; en pincer pour qn.

spoon[2]. **1.** *v.tr.* (*a*) **to s. (up) one's soup,** manger sa soupe (avec une cuillère); **to s. out the sauce, the peas,** servir la sauce, les petits pois (avec une cuillère); **to s. off the cream,** enlever la crème (avec une cuillère); (*b*) *Fish:* pêcher (le poisson) à la cuillère; (*c*) *Cr: Ten: Golf:* prendre (la balle) en, à la, cuillère. **2.** *F:* (*a*) *v.tr. O:* faire la cour à (qn) (d'une façon sentimentale); faire le galant auprès de (qn); (*b*) *v.i.* (*of couple*) se faire des mamours, des caresses, des cajoleries; filer le parfait amour.

spoonbill ['spu:nbil], *s.* **1.** *Orn:* spatule (blanche); **roseate s.,** spatule rose; **s. sandpiper,** eurynorhynche *m*. **2.** *Ich:* grande spatule.

spoondrift ['spu:ndrift], *s.* embrun(s) *m*(*pl*); poussière *f* d'eau; poudrin *m*.

spoonerism ['spu:nərizm], *s.* contrepèterie *f*, lapsus *m*.

spoonfeed ['spu:nfi:d], *v.tr.* (*p.t.* & *p.p.* **-fed** [fed]) (*a*) nourrir (qn) à la cuillère; (*b*) mâcher (le travail, la besogne) (à qn); subventionner (une industrie, etc.).

spoonful ['spu:nful], *a.* cuillerée *f*; **two dessert spoonfuls,** deux cuillerées à dessert.

spoony ['spu:ni]. *F: O:* **1.** *a.* (*a*) nigaud, niais, sot; (*b*) amoureux; langoureux; cajoleur, caressant; **to be s. on s.o.,** être coiffé de qn; avoir le béguin pour qn; en pincer pour qn. **2.** *s.* nigaud, -aude; niais, -aise; sot *m*, sotte *f*.

spoor[1] ['spuər], *s. Ven:* foulées *fpl*, piste *f*, erres *fpl*, empreintes *fpl* (d'un cerf, etc.).

spoor[2]. *Ven:* **1.** *v.tr.* suivre (une bête) à la piste. **2.** *v.i.* suivre la piste, les foulées.

sporadic [spə'rædik], *a.* **1.** *Nat.Hist: Med:* sporadique. **2.** (*of action, etc.*) sporadique; isolé; rare.

sporadically [spə'rædik(ə)li], *adv.* **1.** *Nat.Hist: Med:* sporadiquement. **2.** sporadiquement; dans des cas isolés; par-ci par-là.

sporadosiderite [spərædou'sidərait], *s. Miner:* sporadosidérite *f*.

sporangiole [spɔ(:)'rændʒioul], *s. Fung:* sporangiole *m*.

sporangiophore [spɔ(:)'rændʒioufɔ:r], *s. Bot:* sporangiophore *m*.

sporangium, *pl.* **-ia** [spɔ(:)'rændʒiəm, -iə], *s. Nat.Hist:* sporange *m*.

sporation [spɔ(:)'reiʃ(ə)n], *s. Nat.Hist:* sporulation *f*.

spore [spɔ:r], *s.* spore *f*; **s. case,** sporange *m*.

spored [spɔ:d], *a. Bot:* sporé; **eight-s. ascus,** asque à huit spores.

sporidium [spɔ(:)'ridiəm], *s. Bot:* sporidie *f*.

sporiferous [spɔ(:)'rifərəs], *a. Bot:* sporifère.

sporo- ['spɔ(:)rou, spɔ(:)'rɔ], *pref.* sporo-.

sporoblast ['spɔ(:)roublæst], *s. Prot:* sporoblaste *m*.

Sporobolus [spɔ(:)'rɔbələs], *s. Bot:* sporobolus *m*.

sporocarp ['spɔ(:)roukɑ:p], *s. Bot:* sporocarpe *m*.

sporocyst ['spɔ(:)rousist], *s. Bot: Prot: Ann:* sporocyste *m*.

sporoduct ['spɔ(:)roudʌkt], *s. Prot:* sporoducte *m*.

sporogonium [spɔ(:)rou'gouniəm], *s. Moss:* sporogone *m*.

sporogony [spɔ(:)'rɔgəni], *s. Prot:* sporogonie *f*.

sporophore ['spɔ(:)roufɔ:r], *s. Bot:* sporophore *m*.

sporophyl(l) ['spɔ(:)roufil], *s. Bot:* sporophylle *m*.

sporophyte ['spɔ(:)roufait], *s. Bot:* sporophyte *m*.

sporothrix ['spɔ(:)rouθriks], *s. Fung:* sporotrichum *m*, sporotriche *m*.

sporotrichosis [spɔ(:)routrai'kousis], *s. Med: Vet:* sporotrichose *f*.

sporotrichotic [spɔ(:)routrai'kɔtik], *a. Med: Vet:* sporotrichosique.

sporotrichum [spɔ(:)'rɔtrikəm], *s. Fung:* sporotrichum *m*, sporotriche *m*.

sporozoite [spɔ(:)rou'zouait], *s. Prot:* sporozoïte *m*.

sporozoon, *pl.* **-oa** [spɔ(:)rou'zouən, -ouə], *s. Prot:* sporozoaire *m*.

sporran ['spɔrən], *s. Scot:* aumônière en cuir brut (pendue sur le devant du kilt); sporran *m*.

sport[1] [spɔ:t], *s.* **1.** (*a*) jeu *m*, divertissement *m*, amusement *m*; **in s.,** pour jouer, pour s'amuser, pour rire; par plaisanterie, par badinage; en badinant; **to make s. of sth.,** s'amuser, se moquer, se jouer, se faire un jeu, de qch.; **to make a s. of doing sth.,** se faire un jeu de faire qch.; (*b*) **to have good s.,** (i) (*in hunting*) faire bonne chasse; (ii) (*in fishing*) faire bonne pêche, bonne prise. **2.** sport *m*; **athletic sports,** sports athlétiques; **aquatic sports,** sports nautiques; **winter sports,** sports d'hiver; **the s. of kings** = les courses *f* (de chevaux); **to go in for sport(s),** s'adonner aux sports; faire du sport; **fond of s., devoted to s.,** sportif; **sports day, school sports,** fête sportive; **sports ground,** terrain de sport, de jeux; stade *m*; *Com:* **sports equipment,** accessoires *mpl*, fournitures *fpl*, articles *mpl*, de sport; **sports jacket, coat,** veston *m* sport; *Journ:* **sports edition,** édition sportive; **sports page,** rubrique sportive; (*as headline*) sports; **sports editor,** rédacteur sportif; *T.V: etc:* **sports results,** résultats sportifs. **3.** *Lit:* **to be the s. of fortune, of circumstances, of every wind,** être le jouet, le jeu, de la fortune, des circonstances, des vents. **4.** *Biol:* variété anormale, type anormal. **5.** *F:* **a (good, real) s.,** (i) un beau joueur; (ii) une personne sympathique; un bon, chic, type; une bonne nature; **come on, be a s.!** voyons, sois chic! *esp. Austr:* **hello, (old) s.!** salut, mon vieux, mon pote!

sport[2]. **1.** *v.i.* (*a*) *O:* jouer; se divertir, s'amuser; folâtrer; **to s. with s.o.,** (i) se divertir avec qn; (ii) se moquer, se jouer, de qn; (*b*) *Biol:* (*of plants, animals*) produire une variété anormale. **2.** *v.tr.* porter (qch. de très voyant); arborer (une cravate rouge, etc.); étaler, exhiber (un manteau de fourrure, etc.); **he was sporting all his medals,** il avait mis toutes ses médailles.

sporting[1] ['spɔ:tiŋ], *a.* **1.** amateur de la chasse, de la pêche. **2.** de sport; sportif; **s. man,** (i) amateur de sport; (ii) turfiste; (iii) *Pej:* parasite du turf; **in a s. spirit,** avec un esprit sportif; sportivement; **he hasn't got the s. spirit,** il n'a pas l'esprit sportif; *F:* **it's very s. of him (to . . .),** c'est très chic de sa part (de . . .); **you've a s. chance,** il vaut la peine d'essayer le coup; vous pourriez réussir, par coup de veine; **I'll make you a s. offer,** je vais vous faire une offre qui vous mettra sur le velours, une offre à laquelle vous ne perdrez rien. **3.** *Biol:* (*of breed, variety*) ayant tendance à produire des variétés anormales.

sporting[2], *s.* **1.** (*a*) **s. gun,** fusil *m* de chasse; (*b*) *U.S:* **s. editor,** rédacteur sportif; **s. page,** rubrique sportive; (*c*) *U.S: F:* **s. house,** maison *f* de prostitution. **2.** *Biol:* production *f* de variétés anormales.

sportive ['spɔ:tiv], *a.* (*a*) *O:* badin; folâtre; (*b*) *Z:* **s. lemur,** lépilémure *m*, lépilemur *m*.

sportsman, *pl.* **-men** ['spɔ:tsmən], *s.m.* **1.** chasseur, pêcheur. **2.** amateur de sport(s); sportif; **a keen s.,** un ardent sportif. **3. he's a real s.,** il est animé de l'esprit sportif; c'est un beau joueur; **they're not sportsmen,** ils n'ont pas l'esprit sportif.

sportsmanlike, sportsmanly ['spɔ:tsmənlaik, -li], *a.* **1.** de chasseur; de pêcheur; de sportif. **2.** animé de l'esprit sportif.

sportsmanship ['spɔ:tsmənʃip], *s.* **1.** habileté *f*, qualités *fpl*, de sportif; pratique *f* des sports, de la chasse, de la pêche, etc. **2.** esprit sportif; sportivité *f*.

sportswear ['spɔ:tswɛər], *s. Com:* vêtements *mpl* (de) sport.

sportswoman, *pl.* **-women** ['spɔ:tswumən, -wimin], *s.f.* **1.** femme amateur de la chasse, de la pêche, etc. **2.** (femme) sportive; femme amateur du sport.

sportula ['spɔ:tjulə], *s. Rom.Ant:* sportule *f*.

sporty ['spɔ:ti], *a.* **1.** *F:* (*a*) sportif; (*b*) qui se vante de son allure sportive; (*c*) *O:* **it's awfully s. of you to . . .,** c'est très chic de votre part de . . .. **2.** *F:* (*a*) *O:* **the s. set,** les (bons) viveurs; (*b*) (veston, etc.) de couleurs criardes, voyantes. **3.** (*of dog*) **a s. little fellow,** un petit chien courageux, résolu.

sporulated ['spɔrjuleitid], *a. Nat.Hist:* sporulé.

sporulation [spɔrjulei'ʃ(ə)n], *s. Nat.Hist:* sporulation *f*.

spot[1] [spɔt], *s.* **1.** (*a*) endroit *m*, lieu *m*; **the finest s. in the town,** le plus bel endroit de la ville; **remote s.,** endroit écarté, isolé; **to drop sth. on a precise s.,** laisser tomber qch. à un endroit précis; **X marks the s.,** la croix indique le lieu (du crime, etc.); **I was on the (very) s.,** j'étais sur le lieu (même), sur les lieux (mêmes); **the police are on the s.,** la police est sur les lieux; **the manager should always be on the s.,** le gérant doit toujours être là; **rely on the man on the s.,** remettez-vous-en, faites confiance, à la personne qui est sur place; *F:* **to put s.o. on the s.,** (i) mettre qn dans une situation difficile; embarrasser qn; (ii) *esp. NAm:* décider d'assassiner, de descendre, d'exécuter, qn; *F:* **to be on the s.,** (i) être alerte, vif, éveillé, actif; être sur le qui-vive; (ii) *esp. NAm:* être dans une situation dangereuse; **to be on the s. (in an emergency),** se montrer à la hauteur d'une situation imprévue; *F:* **to hit the high spots,** faire la noce; *F:* **to be in a tight s., in a (bit of a) s.,** (i) être dans une situation difficile; être dans le pétrin; (ii) avoir des ennuis pécuniaires; **night s.,** boîte *f* de nuit; **s. check,** contrôle-surprise *m*; vérification *f* sur place; **to s.-check sth.,** contrôler, vérifier, qch. à l'improviste, à intervalles irréguliers; *F:* **s. on,** exact, au point; **it's s. on,** c'est juste ce qu'il faut; **to be s. on,** mettre dans le mille; faire mouche; *Surv:* **s. height,** point coté; **s. level,** cote *f* (de nivellement, de niveau); *Journ:* **s. news,** (édition *f* de) dernière heure; (*b*) *adv.phr.* **on the s.,** sur-le-champ, sur le coup; immédiatement; **to be killed on the s.,** être tué sur le coup; être tué net, raide; *F:* y rester; **a bullet killed him on the s.,** une balle l'a étendu mort; **to fall dead on the s.,** tomber raide mort; **to do sth. on the s.,** faire qch. sur place, sur-le-champ; (*c*) poste *m*, place *f*, position *f*, rang *m* (dans une organisation, dans une hiérarchie); (*d*) *T.V: W.Tel:* créneau (réservé à la publicité, à une personne, etc.); **s. announcement,** bref message publicitaire; *F:* spot *m* publicitaire; (*e*) *Com:* **s. cash,** (argent) comptant *m*; *St.Exch:* **s. transaction, deal,** opération au comptant; **s. market,** marché du disponible, du comptant; **s. price, rate,** cours du comptant, du disponible; **s. cotton, wheat,** coton, blé, au comptant; **s. goods,** marchandises disponibles; (*f*) **to put one's finger on a weak s.,** mettre le doigt sur un point faible; **to find s.o.'s weak s.,** trouver le défaut dans la cuirasse de qn; **the sore s.,** l'endroit sensible; *F:* **to hit, touch, the s.,** être exactement ce qu'il faut. **2.** (*a*) tache *f*, macule *f*; souillure *f*; (*on fruit, etc.*) tavelure *f*; **s. remover,** détachant *m*; *Paint:* **s. glaze,** glacis *m* pour taches; (*b*) (*on face, etc.*) bouton *m*; (*c*) *Th: Cin:* **flare s.,** *U.S:* **hot s.,** tache lumineuse (due à la réflexion). **3.** (*a*) pois *m* (de couleur, de broderie); **blue tie with red spots,** cravate bleue à pois rouges; **a panther's spots,** la tacheture, la moucheture, d'une panthère; *F:* **to knock spots off s.o.,** battre qn à plate(s) couture(s); l'emporter sur qn; rendre des points à qn; (*b*) **blind s.,** (i) *Anat:* papille *f* optique; point *m* aveugle; punctum *m* cæcum; tache de Mariotte; (ii) *Aut:* angle *m* aveugle; *F:* **that's your blind s.,** c'est là où vous refusez de voir clair; *Anat:* **yellow s.,** tache jaune (de la rétine); (*c*) point (sur une carte à jouer, etc.); *Bill:* mouche *f* (sur la bille, sur la table); **s. (ball),** bille marquée d'une mouche; (*d*) *Med:* (*radiography*) **a s. on the lung,** un voile au poumon; (*e*) *Th: Cin:* projecteur (orientable, intensif); **baby s.,** projecteur directif; spot; (*f*) *Elcs: T.V:* spot; **scanning s.,** spot explorateur; **flying s.,** spot mobile; (*of recording apparatus, etc.*) **light s.,** spot lumineux; (*g*) **s. welding,** soudure *f* par points; **s. welder,** (i) (*pers.*) soudeur, -euse, par points; (ii) machine *f* à souder, soudeuse *f*, par points. **4.** (*a*) goutte *f* (de pluie, de vin); (*b*) *F:* **a s. of whisky,** un (tout petit) peu, un coup, deux doigts, de whisky; **what about a s. of lunch?** si nous allions déjeuner? **to do a s. of work,** faire un peu de travail; **a s. of bother, of trouble,** un petit ennui; une petite difficulté; une anicroche; **to get into a s. of bother,** avoir des ennuis; être dans de beaux, de mauvais, draps.

spot[2], *v.tr.* **(spotted) 1.** (*a*) tacher, souiller (qch.); (*with passive force*) **material that spots easily,** tissu qui se tache facilement; (*b*) tacheter, moucheter (qch.); *Phot:* **to s. a print,** repiquer une épreuve; (*with passive force*) **these prints are beginning to s.,** ces photos commencent à se moucheter; **it's spotting (with rain),** il commence à pleuvoir; (*c*) *Bill:* mettre (la bille) sur la mouche. **2.** *F:* (*a*) repérer, apercevoir, remarquer (qn, qch.); **I spotted him in the crowd,** je l'ai repéré, distingué, au milieu de la foule; **he spotted me from his box,** il m'a repéré de sa loge; (*b*) reconnaître; **I spotted him as a German,** je l'ai reconnu pour, comme, allemand; (*c*) *Turf:* etc: **to s. the winner,** prédire, repérer, le gagnant; (*d*) *Mil:* repérer, observer (des emplacements ennemis, etc.); (*e*) repérer (des différents modèles de trains, d'avions, etc.); (*f*) dénicher (du talent). **3.** *Metalw: Mec.E:* marquer, centrer (un trou).

spotbill ['spɔtbil], *s. Orn:* canard *m* à bec tacheté.

spot(-)face [spɔt'feis], *v.tr. Tchn:* lamer.

spotless ['spɔtlis], *a.* sans tache, sans macule; immaculé; pur; **s. snow,** neige immaculée, vierge; **s. kitchen,** cuisine d'une propreté irréprochable; **s. conscience,** conscience pure, nette.

spotlessly ['spɔtlisli], *adv.* **s. white,** d'une blancheur immaculée, parfaite; immaculé; **s. clean,** d'une propreté irréprochable.

spotlessness ['spɔtlisnis], *s.* propreté *f*; netteté *f*; pureté *f*.

spotlight[1] ['spɔtlait], *s.* (*a*) *Th: Cin:* lumière *f* de projecteur; (*b*) *Th: Cin:* projecteur (orientable, intensif); **(baby) s.,** projecteur directif; spot *m*; **to hold the s.,** (i) *Th:* occuper le centre de la scène (dans la lumière du projecteur); (ii) avoir, tenir, la vedette; être en vedette; **to direct, turn, put, the spotlights on sth.,** (i) *Th:* diriger les projecteurs sur qch.; (ii) mettre qch. en vedette; (*c*) *Aut:* projecteur auxiliaire orientable.

spotlight[2], *v.tr.* (*a*) *Th:* diriger les projecteurs sur (qn, qch.); (*b*) mettre (qn, qch.) en vedette; mettre (qch.) en relief; souligner (qch.).

spotlighting ['spɔtlaitiŋ], *s. Th: Cin:* éclairage *m* à effet.

spotted ['spɔtid], *a.* **1.** tacheté, moucheté; (cravate, etc.) à pois; *Nat.Hist:* taché, tacheté, maculé; (fruit, etc.) tavelé; (bois) madré; (chien, etc.) truité. **2.** *F:* **s. Dick, dog,** (i) petit danois, chien de Dalmatie; (ii) *Cu:* pudding *m* aux raisins secs.

spotter ['spɔtər], *s.* **1.** *Mil: Av:* (*a*) observateur *m* (d'emplacements ennemis, de défense contre avions); (*b*) avion *m* d'observation, de réglage de tir. **2.** (*a*) **train, aeroplane, s.,** personne *f* qui regarde passer des trains, des avions (pour repérer les différents modèles); (*b*) dénicheur, -euse (de talent). **3.** *N Am:* détective privé.

spotting ['spɔtiŋ], *s.* **1.** taches *fpl*; tachetures *fpl*. **2.** *Phot:* repiquage *m*, repiquement *m* (des épreuves). **3.** (*a*) repérage *m* (de trains, d'avions, etc.); (*b*) *Mil: Av:* observation *f*, repérage (d'emplacements ennemis, etc.); *Artil:* réglage *m* du tir; **s. mission,** mission de repérage (d'avions, etc.); *Mil: Navy:* **s. officer,** observateur du but; officier spotteur. **4.** *Mec.E:* centrage *m* (d'un trou); **s. tool,** outil à centrer, à marquer. **5.** *Med:* menstruation peu abondante (entre deux règles normales).

spotty ['spɔti], *a.* **1.** moucheté, tacheté; couvert de taches; (visage, etc.) couvert de boutons, boutonneux; (verre) galeux. **2.** *F:* (travail, exécution, etc.) qui manque d'ensemble, d'unité; inégal, -aux; irrégulier.

spousals ['spauz(ə)lz], *s.pl. A:* mariage *m*; épousailles *fpl*.

spouse [spauz], *s.* (*a*) *A: & Lit:* époux, *f.* épouse; (*b*) *Adm: Jur:* conjoint, -ointe.

spout[1] [spaut], *s.* **1.** (*a*) *Const:* **rainwater s.,** (i) tuyau *m* de décharge, de descente; canon *m*; (ii) gargouille *f*, chantepleure *f* (de gouttière); (*b*) bec *m* (de théière, de bouilloire, etc.); canon, goulot *m* (d'arrosoir); jet *m*, dégorgeoir *m* (de pompe); goulotte *f*, anche *f* (de trémie); **s. hole,** (i) lumière *f* (de pompe); (ii) *Z:* évent *m* (de baleine); (*c*) *Mill: etc:* trémie *f*; **boiler coal s.,** trémie de chargement de chaudière. **2.** (*a*) *A:* monte-charge *m* (de bureau de prêt sur gage); *F:* **to put one's watch up the s.,** mettre sa montre au clou, chez ma tante; (*b*) *F:* **up, down, the s.,** irrécupérable; perdu, fichu, foutu. **3.** *Meteor:* trombe *f*.

spout[2]. **1.** *v.i.* (*a*) (*of liquid*) jaillir, rejaillir; gicler; (*b*) (*of whale*) lancer un jet d'eau, d'air; souffler; (*c*) *F:* (*of pers.*) parler à jet continu; dépenser beaucoup de salive; dégoiser, déblatérer; pérorer; laïusser. **2.** *v.tr.* (*a*) faire jaillir, lancer (de l'eau, etc.); (*b*) *F:* dégoiser, débiter à jet continu (des discours, des injures, des sottises); **to s. Latin,** dégoiser du latin; (*c*) *F: A:* mettre au clou (de l'argenterie, etc.).

spouter ['spautər], *s.* **1.** *Petr: etc:* puits jaillissant. **2.** *F:* déclamateur, -trice; laïusseur, -euse; péroreur *m*.

spouting ['spautiŋ], *s.* **1.** jaillissement *m* (d'eau, etc.). **2.** *F:* déclamation *f*.

sprag[1] [spræg], *s.* **1.** *Min:* cale *f*, tasseau *m*. **2.** *Veh:* (*a*) cale, bâton *m* (pour enrayer les roues); (*b*) *Aut: U.S: A:* béquille *f* à décrochage; béquille de recul; **to drop the s.,** décrocher la béquille; **the car leapt the s.,** la voiture a grimpé sur la béquille.

sprag[2], *v.tr.* **(spragged) 1.** *Min:* soutenir (la masse de houille) au moyen de cales. **2.** *Veh:* caler, enrayer (une roue).

sprain[1] [sprein], *s.* entorse *f*, foulure *f*; *Vet:* nerf-foulure *f*, *pl.* nerfs-foulures.

sprain[2], *v.tr.* se fouler (la cheville, le poignet); se donner, se faire, une entorse (au pied, au poignet); **sprained ankle,** foulure *f* au pied, entorse; *Vet:* nerf-foulure *f*, *pl.* nerfs-foulures.

spraints [spreints], *s.pl. Ven:* épreintes *f* (de la loutre).

sprat [spræt], *s.* **1.** *Ich:* sprat *m*, harenguet *m*, anchois *m* de Norvège; esprot *m*, melet *m*, melette *f*; *F:* **it's a s. to catch a herring, a mackerel, a whale,** c'est donner un œuf pour avoir un bœuf; c'est donner un pois pour avoir une fève. **2.** *F:* gringalet *m*; mauviette *f*.

sprawl[1] [sprɔ:l], *s.* (attitude *f* de qn qui est étalé par terre, sur un lit, etc.) position abandonnée; **lying in a s. on the grass,** vautré sur l'herbe.

sprawl[2], *v.i.* **1.** (*a*) s'étendre, s'étaler; *F:* faire le veau; **to s. on a sofa,** s'étaler, se vautrer, sur un divan; (*b*) **to send s.o. sprawling,** envoyer rouler qn de tout son long; **to go sprawling,** s'étaler par terre; tomber les quatre fers en l'air; ramasser une pelle; **sprawling on his back,** étendu les quatre fers en l'air. **2.** (*a*) *O:* se traîner, ramper, à plat ventre; (*b*) **the name sprawled over the whole page,** le nom couvrait toute la page d'une écriture informe; **there were plants sprawling all over the place,** il y avait des plantes qui rampaient, qui s'étendaient, de tous côtés.

sprawling ['sprɔ:liŋ], *a.* **1.** (*a*) vautré; (*b*) étendu les quatre fers en l'air. **2. s. handwriting,** grosse écriture informe; gribouillage *m* **s. town,** ville informe, tentaculaire.

spray[1] [sprei], *s.* brin *m*, brindille *f*, ramille *f*; **s. of flowers,** (i) branche *f* de fleurs; rameau fleuri; (ii) *Arch: Needlew: etc:* chute *f* de fleurs; **s. of diamonds,** aigrette *f* de diamants.

spray[2], *s.* **1.** embrun *m*, poudrin *m*; écume *f*; *Agr:* **s. drift,** entraînement *m* par le vent. **2.** (*a*) poussière *f* d'eau, eau vaporisée, eau pulvérisée; *Mch: Ind:* **s. cooling,** rafraîchissement *m* par pulvérisation; refroidissement *m* par atomisation; (*b*) jet pulvérisé (de parfum, d'essence, etc.); **s. painting,** peinture *f* au pistolet, au vaporisateur, au pulvérisateur; **s. gun,** pistolet, pulvérisateur (à peinture, à insecticide, etc.); *I.C.E:* **s. nozzle,** gicleur *m*. **3.** (*a*) liquide *m* pour vaporisation; **hair s.,** laque *f*; **s. deodorant, deodorant s.,** désodorisant en nébuliseur, en atomiseur, en bombe; (*b*) coup *m* de vaporisateur; giclée *f*, jet (de peinture, de parfum, etc.); (*c*) (*atomizer*) atomiseur *m*, vaporisateur; pulvérisateur; **s. (canister),** bombe *f* (aérosol) (à laque, à peinture, etc.); **perfume s.,** atomiseur, vaporisateur, nébuliseur *m*, à parfum; *Med:* **nasal s.,** nébuliseur.

spray[3], *v.tr.* **1.** atomiser, pulvériser, vaporiser (un liquide); **to s. a solution up one's nostrils,** se vaporiser un liquide dans le nez; *Ind:* **to s. dry,** sécher (du lait, etc.) par atomisation; **s. drying,** séchage *m* (du lait, etc.) par atomisation; **s.-dried milk,** poudre *f* de lait. **2.** asperger, arroser; bassiner (des plants, des semis); peindre (qch.) au pistolet; *F:* pistoler (qch.); **to s. oneself with perfume,** se parfumer à l'atomiseur, au vaporisateur; **to s. sth. with machine-gun fire,** arroser, seringuer, qch. à la mitrailleuse; *Hort:* **to s. a tree,** passer un arbre au vaporisateur.

sprayer ['spreiər], *s.* **1.** (*a*) *Hort: etc:* vaporisateur *m*, pulvérisateur *m* (à insecticide, etc.); atomiseur *m*; **bivert, bifluid, s.,** pulvérisateur à émulsions inverties multiphases; *Av:* **crop s.,** avion *m*, hélicoptère *m*, agricole; (*b*) *Nau: etc:* brûleur *m* (de mazout); (*c*) pistolet *m*, pulvérisateur (à peinture); (*d*) **foam s.,** extincteur *m* à mousse. **2.** arroseuse *f*.

spraying ['spreiiŋ], *s.* **1.** pulvérisation *f*, vaporisation *f*, atomisation *f* (d'un liquide); **metal s.,** métallisation *f* par projection; *Vit:* **s. mixture,** bouillie *f*. **2.** arrosage *m*, arrosement *m*; bassinage *m* (de semis, etc.).

spread[1] [spred], *s.* **1.** (*a*) étendue *f* (de pays, etc.); **boats with a s. of white sails,** barques tendues de voiles blanches; (*b*) (*of bird's wings, of sails, of aircraft*) envergure *f*; **s. of a tree,** développement *m* du branchage; **s. of compass legs,** ouverture *f* d'un compas; *Nau:* **s. of the shrouds,** épatement *m*; *F:* **middle-age(d) s.,** embonpoint *m* de la maturité; *Ind:* **s. over,** répartition *f* sur la semaine entière, selon les exigences du service, d'un nombre fixe d'heures de travail; (*c*) *Com:* différence *f* (entre le prix de fabrique et le prix de vente, entre deux tarifs, etc.); (*d*) *St.Exch: esp. U.S:* opération *f* à cheval; (*e*) *NAm:* ranch *m*. **2.** (*a*) diffusion *f* (de l'éducation); propagation *f*, extension *f*, diffusion (d'une doctrine, d'une maladie); expansion *f*, dissémination *f* (des idées); (*b*) dispersion latérale (d'un phare); *Ball:* dispersion (du tir). **3.** couverture *f* de lit; dessus-de-lit *m inv*; couvre-lit *m*, *pl.* couvre-lits; courtepointe *f*. **4.** *F:* festin *m*, repas somptueux; gueuleton *m*; **cold s.,** repas froid; **to make a great s.,** mettre les petits plats dans les grands. **5.** *Journ: etc:* **double page s.,** annonce *f*, article *m*, etc., sur deux pages. **6.** fromage *m*, pâte *f* de viande, de poisson, etc., à tartiner.

spread[2], *v.* (*p.t. & p.p.* **spread**)

I. *v.tr.* **1.** (*a*) étendre; **to s. a cloth on, over, a table,** étendre une nappe sur une table; **to s. a net,** tendre, appareiller, un filet; **to s. the sails,** déployer, établir, mettre dehors, les voiles; **the trees s. (out) their branches,** les arbres étendent leurs branches; **the bird spreads (out) its wings,** l'oiseau étend, déploie, ses ailes; **a bird with its wings s. (out),** un oiseau aux ailes étendues, déployées; **to s. out a map, a handkerchief,** déployer, étaler, une carte, un mouchoir; **a map, a fan, lay s. out on the table,** il y avait sur la table une carte déployée, étalée, un éventail ouvert; **to s. out goods for sale,** étaler, déplier, déballer, des marchandises; **to s. (out) one's fingers,** écarter ses doigts; **to s. (oneself) out,** s'étendre, s'allonger (sur un divan, etc.); **to s. oneself,** (i) se prodiguer; dépenser de l'argent à profusion; faire le généreux; (ii) se donner des airs; plastronner, parader; **to s. oneself on a subject,** s'étendre sur un sujet; **patrol boats s. in search,** vedettes déployées en recherche; *Mus:* **to s. a chord,** arpéger un accord; **s. chord,** accord arpégé; arpège *m*; (*b*) **s. eagle,** (i) *Her:* aigle éployée; (ii) *Hist:* personne assujettie jambes et bras écartés (pour la peine du fouet); (iii) (*skating*) grand aigle; (iv) *Cu: A:* poulet *m*, poussin *m*, à la crapaudine; *U.S: F:* **s. eagle oratory,** éloquence chauviniste, grandiloquente; **s.-eagleism,** chauvinisme américain; **to s.-eagle,** (i) *Hist:* assujettir (qn) jambes et bras écartés (pour la peine du fouet); (ii) se répandre, se propager, dans (un pays, etc.); (iii) (*skating*) faire le grand aigle; **sunbathers lying s.-eagled on the sand,** baigneurs étalés, vautrés, sur la plage; *Her:* **s. eaglet,** alérion *m*. **2.** (*a*) répandre (du sable, de la paille); épandre (du fumier); semer (la terreur); répandre, colporter, rapporter (un bruit, des nouvelles); propager (une maladie); **there is a rumour being s. around that. . .,** il se répand que . . .; le bruit court que . . .; **to s. s.o.'s fame (abroad),** faire connaître, répandre, la réputation de qn; (*b*) **the payments are s. over several months,** les paiements sont échelonnés, étalés, répartis, sur plusieurs mois; **my friends are s. all over the country,** mes amis sont dispersés par tout le pays. **3.** (*a*) **to s. butter on a slice of bread,** étendre, étaler, du beurre sur une tranche de pain; tartiner une tranche de pain; **the river s. its waters over the countryside,** le fleuve a répandu ses eaux dans la campagne; **to s. ointment on a burn,** badigeonner une brûlure avec de l'onguent; appliquer de l'onguent sur une brûlure; *Nau:* **to s. oil on a rough sea,** filer de l'huile sur une mer démontée; (*b*) *U.S:* **to s. sth. on the records,** consigner qch. au procès-verbal; noter qch. sur les archives. **4.** (*a*) **to s. a surface with sth.,** recouvrir, enduire, une surface de qch.; (*b*) *O: & NAm:* **to s. the table,** dresser, mettre, la table; mettre le couvert; **table s. with dishes,** table couverte de plats; **lunch was s.,** le déjeuner était servi; (*c*) *Lit:* **the meadows were s. with daisies,** les prés étaient (par)semés, émaillés, de pâquerettes.

II. *v.i.* **1.** s'étendre, s'étaler; **on every side spreads a vast desert,** de chaque côté s'étale, s'étend, un vaste désert; **here the river spreads out,** ici la rivière s'élargit, s'étale. **2.** (*of rumour, news, ideas, etc.*) se répandre, se propager; se disséminer; (*of disease, fire, theory, etc.*) se propager; (*of custom, habit*) se répandre, se généraliser; (*of smell, smoke, sound*) se répandre; (*of evil, epidemic, fame*) s'étendre; (*of evil, cancer*) se généraliser; *Typ:* (*of type, etc.*) bavocher; **the fire is spreading,** l'incendie gagne (du terrain); **the fire s. to the next house,** l'incendie a gagné la maison voisine; **to stop a fire from spreading,** couper chemin à un incendie; **a sudden flush s. over her face,** une rougeur subite se répandit sur son visage; **his ideas are spreading,** ses idées font tache d'huile; **the pain was spreading on the left side,** la douleur irradiait du côté gauche; **the swelling has s. to the throat,** l'enflure a gagné la gorge; **the mutiny s. to the other regiments,** la révolte a gagné les autres régiments; **the rumour was spreading,** la rumeur grandissait; **a rumour has s. that. . .,** un bruit s'est répandu que . . .; **terror s. among the nations,** la terreur se répandit parmi les peuples; **terror s. everywhere,** l'épouvante se mit partout. **3.** (*of group of people, of small shot*) s'écarter, se disperser; **the birds rose and s. (out),** les oiseaux s'envolèrent en gerbe, en s'égaillant; **the roads that s. round Paris,** les routes qui sillonnent, qui irradient, autour de Paris.

spreader ['spredər], *s.* **1.** *Tchn:* (*a*) étendeur, -euse; (*b*) *Tex:* étaleur, -euse (des mèches). **2.** propagateur, -trice (d'une idée, d'un bruit, de nouvelles); colporteur, -euse, rapporteur, -euse (de nouvelles, d'un bruit); semeur, -euse (de discordes, etc.). **3.** (*a*) arrosoir *m* (d'une machine à arroser); éventail *m* (d'une lance d'arrosage); (*b*) *Agr: Civ.E:* épandeur *m*, épandeuse *f*. **4.** *Tls: Carp:* couteau fendeur. **5.** (*a*) tendeur *m*, extenseur *m*; barre *f* d'écartement (d'un hamac, etc.); (*b*) *Min:* étrésillon *m*. **6.** *Tex:* (*a*) table *f* à étaler; étaleuse; (*b*) élargisseuse *f*; épandeuse *f*.

spreading[1] ['sprediŋ], *a.* étendu; qui s'étend, qui se répand; **s. oak,** chêne touffu; **under a s. chestnut tree,** sous un châtaignier rameux.

spreading[2], *s.* **1.** (*a*) déploiement *m*, développement *m*; *Mus:* arpègement *m* (d'accords); *Ent:* **s. board,** planche à épingler; (*b*) colportage *m* (de nouvelles); propagation *f* (d'une maladie, d'une doctrine); expansion *f*, dissémination *f* (d'idées); diffusion *f* (de l'éducation); (*c*) étendage *m* (de la peinture, du vernis); répandage *m* (du goudron sur la chaussée, etc.); *Tex:* **s. machine,** élargisseuse *f*; (*d*) *O: & NAm:* **s. of the table,** mise *f* du couvert. **2.** (*a*) extension *f* (de territoire, d'une industrie); (*b*) disperson *f* (d'un groupe de personnes, etc.); *Ven:* **s. of the shot,** écart *m* du plomb.

spree [spri:], *s. F:* partie *f* de plaisir; (partie de) rigolade *f*; bombe *f*, bamboche *f*; **to have a s., to go (out) on a s.,** faire la noce, la bombe, la bringue, la bamboula, la java; faire bamboche, bombance; bambocher; partir en java; *Nau:* courir, tirer, une bordée; **to be on the s.,** être en bombe, faire la nouba; **to go on a shopping, spending, s.,** faire des achats extravagants.

sprig[1] [sprig], *s.* **1.** (*a*) brin *m*, brindille *f*; menue branche; (*b*) *Needlew:* ramage *m*; **s. muslin,** mousseline à ramages; (*c*) aigrette *f* (de diamants). **2. s. (nail),** pointe *f* (de Paris); cheville *f*; semence *f* (de tapissier); **glazier's s.,** clou *m* de vitrier. **3.** *usu. Pej:* (*a*) rejeton *m* (d'une race illustre); (*b*) *A:* jeune homme.

sprig[2], *v.tr.* **(sprigged) 1.** border des ramages sur (qch.). **2.** cheviller (qch.).

sprigged [sprigd], *a.* (tissu) à ramages, à branches, à fleurs.

sprightliness ['spraitlinis], *s.* vivacité *f*, enjouement *m*, entrain *m*; pétillement *m* (de l'esprit).

sprightly ['spraitli], *a.* éveillé, enjoué, vif, actif, sémillant; **s. wit,** esprit pétillant; **to be as s. as a two-year-old,** avoir des jambes de vingt ans.

sprigtail ['sprigteil], *s. Orn:* pilet *m*.

spring[1] [spriŋ], *s.* **1.** (*a*) source *f* (d'eau); fontaine *f*, point *m* d'eau; **hot, thermal, spring(s),** source thermale; eaux thermales; **mineral s.,** source d'eau minérale; **living s.,** source d'eau vive; source, eau, vive; **sprouting, gushing, s.,** source jaillissante; **s. well,** fontaine jaillissante; *Lit:* **the living springs of his influence have not run dry,** les sources vives de son influence ne sont pas taries; **to intercept, divert, a s.,** couper une source; (*b*) source, origine *f* (d'une coutume, etc.); (*c*) *Arch:* naissance *f*, retombée *f* (d'un arc, d'une voûte). **2.** printemps *m*; **in (the) s.,** au printemps; **in early s.,** dans les premiers jours de printemps; **a lovely s. evening,** une belle soirée de printemps; **s. is in the air,** on respire le printemps dans l'air; on sent dans l'air les effluves du printemps; **s. tide,** grande marée; (marée de) vives-eaux *fpl*; marée de syzygie; vive-eau *f*; vif *m* de la marée, de l'eau; maline *f*; **to have s. fever,** être amoureux; *Fr.C:* avoir la fièvre du printemps; **s. flowers,** fleurs printanières; *Bot:* **s. grass,** flouve odorante; **s. vegetables,** primeurs *m*; **s. greens,** variété *f* précoce de choux; *Cu:* **s. chicken,** poussin *m*; *F:* **she's no s. chicken,** elle n'est plus jeune; **s. materials,** tissus de demi-saison, tissus printaniers; **to s.-clean,** nettoyer à fond (une maison) (au printemps); *Fr.C:* faire le grand ménage; **s.-cleaning,** grand nettoyage (fait au printemps); nettoyage à fond; *Fr.C:* grand ménage. **3.** saut *m*, bond *m*; **to take a s.,** prendre son élan; faire un bond; **to rise with a s.,** se lever d'un bond. **4.** élasticité *f*; **the s. of a bow,** la force, la souplesse, d'un arc; **his muscles have no s. in them,** ses muscles manquent d'élasticité. **5.** (*a*) ressort *m*; **s. bed,** (lit à) sommier (i) métallique, (ii) à ressorts; **(interior) s. mattress,** matelas à ressorts, semi-métallique; **box s. mattress,** sommier métallique; *Mec.E: etc:* **spiral s.,** ressort à spires, en spirale; ressort à, en, boudin; **flat s.,** lame-ressort *f*, *pl.* lames-ressorts; **(semi-)elliptic s.,** ressort (semi-)-elliptique; **helical s.,** ressort hélicoïdal; **volute s.,** ressort en volute; **cantilever s.,** ressort cantilever; **laminated, leaf, plate, s.,** ressort à feuilles, à lames (étagées); **leaf s. clip,** bride *f* de ressort; **leaf s. opener,** écarte-lames *m inv*; **s. leaf, plate,** lame de ressort; **liquid s.,** ressort hydraulique; **compression s.,** ressort de compression; **release, return, restoring, s.,** ressort de rappel; **buffer s., shock-absorbing s.,** ressort amortisseur; **follow-up s.,** ressort d'asservissement; **tension s.,** ressort de tension; **torsion(al) s.,** ressort de torsion; **draft, drag, s.,** ressort de traction; **main s.,** ressort moteur, grand ressort; (*of machine gun*) **recoil, return, s.,** ressort récupérateur; *Sm.a:* **sear s.,** ressort de gâchette, petit ressort; **constant effort s.,** ressort régulateur; **s. bridle, buckle,** bride de ressort; **s. camber,** flèche de ressort; **s. guide,** guide de ressort; **s. guide tube,** tube guide de ressort; **s. shackle,** jumelle, étrier, de ressort; **s. seat, clamp,** logement, boîtier, de ressort; **s.-loaded latch, s. bolt,** verrou à ressort; **s. gun,** piège *m* à fusil; *Cin:* **s. motor,** moteur à ressort; **to act as a s.,** faire ressort; **the springs of human action,** les mobiles qui font agir les hommes; **to compress, set, a s.,** comprimer, tendre, un ressort; **to relax, release, a s.,** détendre un ressort; **to work a s.,** faire jouer un ressort; **s.-loaded, -driven, -actuated,** à ressort; actionné, mû, par ressort; **s. bracket,** support de ressort; **s. lock,** serrure à ressort, à fouillot; housset *m*, houssette *f*; (serrure) bec-de-cane *m*; serrure demi-tour; **s. bolt,** pêne coulant, à ressort; pêne demi-tour; **s. balance,** balance, peson, à ressort; dynamomètre *m*; *Metalw:* **s. beam (of drop hammer),** rabat *m*; *Clockm: etc:* **s. barrel, box, drum,** barillet *m*; boîte à ressort; douille de ressort; *Gym:* **s. grip,** crispateur *m*; *Tp:* **s. band,** ressort (de casque téléphonique); *Ent:* **s. beetle,** taupin *m*; maréchal *m*; tape-marteau *m*, *pl.* tape-marteaux; (*b*) *Veh: etc:* **springs, s. suspension,** suspension *f* à ressort(s) (d'une voiture, etc.); **vehicle on springs,** véhicule suspendu; **carriage s.,** ressort de voiture; **underslung s.,** ressort sous l'essieu; *Rail:* **bearing s.,** ressort de suspension; **s. carrier,** porte-ressort *m*, *pl.* porte-ressorts; **s. carrier arm,** main de ressort; **front, rear, s. carriers,** mains avant, arrière; **s. eye,** rouleau de ressort; *A:* **s. cart,** voiture suspendue; maringot(t)e *f*, jardinière *f*; **s. van,** tapissière *f*; *Cy:* **s. fork,** fourche élastique. **6.** *Bootm:* courbure *f* (du dessous de la forme). **7.** craqûre *f* (d'un espar). **8.** *Nau:* embossure *f*, croupiat *m*, traversier *m*; **fore s., back s.,** garde montante, descendante; *N.Arch:* **s. beam,** élongis *m* de tambour; traversin *m* des roues.

spring[2], *v.* **(sprang** [spræŋ]; **sprung** [sprʌŋ])

I. *v.i.* **1.** (*a*) bondir, sauter; **to s. up,** (i) sauter en l'air; (ii) se lever précipitamment, d'un bond; **to s. to one's feet,** se lever vivement, d'un bond, d'une secousse; **to s. over a ditch,** sauter un fossé; **to s. aside, to one side,** s'écarter brusquement; faire un bond de côté; **to s. back,** (i) faire un bond en arrière; (ii) faire ressort; **the branch sprang back,** la branche s'est redressée; **to s. forward,** s'élancer, se précipiter, en avant; **to s. to s.o.'s help,** se précipiter, voler, au secours de qn; **to s. to the attack,** bondir à l'assaut; *Lit:* **to s. to arms,** voler aux armes; **to s. into the saddle,** sauter en selle; **to s. out of bed,** sauter du lit; **to s. at s.o.,** s'élancer, se jeter, sur qn; (*b*) se mouvoir sous l'action (subite) d'un ressort; **to s. out,** (i) (*of cork, etc.*) sauter; sortir d'un bond; (ii) sortir sous l'action d'un ressort; **the lid sprang open,** le couvercle a sauté. **2.** (*a*) (*of water, etc.*) jaillir, filtrer, sourdre; **water springing from a fountain,** eau qui jaillit d'une fontaine; (*b*) **the blood sprang to his cheeks,** une rougeur subite lui monta aux joues; **hope springs eternal,** l'espérance reste toujours vivace; **to s. into existence,** naître, surgir; (ap)paraître (soudainement); (*c*) *A:* **to be sprung from a noble family,** descendre, sortir, d'une famille noble; **sprung from royal blood,** issu de sang royal; *F:* **where did you s. from?** d'où sortez-vous? (*d*) *Lit:* **what will s. from these events?** que verra-t-on sourdre de ces événements? **his genius springs from strong passions,** son génie a sa source dans de fortes passions; (*e*) (*of plant, etc.*) **(to begin to) s. (up),** (commencer à) pousser, poindre, croître; commencer à) sortir de terre; (*f*) **a breeze sprang up,** une brise s'est levée; **the belief has sprung up that. . .,** la croyance s'est formée, a pris naissance, que . . .; **an intimacy sprang up between them,** l'intimité s'est établie entre eux; **a doubt sprang up in his mind,** un doute a germé dans son esprit. **3.** (*a*) (*of wood*) gauchir; se déformer, se déjeter; (*b*) (*of mast, pole*) craquer; se fendre.

II. *v.tr.* **1.** (*a*) fendre (une raquette); faire craquer (un mât, un aviron); gauchir, déformer (une planche, etc.); (*b*) *Nau:* **to s. a butt,** faire sauter un about. **2.** (faire) lever (une perdrix, etc.). **3.** (*a*) faire jouer (un piège); faire sauter (une mine); (*b*) **to s. a question, a request, on s.o.,** poser à qn une question inattendue; demander qch. à brûle-pourpoint; **to s. a surprise on s.o.,** prendre qn à l'improviste; faire une surprise à qn. **4.** munir (une voiture) de ressorts. **5.** *F:* (i) faire échapper (qn) de prison; larguer (qn); (ii) *NAm:* faire libérer (qn) de prison, cautionner (qn).

springboard ['spriŋbɔ:d], *s.* (*a*) *Gym: Swim:* tremplin *m*; (*b*) *Fig:* source *f*.

springbok ['spriŋbɔk], *s.* **1.** *Z:* springbok *m*. **2.** *F:* **the Springboks,** (i) les Sud-Africains; (ii) *Sp:* l'équipe sud-africaine de rugby, etc.

springe[1] [sprin(d)ʒ], *s.* (*for rabbits, etc.*) lacet *m*, lacs *m*, collet *m*; (*for birds*) arbalète *f*, mésangette *f*.

springe[2], *v.tr.* piéger (un lapin, un oiseau); prendre (un lapin) au collet, au lacet.

springer ['spriŋər], *s.* **1.** (*pers.*) sauteur, -euse; *Navy: F:* maître *m* de gymnastique. **2.** (*a*) **S. (spaniel),** épagneul springer (anglais); (*b*) *Z:* springbok *m*. **3.** *Arch:* sommier *m*, imposte *f* (d'une arcade); claveau *m* (d'une voûte).

springhaas ['spriŋhɑ:s], *s. Z:* (*S. Africa*) lièvre sauteur, pédète *f*.

springhalt ['spriŋhɔ:lt], *s. Vet:* éparvin, épervin, sec.

springhead ['spriŋhed], *s.* source *f*, fontaine *f*; point *m* d'eau.

springiness ['spriŋinis], *s.* élasticité *f* (d'un matelas, etc.); effet *m* de ressort; liant *m*, ressort *m*.

springing[1] ['spriŋiŋ], *a*. **1.** *Lit:* **s. corn,** blé qui lève. **2. s. step,** pas dansant, élastique. **3.** *Her:* (cerf) élancé.

springing[2], *s*. **1.** bonds *mpl*, sauts *mpl*. **2.** (*a*) jaillissement *m* (d'une source); (*b*) germination *f* (de plantes). **3.** (*a*) craquement *m* (d'un mât, etc.); (*b*) gauchissement *m* (d'une planche, etc.). **4.** suspension *f* (d'une voiture, d'un lit, etc.). **5.** *Arch:* **s. (of a vault),** naissance *f*, retombée *f* (d'une voûte); **s. course,** assise de retombée; **s. line,** ligne de naissance; *Arch: Civ.E:* (*on pier*) **s. stones,** tas *m* de charge.

springless ['spriŋlis], *a*. sans ressort(s); **s. step,** démarche lourde.

springlet ['spriŋlit], *s. Lit:* petite source.

springlike ['spriŋlaik], *a*. printanier; de printemps; vernal.

springtail ['spriŋteil], *s. Ent:* podure *m*, podurelle *f*.

springtide ['spriŋtaid], *s*. = SPRINGTIME.

springtime ['spriŋtaim], *s*. printemps *m*; *A: & Lit:* renouveau *m*; **she died in the s. of life,** elle est morte dans le printemps de sa vie.

springwater ['spriŋwɔ:tər], *s*. eau *f* de source; eau de fontaine; eau, source, vive.

springwood ['spriŋwud], *s. Arb:* bois *m* de printemps.

springy ['spriŋi], *a*. **1.** élastique, qui fait ressort; liant, flexible; (corps) à ressort; **s. carpet,** tapis moelleux. **2. to walk with a s. step,** marcher d'un pas leste, léger, alerte.

sprinkle[1] ['spriŋkl], *s*. (*a*) petite averse; **a s. of rain,** quelques gouttes *f* de pluie; (*b*) **a s. of salt,** quelques grains *m* de sel; une pincée de sel.

sprinkle[2], *v.tr*. (*a*) répandre, jeter (de l'eau, du sel, du gravier); (*b*) asperger, arroser, bassiner (**with water,** d'eau); saupoudrer (**with salt,** de sel); **to s. the floor with sand,** répandre du sable par terre; **lawn sprinkled with daisies,** gazon parsemé de pâquerettes; **writings sprinkled with quotations,** écrits semés, lardés, truffés, de citations; (*c*) *Bookb:* jasper (les tranches).

sprinkler ['spriŋklər], *s*. **1.** (*for lawns, etc.*) appareil *m* d'arrosage; arroseuse *f* à jet tournant; arroseur (rotatif); tourniquet *m* hydraulique, de jardinier; rampe *f* d'arrosage; (*extinguisher*) (**automatic**) **fire s.,** extincteur *m* (automatique) d'incendie; **s. system,** noyage *m* en pluie. **2.** *Ecc:* aspergès *m*, goupillon *m*, aspersoir *m*.

sprinkling ['spriŋkliŋ], *s*. **1.** aspersion *f*, arrosage *m*, arrosement *m*; (*with sugar, etc.*) saupoudrage *m*; *U.S:* **s. can,** arrosoir *m*; **s. cart,** tonneau *m* d'arrosage; arroseuse *f* (automobile); *Ecc:* **s. of holy water,** aspergès *m*, aspersion. **2.** (*a*) **a s. of gravel,** légère couche de gravier; (*b*) **a s. of knowledge,** quelques connaissances; **a fair s. of foreign words,** un assez grand nombre, un nombre respectable, de mots étrangers. **3.** *Bookb:* jaspure *f*. **4.** *Mil:* **s. fire,** tir d'arrosage.

sprint[1] [sprint], *s*. (*a*) **s. (race),** course *f* de vitesse; (*b*) pointe *f* de vitesse; rush *m* (de fin de course); sprint *m*.

sprint[2]. **1.** *v.i.* faire une course de vitesse; sprinter; **to s. past one's opponent,** dépasser, *F:* gratter, griller, son adversaire. **2.** *v.tr.* **the 100 metres is always sprinted,** le 100 mètres est toujours couru en vitesse.

sprinter ['sprintər], *s*. coureur, -euse, de vitesse; sprinter *m*.

sprinting ['sprintiŋ], *s*. courses *fpl* de vitesse.

sprit [sprit], *s. Nau:* livarde *f*, baleston *m*; **s. topsail,** contre-civadière *f*, *pl*. contre-civadières.

sprite [sprait], *s*. lutin *m*; esprit (follet); fée *f*; farfadet *m*; elfe *m*.

spritsail ['spritseil, *Nau:* 'sprits(ə)l], *s. Nau:* (i) voile *f* à livarde; voile à baleston; (ii) *A:* civadière *f* (sous le mât de beaupré).

sprocket ['sprɔkit], *s. Mec.E:* **1.** dent *f* (de pignon). **2. s. wheel,** pignon *m* de chaîne; couronne *f* à empreintes; roue *f* à cames, à réas; barbotin *m*; hérisson *m*; *Cy:* **chain s.,** pignon de chaîne; **s. chain,** chaîne à barbotins; chaîne Galle; *Cin:* **s. (wheel),** galet *m*, tambour *m*; **top s. wheel (of projector),** débiteur *m*; **feed s.,** tambour dérouleur.

sprog [sprɔg], *s. F:* **1.** recrue *f*, conscrit *m*, bleu *m*. **2.** enfant *m*, mioche *m*, moutard *m*.

sprout[1] [spraut], *s. Bot:* **1.** (*a*) jet *m*, rejet *m*, rejeton *m*, pousse *f*; (*b*) germe *m*, bourgeon *m*. **2. Brussels sprouts,** *F:* **sprouts,** choux *m* de Bruxelles.

sprout[2]. **1.** *v.i.* (*a*) (*of plant*) pousser, pointer; **to s. from the base,** rejeter, rejetonner; émettre des rejets, des rejetons; (*b*) (*of branch, shrub*) bourgeonner; (*c*) (*of seed*) pousser des germes; germer; **sprouted barley,** orge germé, levé; (*d*) *Metall:* (*of silver, etc.*) rocher. **2.** *v.tr.* (*of animal*) **to s. horns,** pousser des cornes; *F:* (*of pers.*) **to s. a moustache,** laisser pousser sa moustache.

sprouting ['sprautiŋ], *s*. **1.** *Bot:* (*a*) germination *f*, bourgeonnement *m*, pousse *f*; (*b*) (**purple**) **s.,** chou-fleur *m* d'hiver; **s. broccoli,** brocoli *m*. **2.** *Metall:* rochage *m*.

spruce[1] [spru:s], *a*. paré, pimpant; soigné; tiré à quatre épingles.

spruce[2], *v.tr.* **to s. oneself up,** se parer; se faire beau, belle; **all spruced up,** sur son trente et un.

spruce[3], *s*. (*a*) *Bot:* **s. (fir),** (sapin *m*) épicéa *m*; épinette *f*, pignet *m*, spruce *m*; **white, black, s.,** sapinette blanche, noire; épinette blanche, noire; **Norway s.,** sapin de Norvège, sapin blanc; **Sitka s.,** épicéa de Sitka; **Douglas s.,** pseudotsuga *m* de Douglas; (*b*) **s. beer,** sapinette; bière d'épinette, de spruce, de pin.

spruceness ['spru:snis], *s*. air pimpant; mise pimpante, soignée.

sprue[1] [spru:], *s. Med:* sprue *f*, psilosis *m*.

sprue[2], *s. Metall:* **1. s. (gate),** trou *m* de coulée. **2.** baguette *f* de coulée. **3.** masselotte *f*; jet *m* de coulée.

Sprue[3], *s. Hort:* asperges *fpl* de qualité inférieure.

spruit [spru:t], *s*. (*S. Africa*) cours *m* d'eau; ruisseau *m*.

sprung [sprʌŋ], *a*. **1. s. carriage,** voiture suspendue; **s. weight,** poids suspendu. **2.** (*a*) *Nau:* **s. mast,** mât craqué; (*b*) **s. spindle,** fusée faussée, fléchie. **3.** *Pros:* **s. rhythm,** mètre *m* imitant le rythme naturel de la parole. **4.** *U.S: F:* ivre, raide, rond.

spry [sprai], *a*. (**spryer, spryest**) **1.** vif, actif; (plein d')allant; plein d'entrain. **2.** *A: Dial:* = SPRUCE[1].

spud[1] [spʌd], *s*. **1.** (*a*) *Agr: Hort:* petite bêche; sarcloir *m*; sarclette *f*; houlette *f*, arrache-racine(s) *m*; (*b*) *F: O:* personne dodue, trapue, de taille ramassée; objet court et renflé; (*c*) *O:* menotte potelée (d'un enfant). **2.** (*dredging*) piquet *m*. **3.** *F:* pomme *f* de terre; patate *f*; *Mil:* **s. basher,** éplucheur de patates; **s. bashing,** corvée de patates, (corvée de) pluches *fpl*.

spud[2], *v.tr.* (**spudded**) *Agr: Hort:* sarcler, bêcher (la terre).

spudding ['spʌdiŋ], *s. Min:* battage *m* au cable; **s. bit,** trépan *m* de battage, d'attaque.

spuddy ['spʌdi], *a. F: O:* (*of pers.*) dodu, trapu, ramassé; (*of hand*) potelé.

spue[1,2] [spju:], *s. & v.* = SPEW[1,2].

spume[1] [spju:m], *s*. (*a*) *A: & Lit:* écume *f* (de la mer); (*b*) *Med:* spume *f*.

spume[2], *v.i.* écumer.

spumescence [spju:'mes(ə)ns], *s*. spumosité *f*.

spumescent [spju:'mes(ə)nt], *a*. spumescent.

spumous ['spju:məs], **spumy** ['spju:mi], *a. A: & Lit:* écumeux; spumeux.

spun [spʌn], *a*. (*a*) *Tex:* câblé; **s. silk,** soie filée; (*b*) *Metalw:* **s. copper,** cuivre repoussé.

spungoid ['spʌŋgɔid], *a. Anat: Med:* (tissu, inflammation) spongoïde.

spunk [spʌŋk], *s*. **1.** (*a*) amadou *m*; (*b*) *Scot: F:* allumette *f*. **2.** *F:* (*a*) courage *m*, cran *m*; **to have plenty of s.,** avoir du cran; **to put fresh s. into s.o.,** mettre, remettre, du cœur au ventre à qn; (*b*) *U.S:* colère *f*, emportement *m*; mauvaise humeur.

spunky ['spʌŋki], *a. F:* (*a*) courageux; qui a du cran; (*b*) *U.S:* irascible, coléreux.

spur[1] [spə:r], *s*. **1.** éperon *m*; **s. maker,** éperonnier *m*; **to win one's spurs,** (i) *Hist:* gagner ses éperons; (ii) *Fig:* faire ses preuves; se faire un nom, une réputation; gagner ses éperons; **to set, put, spurs to one's horse,** donner de l'éperon à son cheval; éperonner son cheval; donner du talon à son cheval; presser son cheval du talon, de l'éperon; piquer de l'éperon, des éperons; piquer des deux; (*of horse*) **s. wise,** sensible à l'éperon, qui a l'éperon délicat, qui connaît les talons; **to put on, take off, one's spurs,** chausser, déchausser, ses éperons; **s. leather,** monture d'éperon; *Hist:* **the battle of the Spurs,** la Journée des éperons; **the s. of Italy,** l'éperon de la botte (de l'Italie); *Her:* **s. rowel,** molette *f*. **2.** coup *m* d'éperon; stimulant *m*; **to do sth. on the s. of the moment,** faire qch. sous l'impulsion, sous l'inspiration, du moment; faire qch. par coup de tête, de but en blanc, à l'improviste; **to give a s. to s.o.'s efforts,** stimuler les efforts de qn. **3.** (*a*) ergot *m* (de coq); (*b*) éperon (d'un coq de combat). **4.** (*a*) éperon, contrefort *m*, rameau *m* (d'une chaîne de montagnes); (*b*) épi *m* (de chemin de fer). **5. climbing spurs,** grappins *m*, griffes *f*, crampons *m*. **6.** *Bot:* éperon; *Hort:* **fruit s.,** dard *m*. **7.** (*a*) *Mec.E: etc:* **s. chuck,** mandrin *m* à pointes; griffe; **s. gear, wheel,** (roue d')engrenage cylindrique, droit; roue droite, dentée; **s. gearing, pinion,** pignon droit; (*b*) *Carp: Const:* contre-fiche *f*, *pl*. contre-fiches; arc-boutant *m*, *pl*. arcs-boutants; entretoise *f*; *Const:* **s. stone,** chasse-roue(s) *m*, bouteroue *f*; (*c*) *N.Arch:* arc-boutant de soutien. **8.** *Fort:* éperon. **9.** *A. Navy:* éperon (de proue).

spur[2], *v.tr.* (**spurred**) **1.** éperonner, talonner (un cheval); presser (un cheval) du talon, de l'éperon; *v.i.* **to s. on, forward,** jouer des éperons; piquer des deux. **2. to s. s.o. on,** aiguillonner, stimuler, qn; **to s. s.o. on to do sth.,** stimuler, exciter, inciter, pousser, qn à faire qch.; **spurred on by the desire, the wish, to . . .,** fouetté par le désir de . . .. **3.** éperonner (un cavalier, un coq de combat); chausser les éperons à (un cavalier). **4.** *Hort:* tailler, pincer (une plante, un arbre).

spurge [spə:dʒ], *s. Bot:* euphorbe *f*, épurge *f*; cierge (amer, laiteux); **cypress s.,** lait *m* de couleuvre; **s. laurel,** (daphné *m*) lauréole *f*; laurier *m* des bois; **s. olive,** bois gentil; garou *m* des bois; **s. flax,** sainbois *m*, garou.

spurious ['spjuəriəs], *a*. **1.** faux, *f*. fausse; controuvé; falsifié; **s. coin,** pièce de monnaie fausse, falsifiée; **s. love,** amour d'emprunt; amour simulé; **s. drug,** drogue falsifiée; *Meteor:* **s. rainbow,** arc surnuméraire; *W.Tel:* **s. oscillations,** oscillations parasites. **2.** (*of writings*) apocryphe; (*of edition*) de contrefaçon. **3.** *Nat.Hist:* (*of organ, limb, etc.*) faux. **4.** *A:* (*of pers.*) illégitime, bâtard.

spuriously ['spjuəriəsli], *adv*. faussement, par contrefaçon.

spuriousness ['spjuəriəsnis], *s*. **1.** fausseté *f*; nature falsifiée (**of,** de). **2.** caractère *m* apocryphe (d'un texte). **3.** *A:* illégitimité *f*, bâtardise *f*.

spurn[1] [spə:n], *s*. **1.** coup *m* de pied pour écarter, repousser, qch. **2.** refus méprisant d'une offre, d'une offrande; rebuffade *f*.

spurn[2], *v.tr.* **1.** repousser, écarter, (qch.) du pied; *Lit:* **to s. the proffered gifts,** repousser du pied les dons offerts. **2.** rejeter (une offre) avec mépris; repousser (qn, les avances de qn) avec mépris; mépriser (qn); traiter (qn) avec mépris.

spurner ['spə:nər], *s*. contempteur, -trice (**of,** de).

spurred ['spə:d], *a*. **1.** éperonné. **2.** *Orn:* ergoté. **3.** (*a*) *Bot:* (fleur) calcarifère; (*b*) (*of rye, etc.*) ergoté, cornu.

spurr(e)y ['spʌri], *s. Bot:* spergule *f*, spargoule *f*, spargoute *f*, sporée *f*; **corn s.,** spargoute des champs; **sand s.,** spergularia *m*, spergulaire *f*.

spurrier ['spʌriər], *s*. éperonnier *m*.

spurring ['spə:riŋ], *s*. **1.** coups *mpl* d'éperon. **2.** stimulation *f*, excitation *f*.

spurt[1] [spə:t], *s*. **1.** jaillissement *m*; rejaillissement *m*; jet *m*; **s. of petrol,** giclée *f* d'essence; **s. of fire,** jaillissement de flamme. **2.** (*a*) effort soudain; coup *m* de collier; poussée *f* d'énergie; (*b*) *Sp:* effort de vitesse; pointe *f* de vitesse, emballage *m*, démarrage *m*, échappée *f*, rush *m* (de fin de course); *Row:* enlevage *m*; **to put on a s.,** démarrer, emballer; **final s.,** pointe finale.

spurt[2]. **1.** *v.i.* **to s. (up, out),** jaillir, rejaillir; gicler. **2.** *v.tr.* (*a*) **to s. (out) a liquid,** faire jaillir, faire gicler, un liquide; (*b*) (*of pen*) couler, cracher, gicler (de l'encre). **3.** *v.i. Sp:* démarrer; faire un effort de vitesse; faire un emballage.

spurting ['spə:tiŋ], *s*. giclement *m* (de sang, etc.); jaillissement *m*, rejaillissement *m* (d'eau).

sputnik ['sputnik], *s. Space:* spoutnik *m*, satellite artificiel.

sputter[1] ['spʌtər], *s*. = SPUTTERING.

sputter[2]. **1.** *v.tr.* dire (qch.) en bredouillant, en lançant des postillons. **2.** *v.i.* (*a*) lancer des postillons en parlant, postillonner; bredouiller, bafouiller; (*b*) (*of pen*) cracher; (*c*) (*of electric arc*) cracher, crachoter; crépiter, (*of kindling wood*) pétiller; (*of meat on grill*) grésiller; (*of flame*) grésiller, crépiter; **the candle sputtered out,** la bougie s'est éteinte, est morte, en grésillant.

sputtering ['spʌt(ə)riŋ], *s*. **1.** bredouillement *m*, bredouillage *m*, bafouillage *m*. **2.** crachement *m*, crachotement *m* (d'un stylo). **3.** crachement, crachotement, crépitement *m*, crépitation *f* (d'un arc électrique); pétillement *m* (du bois); grésillement *m* (de la friture, d'une bougie).

sputum, *pl*. **-a** ['spju:təm, -ə], *s. Med:* salive *f*; crachat *m*, crachement *m*; expectoration *f*.

spy[1], *pl*. **spies** [spai, spaiz], *s*. espion, -onne; *F:* mouchard, -arde, cafard, -arde.

spy[2], *v*. (**spied; spying**) **1.** *v.tr.* apercevoir, voir, reconnaître, remarquer; **he spied him approaching,** il l'a vu s'approcher; **to s. out the ground,** explorer le terrain; **I s.,** jeu *m* d'enfant dans lequel on devine un objet visible par l'initiale de son nom. **2.** *v.i.* espionner; *F:* moucharder, cafarder; **to s. on s.o., on s.o.'s movements,** épier, espionner, guetter, qn, les mouvements de qn.

spyglass ['spaiglɑ:s], *s*. (*a*) lunette *f* d'approche; longue-vue *f*, *pl*. longues-vues; (*b*) (*in door*) œilleton *m*.

spyhole ['spaihoul], *s*. (*a*) trou *m* (dans un rideau, etc.); fente *f* (dans une clôture, etc.); (*b*) judas *m*, guichet *m* (de porte); (*c*) regard *m* (de machine, etc.).

spying ['spaiiŋ], *s*. espionnage *m*.

squab[1] [skwɔb], *s*. **1.** pigeonneau *m* sans plumes; **s.**

chick(en), poussin *m* (sans plumes); *Cu:* **s. pie** = (i) croustade *f* de pigeonneaux; (ii) tourte composée de mouton, de porc, d'oignons et de pommes. **2.** *O:* petite personne grassouillette, dodue, trapue; boulot, -otte. **3.** (*a*) coussin capitonné; (*b*) *Aut:* coussin (de siège). **4.** (*a*) canapé rembourré; ottomane *f*; (*b*) pouf *m*.

squab[2], *a. O:* boulot, -otte; courtaud; grassouillet, -ette; rondelet, -ette; trapu.

squabble[1] ['skwɔbl], *s.* querelle *f*, dispute *f*, altercation *f*, chamaillerie *f*; prise *f* de bec; accrochage *m*.

squabble[2]. **1.** *v.i.* (*a*) se quereller, se disputer, se chamailler, se chicaner (**with,** avec); (*b*) *Typ:* (*of type*) (se) chevaucher. **2.** *v.tr. Typ:* faire chevaucher (les caractères); **squabbled type,** caractères qui chevauchent.

squabbler ['skwɔblər], *s.* querelleur, -euse; chamailleur, -euse.

squabbling ['skwɔbliŋ], *s.* querelles *fpl*; chamaillerie *f*.

squad[1] [skwɔd], *s.* **1.** *Mil: etc:* (i) escouade *f*; (ii) peloton *m*; **punishment, defaulters', s.,** peloton de punition, de discipline, des punis; *F:* pelote *f*; **firing s.,** peloton d'exécution; *Artil:* **gun s.,** peloton de pièce. **2.** (*a*) brigade *f*, équipe *f* (de cheminots, etc.); **rescue s.,** équipe de secours; *Ind:* **duty s.,** équipe de service; (*b*) **the Flying S. (of Scotland Yard),** l'équipe volante; **the Vice S.** = la police mondaine, des mœurs; la mondaine, les mœurs *f*; **s. car,** voiture *f* de police; (*c*) *Sp:* équipe.

squad[2], *v.tr.* (**squadded**) *esp. Mil:* former (des hommes) en escouades, en pelotons, en brigades, en équipes.

squaddie, squaddy ['skwɔdi], *s. F: A:* (simple) soldat *m*; bidasse *m*, fantassin *m*, troufion *m*.

squadron ['skwɔdrən], *s.* **1.** (*a*) *Mil:* escadron *m*; groupe *m* de combat; **armoured s.,** escadron de chars; **headquarters,** *U.S:* **service, s.,** escadron de commandement et des services; *U.S:* **half s.,** demi-groupe *m*, *pl.* demi-groupes; (*b*) *Mil.Av:* escadron, escadrille *f*; groupe d'aviation (d'avions de transport); **fighter, bomber, s.,** escadron de chasse, de bombardement; (*rank*) **s. leader** = commandant *m*; **s. commander,** chef *m* d'escadre *f*. **2.** *Navy:* escadre; (*in Fleet Air Arm*) flottille *f*; **battleship s., cruiser s.,** escadre de bâtiments de ligne, de croiseurs; **the van s.,** l'avant-garde *f*; **the rear s.,** l'arrière-garde *f*; **blockading s.,** escadre de blocus.

squails [skweilz], *s.pl.* (sorte *f* de) jeu *m* de galet *m*.

Squali ['skweilai], *s.pl. Ich:* squales *m*.

squalid ['skwɔlid], *a.* sale, malpropre, crasseux; misérable, sordide; dégoûtant.

Squalidae ['skweilidi:], *s.pl. Ich:* squalidés *m*.

squalidity [skwɔ'liditi], **squalidness** ['skwɔlidnis], *s.* = SQUALOR.

squalidly ['skwɔlidli], *adv.* misérablement, sordidement; d'une façon misérable, sordide.

squall[1] [skwɔ:l], *s.* cri *m* (rauque, discordant, qui écorche les oreilles).

squall[2]. **1.** *v.i.* crier, brailler, piailler; pousser des cris rauques, discordants. **2.** *v.tr.* **to s. (out) sth.,** brailler, crier, qch.

squall[3], *s. Nau:* grain *m*; coup *m* de vent; bourrasque *f*; rafale *f*; *F:* coup de chien, de tabac; **light s.,** risée *f*; **thick s.,** grain épais; **black s., white s.,** grain noir, grain blanc; **sudden s.,** coup de temps; **the wind was blowing in squalls,** le vent soufflait par rafales; **to meet with, encounter, a s.,** essuyer, recevoir, un grain; **to prepare to meet a s., to reduce sail for a s.,** parer, saluer, un grain; **line s.,** ligne de grains; **s. kink,** crochet *m* de grain; *Fig:* **look out for squalls!** veille, pare, au grain! il va y avoir du grabuge!

squaller ['skwɔ:lər], *s.* criard, -arde; braillard, -arde; brailleur, -euse; piaillard, -arde.

squalling[1] ['skwɔ:liŋ], *a.* criard, braillard, piaillard.

squalling[2], *s.* criaillerie *f*, braillement *m*, piaillement *m*, piaillerie *f*.

squally ['skwɔ:li], *a.* (temps) à grains, à rafales; **the weather is becoming s.,** il fait un temps à grains.

squaloid ['skweilɔid]. *Ich:* **1.** *s.* squalidé *m*, squale *m*. **2.** *a.* squalidé.

Squaloidea [skwei'lɔidiə], *s.pl. Ich:* squaloïdes *m*.

squalor ['skwɔlər], *s.* saleté *f*; malpropreté *f*; misère *f*; **born in s.,** né dans la crasse; **to die in s.,** mourir sur le fumier; **the s. of these streets,** l'aspect *m* sordide de ces rues.

squama, *pl.* **-ae** ['skweimə, -i:], *s.* **1.** *Z:* squame *f*. **2.** *Bot:* écaille *f*. **3.** *Med:* squame.

squamaria [skwə'mɛəriə], *s. Bot:* squamarie *f*.

squamate ['skweimeit], *a. Nat.Hist:* squameux.

squamation [skwə'meiʃ(ə)n], *s. Nat.Hist:* **1.** squamosité *f*. **2.** disposition *f*, arrangement *m*, (i) *Z:* des squames, (ii) *Bot:* des écailles.

squamella, *pl.* **-ae** [skwə'melə, -i:], *s. Z:* squamule *f*; *Bot:* petite écaille.

squam(ell)iferous [skweimə'lifərəs, skwə'mifərəs], *a. Nat.Hist:* squam(ell)ifère.

squamifoliate [skweimi'foulieit], *a. Bot:* squamifolié.

squamiform ['skweimifɔ:m], *a. Nat.Hist:* squamiforme.

Squamipennes [skweimi'peni:z], *s.pl. Ich:* squamipennes *m*.

squamose, squamous ['skweimous, -əs], *a. Nat.Hist:* squameux.

squamula, *pl.* **-ae, squamule** ['skweimjulə, -i:, -ju:l], *s.* = SQUAMELLA.

squamulose ['skweimjulous], *a. Nat.Hist:* squam(ell)ifère; squameux.

squander ['skwɔndər], *v.tr.* gaspiller, prodiguer (de l'argent); dissiper, gaspiller, dilapider, manger, dévorer, *F:* claquer, croquer (une fortune); gaspiller (son temps); **to s. one's money,** jeter son argent par la fenêtre; croquer son argent.

squanderer ['skwɔndərər], *s.* gaspilleur, -euse; prodigue *mf*; dissipateur, -trice; dilapidateur, -trice; dépensier, -ière; *F:* panier percé.

squandering[1] ['skwɔndəriŋ], *a.* gaspilleur, prodigue; dissipateur, -trice; dilapidateur, -trice; dépensier.

squandering[2], *s.* gaspillage *m* (d'argent, de temps); prodigalité *f* (d'argent); dissipation *f*, dilapidation *f* (d'une fortune).

square[1] [skwɛər], *s., a. & adv.*

I. *s.* **1.** (*a*) *Mth: etc:* carré *m*; **magic s.,** carré magique; **word s.,** mots carrés; *A:* **oblong s.,** carré long; rectangle *m*; (*b*) *Mil.Hist:* (formation *f* en) carré; **hollow s.,** carré creux, vide; **to form (in) s.,** former le carré, se former en carré(s); **to break up the enemy squares,** enfoncer les carrés ennemis. **2.** (*a*) carreau *m* (de figure quadrillée, etc.); case *f*, compartiment *m* (d'échiquier, etc.); **to divide a map into squares,** quadriller, graticuler, une carte; (*for enlargement, etc., of maps and plans*) **framework of squares,** graticule *m*; **reducing squares,** carreaux de réduction; *Surv:* (*on map*) **(reference) s.,** carreau-module *m*, *pl.* carreaux-modules; **to be back at s. one,** revenir à son point de départ; repartir à zéro; (*b*) *A:* carreau (de verre); (*c*) **(silk) s.,** carré, foulard (de soie); (*d*) **squares,** (i) *Bookb:* chasses *f* (des plats); (ii) *Metalw:* fers carrés; (*e*) *Fish:* grand-dos *m*, ciel *m* de chalut. **3.** (*a*) (*of town, village*) place *f*; (*with garden*) square *m*; (*in front of church*) parvis *m*; (*b*) *Mil:* terrain *m* de manœuvre(s); **to be on the s.,** être passé en revue; *F:* **s. bashing** = l'exercice *m*; (*c*) *NAm:* bloc *m*, pâté *m*, de maisons (entre quatre rues). **4.** équerre *f*; **set s.,** équerre à dessin; **T s.,** équerre en T; té *m* (à dessin); double équerre (à dessin); **centre s.,** équerre à centrer; *Surv:* **optical s.,** équerre d'arpenteur; *Rail:* **rail s.,** équerre de pose; **to cut sth. on the s.,** couper qch. à angles droits; **out of s.,** hors d'équerre; hors d'aplomb; **to cut sth. out of s.,** couper qch. à fausse équerre; *F:* **to be on the s.,** (i) agir carrément, honnêtement; jouer franc jeu; être honnête; (ii) être franc-maçon; **our business is all on the s.,** nous jouons franc jeu. **5.** *Mth:* carré (d'un nombre, d'une expression); **perfect s.,** carré parfait; **mean s.,** carré moyen; **mean s. convergence,** convergence *f* en moyenne quadratique; **mean s. error,** écart quadratique moyen; **least squares,** moindres carrés; **least squares method,** méthode *f* des moindres carrés; **least squares adjustment,** compensation *f* par méthode des moindres carrés; **inverse s. law,** loi *f* de l'inverse carré. **6.** *Const: etc: A:* unité *f* de mesure de cent pieds carrés. **7.** *F: O:* **he's a s.,** il est tout à fait vieux jeu.

II. *a.* **1.** carré; (*a*) **s. table,** table carrée; **s. ruler,** carrelet *m*, réglette *f*; règle *f* quadrangulaire; **s. game,** partie *f* à quatre; **s. dance,** danse *f* à quatre; *Nau:* **s. sail,** voile carrée; *N.Arch:* **s. (transom) stern,** arrière carré; *Mil:* **s. division,** division quaternaire; **s. measure,** mesure *f* de surface, de superficie; **s. metre, centimetre,** mètre, centimètre, carré; **nine s. metres,** neuf mètres carrés; **nine metres s.,** de neuf mètres carrés; formant un carré de neuf mètres de côté; (*b*) **s. shoulders,** épaules carrées; **s.-shouldered,** aux épaules carrées; **s.-built,** (i) bâti en carré; (ii) (*of pers.*) aux épaules carrées; de belle carrure; trapu; **s. chin, jaw,** menton carré; **s.-jawed,** au menton carré; **s. toe,** carre *f* (de chaussure); **s.-toed shoes,** chaussures à bouts carrés; *F: O:* **to be s.(-toed),** être très collet monté, très vieux jeu, très guindé; *Cost:* **s. neck,** encolure carrée; décolleté (en) carré; **s.-necked dress,** robe à décolletage carré, à encolure carrée; **s.-cut bodice,** corsage à encolure carrée; (*c*) plat; *Carp:* **s. joint,** assemblage à plat. **2.** (*a*) **line s. with another,** ligne à angle droit, d'équerre, avec une autre; **s. corner,** coin en angle droit; coin formant un angle droit, un angle rectangulaire; *Cr:* **s. leg,** (i) chasseur *m* à gauche (du batteur) dans le prolongement du guichet; (ii) l'endroit *m* où ce chasseur se tient; (*b*) *N.Arch:* **s. body,** maîtresse partie; **s. frame,** couple droit; **s. rig(ging),** gréement carré, à traits carrés; **s.-rigged ship,** navire gréé en carré; **s.-rigged threemaster,** trois-mâts carré; **s. yards,** vergues brassées carré; (*c*) *Mec.E: etc:* (*of a screw*) **s. thread,** filet carré, filet rectangulaire; pas carré; **s.-thread(ed) screw,** vis à filet carré, à filet rectangulaire, à pas carré; **s.-thread tap,** taraud à filet carré, à pas carré; **s.-headed,** à tête carrée; **s.-tipped,** à bout carré; (*d*) *Elcs: etc:* **s. signal,** signal carré, signal rectangulaire; **s. wave,** (i) onde carrée, (onde) rectangulaire *f*; (ii) *Rad:* créneau *m*, impulsion *f* de fixation (sur l'écran); **s. wave (modulated) oscillator,** oscillateur modulé en ondes rectangulaires, en signaux carrés; **s. wave response,** réponse en rectangulaires, en transitoires. **3.** *Mth:* **s. root,** racine carrée; **s. number,** nombre carré; *Elcs;* **s. detector,** détecteur *m* quadratique; **s. law,** loi quadratique, loi de Lambert; **s. law condenser,** condensateur à variation linéaire de longueur d'onde; **s. law detection,** détection quadratique, parabolique; **s. law distortion,** distorsion quadratique. **4.** (*a*) **to get things s.,** (i) arranger les choses; (ii) mettre tout en ordre; **to make an account s.,** régler un compte; (*b*) **s. refusal,** refus net, catégorique; **s. meal,** repas copieux, solide; ample repas; (*c*) **a s. deal,** une affaire honnête; un coup régulier; **he always gives you a s. deal,** il est toujours loyal en affaires; **to play a s. game,** jouer franc jeu; (*d*) **to be s. with s.o.,** être quitte envers qn; **to be (all) s.,** (i) *Golf: etc:* être à égalité; (ii) (*of two people*) être quittes; **to call it s.,** faire une cote mal taillée; **let's call it s.,** je vous tiens quitte; **to get s. with s.o.,** (i) se venger de qn; régler son compte à qn; (ii) être quitte envers qn; tenir qn quitte.

III. *adv.* **1.** à angles droits (**to, with,** avec); d'équerre (**to, with,** avec); **set s. upon its base,** d'aplomb sur sa base; **to run s. into a ship,** aborder un navire de bout en plein; **the bullet struck him s. in the chest,** la balle l'a frappé en pleine poitrine; **he hit him (fair and) s. on the jaw,** il l'a frappé en plein menton. **2.** (agir) honnêtement, correctement; **fair and s.,** loyalement, carrément.

square[2], *v.*

I. *v.tr.* **1.** (*a*) carrer, équarrir, dresser (un bloc de marbre); équarrir, équerrer (du bois); araser (une planche); **to s. off, up, the end of a plank,** mettre d'équerre, équarrir, le bout d'une planche; *Const:* **squared stone,** pierre carrée; (*b*) *Nau:* **to s. the yards,** brasser carré; mettre (les vergues) en croix; (*c*) **to s. one's shoulders,** (i) se carrer (en face de qn); se mettre droit; (ii) raidir sa volonté; faire face à des difficultés. **2.** (*a*) **to s. one's practice with one's principles,** accorder, faire cadrer, ses actions avec ses principes; **how do you s. it with your conscience?** comment arrangez-vous cela avec votre conscience? (*b*) balancer, égaliser, régler (un compte); **we must s. accounts,** il faut régler nos comptes; *F:* **to s. accounts with s.o.,** (i) régler ses comptes avec qn; (ii) se venger de qn; régler son compte à qn; **to s. matters,** arranger les choses; mettre tout le monde d'accord; (*c*) *F:* acheter, soudoyer, suborner (qn); graisser la patte à (qn); **he has been squared to keep quiet,** on a acheté, payé, son silence; (*d*) *NAm:* **to s. books away,** ranger des livres; **to s. away a bedroom,** préparer, arranger, une chambre. **3. to s. the circle,** (i) chercher à carrer le cercle; (ii) s'efforcer de faire l'impossible; tenter l'impossible. **4.** *Mth:* élever, mettre, porter, (un nombre, une expression) au carré; carrer (un nombre); **four squared,** quatre au carré. **5. to s. (off) a piece of paper,** quadriller une feuille de papier; **squared paper,** papier quadrillé, à carreaux; **to s. (up) a sketch for enlargement,** mettre un croquis au carreau.

II. *v.i.* **1.** (*a*) **the end and the side should s. with each other, should s. together,** le bout et le côté doivent se carrer, se raccorder; (*b*) **to s. up to s.o.,** *NAm:* **to s. (off, away) to s.o.,** s'avancer vers qn, se mettre en posture de combat; être prêt à se battre; **to s. up to the difficulties,** faire face aux difficultés; raidir sa volonté; *NAm:* **to s. away,** tout remettre en place. **2. his practice does not s. with his principles,** ses actions ne s'accordent pas, ne cadrent pas, ne sont pas d'accord, avec ses principes; **the theory does not s. with the facts,** la théorie ne correspond pas aux faits. **3.** (*a*) *v. tr. Golf: etc:* **to s. the match,** égaliser la marque; (*b*) **to s. (up) with s.o.,** (i) régler ses comptes avec qn; (ii) se venger de qn; régler son compte à qn.

squarehead ['skwɛəhed], *s. A:* **1.** *U.S:* colon allemand, hollandais, scandinave. **2.** (1914–18) Boche *m*.

squarely ['skwɛəli], *adv.* **1.** carrément; **s. built,** (i) bâti en carré; (ii) (*of pers.*) aux épaules carrées; de belle carrure; trapu. **2.** carrément, honnêtement; **to act s.,** agir carrément, loyalement.

squareness ['skwɛənis], *s.* **1.** forme carrée. **2.** honnêteté *f*, loyauté *f* (dans les affaires). **3.** *F: O:* conservatisme *m* (d'une personne vieux jeu).

squaring ['skwɛəriŋ], *s.* **1.** équarrissage *m*, équarrissement *m*, dressage *m* (d'un bloc de pierre, etc.); mise *f* en équerre. **2.** quadrature *f* (du cercle). **3.** quadrillage *m*, carroyage *m* (d'une carte, etc.); **s. up of a sketch (for enlargement on canvas),** mise au carreau d'un croquis; *Tex:* **s. of a design,** carreautage *m* d'un dessin.

squarish ['skwɛəriʃ], *a.* (*a*) plutôt carré; (*b*) (*of pers.*) trapu.

squarrose ['skwærous, 'skwɔr-], *a. Nat.Hist:* squarreux.

squash[1] [skwɔʃ], *s.* **1.** écrasement *m*, aplatissement *m*; *O:* **s. hat,** (i) chapeau mou; (ii) (chapeau) claque *m*, (chapeau) gibus *m*. **2.** (*a*) cohue *f*; foule *f*; **there was a dreadful s. at the doors,** la foule s'écrasait aux portes; **it's a bit of a s.!** c'est un peu juste! (*b*) *F:* réception mondaine (où l'on s'écrase). **3.** (*a*) pulpe *f*; *F:* **his hand was just a s.,** sa main était en capilotade; (*b*) **orange, lemon, s.,** (i) sirop *m* d'orange, de citron; (ii) orangeade, limonade, non gazeuse (faite avec (i)). **4.** *Sp:* **s. (rackets),** squash(-rackets) *m*; **s. court,** terrain de squash; *NAm:* **s. tennis,** squash-tennis *m*.

squash[2]. **1.** *v.tr.* (*a*) écraser, aplatir, faire gicler, *F:* écrabouiller (un fruit, etc.); **the boxer had a squashed nose,** le boxeur avait le nez en marmelade; (*b*) écraser, étouffer (une révolte, etc.); (*c*) *F:* couper le sifflet à (qn); clore, clouer, le bec à (qn); remettre (qn) à sa place; rembarrer (qn); envoyer promener (qn). **2.** *v.i.* (*a*) (*of fruit, etc.*) s'écraser, s'aplatir, *F:* s'écrabouiller; (*b*) **to s. (up),** se serrer, se presser; **to s. into a lift,** entrer de force dans un ascenseur; **to s. through a gate,** se bousculer à une barrière; entrer en cohue.

squash[3], *s. Hort:* (*a*) gourde *f*, pâtisson *m*; **s. melon,** bonnet *m* de prêtre; artichaut *m* d'Espagne; pâtisson; (*b*) *esp. NAm:* courge *f* (calebasse); courgette *f*; **(winter) s.,** (courge) potiron *m*.

squashy ['skwɔʃi], *a.* mou et humide; qui s'écrase facilement; **s. plums,** prunes à pulpe molle; **s. ground,** terrain bourbeux, détrempé, qui gicle, gargouille, sous le pas.

squat[1] [skwɔt], *s.* **1.** accroupissement *m*; posture accroupie. **2.** *F:* terrain, appartement, etc., occupé par un squatter.

squat[2], *v.i.* **(squatted) 1.** (*a*) **to s. (down),** s'accroupir; **she was squatting by the fire,** elle était accroupie au coin du feu; (*b*) *Ven:* (*of game*) se tapir; (*of rabbit, etc.*) se terrer; (*of partridge, etc.*) se raser; (*of hare, wolf*) se flâtrer; (*c*) *Nau:* (*of ship*) tanguer en arrière. **2.** (*a*) *NAm:* **to s. upon a piece of land,** (i) *Hist:* s'établir sur un terrain (vierge, qui n'a pas été concédé); s'approprier un terrain; (ii) s'établir sur un terrain commun (avec titre légal de propriété); (*c*) *F:* s'installer, s'établir comme squatter, dans une maison inoccupée.

squat[3], *a.* **1.** accroupi; assis sur ses talons. **2.** (*a*) (*of pers.*) ramassé, trapu; ragot, -ote, courtaud; (*b*) (*of object, building, etc.*) écrasé; **s. letters,** lettres écrasées; **s. arch,** arc surbaissé; (*c*) *Crust:* **s. lobster,** galat(h)ée *f*.

Squatinidae [skwɔ'tinidi:], *s.pl. Ich:* squatinidés *m*.

squatter ['skwɔtər], *s.* **1.** *F:* squatter *mf.* **2.** (*a*) personne accroupie; (*b*) *Ven:* bête tapie, qui se rase.

squatting ['skwɔtiŋ], *s.* **1.** accroupissement *m*. **2.** occupation *f* d'un terrain, d'une maison, en qualité de squatter; squatting *m*.

squaw [skwɔ:], *s.f.* (*a*) squaw; femme peau-rouge; (*b*) *Orn:* **old s.,** harelde *f*, canard *m*, de Miquelon, *Fr.C:* canard kakawi.

squawk[1] [skwɔ:k], *s.* **1.** cri *m* rauque, couic *m* (de certains oiseaux, *F:* de qn); couac *m*, canard *m* (sur la clarinette, etc.); *F:* **s. box,** haut-parleur *m*, *pl.* haut-parleurs. **2.** *esp. NAm: F:* rouspétance *f*.

squawk[2], *v.i.* **1.** (*of bird, F: of pers.*) pousser des cris rauques; faire couac; (*on reed instrument*) faire des couacs. **2.** *esp. NAm: F:* rouspéter, rouscailler.

squawker ['skwɔ:kər], *s. esp. NAm: F:* rouspéteur, -euse.

squeak[1] [skwi:k], *s.* **1.** petit cri aigu; couinement *m*; couic *m*, vagissement *m* (d'un animal); crissement *m*, grincement *m* (de choses mal huilées); canard *m*, couac *m* (sur une clarinette, etc.); *F:* **I don't want to hear another s. out of you,** je ne veux pas entendre le moindre murmure. **2.** *F:* **to have a narrow s.,** l'échapper belle, revenir de loin; **that was a near s.,** nous l'avons échappé belle; il était moins cinq!

squeak[2]. **1.** *v.i.* (*a*) (*of pers.*) pousser des cris aigus; couiner; (*of animal*) faire couic; vagir; (*of mouse*) guiorer; (*of bat*) grincer; (*of machine part, etc.*) crier, grincer, crisser; (*of shoes*) craquer, couiner; (*of musical instrument*) faire des couacs; **chalk that squeaks on the blackboard,** craie qui grince, qui crisse, sur le tableau; (*b*) *F:* vendre la mèche; casser, manger, le morceau; moucharder. **2.** *v.tr.* **to s. (out) sth.,** crier qch. d'une petite voix aiguë.

squeaker ['skwi:kər], *s.* **1.** (*a*) celui, celle, qui pousse des petits cris; (*b*) *F:* dénonciateur, -trice; mouchard, -arde, cafard, -arde. **2.** (*a*) jeune oiseau *m*; pigeonneau *m*; (*b*) cochonnet *m*; cochon *m* de lait. **3.** (*device*) pratique *f* (de montreur de marionnettes).

squeaking ['skwi:kiŋ], *s.* couics *mpl*, couinements *mpl*; **the s. of the chalk on the blackboard,** le grincement, le crissement, de la craie sur le tableau.

squeaky ['skwi:ki], *a.* criard, qui crie; **s. shoes,** chaussures qui craquent, qui couinent; *Veh:* **s. springs,** ressorts qui grincent; **s. voice,** petite voix aiguë.

squeal[1] [skwi:l], *s.* (*a*) cri aigu; cri perçant (d'un animal); (*b*) grincement *m*, crissement *m* (de pneus, de freins).

squeal[2]. **1.** *v.i.* (*a*) pousser des cris aigus; couiner; (*of birds, children*) piailler; (*of tyres, brakes*) grincer, crisser; **to s. like a pig,** crier comme un porc qu'on égorge, comme un sourd; (*b*) *F:* protester; réclamer; jeter les hauts cris; (*c*) *F:* vendre la mèche; casser, manger, le morceau; moucharder; **to s. on s.o.,** dénoncer qn; moucharder, cafarder, qn. **2.** *v.tr.* **to s. (out) sth.,** crier qch. d'une voix aiguë, perçante.

squealer ['skwi:lər], *s.* **1.** (*a*) personne criarde; (*b*) *F:* protestataire *mf.* **2.** *F:* dénonciateur, -trice; mouchard, -arde, cafard, -arde. **3.** jeune oiseau *m*; pigeonneau *m*.

squealing[1] ['skwi:liŋ], *a.* criard; qui crie, qui piaille.

squealing[2], *s.* (*a*) cris aigus; hauts cris; (*b*) crissement *m*, grincement *m* (de pneus, de freins).

squeamish ['skwi:miʃ], *a.* **1.** sujet aux nausées; **s. stomach,** estomac délicat; **to feel s.,** avoir, se sentir, envie de vomir; avoir des nausées; avoir mal au cœur; se sentir mal; avoir le cœur, l'estomac, barbouillé. **2.** (*a*) difficile, exigeant, délicat, dégoûté; (*b*) scrupuleux à l'excès; (*c*) pudique à l'excès; **don't be so s.!** pas tant de délicatesses! ne faites pas le dégoûté! ne faites pas tant de façons! **don't be s. about telling me,** ne vous embarrassez pas pour me le dire; **the songs were coarse, but the audience was not s.,** les chansons étaient plutôt lestes, mais l'auditoire ne s'en effarouchait pas, ne s'en offusquait pas.

squeamishness ['skwi:miʃnis], *s.* **1.** disposition *f* à avoir des nausées. **2.** délicatesse exagérée; goût *m* difficile.

squeegee[1] ['skwi:dʒi:], *s.* **1.** balai *m* en caoutchouc; raclette *f*, racloir *m*; *Nau:* râteau *m* de pont. **2.** *Phot: etc:* raclette *f*; **roller s.,** rouleau *m* en caoutchouc.

squeegee[2], *v.tr.* **1.** balayer, goudronner (une rue) avec une raclette. **2.** *Phot:* passer la raclette, le rouleau, sur (une épreuve).

squeezable ['skwi:zəbl], *a.* **1.** comprimable, compressible. **2.** (*of pers.*) à qui l'on peut arracher, extorquer, de l'argent.

squeeze[1] [skwi:z], *s.* **1.** (*a*) compression *f*; serrage *m*; serrement *m* (de main); **he gave her cheek a little s.,** il lui a pincé la joue; **s. bottle,** flacon pulvérisateur; (*b*) étreinte *f*; **to give s.o. a s.,** serrer qn dans ses bras; embrasser, enlacer, qn; (*c*) *Pol.Ec:* mesures *fpl* d'austérité; **credit s.,** restriction *f*, resserrement *m*, du crédit; (*d*) *Min:* **roof undergoing s.,** toit qui charge; (*e*) *Metalw:* **s. time,** temps d'accostage; (*f*) *Cin:* **s. track,** piste *f* sonore à densité et largeur variables. **2.** foule *f*, cohue *f*; **it was a tight s.,** on tenait tout juste; nous étions serrés comme des sardines. **3. a s. of lemon,** quelques gouttes *f* de citron. **4.** (*a*) exaction *f*; **to put the s. on s.o.,** forcer la main à qn; (*b*) tantième *m*, pot-de-vin *m* (exigé par les fonctionnaires et les domestiques en Orient). **5.** estampage *m*, empreinte *f* au carton mouillé (d'une médaille, d'une inscription, etc.). **6. s. (play),** (i) *Cards:* (*at bridge*) squeeze *m*; (ii) (*baseball*) jeu risqué.

squeeze[2], *v.tr.* **1.** (*a*) presser (une éponge, un citron); pressurer (un citron, etc.); **to s. s.o.'s hand,** serrer la main à qn; **to s. the waist in,** comprimer la taille; **he was squeezed to death in the crowd,** il a été étouffé dans la foule; (*b*) embrasser, étreindre, enlacer (qn); serrer (qn) contre son cœur; presser (qn) dans, entre, ses bras. **2.** (*a*) **to s. sth. into a box,** faire entrer qch. de force dans une boîte; **to s. the juice out of a lemon, to s. out the juice of a lemon,** exprimer, extraire, le jus d'un citron; **to s. the water out of a sponge,** exprimer l'eau d'une éponge; exprimer une éponge; **to s. out a tear,** y aller de sa (petite) larme; verser un pleur; **to s. (oneself) through a hole in the fence,** se faufiler, se glisser, par un trou dans la clôture; (*b*) *v.i.* **to s. through the crowd,** fendre la foule; se frayer un passage à travers la foule; **to s. into a crowded train,** entrer de force dans un train bondé; **to s. up (together),** se serrer (les uns contre les autres); **by squeezing a little you will all be able to sit down,** en vous serrant, en vous gênant, un peu, vous pourrez tous vous asseoir. **3.** (*a*) exercer une pression sur (qn, le gouvernement, etc.); forcer la main à (qn); (*b*) pressurer (qn); **to s. money out of s.o.,** extorquer, arracher, de l'argent à qn. **4. to s. a coin, an inscription,** estamper une pièce de monnaie, une inscription; prendre l'empreinte d'une pièce de monnaie, d'une inscription. **5.** *Metall:* macquer (le fer puddlé). **6.** *Cards:* (*at bridge*) squeezer (son adversaire).

squeezebox ['skwi:zbɔks], *s. F:* accordéon *m*, concertina *m*.

squeezer ['skwi:zər], *s.* **1.** (*pers.*) extorqueur *m*, oppresseur *m*. **2.** (*a*) machine *f*, appareil *m*, à compression; presse *f*; **cork s.,** mâche-bouchon(s) *m inv*; (*b*) *Metall:* ma(c)que *f*; machine *f* à macquer; cingleur (rotatif); marteau *m* à cingler; **crocodile s.,** presse à cingler.

squeezerman, *pl.* **-men** ['skwi:zəmən], *s.m. Metall:* cingleur.

squeezing ['skwi:ziŋ], *s.* **1.** (*a*) compression *f*; serrage *m*; (*b*) étreinte *f*; serrement *m* (de main). **2.** expression *f* (du jus d'un citron, etc.). **3.** extorsion *f*, exaction *f*. **4.** *Metall:* macquage *m* (du fer puddlé).

squelch[1] [skwel(t)ʃ], *s.* **1.** giclement *m* (de boue); gargouillement *m*, gargouillis *m* (de chaussures détrempées, etc.). **2.** lourde chute (sur qch. de mou). **3.** *W.Tel:* **s. circuit,** éliminateur *m* de bruit de fond; circuit *m* de réglage silencieux.

squelch[2]. **1.** *v.tr.* (*a*) écraser (qch.) (en le faisant gicler); (*b*) *F:* faire taire (qn); river le clou à (qn); réprimer, étouffer (une rébellion, etc.). **2.** *v.i.* (*a*) **to s. in the mud,** écraser la boue liquide avec un bruit de succion; **to s. through the mud,** patauger dans la boue; (*b*) gargouiller; **the water squelched in his shoes,** l'eau gargouillait dans ses chaussures.

squib[1] [skwib], *s.* **1.** *Pyr:* pétard *m*, serpenteau *m*, crapaud *m*; **to let off a s.,** faire partir un pétard; *Fig:* **damp s.,** affaire ratée. **2.** *Exp:* amorce *f* électro-pyrotechnique. **3.** satire *f*, pasquinade *f*, brocard *m*; **to launch squibs at s.o.,** brocarder qn.

squib[2], *v.tr.* **(squibbed)** *O:* lancer, écrire, publier, des satires, des brocards, contre (qn); brocarder, satiriser (qn).

squid[1] [skwid], *s.* **1.** *Moll:* calmar *m*, calmaret *m*, calamar *m*, encornet *m*; **the Squids,** les mollusques *m* céphalopodes. **2.** *Fish:* calmar (employé comme appât).

squid[2], *v.i.* **(squidded)** pêcher en employant le calmar comme appât.

squiffed [skwift], **squiffy** ['skwifi], *a. F: O:* un peu ivre; gris, éméché, gai, pompette.

squiffer ['skwifər], *s. Mus: F:* concertina *m*.

squiggle[1] ['skwigl], *s. F:* (*a*) trait *m*, ligne *f*, en paraphe, en parafe; enjolivure *f*, enjolivement *m*; (*b*) écriture *f* illisible.

squiggle[2], *v.i. F:* se tortiller.

squiggly ['skwigli], *a. F:* tortueux, sinueux.

squill [skwil], *s.* **1.** (*a*) *Bot:* scille *f*; squille *f*; **red s.,** scille rouge; (*b*) *Pharm:* scille. **2.** *Crust:* **s. (fish),** squille; cigale *f*, sauterelle *f*, mante *f*, de mer.

squilla ['skwilə], *s. Crust:* = SQUILL 2.

Squillidae ['skwilidi:], *s.pl. Crust:* squilidés *m*.

squinancy ['skwinənsi], *s.* **1.** *A.Med:* (e)squinancie *f*. **2.** *Bot:* **s. (wort),** herbe *f* à l'esquinancie; rubéole *f*; petite garance; garance de chien.

squinch [skwin(t)ʃ], *s. Arch:* trompe *f*.

squint[1] [skwint], *s.* **1.** strabisme *m*, louchement *m*, loucherie *f*; yeux *mpl* qui louchent; **he has a slight s.,** il louche légèrement; **he has a s. in his left eye,** il louche de l'œil gauche; **angle of s.,** angle strabique. **2.** regard *m* louche, de côté, de travers; coup d'œil furtif; **I had a s. at his paper,** j'ai jeté un coup d'œil oblique sur son journal. **3.** *F:* regard; coup d'œil; **let's have a s. at it!** faites voir! **take a s. at that!** zyeutez-moi ça! **4.** inclination *f*, penchant *m* (to, towards, vers). **5.** *Ecc.Arch:* **(lepers') s.,** guichet *m* (des lépreux).

squint[2], *v.i.* **1.** loucher; *F:* avoir un œil qui dit zut à l'autre; avoir les yeux qui se croisent les bras. **2. to s. at sth., at s.o.,** (i) regarder qch., qn, en louchant; (ii) regarder qch. qn, de côté, de travers, furtivement; jeter à qn un regard louche.

squint[3], *a.* **1. s. eyes,** yeux louches; **s.-eyed,** (i) au regard louche; strabique; *F:* bigleux; (ii) au regard malveillant. **2.** oblique, incliné, de, en, biais.

squinter ['skwintər], *s.* loucheur, -euse; *F:* louchon, -onne; *Med:* strabique *mf.*

squinting[1] ['skwintiŋ], *a.* strabique, louche.

squinting[2], *s.* strabisme *m*, louchement *m*, loucherie *f*.

squirage ['skwaiəridʒ], *s. A:* **1. the s.,** les propriétaires terriens; la petite noblesse. **2.** annuaire *m* des propriétaires terriens.

squire[1] ['skwaiər], *s.m.* **1.** (*a*) *Hist:* écuyer (attaché à un chevalier); (*b*) *A: & Lit:* **s. of dames,** cavalier, chevalier servant; galant. **2.** *A:* (*a*) propriétaire terrien, foncier; (*b*) châtelain; seigneur du village. **3.** *U.S:* juge de paix; magistrat.

squire², *v.tr. A: & Lit:* servir de cavalier à, escorter (une dame).
squir(e)archy ['skwaiərɑːki], *s. A:* **1.** corps *m* des gros propriétaires fonciers (en tant que puissance politique et sociale). **2.** coterie *f* de la noblesse terrienne. **3.** gouvernement *m* par les propriétaires terriens.
squireen [skwaiə'riːn], *s.m. esp. Irish: A:* hobereau, gentillâtre.
squirm¹ [skwəːm], *s.* tortillement *m* (de douleur, de honte, etc.).
squirm², *v.i.* (*a*) (*of worm, etc.*) se tordre, se tortiller; (*b*) éprouver de l'embarras; être mal à l'aise; être au supplice; **to make s.o. s.,** mettre qn au supplice.
squirming ['skwəːmiŋ], *s.* tortillement *m*, tortillage *m*.
squirrel¹ ['skwir(ə)l], *s.* **1.** (*a*) *Z:* écureuil *m*; **Siberian s.,** petit-gris *m, pl.* petits-gris, de Sibérie; **grey s.,** écureuil du Canada, de Virginie; **red s.,** écureuil roux; **African ground s.,** écureuil fossoyeur africain, rat *m* palmiste; **Gambian tree s.,** écureuil gris; **striped Indian s.,** écureuil rayé indien, écureuil de terre; **spiny-tailed s.,** anomalure *m*; **s. monkey,** sagouin *m*, saïmiri *m*; (*b*) **s. cage,** (i) cage *f* d'écureuil; tournette *f*; (ii) *El:* cage d'écureuil; *El:* **s. cage rotor,** induit *m* à cage d'écureuil. **2.** *Com:* **s. (fur),** petit-gris.
squirrel², *v.tr.* accumuler, amasser (des provisions, etc.); **wine that's been kept squirrelled away,** vin de derrière les fagots.
squirrelfish ['skwir(ə)lfiʃ], *s. Ich:* holocentridé *m*, poisson-soldat *m, pl.* poissons-soldats.
squirreltail ['skwir(ə)lteil], *s. Bot:* orge *f*.
squirt¹ [skwəːt], *s.* **1.** seringue *f*; **s. gun,** (i) jouet *m* en forme de seringue; pistolet *m* à eau; (ii) injecteur *m*, pistolet, à graisse; pistolet graisseur. **2.** jet *m*, giclée *f* (de liquide). **3.** *F:* freluquet *m*, merdaillon *m*.
squirt². **1.** *v.tr.* faire (re)jaillir, faire gicler, lancer en jet, seringuer (un liquide, etc.); injecter (un liquide, etc.) avec une seringue; **to s. soda water into a glass,** faire gicler du soda dans un verre; **to s. in oil, petrol,** injecter de l'huile, de l'essence. **2.** *v.i.* (*of liquid, etc.*) (re)jaillir, gicler.
squirting ['skwəːtiŋ], *s.* **1.** seringage *m*; injection *f* avec une seringue. **2.** (re)jaillissement *m*, giclement *m*.
squish¹ [skwiʃ], *s.* **1.** giclement *m* (d'un liquide). **2.** *F: A:* (*a*) *Sch:* marmelade *f* d'orange; (*b*) bêtises *fpl*, sottises *fpl*, niaiseries *fpl*.
squish², *v.i.* (*of liquid*) gicler.
squishy ['skwiʃi], *a. F:* détrempé; mou; qui gicle sous la pression; **the ground's s. underfoot,** le sol gargouille sous les pas.
squit [skwit], *s. P:* freluquet *m*, merdaillon *m*.
squitters ['skwitəz], *s.pl. P:* diarrhée *f*, courante *f*; **to have the s.,** avoir la chiasse.
squiz [skwiz], *s. Austr: N.Z: F:* regard furtif.
st [st], *int.* chut! paix!
stab¹ [stæb], *s.* **1.** (*a*) coup *m* de poignard, de couteau; **s. in the back,** (i) coup porté dans le dos; (ii) = coup de Jarnac; attaque déloyale; *Med:* **s. of pain,** élancement *m*, clou *m*; (*b*) **s. (wound),** coup d'estoc, de pointe; estocade *f*; *F:* **to have a s. at sth.,** essayer de faire qch.; essayer le coup. **2.** *Games:* **s. shot,** coup sec.
stab², *v.* **(stabbed) 1.** *v.tr.* (*a*) poignarder; donner un coup de couteau à (qn); percer (qn) d'un coup de couteau, etc.; **to s. s.o. to the heart,** percer le cœur à qn; frapper qn au cœur; **this reproach stabbed him to the heart,** ce reproche lui a traversé le cœur; **to s. s.o. to death,** porter un coup mortel à qn; frapper qn mortellement; tuer qn d'un coup de poignard, à coups de poignard; **to s. s.o. in the back,** (i) poignarder qn dans le dos; (ii) calomnier qn; (*b*) *Bookb:* piquer (un cahier); **stabbed pamphlet,** piqûre *f*; (*c*) *Const:* piquer, repiquer (une surface destinée à recevoir un enduit). **2.** *v.i.* **to s. at s.o.,** porter un coup de couteau, de poignard, à qn; *O:* **to s. at s.o.'s reputation,** porter un coup à la réputation de qn.
stab³, *s. Typ: O:* **s. work,** travail régulier, payé à la semaine.
stabat(mater) ['stɑːbæt('mɑːtər)], *s. Ecc.Mus:* stabat *m*.
stabber ['stæbər], *s.* **1.** assassin *m*, meurtrier *m*, poignardeur, -euse. **2.** *Tls:* (*a*) poinçon *m* (de voilier); (*b*) tire-point *m, pl.* tire-points.
stabbing¹ ['stæbiŋ], *a. Med:* **s. pain,** élancement *m*; douleur lancinante.
stabbing², *s.* **1.** (*a*) coups *mpl* de poignard, de couteau; (*b*) assassinat *m* à coups de poignard, de couteau; (*c*) *Tls:* **s. awl,** tire-point *m, pl.* tire-points **2.** *Bookb:* piqûre *f* métallique.
Stabiae ['stæbiiː]. *Pr.n. A.Geog:* Stabies.
stability [stə'biliti], *s.* (*a*) stabilité *f*, solidité *f* (d'une construction); (*b*) stabilité (d'un avion, d'un navire, etc.); **curve of s., s. curve,** courbe *f* de stabilité; **dynamic, static, s.,** stabilité dynamique, statique; **inherent s.,** stabilité inhérente, propre; **lateral s., rolling s., transversal s.,** stabilité latérale, stabilité en roulis; **longitudinal s.,** stabilité longitudinale; **neutral s.,** stabilité indifférente, équilibre indifférent; **range of s.,** limite *f* de stabilité; *Av: Ball:* **s. about the yaw,** stabilité en lacet, par rapport à l'axe de lacet; *Av:* **directional s.,** stabilité de route, stabilité en lacet; **directional and lateral s.,** stabilité en lacet et en roulis; **automatic s.,** stabilité automatique; (*c*) *Ch: Ph:* **chemical s.,** stabilité chimique; **atom s.,** stabilité de l'atome; **nuclear s.,** stabilité nucléaire; **phase s.,** stabilité de phase; **radiation s.,** stabilité de rayonnement; **s. constant,** constante *f* de stabilité; **s. limit,** seuil *m* d'instabilité; **s. parameter,** paramètre *m* de stabilité; **thermal s.,** stabilité thermique; (*d*) **economic s.,** stabilité économique; **price s.,** stabilité des prix; **political s.,** stabilité politique; **man of no s., without s.,** homme inconstant, irrésolu.
stabilization [steibilai'zeiʃ(ə)n], *s.* (*a*) stabilisation *f* (du sol, d'un navire, d'un avion, etc.); **automatic s.,** stabilisation automatique; **gravity-gradient s.,** stabilisation par gradient de gravité; **gyro(scopic) s.,** stabilisation gyroscopique; **spin s.,** stabilisation (d'un projectile, d'un satellite) par rotation; *Ph: El:* **phase s.,** stabilisation de phase; **self-s. of phase,** stabilisation automatique de phase; **s. circuit,** circuit *m* de stabilisation; **voltage s.,** stabilisation de (la) tension; (*b*) *Fin:* stabilisation, valorisation *f* (des cours, etc.); **s. of currency, of prices,** stabilisation de la monnaie, des prix; **s. fund,** fonds *m* de stabilisation; **s. loan,** emprunt *m* de stabilisation.
stabilize ['steibilaiz]. **1.** *v.tr.* stabiliser (le sol, un navire, un avion, le cours du change, etc.); *El: Elcs:* caler (une fréquence). **2.** *v.i.* se stabiliser.
stabilized ['steibilaizd], *a.* stabilisé; **fin-s. projectile,** projectile stabilisé (sur sa trajectoire) au moyen d'ailettes, d'un empennage; **gravity-gradient-s.,** stabilisé par gradient de gravité; **spin-s. projectile, satellite,** projectile, satellite, stabilisé par rotation; **s. platform,** plate-forme stabilisée; **s. food product,** produit alimentaire stabilisé; **s. steel,** acier stabilisé; *Elcs:* **s. amplifier tube,** tube amplificateur stabilisé; *W.Tel:* **s. antenna,** antenne stabilisée; **s. frequency,** fréquence calée; *El:* **s. phase,** phase stabilisée; **s. voltage,** tension stabilisée.
stabilizer ['steibilaizər], *s.* **1.** *Nau: Av:* stabilisateur *m*; *Av:* empennage *m*; *Nau:* **fin s.,** stabilisateur à ailerons; **automatic s.,** stabilisateur automatique; **gyro(scopic) s.,** stabilisateur gyroscopique; *El:* **s. circuit,** circuit stabilisateur; **voltage s.,** stabilisateur de tension; *Elcs:* **s. tube, s. valve,** tube stabilisateur. **2.** stabilisant *m* (de produits alimentaires, d'explosifs, etc.).
stabilizing¹ ['steibilaiziŋ], *a.* **1.** (*a*) stabilisateur, -trice; compensateur, -trice; **s. gyro(scope),** gyroscope stabilisateur; *Aut: Av:* **s. fin,** plan *m* de dérive (d'une voiture de course, d'un avion); *Rail:* **s. device,** dispositif *m* anti-lacet; *El:* **s. winding,** enroulement *m* d'équilibrage; (*b*) *Pol.Ec:* **to have, exert, a s. effect on prices,** exercer une action stabilisatrice sur les prix. **2. s. agent,** agent stabilisant (pour produits alimentaires, etc.).
stabilizing², *s.* = STABILIZATION.
stable¹ ['steibl], *s.* **1.** (*a*) (*for horses*) écurie *f*; **to shut, lock, the s. door after the horse is stolen, has bolted,** fermer la cage quand les oiseaux se sont envolés; (*b*) *occ.* (*for cattle*) étable *f*. **2.** chevaux *mpl* (d'une certaine écurie); *Turf: Aut: etc:* écurie; *Com:* série *f*, gamme *f*, de produits (d'une entreprise); **racing s.,** écurie de courses; **s. companion, s. mate,** (i) cheval, -aux *m*, de la même écurie; (ii) *F:* boxeur lié contractuellement au même promoteur; (iii) *F:* membre *m* de la même entreprise, de la même école, etc. **3.** *Mil: A:* **stables,** pansage *m* (corvée ou sonnerie); **evening stables,** souper *m*.
stable². **1.** *v.tr.* (*a*) loger (un cheval) dans une écurie; mettre (un cheval) à, dans, l'écurie; **we can s. three horses,** nous avons de la place pour trois chevaux; (*b*) *F:* loger, abriter, garer (un véhicule); **garage to s. two cars,** garage conçu pour (loger, abriter) deux voitures. **2.** *v.i.* *O:* (*of horse*) loger (dans telle ou telle écurie).
stable³, *a.* **1.** stable, solide, fixe; permanent; *Ch: Ph:* **s. body, s. element,** corps *m*, élément *m*, stable; **s. equilibrium,** équilibre *m* stable; **s. isotope, s. particle,** isotope *m*, particule *f*, stable; **s. (atomic) nucleus,** noyau *m* (atomique) stable; **s. oscillation,** oscillation *f* qui tend à décroître, oscillation stable; **s. state,** état *m* stable, état de stabilité; *Pol.Ec:* **s. currency,** monnaie *f* stable; **the government is becoming more s.,** le gouvernement se consolide, se raffermit; **s. job,** emploi stable, permanent. **2.** (*of pers.*) constant, ferme; *F:* **he's perfectly s.,** il est parfaitement sain d'esprit.
stableman, *pl.* **-men** ['steiblmən], *s.m.* palefrenier.
stabling ['steibliŋ], *s.* **1.** logement *m*, installation *f*, (de chevaux) dans une écurie; stabulation *f* (des chevaux). **2.** *coll.* écuries *fpl*; (*for cattle*) étables *fpl*; **we have plenty of s.,** nous ne manquons pas de place aux écuries.
stably ['steibli], *adv.* stablement, d'une manière stable.
staccato [stə'kɑːtou], *a. adv. & s.* (*a*) *Mus:* staccato (*m*); **s. note,** note piquée; **s. bowing,** détaché *m*; **light s. (with the point of the bow),** petit détaché; **to play the notes s.,** détacher les notes; (*b*) **s. style,** style haché; **in a s. voice,** d'une voix saccadée.
stachyose ['stækious], *s. Ch:* stachyose *m*.
stack¹ [stæk], *s.* **1.** (*a*) meule *f*, moie *f* (de foin, etc.); (*of cereals*) gerbier *m*; (*b*) pile *f*, tas *m* (de bois, de charbon, d'assiettes); *F:* **I've stacks of work, a whole s. of work, to do,** j'ai de quoi faire; **to make stacks of money,** gagner des mille et des cents; ramasser l'argent à la pelle; **I've stacks of it,** j'en ai des tas; (*c*) (*in library*) **stacks,** rayonnages *m*; **s. room,** réserve *f*; (*d*) *Cmptr:* pile *f* (de cartes, etc.); empilage *m* (de relais); **stacks,** archives *f*; **memory s.,** empilage de plans de tores; (*e*) faisceau *m* (d'armes); (*f*) *A:* mesure *f* de 108 pieds cubes (de bois de chauffage, de charbon); *A:* corde *f* (de bois). **2.** (*a*) souche *f*, corps *m* (de cheminée); (*b*) cheminée *f* (d'une locomotive, etc.); (*c*) (*for vineyards, etc.*) **s. heater,** réchauffeur à cheminée; (*d*) *Aut: U.S:* tuyau *m* d'échappement; (*e*) **s. pipe,** tuyau de descente, descente *f* d'eau (d'une gouttière). **3.** *Geog:* haut rocher (au large d'une côte). **4.** *Av:* (*a*) circuit *m* d'attente; (*b*) avions en attente (échelonnés en altitude).
stack², *v.tr.* **1.** emmeuler, ameulonner (le foin); mettre (le foin) en meule. **2. to s. (up),** empiler, entasser, mettre en tas (du bois, du charbon, des assiettes, etc.); **the library is stacked with books,** la bibliothèque regorge de livres; *F:* **she's well stacked,** il y a du monde au balcon. **3. to s. arms,** mettre les armes en faisceaux; former les faisceaux. **4. to s. sth. away,** ranger qch.; mettre qch. en lieu sûr. **5.** *Av:* échelonner en altitude (les avions en attente).
stackable ['stækəbl], *a.* gerbable; empilable.
stacker ['stækər], *s.* (*a*) empileur, -euse (de bois, etc.); gerbeur *m* (de tonneaux); (*b*) (*machine*) gerbeur.
stacking ['stækiŋ], *s.* **1.** emmeulage *m*, mise *f* en meule (du foin). **2. s. (up),** empilage *m*, empilement *m*, entassement *m*, mise en tas (du bois, du charbon, etc.); **s. machine,** gerbeur *m*; *Furn:* **s. chairs,** chaises *f* superposables. **3.** mise en faisceaux (des armes). **4.** *Av:* échelonnement *m* en altitude (des avions en attente).
stactometer [stæk'tɔmitər], *s. Ph:* stalagmomètre *m*; compte-gouttes *m inv*.
staddle¹ ['stædl], *s.* **1.** *For:* baliveau *m*, lais *m*. **2.** (*a*) *Agr:* support *m* de meule; (*b*) support, appui *m*.
staddle², *v.tr. For:* baliver (un taillis).
staddling ['stædliŋ], *s. For:* balivage *m*.
stadia ['steidiə], *s. Surv:* stadia *m*.
stadimeter [stæ'dimitər], *s. Surv:* stadimètre *m*.
stadiometer [steidi'ɔmitər], *s. Surv:* stadiomètre *m*.
stadium, *pl.* **-iums, -ia** ['steidiəm, -iəmz, -iə], *s. Sp: etc:* stade *m*; **Olympic s.,** stade olympique.
stadtholder ['stæthouldər], *s. Hist:* stathouder *m*.
staff¹ [stɑːf], *s.* **1.** (*a*) bâton *m*; **pilgrim's s.,** bourdon *m* de pèlerin; **bread is the s. of life,** le pain est le soutien de la vie; (*b*) *Ecc:* **pastoral s.,** bâton pastoral; (*c*) hampe *f* (de bannière, de lance); *Nau:* mât *m* (de pavillon); mâtereau *m*; *U.S:* (*of flag*) **at half s.,** en berne; (*d*) *Tls: Metall:* crochet *m*, ringard *m*; (*e*) *Rail: O:* bâton pilote; (*f*) *Surv:* jalon *m*, mire *f*; (*g*) *Med:* sonde cannelée. **2.** (*a*) *Mil: etc:* état-major *m, pl.* états-majors; **general s.,** état-major général; **chief of s.,** chef d'état-major; (*of a commander-in-chief in the field*) major général; **deputy chief of s.,** sous-chef d'état-major; *U.S:* **assistant chief of s.,** chef de bureau (d'état-major); **joint chiefs of s.,** état-major interarmées; **s. duty,** service *m* d'état-major; **s. officer,** officier d'état-major; **S. College** = École supérieure de guerre; (*b*) *Com: Ind: etc:* personnel *m*; **domestic s.,** les domestiques *m*; **hotel s.,** personnel de l'hôtel; *Journ:* **editorial s.,** la rédaction; les rédacteurs *m*; les collaborateurs *m*; *Sch:* **teaching s.,** personnel enseignant; **s. room,** salle *f* des professeurs; **nursing s.,** les infirmiers, les infirmières; **office s.,** personnel de bureau; **supervisory s.,** cadres *mpl* de maitrise; **senior, managerial, s.,** les cadres supérieurs; **s. management,** direction *f* du personnel; **to dismiss one's s.,** congédier son personnel, *F:* congédier tout son monde; **I'm on the s. of. . .,** je travaille chez . . .; (*c*) *Med: F:* = infirmière diplômée. **3.** *Mus:* (*pl.* **staves** [steivz]) portée *f*; **s. notation,** notation figurée sur la portée; notation ordinaire (par opposition à la notation chiffrée, etc.). **4.** *Bot:* **s. tree,** célastre *m*.
staff², *v.tr.* (*a*) fournir, pourvoir (un bureau, etc.) de personnel, d'employés; **this hotel is badly staffed,** le per-

sonnel de cet hôtel laisse à désirer; **it's difficult to s. such a large house,** il est difficile de trouver un personnel suffisant pour une maison de cette importance; (*b*) **army staffed with brilliant generals,** armée dont l'état-major se compose de généraux remarquables.

staff[3], *s. Const:* staff *m*; **worker in s.,** staffeur *m*.

staffelite ['stæfəlait], *s. Miner:* staffélite *f*.

staffer ['stæfər], *s. U.S: Journ:* rédacteur *m*.

staffman, *pl.* **staffmen** ['stɑːfmən], *s.m. Surv:* jalonneur.

stag[1] [stæg], *s.* **1.** *Z:* (*a*) cerf *m*; **ten-point s.,** dix-cors *m*; **s. hunt(ing),** chasse *f* au cerf; chasse à courre; **s. hunting season,** cervaison *f*; (*b*) **s.-headed,** (i) (animal) à tête de cerf; (ii) (arbre) couronné, mort en cime; (*c*) *Ent:* **s. beetle,** lucane *m*; cerf-volant *m*, *pl.* cerfs-volants; *F:* cornard *m*. **2.** (*a*) bœuf, etc. (châtré après pleine croissance); (*b*) jeune coq *m* de combat; (*c*) *Scot:* poulain non dressé. **3.** *St.Exch: F:* (*premium hunter*) loup *m*. **4. s. party, dinner,** réunion pour hommes seulement, *F:* un P.H.S.

stag[2], *v.tr. St.Exch:* spéculer (sur des valeurs).

stage[1] [steidʒ], *s.* **1.** (*a*) estrade *f*, échafaud *m*, échafaudage *m*; *Const: etc:* **hanging s.,** échafaud volant; plate-forme suspendue; pont volant; **tipping s.,** pont de décharge, à chariots culbuteurs; plate-forme de déversement; *Nau:* **floating s.,** plate-forme flottante; ras *m* (de carène); plate *f*; **landing s.,** débarcadère *m*; embarcadère (flottant); ponton *m*; (*b*) platine *f* (d'un microscope); **s. forceps,** porte-objet *m inv* (pour microscope); (*c*) étage *m* (d'une fusée, d'un engin spatial). **2.** (*a*) *Th:* scène *f*; tréteaux *mpl* (de saltimbanque); **(floor of the) s.,** plateau *m*; **front of the s.,** avant-scène *f*; **revolving s.,** plateau tournant; **to come on the s.,** entrer en scène; **to keep, hold, the s.,** tenir la scène; **to set the s.,** (i) monter les décors; (ii) *Fig:* exposer la situation; **s. directions,** indications *f* scéniques; **s. lighting,** éclairage *m* scénique, de la scène; **s. lights,** herses *f*; **s. effects,** effets *m* scéniques; **s. manager,** régisseur *m*; **s. carpenter,** machiniste *m*; **s. name,** nom *m* de théâtre; **s. whisper,** aparté *m*; **in a s. whisper,** en aparté; **s. fright,** trac *m*; **s. door,** entrée *f* des artistes; (*b*) **the s.,** le théâtre; **the French s.,** le théâtre français; **to go on the s.,** devenir, se faire, acteur, actrice; **to retire from the s.,** se retirer du théâtre; quitter la scène; **to write for the s.,** écrire pour le théâtre; **s. rights,** droits *m* de production (d'une pièce); **s. slang,** argot *m* des coulisses, de la coulisse; (*c*) *Fig:* théâtre, champ *m*. **3.** phase *f*, période *f*, stade *m*, étape *f*, degré *m*, palier *m*, étage; **the stages of an evolution,** les étapes, les stades, d'une évolution; *Surg:* **the successive stages in an operation,** les temps successifs d'une opération; *Elcs: etc:* **s. of amplification,** étage d'amplification; **input s.,** étage d'entrée; **bridging s.,** étage intermédiaire; **terminal s.,** étage de sortie; **to reach a critical s.,** arriver à une phase, à une période, critique; **at this s. there was an interruption,** à ce point, à ce moment, il y a eu une interruption; **at this s. of the illness,** au point où en est la maladie; **to be in the last stages of tuberculosis,** être sur le point de mourir de la tuberculose; **to pass through all the stages,** passer par tous les degrés; **to be in the larval s.,** être à l'état de larve; **to do sth. in successive stages,** faire qch. par reprises; **to rise by successive stages,** monter par échelons; **at what s. in its development?** à quel moment de son développement? **4.** (*a*) étape; **s. by s.,** d'étape en étape; **we did the journey in easy stages,** nous avons fait le voyage en petites étapes, sans nous presser; (*b*) *A:* relais *m*; **to change horses at each s.,** changer de chevaux à chaque relais; **s. (coach),** diligence *f*; (*c*) **fare s.,** (changement *m* de) section *f* (de l'itinéraire d'un autobus). **5.** (*a*) *Geol:* étage; (*b*) *Min:* (i) étage, niveau *m*; (ii) (*of ladderway*) palier *m*, plancher *m*, de repos.

stage[2]. **1.** *v.tr.* (*a*) monter (une pièce), mettre (une pièce) sur la scène; (*with passive force*) **this play does not s. well,** cette pièce ne rend pas sur la scène; (*b*) organiser, faire (une manifestation, etc.); monter (un coup); (*c*) **carefully staged reduction of nuclear weapons,** réduction soigneusement étagée des armes nucléaires. **2.** *v.i. A:* voyager (i) en diligence, (ii) par étapes.

stagecraft ['steidʒkrɑːft], *s. Th:* art *m* de la mise en scène; technique *f* de la scène.

staged ['steidʒd], *a. Const:* bâti en étages.

stagehand ['steidʒhænd], *s. Th:* machiniste *m*.

stager ['steidʒər], *s.* **old s.,** vieux routier, vieux madré.

stagestruck ['steidʒstrʌk], *a.* enamouré, féru, fou, *f.* folle, du théâtre.

staggard ['stægəd], *s.* cerf *m* de quatre ans.

stagger[1] ['stægər], *s.* **1.** (*a*) chancellement *m*, titubation *f*; (*b*) allure chancelante, pas chancelant(s). **2.** *Vet:* **(blind) staggers,** (i) (*of sheep*) lourd vertige; avertin *m*; tournis *m*; (ii) (*of horse*) vertigo *m*; **s. worm,** ver-coquin *m*, *pl.* vers-coquins; **grass staggers,** tétanie *f* d'herbage; *Bot:* **s. bush,** andromède *f*; *F:* (*of pers.*) **to have the staggers,** tituber (d'ivresse).

stagger[2]. **1.** *v.i.* chanceler, tituber; **to s. along,** marcher, avancer, en chancelant, en titubant, à pas chancelants; vaciller (en marchant); **to s. in, out,** entrer, sortir, en chancelant, d'un pas mal assuré; **to s. from one side of the road to the other,** battre les murs; **to s. to one's feet,** se relever en chancelant, avec difficulté. **2.** *v.tr.* confondre, consterner, renverser (qn); **to be staggered,** être saisi d'étonnement; être désarçonné; **his impudence staggered me,** son impudence m'a renversé. **3.** *v.tr.* (*a*) *Av:* décaler (les ailes); (*b*) *Mec.E:* disposer (des rivets, des joints, etc.) en quinconce, en chicane, en zigzag; placer (des rivets) alternativement; alterner, étager (des rivets); *Mch.Tls:* **to s. the cutters,** étager les lames; (*c*) *El:* échelonner (les balais); disposer (les balais) en quinconce; (*d*) échelonner (les heures de travail); étaler, échelonner (les vacances).

staggered ['stægəd], *a.* (*a*) décalé; (*of rivets*) en quinconce, en chicane, en zigzag; (*of cutters*) étagé; *El:* (*of poles*) alterné, en quinconce; (*b*) (*of holidays, etc.*) échelonné.

staggerer ['stægərər], *s. F:* **that was a s.!** ça m'a (complètement) renversé!

staggering[1] ['stægəriŋ], *a.* (*a*) **s. blow,** coup *m* de massue, d'assommoir; (*b*) (*of news, etc.*) renversant, désarçonnant, atterrant; **s. increase in prices,** hausse vertigineuse des prix; **s. majority,** majorité écrasante.

staggering[2], *s.* **1.** chancellement *m*, titubation *f*. **2.** (*a*) *Av:* décalage *m* (des ailes); **s. forward, backward,** décalage vers l'avant, vers l'arrière; (*b*) *Mec.E: etc:* disposition *f* en quinconce; *I.C.E:* tierçage *m* (des segments de piston); (*c*) *El:* échelonnage *m* (des balais); (*d*) échelonnage, échelonnement *m*, étalement *m* (des vacances, des heures de travail).

staghorn ['stæghɔːn], *s.* **1.** corne *f* de cerf. **2.** *Bot:* **s. (sumac),** sumac *m* de Virginie; **s. (moss),** lycopode *m* en massue; soufre végétal; mousse *f* terrestre; **s. fern,** platycérium *m*, *F:* cornes *fpl* d'élan. **3.** *Nau:* bitte *f* en crosse.

staghound ['stæghaund], *s.* chien courant (pour la chasse au cerf).

staginess ['steidʒinis], *s.* caractère théâtral.

staging ['steidʒiŋ], *s.* **1.** (*a*) échafaud *m*, échafaudage *m*; (*b*) *Nau:* appontement *m* (d'un quai). **2.** mise *f* à la scène (d'une pièce); **multiple s.,** décor simultané. **3.** *A:* **s. house, s. post,** relais *m* (de diligences).

Stagira, Stagirus [stæ'dʒaiərə, -əs], *Pr.n. A.Geog:* Stagire.

stagnancy ['stægnənsi], *s.* stagnation *f*.

stagnant ['stægnənt], *a.* stagnant; (*of trade, business*) en stagnation; **s. water,** eau stagnante, morte, dormante, croupie; eaux croupissantes.

stagnate [stæg'neit], *v.i.* (*of water, trade*) être, devenir, stagnant; être dans un état de stagnation.

stagnating [stæg'neitiŋ], *a.* stagnant; dans un état de stagnation; dans le marasme.

stagnation [stæg'neiʃ(ə)n], *s.* stagnation *f*; marasme *m* (des affaires).

stagnicolous [stæg'nikələs], *a. Nat.Hist:* stagnicole.

stagy ['steidʒi], *a.* théâtral, -aux; histrionique.

staid [steid], *a.* posé, sérieux, sage; peu démonstratif; (esprit) rassis, grave.

staidly ['steidli], *adv.* posément, sérieusement, sagement.

staidness ['steidnis], *s.* caractère posé, sérieux, sage; air posé, sérieux.

stain[1] [stein], *s.* **1.** (*a*) tache *f*, souillure *f*; **to take out, remove, a s.,** enlever une tache **(from,** de); **s. remover,** détachant *m*, détacheur *m*; **s.-resisting,** antitache; (*b*) **he came out of it without a s. on his character,** il est sorti de l'affaire sans atteinte à sa réputation, blanc comme neige. **2.** (*a*) couleur *f*, colorant *m*; **(wood) s.,** teinture *f* (pour bois); (*b*) *Bac:* gram *m*. **3.** *For:* échauffure *f*.

stain[2], *v.tr.* **1.** (*a*) tacher; souiller, salir **(with,** de); **hands stained with blood,** mains tachées, souillées, de sang; mains ensanglantées; (*with passive force*) **material that stains easily,** tissu *m* qui se tache, se salit, facilement; tissu salissant; (*b*) tacher, entacher, souiller, ternir (la réputation de qn); **he would have accepted nothing that stained his honour,** il n'aurait pas accepté de ternissure. **2.** (*a*) teindre, teinter, mettre en couleur (le bois); teindre, imprimer (des tissus); peindre (le verre); (*b*) *Bac:* teinter, colorer (des microbes); (*with passive force*) (*of microbes*) prendre le gram.

stainable ['steinəbl], *a. Bac:* (microbe, etc.) qui peut se teinter, se colorer, qui prend le gram.

stained [steind], *a.* **1.** taché, souillé. **2.** (*a*) teinté, mis en couleur; **s. floor,** parquet teinté; **s. paper,** papier peint, teinté; papier de couleur; (*b*) *Bac:* teinté, coloré.

stainer ['steinər], *s.* teinturier, -ière; peintre *m*; metteur *m* en couleur.

staining ['steiniŋ], *s.* **1.** souillure *f*. **2.** (*a*) teinture *f*; coloration *f*; (*b*) *Bac:* coloration.

stainless ['steinlis], *a.* **1.** sans tache; immaculé, pur. **2. s. steel,** acier *m* inoxydable.

stair [stɛər], *s.* **1.** marche *f*, degré *m* (d'un escalier); **the bottom s.,** la marche du bas; **corner s.,** marche d'angle. **2. (flight of) stairs,** escalier; **spiral stairs,** escalier tournant, en vis; **box s.,** escalier entre murs; **back stairs,** escalier de service; **to run up, down, the stairs,** monter, descendre, l'escalier en courant; **to meet s.o. on the stairs,** rencontrer qn dans l'escalier; *O:* **below stairs,** au sous-sol, (c.-à-d.) chez les domestiques; à l'office.

staircarpet ['stɛəkɑːpit], *s.* tapis *m* d'escalier.

staircase ['stɛəkeis], *s.* **1.** (i) cage *f* d'escalier; passage *m* d'escalier; (ii) escalier; **external s., turret s.,** escalier hors d'œuvre; **spiral s.,** escalier tournant, hélicoïdal; escalier en vis, à vis; escalier en spirale, en (co)limaçon; **service s.,** escalier de service; **secret s.,** escalier dérobé. **2.** *Moll:* **s. shell,** scalaire *f*.

stairhead ['stɛəhed], *s.* haut *m* de l'escalier; palier *m*.

stairway ['stɛəwei], *s.* = STAIRCASE.

stairwell ['stɛəwel], *s.* cage *f* d'escalier.

staithe [steið], *s. O:* **1.** quai *m* (à charbon). **2.** entrepôt *m* (à charbon) (le long du quai).

stake[1] [steik], *s.* **1.** (*a*) (*post*) pieu *m*, poteau *m*; (*rod*) jalon *m*, fiche *f*; piquet *m* (de tente); *Hort:* tuteur *m*; échalas *m* (de vigne); *Const:* **panel s.,** palançon *m*; *Fish:* **s. net,** étente *f*, gord *m*; (*b*) *Surv:* jalon, jalonnette *f*, piquet; *Artil:* **ranging s.,** piquet *m* de mire; *Sp: Row:* **s. boat,** bateau *m* de ligne de départ; bateau jalon; (*c*) *NAm: F:* **to pull up stakes,** partir; déménager. **2.** (poteau du) bûcher (d'un(e) martyr(e), d'un(e) criminel(le)); **to condemn s.o. to the s.,** condamner qn à monter sur le bûcher, à être brûlé vif; **to die, be burned, at the s.,** mourir sur le bûcher. **3.** (*a*) **s. (anvil),** tas *m*, tasseau *m*, enclumette *f* (de ferblantier, de zingueur); (*dome head*) boule *f*; (*b*) *Leath:* palisson *m*. **4.** (*a*) *Gaming:* mise *f*, enjeu *m*; **to lay the stakes,** faire le jeu; **the stakes are down,** les jeux sont faits; **to play one's last s.,** jouer (de) son reste; **to hold the stakes,** tenir les enjeux; **to play for high stakes,** jouer gros jeu; **the stakes are fifty pence,** il y va de cinquante pence; **the interests at s.,** les intérêts *m* en jeu; **our honour is at s.,** il y va, il s'agit, de notre honneur; notre honneur est en jeu; **his life is at s. (in this struggle),** c'est sa vie qui est l'enjeu (de cette lutte); il y va de sa tête; **to have large sums at s. in an enterprise,** avoir de fortes sommes engagées dans une entreprise; **to have a s. in sth.,** avoir des intérêts dans une affaire; *Fin:* **he has a ten per cent s. in the company,** il tient dix pour cent des actions de la société; (*b*) *Turf:* **stakes,** prix *m*; **maiden stakes,** prix de l'avenir; poule *f* d'essai.

stake[2], *v.tr.* **1. to stake (off, out),** (i) jalonner, piqueter, borner (une concession, etc.); enclore (une concession) de pieux; (ii) *Surv:* jalonner, bornoyer (une ligne, une route, etc.); **to s. a claim,** (i) *Min:* jalonner une concession; (ii) *Fig:* établir, faire valoir, ses droits. **2.** (*a*) garnir (qch.) de pieux; soutenir (qch.) avec des pieux; échalasser (une vigne, etc.); ramer (des haricots, etc.); tuteurer (des tomates); (*b*) attacher (une chèvre, etc.) à un pieu. **3.** (*a*) *Hist:* (*of pers.*) **to be staked through the body,** être empalé; (*b*) (*of horse*) **to be staked on a jump,** s'éventrer sur une haie. **4.** *Leath:* palissonner (les peaux). **5.** mettre (une somme) en jeu, au jeu; jouer, risquer, hasarder (une somme); **to s. twenty francs,** miser vingt francs; **to s. heavily,** coucher gros; **to s. everything, one's all,** jouer son va-tout; mettre tout en jeu; mettre, risquer, le tout pour le tout; y aller de son reste; **I'd s. my life on it,** j'y mettrais, j'en gagerais, ma tête à couper. **6.** *NAm: F:* fournir (qn) d'argent; fournir aux besoins de (qn).

stakeholder ['steikhouldər], *s.* dépositaire *mf* d'enjeux.

staker ['steikər], *s. Leath:* palissonneur *m*.

stakhanovite [stæk'hɑːnouvait], *a.* & *s.* stakhanoviste (*mf*).

staking ['steikiŋ], *s.* **1. s. (off, out),** jalonnement *m*, bornage *m*, piquetage *m* (d'une concession, etc.). **2.** échalassage *m* (d'une vigne); tuteurage *m* (des tomates). **3.** mise *f* (en jeu) (d'une somme).

stalactite ['stæləktait, *NAm: also* stə'læktait], *s. Geol:* stalactite *f*.

stalactitic [stælək'titik], *a.* stalactitique, stalactifère.

stalagmite ['stæləgmait, *NAm: also* stə'lægmait], *s. Geol:* stalagmite *f*.

stalagmitic [stæləg'mitik], *a.* stalagmitique.

stalagmometer [stælæg'mɔmitər], *s. Pharm:* stalagmomètre *m*.

stalagmometric [stælægmou'metrik], *a.* stalagmométrique.

stalagmometry [stælæg'mɔmitri], *s.* stalagmométrie *f*.

stale[1] [steil], *a.* **1.** (*a*) (pain, gâteau) rassis; (*b*) (œuf, etc.)

qui n'est pas frais; (vin) éventé, plat; (*c*) (air) vicié, croupi; **s. smell,** odeur *f* de renfermé (d'une chambre); **s. smell of. . .,** relent *m* de . . .; **to smell s.,** (*of beer, etc.*) sentir l'évent; (*of room, etc.*) sentir le renfermé. **2.** (*a*) vieux, *f.* vieille; vieilli, passé, usé; **s. goods,** articles défraîchis; **s. joke,** vieille plaisanterie; plaisanterie surannée, rebattue; **s. news,** nouvelle déflorée, défraîchie; **that's s. news!** c'est du réchauffé! (*b*) *Fin:* **s. market,** marché lourd, plat; (*c*) *Jur:* périmé; **s. cheque,** chèque prescrit. **3.** fatigué, éreinté; (*of athlete, etc.*) **to go s.,** se surentraîner; se surmener; **I'm s.,** je n'ai plus d'enthousiasme; rien ne va, ne marche, plus; *F:* **it's gone s. on me,** ça ne me plaît plus; je n'arrive plus à m'y mettre.

stale[2], *v.i.* (*a*) (*of beer, etc.*) s'éventer; (*b*) (*of news, etc.*) perdre son intérêt; **pleasure that never stales,** plaisir toujours nouveau.

stale[3], *s.* urine *f* (du bétail, des chevaux).

stale[4], *v.i.* (*of cattle, horses*) uriner.

stalemate[1] ['steilmeit], *s.* (*a*) *Chess:* pat *m*; (*b*) **negotiations have reached a s.,** les négociations sont arrivées au point mort, ont abouti à une impasse.

stalemate[2], *v.tr. Chess:* faire pat (son adversaire).

staleness ['steilnis], *s.* **1.** (*a*) état rassis (du pain); (*b*) évent *m* (de la bière, etc.); (*c*) relent *m* (d'un aliment, d'une pièce); odeur *f* de renfermé. **2.** manque *m* de fraîcheur (d'une nouvelle); banalité *f* (d'une plaisanterie).

Stalin ['stɑ:lin], *Pr.n.* Staline.

Stalinism ['stɑ:linizm], *s.* stalinisme *m.*

Stalinist ['stɑ:linist], *a. & s.* stalinien, -ienne.

stalk[1] [stɔ:k], *s.* **1.** (*a*) pas mesuré; démarche majestueuse, dédaigneuse; (*b*) marche *f* à grandes enjambées. **2.** *Ven:* chasse *f* à l'approche.

stalk[2], **1.** *v.i.* **to s. (along),** (i) marcher, s'avancer, d'un pas majestueux, à pas comptés; (ii) marcher à grands pas; **to s. away,** s'éloigner (i) d'un pas majestueux, d'un air dédaigneux, (ii) à grands pas; **to s. out of a room,** sortir d'une pièce d'un air dédaigneux. **2.** *v.tr.* (*a*) *Ven:* chasser (le daim) à l'approche; (*b*) suivre furtivement (qn); filer (qn).

stalk[3], *s.* **1.** tige *f* (de plante, de fleur); queue *f* (de fruit, de fleur); chaume *m*, tige (de blé); tuyau *m* (de blé, d'herbe); pied *m* (de rejeton); rafle *f*, râpe *f* (de grappe de raisins); trognon *m* (de chou); chènevotte *f* (du chanvre); *Nat.Hist:* pédoncule *m*; **s.-eyed,** podophthalme, podophthalmaire; aux yeux pédonculés. **2.** pied (de verre à vin).

stalk[4], *v.tr.* égrapper (des raisins); équeuter (des cerises, etc.).

stalked [stɔ:kt], *a.* **1.** à tige. **2.** (*a*) *Bot:* (feuille) pétiolée; (champignon) stipité; (*b*) *Nat.Hist:* (*of flower, fruit, eye*) pédonculé.

stalker ['stɔ:kər], *s.* (*a*) *Ven:* chasseur *m* à l'approche; (*b*) (*pers. following s.o.*) fileur, -euse.

stalking ['stɔ:kiŋ], *s. Ven:* chasse *f* à l'approche; **s. horse,** (i) *Ven:* cheval *m* d'abri; (ii) *Ven:* abri *m* en forme de cheval; (iii) prétexte *m*, masque *m*, paravent *m.*

stalklet ['stɔ:klit], *s. Bot:* pédicelle *m.*

stall[1] [stɔ:l], *s.* **1.** (*a*) stalle *f* (d'écurie); case *f* (d'étable); loge *f*, box *m* (de porcherie); (*b*) étable *f.* **2.** étalage *m* (en plein vent); échoppe *f*, éventaire *m*; étal, -aux *m* (de boucher); (*at bazaar*) étalage; (*at exhibition, etc.*) stand *m*; **(market) s.,** place *f*, emplacement *m* (au marché); **newspaper s.,** kiosque *m*; **s. rent,** droits *mpl* de place (au marché, etc.). **3.** (*a*) *Ecc.Arch:* stalle; *O:* **how long has he had his s.?** depuis combien de temps est-il chanoine? (*b*) *Th:* **(orchestra) stalls,** fauteuils *mpl* d'orchestre. **4.** *Min:* taille *f*; **s. road,** allée *f* de desserte; galerie *f* desservant la taille. **5. finger s.,** doigtier *m.* **6.** *Aut: etc:* calage *m*, blocage *m* (du moteur); *Av:* ralentissement *m* (au-dessous de la vitesse critique); **s. dive,** abattée *f.*

stall[2], *v.* **1.** *v.tr.* (*a*) établer, mettre à l'étable (du bétail); mettre (des chevaux) à l'écurie; (*b*) aménager (une écurie) en stalles. **2.** *v.tr. & i. Aut:* caler, bloquer (le moteur); (*of engine*) (se) caler, se bloquer; *Av:* ralentir (l'appareil) au-dessous de la vitesse critique; se mettre en perte de vitesse. **3.** *v.i.* s'embourber, s'enliser; s'enfoncer dans la boue, *NAm:* dans la neige.

stall[3], *s. F:* complice *mf* (d'un pickpocket).

stall[4]. **1.** *v.tr.* (*a*) **to s. sth. off,** repousser, écarter, qch.; **to s. s.o. off,** (i) repousser, faire attendre, qn; (ii) duper qn; donner le change à qn; (*b*) (*of accomplice*) masquer (un pickpocket). **2.** *v.i.* chercher à gagner du temps.

stallage ['stɔlidʒ], *s.* droits *mpl* d'étalage, de place, d'emplacement (au marché, etc.).

stalled [stɔld], *a.* **1.** (écurie, etc.) à stalles. **2.** (*of cattle, etc.*) établé; mis à l'étable. **3.** (*of vehicle*) embourbé; enfoncé dans la boue. **4.** (*a*) *I.C.E:* (moteur) calé, bloqué; (*b*) *Av:* (avion) en perte de vitesse.

stall-feed ['stɔ:lfi:d], *v.tr.* (**stall-fed** [-fed]) nourrir, engraisser (du bétail) à l'étable.

stallholder ['stɔ:lhouldər], *s.* **1.** (*also* **stallkeeper**) étalagiste *mf*; hallier *m*; marchand, -ande, en plein vent. **2.** (*at charity bazaar*) vendeuse *f.*

stalling ['stɔ:liŋ], *s.* **1.** stabulation *f* (des bêtes). **2.** (*a*) *Aut: etc:* calage *m*, blocage *m* (du moteur); arrêt *m* (du moteur); (*b*) *Av:* perte *f* de vitesse; **s. speed, s. point,** vitesse *f* minimum de sustentation critique; vitesse de décrochage; **s. angle,** angle *m* critique.

stallion ['stæliən], *s.* étalon *m*; cheval entier.

stalwart ['stɔ:lwət], *a.* **1.** robuste, vigoureux. **2.** vaillant, résolu, ferme; *s.* **one of the old stalwarts,** un vieux de la vieille.

stamen ['steimen], *s. Bot:* étamine *f.*

stamened ['steimend], *a. Bot:* staminé.

stamina ['stæminə], *s.* force vitale; vigueur *f*, résistance *f*; **to have great s.,** être bien trempé, d'une bonne trempe; avoir du fond; **to lack s.,** manquer de résistance, de fond, de nerf; **to lose one's s.,** s'avachir.

staminal ['stæmin(ə)l], *a.* **1.** *Bot:* staminaire; staminal, -aux. **2.** *Med:* fortifiant.

staminate ['stæmineit], *a. Bot:* staminé; (fleur *f*) mâle.

stamineal [stə'miniəl], *a. Bot:* stamineux.

stamineous [stə'miniəs], *a. Bot:* staminaire; staminal, -aux; stamineux.

staminiferous [stæmi'nifərəs], *a. Bot:* staminifère.

staminode ['stæminoud], **staminodium,** *pl.* **-ia** [stæmi'noudiəm, -iə], *s. Bot:* staminode *m.*

stammer[1] ['stæmər], *s.* (i) bégaiement *m*; (ii) balbutiement *m*; ânonnement *m*; **man with a s.,** homme *m* qui bégaie; homme bègue.

stammer[2]. **1.** *v.i.* (i) bégayer; (ii) balbutier. **2.** *v.tr.* bégayer, balbutier, bafouiller (qch.); **to s. (out) an excuse,** bégayer une excuse; **to s. (through) a few phrases in French,** bégayer quelques phrases françaises.

stammerer ['stæmərər], *s.* bègue *mf*; bégayeur, -euse.

stammering[1] ['stæməriŋ], *a.* (homme) bègue, qui bégaie; bégayant, bégayeur, -euse; **s. speech,** bégaiement *m.*

stammering[2], *s.* = STAMMER[1].

stammeringly ['stæməriŋli], *adv.* en bégayant; en balbutiant; avec hésitation.

stamp[1] [stæmp], *s.* **1.** (*a*) battement *m* de pied (d'impatience, de colère); trépignement *m*; **with a s. (of the foot),** en frappant du pied; (*b*) **ceaseless s. of feet,** piétinement perpétuel; bruit continuel de pas. **2.** (*a*) timbre *m*, empreinte *f*; **signature s.,** griffe *f*; **date s.,** timbre à date; (timbre) dateur *m*; **date and signature s.,** griffe à date; **rubber s.,** timbre humide; **self-inking s.,** timbre à encrage automatique; **numbering s.,** numéroteur *m*; (*b*) découpoir *m* (à emporte-pièce); (*c*) estampe *f*, étampe *f*, poinçon *m*; **figure s.,** poinçon à chiffrer; (*d*) (*minting*) coin *m.* **3.** (*a*) timbre; marque (apposée); *Ind:* estampille *f*, marque, de contrôle (apposée sur le matériel réceptionné); **(hallmark) s.,** poinçon (de contrôle) (marquant l'or, l'argent); **official s.,** estampille officielle; **government s.,** marque de l'État; **customs s.,** marque de la douane; (*b*) **to bear the s. of genius,** porter l'empreinte, la marque, le sceau, le cachet, du génie; être marqué au coin du génie; *O:* **a man of his s.,** un homme de sa trempe. **4. (postage) s.,** timbre(-poste) *m* (*pl.* timbres-poste); **postage-due s.,** timbre-taxe *m*, *pl.* timbres-taxe; **s. album,** album *m*, classeur *m*, de timbres-poste (de collectionneur); **s. collector,** philatéliste *mf*; collectionneur, -euse, de timbres-poste; **s. dealer,** marchand, -ande, de timbres-poste pour philatélistes; **s. machine,** distributeur *m* automatique de timbres-poste; **revenue s.,** timbre fiscal, du fisc; **duty s.,** timbre d'effets; **s. duty,** impôt *m* du timbre; droit *m* de timbre; **exempt from s. duty,** exempt du timbre; **liable to s. duty,** soumis au droit de timbre; **the S. Act,** la Loi sur le, du, timbre; **ad valorem s.,** timbre proportionnel; **adhesive s.,** timbre mobile, adhésif; **embossed s., impressed s.,** timbre à empreinte; timbre fixe, sec. **5.** *Metalw:* étampeuse *f*, estampeuse *f*, emboutisseuse *f*, emboutissoir *m.* **6.** *Min: etc:* **s. (mill),** bocard *m*; **s. milling,** broyage *m* au bocard; bocardage *m*; **s. battery,** batterie *f* de bocards, de pilons; **s. block,** pilon *m*; broyeuse *f*; **gravitation s.,** pilon à chute libre; *Paperm:* **s. machine,** pile défileuse.

stamp[2], *v.*

I *v.tr. & i.* **1.** (*a*) **to s. one's foot,** frapper du pied, du talon; **to s. one's feet,** *v.i.* **to s. about,** (i) trépigner, piétiner; (ii) (*for warmth*) battre la semelle; **to s. the snow from one's feet,** secouer la neige en frappant du pied; (*b*) *v.i.* **to s. with rage,** trépigner de colère; **to s. on sth.,** piétiner qch.; fouler qch. aux pieds; **to s. upstairs,** monter l'escalier à pas bruyants. **2.** frapper, imprimer, une marque sur (qch.); marquer (du beurre, du papier, etc.); contrôler, poinçonner (l'or, l'argent); frapper, estamper (la monnaie, une médaille, le cuir, du papier-tenture); gaufrer (le cuir); frapper (le velours); signer (de la bijouterie); **to have one's initials stamped on sth.,** faire frapper ses initiales sur qch. **3.** timbrer (un document, un effet, un reçu); apposer un visa à, viser (un passeport); timbrer, afranchir (une lettre); estampiller (un document, des marchandises); *Rail:* viser (un billet circulaire, etc.); **the letter is insufficiently stamped,** l'affranchissement est insuffisant. **4.** *Metalw:* travailler (le métal) à la presse; étamper, estamper, emboutir, matricer (des objets en métal). **5.** *Min:* broyer, briser, concasser, bocarder (le minerai); pilonner (le minerai). **6.** *O:* **to s. s.o., sth., (as) . . .,** donner à qn, qch., le caractère de . . .; déclarer, indiquer, que qn, qch., est . . ..

II. (*compound verb*) **stamp out,** *v.tr.* **1.** *Metalw:* découper (des tôles) à la presse, à l'emporte-pièce; matricer (des barres). **2. to s. out the fire,** piétiner sur le feu pour l'éteindre; éteindre le feu en piétinant dessus, en le piétinant; **to s. out a rebellion,** écraser une rébellion; **to s. out an epidemic,** étouffer, écraser, une épidémie; venir à bout d'une épidémie; **to s. out a disease,** éliminer une maladie (d'un pays, etc.).

stamped [stæmpt], *a.* **1.** (*a*) broyé, concassé; (*b*) **s. earth,** terre piétinée, battue. **2.** (*a*) timbré; **s. document,** document timbré; **s.-addressed envelope,** enveloppe timbrée; (*b*) estampillé, marqué, poinçonné, contrôlé; **s. gold, silver,** or, argent, contrôlé. **3.** (*a*) *Metalw:* embouti, étampé, estampé, matricé; **s. hole,** trou embouti; **s. ring,** cerce emboutie; **s. steel,** acier estampé; (*b*) (cuir) gaufré; (velours) frappé.

stampede[1] [stæm'pi:d], *s.* **1.** (*a*) fuite précipitée (causée par une terreur panique); panique *f*; (*b*) débandade *f* (de troupes, de chevaux, etc.); **general s.,** sauve-qui-peut général; débandade générale. **2.** ruée *f*; **there was a s. for the door,** on s'est précipité vers la porte.

stampede[2]. **1.** *v.i.* (*a*) fuir en désordre, à la débandade; être pris de panique; s'affoler; (*b*) se ruer, se précipiter **(for, towards,** vers, sur). **2.** *v.tr.* (*a*) jeter la panique parmi (des bêtes, des personnes); mettre en fuite (des bêtes, des personnes); (*b*) **to s. a nation into war,** précipiter un peuple dans la guerre; *U.S:* **to s. the voters,** précipiter les voteurs en faveur d'un certain candidat.

stamper ['stæmpər], *s.* **1.** (*pers.*) (*a*) timbreur, -euse; estampilleur, -euse; (*b*) estampeur, -euse; étampeur, -euse; emboutisseur, -euse; (*c*) frappeur, -euse (de monnaie, de médailles, etc.). **2.** (*machine*) (*a*) estampeuse *f*; poinçonneuse *f*; (*b*) *Rec:* poinçon *m*; (*c*) pilon *m*, bocard *m.*

Stampian ['stæmpiən], *a. & s. Geol:* stampien (*m*).

stamping ['stæmpiŋ], *s.* **1.** piétinement *m*; trépignement *m*; *F:* **our favourite s. ground,** l'endroit où nous nous plaisons le mieux; **a s. ground of bandits,** un lieu infesté de bandits; *Med:* **s. out,** éradication *f* (d'une maladie). **2.** (*a*) timbrage *m* (des documents, etc.); estampillage *m* (des marchandises, etc.); affranchissement *m* (des lettres); (*b*) poinçonnage *m* (de l'or, etc.); (*c*) *Metalw:* estampage *m*, étampage *m*, emboutissage *m*, matriçage *m*; **sheet s.,** estampage des tôles; **hand s.,** repoussage *m*; **s. die,** matrice *f* pour emboutissage; **s. press,** estampeuse *f*, étampeuse *f*, emboutisseuse *f*, emboutissoir *m*; machine *f* à étamper; presse *f* à estamper, à matricer; presse à percussion; balancier *m*; (*d*) **s. (out),** découpage *m* à la presse, à l'emporte-pièce; (*e*) *Min:* bocardage *m*, broiement *m* (du minerai); pilonnage *m*; **s. mill,** moulin *m* à bocards; bocard *m.* **3.** *Metalw:* pièce estampée, matricée, emboutie; *Aut:* **body s.,** embouti *m*, pièce emboutie, pour carrosserie.

stance [stæns], *s. Golf: Cr: etc:* position *f* des pieds, posture *f* (du joueur); **to take up one's s.,** se mettre en posture (pour jouer).

stanch, *v.tr.* = STAUNCH[2].

stanchion[1] ['stɑ:nʃ(ə)n], *s.* colonnette *f* de soutien. **1.** (*a*) étançon *m*, étance *f*; étai *m*, appui *m*, béquille *f*, jambette *f*; (*b*) accore *m* (de bateau en construction). **2.** *Nau:* (*a*) épontille *f* (de cale, d'entrepont); (*b*) montant *m* (de tente); chandelier *m.* **3.** *Rail:* ranchet *m* (de wagon, etc.).

stanchion[2], *v.tr.* **1.** étayer, accorer, épontiller. **2.** garnir de montants. **3.** attacher (une bête) à un montant.

stand[1] [stænd], *s.* **1.** (*a*) manière *f* de se tenir (debout); **horse with a good s.,** cheval qui a un aplomb régulier; **to take a firm s.,** (i) se camper solidement, se planter, sur ses jambes; s'assurer sur ses pieds, sur ses jambes; s'assurer un solide aplomb; (ii) ne pas transiger; (*b*) arrêt *m*, halte *f*, pause *f*; **to come, be brought, to a s.,** s'arrêter, être forcé de s'arrêter; demeurer court; **to put, bring, s.o. to a s.,** acculer qn; *A:* **to be at a s.,** être acculé; *Mil:* **to be compelled to make a s.,** se laisser accrocher; (*c*) *Th:* arrêt (dans une ville); séjour *m* (d'une troupe en tournée); **one-night s.,** soirée *f*, représentation *f*, unique. **2.** résistance *f*; **to make a s. against the enemy,** s'accrocher au sol; résister à l'ennemi; tenir bon; **to make a s. against s.o.,** résister à qn; **to make a s. against an abuse,** s'opposer résolument à un abus; s'élever contre un abus; se dresser en face d'un abus. **3.** situation *f*, place *f*, position *f*; (*a*) **to take one's s. near the door,** se placer, se poster, se planter, prendre position, près de la porte; (*b*) **to take one's s. on a principle,** s'en tenir à, se fonder sur, un principe. **4.** station *f*, stationnement *m* (de taxis). **5.** support *m*, colonne *f*, pied *m*, socle *m* (de lampe, etc.); affût *m* (de télescope); statif *m* (de microscope); râtelier *m* (pour bouteilles, etc.); valet *m* (de laboratoire); étagère *f* (pour objets divers); dessous *m* (de plat, de carafe); présentoir *m* (pour un vase, etc.); **(dish) s.,** porte-plat *m*; **milliner's s.,** champignon *m*; (*for books, postcards, etc.*) **revolving s.,** tourniquet *m*; **(bee)hive stand,** tablier *m* de ruche; *Motor-Cy:* **back-wheel stand,** béquille *f* de démarrage, support-béquille *m*, *pl.* supports-béquilles. **6.** (*a*) étalage *m*, étal *m*, boutique *f* (en plein air); (*at an exhibition, etc.*) stand *m*; (*b*) *Com:* **broker's s.,** emplacement *m*, poste *m* (de vente à la criée). **7.** (*a*) *Sp: Rac: etc:* tribune *f*; stand; **the stands,** les tribunes; (*b*) estrade *f*. **8.** (*a*) *Agr:* récolte *f* sur pied; (*b*) *For:* peuplement *m*; **mixed s.,** peuplement mélangé. **9.** *Mil: A:* **s. of arms,** armement *m* (d'un soldat); **s. of colours,** drapeau *m*. **10.** *Jur: U.S:* barre *f* des témoins.

stand[2], *v.* (*p.t. & p.p.* **stood** [stud]) **I.** *v.i.* **1.** (*a*) (*have, maintain, upright position*) être debout; se tenir debout; rester debout; **horse that stands well,** cheval qui a de beaux aplombs; cheval bien placé; **table that stands firm,** table qui pose bien sur ses pieds; **to be, to keep, standing,** être, rester, debout; **I stood there so long that I nearly fainted,** je suis resté là debout si longtemps que j'ai failli m'évanouir; **I was too weak to s.,** j'étais trop faible pour me tenir debout; **I could hardly s.,** je pouvais à peine me tenir; je me soutenais à peine; **to s. on one's feet,** se soutenir sur ses pieds; être debout; **the chair will not s. on three legs,** la chaise ne tient pas sur trois pieds; **to s. on one's own legs, feet,** ne dépendre que de soi; voler de ses propres ailes; **I didn't leave him a leg to s. on,** j'ai détruit, démoli, ses arguments de fond en comble; *F:* je lui ai rivé son clou; **he hasn't a leg to s. on,** il est absolument sans excuse; il est entièrement dans son tort; son argument est détruit de fond en comble; *For:* **to leave a tree standing,** réserver un arbre; **I've lost everything but what I s. up in,** j'ai tout perdu sauf ce que j'ai sur le dos; (*b*) **to s. six feet high,** avoir six pieds de haut; mesurer six pieds; (*c*) (*assume upright position*) se lever; *Sch:* **stand!** levez-vous! **2.** (*a*) (*be situated; be*) se trouver; être; se dresser, s'élever; **there was a bookcase standing in one corner,** il y avait une bibliothèque dans un des coins; **a chapel stands at the top of the hill,** une chapelle se dresse au sommet de la colline; **a large yew tree stands in front of the house,** un grand if s'élève devant la maison; **a car was standing at the door,** il y avait une voiture à la porte; **I found the door standing open,** j'ai trouvé la porte ouverte; **the tears stood in his eyes,** il avait les larmes aux yeux; **the sweat stood on his forehead,** la sueur perlait sur son front; **to let sth. s. in the sun,** laisser qch. exposé au soleil; **after standing in the sun,** après avoir été exposé au soleil; **to buy the house as it stands,** acheter la maison telle quelle; **nothing stands between you and success,** rien ne s'oppose à votre succès; (*b*) **a man stood in the doorway,** un homme se tenait à la porte; **I stood and looked at him, I stood looking at him,** je suis resté à le regarder; **she stood at the window watching me,** elle se tenait à la fenêtre et m'observait; **she stood looking over my shoulder,** elle regardait par-dessus mon épaule; **to s. talking,** rester à parler; **don't s. there arguing!** ne restez pas là à discuter! **don't s. in the rain,** ne restez pas à la pluie; **don't s. about, in, the gangway!** n'encombrez pas la passerelle! **I left him standing at the door,** je l'ai laissé à la porte; **to leave s.o. standing (there),** laisser qn planté (là); *Sp: etc:* **to be left standing,** être laissé sur place; *Turf:* **to leave the field standing,** faire cavalier seul; *Rac:* **to leave a competitor standing,** brûler, griller, un concurrent; *Typ:* **to keep the type standing,** conserver la composition; mettre la composition en conserve; **I kissed her where she stood,** je l'ai embrassée tout de go; **a lot of people were standing about, around,** beaucoup de gens s'y trouvaient, restaient à regarder; il y avait là beaucoup de flâneurs. **3.** (*take up a stationary position*) s'arrêter; faire halte; **stand!** halte (là)! **s. and deliver!** la bourse ou la vie! **he came out of the crowd and stood in front of me,** il est sorti de la foule et s'est arrêté devant moi; **to s. still,** rester immobile, sans bouger. **4.** (*maintain position*) rester, durer; **the house will s. for another century,** la maison durera encore un siècle; **to s. fast, firm,** tenir pied; tenir ferme; tenir bon; tenir; **to s. or fall,** se maintenir ou succomber; tenir (bon) ou succomber; **we s. or fall together,** nous sommes solidaires (les uns des autres); **these doctrines s. or fall together,** ces doctrines sont étroitement liées; **I shall s. or fall by the issue,** je suis prêt à engager ma fortune sur le résultat. **5.** (*remain valid*) tenir, se maintenir; **the passage must stand,** le passage doit rester comme il est, tel quel, sans modification; il faut maintenir le passage; **the contract stands,** le contrat tient, est valide; **the bargain, the bet, stands,** le marché, le pari, tient; **the objection stands,** cette objection subsiste; **the same remark stands,** la même observation est applicable. **6.** (*a*) (*be in certain position*) être, se trouver; **to s. convicted of . . .,** être déclaré coupable de . . .; être convaincu de . . .; **to s. convicted of lying,** être convaincu d'un mensonge; **to s. in need of . . .,** avoir besoin de . . .; manquer de . . .; **you s. in danger of getting killed,** vous vous exposez au danger de vous faire tuer; vous risquez de vous faire tuer; **I s. dishonoured,** je suis déshonoré; **to s. to lose £100,** risquer de perdre £100; **to s. to lose nothing,** n'avoir rien à perdre; **I s. to win, to lose, if . . .,** je gagne, je perds, si. . .; **we s. to lose, whereas you s. to gain,** nous courons le risque d'y perdre, tandis que vous avez des chances d'y gagner; (*b*) **to s. as security for a debt,** assurer une créance; **to s. as candidate,** se porter candidat, se présenter comme candidat, poser sa candidature (**for,** à); **to s. (as candidate) for Parliament,** se présenter, se porter candidat, à la députation; (*c*) **he stands first on the list,** il est le premier, il vient en tête, de la liste; **the thermometer stood at 30°,** le thermomètre marquait 30°; (*d*) **securities standing in the company's books at so much,** titres portés pour tant dans les livres de la société; **the house does not s. in his name,** la maison n'est pas portée à son nom; (*e*) **the balance stands at £50,** le reliquat de compte est de cinquante livres; **the amount standing to your credit,** votre solde créditeur; **how do we s.?** où en sont nos comptes? **how do we s. for ready money?** combien d'argent liquide avons-nous? **as matters s., as it stands,** au point où en sont les choses; dans l'état actuel des choses; **to know how things s.,** être au fait de la question; **as the case stands,** étant donné(s) les faits de la cause; **I don't know where I s.,** j'ignore quelle est ma situation, ma position; je ne sais plus où j'en suis; **this is how I s.,** voici ma position; **we are going to take stock in order to see how we s.,** nous allons faire l'inventaire pour nous rendre compte de notre position, pour voir où nous en sommes; **how do you s. with him?** quelle est votre position vis-à-vis de lui? sur quel pied êtes-vous avec lui? comment êtes-vous avec lui? **to s. well with s.o.,** être estimé de qn. **7.** (*move to and remain in certain position*) se tenir, se mettre; **I'll s. here,** je me tiendrai ici; **I'll s. at, by, near, the window,** je me mettrai à la fenêtre; **I didn't know where to s.,** je ne savais où me mettre; **to s. against a wall,** se mettre contre un mur; *Nau:* **to s. upon the course,** porter à route; **to s. to the south,** avoir, mettre, le cap au sud; **to s. inshore,** rallier la terre; **you're standing into danger,** vous courez sur un danger. **8.** (*remain motionless*) **the water appears to s. here,** il semble qu'ici il n'y ait pas de courant; ici l'eau paraît être stagnante; **to allow a liquid to s.,** laisser reposer, laisser déposer, un liquide; **to let the tea s.,** laisser infuser le thé; **trucks standing in a siding,** wagons en station sur une voie de garage.

II. *v.tr.* **1.** (*place upright*) mettre, poser, placer; **to s. sth. on the table,** mettre, poser, qch. sur la table; **to s. sth. against the wall,** dresser qch. contre le mur; **to s. sth. on end, upright,** faire tenir qch. debout; mettre qch. debout; **to s. sth. in a corner,** mettre, placer, qch. dans un coin; **if Tom does it again he will be stood in the corner,** si Tom recommence, il sera mis au coin, il sera mis en pénitence dans le coin. **2. to s. one's ground,** tenir bon, ferme; tenir pied; ne pas reculer; ne pas lâcher pied; **stand your ground!** ne reculez pas d'une semelle! accrochez-vous au sol! **3.** (*endure*) supporter, soutenir, subir; **to s. cold, fatigue,** supporter le froid, la fatigue; résister au froid, à la fatigue; **plant that cannot s. a damp soil,** plante *f* qui redoute un sol humide; **he can't s. drink,** il ne soutient pas la boisson; **it would be more than nature could s. to . . .,** il serait outre nature de . . .; **to s. a shock,** soutenir un choc; (*of car, etc.*) **to s. rough handling,** résister à des manipulations brutales; être solide; **we had to s. the loss,** la perte a porté sur nous; *Mil:* **to s. fire,** soutenir le feu; **argument that does not s. investigation,** argument qui ne supporte pas l'examen; **he can't stand her,** il ne peut pas la souffrir, la sentir; *F:* **I can't s. him at any price!** je ne peux pas le sentir; **I can't s. his professorial attitude,** je n'encaisse pas son air professoral; **I won't stand such behaviour,** je ne supporterai pas une pareille conduite; **I can't s. it any longer,** je n'y tiens plus; j'en ai assez; j'en ai pardessus la tête. **4.** *F:* payer, offrir; **to s. s.o. a drink,** payer à boire à qn; **to s. a round (of drinks),** payer une tournée; **I'm standing this one,** c'est ma tournée; **he stood us a couple of bottles,** il y est allé de deux bouteilles; **to s. s.o. a dinner,** payer un dîner à qn; **to s. oneself a good dinner,** s'offrir un bon dîner.

III. (*compound verbs*) **1. stand aside,** *v.i.* (*a*) se tenir à l'écart; **to s. aside when something is to be done,** s'abstenir lorsqu'il s'agit de faire quelque chose; (*b*) s'écarter, se ranger; **to s. aside to let s.o. pass,** s'effacer pour laisser passer qn; (*c*) **to s. aside in favour of s.o.,** se désister en faveur de qn.

2. stand away, *v.i.* (*a*) s'éloigner, s'écarter (**from,** de); **s. away from the gates!** écartez-vous de la grille! *Nau:* **to s. away from shore,** s'éloigner de la côte; prendre le large; (*b*) *Nau:* prendre chasse; soutenir la chasse.

3. stand back, *v.i.* (i) se tenir en arrière; (ii) (se) reculer; (iii) être situé en retrait; **house standing back from the road,** maison écartée du chemin; maison en retrait (de la route).

4. stand by, *v.i.* (*a*) (i) se tenir prêt; *Mil:* **the troops are standing by,** les troupes sont consignées, sont en état d'alerte; (ii) *Nau:* se tenir paré; veiller; **s. by!** paré! attention! (iii) *Ind:* (*of furnace, etc.*) être au repos; (iv) se tenir là (sans intervenir); **would you have stood by and let her drown?** est-ce que vous seriez resté à la regarder se noyer? **all I could do was to s. by,** tout ce que je pouvais faire c'était de rester à veiller; (*b*) (i) se tenir près de, à côté de (qn); (ii) soutenir, défendre (qn); se ranger du côté de (qn); faire cause commune avec (qn); (iii) rester fidèle à (sa promesse); **I s. by what I said,** je me tiens, je m'en tiens, à ce que j'ai dit.

5. stand down, *v.i.* (*a*) (*of witness*) quitter la barre; **you may s. down,** vous pouvez vous retirer; (*b*) *Sp:* se retirer (du jeu, d'une équipe); (*of candidate*) retirer sa candidature, se retirer, se désister (**in favour of,** en faveur de); (*c*) *Mil:* quitter son service; descendre de garde.

6. stand for, *v. ind. tr.* (*a*) défendre, soutenir (qn, une cause); (*b*) remplacer, tenir lieu de (qn, qch.); *Jur: Pol:* représenter (qn); (*c*) signifier, vouloir dire (qch.); **to s. for nothing,** ne compter pour rien; **Union Street stands for modern ideas,** Union Street est un exemple parfait d'une rue d'après les idées modernes; (*d*) supporter, tolérer (qch.); **I won't s. for that any longer,** je ne supporterai plus cela.

7. stand forward, *v.i.* (*a*) se tenir en avant; (*b*) se mettre en avant; s'avancer; *Mil: etc:* sortir du rang.

8. stand in, *v.i.* (*a*) *Nau:* **to s. in for a port,** mettre le cap sur un port; courir vers un port; **to s. in to land, for (the) land,** courir, porter, à terre; (*b*) **to s. in for s.o.,** remplacer qn, *Cin:* doubler un acteur; **as he was ill I had to s. in,** j'ai dû le remplacer parce qu'il était malade.

9. stand off. (*a*) *v.i.* (i) se tenir éloigné, à l'écart; (ii) s'éloigner; *Nau:* courir au large; avoir le cap au large; (*b*) *v.tr.* (*of employer*) congédier (des ouvriers).

10. stand on, *v.i. Nau:* faire route; continuer sa route.

11. stand out, *v.i.* (*a*) résister (**against,** à); tenir bon, ferme (**against,** contre); s'opposer (**against,** à); (*b*) **to s. out for sth.,** s'obstiner à demander qch.; **to s. out for one's claims,** insister sur ses demandes; (*c*) faire saillie; être en saillie; avancer; **his house stands out from the others,** sa maison avance dans la rue, se détache des autres; **to s. out in relief,** ressortir, se détacher, se découper, s'accuser; faire vedette; **to s. out against sth.,** faire contraste avec qch.; **the statue stands out against a dark background,** la statue se détache, tranche, sur un fond sombre; la statue se distingue contre un fond sombre; **mountains that s. out against the horizon,** montagnes qui se dessinent, se profilent, se silhouettent, à l'horizon, sur l'horizon; montagnes qui se projettent sur l'horizon; **to make a figure s. out in a picture,** détacher une figure dans un tableau; **the qualities that s. out in his work,** les qualités marquantes de son œuvre; les qualités qui s'affirment, qui ressortent, dans son œuvre; **among so many canvases a small masterpiece stands out,** parmi tant de toiles se distingue un petit chef-d'œuvre; **characteristics that make him s. out in the crowd,** traits qui le détachent de la foule; *Th:* **the son's part does not s. out as it should,** le rôle du fils ne ressort pas assez; (*d*) *Nau:* **to s. out to sea,** (i) gagner le large; mettre le cap au large; (ii) se tenir au large.

12. stand over, *v.i.* (*a*) rester en suspens; **to let a question s. over, to allow a question to s. over,** remettre une question à plus tard; laisser une question en suspens; **we'll let it s. over until next week,** nous laisserons cela jusqu'à la semaine prochaine; **to let an account s. over,** laisser traîner un compte; (*b*) **to s. over s.o. while he does sth.,** (i) se pencher sur qn, (ii) surveiller qn de près, pendant qu'il fait qch.; **if I don't s. over him he does nothing,** si je ne suis pas toujours sur son dos il ne fait rien.

13. stand to, *v.i.* (*a*) *Nau:* **to s. to the south,** avoir le cap au sud; (*b*) *Mil: etc:* être prêt, être en état d'alerte; **to s. to one's arms,** se tenir sous les armes; **s. to!** aux armes! (*c*) **to s. to one's promise,** ne pas renier sa promesse.

14. stand up. (*a*) *v.i.* (i) se lever; se mettre debout; **s. up!** levez-vous! debout! **and now we've got to s. up again!** et maintenant il nous faut nous relever, nous remettre debout! *A:* **to s. up with a lady,** danser avec une dame; *NAm: F:* **to s. up with s.o.,** être garçon d'honneur, demoiselle d'honneur (à un mariage); **well-known actresses don't want to s. up and be counted,** une actrice bien connue ne veut pas se déclarer publiquement pour, contre, une question discutable; *F:* **to take it standing up,** ne pas broncher; encaisser le coup; (ii) **to s. up against (s.o., sth.),** résister à (qn, qch.); tenir tête à (qn); **to s. up for s.o.,** défendre, soutenir, qn; prendre le parti de qn; prendre fait et cause pour qn; **to s. up to s.o.,** tenir pied à qn; affronter courageusement qn; ne pas se laisser démonter par qn; **he couldn't s. up to it,** il n'a pas tenu le coup; **steel that stands up well to high temperatures,** acier qui résiste aux hautes températures, dont la tenue est bonne aux hautes températures; (*of machine, etc.*) **to stand up to rough handling, treatment,** résister à des manipulations brutales, à un traitement brutal; être bien solide; (*b*) *v.tr.* (i) **to s. sth. up,** mettre qch. debout; **to s. a child up (again),** (re)mettre un enfant sur ses pieds; (ii) *F:* **to s. s.o. up,** (α) lâcher, planter là, qn; (β) tromper, refaire qn.

standage ['stændidʒ], *s. Min:* puisard *m.*

standard ['stændəd], *s.* **1.** (*a*) bannière *f*; *Mil:* étendard *m*; *Nau:* pavillon *m*; **the Royal S.,** la bannière royale; *Mil:* **s. bearer,** (i) porte-étendard *m inv*; (ii) *A:* porte-drapeau *m inv*; (*b*) *Bot:* pavillon, étendard (d'une papilionacée); (*c*) *Orn:* **s. wing,** (i) (*New Guinea*) semioptère *m*, paradisier *m* de Wallace; (ii) (*Africa*) engoulevent *m* porte-étendard. **2.** *Meas: etc:* étalon *m*; type *m* (de poids, de mesures, etc.); **the metre is the s. of length,** le mètre est le module des longueurs; **legal s.,** étalon légal; *Fin:* **gold, silver, s.,** étalon (d')or, d'argent; **double s.,** double étalon; bimétallisme *m*; *attrib.* **s. measure,** mesure-étalon *f, pl.* mesures-étalons; **s. metre,** étalon du mètre; **s. weight,** (i) poids *m* étalon; (ii) poids normal; **s. weights,** poids unifiés; **s. coin,** pièce droite; **s. copper,** cuivre *m* type; **s. gold, silver,** or *m*, argent *m*, au titre; *Com:* **(British) s. specifications,** normes *fpl*; **British Advertising Standards Authority** = Bureau *m* de Vérification de la Publicité; **s. price,** prix régulateur; **s. shape,** forme *f* type (d'un outil, etc.); **s. thickness,** épaisseur type, courante (du fer, etc.); **s. dimensions,** dimensions, cotes, normales; **of s. size, make,** de taille, de marque, courante; (*of car*) **s. model,** voiture *f* de série; **s. equipment,** équipement *m* standard; **headrests are s. (equipment),** les appuis-tête sont montés en série; *Rail:* **s. gauge,** voie normale; écartement normal; *Tchn:* **s. nut,** écrou *m* ordinaire; *Ch:* **s. paper,** papier *m* à réactif; **British s. time,** heure légale anglaise; *Psy:* **s. test,** test étalonné. **3.** (*a*) modèle *m*, type, niveau *m*, norme; **s. of living,** niveau de vie; **high s. of taste,** bon goût; goût raffiné; **there is no absolute s. of morality,** il n'y a pas d'étalon des mœurs; **everyone has his own standards,** tout homme a sa manière de voir; **other times, other standards,** autres temps autres mœurs; (*b*) qualité *f*; aloi *m*; niveau; **a high s. of intelligence,** un niveau élevé de capacité intellectuelle; **this school has low academic standards,** le niveau des études à cette école laisse à désirer; **to aim at, to reach, a high s.,** viser à, atteindre, un niveau élevé; **not to come up to s.,** ne pas atteindre le niveau exigé; ne pas avoir toutes les qualités requises; (*c*) *attrib.* **s. authors,** auteurs *m* classiques; **s. edition;** édition courante (d'un auteur); **a s. French dictionary,** un dictionnaire général de la langue française; **s. English,** l'anglais des gens cultivés; **one of his s. jokes,** une de ses plaisanteries classiques, habituelles; (*d*) **s. (of purity) of gold, silver,** titre *m* de l'or, de l'argent; *Ch:* **s. of a solution,** titre, teneur *f*, d'une solution. **4.** *Sch: A:* classe *f* (dans une école primaire). **5.** (*a*) *Tchn:* bâti *m*; pied *m*, support *m* (d'un instrument scientifique, etc.); montant *m* (d'une machine, d'une palissade, etc.); chandelle *f*, jambe *f* (d'un bâti); jambage *m* (d'un marteau-pilon); **windlass standards,** poteaux *m* de treuil; *Mec.E:* **standards of a rolling mill,** colonnes *f* d'un laminoir; **s. of a jack,** fût *m* d'un cric, d'un vérin; **shafting s.,** chaise *f* sur le sol pour transmission; (*b*) *Const:* écoperche *f*; échasse *f* d'échafaud; baliveau *m*; (*c*) pylône *m* d'éclairage; réverbère *m* électrique; (*d*) *Furn:* **s. lamp,** lampadaire *m*; (*e*) *Mus:* pique *f* (de violoncelle). **6.** (*a*) *Hort:* **s. (tree),** arbre *m* de plein vent; **tall standards,** (arbres à) hautes tiges; **s. rose (tree),** rosier *m* sur tige; **half s.,** demi-tige *f*; (*b*) *For:* baliveau *m.*

standardization [stændədai'zeiʃ(ə)n], *s.* étalonnage *m*, étalonnement *m* (des poids, d'un galvanomètre, etc.); unification *f*, uniformisation *f* (des méthodes d'essai, des objets de commerce, etc.); *Ind:* standardisation *f*; mise *f* en série (d'une machine, etc.); *Cin:* standardisation (des films, de la perforation); *Ch:* titrage *m*; *Rail:* **s. of freight charges, of tariffs,** péréquation *f* des prix, des tarifs.

standardize ['stændədaiz], *v.tr.* étalonner, unifier, uniformiser (des méthodes d'essai, des objets de commerce, etc.); normaliser (une condition); *Ind:* standardiser; mettre en série (des voitures, etc.); *Ch:* titrer (une solution); *Psy:* étalonner (un test); **standardized production,** fabrication *f* en (grande) série; **standardized products,** produits typifiés.

standardizing ['stændədaiziŋ], *s.* = STANDARDIZATION.

standaway ['stændəwei], *a. Cost:* **s. neck,** encolure décollée, loin du cou.

standby ['stændbai], *s.* **1.** personne sur qui l'on peut compter; appui *m*, soutien *m* (**of s.o.,** de qn). **2.** ressource *f*; **to have a sum in reserve as a s.,** avoir une somme en réserve comme en-cas. **3.** *attrib.* **s. machine, dynamo,** machine *f*, dynamo *f*, de secours, de réserve, de pointe; **s. engine,** locomotive *f* de réserve. **4.** *Av: etc:* (*of pers.*) **to be on s.,** attendre une place libre.

stand-easy [stænd'i:zi], *s. Mil:* repos *m.*

standee [stæn'di:], *s. esp. NAm:* (*in bus, etc.*) voyageur, -euse, debout; *Th: etc:* spectateur, -trice, debout; **standees not allowed,** il est défendu, defense, de rester, de voyager, debout.

stand-in ['stændin], *s.* **1.** *NAm: F:* entente *f*; **to have a s.-in with s.o.,** être bien avec qn. **2.** (*pers.*) remplaçant, -ante; *Th: etc:* doublure *f.*

standing[1] ['stændiŋ], *a.* **1.** (*a*) (qui se tient) debout; **s. passengers,** voyageurs debout; **s. spectator,** spectateur, -trice, debout; **s. statue,** statue *f* en pied; *Prehist:* **s. stone,** pierre levée; menhir *m*; (*b*) **s. crops,** récoltes *f* sur pied; *Jur:* fruits pendants par (les) racines; **to sell a crop s.,** vendre une récolte sur pied; **a hundred s. trees,** cent pieds *m* d'arbres; (*c*) *Typ:* **s. press,** verticale. **2.** (*a*) **s. water,** eau stagnante, dormante; (*b*) **s. engine,** machine *f* en chômage; machine inactive; (*c*) *Typ:* **s. type,** conservation *f*; **to keep the type standing,** conserver la composition; mettre la composition en conserve. **3.** (*a*) *Mil:* **s. army,** armée permanente; **s. camp,** camp permanent, de séjour; (*b*) *Tchn:* **s. block,** poulie *f* fixe; **s. bolt,** boulon prisonnier; *Nau:* **s. rope,** manœuvre *f* fixe; **s. part of a rope,** dormant *m* d'une manœuvre. **4.** *adv.phr. Nau:* **all s.,** (i) tout étant en bon état; (ii) sans désarmer; **to be brought up all s.,** (i) faire chapelle, faire panne, toutes voiles dehors; (ii) *Fig:* se heurter rudement à un obstacle; se trouver immobilisé, désemparé; rester en panne. **5.** (*a*) **s. price,** prix *m* fixe; *Ind: Com:* **s. expenses,** frais généraux; dépenses *f* de maison; (*b*) **s. rule,** règle *f* fixe, invariable, immuable; **s. joke,** plaisanterie habituelle, courante, traditionnelle, classique; **I have a s. invitation,** j'ai mes entrées libres (dans cette famille); je suis invité chez eux quand je suis libre.

standing[2], *s.* **1.** (*a*) fait *m* de se tenir debout; station *f* debout; (*b*) *Rail: Th: etc:* **s. room,** place(s) *f*(*pl*) debout; **s. (room) only!** debout seulement! **no s.!** défense de rester, de voyager, debout; (*c*) *U.S: P.N: Aut:* **no s.,** défense de stationner. **2.** durée *f*; **friends of long s.,** amis de longue date, de vieille date; **friend of twenty years' s.,** ami de vingt ans; *Com: etc:* **connection of long s.,** relations *fpl* de longues années, de vieille date. **3.** rang *m*, position *f*, importance *f*, considération *f*, *F:* standing *m*; **social s.,** position sociale; **it would mean losing one's s.,** ce serait déchoir; **the firm's s.,** l'importance de la maison; **financial s.,** situation financière; **firm of recognized s.,** entreprise d'une solidité reconnue; (*of trade union, etc.*) **(member) in good s.,** (membre) en règle.

stand-off ['stændɔf], *a. Rugby Fb:* **s.-o. half,** demi *m* d'ouverture.

stand-offish [stænd'ɔfiʃ], *a. F:* (*of pers.*) peu accessible, peu communicatif, peu abordable; distant, raide, réservé; peu liant; (*of attitude*) raide; **to be s.-o.,** se mettre, se tenir, sur son quant-à-soi; prendre, tenir, garder, son quant-à-soi; **don't be so s.-o.,** ne faites pas le réservé, la réservée.

stand-offishness [stænd'ɔfiʃnis], *s. F:* raideur *f*, réserve *f*; morgue *f.*

standout ['stændaut], *s. NAm: F:* **he's, it's, a s.!** il est, c'est, hors concours!

standpat, *a. & s.,* **standpatter,** *s.* ['stændpæt(ər)], *N Am: Pol: F:* immobiliste (*mf*).

standpipe ['stændpaip], *s.* (*a*) tuyau vertical, de chute; conduite *f* en élévation; colonne montante; colonne d'alimentation (d'eau, etc.); (*b*) réservoir *m* cylindrique (de hauteur plus grande que son diamètre).

standpoint ['stændpɔint], *s.* point *m* de vue; position *f.*

standstill ['stændstil], *s.* **1.** (*a*) arrêt *m*, immobilisation *f*; **to come to a s.,** s'arrêter, s'immobiliser; (*of car, etc.*) rester en panne; **matters have come to a (dead) standstill,** les choses *f* n'avancent plus; il y a arrêt complet; on est arrivé à un point mort; **to bring a train to a s.,** arrêter un train; **trade is at a s.,** le commerce ne va plus; les affaires ne marchent pas, sont au calme plat; les affaires sont enrayées, dans un état de stagnation; **business is at an absolute s.,** il y a arrêt complet dans les affaires; **many factories are at a s.,** beaucoup d'usines chôment; **all our plans are at a s.,** tous nos projets restent en souffrance; (*b*) *Mil:* (période *f* de) stabilisation *f* (dans la guerre de tranchées). **2.** *attrib.* **s. order,** immobilisation du cheptel, interdiction *f* de transport des bêtes (dans une région où sévit une épizootie).

stand-to ['stændtu:], *s. Mil:* (état *m* d')alerte *f.*

stand-up ['stændʌp], *a.* **1.** *Cost:* (col) droit, montant, relevé. **2.** (repas) pris debout. **3.** **s.-up fight,** (i) combat *m* en règle; (ii) bataille rangée.

stang [stæŋ], *s.* perche *f*, bâton *m.*

stanhope ['stænəp], *s.* **1.** *A. Veh:* stanhope *m*; cabriolet léger (et découvert). **2.** *Typ:* **s. press,** stanhope *f.*

staniel ['stænjəl], *s. Orn: O:* crécerelle *f.*

stank [stæŋk], *s. Dial:* étang *m.*

stannary ['stænəri], *s.* (*a*) *A:* mine *f* d'étain; (*b*) *Hist:* **the Stannaries,** la région stannifère des Cornouailles et du Devon.

stannate ['stæneit], *s. Ch:* stannate *m.*

stannic ['stænik], *a. Ch:* stannique; **s. chloride,** stannichlorure *m.*

stanniferous [stæ'nifərəs], *a.* stannifère.

stannite ['stænait], *s. Miner:* stannine *f*, stannite *f.*

stannous ['stænəs], *a. Ch:* stanneux; **s. chloride,** stannochlorure *m.*

stanza[1], *pl.* **-as** ['stænzə, -əz], *s. Pros:* stance *f*, strophe *f*; **sapphic s.,** strophe saphique; **in three stanzas,** (poème) à trois stances, à trois strophes.

stanza[2], *pl.* **-e** ['stæntsə, -ei], *s. Arch:* portique *m* en avant-corps; loge *f*; **Raphael's stanze in the Vatican,** les loges du Vatican par Raphaël.

stapedial [stæ'pi:diəl], *a. Anat:* stapédien.

stapedius [stæ'pi:diəs], *s. Anat:* **s. (muscle),** stapédien *m.*

stapelia [stæ'pi:liə], *s. Bot:* stapélie *f.*

staper ['steipər], *s.* machine *f* à tailler les engrenages à mouvement alternatif de l'outil.

stapes ['steipi:z], *s. Anat:* étrier *m* (de l'oreille); stapéal *m.*

staphisagria [stæfi'seigriə], *s. Bot:* staphisaigre *f.*

staphyline ['stæfilain], *a. Anat:* staphylin.

staphylinid [stæfi'linid], *s. Ent:* staphylinide *m.*

Staphylinidae [stæfi'linidi:], *s.pl. Ent:* staphylinides *m*, staphylinidés *m.*

Staphylinoidea [stæfili'nɔidiə], *s.pl. Ent:* staphylinoïdes *m.*

staphylinus [stæfi'lainəs], *s. Ent:* staphylin *m.*

staphylococcia [stæfilou'kɔksiə], *s. Med:* staphylococcie *f.*

staphylococcic [stæfilou'kɔksik], *a. Bac:* staphylococcique.

staphylococcus, *pl.* **-cocci** [stæfilou'kɔkəs, -'kɔksai], *s. Bac:* staphylocoque *m.*

staphylocosis [stæfilou'kousis], *s. Med:* staphylococcie *f.*

staphyloma [stæfi'loumə], *s. Med:* staphylome *m.*

staphylomatous [stæfi'loumətəs], *a. Med:* staphylomateux.

staphyloplasty [stæfilou'plæsti], *s. Surg:* staphyloplastie *f.*

staphylorr(h)aphy [stæfilou'ræfi], *s. Surg:* staphylorraphie *f.*

staphylotomy [stæfi'lɔtəmi], *s. Surg:* staphylotomie *f.*

staple[1] ['steipl], *s.* **1.** (*a*) crampon *m* (à deux pointes); crampe *f*, crampillon *m*; agrafe *f* (métallique de jonction); **s. gun,** agrafeuse *f*; **s. remover, extractor,** dégrafeuse *f*; **wall s.,** harpon *m*, agrafe; **wire s.,** (i) (clou) cavalier *m* en fil de fer, clou à deux pointes; (ii) *Bookb: etc:* broche *f* (en fil métallique); **s. press,** brocheuse *f*; *El:* **insulated s.,** cavalier isolant; (*b*) *Carp:* **s. of a bench,** valet *m* d'établi; *Hyd.E:* **s. post,** potille *f*;

poteau *m* de vanne. **2. s. (of lock),** cramponnet *m*, picolet *m*; **(bolt) s.,** gâche *f*, gâchette *f*, verterelle *f*, vertevelle *f*; auberon *m* (de la serrure d'une malle, etc.); **s. plate,** auberonnière *f*.

staple[2], *v.tr.* **1.** *Const: etc:* fixer, attacher (qch.) avec un crampon, une agrafe, à l'aide de crampons, d'agrafes; agrafer, cramponner. **2.** *Bookb:* brocher (des feuilles) au fil de fer.

staple[3], *s.* **1.** *Hist:* étape *f*; entrepôt *m*, comptoir *m*; **the S.,** l'Étape de Calais; **wool s.,** marché *m* aux laines. **2.** (*a*) produit principal (d'un pays); **s. commodities,** produits de première nécessité; **s. diet,** régime *m*, nourriture *f*, de base; **s. trade,** commerce régulier; **s. industry,** industrie principale; (*b*) matière première, matière brute.

staple[4], *s. Tex:* brin *m*, fibre *f* (de laine, de lin, de chanvre); soie *f* (de coton); **long s., short s., cotton,** coton *m* (de) longue, (de) courte, soie; coton à fibres longues, courtes.

stapler ['steiplər], *s.* **1.** (*pers.*) (*a*) **(wool) s.,** négociant *m* en laine; marchand *m* de laine; (*b*) *Hist:* membre *m* du corps des marchands de l'Étape. **2.** (*device*) agrafeuse *f*.

stapling ['steipliŋ], *s.* (i) fixage *m* à l'aide de crampons, d'agrafes; agrafage *m*; (ii) *Bookb:* brochage *m* au fil de fer; **s. machine,** (i) agrafeuse *f*; (ii) *Bookb:* machine *f* à brocher (au fil de fer); brocheuse *f* mécanique.

star[1] [stɑːr], *s.* **1.** (*a*) *Astr:* étoile *f*; astre *m*; **fixed s.,** étoile fixe; **shooting s., falling s.,** étoile filante, tombante; **s. shower,** pluie *f*, essaim *m*, d'étoiles filantes; **radio s.,** radio-étoile *f*, *pl.* radio-étoiles; **temporary s.,** nova *f*, *pl.* novae; **the morning s.,** l'étoile du matin; l'étoile matinière; Lucifer *m*; **the evening s.,** l'étoile du soir; l'étoile du berger; Vesper *f*; **the pole s., the north s.,** l'étoile polaire; la polaire; l'étoile du nord; **s. cluster,** étoiles groupées; **s. worship,** astrolâtrie *f*; **s. worshipper,** astrolâtre *mf*; *Hist:* **the S. Chamber,** la Chambre étoilée; **to be born under a lucky s.,** naître sous une bonne étoile, sous une étoile propice, sous une heureuse planète; naître coiffé; **you may thank your stars you weren't there,** vous pouvez vous estimer heureux de ne pas avoir été là; **I thank my stars that . . .,** je bénis mon étoile de ce que + *ind.*; **to reach for the stars,** demander la lune; *F:* **to see stars,** voir les étoiles en plein midi; voir trente-six chandelles; **to make s.o. see stars,** faire voir des chandelles à qn; étourdir qn; *O:* **my stars!** grands dieux! *B:* **the s. of Bethlehem, the s. in the east,** l'étoile de Bethléhem; *Bot:* **s. of Bethlehem,** ornithogale *m* (à ombelle); *F:* belle *f*, dame *f*, d'onze heures; *F:* **there's a s. in the east,** votre braguette est déboutonnée; (*b*) (i) *Bot:* **s. grass,** alétris *m*, hypoxis *m*; **s. thistle,** chardon étoilé; chausse-trape *f*, *pl.* chausse-trapes; **s. pine,** pin *m* maritime, pinastre *m*; *Fung:* **earth s.,** étoile de terre, géaster *m*, géastre *m*; *Algae:* **s. jelly,** nostoc *m*; nodulaire *f*; crachat *m* de lune; (ii) *Echin:* **basket s.,** euryale *m*; **mud s.,** luidia *m*; **sun s.,** solaster *m*. **2.** (*a*) **s. of an order,** plaque *f* d'un ordre; décoration *f*; (*b*) *Mil:* étoile (portée sur l'épaule et servant à indiquer les grades de sous-lieutenant, de lieutenant et de capitaine dans l'armée britannique); (*c*) **S. of David,** étoile de David, *Pol:* étoile jaune; (*d*) **three s. brandy,** cognac *m* trois étoiles; **three s. hotel,** hôtel *m* à trois étoiles. **3.** (*a*) *Her:* étoile; **blazing s.,** comète *f*; *U.S:* **the stars and stripes,** la bannière étoilée; (*b*) (*on horse's forehead*) étoile, pelote *f*, marque *f*; (*c*) (*star-shaped crack*) étoile, étoilement *m*; (*d*) *Typ:* étoile; astérisque *m*; (*e*) *Mec.E:* étoile, croix *f*; **s.-and-cam movement,** croix de Malte; **s. handle, s. wheel,** croisillon *m* (à poignées); *El:* **s. connection,** montage *m* en étoile; groupement *m*, couplage *m*, en étoile. **4.** *Cin: Th: etc:* (*pers.*) étoile, vedette *f*, star *f*; **s. part,** rôle de vedette; **s. turn,** (i) numéro *m* de premier ordre; (ii) *F:* clou *m* (d'une fête, etc.).

star[2], *v.* **(starred) 1.** *v.tr.* (*a*) étoiler (qch.); (par)semer (qch.) d'étoiles; **grass starred with daisies,** herbe semée de pâquerettes; (*b*) étoiler, fêler (une glace, une vitre); (*c*) *Typ: etc:* marquer (un mot) d'une étoile, d'un astérisque. **2.** *v.i.* (*a*) (*of glass*) se fêler, s'étoiler; (*b*) *Th: etc:* être en vedette; avoir un rôle de vedette; jouer les rôles de vedette; tenir le premier rôle.

starblind ['stɑːblaind], *a.* à moitié aveugle; presque aveugle.

starboard[1] ['stɑːbəd], *s. Nau:* tribord *m*; **the s. side,** le côté de tribord; **on the s. side, to s.,** à tribord; **to alter course to s.,** changer de route sur la droite; **s. tack,** tribord amures; **on the s. bow,** par tribord devant; **the s. watch,** la bordée de tribord; les tribordais *m*; **hard a-starboard!** à droite toute! tribord toute!

starboard[2]. *Nau:* **1.** *v.tr.* **to s. the helm,** mettre la barre à tribord; **s. (the helm)!** à droite! **2.** *v.i.* (*of ship*) venir sur tribord.

starch[1] [stɑːtʃ], *s.* **1.** (*a*) amidon *m*; **rice s., wheat s.,** amidon de riz, de blé; **potato s.,** fécule *f* de pommes de terre; **unmodified s., regular s., thick-boiling s., prime s., raw s.,** amidon cru, amidon natif; **pre-cooked s., pregelatinized s.,** amidon gonflant; **flash-dried s.,** amidon pulvérisé; **soluble s.,** amidon soluble; **thin-boiling s.,** amidon fluide; **waxy s.,** amidon glutineux, amidon de grain cireux; **mill s.,** amidon industriel; **s. factory,** amidonnerie *f*; **s. manufacturer,** amidonnier *m*; (*b*) **laundry s.,** empois *m* (d'amidon); **s. (paste),** empois; colle *f* d'amidon; *Tex:* chas *m*, apprêt *m*; *Med:* **s. bandage, s. splint,** appareil amidonné. **2.** *F:* (*a*) manières empesées, guindées; raideur *f*; (*b*) *O:* **to take the s. out of s.o.,** démonter qn.

starch[2], *v.tr. Laund:* empeser, amidonner (le linge).

starched [stɑːtʃt], *a.* **1.** empesé, amidonné. **2.** *F: O:* = STARCHY 2.

starcher ['stɑːtʃər], *s.* **1.** empeseur, -euse. **2.** empeseuse *f*; machine *f* à apprêter.

starchily ['stɑːtʃili], *adv. F:* raidement; d'un air, d'un ton, guindé.

starchiness ['stɑːtʃinis], *s. F:* manières empesées, compassées, guindées; raideur *f*.

starching ['stɑːtʃiŋ], *s. Laund:* empesage *m*; amidonnage *m*; **s. machine** = STARCHER 2.

starchy ['stɑːtʃi], *a.* **1.** *Ch:* amylacé, amyloïde; féculent; **s. foods,** féculents *m*. **2.** *F:* (*of pers., manner*) empesé, gourmé, guindé; raide.

stardom ['stɑːdəm], *s. Cin: etc:* **to rise to s.,** devenir une vedette.

stardrift ['stɑːdrift], *s. Astr:* mouvements *m* propres des étoiles.

stardust ['stɑːdʌst], *s. Astr:* amas *m* stellaire.

stare[1] ['stɛər], *s.* regard fixe; regard appuyé, qui appuie; **glassy s.,** regard terne, vitreux; **set s.,** regard fixe; **stony s.,** regard dur, torve; **vacant s.,** regard vague, qui ne voit pas; regard ahuri; **to give s.o. a s.,** dévisager qn; appuyer sur qn un regard inquisiteur; **with a s. of astonishment,** les yeux écarquillés; les yeux ébahis.

stare[2]. **1.** *v.i.* (*a*) regarder fixement; **to s. into the distance,** regarder au loin; (*b*) **he stared into the room,** il a plongé dans la salle un regard inquisiteur; **to s. in s.o.'s face,** dévisager qn; (*c*) écarquiller les yeux; ouvrir de grands yeux; **everybody stared with astonishment,** tout le monde écarquillait les yeux, regardait d'un air ébahi; **it's (done) to make the passers by s.,** c'est pour ébahir les passants. **2.** *v.ind.tr.* **to s. at s.o., sth.,** (i) regarder qn, qch. fixement; fixer ses yeux, braquer les yeux, sur qn, qch.; appuyer son regard sur qn; fixer qn; (ii) regarder qn effrontément; dévisager qn; (iii) regarder qn d'un air hébété; **they were staring rudely at each other,** ils se regardaient en chiens de faïence; **she doesn't like to be stared at,** elle n'aime pas (i) à ce qu'on la dévisage; (ii) à ce que tous les yeux soient braqués sur elle. **3.** *v.tr.* **to s. s.o. in the face,** dévisager qn; **ruin stares him in the face,** il voit s'approcher le spectre de la ruine; sa ruine est imminente; *F:* **it's staring you in the face,** ça vous saute aux yeux; ça vous crève les yeux; **to s. s.o. up and down,** toiser qn du regard; **to s. s.o. into silence,** imposer du regard le silence à qn; *O:* **to s. s.o. down,** faire baisser les yeux à qn. **4.** *v.i.* (*of animal's coat*) se hérisser.

starer ['stɛərər], *s.* **1.** curieux, -euse; badaud, -aude. **2.** *F: A:* **starers,** lorgnon *m*; face-à-main *m*, *pl.* faces-à-main.

starfish ['stɑːfiʃ], *s. Echin:* astérie *f*, étoile *f* de mer; **spiny s.,** astérie épineuse; **small s.,** astérine *f*; **sun s.,** étoile de mer à bras multiples rouges, solaster *m*; **duck's foot s.,** étoile palmée.

starflower ['stɑːflauər], *s. Bot:* **1.** ornithogale *m*; dame *f* d'onze heures. **2.** stellaire *f*.

stargaze ['stɑːgeiz], *v.i. F:* **1.** faire de l'astronomie. **2.** (*a*) bayer aux étoiles, aux corneilles; rêvasser; (*b*) (*of horse*) porter le nez au vent.

stargazer ['stɑːgeizər], *s.* **1.** *F:* (*a*) astronome *mf*; astrologue *m*; (*b*) rêveur, -euse; rêvasseur, -euse. **2.** *Ich:* (*a*) uranoscope *m*; *F:* rascasse blanche, raspecon *m*, rat *m*; (*b*) anableps *m*; gros-œil *m*, *pl.* gros-œils. **3.** *Nau:* (*sail*) papillon *m*; aile *f* de pigeon.

stargazing ['stɑːgeiziŋ], *s.* **1.** *F:* astronomie *f*. **2.** rêvasserie(s) *f(pl)*.

staring[1] ['stɛəriŋ], *a.* **1. s. eyes,** (i) yeux *m* fixes; (ii) yeux grands ouverts; yeux effarés; regard ébahi; **s. crowd,** foule *f* d'observateurs (i) attentifs, (ii) gênants. **2.** (*a*) voyant, tranchant; criard; (*b*) **stark s. mad,** fou, folle, à lier; complètement fou.

staring[2], *s.* regards *m* fixes; regards effrontés.

stark [stɑːk]. **1.** *a. esp. Lit:* (*a*) raide, rigide; **he lay s. in death,** il gisait dans la rigidité de la mort; (*b*) fort, vigoureux; (*c*) résolu, inflexible; (*d*) **s. madness,** folie pure; **s. nonsense,** pure bêtise; **the s. desolation of the whole region,** l'absolue désolation de toute cette région; (*e*) **the s. towns of the North,** les mornes villes du Nord; (*f*) **s. light,** lumière crue; (*g*) tout nu; **they stripped him s.,** on le dépouilla de tous ses vêtements. **2.** *adv.* **s. naked,** tout nu; complètement, entièrement, nu; nu comme un ver, comme la main.

starkers ['stɑːkəz], *a.* & *adv. F:* tout nu; nu comme un ver; complètement à nu; **I prefer bathing s.,** je préfère me baigner tout(e) nu(e).

starkly ['stɑːkli], *adv.* **1.** raidement, rigidement. **2.** nûment; pauvrement (meublé, etc.).

starkness ['stɑːknis], *s.* **1.** raideur *f*; rigidité *f*. **2. in the s. of their ignorance,** dans la profondeur de leur ignorance. **3.** nudité *f*; **the s. of the mountains,** l'aspect morne des montagnes.

starless ['stɑːlis], *a.* (*a*) sans étoiles; (*b*) *Th: etc:* sans vedettes.

starlet ['stɑːlit], *s.* **1.** *Cin: etc:* starlette *f*, starlet *f*. **2.** *Echin:* astérine *f*.

starlight ['stɑːlait], *s.* **1.** lumière *f* des étoiles; lumière stellaire; **in the s., by s.,** à la lumière, à la lueur, à la clarté, des étoiles. **2. a s. night,** une nuit étoilée.

starling[1] ['stɑːliŋ], *s. Orn:* étourneau *m* (sansonnet); *F:* sansonnet *m*; **spotless s.,** étourneau unicolore; **military s.,** étourneau militaire; **glossy s.,** lamprocoliou *m*, merle *m* métallique, spréo *m*; **superb s.,** spréo superbe; **rose(-coloured) s., crested s.,** (martin *m*) roselin *m*; martin rose, merle *m* rose.

starling[2], *s. Hyd.E:* bec *m*, éperon *m* (de môle, de pile de pont); brise-glace *m*, *pl.* brise-glace(s) (en pilotis); **back s.,** bec d'aval; arrière-bec *m*; **fore s.,** bec d'amont; avant-bec *m*.

starlit ['stɑːlit], *a.* (ciel) étoilé, (par)semé d'étoiles; **s. night,** nuit étoilée.

starnose ['stɑːnouz], *s. Z:* taupe étoilée.

starred [stɑːd], *a.* **1.** étoilé; parsemé d'étoiles. **2.** (*a*) étoilé; en forme d'étoile; (*b*) (*of bottle, windowpane*) étoilé, fêlé. **3. ill-s.,** né sous une mauvaise étoile. **4.** *Typ: etc:* marqué d'une étoile, d'un astérisque; *Hist:* (1914–18) **s. profession,** profession exemptée du service militaire.

star-ribbed ['stɑːribd], *a. Bot:* (*of leaf*) stellinervé.

starry ['stɑːri], *a.* **1.** (ciel) étoilé, (par)semé d'étoiles; **s. night,** nuit étoilée. **2.** *Lit:* étincelant, brillant; beau comme les étoiles. **3.** *Bot:* étoilé; en forme d'étoile.

starry-eyed [stɑːri'aid], *a.* (*a*) extasié, qui voit les choses en rose; (*b*) rêveur, -euse, dans la lune; (*c*) visionnaire; **a s.-e. scheme,** un projet utopique.

starshake ['stɑːʃeik], *s.* (*in timber*) fente rayonnante; cadran(n)ure *f*, maille *f*.

starshell ['stɑːʃel], *s. Mil:* obus éclairant; obus à étoiles.

star-spangled ['stɑːspæŋgld], *a.* étoilé; (par)semé d'étoiles; piqué d'étoiles; (ciel) constellé d'étoiles; **the s.-s. banner,** la bannière étoilée (des États-Unis).

starstone ['stɑːstoun], *s. Miner:* astérie *f*.

start[1] [stɑːt], *s.* **1.** (*a*) tressaillement *m*, sursaut *m*, soubresaut *m*; **to wake with a s.,** se réveiller en sursaut; **he gave a s.,** il a tressailli, a sursauté; il a eu un haut-le-corps; **to give a s. of joy,** tressaillir de joie; **he gave a s. of surprise,** il a eu un mouvement de surprise; il a sursauté d'étonnement; **to give s.o. a s.,** faire tressaillir qn; **the news gave me a s.,** la nouvelle m'a donné un soubresaut; (*of horse*) **sudden s.,** contrecoup *m*; (*b*) saut *m*; mouvement brusque. **2.** (*a*) commencement *m*, début *m*; **to make an early s.,** commencer de bonne heure; **for a s.,** pour débuter, pour commencer; **at the s.,** au début; **at the very s.,** de prime abord; **from s. to finish,** du commencement (jusqu')à la fin; **he had a good s. in life,** il a bien débuté dans la vie; **to give s.o. a s.,** lancer qn (dans les affaires, etc.); **to make a good s.,** bien commencer; **to make a fresh s. (in life),** recommencer (sa carrière, sa vie); repartir sur (de) nouveaux frais; (*b*) départ *m*; *Aut:* démarrage *m*; *Av:* envol *m*; *Sp:* start *m* (d'une course de bicyclettes, etc.); **to make an early s.,** partir de bonne heure; *Aut:* **cold s.,** démarrage à froid; *Rac:* **flying s.,** départ lancé; **standing s.,** départ arrêté; **false s.,** faux départ; (*c*) *Sp:* **to give s.o. a s.,** laisser qn partir le premier; donner un peu d'avance à qn; **to give s.o. a 60 metre(s) s.,** donner à qn 60 mètres d'avance. **3.** *P: A:* **rum s.,** chose *f* bizarre; drôle d'événement *m*.

start[2], *v.*

I. *v.i.* **1.** (*a*) tressaillir, tressauter, sursauter, sauter; avoir, faire, un sursaut; avoir un haut-le-corps; (*of horse, etc.*) soubresauter; **the report made him s.,** la détonation l'a fait sursauter; **he started at the sound of my voice,** il a tressailli au son de ma voix; **he started with surprise,** il a eu un mouvement de surprise; il a sursauté d'étonnement; **to s. up from, s. out of, one's sleep,** se réveiller en sursaut; (*b*) se déplacer brusquement; **to s. aside,** se jeter de côté; s'écarter brusquement; (*of horse*) faire un écart brusque; **to s. back,** se jeter en arrière; reculer vivement; avoir un mouvement de recul; (*of horse*) se rejeter (en arrière); **to s. to one's feet,** se lever tout à coup, d'un bond; **tears started from his eyes,** les larmes ont jailli de ses yeux; **his eyes were starting out of his head,** les yeux lui sortaient de la tête; il avait les yeux hors de la tête. **2.** (*of timber*) se déjeter; (*of planks*) se disjoindre, se détacher; (*of rivets*) se détacher; sauter; *Nau:* (*of ship's seams*) se délier, s'ouvrir; (*of ship*) **to s. at the seams,** cracher ses étoupes. **3.** (*a*) commencer; débuter; **starting Monday,** à partir de lundi; **to s. with soup,** commencer par un potage; **the play starts with a prologue,** la pièce débute par un prologue; **negotiations have started well,** les négociations sont en bon train; **to s. at the beginning,** commencer par le commencement; **to s. again,** (i) recommencer; (ii) se ranger; refaire sa vie; (iii) (*after a failure, etc.*) recommencer sur (de) nouveaux frais; **to s. in life,** débuter dans la vie; **he had started as a doctor,** il avait commencé par être médecin; il avait débuté dans la médecine; **to s. at £30 a week,** débuter à £30 par semaine; **to s. in business,** se mettre, se lancer, dans les affaires; **there were only six members to s. with,** il n'y avait que six membres au début; **to s. with, you ought not to be here,** et (tout) d'abord, vous n'avez que faire ici; **to s. with we must . . .,** en premier lieu il va falloir . . .; **to s. on a job,** commencer, entamer, un travail; **I can't s. on it just now,** je ne peux pas m'y mettre à présent; **to s. by doing sth.,** commencer par faire qch.; (*b*) **to s. (off, out, on one's way),** partir; se mettre en route; **to s. (off, out) on a journey,** commencer un voyage; **we s. tomorrow,** nous partons demain; **just as he was starting,** au moment de son départ; **to be on the point of starting,** être sur son départ; **to s. again,** repartir; se remettre en route; **he started back the next day,** il a repris le chemin de la maison le lendemain; **he started out to write a novel,** il a eu (d'abord) l'idée d'écrire un roman; *Rac:* **only six horses started,** six chevaux seulement sont partis; (*c*) **to s. (off),** (*of car*) démarrer; se mettre en route; (*of train*) partir, s'ébranler; **to s. off smoothly,** démarrer doucement; (*d*) **to s. (up),** (*of engine*) démarrer; se mettre en marche, en train; (*of injector, dynamo*) s'amorcer; **the engine won't s.,** le moteur refuse de partir, de démarrer; **I can't get it to s.,** je ne peux pas le faire marcher; **the engine started first time, straight away,** le moteur a parti, est parti, au premier tour.

II. *v.tr.* **1.** commencer (un travail, etc.); amorcer (un bâtiment, un sujet, etc.); entamer (une conversation, etc.); **to s. negotiations,** entamer, engager, des négociations; **to s. a conversation with s.o.,** lier conversation avec qn; **to s. a topic,** entamer un sujet; **you started it,** c'est vous qui avez commencé; **to s. an attack,** amorcer une attaque; **to s. doing sth., to s. to do sth.,** commencer, se mettre, à faire qch.; **to s. crying again,** se remettre à pleurer; **it's just started raining,** voilà la pluie qui commence; voilà qu'il commence à pleuvoir; **the flowers are starting to bloom,** les fleurs commencent d'éclore. **2.** (*a*) **to s. a horse at a gallop, at a trot,** faire partir un cheval au galop, au trot; (*b*) *Rac:* donner le signal du départ à (des coureurs, etc.); (*c*) *Ven:* lancer (un cerf, un sanglier); lever, mettre debout, déloger (un lièvre); faire partir (une perdrix, etc.). **3.** (*a*) lancer, donner le branle à (une entreprise); fonder (un commerce); fonder, lancer (un journal); ouvrir (une école); mettre en train (une affaire); **to s. a fund,** lancer une souscription; *F:* **now you've started something!** en voilà une affaire! (*b*) **to s. a fire,** provoquer un incendie; **to get a fire started,** (arriver à) allumer un feu (dans la cheminée). **4.** (*a*) mettre en marche, faire marcher (une horloge); (*b*) **to s. (up) a machine,** mettre une machine en marche, en train, en mouvement; lancer une machine; **to s. (up) an injector, a pump,** amorcer un injecteur; amorcer, *F:* allumer, une pompe; *Aut:* **the engine is hard to s.,** le moteur est dur à démarrer. **5. if you s. him on this subject he will never stop,** si vous le lancez sur ce sujet il ne tarira pas; **once you s. him talking,** quand on le met à parler; **to s. s.o. in business,** lancer qn dans les affaires. **6.** disjoindre (des planches, des tôles); faire craquer (les coutures d'un vêtement); délier (les coutures d'un navire).

starter ['stɑːtər], *s.* **1.** (*a*) **to be an early s.,** partir, commencer son travail, de bonne heure; (*b*) *Sp:* partant *m*; *Turf:* **probable starters and jockeys,** partants et montes probables. **2.** (*a*) starter *m* (*Sp:* qui donne le signal du départ; *Av:* du contrôle de la circulation aérienne); (*b*) auteur *m* (d'un projet, etc.); inventeur, -trice (d'une calomnie, etc.); lanceur *m* (d'une affaire, etc.). **3.** (*device*) (*a*) *Mec.E: I.C.E:* démarreur *m*; dispositif *m* de mise en marche; **automatic s., self s.,** démarreur automatique; **recoil s.,** lanceur *m* à rappel; **s. motor,** moteur *m* auxiliaire de démarrage; démarreur mécanique; *Mec.E:* **s. pedal,** pédale *f* de démarrage, de mise en marche; (*b*) *El:* (rhéostat *m*) démarreur; rhéostat de démarrage; (*c*) *Tls:* repoussoir *m*. **4.** (*a*) inducteur *m* (d'une réaction chimique, physiologique); **anaesthesia s.,** inducteur d'anesthésie; (*b*) *Ap:* **foundation s.,** amorce *f*. **5.** *Cu: F:* = hors-d'œuvre *m inv* (ou potage *m*); **what will you have for a s.?** qu'est-ce que vous prendrez pour commencer?

starting ['stɑːtiŋ], *s.* **1.** tressaillement *m*; sursaut *m*, soubresaut *m*. **2.** (*a*) commencement *m*, début *m*; **s. salary,** traitement initial, de début; **s. phase,** phase initiale (d'un phénomène, etc.); **s. price,** (i) *St.Exch: etc:* prix initial; (ii) *Turf:* dernière cote avant le départ; (*b*) départ *m*; **s. place,** point *m* de départ; **s. signal,** signal *m* de, du, départ; *Sp:* **s. line, block,** ligne *f*, bloc *m*, de départ; **s. post,** poteau *m* de départ; barrière *f*; **s. pistol,** pistolet *m* de starter; *Ski:* **s. slope,** piste *f* de départ, d'élan. **3.** (*a*) mise *f* en route, en train, ouverture *f* (d'une entreprise, des travaux, etc.); (*b*) **s. (up),** mise en marche, en route, en train, démarrage *m* (d'une machine, etc.); lancement *m* (d'un moteur); déclenchement *m* (d'un mécanisme); amorçage *m*, démarrage (d'une dynamo, d'un moteur électrique); *Atom.Ph:* mise en fonctionnement (d'un réacteur); **automatic s., self s.,** démarrage automatique; **s. motor, engine,** moteur *m* de démarrage, de lancement, d'amorçage; démarreur *m* mécanique; (*of diesel engine*) **s. air,** air *m* de lancement; *Aut: O:* **s. handle,** manivelle *f* (de mise en marche); *Tls:* **s. bolt,** repoussoir *m*; (*electroplating*) **s. bath,** amorce *f*; *El:* **s. current,** intensité *f* au démarrage; **s. resistance,** résistance *f* de démarrage; **split-phase s.,** démarrage par enroulement auxiliaire; *Aut:* **to have s. trouble,** avoir une panne de démarrage, des difficultés à démarrer; (*c*) *Ven:* lancer *m* (du gibier).

startle ['stɑːtl], *v.tr.* effrayer, alarmer (qn); faire tressaillir, faire sursauter (qn); **to s. s.o. out of his sleep,** éveiller qn en sursaut; **she was startled to see him so pale,** elle a été saisie, cela lui a donné un tour, de le voir si pâle; *F:* **he wants to s. the old fogeys,** il veut épater le bourgeois; **to s. an admission out of s.o.,** arracher un aveu à qn par surprise; **to s. s.o. into deciding sth.,** forcer qn à décider qch. en toute hâte, ne lui laissant pas le temps de réfléchir.

startled ['stɑːtld], *a.* effrayé, alarmé; **a s. shout,** un cri d'alarme, d'effroi; **she was quite s.,** elle est restée toute saisie.

startler ['stɑːtlər], *s. F:* chose, nouvelle, sensationnelle; **that's a bit of a s.!** et voilà quelque chose de bouleversant!

startling ['stɑːtliŋ], *a.* (*of news, discovery, etc.*) effrayant, saisissant; renversant, foudroyant, atterrant; **s. events,** événements sensationnels, à sensation; **s. resemblance,** ressemblance saisissante; *F:* **that hat's a bit s.!** quel chapeau!

start-up ['stɑːtʌp], *s.* démarrage *m*; mise *f* en marche, en route, en train.

starvation [stɑː'veiʃ(ə)n], *s.* privation *f*, manque *m*, de nourriture; famine *f*; *Med:* inanition *f*; **night s.,** fringale *f* nocturne; **to die of s.,** mourir de faim, d'inanition; **s. wages,** salaire *m* de famine.

starve [stɑːv]. **1.** *v.i.* (*a*) **to s. (to death),** mourir de faim, d'inanition; (*b*) manquer de nourriture; endurer la faim; **wolves can s. for a long time,** les loups supportent longtemps la faim; **I'm starving,** je meurs, je crève, de faim; **I would rather s.!** je ne mange pas de ce pain-là! (*c*) *A: & Dial:* mourir de froid; *F:* **to be starving with cold,** être tout transi (de froid); être gelé; (*d*) (*of tree, plant*) dépérir; s'étioler. **2.** *v.tr.* (*a*) faire mourir (qn) de faim; **to s. s.o. out,** couper les vivres à qn; **to s. out a town, a garrison,** affamer une ville, une garnison; prendre, réduire, une ville par la famine; **to s. a garrison into surrender,** réduire une garnison par la faim; (*b*) priver (qn) de nourriture; *Med:* soumettre (un malade) à un régime affamant; **to s. a cold,** traiter un rhume par la diète; (*c*) *A: & Dial:* faire mourir (qn) de froid.

starved [stɑːvd], *a.* **1.** (*a*) affamé; famélique; **he looks half s.,** il a l'air famélique; (*b*) **s. of affection,** privé d'affection. **2.** *F:* gelé; transi; **you look s. to death,** tu as l'air tout transi. **3.** (*of plant*) languissant; étiolé.

starveling ['stɑːvliŋ]. **1.** *s.* affamé, -ée; famélique *mf*. **2.** *a.* (*a*) affamé, famélique; **little s. kitten,** petit chaton famélique; (*b*) *O:* (salaire, conditions, etc.) de famine.

starving[1] ['stɑːviŋ], *a.* mourant de faim; affamé; famélique.

starving[2], *s.* **1.** inanition *f*. **2.** privation *f* de nourriture; *Med:* régime affamant; diète absolue.

starweed ['stɑːwiːd], *s. Bot:* corne *f* de cerf.

starwort ['stɑːwəːt], *s. Bot:* stellaire *f*; **sea s.,** aster *m*; **water s.,** callitriche *m*.

stash [stæʃ], *v.tr. F:* cacher, planquer (qch.); **s. it in the corner, in your pocket,** mettez-le, fourrez-le, dans le coin, dans votre poche; **to s. sth. away,** mettre qch. à l'abri; planquer qch.; **he must have a lot of money stashed away,** il doit avoir je ne sais combien d'argent mis de côté.

stasis ['steisis], *s. Med:* stase *f*.

statant ['steitənt], *a. Her:* (lion) posé.

state[1] [steit], *s.* **1.** (*a*) état *m*, condition *f*; situation *f*; **in a good s.,** en bon état; en bonne condition; **bad s. of the packing,** mauvais conditionnement des emballages; **I want to know the real s. of things,** je voudrais savoir ce qu'il en est; **here's a nice, a pretty, s. of affairs,** nous voilà bien! c'est du joli, du propre! *F:* **what a s. you're in!** vous voilà dans de beaux draps! (*b*) état; **body in a s. of rest,** corps à l'état de repos; corps au repos; **s. of health,** état de santé; **I am not in a fit s. to travel,** je ne suis pas en état de voyager; **in a s. of intoxication,** en état d'ivresse; **in a s. of siege,** en état de siège; **the married s.,** le mariage; **the single s.,** le célibat; **s. of mind,** disposition *f* d'esprit; *F:* **to be in a great s., in a terrible s.,** être dans tous ses états; **he was in quite a s. about it,** ça l'avait bien bouleversé; **he will work himself into such a s. that. . .,** il va se mettre dans un tel état que . . .. **2.** (*a*) rang *m*, dignité *f*; **he lived in a style befitting his s.,** il vivait sur un pied digne de son rang; (*b*) pompe *f*, parade *f*, apparat *m*; *Adm:* représentation *f* (d'un ambassadeur, etc.); **to keep great s.,** to **live in s.,** mener grand train; **to travel in s.,** voyager en grand apparat, en grand appareil, en grand équipage; **to dine in s.,** dîner en grand gala; (*of body*) **to lie in s.,** être exposé (sur un lit de parade); **lying in s.,** exposition *f* (d'un corps); **the proprietress sat in s. at the counter,** la patronne trônait au comptoir; **to escort s.o. in s.,** escorter qn en grande cérémonie; **to receive an ambassador in s.,** recevoir solennellement un ambassadeur; **he was in his robes of s.,** il était en costume d'apparat; **chair of s.,** fauteuil *m* d'apparat; trône *m*; **bed of s.,** lit *m* de parade; (*c*) *attrib.* **s. carriage, s. coach,** voiture *f* d'apparat; voiture de cérémonie officielle; voiture de gala; **s. reception of a prince,** réception solennelle d'un prince; **s. ball,** grand bal officiel; grand bal de cour; **s. apartments,** grands appartements; salons *m* d'apparat. **3.** (*a*) *Fr.Hist:* **the States General,** les États généraux; (*b*) (*Channel Islands*) **the States,** l'Assemblée législative. **4.** (*a*) *Pol:* **the S.,** l'État; **Church and S.,** l'Église et l'État; **Secretary of S.,** (i) secrétaire *m* d'État; (ii) *U.S:* = Ministre *m* des Affaires étrangères; *U.S:* **S. Department** = Ministère *m* des Affaires étrangères; **affairs of S., S. affairs,** affaires *f* d'État; **foreign Heads of S.,** chefs d'État étrangers; **s. documents, papers,** documents officiels; papiers *m* d'État; **s. trial,** procès *m* politique; **s. church,** église *f* d'État; **s. socialism,** (i) socialisme *m* d'État; (ii) étatisme *m*; **s. control,** étatisme; **to bring an industry under s. control,** étatiser une industrie; **s.-aided, s.-controlled, industry,** industrie subventionnée par l'État, étatisée; **s. forest,** forêt domaniale; forêt d'État; (*b*) état, nation *f*; **the United States of America,** *F:* **the States,** les États-Unis (d'Amérique); (*c*) *U.S:* **s. legislature,** chambre législative (d'un État); **s. legislator,** membre d'une chambre législative.

state[2], *v.tr.* **1.** (*a*) énoncer, déclarer, affirmer, faire connaître (qch.); **this condition was definitely, precisely, expressly, stated,** cette condition était spécifiée, était précisée, était énoncée, déclarée, expressément; *Com:* **to s. an account,** spécifier un compte; **the receipt should s. the source of payment,** la quittance doit énoncer l'origine de l'argent; **please s. below . . .,** veuillez noter en bas . . .; **as stated above,** (i) comme on a dit plus haut; (ii) (*on official form*) voir déclaration ci-dessus; **it should also be stated that . . .,** nous devons ajouter que . . .; **he did not s. why . . .,** il n'a pas dit pourquoi . . .; **he stated that the arrangements were complete,** il a déclaré que les préparatifs étaient terminés; **I have stated my opinion,** j'ai donné mon opinion; **he stated all the facts,** il présenta, *Jur:* relata, articula, tous les faits; **he states positively that he heard it,** il affirme l'avoir entendu; **I have seen it stated that . . .,** j'ai lu quelque part que . . .; *Mil:* **it is stated in orders that. . .,** la décision porte que . . .; (*b*) exposer (une réclamation, etc.); *Jur:* **to s. the case,** faire l'exposé des faits; **to s. a case,** soumettre les faits au tribunal; **the plaintiff stated his case,** le plaignant a exposé sa réclamation; (*c*) *Mth:* poser, énoncer (un problème). **2.** régler, arrêter, fixer (une heure, une date).

statecraft ['steitkrɑːft], *s.* (*a*) art *m* de gouverner; habileté *f* politique; (*b*) *Pej:* finasserie *f* politique.

stated ['steitid], *a.* **1.** réglé, fixé; fixe; **at s. intervals,** à des époques fixées; à intervalles réglés; **on s. days,** à jours fixes. **2.** *Jur:* **s. case,** énoncé *m* des faits (soumis à la cour ou à un arbitre).

statehouse ['steithaus], *s. U.S:* chambre législative (d'un état).

stateless ['steitlis], *a. Jur:* apatride; **s. person,** apatride *mf.*

statelessness ['steitlisnis], *s. Jur:* apatridie *f.*

stateliness ['steitlinis], *s.* majesté *f*; aspect imposant; grandeur *f*; dignité *f.*

stately ['steitli], *a.* **1.** majestueux; imposant; **the s. homes of England,** les châteaux et manoirs historiques de l'Angleterre. **2.** plein de dignité; noble, élevé; soutenu; **s. bearing,** allure pleine de majesté; **s. grace,** beauté fière.

statement ['steitmənt], *s.* **1.** (*a*) exposition *f*, exposé *m*, énoncé *m* (des faits, de la situation, etc.); rapport *m*, compte rendu, relation *f*; **official s. (to the press),** communiqué *m*; **certified s.,** constatation *f*; **to make, publish, a s.,** émettre une déclaration; **to draw up a s.,** rédiger un exposé; dresser un mémoire; **he made the following s. . . .,** il a déclaré que . . .; **s. of conclusions arrived at,** exposé des décisions prises; **full s. of the position,** exposé complet de la situation; **bare s. of the facts,** simple énoncé des faits; **according to the s. of . . .,** d'après la déclaration de . . ., d'après le rapport de . . ., d'après le témoignage de . . .; à ce que dit . . .; au dire de . . .; aux dires de . . .; d'après les dires de . . .; **according to his own s.,** suivant sa propre déclaration; *Jur:* **the statements made by the witnesses,** les dépositions *f* des témoins; **written s. of a case,** instruction écrite; mémoire *m*; **official s. of facts,** constat *m*; **s. of grounds of an appeal,** grief *m*; **s. of defence,** exposé des moyens de fait et de droit du défendeur; (*b*) assertion *f*, affirmation *f*; **to contradict a s.,** nier une affirmation; **a s. appeared in the press to the effect that . . .,** il fut affirmé dans la presse que . . .. **2.** *Com:* **s. of account,** état *m* de compte; relevé *m*, relèvement *m*, de compte; bordereau *m* de compte; **monthly s.,** fin *f* de mois; **to send s.o. a s. of the amount owing to him,** fournir à qn un état des sommes qui lui sont dues; **s. of expenses,** état, montant *m*, des frais; *Jur:* **s. of costs,** état de frais; mémoire; *Fin:* **bank s.,** (i) relevé de compte; (ii) situation *f* de la Banque (d'Angleterre); **the Bank weekly s.,** le bilan hebdomadaire de la Banque; **s. of affairs (in bankruptcy),** bilan de liquidation.

stater ['steitər], *s. M.Ins:* **average s.,** répartiteur *m* d'avaries; dispacheur *m.*

stateroom ['steitru:m], *s.* **1.** chambre *f* d'apparat; grand appartement. **2.** (*a*) *Nau:* cabine *f* (de luxe); (*b*) *NAm: Rail: O:* (compartiment *m* de) wagon-lit *m.*

statesman, *pl.* **-men** ['steitsmən], *s.* **1.** homme d'État. **2.** *NAm:* homme politique; = député *m.*

statesmanlike, statesmanly ['steitsmənlaik, -li], *a.* (*of attitude, etc.*) d'homme d'État; diplomatique.

statesmanship ['steitsmənʃip], *s.* l'art *m* de gouverner; la politique.

static, *occ.* **statical** ['stætik(l)], *a.* **1.** statique; **s. electricity,** électricité *f* statique; **s. friction,** frottement *m* au départ; **s. moment,** moment *m* d'une force; **s. transformer,** transformateur *m* statique; *Av:* **s. testing, (of aircraft),** essais *m* statiques. **2.** statique; immuable; immobile; qui n'évolue pas; **the situation remains s.,** la situation n'a pas changé.

statically ['stætik(ə)li], *adv.* statiquement; **s. balanced,** équilibré statiquement; *Civ.E:* **s. determinate system,** système *m* isostatique.

statice ['stætis(i)], *s. Bot:* (*a*) statice *m*; armérie *f* maritime; immortelle bleue, lavande *f* de mer; (*b*) **(mountain) s.,** gazon *m* d'Olympe.

statics ['stætiks], *s.pl.* **1.** *Mec:* (*usu. with sg. const.*) la statique. **2.** (*a*) *W.Tel:* perturbations *f* atmosphériques; parasites *m* atmosphériques; (*b*) *Cin:* effluves *m* (striant le film).

stating ['steitiŋ], *s.* déclaration *f*, énoncé *m* (des faits, etc.); exposition *f.*

station[1] ['steiʃ(ə)n], *s.* **1.** (*a*) position *f*, place *f*; poste *m*; emplacement *m*; **to take up one's s.,** prendre sa place; se placer; se rendre à son poste; *Nau: etc:* **take your stations!** à vos postes! **anchor s.,** poste de mouillage; **fire s.,** poste d'incendie; **s. bill,** rôle *m* de manœuvre; *Mil: Navy: etc:* **action stations,** postes de combat; (*of ship*) **to be in, out of, s.,** être, ne pas être, à son poste; **to be ahead of s.,** être à l'avance de son poste; (*b*) station *f*, poste; *Navy:* **naval s.,** station navale; port *m* militaire, port de guerre; **outlying s.,** point *m* d'appui (de la flotte); **to be on s.,** être en station; **s. ship,** stationnaire *m*; *Mil:* **military s.,** poste militaire; garnison *f*; **to change s.,** changer de garnison; **s. hospital,** hôpital *m* de garnison; **checking s.,** poste de contrôle (d'identité, etc.); **field dressing s.,** *U.S:* **regimental collecting s.,** poste de secours; **casualty clearing s.,** hôpital d'évacuation; **Red Cross s.,** poste de la Croix Rouge; *Av:* **(air) s.,** base aérienne, base d'aviation; escadre aérienne; **sea-plane s.,** base d'hydravions; **aerodrome control s.,** station de contrôle d'aérodrome; (*c*) *Nau: etc:* **coastguard s.,** station garde-côte; **lifeboat s.,** station de sauvetage; **quarantine s.,** station de quarantaine; (*d*) *Meteor:* **meteorological,** *F:* **met, s., weather s.,** station météo(rologique); **upper air s.,** station (d'observation) en altitude; (*e*) *Surv:* **triangulation s.,** station de triangulation; **plane table s.,** station de planchette; **traversing s.,** point *m* de cheminement; (*f*) **police s.,** *F:* **the s.,** commissariat *m*, poste, de police; *F:* **you'll have to come along to the s. with me,** je t'amène au poste; **fire s.,** poste, caserne *f*, de sapeurs pompiers; *esp. U.S:* **s. house,** (i) poste de police; (ii) poste de sapeurs pompiers; (iii) petite gare de campagne; (*g*) **power s.,** centrale *f* électrique; **atomic power s.,** centrale atomique; **transformer s.,** poste abaisseur de courant; **booster s.,** station auxiliaire; (*h*) *Elcs: W.Tel: etc:* **broadcasting s.,** poste émetteur, d'émission, de radiodiffusion; **link s., relay s., repeater s.,** station relais; *Space:* **earth s., terrestrial s.,** station terrestre; *Cmptr:* **subscriber s.,** poste de réseau; **punch(ing) s.,** poste de perforation; **inquiry s.,** poste d'interrogation (-réponse); **tape s.,** dérouleur *m* de bande magnétique; (*i*) *Hyd.E:* **pumping s.,** central de pompage; station d'épuisement, de pompes; usine *f* élévatoire; (*j*) *Petr:* **barrelling s.,** dépôt emplisseur (en conditionné); **filling s.,** dépôt de remplissage; *Aut:* **petrol s., filling s., service s.,** *NAm:* **gas s.,** poste d'essence; station-service *f*, *pl.* stations-service; (*k*) *U.S: Post:* recette *f* auxiliaire; (*l*) *Nat.Hist:* habitat *m* (d'un animal, d'une plante); (*m*) *Ecc:* **the stations of the Cross,** le chemin de la Croix. **2.** *Austr: N.Z:* ferme *f* (et ses dépendances); **sheep s.,** élevage *m* de moutons. **3.** position, condition *f*; rang *m*; **s. in life,** situation sociale; *O:* **to marry below one's s.,** se mésallier. **4.** (*a*) **(railway) s.,** gare *f*; **underground s.,** station de métro; **passenger s., goods s.,** gare de voyageurs, de marchandises; **frontier s.,** gare frontière; **harbour, maritime, s.,** gare maritime; **Paddington s.,** la gare de Paddington; **s. manager,** chef *m* de gare; **s. hotel,** hôtel *m* de la gare; (*b*) **bus s., coach s.,** gare routière; (*c*) *Aut:* **s. wagon,** canadienne *f*, familiale *f.*

station[2], *v.tr.* (*a*) placer, mettre (qn dans un endroit); **he was stationed behind a door, behind a tree,** il s'est posté derrière une porte, derrière un arbre; (*b*) **to s. troops,** poster des troupes; **to s. the officers and men,** désigner leurs postes aux officiers et aux hommes; (*c*) **to be stationed at . . .,** (i) *Mil:* être stationné, être en garnison, à . . .; (ii) *Navy:* être en station à . . .; **fleet stationed abroad,** flotte stationnée à l'étranger.

stational ['steiʃən(ə)l], *a. Ecc: O:* (messe, etc.) stationale.

stationary ['steiʃən(ə)ri], *a.* **1.** stationnaire; immobile; **to remain s.,** rester stationnaire, immobile; **a s. period in technology,** une période de stagnation en technologie; **s. car,** voiture en stationnement; *Meteor:* **s. front,** front *m* stationnaire; *Mil:* **s. target,** cible *f* fixe; objectif *m* fixe, stationnaire; *Ph:* **s. field, s. phase,** champ *m*, phase *f*, stationnaire; **s. wave,** onde *f* stationnaire; *Atom.Ph:* **s. nucleus,** noyau *m* stationnaire; **s. reactor,** pile *f*, réacteur *m*, en régime stationnaire. **2.** (*a*) fixe; installé à demeure; *El:* **s. armature,** induit *m* fixe; **s. battery,** batterie *f* fixe; **s. winding,** enroulement *m* (de champ) fixe; *Mch: Mec.E:* **s. boiler,** chaudière *f* fixe, chaudière placée à demeure; **s. engine,** machine fixe, moteur *m* fixe; **s. gear,** couronne *f* fixe; *Mec.E: Ind:* **s. plant,** outillage *m* fixe, matériel fixe; **s. shaft,** arbre *m* fixe; **s. vane, s. blade,** aube *f* fixe, aube de stator (de turbine); *Artil:* **s. carriage,** affût *m* fixe; (*b*) *Mil:* **s. troops,** troupes *f* sédentaires; (*c*) *Med:* **s. disease (prevalent in a district),** maladie *f* stationnaire.

stationer ['steiʃənər], *s.* (*a*) *A:* libraire *m*; libraire-éditeur *m*; (*b*) papetier *m*; **stationer's shop,** papeterie *f*; **Stationers' Hall,** Hôtel *m* de la Corporation des libraires, relieurs, et papetiers (à Londres); *Adm:* **entered at Stationers' Hall,** (livre) déposé.

stationery ['steiʃən(ə)ri], *s.* papeterie *f*; **office s., school s.,** fournitures *fpl* de bureau, d'école; *Adm:* **the S. Office,** le Service des fournitures et des publications de l'Administration.

stationman, -woman, *pl.* **-men, -women** ['steiʃənmæn, -wumən; -men, -wimin], *s.* employé(e) de station de métro.

station-master ['steiʃənma:stər], *s.m.* chef de gare; **deputy s.,** sous-chef, *pl.* sous-chefs, de gare.

statism ['steitizm], *s. Pol:* étatisme *m.*

statist ['steitist], *s.* **1.** *esp. NAm:* statisticien, -ienne. **2.** étatiste *mf.*

statistic [stə'tistik], *s.* élément *m* d'un tableau statistique.

statistical [stə'tisk(ə)l], *a.* statistique; **s. analysis,** analyse *f* statistique; **s. tables,** statistiques *f.*

statistically [stə'tistik(ə)li], *adv.* statistiquement.

statistician [stætis'tiʃ(ə)n], *s.* statisticien, -ienne.

statistics [stə'tistiks], *s.pl.* (*a*) (*considered as a science*) (*with sg. or pl. const.*) la statistique; (*b*) **s. for 1980,** statistiques pour 1980; **vital s.,** (i) statistiques démographiques; statistiques de l'état civil; (ii) *F:* mensurations *fpl* (d'une femme).

statocyst ['stætousist], *s. Z: Coel:* statocyste *m.*

statolith ['stætouliθ], *s. Nat.Hist:* statolithe *m.*

stator ['steitər], *s. Mch: El:* stator *m* (d'une turbine, d'un moteur électrique); *El:* induit *m* fixe.

statoscope ['stætouskoup], *s. Meteor: Av:* statoscope *m.*

statuary ['stætjuəri]. **1.** *a.* (art, etc.) statuaire; **s. marble,** marbre *m* statuaire. **2.** *s.* (*pers.*) statuaire *mf.* **3.** *s.* (*a*) la statuaire; l'art *m* statuaire; (*b*) *coll.* statues *fpl.*

statue ['stætju:], *s.* statue *f*; **don't stand there like a s.!** ne reste pas là comme une souche!

statuesque [stætju(:)'esk], *a.* sculptural, -aux; plastique; **s. beauty,** beauté *f* plastique.

statuette [stætju(:)'et], *s.* statuette *f.*

stature ['stætjər], *s.* stature *f*; taille *f*; **to be short of s.,** avoir la taille courte, être petit; (*of author, etc.*) **it will increase his s.,** sa réputation y gagnera.

status ['steitəs], *s.* **1.** (*a*) statut légal (de qn); **personal s.,** statut personnel; **the s. of women,** le statut des femmes; (*b*) *Adm:* **civil s.,** état civil; *Jur:* **action of legitimate child to claim his s.,** action *f* en réclamation d'état; (*c*) condition *f*, position *f*, rang *m*; **social s.,** rang social; **s. symbol,** signe extérieur de situation sociale, de prestige, *F:* de standing; **with no official s.,** sans titre officiel. **2.** (*a*) *Med:* état; (*b*) état, situation *f*; **what is the present s. of broadcasting?** où en est la radiodiffusion?

status quo ['steitəs'kwou], *s.* statu quo *m inv.*

statutable ['stætju(:)təbl], *a.* **1.** autorisé (par la loi); réglementaire. **2.** (délit) prévu par la loi.

statute ['stætju:t], *s.* **1.** (*a*) *Jur:* acte *m* du Parlement; loi *f*, ordonnance *f*; **the S. of Limitations,** la loi de prescription; **to bar a debt by the S. of Limitations,** prescrire une dette; **debt barred by the S. of Limitations, s.-barred debt,** dette prescrite; dette caduque; **s. fair,** foire légale; **s. measure,** mesure légale; **s. law,** droit écrit; jurisprudence *f*; **s. book,** code *m* (des lois); (*b*) **the statutes of God,** les ordonnances de Dieu. **2. statutes,** statuts *m*, règlements *m* (d'une société, d'une compagnie). **3.** *Jur:* **personal s., real s.,** statut personnel, réel.

statutory ['stætjut(ə)ri], *a.* **1.** établi, fixé, imposé, par la loi; réglementaire; (*of offence*) prévu par la loi; **s. holiday,** fête légale; **s. declaration,** (i) attestation *f* (en lieu de serment); (ii) attestation (par un homme de loi) que certaines formalités ont été accomplies; (iii) acte *m* de notoriété; **s. company,** compagnie créée par législation spéciale pour assurer une entreprise de service public; **s. services,** services publics, gouvernementaux; **s. authority,** autorité publique; **s. regulations,** règlements *m* statutaires; **s. rape,** viol *m* d'une fille qui n'a pas atteint l'âge nubile. **2.** statutaire; conforme aux statuts.

staunch[1] [stɔ:n(t)ʃ], *a.* **1.** (*of pers.*) sûr, dévoué; ferme; **s. friend,** ami à toute épreuve; ami solide; **s. socialist,** socialiste convaincu(e); **s. courage,** courage *m* inébranlable. **2.** (*a*) (*of ship, etc.*) étanche; (*b*) *A:* (*of wall, etc.*) solide, ferme.

staunch[2] [stɔ:n(t)ʃ, sta:n(t)ʃ], *v.tr.* **1.** étancher (le sang). **2. to s. a wound,** étancher le sang d'une blessure.

staunching ['stɔ:n(t)ʃiŋ], *s.* étanchement *m* (du sang).

staunchly ['stɔ:n(t)ʃli], *adv.* avec fermeté; avec résolution; avec dévouement.

staunchness ['stɔ:n(t)ʃnis], *s.* **1.** fermeté *f*; dévouement *m.* **2.** (*a*) étanchéité *f*; (*b*) *A:* solidité *f.*

staurolite ['stɔ:roulait], *s. Miner:* staurolite *f*, staurotide *f*; pierre *f* de croix.

Stauromedusae [stɔ:roume'dju:zi], *s. Coel:* lucernaridés *m.*

stauroscope ['stɔ:rouskoup], *s. Opt:* stauroscope *m.*

staurotide ['stɔ:routaid], *s. Miner:* staurotide *f*, staurolite *f.*

stave[1] [steiv], *s.* **1.** (*a*) *Coop:* **barrel staves,** douves *f*, longailles *f*, pour tonneaux; **s. wood,** bourdillon *m*, merrain *m*; (*b*) bâton *m*; (*c*) échelon *m* (d'une échelle); hampe *f* (d'une hallebarde); *Dial:* bâton de chaise; *Mec.E:* **s. of a trundle,** fuseau *m* de lanterne. **2.** *Pros:* stance *f*, strophe *f*, couplet *m* (d'un poème). **3.** *Mus:* (*a*) portée *f*; (*b*) (barre *f* de) mesure *f*; **the first staves,** les premières mesures (du morceau).

stave[2], *v.* (*p.t.* **staved;** *p.p.* **staved,** *esp. Nau:* **stove** [stouv])

I. *v.tr. & i.* **1.** *v.tr. Coop;* garnir (un tonneau) de douves; assembler les douves (d'un tonneau). **2.** (*a*) *v.tr.* **to s. (in),** défoncer, enfoncer, crever, effondrer (une barrique, un bateau, etc.); *Aut:* **the radiator was**

staved, stove, in, le radiateur a été embouti, faussé; (*b*) *v.i.* (*of boat, ship*) se défoncer, se disjoindre, s'effondrer.
II. (*compound verbs*) **1. stave off,** *v.tr.* (*a*) *A:* écarter, chasser (un chien, etc.) avec un bâton; (*b*) détourner, écarter (un ennui, etc.); prévenir (un danger, une maladie); conjurer (un désastre); parer à (un danger); **to s. off hunger,** tromper la faim; **to s. off bankruptcy,** doubler le cap de l'imminente faillite.
2. stave up, *v.tr. Metalw:* **to s. up the head of a bolt,** refouler la tête d'un boulon.

staved [steivd], *a. Arch:* (*of column*) rudenté.

stavesacre ['steivzeikər], *s. Bot:* staphisaigre *f*; *F:* herbe *f* aux poux.

staving ['steiviŋ], *s. Coop:* merrain *m.*

stay[1] [stei], *s.* **1.** séjour *m* (dans une ville, etc.); visite *f* (chez un ami); **fortnight's s.,** séjour de quinze jours; **to be making only a short s. in a place,** être de passage dans un lieu. **2.** (*a*) *A:* & *Lit:* retard *m*; entrave *f*; **he will endure no s.,** il ne supportera aucun retard; **a s. upon his activity,** une entrave à son activité; (*b*) *Jur:* suspension *f*; **s. of proceedings,** suspension d'instances; **s. of execution,** sursis *m*; ordonnance *f* de surseoir (à un jugement); **judgment liable to s. of execution,** jugement susceptible d'opposition; **an appeal is not a s.,** un appel n'est pas suspensif.

stay[2], *v.*
I. *v.i.* **1.** (*a*) *A:* s'arrêter; (*b*) (*in imper.*) **s.! you have forgotten something,** attendez! vous avez oublié quelque chose. **2.** (*a*) rester; demeurer sur les lieux; **s. here until I come back,** restez ici jusqu'à ce que je revienne, jusqu'à mon retour; **s. there!** tenez-vous là! **it won't s. where it's put,** ça ne veut pas rester où on le met; *F:* **to s. put,** (i) rester à la même place; rester en place; refuser de bouger; occuper un lieu; (ii) ne plus changer; **I shall s. put,** j'y suis j'y reste; **to s. at home,** se tenir chez soi; **on wet days we s. at home,** les jours de pluie nous restons à la maison, nous gardons la maison; **to s. in bed,** rester au lit; garder le lit; **to s. to dinner, for dinner,** rester à dîner; rester dîner; **won't you s. to lunch?** restez donc à déjeuner; **to make s.o. s. to lunch,** retenir qn à déjeuner; **shall I s. with you?** voulez-vous de ma compagnie? **he has come to s.,** il est venu (i) passer quelques jours chez nous, (ii) habiter chez nous; **it was said that jazz had come to s.,** on prétendait que le jazz avait pris racine, était entré définitivement dans nos mœurs; **book that has come to s.,** livre qui restera; **foreign words that come to s.,** mots étrangers qui entrent dans la langue; (*b*) séjourner, demeurer quelque temps (**in a place,** dans un endroit); **I stayed in London last summer,** j'ai passé, je suis resté, quelque temps à Londres l'été dernier; **to s. at a hotel,** (i) descendre à un hôtel; (ii) être installé à un hôtel; **to s. with s.o.,** faire une visite à qn; passer quelque temps, quelques jours, chez qn; **we are staying with relations,** nous sommes chez des parents. **3.** *Rac:* **he wasn't able to s.,** il n'a pas pu soutenir l'allure; **he can s. five kilometres,** il peut fournir une course de cinq kilomètres; **horse that can s., that stays for ever,** cheval qui a du fond, de la tenue.
II. *v.tr.* **1.** *A:* arrêter (le progrès de qn, etc.); **to s. the inroads, the progress, of an epidemic,** barrer la route à une épidémie; enrayer une épidémie; **to s. the course of events,** endiguer la marche des événements; **if one could s. the progress of old age,** si l'on pouvait résister à l'action de la vieillesse; **to s. s.o.'s arm, s.o.'s hand,** retenir le bras de qn; **to s. one's hand,** se retenir; *F:* **to s. one's stomach,** tromper la faim. **2.** *Jur: etc:* remettre, ajourner (une décision, etc.); suspendre (son jugement, etc.); **to s. judgment,** surseoir à un jugement.
III. (*compound verbs*) **1. stay away,** *v.i.* ne pas venir; s'absenter; **to s. away from school,** (i) ne pas aller en classe (à cause d'une maladie, etc.); (ii) faire l'école buissonnière.
2. stay down, *v.i. Sch:* redoubler (une classe).
3. stay in, *v.i.* (*a*) ne pas sortir; rester à la maison; (*b*) *Sch:* être consigné; être en retenue.
4. stay on, *v.i.* rester encore quelque temps; **I'm staying on here for a week,** je reste encore huit jours ici.
5. stay out, *v.i.* (*a*) rester dehors; ne pas rentrer; **to s. out all night,** découcher; (*b*) *Ind:* **it was decided to s. out,** on a décidé que la grève continuerait.
6. stay up, *v.i.* (*a*) (i) ne pas se coucher; veiller; **to s. up late,** veiller tard; (ii) (*of child*) se coucher plus tard que d'habitude; (*b*) *Sch:* **he had to s. up to sit an exam after everyone else had gone down,** il a dû rester à l'université pour passer un examen quand tous les autres étaient en vacances.

stay[3], *s.* **1.** (*a*) support *m*, soutien *m*; montant *m*; *Arb:* **sapling s.,** tuteur *m*, écuyer *m*, d'un plant; *A:* **the s. of his old age,** le soutien de sa vieillesse; son bâton de vieillesse; (*b*) *Const: Mec.E: etc:* support, appui *m*, étai *m*, étançon *m*; arc-boutant *m*, *pl.* arcs-boutants; pointal *m*, -aux; *N.Arch:* accore *m* (de navire en construction); **s. (bar), s. rod,** jambe *f* de force; contre-fiche *f*; *Mec.E:* **s. plate,** gousset *m.* **2.** (*brace, tie*) (*a*) tirant *m* (de chaudière, de machine); *Mch:* ancre *f* (d'une chaudière); entretoise *f*; **s. bar, s. rod,** tige *f* de rappel; tirant de fixation; entretoise; **s. tube,** tube-tirant *m*, *pl.* tubes-tirants (d'une chaudière); *Mec.E: etc:* **s. bolt,** boulon *m* d'ancrage, d'entretoisement; entretoise; tirant; *Civ.E: etc:* **s. anchor,** ancre; *Mch:* **bridge stays,** armature *f* de la boîte à feu; (*b*) *N.Arch:* **bulwark, coaming, s.,** jambette *f* de pavois, d'hiloire. **3.** *Cost: O:* **stays,** corset *m.*

stay[4], *v.tr. Const: etc:* **1. to s. (up) sth.,** étayer, étançonner, accorer, arc-bouter (un mur, une maison); accorer, accoter (un navire, etc.). **2.** entretoiser (un mur, etc.); ancrer (une cheminée, etc.); affermir (une chaudière, etc.) par des ancres.

stay[5], *s.* **1.** (*a*) *Nau:* étai *m* (de mât); **cap s.,** étai de chouque; **jib s.,** draille *f* de foc; (*b*) **chain s.,** hauban-chaîne *m.* **2.** *Nau:* (*a*) (*of ship*) **to be in stays, to hang in stays,** être pris vent devant; dépasser le lit du vent; **to be slack in stays,** être lent à virer (de bord); **to miss stays,** manquer à virer; (*b*) (*of anchor*) **to be at short s., at long s.,** être à pic, à long pic.

stay[6]. **1.** *v.tr.* tenir (un mât) en étai; hauban(n)er (un mât, un poteau, etc.); rappeler (un mât) avec un câble. **2.** *Nau:* (*a*) *v.tr.* faire virer de bord (un navire) vent devant; (*b*) *v.i.* (*of ship*) virer de bord vent devant.

stay-at-home ['steiət(h)oum]. **1.** *s.* casanier, -ière; homme *m* d'intérieur; cendrillon *f.* **2.** *a.* casanier.

stayed [steid], *a.* hauban(n)é; **s. mast,** mât haubanné; **s. pole,** poteau haubanné; *Tg:* appui haubanné, appui consolidé.

stayer ['steiər], *s.* **1.** *F:* **he's a terrible s.,** il s'incruste chez nous (quand il vient). **2.** *Sp:* (*a*) coureur *m* de fond; stayer *m*; (*b*) cheval *m* de longue haleine; cheval capable de fournir une longue course; **horse that is a good s.,** cheval qui a du fond, de la tenue.

stay-in ['steiin], *attrib.* **s.-in strike,** grève *f* sur le tas, grève des bras croisés.

staying[1] ['steiiŋ], *s.* **1.** résistance *f*; **s. power,** résistance; endurance *f*; fond *m*; (*of horse*) **to have good s. power,** avoir du fond, de la tenue; **this job needs s. power,** ce travail est de longue haleine. **2.** (*a*) *A:* arrêt *m* (du progrès de qch., etc.); enrayage *m*, enrayement *m* (d'une épidémie, etc.); (*b*) *Jur: etc:* remise *f*, ajournement (d'une décision, etc.).

staying[2], *s. Civ.E: Const: etc:* **1.** (*a*) étayage *m*, étaiement *m*, arc-boutement *m*; renforcement *m*; *Min:* **s. of the roof,** consolidation *f* du ciel; (*b*) ancrage *m.* **2.** entretoisage *m*, entretoisement *m.*

staying[3], *s.* hauban(n)age *m*, étayage *m*, étaiement *m* (d'un mât).

staysail ['steisl], *s. Nau:* voile *f* d'étai; **main s.,** grand-voile d'étai; pouillousse *f*; **fore s.,** petit foc; **fore-topmast s.,** trinquette *f*; **mizzen-topmast s.,** foc d'artimon; diablotin *m*; marquise *f.*

stead [sted], *s. Lit:* **1. to stand s.o. in good s.,** être d'une grande utilité, être fort utile, à qn; être d'un grand secours à qn; beaucoup aider qn. **2. in s.o.'s s.,** à la place de qn; au lieu de qn; **to act in s.o.'s s.,** remplacer qn.

steadfast ['stedfɑːst], *a. esp. Lit:* ferme, stable; inébranlable, qui ne bronche pas; **s. in danger,** ferme en face du danger; **s. in love, in adversity,** constant en amour, dans l'adversité; **s. policy,** politique suivie.

steadfastly ['stedfɑːstli], *adv. esp. Lit:* fermement; avec constance; **we s. refuse,** nous refusons obstinément, absolument; **to look s. at s.o.,** regarder fixement qn.

steadfastness ['stedfɑːstnis], *s. esp. Lit:* fermeté *f* (d'esprit); stabilité *f*; constance *f*; **s. of purpose,** ténacité *f* de caractère; **to lack s. of purpose,** manquer de fond.

steadily ['stedili], *adv.* **1.** solidement, fermement; **vases that do not stand s.,** vases *m* qui ne sont pas en équilibre stable; **to walk s.,** marcher d'un pas ferme; marcher d'aplomb. **2.** (*a*) régulièrement; continuellement; sans arrêt, sans cesse; toujours; **s. increasing output,** rendement *m* augmentant régulièrement, de façon soutenue; **his health grows s. worse,** sa santé va (en) empirant; (*b*) uniment; sans à-coups; **horse that gallops s.,** cheval qui galope uniment; cheval au galop uni. **3.** fermement; avec fermeté; assidûment; **to work s. at sth.,** travailler fermement, assidûment, d'arrache-pied, à qch.; **to refuse s. to do sth.,** refuser fermement de faire qch. **4.** (se conduire) d'une manière rangée, posée; avec sagesse.

steadiness ['stedinis], *s.* **1.** fermeté *f*, sûreté *f*; **s. of hand,** sûreté de main. **2.** fermeté (d'esprit); assiduité *f*, persévérance *f*, application *f*; **s. in doing sth.,** assiduité à faire qch.; **s. of gaze,** fermeté *f*, fixité *f*, du regard. **3.** (*a*) régularité *f* (de mouvement, d'action); (*b*) stabilité *f*; *St.Exch:* **s. of prices,** tenue *f* des prix; (*c*) fixité *f*, rigidité *f*. **4.** (*of pers.*) conduite rangée, posée; sagesse *f.*

steading ['stediŋ], *s. Scot:* (*a*) ferme *f* et ses dépendances; (*b*) dépendances *f* (d'une ferme).

steady[1] ['stedi]. **1.** *a.* (*a*) ferme, solide; fixe, rigide; **s. rest,** support *m* fixe; **to make a table s.,** mettre une table en bon équilibre; caler une table; **to make a beam steadier,** donner plus de fixité à une poutre; assurer une poutre; **to keep s.,** ne pas bouger; rester en place; **to have a s. hand,** avoir la main sûre; **with a s. hand, step,** d'une main assurée, ferme; d'un pas assuré, ferme; **to be s. on one's legs,** *F:* **on one's pins,** être d'aplomb sur ses jambes; *F:* être ferme sur ses piliers; *Equit:* **to have a s. seat,** être ferme à cheval, sur ses étriers; avoir une bonne assiette; **s. horse,** cheval *m* calme; **horse s. under fire,** cheval docile au feu; **ship s. in a sea, in a breeze,** navire *m* qui tient bien la mer, le vent; (*b*) continu, soutenu; persistant; régulier; *Sp: etc:* **to play a s. game,** avoir un jeu régulier; **s. increase,** augmentation soutenue; **s. progress,** progrès ininterrompus, soutenus; **s. pace,** allure modérée, réglée; **s. trot,** trot soutenu; **s. movements,** mouvements mesurés; **s. pulse,** pouls égal; **s. light,** lumière *f* stable; **s. fire,** feu nourri; **s. weather,** temps établi; **s. breeze,** brise faite (et forte); brise étale, franche; **s. downpour,** pluie persistante; **s. barometer,** baromètre *m* stationnaire; *Nau:* **s. compass,** compas *m* tranquille; *Mch:* **s. governor,** régulateur stabilisé; *Mec.E:* **s. load,** charge constante; *Com:* **s. demand for . . .,** demande suivie pour . . .; **s. market,** marché soutenu; (*of market, etc.*) **to grow s.,** se stabiliser; **s. prices,** prix *m* fixes; (*c*) (*of pers.*) ferme, constant; assidu; **s. worker,** travailleur appliqué, assidu, régulier; (*d*) (*of pers.*) rangé, posé; sérieux, sage; **to become s.,** se ranger; s'assagir. **2.** *adv.* & *int.* (*a*) **s.!** (i) ne bougez pas! (ii) *Ven:* (*to dog*) tout beau! (iii) *Mil:* fixe! (iv) attention (de ne pas tomber)! *F:* **s. (on)!** doucement! du calme! ne vous pressez pas! (*b*) *Nau:* comme ça! (*c*) *adv. P:* (*of young man and woman*) **to be going s.,** être de bons amis (qui espèrent se marier plus tard). **3.** *s.* (*a*) support *m* (pour la main, etc.); (*b*) *Mec.E:* **s. (rest),** lunette *f* (d'un tour, etc.); **fixed s. rest,** lunette fixe; (*c*) *F:* **my s.,** mon ami(e) attitré(e) (avec qui je sors régulièrement).

steady[2]. **1.** *v.tr.* (*a*) raffermir, affermir; assurer; **to s. a table leg,** caler le pied d'une table; **to s. one's hand,** assurer sa main; **to s. oneself against sth.,** s'étayer contre qch.; **to s. the running of a machine,** régulariser, stabiliser, la marche d'une machine; **to s. the nerves,** raffermir, calmer, détendre, les nerfs; *Nau:* **to s. a ship,** appuyer un navire; **to s. the ship against a sea,** tenir barre à la vague; (*b*) assagir (un jeune homme, etc.); **marriage has steadied him,** le mariage l'a rangé. **2.** *v.i.* **to s. (down),** se raffermir; reprendre son aplomb; **the boat steadied,** le bateau retrouva son équilibre; **prices are steadying,** les prix *m* se raffermissent; **the market has steadied (down),** le marché a repris son aplomb.

steadying ['stediiŋ], *s.* affermissement *m*; raffermissement *m*; **s. rope,** retenue *f*; *Com: Ind:* (*in production*) **s. force, s. factor,** volant *m.*

steak [steik], *s. Cu:* (*a*) tranche *f* (de viande, de poisson); darne *f* (de saumon); côtelette *f* (de porc); (*b*) bifteck *m*, steak *m*, steck *m*; filet *m* de bœuf; (*cut from the ribs*) entrecôte *f*; **fillet s.,** tournedos *m*; **veal s., bear s., horse s.,** bifteck de veau, d'ours, de cheval; (*c*) **s. tartare,** steak tartare, *Belg:* filet américain; **s. and chips,** steak frites.

steal[1] [stiːl], *v.* (*p.t.* **stole** [stoul]; *p.p.* **stolen** ['stoul(ə)n]) **1.** *v.tr.* (*a*) voler, dérober, soustraire (**sth. from s.o.,** qch. à qn); **to s. money from the till,** voler de l'argent dans la caisse; **I've had my purse stolen,** on m'a volé mon porte-monnaie; *B:* **thou shalt not s.,** tu ne déroberas point; (*b*) **to s. s.o.'s heart,** séduire le cœur de qn; **to s. a few hours from one's studies,** dérober quelques heures à ses études; (*c*) **to s. a glance at s.o.,** jeter furtivement un regard à qn; jeter un coup d'œil furtif à qn; jeter vers, sur, qn un regard à la dérobée; regarder qn à la dérobée, d'un œil furtif, furtivement; (*d*) **to s. a march on the enemy,** gagner une marche sur l'ennemi; **to s. a march on s.o.,** prendre les devants sur qn; devancer qn; circonvenir qn; gagner, prendre, qn de vitesse. **2.** *v.i.* **to s. away, down, in, out,** s'en aller, descendre, entrer, sortir, à la dérobée, furtivement, à pas furtifs, à pas de loup, en tapinois; **he stole away,** (i) il s'est éloigné à pas feutrés; (ii) il s'est esquivé; **he stole into the room,** il s'est faufilé, s'est glissé, dans la pièce; **to s. along,** marcher à pas de loup; **he felt sleep stealing in on him,** il se sentait gagné par le sommeil; **he felt a vague apprehension stealing over him,** il se sentait sous le coup d'une vague appréhension; **a tear stole down her**

cheek, une larme coulait doucement le long de sa joue; **the mist stole over the valley,** le brouillard gagnait insensiblement la vallée; **the light was stealing through the chinks,** la lumière filtrait par les fissures.

steal[2], *s. F: NAm:* (*a*) vol *m*; (*b*) objet volé; (*c*) **at that price it's a s.!** à ce prix-là c'est vraiment donné! (*d*) transaction *f* malhonnête; filouterie *f*; plagiat *m* **(from,** fait à).

stealer ['sti:lər], *s.* voleur, -euse **(of,** de); **sheep s.,** voleur de moutons.

stealing ['sti:liŋ], *s.* vol *m*; **s. by finding,** vol commis par l'appropriation d'un objet trouvé.

stealth [stelθ], *s.* (*only in the phr.*) **by s.,** à la dérobée; furtivement; en tapinois; **to do sth. by s.,** faire qch. sous main, en cachette.

stealthily ['stelθili], *adv.* à la dérobée; furtivement, subrepticement; en tapinois, en catimini; **to creep in s.,** entrer à pas de loup; **to look at s.o. s.,** regarder qn furtivement, en dessous.

stealthiness ['stelθinis], *s.* caractère furtif (d'une action, etc.).

stealthy ['stelθi], *a.* furtif; **s. glance,** regard dérobé; regard à la dérobée; **with a s. step,** d'un pas furtif; à pas de loup, à pas feutrés.

steam[1] [sti:m], *s.* (*a*) vapeur *f* (d'eau); buée *f*; **the kitchen was full of s.,** la cuisine était remplie de buée; **windowpane covered with s.,** vitre couverte de buée; *Dom.Ec:* **s. cooking,** cuisson *f* à la vapeur; **s. ironing,** repassage *m* à la vapeur; **s. iron,** fer *m* à vapeur; *Med: etc:* **s. tent,** tente *f* de vapeur; **s. kettle,** bouilloire *f* pour humidifier l'atmosphère; **s. bath,** bain *m* de vapeur; **s. heating,** chauffage *m* à la vapeur; *Paperm:* **s. finish,** humectage *m* à la vapeur; (*b*) *Ph: Mch:* vapeur; **dry s.,** vapeur sèche; **wet s.,** vapeur humide, mouillée, aqueuse; **saturated, non-saturated, s.,** vapeur saturée, non saturée; **condensed s.,** vapeur condensée; **superheated s.,** vapeur surchauffée; **s. production, generation,** production *f*, génération *f*, de vapeur; vaporisation *f*; **s. generator,** générateur *m* de vapeur; **s. power,** la vapeur (en tant qu'énergie, que force motrice); **s. pressure,** pression *f*, tension *f*, de vapeur; **s. gauge,** jauge *f* de vapeur; manomètre *m* à vapeur, de pression de vapeur; **s. engine,** machine *f* à vapeur; **s. boiler,** chaudière *f* à vapeur; **s. coal,** charbon *m* à vapeur; houille *f* de chaudière; **s. jacket,** chemise *f*, enveloppe *f*, de vapeur; chapelle *f*; cylindre-enveloppe *m*, *pl.* cylindres-enveloppes; **s. box, s. chamber,** boîte *f* à vapeur, à tiroir(s); chapelle *f* du tiroir; boîte de distribution de vapeur; *Ind:* **s. distillation,** distillation *f* à la vapeur; *Petr:* **s. cracking,** craquage *m* à la vapeur, vapocraquage *m*; *F:* **s. radio,** la radio (par opposition à la télévision); *Mch: etc:* **to get up s., to raise s.,** mettre (une chaudière) sous pression; chauffer (une machine à vapeur); faire monter la pression; pousser les feux; (*of pers.*) **to get up s.,** faire appel à, rassembler, toutes ses forces, toute son énergie; *Nau:* **engine under s.,** machine sous pression, en pression; **at full s.,** à toute vapeur; en pleine vapeur; *Nau:* **full s. ahead!** en avant toute! **to keep up s.,** (i) tenir (de) la pression; rester, tenir, sous pression; (ii) *F:* (*of pers.*) ne pas se relâcher; travailler ferme; **to run out of s.,** (i) *Mch:* ne plus être sous pression; (ii) *F:* (*of pers.*) être épuisé; *Turf:* **horse that runs out of s.,** cheval qui ne peut pas soutenir l'allure, qui n'a pas de fond, de la tenue; *St.Exch: F:* **these shares still have s. in them,** ces actions montrent toujours une tendance à la hausse; **to let off, blow off, s.,** (i) *Mch:* lâcher, laisser échapper, larguer, (de) la vapeur; (ii) *F:* (*of pers.*) dépenser son trop-plein d'énergie; (iii) *F:* (*of pers.*) donner libre cours à ses sentiments, épancher sa bile; (*of damaged ship*) **to proceed under its own s.,** marcher par ses seuls moyens; **I'll come under my own s.,** je viendrai par mes propres moyens; **I can do it under my own s.,** je puis le faire tout seul, sans aide.

steam[2]. **1.** *v.tr.* (*a*) *Cu:* cuire (des légumes, etc.) à la vapeur, à l'étuvée; **steamed potatoes,** pommes *f* vapeur; (*b*) passer (qch.) à la vapeur, à l'étuve, étuver (qch.); vaporiser (un vêtement, du drap); *Tex:* délustrer (le drap); **to s. open an envelope,** décacheter une lettre à la vapeur; (*c*) *Tex:* fixer (un colorant) à la vapeur. **2.** *v.i.* (*a*) jeter, exhaler, de la vapeur; fumer; (*of hot pastry, etc.*) buer; **the soup is steaming on the table,** la soupe fume sur la table; **horses steaming with sweat,** chevaux *m* fumants (de sueur); **to s. away,** s'évaporer; (*b*) marcher (à la vapeur); **to s. ahead,** (i) avancer (à la vapeur); (ii) *F:* faire des progrès rapides; **the train steamed out of the station,** le train a quitté la gare; *Nau:* **to s. at ten knots,** filer dix nœuds; (*c*) *Mch:* **to s. up,** mettre la vapeur; pousser les feux; (*of window, windscreen*) **to s. (up),** s'embuer; se couvrir de buée; **all steamed over,** tout embué; *F:* (*of pers.*) **to get (all) steamed up,** perdre son sang-froid; se laisser emporter (par la colère); s'énerver; se mettre dans tous ses états.

steamboat ['sti:mbout], *s.* (bateau *m* à) vapeur *m.*

steamer ['sti:mər], *s.* **1.** *Nau:* vapeur *m.* **2.** *Dom.Ec:* marmite *f* à vapeur.

steamhammer ['sti:mhæmər], *s.* marteau-pilon *m*, *pl.* marteaux-pilons (à vapeur); pilon *m* mécanique; *F:* **to use a s. to crack a nut,** enfoncer une porte ouverte; se servir d'un marteau-pilon pour enfoncer un clou.

steaming[1] ['sti:miŋ], *a.* fumant; qui s'évapore; *a.phr.* **s. hot,** tout chaud.

steaming[2], *s.* (*a*) *Cu:* cuisson *f* à la vapeur, à l'étuvée; (*b*) étuvage *m*, injection *f* de vapeur; (*c*) *Tex:* fixation *f* à la vapeur (du colorant).

steamroller[1] [sti:m'roulər], *s.* (*a*) *Civ.E: O:* rouleau *m* compresseur; (*b*) *F:* force *f* irrésistible, qui écrase toute opposition.

steamroller[2], *v.tr.* (*a*) *Civ.E: A:* cylindrer (une route); (*b*) *F:* écraser toute opposition.

steamship ['sti:mʃip], *s.* vapeur *m.*

steamtight ['sti:mtait], *a.* étanche (à la vapeur).

steamy ['sti:mi], *a.* plein de vapeur; plein, couvert, de buée; **s. atmosphere,** atmosphère humide.

stearate ['stiəreit], *s. Ch:* stéarate *m.*

stearic [sti'ærik], *a. Ch:* (acide) stéarique.

stearin(e) ['stiərin], *s. Ch:* stéarine *f*; **s. candle,** bougie *f* stéarique.

stearyl ['stiəril], *s. Ch:* stéaryle *m.*

steatite ['stiətait], *s. Miner:* stéatite *f.*

steatitic [stiə'titik], *a. Geol:* stéatiteux.

steatocele [sti(:)'ætousi:l], *s. Med:* stéatocèle *f.*

steatoma [stiə'toumə], *s. Med:* stéatome *m.*

steatopyga [stiətou'paigə], **steatopygia** [stiətou'pidʒiə], **steatopygy** [stiə'tɔpidʒi], *s. Med:* stéatopygie *f.*

steatopygous [stiə'tɔpigəs], *a. Med:* stéatopyge.

Steatornithidae [stiətɔ:'niθidi:], *s.pl. Orn:* steatornithidés *m.*

steatosis [stiə'tousis], *s. Med:* stéatose *f.*

steed [sti:d], *s. Lit:* coursier *m*, destrier *m.*

steel[1] [sti:l], *s.* **1.** *Metall:* acier *m*; **basic s.,** acier Thomas; **Bessemer s.,** acier Bessemer; **open-hearth s.,** acier Martin; **rolled s.,** acier laminé; **high grade s.,** acier fin, à haute teneur; **high speed s.,** acier (à coup) rapide; **cold-rolled s.,** acier laminé à froid, écroui; **cold-drawn s.,** acier étiré à froid; **cast s.,** acier coulé, fondu, moulé; fonte *f* d'acier; **s. casting,** moulage *m* d'acier; acier moulé; **case-hardened s.,** acier de cémentation; **precision ground s.,** acier en barres rectifiées avec précision; **forged s.,** acier forgé; **drop-forged s.,** acier matricé; **rolled s.,** acier laminé; **pressed s.,** acier embouti; **puddled s.,** acier puddlé; **killed s.,** acier calmé; **pot s.,** acier au creuset; **alloy s.,** acier allié, spécial; **lead-alloy s.,** acier allié au plomb; **carbon s.,** acier au carbone; **chrome, chromium, s.,** acier chromé; **manganese, molybdenum, s.,** acier au manganèse, au molybdène; **nickel s.,** acier au nickel; **silicon, titanium, vanadium, s.,** acier au silicium, au titane, au vanadium; **hard s.,** acier dur; **hardened, tempered, s.,** acier trempé, revenu; **soft s.,** acier doux; **softened s.,** acier adouci; **s. plate,** (i) tôle *f* d'acier; (ii) *Engr:* planche *f* d'acier; **s. engraving,** gravure *f*, estampe *f*, sur acier; **s. plated,** cuirassé; **s. foundry,** fonderie *f* d'acier; **s. manufacturer,** aciériste *m*; **the iron and s. industry,** l'industrie *f* sidérurgique; la sidérurgie; **a grip, a will, of s.,** une poigne, une volonté, de fer; **nerves of s.,** nerfs *m* d'acier. **2.** *A: & Lit:* fer *m*, épée *f*; lame *f*; **to fight with cold s.,** se battre à l'arme blanche. **3.** (*a*) (*for sharpening knives*) affiloir *m*; fusil *m*; (*b*) *A:* (*for striking light*) briquet *m*; **flint and s.,** briquet à silex. **4.** *Cost: A:* baleine *f*, busc *m* (de corset). **5.** *Pharm: A:* **tincture of s.,** teinture *f* de perchlorure de fer; **s. pills,** pillules ferrugineuses; **s. wine,** vin chalybé, ferrugineux.

steel[2], *v.tr.* **1.** (*a*) *Metalw:* aciérer, acérer, armer (un outil); (*b*) *Ch:* **to s.(-face) a copper plate,** aciérer une plaque de cuivre. **2.** *Metall:* aciérer (le fer). **3. to s. oneself, to s. one's heart, to sth., to do sth.,** (i) s'endurcir à qch., à faire qch.; (ii) s'armer de courage pour faire qch.; **to s. oneself against sth.,** se raidir, se cuirasser, contre qch.; **to s. one's heart against pity,** se cuirasser contre la pitié.

steelclad ['sti:lklæd], *a.* couvert, revêtu, d'acier, de fer; à revêtement d'acier; (*of ancient knight*) bardé de fer.

steeled [sti:ld], *a.* **1.** (*a*) *Metall:* (outil) aciéré, acéré, armé; (*b*) *Metalw:* **s. iron,** fer aciéré; fer étoffé; (*c*) (cœur) dur, de fer. **2.** *Pharm:* chalybé, ferrugineux.

steeliness ['sti:linis], *s.* dureté *f*; inflexibilité *f* (de caractère, etc.).

steeling ['sti:liŋ], *s.* **1.** (*a*) aciérage *m*, acérage *m* (d'un outil); (*b*) *Ch:* aciérage, aciération *f.* **2.** *Metall:* aciérage, aciération, étoffage *m* (du fer).

steelwork ['sti:lwə:k], *s.* **1.** (*a*) **constructional s.,** profilés *mpl* pour constructions; (*b*) *Aut: etc:* tôleries *fpl.* **2.** (*usu. with sg. const.*) **steelworks,** aciérie *f.*

steely ['sti:li], *a.* **1.** d'acier; *Metall:* **s. iron,** fer aciéreux, fer acérain. **2.** d'acier; dur, inflexible; **a s. glance, look,** un regard d'acier.

steelyard ['sti:ljɑ:d, 'stiljəd], *s.* (balance) romaine *f*; peson *m* à contrepoids; crochet-bascule *m*, *pl.* crochets-bascules.

steenbok ['sti:nbɔk], *s. Z:* steinbock *m.*

steening ['sti:niŋ], *s. Hyd.E:* muraillement *m* (de puits).

steep[1] [sti:p]. **1.** *a.* (*a*) escarpé; pic; raide; **s. hill,** colline escarpée; pente rapide; **s. gradient,** forte pente; pente raide, rapide; **s. descent,** forte descente; **the slopes grow steeper,** les pentes s'escarpent; **slopes less s.,** des pentes moins déclives; **s. path,** chemin à forte pente; chemin en forte descente; chemin ardu; **s. climb,** rude montée *f*; montée rude, raide; *Nau:* **s. shore,** côte *f* accore; *Av:* **s. start,** départ *m* en chandelle; **too s. a dive,** descente trop piquée; **s. rise in prices,** hausse considérable des prix; (*b*) *F:* fort, raide; **that's a bit s.!** c'est un peu fort! c'est un peu raide! **s. price,** prix exorbitant; prix salé. **2.** *s. Lit:* pente rapide; escarpement *m*; à-pic *m.*

steep[2], *s. Ind:* **1.** = STEEPING; **to put sth. in s.,** mettre qch. en trempe. **2.** (*a*) bain *m* (de macération); *Tan:* **alum s.,** mégis *m*; (*b*) *Paperm:* **the steeps,** les caisses *f* de macération.

steep[3]. **1.** *v.tr.* (*a*) *Ind: etc:* baigner, tremper; mettre (qch.) en trempe, à macérer; mouiller (le linge); infuser (des herbes) à froid; **to s. gherkins in vinegar, roots in alcohol,** macérer des cornichons dans du vinaigre, des racines dans l'alcool; **to s. flax,** rouir le lin; *Tan:* **to s. skins,** tremper, confire, les peaux; (*b*) saturer, imbiber (qch. de qch.); **terrace steeped in sunshine,** terrasse inondée, baignée, de soleil; **steeped in ignorance,** pétri d'ignorance; **steeped in prejudice,** imbibé de préjugés; **to be steeped in vice,** être plongé dans le vice; baigner dans le vice; **to s. oneself in the atmosphere of the Middle Ages,** se tremper, se plonger, dans l'atmosphère du moyen âge. **2.** *v.i.* (*of skins, soiled linen, etc.*) tremper; (*of flax, etc.*) rouir; (*of herbs*) infuser (à froid).

steepen ['sti:p(ə)n], *v.i.* (*of slope, etc.*) devenir plus raide; s'escarper; (*b*) (*of prices*) augmenter; être à la hausse.

steepening[1] ['sti:p(ə)niŋ], *a.* **s. prices,** prix en hausse, à la hausse; **s. path,** sentier qui devient plus raide.

steepening[2], *s.* augmentation *f* (des prix).

steeper ['sti:pər], *s. Ind:* trempoire *f*, cuve *f.*

steeping ['sti:piŋ], *s. Ind: etc:* trempage *m*, macération *f*, trempe *f*; mouillage *m* (du linge); rouissage *m*, roui *m* (du chanvre); infusion *f* à froid; **s. vat, trough,** trempoire *f*, cuve *f.*

steepish ['sti:piʃ], *a.* (*of gradient, etc.*) assez raide; assez rude; (*of price*) plutôt raide.

steeple ['sti:pl], *s.* (*a*) clocher *m*; (*b*) flèche *f* (de clocher).

steeplechase[1] ['sti:pltʃeis], *s.* steeple-chase *m*, *pl.* steeple-chases; *F:* steeple *m*; course *f* d'obstacles (à cheval).

steeplechase[2], *v.i.* monter en steeple-chase.

steeplechaser ['sti:pltʃeisər], *s.* **1.** cavalier *m* qui monte en steeple-chases; jockey *m* d'obstacles. **2.** (*horse*) steeple-chaser *m.*

steeplechasing ['sti:pltʃeisiŋ], *s.* steeple-chases *mpl*; courses *fpl* d'obstacles (à cheval).

steeplejack ['sti:pldʒæk], *s.* réparateur *m* de clochers, de cheminées d'usines.

steeply ['sti:pli], *adv.* en pente rapide; à pic; abruptement; **the cliff falls s. into the sea,** la falaise tombe à pic dans la mer; **road that climbs s.,** route à forte pente.

steepness ['sti:pnis], *s.* **1.** raideur *f*, rapidité *f*, escarpement *m* (d'une pente); *Mth:* **s. of a curve,** degré *m* d'inclinaison d'une courbe. **2.** pente raide; pente rapide; raidillon *m.*

steepwater ['sti:pwɔ:tər], *s. Agr:* eau *f* de trempage, de trempe.

steer[1] ['stiər], *v.tr. & i. Nau:* gouverner (un navire); tenir la barre, le gouvernail; barrer (un yacht); cingler; *Row:* barrer; *Aut:* conduire, diriger (une voiture); **to s. by the sea, by the wind,** gouverner à la lame, d'après le vent; **to s. a northerly course, to s. north,** faire route au nord; mettre le cap sur le nord; **to s. clear of sth., s.o.,** éviter qch., qn; (*with passive force*) **ship that steers well, badly,** navire qui gouverne, qui manœuvre, bien, mal.

steer[2], *s.* (*a*) jeune bœuf *m*; bouveau *m*, bouvelet *m*, bouvillon *m*; (*b*) bœuf.

steerage ['stiəridʒ], *s. Nau:* **1.** *A:* manœuvre *f* de la barre. **2.** *A:* emménagements *mpl* pour passagers de troisième classe, pour émigrants; entrepont *m*; **to go s., to travel s.,** voyager dans l'entrepont; faire la traversée en troisième classe.

steerageway ['stiəridʒwei], *s.* vitesse *f* nécessaire pour gouverner; erre *f* (pour gouverner).

steering ['stiəriŋ], *s.* **1.** (*a*) direction *f*, conduite *f* (d'un bateau, d'une voiture; *Aut:* **power (assisted) s.,** direction assistée; (*b*) **s. (gear),** organes *m* de transmission d'un moteur; *Aut:* (i) timonerie *f*; (ii) boîte *f* de direction; *Nau:* appareil *m* à gouverner; *Av:* direction; *Nau:* **s. engine,** servo-moteur *m* du gouvernail; *Aut:* **differential s.,** direction par vis différentielle; **s. wheel,** (i) *Nau:* roue *f* du gouvernail; (ii) *Aut:* volant *m* (de direction); *Aut:* **s. column,** colonne *f*, pilier *m*, de direction; **collapsible, impact absorbing s. column,** colonne de direction à absorption d'énergie; (*c*) **s. committee,** comité *m* de direction, d'organisation. **2.** *Nau:* manœuvre *f* de la barre; **good, bad, s.,** bon, mauvais, coup de barre; (*of ship*) **to have lost s. control,** ne plus être maître de sa manœuvre.

steersman, *pl.* **-men** ['stiəzmən], *s.m. Nau:* homme de barre; timonier.

steeve[1] [sti:v], *s. Nau:* apiquage *m* (du beaupré, etc.).

steeve[2], *Nau:* **1.** *v.tr.* apiquer (le beaupré). **2.** *v.i.* (*of bowsprit*) être apiqué.

steeve[3], *v.tr. Nau:* estiver, comprimer, tasser (la cargaison dans la cale).

Stegocephalia [stegouse'feiliə], *s.pl.* stégocéphales *m.*

stegocephalian [stegouse'feiliən], *a.* & *s. Paleont:* stégocéphalien (*m*); *s.* stégocéphale *m.*

stegodon ['stegoudən], *s. Paleont:* stégodon *m.*

Steinkirk ['stainkə:k]. *Pr.n. Geog:* Steinkerque.

stele, *pl.* **-ae** ['sti:li, -i:], *s.* **1.** stèle *f.* **2.** *Bot:* (*also* [sti:l]) stèle.

stellar ['stelər], *a.* stellaire; *Astr:* **blue s. objects,** galazie bleue.

stellaria [ste'lɛəriə], *s. Bot:* stellarie *f.*

stellate ['steleit], **stellated** [ste'leitid], *a. Nat.Hist:* étoilé; en étoile; radié.

Stelleroidea [stelə'rɔidiə], *s.pl. Echin:* stellérides *m.*

stelliform ['stelifɔ:m], *a.* stelliforme.

Stelliformia [steli'fɔ:miə], *s.pl. Echin:* stellérides *m.*

stellion ['steliən], *s. Rept:* stellion *m.*

stellionate ['steliəneit], *s. Jur:* stellionat *m.*

stellular, stellulate ['steljulər, -leit], *a. Nat.Hist:* stellulé.

stem[1] [stem], *s.* **1.** (*a*) *Bot:* tige *f* (de plante, de fleur); queue *f* (de fruit, de feuille); pétiole *m*, pédoncule *m*, hampe *f* (de fleur); tronc *m*, souche *f*, caudex *m* (d'arbre); stipe *m* (de palmier); (*b*) régime *m* (de bananes); (*c*) dague *f* (de cerf de deux ans). **2.** (*a*) pied *m*, patte *f*, jambe *f* (de verre à boire); tige, queue (de soupape); tige (de vis); tige, branche *f* (de clef); broche *f* (de serrure); tuyau *m* (de pipe de fumeur); arbre *m* (de grue); *Cy:* potence *f* (du guidon); *Petr:* **grief s.,** tige carrée d'entraînement; (*b*) haste *f* (des lettres, t, f, etc.); (*c*) *Mus:* queue (d'une note). **3.** (*a*) souche, tronc (de famille); **descended from an ancient s.,** rejeton *m* d'une souche ancienne; (*b*) *Ling:* thème *m* (étymologique), radical *m* (d'un mot). **4.** *N.Arch:* étrave *f*, avant *m*; **cutwater s.,** étrave à guibre; **from s. to stern,** de l'avant à l'arrière; de l'étrave à l'étambot; de bout en bout.

stem[2], *v.* **(stemmed) 1.** *v.tr.* égrapper (des raisins); écôter (des feuilles de tabac). **2.** *v.i.* **to s. from (sth.);** être issu de, descendre de, provenir de (qch.); **the economic benefits that stemmed from this,** les avantages économiques qui en résultaient; **much harm stemmed from it,** il en est résulté beaucoup de mal.

stem[3]. **1.** *v.tr.* (*a*) contenir, arrêter, endiguer (un cours d'eau, etc.); enrayer (une épidémie); **to s. the course of events,** endiguer la marche des événements; (*b*) aller contre, lutter contre (la marée); refouler, remonter, rencontrer (le courant); (*of ship*) étaler (le courant); refouler, résister à (une attaque); **to s. the tide of public indignation,** endiguer, arrêter, le flot de l'indignation publique; (*c*) *Min:* bourrer (un trou de mine). **2.** *v.i. Ski:* faire un stemm.

stembogen ['stembouɡ(ə)n], *s. Ski:* (*also* **stem turn**) stembogen *m.*

stemless[1] ['stemlis], *a. Bot:* sans tige(s); acaule.

stemless[2], *a. Lit:* (flot, etc.) qu'on ne peut pas arrêter.

stemlet ['stemlit], *s. Bot:* petite tige.

stemma, *pl.* **-ata** ['stemə, -ətə], *s.* **1.** *Nat.Hist:* stemmate *m*, ocelle *m.* **2.** arbre *m* généalogique.

stemmed [stemd], *a.* **1.** (fleur, etc.) à tige, à queue; (verre) à pied, à patte. **2.** *Bot:* (*with adj. prefixed, e.g.*) **long-s.,** longicaule; **thick-s.,** crassicaule; **many-s.,** multicaule.

stemmer ['stemər], *s. Tls: Min:* bourroir *m.*

stemming ['stemiŋ], *s.* **1.** refoulement *m* (de la marée, etc.). **2.** *Min:* bourrage *m* (d'un trou de mine). **3.** *Ski:* freinage *m*; **single s.,** freinage unilatéral.

stemson ['stems(ə)n], *s. N.Arch:* marsouin *m* (de l')avant (d'un navire en bois).

stench [sten(t)ʃ], *s.* (*a*) odeur empoisonnante; odeur infecte; puanteur *f*; **what a s.!** c'est une infection ici! ce que ça empeste ici! *F:* que ça pue! (*b*) *Const:* **s. pipe,** ventilateur *m*; **s. trap,** siphon *m* (d'évier, etc.).

stencil[1] ['stensl], *s.* **1.** (*a*) patron (ajouré); poncif *m*, pochoir *m*; **s. plate,** pochoir; **s. brush,** pochon *m*; **s. letter,** lettre *f* à jour; **s. painting,** coloriage *m* au patron; **coloured by s.,** colorié au patron; (*b*) **cipher s.,** grille *f.* **2.** peinture *f*, décoration *f*, travail *m*, au poncif, au pochoir; tracé *m.* **3.** *Typewr: etc:* cliché *m*; stencil *m*; **s. paper,** papier *m* stencil.

stencil[2], *v.tr.* **(stencilled)** (*a*) peindre, marquer, imprimer, (qch.) au poncif, au patron, au pochoir; poncer, pocher, patronner (qch.); passer (un dessin) au pochoir; *Ind: Com:* marquer (une caisse, un ballot); (*b*) polycopier (une circulaire, etc.); tirer (une circulaire) au stencil.

stenciller ['stensələr], *s.* peintre *m* au pochoir; marqueur *m* (de caisses, de ballots).

stencilling ['stensiliŋ], *s.* peinture *f*, travail *m*, au pochoir; patronage *m.*

sten-gun ['stengʌn], *s.* mitraillette *f* sten.

stenocardia [stenou'kɑ:diə], *s. Med:* sténocardie *f.*

stenoderm ['stenoudə:m], *s. Z:* sténoderme *m.*

stenographer, *U.S:* **stenographist** [stə'nɔgrəfər, -fist], *s.* sténographe *mf*; *F:* sténo *mf.*

stenographic(al) [stenə'græfik(l)], *a.* sténographique.

stenographically [stenə'græfik(ə)li], *adv.* sténographiquement.

stenography [stə'nɔgrəfi], *s.* sténographie *f.*

stenohaline [stenou'heili:n], *a. Biol:* sténohalin; **s. habits, conditions,** sténohalinité *f.*

stenopaeic [stenou'pi:ik], *a. Opt:* (fente *f*, etc.) sténopéique.

stenophagous [ste'nɔfəgəs], *a. Ent:* sténophage.

stenosis [ste'nousis], *s. Med:* sténose *f.*

stenothermal, stenothermic [stenou'θə:m(ə)l, -'θə:mik], *a. Biol:* sténotherme.

stenothermy ['stenouθə:mi], *s. Biol:* sténothermie *f.*

stenotype ['stenoutaip], *s.* sténotype *m.*

stenotyping ['stenətaipiŋ], *s.* sténotypie *f.*

stenotypist ['stenətaipist], *s.* sténotypiste *mf.*

stenotypy ['stenətaipi], *s.* sténotypie *f.*

stenter ['stentər], *s. Tex:* élargisseur *m.*

Stentor ['stentɔ:r]. **1.** *Pr.n.m. Gr.Lit:* Stentor. **2.** *s.* (*a*) *Prot:* stentor *m*; (*b*) *Z:* **s. (monkey),** stentor.

stentorian [sten'tɔ:riən], *a.* (voix *f*) de Stentor.

step[1] [step], *s.* **1.** pas *m*; **to take a s.,** faire un pas; **to take a s. back, forward,** faire un pas en arrière, en avant; **you shan't stir a s.,** je vous défends de bouger d'un pas; **to turn one's steps towards a place,** se diriger, diriger ses pas, vers un lieu; **at every s.,** à chaque pas; **s. by s.,** pas à pas; par échelons; petit à petit; graduellement; de proche en proche; **to fall back s. by s.,** reculer pied à pied; *El:* **s.-by-s. relay,** relais graduel; **within a few steps of the house,** à deux pas de la maison; **it's only a s. to my house,** je n'ai que deux pas à faire d'ici chez moi; je suis, vous êtes, à deux pas de chez moi; **it's a good s.,** c'est un bon bout de chemin; il y a une bonne trotte jusque-là, d'ici là; **that's a great s. forward,** c'est déjà un grand pas de fait; **a s. towards one's goal,** un acheminement vers le but désiré; **do you hear a s.?** entendez-vous un pas? **with a rapid s.,** d'un pas rapide; **to tread in s.o.'s steps,** marcher sur les traces de qn. **2.** (*a*) pas, cadence *f*; *Mil: Mus:* **quick s.,** pas redoublé; pas accéléré, cadencé; **marching s.,** pas ordinaire; **to keep s., to be in s.,** marcher au pas; être au pas; tenir la cadence; **to fall into s.,** se mettre au pas; prendre le pas cadencé; **to fall into s. with s.o.,** emboîter le pas à, sur, qn; **I knew him by his s.,** (i) je l'ai reconnu à son allure; (ii) j'ai reconnu son pas; **to change s.,** changer de pas; **to break s.,** rompre le pas; **to fall out of s.,** (i) perdre le pas; (ii) *Danc:* sortir de cadence; **to be out of s.,** ne pas être au pas; marcher à contre-pas de qn; (*b*) *El:* **alternators in s.,** alternateurs accrochés, en phase, synchronisés; **alternators out of s.,** alternateurs hors de synchronisme, déphasés, décrochés; **to put alternators into s.,** accrocher les alternateurs; **to come, fall, into s.,** accrocher les oscillations; s'accrocher; se mettre en phase; atteindre le synchronisme; *W.Tel:* accrocher la longueur d'onde; **falling into s.,** accrochage *m*; **to fall out of s.,** tomber hors de phase; se décrocher; **to run in s.,** marcher en synchronisme; (*c*) **waltz s.,** pas de valse. **3.** (*a*) démarche *f*, mesure *f*; **a s. in the right direction,** un pas dans la bonne voie; **false s.,** fausse démarche; **ill-timed s.,** démarche inopportune; **to take a decisive, decided, s.,** sauter le pas; **to take a rash s.,** prendre une décision téméraire, commettre une imprudence; **if you take such a s.,** si vous agissez de la sorte; **the s. that we are about to take,** la mesure, la décision, que nous allons prendre; **to take the necessary steps,** faire, entreprendre, les démarches nécessaires; prendre toutes dispositions utiles; **what steps have been taken?** quelles mesures a-t-on adoptées? **to take steps to do sth.,** prendre des mesures pour faire qch.; aviser, se préparer, à faire qch.; **to take steps to meet a contingency,** pourvoir à une éventualité; **I shall take no steps until. . .,** je m'abstiendrai de toute démarche, je ne ferai rien, jusqu'à ce que . . .; **the first s. will be to . . .,** la première chose à faire, ce sera de . . .; (*b*) *F:* **to go up a s.,** avancer en grade. **4.** (*a*) marche *f*, degré *m*, montée *f*, pas (d'un escalier); échelon *m*, marche, barreau *m* (d'une échelle); marchepied *m* (d'un véhicule, d'une bicyclette); *A.Veh:* **drop s.,** marchepied pliant; abattant *m*; **cellar steps,** descente *f*; **top s. (of a stair),** marche palière; palière *f*; **the steps of the altar,** le marchepied de l'autel; **the steps of the throne,** les marches du trône; **stone steps,** escalier de pierre; **flight of steps,** (i) escalier; (ii) perron *m*; **landing steps (of a jetty),** échelle de débarquement; (*b*) gradin *m*, étage *m* (de cône-poulie); *Metall:* **s. grate,** grille *f* à gradins, à étages; (*c*) banquette *f* (de cale sèche); (*d*) *Carp:* **s. joint,** (i) assemblage *m*, joint *m*, à recouvrement; (ii) assemblage, entaille *f*, à mi-bois; (*e*) *Geol:* **rock s.,** ressaut *m*; *Mount:* **to cut steps,** tailler; **s. cutting,** taille *f.* **5. (pair, set, of) steps,** escabeau *m*, échelle double; **folding steps,** échelle brisée; *Av:* **steps,** passerelle *f.* **6.** (*a*) cran *m*; **steps of a key,** dents *f* d'une clef; *Mec.E:* **collar s.,** grain *m* annulaire (de crapaudine); bague *f* de fond; *Nau:* **s. of a mast,** collet *m* de pied de mât; (*b*) *N.Arch:* redan *m* (d'hydroglisseur); *Av:* retrait *m* (de flotteur d'hydravion). **7.** (*a*) *N.Arch:* emplanture *f* (qui reçoit le mât); (*b*) *Mec.E:* **s. (bearing),** palier *m* de pied (d'un arbre vertical); crapaudine *f*, bourdonnière *f.*

step[2], *v.* **(stepped** [stept])

I. *v.i.* (*a*) faire un pas, des pas; marcher pas à pas; marcher, aller; **to s. on s.o.'s foot,** marcher sur le pied de qn; **to s. short,** (i) faire un pas trop court; (ii) raccourcir le pas; (*of horse*) **to s. high, well,** stepper; **s. this way,** venez par ici; *esp. U.S: F:* **s. lively!** grouillez-vous! (*b*) **to s. back, forward,** faire un pas en arrière, en avant; se reculer, s'avancer; **to s. aside to let s.o. pass,** s'écarter pour laisser passer qn; **the car drew up and he stepped in, out,** la voiture s'est arrêtée et il y est monté, en est descendu; **s. in(side) for a moment,** entrez pour un moment; **s. over to my place,** venez chez moi; **I'll just s. across, over, to the grocer's,** je vais faire un saut jusque chez l'épicier; **to s. over a ditch,** franchir, enjamber, un fossé; **to s. out briskly,** allonger le pas; marcher avec entrain; **I haven't stepped outside all day,** je ne suis pas sorti toute la journée; **to s. up to s.o.,** s'approcher de qn; *F:* **to s. into a job,** trouver un emploi sans la moindre difficulté.

II. *v.tr.* **1.** (*a*) **to s. (off, out) a distance,** mesurer une distance au pas; compter les pas pour mesurer une distance; (*b*) *A:* **to s. a minuet,** danser un menuet; *F:* **to s. it with s.o.,** danser avec qn. **2.** disposer en échelons; échelonner; recouper (un mur, un parapet). **3.** *Nau:* dresser, arborer (un mât); mettre (un mât) dans son emplanture.

III. (*compound verbs*) (*s.a.* **I.** *v.i. for some adverbial uses*)

1. step down. (*a*) *v.tr. El:* **to s. down the current, the voltage,** réduire la tension; dévolter le courant; *Mec.E:* **to s. down the gear,** démultiplier la transmission; (*b*) *v.i.* démissionner.

2. step in, *v.i.* intervenir; s'interposer.

3. step off, *v.i. F:* **I'll soon tell him where he steps off,** je n'hésiterai pas à lui dire son fait, à le remettre à sa place.

4. step on, *v.i. F:* **to s. on the gas, to s. on it,** (i) *Aut:* appuyer sur, écraser, l'accélérateur, le champignon; (ii) se dépêcher, se grouiller; **to s. on the brakes,** donner un coup de frein brusque.

5. step out, *v.i.* (*a*) sortir (de la maison, etc.); (*b*) allonger, forcer, le pas; marcher rapidement, avec entrain.

6. step up, *v.tr.* (*a*) *El:* **to s. up the current,** survolter le courant; augmenter la tension du courant; (*b*) **to s. up production,** augmenter la production.

step-and-repeat [stepəndri'pi:t], *a.* **s.-a.-r. machine,** machine *f* à report photo(graphique).

step-back ['stepbæk], *attrib. El:* **s.-b. relay,** relais *m* de rappel.

stepbrother ['stepbrʌðər], *s.m.* (*a*) frère consanguin, utérin; demi-frère, *pl.* demi-frères; (*b*) fils né d'un mariage antérieur de son beau-père, de sa belle-mère.

stepchild, *pl.* **-children** ['steptʃaild, -tʃildrən], *s.* enfant *mf* d'un autre lit, né(e) d'un mariage antérieur; beau-fils, *pl.* beaux-fils; belle-fille, *pl.* belles-filles.

stepdancer ['stepdɑ:nsər], *s.* danseur, -euse, de danses de caractère.

stepdaughter ['stepdɔ:tər], *s.f.* belle-fille (née d'un lit antérieur), *pl.* belles-filles.
step-down ['stepdaun], *attrib. El:* **s.-d. transformer,** transformateur réducteur, transformateur abaisseur (de tension); *Elcs:* **s.-d. amplifier,** amplificateur *m* de seuil à anode négative.
stepfather ['stepfɑ:ðər], *s.m.* beau-père (second mari de la mère), *pl.* beaux-pères.
stepgranddaughter ['stepgrænd(d)ɔ:tər], *s.f.* belle-petite-fille, *pl.* belles-petites-filles.
stepgrandson ['stepgrændsʌn], *s.m.* beau-petit-fils, *pl.* beaux-petits-fils.
stephanian [ste'feiniən], *a. & s. Geol:* stéphanien (*m*).
stephanion [ste'feiniən], *s. Anthr:* stéphanion *m.*
stephanite ['stefənait], *s. Miner:* stéphanite *f.*
Stephen ['sti:vn], *Pr.n.m.* Étienne; *Hist:* **King S.,** Étienne de Blois, roi d'Angleterre.
step-in ['stepin], *a. & s.* (vêtement *m*) à enfiler.
stepladder ['steplædər], *s.* escabeau *m*; échelle *f* double.
stepmother ['stepmʌðər], *s.f.* belle-mère (seconde femme du père), *pl.* belles-mères; **Cinderella was ill-treated by her (wicked) s.,** Cendrillon a été maltraitée par sa marâtre.
steppe [step], *s. Geog:* steppe *f.*
stepped [stept], *a.* à gradins, en gradins, à étages; échelonné, en échelons; **s. gear(ing),** engrenage échelonné, en échelon; **s. grate,** grille *f* à gradins, à étages; *I.C.E:* **s. piston ring,** segment *m* à extrémités à recouvrement; *Arch:* **s. gable,** pignon *m* à redans.
stepper ['stepər], *s.* (*of horse*) stepper *m*, steppeur *m*; **clean s.,** cheval *m* au trot bien articulé; (*of horse*) **to be a good s.,** avoir de l'action, de l'allure; (*of horse, pers.*) **to be a high s.,** avoir de l'allure.
stepping ['stepiŋ], *s.* **1.** marche *f*, pas *mpl.* **2.** échelonnement *m*, étagement *m*; **s. down,** (i) *El:* dévoltage *m*, réduction *f* de tension; (ii) *Mec.E:* démultiplication *f* (de la transmission); **s. up,** (i) *El:* survoltage *m*; (ii) *Mec.E:* multiplication *f* (d'un engrenage); (iii) accélération *f* (de rythme de production, etc.); augmentation *f* (de production).
stepsister ['stepsistər], *s.f.* (*a*) sœur consanguine, utérine; demi-sœur, *pl.* demi-sœurs; (*b*) fille née d'un mariage antérieur de son beau-père, de sa belle-mère.
stepson ['stepsʌn], *s.m.* beau-fils (né d'un lit antérieur), *pl.* beaux-fils.
step-up ['stepʌp]. **1.** *attrib. El:* **s.-up transformer,** transformateur élévateur (de tension); survolteur *m*; *Elcs:* **s.-up ratio (of a signal),** accroissement *m* d'oscillation (d'un signal). **2.** *s.* multiplication *f* (d'un engrenage).
stercoraceous [stə:kə'reiʃəs], **stercoral** ['stə:kərəl], *a.* **1.** *Nat.Hist:* stercoraire. **2.** *Med:* stercoraire; stercoral, -aux; **s. fistula,** fistule stercorale, stercoraire.
Stercorariidae [stə:kərə'raiidi:], *s.pl. Orn:* stercorariidés *m.*
stercorary ['stə:kərəri], **stercoricolous** [stə:kə'rikələs], *a. Ent:* stercoraire, merdicole.
stercorite ['stə:kərait], *s. Miner:* stercorite *f.*
stercorvorous [stə:'kɔ:vərəs], *a.* merdivore, scatophage.
Sterculiaceae [stə:kjuli'eisii:], *s.pl. Bot:* sterculiacées *f.*
stere ['stiər], *s. Meas:* stère *m.*
stereo, *pl.* **-os** ['stiəriou, -ouz; 'ste-], *s. F:* **1.** = STEREOTYPE 1. **2.** = STEREOSCOPE. **3.** *Rec:* (*a*) *a.* stéréo *inv*; (*b*) *s.* (appareil *m*) stéréo *f.*
stereo- ['stiəriou, -iə; stiəri'ɔ; 'steriou, -iə; steri'ɔ], *comb.fm.* stéréo-.
stereoautograph [steriou'ɔ:təgræf], *s. Surv.* stéréoautographe *m.*
stereochemistry [steriou'kemistri, -'stiər-], *s.* stéréochimie *f.*
stereochromy [steriou'kroumi, stiər-], *s.* stéréochromie *f.*
stereocomparagraph, stereocomparator [stiəriou'kɔmpərəgræf, -'kɔmpəreitər; ster-], *s. Astr: Phot:* stéréocomparateur *m.*
stereogram ['stiərougræm, ster-], *s. Opt: Phot:* stéréogramme *m.*
stereograph ['stiəriougræf, ster-], *s.* **1.** stéréographe *m.* **2.** stéréogramme *m*, vue *f* stéréographique.
stereographic [stiəriou'græfik, ster-], *a.* stéréographique.
stereographically [stiəriou'græfik(ə)li, ster-], *adv.* stéréographiquement.
stereography [stiəri'ɔgrəfi, ster-], *s.* stéréographie *f.*
stereome ['stiərioum, ster-], *s. Bot:* stéréome *m.*
stereometer [stiəri'ɔmitə, ster-], *s. Ph:* stéréomètre *m.*
stereometric [stiəriou'metrik, ster-], *a.* stéréométrique.
stereometry [stiəri'ɔmitri, ster-], *s.* stéréométrie *f.*
stereophonic [stiəriə'founik, ster-], *a.* stéréophonique.
stereophony [stiəri'ɔfəni, ster-], *s.* stéréophonie *f.*
stereophotogrammetry [stiəarioufoutou'græmitri, ster-], *s. Surv:* stéréophotogrammétrie *f.*
stereophotography [stiərioufə'tɔgrəfi, ster-], *s.* stéréophotographie *f.*
stereoscope ['stiəriəskoup, 'ster-], *s. Opt:* stéréoscope *m.*
stereoscopic [stiəriou'skɔpik, ster-], *a.* stéréoscopique; **s. camera,** appareil *m* stéréoscopique; **s. telemeter,** stéréotélémètre *m.*
stereostatics [stiəriou'stætiks, ster-], *s.pl.* (*usu. with sg. const.*) stéréostatique *f.*
stereotaxis, stereotaxy [stiəriou'tæksis, -'tæksi; ster-], *s. Biol:* thigmotaxie *f.*
stereotomic [stiəriou'tɔmik, ster-], *a.* stéréotomique.
stereotomy [stiəri'ɔtəmi, ster-], *s.* stéréotomie *f.*
stereotriangulation [stiəriouttraiæŋgu'leiʃ(ə)n, ster-], *s.* aérotriangulation *f.*
stereotropism [stiəriou'trɔpizm, ster-], *s. Biol:* thigmotropisme *m.*
stereotype[1] ['stiəriətaip, ster-]. *Typ:* **1.** *s.* cliché *m.* **2.** *a.* stéréotypé, cliché; **s. printing,** stéréotypie *f*; **s. plate,** cliché, stéréotype *m.*
stereotype[2], *v.tr. Typ:* stéréotyper, clicher.
stereotyped ['stiəriətaipt, ster-], *a.* (*a*) *Typ:* stéréotypé; (*b*) **s. phrase,** expression stéréotypée; cliché *m.*
stereotyper, stereotypist [stiəriou'taiper, -'taipist; ster], *s.* stéréotypeur *m.*
stereotyping ['stiərioutaipiŋ, ster-], *s.* **1.** *Typ:* stéréotypage *m*, clichage *m.* **2.** stéréotypie *f.*
stereotypy ['stiərioutaipi, ster-], *s. Typ:* stéréotypie *f.*
steric ['stiərik], *a. Ch:* stérique.
sterile ['sterail], *a.* **1.** (terre, femelle, discussion) stérile; (plante) acarpe; **s. mare,** jument stérile, bréhaigne. **2.** *Bac:* stérile, aseptique.
sterility [ste'riliti], *s.* stérilité *f.*
sterilization [sterilai'zeiʃ(ə)n], *s.* **1.** *Surg:* stérilisation *f* (d'un homme, etc.). **2.** stérilisation (d'un pansement, des instruments de chirurgie, du lait, etc.).
sterilize ['sterilaiz], *v.tr.* **1.** *Surg:* stériliser (un homme, etc.). **2.** *Med: etc:* stériliser (un pansement, etc.); (*in flame*) flamber (une aiguille); **sterilized gauze,** gaze stérilisée; **sterilized instruments,** instruments stérilisés, stériles; **sterilized milk,** lait stérilisé.
sterilizer ['sterilaizər], *s.* stérilisateur *m*; étuve *f* à stérilisation; autoclave *m.*
sterilizing ['sterilaiziŋ], *s.* stérilisation *f.*
sterlet ['stə:lit], *s. Ich:* sterlet *m.*
sterling ['stə:liŋ]. **1.** *a.* (*a*) (monnaie, or, argent) de bon aloi, d'aloi; (*b*) de bon aloi, vrai, véritable, solide; **s. qualities,** qualités *f* solides; **man of s. worth,** homme de valeur. **2.** *s.* (livre *f*) sterling *m*; **s. area,** zone *f* sterling; **to pay in s.,** payer en livres sterling.
stern[1] [stə:n], *a.* sévère, rigide, dur; **s. look,** regard *m* sévère; **s. teacher,** professeur rigoureux, sévère; **s. countenance,** visage *m* austère; **the sterner sex,** le sexe fort.
stern[2], *s.* **1.** *Nau:* (*a*) arrière *m*; **flat, square, s.,** arrière carré; (*of ship*) **to sink s. foremost,** couler par l'arrière, par le cul; **to go out s. first,** appareiller en culant; **to steam s. to the sea,** prendre la mer par arrière, en marche arrière; **to anchor by the s.,** mouiller en croupière; **to be down by the s.,** être enfoncé par l'arrière; être acculé; **ship heavy by the s.,** navire à queue lourde; **s. sheets,** chambre *f* (d'une embarcation); **s. ladder,** échelle *f* de poupe; **s. frame,** arcasse *f*; **s. light,** feu *m* d'arrière, de poupe; ratière *f*; **s. board,** manœuvre *f* en culant; **to make a s. board,** (i) appareiller en culant; (ii) virer de bord en culant; **s. fast,** amarre *f* (de l')arrière; (*b*) arrière-bec *m* (d'un ponton). **2.** (*a*) *F:* (*of pers.*) postérieur *m*, derrière *m*; (*b*) *Ven:* queue *f* (d'un chien courant, d'un loup).
sternal ['stə:n(ə)l], *a. Anat:* sternal, -aux.
sternalgia [stə:'nældʒiə], *s. Med:* sternalgie *f.*
sternbergite ['stə:nbə:dʒait], *s. Miner:* sternbergite *f.*
sternly ['stə:nli], *adv.* sévèrement, rigoureusement, durement; **to look s. at s.o.,** faire les gros yeux à qn.
sternmost ['stə:nmoust, -məst], *a.* le plus à l'arrière ((i) à bord, (ii) de l'escadre).
sternness ['stə:nnis], *s.* sévérité *f*; austérité *f*; dureté *f.*
sternoclavicular [stə:noukla'vikjulər], *a. Anat:* sterno-claviculaire, *pl.* sterno-claviculaires.
sternocleidomastoid [stə:nouklaidou'mæstɔid], *a. & s. Anat:* sterno-cléido-mastoïdien (*m*), *pl.* sterno-cléido-mastoïdiens.
sternocostal [stə:nou'kɔstəl], *a. Anat:* sterno-costal, -aux.
sternohyoid [stə:nou'haiɔid], *a. & s. Anat:* sterno-hyoïdien (*m*), *pl.* sterno-hyoïdiens.
sternomastoid [stə:nou'mæstɔid], *a. & s.* = STERNOCLEIDOMASTOID.
Sternotherae [stə:nou'θeri:], *s.pl. Rept:* sternothères *m.*
sternothyroid [stə:nou'θairɔid], *a. & s. Anat:* sterno-thyroïdien (*m*), *pl.* sterno-thyroïdiens.
sternpost ['stə:npoust], *s. Nau:* étambot *m*; **outer s.,** étambot arrière; **inner s., false s.,** faux étambot, contre-étambot *m*; étambot avant.
sternson ['stə:ns(ə)n], *s. N.Arch:* marsouin *m* arrière.
sternum, *pl.* **-a, -ums** ['stə:nəm, -ə, -əmz], *s. Anat:* sternum *m.*
sternutation [stə:nju'teiʃ(ə)n], *s.* sternutation *f*, éternuement *m.*
sternutative, sternutatory [stə:'nju:tətiv, -'nju:tət(ə)ri], *a. & s.* sternutatoire (*m*).
sternway ['stə:nwei], *s. Nau:* marche *f* arrière; culée *f*, acculée *f*; **to make, gather, s.,** culer; aller de l'arrière.
steroid ['stiərɔid], *s. Bio-Ch:* stéroïde *m.*
sterol ['stiərɔl], *s. Bio-Ch:* stérol *m.*
stertor ['stə:tɔ:r], *s. Med:* stertor *m*; respiration stertoreuse.
stertorous ['stə:tərəs], *a. Med:* stertoreux, ronflant.
stet[1] [stet]. *Lt.imp. Typ:* bon; à maintenir.
stet[2], *v.tr.* (**stetted**) maintenir (un mot sur l'épreuve, etc.).
stethograph ['steθəgræf], *s. Med:* pneumographe *m.*
stethometer [ste'θɔmitər], *s. Med:* stéthomètre *m.*
stethoscope ['steθəskoup], *s. Med:* stéthoscope *m.*
stethoscopic [steθə'skɔpik], *a. Med:* stéthoscopique.
stethoscopy [ste'θɔskəpi], *s. Med:* stéthoscopie *f.*
stetson ['stets(ə)n], *s. Cost:* chapeau mou à larges bords; stetson *m.*
stevedore[1] ['sti:v(ə)dɔ:r], *s.* **1.** (*labourer*) docker *m*; arrimeur *m*, déchargeur *m*; **foreman s.,** chef arrimeur. **2.** entrepreneur *m* de chargement, de déchargement.
stevedore[2], *v.tr. Nau:* charger, décharger (un navire); arrimer la cargaison (d'un navire).
stew[1] [stju:], *s.* **1.** *A:* (*a*) maison *f* de bains; thermes *mpl*; (*b*) **stews,** lieu *m* de débauche; lupanar *m*; (*c*) *P:* putain *f.* **2.** (*a*) *Cu:* ragoût *m*; civet *m* (de chevreuil, etc.); **Irish s.,** ragoût de mouton à l'irlandaise; (*b*) *F:* trouble *m* (de qn); émoi *m*, bouleversement *m*; **to be in a s.,** être sur des charbons ardents; être sur le gril; être dans tous ses états; (*c*) *F: O:* **what a s.!** quelle chaleur ici! on étouffe ici! quelle étuve! **3.** *F: O:* (*pers.*) piocheur *m*, bûchard *m.*
stew[2]. **1.** *v.tr. Cu:* faire cuire (la viande) en ragoût, à l'étouffée, à la casserole; faire un ragoût de (qch.); **to s. a rabbit,** fricasser un lapin; **to s. fruit,** faire une compote de fruits; faire cuire des fruits en compote; **s. for an hour,** laisser mijoter pendant une heure. **2.** *v.i.* (*a*) *Cu:* (*of meat, etc.*) cuire à la casserole; mijoter; *F:* **to let s.o. s. in his own juice,** laisser qn cuire, mijoter, dans son jus; laisser mariner qn; (*b*) *F: O:* (*of pers.*) étouffer; manquer d'air; (*c*) *F: A:* (*of pers.*) piocher, bûcher.
stew[3], *s.* **1.** vivier *m.* **2.** huîtrière *f*; parc *m* à huîtres.
steward ['stjuəd], *s.* **1.** économe *m*, régisseur *m*, intendant *m*, administrateur *m* (d'une propriété); homme *m* d'affaires; *B:* **the unjust s.,** l'économe infidèle. **2.** (*a*) économe (d'un collège); maître *m* d'hôtel (d'un cercle, etc.); (*b*) *Nau:* distributeur *m*; commis *m*, agent *m*, aux vivres; **steward's mate,** cambusier *m*; **steward's room,** cambuse *f*; (*c*) *Nau:* garçon *m* (de bord, de cabine); steward *m*; **deck s.,** garçon de pont; **chief s.,** maître d'hôtel; *Navy:* **officers' s.,** maître d'hôtel. **3.** commissaire *m* (d'une réunion sportive, d'un bal); garçon de la fête. **4.** *Ind:* **shop s.,** délégué *m* d'atelier, d'usine, du personnel.
stewardess [stjuə'des], *s.f. Nau:* femme de chambre (de bord); stewardess; *Av:* **air s.,** hôtesse de l'air.
stewardship ['stjuədʃip], *s.* économat *m*, intendance *f*; charge *f* de régisseur, d'intendant; *F:* **to give an account of one's s.,** rendre compte de son administration, de sa gestion.
stewed [stju:d], *a.* **1.** *Cu:* (*a*) en ragoût, en compote; **s. mutton, s. beef,** ragoût de mouton, de bœuf; bœuf *m* (à la) mode; bœuf en daube, à la daube; **s. fruit,** compote *f* de fruits, fruits *mpl* en compote; (*b*) **s. tea,** thé trop infusé. **2.** *F:* ivre; qui a sa cuite.
stewing ['stju:iŋ], *s.* cuisson *f* à la casserole; **s. beef,** bœuf *m* pour ragoût; **s. pears,** poires *f* à cuire; **s. pan** = STEWPAN.
stewpan ['stju:pæn], *s.* (grande) casserole.
stewpot ['stju:pɔt], *s.* braisière *f*, daubière *f*, cocotte *f*, fait-tout *m inv.*
sthenic ['sθenik], *a. Med:* sthénique.
stibine ['stibain], *s.* **1.** *Miner:* antimoniure *m* d'hydrogène. **2.** *Ch:* stibine *f.*
stibium ['stibiəm], *s.* **1.** antimoine *m.* **2.** stibine *f.*
stibnite ['stibnait], *s. Miner:* stibine *f.*
stichomythia [stikou'miθiə], *s. Gr. Pros:* stichomythie *f.*
stick[1] [stik], *s.* **1.** (*a*) bâton *m*; **to cut a s. from the hedge,** se couper un bâton, une canne, dans la haie; *F: O:* **to cut one's s.,** décamper, filer, déguerpir, se sauver; **in a**

cleft s., dans une impasse; **you're giving him a s. to beat you with,** vous lui donnez des verges pour vous fouetter; **to get the s.** recevoir des coups de bâton, être sévèrement grondé; **give it some s.!** frappez fort! allez-y! **to take a lot of s.**, être pilonné; **the big s.**, la manière forte; (la politique de) la force; *F:* la trique; **to use big s. methods,** avoir recours à la trique; *Rac:* **horse that is good over the sticks,** cheval bon dans les courses d'obstacles; *Hort:* **pea sticks,** rames *f*; **hop sticks, vine sticks,** échalas *m*; (*b*) (**walking**) **s.**, canne *f*; **loaded s.**, canne plombée; casse-tête *m inv*; (*c*) manche *m* (à balai); canne, manche (de parapluie); verge *f*, baguette *f* (de fusée volante); *F:* levier *m* (de changement de vitesse); baguette (de chef d'orchestre); **s. of a violin bow,** fût *m*, baguette, d'archet; **rack(ing) s.**, tordoir *m*, garrot *m*; *Av:* **controls s.**, *F:* **(joy)stick,** manche à balai; **s. full back, back on the s.**, manche au ventre; **to ease the s.**, rendre la main; **to ease the s. back,** tirer sur le manche; (*d*) *Sp:* (**hockey, etc.**) **s.**, crosse *f*; **s. fault, sticks,** stick *m*; **to give sticks,** couper; donner des crosses; (*e*) morceau *m* de bois; **to gather sticks,** ramasser du bois sec, du petit bois, (aller) faire du bois; **cocktail, cherry, s.**, bâtonnet *m* (pour cerise de cocktail); **swizzle s.**, agitateur *m* (pour cocktails, etc.); *F:* **not a s. was saved,** on n'a pas sauvé une allumette; **not a s. was left standing,** tout était rasé; **without a s. of furniture,** sans un meuble; **my few sticks of furniture,** mes quelques meubles; **to have one's own sticks,** être dans ses meubles; *A:* **to beat s.o. all to sticks,** battre qn à plate couture; *F:* **the sticks,** (i) *Nau:* la mâture; (ii) *Fb:* le but; (iii) *Cr:* le guichet; *Ent:* **s. insect,** phasme *m*, insecte-brindille *m*; **s. figure,** bonhomme dessiné, personnage composé de bâtonnets; (*f*) *Min:* **s. of timber,** poteau *m*, étai *m*, de mine; (*g*) *Typ:* (**setting, composing**) **s.**, composteur *m*; (*h*) *F:* **the sticks,** la brousse; **he lives out in the sticks,** il habite un trou perdu, il vit dans la brousse. **2.** *F: O:* (*of pers.*) (*a*) **poor s.**, pauvre diable *m*; **rum, queer, s.**, drôle de type, drôle de paroissien, drôle d'oiseau; **old s.**, vieille perruque; (*b*) personne *f* sans entrain, sans talent; acteur *m* au jeu raide; *P:* godiche *mf*; bûche *f*, mazette *f*. **3.** bâton (de sucre d'orge, de cire à cacheter, etc.); barre *f* (de chocolat); bâton, canon *m* (de soufre); crayon *m* (de potasse); *El:* baguette *f* (de charbon), bâtonnet *m* (de dynamite); **s. sulphur,** soufre *m* en canons, en bâtons; **s. potash,** potasse *f* en crayons. **4.** *Cu:* **s. of celery,** branche *f* de céleri; **s. of rhubarb,** tige *f* de rhubarbe; **s. of asparagus,** asperge *f*. **5.** *Mil: Av:* **s. of bombs,** chapelet *m* de bombes; **s. (of parachutists),** stick *m* (de parachutistes).

stick[2], *v.* (*p.t.* & *p.p.* **stuck** [stʌk])

I. *v.tr.* **1.** (*a*) piquer, enfoncer (**sth. into sth.**, qch. dans qch.); **to s. a dagger into s.o.**, percer qn d'un coup de poignard; **to s. a pin into sth.**, ficher une épingle dans qch.; **to s. a stake in the ground,** ficher un pieu en terre; **he stuck the spade into the ground,** il a planté la bêche dans le sol; **to s. a pin through sth.**, passer une épingle à travers qch.; **he stuck a needle through my ear,** il m'a percé l'oreille avec une aiguille; **cushion stuck full of pins,** pelote pleine d'épingles; **cake stuck (over) with almonds,** gâteau garni d'amandes; **to get stuck in,** se mettre (i) à travailler, (ii) à manger; **get stuck in!** mets-y toi! (*b*) *P:* **to s. s.o.**, poignarder qn; *P:* **to s. s.o. with a bayonet,** enfoncer, planter, une baïonnette dans le corps de qn; **to s. pigs,** (i) (*of butcher*) égorger, saigner, les porcs; (ii) *Ven:* chasser le sanglier à l'épieu; (*c*) planter, fixer (**sth. on a spike,** qch. sur une pointe); **traitors' heads were stuck on the city gates,** on plantait, on fichait, les têtes des traîtres aux portes de la ville. **2.** *F:* (*meaning little more than* **put, place**) **to s. a rose in one's buttonhole,** mettre une rose à sa boutonnière; **she stuck a flower in her belt,** elle piqua, passa, une fleur dans sa ceinture; **to s. a pen behind one's ear,** mettre, ficher, une plume derrière son oreille; **to s. one's hat on one's head,** mettre, planter, *F:* camper, son chapeau sur sa tête; **to s. a candle in a bottle,** fixer, ficher, une bougie dans une bouteille; **s. it in your pocket,** fourrez-le dans votre poche; **don't s. your hands in your pockets!** ne mets pas les mains dans tes poches! **s. it in the corner, on the table,** collez ça dans le coin, mettez ça sur la table; **s. in a few commas,** insérez quelques virgules; *P:* **as for your generous offer, you can s. it,** quant à ton offre généreuse, moi je me la mets quelque part. **3.** coller, attacher; **to s. sth. on (to) sth.**, coller qch. à, sur, qch.; **to s. photographs in an album,** fixer, coller, des photographies dans un album; **to s. two sheets of paper together,** attacher deux feuilles ensemble (avec de la colle); **to s. sth. back together,** recoller qch., réparer qch. à la colle; **to s. a stamp on a letter,** timbrer une lettre; *Med:* **to s. together the edges of a wound,** conglutiner les bords d'une plaie; **trunk stuck all over with labels,** malle bardée d'étiquettes. **4.** *F:* supporter, endurer, souffrir (qn, qch.); **to s. it,** tenir le coup; tenir; **how long can you s. it?** combien de temps pouvez-vous durer? **I can't s. it any longer,** je n'y tiens plus; **I can't s. him,** je ne peux pas le sentir; je ne peux pas le voir en peinture. **5.** *U.S: P:* refaire, voler, rouler (qn). **6.** *Hort:* ramer (des pois, etc.); mettre des tuteurs à (des plantes).

II. *v.i.* **1.** se piquer, s'enfoncer, se ficher, se planter; **the arrows s. in the target,** les flèches se piquent, se plantent, se fixent, dans la cible; **sewing left with a needle sticking in it,** ouvrage laissé avec une aiguille piquée dedans; **the buckle sticks into me,** la boucle me pique, me gêne. **2.** (*a*) (se) coller, s'attacher, tenir, adhérer, s'attraper (**to, à**); **the envelope won't s.**, impossible de coller cette enveloppe; **the stamp won't s.**, le timbre ne tient pas; **his shirt stuck to his back,** il avait la chemise collée au dos; *Cu:* **The stew has stuck (to the pan),** le ragoût a attaché; **the name stuck (to him),** ce nom lui est resté; **the slur has stuck to his name,** sa réputation en est restée souillée; **money sticks to his fingers,** c'est un accrocheur d'argent, il a les doigts crochus, il a de la poix, de la glu, aux mains; **whatever he touches, some of it sticks to his fingers,** il tond sur tout; **it sticks like pitch,** cela colle comme poix; **to s. by, to, a friend,** ne pas abandonner un ami; **he has stuck to me,** il m'est resté fidèle; **friends should s. together,** les amis doivent se serrer les coudes, doivent rester unis; **to s. like a limpet, like a leech, like glue, like a burr (to s.o.),** se cramponner (à qn); cramponner (qn); s'accrocher (à qn); être crampon *inv.*; **s. tight!** n'abandonnez pas les étriers! cramponnez-vous! **to s. to one's post,** rester à son poste; **to s. to one's duty,** s'attacher à remplir son devoir; **to s. to one's promise,** tenir sa promesse; **s. to it!** persévérez! ne lâchez pas! **to s. to one's purpose,** rester fidèle à son dessein; **to s. to a resolve,** persévérer dans une résolution; *F:* **to s. to one's guns, to one's opinions,** ne pas en démordre; défendre mordicus son opinion; **to s. to an opinion,** maintenir une opinion, ne pas démordre d'une opinion; **to s. to (the) facts,** s'en tenir, s'attacher, aux faits; **to s. to old friendships,** s'en tenir à des amitiés de longue date; **to s. to the point,** ne pas s'écarter de la question; **to s. to the text,** serrer le texte de près; **he did not s. to the programme,** il s'est écarté du programme; **I s. to what I said,** j'en suis pour ce que j'ai dit; **he sticks to his point,** il ne sort pas de là, il n'en sort pas; **he sticks to it,** il (y) persiste, il s'y tient; il ne veut pas en démordre; **to stick with,** (i) se contenter de; (ii) rester fidèle à; (*b*) **to s. to sth.**, garder qch. pour soi; **s. to what you've got!** gardez vos biens! ne lâchez pas ce que vous avez; (*c*) *F:* rester; (*of newspaper, magazine*) bouillonner, rester invendu; **here I am and here I s.**, j'y suis, j'y reste; **are you going to s. in all day?** est-ce que vous allez rester enfermé toute la journée? **he sticks to his room,** il ne sort pas de sa chambre; **he stuck around the house all day,** il a traîné dans la maison toute la journée; (*d*) *F:* **I'm stuck with it, him,** je ne peux pas m'en débarrasser; je l'ai sur le dos; **we're stuck with it,** il faut s'y résigner; (*e*) *F: O:* **he's stuck on her,** il est entiché d'elle. **3.** (*a*) **to s., to be stuck, to become stuck,** être pris, être engagé; (*in mud, etc.*) s'embourber, être embourbé, s'ensabler, s'enliser; **car stuck in the mud,** voiture enlisée dans la boue; **to get stuck in a bog,** s'embourber dans un marécage; *F:* **he's an old s.-in-the-mud,** c'est un vieux plumeau; il retarde sur son siècle; c'est un vieux routinier; **old S.-in-the-Mud,** Machin *m*, Chose *m*; (*of boat*) **to s. fast,** s'enliser (sur un banc de sable, dans la vase); **we got stuck at Aix,** (i) on n'a pas pu aller plus loin qu'Aix; (ii) nous nous sommes trouvés en panne à Aix; **here I am stuck in hospital for six weeks,** me voilà cloué à l'hôpital pour six semaines; **I'm stuck,** je n'avance plus; je suis en panne; **the book's finished but I'm stuck for a title,** le livre est fini mais je ne trouve pas de titre; **stuck for money,** en panne d'argent; **to s., to be stuck (in a speech),** *F:* rester en carafe, en panne; (*b*) (*to be caught, jammed*) être pris, être engagé, rester pris, rester engagé, s'enfoncer, s'empêtrer; (*of machine parts*) (se) coincer, gommer; *Aut:* (*of valve, cut-out*) rester collé; **the ball got stuck on the roof,** la balle s'est logée sur le toit; **the words stuck in his throat,** les mots lui restèrent dans la gorge; **it sticks in my throat,** je ne peux pas avaler ça, digérer ça; **the lift has stuck,** l'ascenseur est coincé, en panne; **piston that sticks,** piston *m* qui se cale, qui ne coule pas; **the pointer sticks,** l'aiguille (du manomètre, etc.) reste coincée, collée; *Aut:* **the cut-out was stuck,** le conjoncteur était collé.

III. (*compound verbs*) **1. stick around,** *v.i., F:* attendre; **s. a.! I'll be back in ten minutes,** bouge pas! je reviens dans dix minutes; **he always sticks around,** lui, c'est la colle! ce qu'il est collant! quel pot de colle!

2. stick at, *v.tr.* (*a*) **to s. at a difficulty,** s'arrêter devant, achopper contre, une difficulté; *F:* rester en panne devant une difficulté; **to s. at doing sth.**, se faire scrupule de faire qch.; *F:* rechigner à faire qch.; **to s. at nothing,** n'être retenu par rien, ne pas connaître de scrupules, ne reculer devant rien; **he sticks at nothing,** il n'hésite devant rien, rien ne l'arrête, il ne s'embarrasse d'aucun scrupule, il n'a pas froid aux yeux; **he would s. at nothing to win,** il est capable de tout, rien ne lui coûtera, pour gagner; (*b*) **to s. at a task for six hours,** s'acharner à une tâche pendant six heures; travailler à qch. pendant six heures d'arrache-pied.

3. stick down, *v.tr. F:* (*a*) **s. it down anywhere,** mettez-le, collez-le, fichez-le, n'importe où; **he stuck it (down) on the table,** il le mit, le posa, sur la table; **to s. sth. down in a notebook,** inscrire qch. sur un carnet; **s. my name down for a fiver,** inscrivez-moi pour £5; (*b*) **to s. down an envelope,** fermer, coller, une enveloppe.

4. stick on. (*a*) *v.tr.* (i) coller, fixer (un timbre, etc.); (ii) *F:* **to s. it on,** exagérer; charrier dans les bégonias; **to s. it on (the bill),** saler la note; (*b*) *v.i.* (*prep. use*) **can you s. on a horse?** pouvez-vous tenir à cheval? (*c*) *v.i.* (*adv. use*) rester collé; adhérer.

5. stick out. (*a*) *v.tr.* (i) faire dépasser (qch.); sortir (qch.); **to s. out one's tongue,** tirer la langue; **to s. out one's chest, one's figure,** bomber la poitrine; cambrer la taille; **he stuck his head out (of the window),** il a passé la tête en dehors; *F:* **to s. one's neck out,** prendre des risques; **I stuck my neck out,** je l'ai cherché; je me suis avancé trop loin; **it sticks out a mile,** c'est clair comme le jour; (ii) *F:* **to s. it out,** tenir jusqu'au bout; (*b*) *v.i.* (i) faire saillie, ressortir; **to s. out (beyond sth.),** dépasser (qch.); (ii) **his ears s. out,** il a les oreilles décollées; **her teeth s. out,** elle a les dents saillantes; **his handkerchief stuck out of his pocket,** son mouchoir dépassait de sa poche; (iii) *F:* ne pas céder; se montrer intraitable; persister; tenir bon; **to s. out for sth.**, s'obstiner à demander qch.; **I offered him eight pounds but he stuck out for ten,** je lui ai offert huit livres, mais il a continué à en exiger dix.

6. stick up. (*a*) *v.tr.* (i) *F:* dresser (une cible, etc.); *P:* **s. 'em up!** haut les mains! (ii) *U.S: P:* **to s. up a bank,** attaquer une banque à main armée; (iii) **to s. up a bill, a notice,** *F:* **a painting,** afficher un avis, pendre un tableau; (iv) *P: A:* **to s. s.o. up,** démonter qn; réduire qn à quia; (*b*) *v.i.* (i) se dresser; se tenir droit; se tenir debout; **his hair sticks straight up,** il a les cheveux récalcitrants; **the end keeps sticking up,** le bout persiste à se relever; (ii) *F:* **to s. up for s.o.**, prendre la défense de qn; prendre fait et cause pour qn.

sticker ['stikər], *s.* **1.** tueur *m* (de porcs). **2.** (*a*) couteau *m* de boucher; (*b*) couteau de chasse; (*c*) *P: A:* couteau; (*d*) *Fish:* gaffe *f*; harpon *m*. **3.** colleur, -euse (d'affiches, etc.). **4.** *F:* adhérent *m* (**to, à**); partisan (**to, de**). **5.** (*a*) *F:* **sticker** (*A:* **in**), rude travailleur; (*b*) *Cr:* batteur prudent, qui ne risque rien, qu'on ne peut pas déloger du guichet. **6.** *F:* (*pers.*) crampon *m*; personne collante. **7.** *Sch: etc: F: O:* colle *f*. **8.** (*a*) *U.S: F:* affiche *f*; placard électoral; (*b*) étiquette gommée.

stickiness ['stikinis], *s.* viscosité *f*; nature gluante (d'un produit); adhésivité *f*; ténacité *f* (de la poix, etc.).

sticking[1] ['stikiŋ], *a.* collant, adhésif.

sticking[2], *s.* **1.** adhérence *f*, adhésion *f* (**to, à**); collage *m*; collement *m* (de deux choses). **2.** arrêt *m*, coincement *m*; *Mch:* blocage *m* (d'une soupape); *I.C.E:* gommage *m*, calage *m* (du piston); grippage *m* (du moteur); **s. point,** point *m* d'arrêt; point de refus (d'une vis); **to screw one's courage to the s. point,** rassembler tout son courage; s'armer de résolution.

stickjaw ['stikdʒɔː], *s. P:* bonbons collants; caramels *mpl.*

stickleback ['stiklbæk], *s. Ich:* épinoche *f*, cordonnier *m*; **fifteen-spined s.**, épinoche de mer.

stickler ['stiklər], *s.* rigoriste *mf* (**for sth.**, au sujet de qch., à l'égard de qch.); **to be a s. for etiquette,** être à cheval sur l'étiquette; être très cérémonieux; **to be a s. over trifles,** être tatillon.

stick-on ['stikɔn], *a.* **s.-on label,** étiquette adhésive; *Bootm:* **s.-on soles,** semelles autocollantes.

stickpin ['stikpin], *s. N.Am:* (*a*) épingle droite, simple; (*b*) épingle de cravate.

stick-up ['stikʌp], *s. esp. U.S: F:* attaque *f* à main armée.

stickwork ['stikwəːk], *s. Sp:* maniement *m* de la crosse, de la batte.

sticky[1] ['stiki], *a. Bot:* (*of plant*) ligneux.

sticky[2], *a.* **1.** collant, gluant, visqueux, adhérent, adhésif, prenant; **s. road,** chemin pâteux; **s. valve,** soupape *f* qui a tendance à coller; **to make one's hands s.**, s'engluer, s'empâter les mains; **it makes one's fingers s.**, cela vous glue les mains; *F:* **to have s. fingers (in money matters),**

avoir de la poix aux mains; **s. weather,** temps mou, lourd; *Cr:* **s. wicket,** terrain *m* (de guichet) qui ne rend pas; *F:* **to be on a s. wicket,** être dans une situation difficile. **2.** *F:* (*a*) peu accommodant; difficile, désagréable; **he's very s. about these things,** il est peu accommodant, il fait le difficile, sur ces choses; **the bank was very s. about an overdraft,** la banque s'est montrée très raide, a fait des histoires, pour consentir un découvert; (*b*) **I had a s. ten minutes,** j'ai passé un mauvais quart d'heure; **he will come to a s. end,** il finira mal; (*c*) (problème) difficile, troublant.

stickybeak ['stikibi:k], *s. Austr: F:* fouineur, -euse, fouinard, -arde.

stiff [stif], *a.* & *s.*

I. *a.* **1.** (*a*) raide, rigide, dur, inflexible; **s. cardboard,** carton *m* raide; **s. shirt front,** plastron empesé; **book bound in s. cover,** livre relié en carton; *Phot:* **s. film,** film *m* rigide; **s. brush,** brosse dure, rude; *Nau:* **s. rope,** filin engourdi; **dress s. with embroidery,** robe raidie par la broderie; *F:* **the place is s. with them,** il y en a partout; **the town is s. with tourists,** cette ville grouille, est bondée, de touristes; (*of rubber, etc.*) **to get s.,** devenir raide; se raidir; (*b*) **s. joint,** articulation ankylosée; (*of joint*) **to grow s.,** s'ankyloser; **to have a s. leg,** avoir la jambe raide, percluse; **s. neck,** torticolis *m*; **s. necked,** obstiné, entêté, intraitable; *B:* au cou raide; **s.-n. opposition,** opposition *f* intraitable; **to be quite s.,** (i) (*with sitting still*) être engourdi, avoir les jambes engourdies; (ii) (*after exercise*) être tout courbaturé; (*of horse*) **s. shoulders,** épaules froides; *F:* (*of pers.*) **s. as a poker,** raide, droit, comme un piquet, comme un manche à balai; **the body was already s.,** le cadavre était déjà raide; *P:* **a s. 'un,** un cadavre; *P:* un macchabée; *F:* **exams scare me s.,** j'ai une peur bleue des examens; (*c*) (*of pers., bearing, manners*) raide, contraint, guindé, empesé, compassé; **s. manners,** manières contraintes, apprêtées; **s. bow,** salut contraint, froid; **he is very s.,** il est d'un abord difficile; *Lit:* **s. style,** style guindé, tendu, empesé; **s. handwriting,** écriture *f* raide; (*d*) (*of pers.*) raide, inflexible, obstiné; **to offer a s. resistance,** (*of pers.*) résister opiniâtrement; (*of thg*) tenir ferme; *Nau:* **s. ship,** navire très stable, navire fort de côté; **boat s. in a seaway,** bateau dur à la mer; (*e*) *Com: Fin:* (*of market, commodity*) ferme, raffermi, tendu. **2.** (*a*) (*of door-handle, hinge, etc.*) qui fonctionne mal; **the handle is s.,** le bouton est dur; (*b*) (*of paste, batter*) épais, *f.* épaisse; ferme; (*of lubricant*) consistant; (*of soil*) tenace; **s. clay, s. soil,** argile *f,* sol *m,* tenace; sol glaiseux; (*c*) *Nau:* **s. wind,** forte brise, brise carabinée. **3.** (*a*) raide, pénible; **s. climb,** montée *f* rude, pénible, raide; **s. examination,** examen *m* difficile; **s. battle,** dure bataille; rude combat *m*; **s. piece of work,** rude besogne; grosse besogne; besogne ardue; **the book is very s. reading,** ce livre fait appel à toutes les facultés du lecteur, est dur à lire; **I had a s. job to get it,** j'ai eu fort à faire pour l'obtenir; (*b*) *F:* **s. price,** prix exagéré; prix salé, poivré; **that's a s. price,** c'est bien payé; **s. bill,** note salée; **s. sentence,** peine salée; **he tells some s. yarns,** il en raconte de raides; *F:* **pour me out a s. one, something s., a s. drink,** versez-moi quelque chose de fort, de raide, de bien tassé.

II. *s. P:* **1.** lettre *f* de change, billet *m* à ordre. **2.** cadavre *m*; macchabée *m*; *Med:* **to carve a s.,** faire une dissection. **3. big s.,** grand nigaud; grand bêta.

stiffen ['stif(ə)n], *v.*

I. *v.tr.* **1.** (*a*) raidir, renforcer (une plaque, un mur, une poutre, etc.); donner plus de rigidité, de raideur, à (qch.); *Laund:* **to s. a shirt front,** empeser un plastron; *Tex:* **to s. cloth,** bougraner (la toile, etc.); donner de l'empois à un tissu; **stiffened with dressing,** apprêté; *Dressm:* **stiffened bodice,** corsage baleiné; *Aut:* **to s. the suspension,** donner plus de raideur à la suspension; durcir la suspension; (*b*) **age has stiffened his joints,** l'âge lui a noué les membres; (*c*) raidir, rendre obstiné (qn); (*d*) *Nau:* **to s. a ship,** lester un navire; (*e*) *Mil:* **to s. a battalion,** renforcer un bataillon avec des éléments aguerris. **2.** (*a*) rendre ferme, donner de la consistance à (une pâte); lier (une sauce); (*b*) **to s. a drink,** corser une boisson. **3.** rendre (un examen) plus difficile, plus dur.

II. *v.i.* **1.** (*a*) (se) raidir, devenir raide; **their arms s. to the oars,** leurs bras se raidissent sur les rames; **the body had stiffened,** le cadavre avait raidi, était déjà raide; (*b*) (*of pers.*) se raidir; se guinder; **opposition (to the scheme) is stiffening,** l'opposition se montre de plus en plus intransigeante; (*c*) *Fin:* (*of rates*) se tendre. **2.** (*a*) (*of paste, etc.*) devenir ferme; prendre de la consistance; (*b*) *Nau:* (*of wind*) fraîchir. **3.** (*of examination*) devenir plus difficile, plus dur.

stiffener ['stifnər], *s.* **1.** (pièce *f* de) renfort *m*; entretoise *f.* **2.** *F:* verre *m* d'eau-de-vie; verre qui ravigote; remontant *m.*

stiffening ['stif(ə)niŋ], *s.* **1.** raidissement *m,* renforcement *m,* consolidation *f* (de qch.); **s. of enemy resistance,** durcissement *m* de la résistance ennemie; **s. of the joints,** ankylose *f*; *Aut:* **s. of the suspension,** durcissement *m* de la suspension; *Tex:* **s. of fabrics,** apprêt *m* des étoffes; *Mec.E: etc:* **s. piece, stiffening plate,** plaque *f,* tôle *f,* de renfort; **s. girder,** poutre *f* de renfort; **s. rib,** nervure *f* de renforcement, de consolidation; *Bootm:* **s. tip,** pièce *f* de renfort. **2.** (*a*) empois *m*; (*for cloth*) cati *m*; (*b*) *Tail:* entoilage *m* (du col d'un habit); *Bootm:* contrefort *m* (de soulier); (*c*) *Carp:* liernes *fpl,* étrésillons *mpl,* entretoises *fpl*; (*d*) *Nau:* lest *m* de stabilité (des navires à voiles).

stiffish ['stifiʃ], *a.* **1.** assez raide; plutôt raide. **2. s. examination paper,** composition *f* assez difficile.

stiffly ['stifli], *adv.* **1.** raidement, avec raideur; *Equit:* (*of horse*) **to trot s.,** trotter des épaules. **2.** d'un air guindé. **3.** (résister, etc.) obstinément. **4.** sévèrement.

stiffness ['stifnis], *s.* **1.** (*a*) raideur *f,* rigidité *f* (d'une poutre, des membres, etc.); dureté *f* (d'un ressort, etc.); **s. of the legs,** (*after exercise*) courbatures *f* dans les jambes, (*after sitting*) engourdissement *m*; **that will take the s. out of your legs,** cela vous dégourdiva les jambes; (*b*) **s. of manner,** raideur, contrainte *f,* compassement *m*; air guindé, apprêté; (*c*) obstination *f,* opiniâtreté *f*; (*d*) fermeté *f,* tension *f* (du marché). **2.** fermeté, consistance *f* (d'une pâte); ténacité *f* (du sol). **3.** (*a*) raideur (d'une pente); (*b*) difficulté *f* (d'un examen).

stifle[1] [staifl]. **1.** *v.tr.* (*a*) étouffer, suffoquer (qn); **to be stifled by the smoke,** être asphyxié par la fumée; **to feel as though one is being stifled, to feel stifled,** éprouver une sensation d'étouffement; **to s. a revolt at birth,** étouffer une révolte dans son germe; (*b*) étouffer (un son, les cris de qn, etc.); **to s. a scandal,** étouffer, cacher, étrangler, un scandale; (*c*) réprimer (une émotion, un éternuement, un juron, etc.); **to s. a cry,** retenir un cri; **to s. one's laughter,** pouffer dans son mouchoir; **to s. one's grief,** faire taire sa douleur; **to s. a yawn,** étouffer un bâillement. **2.** *v.i.* suffoquer, étouffer; se sentir près d'étouffer.

stifle[2], *s.* **1. s. (joint),** grasset *m*; **s. bone,** os *m* du grasset. **2.** *Vet:* affection *f* du grasset; vessigon *m* du grasset.

stifled[1] ['staifld], *a.* (cri, etc.) étouffé; **with a s. voice,** d'une voix éteinte.

stifled[2], *a. Vet:* qui a une affection du grasset.

stifling[1] ['staifliŋ], *a.* **1.** étouffant, suffocant; **it is s. here!** on étouffe ici! **2.** (sensation *f*) d'étouffement.

stifling[2], **stiflingly** ['staifliŋli], *adv.* **it was s. hot,** on étouffait de chaleur.

stigma, *pl.* **-as, -ata** ['stigmə, -əz, 'stigmətə, stig'mɑ:tə], *s.* **1.** (*pl. usu.* **stigmas**) (*a*) *A:* stigmate *m* (marque d'un esclave, etc.); flétrissure *f* (au fer rouge); (*b*) stigmate, tache *f*; flétrissure (morale); **branded with the s. of illegitimacy,** entaché de bâtardise; **there is no longer any s. attached to being out of work,** il n'y a plus de honte à être, il n'est plus infamant d'être, sans travail. **2.** (*pl.* **stigmata**) (*a*) *Nat.Hist:* stigmate (d'un insecte, etc.); (*b*) *Med:* stigmate (de l'hystérie); (*c*) *pl. Rel.H:* stigmates (d'un saint). **3.** *Bot:* (*pl.* **stigmas**) stigmate (du pistil).

stigmatic [stig'mætik]. **1.** *a.* (*a*) *Opt:* (objectif *m*) stigmatique, anastigmate, anastigmatique; (*b*) *Bot:* stigmatique. **2.** *a.* & *s. Rel.Hist:* stigmatisé, -ée.

stigmatism ['stigmətizm], *s. Opt:* anastigmatisme *m.*

stigmatist ['stigmətist], *s. Rel.Hist:* stigmatisé, -ée.

stigmatization [stigmətai'zeiʃ(ə)n], *s.* **1.** *Med: etc:* stigmatisation *f.* **2.** stigmatisation, flétrissure *f.*

stigmatize ['stigmətaiz], *v.tr.* **1.** marquer de stigmates. **2.** (*a*) stigmatiser, flétrir (qn); **stigmatized as a coward, as illegitimate,** marqué d'infamie comme lâche; entaché de bâtardise; (*b*) qualifier (**s.o. as sth.,** qn de qch.).

stigmatose ['stigmətous], *a.* **1.** *Bot:* stigmatophore. **2.** (*of pers.*) stigmatisé; affligé de stigmates.

stigmula ['stigmjulə], *s. Bot:* stigmule *m.*

stilb [stilb], *s. Ph:* stilb *m.*

stilbene ['stilbi:n], *s. Ch:* stilbène *m.*

stilbite ['stilbait], *s. Miner:* stilbite *f.*

stilbœstrol [stil'bi:strəl], *s. Bio-Ch:* stilbœstrol *m.*

stile[1] [stail], *s.* (*a*) échalier *m,* échalis *m*; (*b*) tourniquet *m,* moulinet *m.*

stile[2], *s.* montant *m* (de porte, etc.).

stiletto, *pl.* **-os, -oes** [sti'letou, -ouz], *s.* **1.** (*dagger*) stylet *m*; **s. heels,** talons *m* aiguille; *Ent:* **s. fly,** thereva *m.* **2.** *Needlew: etc:* poinçon *m.*

still[1] [stil]. **1.** *a.* tranquille; (*a*) immobile; **to keep s.,** ne pas bouger; se tenir, rester, tranquille; se tenir en repos; **she couldn't keep s.,** elle ne pouvait tenir en place; **sit s.,** restez tranquille; restez tranquillement assis; **to stand s.,** (i) ne pas bouger; se tenir tranquille; rester inactif; (ii) s'arrêter, s'immobiliser; (*of science, etc.*) rester stationnaire; *Prov:* **there is no standing s.,** qui n'avance pas recule; **his heart stood s.,** son cœur cessa de battre; **as s. as death, as s. as the grave,** immobile, silencieux, comme la mort; **she lay as s. as s.,** elle reposait dans une immobilité absolue; (*b*) silencieux; *NAm:* **s. hunt** = STALK[1] 2; *B:* **peace, be s.,** tais-toi, sois tranquille; **to keep a s. tongue in one's head,** se taire; **in the s. watches of the night,** pendant les veilles silencieuses de la nuit; *Lit:* **the voices that are s.,** les voix qui se sont tues (à jamais); (*c*) calme, silencieux; **s. water,** eau tranquille, calme, paisible; eau dormante, eau morte; **s. evening, s. woods,** soir, bois, silencieux; *B:* **and after the fire a s. small voice,** après le feu venait un son doux et subtil; **the s. small voice,** la voix de la conscience; (*d*) **s. wines,** vins non mousseux; **s. champagne,** champagne nature; (*e*) *Art:* **s. life,** *pl.* **s. lifes,** nature morte. **2.** *s.* (*a*) **in the s. of the night,** dans le calme de la nuit; (*b*) *Cin:* photo (empruntée au film).

still[2]. **1.** *v.tr.* (*a*) tranquilliser, calmer, apaiser; **to s. s.o.'s fears,** calmer les craintes de qn; **to s. the winds,** faire taire les vents; (*b*) **to s. one's songs,** taire, cesser, ses chants. **2.** *v.i. Lit:* (*a*) se calmer; **the storm had stilled,** la tempête s'était apaisée; (*b*) **that mighty pen is stilled for ever,** cet écrivain génial s'est tu à jamais.

still[3]. **1.** *adv.* (*a*) encore; **he is s. here,** il est encore, toujours, ici; *Manon Lescaut* **is s. an admirable work,** *Manon Lescaut* est encore aujourd'hui une œuvre admirable; **I am s. looking for an explanation,** j'en suis encore à chercher une explication; **I s. have 500 francs,** il me reste 500 francs; **I have s. to thank you,** il me reste à vous remercier; **in spite of his faults, I love him s.,** malgré ses fautes je l'aime toujours; (*b*) **s. more, s. less,** encore plus, encore moins; **that would be s. worse,** ce serait encore pis; **if you can reduce the price s. further,** si vous pouvez réduire encore le prix; (*c*) *A:* (i) constamment; (ii) de plus en plus. **2.** *conj.* cependant, pourtant, néanmoins, encore, toutefois, malgré cela; **s. the fact remains that . . .,** toujours est-il que . . .; **s. I did see her,** toujours est-il que je l'ai vue; **he neglects her but still he loves her,** il la néglige et néanmoins il l'aime; **I detest him but still I'll help him,** malgré que je le déteste je l'aiderai; **but s., if he** ***did*** **accept!** mais enfin, s'il acceptait!

still[4], *s.* alambic *m,* cornue *f*; **secondary s.,** appareil *m* de redistillation; **water s.,** appareil à eau distillée; alambic; *Petr:* **topping s.,** four *m* de fractionnement; **tar s.,** cornue à goudron; **oil s.,** purificateur *m* d'huile.

stillage ['stilidʒ], *s.* **1.** banc *m* de peu de hauteur. **2.** = STILLING.

Stillbay ['stilbei], *a.* & *s. Prehist:* stillbayien (*m*).

stillbirth ['stilbə:θ], *s.* mortinaissance *f*; mise *f* au monde d'un enfant mort-né; **rate of stillbirths,** mortinatalité *f.*

stillborn ['stilbɔ:n], *a.* mort-né, -ée, *pl.* mort-nés, -ées; *Fig:* avorté, mort-né.

still-hunt ['stilhʌnt], *v.tr. NAm:* = STALK[2] 2.

still-hunter ['stilhʌntər], *s. NAm:* = STALKER.

stilling[1] ['stiliŋ], **stillion** ['stiliən], *s.* chantier *m* (pour fûts); porte-fût(s) *m inv.*

stilling[2], *s. esp. U.S:* distillation *f* (sans licence).

stillness ['stilnis], *s.* tranquillité *f,* calme *m,* repos *m*; silence *m,* paix *f.*

stillroom ['stilru:m], *s.* **1.** *A:* laboratoire *m* de distillerie. **2.** office *f.*

stilly[1] ['stili], *a. Lit:* silencieux, calme, tranquille, paisible.

stilly[2] ['stilli], *adv.* silencieusement, tranquillement; avec calme.

stilpnosiderite [stilpnou'sidərait], *s. Miner:* stilpnosidérite *f.*

stilt[1] [stilt], *s.* **1.** échasse *f*; *Bot:* **s. root,** racine-échasse *f.* **2.** *Civ.E:* pilotis *m,* pieu *m.* **3.** manche *m,* mancheron *m* (de charrue). **4.** *Arch:* surhaussement *m,* exhaussement *m* (d'une voûte). **5.** *Orn:* (*a*) **s. (bird), s. plover,** échasse; **black-winged s.,** échasse blanche; **black-necked s.,** échasse américaine; (*b*) **the s. birds, s. walkers,** les échassiers *m.*

stilt[2], *v.tr.* **1.** *A:* monter (qn) sur des échasses. **2.** *Arch:* surhausser, surélever (une voûte).

stilted ['stiltid], *a.* **1.** *A:* monté sur des échasses. **2.** *Arch:* (arc) surhaussé, surélevé. **3.** (*of style, etc.*) guindé, tendu.

stiltedness ['stiltidnis], *s.* manière guindée; air, ton, style, guindé, emphatique, ampoulé; emphase *f.*

stilting ['stiltiŋ], *s.* **1.** *A:* marche *f* avec des échasses. **2.** *Arch:* surhaussement *m* (d'une voûte).

Stilton ['stilt(ə)n], *s.* fromage *m* de Stilton; stilton *m.*

stimulant ['stimjulənt]. **1.** *a.* & *s. Med:* stimulant (*m*); remontant (*m*); **heart s.,** tonicardiaque *m.* **2.** *s.* surexcitant *m*; *F:* **he never takes stimulants,** il ne boit jamais d'alcool.

stimulate ['stimjuleit], *v.tr.* (*a*) stimuler (qn, le zèle de qn); aiguillonner, activer, exciter (**to,** à); aiguiser (l'esprit, l'appétit, etc.); **to be stimulated by opposition,** se piquer au jeu; **to s. s.o. to do sth.,** encourager qn à faire qch.; *F:* aiguillonner qn; **to s. the conversation,** meubler la conversation; *Ind:* **to s. production,** encourager, activer, la production; (*b*) *Med:* stimuler (le foie, etc.).

stimulating ['stimjuleitiŋ], *a.* **1.** stimulant, encourageant; (désir) aiguillonnant; (musique) entraînante; (livre) qui donne à penser; (travail) rémunérateur, qui en vaut la peine. **2.** *Med:* (régime, etc.) stimulant, excitant, remontant.

stimulation [stimju'leiʃ(ə)n], *s.* stimulation *f.*

stimulative ['stimulətiv], *a.* stimulateur, -trice.

stimuline ['stimjulin], *s. Biol:* stimuline *f.*

stimulose ['stimjulous], *a. Bot:* stimuleux; à poils piquants; à stimules.

stimulus, *pl.* **-i** ['stimjuləs, -ai], *s.* **1.** (*a*) stimulant *m*; aiguillon *m*; **to give a stimulus to trade,** donner de l'impulsion *f* au commerce; *F:* **to give a s. to the circulation,** donner un coup de fouet à la circulation; **ambition is his only s.,** l'ambition est le seul ressort de son activité; (*b*) *Physiol:* stimulus *m inv*; **to apply a s. to a muscle,** exciter un muscle; (*of nerve, etc.*) **to respond to a s.,** s'exciter. **2.** *Bot:* stimule *m.*

sting[1] [stiŋ], *s.* **1.** (*a*) dard *m*, aiguillon *m* (d'abeille); (*b*) dard, stimule *m*; poil piquant (d'ortie); poil urticant; (*c*) crochet venimeux (d'un serpent). **2.** (*a*) piqûre *f* (de guêpe, etc.); **face covered with stings,** visage couvert de piqûres; (*b*) pointe *f* (d'une épigramme); mordant *m*; **joke with a s. in it, in the tail,** plaisanterie mordante, piquante; *Lit:* **the s. of remorse,** l'aiguillon du remords; (*c*) douleur cuisante (d'une blessure); cinglure *f* (d'une lanière, d'une insulte); (*d*) vigueur *f*, mordant (d'une attaque); *Ten:* **service with no s. in it,** service mou.

sting[2], *v.* (*p.t. & p.p.* **stung** [stʌŋ]) **1.** *v.tr.* (*a*) (*of bees, nettles, etc.*) piquer; **a bee stung his finger, stung him on the finger,** une abeille lui a piqué le doigt; **bees which do not s.,** abeilles qui ne piquent pas; mélipones *f*; **his conscience stings him,** sa conscience le tourmente; **the blow stung him,** le coup le cingla; **that reply stung him (to the quick),** cette réponse l'a piqué (au vif); *Prov:* **nothing stings like the truth,** il n'y a que la vérité qui offense; **smoke that stings the eyes,** fumée qui picote les yeux; (*b*) *F:* **to s. s.o. for sth.,** faire payer qch. à qn un prix exorbitant; **to be stung,** être salé, essuyer le coup de fusil. **2.** *v.i.* (*of parts of the body*) cuire; sentir des élancements; **my eyes were stinging,** les yeux me cuisaient.

stingaree ['stiŋgəri:], *s. Ich:* pastenague *f* (de l'océan Pacifique).

stinger ['stiŋər], *s. F:* coup bien appliqué; coup douloureux; coup raide, qui cingle; **to get a regular s.,** recevoir une fameuse gifle.

stingfish [stiŋfiʃ], *s. Ich:* **1.** vive *f*; dragon *m* de mer. **2.** diable *m* de mer.

stingily ['stindʒili], *adv.* chichement, mesquinement; en ladre.

stinginess ['stindʒinis], *s.* mesquinerie *f*, ladrerie *f*, avarice *f*; pingrerie *f.*

stinging ['stiŋiŋ], *a.* piquant, cuisant, mordant; **s. plant,** plante piquante; plante brûlante, urticante; **s. blow,** coup cinglant, coup raide comme une balle; **s. answer,** réponse cinglante; réponse raide; **s. remark,** remarque blessante, offensante; **s. tongue,** langue acérée, mordante.

stingless ['stiŋlis], *a. Ent:* **s. bees,** mélipones *f.*

stingo ['stiŋgou], *s. P:* **1.** *O:* bière forte. **2.** *A:* (*a*) verve *f*, entrain *m*, brio *m*; (*b*) **to give s.o. s.,** laver la tête à qn; tancer qn d'importance.

stingray ['stiŋrei], *s. Ich:* **whip-tailed s.,** pastenague *f.*

stingy ['stindʒi], *a.* mesquin, avaricieux, chiche, ladre, regardant; *P:* chien; **s. person,** personne dure à la détente, à la desserre; pingre *mf*; **a bit s.,** *P:* un peu radin; **don't be so s. with sugar!** ne soyez pas si chiche de sucre, si regardant avec le sucre! ne ménagez pas tant le sucre!

stink[1] ['stiŋk], *s.* **1.** (*a*) puanteur *f*; odeur *f* fétide; mauvaise odeur; **what a s.!** c'est une infection ici! **s. trap,** siphon *m* (d'évier, etc.); (*b*) *P:* **to raise a s., (about sth.),** crier au scandale (à propos de qch.); faire de l'esclandre. **2.** *pl. Sch: F:* **stinks,** la chimie.

stink[2], *v.* (*p.t.* **stank** [stæŋk], **stunk** [stʌŋk]; *p.p.* **stunk**) **1.** *v.i.* puer, sentir mauvais; *F:* empester; blairer; **it stinks in here,** c'est une infection ici; **corpse that stinks,** cadavre *m* qui sent, qui infecte; **to s. of wine, of garlic,** puer le vin, l'ail; *P:* **to s. of money,** avoir un argent fou; *P:* **what do you think of it?—it stinks!** qu'en dis-tu?—c'est moche! **2.** *v.tr.* (*a*) **to s. s.o. out,** chasser qn par la mauvaise odeur; **to s. out a fox,** déloger, enfumer, un renard; (*b*) *F:* sentir, flairer (qch.).

stink-albe ['stiŋkælb], *s. Bot:* roupala *m.*

stink-alive ['stiŋkəlaiv], *s. Ich:* tacaud *m.*

stinkard ['stiŋkəd], *s.* **1.** *Z: F:* télédu *m*, télagon *m.* **2.** *F:* = STINKER **1.**

stinkball ['stiŋkbɔ:l], *s. Pyr:* pot *m* à feu.

stinkbomb ['stiŋkbɔm], *s. F:* obus *m* à gaz; *Sch:* boule puante.

stinkbug ['stiŋkbʌg], *s. Ent:* punaise *f* des bois.

stinker ['stiŋkər], *s. F:* **1.** (*a*) individu *m* méprisable; goujat *m*; salaud *m*; (*b*) individu qui pue. **2.** (*a*) **to write s.o. a s.,** écrire une lettre carabinée, d'engueulade, à qn; (*b*) **the algebra paper was a s.,** on a eu une sale composition d'algèbre; la composition d'algèbre était rosse; (*c*) (*of play, etc.*) navet *m.* **3.** *Orn:* fulmar *m.*

stinkhorn ['stiŋkhɔ:n], *s. Fung:* phallus *m* impudique, satyre puant.

stinking[1] ['stiŋkiŋ], *a.* **1.** (*a*) puant, nauséabond, fétide, empesté, infect; (*b*) *P:* dégoûtant, dégueulasse; (*c*) *P:* soûl comme un cochon. **2.** *Bot: Z:* puant; **s. nettle,** galéopsis *m*; **s. badger,** mydaüs *m*, télédu *m*, télagon *m.*

stinking[2], **stinkingly** ['stiŋkiŋli], *adv. F:* **to be s. rich,** avoir un argent fou; **a s. bad meal,** un repas infect; **stinking drunk,** soûl comme un cochon; **he behaved stinkingly to his friends,** il a été infect avec ses amis.

stinkpot ['stiŋkpɔt], *s.* **1.** *Pyr:* pot *m* à feu. **2.** *F:* individu *m* méprisable.

stinkweed ['stiŋkwi:d], *s. Bot:* **1.** diplotaxis *m.* **2.** *U.S:* stramoine *f.*

stinkwood ['stiŋkwud], *s. Bot:* ocotea *m* bullata.

stinky ['stiŋki], *a. Sch: P:* infect; qui pue.

stint[1] [stint], *s.* **1.** restriction *f*; **without s.,** sans restriction; sans limite, sans bornes, sans ménagement, à volonté, à discrétion; **to spend money without s.,** dépenser sans compter. **2.** *A:* ration *f*, portion *f*, part *f*, quantité *f* (**of,** de). **3.** besogne assignée; **to do one's daily s.,** accomplir sa tâche quotidienne. **4.** temps *m*, période *f*; **he had a two-year s. in the army,** il a fait ses deux ans dans l'armée.

stint[2], *v.tr.* **1.** imposer des restrictions à (qn); réduire (qn) à la portion congrue; **to s. oneself,** se restreindre; se refuser le nécessaire; **don't s. yourself on food,** ne lésine pas sur la nourriture; **to s. oneself for one's children,** se priver pour ses enfants; **to s. s.o. of sth.,** priver qn de qch., refuser qch. à qn, rationner qch. à qn. **2.** réduire (la nourriture); épargner (l'argent, la peine); être chiche de (qch.); lésiner sur (qch.); **to give without stinting,** donner sans compter.

stint[3], *s. Orn:* **little s.,** bécasseau *m* minute; **American s.,** bécasseau minuscule; **Temminck's s.,** bécasseau de Temminck.

stinting ['stintiŋ], *s.* restriction *f*, épargne *f*; lésinerie *f*, lésine *f*; **there was no s.,** on ne regardait pas à la dépense.

stintless ['stintlis], *a. O:* abondant, sans restriction.

stipe [staip], *s. Bot:* stipe *m.*

stipel ['staip(ə)l], **stipella** [sti'pelə], *s. Bot:* stipelle *f.*

stipellate [sti'peleit], *a. Bot:* stipellé.

stipend ['staipend], *s.* traitement *m*, appointements *mpl* (d'un ecclésiastique, d'un magistrat).

stipendiary [stai'pendjəri], *a.* appointé; qui reçoit des appointements fixes, un traitement; **s. magistrate,** *s.* **stipendiary,** juge *m* d'un tribunal d'instance (à Londres et dans les grandes villes).

stipes, *pl.* **-ites** ['staipi:z, 'stipiti:z], *s. Bot:* stipe *m.*

stipiform ['staipifɔ:m], *a. Bot: Z:* stipiforme.

stipitate ['stipiteit], *a. Bot:* stipité.

stipple[1] [stipl], *s. Art:* pointillé *m*; *Engr:* grenure *f.*

stipple[2], *v.tr.* (*a*) figurer (un dessin) en pointillé; pointiller (un dessin); (*b*) *Engr:* graver (un dessin) au pointillé; granuler, grener (une planche).

stippled ['stipld], *a.* pointillé; gravé au pointillé; **s. design,** dessin *m* au pointillé.

stippler ['stiplər], *s.* graveur *m* au pointillé.

stippling ['stipliŋ], *s.* **1.** pointillage *m*; grenure *f.* **2.** pointillé *m*; grenure.

stipula, *pl.* **-ae, -as** ['stipjulə, -i:, -əz], *s. Bot:* stipule *f.*

stipulaceous [stipju'leiʃəs], *a. Bot:* stipulacé.

stipular ['stipjulər], *a. Bot:* stipulaire.

stipulate[1] ['stipjuleit], *a. Bot:* stipulé.

stipulate[2]. **1.** *v.i.* **to s. for sth.,** stipuler, énoncer, expressément (une condition obligatoire); convenir de (certaines conditions); **to s. for a reward of a hundred pounds,** stipuler une récompense de cent livres. **2.** *v.tr.* **to s. (in writing) that. . .,** stipuler (par écrit) que . . .; **to s. that the tenant is responsible for all repairs,** stipuler que toutes les réparations seront, soient, à la charge du locataire; **it is stipulated that delivery shall be effected this year,** il est stipulé que la livraison devra être faite cette année; **within the period stipulated,** dans le délai prescrit.

stipulated ['stipjuleitid], *a.* stipulé, convenu; **the s. quality,** la qualité prescrite; *Jur:* **s. jointure,** douaire préfix.

stipulation [stipju'leiʃ(ə)n], *s.* (*a*) *Jur:* stipulation *f* (d'une condition); (*b*) **the only s. I make is that you shall be in by ten o'clock,** la seule condition que je pose c'est que vous soyez rentré à dix heures; **on the s. that . . .,** à condition que . . ..

stipulator ['stipjuleitər], *s. Jur:* stipulant *m.*

stipule ['stipju:l], *s. Bot:* stipule *f.*

stipuled ['stipju:ld], *a. Bot:* stipulé.

stipulose ['stipjulous], *a. Bot:* stipuleux.

stir[1] [stə:r], *s.* **1.** remuement *m*; **to give one's coffee, the fire, a stir,** remuer son café; tisonner le feu. **2.** mouvement *m*; **stir of warm wind,** souffle *m* d'air chaud. **3.** (*a*) mouvement, remue-ménage *m inv*; **place full of s. and movement,** endroit plein de vie et de mouvement; **the s. of a great town,** le mouvement d'une grande ville; **there was a great s.,** il y eut un grand remue-ménage; (*b*) agitation *f*, émoi *m*; **to make a s.,** faire du bruit, de l'éclat; faire événement; faire sensation; **the news caused a s. in the town,** la nouvelle a mis la ville en émoi, en rumeur, a provoqué des remous; **to create little, s.,** avoir peu de retentissement.

stir[2], *v.* (**stirred**) **1.** *v.tr.* (*a*) remuer, mouvoir; (*usu. neg.*) **not a breath stirs the leaves, the lake,** pas un souffle ne remue, ne fait trembler, les feuilles; pas un souffle ne ride le lac; **he could not s. a foot,** (i) il était incapable de faire un pas; (ii) on ne lui laissait aucune liberté; **I will not s. a foot,** je ne bougerai pas d'ici; (*b*) activer, attiser, tisonner, remuer, fourgonner (le feu); agiter (un mélange, etc.); *Cu:* tourner (une crème); **to s. one's tea,** remuer son thé; *Tchn:* **to s. puddled iron,** brasser le fer puddlé; *Glassm;* **to s. glass,** macler le verre; *Brew:* **to s. the mash with the oar,** vaguer le fardeau; (*c*) émouvoir, remuer, troubler (qn); éveiller, susciter (des souvenirs); **stirred,** agité, troublé; ému; **to s. s.o.'s wrath,** exciter, animer, la colère de qn; **to s. s.o. to pity,** émouvoir la compassion de qn; **to s. s.o.'s passions, blood,** agiter, émouvoir, les passions de qn; **the country was stirred by a deep emotion,** une émotion intense souleva le pays; **events that s. the soul,** événements qui remuent l'âme; **scents that s. the senses,** parfums qui troublent les sens; *F:* **to s. it,** fomenter la discorde; *P:* **s. yourself, your stumps!** grouille-toi! **2.** *v.i.* bouger, remuer; se mettre en mouvement; (*usu. neg.*) **to sit without stirring,** rester assis sans bouger, dans une complète immobilité, sans faire le moindre mouvement; **don't s.!** ne bougez pas! **don't s. from here,** ne bougez pas d'ici; *F:* ne démarrez pas d'ici; **he did not s. out of the house,** il n'est pas sorti de la maison; **he settled in Brighton and never stirred from there,** il s'est fixé à Brighton et n'en a plus bougé; **he is not stirring yet,** il n'est pas encore levé, debout; **to s. about,** se remuer; **there is not a breath of air stirring,** on ne sent pas un souffle d'air; *O:* **there is no news stirring,** il n'y a point de nouvelles. **3.** *v.tr.* **to s. up,** remuer, agiter, tourner, *F:* touiller (un liquide); ranimer, activer (le feu). **4.** fomenter (une sédition, les dissensions); remuer, ameuter (le peuple); exciter, animer (la curiosité, l'émotion); susciter (l'admiration); allumer (la guerre); *F:* travailler (des ouvriers); **to s. up hatred,** attiser les haines; **to s. up s.o.'s courage, s.o.'s enthusiasm,** réchauffer, exciter, le courage, le zèle, de qn; **to s. up trouble,** *F:* **to s. it up,** fomenter la discorde; **stirred up,** agité, troublé; en émoi; **to s. up s.o. to mutiny,** exciter, pousser, qn à la sédition; **he wants stirring up,** il a besoin d'être secoué; il a besoin qu'on l'aiguillonne.

stir[3], *s. P:* prison *f*, taule *f.*

stirabout ['stə:rəbaut], *s.* **1.** *Cu:* bouillie *f* (de farine d'avoine), porridge *m.* **2.** remuse-ménage *m inv.* **3.** personne remuante.

stirk [stə:k], *s. Dial:* bœuf *m*, vache *f*, d'un an; bouvillon *m.*

stirless ['stə:lis], *a. A:* immobile; sans mouvement.

stirps, *pl.* **stirpes** [stə:ps, 'stə:pi:z], *s.* **1.** *Jur:* souche *f*; **succession per stirpes,** descente *f* par souche. **2.** *Z:* groupe *m* ou famille *f.*

stirrer ['stə:rər], *s.* **1.** (*pers.*) **s.(-up),** incitateur, -trice; instigateur, -trice (**of,** de); **s. of sedition,** fauteur *m* de sédition; **s.-up of strife, of trouble,** fomentateur, -trice, de dissensions; remueur, -euse, de discorde. **2.** (*device*) *Ch: Phot:* agitateur *m*, remueur *m*; *Ind:* barboteur *m*; *Dy: Glassm:* râble *m*; *Cu:* mouvette *f.* **3.** (*pers.*) **to be an early s.,** être matinal; être toujours debout de grand matin.

stirring[1] ['stəriŋ], *a.* **1.** actif, remuant; (enfant) turbulent; **to lead a s. life,** mener une vie très active; **s. times,** époque mouvementée. **2.** émouvant, empoignant; **s. events,** événements sensationnels, à sensation; **s. speech,** discours vibrant, entraînant.

stirring[2], *s.* **1.** remuement *m*; agitation *f*; *Brew:* vaguage *m* (du fardeau), brassage *m*; *Glassm:* maclage *m* (du verre); **s. device,** remueur *m*; *Ch: Phot:* **s. rod,** agitateur *m*; *Paperm: etc:* spatule *f*, brasseur *m*. **2. s. up,** excitation *f*; mise *f* en émoi; attisage *m*, attisement *m*.

stirringly [ˈstəːriŋli], *adv.* d'une façon émouvante, entraînante.

stirrup [ˈstirəp], *s.* **1.** *Harn:* étrier *m*; **to put one's feet in the stirrups,** chausser les étriers; **to lose one's stirrups,** perdre les étriers; **to ride with long stirrups,** chevaucher long; **to ride with short stirrups,** chevaucher court; monter à la genette; **s. foot,** pied *m* de l'étrier, pied gauche; **s. leather, strap,** étrivière *f*; **to lower the s. leathers,** rallonger les étrivières; **s. (iron),** étrier; **s. oil,** fouettée *f*. **2.** *Nau:* étrier (de marchepied de vergue). **3.** tire-pied *m*, *pl.* tire-pieds (de cordonnier). **4.** *Surg:* étrier (de la table d'opération). **5.** (*a*) *Const:* **s. (piece, strap),** étrier (de fixation); lien *m* en fer à U; bride *f*; armature *f* en étrier; (*b*) (*of rowlock*) lyre *f*; (*c*) (*of* (*leaf-*)*spring*) bride de ressort. **6.** *Phot:* **s. lens-panel,** porte-objectif *m inv* en U. **7.** *Anat:* **s. (bone),** stapéal *m*, étrier.

stitch¹ [stitʃ], *s.* **1.** (*a*) *Needlew:* point *m*; **(machine) s.,** piqûre (à la machine); **darning s.,** point de reprise; **knot s.,** point noué; **pin s.,** point turc; **whipping s.,** point roulé; (*in tapestry*) **Holbein s., Italian s.,** point de Holbein; point droit; *Leath:* **s. wheel,** roulette *f*; molette *f* à piquer le cuir; **to put a few stitches in a garment,** faire un point à un vêtement; *Prov:* **a s. in time saves nine,** un point à temps en épargne cent; un point fait à temps en vaut mille; *Nau:* **with every s. of canvas set,** couvert de toile; avec tout dessus; toutes voiles dehors; *F:* **he has not a dry s. on him,** il est complètement trempé; **without a s. on,** complètement nu; (*b*) (*in knitting, crochet*) maille *f*; **to drop a s.,** sauter une maille; **dropped s.,** maille coulée; **to take up a s.,** reprendre une maille; **to make a s.,** faire une augmentation; (*c*) *Surg:* (point de) suture *f*; **to put stitches in a wound,** suturer, faire une suture à, une plaie. **2. s. (in the side),** point de côté; **I've got a s., the s.,** j'ai un point; *F:* **we were in stitches,** nous nous fendions la pipe; on se tordait de rire.

stitch², *v.tr.* **1.** (*a*) coudre (un vêtement, etc.); **to (machine) s.,** piquer (à la machine); **to s. two pieces together,** joindre deux morceaux; **to s. down,** rabattre (une couture, etc.); **to s. sth. on to sth.,** coudre qch. sur qch.; appliquer (une poche, etc.); coudre (qch.) en place; *Av: A:* **to s. on the wing coverings,** larder les toiles; **to s. up a tear, a garment,** recoudre une déchirure, un vêtement; faire un point à qch.; (*b*) **to s. leather,** piquer le cuir. **2.** *Surg:* **to s. (up) a wound,** suturer une plaie. **3.** *Bookb:* brocher (un livre).

stitcher [ˈstitʃər], *s.* couseur, -euse; *Leath:* piqueur, -euse; *Bookb:* brocheur, -euse.

stitching [ˈstitʃiŋ], *s.* **1.** (*a*) *Needlew:* couture *f*; *Leath:* piqûre *f*; *Dressm:* **line of s.,** piqûre; (*b*) *Surg:* suture *f*; (*c*) *Bookb:* brochage *m*, brochure *f*. **2.** points *mpl*, piqûres; **ornamental s.,** broderie *f*; (*on back of glove*) baguettes *fpl*; **saddle s.,** piqûres sellier.

stitchwork [ˈstitʃwəːk], *s.* broderie *f*, tapisserie *f*.

stitchwort [ˈstitʃwəːt], *s. Bot:* stellaire *f* holostée; collerette *f* de la Vierge.

stithy [ˈstiði], *s. A. & Poet:* forge *f*.

stiver [ˈstaivər], *s. F: O:* sou *m*; **he hasn't a s.,** il n'a pas le sou; *P:* il n'a pas un radis; **I wouldn't give a s. for it,** je n'en donnerais pas quatre sous.

stoa, *pl.* **-ae, -as** [ˈstouə, -iː, -əz], *s. Gr.Ant:* portique *m*.

stoat¹ [stout], *s. Z:* hermine *f* d'été.

stoat², *v.tr. Tail:* faire une reprise perdue à (une déchirure).

stochastic [stəˈkæstik], *a. Stat: etc:* (processus, variable, etc.) stochastique.

stock¹ [stɔk], *s.* **1.** (*a*) *Bot:* tronc *m*, caudex *m* (d'arbre); (*b*) souche *f*, estoc *m* (d'arbre); souche (d'iris, etc.); bûche *f*, bloc *m*; billot *m* (d'enclume); *F: O:* **to stand like a s.,** demeurer, rester planté, comme une souche; **stocks and stones,** objets inanimés; personnes stupides, rois soliveaux; empotés *m*; *Tls:* **s. saw, gang,** scie alternative à plusieurs lames; scie multiple; (*c*) *Geol:* petit batholit(h)e; mamelon *m*; (*d*) *Hort:* sujet *m*, ente *f*; porte-greffe *m inv*; *Vit:* cep *m* (de vigne); *Arb:* **paradise s.,** paradis *m*; (*e*) race *f*, famille *f*, lignée *f*, tige *f*; **true to s.,** fortement racé; **of good stock,** de bonne lignée; **he comes of good, sound, s.,** il descend d'une bonne famille; il vient de bonne souche; il a de qui tenir; *A: & Lit:* il est de bon estoc. **2.** (*a*) fût *m*, bois *m*, monture *f* (de fusil); manche *m* (de fouet); mancheron *m* (de charrue); sommier *m*, mouton *m* (de cloche); boîte *f* de bois (enfermant une serrure); **anchor s.,** *Nau:* jas *m* d'ancre, *Her:* trabe *f*; **to take the s. off the anchor,** déjaler l'ancre; *Locksm:* **s. lock,** serrure *f* à pêne dormant enfermée dans une boîte de bois; *Sm.a:* **s. plate,** plaquette *f* (de revolver); (*b*) **screw s., die s.,** porte-filière *m*, *pl.* porte-filières; **s. and die,** filière *f*; **screw s. and dies,** filière double. **3.** *pl. A:* **stocks,** ceps *mpl*, pilori *m* (en place publique); **to put s.o. in the stocks,** mettre qn aux ceps. **4.** *N.Arch:* **stocks,** (i) chantier *m*; cale *f* de construction; (ii) (*on slips*) tins *m*; **ship on the stocks,** navire en construction, sur cales; *Fig:* **to have a piece of work on the stocks,** avoir un ouvrage sur le métier, sur le chantier, en chantier. **5.** (*a*) provision *f*, approvisionnement *m*; **s. of wood,** provision de bois; **s. of plays,** répertoire *m*; **to have a great s. of information about sth.,** avoir, posséder, beaucoup de renseignements au sujet de qch.; **to lay in a s. of food,** faire (une) provision de vivres; s'approvisionner de vivres; **to lay in one's autumn s.,** faire ses approvisionnements pour l'automne; **to lay in a good s. of linen,** se monter en linge; **to lay in a good s. of books for the holidays,** s'assortir de livres pour les vacances; **I'm at the end of my s. of wine,** je n'ai plus de vin en cave; (*b*) *Com:* (i) **s. (in trade),** marchandises *fpl* (en magasin); stock *m*; **new s., fresh s.,** rassortiment *m*; **old s., dead s.,** fonds *mpl* de boutique; vieux rossignols; **surplus s.,** soldes *mpl*; **s. in hand,** marchandises en magasin; stock, existences *fpl* (en magasin); **to buy the whole s. of a business,** acheter un fonds en bloc; **to carry heavy s.,** faire de grosses immobilisations (de capitaux); **to take s.,** faire, dresser, l'inventaire; *Fig:* **to take s. of s.o., of a place,** scruter, toiser, qn; examiner attentivement un endroit; **he kept s. of everything around him,** il observait tout autour de lui; **to take s. (of the situation),** faire le bilan de la situation; faire le point; **opening s.,** stock initial, en début d'exercice; **closing s.,** stock final, en fin d'exercice; *Book-k:* **s. account,** compte *m* de capital; **s. book,** livre *m* de magasin; magasinier *m*; **s. control,** gestion *f* des stocks; **s. keeper,** magasinier *m*; **s. list,** inventaire *m*; **s. room,** magasin *m*; (*in hotel*) salle *f* de montre (des marchandises d'un commis voyageur); **in s.,** en magasin, en stock, en dépôt, en rayon; **spare parts always in s.,** pièces de rechange toujours en stock, disponibles; (*of goods*) **to be out of s.,** manquer en magasin; **this item is out of s.,** nous sommes désassortis de cet article; *Publ:* **book temporarily out of s.,** livre qui manque, est temporairement épuisé; (ii) **working s.,** matériel *m* (d'une usine); (*c*) (*at cards, dominoes*) talon *m*; (*at dominoes*) **to draw from the s.,** piocher; (*d*) *Husb:* (*livestock*) **grazing s.,** bétail *m*, bestiaux *mpl*; animaux *m* sur pied; *Jur:* cheptel *m*; **fat s.,** bétail de boucherie; **dead s.,** matériel; mobilier mort; **s. book,** livre d'origines (des chevaux, etc.); **s. farm,** élevage *m*; **s. farmer, breeder, raiser,** éleveur *m*; **s. farming, breeding, raising,** élevage; **s. market,** (i) marché *m* aux bestiaux; (ii) commerce *m* des bestiaux; **s. mare,** jument *f* de haras; *NAm:* **s. horse,** cheval *m* de ranch; **s. saddle,** selle *f* de cowboy; *Austr:* **s. rider,** cowboy *m*; **s. whip,** fouet *m* de bouvier (à manche court); (*e*) *For:* peuplement *m*; (*f*) *Ind:* dotation *f*; *Rail:* **locomotive s.,** effectif *m*, dotation, en locomotives; (*g*) *Cin:* **(film) s.,** film *m* vierge; films, bandes *f*, vierges; *F:* **non-flam s.,** bandes ininflammables; (*h*) charge *f* (de haut fourneau). **6.** (*a*) *Ind:* matières premières (de pâte à papier, de savon, etc.); (*b*) *Cu:* **soup s.,** consommé *m*; **meat s.,** bouillon (concentré); blond *m*; **vegetable s.,** bouillon de légumes. **7.** *Fin:* fonds *mpl*, valeurs *fpl*, actions *fpl*; **government s.,** fonds d'État; fonds, effets, publics; rentes *fpl* (sur l'État); **corporation s.,** emprunt(s) *m*(*pl*) de ville(s); **bank s.,** valeurs de banque; **s. exchange,** bourse *f* (des valeurs); **the S. Exchange,** la Bourse (de Londres); **common s.,** actions ordinaires; **stocks and shares,** valeurs mobilières; valeurs de bourse; titres *m* (c.-à-d. rentes, actions et obligations); **he has all his fortune in stocks and shares,** il a toute sa fortune en portefeuille; **to take delivery of s.,** prendre livraison des titres; *St.Exch:* **to take in, borrow, carry, s.,** (faire) reporter des titres; prendre des actions en report; **s. taken in, carried over,** titres en report; **to take in s. for a borrower,** (faire) reporter un emprunteur; *Fin:* **s. register,** grand-livre, *pl.* grands-livres, des titres; *St.Exch:* **s. list,** bulletin *m* de la cote; **s. market,** marché des titres, de valeurs; marché financier; *Fig:* **his s. is going up, down,** ses actions sont en hausse, en baisse; **his s. stands high,** il est très estimé, prisé; *NAm:* **to take s., no s., in s.o., sth.,** faire grand cas, peu de cas, de qn, qch. **8.** *Bot:* **s. (gillyflower),** matthiole *f*; giroflée des jardins, grande giroflée; violier *m*; **ten-week s.,** giroflée quarantaine; **Virginia(n) s.,** malcolmie *f*, julienne *f* de Mahon. **9.** *Cost:* (*a*) cravate *f* ample, en écharpe; (*b*) *Mil: A:* col droit (d'uniforme); *F:* cancan *m*; (*c*) colcravate *m* (d'équitation), *pl.* cols-cravates; (*d*) plastron *m* en soie noire (des ecclésiastiques anglais). **10.** (*a*) normal; **s. sizes,** tailles courantes; **s. bricks,** briques *f* de campagne; *Aut:* **s. car,** (i) voiture *f* de série; vieille voiture que l'on force jusqu'au bout; (ii) stock-car *m*, *pl.* stock-cars; **s.-car racing, races,** courses *f* de stock-cars; (*b*) *Th:* **s. play, piece,** pièce *f* de, du, répertoire; *NAm:* **to play s.,** jouer les pièces de répertoire; **s. company,** troupe *f* à demeure (dans une ville); (*c*) **he has three s. speeches,** il a un répertoire de trois discours; **s. joke,** plaisanterie courante, classique; **s. phrase,** phrase toute faite; expression consacrée; locution figée; cliché *m*; **s. argument,** argument habituel, bien connu; **s. answer,** réponse régulière; **it's the s. trick, dodge,** c'est le coup régulier, classique; (*d*) *Ch: Phot:* **s. solution,** solution concentrée (et de bonne garde).

stock², *v.tr.* **1.** (*a*) monter (un fusil); (*b*) *Nau:* jaler, enjaler (une ancre); **stocked anchor,** ancre de l'Amirauté, à jas fixe. **2.** monter, garnir, assortir, stocker (un magasin) **(with,** de); meubler (une ferme) **(with,** de); monter (une ferme) de bétail; approvisionner (une maison) **(with,** de); empoissonner (un étang); enherber (un pré, un terrain); boiser (un terrain); peupler (une forêt) **(with,** de); peupler (un parc à cerfs); **to s. one's garden,** planter son jardin; **to s. a warehouse (with goods),** garnir, pourvoir, un magasin de marchandises; **I want to s. my cellar a bit,** je voudrais remplir un peu, remonter, ma cave; **this shop is well stocked,** ce magasin est bien monté, bien approvisionné, bien achalandé; **to have a well-stocked cellar,** avoir une cave bien montée. **3.** avoir, tenir, garder, (des marchandises) en magasin, en dépôt; stocker (des marchandises); mettre en grenier (une récolte); **I don't s. this article,** je ne tiens pas cet article; je n'ai pas cet article en magasin; **stocked by all first-class chemists,** dans toutes les bonnes pharmacies. **4.** *v.i.* **to s. up with sth.,** bien s'approvisionner en, de, qch. **5.** *A:* = mettre (un malfaiteur) au pilori. **6.** *Tan:* triballer (des peaux).

stockade¹ [stɔˈkeid], *s.* **1.** palissade *f*, palanque *f*. **2.** *Hyd.E:* estacade *f*. **3.** *U.S:* terrain palissadé pour prisonniers.

stockade², *v.tr.* **1.** palissader, palanquer. **2.** *Hyd.E:* garnir (une berge, etc.) d'une estacade.

stockbroker [ˈstɔkbroukər], *s.* agent *m* de change; courtier *m* de bourse; **outside s.,** coulissier *m*; **the outside stockbrokers,** la coulisse.

stockbroking [ˈstɔkbroukiŋ], *s.* profession *f* d'agent de change; **to take up s.,** se faire agent de change.

stockcar [ˈstɔkkaːr], *s. Rail: NAm:* wagon *m* à bestiaux.

stockdove [ˈstɔkdʌv], *s. Orn:* petit ramier; colombin *m*, pigeon bleu.

stocker [ˈstɔkər], *s.* **1.** monteur *m* (de fusils). **2.** stockiste *m* (de pièces détachées d'automobiles, etc.). **3.** *NAm:* (*a*) bête *f* de boucherie; (*b*) bête choisie pour l'élevage.

stockfish [ˈstɔkfiʃ], *s.* stockfisch *m*, morue séchée, merluche *f*; *Nau:* bacaliau *m*.

stockholder [ˈstɔkhouldər], *s.* actionnaire *mf*; porteur *m*, détenteur *m*, de titres; sociétaire *mf*.

stockiness [ˈstɔkinis], *s.* apparence trapue, costaude.

stockinet(te) [stɔkiˈnet], *s. Tex:* **wool, silk, cotton, s.,** jersey *m* tubulaire de laine, soie, coton.

stocking¹ [ˈstɔkiŋ], *s.* **1.** montage *m* (d'un fusil). **2.** montage, stockage *m* (d'un magasin); approvisionnement *m* (d'une maison); empoissonnement *m*, alevinage *m* (d'un étang); peuplement *m* (d'un parc à cerfs); mise *f* en grenier (d'une récolte).

stocking², *s.* **1.** *Cost:* bas *m*; **ribbed stockings,** bas à côtes; **knitted stockings,** bas tricotés; *Med:* **elastic s.,** bas pour varices; jambière *f*; **to stand six feet in one's stockings, one's s. feet,** mesurer six pieds à pied plat, sans chaussures; **body s.,** combinaison *f* (une pièce); *Fig:* **a well-lined, fat, s.,** un bas de laine bien garni; **s. filler,** petit cadeau de Noël supplémentaire (pour enfant); **s. mask,** bas utilisé par des bandits, et qui forme masque; *Knit:* **s. stich,** point *m* (de) jersey; *Tex:* **s. frame, loom,** métier *m* à bas. **2.** (*of horse*) **white s.,** balzane *f*; **horse with white stockings,** cheval balzan.

stockinged [ˈstɔkiŋd], *a.* **in one's s. feet,** à pieds de bas (sans chaussures).

stockist [ˈstɔkist], *s. Com:* stockiste *m*; **we have stockists in most towns,** nous avons des points *m* de vente dans la plupart des villes.

stockless [ˈstɔklis], *a.* (ancre) sans jas, à pattes articulées; (ancre) brevetée.

stockman, *pl.* **-men** [ˈstɔkmən], *s.m.* **1.** *Austr:* gardeur de bestiaux; bouvier. **2.** *NAm:* éleveur (de bestiaux). **3.** *NAm:* magasinier.

stockpile¹ [ˈstɔkpail], *s.* (*a*) tas *m* (de matériaux d'empierrement pour routes, etc.); (*b*) stocks *mpl* de réserve, de sécurité.

stockpile², *v.tr.* (*a*) stocker (des marchandises, etc.); (*b*) entasser, accumuler (le matériel de guerre, etc.).

stockpiling [ˈstɔkpailiŋ], *s.* stockage *m*, constitution *f* de réserves.

stockpot ['stɔkpɔt], *s. Cu:* pot *m* à bouillon; pot-au-feu *m inv.*

stockstone ['stɔkstoun], *s. Leath:* pierre *f* à poncer.

stocktake ['stɔkteik], *s.* (établissement *m*, levée *f* d')inventaire *m.*

stocktaking ['stɔkteikiŋ], *s. Com: Ind:* (établissement *m*, levée *f* d')inventaire *m*; **s. sale,** solde *m* avant, après, inventaire; **s. inventory,** inventaire intra-comptable.

stocky ['stɔki], *a.* trapu, ragot, -ote, étoffé, courtaud; (cheval) goussaut, bouleux, ragot.

stockyard ['stɔkjɑːd], *s.* **1.** parc *m* à bétail, à bestiaux. **2.** parc à matériau.

stodge[1] [stɔdʒ], *s. F:* **1.** *(a)* aliment bourrant; *esp. Sch:* *(b)* littérature *f* indigeste; *(c) O:* tâche ingrate; corvée *f.* **2.** *O:* *(a)* empiffrerie *f*, bâfrerie *f*; *(b)* bâfrée *f*; **to have a good s.,** s'en fourrer jusque-là. **3.** personne *f* à l'esprit lourd; lourdaud, -aude.

stodge[2], *v.i. & pr. F: O:* se caler les joues; s'empiffrer, se gorger, se bourrer de nourriture; bâfrer; **to s. oneself with cakes,** se bourrer de gâteaux.

stodgy ['stɔdʒi], *a.* **1.** (repas) lourd; (pain) pâteux; (aliment) qui bourre. **2.** *(a)* (livre) indigeste; (style) lourd; *(b) (of pers.)* à l'esprit lourd; lourdaud.

stoep [stuːp], *s. (in S. Africa)* véranda *f.*

stogy ['stougi], *s. U.S:* **1.** gros soulier; godillot *m.* **2.** cigare long et fort à bouts coupés.

stoic ['stouik], *a. & s.* **1.** *Gr.Phil:* **Stoic,** stoïcien *(m)*, stoïque *(m)*; **the S. body,** le Portique. **2. stoic,** stoïque *(mf)*, stoïcien, -ienne.

stoical ['stouikl], *a.* stoïque.

stoically ['stouik(ə)li], *adv.* stoïquement.

stoich(e)iometric [stɔikiou'metrik], *a. Ch:* stœchiométrique.

stoich(e)iometry [stɔiki'ɔmitri], *s. Ch:* stœchiométrie *f.*

stoicism ['stouisizm], *s.* stoïcisme *m.*

stoke ['stouk]. **1.** *v.tr.* **to s. (up),** charger (un foyer); chauffer (un four); entretenir, alimenter, le feu (d'un four); chauffer le foyer (d'une machine à vapeur). **2.** *v.i.* **to s. up,** (i) conduire la chauffe; pousser les feux; (ii) *F:* manger, bouffer, bâfrer.

stokehold ['stoukhould], *s. Nau:* chaufferie *f*, chambre *f* de chauffe.

stokehole ['stoukhoul], *s.* **1.** *(a)* ouverture *f* de foyer; trou *m* de chargement; tisard *m*, tisart *m*; *(b) Nau:* enfer *m* (devant la chaudière). **2.** = STOKEHOLD.

stoker ['stoukər], *s. Nau: Rail: etc:* **1.** *(pers.)* chauffeur *m*; chargeur *m* (d'un foyer); **chief s.,** chef *m* de chauffe; *Navy: A:* **leading s.,** chauffeur breveté. **2. mechanical s.,** chauffeur automatique; foyer *m*, chargeur, mécanique; grille *f* mécanique; stoker *m.*

Stokes[1] [stouks], *Pr.n. Ph:* **Stokes' law,** loi *f* de Stokes.

stokes[2], *s. Ph:* stokes *m.*

stoking (up) ['stoukiŋ(ʌp)], *s.* chauffage *m*, chauffe *f*; alimentation *f* (d'un foyer); **mechanical s.,** chauffage mécanique; **s. of the boilers,** conduite *f* du feu, des feux.

stole[1] [stoul], *s.* **1.** *Rom.Ant:* stole *f.* **2.** *Ecc:* étole *f.* **3.** *Cost:* étole (de vison, etc.).

stole[2], *s.* = STOLON.

stole[3], *s. A:* chaise percée; garde-robe *f*, *pl.* garde-robes; *Hist:* **groom of the s.,** premier gentilhomme de la Chambre (du roi).

stolid ['stɔlid], *a.* lourd, lent, flegmatique, impassible.

stolidity [stɔ'liditi], **stolidness** ['stɔlidnis], *s.* flegme *m.*

stolidly ['stɔlidli], *adv.* flegmatiquement; avec une lenteur impassible.

stolon ['stoulən], *s. Nat.Hist:* stolon *m*, stolone *f*; *Bot: F:* traînant *m*, coulant *m.*

stolonate ['stouləneit], **stoloniferous** [stoulə'nifərəs], *a. Nat.Hist:* stolonifère.

stolzite ['stoulzait], *s. Miner:* stolzite *f.*

stoma, *pl.* **-ata,** *occ.* **-as** ['stoumə, -ətə, -əz], *s. Nat.Hist:* stomate *m.*

stomach[1] ['stʌmək], *s.* **1.** *(a)* estomac *m*; **pain in the s.,** douleur *f*, mal *m*, d'estomac; **disordered, upset, s., s. upset,** troubles *mpl* de digestion; **to satisfy one's s.,** apaiser sa faim; *Pharm:* **to be taken on an empty s.,** à prendre à jeun; **on a full s.,** aussitôt après un repas; au moment de la digestion; **to turn s.o.'s s.,** soulever, retourner, le cœur, porter sur le cœur, à qn; écœurer qn; **it makes my s. turn,** cela me donne des nausées; me soulève le cœur; **to have a strong s.,** bien digérer; *F:* avoir le cœur bien accroché; **to have a cast iron s.,** avoir un estomac d'autruche; *Z: (of ruminants)* **first s.,** panse *f*; **second s.,** bonnet *m*; **third s.,** feuillet *m*, mellier *m*; **fourth, true, s.,** caillette *f*; *(b)* (euphémisme pour désigner le) ventre; **to crawl on one's s.,** ramper à plat ventre; **to have a large s.,** être pansu, ventru; *(c) attrib.* **s. ache,** (i) douleurs d'estomac; (ii) *F:* mal de ventre; **to have (the) s. ache,** avoir mal au ventre; avoir la colique; **s. complaint,** maux d'estomac; **s. cough,** toux *f* gastrique; **s. pump,** pompe stomacale; **s. tube,** sonde stomacale, œsophagienne; **s. tooth,** canine inférieure (d'enfant) (dont l'éruption est souvent accompagnée de troubles de digestion); **s. worm,** ascaride *m* lombricoïde; *Hort:* **s. insecticide,** insecticide *m* toxique par ingestion; *Paleont:* **s. stone,** gastrolithe *m.* **2.** *(a)* appétit *m*; **to have no s. for one's food,** ne pas avoir d'appétit; être sans appétit; *(b) O:* envie *f*, goût *m* **(for,** de); inclination *f* **(for,** pour); cœur, courage *m* (pour faire qch.); **it will put some s. into them,** cela leur mettra du cœur au ventre; **he had no s. for a fight,** il ne se sentait pas d'humeur à se battre; il n'avait aucune envie de se battre; *A:* **men of s.,** hommes de cœur; hommes qui n'ont peur de rien; *(c) A:* **to be of a proud, of a high, s.,** être plein de morgue.

stomach[2], *v.tr.* **1.** manger avec appétit; bien digérer (qch.); **I can't s. oysters,** (i) je ne digère pas les huîtres; les huîtres ne me vont pas; (ii) je n'aime pas, je déteste, les huîtres. **2.** endurer, supporter, tolérer (qch.); *F:* digérer (une insulte, etc.); **he could never s. maths,** il n'a jamais pu se mettre aux math; **I can't s. it any longer,** j'en ai plein le dos; **he won't s. that insult,** il n'avalera pas, ne digérera pas, cet affront; **I can hardly s. that,** ça c'est dur à avaler.

stomachal ['stʌməkl], *a.* stomacal, -aux.

stomacher ['stʌməkər], *s. A.Cost:* pièce *f* d'estomac (d'un corsage de femme).

stomachful ['stʌməkful], *s.* plein estomac (de nourriture, etc.); *P:* **I've had a s. of it,** j'en ai soupé.

stomachic [stɔ'mækik], *a. & s. Pharm:* stomachique *(m)*, stomacal *(m)*, -aux.

stomatal ['stoumətl], **stomate**[1] ['stoumeit], *a. Nat.Hist:* **1.** qui a rapport aux stomates. **2.** à stomates.

stomate[2], *s. Bot:* = STOMA.

stomatitis [stoumə'taitis], *s. Med:* stomatite *f*; *Vet:* **aphthous s.,** fièvre aphteuse; **angular s.,** perlèche *f*, pourlèche *f.*

stomato- ['stoumətou], *comb.fm. Z: etc:* stomato-.

stomatology [stoumə'tɔlədʒi], *s. Med:* stomatologie *f.*

stomatoplasty [stoumətou'plæsti], *s. Surg:* stomatoplastie *f.*

stomatopod ['stoumətoupɔd], *s. Crust:* stomatopode *m.*

stomatose ['stoumətous], **stomatous** ['stoumətəs], *a.* qui a des stomates; à stomates.

stomiatid [stoumi'ætid], *s. Ich:* stomiatidé *m.*

Stomiatidae [stoumi'ætidiː], *s. pl. Ich:* stomiatidés *m*, stomiatides *m.*

stomiatoid ['stoumiətɔid], *a. & s. Ich:* (poisson) stomiatide *(m).*

stomium, *pl.* **-ia, -iums** ['stoumiəm, -iə, -iəmz], *s. Bot:* stomium *m.*

stomp[1] [stɔmp], *s.* jazz *m* à temps fortement accentué que les danseurs accompagnent en frappant du pied.

stomp[2], *v.i.* **1.** frapper du pied; **to s. out of the room,** quitter la pièce d'un pas lourd. **2.** danser le *stomp, q.v.*

stone[1] [stoun], *s.* **1.** *(a)* pierre *f*; **(pebble) s.,** caillou, -oux *m*; **meteoric s.,** aérolithe *m*; **shower, fall, of stones,** avalanche *f* de pierres; éboulement *m*; *Civ.E:* **paving with stones,** empierrement *m*, cailloutage *m*; **to leave no stone unturned,** mettre tout en œuvre, en jeu, remuer ciel et terre, faire l'impossible, remuer toutes choses **(to do sth.,** pour accomplir qch.); faire jouer tous les ressorts; faire flèche de tout bois; employer le vert et le sec; *B:* **let him that is without sin among you cast the first s.,** que celui d'entre vous qui est sans péché lui jette la première pierre; **to throw, cast, stones at s.o.,** (i) lancer des pierres sur, à, qn; (ii) *Fig:* jeter des pierres dans le jardin de qn; **to throw stones at a dog,** jeter des pierres à un chien, lapider un chien; **within a stone's throw,** à un jet de pierre; à quelques, deux, pas; **it's only a stone's throw away,** il n'y a qu'un saut d'ici là; **we must mark that with a white s.,** il faut faire une croix à la cheminée; **to break stones,** (i) casser des pierres; (ii) *F:* être dans la dèche; **to clear ground of stones,** épierrer un terrain; *(b) Const: etc:* mœllon *m*, pierre de taille; **not to leave a s. standing,** ne pas laisser pierre sur pierre; *(c) (flagstone)* dalle *f*; *(gravestone)* pierre tumulaire, funéraire, tombale; *(d) Typ:* **(imposing, press) s.,** marbre *m*; *(e)* **scouring s.,** brique anglaise; *(f)* meule *f* (à repasser, de moulin); **honing s.,** pierre à huile. **2.** *(a)* **precious stones,** pierres précieuses; pierreries *f*; **Bristol s.,** cristal *m* de roche; *(b) Com: F:* diamant *m*; *(c) Clockm:* rubis *m.* **3.** *(material)* pierre (à bâtir, etc.); grès *m*; **broken s.,** pierraille *f*, cailloutis *m*; **Cornish s.,** kaolin *m*; terre *f* à porcelaine. **4.** *Med:* *(a)* calcul *m*, pierre (de la vessie, du rein); *(b)* lithiase *f*; **he frequently suffered from s.,** il était sujet à la lithiase. **5.** *(a)* noyau *m* (de fruit); pépin *m* (de raisin); *(b) pl. P:* testicules *m*; *(c) (domino)* dé *m.* **6.** *inv. Meas:* stone *m* (= 6·348 kg); **he weighs 12 s.,** il pèse 76 kilos; *Rac:* **colt that could give a s. to any other in the field,** poulain qui pourrait donner un avantage de 6 kilos à n'importe quel autre. **7. s. blind,** complètement aveugle; *F:* **s. broke,** sans le sou, à sec, dans la dèche, la débine; **s. cold,** froid comme (le) marbre; **the tea is s. cold,** le thé est complètement froid; *P:* **I've got him s. cold,** je l'ai à ma merci; **s. dead,** raide mort; **s. deaf,** complètement sourd; *F:* sourd comme un pot. **8.** *attrib.* *(a)* **s. axe,** (i) hache *f* de pierre; (ii) *Const:* marteau *m* à dresser; **s. barrow,** bard *m*, bayart *m*; *Laund:* **s. blue,** bleu *m* (d'empois); indigo *m*, azur *m*; *Agr: etc: NAm:* **s. boat,** traîneau *m*; *Archeol:* **s. bow,** arbalète *f* à jalet; *Miner:* **s. butter,** beurre *m* de pierre, de roche, de montagne; *Bot:* **s. cell,** sclérite *f*; *Paleont:* **s. circle,** cromlech *m*; **s. coal,** anthracite *m*; **s. colour,** couleur *f* pierre; **s.-coloured,** (de) couleur pierre *inv*; *Civ.E:* **s. crusher,** casse-pierre(s) *m inv*; concasseur *m*; **s. cutter,** tailleur *m*, équarrisseur *m*, de pierres; **s. cutter's tools,** outils *m* de taille; **s. cutter's hammer,** marteau de tailleur de pierres; polka *f*; **s. cutting,** taille *f* des pierres; **s. dresser,** équarrisseur de pierres; **s. dressing,** dressage *m*, taille, des pierres; **s. dressing pick,** pic *m* de tailleur de pierres; *NAm: F:* **s. fence,** boisson composée de whisky et de cidre; *Aut:* **s. guard,** pare-radiateur *m*, *pl.* pare-radiateurs; protège-radiateur *m*, *pl.* protège-radiateurs; **s. hammer,** casse-pierre(s); marteau à concasser la pierre; **s. mill,** casse-pierre(s); concasseur; **s. oil,** pétrole *m*; **s. pit, quarry,** carrière *f* de pierre; *Med:* **s. pock,** goutte *f* rose; *Archeol:* **s. robbing,** utilisation *f* de vieux bâtiments comme carrières; **s. saw,** scie *f* à pierre, de carrier; scie passe-partout; **s. sawyer,** scieur *m* de pierres; **s. slide,** (i) traînée *f* d'éboulis, de cailloux roulés; (ii) éboulement *m*; avalanche *f* de pierres; *(b) Nat.Hist:* (i) *Bot:* **s. break,** saxifrage *f*; *F:* casse-pierre(s) *m inv*; **s. fern,** cétérac(h) *m*; **s. parsley,** sison *m* (amomum), faux amome; **s. seed, weed,** grémil *m*, herbe *f* aux perles; (ii) *Ent:* **s. fly,** perle *f*; **the S. flies,** les perloïdes *m*; (iii) *Ich:* **s. bass,** cernier *m*; (iv) *Moll:* **s. borer,** pholade *f*, saxicave *f*; (v) *Orn:* **s. curlew, plover, snipe,** œdicnème (criard); courlis *m* de terre; **s. falcon, hawk,** faucon *m* émerillon; **s. hatch,** pluvier *m* à collier, gravière *f*; (vi) *Paleont:* **s. lily,** encrinite *m*; *(c)* de grès, en grès; **s. jug,** cruche *f* de grès; **s. china,** porcelaine (anglaise) opaque; *(d)* **s. fruit,** fruit *m* à noyau; drupe *m or f.*

stone[2], *v.tr.* **1.** lapider (qn); assaillir (qn) à coups de pierres; **to s. s.o. to death,** tuer qn à coups de pierres; lapider qn; **to s. s.o. out of a place,** chasser qn d'un endroit à coups de pierres; *P:* **s. the crows!** ça alors! **2. to s. fruit,** ôter, enlever, les noyaux des fruits; dénoyauter, énucléer, les fruits; **to s. raisins,** épépiner les raisins secs. **3.** *Const:* revêtir de pierres (un édifice, etc.); paver de pierres (une allée, une cave). **4.** empierrer, caillouter (une route). **5.** *(a) Leath:* **to s. (out) a skin,** poncer une peau; *(b)* **to s. (down) a tool,** passer un outil à la pierre.

stonechat ['stountʃæt], *s. Orn:* **1.** tarier *m* pâtre, traquet *m* pâtre. **2.** *F: Dial:* = *wheatear.*

stonecrop ['stounkrɔp], *s. Bot:* orpin *m*; joubarbe *f* des vignes; reprise *f*; **white s.,** orpin blanc; petite joubarbe; trique-madame *f inv*; **biting yellow s.,** orpin âcre; vermiculaire *f* âcre; poivre *m* de muraille; **ditch s.,** penthore *m.*

stoned [stound], *a.* **1.** (chemin) pavé, revêtu, de pierres. **2.** *(of fruit)* dénoyauté; *(of raisins)* épépiné; dont on a ôté le noyau, les pépins. **3.** *P:* **to be s.,** être chargé, (i) soûl, bourré, rond, (ii) drogué.

stoneless ['stounlis], *a.* (raisins secs) sans pépins.

stoneman, *pl.* **-men** ['stounmən], *s.m.* **1.** *Min:* mineur au rocher. **2.** maçon.

stonemason ['stounmeis(ə)n], *s.* maçon *m*; *O:* **stonemason's disease,** phthisie *f* des tailleurs de pierre; chalicose *f*, cailloute *f.*

stoner ['stounər], *s.* **1.** lapidateur, -trice. **2.** *(thg)* dénoyauteur *m* (de fruits); chasse-noyaux *m inv.*

stonewall ['stoun'wɔːl], *v.i.* **1.** *(a) Cr:* jouer un jeu prudent pour tenir jusqu'à la fin; *(b) Fenc:* parer au mur. **2.** *(a)* se montrer intransigeant; *(b) Parl:* faire de l'obstruction.

stonewaller ['stoun'wɔːlər], *s.* **1.** *Cr:* joueur prudent qui ne risque rien. **2.** *Parl:* obstructionniste *mf.*

stonewalling ['stoun'wɔːliŋ], *s.* **1.** *Cr:* jeu prudent. **2.** *(a)* intransigeance *f*; *(b) Parl:* obstructionnisme *m.*

stoneware ['stounwɛər], *s. Cer:* grès *m* (cérame), poterie *f* de grès; **fine s.,** faïence cailloutée; cailloutage *m.*

stonework ['stounwəːk], *s.* **1.** maçonnerie *f*; (i) maçonnage *m*; (ii) ouvrage *m* en pierre; **the s. is in poor condition,** la maçonnerie est en mauvais état. **2.** *Min:* travail *m* au rocher. **3.** *Typ:* *(a)* correction *f* sur le marbre; *(b)* imposition *f.*

stonewort ['stounwəːt], *s. Bot:* **1.** sison *m* (amome); faux amome. **2.** chara *m*, charagne *f*; **the Stoneworts,** les characées *f.*

stonily ['stounili], *adv.* **to look s. at s.o.,** regarder qn d'un air glacial, froid; jeter un regard glacé à qn.

stoniness ['stouninis], *s.* **1.** nature pierreuse (du sol, d'une poire). **2.** dureté *f* (de cœur); insensibilité *f*; froideur *f* (du regard de qn, etc.).

stoning ['stouniŋ], *s.* **1.** lapidation *f.* **2.** empierrement *m* (des routes). **3.** énucléation *f* (des abricots, etc.), épépinage *m* (des raisins secs). **4.** pierrage *m* (d'un outil tranchant, etc.).

stonker ['stɔŋkər], *v.tr. esp. Austr: P:* déjouer, contrecarrer, les plans, manœuvres, de (qn); **I was stonkered,** je me trouvais dans une impasse; j'étais tout désemparé.

stony ['stouni], *a.* **1.** (*a*) pierreux; couvert, rempli, de pierres; pétré; rocailleux; **s. meteorites,** météorites pierreuses; (*b*) **s. pear,** poire pierreuse. **2.** (*a*) de, en, pierre; (*b*) dur comme la pierre; **s. concretion,** concrétion pierreuse, très dure. **3.** froid, dur, insensible; glacial, -ials; **s. heart,** cœur de roche, de marbre; **s. look,** regard glacial, glacé, froid; **s. politeness,** politesse glacée. **4.** (*of fear, grief*) paralysant. **5.** *F:* **s. (broke),** sans le sou; à sec; dans la dèche, la débine; **I'm s. (broke),** je n'ai pas le sou.

stony-hearted [stouni'hɑːtid], *a.* au cœur de roche, de marbre; dur, insensible, dénaturé.

stooge[1] [stuːdʒ], *s. F:* (*a*) *Th:* faire-valoir *m inv* (d'un comique); (*b*) souffre-douleur *mf inv*; (*c*) (i) subalterne *m*, nègre *m* (ii) pantin *m*; **he's only a s.,** ce n'est qu'un comparse; **I'm only a s. round here,** c'est à moi qu'on donne toutes les besognes ingrates; (*d*) espion, -ionne; **police s.,** casserole *f.*

stooge[2], *v.i. F:* **1. to s. for s.o.,** (i) *Th:* servir de faire-valoir à (un comique); (ii) faire le nègre de qn. **2. to s. around,** faire un tour, flâner; *Av:* **to s. around, about,** attendre pour atterrir, patrouiller sans s'en faire; **to s. around the target,** rôder autour de l'objectif; *Fig:* **to s. around the office,** bricoler au bureau.

stook[1] [stuːk], *s.* **1.** *Agr:* tas *m* de gerbes; meulette *f*, moyette *f.* **2.** *Min:* = STOOP[3]. **3.** *Min:* (*wedge*) **s. and feathers,** aiguille infernale; aiguille-coin *f, pl.* aiguilles-coins.

stook[2], *v.tr. Agr:* mettre (les gerbes) en meulettes, en moyettes.

stool[1] [stuːl], *s.* **1.** (*a*) tabouret *m*; (*wooden, usu. with three legs*) escabeau *m*; **milking s.,** tabouret de vacher, sellette *f* à traire; **folding s.,** pliant *m*; **piano s., music s.,** tabouret de piano; **s. of repentance,** sellette; *Fig:* **to fall between two stools,** demeurer entre deux selles (le cul à terre); **to be in danger of falling between two stools,** se trouver entre deux selles; (*b*) **prayer s.,** prie-Dieu *m inv.* **2.** (*a*) *A:* garde-robe *f, pl.* garde-robes; *still used in:* **to go to s.,** aller à la selle, *F:* où le roi va à pied, en personne; **to strain at s.,** faire de grands efforts pour déféquer; (*b*) *Med:* **stools,** selles, fèces *f.* **3.** (*a*) souche *f*; **s. shoot,** rejet *m* de souche; (*b*) *Hort: Agr:* talle *f*, tige *f* adventice; **the stools,** le tallage; (*c*) *Hort: Agr:* pied *m* mère, plante *f* mère. **4.** *Ven:* poteau *m* qui porte un appelant; **s. (pigeon),** (*a*) pigeon appelant; appeau *m*, appelant, chanterelle *f*; (*b*) *F:* (i) canard privé (de la police, etc.); (ii) compère *m* (d'un escroc, etc.); (iii) *NAm:* mouchard *m*, indicateur, -trice (de police). **5.** *Const:* tablette *f*, appui *m*, rebord *m* (de fenêtre).

stool[2], *v.i.* **1.** *Agr:* pousser des rejetons, donner des rejets, taller; **corn that is stooling well,** blé qui gerbe bien. **2.** *Med:* aller à la selle. **3.** *NAm: F:* moucharder, cafarder; **to s. on an accomplice,** dénoncer, moutonner, un complice.

stoolball ['stuːlbɔːl], *s. Games:* balle *f* au camp.

stooling ['stuːliŋ], *s.* **1.** *Agr: Hort:* tallage *m*, multiplication *f* par rejetons; **s. stage,** stade *m* du tallage. **2.** *Med:* évacuation *f* (de selles).

stoop[1] [stuːp], *s.* **1.** inclination *f* en avant (du corps), penchement *m* en avant; *NAm: Agr:* **s. crop,** culture *f* qui demande qu'on se courbe en y travaillant; **s. labour,** travail *m* qui demande un penchement en avant pour le faire. **2.** dos rond; épaules voûtées; attitude voûtée; **to walk with a s.,** marcher le dos voûté; marcher penché; **he has a slight s.,** il a le dos légèrement voûté; **age brings a s.,** l'âge voûte la taille.

stoop[2]. **1.** *v.i.* (*a*) se pencher, se baisser; **he had to s. in order to get into the car,** il lui fallait se baisser pour monter dans la voiture; **he stooped to pick up the pin,** il s'est baissé pour ramasser l'épingle; (*b*) (i) s'abaisser, s'avilir, descendre (**to do sth.,** à, jusqu'à, faire qch.); (ii) daigner (**to do sth.,** faire qch.); **he wouldn't s. to a lie,** il ne descendrait pas jusqu'au mensonge; **man who would s. to anything,** homme prêt à toutes les bassesses; **you would not s. to that,** vous ne vous ravaleriez pas jusque-là; **I refuse to s. to such a thing,** je ne veux pas déroger jusqu'à faire une chose pareille; *Lit:* **to s. to conquer,** s'abaisser pour triompher; (*c*) *occ.* s'incliner, se plier (**to s.o.,** devant qn); (*d*) se tenir courbé; avoir le dos rond; être voûté; pencher les épaules; **to s. in walking,** marcher courbé; **to begin to s.,** se voûter; (*e*) *Poet: Ven: A:* (*of hawks, etc.*) s'abattre, fondre (**at, on,** sur); **the falcon stoops on its prey,** le faucon s'abat sur sa proie. **2.** *v.tr.* pencher, incliner, courber (la tête); courber, arrondir (le dos).

stoop[3], *s. Dial: Min:* pilier *m*, massif *m*; **s.-and-room system,** méthode *f* des piliers et galeries.

stoop[4], *s. NAm:* porche *m* (avec perron); terrasse surélevée (devant une maison).

stoop[5], *s.* = STOUP.

stoop-gallant ['stuːp'gæləntl], *s. Med: A:* trousse-galant *m inv*, suette *f.*

stooping[1] ['stuːpiŋ], *a.* penché, courbé; voûté.

stooping[2], *s.* = STOOP[1]; **in a s. position,** penché en avant.

stop[1] [stɔp], *s.* **1.** (*a*) arrêt *m*, interruption *f*, empêchement *m*; **to put a s. to sth.,** arrêter, faire cesser, suspendre, qch.; mettre un terme à, mettre fin à, mettre ordre à, qch.; **one ought to put a s. to it,** il faudrait y mettre fin; **I shall put a s. to it,** j'y mettrai bon ordre; **that put a s. to everything,** cela a tout arrêté; **to be at a s.,** se trouver arrêté; être aheurté à un obstacle; (*b*) arrêt, halte *f*, pause *f*; **short s.,** moment *m* d'arrêt; **ten minutes' s.,** dix minutes d'arrêt; **her tongue ran on without a s.,** sa langue marchait sans arrêt; **to make a s., to come to a s.,** s'arrêter; faire halte; faire une pause; (*of car, etc.*) stopper; **to make a sudden s.,** s'arrêter, stopper, brusquement; **business is at a s.,** les affaires ne marchent plus; **to bring sth. to a s.,** arrêter qch.; (*c*) **bus s.,** (point *m* d')arrêt d'autobus; halte; **route with frequent stops,** parcours à arrêts fréquents; **regular s.,** arrêt fixe; **request s.,** arrêt facultatif; (*d*) *Av:* (*in flight*) escale *f.* **2.** signe *m* de ponctuation; point *m*; **to put in the stops correctly,** mettre les points et virgules. **3.** *Mus:* (*a*) jeu *m*, registre *m* (d'orgue); **s. (key, knob),** bouton *m* d'appel; **to pull out a s.,** tirer un registre; *F:* **to pull out, put on, the sentimental s.,** se lancer dans la sensiblerie, faire de la sensiblerie; **to pull out all the stops,** faire l'impossible (**to achieve sth.,** pour accomplir qch.); y aller à plein; (*b*) trou *m* (de flûte, etc.); (*c*) clé *f* (de clarinette, etc.); (*d*) touche *f*, touchette *f* (de la guitare); (*e*) barré *m* (sur la guitare, le violon, le violoncelle). **4.** *Carp: Mec.E: etc:* dispositif *m* de blocage; arrêt, taquet *m*, butée *f*, toc *m*; heurtoir *m* (d'une porte, etc.); arrêtoir *m* (de vis, de boulon); (*on moving part of machine*) mentonnet *m*; (*in lock, etc.*) repos *m*; *Mec.E:* butoir *m* (de bout de course); *Aut: etc:* **shackle s.,** butée de jumelle; *Carp:* **bench s.,** crochet *m*, mentonnet, griffe *f*, d'établi; *Rail:* **automatic s.,** crocodile *m*; *Typew:* **margin(al) s.,** curseur *m*, régulateur *m*, de marge; margeur *m* (réglable). **5.** (*a*) *Cards:* (carte *f* d')arrêt; (*b*) *Box:* coup bloqué. **6.** *Opt: Phot:* diaphragme *m* (d'objectif); **s. scale,** échelle *f* des diaphragmes; *Phot:* **s. ring,** anneau *m* de réglage du diaphragme. **7. cattle s.,** tranchée couverte d'une grille (pour bloquer le passage du bétail). **8.** *Ling:* plosive *f*, explosive *f.* **9.** *Nau:* (*a*) (*frapping*) genope *f*; **to break the stops,** casser les genopes (d'un drapeau); (*b*) raban *m* de ferlage. **10.** *Z:* cassure *f* du nez (d'un chien). **11.** *NAm: P:* receveur *m.* **12.** *attrib. Phot: etc:* **s. bath,** bain *m* d'arrêt, bain acide pour arrêt (du développement); **s. bolt,** arrêt, arrêtoir *m*; cheville *f*, goupille *f*, d'arrêt (d'un essieu, etc.); **s. butt,** butte *f* (de champ de tir); *Mec.E:* **s. collar,** collier *m*, bague *f*, d'arrêt; bague de butée; **s. drill,** foret *m* à repos; **s. gear, s. motion,** appareil *m* d'arrêt; organes *mpl* d'arrêt; **automatic s. gear,** arrêt de secours (d'une presse d'imprimerie, etc.); *Fenc:* **s. hit, thrust,** coup *m* d'arrêt; *Ten:* **s. netting,** grillage *m*; *St.Exch:* **s. order,** ordre *m* stop (spécifiant la vente ou le rachat de titres si le cours varie au delà d'une certaine cote); **s. piece, pin,** broche *f*, cheville *f*, goupille *f*, de butée; ergot *m* d'arrêt; butoir *m*; *Aut:* étoquiau *m*, -aux (de ressort à lames); *Hyd.E:* **s. plank,** hausse *f* (de vanne, de barrage de retenue); *Aut:* **s. screw,** vis-butoir *f, pl.* vis-butoirs; vis *f* de butée, d'arrêt (de pédale d'embrayage); **s. shoulder,** saillie *f* d'arrêt; **s. signal,** *Aut:* stop *m*; *Rail:* signal *m* -aux d'arrêt; *NAm:* **s. street,** rue *f* avec un stop au débouché; **s. valve,** (i) *Mch: etc:* soupape *f*, robinet *m*, d'arrêt; obturateur *m*; **sliding s. valve,** diaphragme *m*; (ii) *Hyd.E: etc:* clapet *m* de retenue; *Ten:* **s. volley,** volée amortie.

stop[2], *v.* **(stopped)**

I. *v.tr.* **1.** boucher, aveugler, étancher, tamponner (une voie d'eau); plomber, obturer (une dent); (*with gold*) aurifier (une dent); *A:* étancher (une blessure); **to s. (up),** boucher, fermer (un trou); obstruer, obturer (un tuyau); (*of pipe, etc.*) **to get stopped (up),** super, s'obstruer; **to s. one's ears,** se boucher les oreilles; *Fig:* **to s. one's ears against entreaties,** rester sourd aux requêtes; *P:* **I'll s. his mouth for him,** je vais le faire taire; **to s. a gap,** (i) boucher, combler, un trou; (ii) combler une lacune; **to s. the way,** fermer, barrer, le passage; **to s. a crack,** reboucher une fente; (*with putty*) mastiquer une fente; (*with plaster or cement*) gobeter une fente; **to s. the draught round a door,** calfeutrer une porte. **2.** (*a*) arrêter (un cheval qui court, une balle qui roule, etc.); **to s. s.o. short,** arrêter qn (tout) court; **s. thief!** au voleur! **to s. the traffic,** interrompre la circulation; **to s. s.o.'s breath,** couper la respiration à qn; *Fb:* **to s. an opponent,** arrêter un adversaire; **to s. a rush,** endiguer une attaque; **to s. a blow,** parer un coup; *Box:* bloquer; *Fb:* **to s. the ball,** bloquer; *Mil: P:* **to s. a bullet,** être atteint d'une balle; *Adm:* **goods stopped at the customs house,** marchandises en consigne à la douane; **goods stopped by the customs house,** marchandises consignées par la douane; **walls that s. sounds,** murs qui étouffent, qui amortissent, le son; **curtains that s. the light,** rideaux qui interceptent la lumière; *Cards:* **I could s. hearts,** j'avais une carte d'arrêt à cœur; (*b*) **to s. s.o.'s doing sth., s.o. from doing sth.,** empêcher qn de faire qch.; **to s. sth. being done,** empêcher que qch. (ne) se fasse; **I can't s. it happening,** je ne peux pas l'empêcher; **there's no one to s. him,** il n'y a personne pour l'en empêcher; **nothing will s. him,** rien ne l'arrêtera; **what's stopping you?** quel obstacle vous arrête? qu'est-ce qui vous retient? **s. me if I talk too much,** arrêtez-moi, faites-moi taire, si je parle trop; *Com:* **to s. (payment of) a cheque,** arrêter, suspendre, le paiement d'un chèque; bloquer, stopper, un chèque; mettre arrêt à un chèque; frapper un chèque d'opposition; (*c*) arrêter (une pendule); arrêter, stopper (une machine); *Mch:* **to s. an injector,** désamorcer un injecteur; *Nau:* (*to engine room*) **s. both engines,** stoppez partout; (*d*) mettre fin à (qch.); enrayer (un abus, une grève, de mauvaises habitudes); **it ought to be stopped,** il faudrait y mettre fin; **rain stopped the game,** la pluie a arrêté la partie; *Jur:* **to s. a case,** mettre arrêt à, arrêter, un procès; **to s. bankruptcy proceedings,** suspendre la procédure de faillite. **3.** (*a*) cesser (ses efforts, ses visites, son travail); *Com:* **to s. payment,** cesser ses paiements; **to s. doing sth.,** s'arrêter de faire qch.; **to s. playing,** cesser de jouer; **we stopped talking,** nous avons cessé de causer; nous avons fait silence; **she never stops talking,** elle n'arrête jamais de parler; elle ne cesse pas de parler; elle parle sans cesse; **s. that noise!** assez de vacarme! assez de bruit! **s. it!** assez! finissez! **stop fooling!** assez de blagues! (*b*) *impers.* **it has stopped raining,** il a cessé de pleuvoir; la pluie a cessé. **4. to s. s.o.'s supply of electricity,** couper l'électricité à qn; **to s. s.o.'s wages,** retenir les gages de qn; **to s. so much out of s.o.'s wages,** retenir tant, faire une retenue de tant, sur les gages de qn; **to s. s.o.'s pension,** rayer, supprimer, la pension de qn; **to s. s.o.'s allowance,** couper les vivres de qn; *Mil:* **all leave is stopped,** toutes les troupes sont consignées; toutes les permissions sont suspendues, sont supprimées. **5.** *Hort:* pincer (une plante). **6.** *Mus:* (*a*) **to s. (down) a string,** presser une corde; (*b*) **to s. a flute,** boucher les trous d'une flûte (avec les doigts, les clés). **7.** *Opt: Phot:* **to s. (down),** diaphragmer (l'objectif, etc.). **8.** *Nau:* genoper (un amarrage).

II. *v.i.* **1.** (*a*) s'arrêter; (*of ship, car*) stopper; **to s. dead,** (i) (*of pers.*) *also* **to s. short,** s'arrêter (tout) court, s'arrêter net, *F:* pile; (ii) *Cmptr:* (*of programme*) se bloquer; **to s. in the middle of one's course,** se retenir, s'arrêter, au milieu de sa course, carrière; **they stopped to look at the view,** ils s'arrêtèrent pour regarder, contempler, le paysage; **to do a hundred kilometres without stopping,** faire cent kilomètres sans s'arrêter, sans arrêt, tout d'une traite; (*of car*) **to s. at the kerb,** s'arrêter, stopper, le long du trottoir; **all buses s. here,** arrêt fixe; **buses s. by request,** arrêt facultatif; (*sign inside bus*) **bus stopping,** arrêt demandé; **how long do we s. at Crewe?** combien d'arrêt à Crewe? **to pass a station without stopping, not to s. at a station,** brûler une gare; *Nau:* **to s. at a port,** faire escale à un port; (*to engine room*) **s.!** stop! stoppez! (*b*) cesser (de parler, fonctionner, etc.); **my watch has stopped,** ma montre (s')est arrêtée, ne marche plus; **to work fifteen hours without stopping,** travailler pendant quinze heures d'arrache-pied, sans arrêt, de suite; **to s. short in one's speech,** rester court dans son discours; **he stopped in the middle of a sentence,** il s'arrêta au milieu d'une phrase; **once on this subject he never stops,** une fois sur ce sujet il ne tarit pas; **he never stops to think,** il ne prend jamais le temps de réfléchir; **I can't s. to argue the matter,** je ne peux pas m'arrêter à discuter la question; **he will not s. till he has succeeded,** il n'aura pas de cesse qu'il n'ait réussi; **he did not s. at that,** il ne s'en tint pas là; **he'll s. at nothing,** rien, aucune considération, ne l'arrêtera; **to s. for s.o.,** (rester à) attendre qn; **s.!** tout beau! (*to speaker*) assez! **s. a moment,** arrêtez un instant; **s. there!** (i) restez-en là! (ii) demeurez-là! restez là! **the matter will not s. there,** l'affaire n'en demeurera pas là; **all their knowledge stops there,** toute leur science se borne à cela; (*c*) (*of noise, etc.*) cesser; **the rain has stopped,** la pluie a cessé. **2.** (*stay*) rester; **to s. at home,** rester à la maison; **won't you s. for lunch?** restez donc à déjeuner; **he's stopping with us for a few days,** il est venu passer quelques jours chez nous; **to s. at a hotel,** descendre, séjourner, à un hôtel.

III. (*compound verbs*) **1. stop away,** *v.i.* (*a*) ne pas venir; ne pas y aller; (*b*) s'absenter.

2. stop by, *v.i. NAm: F:* faire une petite visite, un bout de visite, (à la improviste) chez qn.

3. stop down, *v.tr. & i. Phot:* **to s. down (the lens),** diaphragmer l'objectif.

4. stop off, *v.i. NAm:* faire étape (**at London,** à Londres).

5. stop out. (*a*) *v.tr.* (i) reboucher (une fente, etc.); (ii) *Engr:* recouvrir de vernis (un faux trait); réserver (certaines parties de la planche); (*b*) *v.i.* **to s. out all night,** ne pas rentrer toute la nuit.

6. stop up. (*a*) *v.tr. see* STOP¹ I.1.; (*b*) *v.i.* **to s. up late,** veiller tard.

stop-(and-)go ['stɔp(nd)'gou], *a.* (conduite d'automobile) avec coups de frein et d'accélérateur alternés; (politique) de coups de frein et d'accélérateur alternés.

stopblock ['stɔpblɔk], *s.* **1.** *Rail:* taquet *m* d'arrêt, tampon *m.* **2.** blochet *m* d'arrêt (d'un frein).

stopcock ['stɔpkɔk], *s.* robinet *m* d'arrêt, de fermeture; obturateur *m.*

stope¹ [stoup], *s. Min:* **1.** gradin *m;* **underhand stopes,** gradins droits; **back, overhand, stopes,** gradins renversés. **2.** chantier *m* en gradins; chantier d'abattage.

stope², *v.tr. Min:* **1.** exploiter (une mine) en gradins. **2.** abattre (le minerai).

stopgap ['stɔpgæp], *s.* bouche-trou *m, pl.* bouche-trous; **it will serve as a s.,** cela servira à boucher un trou.

stoping ['stoupiŋ], *s. Min:* **1.** abattage *m,* exploitation *f,* en gradins. **2.** abattage (du minerai).

stoplight ['stɔplait], *s. Aut:* **1. the s.,** le feu rouge, le signal d'arrêt; le stop. **2.** (*on car*) stop *m.*

stopoff ['stɔpɔf], *s. NAm:* escale *f,* arrêt *m;* **a good s.-o. for travellers,** une bonne étape pour voyageurs.

stopover ['stɔpouvər], *s.* **1.** *Rail: NAm:* (*a*) faculté *f* d'arrêt; **s. ticket,** billet *m* avec (faculté d')arrêt; (*b*) étape *f.* **2.** *Av:* escale *f;* **flight with no stopovers,** vol *m* sans escale.

stoppage ['stɔpidʒ], *s.* **1.** (*a*) arrêt *m;* mise *f* au repos; suspension *f; Med:* suppression *f* (de la sudation, etc.); **s. of the traffic,** suspension de la circulation; **s. of business,** arrêt des affaires commerciales; **s. of payments,** suspension, cessation *f,* de paiements; *Mil: etc:* **s. of pay,** suppression de solde; **s. of leave,** suppression des permissions; consigne *f; Com:* **s. in transit,** droit *m* de suite; (*b*) **stoppages of pay,** retenues *f* sur les appointements; (*c*) (i) arrêt, pause *f,* halte *f,* interruption *f* (du travail); **sudden s. of a machine,** à-coup *m, pl.* à-coups, d'une machine; (ii) (*by discontented employees*), débrayage *m.* **2.** obstruction *f,* engorgement *m* (d'un tuyau, etc.); *Med:* **intestinal s.,** obstruction, occlusion, intestinale; (*by torsion*) volvulus *m.*

stopped [stɔpt], *a.* **1.** (*a*) **s. (up),** bouché, obstrué, obturé, engorgé; (*b*) *I.C.E:* **ring with s. ends,** segment *m* à joint à baïonnette. **2.** arrêté. **3.** *Ling:* **s. consonant,** plosive *f.* **4.** *Mus:* **s. note,** son bouché.

stopper¹ ['stɔpər], *s.* **1.** (*a*) bouchon *m* (*esp.* en verre); **ground (glass) s.,** bouchon à l'émeri; **screw s.,** fermeture *f* à vis; (*b*) obturateur *m* (de tuyau, etc.); pointeau *m* d'arrêt (de réservoir, citerne); (*c*) tampon *m* (de cornue, etc.); *Metall:* **s. rod,** quenouille *f* (de poche à couler). **2.** (*a*) *Mec.E:* taquet *m* (d'arrêt de mouvement); *Fig:* **to put a s. on s.o.'s activities,** enrayer les activités, menées, de qn; (*b*) *Nau:* bosse *f,* arrêtoir *m;* **cathead s.,** bosse de bout; **(chain) s.,** stoppeur *m;* bosse à chaîne; **to take the s. off a cable,** débosser un câble; **s. knot,** nœud *m* de ride. **3.** *Box:* coup *m* qui met knockout. **4.** *Cards:* carte *f* d'arrêt.

stopper², *v.tr.* **1.** boucher (un flacon). **2.** *Nau:* bosser (un câble).

stoppered ['stɔpəd], *a.* (*of bottle, etc.*) bouché à l'émeri.

stopping¹ ['stɔpiŋ], *a.* qui s'arrête; *Rail:* **s. train,** train *m* omnibus.

stopping², *s.* **1.** (*a*) arrêt *m;* **s. device,** dispositif *m* d'arrêt (de mouvement); *Aut:* **no s.,** arrêt interdit; **s. place,** (point *m* d')arrêt; halte *f; Av:* escale *f;* (*b*) suspension *f;* cessation *f;* **s. of a train, of a service,** suppression *f* d'un train, d'un service; (*c*) **s. of a cheque,** arrêt de paiement d'un chèque; (*d*) **s. (up),** obturation *f,* bouchage *m,* obstruction *f,* occlusion *f;* capture *f* (d'une voie d'eau, etc.); **s. of a tooth,** plombage *m,* obturation, d'une dent; (*with gold*) aurification *f;* **s. of a crack,** rebouchage *m* d'une fente; (*with putty*) mastiquage *m* d'une fente; (*with plaster or cement*) gobetage *m* d'une fente; **s. of the chink round a door,** calfeutrage *m* d'une porte; **s. knife,** couteau *m* à mastiquer; (*e*) *Gram: U.S:* ponctuation *f.* **2.** (*a*) bouchon *m,* tampon *m;* (*b*) mastic *m* (à reboucher); *Dent:* plombage *m,* mastic; **to remove the s. from a tooth,** déplomber une dent; *Cy:* **tyre s.,** mastic pour enveloppes. **3.** (*compound nouns*) (*a*) **s. down,** diaphragmation *f* (d'une lentille); (*b*) **s. out,** (i) rebouchage *m* (d'une fente, etc.); **s.-out wax,** mastic à reboucher; (ii) *Engr:* recouvrement *m* (de parties de la planche).

stopple¹ ['stɔpl], *s.* **1.** *A:* bouchon *m.* **2.** *NAm:* protège-tympan *m inv.*

stopple², *v.tr. A:* boucher.

stop-press ['stɔppres], *a. Journ:* **s.-p. news,** informations de dernière heure (insérées après interruption du tirage).

stopwatch ['stɔpwɔtʃ], *s.* chronomètre *m* (à déclic); montre *f* à arrêt.

storable ['stɔ:rəbl], *a.* **1.** (comestible etc.) qui se laisse conserver; de (bonne) garde. **2.** *Cmptr:* (*of data*) enregistrable.

storage ['stɔ:ridʒ], *s.* **1.** (*a*) emmagasinage *m,* emmagasinement *m,* entreposage *m;* **to take the lawn mower out of s.,** remettre la tondeuse à gazon en service; **to take goods out of s.,** sortir des marchandises; **wall safe for the s. of valuables,** armoire de fer pour la resserre des objets précieux; **the kitchen has plenty of s. space,** la cuisine a un grand volume de rangement; *Furn:* **s. unit,** meuble *m,* élément *m,* de rangement; **s. bin,** coffre *m,* récipient *m;* **s. tank,** réservoir *m,* cuve *f,* de magasinage, de stockage; (*b*) *El: Hyd.E: etc:* accumulation *f; El:* emmagasinage, emmagasinement; *Hyd.E:* **bank s.,** eau accumulée; **s. basin,** réservoir de bassin; *El:* **s. cell,** élément d'accumulateur; **s. heating,** chauffage *m* par accumulation; **(night) s. heater,** radiateur à accumulation (chauffé pendant la nuit); (*c*) *Cmptr:* stockage *m,* rangement *m,* mémorisation *f,* mise *f* en mémoire (de données). **2.** espace *m* disponible (en magasin, pour rangement, etc.); caves *fpl,* greniers *mpl* (d'une maison particulière); entrepôts *mpl,* magasins *mpl* (d'une maison de commerce). **3.** frais *mpl* d'entrepôt; magasinage *m.* **4.** *Cmptr:* mémoire *f;* **auxiliary, secondary, s.,** mémoire auxiliaire; **beam s.,** mémoire à faisceau(x); **main, primary, s.,** mémoire centrale, principale; **one-core-per-bit s.,** mémoire à un tore par bit; **read-only s.,** mémoire fixe, morte; **fast, sequential, access s.,** mémoire à accès rapide, séquentielle; **volatile, non-volatile, s.,** mémoire non rémanente, rémanente; **working s.,** mémoire de travail; mémoire, zone *f,* de manœuvre; **s. key,** indicatif *m* de protection de mémoire; **s. keyboard,** clavier *m* à transfert; **s. medium,** support *m* de mémoire.

storax ['stɔ:ræks], *s.* **1.** *Bot:* styrax *m; F:* aliboufier *m.* **2.** *Com: Pharm:* (baume *m*) styrax, storax *m.*

store¹ [stɔ:r], *s.* **1.** (*a*) provision *f,* approvisionnement *m;* **to have (a) good s., to have stores, of wine,** avoir une bonne provision de vin; *Ind:* **s. of energy,** énergie *f* disponible; **s. of money,** pécule *m;* **to have a s. of courage,** avoir un bon fonds de courage; **to lay in a s. of sth.,** faire une provision de qch.; s'approvisionner de qch.; **to lay in stores,** s'approvisionner; *Prov:* **s. is no sore,** abondance de biens ne nuit pas; (*b*) **to hold, keep, sth. in s.,** tenir, garder, qch. en réserve; réserver qch.; **what the future holds in s. for us,** ce que l'avenir nous réserve; *F:* ce qui nous pend au nez; **the disappointments in s. for you,** les déceptions qui vous sont réservées, qui vous attendent; **to have a hearty welcome in s. for s.o.,** réserver à qn un accueil cordial; **I have a surprise in s. for him,** je lui ménage une surprise; **that's a treat in s.,** c'est un plaisir à venir; **success was in s. for him,** il lui était réservé de réussir; (*c*) **to set great s. by sth.,** faire grand cas de qch.; attacher (un) grand prix, beaucoup de prix, à qch.; tenir beaucoup à qch.; **to set little s. by sth.,** faire peu de cas de qch.; (*d*) **s. cattle,** bétail *m* à l'engraissage. **2. stores,** provisions, approvisionnements, vivres *m; Nau:* approvisionnements, armement *m;* **war stores,** munitions *f,* matériel *m,* de guerre; **small stores,** assortiments *m;* **s. ship,** ravitailleur *m;* transport *m;* **marine stores,** (i) approvisionnements, matériel, de navires; (ii) *F: O:* friperie *f,* ferraille *f;* (iii) magasin *m,* maison *f,* d'approvisionnements de navires; **marine s. dealer,** (i) approvisionneur, -euse; (ii) marchand, -ande, de ferraille; fripier, -ière. **3.** (*a*) *Com: Ind:* entrepôt *m,* magasin, réserve *f;* (*for furniture*) garde-meuble *m, pl.* garde-meubles; *Mil: Navy:* (*in barracks, etc.*) magasin; (*for whole district*) manutention *f; Ind:* **contractor's s.,** gare *f* dépôt de matériaux; *Cust:* **bond s.,** entrepôt en douane; (*b*) (i) **(small) general s.,** épicerie *f,* bazar *m;* **the village, corner, s.,** l'épicerie, l'alimentation *f,* du village, du coin; (ii) *esp. NAm:* boutique *f,* magasin; **toy s.,** magasin de jouets; (*c*) **(department, big) stores,** les grands magasins; **chain s.,** (i) magasin à succursales (multiples); (ii) succursale *f* (de grand magasin); *attrib. NAm:* **s. cheese,** (fromage *m* de) cheddar *m;* **s. clothes,** confections *f;* **s. furniture,** meubles *m* provenant des grands magasins; **s. teeth,** fausses dents. **4.** *Cmptr:* = STORAGE 4.

store², *v.tr.* **1.** pourvoir, munir, approvisionner (**with,** de); **to s. one's mind with knowledge,** enrichir son esprit de connaissances; **to have a well-stored mind,** avoir la tête bien meublée; avoir l'esprit bien meublé. **2. to s. sth. (up),** amasser, accumuler, qch.; mettre qch. en réserve; **to s. up electricity, heat,** emmagasiner l'électricité, la chaleur. **3.** (*a*) emmagasiner, magasiner, mettre en grange (le foin, le blé, etc.); mettre en silo (des betteraves, etc.); **the crop was not yet stored,** la récolte n'était pas encore rentrée; **squirrels s. food for the winter,** les écureuils organisent des réserves de vivres pour l'hiver; *v.i.* **goods that don't s. well,** marchandises qui ne se conservent, se gardent, pas bien; *Fig:* **dates stored away in the memory,** dates emmagasinées dans la mémoire; (*b*) (i) prendre, (ii) mettre, (des meubles, etc.) en dépôt; **stored furniture,** mobilier au garde-meuble; *Ind: etc:* **stored plant,** machines en dépôt. **4.** *Cmptr:* mettre, ranger, en mémoire; mémoriser, stocker (des données); **stored programme,** programme enregistré; **permanently stored,** en mémoire fixe, permanente; **stored programme computer,** calculateur *m* à programme enregistré; ordinateur *m.*

storefront ['stɔ:frʌnt], *s. NAm:* devanture *f* de magasin; **s. office,** bureau situé dans la devanture d'un magasin.

storehouse ['stɔ:haus], *s.* magasin *m,* entrepôt *m,* dépôt *m; Mil:* (*for whole district*) manutention *f; Fig:* (*of pers., book, etc.*) **a s. of information,** une mine de renseignements.

storekeeper ['stɔ:ki:pər], *s.* **1.** (*a*) garde-magasin *m, pl.* gardes-magasin(s), magasinier *m; Ind: etc:* chef *m* de matériel, manutentionnaire *mf;* (*b*) (*in hospital, convent, etc.*) dépensier, -ière; *Nau:* cambusier *m,* magasinier. **2.** *NAm:* marchand, -ande; boutiquier, -ière.

storer ['stɔ:rər], *s.* **furniture s.,** propriétaire *mf* d'un garde-meuble.

store(-)room ['stɔ:ru:m], *s.* **1.** (*a*) (*in private house*) office *f,* resserre *f,* dépense *f;* (*b*) *Ind:* halle *f* de dépôt; (*c*) *Nau:* (i) soute *f* aux vivres, à provisions, magasin *m,* coqueron *m;* (ii) cambuse *f;* (*d*) (*in library, museum*) réserve *f.* **2.** *NAm:* (chambre *f* de) débarras *m.*

storewide ['stɔ:waid], *a. NAm:* dans l'ensemble du magasin; **s. clearance,** liquidation complète.

storey ['stɔ:ri], *s.* **1.** étage *m* (d'un bâtiment); **to add a s. to a house,** exhausser une maison d'un étage; **on the third s.,** *NAm:* **on the fourth s.,** au troisième étage; **single, one, s. house,** maison sans étage, de plain-pied. **2.** *For:* étage (d'essences); **lower s.,** sous-étage *m, pl.* sous-étages.

storeyed ['stɔ:rid], *a.* **1.** à étage(s); **two-s. house,** maison à un étage, *NAm:* à deux étages; **one-s., single-s., house,** maison sans étage, de plain-pied. **2.** *For:* (forêt) à arbres d'âges différents; **two-s. forest,** futaie à double étage.

storiated ['stɔ:rieitid], *a. Typ:* (titre) enjolivé d'ornements, historié.

storied¹ ['stɔ:rid], *a.* **1.** historié; **s. urn,** urne historiée; *Arch:* **s. window,** vitrail historié. **2.** *A: & Lit:* célébré dans l'histoire, dans la légende.

storied², *a.* = STOREYED.

storing ['stɔ:riŋ], *s.* **1.** approvisionnement *m* (**with,** en). **2. s. (up),** accumulation *f,* amassage *m* (**of,** de). **3.** emmagasinage *m,* emmagasinement *m* (**of,** de). **4.** *Cmptr:* mise *f* en mémoire; mémorisation *f,* stockage *m,* rangement *m* (de données).

stork [stɔ:k], *s.* **1.** *Orn:* cigogne *f;* **black s.,** cigogne noire; **white s.,** cigogne blanche; **black-necked, saddle-billed, s.,** jabiru *m,* cigogne à selle; **open-billed s.,** (cigogne) bec-ouvert *m, pl.* becs-ouverts; anastome *m;* **painted s.,** tantale *m* asiatique; **South American, maguari, s.,** cigogne maguari; **shoe-billed, whale-headed, s.,** balæniceps *m,* baléniceps *m,* bec-en-sabot *m, pl.* becs-en-sabot; **white-bellied s.,** cigogne d'Abdimi; **wood s.,** tantale d'Amérique; *Fr.C:* cigogne américaine; **woolly-necked s.,** cigogne épiscopale; *F: O:* **a visit from the s.,** une naissance, l'arrivée *f* d'un bébé. **2.** *Bot:* **stork's bill,** bec-de-grue *m, pl.* becs-de-grue; (i) érodium *m;* (ii) pélargonium *m.*

storm[1] [stɔ:m], *s.* **1.** orage *m*; (*windstorm*) tempête *f*; (*a*) **rains s.,** tempête de pluie, pluie *f* d'orage; *Nau:* fort grain de pluie; **magnetic s.,** orage magnétique; **there's a s. coming,** le temps est à l'orage; **a s. was raging,** la tempête faisait rage; *Prov:* **after a s. comes a calm,** après la pluie le beau temps; *Fig:* **a s. in a teacup,** une tempête dans un verre d'eau; **political s.,** ouragan *m*, tourmente *f*, politique; **to stir up a s.,** soulever une tempête; **to bring a s. about one's ears,** s'attirer une véritable tempête d'ennuis, d'indignation; soulever un tollé général; (*b*) *attrib.* **s. bell,** tocsin *m*; **s. cone, drum,** cône *m*, cylindre *m*, de tempête; **s. damage,** dommage causé par l'orage, la tempête; **s. door,** deuxième porte (à l'extérieur d'une porte de maison); **s. window,** (i) contre-fenêtre *f*, *pl.* contre-fenêtres; (ii) petite (fenêtre en) mansarde; *NAm:* **s. cellar,** caveau aménagé en abri (contre les cyclones, etc.); **s. lantern,** lampe-tempête *f*, *pl.* lampes-tempêtes; **s. signal,** signal *m*, -aux, de tempête; *Meteor:* **s. area,** étendue *f* d'une tempête; **s. belt, zone,** zone *f* des tempêtes; **s. centre,** (i) centre *m* de la tempête, du cyclone; (ii) *Fig:* foyer *m* d'agitation, de troubles, de sédition, d'intrigues, etc.; **s. cloud,** (i) nuée *f* d'orage; (ii) nuage à l'horizon, nuage menaçant; **the s. cloud has burst,** la nuée a crevé (sur le pays, etc.); *Civ.E:* **s. drain,** fossé *m* d'évacuation; *Nau:* **s. sail,** voile *f* de cape, de mauvais temps; dériveur *m*; *Orn:* **s. bird,** oiseau *m* des tempêtes; *esp.* pétrel *m* tempête; **s. cock,** (grive *f*) draine *f*, grive de gui. **2.** pluie (de projectiles, etc.); bordée *f* (d'injures); **s. of applause, protests,** tempête d'applaudissements, de protestations; **to raise a s. of laughter,** déchaîner l'hilarité générale. **3.** *Mil:* assaut *m*; **to take a stronghold by s.,** prendre d'assaut une place forte; *Fig:* **to take the audience by s.,** emporter, soulever, l'auditoire; **s. troops,** (i) troupes *f* d'assaut; (ii) *German Hist:* sections *f* d'assaut; **s. trooper,** membre des sections d'assaut.

storm[2]. **1.** *v.i.* (*a*) (*of wind, rain*) se déchaîner; faire rage; (*b*) **it is storming,** il fait de l'orage; (*c*) (*of pers.*) tempêter, pester; **to s. at s.o.,** s'emporter contre qn; faire essuyer une algarade à qn; (*d*) **to s. into, out of, the room,** entrer dans, quitter, la salle violemment, furieusement. **2.** *v.tr. Mil:* (i) donner, livrer, l'assaut à (une place forte); (ii) prendre d'assaut, emporter d'assaut, enlever (une place forte).

storm-beaten ['stɔ:mbi:t(ə)n], *a.* battu par la tempête, les tempêtes.

stormbound ['stɔ:mbaund], *a.* retenu par une tempête; en relâche forcée.

stormily ['stɔ:mili], *adv.* orageusement, tempestueusement.

storminess ['stɔ:minis], *s.* caractère orageux (du temps, d'une réunion, etc.).

storming ['stɔ:miŋ], *s.* **1.** violence *f*, emportements *mpl.* **2.** *Mil:* (i) assaut *m*; (ii) prise *f* d'assaut, enlèvement *m*; **s. party,** troupes *fpl*, colonne *f*, d'assaut.

stormproof ['stɔ:mpru:f], *a.* **1.** à l'épreuve de la tempête, des tempêtes; résistant au vent. **2.** *Mil:* (forteresse, etc.) inexpugnable.

storm-tossed ['stɔ:mtɔst], *a.* ballotté par la tempête; (navire) battu par la tempête.

stormy ['stɔ:mi], *a.* (temps, ciel) orageux, d'orage; **the weather is s.,** le temps est à l'orage; (*on barometer*) **s.,** tempête; **s. sea,** mer démontée; **s. wind,** fort vent, vent tempétueux; **s. coast,** côte orageuse; *Fig:* **s. discussion,** discussion orageuse; **s. meeting,** réunion houleuse; **s. life,** vie tumultueuse, orageuse.

story[1] ['stɔ:ri], *s.* **1.** (*a*) histoire *f*, récit *m*, conte *m*; **to tell a s.,** raconter, conter, une histoire; faire un conte; **they all tell the same s.,** ils racontent tous la même histoire; **according to his s.,** à croire ce qu'il dit, ce qu'il raconte; d'après lui; **there is a s. that. . .,** on raconte que . . .; **as the s. goes,** à ce que dit l'histoire; à ce que l'on raconte; d'après ce que l'on dit; *F:* **that is quite another s.,** ça c'est une autre histoire; ça c'est une autre paire de manches; **it is quite another s. now,** c'est maintenant une autre chanson, une tout autre histoire; **it's the (same) old s., the old, old s.,** c'est toujours la même histoire, la même rengaine, la vieille rengaine, la même chanson, c'est le refrain de la ballade; **it's the old s. of the only child,** c'est l'histoire bien connue de l'enfant unique; **it's a long s.,** c'est toute une histoire; **the best of the s. is that he missed the train,** le plus beau de l'histoire c'est qu'il a manqué le train; **these bruises tell their own s.,** ces meurtrissures en disent long; (*b*) anecdote *f*; **funny, good, s.,** bonne histoire; **he can tell a good s.,** il en sait de bonnes; (*c*) histoire (de qn, qch.); **have you read the s. of his life?** avez-vous lu l'histoire de sa vie? **his s. is an eventful one,** son passé a été plein d'aventures; **the s. of printing,** l'histoire de l'imprimerie. **2. short s.,** nouvelle *f*, conte; **short s. writer,** (i) nouvelliste *mf*; (ii) *U.S:* *P:* faussaire *m* de chèques bancaires; **film s.,** ciné-roman *m*, *pl.* ciné-romans. **3.** intrigue *f* (d'un roman, d'une pièce de théâtre); **he reads novels only for the s.,** il ne lit les romans que pour l'action; **the s. of the film is Shakespeare's Romeo and Juliet,** on a fait le film d'après Roméo et Juliette de Shakespeare; **have you read the s. of the film?** avez-vous lu le roman d'après lequel on a fait ce film? **4.** *Journ:* *F:* article *m*; **to make a s. out of a trivial event,** faire un article, *F:* un papier, une nouvelle, d'un événement sans importance. **5.** *F:* (*esp. when speaking to children*) (*a*) conte; mensonge *m*, menterie *f*; **to tell stories,** dire des mensonges; **what a s.!** quel mensonge! (*b*) *O:* **oh you s.!** oh, le petit menteur, la petite menteuse! **6.** *A:* l'histoire, la légende; **famous in s.,** célèbre dans l'histoire, la fable.

story[2], *s. esp. NAm:* = STOREY.

storybook ['stɔ:ribuk], *s.* livre *m* de contes; livre d'histoires; *attrib.* **it looks like a s. castle,** cela ressemble au château d'un conte de fées; **our meeting was quite a s. affair,** l'histoire de notre rencontre est tout un roman.

storyteller ['stɔ:ritelər], *s.* **1.** conteur, -euse. **2.** *F:* *O:* (*esp. said to children*) menteur, -euse.

storytelling[1] ['stɔ:riteliŋ], *a.* **1.** (personne) qui se plaît à raconter; **s. old age,** vieillesse raconteuse. **2.** *F:* *O:* (*of child*) menteur, -euse.

storytelling[2], *s.* **1.** l'art *m* de conter; **to be good at s.,** avoir le talent de raconter des histoires. **2.** *F:* *O:* mensonges *mpl.*

stoup ['stu:p], *s.* **1.** *A:* cruche *f*. **2.** *Ecc:* **(holy water) s.,** bénitier *m*.

stoupful ['stu:pful], *s.* cruchée *f*.

stout[1] [staut], *a.* **1.** (i) fort, vigoureux; (ii) brave, vaillant; (iii) ferme, résolu; **s. fellow,** (i) homme vaillant, courageux; (ii) gaillard *m* solide; solide gaillard; **to call for a few s. men,** faire appel à des hommes de bonne volonté; *F:* **s. fellow!** bravo! **to make, put up, a s. resistance,** faire une résistance opiniâtre; se défendre vaillamment; **s. heart,** cœur vaillant; **to work with a s. heart,** être courageux au travail. **2.** (*of thg*) fort, solide; (*of cloth, etc.*) renforcé; (*of material*) résistant; **s. sole,** semelle forte; **s. ship,** navire solide; **s. glass,** verre épais. **3.** (*a*) gros, *f.* grosse; corpulent, fort, puissant; **to grow s.,** devenir adipeux; **to be getting, growing, s.,** engraisser; prendre de l'embonpoint, du corps, du ventre; *F:* s'empâter; **to grow s. again,** rengraisser; (*b*) (cheval) étoffé.

stout[2], *s.* stout *m*; bière brune forte.

stouthearted ['staut'hɑ:tid], *a.* courageux, intrépide, vaillant.

stoutheartedly ['staut'hɑ:tidli], *adv.* courageusement, intrépidement, vaillamment.

stoutheartedness ['staut'hɑ:tidnis], *s.* courage *m*, intrépidité *f*.

stoutish ['stautiʃ], *a.* **1.** assez gros, assez corpulent; replet, -ète. **2.** (*of door, box, etc.*) assez solide.

stoutly ['stautli], *adv.* **1.** fortement, vigoureusement, vaillamment, résolument; (travailler) ferme; **to deny sth. s.,** nier qch. (fort et) ferme; **he s. maintained that he was not there,** il affirmait énergiquement qu'il n'était pas là. **2.** (bâti, etc.) fortement, solidement.

stoutness ['stautnis], *s.* **1.** fermeté *f*, vigueur *f* (de la résistance, etc.). **2.** solidité *f*; **of sufficient s. to last a long time,** assez solide, résistant, pour durer longtemps. **3.** embonpoint *m*, corpulence *f*; **a tendency to s.,** une tendance à engraisser.

stovaine ['stouvein], *s.* *Pharm:* stovaïne *f*; *Med:* **to anaesthetize with s.,** stovaïn(is)er.

stove[1] [stouv], *s.* **1.** poêle *m*, fourneau *m*; (*a*) **slow-combustion s.,** poêle à feu continu; calorifère *m*, salamandre *f*; (*of enamelled iron*) cheminée prussienne; *O:* **oil s.,** (i) (*burning paraffin*) poêle à pétrole; (ii) (*burning heavy oil*) calorifère à mazout; **s. setter,** poseur *m* de poêles, poêlier-fumiste *m*, *pl.* poêliers-fumistes; (*b*) fourneau de cuisine; cuisinière *f*; (*small, portable*) réchaud *m*; **electric, gas, s.,** cuisinière électrique, à gaz. **2.** (*a*) *Ch:* *Ind:* étuve *f*, four *m*; (*b*) *Metall:* **Cowper s.,** récupérateur *m* cylindrique. **3.** *Hort:* *A:* **s. (house),** serre chaude; forcerie *f*; **s. plants,** plantes *f* de serre chaude.

stove[2], *v.tr.* **1.** (*a*) étuver (des émaux, *Metall:* des moules, etc.); (*b*) étuver, désinfecter (des vêtements, etc.); les passer à l'étuve. **2.** *Hort:* élever (des plantes) en serre chaude.

stove[3], *v.tr. occ.* **to s. in,** défoncer, crever (une barrique, un bateau, etc.).

stove-enamelled ['stouvinæmld], *a.* émaillé au four.

stovepipe ['stouvpaip], *s.* **1.** tuyau *m* de poêle. **2.** *F:* *O:* **s. hat,** chapeau haut de forme; *F:* huit-reflets *m inv.* **3.** *NAm:* *Mil:* *F:* (*a*) avion *m* de chasse à réaction; (*b*) mortier *m* de tranchée.

stover ['stouvər], *s.* *Dial:* & *NAm:* fourrage *m* (de paille).

stoving ['stouviŋ], *s.* **1.** étuvage *m*, étuvement *m*. **2.** *Hort:* élevage *m* en serre chaude.

stow [stou], *v.tr.* **1.** **to s. (away),** mettre en place, ranger, serrer (des objets); *F:* **we were stowed in the attic,** on nous avait fourrés dans la mansarde; **to s. away a huge meal,** bouffer, avaler, expédier, un repas énorme; *P:* **s. it!** (i) la ferme! (ii) ça suffit! (il) y en a marre! **2.** *Nau:* arrimer, installer (des marchandises, etc.); **to s. the cargo,** faire l'arrimage; **to s. the anchor, the boats,** mettre à poste, saisir, l'ancre; saisir les canots; **to s. a sail,** ferler, serrer, amarrer, une voile. **3.** *v.i.* **to s. away (on board a ship, a plane),** s'embarquer clandestinement (à bord d'un navire, d'un avion). **4.** (*a*) **to s. sth. full of sth.,** remplir qch. de qch.; **to s. a waggon,** charger une charrette; (*b*) *Min:* remblayer (de vieux chantiers).

stowage ['stouidʒ], *s.* **1.** *Nau:* (*a*) arrimage *m*; **to avoid broken s.,** pour éviter les pertes, les vides, d'arrimage; (*b*) capacité *f* utilisable pour marchandises; espace *m* utile; (*c*) frais *mpl* d'arrimage. **2.** magasinage *m*.

stowaway ['stouəwei], *s.* **1.** *Nau:* *Av:* voyageur, -euse, de fond de cale; passager, voyageur, clandestin; stowaway *m*. **2.** endroit *m* où l'on peut fourrer des objets; (*secret*) cachette *f*.

stower ['stouər], *s.* **1.** *Nau:* arrimeur *m*. **2.** *Min:* remblayeur *m*, restapleur *m*.

stowing ['stouiŋ], *s.* **1. s. (away),** rangement *m*, mise *f* en place. **2.** *Nau:* arrimage *m*, installation *f* (de la cargaison). **3.** *Min:* remblayage *m*.

strabismal [stræ'bizm(ə)l], **strabismic** [strə'bizmik], *a.* *Med:* strabique.

strabismometer [stræbiz'mɔmitər], *s.* *Med:* strabomètre *m*.

strabismus [stræ'bizməs], *s.* *Med:* strabisme *m*; **convergent, internal, s.,** strabisme convergent; **divergent, external, s.,** strabisme divergent.

Strabo ['streibou]. *Pr.n.m. Gr.Lit:* Strabon.

strabotomy [stræ'bɔtəmi], *s.* *Surg:* strabotomie *f*.

Strad [stræd], *s.* *Mus:* *F:* stradivarius *m*.

straddle[1] ['strædl], *s.* **1.** (*a*) écartement *m*, écarquillement *m*, des jambes; (*b*) position *f* à califourchon; (*c*) *Sp:* rouleau ventral; (*d*) **s. carrier, truck,** charrette *f* en contrebas. **2.** *Artil:* encadrement *m* (du but). **3.** (*a*) *St.Exch:* opération *f* à cheval; (*b*) *Cards:* (*at poker*) mise doublée; (*c*) *NAm:* *Pol:* refus *m* de se compromettre (entre deux partis).

straddle[2]. **1.** *v.i.* (*a*) (i) écarter, écarquiller, les jambes; se tenir, marcher, les jambes écartées; (ii) *Sp:* sauter en rouleau ventral; (*b*) éviter de se compromettre, de se prononcer; (*c*) *Artil:* tirer à la fourchette. **2.** *v.tr.* (*a*) enfourcher (un cheval); se mettre, être, à califourchon sur (une chaise, etc.); chevaucher (un mur, une chaise); *Mil:* **to s. a river, a railway,** achevaler, être à cheval sur, un fleuve, une ligne de chemin de fer; (*b*) *Pol:* *NAm:* **to s. a question, an issue,** refuser de se compromettre sur une question; **to s. the fence,** ménager la chèvre et le chou; (*c*) *Artil:* **to s. the target,** encadrer l'objectif; (*d*) *Cards:* (*at poker*) doubler (la mise); (*e*) **to s. (out) one's legs,** écarter, écarquiller, les jambes.

straddle-legged ['strædl'legd], *a.* (qui a) les jambes écartées; **to sit s.-l. on a form,** être à califourchon sur, chevaucher, une banquette.

straddle-legs ['strædllegz], *adv.* à califourchon.

straddler ['strædlər], *s.* *NAm:* **1.** politicien *m* qui refuse de se compromettre. **2.** *Cards:* (*at poker*) joueur *m* qui double la mise.

straddling ['strædliŋ], *s.* **1.** écartement *m*, écarquillement *m*, des jambes. **2.** *Artil:* tir *m* à la fourchette.

stradiot ['strædiɔt], *s.* *A.Mil:* estradiot *m*, stradiot *m*.

Stradivarius [strædi'vɛəriəs, -vɑ:riəs], *s.* **S. (violin),** stradivarius *m*.

strafe[1] [streif], *s.* *F:* **1.** *Mil:* (i) bombardement *m*; *F:* marmitage *m*; (ii) mitraillage *m* en rase-mottes. **2.** verte semonce, bonne correction; *P:* engueulade *f*.

strafe[2], *v.tr.* *F:* **1.** *Mil:* (i) faire subir à (l'ennemi) un bombardement en règle; *F:* marmiter (l'ennemi); (ii) mitrailler (l'ennemi) en rase-mottes. **2.** (*a*) rosser (qn); (*b*) semoncer, *P:* engueuler (qn).

strafing ['streifiŋ], *s.* = STRAFE[1].

straggle ['strægl], *v.i.* **1.** **to s. (along),** marcher sans ordre, à la débandade; *Mil:* rester en arrière; traîner; **the guests straggled away, off,** les invités s'en allaient par petits groupes, se dispersaient lentement. **2. houses that s. round the lake,** maisons qui s'éparpillent autour du lac; **his hair straggled over his collar,** ses cheveux traînaient en désordre sur le col de son veston. **3.** *Hort:* (*of plant*) traîner.

straggler ['stræglər], *s.* **1.** traînard, -arde; *Nau:* (*ship, sailor*) retardataire *m*. **3.** *Arb:* branche *f* qui traîne; (*of fruit tree*) branche gourmande, gourmand *m*.

straggling[1] ['strægliŋ], *a.* **1.** disséminé; **a few s. houses,**

quelques maisons éparpillées, isolées; **s. village,** village aux maisons éparses; **s. hairs,** cheveux épars, mal plantés; **s. beard,** barbe *f* maigre; quelques poils *m* de barbe incultes. **2. s. plants,** plantes *f* qui traînent.

straggling², *s.* marche *f* à la débandade.

stragglingly ['stræglinli], *adv.* à la débandade, en désordre; confusément; çà et là.

straggly ['strægli], *a.* (*of branches, hair, etc.*) épars.

straight [streit], *a., s. & adv.*

I. *a.* **1.** (*a*) droit, rectiligne; **s. as a ramrod,** droit comme un i, un jonc, un cierge; **to hold oneself s. as a post, ramrod,** se tenir droit comme une quille, un piquet; **s. line,** (ligne) droite (*f*); **perfectly s. line, line s. as a bowstring,** ligne tirée au cordeau; *Com:* **s.-line depreciation,** amortissement *m* en ligne droite; *Cmptr:* **s.-line coding,** codage *m* en succession; **s. garden path,** allée tirée au cordeau; **the straightest way to get there,** le chemin le plus direct pour y aller; **to have a s. eye,** avoir l'œil juste; (*of figure*) **s. up and down,** tout d'une venue; **s. back, legs,** dos droit, jambes droites; **with a s. knee,** la jambe tendue, le jarret tendu; **s. hair,** cheveux (i) raides, (ii) plats; **s. flight of stairs,** volée droite; *Tls:* **s. edge,** règle *f* (à araser); limande *f*; (*of drill*) **s. shank,** queue *f* cylindrique; **s. lever,** levier droit; *Arch:* **s. arch,** arc droit, en plate-bande; *Carp:* **s. joint,** assemblage *m* à plat; *Geom:* **s. angle,** angle plat; *Aut:* **s. eight engine,** moteur *m* à huit cylindres en ligne; *P:* **s. drinking,** consommation *f* debout devant le bar; **I don't like s. drinking,** je n'aime pas boire le verre sur le zinc; (*b*) (mouvement) en ligne droite; **to fly s. as a dart, an arrow,** voler droit comme une flèche; *Fenc:* **s. thrust,** coup droit; *Box:* **s. right, left,** direct *m* du droit, gauche; (*c*) *Turf: Fin:* **s. tip,** tuyau sûr, de la source; (*d*) de suite; *Ten:* **to win in three s. sets,** gagner par trois sets de suite; *NAm:* **six s. days,** six jours consécutifs, de suite. **2.** (*a*) juste, honnête; loyal, -aux; franc, *f.* franche; **s. as a die,** d'une droiture absolue; **s. dealings,** procédés *m* honnêtes; rondeur *f* en affaires; **man perfectly s. in his dealings, who does a s. deal,** homme sérieux et rond en affaires; homme qui est toujours loyal en affaires; **she'll keep him s.,** elle le fera marcher droit, elle l'aidera à marcher droit; **s. answer,** réponse franche; réponse sans équivoque; **to be s. with s.o.,** agir loyalement avec qn, envers qn; **to play a s. game,** jouer bon jeu bon argent; *F:* **s. girl,** fille honnête; (*b*) *F:* normal, hétérosexuel. **2.** net, *f.* nette; tout simple; **s. definition,** définition claire et précise; *Swim:* **s. dive,** plongeon *m* classique; *Th:* **s. play,** pièce de théâtre proprement dite; **s. part,** rôle sérieux, sans complications; **s. actor,** comédien *m* dramatique; (*comedian's*) **s. man,** faire-valoir *m inv*; *Pol:* **s. fight,** campagne électorale à deux candidats; *U.S:* **s. democrat,** démocrate bon teint; bon démocrate; **s. ticket,** (i) programme *m* (du parti) sans modification aucune; (ii) voix donnée à tous les candidats d'un parti; **s. A student,** élève *mf* qui a un curriculum vitae irréprochable; *F:* **s. whisky,** whisky sec; **to drink one's whisky s.,** boire son whisky sec, sans eau. **4.** (*a*) droit; d'aplomb; **are the pictures s.?** les tableaux sont-ils droits? sont-ils d'aplomb? **to put sth. s.,** redresser, ajuster, qch.; **your tie isn't s.,** votre cravate est (tout) de travers; **to set one's tie s.,** rajuster, arranger, sa cravate; (*b*) en ordre; **to put the room s.,** remettre de l'ordre dans la pièce; **to put one's hair s.,** rajuster sa coiffure; s'arranger les cheveux; **to put things, matters, s.,** arranger les choses; débrouiller l'affaire; **I'll try to make things s.,** je vais essayer d'arranger les choses; **let's try to get things s.,** (i) tâchons d'y mettre de l'ordre; (ii) essayons d'y voir clair; *F:* **get this s.!** comprends-moi bien! **the accounts are s.,** les comptes sont en ordre; **I need five hundred pounds to get me s.,** il me faut cinq cents livres pour me remettre d'aplomb. **5.** (*in compounds*) **s.-boled,** (arbre) à fût droit; *Breed:* **s.-bred,** de race pure; **s.-edged,** à tranchant droit; **s.-faced,** (personne) qui ne sourit pas; impassible; **s.-haired,** aux cheveux (i) plats, (ii) raides; **s.-lined,** rectiligne.

II. *s.* **1.** (*a*) aplomb *m*; **to be out of (the) s.,** n'être pas d'aplomb; être de travers; **that building is out of the s.,** il y a du biais dans ce bâtiment; **door hung off the s.,** porte gondée à faux; **shoulders off the s.,** épaules déjetées; **to cut a material on the s.,** couper une étoffe de droit fil; (*b*) *F:* **to be on the s.,** vivre honnêtement; **to act on the s.,** agir loyalement. **2.** (*a*) *Rac:* **the s.,** la ligne droite; **coming into the s.,** à l'entrée de la ligne droite; (*b*) *Rail:* alignement (droit); **the straights and the curves,** les alignements droits et les courbes. **3.** *Cards:* (*at poker*) séquence *f* (de cinq); quinte *f.* **4.** *P:* (*a*) personne honnête (et vieux jeu); bourgeois, -oise; (*b*) personne normale, hétérosexuelle.

III. *adv.* **1.** droit; **to shoot s.,** tirer juste; **to go s.,** (i) aller droit; (ii) vivre honnêtement; (iii) (*of drug addict*) se désintoxiquer; **keep s. on,** continuez tout droit; **to go s. on,** aller, continuer, sans s'arrêter; **the bullet went s. through his leg,** la balle lui a traversé la jambe de part en part; **to read a book s. through,** lire un livre d'un bout à l'autre; **s.-cut tobacco,** *s.* **s. cut,** (tabac *m*) en tranches coupées dans la longueur des feuilles. **2.** directement; **it comes s. from Paris,** ça vient directement, tout droit, de Paris; *Turf:* **tip s. from the course,** tuyau sûr, de la source; **I'll come s. back,** je ne ferai qu'aller et (re)venir; *Ven:* **to ride s.,** suivre exactement la piste des chiens; **on leaving school he went s. into business,** sitôt après l'école, il entra dans les affaires; **he was sent s. home to his people,** on l'a renvoyé tout droit chez ses parents; **to come, go, s. to the point,** aller, venir, droit au fait; parler sans tourner autour du pot, sans circonlocutions; **he goes s. to the point,** il n'y va pas par quatre chemins, par trente-six chemins; **to drink s. from the bottle,** boire à même la bouteille; **to walk s. in,** entrer sans frapper; **s. away,** immédiatement, aussitôt; tout de suite; d'emblée; **to guess s. away,** deviner du premier coup; **to take a piece of news s. away to s.o.,** porter une nouvelle toute chaude, tout chaud, à qn; **I'm going s. away,** je m'en vais de ce pas; **to get an important job s. away,** arriver de plein saut à une position élevée; **s. off,** sur-le-champ; tout de suite; au pied levé; d'emblée; **I can't tell you s. off,** je ne peux pas vous le dire tout de suite; **to answer s. off,** répondre tout de go; *Cards:* **five tricks s. off,** cinq levées franches. **3.** tout droit; directement; **to go s. across the road,** traverser la rue tout droit; **it is s. across the road,** c'est juste en face; **s. above sth.,** juste au-dessus de qch.; **to look s.o. s. in the face,** regarder qn dans le blanc des yeux, entre les deux yeux; regarder qn bien en face; *F:* **to let s.o. have it s.,** dire son fait à qn; **I told him s. (out) what I thought of it,** je lui ai dit carrément, franchement, tout net, sans détours, sans ambages, ce que j'en pensais; **he called me a fool s. out,** il m'a traité carrément d'imbécile; **a s.-out lie,** un mensonge pur et simple; *U.S: Pol:* **a s.-out republican,** un républicain intransigeant. **4.** (*a*) honnêtement; **to deal s. with people,** être loyal en affaires; **to play s.,** jouer beau jeu; **that's not playing s.,** ce n'est pas de jeu; *F:* **s.!** vrai de vrai! sans blague! (*b*) *Th:* **to play a part s.,** jouer un rôle sans complications.

straight-arm ['streitɑ:m], *v.tr. NAm: Sp:* écarter (un adversaire) avec le plat de la main et le bras tendu.

straightaway ['streitəwei], *NAm:* **1.** *a.* (*a*) (*of course, direction, etc.*) en ligne droite; (*b*) (*of line, etc.*) droit; (*c*) (*of style, language, etc.*) simple, sans détours, qui va droit au but; (*d*) (*of result, etc.*) immédiat. **2.** *s. Turf:* ligne droite. **3.** *adv.* = **straight away** *q.v. under* STRAIGHT III. 2.

straighten ['streit(ə)n]. **1.** *v.tr.* (*a*) rendre (qch.) droit, (re)dresser (qch.); **to s. one's back,** se redresser; cambrer la taille, les reins; **to s. the alignment of a road,** rectifier le tracé d'une route; **to s. (out) an iron bar,** défausser, dégauchir, une barre de fer; **to s. an axle shaft,** redresser un essieu; *F:* **to s. out the traffic,** canaliser les véhicules; (*b*) **to s. (up),** ranger, mettre en ordre; **to s. one's tie,** arranger sa cravate; **to s. (up) a room,** ranger une chambre; **to s. (out) one's affairs,** arranger ses affaires; mettre ses affaires en ordre; **to s. out a business,** régulariser une affaire; **I will try to s. things out,** je vais essayer d'arranger les choses. **2.** *v.i.* (*a*) se redresser; devenir droit; (*of pers.*) **to s. up,** (i) se redresser; cambrer la taille, les reins; (ii) (*of debauchee, etc.*) se ranger; **his figure has straightened (out),** sa taille s'est redressée; **I expect things will s. out,** je pense que ça se rangera, *F:* se tassera; (*b*) *Av:* **to s. up, out,** se redresser, reprendre le vol horizontal.

straightener ['streit(ə)nər], *s.* **1.** (*pers.*) redresseur, -euse. **2.** (*a*) machine *f* à équerrer, redresser; banc *m* de redressage; équerreur *m*; (*b*) *Aer:* grille *f* (de tunnel aérodynamique).

straightening ['streitniŋ], *s.* redressement *m*, redressage *m*, dégauchissement *m*, dégauchissage *m*, équerrage *m*; *Metalw:* **s. press,** presse *f* à dresser.

straightforward [streit'fɔ:wəd], *a.* **1.** (*of movement, vision, etc.*) droit, direct. **2.** (*of pers., conduct, etc.*) loyal, -aux; franc, *f.* franche; sans détours; **s. man,** homme tout rond; **to give a s. answer to a question,** répondre sans détours à une question; **s. language,** langage franc, sincère; **to be quite s. about it,** y aller de franc jeu.

straightforwardly [streit'fɔ:wədli], *adv.* (agir) avec droiture, franchement, loyalement; (parler) carrément, franchement, nettement, sincèrement, sans détours; **to act s.,** jouer cartes sur table.

straightforwardness [streit'fɔ:wədnis], *s.* droiture *f*, honnêteté *f*, franchise *f*; *F:* rondeur *f*.

straightness ['streitnis], *s.* **1.** rectitude *f* (d'une ligne), rectilignité *f*. **2.** droiture *f*, rectitude (de conduite); honnêteté *f*, loyauté *f*.

straightway ['streitwei]. **1.** *adv.* (*a*) *A: & Lit:* immédiatement; tout de suite; *A:* (tout) d'abord; (*b*) *NAm:* directement, en ligne droite. **2.** *a. NAm:* (conduit, etc.) droit, non coudé.

strain¹ [strein], *s.* **1.** (*a*) (i) tension *f*, surtension *f*; effort *m*, contrainte *f*; (ii) *Ph:* rapport *m* de la déformation, allongement *m* unitaire; **the s. on the rope,** la tension de la corde; **to bring, put, a s. on a cable,** faire force sur un câble; **to relieve the s. on, take the s. off, a beam,** soulager une poutre; **to impose a s. on a machine,** fatiguer une machine; *Mec.E:* **breaking s.,** force *f*, contrainte, à la rupture; effort de rupture; tension de rupture; **bending s.,** effort à la flexion; **spreading s.,** effort tendant à ouvrir (un ressort); **parts under s.,** pièces de contrainte; **beam that bears a heavy s.,** poutre qui fatigue; (*of beam*) **to take the s.,** (i) (*also* **to come under s.**) être soumis à la tension; (ii) supporter la tension; **s. gauge, indicator,** (i) indicateur *m* de contrainte, d'effort, (ii) extensomètre *m*; *Nau:* **s. band,** bande *f* de renfort; barate *f*; (*b*) **it would be, put, too great a s. on my purse,** ce serait trop demander à ma bourse, ce serait au-dessus de mes moyens; **it was a great s. on my attention, credulity,** c'était demander beaucoup à mon attention, à ma crédulité; **the s. of a prolonged match,** l'effort soutenu d'un match prolongé; **the s. of modern life,** la tension de la vie moderne; **the s. of business,** la fatigue des affaires; **mental s.,** surmenage *m*; **he couldn't stand, take, the s.,** il n'a pu supporter la tension. **2.** (*a*) *Med:* entorse *f*, foulure *f*; claquage *m* (d'un muscle); **s. in the back,** tour *m*, effort *m*, de reins; (*b*) déformation; **bending s.,** déformation par flexion; **tensile s.,** déformation due à la traction; **torsion(al) s.,** déformation par tension; gauchissement *m*. **3.** *Poet:* (*usu. pl.*) accents *mpl*; **sweet strains,** doux accords. **4.** ton *m*, sens *m* (d'un discours, etc.); **he went on in quite another s.,** il a continué sur un tout autre ton; **he said much more in the same s.,** il s'est étendu longuement dans ce sens.

strain², *v.*

I. *v.tr.* **1.** (*a*) tendre, surtendre (un câble, etc.); **beam that is strained,** poutre qui fatigue; **the deck, the yard, is strained,** le pont, la vergue, fatigue; **to s. one's ears,** tendre l'oreille; **to s. one's eyes,** se fatiguer, s'abîmer, se gâter, les yeux, la vue (**doing sth.,** à faire qch.); **these glasses s. my eyes,** ces lunettes me fatiguent les yeux; **to s. one's voice,** se fatiguer la voix; forcer sa voix; **to s. one's powers,** pousser trop loin l'exercice de ses pouvoirs; **to s. the law,** faire violence, donner une entorse, à la loi; forcer la loi; **to s. relations,** tendre les rapports (**between,** entre); **to s. s.o.'s friendship,** exiger trop de l'amitié de qn; **to s. the meaning of a word,** presser, forcer, le sens d'un mot; **to s. a point,** forcer les choses; faire une exception, une concession; faire violence à ses principes; **to s. one's resources,** grever ses ressources jusqu'à la limite; **the island's accommodation has been strained to the limit,** tout a été fait pour assurer le logement aux visiteurs de l'île; (*b*) tendre (un hauban); rappeler (un poteau télégraphique, etc.). **2.** (*a*) fouler, forcer (un membre); **to s. one's back,** se donner un tour de reins, un effort de reins; **to s. one's heart, one's shoulders,** se forcer le cœur; se forcer, se fouler, l'épaule; **he has strained his foot,** il s'est foulé le pied; **to s. a muscle,** se froisser un muscle; faire un faux mouvement; *Vet:* (*of horse, etc.*) **to s. its shoulder,** se donner un écart; (*b*) forcer (un mât, une poutre); *Mec.E:* déformer (une pièce); (*c*) **to s. oneself,** (i) se surmener, *F:* s'éreinter (**doing sth.,** à faire qch.); (ii) faire un faux mouvement; se donner un effort; **he doesn't (exactly) s. himself,** il ne se fait pas d'ampoules aux mains. **3.** (*a*) filtrer, passer, couler (un liquide) (à travers un linge, etc.); passer (un liquide) au tamis; tamiser; **to s. the soup,** passer le bouillon; (*b*) **to s. sth. out (of a liquid),** enlever, ôter, extraire, qch. d'un liquide (en se servant d'une passoire); **to s. the vegetables,** faire égoutter les légumes; (*c*) *A:* extorquer (de l'argent, etc.); **the quality of mercy is not strained,** la clémence ne s'obtient pas par contrainte.

II. *v.i.* **1.** faire un (grand) effort; peiner; **to s. at a rope, at the oars,** tirer sur une corde; tirer, forcer, sur les rames; **to s. under a load,** se raidir sous une charge; **to s. after sth.,** faire tous ses efforts pour atteindre qch.; **the author doesn't s. after effect,** l'auteur ne s'évertue pas à produire de l'effet, ne vise pas à l'effet; **to s. to do sth.,** faire de grands efforts pour accomplir qch.; (*of dog*) **to s. at the leash,** tirer sur la laisse; *Ven:* bander sur le trait. **2.** (*of beam, etc.*) fatiguer, travailler; (*of rope*) être trop tendu; *Nau:* (*of ship*) **to s. in a seaway,** fatiguer, bourlinguer, par une mer dure. **3.** *Mec.E:* (*of* *machine part*) se déformer; gauchir; se fausser. **4. to s. at sth., at doing sth.,** se faire scrupule de qch., de faire qch. **5.** (*of liquid*) filtrer (**through,** à travers).

strain[3], *s.* **1.** qualité héritée, inhérente; disposition naturelle; tendance (morale); **a s. of weakness, ferocity,** un héritage, fond, de faiblesse, de férocité; **there is a s. of mysticism in his nature,** il y a une tendance au mysticisme, il y a du mysticisme, dans sa nature. **2.** (*a*) race *f*, lignée *f*; *A:* **of noble s.,** de race noble; **spaniel of good s.,** épagneul de bonne lignée, de bonne race; (*b*) *Biol:* souche *f* (d'un virus); variété *f* (de graine).

strained [streind], *a.* **1.** (*a*) (*of rope, etc.*) tendu; trop tendu; **s. nerves,** nerfs tendus; **s. relations,** rapports tendus; (*b*) **s. ankle,** cheville foulée; **s. heart,** cœur forcé, fatigué, claqué; (*of athlete*) claquage sportif; **horse with a s. tendon,** cheval claqué. **2.** (*a*) (*of conduct, demeanour*) forcé, contraint, guindé; **s. laugh,** rire forcé, contraint; (*b*) (*of language, interpretation*) forcé, exagéré; poussé trop loin; *F:* tiré par les cheveux. **3.** filtré; tamisé.

strainer ['streinər], *s.* **1.** (*pers.*) tamiseur, -euse. **2.** (*device*) (*a*) (i) filtre *m*; (ii) tamis *m*; *Cu:* passoire *f*, couloire *f*; **conical s.,** chinois *m*; **soup s.,** passe-bouillon *m inv*; **tea s.,** passe-thé *m inv*; **milk s.,** passe-lait *m inv*; **gauze s. for a funnel,** tamis métallique pour un entonnoir; (*b*) *Ind: etc:* épurateur *m* (d'air, etc.); **centrifugal s.,** épurateur, classeur *m*, centrifuge; (*c*) *Hyd.E: etc:* crépine *f*, aspirant *m*, grenouillère *f* (d'une pompe); (*over drainpipe*) pommelle *f*; *Mch:* reniflard *m* (de chaudière à vapeur). **3.** (*stretcher*) tendeur *m*, tenseur *m*, raidisseur *m*.

straining ['streiniŋ], *s.* **1.** (*a*) tension *f*, effort *m*, fatigue *f*; (*excessive*) surtension *f*; **s. of a beam,** fatigue d'une poutre; *Const:* **s. piece, tie,** entrait (retroussé), poutre traversière (d'un comble); (*b*) **s. screw,** tendeur *m* à vis; vis *f* de tension; **s. stay, tie,** hauban raidisseur, de rappel; **s. wire,** fil de rappel. **2.** fatigue (des yeux, de la voix). **3.** grands efforts (**to do sth.,** pour faire qch.). **4.** interprétation forcée, tirée par les cheveux; violence faite (**of the law, a text,** à la loi, à un texte). **5.** filtrage *m*, égouttage *m*; *Pharm:* colature *f*; **s. bag,** chausse *f* (à vin, etc.); *Paperm: etc:* **s. chest,** cuve *f* d'égouttage; *Ind:* **s. press,** presse *f* à passoire.

strainless ['streinlis], *a.* fait sans effort.

strainometer [strei'nɔmitər], *s. Ph:* extensomètre *m*.

strait [streit]. **1.** *a.* (*a*) *A:* étroit; *B:* **the s. gate,** la porte étroite; **to leave the s. and narrow (way),** quitter la bonne voie, le droit chemin; **to keep to the s. and narrow (way),** cheminer droit; *Min:* **s. work,** galeries d'avancement étroites; (*b*) **s. jacket, waistcoat,** camisole *f* de force; **to put s.o. into a s. jacket, to put a s. jacket on s.o.,** (i) passer une camisole de force à qn; (ii) *Fig:* enlever à qn toute liberté d'action, lier les mains à qn; (*c*) *A:* **the straitest sect of their religion,** la secte la plus rigoriste de leur religion. **2.** *s.pl.* (*a*) *Geog:* (*with proper name*) détroit *m*; **the Straits of Gibraltar,** le détroit de Gibraltar; **the Straits of Dover,** le Pas de Calais; *Hist:* **the Straits Settlements,** les Établissements *m* des Détroits; *Num: A:* **Straits dollar,** dollar *m* des Établissements des Détroits; (*b*) *Anat:* **straits of the pelvis,** détroits du bassin; (*c*) **to be in great, dire, desperate, straits,** être dans l'embarras, dans une situation critique, dans la (plus grande) gêne, dans la plus grande détresse, aux abois.

straiten ['streit(ə)n], *v.tr.* **1.** mettre (qn) dans la gêne; réduire (qn) à la portion congrue; **straitened by debt,** gêné, embarrassé, par ses dettes; **they were straitened for provisions,** les provisions leur faisaient défaut. **2.** *A:* (*a*) rétrécir; (*b*) resserrer (un nœud, les liens de qn).

straitened ['streit(ə)nd], *a.* **s. circumstances,** gêne *f* pécuniaire; **to be in s. circumstances,** être dans la gêne, dans le besoin, dans la nécessité, dans l'adversité, dans l'embarras; être gêné d'argent; **s. household,** ménage pauvre.

straitjacket ['streitdʒækit], *v.tr.* **1.** passer une camisole de force à (qn). **2.** enlever toute liberté d'action à (qn), lier les mains à (qn).

straitlaced ['streit'leist], *a.* **1.** *A:* (*of woman*) serré(e) dans son corset, étranglé(e) par son corset. **2.** *Fig:* prude, bégueule; collet monté *inv*.

straitly ['streitli], *adv. A:* **1.** étroitement. **2.** rigoureusement, strictement.

straitness ['streitnis], *s. A:* **1.** (*a*) étroitesse *f*; (*b*) manque *m* de place. **2.** rigueur *f*. **3.** gêne *f*, embarras *m*.

strake [streik], *s. N.Arch:* virure *f*; lisse *f*; liston *m*; ceinture *f*.

stramonium [strə'mouniəm], *s.* **1.** *Bot:* (*also* **stramony** ['stræməni]) stramoine *f*, (datura) stramonium *m*. **2.** *Pharm:* stramonine *f*.

strand[1] [strænd], *s.* **1.** (*a*) *Lit:* rive *f*, plage *f*, grève *f*; *Bot:* **s. plants,** plantes littorales; (*b*) *Nau:* estran(d) *m*. **2. the S.,** le Strand (rue de Londres).

strand[2]. **1.** *v.tr.* échouer (un navire), jeter (un navire) à la côte. **2.** *v.i.* (*of ship, whale*) (s')échouer.

strand[3], *s.* **1.** (*a*) brin *m*, toron *m* (de cordage); cordon *m* (d'aussière); *Needlew:* brin (de fil à coudre); **wire s.,** toron métallique; **central s.,** âme *f* (d'un câble); (*b*) brin, corde *f*; **four-s. pulley block,** palan *m* à quatre brins; (*c*) fil *m* (d'un tissu); *Fig:* **to unravel the strands of a complicated affair,** démêler les fils d'une affaire compliquée; (*d*) fibre (animale, végétale). **2.** fil (de perles); tresse *f* (de cheveux).

strand[4], *v.tr.* **1.** (*a*) toronner (un cordage); (*b*) **to s. a coloured thread into a piece of cloth,** introduire un fil de couleur dans la trame d'une étoffe. **2.** décorder (un câble). **3. to s. a rope,** rompre les torons d'un cordage.

stranded[1] ['strændid], *a.* **1.** (navire) échoué, gisant; (*neaped*) au plein; **s. whale,** baleine échouée à la côte. **2.** (*a*) (*of pers.*) à bout de ressources; (*b*) laissé en arrière; abandonné; **to leave s.o. s.,** laisser qn en plan; laisser qn le bec dans l'eau; **to be s.,** (i) être (mis) sur le sable; être dans la gêne, dans l'embarras; (ii) rester en arrière, sur le carreau; rester le bec dans l'eau; être, rester, de panne.

stranded[2], *a.* **1.** à torons, à brins; **three-s. rope,** filon commis en trois, corde à trois cordons, à trois torons. **2.** *Nau:* (manœuvre) qui a des torons rompus, coupés.

stranding[1] ['strændiŋ], *s.* échouement *m*, échouage *m*.

stranding[2], *s.* toronnage *m* (d'une corde); *Ropem:* **s. machine,** toronneuse *f*.

strandline ['strændlain], *s.* (ligne *f* du) rivage.

strange [strein(d)ʒ], *a.* **1.** (*a*) *A:* étranger; **in a s. land,** dans un pays étranger; **I'm s. here,** je suis étranger ici; **a s. man,** un étranger; (*b*) **to play on a s. ground,** jouer sur un terrain qui n'est pas le sien; **I can't work with s. tools,** je ne peux pas travailler avec des outils qui ne sont pas les miens, d'autres outils que les miens; **this handwriting is s. to me,** je ne connais pas cette écriture; **new and s. words,** mots nouveaux et insolites; **we go back to the old school to find many s. faces,** quand on retourne à son ancienne école on y trouve beaucoup de visages nouveaux, inconnus; **it feels s. to have a holiday while others are working,** il me paraît bien étrange, cela me fait un drôle d'effet, d'être en congé pendant que les autres travaillent; **I felt s. in those surroundings,** je me sentais étranger, dépaysé, dans ce milieu; **I felt a bit s. that morning,** ce matin je n'étais pas dans mon assiette; **suddenly I felt very s.,** tout à coup j'ai eu des vertiges. **2.** singulier, bizarre, extraordinaire, remarquable; **s. beasts,** bêtes curieuses; **s. behaviour,** conduite inexplicable; **she wears the strangest clothes,** elle porte les vêtements les plus étranges, les plus singuliers, les plus bizarres; **it's a s. thing,** c'est une chose étrange, curieuse; **s. to say, I've never met him,** chose étrange (à dire), je ne l'ai jamais rencontré; **strangest of all, he was usually very generous,** le plus étrange, c'est que d'ordinaire il était très libéral; **it's s. that he has not, should not have, arrived yet,** il est singulier qu'il ne soit pas encore arrivé; **it's s. that you should not have, haven't, heard of it,** il est étonnant que vous ne l'ayez pas appris; **it would be s. if he submitted to this demand,** il ferait beau voir qu'il se soumette à cette exigence. **3. I'm s. to this work,** je suis nouveau dans ce métier; **he was s. to that way of life,** ce genre de vie lui était nouveau. **4.** *Ph:* **s. particles,** particules *f* étranges.

strangely ['strein(d)ʒli], *adv.* étrangement, singulièrement; **s. enough, he felt nothing,** chose étrange, il n'a rien senti.

strangeness ['strein(d)ʒnis], *s.* **1.** étrangeté *f*, singularité *f*, bizarrerie *f*. **2.** étrangeté, nouveauté *f*; **the s. of the work,** l'étrangeté du travail. **3.** *Ph:* étrangeté.

stranger ['strein(d)ʒər], *s.* **1.** (*a*) étranger, -ère, inconnu, -ue; **I'm a s. here,** je suis étranger ici, je ne suis pas d'ici; **they're strangers (to us),** nous ne les connaissons pas; ils ne sont pas de chez nous; **he's a complete s. to me,** il m'est tout à fait étranger, inconnu; **to take the umbrella of a perfect s.,** prendre le parapluie d'un tiers (qui vous est inconnu); **what! lend money to a perfect s.!** quoi, prêter de l'argent à un inconnu! **you're quite a s.,** vous devenez rare comme les beaux jours; c'est une rareté, une nouveauté, que de vous voir; on ne vous voit plus; vous vous faites rare; quel revenant vous faites! **to become a s. to s.o., sth.,** s'aliéner de qn, qch.; **to make a s. of s.o.,** traiter qn en, comme un, étranger; **to make no s. of s.o.,** traiter qn en ami; **he's a s., no s., to fear,** il ne connaît pas, il connaît bien, la peur; (*in House of Commons*) **I spy strangers!** je demande le huis clos! *F: O:* **the little s.,** le nouveau-né; *U.S:* **say s.!** pardon monsieur! (*b*) *Jur:* celui qui n'est pas partie (**to an act,** à un fait); tiers *m*. **2.** *F:* (*a*) (*in candle*) champignon *m*; (*b*) (*in cup of tea*) chinois *m*.

strangle ['stræŋgl]. **1.** *v.tr.* étrangler (qn); serrer le cou à (qn); **my collar is strangling me,** mon faux col m'étrangle; *Fig:* **to s. the press,** étrangler la presse; **to s. a laugh,** étouffer un rire; **to s. a sneeze,** réprimer un éternuement; **to s. evil at birth,** étrangler, étouffer, le mal au berceau; **strangled voice,** vois étranglée, strangulée. **2.** *v.i.* s'étrangler; **a cat that has to wear a collar can s.,** un chat à qui on fait porter un collier peut s'étrangler.

stranglehold ['stræŋglhould], *s.* **1.** *Wr:* étranglement *m*. **2. to have a s. on s.o.,** tenir qn à la gorge; **economic, linguistic, s.,** mainmise *f* économique, linguistique; **the s. of restrictions,** l'étau *m* des restrictions.

strangler ['stræŋglər], *s.* **1.** (*a*) (*pers.*) étrangleur, -euse; (*b*) *Bot:* **ivy and other stranglers,** le lierre et autres étrangleurs. **2.** *I.C.E:* (*device*) étrangleur.

strangles ['stræŋglz], *s.pl.* (*with sg. or pl. const.*) *Vet:* gourme *f*; étranguillon *m*.

strangling ['stræŋgliŋ], *s.* étranglement *m*; *Jur:* strangulation *f*.

strangulate ['stræŋgjuleit]. *Med:* **1.** *v.tr.* étrangler (l'intestin, etc.). **2.** *v.i.* (*of hernia, intestine, etc.*) devenir étranglé.

strangulated ['stræŋgjuleitid], *a.* étranglé; *Med:* **s. hernia,** hernie étranglée.

strangulation [stræŋgju'leiʃ(ə)n], *s.* étranglement *m*, strangulation *f*; *Fig:* **economic s.,** asphyxie *f* économique; *Med:* **s. of a hernia,** étranglement herniaire.

strangury ['stræŋgjuri], *s. Med:* strangurie *f*.

strap[1] [stræp], *s.* **1.** (*a*) courroie *f*; **buckle s., s. and buckle,** courroie à boucle; **carrying s.,** courroie de portage, sangle *f* de transport; **tie-down s.,** sangle d'amarrage; **tension s.,** courroie de tension; **tightening s.,** courroie de serrage; **luggage s.,** courroie porte-paquets *inv*; **watch s.,** bracelet *m* (en cuir) pour montre; **toe s. (of ski),** courroie avant (de ski); *Harn:* **stirrup s.,** étrivière *f*; **lip s.,** fausse gourmette; **breeching s.,** courroie d'arrêt; **strengthening s.,** blanchet *m*; **breast s.,** bricole *f*; **girth s.,** contre-sanglef, *pl.* contre-sangles; **hip s.,** croupière *f*; courroie d'attelle; **loin s.,** surdos *m*; **hame s.,** courroie d'attelle; **lashing s.,** courroie de brêlage; (*b*) martinet *m*; *F: O:* **s. oil,** huile de cotret; **to give s.o. a little s. oil,** administrer une raclée à qn. **2.** (*a*) bande *f*, sangle (de cuir, de toile, etc.); (*for lid of suitcase*) **retaining s.,** attachot *m*; **hoisting s.,** brayer *m*; *Mec.E:* **driving s.,** courroie d'entraînement; (*b*) *Veh:* courroie à main, courroie de fermeture, de portière; **window s.,** tirant *m* de fenêtre, de vitre; (*in underground, etc.*) **(standing passengers') s.,** courroie, poignée *f* d'appui; (*c*) *Nau:* **block (binding) s.,** estrope *f* de moufle, de poulie; **rope s.,** estrope de cordage; **selvagee s.,** erse *f* en bitord; (*d*) *Cost:* bande, patte *f* (d'étoffe); bretelle *f*; *Bootm:* barrette *f* (de soulier); **trouser s.,** sous-pied *m*, *pl.* sous-pieds, (de pantalon); *Equit:* **instep s.,** suspied *m* d'éperon; **spur s.,** courroie d'éperon. **3.** *Tchn:* (*a*) attache *f*, lien *m* (en métal); armature *f*, étrier *m* (de renfort); **s. bolt,** lien (en U); **to strengthen a frame, a plate, with straps,** renforcer une charpente, une plaque, par des armatures; *Veh:* (*over carriage door*) gouttière *f*; *Rail: U.S:* **s. rail,** rail méplat; (*b*) *Mch:* chape *f*, bride *f* (de bielle); collier *m*, bague *f* (d'excentrique); **backward, forward, eccentric s.,** collier d'excentrique de marche arrière, de marche avant; *Tls:* **s. wrench,** clef à ruban; (*c*) *Metall:* ruban *m* (métallique); **straps,** feuillard *m*; **s. iron,** feuillard de fer, fer feuillard; (*d*) *Mec.E: etc:* bande, ruban; **brake s.,** ruban de frein; **clamping s.,** bande de serrage; **butt s.,** bande (de recouvrement); éclisse *f*; plaque *f* d'éclissage; couvre-joint *m*, *pl.* couvre-joints; **s. brake,** frein à bande, à ruban, à collier; **s. clutch,** embrayage à ruban; **s. fork,** fourche de débrayage (de courroie de transmission); **s. bearing,** coussinet-bague *m*, *pl.* coussinets-bagues; (*e*) *El:* barrette *f*; **connecting s.,** barrette de connexion; **s.-braided conductor,** conducteur méplat. **4.** *Bot:* ligule *f*; *Ann:* **s. worm,** bothriocéphale *m*; ligule (des poissons, des oiseaux).

strap[2], *v.tr.* (**strapped** [stræpt]) **1.** (*a*) **to s. sth. (up),** mettre une courroie à qch.; attacher, lier, fixer, qch. avec une courroie; boucler (une malle); ceinturer (une caisse, etc.); sangler (un paquet); (*b*) *Cost:* **strapped trousers,** pantalon à sous-pieds. **2.** administrer une correction à (un enfant, etc.) avec le bout d'une courroie, avec un martinet. **3.** *Med:* (*a*) mettre des bandelettes, de l'emplâtre, un pansement adhésif, sur (une blessure); (*b*) maintenir (un membre cassé, etc.) au moyen de bandages. **4.** *Nau:* estroper (une moufle). **5.** *Metalw:* polir (une pièce) à la bande de toile (d')émeri. **6.** *F: O:* **to be strapped,** être sans le sou.

straphang ['stræphæŋ], *v.i.* voyager debout (en se tenant à la courroie, à la poignée).

straphanger ['stræphæŋər], *s.* voyageur, -euse, debout (dans le métro, etc.).

strapless ['stræplis], *a.* sans bretelles, sans épaulettes; **s. bra,** bustier *m*; soutien-gorge sans bretelles.

strappado [strə'peidou], *s. Hist:* estrapade *f.*

strapper ['stræpər], *s.* **1.** *O:* grand gaillard, grande gaillarde. **2.** garçon *m* d'écurie; personne *f* qui soigne les chevaux.

strapping[1] ['stræpiŋ], *a.* solide, robuste; **s. fellow,** grand gaillard; gaillard robuste, bien bâti, râblé; jeune homme bien découplé; **tall s. girl,** grande jeune fille bien découplée; fille grande et faite; beau brin de fille.

strapping[2], *s.* **1.** action *f* de boucler, de sangler (un colis, etc.). **2.** correction (administrée sur la paume de la main avec une courroie, avec un martinet). **3.** *coll.* (*a*) courroies *fpl*, liens *mpl*, armatures *fpl*; (*b*) *Med:* emplâtre *m*, pansement *m*, adhésif *m*; (*c*) *Dressm:* bandes *fpl.* **4.** *Metalw:* polissage *m* à la bande de toile (d')émeri. **5.** (*a*) *El:* câblage *m*, connexion *f*, en fils nus; (*b*) *Elcs:* court-circuit *m, pl.* courts-circuits (dans un magnétron); jumelage (d'un magnétron à cavités).

strapwork ['stræpwɔ:k], *s.* (*in embroidery, architecture, etc.*) entrelacs *m*, tresse *f.*

strapwort ['stræpwɔ:t], *s. Bot:* corrigiole *f.*

strass [stræs], *s.* stras(s) *m.*

stratagem ['strætədʒəm], *s.* **1.** *Mil:* ruse *f* de guerre; stratagème *m.* **2.** stratagème, ruse (pour atteindre son but, etc.).

strategic [strə'ti:dʒik], *a.* stratégique; *Mil:* **s. point,** point stratégique; **s. materials,** matières *f* stratégiques; **s. bombing,** bombardement(s) *m* stratégique(s); **s. nuclear weapons,** armements *m* nucléaires stratégiques.

strategical [strə'ti:dʒikl], *a.* stratégique.

strategically [strə'ti:dʒik(ə)li], *adv.* stratégiquement.

strategics [strə'ti:dʒiks], *s.pl.* (*usu. with sg. const.*) stratégie *f.*

strategist ['strætidʒist], *s.* stratège *m*; *O:* stratégiste *m.*

strategus, *pl.* **-gi** [strə'ti:gəs, -dʒai], *s. Gr.Hist:* stratège *m.*

strategy ['strætidʒi], *s.* stratégie (employée pour gagner une bataille, une élection, etc.).

strath [stræθ], *s. Scot:* vallée *f.*

strathspey [stræθ'spei], *s. Danc: Mus:* branle écossais (dansé par deux personnes).

straticulate [stræ'tikjuleit], *a. Geol:* en couches minces.

stratification [strætifi'keiʃ(ə)n], *s. Geol:* stratification *f*; **diagonal s.,** stratification entrecroisée.

stratified ['strætifaid], *a.* (formation, etc.) en couches, en strates; *Stat:* **s. sampling,** sondages stratifiés, par strates.

stratiform ['strætifɔ:m], *a. Anat: etc:* stratiforme.

stratify ['strætifai]. **1.** *v.tr.* stratifier; *Hort:* **to s. seeds,** stratifier des semences. **2.** *v.i.* se stratifier.

stratigrapher [strə'tigrəfər], *s. Geol:* stratigraphe *mf.*

stratigraphic(al) [stræti'græfik(l)], *a.* stratigraphique.

stratigraphy [strə'tigrəfi], *s.* stratigraphie *f.*

stratiomy(i)id [strætiou'mai(i)id]. *Ent:* **1.** *a.* (insecte) stratiomyide. **2.** *s.* stratiomyide *m*, stratiome *m*, stratiomys *m.*

stratiotes [stræti'outi:z], *s. Bot:* stratiote *f.*

Strato ['streitou], *Pr.n.m. Gr.Phil:* Straton.

stratocirrus [strɑ:tou'sirəs, strei-], *s. Meteor:* cirrostratus *m.*

stratocracy [stræ'tɔkrəsi], *s.* stratocratie *f*, gouvernement *m* militaire.

stratocruiser ['strætoukru:zər], **stratoliner** ['strætoulainər], *s.* avion *m* (de ligne) stratosphérique.

stratocumulus [strɑ:tou'kju:mjuləs, streitou-], *s. Meteor:* cumulo-stratus *m.*

stratopause ['strætoupɔ:z], *s. Meteor:* stratopause *f.*

stratose ['streitous], *a. Bot:* en couches.

stratosphere ['strætəsfiər], *s.* stratosphère *f*; **s. explorer, balloonist,** stratonaute *m.*

stratospheric [strætə'sferik], *a.* stratosphérique.

stratovision [strætou'viʒən], *s. T.V:* stratovision *f.*

stratum, *pl.* **-a** ['strɑ:təm, strei-, -ə], *s.* (*a*) *Geol:* strate *f*, couche *f*, gisement *m*, assise *f*; gîte *m* (de minerai); *Hyd.E:* **foundation s.,** sol *m* de fondation; (*b*) couche (d'air, etc.); **the various strata of society,** les différentes couches sociales; *Bot:* **s. society,** association (de plantes) limitée à un seul étage.

stratus ['strɑ:təs, -eit-], *s. Meteor:* stratus *m*; nuage *m* en bandes.

straw[1] [strɔ:], *s.* **1.** paille *f*; **loose s.,** paille de litière; **rice s.,** paille de riz; paille d'Italie; **bundle, truss, of s.,** botte *f* de paille; *Fig:* **man of s.,** *NAm:* **s. man,** (i) homme de paille, de carton; (ii) prête-nom *m, pl.* prête-noms; **s. bed,** lit *m* de paille; **s. case,** paillon *m* (de bouteille); **s. mattress,** paillasse *f*; **s. mat,** paillasson *m*; **s. hat,** chapeau *m* de paille; (*boater*) canotier *m*, régate *f*; *NAm:* **s. hat theatre,** théâtre *m* pour estivants; *Paperm:* **s. pulp,** pâte *f* de paille; **s. roof,** toiture *f* en paille; **s. rope,** corde *f* en paille; torche *f*; **s. wine,** vin *m* de paille; *Agr:* **s. cutter,** hache-paille *m inv*; **s. loft,** pailler *m* (d'écurie); **s. yard,** pailler; *NAm: P:* **s. boss,** aide *m* du contremaître (dans un atelier); **s. colour, s. yellow,** couleur *f* paille *inv*; jaune *m* paille *inv*; **s.-coloured,** (jaune) paille *inv*; **s.-coloured mane,** crinière paillée; **s.-bottomed,** à fond de paille; **s.-bottomed chair,** chaise de paille, paillée; **s.-stuffed,** bourré de paille, empaillé. **2.** (*a*) paille, chalumeau *m*, fétu *m*; **to drink lemonade through a s.,** boire de la limonade avec une paille; **to play long straws,** tirer à la courte paille; **to split straws,** ergoter, chicaner; **s. splitter,** ergoteur *m*, chicaneur *m*; **s. splitting,** ergotage *m*, chicane(rie) *f*, distinctions subtiles, subtilités *fpl*; **it's not worth a s.,** cela ne vaut pas un fétu, quatre sous, tripette; **I don't care a s.,** je m'en soucie comme d'un fétu, de l'an quarante; **to clutch at any s.,** se raccrocher à n'importe quoi; **to be blown along like a s. in the wind,** être emporté comme un fétu; **straws in the wind,** indications *f* d'où vient le vent; indications de l'opinion publique; **s. vote,** sondage *m* d'opinion publique (à un meeting, etc.); *Prov:* **it's the last s. that breaks the camel's back,** la surcharge abat l'âne; une goutte d'eau suffit pour faire déborder le vase; **it's the last s.!** ça c'est le comble! il ne manquait plus que cela! **as a last s., it started raining,** pour comble de malheur la pluie a commencé; **that would be the last s.!** ça serait le comble! **this bad news was the last s.,** cette mauvaise nouvelle m'a achevé, a fait déborder le vase; *Bot:* **s.-bearing plant,** plante *f* culmifère; (*b*) *Ent:* **s. worm,** larve *f* de phrygane; *Fish:* (*for bait*) (ver) caset (*m*); (*c*) *Vet:* paillette *f* (pour semence).

straw[2], *v.tr.* **1.** pailler, couvrir de paille (le plancher, la cour, etc.); **to s. down the horses,** faire la litière des chevaux. **2.** pailler, rempailler (une chaise).

straw[3], *v.tr. A:* = STREW.

strawberry ['strɔ:b(ə)ri], *s.* **1.** (*a*) *Bot:* fraise *f*; **wild s., wood s.,** *NAm:* **field s.,** (petite) fraise des bois; **pine s.,** fraise ananas; **s. jam,** confiture *f* de fraises; **s. ice,** glace *f* aux fraises, à la fraise; (*b*) **s. (plant),** fraisier *m*; **barren s.,** faux fraisier, fraisier stérile; **s. bed,** planche *f*, plant *m*, de fraisiers; **s. field,** plantation *f* de fraisiers, fraiseraie *f*; **s. grower,** fraisier *m*; *F:* **the s. leaves,** la couronne ducale; (*c*) **s. colour,** fraise *inv*; **crushed s. ribbons,** rubans *m* fraise écrasée; **s. roan,** (cheval) aubère clair; *NAm:* **s. blond,** blond ardent; **she's a s. blonde,** elle a les cheveux (d'un) blond ardent; **s. mark,** fraise sur la peau; tache *f* de vin (congénitale); *Med:* **s. tongue,** langue framboisée. **2.** *Bot:* **s. bush,** fusain *m* d'Amérique; **s. pear,** (fruit *m* du) cierge; **s. shrub,** calycanthe *m*; **s. tree,** arbousier commun; arbre *m* à fraises.

strawboard ['strɔ:bɔ:d], *s.* carton *m* paille.

strawy ['strɔ:i], *a.* **1.** de paille; qui contient de la paille; **s. manure,** fumier pailleux. **2.** (jaune) paille *inv.*

stray[1] [strei], *a.* & *s.*

I. *s.* **1.** (*a*) animal égaré, bête perdue, animal errant; *Jur:* bête épave; (*b*) **waifs and strays,** enfants abandonnés; (*c*) objet égaré; exemple, spécimen, etc., isolé. **2.** *El:* (*a*) dispersion *f*; **magnetic s. field,** champ *m* de dispersion magnétique; **s. lines,** lignes *f* de dispersion; **s. induction,** induction *f* par dispersion; **s. flux,** flux *m* de fuite; (*b*) *pl. W.Tel:* **strays,** bruissements *m* parasites; (bruits *m* de) friture *f*; crissements *m*, crachements *m.* **3.** *Cin:* **s. angle of the screen,** angle *m* de diffusion de l'écran. **4.** *Nau:* **s. (line),** houache *f* (de loch). **5.** *P:* **to have a bit of s.,** faire l'amour hors du ménage; prendre un petit à-côté.

II. *a.* **1.** (*of animal*) égaré, errant, perdu; *Jur:* épave. **2.** (*a*) égaré, isolé; **s. bullets,** balles égarées, perdues; **s. thoughts,** pensées détachées; **a few s. houses,** quelques maisons isolées, espacées, éparses; **we had no friends, only a few s. acquaintances,** nous n'avions pas d'amis, seulement quelques connaissances de hasard, de passage; **a s. beam of sunshine,** une coulée de soleil; (*b*) *Opt: Cin: etc:* **s. light,** lumière diffuse.

stray[2], *v.i.* (*a*) s'égarer, errer, vaguer; (*of sheep, etc.*) s'écarter du troupeau; **to s. from the right path,** s'écarter du bon chemin; se dévoyer; **to s. from the strait and narrow way,** quitter le droit chemin; **to let one's thoughts s.,** laisser vaguer, laisser errer, laisser vagabonder, ses pensées; **to s. from the point,** sortir du sujet; (*b*) *El:* (*of current*) se disperser.

strayed [streid], *a.* égaré, isolé, détaché; perdu.

strayer ['streiər], *s.* égaré, -ée.

straying[1] ['streiiŋ], *a.* égaré, errant, perdu; dévoyé (du bon chemin, du droit chemin).

straying[2], *s.* **1.** égarement *m*; sortie *f* (i) du bon chemin, (ii) du droit chemin. **2.** *Magn:* dispersion *f* (magnétique).

strayless ['streilis], *a. Magn:* sans dispersion.

streak[1] [stri:k], *s.* **1.** raie *f*, rayure *f*, bande *f*, strie *f*; (*on flowers, leaves*) panache *m*, panachure *f*; sillon *m* (de feu); traînée *f* (de brume, de vapeur); **s. of light,** trait *m*, bande, sillon, filet *m*, filtrée *f*, de lumière; *Ball:* **s. photography,** strioscopie *f*; **s. of sunlight,** coulée *f* de soleil; **the sun cast streaks of light on the floor,** le soleil zébrait le plancher; **the first s. of dawn,** la première lueur du jour, le point du jour; **streaks of smoke drifted across the sky,** des fumées *f* se traînaient dans le ciel; *Phot:* **black streaks on a negative,** vermicelles noirs sur un cliché; **like a s. of lightning,** comme un éclair; **to run like a s.,** partir comme l'éclair; **we made a s. for the house,** nous nous sommes élancés vers la maison; *F:* **to do a s.,** courir nu (en public). **2. s. of ore,** bande, filon *m*, de minerai; (*in oilstone*) **soft s.,** moulière *f*; *F:* **I've had a s. of luck,** je tiens le filon; **winning s.,** suite *f* de victoires; **to have hit a winning s.,** être en veine; **there's a s. of Irish blood in him,** il y a en lui une trace de sang irlandais; **there was a s. of cowardice, a yellow s., in him,** il y avait de la lâcheté dans sa nature; **s. of irony,** pointe *f*, filet, d'ironie; **s. of eccentricity,** légère dose d'excentricité. **3.** *Ch: Miner:* trait de couleur (laissé par un minéral dans un essai à la touche); **s. plate,** plaque *f* de biscuit (de porcelaine) pour essais à la touche.

streak[2]. **1.** *v.tr.* (*a*) rayer, strier, barioler, panacher, vergeter, zébrer; **the sky is streaked with smoke,** des fumées se traînent dans le ciel; **coat streaked with black,** pelage rayé de bandes sombres; **sky streaked with shooting stars,** ciel sillonné d'étoiles filantes; **wall streaked with damp,** mur couturé d'humidité; **panes streaked with water,** vitres hachurées d'eau; **white marble streaked with red,** marbre blanc veiné de rouge; (*b*) (*with passive force*) se rayer, se panacher. **2.** *v.i. F:* (*a*) **to s. along, past,** aller, passer, comme un éclair; **to s. off,** se sauver à toutes jambes; (*b*) courir nu (en public).

streaked [stri:kt], *a.* **1.** rayé, strié, bariolé, panaché; (bois) filandreux. **2.** *NAm:* (*of pers.*) agité, énervé.

streaker ['stri:kər], *s. F:* coureur, -euse, nu(e) (en public); nudiste galopant(e).

streakiness ['stri:kinis], *s.* état rayé, strié; vergeure *f* (d'un tissu); *Paint:* embus *mpl.*

streaking ['stri:kiŋ], *s.* **1.** raies *fpl*, rayures *fpl*, bandes *fpl*, stries *fpl*; *Hairdr:* effet de rayure (obtenu en colorant une mèche); *T.V:* traînage *m.* **2.** *F:* course *f* de nudiste (devant le public).

streaky ['stri:ki], *a.* **1.** (nuage, etc.) en raies, en bandes. **2.** rayé, strié, bariolé, zébré, panaché; *Tex:* vergé; *Miner:* rubané, zoné; **s. complexion,** teint vergeté. **3.** (*of bacon, etc.*) entrelardé. **4.** *NAm:* (*of pers.*) (*a*) nerveux; (*b*) volage.

stream[1] [stri:m], *s.* **1.** (*a*) cours *m* d'eau; fleuve *m*, rivière *f*; *Min:* **s. gold,** or *m* alluvionnaire; or alluvien; or de lavage; **s. tin,** étain *m* d'alluvion; *Hyd.E:* **s. power,** énergie hydraulique; *F:* houille verte; (*b*) ruisseau *m*; **mountain s.,** torrent *m*; *Prov:* **little streams make great rivers,** les petits ruisseaux font les grandes rivières; (*c*) flot *m* (d'eau); ruissellement *m* (d'eau, etc.); **heavy s. of water,** fort jet d'eau; **in a thin s.,** en mince filet; (*d*) *Sch:* **three-s. school,** école où les classes sont réparties sur trois niveaux différents. **2.** coulée *f* (de lave); flot(s) *m(pl)*, torrent, jet (de lumière, de sang); flux *m*, torrent (de larmes, de paroles); flots (de gens); averse *f* (de félicitations); **people entered in streams,** les gens entraient à flots; **unceasing s. of immigrants,** flux continu d'immigrants; **s. of cars,** défilé ininterrompu de voitures; **streams of fire,** des rivières de feu; **to hold up the s. of traffic,** arrêter le flot de voitures; **in one continuous s.,** à jet continu; *Cmptr:* **s. of data,** flot, chaîne *f*, suite *f*, train *m*, de données; *Min: Ind:* (*of oil well, factory, etc.*) **to be on s.,** travailler à plein rendement; **to go, come, on s.,** entrer en service; commencer la production. **3.** courant *m*; *Nau:* lit *m* du courant; **with the s.,** dans le sens du courant; au fil de l'eau; **against the s.,** contre le courant, à contre-courant; **to let a boat run with the s.,** lâcher un bateau à la lancée; **to go with the s.,** suivre le courant (du fleuve, *Fig:* de l'opinion); suivre le mouvement; **the main s. of public opinion,** le courant de l'opinion publique; **in the main s. of French tradition,** en plein dans l'axe de la tradition française; **s. of consciousness,** *Lit: & Psy:* monologue intérieur; *Nau:* **s. cable,** câble *m* d'embossage.

stream[2]. **1.** *v.i.* (*a*) (*of liquid*) couler à flots; ruisseler; **blood was streaming from, out of, his mouth,** le sang lui jaillissait de la bouche; **people were streaming over the bridge,** les gens traversaient le pont à flot continu; **the guests streamed in, out,** les invités entraient, sortaient, à flots; **the sunlight streams in(to the room),** le soleil pénètre à flots (dans la chambre); (*b*) (*of surface*) ruisseler (**with,** de); **her eyes were streaming with tears,**

ses yeux ruisselaient de larmes, ses larmes coulaient à flots; **he was streaming with perspiration,** il ruisselait par tous les pores; il était en nage, trempé de sueur; (*c*) (*of hair, garment, banner*) flotter (au vent); **her hair streamed on the breeze,** ses cheveux flottaient au gré du vent. **2.** *v.tr.* (*a*) verser, laisser, couler, (un liquide) à flots; **the river streamed blood,** la rivière coulait rouge; (*b*) *Nau:* mouiller (une bouée); **to s. the log,** jeter, filer, le loch; (*c*) *Min:* laver, débourber (le minerai); (*d*) *Sch:* **to s. pupils,** répartir les élèves en sections de force homogène.

streamer ['stri:mər], *s.* **1.** (*a*) banderole *f*; *Nau:* flamme *f*; **(paper) streamers,** serpentins *m* (de carnaval, etc.); (*b*) *Journ:* titre flamboyant. **2.** *Meteor:* **streamers,** (i) lumière *f* polaire, aurore boréale; (ii) flèches *f* de la couronne solaire (pendant une éclipse). **3.** *Min:* (*pers.*) laveur *m* de minerai.

streaming[1] ['stri:miŋ], *a.* **1.** (*a*) (liquide) qui coule, jaillissant; *F:* **to have a s. cold,** avoir un fort rhume de cerveau; (*b*) (*of surface, umbrella*) ruisselant. **2.** flottant au vent; **s. hair,** cheveux épars au vent.

streaming[2], *s.* **1.** *Min:* lavage *m* (du minerai). **2.** *Sch:* répartition *f* (des élèves) en sections de force homogène.

streamless ['stri:mlis], *a.* **1.** (*of water*) sans courant. **2.** (*of district*) sans cours d'eau.

streamlet ['stri:mlit], *s.* petit ruisseau; ruisselet *m*.

streamline[1] ['stri:mlain], *s.* **1.** *Ph:* courant naturel (d'un fluide); **s. flow,** écoulement *m* laminaire. **2.** *Aut: Av: etc:* ligne fuyante, fuselée; **body s.,** ligne profilée, aérodynamique, de carrosserie; **s. body,** carrosserie profilée, carénée; carène *f*.

streamline[2], *v.tr.* **1.** caréner (une voiture, etc.). **2.** simplifier, rationaliser (une méthode); réduire (l'économie) à l'essentiel; **he streamlined rearing methods,** il a modernisé, affiné, la méthode d'élevage; **we have streamlined our catalogue,** nous avons rénové, allégé, refondu, notre catalogue.

streamlined ['stri:mlaind], *a.* **1.** (*a*) *Aut: Av:* caréné, fuselé, profilé, effilé; **s. fuselage,** fuselage *m* aérodynamique; **s. cowling,** capotage *m* à avant profilé; *Aut:* **s. coachwork,** carrosserie carénée, aérodynamique; *Rail:* **s. railcar,** autorail *m* aérodynamique; (*b*) (*of fish, ship's hull, etc.*) hydrodynamique. **2.** (*of system, etc.*) rationalisé; **s. economy,** économie réduite à l'essentiel.

streamlining ['stri:mlainiŋ], *s.* **1.** carénage *m*, profilage *m* (de la carrosserie). **2.** simplification *f*, rationalisation *f* (d'un système, etc.); réduction *f* (de l'économie) à l'essentiel.

streamway ['stri:mwei], *s.* chenal *m*, *pl.* -aux, de cours d'eau.

streek [stri:k], *v.tr. Scot:* **to s. a body,** faire la toilette d'un mort.

street [stri:t], *s.* (*a*) rue *f*; **back s.,** petite rue écartée; *Pej:* rue pauvre, mal fréquentée; **the back streets of a town,** les bas quartiers d'une ville; **cross s.,** (i) rue transversale, de traverse; (ii) rue latérale; **the main traffic s. of the town,** la grande artère de la ville; **the High S.,** la Grande rue, la Grand-rue; **the High S. banks,** les succursales (provinciales, etc.) d'une banque; **they live in,** *N Am:* **on, the same s.,** ils habitent la même rue; **to turn, throw, s.o. (out) into the s.,** jeter qn à la rue, mettre qn sur le pavé; **to find oneself (out) on the s.,** être à la rue; **to walk the streets,** courir les rues, battre le pavé; (*of prostitute*) (*also* **to be on the streets),** faire le trottoir, le raccroc, la retape; **s. walker,** fille *f* de trottoir; raccrocheuse *f*, racoleuse *f*; **s. walking,** prostitution *f* sur la voie publique; **the man in the s.,** l'homme moyen, ordinaire; Monsieur Tout-le-Monde; l'homme de la rue; le bon, gros, grand, public; le premier venu; *F:* **not to be in the same s. with s.o.,** ne pas être de taille avec qn, être de beaucoup inférieur à qn; *Turf:* **to come in streets ahead of, behind, the rest,** arriver de beaucoup le premier, gagner de beaucoup; arriver de beaucoup le dernier; **he's streets ahead of his competitors,** il a devancé de beaucoup, dépassé de tout en tout, ses concurrents; **they are streets behind him,** ils lui sont nettement inférieurs; **that's not up his s. at all,** (i) cela est tout à fait hors de sa compétence; (ii) cela n'est pas dans ses goûts; **that's right up my s.,** c'est mon rayon, dans ma ligne; **s. accidents,** accidents *m* de la circulation; **s. cries, calls,** cris *m* des marchands ambulants, etc.; cris des rues; **s. door,** porte *f* sur la rue, de (la) rue; **s. dress,** costume *m* de ville; **s. fighting,** bataille *f* de rues; **s. guide,** indicateur *m* des rues; **s. lamp, light,** réverbère *m*; **s. lighting,** éclairage des rues; **s. level,** rez-de-chaussée *m inv*; **s. market,** (i) marché *m* en plein air (dans une rue); (ii) *St.Exch:* marché après Bourse; **s. musician,** musicien, -ienne, des rues, de carrefour; **s. porter,** commissionnaire *m*; **s. sweeper,** (i) (*pers.*) balayeur *m* de rues; (ii) (*machine*) balayeuse *f* (de rues); *U.S:* **s. railway,** tramway *m*; (*b*) (habitants *mpl* de la) rue; **the whole s. heard the row,** toute la rue a entendu le chahut; *F:* **the S.,** (i) *Journ:* **(Fleet S.),** le monde des journalistes; (ii) *U.S:* **(Wall S.),** le monde financier; (*c*) (*opposed to footway*) la chaussée.

streetcar ['stri:tkɑ:r], *s. NAm:* tramway *m*.

strength [streŋθ], *s.* **1.** (*a*) force(s) *f*(*pl*); **s. of a man, of a horse,** force d'un homme, d'un cheval; **s. of body,** force corporelle; **s. of a current,** force, *El:* intensité *f*, d'un courant; *Art:* **s. of a colour,** intensité d'une couleur; **s. of a wine, of an acid,** force d'un vin, d'un acide; **s. of the tea,** degré *m* d'infusion du thé; **alcoholic s.,** teneur *f* en alcool, degré d'alcool, degré alcoolique (d'un vin, etc.); *St.Exch:* **the s. of the market for government stock, the s. of government stock on the market,** le cours, la valeur boursière, des fonds publics; *Ch:* **s. of a solution,** titre *m*, teneur, d'une solution; **solution at full s., full-s. solution,** solution concentrée; **solution below full s.,** solution diluée; **s. of mind,** fermeté *f* d'esprit; force de caractère; **s. of will,** résolution *f*; **s. of intellect,** vigueur intellectuelle; **by s. of arm,** à force de bras; **by sheer s.,** de vive force; de haute lutte; à force de bras; **that is too much for my s.,** c'est au-dessus de mes forces; **to recover, regain, s., to recruit, revive, one's s., to acquire new s.,** se rétablir, se remonter; reprendre des forces; recouvrer ses forces; reprendre vigueur; se retremper; *F:* se remettre d'aplomb; **you must keep up your s.,** il faut vous sustenter; **to build up one's s. again,** se reconstituer; **to lose s.,** s'affaiblir; **the patient is losing s.,** le malade baisse; **he hasn't the s. left to speak,** il n'a plus la force de parler; **to do sth. on the s. of what one has been told,** faire qch. sur la foi de, en se fiant à, en s'appuyant sur, fort de, ce qu'on vous a dit; **promoted to a directorship on the s. of his father's millions,** promu au conseil d'administration de par les millions de son père; **he got a good job on the s. of his qualifications,** il a obtenu un bon emploi grâce à ses diplômes; **it is impossible to negotiate on the s. of samples,** on ne peut pas se baser sur des échantillons pour négocier; (*b*) solidité *f*, rigidité *f*, résistance *f* (d'une poutre, d'une corde); ténacité *f* (du papier, etc.); robustesse *f* (d'un meuble, etc.); **s. of a building, of a scaffolding,** solidité d'un bâtiment, d'un échafaudage; **s. of a friendship,** solidité d'une amitié; *Mec:* **s. of materials,** résistance des matériaux; **bending s.,** résistance à la flexion; **tensile s.,** (force de) résistance à la tension; limite *f* élastique à la traction; **breaking s., ultimate s.,** résistance à la rupture; résistance extrême; résistance limite; ténacité extrême; **crushing s., compressive s.,** résistance à l'écrasement; **bursting s.,** résistance à l'éclatement; **seal s.,** étanchéité *f*; (*c*) force (d'un joueur, etc.); **his s. lies in his wealth,** sa richesse est son point fort; **to go from s. to s.,** aller de mieux en mieux; avancer à pas de géant. **2. to be present in great s.,** être présents en grand nombre; **to be there in full s.,** assister (à la cérémonie, etc.) au grand complet. **3.** *Mil:* effectif(s) *m*(*pl*) (d'un régiment); **war s., peace s.,** effectif de guerre, de paix; **under s.,** incomplet, à effectif insuffisant; **to bring a battalion up to s.,** compléter, recruter, un bataillon; **bringing up to s.,** complètement *m*, recomplètement *m*; **battalion at full s.,** bataillon à effectifs complets; *Navy:* **squadron at full s.,** escadre au grand complet; **to be taken on the s.,** être porté sur les contrôles *m*; **to be on the s.,** figurer sur les contrôles; **not on the s.,** hors cadre; **to bring men on to the s.,** incorporer des soldats; **to strike s.o. off the s.,** rayer qn des cadres, des contrôles; désenrôler qn.

strengthen ['streŋθ(ə)n]. **1.** *v.tr.* consolider, assurer (un mur, une maison); renforcer (une poutre, une garnison); fortifier (qn, le corps); assurer (la main de qn); (r)affermir (l'autorité de qn); **to s. the hand of the government,** rendre le gouvernement plus fort, renforcer la position du gouvernement; **it would s. my hand, position,** cela raffermirait ma position; **to s. a law,** renforcer une loi; **trunk with strengthened corners,** malle à coins renforcés; **his answer strengthened my opinion,** sa réponse renforça, accentua, mon opinion; **to s. a solution,** augmenter la concentration d'une solution; *Typ:* **to s. a colour,** charger une couleur. **2.** *v.i.* (*a*) se fortifier, se renforcer, s'affermir; (*b*) prendre, reprendre, des forces.

strengthener ['streŋθ(ə)nər], *s.* **1.** renfort *m*, liaison *f*; affermissement *m*. **2.** *Med:* fortifiant *m*.

strengthening[1] ['streŋθ(ə)niŋ], *a.* fortifiant; (*of drink*) réconfortant.

strengthening[2], *s.* renforcement *m*, renforçage *m*, consolidation *f*, (r)affermissement *m*; armement *m* (d'une poutre, etc.); *El:* renforcement (du courant); *Mec.E: etc:* **s. piece,** renfort *m*; *Nau:* **s. band,** bande *f* de renfort (d'une voile).

strengthless ['streŋθlis], *a.* faible, sans forces; qui n'a pas de résistance.

strenuous ['strenjuəs], *a.* **1.** (*of pers.*) actif, agissant, énergique; zélé. **2.** (*of conflict, etc.*) acharné; (*of effort*) tendu; (*of work*) ardu; (*of resistance*) opiniâtre; **s. profession,** métier dur, pénible, où l'on peine beaucoup; **s. life,** vie toute d'effort; **the s. life,** la vie intense; **to make s. efforts to get sth. done,** tendre tous ses efforts vers l'accomplissement de qch.; **through much s. work,** à force de labeur, à force d'énergie.

strenuously ['strenjuəsli], *adv.* vigoureusement, avec zèle, avec acharnement; **to work s. to reach an agreement,** travailler énergiquement, d'arrache-pied, afin d'obtenir un accord.

strenuousness ['strenjuəsnis], *s.* (*of pers.*) ardeur *f*, vigueur *f*, zèle *m*; (*of work*) dureté *f*; (*of opposition*) acharnement *m*, opiniâtreté *f*.

strep [strep], *F:* **1.** *s.* streptocoque *m*. **2.** *a.* (infection) streptococcique; **s. throat,** gorge atteinte d'une infection streptococcique.

strepera ['strepərə], *s. Orn:* strépère *m*, réveilleur *m*.

strepitous ['strepitəs], *a. Lit:* bruyant, tumultueux.

Strepsitera [strep'sitərə], *s.pl. Ent:* strepsitères *m*.

streptobacillus [streptoubə'siləs], *s. Bac:* streptobacille *m*.

streptococcal [streptou'kɔkl], **streptococcic** [streptou'kɔk(s)ik], *a. Bac:* streptococcique.

streptococcosis [streptoukɔ'kousis], *s. Med:* streptococcie *f*.

streptococcus, *pl.* **-cocci** [streptou'kɔkəs, -'kɔk(s)ai], *s. Med:* streptocoque *m*.

streptomycin [streptou'maisin], *s. Med:* streptomycine *f*.

Streptoneura [streptou'nju:rə], *s.pl. Moll:* streptoneures *m*, prosobranches *m*.

streptoseptic(a)emia ['streptousepti'si:miə], *s. Med:* streptococcémie *f*.

streptothricin [streptou'θraisin, -'θrisin], *s. Med:* streptothricine *f*.

streptotrichosis [streptoutri'kousis], *s. Med:* streptotrichose *f*.

stress[1] [stres], *s.* **1.** force *f*, contrainte *f*; **s. of weather** violence *f* du temps, gros temps, *Nau:* temps forcé; **compelled by s. of weather to shelter,** forcé par le gros temps de s'abriter. **2.** (*a*) *Mec.E: Mec:* tension *f*, travail *m*, contrainte; **tractive s.,** sollicitation *f* (d'une force); **tension s.,** contrainte à la traction; **diagram of stresses, s. diagram,** épure *f* des contraintes; **allowable s., working s.,** contrainte admissible en pratique, résistance *f* pratique; **working unit s.,** effort unitaire admissible; **ultimate breaking s.,** contrainte de rupture; limite *f*, résistance, de rupture; **bending s.,** contrainte de flexion, moment *m* de flambage; **yield s.,** limite, résistance, élastique; *Metall:* **casting s.,** tension de coulée; **internal stresses of a cooling body,** tensions au sein d'un corps qui se refroidit; (*of beam*) **to be in s.,** travailler; **subjected to great s.,** assujetti à des efforts considérables; **bearing s.,** charge *f* du palier; **s. limit,** limite de travail, de fatigue; **s. unit,** unité *f* de charge; **s.-bearing,** travaillant; (*b*) **times of slackness and times of s.,** temps de relâchement et temps d'effort; **period of storm and s.,** période *f* de trouble et d'agitation; (*c*) **(inner) s.,** tension, état tendu, des nerfs, de l'esprit, *Med:* stress *m*; **nervous s.,** tension nerveuse; **in a moment of s. he committed murder,** dans une crise de tension nerveuse il a commis un assassinat. **3.** (*a*) insistance *f*; **to lay s. on a fact,** insister sur un fait; s'arrêter à, sur, un fait; attacher de l'importance à un fait; faire ressortir un fait; **to lay s. on a word,** insister, peser, sur un mot; souligner un mot; **to lay s. on a syllable,** appuyer sur une syllabe; (*b*) *Ling:* **s. (accent),** accent *m* (d'intensité); accent tonique; *Pros:* temps marqué; **s. on a syllable,** appui *m* de la voix sur une syllabe; **the s. falls on the last syllable,** l'accent tonique tombe sur la dernière syllabe; **the laws of s. in English,** les lois de l'accentuation *f* en anglais; la tonétique anglaise; **s. mark,** accent écrit; **s. verse,** vers *m* métriques.

stress[2], *v.tr.* **1.** *Mec.E:* charger, fatiguer, faire travailler (une poutre, etc.); (*of beam*) **to be stressed,** travailler. **2.** appuyer, insister, mettre l'accent, sur (qch.); souligner, peser sur (un mot); appuyer sur, accentuer (une syllabe); **he stressed (the point) that nobody was to blame,** il a fait valoir que, a fait ressortir ce fait que, personne n'était blâmable; *Mus:* **to s. the melody,** faire sentir la mélodie; faire ressortir le chant.

stressed [strest], *a.* **1.** *Mec.E:* chargé, travaillant; *Av:* **s. skin,** revêtement travaillant. **2.** *Ling:* (*of syllable*) accentué.

stressing ['stresiŋ], *s.* **1.** *Mec.E:* chargement *m* (d'une poutre, etc.); **alternate s.,** effort *m* de rupture. **2.** (*a*) soulignement *m* (d'un mot), insistance *f* (**of a word,** sur un mot); (*b*) accentuation *f* (d'une syllabe).

stretch[1] [stretʃ], *s.* **1.** (*a*) allongement *m*, extension *f*; **s. (out) of the wings,** déploiement *m* des ailes; **s. (out) of the arm,** extension du bras; **with a yawn and a s.,** en bâillant et en s'étirant; *Rac:* **at full s.,** à toute allure, ventre à terre; (*b*) allongement par traction; élargissement *m* par traction; tension *f* étirage; **cable wire s.,** allongement d'un câble métallique; **percentage of s.,** coefficient *m* d'allongement; **by a s. of the imagination,** par un effort d'imagination; **by no s. of the imagination could I conceive that. . .,** il me serait absolument impossible de croire que. . .; **with every faculty on the s.,** avec toutes ses facultés tendues; (*c*) étendue *f*, portée *f* (du bras, du sens d'un mot); **s. of wing,** envergure *f*; *Mus:* **s. of the fingers,** écart *m* des doigts (au piano); (*d*) élasticité *f*; (*of elastic fabric*) **with two-way s.,** extensible dans les deux sens; *Obst:* **s. mark,** vergeture *f*; *Mec:* **s. modulus,** module *m*, coefficient *m*, d'élasticité; (*e*) *a.* **s. fabric,** tissu extensible. **2.** (*a*) étendue (de pays, d'eau, etc.); bande *f* (de terrain); **s. of road,** section *f* de route; **long s. of straight road,** long ruban rectiligne; **level s.,** palier *m*; *Rac:* **the (home)s.,** la ligne droite; *Nau:* **to make a long s.,** courir une longue bordée; (*b*) **for a long s. of time,** longtemps; *F:* **at a s., at one s.,** (tout) d'un trait, (tout) d'une traite; tout d'une haleine, tout d'une trotte; d'arrache-pied, d'affilée; sans débrider; **he has been working for hours at a s.,** voilà des heures qu'il travaille sans désemparer, sans discontinuer; **to ride ten kilometres at a s.,** faire dix kilomètres d'une chevauchée, d'une seule traite; *P:* **he's doing his s.,** il tire, fait, de la prison, fait de la taule; **to do a long s.,** faire de longues années de prison. **3.** *F:* **to have a s.,** (i) se dégourdir; (ii) faire une petite promenade. **4.** *Min:* direction *f* (d'un filon).

stretch[2], *v.*

I. *v.tr.* (*a*) tendre (de l'élastique); tendre, tirer, bander (une courroie, un câble, un ressort); retendre (une courroie); étendre, élargir (des souliers, gants); renformer (des gants); détirer (le linge, cuir); *Art:* **to s. the canvas on the frame,** tendre la toile sur le châssis; **to s. a bow,** tendre, bander, un arc; **to s. one's shoes by use,** faire ses souliers; **to s. one's trousers,** mettre son pantalon sur tendeur; **how far can I s. this dish?** pour combien de portions ce plat suffira-t-il au besoin? *F: O:* **it made me s. my eyes,** cela m'a fait écarquiller les yeux; (*b*) **to s. oneself,** *v.i.* **to s.,** s'étirer; se détirer; **I can s. for it,** c'est à portée de ma main; **I can get it if I s. hard,** avec tous mes efforts je peux l'atteindre; **to s. (out) one's arm,** allonger, développer, le bras; **to s. out one's hand,** tendre, avancer, la main; **to s. one's neck to see sth.,** allonger le cou pour voir qch.; **to s. one's legs,** (i) allonger les jambes; (ii) se dégourdir, se dérouiller, les jambes; **I'm going to s. my legs before it gets dark,** je vais faire une petite promenade avant que la nuit tombe; **to lie stretched (out) on the ground,** être étendu de tout son long par terre; (*of bird*) **to s. its wings,** déployer ses ailes; (*c*) **to s. s.o.'s patience,** éprouver, exercer, la patience de qn; (*d*) forcer (le sens d'un mot, etc.); **to s. the law,** faire violence à la loi; donner une entorse au code; **to s. the truth, veracity, too far,** outrepasser les bornes de la vérité; exagérer, hâbler; **to s. a point,** faire une concession, une exception (**for s.o.,** en faveur de qn); *F:* **that's stretching it a bit!** c'est le tirer par les cheveux; (*e*) **to s. a rope across a room,** tendre une corde à travers une pièce; **to s. an awning over the deck,** établir une tente sur le pont.

II. *v.i.* **1.** (*a*) s'étirer ((i) s'élargir; (ii) s'allonger); (*of elastic*) s'étendre, s'allonger; (*of rope*) rendre; (*of gloves, etc.*) s'étendre, s'élargir; **material that stretches,** étoffe qui prête; **rope that has stretched,** corde qui a pris de l'allongement, qui s'est détendue; *Nau:* **canvas that stretches,** toile qui adonne; (*b*) être susceptible d'extension. **2.** (*a*) s'étendre; **the valley stretches southward,** la vallée s'étend vers le sud; **the road stretches away into the distance,** la route se déroule au loin; **his mouth stretches from ear to ear,** il a la bouche fendue jusqu'aux oreilles; (*b*) **to s. out,** (i) (*of line of runners, etc.*) s'étirer; (ii) (*of racehorse*) aller ventre à terre; (iii) *Row:* souquer sur les avirons. **3. my resources won't s. to that,** mes moyens (pécuniaires) ne vont pas jusque-là; **the dish will s. to six helpings,** au besoin on peut faire six portions de ce plat.

stretchable ['stretʃəbl], *a.* extensible.

stretched [stretʃt], *a.* **1.** (*a*) (corde, etc.) raide; (*b*) (*of language, etc.*) forcé, exagéré; poussé trop loin. **2.** (élastique) qui a perdu son élasticité; allongé; (ressort) fatigué, détendu.

stretcher ['stretʃər], *s.* **1.** *Tex:* (*pers.*) étireur, -euse (de soie, etc.). **2.** (*a*) tendeur *m*; tenseur *m* (de hauban, etc.); **trouser-s.,** tendeur, extenseur *m*, de pantalons; **shoe stretchers,** tendeurs (pour chaussures); conformateurs *m*; *Mec.E:* **s. pulley,** tendeur *m* de courroie; (*b*) *Art:* **canvas s.,** châssis *m* (de toile d'artiste); (*c*) *Leath:* étire *f*. **3.** (*a*) bois *m* d'écartement (de hamac); traverse *f* (de tente); arc-boutant *m*, *pl.* arcs-boutants (d'un parapluie); *Rail:* **s. rod,** tringle *f* d'écartement (des aiguilles); (*b*) barreau *m*, bâton *m* (de chaise); sommier *m* (de scie à châssis); *Const:* (*tie beam*) tirant *m*, entrait *m* (de comble). **4.** (*a*) brancard *m*, civière *f*; **to carry s.o. on a s.,** porter qn sur une civière; *F:* brancarder qn; **s. bearer,** brancardier *m*, ambulancier *m*; **s. party,** détachement *m*, équipe *f*, de brancardiers; (*b*) *O:* lit *m* de camp, de sangle. **5.** *Nau:* marchepied *m* de nage, barre *f* des pieds, traversin *m* (d'une embarcation). **6.** *Const:* (*in masonry, brickwork*) carreau *m*, panneresse *f*; **s. bond,** appareil en panneresses. **7.** *U.S: F: O:* histoire *f* difficile à avaler; histoire un peu forte de café.

stretching ['stretʃiŋ], *s.* **1.** (*a*) tension *f*; **s. frame,** stirator *m* (de dessinateur); *Leath:* **s. iron,** étire *f*; *Ind:* **s. roll(er),** rouleau tendeur; **s. screw,** tendeur *m*; vis *f* de serrage; (*b*) baguettage *m* (de gants). **2.** allongement *m*, élargissement *m*. **3.** *Const:* **s. bond, course,** appareil *m*, assise *f*, en panneresses.

stretchy ['stretʃi], *a. F:* élastique, qui prête.

stretto, *pl.* **-ti** ['stretou, -ti:], *s. Mus:* strette *f* (d'une fugue).

strew [stru:], *v.tr.* (*p.p.* **strewed** [stru:d] *or* **strewn** [stru:n]) **1. to s. sand over the floor,** jeter, répandre, du sable sur le plancher; **they strewed flowers in his path,** on éparpillait, on répandait, des fleurs sur son passage; on faisait une jonchée de fleurs sur son passage; **fragments of the statue lie strewn about the pavement,** des débris de la statue jonchent le pavé; **toys were strewn over, around, on, the floor,** des jouets étaient éparpillés sur le plancher. **2. to s. the floor with sand, with flowers,** couvrir le plancher de sable; joncher, parsemer, le plancher de fleurs; **they strewed his path with flowers,** on répandait des fleurs sur son passage; **the ground was strewn with rushes, with dead,** une jonchée de roseaux, de morts, recouvrait le sol.

strewth [stru:θ], *int. P:* = STRUTH.

stria, *pl.* **-ae** ['straiə, -i:], *s.* **1.** strie *f*, striure *f*; (*a*) bande *f* de couleur; **s. of light,** raie lumineuse; (*b*) *Bot:* **striae on the stem of a plant,** stries, striures, cannelures *f*, sur la tige d'une plante; *Geol:* **glacial striae,** stries glaciaires. **2.** *Arch:* listel *m*, *pl.* -eaux, listeau *m* (de colonne).

striate[1] ['straieit], **striated** [strai'eitid], *a. Nat.Hist: Geol: etc:* strié; **striated muscle,** muscle strié.

striate[2], *v.tr.* strier.

striation [strai'eiʃ(ə)n], *s. Nat.Hist: Geol: etc:* striation *f*.

strick [strik], *s. Tex:* poignée *f* de chanvre, lin, jute, peigné.

stricken ['strik(ə)n], *a. Lit:* **1.** (*a*) *Ven:* (daim) blessé; (*b*) frappé; *A:* **for three stricken hours,** pendant trois heures d'horloge, trois mortelles heures. **2.** (*a*) (*of pers.*) affligé; éprouvé; **s. with grief,** accablé de douleur; en proie à la douleur; **s. with fever,** atteint d'une fièvre; **s. by a disease,** frappé d'une maladie; (*b*) **the s. city,** la ville sinistrée; **the s. vessel,** le vaisseau en détresse, naufragé. **3.** *A:* **s. in years,** avancé en âge; chargé d'années; écrasé sous le poids des années, *Lit:* des ans. **4.** *A:* **s. field,** (i) bataille rangée; (ii) champ *m* de bataille, de carnage. **5. s. measure,** mesure rase (de blé, etc.).

strickle[1] ['strikl], *s.* **1.** *Meas:* racloire *f*. **2.** *Metall:* **s. (board),** trousseau *m*, trousse *f*, gabarit *m*. **3.** *Agr:* pierre *f* à (aiguiser les) faux.

strickle[2], *v.tr. Metall:* trousser (le moule).

strickling ['strikliŋ], *s. Metall:* troussage *m* (du moule).

strict [strikt], *a.* **1.** exact, strict; (*a*) précis; **the s. minimum,** le strict minimum; **in the s., the strictest, sense of the word,** au sens précis, rigoureux, du mot; dans le sens strict, exact, dans le sens le plus étroit, du mot; (*b*) rigoureux; **to observe s. neutrality,** observer une neutralité rigoureuse; **he lives in s. seclusion,** il vit dans une retraite rigoureuse, absolue; **it was told me in strictest confidence,** on me l'a dit à titre tout à fait confidentiel, sous le sceau du secret le plus strict; *Com:* **s. cost price,** prix de revient calculé au plus juste. **2.** (règlement, etc.) étroit, rigide; *Jur:* (délai) péremptoire; **he gave s. orders,** il a donné des ordres formels, rigoureux; **s. prohibition,** défense formelle; **s. obligation,** obligation stricte; **s. discipline,** discipline sévère; **s. etiquette,** étiquette rigide; **s. censorship,** censure sévère, rigoureuse; **s. code of laws,** code de lois sévère, rigoureux; **s. diet,** régime exact; **s. fast,** jeûne austère, sévère; **s. morals,** morale stricte, rigide; mœurs sévères; **S. Protestant,** protestant rigide; **s. Moslem,** musulman de stricte obédience; **s. in business,** strict en affaires; **to keep a s. watch over s.o.,** exercer sur qn une surveillance rigoureuse, sévère. **3.** (*of pers.*) sévère; **to be s. with s.o.,** être sévère avec, envers, pour, qn; traiter qn avec beaucoup de rigueur; **to keep a s. hand over s.o.,** traiter qn avec sévérité; tenir à qn la bride courte. **4.** *Bot:* (*of stem, etc.*) dressé, raide.

striction ['strikʃ(ə)n], *s. Mth:* **curve, line, of s.,** ligne *f* de striction *f*.

strictly ['striktli], *adv.* **1.** exactement, rigoureusement; **to define one's terms s.,** définir ses termes avec précision; **to correspond s. to the description,** correspondre exactement à la description; **s. speaking,** à proprement parler, à parler rigoureusement; rigoureusement, strictement, parlant; à vrai dire, à dire vrai. **2.** étroitement, strictement; **smoking (is) s. prohibited,** défense formelle, expresse, de fumer; **it is s. forbidden,** c'est absolument défendu; **s. confidential,** strictement confidentiel; **to adhere s. to a clause,** se montrer irréductible sur un article; **applications must be submitted before September 10; this date will be s. adhered to,** les demandes devront être remises avant le 10 septembre, terme de rigueur; **to guard s.o. s.,** surveiller étroitement qn. **3.** sévèrement; (traité, élevé) avec rigueur.

strictness ['striktnis], *s.* **1.** exactitude rigoureuse, précision *f* (d'une traduction, etc.). **2.** rigueur *f* (des règles, etc.). **3.** sévérité *f* (de la discipline, etc.).

stricture ['striktjər], *s.* **1.** (*a*) *Med:* rétrécissement *m* (du canal de l'urètre, de l'œsophage); étranglement *m* (de l'intestin); (*b*) *NAm:* restriction *f*, limitation *f*. **2.** (*usu. pl.*) **to pass strictures (up)on s.o., sth.,** diriger ses critiques contre qn, qch.; trouver à redire à qch.

strictured ['striktjəd], *a. Med:* (canal, etc.) rétréci.

stricturotomy [striktjə'rɔtəmi], *s. Surg:* stricturotomie *f*.

stride[1] [straid], *s.* **1.** (grand) pas; enjambée *f*; **to walk with, take, long strides,** marcher à grands pas, à grandes enjambées; **to shorten, lengthen, one's s.,** raccourcir, allonger, le pas, *Sp:* la foulée; **horse with a good length of s.,** cheval au trot allongé; *Fig:* **to make great strides,** faire de grands progrès; **the mining industry has made great strides,** l'industrie minière a pris un grand essor; **science has made great, rapid, strides,** la science a réalisé de sérieux progrès, des progrès rapides; *Sp:* **to take the hurdles in one's s.,** franchir chaque haie d'une enjambée, sans changer d'allure; *Fig:* **to take sth. in one's s.,** *U.S:* **in s.,** faire qch. sans le moindre effort; **to get into one's s.,** prendre son allure normale; attraper la cadence (d'un travail, etc.); aller de l'avant; **wait till he has got into his s.,** attendez qu'il soit lancé; **to be thrown out of one's s.,** être déconcerté, dérouté. **2.** *Austr: F:* **strides,** pantalon *m*.

stride[2], *v.* (*p.t.* **strode** [stroud]; *p.p.* **stridden** ['stridn]. **1.** *v.i.* (*a*) marcher à grands pas, à grandes enjambées; **to s. along, to s. out,** avancer à grands pas, à grandes enjambées; **to s. away,** s'éloigner à grands pas; **to s. out of the room,** sortir de la pièce d'un pas digne; **to s. over the fields,** parcourir les champs à longues foulées; **to s. up and down a room,** arpenter une pièce; **to s. up to s.o.,** avancer à grands pas vers qn; **science is striding further ahead each year,** la science avance, progresse, à pas de géant d'année en année; (*b*) **to s. over sth.,** enjamber qch. **2.** *v.tr.* (*a*) *A:* arpenter (les rues, etc.); (*b*) *Lit:* enjamber (un fossé, etc.); (*c*) *occ.* (i) enfourcher (un cheval, etc.); (ii) se tenir à califourchon sur (une branche, etc.); être à cheval sur (une bête).

stridency ['straidənsi], *s.* stridulence *f*.

strident ['straid(ə)nt], *a.* strident.

stridently ['straid(ə)ntli], *adv.* stridemment.

stridor ['straidɔ:r], *s. Med:* stridor *m or f*, bruits striduleux.

stridulant ['stridjulənt], *a. Ent:* stridulant.

stridulate ['stridjuleit], *v.i. Ent:* striduler.

stridulation [stridju'leiʃ(ə)n], *s.* stridulation *f*.

stridulator ['stridjuleitər], *s. Ent:* (i) insecte stridulant; (ii) appareil *m* stridulatoire.

stridulatory ['stridjulət(ə)ri], *a. Ent:* (appareil, etc.) stridulatoire.

stridulous ['stridjuləs], *a. Med: etc:* striduleux.

strife [straif], *s.* lutte *f*, contestation *f*, différends *mpl*; **domestic s.,** querelles *fpl* de ménage; *Lit:* **to be at s.,** être en conflit, en lutte (**with,** avec); **to cease from s.,** mettre bas les armes.

striga, *pl.* **-gae** ['straigə, -dʒi:], *s.* **1.** *Ent:* strie *f*, rayure transversale. **2.** *pl. Bot:* **strigae,** poils raides et appressés.

Strigidae ['stridʒidi:], *s.pl. Orn:* strigidés *m*.

Strigiformes [stridʒi'fɔ:mi:z], *s.pl. Orn:* strigiformes *m*.

strigil ['stridʒil], *s. Gr. & Rom.Ant:* strigile *m*.

strigose ['straigous], *a.* **1.** *Ent:* strié. **2.** *Bot:* hérissé.

strigovite ['straigəvait], *s. Miner:* strigovite *f*.

strike[1] [straik], *s.* **1.** (*a*) coup *m*; (*of snake*) **to make a s. at s.o.,** darder un coup de dents à qn; **to listen for the s. (of**

the clock), écouter pour entendre sonner l'horloge; *Locksm:* **s. box, plate,** gâche *f* (de pêne coulant); *Mec.E:* **s. gear,** passe-courroie *m, pl.* passe-courroies; (i) débrayeur *m*, (ii) embrayeur *m* (de courroie); (*b*) *Fish:* saccade (donnée à la ligne par le poisson); (*c*) *NAm: Games:* (i) (*baseball*) balle manquée (par le batteur); *Fig:* **it was a s. against him,** c'était un mauvais point pour lui; (ii) (*at tenpin bowling*) honneur *m* double; (*d*) *Mil:* attaque *f*; **pre-emptive s.,** attaque à priori; **atomic s.,** frappe *f* atomique; **air s.,** (i) raid *m*, intervention aérienne, opération *f* de soutien aérien; (ii) escadron *m* d'assaut; **s. aircraft,** avions *mpl* d'assaut. **2.** *Ind: etc:* grève *f*; **unofficial s.,** grève désapprouvée par les autorités syndicales; **staggered, selective, s.,** grève tournante; **go-slow s.,** grève perlée; **lightning s.,** grève surprise; **sit-down, stay-in, s.,** grève sur le tas; **sympathy s.,** grève de solidarité; **bottleneck s.,** grève bouchon; **to go, come out, on s., to take s. action,** se mettre en grève; *F:* débrayer; (*of prisoner*) **to go on hunger s.,** faire la grève de la faim; **s. breaker,** briseur, -euse, de grève; *F:* renard *m*, jaune *m*; *Ins:* **s. clause,** clause *f* pour cas de grève; **s. pay,** allocation *f* de grève. **3.** *Min:* rencontre *f* (de minerai, pétrole); découverte *f* (d'un gisement); **the importance of the new s.,** l'importance du nouveau filon: *F:* **lucky s.,** coup de veine. **4.** *Artil:* souille *f* (d'un projectile rasant le sol). **5.** *Geol: Min:* direction *f* (d'un filon). **6.** (*a*) *Typ:* matrice (frappée); (*b*) (*minting coins*) (campagne *f* de) frappe *f*. **7.** (*a*) *Meas:* racloire *f*; **s. measure,** (i) mesurage *m* (du blé, etc.) à l'aide d'un racloir; (ii) mesure rase; (*b*) *Metall:* trousseau *m*, trousse *f*, gabarit *m*.

strike[2], *v.* (*p.t.* **struck** [strʌk]; *p.p.* **struck,** *A:* **stricken** ['strik(ə)n])

I. *v.tr. & ind. tr.* **1.** (*a*) frapper (qn, qch.); *Jur:* porter la main sur (qn); **to s. s.o. in the face, on the mouth,** frapper qn à la figure, à la bouche; **to s. a blow at s.o., to s. at s.o., to s. s.o. a blow,** porter un coup à qn; assener un coup à qn; **without striking a blow,** sans coup férir; **ready to s. a blow for freedom of speech,** prêt à se battre pour défendre la liberté de parole; **to be struck by a stone,** être frappé d'une pierre; (*of ship*) **to be struck by a heavy sea,** essuyer un coup de mer; *v.i.* **to s. home,** frapper juste, *F:* dans le mille; **to s. a weapon aside,** écarter une arme (d'un revers de main, etc.); *Fenc:* écarter l'épée d'une parade; **the hammer strikes (on) the metal,** le marteau frappe sur le métal; **to s. one's fist on the table,** frapper du poing sur la table; frapper la table du poing; *Prov:* **s. while the iron is hot,** il faut battre le fer quand il est chaud; *F:* il faut chauffer l'affaire; (*b*) frapper (une monnaie, une médaille, *Typ:* une matrice); (*c*) *Mus:* frapper (les touches du piano, une note); toucher de (la harpe); **to s. a chord,** plaquer un accord; *Fig:* **that strikes a familiar note,** cela fait l'effet du déjà vu, du déjà entendu; (*d*) *A:* **to s. hands,** toucher dans la main (**with s.o.,** à qn); se toucher dans la main; **s. hands on it!** touchez là! tope là! (*e*) **to s. a bargain,** faire, conclure, un marché; toper. **2.** (*a*) **to s. sparks out of, from, a flint,** faire jaillir des étincelles d'un silex; tirer du feu d'un caillou; *Fig:* **to s. a spark out of s.o.,** tirer de qn une lueur d'intelligence, un peu d'animation; **to s. a match, a light,** allumer, enflammer, frotter, craquer, une allumette; *P:* **s. a light!** nom d'un nom! nom d'une pipe! (*with passive force*) **matches that won't s.,** allumettes qui ne prennent pas, qui ne veulent pas prendre feu; (*b*) *El:* **to s. the arc,** amorcer l'arc, produire l'arc (entre les charbons); **to s. a vapour lamp,** amorcer une lampe à vapeur de mercure. **3.** (*a*) **to s. a knife into s.o.'s heart,** enfoncer un couteau dans le cœur de qn; donner à qn un coup de couteau en plein cœur; *v.i.* (*of serpent*) **to s.,** foncer; **to s. terror into s.o.,** frapper qn de terreur; **the plant strikes its roots into the soil,** la plante enfonce ses racines dans le sol; **the plant strikes root,** *v.i.* **strikes,** la plante prend racine, jette des racines, pousse des racines; la plante prend; **slip that has struck,** greffe qui a pris, qui a bien repris; **to s. a cutting,** réussir une bouture; **to s. cuttings of a plant,** bouturer une plante; (*b*) *Fish:* ferrer, piquer (le poisson). **4.** (*a*) **house, tree, struck by lightning,** maison frappée par la foudre; arbre foudroyé; **lightning had struck the house,** la foudre était tombée sur la maison; (*b*) **to s. s.o. with surprise,** frapper qn d'étonnement; **struck with terror,** frappé de terreur; saisi d'effroi; **struck with panic, with dizziness,** saisi, pris, de panique, de vertige; (*of lightning*) **to s. s.o. dead, blind,** foudroyer qn; frapper qn de cécité; *P:* **s. me dead, blind, if I'm not telling the truth,** je veux bien être pendu si je mens; *O:* **s. me pink if it wasn't my friend!** du diable, s'il n'était pas mon ami! **5.** percer; **the rays s. through the mist,** les rayons percent le brouillard; **the cold strikes (in)to one's very bones,** le froid vous pénètre jusqu'à la moelle des os. **6.** (*a*) **to s. (against) sth.,** frapper, heurter, donner, contre qch.; se cogner à, contre, qch.; buter contre qch.; **to s. one's head against the wall,** se cogner, se heurter, la tête, donner de la tête, contre le mur; **his head struck (against) the pavement,** sa tête a porté sur le trottoir; *Veh:* **the body strikes the axle,** la caisse talonne l'essieu, talonne sur l'essieu; (*of ship*) **to s. (the) bottom,** *v.i.* **to s.,** toucher (le fond); talonner; **to s. an obstruction,** rencontrer un obstacle; (*of ship*) **to s. a mine,** heurter une mine; **the ship strikes (on) the rocks,** le navire donne, touche, sur les écueils; **to s. another ship,** aborder un autre navire; (*of car*) **to s. a pedestrian,** heurter, tamponner, un piéton; **the light strikes (on) an object,** la lumière frappe un objet; **a sound struck my ear,** un bruit me frappa l'oreille, frappa mon oreille; **a bright idea struck me,** il m'est venu une idée lumineuse; **the thought struck me that it could happen to me,** l'idée m'est venue, il m'est venu à l'idée, à l'esprit, que cela peut m'arriver; (*a*) faire une impression (quelconque) sur (qn); **how does, did, she s. you?** quelle impression vous a-t-elle faite? **he strikes me as (being) sincere,** il me paraît sincère; il me fait l'effet d'être sincère; **the place struck him as familiar,** l'endroit lui paraissait familier; **that is how it struck me,** voilà l'effet que cela m'a fait; **as it strikes me,** à mon avis; à ce qu'il me semble; **it strikes me (that) he doesn't like work,** il me semble, me paraît, m'est avis, j'ai l'idée, qu'il n'aime pas travailler; **it strikes me very forcibly that he's crooked,** il me semble plus que probable qu'il n'est pas honnête; **did it never s. you that you weren't wanted there?** ne vous est-il jamais venu à l'esprit que vous étiez de trop? (*b*) faire impression à (qn); impressionner (qn); frapper (l'œil, l'imagination); attirer (l'œil); **what struck me was his brazen impudence,** ce qui m'a frappé, c'est son effronterie cynique; **I was greatly struck,** j'ai été très impressionné; *P:* **to be struck on s.o.,** avoir un béguin pour qn; **to get struck on s.o.,** s'enticher de qn. **7.** tomber sur, découvrir (une piste, etc.); découvrir (un filon d'or); **to s. oil,** (i) atteindre une nappe pétrolifère; rencontrer, toucher, le pétrole; (ii) avoir du succès; faire une bonne affaire; trouver le filon; dénicher le bon filon; **he has struck oil,** *F:* **he has struck it rich,** il tient le filon; **an idea struck me,** j'ai eu une idée; une idée m'est venu à l'esprit. **8.** (*a*) *Nau:* amener, caler (une voile); abaisser, dépasser (un mât); **to s. one's flag, one's colours,** *v.i.* **to s.,** *Nau:* amener, *Navy:* rentrer, haler bas, son pavillon; mettre pavillon bas; (*of town, etc.*) se rendre; **the admiral strikes his flag,** l'amiral rentre sa marque; (*b*) **to s. a tent,** démonter une tente; **to s. tents,** abattre les tentes; **to s. camp,** lever le camp; (*c*) *Civ.E: Const:* **to s. the centre of an arch,** décintrer une voûte, un arc; **to s. the form(work),** décoffrer. **9.** *Ind: etc: O:* **to s. work,** *v.i.* **to s.,** se mettre en grève; *F:* débrayer. **10. to s. an attitude,** prendre une attitude dramatique; poser. **11.** (*a*) tirer (une ligne), décrire (un cercle); (*b*) **to s. an average,** établir, prendre, une moyenne; (*c*) **to s. a committee,** former, constituer, une commission; *Jur:* **to s. a jury,** constituer un jury (après élimination des jurés récusés). **12.** *Meas: Com:* rader, raser (une mesure). **13.** *Glassm:* thermocolorer. **14.** *Tan:* rebrousser (les peaux).

II. *v.i.* **1.** (*a*) attaquer; **don't wait for the enemy to s.,** n'attendez pas que l'ennemi attaque; (*b*) **to s. at the very foundations of civilization,** menacer les assises mêmes de la civilisation. **2.** (*of clock*) sonner; (*with cogn. acc.*) **to s. the hour,** sonner, *Nau:* piquer, l'heure; **the clock strikes, is striking, five,** l'horloge sonne cinq heures, cinq coups; **it has struck ten,** dix heures viennent de sonner; **twelve o'clock struck some minutes ago,** midi est sonné depuis quelques minutes; **his hour has struck,** son heure est sonnée, a sonné. **3.** prendre (une certaine direction); **to s. across a field,** traverser un champ; **to s. across country,** prendre à travers champs; **to s. for the shore,** (i) ramer, (ii) nager, dans la direction du rivage; **to s. into the jungle,** s'enfoncer, pénétrer, dans la jungle; **we struck (off) to the left,** nous avons pris à gauche; **the road strikes (off) to the right,** la route tourne à droite. **4.** (*of roots, etc.*) s'enfoncer (**into sth.,** dans qch.); (*of cutting*) prendre (racine), reprendre. **5.** *Fish:* (*of fish*) mordre (à l'hameçon).

III. (*compound verbs*) **1. strike back.** (*a*) *v.tr.* **to s. s.o. back,** répondre au coup de qn; **if anyone strikes me I s. (him, them) back,** si quelqu'un me frappe je rends le coup; (*b*) *v.i.* (i) rebrousser chemin; (ii) (*of gas burner*) avoir un retour de flamme.

2. strike down, *v.tr.* abattre, renverser (qch., qn) (d'un coup de poing, etc.); rabattre (la lame de l'adversaire, etc.) d'un coup sec; **he was struck down by apoplexy,** l'apoplexie l'a foudroyé; **struck down by disease,** terrassé par la maladie.

3. strike in. (*a*) *v.tr.* enfoncer (un clou); (*b*) *v.i.* (i) *Med:* (*of gout*) rentrer; (ii) s'interposer (dans une querelle); intervenir; interrompre; **she struck in with the remark that it was no concern of ours,** elle est intervenue pour faire observer que ce n'était pas notre affaire.

4. strike off, *v.tr.* (*a*) trancher, abattre, faire tomber, *F:* faire voler (la tête de qn); briser (les fers d'un prisonnier); **to s. off the heads of piles,** couper, araser, les têtes des pieux; (*b*) **to s. off a name from a list, to s. a name off a list,** biffer, rayer, radier, retrancher, éliminer, un nom d'une liste; **to s. off a solicitor, doctor,** radier un avoué, médecin; *Mil:* **to s. s.o. off the strength,** rayer qn des contrôles; (*c*) *Com:* (*deduct*) **to s. off 5%,** déduire 5%; faire une réduction de 5%; (*d*) *Typ:* tirer (tant d'exemplaires).

5. strike out. (*a*) *v.tr.* rayer, radier, biffer, raturer, barrer (un mot); tirer un trait sur (un mot); **to s. a passage out of a book,** retrancher un passage d'un livre; (*b*) *v.i.* (i) **to s. out at s.o.,** allonger un coup à qn; porter un coup à qn; **to s. out right and left,** frapper à droite et à gauche; *Box:* **to s. out from the shoulder,** porter un coup droit (**at,** à); (ii) (*of swimmer*) **to s. out with one's arms,** lancer les bras en avant; (iii) (*of swimmer, skater*) s'élancer; partir rapidement; **I struck out for the shore,** j'ai commencé à nager dans la direction du rivage; (iv) *Fig:* **to s. out for oneself,** voler de ses propres ailes; s'installer à son propre compte; **it is time I struck out for myself,** il est temps de songer à me faire une position; (v) *Sp:* (*baseball*) (*of batter*) s'éliminer en manquant trois balles de suite.

6. strike through, *v.tr.* = **strike out** (*a*).

7. strike up, *v.tr.* (*a*) entonner (une chanson); commencer de jouer (un morceau); **the band strikes up a march,** l'orchestre attaque une marche; *v.i.* **on his arrival the band struck up,** à son arrivée la fanfare attaqua un morceau; (*b*) conclure, nouer (une alliance); contracter (une amitié); **to s. up an acquaintance, a friendship, with s.o.,** lier connaissance avec qn; se lier, se prendre, d'amitié avec qn; **to s. up a conversation with s.o.,** entrer en conversation avec qn; (*c*) *Fenc: etc:* relever (l'épée de l'adversaire) d'un coup sec; (*d*) *Metall:* trousser (le moule).

strike-a-light ['straikəlait], *s. A:* briquet *m* (à silex); pierre *f* à feu.

strikebound ['straikbaund], *a. Ind: etc:* paralysé par une grève.

strikeout ['straikaut], *s. Sp:* (*baseball*) élimination *f* (du batteur pour trois balles manquées).

striker ['straikər], *s.* **1.** (*pers.*) (*a*) *Metalw: etc:* frappeur, -euse; (*b*) harponneur *m*; (*c*) *Tan:* rebrousseur *m*; (*d*) *Sp:* (i) *Ten:* **s.(-out),** relanceur, -euse; (ii) *Baseball:* batteur *m*. **2.** *Ind: etc:* gréviste *mf*. **3.** (*device*) (*a*) frappeur; (*of clock*) marteau *m*; (*of firearm*) percuteur *m*; (*of fuse*) rugueux *m*; (*of torpedo*) (i) antenne *f*, (ii) percuteur; *Aut:* **s. rod,** tige *f*, tringle *f*, d'embrayage; (*b*) *Mec.E:* passe-courroie *m, pl.* passe-courroies; (i) embrayeur *m*, (ii) débrayeur *m* (de courroie).

striking[1] ['straikiŋ], *a.* **1. s. clock,** pendule *f* à sonnerie, horloge sonnante. **2.** (spectacle, etc.) frappant, saisissant; (trait) saillant; **he was a s. figure,** il était impressionnant; **s. situation,** situation dramatique.

striking[2], *s.* **1.** (*a*) frappement *m*; coups *mpl*; **within s. distance,** à portée, à (la) portée de la main; *B.Hist:* **the s. of the rock,** le frappement du rocher; *Row:* **rate of s.,** cadence *f* de nage; *Locksm:* **s. box, plate,** gâche *f* (de pêne coulant); *Mec.E:* **s. gear,** passe-courroie *m, pl.* passe-courroies; (i) embrayeur *m*, (ii) débrayeur *m* (de courroie); (*b*) *Mil:* frappe *f*; **s. power,** puissance *f* de frappe; **s. force,** force *f* de frappe; **s. force(s),** masse *f* de manœuvre; (*c*) frappe (de la monnaie); (*d*) frottement *m* (d'une allumette); **s. surface,** frottoir *m*; (*e*) *El:* amorçage *m* (de l'arc). **2.** *Hort:* **s. (root),** reprise *f* (d'une bouture, etc.). **3.** (*a*) *Nau:* calage *m* (d'une voile); (*b*) *Mil:* **s. camp,** levée *f* du camp; décampement *m*. **4.** établissement *m* (d'une moyenne, d'un bilan). **5.** sonnerie *f* (d'une horloge); (*of clock with double chime*) **second s.,** réplique *f*; **s. mechanism,** sonnerie. **6.** *Ind:* grèves *fpl*. **7.** (*compound nouns*) (*a*) **s. down,** abattage *m*, renversement *m*; (*b*) **s. off,** (i) rayure *f*, radiation *f* (d'un nom, etc.); radiation (d'un avoué, d'un médecin); (ii) *Typ:* tirage *m* (à tant d'exemplaires); (*c*) **s. out,** rayure, radiation, biffage *m* (d'un mot, etc.).

strikingly ['straikiŋli], *adv.* d'une manière frappante, saisissante; **s. beautiful,** d'une beauté frappante.

strikingness ['straikiŋnis], *s.* caractère frappant, saisissant (d'un spectacle, etc.).

string[1] [striŋ], *s.* **1.** (*a*) (i) ficelle *f*; (ii) corde *f*, cordon *m*; **ball of s.,** pelote *f* de ficelle; **cotton s.,** ficelle de coton; **hemp s.,** corde de chanvre; **bonnet strings,** cordons, brides *f*, de bonnet; *Cu:* **trussing s.,** bride; **to lead a dog by a s.,** mener un chien en laisse; *F:* **to have s.o. on a s.,** (i) tenir qn en lisière; (ii) mener qn par le bout du nez; (iii) se payer la tête de qn, faire marcher qn, monter le coup à qn; **to keep s.o. on a s.,** tenir qn le bec dans l'eau; *NAm:* **to have a s. on s.o.,** avoir prise sur qn; **investigation with a s. tied to it,** enquête limitée; **acceptance with a s. tied to it,** acceptance sous condition; **with no strings (attached), without strings,** sans conditions, sans condition aucune; **s. bag,** filet *m* (à provisions); (*b*) **the strings of a marionette,** les fils *m* d'une marionnette; *Fig:* **to pull the strings,** tenir les fils, tirer les ficelles; être dans la coulisse; **to pull strings,** faire jouer ses relations, *F:* le piston; **to pull every possible s. to attain one's ends,** faire jouer tous les ressorts pour parvenir à ses fins; *Sp:* (*baseball*) **to pull the s.,** lancer une balle lente; (*c*) *Surg: F:* ligature *f.* **2.** (*a*) fibre *f,* filament *m* (de plante, etc.); **strings in beans, meat,** fils des haricots, filandres *f* de la viande; **s. bean,** (i) *Hort:* haricot vert; (ii) *NAm: F:* (*pers.*) asperge (montée), grand échalas; *NAm:* **s. pea,** (pois *m*) mange-tout *m inv;* (*b*) *Anat:* filet *m,* frein *m* (de la langue); fibre (de l'œil). **3.** (*a*) *Mus:* corde (de violon, piano, etc.); **(cat)gut s.,** corde à boyau; **covered s.,** corde filée; **wire, steel, s.,** corde acier; (*of violin*) **first, highest, E, s.,** (le) mi, (la) chanterelle; **lowest s.,** grosse corde; **the strings of a violin,** la monture d'un violon; (*in orchestra*) **the strings,** les (instruments, joueurs des instruments, à) cordes; **s. orchestra, s. band,** orchestre *m* à cordes; **s. quartet,** quatuor *m* à cordes; *NAm:* **s. bass,** contrebasse *f;* **s. pin,** cheville *f* (de piano); **s. plate,** sommier *m* (de piano); *Fig:* **to touch a s. in s.o.'s heart,** faire vibrer une corde dans le cœur de qn; *Lit:* **to add a s. to one's bow,** ajouter une corde à sa lyre; (*b*) corde (d'un arc, etc.); **strings of a tennis racket,** cordes, cordage *m,* d'une raquette de tennis; *El:* **s. galvanometer,** galvanomètre *m* à corde; (*c*) *Sp:* **first s.,** meilleur athlète (sélectionné pour une épreuve); *Turf:* premier champion (d'une écurie); **second s.,** second athlète sélectionné; *Turf:* second champion; *F:* **he's not the first s. of our sales staff,** ce n'est pas notre premier, meilleur, vendeur. **4.** (*a*) **s. of beads,** (i) collier *m;* (ii) *Ecc:* chapelet *m;* **s. of onions,** chapelet, rang *m,* d'oignons; **s. of islands,** chapelet d'îles; **s. of tools,** chapelet, attirail *m,* jeu *m,* d'outils; *Min:* **s. of drill pipes,** train *m* de tiges de forage; **s. of medals,** brochette *f* de décorations; **s. of vehicles, of waggons,** file *f* de véhicules; rame *f* de wagons; **s. of barges,** train de péniches; **a long s. of tourists,** une longue procession de touristes; **a whole s. of children, of names,** toute une kyrielle d'enfants, de noms; **s. of words,** suite *f,* série *f,* de mots; **s. of oaths,** séquelle *f* de jurons; (*b*) *Cmptr:* **character, symbol, s.,** chaîne *f* de caractères, symboles; **null s.,** chaîne vide; **s. break,** rupture *f* de monotonie; **s. building,** constitution *f* de monotonie; (*c*) *Turf:* **Lord Derby's s. (of horses),** l'écurie *f* de Lord Derby. **5.** (*a*) *Arch:* **s. course, moulding,** bandeau *m,* cordon *m;* (*b*) *Const:* **s. board, face s.,** limon *m* (d'escalier); **s. piece,** longeron *m,* longrine *f;* **s. wall,** (parpaing *m* d'échiff(r)e *m* (d'escalier). **6.** *Bill:* (*a*) boulier *m,* marque *f;* (*b*) ligne *f* de départ. **7.** *Min: Geol:* filet (de houille, etc.); petite veine (de minerai).

string², *v.* (*p.p. & p.t.* **strung** [strʌŋ])

I. *v.tr.* **1.** (*a*) mettre une ficelle, une corde, à (qch.); ficeler (un paquet, etc.); (*b*) garnir, munir, (qch.) de cordes; corder (une raquette de tennis, etc.); **to s. a violin,** mettre les cordes à, monter, un violon; **to s. a piano,** monter les cordes d'un piano; (*c*) accouer (des chevaux). **2.** bander (un arc); (*of pers.*) **to be highly strung,** être nerveux, impressionnable. **3.** enfiler (des perles, etc.); **to s. fairy lamps across a garden,** accrocher des guirlandes de lampions dans un jardin; *Fig:* **to s. sentences together,** enfiler des phrases. **4.** *Cu:* **to s. beans,** ôter les fils des haricots. **5.** *NAm: F:* **to s. s.o. (on, along),** (i) tenir qn en suspens, *F:* le bec dans l'eau; (ii) duper, tromper, qn, *F:* monter un bateau, le coup, à qn.

II. *v.i.* **1.** (*of glue, etc.*) filer. **2.** *Bill:* débuter par un coup préliminaire (pour l'honneur).

III. (*compound verbs*) **1. string along.** (*a*) *v.tr. see* **string² I. 5;** (*b*) *v.i. F:* **to s. along with s.o.,** (i) accompagner, faire route avec, qn; (ii) être copain avec qn. **2. string out.** (*a*) *v.i.* s'espacer (à la file); **hounds strung out on the scent,** chiens allongés sur la piste; **the field strung out behind,** le peloton des coureurs s'égrenait, s'allongeait, derrière; (*b*) *v.tr.* faire traîner (qch.) en longueur.

3. string up, *v.tr.* (*a*) pendre (qn) haut et court; *A:* **s. him up!** à la lanterne! (*b*) *F:* (i) *O:* **to s. up one's resolution, to s. oneself up, to do sth.,** tendre toute sa volonté pour faire qch.; (ii) **to get (oneself) strung up,** s'en faire, s'énerver (**about sth.,** à propos de qch.).

stringed [striŋd], *a. Mus:* (instrument) à cordes.

stringency ['strin(d)ʒənsi], *s.* **1.** rigueur *f,* sévérité *f* (des règles, etc.). **2.** force *f,* puissance *f* (d'un argument). **3.** *Fin:* resserrement *m* (de l'argent).

stringendo [strin'dʒendou], *adv. Mus:* stringendo, en serrant.

stringent ['strin(d)ʒ(ə)nt], *a.* **1.** (règlement, etc.) rigoureux, strict; **to make a rule less s.,** élargir, assouplir, une règle. **2.** (argument) convaincant, incontestable, serré. **3.** *Fin:* (argent) serré; (marché) tendu.

stringently ['strin(d)ʒ(ə)ntli], *adv.* **1.** rigoureusement, strictement. **2.** avec force, puissamment.

stringer ['striŋər], *s.* **1.** (*pers.*) (*a*) fabricant *m* de cordes, cordier *m;* (*b*) monteur *m* de cordes (de piano, etc.); (*c*) **first s.,** athlète *mf, etc:* de première classe; champion, -onne; **second s.,** second champion, seconde championne; (*d*) *Journ:* reporter local. **2.** (*a*) *Const: Civ.E:* longrine *f,* longeron *m,* sommier *m,* travon *m* (d'une charpente); *Civ.E:* sommier (d'un pont); *Const:* tirant *m,* entrait *m* (de ferme de comble); limon *m* (d'escalier); *Aut: Av:* longeron (du châssis, de l'aile); (*b*) *N.Arch:* gouttière renversée; ceinture *f* de cloison. **3.** *Geol: Min:* filet *m,* veinule *f* (de minerai); cordon *m,* crin *m* (de quartz, etc.). **4.** *pl. P:* **stringers,** menottes *f* (aux mains d'un prisonnier).

stringhalt ['striŋhɔːlt], *s. Vet:* éparvin sec.

stringiness ['striŋinis], *s.* **1.** caractère fibreux, filandreux (de la viande, etc.). **2.** viscosité *f* (d'un liquide). **3.** caractère filiforme (du pouls).

stringing ['striŋiŋ], *s.* **1.** (*a*) montage *m* (d'un violon); cordage *m* (d'une raquette); (*b*) bandage *m* (d'un arc); (*c*) enfilement *m* (de perles). **2.** cordage, cordes *fpl* (d'une raquette).

stringy ['striŋi], *a.* **1.** (*of vegetables, etc.*) fibreux, filandreux; **s. meat,** viande tendineuse, filandreuse. **2.** (liquide) visqueux, qui file. **3.** *Med:* (pouls) filiforme.

striola, *pl.* **-ae** ['straiələ, -iː], *s. Biol:* striole *f.*

striolate ['straiəleit], *a. Biol:* striolé.

striometer [strai'əmitər], *s. Opt:* striomètre *m.*

strioscopic [straiə'skɔpik], *a. Opt:* strioscopique.

strioscopy [strai'ɔskəpi], *s. Opt:* strioscopie *f.*

strip¹ [strip], *s.* **1.** bande *f* (de tissu, de papier, etc.); lambeau *m* (de tissu); balayeuse *f* (au bas d'une jupe); *F:* **to tear s.o. off a s.,** laver la tête à qn; donner, passer, un savon à qn; attraper qn; **narrow s.,** bandelette *f;* *Med:* **dressing s.,** bande à pansement; **s. of metal, metal s.,** bande, lame *f,* lamelle *f,* languette *f,* de métal; *Metall:* ruban *m* métallique; feuillard *m;* **s. iron,** feuillard de fer; fer *m* feuillard; **s. steel,** feuillard d'acier, acier *m* feuillard; **s. mill,** (i) usine *f* de laminage; (ii) train *m,* laminoir *m,* à feuillards; *Exp:* **s. powder,** poudre en lamelle; *Artil:* **s.-wound gun,** canon rubané; (*of machine gun*) **feeding, loading, s.,** bande-chargeur *f, pl.* bandes-chargeurs; bande rigide; (*supporting shelf*) **wooden s.,** tasseau *m;* **celluloid s.,** bande, lamelle, de celluloïde; **small s. of rubber,** lamelle de caoutchouc; **s. light,** rampe *f* au néon; rampe fluorescente; **s. lighting,** éclairage *m* au néon; éclairage fluorescent; *Arch:* **pilaster s.,** (*XIth, XIIth c.*) bande lombarde; *Av: etc:* **lining s.,** bande à maroufler; *Journ:* **s. cartoon, comic s.,** bande dessinée, illustrée; comics *mpl;* *Cin:* **picture s.,** bande d'images; *Av:* **photograph s.,** bande photographique; **s. map,** carte *f* en rouleau (pour itinéraire); **s. mosaic,** mosaïque *f* photographique; *El:* **connecting s.,** barrette *f* de connexion; *Tp:* **connecting s., terminal s.,** réglette *f* de raccordement; **s. of keys,** réglette de clefs; *Cmptr: etc:* **s. printer,** imprimante *f* sur bande; **s. printing,** (i) *Cmptr: etc:* impression *f* sur bande; (ii) *Phot:* tirage *m* des épreuves sur bande (de papier); *Elcs:* **peaker s.,** bande écrêteuse; **s. of land,** bande, langue *f,* de terrain; *Hort:* **s. of onions,** planche *f* d'oignons; *Agr:* **s. farming,** culture *f* en bandes (de niveau); *For:* **s. felling,** coupe *f* par bandes; *Aut:* **centre s.,** *NAm:* **median s.,** terre-plein central; *Av:* **(landing) s.,** bande (d'atterrissage); piste *f* (de fortune); **take-off s.,** bande d'envol; **taxying s.,** bande, piste, de roulement; **fighter s.,** piste pour avions de chasse, pour chasseurs; **s. lights,** feux *m* de bande. **2.** *Ch: Ind:* solution *f* de décapage, de lavage. **3.** *Sp: F:* vêtements *mpl,* couleurs *fpl* (d'une équipe de football, etc.).

strip², *v.tr.* **(stripped)** découper (du cuir, etc.) en bandes, en lanières.

strip³, *s.* **to do a s.,** se déshabiller (en public); **s. show,** (spectacle *m* de) strip-tease *m;* effeuillage *m;* *Cards:* **s. poker,** poker *m* dans lequel celui qui perd le jeu est obligé d'enlever un vêtement; strip-tease-poker *m.*

strip⁴, *v.* **(stripped)**

I. *v.tr.* **1.** mettre (qn) tout nu; déshabiller, dévêtir (qn); dépouiller (qn) de ses vêtements; **to s. s.o. to the skin,** mettre qn à poil; **stripped to the waist,** nu jusqu'à la ceinture; torse nu. **2.** (*a*) **to s. s.o., sth., of sth.,** dépouiller, dégarnir, déposséder, dénuder, qn, qch., de qch.; **to s. s.o. of his clothes,** dépouiller qn de ses vêtements; **trees stripped of their leaves, of their bark,** arbres dépouillés de leurs feuilles, dépouillés, dénudés, de leur écorce; *Agr:* **to s. a plant of superfluous leaves,** effaner une plante; **nobility stripped of all authority,** noblesse dépossédée, dépouillée, de toute autorité; **to s. s.o. of his money,** dépouiller qn de son argent; dévaliser qn; **stripped of all his worldly goods,** dépouillé de tous ses biens; (*b*) défaire (un lit); dégarnir, démeubler (un appartement, une maison); *Nau:* déshabiller, décapeler (un mât, une vergue); dégréer (un mât, un navire); *El: etc:* dénuder, dépouiller (un câble); *Trans:* décharger (un container); *Petr:* distiller (les fractions légères du pétrole); stripper (un liquide); rectifier (du gaz); **to s. a tree,** (i) effeuiller un arbre; (ii) écorcer un arbre; (iii) ébrancher un arbre; (iv) défruiter un arbre (fruitier); **to s. a wall,** arracher le papier d'un mur; **thieves have stripped the house bare,** des cambrioleurs ont complètement vidé, dévalisé, la maison; **to s. a dog to its undercoat,** déshabiller un chien jusqu'au sous-poil; **to s. tobacco,** écôter le tabac; *Tex:* **to s. flax,** teiller, tiller, le lin; **to s. a carding machine,** débourrer une cardeuse; *Mil: F:* **to s. an N.C.O.,** dégrader un sous-officier; **colonels stripped of their rank,** des colonels destitués; *Mec.E:* **to s. a nut,** arracher le filet d'un écrou; (faire) foirer un écrou; *Aut:* **to s. the gears,** arracher les dents de l'engrenage; endommager le pignon; **to s. a brake shoe,** dégarnir un segment de frein; **to s. (down) an engine, a gun,** démonter un moteur, un fusil; *Aut:* **stripped chassis,** châssis nu; *Metall:* **to s. a casting,** démouler, décocher, une pièce coulée; *Phot:* **to s. a negative,** pelliculer un cliché; *Com:* **to (cancel and) s. a file,** purger un dossier; *Cmptr:* **stripped down version,** version réduite; *Atom Ph:* **stripped atom,** atome dépouillé d'électrons; **stripped fraction,** fraction épuisée; **stripped output,** rendement appauvri (de produits de fission, etc.). **3.** (*a*) **to s. sth. off, from, sth.,** enlever, ôter, qch. à, de, qch.; **to s. the paint off a wall,** enlever, gratter, la peinture d'un mur; *Mec.E:* **to s. the thread off a screw,** arracher le filet d'une vis; (faire) foirer une vis; *Phot:* **to s. the emulsion from a film,** enlever la couche sensible d'un film; pelliculer un film; (*b*) *Phot:* **to s. off a carbon tissue,** dépouiller un papier au charbon; *El:* **to s. off the insulation,** détacher l'isolement; *Min:* **to s. (off) the overburden,** dépouiller, décapeler, le gîte; pratiquer la découverte.

II. *v.i.* **1.** (*of pers.*) **to s. (off),** se déshabiller; se dévêtir; se dépouiller de ses vêtements; dépouiller, ôter, ses vêtements; **to s. to the skin,** se mettre tout nu; se mettre à poil; **to s. to the waist,** se mettre nu jusqu'à la ceinture. **2.** (*of screw*) perdre son filet; s'araser; foirer. **3.** (*a*) (*of tree*) perdre son écorce; (*b*) (*of bark, negative, film, etc.*) **to s. (off),** s'enlever, se détacher.

strip⁵, *v.tr.* égoutter, traire (une vache) à fond, jusqu'à la dernière goutte.

stripclub ['stripklʌb], *s.* strip-tease *m, pl.* strip-teases.

stripe¹ [straip], *s.* **1.** (*a*) raie *f,* bande *f,* filet *m,* barre *f* (d'un tissu, etc.); raie, rayure *f,* zébrure *f* (sur le pelage d'une bête, etc.); *Hort:* panache *m* (sur une fleur, etc.); *Paint:* **colour s., gold s.,** filet de peinture, d'or; **black with a red s.,** noir à raie rouge; noir rayé de rouge; **table linen with coloured stripes,** linge de table à liteaux *m;* **to mark sth. with stripes,** rayer, zébrer, qch.; (*b*) bande (de pantalon); (*c*) *Mil: etc:* galon *m, F:* ficelle *f;* **long service s.,** chevron *m;* **to give a soldier a s.,** donner du galon à un soldat; **to get, lose, a s.,** être promu, dégradé; (*d*) *U.S:* uniforme rayé d'un prisonnier. **2.** *NAm:* **of the same political s.,** de la même nuance politique; **a man of that s.,** un homme de ce genre, de cet acabit.

stripe², *v.tr.* rayer, barrer (un tissu, etc.); *Paint:* tirer des filets sur, réchampir (une surface).

stripe³, *s. A:* **1. stripes,** coups *m* de fouet. **2.** marque *f,* zébrure *f* (occasionnée par un coup de cravache, etc.).

striped [straipt], *a.* (*a*) (chaussettes, etc.) à raies, à rayures, à barres; (tigre, pelage, etc.) rayé; *Nat.Hist:* zébré, rubané; **card s. with red and blue lines,** carte striée de traits rouges et bleus; **red and blue s. jacket,** veston rayé rouge et bleu; (*b*) *Anat:* (muscle) strié.

striping ['straipiŋ], *s.* rayage *m* (d'un tissu, etc.); *Paint:* réchampissage *m* (d'une surface); *Mapm:* baguettage *m.*

stripling ['stripliŋ], *s.* tout jeune homme; adolescent *m;* *Lit:* jouvenceau *m.*

stripper ['stripər], *s.* **1.** (*pers.*) (*a*) *Tex:* teilleur, -euse (de lin, de chanvre); (*b*) écôteur, -euse (de feuilles de tabac); (*c*) *Hort:* effeuilleur, -euse (d'arbres); (*d*) *Metall:* démouleur *m;* (*e*) *Tex:* débourreur, -euse (de carde); (*f*) strip-teaseuse *f;* effeuilleuse; **male s.,** homme qui pratique le strip-tease; (*g*) *Com:* **asset s.,** personne *f* qui achète une société pour profiter de la réalisation de l'actif. **2.** (*a*) *Tex:* débourreur *m* mécanique; (*b*) *Metall:* (appareil *m*) démouleur *m*; (machine *f*) démouleuse *f*; **s. plate,** plaque *f* d'éjection, plaque dévêtisseuse (d'une emboutisseuse); (*c*) *El:* **(wire) stripper(s),** outil *m*, machine, à dénuder des câbles, des fils; (*d*) *Petr:* rectificateur *m*; (*e*) *Atom.Ph:* séparateur *m* d'extraction, d'épuisement. **3.** *Ch: etc:* décapant *m*; **s. tank,** cuve *f* électrolytique. **4.** *Petr:* puits marginal à faible production.

stripping ['stripiŋ], *s.* **1.** (*of pers.*) déshabillage *m*, déshabillement *m*; (*in hospital*) **s. room,** salle *f* d'attente (où l'on se déshabille); salle de déshabillage; vestiaire *m*. **2.** (*a*) dégarnissement *m* (d'un lit, etc.); déshabillage, dénudation *f*, dépouillement *m* (d'un câble, etc.); effeuillage *m* (d'un arbre); écôtage *m* (des feuilles de tabac); teillage *m*, tillage *m* (du chanvre, du lin); *Trans:* déchargement *m* (d'un container); *Mec.E:* arrachement *m* du filet, foirage *m* (d'une vis, d'un écrou); arrachement (des dents d'un engrenage); *Atom.Ph:* stripage *m* (d'un noyau projectile par un noyau cible); **s. (down) of an engine, a rifle,** démontage *m* d'un moteur, d'un fusil; *Com:* **asset s.,** réalisation *f* (d'une partie) de l'actif d'une société; (*b*) *Ch: etc:* grattage *m*, décapage *m* (d'une surface); **s. acid,** acide décapant; **s. solution,** solution décapante; (*c*) *Nau:* décapelage *m*, déshabillage (d'un mât, d'une vergue); dégréement *m* (d'un mât, d'un navire); **s. line,** collecteur *m* d'assèchement; **s. pump,** pompe *f* d'assèchement; (*d*) *Metall:* démoulage *m*, décochage *m* (d'une pièce coulée); **s. bar,** pince à décocher; (*in foundry*) **s. machine,** (machine *f*) démouleuse *f*; (*e*) *Phot:* pelliculage *m* (d'un cliché); **s. emulsion, film,** émulsion pelliculable; **s. negative,** négatif pelliculable; **s. off of carbon tissue,** dépouillement des papiers au charbon; (*f*) *Atom.Ph:* épuisement *m* (du combustible); **s. cascade,** cascade *f* d'épuisement; **s. column,** colonne *f* d'épuisement *m*. **3.** *Petr:* rectification *f*; désessenciement *m*, stripping *m*; **s. tower,** tour *f* de rectification.

striptease [strip'ti:z], *s.* (spectacle *m* de) strip-tease *m*; effeuillage *m*; **s. artist,** strip-teaseuse *f*, effeuilleuse *f*; homme qui pratique le strip-tease.

stripy ['straipi], *a.* rayé; zébré; à rayures.

strive [straiv], *v.i.* (*p.t.* **strove** [strouv]; *p.p.* **striven** [striv(ə)n]) **1. to s. to do sth.,** tâcher, s'efforcer, de faire qch.; faire des efforts pour faire qch.; **he is striving hard to succeed,** il se démène pour réussir; **to s. for sth.,** essayer d'obtenir qch.; **what are you striving after?** à quoi tendent vos efforts? **to s. after effect,** pousser à l'effet; rechercher (de) l'effet; **to s. after wit,** rechercher l'esprit. **2. to s. with, against, s.o., sth.,** lutter, se débattre, contre qn, qch.

striving ['straiviŋ], *s.* **1.** efforts *mpl*. **2.** lutte *f*.

strobe [stroub], *s.* *Ph: etc: F:* stroboscope *m*; **radar s.,** pinceau *m* radar.

strobic ['stroubik], *a.* *Opt:* strobique.

strobila, *pl.* **-ae** [strou'bailə, -i:; strɔ-], *s.* *Z:* strobile *m*.

strobilaceous [strɔbi'leiʃəs], **strobilar** ['strɔbilər], **strobilate** ['strɔbileit], *a.* *Bot:* strobilacé.

strobilation [strɔbi'leiʃ(ə)n], *s.* *Biol:* strobilation *f*.

strobile ['stroubail, 'strɔ-], *s.* *Bot:* strobile *m* (du pin, houblon, etc.).

strobiliferous [stroubi'lifərəs, strɔ-], *a.* *Bot:* strobilifère.

strobiliform [strou'bilifɔ:m, strɔ-], *a.* *Nat.Hist:* strobiliforme.

strobilus, *pl.* **-i** [strou'bailəs, -ai; strɔ-], *s.* *Bot: Z:* strobile *m*.

stroboscope ['strɔbouskoup, 'strou-], *s.* *Opt: etc:* stroboscope *m*.

stroboscopic [strɔbou'skɔpik, 'strou-], *a.* stroboscopique.

stroboscopy [strɔ'bɔskəpi], *s.* *Opt:* stroboscopie *f*.

strobotron ['strɔbətrɔn, 'strou-], *s.* tube *m* électronique à cathode froide (pour fournir la lumière stroboscopique).

stroke¹ [strouk], *s.* coup *m*. **1.** (*a*) **to receive twenty strokes,** recevoir vingt coups (de férule, etc.); **with one s. of his sword,** d'un coup de son épée; **to fell s.o., a tree, at a s.,** abattre qn, un arbre, d'un seul coup; **work done at one s.,** travail fait d'un seul jet; **to abolish a practice at a, one, s.,** abolir un usage d'un seul coup; **finishing s.,** (i) dernier coup; (ii) coup de grâce; *Prov:* **little strokes fell great oaks,** petit à petit l'oiseau fait son nid; (*b*) **s. of lightning,** coup de foudre. **2.** (*normal movement*) (*a*) coup (d'aile, d'aviron, etc.); coup, trait *m* (de lime, etc.); frappe *f* (au clavier, etc.); *Mus:* **s. of the bow,** coup d'archet; (*at billiards, etc.*) **whose s. is it?** à qui de jouer? *Golf:* **s. play, competition,** concours *m* par coups; *Row:* **one s. (ahead),** avant un coup; **to row a long s.,** nager de long; allonger la nage; **to lengthen the s.,** allonger la nage; **to keep s.,** nager ensemble; ramer, aller, en mesure; garder la cadence; **'keep s.!'** 'nagez ensemble!' 'accordez!'; *F:* **to be off one's s.,** être mal en train; **to put s.o. off his s.,** déconcerter qn; (*b*) *Swim:* brassée *f*; (i) **breathe after each s.,** respirez après chaque brassée, après chaque coup; (ii) **the swimming strokes,** les nages *f*; **stroke's length,** nagée *f*; **arm s.,** brassée; (*c*) *Mec.E:* mouvement *m*, course *f*, excursion *f* (du piston); **power s.,** course motrice, (course de) détente *f*; temps moteur; **piston at half s.,** piston à mi-course; *I.C.E:* **two-s. engine, four-s. engine,** moteur *m* à deux, à quatre, temps; **long-s. engine,** moteur à longue course; moteur long; **s.-bore ratio,** rapport *m* de la course à l'alésage; (*d*) *F:* **not to do a s. of work,** ne rien faire; *P:* n'en pas ficher un coup; **he has not done a s. of work,** il n'a pas fait œuvre de ses dix doigts; il n'a pas fait une panse d'a; (*e*) **s. of good luck,** coup de bonheur, de fortune; aubaine *f*; **s. of wit, of genius,** trait d'esprit, de génie; **bold s.,** coup hardi; **he has done a good s. of business,** il a fait une bonne affaire. **3.** coup (d'horloge, etc.); battement *m* (du cœur); **on the s. of nine,** sur le coup de neuf heures; à neuf heures sonnant(es), *F:* battant, tapant; **the clock is on the s. of nine,** l'horloge va sonner neuf heures; **to arrive on the s. (of time),** arriver à l'heure juste, à la seconde sonnant, *F:* à l'heure tapante. **4.** *Med:* **s. of apoplexy, of paralysis, (apoplectic, paralytic) s.,** coup de sang; attaque *f* d'apoplexie; apoplexie (foudroyante); transport *m* au cerveau; congestion cérébrale; **to have a s.,** tomber en apoplexie; être frappé d'apoplexie; *F:* avoir une attaque. **5.** trait; barre *f*; coup de crayon, de pinceau; trait de plume; **up s.,** *Typ:* **thin s.,** délié *m* (d'une lettre); **down s.,** plein *m*, jambage *m*; *Typ:* **thick s.,** plein; **oblique s.,** barre transversale, barre de fraction; **with a s. of the pen,** d'un trait de plume; *Fig:* **to give the finishing strokes to one's work,** faire les dernières retouches, mettre la dernière main, à son travail; mettre son travail au point; *Engr:* **s. engraving,** gravure *f* au burin. **6.** *Row:* (*a*) (*pers.*) chef *m* de nage; nageur, -euse, de l'arrière; (*b*) **to row s., to pull s.,** donner la nage; être chef de nage; **s. oar,** (i) aviron *m* du chef de nage, de l'arrière; (ii) chef de nage; **s. side,** bâbord *m*.

stroke². **1.** *Row:* (*a*) *v.tr.* **to s. a boat,** être chef de nage d'un canot; donner la nage; (*b*) *v.i.* **to s. thirty (per minute),** nager à trente coups par minute. **2.** *v.tr.* marquer (qch.) d'un trait; **to s. out a word,** barrer, biffer, un mot.

stroke³, *s.* caresse *f* de la main; **to give the cat a s.,** passer la main sur le dos du chat, caresser le chat de la main.

stroke⁴, *v.tr.* passer la main sur, lisser avec la main, caresser de la main (une fourrure, les cheveux de qn, etc.); **to s. one's chin,** se flatter le menton de la main; **to s. out one's beard,** se peigner la barbe avec les doigts; **to s. the cat the wrong way,** caresser le chat à contre-poil; lui rebrousser le poil; *Fig:* **to s. s.o., s.o.'s hair, the wrong way,** prendre qn à contre-poil, à rebrousse-poil; **to s. s.o. down,** (i) apaiser la colère de qn; (ii) câliner, cajoler, qn.

stroking ['stroukiŋ], *s.* caresses *fpl* (de la main).

stroll¹ [stroul], *s.* petit tour, flânerie *f*, bout *m* de promenade; *F:* balade *f*; **to take, go for, a s.,** (aller) faire un tour.

stroll². **1.** *v.i.* errer, aller, à l'aventure; flâner; déambuler; *F:* se balader. **2.** *v.tr.* **to s. the streets,** se promener dans les rues.

stroller ['stroulər], *s.* **1.** flâneur, -euse; promeneur, -euse. **2.** = **strolling-player** *q.v. under* STROLLING¹. **3.** *NAm:* poussette *f* (d'enfant).

strolling¹ ['strouliŋ], *a.* vagabond, errant; **s. player,** comédien ambulant, comédienne ambulante; acteur forain, actrice foraine; **s. players,** troupe ambulante.

strolling², *s.* flânerie *f*, promenades *fpl*.

stroma, *pl.* **-ata** ['stroumə, -ətə], *s.* *Nat.Hist:* stroma *m*.

stromateus [stroumə'ti:əs], *s.* *Ich:* stromatée *m*.

stromatic [strou'mætik], **stromatiform** [strou'mætifɔ:m], **strom(at)oid** ['stroum(ət)ɔid], **stromatous** ['stroumətəs], *a.* *Nat.Hist:* stromatique.

stromatolite [strou'mætəlait], *s.* *Paleont:* stromatolithe *f*.

Stromatoporidae [stroumətə'pɔridi:], *s.pl.* *Paleont:* stromatoporidés *m*.

stromb [strɔm(b)], *s.* *Moll:* strombe *m*.

Strombidae ['strɔmbidi:], *s.pl.* *Moll:* strombidés *m*.

Strombolian [strɔm'bouliən], *a.* *Geog:* strombolien.

stromeyerite ['stroumaiərait], *s.* *Miner:* stromeyérite *f*.

strong [strɔŋ], *a.* **(stronger** ['strɔŋgər], **strongest** ['strɔŋgist]) fort. **1.** (*a*) solide, résistant, ferme, robuste; **s. cloth,** drap fort, solide, résistant, qui a du corps; **s. shoes,** chaussures de fatigue; **s. stick,** bâton solide; **s. china,** porcelaine solide; **a building is only as s. as its foundations,** un édifice n'est pas plus solide que le fondement; **s. room,** cave forte, chambre blindée, salle blindée; cave des coffres-forts; *Nau:* soute à, aux, valeurs; **s. fortress,** forteresse bien défendue; **s. conviction,** ferme conviction; **s. faith,** foi solide, robuste; *Com:* **s. market,** marché ferme; **s. character,** caractère fort, ferme; (*of faith, etc.*) **to get stronger,** s'affermir; (*b*) **s. constitution,** forte constitution; tempérament *m* robuste; **s. nerves,** nerfs bien équilibrés; **s. in health,** de santé robuste; **he is not very s.,** il est peu robuste; **I am still far from s.,** je suis encore peu solide; **to grow stronger,** reprendre des forces; se renforcer; **his legs are growing stronger again,** ses jambes se raffermissent; **are you quite s. again?** avez-vous repris toutes vos forces? êtes-vous entièrement remis? *s.* **the s.,** (i) les gens bien portants; (ii) les forts, les puissants. **2.** (*a*) **s. fellow,** gaillard solide, solide gaillard; *F:* costaud; **(professional) s. man,** hercule *m* de foire; **s. horse,** cheval vigoureux; **he's as s. as a horse, an ox,** il est fort comme un cheval, un Turc; **s. eyes,** vue forte; bons yeux; **s. voice,** voix forte, puissante; **s. memory,** bonne mémoire; **s. mind,** forte tête; (i) esprit solide; (ii) esprit décidé, énergique; **s. arms,** bras solides; **the s. arm of the law,** l'autorité publique; **to be s. in the arm,** avoir le bras fort; **by the s. arm, hand,** de force, par force; **to have recourse to s. action,** recourir à la manière forte; **s. measures,** mesures énergiques; **he is s. enough to overthrow you,** il est de force, de taille, à vous renverser; **he is a s. man,** c'est un homme à poigne, de poigne; **to be up against a s. man,** avoir affaire à forte partie; **s. candidate,** candidat sérieux; **s. in the popularity he enjoyed,** fort de la popularité dont il jouissait; **s. in Greek,** fort en grec; **politeness is not his s. point,** la politesse n'est pas son fort; **strong in numbers,** en grand nombre; **to be on the strongest side,** *F:* être du côté du manche; **to give s. support to s.o., a measure,** donner un grand appui à, appuyer fortement, qch., une mesure; *Cards:* **s. suit,** (couleur) longue (*f*); **to indicate one's s. suit,** révéler, indiquer, la force de son jeu; **s. partisan,** partisan ardent, chaud partisan; **he's s. against censorship,** il est tout à fait opposé, s'oppose énergiquement, à la censure; **s. army,** armée forte; **company two hundred s.,** compagnie forte de deux cents hommes; **s. evidence,** preuves convaincantes; fortes preuves; **the evidence is very s.,** les témoignages sont irréfutables; **s. argument,** argument puissant; **s. reason,** raison majeure; forte raison; **s. likeness,** grande ressemblance; **I have a s. recollection of it,** j'en ai gardé un vif souvenir; **s. attraction,** attrait puissant; **s. features,** traits accusés; **s. (literary) style,** style vigoureux; **s. novel, s. play,** roman corsé; pièce corsée; **the word 'veneration' is stronger than the word 'respect,'** le mot 'vénération' renchérit sur le mot 'respect'; **to write in s. terms to s.o.,** écrire une lettre énergique à qn; **s. spring,** ressort puissant; **s. grip of a vice,** serrage énergique d'un étau; **s. ventilation,** aérage intensif; **s. wind,** grand vent; vent violent; fort vent; **the wind is growing stronger,** le vent renforce; *Nau:* **s. gale,** gros vent; vent carabiné; **s. tide,** grande marée, forte marée; *Can:* **s. wood(s),** bois forts; *El:* **s. current,** courant intense; *Atom.Ph:* **particle with s. interactions,** particule à fortes interactions; *Mus:* **s. beat,** temps fort; (*b*) **s. drink,** boisson(s) forte(s); **s. wine,** vin (i) fort, corsé, (ii) capiteux; **s. solution,** solution forte, concentrée; **s. light,** lumière forte, vive lumière; **s. colour,** couleur forte; (*c*) (i) **s. cheese,** fromage qui pique; (*of food*) **to have a s. smell,** sentir fort; **their cooking has a s. smell of oil,** leur cuisine a une forte odeur d'huile; *Fig:* **I found the book rather s. meat,** j'ai trouvé ce livre assez corsé; (ii) **s. butter,** beurre rance; **he has s. breath,** il a l'haleine forte. **3.** *Gram:* **s. verb,** verbe fort; *Gr.Gram:* **s. aorist,** second aoriste. **4.** *adv.* *F:* **things are going s.,** les choses avancent, tout marche à merveille; **going s.?** ça marche? ça colle? **he's going s.,** il est toujours d'attaque, solide au poste; **how's grandfather?—still going s.,** comment va le grand-père?—toujours solide.

strong-arm¹ ['strɔŋɑ:m], *a.* (*a*) **to believe in s.-a. tactics,** se fier à la main forte; **to do sth. by s.-a. methods,** faire qch. de vive force; (*b*) **s.-a. man,** (i) homme fort, *F:* fortiche; (ii) *NAm:* (*also* **s. s.-a.**) homme de main, brute *f*, battant *m*.

strong-arm², *v.tr.* *NAm:* *F:* (i) rouer (qn) de coups; *F:* tabasser (qn); (ii) voler (qn) avec violence; détrousser (qn).

stronghold ['strɔŋhould], *s.* forteresse *f*; place forte; redoute *f*; **s. of trade unionism,** citadelle *f* du syndicalisme.

strongish ['strɔŋiʃ], *a.* assez fort.

strongly ['strɔŋli], *adv.* **1.** fortement, solidement, fermement; **s. built bicycle,** bicyclette robuste. **2.** fortement, vigoureusement, énergiquement; **to be s. in**

favour of nationalization, être chaud partisan de la nationalisation; **s. worded letter,** lettre en termes énergiques; **s. marked differences,** différences accentuées, prononcées; **I don't feel s. about it,** je n'y attache pas une grande importance.

strong-minded [strɔŋ'maindid], *a.* à l'esprit solide, résolu, décidé; **s.-m. person,** forte tête.

strong-mindedly [strɔŋ'maindidli], *adv.* avec décision.

strong-mindedness [strɔŋ'maindidnis], *s.* force *f* de caractère; résolution *f.*

strongyle ['strɔndʒil], *s. Ann:* strongle *m*, strongyle *m.*

Strongylidae [strɔn'dʒilidi:], *s.pl. Ann:* strongyloïdés *m.*

strongylosis [strɔndʒi'lousis], *s. Vet:* strongylose *f.*

strontia ['strɔnʃiə], *s. Ch:* strontiane ((i) vive, (ii) éteinte).

strontian ['strɔnʃiən], *s.* **1.** *Miner:* strontianite *f.* **2. s. yellow,** jaune *m* de strontium.

strontianite ['strɔnʃiənait], *s. Miner:* strontianite *f*, strontiane carbonatée.

strontic ['strɔntik], *a. Ch:* strontique.

strontium ['strɔnʃiəm], *s. Ch:* strontium *m*; **radioactive s., s. 90,** strontium radioactif; **s. yellow,** jaune *m*, chromate *m*, de strontium.

strop[1] [strɔp], *s.* **1. (razor) s.,** cuir *m* (à repasser, à rasoir); affiloir *m*; **belt s.,** lanière *f* de cuir (pour affûter les rasoirs). **2.** *Nau:* estrope *f*, erse *f* (de poulie).

strop[2], *v.tr.* **(stropped** [strɔpt]**) 1.** affiler, repasser, affûter, (un rasoir) sur le cuir. **2.** *Nau:* estroper (une poulie); **stropped block,** poulie à estrope.

strophanthin [strə'fænθin], *s. Pharm:* strophantine *f.*

stropharia [strə'fɛəriə], *s. Fung:* strophaire *m.*

strophe ['stroufi, strɔf], *s.* **1.** *Gr.Lit:* strophe *f.* **2.** *Pros:* strophe, stance *f.*

strophic ['strɔfik, strou-], *a.* qui a rapport à la strophe, aux strophes; (*of verse, song*) (divisé, composé) en strophes.

strophiola [strɔfi'oulə], **strophiole** ['strɔfioul], *s. Bot:* strophiole *m.*

strophism ['strɔfizm], *s. Bot:* strophisme *m.*

strophoid ['strɔfɔid], *s. Mth:* strophoïde *f.*

strophoidal [strə'fɔidl], *a. Mth:* **s. curve,** strophoïde *f.*

strophulus ['strɔfjuləs], *s. Med:* strophulus *m.*

stropping ['strɔpiŋ], *s.* affilage *m*; **s. machine,** affûteur *m* automatique, aiguiseur *m*, repasseur *m.*

stroppy ['strɔpi], *a. P:* de mauvaise humeur; maussade.

structural ['strʌktjərəl], *a.* **1.** de construction; **s. iron, steel,** fer, acier, de construction; charpentes *fpl* métalliques; **s. iron and steel work of a building,** constructions *fpl* en fer et en acier, charpente *f* métallique, d'un édifice; **s. engineer,** (ingénieur) constructeur, -trice. **2.** structural, -aux; structurel; de structure; **s. psychology,** psychologie structurale; **s. linguistics,** linguistique structurale; **s. geology,** géologie structurale; tectonique *f*; **s. disequilibrium,** déséquilibre structural; *Ch:* **s. formula,** formule de constitution.

structuralism ['strʌktjərəlizm], *s. Psy: Ling:* structuralisme *m.*

structuralist ['strʌktjərəlist], *a. & s. Psy: Ling:* structuraliste (*mf*).

structuralization [strʌktjərəlai'zeiʃ(ə)n], *s.* structuration *f.*

structuralize ['strʌktjərəlaiz], *v.tr.* structurer.

structurally ['strʌktjərəli], *adv.* d'une manière structurale, structurelle; structuralement, structurellement.

structuration [strʌktjə'reiʃ(ə)n], *s.* structuration *f.*

structure[1] ['strʌktjər], *s.* **1.** structure *f* (d'un corps, d'une plante, d'un atome, d'un poème, etc.); facture *f* (d'un poème, d'une pièce de théâtre, d'une symphonie); agencement *m* (de vers, d'un récit, etc.); construction *f* (d'un bâtiment). **2.** (*a*) construction, édifice *m*; bâtiment; **the social s.,** l'édifice social; **the whole s. of his argument collapsed,** tout l'échafaudage de son argument s'est écroulé; (*b*) *Civ.E:* ouvrage *m*, travail, -aux *m*, d'art; (*c*) *Rail:* **maximum s.,** gabarit *m* (du matériel roulant); **s. gauge,** gabarit de libre passage; (*d*) *Geol:* **imbricate s.,** structure à, en, écailles; (*in igneous rocks*) **alliotriomorphic s.,** structure alliotriomorphe; **subhedral, hypidiomorphic, s.,** structure hypidiomorphe; **mullion s.,** structure linéaire (dans des roches plissées); **banded s.,** structure stratifiée; (*e*) *Atom.Ph:* **s. of nucleus,** structure du noyau; (*of reactor*) **lattice s.,** structure du réseau; (*f*) *St.Exch:* **cross rate s.,** structure des taux de change; *Pol.Ec:* **price s.,** structure des prix.

structure[2], *v.tr.* (*a*) structurer (une organisation, une situation, etc.); (*b*) architecturer (une œuvre d'art).

structured ['strʌktjəd], *a.* à structure; structuré; agencé; charpenté.

structureless ['strʌktjəlis], *a. Geol: etc:* amorphe; *Biol:* homogène.

struggle[1] ['strʌgl], *s.* **1.** lutte *f*; **desperate s.,** lutte désespérée; combat acharné; **desperate hand-to-hand s.,** corps-à-corps acharné; **there was a general s.,** il y eut une mêlée générale; **he gave in without a s.,** il n'a fait aucune résistance; il s'est rendu sans se débattre; **in the death s.,** à l'agonie; dans les affres *f* de l'agonie, de la mort; **the class s.,** la lutte des classes; **s. for freedom,** lutte pour la liberté. **2.** lutte, effort *m*; **the s. for life, for existence,** la lutte pour la vie, pour l'existence; sélection naturelle (des espèces); efforts *mpl* pour survivre.

struggle[2], *v.i.* (*a*) lutter (**with, against, for,** avec, contre, pour); se débattre, se démener; **the child struggled and kicked,** l'enfant se débattait des pieds et des mains; **he was struggling with his umbrella,** il se débattait pour ouvrir, pour fermer, son parapluie; il luttait avec son parapluie; **he struggled to his feet,** il a réussi à se relever; il s'est levé avec difficulté, péniblement; **we struggled (up) to the top of the hill,** nous nous sommes hissés avec peine, péniblement, jusqu'au sommet de la colline; **to s. along,** marcher, avancer, péniblement; **his business is struggling along,** ses affaires vont tant bien que mal, vont cahin-caha; **we are struggling along,** on se défend; **to s. in, out, through,** se frayer un passage (avec difficulté); **we struggled through,** nous avons surmonté tous les obstacles; (*b*) *Lit:* **to be struggling with adversity,** lutter contre l'adversité; être aux prises avec l'adversité; **to s. against circumstances, against fate,** nager contre le courant; **to s. with death,** lutter contre la mort.

struggler ['strʌglər], *s. esp. Lit:* lutteur, -euse; **the strugglers against fate,** ceux qui se débattent contre le sort.

struggling[1] ['strʌgliŋ], *a.* (artiste, etc.) qui vit péniblement, qui cherche à percer.

struggling[2], *s.* lutte *f*; grands efforts; débattement *m.*

strum[1] [strʌm], *s. Min: Nau:* crépine *f* (de pompe, etc.).

strum[2], *s.* son *m*, bruit *m* (d'une guitare, etc., dont on pince les cordes); pianotage *m*, tapotement *m*, tambourinage *m*, tambourinement *m* (des doigts).

strum[3], *v.tr. & i.* **(strummed) to s. (on) a guitar, a banjo,** pincer (distraitement) les cordes d'une guitare, d'un banjo; pincer, gratter, de la guitare, du banjo; **to s. a tune,** (i) jouer (distraitement) un air (à la guitare, etc.); (ii) tapoter un air (au piano); **his fingers strummed (on) the table,** ses doigts pianotaient, tapotaient, tambourinaient, sur la table.

struma, *pl.* **-ae** ['stru:mə, -i:], *s.* **1.** *Med:* (*a*) *A:* strume *f*, scrofules *fpl*; écrouelles *fpl*; (*b*) goitre *m.* **2.** *Bot:* goitre.

strummer ['strʌmər], *s.* (*a*) joueur, -euse, médiocre (de guitare, etc.); (*b*) tapoteur, -euse (de piano).

strumming ['strʌmiŋ], *s.* (*a*) = STRUM[2]; (*b*) pincement (distrait) (de la guitare, etc.); (*c*) pianotage *m*, tapotage *m.*

strumous ['stru:məs], *a.* **1.** *Med:* (*a*) *A:* strumeux, scrofuleux; (*b*) goitreux. **2.** *Bot:* goitreux.

strumpet ['strʌmpit], *s.f. A: & Lit:* prostituée; catin.

strut[1] [strʌt], *s.* démarche affectée, fière; pas mesuré.

strut[2], *v.i.* **(strutted) to s. (about),** se pavaner, parader; faire la roue; se rengorger; plastronner; bomber le torse; **to s. in, out,** entrer, sortir, d'un pas mesuré, d'un air important.

strut[3], *s.* entretoise *f*, étrésillon *m*; pièce comprimée; montant *m*, cale *f*, support *m*, étai *m*, traverse *f*, pointal, -aux *m*; (*spur*) arc-boutant *m*, *pl.* arcs-boutants; jambe *f* de force; (*of roof truss*) contre-fiche *f*, *pl.* contre-fiches; blochet *m*; (*of iron roof*) bielle *f*; (*placed across an angle*) aisselier *m*, esselier *m*; *Av:* pilier *m*, mât *m*; **compression s.,** traverse (de l'aile); **oleo s.,** jambe pneumatique; *Civ.E:* **s. bracing,** poutre *f* en U; *Phot:* **struts,** compas *mpl*, tendeurs *m* (d'un appareil pliant).

strut[4], *v.tr.* **(strutted)** *Const: etc:* entretoiser, étrésillonner; moiser (une charpente, etc.); étayer (une tranchée).

Struthionidae [stru:θi'ɔnidi:], *s.pl. Orn:* struthionidés *m.*

Struthioniformes [stru:θiɔni'fɔ:mi:z], *s.pl. Orn:* struthioniformes *m.*

strutter ['strʌtər], *s.* personne *f* à la démarche affectée; prétentieux, -euse; *F:* crâneur, -euse.

strutting[1] ['strʌtiŋ], *s.* = STRUT[1].

strutting[2], *s.* **1.** entretoisement *m*; renforcement *m* par contre-fiches; étrésillonnement *m*; étaiement *m.* **2.** contre-fiches *fpl*; **s. beam, piece,** lierne *f*, entretoise *f*, étrésillon *m.*

s'truth [stru:θ], *int. P:* eh ben alors! mince alors! ça alors!

struthious ['stru:θiəs], *a.* (qui tient) de l'autruche.

struvite ['stru:vait], *s. Miner:* struvite *f.*

strychnic ['striknik], *a. Med:* strychnique.

strychnine[1] ['strikni:n], *s.* strychnine *f*; **to treat a patient with s.,** strychniser un malade.

strychnine[2], *v.tr. Med:* strychniser (un malade).

strychn(in)ism ['strikn(i:n)izm], *s. Med:* strychnisme *m.*

Strychnos ['striknɔs], *s. Bot:* strychnos *m.*

Strymon ['straimɔn], *s. Ent:* thècle *m*, thécla *m.*

stub[1] [stʌb], *s.* **1.** souche *f* (d'arbre); chicot *m* (d'arbre, de dent); bout *m* (de crayon, de cigarette, de cigare, etc.); tronçon *m* (de mât, de queue de chien, etc.); *F:* mégot *m* (de cigarette, de cigare); *W.Tel:* **s. aerial,** antenne courte; **s. mast,** mât (d'antenne) tronqué; *Mec.E:* **s. pipe,** (i) tuyau court; (ii) pipe *f* d'échappement; **s. shaft,** arbre court, bout d'arbre; **s. teeth,** denture tronquée (d'engrenage); *Mch:* **s. end,** tête *f* de bielle; *Veh:* **s. axle,** fusée *f* (d'essieu); *Carp:* **s. mortise,** mortaise *f* aveugle; **s. tenon,** tenon *m* invisible; **s. nail,** caboche *f*; *Metall:* **s. iron,** fer *m* de riblons; *Av:* **s. plane,** amorce *f* d'aile (sur le fuselage); emplanture *f*; **s. tank,** réservoir *m* d'emplanture; **s. wing,** (i) emplanture d'aile; (ii) (*of seaplane*) nageoire porteuse; **s. wing stabilizer,** ballonnet *m* de bout d'aile. **2.** *Tchn:* mentonnet *m*, ergot *m* de détente (d'une serrure). **3.** (*a*) *Com:* talon *m*, souche (de chèque, etc.); (*b*) *Cmptr:* talon (de carte, etc.); **s. card,** carte à talon; **s. edge,** côté *m* reliure (d'un feuillet, etc.).

stub[2], *v.tr.* **(stubbed) 1. to s. (up) roots,** arracher, extirper, des racines. **2.** *Agr:* **to s. (out) a field,** essoucher un champ. **3. to s. out one's cigarette,** éteindre sa cigarette en l'écrasant (par le bout). **4. to s. one's toe, one's foot, against sth.,** heurter, se cogner, le pied contre qch.; buter contre qch.

stubbed [stʌbd], *a.* **1.** (arbre) tronqué. **2.** (terrain) plein de chicots.

stubbing ['stʌbiŋ], *s. Min:* raboutage *m* (des masses-tiges de forage).

stubble[1] [stʌbl], *s.* **1.** (*a*) chaume *m*, éteule *f*; **to clear a field of s.,** (dé)chaumer un champ; **s. plough,** déchaumeuse *f*; **s. ploughing,** (dé)chaumage *m*; (*b*) **s. (field),** chaume. **2.** (*a*) barbe piquante (de plusieurs jours); (*b*) cheveux *mpl* en brosse.

stubble[2], *v.tr. Agr:* (dé)chaumer (un champ).

stubbling ['stʌbliŋ], *s. Agr:* (dé)chaumage *m.*

stubbly ['stʌbli], *a.* **1.** (champ) couvert de chaume, d'éteule; **s. field,** chaume *m.* **2. s. beard,** barbe piquante (de plusieurs jours); **s. chin, cheeks,** menton piquant, joues piquantes; **s. hair,** cheveux courts et raides; cheveux en brosse.

stubborn ['stʌbən], *a.* **1.** obstiné, opiniâtre, entêté, têtu, inflexible, tenace; cabochard; **s. nature,** caractère buté; **s. horse,** cheval rétif, ramingue; *F:* **as s. as a mule,** têtu, entêté, comme un mulet, comme une mule, comme un âne. **2.** (*of thg*) réfractaire, rebelle; **s. ore,** minerai réfractaire; **s. fever,** fièvre rebelle; **s. soil,** sol ingrat; terre ingrate.

stubbornly ['stʌbənli], *adv.* obstinément, opiniâtrement, avec entêtement; **he s. refuses to eat,** il s'entête à ne pas vouloir manger.

stubbornness ['stʌbənnis], *s.* entêtement *m*, obstination *f*, opiniâtreté *f*; ténacité *f* (de volonté).

stubby ['stʌbi], *a.* **1.** (*of plant, etc.*) tronqué; (*of pers.*) trapu. **2.** (terrain) couvert de chicots.

stucco[1] ['stʌkou], *s. Const:* stuc *m*; **fine s.,** stucatine *f*; **s. work,** stucage *m*; **s. worker,** stucateur *m.*

stucco[2], *v.tr.* **(stuccoed; stuccoing)** stuquer; enduire de stuc.

stuck-up ['stʌk'ʌp], *a. F:* prétentieux, gourmé, guindé, poseur; **there's nothing s.-up about him,** il n'est pas prétentieux pour un sou; **what a s.-up woman!** quelle mijaurée!

stud[1] [stʌd], *s.* **1.** (*a*) clou *m* à grosse tête; clou (doré) (pour ornement, etc.); (*b*) (*on football boots, etc.*) **studs,** crampons *m*; (*c*) clou (de passage clouté). **2.** bouton *m* (double) (de chemise de soirée, etc.); **collar s.,** bouton de col; **s. hole,** boutonnière *f.* **3.** *Tchn:* (*a*) (*short pin*) goujon *m*; pion *m*; tourillon *m*; **locating s.,** pion de centrage; **locking s.,** ergot *m* d'arrêt; téton *m* de blocage; **movable s.,** goujon mobile; **spring s.,** bonhomme *m* à ressort; (*releasing camera front, etc.*) piston *m*; **to remove the stud(s) from sth.,** dégoujonner qch.; **s. link,** maille *f* à étai; maille étançonnée (d'un câble); **s. link chain,** chaîne *f* à étais; **s. chain,** chaîne à fuseaux; **s. wheel,** roue *f* intermédiaire; roue parasite; (*b*) **s. (bolt),** goujon; (goujon) prisonnier *m*; **cotter s. (bolt),** prisonnier à clavette; (*c*) *Metall:* **s. (chaplet),** support *m* double (d'âme); (*d*) *El:* plot *m* (de contact); contact *m*; goutte-de-suif *f*, *pl.* gouttes-de-suif; (*e*) tenon *m*; **cross s., distance s., stand-off s.,** entretoise *f*, tenon d'écartement; **hold-down s.,** tenon de fixation; **safety s.,** tenon de sûreté; *Sm.a:* **bayonet s.,** tenon de baïonnette; **band s.,** tenon de grenadière (de fusil); (*f*) *Nau:* étai *m* (d'une maille, d'un maillon de chaîne); ergot goujon. **4.** *Const:* (*a*) poteau *m*, montant *m*, tournisse *f* (de cloison, de pan de bois); (*b*) *coll.* = STUDDING 1.

stud[2], *v.tr.* (**studded**) **1.** garnir de clous; clouter; **studded door,** porte garnie de clous, cloutée; *A:* **studded tyre,** pneu ferré; *N.Arch:* **to s. the hull of a ship,** mailleter la coque d'un navire; **studded rope,** câble à étais. **2.** *esp. Lit:* **meadow studded with daisies,** pré (par)semé, émaillé, de pâquerettes; **sky studded with stars, star-studded sky,** ciel criblé, (par)semé, d'étoiles; **her dress was studded with jewels,** sa robe était constellée de pierreries; **the darkness was studded with red points,** la nuit se piquait de points rouges. **3.** *Const:* soutenir au moyen de poteaux; établir la charpente (d'une cloison).

stud[3], *s.* **1.** écurie *f* (de chasse, etc.); **racing s.,** écurie de courses. **2.** (**breeding**) **s., s. farm, stable,** haras *m* (de pur-sang); **mule and horse studs,** élevages chevalins et mulassiers; **to be at s., in s.,** (i) (*of horse, etc.*) être en haras; (ii) (*of dog, etc.*) faire saillies; **to place a stallion, a mare, at s., in s.,** élever un étalon, une jument, par la reproduction; **s. book,** livre d'origines, livre généalogique; registre *m* (d'un haras, des chevaux, etc.); stud-book *m, pl.* stud-books; **s. farmer,** éleveur, -euse, de chevaux; **s. mare,** (jument) poulinière *f*. **3.** étalon *m*.

studding ['stʌdiŋ], *s.* **1.** *Const:* (*a*) lattage *m*; (*b*) lattis *m*; charpente *f*. **2.** (*a*) cloutage *m* (d'une boîte, etc.); (*b*) *Nau:* mailletage *m* (de la coque). **3.** *Nau:* **s. sail** ['stʌnsl], bonnette *f*; **lower s. sail,** bonnette basse; **s. sail boom,** bout-dehors *m* de bonnette.

student ['stju:d(ə)nt], *s.* **1.** (*a*) étudiant, -ante; **law s., medical s., arts s.,** étudiant en droit, en médecine, en lettres; **external s.,** étudiant libre; **he is a s.,** (i) il est étudiant; (ii) c'est un homme studieux, qui aime l'étude; **s. life,** la vie d'étudiant; la vie étudiante; la vie estudiantine; **s. organizations,** organisations étudiantes, estudiantines; **s. accommodation,** logement des étudiants; **the s. body,** les étudiants; *NAm:* **beginning s.,** personne *f* qui commence à faire des études (**in** sth., de qch.); (*b*) (*esp. at Christ Church, Oxford*) boursier, -ière (chargé(e) de cours). **2. he is a great s.,** il est très studieux; il étudie beaucoup; il aime beaucoup l'étude; **s. of psychic phenomena,** investigateur, -trice, de phénomènes psychiques.

studhorse ['stʌdhɔ:s], *s.* étalon *m*.

studied ['stʌdid], *a.* **1.** étudié, recherché; prémédité, calculé, voulu; **s. carelessness,** négligence voulue; **s. grace,** grâce étudiée; **dress of s. elegance,** toilette (d'une élégance) recherchée; **s. manners,** manières concertées; **all his gestures are s.,** tous ses gestes sont compassés. **2.** *O: & Lit:* (*of pers.*) instruit, versé (**in,** dans); **he is a very well s. man,** c'est un homme très érudit, très cultivé.

studio ['stju:diou], *s.* atelier *m*, studio *m* (d'artiste, de photographe, etc.); (**film**) **s.,** studio (de cinéma); **broadcasting s.,** studio d'émission; auditorium *m*; **recording s.,** studio d'enregistrement; auditorium; **s. audience,** public qui assiste à une émission (de radio, de télévision); **s. flat,** studio; **s. couch,** lit *m* canapé.

studious ['stju:diəs], *a.* **1.** (*a*) (*of pers.*) studieux, appliqué; adonné à l'étude; (*b*) (habitudes) studieuses; **person of s. habits,** personne adonnée à l'étude. **2. with s. politeness,** avec une politesse étudiée; **with s. attention,** avec une attention réfléchie; *A:* **to be s. to do sth., of doing sth.,** être attentif à, soigneux de, empressé à, faire qch.; s'appliquer à faire qch.

studiously ['stju:diəsli], *adv.* **1.** studieusement. **2.** attentivement, soigneusement; avec attention, avec empressement; **he s. avoided me,** il s'ingéniait à m'éviter. **3. he was s. polite,** il était d'une politesse étudiée.

studiousness ['stju:diəsnis], *s.* **1.** amour *m* de l'étude; attachement *m* à l'étude. **2.** *O:* empressement *m*, attention *f*, zèle *m* (**to do sth., in doing sth.,** à faire qch.).

studwork ['stʌdwə:k], *s. Arch:* colombage *m* (de cloison).

study[1] ['stʌdi], *s.* **1.** *A:* soin(s) *m*(*pl*), attention *f*; **this has been my only s.,** voilà ma seule préoccupation; **he made a s. of my health,** il apportait tous ses soins à ma santé; il s'occupait soigneusement de ma santé; **he makes it his s. to please,** il s'étude, il travaille, à plaire. **2.** (**brown**) **s.,** rêverie *f*; **to be (lost) in a brown s.,** être plongé, absorbé, dans ses réflexions, dans de vagues rêveries, dans la méditation, dans la songerie; être, se perdre, dans les nuages; être dans la lune; **to fall into a brown s.,** s'abandonner au vague de ses pensées. **3.** (*a*) étude *f*; **the s. of mathematics, of history,** l'étude des mathématiques, de l'histoire; **to make a s. of sth.,** s'appliquer à l'étude de qch.; étudier qch.; **to make a special s. of sth.,** faire son étude de qch.; mettre son étude à qch., à faire qch.; **revising the dictionary was his life s.,** la révision du dictionnaire a été le travail de sa vie; **preliminary, pilot, s.,** étude préliminaire; **feasibility, profitability, s.,** étude de faisabilité, de rentabilité; **field s.,** étude(s) sur le terrain; **home s. course,** programme *m* d'études chez soi; **s. group,** groupe de travail; **s. bedroom,** chambre d'étudiant(e); (*b*) *pl.* études; **my studies have convinced me of it,** mes études m'en ont convaincu; **to finish one's studies,** achever ses études; (*c*) **his face was a s.,** ses sentiments se reflétaient sur son visage; il fallait voir son visage! **4.** *Art: Mus:* étude; **violin s.,** étude pour violon; **s. of a head,** étude d'une tête; **s. from the nude,** étude de nu. **5.** *Th:* (*of pers.*) **to be a good, a slow, s.,** apprendre vite, lentement, ses rôles. **6.** (*a*) cabinet *m* de travail; bureau *m*; (*b*) *Sch:* salle *f* d'étude.

study[2], *v.* (**studied; studying**)

I. *v.tr.* **1.** étudier (une langue, la musique, un auteur, un rôle, le caractère de qn); observer (le terrain, les astres); faire des études de (français, de droit, etc.); examiner, étudier (des plans, etc.); **to s. a question,** procéder à l'étude d'une question; mettre une question à l'étude. **2.** *O:* s'occuper de, se préoccuper de, être soigneux de (qn, qch.); **to s. one's own interests,** s'occuper de, rechercher, ses propres intérêts. **3.** *O:* s'étudier, s'appliquer, chercher, viser (**to do sth.,** à faire qch.); **he was studying how he could help her,** il se demandait comment il pourrait l'aider.

II. *v.i.* **1.** faire ses études; étudier; **he's studying,** (i) il fait ses études; (ii) il travaille; **he's studying to be a doctor, for the medical profession,** il fait des études de médecine; **he had studied under Professor X,** il avait suivi les cours du professeur X; **to s. for an examination,** préparer un examen; se préparer à un examen; **to s. hard,** travailler ferme, sérieusement. **2.** *esp. U.S:* être plongé dans des réflexions, dans la méditation.

studying ['stʌdiiŋ], *s.* études *fpl*.

stuff[1] [stʌf], *s.* **1.** (*a*) matière(s) *f*(pl), matériaux *mpl*, substance *f*, étoffe *f*; *Paperm:* pâte *f* (à papier); *N.Arch:* **thick s.,** planches *fpl* de doublage; *Nau:* **small s.,** lusin *m*, merlin *m*; *A:* **household s.,** mobilier *m*, effets *mpl*; **he is of the s. that heroes are made of,** il est du bois, de l'étoffe, dont sont faits les héros; **we must see what s. he is made of,** il faut voir ce qu'il a dans le corps, dans le ventre; **I'll show them what s. I'm made of,** je leur ferai voir de quel bois je me chauffe; *F:* **he writes good s.,** il écrit bien; (*b*) *F:* **this wine is good s.,** ce vin est excellent; **I don't like that s. you gave me,** je n'aime pas ce que vous m'avez donné là; **drink some of that s.,** buvez-moi un peu de ça; **let's have a look at your s.,** faites voir votre camelote *f*; **come on, do your s.!** allons, montre-nous ce que tu sais faire, déballe tes connaissances! **to know one's s.,** être capable, à la hauteur; **he knows his s.,** il s'y connaît; **that's the s.!** voilà ce qu'il faut! *P:* **a nice bit of s.,** une belle pépée, une jolie môme; (*c*) *P:* (i) héroïne *f*, jus *m*; (ii) came *f*; (*d*) fatras *m*; **old s.,** vieilleries *fpl*; **silly s.,** sottises *fpl*, balivernes *fpl*; *O:* **s. and nonsense!** ça c'est de la bêtise! quelle bêtise! allons donc! **2.** *Tex:* étoffe, tissu *m* (de laine); *Jur: A:* **s. gown,** (i) robe d'étoffe; (ii) jeune avocat, avocat en second (qui ne porte pas de soie).

stuff[2], *v.tr.* **1.** (*a*) bourrer (**with,** de); rembourrer (un meuble, un coussin) (**with,** de); garnir (une chaise, etc.); *Trans:* charger (un container); **his pockets are stuffed with sweets,** il a des bonbons plein les poches; il a les poches bourrées de bonbons; **to s. s.o.,** bourrer, gorger, qn de nourriture; gaver qn; *F:* **I'm stuffed full,** j'en ai jusque-là; **to s. oneself,** manger avec excès; se bourrer; s'empiffrer, se gaver; **head stuffed with romantic ideas,** tête bourrée, farcie, d'idées romanesques; (*b*) *Cu:* farcir (un poulet, etc.); *F:* **stuffed shirt,** individu suffisant, prétentieux; crâneur, -euse; collet monté *m inv*; (*c*) empailler, naturaliser (un spécimen zoologique, etc.); (*d*) *V:* coïter avec (une femme); (*e*) *P:* **get stuffed! you can s. it!** va te faire foutre! **he can go and get s.! he can s. it!** je l'emmerde; **s. the job, etc.!** merde pour le boulot, etc.! **2.** *F: O:* **to s. s.o. (up),** bourrer le crâne de qn; faire marcher qn; en faire accroire à qn. **3. to s. (up) one's ears with cotton wool,** se boucher les oreilles avec de l'ouate; **to s. up a hole,** boucher un trou; **my nose is stuffed up,** se suis enchifrené. **4. to s. sth. into sth.,** fourrer, serrer, qch. dans qch.; **to s. one's fingers in one's ears,** se boucher les oreilles (avec les doigts).

stuffer ['stʌfər], *s.* **1.** personne *f* qui bourre, qui rembourre (des coussins, etc.). **2.** empailleur, -euse (d'animaux). **3.** (*device*) rembourroir *m*; **sausage s.,** poussoir *m*.

stuffiness ['stʌfinis], *s.* **1.** manque *m* d'air; odeur *f* de renfermé. **2.** enchifrènement *m*. **3.** préjugés vieillots.

stuffing ['stʌfiŋ], *s.* **1.** (*a*) bourrage *m*, rembourrage *m*; empaillage *m* (d'animaux); poussage *m* en boyau (de saucisses); *Trans:* chargement *m* (d'un container); (*b*) *F:* gavage *m*, bâfrerie *f*. **2.** (*a*) bourre *f*; rembourrage; (*for furniture*) paille *f* de fer; **horsehair s.,** matelassure *f* de crin; *Mch:* **s. (piece),** garniture *f*, étoupe *f*; **s. box,** boîte à garniture, à étoupe; presse-étoupe(s) *m inv*; boîte à bourrage; *F:* **to knock, beat, the s. out of s.o.,** (i) flanquer une tripotée à qn; battre qn à plate(s) couture(s); (ii) désarçonner, dégonfler, qn; (*b*) *Cu:* farce *f*.

stuffy ['stʌfi], *a.* **1.** privé d'air; mal ventilé, mal aéré; sans air; **s. room,** pièce qui sent le renfermé; **it's a bit s. in here,** cela manque d'air ici. **2.** *F:* fâché; en rogne. **3.** *F:* collet monté; aux préjugés vieillots; **don't be so s.,** il n'y a pas de quoi te scandaliser, il n'y a pas de quoi faire un scandale! **4. to feel s.,** se sentir enchifrené.

stulm [stʌlm], *s. Min:* galerie *f* (d'accès) à flanc de coteau.

stultification [stʌltifi'keiʃ(ə)n], *s.* **1.** invalidation *f* (d'un décret, etc.). **2.** action de ridiculiser (qn, qch.), de rendre (qn, qch.) ridicule.

stultify ['stʌltifai], *v.tr.* **1.** enlever toute valeur à (un argument, un témoignage); invalider, infirmer (un décret, etc.); rendre (une mesure) inutile; confondre, rendre vains (les projets de qn). **2.** ridiculiser (qn, qch.), rendre (qn, qch.) ridicule; faire ressortir la sottise, l'absurdité (d'une action); **to s. oneself,** (i) *Jur:* (*of witness*) se contredire, se démentir; (ii) *Jur:* exciper de sa faiblesse d'esprit; (iii) se rendre ridicule.

stum[1] [stʌm], *s. Wine-m:* moût *m* (de raisin).

stum[2], *v.tr.* (**stummed**) *Wine-m:* soufrer, muter (le vin, un fût).

stumble[1] ['stʌmb(ə)l], *s.* trébuchement *m*, faux pas; bronchement *m* (d'un cheval).

stumble[2], *v.i.* **1.** trébucher; faire un faux pas; (*of horse*) broncher; **to s. along,** marcher, avancer, en trébuchant; **to s. against sth.,** se heurter, buter, contre qch.; *Prov:* **it's a good horse that never stumbles,** il n'y a si bon cheval qui ne bronche. **2. to s. in one's speech,** (i) hésiter en parlant; (ii) patauger, s'embrouiller, en prononçant son discours. **3. to s. across, on, s.o., sth.,** rencontrer qn, qch., par hasard; tomber sur qn, qch.

stumbling[1] ['stʌmbliŋ], *a.* qui trébuche; (*of horse*) qui bronche; (*of speech*) hésitant.

stumbling[2], *s.* **1.** trébuchement *m*, faux pas; bronchement *m* (d'un cheval); **s. block,** pierre *f* d'achoppement. **2.** hésitation *f*; ânonnement *m*.

stumer ['stju:mər], *s. F:* **1.** (*a*) chèque *m* sans valeur, sans provision; (*b*) faux billet de banque, fausse monnaie. **2.** personne *f*, chose *f*, qui ne vaut rien; (*of pers.*) raté, -ée.

stumming ['stʌmiŋ], *s. Wine-m:* soufrage *m*, mutage *m* (du vin, d'un fût).

stump[1] [stʌmp], *s.* **1.** (*a*) tronçon *m*, souche *f*, chicot *m* (d'arbre); chicot, racine *f* (de dent); moignon *m* (de bras, de jambe); bout *m* (de cigare, de crayon); *F:* mégot *m* (de cigare); tronçon (de queue, de colonne, de mât); trognon *m* (de chou); **to remove the stumps of branches, of trees,** échicoter des branches, des arbres; **to stub up the tree stumps (from the land),** essoucher un terrain; **s.-pulling machine, s. puller,** essoucheur *m*; *Austr: F:* **beyond the black s.,** loin d'ici; *NAm: F:* **to be up a s.,** être incapable de répondre; être réduit à quia; (*b*) jambe *f* de bois. **2.** *F:* **stumps,** jambes; gigues, quilles *f*; **stir your stumps!** remuez-vous! trémoussez-vous! (dé)grouillez-vous! **3.** *Pol: F:* **to be on the s.,** être en tournée électorale; faire des harangues politiques; **s. orator,** *NAm:* **s. speaker,** orateur de carrefour; **s. oratory,** *NAm:* **s. speaking,** éloquence *f* de carrefour; **s. speech,** harangue *f* en plein air. **4.** *Cr:* piquet *m* (du guichet); **stumps are pitched at eleven o'clock,** le match commence à onze heures; **to draw stumps,** enlever les piquets; cesser le match. **5.** *Draw:* estompe *f*; **s. drawing,** (dessin à l')estompe.

stump[2]. **1.** *v.i.* (*a*) **to s. along,** marcher, avancer, en clopinant; clopiner; (*b*) *Pol: F:* faire des harangues politiques; faire une tournée électorale; (*c*) *F:* **to s. up,** payer, casquer; abouler son argent. **2.** *v.tr.* (*a*) *F:* coller (un candidat); poser une colle à (qn); faire sécher (qn) (sur un sujet); mettre, réduire, (qn) à quia; **to be stumped,** rester bouche bée; ne savoir plus que faire; sécher, piquer une sèche; **this stumped me,** sur le coup je n'ai su que répondre; cela m'a désarçonné; (*b*) *F:* **to s. up the money,** payer, casquer; abouler son argent; (*c*) *Cr: etc:* mettre hors jeu (un batteur qui est sorti de son camp) en abattant le guichet avec la balle tenue à la main; (*d*) *Draw:* estomper (un dessin).

stumper ['stʌmpər], *s.* **1.** *F:* question embarrassante; colle *f*. **2.** *Cr: F:* (*pers.*) garde-guichet *m, pl.* gardes-guichet. **3.** *Agr:* dessoucheur *m*.

stumpiness ['stʌmpinis], *s.* aspect trapu, ragot (de qn, d'un cheval); peu *m* de longueur (de la queue d'un chien).

stumpwood ['stʌmpwud], *s.* bois *m* de souche.

stumpy ['stʌmpi], *a.* **1.** trapu, ragot, ramassé; **s. man,** homme gros et court; **s. umbrella,** tom-pouce *m, pl.* tom-pouces; **s. pencil,** petit bout de crayon. **2.** (*of ground*) plein de souches, de chicots.

stun [stʌn], *v.tr.* (**stunned**) **1.** étourdir, assommer. **2.** renverser, abasourdir; **the news stunned us,** c'était un coup de massue; **stunned with surprise,** figé par la surprise; stupéfié; frappé de stupeur.

stunner ['stʌnər], *s. F:* **1.** type épatant; **he's a s., she's a s.,** il est épatant, elle est épatante. **2.** chose épatante, renversante.

stunning ['stʌniŋ], *a.* **1.** (*a*) (coup) étourdissant, abrutissant; (*b*) (malheur) accablant, bouleversant. **2.** *F:* renversant, abasourdissant; formidable, épatant, sensas; **she's really s.,** c'est une beauté; elle est ravissante.

stunningly ['stʌniŋli], *adv.* **1.** d'une façon étourdissante. **2.** *F:* admirablement, épatamment.

stunt[1] [stʌnt], *s.* **1.** arrêt *m* dans la croissance. **2.** *Nat.Hist:* avorton *m.*

stunt[2], *v.tr.* empêcher (qn, qch.) de croître; arrêter (qn, qch.) dans sa croissance; rabougrir; **to become stunted,** se rabougrir; **stunted tree,** arbre rabougri, avorté, chétif; **stunted mind,** esprit noué.

stunt[3], *s.* **1.** coup *m* d'épate; affaire *f* de publicité, de pure réclame; **the Zinoviev letter s.,** le coup de la lettre Zinovieff; **that's a good s.!** ça, c'est une bonne idée! **2.** (*a*) tour *m* de force; *Av:* **s. flying,** vol *m* de virtuosité; **s. pilot,** pilote *m* de voltige; **to perform stunts,** faire des acrobaties (en vol); (*b*) *Cin:* acrobatie *f*; **s. man,** cascadeur *m*; (*c*) *Mil: F:* journée *f* de combat; affaire *f*; attaque *f.*

stunt[4], *v.i. Av:* faire des acrobaties (en vol).

stuntedness ['stʌntidnis], *s.* rabougrissement *m.*

stunter ['stʌntər], *s. Av:* as *m* de l'acrobatie aérienne.

stunting ['stʌntiŋ], *s.* rabougrissement *m*, étiolement *m.*

stupa ['stju:pə], *s. Arch:* stupa *m*, stoupa *m.*

stupe[1] [stju:p], *s. Med:* compresse *f*, cataplasme *m*, pour fomentation.

stupe[2], *v.tr. Med:* appliquer une compresse, un cataplasme, sur (une plaie).

stupe[3], *s. F: A:* imbécile *mf*, idiot, -ote.

stupefacient [stju:pi'feiʃ(ə)nt], *a. & s.* abrutisseur (*m*); *Med:* stupéfiant (*m*).

stupefaction [stju:pi'fækʃ(ə)n], *s.* stupéfaction *f*; (*astonishment*) abasourdissement *m*, stupeur *f*, ahurissement *m.*

stupefactive [stju:pi'fæktiv], *a. & s.* abrutisseur (*m*); *Med:* stupéfiant (*m*).

stupefier ['stju:pifaiər], *s.* abrutisseur *m*; *Med:* stupéfiant.

stupefy ['stju:pifai], *v.tr.* **1.** (*a*) *Med:* stupéfier, engourdir; (*b*) hébéter, abrutir; **stupefied with opium,** stupéfié, abruti, par l'opium; **stupefied with grief,** hébété par la douleur; **to be stupefied,** être frappé de stupeur. **2.** abasourdir, stupéfier; **I'm absolutely stupefied (by what has happened),** je n'en reviens pas; j'en reste médusé; les bras m'en tombent.

stupefying[1] ['stju:pifaiiŋ], *a.* **1.** *Med:* stupéfiant. **2.** abasourdissant, stupéfiant.

stupefying[2], *s.* (*a*) stupéfaction *f*; engourdissement *m*; (*b*) abrutissement *m.*

stupendous [stju(:)'pendəs], *a.* prodigieux; *F:* formidable.

stupendously [stju(:)'pendəsli], *adv.* prodigieusement.

stupendousness [stju(:)'pendəsnis], *s.* nature prodigieuse, caractère prodigieux (d'un phénomène, etc.).

stupeous ['stju:piəs], *a.* laineux.

stupid ['stju:pid], *a.* **1.** *A: & Lit:* stupide; frappé de stupeur. **2.** (*a*) stupide, sot, *f.* sotte; bête; **my pupils are very s.,** mes élèves ont la tête dure; *F:* j'ai une classe de crétins; *s. F:* **I was only teasing, s.!** c'était pour te taquiner, gros bêta! **he's as s. as anything,** il est bête comme tout, comme ses pieds, comme une oie; il est bête, sot, comme un panier (percé); **I did a s. thing,** j'ai fait une bêtise, une chose stupide; j'ai commis une sottise, une balourdise, une boulette; **don't be s.!** ne faites pas la bête, l'idiot; **how s. of me!** que je suis bête! **he's not s. enough to believe that,** il n'est pas si bête pour le croire; **a s. question, answer,** sotte demande, sotte réponse; **to give a s. answer,** répondre par une stupidité; répondre en dépit du bon sens; **why did you go on that s. journey?** pourquoi avez-vous fait ce bête de voyage? **what a s. place to put it in!** c'est idiot de l'avoir mis là! **to drink oneself s.,** s'hébéter, s'abrutir, à force de boire; (*b*) insipide, ennuyeux.

stupidity [stju:'piditi], *s.* stupidité *f*; (*a*) *A: & Lit:* lourdeur *m* d'esprit; (*b*) sottise *f*, niaiserie *f*, bêtise *f*, ânerie *f*; **it's crass s.!** c'est idiot!

stupidly ['stju:pidli], *adv.* stupidement, sottement, bêtement.

stupor ['stju:pər], *s.* stupeur *f*; **in a drunken s.,** abruti par la boisson.

stuporous ['stju:pərəs], *a.* **1.** (*of pers.*) dans un état de léthargie, de stupeur. **2.** *Med:* stuporeux; caractérisé par la stupeur, par la léthargie.

sturdily ['stə:dili], *adv.* **1.** fortement, vigoureusement; avec robustesse. **2.** hardiment, fortement, fermement, résolument.

sturdiness ['stə:dinis], *s.* **1.** vigueur *f*, robustesse *f.* **2.** hardiesse *f*, résolution *f*, fermeté *f.*

sturdy ['stə:di]. **1.** *a.* (*a*) vigoureux, robuste, fort; **s. fellow,** gaillard robuste; (*b*) (*of opposition, resistance, etc.*) hardi, résolu, ferme; (*c*) *A:* **s. beggar,** mendiant effronté; truand, -ande. **2.** *s. Vet:* tournis *m.*

sturgeon ['stə:dʒ(ə)n], *s. Ich:* esturgeon *m*; **Chinese s.,** spatule *f.*

sturnella [stə:'nelə], *s. Orn:* sturnelle *f.*

Sturnidae ['stə:nidi:], *s.pl. Orn:* sturnidés *m.*

stutter[1] ['stʌtər], *s.* bégaiement *m*; **he has a terrible s.,** il est affecté d'un bégaiement insupportable; **the s. of the machine guns,** le feu répété des mitrailleuses.

stutter[2]. **1.** *v.i.* bégayer, bredouiller. **2.** *v.tr.* **to s. sth.,** bégayer, bredouiller, balbutier, qch.

stutterer ['stʌtərər], *s.* bègue *mf.*

stuttering[1] ['stʌt(ə)riŋ], *a.* bègue.

stuttering[2], *s.* bégaiement *m*, bredouillement *m*, balbutiement *m.*

stutteringly ['stʌt(ə)riŋli], *adv.* en bégayant.

sty[1], *pl.* **sties** [stai, staiz], *s.* (*a*) étable *f* (à porcs); porcherie *f*; (*b*) taudis *m.*

sty[2], *v.tr.* (**stied**) mettre, enfermer (des porcs) dans leur étable, dans la porcherie.

sty[3], **stye** [stai], *s. Med:* orgelet *m*, chalazion *m*; *F:* compère-loriot *m*, *pl.* compères-loriots; grain-d'orge *m*, grains-d'orge.

Stygian ['stidʒiən], *a. Lit:* (*a*) stygien, stygial; **to visit the S. shores,** visiter les rives du Styx; **to swear the S. oath,** jurer par le Styx; (*b*) **S. gloom,** (i) nuit noire, (ii) humeur noire, comme le Styx; (*c*) infernal, -aux.

stylar ['stailər], *a. Nat.Hist:* stylaire.

stylate ['staileit], *a. Nat.Hist:* stylé; muni d'un style.

style[1] [stail], *s.* **1.** (*a*) *Ant: etc:* style *m* (pour écrire); poinçon *m* (en métal, en ivoire); (*b*) *Engr:* burin *m*; (*c*) (*of sundial*) style, gnomon *m*; (*d*) *Bot:* style. **2.** (*a*) style, manière *f*, façon *f*, genre *m*; **s. of living,** manière de vivre; genre, train, de vie; **the s. in which they live,** le train qu'ils mènent; **to live in (grand, great) s.,** mener grand train; **they arrived in s.,** ils ont fait leur entrée en grande pompe; **in the grand s.,** dans le grand style; dans le grand genre; **good, bad, s.,** bon, mauvais, genre; bon, mauvais, goût, ton; **let's do things in s.,** faisons bien les choses; **that's the s.!** c'est cela! bravo! à la bonne heure! (*b*) *Art: Arch: etc:* **in the s. of Rubens,** dans le style de Rubens; **Gothic, Byzantine, s.,** style gothique, byzantin; **building in the classical s.,** bâtiment de style classique; **built in the s. of the last century,** construit dans le goût du siècle dernier; (*c*) style, genre; type *m*, modèle *m* (d'une voiture, etc.); **made in three styles,** fabriqué en trois catégories *f*, sur trois modèles; (*d*) **aristocrat of the old s.,** aristocrate de la vieille école; **that's not my s.,** ce n'est pas mon genre; **something in that s.,** quelque chose de ce genre; quelque chose dans ce genre, dans ce goût-là; (*e*) *Cost: etc:* mode *f*; **in the latest s.,** à la mode; *F:* dernier cri. **3.** (*a*) style, ton; manière d'écrire; **written in a humorous s.,** écrit sur un ton de plaisanterie; **written in an unoriginal s.,** écrit d'un, dans un, style peu original; **biblical s.,** style biblique; style de l'Écriture; **judicial s.,** style judiciaire; style du palais; (*b*) (*good style*) **this writer lacks s.,** cet écrivain n'a pas de style. **4.** chic *m*, cachet *m*, ton *m*; **she has s.,** elle a de l'allure, du chic, du genre, de la distinction; elle est distinguée; **she has no s.,** elle n'a pas de chic; elle n'a aucun cachet. **5.** *Chr:* (*of calendar*) **old, new, s.,** vieux, nouveau, style. **6.** *O:* titre *m*, nom *m*; *Com:* raison sociale; nom commercial; firme *f*; **he had assumed the s. of colonel,** il s'était intitulé colonel.

style[2], *v.tr.* **1.** *O:* dénommer; appeler; **to s. s.o. baron,** qualifier qn de baron; donner à qn le titre de baron; **to s. oneself doctor,** se donner le titre de docteur; s'intituler, se faire appeler, docteur. **2.** *Cost: etc:* créer; **dress styled by X,** robe créée par X; **hair styled by X,** coiffé(e) par X.

style[3], *s. A:* STILE[1,2].

stylet ['stailit], *s.* **1.** *A:* (*dagger*) stylet *m.* **2.** *Surg:* stylet. **3.** *Z:* stylet, rostre *m.*

styliform ['stailifɔ:m], *a. Bot:* styliforme.

styling ['stailiŋ], *s.* (*a*) ornementation tracée au style; (*b*) (**hair**) **s.,** coiffure *f* (d'art).

stylish ['stailiʃ], *a.* élégant, chic; coquet, *f.* coquette; qui a du cachet; (chapeau, etc.) habillé, à la mode, qui a du chic; **it looks more s.,** cela fait plus élégant, plus habillé.

stylishly ['stailiʃli], *adv.* élégamment; avec chic; coquettement; à la mode.

stylishness ['stailiʃnis], *s.* élégance *f*, chic *m*, coquetterie *f*; souci *m* de la mode.

stylism ['stailizm], *s. Lit: Cost: etc:* stylisme *m.*

stylist ['stailist], *s.* (*a*) *Lit:* styliste *mf*; (*b*) *Cost: etc:* styliste; **hair s.,** (i) coiffeur, -euse (d'art); artiste capillaire; (ii) (*shop sign*) = coiffure *f* (d'art); *F:* tifferie *f.*

stylistic [stai'listik], *a.* stylistique; du, de, style.

stylistics [stai'listiks], *s.pl.* (*usu. with sg. const.*) stylistique *f.*

stylite ['stailait], *s. & a. Rel.H:* stylite (*m*).

Stylites [stai'laiti:z]. *Pr.n.m. Rel.H:* **Saint Simeon S.,** Saint Siméon Stylite.

stylization [stailai'zeiʃ(ə)n], *s.* stylisation *f.*

stylize ['stailaiz], *v.tr. Art:* styliser (son art).

stylized ['stailaizd], *a.* stylisé; **s. flowers,** fleurs stylisées.

stylo- ['stailou, -ə], *comb.fm. Anat: Bot: etc:* stylo-.

stylo ['stailou], *s. F:* = STYLOGRAPH.

stylobate ['stailoubeit], *s. Arch:* stylobate *m*; soubassement *m* (de colonnade).

styloglossal [stailou'glɔsəl], *a. Anat:* stylo(-)glosse.

styloglossus, *pl.* **-i** [stailou'glɔsəs, -ai], *s. Anat:* stylo(-)glosse *m.*

stylograph ['stailəgræf], *s.* stylographe *m*, *F:* stylo *m.*

stylographic [stailə'græfik], *a.* stylographique.

stylohyoid [stailou'haiɔid], *a. & s. Anat:* stylo-hyoïdien (*m*).

styloid ['stailɔid], *a. Anat:* styloïde; **the s. process,** *s.* **the s.,** l'apophyse *f* styloïde.

stylolite ['stailoulait], *s. Geol:* stylolite *m.*

stylomastoid [stailou'mæstɔid], *a. Anat:* (trou) stylomastoïdien.

stylomaxillary [stailoumæk'siləri], *a. Anat:* stylomaxillaire.

stylometric [stailou'metrik], *a. Arch:* stylométrique.

stylometry [stai'lɔmitri], *s. Arch:* stylométrie *f.*

Stylommatophora [stailɔmə'tɔfərə], *s.pl. Moll:* stylommatophores *m.*

stylopodium, *pl.* **-ia** [stailou'poudiəm, -iə], *s. Bot:* stylopode *m.*

stylospore ['stailouspɔ:r], *s. Fung:* stylospore *f.*

stylus, *pl.* **-i, -uses** ['stailəs, -ai, -əsiz], *s.* (*a*) *Ant: Engr:* style *m*; (*b*) *Rec:* style; aiguille *f.*

stymie ['staimi], *v.tr.* (*a*) *Golf: A:* barrer le trou à (son adversaire); (*b*) *F:* **to be stymied,** être dans une impasse.

Stymphalian [stim'feiliən], *a. Myth:* **the S. birds,** les oiseaux du lac Stymphale.

Stymphalus [stim'feiləs], *Pr.n. A. Geog:* Stymphale.

styphnate ['stifneit], *s. Ch:* styphnate *m*, tricinate *m*, trinitrorésorcinate *m.*

styphnic ['stifnik], *a. Ch:* **s. acid,** acide styphnique; trinitrorésorcine *f*, trinitrorésorcinol *m.*

styptic ['stiptik], *a. & s. Med:* styptique (*m*), astringent (*m*); **s. pencil,** pierre d'alun.

stypticity [stip'tisiti], *s. Med:* stypticité *f*, astringence *f.*

Styracaceae [staiərə'keisii:], *s.pl. Bot:* styra(ca)cées *f.*

styrax ['staiəræks], *s. Bot:* styrax *m*, aliboufier *m.*

styrene ['staiəri:n], *s. Ch:* styrène *m*; styrol(ène) *m*; vinylbenzène *m.*

Styria ['stiriə], *Pr.n. Geog:* Styrie *f.*

Styrian ['stiriən]. *Geog:* (*a*) *a.* styrien; (*b*) *s.* Styrien, -ienne.

styrol(ene) ['stai(ə)rɔl(i:n)], *s. Ch:* styrol(ène) *m*; styrène *m*; vinylbenzène *m.*

Styx [stiks], *Pr.n. Gr.Myth:* Styx *m*; *Poet:* l'Onde noire; **to cross the S.,** traverser, franchir, le Styx.

suable ['sju:əbl], *a. Jur:* poursuivable en justice.

suasion ['sweiʒ(ə)n], *s. A:* persuasion *f*; **to subject s.o. to moral s.,** agir sur la conscience de qn.

suasive ['sweisiv], *a. A:* persuasif.

suave [swɑ:v], *a.* **1.** *A:* (parfum, etc.) suave. **2.** (*a*) *O:* (accueil) affable; (*b*) *Pej:* mielleux; (trop) courtois; **s. manners,** manières doucereuses.

suavely ['swɑ:vli], *adv.* (*a*) *O:* avec affabilité; (*b*) *Pej:* doucereusement.

suaveness ['swɑ:vnis], **suavity** ['swɑ:viti], *s.* **1.** *A:* suavité *f* (d'un parfum). **2.** (*a*) affabilité *f*; douceur *f*; (*b*) *Pej:* politesse mielleuse.

sub[1] [sʌb], *s. F:* **1.** = SUBORDINATE[1] 2. **2.** = SUBALTERN 2. **3.** = SUBSCRIPTION 2, 3. **4.** allocation *f* de séjour. **5.** = SUBSTITUTE[1] 1. **6.** = SUBMARINE 2. **7.** = SUB-EDITOR. **8.** *Phot:* = SUBSTRATUM.

sub[2], *v.* (**subbed**) *F:* **1.** *v.tr.* payer un acompte sur le salaire de (qn); prêter de l'argent à (qn). **2.** *v.i.* (= *substitute*) **to s. for s.o.,** remplacer qn, se substituer à qn; faire l'intérim de qn; *abs.* assurer l'intérim. **3.** *v.tr. & i. Journ:* mettre (un article) au point, être secrétaire à la rédaction.

sub- [sʌb], *pref.* **1.** sub-. **2.** sous-. **3.** (*a*) presque; (*b*) moins de.

sub-account ['sʌbəkaunt], *s.* sous-compte *m.*
subacetate [sʌb'æsiteit], *s. Ch:* sous-acétate *m.*
subacid [sʌb'æsid], *a.* **1.** aigrelet, -ette; acidule; légèrement acide. **2.** (ton) aigre-doux; (réponse) aigre-douce, *pl.* aigres-doux, -douces.
subacute [sʌbə'kju:t], *a. Med:* subaigu, -uë.
subaerial [sʌb'ɛəriəl], *a. Geol: Bot:* subaérien.
sub-agency [sʌb'eidʒənsi], *s.* sous-agence *f.*
sub-agent [sʌb'eidʒənt], *s.* sous-agent *m.*
subalary [sʌb'eiləri], *a. Orn:* subalaire.
subalkaline [sʌb'ælkəlain], *a. Ch: Geol:* subalcalin.
subalpine [sʌb'ælpain], *a.* subalpin.
subaltern ['sʌbəltə:n]. **1.** *a.* subalterne, subordonné; *Log:* **s. proposition,** proposition *f* subalterne. **2.** *s.* (*a*) subalterne *m*, subordonné *m*; (*b*) *Mil:* lieutenant *m*; sous-lieutenant *m*; subalterne *m.*
subalternation [sʌbɔ:ltə'neiʃ(ə)n], *s. Log:* subalternation *f.*
subaponeurotic [sʌbæpounju:'rɔtik], *a. Anat:* sous-aponévrotique.
subaqua [sʌb'ækwə], *a.* (sport) subaquatique.
subaquatic [sʌbə'kwætik], **subaqueous** [sʌb'eikwiəs], *a.* (lumière, exploration, etc.) subaquatique.
subarachnoid [sʌbæ'ræknɔid], *a. Anat:* sous-arachnoïdien.
subarctic [sʌb'ɑ:ktik], *a. Geog:* (région, latitude) presque arctique.
sub-assembly ['sʌbəsembli], *s. Mec.E: etc:* préassemblage *m*; bloc *m*; élément *m*; ensemble partiel; *Cmptr:* sous-ensemble *m.*
subastragalar [sʌbæ'strægələr], **subastragaloid** [sʌbæ'strægəlɔid], *a. Anat:* sous-astragalien.
subastral [sʌb'æstrəl], *a.* terrestre, sublunaire.
subatomic [sʌbə'tɔmik], *a.* subatomique.
sub-audio [sʌb'ɔ:diou], *a.* infra-acoustique.
subaxillary [sʌbæk'siləri], *a.* **1.** *Z:* sous-axillaire; *Orn:* axillaire. **2.** *Bot:* infra-axillaire, sous-axillaire.
sub-band ['sʌbbænd], *s. Cmptr:* sous-bande *f.*
subbituminous [sʌbbi'tju:minəs], *a.* subbitumineux; **s. coal,** lignite *m.*
subcalibre [sʌb'kælibər], *a. Artil:* (projectile) sous-calibré.
subcarbonate [sʌb'kɑ:bəneit], *s. Ch:* sous-carbonate *m.*
subcarrier [sʌb'kæriər], *s. Elcs:* (onde) sous-porteuse *f.*
subcaudal [sʌb'kɔ:d(ə)l], *a. Z: Orn:* subcaudal, -aux, sous-caudal, -aux.
subcentre ['sʌbsentər], *s. Cmptr:* sous-centre *m.*
subchanter ['sʌbtʃɑ:ntər], *s. Ecc:* sous-chantre *m.*
sub-charter[1] [sʌb'tʃɑ:tər], *s.* sous-affrètement *m.*
sub-charter[2] [sʌb'tʃɑ:tər], *v.tr.* sous-affréter (un navire).
sub-charterer [sʌb'tʃɑ:tərər], *s.* sous-affréteur *m.*
sub-chartering [sʌb'tʃɑ:təriŋ], *s.* sous-affrètement *m.*
subchloride [sʌb'klɔ:raid], *s. Ch:* sous-chlorure *m.*
subclass ['sʌbklɑ:s], *s. Nat.Hist:* sous-classe *f.*
subclause ['sʌbklɔ:z], *s. esp. Jur:* paragraphe *m* (d'un contrat).
subclavian [sʌb'kleiviən], *a. Anat:* sous-clavier.
subclavicular [sʌbklæ'vikjulər], *a. Anat:* sous-claviculaire.
subcommission [sʌbkə'miʃ(ə)n], *s.* sous-commission *f.*
subcommissioner [sʌbkə'miʃ(ə)nər], *s.* sous-commissaire *m.*
subcommittee ['sʌbkəmiti], *s.* sous-comité *m*; sous-commission *f.*
sub-compartment [sʌbkəm'pɑ:tmənt], *s. For:* sous-parcelle *f.*
subconjunctival [sʌbkɔndʒʌŋk'taiv(ə)l], *a. Anat:* sous-conjonctival, -aux.
subconscious [sʌb'kɔnʃəs], *a. & s. Psy:* subconscient (*m*).
subconsciously [sʌb'kɔnʃəsli], *adv.* subconsciemment.
subconsciousness [sʌb'kɔnʃəsnis], *s. Psy:* subconscience *f.*
subcontract[1] [sʌb'kɔntrækt], *s.* sous-traité *m.*
subcontract[2] [sʌbkən'trækt], *v.tr.* sous-traiter (une affaire).
subcontracting [sʌbkən'træktiŋ], *s.* sous-traitance *f.*
subcontractor [sʌbkən'træktər], *s.* sous-entrepreneur *m*, sous-traitant *m*; *Const: etc:* tâcheron *m.*
subcoracoid [sʌb'kɔrəkɔid], *a. Anat:* sous-coracoïdien.
subcortical [sʌb'kɔ:tikl], *a. Bot:* subcortical, -aux; *Anat:* sous-cortical, -aux.
subcostal [sʌb'kɔst(ə)l], *a. Anat: Ent:* sous-costal, -aux; subcostal, -aux.
subcrepitant [sʌb'krepitənt], *a. Med:* sous-crépitant.
subcritical [sʌb'kritikl], *a. Atom.Ph: etc:* sous-critique.
subculture[1] [sʌb'kʌltjər], *s.* **1.** *Bac:* repiquage *m*; culture *f* secondaire. **2.** groupe culturel secondaire.
subculture[2], *v.tr. Bac:* repiquer.
subcutaneous [sʌbkju(:)'teiniəs], *a.* sous-cutané; **s. parasite, s. larva,** parasite *m*, larve *f*, cuticole; **s. injection,** injection sous-cutanée.
subdeacon [sʌb'di:kən], *s. Ecc:* sous-diacre *m.*
subdeaconate [sʌb'di:kənet], **subdeaconry** [sʌb'di:kənri], *s.* = SUBDIACONATE.
subdean [sʌb'di:n], *s. Ecc:* sous-doyen *m.*
subdeanery [sʌb'di:nəri], *s.* sous-doyenné *m*, sous-décanat *m.*
subdecuple [sʌb'dekjupl], *a. Mth:* sous-décuple.
subdelegate[1] [sʌb'deligeit], *s.* subdélégué, -ée, sous-délégué, -ée.
subdelegate[2], *v.tr.* subdéléguer.
subdelegation [sʌbdeli'geiʃ(ə)n], *s.* subdélégation *f*, sous-délégation *f.*
sub-derivative [sʌbdi'rivətiv], *s. Ling:* dérivé *m* secondaire.
subdiaconate [sʌbdai'ækəneit], *s. Ecc:* sous-diaconat *m.*
subdiaphragmatic [sʌbdaiəfræg'mætik], *a. Anat:* sous-diaphragmatique.
subdirector [sʌbd(a)i'rektər], *s.* sous-directeur, -trice.
sub-district [sʌb'distrikt], *s. Adm:* sous-division (régionale).
subdivide [sʌbdi'vaid]. **1.** *v.tr.* subdiviser, sous-diviser. **2.** *v.i.* se subdiviser.
subdivisible [sʌbdi'vizibl], *a.* subdivisible.
subdivision [sʌbdi'viʒ(ə)n], *s.* subdivision *f.* **1.** morcellement *m* (du terrain); sous-répartition *f* (d'une action financière); fractionnement *m*; sectionnement *m.* **2.** (*a*) sous-division *f*; fraction *f*; (*b*) *Z: etc:* sous-classe *f*; (*c*) *Navy:* section *f* (d'une flotte).
subdivisional [sʌbdi'viʒən(ə)l], **subdivisionary** [sʌbdi'viʒənri], *a. Adm:* subdivisionnaire.
subdominant [sʌb'dɔminənt], *s. Mus:* sous-dominante *f.*
subdual [səb'dju:əl], *s.* subjugation *f* (d'un peuple rebelle).
subdue [səb'dju:], *v.tr.* **1.** subjuguer, soumettre, réduire, assujettir (une tribu, etc.); maîtriser (un incendie); dompter, réprimer (un mouvement de colère); asservir (ses passions). **2.** adoucir, réduire la force de (la lumière, la chaleur, la voix); assourdir (une couleur); tamiser, assourdir (la lumière); amortir, atténuer (la lumière, la fièvre, la douleur); baisser (la voix).
subdued [səb'dju:d], *a.* **1.** (*of pers.*) sous le coup d'un événement attristant; préoccupé; déprimé. **2.** (*of heat, light, sound, etc.*) adouci; **s. light,** demi-jour *m*; lumière tamisée, atténuée; **s. colours,** couleurs sobres, peu voyantes; **s. conversation,** causerie discrète; conversation *f* à voix basse; **in a s. tone, voice,** (i) d'un ton radouci; (ii) d'une voix étouffée; à voix basse; à mi-voix; à demi-voix; **with an air of s. satisfaction,** avec un air de satisfaction contenue.
subduer [səb'dju:ər], *s.* vainqueur *m*, dompteur *m.*
subduing [səb'dju:iŋ], *s.* **1.** subjugation *f*, réduction *f* (d'une tribu, etc.). **2.** adoucissement *m*, amortissement *m*, atténuation *f*, assourdissement *m* (de la lumière, etc.).
subduple [sʌb'dju:pl], *a. Mth:* (*of progression*) sous-double.
subduplicate [sʌb'dju:plikət], *a. Mth:* sous-doublé; **in s. ratio,** en raison sous-doublée.
subedit [sʌb'edit], *v.tr. & i. Journ:* corriger, mettre au point (un article); *Publ:* être secrétaire à la rédaction.
subediting [sʌb'editiŋ], *s. Journ:* mise *f* au point, *F:* cuisine *f* (d'un article).
subeditor [sʌb'editər], *s.* (*a*) *Journ:* secrétaire *m* de la rédaction; **assistant s.,** secrétaire adjoint; (*b*) *Publ:* rédacteur, -trice.
subeditorial [sʌbedi'tɔ:riəl], *a. Journ: Publ:* (travail) de mise au point.
subepidermal, subepidermic [sʌbepi'də:ml, -mik], *a.* sous-épidermique.
sub-equatorial [sʌbekwə'tɔ:riəl], *a. Geog:* subéquatorial, -aux.
suber ['sju:bər], *s. Bot:* suber *m*; liège *m.*
suberate ['sju:bəreit], *s. Ch:* subérate *m.*
suberic [sju'berik], *a. Ch:* subérique.
suberification [sjuberifi'keiʃ(ə)n], *s. Ch:* subérification *f.*
suberin ['sju:bərin], *s. Ch:* subérine *f.*
Suberites [sjubə'raiti:z], *s. Spong:* subérite *f.*
suberize ['sju:bəraiz], *v.tr. Bot:* subériser.
suberose ['sju:bərous], **suberous** ['sju:bərəs], *a. Bot:* subéreux.
subfamily ['sʌbfæmili], *s. Nat.Hist:* sous-famille *f.*
sub-farm ['sʌbfɑ:m], *s. Hist:* sous-ferme *f.*
subfebrile [sʌb'fi:brail], *a. Med:* subfébrile.
subfeu ['sʌbfju:], *v.tr. A.Jur:* afféager (une terre).
sub-fief ['sʌbfi:f], *s. A.Jur:* arrière-fief *m*, *pl.* arrière-fiefs.
sub-foundation [sʌbfaun'deiʃ(ə)n], *s. Arch:* soubassement *m.*
sub-frame ['sʌbfreim], *s. Aut:* soubassement *m*, faux châssis.
subfusc [sʌb'fʌsk], *a.* (*of clothing, etc.*) sombre.
subgenus, *pl.* **-genera** ['sʌbdʒi:nəs, -dʒenərə], *s. Nat.Hist:* sous-genre *m.*
subglacial [sʌb'gleisiəl, -ʃəl], *a. Geog:* sous-glaciaire.
subgrade ['sʌbgreid], *s. Civ.E:* hérisson *m* (d'une chaussée).
subgranular [sʌb'grænjulər], *a.* subgranulaire, subgranuleux.
sub-group ['sʌbgru:p], *s. Nat.Hist: Mth:* sous-groupe *m.*
subhead[1] ['sʌbhed], **subheading** ['sʌbhediŋ], *s.* sous-titre *m.*
subhead[2], *v.tr.* sous-titrer.
subhepatic [sʌbhe'pætik], *a. Anat:* sous-hépatique.
subhuman [sʌb'hju:mən], *a.* **1.** pas tout à fait humain; moins qu'humain; *F:* **he's positively s.,** il est bête comme ses pieds. **2.** presque humain.
subhyoid(ean) [sʌb'haiɔid, sʌbhai'ɔidiən], *a. Anat:* sous-hyoïdien.
subincision [sʌbin'siʒ(ə)n], *s.* subincision *f.*
subinfeudate [sʌb'infju(:)deit], *v.tr. Jur: A:* (*of fief*) **to be subinfeudated,** mouvoir (**to,** de).
subinfeudation [sʌbinfju(:)'deiʃ(ə)n], *s. Jur:* mouvance *f* (**to,** de); sous-inféodation *f*; afféagement *m.*
subintrant [sʌb'intrənt], *a. Med:* subintrant.
subirrigation [sʌbiri'geiʃ(ə)n], *s.* subirrigation *f.*
subjacent [sʌb'dʒeis(ə)nt], *a. Anat: Bot: Geol: etc:* sous-jacent.
subject[1] ['sʌbdʒikt], *s.* **1.** sujet, -ette (d'un souverain); **British s.,** sujet britannique. **2.** *Gram:* sujet (du verbe); **the logical s.,** le sujet logique. **3.** (*a*) sujet (de conversation, d'un livre, d'un tableau, d'un discours); motif *m* (d'un paysage); objet *m* (d'un litige, de méditation); **a fine s. for a novel,** un beau sujet de roman; **this will be the s. of my next lecture,** cela fera l'objet de ma prochaine conférence; **s. matter,** contenu *m* (d'une lettre); sujet (d'un livre); objet *m* (d'un contrat réel); **literary s. matter,** thèmes *m* littéraires; **a s. picture,** un tableau, une peinture, de genre; **to come to one's s.,** entrer en matière; **to lead s.o. on to the s. of . . .,** porter qn sur le propos de . . .; **to wander from the s.,** sortir de la question; **to come back to our s.,** revenons au sujet, à notre texte, à nos moutons; **while we are on the s.,** à ce propos; pendant que nous sommes sur ce sujet; **enough on this s.,** laissons là cet article; **on the s. of,** au sujet de; **we will now return to the s. of Mr X,** revenons maintenant à M. X; **to change the s.,** parler d'autre chose; changer de sujet; (*abruptly*) rompre les chiens; (*b*) *Mus:* **s. of a fugue,** sujet d'une fugue; demande *f*; (*c*) *Sch:* **what subjects do you teach?** quelles matières enseignez-vous? **4.** (*a*) **the s. (of an experiment),** le sujet (d'une expérience); **to be a s. of experiment,** servir de sujet d'expérience; **to be a s. for pity,** être un sujet, un objet, de pitié; provoquer la pitié; (*b*) *Med:* sujet, malade *mf* (que l'on traite).
subject[2], *a.* **1.** (État, pays) assujetti, soumis (**to,** à); sous la dépendance (**to,** de); **s. provinces,** provinces sujettes; **country held s. by another,** pays tenu en sujétion par un autre; **to be s. to the laws of nature,** être soumis aux lois de la nature; **s. to military laws,** justiciable des tribunaux militaires. **2.** (*liable*) (*a*) sujet (au rhumatisme); porté (à l'envie, etc.); **he is s. to extraordinary whims,** il lui prend des lubies impossibles; **votes of credit s. to delays,** crédits soumis à des retards; **the evils to which we might be s.,** les maux *m* qui pourraient nous atteindre; **gods s. to human passions,** dieux assujettis aux passions humaines; (*b*) **prices s. to 5% discount,** prix bénéficiant d'une remise de 5%; **transaction s. to a commission of 5%,** opération *f* passible d'un courtage de 5%; **s. to stamp duty,** passible du droit de timbre; soumis au timbre; sujet au droit de timbre; **the plan is s. to modifications,** ce projet pourra subir des modifications. **3.** (*conditional*) **s. to . . .,** sauf . . .; sous réserve de . . .; **s. to your consent,** sauf votre consentement; sauf votre agrément; *Com:* **s. to your order,** à votre ordre; **s. to inspection, to ratification,** sous réserve d'inspection, de ratification; **s. to the provisions of . . .,** sous la réserve des provisions de . . .; **s. to alteration, to revision,** sauf nouvel avis; sauf à corriger; sauf correction.
subject[3] [səb'dʒekt], *v.tr.* **1.** soumettre, assujettir, subjuguer (un peuple). **2.** soumettre, exposer, assujettir (**s.o., sth., to sth.,** qn, qch., à qch.); **to s. s.o. to criticism,** critiquer qn; **to s. s.o. to heavy work,** astreindre qn à un labeur; **to s. s.o. to torture,** mettre qn à la torture; **to s. s.o., sth., to an examination,** faire subir un examen à qn; soumettre qch. à un examen; **to be subjected to much criticism,** être en butte à de nombreuses

critiques; **metal subjected to great heat,** métal exposé à une grande chaleur.

subjection [səb'dʒekʃ(ə)n], *s.* sujétion *f,* soumission *f,* assujettissement *m* (**to,** à); **in a state of s.,** dans la sujétion; **to hold, keep, s.o. in s.,** (i) tenir qn sous sa dépendance; (ii) tenir qn en captivité; **to be in s. to s.o.,** être soumis à qn; **to bring into s.,** soumettre, assujettir (qn); soumettre (une province, ses passions).

subjective [sʌb'dʒektiv], *a.* subjectif; *Gram:* **s. genitive,** génitif subjectif; **the s. case,** le cas subjectif, le nominatif.

subjectively [səb'dʒektivli], *adv.* subjectivement.

subjectivism [səb'dʒektivizm], *s. Phil:* subjectivisme *m.*

subjectivist [səb'dʒektivist], *s.* subjectiviste *mf.*

subjectivity [sʌbdʒek'tiviti], *s.* subjectivité *f.*

subjoin [sʌb'dʒɔin], *v.tr.* ajouter, adjoindre (une liste, une explication); **the subjoined details,** les détails ci-joints.

sub judice ['sʌb'dʒu:disi]. *Lt.phr. Jur:* **the case is s. j.,** l'affaire n'est pas encore jugée, est encore devant les tribunaux.

subjugate ['sʌbdʒugeit], *v.tr.* subjuguer, soumettre, assujettir, asservir, réduire (un peuple); dompter (un animal); captiver (ses passions).

subjugation [sʌbdʒu'geiʃ(ə)n], *s.* subjugation *f,* assujettissement *m.*

subjugator ['sʌbdʒugeitər], *s.* asservisseur *m.*

subjunctive [səb'dʒʌŋktiv], *a. & s. Gram:* subjonctif (*m*); **in the s. (mood),** au subjonctif.

sub-king ['sʌbkiŋ], *s. Hist:* sous-roi *m*; petit roi; chef *m.*

subkingdom ['sʌbkiŋdəm], *s. Nat.Hist:* embranchement *m.*

sublacustrine [sʌblæ'kʌstrain], *a.* sous-lacustre.

sublapsarian [sʌblæp'sɛəriən], *s. Rel.H:* infralapsaire *m.*

sublapsarianism [sʌblæp'sɛəriənizm], *s. Rel.H:* infralapsarisme *m.*

sublease[1] ['sʌbli:s], *s.* sous-bail *m, pl.* sous-baux; sous-location *f*; *Husb:* sous-ferme *f.*

sublease[2] [sʌb'li:s], *v.tr.* sous-louer (un appartement); sous-(af)fermer (une terre); (*a*) donner en sous-location, à sous-ferme; (*b*) prendre en sous-location, à sous-ferme.

subleasing [sʌb'li:siŋ], *s.* (*a*) sous-location *f*; (*b*) amodiation *f* (de droits d'exploitation minière).

sub-lessee [sʌble'si:], *s.* **1.** sous-locataire *mf* (à bail); sous-fermier, -ière; sous-preneur *m.* **2.** sous-traitant *m* (d'un travail à l'entreprise).

sub-lessor [sʌb'lesɔr], *s.* sous-bailleur, -bailleresse.

sublet[1] ['sʌblet], *s.* sous-bail *m, pl.* sous-baux; sous-location *f.*

sublet[2] [sʌb'let], *v.tr.* (*p.t. & p.p.* **-let;** *pr.p.* **-letting**) **1.** sous-bailler; sous-louer (un appartement); sous-affermer (une terre). **2.** sous-traiter (un travail à l'entreprise).

sublethal [sʌb'li:θəl], *a.* sublétal, -aux.

subletter [sʌb'letər], *s.* sous-bailleur, -bailleresse.

subletting [sʌb'letiŋ], *s.* **1.** sous-location *f.* **2.** sous-traitance *f.*

sub-librarian [sʌblai'brɛəriən], *s.* sous-bibliothécaire *mf.*

sub-lieutenancy [sʌblef'tenənsi], *s.* **1.** *Navy:* grade *m* d'enseigne de vaisseau. **2.** *Mil: A:* grade de sous-lieutenant.

sub-lieutenant [sʌblef'tenənt], *s.* **1.** *Navy:* enseigne *m* (de vaisseau) première classe. **2.** *Mil: A:* sous-lieutenant *m.*

sublimable [sʌ'blaiməbl], *a. Ch:* sublimable.

sublimate[1] ['sʌblimeit], *s. Ch:* sublimé *m,* sublimat *m*; **corrosive s.,** chlorure *m* mercurique; sublimé corrosif; *Pharm:* **corrosive s. gauze,** gaze *f* au sublimé.

sublimate[2], *v.tr.* **1.** sublimer (un solide). **2.** raffiner, idéaliser (un sentiment, etc.); *Psy:* (*of instinct*) **to become sublimated,** se sublimiser.

sublimating ['sʌblimeitiŋ], **sublimation** [sʌbli'meiʃ(ə)n], *s. Ch: Psy:* sublimation *f*; **sublimating vessel,** sublimatoire *m.*

sublimatory [sʌb'limət(ə)ri], *a. & s. Ch:* sublimatoire (*m*).

sublime[1] [sə'blaim]. **1.** *a.* sublime; (*a*) (pensée *f,* poète *m,* etc.) sublime; (*b*) **s. indifference,** suprême indifférence *f*; **s. impudence,** impudence sans pareille, sans égale; (*c*) **s. muscles,** muscles *m* à fleur de peau. **2.** *s.* **the s.,** le sublime; **to pass from the s. to the ridiculous,** passer du sublime au terre à terre.

sublime[2]. **1.** *v.tr.* (*a*) *Ch:* sublimer (un solide); (*b*) idéaliser (une idée, etc.); rendre sublime. **2.** *v.i. Ch:* (*of solid*) se sublimer.

sublimely [sə'blaimli], *adv.* **1.** sublimement. **2. to be s. unconscious of. . .,** être dans une ignorance absolue de. . ..

sublimeness [sə'blaimnis], *s.* sublimité *f.*

subliminal [sʌb'limin(ə)l], *a. Psy:* subliminal, -aux, subliminaire; **s. advertising,** publicité *f* subliminaire.

sublimity [sʌ'blimiti], *s.* sublimité *f.*

sublinear [sʌb'liniər], *a.* sublinéaire.

sublingual [sʌb'liŋgwəl], *a. Anat:* sublingual, -aux; sous-lingual, -aux.

sublunary [sʌb'lu:nəri], *a.* sublunaire; (corps *m*) terrestre.

subluxation [sʌblʌk'seiʃ(ə)n], *s. Med:* subluxation *f.*

sub-machine-gun [sʌbmə'ʃi:ngʌn], *s.* mitraillette *f.*

submammary [sʌb'mæməri], *a. Anat:* sous-mammaire.

subman, -men ['sʌbmæn, -men], *s.m.* sous-homme.

sub-manager [sʌb'mænidʒər], *s.* sous-directeur *m,* sous-gérant *m,* sous-chef *m.*

sub-manageress [sʌbmænidʒə'res], *s.f.* sous-directrice, sous-gérante.

submarginal [sʌb'mɑ:dʒin(ə)l], *a. Z: Ent:* submarginal.

submarine ['sʌbməri:n]. **1.** *a.* (câble, volcan) sous-marin; *Cin:* **s. shooting,** prise de vues sous-marine; *Bot:* **s. plants,** plantes plongées. **2.** *s.* sous-marin *m*; **fleet s.,** sous-marin d'escadre; **midget, pocket, s.,** sous-marin de poche; **nuclear-powered s., Polaris s.,** sous-marin nucléaire; **missile-armed s.,** sous-marin lance-engins; **s.-launched missile,** missile lancé en plongée.

submariner [sʌb'mærinər], *s.* sous-marinier *m.*

submaxillary [sʌbmæk'siləri], *a. Anat:* sous-maxillaire.

submediant [sʌb'mi:diənt], *s. Mus:* sus-dominante *f.*

submental [sʌb'ment(ə)l], *a. Anat:* submental, -aux.

submentum [sʌb'mentəm], *s. Ent:* sous-menton *m.*

submerge [səb'mə:dʒ]. **1.** *v.tr.* (*a*) submerger, immerger, noyer; plonger, enfoncer, (qch.) sous l'eau; (*b*) inonder, noyer (un champ, etc.). **2.** *v.i.* plonger; (*of submarine*) effectuer sa plongée.

submerged [səb'mə:dʒd], *a.* **1.** (*a*) submergé, noyé; **s. concrete,** béton immergé; **s. turbine,** turbine noyée; *I.C.E:* **the jet is s.,** le gicleur est noyé; **s. vessel,** vaisseau englouti par les flots; **wreck s. at high tide,** épave submergée à (la) haute marée; (*b*) **s. submarine,** sous-marin *m* en plongée; **s. speed,** vitesse *f* en immersion, en plongée (d'un sous-marin); (*c*) **s. reef,** écueil sous-marin; *Bot:* **s. plant, leaf,** plante *f,* feuille *f,* submersible, qui pousse sous l'eau. **2.** *a. & s.* **the s. (tenth),** les déclassés *m,* les nécessiteux *m.*

submergence [səb'mə:dʒəns], *s.* submersion *f*; plongée *f* (d'un sous-marin); affaissement *m* (d'un banc de corail).

submersed [səb'mə:st], *a. Bot:* submergé, submersible.

submersibility [səbmə:si'biliti], *s.* submersibilité *f.*

submersible [səb'mə:sibl], *a. & s.* (bateau *m*) submersible (*m*); sous-marin (*m*).

submersion [səb'mə:ʃ(ə)n], *s.* submersion *f,* plongée *f*; *I.C.E:* **s. of the jet,** noyage *m* du gicleur.

subminiature [sʌb'minjətjər], *a. Elcs:* subminiature.

subminiaturization [sʌbminjətjərai'zeiʃn], *s. Elcs:* subminiaturisation *f.*

submission [səb'miʃ(ə)n], *s.* **1.** (*a*) soumission *f* (à la volonté de qn, à une autorité); résignation *f* (à une défaite, etc.); *Wr:* abandon *m*; **to starve s.o. into s.,** réduire qn par la famine; **the dukes made their s. to Henry IV,** les ducs firent leur soumission à Henri IV; (*b*) docilité *f*; humilité *f.* **2.** soumission (d'une question à un arbitre, d'une signature à un expert); **s. of proofs of identity,** présentation *f* de pièces d'identité. **3.** *Jur:* plaidoirie *f*; **in my submission. . .,** selon la théorie que je soutiens dans ma plaidoirie. . ., selon ma thèse. . ..

submissive [səb'misiv], *a.* (ton, air) soumis, humble, résigné; (personne *f*) docile; **s. to advice,** docile aux conseils donnés.

submissively [səb'misivli], *adv.* d'un ton, d'un air, soumis; avec soumission; humblement; avec docilité; avec résignation.

submissiveness [səb'misivnis], *s.* soumission *f,* docilité *f,* humilité *f*; **s. to the will of God,** soumission à la volonté de Dieu; résignation *f*; **in all s. he owned that. . .,** très humblement il reconnaissait que. . ..

submit [səb'mit], *v.* (**submitted**) **1.** *v.i. & pr.* se soumettre (à qn, au joug, à la volonté de qn, à une force supérieure); se plier (à une nécessité); s'astreindre, s'asservir (à la discipline); se résigner (à un malheur, à supporter qch.); *Wr:* abandonner; **to s. to authority,** se subordonner; **I have submitted to your insolence for an hour,** j'ai supporté votre insolence pendant une heure; **it is for them to s.,** c'est à eux de se soumettre, d'accepter la loi, de plier la tête. **2.** *v.tr.* (*a*) soumettre; **to s. sth. to s.o.,** mettre qch. sous les yeux de qn; **to s. sth. for s.o.'s approval to s.o.'s judgment, to s.o.'s inspection,** soumettre, présenter, qch. à l'approbation de qn, au jugement, à l'inspection, de qn; **to s. proofs of identity,** présenter des pièces d'identité; **to s. a question to a court,** saisir un tribunal d'une question; **to s. the case to the court,** en référer à la cour; (*of bankrupt*) **to s. a statement of one's affairs,** déposer son bilan; (*b*) **to s. that. . .,** représenter, alléguer, que. . .; poser en thèse que. . .; *Jur:* **I s. that there is no case against my client,** je plaide le non-lieu.

sub-model ['sʌbmɔd(ə)l], *s.* sous-modèle *m.*

submucosa [sʌbmju:'kousə], *s. Anat:* tissu sous-muqueux.

submucous [sʌb'mju:kəs], *a. Anat:* sous-muqueux.

submultiple [sʌb'mʌltipl], *a. & s. Mth:* sous-multiple (*m*) (**of,** de).

subnasal [sʌb'neiz(ə)l], *a. Anat:* sous-nasal, -aux.

subnitrate [sʌb'naitreit], *s. Ch:* sous-nitrate *m,* sous-azotate *m.*

subnormal [sʌb'nɔ:məl]. **1.** *a.* subnormal, -aux; (température *f,* etc.) au-dessous de la normale; (*of pers.*) faible d'esprit; **educationally s.,** arriéré. **2.** *s. Geom:* sous-normale *f,* sous-perpendiculaire *f* (d'une courbe).

suboccipital [sʌbɔk'sipit(ə)l], *a. Anat:* sous-occipital, -aux, suboccipital, -aux.

sub-office ['sʌbɔfis], *s. Com:* succursale *f* (d'une banque, etc.); filiale *f*; bureau *m* auxiliaire.

suborbital [sʌb'ɔ:bit(ə)l], *a.* **1.** *Anat:* sous-orbitaire. **2.** *Space:* sous-orbital, -aux, suborbital, -aux.

suborder ['sʌbɔ:dər], *s. Nat.Hist:* sous-ordre *m.*

subordinary [sʌb'ɔ:dinəri], *s. Her:* menue pièce.

subordinate[1] [sə'bɔ:dinət]. **1.** *a.* (*a*) (rang, etc.) inférieur, subalterne; **he plays a s. part,** il joue un rôle accessoire; **s. interests,** intérêts *m* secondaires; *Mil:* **s. commander,** commandant *m* subalterne; (*b*) subordonné (**to,** à); *Gram:* **s. clause,** proposition subordonnée; **syntax of s. clauses,** syntaxe *f* de dépendance; (*c*) *Geol:* sous-jacent; (*d*) **s. (mountain) chain,** rameau *m* (d'une chaîne de montagnes). **2.** *s.* subordonné, -ée; subalterne *mf.*

subordinate[2] [sə'bɔ:dineit], *v.tr.* subordonner (**to,** à).

subordinately [sə'bɔ:dinətli], *adv.* d'une façon secondaire; en sous-ordre; subordonnément.

subordinating [sə'bɔ:dineitiŋ], *a. Gram:* **s. conjunction,** conjonction subordonnante, de subordination.

subordination [səbɔ:di'neiʃ(ə)n], *s.* **1.** subordination *f* (**to,** à). **2.** (*a*) soumission *f* (**to,** à); (*b*) *A:* discipline *f.*

suborn [sʌ'bɔ:n], *v.tr. Jur:* suborner, corrompre, séduire (un témoin).

subornation [sʌbɔ:'neiʃ(ə)n], *s.* subornation *f,* corruption *f,* séduction *f* (de témoins).

suborner [sʌ'bɔ:nər], *s.* suborneur, -euse, corrupteur, -trice (de témoins).

suboxide [sʌb'ɔksaid], *s. Ch:* sous-oxyde *m.*

sub-paragraph [sʌb'pærəgræf], *s.* sous-alinéa *m.*

subperiosteal [sʌbperi'ɔstiəl], *a. Anat:* sous-périosté.

subperitoneal [sʌbperitou'niəl], *a. Anat:* sous-péritonéal.

sub-permanent [sʌb'pə:mənənt], *a.* quasi-permanent; (magnétisme) rémanent.

subperpendicular [sʌbpə:pən'dikjulər], *s.* sous-perpendiculaire.

sub-persistent [sʌbpə'sistənt], *a. Bot:* (organe) marcescent.

subphrenic [sʌb'frenik], *a. Anat:* sous-phrénique.

subphylum [sʌb'failəm], *s. Nat.Hist:* sous-embranchement *m.*

sub-plot ['sʌbplɔt], *s. Lit: Th:* intrigue *f* secondaire.

subpoena[1] [sʌb'pi:nə, sə'pi:nə], *s. Jur:* citation *f,* assignation *f* (de témoins) (sous peine d'amende).

subpoena[2], *v.tr.* (**subpoenaed**) **to s. s.o. to appear,** citer, assigner, qn à comparaître (sous peine d'amende); **to s. s.o. as witness,** assigner qn comme témoin; **to s. a witness,** signifier, faire, donner, envoyer, une assignation à un témoin.

sub-polar [sʌb'poulər], *a.* **1.** (climat *m,* etc.) subpolaire. **2.** *Astr:* au-dessous du pôle céleste.

sub-prefect [sʌb'pri:fekt], *s. Fr.Adm:* sous-préfet *m.*

subprefectorial [sʌbpri:fek'tɔ:riəl], *a.* sous-préfectoral, -aux.

subprefecture [sʌb'pri:fektjuər], *s. Fr.Adm:* sous-préfecture (la fonction ou l'immeuble).

subprioress [sʌb'praiəres], *s.f. Ecc:* sous-prieure.

subprogram(me) [sʌb'prougræm], *s. Cmptr:* sous-programme *m.*

sub-pubic [sʌb'pju:bik], *a. Anat:* sous-pubien.

subquadruple [sʌb'kwɔdrupl], *a. & s. Mth:* sous-quadruple (*m*).

subquintuple [sʌb'kwintjupl], *a. & s. Mth:* sous-quintuple (*m*).

subrace ['sʌbreis], *s. Z:* sous-race *f.*

sub-range [sʌb'reindʒ], *s. Ph: etc:* sous-gammes *f inv.*

sub-rector [sʌb'rektər], *s.m. Sch:* vice-recteur.

subrent [sʌb'rent], *v.tr.* sous-louer; prendre (un appartement, etc.) en sous-location.

subreption [sʌb'repʃ(ə)n], *s. Jur:* subreption *f.*

subrogate ['sʌbrəgeit], *v.tr. Jur:* subroger.

subrogation [sʌbrə'geiʃ(ə)n], *s. Jur:* subrogation *f* (d'un créancier); substitution *f* (de créancier); **act of s.,** acte subrogatoire, subrogateur.

sub rosa ['sʌb'rouzə]. *Lt. adv.phr.* secrètement, confidentiellement; sous le manteau; en cachette; sub rosa.

subroutine [sʌbru:'ti:n], *s. Cmptr:* sous-programme *m*; **nesting subroutines,** sous-programmes emboîtés.

subsalt ['sʌbsɔ:lt], *s. Ch:* sous-sel *m.*

subscale ['sʌbskeil], *s. Metalw:* sous-couche oxydée, d'oxydation.

subscapular [sʌb'skæpjulər], *a. & s. Anat:* sous-scapulaire (*m*).

subscribe [səb'skraib], *v.tr. & i.* **1.** (*a*) souscrire (son nom); signer (un document); souscrire (une obligation); **to s. one's name to a document,** apposer sa signature à un document; signer un document; (*b*) **to s. to an opinion,** souscrire à une opinion; **I cannot s. to that,** je ne peux pas consentir à cela. **2.** (*a*) **to s. ten pounds,** souscrire pour (la somme de) dix livres; donner dix livres; **to s. for a publication, towards a monument,** souscrire à une publication, à un monument; **to s. a thousand francs to a charity,** souscrire mille francs pour une œuvre de charité; *Fin:* **to s. shares,** souscrire des actions; **to s. for ten shares in a company,** souscrire à dix actions d'une société; **to s. to a loan, to an issue,** souscrire à un emprunt, à une émission; **subscribed capital,** capital souscrit; (*b*) **to s. to a newspaper,** (i) s'abonner, prendre un abonnement, à un journal; (ii) être abonné à un journal; **to give up subscribing,** cesser son abonnement; se désabonner; **to s. ten pounds to a club,** payer une cotisation de dix livres à un club; (*c*) *Publ:* **to s. a book,** (i) (*of publisher*) offrir un livre en souscription; (ii) (*of bookseller*) acheter un livre en souscription.

subscriber [səb'skraibər], *s.* **1. s. to, of, a document,** signataire *mf,* souscripteur *m,* d'un document; **the s.,** (i) le soussigné; (ii) le contractant. **2. s. to a charity, for shares, to a new publication,** souscripteur *m* à une œuvre de charité, à des actions, à une nouvelle publication; cotisant *m* d'une œuvre de charité. **3.** abonné, -ée (à un journal, etc.); **telephone s.,** titulaire *mf* d'un abonnement au téléphone; abonné au téléphone; **s. trunk dialling,** (téléphone) automatique *m.*

subscribing [səb'skraibiŋ], *s.* (*a*) souscription *f*; (*b*) abonnement *m.*

subscript ['sʌbskript], *a. Gr.Gram:* (iota) souscrit.

subscription [sʌb'skripʃ(ə)n], *s.* **1.** (*a*) souscription *f* (de son nom); signature *f*; **s. to a document,** souscription d'un document; (*b*) adhésion *f* (**to,** à); approbation *f* (**to,** de); **s. to an article of faith,** adhésion à un article de foi. **2. s. to a charity,** souscription à une œuvre de bienfaisance; **to pay a s.,** verser une cotisation; **to get up a s.,** (i) se cotiser; (ii) demander des cotisations (à une œuvre de charité, etc.); **we got up a s. for the flood victims,** nous avons fait la quête pour les inondés; **monument erected by public s.,** monument élevé par souscription publique; *Fin:* **s. to a loan,** souscription à un emprunt; **s. in cash,** souscription en espèces; **s. by conversion of securities,** souscription en titres; **s. list,** liste *f* de souscription; liste des souscripteurs; **s. form,** bulletin *m* de souscription; **s. dance,** bal *m* par souscription. **3.** abonnement *m* (à un journal, etc.); **to take out a s. to a paper,** s'abonner à un journal; souscrire un abonnement; **to take out a s. to a paper in favour of s.o.,** abonner qn à un journal; **subscriptions to be paid in advance,** on doit s'abonner, payer son abonnement, d'avance; **to withdraw one's s.,** cesser son abonnement; se désabonner; **s. to a club,** cotisation (annuelle) à un cercle, comme membre d'un cercle; **to pay one's s.,** payer sa cotisation (**to,** à). **4.** *Publ:* souscription.

subsection ['sʌbsekʃ(ə)n], *s.* subdivision *f*; paragraphe *m.*

subsellium, *pl.* **-ia** [sʌb'seliəm, -iə], *s.* **1.** *Rom.Ant:* place assise (dans l'amphithéâtre). **2.** *Ecc.Arch:* miséricorde *f* (de stalle).

subseptuple [sʌb'septjupl], *a. & s. Mth:* sous-septuple (*m*).

subsequence ['sʌbsikwəns], *s.* **1.** postériorité *f.* **2.** événement subséquent; conséquence *f.*

subsequent ['sʌbsikwənt], *a.* (chapitre, etc.) subséquent, qui suit ou qui suivra; **at a s. meeting,** dans une séance ultérieure; quand nous nous sommes, quand ils se sont, rencontrés plus tard; **the s. ratification of the treaty,** la ratification ultérieure du traité; **s. to . . .,** postérieur, consécutif, à . . .; *Book-k:* **s. entry,** écriture *f* complémentaire; *Geol:* **s. stream,** cours *m* d'eau subséquent.

subsequently ['sʌbsikwəntli], *adv.* plus tard; par la suite; dans la suite; subséquemment; postérieurement (**to,** à).

subserous [sʌb'si:ərəs], *a. Anat: Med:* sous-séreux.

subserve [sʌb'sə:v], *v.tr.* aider à, favoriser (un but, une fonction).

subservience [sʌb'sə:viəns], **subserviency** [sʌb'sə:viənsi], *s.* **1.** utilité *f* (**to,** à). **2.** *A:* subordination *f* (**to,** à). **3.** soumission *f,* obséquiosité *f,* servilité *f*; **s. to fashion,** assujettissement *m,* asservissement *m,* à la mode.

subservient [sʌb'sə:viənt], *a.* **1.** utile, qui contribue, qui aide (**to,** à); **to make sth. s. to sth.,** faire servir qch. à qch. **2.** subordonné (**to,** à). **3.** obséquieux; servile.

subsextuple [sʌb'sekstjupl], *a. & s. Mth:* sous-sextuple (*m*).

subside [səb'said], *v.i.* **1.** (*a*) (*of sediment*) tomber au fond; se précipiter; (*b*) (*of liquid*) déposer. **2.** (*a*) (*of ground, building*) s'affaisser, se tasser, s'enfoncer, se déniveler; **the ground has subsided,** le terrain s'est abaissé; (*b*) s'effondrer, s'écrouler; **to s. into an armchair,** s'affaler, s'effondrer, dans un fauteuil. **3.** (*of water, etc.*) baisser, s'abaisser, diminuer; (*of blister*) se dégonfler; **the flood is subsiding,** la crue diminue. **4.** (*a*) (*of storm, excitement, fever, tumult, etc.*) s'apaiser, se calmer, tomber; (*of wind*) s'abattre; **the fever is subsiding,** la fièvre commence à céder; (*b*) *F:* (*of pers.*) se taire; fermer le bec.

subsidence ['sʌbsidəns], *s.* **1.** (*a*) subsidence *f*; affaissement *m* (d'un édifice, d'une montagne); dénivellation *f,* dénivellement *m* (d'un pont, d'un bâti); effondrement *m,* tombée *f* (d'un toit de mine); abaissement *m* (du terrain); tassement *m* (du terrain, des fondations); (*b*) décrue *f,* baisse *f* (d'une rivière, etc.); (*c*) *Med:* délitescence *f* (d'une tumeur, etc.); (*d*) apaisement *m* (d'une fièvre, d'une passion). **2.** *Geol:* effondrement; fondis *m,* cloche *f* (dans le terrain).

subsidiarily [səb'sidjərili], *adv.* subsidiairement; en second lieu.

subsidiary [sʌb'sidjəri], *a.* subsidiaire, auxiliaire; **s. coinage,** monnaie *f* d'appoint; *Book-k:* **s. journal,** journal *m* auxiliaire; **s. account,** sous-compte *m*; *Fin:* **s. company,** *s.* **subsidiary,** filiale *f*; *Mil:* **s. troops,** *s.* **subsidiaries,** auxiliaires *m.*

subsidization [sʌbsidai'zeiʃ(ə)n], *s.* fait *m* de fournir une subvention ou des subsides (**of s.o.,** à qn).

subsidize ['sʌbsidaiz], *v.tr.* subventionner (un théâtre, un journal); primer (une industrie, etc.); donner, fournir, des subsides à (un prince, un État); **to be subsidized by the State, the government,** recevoir une subvention de, être subventionné par, l'État; **journalists subsidized out of secret funds,** journalistes qui émargent aux fonds secrets; **subsidized agents,** agents stipendiés; **subsidized industry,** industrie primée; **subsidized troops,** mercenaires *m,* auxiliaires *m.*

subsidy ['sʌbsidi], *s.* **1.** subvention *f*; *Ind:* prime *f*; **s. quota,** contingent *m* subventionnable; *Av: Nau:* **mail s.,** subvention postale. **2.** *Hist:* subside (accordé au souverain, exigé par le souverain, fourni à une puissance alliée).

subsist[1] [səb'sist], *s.* acompte *m* sur le salaire (d'un ouvrier).

subsist[2]. **1.** *v.i.* (*a*) subsister; continuer d'être; **custom that still subsists,** coutume qui existe encore, qui a persisté; (*b*) s'entretenir, vivre (**on,** de); **to s. by begging,** ne vivre que de (la) mendicité; **to s. on charity,** subsister d'aumônes. **2.** *v.tr.* entretenir (un corps d'armée, etc.); assurer la subsistance (des troupes).

subsistence [səb'sistəns], *s.* **1.** existence *f.* **2.** subsistance *f,* entretien *m,* vivres *mpl*; **means of s.,** moyens *m* de subsistance; **a bare s. wage,** un salaire à peine suffisant pour vivre; **s. farming,** autoconsommation *f.* **3. s. allowance, money,** prestation *f*; frais *mpl* de subsistance; allocation *f* de séjour.

subsistent [səb'sist(ə)nt], *a.* **1.** qui existe. **2.** qui existe encore; qui a persisté.

subsoil[1] ['sʌbsɔil], *s.* (*a*) *Geol: etc:* sous-sol *m*; **chalky s.,** tuf *m* calcaire; **to sell soil and s.,** vendre le fonds et le tréfonds; **owner of the (soil and) s.,** tréfoncier *m*; (*b*) *Civ.E:* **s. attachment,** accessoire *m* pour fouiller.

subsoil[2], *v.tr. Agr: etc:* sous-soler (la terre).

subsoiler ['sʌbsɔilər], *s. Civ.E: Agr:* fouilleuse *f*; sous-soleuse *f.*

subsoiling ['sʌbsɔiliŋ], *s.* sous-solage *m.*

subsong ['sʌbsɔŋ], *s. Orn:* chant *m* juvénile.

subsonic [sʌb'sɔnik], *a. Av:* subsonique.

subspace ['sʌbspeis], *s. Mth:* sous-espace *m.*

subspecies [sʌb'spi:ʃi:z], *s. Nat.Hist:* sous-espèce *f.*

substage ['sʌbsteidʒ], *s. Geol:* sous-étage *m.*

substance ['sʌbstəns], *s.* **1.** (*a*) *Phil:* substance *f,* matière *f*; *Ch:* **stable s.,** corps *m* stable; **pure s.,** corps pur; **to throw away the s. for the shadow,** lâcher la proie pour l'ombre; (*b*) *Theol:* substance (spirituelle, corporelle); **the Son is of one s. with the Father,** le Fils est consubstantiel au Père, avec le Père. **2.** substance, fond *m,* essentiel *m* (d'un article, d'un argument, d'une lettre); **I agree in s.,** en substance, je suis d'accord. **3.** solidité *f*; **this material has some s.,** ce tissu a du corps; **paper with some s.,** papier *m* qui a de la main; **book of s.,** livre *m* solide; **his argument has little s.,** son argument n'a rien de solide. **4.** avoir *m,* bien *m,* fortune *f*; **to waste one's s.,** gaspiller, dissiper, son bien; **he's a man of s.,** il a de quoi, du bien.

substandard [sʌb'stændəd], *a.* **1.** (*a*) au-dessous de la moyenne, de la norme; de qualité inférieure; (*b*) *Ins:* **s. risk,** risque douteux. **2.** *Cin:* étroit, (de format) réduit.

substantial [səb'stænʃ(ə)l], *a.* **1.** substantiel, réel. **2.** (point) important; (progrès *m, Com:* réduction *f*) considérable; **s. reasons,** raisons sérieuses; **s. proof,** preuve concluante, valable; **these troops brought immediate and s. aid,** ces troupes ont apporté une aide immédiate et massive; **this makes a s. difference,** cela fait une différence appréciable, sensible. **3.** (*a*) **s. food,** nourriture substantielle; **s. meal,** repas substantiel, copieux, solide; (*b*) (construction *f,* livre *m*) solide; (drap) résistant; **s. furniture,** (i) ameublement *m* solide et riche; (ii) ameublement massif; **man of s. build,** homme bien taillé; homme solide, robuste. **4.** (bourgeois) qui a de quoi, qui a des écus; (maison de commerce) riche, solide, bien assise; **s. landlord,** gros propriétaire.

substantialism [səb'stænʃəlizm], *s. Phil:* substantialisme *m.*

substantialist [səb'stænʃəlist], *s. Phil:* substantialiste *mf.*

substantiality [səbstænʃi'æliti], *s.* **1.** *Phil:* substantialité *f*; existence réelle. **2.** solidité *f* (d'une construction).

substantially [səb'stænʃəli], *adv.* **1.** substantiellement, réellement, effectivement; en substance. **2.** solidement, substantiellement; **s. built,** (homme) bien taillé; (ameublement) solide; **to dine s.,** faire un dîner solide; dîner copieusement. **3.** fortement, considérablement; **this contributed s. to our success,** cela a contribué pour une grande part à notre succès.

substantiate [səb'stænʃieit], *v.tr.* établir, prouver, justifier (une affirmation, etc.); **to s. a charge,** apporter des faits à l'appui d'une accusation; établir une accusation; **to s. a claim,** prouver, établir, le bien-fondé d'une réclamation.

substantiation [səbstænʃi'eiʃ(ə)n], *s.* justification *f* (d'une affirmation); énumération *f* des faits à l'appui (d'une accusation).

substantification [səbstæntifi'keiʃ(ə)n], *s.* substantification *f.*

substantify [səb'stæntifai], *v.tr.* substantifier.

substantival [sʌbstən'taiv(ə)l], *a. Gram:* qui fait fonction de substantif; substantival, -aux.

substantivally [sʌbstən'taivəli], *adv. Gram:* comme nom; substantivement.

substantivate [səb'stæntiveit], *v.tr.* = SUBSTANTIVIZE.

substantivation [səbstænti'veiʃ(ə)n], *s. Gram:* substantivation *f.*

substantive ['sʌbst(ə)ntiv]. **1.** *a.* (*a*) *Gram:* substantif; *A:* **the s. verb,** le verbe substantif; (*b*) (*occ.* [səb'stæntiv]) réel, indépendant; **to raise a colony to the status of a s. nation,** élever une colonie au rang d'une nation indépendante, autonome; **nation that has no s. existence,** nation qui n'a pas d'existence propre; *Jur:* **s. law,** droit positif. **2.** *s. Gram:* substantif *m,* nom *m.*

substantively [səb'stæntivli], *adv. Gram:* substantivement, comme nom.

substantivization [səbstæntivai'zeiʃ(ə)n], *s. Gram:* substantivation *f.*

substantivize [səb'stæntivaiz], *v.tr. Gram:* substantiver (une expression, etc.).

substation ['sʌbsteiʃ(ə)n], *s. El: etc:* sous-station *f*; poste *m* de réseau.

substernal [sʌb'stə:n(ə)l], *a. Anat: etc:* sous-sternal, -aux.

substituent [səb'stitjuənt], *s. Ch:* substituant *m.*

substitute[1] ['sʌbstitju:t], *s.* **1.** (*pers.*) (*a*) remplaçant, -ante, suppléant, -ante; intérimaire *mf*; *Sp:* remplaçant; *Jur: Ecc:* substitut *m*; **as a s. for . . .,** en remplacement de . . ., pour remplacer . . .; **to act as a s. for s.o., sth.,** remplacer qn, se substituer à qn, à qch.; **to find a s. (for oneself),** se faire suppléer; **we can easily find a s.,** nous pouvons facilement vous, le, remplacer; **to be appointed s.o.'s s.,** obtenir la suppléance de qn; être désigné pour remplacer qn; **s. delegate,** remplaçant d'un délégué; (*b*) mandataire *m*; représentant, -ante. **2.** (*a*) (*of foodstuffs, drugs, etc.*)

succédané *m*, factice *m*; ersatz *m*, produit *m* de remplacement; **as a s. for . . .**, comme succédané de . . .; **margarine was used as a s. for butter,** la margarine a remplacé le beurre; **coffee s.,** ersatz de café; (*b*) (*imitation*) contrefaçon *f*; **beware of substitutes,** se méfier des contrefaçons, des imitations *f*; (*c*) *Gram:* (verbe, etc.) suppléant; (*d*) *Cmptr:* **s. character,** caractère *m* de substitution.

substitute[2]. **1.** *v.tr.* (*a*) substituer; *Jur:* subroger; **to s. margarine for butter,** substituer la margarine au beurre; remplacer le beurre par la margarine; **trainees are being substituted for experts,** on remplace les experts par des stagiaires, on substitue des stagiaires aux experts; (*b*) *Jur:* nover (une dette). **2.** *v.i.* **to substitute for s.o.,** remplacer, suppléer, qn; faire la suppléance ou l'intérim de qn.

substitution [sʌbsti'tju:ʃ(ə)n], *s.* (*a*) substitution *f*, remplacement *m*; **s. of margarine for butter,** remplacement du beurre par la margarine; substitution de la margarine au beurre; *Ch:* **s. of chlorine for hydrogen,** substitution du chlore à l'hydrogène; **double s.,** double décomposition *f*; **to react by s.,** agir par substitution; (*b*) *Mth:* substitution; **method of successive substitutions,** méthode *f* des approximations successives; *Jur:* **s. (of debt),** novation *f* de créance; (*c*) *Cmptr:* **address s.,** substitution d'adresse; (*d*) *Jur:* subrogation *f*; **act of s.,** acte subrogateur, subrogatoire.

substrate ['sʌbstreit], *s. Phot: Biol: Cmptr:* substrat *m*.

substratum, *pl.* **-a, -ums** [sʌb'streitəm, -ə, -əmz], *s.* **1.** couche inférieure; sous-couche *f*; *Geol:* substrat(um) *m*; *Agr:* sous-sol *m*; **a s. of truth,** un fond de vérité. **2.** *Phil: Ling:* substrat(um).

substruction [səb'strʌkʃ(ə)n], **substructure** ['sʌbstrʌktjər], *s.* sous-structure *f*, substructure *f*; *Const:* substruction *f*, fondement *m*, jambage *m* (d'un édifice); *Civ.E:* infrastructure *f* (d'un pont roulant, d'une route); **the social s.,** le soubassement social; les bases *f* de la société.

substructural [sʌb'strʌktjərəl], *a.* substructural, -aux.

substyle ['sʌbstail], *s.* soustylaire *f* (d'un cadran solaire).

subsume [səb'sju:m], *v.tr. Phil: etc:* subsumer.

subsumption [səb'sʌmpʃ(ə)n], *s. Phil: etc:* subsomption *f*.

subsystem [sʌb'sistəm], *s.* sous-système *m*.

subtangent [sʌb'tændʒənt], *s. Mth:* sous-tangente *f*.

subtenancy [sʌb'tenənsi], *s.* sous-location *f*.

subtenant [sʌb'tenənt], *s.* sous-locataire *mf*.

subtend [səb'tend], *v.tr. Mth:* sous-tendre (un arc).

subtense [səb'tens], *s. Mth:* sous-tendante *f*, corde *f* (d'un arc).

subterfuge ['sʌbtəfju:dʒ], *s.* **1.** subterfuge *m*; faux-fuyant *m*, *pl.* faux-fuyants; **to resort to s.,** user de subterfuge. **2.** *A:* moyen *m* d'évasion **(from,** de). **3.** *A:* lieu *m* de refuge.

subterranean [sʌbte'reiniən], *a.* souterrain; *Bot:* interrané.

subterrestrial [sʌbte'restriəl], *a. Oc: Geol:* subterrestre.

subtile ['sʌtl], *a. A:* = SUBTLE.

subtility [sʌb'tiliti], *s. A:* = SUBTLETY.

subtilization [sʌtilai'zeiʃ(ə)n], *s.* **1.** *A.Ch: etc:* subtilisation *f*; sublimation *f*. **2.** tendance *f* à subtiliser; raffinement *m*, ergotage *m*.

subtilize ['sʌtila:iz]. **1.** *v.tr.* subtiliser; (*a*) *A.Ch:* sublimer; (*b*) donner de la subtilité à (une pensée, son style); raffiner (son style); *Pej:* alambiquer (sa pensée, son style). **2.** *v.i.* (*a*) *A.Ch:* se subtiliser, se sublimer; (*b*) subtiliser, raffiner; ergoter.

subtilty ['sʌt(ə)lti], *s. A:* = SUBTLETY.

subtitle[1] ['sʌbtaitl], *s. Typ: Cin:* sous-titre *m*; intertitre *m*; **film with English subtitles,** film sous-titré en anglais.

subtitle[2], *v.tr. Cin:* sous-titrer.

subtitling ['sʌbtaitliŋ], *s.* sous-titrage *m*.

subtle [sʌtl], *a.* subtil. **1.** (*a*) (parfum, poison) pénétrant; (*b*) (art, charme) évasif, mystérieux, qui échappe à l'analyse; **s. distinction,** distinction ténue, subtile. **2.** (*a*) (esprit, raisonnement) fin, raffiné. **s. policy,** politique raffinée; **s. observer,** observateur subtil; **s. remark,** observation subtile; **s. device,** dispositif ingénieux; **s. irony,** fine ironie; **you are being too s.,** vous raffinez; (*b*) *A:* **s. fingers,** doigts expérimentés, habiles; (*c*) rusé, astucieux, artificieux, fin; *B:* **now the serpent was more s. than any beast of the field,** or le serpent était le plus fin de tous les animaux des champs.

subtleness ['sʌtlnis], **subtlety** ['sʌt(ə)lti], *s.* **1.** (*a*) subtilité *f* (de l'esprit, d'un raisonnement); raffinement *m*, finesse *f* (d'une politique); (*b*) **subtlety,** subtilité; distinction subtile; **his thought strays into subtleties,** sa pensée se perd dans des subtilités. **2.** subtilité, ténuité *f* (d'une distinction). **3.** *O:* ruse *f*, astuce *f*.

subtly ['sʌtli], *adv.* subtilement; avec finesse; **s. different,** avec une différence à peine perceptible.

subtonic [sʌb'tɔnik], *s. Mus:* note *f* sensible; la sensible.

subtopia [sʌb'toupiə], *s. F: Pej:* la banlieue.

subtotal [sʌb'toutl], *s.* total partiel.

subtract [sʌb'trækt], *v.tr. Mth:* soustraire, retrancher **(from,** de).

subtracter [səb'træktər], *s. Mth: etc:* soustracteur *m*.

subtraction [səb'trækʃ(ə)n], *s. Mth:* soustraction *f* **(from,** de).

subtractive [səb'træktiv], *a. Mth:* soustractif; à soustraire; affecté du signe – ; *Phot:* soustractif.

subtrahend ['sʌbtrəhend], *s. Mth:* quantité *f* à soustraire.

subtriple ['sʌbtripl], *a. Mth:* sous-triple.

subtriplicate [sʌb'triplikeit], *a. Mth:* sous-triplé; **in s. ratio,** en raison sous-triplée.

subtrochanteric [sʌbtrɔkæn'terik], *a. Anat:* sous-trochantérien.

subtropical [sʌb'trɔpik(ə)l], *a.* subtropical, -aux.

subtype ['sʌbtaip], *s. Nat.Hist:* sous-classe *f*.

subulate ['sju:bjuleit], *a. Nat.Hist:* subulé; *Bot:* **s. leaf,** feuille alénée; **with s. leaves,** subulifolié.

subungual [sʌb'ʌŋgwəl], *a. Anat:* sous-ongulaire, sous-unguéal, -aux.

suburb ['sʌbə:b], *s.* banlieue *f*; **in the suburbs,** dans la banlieue, en banlieue; **garden s.,** cité-jardin *f*, *pl.* cités-jardins.

suburban [sə'bə:bən], *a.* (*a*) suburbain; (maison, train) de banlieue; (quartier *m*) excentrique, extra-muros; (*b*) *Pej:* (*of pers.*) à l'esprit étroit et bourgeois.

suburbanite [sə'bə:bənait], *s. F:* banlieusard, -arde.

suburbanization [səbə:bənai'zeiʃ(ə)n], *s.* **the s. of the Thames valley,** le développement de la banlieue dans la vallée de la Tamise.

suburbanize [sə'bə:bənaiz], *v.tr.* **to become suburbanized,** (*of town, etc.*) prendre un air de banlieue; (*of pers.*) devenir banlieusard.

Suburbia [sə'bə:biə]. *Pr.n. F:* la banlieue.

Suburra (the) [ðəsu'bʌrə], *s. Rom. Ant:* la Subur(r)e.

subvariant [sʌb'vɛəriənt], *s. Biol:* sous-variant *m*.

subvariety ['sʌbvəraiəti], *s. Hort: etc:* sous-variété *f*.

subvassal ['sʌbvæs(ə)l], *s. Hist:* sous-vassal, -aux *m*; sous-tenant *m*.

subvention [səb'venʃ(ə)n], *s.* **1.** subvention *f*; *Ind:* prime *f*. **2.** octroi *m* d'une subvention.

subventionary [səb'venʃənəri], *a.* subventionnel.

subversion [səb'və:ʃ(ə)n], *s.* subversion *f* (des lois, de l'État, de la moralité); renversement *m* (d'une religion, d'un État, d'un système).

subversive [səb'və:siv]. **1.** *a.* subversif **(of,** de); **s. of morality,** propre à ébranler la moralité; subversif de toute morale. **2.** *s.* = SUBVERTER.

subversively [səb'və:sivli], *adv.* subversivement.

subvert [səb'və:t], *v.tr.* renverser, subvertir.

subverter [səb'və:tər], *s.* destructeur, -trice, renverseur, -euse (d'un système, d'une religion, d'un gouvernement).

subway ['sʌbwei], *s.* **1.** (*a*) passage, couloir, souterrain; passage en dessous; passage inférieur; souterrain *m*; (*b*) *El:* **cable s.,** tunnel *m* de câbles. **2.** *esp. NAm:* chemin de fer souterrain; le métro.

sub-zero [sʌb'ziərou], *a.* (température) au-dessous de zéro.

succedaneous [sʌksi'deiniəs], *a. Pharm: Ind:* succédané.

succedaneum, *pl.* **-ea** [sʌksi'deiniəm, -iə], *s. Pharm: etc:* succédané *m*.

succeed [sək'si:d], *v.tr. & i.* **1.** (*a*) *v.tr.* **to s. s.o.,** succéder à qn; **George III was succeeded by George IV,** George IV succéda à, fut le successeur de, George III; George III eut pour successeur George IV; **to s. a minister,** prendre la succession d'un ministre; *NAm:* **to s. oneself,** être réélu (à la Chambre, etc.); (*b*) *v.i.* **to s. to the throne, to the Crown,** succéder à, recueillir, la couronne; **a nephew succeeded to the throne,** le trône est échu à un neveu; **to s. to an office, estate,** hériter d'une fonction; hériter une propriété, d'une propriété; **to s. to a business,** prendre la suite des affaires d'une maison; *Jur:* **right to s.,** droits successifs; (*c*) *v.tr.* **day succeeds day,** un jour suit l'autre; les jours se suivent; **winter is succeeded by spring,** le printemps suit l'hiver; après l'hiver vient le printemps. **2.** *v.i.* réussir; atteindre son but; aboutir, arriver; venir à bien; **the plan succeeded,** le projet a réussi; **hard workers always s.,** les grands travailleurs arrivent toujours; *Prov:* **nothing succeeds like success,** rien ne réussit comme le succès; (i) ce qui réussit est toujours approuvé; (ii) un succès en entraîne un autre; **there is no means of succeeding in this,** il n'y a pas moyen d'y aboutir; **how to s.,** le moyen de parvenir; **young man who will s.,** jeune homme qui ira loin, qui arrivera; **to s. in doing sth.,** réussir, parvenir, arriver, à faire qch.; venir à bout de faire qch.

succeeding[1] [sək'si:diŋ], *a.* **1.** suivant, subséquent. **2.** à venir; **all s. ages,** tous les siècles à venir, futurs. **3.** successif; **each s. year,** chaque année successive.

succeeding[2], *s.* succès *m*, réussite *f*.

succentor [sək'sentər], *s. Ecc:* succenteur *m*; sous-chantre *m*, *pl.* sous-chantres.

succenturiate [sʌksen'tju:rieit], *a. Z:* succenturié; *Orn:* **s. lobe,** ventricule succenturié.

success [sək'ses], *s.* **1.** *A:* succès *m*, issue *f* (d'une affaire, etc.); **good s.,** (bon) succès; issue heureuse; **a second attempt met with no better s.,** une seconde tentative n'eut pas plus de succès. **2.** (*a*) succès, réussite *f*; issue heureuse; **we wish you s.,** bonne chance! **to meet with s., to achieve s.,** avoir, obtenir, remporter, du succès; réussir; **man who has achieved s.,** homme qui a abouti; **he is far from having achieved s.,** il est loin d'être arrivé; **his s. was due to chance,** c'est un hasard qu'il ait réussi; **a factor for, in, s.,** un facteur de succès; **what s. did you have in your research?** dans quelle mesure avez-vous réussi dans vos recherches? **without s.,** sans succès; sans y parvenir; **to score a s.,** remporter, avoir, un succès; (*b*) (*of play, venture*) **to be, turn out, a s.,** réussir; (*of play*) avoir du succès; **his visit was not a s.,** sa visite a laissé tout le monde froid; sa visite a été un four; **the portrait is a s.,** le portrait est très réussi; **the evening was a great s.,** la soirée a été très réussie; **it was a huge, great, s.,** c'était un succès fou; **he was a great s. as Hamlet,** il était excellent dans le rôle de Hamlet; **he was not a s. in business,** il n'a pas réussi dans les affaires; **he was a failure as a barrister, but a s. as an officer,** il a fait un mauvais avocat mais un excellent officier; **he was the s. of the evening,** il a été le clou, la joie, de la soirée; **to make a s. of sth.,** réussir qch.; **s. story,** histoire d'un pauvre garçon, d'une pauvre fille, qui a réussi, histoire d'une réussite.

successful [sək'sesful], *a.* (projet) couronné de succès; (résultat) heureux; (portrait) réussi; **s. play,** pièce qui a du succès; **that trick is always s.,** ce truc-là prend toujours; **to bring an operation to a s. conclusion,** mener une opération à bonne fin, à bien; **s. outcome,** succès *m*; **to be entirely s.,** remporter un succès complet, un plein succès; **I believe he will be s.,** je crois (i) à sa réussite, (ii) (*in life*) qu'il réussira; **to be s. in doing sth.,** réussir à faire qch.; **he is s. in everything,** il est toujours heureux; tout lui réussit; il met toujours dans le mille; **a s. business man,** un homme d'affaires réussi, arrivé; **to be s. at the polls,** sortir victorieux du scrutin; **s. candidates,** (i) candidats élus; (ii) *Sch:* candidats reçus; *Mil: Navy:* **the action was s.,** l'engagement a été heureux.

successfully [sək'sesfuli], *adv.* avec succès; heureusement; **he got through s.,** il s'en est tiré avec succès; **to undergo a test s.,** sortir vainqueur d'une épreuve; **to deal s. with a task,** mener une tâche à bonne fin.

succession [sək'seʃ(ə)n], *s.* succession *f*. **1.** (*a*) suite *f*; **in s.,** consécutivement, successivement; à la file; tour à tour; **for two years in s.,** pendant deux années successives, consécutives; pendant deux années de suite; **in close s.,** se succédant de près; à intervalles rapprochés; **in rapid s.,** coup sur coup; *Navy:* **alteration of course (16 points) in s.,** mouvement successif; *Agr:* **the s. of crops,** la rotation des récoltes; **s. states,** états provenant de la dissolution d'un empire; (*b*) série *f*, suite ininterrompue (de victoires, etc.); **after a s. of losses,** après des pertes successives, une série de pertes; **s. of successes and failures,** succession, suite, alternative *f*, de succès et d'échecs; **long s. of kings,** longue suite de rois; **France has had a s. of revolutions,** les révolutions se sont succédé en France; la France a eu à souffrir d'une succession de révolutions; (*c*) *Bot:* succession (d'associations). **2.** (*a*) succession (à la couronne, etc.); **to settle the s.,** régler la succession; désigner le successeur; **at the time of his s. to the throne,** au moment de son avènement *m*; **in s. to s.o.,** en remplacement de qn; *Hist:* **the Wars of S.,** les guerres de succession; **the War of the Austrian S.,** la guerre de la succession d'Autriche; (*b*) *Jur:* succession; **title by s.,** titre *m* par droit de succession; **law of s.,** droit successif; **right of s.,** droits successifs; **by right of s.,** patrimonialement; **s. duties,** droits de succession, de mutation; (*c*) héritage *m*; *Jur:* hoirie *f*; (*d*) lignée *f*; descendance *f*, descendants *mpl*; **left to him and his s.,** légué à lui et à ses descendants; légué à sa postérité; *Ecc:* **apostolic s.,** succession apostolique.

successional [sək'seʃənl], *a.* **1.** *Jur:* successoral, -aux. **2.** successif, qui suit, qui vient après.

successive [sək'sesiv], *a.* successif, consécutif.

successively [sək'sesivli], *adv.* successivement, consécutivement ((i) à mesure; (ii) tour à tour).

successiveness [sək'sesivnis], **successivity**

[səkse'siviti], *s.* successivité *f.*

successor [sək'sesər], *s.* successeur *m* (to, à); **my first car and its successors,** ma première voiture et celles qui lui ont succédé, qui sont venues ensuite, qui l'ont remplacée.

succin ['sʌksin], *s. O:* succin *m*; ambre *m* (jaune).

succinamide [sʌk'sinəmaid], *s. Ch:* succinamide *m.*

succinate ['sʌksineit], *s. Ch:* succinate *m.*

succinct [sʌk'siŋ(k)t], *a.* (récit, etc.) succinct, concis; (écrivain, etc.) succinct.

succinctly [sʌk'siŋ(k)tli], *adv.* succinctement; en peu de mots.

succinctness [sʌk'siŋ(k)tnis], *s.* concision *f,* brièveté *f.*

succinic [sʌk'sinik], *a. Ch:* succinique; *Bio-Ch:* **s. dehydrogenase,** succino-déhydrase *f.*

succinite ['sʌksinait], *s.* **1.** *Miner:* succinite *f.* **2.** succin *m*, ambre *m* jaune.

succinyl ['sʌksinil], *s. Ch:* succinyle *m.*

succory ['sʌkəri], *s. Bot:* chicorée *f* sauvage, herbe-de-capucin *f.*

succotash ['sʌkətæʃ], *s. NAm: Cu:* purée *f* de maïs et de fèves.

Succoth ['sʌkəθ], *s. Jew.Rel:* Succot *m.*

succour[1] ['sʌkər], *s.* **1.** *Lit:* secours *m*, aide *f.* **2.** *Mil: A:* renforts *mpl.*

succour[2], *v.tr. Lit:* secourir, soulager (les pauvres, etc.); aider, assister (qn); venir en aide à (qn), venir à l'aide de (qn).

succuba, *pl.* **-ae** ['sʌkjubə, -i:], **succubus,** *pl.* **-i** ['sʌkjubəs, -ai], *s.* succube *m.*

succubous ['sʌkjubəs], *a. Bot:* (feuille) succube.

succulence, succulency ['sʌkjuləns, -lənsi], *s.* succulence *f.*

succulent ['sʌkjulənt]. **1.** *a.* (*a*) (*of food, etc.*) succulent; (*b*) *Bot:* **s. leaf,** feuille succulente, charnue. **2.** *s. Bot:* plante grasse, succulente.

succumb [sə'kʌm], *v.i.* succomber; céder; **to s. to temptation,** succomber à la tentation; **to s. to odds, to force,** succomber sous le nombre; **to s. to sleep,** céder au sommeil; **to s. to flattery,** se laisser prendre aux flatteries; **to s. to one's injuries,** succomber à, mourir de, ses blessures; **to s. to the heat,** être frappé d'insolation; **we have all succumbed to her charm,** son charme nous a tous conquis.

succursal [sə'kə:s(ə)l]. **1.** *a. Ecc:* **s. church, chapel,** église succursale; succursale *f.* **2.** *s. Com: etc:* succursale.

succuss [sʌ'kʌs], *v.tr. Med:* explorer (le thorax, etc.) par succussion.

succussion [sʌ'kʌʃ(ə)n], *s.* secousse *f*; *esp. Med:* succussion *f.*

such [sʌtʃ], *a. & pron.*

I. *a.* tel, pareil, semblable. **1.** (*a*) **poets s. as Keats, s. poets as Keats,** des poètes tels que Keats; **an actress s. as Sarah Bernhardt,** une actrice telle Sarah Bernhardt; **beasts of prey s. as the lion or the tiger,** des bêtes fauves telles que, comme (par exemple), le lion ou le tigre; **s. men as he and I,** des gens comme lui et moi; **s. countries as Spain,** des pays tels que l'Espagne; **s. books as these are always useful,** les livres de ce genre sont toujours utiles; **s. food is very unwholesome,** les aliments de cette nature sont très malsains; **tiredness s. as one feels on a stormy day,** une lassitude telle qu'on en éprouve par un jour orageux; **s. a plan as, a plan s. as, he would never have thought of himself,** un projet auquel il n'aurait jamais songé par lui-même; **s. a man,** un tel homme; **s. things,** de telles choses; **in s. cases,** en pareils cas; **on s. an occasion,** en semblable occasion; **in s. weather,** (i) par un temps pareil; (ii) par le temps qu'il fait; **why do you ask s. a question!** pourquoi faire une question pareille! **she never sings s. songs,** elle ne chante jamais des chansons de ce genre; **how can you tell s. lies?** comment pouvez-vous mentir de cette façon, mentir de la sorte? **did you ever see s. a thing!** a-t-on jamais vu chose pareille! **all s. errors are to be avoided,** toutes les erreurs de ce genre sont à éviter; **s. transactions need capital,** pour de telles transactions il faut des capitaux; **some s. plan was in my mind,** j'avais dans l'esprit un projet de ce genre; **no s. body exists,** il n'existe aucun corps de cette nature; **there is no s. thing,** cela n'existe pas; **there are no s. things as fairies,** les fées n'existent pas; **if there were no s. thing as money,** si l'argent n'existait pas; **you know there is s. a thing as gratitude,** vous savez que la gratitude existe; **do no s. thing!** n'en faites rien! **I said no s. thing,** je n'ai rien dit de semblable, de la sorte; **no s. thing!** il n'en est rien! il n'en est pas ainsi! pas du tout! pas le moins du monde! *Jur:* **persons guilty of s. offences,** personnes coupables des délits susmentionnés; (*b*) **s. is not my intention,** ce n'est pas là mon intention; **if s. were the case,** à ce compte-là, s'il en était ainsi; **s. is not the case,** il n'en est pas ainsi; il n'en est rien; **s. is our present position,** telle est la situation actuelle; voilà ou nous en sommes; *O:* **s. is the world!** ainsi va le monde! **the village boasts a bus, s. as it is,** le village a un autobus, si l'on peut dire; **you may use my typewriter, s. as it is,** vous pouvez vous servir de ma machine à écrire, bien qu'elle ne vaille pas grand-chose. **2. on s. (and s.) a day in s. (and s.) a place,** tel jour en tel endroit; **we are told that on s. a date he lived at number so and so of s. and s. a street,** on nous dit qu'à une certaine date il demeurait à numéro tant de telle et telle rue; **your letter of s. and s. a date,** votre lettre de tant; **s. and s. results will follow s. and s. causes,** tels ou tels résultats suivront telles ou telles causes; **s. a one,** un tel, une telle. **3. he arranges things in s. a way that he is free on Saturdays,** il s'arrange de manière, de façon, qu'il soit libre les samedis; **he speaks in s. a way that I don't understand him,** il parle de telle sorte que je ne le comprends pas; **her kindness was s. as to make us feel ashamed,** sa bonté était telle que nous en étions confus; **his pain was s. that he fainted,** telle était sa douleur qu'il s'est évanoui; **he would fell you with one blow, s. is his strength,** il vous assommerait d'un coup de poing, tant il est fort; **he bore himself with s. gallantry as to deserve special mention,** il s'est conduit avec une bravoure qui lui a valu une citation; **to take s. steps as shall be considered necessary,** prendre toutes mesures qui paraîtront nécessaires; **s. conversation as took place during the meal came from their host,** le peu de conversation qui avait lieu pendant le repas, c'était leur hôte qui en faisait les frais; **until s. time as is convenient to me,** jusqu'à ce que cela me convienne. **4.** (*intensive*) **s. large houses,** de si grandes maisons; **I don't want s. big potatoes,** je ne veux pas de pommes de terre aussi grandes que celles-ci; **I had never heard s. good music,** je n'avais jamais entendu d'aussi bonne musique; **s. a clever man,** un homme si habile; **s. courage,** un tel courage; tant de courage; **s. filthy language,** de si vilains mots; **I am not s. a simpleton as to believe you,** je ne suis pas assez simple pour vous croire; **s. an industrious person as yourself,** une personne aussi travailleuse que vous; **it was s. a long time ago,** il y a si longtemps de cela; **he is s. a liar,** il ment tellement; il est si menteur, tellement menteur; **s. an enjoyable day,** une journée si agréable; **we had s. a good time,** on s'est si bien amusé(s); **I never came across s. a fool,** je n'ai jamais vu un imbécile de son acabit; **it's s. a pity he can't come,** je regrette bien qu'il ne puisse pas venir; **don't be in s. a hurry,** ne soyez pas si pressé; ce n'est pas la peine de tant vous presser; **there's s. a draught down my back!** si vous sentiez le courant d'air qui me donne dans le dos! **you gave me s. a fright!** vous m'avez fait une peur! **I had s. a fright!** j'ai eu tellement peur! j'ai eu une peur bleue! **I've got s. a thirst!** j'ai une de ces soifs! **I wrote him s. a letter,** je lui ai écrit une de ces lettres; **you do use s. expressions!** vous avez de ces expressions! **he has s. ideas!** il a de ces idées!

II. *pron.* **1. down with traitors and all s.,** à bas les traîtres et tous ceux qui leur ressemblent; **he enjoys cakes, ices and s.,** il mange avec plaisir des gâteaux, des glaces et des choses de ce genre; **dance bands and s.,** orchestres de danse et choses dans ce goût-là. **2.** (*a*) *O: & Lit:* **s. only who have lived in that country can appreciate it,** seuls ceux qui ont vécu dans ce pays savent l'apprécier; **let (all) s. as are of my opinion lift up their hands,** que (tous) ceux qui sont de mon opinion lèvent la main; **that's not for s. as you,** cela n'est pas pour quelqu'un comme toi; **I have not many, but I will send you s. as I have,** je n'en ai pas beaucoup, mais ce que j'en ai je vous les enverrai. **3. he was a very gallant man and well known as s.,** il était très crâne et connu pour tel; **he was a foreigner and was regarded as a s.,** il était étranger et était considéré comme tel; **history as s. is too often neglected,** l'histoire en tant que telle est trop souvent négligée.

suchlike ['sʌtʃlaik], *F:* **1.** *a.* semblable, pareil; de ce genre; **did you ever see s. going-on!** a-t-on jamais vu la pareille! **2.** *pron.* **beggars, tramps, and s.,** mendiants, chemineaux et autres gens de la sorte, de cette espèce; **her income left her a good margin for concerts, theatres, and s.,** ses revenus lui laissaient de la marge pour concerts, théâtres, et autres choses de ce genre.

suck[1] [sʌk], *s.* **1.** (*a*) action *f* de sucer; **to have, take, a s. at a sweet,** sucer, suçoter, un bonbon; **to have, take, a s. at one's pipe,** sucer sa pipe; tirer sur sa pipe; (*b*) *Hyd.E:* succion *f,* aspiration *f* (d'un déversoir, d'une pompe). **2. to give a child s.,** donner à téter, la tétée, à un enfant; allaiter un enfant; donner le sein à un enfant; **child at s.,** enfant au sein. **3.** *F:* petite gorgée (de boisson). **4.** *Sch: P: O:* **sucks,** bonbons *m.* **5.** *P:* (*a*) **what a s.(-in)!** quelle attrape! (*b*) **sucks (to you)!** je me fiche de vous!

suck[2], *v.tr. & i.*

I. *v.tr.* **1.** sucer (le lait, etc.); (*of bees*) sucer, butiner (les fleurs); (*of flowers*) absorber, boire (la rosée); **to s. the marrow out of a bone,** sucer la moelle d'un os; (*of horse*) **to s. wind,** avaler de l'air. **2.** (*a*) sucer (la mamelle, un os, etc.); sucer, suçoter (une orange, des bonbons); mordiller (le coin de son mouchoir); sucer, tirer sur (sa pipe); **to s. one's fingers, one's teeth,** se sucer les doigts, les dents; **to s. one's thumb,** sucer son pouce; *P:* **s. it and see!** essaie et tu verras! **to s. an orange dry,** sucer une orange jusqu'à la dernière goutte; *Fig:* **to s. s.o. dry,** sucer qn jusqu'à la moelle, jusqu'au dernier sou; vider qn; **to s. a raw egg,** gober un œuf; *F:* **go and teach your grandmother to s. eggs,** c'est Gros-Jean qui en remontre à son curé; ce n'est pas aux vieux singes qu'on apprend à faire des grimaces; on n'apprend pas aux poissons à nager; **to s. s.o.'s brains,** exploiter les connaissances, l'intelligence, de qn; (*b*) *Med:* **to s. a wound,** sucer une plaie; pratiquer la succion d'une plaie. **3. the dust is sucked into the bag,** la poussière est aspirée dans le sac; *Fig:* **to get sucked into a conspiracy,** être entraîné dans une conspiration. **4.** *Nau:* affranchir (une pompe).

II. *v.i.* **1.** (*of child, etc.*) sucer le lait; téter (le lait); **the child won't s.,** l'enfant ne prend pas le sein; *Lit:* **where the bee sucks,** là où butine l'abeille. **2. to s. at sth.,** sucer, suçoter (un bonbon, etc.); sucer, tirer sur (sa pipe). **3.** (*of pump*) super; (*of ship's pump*) être franche. **4.** *NAm: F:* **to s. around s.o.,** tourner autour de qn (d'importance); **candidates sucking around for votes,** candidats à la recherche de voix.

III. (*compound verbs*) **1. suck down,** *v.tr.* engloutir; entraîner au fond; **whirlpool that sucks down boats,** tourbillon qui attire les canots au fond; **to be sucked down by a sinking ship,** être aspiré par un navire en train de sombrer.

2. suck in, *v.tr.* (*a*) sucer, absorber; aspirer, avaler; absorber (des connaissances); (*of air pump*) aspirer (l'air); **to s. in the morning air,** aspirer, humer, l'air frais du matin; **to s. in sth. with one's mother's milk,** sucer avec le lait, recevoir dès l'enfance, une doctrine, une qualité, etc.; **to s. in s.o.'s words,** boire les paroles de qn; (*b*) engloutir (dans un tourbillon); (*c*) faire rentrer (ses joues); (*d*) *P: O:* duper, rouler, refaire (qn); **you got sucked in,** on vous a refait.

3. suck out, *v.tr.* sucer (du jus, etc.); tirer (qch.) en suçant; **to s. out the poison from the wound,** aspirer, sucer, le poison de la blessure.

4. suck up. (*a*) *v.tr.* sucer, aspirer, pomper (un liquide, de l'air); (*of sponge, etc.*) **to s. up water,** absorber, boire, l'eau; s'imbiber d'eau; (*b*) *P: v.i.* **to s. up to s.o.,** faire (de) la lèche à qn; lécher les bottines, *V:* le cul, à qn.

sucker[1] ['sʌkər], *s.* **1.** suceur, -euse. **2.** animal *m* qui tette; *esp.* (i) baleineau *m* qui tette encore; (ii) cochon *m* de lait. **3.** (*a*) *P:* gogo *m*, poire *f,* niais *m*, blanc-bec *m*, *pl.* blancs-becs; **to be a s. for sth.,** raffoler de qch.; (*b*) écornifleur, -euse; parasite *mf.* **4.** (*a*) *Nat.Hist:* suçoir *m* (de pou, etc.); ventouse *f* (de sangsue, pieuvre, etc.); (*b*) **(rubber fixing) s.,** ventouse (de tapis antidérapant de baignoire, etc.); (*c*) piston *m* (de pompe aspirante); (*d*) *Sug.-R:* sucette *f* (pour faire écouler le sirop). **5.** *Ich:* (i) échénéide *m*; *F:* rémora *m*; **(Cornish) s.,** lépadogastre *m*; *F:* porte-écuelle *m inv*; (ii) *NAm:* poisson suceur; catostomide *m.* **6.** *F:* bonbon *m.* **7.** *Hort:* rejeton *m*, rejet *m* (d'une plante); bion *m*, accru *m*; drageon *m*, surgeon *m*; talle *f* (d'arbre); œilleton *m* (d'artichaut, d'ananas); stolon *m*, stolone *f* (de fraisier); **stem s.,** bouture *f*; (*of tree*) **to throw out suckers,** drageonner, surgeonner; pousser des drageons, des surgeons; taller; **throwing out of suckers,** tallage *m*, drageonnement *m*; **to plant the suckers of artichokes,** bionner des artichauts.

sucker[2]. **1.** *v.tr.* (*a*) *Hort:* enlever les drageons, surgeons, de; ébouturer (un arbre); enlever les branches gourmandes, les gourmands de (qch.); (*b*) *NAm: P:* duper, rouler, refaire (qn). **2.** *v.i.* (*of bush*) rejetonner; (*of tree*) pousser des drageons, surgeons; drageonner, surgeonner, taller.

suckering ['sʌkəriŋ], *s.* drageonnement *m*; tallage *m.*

sucking[1] ['sʌkiŋ], *a.* **1.** (animal) qui tette, qui n'est pas encore sevré; **s. calf, pig,** veau *m*, cochon *m*, de lait; **s. child,** enfant *mf* à la mamelle; nourrisson *m*; **s. dove,** jeune colombe *f* (qui n'a pas encore quitté sa mère). **2.** *Ich:* **s. fish** = SUCKER[1] 5. **3.** *NAm: Ent:* **s. lice,** anoploures *m.*

sucking[2], *s.* **1.** succion *f*; aspiration *f*; **s. motion,** mouvement *m* de succion; **s. tube,** tuyau aspirant, d'aspiration; *Nat.Hist:* **s. disc,** ventouse *f* (de céphalopode, etc.). **2. sucking up:** (*a*) aspiration (d'un liquide, etc.); (*b*) *P:* flagornerie *f.*

suckle ['sʌkl], *v.tr.* (*a*) allaiter (un enfant, un petit); donner le sein, donner à téter, à (un enfant); (*b*) *Lit:* **suckled in luxury,** élevé dans le luxe.

suckling[1] ['sʌkliŋ], *s.* allaitement *m.*

suckling[2], *s.* (*a*) nourrisson, -onne; enfant *mf* au sein; (*b*) jeune animal *m* qui tette encore; **s. pig,** cochon *m* de lait.

sucrase ['s(j)u:kreis], *s. Ch:* sucrase *f,* invertase *f.*

sucrate ['s(j)u:kreit], *s. Sug.-R:* sucrate *m.*

sucrose ['s(j)u:krous], *s. Ch:* saccharose *m,* hexobiose *f.*

suction ['sʌkʃ(ə)n], *s.* succion *f*; aspiration *f* (de l'eau dans une pompe, etc.); aspiration, appel *m* (d'air); *I.C.E:* **s. of fresh gas,** appel de gaz frais; **to adhere by s.,** faire ventouse; *Ch:* **to filter with s.,** filtrer dans le vide, à la trompe; **s. apparatus,** appareil aspirateur; *Ch:* **s. flask,** fiole *f* à vide; *Ind:* **s. conveyor,** aspirateur *m*; **s. box,** (i) *Hyd.E:* chambre *f* d'aspiration; (ii) *Paperm:* caisse aspirante; *F:* sucette *f* (sous la toile métallique); **s. pipe,** *Hyd.E:* tuyau *m,* tubulaire *f,* d'aspiration, de prise de vide; *I.C.E:* exhausteur *m*; **s. valve,** clapet *m* d'aspiration (d'une pompe, etc.); *Hyd.E:* **s. head, lift,** (i) hauteur *f* d'aspiration (d'une turbine); (ii) hauteur à l'aspiration (pour une pompe); *I.C.E:* **s. stroke,** temps *m* de l'aspiration; *Min:* **s. shaft,** puits *m* d'appel d'air; *Aut: etc:* **s.-grip ashtray,** cendrier *m* à ventouse; **s. cup,** ventouse *f.*

suctorial [sʌk'tɔ:riəl], *a. Nat.Hist:* suceur; **s. organ,** organe suceur, ventousaire; suçoir *m.*

sudamina [s(j)u:'dæminə], *s.pl. Med:* sudamina *mpl* (dans la fièvre typhoïde).

Sudan (the) [ðəsu:'dɑ:n, -'dæn], *Pr.n. Geog:* le Soudan; *Hist:* **the Anglo-Egyptian S.,** le Soudan anglo-égyptien.

Sudanese [su:də'ni:z]. *Geog:* **1.** *a.* soudanais, soudanien. **2.** *s.* Soudanais, -aise; Soudanien, -ienne.

sudarium [s(j)u:'dɛəriəm], *s. Rel.Hist:* suaire *m*; véronique *f.*

sudation [s(j)u:'deiʃ(ə)n], *s. Med: etc:* sudation *f.*

sudatorium, *pl.* **-ia** [s(j)u:də'tɔ:riəm, -iə], *s. Rom.Ant:* sudatoire *m*; bains *mpl* de vapeur (des thermes).

sudatory ['s(j)u:dət(ə)ri]. **1.** *a.* sudatoire. **2.** *s.* = SUDATORIUM.

sudd [sʌd], *s.* amas encombrant de végétation aquatique (dans le Nil blanc).

sudden ['sʌdn]. **1.** *a.* (*a*) soudain, subit; **s. hush,** silence subit; **s. shower,** averse inopinée, intempestive; **s. death,** (i) mort soudaine, (ii) *Sp: etc:* (*deciding game*) la belle; (iii) *Sp: etc:* jeu pour décider d'un match nul (dans lequel celui qui marque le premier point est le gagnant); **the best of three or s. death?** en deux manches ou coup sec? **this is rather s.,** je ne m'y attendais pas; (*b*) (mouvement) brusque; **s. turning,** tournant *m* brusque; **very s. stop,** arrêt brutal; **to take a s. decision,** prendre une brusque résolution; **he's very s. in his movements,** ses mouvements sont très brusques. **2.** *adv.phr.* **all of a s.,** *A: & Lit:* **on a s.,** soudain, subitement; tout à coup.

suddenly ['sʌdənli], *adv.* (*a*) soudain, soudainement, subitement; tout à coup; subito; **he died s.,** il est mort soudainement; sa mort a été soudaine; **s. the door opened,** soudain la porte s'est ouverte; (*b*) brusquement; **he stood up s.,** il s'est mis debout brusquement; **the door s. opened,** la porte s'est ouverte brusquement.

suddenness ['sʌdənnis], *s.* (*a*) soudaineté *f*; **with startling s.,** en coup de théâtre; (*b*) brusquerie *f* (d'une résolution, etc.).

Sudeten [su'deitən], *a. Geog:* **the S. Mountains,** les (monts *m*) Sudètes *m*; *Hist:* **the S. Germans,** les Allemands des Sudètes.

sudoriferous [s(j)u:də'rifərəs], **sudoriparous** [s(j)u:də'ripərəs], *a.* (glande) sudorifère, sudoripare.

sudorific [s(j)u:də'rifik], *a. & s. Med:* sudorifique (*m*), diaphorétique (*m*).

Sudra ['su:drə], *s.* (*in India*) s(h)oudra *m,* çoudra *m.*

suds [sʌdz], *s.pl.* **1.** **(soap) s.,** eau *f* de savon; lessive *f* (qui mousse). **2.** *NAm: P:* bière moussante.

sue[1] [s(j)u:]. **1.** *v.tr. Jur:* (*a*) **to s. s.o. at law,** intenter un procès à qn; poursuivre qn en justice; appeler, contraindre, traduire, qn en justice; actionner qn; agir (civilement) contre qn; se porter partie civile contre qn; porter plainte, donner plainte, déposer une plainte, contre qn; **to s. s.o. for damages,** poursuivre qn en dommages-intérêts; **liable to be sued,** assignable; **to s. s.o. for civil injury,** se porter partie civile (dans une affaire au criminel); **to s. s.o. for infringement of patent,** assigner qn en contrefaçon; (*b*) **to s. out a pardon for s.o.,** obtenir la grâce de qn (à la suite d'une requête). **2.** *v.i.* (*a*) **to s. for a separation,** plaider en séparation; **to s. for libel,** attaquer en diffamation; **to s. in a civil action,** ester en justice; **to s. in forma pauperis,** intenter une action avec assistance judiciaire; (*b*) **to s. for a writ,** obtenir une ordonnance de la cour; (*c*) **to s. to s.o. for sth.,** solliciter qch. de qn; *O:* **to s. for a woman's hand,** solliciter, demander, une femme en mariage; demander la main d'une femme; (*d*) **to s. for peace,** demander la paix.

sue[2]. *Nau:* **1.** *v.tr.* laisser (un navire) au sec; **sued up,** au sec, à sec. **2.** *v.i.* (*of ship*) **to s. (up),** déjauger; **sued two feet,** déjaugé de deux pieds.

Sue[3]. *Pr.n.f.* (*dim. of Susan*) Suzette, Suzon.

sueable ['s(j)u:əbl], *a.* poursuivable en justice.

suede, suède[1] [sweid], *s. Leath:* (i) (*for shoes*) daim *m*; (ii) (*for gloves, etc.*) peau *f* de suède; peau suédée; agneau suédé; suède *m*; **s. gloves,** gants *m* de suède; **s. shoes,** souliers *m* en daim; **s. cloth,** suédine *f.*

suede, suède[2], *v.tr. Tan:* finir (un cuir) en daim, en peau de suède.

suedette, suedine [swei'det, -'di:n], *s. Tex:* suédine *f.*

suet ['s(j)u:it], *s. Cu:* graisse *f* de rognon; gras *m* de rognon; **beef s.,** graisse (de rognon) de bœuf; **s. pudding,** pouding fait avec de la farine et de la graisse de bœuf, roulé dans une serviette et cuit à l'eau; *F:* **s. face,** visage (i) pâle, terreux, blafard, (ii) adipeux.

Suetonius [swi(:)'touniəs]. *Pr.n.m. Lt.Lit:* Suétone.

suety ['s(j)u:iti], *a.* qui ressemble à la graisse de rognon; qui a un goût de graisse, contient beaucoup de graisse; *F:* **s. face,** visage (i) pâle, terreux, blafard, (ii) adipeux.

Suevi ['swi:vai], *s.m.pl. Hist:* Suèves.

Suevian ['swi:viən]. *Hist:* **1.** *a.* suève. **2.** *s.* Suève *mf.*

Suez ['sju(:)iz, 'su(:)iz]. *Pr.n. Geog:* Suez; **the S. Canal,** le canal de Suez.

suffer ['sʌfər], *v.*

I. *v.tr.* **1.** éprouver, subir, souffrir (une perte, etc.); endurer, ressentir (une douleur); subir (une peine, etc.); **to s. hunger,** souffrir, pâtir, la faim; **to s. defeat,** essuyer, subir, une défaite; **to s. death, the death penalty,** subir la peine de mort. **2.** permettre, supporter, tolérer; souffrir; **he does not s. fools gladly,** il ne peut pas supporter les imbéciles; *Lit:* **to s. sth. to be done, to s. s.o. to do sth.,** tolérer, souffrir, qu'on fasse qch.; *B:* **s. little children to come unto me,** laissez venir à moi les petits enfants.

II. *v.i.* **1.** (*of pers.*) (*a*) souffrir; **to s. acutely,** souffrir cruellement; **to s. (greatly) from rheumatism,** souffrir (beaucoup) de rhumatismes; être affligé de rhumatismes; **to s. for one's misdeeds,** supporter la conséquence de ses méfaits; **if I eat lobster I am sure to s. for it,** si je mange du homard j'en pâtirai à coup sûr; **you'll s. for it,** il vous en cuira; (*b*) *O:* subir la peine de mort; souffrir le martyre. **2.** **to s. from neglect,** pâtir d'un manque de soins; **country suffering from labour troubles,** pays en proie à l'agitation ouvrière; **author who suffers from the fact that he is still alive,** auteur qui a le démérite d'être vivant; **his good name has suffered,** il a souffert dans sa réputation. **3.** subir une perte, un dommage; **the battalion suffered severely,** le bataillon a essuyé de fortes pertes, a été fort malmené; **the engine suffered severely,** la machine a grandement souffert, a éprouvé de grands dommages; **the vines have suffered from the frost,** les vignes ont souffert de la gelée; **this rose suffers from mildew,** ce rosier est sujet au mildiou.

sufferance ['sʌf(ə)rəns], *s.* **1.** tolérance *f,* souffrance *f* (**of,** de); permission *f* (tacite); **the s. of evil,** la souffrance du mal; *esp.* **on s.,** par tolérance; **children are admitted on s.,** l'entrée des enfants est tolérée; *Cust:* **bill of s.,** lettre *f* d'exemption des droits de douane dans un entrepôt déterminé. **2.** *A:* (*a*) endurance *f,* patience *f*; *A:* souffrance *f*; (*b*) douleur *f,* misère *f.*

sufferer ['sʌfərər], *s.* (*a*) **to be a s. from ill health,** souffrir d'une mauvaise santé; **sufferers from asthma, migraine,** personnes sujettes à l'asthme, la migraine; **sufferers from a calamity,** victimes *f* d'une calamité; sinistrés *m*; (*from accident*) accidentés *m*; (*from fire*) incendiés *m,* sinistrés; (*b*) *A:* (*person undergoing torture*) patient *m.*

suffering[1] ['sʌfəriŋ], *a.* **1.** *A:* (*longsuffering*) (*a*) patient, endurant; (*b*) longanime, indulgent. **2.** souffrant; qui souffre.

suffering[2], *s.* **1.** *A:* (*longsuffering*) (*a*) patience *f,* endurance *f*; (*b*) longanimité *f,* indulgence *f.* **2.** (*a*) souffrance *f*; **cheerful in spite of his s.,** gai malgré ses souffrances; (*b*) **sufferings,** souffrances, douleurs *f.*

suffete ['sʌfi:t], *s. A.Hist:* suffète *m.*

suffice [sə'fais]. **1.** *v.i.* suffire; **your word will s.,** votre parole suffit; **that will s. for me,** cela me suffira; **to s. to a purpose,** suffire, être suffisant, pour l'objet en vue; **that suffices to prove it,** cela suffit pour le prouver; **s. it to say that I had nothing out of it,** qu'il (nous) suffise de dire que, *F:* suffit que, je n'en ai rien obtenu. **2.** *v.tr.* suffire à (qn); être suffisant pour (qn); **one meal a day suffices him,** un repas par jour lui suffit; il lui suffit d'un repas par jour; **an apology will not s. him,** il ne se contentera pas d'un mot d'excuses.

sufficiency [sə'fiʃ(ə)nsi], *s.* (*a*) suffisance *f*; **to have a s. of sth.,** avoir assez de qch.; (*b*) fortune suffisante; aisance *f*; **to have a s.,** jouir de l'aisance; être dans l'aisance; **to have no more than a s., a bare s.,** avoir tout juste de quoi vivre.

sufficient [sə'fiʃ(ə)nt]. **1.** *a.* assez, suffisant; **this sum is s. for the journey,** cette somme est suffisante, suffit, pour les frais de voyage; **lack of s. food,** insuffisance *f* d'alimentation; **this is s. to feed them,** cela suffit pour les nourrir; **he has s. courage for anything,** son courage est suffisant pour n'importe quoi; **a hundred francs will be s.,** j'aurai assez de cent francs; **one light will be s.,** il suffira d'une lampe; **there was just s. water for drinking,** il y avait juste assez d'eau pour boire; **isn't my word s.?** n'est-ce pas assez de ma parole? est-ce que ma parole ne vous suffit pas? *Prov:* **s. unto the day is the evil thereof,** à chaque jour suffit sa peine, sa tâche, son mal; à nouvelles affaires nouveaux conseils; *Phil:* **s. reason,** raison suffisante; *Theol:* **s. grace,** grâce suffisante. **2.** *s.* assez; *O:* **have you s. of it?** en avez-vous assez? **have you had s. (to eat)?** avez-vous mangé à votre faim? êtes-vous rassasié? **I've had s.,** cela me suffit.

sufficiently [sə'fiʃ(ə)ntli], *adv.* suffisamment, assez; **I'm not s. influential to help you,** je n'ai pas assez d'influence pour vous aider; **he's not s. a friend of mine for me to suggest it,** il n'est pas assez de mes amis pour que je puisse le lui suggérer.

sufficing [sə'faisiŋ], *a.* suffisant (**for,** pour).

sufficingly [sə'faisiŋli], *adv.* suffisamment; d'une manière satisfaisante.

suffix[1] ['sʌfiks], *s.* **1.** *Gram:* suffixe *m.* **2.** *Mth: Cmptr:* indice inférieur.

suffix[2] ['sʌfiks, sʌ'fiks], *v.tr. Gram:* suffixer; pourvoir d'un suffixe.

suffixal ['sʌfiksəl], *a. Gram:* suffixal, -aux.

suffixation [sʌfik'seiʃ(ə)n], *s. Gram:* suffixation *f.*

suffixed ['sʌfikst, sʌ'fikst], *a. Gram:* (lettre, particule) suffixe.

suffocate ['sʌfəkeit]. **1.** *v.tr.* (*a*) (*to death*) étouffer (qn); (*b*) (*of smell, etc.*) étouffer, suffoquer, asphyxier (qn); **in a suffocated voice,** d'une voix étranglée; (*c*) *Fig:* **all signs of initiative were suffocated,** toute indication d'initiative était étouffée. **2.** *v.i.* étouffer, suffoquer (**with rage,** etc., de colère, etc.).

suffocating ['sʌfəkeitiŋ], *a.* suffocant, étouffant, asphyxiant; **it's s. (in) here,** on étouffe ici.

suffocatingly [sʌfə'keitiŋli], *adv.* **it was s. hot,** il faisait chaud à étouffer; on étouffait.

suffocation [sʌfə'keiʃ(ə)n], *s.* suffocation *f,* étouffement *m,* asphyxie *f*; **it was hot to s.,** il faisait chaud à étouffer.

suffocative ['sʌfəkeitiv], *a.* qui suffoque; *esp. Med:* **s. catarrh,** catarrhe suffocant; bronchite *f* capillaire.

suffragan ['sʌfrəgən], *a. & s. Ecc:* **s. (bishop), (bishop) s.,** (évêque) suffragant (*m*); **s. see,** évêché suffragant (**to,** de).

suffrage ['sʌfridʒ], *s.* **1.** *Pol:* suffrage *m*; (*a*) vote *m,* voix *f*; **to give one's s. to s.o.,** donner sa voix à qn; accorder son suffrage à qn; (*b*) droit *m* de vote; **manhood s.,** droit de vote restreint aux hommes adultes; **woman, women's, female, s.,** droit de vote pour les femmes; **universal s.,** suffrage universel; **one-man-one-vote s.,** suffrage universel pur et simple. **2.** *Ecc:* suffrage. **3.** approbation *f,* suffrage, préférence *f.*

suffragette [sʌfrə'dʒet], *s.f. Pol.Hist:* suffragette, militante.

suffragist ['sʌfrədʒist], *s. Pol.Hist:* partisan, -ane, du droit de vote pour les femmes.

suffrutescent [sʌfru'tes(ə)nt], *a. Bot:* suffrutescent, sous-frutescent.

suffrutex, *pl.* **suffrutices** ['sʌfruteks, sʌ'frutisi:z], *s. Bot:* sous-arbrisseau *m, pl.* sous-arbrisseaux.

suffuse [sə'fju:z], *v.tr.* (*of light, colour, tears*) se répandre sur (qch.); **a blush suffused her cheeks,** une rougeur s'est répandue sur ses joues; *Lit:* ses joues s'empourprèrent; **eyes, cheeks, suffused with tears,** yeux noyés, baignés, de larmes; joues mouillées, inondées, de larmes; **suffused with light,** inondé de lumière; **sky delicately suffused with amber,** ciel délicatement coloré d'ambre.

suffusion [sə'fju:ʒ(ə)n], *s.* **1.** *Med:* suffusion *f* (de sang, de bile). **2.** (*a*) **the s. of the eyes with tears,** le flot de larmes qui inonde les yeux; (*b*) coloration *f*; rougeur *f* (sur la peau).

Sufi ['su:fi], *s. Moslem.Rel:* souff *m*; sufi *m.*

sugar[1] ['ʃugər], *s.* **1.** sucre *m*; **crude s.,** sucre brut; **refined s.,** sucre raffiné; raffinade *f*; **granulated s.,** sucre cristallisé; **lump s.,** sucre en morceaux, en dominos;

sucre cassé; **lump, cube, of s.,** morceau *m*, *Fr.Can:* cube *m*, de sucre; **soft s.,** (i) sucre en poudre; (ii) cassonade *f*; **caster s.,** sucre en poudre; sucre semoule; **icing s.,** sucre farine; sucre glace, à glacer; **brown s., moist s.,** cassonade *f*; **Barbado(e)s s.,** cassonade en petits cristaux; **(piece of) s.,** (morceau de) sucre; **help yourself to s.,** prenez du sucre, *F:* sucrez-vous; **to sweeten a dish with s.,** sucrer un plat; **cake with too much s. (in it),** gâteau trop sucré; **to make one's fortune in s.,** faire sa fortune dans les sucres; *F:* **I'm neither s. nor salt,** je ne fondrai pas sous la pluie; *Cu:* **burnt s.,** caramel *m*. **2.** (a) **s. mouse,** souris *f* en sucre; **s. almond,** dragée *f*, amande lissée; **s. basin, bowl,** sucrier *m*; **s. dredger, sifter, shaker,** saupoudroir *m* à sucre; *Cu:* glaçoire *f*; passoire *f* à sucre; **(pair of) s. tongs,** pince *f* à sucre; **s. merchant,** marchand *m* de sucre; **s. industry,** industrie sucrière, industrie saccharine; **s. boiler, maker,** fabricant *m* de sucre, sucrier *m*; **s. refiner,** raffineur *m* de sucre; sucrier; **s. refining,** raffinage *m* (du sucre); **s. refinery, mill,** raffinerie *f* (de sucre); sucrerie *f*; **s. cutting machine,** casse-sucre *m inv*; *F:* **s. daddy,** protecteur âgé; papa gâteau; **she's got a s. daddy,** elle a un vieux; (b) **s. plant,** plante sucrière; **s. beet,** betterave *f* à sucre; **s. beet factory,** fabrique *f* de sucre de betterave; **s. cane,** canne *f* à sucre; *F:* can(n)amelle *f*; **Chinese, African, s. cane,** sorg(h)o sucré; **s. plantation,** plantation *f* de cannes à sucre; **s. planter,** planteur *m* (de cannes à sucre); **s. mill,** moulin *m* à broyer la canne à sucre; moulin à cannes; **s. maple,** érable *m* à sucre; *NAm:* **s. bush, s. orchard,** (i) bosquet *m*, (ii) plantation *f*, d'érables à sucre; **s. palm,** palmier *m* à sucre; (c) *Hort:* **s. pea,** mange-tout *m inv*; *Can:* **s. corn,** maïs doux, vert; (d) *Bot:* **s. apple,** anone écailleuse, corossol écailleux; **s. bean,** haricot *m* de Lima; **s. grass,** sorg(h)o sucré, à sucre; *Algae:* **s. wrack,** baudrier *m* de Neptune. **3.** (a) *A.Ch:* **s. of lead,** acétate *m* de plomb; *A:* sucre de saturne; (b) **s. of milk, milk s.,** sucre de lait; lactose *f*; *Physiol:* **blood s.,** glucose sanguin. **4.** douceur affectée; langage sucré, mielleux; flatterie *f*; **she was all s.,** elle avait pris un air sucré. **5.** *NAm: P:* (a) (i) galette *f*, pognon *m*; (ii) pot *m* de vin; (b) (i) belle fille; (ii) petite amie; (c) drogue *f*, narcotique *m*.

sugar². **1.** *v.tr.* (a) sucrer (son café, etc.); saupoudrer (un gâteau) de sucre; recouvrir (une pilule) de sucre; dragéifier, lisser (des amandes); *Wine-m:* chaptaliser, sucrer (les moûts); *Fig:* **to s. the pill,** dorer la pilule; dorer la dragée; emmieller un refus; **to s. one's words,** sucrer ses paroles; (b) *Hort:* enduire (des arbres, etc.) de bière, de gomme sucrée (pour attraper les phalènes); (c) *F:* flatter (qn); (d) *P: esp. NAm:* (i) donner de l'argent à (qn); **her last daddy sugared her nicely,** son dernier protecteur a été très généreux; (ii) soudoyer, acheter (qn). **2.** *v.i.* (a) (*of jam, etc.*) tourner au, en, sucre; cristalliser; (b) *P: O:* tirer au flanc; *esp. Row:* carotter (en faisant semblant de souquer ferme); ne pas se la fouler. **3.** *Sug.-R:* **to s. off,** (i) *v.tr.* faire cristalliser (le sirop); (ii) *v.i.* (*of syrup*) cristalliser.

sugarberry ['ʃugəberi], *s. NAm: Bot:* micocoulier occidental.

sugarbird ['ʃugəbəːd], *s. Orn:* sucrier *m*, souïmanga *m*, nectarine *f*.

sugar-coat ['ʃugəkout], *v.tr.* recouvrir (une pilule, etc.) de sucre; dragéifier (une pilule); lisser (des amandes); *Fig:* sucrer (ses mots, une décision fâcheuse, etc.); emmieller (un refus).

sugar-coated [ʃugə'koutid], *a.* recouvert de sucre; (*of almond*) lissé; **s.-c. pill,** pilule dragéifiée; dragée *f*; *Fig:* **s.-c. criticism,** critique sucrée, édulcorée.

sugared ['ʃugəd], *a.* (a) (*of drink, etc.*) sucré; (b) (*of cake, etc.*) saupoudré de sucre; (c) = SUGAR-COATED.

sugarer ['ʃugərər], *s. F: esp. Row:* tireur *m* au flanc.

sugarhouse ['ʃugəhaus], *s. NAm:* sucrerie *f*; *esp.* raffinerie *f* de sucre d'érable.

sugariness ['ʃugərinis], *s.* (a) goût sucré (d'un fruit, etc.); (b) douceur mielleuse (d'un discours, sourire, etc.).

sugaring ['ʃugəriŋ], *s.* **1.** *Wine-m:* sucrage *m* (des moûts); chaptalisation *f*. **2.** *Sug.-R:* **s. off,** cristallisation *f* (du sirop); *Can:* **s. (off) party,** partie *f* de sucre (*Fr.C.*).

sugarloaf ['ʃugəlouf], *s.* pain *m* de sucre; *F:* **s. hat,** chapeau pointu; *F:* pain de sucre; **s. mountain,** montagne *f* en pain de sucre; *Nau:* **s. sea,** mer clapoteuse.

sugarplum ['ʃugəplʌm], *s.* **1.** *A:* bonbon *m*. **2.** *NAm: Bot:* corme *f*, sorbe *f*.

sugary ['ʃugəri], *a.* **1.** (a) sucré; **s. cakes,** gâteaux saupoudrés de sucre; (b) trop sucré; (c) (*of jam, etc.*) **to go s.,** cristalliser. **2.** (sourire, ton) mielleux, sucré; (ton) doucereux; **s. eloquence,** éloquence melliflue.

sugent ['sudʒ(ə)nt], **sugescent** [su'dʒes(ə)nt], *a. Z:* (organe, etc.) suceur.

suggest [sə'dʒest], *v.tr.* **1.** (a) suggérer, proposer (qch. à qn); **can you s. a better plan?** pouvez-vous suggérer une meilleure méthode? **he suggested my following him, that I should follow him,** il a suggéré, a proposé, que je le suive; **he suggested going for a walk,** il a suggéré de faire une promenade; **I shall do as you s.,** je ferai comme vous le suggérez; je vais suivre votre conseil; **to s. (that) the meeting be fixed for September 9th,** proposer de fixer la réunion au 9 septembre; proposer que la réunion soit fixée au 9 septembre; **this, I s., is what happened,** d'après moi, cela s'est produit ainsi; **a solution suggested itself to me,** une solution m'est venue à l'esprit, s'est présentée à mon esprit; (b) *Med: Psy:* suggérer (une idée, une action). **2.** inspirer, faire naître (une idée, etc.); **what suggested that thought?** qu'est-ce qui a inspiré cette pensée? **that suggested to me the idea of travelling,** cela a fait naître en moi l'idée de voyager; **prudence suggests a retreat,** la prudence conseille la retraite. **3.** insinuer; **do you s. that I am lying?** est-ce que vous insinuez que je mens? **are eggs as scarce as the price would s.?** les œufs sont-ils aussi rares que le prix le laisse supposer? *Jur:* **I s. that you were not there at that time,** n'est-il pas vrai que vous étiez absent à ce moment-là? **4.** évoquer; **his nose and ears s. a rabbit,** son nez et ses oreilles donnent, évoquent, l'idée d'un lapin; **the look on his face suggested fear,** l'expression de son visage donnait l'idée, faisait penser, qu'il avait peur; son visage exprimait la crainte.

suggester [sə'dʒestər], *s.* suggesteur, -trice; inspirateur, -trice (d'un projet, etc.).

suggestibility [sədʒesti'biliti], *s.* suggestibilité *f*.

suggestible [sə'dʒestibl], *a.* **1.** (projet, etc.) proposable, que l'on peut suggérer. **2.** (sujet) influençable par la suggestion (hypnotique); (sujet) suggestible.

suggestion [sə'dʒestʃ(ə)n], *s.* **1.** suggestion *f*; (a) **the mere s. of it makes him furious,** on n'a qu'à le suggérer pour qu'il s'emporte; **to give way to s.,** se laisser suggérer; **to be open to s.,** être prêt à accueillir des suggestions; **at his s. I stayed at home,** suivant son conseil je suis resté chez moi; **hypnotic s.,** suggestion hypnotique; (b) **to make, offer, a s.,** faire une suggestion, proposition; **I have no s. to offer,** je n'ai rien à suggérer; **practical s.,** conseil *m* pratique; **suggestions for improvement,** suggestions, propositions, en vue d'une amélioration; **suggestion(s) book, box,** cahier *m*, boîte *f*, pour les suggestions d'amélioration (offertes par les employés, les visiteurs, etc.); **to be full of suggestions,** être fécond en idées, en conseils; **to make (indecent) suggestions to a girl,** faire des propositions inconvenantes à une jeune fille; (c) *Jur:* **my s. is that you were not there at the time,** n'est-il pas vrai que vous étiez absent à ce moment-là? **2. blue with no s. of green,** bleu sans la moindre trace de vert; **to speak with just a s. of a foreign accent,** parler avec une pointe d'accent étranger; **s. of regret, contempt,** nuance *f* de regret, mépris.

suggestionist [sə'dʒestʃənist], *s. Med:* suggestionneur *m*.

suggestive [sə'dʒestiv], *a.* suggestif; (i) évocateur, -trice; **s. of sth.,** qui évoque qch.; qui donne, évoque, l'idée de qch.; (ii) **s. joke,** plaisanterie suggestive, grivoise.

suggestiveness [sə'dʒestivnis], *s.* caractère suggestif (d'un dessin, etc.); **s. is worse than frank obscenity,** les plaisanteries suggestives sont pires que la franche obscénité.

suggillation [sʌ(g)dʒi'leiʃ(ə)n], *s. Med:* sugillation *f*.

suicidal [s(j)uːi'saidl], *a.* (malade, etc.) suicidaire; **s. tendencies,** tendances *f* suicidaires, au suicide; **s. mania,** manie *f* du suicide; suicidomanie *f*; **s. maniac,** suicidomane *mf*; *Fig:* **it would be s. (to do it),** ce serait un véritable suicide, ce serait courir à la ruine, (d'agir de la sorte).

suicidally [s(j)uːi'saidəli], *adv.* (agir, etc.) d'une façon suicidaire; **s. inclined,** enclin au suicide.

suicide¹ ['s(j)uːisaid], *s.* (*pers.*) suicidé, -ée.

suicide², *s.* (crime *m* du) suicide; **to commit s.,** se suicider, se donner la mort; (*of murderer*) se faire justice; **to attempt s.,** attenter à ses jours; **attempted s.,** tentative *f* de suicide; **racial s.,** la mort, l'extinction *f*, de la race; **to commit political s.,** se suicider, se couler, politiquement; **it would be s. to go there,** ce serait un véritable suicide d'y aller; *Hist:* **s. plane,** avion *m* suicide.

Suidae ['s(j)uːidiː], *s.pl. Z:* suidés *m*.

Suiformes [s(j)uːi'fɔːmiːz], *s.pl. Z:* suiformes *m*.

suing ['s(j)uːiŋ], *s.* **1.** poursuite *f* en justice. **2.** sollicitation *f*; prière *f*.

suint [swint], *s.* suin(t) *m*.

suit¹ [s(j)uːt], *s.* **1.** *Jur:* **s. at law,** procès (civil); poursuites *fpl* (en justice); instance *f*; cause *f*; **s. in chancery,** poursuite(s) devant la chancellerie; **criminal s.,** action *f*, procès, au criminel; **to bring, institute, a s. against s.o.,** intenter un procès à, contre, qn; (*of lawyer*) **to conduct the s.,** occuper pour le demandeur; postuler; **to be a party in a s.,** être en cause. **2.** *O:* prière *f*, demande *f*, requête *f*; **at the s. of s.o.,** à la requête, *Jur:* à la diligence, de qn; **to press one's s.,** faire valoir ses droits; appuyer sa requête. **3.** *O:* recherche *f*, demande, en mariage; **to plead, press, one's s. with a girl,** faire une cour assidue à une jeune fille, courtiser une jeune fille avec ardeur. **4.** *Cost:* (a) costume *m*, ensemble *m*; (i) (*man's*) complet *m*, **two-piece, three-piece, s.,** complet en deux, trois, pièces; **lounge s.,** complet veston; **he was wearing a lounge s.,** il était en veston; **business s.,** complet de bureau; *NAm:* complet veston; **his best s.,** son costume de dimanche; **dressed in a dark s.,** vêtu d'un complet sombre; (ii) (*woman's*) tailleur *m*; *O:* **travelling s.,** ensemble, costume, de voyage; **child's woolly s.,** (costume) esquimau *m* pour enfant; (b) *Av: Space:* **flying, flight, s.,** combinaison *f* de vol; **moon s.,** tenue *f* lunaire; **pressure s.,** combinaison pressurisée; **(anti-)G s.,** combinaison anti-g. **5.** *Nau:* **s. of sails,** jeu *m* de voiles; **new s. of sails,** voilure neuve. **6.** *Cards:* couleur *f*; **the four suits,** les quatre couleurs; **the three plain suits,** les trois couleurs (par opposition à l'atout); **s. call,** demande en couleurs (par opposition avec sans-atout); **long, strong, s.,** couleur longue; **to lead from one's long s.,** attaquer dans sa longue; **the highest card of one's longest s.,** la plus haute carte de sa longue; **politeness is not his long s.,** la politesse n'est pas son fort; **to have a short s. in trumps,** avoir une main courte; **to follow s.,** (i) fournir à la couleur (demandée); (ii) *Fig:* en faire autant, faire de même; **the others followed s.,** les autres ont suivi le mouvement, ont emboîté le pas; **to fail to follow s.,** renoncer; **inability to follow s.,** renonce *f*.

suit². **1.** *v.tr.* (a) accommoder, adapter, approprier (**sth. to sth.,** qch. à qch.); **to s. one's style to one's audience,** adapter son style à son public; **to s. one's conversation to the company,** se mettre au diapason de la compagnie; **to be suited to, for, sth.,** être adapté, apte, à qch.; être fait pour qch.; **the premises are not suited for display purposes,** le local ne se prête pas à l'étalage; **he is not suited for, to be, a parson,** il n'est pas fait pour être prêtre; la prêtrise n'est pas sa vocation; **he is ill suited to these parts,** ces rôles ne lui conviennent pas; il n'est pas fait pour ces rôles; **they are suited to each other,** ils sont faits l'un pour l'autre; **we are not suited to one another,** nous ne sommes pas faits pour nous entendre; (b) convenir à, aller à, accommoder (qn); **a small job in the country would s. me very well,** un petit emploi en province m'irait, me conviendrait, très bien; **the house does not s. me,** la maison n'est pas à ma convenance; **he found a house that suited him,** il a trouvé une maison à son gré; **I have not yet found a job to s. me,** je n'ai pas encore trouvé un emploi qui me convienne; *F:* je n'ai pas encore trouvé chaussure à mon pied; **marriage suits you,** le mariage vous réussit; **acting is what suits him best,** le théâtre est son affaire; **that suits me best,** c'est ce qui m'arrange le mieux, ce qui m'accommode le mieux; **I have something that would s.,** j'ai quelque chose qui ferait l'affaire; **I am not easily suited,** je suis difficile à satisfaire; **anything suits me,** je m'accommode de tout; **that just suits me, it suits me all right,** ça me va à merveille; **I shall do it if it suits me,** je le ferai si ça me chante, si ça me dit; **I shall do it when it suits me,** je le ferai quand cela me conviendra; je le ferai à mon temps, à mon heure; **would that s. you?** cela ferait-il votre affaire? ceci vous accommoderait-il? **it would s. me to have today free,** cela m'arrangerait d'avoir ma journée libre; **that suits me down to the ground,** c'est juste mon affaire; **s. yourself,** arrangez cela à votre gré; faites comme vous voudrez; **this climate, this food, does not s. me,** ce climat, cette nourriture, ne me va pas, ne me vaut rien; **that colour does not s. your complexion,** cette couleur ne va pas bien, ne s'accorde pas, avec votre teint; **this hat suits you,** ce chapeau vous va, vous coiffe bien; (c) *A:* **to s. oneself with sth.,** se pourvoir de qch.; **are you suited with a cook?** avez-vous trouvé une cuisinière qui vous convient? **to be suited with a situation,** avoir une place; (d) *NAm:* habiller (qn) d'un costume. **2.** *v.i.* (a) **that date does not s.,** cette date ne convient pas; (b) **and a hat to s.,** et un chapeau à l'avenant; (c) *NAm:* mettre ses vêtements (protecteurs, etc.).

suitability [s(j)uːtə'biliti], **suitableness** ['s(j)uːtəbəlnis], *s.* convenance *f* (d'une date, etc.); à-propos *m* (d'une remarque, d'une expression); accord *m*, rapport *m* (de caractères); **s. of a candidate to, for, a post,** aptitude *f* d'un candidat à un poste.

suitable ['s(j)uːtəbl], *a.* **1.** (sujet, travail, moyen) convenable, qui convient; (exemple, etc.) apte; **s. expres-**

sion, reply, expression, réponse, pleine d'à-propos, pertinente, appropriée; **s. marriage,** union bien assortie; **he is of a s. age to sign,** il est d'un âge compétent pour signer; **we have found nothing s.,** nous n'avons rien trouvé à notre convenance; **most s. plan,** plan qui offre les plus grands avantages; **the most s. date,** la date qui conviendrait le mieux; **wherever you think s.,** où bon vous semblera; **it seemed more s. to laugh,** il semblait plus à propos de rire; **first he introduced his father, as seems s.,** d'abord il a présenté son père, comme il sied. **2. s. to, for, sth.,** bon à qch.; propre, approprié, applicable, adapté, à qch.; **s. to the occasion,** qui convient à la circonstance; en accord avec l'occasion; **reading s. to his age,** lectures de son âge, en rapport avec son âge; **is it a book s. for children?** est-ce un livre à mettre entre les mains de la jeunesse? **to make sth. s. for sth.,** adapter qch. à qch.

suitably ['s(j)u:təbli], *adv.* **1.** convenablement; **to answer s.,** répondre à propos; **to act s.,** agir comme il convient; **to be s. impressed,** être impressionné comme il convient; **s. matched,** bien assortis. **2. s. to the occasion,** d'une manière appropriée à l'occasion; **s. to your wishes,** conformément à vos désirs; en conformité avec vos désirs.

suitcase ['s(j)u:tkeis], *s.* mallette *f*, valise *f*; (*fitted with hangers*) porte-habit(s) *m inv.*

suite [swi:t], *s.* **1.** suite *f*, cortège *m* (d'un prince, etc.). **2. s. (of rooms),** appartement *m*; pièces *fpl* en enfilade; **s. (of furniture),** ameublement *m*, ensemble *m*; **three-piece s.,** canapé *m* avec deux fauteuils assortis; salon *m* (en) trois pièces; **lounge s., drawing room s.,** (mobilier *m* de) salon; **dining room s.,** salle *f* à manger; **bedroom s.,** chambre *f* à coucher; **bathroom s.,** salle de bains; *Plumb:* **low-down, low level, s.,** W.C. à aspiration, à action siphonique. **3.** *Mus:* suite; **orchestral s.,** suite d'orchestre.

suiting ['s(j)u:tiŋ], *s.* **1.** adaptation *f*, appropriation *f* (**of sth. to sth.,** de qch. à qch.). **2.** *Com:* tissu *m* de confection; **men's suitings,** étoffes *f*, tissus, pour complets.

suitor ['s(j)u:tər], *s.* **1.** *Jur:* (i) plaideur, -euse; (ii) requérant, -ante. **2.** (*a*) *A:* pétitionnaire *m*; (*b*) prétendant *m*, soupirant *m*; **her suitors,** les aspirants à sa main.

suk(h) [su(:)k], *s.* souk(h) *m*.

sulcate ['sʌlkeit], *a. Nat.Hist:* sulcifère.

sulciform ['sʌlsifɔ:m], *a. Nat.Hist:* sulciforme; en forme de sillon.

sulcus, *pl.* **-ci** ['sʌlkəs, -sai], *s. Nat.Hist:* sillon *m*; sulcature *f* (du cerveau).

sulf(o)- ['sʌlf(ou)], *comb.fm. U.S:* = SULPH(O)-. NOTE: *the spelling* **sulf(o)-** *may gradually replace* **sulph(o)-** *in international scientific use.*

sulfate, sulfur, etc. *see* SULPHATE, SUPLHUR, ETC.

Sulidae ['s(j)u:lidi:], *s. Orn:* sulidés *m*.

Suliote ['s(j)uliout]. *Ethn:* **1.** *a.* souliote. **2.** *s.* Souliote *mf*.

sulk[1] ['sʌlk], *s. usu.pl.* bouderie *f*; **to be in, have (a fit of), the sulks,** bouder; faire la mine.

sulk[2], *v.i.* bouder; faire la mine; être maussade; **why are you sulking (about it)?** pourquoi boudez-vous? *Lit:* **to s. in one's tent,** se retirer dans sa tente (comme Achille).

sulkily ['sʌlkili], *adv.* en boudant; d'un ton, d'un air, boudeur, maussade.

sulkiness ['sʌlkinis], *s.* bouderie *f*, maussaderie *f*.

sulky[1] ['sʌlki], *a.* boudeur, maussade; **to be s.,** bouder; **to look s.,** avoir un air boudeur; faire la mine; **s. as a bear,** grognon comme un ours; **to be s. with s.o.,** bouder (contre) qn; *F:* faire la tête à qn.

sulky[2], *s. Veh:* sulky *m*; *Agr:* **s. plough,** charrue *f* tilbury.

sullage ['sʌlidʒ], *s.* **1.** (*a*) eaux *fpl* d'égout, eaux usées; **s. pipe,** égout *m*; (*b*) vase *f* d'alluvion; limon *m*. **2.** *Metall:* scories *fpl*, crasses *fpl*; **s. piece,** masselotte *f*.

sullen ['sʌlən], *a.* (*of pers.*) maussade, renfrogné, morose; (*of horse*) rétif; (*of outlook, etc.*) sombre, triste, morne, lugubre; **s. silence,** silence obstiné, buté; *O:* **to have the sullens,** être d'humeur maussade.

sullenly ['sʌlənli], *adv.* d'un air maussade; maussadement; d'un air renfrogné, sombre; **to obey s.,** obéir de mauvaise grâce.

sullenness ['sʌlənnis], *s.* (*a*) maussaderie *f*; air renfrogné; (*b*) obstination *f* à ne pas parler.

sullied ['sʌlid], *a.* souillé, sali, terni.

sully ['sʌli], *v.tr.* souiller, salir, ternir; flétrir, tacher (sa réputation, etc.).

sulph(o)- ['sʌlf(ou)], *comb.fm.* sulf(o)-.

sulpha, sulfa ['sʌlfə], *s. Pharm:* **the s. series,** la série des sulfamides; **s. drug,** sulfamide *f*.

sulphadiazine, sulf- [sʌlfə'daiəzain], *s. Pharm:* sulfadiazine *f*.

sulph(a)emoglobin, sulf- ['sʌlfi:mə'gloubin], *s. Physiol:* sulfhémoglobine *f*.

sulphaguanidine, sulf- [sʌlfə'gwænidi:n], *s. Pharm:* sulfaguanidine *f*.

sulphamate, sulf- ['sʌlfəmeit], *s. Ch:* sulfamate *m*.

sulphamic, sulf- [sʌl'fæmik], *a. Ch:* (acide) sulfamique.

sulphamide, sulf- ['sʌlfəmaid], *s. Ch:* sulfamide *m*.

sulphanilamide, sulf- [sʌlfə'niləmaid], *s. Ch:* sulfanilamide *m or f*.

sulphanilic, sulf- [sʌlfə'nilik], *a. Ch:* (acide) sulfanilique.

sulpharsenic, sulf- [sʌlfɑ:'senik], *a. Ch:* (acide) sulfarsénique.

sulpharsenide, sulf- [sʌl'fɑ:sənaid], *s. Ch:* sulfarséniure *m*.

sulphatase, sulf- ['sʌlfəteis], *s. Bio-Ch:* sulfatase *f*.

sulphate[1], **sulf-** ['sʌlfeit], *s.* **1.** *Ch:* sulfate *m*; **iron s., ferrous s.,** sulfate ferreux, de fer; vitriol vert; couperose verte; **zinc s.,** sulfate de zinc; couperose blanche; vitriol blanc; **copper s.,** sulfate de cuivre; vitriol bleu; couperose bleue; **s. of ammonia,** sulfate d'ammonium; *Agr:* crude ammoniac *m*; **to treat, dress, vines with (copper) s.,** sulfater des vignes; **treating, dressing, with s.,** sulfatage *m*. **2.** *Com:* sulfate de soude; *Paperm:* **s. process,** procédé *m* au sulfate.

sulphate[2], **sulf-.** **1.** *v.tr. Ch: Ind:* sulfater. **2.** *v.i. El:* (*of accumulator*) se sulfater.

sulphated, sulf- ['sʌlfeitid], *a.* **1.** (*of lime, mineral water, etc.*) sulfaté. **2.** *El:* (*of accumulator plate*) sulfaté; encrassé de sulfate.

sulphating, sulf- ['sʌlfeitiŋ], *s.* **1.** *Ch: Ind:* sulfatage *m*. **2.** *El:* sulfatation *f* (des plaques d'accumulateur).

sulphatization, sulf- [sʌlfətai'zeiʃ(ə)n], *s. Metall:* sulfatisation *f*.

sulphide, sulf- ['sʌlfaid], *s. Ch:* sulfure *m*; **hydrogen s.,** hydrogène sulfuré; acide *m* sulfhydrique; *F:* gaz puant; **lead s.,** sulfure de plomb; *Miner:* **s. of lead, lead s.,** galène *f*; sulfure de plomb; plomb sulfuré; **red s. of antimony,** pentasulfure *m* d'antimoine; *Phot:* **s. toning,** virage *m* au sulfure; virage sépia; **to treat, dress, vines with s.,** sulfurer les vignes; **treating, dressing, with s.,** sulfurage *m*.

sulphiding, sulf- ['sʌlfaidiŋ], *s. Agr: Vit:* sulfurage *m*.

sulphinic, sulf- [sʌl'finik], *a. Ch:* (acide) sulfinique.

sulphinuzing, sulf- ['sʌlfinju:ziŋ], *s. Metall:* sulfinusation *f*, sulfinuzation *f*.

sulphinyle, sulf- ['sʌlfinil], *s. Ch:* sulfinyle *m*.

sulphitation, sulf- [sʌlfi'teiʃ(ə)n], *s. Sug.-R.* sulfitation *f*.

sulphite[1], **sulf-** ['sʌlfait], *s. Ch:* sulfite *m*; **sodium s.,** sulfite de sodium, de soude; **to treat wines with s.,** sulfiter les vins; **treating with s.,** sulfitage *m*; *Paperm:* **s. process,** procédé *m* au sulfite, au bisulfite; **s. pulp,** pâte *f* bisulfitique.

sulphite[2], **sulf-,** *v.tr.* sulfiter (les vins).

sulphiting, sulf- ['sʌlfaitiŋ], *s.* sulfitage *m* (des vins).

sulpho, sulfo, acid ['sʌlfou'æsid], *s. Ch:* sulfacide *m*.

sulphocyanate, sulphocyanide, sulf- [sʌlfou'saiəneit, -naid], *s.* **1.** *Ch:* sulfocyanate *m*, sulfocyanure *m*. **2. ammonium sulphocyanide,** *Phot: F:* **sulphocyanide,** sulfocyanure d'ammonium.

sulphocyanic, sulf- [sʌlfousai'ænik], *a. Ch:* sulfocyanique.

sulphonal, sulf- ['sʌlfənəl], *s. Pharm:* sulfonal *m*.

sulphonamide, sulf- [sʌl'fənəmaid], *s. Pharm:* sulfamide *m*.

sulphonate, sulf- ['sʌlfəneit], *s. Ch:* sulfonate *m*.

sulphonated, sulf- ['sʌlfəneitid], *a.* sulfoné.

sulphonation, sulf- [sʌlfə'neiʃ(ə)n], *s.* sulfonation *f*.

sulphone, sulf- ['sʌlfoun], *s. Ch:* sulfone *f*.

sulphonic, sulf- [sʌl'fənik], *a. Ch:* sulfonique, sulfoné.

sulphonium, sulf- [sʌl'founiəm], *s. Ch:* sulfine *f*.

sulphonyl, sulf- ['sʌlfənil], *s. Ch:* sulfonyle *m*.

sulphoricinate, sulf- [sʌlfou'risineit], *s. Ch:* sulforicinate *m*.

sulphosalicylate, sulf- [sʌlfousə'lisileit], *s. Ch:* **mercury s.,** sulfosalicylate *m* de mercure.

sulphosalicylic, sulf- [sʌlfousæli'silik], *a. Ch:* sulphosalicylique.

sulpho, sulfo, salt ['sʌlfousɔlt], *s. Ch:* sulfosel *m*.

sulphovinic, sulf- [sʌlfou'vinik], *a. Ch:* sulfovinique.

sulphur[1], **sulf-** ['sʌlfər], *s.* **1.** soufre *m*; **roll s., stick s.,** soufre en canon, en bâtons; **plastic s.,** soufre mou; **drop s.,** soufre granulé; **native s.,** soufre de mine; **virgin s.,** soufre vierge, vif; **flowers of s.,** fleur(s) *f* de soufre, crème *f* de soufre; soufre en fleur(s), en poudre; soufre pulvérulent, pulvérisé, sublimé; **milk of s.,** lait *m* de soufre; **to treat with s.,** soufrer; **to dip matches in s.,** soufre des allumettes; **s. dioxide,** anhydride sulfureux; **s. trioxide,** anhydride sulfurique; *Hort:* **lime s.,** bouillie *f* sulfocalcique; **s. match,** allumette soufrée; *Geol:* **s. spring,** source sulfureuse; solfatare *f*; **s. water,** eau sulfureuse; **s. mine,** soufrière *f*; **s. ore,** pyrite *f*; sulfure *m* de fer; **s. bacteria,** sulfobactéries *f*. **2.** (*a*) *Ent:* **s. (butterfly),** (i) soufré *m*; (ii) coliade *f*, colias *m*; **giant Arctic s.,** colias géant; (*b*) *Z:* **s. bottom (whale),** baleine bleue; (*c*) *Bot:* **s. root,** fenouil *m* de porc. **3.** *a.* **s. (coloured),** couleur de soufre *inv*; soufré.

sulphur[2], **sulf-,** *v.tr.* soufrer (la laine, un tonneau, etc.).

sulphurate, sulf- ['sʌlfjureit], *v.tr.* sulfurer (un métal, etc.); soufrer (la laine).

sulphurated, sulf- ['sʌlfjureitid], *a. Ch:* sulfuré.

sulphuration, sulf- [sʌlfju'reiʃ(ə)n], *s.* (*a*) sulfuration *f*, sulfurisation *f*, sulfurage *m* (des vignes); (*b*) *Tex:* blanchiment *m* au soufre; soufrage *m*.

sulphurator, sulf- ['sʌlfjureitər], *s.* **1.** *Hort: Vit:* soufreuse *f*. **2.** *Tex:* soufroir *m* (pour laine).

sulphureous, sulf- [sʌl'fju:riəs], *a.* **1.** (*a*) sulfureux; qui contient du soufre; (*b*) couleur de soufre *inv*; soufré. **2.** (*a*) qui sent le soufre (en train de brûler); **s. exhalations,** exhalaisons sulfureuses; (*b*) bleuâtre (comme le soufre qui brûle).

sulphuret, sulf- ['sʌlfjuret], *s. Ch:* sulfure *m*.

sulphuretted, sulf- ['sʌlfjuretid], *a. Ch:* sulfuré; **s. hydrogen,** hydrogène sulfuré; acide sulfhydrique; sulfure *m* d'hydrogène.

sulphuric, sulf- [sʌl'fju:rik], *a. Ch:* sulfurique; **s. acid,** acide *m* sulfurique, vitriolique; (huile *f* de) vitriol *m*.

sulphuring, sulf- ['sʌlfəriŋ], *s.* soufrage *m*; *Tex: etc:* **s. chamber, room,** soufroir *m*; *Hort:* **s. apparatus,** soufreuse *f*.

sulphurization, sulf- [sʌlfjurai'zeiʃ(ə)n], *s.* sulfuration *f*, sulfurisation *f* (d'un métal, etc.); soufrage *m* (de la laine, etc.).

sulphurize, sulf- ['sʌlfjuraiz], *v.tr.* sulfurer (un métal, etc.); soufrer (la laine, etc.).

sulphurous, sulf- ['sʌlfərəs, -jur-], *a.* **1.** (*a*) = SULPHUREOUS; (*b*) *usu.* **sulphurous,** diabolique, infernal; **s. criticism,** critique *f* au vitriol. **2.** *Ch:* [sʌl'fjurəs] (acide, etc.) sulfureux.

sulphurwort ['sʌlfəwə:t], *s. Bot:* fenouil *m* de porc.

sulphury, sulf- ['sʌlfəri], *a.* (*of smell, etc.*) sulfureux, de soufre.

sulphuryl, sulf- ['sʌlfjuril], *s. Ch:* sulfuryle *m*.

sulphydrate, sulf- [sʌlf'(h)aidreit], *s. Ch:* sulfhydrate *m*.

sulphydric, sulf- [sʌlf'(h)aidrik], *a. Ch:* sulfhydrique.

Sulpice ['sʌlpis]. *Pr.n.m. Rel.H:* (saint) Sulpice.

Sulpicius [sʌlpiʃiəs]. *Pr.n.m.* **1.** *Rel.H:* **S. Severus,** Sulpice-Sévère. **2.** *Rom.Hist:* Sulpicius.

sultam ['sʌltæm], *s. Ch:* sultame *f*.

sultan ['sʌltən], *s.* **1.** sultan *m*. **2.** *Bot:* **sweet s.,** ambrette *f* (jaune); centaurée musquée. **3.** (*a*) *Husb:* race *f* de poules blanches; (*b*) *Orn:* poule sultane.

sultana [sʌl'tɑ:nə], *s.* **1.** sultane *f*. **2.** *Cu:* raisin sec de Smyrne. **3.** *Orn:* **s. (bird),** poule *f* sultane.

sultanate ['sʌltəneit], *s.* sultanat *m*.

sultane [sʌl'tɑ:n], *s. Furn:* sultane *f*.

sultaness ['sʌltənes], *s.f.* sultane.

sultone ['sʌltoun], *s. Ch:* sultone *f*.

sultriness ['sʌltrinis], *s.* chaleur étouffante; lourdeur *f* (de l'atmosphère).

sultry ['sʌltri], *a.* **1.** (*of heat, atmosphere, etc.*) étouffant, suffocant, accablant, embrasé; **s. weather,** temps lourd, orageux; **it is s.,** il fait très lourd. **2.** *Fig:* (*a*) (*of passions, voice, etc.*) chaud; (*b*) (*of language, story, etc.*) salé, épicé, poivré; (*c*) sensuel, aguichant, provocant.

Sulu ['su:lu:], *Pr.n. Geog:* **the S. Islands,** les îles *f* Soulou.

sulvanite ['sʌlvənait], *s. Miner:* sulvanite *f*.

sum[1] [sʌm], *s.* **1.** (*a*) somme *f*, total *m*; montant *m* (d'un compte); **to mount up to the s. of 500, of £500,** s'élever à une somme de 500, à un montant de £500; **s. total,** somme totale, montant total; *Mth:* **to find the s. of the terms of a series,** sommer les termes d'une série; *Cmptr:* **logical s.,** somme logique; **s. check,** contrôle *m* par totalisation; **check s.,** total de contrôle; (*b*) **the s. of my wishes is to be left alone,** la somme de mes désirs est d'être laissé en paix; **the s. and substance of the matter, of his complaint,** le fond, la substance, l'essence *f*, de l'affaire; le fond de sa réclamation; **the s. total of his speech was that he has no intention of resigning,** son discours se résumait en ceci: il n'a aucune intention de démissionner; **in s. there's nothing we can do about it,** en somme, somme toute, on ne peut rien y faire; (*c*) **s. (of money),** somme (d'argent); **large s.,** grosse somme, forte somme; **nice little s.,** somme rondelette. **2.** problème *m*, exercice *m* (d'arithmétique); **a multiplication s.,** une multiplication; **to set a child a s.,** poser un problème d'arithmétique à un enfant; **to do a s. in one's head,** faire un calcul de tête; **to do sums,** faire du calcul, de l'arithmétique, des problèmes; **I was very bad at sums,** j'étais très faible en calcul, en arithmétique.

sum², *v.* (**summed**) **1.** (*a*) *v.tr.* additionner (des nombres, etc.); *Mth:* sommer (une série); (*b*) *v.i. NAm:* **the assets s. to ten million,** l'actif se totalise par dix millions. **2.** *v.tr. & i.* **to s. up:** (*a*) **to s. up ten numbers,** faire la somme de, totaliser, dix nombres; (*b*) résumer, faire un résumé de, récapituler (les faits); **to s. up (the matter) I will say that the firm can survive,** en résumé, en dernière analyse, je dirai que l'entreprise est viable; **to s. up (what one has said before),** se résumer; résumer les faits; (*c*) *Jur:* (*of judge*) **to s. up (the case, the evidence),** résumer l'affaire, les débats (avant la délibération du jury); **to s. up for, against s.o.,** résumer les débats dans un sens favorable, défavorable, à qn; (*d*) **to s. up the situation at a glance,** se rendre compte de la situation d'un coup d'œil; **to s. s.o. up,** juger, classer, qn.

sumac(h) ['s(j)u:mæk, 'ʃu:-], *s.* **1.** *Bot:* sumac *m*; **smooth s.,** sumac blanc; **staghorn, Virginia s.,** sumac de Virginie; **tanner's, tanning, Sicilian, s.,** sumac des corroyeurs, de Sicile; *F:* vinaigrier *m*; **myrtle-leaved (tanner's) s.,** redoul *m*; **poison s.,** sumac vénéneux; toxicodendron *m*; **Venetian s.,** (sumac) fustet *m*; sumac à perruque; arbre *m* à la perruque. **2.** *Tan:* sumac.

sumatra [su:'mɑ:trə], *s. Meteor:* coup *m* de vent du sud-ouest (au détroit des Moluques).

Sumatran [su:'mɑ:trən]. *Geog:* **1.** *a.* sumatrien. **2.** *s.* Sumatrien, -ienne.

Sumerian [s(j)u:'miəriən]. **1.** *A.Geog:* (*a*) *a.* sumérien; (*b*) *s.* Sumérien, -ienne. **2.** *s. Ling:* sumérien *m.*

Sumerologist [s(j)u:mi'rɔlədʒist], *s.* sumérologue *mf.*

summa, *pl.* **-ae** ['sʌmə, -i:], *s. Lit: etc:* somme *f*; *Theol:* **the S. Theologica,** la Somme théologique (de saint Thomas d'Aquin).

summarily ['sʌmərili], *adv.* sommairement; (i) succinctement, en peu de mots; (ii) avec peu de formalités.

summarize ['sʌməraiz], *v.tr.* résumer sommairement (un ouvrage, etc.); récapituler (les débats, etc.); *Cmptr:* **summarizing punch,** perforation récapitulative.

summarized ['sʌməraizd], *a.* (*of report, etc.*) compendieux; en résumé.

summary ['sʌməri]. **1.** *a.* (examen, etc.) sommaire; **s. account,** (i) récit sommaire, succinct; récit en peu de mots; (ii) récit récapitulatif; *Jur:* **s. procedure,** procédure *f* sommaire; référé *m*; **s. proceedings,** affaire *f* sommaire; **s. offences,** délits qui peuvent être jugés en procédure sommaire; **to sit in cases of s. procedure,** statuer en procédure sommaire; **to make a ruling by s. process,** statuer sommairement. **2.** *s.* (*a*) sommaire *m*, résumé *m*, aperçu *m*; argument *m* (d'un livre); récapitulation *f*, relevé *m*, liste *f* (d'opérations commerciales, etc.); relevé (des naissances); *Jur:* **s. of leading cases and decisions,** répertoire *m* de jurisprudence; *Mil: Jur:* **to take a s. of evidence,** prendre des informations; (*b*) *Cmptr:* résumé, récapitulation *f*; **s. card,** carte récapitulative; **s. punch,** perforateur récapitulateur; poinçonneuse *f.*

summate ['sʌmeit], *v.tr. NAm:* additionner.

summation [sʌ'meiʃ(ə)n], *s.* **1.** (*a*) sommation *f*, addition *f*; *Ind: etc:* **s. diagram,** diagramme *m* d'addition; **s. counter,** compteur totalisateur; (*b*) *Physiol:* sommation (de stimulations). **2.** somme *f*, total *m*. **3.** *NAm: Jur:* résumé de l'affaire fait par le juge.

summer¹ ['sʌmər], *s.* été *m*; **in s.,** en été; **a summer('s) day,** un jour d'été; **winter and s. alike, I live in the country,** hiver comme été j'habite la campagne; **we shall see him again next s., in the s.,** on le reverra l'été prochain, cet été; **they only spend the s. here,** ce sont des estivants; **St Martin's s., Indian s.,** été de la Saint-Martin; **St Luke's s.,** été de la Saint-Denis; *Fig:* **the Indian s. of an elderly man,** l'été de la Saint-Martin d'un homme d'un certain âge; *Poet:* **maiden of twenty summers,** jeune fille de vingt printemps; **s. clothes,** habits d'été; **to put on one's s. clothes,** se mettre en été; **s. residence,** résidence estivale; résidence d'été; **s. resort,** station estivale; **s. visitor,** estivant, -e; **the s. holidays,** les grandes vacances; **s. time,** l'heure *f* d'été; *Cu:* **s. pudding,** pudding composé d'une compote de groseilles, etc., enveloppée de biscuit ou de pain; *Hort:* **s. roses,** rosiers non remontants.

summer². **1.** *v.i.* passer l'été, estiver (au bord de la mer, etc.); (*b*) (*of cattle*) estiver. **2.** *v.tr.* estiver (le bétail).

summer³, *s. Const:* (*a*) **s. (beam, tree),** poutre *f* de plancher; (*b*) **(breast)s.,** poitrail *m*, sommier *m*; linteau *m* (de baie).

summer⁴, *s. Cmptr:* additionneur *m* analogique.

summerhouse ['sʌməhaus], *s.* pavillon *m*, gloriette *f*; kiosque *m* de jardin.

summersault¹,² ['sʌməsɔ:lt], *s. & v.i.* SOMERSAULT¹,².

summertime ['sʌmətaim], *s.* (saison *f* d')été *m.*

summerwood ['sʌməwud], *s. Arb:* bois *m* d'été, d'automne.

summery ['sʌməri], *a.* estival, -aux; d'été; **we had a fine s. Easter,** nous avons eu pour Pâques un beau temps d'été.

summing ['sʌmiŋ], *s.* **1.** *Mth:* addition *f*, sommation *f*; *Cmptr:* **s. amplifier,** additionneur *m*; **s. integrator,** intégrateur additionneur. **2. s. up,** (i) résumé de l'affaire (fait par le juge avant que les jurés se retirent pour délibérer); résumé des débats; (ii) évaluation *f* (de la situation, etc.).

summit ['sʌmit], *s.* sommet *m*, cime *f*, faîte *m* (d'une montagne); *Nau: Oc:* **rock s.,** tête *f* de roche; **the s. of greatness,** le faîte, comble, sommet, des grandeurs; **the s. of happiness,** le summum de la félicité; **to be at the s. of power, fame,** être au pinacle; *Pol:* **conference, talks, at s. level, s. (conference, meeting),** conférence *f* au sommet; *Civ.E:* **s. level,** (i) *also* **s.,** point *m* de partage (d'un canal); (ii) bief *m* de partage.

summon ['sʌmən], *v.tr.* **1.** (*a*) appeler, faire venir (un domestique, etc.); convoquer (une assemblée, qn à une réunion); **to s. the shareholders,** convoquer les actionnaires; **business summoned him back to London,** les affaires l'ont rappelé à Londres; **to be summoned to high office,** être appelé à une haute fonction; **to s. help,** appeler au secours; (*b*) *Jur:* sommer (qn) de comparaître; **to s. a defendant, a witness, to attend,** citer, assigner, appeler, ajourner, un défendeur, un témoin; **to s. s.o. for debt,** assigner qn en paiement d'une dette; **to s. the parties,** citer, assigner, les parties; *Mil:* **to s. a man before a court martial,** traduire un homme en conseil de guerre. **2.** sommer, requérir; **to s. a fortress to surrender,** sommer une place forte; **to s. the rebels to disperse,** sommer les rebelles de se disperser; **to s. s.o. to perform a contract,** mettre qn en demeure d'exécuter un contrat. **3. to s. (up) all one's strength,** faire appel à, rassembler, toutes ses forces; **to s. up one's courage,** faire appel à, s'armer de, tout son courage; prendre son courage à deux mains; **I couldn't s. up courage to tell him about it,** je n'ai pas eu le courage de le lui dire.

summoner ['sʌmənər], *s.* **1.** convocateur, -trice (d'une assemblée). **2.** *Jur: A:* huissier *m.*

summoning ['sʌməniŋ], *s.* **1.** (*a*) appel *m*, convocation *f* (d'une assemblée); (*b*) *Jur:* (i) citation *f*, assignation *f* (d'un témoin, etc.); (ii) sommation *f* (**to do sth.,** de faire qch.). **2. s. of help,** appel au secours.

summons¹, *pl.* **-ses** ['sʌmənz, -ziz], *s.* **1.** appel (fait d'autorité); convocation urgente; *Mil: A:* **the town surrendered at the first s.,** la ville se rendit à la première sommation. **2.** *Jur:* (i) citation *f* (à comparaître); assignation *f*; sommation *f*; (ii) mandat *m* de comparution; ajournement *m*; billet *m* d'avertissement; *F:* procès-verbal *m*, *pl.* procès-verbaux; *Aut:* (*stuck on windscreen*) *F:* papillon *m*; **cross s.,** contre-citation *f*, citation *f* au contraire; **to issue a s.,** lancer une assignation; **to serve a s. on s.o.,** signifier une citation, assignation, à qn; faire, envoyer, une assignation à qn; assigner qn; **to take out a s. against s.o.,** faire assigner qn; **s. for a motoring offence,** contravention *f* pour infraction au code de la route; **to make oneself liable for a s.,** s'attirer une contravention; **you'll be getting another s.,** *F:* vous allez recevoir encore du papier timbré.

summons², *v.tr. Jur:* citer (qn) à comparaître; assigner (qn); appeler (qn) en justice.

sump [sʌmp], *s.* **1.** (*a*) *Min: etc:* puisard *m*; (*b*) fosse *f* d'aisance. **2.** *Mec.E: I.C.E:* **(oil) s.,** carter *m* à huile; puisard *m* (d'huile); fond *m* de carter, carter inférieur; cuvette *f* d'égouttage; **dry s.,** carter sec; *Aut:* **to drain the s.,** faire la vidange.

sumpitan ['sʌmpitən], *s.* sarbacane *f* (des Malais).

sumpman, *pl.* **-men** ['sʌmpmən], *s.m. Min:* puisatier.

sumpter ['sʌm(p)tər], *s. A:* bête *f* de somme, de charge; **s. horse, mule,** cheval, -aux *m*, mulet *m*, de somme, de charge; **s. cloth,** housse *f* de bête de somme.

sumptuary ['sʌm(p)tjuəri], *a.* (*of law, etc.*) somptuaire.

sumptuosity [sʌm(p)tju'ɔsiti, sʌm(p)tʃu-], *s.* somptuosité *f.*

sumptuous ['sʌm(p)tjuəs, -tʃuəs], *a.* somptueux, fastueux.

sumptuously ['sʌm(p)tjuəsli, -tʃuəsli], *adv.* somptueusement, fastueusement.

sumptuousness ['sʌm(p)tjuəsnis, -tʃu-], *s.* somptuosité *f*, faste *m*; richesse *f* (du mobilier).

sun¹ [sʌn], *s.* (*a*) soleil *m*; **the s. is shining,** il fait (du) soleil; le soleil brille; **the s. was shining brightly,** il faisait grand soleil; **there is nothing new under the s.,** il n'y a rien de nouveau sous le soleil; **the s. rises, sets,** le soleil se lève, se couche; **rising, setting, s.,** soleil levant, couchant; **to worship the rising s.,** adorer le soleil levant; *Lit:* **his s. is set,** son soleil est couché; son étoile *f* a pâli; *Nau: F:* **to take, shoot, the s.,** relever le soleil; faire, prendre, une observation; observer le soleil; faire le point; **against the s.,** dans le soleil; **with the s.,** dans le sens des aiguilles d'une montre; **with the s., against the s.,** de gauche à droite, de droite à gauche; *B:* **the S. of righteousness,** le soleil de justice; *Astr:* **fictitious s.,** soleil apparent, fictif; **mean s.,** soleil moyen; (*b*) **to have a place in the s.,** avoir une place au soleil; **(full) in the s.,** au (grand) soleil; en plein soleil; **to take the s., to bask in the s.,** prendre le soleil; se chauffer, s'exposer, au soleil; *F:* faire le lézard, lézarder; **to get a touch of the s.,** prendre, attraper, un coup de soleil; (*c*) *Pyr:* **fixed s.,** gloire *f*; (*d*) **s. hat,** chapeau *m* de soleil; capeline *f*; (*for men*) panama *m*; **(baby's) s. bonnet,** capeline; **s. helmet,** casque (colonial) (à couvre-nuque); **s. top,** haut *m* bain de soleil; **s. shield,** parasoleil *m*, pare-soleil *m inv* (de télescope, d'un objectif, etc.); *Aut:* **s. visor, shield,** pare-soleil; **s. awning,** store *m*; **s. curtain,** (i) rideau *m* contre le soleil; (ii) couvre-nuque *m*, *pl.* couvre-nuques; coiffe *f* (de casque colonial); **s. oil, lotion, cream,** huile, lotion, crème, solaire; **s. lamp,** (i) *Cin:* grand projecteur; sunlight *m*; (ii) lampe *f* à bronzer; lampe ultra(-)violette (pour le bronzage); *Med:* **s. lamp treatment,** traitement par rayons ultra(-) violets; **s. trap,** coin très ensoleillé; solarium *m*; **s. lounge,** *NAm:* **s. parlor, porch,** solarium; véranda *f*; *Nau:* **s. deck,** pont-promenade *m*, *pl.* ponts-promenades; pont *m* d'ensoleillement; **s. worship,** culte *m* du soleil; **s. worshipper,** adorateur, -trice, du soleil; **s.-loving,** héliophile; **s. myth,** mythe *m* solaire; **s. god,** dieu *m* solaire; *Meteor:* **s. dog,** par(h)élie *m*; faux soleil; **s. pillar,** pilier *m* solaire; (*in ground, etc.*) **s. crack,** fente *f* d'insolation; *Mec.E:* **s. and planet motion, wheel,** mouvement satellite; **s. and planet gear,** engrenage à satellites; *Orn:* **s. bittern,** caurale *m*, *F:* râle-soleil *m*; **s. grebe,** grébifoulque *m*, héliornis *m*; *Bot:* **s. spurge,** réveille-matin *m inv*; *Echin:* **s. star,** solaster *m.*

sun², *v.tr.* (**sunned**) exposer au soleil; insoler, ensoleiller; **to s. oneself,** prendre le soleil; se chauffer, s'exposer, au soleil; *F:* faire le lézard, lézarder.

sunbaked ['sʌnbeikt], *a.* brûlé par le soleil; cuit au soleil.

sunbath ['sʌnbɑ:θ], *s. O:* bain *m* de soleil.

sunbathe ['sʌnbeið], *v.i.* prendre le soleil, des bains de soleil; se chauffer, s'exposer, au soleil; *F:* faire le lézard, lézarder.

sunbather ['sʌnbeiðər], *s.* personne *f* qui prend des bains de soleil.

sunbathing ['sʌnbeiðiŋ], *s.* bains *mpl* de soleil.

sunbeam ['sʌnbi:m], *s.* rayon *m* de soleil; rayon solaire.

sunbird ['sʌnbə:d], *s. Orn:* souï(-)manga *m*, sucrier *m*; **scarlet-breasted s.,** souï(-)manga du Sénégal; **the sunbirds,** les nectarini(i)dés *m.*

sunblind ['sʌnblaind], *s.* store *m.*

sunbow ['sʌnbou], *s.* arc irisé (produit par le soleil dans un jet d'eau, etc.).

sunburn ['sʌnbə:n], *s.* **1.** *Med:* coup *m* de soleil. **2.** hâle *m*, bronzage *m*, teint *m* bronzé.

sunburnt, sunburned ['sʌnbə:nt, -bə:nd], *a.* (i) brûlé par le soleil; (ii) bronzé, hâlé, basané; **to get s.,** (i) attraper, prendre, un coup de soleil; (ii) (se) bronzer, se hâler, se basaner, se brunir.

sunburst ['sʌnbə:st], *s.* (*a*) échappée *f* de soleil; (*b*) bijou *m* (en forme de) soleil.

Sunda ['sʌndə], *Pr.n. Geog:* **the S. Islands,** les îles *f*, l'archipel *m*, de la Sonde.

sundae ['sʌndei], *s.* glace aux fruits recouverte de noix, de crème, etc.

Sundanese [sʌndə'ni:z]. *Geog:* **1.** *a.* so(u)ndanais. **2.** *s.* (*a*) *Geog:* So(u)ndanais, -aise; (*b*) *Ling:* so(u)ndanais *m*, sondéin *m*, sondéen *m.*

Sunday ['sʌnd(e)i], *s.* dimanche *m*; **come and see me on S.,** venez me voir dimanche; **I expect him on S., this (coming) S.,** je l'attends dimanche; **he comes on Sundays,** il vient le dimanche, *occ.* les dimanches; **he comes every S.,** il vient tous les dimanches; *F:* **when two Sundays come in one week,** la semaine des quatre jeudis; **S. rest,** le repos dominical; **S. paper,** journal du dimanche; **in one's S. clothes, one's S. best,** *O:* **one's S. go-to-meeting clothes,** dans ses habits du dimanche; sur son trente et un; endimanché; **to put on one's S. best,** s'habiller en dimanche, s'endimancher; se mettre sur son trente et un; **Laetare, Mid-Lent, S.,** lætare *m*; quatrième dimanche du carême.

Sundayfied ['sʌndifaid], *a. F: O:* (*of pers., etc.*) endimanché.

sunder¹ ['sʌndər], *s. A: & Lit:* **in s.** = ASUNDER.

sunder². *A: & Lit:* **1.** *v.tr.* (*a*) **to s. sth. from sth.,** séparer, disjoindre, qch. de qch.; (*b*) couper, fendre (qch.) en deux. **2.** *v.i.* (*a*) se séparer; (*b*) se briser.

sundering ['sʌndəriŋ], *s. A: & Lit:* séparation *f*, disjonction *f.*

sundew ['sʌndju:], *s. Bot:* drosera *m*; rosée *f* du soleil;

attrape-mouche *m*, *pl.* attrape-mouche(s), gobe-mouches *m inv*.
sundial ['sʌndaiəl], *s.* cadran *m* solaire; gnomon *m*.
sundown ['sʌndaun], *s.* **1.** coucher *m* du soleil. **2.** *U.S:* chapeau *m* à larges bords (de femme).
sundowner ['sʌndaunər], *s. F:* **1.** *Austr:* clochard *m* (qui règle sa journée pour arriver à une habitation au soleil couchant). **2.** boisson prise au coucher du soleil.
sundress ['sʌndres], *s.* robe *f* de plage, robe bain de soleil.
sundried ['sʌndraid], *a.* (*a*) (des)séché au soleil; (*b*) (fruit) confit au soleil.
sundriesman, *pl.* **-men** ['sʌndrizmən], *s.m. O:* **horticultural s.,** fournisseur d'articles pour l'horticulture.
sundry ['sʌndri]. **1.** *a.* divers; **s. expenses,** frais divers; **on s. occasions,** à différentes occasions; **he showed us s. samples,** il nous a montré divers échantillons. **2.** *s.* (*a*) **all and s.,** tous sans exception; **to invite all and s.,** inviter tout le monde et son père; convoquer le ban et l'arrière-ban; **all and s. knew him,** il était connu de tous, de tout le monde; **for all and s.,** pour chacun et pour tous; **he informed all and s. that. . .,** il a annoncé à qui voulait l'entendre que. . .; **he told all and s. about it,** il le racontait à tout venant; **I have applied to all and s.,** je me suis adressé aux uns et aux autres, au tiers et au quart; (*b*) **sundries,** (i) articles divers; (ii) frais divers; faux frais.
sunfast ['sʌnfɑːst], *a. Tex:* (tissu) inaltérable au soleil.
sunfish[1] ['sʌnfiʃ], *s. Ich:* môle *f*; poisson-lune *m*, *pl.* poissons-lunes; perche *f* soleil; **(freshwater) s.,** perche d'Amérique (du Nord).
sunfish[2], *v.i. U.S: F:* (*of horse*) rouler les épaules (pour désarçonner le cavalier).
sunflower ['sʌnflauər], *s. Bot:* hélianthe *m*, hélianthus *m*; soleil *m*, tournesol *m*; girasol *m*; **s. (seed) oil,** huile de tournesol; **ditch, tickseed, s.,** (espèce *f* de) bidens *m*; *U.S:* **the S. State,** le Kansas.
Sungari [sʌŋ'gɑːri], *Pr.n. Geog:* Soungari *m*.
sunglasses ['sʌnglɑːsiz], *s.pl.* lunettes *f* de soleil; lunettes solaires, fumées, noires; verres fumés.
sunglow ['sʌnglou], *s. Meteor:* couronne *f* solaire.
sunken ['sʌŋk(ə)n], *a.* (*a*) (rocher, etc.) noyé, sous l'eau, submergé, immergé **s. wreck,** épave sous-marine; (*b*) affaissé, enfoncé; **s. cheeks,** joues hâves, creuses, rentrées; **s. eyes,** yeux caves, (r)enfoncés, creux, rentrés; (*c*) **s. road,** route creuse, encaissée; route en déblai; chemin creux; cavée *f*; **s. garden,** jardin encaissé, enterré, en contrebas.
sunless ['sʌnlis], *a.* sans soleil.
sunlight ['sʌnlait], *s.* lumière *f* du soleil; lumière solaire; **in the s.,** au (grand) soleil, en plein soleil; *Med:* **s. treatment,** héliothérapie *f*; traitement *m* solaire; *Cin:* **s. lamp,** sunlight *m*.
sunlit ['sʌnlit], *a.* éclairé par le soleil; ensoleillé.
sunn [sʌn], *s. Bot:* **s. (hemp),** crotalaria *f*.
Sunna(h) ['sʌnə], *s. Rel:* sunna *f*, sounna *f*.
Sunni ['sʌni], **Sunnite** ['sʌnait], *s. Rel:* sunnite *mf*.
sunnily ['sʌnili], *adv.* radieusement, joyeusement; **to smile s.,** sourire gaiement, radieusement.
sunniness ['sʌninis], *s.* **1.** situation ensoleillée (d'un endroit, etc.). **2.** gaieté *f* (de caractère); rayonnement *m* (du visage, du sourire).
sunning ['sʌniŋ], *s.* ensoleillement *m*.
sunnud ['sʌnʌd], *s. Jur:* (*in India*) charte *f*, brevet *m*.
sunny ['sʌni], *a.* **1.** (journée, etc.) de soleil; (endroit) ensoleillé; (bâtiment) rempli de soleil; (côté) exposé au soleil; **it's s.,** il fait (du) soleil; **the s. side of a valley,** l'adret *m* d'une vallée; *F:* **the s. side of the picture,** le bon côté de l'affaire; *esp: NAm:* **s. side up,** (œuf sur le plat) cuit d'un seul côté. **2.** (visage) radieux, rayonnant, riant; (caractère) heureux.
sunproof ['sʌnpruːf], *a. Tex: etc:* (tissu) inaltérable au soleil.
sunray ['sʌnrei], *s.* rayon *m* de soleil; rayon solaire; *Med:* **s. treatment,** héliothérapie *f*; traitement *m* solaire; **s. lamp,** lampe à bronzer, lampe ultra(-)violette (pour le bronzage).
sunrise ['sʌnraiz], *s.* lever *m* du soleil; **at s.,** au soleil levant; au lever du soleil.
sunroof ['sʌnruːf], *s. Aut:* toit ouvrant.
sunrose ['sʌnrouz], *s. Bot:* hélianthème *m*.
sunscald ['sʌnskɔːld], *s. Hort: Arb:* insolation *f*.
sunscalded ['sʌnskɔːldid], *a. Hort: Arb:* brûlé par le soleil.
sunset ['sʌnset], *s.* coucher *m* du soleil; **at s.,** au soleil couchant; au coucher du soleil; à soleil couché; *Lit:* **the s. of life, of an empire,** le déclin de la vie, d'un empire; *Moll:* **s. shell,** telline *f*; flion *m*.
sunshade ['sʌnʃeid], *s.* **1.** ombrelle *f*; (*for table, etc.*) parasol *m*. **2.** parasoleil *m*, pare-soleil *m inv* (de télescope, d'un objectif, etc.). **3.** *Aut:* pare-soleil.
sunshine ['sʌnʃain], *s.* **1.** (clarté *f*, lumière *f*, du) soleil; **in the s.,** au soleil; **in the bright, the brilliant, s.,** au grand soleil; en plein soleil; au beau soleil; **I like the woods in the s.,** j'aime les bois quand il fait du soleil; **the afternoon broke into s.,** l'après-midi s'est ensoleillé; **period of s.,** période d'ensoleillement; *Meteor:* **s. recorder,** héliographe enregistreur; *Med:* **s. treatment,** traitement *m* solaire; héliothérapie *f*. **2.** bonheur *m*, gaieté *f*, rayonnement *m* (du visage, de la vie, etc.); **life was all s. for him,** la vie n'avait pour lui que des sourires; **she sheds s. all around her,** elle ensoleille tout autour d'elle.
sunshiny ['sʌnʃaini], *a. F:* = SUNNY.
sunspot ['sʌnspɔt], *s. Astr:* tache *f* solaire; tache du soleil; macule *f*.
sunstone ['sʌnstoun], *s. Miner:* aventurine *f*.
sunstroke ['sʌnstrouk], *s. Med:* insolation *f*; coup *m* de soleil; **to get (a touch of) s.,** attraper, prendre, un coup de soleil.
sunstruck ['sʌnstrʌk], *a. Med:* frappé d'insolation.
sunsuit ['sʌns(j)uːt], *s. Cost:* costume *m* bain de soleil.
suntanned ['sʌntænd], *a.* bronzé, hâlé, basané.
suntan(ning) ['sʌntæn(iŋ)], *s.* bronzage *m*, hâle *m*; **suntan cream, lotion, oil,** crème, lotion, huile, solaire.
sunup ['sʌnʌp], *s. NAm:* lever *m* du soleil.
sup[1] [sʌp], *s. esp. Scot:* petite gorgée; goutte *f* (de liquide); **to take a s. of soup,** prendre une goutte de bouillon.
sup[2], *v.* **(supped** [sʌpt]) **1.** *v.tr.* (*a*) *esp. Scot:* boire à petites gorgées; **to s. up a bowl of soup,** avaler une assiette de soupe à petites gorgées; (*b*) *A:* donner à souper à (qn). **2.** *v.i. O:* souper **(off, on,** de); **I supped with a friend,** j'ai soupé (i) avec un ami, (ii) chez un ami.
super ['s(j)uːpər], *a. & s.* **1.** *s. F:* surnuméraire *m*; (*a*) employé *m* supplémentaire; (*b*) *Th: Cin:* figurant, -ante; comparse *mf*; bouche-trou *m*, *pl.* bouche-trous. **2.** *s. F:* (*a*) directeur, -trice; surveillant, -ante; chef *m* (des travaux, etc.); surintendant *m*; (*b*) = commissaire *m* (de police). **3.** *s. Ap:* hausse *f* (de ruche). **4.** *s. Ch: Agr:* superphosphate *m*. **5.** *a.* superficiel; *Meas:* carré. **6.** *a. Com:* superfin, surfin. **7.** *a. F:* **s.(-duper),** superbe, formidable, magnifique, sensationnel; sensass.
super- [s(j)uːpər], *pref.* **1.** super-. **2.** sur-. **3.** sus-. **4.** supra-.
superable ['s(j)uːpərəbl], *a.* surmontable.
superabound [s(j)uːpərə'baund], *v.i.* surabonder, redonder **(in, with,** de, en); foisonner **(in, with,** de).
superabundance [s(j)uːpərə'bʌndəns], *s.* surabondance *f*, foisonnement *m*, pléthore *f* **(of,** de).
superabundant [s(j)uːpərə'bʌndənt], *a.* surabondant, pléthorique.
superabundantly [s(j)uːpərə'bʌndəntli], *adv.* surabondamment.
superaerodynamics [s(j)uːpərɛəroudai'næmiks], *s.pl.* (*with sg. const.*) superaérodynamique *f*.
superaltar ['s(j)uːpərɔ(ː)ltər], *s. Ecc:* (*a*) autel (portatif); (*b*) retable *m*.
superannuate [s(j)uːpər'ænjueit]. **1.** *v.tr.* (*a*) mettre (qn) à la retraite, en retraite; retraiter (qn); (*b*) *Sch:* faire retirer de l'école (un élève qui a dépassé l'âge normal de sa classe); (*c*) mettre au rancart, remiser (un vieux chapeau, etc.). **2.** *v.i.* (*of pers.*) arriver à l'âge de la retraite.
superannuated [s(j)uːpər'ænjueitid], *a.* **1.** suranné; désuet; (*of car, etc.*) démodé. **2.** (mis) en, à la, retraite; retraité.
superannuation [s(j)uːpərænju'eiʃ(ə)n], *s.* retraite *f* par limite d'âge; **s. fund,** caisse des retraites; **s. contribution,** retenue pour la retraite; **s. benefit,** pension de retraite.
superaudible [s(j)uːpər'ɔːdibl], *a. Ph:* (fréquence, etc.) superaudible, ultrasonore.
superb [s(j)uː'pəːb], *a.* superbe, magnifique, sensationnel.
superbly [s(j)uː'pəːbli], *adv.* superbement, magnifiquement.
supercalender[1] [s(j)uːpə'kælindər], *s. Paperm:* calandre *f* (à glacer).
supercalender[2], *v.tr. Paperm:* calandrer, glacer (le papier).
supercargo ['s(j)uːpəkɑːgou], *s. Nau:* subrécargue *m*.
supercharge ['s(j)uːpətʃɑːdʒ], *v.tr. I.C.E:* suralimenter, surcomprimer (un moteur, etc.); **supercharged engine,** moteur suralimenté, surcomprimé, à compresseur.
supercharger ['s(j)uːpətʃɑːdʒər], *s. I.C.E:* compresseur *m*, surpresseur *m*; soufflante *f* de suralimentation; **multi-speed s.,** compresseur à plusieurs vitesses; **exhaust-driven s.,** compresseur commandé par l'échappement.
supercharging ['s(j)uːpətʃɑːdʒiŋ], *s. I.C.E:* suralimentation *f*, surcompression *f*.
superciliary [s(j)uːpə'siliəri], *a. Anat:* sourcilier; **s. arch, ridge,** arcade sourcilière.
supercilious [s(j)uːpə'siliəs], *a.* sourcilleux, hautain; (air) pincé, dédaigneux.
superciliously [s(j)uːpə'siliəsli], *adv.* d'un air sourcilleux; avec hauteur; **to treat s.o. s.,** traiter qn de haut en bas, avec dédain.
superciliousness [s(j)uːpə'siliəsnis], *s.* hauteur *m*, dédain *m*; air sourcilleux, dédaigneux.
superconducting [s(j)uːpəkən'dʌktiŋ], *a. Ph: El:* = SUPERCONDUCTIVE.
superconduction [s(j)uːpəkən'dʌkʃ(ə)n], *s. Ph: El:* = SUPERCONDUCTIVITY.
superconductive [s(j)uːpəkən'dʌktiv], *a. Ph: El:* supraconducteur, -trice.
superconductivity [s(j)uːpəkɔndʌk'tiviti], *s. Ph: El:* supraconduction *f*, supraconductivité *f*, supraconductibilité *f*.
superconductor [s(j)uːpəkən'dʌktər], *s. Ph: El:* supraconducteur *m*.
supercool ['s(j)uːpəkuːl], *v.tr. Ph:* surfondre.
supercooling ['s(j)uːpə'kuːliŋ], *s. Ph:* surfusion *f*, sous-refroidissement *m*.
supercritical [s(j)uːpə'kritik(ə)l], *a. Atom.Ph:* supercritique, surcritique.
superdominant [s(j)uːpə'dɔminənt], *s. Mus:* sus-dominante *f*, *pl.* sus-dominantes.
superego [s(j)uːpər'iːgou], *s. Psy:* surmoi *m*.
superelevation [s(j)uːpəreli'veiʃ(ə)n], *s. Civ.E: Rail: etc:* surhaussement *m*; surélèvement *m*; dévers *m* (de la voie, d'une route).
supereminence [s(j)uːpər'eminəns], *s.* suréminence *f*, prééminence *f*.
supereminent [s(j)uːpər'eminənt], *a.* suréminent, prééminent.
supererogation [s(j)uːpərerou'geiʃ(ə)n], *s.* surérogation *f*; superfétation *f*; *Ecc:* **works of s.,** œuvres de surérogation.
supererogatory [s(j)uːpəri'rɔgət(ə)ri], *a.* surérogatoire; superfétatoire; **it would be s. to sing his praises,** son éloge n'est plus à faire.
superfatted ['s(j)uːpə'fætid], *a.* (savon) contenant des produits insaponifiés.
superfecundation [s(j)uːpəfikʌn'deiʃ(ə)n], *s. Physiol:* superfécondation *f*, superimprégnation *f*.
superfetation [s(j)uːpəfiː'teiʃ(ə)n], *s. Physiol:* superfétation *f*, superfécondation *f*.
superficial [s(j)uːpə'fiʃ(ə)l], *a.* superficiel. **1. s. measurement,** mesure de superficie; **s. foot,** pied carré. **2.** (*a*) **s. wound,** blessure superficielle; *Geol:* **s. deposit,** placage *m*; (*b*) **s. learning,** science d'emprunt; teinture *f* de science; **to have a s. knowledge of sth.,** avoir des connaissances superficielles, une teinture, de qch.; **his knowledge is entirely s.,** son savoir est tout en superficie, tout en surface; **she has a s. mind,** elle manque de profondeur.
superficiality [s(j)uːpəfiʃi'æliti], *s.* superficialité *f*.
superficially [s(j)uːpə'fiʃəli], *adv.* superficiellement; en surface; en superficie.
superficiary [s(j)uːpə'fiʃəri]. *Jur:* **1.** *a.* superficiaire. **2.** *s.* propriétaire *m* superficiaire.
superficies [s(j)uːpə'fiʃiiːz], *s. inv.* superficie *f*.
superfine ['s(j)uːpəfain], *a.* **1.** *Com: etc:* superfin, surfin. **2.** *Metalw:* **s. file cut,** taille très douce. **3. s. wit,** esprit raffiné.
superfinish [s(j)uːpə'finiʃ], *v.tr. Metall: Tchn:* superfinir.
superfinishing [s(j)uːpə'finiʃiŋ], *s. Metall: Tchn:* superfinition *f*.
superfluid ['s(j)uːpəfluːid], *s. Cu:* superfluide *m*.
superfluidity [s(j)uːpəfluː'iditi], *s. Ch:* superfluidité *f*.
superfluity [s(j)uːpə'fluːiti], *s.* superfluité *f*; **s. of good things,** embarras *m* de richesses; **s. of words,** superfétation *f* de paroles; **to take a s. of luggage,** s'encombrer de bagages inutiles.
superfluous [s(j)uː'pəːfluəs], *a.* superflu; superfétatoire; **it is s. to say. . .,** il est inutile, superflu, de dire. . ..
superfluously [s(j)uː'pəːfluəsli], *adv.* d'une manière superflue; inutilement.
superfluousness [s(j)uː'pəːfluəsnis], *s.* superfluité *f*.
superfoetation [s(j)uːpəfiː'teiʃ(ə)n], *s. Physiol:* superfétation *f*, superfécondation *f*.
superfusibility [s(j)uːpəfjuːzi'biliti], *s. Ph:* surfusibilité *f*.
superfusible [s(j)uːpə'fjuːzibl], *a. Ph:* surfusible.
superfusion [s(j)uːpə'fjuːʒ(ə)n], *s. Ph:* surfusion *f*.
superheat[1] ['s(j)uːpəhiːt], *s. Ph:* surchauffe *f*.
superheat[2], *v.tr. Ph:* surchauffer; **superheated steam,** vapeur surchauffée.
superheater ['s(j)uːpəhiːtər], *s. Ph:* surchauffeur *m* (de vapeur).

superheating ['s(j)u:pəhi:tiŋ], *s. Ph:* surchauffage *m*, surchauffe *f*; **s. calorimeter,** calorimètre à surchauffe.
superhet ['s(j)u:pəhet], *s. F:* = SUPERHETERODYNE.
superheterodyne [s(j)u:pə'het(ə)rədain], *s. W.Tel:* superhétérodyne *m.*
superhighway ['su:pəhaiwei], *s. NAm:* autoroute *f.*
superhive ['s(j)u:pəhaiv], *s. Ap:* hausse *f* (de ruche).
superhuman [s(j)u:pə'hju:mən], *a.* surhumain.
superhumanly [s(j)u:pə'hju:mənli], *adv.* de façon surhumaine, sur le plan surhumain.
superimposable [s(j)u:pərim'pouzəbl], *a.* superposable.
superimpose [s(j)u:pərim'pouz], *v.tr.* superposer, surimposer; *Phot: Cin:* faire une surimpression; surimprimer; **to s. sth. on sth.,** superposer qch. à qch.; poser qch. sur qch.; **to s. colours,** superposer des couleurs; *Cin: T.V:* **superimposed title,** titre superposé, surimpressionné, surimprimé.
superimposition [s(j)u:pərimpə'ziʃ(ə)n], *s. (a)* superposition *f* (de couleurs, etc.); *(b) Phot: Cin:* surimpression *f*; *(c) Geol:* surimposition *f*; épigénie *f.*
superincumbent [s(j)u:pərin'kʌmbənt], *a.* superposé.
superinfection [s(j)u:pərin'fekʃ(ə)n], *s. Med:* superinfection *f*, surinfection *f.*
superintend [s(j)u:pərin'tend], *v.tr.* diriger, surveiller; **to s. the work personally,** diriger soi-même les travaux; **to s. an election,** présider au scrutin.
superintendence [s(j)u:pərin'tendəns], *s.* direction *f*, surveillance *f*, contrôle *m*; direction technique (d'une usine); conduite *f* (des travaux); surintendance *f.*
superintendent [s(j)u:pərin'tendənt], *s.* **1.** directeur, -trice; surveillant, -ante; chef *m* (des travaux, etc.); surintendant *m.* **2.** *(a)* **naval s.,** préfet *m* maritime; *(b)* **(police) s.** = commissaire *m* (de police); *(c) Rail:* **(railway) s.,** (i) inspecteur *m* des chemins de fer; (ii) chef de division des chemins de fer; **signal s.,** chef du service des signaux.
superintendentship [s(j)u:pərin'tendəntʃip], *s. (a)* direction *f*; surveillance *f*, surintendance *f.*
superior [s(j)u:'piəriər]. **1.** *a. (a) (of position, officer, quality, etc.)* supérieur; **to be s. in numbers to the enemy,** être supérieur en nombre à l'ennemi; avoir la supériorité du nombre sur l'ennemi; **they were overcome by s. numbers,** ils ont été vaincus par le nombre; **the s. classes of society,** les classes supérieures de la société; **thanks to your s. wealth,** grâce à la supériorité de vos richesses; **to be s. to flattery,** être au-dessus de la flatterie; être insensible à la flatterie; **to rise s. to temptation,** s'élever au-dessus de la tentation; *Com:* **article of s. quality,** article riche, de qualité supérieure; *(b) (of pers., etc.)* sourcilleux, orgueilleux, superbe; **with a s. smile,** avec un sourire suffisant, condescendant; **s. air,** air supérieur, de supériorité; **she looked very s.,** elle avait l'air très digne; *(c) Astr:* **the s. planets,** les planètes supérieures; *(d) Bot:* (ovaire, etc.) supère; *(e) Typ:* **s. letter,** lettre supérieure; lettrine *f*; **s. number,** chiffre supérieur; exposant *m*; **s. figure,** appel *m* de note; *(f) Geog:* **Lake S.,** le lac Supérieur. **2.** *s. (a)* supérieur, -eure; **he is your s.,** il est votre supérieur; **his superiors in rank,** (i) ses supérieurs hiérarchiques; (ii) ses supérieurs (en degré social); **to be s.o.'s s. in courage,** être supérieur en courage à qn; *(b)* supérieur, -eure (d'une communauté religieuse); **the Father S.,** le père supérieur; **the Mother S.,** la mère supérieure.
superiority [s(j)u:piəri'ɔriti], *s.* supériorité *f*; **s. in talent,** supériorité de talent; *Mil: etc:* **s. in men and materials,** supériorité en hommes et en matériel; *F:* **s. complex,** complexe de supériorité.
superiorly [s(j)u:'piəriəli], *adv.* **1.** *Bot: etc:* **s. placed,** placé plus haut, au-dessus; supère. **2.** d'une manière supérieure; **s. armed,** mieux armé. **3.** d'un air suffisant; d'un air de condescendance; avec un air de supériorité, de dignité.
superjacent [s(j)u:pə'dʒeis(ə)nt], *a. Geol:* surjacent.
superlative [s(j)u:'pə:lətiv]. **1.** *a.* suprême; d'une excellence suprême; superlatif. **2.** *a. & s. Gram:* superlatif (*m*); **adjective in the s.,** adjectif au superlatif; **absolute, relative, s.,** superlatif absolu, relatif; **to speak in superlatives,** se répandre en éloges dithyrambiques.
superlatively [s(j)u:'pə:lətivli], *adv.* superlativement; au suprême degré; au superlatif; **s. handsome,** d'une beauté sans pareille.
superlunar(y) [s(j)u:pə'lu:nər(i)], *a.* surlunaire; supramondain.
superman, *pl.* **-men** ['s(j)u:pəmæn, -men], *s.m.* surhomme.
supermarket ['s(j)u:pəma:kit], *s. Com:* supermarché *m.*
supermundane [s(j)u:pə'mʌndein], *a.* supramondain.
supernaculum [s(j)u:pə'nækjuləm]. **1.** *adv.* **to drink s.,** faire rubis sur l'ongle. **2.** *s.* vin *m* de choix.
supernal [s(j)u:'pə:n(ə)l], *a.* **1.** céleste. **2.** d'une excellence suprême, divine.
supernatant [s(j)u:pə'neit(ə)nt], *a.* surnageant.
supernational [s(j)u:pə'næʃən(ə)l], *a.* supranational, -aux.
supernationalism [s(j)u:pə'næʃənəlizm], *s.* supranationalisme.
supernatural [s(j)u:pə'nætjərəl], *a. & s.* surnaturel (*m*).
supernaturalism [s(j)u:pə'nætjərəlizm], *s. Rel: Phil:* surnaturalisme *m*, supernaturalisme *m*, supranaturalisme *m.*
supernaturalist [s(j)u:pə'nætjərəlist], *a. & s. Rel: Phil:* surnaturaliste (*mf*), supernaturaliste (*mf*), supranaturaliste (*mf*).
supernaturality [s(j)u:pənætjə'ræliti], **supernaturalness** [s(j)u:pə'nætjərəlnis], *s.* surnaturalité *f*; caractère surnaturel (d'une apparition, etc.).
supernaturalize [s(j)u:pə'nætjərəlaiz], *v.tr.* surnaturaliser.
supernaturally [s(j)u:pə'nætjərəli], *adv.* surnaturellement.
supernormal [s(j)u:pə'nɔ:m(ə)l], *a.* au-dessus de la normale; extraordinaire.
supernova [s(j)u:pə'nouvə], *s. Astr:* supernova *f.*
supernumerary [s(j)u:pə'nju:mərəri]. **1.** *a.* surnuméraire; en surnombre; *Mil:* **s. officer,** officier à la suite. **2.** *s. (a)* surnuméraire *m*; *(b) Th: Cin:* figurant, -ante; comparse *mf*; bouche-trou *m, pl.* bouche-trous.
superorder ['s(j)u:pərɔ:dər], *s. Nat.Hist:* super-ordre *m, pl.* super-ordres.
superovulation [s(j)u:pərɔvju'leiʃ(ə)n], *s. Biol:* superovulation *f.*
superphosphate [s(j)u:pə'fɔsfeit], *s.* superphosphate *m.*
superposable [s(j)u:pə'pouzəbl], *a.* superposable.
superpose [s(j)u:pə'pouz], *v.tr.* superposer (**upon, on,** à); étager (des planches, etc.); *Mth:* **to s. two triangles,** superposer deux triangles.
superposition [s(j)u:pəpə'ziʃ(ə)n], *s.* superposition *f*; application *f* (**of sth. on sth.,** de qch. à, sur, qch.).
superpower ['s(j)u:pəpauər], *s. Pol:* superpuissance *f.*
superregeneration [s(j)u:pəri(:)'dʒenə'reiʃ(ə)n], *s. W.Tel:* superréaction *f.*
superregenerative [s(j)u:pəri(:)'dʒenərətiv], *a. W.Tel:* **s. reception,** réception à superréaction.
supersalt ['s(j)u:pəsɔlt], *s. Ch:* sursel *m.*
supersaturate [s(j)u:pə'sætjəreit], *v.tr.* sursaturer.
supersaturation [s(j)u:pəsætjə'reiʃ(ə)n], *s.* sursaturation *f.*
superscribe ['s(j)u:pəskraib], *v.tr.* **1.** marquer (qch.) d'une inscription, d'une suscription; suscrire. **2.** *(a)* écrire son nom en tête (d'un document); *(b)* mettre l'adresse sur (une lettre).
superscript ['s(j)u:pəskript], *s. Mth: etc:* exposant *m.*
superscription [s(j)u:pə'skripʃ(ə)n], *s. (on stone, coin)* inscription *f*; *(on coin)* légende *f*; *(on letter)* adresse *f*, suscription *f*; *(on document, etc.)* en-tête *m, pl.* en-têtes.
supersede [s(j)u:pə'si:d], *v.tr. (a)* remplacer; **to s. an old machine (by a new one),** remplacer une vieille machine par une nouvelle; **this catalogue supersedes previous issues,** ce catalogue annule les précédents; **to s. an official,** remplacer un employé; relever un employé de ses fonctions; **to s. an officer,** démonter un officier; **to s. a system,** détrôner un système; **method now superseded,** méthode périmée; *(b)* prendre la place de (qn); supplanter (qn); **to be superseded by s.o.,** être évincé par qn.
supersedeas [s(j)u:pə'si:diæs], *s. Jur:* **(writ of) s.,** acte suspensif d'instance; ordonnance de suspension d'instance; sursis *m.*
supersedure [s(j)u:pə'siædʒər], *s.* = SUPERSESSION.
supersensible [s(j)u:pə'sensibl], *a. Metaph:* suprasensible.
supersensitive [s(j)u:pə'sensitiv], *a.* hypersensible; d'une sensitivité extrême.
supersensitiveness [s(j)u:pə'sensitivnis], *s.* hypersensibilité *f.*
supersession [s(j)u:pə'seʃ(ə)n], *s.* **1.** remplacement *m* (d'un employé, d'une règle, etc.); annulation *f* (d'un catalogue, etc.). **2.** évincement *m* (d'un collègue, etc.).
supersonic [s(j)u:pə'sɔnik], *a.* **1.** ultrasonore, ultrasonique. **2.** supersonique, sonique; **s. boom, bang,** détonation *f* sonique, bang *m*; **s. aircraft,** avion supersonique; **s. speed,** vitesse supersonique.
superspeed ['s(j)u:pəspi:d], *a. Cin: T.V:* **s. camera,** caméra (à) grande vitesse; **s. shooting,** prise de vues à haute fréquence.
superstage ['s(j)u:pəsteidʒ], *s.* surplatine *f* (de microscope).
superstar ['s(j)u:pəsta:r], *s. Cin: etc:* super vedette *f.*
superstition [s(j)u:pə'stiʃ(ə)n], *s.* superstition *f.*
superstitious [s(j)u:pə'stiʃəs], *a.* superstitieux.
superstitiously [s(j)u:pə'stiʃəsli], *adv.* superstitieusement.
superstore ['s(j)u:pəstɔ:r], *s. Com:* hypermarché *m*; grand supermarché.
superstratum, *pl.* **-a** ['s(j)u:pəstreitəm, -ə], *s. Geol:* couche supérieure.
superstructure ['s(j)u:pəstrʌktjər], *s.* **1.** *(a) Civ.E: Const:* superstructure *f*; *(b)* tablier *m* (d'un pont). **2.** *N.Arch:* *(a)* superstructure, accastillage *m*; *(b) (deckhouse)* rouf *m.* **3.** *Phil:* superstructure.
supersubtle [s(j)u:pə'sʌtl], *a.* d'une subtilité excessive.
supersulphated [s(j)u:pə'sʌlfeitid], *a. Civ.E:* **s. cement,** ciment métallurgique sursulfaté.
supertanker ['s(j)u:pətæŋkər], *s. Nau:* pétrolier géant; supertanker *m.*
supertax ['s(j)u:pətæks], *s. Adm: A:* surtaxe *f*; impôt *m* supplémentaire sur le revenu (à partir d'un certain chiffre).
superterranean [s(j)u:pəte'reiniən], **superterrestrial** [s(j)u:pəte'restriəl], *a.* **1.** supramondain, céleste, supraterrestre. **2.** situé à la surface de la terre.
supertonic [s(j)u:pə'tɔnik], *s. Mus:* sous-médiante *f, pl.* sous-médiantes; sus-tonique *f, pl.* sus-toniques.
supervene [s(j)u:pə'vi:n], *v.i.* survenir; *esp. Med:* **if no complications s.,** s'il ne survient pas de complications.
supervening[1] [s(j)u:pə'vi:niŋ], *a.* survenant.
supervening[2], *s.* = SUPERVENTION.
supervention [s(j)u:pə'venʃ(ə)n], *s.* survenance *f*, survenue *f.*
supervise ['s(j)u:pəvaiz], *v.tr.* **1.** superviser, surveiller (une entreprise, etc.). **2.** diriger, conduire (une entreprise).
supervision [s(j)u:pə'viʒ(ə)n], *s.* **1.** surveillance *f*; supervision *f*; **to be under police s.,** être sous la surveillance de la police; **to keep s.o. under strict s.,** exercer une surveillance sévère sur la conduite de qn; surveiller qn de très près. **2.** direction *f* (d'une entreprise).
supervisor ['s(j)u:pəvaizər], *s.* **1.** surveillant, -ante; directeur, -trice; superviseur *m*; **to act as s. (on playground, in factory, etc.),** exercer la surveillance; *Tp:* **chief s.,** chef de central; *Cmptr:* **overlay s.,** superviseur de segments de recouvrement. **2.** *U.S:* **(chief) s.,** président *m* du conseil d'administration (d'une commune).
supervisory [s(j)u:pə'vaizəri], *a.* (comité, etc.) de surveillance; **s. staff,** cadre de maîtrise; *El:* **s. control,** appareillage de surveillance; *Cmptr:* **s. state,** état superviseur; **s. routine,** programme superviseur; **s. relay,** relais de supervision; **s. signal,** signal de supervision; **s. channel,** voie de supervision.
supinate ['s(j)u:pineit], *v.tr.* tourner (la main) la paume en avant, en dessus; tourner (la jambe) en dehors.
supination [s(j)u:pi'neiʃ(ə)n], *s.* supination *f.*
supinator ['s(j)u:pineitər], *s. Anat:* supinateur *m.*
supine[1] ['s(j)u:pain], *a.* **1.** *(of pers.)* couché, étendu, sur le dos; *Med: (of pers., limb, etc.)* en supination; **s. position,** décubitus dorsal. **2.** *(of pers., life, etc.)* mou, *f.* molle; indolent, inerte, nonchalant.
supine[2], *s. Lt.Gram:* supin *m*; **first s.,** supin actif; **second s.,** supin passif; **in the s.,** au supin.
supinely ['s(j)u:painli], *adv.* **1.** (couché) sur le dos. **2.** indolemment, avec indolence; mollement; nonchalamment, avec nonchalance.
supineness ['s(j)u:painnis], *s.* mollesse *f*, indolence *f*, inertie *f.*
suppedaneum, *pl.* **-ea** [sʌpə'deiniəm, -iə], *s.* soutien-pieds *m inv* (d'une croix de crucifiement).
supper ['sʌpər], *s.* souper *m*; dîner *m*; **to have s.,** souper; dîner; **to have salad for s.,** souper d'une salade; **s. dance,** (i) danse qui précède le souper; (ii) souper dansant; **s. party,** (i) souper, dîner, par invitation; (ii) les convives *m*; **to have a s. party,** avoir du monde à souper, à dîner; **the Last S.,** la (Sainte) Cène; *Ecc:* **the Lord's S.,** la communion, la cène, l'eucharistie *f.*
supperless ['sʌpəlis], *a.* qui n'a pas soupé; **to go to bed s.,** se coucher sans souper.
suppertime ['sʌpətaim], *s.* heure *f* du souper.
supplant [sə'pla:nt], *v.tr.* supplanter; prendre la place de (qn); remplacer (qn, qch.); évincer (qn); *F:* dégommer (qn).
supplantation [sʌpla:n'teiʃ(ə)n], *s.* supplantation *f*, supplantement *m*, évincement *m.*
supplanter [sə'pla:ntər], *s.* supplanteur, -euse; supplantateur, -trice.
supplanting [sə'pla:ntiŋ], *s.* = SUPPLANTATION.
supple[1] [sʌpl], *a.* **1.** souple, pliable, flexible; (cordage) maniable; **s. figure,** taille souple, déliée; **to make sth. s.,** assouplir qch.; **to make s.o.'s limbs more s.,** dénouer les membres à qn; **to become s.,** s'assouplir; **s. limbed,** aux membres souples. **2.** obséquieux, complaisant, souple; **s. minded,** à l'esprit souple; complaisant.

supple[2], *v.tr.* **1.** *O:* assouplir (un membre, l'esprit, un cheval, etc.); dresser (un cheval). **2.** *Leath:* meurtrir, corroyer (le cuir).

supplejack ['sʌpldʒæk], *s.* **1.** (*a*) *Bot:* paullinia *f*, paullinie *f*; liane *f* à scie; (*b*) canne *f* souple; jonc *m*. **2.** *U.S:* pantin *m*, polichinelle *m*.

supplement[1] ['sʌplimənt], *s.* supplément *m*; appendice *m*, annexe *f* (d'un livre, etc.); supplément (d'un journal); *Jur: Scot:* **oath in s.,** serment *m* supplétoire; *Mth:* **s. of an angle,** supplément d'un angle.

supplement[2] [sʌpli'ment], *v.tr.* ajouter un supplément à (un livre, etc.); **to s. one's income by writing articles,** augmenter ses revenus en écrivant des articles; **to s. a scanty meal with cheese,** compléter avec du fromage un repas sommaire.

supplemental [sʌpli'ment(ə)l], *a.* **1.** *Mth:* (angle) supplémentaire (**to, of,** de); **angle s. to another,** angle supplément d'un autre. **2.** *Physiol:* **s. air,** air résiduel (des poumons).

supplementarily [sʌpli'ment(ə)rili, *NAm:* sʌplimen'teərili], *adv.* (ajouté, etc.) comme supplément, en complément.

supplementary [sʌpli'ment(ə)ri], *a.* supplémentaire (**to,** de); additionnel (**to,** à); **s. income,** revenus annexes; **s. maintenance,** entretien *m* supplémentaire; *Book-k:* **s. entry,** écriture *f* complémentaire; *Mth:* **s. angle,** angle *m* supplémentaire.

suppleness ['sʌpəlnis], *s.* **1.** souplesse *f*, flexibilité *f* (du corps, etc.). **2.** complaisance *f*, obséquiosité *f*.

suppletive [sə'pli:tiv], *a.* (mot) supplétif.

suppletory ['sʌplitəri], *a. Jur:* (serment) supplétoire.

suppliant ['sʌpliənt]. **1.** *a.* suppliant; de supplication. **2.** *s.* suppliant, -ante.

suppliantly ['sʌpliəntli], *adv.* d'une manière suppliante; en suppliant; en signe de supplication.

supplicant ['sʌplikənt], *s.* suppliant, -ante.

supplicate ['sʌplikeit]. **1.** *v.i.* supplier, prier avec instance. **2.** *v.tr.* (*a*) **to s. s.o. for sth.,** supplier qn pour obtenir qch.; **to s. s.o. to do sth.,** supplier qn de faire qch.; (*b*) **to s. protection,** solliciter humblement la protection de qn.

supplicating ['sʌplikeitiŋ], *a.* suppliant.

supplicatingly ['sʌplikeitiŋli], *adv.* d'un air, d'un ton, suppliant.

supplication [sʌpli'keiʃ(ə)n], *s.* **1.** supplication *f*. **2.** supplique *f*.

supplicatory [sʌ'plikət(ə)ri, sʌpli'keitəri], *a.* (prière, etc.) supplicatoire, de supplication.

supplier [sə'plaiər], *s.* fournisseur, -euse; pourvoyeur, -euse (**of,** de); approvisionneur, -euse (**of,** en, de).

supply[1] [sə'plai], *s.* **1.** (*a*) approvisionnement *m*, fourniture *f*; **s. of a town with food,** alimentation *f* d'une ville; *Mil: etc:* **food supplies,** approvisionnement en vivres; *Mil:* **s. of the army with food,** ravitaillement *m* de l'armée; **ammunition s.,** ravitaillement en munitions; **s. column,** convoi administratif; convoi de ravitaillement; *Artil:* échelon *m*; **axis of s., main line of s., main s. route,** axe (principal) de ravitaillement; *Artil:* **s. number,** pourvoyeur *m* (de la pièce); *Navy:* **s. ship,** (transport) ravitailleur *m*; **districts of s. of an industrial area,** greniers *m* d'un centre industriel; *Ind:* **power s.,** cession *f* de force motrice; **electric s. service,** service de courant; alimentation électrique; **the local s. circuit,** le secteur; **s. main,** câble de distribution; **s. pressure,** tension de distribution, de consommation, d'utilisation; *Hyd.E:* **s. main, pipe,** canalisation *f*; tuyau *m* d'alimentation, d'amenée; (canal) adducteur *m*; *Sm.a: etc:* **s. magazine,** magasin débiteur; (*b*) *Parl:* **bill of s.,** projet de crédit supplémentaire; **committee of s.,** commission du budget; **monthly s. vote,** les douzièmes *m* provisoires; **to vote supplies,** voter des crédits *m*; (*c*) **s. (post),** occupation *f* (d'une place) par intérim; suppléance *f*; **to be, go, on s.,** occuper une place par intérim; suppléer à un poste. **2.** (*a*) provision *f*; **to take in, lay in, a s. of sth.,** se faire une provision, s'approvisionner, faire un approvisionnement, de qch.; **a good s. of books,** une bonne provision de livres; **inexhaustible s.,** provision inépuisable (de vin, etc.); fonds *m* inépuisable (d'argent, etc.); **fresh s. of troops,** nouveaux renforts; **to get (in) a fresh s. of sth.,** se remonter en qch.; **I must get a new s. of cigars,** il faut que je me r(é)assortisse en cigares; *Pol.Ec:* **s. and demand,** l'offre *f* et la demande; **s. control,** régulation des marchés *m*; *Mil:* **s. officer,** officier d'approvisionnement; *Navy:* commissaire *m*; (*b*) **supplies,** fournitures (de photographie, de bureau, etc.); **supplies of money,** fonds, ressources *f*; **supplies of an army, of a town,** approvisionnement d'une armée, d'une ville; **food supplies,** vivres *m*; **military supplies,** subsistances *f* militaires; *Mil:* **expendable supplies,** approvisionnements de consommation courante: **non-expendable supplies,** approvisionnements non consommables, d'usage courant; **common (user) supplies,** approvisionnements d'usage commun; **to get one's supplies from the grocer,** s'approvisionner, se fournir, chez l'épicier; **to give s.o. supplies,** approvisionner qn; **to cut off, stop, the enemy's supplies,** couper les vivres à l'ennemi; (*c*) prêtre *m*, professeur *m*, etc., qui occupe une place par intérim; **s. teacher,** suppléant, -ante; remplaçant, -ante; **to do some s. teaching,** occuper une place par intérim; suppléer à un poste; **to arrange for a s.,** se faire suppléer.

supply[2] [sə'plai], *v.tr.* (**supplied**) **1.** (*a*) fournir, pourvoir, munir, approvisionner (**s.o. with sth.,** qn de qch.); alimenter (un marché); **to s. oneself with sth.,** s'approvisionner en qch.; **to s. s.o. with food,** alimenter qn; **to s. an army, a town (with provisions),** approvisionner, ravitailler, amunitionner, une armée, une ville; **well supplied town,** ville de ressource(s); **the tradesmen who s. us,** nos fournisseurs *m*; (*of tradesmen*) **we s. him,** il se fournit chez nous; *Com:* **families supplied daily,** livraisons *fpl* à domicile tous les jours; **region supplied by an electricity board,** région desservie par une compagnie d'électricité; *El:* **to s. a factory with current,** alimenter une usine en courant; **to s. a machine (with material, etc.),** alimenter une machine; **river that supplies a mill,** rivière qui alimente un moulin; **the arteries that s. the arms (with blood),** les artères qui amènent le sang aux bras; (*b*) **to s. sth.,** fournir, apporter, qch.; amener (l'eau, le gaz, etc.); **to s. proof(s),** fournir des épreuves; **to keep a paper supplied with news,** alimenter un journal. **2.** (*a*) réparer (une omission); remplir (une vacance); combler, pourvoir à (un déficit); répondre à (un besoin); **to s. a defect in manufacture,** corriger un défaut de fabrication; remédier à une imperfection; **to s. s.o.'s needs,** fournir, pourvoir, subvenir, aux besoins de qn; **to s. the deficiency of sth.,** suppléer à qch.; (*b*) **to s. s.o.'s place,** occuper la place de qn par intérim; remplacer, suppléer, qn; **to s. for s.o.,** faire une suppléance; assurer l'intérim.

supply[3] ['sʌpli], *adv.* souplement; avec souplesse.

support[1] [sə'pɔ:t], *s.* **1.** (*a*) appui *m*, soutien *m*; **moral s.,** appui, soutien, moral; **to solicit s.o.'s s.,** solliciter l'appui, l'aide, de qn; **to give s. to the proposal,** venir à l'appui de, appuyer, la proposition; **to give s.o. effectual s.,** fournir, prêter, à qn un appui efficace; **to get, obtain, no s.,** ne trouver aucun appui; **to receive the sympathy and s. of all,** rallier la sympathie active de tous; **in s.,** en renfort; à l'appui; en soutien; **to produce documents in s. of an allegation,** produire des pièces à l'appui d'une allégation, pour soutenir, appuyer, étayer, une allégation; *Jur:* fournir les pièces au soutien; **in s. of this theory,** en appui à, pour corroborer, cette théorie; **proofs in s. of a case,** preuves à l'appui d'une cause; **collection in s. of a charity,** quête à l'intention, au profit, d'une œuvre (de charité); *Mil: etc:* **artillery s.,** appui d'artillerie; **air s.,** appui d'aviation; appui, soutien, aérien; **fire s.,** appui de feu; **close,** *NAm:* **direct, s.,** appui direct; accompagnement *m*; **close s. weapons, aviation,** engins, aviation, d'accompagnement; **close air s.,** accompagnement aérien; **logistic(al) s.,** soutien logistique; **logistic s. equipment,** matériel de soutien logistique; **to send up two divisions in s. of the first army,** envoyer deux divisions en renfort de la première armée; **to go in s. of a battalion, of a ship,** se porter au secours d'un bataillon, d'un navire; aller soutenir un bataillon, un navire; **s. unit,** unité de soutien; **s. line, trench,** ligne, tranchée, de soutien; (*b*) soutènement *m* (d'une voûte, etc.); *Ph:* **basis of s.,** base, trapèze, de sustentation (d'un corps); (*c*) **insufficient air for the s. of life,** air insuffisant pour entretenir la vie; **they depended on their son for s.,** ils n'avaient que leur fils pour les faire vivre; **to be without means of s.,** être sans ressources; *Jur:* **found without visible means of s.,** trouvé sans moyens d'existence connus. **2.** (*a*) soutien; **the sole s. of his old age,** son seul soutien dans sa vieillesse; **he is the s. of the family,** c'est lui le soutien de la famille; **to find a firm s. in religion,** trouver un support certain dans la religion; (*b*) appui, support, soutien (d'une voûte, etc.); pied *m* (de sustentation); console *f*, soupente *f* (de treuil de poulie); assiette *f* (d'une poutre, etc.); potence *f*; *Phot: Cin:* support (de la couche sensible); *Hort:* tuteur *m*; *Mec.E:* chaise *f*; **cushioned, shock-absorbing, s.,** support amortisseur, support antivibrateur, support antivibratoire; **elastic s.,** support élastique; **pivoting s.,** support à pivot; **floating s.,** support flottant; **loose, free, s.,** support libre; **fixed s.,** support fixe; **square s.,** support en équerre; **s. plate,** plaque support; *Mch:* **gland s.,** support de presse-étoupe; *El:* **electrode s.,** support d'électrode; *Artil:* **bipod s.,** affût-bipied *m, pl.* affûts-bipieds; *Aer:* **(wire) car supports,** balancines *f* (d'un dirigeable); (*c*) *Cost:* **(athletic) s.,** slip *m* de soutien (pour sportifs); support athlétique; **knee s.,** genouillère *f*; **s. stockings, tights,** bas, collant, à varices. (*d*) *U.S:* **price supports,** subventions *f*.

support[2], *v.tr.* **1.** (*a*) supporter, soutenir, appuyer, maintenir, buter (une voûte, etc.); *Hort:* tuteurer (un arbuste, etc.); **gallery supported by pillars,** galerie appuyée sur des colonnes; **this pillar supports the whole building,** cette colonne soutient tout le bâtiment; **I supported him with my arm,** je lui ai prêté l'appui de mon bras; je l'ai soutenu du bras; **I supported him by the arm,** je lui ai pris le bras; **he had to be supported home,** il lui a fallu s'appuyer sur qn pour rentrer chez lui; (*b*) *Mec.E:* supporter, résister à (un effort, une charge, etc.). **2.** appuyer (qn, une pétition, etc.); soutenir, corroborer (une théorie); apporter son soutien à (un gouvernement, etc.); seconder les efforts de (qn); patronner (qn, un bal de charité); faire une donation à (une œuvre de charité, etc.); *Sp:* supporter (une équipe, etc.); *Mil: etc:* soutenir (des troupes); **to s. the advance of the infantry,** appuyer la progression de l'infanterie; **accusation supported by proofs,** accusation avec preuves à l'appui; **proofs that s. a case,** preuves à l'appui d'une cause; **theory supported by experience, by facts,** théorie affirmée par l'expérience, appuyée sur des faits, corroborée par des faits; *Parl: etc:* **to s. the motion,** soutenir la motion; **he supported my statement,** il est venu à l'appui de mon affirmation; **to be supported by s.o. (in a proposal, etc.),** être secondé par qn; **the mayor, supported by the clergy and the officers of the garrison,** monsieur le maire, entouré du clergé et des officiers de la garnison; *Th:* **to s. the leading actor,** donner la réplique au premier rôle; avoir le second rôle. **3.** entretenir (la vie, la combustion, etc.); subvenir à l'entretien de (qn); faire vivre, faire subsister (qn); **to have a wife and three children to s.,** avoir une femme et trois enfants à nourrir; **hospital supported by voluntary contributions,** hôpital entretenu par souscriptions volontaires; **to s. oneself,** se suffire (à soi-même); gagner sa vie. **4.** supporter, tolérer, endurer (une injure, etc.). **5.** *O:* soutenir (un rôle, un caractère).

supportable [sə'pɔ:təbl], *a.* **1.** supportable, tolérable. **2.** (*of theory, etc.*) soutenable.

supporter [sə'pɔ:tər], *s.* **1.** (*device*) soutien *m*, support *m*; *Cost:* **athletic s.,** slip *m* de soutien (pour sportifs); support athlétique; **knee s.,** genouillère *f*. **2.** (*pers.*) défenseur *m*, tenant, -ante (d'une opinion); adhérent, -ente (d'un parti); partisan, -ane (d'un homme politique, d'une coutume, etc.); suppôt *m* (d'un tyran); *Sp:* supporter *m* (d'une équipe, etc.). **3.** *Her:* (i) (*animal*) support, (ii) (*human*) tenant (de l'écu).

supporting[1] [sə'pɔ:tiŋ], *a.* (mur, point) d'appui, de soutènement; **s. pillar,** pilier de soutènement; **s. beam of a winch,** soupente *f* (d'un treuil); *Ph:* **s. base,** base, trapèze, de sustentation (d'un corps); *Th:* **the s. cast,** la troupe qui seconde les premiers rôles; *Cin:* **s. film, programme,** film *m*, programme *m*, supplémentaire; *Mil:* **s. troops,** troupes de soutien.

supporting[2], *s. Const: etc:* soutènement *m*, soutien *m*, appui *m* (d'un mur, etc.).

supportive [sə'pɔ:tiv], *a.* soutenant; **s. treatment,** traitement (thérapeutique) de soutien; **to give s. action,** (i) prêter son appui, venir à l'appui; (ii) faire une grève de solidarité, de sympathie.

supposable [sə'pouzəbl], *a.* supposable.

supposal [sə'pouz(ə)l], *s. A:* supposition *f*.

suppose[1] [sə'pouz], *s. F:* supposition *f*; idée *f* en l'air.

suppose[2], *v.tr.* supposer; (*a*) admettre par hypothèse; **s. yourself in my place,** mettez-vous à ma place; **let us s. the two things equal,** supposons les deux choses égales; **s. ABC an equilateral triangle,** soit ABC un triangle équilatéral; **(let us) s. (that) you're right, supposing (that) you're right,** supposons, supposé, que vous ayez raison; mettons que vous ayez raison; en supposant, à supposer, que vous ayez raison; dans la supposition que vous ayez raison; admettons, en admettant, que vous ayez raison; **s., supposing, you were ill,** supposez que vous soyez malade; **s. that Napoleon had won the battle of Waterloo,** supposons que Napoléon ait gagné la bataille de Waterloo; **supposing that (that) is the case,** posons le cas que cela soit, que cela soit ainsi, qu'il en soit ainsi; le cas posé que cela soit; admettons que cela soit le cas; **supposing, s., he came back,** si par supposition il revenait; **yes, but s. I were to die,** oui, mais si je venais à mourir; **well, supposing I did?** eh bien! et puis après? **s. he is,** *Lit:* **he be, guilty,** à supposer qu'il soit coupable; *F:* **s. we change the subject,** si nous changions de sujet; (*b*) (*postulate*) **the creation supposes the creator,** la création suppose le créateur; **that supposes the ultimate perfectibility of man,** cela présuppose l'ultime perfectibilité humaine; (*c*) s'imaginer; croire, penser, supposer; **you mustn't s. that . . .,** il ne faut pas vous imaginer que . . .; **I s. you'll do it, you'll do it, I s.,** je suppose que vous le ferez; **I don't s. he'll do it,** je ne suppose pas qu'il le fasse; il est peu probable qu'il le fasse; **do you s. he'll do it?** supposez-vous qu'il le fasse? **I don't s. for one minute, for a moment, that I'll get the prize,** je n'ai pas la moindre prétention de remporter le prix; **will you go?—I s. so,** irez-vous?—probablement; sans doute; **is she beautiful?—I s. so,** est-ce qu'elle est belle?—sans doute; il faut le croire; **I don't think he'll come—no, I s. not, I don't s. so,** je ne crois pas qu'il viendra—non, sans doute; probablement pas; **I may do what I like, I s.!** j'ai le droit de faire ce que je veux, peut-être! **I don't s. I've been on a bus for two years,** autant que je sache, voilà deux ans que je n'ai pas pris l'autobus; **I don't s. you remember me,** vous ne vous souvenez pas de moi sans doute; **he is supposed to be wealthy, in London,** on le suppose riche, à Londres; on suppose qu'il est riche, qu'il est à Londres; il est censé être riche, être à Londres; **he's supposed to have a chance,** on lui croit des chances; **it is supposed to be authentic,** cela passe pour authentique; **there is supposed to be a well in the garden,** on dit qu'il y a un puits dans le jardin; **the sum that is supposed to be due to him,** la somme qu'on suppose lui être due, qui est censée lui être due; (*d*) **to be supposed to do sth.,** être censé faire qch.; **he is supposed to be the master,** il est censément le maître; **I'm not supposed to do it,** je ne suis pas censé le faire; ce n'est pas à moi de le faire; **I'm not supposed to know,** je ne suis pas censé le savoir; **I'm supposed not to know,** je suis censé ne pas le savoir.

supposed [sə'pouzd], *a.* supposé, prétendu; soi-disant; **the s. culprit,** le présumé coupable.

supposedly [sə'pouzidli], *adv.* par supposition; censément; **he went away, s. to fetch help,** il est parti soi-disant pour chercher de l'aide.

supposit [sə'pɔzit], *s. Log: Phil:* suppôt *m.*

supposition [sʌpə'ziʃ(ə)n], *s.* supposition *f,* hypothèse *f;* (*a*) **to make suppositions,** faire des hypothèses; **unfounded s.,** supposition gratuite; **why (do you) make that s.?** pourquoi irez-vous supposer cela? pourquoi supposez-vous cela? **on the s. that . . .,** supposé que + *sub.*; (*b*) **on s.,** par supposition, par conjecture; **on the s. that. . .,** dans l'hypothèse que . . ..

suppositional [sʌpə'ziʃən(ə)l], *a.* hypothétique; supposé, imaginaire.

suppositious [sʌpə'ziʃəs], *a.* **1.** faux, *f.* fausse. **2.** hypothétique; supposé, imaginaire.

supposititious [səpɔzi'tiʃəs], *a.* **1.** faux, *f.* fausse; **s. name,** nom supposé; faux nom. **2.** *Jur:* (enfant) supposé, substitué; **s. will,** testament supposé. **3.** hypothétique; supposé, imaginaire.

supposititiously [səpɔzi'tiʃəsli], *adv.* par supposition; faussement; par substitution.

suppositive [sə'pɔzitiv], *a.* **1.** = SUPPOSITIONAL. **2.** *Gram:* suppositif.

suppository [sə'pɔzitəri], *s. Pharm:* suppositoire *m.*

suppositum, *pl.* **-a** [sə'pɔzitəm, -ə], *s. Log: Phil:* suppôt *m.*

suppress [sə'pres], *v.tr.* **1.** (*a*) réprimer, étouffer (une révolte, etc.); (*b*) supprimer (un journal, une association, etc.); faire disparaître (un abus, etc.); supprimer, retrancher, caviarder (un article de journal, etc.); supprimer, interdire (une publication); arrêter (une hémorragie); **to s. s.o.'s pension,** supprimer, rayer, la pension de qn. **2.** étouffer (une toux, un bâillement, un scandale); étouffer, ravaler (un sanglot); réprimer, refouler (ses sentiments); dominer (une émotion); faire taire (sa conscience, un interrupteur, etc.); **to s. one's feelings,** se contenir. **3.** cacher, dissimuler (qch.); passer (qch.) sous silence; ne pas révéler (un fait); taire, ne pas donner (un nom); *Jur:* supprimer (un fait, une circonstance). **4.** *W.Tel: El: etc:* antiparasiter (un appareil).

suppressed [sə'prest], *a.* **1.** réprimé; supprimé. **2.** étouffé, réprimé; **s. anger,** colère réprimée, rentrée, refoulée; **s. excitement,** agitation contenue; **s. voice,** voix étouffée; *For:* **s. undergrowth,** sous-bois étouffé. **3.** *Bot:* (organe) qui manque, qui fait défaut.

suppressible [sə'presibl], *a.* **1.** supprimable. **2.** réprimable. **3.** que l'on peut passer sous silence.

suppression [sə'preʃ(ə)n], *s.* **1.** répression *f* (d'une émeute, d'un abus, etc.); suppression *f* (d'un livre, etc.). **2.** (*a*) étouffement *m* (d'un scandale); refoulement *m* (des émotions); (*b*) *Med:* suppression (de transpiration, d'urine); (*c*) *For:* étouffement (du sous-bois). **3.** suppression (d'un fait, etc.); dissimulation *f* (de la vérité). **4.** (*a*) *W.Tel: El:* antiparasitage *m*; *T.V:* **beam s.,** suppression du faisceau; *Cmptr:* **space s.,** suppression d'espaces; **zero s.,** suppression de zéros; **transmission with partial sideband s.,** transmission avec bande latérale partiellement supprimée.

suppressive [sə'presiv], *a.* suppressif, répressif; **s. measures,** mesures de répression.

suppressor [sə'presər], *s.* **1.** (*a*) étouffeur, -euse (d'une émeute, etc.); **he was the s. of the revolt,** c'est lui qui a réprimé la révolte; (*b*) dissimulateur, -trice (d'un fait). **2.** *W.Tel: Aut: etc:* (dispositif *m*, appareil *m*, filtre *m*) antiparasite *m*; *W.Tel:* **s. grid,** grille de freinage.

suppurate ['sʌpjureit], *v.i.* (*of wound, sore*) suppurer.

suppurating ['sʌpjureitiŋ], *a.* (abcès, etc.) suppurant.

suppuration [sʌpju'reiʃ(ə)n], *s.* suppuration *f* (d'un abcès, etc.).

suppurative ['sʌpjurətiv], *a.* suppuratif.

supra ['s(j)u:prə], *adv.* supra.

supra- ['s(j)u:prə], *pref.* **1.** supra-. **2.** sus-. **3.** sur-.

supra-axillary [s(j)u:præk'siləri], *a. Bot:* supra-axillaire.

supraconductive [s(j)u:prəkɔn'dʌktiv], *a. Ph: El:* supraconducteur.

supraconductivity [s(j)u:prəkɔndʌk'tiviti], *s. Ph: El:* supraconductivité *f,* supraconductibilité *f,* supraconduction *f.*

supraconductor [s(j)u:prəkɔn'dʌktər], *s. Ph: El:* supraconducteur *m.*

supracoracoideus [s(j)u:prəkɔrə'kɔidiəs], *s. Anat:* supracoracoïde *f.*

supracostal [s(j)u:prə'kɔst(ə)l], *a. Anat:* surcostal, -aux.

supracretaceous [s(j)u:prəkri'teiʃəs], *a. Geol:* supracrétacé.

suprahepatic [s(j)u:prəhi'pætik], *a. Anat:* sus-hépatique.

supraliminal [s(j)u:prə'limin(ə)l], *a. Psy:* supraliminal, -aux.

supramundane [s(j)u:prə'mʌndein], *a.* supramondain.

supranational [s(j)u:prə'næʃən(ə)l], *a.* supranational, -aux.

supranatural [s(j)u:prə'nætjərəl], *a.* surnaturel.

supranaturalism [s(j)u:prə'nætjərəlizm], *s. Rel: Phil:* supranaturalisme *m*, surnaturalisme *m*, supernaturalisme *m.*

supranaturalist [s(j)u:prə'nætjərəlist], *a.* & *s. Rel: Phil:* supranaturaliste (*mf*), surnaturaliste (*mf*), supernaturaliste (*mf*).

supraoccipital [s(j)u:prəɔk'sipit(ə)l], *a. Anat:* sus-occipital, -aux.

supraorbital [s(j)u:prə'ɔ:bit(ə)l], *a. Anat:* sus-orbitaire.

supraprotest [s(j)u:prə'proutest], *s. Com: Jur:* acceptation *f* sous protêt, par intervention.

suprarenal [s(j)u:prə'ri:n(ə)l], *a. Anat:* surrénal, -aux.

suprasegmental [s(j)u:prəseg'ment(ə)l], *a. Ling:* suprasegmental, -aux.

suprasensible [s(j)u:prə'sensibl], *a. Metaph:* suprasensible.

supraspinal [s(j)u:prə'spain(ə)l], *a. Anat:* surépineux, sus-épineux.

suprathoracic [s(j)u:prəθɔ:'ræsik], *a. Anat:* suprathoracique.

supravital [s(j)u:prə'vait(ə)l], *a. Biol:* supravital, -aux.

supremacy [s(j)u(:)'preməsi], *s.* suprématie *f,* hégémonie *f*; *Hist:* **Act of S.,** acte de Suprématie; **the Oath of S.,** le serment de suprématie.

supreme[1] [s(j)u(:)'pri:m], *a.* suprême; **the S. Being,** l'Être suprême; **to reign s.,** régner en maître, en souverain absolu; **to make the s. sacrifice,** mourir (pour qn, pour son pays); *Jur:* **S. Court (of Judicature),** cour souveraine, suprême; *Pol:* **the S. Soviet,** le Soviet suprême; *Ecc:* **the S. Pontiff,** le souverain pontife, le Pape; *Hist:* **the S. War Council,** le conseil supérieur interallié; *Phil:* **the s. good,** le souverain bien; **s. happiness,** bonheur suprême; souverain bonheur; **to hold s.o. in s. contempt,** avoir un souverain mépris pour qn; *Lit:* **the s. hour, moment,** l'heure, l'instant, suprême.

supreme[2], *s. Cu:* (i) sauce suprême, veloutée; (ii) (*dish*) suprême *m* (de volaille, etc.).

suprême [s(j)u(:)'prem], *s.* = SUPREME[2].

supremely [s(j)u(:)'pri:mli], *adv.* suprêmement; au suprême degré; **we are s. happy,** notre bonheur est sans mélange; nous jouissons d'un bonheur suprême.

supremo, *pl.* **-s** [s(j)u(:)'pri:mou, -mouz], *s.* commandant *m*, chef *m*, suprême; souverain absolu.

sura(h)[1] ['sjuərə], *s.* s(o)urate *f* (du Coran).

surah[2], *s. Tex:* surah *m.*

sural ['sjuərəl], *a. Anat:* (*of artery, etc.*) sural, -aux.

suranal [sju'reinəl], *a. Ent:* suranal, -aux.

Surat [sju'ræt], *Pr.n. Geog:* S(o)urate; *Tex:* **s. (cotton),** coton *m*, cotonnade *f,* de S(o)urate.

surbase[1] ['sə:beis], *s. Arch:* **1.** corniche *f* (de piédestal). **2.** moulure *f* de la plinthe (d'un lambris).

surbase[2] [sə:beis], *v.tr. Arch:* surbaisser (une arcade, une voûte); **surbased arch,** arc surbaissé.

surbasement [sə:'beismənt], *s. Arch:* surbaissement *m* (d'un arc, etc.).

surbed [sə:'bed], *v.tr.* (**surbedded**) *Const:* déliter (une pierre).

surbedding [sə:'bediŋ], *s. Const:* délitage *m*, délitement *m*, délitation *f* (d'une pierre).

surcease [sə:'si:s], *s. A:* répit *m.*

surcharge[1] ['sə:tʃɑ:dʒ], *s.* **1.** (*overload*) surcharge *f*; charge excessive. **2.** (*a*) prix excessif; (*b*) droit *m* supplémentaire; majoration *f* d'impôt (par pénalisation); **s. on a letter,** surtaxe d'une lettre; taxe *f* supplémentaire; (*c*) *Adm:* débours injustifié porté à la charge du responsable; (*d*) *Jur:* somme omise dans les frais de justice. **3.** *Post:* surcharge (sur un timbre).

surcharge[2], *v.tr.* **1.** (*overload*) surcharger (**with,** de). **2.** (*a*) faire payer (qn) trop cher; surimposer (les contribuables, etc.); (*b*) majorer (un impôt); (*c*) (sur)taxer (une lettre, etc.); (*d*) *Adm:* (i) faire supporter (au responsable) une erreur de paiement; (ii) montrer une erreur de crédit dans un arrêté de comptes. **3.** *Post:* surcharger (un timbre).

surcingle ['sə:siŋgl], *s.* **1.** *Harn:* surfaix *m*; sous-ventrière *f, pl.* sous-ventrières. **2.** *A:* ceinture *f* (de soutane).

surcoat ['sə:kout], *s. A.Cost:* surcot *m*; casaque *f*; houppelande *f.*

surd [sə:d]. **1.** *a.* (*a*) *Mth:* (*of quantity*) irrationnel, incommensurable; (*b*) *Ling:* (son) sourd, dévoisé. **2.** *s.* (*a*) *Mth:* quantité *f* incommensurable; racine irrationnelle; (*b*) *Ling:* (consonne) sourde *f.*

surdity ['sə:diti], *s.* surdité *f.*

surdomutism [sə:dou'mju:tizm], *s. Med:* surdi-mutité *f.*

sure ['ʃuər]. **1.** *a.* sûr, certain; (*a*) **to be s. of, about, sth.,** être sûr, certain, de qch.; **I'm s. of my facts, of what I'm saying,** je suis sûr de mon fait; **I'm s. of it,** j'en suis certain; j'en suis convaincu; j'en ai la certitude; **I'm not so s. of, about, that,** je n'en suis pas bien sûr, certain; je n'en sais trop rien; je ne suis trop; **I'm not s. whether he agrees with me or not,** je ne suis pas sûr s'il est de mon avis (ou non, ou pas); **I'm s. (that) you're mistaken,** je suis sûr que vous vous trompez; **he's s. he will succeed, he's s. of succeeding,** il a la conviction qu'il réussira; il est certain, sûr, de réussir; il se flatte de réussir; **he's s. he heard it,** il est sûr de l'avoir entendu; **are you perfectly s. you will see him again?** avez-vous la pleine assurance, êtes-vous certain, de le revoir? **are you quite s. he hasn't left yet?** êtes-vous bien sûr qu'il n'est pas encore parti? **I'm s. you don't know the answer,** vous ne savez assurément pas la réponse; **it's the wallet which I was s. I had left in the drawer,** c'est le portefeuille que j'étais persuadé avoir laissé dans le tiroir; **you're s. that book is mine?** il est bien à moi, ce livre? **to be s. of oneself,** être sûr de soi(-même); **I'm not s. myself,** moi, je n'en suis pas bien certain; **I don't know, I'm sure,** ma foi, je ne sais pas, je n'en sais rien; je ne sais vraiment pas; **to make s. of sth.,** s'assurer de qch.; **make s. (that) the door is shut,** assurez-vous que la porte est fermée; **after making s. which was my carriage,** après avoir repéré mon wagon; **to make s. of a seat,** s'assurer une place; **don't be too, so, s.!** vous êtes trop sûr de vous! (*b*) infaillible; (jugement, tireur, etc.) sûr; (asile) assuré; (remède) sûr, infaillible; **s. step,** pas assuré; **with a s. hand,** d'une main assurée; **s. sighted,** à l'œil juste; **to be s. sighted,** avoir du coup d'œil; **there is only one s. way of doing it,** il n'y a qu'un moyen sûr de le faire; (*c*) indubitable; (bénéfice, succès) sûr, assuré; **(it's a) s. thing,** c'est une certitude, c'est une chose certaine; c'est sûr et certain; *NAm: F:* **s. thing!** mais oui! bien sûr! pour sûr! d'accord! **I don't know for s.,** je n'en suis pas bien sûr; **tomorrow for s.,** demain sans faute; **he won't come today, that's for s.,** il ne viendra certainement pas aujourd'hui; c'est sûr qu'il ne viendra pas aujourd'hui; **he'll be killed for s.,** à coup sûr il sera tué; (*d*) **it's s. to be fine,** il fera sûrement beau; **there are s. to be some changes,** il va sûrement y avoir des changements; **he's s. to come,** il viendra à coup sûr; il viendra sûrement; **be s. to come early, be s. and come early,** ne manquez pas d'arriver de bonne heure; **be s. not to lose it,** gardez-vous, prenez garde, de le perdre; *O:* **(yes,) to be s.!** mais oui! assurément! certainement! bien sûr! pour sûr! oui certes! *O:* **well, to be s.!** tiens, tiens! par exemple! **2.** *adv.* (*a*) *A:* vraiment; certainement; indubitablement; *NAm: F:* **it s. is cold,** il fait vraiment froid; il fait un froid de canard; (*b*) **as s. as fate, as s. as eggs are eggs, as s. as eggs is eggs,** aussi vrai qu'il fait jour; aussi sûr que deux et deux font quatre; tout ce qu'il y a de plus sûr; **s. enough he was there,** il était bien là; c'était bien lui; **I thought he would come and s. enough he did,** je pensais bien qu'il viendrait, et il est venu effectivement; **he will come s. enough,** il viendra à coup sûr; **s. enough!** c'est (bien) vrai! sans doute! bien sûr! assurément! *F:* **for s.!** *NAm:* **s.!** mais oui! d'accord! bien sûr! pour sûr!

surefooted [ʃuə'futid], *a.* au pied sûr, aux pieds sûrs; **to be s.,** avoir le pied sûr.

surely ['ʃuəli], *adv.* **1.** sûrement; **to work slowly but s.,** travailler lentement mais sûrement. **2.** (*a*) assurément; sans doute; vraiment, en vérité; **he will s. come,** il viendra assurément, sûrement; (*b*) **s. you don't believe that!** n'allez pas me dire que vous croyez cela! vous ne croyez pas cela, voyons! **s. you have read that,** vous l'avez certainement lu; **s. we have met before,** nous nous sommes déjà rencontrés, n'est-ce pas? **s. you're not going to leave us?** vous n'allez pourtant pas nous quitter? **that isn't true, s.,** ce n'est sûrement pas vrai; *O:* **s. to goodness!** assurément! parbleu! (*c*) *O:* **will you help me?—s.!** voulez-vous m'aider?—bien sûr! certes!

sureness ['ʃuənis], *s.* **1.** sûreté *f* (de main, etc.). **2.** certitude *f.*

surety ['ʃuəti], *s.* **1.** *A:* sûreté *f,* certitude *f*; **for, of, a s.,** sûrement, certainement. **2.** (*a*) *A:* garantie *f,* sûreté, cautionnement *m*; (*b*) *Jur:* (*pers.*) caution *f*; garant, -ante; répondant, -ante; *Com:* donneur *m* d'aval, de caution; avaliseur *m,* avaliste *m*; **to stand s. for s.o.,** se porter caution pour qn; se rendre, se porter, garant de qn; répondre de, pour, qn; cautionner qn; appuyer qn de sa garantie; **s. for a debt,** garant d'une dette; **s. for a s.,** arrière-caution *f, pl.* arrière-cautions; **s. bond,** (contrat de) cautionnement *m*; garantie; **to enter into a s. bond,** s'engager par cautionnement.

suretyship ['ʃuətiʃip], *s. Jur: Com:* cautionnement *m*; garantie *f.*

surf[1] [sə:f], *s.* barre *f* de plage; ressac *m*; brisants *mpl* sur la plage; déferlement *m*; **s. bathing,** (i) (*esp. in Austr.*) bains *mpl* dans les brisants (de la plage); (ii) surfing *m,* surf *m*; **s. rider,** (i) amateur *m* du surfing; (ii) aquaplaniste *mf*; **s. riding,** (i) surfing, surf; (ii) (sport *m* de) l'aquaplane *m.*

surf[2], *v.i.* (*a*) se baigner dans les brisants; (*b*) faire du surfing.

surface[1] ['sə:fis], *s.* **1.** surface *f*; (*a*) **the earth's s.,** la surface, la superficie, de la terre; **to rise to the s. of the water,** remonter, revenir, sur l'eau; (*of submarine*) **to rise, come, to the s.,** revenir en surface; **to break s.,** faire surface; **s. attack,** attaque *f* en surface; **s. speed,** vitesse *f* en surface (d'un sous-marin); *Nau:* **s. craft,** vaisseaux *m* de surface, non-submersibles; *Min:* **to bring ore (up) to the s.,** monter du minerai à la surface, au jour; **s. work,** travail *m* au jour; **s. worker,** ouvrier *m* du jour; **s. mine,** minière *f*; **s. temperature,** température *f* de la surface; *Post:* **to send a letter by s. mail,** envoyer une lettre par voie de terre, de mer; **s. drain,** *Civ.E:* tranchée *f* à ciel ouvert; *Agr:* saignée *f* d'irrigation; **s. water,** eau superficielle, eaux de surface; eau du jour, folle; *Meteor:* **s. wave,** onde *f* de surface (d'un tremblement de terre); *NAm:* **s. car,** tramway *m*; (*b*) **smooth, even, s.,** surface lisse, unie; *Carp:* **s. planing,** dégauchissage *m* (d'une planche); *Mec.E:* **s. plate,** marbre *m* à dresser; planomètre *m*; plaque *f* de dressage; **bearing s., working s.,** surface d'appui, de frottement, frottante; portée *f* (d'un coussinet); **s. grinding machine,** machine *f* à dresser à la meule; *Rec:* **s. scratching, noise,** bruit *m* de surface; *Ph:* **s. tension,** tension superficielle, de surface; *Typ:* **s. printing,** impression *f* sur planches gravées en relief; (*c*) extérieur *m,* dehors *m*; **on the s. everything was going well,** tout allait bien en apparence; **his politeness is only on the s.,** sa politesse est toute de surface, toute en superficie; il n'a qu'un vernis de politesse; **meaning that lies below the s.,** signification cachée; **he never goes below the s.,** il s'arrête à la surface des choses; il ne va jamais au fond des choses; **one never gets below the s. with him,** on n'arrive jamais à lire dans son âme, à pénétrer sous le masque. **2.** (*a*) *Mth:* **s. of revolution,** surface de révolution, de rotation; (*b*) aire *f,* étendue *f,* superficie *f*; **working s.,** plan *m* de travail, surface utile (d'un bureau, etc.); *Av:* **lifting s.,** surface portante, de sustentation; *Mch:* **heating s.,** surface de chauffe. **3.** (*a*) revêtement *m* (d'une route); **temporary s.,** chaussée *f* provisoire; (*b*) *Agr: For:* couverture *f* du sol; *Agr:* **s. soil,** terre végétale; *For:* **s. fire,** incendie *m* dans la couverture du sol.

surface[2]. **1.** *v.tr.* (*a*) apprêter, polir, lisser, la surface de (qch.); (*b*) dresser, dégauchir (une planche); (*c*) *Paperm:* calandrer, glacer, satiner (le papier); (*d*) *Civ.E:* revêtir (une route) **(with,** de); **to s. a road with macadam,** établir une chaussée en macadam; (*e*) *Paint:* apprêter (une surface); (*f*) *Navy:* faire revenir (un sous-marin) en surface. **2.** *v.i.* (*a*) *Navy:* (*of submarine*) faire surface; revenir en surface; *F:* **after disappearing for some months he surfaced in California,** après s'être caché pendant quelques mois il est réapparu en Californie; (*b*) *F:* (*of pers.*) reprendre connaissance; *F:* faire surface.

surface-active ['sə:fis'æktiv], *a. Ch:* tensio-actif.

surface-coated ['sə:fis'koutid], *a. Paperm:* (papier) couché.

surfaceman, *pl.* **-men** ['sə:fismən], *s.m.* **1.** *Min:* ouvrier du jour. **2.** *Rail:* cheminot *m.*

surfacer ['sə:fisər], *s.* **1.** machine *f* à surfacer, à polir; surfaceuse *f.* **2.** *Carp:* dégauchisseuse *f*; machine à dégauchir, à surfacer.

surface-sized ['sə:fissaizd], *a. Paperm:* collé en surface.

surfacing ['sə:fisiŋ], *s.* **1.** (*a*) apprêtage *m,* polissage *m,* de la surface (de qch.); surfaçage *m*; *Paperm:* calandrage *m,* glaçage *m,* satinage *m*; (*b*) *Carp:* dégauchissage *m* (d'une planche); **s. machine** = SURFACER 2. **2.** (*a*) *Civ.E:* revêtement *m* (d'une route); (*b*) *Paint:* **s. coat,** couche *f* d'apprêt.

surfactant [sə:'fæktənt], *s. Ch:* tensio-actif *m.*

surfbird ['sə:fbə:d], *s. Orn: NAm:* échassier *m* (du littoral du Pacifique); *Fr.C:* échassier du ressac.

surfboard ['sə:fbɔ:d], *s. Sp:* (*a*) planche *f* de surfing; (*b*) aquaplane *m.*

surfboat ['sə:fbout], *s.* pirogue *f* de barre (des Hawaïens); surf-boat *m, pl.* surf-boats.

surfeit[1] ['sə:fit], *s.* **1.** surabondance *f*; **there is a s. of gold in the market,** il y a sur le marché une surabondance d'or. **2.** (*a*) réplétion *f* (d'aliments); satiété *f*; **to have a s. of oysters, of music,** être rassasié d'huîtres, de musique; **to die of a s. of sth.,** mourir d'une indigestion de qch.; (*b*) dégoût *m*; nausée *f*; **to eat sth. to (a) s.,** manger de qch. jusqu'à s'en dégoûter, jusqu'à la nausée.

surfeit[2]. **1.** *v.i.* se gorger; se repaître. **2.** *v.tr.* gorger, rassasier (qn de qch.); blaser (qn); **to s. oneself with sth.,** se gorger, se repaître, de qch. jusqu'à s'en dégoûter, jusqu'à la nausée; **surfeited with pleasure,** blasé de plaisirs; écœuré par les plaisirs.

surfer ['sə:fər], *s.* amateur *m* du surfing.

surfing ['sə:fiŋ], *s. Sp:* surfing *m,* surf *m.*

surfman, *pl.* **-men** ['sə:fmən], *s.m.* spécialiste, fervent, du surfing.

surge[1] [sə:dʒ], *s.* **1.** (*a*) *Nau:* (i) levée *f* de la lame; houle *f*; (ii) lame de fond; grosse lame de houle; (iii) **the barrier didn't stand up to the s. of the crowd,** la barrière a cédé aux remous de la foule; (*b*) poussée *f* (d'activité, etc.); accès *m* (d'enthousiasme, colère, etc.); **he felt a s. of anger,** un flot, une vague, de colère est monté(e) en lui; (*c*) irrégularité *f* (dans la marche d'une machine, etc.); *Ph:* coïncidence *f* de vibrations, d'oscillations; battement *m*; *El:* **s. of current,** vague, à-coup *m,* impulsion *f,* de courant; surintensité *f*; **s. of voltage,** surtension *f*; **s. absorber,** parasurtension *m*; (*d*) *Hyd.E:* **s. tank, chamber,** réservoir *m* amortisseur; réservoir tampon; **s. tank, shaft,** cheminée *f* d'équilibre (d'un barrage). **2.** *Nau:* saut *m* (d'un cordage); choc *m,* coup *m* de fouet (au cabestan).

surge[2], *v.i.* **1.** (*of ship*) monter sur la vague. **2.** (*a*) (*of sea*) être houleux; devenir houleux; (*of waters*) se soulever, rebondir; (*b*) **lava surged out of the crater,** des vagues de lave débordaient du cratère; **the crowd surged along the street, into the building, on to the pitch,** la foule s'est répandue en flots dans la rue, s'est engouffrée dans l'édifice, a inondé le terrain; **the crowd surged back,** la foule a reflué; **anger surged (up) within her,** un flot de colère est monté en elle; **the blood surged to her cheeks,** le sang lui a reflué au visage. **3.** *I.C.E: etc:* **the engine surges,** le moteur tourne irrégulièrement, pompe, galope; *El:* **the current surges,** il y a des à-coups de courant; **the voltage surges,** il y a des surtensions. **4.** (*a*) (*of wheel, etc.*) glisser; *Nau:* (*of cable*) choquer brusquement; (*b*) *v.tr. Nau:* dériver, filer (un câble); **to s. a rope round the capstan,** choquer (brusquement) une amarre au cabestan.

surgeon ['sə:dʒən], *s.* **1.** chirurgien, -ienne. **2.** *Mil: A:* médecin *m* militaire; chirurgien-major *m, pl.* chirurgiens-majors; *Navy:* médecin. **3.** *U.S:* **s. general,** (i) *Mil:* chef *m* du service de santé militaire; (ii) = médecin inspecteur (du service de santé publique). **4.** (*a*) *Ich:* **s. (fish),** chirurgien, acanthure *m*; (*b*) *Orn:* **s. (bird),** jacana *m*; (oiseau) chirurgien.

surgery ['sə:dʒəri], *s.* **1.** chirurgie *f*;, médecine *f* opératoire; **major s.,** grande chirurgie; **minor s.,** petite chirurgie, chirurgie ministrante; **bone s.,** chirurgie osseuse; **oral s.,** chirurgie buccale; **heart s.,** chirurgie du cœur; *Arb:* **tree s.,** chirurgie végétale, arboricole. **2.** cabinet *m* de consultation (chez un médecin); cabinet (de dentiste); **s. (hours),** heures *f* de consultation.

surgical ['sə:dʒikl], *a.* chirurgical, -aux; **s. instruments,** instruments *m* de chirurgie; **s. case,** (i) cas *m* relevant du chirurgien; (ii) trousse *f* de chirurgien; **s. appliances,** (i) appareils chirurgicaux; (ii) appareils orthopédiques; **s. boot,** chaussure *f* orthopédique; **s. spirit,** alcool *m* à 90°; *Mil:* **mobile s. unit,** ambulance chirurgicale.

surging[1] ['sə:dʒiŋ], *a.* **s. sea,** mer houleuse; **s. crowds,** foules houleuses; **a s. mass of people,** un flot (pressé) d'êtres humains.

surging[2], *s.* **1.** (*a*) **the s. of a torrent,** les rebonds *m* d'un torrent; **the s. of the crowd,** les remous *m* de la foule; **s. back,** reflux *m* (de la foule, etc.); *Hyd.E:* **s. of water in a pipe,** contre-foulement *m* de l'eau dans une conduite; (*b*) *El:* coïncidence *f* d'oscillations; battement *m.* **2.** *Nau:* = SURGE[1] 2.

Suricata [sjuəri'keitə], *s.pl. Z:* suricates *m.*

suricate ['sjuərikeit], *s. Z:* suricate *m.*

Surinam [suəri'næm]. *Pr.n. Geog:* Surinam *m*; *Amph:* **S. toad,** pipa *m.*

surlily ['sə:lili], *adv.* (*a*) d'un air bourru; d'un ton bourru; (*b*) hargneusement; d'un ton revêche; d'un air revêche.

surliness ['sə:linis], *s.* (*a*) air bourru; caractère *m,* humeur *f,* maussade; maussaderie *f*; (*b*) ton bourru.

surly ['sə:li], *a.* (*a*) (ton, air) bourru; (*b*) hargneux, maussade, revêche; **s. disposition,** caractère *m* désagréable; humeur rébarbative; **he's as s. as a bear,** c'est un vrai ours.

surmise[1] ['sə:maiz, sə:'maiz], *s.* conjecture *f,* supposition *f*; **to be right in one's surmises,** avoir deviné juste.

surmise[2] [sə:'maiz], *v.tr.* conjecturer, soupçonner, deviner; **I surmised as much,** je m'en doutais bien; **as I surmised,** comme je m'en doutais (bien).

surmount [sə(:)'maunt], *v.tr.* **1.** surmonter; **column surmounted by a cross,** colonne surmontée d'une croix. **2.** surmounter (un obstacle, une difficulté, etc.); surmonter, maîtriser (son chagrin, etc.); triompher (d'une passion, d'une difficulté).

surmountable [sə(:)'mauntəbl], *a.* (obstacle, etc.) surmontable.

surmounted [sə(:)'mauntid], *a.* **1.** *Arch:* (arc) surhaussé. **2.** *Her:* (écu) sommé.

surmullet [sə:'mʌlit], *s. Ich:* surmulet *m*; mulle barbu; rouget *m* (barbet).

surname ['sə:neim], *s.* **1.** nom *m* de famille; nom patronymique; **s. and Christian, first, names,** nom et prénoms. **2.** *A:* surnom *m.*

surpass [sə(:)'pɑ:s], *v.tr.* **1.** surpasser (qn); devancer (ses rivaux, etc.); **to s. s.o. in eloquence,** surpasser qn, l'emporter sur qn, en éloquence; **to s. s.o. in intelligence,** surpasser qn par intelligence; **to s. s.o. in kindness,** renchérir sur la bonté de qn; **he has surpassed himself,** il s'est surpassé. **2.** dépasser, excéder; **the result surpassed my hopes,** le résultat a excédé mes espérances, a dépassé mon attente; **filth that surpasses description,** saleté qui dépasse toute description, indescriptible.

surpassable [sə(:)'pɑ:səbl], *a.* surpassable.

surpassing [sə(:)'pɑ:siŋ]. **1.** *a.* sans égal, sans pareil; prééminent; **of s. beauty,** d'une beauté incomparable, extraordinaire. **2.** *adv. A: & Poet:* = SURPASSINGLY; **she was s. fair,** elle était d'une beauté nonpareille.

surpassingly [sə(:)'pɑ:siŋli], *adv.* extrêmement, excessivement; incomparablement, extraordinairement; **s. ugly,** d'une laideur sans égale.

surplice ['sə:plis], *s. Ecc:* surplis *m*; *F: O:* **s. fees,** casuel *m.*

surpliced ['sə:plist], *a. Ecc:* en surplis; vêtu d'un surplis.

surplus ['sə:pləs], *s.* surplus *m,* excédent *m*; **to have a s. of sth.,** avoir qch. en excès; avoir (des livres, etc.) en surnombre; **budget s.,** excédent budgétaire; **tax s.,** plus-value *f, pl.* plus-values, des contributions; **s. population, products,** surplus, excédent, de la population, des produits; **s. provisions,** vivres de surplus, en surplus; *Com:* **s. stock,** surstock *m*; **sale of s. stock,** vente de soldes *mpl*; **government s. (stock),** les surplus du gouvernement; *Bookb:* **s. sheets,** défets *m*; *Publ:* **s. copies,** exemplaires *m* de passe; *Com: Ind:* **s. profits,** superbénéfices *m*; *Fin:* **s. dividend,** superdividende *m*; *Pol.Ec:* **s. value,** plus-value.

surprise[1] [sə'praiz], *s.* surprise *f.* **1. to take s.o. by s.,** prendre qn à l'improviste, au dépourvu; surprendre qn; *Mil:* **to take a town by s.,** enlever une ville par surprise, par un coup de surprise, par un coup de main; **s. attack,** attaque brusquée; attaque par surprise; coup de main; **s. party,** surprise-partie *f, pl.* surprises-parties; **s. visit,** visite *f* à l'improviste; **to pay a s. visit to s.o.,** aller surprendre qn chez lui. **2. to give s.o. a s.,** faire une surprise à qn; **it was a great s. to me,** j'en ai été grandement surpris; **what a s. to see you here!** je m'étonne de vous rencontrer ici; **what a pleasant s.!** quelle bonne surprise! **to give s.o. the s. of his life,** faire une surprise inouïe à qn; **he's in for a bit of a s.!** s'il savait ce qu'on lui prépare! (*at bazaar, etc.*) **s. packet,** surprise; *F:* **that**

was a s. packet for him, il ne s'attendait guère à cela; cela lui est tombé des nues. **3.** étonnement *m*; **struck with s.,** saisi d'étonnement; **to my great s., much to my s. he spoke to me,** à ma grande surprise il m'a adressé la parole; **I paused in s.,** je me suis arrêté surpris; **I watched them in s.,** surpris, je les regardais; **he started up in s.,** la surprise l'a fait tressauter, l'a fait bondir.

surprise[2], *v.tr.* **1.** (*a*) surprendre (une armée, etc.); prendre (une place) par surprise, par coup de main; (*b*) **to s. s.o. in the act,** surprendre qn en flagrant délit; prendre qn sur le fait; **to s. s.o. into admitting sth.,** arracher un aveu à qn par surprise; (*c*) surprendre, dérober (un secret). **2.** (*a*) surprendre, étonner; **what surprises me is that I should have been chosen,** ce qui me surprend, ce qui m'étonne, c'est qu'on m'ait choisi; **nothing surprises him,** il ne s'épate de rien; (*b*) **to be surprised at sth.,** être surpris de qch.; **I am surprised to see you, at seeing you,** je m'étonne de vous voir; je suis surpris de vous voir; **I should be surprised if he came back,** cela me surprendrait qu'il revienne, s'il reviendrait; **I should not be surprised if he were in the plot,** cela ne me surprendrait pas, je ne serais pas surpris, rien de surprenant, s'il était du complot; **it doesn't s. me in the least,** ce n'est pas pour me surprendre; **well I *am* surprised!** vous me mettez au comble de la surprise; **I was agreeably surprised,** j'ai été agréablement surpris; **I'm surprised at you!** vous m'étonnez! je n'aurais pas cru cela de vous! vous n'avez-pas honte?

surprised [sə'praizd], *a.* (regard, etc.) étonné, surpris; (air, etc.) de surprise.

surprising [sə'praiziŋ], *a.* surprenant, étonnant; **his energy is s.,** il est surprenant d'énergie; **it's s. that you (should) know of it,** il est surprenant que vous le sachiez; il est surprenant que vous le sachiez; **it's s. to learn that he's only fifty,** il est surprenant d'apprendre qu'il n'a que cinquante ans; **it wouldn't be s. if he was in the plot,** rien de surprenant s'il était du complot; **that's s. coming from him,** cela surprend de sa part.

surprisingly [sə'praiziŋli], *adv.* étonnamment; d'une manière surprenante; **I found him s. young,** j'ai été surpris de lui trouver l'air si jeune.

surra ['surə], *s. Vet:* surra *m.*

surreal [sə:'riəl]. **1.** *a.* surréal, -aux. **2.** *s.* **the s.,** le surréal.

surrealism [sə:'riəlizm], *s. Lit: Art:* surréalisme *m.*

surrealist [sə:'riəlist], *a. & s. Lit: Art:* surréaliste (*mf*).

surrealistic [sə:riə'listik], *a. Lit: Art:* surréaliste; *Fig:* **the s. atmosphere of the meeting,** l'atmosphère surréaliste de la réunion.

surrebutter [sʌri'bʌtər], *s. A.Jur:* triplique *f.*

surrejoinder [sʌri'dʒɔindər], *s. A.Jur:* duplique *f.*

surrenal [sʌ'ri:n(ə)l], *a. Anat:* (*of artery, etc.*) surrénal, -aux.

surrender[1] [sə'rendər], *s.* **1.** (*a*) *Mil:* reddition *f* (d'une forteresse); (*b*) action *f* de se rendre; **no s.!** on ne se rend pas! (*c*) *Jur:* **s. of a defendant to his bail,** décharge *f* de ses cautions par un accusé (libéré sous caution). **2.** abandon *m*, abandonnement *m*, cession *f* (de biens, de droits); restitution *f* (d'un droit de propriété); abdication *f* (de droits, de l'autorité); *Jur:* **compulsory s. (of real estate),** expropriation *f*; **s. of a bankrupt's property,** abandon des biens d'un failli à ses créanciers; **s. of payment made in error,** restitution *f* d'indu; *Mil: etc:* **to demand the s. of firearms, of a ship,** demander la remise des armes à feu, d'un navire; *Fig:* **to make a s. of principle(s),** transiger avec ses principes; abdiquer ses principes. **3.** *Ins:* rachat *m* (d'une police); **s. value,** valeur *f* de rachat.

surrender[2]. **1.** *v.tr.* (*a*) *Mil: etc:* rendre, livrer (une forteresse, etc.); (*b*) *Jur: etc:* abandonner, céder (un droit, ses biens, etc.); abdiquer (un droit); se désister (d'un droit); **to s. one's office,** démissionner; **to s. one's goods to one's creditors,** abandonner, livrer, ses biens à ses créanciers; faire l'abandon, faire cession, de ses biens à ses créanciers; *Fig:* **to s. all hope of sth.,** abandonner, renoncer à, tout espoir de qch.; (*c*) *Ins:* racheter (une police d'assurances). **2.** *v.pr. & i.* **to s. (oneself),** se rendre; *Mil:* faire (sa) soumission; rendre les armes; **to s. on terms,** se rendre par capitulation; **to s. (oneself) to justice,** se livrer à la justice; **to s. to the police,** se constituer prisonnier; **to s. to one's bail,** décharger ses cautions; comparaître en jugement.

surreptitious [sʌrəp'tiʃəs], *a.* subreptice, clandestin.

surreptitiously [sʌrəp'tiʃəsli], *adv.* subrepticement, clandestinement, furtivement; à la dérobée; sans faire semblant de rien.

surreptitiousness [sʌrəp'tiʃəsnis], *s.* caractère *m*, nature *f*, subreptice; clandestinité *f.*

surrogate ['sʌrəgət], *s.* **1.** (*pers.*) (*a*) suppléant, -ante; substitut *m*; *Ecc: Jur:* subrogé, -ée; **s. guardian,** subrogé tuteur; (*b*) *NAm:* juge *m* qui a charge d'homologuer les testaments; **s. court,** tribunal chargé d'homologuer les testaments. **2.** succédané *m* (**for, of, sth.,** de qch.).

surrogation [sʌrə'geiʃ(ə)n], *s.* substitution *f* (de documents par d'autres dans un bureau d'information).

surrosion [sə'rouʒ(ə)n], *s. Ch:* augmentation de poids (due à la corrosion).

surround[1] [sə'raund], *s.* encadrement *m*, bordure *f*; **s. of a carpet,** bordure entre le tapis et le mur; **turf s. of a flower bed,** encadrement de gazon d'un parterre; **wire netting s. of a tennis court,** clôture *f* en grillage d'un court de tennis; *Rec:* **s. sound,** quadrosound *m.*

surround[2], *v.tr.* entourer; (*a*) **to s. a town with walls,** entourer, ceinturer, ceindre, une ville de murs; **the crowd surrounded the carriage,** la foule assiégeait la voiture; **surrounded by, with, dangers, friends,** entouré, environné, de dangers, d'amis; (*b*) *Mil:* entourer, cerner (l'ennemi, etc.); investir (une ville, etc.).

surrounding [sə'raundiŋ], *a.* (*a*) entourant, environnant; **the s. country,** le pays d'alentour, à l'entour; **the town with its s. walls,** la ville et les murs qui l'entourent; (*b*) **the s. air,** l'air ambiant.

surroundings [sə'raundiŋz], *s.pl.* **1.** entourage *m*, milieu *m*, ambiance *f*; cadre *m*, environnement *m*; **to see an animal in its proper s.,** voir une bête dans son propre milieu; **to be in familiar s.,** être en pays de connaissance. **2.** environs *mpl*, alentours *mpl*; abords *mpl*, pourtour *m* (d'une ville, etc.).

surtax[1] ['sə:tæks], *s. Adm:* surtaxe *f*; *esp.* surtaxe progressive sur le revenu.

surtax[2], *v.tr.* surtaxer.

surtout ['sə:tu:], *s. Cost: A:* (*a*) (i) pardessus *m*, surtout m (d'homme); (ii) redingote *f*; (*b*) pèlerine *f*, cape *f* (de femme).

surveillance [sə(:)'veiləns], *s. Adm:* surveillance *f*, contrôle *m*; **to be under s.,** être en surveillance.

survey ['sə:vei], *s.* **1.** (*a*) aperçu *m*; regard *m*, vue *f*; **general s. of a subject,** aperçu, exposé *m* sommaire, d'un sujet; (*b*) examen attentif; étude *f* (de la situation); enquête *f*; **to take, make, a s. of sth.,** (i) jeter un coup d'œil sur qch.; (ii) étudier (une question); faire un tour d'horizon. **2.** *Surv:* (*a*) levé *m* des plans; relevé *m*; *Const: etc:* métrage *m* des travaux; (*b*) plan *m*, levé, lever *m* (du terrain, du littoral, d'un édifice); *Civ.E:* étude; **trigonometrical s.,** levé trigonométrique; **skeleton s.,** levé du canevas; **contoured s.,** lever dénivelé; **aerial s.,** levé aérophotogrammétrique; **to make, effect, a s.,** lever un plan; **to make a s. of an estate,** relever un domaine; **to make a harbour s.,** faire le levé d'un port; **s. department,** service *m* topographique; *Adm:* (*for rating purposes*) cadastre *m*; *Nau:* service hydrographique; **s. vessel,** navire *m* hydrographique; (*c*) **quantity s.,** métrage *m*; métré *m*; toisé *m*. **3.** (*a*) inspection *f*, visite *f*; expertise *f* (d'un vaisseau, etc.); **to carry through a s.,** faire une expertise; expertiser; **certificate of s.,** procès-verbal *m*, *pl.* procès-verbaux, de visite; **s. repairs,** révisions *f*; (*b*) (i) rapport *m* d'un expert; expertise; (ii) inventaire *m* (de monuments, tableaux, etc.).

survey[2] [sə(:)'vei], *v.tr.* **1.** (*a*) regarder, contempler, promener ses regards sur (le paysage, etc.); (*b*) examiner attentivement; mettre (une question) à l'étude; **to s. the situation,** procéder à l'étude de la situation; passer la situation en revue; se rendre compte de la situation; (*of politician, etc.*) faire un tour d'horizon. **2.** *Surv:* relever, faire le (re)levé de, lever le(s) plan(s) de (la ville, la propriété, etc.); faire l'arpentage de, arpenter (un champ, etc.); **to s. a railway,** faire les études d'une ligne de chemin de fer; **to s. a coast,** hydrographier une côte; faire l'hydrographie d'une côte; relever le littoral; *Adm:* **to s. and value a district,** cadastrer une commune; *Civ.E: Const:* **to s. for quantities, for work done,** métrer, toiser, un immeuble, le travail accompli. **3.** inspecter; visiter; faire l'expertise de l'état (d'un navire, d'un immeuble, etc.); expertiser (un navire, etc.); surveiller (la voirie, etc.); **to have a house surveyed,** faire inspecter un immeuble par un (architecte) expert.

surveying [sə(:)'veiiŋ], *s.* **1.** (*a*) *Surv:* levé *m* de plans; **(land) s.,** arpentage *m*, aréage *m*; géodésie *f*; topographie *f*; **naval s.,** hydrographie *f*; **photographic s.,** photogrammétrie *f*; **s. instruments,** instruments *m* topographiques; **s. compass,** boussole *f*; **s. wheel,** compte-pas *m inv*; **s. ship,** navire *m* hydrographique; (*b*) **quantity s.,** métrage *m*, métré *m*, toisé *m*. **2.** inspection *f*, visite *f*, expertise *f* (d'un navire, etc.); surveillance *f* (de la voirie, etc.).

surveyor [sə(:)'veiər], *s.* **1.** (*a*) **(land) s.,** géomètre expert; arpenteur *m* (géomètre); ingénieur *m* géographe; *Mil:* ingénieur topographe; **naval s.,** (ingénieur) hydrographe; **surveyor's table,** planchette *f*; *Adm:* **land s. and valuer, district s.,** cadastreur *m*; **highways, road, s.,** fonctionnaire chargé de la voirie; (*b*) **quantity s.,** métreur vérificateur. **2.** (*a*) *Adm:* surveillant, -ante; inspecteur, -trice; contrôleur, -euse; (*b*) *Nau:* **ship s.,** visiteur *m*, inspecteur, de navires; expert *m*; **the surveyors,** la commission de surveillance; (*c*) **property s.,** (architecte) expert.

surveyorship [sə(:)'veiəʃip], *s.* office *m*, fonction *f*, de contrôleur, d'inspecteur, etc.

survival [sə(:)'vaiv(ə)l], *s.* **1.** (*a*) survivance *f* (de l'âme, d'une coutume, etc.); *Nat.Hist:* **the s. of the fittest,** la survivance des mieux adaptés, du plus apte; (*b*) survie *f* (d'un accidenté, *Fig:* d'une émotion); **s. kit,** équipement *m* de survie; **s. at sea,** survie en mer; *Jur:* **presumption of s.,** (présomption *f* de) survie. **2.** restant *m* (d'une ancienne coutume, d'une croyance, etc.); **a s. of times past,** une survivance des temps passés.

survivance [sə(:)'vaiv(ə)ns], *s. Jur:* succession *f* (en cas de survivance).

survive [sə(:)'vaiv]. **1.** *v.i.* (*a*) survivre; demeurer en vie; (*of custom, etc.*) subsister, passer à la postérité; **those who survived,** les survivants *m*; (*b*) *Jur:* (*of estate, etc.*) **to s. to s.o.,** passer aux mains de qn (qui est le survivant). **2.** *v.tr.* (*a*) survivre à (qn); **he was survived only three years by his son,** son fils ne lui a survécu que de trois ans; **he will s. us all,** il nous enterrera tous; **custom that has survived the need for it,** coutume qui n'est plus nécessaire; (*b*) **to s. an injury,** survivre à une blessure; **to s. an illness, shipwreck, financial crash,** réchapper d'une maladie, d'un naufrage; surnager à un naufrage, un krach.

surviving [sə(:)'vaiviŋ], *a.* survivant.

survivor [sə(:)'vaivər], *s.* survivant, -ante; **he is the sole s. of his family,** il est le seul qui reste de sa famille; **the survivors of the disaster, of the wreck,** les rescapé(s).

survivorship [sə(:)'vaivəʃip], *s. Jur:* survie *f*; **right of s. (between husband and wife),** gain *m* de survie; **presumption of s.,** (présomption *f* de) survie; *Ins:* **s. annuity,** rente viagère avec réversion.

Surya ['su:riə]. *Pr.n.m. Hindu Myth:* Sourya.

Susa ['su:zə]. *Pr.n. Geog:* **1.** *A:* (*in Persia*) Suse. **2.** (*in Italy*) Suse. **3.** (*in Tunis*) Sousse.

Susan ['su:z(ə)n]. *Pr.n.f.* Suzanne.

Susanna(h) [su(:)'zænə]. *Pr.n.f.* Suzanne.

susannite [su(:)'zænait], *s. Miner:* susannite *f.*

susceptance [sə'septəns], *s. El:* susceptance *f.*

susceptibility [səsepti'biliti], *s.* **1.** (*a*) susceptibilité *f*; *El:* **magnetic s.,** susceptibilité magnétique (du nickel, etc.); (*b*) **s. to a disease,** prédisposition *f* à une maladie; **s. to impressions, to hypnotic influences,** suggestibilité *f*; **s. to pain,** sensibilité *f* à la douleur. **2.** sensibilité, susceptibilité; **these people have their susceptibilities,** ces gens-là ont leurs délicatesses *f*; **words that wound susceptibilities,** mots qui blessent les susceptibilités; mots qui choquent; mots blessants.

susceptible [sə'septibl], *a.* **1.** susceptible; (*a*) **s. of proof,** susceptible d'être prouvé; (*b*) **s. to a disease,** prédisposé à une maladie; susceptible d'attraper une maladie; **conduct s. to being misunderstood,** conduite susceptible d'être mal interprétée. **2.** (*a*) sensible, impressionnable; **to be s.,** avoir la fibre sensible; **s. to female beauty,** sensible à la beauté féminine; **a very s. young man,** un jeune homme sensible à l'attrait des femmes; **s. to good influences,** ouvert, sensible, accessible, aux bonnes influences; **very s. to pain,** très sensible à la douleur; **s. to cold,** frileux; (*b*) qui se froisse facilement; susceptible.

susception [sə'sepʃ(ə)n], *s. Ecc:* susception *f* (de la couronne, de la croix).

susceptive [sə'septiv], *a.* **1.** (facultés) de susception. **2.** susceptible (**of, de**). **3.** sensible, impressionnable.

susceptivity [sʌsep'tiviti], *s.* susceptibilité *f*; (*to hypnotism, etc.*) suggestibilité *f.*

suslik ['sʌslik], *s. Z:* souslik *m.*

suspect[1] ['sʌspekt], *a. & s.* suspect, -e; **to hold s.o. s., consider s.o. as s.,** tenir qn pour suspect.

suspect[2] [sə'spekt], *v.tr.* (*a*) **to s. s.o. of a crime,** soupçonner qn d'un crime; suspecter qn; **to be suspected,** être en suspicion; être incriminé; **to be suspected of treachery,** être suspect de perfidie; **to be suspected by s.o. of sth., of doing sth.,** être suspect à qn de qch., de faire qch.; **I s. him of drinking,** je le soupçonne d'être ivrogne; j'ai dans l'idée, je suspecte, qu'il boit; **to begin to s. s.o.,** concevoir des soupçons à l'égard de qn; (*b*) **to s. the authenticity of a work,** suspecter l'authenticité d'une œuvre; (*c*) soupçonner, s'imaginer (qch.); se douter de (qch.); **I s. that he is the perpetrator of the joke,** j'ai idée que c'est lui l'auteur de cette farce; je le soupçonne d'être l'auteur de cette farce; **I suspected as much,** je m'en doutais; j'en avais le soupçon; **book which I s. to be mine,** livre que je soupçonne être (le) mien; **to s. danger,** flairer, subodorer, le danger; **to s. a hoax,** flairer une mystification; **he suspects nothing,** il ne se doute de rien; **I never suspected it for a moment,** je n'en avais pas le moindre soupçon; **he showed qualities that no one would have suspected him to possess,** il a fait preuve de qualités qu'on ne lui aurait pas soupçonnées; **I s. he is inclined to be selfish,** je lui soupçonne un peu d'égoïsme; **I s. you're right,** je crois bien que vous avez raison.

suspectable [sə'spektəbl], *a.* suspect, soupçonnable.

suspected [sə'spektid], *a.* **a s. person,** un suspect, une suspecte; **s. traitor,** personne accusée, suspectée, de trahison, en suspicion de trahison; *Med:* **s. case of smallpox,** cas présumé de petite vérole; **s. fracture,** crainte *f* de fracture.

suspend [sə'spend], *v.tr.* suspendre. **1.** pendre; appendre (un trophée, etc.); **to s. sth. from the ceiling,** suspendre, pendre, qch. au plafond. **2. to s. the traffic, a bus service,** suspendre, interrompre, la circulation, un service d'autobus; **to s. work, operations, for two days,** suspendre le travail, les activités, pour deux jours; **to s. (one's) judgment,** suspendre son jugement; *Jur:* **to s. judgment,** surseoir au jugement; **to s. proceedings,** suspendre les poursuites; *Com:* **to s. payment,** suspendre ses, les, paiements. **3.** (*a*) suspendre (**s.o. from his office,** qn de ses fonctions); interdire (qn); mettre (un officier) en non-activité; mettre (un jockey, etc.) à pied; *Parl:* exclure temporairement (un député); **to s. a barrister from (practice at) the bar,** suspendre un avocat du barreau; **to s. a pupil (from school),** renvoyer un élève (provisoirement); *Sp:* **to s. a player indefinitely,** exécuter un joueur; *Adm:* **suspended on full pay,** suspendu sans suppression de traitement, *Mil:* de solde; (*b*) **to s. a newspaper,** mettre un embargo sur, suspendre, un journal; *Aut:* **to s. a driving licence,** suspendre un permis de conduire.

suspended [sə'spendid], *a.* suspendu; (*a*) **s. particles (of dust),** particules en suspension; (*b*) (*of traffic, etc.*) interrompu; *Jur:* (*of proceedings, judgment*) en suspens; suspendu; **he was given a s. prison sentence of six months,** il a été condamné à six mois de prison avec sursis; *Med:* **s. animation,** arrêt momentané des fonctions vitales; syncope *f*; *Fig:* **the scheme is in a state of s. animation,** le projet est en suspens; (*c*) *Mus:* **s. cadence,** cadence suspendue.

suspender [sə'spendər], *s.* (*a*) suspensoir *m*; (*b*) **(women's) stocking suspenders,** jarretelles *f*; **(men's) sock suspenders,** jarretelles, supports-chaussettes *m*; (*c*) *NAm:* **(pair of) suspenders,** (paire *f* de) bretelles *f*.

suspending [sə'spendiŋ], *s.* = SUSPENSION; *Civ.E:* **s. rod,** suspensoir *m* (de pont suspendu, etc.); *Aer:* **s. ropes,** suspente *f* (d'une nacelle de ballon).

suspense [sə'spens], *s.* **1.** (*a*) suspens *m*; **after a long period of s.,** après une longue incertitude; **to keep, hold, s.o. in s.,** tenir, garder, qn en suspens, en balance, en haleine; *F:* tenir qn le bec dans l'eau; (*b*) **the question remains in s.,** la question reste pendante; *Com:* **bills in s.,** effets en suspens, en souffrance *f*; *Book-k:* **s. account,** compte d'ordre; **s. item,** suspens; *Cmptr: etc:* **s. file,** fichier *m* d'attente. **2.** *Lit: etc:* suspens, suspense *m*; **author who has used s. to good effect,** auteur qui s'est bien servi du suspens(e). **3.** *Jur:* surséance *f* (d'un jugement).

suspension [sə'spenʃ(ə)n], *s.* suspension *f*. **1.** (*a*) *Mec.E: etc:* **points of s.,** points *m* de suspension, de montage *m*; **s. chain, hook,** chaîne *f*, croc *m*, de suspension; **s. cable,** câble porteur; **semi-elliptic spring s.,** suspension par ressorts semi-elliptiques; **Cardan s.,** suspension à la Cardan; *Civ.E:* **s. bridge,** pont suspendu; (*b*) *Ch:* **(substance in) s.,** (substance *f* en) suspension. **2.** (*a*) suspension (de la circulation, d'une séance, etc.); **s. of hostilities, arms,** suspension des hostilités, d'armes; armistice *m*; **to the s. of all other business,** toutes choses cessantes; toute affaire cessante; **s. of judgment,** suspension de jugement; *Jur:* surséance *f* de jugement; (*b*) *Com:* suspension de paiements; (*c*) *Gram:* **points of s.,** points de suspension; (*d*) *Mus:* suspension. **3.** suspension (d'un fonctionnaire, d'un journal, etc.); mise *f* en non-activité (d'un officier); mise à pied (d'un jockey); *Ecc: A:* suspense *f* (d'un bénéficier); *Parl:* exclusion *f* temporaire (d'un député); *Sp:* **indefinite s. of a player,** exécution *f* d'un joueur; **s. of a licence,** retrait *m* temporaire d'une patente; *Aut:* retrait temporaire, suspension, d'un permis de conduire.

suspensive [sə'spensiv], *a.* (veto, etc.) suspensif.

suspensoid [sə'spensɔid], *s. Ch:* suspensoïde *m*.

suspensor [sə'spensər], *s.* **1.** *Surg: A:* suspensoir *m*. **2.** *Bot:* suspenseur *m*.

suspensory [sə'spensəri], *a.* **1.** (*a*) *Anat:* (*of ligament, etc.*) suspenseur *m*; (*b*) *Med:* **s. bandage,** suspensoir *m*. **2.** (période, etc.) de suspension.

suspicion[1] [sə'spiʃ(ə)n], *s.* **1.** soupçon *m*; *Jur:* suspicion *f*; **not the shadow, ghost, of a s.,** pas l'ombre d'un soupçon; **I resent such suspicions on your part,** cette suspicion de votre part me blesse; **to look at s.o. with s.,** regarder qn avec défiance; **to have (one's) suspicions about s.o., attach s. to s.o.,** avoir des doutes sur qn; soupçonner qn; **I always had my suspicions about him,** je me suis toujours méfié de lui; **to hold s.o. in s.,** tenir qn pour suspect; **held in s.,** mal vu; suspecté; **to form suspicions regarding s.o.,** concevoir des soupçons à l'égard de qn; **to cast s. on s.o.'s good faith,** suspecter la loyauté de qn; **to lay oneself open to s.,** s'exposer aux soupçons; **to arouse s.,** éveiller, faire naître, les soupçons; devenir suspect; **to arouse, awaken, s.o.'s suspicions,** éveiller la défiance de qn; donner l'éveil à qn; **his conduct aroused no suspicions,** sa conduite n'a suscité de soupçons; **to incur s.o.'s s.,** devenir suspect à qn; **liable to s.,** soupçonnable; **to lull s.,** endormir les soupçons; **to clear s.o. from s.,** disculper qn d'un soupçon; **above s.,** au-dessus de tout soupçon; **his case is not above s.,** son cas n'est pas net; **Caesar's wife must be above s.,** la femme de César ne doit pas même être soupçonnée; **his reputation is beyond s.,** sa réputation est hors d'atteinte; **evidence not beyond s.,** témoignages sujets à caution; **praise free from any s. of flattery,** louanges aucunement suspects de flatterie; **magistrate under s. of partiality,** magistrat suspect de partialité; **s. falls on him,** les soupçons tombent sur lui; **to be right in one's suspicions,** soupçonner juste; *Jur:* **to arrest, detain, s.o. on s.,** arrêter, détenir, qn préventivement; **to arrest s.o. on a mere s.,** arrêter qn sur un soupçon; **detention on s.,** détention préventive; prévention *f*. **2. I had my suspicions about it,** je m'en doutais; **I had no s. of it,** je n'en avais pas le moindre soupçon; **I had no s. he was there,** je ne me doutais pas, je ne soupçonnais pas, qu'il fût là; **to have no s. of what occurred,** ne pas soupçonner ce qui est arrivé; **my s. is (that) he's not honest,** je soupçonne, j'ai (l')idée, j'ai dans l'idée, qu'il n'est pas honnête. **3.** très petite quantité; soupçon, (un) tout petit peu; **the s. of a smile,** l'ébauche *f* d'un sourire; **s. of irony, malice,** légère dose, pointe, d'ironie, de malice.

suspicion[2], *v.tr. esp U.S: F:* soupçonner **(that,** que + *ind.*).

suspicious [sə'spiʃəs], *a.* **1.** soupçonnable, suspect; (*of conduct, etc.*) louche, équivoque; **to look s.,** avoir l'air louche, suspect; **it looks s.,** cela me paraît louche; **s. character,** (i) individu *m* louche; (ii) *Adm:* sujet noté; **his conduct is s.,** sa conduite n'est pas claire; **he died in s. circumstances,** il est mort dans des circonstances équivoques. **2.** méfiant, soupçonneux; **s. look,** regard méfiant; **s. person,** soupçonneur, -euse; **we are apt to be s. when we are not happy,** on soupçonne aisément quand on n'est pas heureux; **to be, feel, s. about s.o., sth., of s.o., sth.,** avoir des soupçons à l'endroit de qn, à l'égard de qn, sur qch.; tenir qn pour suspect; *F:* avoir la puce à l'oreille au sujet de qch.; **his behaviour made me s.,** sa conduite a éveillé ma défiance; **animals are s. of anything unusual,** les animaux se méfient de toute chose anormale; **public opinion is s. of unusual ideas,** l'opinion publique est ombrageuse à l'endroit des idées qui sortent de l'ordinaire.

suspiciously [sə'spiʃəsli], *adv.* **1.** (*a*) d'une manière suspecte, équivoque, louche; (*b*) **it looks s. like measles (to me),** cela ressemble étrangement à la rougeole. **2.** d'un air méfiant; soupçonneusement; **to eye s.o. s.,** regarder qn avec méfiance, défiance.

suspiciousness [sə'spiʃəsnis], *s.* **1.** caractère suspect, louche, équivoque. **2.** caractère soupçonneux; méfiance *f*; **I dislike this s. on your part,** cette suspicion de votre part me déplaît.

suspiration [sʌspi'reiʃ(ə)n], *s. Lit: Poet:* **1.** soupir *m*. **2.** expiration *f* (de son haleine).

suspire [sə'spaiər], *v.i. A: & Lit:* **1.** soupirer. **2.** expirer (son haleine), souffler.

suss [sʌs], *v.tr. P:* soupçonner (qn); **to s. s.o. out,** savoir ce que vaut qn, *P:* cataloguer qn.

sussexite ['sʌsəksait], *s. Miner:* sussexite *f*.

sussultatory [sʌ'sʌltət(ə)ri], *a.* sussultoire.

sustain [sə'stein], *v.tr.* soutenir, supporter. **1.** (*a*) **hope sustains us,** l'espoir nous soutient; **enough to s. life,** de quoi entretenir la vie; de quoi vivre; **to s. the body,** soutenir, sustenter, le corps; **to s. oneself,** se sustenter; **enough to s. the whole village,** de quoi faire vivre tout le village; **evidence to s. an assertion,** témoignages pour soutenir, appuyer, corroborer, une affirmation; **to s. the emotions at the highest point,** soutenir, maintenir, les émotions à leur plus haut point; *Th:* **to s. a part,** soutenir, tenir, remplir, un rôle; *Mus:* **to s. a note,** soutenir, prolonger, une note; appuyer (sur) une note; (*b*) *Jur:* (*of court*) **to s. an objection,** admettre une réclamation; **objection sustained,** réclamation admise; **to s. s.o. in a claim,** faire droit à la demande de qn; admettre la validité d'une réclamation. **2.** (*a*) *Mil:* **to s. an attack,** soutenir une attaque; **to s. the shock of the charge,** soutenir, supporter, le choc de la charge; (*b*) **to s. a loss,** éprouver, essuyer, souffrir, subir, faire, une perte; **to s. an injury,** recevoir une blessure; être blessé.

sustainable [sə'steinəbl], *a.* soutenable.

sustained [sə'steind], *a.* (*of effort, reasoning, attention, etc.*) soutenu; **s. applause,** applaudissements prolongés, nourris; **s. eloquence,** éloquence continue; *Mil:* **s. fire,** feu soutenu, nourri; *Ph: W.Tel:* **s. oscillations,** oscillations entretenues; *Mus:* **s. note,** tenue *f*.

sustainer [sə'steinər], *s.* **1.** (*pers., thg*) soutien *m*. **2.** *Space:* groupe(s) moteur(s) (d'une fusée).

sustaining[1] [sə'steiniŋ], *a.* (*of power, etc.*) soutenant; **s. food,** nourriture qui soutient (bien), fortifiante; *Mec:* **s. force,** force portante; *Arch: Const:* **s. wall,** mur *m* de soutènement.

sustaining[2], *s.* **1.** *Arch: Const:* soutènement *m* (d'un mur, etc.). **2.** prolongement *m* (d'un son, etc.).

sustenance ['sʌstinəns], *s.* (*a*) sustentation *f*; **necessary for the s. of our bodies,** nécessaire à notre subsistance *f*; **there is no s. in tea,** le thé n'a aucune valeur nutritive; **there is more s. in cocoa,** le cacao est plus nourrissant; **means of s.,** moyens de subsistance; moyens de vivre; (*b*) aliments *mpl*, nourriture *f*; *A:* **to earn a scanty s.,** gagner tout juste de quoi vivre.

sustentation [sʌsten'teiʃ(ə)n], *s.* **1.** entretien *m* (de la maison); maintien *m* (de la paix, etc.); **s. fund,** caisse *f*, fonds *m*, de réserve (de l'Église libre d'Écosse). **2.** *Physiol:* sustentation *f* (du corps).

sustention [sə'stenʃ(ə)n], *s.* **1.** maintien *m* à un haut niveau (de l'éloquence, etc.). **2.** *Mus:* prolongement *m* (d'une note).

susu ['su:su:], *s. Z:* sousouc *m*.

susurrant [sju'sʌrənt], *a. Lit:* susurrant; (feuillage, etc.) murmurant.

susurrate [sju'sʌreit], *v.i. Lit:* (*of wind, etc.*) susurrer, murmurer.

susurration [sjusʌ'reiʃ(ə)n], **susurrus** [sju'sʌrəs], *s. Lit:* susurration *f*, susurrement *m*, murmure *m*.

Sutlej (the) [ðə'sʌtledʒ], *Pr.n. Geog:* le Satledj, Sutledj.

sutler ['sʌtlər], *s. Mil: A:* cantinier, -ière; vivandier, -ière; *P:* mercanti *m*.

Sutra ['su:trə], *s.* (*Sanscrit Lit.*) Soûtra *m*; **the Soutras,** le Soûtra.

suttee ['sʌti:], *s. Hindu Rel:* **1.** (*practice*) sâti *m*, suttee *m*. **2.** (*widow*) sâti *f*, suttee *f*, suttie *f*.

sutteeism ['sʌti:izm], *s.* sâti *m*.

sutural ['su:tjərəl, sju:-], *a. Anat: Surg: etc:* sutural, -aux; de suture.

suture[1] ['su:tjər, 'sju:-], *s.* **1.** *Anat: Bot: etc:* suture *f*; *Anat:* **serrated s.,** engrenure *f* (du crâne). **2.** *Surg:* (*a*) (*action*) suture; (*b*) (*stitch*) point *m* de suture; (*c*) fil *m* pour sutures.

suture[2], *v.tr. Surg:* suturer (une plaie).

suzerain ['su:zərein]. **1.** *a.* suzerain, -aine; *Jur:* **s. (state),** suzerain. **2.** *s.m.* suzerain.

suzeraine ['su:zərein], *s.f.* suzeraine.

suzerainty ['su:zəreinti], *s.* suzeraineté *f*; **region under the s. of a neighbouring country,** région vassale d'un pays voisin.

svanbergite ['svɔnbə:gait], *s. Miner:* svanbergite *f*.

svelte [svelt], *a.* svelte.

swab[1] [swɔb], *s.* **1.** (*a*) *Dom.Ec:* torchon *m*; toile *f* à laver; serpillière *f*, wassingue *f*; *Fr.C:* vadrouille *f*; *Nau:* **(deck) s.,** faubert *m*, vadrouille; (*b*) *Metall:* mouillette *f*, mouilleur *m*; (*c*) *Artil: Med:* écouvillon *m*; (*d*) *Med:* **s. of cotton wool,** tampon *m* d'ouate; **to take a s. of s.o.'s throat,** faire un prélèvement dans la gorge de qn. **2.** *P:* lourdaud *m*, andouille *f*; propre *m* à rien; *Nau:* marin *m* d'eau douce. **3.** *P:* (*a*) *Navy:* épaulette *f* (d'officier); (*b*) *U.S:* (i) *Navy:* matelot *m*; (ii) *Nau:* marin *m*. **4. to give sth. a s. (down),** (i) nettoyer, essuyer, qch. avec un torchon; (ii) laver (une cour, etc.) à grande eau.

swab[2], *v.tr.* **(swabbed) 1.** nettoyer, essuyer (avec un torchon, etc.); *Nau:* essarder (le pont). **2. to s. (out),** écouvillonner (*Artil:* une pièce, *Med:* la matrice). **3. to s. (down),** nettoyer, essuyer (l'égouttoir de l'évier, etc.) (avec un torchon); laver (la cour, etc.) à grande eau. **4. to s. up,** éponger (une flaque d'eau, etc.).

swabber ['swɔbər], *s.* **1.** (*pers.*) nettoyeur, -euse; *Nau:* (i) marin *m* qui essarde le pont; (ii) *F:* marin. **2.** (*mop*) vadrouille *f*.

swabbing ['swɔbiŋ], *s.* **1.** nettoyage *m* (à grande eau). **2. s. (out),** écouvillonnage *m*. **3. s. up,** épongeage *m*.

Swabia ['sweibiə], *Pr.n. Geog:* la Souabe.

swaddle[1] ['swɔdl], *s. NAm:* = SWADDLING CLOTHES.

swaddle², *v.tr.* emmailloter (**with**, de).
swaddling ['swɔdliŋ], *s.* emmaillotement *m*; *A:* **s. clothes, s. bands,** maillot *m*, langes *m*; *P:* **he's not out of s. clothes,** si on lui pressait le nez il en sortirait du lait.
swag¹ [swæg], *s.* **1.** *Furn: Arch:* bouillon *m*, guirlande *f.* **2.** (*a*) *A:* balancement *m*; ballottement *m*; (*b*) effondrement *m*, creux *m* (de terrain). **3.** *F:* (*a*) rafle *f*, butin *m* (d'un cambrioleur); (*b*) grande quantité; grand nombre; tas *m*; (*c*) *Austr:* baluchon *m*, paquet *m* (de chemineau).
swag², *v.* (**swagged**) **1.** *v.i.* (*a*) ballotter, se balancer, osciller; (*b*) pendre; faire guirlande; fléchir. **2.** *v.tr.* (*a*) faire osciller; balancer; ballotter; (*b*) arranger (de l'étoffe) en bouillons, en guirlandes; (*c*) *Austr: F:* porter (ses effets) en baluchon; **to s. it,** porter son baluchon sur le dos.
swag belly ['swæg'beli], *s.* **1.** *Med:* enflure *f* du ventre. **2.** *F:* grosse panse; bedaine *f*, bedon *m.*
swage¹ [sweidʒ], *s.* **1.** *Metalw:* (*a*) *Tls:* étampe *f*, emboutissoir *m*; mandrin *m*, matrice *f*; **bottom s.,** dessous *m* d'étampe; sous-chasse *f*, *pl.* sous-chasses; **s. hammer,** étampe supérieure; **s. block,** tas-étampe *m*, *pl.* tas-étampes; (*b*) cannelure *f*, rainure *f* circulaire (d'un chandelier en cuivre, etc.). **2.** *Carp:* tourne-à-gauche *m inv* (pour scies circulaires).
swage², *v.tr.* **1.** *Metalw:* étamper, emboutir, suager (une tôle, etc.). **2.** *Carp:* avoyer (une scie).
swagger¹ ['swægər], *a.* (*a*) d'une élégance tapageuse; (*b*) élégant, ultra-chic.
swagger², *s.* **1.** (*a*) air important, avantageux; **to walk with a s.,** marcher avec un air avantageux; se pavaner; faire la roue; faire de l'épate; (*b*) air cavalier, désinvolte; (*c*) (i) *Cost: O:* **s. coat,** manteau *m* raglan trois-quarts (pour dame); (ii) *Mil:* **s. stick, cane,** jonc *m*, stick *m*; (*short*) badine *f.* **2.** rodomontades *fpl*; crâneries *fpl*; fanfaronnades *fpl.*
swagger³. **1.** *v.i.* (*a*) crâner, se pavaner; faire le glorieux, le beau; faire la roue; plastronner; se rengorger; faire de l'épate; poser (insolemment); (*b*) fanfaronner; faire de l'esbrouffe; (*c*) **to s. about,** se promener d'un air conquérant, en se rengorgeant; **to s. in, out,** entrer, sortir, d'un air important, glorieux; **to s. along,** se carrer en marchant; (*d*) **to s. about sth.,** se faire gloire, se vanter, de qch. **2.** *v.tr.* intimider (qn).
swagger⁴, *s. Austr: F:* = SWAGMAN.
swaggerer ['swægərər], *s.* crâneur, -euse; fanfaron, -onne; rodomont *m.*
swaggering¹ ['swægəriŋ], *a.* (air, etc.) important, crâneur, glorieux, conquérant.
swaggering², *s.* = SWAGGER².
swaggeringly ['swægəriŋli], *adv.* d'un air important, crâneur, glorieux.
swaggie ['swægi], *s.m. Austr:* = SWAGMAN.
swaging ['sweidʒiŋ], *s. Metalw:* étampage *m*, emboutissage *m.*
swagman, *pl.* **-men** ['swægmən], *s.m. Austr: F:* (*a*) chemineau (qui porte son baluchon); trimardeur; (*b*) marchand forain, ambulant; colporteur; (*c*) homme de peine ambulant.
Swahili [swɑː'hiːli]. **1.** *Ethn:* (*a*) *a.* souahéli, swahéli; (*b*) *s.* (*pl.* **Swahili(s)**), Souahéli, -ie, Swahéli, -ie; *pl.* -i(s). **2.** *s. Ling:* le souahéli, swahéli.
swain [swein], *s.m.* **1.** *A:* berger; villageois. **2.** (*a*) *A: & Poet:* jeune berger; amoureux (de pastorale); pastoureau; (*b*) *Hum: O:* soupirant; **she always has two or three swains in attendance,** elle a toujours à sa suite deux ou trois petits jeunes gens.
swale¹ [sweil], *s.* **1.** *Dial:* creux *m* de terre; bas-fond *m*, *pl.* bas-fonds. **2.** *NAm:* dépression marécageuse.
swale², *v.tr. Agr:* écobuer (les ajoncs, etc.).
swallet ['swɔlit], *s. Dial:* **1.** *Geol:* = SWALLOW¹ 3. **2.** *Min:* nappe d'eau souterraine (susceptible d'inonder la mine).
swallow¹ ['swɔlou], *s.* **1.** gosier *m*, gorge *f.* **2.** gorgée *f* (d'eau, etc.); **to drink sth. at one s.,** boire qch. d'un seul coup, d'un seul trait, d'un coup de gosier. **3.** *Geol:* **s. (hole),** (i) aven *m*, gouffre *m*, abîme *m*, puits naturel, bétoire *f*; (ii) perte *f* (d'un fleuve). **4.** *Mec.E:* gorge, *Nau:* clan *m* (de poulie).
swallow². **1.** *v.tr.* (*a*) **to s. sth. (down),** (i) avaler, ingurgiter, *Physiol:* déglutir, qch.; (ii) gober (une huître); **to s. the bait,** (i) (*of fish*) avaler l'appât; (ii) *F:* (*of pers.*) se laisser prendre à l'appât; avaler le goujon; **to s. a story,** gober, avaler, une histoire; **he'll s. anything,** il est très gobeur; il avale toutes les bourdes qu'on lui raconte; **I told her a lie and she swallowed it,** je lui ai raconté un mensonge et elle a marché; **he swallowed it hook, line and sinker,** il a donné dans le panneau, a gobé le morceau, a avalé la pilule; **story hard to s.,** histoire invraisemblable; **that's hard to s.,** ça c'est un peu raide; *P:* ça c'est un peu fort; **insult hard to s.,** insulte dure à digérer, de dure digestion; **to s. an affront,** avaler, boire, un affront; **to s. one's tears,** (r)avaler ses larmes; **to s. one's pride,** mettre son orgueil dans sa poche; **to s. one's anger,** retenir, rentrer, sa colère; **to s. one's words,** (i) parler vite et indistinctement; (ii) se rétracter, se dédire; ravaler ses paroles; **to make s.o. s. his words,** faire rentrer à qn les paroles dans la gorge; (*b*) **to s. sth. (up),** dévorer, avaler, qch.; (*of the sea, etc.*) engloutir, engouffrer, qch.; **to be swallowed up by the sea, the darkness,** s'abîmer dans les flots; s'enfoncer dans l'ombre; **gambling has swallowed up all his fortune,** le jeu a englouti toute sa fortune. **2.** *v.i.* avaler; **to s. hard,** avaler sa salive (pour faire passer une émotion).
swallow³, *s.* **1.** *Orn:* (*a*) hirondelle *f*; *Prov:* **one s. doesn't make a summer,** une hirondelle ne fait pas le printemps; une fois n'est pas coutume; (**common**) **s.,** *NAm:* **barn s.,** hirondelle de cheminée, *Fr.C:* hirondelle des granges; **red-rumped s.,** hirondelle rousseline; *NAm:* **bank s.,** hirondelle de rivage, *Fr.C:* hirondelle des sables; **cliff s.,** hirondelle à front blanc; **rough-winged s.,** hirondelle à ailes hérissées; **tree s.,** hirondelle bicolore; **violet-green s.,** hirondelle à face blanche; (*b*) **wood s.,** langrayen *m.* **2.** *attrib.* (*a*) *Orn:* **s. hawk,** élane *m*, élanion *m*; *Ich:* **s. fish,** hirondelle de mer; (i) trigle *m* hirondelle, *F:* perlon *m*; (ii) *A:* poisson volant; (*b*) *Swim:* **s. dive,** saut *m* de l'ange; plongeon *m* en ange.
swallow-dive ['swɔloudaiv], *v.i. Swim:* faire un saut de l'ange.
swallower ['swɔlouər], *s.* (*a*) avaleur, -euse; **sword s.,** avaleur de sabres; (*b*) *Fig:* gobeur, -euse (de fausses nouvelles, etc.).
swallowing ['swɔlouiŋ], *s.* **1.** (*a*) **s. (down),** avalement (de qch.); (*b*) *Physiol:* déglutition *f.* **2. s. (up),** engloutissement *m*, engouffrement *m.*
swallowtail ['swɔlouteil], *s.* **1.** queue fourchue; queue d'hirondelle. **2.** *Cost: F: O:* (*often pl.*) queue-de-morue *f*, *pl.* queues-de-morue; queue-de-pie *f*, *pl.* queues-de-pie; **everybody was in swallowtails,** tout le monde était en habit. **3.** *Mil: Nau:* flamme *f* à deux pointes. **4.** *Join:* queue-d'aronde *f*, *pl.* queues-d'aronde. **5.** *Ent:* **s. (butterfly),** (grand) porte-queue *inv*, machaon *m*; **scarce s.,** flambé *m.*
swallow-tailed ['swɔlou'teild], *a.* **1.** à queue fourchue, à queue d'hirondelle. **2.** (guidon, flamme) à deux pointes. **3. s.-t. coat** = SWALLOWTAIL 2. **4. s.-t. butterfly** = SWALLOWTAIL 5.
swallowwort ['swɔlouwəːt], *s. Bot:* **1.** (*a*) (**white**) **s.,** dompte-venin *m inv*; (*b*) herbe *f* à ouate; ouatier *m*; coton *m* sauvage; asclépiade *f* à ouate, de Syrie; plante *f* à soie; (*c*) apocyn *m* à ouate soyeuse. **2.** grande éclaire; grande chélidoine.
swamp¹ [swɔmp], *s.* marais *m*, marécage *m*, bas-fond *m*, *pl.* bas-fonds; terrain *m* uliginaire; **s. plants,** plantes des marais; *Med: A:* **s. fever,** fièvre paludéenne; paludisme *m.*
swamp². **1.** *v.tr.* (*a*) inonder, submerger (un pré); inonder (une pièce, la cave); (*b*) remplir d'eau (une embarcation); **a wave swamped the boat,** une vague a rempli d'eau l'embarcation, a fait sombrer, a englouti, a submergé, l'embarcation; l'embarcation a été capelée par une lame; (*c*) *F:* **party swamped by its opponents,** parti écrasé par le nombre de ses adversaires; **the local team was swamped by the visitors,** l'équipe locale a été écrasée par les visiteurs; **to be swamped with work,** être débordé de travail; (*d*) *NAm:* débroussailler (une route, etc.). **2.** *v.i.* (*of boat*) se remplir d'eau.
swampy ['swɔmpi], *a.* (terrain) marécageux, uligineux, palustre; **s. ground,** molets *mpl*; fondrière *f.*
swan¹ [swɔn], *s.* **1.** (*a*) cygne *m*; **mute s.,** cygne commun, muet, tuberculé; **whooper s.,** cygne sauvage, chanteur; **Bewick's s.,** cygne nain, de Bewick; **black s.,** cygne noir; **trumpeter s.,** cygne trompette; **whistling s.,** cygne siffleur; (*b*) *Lit:* **the S. of Avon,** Shakespeare. **2.** *attrib.* (*a*) **s. song,** chant *m* du cygne; *Fig:* **it was his s. song,** ce fut pour lui le chant du cygne; *Ven:* **s. shot,** plomb *m* pour cygne; gros plomb; *Myth:* **s. maiden,** jeune fille *f* qui savait se transformer en cygne; *Lit:* **the S. Knight,** le Chevalier au Cygne; (*b*) *Swim: NAm:* **s. dive,** saut *m* de l'ange; plongeon *m* en ange; (*c*) *Bot:* **s. flower,** cycnoche *m*; (*d*) **s. neck,** (i) *Mec.E:* cou *m*, col *m*, de cygne; (ii) *Nau:* aiguillot *m* (de gui); (iii) *Bot:* cycnoche.
swan², *v.i.* (**swanned**) **to s. around,** se pavaner.
swanherd ['swɔnhəːd], *s.* (i) gardien *m* de cygnes; (ii) (*also* **swan master**) gardien des cygnes royaux de la Tamise.
swank¹ [swæŋk], *F:* **1.** *s.* (*a*) prétention *f*, gloriole *f*, épate *f*; (*b*) épateur, -euse; poseur, -euse; crâneur, -euse; esbrouffeur, -euse. **2.** *a.* (restaurant, etc.) élégant; (dîner, etc.) chic.
swank², *v.i. F:* se donner des airs; crâner; le faire à la pose; faire le flambard, le fier; faire du chiqué, de la gomme, de l'épate; **he used to s. with an expensive car,** il faisait le malin avec une voiture qui avait coûté cher.
swanker ['swæŋkər], *s. F:* épateur, -euse; poseur, -euse; crâneur, -euse; esbrouffeur, -euse.
swanky ['swæŋki], *a. F:* (*a*) (*of pers.*) prétentieux, poseur; (*b*) (restaurant, etc.) élégant; (dîner, etc.) chic; **that's very s.,** ça fait très snob.
swan-necked ['swɔnnekt], *a.* **1.** au cou de cygne. **2.** *Tls: etc:* en col de cygne.
swannery ['swɔnəri], *s.* endroit aménagé pour l'élevage des cygnes.
swansdown ['swɔnzdaun], *s.* **1.** duvet *m* de cygne (pour garnitures, etc.); cygne *m.* **2.** *Tex:* molleton *m.*
swanskin ['swɔnskin], *s.* **1.** peau *f* de cygne. **2.** *Tex:* molleton *m.*
swan-upping ['swɔnʌpiŋ], *s.* recensement annuel des cygnes de la Tamise.
swap¹ [swɔp], *s.* (*a*) troc *m*, échange *m*; **to do a s.,** faire un troc; *Cmptr:* remplacer un programme par un autre; *Cmptr:* **s. time,** temps de transfert; *Fin:* **s. facilities,** facilités de crédit réciproques; (*b*) objet *m*, article *m*, à échanger, qu'on a échangé; **he took my old car as a s. for this one,** il a pris ma vieille voiture en échange de celle-ci; (*in stamp collecting, etc.*) **swaps,** doubles *m.*
swap², *v.* (**swapped**) **1.** *v.tr.* (*a*) *F:* **to s. sth. for sth.,** échanger, troquer, qch. contre, pour, qch.; faire un échange de qch. contre, pour, qch.; **to s. places with s.o.,** changer de place avec qn; **to s. mounts,** troquer de monture; **to s. bad for worse,** échanger un cheval borgne contre un aveugle; **to s. stories,** échanger ses impressions; (*b*) *Cmptr:* **to s. a programme,** remplacer un programme par un autre; **to s. tape handlers,** faire une bascule de dérouleurs; **to s. out a programme,** transférer un programme sur mémoire auxiliaire; **to s. in a programme,** introduire un programme d'une mémoire auxiliaire en mémoire centrale. **2.** *v.i. F:* faire du troc; **shall we s.?** si nous faisons un échange?
swapping ['swɔpiŋ], *s.* **1.** *F:* échange *m*, troc *m*; **wife s.,** échange de femmes entre maris. **2.** *Cmptr:* bascule *f* (de dérouleurs); remplacement *m* (d'un programme); **s. routine,** sous-programme *m* de transfert.
sward¹ [swɔːd], *s. Lit:* (tapis *m* de) gazon *m*; pelouse *f*; prairies gazonnées.
sward², *v.tr. Lit:* gazonner.
swarded ['swɔːdid], *a. Lit:* gazonné, gazonneux.
swardy ['swɔːdi], *a. Lit:* gazonneux.
swarf [swɔːf], *s.* **1.** *A:* boue *f* de meule, d'émoulage. **2.** copeaux *mpl* (de bois, métal, etc.); limaille *f* (de métal); riblons *mpl* (de ferraille); *Rec:* fils de cire (enlevés à la gravure d'un disque).
swarm¹ [swɔːm], *s.* **1.** essaim *m* (d'abeilles, d'insectes, de gens, d'étoiles filantes, etc.); (*a*) **s. of locusts,** vol *m* de sauterelles; **s. of midges, of earwigs,** nuée *f* de moucherons, pullulement *m* de perce-oreilles; **s. of small boats,** fourmillement *m* de petites embarcations; **s. of barbarians,** nuée de barbares; **s. of children,** essaim, troupe *f*, *F:* ribambelle *f*, légion *f*, d'enfants; (*b*) (**new**) **s. of bees,** jeton *m* d'abeilles; (*of bees*) **to send out a s.,** jeter un essaim; *Ap:* **s. catcher,** cueille-essaim *m inv*; *Ent:* **s. year,** année d'essaimage (des coléoptères). **2.** *Biol:* amas *m* (de zoospores); **s. cell, spore,** zoospore *f.*
swarm², *v.* **1.** *v.i.* (*a*) (*of bees*) essaimer; faire l'essaim; (*b*) *Biol:* (*of swarm spores*) se libérer (du zoosporange); (*c*) (*of pers.*) accourir en foule, se presser (**round, in,** autour de, dans); **the crowd swarmed over the (football) pitch,** la foule a inondé, a fait irruption, sur le terrain; (*d*) *Fig:* pulluler, grouiller; **children s. in these districts,** dans ces quartiers les enfants pullulent; (*e*) *Cin:* (*of image*) grouiller. **2.** *v.i.* fourmiller, grouiller (**with,** de); **the roads were swarming with people,** les rues grouillaient, regorgeaient, fourmillaient, de monde; **the river swarmed with alligators,** le fleuve était infesté d'alligators; **London always swarms with foreigners,** toujours Londres regorge d'étrangers. **3.** *v.tr. NAm:* **the passengers swarmed the deck,** les voyageurs se serraient sur le pont.
swarm³, *v.tr. & i.* **to s. (up) a tree, mast, cliff,** grimper à un arbre, à un mât, escalader une falaise (en s'aidant des bras et des genoux).
swarmer ['swɔːmər], *s.* **1.** (*a*) (i) abeille *f* qui fait l'essaim; (ii) ruche prête à essaimer; (*b*) *Biol:* zoospore *f.* **2.** *Ap:* ruche pour cueillir l'essaim.
swarming ['swɔːmiŋ], *s.* **1.** *Ap:* essaimage *m*, essaimement *m*; **s. time,** essaimage. **2.** *Cin:* grouillement *m* (de l'image).
swart [swɔːt], *a. A: & Poet:* = SWARTHY.
swarthiness ['swɔːðinis], *s.* teint basané, bistré, boucané.

swarthy ['swɔ:ði], *a.* (*of complexion*) basané, bistré, boucané; (*of pers.*) brun, noiraud.

swash[1] [swɔʃ], *s.* **1.** clapotage *m*, clapotement *m*, clapotis *m* (des vagues). **2.** (*a*) jet *m* de rive (d'une vague); (*b*) *NAm:* chenal *m*, -aux, derrière un banc de sable.

swash[2]. **1.** *v.i.* (*of water*) clapoter. **2.** *v.tr.* (*a*) faire jaillir, faire gicler (l'eau, etc.); (*b*) (*of water*) **to s. the rocks,** clapoter contre les rochers; lécher les rochers en clapotant.

swash[3], *a.* **1.** *Mec.E:* incliné sur l'axe (du tour); de biais; **s. plate,** plateau oscillant, basculant (pour la transformation d'un mouvement circulaire en mouvement rectiligne alternatif); **s. work,** façonnage *m* (au tour) des surfaces obliques. **2.** *Typ:* **s. letters,** (lettres *f* italiques) majuscules avec fioritures.

swashbuckler ['swɔʃbʌklər], *s.* rodomont *m*, bretailleur *m*, bretteur *m*; bravache *m*, fanfaron *m*; traîneur *m* de sabre, d'épée, de rapière; matamore *m*; ferrailleur *m*; batteur *m* de fer.

swashbuckling[1] ['swɔʃbʌkliŋ], *a.* fanfaron, bravache; **s. fellow,** bretailleur *m*, bretteur *m*; **s. life,** vie de bretteur.

swashbuckling[2], *s.* rodomontades *fpl*; fanfaronnades *fpl*; manières *fpl*, allures *fpl*, de bravache, de bretteur.

swashing ['swɔʃiŋ], *a.* **1.** (coup) violent, assommant. **2.** (*of liquid*) clapotant, clapoteux.

swastika ['swɔstikə], *s.* svastika *m*, croix gammée.

swat[1] [swɔt], *s.* **1.** (*a*) (i) coup sec; tape *f*; (ii) *NAm:* (*at baseball*) frappe *f*; **s. stick,** batte *f*; (*b*) (**fly**) **s.,** (tapette *f*) tue-mouches *m inv.* **2.** = SWOT[1].

swat[2], *v.* (**swatted**) *F:* **1.** *v.tr.* frapper, taper, cogner sur (qn, qch.); **s. that fly!** écrasez donc cette mouche! **2.** *v.tr. & i.* = SWOT[2].

swatch ['swɔtʃ], *s. Com:* (i) échantillon *m*; (ii) album *m* d'échantillons (de tissus).

swath [swɔ:θ], *s.* = SWATHE[3].

swathe[1] [sweið], *s.* **1.** bandage *m*, bandelette *f.* **2.** *A:* lange *m*.

swathe[2], *v.tr.* **1.** emmailloter, envelopper; **head swathed in bandages,** tête enveloppée de linges; **woman swathed in a shawl, in warm clothes,** femme enveloppée, entourée, d'un châle, emmaillotée de vêtements chauds. **2.** rouler (qch. autour de qch.).

swathe[3], *s. Agr:* andain *m*, ondain *m*, javelle *f*; **s. layer,** javeleur, -euse.

swathing ['sweiðiŋ]. **1.** emmaillotement *m*, enveloppement *m*; *A:* **s. bands,** langes *mpl*, maillot *m*. **2.** **swathings,** bandages *m*; bandelettes *f* (de momie).

swatter ['swɔtər], *s.* (**fly**) **s.,** (tapette *f*) tue-mouches *m inv.*

sway[1] [swei], *s.* **1.** balancement *m*, oscillation *f*; mouvement *m* de va-et-vient; *Rail:* mouvement de lacet (des wagons); *Aut:* roulis *m* (de la voiture); *Veh:* **s. bar,** sassoire *f*; *Civ.E:* **s. bracing,** contreventement *m*. **2.** empire *m*, domination *f*; **the s. of fashion,** le règne, l'empire, de la mode; **under his s.,** sous son empire; sous son influence; **peoples under the s. of Rome,** peuples soumis à Rome; **to bring a people under one's s.,** réduire un peuple sous sa puissance; **to be under the s. of a passion,** être sous l'empire d'une passion; subir le joug d'une passion; **to have, hold, bear, s. over a people,** régner sur un peuple; avoir, exercer, le pouvoir sur un peuple; **to hold s. over a country,** tenir un pays en souveraineté; **these laws hold s. in all natural sciences,** ces lois s'exercent dans toutes les sciences naturelles; **to have lost one's s. over public opinion,** avoir perdu son empire sur l'opinion publique; **to have great s. in the House,** jouir d'une grande influence à la Chambre; *Lit:* **she held s. over his heart,** elle régnait sur son cœur.

sway[2]. **1.** *v.i.* (*a*) se balancer; osciller; ballotter; (*of drunkard*) vaciller; (*of trees*) **to s. in the wind,** se balancer au vent; **trees swaying in the wind,** arbres que berce le vent; (*b*) rester indécis, balancer, vaciller; (*c*) **after the earthquake the wall swayed outwards,** après le tremblement de terre le mur penchait en dehors. **2.** *v.tr.* (*a*) faire osciller; balancer, agiter (les arbres, etc.); **heart swayed between hope and fear,** cœur suspendu entre l'espoir et la crainte; (*b*) *Poet:* (i) porter, tenir (le sceptre); (ii) régner sur (un pays); (*c*) gouverner, diriger, influencer; influer sur (qn, qch.); **considerations that s. our opinions,** considérations qui font pencher, qui influencent, nos opinions; **his advice sways the whole council,** son avis entraîne l'opinion de tout le conseil; (*d*) **to s. s.o. from his course,** détourner qn de ses projets; **to refuse to be swayed,** rester inflexible; (*e*) *Nau:* **to s. up,** hisser, guinder (un mât de hune, etc.); **s. away!** hissez!

swayback ['sweibæk], *s.* ensellure *f* (d'un cheval); *Med:* ensellure lombaire.

swaybacked ['sweibækt], *a.* (*of horse, pers.*) ensellé.

sway-brace ['sweibreis], *v.tr. Civ.E:* contreventer (un pont, etc.).

swaying[1] ['sweiiŋ], *a.* qui se balance de-ci de-là; oscillant; **s. gait,** déhanchement *m* en marchant, dandinement *m*; **to walk with a s. gait,** tanguer en marchant; **s. crowd,** foule ondoyante.

swaying[2], *s.* balancement *m*, oscillation *f*; mouvement *m* de va-et-vient; *Rail:* mouvement de lacet (des wagons); *Aut:* roulis *m* (de la voiture).

Swazi ['swɑ:zi]. **1.** *Geog:* (*a*) *a.* souazi; (*b*) *s.* Souazi(e). **2.** *s. Ling:* le dialecte souazi.

Swaziland ['swɑ:zilænd], *Pr.n. Geog:* le Souaziland.

sweal [swi:l], *v.tr. Dial: Agr:* écouber (les ajoncs, etc.).

swear[1] ['swɛər], *s.* **1.** jurons *mpl*; **to have a good s.,** lâcher une bordée de jurons. **2.** **s. (word),** gros mot; juron *m*.

swear[2], *v.* (*p.t.* **swore** [swɔ:r], *A:* **sware** [swɛər]; *p.p.* **sworn** [swɔ:n]).

I. *v.tr.* **1.** jurer; **to s. an oath,** faire un serment; jurer; **to s. sth. on the Bible,** jurer qch. sur la Bible; **to s. to do sth., that one will do sth.,** jurer de faire qch.; **we could have sworn we heard a shout,** on aurait juré entendre un cri; **to s. fealty to s.o.,** faire, prêter, serment de féauté à qn; jurer la féauté à qn; **the allegiance that they had sworn to him,** le serment de fidélité à lui prêté par eux; **he broke the peace he had sworn,** il rompit la paix par lui jurée; **to s. eternal hatred,** jurer une haine éternelle (**against,** contre); **to s. revenge,** jurer, faire serment, de se venger. **2.** **to s. (in) a witness, a jury,** faire prêter serment à, déférer le serment à, assermenter, un témoin, un jury; (*of juryman*) **to be sworn (in),** prêter serment; **to s. s.o. to secrecy,** faire jurer le secret à qn; **I s. you to secrecy,** vous me jurez le secret. **3.** déclarer (qch.) sous (la foi du) serment; **to s. an estate at £100,000,** évaluer un bien à £100,000 sous la foi du serment; **to s. treason against s.o.,** jurer que qn est coupable de trahison.

II. *v.i.* **1.** (i) jurer, sacrer, blasphémer; renier Dieu; (ii) proférer, lâcher, un juron, des jurons; **to s. at s.o.,** maudire, injurier, qn; jurer après qn; **to s. about s.o., sth.,** pester contre qn, qch.; **to s. like a trooper, bargee,** jurer comme un charretier (embourbé), un templier, un démon, tous les diables; **it's enough to make a saint s.,** il y a de quoi faire jurer un saint; cela fera damner un saint. **2.** (*of cat*) gronder. **3.** **colours that s. at each other,** couleurs qui jurent ensemble, l'une avec l'autre.

III. (*compound verbs*) **1. swear away,** *v.tr.* **to s. away s.o.'s freedom, good name,** envoyer qn en prison, perdre qn de réputation, en portant un faux témoignage.

2. swear by. (*a*) *v.tr. & i.* **he swore by Apollo to avenge his father,** il jura par Apollon de venger son père; **to s. by one's honour,** jurer sa foi; **to s. by all that one holds sacred,** jurer ses grands dieux; (*b*) se fier à (qn, qch.); **he swears by his boss,** il ne jure que par son patron; **I s. by aspirin for a headache,** pour moi il n'y a rien de tel que l'aspirine pour un mal de tête.

3. swear off, *v. ind.tr.* jurer de renoncer à (l'alcool, etc.); **I've sworn off bridge,** j'ai renoncé au bridge.

4. swear out, *v.tr. NAm:* obtenir (un mandat d'arrêt) en faisant une accusation sous serment.

5. swear to, *v. ind.tr.* attester, certifier, (qch.) sous serment; **she swore to having paid him,** elle déclara sous serment l'avoir payé; **I s. to it,** j'en lève la main; **I would s. to it,** j'en jurerais; *F:* j'en mettrais la main au feu, à couper; **I will s. to it on my life,** *F:* je vous le signerai de mon sang; **I would have sworn to him,** j'aurais juré que c'était lui.

swearer ['swɛərər], *s.* **1.** celui, celle, qui prête serment; *Jur: A:* jureur *m*. **2.** personne mal embouchée.

swearing ['swɛəriŋ], *s.* **1.** (*a*) attestation *f* sous serment; (*b*) prestation *f* de serment. **2.** **s. (in) of the jury,** assermentation *f* du jury. **3.** jurements *mpl*, jurons *mpl*; gros mots. **4.** grondement *m* (d'un chat).

sweat[1] [swet], *s.* **1.** (*a*) sueur *f*, transpiration *f*; **forehead, hands, wet with s.,** front couvert, mains moites, de sueur; **night sweats,** sueurs nocturnes; **bloody s.,** sueur de sang; *B:* **in the s. of thy face shalt thou eat bread,** tu mangeras le pain à la sueur de ton visage; **by the s. of one's brow,** à la sueur de son front; **to be in a s.,** *F:* **all of a s.,** (i) être trempé de sueur; suer à grosses gouttes; être tout en nage; (ii) être tout en émoi; ne savoir où donner de la tête; **to be in a s. about sth.,** s'inquiéter de qch.; **to work oneself (up) into a s.,** s'énerver (**about sth.,** de qch.); se faire de la bile; **to be in a s. of fear,** suer de terreur; **a cold s. came over him, he came out in a cold s.,** il a été pris d'une sueur froide; *Anat:* **s. duct,** canal excréteur (d'une glande sudoripare); conduit *m* sudorifère; **s. gland,** glande sudoripare; *Harn:* **s. cloth,** tapis *m* de selle; **s. flap,** quartier *m* de selle; *Sp:* **s. shirt,** blouson *m* de sport, d'entraînement; **s. suit,** survêtement *m*; (*b*) *Med: Vet:* suerie *f*, suée *f*; **to give a horse a s.,** donner une suée à un cheval (soumis à l'entraînement); (*c*) *F:* corvée *f*, travail *m* pénible; **it's an awful s.,** c'est une suée, un drôle de travail, un fichu travail; *NAm:* **no s.,** il n'y a pas de difficulté; c'est simple comme bonjour; c'est du gâteau; (*d*) *Mil: P:* **old s.,** vieux troupier; vétéran *m*. **2.** (*a*) *Bot: etc:* transudation *f*; (*b*) condensation *f*; suintement *m* (des murs, etc.). **3.** (*a*) *Metall:* ressuage *m* (du minerai); (*b*) *Tan: etc:* échauffe *f*.

sweat[2], *v.*

I. *v.i.* **1.** (*a*) suer, transpirer; **to s. profusely, like a bull, a horse,** suer à grosses gouttes, comme un phoque; *F:* être en nage; *F:* **only to look at surgical instruments makes me s.,** rien que de voir des instruments de chirurgie, ça me donne des sueurs froides; (*b*) (*of worker*) peiner; travailler comme un nègre; turbiner; **schoolboy sweating over his lessons,** élève qui bûche, potasse, ses devoirs; **to s. up a hill, along the road,** gravir péniblement une colline; cheminer péniblement; (*c*) *F:* s'inquiéter; se faire de la bile; **to be sweating on the top line,** être très agité, sur des charbons ardents. **2.** (*of walls, etc.*) suer, ressuer, suinter.

II. *v.tr.* **1.** (*a*) suer; **to s. blood,** (i) suer du sang; (ii) *Fig:* suer sang et eau; *P:* **to s. one's guts out,** s'échiner; (*b*) faire suer (qn, un cheval); *Med:* faire transpirer (un malade); *Turf:* suer (un cheval); (*c*) exploiter, *P:* usiner (la main-d'œuvre); (*d*) *NAm: F:* cuisiner (un suspect). **2.** **to s. a horse,** enlever la sueur d'un cheval; bouchonner un cheval. **3.** *A:* frayer (la monnaie d'or). **4.** *Metall:* suer, faire ressuer (le minerai). **5.** *Metalw:* **to s. sth. into, on to, sth.,** souder qch. à qch. à l'étain, à la soudure tendre; **to s. a joint,** ressuer une jointure. **6.** (*a*) *Tan:* passer à l'échauffe, étuver (les peaux); (*b*) faire fermenter (les feuilles de tabac).

III. (*compound verbs*) **1. sweat away, off,** *v.tr.* **to s. away, off, ten kilos,** réduire son poids de dix kilos (i) par bains de vapeur, (ii) en se faisant suer.

2. sweat out. (*a*) *v.tr.* (i) **to s. out the moisture from a wall,** faire exsuder l'humidité d'un mur; (ii) chasser, guérir (un rhume par des sudorifiques); (iii) *F:* **I could only s. it out,** je n'avais qu'à endurer jusqu'à la fin; **I was left to s. it out in the waiting room,** on m'a laissé faire le pied de grue dans la salle d'attente; (*b*) *v.i.* (*of moisture*) exsuder.

sweatband ['swetbænd], *s. Hatm:* cuir intérieur (d'un chapeau); cuiret *m*.

sweatbox ['swetbɔks], *s. Tan:* échauffe *f*, étuve *f*.

sweated ['swetid], *a.* **s. labour,** travail exténuant et mal rétribué; travail d'esclave; **s. goods,** articles produits à la sueur des ouvriers, ouvrières.

sweater ['swetər], *s.* **1.** *Cost:* pullover *m*, chandail *m*, tricot *m*, sweater *m*; *NAm: P:* **s. girl,** jeune femme bien moulée (qui porte un pullover collant). **2.** *Pej:* exploiteur, -euse (de main-d'œuvre).

sweathouse ['swethaus], *s.* **1.** (*a*) *Tan:* échauffe *f*, étuve *f*; (*b*) (*for tobacco*) suerie *f.* **2.** *NAm:* étuve (de Peaux-Rouges).

sweatiness ['swetinis], *s.* moiteur *f* (du corps); humidité (d'un vêtement) due à la transpiration.

sweating[1] ['swetiŋ], *a.* **1.** (*a*) en sueur; suant; (*b*) (mur, etc.) suintant. **2.** (*a*) (travail) exténuant et mal rétribué; (*b*) (patron) qui exploite ses ouvriers.

sweating[2], *s.* **1.** (*a*) transpiration *f*; *Med:* sudation *f*; *Med: A:* **s. sickness,** suette anglaise; *A:* trousse-galant *m*; (*b*) ressuage *m*, suintement *m* (d'un mur, etc.). **2.** (*a*) *Med: etc:* suée *f*, suerie *f*; **s. bath,** bain turc; **s. room,** étuve *f*; salle *f* de sudation (d'un hammam); sudatoire *m*; (*b*) exploitation *f*, *F:* usinage *m* (de la main-d'œuvre, etc.); **the s. system,** l'exploitation patronale; (*c*) *NAm: F:* cuisinage *m* (d'un prisonnier). **3.** enlèvement *m* de la sueur (d'un cheval); bouchonnage *m*; **s. iron,** couteau *m* de chaleur. **4.** *A:* frai artificiel (des pièces d'or). **5.** (*a*) *Metall:* ressuage *m* (du minerai); **s. heat,** chaude suante; (*b*) *Metalw:* soudure *f* à l'étain; ressuage. **6.** *Tan:* étuvage *m*, échauffe *f*; **s. room, pit,** étuve, échauffe.

sweatshop ['swetʃɔp], *s.* atelier *m* où les ouvriers sont exploités; *F:* vrai bagne.

sweaty ['sweti], *a.* **1.** couvert de sueur; en sueur; **s. hands,** mains moites. **2.** **s. afternoon,** après-midi d'une chaleur humide; **s. work,** travail qui fait transpirer. **3.** **s. clothes,** vêtements imprégnés de sueur; **s. smell,** odeur de sueur.

Swede [swi:d], *s.* **1.** *Geog:* Suédois, -oise. **2.** *Agr:* **swede,** rutabaga *m*; navet *m* de Suède; chou-navet *m*, *pl.* choux-navets; **s. rape,** colza (vrai).

Sweden ['swi:d(ə)n], *Pr.n. Geog:* Suède *f.*

Swedenborgian [swi:d(ə)n'bɔ:dʒiən], *a. & s. Rel.H:* Swedenborgien, -ienne.

Swedish ['swi:diʃ]. **1.** *a.* suédois; **S. gymnastics, exercises, movements,** gymnastique suédoise. **2.** *s. Ling:* suédois *m*.

sweeny ['swi:ni], *s. Vet: NAm:* atrophie *f* musculaire (*esp.* de l'épaule chez le cheval).

sweep[1] [swi:p], *s.* **1.** (*a*) coup *m* de balai, de pinceau, de faux; **at one s.,** d'un seul coup; (*b*) balayage *m*; **to give a room a good s. (out),** donner à une pièce un bon coup de balai; balayer une chambre à fond; *F:* **to have a s. up,** balayer, ramasser, la poussière, les débris, etc.; *Fig:* **to make a clean s. of one's old furniture, of one's staff,** faire place nette de ses vieux meubles, de son personnel; faire maison nette; *F:* balayer son personnel; **to make a clean s. of a gang of thieves,** faire une rafle complète d'une bande de voleurs; rafler une bande; **to make a clean s. of the table,** faire table rase; **to make a clean s. of one's prejudices,** faire table rase de ses préjugés; **to make a clean s. of the provisions,** faire main basse sur les vivres; **the thieves made a clean s.,** les voleurs ont tout enlevé, tout raflé; **it was a clean s.,** ç'a été la rafle totale; *Gaming:* **to make a clean s.,** faire rafle; rafler le tout. **2.** (*a*) mouvement *m* circulaire (du bras, etc.); **with a wide s. of the arm,** d'un geste large; **with a s. of the hand he caught the rope,** dans un ramassement de main il a attrapé la corde; **s. of the eye,** regard *m* circulaire; *Danc:* **s. of the leg,** rond *m* de jambe; *Paint:* **s. brush,** brosse *f* à coller; (*b*) *Fish:* **to make a s.,** faire une pêche à la seine; **within the s. of the net,** dans le cercle du filet; **s. net, s. seine,** seine *f*, senne *f*; (*c*) *Mil: Av:* balayage; opération offensive de chasse lointaine en territoire ennemi. **3.** (*a*) zone *f* de jeu (d'une manivelle, etc.); **door s.,** ouverture *f* de porte; *Aut: etc:* **fan s.,** région couverte par le ventilateur; (*b*) *Artil: etc:* (i) battage *m*, (ii) portée *f* (d'une pièce); portée (d'un phare); **the convoy was beyond, within, the s. of the guns,** le convoi était hors de portée, à portée; **to bring one's arguments within the s. of one's audience,** mettre son raisonnement à la portée de son auditoire; (*c*) envergure *f* (des ailes, *Fig:* d'un génie); portée (d'un raisonnement, principe). **4.** *Rad: Elcs:* **scan(ning) s.,** balayage; **s. circuit, frequency, generator,** circuit *m*, fréquence *f*, générateur *m*, de balayage. **5.** (*a*) course *f* rapide (d'un fleuve, etc.); **s. by,** passage *m* rapide (d'une voiture, d'un grand oiseau, etc.); (*b*) *Phot:* **to cover the plate with the developer at one s.,** répandre le révélateur sur la plaque d'un seul coup. **6.** (*a*) courbe *f*, courbure *f*; boucle *f* (d'une rivière); *Arch:* courbure (d'un arc); **to make, take, a s.,** (*of river, etc.*) décrire une courbe; (*of ship*) prendre du tour; **the car took a big s.,** la voiture a pris un virage large; **to make a wide s. to take a bend,** prendre du champ pour effectuer un virage; **s. of a hill,** versant incurvé d'une colline; **s. of a car's lines,** galbe *f* d'une voiture; **up s. of the chassis,** surélévation *f* du châssis; *N.Arch:* **s. (of the lines) of a ship,** courbure, façons *fpl*, d'un navire; *Tls:* **s. saw,** scie *f* à chantourner; (*b*) *Av:* **s. (back),** flèche *f*; **s. forward,** flèche inversée, négative; (*c*) **a large s. leads to the house,** une grande allée en demi-cercle conduit à la maison; **a fine s. of grass, of country,** une belle étendue de gazon, de pays. **7.** (*a*) (i) aviron *m* (de chaland); (ii) aviron de queue (d'une embarcation, etc.); (*b*) aile *f* (de moulin); (*c*) flèche *f* (d'un manège); (*d*) balancier *m* (de pompe, de porte d'écluse); (*e*) bascule *f* (pour tirer l'eau d'un puits); (*in Egypt, etc.*) chadouf *m*; (*f*) *N.Arch:* tamisaille *f* (du gouvernail). **8.** (*a*) *Metall:* **s. (board),** trousseau *m*; calibre *m* de moulage; (*b*) *Draw:* compas *m* à verge. **9.** *Clockm:* **seconds s., s. second(s) (hand),** trotteuse centrale. **10.** *Nau:* câble balayeur; drague *f* (pour mines). **11.** (*pers.*) (*a*) **(chimney) s.,** ramoneur *m*; (*b*) *P:* sale type *m*; *P:* cochon *m*. **12.** *F:* sweepstake *m*.

sweep[2], *v.* **(swept)**

I. *v.tr.* **1.** (*a*) balayer (une pièce, etc.); ramoner (une cheminée); ébouer (les rues); *B:* **he findeth it empty, swept and garnished,** il la trouve vide, balayée et parée; **dress that sweeps the ground,** robe qui balaie le sol; **a storm swept the town,** un orage ravagea la ville; **to s. the ground with shrapnel fire,** arroser le terrain; **region swept by machine-gun fire,** région balayée, battue, par les mitrailleuses; **the deck was swept by a sea,** une grosse vague balaya le pont; **to s. the strings of a harp,** effleurer les cordes d'une harpe; arpéger; **to s. the horizon with a telescope,** parcourir, interroger, scruter, l'horizon avec une lunette; **to s. the room with a glance,** promener un regard circulaire sur la salle; **his eye swept the sea,** son œil parcourait la mer; **to s. the seas,** battre, parcourir, balayer, les mers; **to s. the seas of one's enemies, of pirates,** purger la mer de ses ennemis, des pirates; **to s. the board,** (i) *Gaming:* faire rafle; rafler le tout; faire table rase; nettoyer le tapis; (ii) *F:* remporter un succès complet; *Pol:* **to s. the country with a programme,** recueillir l'approbation de tout le pays pour son programme; **the latest craze to s. the country,** la dernière chose qui fait fureur partout dans le pays; (*b*) *Nau:* **to s. a channel,** draguer un chenal; *v.i.* **to s. for mines, for an anchor,** draguer des mines, une ancre; **to s. for a cable,** pêcher un câble. **2.** (*a*) balayer (la poussière); **to s. the dust into a corner,** refouler la poussière dans un coin (avec le balai); (*b*) emporter, entraîner; **a wave swept him overboard,** une lame le jeta à la mer; **we were swept into the road by the crowd,** nous fûmes entraînés dans la rue par la foule; **to be swept out of sight,** être emporté, entraîné, hors de vue; **everything he can lay hold of is swept into his net,** il ramasse tout sur quoi il peut mettre le grappin; **to be swept off one's feet by the tide,** être entraîné par la marée; perdre pied; (*of the crowd*) **to s. s.o. off his feet,** soulever qn de la terre; entraîner qn; *F:* **to be swept off one's feet by s.o.,** s'emballer, être emballé, pour qn. **3.** **to s. one's hand over sth.,** (i) passer la main sur qch.; (ii) passer la main sur qch. d'un geste circulaire; **to s. one's hand over one's hair,** se passer la main sur les cheveux; **to s. one's eyes along the horizon,** interroger, scruter, l'horizon d'un regard circulaire; **to s. one's eyes over s.o.,** envelopper qn d'un regard. **4.** tracer (une courbe). **5.** *Metall:* mouler au trousseau, au calibre; **to s. the mould,** calibrer, trousser, le moule.

II. *v.i.* **1.** (*extend widely*) s'étendre, s'étaler; **the plain sweeps (away) towards the north,** la plaine s'étend vers le nord. **2.** **to s. (along),** avancer rapidement; avancer avec un mouvement rapide et uni; **she swept in(to the room), out (of the room),** elle est entrée dans, sortie de, la salle d'un air majestueux, avec un port de reine; **she swept by the waiting crowd,** elle est passée (i) majestueusement, (ii) dédaigneusement (devant la foule qui l'attendait); (*of car, etc.*) **to s. round the corner,** tourner le coin de la rue en faisant un large virage; **the wind sweeps along the road,** le vent balaye la rue; **the crowd swept over the pitch,** la foule envahit le terrain de jeu; **the plague swept over Europe,** la peste parcourut toute l'Europe; **the beam swept across the sea,** le faisceau lumineux balaya la mer; **the road sweeps round the lake,** la route décrit une courbe autour du lac; **the opposition swept home,** l'opposition a remporté un succès complet.

III. (*compound verbs*) **1. sweep along,** *v.tr.* (*a*) (*of current, etc.*) entraîner, emporter (qch.); **speaker who sweeps his audience along with him,** orateur qui entraîne son auditoire; (*b*) faire avancer (un chaland) avec les avirons, en souquant.

2. sweep aside, *v.tr.* écarter (les rideaux, etc.) d'un geste large; **to s. aside opposition,** écarter brusquement, de haute main, l'opposition.

3. sweep away, *v.tr.* balayer (la neige, les nuages, etc.); supprimer, détruire (un abus); **the storm swept everything away,** la tempête a tout balayé, *F:* a tout moissonné; **bridge swept away by the torrent,** pont emporté, balayé, entraîné, par le torrent.

4. sweep by, *v.i.* (*of traffic, etc.*) passer avec vitesse; (*of pers.*) passer (i) majestueusement, (ii) dédaigneusement.

5. sweep down. (*a*) *v.tr.* **the current sweeps the logs down with it,** le courant emporte, entraîne, charrie, le bois; (*b*) *v.i.* (i) **the enemy, the storm, swept down upon us,** l'ennemi, l'orage, s'abattit sur nous; l'ennemi fondit, fonça, sur nous; (ii) **hills sweeping down to the sea,** collines qui descendent, qui dévalent, vers la mer.

6. sweep in, (*a*) *v.i.* **the wind sweeps in,** le vent s'engouffre par la porte; **the opposition swept in,** l'opposition a remporté un succès complet; (*b*) *v.tr. Veh:* **chassis swept in at the front,** châssis rétréci vers, à, l'avant.

7. sweep off, *v.tr.* (*a*) enlever, emporter, avec violence; **the plague swept off thousands,** la peste emporta des milliers de personnes; (*b*) *O:* **to s. off one's hat,** faire un large salut.

8. sweep on, *v.i.* (*of flood, etc.*) avancer d'un flot régulier; continuer d'avancer (irrésistiblement).

9. sweep out. (*a*) *v.tr.* balayer (une pièce) (à fond); débarrasser (une chambre) de sa poussière; (*b*) *v.i.* **she swept out (of the room),** elle est sortie (de la pièce) d'un air dédaigneux, impérieusement.

10. sweep past, *v.i.* = SWEEP BY.

11. sweep round, *v.i. Nau:* virer.

12. sweep up. (*a*) *v.tr.* balayer, ramasser (la poussière); ramasser (la poussière, etc.) en tas; *Aut:* **swept up chassis,** châssis surélevé (à l'arrière, etc.); (*b*) *v.i.* **the car swept up to the door,** la voiture a roulé jusqu'à la porte.

sweepback ['swi:pbæk], *s. Av:* (angle *m* de) flèche *f* (des ailes).

sweeper ['swi:pər], *s.* **1.** (*pers.*) balayeur, -euse. **2.** (*machine*) balayeuse; balai *m* (mécanique); ébouеuse *f*; **(motor) street s.,** autobalayeuse *f*; **s. and sprinkler,** balayeuse-arroseuse *f*, *pl.* balayeuses-arroseuses; *Hort:* **lawn s.,** balayeuse mécanique pour pelouses.

sweeping[1] ['swi:piŋ], *a.* **1.** (*of stream, etc.*) rapide, impétueux. **2.** (*a*) **s. plain,** vaste plaine, vaste étendue; **s. gesture,** geste large; **s. curtsy,** révérence profonde; **s. glance,** regard circulaire, qui embrasse toute l'assemblée; **s. motion,** mouvement circulaire; (*b*) (mouvement) balayant; **s. flight,** vol plané (des grands oiseaux); *Mil:* **s. fire,** tir fauchant, de fauchage; (*c*) *Art: etc:* **s. line,** ligne allongée, élancée, fuyante; **the s. lines of the drapery,** les lignes dégagées des draperies; *Veh:* **low s. lines,** lignes basses et allongées. **3.** **s. statement, s. generalization,** déclaration par trop générale; généralisation par trop absolue; **s. reform,** réforme complète, intégrale, radicale; **s. changes,** changement de fond en comble; *Com:* **s. reductions,** (i) rabais incroyables; (ii) rabais sur tous les articles.

sweeping[2], *s.* **1.** (*a*) balayage *m* (d'une chambre); ramonage *m* (d'une cheminée); ébouage *m* (d'une rue); **s. machine,** balayeuse *f* mécanique, (*for roads*) éboueuse *f*; **s. and watering machine,** balayeuse-arroseuse *f*, *pl.* balayeuses-arroseuses; (*b*) balayage *m* (d'un projecteur, etc.); *Mil:* fauchage *m* (d'une arme à feu); *Elcs:* **s. circuit,** circuit de balayage. **2.** **sweepings,** balayures *f*, ordures *f*; *Metall:* sarrasin *m*; **heap of street sweepings,** tas d'ordures, de raclons *m*; *Fig:* **the sweepings of society,** le rebut de la société. **3.** (*compound nouns*) (*a*) **s. away,** balayage (de la neige, etc.); suppression *f* (d'un abus); (*b*) *Nau:* **s. round,** virage *m*; (*c*) **s. up,** balayage, ramassement *m*.

sweepingly ['swi:piŋli], *adv.* **1.** rapidement. **2.** sans distinction; **actors were s. denounced as rogues,** les acteurs étaient traités de fripons par une généralisation par trop absolue.

sweepstake ['swi:psteik], *s.* sweepstake *m*.

sweet [swi:t].

I. *a.* doux, *f.* douce. **1.** sucré; **as s. as honey,** doux comme (le) miel; **to taste s.,** avoir une saveur douce; **s. apple,** pomme douce, sucrée; **s. biscuit,** biscuit sucré; **s. wine,** vin sucré; **s. stuff,** bonbons *mpl*, douceurs *fpl*, friandises *fpl*; **my tea is too s.,** mon thé est trop sucré; **to have a s. tooth,** aimer les douceurs, le sucre, les sucreries; être friand de sucreries; *F:* avoir la bouche sucrée; *F:* **s. morsel,** morceau succulent; *Cu:* **s. corn,** maïs doux, vert; *Pharm:* **s. root,** réglisse *f*; *Cu:* **s. and sour sauce,** sauce aigre-douce. **2.** (*of flower, etc.*) parfumé, odorant; **s. violet,** violette odorante; **to smell s.,** sentir bon; avoir une douce odeur; (*of rose, etc.*) embaumer; *F:* **it doesn't smell exactly s.,** ça ne sent pas la rose; **the air was s. with the odours of spring,** l'air sentait bon le printemps. **3.** *Bot:* **s. cherry,** merisier *m*; **s. clover,** mélilot *m*; **s. grass,** glycérie *f*; **s. william,** œillet *m* de(s) poète(s); jalousie *f*; fleur *f* d'Arménie; NOTE: *for other plant names see the nouns.* **4.** (*of food, air, etc.*) frais, *f.* fraîche; **s. water,** (i) eau bonne à boire; eau potable; (ii) eau douce; **is the ham still s.?** est-ce que le jambon est encore bon? **to keep the ham s.,** empêcher le jambon de se corrompre; **to keep a stable s. and clean,** maintenir une écurie nette et saine, sans odeur; **s. breath,** haleine saine, pure, fraîche; *Agr:* **s. earth,** sol sain; *Min:* **s. air,** air non grisouteux. **5.** (son) doux, mélodieux, suave; **s. singer,** chanteur à la voix douce; **her voice sounds s.,** elle a la voix douce; **flattery that sounds s., is s. to hear,** flatteries douces aux oreilles. **6.** (*a*) agréable; **s. repose,** doux repos; **s. temper,** caractère doux, aimable; **revenge is s.,** la vengeance est douce; **it is s. to know that one is loved,** c'est une grande douceur de se savoir aimé; *F:* **to keep s.o. s.,** cultiver la bienveillance de qn; (*b*) charmant, gentil, -ille; gentillet, -ette; **s. old lady,** vieille dame charmante, exquise; **s. girl,** gentille jeune fille; **she's perfectly s.,** elle est gentille, mignonne, à croquer; **she was s. and twenty,** c'était une délicieuse jeune fille de vingt printemps; **what a s. kitten!** quel petit chat adorable! **s. smile,** sourire doux; **s. manners,** manières gracieuses, aimables; **my sweet(est)!** *O:* **s. one!** ma chérie! ma douce amie! **that's very s. of you,** c'est bien gentil à vous, c'est trop gentil de votre part; **a s. little dress,** une gentille petite robe; une petite robe exquise; **to say s. nothings to s.o.,** conter fleurette à qn; dire des gentillesses, des douceurs, à qn; *NAm: F:* **s. talk,** flatterie *f*; parler mielleux; boniment *m*, barat(t)in *m*; pommade *f*; **to hand a girl a s. line,** barat(t)iner une fille. **7.** *F:* **to be s. on s.o.,** être amoureux de qn; avoir un béguin, caprice, pour qn; *O:* **I'm not very s. on the proposition,** cette proposition ne me dit rien. **8.** **s. running,** fonctionnement doux, sans à-coups (d'une machine); *Nau:* **s. ship,** navire maniable. **9.** **s. oil,** (*a*) huile douce, *esp.* huile d'olive; (*b*) (i) huile de colza, (ii) huile de navette. **10.** *F:* **you can bet your s. life (on it),** tu peux en mettre la main au feu, la main à couper.

II. *s.* **1.** (*a*) bonbon *m*; **sweets,** (i) sucreries *f*, confiserie *f*, douceurs *f*, friandises *f*; (ii) *P:* amphétamines *f*; (*b*) (*at dinner*) entremets sucré. **2.** **sweets:** (*a*) douceurs (de la vie, des fonctions publiques, etc.); **the sweets of life,** les joies *f* et les plaisirs *m* de ce monde; les délices *f* de ce monde; (*b*) (i) vins sucrés; (ii) *Wine-m:* liqueur *f* d'expédition; (*c*) *Poet:* doux parfums (des fleurs, etc.).

sweetbread ['swi:tbred], *s. Cu:* (**throat, neck**) **s.,** ris *m* (de veau, d'agneau); **belly s.,** pancréas *m.*

sweeten ['swi:tn]. **1.** *v.tr.* (*a*) adoucir (une boisson amère); sucrer (un plat, une boisson, etc.); édulcorer (une potion); (*b*) épurer (l'eau, etc.); assainir, rafraîchir (l'air); purifier (l'air, l'eau); assainir (une écurie, le sol, etc.); déodoriser (l'air, l'haleine, etc.); (*c*) adoucir, rendre plus agréable (un son, la vie, l'humeur de qn); (*d*) *F:* **to s. s.o. (up),** (i) flatter, pommader, qn; (ii) graisser la patte à qn; (*e*) *Cards: NAm:* **to s. the jackpot,** augmenter le jackpot d'un enjeu (avant la donne); (*f*) *Mec.E:* **to s. the gears,** permettre aux engrenages de se faire. **2.** *v.i.* (*a*) s'adoucir; (*b*) (*of soil*) s'assainir; (*c*) *Mec.E:* (*of gears*) se faire.

sweetener ['swi:t(ə)nər], *s.* **1.** *Cu: etc:* édulcorant *m*; *Wine-m:* liqueur *f* d'expédition. **2. the sweeteners of life,** les choses qui rendent la vie douce. **3.** *F:* **to give s.o. a s.,** graisser la patte à qn.

sweetening ['swi:t(ə)niŋ], *s.* **1.** (*a*) adoucissement *m*; sucrage *m*; édulcoration *f*; (*b*) assainissement *m* (du sol, d'une écurie, etc.); déodorisation *f* (de l'air, de l'haleine); (*c*) *Ind: Ch: Petr:* adoucissement; **air s., copper s.,** adoucissement à l'air, au cuivre; (*d*) adoucissement (du travail, de l'humeur de qn). **2.** substance *f* pour sucrer; **what s. did you use?** avec quoi (l')avez-vous sucré?

sweetheart[1] ['swi:thα:t], *s.* **1.** amoureux, -euse; bien-aimé, -ée; (**my**) **s.!** mon amour! mon cœur! ma chérie! **he's off to see his s.,** il va voir celle qu'il aime, sa belle; **they have been sweethearts since childhood,** ils s'adorent depuis leur enfance. **2.** fiancé, -ée.

sweetheart[2], *v.tr. A:* courtiser (qn).

sweetie ['swi:ti], *s. F:* **1.** bonbon *m.* **2. s. (pie),** chéri, -e; chouchou, -oute.

sweeting ['swi:tiŋ], *s.* **1.** *A:* douce amie; chérie *f.* **2.** pomme douce.

sweetish ['swi:tiʃ], *a.* assez doux, *f.* douce; douceâtre; au goût un peu sucré.

sweetly ['swi:tli], *adv.* **1.** (*a*) doucement; avec douceur; (*b*) (chanter, etc.) mélodieusement. **2.** agréablement, *F:* gentiment. **3.** (*of machine*) **to run s.,** fonctionner sans chocs, sans à-coups; avoir une allure douce.

sweetmeat ['swi:tmi:t], *s.* bonbon *m*; **sweetmeats,** sucreries *f*, confiserie *f*, douceurs *f*; **s. box,** bonbonnière *f.*

sweetness ['swi:tnis], *s.* **1.** douceur *f* (du miel, etc.). **2.** fraîcheur *f* (d'un jambon, de l'air, etc.); **s. of the soil,** bon état du sol. **3.** (*a*) gentillesse *f*, charme *m*; (*b*) **she's all s. when you are there,** elle fait la sucrée quand vous êtes là; (*c*) **s. and light,** amabilité *f* et intelligence *f.* **3.** *F:* **my s.,** ma chérie, mon petit chou.

sweet-scented, -smelling ['swi:t'sentid, -'smeliŋ], *a.* qui sent bon, qui a une douce odeur, qui embaume; au parfum délicieux; odorant.

sweetshop ['swi:tʃɔp], *s.* confiserie *f.*

sweetsop ['swi:tsɔp], *s. Bot:* **1.** atte *f*; anone écailleuse; corossol écailleux. **2.** attier *m.*

sweet-spoken ['swi:t'spouk(ə)n], *a.* **1.** au doux parler. **2.** *Pej:* au parler mielleux.

sweet-talk ['swi:t'tɔ:k], *v.tr. NAm: F:* flagorner, flatter (qn); *F:* bonimenter (qn).

sweet-tempered ['swi:t'tempəd], *a.* doux, *f.* douce; au caractère doux; aimable de caractère.

sweet-toothed ['swi:t'touθt], *a.* qui aime les douceurs, le sucre; qui a la bouche sucrée.

sweety ['swi:ti], *s.* = *F:* SWEETIE.

swell[1] [swel], *s. & a.*

I. *s.* **1.** (*a*) bosse *f*; bombement *m*; renflement *m* (d'une colonne, d'un canon, etc.); bouge *m* (du moyeu d'une roue); gros *m* (de l'avant-bras, etc.); saillie *f* (du mollet); *Artil:* **s. of the muzzle,** bourrelet *m* en tulipe; (**strengthening**) **s. of the gun barrel,** bossage *m* du canon; *Mec.E:* **s. of the cam,** doigt *m*, ressaut *m*, de la came; *Typ:* **s. rule,** filet anglais; (*b*) **s. of ground,** élévation *f* de terrain; éminence *f*, ondulation *f*; (*c*) *A:* crue *f* (d'un cours d'eau); (*d*) augmentation *f* d'un son); *Mus:* crescendo *m* et diminuendo; **s. on sustained note,** mise *f* de voix; *Lit:* **the majestic s. of the organ,** les accents majestueux du grand orgue. **2.** *Nau:* houle *f*; levée *f* (de la lame); **ground s.,** mer *f*, houle, de fond; mer du fond; **land s.,** mer sur les bas-fonds; **there is a s.,** il y a de la levée; **there is a heavy s.,** il y a beaucoup de houle, une forte houle, une grosse houle. **3.** *Mus:* soufflet *m* (d'un orgue); **Venetian s.,** jalousies *fpl;* **s. box,** boîte expressive; boîte, caisse *f*, d'expression; récit *m*; **s. manual,** clavier expressif, de récit; **s. organ,** (i) (jeux *mpl* de) récit; (ii) = **s. manual; s. pedal,** pédale expressive. **4.** *F: O:* (*a*) élégant *m*; (*b*) grosse légume; aristo *m*; **the swells,** les gens chics; les gens huppés.

II. *a. F:* (*a*) *O:* chic *inv*, élégant; **you look very s. this morning,** comme vous voilà beau ce matin! (*b*) *O:* (artiste, etc.) de premier ordre; (*c*) *NAm:* épatant, bath; **a s. guy,** un chic type.

swell[2], *v.* (*p.t.* **swelled;** *p.p.* **swollen** ['swoul(ə)n], *occ.* **swelled**). **1.** *v.tr.* (*a*) (r)enfler, gonfler; **river swollen by the rain,** rivière grossie, enflée, par la pluie; **the Rhône, swollen by the Saône, turns south,** le Rhône, grossi de la Saône, se dirige vers le midi; **eyes swollen with tears,** yeux gonflés de larmes; **to s. the crowd,** enfler, augmenter, la foule; **all this has helped to s. the ranks of the unemployed,** tout cela a augmenté le nombre de chômeurs; (*b*) *Mus:* enfler (une note). **2.** *v.i.* (*a*) **to s. (up),** (s')enfler, se gonfler; (*of part of the body*) se tuméfier; (*of plaster*) bouffer; (*of dough, etc.*) lever; (*of earth, lime*) foisonner; (*of number, debt, crowd, sound*) augmenter, grossir; **vegetables that s. in cooking,** légumes qui gonflent à la cuisson; **his arm is swelling (up),** son bras enfle; **the murmur swells into a roar,** le murmure s'enfle jusqu'à devenir un rugissement; **his heart swelled with pride,** son cœur s'enflait, se gonflait, d'orgueil; **to s. with importance,** *F:* **to s. like a turkey cock,** s'enfler d'orgueil; enfler, gonfler, le jabot; faire jabot; (*b*) (*of sea*) se soulever; **hate swelled up within him,** la haine montait en lui; (*c*) **to s. out,** être bombé, être renflé; bomber; **the sails s. (out),** les voiles se gonflent, se bombent.

swelled [sweld], *a.* **s. head** = **swollen head** *q.v. under* SWOLLEN.

swellfish ['swelfiʃ], *s. Ich:* **1.** diodon *m*, orbe épineux, poisson-boule *m*, *pl.* poissons-boules. **2.** tétrodon *m.* **3.** triodon *m.* **4.** môle *f.*

swellhead ['swelhed], *s. NAm:* **1.** *Med:* sinusite infectieuse. **2.** *F:* faraud *m*; prétentieux, -euse; vaniteux, -euse.

swellheaded [swel'hedid], *a. NAm:* vaniteux, suffisant, prétentieux; **to be s.,** se faire accroire; se gober.

swelling[1] ['sweliŋ], *a.* (*a*) qui s'enfle, se gonfle; (*of sail, etc.*) enflé, gonflé; (foule) qui va en s'augmentant; *Med:* tumescent; *Poet:* **the s. tide,** la marée montante; (*b*) (style) boursouflé; (*of pers.*) **s. with importance,** gonflé d'importance; (*c*) *Arch:* **s. column,** colonne renflée.

swelling[2], *s.* **1.** (*a*) enflement *m*, gonflement *m* (d'un fleuve, etc.); crue *f* (d'un fleuve); soulèvement *m* (des vagues); gonflement, bombement *m*, ballonnement *m* (des voiles, etc.); (*b*) renflement *m* (d'une colonne, etc.); *Furn:* bourrelet *m.* **2.** (*a*) *Med:* tuméfaction *f*, turgescence *f*; gonflement, boursouflement *m* (du visage, etc.); engorgement *m* (des seins); (*b*) foisonnement *m* (de la chaux, etc.). **3.** bosse *f*, enflure *f* (au front, etc.); tumescence *f*, tumeur *f*; fluxion *f* (à la joue); **to have a s. on the neck,** avoir une grosseur au cou; **dropsical s.,** bourrelet; **white s.,** tumeur blanche (tuberculeuse).

swelter[1] ['sweltər], *s.* **1.** chaleur étouffante, lourde et humide. **2.** état *m* de transpiration; **to be in a s.,** étouffer de chaleur; être en nage; *Fig:* **to be in a s. about sth.,** se faire du mauvais sang au sujet de qch.

swelter[2], *v.i.* **1.** étouffer, être accablé de chaleur. **2.** suer à grosses gouttes; être en nage.

sweltering ['sweltəriŋ], *a.* **1.** (*of pers., etc.*) en nage. **2. s. heat,** chaleur étouffante, accablante; **s. day,** journée embrasée; **s. office,** bureau étouffant (de chaleur).

swerve[1] [swə:v], *s.* écart *m*, déviation *f*; incartade *f* (d'un cheval); *Fb:* crochet *m*; *Aut:* embardage *m*, embardée *f*, embardement *m*; *Ten: Cr:* courbe latérale (décrite par la balle).

swerve[2]. **1.** *v.i.* faire un écart, un crochet; dévier (de sa trajectoire, de son chemin); (*of horse*) se dérober; (*of motor car*) embarder, faire une embardée; (*of footballer*) crocheter; *Fig:* **to s. from the straight path,** quitter le droit chemin; **he never swerves from his duty,** il ne s'écarte, ne s'éloigne, jamais de son devoir. **2.** *v.tr.* faire écarter (qn, qch.); faire dévier (une balle, etc.); faire faire une embardée à (une auto).

swift[1] [swift]. **1.** *a.* (*a*) rapide; *Sp:* (coureur, cheval) vite; **s. flight,** vol à tire-d'aile; **as s. as an arrow, as s. as thought,** vif comme l'éclair; rapide comme la pensée, comme la poudre; **child s. in its movements,** enfant aux mouvements vifs; **he is swifter than I,** il court plus vite que moi; *Lit:* **s. of foot,** rapide à la course; aux pieds rapides; (*b*) prompt; **s. of wit,** vif d'esprit; à l'esprit vif; à la repartie prompte; **s. to anger,** toujours prêt à s'emporter; irascible; **s. to action,** prompt à agir; **to be s. to imagine sth.,** être toujours prêt à imaginer qch.; **epidemic s. to spread,** épidémie rapide à se propager. **2.** *adv.* (*a*) *O:* vite, rapidement; **arrows fell as s. as rain,** les flèches tombaient rapides comme la pluie; (*b*) (*forming compound adjs.*) **s.-flowing,** (rivière) au cours rapide; **s.-footed,** aux pieds rapides; au pied léger; **s.-running,** (i) (*of pers.*) rapide à la course; (ii) (*of stream*) au cours rapide; **s.-tongued,** à la repartie prompte; **s.-winged,** au vol rapide. **3.** *s.* (*a*) *Orn:* (**black**) **s.,** martinet (noir); **alpine s.,** martinet alpin, à ventre blanc; **chimney s.,** *Fr.C:* martinet ramoneur; **Indian crested s.,** martinet huppé de l'Inde; **needle-tailed s.,** martinet épineux; **pallid s.,** martinet pâle; **palm s.,** martinet des palmes; **tree s.,** martinet arboricole; **Vaux's s.,** *Fr.C:* martinet occidental; **white-rumped s.,** martinet à dos blanc; **white-throated s.,** *Fr.C:* martinet à gorge blanche; (*b*) *Ent:* hépiale *m*; (*c*) *Rept: NAm:* scélopore *m.* **4.** *s. Tex: etc:* dévidoir *m.*

swift[2], *v.tr. Nau:* **1.** raidir, trélinguer (les haubans). **2.** ceintrer une embarcation. **3. to s. the capstan bars,** mettre les rabans aux barres du cabestan; rabaner le cabestan.

swifter ['swiftər], *s. Nau:* **1.** hauban bâtard. **2.** ceinture *f*, ceintre *m* (d'embarcation). **3.** raban *m* (de barre de cabestan).

swifting ['swiftiŋ], *s. Nau:* **1.** raidissement *m* (des haubans, etc.); **s. tackle,** pantequière *f.* **2.** ceintrage *m* (d'une embarcation).

swiftlet ['swiftlit], *s. Orn:* salangane *m.*

swiftly ['swiftli], *adv.* vite, rapidement; **to fly s. away,** s'envoler à tire-d'aile; **events followed s. on one another,** les événements se suivaient de près.

swiftness ['swiftnis], *s.* **1.** rapidité *f*, vitesse *f*, célérité *f.* **2.** promptitude *f* (d'une réplique, *Fenc:* d'une riposte, etc.).

swig[1] [swig], *s. Nau:* **1.** palan *m* (dont les garants ne sont pas parallèles). **2. to take a s. on a halyard,** tirer sur une drisse; raidir une drisse en abattant sur le double.

swig[2], *v.tr.* (**swigged**) **1.** *Husb:* fouetter (un bélier); châtrer (un bélier) par ligature. **2.** *Nau:* raidir (une drisse).

swig[3], *s. P:* grand trait, grand coup, lampée *f* (de bière, etc.); **to take a s. at the bottle,** boire un grand coup à la bouteille; boire à même la bouteille; s'en jeter un derrière la cravate.

swig[4], *v.tr. P:* boire (un verre) à grands traits, à grands coups; *v.i.* lamper, pinter, bidonner; **to s. off a glass,** boire un verre d'un seul coup, d'un trait; lamper, flûter, sabler, siffler, un verre; s'en jeter un derrière la cravate.

swill[1] [swil], *s.* **1.** lavage *m* à grande eau; **to give a pail a s. out,** laver, rincer, un seau à grande eau. **2.** (*a*) pâtée *f*, soupe *f*, pour les porcs; eaux grasses; (*b*) *P:* mauvaise boisson, rinçure *f*, vinasse *f*; (*c*) *P:* bêtises *fpl*; **a proper load of s.,** un vrai tissu d'âneries. **3.** *P:* ribote *f.*

swill[2], *v.tr.* **1.** laver (le plancher, etc.) à grande eau; **to s. out a basin,** rincer une cuvette. **2.** *P:* (*a*) boire avidement (qch.); s'entonner (de la bière, etc.) dans le gosier; **to s. tea,** s'enfiler des tasses de thé; (*b*) *v.i.* boire comme une éponge; riboter, pinter, chopiner.

swiller ['swilər], *s. P:* ivrogne *m*; poivrot *m.*

swilling ['swiliŋ], *s.* **1.** (*a*) lavage *m* à grande eau; (*b*) *P:* ribote *f.* **2. swillings,** eaux grasses (pour les porcs).

swim[1] [swim], *s.* **1.** (*a*) **to have, take, a s.,** nager un peu; **to go for a s.,** aller se baigner; **a s. across the river,** une traversée du fleuve à la nage; (*b*) *Swim: NAm:* **s. fin,** palme *f* (d'homme grenouille); *Ich:* **s. (bladder),** vessie *f* natatoire. **2.** *F:* **to be in the s.,** être dans le mouvement, dans le train, à la page, à la coule; être lancé; nager en grandes eaux; *Pej:* **to be in the s. with the underworld,** être de mèche avec les bas-fonds de la société; **out of the s.,** hors du coup; pas à la page. **3.** *Fish:* partie *f* de la rivière où le poisson abonde; **roach and dace are often found in the same s.,** on trouve souvent le gardon et la vandoise dans les mêmes eaux. **4.** étourdissement *m*, vertige *m*; *F:* **my head is all of a s.,** la tête me tourne.

swim[2], *v.* **swam** [swæm]; **swum** [swʌm]; *pr.p.* **swimming**)

I. *v.i.* nager. **1.** (*a*) *F:* **to s. like a fish,** nager comme un poisson; **to s. like a brick, a stone,** nager comme un caillou, une meule de moulin, un chien de plomb; **to s. under water,** nager sous l'eau, entre deux eaux; **to s. for one's life,** *F:* **for it,** se sauver à la nage; **to s. for the shore,** nager dans la direction du rivage; **to s. to the shore,** gagner le rivage à la nage; **to s. over, across, a stream,** traverser une rivière à la nage; **to s. with the tide,** (i) nager dans le sens du courant; (ii) *F:* se ranger à l'opinion générale; aller dans le sens de la foule; **to s. against the tide, against the stream,** (i) nager contre le courant; (ii) *F:* entrer en lutte avec l'opinion générale; aller contre le courant des idées; (*b*) *with cogn. acc.* **to s. a stroke,** faire une brasse; **to s. the breast stroke,** nager (à) la brasse; **he can't s. a stroke,** il nage comme un chien de plomb, comme un caillou; **to s. a race,** faire une course de natation (**with s.o.,** contre qn); (*c*) **meat swimming in gravy,** viande noyée, nageant, dans la sauce; **moon swimming in a cloudy sky,** lune baignée dans un ciel de nuages; (*d*) surnager, flotter; **the fat**

was swimming on the soup, sur le potage la graisse surnageait; (*e*) **clouds swimming slowly across the sky,** des nuages glissant à travers le ciel. **2.** être inondé (**in, with,** de); **eyes swimming with tears,** yeux inondés de larmes; **floor swimming in blood,** plancher inondé de sang; *F:* **to be swimming in money,** nager dans l'opulence; être riche à crever. **3.** (*a*) (*of head*) tourner; (*of eyes, vision*) se brouiller; **to make s.o.'s head s.,** faire tourner la tête à qn; étourdir qn; donner des étourdissements, le vertige, à qn; **my head is swimming,** la tête me tourne; j'ai le vertige; (*b*) **everything swam before my eyes,** tout semblait tourner autour de moi.

II. *v.tr.* **1.** traverser, passer (une rivière, etc.) à la nage. **2.** faire nager (un cheval, etc.); **to s. one's horse across the river,** faire traverser à son cheval la rivière à la nage. **3.** lutter de vitesse avec (qn) à la nage; **I'll s. anyone a hundred metres,** je défie n'importe qui à la nage pour une course de cent mètres.

swimmable ['swiməbl], *a.* (rivière, etc.) traversable à la nage.

swimmer ['swimər], *s.* **1.** (*pers.*) nageur, -euse. **2.** *Fish:* bouchon *m*. **3.** *Ich:* vessie *f* natatoire.

swimmeret ['swimərət], *s.* patte *f* natatoire (de crustacé).

swimming[1] ['swimiŋ], *a.* **1.** (animal) nageant, qui nage. **2. s. eyes,** yeux noyés, inondés, de larmes; **s. head,** tête qui tourne.

swimming[2], *s.* **1.** nage *f*, natation *f*; **to enjoy s.,** aimer la natation, à nager; **s. bath,** piscine *f*; **public s. baths,** école *f* de natation; **s. pool,** piscine (en plein air); **s. belt,** ceinture *f* de natation; **s. match,** concours *m* de natation; *Ich:* **s. bladder,** vessie *f* natatoire; *Coel:* **s. bell,** cloche *f* natatoire (de siphonophore); ombrelle *f* (de méduse); **s. plate,** palette *f* (de cténaire); *Moll:* **s. funnel,** entonnoir *m*, siphon *m* (de céphalopode). **2. s. of the head,** vertige *m*, étourdissement *m*.

swimmingly ['swimiŋli], *adv. F:* au mieux, à merveille; le mieux du monde; **everything is going s.,** tout va comme sur des roulettes, marche à souhait.

swimmy ['swimi], *a. F:* **to feel s.,** avoir des étourdissements, le vertige; **my eyes were s.,** mes yeux se brouillaient.

swimsuit ['swims(j)uːt], *s.* costume *m*, maillot *m*, de bain(s) (pour dames).

swindle[1] ['swindl], *s.* **1.** escroquerie *f*, filouterie *f*; *P:* flouerie *f*; *F:* **s. sheet,** note *f* des frais (d'un commis voyageur, etc.); indemnité *f* pour frais professionnels. **2.** duperie *f*.

swindle[2], *v.tr.* escroquer, filouter (qn); duper (qn); *P:* flouer, charrier, rouler (qn); **I'm not easily swindled,** je ne me laisse pas duper; **to s. s.o. out of sth., sth. out of s.o.,** escroquer qch. à qn; filouter, *P:* flouer, qn de qch.

swindler ['swindlər], *s.* filou *m*, escroc *m*; *P:* chevalier *m* d'industrie; aigrefin, -ine; *P:* floueur, -euse, charrieur, -euse, empileur, -euse.

swindling[1] ['swindliŋ], *a.* qui fait de l'escroquerie; (*of firm, etc.*) d'escrocs.

swindling[2], *s.* escroquerie *f*; filoutage *m*; *P:* flouerie *f*, carottage *m*, charriage *m*; *Jur:* manœuvres frauduleuses.

swine [swain], *s. inv. in pl.* **1.** cochon *m*, porc *m*; pourceau *m*; *Z:* **the s.,** les suidés *m*; *F:* **to behave like a s.,** se conduire comme un pourceau; **to eat like a s.,** manger comme un porc; goinfrer; *A: & Lit:* **s. maiden,** porchère *f*; *Vet:* **s. fever,** peste porcine; **s. influenza,** grippe porcine; influenza *f* du porc; **s. plague,** septicémie *f*, pasteurellose *f*, hémorragique; **s. pox,** variole *f* du porc. **2.** *P:* salopard *m*; **dirty s.!** sale cochon! charogne! salaud! **he's a s.,** c'est un salaud; **he looks a s.,** il a l'air chien; **to be a s. to s.o.,** être vache avec qn; **it's a s.,** *P:* c'est emmerdant. **3.** *Bot:* **s. cress,** coronope *m*; **s. succory,** chicorée *f* sauvage; herbe-de-capucin *f*.

swineherd ['swainhəːd], *s.m. A: & Lit:* porcher; gardeur de cochons.

swinery ['swainəri], *s.* porcherie *f*.

swinestone ['swainstoun], *s. Miner:* roche puante; stinkal *m*.

swing[1] [swiŋ], *s.* **1.** (*a*) balancement *m*; **to give a hammock a s.,** balancer, remuer, faire aller, un hamac; **to give a child a s.,** (i) (*on a swing*) pousser un enfant sur une balançoire, une escarpolette; mettre l'escarpolette en branle; (ii) (*by its arms*) balancer un enfant (en le tenant par les bras); (*b*) tour *m*; *I.C.E:* **to give the starting handle a s.,** donner un tour à la manivelle; **the engine started at the first s.,** le moteur est parti au premier tour de manivelle, du premier coup; (*c*) coup balancé; *Box: Golf:* swing *m*; *F:* **to take a s. at s.o.,** lancer un coup de poing à qn; *Golf:* **full s.,** plein ballant; **up(ward), down(ward), s.,** ballant ascendant, descendant; **flat s.,** ballant horizontal; **s. back,** (i) *Row:* temps de nage pendant lequel le tireur revient en arrière; (ii) *Ten:* retour *m* en arrière (de la raquette); *Row:* **s. forward,** retour sur l'avant. **2.** (*a*) oscillation *f*, va-et-vient *m* (d'un pendule); *Pol:* **the s. of the pendulum,** le flux et le reflux des partis; *F:* le jeu de bascule (entre les partis); *Fig:* **to give full s. to one's imagination,** donner libre cours, libre carrière, à son imagination; **to be in full s.,** (*of fête, etc.*) battre son plein; (*of organization, etc.*) être en pleine activité; (*of factory, etc.*) être en plein travail; **when the season is in full s.,** en pleine saison, quand la saison bat son plein; (*b*) **single s. of a pendulum,** oscillation simple, battement *m*, d'un pendule; *Fig:* **sudden s. of public opinion,** revirement inattendu de l'opinion publique; *Pol:* **s. to the left,** glissement *m* à gauche, vers la gauche, au profit des gauches; **at the election there was a s. back to the opposition,** aux élections il y avait un revirement vers l'opposition; *Pol.E: Com: etc:* **seasonal swings,** variations saisonnières; **cyclical swings,** oscillations cycliques; (*c*) *Cmptr:* **frequency s.,** excursion *f* de fréquence; (*d*) *Navy:* **s. to port,** crochet exécuté sur la gauche (par la flotte); (*e*) *NAm:* **s. (around the circle),** tournée électorale (dans une région). **3.** (*a*) amplitude *f* (d'une oscillation); **to give a shop sign a s. of 90°,** laisser 90° de jeu à une enseigne (pour qu'elle puisse se balancer); **s. of a door,** ouverture *f* d'une porte; *Mec.E:* **s. of a lathe,** hauteur *f* de pointe, diamètre *m*, d'un tour; (*b*) *Nau:* évitage *m* (d'un navire à l'ancre). **4.** (*a*) mouvement rythmé; **to walk with a s.,** marcher d'un pas rythmé, d'un pas dégagé; **to walk with a s. of one's shoulders,** marcher des épaules; **to row with a steady s.,** ramer en cadence; ramer d'un mouvement rythmé; **song that goes with a s.,** chanson très rythmée; chanson entraînante, enlevante; *F:* **everything went with a s.,** tout a très bien marché; tout le monde s'est montré plein d'entrain; **the team played with a fine s.,** l'équipe a montré un bel élan; **s. of a passage,** rythme *m*, eurythmie *f*, d'un passage; *F:* **to get into the s. of the work,** se mettre au courant du travail; **when you have got into the s. of things,** quand vous serez au courant; (*b*) *Mus:* **s. (music),** swing; **s. band,** orchestre *m* de swing. **5.** escarpolette *f*, balançoire *f*. **6.** *attrib.* (*a*) *Phot:* **s. back,** bascule *f* (arrière) (de l'appareil); **s. front,** bascule avant, antérieure; **s. bar,** (i) *Veh:* palonnier *m*, volée *f*, bacul *m*; (ii) *Av:* palonnier (du gouvernail) de direction; **s. bob,** contrepoids *m*; **s.-bob lever,** levier *m* à contrepoids; (*at fair*) **s. boat,** (bateau *m*) balançoire; **s. bridge,** pont tournant, pivotant; **s. cart,** charrette suspendue; **s. cot,** bercelonnette *f*; **s. frame,** tête *f* de cheval (de tour à fileter); **s. handle,** anse *f* mobile; **s. glass, mirror,** miroir *m* à bascule, (*full length*) psyché *f*; **s. sign,** enseigne pendante; *Agr:* **s. plough,** araire *m*, sochet *m*; *Clockm:* **s. wheel,** balancier *m* (d'une montre); roue *f* de rencontre (d'une horloge); *Av:* **s. wings,** voilure *f* mobile; **s.-wing aircraft, s.-winger,** avion *m* à géométrie variable; (*b*) *NAm: Ind:* **s. shift,** (i) équipe *f* (d'ouvriers) assurant la relève (*esp.* entre celle de jour et celle de nuit); (ii) journée *f* de travail mi-jour mi-nuit.

swing[2], *v.* (*p.t.* **swung** [swʌŋ], *occ.* **swang** [swæŋ]; *p.p.* **swung**)

I. *v.i.* **1.** (*a*) **to s. to and fro,** se balancer; (*of bell, etc.*) brimbaler; (*of pendulum*) osciller; **to s. free,** osciller librement; **shop sign that swings to and fro in the wind,** enseigne de magasin qui ballotte au vent; **lamp that swings from the ceiling,** lampe suspendue au plafond; suspension *f*; *P:* **to s. for a crime,** être pendu pour un crime; (*b*) **to s. on, round, an axis,** tourner, pivoter, sur un axe; (*of mirror, etc.*) basculer; **to s. through an angle of 90°,** se déplacer d'un angle de 90°; **the door swings on its hinges,** la porte tourne sur ses gonds; (*of door*) **to s. open,** s'ouvrir; **to s. to,** se refermer; (*c*) (*of ship*) **to s. (at anchor),** éviter (sur l'ancre); **to s. to the anchor,** rappeler sur son ancre; (*d*) jouer à la balançoire, se balancer (sur l'escarpolette). **2.** faire un mouvement de conversion; changer de direction; tourner; (*a*) **to s. round,** faire volte-face; **he swung round and faced me,** il tourna vivement sur ses talons, il se retourna vivement, et me fit face; **the car swung round,** l'auto vira, fit un virage; **the car swung right round,** la voiture a fait un tête-à-queue; (*b*) *Mil:* **the whole line swung to the left,** toute la ligne fit une conversion vers la gauche; **to s. inwards,** se rabattre sur le flanc de l'ennemi; *Nau:* (*of fleet*) **to s. to starboard,** faire un crochet sur la droite; (*c*) *NAm:* **to s. round the circle,** faire le tour de sa circonscription électorale. **3.** (*a*) **to s. along,** avancer en scandant le pas; marcher d'un pas rythmé, d'une allure dégagée; scander le pas; **the column swung in through the gateway,** la colonne franchit le portail d'une allure rapide, d'un pas martial; (*b*) *Row:* **to s. forward,** revenir sur l'avant. **4.** (*a*) *Mus:* jouer le swing; (*b*) *F:* être dans le mouvement; être dynamique, être swing.

II. *v.tr.* **1.** (*a*) (faire) balancer (qch.); faire osciller (un pendule, etc.); **to s. the bells,** mettre les cloches en branle; **to s. one's arms,** balancer les bras (en marchant, etc.); **to s. the hips (in walking),** se dandiner; *P:* tortiller des hanches; **to s. Indian clubs,** manier des mils; *Box:* **to s. a blow,** balancer un coup; **to s. one's stick about one's head,** faire le moulinet avec sa canne; (*b*) *P:* **to s. it, a fast one, on s.o.,** duper, essayer de duper, qn; tirer une carotte à qn. **2.** (*a*) *Nau:* **to s. the cargo ashore,** décharger la cargaison; **to s. the davits,** faire tourner les bossoirs; **boat swung out,** embarcation parée au dehors; (*b*) *Aut:* **to s. the front wheels,** braquer les roues avant; *Bill:* **to s. the cue,** faucher; (*c*) **to s. a car right round,** faire faire un brusque virage à une auto; **to s. a car right round,** faire faire (un) tête-à-queue à une auto; *Nau:* **to s. ship (for compass adjustment),** faire un tour d'horizon (pour régler le compas); faire le tour; (*d*) *Cr:* **to s. the ball,** faire dévier la balle en l'air. **3.** faire tourner (qch.); *Av:* **to s. the propeller,** lancer, brasser, l'hélice; tourner l'hélice à la main; mettre en marche à l'hélice; *Nau:* **to s. the engines,** balancer la machine. **4. to s. the voting in favour of s.o.,** faire balancer les votes en faveur de qn; *NAm: F:* **to s. a deal,** mener une affaire à bien. **5.** suspendre (qch.); **lamp swung from the ceiling,** lampe suspendue au plafond; **to s. a hammock,** pendre, (ac)crocher, un hamac. **6.** *v.pr. & i.* **to s. (oneself) into the saddle,** monter vivement à cheval, en selle; **the guard swings into the train,** le chef de train monte à la marche; **to s. (oneself) from branch to branch,** se balancer d'une branche à une autre; **to s. oneself along a rope,** se gambiller le long d'un cordage; **to s. into action,** passer (vivement) à l'action. **7.** *Mus:* interpréter (une mélodie, etc.) en swing.

III. (*compound verbs*) **1. swing back,** *v.i.* (*a*) (*of door, etc.*) basculer; se rabattre; (*b*) (*of pendulum, etc.*) revenir; **public opinion swung back,** il y eut un revirement d'opinion.

2. swing over, *v.i.* (*of boat's boom, etc.*) battre d'un bord à l'autre; (*of public opinion*) revirer de bord.

3. swing up. (*a*) *v.tr.* hisser (qch.); **to s. up a heavy load with a crane,** hisser une lourde charge avec une grue; (*b*) *v.i.* **the (loft) ladder swings up to the ceiling,** l'échelle remonte au plafond.

swinge [swin(d)ʒ], *v.tr. A:* fouetter, cingler, rosser.

swingeing ['swin(d)ʒiŋ], *a.* **1. s. blow,** coup bien envoyé. **2.** énorme, épatant; **s. majority,** majorité énorme, écrasante; **s. damages,** forts dommages-intérêts.

swinger ['swiŋər], *s.* **1.** personne *f* qui balance qch. **2.** personne qui se balance. **3.** chacun des chevaux du milieu (d'un attelage de six). **4.** *F:* **horse with three legs and a s.,** cheval qui a trois bonnes jambes et une qui traîne. **5.** *Rec:* disque mal centré.

swinging[1] ['swiŋiŋ], *a.* **1.** (*a*) balançant; oscillant; **with s. arms,** les bras ballants; (*b*) (miroir, etc.) à bascule; **s. door,** porte battante; *Mch:* **s. valve,** distributeur oscillant; *Mec.E:* **s. arm,** potence *f*, grue pivotante (de perceuse, etc.). **2.** (*a*) **s. stride,** allure rythmée, cadencée, dégagée; **s. blow,** coup balancé; **s. tune,** air enlevant, entraînant; (*b*) *F:* (*of pers.*) (i) plein d'entrain, de ressort; (ii) dans le vent, avant-garde *inv*, swing; (*of girl*) aguichant, sexy; **s. London,** le Londres d'avant-garde.

swinging[2], *s.* **1.** (*a*) balancement *m*, oscillation *f*; *Games:* jeu *m* de la balançoire; **s. motion,** mouvement *m* pendulaire; balancement *m*; (*b*) mouvement *m* de bascule, de rotation; **s. open,** ouverture *f* (d'une porte); **s. to,** rabattement *m* (d'une porte); (*c*) *Nau:* évitage *m*; **s. berth,** évitage, évitée *f*; (*d*) **s. round,** (i) virage *m*, (ii) tête-à-queue *m inv* (d'une voiture). **2.** *Av:* lancement *m* (de l'hélice).

swingingly ['swiŋiŋli], *adv.* avec rythme; d'un pas cadencé; avec entrain.

swinish ['swainiʃ], *a.* de cochon, de pourceau; (i) sale, bestial, -aux; (ii) glouton, -onne, goulu; **s. behaviour,** sale conduite.

swinishly ['swainiʃli], *adv.* salement, bestialement; **to eat s.,** manger comme un pourceau, en goinfre; goinfrer; **s. drunk,** soûl comme un cochon.

swinishness ['swainiʃnis], *s.* **1.** saleté *f*, grossièreté *f*. **2.** goinfrerie *f*, gloutonnerie *f*.

swingle[1] ['swiŋgl], *s.* **1.** *Tex:* écangue *f*, écang *m*. **2.** *Husb:* battoir *m* (d'un fléau). **3.** *Veh:* **s. tree, bar,** palonnier *m*, volée *f*, bacul *m*.

swingle[2], *v.tr. Tex:* teiller, écanguer (le lin, chanvre).

swingling ['swiŋgliŋ], *s. Tex:* teillage *m*, écangage *m*.

swing-to ['swiŋ'tou], *s.* rabattement *m* (d'une porte).

swipe[1] [swaip], *s.* **1.** (*a*) *Cr: Golf:* coup *m* à toute volée; (*b*) *F:* **to take a s. at s.o.,** (i) lâcher un coup (de poing, etc.) à qn; (ii) *Fig:* lâcher un coup de patte à qn; **to take a s. at a job,** se lancer dans une besogne. **2.** *NAm:* valet *m* d'écurie. **3.** (*a*) bascule *f* (pour tirer l'eau d'un puits); chadouf *m*; (*b*) balancier *m* (de pompe, de porte d'écluse); **s. beam,** flèche *f* (de pont-levis).

swipe[2]. **1.** *v.i. Cr: etc:* **to s. at the ball,** lancer un coup à la balle à toute volée. **2.** *v.tr.* (*a*) *Cr: etc:* frapper (la balle) à toute volée; (*b*) *F:* donner un coup de poing, de bâton, etc., à (qn); **to s. the heads off the thistles with one's stick,** faire sauter les têtes des chardons avec sa canne; (*c*) *P:* chiper, chaparder, faucher (qch.).

swipes [swaips], *s.pl. F: O:* petite bière; bibine *f.*

swipple ['swipl], *s. Husb:* battoir *m* (d'un fléau).

swirl[1] [swəːl], *s.* **1.** remous *m* (de l'eau); tournoiement *m* (des vagues, etc.); tourbillonnement *m*, brassage *m* (d'un mélange gazeux); **a s. of dust,** un tourbillon de poussière; *Fig:* **the s. of modern life,** le tourbillon de la vie moderne. **2.** (*a*) spirale *f*, volute *f*; *Carp:* ronce *f* (dans le bois); (*b*) *A:* tresse de cheveux, bande de crêpe, roulée autour de la tête, du chapeau.

swirl[2]. **1.** *v.i.* tournoyer, tourbillonner; (*of dust, etc.*) **to s. up,** monter en tourbillons; s'élever en tourbillonnant; **my head is swirling,** la tête me tourne. **2.** *v.tr.* faire tournoyer (qch.); **to s. the dust away,** emporter la poussière dans un tourbillon; soulever un tourbillon de poussière.

swirling[1] ['swəːliŋ], *a.* tourbillonnant.

swirling[2], *s.* tourbillonnement *m.*

swish[1] [swiʃ], *s.* **1.** bruissement *m*, susurrement *m* (de l'eau); froufrou *m* (d'une robe); sifflement *m* (d'un fouet); bruit *m* rêche, crissement *m* (d'une faux). **2.** coup *m* de fouet; coup de badine. **3.** *NAm: P:* pédé(raste) *m*, tapette *f*, tante *f.*

swish[2]. **1.** *v.i.* (*of water, etc.*) bruire; susurrer; (*of silk*) froufrouter; (*of whip, etc.*) siffler; (*of pers.*) **to s. in, out,** entrer, sortir, dans un froufrou (de soie, etc.). **2.** *v.tr.* (*a*) fouetter (qn, qch.); houssiner (des meubles); (*b*) faire siffler (sa canne, une badine); (*c*) (*of animal*) **to s. its tail,** battre l'air de sa queue; (*d*) **to s. off the head of a thistle,** faire sauter la tête d'un chardon (d'un coup de badine, etc.).

swish[3], *a. P: A:* élégant, chic.

swishing ['swiʃiŋ], *s. Sch: P:* **to get a s.,** recevoir une bonne correction.

Swiss [swis]. **1.** *a.* suisse; **the S. government,** le gouvernement helvétique; **the S. Guards,** (i) les gardes *m* suisses (du Vatican); (ii) *Fr.Hist:* les cent-Suisses *m*; *P:* **S. admiral,** (i) amiral *m* suisse; marin *m* d'eau douce; (ii) soi-disant officier de marine. **2.** *s. inv. in pl.* Suisse *m*; **she's a S.,** c'est une dame suisse; *Pej:* une Suissesse.

switch[1] [switʃ], *s.* **1.** (*a*) baguette *f*, badine *f*; (*for caning pupil, etc.*) canne *f*; (**riding**) **s.,** petite cravache; stick léger; gaulette *f*; (*b*) coup *m* de baguette. **2.** (*a*) *Rail:* aiguille *f* (de raccordement, de changement de voie); **automatic s.,** aiguille automatique; **safety s.,** aiguille de sûreté; **derailing s.,** aiguille de déraillement; **bolted s.,** aiguille verrouillée; **symmetrical s.,** changement *m* symétrique; **compound s.,** traversée-jonction *f, pl.* traversées-jonctions; **s. lock,** verrou *m* de blocage des aiguilles; *s.a.* **3. for s. key, lever;** (*b*) *Rail: U.S:* voie *f* de raccordement, de garage; (*c*) changement *m* (d'une chose à une autre); *Mil:* **s. line, s. trench,** bretelle *f*; **s. position,** position *f* en bretelle; *Cards:* **s. (bid),** changement de couleur (dans les annonces); (*d*) *Cmptr:* aiguillage *m* (des éléments d'un programme); **s. point,** point *m* d'aiguillage; **breakpoint s.,** (i) bouton *m* de commande d'aiguillage; (ii) commutation *f*; **s. core,** tore *m* magnétique de commutation. **3.** *El: etc:* commutateur *m*, interrupteur *m*, bouton (commutateur); conjoncteur *m*, disjoncteur *m*; contacteur *m*; inverseur *m*; **master s.,** interrupteur général; coupe-tout *m inv*; **safety s.,** interrupteur de sécurité; **automatic s.,** commutateur, interrupteur, automatique; **charge s.,** commutateur de charge; **on-off s.,** interrupteur marche-arrêt; **to set the s. to** *on,* **to** *off,* mettre l'interrupteur, l'inverseur, sur *marche,* sur *arrêt*; **changeover s., selector s.,** (commutateur) sélecteur *m*; **control s.,** (i) interrupteur; bouton, de commande; (ii) *Tp:* commutateur de contrôle; **closing s.,** (commutateur) conjoncteur; **cut-out s.,** disjoncteur; **single-pole, single-way, s.,** interreupteur, inverseur, monopolaire, unipolaire; **double-pole, double-throw, two-pole, s.,** interrupteur bipolaire; **two-way s.,** commutateur à deux directions; interrupteur d'escalier; **double-bladed s.,** interrupteur à deux lames, à deux couteaux; **earth s.,** *NAm:* **ground s.,** commutateur de mise à la terre; **isolating s.,** interrupteur d'isolement de ligne; sectionneur *m*; **rotary s.,** commutateur rotatif; **reversing s., throw-over s.,** (commutateur) inverseur; **sequence s.,** commutateur séquentiel; **time-delay s.,** interrupteur temporisé; **mercury s.,** interrupteur à mercure; **oil s.,** commutateur à bain d'huile; **tumbler s.,** commutateur, inverseur, à bascule, à culbuteur; **float s.,** interrupteur à flotteur; **key s.,** commutateur à touches; **pressure s.,** pressostat *m*; *I.C.E:* **ignition s.,** interrupteur d'allumage; *W.Tel:* **wave-band s.,** commutateur de gamme d'ondes; **s. gear,** appareillage *m* de commutation, de distribution; **s. key,** (i) *El: Aut:* clef *f* de contact; (ii) *Rail:* clef de blocage d'aiguilles; **s. lever,** (i) *El:* manette *f* d'interrupteur; (ii) *Rail:* levier *m* d'aiguilles, de manœuvre des aiguilles; **s. blade,** (i) lame *f*, couteau *m*, d'interrupteur, de commutateur; (ii) couteau automatique. **4.** tresse *f* de cheveux postiches; crêpé *m*; postiche *m.*

switch[2], *v.*

I. *v.tr.* **1.** (*a*) donner un coup de badine à (qn, qch.); fouetter, cingler (qn, qch.); (*b*) **the cow was switching its tail,** la vache agitait sa queue, battait l'air de sa queue. **2.** faire mouvoir brusquement; **he switched his head round,** il a tourné vivement la tête; **she switched the cloth off the table,** elle a retiré la nappe de la table d'un mouvement brusque. **3.** (*a*) *Rail:* aiguiller (un train); **to s. a train on to a branch line,** aiguiller, dériver, un train sur un embranchement; (*b*) *U.S:* manœuvrer (un train); (*c*) **to s. the conversation to another subject,** faire tourner, aiguiller, la conversation vers un autre sujet, sur une autre voie; (*d*) changer la position (d'une manette, d'un levier, etc.); (*e*) *Artil:* effectuer, opérer, un transport de tir. **4.** *El:* commuter (le courant); *Cmptr:* basculer (un dérouleur, un tore magnétique).

II. (*compound verbs*) **1. switch in,** *v.tr. El:* intercaler (une résistance); mettre (une résistance) en circuit.

2. switch off, *v.tr. & i.* (*a*) *El:* interrompre, couper (le courant); ouvrir (le circuit); rompre, couper, enlever (le contact); **s. (the light) off when you go out!** fermez l'électricité quand vous sortez! *I.C.E:* **to s. off the ignition, the engine,** couper l'allumage; **to s. off the radio, the television,** arrêter la radio, la télévision; *F:* (*of pers.*) **to s. off (completely),** cesser d'écouter; couper l'allumage.

3. switch on, *v.tr. & i. El:* mettre (une lampe, etc.) en circuit; donner (du courant); fermer (le circuit); établir, mettre (le contact); allumer (l'électricité); allumer, mettre en marche (un projecteur); *I.C.E:* **to s. on the ignition, the engine,** mettre le contact (d'allumage); **to s. on the radio, the television,** mettre la radio, la télévision, en marche; (*of pers.*) **to be switched on,** (i) *F:* écouter avec attention; être bien au courant de ce qui se passe; (ii) *P:* être chargé (par des drogues); fumer de la marijuana.

4. switch over, *v.tr. & i. El:* commuter (le courant); *W.Tel: T.V:* **to s. over to another wavelength, to another channel,** changer de réglage; *Sch:* **to s. over to modern languages,** réorienter ses études vers les langues vivantes.

switchback ['switʃbæk], *s.* (*at fair*) montagnes russes; **s. road,** route *f* qui monte et descend; route en montagnes russes.

switchboard ['switʃbɔːd], *s.* (*a*) panneau *m*, tableau *m*, de commutation, de commande; (*b*) *Tp: El:* tableau (commutateur, de distribution); table *f* (d'opérateur, d'opératrice); (*in office, etc.*) standard *m*; **s. operator,** standardiste *mf.*

switchbox ['switʃbɔks], *s.* **1.** *El:* boîte *f* de commutation. **2.** *Rail: U.S:* boîte de manœuvre des aiguilles.

switchdesk ['switʃdesk], *s.* (*a*) *Tchn:* pupitre *m* de commande; (*b*) *Th: etc:* pupitre de distribution, de commutation (de la lumière).

switcher ['switʃər], *s. U.S:* **1.** = SWITCHMAN. **2.** locomotive *f* de manœuvre.

switching ['switʃiŋ], *s.* **1.** fouettement *m.* **2.** *Rail:* (*a*) aiguillage *m*; *U.S:* **s. tower,** poste *m* à signaux; cabine *f* d'aiguillage; (*b*) *U.S:* triage *m*; **gravity s.,** triage par gravité; **s. engine** = SWITCHER 2; **s. track,** voie *f* de manœuvre; **s. yard,** gare *f*, centre *m*, de triage. **3.** *Trans:* **s. point,** centre de transit.

switchman, *pl.* **-men** ['switʃmən, -men], *s.m. Rail: U.S:* aiguilleur.

swither[1] ['swiðər], *s. Scot:* **1.** agitation *f*, bouleversement *m*, émoi *m.* **2.** hésitation *f*, indécision *f.*

swither[2], *v.i.* être indécis; hésiter.

Swithin ['swiðin], *Pr.n.m.* **St Swithin's day** (*15th July*) = la Saint-Médard (*8th June*).

Switzer ['switsər], *s. A:* Suisse *mf*; *Hist:* **Switzers,** mercenaires *m* suisses.

Switzerland ['switsələnd], *Pr.n. Geog:* la Suisse; *Adm:* la Confédération helvétique; **German S.,** la Suisse alémanique; **French(-speaking) S.,** la Suisse romande, française; **Italian(-speaking) S.,** la Suisse italienne.

swivel[1] ['swivl], *s.* **1.** (*a*) émerillon *m*, maillon tournant (de câble-chaîne); *Nau:* **mooring s.,** émerillon *m* d'affourche; *Mil:* **carbine s.,** porte-mousqueton *m inv* (de bandoulière); (*b*) pivot *m*; tourillon *m*; rotule *f*; **ball s.,** pivot à rotule; *Aut:* **s. pin,** pivot de fusée, axe *m* de pivotement. **2.** *attrib.* (*a*) pivotant, tournant; à pivot; à rotule; orientable; **s. chair, seat,** siège tournant; **s. block,** poulie *f* à émerillon; **s. clip,** collier tournant; **s. connection,** raccord *m* orientable; **s. hook,** croc *m* à émerillon; crochet *m* mobile; **s. joint,** (joint *m* à) rotule; *Nau:* **s. piece,** étalingure *f* (d'ancre); **s. slide rest,** support de chariot (de tour) pivotant; **s. gun,** (i) *Artil:* canon *m* à pivot, *A:* pierrier *m*; (ii) *Ven:* canardière *f*; (*b*) *F:* **s. eye,** œil *m* louche. **3.** *NAm: Ven:* canardière.

swivel[2], *v.* (**swivelled**) **1.** *v.i.* pivoter, tourner; être articulé; **free to s.,** à orientation libre; **to s. round on one's heels,** pivoter sur ses talons. **2.** *v.tr.* (*a*) **to s. sth. to sth.,** attacher qch. à qch. avec un émerillon; (*b*) faire pivoter (une mitrailleuse, etc.); **to s. one's eyes round,** tourner les yeux de côté.

swivel-eyed ['swivəlaid], *a. F:* louche, strabique.

swivelling ['swivəliŋ], *a.* pivotant, tournant; à pivot; **s. union,** raccord *m* orientable, à orientation libre; *Rail:* **s. truck,** bogie pivotant.

swivet ['swivit], *s. NAm: P:* **to be in a s.,** être tout en émoi, tout bouleversé.

swiz(z) [swiz], *s. Sch: P:* **1.** duperie *f*, flouerie *f.* **2.** déception *f.*

swizzle[1] ['swizl], *s.* **1.** *NAm: F:* cocktail *m*; **s. stick,** fouet *m*, marteau *m*, à champagne. **2.** *P:* = SWIZ(Z).

swizzle[2]. **1.** *v.i. F:* boire à l'excès. **2.** *v.tr.* mélanger, fouetter (un cocktail).

swob[1,2] [swɔb], *s. & v.tr.* = SWAB[1,2].

swollen ['swoulən], *a.* enflé, gonflé. **1.** (*a*) **the river is s.,** la rivière est enflée, grosse; la rivière est en crue; **s. budget,** budget *m* pléthorique; (*b*) **to have a s. face,** (i) avoir le visage bouffi; (ii) avoir une fluxion à la joue; *Vet:* **s. leg,** jambe gorgée (d'un cheval). **2.** (*also* **swelled**) *F:* **to suffer from a s. head, have a s. head,** être bouffi d'orgueil, pénétré de sa propre importance; *F:* se gober, s'en faire accroire.

swollen-headed ['swoulən'hedid], *a. F:* vaniteux, suffisant, prétentieux; **to be s.-h.,** s'en faire accroire; se gober.

swoon[1] [swuːn], *s. O:* évanouissement *m*, pâmoison *f*, défaillance *f*; *Med:* syncope *f*; **to go off in, fall into, a s.,** s'évanouir, se pâmer; tomber évanoui, en défaillance, en pâmoison, en syncope.

swoon[2], *v.i. O:* s'évanouir, se pâmer; défaillir; se trouver mal; *Med:* avoir une syncope.

swooning[1] ['swuːniŋ], *a. O:* (*a*) défaillant; (*b*) évanoui; en pâmoison, en défaillance.

swooning[2], *s. O:* syncope *f*, évanouissement *m.*

swoop[1] [swuːp], *s.* abat(t)ée *f* (d'un avion etc.) (**upon,** sur); descente *f* (du faucon qui fond sur sa proie); attaque brusquée, inattendue; **police s.,** descente de police (sur une boîte de nuit, etc.); *F:* **at one (fell) s.,** d'un seul coup.

swoop[2], *v.i.* (*of hawk, pers.*) **to s. down on sth.,** s'abattre, foncer, fondre, sur qch.; *Av:* **to s. down on an enemy plane,** piquer de haut, foncer, sur un avion ennemi; **the police swooped down on the district,** la police a fait une descente sur le quartier.

swop[1,2] [swɔp], *s. & v.tr.* = SWAP[1,2].

sword [sɔːd], *s.* **1.** (*a*) épée *f*; *A: & Poet:* glaive *m*; **two-handed s.,** épée à deux mains; espadon *m*; **duelling s.,** épée de combat; **fencing s.,** arme *f*, épée, d'escrime; **dress s.,** épée de parade; **to wear, carry, a s.,** porter l'épée; **to fight with the s., with swords,** se battre à l'épée; **to draw one's s.,** tirer son épée; dégainer; **to draw the s.,** commencer les hostilités; *Lit:* tirer le glaive; **to put up the s.,** remettre l'épée au fourreau; rengainer; **to measure, cross, swords with s.o.,** (i) croiser l'épée, le fer, avec qn; (ii) mesurer ses forces avec qn; se mesurer contre, avec, qn; **to deliver one's s. to the victor,** rendre son épée au vainqueur; **to put the inhabitants to (the edge of) the s.,** passer les habitants au fil de l'épée, par les armes; **s. in hand,** l'épée à la main; *NAm: F:* **to be at swords' points,** être à couteaux tirés; *Lit:* **the S. of Justice,** le glaive de la Justice; (*b*) *Mil: Navy:* sabre *m*; **cavalry s.,** sabre de cavalerie; **back of the s.,** faux tranchant du sabre; **draw swords!** sabre main! **return swords!** remettez sabre! **to draw one's s.,** tirer sabre au clair; dégainer; **with drawn s.,** le sabre au clair; (*c*) *attrib.* **s. arm,** (i) bras droit; (ii) *Lit:* puissance *f* du glaive; **s. bearer,** officier (*esp.* municipal) qui porte le glaive; **s. blade,** lame *f* d'épée, de sabre; **s. bayonet,** épée-baïonnette *f, pl.* épées-baïonnettes; épée-sabre *f, pl.* épées-sabres; **s. cane, stick,** canne *f* à épée; **s. cut,** (i) coup *m* de sabre; (ii) blessure faite avec le sabre; (*on face*) balafre *f*; **s. cutler,** fabricant *m* d'épées; armurier *m*; **s. dance,** danse *f* du sabre; **s. fight,** combat *m* à l'épée; **s. hand,** main *f* de l'épée, main droite; **s. knot,** dragonne *f*, porte-épée *m inv*; **s. side,** côté *m* des mâles, ligne *f* mâle (dans la descendance); **s. stroke,** coup d'épée, de sabre; **s. thrust,** coup de pointe, d'épée; *Bot:* **s. flag, s. grass,** glaïeul *m*, iris *m*, des marais; **s. grass,** graminée ensifoliée; **s. lily,** glaïeul. **2.** *Tex:* **lathe s.,** épée de chasse.

swordbelt ['sɔ:dbelt], *s.* ceinturon *m.*

swordbill ['sɔdbil], *s. Orn:* oiseau-mouche *m, pl.* oiseaux-mouches, porte-épée *m inv.*

swordcraft ['sɔ:dkrɑ:ft], *s.* escrime *f* à l'épée; art *m* de tirer les armes.

swordfish ['sɔ:dfiʃ], *s.* **1.** *Ich:* espadon *m*; sabre *m*; épée *f* de mer; poisson-épée *m*, xiphias *m*; *F:* coutelas *m*, glaive *m.* **2.** *Astr:* **the S.,** la Dorade.

sword-leaved ['sɔ:dli:vd], *a. Bot:* aux feuilles en forme d'épée; ensifolié.

swordplay ['sɔ:dplei], *s.* **1.** maniement *m* de l'épée; escrime *f* (à l'épée). **2. (back)sword play,** escrime (i) au sabre, (ii) au bâton. **3. verbal s.,** joute *f* oratoire.

sword-shaped ['sɔ:dʃeipt], *a.* ensiforme; *Anat:* xiphoïde.

swordsman, *pl.* **-men** ['sɔ:dzmən], *s.m.* **1.** épéiste, tireur d'épée; **fine s.,** fine lame, bonne épée. **2.** *NAm: P:* libertin, trousseur de jupons.

swordsmanship ['sɔ:dzmənʃip], *s.* maniement *m* de l'épée; escrime *f* (à l'épée).

swordtail ['sɔ:dteil], *s.* **1.** *Ich:* porte-épée *m inv.* **2.** *Crust:* limule *m*, crabe *m* des Moluques.

sworn [swɔ:n], *a.* **1.** juré, assermenté; **s. official,** agent, fonctionnaire, assermenté; **s. broker,** courtier assermenté; *Hist:* **s. man,** homme lige; **s. enemies,** ennemis jurés, acharnés; **they are s. friends,** entre eux c'est à la vie à la mort; ils sont amis à la vie à la mort. **2. s. witness,** (i) témoin *m* qui a prêté serment; (ii) témoignage *m* sous serment; **s. statement,** déclaration *f* sous serment.

swot[1] [swɔt], *s. F:* **1.** (*a*) *Sch:* travail *m* intense; turbin *m*; (*b*) travail de chien; turbin, corvée *f.* **2.** (*pers.*) bûcheur, -euse, potasseur *m*, piocheur, -euse.

swot[2], *v.tr. & i.* **(swotted)** *Sch: F:* bûcher, potasser. piocher, turbiner; **to s. for an exam,** bûcher, chauffer, potasser, un examen; **to s. (at) maths, to s. up one's maths,** potasser, piocher, bûcher, les math.

sybarite ['sibərait], *a. & s.* sybarite (*mf*).

sybaritic [sibə'ritik], *a.* sybaritique, sybarite.

sybaritism ['sibəritizm], *s.* sybaritisme *m.*

Sybil ['sibil], *Pr.n.f.* Sibylle.

sycamine ['sikəmain], *s. A: & B:* mûrier noir.

sycamore ['sikəmɔ:r], *s. Bot:* **1.** (*a*) **s. (tree, maple),** (érable *m*) sycomore *m*, faux platane, faux plane; (*b*) *NAm:* platane. **2. Egyptian, oriental, s. (tree), s. fig,** figuier *m* sycomore, d'Égypte.

syce [sais], *s. A:* (*in India*) (i) palefrenier *m*; (ii) domestique monté.

sycon ['sikɔn], *s. Spong:* sycon *m.*

syconium, *pl.* **-ia** [sai'kouniəm, -iə], *s. Bot:* sycone *m.*

sycophancy ['sikəfənsi], *s.* adulation *f*, flagornerie *f.*

sycophant ['sikəfənt], *s.* **1.** *Gr.Ant:* sycophante *m.* **2.** *A:* sycophante, délateur *m.* **3.** adulateur, -trice; flagorneur *m*; *F:* chattemite *f.*

sycophantic [sikə'fæntik], *a.* adulateur, -trice; fourbe.

sycophantically [sikə'fæntik(ə)li], *adv.* bassement.

sycosis [sai'kousis], *s. Med:* sycosis *m*; *esp.* mentagre *f.*

syenite ['saiənait], *s. Miner:* syénite *f.*

syenitic [saiə'nitik], *a. Miner:* syénitique.

syenodiorite ['saiənou'daiərait], *s. Miner:* monzonite *f.*

syllabic [si'læbik], *a.* syllabique.

syllabicate [si'læbikeit], *v.tr.* syllabiser (un mot).

syllabi(fi)cation [silæbi(fi)'keiʃ(ə)n], *s.* syllabisation *f.*

syllabify [si'læbifai], *v.tr.* syllabiser (un mot).

syllabism ['siləbizm], *s.* syllabisme *m.*

syllabize ['siləbaiz], *v.tr.* syllabiser (un mot).

syllable ['siləbl], *s.* syllabe *f*; *Pros:* **short s.,** brève *f*; **long s.,** longue *f*; *F:* **he didn't say a s.,** il n'a pas prononcé une syllabe; **to explain sth. in words of one s.,** expliquer qch. en termes très simples; **I gave my opinion of it in words of one s.,** j'ai donné mon opinion à ne s'y méprendre.

-syllabled ['siləbld], *a.* (*with num. prefixed*) **two-s., three-s., word,** mot *m* de deux, trois, syllabes.

syllabub ['siləbʌb], *s. Cu:* = sabayon *m.*

syllabus, *pl.* **-i, -uses** ['siləbəs, -ai, -əsiz], *s.* **1.** programme *m*, sommaire *m* (d'un cours). **2.** *R.C.Ch:* syllabus *m.*

syllepsis, *pl.* **-es** [si'lepsis, -i:z], *s. Rh:* syllepse *f.*

sylleptic [si'leptik], *a.* sylleptique.

syllid ['silid], **syllis** ['silis], *s. Ann:* syllide *m*, syllis *m.*

syllidian [si'lidiən], *s. Ann:* syllidien *m.*

syllogism ['silədʒizm], *s. Log:* syllogisme *m.*

syllogistic [silə'dʒistik], *a. Log:* syllogistique.

syllogistically [silə'dʒistik(ə)li], *adv.* (argumenter) par syllogismes.

syllogize ['silədʒaiz], *v.i.* syllogistiquer.

sylph [silf], *s.* **1.** sylphe *m*, sylphide *f.* **2.** (*applied to woman*) sylphide; *F:* **she's no s.,** elle prend de la place. **3.** *NAm: Orn:* (espèce *f* de) colibri *m.*

sylphid ['silfid], *s.* jeune sylphe *m*, jeune sylphide *f.*

sylph-like ['silflaik], *a.* (taille, etc.) de sylphide.

sylva ['silvə], *s.* flore *f* sylvestre; forêts *fpl* (d'une région).

sylvan ['silvən]. **1.** *s.* (*a*) *Myth:* sylvain *m*; (*b*) homme, oiseau, animal, etc. sylvain. **2.** *a.* (*a*) sylvestre; (*b*) (oiseau, etc.) sylvain; (*c*) (plante) sylvatique, sylvestre.

sylvanite ['silvənait], *s. Miner:* sylvanite *f*, or *m* graphique.

Sylvanus [sil'veinəs], *Pr.n.m. Rom.Myth:* Silvain, Sylvain.

sylvatic [sil'vætik], *a.* **1.** = SYLVAN 2. **2. s. diseases,** maladies répandues par les animaux sylvains.

Sylvester [sil'vestər], *Pr.n.m.* Sylvestre.

sylvestrene [sil'vestri:n], *s. Ch:* sylvestrène *f.*

Sylvestrian [sil'vestriən], *a. & s. Ecc.Hist:* **S. (Benedictine),** sylvestrin (*m*).

Sylvia ['silviə]. **1.** *Pr.n.f.* Sylvie. **2.** *s. Orn:* **sylvia,** sylvie *f.*

sylvian ['silviən], *a. Anat:* sylvien; de Sylvius; **s. fissure,** scissure *f* de Sylvius; *Z:* **s. aqueduct,** aqueduc *m* de Sylvius.

sylviculture ['silvikʌltʃər], *s.* sylviculture *f.*

sylviculturist [silvi'kʌltʃərist], *s.* silviculteur *m.*

sylviid ['silviid], *s. Orn:* sylviette *f.*

Sylviidae [sil'vi:idi:], *s.pl. Orn:* sylviidés *m.*

sylvine ['silvi:n], **sylvite** ['silvait], *s. Miner:* sylvine *f*, sylvite *f.*

sylvinite ['silvinait], *s. Miner:* sylvinite *f.*

symbion(t) ['simbiɔn(t)], *s. Biol:* symbio(n)te *m.*

symbiosis, *pl.* **-ses** [simb(a)i'ousis, -i:z], *s. Biol:* symbiose *f*, commensalisme *m*; **antagonistic s.,** symbiose dysharmonique; antibiose *f*; parasitisme *m.*

symbiote ['simb(a)iout], *s. Biol:* symbio(n)te *m.*

symbiotic [simb'(a)i'ɔtik], *a. Biol:* symbiotique; (*of association, etc.*) de symbiotes; (*of plant, etc.*) associé en symbiote.

symbiotically [simb(a)i'ɔtik(ə)li], *adv.* (vivre, etc.) en symbiote.

symblepharon [sim'blefərɔn], *s. Med:* symblépharon *m.*

symbol[1] ['simb(ə)l], *s.* **1.** symbole *m*, emblème *m*; signe *m*; attribut *m* (de la puissance souveraine, etc.); **picture s.,** idéogramme *m*; *NAm:* **road symbols,** pictogrammes routiers; **system of symbols,** symbolique *f*; *Cmptr:* **breakpoint s.,** symbole de point d'interruption; **check s.,** symbole de contrôle; **terminating s.,** marque *f* de fin de bloc; borne *f*, indication *f*, de fin d'information; **s. string,** chaîne *f* de symboles. **2.** *Ch: Mth: etc:* symbole. **3.** *Theol:* symbole (de saint Athanase, etc.).

symbol[2], *v.tr.* **(symbolled)** *NAm:* = SYMBOLIZE.

symbolic [sim'bɔlik], *a.* **1.** (*also* **symbolical** [sim'bɔlikl]), (geste, etc.) symbolique. **2.** *Cmptr:* (*of code, logic, address, language, programming, etc.*) symbolique. **3.** *Ecc:* **s. theology,** symbolique *f.*

symbolics [sim'bɔliks], *s.pl.* (*usu. with sg. const.*) la symbolique.

symbolism ['simbəlizm], *s.* symbolisme *m.*

symbolist ['simbəlist], *a. & s.* symboliste (*mf*).

symbolistic(al) [simbə'listik(l)], *a.* symboliste.

symbolization [simbəlai'zeiʃ(ə)n], *s.* symbolisation *f.*

symbolize ['simbəlaiz], *v.tr.* symboliser. **1.** être le symbole de (qch.); représenter (qch.). **2.** représenter (qch.) sous la forme d'un symbole. **3.** *v.i.* parler par symboles. **4.** *Theol:* mettre en symbole (les principaux articles de foi).

symbolizing ['simbəlaiziŋ], *s.* symbolisation *f*; mise *f* en symbole, en symboles.

symbology [sim'bɔlədʒi], *s.* **1.** (*system of symbols*) symbolique *f.* **2.** (*expression in symbols*) symbolisation *f.* **3.** (*science of symbols*) symbolisme *m.*

Symbranchidae [sim'bræŋkidi:], *s.pl. Ich:* symbranchidés *m.*

Symmachus ['siməkəs], *Pr.n.m. Rom. Hist:* Symmaque.

symmetrical [si'metrikl], *a.* symétrique (**about sth.,** par rapport à qch.); *Elcs:* **s. cyclical magnetized condition,** magnétisation cyclique symétrique.

symmetrically [si'metrik(ə)li], *adv.* symétriquement; **to be arranged s. with sth.,** symétriser avec qch.

symmetrization [simitrai'zeiʃ(ə)n], *s.* symétrisation *f.*

symmetrize ['simitraiz], *v.tr.* rendre symétrique; symétriser.

symmetry ['simitri], *s.* symétrie *f*; *Geom:* **s. axis,** axe *m* de symétrie; **plane of s.,** plan *m* de symétrie; **plane s.,** symétrie par rapport à un plan (donné).

sympathectomy [simpə'θektəmi], *s. Surg:* sympath(ic)ectomie *f.*

sympathetic [simpə'θetik], *a.* **1.** (*a*) *Anat: Physiol: etc:* (*of pain, nerve*) sympathique; **the s. nerve,** le (nerf) grand sympathique; **the s. (nervous system),** le (système nerveux) sympathique; (*b*) *Ph:* **s. vibration,** vibration due à la résonance; **s. string,** corde qui vibre par résonance; (*c*) **s. landscape,** paysage évocateur; (*d*) **s. ink,** encre sympathique; (*e*) **s. magic,** envoûtement *m.* **2.** (*a*) qui marque la sympathie; **s. glance, smile,** regard, sourire, de sympathie; (*b*) **s. audience,** auditoire bien disposé, prompt à comprendre, sympathique; **he's always very s.,** il est toujours prêt à vous écouter; **to be s. to a proposal,** être en sympathie avec une proposition; regarder, voir, une proposition d'un bon œil; (*c*) compatissant; **s. heart,** cœur compatissant; **s. words, letter,** paroles, lettre, de condoléances, de sympathie; (*d*) **s. strike,** grève de solidarité, de sympathie. **3.** (*as Gallicism*) (*of pers., face, talent*) qui évoque la sympathie; sympathique.

sympathetically [simpə'θetik(ə)li], *adv.* **1.** sympathiquement; avec sympathie; par sympathie; *Ph:* **to vibrate s.,** vibrer par résonance. **2.** d'une manière compatissante.

sympathin ['simpəθin], *s. Physiol:* sympathine *f.*

sympathize ['simpəθaiz], *v.i.* **1. to s. with s.o. (in his sorrow, in his loss, etc.),** (i) sympathiser avec qn; (ii) avoir de la compassion pour qn; compatir aux malheurs de qn; se montrer sensible à la douleur, aux malheurs, de qn; **I s. with you in your anxiety,** je partage votre inquiétude; **the Martins called to s.,** les Martin sont venus exprimer leurs condoléances; **I s. with you in your recent bereavement,** je suis de cœur avec vous dans votre deuil récent. **2.** (*a*) **to s. with s.o.'s point of view,** comprendre le point de vue de qn; **I can s. with his being angry,** je peux bien comprendre qu'il soit en colère; (*b*) **to s. with s.o.,** s'associer (de cœur) aux sentiments de qn.

sympathizer ['simpəθaizər], *s.* **1. to be a s. with s.o.,** (i) sympathiser avec qn; (ii) ressentir de la compassion pour qn; **to be a s. in s.o.'s grief,** compatir au chagrin de qn. **2.** sympathisant, -e (**with a cause,** d'une cause).

sympathizing ['simpəθaiziŋ], *a.* compatissant, sympathisant.

sympatholytic [simpæθə'litik], *a. Physiol:* sympatholytique.

sympathomimetic ['simpəθoumi'metik], *a. Physiol:* sympath(ic)omimétique.

sympathy ['simpəθi], *s.* **1.** compassion *f*; condoléances *fpl*; **accept my deep s.,** agréez mes condoléances; **to arouse s. for the oppressed,** éveiller de la sympathie, compassion, pour les opprimés; **he claims our s.,** (i) il a droit à notre sympathie; (ii) il veut à toute force être plaint. **2.** (*a*) sympathie *f* (**for s.o.,** pour qn); **to feel a s. for s.o.,** se sentir de l'attrait pour qn; **popular sympathies are on his side,** il a l'opinion pour lui; **man of active sympathies,** homme sensible; **to view a proposal with s.,** regarder une proposition d'un bon œil; **to be in s. with s.o.'s ideas,** être en sympathie avec les, sympathique aux, idées de qn; **my s. is, my sympathies are, with the opposition,** je partage les opinions de l'opposition; **I known you are in s. with them,** je sais que vous êtes de leur côté; **to strike, come out (on strike), in s.,** se mettre en grève de solidarité (**with,** avec); **s. strike, strike in s.,** grève de solidarité, de sympathie; **he had no s. with the Liberal party,** il était l'adversaire déclaré du parti libéral; (*b*) **prices went up in s.,** les prix sont montés par contrecoup; (*c*) *Ph:* **string that vibrates in s.,** corde qui vibre par résonance; (*d*) *Med: Physiol:* (*between organs*) sympathie.

sympatric [sim'pætrik], *a. Nat.Hist:* sympatrique.

Sympetalae [sim'petəli:], *s.pl. Bot:* sympétales *f*, gamopétales *f.*

sympetalous [sim'petələs], *a. Bot:* sympétale, gamopétale.

symphile ['simfail], *s. Ent:* symphile *m.*

symphonic [sim'fɔnik], *a. Mus:* (musique, poème) symphonique.

symphonically [sim'fɔnik(ə)li], *adv.* symphoniquement.

symphonious [sim'founiəs], *a.* harmonieux.

symphonist ['simfənist], *s.* symphoniste *m*; (i) compositeur *m* de symphonies; (ii) membre *m* d'un orchestre symphonique.

symphony ['simfəni], *s. Mus:* symphonie *f*; **composer of symphonies,** symphoniste *m*; **s. orchestra,** orchestre *m* symphonique; **s. concert,** concert *m* symphonique.

Symphorian [sim'fɔ:riən], *Pr.n.m. Ecc.Hist:* (saint) Symphorien.

symphoricarpos [simfəri'kɑ:pəs], *s. Bot:* symphorine *f.*

Symphyla ['simfilə], *s.pl. Z:* symphyles *m.*

symphysectomy [simfi'zektəmi], **symphysiotomy** [simfizi'ɔtəmi], *s. Surg:* symphyséotomie *f.*

symphysial [sim'fiziəl], *a. Anat:* de la, d'une, symphyse.

symphysis ['simfisis], *s. Anat:* symphyse *f.*

sympiesometer [simpie'sɔmitər], *s. Ph:* sympiézomètre *m.*

symplast ['simplæst], *s. Biol:* symplaste *m.*

symplectic [sim'plektik], *a. Anat:* symplectique.

symploce [sim'plousi], *s. Rh:* symploque *f.*

sympode ['simpoud], *s. Bot:* sympode *m.*

sympodial [sim'poudiəl], *a. Bot:* sympodique.
sympodite ['simpədait], *s. Z:* sympodite *m.*
sympodium, *pl.* **-ia** [sim'poudiəm, -iə], *s. Bot:* sympode *m.*
symposiarch [sim'pouziɑːk], *s.* **1.** *Gr.Ant:* symposiarque *m.* **2.** président *m* d'un symposium, d'une conférence.
symposium, *pl.* **-ia, -iums** [sim'pouziəm, -iə, -iəmz], *s.* **1.** *(a) Gr.Lit: etc:* symposium *m;* **Plato's S.,** la Banquet de Platon; *(b) F:* réunion *f* de convives; festin *m.* **2.** *(a)* conférence *f,* discussion *f* (académique); colloque *m,* symposium, *F:* échange *m* de vues; *(b)* recueil *m* d'articles (sur un sujet du jour).
symptom ['sim(p)təm], *s. Med: etc:* symptôme *m;* indice *m;* **premonitory s.,** symptôme prémonitoire; **to show symptoms of discontent,** présenter des indices du mécontentement.
symptomatic [sim(p)tə'mætik], *a.* symptomatique; **feverishness s. of tuberculosis,** état fiévreux qui est symptomatique, est un des symptômes, de la tuberculose; **events s. of social unrest,** événements symptomatiques du malaise social, qui indiquent le malaise social.
symptomatically [sim(p)tə'mætik(ə)li], *adv.* symptomatiquement.
symptomatize ['sim(p)təmətaiz], *v.tr.* être un symptôme, un indice, de (la maladie, la révolte, etc.).
symptomatologic(al) [sim(p)təmætə'lɔdʒik(l)], *a.* symptomatologique.
symptomatology [sim(p)təmə'tɔlədʒi], *s. Med:* symptomatologie *f.*
synaeresis [si'niərisis], *s. Ling: Ph:* synérèse *f.*
synaesthesia, *pl.* **-iae** [sinis'θiːziə, -iiː], *s. Psy: Physiol:* synesthésie *f.*
synagogal [sinə'gɔgl], **synagogical** [sinə'gɔgikl, -'gɔdʒ-], *a.* synagogal, -aux.
synagogue ['sinəgɔg], *s.* synagogue *f.*
synalgia [sin'ældʒiə], *s. Med:* synalg(és)ie *f.*
synallagmatic [sinælæg'mætik], *a. Jur:* (contrat) synallagmatique, bilatéral, -aux.
synal(o)epha [sinə'liːfə], *s. Gram:* synalèphe *f.*
synangium, *pl.* **-ia** [si'nændʒiəm, -iə], *s. Bot:* synange *m.*
synanthereous [sinæn'θeriəs], **synantherous** [si'nænθərəs], *a. Bot: (of plant)* synanthéré.
synanthous [si'nænθəs], *a. Bot: (of plant)* synanthé.
synanthropic [sinæn'θrɔpik], *a. Bot:* **s. species,** plante *f* sauvage qui pousse surtout dans les terres cultivées et les lieux habités.
synanthy [si'nænθi], *s. Bot:* synanthie *f.*
synapse ['sainæps, si'næps], *s. Anat:* synapse *f.*
synapsis, *pl.* **-apses** [si'næpsis, -æpsiːz], *s. Biol: Anat:* synapse *f.*
synaptic [si'næptik], *a. Anat:* synaptique.
Synaptidae [si'næptidiː], *s.pl. Echin:* synaptidés *m.*
synarchical [si'nɑːkikl], *a.* synarchique.
synarchy ['sinɑːki], *s.* synarchie *f.*
synarthrodial [sinɑː'θroudiəl], *a. Anat:* synarthrodial, -aux.
synarthrosis, *pl.* **-oses** [sinɑː'θrousis, -ousiːz], *s. Anat:* synarthrose *f.*
Synbranchidae [sin'bræŋkidiː], *s.pl. Ich:* symbranchidés *m.*
sync [siŋk], *s. Cmptr: etc:* **1.** synchronisation *f;* **s. bits,** bits *m* de synchronisation. **2.** *NAm:* signal *m,* -aux, de début de bloc.
syncarp ['sinkɑːp], *s. Bot:* syncarpe *m;* fruit syncarpé.
syncarpous [sin'kɑːpəs], *a. Bot:* syncarpé, gamocarpellé.
syncaryon [siŋ'kæriən], *s. Biol:* syncarion *m.*
syncategorematic [sin'kætigɔri'mætik], *a. Log:* syncatégorématique.
synch [siŋk], *s. Cmptr:* = SYNC.
synchondrosis, *pl.* **-oses** [siŋkɔn'drousis, -ousiːz], *s. Anat:* synchondrose *f.*
synchro ['siŋkrou], *s. El:* synchromachine *f, F:* synchro *f inv.*
synchrocyclotron [siŋkrou'saiklətrɔn], *s. Atom.Ph:* synchrocyclotron *m.*
synchroflash ['siŋkrouflæʃ], *s. Phot:* **s. (device),** (dispositif) synchroflash *m.*
synchromesh ['siŋkroumeʃ], *s. Aut:* **s. (gear),** (boîte *f* de vitesses) synchromesh *m.*
synchronal [siŋ'krounl], *a.* synchrone.
synchronality [siŋkrə'næliti], *s.* synchronisme *m.*
synchronic [siŋ'krɔnik], *a. Ling: etc:* synchronique.
synchronically [siŋ'krɔnik(ə)li], *adv.* synchroniquement.
synchronism ['siŋkrənizm], *s.* synchronisme *m;* **in s.,** en synchronisme; *El:* en phase; **out of s.,** hors de synchronisme, *El:* hors de phase; *T.V:* **irregular s.,** drapeau *m.*
synchronistic [siŋkrə'nistik], *a.* (tableau) synchronique.
synchronization [siŋkrənai'zeiʃ(ə)n], *s.* synchronisation *f; Cin: T.V:* **s. of sound and image,** synchronisation du son et de l'image; *El:* **s. of an alternator,** accrochage *m* d'un alternateur.
synchronize ['siŋkrənaiz]. **1.** *v.tr.* *(a)* synchroniser (deux mouvements, deux horloges, etc.; **sth. with sth.,** qch. avec qch.); *El:* coupler (deux générateurs) en phase; accrocher (un alternateur); *T.V:* **to s. sound and image,** synchroniser le son et l'image; *Cin:* **to s. the clapstick signals (on the picture film and the sound track),** repérer; *(b)* établir le synchronisme de (différents événements); *(c)* faire coïncider (par anachronisme) (des événements, etc., de dates différentes). **2.** *v.i.* *(a) (of events)* arriver, avoir lieu, simultanément; *(b)* **clocks that s.,** horloges qui marchent en synchronisme, qui marquent la même heure; *El:* **when the generators s.,** lorsque les générateurs sont en phase.
synchronized ['siŋkrə'naizd], *a.* synchronisé; *El:* **s. generators,** générateurs synchronisés, en phase.
synchronizer ['siŋkrənaizər], *s.* synchronisateur *m;* dispositif *m,* mécanisme *m,* de synchronisation; *El:* synchroniseur *m; Av:* **gun s.,** mécanisme de synchronisation de la mitrailleuse; *Cin:* **film s.,** synchroniseuse *f.*
synchronizing ['siŋkrənaiziŋ], *s.* synchronisation *f; El:* accrochage *m* en phase; *T.V:* **s. of sound and image,** synchronisation du son et de l'image; *Cin:* **s. of the picture film and the sound track,** repérage *m* de la piste sonore sur la bande des images; **s. mark,** (point *m* de) repère *m; Elcs:* **s. pulse, pilot,** impulsion *f,* onde *f* pilote, de synchronisation; *Av:* **s. gear,** mécanisme *m* de synchronisation (de la mitrailleuse).
synchronological [siŋkrənə'lɔdʒikl], *a.* qui appartient à la synchronologie; (tableau) synchronique.
synchronology [siŋkrə'nɔlədʒi], *s.* synchronologie *f.*
synchronoscope ['siŋkrɔnəskoup], *s. Elcs:* synchronoscope *m.*
synchronous ['siŋkrənəs], *a.* synchrone (**with,** de); *El: (of alternator)* en phase; *Cmptr: (of computer, system, transmission, working, etc.),* synchrone; *Space:* **s. orbit,** orbite *f* synchrone (d'un satellite).
synchronously ['siŋkrənəsli], *adv.* synchroniquement.
synchrony ['siŋkrəni], *s.* **1.** synchronisme *m; Cin:* **s. mark,** marque *f,* signal *m,* de synchronisme; repère *m.* **2.** *Ling:* synchronie *f.*
synchroscope ['siŋkrəskoup], *s. El:* synchroscope *m.*
synchrotron ['siŋkrətrɔn], *s. Atom.Ph:* synchrotron *m;* **electron, proton, s.,** synchrotron à électrons, à protons; **strong focussing s.,** synchrotron à focalisation forte; **alternating gradient s.,** synchrotron à gradient alterné.
synchysis ['siŋkisis], *s.* **1.** *Gram:* synchyse *f.* **2.** *Med:* synchysis *m;* **sparkling s.,** synchysis étincelant (de l'œil).
synclinal [siŋ'klainl], *a. Geol:* synclinal, -aux; **s. fold,** charnière inférieure (d'un plissement).
syncline ['siŋklain], *s. Geol:* synclinal *m.*
synclinorium, *pl.* **-ia** [siŋklai'nɔːriəm, -iə], *s. Geol:* synclinorium *m.*
synclitism [siŋ'klitizm], *s. Med:* synclitisme *m.*
Syncom ['siŋkɔm], *s. R.t.m. Space:* Syncom.
syncopal ['siŋkəpl], *a. Med:* syncopal, -aux.
syncopate ['siŋkəpeit], *v.tr. Gram: Mus:* syncoper.
syncopated ['siŋkəpeitid], *a.* syncopé; *Mus:* **s. notes,** notes syncopées; notes liées; **s. music,** musique syncopée, à contre-temps.
syncopation [siŋkə'peiʃ(ə)n], *s. Mus:* syncope *f.*
syncope ['siŋkəpi], *s.* **1.** *Med:* syncope *f;* perte *f* de connaissance; évanouissement *m.* **2.** *Gram:* syncope; retranchement *m* d'une lettre, syllabe.
syncotyledonous [siŋkɔti'liːdənəs], **syncotylous** [siŋ'kɔtiləs], *a. Bot:* syncotylédoné.
syncotyly [siŋ'kɔtili], *s. Bot:* état syncotylédoné.
syncraniate [siŋ'kreiniət], *a. Anat:* syncrânien.
syncretic [siŋ'kriːtik, -'kre-], *a. Phil: Theol:* syncrétique.
syncretism ['siŋkritizm], *s. Phil: Theol:* syncrétisme *m.*
syncretist ['siŋkritist], *a. & s. Phil: Theol:* syncrétiste *(m).*
syncretistic [siŋkri'tistik], *a. Phil: Theol:* syncrétistique.
syncretize ['siŋkritaiz], *v.tr.* (chercher à) concilier (des sectes diverses, etc.).
syncytium [sin'siʃiəm], *s. Biol:* syncytium *m.*
syndactyl(ous) [sin'dæktil(əs)], *a. Z:* syndactyle.
syndactylism, syndactyly [sin'dæktilizm, -tili], *s. Z:* syndactylie *f.*
syndesis ['sindisis], *s. Biol:* synpase *f.*
syndesmosis [sindes'mousis], *s. Anat:* syndesmose *f,* synnévrose *f.*
syndic ['sindik], *s.* syndic *m.*
syndical ['sindikl], *a.* syndical, -aux.
syndicalism ['sindikəlizm], *s.* syndicalisme *m.*
syndicalist ['sindikəlist], *s. & a.* syndicaliste *(mf).*
syndicalistic [sindikə'listik], *a.* syndicaliste.
syndicate[1] ['sindikət], *s.* **1.** *(a) Com: Fin:* syndicat *m,* consortium *m;* **financial s.,** syndicat financier; **underwriting s.,** syndicat de garantie; **member of a s.,** syndicataire *m; (b) NAm:* association *f* de malfaiteurs. **2.** conseil *m* de syndics.
syndicate[2] ['sindikeit]. **1.** *v.tr.* *(a)* syndiquer (des personnes, une profession, etc.); *(b)* publier (un article) simultanément dans plusieurs journaux. **2.** *v.i.* se syndiquer.
syndication [sindi'keiʃ(ə)n], *s.* **1.** mise *f* en syndicat. **2.** publication simultanée (d'un article) dans plusieurs journaux.
syndrome ['sindroum], *s. Med:* syndrome *m;* **dumping s.,** syndrome de vidange; dumping-syndrome *m;* **Down's s.,** mongolisme *m;* **Adams-Stokes, Stokes-Adams, s.,** syndrome, maladie *f,* d'Adams-Stokes; pouls lent permanent.
synecdoche [si'nekdəki], *s. Rh:* synecdoche *f,* synecdoque *f.*
synechia [si'nekiə], *s. Med:* synéchie *f.*
synecology [sini'kɔlədʒi], *s. Biol:* synécologie *f.*
synecphonesis [sinekfə'niːsis], *s. Gram:* synecphonèse *f.*
synectics [si'nektiks], *s.pl. (usu. with sg. const.)* synectique *f.*
synema ['sinimə], *s. Bot:* sinème *m.*
syneresis [si'niərisis], *s. Gram: NAm:* synérèse *f.*
synergetic [sinə'dʒetik], *a. Physiol:* synergique.
synergia [si'nəːdʒiə], *s. Physiol:* synergie *f.*
synergic [si'nəːdʒik], *a. Physiol:* synergique.
synergid [si'nəːdʒid], **synergida,** *pl.* **-ae** [si'nəːdʒidə, -iː], *s. Bot:* synergide *f.*
synergism ['sinədʒizm], *s.* **1.** *Theol:* synergisme *m.* **2.** *Biol:* synergie *f.*
synergist ['sinədʒist], *s.* **1.** *(pers.)* synergiste *m.* **2.** *Biol: (substance)* synergiste *m.*
synergistic [sinə'dʒistik], *a. Theol: Biol:* synergique.
synergy ['sinədʒi], *s.* synergie *f.*
synesthesia [sinis'θiːziə], *s. Med:* synesthésie *f.*
synform ['sinfɔːm], *s. Geol:* fond *m* de bateau; auge *f.*
syngameon [siŋ'gæmiən], *s. Biol:* syngaméon *m.*
syngamiasis [siŋgə'maiəsis], *s. Husb:* syngamose *f.*
syngamous ['siŋgəməs], *a. Biol:* syngamique.
syngenesia [sindʒi'niːziə], *s. A.Bot:* syngénésie *f,* syngénèse *f.*
syngenesious [sindʒi'niːʃ(i)əs], *a. Bot: (of stamens)* synanthéré.
syngenesis [sin'dʒenisis], *s. Biol:* syngénésie *f,* syngénèse *f.*
syngenetic [sindʒi'netik], *a. Biol: Miner:* syngénésique.
syngenite ['sindʒinait], *s. Miner:* syngénite *f.*
syngnathid [siŋ'(g)næθid], *s. Ich:* syngnathe *m.*
Syngnathidae [siŋ'(g)næθidiː], *s.pl. Ich:* syngnathidés *m,* syngnathes *m.*
syngnathous ['siŋ(g)nəθəs], *a. Ich:* syngnathe.
synizesis [sini'ziːsis], *s. Biol:* synizésis *f.*
synkaryon [siŋ'kæriən], *s. Biol:* syncarion *m.*
synod ['sinəd], *s.* *(a) Ecc:* synode *m,* concile *m;* *(in Presbyterian Ch.)* assemblée supérieure au consistoire; **the General S.,** le conseil d'administration de l'Église anglicane; *(b)* assemblée, convention *f.*
synodal ['sinədl], *a.* synodal, -aux.
synodic(al) [si'nɔdik(l)], *a.* *(a) Ecc: (of proceedings, etc.)* synodique, synodal, -aux; *(b) Astr: (usu.* **synodic)** **s. period,** période *f,* révolution *f,* synodique; **s. month,** mois *m* synodique, de consécution; lunaison *f.*
synoecete [si'niːsiːt], *s. Ent:* synœcète *m.*
synoecious [si'niːʃəs], *a.* *(a) Bot:* monœcique, monoïque; *(b) Nat.Hist:* (espèce) qui vit en synœcie.
synoecology [siniː'kɔlədʒi], *s. Biol:* synécologie *f.*
synoecy [si'niːsi], *s. Nat.Hist:* synœcie *f,* synécie *f;* **habitat s.,** synœcie d'habitat.
synonym ['sinənim], *s.* **1.** synonyme *m.* **2.** *Nat.Hist:* ancien nom, ancien terme.
synonymic [sinə'nimik], *a.* synonymique.
synonymics [sinə'nimiks], *s.pl. (usu. with sg. const.)* la synonymique.
synonymity [sinə'nimiti], *s.* synonymie *f.*
synonymize [si'nɔnimaiz]. **1.** *v.tr.* **to s. a word,** donner les synonymes d'un mot. **2.** *v.i.* s'exprimer par synonymes.
synonymous [si'nɔniməs], *a.* synonyme (**with,** de).
synonymy [si'nɔnimi], *s.* **1.** *(synonymity)* synonymie *f.* **2.** *(study)* synonymique *f.* **3.** dictionnaire *m,* liste *f,* de synonymes.
synopsis, *pl.* **-pses** [si'nɔpsis, -psiːz], *s.* résumé *m,* sommaire *m,* argument *m;* tableau *m* synoptique; synopsis

f (d'une science); *Sch:* (*examination*) **s. of chemistry, of history,** mémento *m* de chimie, d'histoire; **s. of the Gospels,** synopse *f*; *Cin:* **brief s. of a film,** plan *m* d'ensemble d'un film; résumé du scénario; synopsis.

synoptic [si'nɔptik]. **1.** *a.* synoptique; (*a*) **the S. Gospels,** les Évangiles *m* synoptiques; **s. table of the Gospels,** synopse *f*; (*b*) *Meteor:* **s. chart,** carte *f* synoptique. **2.** *s.* auteur *m* d'un des Évangiles synoptiques.

synopticist [si'nɔptisist], *s.* = SYNOPTIC 2.

synorogenic [sinɔrou'dʒenik], *a. Geol:* synorogénique.

synosteology [sinɔsti'ɔlədʒi], *s. Anat:* synostéologie *f*.

synostosis, *pl.* **-es** [sinɔ'stousis, -i:z], *s. Anat:* synostose *f*.

synovectomy [sinou'vektəmi, sai-], *s. Surg:* synovectomie *f*.

synovia [si'nouviə, sai-], *s. Physiol: Anat:* synovie *f*.

synovial [si'nouviəl, sai-], *a.* (*of gland, membrane*) synovial, -aux.

synovitis [sinə'vaitis, sai-], *s. Med:* synovite *f*.

synsacrum ['sinseikrəm], *s. Orn:* synsacrum *m*.

synsepalous [sin'sepələs], *a. Bot:* gamosépale.

syntactic(al) [sin'tæktik(l)], *a. Gram: etc:* syntactique, syntaxique.

syntactician [sintæk'tiʃ(ə)n], *s.* syntacticien, -ienne.

syntagm ['sintæm], **syntagma,** *pl.* **-s, -ata** [sin'tægmə, -z, -ətə], *s. Ling:* syntagme *m*.

syntagmatic [sintæg'mætik], *a. Ling:* syntagmatique.

syntax ['sintæks], *s.* syntaxe *f*.

syntectonic [sintek'tɔnik], *a. Geol:* syntectonique.

syntexis [sin'teksis], *s. Geol:* fusion *f*.

synthesis, *pl.* **-es** ['sinθisis, -i:z], *s.* synthèse *f*.

synthesist ['sinθisist], *s.* chimiste *mf*, philosophe *mf*, qui procède par synthèse; chirurgien expert dans la synthèse.

synthesize ['sinθəsaiz], *v.tr.* synthétiser (des éléments); **to s. a product,** faire la synthèse d'un produit.

synthetic [sin'θetik]. **1.** *a.* synthétique; **s. language,** (i) *Ling:* langue *f* synthétique; (ii) *Cmptr:* langage *m* synthétique; **s. stone,** pierre *f* de synthèse; **s. rubber,** caoutchouc *m* synthétique, de synthèse; **s. fabrics,** matières *f* synthétiques; **s. foods,** aliments artificiels; *Cmptr:* **s. address,** adresse générée; *F:* **s. smile,** sourire factice, artificiel. **2.** *s. usu.pl.* **synthetics,** (matières) plastiques (*f*).

synthetical [sin'θetikl], *a.* synthétique.

synthetically [sin'θetik(ə)li], *adv.* synthétiquement.

synthetist ['sinθitist], *s.* = SYNTHESIST.

synthetize ['sinθitaiz], *v.tr.* = SYNTHESIZE.

synthetizer ['sinθitaizər], *s.* **1.** (*pers.*) = SYNTHESIST. **2.** *Elcs:* synthétiseur *m*; **digital s.,** synthétiseur numérique.

synthol ['sinθɔl], *s. Ch:* synthol *m*.

Syntomidae [sin'tɔmidi:], *s.pl. Ent:* syntomides *m*, euchromides *m*.

syntone ['sintoun], *a. Psy:* syntone.

syntonic [sin'tɔnik], *a. W.Tel:* (transmetteur, récepteur) syntonique.

syntonin ['sintənin], *s. Bio-Ch:* syntonine *f*.

syntonism ['sintənizm], *s. W.Tel:* syntonie *f*, accord *m*.

syntonization [sintənai'zeiʃ(ə)n], *s. W.Tel:* syntonisation *f*, accordage *m*.

syntonize ['sintənaiz], *v.tr. W.Tel:* syntoniser, accorder.

syntonous ['sintənəs], *a. A.Mus:* syntonique.

syntony ['sintəni], *s. W.Tel: Psy:* syntonie *f*.

syntype ['sintaip], *s. Biol:* syntype *m*.

synusia [si'nju:ziə], *s. Biol:* synusie *f*.

sypher ['saifər], *v.tr. Carp:* assembler à mi-bois.

sypher-joint ['saifədʒɔint], *s. Carp:* assemblage *m* à mi-bois.

syphilide ['sifilaid], *s. Med:* syphilide *f*; éruption *f* syphilitique; **macular s.,** syphilide pigmentaire.

syphilis ['sifilis], *s. Med:* syphilis *f*; **congenital s.,** syphilis congénitale, héréditaire; **occupational s.,** syphilis extra-génitale; **Wassermann s. test,** réaction *f* de (Bordet-)Wassermann.

syphilitic [sifi'litik], *a. & s. Med:* syphilitique (*mf*); *F:* taré; **s. infection,** infection *f* syphilitique; *F:* avarie *f*.

syphilization [sifilai'zeiʃ(ə)n], *s. Med:* syphilisation *f*.

syphilize ['sifilaiz], *v.tr. Med:* syphiliser.

syphiloid ['sifilɔid], *a. Med:* syphiloïde.

syphiloma [sifi'loumə], *s. Med:* syphilome *m*.

syphilophobia [sifilə'foubiə], *s.* syphilophobie *f*.

syphilosis [sifi'lousis], *s. Med:* syphilisme *m*.

syphon[1,2] ['saif(ə)n], *s. & v.* = SIPHON[1,2].

Syracusan ['saiərəkju:z(ə)n]. *Geog:* **1.** *a.* syracusain. **2.** *s.* Syracusain, -aine.

Syracuse ['saiərəkju:z], *Pr.n. Geog:* Syracuse *f*.

syren ['saiərən], *s.* = SIREN.

Syria ['siriə], *Pr.n. Geog:* Syrie *f*.

Syriac ['siriæk]. *Ling:* **1.** *a.* syriaque. **2.** *s.* le syriaque.

Syrian ['siriən]. *Geog:* **1.** *a.* (*a*) syrien; (*b*) *Com:* **S. garnet,** grenat almandin. **2.** *s.* Syrien, -ienne.

syringa [si'riŋgə], *s. Bot:* **1.** syringa *m*. **2.** *F:* seringa(t) (commun); jasmin *m* en arbre.

syringe[1] ['sirindʒ, si'rindʒ], *s.* **1.** seringue *f*; **enema s.,** seringue à lavement; **hypodermic s.,** seringue hypodermique, à injections, de Pravaz; *Hort:* **garden s.,** pompe *f*, seringue, de jardin; **fine-spraying s.,** seringue bruineuse. **2.** *Ph:* **fire s.,** briquet *m* pneumatique, à air.

syringe[2], *v.tr.* **1.** seringuer (une plaie, etc.); *Hort:* bassiner (des fleurs); *Med:* **to s. (out) the ears,** laver les oreilles avec une seringue. **2. to s. a liquid into a cavity,** injecter un liquide dans une cavité.

syringeal [si'rindʒiəl], *a. Orn:* (muscle, etc.) de la syrinx.

syringing ['sirindʒiŋ, si'rin-], *s.* seringage *m*; *Hort:* bassinage *m*.

syringitis [sirin'dʒaitis], *s. Med:* inflammation *f* de la trompe d'Eustache.

syringobulbia [siriŋgou'bʌlbiə], *s. Med:* syringobulbie *f*.

syringomyelia [siriŋgoumai'i:liə], *s. Med:* syringomyélie *f*; maladie *f* de Morvan.

syringomyelic [siriŋgoumai'i:lik]. *a. Med:* syringomyélique.

syringotomy [siriŋ'gɔtəmi], *s. Surg:* syringotomie *f*; incision *f* d'une fistule.

syrinx, *pl.* **-xes, -inges** ['siriŋks, -ksiz, si'rindʒi:z], *s.* **1.** syringe *f*, syrinx *f*; flûte *f* de Pan. **2.** *Archeol:* syrinx, syringe (des rois égyptiens). **3.** *Anat:* trompe *f* d'Eustache. **4.** *Orn:* organe phonateur, syrinx. **5.** *Med:* fistule *f*.

Syro-Chaldaic ['sairoukæl'deiik]. *Ling:* **1.** *a.* syro-chaldaïque. **2.** *s.* syro-chaldaïque *m*.

syrphid ['sə:fid], *s. Ent:* syrphidé *m*.

Syrphidae ['sə:fidi:], *s.pl. Ent:* syrphidés *m*.

syrphus, *pl.* **-phi** ['sə:fəs, -fai], *s. Ent:* **s. (fly),** syrphe *m*.

syrtis, *pl.* **-tes** ['sə:tis, -ti:z], *s. Geog:* **1.** *A:* (*quicksand*) syrte *f*. **2. the Major, Minor, S.,** la Grande, Petite, Syrte.

syrup[1] ['sirəp], *s.* **1.** sirop *m*; **red currant s.,** sirop de groseilles; *Med:* **cough s.,** sirop pectoral. **2. golden s.,** mélasse raffinée; sirop de sucre. **3.** *F:* douceur affectée; langage sucré, mielleux.

syrup[2], *v.tr.* (**syruped**) **1.** couvrir de sirop. **2.** réduire en sirop.

syrupy ['sirəpi], *a.* **1.** sirupeux. **2.** *F:* (ton) mielleux, doucereux; **s. eloquence,** éloquence melliflue.

syssarcosis [sisɑ:'kousis], *s. Anat:* syssarcose *f*.

systaltic [sis'tæltik], *a. Physiol:* (pulsation) systaltique.

system ['sistəm], *s.* **1.** (*a*) système *m* (de philosophie, etc.); **s. of support,** mode *m* de soutènement (d'un pont, etc.); **to establish sth. on a s.,** établir qch. d'après un système; **to act according to, on, a s.,** agir par système; **the feudal s.,** le régime féodal; *Jur:* **married under the dotal s.,** marié sous le régime dotal; *F:* **the s.,** l'ordre établi; *Cmptr:* **basic operating s.,** système d'exploitation de base; **teleprinter s.,** système de téléimprimeurs, liaison *f* par téléimprimeurs; **two-way s.,** liaison bilatérale; **s. library,** bibliothèque *f* d'une installation; **systems analysis,** analyse de systèmes, fonctionnelle; **systems analyst,** analyste de systèmes, fonctionnel; **systems design,** analyse organique; **systems designer,** analyste organique; *Sch:* **block s.,** enseignement groupé; *Const:* **s. building,** préfabrication *f*; **s. built,** préfabriqué; (*b*) *Astr:* **the solar s.,** le système solaire; (*c*) *Anat:* **nervous s., muscular s.,** système nerveux, musculaire; **the digestive s.,** l'appareil digestif; **bad for the s.,** mauvais pour l'organisme; *F:* **to get a phobia out of one's s.,** se libérer d'une phobie. **2.** (*a*) réseau (télégraphique, etc.); réseau ferré (d'un chemin de fer); **road s.,** réseau routier; **river s.,** réseau fluvial; *Mil:* **s. of mines,** dispositif *m* de mines; (*b*) **s. of pulleys,** système de poulies; **central heating s.,** installation *f* de chauffage central. **3.** méthode *f* (de travail, etc.); **to lack s.,** manquer de méthode, d'organisation; **to work without s.,** travailler sans méthode. **4.** *Mus:* (*a*) distribution *f* de la partition (d'orchestre, etc.); (*b*) pupitre *m* (d'instruments, dans une partition).

systematic [sistə'mætik], *a.* systématique, méthodique; **s. orders,** ordres coordonnés; **he's very s.,** il a de l'ordre, de la méthode.

systematically [sistə'mætik(ə)li], *adv.* systématiquement, méthodiquement; **she does her work s.,** elle travaille avec méthode; **gang of thieves working s. through a district,** bande de voleurs qui met un quartier en coupe réglée.

systematics [sistə'mætiks], *s.pl.* (*usu. with sg. const.*) systématique *f*.

systematist ['sistəmətist], *s.* classificateur, -trice.

system(at)ization [sistəm(ət)ai'zeiʃ(ə)n], *s.* systématisation *f*.

system(at)ize ['sistəm(ət)aiz], *v.tr.* réduire en système, systématiser; **he'd systematized crime,** il avait réduit le crime en système.

systematizer ['sistəmətaizər], *s.* systématiseur *m*.

systemic [si'stemik, -'sti:m-], *a. Physiol:* du système, de l'organisme; **s. circulation,** circulation générale; *Z: Orn:* **s. heart,** auricule *m* et ventricule *m* gauches du cœur; *Hort: etc:* **s. insecticides,** systémiques *m*.

systole ['sistəli], *s. Physiol: Pros:* systole *f*.

systolic [si'stɔlik], *a. Physiol:* systolique.

systyle ['sistail], *a. & s. Arch:* systyle (*m*); **s. temple,** temple *m* systyle.

syzygy ['sizidʒi], *s. Astr:* syzygie *f*.

T

T, t [ti:], *s.* **1.** (la lettre) T, t, té *m*; *Tp:* **T for Tommy,** T comme Thérèse; **to cross one's t's,** (i) barrer ses t; (ii) *F:* mettre les points sur les i, observer les longues et les brèves; *Navy:* **to cross the T,** barrer le T; *adv.phr.* **to a T,** exactement; trait pour trait; parfaitement, à la perfection; **that's you to a T,** c'est absolument vous; **to fit, suit, to a T,** aller comme un gant; **that suits me to a T,** cela me va à merveille; *P:* ça fait mon blot; ça me botte. **2.** (*a*) *Mec.E: etc:* **union T,** raccord *m* en T; *Av:* **landing T,** T d'atterrissage; (*b*) **T(-shaped),** en forme de) T; à T; à, en, té; en potence; *Surg:* **T bandage,** bandage *m* en té; *Mec.E:* **T section, bar, iron,** fer *m* à, en, T; profilé *m* à, en, té; **T branch,** tube *m*, tuyau *m*, en T; *W.Tel:* **T aerial,** antenne *f* en T; (*of roads*) **T junction,** tête *f* de carrefour; *Cost:* **T shirt,** T-shirt *m*, tee-shirt *m*.

't [t], (*abbr. of* **it**) **'twas, 'tis,** c'était, c'est.

t' [tə], *def.art. Dial:* = THE.

ta [tɑ:], *s. & int.* (*Nursery speech and*) *P:* merci (*m*).

Taal [tɑ:l], *s. Ling:* **the t.,** le patois hollandais (parlé au Cap).

tab[1] [tæb], *s.* **1.** (*a*) patte *f* (de vêtement, etc.); *Mil:* patte du collet; écusson *m*, insigne *m* (d'officier d'état-major); (*b*) **ear tabs,** oreillettes *f*, oreillons *m* (de casquette); (*c*) **shoelace t.,** ferret *m* de cordon de soulier; (*d*) (*for hanging up coat, pulling on boots etc.*) attache *f*; (*e*) patte *f* (de carton de classement); onglet *m* (de dictionnaire, fichier, etc.); (*f*) *Av:* **trimming t.,** compensateur *m*, volet *m*, flettner *m*. **2.** étiquette *f* (pour bagages); *Fig:* **to keep tabs on s.o., sth.,** tenir qn, qch., à l'œil; ne pas perdre qn, qch., de vue; ne pas oublier qch.; **to keep tabs on the expenditure,** contrôler les dépenses. **3.** *NAm: F:* facture *f*, note *f*.

tab[2], *v.tr.* (**tabbed**) mettre un onglet, une patte, à (une fiche, etc.).

tab[3], *s. F: Typewr: Cmptr:* (= TABULATING) **t. key,** tabulateur *m*; **t. card,** carte *f* mécanographique; **t. form,** imprimé *m* mécanographique; **t. equipment, gear,** matériel *m* mécanographique classique (à cartes perforées).

tab[4], *s. Th: F:* (= TABLEAU) **t. (curtain),** rideau *m* à l'italienne.

Tabanidae [tə'bænidi:], *s.pl. Ent:* tabanidés *m*.

tabard ['tæbəd], *s. Cost:* **1.** tabar(d) *m* (de héraut, *Hist:* de chevalier). **2.** chasuble *m*; tunique grecque.

tabaret ['tæbəret], *s. Tex:* satin rayé (d'ameublement).

Tabasco [tə'bæskou], *s. R.t.m.* sorte *f* de sauce piquante au piment rouge.

tabasheer [tæbə'ʃiər], *s.* tabas(c)hir *m*.

tabbed [tæbd], *a.* (*of garment, index card, etc.*) garni de pattes, d'une patte.

tabbing ['tæbiŋ], *s. Typewr: Cmptr: F:* tabulation *f*.

tabby[1] ['tæbi], *s.* **1.** *Tex:* (*a*) *A:* tabi(s) *m*; soie moirée; moire *f*; (*b*) **t. weave,** armure *f* toile. **2. t. (cat),** (*a*) (i) chat tigré, moucheté, tacheté, rayé; (ii) *F:* chatte *f*; (*b*) *F:* vieille fille cancanière; vieille teigne, vieille chipie. **3.** *Ent:* teigne *f* de la graisse.

tabby[2], *v.tr.* (**tabbied**) *Tex:* tabiser (la soie, etc.).

tabellion [tə'beljən], *s. Jur: A:* tabellion *m*.

tabernacle ['tæbənækl], *s.* **1.** *Ecc:* (*a*) tabernacle *m* (pour abriter l'hostie); (*b*) stalle *f* à dais. **2.** *Jew.Rel:* tabernacle, tente *f*; **the Feast of Tabernacles,** la fête des Tabernacles. **3.** *Ecc: Pej:* temple (dissident); **tin t.,** petit temple, petite chapelle, à toit en tôle ondulée. **4.** *Nau:* cornet *m* (d'un mât).

tabes ['teibi:z], *s. Med:* tabes *m*, tabès *m*; **dorsal t.,** ataxie locomotrice progressive.

tabescence [tə'bes(ə)ns], *s. Med:* tabescence *f*; émaciation *f*; marasme *m*.

tabescent [tə'bes(ə)nt], *a. Med:* tabescent.

tabetic [tə'betik], *a. & s. Med:* tabétique (*mf*).

tabinet ['tæbinit], *s.* popeline *f* d'Irlande.

Tabitha ['tæbiθə], *Pr.n.f. B:* Tabithe.

tablature ['tæblətʃər], *s.* **1.** *Mus: A:* tablature *f*. **2.** (*a*) image mentale; (*b*) description *f* graphique.

table[1] ['teibl], *s.* table *f*. **1.** (*a*) *Furn:* **extending t., draw t.,** table à rallonges; **drop leaf, gate-legged, t.,** table à abattants; **pedestal t., t. on pillar and claw,** guéridon *m*, table à pied central; **cross t.,** table en potence; **collapsible, folding, t.,** table pliante; **card, gaming, t.,** table de jeu; **nest of tables,** table gigogne; **to bring opposing sides to the (conference, peace, negotiating) t.,** amener les partis opposés à la table des conférences; *F:* **to give s.o. sth. under the t.,** donner qch. à qn clandestinement, sous la table; *Parl:* **to lay a measure on the t.,** déposer un projet de loi sur le bureau; **to allow a bill to lie on the t.,** ajourner un projet de loi; **to lay papers on the t.,** communiquer à la Chambre les documents relatifs à l'affaire; *Psychics:* **t. rapping,** (phénomène *m* des) tables frappantes, parlantes; **t. turning,** (phénomène des) tables tournantes; (*b*) **the (meal, breakfast, dinner) t.,** la table; **to lay, set, the t.,** mettre, dresser, la table; mettre le couvert; **t. laid for twelve people,** table de douze couverts; **to clear the t.,** desservir; **to sit down to t.,** se mettre à table; **to rise from t., leave the t.,** se lever, sortir, de table; **to be (seated) at t.,** être à table, être attablé; **to wait at t.,** servir à table; (*in restaurant*) **separate tables,** (service *m* par) petites tables; (*at banquet, etc.*) **high t., head t.,** *F:* **top t.,** table d'honneur; **the pleasures of the t.,** les plaisirs de la table; la bonne chère; **to be fond of the t.,** aimer la table, la bonne chère; **to keep a good t.,** avoir une bonne table; faire bonne chère; manger bien; *F:* **to drink s.o. under the t.,** mettre qn sous la table; **he finished up under the t.,** à la fin il était ivre mort; **I was the only stranger at the t.,** j'étais le seul convive étranger; **she kept the whole t. amused,** elle faisait rire toute la table, tous les convives; **his t. manners leave much to be desired,** sa façon de manger laisse beaucoup à désirer; **t. talk,** (i) propos *m* de table; (ii) propos familiers; **t. fork,** fourchette *f* (de table); **t. knife,** couteau *m* de table; **t. wine,** vin *m* de table; **t. centre,** rond *m*, carré *m*, de table; **t. runner,** chemin *m*, jeté *m*, de table; **t. cover,** tapis *m* de table; *Tex:* **t. length,** tablée *f* d'étoffe; **t. linen,** linge *m* de table; **t. mat,** (i) dessous *m* d'assiette; porte-assiette *m*, *pl.* porte-assiettes; (ii) napperon individuel, garde-nappe *m*, *pl.* garde-nappe(s); **t. licence,** licence *f* permettant la vente des boissons alcooliques exclusivement avec les repas; **t. money,** (i) *Mil: etc:* frais *mpl* de table; (indemnité *f* pour) frais de représentation; (ii) taxe payée (dans certains clubs) pour la permission de se servir de la salle à manger; *Ecc:* **the Lord's T., the communion t.,** la Sainte Table; (*c*) *Geog:* **T. Mountain,** la Montagne de la Table; **T. Bay,** la baie de la Table. **2.** *Games: A:* table (de tablier de trictrac); **tables,** trictrac; *Fig:* **to turn the tables on s.o.,** retourner un argument contre qn; renvoyer la balle à qn; reprendre l'avantage sur qn; retourner la situation; **the tables are turned,** les rôles sont renversés, la chance a tourné. **3.** *Tchn:* console *f*, plateau *m* (de machine-outil); entablement *m* (de laminoir); banc *m*, table (de machine à percer); **tracing t.,** marbre *m* à tracer; *Geog:* **orientation, panoramic, t.,** table d'orientation (à un belvédère). **4.** (*a*) *Lap:* (i) table (d'un diamant); **t. cut,** (taillé) en table; (ii) diamant (taillé) en table; (*b*) semelle *f* (de poutre); surface *f* (de rail); tablier (de pont à bascule); (*c*) *Anat:* **inner t., vitreous t.,** table interne, vitrée (du crâne); **outer t.,** table externe (du crâne); (*d*) *Farr:* table (d'une incisive usée); (*e*) (*in palmistry*) quadrilatère *m* (de la paume de la main). **5.** plaque *f*, tablette *f* (de marbre, d'ivoire); *B.Hist:* **the Tables of the Law, the two Tables,** les Tables de la loi; *Rom.Jur:* **the Twelve Tables,** les douze Tables. **6.** *Arch:* **ground t. of a wall,** embasement *m*. **7.** *Geog:* plateau *m*. **8.** (*list*) table, tableau *m*, répertoire *m*; **synoptic t. of a science,** tableau synoptique d'une science; **t. of weights and measures,** table de poids et de mesures; **alphabetical t.,** table alphabétique; **t. of contents,** table des matières; **t. of saints, of festivals,** canon *m* des saints, des fêtes; **t. of births,** relevé *m* des naissances; *Mth:* **multiplication t.,** table de multiplication; **nine times t.,** table de multiplication par neuf; **to learn one's tables,** apprendre la table de multiplication; **log(arithmic) tables,** tables logarithmiques; **astronomical tables,** tables astronomiques; éphémérides *f*; *Artil:* **range t.,** table de tir; *Aut:* **inflation t.,** tableau de gonflage; *Ch:* **t. of chemical equivalents,** abaque des équivalents chimiques; *Nau:* **tide t.,** annuaire *m*, indicateur *m*, des marées; *Rail: etc:* **t. of fares, of charges,** barême *m* des prix; *Typ:* **t. work,** tableaux; ouvrage *m* à filets et à chiffres; **compositor on t. work,** tableautier *m*. **9.** *Cmptr:* **decision t.,** table de décision; **header t.,** table des en-têtes; **symbol t.,** table des symboles; **truth t.,** table de vérité; **output, plotting, t.,** table traçante; traceur *m* de courbes.

table[2], *v.tr.* **1.** (*a*) *Parl:* **to t. a bill,** (i) saisir la Chambre d'un projet de loi; déposer un projet de loi sur le bureau; (ii) *U.S:* ajourner (indéfiniment) un projet de loi; **to t. a motion,** présenter une motion; **to t. a motion of confidence,** poser la question de confiance; (*b*) *Cards:* jouer (une carte); *Fig:* **to t. one's cards,** jouer cartes sur table. **2.** *Carp:* emboîter, assembler (deux poutres, etc.). **3.** *Nau:* doubler les bords (d'une voile); renforcer, gainer (une voile).

tableau, *pl.* **-eaux** ['tæblou, -ouz], *s. Th:* tableau *m*; **tableaux vivants,** tableaux vivants; **t. curtain,** rideau *m* à l'italienne; *F:* **at that moment the manager walked in; t!** à ce moment le gérant est entré; tableau!

tablecloth ['teiblklɔθ], *s.* (*a*) tapis *m* (de table); (*b*) (*of linen*) nappe *f*; **t. material,** nappage *m*; (*c*) (*in S. Africa*) **the t.,** nappe de nuages (qui cache souvent la Montagne de la Table).

table d'hôte ['tɑ:blə'dout], *s.* table *f* d'hôte; **t. d'h. dinner,** (i) dîner *m* à la table d'hôte; (ii) dîner à prix fixe; **the t. d'h. meal,** le menu à prix fixe.

tableful ['teiblful], *s.* tablée *f*.

tableland ['teibllænd], *s. Geog:* plateau *m*.

tablespoon ['teiblspu:n], *s.* cuiller *f*, cuillère *f*, à servir.
tablespoonful ['teiblspu:nful], *s.* cuillerée *f* (à servir).
tablet ['tæblit], *s.* **1.** (*a*) (i) *A:* tablette *f* (pour écrire); (ii) *NAm:* bloc(-notes) *m*, *pl.* blocs-notes; (*b*) plaque commémorative; **votive t.**, (i) *Rom.Ant:* tablette votive; (ii) *Ecc:* ex-voto *m inv.* **2.** *Pharm:* comprimé *m.* **3. t. of soap,** pain *m* de savon, savonnette *f*; **t. of chocolate,** tablette *f* de chocolat. **4.** *Arch:* entablement *m* (d'un mur).
tableware ['teiblwɛər], *s.* articles *mpl* de table.
tabling ['teibliŋ], *s.* **1.** (*a*) *Carp:* assemblage *m*, emboîtement *m* (de deux poutres, etc.); (*b*) *Parl:* **t. of a bill,** (i) dépôt *m* d'un projet de loi (sur le bureau); (ii) *U.S:* ajournement *m* d'un projet de loi. **2.** *Nau:* gaine *f*, doublage *m*, tablir *m* (d'une voile). **3.** nombre *m* de tables dont on peut disposer; **t. for twenty people,** places *fpl*, couverts *mpl*, pour vingt personnes.
Tabloid ['tæblɔid], *s.* **1.** *Pharm:* (*R.t.m. of drugs manufactured by Burroughs Wellcome & Co.*) tabloïd *m.* **2.** *F:* (*a*) **to put a report in t. form,** donner un résumé d'un compte-rendu; *Journ:* **news in t. form,** nouvelles *fpl* en une ligne; (*b*) **t. (newspaper),** journal *m*, -aux, de petit format; tabloïd, *Pej:* journal de concierge, feuille *f* de chou.
taboo[1] [tə'bu:]. **1.** *s. Anthr: etc:* tabou *m*, *pl.* -ous. **2.** *a.* tabou (*often inv. in pl.*); (*a*) *Anthr:* **to declare s.o., sth., t.,** déclarer qn, qch., tabou; tabouer qn, qch.; (*b*) interdit, proscrit; **these subjects (of conversation) are t.,** ces sujets sont tabou(s); **t. word,** mot tabou; **it's t.,** c'est une chose qui ne se fait pas.
taboo[2], *v.tr.* **1.** *Anthr:* tabouer (qn, qch.); déclarer (qn, qch.) tabou. **2.** proscrire, interdire (qch.).
tabooing [tə'bu:iŋ], *s.* **1.** *Anthr:* tabouisation *f* (de qch.); déclaration *f* que qch. est tabou. **2.** interdiction *f*, proscription *f* (de qch.); mise *f* d'un ban sur (qn).
tabor ['teibər], *s. Mus: A:* tambourin *m*, tambour *m* de Basque.
taborer ['teibərər], *s.* tambourinaire *m.*
taboret ['tæbəret], *s. NAm:* tabouret *m.*
Taborites ['tæbəraits], *s.pl. Rel.H:* taborites *m.*
tabouret ['tæbəret], *s.* **1.** tabouret *m.* **2.** tambour *m* à broder.
tabu[1] [tə'bu:]. *Anthr:* **1.** *s.* tabou *m*, *pl.* -ous. **2.** *a.* tabou (*often inv. in pl.*).
tabu[2], *v.tr. Anthr:* tabouer (qch.), déclarer (qch.) tabou.
tabula, *pl.* **-ae** ['tæbjulə, -i:], *s.* **1.** *Anat:* table *f* (du crâne). **2. t. rasa,** table rase.
tabular ['tæbjulər], *a.* **1.** tabulaire, disposé en table(s), en tableau(x); **statistics in t. form,** statistique sous forme de tableau; *Typ:* **t. matter,** tableaux *mpl*, ouvrage *m* à filets et à chiffres. **2.** (*a*) (*of surface, crystal*) tabulaire; (*of rock, hill*) aplati; (*b*) disposé en lamelles; *Miner:* **t. spar,** wollastonite *f*.
tabulate[1] ['tæbjuleit], *v.tr.* disposer (des chiffres, des faits) en forme de table(s), de tableau(x); digérer (des lois, etc.); classifier (des résultats); cataloguer (des marchandises).
tabulate[2], *a. Paleont:* (coralliaire) tabulé.
tabulated ['tæbjuleitid], *a.* **1.** (*a*) en forme de plateau; en table; (*b*) en lamelles. **2.** (*of data, statistics, etc.*) arrangé en tableau(x).
tabulating ['tæbjuleitiŋ], *s.* = TABULATION; *Typew:* **t. key,** tabulateur *m*; *Cmptr:* **t. card,** carte *f* mécanographique; **t. equipment,** matériel *m* classique; **t. machine,** tabulatrice *f*; **t. room,** (salle *f* de la) mécanographie.
tabulation [tæbju'leiʃ(ə)n], *s.* arrangement *m*, disposition *f*, (des résultats, etc.) en tables, en tableau(x); classification *f* (des résultats); *Typew: Cmptr:* tabulation *f*; *Typew:* **t. stop,** taquet *m* de tabulation; *Cmptr:* **t. character,** caractère *m* de tabulation.
tabulator ['tæbjuleitər], *s.* **1.** *Typ:* (*pers.*) tableautier *m.* **2.** *Typewr:* tabulateur *m* (d'une machine à écrire); *Cmptr:* tabulatrice *f*; **digital t.,** tabulatrice numérique.
tacamahac ['tækəməhæk], *s.* **1.** *Pharm:* tacamaque *m*; baume vert, de Marie. **2.** *Bot:* peuplier *m* de Giléad, peuplier baumier.
tacan ['tækæn], *s. Av:* tacan *m.*
tac-au-tac ['tækou'tæk], *s. Fenc:* **t.-au.-t. riposte,** riposte *f* du tac au tac.
tacca ['tækə], *s. Bot:* tacca *m.*
tace [teis], *s. A.Arm:* tassette *f*.
tache [tɑ:ʃ], *s. A: & B:* fermoir *m*, agrafe *f*.
tacheometer [tæki'ɔmitər], *s. Surv:* tachéomètre *m.*
tacheometry [tæki'ɔmitri], *s. Surv:* tachéométrie *f*.
tachina ['tækinə], *s. Ent:* **t. (fly),** tachine *m occ. f*, tachinaire *m occ. f*.
tachinid ['tækinid], *a. & s. Ent:* **t. (fly),** tachine *m occ. f*, tachinaire *m occ. f*.
tachism(e) ['tæʃizm], *s. Art:* tachisme *m.*
tachist ['tæʃist], *a. & s. Art:* tachiste (*mf*).
tachistoscope [tæ'kistouskoup], *s. Opt:* tachistoscope *m.*
tachograph ['tækougræ:f], *s. Mec.E:* tachygraphe *m.*
tachometer [tæ'kɔmitər], *s. Mec.E: etc:* tachymètre *m*, cinémomètre *m*, compte-tours *m inv*; **recording t.,** tachygraphe *m*, tachymètre enregistreur.
tachometric [tækə'metrik], *a. Mec.E: etc:* tachymétrique.
tachometry [tæ'kɔmitri], *s. Mec.E: etc:* tachymétrie *f*.
tachycardia [tæki'kɑ:diə], *s. Med:* tachycardie *f*.
tachygenesis [tæki'dʒenisis], *s. Biol:* tachygénèse *f*.
tachygenetic [tækidʒi'netik], *a. Biol:* (phénomène, etc.) de tachygénèse.
tachygraph, tachygrapher, tachygraphist ['tækigræf, tæ'kigrəfər, -fist], *s. Rom. & Gr.Ant:* tachygraphe *m.*
tachygraphical [tæki'græfikl], *a.* tachygraphique.
tachygraphy [tæ'kigrəfi], *s. Ant:* tachygraphie *f*.
tachylite, -lyte ['tækilait], *s. Miner:* tachylite *f*.
tachymeter [tæ'kimitər], *s. Surv.* tachéomètre *m.*
tachymetry [tæ'kimitri], *s. Surv.* tachéométrie *f*.
tachyon ['tækiɔn], *s. Atom.Ph:* tachyon *m.*
tachyph(a)emia [tæki'fi:miə], *s. Med:* tachyphémie *f*.
tachyphagia [tæki'feidʒiə], *s. Med:* tachyphagie *f*.
tachypn(o)ea [tæki'pni:ə], *s. Med:* tachypnée *f*.
tacit ['tæsit], *a.* (consentement, aveu) tacite, implicite; *Jur:* **renewal by t. agreement, t. renewal,** reconduction *f* tacite.
tacitly ['tæsitli], *adv.* tacitement.
taciturn ['tæsitə:n], *a.* taciturne; économe de paroles; qui parle peu.
taciturnity [tæsi'tə:niti], *s.* taciturnité *f*.
taciturnly ['tæsitə:nli], *adv.* d'une manière taciturne.
Tacitus ['tæsitəs], *Pr.n.m. Lt.Lit:* Tacite.
tack[1] [tæk], *s.* **1.** (*a*) petit clou; clou de bouche; pointe *f*; broquette *f*; *pl.* semence *f* (de tapissier); **t. claw, t. drawer,** arrache-pointes *m inv*; **t. hammer,** marteau *m* de tapissier; *F:* **to come, get, down to brass tacks,** en venir au fait; arriver à la réalité, aux faits; **let's get down to brass tacks,** parlons peu et parlons bien; (*b*) *NAm:* punaise *f* (pour planche à dessin, etc.); **t. board,** tableau *m* d'annonces; porte-affiches *m inv.* **2.** *Needlew:* point *m* de bâti; **to take out the tacks,** enlever la faufilure; **to put a t. in a garment,** faire un point à un vêtement. **3.** *Nau:* (*a*) (*clew line*) amure *f*; **main t.,** grande amure; amure de grand-voile; (*b*) (*of a sail*) point d'amure (d'une voile); **t. of a flag,** queue *f* d'un pavillon; (*c*) bord *m*, bordée *f*; **to make a t.,** tirer un bord, une bordée; **to be, sail, run, on the starboard, the port, t.,** être, courir, faire route, tribord amures, bâbord amures; **to be on the opposite t.,** naviguer à bord opposé; **to sail on opposite tacks,** courir à contrebord; **to change t.,** changer d'amures; **to take short tacks,** louvoyer à petits bords; *F:* **to be on the right t.,** être sur la bonne voie; **to be on the wrong t.,** faire fausse route; suivre une fausse piste; être fourvoyé. **4.** *Parl:* clause additionnelle (d'un projet de loi).
tack[2]. **1.** *v.tr.* (*a*) **to t. sth. (down),** clouer qch. avec des semences, de la broquette; **to t. up hangings on a wall,** clouer une tenture au mur; **to t. the webbing to an armchair,** sangler un fauteuil; *F:* **to t. sth. (on) to sth.,** attacher, joindre, annexer, qch. à qch.; *Parl:* **to t. a clause on, to, a bill,** ajouter une clause à un projet de loi; (*b*) *Needlew:* faufiler, bâtir, baguer (un vêtement); pointer (une couture); **to t. (down) folds,** empointer des plis; **to t. in a lining,** bâtir une doublure. **2.** *v.i. Nau:* (*a*) virer de bord vent devant; **to t. to port,** virer (de bord) sur bâbord; (*b*) tirer des bordées; louvoyer; (*c*) *F:* (*of pers.*) **to t. (about),** changer de tactique; donner un coup de barre. **3.** *v.i. F:* (*of pers.*) **to t. on to s.o.,** se coller à qn.
tack[3], *s. F:* **1.** nourriture *f*, aliment *m*; **hard t.,** biscuit *m* de mer. **2.** *O:* fatras *m*, bêtises *fpl.*
tack[4], *s.* (*a*) *Equit:* sellerie *f*; (*b*) **t. room,** sellerie.
tack[5], *s. Scot:* **1.** (tenure *f* par) bail *m.* **2.** prise *f* de poisson; coup de filet heureux.
tackiness[1] ['tækinis], *s.* viscosité *f*; adhésivité *f*.
tackiness[2], *s. NAm: F:* apparence *f* minable, pauvre.
tacking ['tækiŋ], *s.* **1.** (*a*) clouage *m*; (*b*) *Needlew:* bâtissage *m*; faufilure *f*; **to take out the t.,** défaufiler; *Metalw:* **t. rivet,** rivet *m* provisoire; (*c*) *Jur:* jonction *f*, rattachement *m*, d'une seconde avance d'argent à la première par un créancier hypothécaire, lorsque dans l'intervalle le débiteur a contracté un second emprunt hypothécaire sans en avertir le premier créancier. **2.** (*a*) *Nau:* virement *m* de bord; **t. (about),** louvoiement *m*, louvoyage *m*; (*b*) *F:* (i) changement *m* de tactique; (ii) conduite ambiguë.
tackle[1] ['tækl], *s.* **1.** (*a*) attirail *m*, appareil *m*, engins *mpl*, ustensiles *mpl*; **fishing t.,** engins, appareil, de pêche; *Com:* articles *mpl* de pêche; *Mec.E:* **screwing t.,** appareil de vissage; (*b*) *Paperm:* garniture *f* (du cylindre porte-lames); (*c*) *Equit:* sellerie *f*. **2.** appareil de levage; *Jur:* agrès *mpl* et apparaux; (*a*) *Nau: etc:* apparaux; palan *m*; **single t.,** palan simple; **purchase t.,** caliorne *f*; **deck t.,** marguerite *f*; **lift t.,** palan d'apiquage; **stay t.,** palan de charge, d'étai; **t. block,** moufle *m or f*; poulie *f*; (*b*) **t. (fall),** courant *m* de palan; garant *m*; **boat's fall t.,** garants de canot. **3.** action *f* de saisir (qn); *Fb:* arrêt *m*; *Rugby Fb:* plaquage *m*; (*hockey, etc.*) interception *f*; accrochage *m.*
tackle[2], *v.tr.* **1.** (i) atteler, (ii) harnacher (un cheval). **2.** (*a*) empoigner; saisir (qn) à bras-le-corps; *Sp:* intercepter (un adversaire); *Rugby Fb:* **to t. an opponent (and bring him down),** plaquer un adversaire; *Fig:* **to t. s.o. about sth.,** entreprendre qn sur qch.; (*b*) attaquer, s'attaquer à (sa nourriture, une question, une corvée); aborder (un problème, une question, la lecture d'un livre); **I don't know how to t. it,** je ne sais pas comment m'y prendre; **to t. the job oneself,** s'atteler soi-même à la besogne, mettre la main à la pâte; **he tackles the job very well,** il s'y prend très bien. **3.** *v.i.* **to t. to,** s'atteler, se mettre, à la besogne.
tackler ['tæklər], *s. Sp:* (*hockey, etc.*) intercepteur, -trice; *Rugby Fb:* plaqueur *m.*
tackling ['tækliŋ], *s.* (*a*) attaque *f*; *Sp:* arrêt *m* sur un homme; *Rugby Fb:* plaquage *m*; (*b*) entreprise *f* (d'une besogne).
tacky[1] ['tæki], *a.* collant; (vernis) presque sec; **to allow the adhesive to get t.,** attendre que l'adhésif soit prêt à coller.
tacky[2], *a. NAm: F:* (*of house, appearance, etc.*) piteux, minable; (*of pers.*) chétif, piètre (de sa personne).
tact [tækt], *s.* tact *m*; entregent *m*, savoir-vivre *m*; adresse *f*, doigté *m*, savoir-faire *m*; **to have t., great t.,** avoir beaucoup de tact; **to show t.,** faire preuve de tact; **a matter requiring t.,** une question de doigté; **to use words with t.,** ménager ses paroles; **to use t. in dealing with s.o.,** ménager qn; **if you use t. he will accept,** si vous y mettez des formes il acceptera; **the job requires t. (in handling people),** cet emploi demande de l'entregent; **to be lacking in t.,** manquer de tact, de doigté.
tactful ['tæktful], *a.* (homme) de tact; **to be t.,** avoir du tact; être plein de tact; **very t. speech,** discours plein de tact; **I'll drop him a t. hint,** je vais lui en toucher quelques mots délicats.
tactfully ['tæktfuli], *adv.* avec tact; avec délicatesse; avec ménagement(s); délicatement; **to deal t. with s.o.,** ménager qn.
tactfulness ['tæktfulnis], *s.* (*of pers.*) tact *m*; (*of behaviour*) délicatesse *f*.
tactic ['tæktik], *s.* tactique *f*, manœuvre *f*.
tactical ['tæktikl], *a.* **1.** tactique; *Mil: etc:* **t. exercises,** évolutions *f* tactiques; **t. bombing,** bombardement *m* tactique; **t. methods,** procédés *m* de combat; **t. aircraft,** avions *m* tactiques; **t. mistake,** erreur *f* (de) tactique. **2.** (*of pers., conduct*) adroit; qui fait preuve de bonne tactique.
tactically ['tæktik(ə)li], *adv.* en (bonne) tactique; **t. speaking it was wrong, it was wrong t.,** du point de vue de la tactique, c'était une erreur.
tactician [tæk'tiʃ(ə)n], *s. Mil: etc:* tacticien, -ienne.
tactics ['tæktiks], *s.pl.* (*usu. with sg. const.*) *Mil: etc:* tactique *f*; **combined arms t.,** tactique générale; **harassing t.,** tactique de harcèlement; **to resort to new t.,** avoir recours à une tactique nouvelle; **it was the wrong t.,** c'était une erreur de tactique.
tactile ['tæktail], *a.* **1.** (perception, corpuscule, poil, etc.) tactile. **2.** tactile, tangible.
tactility [tæk'tiliti], *s.* tactilité *f*.
tactism ['tæktizm], *s. Biol:* tactisme *m.*
tactless ['tæktlis], *a.* (*a*) (*of pers.*) dépourvu de tact, sans tact; qui manque de savoir-faire, d'entregent, de doigté; indiscret; (*b*) **t. question,** question indiscrète.
tactlessly ['tæktlisli], *adv.* sans tact, indiscrètement.
tactlessness ['tæktlisnis], *s.* manque *m* de tact; indiscrétion *f*, indélicatesse *f*.
tactual ['tæktjuəl], *a.* tactuel, tactile.
tactuality [tæktju'æliti], *s.* tactualité *f*.
tactually ['tæktjuəli], *adv.* par le toucher.
tadpole ['tædpoul], *s. Amph:* têtard *m.*
tael [teil], *s. Num:* tael *m.*
Taenarus ['ti:nərəs], *Pr.n. A.Geog:* **Cape T.,** le cap Ténare.
taenia, *pl.* **-iae** ['ti:niə, -ii:], *s.* **1.** *Med:* ténia *m*, tænia *m*, ver *m* solitaire. **2.** *Arch:* ténie *f*. **3.** *Gr.Ant:* ténia; bandeau *m* (pour les cheveux). **4.** *Surg:* ligature *f* en ruban.
taeniasis [ti:'naiəsis], *s. Med:* téniasis *m.*
taeni(i)cide ['ti:ni(i)said], **taenifuge** ['ti:nifju:dʒ], *a. & s. Med:* (médicament) ténifuge (*m*).
Taenioglossa [ti:niou'glɔsə], *s.pl. Moll:* ténioglosses *m.*

taenite ['ti:nait], *s. Miner:* ténite *f.*

taffeta ['tæfitə], *s. Tex:* taffetas *m;* **grained t.,** poult-de-soie *m;* **t. dress,** robe de, en, taffetas.

taffrail ['tæfreil], *s. N.Arch:* (lisse *f* de) couronnement *m* (de la poupe).

taffy[1] ['tæfi], *s. NAm:* **1.** (pâte à) berlingot(s) (fait(s) avec de la mélasse). **2.** *P:* flagornerie *f,* eau bénite de cour.

Taffy[2], *s. F:* Gallois *m.*

tafia ['tæfi:ə], *s.* tafia *m.*

tag[1] [tæg], *s.* **1.** (*a*) morceau *m* (de ruban, d'étoffe, de draperie) qui pend; *Husb:* flocon souillé (de la toison d'un mouton); *Tex:* **t. wool,** bourre *f* de laine; (*b*) attache *f;* tirant *m* (de botte); (*c*) (i) (*showing price, name, size, etc.*) fiche *f,* étiquette *f* mobile; *U.S:* **(parking) t.,** contravention *f, F:* papillon *m;* (ii) *U.S:* **dog t.,** plaque *f* d'identité d'un chien; *F:* d'un militaire; *Aut:* **license t.,** plaque d'immatriculation; (*d*) *NAm:* insigne *m,* cocarde *f;* **t. day,** jour *m* de vente d'insignes, jour de quête, pour une œuvre de bienfaisance; (*e*) *Cmptr:* **t. bit,** bit *m* drapeau; (*f*) ferret *m,* fer *m* (de lacet, etc.); (*g*) (bout *m* de la) queue (d'un animal); *Vet:* **t. sore,** excoriation pustuleuse (sur les queues des moutons); (*h*) *NAm: Fish:* bout d'oripeau, etc., attaché au leurre. **2.** (*a*) *Th:* (i) discours adressé au public après la représentation; (ii) *F:* **t. (line),** mot *m* de la fin; (*b*) *Lit:* cheville (ajoutée à un vers). **3.** (*a*) citation banale; aphorisme *m;* cliché *m;* **old t.,** vieille rengaine; **as the old t. has it,** comme dit le vieux dicton; **one of his favourite tags,** une de ses expressions favorites; (*b*) *NAm: Com:* devise *f,* slogan *m;* (*c*) refrain *m* (d'une chanson, d'un poème). **4. t. end,** (i) bout (d'un morceau d'étoffe, etc.); bout décommis (d'un cordage); témoin *m* (d'un cordage neuf); mouchure (coupée d'un cordage); *F:* restes *mpl* (d'un gigot, etc.); (ii) queue (de l'hiver, d'une affaire, etc.); bribes *fpl* (d'une conversation).

tag[2], *v.* **(tagged) 1.** *v.tr.* (*a*) aiguilleter, ferrer (un lacet); (*b*) attacher une fiche à (un paquet); étiqueter (des marchandises, un politicien, etc.); **tagged teabag,** sachet de thé à fiche, à étiquette; *Atom.Ph:* **to t. an atom,** marquer un atome; *U.S:* **to t. a car,** attacher une contravention, *F:* un papillon, à une voiture; *U.S: P:* (*of criminal*) **to get tagged,** se faire pincer, choper; (*c*) *F:* **to t. sth. on to sth.,** attacher, ajouter, qch. à qch.; **a few old (newspaper) articles tagged together,** quelques vieux articles cousus ensemble, cousus de gros fil; (*d*) *Husb:* enlever les flocons souillés à (un mouton). **2.** *v.i.* **to t. along,** traîner **(behind s.o.,** derrière qn); **to t. at s.o.'s heels, after s.o.,** suivre qn (de près), être sur les talons de qn; **to t. on to s.o.,** s'attacher, *F:* coller, à qn; **to t. around with s.o.,** rouler sa bosse avec qn.

tag[3], *s.* (jeu *m* de) chat *m;* **to play t.,** jouer à, au, chat; **cross t.,** chat coupé; **long t.,** chat perché; **ball t.,** balle *f* au chasseur.

tag[4], *v.tr.* **(tagged)** toucher (qn) au jeu de chat; *Baseball:* éliminer (un coureur) en le touchant avec la balle.

tagetes [tæ'dʒi:ti:z], *s. Bot:* tagète *m;* tagetes *m,* tagette *m.*

tagger[1] ['tægər], *s.* poursuivant, -ante, chat *m* (au jeu de chat).

tagger[2], *s.* tôle de fer étamée; **black t.,** tôle noire.

tagging ['tægiŋ], *s. Games:* (*baseball*) élimination *f* (d'un coureur en le touchant avec la balle).

tagliatelli [tɑ:ljɑ:'teli:], *s.pl. Cu:* tagliatelles *f.*

tagma, *pl.* **-mata** ['tægmə, -mətə], *s. Nat.Hist:* tagme *m; Ent:* **cephalic t.,** tagme céphalique; *F:* tête *f.*

taguan ['tɑ:gwɑ:n], *s. Z:* pétauriste *m,* taguan *m.*

Tagus (the) [ðə'teigəs], *Pr.n. Geog:* le Tage.

Tahiti [tɑ:'hi:ti], *Pr.n. Geog:* Tahiti *m.*

Tahitian [tɑ:'hi:ʃən]. **1.** *Geog:* (*a*) *a.* tahitien; (*b*) *s.* Tahitien, -ienne. **2.** *s. Ling:* tahitien *m.*

tahr [tɑ:r], *s. Z:* tahr *m;* **Himalayan, Nilgiri, Arabian, t.,** tahr de l'Himalaya, des Nilgiris, d'Oman.

tai [tai], *s. Ich:* taï *m.*

taiga ['taigɑ:], *s. Geog:* taïga *f.*

tail[1] [teil], *s.* **1.** (*a*) queue *f* (d'animal, de poisson, etc.), balai *m* (de faucon); (*of peacock*) **to spread its t.,** faire la roue; **dog's t.,** queue, *Ven:* fouet *m,* du chien; **the dog's wagging his t.,** le chien agite sa queue; *F:* **the tail's wagging the dog,** les subordonnés l'emportent sur les chefs; **with his t. between his legs,** (i) (*of dog*) la queue entre les jambes; (ii) (*of pers.*) en serrant les fesses; l'oreille basse; tout penaud; *F:* (*of pers.*) **sitting on his t.,** assis sur son derrière, sur ses fesses; **to keep one's t. up,** ne pas se laisser abattre; ne pas se décourager; garder le sourire; **to have one's t. up,** être plein d'entrain; **to turn t.,** s'enfuir; tourner, montrer, les talons; prendre fuite; montrer, tourner, le dos à l'ennemi; **the sting is in the t.,** à la queue gît le venin; **story with a sting in the t.,** histoire avec une méchanceté finale; *Anat: Z:* **t. base,** croupion *m;* **t. bone,** coccyx *m; Orn:* **t. feather,** (penne) rectrice *f; Z:* **t. flukes,** nageoire caudale de la queue (d'une baleine); *Harn:* **t. case, leather,** trousse *f,* trousse-queue *m inv* (de cheval); (*b*) queue (de cerf-volant, d'aile de papillon, de lettre, de note musicale); queue d'orientation (d'un moulin à vent); mancherons *mpl* (d'une charrue); natte *f* (de cheveux); chevelure *f* (de comète); *Cost:* **t. of a skirt,** queue, traîne *f,* d'une jupe; **t. of a shirt,** pan *m* de chemise; **tails of a coat, coat tails,** queue, basques *f,* pans, d'un habit; **to wear tails,** porter l'habit à queue; *F:* mettre sa queue-de-morue; (*c*) *Av:* queue (d'un avion); **t. slide, dive,** glissade *f* sur la queue, sur l'empennage; **t. spin,** (descente *f* en) vrille *f; F:* (*of pers.*) **to go, get, into a t. spin,** s'affoler, paniquer; **t. boom,** longeron *m* de fuselage; **t. fin,** (plan *m* de) dérive *f;* **t. plane,** plan fixe horizontal; **t. unit,** empennage *m;* **t. wheel,** roulette *f* de queue; (*d*) arrière *m* (d'une voiture, d'un ski, etc.); **to walk at the t. of the cart,** marcher derrière la charrette; **there was another car close on my t.,** une autre voiture me suivait de près; **to be on s.o.'s t.,** (i) suivre qn de près; (ii) (*of detective*) filer qn; **vessel heavy by the t.,** vaisseau à queue lourde; **we caught only the t. of the storm,** nous n'avons essuyé que la fin de l'orage; **t. of a procession,** queue d'un défilé; **t. end,** extrémité *f* arrière, queue (d'un défilé, etc.); fin (d'un orage); *Turf:* **to come in at the t. end,** arriver en queue, *F:* dans les choux; **t. wind,** vent arrière; **t. light,** (i) *Aut:* lanterne *f* arrière; (ii) *Rail:* (*also* **t. lamp),** feu *m* (d')arrière; lanterne à feu rouge; lanterne, fanal *m,* de queue; *Min: etc:* **t. rope,** câble-queue *m, pl.* câbles-queues, câble *m* de queue (d'un wagonnet, etc.); **t. pipe,** (i) *Hyd.E:* tubulure *f* d'aspiration (d'une pompe); (ii) *Aut:* tuyau *m* de sortie (des gaz d'échappement); *I.C.E:* (*of jet engine*) tuyère *f* d'échappement; *Mus:* **t. pin,** bouton *m* (de queue de violon); *Mch:* **t. rod,** tige de piston prolongée; guide *m* de piston; *Mec.E:* **t. stock, block,** poupée *f* mobile, contre-pointe *f, pl.* contre-pointes (de tour); **t. end (of a lathe),** fusée *f* de l'arbre; *N.Arch:* **t. shaft,** extrémité de l'arbre; **t. shaft bracket,** porte-hélice *m inv;* (*e*) pied *m* (d'une page, etc.); *Bookb:* **t. margin,** marge inférieure; *Const:* **t. of a slate,** chef *m* de base d'une ardoise; **t. of a masonry block,** queue d'un moellon; (*f*) **the t. of one's eye,** le coin de l'œil; *O:* **to look at s.o. out of the t. of one's eye,** regarder qn de côté; (*g*) *Hyd.E:* aval *m* (d'une écluse); **t. bay,** bief *m* d'aval, de fuite; **t. gate,** porte *f* d'aval; **t. lock,** écluse de fuite; **t. water,** eau *f* d'aval; (*h*) suite *f,* escorte *f* (d'un chef de clan); adhérents *mpl* (d'un chef politique); (*i*) **the t. of the class, of the team,** la queue de la classe, de l'équipe; les faiblards. **2.** *F:* fileur *m;* **we've got a t.,** quelqu'un nous file. **3.** (*of coin*) pile *f,* revers *m.*

tail[2], *v.tr. & i.*

I. *v.tr.* **1.** (*a*) mettre une queue à (un cerf-volant, etc.); (*b*) **to t. sth. on to sth.,** attacher qch. derrière qch. **2.** (*a*) couper la queue à (un agneau); (*b*) enlever, ôter, les queues (des groseilles, etc.); équeuter (des cerises, etc.); égrapper (des groseilles). **3.** *F:* (*of detective, etc.*) filer (qn).

II. *v.i.* **1. to t. after s.o.,** (i) suivre qn de près; (ii) (*of several persons*) suivre qn à la queue leu leu. **2. to t. on a rope,** se mettre sur, à, une manœuvre (derrière les autres).

III. (*compound verbs*) **1. tail away,** *v.i.* (*a*) (*of competitors in a race, etc.*) s'espacer, s'égrener; (*of column on the march*) s'allonger; (*b*) diminuer, décroître, s'amoindrir; **her voice tailed away dismally,** sa voix s'éteignit en accents mornes; (*c*) (*of novel, etc.*) finir en queue de poisson.

2. tail in. (*a*) *v.tr.* encastrer (une poutre); (*b*) *v.i.* (*of beam*) s'encastrer.

3. tail off, *v.i.* (*a*) = TAIL AWAY; (*b*) s'enfuir.

4. tail on, *v.i.* se mettre à la queue, prendre la queue.

5. tail out, *v.i.* (*of runners, etc.*) s'espacer, s'égrener.

6. tail up, *v.i.* (*of aircraft*) piquer du nez; (*of whale*) faire la sonde, sonder.

tail[3], *Jur:* **1.** *s.* clause *f* de substitution; **heir, estate, in t.,** héritier *m* par substitution ; bien substitué. **2.** *a.* **estate t.,** bien substitué.

tail[4], *v.tr. Jur:* **to t. an estate (on s.o.),** substituer un bien (au profit de qn); **tailed estate,** majorat *m;* bien substitué; bien indisponible, grevé, majoraté.

tailboard ['teilbɔ:d], *s.* layon *m,* planche *f,* marchepied *m* (d'une charrette).

tailed [teild]. **1.** (*a*) *Nat.Hist:* caudifère, caudé; à queue; (*b*) (*with adj. or num. prefixed, e.g.*) **long-t.,** à longue queue; longicaude; (*c*) *Her:* caudé. **2.** *Pros:* **t. rhyme,** rime couée.

tailer ['teilər], *s. NAm: F:* fileur *m.*

tailgate[1] ['teilgeit], *s.* (*a*) porte *f* à rabattement arrière (d'un camion); (*b*) hayon *m* arrière (relevable) (d'une voiture).

tailgate[2], *v.tr. NAm: F:* suivre (une voiture) de (trop) près; *F:* coller (une voiture).

tail-in ['teilin], *s. Const:* encastrement *m* (d'une poutre, etc.).

tailing ['teiliŋ], *s.* **1.** (*a*) (i) coupe *f* des queues (aux agneaux); (ii) équeutage *m* (des cerises); égrappage *m* (des groseilles); (*b*) *Petr:* **t. out,** équeutage. **2.** *Const:* bout *m* (d'une pierre) en saillie. **3. tailings,** (i) *Min: etc:* résidus *m,* schlamms *mpl,* queue *f;* refus *m* de broyage; (ii) *Mill:* grenailles *f;* (iii) *Dist: etc:* produits *m* de queue.

tailless ['teillis], *a.* (*a*) sans queue; *Nat.Hist:* écaudé, acaudé, anoure; (*b*) *Her:* (lion, etc.) diffamé.

tailor[1] ['teilər], *s.* **1.** tailleur *m* (d'habits); **tailor's workshop,** atelier *m* de confection; **ladies' t.,** tailleur pour dames; **tailor's chalk,** craie *f* de tailleur, de Meudon; *Anat:* **tailor('s) muscle,** couturier *m.* **2.** *O:* = TELLER 4.

tailor[2]. **1.** *v.i.* exercer le métier de tailleur. **2.** *v.tr.* (*a*) faire, façonner (un complet, etc.); **well tailored overcoat,** pardessus de facture soignée; **(woman's) tailored suit,** (costume *m*) tailleur *m;* **tailored dress,** robe de coupe simple et bien ajustée; **tailored (fitting) shirt,** chemise cintrée; (*b*) *O:* **to be tailored by a reliable firm,** être habillé par un tailleur de confiance; (*c*) **cloth difficult to t.,** drap difficile à travailler; (*with passive force*) **material that tailors well,** tissu qui se façonne bien; (*d*) **to t. sth. for a special purpose,** faire, façonner, qch. pour un usage spécial; **tailored to suit the customer,** fait sur commande, sur demande; *F:* **it's just tailored for the job,** cela fera l'affaire à merveille. **3.** *v.tr. Ven: F: A:* abîmer (le gibier en l'abattant).

tailorbird ['teiləbə:d], *s. Orn:* fauvette couturière; couturier *m;* cisticole couturière.

tailoress [teilə'res], *s.f.* tailleuse-couturière, *pl.* tailleuses-couturières.

tailoring ['teiləriŋ], *s.* **1.** métier *m* de tailleur; **he went in for t.,** il s'est fait tailleur. **2.** ouvrage *m* de tailleur; **to do dressmaking and t.,** faire le flou et le tailleur.

tailormade ['teiləmeid], *a.* (*of suit, etc.*) fait sur mesure; **(woman's) t. (suit),** (costume *m*) tailleur *m;* (*b*) adapté aux besoins particuliers de l'utilisateur; (outil) spécial, façonné pour un usage spécial.

tailpiece ['teilpi:s], *s.* **1.** queue *f;* contre-tige *f, pl.* contre-tiges (de piston); crépine *f* (de pompe); traverse *f* (d')arrière (de locomotive). **2.** *Mus:* cordier *m* (de violon, etc.). **3.** *Typ:* cul-de-lampe *m* (en fin de chapitre), *pl.* culs-de-lampe; vignette *f.*

tailrace ['teilreis], *s. Hyd.E:* bief *m,* biez *m,* d'aval, de fuite (d'un moulin); écluse *f* de fuite.

tain [tein], *s.* tain *m* (de miroir).

taint[1] [teint], *s.* **1.** (*a*) corruption *f,* infection *f;* (*b*) **the t. of sin,** la tache, la souillure, du péché; **free from t.,** pur; sans péché. **2.** tare *f* héréditaire (d'insanité, etc.). **3.** trace *f* (d'infection, etc.); **book with no t. of bias,** livre sans trace de préjugés. **4. boar t.,** odeur sexuelle du verrat.

taint[2]. **1.** *v.tr.* infecter (l'air); infecter, vicier, corrompre (les esprits, les mœurs); souiller (l'âme); gâter, corrompre, altérer (la nourriture); **stock that is tainted with insanity,** sang qui est touché, atteint, a une tare, d'insanité. **2.** *v.i.* se corrompre; se gâter; s'altérer; **fish taints quickly,** le poisson s'altère vite.

tainted ['teintid], *a.* (*a*) infecté, corrompu; **t. heredity,** hérédité chargée; **born of t. stock,** né d'un sang impur; *Jur:* **t. with fraud,** entaché de dol; (*b*) (*of meat*) qui a un mauvais goût, faisandé; **t. milk,** lait qui a une odeur, saveur, anormale; (*c*) *Ind:* **t. goods,** marchandises issues de main-d'œuvre non-syndiquée.

taintless ['teintlis], *a.* sans tache; pur, immaculé.

taipan ['taipæn], *s. Rept:* taipan *m.*

taira ['tairə], *s. Z:* taïra *m.*

Taiwan [tai'wɑ:n], *Pr.n. Geog:* (l'île de) Taïwan.

Taiwanese [taiwə'ni:z], *a. & s. Geog:* (originaire, natif) de Taïwan.

takahe ['tɑ:kəhi], *s. Orn:* notornis *m.*

take[1] [teik], *s.* **1.** (*a*) *Cin:* prise *f* de vues; (*b*) *NAm: F:* **to be on the t.,** être à la recherche (i) de choses à chiper, (ii) de la chance de prendre qn au dépourvu. **2.** (*a*) prise (de gibier, poisson); (*b*) *NAm:* recette *f,* produit *m* (d'un magasin, etc.). **3.** *Typ:* (*a*) paquet *m* (de composition); (*b*) pige *f* (de copie à composer). **4.** *Hort: Surg:* greffe *f,* inoculation *f,* qui a pris.

take[2], *v.* (*p.t.* **took** [tuk]; *p.p.* **taken** ['teik(ə)n]) prendre.

I. *v.tr.* **1.** (*a*) **to t. sth. in one's hand,** prendre qch. dans la main; **to t. sth. on one's back,** prendre, charger, qch. sur son dos; **to t. sth. again,** reprendre qch.; (*b*) **to t. sth. from s.o.,** enlever, prendre, ôter, qch. à qn; **someone has taken my umbrella,** on m'a pris mon parapluie; **excuse me, but haven't you taken my hat?** pardon, monsieur, est-ce que vous ne vous êtes pas trompé de chapeau? **to t. one number from another,** ôter, retrancher, soustraire, un nombre d'un autre; **to t. sth. from the table, from under a chair,** prendre qch. sur la table, sous une chaise; **to t. sth. from, out of, a drawer,** retirer qch. d'un tiroir; prendre qch. dans un tiroir; **to t. a saucepan off the fire,** retirer une casserole du feu; **to t. the lid off sth.,** enlever, ôter, le couvercle de qch.; **here's a five-pound note, t. it out of that,** voici un billet de cinq livres, payez-vous; **t. your hands out of your pockets,** ôtez, sortez les mains de vos poches; **books must not be taken out of the reading room,** il est défendu de sortir les livres de la salle de lecture; (*c*) **to t. (hold of) s.o., sth.,** saisir, empoigner, mettre la main sur, se saisir de, s'emparer de, qn, qch.; **to take s.o. by the throat,** saisir qn à la gorge; **she took my arm,** elle m'a pris le bras; **he took her in his arms,** il l'a prise dans ses bras; *F:* **to t. a woman,** prendre une femme; **to t. one's courage in both hands,** prendre son courage à deux mains; **to t. an opportunity,** saisir, prendre, une occasion; **to t. the opportunity to do sth., of doing sth.,** profiter de l'occasion pour faire qch.; saisir, prendre, l'occasion de faire qch.; prendre occasion pour faire qch.; **to t. a chance,** risquer les chances; **to t. one's chance,** saisir l'occasion; (*d*) prendre (une ville, forteresse); **to t. a fish, rabbit,** prendre, attraper, un poisson, lapin; **to t. s.o. prisoner,** faire qn prisonnier; **no prisoners were taken,** on n'a pas fait de prisonniers; **to t. s.o. in the act,** prendre qn en flagrant délit, sur le fait, *F:* la main dans le sac; **to t. s.o. by surprise,** prendre qn à l'improviste, surprendre qn; **the devil t. him,** que le diable l'emporte! *Chess: etc:* **to t. a piece,** prendre une pièce; **piece in a position to be taken,** pièce en prise; **to be taken with a fit of laughter,** être pris d'un accès de rire; **to be taken ill,** tomber malade; **he was very much taken with the idea,** l'idée lui souriait beaucoup, l'enchantait; **I was not taken with him,** il ne m'a pas plu; il ne m'a pas été sympathique; il ne m'a pas fait bonne impression; (*e*) **to t. a passage from a book,** emprunter un passage à un livre; **word taken from the Latin,** mot emprunté du latin; **to t. an idea from an author,** puiser une idée chez un auteur. **2.** (*a*) louer (une maison), prendre, louer (une voiture); **to t. lodgings,** prendre un appartement garni; (*b*) **to t. tickets,** prendre des billets; **all the seats are taken,** toutes les places sont prises; (*in railway compartment*) le compartiment est au complet; (*of seat, table*) **taken,** occupé; **to t. a secretary,** prendre un, une, secrétaire; **to t. a paper,** prendre (régulièrement) un journal; (*of yearly subscriber, etc.*) être abonné à un journal; **what paper do you t.?** quel journal lisez-vous? **to t. paying guests,** recevoir, prendre, des pensionnaires; **to t. pupils,** (i) prendre des élèves (en pension); (ii) donner des leçons particulières; (*c*) prendre (le train, le bateau); **to t. a seat,** prendre un siège; s'asseoir; **t. your seats!** prenez vos places! *Rail:* en voiture! (*d*) **he took the road to London,** il a pris la route de Londres; **the procession took the Mall,** le cortège emprunta le Mall; **t. the first street to the right,** prenez la première rue à droite; **t. the turning on the left,** prenez à gauche; **to t. the wrong road,** se tromper de chemin; *Sp:* **to t. an obstacle,** franchir, sauter, un obstacle; **to t. a corner at full speed,** prendre un virage à toute vitesse; (*e*) **to t. information,** prendre des renseignements; **to t. legal advice,** consulter un avocat, un avoué; prendre conseil; (*f*) **to t. holy orders,** recevoir les ordres. **3.** (*a*) gagner, remporter (le prix); **to t. the first prize in Latin,** obtenir le premier prix de latin; *Cards:* **to t. a trick, the odd trick,** faire une levée; faire le trick; (*b*) (i) **to t. one's degree,** passer son examen de licence; **to t., be taking, law,** faire son droit; **I didn't t. Latin at school,** je n'ai pas fait de latin au lycée; **to t. an examination,** se présenter à un examen; passer un examen; (ii) **to t. a good degree** = être reçu avec mention; (*c*) *Com: etc:* **to t. so much a week,** se faire tant, faire une recette de tant, par semaine. **4.** prendre (de la nourriture, du poison); (*of fish*) **to t. the hook, the bait,** prendre l'hameçon; **to t. something to drink,** prendre quelque chose à boire; **just t. a sip of that,** goûtez-moi ça; **to t. a meal,** faire un repas; **he takes his meals in a hotel,** il prend ses repas à l'hôtel; **do you t. sugar?** prenez-vous du sucre? **I can't t. whisky,** je ne supporte pas le whisky; *F:* **he can't t. his drink,** il ne sait pas boire; **he can t. his drink,** il a la tête solide, porte bien le vin; **to t. medicine,** prendre un médicament; **to be well shaken before taking,** agiter la bouteille avant de s'en servir; **not to be taken internally,** médicament pour usage externe; *P:* **I'm not taking any!** je ne marche pas! très peu pour moi! on ne me la fait pas! **5.** (*a*) **to t. a walk, journey,** faire une promenade, un voyage; **to t. a nap,** faire un petit somme; **to t. a bath,** prendre un bain; **to t. a holiday,** prendre un congé; partir en vacances; **to t. three days' holiday,** prendre trois jours de congé; **to t. a few steps,** faire quelques pas; *Fb:* **penalty shot taken by X,** penalty botté par X; **to t. a cast of a medal,** tirer un plâtre d'une médaille; **to t. a print from a negative,** tirer une épreuve d'un cliché; **to t. notes,** prendre des notes; (*of secretary*) **to t. letters, dictation,** prendre des lettres (en sténo); **to t. barometer readings,** faire des lectures barométriques; *Surv: etc:* **to t. an angle,** observer un angle; **to t. breath,** reprendre haleine; **to t. fire,** prendre feu; s'allumer, s'enflammer; **to t. effect,** produire son effet; (*b*) **to t. a photograph,** prendre une photo(graphie); **to have one's photograph taken,** se faire photographier; (*with passive force*) **he doesn't t. well,** il n'est pas photogénique; **colour that doesn't t. well,** couleur qui ne réussit pas en photo; (*c*) **to t. sth. apart, to pieces,** démonter qch. **6.** *Ecc:* **to t. a service,** diriger un office; *Sch:* **he takes them in English,** il fait la classe d'anglais; **he's taking English,** il suit le cours d'anglais; **Mr Martin is taking the sixth form,** Monsieur Martin prend la classe de première. **7.** (*a*) prendre, accepter, recevoir; *Ten:* **to t. the service,** recevoir le service; **to t. a volley low,** reprendre une volée près du sol; **t. what he offers you,** prenez ce qu'il vous offre; **I'll t. it,** je suis preneur; **t. it or leave it!** c'est à prendre ou à laisser; **anyone will t. money,** tout le monde accepte de l'argent; **to t. a blow on one's arm,** recevoir un coup sur le bras; **to take a beating, a hiding, a thrashing,** recevoir une rossée, raclée; **t. that (and that)!** attrape (ça et ça)! **if The** *Times* **takes my article,** si le *Times* accepte mon article; **to t. no denial,** ne pas accepter de refus; (*at bank*) **will you t. it in five pound notes or singles?** voulez-vous toucher cette somme en billets de cinq livres ou d'une livre? **how much less will you t.?** combien voulez-vous en rabattre? **what will you t. for it?** combien en voulez-vous? *St. Exch:* **to t. for the call,** vendre à prime; **to t. a bet,** tenir un pari; **to t. all responsibility,** assumer, prendre sur soi, se charger de, toute la responsabilité; **to t. responsibility for an action,** avouer une action; **I took it upon myself to do it,** j'ai pris la responsabilité de le faire; **taking one thing, year, with another,** l'un dans l'autre, une année dans l'autre; **taking all in all,** à tout prendre; **we must t. things as we find them, as they come,** il faut prendre les choses comme elles sont; **you must t. me as I am,** il faut me prendre comme je suis; **you can t. it from me that it will never happen,** je suis à même de vous affirmer que cela n'arrivera jamais; **t. it from me!** croyez-m'en! puisque je vous le dis! **we must t. it at that,** il faut bien vous en croire; **to t. s.o. seriously,** prendre qn au sérieux; **to t. s.o. the wrong way,** mal comprendre qn, comprendre qn à rebours; **one doesn't know how to t. him,** on ne sait jamais comment il faut prendre ce qu'il dit; **I wonder how he'll t. it,** je me demande quelle tête il fera; **he can't t. a joke,** il n'entend pas la plaisanterie; *F:* **he can't t. it,** il manque de cran, n'est pas capable de tenir le coup; **he can t. it,** il sait encaisser, il tient le coup; **I can't t. any more,** je ne peux plus; **I can't t. any more of him,** je ne peux plus le supporter; **expression that may be taken in the wrong sense,** expression qui peut se prendre en mauvaise part; *F:* **I don't t. you, your meaning,** je ne saisis pas votre pensée, je ne vous saisis pas bien; (*b*) **parchment that will not t. the ink,** parchemin qui ne prend pas l'encre; **cotton does not t. dyes well,** le coton est réfractaire à la teinture; **surface that will t. a high polish,** surface qui prend un beau poli; **wood that takes the nails easily,** bois qui accueille bien le clou; (*c*) (*of mare*) **to t. the stallion,** souffrir l'étalon; (*d*) **bus that takes twenty passengers,** autobus qui tient vingt voyageurs; **the car only takes five,** on ne tient pas plus de cinq dans la voiture; **the petrol tank takes 40 litres,** le réservoir à essence a une capacité de 40 litres; **typewriter that takes large sizes of paper,** machine à écrire qui emploie de grands formats; (*of crane, engine, etc.*) **to t. heavy loads,** supporter de fortes charges; **recess to t. the end of a beam,** renfoncement pour loger une poutre; encastrement d'une poutre; **mortises to t. tenons,** mortaises pour recevoir des tenons; *Mec.* **to t. a stress,** résister à une tension, à un effort. **8.** (*a*) prendre, *F:* attraper (une maladie, un rhume); contracter (une maladie); (*b*) **to t. a dislike to s.o.,** prendre qn en aversion, en grippe; **to t. a decision about sth.,** prendre une décision touchant, quant à, qch. **9.** (*a*) **t. (for example) the pensioners,** prenez (par exemple) les, le cas des, retraités; **we'll t. the will for the deed,** l'intention est réputée pour le fait; **to t. the news as, to be, true,** tenir la nouvelle pour vraie; **what time do you t. it to be?** quelle heure pensez-vous qu'il soit? **how old do you t. him to be?** quel âge lui donnez-vous? **I t. it that you agree,** je suppose que vous êtes d'accord; **as I t. it,** selon moi; à mon idée; **let us t. it that it is so,** prenons, mettons, qu'il en soit ainsi; supposons qu'il en soit ainsi; **the French romantic movement, which we may t. to begin about 1820,** le romantisme français, dont nous fixerons les débuts à 1820; (*b*) **to t. one person, one thing, for another,** prendre une personne, une chose, pour une autre; **I took, had taken, you for an Englishman,** je vous croyais anglais; **I am not the person you t. me for,** je ne suis pas la personne que vous croyez; *F:* **what do you t. me for?** pour qui me prenez-vous? **it might be taken for a water colour,** on dirait une aquarelle; **I took her to be our hostess,** je l'ai prise pour notre hôtesse; **I took his silence for consent,** de son silence j'ai présumé son consentement. **10.** (*require*) (*a*) **these old engines t. a great deal of coal,** ces vieilles machines usent, mangent, consument, beaucoup de charbon; **that will t. some explaining,** voilà qui va demander des explications; **the work took some doing,** le travail a été difficile, dur; **it took some finding,** cela a été difficile à trouver; **he takes a lot of coaxing to go out in the evening,** il se fait tirer l'oreille pour sortir le soir; **that will t. a long time,** cela prendra longtemps; **the journey takes five days,** le voyage prend, demande, cinq jours; **it will t. a week,** il faut compter une huitaine; cela prendra huit jours; **it won't t. long,** ce sera tôt fait; cela ne demandera pas longtemps; **it will t. him two hours,** il en a, en aura, pour deux heures; **how long does it t. to go there?** combien de temps faut-il pour y aller? **it would t. volumes, hours, to relate,** il faudrait des volumes, des heures, pour le raconter; **it took us two hours to reach the shore,** nous avons été deux heures à gagner le rivage; **he took three years to write it,** il fut trois ans à l'écrire; **it took me, I took, two years to do it,** j'ai mis deux ans à, pour, le faire; cela m'a pris, m'a demandé, il m'a fallu, deux ans pour le faire; **she takes, it takes her, hours to dress,** elle demeure des heures à s'habiller; il lui faut des heures, elle prend des heures, pour s'habiller; **it took four men to hold him,** il a fallu le tenir à quatre; **it takes a clever man to do that,** bien habile qui peut le faire; **it takes a poet to translate poetry,** pour traduire la poésie il faut un poète, il n'y a qu'un poète; *F:* **he hasn't got what it takes to be a leader,** il lui manque ce qu'il faut pour être un chef; *F:* **she's got what it takes,** elle a du sex-appeal; (*b*) *Gram:* **verb that takes a preposition,** verbe qui veut la préposition; **noun that takes an "s" in the plural,** nom qui prend un "s" au pluriel; (*c*) **to t. tens in shoes,** chausser du dix; **I take sixes (in gloves, etc.),** j'ai six de pointure. **11.** (*a*) (*lead*) conduire, mener, emmener; prendre (qn avec soi); **to t. s.o. somewhere,** mener, conduire, qn dans un endroit; **the bus, this street, will t. you to the station,** l'autobus, cette rue, vous mènera à la gare; **to t. s.o. to his room,** mener qn à sa chambre; **to t. s.o. into a corner,** prendre qn dans un coin; **to t. oneself to bed,** aller se coucher; **he was taken to the police station,** il a été conduit au poste; **to t. s.o. into a place,** faire entrer qn à, dans, un endroit; **to t. s.o. abroad,** emmener qn à l'étranger; **to t. the dog for a walk,** promener le chien; **to t. s.o. (along) with one,** prendre, emmener, qn avec soi; **t. someone with you,** faites-vous accompagner; *F:* **he'll do to t. along,** (i) c'est un homme sûr; (ii) c'est un costaud qui ne reculera devant rien; **to t. s.o. to see sth.,** mener qn voir qch.; **to t. s.o. over a house,** faire visiter une maison à qn; **to t. s.o. over, round, a museum,** faire faire la visite d'un musée à qn; **to t. s.o. across the road,** conduire qn de l'autre côté de la rue; **to t. s.o. out of his way,** écarter qn de sa route; *F:* **what (ever) took him there?** qu'allait-il faire dans cette galère? **to t. s.o. through the first two books of the Aeneid,** faire étudier à qn les deux premiers livres de l'Énéide; (*b*) (*carry*) (i) **to t. sth. to s.o., to t. sth. somewhere,** porter qch. à qn, à, dans, un endroit; **I'll t. the book (along) to his house,** je vais porter le livre chez lui; **to t. provisions (with one),** emporter des provisions, de quoi manger; **to have one's luggage taken to the station,** faire porter ses bagages à la gare; (*of ambulance*) **to t. s.o. to hospital,** transporter qn à l'hôpital; **it was I who took the news to him,** c'est moi qui lui ai porté la nouvelle; **main that takes water to a district,** conduit qui amène l'eau dans un quartier; **to t. a road across the desert,** construire une route à travers le désert; *F:* **you can't t. it with you,** vous n'emporterez pas votre fortune avec vous; (ii) **to t. a hammer to sth.,** donner des coups, un coup, de marteau à qch.; **his father took a stick to him,** son père lui a donné des coups de bâton.

II. *v.i.* **1.** (*a*) avoir du succès; réussir; prendre; **his last novel didn't t.,** son dernier roman n'a pas eu de succès, n'a pas pris; **this play won't t.,** cette pièce ne prendra pas, ne passera pas la rampe; (*b*) *Med:* **the vaccine has not taken,** le vaccin n'a pas pris; *Hort:* **before the graft has taken,** avant que la greffe ait pris; (*c*) **the fire took at once,** le feu a pris tout de suite; *Cu:* **the mayonnaise hasn't taken,** la mayonnaise n'a pas pris; *NAm:* **the pond has taken,** l'étang a gelé, a pris (*esp.* à une épaisseur suffisante pour porter des patineurs). 2. (*of sails*) prendre le vent.

III. (*compound verbs*) **1. take about,** *v.tr.* promener, escorter (qn).

2. take after, *v.i.* **to t. after s.o.,** ressembler à qn, tenir de qn; **his son doesn't t. after him in any way,** son fils n'a rien de lui.

3. take away, *v.tr.* (*a*) enlever, emporter (qch.); soustraire (un document, etc.); emmener (qn); **sandwiches to t. away,** sandwichs à emporter; (*on book in library*) **not to be taken away,** exclu du prêt; (*b*) **to t. away a knife from a child,** ôter un couteau à un enfant; (*c*) **to t. away sth. from sth.,** ôter, retrancher, qch. de qch.; (*d*) **his pension has been taken away,** on lui a retiré sa retraite; (*e*) **to t. a child away from school,** retirer un enfant du collège; (*f*) **what takes you away so soon?** qu'est-ce qui vous fait partir de si bonne heure? **if your father should be taken away (from you),** si votre père venait à vous manquer, venait à mourir.

4. take back, *v.tr.* (*a*) reconduire, remmener (qn, un cheval, etc.); **he was taken back to prison,** il fut remmené en prison; **the boatman will t. us back,** le batelier nous repassera; **that takes me back to my childhood,** cela me rappelle mon enfance; (*b*) **to t. a book back to s.o.,** reporter un livre à qn; (*c*) *Typ:* transférer (un mot) à la ligne précédente; (*d*) reprendre (un ancien employé, un cadeau, *Com:* les invendus); (*e*) **to t. back one's word,** retirer sa parole; revenir sur sa parole, sa promesse; **I t. back what I said,** je retire ce que j'ai dit; **I t. it all back,** mettons que je n'aie rien dit.

5. take down, *v.tr.* (*a*) **to t. down a pot of jam from a shelf,** prendre un pot de confiture sur une planche; **to t. down a picture, a curtain,** descendre, décrocher, un tableau; enlever, décrocher, un rideau; **to t. down s.o.'s trousers,** baisser le pantalon à qn; **to t. down the Christmas decorations,** enlever les décorations de Noël; **to t. down a flagstaff,** abattre un mât de drapeau; **to t. down a wall,** démolir un mur; *Nau:* **to t. down the booms,** amener les mâts de charge; (*b*) démonter, désassembler, déséquiper (une machine); dégréer, désappareiller (une grue); (*c*) *Typ:* **to t. a word down (to the next line),** transférer un mot à la ligne suivante; (*d*) *F:* **to t. s.o. down (a peg or two),** remettre qn à sa place, faire baisser le ton à qn, faire baisser qn de ton, rabattre le caquet à qn, faire mettre de l'eau dans le vin à qn; (*e*) **to t. down s.o.'s name and address,** prendre par écrit, coucher par écrit, noter, inscrire, le nom et l'adresse de qn; **to t. down the number of a car,** relever le numéro d'une voiture; **to t. down a few notes,** prendre quelques notes; **to t. down a letter in shorthand,** prendre une lettre en sténo(graphie), sténographier une lettre; *Jur:* **to t. down an answer,** consigner une réponse par écrit.

6. take in, *v.tr.* (*a*) faire entrer (qn); **to t. a lady in to dinner,** offrir le bras à une dame pour la conduire à table, pour passer à la salle à manger; **to t. in s.o.'s card,** faire passer la carte de qn; (*b*) rentrer (les chaises, le linge, etc.); **to t. in the harvest,** rentrer la moisson; **to t. in coal for the winter,** faire provision de charbon pour l'hiver; *Nau:* (i) **to t. in (a supply of) water,** faire de l'eau; embarquer son eau; (ii) (*of boat*) **to t. in water,** faire eau; avoir une voie d'eau; **my shoes t. in water,** mes souliers prennent l'eau, boivent; *Nau:* **to t. in the boats,** mettre les embarcations en drome; (*c*) (*admit, receive*) **to t. in a refugee, an orphan,** recueillir, donner un asile à, un réfugié, un orphelin; **can you t. me in for a day or two?** pouvez-vous me prendre chez vous, m'héberger, me loger, me recevoir, pour un ou deux jours? **to t. in lodgers, paying guests,** prendre des locataires, des pensionnaires; **to t. in washing,** faire des lessives; (*d*) *A: & NAm:* **to t. in a paper,** prendre (régulièrement) un journal; (*of yearly subscriber, etc.*) être abonné à un journal; (*e*) *St.Exch:* **to t. in stock,** reporter des titres; (*f*) *NAm:* **to t. in money,** encaisser de l'argent; (*g*) **to t. in a seam,** rentrer, reprendre, une couture; **to t. in a sleeve,** serrer une manche; **to t. in a dress,** reprendre une robe; **to t. in a dress at the waist,** rentrer une robe à la taille; *Knit:* **to t. in a round,** diminuer un rang; (*h*) *Nau:* **to t. in a sail,** carguer, ramasser, serrer, rentrer, une voile; **to t. in a reef,** prendre un ris; **to t. in the slack,** embraquer le mou; **to t. in sail,** (i) diminuer de voile(s), carguer la voilure; (ii) *F:* mettre de l'eau dans son vin; (*i*) comprendre, inclure, englober; **inventory that takes in all the contents of the room,** inventaire qui comprend tout ce qu'il y a dans la pièce; **tour which takes in all the important towns of the west country,** excursion qui passe par toutes les villes importantes de l'ouest; **the empire took in all these countries,** l'empire englobait tous ces pays; (*j*) comprendre, se rendre compte de (qch.); **he didn't t. in the full meaning of her words,** il n'a pas très bien compris ce qu'elle voulait dire; **to t. in the situation,** se rendre compte de la situation; juger la situation; **give me time to t. it all in,** donnez-moi le temps de me reconnaître; **to t. in everything at a glance,** tout embrasser d'un coup d'œil; **the eye cannot t. in the whole landscape,** le regard ne peut (pas) embrasser tout le paysage; (*k*) *F:* (*believe*) **he takes it all in,** il prend tout ça pour argent comptant; il avale ça doux comme le lait; il boit ça comme du petit-lait; il gobe tout ce qu'on lui dit; (*l*) *F:* (*cheat*) mettre (qn) dedans; attraper (qn); rouler (qn); monter le coup, un bateau, à (qn); faire une attrape à (qn); en conter (de belles, de fortes) à (qn); empaumer (qn); **to t. in a customer,** tromper un client; **to be taken in,** se laisser attraper; se laisser monter le coup; **I've been taken in,** on m'a mis dedans; on m'a roulé; **I told her a lie and she was taken in by it,** je lui ai dit un mensonge et elle a marché; **he is not a man to be taken in,** on ne la lui fait pas; **he's easily taken in,** il est très jobard; **I'm not taken in!** ça ne mord pas, ne prend pas! **I'm not (to be) taken in by your lies,** je ne suis pas dupe de vos mensonges; **to allow oneself to be taken in,** se laisser duper, tromper; **to let oneself be taken in by the sales talk of a canvasser,** se laisser prendre au bagout d'un démarcheur; **he was absolutely, properly, taken in,** il a gobé ça comme un œuf; **to be taken in again by the same trick,** remordre à l'hameçon; **to be taken in by appearances,** se laisser tromper aux apparences.

7. take off. (*a*) *v.tr.* (*prep. use*) **to t. s.o.'s attention, s.o.'s mind, off sth.,** distraire l'attention de qn; **to t. s.o. off his work,** distraire qn de ses travaux; **to t. one's eye off sth.,** quitter qch. des yeux, du regard; **he never took his eyes off us, off his book,** ses yeux ne nous quittaient pas; il n'a pas levé les yeux de (sur) son livre; **to t. a ship off the active list,** rayer un bâtiment de l'activité; (*b*) *v.tr.* (*adv. use*) (i) enlever, ôter, emporter, retirer (qch.); **to t. off the lid,** enlever, ôter, retirer, le couvercle; **to t. off one's clothes,** quitter ses vêtements; se déshabiller; se dévêtir; **to t. off one's gloves,** se déganter; **to t. off one's overcoat,** enlever son pardessus; se débarrasser de son pardessus; **to t. off a tyre,** déjanter un pneu; (*of surgeon*) **to t. off a leg,** amputer une jambe; **a grenade had taken off his leg,** une grenade lui avait emporté la jambe; **to t. off one's moustache,** se raser la moustache; *Nau:* **passengers are taken off by tender,** les voyageurs sont débarqués au moyen de bateaux annexes; **to t. off the survivors from a wreck,** recueillir les survivants d'un naufrage; *Tp:* **to t. off the receiver,** décrocher le récepteur; *Aut: etc:* **to t. off the brake,** dégager, desserrer, le frein; (ii) emmener (qn); **he was taken off to gaol,** il fut emmené en prison; **to t. oneself off,** s'en aller, s'éloigner; *F:* décamper, filer, détaler; prendre ses cliques et ses claques; **t. yourself off!** ôtez-vous de là! filez! fichez-moi le camp! *NAm:* **he was taken off by a stroke,** il a été emporté par un coup de sang; (iii) **to t. off £10 from the total,** défalquer dix livres du total; **to t. so much off (the price of sth.),** rabattre tant (sur le prix de qch.); **I can't t. a penny off,** je ne puis rien rabattre, rien diminuer (sur ce prix); (iv) **a cup of tea takes off the effects of seasickness,** une tasse de thé fait disparaître les effets du mal de mer; **to t. off a train,** supprimer un train; (v) imiter, singer, mimer, parodier, contrefaire (qn); copier les gestes, les manières, de (qn); (vi) **to t. three days off,** prendre, *F:* s'octroyer, trois jours de congé; (*c*) *v.i.* (i) (*of athlete, etc.*) prendre son élan, s'élancer **(from,** de); (ii) *Av:* décoller, partir, s'envoler; prendre son vol, son essor; **we shall t. off from London airport,** nous partirons de l'aéroport de Londres; (iii) *F:* (*of pers.*) s'en aller, s'éloigner, décamper; (iv) *Nau:* (*of wind, tide*) s'affaiblir.

8. take on. (*a*) *v.tr.* (i) se charger de, entreprendre (un travail); assumer (une responsabilité); (ii) accepter le défi de (qn); **I'm ready to t. on all comers,** je suis prêt à me battre, à lutter, avec n'importe qui; à tout venant beau jeu; **to t. s.o. on at tennis,** engager une partie de tennis avec qn; **come along, I'll t. you on at billiards!** allons, je vais vous faire une partie de billard! (iii) engager, embaucher (un ouvrier); (iv) prendre, revêtir, affecter (une couleur, une qualité, l'apparence de qch.); **the word takes on another meaning,** le mot prend une autre signification; (v) (*of train, etc.*) **to t. on passengers,** prendre, laisser monter, des voyageurs; (vi) mener (qn) plus loin; mener (qn) au delà de sa destination; **the train didn't stop at Rugby and I was taken on to Crewe,** le train a brûlé Rugby et m'a mené jusqu'à Crewe; (*b*) *v.i. F:* laisser éclater, laisser échapper, son chagrin; **don't t. on so!** ne vous désolez pas comme ça!

9. take out, *v.tr.* (*a*) **to t. sth. out,** sortir qch. **(of,** de); **to t. out one's luggage (from the left luggage office),** retirer des bagages (de la consigne); **to t. out one's pipe (from one's pocket),** sortir sa pipe; **to t. out a tooth,** arracher une dent; **to t. out a stain,** ôter, enlever, une tache; **to t. out a word,** rayer, biffer, un mot; (*b*) *F:* **to t. it out of s.o.,** (i) épuiser, esquinter, éreinter, qn; (ii) (*also* **to t. it out on s.o.),** se rattraper sur qn; se payer la peau à qn; **I'll t. it out of him, of his hide,** je me vengerai, je me payerai sa peau; **don't t. it out on me,** ne vous en prenez pas à moi; **heat takes it out of me,** la chaleur m'épuise; **it does t. it out of you,** c'est éreintant; **this illness has taken it out of him,** cette maladie l'a mis à plat; (*c*) **to t. s.o. out of himself,** faire oublier soi-même à qn; relever le moral à qn; (*d*) *Cards:* **to t. one's partner out (of the suit he has called),** changer la couleur annoncée par le partenaire; (*e*) *NAm:* **sandwiches to t. out,** sandwichs à emporter; (*f*) faire sortir (qn); **to t. a child out,** emmener un enfant en promenade; **to t. the dog out,** promener, sortir, le chien; **he takes lots of girls out,** il sort beaucoup de jeunes filles; **he's going to t. me out to dinner,** il va m'emmener dîner; (*g*) prendre, obtenir (un brevet, permis, etc.), se faire délivrer (un permis, etc.); **to t. out an insurance policy,** souscrire, prendre, une police d'assurance; *Fin:* **to t. out shares,** acheter des actions; (*h*) *Const: etc:* **to t. out quantities,** faire le devis; (*for earthworks, etc.*) relever le cubage.

10. take over, *v.tr.* (*a*) **to t. over a business,** (i) prendre la suite des affaires; prendre la succession d'une maison de commerce; reprendre une maison de commerce; (ii) racheter une maison (en surenchérissant); **he wants his son to t. over the business,** il voudrait que son fils lui succède; **to t. over a building for public purposes,** exproprier un immeuble pour cause d'utilité publique; **to rent a flat and t. over the furniture,** louer un appartement avec une reprise de meubles; **to t. over the liabilities,** prendre les dettes à sa charge; reprendre le passif; *Fin:* **to t. over an issue,** absorber une émission; **to t. over authority,** prendre possession du pouvoir; *Mil:* **to t. over a trench,** relever une tranchée; *Nau:* **to t. over the watch,** prendre le quart; *v.i.* **to t. over from s.o.,** relever, remplacer, qn (dans ses fonctions); (*b*) (i) transporter (qn, qch.); **I'll t. you over by car,** je vais vous y mener en voiture; (ii) passer (qn) (dans un bateau); transborder (des marchandises); (iii) *W.Tel:* **we are taking you over to Rome,** nous vous mettons en communication avec Rome; (iv) *Typ:* transférer (un mot) à la ligne suivante.

11. take to, *v.i.* (*a*) **to t. to flight,** prendre la fuite; **the guerillas took to the mountains,** les guérilleros se sont réfugiés dans les montagnes; **to t. to the open sea,** prendre le large; **to t. to the woods, to the bush,** gagner le taillis; prendre la brousse, le maquis; **to t. to the road again,** reprendre la route; (*b*) (i) **to t. to bad habits,** s'abandonner à, prendre, de mauvaises habitudes; **to t. to drink, to drinking,** se mettre à boire; s'adonner à la boisson; (ii) **to t. to tennis,** se mettre à faire du tennis; **to t. to writing, to literature (as a career),** se mettre à écrire; se faire écrivain; (*c*) (i) **to t. to s.o.,** éprouver de la sympathie pour qn; se prendre de sympathie pour qn; prendre qn en amitié; concevoir de l'amitié pour qn; **they have taken to each other,** ils se sont plu réciproquement; **I took to him at once,** il me fut sympathique dès l'abord; **I didn't t. to him,** il ne m'était pas sympathique; *F:* il ne me revenait pas; (ii) **to t. to a game, to chemistry,** prendre goût à un jeu, à la chimie; **does he t. to Latin?** mord-il au latin? **I don't t. to the idea,** cette idée ne me dit rien; **I shall never t. to it,** je ne m'y ferai jamais; **he has taken to flying like a duck to water,** il s'est montré aviateur dès son premier essai.

12. take up. (*a*) *v.tr.* (i) relever, ramasser (qch.); **to t. up a stone,** ramasser une pierre; **to t. up a book from the table,** prendre un livre sur la table; **to t. up the hay with a fork,** ramasser, prendre, le foin avec une fourche; (ii) **to t. up a carpet,** enlever, déclouer, un tapis; **to t. up paving stones, rails,** déposer, enlever, des pavés, des rails; **to t. up a street,** dépaver, défoncer, une rue; **to t. up a tree,** déplanter un arbre; *Nau:* **to t. up a buoy,** relever une bouée; (iii) **the porter will t. you up in the lift,** le chasseur vous fera monter (à votre chambre) par l'ascenseur; **there's a lift to t. you up,** vous pouvez monter en ascenseur; (iv) *Rail: etc:* **to stop to t. up passengers,** s'arrêter pour prendre des voyageurs; (*of taxi driver*) **I took up a fare at the station,** j'ai pris un client à la gare; (v) *Dressm:* **to t. up a skirt, sleeve,** raccourcir une jupe, une manche; **to t. up a sleeve at the shoulder,** remonter une manche; (vi) **to t. up the slack in a cable,** retendre un câble; embraquer le mou; mettre un câble au raide; *Mec.E:* **to t. up the backlash,** rattraper, reprendre, le jeu; **to t. up the bearings,** rattraper l'usure des paliers; **to t. up the wear,** rappeler, rattraper, corriger, compenser, l'usure; **device for taking up the play,** (dispositif *m* de) rattrape-jeu *m inv*; *Tex:* **to**

t. up the cloth, enrouler la toile; *Cin:* **to t. up the film,** enrouler la bande; (vii) *Typ:* **to t. up a word to the previous line,** transférer un mot à la ligne précédente; (*b*) *v.tr.* (i) absorber (de l'eau); (ii) *Mec.E:* **to t. up the drive,** (s')embrayer; (*c*) *v.tr.* (i) *Com:* **to t. up a bill,** honorer un effet; retirer une traite; *St.Exch:* **to t. up an option,** lever une prime, consolider un marché à prime; **to t. up shares,** souscrire à des actions; **to t. up stock,** prendre livraison des titres; (ii) **to t. up a challenge,** relever un défi; **to t. up a bet,** tenir un pari; tenir le pari; (iii) **to t. up an idea, a suggestion,** adopter une idée; suivre un conseil; **to t. up an attitude, a stance, on sth.,** prendre, adopter, une attitude à l'égard de qch.; (*d*) *v.tr.* (i) **to t. up a question,** prendre une question en main; aborder la discussion d'une question; **the question would at once be taken up,** la question se poserait, serait abordée, immédiatement; **I will not t. up the matter,** je ne veux pas entrer dans l'affaire; **we took the matter up strongly with them,** nous avons insisté auprès d'eux; **to t. up a matter again,** reprendre une affaire; remettre une affaire en question; **to t. up a statement,** relever une affirmation; (ii) embrasser (une carrière), s'adonner à (une occupation); adopter (une méthode); épouser (une querelle); **he has taken up photography,** il s'est mis à faire de la photographie; **he is taking up physical training,** il s'adonne à la culture physique; il s'est mis à faire de la gymnastique; **to t. up modern languages,** se mettre aux langues vivantes; **to t. up new studies,** aborder de nouvelles études; **to t. up French again,** se remettre au français; **to t. up one's duties again,** reprendre ses fonctions; **to t. up the work where someone else has left off,** continuer le travail du point où un autre l'a quitté; (iii) prendre (qn) sous sa protection; (*e*) *v.tr. O:* (*arrest*) arrêter (qn); **he was taken up by the police,** il a été arrêté; (*f*) *v.tr.* **to t. s.o. up on sth.,** prendre qn au mot; **I'll t. you up on that,** (i) je vous prendrai au mot sur cela; (ii) je vous défie de prouver, justifier, cela; **to t. s.o. up sharply,** reprendre qn vertement, aigrement; relever qn; **to t. s.o. up short,** couper la parole à qn; **his statement was false and I took him up at once,** son affirmation était fausse et je l'ai repris aussitôt; (*g*) *v.tr.* occuper; (i) **to t. up too much room,** occuper trop de place; être encombrant; **you're taking up too much room,** vous tenez trop de place; (ii) **to t. up all s.o.'s attention, time,** absorber l'attention, le temps, de qn; **his work takes up all his time,** son travail l'absorbe; **it takes up all my evenings,** cela remplit, occupe, toutes mes soirées; (iii) (*in the passive*) **he is entirely taken up with his business,** il est tout à son commerce, entièrement absorbé dans son commerce; il ne songe qu'à son commerce; **she is entirely taken up with her own sweet self,** elle n'est occupée que de sa petite personne; (*h*) *v.i.* **to t. up with (s.o.),** se lier d'amitié avec (qn); se mettre à fréquenter (des vauriens, etc.); se mettre (en ménage) avec (qn); *P:* se coller avec (qn).

takeable ['teikəbl], *a.* prenable.

takeaway ['teikəwei], *s. F:* (*a*) magasin *m* qui vend des sandwichs, mets, repas, à emporter; (*b*) sandwich *m*, mets *m*, repas *m*, etc., à emporter.

takedown ['teikdaun], *s.* **1.** *F:* mortification *f*, humiliation *f*, affront *m*. **2.** *attrib.* (machine, etc.) démontable.

take-home ['teik'houm], *a.* **t.-h. pay,** salaire reçu (moins impôt retenu à la source, etc.).

take-in ['teikin], *s. F:* attrape *f*; attrape-nigaud *m*, *pl.* attrape-nigauds; carottage *m*.

takeoff ['teikɔf], *s.* **1.** imitation *f*, caricature *f*, charge *f* (de qn). **2.** (*a*) élan *m*; **to step back to get a better t.,** reculer pour mieux sauter; *Sp:* **jump with a double t.,** saut *m* à pieds joints; (*b*) *Av:* décollage *m*, envol *m*; **rocket-assisted t.,** décollage assisté par fusée; **vertical t.,** décollage vertical; **to make a careful t.,** faire un décollage prudent; **length of t.,** roulement *m* au décollage. **3.** *Sp:* (*a*) point *m*, ligne *f*, de départ; appel *m*; (*b*) tremplin *m*. **4.** *Mec.E: etc:* branchement *m* (d'un tuyau); **power t.,** point *m* de la prise de force. **5.** *attrib. Cin:* **t. sprocket,** roue dentée d'entraînement (de la pellicule); *Cmptr:* **t. spool,** bobine émettrice.

takeout ['teikaut], *s.* **1.** *Cards:* **t. (bid),** enchère *f* pour changer la couleur après l'annonce du partenaire. **2.** *NAm:* (*a*) sandwich *m*, mets *m*, repas *m*, etc. à emporter; (*b*) part *f*, portion *f*, quote-part *f*, *pl.* quotes-parts, de la recette, du produit.

takeover ['teikouvər], *s.* (*a*) prise *f* de possession du pouvoir; (*b*) prise de contrôle, achat *m*, absorption *f*, (d'une maison de commerce); **t. bid,** offre publique d'achat.

taker ['teikər], *s.* **1.** (*a*) preneur *m* (d'un navire ennemi, etc.); (*b*) preneur, -euse (d'un bail, etc.); acceptant, -ante (d'une offre); **at that price there were no takers,** à ce prix on n'a pas trouvé d'acheteurs; **any takers?** est-ce qu'il y a des amateurs? (*c*) *St.Exch:* reporteur *m*, vendeur *m*; **t. of an option,** optant *m*; **t. of a bill,** preneur d'une lettre de change; **t. for a call, a put,** vendeur d'un dont, d'une prime directe; (*d*) **t. of a bet,** tenant *m*, teneur *m*, d'un pari; *Turf:* **takers of odds,** preneurs. **2. taker-in,** *pl.* **takers-in;** (*a*) (*pers.*) trompeur, -euse; carotteur, -euse; (*b*) *Tex:* tambour briseur; (*c*) *Typ:* guide-feuilles *m inv*. **3.** *F:* **taker-off,** *pl.* **takers-off,** imitateur, -trice, singeur, -euse (de qn).

take-up ['teikʌp], *s.* **1.** (*a*) *Mec.E:* rattrapage *m* (du jeu); serrage *m*, compensation *f*; (*b*) *Cin: Cmptr:* enroulement *m*; **t.-up (spool, reel),** bobine réceptrice; enrouleuse *f*; **t.-up magazine,** magasin récepteur; (*c*) *Aut: Mec.E:* embrayage; **clutch with a smooth t.-up,** embrayage doux. **2.** *Mec.E:* tendeur *m*; *Tex:* (le) rouleau et (le) dispositif de tension; (*of sewing machine*) levier tendeur de fil.

takin ['tɑːkin], *s. Z:* takin *m*.

taking[1] ['teikiŋ], *a.* **1.** (style, titre) attrayant; (visage) séduisant; **t. manners, ways,** manières engageantes, qui charment; *Hum: O:* **he, she, has t. ways,** c'est un chapardeur, une chapardeuse. **2.** (*of disease*) qui s'attrape, contagieux.

taking[2], *s.* **1.** (*a*) prise *f* (d'une ville, etc.); arrestation *f* (d'un voleur); (*b*) *Jur:* (acte *m* de) soustraction *f*; (*c*) *Mch:* **t. of a diagram,** relevé *m* d'un diagramme; (*d*) *Med:* prélèvement *m* (de sang, etc.). **2. takings,** recette *f*, produit *m*; *Th:* chambrée *f*; **the day's takings,** la recette, le produit, de la journée; **the takings are good,** la recette est bonne.

takingly ['teikiŋli], *adv.* d'une manière attrayante, engageante, séduisante.

talapoin ['tæləpɔin], *s.* **1.** (*monk, priest*) talapoin *m*. **2.** *Z:* **t. (monkey),** talapoin.

talaria [tə'lɛəriə], *s.pl. Myth:* talonnières *f*, talaires *f* (de Mercure, etc.).

talaric [tə'lærik], *a. Ant:* (toge, tunique) talaire.

talbot ['tɔːlbət], *s. A:* (grand) chien courant; limier *m*.

talbotype ['tɔːlbətaip], *s. A.Phot:* calotype *m*.

talc[1] [tælk], *s.* **1.** (*a*) *Miner:* talc *m*; silicate *m* de magnésie; **t. schist,** talcschiste *m*; (*b*) *Toil:* (poudre *f* de) talc. **2.** *Com:* mica *m*; **t. lamp chimney,** verre *m* de lampe en mica.

talc[2], *v.tr.* **(talcked)** saupoudrer de talc, talquer (des gants, etc.).

talcite ['tælsait], *s. Miner:* talcite *f*.

talcky ['tælki], *a. Miner:* = TALCOSE.

talcomicaceous [tælkoumai'keiʃəs], *a. Miner:* talco-micacé, *pl.* talco-micacés.

talcose ['tælkous], **talcous** ['tælkəs], *a. Miner:* talcaire, talcique, talqueux.

talcum ['tælkəm], *s.* (*a*) *Miner:* talc *m*; (*b*) *Toil:* **t. (powder),** (poudre *f* de) talc.

tale [teil], *s.* **1.** conte *m*; (*a*) récit *m*, histoire *f*; **he listened to my t.,** il a écouté mon récit; **there's a t. that her ghost returned to haunt the palace,** la légende raconte que son spectre est revenu, veut que son spectre soit revenu, hanter le palais; **idle t.,** conte à faire plaisir; **old wives' tales,** contes de bonne femme; **thereby hangs a t.,** il y a là-dessus toute une histoire (que je pourrais vous raconter); **that tells its own t.,** cela est suffisant comme témoignage; cela se passe de commentaire; **his drawn face told the t. of his sufferings,** ses traits tirés en disaient long sur ses souffrances; **his t. is told,** c'en est fait de lui; il est flambé; **he lived to tell the t.,** il a survécu; il est là pour en parler; *F:* **to tell s.o. the t.,** raconter des histoires, des boniments, à qn; **I've heard that t. before,** je connais des paroles sur cet air-là; **tales lose nothing in the telling,** on fait toujours le loup plus gros qu'il n'est; (*b*) *Lit:* nouvelle *f*, conte; **a book of tales,** un livre de contes, de nouvelles; **the Canterbury Tales,** les Contes de Cantorbéry (de Chaucer); **the Winter's Tale,** le Conte d'hiver (de Shakespeare). **2.** *Pej:* (*a*) racontar *m*, potin *m*, on-dit *m inv*; **I've heard some pretty tales about you,** j'en ai appris de belles sur votre compte; **this is the t. that is going about,** voilà ce qu'on raconte; (*b*) rapport *m*, cafardage *m*; **to tell tales (out of school),** (i) rapporter, faire des rapports, cafarder; (ii) dévoiler un secret; **to carry tales to s.o. about s.o.,** desservir qn auprès de qn. **3.** *A: & Lit:* compte *m*, nombre *m*, quantité *f*; **the shepherd was telling the t. of his flocks,** le pasteur dénombrait ses troupeaux.

talebearer ['teilbɛərər], *s.* (i) rapporteur, -euse; (ii) jaseur, -euse; mauvaise langue; **he's a t.,** il rapporte, c'est un rapporteur.

talebearing[1] ['teilbɛəriŋ], *a.* (i) rapporteur, cafard; (ii) cancanier, jaseur.

talebearing[2], *s.* (i) rapportage *m*, cafardage *m*; (ii) potins *mpl*, cancans *mpl*.

talent ['tælənt], *s.* **1.** *Ant:* talent *m*; **gold, silver, t.,** talent d'or, d'argent; *B:* **the parable of the talents,** la parabole des talents. **2.** talent; capacité (naturelle); aptitude *f*; **to have a t. for doing the right thing,** avoir le don d'agir à propos; **he has no t. for business,** il manque de talent, de capacité, pour les affaires; **to have a t. for languages,** avoir une grande facilité pour les langues; avoir le don, le talent, des langues; *Sp:* **t. money,** prime allouée à un professionnel hors de pair. **3.** (*a*) personne bien douée; *Pol: etc:* **to call upon all the talents, to form an administration of all the talents,** faire appel à tous les talents; (*b*) *Coll.* gens *mpl* de talent; **exhibition of local t.,** exposition des œuvres d'artistes régionaux; *F:* **t. scout, spotter,** dénicheur, -euse, de talent(s), de vedettes; *Turf:* **the t.,** les habitués *m*, ceux qui parient en connaissance de cause.

talented ['tæləntid], *a.* qui a du talent; (enfant, etc.) (bien) doué; (écrivain, etc.) de talent, de valeur.

talentless ['tæləntlis], *a.* sans talent.

tales ['teiliːz], *s. Jur:* (i) jurés suppléants; (ii) **to pray a t.,** demander que le jury soit complété en faisant appel aux suppléants (lorsque certains jurés ont été récusés).

talesman, *pl.* **-men** ['teiliːzmən, 'teilzmən], *s. Jur:* juré suppléant; *NAm:* personne qui peut être sélectionnée comme membre du jury.

taleteller ['teiltelər], *s.* **1.** conteur, -euse, d'histoires. **2.** (i) rapporteur, -euse; (ii) jaseur, -euse.

Taliacotian [tæliə'kouʃən], *a. Surg:* **T. operation,** reconstitution *f* du nez par la méthode autoplastique de Tagliacozzi.

talion ['tæliən], *s. Hist:* **the law of t., t. law,** la loi du talion.

taliped ['tæliped], *a.* qui a le pied bot talus.

talipes ['tælipiːz], *s. Med:* pied bot talus.

talipot ['tælipɔt], *s. Bot:* tal(l)ipot *m*.

talisman ['tælizmən], *s.* talisman *m*.

talismanic [tæliz'mænik], *a.* talismanique.

talk[1] [tɔːk], *s.* **1.** (*a*) paroles *fpl*; **we want actions not t.,** il nous faut des actions, non pas des paroles, des mots; **he is all t.,** ce n'est qu'un bavard; il n'a que du caquet; *F:* il n'a que le bec; (*b*) bruit *m*, dires *mpl*, racontages *mpl*; **there is some t. of his returning,** il est question qu'il revienne; il est question de son retour; le bruit court qu'il va revenir; **there has been t. of it,** on en a parlé; il en a été question; **it's all t.,** ce ne sont que des on-dit; tout ça c'est des racontars; **to risk t.,** risquer de faire parler de soi; (*c*) propos *mpl*; bavardage *m*; **disjointed t.,** propos incohérents; **weary of t.,** las de jaser; **idle t.,** papotage *m*; paroles en l'air; balivernes *fpl*; *F:* chansons *fpl*, sornettes *fpl*; **small t.,** menus propos; conversation banale; banalités *fpl*; **to indulge, engage, in small t.,** parler de choses indifférentes, de choses banales; causer de choses et d'autres; parler de la pluie et du beau temps; **to spend an hour in small t.,** passer une heure à dire des riens; **to have plenty of small t.,** ne pas manquer de sujets de conversation; **she has no small t.,** elle ne sait pas parler pour ne rien dire; **double t.,** (i) propos ambigus, nègre blanc; (ii) propos insincères; (*d*) langage *m* (des marins, etc.); **baby t.,** babil enfantin. **2.** (*a*) entretien *m*, conversation *f*; causerie *f*; **to have a t. with,** *F:* **to, s.o.,** causer, s'entretenir, avec qn; avoir un entretien avec qn; **don't go before I have had a t. with you,** ne partez pas que je ne vous aie causé; **they had a long t.,** ils se sont entretenus longuement; **an intimate t.,** une causerie intime; **she came in on Sunday night for a t.,** elle est venue dimanche soir (pour) faire la causette; **to engage s.o. in t.,** lier conversation avec qn; (*b*) *Pol: etc:* **talks,** dialogue *m*, pourparlers *mpl*; **to start talks,** engager le dialogue; entrer en pourparlers; (*c*) causerie; **to give a t. on, about, sth.,** faire une causerie sur qch.; **to give a t. on the radio,** parler à la radio; **weekly t. on motoring,** feuilleton parlé hebdomadaire sur l'automobilisme; *NAm:* **t. show,** programme composé d'un débat, d'une causerie. **3. it's the t. of the town,** c'est la fable, le bruit, de la ville; on ne parle, il n'est bruit, que de cela; tout le monde en jase; cela fait l'étonnement de tout le monde; **this scandal was the t. of the town,** ce scandale a fait du tapage, a eu un grand retentissement; **she's the t. of the town,** elle défraie la chronique.

talk[2], *v.i. & tr.*

I. *v.i.* **1.** (*a*) parler; **to learn to t.,** apprendre à parler; **to t. slowly,** parler lentement; (*b*) parler, discourir; **to t. and t.,** parler sans arrêt; pérorer; n'en pas finir; **to t. for the sake of talking,** parler pour parler; **it was only for the sake of talking,** c'était histoire de parler; **to t. by signs, by looks,** parler par gestes, du regard; **to t. in riddles,** parler par énigmes; **that is a strange way to t.,** vous tenez là un étrange langage; *F:* **that's no way to t.!** (i) en voilà un langage! (ii) il ne faut pas dire des choses pareilles! **he likes to hear himself t.,** il aime à s'entendre parler; il s'écoute parler; c'est un grand discoureur; *F:*

to t. through one's hat, through (the back of) one's neck, (i) parler pour ne rien dire; dire, débiter, des sottises; extravaguer; (ii) blaguer, exagérer; **you're talking through the back of your neck,** *NAm:* **off the top of your head,** ça n'a aucun sens; *do* **t. sense!** tu radotes! **it's easy to t.!** vous êtes magnifique! cela vous plaît à dire! **now you're talking! that's the way to t.!** voilà qui s'appelle parler! à la bonne heure! maintenant tu y es, y viens! *you* **can, can't, t.!** c'est bien à vous de parler! **to t. of, about, sth.,** parler de qch.; **to t. of one thing and another, of this and that,** parler de choses et d'autres; parler de la pluie et du beau temps; **I am not talking of you,** il ne s'agit pas de vous; **the much talked-of revival of the drama,** le renouveau du théâtre dont on parle tant; **talking of that, have you heard the latest?** à propos de cela, à ce propos, avez-vous entendu le plus nouveau? **what are you talking about?** (i) de quoi parlez-vous? (ii) *F:* qu'est-ce que vous racontez? vous me la baillez belle! **he knows what he is talking about,** il parle en connaissance de cause; il s'y connaît; il sait ce qu'il dit; *F:* **t. about luck!** tu parles d'une chance! **t. about books being dear!** vous nous dites que les livres sont chers! (*c*) **to t. of, about, doing sth.,** parler de faire qch.; dire avoir l'intention de faire qch.; (*d*) **to t. on the radio,** parler, faire un discours, à la radio, au micro (**on, about,** sur); (*e*) **to make a prisoner t.,** faire avouer, confesser, *F:* accoucher, un prisonnier; **his accomplices are afraid he'll t.,** ses complices craignent qu'il ne vende la mèche. **2.** (*a*) **to t. to, with, s.o.,** s'entretenir avec qn; parler à, avec, qn; **to talk freely to s.o.,** s'ouvrir à qn; parler librement avec qn; **he never talked to me the whole evening,** il ne m'a pas dit un mot de la soirée; **she has found someone to t. to,** elle a trouvé à qui parler; **ships talking to each other (by wireless),** bâtiments qui s'envoient des messages; **to t. to oneself,** parler tout seul; monologuer, *F:* parler à son bonnet, aux anges; *F:* **who do you think you are talking to!** à qui croyez-vous donc parler? (*b*) **to t. (severely) to s.o.,** faire des remontrances à qn; réprimander, semoncer, gronder, qn; *I'll* **t. to him!** je vais lui dire son fait! je vais le remettre à sa place! (*c*) **money talks,** l'argent veut tout dire. **3.** (*a*) jaser, bavarder, babiller; **she is always talking,** elle bavarde sans cesse; *F:* elle n'a pas la pépie; **grandmother loved to t.,** notre grand'mère aimait à bavarder; (*b*) cancaner; **people will t.,** (i) cela fera scandale; (ii) le monde est cancanier; **people talked and he had to resign,** on jasait, clabaudait, et il a dû démissionner; **to get oneself talked about,** faire parler de soi; **if you go on like that you'll get (yourself) talked about,** si vous continuez de la sorte on jasera sur votre compte; **the whole town was talking about it,** toute la ville en jasait; **the case was greatly talked about, gave people something to t. about, at the time,** ce cas a eu un grand retentissement, défrayait la conversation, à l'époque.

II. *v.tr.* **1.** (*a*) **to t. French, to t. slang,** parler français, parler argot; (*b*) **to t. politics,** parler politique; causer politique; **to t. treason,** tenir des propos séditieux; **to t. (common) sense,** parler raison; **there is a great deal of nonsense talked about this matter,** on a dit beaucoup de sottises à ce sujet. **2.** (*a*) **to t. oneself hoarse,** s'enrouer à force de parler; *F:* **I've talked myself black in the face telling you!** mais je m'époumone à vous le dire! **he talked himself into trouble,** ses discours imprudents finirent par le mettre dans le pétrin; **he talked himself out of the fix,** à force de parler il s'est tiré d'embarras; (*b*) **to t. s.o. into doing sth.,** persuader qn de faire qch.; amener qn à faire qch.; **he was talked into giving his consent,** à force de le sermonner on lui a arraché un assentiment; **to t. s.o. out of doing sth.,** dissuader qn de faire qch.

III. (*compound verbs*) **1. talk at,** *v.i.* **to t. at s.o.,** faire des allusions voilées à qn (qui se trouve présent); persifler qn (au su, à l'insu, de la compagnie).

2. talk away, *v.tr.* (i) passer (le temps, la nuit, etc.) à parler, à bavarder; faire passer (le temps) en bavardant; (ii) **to t. a child's fears away,** chasser les craintes d'un enfant avec des paroles réconfortantes.

3. talk back, *v.i.* (*a*) *W.Tel:* (*on two-way radio*) répondre; (*b*) *NAm:* répondre d'une manière impertinente; répliquer.

4. talk down. (*a*) *v.i.* **to t. down to one's audience,** se mettre à la portée de son auditoire (avec condescendance); (*b*) *v.tr.* (i) faire taire (qn), réduire (qn) au silence (en parlant plus haut et plus longtemps que lui); **I won't allow myself to be talked down,** on ne me fera pas taire; (ii) *Av:* **to t. down an aircraft,** donner des instructions d'atterrissage à un avion.

5. talk out, *v.tr.* (*a*) **I want to t. things out with you,** je voudrais discuter la chose à fond, sous toutes ses faces; je voudrais débattre la question jusqu'à ce que nous tombions d'accord; (*b*) *Parl:* **to t. a bill out,** prolonger les débats de façon qu'un projet de loi ne puisse être voté avant la clôture.

6. talk over, *v.tr.* (*a*) discuter, débattre (une question); **let's t. it over,** discutons la chose; **we can t. it over after lunch,** nous en parlerons, nous en causerons, après déjeuner; **we talked your business over,** nous avons conféré de votre affaire; (*b*) = TALK ROUND.

7. talk round, *v.tr.* enjôler (qn); amener (qn) à changer d'avis; **to t. s.o. round to one's way of thinking,** faire partager à qn sa manière de voir; **I talked them round at last,** j'ai fini par les persuader.

8. talk up, *v.tr. F:* **to t. up a book, an entertainment,** faire du battage, de la publicité, autour d'un livre, d'un spectacle; faire mousser un livre; *St.Exch:* **to t. up stock,** créer une atmosphère de hausse autour d'une valeur.

talkathon ['tɔːkəθən], *s. F:* marathon *m* oratoire.

talkative ['tɔːkətiv], *a.* causeur; jaseur, bavard, babillard; loquace; **she's very t.,** elle a la langue déliée.

talkatively ['tɔːkətivli], *adv.* loquacement.

talkativeness ['tɔːkətivnis], *s.* loquacité *f.*

talk-back ['tɔːkbæk], *s. W.Tel:* émetteur-récepteur *m, pl.* émetteurs-récepteurs.

talkdown ['tɔːkdaun], *s. Av:* atterrissage *m* par contrôle au sol.

talkee-talkee ['tɔːkiː'tɔːkiː], *s. F:* **1.** *Ling:* (parler *m*) petit-nègre (*m*). **2.** pur bavardage; papotage *m.*

talker ['tɔːkər], *s.* **1.** parleur, -euse; **brilliant t.,** beau parleur, personne *f* qui brille dans la conversation. **2.** bavard, -arde; **to be a great t.,** être bavard, avoir la langue bien pendue. **3.** fanfaron, -onne; vantard, -arde; *Prov:* **great talkers are little doers,** les grands diseurs ne sont pas les grands faiseurs.

talkfest ['tɔːkfest], *s. F:* réunion *f* pour échange de vues.

talkie ['tɔːki], *s. Cin: F: O:* film parlant, parlé.

talking[1] ['tɔːkiŋ], *a.* parlant; **t. doll,** poupée parlante; *Cin:* **t. film,** film parlant, parlé; *Rec:* **t. book,** lecture enregistrée d'un livre (*esp.* à l'usage des aveugles); **t. machine,** phonographe *m.*

talking[2], *s.* **1.** discours *mpl*, propos *mpl*, paroles *fpl*; **t. is no use,** on perd ses paroles; **that's enough of t.,** c'est assez parlé; trêve de discours! **t. point,** (i) bonne matière de discussion; (ii) bon argument; *Pej:* **the t. shop,** le parlement. **2.** (*a*) conversation *f*; (*b*) bavardage *m*; **to do all the t.,** faire tous les frais de la conversation; **I don't want to do all the t.,** je ne veux pas parler tout le temps; **there was very little t. at breakfast,** on parlait très peu au petit déjeuner; **no t., please!** pas de bavardage! **3. t.-to,** réprimande *f*, semonce *f*; **to give s.o. a good t.-to,** semoncer qn; donner à qn une verte semonce; tancer qn vertement; arranger qn de la belle manière.

tall [tɔːl], *a.* **1.** (*of pers.*) (*a*) grand; de grande stature, de haute taille; haut de taille; **a t. thin woman,** une grande (femme) maigre; **she's a fine t. girl,** c'est un beau brin de fille; (*b*) **how t. are you?** quelle est votre taille? combien mesurez-vous? **he's two metres t.,** il mesure, *F:* fait, deux mètres; **she's taller than I am,** elle est plus grande que moi; **he was taller by a head, stood a (whole) head taller, than I,** il me dépassait de la tête; **to make oneself look taller by standing on tiptoe,** se grandir en se haussant sur la pointe des pieds; **that dress makes you look taller,** cette robe vous allonge; **she's growing taller,** elle se fait grande; elle s'allonge; **he has grown t.,** il a, est, grandi; **children grow taller as the years pass,** le temps grandit les enfants. **2.** (*of thg*) haut, élevé; **how t. is that mast?** quelle hauteur a ce mât? quelle est la hauteur de ce mât? **tree fifty metres t.,** arbre qui a cinquante mètres de hauteur; *O:* **t. hat,** chapeau haut de forme; **t. glass,** flûte *f* (à champagne, etc.). **3.** *F:* (*a*) (conte, histoire) incroyable, invraisemblable, *F:* raide; **that's a t. story,** cella-là est raide, est dure à avaler; vous m'en contez de belles; **to tell t. stories,** *NAm:* **tales,** raconter des histoires invraisemblables; (*b*) **t. talk,** hâblerie *f*, vantardises *fpl*; (*c*) **that's a t. order,** voilà qui va être difficile, compliqué. **4.** *adv. F: O:* **to talk t.,** se vanter; hâbler; **to walk t.,** être fier.

tallage ['tælidʒ], *s. Hist:* (*a*) taille seigneuriale; (*b*) impôt *m.*

tallboy ['tɔːlbɔi], *s.* **1.** *Furn:* commode *f* (i) de hauteur double (à pieds), (ii) à deux corps superposés. **2.** *Mil:* bombe *f* de gros calibre.

tallish ['tɔːliʃ], *a.* assez grand; grandelet.

tallith ['tæliθ], *s. Jew.Rel:* taleth *m.*

tallness ['tɔːlnis], *s.* (*a*) (*of pers.*) grande taille; (*b*) hauteur *f* (d'un édifice, etc.).

tallow[1] ['tælou], *s.* **1.** suif *m*; (*a*) **raw t.,** suif en branches; **soap t.,** suif à savon; **t. candle,** chandelle *f*; **t. chandler,** chandelier, -ière; (i) fabricant, -ante, (ii) marchand, -ande, de chandelles; **t. chandlery,** chandellerie *f*; (*b*) *Nau:* suif, suage *m.* **2.** (*a*) **vegetable t.,** suif végétal; (*b*) *Bot:* **t. tree,** (i) **Chinese t. tree,** arbre *m* à suif; croton *m*; (ii) arbre à beurre; (iii) vaterie *f.* **3.** *Miner:* **mineral, mountain, t.,** suif minéral, hachettine *f*, gras *m* de cadavre. **4.** *Lap:* **t. drop emerald,** émeraude *f* en cabochon.

tallow[2]. **1.** *v.tr.* suiffer; enduire de suif; *Nau:* suiffer, suager (un navire); *Leath:* mettre (une peau) en suif; **tallowed leather,** cuir suiffé; cuir en suif. **2.** *A:* (*a*) *v.i.* (*of cattle*) engraisser; (*b*) *v.tr.* (*of pasture, etc.*) engraisser (le bétail).

tallow-faced ['tæloufeist], *a.* au visage blême, au teint terreux; *F:* à face de carême.

tallowy ['tæloui], *a.* **1.** suiffeux, graisseux. **2.** (teint) pâle, terreux.

tally[1] ['tæli], *s.* **1.** *A:* (*a*) *Com:* **t. (stick),** taille *f*, marque *f* (de boulanger, etc.); baguette *f* à encoches; **creditor's half of the t.,** échantillon *m* de taille; (*b*) **the t. trade,** le commerce à tempérament; **t. shop,** boutique *f* faisant la vente à tempérament; (*c*) entaille, encoche (faite sur la taille). **2.** pointage *m*; **to keep t. of goods, names,** pointer des marchandises, des noms (sur une liste); **t. clerk, keeper,** pointeur *m*, contrôleur *m*, marqueur *m* (de marchandises, etc.); **t. sheet,** feuille *f* de pointage (à la réception de marchandises, etc.); *NAm: esp:* feuille sur laquelle on marque les votes. **3.** (*a*) compte *m*, calcul *m*, comptage *m*; (*b*) *NAm:* (nombre *m* de) points *mpl* (dans un match, une partie). **4.** (*a*) nombre (de certaines marchandises vendues en paquets) établi par l'usage du métier; (*b*) nombre complet (de paquets livrés, etc.). **5.** (*a*) étiquette *f* (pour plantes, bagages); (*b*) jeton *m* (de présence); marron *m* (de service, de ronde). **6.** (*a*) pendant *m*, pareil *m*; contrepartie *f* (d'un document); (*b*) *P:* **to live t. with a man, a woman,** vivre à la colle avec, être collé(e) à, un homme, une femme.

tally[2]. **1.** *v.tr.* (*a*) *A:* cocher (une taille); (*b*) pointer, contrôler (des marchandises); (*c*) étiqueter (un paquet, etc.); (*d*) *NAm:* calculer, compter; *Games:* compter, marquer (les points). **2.** *v.i.* correspondre (**with,** à); s'accorder, concorder (**with,** avec); cadrer (**with,** avec); **these accounts do not t.,** (i) ces comptes, (ii) ces comptes rendus, ne s'accordent pas; **the theory does not t. with the facts,** la théorie ne s'accorde pas avec les faits, ne correspond pas aux faits; **to make sth. t. with sth.,** mettre qch. d'accord avec qch.

tally-ho[1]. **1.** *int. & s. Ven:* taïaut (*m*). **2.** *s. A.Veh:* (*a*) diligence *f*; (*b*) drag *m*, mail-coach *m*, *pl.* mail-coaches.

tally-ho[2]. **1.** *v.i.* crier taïaut. **2.** *v.tr.* exciter (les chiens) en criant taïaut.

tallying ['tæliiŋ], *s.* pointage *m*, contrôle *m* (de marchandises, etc.); *Nau:* **t. of discharging,** pointage du déchargement.

tallyman, *pl.* **-men** ['tælimən], *s.m.* **1.** marchand qui vend à tempérament. **2.** pointeur, contrôleur, marqueur (de marchandises, etc.).

talmi-gold ['tælmi'gould], *s.* alliage *m* de cuivre et de zinc légèrement plaqué d'or.

Talmud (the) [ðə'tælmud], *s. Jew.Rel:* le Talmud.

Talmudic(al) [tæl'mudik(l)], *a.* talmudique.

Talmudist ['tælmudist], *s.* talmudiste *m.*

talon ['tælən], *s.* **1.** serre *f* (d'oiseau de proie); griffe *f* (de lion, etc.); *F:* **talons,** ongles longs, doigts crochus (d'une personne). **2.** *Locksm:* ergot *m* (de pêne de serrure). **3.** *Arch:* talon *m*, doucine *f.* **4.** *Com:* **t. of a sheet of coupons,** talon de souche. **5.** *Games:* (*at cards, dominoes*) talon.

taloned ['tælənd], *a.* muni de griffes, de serres.

talonic [tə'lɔnik], *a. Ch:* talonique.

talose ['tælous], *s. Ch:* talose *m.*

talpa ['tælpə], *s.* **1.** *Z:* taupe *f.* **2.** *Med:* talpa *f*, testudo *m*; *F:* taupe.

Talpidae ['tælpidiː], *s.pl. Z:* talpidés *m.*

talpoid ['tælpɔid], *a.* talpoïde.

talus[1], *pl.* **-i** ['teiləs, -ai], *s.* **1.** *Anat:* (*a*) astragale *m* (du tarse); (*b*) cheville *f.* **2.** *Med:* pied bot talus.

talus[2], *s.* **1.** *Fort: etc:* talus *m.* **2.** *Geol:* talus; pente *f* d'éboulis.

talweg ['tɑːlveg], *s. Geog:* talweg *m.*

tamable ['teiməbl], *a.* = TAMEABLE.

tamandua [tə'mændjuə], *s. Z:* tamandua *m.*

tamanoir ['tæmənwɑːr], *s. Z:* tamanoir *m.*

tamarack ['tæməræk], *s. Bot:* mélèze *m* d'Amérique; épinette *f* rouge.

Tamaricaceae [tæməri'keisiiː], *s.pl. Bot:* tamaricacées *f.*

tamarillo [tæmə'rilou], *s. Bot: N.Z:* tomate *f* en arbre, cyphomandra *m.*

tamarin ['tæmərin], *s. Z:* tamarin *m*, midas *m*; **silky t.,** marikina *m.*

tamarind ['tæmərind], *s. Bot:* **1.** tamarin *m*; **t. pulp,** tamarin. **2. t. (tree),** tamarinier *m.*

tamarisk ['tæmərisk], **tamarix** ['tæməriks], *s. Bot:* tamaris *m*; **common, French, t.,** tamaris commun.

tambac ['tæmbæk], *s. Metall:* tombac *m*.

tambor ['tæmbuər], *s. Ich:* tambour *m*.

tambour[1] ['tæmbər], *s.* **1.** *Mus:* caisse *f*, *esp.* grosse caisse. **2.** (*a*) *Needlew:* (i) **t. (frame),** métier *m*, tambour *m*, à broder; métier suisse; **t. lace,** dentelle (brodée) sur tulle; (ii) **t. (work),** broderie *f*, tapisserie *f*, au tambour; **to do t. work,** broder sur tambour, sur métier; crocheter sur métier; (*b*) *Arch:* tambour (de colonne, de noyau; (*c*) *Const:* tambour (de vestibule); *Fort:* tambour (à l'entrée d'un ouvrage); (*d*) *NAm:* rideau *m* (de bureau américain, de classeur). **3.** *Ich:* tambour.

tambour[2]. **1.** *v.tr.* broder (une étoffe) au tambour, sur métier. **2.** *v.i.* broder au tambour; crocheter sur métier.

tambourin ['tæmbərin], *s. Mus:* tambourin *m*; **t. player,** tambourineur *m*.

tambourine [tæmbə'ri:n], *s.* **1.** *Mus:* tambour *m* de basque. **2.** *Orn:* **t. (pigeon),** tambour.

tame[1] [teim], *a.* **1.** (*a*) (i) (animal) apprivoisé, domestiqué; (ii) (animal) domestique; **animal that easily grows t.,** animal qui s'apprivoise, se domestique, facilement; **our robin has become very t.,** notre rouge-gorge s'est bien apprivoisé; (*b*) *NAm:* (*of plant, land*) cultivé. **2.** *F:* (*a*) (i) (*of pers.*) soumis, docile, pusillanime; **her husband was a t. little man,** son mari était un petit homme doux; (ii) **we have a t. builder,** nous disposons d'un entrepreneur complaisant; (*b*) anodin, insipide; **the story has a t. ending,** l'histoire se termine sur une note banale, finit en queue-de-poisson.

tame[2]. **1.** *v.tr.* (*a*) apprivoiser (une souris, etc.); (*b*) domestiquer (une bête); *NAm:* cultiver (une plante, un terrain); (*c*) mater (qn, une passion); dompter (un lion, un cheval); brider (le courage, l'ardeur, de qn); (*d*) **to t. (down),** atténuer, adoucir (une couleur, une expression). **2.** *v.i.* (*a*) (*of wild animal, etc.*) s'apprivoiser; (*b*) **here the story begins to t.,** ici l'intérêt ne se soutient pas, l'histoire devient banale; (*c*) (*of pers.*) **to t. (down),** (i) s'adoucir, décolérer; (ii) se ranger, jeter sa gourme.

tameable ['teiməbl], *a.* (animal, etc.) (i) apprivoisable, (ii) domptable.

tamely ['teimli], *adv.* **1.** (se soumettre) sans résistance, lâchement, servilement, docilement. **2.** fadement; (écrire) platement; **to end t.,** avoir un dénouement insipide.

tameness ['teimnis], *s.* **1.** nature apprivoisée, nature douce (d'un animal). **2.** *F:* (*a*) (*of pers.*) manque *m* de courage, de vie; pusillanimité *f*; (*b*) monotonie *f*, fadeur *f* (du style, etc.); insipidité *f*, banalité *f* (d'un conte, du dénouement).

tame-poison ['teimpɔizən], *s. Bot:* dompte-venin *m inv*.

tamer ['teimər], *s.* apprivoiseur, -euse (d'oiseaux, etc.); dompteur, -euse (d'animaux sauvages); **lion t.,** dompteur de lions.

Tamerlane ['tæmə(:)lein], *Pr.n.m. Hist:* Tamerlan.

Tamil ['tæmil]. **1.** *Ethn:* (*a*) *a.* tamoul; tamil (*no f.*); (*b*) *s.* Tamoul, -e; Tamil *m*. **2.** *s. Ling:* tamoul *m*, tamil *m*.

taming ['teimiŋ], *s.* **1.** (*a*) apprivoisement *m*; (*b*) domestication *f*. **2.** domptage *m*. **3. t. (down),** atténuation *f*, adoucissement *m* (du langage, des couleurs).

Tammany ['tæməni], *s. U.S:* (*a*) organisation centrale du parti démocrate de New York (siégeant à Tammany Hall); (*b*) corruption *f*, vénalité *f*, dans l'administration municipale, politique.

Tammanyism ['tæməniizm], *s.* = TAMMANY (*b*).

tammy[1] ['tæmi], *s.* étamine *f*, tamise *f*.

tammy[2], *s. Cu:* (i) passoire *f*, (ii) tamis *m*.

tammy[3], *v.tr. Cu:* tamiser.

tammy[4], *s. F:* béret écossais.

tam-o'-shanter [tæmə'ʃæntər], *s.* béret écossais.

tamp [tæmp], *v.tr.* **1.** *Civ.E:* damer, pilonner, tasser, refouler, bliner (la terre, etc.); damer (du ballast). **2.** bourrer (la charge d'un obus, un fourneau de mine, etc.).

tamper[1] ['tæmpər], *s.* **1.** (*pers.*) bourreur *m*. **2.** *Tls:* dame *f* à fouler; *Min:* bourroir *m*. **3.** *Atom.Ph:* réflecteur *m* de neutrons.

tamper[2], *v.i.* (*a*) **to t. with sth.,** (i) toucher à, *F:* trifouiller (avec) (un mécanisme, etc.); (ii) (*with evil intent*) altérer (un document, une clef, les monnaies); falsifier (un registre); fausser, brouiller (une serrure); *F:* tripatouiller (des comptes, des dépêches); *Post:* spolier (une lettre, un colis); **to t. with the cash,** tripoter, trifouiller, dans la caisse; *Turf:* **to t. with a horse,** donner une boulette à, doper, un cheval; (*b*) **to t. with a witness,** essayer de corrompre un témoin; suborner un témoin; **to t. with the army,** travailler l'armée.

tampering ['tæmpəriŋ], *s.* (*a*) **t. with sth.,** altération *f*, adultération *f* (de documents); falsification *f* (de registres); tripatouillage *m* (de comptes, etc.); spoliation *f* (de colis, etc.); (*b*) **t. with witnesses,** subornation *f* de témoins.

Tampico [tæm'pi:kou], *Pr.n. Geog:* Tampico; *Com:* **T. fibre,** tampico *m*.

tamping ['tæmpiŋ], *s.* **1.** *Civ.E: etc:* damage *m*, pilonnage *m*, refoulement *m*, blinage *m* (de la terre, du gravier). **2.** (*a*) bourrage *m* (d'un fourneau de mine, d'un obus); **t. bar,** refouloir *m*, bourroir *m*, batte *f* à bourrer; (*b*) *Min:* bourre *f* (d'un fourneau de mine).

tampion ['tæmpiən], *s.* bouchon *m*; *Artil:* **(muzzle) t.,** tampon *m*, tape *f*, de bouche; **to put a t. in a gun,** taper un canon.

tampon[1] ['tæmpən], *s.* (*a*) (i) *Surg:* tampon *m* (d'ouate, de gaze); (ii) *Hyg:* tampon périodique; (*b*) *Engr:* tampon (de graveur); (*c*) *Mus:* **bass t.,** tampon, mailloche *f* (de grosse caisse).

tampon[2], *v.tr. Surg:* tamponner (une plaie profonde, le vagin, etc.).

tamponade [tæmpə'neid], **tamponage** ['tæmpənidʒ], *s. Surg:* tamponnement *m* (des fosses nasales, du vagin, etc.).

tam-tam ['tæmtæm], *s. Mus:* tam-tam *m*, *pl.* tams-tams.

tan[1] [tæn]. **1.** *s.* (*a*) *Tan:* tan *m*; **t. bark,** écorce *f* à tan; **spent t. (bark),** tannée *f*; **t. ball, t. turf,** briquette *f*, motte *f*, de tan; **t. litter,** poussier *m* de mottes (pour arènes de cirque, etc.); *Hort:* **t. bed,** couche *f* de tannée; *Tan:* **t. house,** magasin *m* d'écorces; **t. liquor, ooze, pickle,** jus tannant, jusée *f*; **t. pit, vat,** fosse *f* à tan; (*b*) *F:* **the t.,** le cirque, l'arène *f*; *Equit:* la piste; (*c*) couleur *f* du tan; (i) tanné *m*; **leather goods in t.,** maroquinerie *f* en havane; (ii) hâle *m*, teint hâlé (de la peau); **to lose one's t.,** débronzer. **2.** *a.* tanné; tan *inv*; **t. leather shoes,** souliers en cuir jaune, souliers marron, jaunes; **t. leather gloves,** gants en tanné; **black and t. dog,** chien noir et feu *inv*.

tan[2], *v.* **(tanned) 1.** *v.tr.* (*a*) tanner (les peaux, une voile); *F:* **to t. s.o., s.o.'s hide,** tanner (le cuir à) qn; administrer une tannée à qn; rosser, étriller, qn; (*b*) (*of sun, weather*) hâler, bronzer (la peau, le teint). **2.** *v.i.* (*of complexion*) se hâler, se bronzer; **I t. easily,** j'ai une peau qui bronze, je bronze facilement.

tan[3], *s. Mth:* tangente *f*.

tanacetum [tænə'si:təm], *s. Bot:* tanacetum *m*.

tanager ['tænədʒər], *s. Orn:* tangara *m*; **scarlet, cardinal, t.,** tangara rouge; cardinal *m*, -aux, d'Amérique; *Fr.C:* tangara écarlate; **swallow t.,** tersine *f*; **summer t., Cooper's t.,** *Fr.C:* tangara vermillon; **western t.,** *Fr.C:* tangara à tête rouge.

Tanagra ['tænəgrə]. **1.** *Pr.n.A.Geog:* Tanagra, Tanagre. **2.** *s. Archeol: Cer:* **tanagra (statuette, figurine),** tanagra *m or f*, statuette tanagrienne.

Tanagridae [tə'nægridi:], *s.pl. Orn:* tanagridés *m*.

tanagrine ['tænəgrin], *a. Orn:* des tanagridés.

Tananarivo [tænænə'ri:vou], *Pr.n. Geog:* Tananarive.

tandem ['tændəm]. **1.** *s.* (*a*) *Veh:* tandem *m*; (*b*) *Cy:* **t. (bicycle),** tandem (de tourisme); **t. riders,** cyclistes *mf* en tandem; tandémistes *mf*; (*c*) **to harness two horses in t.,** atteler deux chevaux en tandem, en flèche; **to pull two trailers in t.,** traîner deux remorques l'une derrière l'autre; **two political parties working in t. for an end,** deux partis politiques qui travaillent en collaboration, qui concourent, à un but; (*d*) *attrib. Mch:* **t. cyclinders,** cylindres *m* en tandem; **t. engine,** machine *f* à cyclindres en tandem; **t. working,** fonctionnement *m* en tandem; *Cmptr:* **t. exchange, t. central office,** central *m* tandem. **2.** *adv.* **to drive t.,** conduire en flèche, à grandes guides, en tandem; **horses driven t.,** chevaux attelés en flèche, en tandem.

tang[1] [tæŋ], *s.* **1.** (*a*) soie *f* (d'un couteau, ciseau, d'une épée); queue *f* (d'une lime); ardillon *m* (d'une boucle); (*b*) *Sm.a:* talon *m* (de culasse de fusil). **2.** (*a*) goût vif, saveur *f*; montant *m* (d'une épice, etc.); **t. of the sea,** senteur *f* de l'air marin; **t. of the soil, native t.,** goût de terroir; **a t. of irony,** une pointe d'ironie; (*b*) **the t. of the morning air,** le piquant de l'air matinal; **there's a t. in the air,** l'air est vif.

tang[2], *v.tr.* façonner une soie, queue, à (un outil, etc.).

tang[3]. **1.** *v.tr.* (*a*) faire retentir, faire résonner (une cloche, etc.); (*b*) *Ap:* **to t. bees,** empêcher la fuite d'un essaim en faisant du tintamarre, en frappant sur des casseroles. **2.** *v.i.* (*of bell*) rendre un son aigu; retentir.

tang[4], *s.* **1.** son aigu (d'une cloche, d'une corde tendue); tintement *m* (d'une cloche). **2. a t. of displeasure in her voice,** un accent de mécontentement dans sa voix.

tang[5], *s. Dial:* goémon *m*.

tanged [tæŋd], *a.* (couteau, ciseau) à soie; (lime) à queue.

tangelo ['tændʒilou], *s. Hort:* tangelo *m*.

tangency ['tændʒənsi], *s. Mth:* tangence *f*.

tangent ['tændʒənt]. **1.** *a.* tangent, tangentiel (**to,** à); *Mth:* **straight line t. to a curve,** droite tangente à une courbe; **t. line,** ligne tangentielle; tangente *f*; **t. plane,** plan tangent; *Ph:* **t. ray,** rayon rasant; *Atom.Ph:* **t. beam holes,** canaux d'irradiation tangentiels; *Mec.E:* **t. key,** clavette tangentielle; **t. screw,** vis tangentielle, sans fin; **t. plate,** cavalier *m* (d'un tour); **t. paddles,** aubes tangentes; *Cy:* **t. spokes,** rayons tangents; *Artil:* **t. scale, sight,** hausse *f*. **2.** *s.* tangente *f*; (*a*) *Mth:* **to draw a t. to a curve,** tracer une tangente à une courbe; **at a t. to a curve,** tangentiellement à une courbe; *F:* **to fly, go, off at a t.,** (i) décamper subrepticement; *F:* prendre la tangente; (ii) changer brusquement de sujet, passer du coq à l'âne, faire un coq-à-l'âne; (*b*) *Mth:* **t. of an angle, of an arc,** tangente d'un angle, d'un arc; **t. A,** la tangente A, tg. A; *Surv:* **t. of the angle of slope,** pente *f* du terrain.

tangential [tæn'dʒenʃ(ə)l], *a.* **1.** *Mth: etc:* tangentiel, tangent (**to,** à); *Mth:* **t. co-ordinates,** coordonnées tangentielles; **t. equation,** équation tangentielle; **t. point,** point *m* de tangence; *Mec:* **t. acceleration,** accélération tangentielle; **t. component,** (force) composante tangentielle; **t. motion,** mouvement tangentiel (d'un astre, etc.); *Aedcs:* **t. swirl,** turbulence tangentielle; *Mec.E:* **t. flow turbine,** turbine tangentielle; *Elcs:* **t. channel,** canal tangentiel; **t. wave path,** parcours direct, trajectoire directe, d'une onde. **2.** *NAm:* superficiel, qui effleure le sujet.

tangentially [tæn'dʒenʃəli], *adv.* tangentiellement.

Tangerine [tændʒə'ri:n, 'tændʒəri:n]. **1.** *Geog:* (*a*) *a.* de Tanger; tangitan; (*b*) *s.* Tangitan, -ane. **2.** *s.* **tangerine,** orange *f* de Tanger; mandarine *f*, tangerine *f*. **3.** *a.* & *s.* **t. (colour),** mandarine (*m*) *inv*.

tanghin ['tæŋgin], *s.* (*tree, poison*) tanghin *m*, tanghen *m*.

tangibility [tæn(d)ʒi'biliti], **tangibleness** ['tæn(d)ʒiblnis], *s.* **1.** tangibilité *f*, palpabilité *f*. **2.** réalité *f*.

tangible ['tæn(d)ʒibl], *a.* **1.** tangible, palpable; **the t. world,** le monde sensible; *Jur:* **t. assets,** valeurs matérielles; **t. personal property,** biens mobiliers corporels; **t. evidence,** preuve matérielle, tangible. **2.** réel; **t. difference,** différence *f* sensible; **without t. ground of complaint,** sans grief réel.

tangibly ['tæn(d)ʒibli], *adv.* **1.** tangiblement, palpablement. **2.** sensiblement, manifestement.

Tangier [tæn'dʒiər], *O:* **Tangiers** [tæn'dʒiəz], *Pr.n. Geog:* Tanger *m*.

tangle[1], **tangleweed, tanglewrack** ['tæŋgl, -wi:d, -ræk], *s. Algae:* laminaire *f*; (i) baudrier *m* de Neptune; (ii) laminaire digitée.

tangle[2], *s.* embrouillement *m* (de fils, d'affaires); emmêlement *m* (de fils, cheveux); fouillis *m* (de broussailles); **t. of branches, barbed wire,** enchevêtrement *m*, entrelacement *m*, de branches, de barbelés; **t. of briars,** entrelacs *m* de ronces; **to be (all) in a t.,** (*of string, etc.*) être (tout) embrouillé; (*of wool, hair*) être (tout) enchevêtré; *Fig:* (*of pers.*) se trouver désorienté, ne savoir plus où on en est; **to get into a t.,** (*of string, business*) s'embrouiller; (*of wool, hair*) s'enchevêtrer; *F:* (*of pers.*) **to get into a t. with s.o.,** avoir une prise de bec avec qn; **to straighten, comb, out the tangles in one's hair,** démêler ses cheveux; **traffic t.,** enchevêtrement, embarras *m*, de voitures; embouteillage *m*; **the traffic got into a complete t.,** il y eut un embouteillage inextricable; **a nice t. you've made of it!** vous avez fait du beau! **it's a hopeless t.,** *F:* c'est le pot au noir.

tangle[3]. **1.** *v.tr.* **to t. sth. (up),** embrouiller, (em)mêler (des fils, des cheveux); embrouiller (une affaire); **to t. up a lock,** fausser, mêler, une serrure; **to get tangled (up),** (*of thgs*) s'emmêler; (*of thgs, pers.*) s'embrouiller, s'entortiller; (*of pers.*) se mettre dans le pétrin. **2.** *v.i.* s'embrouiller, s'emmêler, s'enchevêtrer; *F: O:* **to t. with s.o.,** avoir une prise de bec avec qn; *NAm:* **to be tangled with a shady business,** se trouver impliqué dans une affaire louche.

tangled [tæŋgld], *a.* embrouillé, emmêlé, entrelacé; **t. brushwood,** broussailles *f* inextricables; **t. hair,** cheveux *m* en désordre; **t. web of intrigue,** trame compliquée d'intrigues; **t. politics,** politique compliquée.

tanglefoot ['tæŋglfut], *s. P:* **1.** *NAm:* whisky *m* de mauvaise qualité; casse-gueule *m*, casse-poitrine *m*, casse-patte *m*. **2.** boisson forte; gnôle *f*.

tangling (up) ['tæŋgliŋ(ʌp)], *s.* embrouillement *m*, emmêlement *m*.

tango[1] ['tæŋgou]. **1.** *s. Danc:* tango *m*. **2.** *a.* tango *inv*; (couleur *f* d')orange *m inv*.

tango[2], *v.i.* danser le tango; *F:* tangoter.

tangram ['tæŋgræm], *s.* casse-tête *inv* chinois.

tanguin ['tæŋgin], *s.* (*tree, poison*) tanghin *m*, tanghen *m*.

tangy ['tæŋi], *a.* **1.** qui a un goût piquant, caractéristique. **2.** qui a un petit goût désagréable.

tanist ['tænist], *s. Hist:* successeur élu d'un chef celtique.

tank[1] [tæŋk], *s.* **1.** réservoir *m*; (*a*) **supply t.,** réservoir d'alimentation; **water t.,** réservoir à eau, d'eau; *Nau:* caisse *f* à eau; (*deep*) cale *f* à eau; (*on deck* *for fresh water*) charnier *m* à eau douce; *Rail:* (*on locomotive, tender*) caisse à eau, soute *f* (à eau); (*along track*) château *m* d'eau; **hot water t.**, réservoir à eau chaude; *Mch:* **(feed) water t.**, réservoir d'eau d'alimentation; bâche *f*; *Fish:* **(live) fish t.**, vivier *m*, boutique *f*; **storage t.**, réservoir d'emmagasinage, de stockage; **petrol,** *NAm:* **gas(oline), (storage) t.**, réservoir à essence, d'essence; **(fuel) oil t.**, réservoir à, de, mazout; **t. cession price,** prix *m* de cession en réservoir; **segmental t.**, réservoir compartimenté; (*b*) *Aut: Av:* **fuel t., petrol t.,** *NAm:* **gas(oline) t.**, réservoir de carburant, de combustible, d'essence; **main t.**, réservoir principal; **auxiliary t., service t.**, réservoir auxiliaire, supplémentaire; *Aut:* nourrice *f*; **gravity feed t.**, réservoir en charge; **t. with vacuum feed,** réservoir à exhausteur; **t. capacity,** contenance *f*, capacité *f*, du réservoir, des réservoirs; *Av:* **belly, ventral, t.**, réservoir ventral; **(wing) tip t.**, réservoir en bout d'aile; **bladder, flexible, t.**, réservoir souple; **built-in, structural, t.**, réservoir structural; **drop(pable), detachable, jettison(able), t.**, réservoir largable; **self-sealing t.**, réservoir auto-étanche, increvable. **2.** (*a*) *Ind: etc:* cuve *f*, bac *m*; **settling t.**, (i) cuve, bac, de décantation; (ii) bassin *m* de colmatage; *Metalw:* **pickling t.**, bac de décapage; **vacuum t.**, cuve à, sous, vide; (*b*) *Phot:* **developing t.**, cuve pour développement; **daylight development t.**, cuve pour développement en plein jour; **washing t.**, cuve à lavage; *Cin:* **cooling t.**, cuvette *f* de refroidissement. **3.** (*a*) *El:* **accumulator t.**, caisse d'accumulateur; **transformer t.**, cuve de transformateur; *Atom.Ph:* **reactor t.**, cuve de la pile, enceinte *f* du réacteur; *Civ.E:* **load t.**, caisson *m* de chargement (de rouleau compresseur); *Nau:* **cargo t.**, citerne *f* de cargaison; (*on cable ship*) **cable t.**, cuve à câbles; (*b*) *Cin: F:* cabine *f* d'enregistrement, cabine insonore; (*c*) *Pol:* **the think t.**, nom familier du *Central Policy Review Staff* (comité d'experts pour conseiller le gouvernement). **4.** compartiment *m* (d'un réservoir, etc.); *Nau:* **double-bottom tanks,** compartiments du double fond (d'un navire). **5.** *N.Arch: Nau:* **trimming t.**, caisse, citerne, d'assiette; **(water ballast) t.**, ballast *m*; (*on submarine*) **to blow the tanks,** chasser aux ballasts; (*on lifeboat, etc.*) **air, buoyancy, t.**, caisson à air, de flottabilité; **watertight t.**, caisson étanche. **6.** (*a*) bassin *m*; *N.Arch: Av:* **experimental, model, trial, t.**, bassin d'essai des carènes; **t. test,** essai *m* au bassin des carènes; (*b*) *NAm:* bassin, réservoir, étang *m*. **7.** *Mil:* char *m* (de combat); *O:* char d'assaut; **the tanks,** les blindés *m*; **the Royal T. Corps,** l'arme blindée; **light, medium, heavy, t.**, char léger, moyen, lourd; **amphibious t.**, char amphibie; **accompanying, close support, t.**, char d'accompagnement; **break-through t.**, char de rupture; **cruiser t.**, char de bataille; **command t.**, char de commandement. **8.** *attrib.* (*a*) **t. barge,** chaland-citerne *m*, *pl.* chalands-citernes; **t. lorry,** *NAm:* **truck,** camion-citerne *m*, *pl.* camions-citernes; **t. trailer,** remorque-citerne *f*, *pl.* remorques-citernes; *Rail:* **t. wagon,** *NAm:* **car,** wagon-citerne *m*, *pl.* wagons-citernes; **t. engine, locomotive,** locomotive *f* tender, machine *f* tender; *Petr:* **t. farm,** dépôt *m* d'hydrocarbure, de carburants; *Agr:* **t. farming,** culture *f* sans sol, aquiculture *f*, culture hydroponique; *Phot:* **t. developing,** développement *m* en cuve; *El:* **t. circuit,** circuit-bouchon *m*, *pl.* circuits-bouchons; circuit résonnant parallèle; (*b*) *Mil:* **t. barrier,** barrière *f* antichar; **t. ditch,** fossé *m* antichar; **t. trap,** piège *m* à char(s); **t. destroyer,** chasseur *m* de chars; **t. commander,** chef *m* de char; **t. carrier, trailer,** remorque *f*, plate-forme *f*, porte-chars; **t. transporter,** porte-chars *m*; **t.-proof,** à l'abri des chars, protégé contre les chars; (terrain, etc.) non accessible aux chars; **t. warfare,** guerre *f* des chars, des blindés; (*c*) *NAm:* **t. town,** patelin perdu, trou perdu, bled *m*.

tank[2]. **1.** *v.tr.* mettre (l'huile, etc.) en réservoir. **2.** *v.i.* **to t. up,** (i) *Aut:* faire le plein (d'essence); (ii) *P:* s'en donner dans le casque, se soûler.

tankage ['tæŋkidʒ], *s.* **1.** (*a*) emmagasinage *m* (d'huile, etc.); (*b*) frais *mpl* d'emmagasinage. **2.** (*a*) contenance *f*, capacité *f*, d'un réservoir; (*b*) ensemble *m*, série *f*, de réservoirs; *Petr:* **field t.**, réservoirs de chantier. **3.** *Husb:* déchets de viande étuvés, farine *f* de viande d'autoclave, farine d'animaux d'équarrissage.

tankard ['tæŋkəd], *s.* **1.** pot *m*, chope *f*, en étain; pot à bière; **a t. of ale,** un pot de bière. **2.** *Agr:* **t. turnip,** navet long.

tanked [tæŋ(k)t], *a.* **1.** (*of oil*) clarifié (par repos prolongé). **2.** *P:* ivre, soûl; **to get t. (up),** s'en donner dans le casque; se soûler.

tanker ['tæŋkər], *s.* **1.** *Nau:* bateau-citerne *m*, *pl.* bateaux-citernes; navire-citerne *m*, *pl.* navires-citernes; bateau-réservoir *m*, *pl.* bateaux-réservoirs; navire *m* pour vrac liquide; **(oil) t.**, (navire) pétrolier (*m*); **butane t.**, butanier *m*; **benzine t.**, benzininer *m*; **methane t.**, méthanier *m*. **2.** (*a*) **t. (lorry, truck),** camion-citerne *m*, *pl.* camions-citernes; **heavy t.**, camion-citerne gros porteur; (*b*) *Rail:* wagon-citerne *m*, *pl.* wagons-citernes; wagon-réservoir *m*, *pl.* wagons-réservoirs. **3.** *Av:* **t. (aircraft),** avion *m* de ravitaillement; avion-citerne *m*, *pl.* avions-citernes. **4.** *Mil:* militaire *m*, soldat *m*, de l'arme blindée; tankiste *m*.

tankette [tæŋ'ket], *s. Mil:* chenillette *f*.

tannage ['tænidʒ], *s.* tannage *m*.

tannate ['tæneit], *s. Ch:* tannate *m*.

tanned [tænd], *a.* **1.** (cuir) tanné. **2.** (teint, visage) basané, hâlé.

tanner[1] ['tænər], *s.* tanneur *m*.

tanner[2], *s. P: A:* (pièce *f* de) six anciens pence.

tannery ['tænəri], *s.* tannerie *f*.

tannic ['tænik], *a. Ch:* (acide) tannique.

tannin ['tænin], *s. Ch:* tan(n)in *m*; **to treat with t.**, tan(n)iser.

tanning ['tæniŋ], *s.* **1.** (*a*) tannage *m* (des peaux, voiles, etc.); **t. bark,** écorce *f* à tan; **t. liquor,** jus tannant; jusée *f*; (*b*) **t. (trade),** tannerie *f*. **2.** *F:* tannée *f*, raclée *f*; **to give s.o. a t.**, administrer une raclée à qn.

tanrec ['tænrek], *s. Z:* tanrec *m*.

tansy ['tænzi], *s. Bot:* tanaisie *f*, barbotine *f*, herbe *f* aux vers.

tantalate ['tæntəleit], *s. Ch:* tantalate *m*.

tantalic [tæn'tælik], *a. Ch:* tantalique.

tantalite ['tæntəlait], *s. Miner:* tantalite *f*.

tantalization [tæntəlai'zeiʃ(ə)n], *s.* tourment *m*, taquinerie *f*.

tantalize ['tæntəlaiz], *v.tr.* infliger le supplice de Tantale à (qn); tourmenter, taquiner, torturer (qn); mettre (qn) au supplice.

tantalizing ['tæntəlaiziŋ], *a.* tentant (mais hors de portée); **it's t.**, c'est un vrai supplice de Tantale; **t. smile,** sourire provocant, aguichant.

tantalizingly ['tæntəlaiziŋli], *adv.* (*a*) cruellement; (*b*) d'un air provocant.

tantalum ['tæntələm], *s. Ch:* tantale *m*; *El:* **t. lamp,** lampe *f* au tantale, à filament de tantale.

Tantalus ['tæntələs]. **1.** *Pr.n.m. Myth:* Tantale; *Ph:* **T. cup,** vase *m* de Tantale. **2.** *s.* cave à liqueurs anglaise. **3.** *s. Orn:* tantale *m*.

tantamount ['tæntəmaunt], *a.* équivalent (**to,** à); **to be t. to sth.**, équivaloir à qch.; **excuse t. to a refusal,** excuse qui équivaut à un refus; **that's t. to saying I'm a liar,** c'est comme si l'on disait, cela revient à dire, de fait c'est dire, que je mens.

tantara ['tæntərə, tæn'tɑːrə], *int. & s.* (*a*) taratata (*m*) (d'une trompette); (*b*) *A:* fanfare *f* (de trompettes).

tantivy [tæn'tivi], *Ven: A:* **1.** *adv.* au galop. **2.** *s.* galop. **3.** *int.* taïaut.

tantra ['tæntrə], *s. Hindu Rel:* tantra *m*.

tantric ['tæntrik], **tantrist** ['tæntrist], *a. Hindu Rel:* tantrique.

tantrism ['tæntrizm], *s. Hindu Rel:* tantrisme *m*.

tantrum ['tæntrəm], *s.* accès *m* de mauvaise humeur, de colère; **to get into a t.**, se mettre en colère; sortir de ses gonds; **to be in a t.**, être énervé; ne pas décolérer; **she's in one of her tantrums this morning,** elle a ses nerfs ce matin.

tantum ergo ['tæntəm'ɜːgou, 'ɛəgou], *s. R.C.Ch:* tantum ergo *m*.

tanyard ['tænjɑːd], *s.* tannerie *f*.

Tanzania [tænzə'niə], *Pr.n. Geog:* Tanzanie *f*.

Taoiseach ['tiːʃəχ], *s.* (*in Eire*) premier ministre.

Taoism ['tɑːouizm], *s. Rel.H:* taôisme *m*.

Taoist ['tɑːouist], *s. Rel.H:* taôiste *mf*.

Taoistic [tɑːou'istik], *a. Rel.H:* taôiste.

Taormina [tɑːɔː'miːnə, teiɔː-], *Pr.n. Geog:* Taormina, Taormine.

tap[1] [tæp], *s.* **1.** (*a*) robinet *m*; (*of cask, tank*) cannelle *f*, cannette *f*; (*of cask*) chantepleure *f*; **cold(-water), hot (-water), t.**, robinet d'eau chaude, d'eau froide; **to turn on, turn off, the t.**, ouvrir, fermer, le robinet; *F:* **to turn on the t.**, pleurer; le faire aux larmes; **to put one's hands under the t.**, se rincer rapidement les mains; **t. water,** eau *f* du robinet, de la ville; **decompression t.**, robinet de décompression; **drip t.**, (robinet) purgeur *m*; **floating-ball t.**, robinet (de réglage) à flotteur; **gauge t.**, robinet de jauge, de hauteur d'eau; **inlet t.**, robinet d'admission; **t. with crutch head,** robinet à béquille, à tête; **t. with square head,** robinet à carré; **water t. with long bend,** chandelier *m* (de paillasse de laboratoire, etc.); (*b*) (*of cask*) **in t.**, en vidange; (*of beer, etc.*) **on t.**, (i) en perce, en vidange; (ii) au tonneau; (*of pers., thg*) **to be on t.**, être (toujours) disponible; *Fin:* **bills on t.**, effets placés de gré à gré. **2.** (*a*) boisson *f*, *esp.* bière *f* (sous pression); **an excellent t.**, une bière excellente; **give me a tankard of the same t.**, tirez-m'en un pot du même fût; (*b*) = TAPROOM; *A:* **t. house,** cabaret *m*, débit *m* de boissons. **3.** (*a*) *El:* prise *f* (intermédiaire); **coil t., transformer t.**, prise de bobine, de transformateur; (*b*) *Tp: U.S:* branchement *m*, bifurcation *f*. **4.** *Tls:* (*a*) **(screw) t.**, taraud *m*; **bottoming t.**, taraud finisseur, taraud pour trou borgne; **entering t.**, taraud amorceur; amorçoir *m*; **expanding t.**, taraud à expansion; **ground-thread t.**, taraud rectifié; **hand t.**, taraud à main; **machine t.**, taraud à machine; **pipe t.**, taraud pour tuyauterie; **reaming t.**, taraud aléseur; **spiral-flute t.**, taraud à rainures hélicoïdales; **square-thread t.**, taraud à filet carré, à pas carré; **taper t.**, taraud conique; ébaucheur *m*; **t. bolt,** boulon taraudé; vis *f* à tête; **t. cutter,** fraise *f* à tarauds; **t. drill,** mèche *f*; **t. holder,** porte-taraud *m*, *pl.* porte-tarauds; **t. handle, t. wrench,** tourne-à-gauche *m inv* pour filière; (*b*) *Coop etc:* **t. auger, t. borer,** (tarière *f*) bondonnière *f*; foret *m*. **5.** *Metall:* coulée *f* (de métal fondu).

tap[2], *v.tr.* **(tapped) 1.** (*a*) mettre une cannelle à (un fût); percer, mettre en perce (un fût, une barrique); (*b*) **to t. a tree (for resin),** inciser, faire une incision à, un arbre; gemmer, saigner, un arbre; *Metall:* **to t. the furnace,** percer le haut fourneau; *Surg:* **to t. a lung,** ponctionner, faire une ponction à, un poumon; **to t. an abscess,** percer, vider, un abcès; **to t. wine,** tirer du vin; *Metall:* **to t. the metal from the furnace,** couler le métal du haut fourneau; **to t. a stream,** faire une prise à, saigner, un cours d'eau; **to t. a (gas, water) main,** faire une prise, un branchement, sur une conduite (de gaz, d'eau); **to t. a telegraph wire,** faire une prise sur un fil télégraphique; capter un message télégraphique; **to t. a telephone conversation,** capter une communication téléphonique; *El:* **to t. a coil,** effectuer, faire, une dérivation à une bobine; faire des prises sur un enroulement; *Com:* **to t. a new market,** exploiter un nouveau marché, créer de nouveaux débouchés; *Fin:* **to t. capital,** drainer les capitaux, faire appel aux capitaux; **to t. talent,** drainer les talents, faire appel au talent; *F:* **to t. s.o. for fifty francs,** taper qn de cinquante francs. **2.** tarauder, fileter (un écrou).

tap[3], *s.* **1.** (*a*) tape *f*; petit coup; coup léger; **t. at the door,** coup léger, discret, à la porte; **there was a t. at the door,** on a frappé doucement, discrètement, à la porte; **the t. (t.) of a blind man's stick,** le tac-tac d'une canne d'aveugle; **a t. of the drum,** on coup de baguette, de tambour; (*b*) (léger) choc; *W.Tel:* **decohering t.**, choc de décohésion. **2.** *Mil:* **taps,** (sonnerie *f* de) (i) la soupe, (ii) *U.S:* l'extinction *f* des feux. **3.** *Danc:* claquette *f*; (*on shoes*) fer *m*; **t. shoes,** chaussures *fpl* à, de, claquettes; claquettes; **t. dance, t. dancing,** danse *f* à claquettes; **t. dancer,** danseur, -euse, de claquettes; **can you do t.?** savez-vous faire des claquettes? **t. routine,** danse à claquettes.

tap[4], *v.* **(tapped) 1.** (*a*) *v.tr.* frapper légèrement; taper, tapoter; **to t. the pavement with one's stick,** frapper le pavé légèrement de sa canne; **she tapped me on the shoulder,** elle m'a frappé (à) l'épaule; **to t. a child on the cheek,** donner des petites tapes sur la joue à un enfant; tapoter la joue à un enfant; (*b*) *v.ind.tr.* **to t. at, on, the door,** frapper, cogner, doucement à la porte; **to t. on a typewriter,** taper (sur) le clavier d'une machine à écrire; **to t. in, out,** enfoncer, chasser (une goupille, etc.) à petits coups secs; **to t. out a message,** émettre un message (en morse); **to t. out one's pipe,** débourrer sa pipe. **2.** *v.tr. Dial: & U.S:* ajouter une couche de cuir à (la semelle d'un soulier); refaire, rectifier (le talon). **3.** *v.i.* **to t. (dance),** faire des claquettes; **can you t.?** savez-vous faire des claquettes?

tap[5], *s. O:* **1.** = TAPNET. **2.** *Com:* **t. figs,** *F:* **taps,** figues *f* de qualité inférieure.

tape[1] [teip], *s.* **1.** (*a*) **(cotton) t., (linen) t.**, ruban *m* de fil, de coton; tresse *f* de coton; cordon *m* de coton; ganse *f*; (*for parcels*) bolduc *m*; (*for covering seams in canvas, etc.*) bande *f* à maroufler; **masking t.**, ruban-cache *m inv*; **paper t., brown-paper t.**, bande de papier gommé; **self-adhesive t.**, ruban adhésif; *Pharm:* **adhesive t.**, sparadrap *m*; *El:* **insulating t.**, ruban isolant; chatterton *m*; (*b*) *Sp:* (*at winning post*) bande d'arrivée; fil *m* (de laine); **to breast the t.**, arriver le premier; *Turf:* (*at starting gate*) **the tapes,** les rubans. **2. t. (measure),** mètre *m* (ruban); centimètre *m* (de couturière); **steel t.**, ruban d'acier; **surveyor's t.**, ruban, roulette *f*, d'arpenteur. **3.** (*a*) *Tg:* bande, ruban, du récepteur; **to watch the news ticking out on the t.**, regarder les nouvelles se dérouler sur la bande; **t. machine,** téléimprimeur *m*; **ticker t.**, bande de téléimprimeur; (*b*) **recording t.**, bande magnétique; **pre-recorded t.**, bande enregistrée; **t. recorder,** enregistreur *m* magnétique sur ruban, sur bande; Magnétophone *m* (*R.t.m.*); **double track, dual track, half track, t.**

recorder, Magnétophone (à) deux pistes, Magnétophone bipiste; **four track, quarter track, t. recorder,** Magnétophone (à) quatre pistes, Magnétophone quadripiste; **t. recording,** enregistrement *m* sur bande. **4.** *Bot:* **t. grass,** vallisnérie spirale.

tape[2], *v.tr.* **1.** (*a*) (i) attacher, ficeler (un paquet, etc.) avec du bolduc; (ii) attacher (un paquet) avec un adhésif; (*b*) *Dressm: etc:* garnir d'une ganse; border (un vêtement); maroufler (une couture); (*c*) guiper, rubaner (un conducteur électrique). **2.** *Bookb:* coudre sur ruban (les cahiers d'un livre). **3.** mesurer (un terrain, etc.) au cordeau; *F:* **it's all taped,** tout est fin prêt; (*of pers.*) **I've got him taped,** j'ai pris sa mesure; je sais ce qu'il vaut. **4.** *Artil:* **to t. the (enemy) battery,** (i) repérer la batterie; (ii) faire taire la batterie. **5.** enregistrer (qch.) sur bande.

taped [teipt], *a.* **1.** (*a*) *El:* (fil) guipé sous ruban; (câble) rubané; (*b*) (couture) marouflée. **2.** *Bookb:* (cahier) cousu sur ruban. **3.** (musique, etc.) enregistrée sur bande.

tapeinocephalic [tæpainouse'fælik], *a. Anthr:* tapinocéphale.

tapeinocephalism, tapeinocephaly [tæpainou'sefəlizm, -'sefəli], *s. Anthr:* tapinocéphalie *f.*

taper[1] ['teipər], *s.* **1.** bougie filée; *Ecc:* cierge *m*, cire *f*; **rolled t.,** pain *m* de bougie; **small wax t.,** queue-de-rat *f*, *pl.* queues-de-rat; **twisted t.,** rat *m* de cave. **2.** *Bot: F:* **Mary's tapers,** perce-neige *m or f inv.*

taper[2], *s. Mec.E: Arch: Const: etc:* conicité *f*, cône *m*; fuseau *m*; délardement *m* (des marches d'un escalier tournant); *Metall:* dépouille *f* (d'un modèle); **with t. fit,** emmanché sur cône.

taper[3], *a.* **1.** *Lit:* (doigt) effilé, fuselé. **2.** *Mec.E: etc:* conique, côné; **t. thread,** pas *m* conique (de vis).

taper[4]. **1.** *v.tr.* effiler; amincir; tailler en pointe, en cône; *Mec.E:* ajuster en cône, côner (une fusée, etc.); *Arch:* fuseler, diminuer (une colonne); contracturer (le fût d'une colonne). **2.** *v.i.* **to t. (off, away),** s'effiler, s'amincir, décroître, diminuer; aller en diminuant; se terminer en pointe; **column that tapers upwards,** colonne qui diminue vers le haut.

tape-record ['teipriko:d], *v.tr.* enregistrer (qch.) sur bande.

tapered ['teipəd], *a.* (*a*) *Mec.E: etc:* (calibre, taraud) conique, côné, diminué; **t. shank,** queue *f* conique (d'un outil); **t. pin,** goupille *f* conique; (*b*) effilé (en forme de fuseau); **t. fingers,** doigts effilés; **t. trousers,** fuseaux *mpl*; pantalon étroit du bas.

tapering[1] ['teip(ə)riŋ], *a.* en pointe; (doigt) effilé, fuselé; (câble) conique, diminué, à section décroissante; *Arch:* **t. column,** colonne diminuée; *Bot:* **t. tree,** arbre *m* à fût décroissant; **non-t. tree,** arbre à fût plein; **t. stalk,** tige atténuée; *Rail:* **t. curve,** courbe *f* de raccordement (entre deux voies).

tapering[2], *s.* (*a*) taille *f* en pointe; effilement *m*, diminution *f*; (*b*) *Hairdr:* technique *f* du dégradé.

tapestried ['tæpistrid], *a.* tapissé; tendu de tapisseries.

tapestry ['tæpistri], *s.* (*a*) tapisserie *f*; **fine(-worked) t., coarse(-worked) t.,** tapisserie au petit point, au gros point; **needle-embroidered t.,** tapisserie à l'aiguille; **to hang a wall with t.,** tendre un mur avec des tapisseries; tapisser un mur; **chair upholstered with t.,** chaise *f* en tapisserie; **t. maker, weaver,** tapissier, -ière; (*b*) *Arach:* **t. weavers,** tapissières.

tapeti ['tæpiti], *s. Z:* tapeti *m.*

tapetum ['tæpitəm], *s. Bot:* tapetum *m*, tapis *m.*

tapeworm ['teipwə:m], *s.* ténia *m*; ver *m* solitaire; **armed t., unarmed t.,** ténia armé, inerme; **the tapeworms,** les cestodes *m*, les cestoïdes *m.*

taphephobia [tæfi'foubiə], *s. Psy:* taphophobie *f*, taphéphobie *f.*

taphole ['tæphoul], *s. Metall:* trou *m* de coulée, de gueuse; percée *f*, pertuis *m*, chio *m.*

taphria ['tæfriə], **taphrina** [tæ'frainə], *s. Fung:* taphrina *m.*

Taphrinaceae [tæfri'neisii:], *s.pl. Fung:* taphrinacées *f.*

Taphrinales [tæfri'neili:z], *s.pl. Fung:* taphrinales *f.*

taping ['teipiŋ], *s.* **1.** (*a*) bordage *m* (d'une robe, etc.); (*b*) marouflage *m*; (*c*) *El:* guipage *m*, rubanage *m* (de câbles, etc.); **t. machine,** rubaneuse *f*. **2.** = TAPE[1] 1. **3.** *Rec:* enregistrement *m* sur bande.

Tapinoma [tæpi'noumə], *s.pl. Ent:* tapinomes *m.*

tapioca [tæpi'oukə], *s.* tapioca *m*; **t. soup,** tapioca au gras; **t. pudding,** tapioca au lait.

tapiolite ['tæpioulait], *s. Miner:* tapiolite *f.*

tapir ['teipər], *s.* (*often inv. in pl.*) *Z:* tapir *m*; **Indian t.,** tapir à chabraque.

tapirid ['teipirid], **tapiridian** [teipi'ridiən], *s. Z:* tapiridé *m.*

Tapiridae [tei'piridi:], *s.pl. Z:* tapiridés *m.*

tapis ['tæpi:], *s. F:* **to be, come, on the t.,** être sur, occuper, le tapis; être, devenir, l'objet de l'entretien.

tapiti ['tæpiti], *s. Z:* tapeti *m.*

tapnet ['tæpnet], *s.* cabas *m* (pour figues).

tapped [tæpt], *a.* **1.** (*a*) (*of cask*) en perce, en vidange; (*of tree*) gemmé; (*b*) (*of gas main, etc.*) branché, ramifié; *Tg: Tp:* capté (par branchement); (*c*) *El:* (*of coil, transformer*) à prises; **t. resistor,** résistance *f* à prises. **2.** (*of bolt, nut*) taraudé, fileté.

tapper ['tæpər], *s.* **1.** tapoteur, -euse. **2.** *Tg:* (*device*) manipulateur *m*, transmetteur *m*. **3.** *W.T: A:* (*device*) décohéreur *m*, frappeur *m*. **4.** *Tls:* taraudeuse *f.*

tappet ['tæpit], *s. Mec:* taquet *m*; poussoir *m*; mentonnet *m* (de came); came *f*; *Mch: I.C.E: etc:* **catch t.,** cliquet *m*; **t. of an ore stamp,** taquet de bocard à minerai; **valve t.,** poussoir de soupape; **rocker arm t.,** poussoir de culbuteur; **roller t.,** poussoir à galet; **t. clearance,** jeu *m* du poussoir, des poussoirs; **t. adjustment,** réglage *m* du poussoir, des poussoirs; **t. gear,** (dispositif *m* de) commande *f* à, par, poussoir, à, par, came; **t. guide,** guide *m* de poussoir; **t. rod, t. stem,** tige-poussoir *f*, *pl.* tiges-poussoirs; **t. stop,** butée *f* de taquet; **t. lever,** basculeur *m.*

tapping[1] ['tæpiŋ], *s.* **1.** (*a*) mise *f* en perce, perçage *m* (d'un tonneau); incision *f*, gemmage *m* (d'un arbre); *Surg:* ponction *f*, paracentèse *f*; (*b*) tirage *m* (du vin); (*c*) prise *f* d'eau (faite sur une rivière); prise, branchement *m* (sur une conduite d'eau); (*d*) prise, soutirage *m* (de gaz, d'électricité); prise, branchement (sur une conduite de gaz); *El:* dérivation *f* (d'une canalisation); prise, branchement (sur le secteur); (*e*) *Tp: Tg:* branchement d'écoute; **(telephone) t.,** captage (clandestin) (des communications téléphoniques); mouchardage *m* électronique; (*f*) *Metall:* coulée *f*; fusion *f*; **t. bar,** pince *f* de débouchage (de trou de coulée); périer *m*; ringard *m* (de fonderie); **t. bed, t. floor,** table *f*, plate-forme *f*, de coulée; **t. hole,** trou *m* de coulée; (*g*) **t. of natural resources,** exploitation *f* des ressources naturelles. **2.** *Mec.E: Tls:* taraudage *m*; **t. attachment,** dispositif *m*, appareillage *m*, de taraudage; **t. machine,** machine *f* à tarauder; taraudeuse *f*; **t. depth,** profondeur *f* de taraudage.

tapping[2], *s.* petits coups; frappement *m*, tapotement *m*; *Tg:* **t. key,** manipulateur *m*, transmetteur *m.*

taproom ['tæpru:m], *s.* bar *m.*

taproot[1] ['tæpru:t], *s. Bot:* racine pivotante; pivot *m*; (*of plant*) **to form, have, a t.,** pivoter.

taproot[2], *v.i. Bot:* pivoter.

tapster ['tæpstər], *s. A:* **1.** garçon *m* de cabaret. **2.** cabaretier *m.*

tar[1] [tɑ:r], *s.* **1.** (*a*) goudron *m*; (*b*) *F:* bitume *m*, brai *m*; poix *f* liquide; **wood t., Swedish t., Stockholm t.,** goudron végétal; goudron de bois; **to extract t. from gas,** dégoudronner le gaz; *F:* **to spoil the ship for a ha'porth of t.,** faire des économies de bouts de chandelle; **t. oil,** huile *f* de goudron; **t. paper,** papier goudronné; **t. remover,** produit *m* anti-goudron; dissolvant *m* de goudron; *Civ.E:* **t. binding material,** liant goudronneux; **t. boiler,** chaudière *f* à bitume, de bitumier; **t. sprayer, spreader, sprinkler,** (i) (*pers.*) goudronneur *m*; (ii) (*machine*) goudronneuse *f*; **t. spraying, t. sprinkling,** goudronnage *m*; **t. spraying machine,** goudronneuse. **2.** *Nau: F:* **(Jack) t.,** loup *m* de mer; mathurin *m*; bourlingueur *m.*

tar[2], *v.tr.* **(tarred)** goudronner (une route); goudronner, coaltarer (un cordage, le bois); bitumer (un trottoir, du carton); *Nau:* goudronner, brayer, caltar(is)er (un navire); *F:* **they're all tarred with the same brush,** on peut les mettre dans le même panier; ils sont tous taillés dans le même drap; ce sont des gens de (la) même farine, du même acabit; ils ne valent pas mieux l'un que l'autre; ils sont du même bateau.

taradiddle[1] ['tærədidl], *s. F:* petit mensonge; craque *f.*

taradiddle[2], *v.i. F:* conter des blagues.

tarantella [tærən'telə], *s. Danc: Mus:* tarentelle *f.*

tarantism ['tærəntizm], *s. Med. Hist:* tarent(ul)isme *m.*

Taranto [tə'ræntou], *Pr.n. Geog:* Tarente *f.*

tarantula [tə'ræntjulə], *s.* **1.** *Arach:* tarentule *f*. **2.** *Ent:* **t. hawk (wasp), t. killer,** pepsis *m.*

Tarantulid [tæ'ræntjulid], *s. Arach:* tarantulidé *m.*

Tarantulidae [tæræn'tju:lidi:], *s.pl. Arach:* tarantulidés *m.*

tarboard ['tɑ:bɔ:d], *s.* carton goudronné.

tarbrush ['tɑ:brʌʃ], *s.* brosse *f* à goudronner; *Nau:* guipon *m*; *F: Pej:* **to have a dash, a touch, of the t.,** avoir un peu de sang nègre dans les veines.

tarbush [tɑ:'bu:ʃ], *s. Cost:* tarbouch(e) *m.*

tarbuttite ['tɑ:bʌtait], *s. Miner:* tarbuttite *f.*

Tardigrada [tɑ:'digrədə], *s.pl. Nat.Hist:* tardigrades *m.*

tardigrade ['tɑ:digreid], *a. & s. Nat.Hist:* tardigrade (*m*).

tardily ['tɑ:dili], *adv.* **1.** *esp. Lit:* (*a*) lentement, paresseusement; (*b*) sans empressement. **2.** (*a*) tardivement; (*b*) *esp. U.S:* en retard.

tardiness ['tɑ:dinis], *s.* **1.** *esp. Lit:* lenteur *f*, nonchalance *f* (**in doing sth.,** à faire qch.). **2.** (*a*) tardiveté *f* (d'un fruit, etc.); (*b*) *esp. U.S:* retard *m*; manque *m* de ponctualité.

tardy ['tɑ:di], *a.* **1.** *esp. Lit:* (*a*) lent; nonchalant; paresseux; **t. to do sth., in doing sth.,** lent à faire qch.; (*b*) peu empressé. **2.** (*a*) tardif; (*b*) *esp. U.S:* en retard.

tare[1] ['tɛər], *s. Bot:* **1.** vesce *f*. **2.** *B:* **tares,** ivraie *f.*

tare[2], *s.* (*a*) *Com:* tare *f*; poids *m* à vide; **real t., actual t.,** tare réelle; **customary t.,** tare d'usage; **average t.,** tare commune, tare par épreuve; **extra t.,** surtare *f*; **to ascertain, to allow for, the t.,** faire la tare; **allowance for t.,** (i) tarage *m*; (ii) la tare; (*b*) poids net (d'un camion).

tare[3], *v.tr. Com:* tarer (un camion, un emballage, etc.); prendre, faire, la tare de (qch.).

Tarentine [tə'rentain]. *Geog:* (*a*) *a.* tarentin; (*b*) *s.* Tarentin, -ine.

Tarentum [tə'rentəm], *Pr.n. A.Geog:* Tarente.

targe [tɑ:dʒ], *s. A.Arm:* targe *f*; bouclier léger.

target[1] ['tɑ:git], *s.* **1.** *A.Arm:* targe *f*; petit bouclier. **2.** (*a*) *Mil: etc:* cible *f*, but *m*, objectif *m*; **moving t.,** but, objectif, mobile, mouvant; **fixed, stationary, t.,** cible, but, objectif, fixe; **floating t.,** cible flottante, but flottant; **towed t.,** cible remorquée; **ground t.,** objectif terrestre; **figure t., silhouette t.,** (cible-)silhouette *f*; **rocket t.,** cible-fusée *f*; **remote-controlled t.,** cible télécommandée, téléguidée; **aerial t.,** cible aérienne, objectif aérien; **sleeve t.,** manche(-cible) *f*, manche remorquée; **t. aircraft,** avion-cible *m*; **t. ship,** bâtiment-cible *m*; **area t.,** objectif sur zone; **t. area,** zone *f* des objectifs; *Artil:* **to straddle a t.,** coiffer un objectif; **t. prediction,** extrapolation *f* de l'objectif; **t. travel,** vecteur *m* d'extrapolation; **to fire, shoot, at a t.,** tirer à la cible; **to shift t.,** changer de cible; **to concentrate fire on a t.,** concentrer son feu sur un objectif; **his enormous nose makes him a sitting t. for caricaturists,** son nez énorme fait de lui une cible facile pour les caricaturistes; *Com: etc:* **t. date,** date *f* limite (de livraison, etc.); **t. figure,** objectif; **what the government did was to reduce the t. figures,** ce que le gouvernement a fait était de réduire les chiffres proposés; (*b*) *Rad:* **t. acquisition,** acquisition *f*, recherche *f*, des objectifs; **t. director post,** poste *m* mobile de contrôle radar; **t. Doppler indicator,** détecteur *m* (d'objectifs) par effet Doppler; **t. tracking,** poursuite *f* de l'objectif, des objectifs; (*c*) *Cmptr:* **t. computer,** calculateur *m* d'exécution; **t. language,** langage *m* d'exécution, langage objet; **t. programme,** programme généré, programme objet; (*d*) *Atom.Ph:* **element t.,** élément-cible *m*, *pl.* éléments-cibles; **isotopic t.,** cible isotopique; **fixed t.,** cible fixée; **liquid t.,** cible liquide; **nuclear t.,** cible nucléaire; **thick t.,** cible épaisse; **thin t.,** cible mince; **tritium, lithium, t.,** cible de tritium, de lithium; **t. area,** aire *f* de cible; **t. nucleus, particle,** noyau *m*, particule *f*, de la cible. **3.** (*a*) *Surv:* voyant *m*; (*over a bench mark*) signal *m*, -aux; (*b*) *Rail: U.S:* disque *m*; **position t.,** signal de position. **4.** *X-rays:* anticathode *f*. **5.** *Cu:* épaulée *f* (d'agneau, de mouton).

target[2], *v.tr.* **1.** désigner, fixer (un objectif, un chiffre) à atteindre; **public works targeted for this year will have to be put off until next,** il faut remettre à l'année prochaine les travaux publics projetés pour cette année; **negotiations targeting an alliance,** négociations visant une alliance. **2.** *Ball:* effectuer expérimentalement la correction de tir (d'une arme à feu).

Targum ['tɑ:gu(:)m], *s. Jew.Rel: Lit:* targum *m.*

Targumic [tɑ:'gu(:)mik], *a. Jew.Rel.Lit:* targumique.

Targumist ['tɑ:gu(:)mist], *s. Jew.Rel.Lit:* targumiste *m.*

tariff[1] ['tærif], *s.* **1.** *Cust: Rail: etc:* tarif *m*; **customs t.,** tarif douanier, tarif d'importation; **reduced t.,** tarif réduit; **full t.,** plein tarif; **t. laws,** lois *f* tarifaires; **t. walls, hostile tariffs,** barrières douanières; **t. reform,** réforme *f* des tarifs douaniers; *esp. U.S:* abolition *f*, réduction *f*, des tarifs douaniers; **t. reformer,** (i) protectionniste *mf*; (ii) *esp. U.S:* anti-protectionniste *mf*. **2.** *Rail: Post: etc:* tableau *m*, liste *f*, des prix.

tariff[2], *v.tr.* tarifer (des marchandises, etc.).

taring ['tɛəriŋ], *s. Com:* tarage *m.*

tarlatan ['tɑ:lætən], *s. Tex:* tarlatane *f.*

tarmac[1] ['tɑ:mæk], *s.* **1.** *Civ.E: R.t.m:* tarmac *m*. **2.** *Av:* aire *f* de stationnement; piste *f* d'envol.

tarmac[2], *v.tr.* tarmacadamiser (une route, etc.).

tarmacadam[1] [tɑ:mə'kædəm], *s. Civ.E:* tarmacadam *m.*

tarmacadam[2], **tarmacadamize** [tɑ:mə'kædəmaiz], *v.tr.* tarmacadamiser (une route, etc.).

tarn [tɑ:n], *s.* petit lac (de montagne).

tarnish[1] ['tɑ:niʃ], *s.* ternissure *f.*

tarnish[2]. **1.** *v.tr.* ternir (la surface d'un métal, d'un

miroir); ternir, flétrir, salir, souiller, tacher, tarer (la réputation de qn); obscurcir la gloire de qn. **2.** *v.i.* (*of metal, etc.*) se ternir; perdre son éclat; (*of gilt*) se dédorer.
tarnishable ['tɑːniʃəbl], *a.* (métal, etc.) qui peut se ternir; qui se ternit facilement.
tarnished ['tɑːniʃt], *a.* (métal) terni; (cadre) dédoré; (nom, honneur) terni, flétri, souillé.
tarnishing ['tɑːniʃiŋ], *s.* ternissure *f*, ternissage *m* (d'un métal, d'une réputation); dédorage *m* (d'un cadre).
taro ['tɑːrou, 'tærou], *s. Bot:* taro *m.*
tarot ['tærou], **taroc** ['tærɔk], *s. Cards:* tarot *m*; **t. cards,** tarots; **to play at tarots,** jouer au tarot.
tarpan ['tɑːpæn], *s. Z:* tarpan *m.*
tarpaulin [tɑː'pɔːlin], *s.* **1.** (*a*) toile goudronnée; toile à bâches, à prélarts; (*b*) bâche *f*; *Nau:* prélart *m*; banne *f*; **to cover a lorry with a t.,** bâcher, banner, un camion; (*c*) *Nau: A:* **t. hat,** chapeau *m* de toile goudronnée. **2.** *F: A:* marin *m*, mathurin *m*; loup *m* de mer.
Tarpeian [tɑː'piːən], *a. Rom.Ant:* **the T. Rock,** la Roche tarpéienne.
tarpon ['tɑːpɔn, -pən], *s.* (*often inv. in pl.*) *Ich:* tarpon *m*; *F:* roi *m* d'argent.
Tarquin ['tɑːkwin], **Tarquinius** [tɑː'kwiniəs], *Pr.n.m. Rom. Hist:* Tarquin; **Tarquinius Priscus,** Tarquin l'Ancien; **Tarquinius Superbus,** Tarquin le Superbe.
tarradiddle[1,2] ['tærədidl], *s. & v.i.* = TARADIDDLE[1,2].
tarragon ['tærəgən], *s. Bot: Cu:* estragon *m.*
Tarragona [tærə'gounə], *Pr.n. Geog:* Tarragone *f.*
tarred [tɑːd], *a.* goudronné; enduit de goudron; **t. rope,** cordage goudronné; **t. felt,** carton bitumé; **t. paper, board,** papier, carton, goudronné; **t. road,** route tarmacadamisée.
tarring ['tɑːriŋ], *s.* goudronnage *m*, bitumage *m*; **cold t.,** goudronnage à froid.
tarry[1] ['tɑːri], *a.* **1.** goudronneux, bitumeux, bitumineux. **2.** couvert, souillé, de goudron; **t. road,** route qui laisse suinter le goudron.
tarry[2] ['tæri], *v.i. A. & Lit:* **1.** rester, demeurer (**at, in, a place,** dans un endroit); *B:* **he tarried behind in Jerusalem,** il demeura dans Jérusalem; **to t. for s.o.,** attendre qn. **2.** tarder, s'attarder, être en retard; **to t. on the way,** s'attarder en route.
tarrying ['tæriiŋ], *s. A: & Lit:* **1.** séjour *m.* **2.** attente *f.* **3.** flânerie *f* en route.
tarsal ['tɑːs(ə)l], *a. Anat:* tarsien; du tarse.
tarsectomy [tɑː'sektəmi], *s. Surg:* tarsectomie *f.*
Tarshish ['tɑːʃiʃ], *Pr.n. B: Geog:* Tarsis.
tarsier ['tɑːsiər], *s. Z:* tarsier *m.*
Tarsiiformes [tɑːsii'fɔːmiːz], *s.pl.* tarsiiformes *m.*
tarsipes ['tɑːsipiːz], *s. Z:* tarsipes *m*; souris *f* à, du, miel.
tarsometatarsal [tɑːsoumetə'tɑːs(ə)l], *a. Anat:* tarso-métatarsien.
tarsometatarsus [tɑːsoumetə'tɑːsəs], *s. Anat:* tarso-métatarse *m.*
tarsoplasty ['tɑːsouplæsti], *s. Surg:* tarsoplastie *f.*
tarsoptosis [tɑːsɔp'tousis], *s. Med:* tarsoptose *f*, tarsalgie *f.*
tarsorrhaphy [tɑː'sɔræfi], *s. Med:* tarsorr(h)aphie *f.*
tarsotomy [tɑː'sɔtəmi], *s. Surg:* tarsotomie *f.*
tarsus[1], *pl.* **-i** ['tɑːsəs, -ai], *s.* (*a*) *Anat: Ent:* tarse *m*; (*b*) *Orn:* tarso-métatarse *m.*
Tarsus[2], *Pr.n. Geog:* (*a*) *A:* Tarse; (*b*) Tarsous.
tart[1] [tɑːt], *s.* **1.** *Cu:* (*a*) (*open*) tarte *f*; **small jam t.,** tartelette *f* aux confitures; **cherry t.,** tarte, galette *f*, cerises; (*b*) (*covered*) tourte *f*; (*c*) **t. dish, plate,** tourtière *f.* **2.** *P:* prostituée *f*, cocotte *f*, poule *f.*
tart[2], *v.tr. P:* **to t. oneself up,** s'affubler, s'attifer; **to t. sth. up,** décorer qch. (avec du tape-à-l'œil); **this dress is too tarted up,** cette robe fait trop le carnaval.
tart[3], *a.* (*a*) au goût âpre, acerbe, acide, aigrelet; (*of wine*) vert, verdelet, piquant; (*b*) (*of answer, tone*) acéré; aigre; mordant, caustique; **somewhat t. manner,** manière un peu aigrelette; **t. disposition,** caractère *m* aigre.
tartan[1] ['tɑːt(ə)n], *s. Tex: Cost:* (*cloth or plaid*) tartan *m*, écossais *m*; **t. shirt,** chemise *f* à carreaux écossais.
tartan[2], **tartane** [tɑː'tæn], *s. Nau:* tartane *f.*
tartar[1] ['tɑːtər], *s.* (*a*) *Ch:* tartre *m*; *Pharm:* **t. emetic,** tartre stibié; tartrate *m* de potasse et d'antimoine; émétique *m* tartrique; (*b*) *Dent:* (*on teeth*) tartre.
Tartar[2]. **1.** (*a*) *a.* tatar, tartare; (*b*) *s.* Tatar, Tartare. **2.** *s.* homme *m* intraitable; (*of woman*) mégère *f*; **to catch a t.,** trouver à qui parler; trouver son maître; **to have caught a t.,** tenir le loup par les oreilles; se trouver en mauvaise passe.
tartarated ['tɑːtəreitid], *a. Ch: Pharm:* = TARTRATED.
Tartarean [tɑː'tɛəriən], *a. Myth:* tartaréen; du Tartare.
tartaric[1] [tɑː'tærik], *a. Ch:* tartarique, tartrique.
Tartaric[2], *a. Geog: Hist:* (région, horde) tartare, tatar.
tartarized ['tɑːtəraizd], *a. Pharm: etc:* tartarisé; **t. antimony,** tartre stibié; tartrate *m* de potasse et d'antimoine; émétique *m* tartrique.
Tartarus ['tɑːtərəs], *Pr.n. Myth:* le Tartare.
Tartary ['tɑːtəri], *Pr.n. A. Geog:* Tartarie *f.*
tartlet ['tɑːtlit], *s. Cu:* tartelette *f.*
tartly ['tɑːtli], *adv.* acrimonieusement; avec aigreur, avec acerbité; d'un ton, d'une voix, acerbe, revêche; d'une manière mordante.
tartness ['tɑːtnis], *s.* acerbité *f*; goût *m* âpre (d'un fruit); verdeur *f* (d'un vin); acidité *f*, aigreur *f*, causticité *f* (du ton, d'une réponse).
tartrate ['tɑːtreit], *s. Ch:* tartrate *m*; **ergotamine t.,** tartrate d'ergotamine.
tartrated ['tɑːtreitid], *a. Ch: Pharm:* tartarisé.
tartrazine ['tɑːtrəziːn], *s. Dy:* tartrazine *f.*
tartronic [tɑː'trɔnik], *a. Ch:* tartronique.
tartronylurea [tɑːtrɔni'ljuːriə], *s. Ch:* tartronylurée *f*; acide *m* dialurique.
tarty ['tɑːti], *a. P:* (*a*) (*of woman*) **to look t.,** avoir l'air d'une prostituée, d'une poule; (*b*) (*of clothes, etc.*) qui font du tape-à-l'œil.
tarweed ['tɑːwiːd], *s. Bot:* madia *m.*
tas-de-charge [tɑːdə'ʃɑːʒ], *s. Arch:* tas *m* de charge.
Tashkend, Tashkent [tæʃ'kend, -'kent], *Pr.n. Geog:* Tachkent *m.*
Tasian ['tɑːsiən], *a. & s. Prehist:* tasien (*m*).
tasimeter [tə'simitər], *s. El:* tasimètre *m*, microtasimètre *m.*
task[1] [tɑːsk], *s.* **1.** tâche *f*; (*a*) *Sch:* (i) devoir *m*; (ii) pensum *m*, punition *f*; **to set a boy at t.,** donner un devoir à un élève; (*b*) travail, -aux *m*; ouvrage *m*, besogne *f*; **t. work,** (i) *Ind:* travail à la tâche; travail aux pièces; (ii) travail dur; **it's a terrible t.,** c'est une véritable corvée; **it's an endless t.,** c'est un travail sans fin, à n'en plus finir; **to set s.o. a t.,** imposer une tâche à qn; **to entrust s.o. with the t. of doing sth.,** confier à qn le soin de faire qch.; **to apply oneself to a t.,** s'atteler à un travail; s'appliquer à faire qch.; **he found it no easy t. to carry on the business alone,** il ne lui a pas été facile de gérer l'affaire tout seul. **2. to take s.o. to t. for sth., for doing sth.,** prendre qn à partie, réprimander, reprocher, semoncer, qn, pour avoir fait qch. **3.** *Mil: etc:* **t. force,** corps *m* expéditionnaire; force *f* tactique, d'intervention.
task[2], *v.tr.* **1.** *A:* assigner, imposer, une tâche à (qn). **2. to t. s.o.'s patience, strength,** mettre à l'épreuve la patience, la force, de qn.
taskmaster, taskmistress ['tɑːskmɑːstər, -mistris], *s.* chef *m* de corvée, surveillant, -ante; **hard t.,** véritable tyran *m.*
taslet ['tæslit], *s. Arm:* tassette *f.*
Tasmania [tæz'meiniə], *Pr.n. Geog:* Tasmanie *f.*
Tasmanian [tæz'meiniən], (*a*) *a.* tasmanien; *Z:* **T. devil,** diable *m* de Tasmanie, diable ourson; sarcophile *m*; (*b*) *s.* Tasmanien, -ienne.
tasmanite ['tæzmənait], *s. Miner:* tasmanite *f.*
tasse [tæs], *s. Arm:* tassette *f.*
tassel[1] ['tæs(ə)l], *s.* **1.** (*a*) *Const: Furn: etc:* gland *m* (de rideau, de dragonne, etc.); gland, houppe *f*, floc *m* (de bonnet de coton); *Needlew:* **t. stitch,** point *m* de houppes; (*b*) *Bookb:* signet *m.* **2.** *Bot:* panicule terminale, épi *m* mâle, aigrette *f* (du maïs).
tassel[2], *v.* (**tasselled**) **1.** *v.tr.* (*a*) garnir (un coussin, etc.) de glands; mettre des houppes à (qch.); (*b*) *Agr:* écimer (le maïs). **2.** *v.i.* (*of maize, etc.*) former des aigrettes; fleurir.
tassel[3], *s. Const:* = TORSEL 2.
tasselled ['tæs(ə)ld], *a.* à glands; à houppes; orné de glands; **t. fringe,** frange *f* à houppes.
tasset ['tæsit], *s. Arm:* tassette *f.*
Tasso ['tæsou], *Pr.n.m. Lit. Hist:* le Tasse.
tastable ['teistəbl], *a.* = TASTEABLE.
taste[1] [teist], *s.* **1.** (*a*) **(sense of) taste,** goût *m*; **keen sense of t.,** sens du goût bien développé; (*b*) saveur *f*, goût; **sweet t., acid t.,** goût sucré, aigre; **the bread had a t. of garlic,** le pain avait un goût d'ail; le pain sentait l'ail; **it has a burnt t.,** cela sent le brûlé; **this drink has no t.,** cette boisson n'a pas de goût, est insipide; (*c*) **a t. of sth.,** un petit peu (de fromage, etc.); une petite gorgée (de vin, etc.); **give me just a t. of cheese,** donnez-moi un rien de fromage; **have a t. of this claret,** goûtez donc à ce bordeaux; (*d*) **he gave us a t. of his bad temper,** il nous a donné un échantillon de sa mauvaise humeur; *F:* **you'll get a t. of it one of these days,** vous en tâterez un de ces jours; **he's already had a t. of prison,** il a déjà tâté de la prison. **2.** goût, penchant particulier, prédilection *f* (**for,** pour); **to have a t. for sth.,** avoir du goût pour qch., avoir le goût de (la musique, etc.); **to have expensive tastes,** avoir des goûts de luxe; **to have no t. for sth.,** ne pas avoir de goût pour qch., le goût de qch.; être fermé à (la musique, etc.); **he has no t. for sweets,** il n'aime pas les sucreries; **career for which I have no t.,** carrière *f* qui n'a pas d'attrait pour moi, qui ne me dit rien; **to acquire, develop, a t. for sth.,** prendre goût à qch.; acquérir un goût pour, le goût de, qch.; **to find sth. to one's t.,** trouver qch. à son goût; **a life like that is not to my t.,** cette vie ne me plait pas, n'est pas de mon goût; *Cu:* **add sugar to t.,** on ajoute du sucre selon son goût, à volonté; **to follow one's natural tastes,** suivre ses penchants; se laisser aller à ses penchants; **it's a matter of t.,** c'est (une) affaire de goût, d'appréciation; *Prov:* **everyone to his t.,** des goûts et des couleurs on ne discute pas; il ne faut pas discuter des goûts; chacun (à) son goût; à chacun son goût. **3.** (*a*) **to have t. in music,** avoir du goût en matière de musique; s'y connaître en musique; **she has excellent t. in dress,** elle s'habille avec (beaucoup de) goût; **people of t.,** les gens de goût; (*b*) **in perfect t.,** d'un goût parfait; **in bad t.,** de mauvais goût, qui manque de goût; **in doubtful t.,** d'un goût douteux; **it would be bad t. to refuse,** il serait de mauvais goût, de mauvaise grâce, de refuser.
taste[2], *v.*
I. *v.tr.* **1.** percevoir la saveur de (qch.); sentir (qch.); **I could not t. any garlic in the salad,** je n'ai pas senti de goût d'ail dans la salade; **one can t. nothing, can't t. anything, when one has a cold,** on ne trouve de goût à rien, on n'a pas de goût, quand on est enrhumé. **2.** (*a*) (*of cook*) goûter (un mets); (*b*) déguster (des vins, des thés, etc.); sonder (un fromage). **3.** (*a*) goûter de, à (qch.); manger un petit morceau (d'un mets); tâter à, de (qch.); boire une petite gorgée (d'un liquide); **I haven't even tasted it,** je n'y ai pas même goûté; **he had not tasted food for three days,** il n'avait pas mangé depuis trois jours; (*b*) **to t. happiness,** *A:* **to t. of happiness,** connaître, goûter, le bonheur; **to t. power,** goûter, tâter, du pouvoir. **4.** *A:* savourer, goûter (une plaisanterie, une bonne histoire, etc.).
II. *v.i.* **to t. of sth.,** avoir le goût de qch.; **the meat tasted of garlic,** la viande avait un goût d'ail, sentait l'ail; **to t. like honey,** goûter du miel; avoir un goût de miel; avoir un goût qui rappelle le miel; **the wine tasted like port,** le vin avait le même goût que le porto, ressemblait au porto; **it tastes like gin,** on dirait du gin; **it makes the food t. bitter,** cela donne un goût amer aux aliments.
tasteable ['teistəbl], *a.* **1.** qu'on peut goûter; qui peut se goûter. **2.** *A:* = TASTY 1.
tasteful ['teistful], *a.* **1.** de bon goût; (ouvrage) fait avec goût; (vêtement) élégant. **2.** (personne) de goût.
tastefully ['teistfuli], *adv.* avec goût.
tastefulness ['teistf(u)lnis], *s.* bon goût.
tasteless ['teistlis], *a.* **1.** (mets, etc.) sans goût, sans saveur; fade, insipide. **2.** (vêtement, etc.) qui manque de goût, de mauvais goût.
tastelessly ['teistlisli], *adv.* (s'habiller, etc.) sans goût.
tastelessness ['teistlisnis], *s.* **1.** insipidité *f*, fadeur *f* (d'un mets, etc.). **2.** manque *m* de goût (dans l'habillement, etc.).
taster ['teistər], *s.* **1.** (*pers.*) dégustateur, -trice; tâteur, -euse (de vins, de thés, etc.). **2.** (*thg*) **wine t.,** tâte-vin *m inv*; **cheese t., butter t.,** sonde *f* à fromage, à beurre; flûte *f.*
tastiness ['teistinis], *s.* **1.** saveur *f*, goût *m* agréable (d'un mets). **2.** *A:* (*a*) = TASTEFULNESS; (*b*) chic *m*, élégance *f.*
tasting ['teistiŋ], *s.* **1.** *Physiol:* gustation *f.* **2.** *Com: etc:* dégustation *f* (de vins, de thés); **t. room,** salle *f* de dégustation.
tasty ['teisti], *a.* **1.** (mets, repas) savoureux; **t. morsel,** morceau succulent. **2.** (*a*) *A:* = TASTEFUL; (*b*) *P: O:* chic, élégant.
tat[1] [tæt], *s. used only in the phr.* **tit for t.,** un prêté pour un rendu; à bon chat bon rat; donnant donnant.
tat[2], *v.tr. & i.* (**tatted**) *Needlew:* faire de la frivolité; **tatted insertion,** entre-deux *m* de frivolité.
ta-ta [tæ'tɑː], *int. P: & child's language,* au revoir! salut!
tatajuba [tɑːtə'ʒuːbə], *s. Bot:* tatajuba *m.*
Tatar ['tɑːtər]. **1.** *a.* tatar, tartare; **T. Republic,** République *f* de Tatarie. **2.** *s.* Tatar *m*, Tartare *m.*
Tatary ['tɑːtəri], *Pr.n. Geog:* Tatarie *f.*
tater ['teitər], *s. P:* pomme *f* de terre, patate *f.*
Tatian ['teiʃ(ə)n], *Pr.n.m. Rel.H:* Tatien.
tatie ['teiti], *s. P:* = TATER.
tatou [tɑ'tuː], *s. Z:* tatou *m*; **t. peba,** tatou à neuf bandes.
tatouay ['tætuːei, tɑːtu'ai], *s. Z:* tatouay *m*; tatou *m* à longues oreilles.
tatt [tæt], *s. F:* **did you ever see such a piece of t.?** a-t-on jamais vu une mocheté pareille?
tatter[1] ['tætər], *s.* lambeau *m*, loque *f*; **garment in tatters,** vêtement *m* en lambeaux, en loques; **to tear s.o.'s reputation to tatters,** éreinter qn; casser du sucre sur le dos de qn.

tatter[2], *v. esp. U.S:* **1.** *v.tr.* réduire en lambeaux, en loques; rendre loqueteux. **2.** *v.i.* tomber en loques, se réduire en loques.

tatterdemalion [tætədi'meiliən], *s.* loqueteux, -euse; déguenillé, -ée; va-nu-pieds *mf inv*; **his t. followers,** les gueux *m* qu'il traîne à sa suite.

tattered ['tætəd], *a.* (vêtement) dépenaillé, en loques, en lambeaux, en pièces, tout déchiré; (homme) déguenillé, loqueteux; **all t. and torn,** en loques et en guenilles; **her reputation is a bit t., she has a rather t. reputation,** elle a plus d'un accroc à sa réputation.

tatting ['tætiŋ], *s.* (*fancywork*) frivolité *f.*

tattle[1] ['tætl], *s.* **1.** bavardage *m*, commérage *m*, jaserie *f.* **2.** cancans *mpl*; commérages.

tattle[2], *v.* **1.** *v.i.* (*a*) bavarder; jaser; commérer; (*b*) cancaner; faire des cancans. **2.** *v.tr.* **to t. s.o.'s secrets,** divulguer les secrets de qn.

tattler ['tætlər], *s.* **1.** bavard, -arde; babillard, -arde; causeur, -euse; jaseur, -euse. **2.** cancanier, -ière. **3.** *Orn:* chevalier *m*, *esp.* chevalier aboyeur; **wandering t.,** chevalier errant; chevalier à pieds courts.

tattling[1] ['tætliŋ], *a.* **1.** babillard, bavard. **2.** cancanier.

tattling[2], *s.* = TATTLE[1].

tattoo[1] [tə'tu:], *s. Mil:* **1.** retraite *f* (du soir); **to beat, sound, the t.,** battre, sonner, la retraite; **t. roll call,** appel *m* du soir; *F:* **to beat the devil's t. (on the table, etc.),** tambouriner, pianoter (sur la table, etc.). **2.** (*a*) **torchlight t.,** retraite aux flambeaux; (*b*) **the Aldershot T.,** le carrousel militaire d'Aldershot.

tattoo[2], *v.i.* tambouriner, pianoter (sur la vitre, etc.).

tattoo[3], *s.* tatouage *m*; **to remove a t. from (s.o.),** détatouer (qn); **t. removing,** détatouage *m.*

tattoo[4], *v.tr.* tatouer (le corps, des dessins sur le corps).

tattooer, tattooist [tæ'tu:ər, -'tu:ist], *s.* tatoueur *m.*

tattooing [tæ'tu:iŋ], *s.* tatouage *m.*

tatty ['tæti], *a. F:* défraîchi; miteux; moche.

tatu [tə'tu:], *s. Z:* tatou *m*; **t. peba,** tatou à neuf bandes.

tau [tɔ:], *s.* (*a*) *Gr.Alph:* tau *m*; (*b*) **t. cross,** croix *f* en tau; croix de Saint-Antoine.

taunt[1] [tɔ:nt], *s.* **1.** reproche méprisant; injure *f* (en paroles); sarcasme *m*, brocard *m.* **2.** *A:* **to be, become, the t. of the public,** être, devenir, l'objet des sarcasmes du public.

taunt[2], *v.tr.* (*a*) accabler (qn) de sarcasmes; se gausser de (qn); (*b*) **to t. s.o. with sth.,** reprocher qch. à qn (avec mépris); **to t. s.o. with cowardice,** traiter qn de lâche.

taunt[3], *a. Nau: A:* (mât) très haut, très élevé; (mât) élancé.

taunter ['tɔ:ntər], *s.* brocardeur, -euse; gausseur, -euse.

taunting[1] ['tɔ:ntiŋ], *a.* (ton *m*, air *m*) de sarcasme, de reproche méprisant; **t. remark,** observation sarcastique, injurieuse.

taunting[2], *s.* reproches méprisants; sarcasmes provocants; brocards *mpl.*

tauntingly ['tɔ:ntiŋli], *adv.* d'un ton, d'un air, de mépris provocant; d'un ton sarcastique, injurieux.

Taurides (the) [ðə'tɔ:ridi:z], *s.pl. Astr:* les Taurides *f.*

taurine[1] ['tɔ:rain], *a.* taurin, tauresque; de taureau.

taurine[2] ['tɔ:ri:n], *s. Ch:* taurine *f.*

taurocholate [tɔ:rou'kouleit], *s. Bio-Ch:* taurocholate *m.*

taurocholic [tɔ:rou'koulik], *a. Bio-Ch:* taurocholique.

Tauroidea [tɔ:'rɔidiə], *s.pl. Z:* tauroïdés *m.*

tauromachian [tɔ:rou'meikiən], *a.* tauromachique.

tauromachy [tɔ:'rɔməki], *s.* tauromachie *f.*

taurotragus [tɔ:'rɔtrəgəs], *s. Z:* taurotrague *m*, antilope *m* éland.

Taurus ['tɔ:rəs], *Pr.n. Astr:* le Taureau.

taut [tɔ:t], *a. Nau: etc:* (*a*) (cordage, câble) tendu, raide, raidi, bandé; (voile *f*) étarque; **to haul a rope t.,** raidir, embraquer, souquer, un cordage; **with one's sinews t.,** (faire qch.) les nerfs tendus; **t. situation,** situation tendue; (*b*) **t. and trim,** (i) (navire) paré, en bon état; (ii) (personne) soignée, tirée à quatre épingles; *Nau:* **t. man,** (officier) rigide pour la discipline.

tauten ['tɔ:t(ə)n], *v.tr.* raidir, roidir, embraquer (un câble, etc.); étarquer (une voile).

tautness ['tɔ:tnis], *s.* raideur *f*, roideur *f* (d'un câble, etc.).

tauto- ['tɔ:tou, tɔ:'tɔ], *comb.fm.* tauto-.

tautochrone ['tɔ:toukroun], *s. Mth:* courbe *f* tautochrone.

tautochronous [tɔ:'tɔkrənəs], *a. Mth:* tautochrone, isochrone.

tautological [tɔ:tə'lɔdʒik(ə)l], *a.* tautologique.

tautology [tɔ:'tɔlədʒi], *s.* tautologie *f*; répétition oiseuse.

tautomer ['tɔ:toumər], *s. Ch:* forme *f* tautomère (d'un composé).

tautomeric [tɔ:tou'merik], *a. Ch:* tautomère.

tautomerism, tautomery [tɔ:'tɔmərizm, -'tɔməri], *s. Ch:* tautomérie *f.*

tautometric(al) [tɔ:tou'metrik(l)], *a.* tautométrique.

tautophony [tɔ:'tɔfəni], *s. Gram:* tautophonie *f*, tautacisme *m.*

tautosyllabic [tɔ:tousi'læbik], *a. Gram:* tautosyllabique.

tavern ['tæv(ə)n], *s. A:* taverne *f*, cabaret *m*; **t. keeper,** cabaretier, -ière.

tavistockite ['tævistɔkait], *s. Miner:* tavistockite *f.*

taw[1] [tɔ:], *s. Games:* **1.** grosse bille (de verre); calot *m.* **2.** (jeu *m* de) rangette *f*; **to have a game of t.,** jouer à la rangette.

taw[2], *v.tr. Tan:* mégir, mégisser, chamoiser (les peaux); passer (les peaux) en mégie; préparer (les peaux) en blanc.

tawdrily ['tɔ:drili], *adv.* avec un faux éclat; sans goût.

tawdriness ['tɔ:drinis], *s.* clinquant *m*; faux brillant, faux éclat (d'un faux bijou, etc.); misère parée, faux luxe (de l'existence de qn).

tawdry ['tɔ:dri], *a.* (vêtement *m*, ornement *m*) d'un mauvais goût criard; **t. jewellery,** clinquant *m*, toc *m*; **t. finery,** oripeaux *mpl*; **t. existence,** misère dorée.

tawed [tɔ:d], *a. Tan:* (cuir) mégis, passé en mégie.

tawer ['tɔ:ər], *s. Tan:* mégissier *m.*

tawery ['tɔ:əri], *s. Tan:* (*works*) mégisserie *f.*

tawing ['tɔ:iŋ], *s. Tan:* mégie *f*, mégisserie *f*; chamoisage *m*; tannage *m* à l'alun.

tawny ['tɔ:ni], *a.* (*a*) *A:* tanné, basané; (*b*) fauve; tirant sur le roux; **t. mane,** crinière *f* fauve; **old t. port,** porto *m* qui a jauni dans le fût; (*c*) *Orn:* **t. eagle,** aigle ravisseur; **t. owl,** chouette *f* hulotte; **t. thrush,** grive *f* de Wilson.

tawse [tɔ:z], *s. Sch:* (*Scot.*) martinet (formé d'une courroie de cuir, à extrémité découpée en lanières, pour corriger les enfants); **to give a child the t.,** corriger un élève avec une courroie.

tax[1] [tæks], *s.* **1.** (*a*) *Adm:* impôt *m*; imposition *f*; taxe *f*; **taxes and dues,** taxes et impôts; **direct, indirect, taxes,** impôts directs, indirects, contributions directes, indirectes; **land t.,** contribution foncière (des propriétés non bâties); impôt foncier; **income t.,** impôt sur le revenu; **the income t. (authorities),** le fisc; **graduated income t.,** impôt progressif; **t. deducted at source,** impôt retenu à la base, à la source; **inspector of taxes,** inspecteur *m* des contributions directes; **collector of taxes, t. collector,** percepteur *m*, receveur *m* (des contributions directes); **t. office,** bureau *m* des contributions; (bureau de) perception *f*; **t. year,** année *f* d'imposition; **t. bracket,** catégorie d'imposition; **capital gains t.,** impôt sur les plus-values; **inheritance t.,** droits *mpl* de succession; **turnover t.,** impôt sur le chiffre d'affaires; **value added t.,** *U.S:* **processing t.,** taxe à la valeur ajoutée; *A:* **purchase t.,** taxe à la production, à l'achat; **entertainment t.,** taxe sur les spectacles; **petrol t.,** impôt sur l'essence; **t. evasion,** fraude fiscale; **to levy a t. on sth.,** mettre un impôt sur qch.; frapper qch. d'un impôt; imposer qch.; **to collect a t.,** lever, percevoir, un impôt, une contribution; **to pay £x in taxes,** payer £x d'impôts; **free of t., t. free,** exempt d'impôts; **t. paid,** net d'impôt; (*b*) *Hist:* taille *f*; **t. on income,** taille personnelle; **property t.,** taille réelle; **t. farmer,** fermier général. **2.** charge *f*; fardeau (imposé à qn).

tax[2], *v.tr.* **1.** *Adm:* (*a*) taxer (les objets de luxe, etc.); frapper (qch.) d'un impôt; mettre un impôt sur (qch.); **to t. income,** imposer (des droits sur) le revenu; **everything is taxed,** tout se taxe; (*b*) imposer (qn); **to be heavily taxed,** être lourdement imposé; (*c*) *Hist:* tailler (qn); (*d*) mettre à l'épreuve (l'adresse, la patience, de qn); **to t. s.o.'s patience to the limit,** pousser à bout la patience de qn; **it would t. his strength too much,** il n'est pas assez fort pour le faire; sa santé est trop faible pour faire face à cette épreuve. **2.** *Jur:* taxer (les dépens d'un procès); **taxed bill of costs,** mémoire taxé (par le juge); **taxing master,** (juge) taxateur *m.* **3. to t. s.o. with sth., with doing sth.,** (i) taxer, accuser, qn de qch., d'avoir fait qch.; (ii) reprocher à qn d'avoir fait qch.; **he taxed me with ingratitude,** il m'a accusé d'ingratitude.

taxable ['tæksəbl], *a.* **1.** (revenu *m*, terrain *m*, etc.) imposable; **t. article, class of goods,** matière *f* imposable; **to make sth. t.,** imposer qch.; **t. year,** année *f* d'imposition; exercice fiscal. **2.** *Jur:* **costs t. to s.o.,** frais *m* à la charge de qn.

Taxaceae [tæk'seisii:], *s.pl. Bot:* taxacées *f.*

taxad ['tæksæd], *s. Bot:* taxacée *f.*

taxation [tæk'seiʃ(ə)n], *s.* **1.** (*a*) imposition *f* (de la propriété, etc.); **the t. authorities,** l'administration fiscale, *F:* le fisc; **t. year,** année *f* d'imposition; exercice fiscal; (*b*) charges fiscales; prélèvement fiscal; **increase of t., supplementary t.,** surimposition *f*; **excessive t.,** fiscalité excessive; **commensurate t.,** équivalence *f* des charges fiscales; **highest scale of t.,** maximum *m* de perception; (*c*) revenu réalisé par les impôts; les impôts *m.* **2.** *Jur:* **t. of costs,** taxation *f*, taxe *f*, des frais (d'un procès).

taxi[1] ['tæksi], *s.* **1.** taxi *m*; **t. rank, stand,** station *f* de taxis; **t. driver,** chauffeur *m* de taxi. **2.** *Av:* **t. track, strip,** piste *f* de roulement, *F:* runway *m*; **t. light,** phare *m* de roulement. **3.** *esp. U.S: F:* **t. girl,** entraîneuse *f.*

taxi[2], *v.i.* (**taxied; taxying**) **1.** aller en taxi. **2.** *Av:* (*of aircraft*) (*a*) rouler au sol; (*b*) **to t. along the water,** hydroplaner.

taxiarch ['tæksiɑ:k], *s. Gr.Ant:* taxiarque *m.*

taxicab ['tæksikæb], *s.* taxi *m.*

Taxidea [tæk'sidiə], *s. Z:* taxidé *m.*

taxidermal [tæksi'də:m(ə)l], *a.* taxidermique.

taxidermist ['tæksidə:mist], *s.* empailleur, -euse; naturaliste *mf*; taxidermiste *m.*

taxidermy ['tæksidə:mi], *s.* taxidermie *f*; naturalisation *f* des animaux.

taxiing ['tæksiiŋ], *s. Av:* roulement *m.*

taximan, *pl.* **-men** ['tæksimən], *s.m.* chauffeur de taxi.

taximeter ['tæksimi:tər], *s.* taximètre *m.*

Taxineae [tæk'sinii:], *s.pl. Bot:* taxinées *f.*

taxinomy [tæk'sinəmi], *s.* taxinomie *f*, taxonomie *f.*

taxiphote ['tæksifout], *s. Phot:* taxiphote *m.*

taxis ['tæksis], *s.* **1.** *Surg:* taxis *m*; manipulation *f* (d'une hernie, etc.). **2.** *Nat.Hist:* taxie *f.*

taxiway ['tæksiwei], *s. Av:* piste *f* de roulement, *F:* runway *m.*

Taxodonta [tæksou'dɔntə], *s.pl. Moll:* taxodontes *m.*

taxology [tæk'sɔlədʒi], *s.* taxologie *f.*

taxon, *pl.* **taxons, taxa** ['tæksɔn, -sɔnz, -sə], *s.* taxon *m*, *pl.* taxons, taxa.

taxonomic [tæksə'nɔmik], *a.* taxonomique, taxologique.

taxonomist [tæk'sɔnəmist], *s.* taxonomiste *mf*, taxologue *mf.*

taxonomy [tæk'sɔnəmi], *s.* taxonomie *f*, taxologie *f.*

taxpayer ['tækspeiər], *s.* contribuable *mf.*

taxridden ['tæksrid(ə)n], *a.* écrasé d'impôts.

taxying ['tæksiiŋ], *s. Av:* roulement *m* (au sol).

Tayacian [tə'jeisiən], *a. & s. Prehist:* tayacien (*m*).

Taygetus [tei'idʒitəs], *Pr.n. Geog:* le Taygète.

Taylorism ['teilərizm], *s. Hist:Ind:* taylorisme *m.*

taylorite ['teilərait], *s. Miner:* taylorite *f.*

tayra ['tairə], *s. Z:* tayra *f.*

tchagra ['tʃægrə], *s. Orn:* tchagra *m.*

te [ti:], *s. Mus:* (*in tonic solfa*) la (note) sensible.

tea [ti:], *s.* **1.** *Bot:* (*a*) thé *m*; **t. plant, t. tree,** arbre *m* à thé; **t. plantation, garden,** plantation *f* de thé; théerie *f*; **t. planter,** planteur *m* de thé; (*b*) **Brigham t., Mormon t.,** ephédra *f*, éphèdre *f*; **Labrador t.,** thé du Labrador; **mountain t.,** thé de montagne, du Canada, *Fr.C:* thé des bois; **Oswego t.,** thé d'Oswego; **Mexican t.,** thé du Mexique; *Austr:* **t. tree,** leptospermum *m*; (*c*) **t. rose,** rose *f* thé. **2.** (*a*) *Com:* thé; **China t.,** thé de Chine; **Indian t.,** thé de Ceylan; **black t.,** thé noir; **green t.,** thé vert; **t. blending,** mélange *m* des thés; **t. factory,** théerie; **t. taster,** dégustateur, -trice, de thés; **t. paper,** empaquetage *m* pour thé; **t. broker,** courtier *m* en thés; **t. merchant,** négociant *m* en thés; **t. chest,** caisse *f* à thé; canasse *f*, canastre *f*; barse *f*; (*b*) **to drink t.,** boire, prendre, du thé; **t. drinker,** buveur, -euse, de thé; **a cup of t.,** une tasse de thé; **t. caddy, canister,** boîte *f* à thé; **t. infuser,** boule *f* à thé; **t. urn,** fontaine *f* à thé; **t. strainer,** passe-thé *m inv*; *Med:* **t. poisoning,** théisme *m*; (*c*) (*as meal*) **(afternoon) t.,** thé; = goûter *m*; **(high) t.,** repas *m* du soir (arrosé de thé); **to ask s.o. to t.,** inviter qn à (venir) prendre le thé; *Austr:* **have you had (your) t.?** est-ce que vous avez dîné, soupé? **(early) morning t.,** tasse de thé servie avant le petit déjeuner; **(mid) morning t.** = pause-café *f*; **t. break,** la pause (du) thé, = pause-café *f*; **children's t. party,** goûter d'enfants; **to give a t. party,** (i) donner, offrir, un thé; (ii) organiser un goûter d'enfants; *F: O:* **t. fight,** goûter copieux (pour des élèves, des membres d'une association, etc.) où il y a cohue; **t. table,** table *f* à thé; **t. trolley, wagon,** table à thé roulante; **t. tray,** plateau *m* à thé; **t. service, set,** *F:* **t. things,** service *m* à thé; **to clear away the t. things,** desservir (le thé); **t. knife** = couteau *m* à dessert; *Cost: O:* **t. gown,** robe *f* d'intérieur. **3.** tisane *f*, infusion *f*; **sage t., mint t.,** infusion de sauge, de menthe. **4.** *P:* marijuana *f*, thé.

tea[2], *v.* (**tea'd; teaing**) *F: O:* **1.** *v.i.* prendre le thé. **2.** *v.tr.* offrir le thé à (qn).

teabag ['ti:bæg], *s.* sachet *m* de thé.

teacake ['ti:keik], *s. Cu:* (espèce de) brioche plate (se mange grillée et beurrée).

teach [ti:tʃ], *v.tr.* (*p.t. & p.p.* **taught** [tɔ:t]) (*a*) enseigner, instruire (qn); enseigner (qch.); **to t. s.o. sth.,** enseigner, apprendre, qch. à qn; **he's being taught all sorts of things,** on lui apprend toutes sortes de choses; **she teaches the young pupils,** elle fait la classe, elle fait l'école, aux petits; **she teaches the piano,** elle est professeur de piano; **he teaches French,** il enseigne, il professe, le français; il est professeur de français; il donne des leçons de français; *v.i.* **to t.,** *NAm:* **to t. school,** enseigner; être dans l'enseignement; **to t. s.o. (how, the way) to do sth.,** apprendre à qn à faire qch.; montrer à qn comment faire qch.; **he taught me to play the piano,** il m'a appris à jouer du piano; **to t. oneself sth.,** apprendre qch. tout seul; **I had been taught never to tell a lie,** on m'avait inculqué qu'il ne faut jamais mentir; (*b*) *F:* **to t. s.o. a lesson,** donner à qn une leçon (qu'il n'oubliera pas si tôt); **that'll t. him!** ça lui apprendra! **to t. s.o. a thing or two,** dégourdir qn; **you can't t. me anything about that,** ça me connaît; **I'll t. you to speak to me like that!** je vous apprendrai à me parler de la sorte!

teachable ['tiːtʃəbl], *a.* **1.** (*of pers.*) qui apprend facilement; docile; à l'intelligence ouverte; **that child's not t.,** voilà un enfant à qui on ne peut rien apprendre. **2.** (sujet) enseignable.

teachableness ['tiːtʃəb(ə)lnis], *s.* **1.** aptitude *f* à apprendre. **2.** nature *f* enseignable (d'un sujet).

teacher ['tiːtʃər], *s.* (i) instituteur, -trice; maître, *f.* maîtresse (d'école); (ii) professeur *m*; (iii) maître (au sens large); **t. of French, of history,** professeur de français, d'histoire; **student t.,** *A:* **pupil t.,** étudiant(e) qui fait un stage comme instituteur (-trice), comme professeur; **to become a t.,** se faire professeur; entrer dans l'enseignement; **she was an excellent t.,** c'était un bon professeur, une bonne institutrice; elle avait le don de l'enseignement; **I hold there are no unteachable children only teachers who can't teach,** j'affirme qu'il n'y a point d'enfants à qui on ne peut rien enseigner, mais seulement des enseignants qui ne peuvent rien enseigner à qui que ce soit; **the t. and his disciples,** le maître et ses disciples.

teach-in ['tiːtʃin], *s.* colloque *m.*

teaching ['tiːtʃiŋ], *s.* **1.** enseignement *m*, instruction *f*; **to go in for t.,** entrer dans l'enseignement; **the t. profession,** (i) le corps enseignant; (ii) l'enseignement; **the t. staff (of a school),** les professeurs, les instituteurs (d'un lycée, d'une école); **t. aids,** matériel *m*, équipement *m*, pédagogique; **t. method,** méthode *f* d'enseignement. **2.** enseignement; leçons *fpl*; **the teachings of experience,** les leçons de l'expérience. **3.** (*a*) doctrine *f*; (*b*) **teachings,** préceptes *m*; **the teachings of Plato,** la doctrine de Platon.

teacloth ['tiːklɔθ], *s.* **1.** nappe *f* à thé; napperon *m.* **2.** torchon *m*, essuie-verres *m inv.*

teacup ['tiːkʌp], *s.* tasse *f* à thé.

teacupful ['tiːkʌpful], *s.* pleine tasse à thé (**of,** de).

teahouse ['tiːhaus], *s.* (*in Japan & China*) salon *m* de thé.

teak [tiːk], *s.* **1.** *Bot:* chêne *m* des Indes; teck *m*, tek *m.* **2.** (bois *m* de) teck.

teal [tiːl], *s.* (*pl. usu.* **teal**) *Orn:* sarcelle *f*; (**winter**) **t.,** *NAm:* **European t.,** sarcelle d'hiver, sarcelle sarcelline, *Fr.C:* sarcelle européenne; **blue-winged t.,** sarcelle soucrourou, *Fr.C:* sarcelle à ailes bleues; **cinnamon t.,** *Fr.C:* sarcelle cannelle; **falcated t., green-winged t.,** sarcelle à faucilles; **Baikal t.,** sarcelle élégante; **cotton t.,** sarcelle de Coromandel.

tealeaf, *pl.* **-leaves** ['tiːliːf, -liːvz], *s.* feuille *f* de thé; **used tealeaves,** marc *m* de thé; **stray t.** (*that has got through the strainer*) chinois *m.*

teallite ['tiːlait], *s.* *Miner:* téallite *f.*

team[1] [tiːm], *s.* **1.** attelage *m* (de chevaux, de bœufs); **tandem t.,** attelage en file; **unicorn t.,** attelage en arbalète; **spare t.,** attelage haut-le-pied; **t. driver,** conducteur *m* d'attelage; charretier *m*; **to walk at the head of the t.,** marcher en tête de l'attelage. **2.** équipe *f* (de joueurs, d'ouvriers); camp *m* (de joueurs); **football t.,** équipe de football; **member of a t., t. member, one of the t.,** équipier *m*; **the players in my t., my t. mates,** mes coéquipiers *m*; mes camarades *mf* d'équipe; **t. games,** jeux *m* d'équipe; **the t. spirit,** l'esprit *m* d'équipe.

team[2], *v.tr.* **1.** atteler (des chevaux, des bœufs); **teamed in pairs,** attelés à deux. **2.** *U.S:* camionner (des marchandises). **3.** *v.i.* **to t. up with s.o.,** faire équipe avec qn, se joindre à qn (pour faire qch.).

teamster ['tiːmstər], *s.* **1.** conducteur *m* (d'attelage); charretier *m.* **2.** *U.S:* camionneur *m*; chauffeur *m* de camion; routier *m.*

teamwork ['tiːmwəːk], *s.* **1.** travail fait avec un attelage; camionnage *m.* **2.** *Sp: etc:* travail en équipe; *Sp:* jeu *m* d'ensemble; **thanks to the t. of the committee,** grâce à la collaboration de tous les membres du comité.

teapot ['tiːpɔt], *s.* théière *f.*

tear[1] ['tiər], *s.* **1.** larme *f*; **to shed (bitter) tears,** pleurer (à chaudes larmes); verser des larmes (amères); **to shed tears of joy,** pleurer de joie; verser des larmes de joie; **to shed, weep, tears of blood,** pleurer des larmes de sang; *P: O:* **to shed a t. for Nelson,** pisser; faire pipi; **on the verge of tears,** au bord des larmes; **to burst into tears,** fondre en larmes; avoir une crise de larmes; **to be easily moved to tears,** avoir la larme facile; **to bring tears to s.o.'s eyes,** faire venir des larmes aux yeux de qn; faire pleurer qn; **she was in tears,** elle pleurait; **crocodile tears,** larmes de crocodile, de commande; **t. duct,** conduit lacrymal; **t. bag,** larmier *m* (de cerf); *Archeol:* **t. bottle,** lacrymatoire *m*; **t. gas,** gaz *m* lacrymogène; **t. (gas) bomb,** bombe *f* lacrymogène. **2.** larme (de résine, etc.).

tear[2] ['tiər], *v.i. esp. U.S:* (*of eyes*) pleurer.

tear[3] ['tɛər], *s.* **1.** (*a*) déchirement *m* (d'un tissu, etc.); (*b*) *Metall:* crique *f.* **2.** déchirure *f*, accroc *m* (dans un vêtement, etc.). **3.** *F:* (*a*) **to go full t.,** aller à toute vitesse, à fond de train; (*b*) *O:* **to be in a t.,** être (i) dans une rage, (ii) (très) agité.

tear[4] ['tɛər], *v.* (*p.t.* **tore** [tɔːr]; *p.p.* **torn** [tɔːn])

I. *v.tr.* & *i.* **1.** *v.tr.* (*a*) déchirer; **I've torn my dress,** j'ai déchiré ma robe; j'ai fait un accroc à ma robe; **to t. sth. in two, in half,** déchirer qch. en deux; **to t. (sth.) open,** ouvrir (qch.) en le déchirant; déchirer vivement (une enveloppe); éventrer (un paquet); **to t. s.o.'s character to shreds,** déchirer qn à belles dents; **to t. a hole in sth.,** faire un trou, faire un accroc, à (un vêtement, etc.); **tool that tears the wood,** outil *m* qui mâche le bois; (*with passive force*) **material that tears easily,** tissu qui se déchire facilement; **it just won't t.,** c'est indéchirable; *Paperm:* **to t. rags,** effilocher les chiffons; (*of pers.*) **to t. a muscle,** claquer un muscle; **torn tendon,** tendon déchiré; *F:* **that's torn it,** il ne manquait plus que ça; c'est la fin de tout; **country torn by civil war,** pays déchiré par la guerre civile; **torn with remorse, with anguish,** déchiré par le remords, par l'angoisse; **torn between two feelings,** tiraillé entre deux émotions; (*b*) **to t. sth. down, away, off, out,** arracher qch. (de qch.); **he tore down the poster from the wall,** il a arraché l'affiche du mur; **to t. a wrapper off a newspaper,** faire sauter la bande d'un journal; **to t. s.o.'s eyes out,** arracher les yeux à qn; **to t. a page out of a book,** arracher une page d'un livre; *F:* **to t. one's hair,** s'arracher les cheveux. **2.** *v.i.* (*a*) **to t. at sth.,** déchirer, arracher, qch. avec des doigts impatients; tirer de toutes ses forces sur qch.; **they tore at the wreckage to release him,** ils faisaient des efforts désespérés pour soulever les débris afin de le dégager; (*b*) **to t. along,** aller, avancer, à toute vitesse, à fond de train; brûler le pavé; (*of horseman*) aller à bride abattue; (*of horse*) aller ventre à terre; **he was tearing along (the road),** il dévorait la route; **the car was tearing along at 150 kilometres an hour,** la voiture filait à 150 à l'heure; **to t. upstairs, downstairs,** monter, descendre, l'escalier quatre à quatre; **to t. about,** courir de tous côtés; **to t. away, off,** partir, s'éloigner, à toute vitesse; **to t. back,** revenir en toute hâte; **to t. down, up, the street,** descendre, monter, précipitamment la rue; **to t. in (to a room),** entrer en coup de vent, entrer en trombe (dans une pièce); **to t. out (of a room),** sortir en toute hâte (d'une pièce); sortir en coup de vent; **to t. through France,** traverser la France à la galopade, à la galope.

II. (*compound verbs*) (*s.a.* **tear** **1**(*b*), **2**) **1. tear away,** *v.tr.* **to t. oneself away,** se décider à partir; **I couldn't t. myself away from the place,** je ne pouvais pas m'arracher de, à, cet endroit.

2. tear off, *v.tr. F:* **to t. s.o. off a strip,** dire son fait à qn, semoncer qn.

3. tear up, *v.tr.* (*a*) déchirer (une lettre, etc.); (*b*) **to t. up a plant by the roots,** déraciner une plante.

tearaway ['tɛərəwei]. *F:* **1.** *s.* casse-cou *m.* **2.** *a.* impulsif.

teardrop ['tiədrɔp], *s.* (*a*) larme *f*; (*b*) *Lap:* pendeloque *f.*

tearful ['tiəful], *a.* éploré; tout en pleurs; *Pej:* larmoyant; **t. eyes,** yeux pleins de larmes; **t. voice,** (i) voix mouillée de larmes; (ii) *Pej:* voix geignarde; **in a t. voice,** (i) avec des larmes dans la voix; (ii) *Pej:* en pleurnichant, d'un ton pleurnicheur, geignard.

tearfully ['tiəfuli], *adv.* en pleurant; les larmes aux yeux; *Pej:* d'un ton pleurnicheur, geignard.

tearfulness ['tiəfulnis], *s.* larmoiement *m.*

tearing ['tɛəriŋ], *s.* **1.** déchirement *m* (d'un tissu, etc.); *Paperm:* effilochage *m* (de chiffons); **t. wire,** fil *m* de coupage (du papier à la forme); **t. of a muscle,** rupture *f* d'un muscle; déchirure *f* musculaire; **t. (up),** déchirement (d'un morceau de papier, etc.). **2. t. away, off, out,** arrachement *m*; *Mec:* **t. stress,** travail *m* à l'arrachement; **t. strength,** résistance *f* à la déchirure; *Paperm: etc:* **t. test,** mesure *f* de la résistance à la déchirure; *F:* **t. rage,** rage *f* à tout casser; **to be in a t. hurry,** être terriblement pressé.

tearjerker ['tiədʒəːkər], *s. F:* histoire larmoyante, film larmoyant, etc.

tearless ['tiəlis], *a.* **t. eyes,** yeux secs; **t. grief,** chagrin *m* sans larmes.

tear-off ['tɛərɔf], *a.* (*of label, etc.*) perforé; **t.-o. calendar,** calendrier *m* éphéméride.

tearoom ['tiːruːm], *s.* salon *m* de thé.

tearproof ['tɛəpruːf], *a.* indéchirable.

tearstained ['tiəsteind], *a.* (visage) portant des traces de larmes, barbouillé de larmes, marbré par les larmes.

tease[1] [tiːz], *s.* **1.** taquin, -ine; **he's a t.,** il est taquin. **2.** *O:* taquinerie *f.*

tease[2], *v.tr.* **1.** (*a*) **to t. (out),** effiler, effilocher, défiler, défilocher (un tissu, etc.); démêler (de la laine); (*b*) = TEASEL[2]; (*c*) carder (la laine, etc.); (*d*) mélanger, touiller (une salade). **2.** (*a*) taquiner, tourmenter (qn); faire des taquineries à (qn); exciter (un chien, etc.); **don't t. your little sister,** ne taquine pas ta petite sœur; **don't t. the cat,** ne tourmentez pas le chat; **to t. s.o. unmercifully,** faire des misères à qn; (*b*) *A:* **to t. s.o. for sth., to do sth.,** tracasser, importuner, qn pour obtenir qch., pour qu'il fasse qch.

teasel[1] ['tiːzl], *s.* **1.** *Bot:* cardère *f*; **wild t.,** cardère sauvage; *F:* cabaret *m* des oiseaux; bain *m* de Vénus; **fuller's t.,** peigne-à-loup *m*; **t. plantation,** chardonnière. **2.** *Tex:* carde *f.*

teasel[2], *v.tr.* (**teaseled**) *Tex:* lainer, chardonner, gratter, garnir, aplaigner (le drap).

teaseler ['tiːzlər], *s. Tex:* laineur, -euse; gratteur, -euse; aplaigneur, -euse; garnisseur, -euse.

teaseling ['tiːzliŋ], *s. Tex:* lainage *m*, garnissage *m*, grattage *m*, aplaignage *m.*

teaser ['tiːzər], *s.* **1.** *Tex:* (*a*) = TEASELER; (*b*) cardeur, -euse. **2.** = TEASE[1] **1. 3.** *Breed:* étalon *m* d'essai; (étalon, bélier) boute-en-train *m inv.* **4.** *F:* problème *m* difficile; colle *f*; question embarrassante; **that really was a t.!** ça m'a donné du fil à retordre! **5.** *El:* contre-enroulement *m* en dérivation.

teashop ['tiːʃɔp], *s.* salon *m* de thé.

teasing[1] ['tiːziŋ], *a.* (ton, etc.) railleur, persifleur.

teasing[2], *s.* **1.** (*a*) **t. (out),** effilage *m*, effilochage *m*, défilage *m* (d'un tissu); démêlage *m* (de la laine); (*b*) = TEASELING; (*c*) cardage *m.* **2.** taquinerie *f*; **he doesn't like t.,** il prend mal les taquineries; il n'aime pas qu'on le taquine.

teasingly ['tiːziŋli], *adv.* d'un ton railleur; pour taquiner.

teaspoon ['tiːspuːn], *s.* cuillère *f*, cuiller *f*, à thé, à café.

teaspoonful ['tiːspuːnful], *s.* cuillerée à thé; petite cuillerée.

teat [tiːt], *s.* **1.** (*a*) mamelon *m*; bout *m* de sein; téton *m*, tétin *m* (de femme); tette *f*, trayon *m* (de vache, etc.); (*b*) tétine *f* (de biberon); *Fb:* tubulaire *m* (de vessie de ballon); *Phot:* **t. of pneumatic release,** raccord *m* de déclenchement. **2.** *Tchn:* **t. screw,** vis *f* à téton.

teatime ['tiːtaim], *s.* l'heure *f* du thé.

teazle[1,2] ['tiːzl], *s.* & *v.tr.* = TEASEL[1,2].

tec [tek], *s. F:* détective (privé).

technetium [tek'niːʃiəm], *s. Ch:* technétium *m.*

technical ['teknik(ə)l], *a.* **1.** technique, technologique; **t. education,** enseignement professionnel, technique; **t. college,** collège *m* technique; **he's a t. man,** c'est un technicien; **t. difficulty, reason,** difficulté *f*, raison *f*, d'ordre technique; **t. hitch,** incident *m* technique; **t. terms,** termes *m* techniques; **t. literacy,** connaissance *f* de termes techniques, du vocabulaire technique; connaissances en technologie; en technique; *Jur:* **t. difficulty,** question *f* de procédure; **judgment quashed on a t. point,** arrêt cassé pour vice de forme, de procédure; *Mil:* **t. arms,** armes spéciales. **2.** *Jur:* **t. offence,** quasi-délit *m*, *pl.* quasi-délits; **t. assault,** quasi-agression *f*; *Box:* **t. knockout,** victoire *f* sur un adversaire qui ne peut pas continuer.

technicality [tekni'kæliti], *s.* **1.** technicité *f* (d'une expression, etc.). **2.** détail *m* technique; terme *m* technique; **to lose oneself in technicalities,** se perdre dans des considérations d'ordre technique; *Jur:* **to lose one's case on a t.,** perdre sa cause pour vice de forme, de procédure.

technically ['teknik(ə)li], *adv.* **1.** techniquement; (s'exprimer) en termes techniques. **2. I suppose he's t. literate,** il sait quand-même lire.

technician [tek'niʃ(ə)n], (*U.S:* *also*) **technicist** ['teknisist], *s.* technicien, -ienne.

Technicolor ['teknikʌlər], *a.* & *s.* *R.t.m. Cin:* Technicolor (*m*).

technics ['tekniks], *s.pl.* (*usu. with sg. const.*) technologie *f.*

technique [tek'niːk], *s.* technique *f* (d'un art, d'un artiste, etc.); **every science has its own (special) t.,** chaque science a sa technique particulière; *Surg:* **operative t.,** technique opératoire; *Mus:* **Chopin's t.,** la technique de Chopin; **his t. is poor,** il manque de technique; *Aut:* **driving t.,** la technique de la conduite.

technocracy [tek'nɔkrəsi], *s. Pol.Ec:* technocratie *f.*

technocrat ['teknəkræt], *s.* technocrate *mf.*
technocratic [teknə'krætik], *a.* technocratique; (*pers.*) technocrate.
technographic [teknə'græfik], *a.* technographique.
technography [tek'nɔgrəfi], *s.* technographie *f.*
technological [teknə'lɔdʒik(ə)l], *a.* technologique.
technologist [tek'nɔlədʒist], *s.* technologue *mf,* technologiste *mf.*
technology [tek'nɔlədʒi], *s.* technologie *f.*
techy ['tetʃi], *a.* = TESTY.
tecoma [te'koumə], *s. Bot:* técoma *m.*
tectibranch ['tektibræŋk], *a. Moll:* tectibranche.
Tectibranchia [tekti'bræŋkiə], *s.pl. Moll:* tectibranches *m,* tectinibranches *m.*
tectiform ['tektifɔ:m]. **1.** *a. Nat.Hist: etc:* en forme de toit, de couvercle. **2.** *s. Prehist:* représentation *f* paléolithique d'un toit, d'une maison.
tectogene ['tektoudʒi:n], *s. Geol:* tectogène *m.*
tectology [tek'tɔlədʒi], *s. Biol:* tectologie *f.*
tectonic [tek'tɔnik]. *Geol:* (*a*) *a. & s.* (dislocation, plissement, etc.) tectonique (*f*); (*b*) *s.pl.* (*with sg. const.*) **tectonics,** la tectonique.
tectorial [tek'tɔ:riəl], *a. Anat:* **t. membrane,** membrane recouvrante (de l'organe de Corti).
tectrix, *pl.* **tectrices** ['tektriks, tek'traisi:z], *s. Orn:* (plume) tectrice (*f*).
ted[1] [ted], *v.tr.* (**tedded**) *Agr:* faner, sauter (le foin).
Ted[2]. **1.** *Pr.n.m.* = TEDDY **1** (*a*). **2.** *s. F: O:* = blouson noir.
tedder ['tedər], *s. Agr:* **1.** (*pers.*) faneur, -euse. **2.** (*machine*) faneuse *f.*
tedding ['tediŋ], *s. Agr:* fanage *m;* **t. machine,** faneuse *f.*
Teddy ['tedi]. (*a*) *Pr.n.m.* (*dim. of Edward, Edmund, Edgar, Theodore*) Édouard, Edmond, Edgar, Théodore; (*b*) *s. F: O:* **t. boy** = blouson noir; (*c*) *s. Toys:* **t. bear,** ours *m* en peluche; **my t.** = mon nounours.
tedious ['ti:diəs], *a.* (*of work, etc.*) fatigant, pénible; (*of speech, etc.*) ennuyeux, fastidieux, rebutant; **t. story,** histoire à dormir debout; (*in book*) **t. passages,** longueurs *f.*
tediously ['ti:diəsli], *adv.* ennuyeusement, fastidieusement.
tediousness, tedium ['ti:diəsnis, -diəm], *s.* ennui *m;* manque *m* d'intérêt (d'un travail, de l'existence).
tee[1] [ti:], *s.* **1.** (la lettre) té *m.* **2.** *Const:* **t. iron,** (simple) té; *Metalw:* **t. joint,** joint *m* de soudure en forme de té; (*of pipes*) **t. piece union,** raccord *m* à T.
tee[2], *s. Golf:* (*a*) dé *m* (de sable); tee *m;* (*b*) tertre *m,* point *m,* de départ.
tee[3], *v.tr. & i. Golf:* surélever (la balle); **to t. up,** placer la balle sur le dé; **to t. off,** jouer sa balle (du tertre de départ).
tee[4], *s. Games:* (*curling*) but *m.*
tee-hee [ti:'hi:], *int., s. & v.i.* = TEHEE[1,2].
teel [ti:l], *s. Bot:* till *m,* teel *m;* sésame *m* de l'Inde; **t. oil,** huile *f* de sésame.
teem [ti:m], *v.i.* abonder (*with,* en); grouiller, fourmiller (*with,* de); **the street is teeming with people,** la rue grouille de monde; **his brain teems with ideas,** il déborde d'idées; **it's teeming with rain,** il pleut à verse.
teenage ['ti:neidʒ], *a.* (de) jeune; d'adolescent.
teenager ['ti:neidʒər], *s.* jeune *mf,* adolescent(e) (de 13 à 19 ans).
teens [ti:nz], *s.pl.* adolescence *f* (de 13 à 19 ans); **she's just out of her t.,** elle a juste 20 ans.
teeny(-weeny) ['ti:ni('wi:ni)], *a. F:* minuscule.
teepee ['ti:pi, ti'pi:], *s.* tente-abri *f, pl.* tentes-abris (des Amérindiens).
teesdalia [ti:z'deiliə], *s. Bot:* teesdalie *f,* teesdalia *m.*
teeshirt ['ti:ʃə:t], *s. Cost:* tee-shirt *m,* T-shirt *m.*
teeter[1] ['ti:tər], *s. esp. U.S: F:* bascule *f,* balançoire *f.*
teeter[2], *v.i.* (*a*) *U.S: F:* se balancer; basculer; (*b*) chanceler.
teethe [ti:ð], *v.i.* (*used only in pr.p. and progressive tenses*) faire ses (premières) dents; **baby's teething,** le bébé fait ses dents.
teething ['ti:ðiŋ], *s.* dentition *f;* poussée *f* dentaire; **t. ring,** anneau *m* de dentition; **t. troubles,** (i) ennuis *m* de dentition; (ii) *F:* difficultés initiales; **the firm's having t. troubles,** la maison a de la peine à démarrer.
teetotal [ti:'tout(ə)l], *a.* antialcoolique; qui ne prend pas de boissons alcooliques.
teetotalism [ti:'toutəlizm], *s.* abstention *f* des boissons alcooliques; antialcoolisme *m.*
teetotaller [ti:'tout(ə)lər], *s.* membre *m* de la ligue antialcoolique; abstinent, -ente; buveur, -euse, d'eau.
teetotum [ti:'toutəm], *s. Games:* (*a*) toton *m;* (*b*) *A:* cochonnet *m.*
tegenaria [tedʒe'nɛəriə], *s. Arach:* tégénaire *f.*
teg(g) [teg], *s. Husb:* (agneau) antennais *m;* (agnelle) antennaise *f.*
tegmen, *pl.* **-mina** ['tegmen, -minə], *s.* **1.** *Bot:* tegmen *m;* tégument *m;* endoplèvre *f.* **2.** *Ent:* aile antérieure (d'une orthoptère); tegmen.
tegu [tə'gu:], *s. Rept:* téju *m,* tégu *m.*
tegula, *pl.* **-ae** ['tegjulə, -i:], *s. Ent:* tégule *f* (de l'aile antérieure).
tegument ['tegjumənt], *s. Nat.Hist:* tégument *m.*
tegumental, tegumentary [tegju'ment(ə)l, -'mentəri], *a. Nat.Hist:* tégumentaire.
tehee[1] [ti:'hi:]. **1.** *int.* hi! hi! **2.** *s. F:* (*a*) ricanement *m;* (*b*) petit rire affecté.
tehee[2], *v.i. F:* (*a*) ricaner; (*b*) faire des petits rires affectés.
Teheran [tɛə'rɑ:n], *Pr.n. Geog:* Téhéran.
teiid ['ti:(j)id], *s. Rept:* téiidé *m.*
Teiidae ['ti:(j)idi:], **Tejidae** ['ti:jidi:], *s.pl. Rept:* téiidés *m,* téjidés *m.*
teju [tə'dʒu:], *s. Rept:* téju *m,* tégu *m;* sauvegarde *m.*
tektite ['tektait], *s. Miner:* tectite *f,* tektite *f.*
telaesthesia [telis'θi:ziə], *s. Psychics:* télesthésie *f.*
telaesthetic [telis'θetik], *a. Psychics:* télesthésique.
Telamon ['teləmən]. **1.** *Pr.n.m. Gr.Myth:* Télamon. **2.** *s.* (*pl.* **telamones** [telə'mouni:z]) *Arch:* atlante *m,* télamon *m.*
telangiectasia, telangiectasis [telændʒiek'teiʒiə, -'ektəsis], *s. Med:* télangiectasie *f.*
Telanthropus [te'lænθrəpəs], *s. Paleont:* télanthrope *m.*
telautogram [te'lɔ:təgræm], *s. Tg:* télautogramme *m,* téléautogramme *m.*
telautograph [te'lɔ:təgræf], *s. Tg:* télautographe *m,* téléautographe *m.*
telautography [telɔ:'tɔgrəfi], *s.* télautographie *f,* téléautographie *f.*
teleammeter [teli'æmitər], *s. El:* téléampèremètre *m.*
teleautogram [teli'ɔ:tougræm], *s.* = TELAUTOGRAM.
teleautography [telio:'tɔgrəfi], *s.* = TELAUTOGRAPHY.
telebreaker ['telibreikər], *s. El:* télérupteur *m.*
telebreaking ['telibreikiŋ], *s. El:* télérupture *f.*
telebriefing ['telibri:fiŋ], *s. Av:* instructions radiotéléphonées avant départ; **t. installation,** téléphone *m* de piste; réseau *m* téléphonique d'ordres de décollage terminal.
telecabin ['telikæbin], *s.* télécabine *f,* télébenne *f.*
telecamera [teli'kæmərə], *s.* caméra *m* de télévision.
telecast[1] ['telikɑ:st], *s.* émission *f* de télévision; programme télédiffusé.
telecast[2], *v.tr.* (*p.t. & p.p.* **telecast**) téléviser; émettre, diffuser, par télévision.
telecaster ['telikɑ:stər], *s.* **1.** émetteur *m* de télévision. **2.** (*pers.*) téléaste *mf.*
telecentre ['telisentər], *s. Cmptr:* centre *m* de télétraitement.
telecine(ma) [teli'sini(mə)], *s.* télécinéma *m.*
telecommunication [telikəmju:ni'keiʃ(ə)n], *s.* télécommunication *f;* **telecommunications engineer,** télémécanicien *m.*
telecontrol [telikən'troul], *s.* télécommande *f,* téléréglage *m;* télécontrôle *m;* téléguidage *m;* commande *f,* réglage *m,* à distance; **to operate by t.,** télécommander (qch.).
telecontrolled [telikən'trould], *a.* télécommandé, téléréglé, commandé, réglé, à distance.
telecourse ['telikɔ:s], *s. U.S:* télévision *f* scolaire; cours télévisé(s).
telecurietherapy [telikjuri'θerəpi], *s. Med:* télécuriethérapie *f.*
teledu ['telidu:], *s. Z:* télédu *m,* télagon *m,* teledon *m.*
teledynamic [telidai'næmik]. *El:* (*a*) *a.* télédynamique, télodynamique; (*b*) *s.pl.* (*usu. with sg. const.*) **teledynamics,** télédynamique *f.*
telefactoring [teli'fæktəriŋ], *s.* mise *f* en œuvre à distance.
teleferic [teli'ferik], *s.* téléphérique *m,* téléférique *m.*
telefilm ['telifilm], *s.* téléfilm *m,* film télévisé.
telegenic [teli'dʒenik], *a.* télégénique.
telegony [ti'legəni], *s. Biol: Breed:* télégonie *f.*
telegram ['teligræm], *s.* télégramme *m;* dépêche *f* (télégraphique); **inland, foreign, t.,** télégramme intérieur, international; **greetings t.,** télégramme de luxe; **code(d) t., t. in code,** télégramme codé; **multiple (-address) t.,** télégramme multiple, à adresses multiples; **press t.,** télégramme de presse; dépêche d'agence (de presse); **repetition-paid t., t. with repetition,** télégramme avec collationnement; **reply-paid t.,** télégramme avec réponse payée; **telephoned t.,** télégramme téléphoné; **radio t.,** radiotélégramme *m;* **to send s.o. a t.,** envoyer un télégramme à qn.
telegraph[1] ['teligræf], *s.* **1.** (*a*) *A:* (**semaphore**) **t.,** télégraphe aérien; télégraphe optique; télégraphe Chappe; sémaphore *m;* (*b*) télégraphe (électrique); **duplex t.,** télégraphe duplex; **Morse t.,** télégraphe Morse; appareil *m* télégraphique Morse; **needle t.,** télégraphe, appareil télégraphique, à cadran; **printing, writing, t.,** télégraphe imprimant, écrivant; typotélégraphe *m;* **recording t.,** télégraphe enregistreur; **bush t.,** téléphone *m* arabe; **to send news by t.,** envoyer des nouvelles par télégramme; **t. form,** formule *f* de télégramme; imprimé *m* à télégramme; **t. line,** ligne *f* télégraphique; **t. pole,** poteau *m* télégraphique; **t. wire,** fil *m* télégraphique; **t. boy,** (jeune) préposé *m* télégraphique. **2.** *Nau:* transmetteur *m* d'ordres (de manœuvre); (**engine-room**) **t.,** chadburn *m.* **3.** *Sp:* **t. (board),** tableau *m* d'affichage (des résultats). **4.** *Bot:* **t. plant,** trèfle oscillant, sainfoin oscillant.
telegraph[2]. **1.** *v.i.* télégraphier; envoyer un télégramme, une dépêche; **they telegraphed for his son,** on a télégraphié pour faire venir son fils; on a appelé son fils par télégramme. **2.** *v.tr.* (*a*) télégraphier (une nouvelle, etc.); **he telegraphed that he would arrive about midday,** il a télégraphié qu'il arriverait vers midi; (*b*) *Box: F:* **to t. a punch,** annoncer un direct.
telegrapher [ti'legrəfər], *s. esp. U.S:* télégraphiste *mf.*
telegraphese [teligræ'fi:z], *s.* langage *m,* style *m,* télégraphique.
telegraphic [teli'græfik], *a.* télégraphique; **t. address,** adresse *f* télégraphique.
telegraphically [teli'græfik(ə)li], *adv.* **1.** télégraphiquement; par télégramme. **2.** en style télégraphique.
telegraphist [ti'legrəfist], *s.* télégraphiste *mf.*
telegraphy [ti'legrəfi], *s.* télégraphie *f;* **duplex t., two-way t.,** télégraphie duplex; **multiplex t.,** télégraphie multiplex; **modulated t.,** télégraphie modulée; **frequency-shift t.,** télégraphie par variation de fréquence; **radio-frequency carrier t.,** télégraphie par porteurs haute-fréquence; **spark t.,** télégraphie à étincelles; **wireless t.,** télégraphie sans fil; radiotélégraphie *f.*
teleguidance [teli'gaidəns], *s.* téléguidage *m.*
tele-irradiation [teliireidi'eiʃ(ə)n], *s. Atom.Ph:* télé-irradiation *f;* **radium t.-i.,** télé-irradiation par radium.
telekinesis [telikai'ni:sis], *s. Psychics:* télékinésie *f.*
telelens ['telilenz], *s. Phot:* téléobjectif *m.*
Telemachus [ti'leməkəs], *Pr.n.m. Gr.Lit:* Télémaque.
telemark ['telimɑ:k], *s. Ski:* télémark *m.*
telemechanics [telimi'kæniks], *s.pl.* (*usu. with sg. const.*) télémécanique *f.*
telemetacarpal [telimetə'kɑ:pəl], *a. Z:* télémétacarpalien.
telemeteorograph [teli'mi:tiərəgræf], *s.* télémétéorographe *m.*
telemeter[1] ['telimi:tər], *s.* (*a*) *Surv: Artil: etc:* télémètre *m;* **stereoscopic t.,** stéréotélémètre *m;* (*b*) appareil *m* de télémesure; **direct-relation t.,** appareil de télémesure à lecture proportionnelle; **position-type t.,** appareil de télémesure à comparaison.
telemeter[2], *v.tr.* (*a*) télémétrer; (*b*) télémesurer.
telemetering ['telimi:t(ə)riŋ], *s.* (*a*) télémétrage *m;* (*b*) télémesure *f;* **pulse-modulated t. device,** appareil *m* de télémesure par impulsions.
telemetric(al) [teli'metrik(l)], *a.* télémétrique.
telemetrist [ti'lemitrist], *s.* télémétreur *m.*
telemetry [ti'lemitri], *s.* (*a*) télémétrie *f;* (*b*) télémesure *f;* **t. transmitter,** émetteur *m* de télémesure; **digital t. system,** système digital de télémesure.
telemotor ['telimoutər], *s. Nau:* **t. (gear),** transmission *f* de barre hydraulique; télémoteur *m.*
telencephalon [telen'sefəlɔn], *s. Anat:* télencéphale *m.*
teleneuron [teli'nju:rɔn], *s. Anat:* téléneurone *m.*
teleobjective [teliɔb'dʒektiv], *s. Phot:* téléobjectif *m.*
Teleoceras [teli'ɔsərəs], *s. Paleont: Z:* teleoceras *m.*
teleological [teliou'lɔdʒik(ə)l], *a. Phil:* téléologique.
teleology [teli'ɔlədʒi], *s. Phil:* téléologie *f.*
teleoroentgenography [telioura:ntge'nɔgrəfi], *s. Med:* téléradiographie *f.*
teleosaur ['teliəsɔ:r], **teleosaurus** [teliou'sɔ:rəs], *s. Paleont:* téléosaure *m,* teleosaurus *m.*
Teleosauridae [teliou'sɔ:ridi:], *s.pl. Paleont: Rept:* téléosauridés *m.*
teleost ['teliɔst], **teleostean** [teli'ɔstiən], *a. & s. Ich:* téléostéen (*m*).
Teleostei [teli'ɔstiai], *s.pl. Ich:* téléostéens *m.*
Teleostomi [teli'ɔstəmai], *s.pl. Ich:* téléostomes *m.*
telepath ['telipæθ], *s.* télépathe *mf.*
telepathic [teli'pæθik], *a.* télépathique; (personne) télépathe.
telepathically [teli'pæθik(ə)li], *adv.* télépathiquement.
telepathist [ti'lepəθist], *s.* télépathe *mf.*
telepathy [ti'lepəθi], *s.* télépathie *f.*
telephone[1] ['telifoun], *s.* téléphone *m;* **automatic t.,** téléphone automatique; **subscriber's t.,** téléphone

d'abonné; **t. subscriber,** abonné *m* au téléphone; **public t., coin-operated t.** = taxiphone *m*; **t. box,** cabine *f* téléphonique; **wall t.,** appareil *m*, poste *m*, (téléphonique) mural; **plug-in t.,** appareil mobile; **house t., room-to-room t.,** téléphone intérieur, d'appartement; **intensifier t.,** téléphone haut-parleur; *Mil:* **field t.,** téléphone de campagne; *Nau:* **ship-to-shore t.,** téléphone bâtiment-terre; **t. transmitter,** émetteur *m* microphonique, radiotéléphonique; *F:* **bush t.,** téléphone arabe, de brousse; **t. line,** ligne téléphonique; **t. channel, circuit, connection,** voie *f*, circuit *m*, liaison *f*, téléphonique; **t. network, system,** réseau *m* téléphonique; **t. wire,** fil *m* téléphonique; **t. operator,** téléphoniste *mf*; standardiste *mf*; **t. answerer, answering device,** répondeur *m* téléphonique; **t. meter,** téléphonomètre *m*; **t. directory, book,** annuaire *m* des téléphones, *Adm:* annuaire officiel des abonnés au téléphone; **to be on the t.,** être abonné au téléphone; **are you on the t.?** avez-vous le téléphone? **what's your t. number?** quel est votre numéro de téléphone? **to speak to s.o. on the t.,** parler à qn au téléphone; **t. call,** appel *m* téléphonique; **t. bell,** sonnerie *f* téléphonique; **you're wanted on the t.,** on vous demande, on vous appelle, au téléphone; **who answered the t.?** qui a répondu au téléphone? **to order sth. by t.,** demander qch. par téléphone; faire une commande téléphonique, par téléphone.

telephone[2]. **1.** *v.i.* téléphoner (to, à); **to t. for the doctor, for a taxi,** appeler le docteur, un taxi (par téléphone); téléphoner pour faire venir le docteur. **2.** *v.tr.* téléphoner (un message).

telephonic [teli'fɔnik], *a.* téléphonique.

telephonically [teli'fɔnik(ə)li], *adv.* téléphoniquement.

telephoning ['telifouniŋ], *s.* téléphonage *m* (d'un télégramme, etc.).

telephonist [ti'lefənist], *s.* téléphoniste *mf.*

telephonograph [teli'founəgræf], *s.* enregistreur *m* téléphonographique.

telephonometry [telifə'nɔmitri], *s.* téléphonométrie *f.*

telephony [ti'lefəni], *s.* téléphonie *f*; **radio t., wireless t.,** téléphonie sans fil; radiotéléphonie *f*; **carrier-current t.,** téléphonie par courant porteur; **multicircuit carrier t.,** téléphonie multivoie par courants porteurs; **ground t.,** téléphonie par le sol.

Telephoridae [teli'fɔridi:], *s.pl. Ent:* téléphoridés *m.*

telephote ['telifout], *s. Tg:* téléphote *m*; **Belin t.,** téléstéréographe *m*; téléphote de Belin.

telephoto [teli'foutou]. **1.** *a.* téléphotographique; **t. lens,** téléobjectif *m*. **2.** *s. Tg:* phototélégraphe *m*; phototélégraphie *f.*

telephotograph [teli'foutəgræf], *s.* **1.** *Phot:* téléphotographie *f*; photographie prise au téléobjectif. **2.** *Tg:* bélinogramme *m*; téléphotographie.

telephotographic [telifoutə'græfik], *a.* **1.** *Phot:* téléphotographique; **t. lens,** téléobjectif *m*. **2.** *Tg:* bélinographique; phototélégraphique; téléphotographique; **t. device,** bélinographe *m*; appareil *m* de phototélégraphie, de téléphotographie.

telephotography [telifə'tɔgrəfi], *s.* **1.** *Phot:* téléphotographie *f*; photographie *f* au téléobjectif. **2.** *Tg:* bélinographie *f*; phototélégraphie *f*; téléphotographie.

teleplasm ['teliplæzm], *s. Psychics:* téléplasme *m*, ectoplasme *m.*

teleportation [telipɔ:'teiʃ(ə)n], *s. Psychics:* téléportation *f.*

teleprinter ['teliprintər], *s.* (i) téléimprimeur *m*, téléscripteur *m*, télétype *m*; **t. operator,** télétypiste *mf*; (ii) Télex *m* (*R.t.m.*); **t. network,** réseau Télex, service Télex; **radio t.,** radiotélétype *m*; **t. perforator,** téléimprimeur-perforateur *m*, *pl.* téléimprimeurs-perforateurs.

teleprinting ['teliprintiŋ], *s.* téléimpression *f*, téléscription *f*, télétypie *f.*

teleprocess ['teliprouses], *v.i. Cmptr:* faire de la télégestion, du télétraitement.

teleprocessing ['teliprousesiŋ], *s. Cmptr:* télégestion *f*; télétraitement *m*; téléinformatique *f*; **t. station,** poste *m* de télégestion; **t. terminal,** terminal *m* de télégestion.

teleprompter ['teliprɔm(p)tər], *s. T.V: R.t.m:* télésouffleur *m.*

teleradiogram [teli'reidiougræm], *s. Med:* téléradiographie *f.*

teleradiography [telireidi'ɔgrəfi], *s. Med:* téléradiographie *f*, *F:* téléradio *f.*

teleran ['teliræn], *s. Av:* navigation *f* par téléradar.

telerecording [teliri'kɔ:diŋ], *s.* émission *f* de télévision enregistrée.

telergy ['telədʒi], *s. Psychics:* force *f* télépathique.

teleroentgenogram [teli'rɔ:ntgenougræm], *s. Med:* téléradiographie *f.*

teleroentgenography [telirɔ:ntgə'nɔgrəfi], *s. Med:* téléradiographie *f.*

telescope[1] ['teliskoup], *s.* (*a*) **(reflecting) t.,** télescope *m* (à réflexion, à miroir); **radio t.,** radiotélescope *m*; **equatorial t.,** (télescope) équatorial *m*, *pl.* équatoriaux; **electron t.,** télescope électronique; *Atom.Ph:* **t. counter,** compteur *m* télescope; (*b*) **(refracting) t.,** lunette *f* (d'approche); longue-vue *f*, *pl.* longues-vues; *Astr:* réfracteur *m*; **astronomical t., zenith t.,** lunette astronomique; **astro-navigation t.,** lunette de navigation astronomique; **bent t., broken t., elbow t.,** lunette coudée; **collimating t.,** lunette à collimation; lunette-collimateur *f*, *pl.* lunettes-collimateurs; **transit t.,** lunette méridienne; **Galilean t.,** lunette de Galilée; **naval t.,** lunette (de) marine; **sighting t.,** (i) *Surv:* lunette-viseur *f*, *pl.* lunettes-viseurs; (ii) *Artil:* lunette de pointage; *Artil: etc:* **tracking t.,** lunette de pointage continu; **to focus a t.,** mettre au point une lunette; (*c*) *Com:* **t. box,** caisse *f* télescope; *Mec.E:* **t. jack,** vérin *m* télescopique; **t. joint,** joint *m* télescopique; (*d*) *Ich:* **t. fish,** poisson *m* télescope.

telescope[2]. **1.** *v.tr.* télescoper (un train, etc.). **2.** *v.i.* (*a*) (*of trains, etc.*) (se) télescoper; (*b*) **parts made to t.,** pièces assemblées en télescope; pièces qui s'emboîtent, à emboîtement.

telescopic [telis'kɔpik], *a.* **1.** (*a*) télescopique; *Surv:* **t. alidade,** alidade *f* à lunette; *Phot:* **t. lens,** téléobjectif *m*; **t. viewfinder,** viseur *m* à lunette, viseur télescopique; **t. magnifier,** téléloupe *f*; (*of firearm*) **t. sight,** appareil *m* de visée à lunette; hausse *f* télescopique; (*b*) (étoile, etc.) visible au télescope. **2.** télescopique; coulissant; (*of drinking cup, etc.*) télescopable; **t. tripod,** trépied *m* télescopique; pied *m* à trois branches coulissantes; **t. leg (of tripod),** branche coulissante, à coulisse (d'un trépied); **t. ladder,** échelle *f* à coulisse; **t. jack,** vérin *m* télescopique; **t. screw,** vis *f* télescopique; *Nau:* **t. mast,** mât *m* télescopique.

telescoping ['teliskoupiŋ], *s.* télescopage *m* (de véhicules, etc.).

telescopy [ti'leskəpi], *s. Astr: etc:* télescopie *f.*

telescreen ['teliskri:n], *s.* écran *m* de télévision; télécran *m*, téléécran *m.*

teleseism ['telisaizm], *s. Geol:* téléséisme *m.*

telespectroscope [teli'spektrəskoup], *s. Astr:* téléspectroscope *m.*

telestereoscope [teli'steriəskoup], *s. Opt:* téléstéréoscope *m.*

telesthesia [teles'θi:ziə], *s.* télesthésie *f.*

telesthetic [teles'θetik], *a.* télesthésique.

teletape ['teliteip], *s.* télébande *f.*

teletherapy [teli'θerəpi], *s. Med:* téléthérapie *f.*

teletype[1] ['telitaip], *s.* télétype *m*, téléimprimeur *m*, téléscripteur *m*; **t. machine,** appareil *m* télétype; **t. operator,** télétypiste *mf.*

teletype[2], *v.tr.* envoyer (un message) par télétype, par téléscripteur.

teletypewrite [teli'taiprait], *v.tr. esp. U.S:* = TELETYPE[2].

teletypewriter [teli'taipraitər], *s. U.S:* **1.** (appareil *m*) télétype *m*. **2.** (*pers.*) télétypiste *mf.*

teletyping ['telitaipiŋ], *s.* télétypie *f*, téléimpression *f*, téléscription *f.*

teletypist ['telitaipist], *s.* télétypiste *mf.*

Teleut ['teliu:t]. *Ethn:* (*a*) *a.* téléoute; (*b*) *s.* Téléoute *mf.*

teleutospore [te'lju:touspɔ:r], *s. Fung:* téleutospore *f*, téliospore *f.*

televiewer ['telivjuər], *s.* téléspectateur, -trice.

televise ['telivaiz], *v.tr.* téléviser; **televised programme,** programme télédiffusé.

television [teli'viʒ(ə)n], *s.* télévision *f*; (*a*) **closed-circuit t.,** télévision à, en, circuit fermé; **stereoscopic t.,** télévision en relief; **colour t.,** télévision (en) couleur; **high-definition, low-definition, t.,** télévision à haute, à basse, définition; **community t.,** télévision par antenne collective; **t. tube,** tube *m* à rayons cathodiques (pour télévision); **t. picture tube,** cinéscope *m*; **t. transmitter,** émetteur *m* de télévision; **t. aerial, antenna,** antenne *f* de télévision; **t. camera,** caméra *f* de télévision; **t. channel,** chaîne *f* de télévision; **t. engineering,** ingénierie *f*, technique *f*, de la télévision; (*b*) **t. (set), t. receiver,** poste *m* de télévision; téléviseur *m*; télérécepteur *m*; **colour t. (set),** téléviseur couleur; **t. screen,** écran *m* de télévision; **to watch t.,** regarder la télévision; **I saw it on t.,** je l'ai vu à la télévision; (*c*) **t. programme,** programme *m*, émission *f*, de télévision; **schools t., t. for schools,** télévision scolaire; **t. interview,** interview télévisée; **t. newscasting,** téléreportage *m*; **t. news,** journal télévisé; **t. serial,** téléroman *m*; **t. version (of a play, etc.),** forme télévisuelle (d'une pièce, etc.); **t. commentary,** téléreportage (d'un match, etc.).

televisor ['telivaizər], *s.* **1.** poste *m* de télévision; téléviseur *m*. **2.** *esp. U.S:* (*a*) émetteur *m* de télévision; (*b*) téléspectateur, -trice.

televisual [teli'vizjuəl], *a.* **1.** télévisuel. **2.** télégénique.

televoltmeter [teli'vɔltmi:tər], *s. El:* télévoltmètre *m.*

telewriter ['teliraitər], *s.* téléimprimeur *m.*

Telex[1] ['teleks], *s. R.t.m:* Telex *m*; **T. tape,** bande *f* Télex; **T. operator,** télexiste *mf*; **T. network, system,** réseau *m* Télex; **T. subscriber,** abonné *m* du Télex; **to send by T.,** télexer (qch.).

telex[2], *v.tr.* envoyer (un message) par Télex; télexer (un message).

Telfairia [tel'fɛəriə], *s. Bot:* telfairia *m*, kouème *m.*

teliospore ['teliouspɔ:r], *s. Fung:* téleutospore *f*, téliospore *f.*

tell[1] [tel], *v.* (*p.t. & p.p.* **told** [tould])

I. *v.tr.* **1.** (*a*) dire; **to t. the truth,** dire la vérité; **to t. a lie,** dire, faire, un mensonge; (*b*) **to t. s.o. sth.,** dire, apprendre, qch. à qn; informer qn de qch.; faire savoir qch. à qn; **can you t. me the way to the station?** pouvez-vous m'indiquer le chemin de la gare? **to t. s.o. the news,** faire part d'une nouvelle à qn; **we weren't told the news until the next day,** ce ne fut que le lendemain que nous avons appris la nouvelle; **please t. him that . . .,** je vous prie de lui dire, de lui faire savoir, que . . .; **you told me that you loved music,** vous m'avez dit que vous adoriez la musique; **I can't t. you how pleased I am,** je ne saurais vous dire combien je suis content; **we are told that. . .,** on nous informe, on nous dit, que . . .; **I have been told that he is saying unkind things about me,** il me revient qu'il dit du mal de moi; **I t. you no!** je vous dis que non! **it's just as I told you,** c'est tout comme je vous l'ai dit; **don't let me have to t. you that again,** tenez-vous cela pour dit; *F:* (*to child*) **I shan't t. you again!** la prochaine fois tu auras une fessée! **I'm not telling you anything you don't know already,** je ne vous apprends rien; *F:* **you can't t. me anything about that!** ça me connaît! **I told you so! didn't I tell you!** je vous l'avais bien dit! quand je vous le disais! **you're telling me!** à qui le dites-vous? **t. me another!** à d'autres! ça, par exemple! **I'll t. you what!** écoutez! **I'll t. you what! let's go out for dinner!** voyons! si on dînait en ville! *esp. U.S: F:* **t. him goodbye (for me)!** dites-lui au revoir de ma part! (*c*) raconter, conter, dire (une histoire, etc.); **the story he told me was untrue,** l'histoire qu'il m'a racontée était fausse; **I'll t. you all about it later,** je vous raconterai cela plus tard; **I'll t. you what happened,** je vais vous raconter ce qui est arrivé; **in less time than it takes to t.,** en moins de temps qu'il n'en faut pour le dire; **t. me something about yourself,** parlez-moi un peu de vous(-même); **his biographer tells us that he was a pupil of Toscanini,** selon son biographe c'était un élève de Toscanini; **he tells me everything that happens to him,** il me met dans toutes ses affaires; **he told us his adventures all over again,** il nous a fait de nouveau le récit de ses aventures; **he told us how he came to be a writer,** il nous a raconté comment il est devenu écrivain; (*d*) *Dial: F:* **to hear t. of . . .,** entendre parler de . . .; **to hear t. that . . .,** entendre dire que . . .; (*e*) annoncer, proclamer, révéler (un fait, etc.); **to t. a secret,** révéler un secret; *F:* **that would be telling!** ça c'est mon secret! (*f*) (*of clock*) **to t. the time,** marquer l'heure; *A:* **the bell was telling the hour,** la cloche sonnait l'heure. **2.** (*a*) **to t. s.o. about s.o.,** parler de qn à qn; **t. me about David,** parlez-moi de David; **he told us about his adventures,** il nous a raconté ses aventures; **he told us about the countries he had visited,** il nous a décrit les pays qu'il avait visités; **he wrote to t. me of his father's death,** il m'a écrit pour me faire part de, pour m'annoncer, la mort de son père; **t. me what you know about it,** dites-moi ce que vous en savez; (*b*) **let me t. you . . .,** permettez-moi de vous dire . . .; **it's not so easy, let me t. you!** ce n'est pas si facile, je vous assure! **he'll be furious, I can t. you!** il va être furieux, je vous en réponds! **it was hot, I can t. you!** il faisait chaud, je vous assure! **3. to t. s.o. to do sth.,** dire, ordonner, commander, à qn de faire qch.; **t. him to come,** dites-lui de venir; **do as you are told,** faites comme on vous dit; **he'll do as he's told,** il marchera; **you can't t. him (anything),** c'est un je-sais-tout; **he was told to leave,** on lui a dit, on lui a demandé, de partir; **t. the children to come in to lunch,** dites aux enfants de rentrer déjeuner; **I told him not to come again,** je lui ai dit de ne pas revenir; je lui ai défendu de revenir; **I told them not to (do it),** je le leur ai défendu, je leur ai dit de ne pas le faire. **4.** (*a*) discerner, distinguer, reconnaître (qn, qch.); **to t. good from bad, right from wrong,** discerner le bon du mauvais, le bien du mal; **you can hardly t. him from his brother,** c'est à peine si on peut le distinguer de son frère; **you (really) can't t. her from her sister,** elle ressemble à sa sœur à s'y tromper; on ne peut pas la distinguer de sa sœur; **one**

can t. him by his voice, on le reconnaît à sa voix; **although he's six he can't t. the time,** quoiqu'il ait six ans il ne sait pas lire l'heure; (*b*) **one can t. that she's intelligent,** on voit bien qu'elle est intelligente; **you can t. he's a detective a mile away,** il sent le policier d'une lieue; **I can t. it from the look in your eyes,** je le lis dans vos yeux; (*c*) savoir; **how can I t. that he'll do it?** quelle certitude ai-je qu'il le fera? **nobody can t. what the future has in store for him,** l'homme est ignorant de sa destinée. **5.** (*a*) *A:* **to t. (over),** compter (son or, un troupeau, etc.); compter, énumérer (les voix); *Lit:* **every shepherd tells his tale,** chaque berger compte son troupeau; *Ecc:* **to t. one's beads,** égrener son chapelet; (*b*) **all told,** tout compris; somme toute; **there were twenty people all told,** il y avait en tout vingt personnes; **I made £100 out of it all told,** tout compte fait j'en ai retiré £100.

II. *v.i.* (*a*) produire son effet; porter (coup); **every little tells,** toutes ces petites choses produisent leur effet; **breeding will t.,** bon sang ne peut mentir; **every blow tells,** l'effet de chaque coup se fait sentir; **his age is beginning to t. on him,** il commence à accuser son âge; **these drugs t. on one in time,** l'effet de ces drogues se fait sentir à la longue; (*b*) **time will t.,** qui vivra verra; **who can t.? there's no telling!** qui sait? on ne sait pas; **you never can t.,** il ne faut (jamais) jurer de rien; on ne sait jamais; **I can't t.,** je n'en sais rien; **how can I t.?** qu'est-ce que j'en sais? comment le saurais-je? **more than words can t.,** plus qu'on ne saurait dire; (*c*) **this tells in his favour,** cela milite en sa faveur; **it will t. against you,** cela vous nuira; **everything was telling against him,** tout témoignait contre lui; (*d*) **to t. of sth.,** annoncer, accuser, révéler, qch.; **the mild air told of the approach of spring,** l'air doux annonçait le printemps; **the lines on his face t. of long suffering,** son visage sillonné de rides accuse, révèle, ses longues souffrances; (*e*) *P:* **to t. on s.o.,** dénoncer qn; rapporter sur le compte de qn; vendre la mèche.

III. (*compound verb*) **tell off,** *v.tr.* (*a*) *Mil: etc:* désigner, affecter, détacher (qn pour une corvée, un service, etc.); (*b*) *F:* rembarrer (qn); remettre (qn) à sa place; dire son fait à (qn); **he told them off in no uncertain terms,** il leur a dit leurs quatre vérités; **I was really, properly, told off!** qu'est-ce que j'ai pris!

tell[2], *s.* **1.** *Archeol:* tell *m.* **2.** *Geog:* **the T.,** le Tell.

teller ['telər], *s.* **1.** raconteur, -euse; conteur, -euse; narrateur, -trice. **2.** (*a*) caissier, -ière, guichetier, -ière (de banque); (*b*) *Parl:* scrutateur *m*; recenseur *m*; (*c*) *Paperm:* compteuse *f* (de feuilles). **3.** *Box: F:* coup bien asséné. **4.** *Ecc:* **tellers,** glas *m* (dont le nombre de tintements annonce si le défunt est un homme, une femme, ou un enfant).

tellina [te'li:nə], *s. Moll:* telline *f.*

telling[1] ['teliŋ], *a.* fort, efficace; impressionnant; qui fait de l'effet; **t. blow,** coup bien asséné, qui porte; **t. style,** style énergique, expressif, qui porte; **with t. effect,** avec un effet marqué; **t. argument,** argument qui porte; **t. look,** regard qui en dit long.

telling[2], *s.* **1.** récit *m*; relation *f*; narration *f* (d'une histoire); **it lost nothing in the t.,** c'était encore mieux quand on l'entendait raconter. **2.** divulgation *f*, révélation *f* (d'un secret, etc.). **3.** (*a*) *A:* **t. (over),** dénombrement *m*; énumération *f* (des votes, etc.); (*b*) *F:* **t. off,** réprimande *f*; (verte) semonce.

tellingly ['teliŋli], *adv.* efficacement; avec effet; d'une manière impressionnante.

Tellinidae [te'linidi:], *s.pl. Moll:* tellinidés *m.*

tell-tale ['telteil], *s.* **1.** (*pers.*) rapporteur, -euse; dénonciateur, -trice; cafard, -arde; *attrib.* **t.-t. tongue,** langue indiscrète; **t.-t. look,** regard dénonciateur, révélateur, qui en dit long. **2.** *Mec.E: etc:* aiguille indicatrice; indicateur *m*; contrôleur *m*; *Mus:* indicateur de vent (d'un orgue); **t.-t. lamp,** lampe témoin, indicatrice, avertisseuse, signalisatrice. **3.** *Nau:* (*a*) axiomètre *m* (du gouvernail); (*b*) **t.-t. compass,** compas renversé.

tellurate ['teljureit], *s. Ch:* tellurate *m.*

tellurhydric [teljuə'haidrik], *a. Ch:* tellurhydrique; **t. acid,** tellurure *m* d'hydrogène; hydrogène telluré.

tellurian [tel'ju:riən], *a.* tellurien.

telluric[1] [tel'ju:rik], *a. Ch: Miner:* tellurique; **t. bismuth,** tétradymite *f.*

telluric[2], *a. Med:* (fièvre) tellurique; *Geol:* **t. currents,** courants *m* telluriques; *Opt:* **t. line,** raie *f* tellurique.

telluride ['teljuraid], *s.* **1.** *Ch:* tellurure *m*; **hydrogen t.,** tellurure d'hydrogène. **2.** *Miner:* telluride *m.*

telluriferous [telju'rifərəs], *a.* tellurifère.

tellurism ['teljurizm], *s.* tellurisme *m.*

tellurite ['teljurait], *s.* **1.** *Miner:* tellurite *f*; tellurine *f.* **2.** *Ch:* tellurite.

tellurium [tel'ju:riəm], *s.* **1.** *Miner:* tellurium *m*; **black t., foliated t., t. glance,** nagyagite *f.* **2.** *Ch:* tellure *m.*

tellurized ['teljuraizd], *a. Ch:* telluré.

tellurometer [telju'rɔmitər], *s. Elcs:* telluromètre *m.*

tellurous ['teljurəs], *a. Ch:* tellureux.

telly ['teli], *s. T.V: F:* télé *f.*

teloblast ['teloublæst], *s. Biol:* téloblaste *m.*

telocentric [telou'sentrik], *a. Biol:* télocentrique.

telodynamic [teloudai'næmik], *a.* = TELEDYNAMIC.

telolecithal [telou'lesiθəl], *a. Biol:* télolécithe.

telome ['teloum], *s. Bot:* télome *m.*

telomere ['teloumiər], *s. Biol:* télomère *m.*

telophase ['teloufeiz], *s. Biol:* télophase *f.*

telpher ['telfər], *s.* **t. (line, railway),** (ligne *f*) téléphérique *m*; téléférique *m*; transporteur *m* monorail; **t. car, carrier,** télébenne *f*, télécabine *f.*

telpherage ['telfəridʒ], *s.* telphérage *m*, téléphérage *m.*

telson ['telsən], *s. Crust: Arach:* telson *m.*

telstar ['telstɑ:r], *s. Telecom:* telstar *m.*

Telugu ['teləgu:], *s. Ling:* télougou *m.*

temenos ['teminɔs], *s.* téménos *m*, enceinte *f* d'un temple.

temerity [ti'meriti], *s.* témérité *f*, audace *f.*

Temnospondyli [temnou'spɔndilai], *s.pl. Amph:* temnospondyles *m.*

temp[1] [temp], *s. F:* secrétaire *mf*, dactylo *mf*, qui fait des remplacements; **I do t. work,** je fais des remplacements.

temp[2], *v.i. F:* travailler comme remplaçant(e) (surtout comme secrétaire).

Tempe ['tempi], *Pr.n. A. Geog:* **the vale of T.,** la vallée de Tempé.

temper[1] ['tempər], *s.* **1.** *Metall:* coefficient *m* de dureté (de l'acier); trempe *f*; **soft t.,** trempe douce; **to draw, let down, the t. of the steel,** recuire, éteindre, faire revenir, laisser revenir, l'acier; (*of steel*) **to lose its t.,** se détremper; **steel that loses its t. (through overheating),** acier *m* qui se pâme; **t. brittleness,** maladie *f* de Krupp. **2.** (*of pers.*) sang-froid *m*, calme *m*; **to keep one's t.,** rester calme; garder, conserver, son sang-froid; se contenir; se posséder; ne pas se fâcher; **to lose one's t.,** perdre son sang-froid; se mettre en colère; s'emporter, se fâcher; perdre patience; **to be out of t.,** être de mauvaise humeur, avoir de l'humeur; **to try s.o.'s t.,** énerver qn; **you must try to control your t.,** il faut tâcher de vous contenir. **3.** humeur *f*; (*a*) caractère *m*, tempérament *m*; **incompatibility of t.,** incompatibilité *f*, opposition *f*, d'humeur; **(habitual) good t.,** placidité *f*; **even t.,** caractère égal, calme; **to have an awkward t.,** avoir l'esprit de travers; **to have a good t.,** avoir bon caractère; **to have a bad t.,** *F:* **to have a t.,** avoir son petit caractère; (*b*) état *m* d'esprit; **to be in a good, a bad, t.,** être de bonne, de mauvaise, humeur; (*c*) colère *f*, irritation *f*; mauvaise humeur; **in an outburst of t.,** d'un mouvement d'humeur; **to be in a t.,** être en colère; **what a t. he's in!** comme il est furieux! **to put s.o. in a t.,** mettre qn en colère; fâcher qn.

temper[2], *v.tr.* **1.** *Tchn:* (*a*) gâcher, délayer, broyer (le mortier, le ciment, etc.); broyer (l'encre, les couleurs, etc.); **to t. hard,** gâcher serré (l'argile, etc.); (*b*) *Metall:* (i) tremper; donner la trempe à (l'acier, une lame); attremper (un creuset); (*with passive force*) (*of steel*) recevoir la trempe; (ii) recuire, faire revenir, adoucir (un métal). **2.** tempérer; (*a*) modérer, adoucir (une action, etc.); *Prov:* **God tempers the wind to the shorn lamb,** à brebis tondue Dieu mesure le vent; (*b*) réprimer; retenir, maîtriser (son chagrin, son ardeur, etc.); modérer (son ardeur, une passion). **3.** *Mus:* accorder (une note, un piano) par tempérament.

tempera ['tempərə], *s. Art:* **t. painting,** peinture *f* a tempera; **to paint in t.,** peindre a tempera.

temperament ['temp(ə)rəmənt], *s.* **1.** (*of pers.*) (*a*) *A:* (*physical*) tempérament *m*, constitution *f*, humeur *f*, complexion *f*; **sanguine t.,** tempérament sanguin; (*b*) (*mental*) caractère *m*, tempérament; (*c*) caractère fantasque, lunatique; caractère émotif. **2.** *Mus:* tempérament; **equal t., even t.,** tempérament égal; (*in piano tuning*) **to set the t.,** accorder par tempérament.

temperamental [temp(ə)rə'ment(ə)l], *a.* **1.** du tempérament, constitutionnel. **2.** (*of pers.*) (*a*) capricieux, fantasque, lunatique; (*b*) qui s'emballe, se déprime, facilement; (*c*) instable; (*machine, etc.*) qui fonctionne irrégulièrement, qui marche mal; *Games: Turf:* (joueur, coureur) inconstant.

temperance ['temp(ə)rəns], *s.* **1.** tempérance *f*; modération, retenue *f* (dans les plaisirs, dans la conduite de la vie). **2.** (*a*) tempérance, sobriété *f* (à table); (*b*) abstention *f* des boissons alcooliques; antialcoolisme *m*; **t. society,** société *f* de tempérance; ligue *f* antialcoolique; **t. hotel,** hôtel où la vente des boissons alcooliques n'est pas autorisée.

temperate ['temp(ə)rət], *a.* **1.** (*a*) (*of pers., etc.*) tempérant, sobre; modéré; **t. habits,** habitudes *f* de sobriété; (*b*) (*of language, etc.*) modéré, mesuré; **to be t.,** garder la mesure (dans ses paroles, etc.). **2.** (*of climate, zone, etc.*) tempéré. **3.** *Mus:* **t. scale,** gamme tempérée.

temperately ['temp(ə)rətli], *adv.* modérément; sobrement; avec modération; avec mesure.

temperateness ['temp(ə)rətnis], *s.* **1.** modération *f*, retenue *f*; sobriété *f.* **2.** douceur *f* (du climat).

temperature ['temp(ə)rətjər], *s.* température *f*; (*a*) **absolute t.,** température absolue; **fall in t., t. drop,** chute *f* de température; refroidissement *m* du temps; **critical t.,** température critique; **average t., mean t., normal t.,** température moyenne; **high t., low t.,** température élevée, basse; **room t.,** température ambiante; **t. gradient,** gradient *m* thermique; **t. coefficient,** coefficient *m* de température; **t. control, regulation,** commande *f*, régulation *f*, de la température; *Atom.Ph:* **Curie t.,** température, point *m*, de Curie; *Nat.Hist:* **t. preference range,** preferendum *m* thermique; **the t. was in the thirties,** le thermomètre marquait plus de trente degrés; (*b*) *Med:* **to take s.o.'s t.,** prendre la température de qn; **to have a high t.,** *F:* **to have, to run, a t.,** avoir de la température, de la fièvre; être fiévreux; **he's got a t. of forty,** il a quarante de fièvre; **t. chart,** feuille *f* de température; *Nat.Hist:* **(automatic) t. regulation,** thermorégulation *f*; (*c*) **to judge the t. of the meeting,** estimer la réaction des auditeurs.

tempered ['tempəd], *a.* **1.** (*a*) (*of clay, etc.*) gâché, délayé, broyé; (*b*) (*of steel, etc.*) trempé; recuit; durci; **oil t.,** trempé à l'huile. **2.** *Mus:* tempéré; **equally t. scale,** gamme tempérée. **3. good t.,** d'une humeur égale; **bad t.,** de mauvaise humeur.

temperer ['tempərər], *s.* (*a*) *Metall:* trempeur *m* (d'acier); (*b*) gâcheur *m* (de mortier, etc.).

tempering ['temp(ə)riŋ], *s.* **1.** (*a*) gâchage *m*, délayage *m* (du mortier, etc.); malaxage *m* (d'argile, etc.); broyage *m* (des couleurs); (*b*) *Metall:* (i) trempe *f*; (ii) recuit *m*, recuite *f*; revient *m*, revenu *m* (après trempe); adoucissage *m*; **water t.,** trempe à l'eau; **oil t.,** trempe à l'huile; revenu au bain d'huile; **t. bath,** bain de revenu; **t. colour,** couleur *f* de revenu; **t. oil, water,** huile *f*, eau *f*, de trempe; **t. furnace,** four *m* à tremper, à recuire. **2.** (*a*) modération *f*, adoucissement *m* (d'une peine, etc.); (*b*) maîtrise *f* (de ses passions, etc.).

tempest ['tempist], *s.* tempête *f*, tourmente *f*; *Lit:* **t. tossed,** ballotté par la tempête.

tempestuous [tem'pestjuəs], *a.* **1.** (*of weather, etc.*) tempétueux; de tempête. **2.** (*of meeting, etc.*) orageux; (*of pers., mood, etc.*) turbulent, impétueux, fougueux, agité, violent.

tempestuously [tem'pestjuəsli], *adv.* tempétueusement.

tempestuousness [tem'pestjuəsnis], *s.* **1.** violence *f* (du temps, etc.). **2.** caractère orageux (d'une réunion, etc.); turbulence *f*, agitation *f*, violence *f* (de la foule, etc.).

templar ['templər], *s.* **1.** *Hist:* **(Knight) T.,** templier *m*; chevalier *m* du Temple. **2.** jurisconsulte *m*, étudiant(e) en droit, du *Temple.* **3. Good Templars, Free Templars,** sociétés de tempérance (quasi secrètes, à l'instar des francs-maçons).

template ['templit], *s.* **1.** (*a*) *Metalw: Carp: etc:* gabarit *m*, calibre *m*, patron *m*, jauge *f*; *Stonew:* cherche *f*; *Mec.E:* **cam t.,** pistolet *m* pour came; **checking t., trim t.,** gabarit de vérification; **contour t.,** gabarit de traçage; **control t.,** gabarit de contrôle; **cutting t.,** gabarit de débit; **drilling t.,** calibre de forage; **drill t.,** gabarit de perçage; **gauge t.,** (i) gabarit, calibre, de référence; (ii) *Rail:* gabarit d'écartement (des voies); **master t.,** gabarit étalon; **rigging t.,** gabarit de réglage; **routing t.,** gabarit de détourage; **t. layout,** schéma coté; (*b*) *Dent:* **occlusal t.,** gabarit d'occlusion. **2.** *Cmptr:* **flowchart t.,** organigraphe *m.* **3.** *Const:* sablière *f.* **4.** *Tex:* = TEMPLE[3].

temple[1] ['templ], *s.* **1.** temple (grec, etc.). **2.** (*a*) *B.Hist:* **the T.,** le Temple; (*b*) *Hist:* **the Knights of the T.,** les chevaliers du Temple, les Templiers; (*in London*) **the T.,** (i) *A:* la maison des Templiers; (ii) nom donné à deux des *Inns of Court* (auxquels appartiennent des avocats); (*c*) *Hist:* **T. Bar,** la barrière du Temple (à l'entrée de Fleet Street et de la Cité de Londres).

temple[2], *s. Anat:* (*a*) tempe *f*; **struck on the t.,** frappé à la tempe; (*b*) larmier *m* (du cheval).

temple[3], *s. usu. pl. Tex:* tempe *f*, tempia *m*, temple *m*, templet *m*, tendoir *m*, rame *f* (du métier).

templet ['templit], *s.* = TEMPLATE.

tempo, *pl.* **-i** ['tempou, -i:], *s.* (*a*) *Mus:* tempo *m*; **t. primo, a t.,** à la mesure; à la même; a tempo; tempo primo; (*b*) *Ind:* **strikes that upset the t. of production,** grèves qui interrompent le rythme de la production.

temporal[1] ['tempər(ə)l]. *Anat:* **1.** *a.* (os, etc.) temporal, -aux; **t. muscle,** muscle temporal; **t. artery,** artère temporale. **2.** *s.* (*bone, muscle*) temporal *m*; (*artery*) temporale *f.*

temporal[2], *a.* **1.** *Jur: etc:* temporel; **the Lords Spiritual and T.,** les lords spirituels et les lords temporels; *Ecc:* **t. power,** pouvoir temporel; **t. affairs,** les affaires séculières. **2.** *(a)* **t. expression,** phrase *f* qui exprime une idée de temps; **t. and spatial existence,** existence *f* dans le temps et dans l'espace; *(b) Gram:* (argument, etc.) temporel.

temporality [tempə'ræliti], *s. Ecc:* revenu *m* d'un bénéfice; temporel *m*; **temporalities,** possessions *f* ecclésiastiques; revenus *m* ecclésiastiques.

temporally ['tempərəli], *adv.* temporellement.

temporalty ['tempərəlti], *s.* **1.** *A:* = TEMPORALITY. **2.** *coll.* **the t.,** les laïques *m.*

temporarily ['temp(ə)rərili], *adv.* *(a)* temporairement, provisoirement; à titre temporaire; par intérim; *(b)* momentanément; pour le moment.

temporariness ['temp(ə)rərinis], *s.* caractère *m* temporaire, provisoire (d'une mesure, etc.); caractère momentané, passager.

temporary ['temp(ə)rəri], *a.* *(a)* temporaire, provisoire, transitoire; **t. measures,** mesures *f* provisoires, transitoires; **t. building,** construction *f* provisoire; *Cust:* **passed for t. importation,** admis en franchise temporaire; **t. committee,** comité *m* provisoire, de circonstance; **t. officer,** officier *m* à titre temporaire; *Hist:* **t. gentleman,** gentleman *m* à titre temporaire (désignation familière des officiers recrutés dans le civil et dans les rangs 1914–1918); **to exercise t. command,** commander par intérim; **on a t. basis,** par intérim; provisoirement; **t. manager,** gérant provisoire; **t. appointment, t. job,** emploi *m* (à titre) temporaire, intérimaire, par intérim; *(esp. of secretary)* (emploi de) remplacement *m*; *Adm:* emploi amovible; **t. accommodation,** logement *m* provisoire; **t. repair,** réparation *f* provisoire; de fortune; *Dent:* **t. filling,** plombage *m* provisoire; *Surg:* **t. ligature,** ligature *f* d'attente; *Rail:* **laying of a t. track,** pose volante; *(b)* momentané, passager; **the improvement is only t.,** l'amélioration n'est que passagère, momentanée; **this will at least give you t. relief,** cela vous soulagera pour le moment.

temporization [tempərai'zeiʃ(ə)n], *s.* **1.** temporisation *f*; **he advised t.,** il nous a conseillé de temporiser, d'essayer de gagner du temps; **policy of t.,** politique de temporisation, d'attente, de compromission. **2.** transaction *f*; compromis *m.*

temporize ['tempəraiz], *v.i.* **1.** temporiser; chercher à gagner du temps. **2.** transiger provisoirement **(with,** avec); se plier aux circonstances.

temporizer ['tempəraizər], *s.* temporisateur, -trice; temporiseur, -euse.

temporizing ['tempəraiziŋ], *s.* = TEMPORIZATION.

temporo- ['tempərou], *comb.fm. Anat:* temporo-.

temporo-auricular [tempərouɔ:'rikjulər], *a. Anat:* temporo-auriculaire.

temporofacial [tempərou'feiʃ(ə)l], *a. Anat:* temporo-facial, -aux.

temporomastoid [tempərou'mæstɔid], *a. & s. Anat:* temporomastoïdien *(m).*

temporomaxillary [tempəroumæk'siləri], *a. Anat:* temporomaxillaire.

temporoparietal [tempəroupə'raiətl], *a. Anat:* temporopariétal, -aux.

tempt [tem(p)t], *v.tr.* tenter. **1.** faire des efforts pour séduire (qn); *B:* **the serpent tempted Eve,** le serpent tenta Ève; **to t. s.o. to do sth.,** induire qn à faire qch.; tenter qn pour lui faire faire qch.; **to t. a patient to eat,** affriander, allécher, un malade; **to let oneself be tempted,** se laisser tenter; céder à la tentation; **I'm tempted by the offer, the offer tempts me,** l'offre est bien tentante; l'offre me séduit, m'attire; **I'm tempted to try,** je suis tenté d'essayer, j'ai envie d'essayer; **the fine weather tempts us to go out,** le beau temps nous invite à sortir, à la promenade. **2.** *(a) A:* *(test)* éprouver (qn); mettre (qn) à l'épreuve; *B:* **God tempted Abraham,** Dieu tenta Abraham; *(b)* **to t. God, providence, fate,** tenter Dieu, la providence, le sort.

temptation [tem(p)'teiʃ(ə)n], *s.* tentation *f*; **the t. to do sth.,** la tentation de faire qch.; **to throw t. in s.o.'s way,** exposer qn à la tentation; **to yield to t.,** succomber, céder, à la tentation; se laisser tenter; **lead us not into t.,** ne nous soumets pas (i) *R.C.Ch:* à la tentation, (ii) *Prot.Ch:* à l'épreuve.

tempter ['tem(p)tər], *s.* tentateur *m*; **the T.,** le Tentateur; le Démon.

tempting ['tem(p)tiŋ], *a.* **1.** qui tente, qui induit au mal. **2.** tentant, alléchant; **t. meal,** repas appétissant; **food isn't very t. when one has a cold,** quand on est enrhumé on n'a guère envie de manger; **I didn't find his offer t.,** son offre ne m'a pas tenté, était peu attrayante, peu tentante.

temptress ['tem(p)tris], *s.f.* tentatrice.

ten [ten], *num. a. & s.* dix *(m)*; **number t.,** le numéro dix; **some, about, t. years ago,** il y a une dizaine d'années; **to count in tens,** compter par dizaines; **three tens are thirty,** trois fois dix font trente; *Turf: etc:* **t. to one,** dix contre un; **t. to one he'll find out,** je vous parie dix, il y a dix à parier, contre un qu'il le découvrira; *Ven:* **hart of t.,** dix-cors *m inv*; *Rec: etc:* **the top t.,** palmarès *m* des dix.

tenable ['tenəbl], *a.* **1.** (position *f*, forteresse *f*) tenable; (théorie *f*) soutenable. **2. appointment t. for three years,** poste auquel on est nommé pour trois ans.

tenace ['teneis], *s. Cards:* tenace *f*; *(in dummy)* fourchette *f*, impasse *f*; **to have, hold, the t.,** être tenace; **to play through a t. in the dummy,** jouer dans les impasses du mort, dans les fourchettes du mort.

tenacious [te'neiʃəs], *a.* tenace. **1.** *(a)* **t. alloy, rock,** alliage *m*, roche *f*, tenace; *(b)* **t. weeds,** herbes *f* tenaces, qui s'accrochent; **t. memory,** mémoire tenace, sûre. **2.** *(of pers.)* *(a)* **to be t. in, of, one's opinion,** adhérer à, tenir à, rester attaché à, son opinion; *(b)* opiniâtre, obstiné; **to be t.,** s'opiniâtrer (dans un projet, etc.).

tenaciously [te'neiʃəsli], *adv.* obstinément; avec ténacité; **to cling t. to,** s'obstiner, s'opiniâtrer, dans (une idée, etc.).

tenaciousness, tenacity [te'neiʃəsnis, -'næsiti], *s.* ténacité *f*. **1.** *(a)* cohésion *f* (d'un métal, etc.); *(b)* sûreté *f* (de la mémoire). **2.** *(a)* attachement *m* (à ses idées, ses droits, etc.); *(b)* obstination *f*, opiniâtreté *f*.

tenail(le) [te'neil], *s. Fort:* tenaille(s) *f(pl)*; **t. line,** tracé tenaillé.

tenaillon [te'naijɔ̃, -ɔn], *s. Fort:* tenaillon *m.*

tenalgia [te'nældʒiə], *s. Med:* ténalgie *f*.

tenancy ['tenənsi], *s.* *(a)* location *f*; **expiration of t.,** expiration *f* de bail; échéance *f* de location; *(b)* **during my t.,** pendant la période de ma location; pendant que j'étais locataire; *(c)* **to hold a life t. of a house,** jouir viagèrement d'une maison.

tenant[1] ['tenənt], *s.* *(a)* locataire *mf*; **quarterly t.,** locataire trimestriel; **sub t.,** sous-locataire *mf*; **t. in possession,** *F:* **sitting t.,** occupant, -ante; **t. at will,** loueur, -euse, bailleur, -euse, dont la location dépend du bon vouloir du locateur; **tenant's repairs,** réparations locatives; **tenant's risks,** risques locatifs; **t. farmer,** cultivateur *m* à bail; *(b) Jur:* **t. for life,** usufruitier, -ière; *Jur: A:* **t. right,** droits *mpl* du tenancier.

tenant[2], *v.tr.* habiter, occuper (une maison, etc.) comme locataire; prendre (une terre) à ferme.

tenantable ['tenəntəbl], *a.* **1.** *(of house, etc.)* habitable; (qui est) dans l'état d'être loué. **2. t. repairs,** réparations locatives.

tenantry ['tenəntri], *s. coll.* *(a)* locataires *mpl*; *(b)* fermiers *m* et tenanciers *m* (d'un domaine).

tench [tenʃ], *s. Ich:* tanche *f*; **sea t.,** brème *f* de mer.

tend[1] [tend]. **1.** *v.tr.* soigner (un malade, etc.); panser (un blessé); surveiller (des enfants, une machine, etc.); garder (les moutons, etc.); entretenir (un jardin); veiller à la chauffe (d'une chaudière); **to t. the fire,** soigner le feu; *U.S: O:* **to t. shop,** tenir boutique. **2.** *v.i. A:* **to t. (up)on s.o.,** servir qn *(esp.* à table).

tend[2], *v.i.* **1.** *(a)* tendre, se diriger, aller, tourner **(towards,** vers); **doctrine that tends towards socialism,** doctrine socialisante; doctrine qui penche vers, qui donne dans, le socialisme; **his portraits t. towards caricature,** ses portraits tournent à la caricature; **blue tending to green,** bleu tirant sur le vert; *(b)* **examples that t. to undermine morality,** exemples qui tendent à ébranler les mœurs; **everything tended to exaggerate the incident,** tout conspirait à grossir l'incident; **speeches tending to prove that . . .,** discours tendant(s) à prouver que . . . . **2. to t. to do sth.,** être susceptible de, être sujet à, faire qch.; **he tends to let his imagination run away with him,** il est enclin à être emporté par son imagination; **your jokes simply t. to annoy him,** vos plaisanteries ne tendent qu'à le fâcher; *(of car)* **to t. to skid,** être sujet à déraper; déraper facilement; **woollens that t. to shrink,** lainages qui sont susceptibles de se rétrécir, qui ont tendance à rétrécir. **3.** *Nau:* *(a) (of ship)* éviter; *(b) v.tr. (of crew)* **to t. the ship,** veiller l'évitage.

tendance ['tendəns], *s. A:* **1.** soin(s) *m(pl).* **2.** suite *f*; serviteurs *mpl.*

tendencious [ten'denʃəs], *a.* = TENDENTIOUS.

tendency ['tendənsi], *s.* tendance *f*, inclination *f*, disposition *f*, penchant *m* **(to,** à); **t. to drink,** penchant à la boisson; **to show a t. to improve,** montrer une tendance à se corriger, *(of weather, etc.)* à s'améliorer; **to have a t. to sth., to do sth.,** avoir une tendance à qch., à faire qch.; **there is a t. for the weak vowels to disappear,** les voyelles faibles tendent à disparaître; **a growing t.,** une tendance de plus en plus marquée; **to have a t. to catch cold,** avoir une disposition à s'enrhumer; *Med:* **rheumatic t.,** diathèse rhumatismale; **where there is a rheumatic t.,** quand le malade est sujet au rhumatisme; **your friend has a great t. to run up debts,** votre ami est très sujet à s'endetter; *Ph:* **t. of bodies (to move) towards a centre,** tendance des corps vers un centre; *Fin:* **tendencies of the market,** tendances du marché; **strong upward t.,** forte poussée vers la hausse.

tendential, tendentious [ten'denʃəl, -əs], *a.* tendanciel, tendancieux; **tendentious book,** livre à tendance; **tendentious interpretation,** interprétation tendancieuse.

tendentiously [ten'denʃəsli], *adv.* tendancieusement; dans un but secret, tendancieux.

tendentiousness [ten'denʃəsnis], *s.* sentiments tendancieux; interprétations tendancieuses; **free from t.,** (histoire, etc.) libre de tendances.

tender[1] ['tendər], *s.* **1.** *(pers.)* *(a)* machiniste *m*; *(b)* garde *m*, gardien *m* (d'un pont à bascule, etc.); *(c)* **(bar) t.,** barman *m*; serveur, -euse; garçon *m* de comptoir. **2.** *(a) Nau:* navire *m* annexe; ravitailleur *m*; *(b) Rail:* tender *m*; **t. engine,** locomotive *f*, machine *f*, à tender séparé.

tender[2], *a.* **1.** tendre; peu résistant; *Cu:* **t. meat,** viande tendre; **to make meat t.,** amortir, attendrir, la viande; *(of meat)* **to become t.,** s'attendrir; **t. porcelain,** porcelaine *f* tendre. **2.** tendre, sensible, susceptible; *(a)* **t. to the touch,** sensible, douloureux, au toucher; **my leg is still t. (where I bruised it),** j'ai toujours la jambe douloureuse; **to touch s.o. on a t. spot,** toucher qn à l'endroit sensible; **to have t. feet,** (i) avoir des pieds qui supportent mal la marche, la fatigue; (ii) avoir les pieds endoloris; **horse with a t. mouth,** cheval qui a la bouche tendre, sensible, délicate, chatouilleuse; **horse t. to the spur,** cheval tendre à l'éperon; *(b)* **t. heart,** cœur tendre, sensible; **t. conscience,** conscience délicate, susceptible; *(c)* (navire *m*) volage, qui manque de stabilité initiale. **3.** *(a) (of plant, etc.)* délicat, fragile; peu résistant (au froid); **this plant is less t. than people used to think,** cette plante résiste mieux l'hiver qu'on a supposé autrefois; *(b)* jeune, tendre; **t. youth,** la tendre, verte, jeunesse; **child of t. years,** enfant en bas âge; **to be of t. age,** être dans la tendresse de l'âge. **4.** *(of colour, light, etc.)* tendre, doux, fin; **the t. green of the first leaves,** le vert tendre des premières feuilles. **5.** *(of pers., sentiment, etc.)* tendre, affectueux; **a t. farewell,** de tendres adieux *m*; **t. parents,** parents aimants, indulgents; **t. look,** regard doux; **to have a t. recollection of s.o.,** conserver un souvenir ému, un doux souvenir, de qn. **6.** soigneux, soucieux, jaloux **(of,** de); **the law is very t. of their rights,** la loi est très soucieuse de leurs droits.

tender[3], *v.tr. Paperm:* affaiblir (le papier, par un blanchiment trop prolongé, etc.).

tender[4], *s.* **1.** *Jur:* offre réelle; **t. of payment,** offre de paiement. **2.** *Com:* soumission *f*, offre; **tenders for loans,** soumissions d'emprunts; **to invite tenders for a piece of work, to put a piece of work out to t.,** mettre un travail en adjudication; **allocation to lowest t.,** adjudication *f* au rabais; **to make, put in, send in, a t. for sth.,** soumissionner, faire une soumission, pour qch.; soumissionner un travail; **by t.,** par voie d'adjudication. **3.** *Jur: Com:* **(legal, lawful, common) t.,** cours légal; monnaie *f* libératoire; instruments de paiement légaux; *(of money)* **to be legal t.,** avoir cours; avoir force libératoire.

tender[5]. **1.** *v.tr.* *(a) Jur:* **to t. money in discharge of debt,** faire une offre réelle; **to t. evidence, a plea,** présenter, avancer, des preuves, une défense; *(b) Jur:* **to t. an oath to s.o.,** déférer le serment à qn; **to t. back an oath, a decisive oath, to s.o.,** référer un serment (décisoire) à qn; *(c)* offrir (ses services, une somme, ses félicitations, etc.); **to t. one's resignation,** offrir de démissionner; **to t. one's apologies,** faire, présenter, ses excuses; *(d) U.S:* offrir, donner (un banquet, etc.); **to t. an ovation to s.o.,** faire une ovation à qn. **2.** *v.i. Com:* **to t. for sth.,** soumissionner (pour) qch.; faire une soumission pour qch.; **to t. for a job,** soumissionner (un travail); **to t. for a contract,** soumissionner à une adjudication; **to t. to the government for a loan,** soumissionner un emprunt; **to t. for the supply of sth.,** soumissionner (pour) la fourniture de qch.

tenderer ['tendərər], *s.* **1.** offreur *m* **(of,** de). **2.** *Com:* soumissionnaire *m*; **allocation to the lowest t.,** adjudication *f* au rabais; **successful t. for a contract,** adjudicataire *m.*

tenderfoot, *pl.* **-foots, -feet** ['tendəfut(s), -fi:t], *s.* *(a) U.S:* nouveau venu (dans un lieu sauvage); *(b) Scout:* novice *mf.*

tenderhearted [tendə'hɑ:tid], *a.* compatissant; au cœur tendre, sensible; **to be too t.,** avoir trop de cœur.

tenderheartedly [tendə'hɑ:tidli], *adv.* avec compassion.

tenderheartedness [tendə'hɑ:tidnis], *s.* sensibilité *f*;

compassion *f*.

tenderize ['tendəraiz], *v.tr.* attendrir (la viande).

tenderizer ['tendəraizər], *s.* attendrisseur *m* (de viande).

tenderizing ['tendəraiziŋ], *s.* attendrissement *m*, rassissement *m* (des viandes).

tenderloin ['tendəlɔin], *s.* **1.** *Cu:* filet *m* (de bœuf, de porc); **double t.,** châteaubriant *m*. **2.** *U.S: F:* quartier *m* des maisons de passe, etc.

tenderly ['tendəli], *adv.* **1.** (toucher, tenir, qch.) doucement, délicatement. **2.** tendrement, affectueusement; avec tendresse.

tender-mouthed [tendə'mauðd], *a.* (cheval *m*) à la bouche chatouilleuse, tendre, délicate.

tenderness ['tendənis], *s.* **1.** *Cu:* tendreté *f* (de la viande). **2.** sensibilité *f* (de la peau, etc.). **3.** délicatesse *f*, fragilité *f* (d'une plante, etc.); manque *m* de résistance au froid; délicatesse (de conscience). **4.** douceur *f*, qualité *f* tendre (de la lumière, etc.). **5.** tendresse *f* (des sentiments); affection *f* (**for,** pour); **to have a t. for s.o.,** avoir du sentiment pour qn.

tendinitis [tendi'naitis], *s. Med:* tendinite *f*, ténosite *f*.

tendinous ['tendinəs], *a.* tendineux.

tendon ['tendən], *s. Anat:* tendon *m*; **t. reflex,** réflexe tendineux.

tendril ['tendril], *s. Bot:* vrille *f*, cirre *m*, anille *f*; nille *f*, griffe *f* (de vigne); **with tendrils,** vrillé, anillé; vrillifère.

tenebrae ['tenibri:], *s.pl. R.C.Ch:* les ténèbres *f*.

tenebrescence [teni'bresəns], *s.* ténébrescence *f*.

tenebrio [ti'nebriou], *s. Ent:* ténébrion *m*.

tenebrionid [tenebri'ɔnid]. *Ent:* (*a*) *a.* (insecte) ténébrionide; (*b*) *s.* ténébrionide *m*, ténébrionidé *m*.

Tenebrionidae [tenebri'ɔnidi:], *s.pl. Ent:* ténébrionides *m*, ténébrionidés *m*.

tenebrous ['tenibrəs], *a. A:* ténébreux.

tenement ['tenimənt], *s.* **1.** *Jur:* (*a*) fonds *m* de terre; (*b*) jouissance *f*, tenure *f* (d'une propriété). **2.** (*a*) *A:* habitation *f*; (*b*) *esp. Scot:* (i) (*also esp. U.S:*) **t. (house),** maison de rapport divisée en appartements; (ii) appartement *m*; (*c*) *Pej:* taudis *m*.

tenesmus [ti'nezməs], *s. Med:* ténesme *m*.

tenet ['tenet, 'ti:-], *s.* (*a*) doctrine *f*, dogme *m*; principe *m*; (*b*) opinion *f*; croyance *f*.

ten-fingered [ten'fiŋgə:d], *a.* à dix doigts; *F:* **a t.-f. typist,** une dactylo experte (qui sait utiliser tous ses doigts).

tenfold ['tenfould]. **1.** *a.* décuple; **of t. strength,** dix fois plus fort; dix fois aussi fort. **2.** *adv.* dix fois autant; au décuple; **to repay s.o. t.,** rendre à qn le décuple de ses avances; rendre à qn dix fois autant; **to increase t.,** décupler.

tenia ['ti:niə], *s.* ténia *m*, tænia *m*.

teniasis [ti:'naiəsis], *s. Med:* téniasis *m*.

tennantite ['tenəntait], *s. Miner:* tennantite *f*.

tenner ['tenər], *s. F:* billet *m* (i) de dix livres, (ii) de dix dollars.

Tennesse(e)an [teni'si:ən], *a. & s. Geog:* (habitant, -ante, originaire) du Tennessee.

tennis ['tenis], *s.* **1.** (*a*) **(lawn) t.,** (lawn-)tennis *m*; **t. court,** (i) court *m* de tennis; (ii) (terrain *m* de) tennis; **to play t.,** jouer au tennis; **t. player,** joueur, -euse, de tennis; **t. ball,** balle *f* de tennis; *Med: F:* **t. arm, t. elbow,** crampe *f* du tennis; (*b*) **table t.,** tennis de table; **deck t.,** deck-tennis *m*. **2. (real, royal) t.,** (jeu *m* de) paume *f*; **court t., close t.,** courte paume; **open-air t.,** longue paume; **t. court,** (salle *f*, terrain, de) jeu de paume; *Hist:* **the T. Court Oath,** le Serment du Jeu de Paume (1789).

tenodesis [tenou'di:sis], *s. Surg:* ténodèse *f*.

tenon[1] ['tenən], *s.* **1.** *Carp:* tenon *m*; (*on foot of post, etc.*) goujon *m*; **through t.,** tenon passant; **end t.,** tenon en about; **barefaced t.,** tenon bâtard; *Nau:* **heel t. (of wooden mast),** tenon d'emplanture. **2.** *Metalw:* ailette *f*; tenon.

tenon[2], *v.tr. Carp: etc:* tenonner (une pièce de charpente, etc.); empatter, assembler à tenon(s) (des pièces de bois, etc.); **to t. and mortise,** assembler à tenon et mortaise.

Tenon[3], *Pr.n. Anat:* **Tenon's capsule,** capsule *f* de Tenon; **Tenon's space,** cavité *f*, espace *m*, de Tenon.

tenoner ['tenənər], *s. Carp:* tenonneuse *f*.

tenoning ['tenəniŋ], *s.* tenonnage *m*; empattement *m*; assemblage *m* à tenon (et mortaise); **t. machine,** machine *f* à (faire les) tenons; tenonneuse *f*.

tenoplasty ['tenouplæsti], *s. Surg:* ténoplastie *f*.

tenor ['tenər], *s.* **1.** (*a*) *Jur:* copie *f* conforme; (*b*) contenu *m*, sens général (d'une lettre, etc.); **the full t. of his words,** la portée de ses paroles; (*c*) cours *m*, marche *f*, progrès *m* (des affaires, de la vie, etc.); **the even t. of his life,** le cours, la teneur, tranquille de sa vie. **2.** *Com:* (terme *m* d')échéance *f* (d'une lettre de change). **3.** *Mus:* (*a*) (*voice or singer*) ténor *m*; **light t.,** ténor léger, ténor d'opéra-comique; **operatic t.,** fort ténor, ténor de grand opéra; **t. voice,** voix *f* de ténor; **t. clef,** clé *f* d'ut quatrième ligne; (*b*) **t. violin,** (i) alto *m*; (ii) violonet *m*; **t. saxhorn,** saxhorn *m* ténor; **t. sax(ophone),** saxo(phone) *m* ténor; ténor; (*c*) **t. (bell),** bourdon *m* (d'une sonnerie).

tenorino, *pl.* **-ni** [tenə'ri:nou, -ni:], *s.m. Mus:* tenorino.

tenorist ['tenərist], *s. Mus:* sax(ophon)iste *m* ténor; saxo *m* ténor.

tenorite ['tenərait], *s. Miner:* ténorite *f*.

tenorman, *pl.* **-men** ['tenəmən], *s.m. Mus:* sax(ophon)iste ténor; saxo ténor.

tenorrhaphy ['tenouræfi], *s. Surg:* ténorrhaphie *f*.

tenosynovitis [tenousainou'vaitis], *s. Med:* ténosynovite *f*.

tenotome ['tenoutoum], *s. Surg:* (*knife*) ténotome *m*.

tenotomy [te'nɔtəmi], *s. Surg:* ténotomie *f*; **t. knife,** ténotome *m*.

tenpence ['tenpəns, -pens], *s.* dix pence *m*; pièce *f* de dix pence; *attrib. F:* **a t. stamp,** un timbre de dix pence.

tenpenny ['tenpəni], *a.* de, à, dix pence; **t. stamp,** timbre *m* de dix pence.

ten-percenter [tenpə'sentər], *s.* agent, -ente, qui prend dix pour cent.

tenpin ['tenpin], *s.* quille *f*; **tenpins, t. bowling,** jeu *m* de quilles, bowling *m*.

ten-pointer [ten'pɔintər], *s. Ven:* (cerf *m*) dix-cors *m inv.*

ten-pounder [ten'paundər], *s.* **1.** (*a*) poisson *m*, balle *f*, etc., pesant dix livres; (*b*) *Ich:* élops *m*. **2.** *A:* canon *m* de dix (livres). **3.** *Pol.Hist: A:* électeur *m* en vertu de l'occupation d'un immeuble d'une valeur locative de dix livres au moins; = censitaire *m*.

tenrec ['tenrek], *s. Z:* tenrec *m*, tanrec *m*, hérisson soyeux; **rice t.,** oryzoryctе *m*.

Tenrecidae [ten'residi:], *s.pl. Z:* tenrécidés *m*.

Tenrecidea [tenre'sidiə], *s.pl. Z:* tenrécoïdes *m*, tenrécoïdés *m*.

tense[1] [tens], *s. Gram:* temps *m*; **verb in the present, the future, t.,** verbe au (temps) présent, futur.

tense[2], *a.* **1.** (*of cord, etc.*) tendu, rigide, raide. **2.** (*of nerves, relations, mind, etc.*) tendu; **t. moment, moment of t. excitement,** moment de forte tension; **t. silence,** silence émotionnant, impressionnant; **t. voice,** voix étranglée (par l'émotion); (*of pers.*) **to be t.,** être contracté, tendu; **t. situation,** situation tendue.

tense[3]. **1.** *v.tr.* **to t. one's muscles,** tendre ses muscles. **2.** *v.i.* **to t. up,** se raidir.

tensely ['tensli], *adv.* **1.** rigidement, raidement; avec tension. **2.** (avec) les nerfs tendus, l'esprit tendu; **nerves t. strung,** nerfs tendus au plus haut point; **crowd t. awaiting the match,** foule tendue dans l'attente du match.

tenseness ['tensnis], *s.* **1.** rigidité *f*; tension *f* (des muscles, etc.). **2.** tension (de relations, etc.); **this meeting has relieved the t. of the situation,** une détente s'est produite dans la situation par suite de cette rencontre.

tensibility [tensi'biliti], *s.* extensibilité *f* (du caoutchouc, etc.).

tensible ['tensibl], *a.* extensible.

tensile ['tensail, -sil], *a.* **1.** extensible, élastique; (*of metal*) ductile. **2.** *Mec: etc:* **t. and impact properties,** propriétés *f* de résistance à la traction et au choc; **t. deformation, t. strain,** déformation due à la traction; **t. stress, load, force,** effort *m*, force *f*, de traction; **(internal) t. stresses of a cooling body,** tensions *f* d'un corps qui se refroidit; **t. test,** essai *m* de traction; **to t. test,** tractionner; **high t. steel,** acier *m* à haute limite élastique; **t. strength,** limite *f* élastique à la traction.

tensileness ['tensailnis], **tensility** [ten'siliti], *s.* extensibilité *f*; (*of metal*) ductibilité *f*.

tension[1] ['tenʃən], *s.* **1.** (*a*) tension *f* (d'une corde, des muscles, etc.); **adjustable t. chain,** chaîne *f* à tension réglable; **belt t.,** tension de courroie; **cable t. compensator,** tendeur *m* automatique de câble; **to adjust the t. of a cable,** régler la tension d'un câble; **t. band,** collier *m* de serrage; *Physiol:* **arterial, muscular, t.,** tension artérielle, musculaire; (*b*) tension, état tendu (de l'esprit, des nerfs, etc.); **period of international t.,** période *f* de tension internationale; **this has eased the t. between the two countries,** une détente s'est produite entre les deux nations; (*c*) *Ph:* tension, force *f* élastique (d'un fluide); *Mch:* pression *f* (de la vapeur); **surface t.,** tension de surface, tension superficielle (d'un liquide, etc.); *Atom.Ph:* **nuclear surface t.,** tension superficielle du noyau; (*d*) *El:* tension, voltage *m*; **cable under t.,** câble sous tension; **normal t.,** tension de régime; **high-t., low-t., circuit,** circuit *m* (de) haute, basse, tension. **2.** *Mec:* (force de) traction *f*; tension (d'un ressort); **axial t.,** traction axiale; **t. bar, t. member, t. piece, t. rod,** raidisseur *m*, tendeur *m*, tirant *m*; **t. block,** renvoi tendeur; **balanced t. block,** contrepoids tendeur; **t. pulley,** galet tendeur, de tension; **t. spring,** ressort *m* de traction; **to be in t., under stress of t.,** être en traction, travailler à la traction. **3.** (*of textile machine, sewing machine, etc.*) tendeur *m*; raidisseur *m*; tenseur *m*; **t. frame** = TEMPLE[3].

tension[2], *v.tr.* **1.** *esp. U.S:* tendre, raidir (un câble, une courroie); tendre (un ressort). **2.** tensionner (une scie, etc.).

tensional ['tenʃən(ə)l], *a.* tensionnel; de tension.

tensioner ['tenʃənər], *s.* tendeur *m*, raidisseur *m*, tenseur *m*.

tensioning ['tenʃəniŋ], *s.* tensionnage *m* (d'une scie, etc.).

tensionless ['tenʃənlis], *a.* sans tension.

tensive ['tensiv], *a. Med:* tensif; **t. pain,** douleur tensive.

tensor ['tensər]. **1.** (*a*) *a. & s. Anat:* **t. (muscle),** (muscle *m*) tenseur (*m*); (*b*) *a. Ph:* tensoriel; **t. field,** champ tensoriel; **t. force,** force tensorielle; **t. interaction,** interaction tensorielle. **2.** *s.* (*a*) *Mth:* tenseur; **zero-order t.,** tenseur d'ordre zéro; (*b*) *Tchn:* = TENSIONER.

tensorial [ten'sɔ:riəl], *a. Mth:* tensoriel; **t. analysis,** analyse tensorielle.

tent[1] [tent], *s.* (*a*) tente *f*; **bell t.,** tente conique; **beach t.,** tente de plage; *Mil:* **shelter t.,** tente-abri *f*, *pl.* tentes-abris; **to pitch, strike, tents,** monter, démonter, les tentes; **to sulk in one's t. (like Achilles),** se retirer dans, sous, sa tente; **t. peg,** piquet *m* de tente; *Mil: A:* **t. pegging,** sport pratiqué dans la cavalerie, où il s'agissait d'enlever au galop, du bout de sa lance, un piquet de tente fiché en terre; **t. rope,** cordon *m*, cordeau *m*, de tirage (d'une tente); (*b*) *Med:* **t. (bed), steam t.,** tente de vapeur(s); **oxygen t.,** tente à oxygène; (*c*) *Needlew:* (*in tapestry*) **t. stitch,** petit point; (*d*) *Ent:* **t. caterpillar,** malacosome *m*.

tent[2], *v.i. F: O:* camper; vivre sous la tente, dans une tente.

tent[3], *s. Surg: A:* mèche *f*, tampon *m*, tente *f*.

tent[4], *v.tr. Surg: A:* mécher, tamponner (une plaie).

tentacle ['tentəkl], *s. Nat.Hist:* (*a*) tentacule *m*; (*b*) cirre *m*.

tentacled ['tentəkld], **tentaculate** [ten'tækjuleit], *a. Nat.Hist:* tentaculé.

tentacular [ten'tækjulər], *a. Nat.Hist:* tentaculaire.

Tentaculifera [tentækju'lifərə], *s.pl. Prot:* tentaculifères *m*.

tentaculite [ten'tækjulait], **Tentaculites** [tentækju'laiti:z], *s. Paleont:* tentaculite *m*.

Tentaculitidae [tentækju'litidi:], *s.pl. Paleont:* tentaculitides *m*.

tentage ['tentidʒ], *s.* matériel *m*, toile *f*, de tente.

tentative ['tentətiv]. **1.** *a.* (*a*) expérimental, -aux; d'essai; **t. move,** démarche expérimentale; **to make t. enquiries,** prendre des renseignements (préliminaires); tâter le terrain; **t. offer,** ouverture *f*; offre *f* préliminaire, d'essai; (*b*) hésitant, indécis; **it's only a t. opinion,** ce n'est qu'un avis à titre de suggestion. **2.** *s.* tentative *f*; essai *m*.

tentatively ['tentətivli], *adv.* à titre d'essai, d'expérience; expérimentalement; avec une certaine hésitation.

tenter[1] ['tentər], *s. Tex:* **1.** = TEMPLE[3]. **2.** (*machine*) élargisseur *m*, élargisseuse *f*.

tenter[2], *v.tr. Tex:* templer, tendre, élargir, ramer (le drap).

tenter[3], *s. Ind:* machiniste *m*; soigneur *m* (de machines); **shaping-machine t.,** toupilleur *m*; **planing-machine t.,** raboteur *m* à la machine.

tenterhook ['tentəhuk], *s.* (*a*) *Tex:* (clou *m* à) crochet *m*; (*b*) **to be on tenterhooks,** être au supplice, sur la braise, sur le gril, sur des charbons ardents; brûler à petit feu; **to keep s.o. on tenterhooks,** faire languir qn; faire mourir qn à petit feu.

tentering ['tentəriŋ], *s. Tex:* élargissage *m*; **t. machine,** élargisseur *m*, élargisseuse *f*.

tenth [tenθ]. **1.** *num. a. & s.* dixième (*mf*); **in the t. place,** en dixième lieu; dixièmement; **to be, come in, t.,** être, arriver, le, la, dixième. **2.** *s.* (*a*) (*fractional*) dixième *m*; **a t. of a millimetre,** un dixième de millimètre; **nine tenths of the voters,** neuf dixièmes, quatre-vingt-dix pour cent, la majeure partie, des électeurs; (*b*) *Hist: Ecc:* dîme *f*. **3.** *s. Mus:* (intervalle *m* de) dixième *f*.

tenthly ['tenθli], *adv.* dixièmement; en dixième lieu; décimo.

Tenthredinidae [tenθre'dinidi:], *s.pl. Ent:* tenthrédinidés *m*.

tenting ['tentiŋ], *s.* toile *f* à tentes.

tentmaker ['tentmeikər], *s.* **1.** fabricant *m* de tentes. **2.** *Ent:* malacosome *m*.

tenuiflorous [tenjui'flɔ:rəs], *a. Bot:* ténuiflore.

tenuifolious [tenjui'fouliəs], *a. Bot:* ténuifolié.

tenuirostrate [tenjui'rɔstreit], *a. Orn:* ténuirostre.

tenuis, *pl.* **-ues** ['tenjuis, -jui:z], *s. Ling:* consonne ténue, non voisée.

tenuity [te'nju:iti], **tenuousness** ['tenjuəsnis], *s.* **1.**

ténuité *f*, finesse *f* (d'un fil). **2.** ténuité (d'un liquide, de l'air); raréfaction *f* (de l'air, d'un gaz); qualité *f* grêle (d'une voix).

tenuous ['tenjuəs], *a.* **1.** ténu; effilé; délié; mince; très fin. **2.** (*a*) (*of gas*) raréfié; (*b*) (*of difference, distinction*) ténu; subtil; (*of voice*) grêle.

tenuously ['tenjuəsli], *adv.* à peine (liés, associés, etc.); **the two ideas are only t. connected,** il y a très peu de connexion entre les deux idées.

tenure ['tenjər], *s.* **1.** *Hist: Jur:* tenure *f*; **feudal t.,** tenure féodale; **military t.,** tenure de chevalier; **system of land t.,** régime foncier. **2.** *Jur:* (période *f* de) jouissance *f*, (d')occupation *f* (d'un office, d'une propriété, etc.); **communal t.,** jouissance en commun (d'un bien); **fixity of t.,** (i) bail assuré; (ii) stabilité *f* (d'un emploi); **during his t. of office,** pendant qu'il exerçait ses fonctions.

tepal ['ti:pl, 'tepl], *s. Bot:* tépale *m.*

tepee ['ti:pi(:)], *s.* tente-abri *f*, *pl.* tentes-abris (des Amérindiens).

tephrite ['tefrait], *s. Miner:* téphrite *f.*

Tephritidae [te'fritidi:], *s.pl. Ent:* téphritidés *m.*

tephritis [te'fraitis], *s. Ent:* téphrite *f.*

tephroite ['tefrouait], *s. Miner:* téphroïte *f.*

tephromyelitis [tefroumaiə'laitis], *s. Med:* téphromyélite *f.*

tepid ['tepid], *a.* (*of water, etc.*) tiède; (*of feelings, etc.*) tiède, qui manque d'ardeur, d'entrain.

tepidity [te'piditi], **tepidness** ['tepidnis], *s.* tiédeur *f.*

tepidly ['tepidli], *adv.* tièdement; sans ardeur, sans entrain.

ter [tə:r], *Lt. adv. Mus:* ter.

Terai ['terai, tə'rai], *Pr.n. Geog:* **the T.,** le Téraï.

teraphim ['terəfim], *s.pl. B:* téraphim *m*, téraphin *m.*

teratogenesis [terətou'dʒenisis], *s.* tératogénèse *f*, tératogénie *f.*

teratogenetic, teratogenic [terətoudʒe'netik, -'dʒenik], *a.* tératogène; tératogénique.

teratoid ['terətɔid]. **1.** *a.* tératoïde. **2.** *s.* tératome *m.*

teratological [terətə'lɔdʒikl], *a.* tératologique.

teratologist [terə'tɔlədʒist], *s.* tératologue *m*, tératologiste *m.*

teratology [terə'tɔlədʒi], *s.* tératologie *f.*

teratoma, *pl.* **-mas, -mata** [terə'toumə, -məz, -meitə], *s. Med:* tératome *m.*

teratoscopy [terə'tɔskəpi], *s.* tératoscopie *f.*

terbic ['tə:bik], *a. Ch:* terbique.

terbium ['tə:biəm], *s. Ch:* terbium *m.*

terce [tə:s], *s. Ecc:* tierce *f.*

tercel(et) ['tə:s(ə)l(et)], *s. Ven:* tiercelet *m*; mâle *m* (d'épervier, de faucon, etc.).

tercentenary [tə:sen'ti:nəri], *a.* & *s.* tricentenaire (*m*).

tercentennial [tə:sen'teniəl], *a.* tricentenaire.

tercet ['tə:sit], *s.* **1.** *Pros:* tercet *m.* **2.** *Mus:* triolet *m.*

terebella [teri'belə], *s. Ann:* térébelle *f.*

Terebellidae [teri'belidi:], *s.pl. Ann:* térébellidés *m*, térébelliens *m.*

terebellum [teri'beləm], *s. Moll:* terebellum *m*, *F:* tarière *f.*

terebene ['teribi:n], *s. Pharm:* térébène *m.*

terebenthene [teri'benθi:n], *s. Ch:* térébenthène *m.*

terebic [ti'rebik], *a. Ch:* (acide) térébique.

terebinth ['teribinθ], *s. Bot:* térébinthe *m.*

Terebinthaceae [teribin'θeisii:], *s.pl. Bot:* térébinthacées *f.*

terebra, *pl.* **-ae, -as** ['teribrə, -i:, -əz], *s.* **1.** *Ent:* tarière *f* (d'insecte). **2.** *Moll:* terebra *m.*

terebrant ['teribrənt]. **1.** *a.* (ver, etc.) térébrant. **2.** *s. Ent:* térébrant *m.*

Terebrantia [teri'brænʃiə], *s.pl. Ent:* térébrants *m.*

terebrate ['teribreit], *v.tr. A:* térébrer; percer (avec une tarière).

terebratula [teri'brætjulə], *s. Moll:* térébratule *f.*

Terebridae [te'rebridi:], *s.pl. Moll:* térébridés *m.*

Teredinidae [teri'dinidi:], *s.pl. Moll:* térédinidés *m.*

teredo, *pl.* **-dines, -dos** [te'ri:dou, -dini:z, -douz], *s. Moll:* taret (naval); perce-bois *m inv*; ver *m* de mer.

terek ['terek], *s. Orn:* térékie *f*, barge *f* de Terek.

Terence ['terəns], *Pr.n.m.* Térence.

terephthalate [te'refθəleit], *s. Ch:* téréphtalate *m.*

terephthalic [teref'θælik], *a. Ch:* téréphtalique.

teres ['tiəri:z], *s. Anat:* **t. major, minor,** grand, petit, rond.

Teresa [te'ri:zə], *Pr.n.f.* Thérèse.

tergal ['tə:g(ə)l], *a. Nat. Hist:* tergal, -aux; dorsal, -aux.

tergeminal, tergeminate [tə:'dʒemin(ə)l, -eit], *a. Bot:* tergéminé, trigéminé.

tergite ['tə:dʒait], *s. Z:* tergite *m.*

tergiversate ['tə:dʒivə:seit], *v.i.* tergiverser.

tergiversation [tə:dʒivə'seiʃ(ə)n], *s.* tergiversation *f.*

tergiversator ['tə:dʒivəseitər], *s.* tergiversateur, -trice.

tergum, *pl.* **-ga** ['tə:gəm, -gə], *s. Z:* tergum *m.*

terlinguaite [tə:'liŋgwait], *s. Miner:* terlinguaïte *f.*

term[1] [tə:m], *s.* **1.** (*a*) *A:* & *Lit:* terme *m*, borne *f*, fin *f*, limite *f*; **the t. of life,** le terme, la fin, de la vie; **to set, put, a t. to sth.,** fixer une limite à qch.; assigner une fin, un terme, à qch.; (*b*) (*of pregnancy*) **to have reached (full) t.,** être à terme; (*c*) *Com:* (terme d')échéance *f* (d'une lettre de change). **2.** (*a*) terme, période *f*, durée *f*; **t. of a lease,** terme, durée, d'un bail; **the loan shall be for a t. of twenty years,** l'emprunt sera conclu pour vingt ans; **to serve a t. of five years (in prison),** faire cinq ans de prison; **during his t. of office,** pendant qu'il exerçait ses fonctions; **t. of notice,** préavis *m* de licencement; **t. of limitation,** délai *m* de prescription; **t. of copyright,** délai, durée, du droit d'auteur; délai de protection (littéraire); *Com:* **t. of payment,** délai de paiement; **long t., medium t., short t., transaction,** opération *f* à long, à moyen, à court, terme; **short t., long t., movements (of capital),** mouvements *m* (de capitaux) à courte, à longue, amplitude; **a long-t. policy,** une politique à longue échéance; (*b*) *Sch:* trimestre *m*; **at the beginning of t.,** à la rentrée; **towards the end of t.,** vers la fin du trimestre; quand le trimestre touchait à sa fin; **in t. time, during t.,** pendant le trimestre; **half t. (holiday),** congé *m* de mi-trimestre; *O:* (*at university*) **to keep one's terms** = prendre ses inscriptions; (*c*) *Jur:* session *f*; (*d*) *Jur:* **to owe a term's rent,** devoir un terme, trois mois de loyer; *Scot:* **t. day,** (jour *m* de) terme. **3.** (*a*) *Com: etc:* **terms,** conditions *f*; clauses *f*, termes, teneur *f* (d'un contrat); **terms under which a ship is chartered,** conditions d'affrètement; *Fin:* **terms of an issue,** conditions d'une émission; **terms and conditions of an issue,** modalités *f* d'une émission; **terms of trade,** taux *m* de l'échange international; prix relatifs des marchandises échangées; prix relatifs des marchandises entrant dans le commerce international; **satisfactory terms,** conditions satisfaisantes; **on these terms I accept,** à ces conditions j'accepte; **on similar terms,** aux mêmes conditions; **I'll take it on your terms,** je le prends à vos conditions, à telles conditions qu'il vous plaira de nommer; **make, name, your own terms,** faites vos conditions vous-même; **what terms do you offer us?** quelles conditions nous faites-vous? **by the terms of article 49 . . .,** aux termes de, en vertu de, l'article 49 . . .; **under the terms of the clause,** sous le bénéfice de la clause; **to dictate terms,** imposer des conditions; **to come to terms, make terms,** en venir à un accommodement; entrer en accommodement, en composition; s'arranger, s'accorder, prendre un arrangement, des arrangements (**with,** avec); **to come to terms with the enemy, with one's creditors,** pactiser avec l'ennemi; transiger avec ses créanciers; **to bring the enemy to terms,** obliger l'ennemi à capituler, à céder; **terms of reference,** attributions *f*, mandat *m* (d'une commission, etc.); (*b*) **terms of payment,** conditions de paiement; **terms strictly cash,** payable au comptant; (*in hotel, etc.*) **weekly terms £x,** pension £*x* par semaine; **inclusive terms,** tout compris; **his terms are £5 a lesson,** il prend £5 par leçon; **I'll give you special terms,** je vous ferai un prix; **on easy terms,** avec facilités de paiement; **not on any terms,** à aucun prix. **4. friendly terms,** relations amicales; relations d'amitié; **to be, live, on friendly, on good, terms with s.o.,** être bien, vivre en bonne intelligence, en bons termes, avec qn; avoir de bons rapports, être en relations d'amitié, avec qn; **we are on good terms,** nous sommes bien ensemble; **to be on bad terms with s.o.,** être en mauvaise intelligence, être mal, avec qn; **to be on the best of terms with s.o.,** être au mieux, le mieux du monde, dans les meilleurs termes, avec qn; **they are not on good terms,** ils ne sont pas bien ensemble; il y a du froid entre eux; ils sont en froid, en brouille. **5.** (*a*) *Mth: Log:* terme (d'une équation, d'un syllogisme); **to express one quantity in terms of another,** exprimer une quantité en fonction d'une autre; **in terms of financial risk,** en ce qui concerne, pour ce qui est, au point de vue, des risques financiers; **to try to calculate happiness in terms of worldly success,** essayer de mesurer le bonheur en fonction du succès; (*b*) **terms of a problem,** énoncé *m* d'un problème. **6.** (*a*) terme, mot *m*, expression *f*, appellation *f*; **nautical t.,** terme de marine; **technical, scientific, t.,** terme, expression, technique, scientifique; (*b*) **he spoke of his colleagues in the most flattering terms,** il a parlé de ses collègues en termes les plus flatteurs; **how dare you address me in such terms?** comment osez-vous me parler de la sorte? **I told him in no uncertain terms,** je le lui ai dit carrément, sans mâcher mes mots. **7.** *Sculp:* terme; dieu *m* Terme.

term[2], *v.tr.* appeler; désigner; nommer; **that is what I would t. a stupid answer,** voilà ce que j'appelle une sotte réponse; **priests attached to a regiment are termed chaplains,** on nomme aumôniers les prêtres attachés à un régiment.

Termagant ['tə:məgənt]. **1.** *Pr.n.m. Lit:* Tervagant. **2.** *s.f.* mégère, virago; **she's a real t.!** c'est un vrai dragon, un vrai gendarme! **his t. of a wife,** sa mégère de femme.

terminable ['tə:minəbl], *a.* (*of annuity, etc.*) terminable; (*of contract, etc.*) résiliable, résoluble.

terminal ['tə:min(ə)l], *a.* & *s.*

I. *a.* **1.** (*of line, mark, etc.*) qui borne, qui termine (une région, etc.); *Sculp:* **t. figure** = TERM[1] 7. **2.** (*a*) *Nat. Hist:* terminal, -aux; distal, -aux; (*b*) *Geol:* **t. moraine,** moraine frontale; (*c*) *Rail: etc:* (gare, etc.) terminus, de tête de ligne; **t. point,** terminus *m*; (*d*) *El: Tg:* (isolateur *m*, poteau *m*) d'arrêt; (*e*) (*of word, letter, market, etc.*) final, -als; dernier; (*f*) *W.Tel: Cin:* **t. amplifier,** amplificateur terminal, final, de sortie; **t. stage,** étage final, de sortie; (*g*) *Mil: etc:* **t. leave,** permission *f* libérable; (*h*) *Med:* **t. cancer, pneumonia,** cancer fatal, pneumonie fatale; **t. case,** malade, cas, condamné; **t. home,** hospice *m.* **3.** *Sch: etc:* trimestriel.

II. *s.* **1.** *El:* borne *f* (de prise de courant); borne d'attache; attache *f*; serre-câble(s) *m inv*; cosse *f* (d'un conducteur); **cable t.,** tête *f*, extrémité *f*, de câble; **screw t.,** borne à vis; **clamp t.,** borne à bouton molleté; **t. cap,** capuchon *m* de borne; **input, output, t.,** borne d'entrée, de sortie; **branch t.,** borne de dérivation, de branchement; **t. voltage,** tension *f* aux bornes. **2.** *Nat. Hist:* distal, -aux *m.* **3.** *Gram:* terminaison *f.* **4.** (*a*) *Rail:* **terminals,** frais *m* de manutention; (*b*) *NAm: Rail: etc:* terminus *m*; gare *f* terminus; (*c*) *Av:* **air-(ways) t.,** aérogare *f*; (*d*) *NAm: Agr:* **grain t.,** marché-gare *m* à céréales; (*e*) *Cmptr:* (poste) terminal *m*; **t. computer,** ordinateur *m* satellite; **t. control unit,** unité *f* de gestion de terminaux; **t. blank, space,** espace *m* à droite; **job-orient(at)ed t.,** terminal spécialisé, spécifique; (*f*) *Petr:* **pipeline t.,** terminal.

terminally ['tə:minəli], *adv. Sch:* tous les trimestres; par trimestre.

terminate[1] ['tə:mineit], *v.tr.* & *i.*

I. *v.tr.* terminer. **1.** (*of boundary, line, etc.*) délimiter (une région, etc.). **2.** (*a*) résoudre, résilier (un contrat, etc.); mettre fin à (un engagement, etc.); **to t. one's work,** terminer son ouvrage; (*b*) être à la fin de (qch.); **the word that terminates the sentence,** le mot qui termine la phrase, qui vient à la fin de la phrase; (*c*) **to have one's pregnancy terminated,** se faire avorter.

II. *v.i.* **1.** (*of word, etc.*) se terminer, finir (**in,** en, par); **words terminating in s, with s,** les mots qui se terminent par s, en s; *Mth:* **terminating decimal,** fraction décimale exacte. **2.** se terminer; aboutir (**in, at,** à).

terminate[2], *a. Mth:* **t. decimal (fraction),** fraction décimale exacte.

termination [tə:mi'neiʃ(ə)n], *s.* **1.** terminaison *f*, fin *f* (d'un procès, etc.); cessation *f* (de relations d'affaires, etc.); *Jur:* extinction *f*, résolution *f*, résiliation *f* (d'une obligation, etc.); **to put a t. to sth., to bring sth. to a t.,** mettre fin à qch. **2.** *Gram:* terminaison, désinence *f.*

terminational [tə:mi'neiʃən(ə)l], *a. Gram:* (changement, etc.) terminatif.

terminator ['tə:mineitər], *s. Astr:* cercle terminateur, ligne terminatrice (de la partie lumineuse de la lune).

terminer ['tə:minər]. *Jur: A:* **oyer and t.,** audition *f* et jugement *m* (d'une cause criminelle).

terminism ['tə:minizm], *s.* **1.** *Theol:* terminisme *m.* **2.** *Phil:* occamisme *m*, terminisme.

terminist ['tə:minist], *s.* **1.** *Theol:* terministe *m.* **2.** *Phil:* occamiste *m*, terministe.

terminological [tə:minə'lɔdʒik(ə)l], *a.* terminologique; **t. inexactitude,** (i) inexactitude *f* de termes; (ii) *Iron: O:* travestissement *m* de la vérité.

terminology [tə:mi'nɔlədʒi], *s.* terminologie *f*; **in an alternative t.,** en d'autres termes.

terminus, *pl.* **-i, -uses** ['tə:minəs, -ai, -əsiz], *s.* **1.** *Rail: etc:* (gare *f*) terminus *m*; (gare de) tête *f* de ligne; **the London railway termini,** les gares terminus de Londres. **2.** *Rom.Myth: Sculp:* terme *m*; dieu *m* Terme.

termitary ['tə:mitəri], **termitarium** [tə:mi'tɛəriəm], *s. Ent:* termitière *f.*

termite ['tə:mait], *s. Ent:* termite *m*; fourmi blanche; **Formosan subterranean t.,** coptoterme *m* de Formose.

Termitidae [tə:'mitidi], *s.pl. Ent:* termitidés *m.*

termitophagous [tə:mi'tɔfəgəs], *a. Nat. Hist:* termitophage.

termitophile [tə:'maitoufail], *s. Nat. Hist:* termitophile *m.*

termless ['tə:mlis], *a. Lit:* illimité; sans limite; sans bornes; sans fin.

termly ['tə:mli]. (*a*) *a.* trimestriel; (*b*) *adv.* trimestriellement; par trimestre; tous les trimestres.

termolecular [tə:mə'lekjulər], *a.* trimoléculaire.

termor ['tɔːmɔr], *s. Jur:* possesseur *m* (i) à terme, (ii) en viager.
tern[1] [tɔːn], *s. Orn:* sterne *f*; **arctic t.,** sterne paradis, sterne arctique; **black t.,** guifette *f* épouvantail, guifette noire, *Fr.C:* sterne noire; **bridled t.,** sterne bridée; **Caspian t.,** sterne caspienne; *NAm:* **common t.,** sterne Pierre-Garin, *Fr.C:* sterne commune; **Forster's t.,** sterne de Forster; **gull-billed t.,** sterne hansel, *Fr.C:* sterne à gros bec; **lesser crested t.,** sterne voyageuse; **little t.,** *NAm:* **least t.,** sterne naine, sterne au front blanc, *Fr.C:* petite sterne; **roseate t.,** sterne de Dougall, *Fr.C:* sterne rosée; **Sandwich t.,** *NAm:* **Cabot's t.,** sterne caugek, *Fr.C:* sterne de Cabot; **sooty t.,** sterne fuligineuse; **whiskered t.,** guifette moustac; **white-winged black t.,** guifette à ailes blanches, guifette leucoptère.
tern[2], *s.* terne *m* (dans une loterie).
ternary ['tɔːnəri], *a. Ch: Mth: etc:* ternaire.
ternate ['tɔːneit], *a. Bot:* terné, ternifolié.
ternately ['tɔːneitli], *adv.* **t. triflorous,** terniflore.
terne(plate) ['tɔːn(pleit)], *s. Metalw:* tôle plombée.
Ternstroemiaceae [tɔːnstriːmi'eisiiː], *s.pl. Bot:* ternstrœmiacées *f*.
terp, *pl.* **-s, terpen** [tɛəp(s), 'tɔːpən], *s. Prehist:* (*in Friesland*) terpan *m*, terpen *m*.
terpene ['tɔːpiːn], *s. Ch:* terpène *m*.
terpenic [tɔː'piːnik], *a. Ch:* terpénique.
terpinene ['tɔːpiniːn], *s. Ch:* terpinène *m*.
terpineol [tɔː'piniɔl, -oul], *s. Ch:* terpinéol *m*.
terpinol ['tɔːpinɔl], *s. Ch:* terpinol *m*.
terpinolene [tɔː'pinouliːn], *s. Ch:* terpinolène *m*.
terpolymer [tɔː'pɔlimər], *s. Ch:* ter-polymère *m*.
Terpsichore [tɔːp'sikəri], *Pr.n.f. Myth:* Terpsichore.
terpsichorean [tɔːpsikə'riːən], *a.* de Terpsichore; de la danse.
terra ['terə], *Lt.s.* terre *f*; *used esp. in* **t. firma,** terre ferme, *F:* le plancher des vaches; *Hist:* **T. Firma,** la Terre-ferme; **t. incognita,** terre inconnue; région inconnue; *Geol:* **t. rossa,** terra-rossa *f*.
terrace[1] ['terəs], *s.* **1.** (*a*) *Const:* terrasse *f*; terre-plein *m*, *pl.* terre-pleins; **lower t.,** contre-terrasse *f*; (*b*) *Geol:* terrasse, plate-forme, *f*, *pl.* plates-formes. **2. t. (houses),** rangée *f* de maisons de style uniforme. **3.** toiture *f* en plate-forme (de maison orientale); terrasse. **4.** terrasse (dans le marbre); partie *f* tendre.
terrace[2], *v.tr.* (*a*) disposer (un jardin, etc.) en terrasse(s); (*b*) terrasser (un flanc de colline, etc.).
terraced ['terəst], *a.* **1.** (*a*) (jardin) suspendu, étagé, en terrasse; **t. hillsides,** collines cultivées en terrasses; (*b*) *Geol:* (dépôt) en terrasse. **2. t. houses,** rangée *f* de maisons de style uniforme.
terracette [terə'set], *s. Geog:* terrassette *f*.
terracing ['terəsiŋ], *s.* construction *f* en terrasses; cultivation *f* en terrasses (d'un flanc de colline).
terracotta ['terə'kɔtə], *s.* terre cuite; terra-cotta *f*; *Art:* **a t.,** une terre cuite.
terrain [tə'rein], *s. Mil: Geog:* terrain *m*; **t. intelligence,** renseignements *m* topographiques (sur une zone déterminée).
terral ['terəl], *s. Nau:* terral *m*; vent *m* de terre.
terramare [terə'mɑːr, -'mɛər], *s.* **t. (deposit),** terramare *f*.
terramycin [terə'maisin], *s. Pharm: R.t.m:* terramycine *f*.
terran ['terən], *a. & s.* terrien, -ienne.
terrapin ['terəpin], *s. Rept:* (*a*) terrapène *m*; (*b*) **(diamondback) t.,** tortue d'eau saumâtre (américaine); tortue diamant; terrapin *m*; **alligator t.,** tortue vorace alligator; **mud t.,** tortue bourbeuse; **musk t.,** tortue musquée.
terraqueous [te'reikwiəs], *a.* terraqué.
terrarium, *pl.* **-ia, -iums** [te'rɛəriəm, -iə, -iəmz], *s.* terrarium *m*.
terrazzo [te'rætsou], *s.* granito *m*.
terrene [te'riːn], *a.* **1.** (*earthy*) terreux. **2.** (animal, etc.) terrestre.
terreplein ['tɛəplein], *s. Fort:* terre-plein *m*, *pl.* terre-pleins (d'un bastion).
terrestrial [ti'restriəl], *a.* (*a*) (*of globe, plant, magnetism, etc.*) terrestre; terrien, -ienne; **t. planet,** planète *f* qui possède les caractéristiques de la terre; (*b*) (*of life, affairs, etc.*) terrestre; de ce monde.
terrestrially [ti'restriəli], *adv.* terrestrement.
terret ['terit], *s.* anneau *m*; *Harn:* anneau d'attelle (de la dossière).
terrible ['teribl]. **1.** *a.* (*a*) terrible; **death is not so t. to Christians,** la mort n'est pas si terrible aux chrétiens; *Hist:* **Ivan the T.,** Ivan le Terrible; (*b*) terrible, affreux, épouvantable; atroce; **to die in t. agonies,** mourir dans d'atroces souffrances; (*c*) **your hat's in a t. state,** ton chapeau est dans un état terrible; **he's a t. talker,** c'est un terrible bavard; **t. prices,** prix exorbitants, formidables; **I'm t. at maths,** en math je suis nul. **2.** *adv. P:* terriblement; **he went on, carried on, something t.,** il a fait une scène de tous les diables.
terribly ['teribli], *adv.* (*a*) terriblement, affreusement, atrocement, épouvantablement; **he was t. wounded,** il a été affreusement blessé; (*b*) **t. dangerous,** excessivement dangereux; **t. rich,** diablement riche; **t. busy,** terriblement occupé; **t. expensive,** hors de prix; **t. important,** de la dernière importance; **t. bad,** (film, etc.) de dernier ordre; **that's t. kind of you,** vous êtes vraiment trop aimable.
terricolous [te'rikələs], *a. Nat.Hist:* terricole.
terrier[1] ['teriər], *s. Hist:* terrier *m*; registre foncier; *Ecc.Hist:* pouillé *m*.
terrier[2], *s.* **1.** (chien *m*) terrier *m*; **bull t.,** bull-terrier *m*, *pl.* bull-terriers. **2.** *Mil: F:* = TERRITORIAL **2.**
terrific [tə'rifik], *a.* **1.** terrifiant, épouvantable. **2.** *F:* terrible; énorme; colossal, -aux; **the heat was t.,** il faisait une chaleur terrible; il faisait une de ces chaleurs! **t. applause,** applaudissements *mpl* à tout casser; **t. pace,** allure vertigineuse; **to eat in t. quantities,** manger à faire trembler; **t.!** magnifique!
terrifically [tə'rifik(ə)li], *adv.* **1.** d'une manière terrifiante. **2.** *F:* terriblement; **it was t. hot,** il faisait terriblement chaud.
terrify ['terifai], *v.tr.* terrifier, effrayer, épouvanter, affoler (qn); frapper (qn) de terreur; **to t. s.o. into doing sth.,** faire faire qch. à qn sous le coup de la peur; **to t. s.o. out of his wits,** rendre qn fou de terreur; **to be terrified of s.o.,** avoir une peur bleue de qn.
terrifying ['terifaiiŋ], *a.* terrifiant, terrible, épouvantable.
terrigenous [tə'ridʒinəs], *a.* **1.** *Lit: A:* né, issu, de la terre, du sol. **2.** *Geol:* (dépôt) terrigène.
terrine [te'riːn], *s.* terrine *f*.
territ ['terit], *s.* = TERRET.
territorial [teri'tɔːriəl]. **1.** *a.* (*a*) (*of possessions, tax, army, etc.*) territorial, -aux; **t. waters,** eaux territoriales; **the T. and Army Volunteer Reserve,** *A:* **the T. Army,** l'armée territoriale, la territoriale; (*b*) terrien, foncier. **2.** *s. Mil:* territorial *m*.
territoriality [teritɔːri'æliti], *s.* territorialité *f*.
territorially [teri'tɔːriəli], *adv.* territorialement.
territory ['terit(ə)ri], *s.* territoire *m* (d'un état, *Nat.Hist:* d'un animal, etc.); *Com:* région assignée (à un représentant); *Geog:* **the Northern T.,** le Territoire du Nord (de l'Australie); *Pol:* **mandated t.,** territoire sous mandat.
terror ['terər], *s.* **1.** terreur *f*, effroi *m*, épouvante *f*; **deadly t.,** épouvantement *m*; **to be in (a state of) t.,** être dans la terreur; être terrifié; **to run away in t.,** se sauver terrifié; **to be in t. of one's life,** craindre pour sa vie; **to go in t. of s.o.,** avoir une peur bleue de qn; *F:* **to have a holy t. of sth.,** craindre qch. comme le feu; *Hist:* **the (Reign of) T.,** la Terreur; **White T.,** Terreur blanche. **2.** (*a*) **he was the t. of the countryside,** c'était la terreur du pays; **he is a t. to his enemies,** il est la terreur de ses ennemis; **to be a t. to all wrongdoers,** se faire redouter de tous les malfaiteurs; (*b*) *F:* **he's a little t., a holy t.,** c'est un enfant terrible, un petit diable; cet enfant est terrible; **he's a t. for being late,** il est d'une inexactitude désespérante.
terrorism ['terərizm], *s.* terrorisme *m*.
terrorist ['terərist], *a. & s.* terroriste (*mf*); **there have been several t. attacks,** les terroristes ont monté plusieurs attaques.
terrorization [terərai'zeiʃ(ə)n], *s.* subjugation *f* (d'un pays, etc.) par le terrorisme.
terrorize ['terəraiz], *v.tr.* terroriser.
terrorstricken, terrorstruck ['terəstrik(ə)n, -strʌk], *a.* saisi de terreur; sous le coup de la terreur; épouvanté; terrifié; **everyone was t.,** partout régnait l'épouvante.
terry ['teri], *a. & s. Tex:* velours *m*, coton *m*, éponge; **t. towelling,** tissu *m* pour serviettes en éponge.
terse [tɔːs], *a.* (*a*) (*of style, language*) concis, net; élégant et précis; (*b*) abrupt, brusque, sec, *f.* sèche.
tersely ['tɔːsli], *adv.* (*a*) d'une façon concise; avec concision; en peu de mots; (*b*) abruptement, brusquement, sèchement.
terseness ['tɔːsnis], *s.* (*a*) concision *f* (du style, du langage); netteté *f* (de style); (*b*) brusquerie *f*.
tertian ['tɔːʃiən], *a. & s. A.Med:* **t. (fever, ague),** fièvre tierce.
tertiary ['tɔːʃiəri]. **1.** *a.* tertiaire; *Med:* **t. syphilis,** syphilis *f* tertiaire; *Pol.Ec:* **t. industries,** secteur *m* tertiaire. **2.** *a. & s. Geol:* tertiaire (*m*). **3.** *R.C.Ch:* tertiaire *mf*; *coll.* **(Franciscan, etc.) Tertiaries,** tiers ordre (de Saint-François, etc.).
tertius ['tɔːʃiəs], *a. Sch: O:* **Martin t.,** Martin (numéro) trois; le plus jeune des trois frères, ou des trois élèves, du nom de Martin.
Tertullian [tɔː'tʌliən], *Pr.n.m. Rel.H:* Tertullien.
tervalent [tɔː'veilənt], *a. Ch:* trivalent.
terylene ['teriliːn], *s. Tex: R.t.m:* térylène *m*.
terza rima [tɔːtsə'riːmə], *s. Pros:* rimes tiercées; tierce-rime *f*.
Teschen ['teʃən], *Pr.n. Geog: Vet:* **T. disease,** maladie *f* de Teschen; méningo-encéphalo-myélite *f* du porc.
Tesla ['teslə]. **1.** *Pr.n. El:* **T. coil,** bobine *f* de Tesla; *F:* (une) Tesla. **2.** *s. Ph.Meas:* tesla *m*.
tessellated ['tesileitid], *a.* **1.** *Const:* (pavage, etc.) en mosaïque, disposé en damier. **2.** *Nat.Hist:* tessellé.
tessellation [tesi'leiʃ(ə)n], *s.* arrangement *m* en damier; mosaïque *f*.
tessera, *pl.* **-ae** ['tesərə, -iː], *s.* **1.** *Rom.Ant:* tessère *f*. **2.** tesselle *f* (de pavage en mosaïque). **3.** *Z:* écaille *f* (du tatou).
tesseral ['tesərəl], *a.* **1.** de tesselles; en tesselles. **2.** *Cryst:* tesséral, -aux.
tessitura [tesi'tjuːrə], *s. Mus:* tessiture *f*.
test[1] [test] *s.* **1.** (*a*) épreuve *f*; **to put s.o., sth., to the t., through a t.,** mettre qn, qch., à l'épreuve, à l'essai; faire l'épreuve de qch.; éprouver qn, qch.; soumettre qch. à un critérium, à un critère; **to undergo a t., to be put through a t.,** subir une épreuve; **when put to the t.,** en face de l'épreuve; **to pass, stand, the t.,** soutenir, supporter, l'épreuve; subir victorieusement l'épreuve; **will this building stand the t. of time?** est-ce que ce bâtiment durera longtemps? **method that has stood the t. of time,** méthode éprouvée; **doctrine that has stood the t. of time,** doctrine devenue classique; **the acid t.,** l'épreuve concluante; **the true t. of civilization,** le signe distinctif de la civilisation; (*b*) essai *m*, épreuve; *Ind: etc:* **acceptance t.,** essai de recette, de réception, d'homologation; **prototype t., type approval t.,** essai en usine; essai d'homologation; **bench t.,** essai en usine; **feasibility t.,** essai probatoire; **control t., check t.,** essai contradictoire; contre-épreuve *f*; contre-essai *m*; **endurance t.,** épreuve d'endurance; **resistance t.,** épreuve d'outrance; **t. requirements, limits,** conditions *fpl* d'essais; **t. bench, t. bed,** banc *m* d'essai, d'épreuve; **t. chamber, laboratory,** chambre *f*, laboratoire *m*, d'essai; **t. room,** salle *f* d'expérimentation; **field t.,** essai sur le terrain; **t. by water, by steam,** épreuve à l'eau, à la vapeur; *Mec.E: etc:* **proof t., running t., working t.,** essai de (bon) fonctionnement (d'un moteur, etc.) (en pleine charge); **t. load,** charge *f* d'essai, d'épreuve; **boiler t.,** épreuve des chaudières; **t. furnace,** fourneau *m* à essais; **t. plate,** timbre *m* (de chaudière); *Metalw:* **t. strip,** barreau plat (pour essais); *Metall:* **t. piece,** éprouvette *f*; **t. ingot,** lingot-éprouvette *m*; **t. portion,** prise *f* d'essai (d'un minerai, etc.); **creep t.,** essai de fluage; *Aut: etc:* **road t.,** essai routier; essais sur route; **t. run,** course *f* d'essai; **t. track,** piste *f* d'essai; *Av:* **t. flight,** vol *m* d'essai; **t. pilot,** pilote *m* d'essai; **vacuum t.,** essai en dépression; **physical t.,** essai mécanique; (*c*) *Ch: etc:* **dry t., wet t.,** essai par la voie sèche, par la voie humide; **t. paper,** papier réactif; **t. tube,** éprouvette; tube *m* à essai(s); *F:* **t.-tube baby,** bébé-éprouvette *m*, *pl.* bébés-éprouvette; (*in analysis*) **flame t.,** essai de coloration; *Atom.Ph:* **nuclear t.,** test *m* nucléaire; *Opt:* **t. object,** test-objet *m*, *pl.* test-objets; (*d*) *Med: etc:* **blood t.,** examen *m* du sang, *F:* prise *f* de sang; **water t.,** examen des urines; **haemoglobin t.,** dosage *m* d'hémoglobine; **Wassermann t.,** réaction *f* de Wassermann; **treponemal immobilization t.,** test, réaction, de Nelson; *Z:* **progeny t.,** test de la descendance; (*e*) *El:* **earth t.,** *NAm:* **ground t.,** essai de masse; **t. plate,** disque *m* d'épreuve; (*f*) *Stat:* **significance t.,** test de signification; épreuve d'hypothèse, de signification; *Jur:* **t. case,** précédent *m*; (*g*) *Cmptr:* **diagnostic t.,** test de diagnostic; **marginal t., high-low bias t.,** test des marges; **leapfrog t.,** test sélectif, test saute-mouton; **t. run,** essai de programme; passage *m* d'essai; **t. case, t. deck, t. pack,** jeu *m* d'essai; *T.V:* **t. pattern,** mire *f*. **2.** (*a*) examen; **eye t.,** examen visuel; examen des yeux; *Aut:* **driving t.,** examen pour permis de conduire; **to fail the driving t.,** échouer à l'examen du permis de conduire; (*b*) *Sch:* **t. (paper)** = composition *f*; **oral t.,** épreuve orale; *Mus:* **t. piece,** morceau imposé (dans un concours, etc.); *Cin: etc:* **screen t.,** bout *m* d'essai; (*c*) *Psy: etc:* test; **self-administered t.,** autotest *m*; **intelligence t.,** test de capacité intellectuelle; **aptitude t.,** test d'intelligence pratique; (*d*) *Cr:* **t. (match),** match international. **3.** *Hist:* **the T.,** le Serment du Test; **the T. Act,** la loi du Test; le Test Act.
test[2], *v.tr. & i.* **1.** (*a*) éprouver (qn, qch.); mettre (qn, qch.) à l'épreuve, à l'essai; (*b*) essayer (un ciment, une machine, etc.); contrôler, vérifier (des poids et mesures, la tension artérielle); examiner (la vue de qn, etc.); expérimenter (un procédé); sonder (une poutre, etc.); analyser (l'eau, etc.); **to t. sth. carefully,** examiner qch. avec soin; passer qch. à l'alambic; **to t. a poison,** faire

l'expérience d'un poison; **to t. a coin for weight,** trébucher une pièce de monnaie; **to t. a wall for straightness,** bornoyer un mur; **to t. a boiler,** éprouver une chaudière; **boiler tested at . . .,** chaudière timbrée à . . .; *v.ind.tr.* **to t. out a scheme,** essayer un projet; **to t. for leaks in a conductor,** déceler les fuites dans un conducteur; (*c*) *Sch:* **to t. a class in algebra,** examiner une classe en algèbre; donner une composition d'algèbre à une classe. **2.** (*a*) *A:* coupeller (l'or); passer (l'or) à la coupelle; (*b*) *Ch:* déterminer la nature (d'un corps) au moyen d'un réactif; **to t. for alkaloids,** faire la réaction des alcaloïdes; **to t. with litmus paper,** faire la réaction au papier de tournesol; **to t. for an element in a compound,** rechercher un élément dans un composé.

test[3], *s. Nat.Hist:* test *m* (d'un oursin, d'une écrevisse); carapace *f*, bouclier *m* testamentaire (du tatou, etc.).

test[4]. **1.** *v.tr. Jur:* (*a*) viser (un document); (*b*) *Scot:* authentiquer, certifier (un document). **2.** *v.i. Scot:* tester; faire son testament.

testa ['testə], *s. Bot:* test *m*, testa *m*.

testacean [tes'teiʃiən], *s. Nat.Hist:* testacé *m*.

testacella [testə'selə], *s. Moll:* testacelle *f*.

testaceous [tes'teiʃəs], *a. Nat.Hist:* **1.** testacé. **2.** couleur brique *inv*.

testament ['testəmənt], *s.* **1. to make one's (last will and) t.,** tester; faire son testament. **2.** *B:* **the Old, the New, T.,** l'Ancien, le Nouveau, Testament.

testamentary [testə'ment(ə)ri], *a.* (*a*) testamentaire; (*b*) **t. capacity,** habilité *f* à tester.

testate ['testeit], *a. & s.* (personne) qui a testé, qui est morte en laissant un testament valable.

testator, *f.* **testatrix,** *pl.* **-trices, -trixes** [tes'teitər; -'teitriks, -trisi:z, -triksiz], *s. Jur:* testateur, -trice.

tester[1] ['testər], *s. A.Furn:* baldaquin *m*, ciel *m* (de lit); **t. bed,** lit *m* à ciel, à baldaquin.

tester[2], *s.* **1.** *Ind:* (*pers.*) essayeur, -euse; vérificateur, -trice; contrôleur, -euse. **2.** (*a*) appareil *m* de contrôle, à essais; (appareil) vérificateur; **oil t.,** machine *f* à essayer l'huile; *El:* **battery t.,** vérificateur d'accus; **armature t.,** vibreur *m* (pour vérification des induits); **coil t.,** vérificateur de bobines; *Tex:* **yarn t.,** dynamomètre *m* pour fil; *Metalw: etc:* **surface finish t.,** rugosimètre *m*; (*b*) échantillon *m* (de cosmétique).

tester[3], *s. Num: A:* (*a*) teston *m*; (*b*) pièce *f* de six pence.

Testicardines [testi'kɑ:dini:z], *s.pl. Nat.Hist:* testicardines *fpl*; articulés *mpl*.

testicle ['testikl], *s. Anat:* testicule *m*.

testicular [tes'tikjulər], *a. Anat:* testiculaire.

testiculate [tes'tikjuleit], *a.* testiculé.

testifier ['testifaiər], *s.* témoin *m*.

testify ['testifai], *v.* **1.** *v.tr.* témoigner (son regret, sa foi, etc.); *Lit:* **work that testifies his deep knowledge of the subject,** œuvre *f* qui fait preuve, qui témoigne, de sa profonde connaissance du sujet. **2.** *Jur:* (*a*) *v.tr.* déclarer, affirmer (qch.) (sous serment); **the witness testified that the accused bore a good character,** le témoin affirma, déclara, déposa, que l'accusé était un homme de bonne vie et mœurs; *v.i.* **to t. in s.o.'s favour,** rendre témoignage en faveur de qn; **to t. against s.o.,** déposer contre qn; (*b*) *v.ind.tr.* **to t. to a fact,** attester, affirmer, un fait; se porter garant d'un fait; témoigner d'un fait; **he testified to having met me,** il attesta m'avoir rencontré; **to t. to the truth,** rendre témoignage, rendre gloire, à la vérité; *A:* **to t. of sth., concerning sth.,** témoigner (de) qch.; rendre témoignage de qch.

testily ['testili], *adv.* d'un air irrité; avec humeur.

testimonial [testi'mouniəl], *s.* **1.** certificat (délivré par une maison, un chef, etc.); lettre testimoniale; (lettre de) recommandation *f*; attestation *f*; **to give a t. to an employee,** donner à un employé un témoignage écrit de ses services. **2.** témoignage d'estime, cadeau (offert à qn par cotisation en reconnaissance de ses services, etc.).

testimony ['testiməni], *s.* **1.** témoignage *m* (des sens, etc.); *Jur:* attestation *f*; déposition *f* (d'un témoin); **to bear t. to sth.,** témoigner de qch.; rendre témoignage de qch.; attester qch.; **to bear t. to the truth,** rendre témoignage à la vérité; **to be called in t.,** être appelé en témoignage; **in t. whereof,** en foi de quoi; *Jur:* **to produce t. of, to, a statement,** apporter des preuves testimonials à l'appui d'une affirmation; *Rel.H:* **to give t.,** affirmer publiquement sa foi. **2.** *B:* **the tables of the T.,** les tables *f* du Témoignage; les tables de la Loi, de l'Alliance; le Décalogue.

testiness ['testinis], *s.* (*a*) irritabilité *f*, irascibilité *f*; (*b*) susceptibilité *f*.

testing ['testiŋ], *s.* (*a*) essai *m*, essayage *m*, épreuve *f* (d'une machine, d'un pont, etc.); contrôle *m*, vérification *f* (des poids et mesures, etc.); **t. for weight,** trébuchage *m* (d'une pièce de monnaie); **t. laboratory,** laboratoire *m* d'essai; **t. bench,** banc *m* d'épreuve; **t. ground,** terrain *m* d'essai; **t. machine,** (appareil) vérificateur *m*; *Tex:* **t. house,** (salle *f* de) conditionnement *m*; la condition; (*b*) *A:* coupellation *f* (de l'or).

testis, *pl.* **testes** ['testis, 'testi:z], *s. Anat:* **1.** testicule *m*. **2. testes,** tubercules quadrijumeaux inférieurs; testes *m*.

teston ['testən], **testoon** [tes'tu:n], *s. Num: A:* teston *m*.

testosterone [tes'tɔstəroun], *s. Physiol: Ch:* testostérone *f*.

testudinaria [testju:di'nεəriə], *s. Bot:* testudinaire *f*, testudinaria *m*.

Testudinata [testju:di'neitə], *s.pl. Rept:* testudinés *m*.

testudinate [tes'tju:dineit], *a. & s.* testudiné (*m*).

testudineous [testju:'diniəs], *a.* testudinaire.

Testudinidae [testju:'dinidi:], *s.pl. Rept:* testudinidés *m*.

testudo [tes'tju:dou], *s.* **1.** *Rept:* testudo *m*, tortue *f*. **2.** *Rom.Ant:* (*a*) tortue (de siège); (*b*) tortue (de boucliers). **3.** *Civ.E: Min:* bouclier *m*. **4.** *Med:* talpa *f*, testudo. *F:* taupe *f*.

testy ['testi], *a.* (*a*) irritable; irascible; (*b*) susceptible.

tetanic [te'tænik], *a. Med:* tétanique; **t. state,** tétanisme *m*; *Pharm: O:* **t. drug,** *s.* **t.,** médicament *m* tétanique.

tetaniform [te'tænifɔ:m], *a.* tétaniforme.

tetanine ['tetəni:n], *s. Med:* tétanine *f*.

tetanization [tetənai'zeiʃ(ə)n], *s. Med:* tétanisation *f*.

tetanize ['tetənaiz], *v.tr. Med:* tétaniser (qn).

tetanoid ['tetənɔid]. *Med:* **1.** *a.* tétaniforme, tétanoïde. **2.** *s.* spasme *m* tétanique, tétaniforme.

tetanolysin [tetənou'laisin], *s.* tétanolysine *f*.

tetanomotor [tetənou'moutər], *s. Physiol:* tétanomoteur *m*.

tetanospasmin [tetənou'spæzmin], *s. Med:* tétanotoxine *f*.

tetanus ['tetənəs], *s. Med:* tétanos *m*; **t. toxin,** tétanotoxine *f*; **t. bacillus,** bacille tétanique.

tetany ['tetəni], *s. Med:* tétanie *f*; tétanos intermittent; *Vet:* **grass t.,** tétanie d'herbage.

tetartohedral [tetɑ:tou'hi:dr(ə)l, -'hed-], *a. Cryst:* tétartoèdre, tétartoédrique.

tetartohedrism [tetɑ:tou'hi:drizm, -'hed-], *s. Cryst:* tétartoèdrie *f*.

tetartohedron [tetɑ:tou'hi:drən, -'hed-], *s. Cryst:* tétartoèdre *m*.

tetchily ['tetʃili], *adv.* **tetchiness** ['tetʃinis], *s.*, **tetchy** ['tetʃi], *a.* = TESTILY, TESTINESS, TESTY.

tête-à-tête ['teitɑ:'teit]. **1.** *adv.* tête-à-tête. **2.** *s.* (*pl.* **tête-à-têtes**) tête-à-tête *m inv.*; **t.-à-t. dinner, talk,** dîner *m*, conversation *f*, en tête-à-tête.

tête-bêche ['teit'beiʃ], *a. Post:* **t.-b. stamps,** timbres *m* tête-bêche.

tether[1] ['teðər], *s. Harn:* longe *f*, attache *f* (d'un cheval, etc.); (*of pers.*) **to be at the end of one's t.,** (i) être à bout de forces; n'en plus pouvoir; (ii) être à bout de ressources; *F:* être au bout de sa corde, de son rouleau; (*of dying man*) **he's near the end of his t.,** il n'en a plus pour longtemps.

tether[2], *v.tr.* attacher, mettre à l'attache (un cheval, etc.); mettre, attacher (un cheval) au piquet.

Tethys ['teθis]. **1.** *Pr.n.f. Myth:* Téthys. **2.** *s. Moll:* téthys *f*, aplysie *f*.

Tethyum ['teθiəm, 'ti:-], *s. Nat.Hist:* cynthia *f*.

tetra- ['tetrə, te'træ], *comb.fm.* tétra-.

tetrabasic [tetrə'beisik], *a. Ch:* tétrabasique, quadribasique.

Tetrabelodon [tetrə'beloudən], *s. Paleont:* tetrabelodon *m*.

tetraborate [tetrə'bɔ:reit], *s. Ch:* tétraborate *m*.

tetrabranch ['tetrəbræŋk], *s. Moll:* tétrabranche *m*.

Tetrabranchia(ta) [tetrə'bræŋkiə, -bræŋki'eitə], *s.pl. Moll:* tétrabranches *m*.

tetrabranchiate [tetrə'bræŋkieit], *a. Moll:* tétrabranche.

tetrabromide [tetrə'broumaid], *s. Ch:* tétrabromure *m*.

tetrabromoethane [tetrəbroumou'eθein], *s. Ch:* tétrabrométhane *m*.

tetrabromoethylene [tetrəbroumou'eθili:n], *s. Ch:* tétrabrométhylène *m*.

tetracaine ['tetrəkein], *s. Pharm:* tétracaïne *f*.

tetracarbonyl [tetrə'kɑ:bənil], *s. Ch:* tétracarbonyle *m*.

tetracerus [te'træsərəs], *s. Z:* tétracère *m*.

tetrachloride [tetrə'klɔ:raid], *s. Ch:* tétrachlorure *m*; **carbon t.,** tétrachlorure de carbone, tétrachlorométhane *m*.

tetrachlor(o)ethane [tetrəklɔ:r(ou)'eθein], *s. Ch:* tétrachloréthane *m*.

tetrachloroethylene [tetrəklɔ:rou'eθili:n], *s. Ch:* tétrachloréthylène *m*.

tetrachloromethane [tetrəklɔ:rou'meθein], *s. Ch:* tétrachlorométhane *m*, tétrachlorure *m* de carbone.

tetrachord ['tetrəkɔ:d], *s. Mus:* tétracorde *m*.

tetrachordal [tetrə'kɔ:d(ə)l], *a. Mus:* tétracordal, -aux.

tetracoccus [tetrə'kɔkəs], *s. Bac:* tétracoque *m*, tétragène *m*.

Tetracoralla [tetrəkə'rælə], *s.pl. Paleont:* tétracorallaires *m*.

Tetractinellida [tetrækti'nelidə], *s.pl. Spong:* tétractinellidés *m*.

tetracycline [tetrə'saiklain], *s. Pharm:* tétracycline *f*.

tetrad ['tetræd], *s.* **1.** *Biol: Ch:* tétrade *f*. **2.** série *f* de quatre.

tetradactyl(ous) [tetrə'dæktil(əs)], *a. Z:* tétradactyle.

tetradymite [te'trædimait], *s. Miner:* tétradymite *f*.

tetradynamous [tetrə'dainəməs], *a. Bot:* tétradyname, tétradynamique.

tetraethyl [tetrə'eθil], *s. Ch:* tétréthyle *m*; **t. lead,** plomb tétréthyle.

tetragenous [te'trædʒənəs], *a. Bac:* **t. bacteria,** tétragène *m*.

tetragon ['tetrəgən], *s.* **1.** *Mth: etc:* tétragone *m*, quadrilatère *m*. **2.** *Astrol:* aspect *m* tétragone.

tetragonal [te'trægən(ə)l], *a. Mth:* tétragone, quadrilatère; *Cryst:* quadratique.

tetragonia [tetrə'gouniə], *s. Bot:* tétragone *f*, tétragonie *f*.

tetragram ['tetrəgræm], *s.* tétragramme *m*.

Tetragrammaton (the) [ðətetrə'græmətən], *s. Rel.H: etc:* le Tétragramme.

tetragynous [tetrə'dʒainəs, -'gainəs], *a. Bot:* tétragyne.

tetrahedral [tetrə'hi:drəl, -'hed-], *a. Mth:* tétraèdre, tétraédrique.

tetrahedrite [tetrə'hi:drait, -'hed-], *s. Miner:* tétraédrite *f*; cuivre gris, panabase *f*.

tetrahedroid [tetrə'hi:drɔid, -'hed-], *s.* tétraédroïde *m*.

tetrahedron [tetrə'hi:drən, -'hed-], *s. Mth:* tétraèdre *m*.

tetrahydrobenzene [tetrəhaidrouben'zi:n, -'benzi:n], *s. Ch:* tétrahydrobenzène *m*.

tetrahydronaphthalene [tetrəhaidrou'næfθəli:n], *s. Ch:* tétrahydronaphtalène *m*, tétraline *f*.

tetraiodofluorescein [tetrəaioudouflu:ɔ'resi:in], *s. Ch:* tétraiodofluorescéine *f*.

tetralin ['tetrəlin], *s. Ch:* tétraline *f*, tétrahydronaphtalène *m*.

tetralogy [te'trælədʒi], *s.* **1.** *Lit: Mus:* tétralogie *f*. **2.** *Med:* **t. of Fallot,** tétralogie de Fallot.

tetramerous [te'træmərəs], *a. Nat.Hist:* tétramère.

tetrameter [te'træmitər], *s. Pros:* tétramètre *m*.

tetramethylene [tetrə'meθili:n], *s. Ch:* tétraméthylène *m*.

tetrandria [te'trændriə], *s. Bot:* tétrandrie *f*.

tetrandrous [te'trændrəs], *a. Bot:* tétrandre.

tetranitroaniline [tetrənaitrou'ænilain], *s. Ch:* tétranitraniline *f*.

tetranitromethane [tetrənaitrou'meθein], *s. Ch:* tétranitrométhane *m*.

tetraodon [te'treioudɔn], *s. Ich:* tétrodon *m*, tétraodon *m*.

Tetraodontidae [tetrəou'dɔntidi:], *s.pl. Ich:* tétrodontidés *m*.

Tetraogallus [tetrəou'gæləs], *s. Orn:* tétraogalle *m*.

Tetraonidae [tetrə'ɔnidi:], *s.pl. Orn:* tétraonidés *m*, lagopèdes *m*.

tetrapetalous [tetrə'petələs], *a. Bot:* tétrapétale.

Tetraphyllidea [tetrəfi'lidiə], *s.pl. Ann:* tétraphyllidiens *m*.

tetraplegia [tetrə'pli:dʒiə], *s. Med:* tétraplégie *f*, quadriplégie *f*.

tetraploid ['tetrəplɔid], *a. & s. Biol:* tétraploïde (*mf*).

tetraploidy ['tetrəplɔidi], *s. Biol:* tétraploïdie *f*.

tetrapneumonous [tetrə'nju:mənəs], *a. Arach:* tétrapneumone.

tetrapod ['tetrəpɔd], *a. & s.* tétrapode (*m*).

tetrapody [te'træpədi], *s.* tétrapodie *f*.

tetrapteron [te'træptərən], *s. Ent:* tétraptère *m*.

tetrapterous [te'træptərəs], *a. Ent: Bot:* tétraptère.

tetrapylon, *pl.* **-pyla** [tetrə'pailən, -'pailə], *s. Arch:* tétrapyle *m*.

tetrarch ['tetrɑ:k], *s. Hist:* tétrarque *m*.

tetrarchate ['tetrɑ:keit], *s. Hist:* tétrarchat *m*.

tetrarchy ['tetrɑ:ki], *s. Hist:* tétrarchie *f*.

Tetrarhynchidea [tetrəriŋ'kidiə], *s.pl. Ann:* tétrarhynques *m*.

tetrasepalous [tetrə'sepələs], *a. Bot:* tétrasépale.

tetrasomic [tetrə'soumik], *a. Biol:* tétrasomique.

tetrasomy ['tetrəsoumi], *s. Biol:* tétrasomie *f*.

tetrasporangium [tetrəspɔ'rændʒiəm], *s. Bot:* tétrasporange *m*.

tetraspore ['tetrəspɔ:r], *s. Bot:* tétraspore *m*.

tetrasporophyte [tetrə'spɔ:roufait], *s. Bot:* tétrasporophyte *m*.

tetrastichous [te'træstikəs], *a. Bot:* tétrastique.

tetrastyle ['tetrəstail], *a. & s. Arch:* tétrastyle (*m*).

tetrasubstituted [tetrə'sʌbstitjutid], *a. Ch:* tétrasubstitué.
tetrasulphide [tetrə'sʌlfaid], *s. Ch:* tétrasulfure *m.*
tetrasyllabic [tetrəsi'læbik], *a. Gram:* tétrasyllabe, tétrasyllabique.
tetrasyllable [tetrə'siləbl], *s. Gram:* mot *m* tétrasyllabe.
tetrathionic [tetrəθai'ɔnik], *a. Ch:* (acide) tétrathionique.
tetratomic [tetrə'tɔmik], *a. Ch:* tétratomique.
tetravalence [tetrə'veiləns], *s. Ch:* tétravalence *f,* quadrivalence *f.*
tetravalent [tetrə'veilənt], *a. Ch:* tétravalent, quadrivalent.
tetrazene ['tetræzi:n], *s. Ch:* tétrazène *m.*
tetrazole ['tetræzoul], *s. Ch:* tétrazole *m.*
Tetrigidae [te'tridʒidi:], *s.pl. Ent:* tétrigidés *m.*
tetrix ['tetriks], *s. Ent:* tétrix *m.*
tetrode ['tetroud], *s. W.Tel: etc:* tétrode *f.*
tetrodon ['tetroudɔn], *s. Ich:* tétrodon *m,* tétraodon *m.*
Tetrodontidae [tetrou'dɔntidi:], *s.pl. Ich:* tétrodontidés *m.*
tetrolic [te'trɔlik], *a. Ch:* (acide) tétrolique.
tetrose [te'trous, -ouz], *s. Ch:* tétrose *m.*
tetroxide [te'trɔksaid], *s. Ch:* tétroxyde *m.*
tetryl ['tetril], *s. Exp:* tétryl *m.*
tetter ['tetər], *s. A: & Dial:* **1.** *Med:* dartre *f;* herpès *m;* impétigo *m;* psoriasis *m.* **2.** *Vet:* bouquet *m.*
tetterwort ['tetəwə:t], *s. Bot:* chélidoine *f,* grande éclaire.
tettigoniid [teti'gouniid], *s. Ent:* tettigoniidé *m.*
Tettigoniidae [tetigə'naiidi:], *s.pl. Ent:* tettigoniidés *m.*
Tettix ['tetiks], *s. Ent:* tettix *m,* tétrix *m.*
Tetuan [tet'wɑ:n], *Pr.n. Geog:* Tétouan, Tétuan.
Teucrian ['tju:kriən]. *Gr.Lit:* **1.** *s.* Troyen, -enne. **2.** *a.* troyen.
Teuthididae [tju:'θididi:], *s.pl. Ich:* teuthididés *m.*
Teuthis ['tju:θis], *s. Ich:* acanthure *m,* (poisson) chirurgien *m.*
Teuton ['tju:tən], *s.* Teuton, -onne.
Teutonic [tju:'tɔnik]. **1.** *a.* teuton, teutonique; *Hist:* **the T. Order (of Knights),** l'ordre Teutonique. **2.** *s. Ling:* teuton *m.*
Teutonism ['tju:tənizm], *s. Ling:* germanisme *m.*
Teutonize ['tju:tənaiz], *v.tr. O:* germaniser (son nom, etc.).
Texan ['teksən]. **1.** *a.* texan. **2.** *s.* Texan, -ane.
Texas ['teksəs]. **1.** *Pr.n. Geog:* Texas *m.* **2.** *s.* (*a*) *U.S:* pont supérieur (d'un vapeur fluvial); (*b*) *Vet:* **T. (cattle) fever,** fièvre du Texas; piroplasmose *f* (du bœuf).
text [tekst], *s.* **1.** texte *m* (d'un manuscrit, d'un auteur); **t. with illustrations, with notes,** texte illustré, annoté; **t. hand,** écriture en gros caractères. **2.** citation tirée de l'Écriture sainte; **t. of a sermon,** texte d'un sermon. **3.** *Cmptr:* **start of t.,** début de texte; **t. mode,** mode de texte; **end-of-t. character,** caractère (de) fin de texte; **t. message,** message avec texte.
textbook ['tekstbuk], *s.* **1.** *Sch: etc:* manuel *m;* **chemistry t.,** manuel de chimie; **t. on physics, on algebra,** physique *f,* algèbre *f;* **t. definitions,** définitions exactes, exemplaires. **2.** recueil *m* de textes sur un sujet spécifique.
textile ['tekstail]. **1.** *a.* textile; **t. fibre,** fibre textile. **2.** *s.* (*a*) tissu *m,* étoffe *f;* **synthetic textiles,** textiles artificiels; **the t. industries,** l'industrie textile; le textile; **t. oil,** huile d'ensimage; (*b*) matière *f* textile; textile *m.*
textorial [teks'tɔ:riəl], *a.* (art, occupation, etc.) textile.
textual ['tekstjuəl], *a.* (*a*) textuel; **t. quotation,** citation textuelle; (*b*) **t. error,** erreur *f* de texte.
textually ['tekstjuəli], *adv.* (*a*) textuellement; (*b*) concernant le texte.
textuary ['tekstjuəri]. **1.** *a.* textuaire. **2.** *s.* personne bien informée sur l'Écriture sainte.
texture ['tekstʃər], *s.* tissage *m,* tissu *m,* tissure *f,* contexture *f* (d'un tissu); texture *f,* grain *m* (de la peau, du bois, etc.); contexture (des os, des muscles); texture (d'un roman, d'une pièce); **close, loose, t. of a material,** tissage serré, lâche, d'un tissu.
textured ['tekstʃəd], *a.* (*with adj. prefixed, e.g.*) **close-t., light-t.,** d'un tissage serré, léger.
Thaddeus [θæ'di:əs], *Pr.n.m. B.Hist:* Thaddée.
Thai [tai]. **1.** *a.* (*of group, languages*) thaï. **2.** *s.* (*a*) *Geog:* Thaïlandais, -aise; (*b*) *Ling:* thaï *m.*
Thailand ['tailænd]. *Geog:* **1.** *Pr.n.* Thaïlande *f.* **2.** *a.* thaïlandais.
Thailander ['tailændər], *s. Geog:* Thaïlandais, -aise.
Thais ['θeiis], *Pr.n.f. A. Hist:* Thaïs.
thalamencephalon [θæləmen'sefələn], *s. Anat:* thalamencéphale *m.*
thalamic [θæ'læmik], *a. Anat:* thalamique.
thalamifloral [θæləmi'flɔ:rəl], **thalamiflorous** [θæləmi'flɔ:rəs], *a. Bot:* thalamiflore.
thalamus, *pl.* **-i** ['θæləməs, -ai], *s. Anat: Bot:* thalamus *m,* thalame *m.*
thalass(a)emia [θælə'si:miə], **thalassan(a)emia** [θæləsæ'ni:miə], *s. Med:* thalassémie *f.*
thalassic [θæ'læsik], *a. Oc:* thalassique.
thalassin [θæ'læsin], *s. Bio-Ch:* thalassine *f.*
thalassocracy [θælə'sɔkrəsi], *s.* thalassocratie *f.*
thalassography [θælə'sɔgrəfi], *s. Oc:* thalassographie *f.*
thalassometer [θælə'sɔmitər], *s. Oc:* thalassomètre *m.*
thalassometry [θælə'sɔmitri], *s. Oc:* thalassométrie *f.*
thalassophobia [θæləsou'foubiə], *s. Med:* thalassophobie *f.*
thalassotherapy [θæləsou'θerəpi], *s. Med:* thalassothérapie *f;* cure marine.
thalattocracy [θælə'tɔkrəsi], *s.* thalassocratie *f.*
thalenite ['θɑ:lənait], *s. Miner:* thalénite *f.*
thaler ['tɑ:lər], *s. Num:* thaler *m;* **Maria Theresa t.,** thaler de Marie-Thérèse.
Thales ['θeili:z], *Pr.n.m. Gr. Phil:* **T. of Miletus,** Thalès de Milet.
Thalia [θə'laiə, 'θeiliə]. **1.** *Pr.n.f. Myth:* Thalie. **2.** *s. Bot:* thalie *f.*
Thaliacea [θeili'eiʃiə], *s.pl. Z:* thaliacés *m.*
thalidomide [θə'lidəmaid], *s. Pharm:* thalidomide *f;* **t. baby,** bébé malformé (à cause de l'emploi de la thalidomide chez la mère).
thallic ['θælik], *a. Ch:* thallique.
thallium ['θæliəm], *s. Ch:* thallium *m.*
thalloid ['θælɔid], *a. Bot:* thalloïde.
thallome ['θæloum], *s. Bot:* thallome *m.*
Thallophyta [θæ'lɔfitə], *s.pl. Bot:* thallophytes *f.*
thallophyte ['θæloufait], *s. Bot:* thallophyte *m & f.*
thallospore ['θælouspɔ:r], *s. Fung:* thallospore *f.*
thallous ['θæləs], *a. Ch:* thalleux.
thallus, *pl.* **-i** ['θæləs, -ai], *s. Bot:* thalle *m.*
thalweg ['tɑ:lveg], *s. Geol:* thalweg *m.*
thameng ['θɑ:meŋ], *s. Z:* thameng *m.*
Thames [temz], *Pr.n. Geog:* **the (river) T.,** la Tamise; **he'll never set the T. on fire,** il n'a pas inventé la poudre; il n'a pas inventé le fil à couper le beurre.
Thames-side ['temzsaid], *s.* le(s) bord(s) *m*(*pl*) de la Tamise; **a T.-s. hotel,** un hôtel au bord de la Tamise.
thamin ['θɑ:min], *s. Z:* thameng *m.*
thamnophile ['θæmnoufail], *s. Orn:* thamnophile *m,* batara *m.*
Thamnophilus [θæm'nɔfiləs], *s. Orn:* thamnophile *m.*
than [*stressed* ðæn; *unstressed* ð(ə)n]. **1.** *conj.* (*a*) (*in comparison of inequality*) que; (*with numbers*) de; **I have more, less, t. you,** j'en ai plus, moins, que vous; **more t. twenty,** plus de vingt; **more t. once,** plus d'une fois; **he's taller t. I (am),** *F:* **t. me,** il est plus grand que moi; **I know you better t. he (does),** je vous connais mieux que lui, mieux qu'il ne vous connaît; **I know you better t. (I know) him,** je vous connais mieux que lui; **they like you better t. anyone else,** on vous préfère à tous les autres; **he does it better t. anyone,** il le fait mieux que personne; **I'd rather phone him t. write,** je préfère lui téléphoner que de lui écrire; **I'd rather starve t. ask him for money,** j'aimerais mieux mourir de faim que de lui demander de l'argent; **she would do anything rather t. let him suffer,** elle ferait n'importe quoi plutôt que de le laisser souffrir; **no sooner had we entered t. the music began,** nous étions à peine entrés que la musique a commencé; (*b*) **any person other t. himself,** tout autre que lui; **it was none other t. his old friend,** ce n'était nul autre que son vieil ami; **it's due to nothing else t. his own obstinacy,** ce n'a pour cause que sa propre obstination. **2.** *quasi-prep. A: & Lit:* **a man t. whom no one was more respected,** un homme qui était plus respecté que personne, que quiconque.
thanatocoenose, thanatocoenosis [θænətou'si:nous, -si'nousis], *s. Paleont:* thanatocénose *f.*
thanatological [θænətə'lɔdʒikl], *a. Biol:* thanatologique.
thanatology [θænə'tɔlədʒi], *s. Biol:* thanatologie *f.*
thanatophidia [θænətou'fidiə], *s.pl. Z:* serpents venimeux.
thanatophobia [θænətou'foubiə], *s. Med:* thanatophobie *f.*
thanatopsis [θænə'tɔpsis], *s.* contemplation *f* de la mort.
thane [θein], *s. Eng. & Scot. Hist:* = baron *m.*
thank [θæŋk], *v.tr.* **1.** (*a*) remercier (qn); faire des remerciements, dire merci, à (qn); rendre grâce(s) à (Dieu); **to t. s.o. for sth.,** remercier qn de, pour, qch.; **he thanked me for helping him,** il m'a remercié de l'avoir aidé; **to t. s.o. sincerely,** faire des remerciements sincères à qn; remercier qn sincèrement; **to t. s.o. effusively,** se confondre en remerciements; **t. God! t. heaven! t. goodness!** Dieu merci! grâce au ciel! le ciel en soit loué! (*b*) **t. you,** *F:* **thanking you,** je vous remercie; merci; **will you have some tea?—no, t. you,** prenez-vous, voulez-vous, du thé?—merci! (non) je vous remercie! **(yes,) t. you,** (i) oui, merci; (ii) s'il vous plaît; **t. you very much,** merci bien, merci beaucoup; **t. you for your letter, for coming,** merci de, pour, votre lettre; merci d'être venu; *F:* **t. you for nothing!** merci de rien! *F:* **he said his t. yous and left,** il a fait ses remerciements et il est parti; **t. you note,** mot de remerciement. **2.** *often Iron: O:* **I'll t. you to close the door,** je vous demanderai de bien vouloir fermer la porte; **I'll t. you to mind your own business!** occupez-vous donc de ce qui vous regarde! **3. to have s.o. to t. for sth.,** devoir qch. à qn; **she has you to t. for that,** c'est à vous qu'elle doit cela; **you have only yourself to t. for it,** c'est à vous seul qu'il faut vous en prendre; il ne faut vous en prendre qu'à vous-même.
thankful ['θæŋkful], *a.* reconnaissant; **to be t. to s.o. for sth.,** être reconnaissant à qn de qch.; savoir gré à qn de qch.; **to be t. that. . .,** être heureux, être bien content, que . . .; **we can be t. for it,** nous pouvons nous en féliciter; **it's something to be t. for,** il y a de quoi nous féliciter.
thankfully ['θæŋkfuli], *adv.* avec reconnaissance; avec gratitude; *Journ: etc:* **t. it never happened,** grâce à Dieu, Dieu merci, cela n'est jamais arrivé.
thankfulness ['θæŋkfulnis], *s.* reconnaissance *f,* gratitude *f.*
thankless ['θæŋklis], *a.* **1.** (*of pers.*) ingrat. **2.** (travail, etc.) mal récompensé, inutile, ingrat; **a t. task,** une tâche ingrate, écœurante; une (vraie) corvée.
thanklessly ['θæŋklisli], *adv.* **1.** avec ingratitude; sans montrer de reconnaissance. **2.** sans récompense; sans satisfaction morale; sans profit.
thanklessness ['θæŋklisnis], *s.* **1.** ingratitude *f* (de qn). **2.** inutilité *f,* caractère ingrat, peu profitable (d'une tâche, etc.).
thankoffering ['θæŋkɔf(ə)riŋ], *s.* (*a*) cadeau *m* de reconnaissance; (*b*) *B:* sacrifice *m* d'actions de grâces.
thanks [θæŋks], *s.pl.* remerciement(s) *m*(*pl*); **give him my t.,** remerciez-le de ma part; **(very) many t.,** *F:* **t. very much, t. awfully,** bien des remerciements! merci bien! merci beaucoup! merci mille fois! mille fois merci! **t.!** merci; *F:* **t. for your letter, for coming,** merci de, pour, votre lettre; merci d'être venu; **t. for nothing!** merci de rien! *F:* **no t.,** (non,) merci; **she smiled her t.,** elle m'a remercié d'un sourire; **to give t. to s.o. for sth.,** remercier qn de, pour, qch.; **to give t.,** dire les grâces (au repas); **to offer, give, t. to God,** rendre grâce à Dieu; **to offer, to express, to extend, one's sincere, heartfelt, t. to s.o.,** présenter, offrir, exprimer, ses remerciements sincères, ses vifs remerciements, à qn; **to propose a vote of t. to s.o.,** voter des remerciements à qn; **t. be to God!** (rendons) grâce à Dieu! **t. to . . .,** grâce à . . .; **I managed, but no t. to you, small t. to you,** je me suis débrouillé, mais ce n'est pas à vous que je le dois, ce n'est pas grâce à vous; **that's all the t. I get!** voilà comme on me remercie! **small,** *Iron:* **much, t. I got for it!** c'était vraiment bien la peine! **what t. do you get?** quel gré vous en sait-on?
thanksgiving [θæŋks'giviŋ], *s.* action *f* de grâce(s); **T. Day,** fête célébrée (i) *U.S:* le 4e jeudi de novembre; (ii) *Can:* le 2e lundi d'octobre, *Fr.C:* le jour de l'action de grâces.
thapsia ['θæpsiə], *s. Bot:* thapsia *m; Pharm:* **t. plaster,** thapsia.
that[1] [ðæt], *dem.pron., a. & adv.*
I. *dem.pron., pl.* **those** [ðouz]. **1.** cela; ce; *F:* ça; (*a*) **give me t.,** donnez-moi cela, ça; **what's t.?** qu'est-ce (que c'est) que cela, que ça? **who's t.?** qui est-ce là? qui est cette personne(-là)? **that's Mr Thomas,** c'est M. Thomas; **is t. you, Anne?** *F:* **t. you, Anne?** est-ce vous, Anne? c'est vous, Anne? **those are my things,** ce sont mes affaires; **those are my orders,** voilà mes ordres; **are those your children?** sont-ce là vos enfants? ce sont vos enfants? **is t. all the luggage you're taking?** c'est tout ce que vous emportez comme bagages? vous n'emportez que ça de bagages? **that's not fair,** cela n'est pas juste; **that's what he told me,** voilà ce qu'il m'a dit; **that's what I've come for,** c'est pour cela que je suis venu; **that's where he lives,** c'est là qu'il habite; voilà où il habite; **that's how I happened to be there,** voilà comment je me suis trouvé là; **that's just like her,** voilà comme elle est; la voilà bien! **that's what you get for telling lies,** voilà ce que c'est (que) de mentir; **that's what they call dancing nowadays,** voilà ce qui s'appelle danser aujourd'hui; **after, before, t.,** après, avant, cela; **t. was two years ago,** il y a deux ans de cela; **with t. she took out her handkerchief,** là-dessus, elle a sorti son mouchoir; **what do you mean by t.?** qu'entendez-vous par là? que voulez-vous dire? **they all think t.,** c'est ce qu'ils pensent tous; **we must get him out of t.,** (i) il faut le tirer de là; (ii) il faut le guérir de ça; **has it come to t.?** les choses en sont-elles arrivées là? **t. is, that's, to say,**

c'est-à-dire; **I'll come with you, t. is if. . .,** je veux bien vous accompagner, si toutefois . . .; (*b*) (*stressed*) **so** *that's* **settled,** alors, c'est décidé; **if anything can please him** *t.* **will,** si quelque chose peut le satisfaire ce sera bien cela; **I've only got two pairs of shoes and those are old,** je n'ai que deux paires de chaussures et encore sont-elles bien usées; **he's a hack writer, and a poor one at t.,** c'est un écrivain besogneux, et encore assez piètre, et qui ne vaut pas grand-chose; **it needs a good actor and an experienced one at t.,** cela demande un bon acteur et de plus, un acteur expérimenté; *F: O:* **will you help me?—t. I will!** voulez-vous m'aider? —volontiers! avec plaisir! *O: & Dial:* **she's very beautiful—she is t.!** elle est très belle—en effet! cela oui! *F:* pour sûr! *O: & Dial:* **I'm really sorry, t. I am,** je le regrette bien, ça pour sûr! **that's right! that's it!** c'est juste! c'est cela! ça y est! **that's all,** voilà tout; *that's* **more like it,** voilà qui est mieux; c'est beaucoup mieux; (*to child*) *that's* **a good boy!** comme tu est gentil! tu es bien gentil! **that's strange!** voilà qui est curieux! *F:* **good stuff, t.!** ça c'est du bon! voilà du bon! **and that's t.! so that's t.!** et voilà! alors voilà qui est fini! c'est terminé! plus rien à dire! *F:* un point c'est tout! **t. will do,** cela, ça, suffit; **that's enough of t.!** en voilà assez! **2.** (*opposed to* **this, these**) celui-là, *f.* celle-là; *pl.* ceux-là, *f.* celles-là; **this is new and that's old,** celui-ci est neuf et celui-là est vieux; **I prefer these to those,** je préfère ceux-ci à ceux-là. **3.** (*indefinite, as antecedent to a relative*) celui, *f.* celle; *pl.* ceux, *f.* celles; **a different colour from t. which I had before,** une couleur différente de celle que j'avais avant; **what's t. (that) you're holding?** qu'est-ce que (c'est que) vous avez dans la main? **all those that I saw,** tous ceux que j'ai vus; **those of whom I speak,** ceux dont je parle; **those who wish to go may do so,** ceux qui veulent s'en aller sont libres de le faire; **one of those who were present,** (l')un de ceux qui étaient présents; un des assistants; **I'm not one of those who . . .,** je ne suis pas de ceux qui . . .; **there are those who maintain it,** certains l'affirment; il y a des gens qui, il y en a qui, l'affirment; *Lit:* **there was t. in her which commanded respect,** il y avait en elle quelque chose qui imposait le respect; (*with relative understood*) **all those present at the wedding,** tous ceux qui ont assisté au mariage; **a house like t. described here,** une maison comme celle qui est décrite ici.

II. *dem.a., pl.* **those;** (*a*) ce, (*before vowel or h mute*) cet; *f.* cette; *pl.* ces; (*for emphasis and in opposition to* **this, these**) ce . . .-là, cet . . .-là, cette . . .-là, ces . . .-là; **t. book, those books,** ce livre(-là), ces livres (-là); **compare t. edition with these two,** comparez cette édition-là avec ces deux-ci; **t. one,** celui-là, celle-là; **would you like a red rose?—no, I prefer t. white one,** voulez-vous une rose rouge?—non, j'aime mieux cette blanche-là; **at t. time, in those days,** en ce temps-là; à cette époque; **everybody is agreed on t. point,** tout le monde est d'accord là-dessus; **t. fool of a gardener,** cet imbécile de jardinier; **it's t. dog again!** c'est encore ce chien! **t. man will get on!** en voilà un qui fera son chemin! **t. clock (over there),** la pendule que voilà; (*indicating goods in shop window*) **I'd like to have a look at t. table (there),** je voudrais voir cette table-là; **how much is t. one (over) there?** combien coûte celui-là, celle-là? *P:* **t. there table,** cette table-là; (*b*) *F:* **well, how's t. leg of yours?** eh bien, et cette jambe? **I don't like t. house of Anne's, t. house of hers,** je n'aime pas la maison d'Anne, cette maison qu'elle a là; **it's t. wife of his who's to blame,** c'est la faute de sa femme; (*c*) **all those flowers that you have there,** toutes ces fleurs que vous avez là; **those people who take an interest in these things,** les gens, ceux, qui s'intéressent à ces choses-là; (*d*) **I have not t. much confidence in him that I would believe all he says,** je n'ai pas assez de foi en lui pour croire tout ce qu'il dit; (*e*) (**that** *with pl. noun;* **those** *with noun sg. coll.*) **what about t., those, five pounds you owe me?** et ces cinq livres que vous me devez? **those clergy who. . .,** ces membres du clergé qui. . ..

III. *dem.adv.* **1.** (*with adj, or adv. of quantity*) aussi . . . que cela; **t. high,** aussi haut que ça; **can you run t. far, as far as t.?** peux-tu courir aussi loin (que ça)? **it's not (all)** *t.* **beautiful,** ce n'est pas tellement beau. **2.** tellement; si; **is he t. tall?** est-il si grand (que ça)? est-il tellement grand? *F:* **it was** *t.* **cold that the lake had frozen,** il faisait si, tellement, froid que le lac avait gelé.

that[2] [ðət], *rel.pron.sg. & pl., standing for pers. or thg to introduce a defining clause* (*sometimes omitted in rapid speech*) **1.** (*for subject*) qui; (*for object*) que; **the house t. stands at the corner,** la maison qui se trouve au coin; **the letter t. came yesterday,** la lettre qui est arrivée hier; **the letter t. I sent you,** la lettre que je vous ai envoyée; **is this the best t. you can do?** c'est le mieux que vous puissiez faire? vous ne pouvez pas faire mieux (que ça)? **it's the only novel of his t. I read with pleasure,** c'est le seul de ses romans que j'ai lu avec plaisir; **you're the only person t. can help me,** vous êtes la seule personne qui puisse m'aider; **he was one of the greatest men t. ever lived,** c'est un des plus grands hommes qui aient jamais vécu; **miser t. he was, he would not consent,** avare comme il était, il n'a pas voulu y consentir. **2.** (*governed by prep., which always follows* **that**) lequel, *f.* laquelle; *pl.* lesquels, *f.* lesquelles; **the envelope t. I put it in,** l'enveloppe dans laquelle je l'ai mis; **the man t. we're talking about,** l'homme dont nous parlons; **the person t. I gave it to,** la personne à laquelle, à qui, je l'ai donné; **the people t. you took it from,** les gens auxquels, à qui, vous l'avez pris; **no one has come t. I know of,** personne n'est venu que je sache. **3.** (*after expression of time*) où; que; **the night t. we went to the theatre,** le soir où nous sommes allés au théâtre; **the time t. I saw him,** la fois, le jour, où je l'ai vu; **during the years t. he had spent in prison,** pendant les années qu'il avait passées en prison.

that[3] [*stressed* ðæt; *unstressed* ðət], *conj.* **1.** (*introducing subordinate clause; often omitted in rapid speech*) que; (*a*) (*of statement, result, reason*) **she said t. she would come,** elle a dit qu'elle viendrait; **he told me t. he was ill,** il m'a dit qu'il était malade; **the idea t. all men are equal,** le concept selon lequel tous les hommes sont égaux; **I'll see to it t. everything is ready,** je veillerai à ce que tout soit prêt; **it is monstrous t. they should treat you so badly,** c'est monstrueux qu'on vous traite si mal; **he's so ill t. he can't work,** il est si malade qu'il est incapable de travailler; **he was so rude t. we refused to see him,** il a été si impoli, que nous avons refusé de le voir; **it is rather t. he hasn't got the time,** c'est plutôt qu'il n'a pas le temps; (*b*) (*of wish + sub. or ind.*) **I wish t. it had never happened,** j'aurai voulu que cela ne soit jamais arrivé; **I hope t. you'll come,** j'espère que vous viendrez; (*c*) (*of purpose +sub.*) (afin) que, pour que, *+sub.*; **they kept quiet so t. he might sleep,** ils ont gardé le silence pour, afin, qu'il puisse dormir; **come nearer so t. I can see you,** approchez, que je vous voie; **I'm telling you, so t. you'll know,** je vous préviens pour que vous soyez au courant; **put it there so t. it won't be forgotten,** mettez-le là pour qu'on ne l'oublie pas. **2.** *esp. Lit:* (*exclamatory*) (*a*) (*expressing sorrow, indignation, etc.*) **t. he should behave like this!** dire qu'il se conduit comme cela! **t. I should live to see such things!** quand je pense que j'aurai vécu pour voir des choses pareilles! (*b*) (*expressing desire +sub.*) **oh t. it were possible!** oh, si c'était possible! plût au Ciel que ce fût possible!

thatch[1] [θætʃ], *s.* (*a*) chaume *m* (de toiture); (*b*) *F:* cheveux *mpl.*

thatch[2], *v.tr.* couvrir (un toit) de, en, chaume; **thatched roof,** toit de chaume; **thatched cottage,** chaumière *f.*

thatcher ['θætʃər], *s.* couvreur *m* en chaume.

thatching ['θætʃiŋ], *s.* **1.** métier *m* de couvreur en chaume. **2.** couverture *f* de chaume.

thaumasite ['θɔːməsait], *s. Miner:* thaumasite *f.*

thaumatrope ['θɔːmətroup], *s. A:* phénakisti(s)cope *m.*

thaumaturge, thaumaturgist ['θɔːmətəːdʒ, -ist], *s.* thaumaturge *m.*

thaumaturgic(al) [θɔːmə'təːdʒik(l)], *a.* thaumaturgique.

thaumaturgy ['θɔːmətəːdʒi], *s.* thaumaturgie *f.*

Thaumetopoea [θɔːmətou'piə], *s. Ent:* thaumetopea *f,* thaumétopée *f.*

thaw[1] [θɔː], *s.* dégel *m;* fonte *f* des neiges; **silver t.,** verglas *m;* **the t. is setting in,** le temps se met, au dégel.

thaw[2]. **1.** *v.tr.* (*a*) dégeler (la neige, etc.); **to t. (out) frozen food,** décongeler, faire dégeler, des aliments congelés; *Aut:* **to t. out the radiator,** dégeler le radiateur; (*b*) **to t. s.o., s.o.'s reserve,** dégeler, dérider, qn; tirer qn de sa réserve. **2.** *v.i.* (*a*) (*of snow, ice*) fondre; (*of frozen food, etc.*) **to t. (out),** se décongeler; dégeler; (*b*) *impers.* **it's thawing,** il dégèle; (*c*) **after dinner he began to t. (out),** après le diner il a commencé à perdre sa froideur, à se dégeler; *F:* **I can't t. out,** je n'arrive pas à me dégeler; **come in and t. out,** entrez et réchauffez-vous.

thawing ['θɔːiŋ], *s.* **1.** dégel *m* (d'un cours d'eau, etc.); fonte *f* (des neiges). **2.** décongélation *f* (d'aliments congelés, etc.).

the[1] [*stressed* ðiː; *unstressed before consonant* ðə; *unstressed before vowel* ði], *def.art.* **1.** le, *f.* la; (*before vowel or h mute*) l'; *pl.* les; (*a*) (*particularizing*) **t. father and (t.) mother,** le père et la mère; **I spoke to t. driver,** j'ai parlé au chauffeur; **give it to t. maid,** donnez-le à la bonne; **t. voice of t. people,** la voix du peuple; **t. roof of t. house,** le toit de la maison; **t. arrival of t. guests,** l'arrivée des invités; **at t. corner,** au coin; **on t. other side,** de l'autre côté; **on t. Monday he fell ill,** le lundi il est tombé malade; **(in) t. year 1939,** (en) l'an 1939; **we went there and back in t. day,** nous avons fait l'aller-retour en un (seul) jour; **far from t. town,** loin de la ville; **t. Greeks,** les Grecs; **t. Bourbons,** les Bourbons; **t. Martins,** les Martin; **t. Emperor William,** l'Empereur Guillaume; **t. poet Keats,** le poète Keats; **Edward t. Seventh,** Édouard Sept; **Alfred t. Great,** Alfred le Grand; **you must be t. Mr Thomas I've heard about,** alors c'est vous le M. Thomas dont j'ai entendu parler; **t. Paris of my youth,** le Paris de ma jeunesse; **t. England of today,** l'Angleterre de nos jours; **she's t. most beautiful woman I know,** c'est la femme la plus belle que je connaisse; **these are t. two oldest books in the library,** voici les deux livres les plus vieux de la bibliothèque; **from t. earliest times,** dès les temps les plus anciens; **it will be finished in a month at t. latest,** on l'aura achevé dans un mois au plus tard; **it's twelve o'clock at t. latest,** c'est tout au plus s'il est midi; **she's t. happiest (one),** c'est elle (qui est) la plus heureuse; **he's, she's t. one!** c'est bien lui, elle! c'est lui, elle, en effet! **she's t. one who works best,** c'est elle qui travaille le mieux; **he's t. one, it's t. man, I told you about,** c'est celui, c'est l'homme, dont je vous ai parlé; **what do you think of t. Rembrandt?** que pensez-vous du Rembrandt? **this incident doesn't lose in t. telling,** cet incident ne perd rien à la narration; **it's very good on the whole, but there is t. occasional mistake,** c'est fort bien en gros, mais il y a quelques petites fautes çà et là; *F:* **well, how's t. throat then?** eh bien, et cette gorge? *P:* **t. wife,** ma femme; ma bourgeoise; *Scot:* **t. McGregor,** le chef du clan McGregor; (*b*) (*with noun in apposition: omitted in Fr.*) **Mr Long, t. manager of the firm,** M. Long, directeur de la maison; (*c*) **you had t. cheek, t. nerve, to tell him so?** vous avez eu l'aplomb de le lui dire? **t. impudence of it!** quelle audace! **I didn't have t. heart to tell him,** je n'ai pas eu le courage de le lui dire; **he hasn't t. patience to wait, t. courage to go on,** il n'a pas la patience d'attendre, assez de courage pour continuer; (*d*) (*used in forming nouns from adjs.*) **t. beautiful,** le beau; **words borrowed from t. French,** mots empruntés au français; **translated from t. Russian,** traduit du russe; **t. poor, t. rich,** les pauvres, les riches; **t. wounded,** les blessés; (*e*) *F:* **he's got t. toothache, t. measles,** il a mal aux dents; il a la rougeole; (*f*) (*generalizing*) **t. dog is a carnivorous mammal,** le chien est un mammifère carnivore; **t. owl sees well at night,** le hibou voit bien la nuit; **who invented t. wheel?** qui a inventé la roue? (*g*) (*distributive*) **to be paid by t. hour,** être payé à l'heure; **eight apples to t. kilo,** huit pommes au kilo; **thirty miles to t. gallon** = dix litres aux cent kilomètres; **my car does thirty (miles) to t. gallon** = ma voiture consomme dix litres au cent. **2.** (*demonstrative in Fr.*) ce, (*before vowel or h mute*) cet, *f.* cette, *pl.* ces; **I was absent at t. time,** j'étais absent à cette époque, à ce moment-là; **it's just what I want at t. moment,** c'est justement ce qu'il me faut en ce moment; **I'll see him in t. summer,** je le verrai cet été; **well, did t. wedding go off all right?** et cette noce, ça s'est bien passé? **do leave t. child alone!** mais laissez-la donc, cette enfant! **he experienced t. feeling that . . .,** il a eu cette sensation que . . .. **3.** (*stressed*) [ðiː] **are you descended from** *t.* **Cromwell, from** *t.* **Wordsworth?** êtes-vous un descendant du Cromwell de l'histoire, du poète Wordsworth? **her father is Professor X,** *t.* **Professor X,** son père est le professeur X, le grand, le célèbre, professeur X; **a certain Charles Dickens—not** *t.* **Charles Dickens,** un certain Charles Dickens—mais non pas le célèbre Charles Dickens; **he's** *t.* **surgeon here,** c'est lui le grand chirurgien ici; **Maurice's is** *t.* **shop for furniture,** la maison Maurice est la meilleure, la seule, pour les meubles; **this is** *t.* **boot for winter wear,** c'est la bottine entre toutes pour la saison d'hiver.

the[2], *adv.* (*preceding an adj. or adv. in the comparative degree*) (*a*) **I am all t. more, the less, surprised because . . ., that. . .,** j'en suis d'autant plus, d'autant moins, surpris que . . .; **he does (all) t. more harm,** il n'en fait que plus de mal; **I can understand it all t. better because . . .,** je le conçois d'autant mieux que . . .; **it will be (all) t. easier for you as you are young,** cela vous sera d'autant plus facile que vous êtes jeune; **he ran all t. faster,** il a couru d'autant plus vite; (*b*) **t. sharper the point t. better the needle,** les aiguilles sont d'autant meilleures que leur pointe est fine; **t. sooner t. better,** le plus tôt sera le mieux; **t. less said about it t. better,** moins on en parlera mieux cela vaudra; **t. fewer the joys of life, t. more we value them,** on attache plus de prix aux joies de la vie qu'elles sont moins nombreuses; **t. more he drinks t. thirstier he gets,** (tant) plus (qu')il boit, (tant) plus il a soif; **t. more famous the novel to be filmed, t. greater the difficulties of adaptation,** plus célèbre est le roman qu'il s'agit de porter à l'écran, plus l'adaptation s'en avère difficile.

theandric [θi:'ændrik], *a. Theol:* théandrique.

thearchy ['θi:ɑ:ki], *s.* théocratie *f.*

Theatine ['θiətain], *s. Ecc:* théatin, -ine.

theatre ['θiətər], *s.* **1.** (*a*) théâtre *m*; salle *f* de spectacle(s); **national t.,** théâtre national; **open air t.,** théâtre de verdure; **t. in the round,** *U.S:* **arena t.,** théâtre en rond; **to go to the t.,** aller au théâtre, au spectacle; **t. bill,** affiche *f* de théâtre; (*b*) *A:* **picture t.,** (grand) cinéma; **news t.,** cinéma où l'on passe des actualités; (*c*) **the t.,** l'art *m* dramatique; le théâtre; **the English t.,** le théâtre anglais; **this play makes very good t.,** cette pièce se joue très bien; c'est une pièce très bien faite. **2.** (*a*) **(lecture) t.,** amphithéâtre *m*; (*b*) **(operating) t.,** salle d'opération; amphithéâtre. **3.** *Mil:* **the t. of war,** le théâtre de la guerre; **t. of operations,** zone *f* d'action; théâtre des opérations.

theatre(-)goer ['θiətəgouər], *s.* amateur, -trice, du théâtre; habitué, -ée, des théâtres.

theatre(-)going ['θiətəgouiŋ], *s.* fréquentation *f* des théâtres; **the t.(-)g. public,** ceux qui vont au théâtre.

theatrical [θi'ætrikl], *a.* **1.** théâtral, -aux; (almanach, etc.) spectaculaire, des spectacles; **t. performance,** représentation théâtrale; **t. company,** troupe d'acteurs; **t. costumier,** costumier de théâtre. **2.** (*of attitude, etc.*) théâtral, histrionique, affecté.

theatrically [θi'ætrik(ə)li], *adv.* **1.** théâtralement. **2.** théâtralement, avec affectation; (parler) d'un ton ronflant, avec emphase.

theatricals [θi'ætriklz], *s.pl.* **1. amateur t.,** spectacle *m* d'amateurs. **2.** *F:* les gens du théâtre.

thebaic[1] [θi:'beiik], *s. Ch: Pharm:* thébaïque; **t. extract,** extrait *m* thébaïque; extrait d'opium.

Thebaic[2], *a. A.Geog:* de Thèbes.

Thebaid [θi:'beiid, 'θi:-], *Pr.n. A.Geog:* Thébaïde *f.*

thebaine [θi:'beii:n, 'θi:-], *s. Pharm:* thébaïne *f.*

thebaism ['θi:beiizm], *s. Med:* thébaïsme *m.*

Theban ['θi:bən]. *A.Geog:* (*a*) *a.* thébain; (*b*) *s.* Thébain, -aine.

Thebes [θi:bz], *Pr.n. A.Geog:* Thèbes *f.*

Thebesian [θi'bi:ʒn], *a. Anat:* **T. vein, vessel, channel,** veine *f* de Thébésius.

theca ['θi:kə], *s.* (*a*) *Bot:* loge *f*; (*b*) *Fung: etc:* asque *m.*

thecal ['θi:k(ə)l], *a. Bot: etc:* thécal, -aux.

Thecamoebae(a) [θi:kə'mi:bi:, -bi:ə], *s.pl. Prot:* thécamibiens *m*, thécamœbiens *m.*

Thecla ['θeklə], *s. Ent:* thècle *m*, thecla *m.*

thecodont ['θi:koudɔnt], *a. & s. Paleont:* thécodonte (*m*).

Thecodontia [θi:kou'dɔn(t)ʃiə], *s.pl. Paleont:* thécodontes *m.*

Thecophora [θi(:)'kɔfərə], *s.pl. Rept:* thécophores *m.*

Thecosomata [θi:kou'soumətə], *s.pl. Moll:* thécosomes *m.*

thé-dansant ['tei'dɑ̃sɑ̃], *s. O:* thé-dansant *m*, *pl.* thés-dansant.

thee[1] [ði:], *pers. pron., objective case A: & Poet:* (*except as used in prayers, etc.*) **1.** (*unstressed*) (*a*) te; (*before a vowel or h mute*) t'; **we beseech t.,** nous te supplions; **I adore t.,** je t'adore; **I will tell t.,** je te le dirai; (*b*) (*refl.*) **get t. gone!** va-t'en! **sit t. down,** assieds-toi. **2.** (*stressed*) toi; **this is for t.,** ceci est pour toi; **he thinks of t.,** il pense à toi.

thee[2], *v.tr. A: & Dial:* **to t. and thou s.o.,** tutoyer qn.

theft [θeft], *s.* vol *m*; *Jur:* **aggravated t.,** vol qualifié; **petty t.,** larcin *m*; **to commit (a) t.,** commettre un vol; **to accuse s.o. of t.,** accuser qn de vol; **t. from a letter, from a parcel,** spoliation *f* d'une lettre, d'un colis.

theftproof ['θeftpru:f], *a.* (véhicule, etc.) muni d'un dispositif antivol, d'un dispositif de sécurité; (serrure, etc.) antivol, de sécurité.

theic ['θi:ik], *s. Med:* buveur, -euse, de thé qui en abuse, qui s'intoxique.

theiform ['θi:ifɔ:m], *a. Bot:* théiforme.

theileriasis [θailə'raiəsis], **theileriosis** [θailiəri'ousis], *s. Vet:* theilériose *f.*

theine ['θi:i(:)n], *s. Ch:* théine *f.*

their ['ðɛər]. *poss.a.* **1.** (*a*) leur, *f.* leur; *pl.* leurs; **t. neighbour(s),** leur(s) voisin(s); **t. idea(s),** leur(s) idée(s); **one of t. friends,** un(e) de leurs ami(e)s; un(e) ami(e) à eux, à elles; **t. father and mother,** leur père et leur mère; leurs père et mère; **they fell on t. backs,** ils sont tombés sur le dos; **t. eyes were torn out,** on leur a arraché les yeux; **there they stood with t. hats on t. heads,** ils étaient là, le chapeau sur la tête; **they've hurt t. feet,** ils se sont fait mal aux pieds; **t. eyes are blue,** ils ont les yeux bleus; **they have a car of t. own,** ils ont leur propre voiture (à eux); (*b*) **T. Majesties,** leurs Majestés. **2. they knew t. Homer from beginning to end,** ils savaient leur Homère d'un bout à l'autre. **3.** (*after indef. pron.*) *F:* **nobody in t. right mind. . .,** personne jouissant de bon sens . . .; **a person can't help t. birth,** on ne peut pas remédier à sa naissance.

theirs ['ðɛəz], *poss.pron.* (*a*) le leur, la leur, les leurs; **here are his books, t. are on the table,** voici ses livres, les leurs sont sur la table; **this house is t.,** cette maison est la leur, est à eux, à elles, leur appartient; **our house has more bedrooms than t.,** notre maison a plus de chambres que la leur; **I wrote to my friends and to t.,** j'ai écrit à mes amis et aux leurs; **a friend of t.,** un ami à eux, à elles; un de leurs amis; **it's no business of t.,** ce n'est pas leur affaire; *Pej:* **that pride of t.,** leur orgueil; cet orgueil dont ils ne peuvent se défaire; (*b*) (*their family*) **I'm interested in them and (in) t.,** je m'intéresse à eux et aux leurs.

theism[1] ['θi:izm], *s. Theol:* théisme *m.*

theism[2], *s. Med:* théisme *m*; intoxication *f* par le thé.

theist ['θi:ist], *s. Theol:* théiste *mf.*

theistic [θi:'istik], *a. Theol:* théiste.

thelitis [θi(:)'laitis], *s. Med:* thélite *f*; inflammation *f* du mamelon.

thelyphonid [θə'lifənid], *a. & s. Arach:* thélyphone (*m*).

Thelyphonidae [θeli'fɔnidi:], *s.pl. Arach:* thélyphonidés *m.*

thelytokous [θə'litəkəs], **thelyotokous** [θeli'ɔtəkəs], *a. Biol:* thélytopque.

thelytoky [θə'litəki], **thelyotoky, thelytocia** [θeli'ɔtəki, -'touʃiə], *s. Biol:* thélytoquie *f.*

them [ðem, ðəm], *pers. pron. pl., objective case.* **1.** (*unstressed*) (*a*) (*direct*) les *mf*; (*indirect*) leur *mf*; **I like t.,** je les aime; **have you seen t.?** les avez-vous vu(e)s? **call t.,** appelez-les; **give t. some,** donnez-leur-en; **she was writing t. a letter,** elle leur écrivait une lettre; **I'll tell t. so,** je le leur dirai; **give it (to) t.,** donnez-le-leur; **he gave t. to t.,** il les leur a donnés; **give t. to t.,** donnez-les-leur; **speak to t.,** parlez-leur; **look at t.,** regardez-les; (*b*) **they took the keys away with t.,** ils ont emporté les clefs avec eux; (*c*) (*refl.*) *A: & Lit:* **they made t. an idol,** ils se sont fait une idole; **then they bethought t. that . . .,** puis ils s'avisèrent que . . .. **2.** (*stressed*) eux, *f.* elles; **he admires his brother more than t.,** il admire son frère plus qu'eux; **I don't like** *t.* **at all,** je ne les aime pas du tout, eux; **I'm thinking of t.,** c'est à eux, à elles, que je pense; **this book belongs to t.,** ce livre est à eux, à elles; *P:* **he's one of** *t.*, c'est un pédé, une tapette. **3.** (*other prep. combinations*) **one or two of t.,** un ou deux d'entre eux; une ou deux d'entre elles; **every one of t. was killed,** ils ont été tous tués; **he's one of t.,** il est de leur bande; **the four of t. went to the cinema together,** tous les quatre sont allés au cinéma ensemble; **there were three of t.,** ils, elles, étaient trois; il y en avait trois; **he's eaten six of t.,** il en a mangé six; **give me half of t.,** donnez-m'en la moitié; **several, many, most, of t.,** plusieurs, nombre, la plupart, d'entre eux; **both of t. saw me,** ils m'ont vu tous (les) deux; **I don't wear all of t., t. all,** je ne les porte pas tous; **neither of t.,** ni l'un ni l'autre; **I didn't see either of t.,** je n'ai vu ni l'un ni l'autre; **none of t.,** aucun d'eux; **I don't like any of t.,** il n'y a pas un seul qui me plait; **it's very kind of t. (to come),** c'est très aimable à eux (d'être venus); **walk in front of t.,** marchez devant eux; **what shall we do with t.?** qu'allons-nous en faire? **lay the tables and put some flowers on t.,** préparez les tables et mettez-y des fleurs; **here are the bottles but there is no wine in t.,** voici les bouteilles mais il n'y a pas de vin dedans; **the committee has devoted great care to the task before t.,** les membres de la commission ont donné beaucoup d'attention à la tâche qui leur incombait. **4.** (*disjunctive nom.*) **it's t.!** c'est eux, elles! ce sont eux, elles! les voilà! **isn't that t. coming to meet us?** est-ce que ce n'est pas eux qui viennent à notre rencontre? **we're not as rich as t.,** nous ne sommes pas si riches qu'eux; *F: O:* **them's my sentiments,** voilà ce que je pense, moi; *P:* **give me t. (there) books,** donne-moi ces livres-là. **5.** (*after indef. pron.*) *F:* **when anyone comes she says to t. . . .,** quand quelqu'un vient elle lui dit . . .; **nobody has so much to worry t.,** personne n'a tant d'ennuis; **even if you dislike a person you must be fair to t.,** même quand on n'aime pas les gens il faut leur rendre justice, il faut agir loyalement avec eux.

thematic [θi:'mætik], *a. Mus: Gram:* thématique; **t. catalogue,** catalogue thématique.

theme [θi:m], *s.* **1.** sujet *m*, thème *m* (d'un discours, etc.); canevas *m*, trame *f* (d'un film, etc.); **t. for discussion, for an essay,** matière *f* d'une discussion, d'une dissertation. **2.** *Sch: & NAm:* dissertation; exercice *m* littéraire. **3.** *Gram:* thème, radical, -aux *m* (d'un mot). **4.** *Mus:* thème, motif *m*; **t. with variations,** air varié; **t. song, tune,** mélodie principale, chanson leitmotiv (d'un film, etc.); indicatif (musical) (d'un artiste, etc.). **5.** *Hist:* thème (de l'Empire byzantin).

Themis ['θemis], *Pr.n.f. Gr.Myth: & Astr:* Thémis.

Themistocles [θi'mistəkli:z], *Pr.n.m. Gr.Hist:* Thémistocle.

themselves [ðəm'selvz, *stressed* ðem-], *pers.pron. pl.* (*a*) (*emphatic*) eux-mêmes, *f.* elles-mêmes; **they did it t.,** ils l'ont fait eux-mêmes; **it was the pilots t. who were against the plan,** c'étaient les pilotes eux-mêmes qui s'opposaient au projet; **they t. are resigned to it,** eux, pour leur part, s'y sont résignés; **they think of nobody but t.,** ils ne pensent qu'à eux; (*after illness, etc.*) **they're not (quite) t. again yet,** ils ne sont pas encore complètement remis; (*b*) (*refl.*) **they've hurt t.,** ils se sont fait mal; **they're working t. to death,** ils se tuent de travail; **they're going to buy t. a new car,** ils vont s'offrir une nouvelle voiture; **they keep t. to t.,** ils sont très casaniers, peu accueillants; (*c*) (*after prep.*) **they were standing in a corner by t.,** ils étaient tout seuls dans un coin; **they've brought it on t.,** ils se le sont attiré; **they were whispering among t.,** ils chuchotaient entre eux; (*d*) (*after indef. pron.*) *F:* **nobody could blame t. if. . .,** personne ne pourrait se le reprocher si . . ..

then [ðen], *adv., conj. & s.*

I. *adv.* **1.** (*a*) alors; en ce temps-là; à cette époque; **I was t. living in London, I was living in London t.,** à ce moment-là, à cette époque, en ce temps-là, je demeurais à Londres; **what were you doing t.?** que faisiez-vous alors? **the t. existing system,** le système qui existait à cette époque, à ce moment-là; **t. and there, there and t.,** séance tenante; sur-le-champ; **I kissed her there and t.,** je l'ai embrassée tout de go; (*b*) (*in space*) **on the left the church, t. a few old houses,** à gauche l'église, puis quelques vieilles maisons. **2.** puis, ensuite, alors; **we'll have soup first (and) t. some fish,** on prendra d'abord du potage (et), ensuite, et puis, du poisson; **they were in France and t. they went to Spain,** ils étaient en France et ensuite ils sont allés en Espagne; **what t.?** et puis? et puis quoi? et (puis) après? et (puis) alors? alors quoi? **3.** d'ailleurs; aussi (bien); et puis; **and t. there are the children to be considered,** et puis, et aussi, il faut penser aux enfants; **I haven't the time, and t. it isn't my business,** je n'ai pas le temps, d'ailleurs, aussi bien, ce n'est pas mon affaire; **it's beautiful material, but t. it is expensive,** c'est une belle étoffe, mais aussi elle coûte cher.

II. *conj.* en ce cas, donc, alors; **if you want to go, well t. go! well, go t.!** si vous voulez partir, eh bien (alors) partez! partez donc! **well t., you're coming?** alors vous viendrez? **t. you'd better stay,** s'il en est ainsi vous feriez mieux de rester; **but t. . . .,** mais c'est que . . .; **(but) t. you should have told him so,** en ce cas vous auriez dû le lui dire; **what's the matter with you t.?** qu'avez-vous donc? **he can't come tonight—what shall we do t.?** il ne peut pas venir ce soir—et alors, nous, qu'est-ce que nous allons faire? **you knew all the time t.?** vous le saviez donc d'avance? **the world, t., was ready for the Messiah,** ainsi le monde était prêt pour le Messie; *Gram: F:* **t. clause,** apodose *f.*

III. *quasi s.* ce temps-là; cette époque-là; **before t.,** avant ce moment-là; avant cette époque; avant cela; **I'll have finished it by t.,** je l'aurai terminé avant ce moment-là, avant cela; **by t. they had gone,** ils étaient déjà partis; ils étaient partis entre-temps, dans l'intervalle; **will you have finished by t.?** est-ce que vous aurez fini d'ici là? **until t.,** (i) jusqu'alors; (ii) jusque-là; **(ever) since t., from t. on,** dès lors; depuis ce temps-là; **between now and t.,** d'ici là; **every now and t.,** de temps en temps; de temps à autre.

thenar ['θi:nər], *s. Anat:* **1.** thénar *m*; **t. eminence, prominence,** (éminence *f*) thénar. **2.** paume *f* (de la main); plante *f* (du pied).

thenardite [θə'nɑ:dait], *s. Miner:* thénardite *f.*

thence [ðens], *adv. A: & Lit:* **1.** de là; **we went to Paris and (from) t. to Rome,** nous sommes allés à Paris et de là à Rome. **2.** pour cette raison; par conséquent; **it would not t. follow that. . .,** il ne s'ensuivrait pas que . . .; il ne faudrait pas en conclure que . . ..

thenceforth, thenceforward ['ðens'fɔ:θ, -'fɔ:wəd], *adv. A: & Lit:* **(from) t.,** dès lors, à partir de ce jour; depuis cette époque; désormais.

theo- ['θi:ou, θi(:)'ɔ], *comb.fm.* théo-.

Theobald ['θi:əbɔ:ld], *Pr.n.m.* Thibau(l)t.

Theobroma [θi:ou'broumə], *s. Bot:* theobroma *m*, théobrome *m.*

theobromine [θi:ou'broumi(:)n], *s. Ch:* théobromine *f.*

theocentric [θi:ou'sentrik], *a. Theol:* théocentrique.

theocentrism [θi:ou'sentrizm], *s. Theol:* théocentrisme *m.*

theocracy [θi:'ɔkrəsi], *s.* théocratie *f.*

theocrat ['θi:əkræt], *s.* théocrate *m.*

theocratic [θi:ə'krætik], *a.* théocratique.

theocratically [θi:ə'krætik(ə)li], *adv.* théocratiquement.
Theocritean [θi:ɔkri'ti:ən], *a.* de Théocrite.
Theocritus [θi:'ɔkritəs], *Pr.n.m. Gr.Lit:* Théocrite.
theodicy [θi:'ɔdisi], *s. Phil:* théodicée *f.*
theodolite [θi:'ɔdəlait], *s. Surv:* théodolite *m*; **transit t.,** théodolite à boussole.
Theodora [θi:ə'dɔ:rə], *Pr.n.f.* (*a*) Théodora; (*b*) **St T.,** sainte Théodore.
Theodore ['θi:ədɔ:r], *Pr.n.m.* Théodore; *Ecc.Hist:* **T. of Tarsus,** Théodore de Cantorbéry.
Theodoric [θi:'ɔdərik], *Pr.n.m.* **1.** *Hist:* **T. the Great,** Théodoric le Grand. **2.** *Fr.Hist:* Thierri, Thierry, Théodoric.
Theodosian [θi:ə'dousiən, -'douʃ(i)ən], *a. Hist:* (code, etc.) théodosien.
Theodosius [θi:ə'dousiəs, -'douʃ(i)əs], *Pr.n.m. Rom.Hist:* Théodose.
Theodotian [θi:ə'douʃ(i)ən], *s. Hist:* théodotien *m.*
theogonic [θi:ə'gɔnik], *a.* théogonique.
theogonist [θi:'ɔgənist], *s.* théogoniste *m.*
theogony [θi:'ɔgəni], *s.* théogonie *f.*
theologal [θi:'ɔləg(ə)l]. *R.C.Ch:* **1.** *a.* théologal, -aux. **2.** *s.* (*pers.*) théologal, -aux *m.*
theologian [θi:ə'loudʒ(i)ən], *s.* théologien *m*; *R.C.Ch:* **canon t.,** théologal, -aux *m.*
theological [θi:ə'lɔdʒikl], *a.* théologique; **the (three) t. virtues,** les (trois) vertus théologales; **t. college,** séminaire *m*; scolasticat *m.*
theologically [θi:ə'lɔdʒik(ə)li], *adv.* théologiquement.
theologus [θi:'ɔləgəs], *s. R.C.Ch:* théologal, -aux *m.*
theology [θi:'ɔlədʒi], *s.* théologie *f.*
theomachy [θi:'ɔməki], *s. Gr.Myth:* guerre *f* des dieux.
theomancy ['θiəmænsi], *s.* théomancie *f.*
theomania [θi:ou'meiniə], *s. Med:* théomanie *f.*
theomaniac [θi:ou'meiniæk], *s. Med:* théomaniaque *mf.*
theomorphic [θi:ou'mɔ:fik], *a.* qui a la forme, l'apparence, de Dieu.
theomythology [θi:oumi'θɔlədʒi], *s.* théomythologie *f.*
Theopaschite [θi:ou'pæskait], *s. Rel.H:* théopaschite *m*, théopathite *m.*
theophany [θi:'ɔfəni], *s.* théophanie *f.*
theophilanthropic [θi:oufilən'θrɔpik], *a. Fr.Hist:* théophilanthropique.
theophilanthropist [θi:oufi'lænθrəpist], *s. Fr.Hist:* théophilanthrope *m.*
theophilanthropy [θi:oufi'lænθrəpi], *s. Fr.Hist:* théophilanthropie *f*, théophilanthropisme *m.*
Theophilus [θi:'ɔfiləs], *Pr.n.m.* Théophile.
theophobia [θi:ou'foubiə], *s.* théophobie *f.*
Theophrastian [θi:ou'fræstiən], *a. Gr.Phil:* de Théophraste.
Theophrastus [θi:ou'fræstəs], *Pr.n.m. Gr.Phil:* Théophraste.
theophylline [θi:ou'fili:n], *s. Ch:* théophylline *f.*
theopneust(ic) ['θi:ɔpnju:st, θi:ɔp'nju:stik], *a.* théopneustique.
theopneusty, -neustia [θi:ɔp'nju:sti, -'nju:stiə], *s.* théopneustie *f.*
theorbo [θi'ɔ:bou], *s. A.Mus:* téorbe *m*, théorbe *m.*
theorem ['θi:ərəm], *s. Mth: Ph: etc:* théorème *m.*
theorematic [θi:ərə'mætik], *a.* théorématique.
theoretical [θi:ə'retikl], *a.* (raisonnement, etc.) théorique; (doctrine, etc.) théorétique; **t. chemistry,** chimie pure; **t. mechanics,** mécanique rationnelle; **t. physics,** physique théorique; **t. physicist,** (i) expert *m*, (ii) étudiant, -ante, en physique théorique; **it's only t.,** ce n'est que de la théorie.
theoretically [θi:ə'retik(ə)li], *adv.* théoriquement.
theoretician [θi:ərə'tiʃ(ə)n], *s.* théoricien, -ienne.
theoretics [θi:ə'retiks], *s.pl.* (*usu. with sg. const.*) théorétique *f*; **t. and practice,** la théorie et la pratique.
theoria [θi:'ɔ:riə], *s. Lit:* perception *f* de la beauté.
theoric [θi:'ɔrik], *a. Gr.Ant:* (impôt, etc.) théorique.
theorician [θi:ə'riʃ(ə)n], **theorist** ['θi:ərist], *s.* théoricien, -ienne.
theorization [θi:ərai'zeiʃ(ə)n], *s.* théorisation *f* (d'une opinion politique, etc.).
theorize ['θi:əraiz]. **1.** *v.i.* théoriser; faire de la théorie, se lancer dans des théories; **to t. about politics,** bâtir, construire, des théories politiques. **2.** *v.tr.* théoriser (une opinion scientifique, etc.).
theorizer ['θi:əraizər], *s.* théoricien, -ienne; homme, femme, à théories.
theorizing ['θi:əraiziŋ], *s.* (*a*) théorisation *f*; création *f* de théories; (*b*) théories *fpl*; idéologie *f.*
theory[1] ['θi:əri], *s.* théorie *f*; **the t. that . . .,** la théorie selon laquelle . . .; **in t.,** en théorie; **this plan is good in t.,** ce plan est excellent en théorie; **he has a t. that we ought to abolish the gold standard,** selon sa thèse il faudrait abolir l'étalon or; *Mth: Cmptr: etc:* **graph t.,** théorie des graphes; **set t.,** théorie des ensembles; **queueing t.,** théorie des files d'attente; **automata t.,** théorie des automates; **decision t.,** théorie de la décision.
theory[2] [θi:'ɔ:ri], *s.* (*a*) *Gr.Ant:* théorie *f*; (*b*) *Lit:* théorie; procession solennelle.
theosophical [θi:ə'sɔfikl], *a.* théosophique.
theosophism [θi:'ɔsəfizm], *s.* théosophisme *m.*
theosophist [θi:'ɔsəfist], *s.* théosophe *mf.*
theosophy [θi:'ɔsəfi], *s.* théosophie *f.*
theralite ['θiərəlait], *s. Miner:* théralite *f.*
Theramenes [θi'ræmini:z], *Pr.n.m. Gr.Hist:* Théramène.
Therapeutae [θerə'pju:ti:], *s.pl. Rel.H:* thérapeutes *m.*
therapeutic [θerə'pju:tik]. **1.** *a.* (*a*) *Med:* thérapeutique; **therapeutic dose,** dose thérapeutique; (*b*) *Rel.H:* thérapeutique; **T. monk,** thérapeute *m.* **2.** *s. Rel.H:* thérapeute, thérapeutride *f.*
therapeutically [θerə'pju:tik(ə)li], *adv. Med:* thérapeutiquement.
therapeutics [θerə'pju:tiks], *s.pl.* (*usu. with sg. const.*) *Med:* thérapeutique *f*, thérapie *f.*
therapeutist [θerə'pju:tist], *s. Med: O:* thérapeute *mf*, thérapeutiste *mf.*
theraphose ['θerəfous], *s. Arach:* théraphose *f*, téraphose *f.*
therapist ['θerəpist], *s.* thérapeute *mf*, thérapeutiste *mf*; **occupational t.,** spécialiste *mf* de thérapie rééducative; **beauty t.,** esthéticien, -ienne.
Therapsida [θə'ræpsidə], *s.pl. Paleont: Rept:* thérapsidés *m.*
therapy ['θerəpi], *s. Med:* thérapeutique *f*, thérapie *f*; **occupational t.,** thérapeutique occupationnelle; thérapie rééducative; **speech t.,** rééducation *f* de la parole; phoniatrie *f*; orthophonie *f*; **cancer t.,** thérapie du cancer; **(deep) X-ray t.,** traitement *m*, thérapie, par rayons X (en profondeur); **myofunctional t.,** thérapeutique fonctionnelle musculaire; myothérapie *f*; **radiation t.,** radiothérapie *f*; *Dent:* **vaccine t.,** vaccinothérapie *f*; **caries t.,** traitement de la carie; *Psy:* **group t.,** sociatrie *f.*
there [*stressed* ðεər, *unstressed* ðər], *adv., int. & s.*
I. *adv.* **1.** (*stressed*) (*a*) là, y; **t. there are rocks** ['ðεə, ðərɑ:, 'rɔks], là il y a des rochers; **the keys aren't t.,** les clefs ne sont pas là, n'y sont pas; **put it t.,** (i) mettez-le là; (ii) *F:* (*when shaking hands*) tope là! **what are you doing t.?** qu'est-ce que vous faites là? **he's t. in the kitchen,** il est là dans la cuisine; **he's still t.,** il est encore là; il y est toujours; **we're still living t.,** nous y habitons toujours; **does he work t.?** c'est là qu'il travaille? **we'll soon be t. now,** nous voilà bientôt arrivés; **we're t.!** nous voilà arrivés! **who's t.?** (i) qui est là? (ii) *Tp:* qui est à l'appareil? **t. or thereabouts,** là ou tout près; **I owe him £6, t. or thereabouts,** je lui dois à peu près, environ, £6; *F:* **to be all t.,** (i) être malin, avisé, débrouillard, dégourdi, dessalé; (ii) avoir toute sa raison; **he's all t.,** c'est un malin, un homme capable; il n'est pas manchot; **he's not all t.,** (i) il n'a pas les yeux en face des trous; il a un (petit) grain; il est marteau; (ii) c'est un minus, un crétin; (*b*) **I'm going t.,** j'y vais; **just to go t. and back,** ne faire qu'aller et revenir; **a hundred kilometres t. and back,** cent kilomètres aller et retour; **you can be t. and back in five minutes, in two days,** tu seras de retour en cinq minutes; tu peux faire l'aller-retour en deux jours; (*c*) *F:* (*emphatic*) (*when appended to noun or pron.*) -là; **give me that book t.,** donnez-moi ce livre-là; **that man t. always comes,** cet homme-là vient toujours; **your friend t.,** votre ami que voilà; **hey! you t.!** hé, vous là-bas! **hello t.!** hé! bonjour! salut! *Nau:* **on deck, t.!** ohé du pont! **hurry up t.!** dépêchez-vous là-bas! **move along t., please!** circulez, s'il vous plaît! (*d*) (*calling attention to s.o., sth.*) **there is, are . . .,** voilà . . .; **there's the bell ringing,** voilà la cloche qui sonne; **t. they are!** les voilà! **t. she comes!** la voilà qui vient! **t. he is coming in,** le voilà qui entre; **the music is about to begin—t. it goes,** la musique va commencer—la voilà; **t. he goes, grumbling again!** voilà qu'il recommence à rouspéter; **there's gratitude for you!** en voilà de la reconnaissance! **there's a good boy!** tu seras bien gentil! **take it, there's a dear!** prends-le, tu seras bien gentil! **t. it is,** le voilà! **ah!** *t.* **you are!** ah! (i) vous voilà! te voilà! (ii) vous voilà enfin! **t. you are!** *F:* **t. you go!** (et) voilà! tenez! tiens! **just press the button and t. you are!** vous n'avez qu'à appuyer sur le bouton et ça y est! **t. you are! what did I tell you?** là! qu'est-ce que je t'avais dit? **2.** (*a*) **t. is, are,** il y a, il est; **t. was,** il y avait, il était; **t. will be,** il y aura; **t. was once a king,** il était, il y avait, une fois un roi; *B:* **God said "let t. be light": and t. was light,** Dieu dit "que la lumière soit": et la lumière fut; **t. was singing and dancing,** on a chanté et dansé; **t. was very little dinner eaten that evening,** ce soir-là on a mangé très peu au dîner; **t. was a lot of talking over breakfast,** on parlait beaucoup au petit déjeuner; **there's a page missing,** il manque une page; **t. is only one,** il n'y en a qu'un; **there's some left,** il y en a qui reste; **there's one slice left,** il en reste une tranche; **t. isn't any,** il n'y en a pas; **there's someone at the door,** il y a quelqu'un à la porte; **t. was a knock at the door,** on a frappé à la porte; **there's no stopping him,** on ne saurait l'arrêter; impossible de l'arrêter; **t. appeared to be someone in the room,** on avait l'impression qu'il y avait quelqu'un dans la pièce; (*b*) **t. comes a time when . . .,** il arrive un moment où . . .; **t. only remains for me to thank Mr X,** il ne me reste qu'à remercier M. X. **3.** (*stressed*) quant à cela; en cela; sur ce sujet; **t. you are mistaken,** quant à cela vous vous trompez; c'est là que vous vous trompez; **t. we differ,** sur ce sujet nous ne sommes pas d'accord; **there's the difficulty,** voilà la difficulté; c'est là qu'est la difficulté; **(well), t. it is,** (i) eh bien, voilà! (ii) rien à faire; pas moyen; il n'y a pas mèche; *F:* **t. you've got me, you have me! you've got me t.!** ça, ça me dépasse.
II. *int.* (*stressed*) voilà! **t. now!** (i) voilà! (ii) là, voyez-vous! allons bon! **t. now, that's done!** là! voilà qui est fait; **t. (now), I was sure it would happen!** ça y est! j'en étais sûr; **t. (you are), I told you so,** là! je vous l'avais bien dit! **t., take this book,** tenez! prenez ce livre; **t.! t.! (now) don't worry!** là là, ne vous inquiétez pas! **I'll do as I like, so t.!** je ferai comme il me plaira, voilà!
III. *quasi s.* (*that place*) **we go to Paris and from t. to Rome,** nous allons à Paris et de là à Rome; **from t. to the village it's 10 km,** de là au village, il y a 10 km; **he left t. last night,** il est parti (de là) hier soir; **I come from t.,** (i) j'en viens; (ii) je suis de là-bas; je suis né là-bas; **they live near Calais, or somewhere round t., near t.,** ils habitent près de Calais ou quelque part par là; **put it over t.,** mettez-le là-bas; **that horse over t.,** le cheval que voilà; **he lives down t., up t.,** il habite là-bas, là-haut; **everything's different out t.,** tout est différent là-bas; **in t.,** là-dedans; là; **on t.,** là-dessus; **under t.,** là-dessous.
thereabouts ['ðεərə'bauts], *adv.* **1.** près de là; dans le voisinage; dans ces parages; **it's the largest house t.,** c'est la plus grande maison du voisinage; **he lives in Brighton or t.,** il demeure à Brighton ou près de là, ou quelque part par là; **somewhere t.,** quelque part par là; dans les environs. **2.** à peu près; environ; **the parcel weighs two kilos or t.,** le colis pèse environ deux kilos; **it's four o'clock or t.,** il est à peu près quatre heures; **a thousand pounds or t.,** quelque mille livres; **she's 35 or t.,** elle a environ 35 ans; elle a 35 ans, par là; *Sp:* **he's always there or t.,** il est toujours parmi les gagnants.
thereafter [ðεər'ɑ:ftər], *adv. A: & Lit:* après (cela); par la suite.
thereat [ðεər'æt], *adv. A: & Lit:* là-dessus; à ce sujet; **they wondered greatly t.,** cela les surprit grandement.
thereby [ðεə'bai *when at the end of clause*; 'ðεəbai *when preceding verb*], *adv.* **1.** par ce moyen; de ce fait; de cette façon; par là; *O:* **he stopped to speak to them and t. missed his train,** il s'est arrêté pour leur parler et de ce fait il a manqué son train; **we've published a pamphlet about our village and hope t. to save it,** nous avons publié une plaquette sur notre village dans l'espoir, par ce moyen, de le sauver. **2.** *A: & Dial:* près de là; **he lived t.,** il demeurait tout près; il habitait dans les environs. **3.** *A:* à ce sujet.
therefor ['ðεə'fɔ:r], *adv. A: & Lit:* pour cela.
therefore ['ðεəfɔ:r], *adv.* donc; par conséquent; aussi; **I think, t. I am,** je pense, donc je suis; **I should t. be grateful if you would . . .,** par conséquent je vous serais reconnaissant de vouloir bien . . ., si vous vouliez bien . . .
therefrom [ðεə'frɔm], *adv. A: & Lit:* de là; **it follows t. that . . .,** il suit de là que . . ..
therein [ðεər'in], *adv. A: & Lit:* **1.** en cela; à cet égard; **t. you are mistaken,** en cela vous vous trompez. **2.** (là-)dedans; **all those that live t.,** tous ceux qui y demeurent.
thereinafter ['ðεərin'ɑ:ftər], *adv. Jur:* plus loin; ci-dessous.
thereinbefore ['ðεərinbi'fɔ:r], *adv. Jur:* plus haut; ci-dessus.
thereinunder ['ðεərin'ʌndər], *adv. Jur:* ci-dessous.
thereof [ðεər'ɔv], *adv. A: & Lit:* de cela; en; **he ate t.,** il en mangea; **in lieu t.,** au lieu de cela; *B:* **great was the fall t.,** grande en a été la ruine.
thereon [ðεər'ɔn], *adv. A: & Lit:* (là-)dessus; **the earth and all that is t.,** la terre et tout ce qu'il y a dessus; **t. hangs your fate,** de là dépend votre destin.
Theresa [tə'ri:zə, -'reizə], *Pr.n.f.* Thérèse.
thereto [ðεə'tu:], *adv.* (*a*) *A: & Lit: & Jur:* à cela; y; **he put his signature t.,** il y apposa sa signature; **the house and the garden pertaining t.,** la maison et le jardin qui y

appartient; (*b*) *A:* en outre.

theretofore [ˈðɛətuːˈfɔːr], *adv. A: & Lit:* jusqu'alors; avant cela.

thereunder [ðɛərˈʌndər], *adv. A: & Lit:* (là-)dessous.

thereupon [ˈðɛərəˈpɔn], *adv.* **1.** sur ce; sur quoi; cela dit; cela fait; là-dessus; **t. he left,** sur quoi il est parti. **2.** *A:* dessus. **3.** *Lit:* **there is much to be said t.,** il y aurait beaucoup à dire là-dessus, à ce sujet.

therevid [θəˈrevid], *s. Ent:* thereva *m.*

Therevidae [θəˈrevidiː], *s.pl. Ent:* thérévidés *m.*

therewith [ðɛəˈwið, -ˈwiθ], **therewithal** [ðɛəwiˈðɔːl], *adv. A : & Lit:* **1.** avec cela. **2.** = THEREUPON 1.

Theria [ˈθiəriə], *s.pl. Z:* thériens *m.*

theriac [ˈθiəriæk], *s. A. Pharm:* thériaque *f.*

theriacal [θiˈraiəkl], *a. A. Pharm:* thériacal, -aux.

theridiid [θəˈridiid], *s. Arach:* théridiidé *m.*

Theridiidae [θeriˈdaiidiː], *s.pl. Arach:* théridiidés *m.*

Theriodonta, -dontia, -donts [θiəriouˈdɔntə, -ˈdɔn(t)ʃ(i)ə, -ˈdɔnts], *s.pl. Paleont: Rept:* thériodontes *m.*

therm[1] [θəːm], *s. Ph: etc:* **1.** (*a*) *A:* petite calorie; (*b*) (*in gas industry*) 100 000 Btu (unités britanniques de chaleur). **2.** *NAm:* (*a*) *A:* grande calorie; kilocalorie *f*; (*b*) *A:* petite calorie; (*c*) 1 000 grandes calories, kilocalories, millithermies *f.*

therm[2], *a. Furn:* **t. foot, leg,** pied carré.

thermae [ˈθəːmiː], *s.pl. Rom.Ant:* thermes *m.*

therm(a)esthesia [θəːməsˈθiːziə], *s. Med:* therm(o)esthésie *f.*

thermal[1] [ˈθəːm(ə)l], *a.* **1.** thermal, -aux; **t. water,** eau thermale; **t. baths,** thermes *m.* **2.** *Ph: etc:* thermal, thermique, calorifique; **t. analysis,** analyse *f* thermique; **t. capacity,** capacité *f* thermique; **t. conduction,** conduction *f* de chaleur; **t. conductivity,** conductibilité *f* calorifique, thermique; **t. cycle,** cycle *m* thermique; **t. cycling,** oscillations *fpl* thermiques; **t. diffusion,** diffusion *f* thermique; thermodiffusion *f*; **t. efficiency,** rendement *m* thermique, calorifique; **t. energy,** énergie *f* thermique, calorifique; **t. equilibrium,** équilibre *m* thermique; **t. inertia,** inertie *f* thermique; **t. insulation,** isolation *f* thermique; **t. stress,** contrainte *f* thermique; **t. unit,** unité *f* thermique; unité de chaleur; **British t. unit,** unité (britannique) de chaleur; = 252 grandes calories, kilocalories; = 1055 joules; **t. alarm (device),** thermo-avertisseur *m, pl.* thermo-avertisseurs; **t. power station,** centrale *f* thermique; **t. equator,** équateur *m* thermique; *Atom.Ph:* **t. column,** colonne *f* thermique; **t. cross section,** section *f* efficace pour les neutrons thermiques; **t. excitation,** agitation *f* thermique; **t. neutron,** neutron *m* thermique; **t. reactor,** pile *f*, réacteur *m*, à neutrons thermiques; **t. shield,** bouclier *m*, écran *m*, thermique; **t. utilization factor,** facteur *m* d'utilisation thermique (d'un réacteur); *Ch:* **t. dissociation,** dissociation *f* thermique; **t. ionization,** ionisation *f* (d'origine) thermique; *Med: etc:* **t. radiation,** radiation *f* thermique; **t. shock,** changement *m* brusque de température; impact *m* thermique; *Elcs:* **t. (agitation) noise,** bruit *m* d'origine thermique; *El:* **t. instability,** instabilité *f* thermique; *Bot:* **t. emissivity,** pouvoir *m* d'échange calorifique; *Petr:* **t. cracking,** craquage *m* catalytique.

thermal[2], *s. Meteor: Av:* thermique *m*; ascendance *f.*

thermalize [ˈθəːməlaiz], *v.tr.* **1.** *Ch:* thermaliser (une eau). **2.** *Atom.Ph:* amener (des neutrons, etc.) à l'état thermique.

therman(a)esthesia [θəːmænisˈθiːziə], *s. Med:* thermoanesthésie *f.*

thermanalgesia [θəːmænəlˈdʒiːziə], *s. Med:* thermoanalgésie *f.*

thermantidote [θəːmˈæntidout], *s.* ventilateur réfrigérateur (pour pays chauds).

thermic [ˈθəːmik], *a. Ph: etc:* thermique; calorifique; thermal, -aux.

Thermidor [ˈθəːmidɔːr], *s. Fr.Hist:* thermidor *m.*

thermion [ˈθəːmiən], *s. Atom.Ph:* thermion *m*; électron *m* thermique.

thermionic [θəːmiˈɔnik], *a. Elcs: W.Tel:* thermionique; thermo-ionique; thermoélectronique; **t. current,** courant *m* thermo-ionique, (thermo)électronique; **t. emission,** émission *f* thermionique, thermoélectronique; **t. oscillator,** oscillateur *m* à tubes électroniques; **t. rectifier,** redresseur *m* à tubes électroniques; **t. valve,** *NAm:* **tube,** lampe *f*, tube *m*, thermionique, thermoélectronique; tube à vide.

thermistor [θəːˈmistər], *s. Elcs:* thermistance *f*, thermistor *m.*

thermite, thermit [ˈθəːmait, -mit], *s. R.t.m.* thermite *f*; *Metalw:* **t. welding,** aluminothermie *f.*

thermo- [ˈθəːmou, ˈθəːmə, θə(ː)ˈmɔ], *comb.fm.* thermo-.

thermo(a)esthesia [θəːmouisˈθiːziə], *s. Med:* therm(o)esthésie *f.*

thermoammeter [θəːmouˈæmitər], *s. El:* ampèremètre *m* thermique.

thermoan(a)esthesia [θəːmouænisˈθiːziə], *s.* = THERMAN(A)ESTHESIA.

thermoanalgesia [θəːmouænəlˈdʒiːziə], *s. Med:* thermoanalgésie *f.*

thermoanalysis [θəːmouəˈnælisis], *s. Ch:* analyse *f* thermique.

thermobalance [ˈθəːmoubæləns], *s. Ch: Ph:* thermobalance *f.*

thermobarometer [θəːmoubəˈrɔmitər], *s. Surv: Meteor:* thermobaromètre *m*; hypsomètre *m.*

thermocautery [θəːmouˈkɔːtəri], *s. Surg:* thermocautère *m.*

thermochemical [θəːmouˈkemikl], *a.* thermochimique.

thermochemist [θəːmouˈkemist], *s.* thermochimiste *mf.*

thermochemistry [θəːmouˈkemistri], *s.* thermochimie *f.*

thermocline [ˈθəːmouklain], *s. Oc: etc:* thermocline *f*, métalimnion *m.*

thermocouple [ˈθəːmoukʌpl], *s. El:* couple *m* thermélectrique; thermocouple *m*; **immersion t.,** thermocouple à immersion; **t. wattmeter,** wattmètre *m* à couple thermoélectrique; **t. thermometer,** thermomètre *m* à couple thermoélectrique; canne *f* thermoélectrique.

thermodiffusion [θəːmoudiˈfjuːʒ(ə)n], *s. Ph:* thermodiffusion *f*; diffusion *f* thermique.

thermodynamic [θəːmoudaiˈnæmik], *a.* thermodynamique; **t. temperature scale,** échelle *f* thermodynamique des températures.

thermodynamics [θəːmoudaiˈnæmiks], *s.pl.* (*usu. with sg. const.*) thermodynamique *f.*

thermoelectric(al) [θəːmouiˈlektrik(l)], *a.* thermoélectrique; électrothermique; **thermoelectric couple,** couple *m* thermoélectrique; thermocouple *m*; **t. junction,** couplage *m* thermoélectrique; **t. power,** tension *f* thermoélectrique.

thermoelectricity [θəːmouilekˈtrisiti], *s.* thermoélectricité *f.*

thermoelectrometer [θəːmouilekˈtrɔmitər], *s. El:* électromètre *m* thermique.

thermoelectron [θəːmouiˈlektrɔn], *s. Atom.Ph:* électron *m* thermique; thermion *m*; **t. emission,** émission *f* thermionique.

thermoelectronic [θəːmouelekˈtrɔnik], *a. Ph:* thermoélectronique.

thermoelement [θəːmouˈelimənt], *s. El:* élément *m* thermoélectrique.

thermofission [θəːmouˈfiʃ(ə)n], *s. Atom.Ph:* thermofission *f.*

thermofusion [θəːmouˈfjuːʒ(ə)n], *s. Atom.Ph:* thermofusion *f.*

thermogalvanometer [θəːmougælvəˈnɔmitər], *s. El:* thermogalvanomètre *m.*

thermogenesis [θəːmouˈdʒenisis], *s.* (*a*) *Ph: Ch:* thermogénie *f*; (*b*) *Physiol:* thermogénèse *f.*

thermogenic [θəːmouˈdʒenik], **thermogenous** [θə(ː)ˈmɔdʒinəs], **thermogenetic** [θəːmoudʒiˈnetik], *a. Physiol: etc:* thermogène.

thermogram [ˈθəːməgræm], *s. Ph:* thermogramme *m.*

thermograph [ˈθəːməgræf], *s. Ph:* thermomètre enregistreur; thermographe *m.*

thermography [θə(ː)ˈmɔgrəfi], *s. Ph:* thermographie *f.*

thermohardening [θəːmouˈhɑːdniŋ], *a. & s.* = THERMOSETTING.

thermojunction [ˈθəːmoudʒʌŋ(k)ʃ(ə)n], *s. El:* couplage *m* thermoélectrique.

thermolabile [θəːmouˈleib(a)il], *a. Biol:* (sérum, etc.) thermolabile.

thermolability [θəːmouləˈbiliti], *s. Biol:* thermolabilité *f* (d'une enzyme, etc.).

Thermologic(al) [θəːməˈlɔdʒik(l)], *a. Ph:* thermologique.

thermology [θə(ː)ˈmɔlədʒi], *s. Ph:* thermologie *f.*

thermoluminescence [θəːmouluːmiˈnes(ə)ns], *s. Ph:* thermoluminescence *f.*

thermoluminescent [θəːmouluːmiˈnes(ə)nt], *a. Ph:* thermoluminescent.

thermolysis [θə(ː)ˈmɔlisis], *s.* thermolyse *f.*

thermomagnetic [θəːmoumægˈnetik], *a. Ph:* thermomagnétique.

thermomagnetism [θəːmouˈmægnitizm], *s. Ph:* thermomagnétisme *m.*

thermomechanical [θəːmoumiˈkænikl], *a. Ph:* thermomécanique.

thermometer [θəˈmɔmitər], *s.* (*a*) thermomètre *m*; **centigrade t.,** thermomètre centigrade; **Celsius t.,** thermomètre de Celsius; **Fahrenheit t.,** thermomètre Fahrenheit; **clinical t.,** thermomètre médical, de clinique; **alcohol, mercury, t.,** thermomètre à alcool, à mercure; **gas t.,** thermomètre à gaz; **(self-)recording, (self-)registering, t.,** thermomètre enregistreur; thermographe *m*; **maximum and minimum t.,** thermomètre à maxima et minima; **differential t.,** thermomètre différentiel; **suppressed zero t.,** thermomètre sans zéro; **resistance t.,** thermomètre à résistance (électrique); thermomètre à sonde; **Beckmann t.,** thermomètre de Beckmann; **Réaumur t.,** thermomètre Réaumur; **sling, whirled, t.,** thermomètre à fronde; **dry bulb t.,** thermomètre sec, à boule sèche; **wet bulb t.,** thermomètre mouillé, à boule mouillée; *Ind:* **alarm t.,** thermomètre avertisseur; thermo-avertisseur *m, pl.* thermo-avertisseurs; **the t. is standing at, registers, 10°(C),** le thermomètre indique 10°(C); **I take the t. reading every morning,** je regarde le thermomètre chaque matin; (*b*) *Orn:* **t. bird,** mégapode *m.*

thermometric(al) [θəːmouˈmetrik(l)], *a.* thermométrique.

thermometrograph [θəːmouˈmetrəgræf], *s. Ph:* thermomètre enregistreur; thermographe *m.*

thermometry [θəˈmɔmitri], *s. Ph:* thermométrie *f.*

thermomolecular [θəːmouməˈlekjulər], *a. Ph:* thermomoléculaire; **t. pressure,** suppression thermomoléculaire.

thermomotive [θəːmouˈmoutiv], *a.* (machine, etc.) à air chaud, thermopropulsé.

thermomotor [θəːmouˈmoutər], *s.* moteur *m* à air chaud, propulsé.

thermonastic [θəːmouˈnæstik], *a. Bot:* thermonastique.

thermonasty [ˈθəːmounæsti], *s. Bot:* thermonastie *f.*

thermonatrite [θəːmouˈneitrait], *s. Miner:* thermonatrite *f.*

thermoneutrality [θəːmounjuːˈtræliti], *s. Ch:* thermoneutralité *f.*

thermonuclear [θəːmouˈnjuːkliər], *a. Atom.Ph:* thermonucléaire.

thermoperiodism [θəːmouˈpiəriədizm], *s. Bot:* thermopériodisme *m.*

thermophil(e) [ˈθəːmoufail, -fil]. *Biol:* (*a*) *a.* (bactérie, etc.) thermophile; (*b*) *s.* bactérie *f*, etc., thermophile.

thermophilic [θəːmouˈfilik], **thermophilous** [θə(ː)ˈmɔfiləs], *a. Biol:* thermophile.

thermophone [ˈθəːməfoun], *s.* (*a*) *Elcs:* thermophone *m*; (*b*) *Ph:* thermotéléphone *m.*

thermophosphorescence [θəːmoufɔsfəˈresəns], *s. Ph:* thermoluminescence *f.*

thermopile [ˈθəːməpail], *s. El:* pile *f* thermoélectrique; thermopile *f.*

thermoplastic [θəːmouˈplæstik], *a. & s.* thermoplastique (*m*); **t. materials, thermoplastics,** (matières *f*) thermoplastiques.

thermoplasticity [θəːmouplæsˈtisiti], *s. Ch: etc:* thermoplasticité *f.*

thermopropulsion [θəːmouprəˈpʌlʃ(ə)n], *s. Av:* thermopropulsion *f*; **t. rocket,** fusée thermopropulsée.

thermopropulsive [θəːmouprəˈpʌlsiv], *a. Av:* thermopropulsif.

Thermopsis [θə(ː)ˈmɔpsis], *s. Bot:* thermopsis *m*, thermopside *f.*

Thermopylae [θə(ː)ˈmɔpili(ː)], *Pr.n. Geog:* **(the Pass of) T.,** les Thermopyles *f.*

thermoregulation [θəːmouregjuˈleiʃ(ə)n], *s. Physiol:* thermorégulation *f.*

thermoregulator [θəːmouˈregjuleitər], *s.* thermorégulateur *m*; thermostat *m.*

thermorelay [θəːmouˈriːlei], *s. Ph:* relais *m* thermique.

Thermos [ˈθəːməs], *s.* (marque déposée désignant les articles fabriqués par Thermos (1925) Limited) **T. (flask),** (bouteille *f*) Thermos *m or f inv.*

thermoscope [ˈθəːməskoup], *s. Ph:* thermoscope *m.*

thermoscopic [θəːməˈskɔpik], *a.* thermoscopique.

thermosensitive [θəːmouˈsensitiv], *a.* sensible aux différences de température; thermosensible.

thermosetting [ˈθəːmousetiŋ]. **1.** *a.* (matière plastique) thermodurcissable. **2.** *s.* thermodurcissage *m* (de matières plastiques).

thermosiphon [θəːmouˈsaif(ə)n], *s.* thermosiphon *m.*

thermosphere [ˈθəːməsfiər], *s. Meteor:* thermosphère *f.*

thermostable [θəːmouˈsteibl], *a. Ch: etc:* thermostab(i)le.

thermostat [ˈθəːməstæt], *s.* thermostat *m*, thermorégulateur *m*; *Dom.Ec:* régulateur *m* de température, d'ambiance; **differential expansion t.,** thermostat à dilatation différentielle; **gas, liquid, expansion t.,** thermostat à dilatation gazeuse, liquide; **t. relay,** relais *m* à thermostat.

thermostatic [θəːməˈstætik], *a.* thermostatique; **t. control,** réglage *m*, régulation *f*, (de la température) par thermostat; commande *f* thermostatique; **t. valve,** régulateur *m* à thermostat.

thermostatically [θəːməˈstætik(ə)li], *adv.* au moyen d'un thermostat, par thermostat; **t. controlled,** commandé, réglé, par thermostat.

thermotaxis [θəːmou'tæksis], *s. Biol:* thermotaxie *f.*

thermotherapy [θəːmou'θerəpi], *s. Med: etc:* thermothérapie *f.*

thermotropic [θəːmou'trɔpik], *a. Biol:* thermotropique.

thermotropism [θəː'mɔtrəpizm], *s. Biol:* thermotropisme *m,* thermotactisme *m.*

thermowelded ['θəːmouweldid], *a.* thermosoudé.

thermowelding ['θəːmouweldiŋ], *s.* thermosoudure *f.*

theroid ['θiərɔid], *a.* à penchants bestiaux; bestial, animal.

therology [θiə'rɔlədʒi], *s.* mammalogie *f.*

Theromorpha [θiərou'mɔːfə], *s.pl. Paleont: Rept:* théromorphes *m,* thérопsidés *m.*

theromorphia, -morphism [θiərou'mɔːfiə, -'mɔːfizm], *s. Biol:* thérmorphie *f.*

therophyte ['θiəroufait], *s. Bot:* thérophyte *f.*

Theropoda [θiə'rɔpədə], *s.pl. Paleont: Rept:* théropodes *m,* thérépodes *m.*

Thersites [θəː'saitiːz], *Pr.n.m. Gr.Lit:* Thersite.

thesaurus, *pl.* **-i** [θi'sɔːrəs, -ai], *s.* (*a*) thesaurus *m*; trésor *m* (de la langue grecque, etc.); recueil *m* de connaissances; (*b*) dictionnaire *m* de synonymes.

these. *See* THIS.

Theseus ['θiːsiəs], *Pr.n.m. Myth:* Thésée.

thesis, *pl.* **theses** ['θiːsis, -iːz], *s.* **1.** *Pros:* thésis *f.* **2.** (*a*) *Sch: Log: etc:* thèse *f*; **doctorate t.,** thèse de doctorat; **to uphold, defend, a t.,** soutenir, défendre, une thèse; (*b*) *Sch:* dissertation *f* (d'étudiant).

Thesium ['θiːziəm], *s. Bot:* thésium *m.*

Thespesia [θes'piːʒ(i)ə], *s. Bot:* thespesia *m.*

Thespiae ['θespiiː], *Pr.n. A.Geog:* Thespies.

Thespian ['θespiən]. **1.** *a.* de Thespis; tragique, dramatique. **2.** *s.* acteur, -trice.

Thespis ['θespis], *Pr.n.m. Gr.Lit:* Thespis.

Thessalian [θe'seiliən]. *Geog:* (*a*) *a.* thessalien; (*b*) *s.* Thessalien, -ienne.

Thessalonian [θesə'louniən]. *A.Geog:* (*a*) *a.* thessalonicien; (*b*) *s.* Thessalonicien, -ienne.

Thessalonica [θesə'lɔnikə], *Pr.n. A.Geog:* Thessalonique *f.*

Thessaly ['θesəli], *Pr.n. Geog:* Thessalie *f.*

theta ['θiːtə], *s. Gr.Alph:* thêta *m.*

thetic ['θiːtik], *a. Phil:* thétique.

Thetis ['θetis], *Pr.n.f. Myth:* Thétis.

theurgic(al) [θi'əːdʒik(l)], *a.* théurgique.

theurgist [θi'əːdʒist], *s.* théurgi(s)te *mf,* théurge *mf.*

theurgy [θi'əːdʒi], *s.* théurgie *f.*

thevetin [θə'viːtin], *s. Ch:* thévétine *f.*

thew [θjuː], *s.* (*a*) tendon *m,* muscle *m*; **he has thews of steel,** il a des nerfs d'acier; (*b*) *Fig:* **thews,** ardeur *f,* vigueur *f.*

they [ðei]. **1.** *pers. pron. nom. pl.* (*a*) (*unstressed*) ils, *f.* elles; **t. are dancing,** ils, elles, dansent; **here t. come,** les voici (qui arrivent); **they're rich,** ils sont riches; ce sont des gens riches; **what are t. doing?** que font-ils, -elles? (*b*) (*stressed*) eux, *f.* elles; **t. alone can . . .,** eux seuls, elles seules, peuvent . . .; **we are as rich as t. are,** nous sommes aussi riches qu'eux, qu'elles; *Lit:* **it is t.,** ce sont eux; **it is t. who told me so, t. told me so themselves,** ce sont eux-mêmes qui me l'ont dit; **I guessed that** *t.* **were the newcomers,** j'ai deviné que c'étaient eux les nouveaux venus; *Lit:* **if I were t.,** (si j'étais) à leur place; si j'étais (d')eux; *t.* **know nothing about it,** quant à eux, ils n'en savent rien; (*c*) (*with dem. force*) ceux, *f.* celles; *Lit:* **t. who believe,** ceux, celles, qui croient; **t. do least who talk most,** ceux-là font le moins qui parlent le plus. **2.** (*a*) *indef. pron.* on; **t. say that . . .,** on dit que . . .; **it may not be true, but that's what t. say, they're saying,** ce n'est pas forcément vrai, mais voilà ce qu'on raconte; (*b*) (*after indef. pron.*) *F:* **nobody ever admits they're wrong,** on ne veut jamais reconnaître ses torts.

thial ['θaiəl], *s. Ch:* thial *m.* thioaldéhyde *m.*

thialdine [θai'ældi(ː)n], *s. Ch:* thialdine *f.*

thiamin(e) ['θaiəm(a)in], *s. Bio-Ch:* thiamine *f,* aneurine *f.*

thianthrene [θai'ænθriːn], *s. Ch:* thianthrène *m.*

thiazine ['θaiəzi(ː)n], *s. Ch:* thiazine *f*; **t. dye,** colorant thiazinique.

thiazole ['θaiəzoul], *s. Ch:* thiazole *m.*

thiazoline [θai'æzəli(ː)n], *s. Ch:* thiazoline *f.*

thick [θik], *a., s. & adv.*

I. *a.* **1.** (*of walls, material, etc.*) épais, *f.* épaisse; (*of book, thread, lips, etc.*) gros, *f.* grosse; (*of coal seam*) puissant; **wall one metre t.,** mur qui a un mètre d'épaisseur, qui a une épaisseur d'un mètre, qui est épais d'un mètre; **the t. end of a stick,** le gros bout d'un bâton; **how t. is the ice?** quelle épaisseur a la glace? **to cut into the thickest part,** couper dans l'épais; **t. lipped,** lippu; à grosses lèvres; **t. skinned,** (i) à la peau épaisse; à l'épiderme peu sensible; (ii) *Fig:* (*of pers.*) peu sensible; qui est peu susceptible; **he's t. skinned,** il a une peau de rhinocéros; *Typ:* **t. stroke,** plein *m*; **t. spaced,** (composition) espacée; *Bot: F:* **t. leaf,** crassule *f.* **2.** (*of wheat, forest, etc.*) épais, dru, serré, touffu; (*of hair*) abondant, fourni, épais; (*of crowd*) compact, serré; **t. eyebrows,** sourcils touffus, épais; **t. beard,** barbe fournie, drue; **the crowd was thickest on the square,** c'est sur la place que la foule était le plus dense. **3.** (*a*) (*of liquid*) épais, consistant; visqueux; pâteux; (*of mist, etc.*) dense, épais; (*of weather*) couvert, bouché; (*of darkness*) profond; **t. mud,** boue grasse; *Cu:* **t. sauce,** sauce courte, épaisse; **air t. with smoke,** air épaissi par la fumée; *F:* **to have a t. head,** (i) être bête, être bouché à l'émeri; (ii) (*hangover*) avoir mal aux cheveux, au crâne; (*b*) (*of voice*) étouffé; **to have a t. voice, to be t. of speech,** avoir le parler gras; avoir la langue épaisse, pâteuse; *Mus:* **t. register,** registre le plus bas de la voix; (*c*) *F:* (*of pers.*) obtus; bouché; à la tête dure; **he's really t., he's as t. as two short planks,** il est bête comme ses pieds, sot comme un panier; c'est une tête de bois; **t. skulled, t. witted,** à la tête dure; à l'esprit étroit, épais, obtus. **4.** *F:* intime, très lié; **to be very t. with s.o.,** être très lié, être de mèche, être à tu et à toi, avec qn; **they're as t. as thieves,** ils s'entendent comme larrons en foire. **5.** *F:* excessif, fort; **that's a bit t.!** ça c'est un peu raide! ça c'est un peu fort! non, mais des fois! ça dépasse les bornes!

II. *s.* **1.** (*a*) partie charnue, gras *m* (de la jambe, etc.); **the t. of the thumb,** le gras du pouce; (*b*) **in the t. of the forest,** au beau milieu de la forêt; **in the t. of it, of things,** en plein dedans; **in the t. of the fight,** au (plus) fort, au vif, de la mêlée; **he plunged into the t. of the discussion,** il est intervenu au vif du débat. **2. to go through t. and thin for s.o.,** courir tous les risques, aller contre vent et marée, pour qn; **to follow s.o., stick to s.o., through t. and thin,** suivre qn à travers tous les dangers, tous les obstacles; rester fidèle à qn à travers toutes les épreuves.

III. *adv.* **1.** en couche épaisse; **snow lay t. on the ground,** une neige épaisse, une épaisse couche de neige, couvrait le sol; **table covered t. with dust,** table couverte d'une épaisse couche de poussière; **don't spread the butter too t.,** ne mettez pas trop de beurre sur les tartines; **to cut the bread t.,** couper le pain en tranches épaisses; *F:* **to lay it on a bit t.,** exagérer. **2.** épais, dru; **to sow t.,** semer épais; **t. sown,** semé épais; **where the grass grew t.,** là où l'herbe poussait dru; **his blows fell t. and fast,** il frappait à coups redoublés; les coups pleuvaient dru. **3.** *A:* (parler, chanter) d'une voix étouffée.

thicken ['θik(ə)n]. **1.** *v.tr.* (*a*) épaissir (un mur, etc.); (*b*) épaissir, lier (une sauce); (*c*) *Mil:* **to t. the fire,** augmenter la densité, le volume, du feu. **2.** *v.i.* (*a*) (*of tree trunk, figure, weather, air, etc.*) (s')épaissir; (*b*) (*of sauce*) se lier, épaissir; **the crowd thickens,** la foule augmente; (*c*) (*of plot*) se compliquer, se corser.

thickener ['θik(ə)nər], *s.* **1.** *Dy: etc:* épaississant *m.* **2.** *Ind:* (*device*) épaississeur *m.*

thickening ['θik(ə)niŋ], *s.* **1.** (*a*) épaississement *m* (d'un mur, de la taille, d'un liquide, etc.); augmentation *f* (de la foule); (*b*) complication *f* (d'une intrigue). **2.** *Cu:* (*for sauces*) liaison *f.*

thicket ['θikit], *s.* bosquet *m,* hallier *m,* fourré *m,* épinier *m*; **thorn t.,** épinaie *f.*

thickhead ['θikhed], *s. F:* lourdaud, -aude; bêta, *f.* bêtasse; crétin, -ine; andouille *f.*

thickheaded [θik'hedid], *a.* **1.** *F:* lourd, lourdaud; bête, stupide; à la tête dure; à l'esprit étroit, épais, obtus. **2.** *Ent:* **t. fly,** conopidé *m.*

thickish ['θikiʃ], *a.* assez épais; (brouillard) assez dense; (*at sea*) (temps) bouché.

thickly ['θikli], *adv.* **1.** en couche épaisse. **2.** épais; dru; **snow fell t.,** la neige tombait dru; **to sow t.,** semer épais. **3.** (parler, chanter) d'une voix étouffée; (*when drunk*) **to speak t.,** avoir la langue épaisse, pâteuse.

thickness[1] ['θiknis], *s.* **1.** (*a*) épaisseur *f* (d'un mur, etc.); grosseur *f* (des lèvres, etc.); puissance *f* (d'une couche de houille); *Const:* **t. of a course,** hauteur *f* d'assise; **excessive t. of a beam,** gras *m* d'une poutre; (*b*) épaisseur; état dru, serré, touffu (d'une forêt, etc.); abondance *f,* état touffu (de la chevelure, etc.); (*c*) consistance *f,* viscosité *f* (d'un liquide); épaisseur (du brouillard); état couvert, bouché (du temps); (*d*) étouffement *m* (de la voix). **2.** couche *f* (de papier, etc.).

thickness[2], *v.tr. Carp:* mettre (une planche, etc.) d'épaisseur.

thicknessing ['θiknisiŋ], *s. Carp:* mise *f* d'épaisseur (d'une planche, etc.).

thickset ['θik'set], *a.* **1.** (*of forest, etc.*) épais, *f.* épaisse; serré, touffu; (*of beard*) dru, fourni. **2.** (*of pers.*) **to be t.,** avoir la taille épaisse; **(short and) t.,** trapu, ramassé; de forte encolure; **t. horse,** cheval renforcé.

thief, *pl.* **thieves** [θiːf, θiːvz], *s.* **1.** voleur, -euse; **hotel t.,** rat *m* d'hôtel; (*female*) souris *f* d'hôtel; **stop t.!** au voleur! *B:* **the penitent, the impenitent, t.,** le bon, le mauvais, larron; *Prov:* **set a t. to catch a t.,** à trompeur, trompeur et demi; à fripon, fripon et demi; **honour among thieves,** loi *f* du milieu. **2.** *Petr:* **oil t.,** échantillon *m* de dosage; (*for storage tank sampling*) **t. rod,** tige voleuse.

thief(-)proof ['θiːfpruːf], *a.* (dispositif) antivol, de sécurité.

thieve [θiːv]. **1.** *v.i.* être voleur, -euse. **2.** *v.tr.* voler (qch.).

thievery ['θiːv(ə)ri], *s.* vol *m.*

thieving[1] ['θiːviŋ], *a.* voleur, -euse.

thieving[2], *s.* vol *m*; **petty t.,** larcin *m.*

thievish ['θiːviʃ], *a.* voleur; malhonnête; adonné au vol.

thievishly ['θiːviʃli], *adv.* en voleur.

thievishness ['θiːviʃnis], *s.* penchant *m* au vol.

thigh [θai], *s.* cuisse *f*; **t. boots,** (bottes) cuissardes *f*; *A.Arm:* **t. piece,** cuissard *m.*

thighbone ['θaiboun], *s. Anat:* fémur *m*; os *m* de la cuisse.

thigmonasty ['θigmənæsti], *s. Bot:* thigmonastie *f.*

thigmotactic [θigmə'tæktik], *a.* thigmotactique.

thigmotaxis, thigmotaxy [θigmə'tæksis, -'tæksi], *s. Biol:* thigmotaxie *f.*

thigmotropism [θig'mɔtrəpizm], *s. Biol:* thigmotropisme *m.*

thill [θil], *s. Veh:* limon *m,* brancard *m*; **t. pin,** attel(l)oire *f*; **t. horse,** limonier *m*; cheval *m* de brancard.

thiller ['θilər], *s.* limonier *m*; cheval *m* de brancard.

thimble ['θimbl], *s.* **1.** *Needlew:* dé *m* (à coudre); **tailor's t.,** dé ouvert; déal *m, pl.* déaux; **t. case,** étui à dé; *Games:* **hunt the t.** = cache-tampon *m inv.* **2.** *Mch: etc:* (*for joining two pipes*) bride *f*; bague *f*; **t. coupling, joint,** bague d'assemblage; virole *f.* **3.** *Nau:* cosse *f* (de câble); **union t.,** cosse baguée.

thimbleful ['θimblful], *s.* doigt *m,* dé *m* à coudre (de cognac, etc.).

thimblerig[1] ['θimblrig], *s.* tour *m* des gobelets.

thimblerig[2], *v.i.* (**thimblerigged**) **1.** jouer le tour des gobelets. **2.** faire de l'escroquerie.

thimblerigger ['θimblrigər], *s.* **1.** joueur, -euse, de gobelets; escamoteur, -euse. **2.** escroc *m.*

thimblerigging ['θimblrigiŋ], *s.* **1.** = THIMBLERIG[1]. **2.** escroquerie *f.*

thin[1] [θin], *a.* (**thinner; thinnest**) **1.** (*a*) (*of paper, steel plate, etc.*) mince, fin; (*of thread, etc.*) ténu, délié, fin; (*of steam, etc.*) menu; (*of material*) fin, mince, léger, clair; **t. trickle of water,** maigre filet d'eau; **t. places,** parties usées (d'un vêtement); **to cut the bread in t. slices,** couper le pain en tranches minces; *Typ:* **t. stroke,** délié *m*; **t. space,** espace fin; *Phot:* **t. negative,** cliché faible; (*b*) (*of pers.*) maigre, mince; sec, *f.* sèche; **t. pale face,** visage maigre et pâle; **long t. figure,** taille fine, élancée; **long t. fingers,** doigts effilés; **t. lipped,** aux lèvres minces; **t. skinned,** (i) à la peau mince; à l'épiderme sensible; (ii) *Fig:* (*of pers.*) susceptible, trop sensible; qui se froisse facilement; **to grow, to become, thinner,** maigrir; s'amaigrir; s'amincir; **dress that makes one look thinner,** robe qui amincit; **as t. as a lath, as a rake,** maigre comme un clou, comme un cent de clous; sec comme un échalas, comme un cotret, comme un hareng. **2.** (*of wheat, hair, etc.*) clair, clairsemé, rare; (*of population, audience*) clairsemé; **t. beard,** barbe peu fournie; barbe rare; **his hair was getting t.,** ses cheveux s'éclaircissaient; **he's going t., he's a bit t., on top,** il devient chauve; **t. on the ground,** peu nombreux; *Th: etc:* **the house is a bit t. (tonight),** l'auditoire est peu nombreux, la salle est peu remplie, ce soir. **3.** (*a*) (*of liquid*) fluide, clair, délayé, peu consistant; (*of wine*) pauvre, sans corps; (*of blood*) appauvri, subtil; (*of hair*) raréfié; *Cu:* **t. sauce,** sauce longue; **t. soup,** potage clair; soupe clairette; (*b*) **t. voice,** voix fluette, grêle. **4. t. argument,** mince argument; argument peu solide, peu convaincant; **t. excuse,** pauvre excuse; **my patience is wearing t.,** je suis presque à bout de patience; *F:* **that's a bit t.!** ça, c'est peu convaincant! **to have a t. time (of it),** (i) s'ennuyer, s'embêter; se raser; (ii) manger de la vache enragée. **5.** *adv.* **to cut t.,** couper (le pain, etc.) en tranches minces; **to cut sth. wafer t.,** couper qch. en tranches fines, ténues; **to butter the bread, to spread the butter, too t.,** mettre trop peu de beurre sur les tartines; (*of wheat, etc.*) **t. sown,** clairsemé; *Art:* **to paint t.,** peindre mince.

thin[2], *v.* (**thinned**) **1.** *v.tr.* (*a*) amincir (qch.); **to t. down a board,** amincir, délarder, dégraisser, amaigrir, démaigrir, amenuiser, étriquer, une planche; (*b*) **to t. (down) the paint, a sauce,** diluer, délayer, la peinture; allonger, éclaircir, une sauce; (*c*) éclaircir (les arbres, etc.); éclaircir, désépaissir (les cheveux); décimer (un peuple); dépeupler, dégarnir (un pays, une forêt, etc.); **to t. out seedlings,** éclaircir, repiquer, des jeunes plants; **to t. out carrots,** éclaircir un plant de carottes; **to t. out (the leaves of) a fruit tree, a vine,** effeuiller, dégarnir, un arbre fruitier; épamprer une vigne. **2.** *v.i.* s'amincir, s'effiler; (*of trees, crowd, place, etc.*) s'éclaircir, se clairsemer; (*of hair*) s'éclaircir; (*of liquid*) devenir fluide, clair; **the crowd began to t. out,** la foule s'est éclaircie; **his hair is thinning,** il perd ses cheveux.

thine [ðain]. *A: & Lit:* (*except as used in prayers, etc.*) **1.** *poss.pron.* (*a*) le tien, la tienne, les tiens, les tiennes; **this book is t.,** ce livre est le tien, est à toi; **a friend of t.,** un de tes amis; un ami à toi; (*b*) **for thee and t.,** pour toi et les tiens; (*c*) **what is mine is t.,** ce qui est à moi est à toi. **2.** *poss.a.* (*used instead of* THY *before a noun or adj. beginning with a vowel or h mute*) **when I look into t. eyes,** quand je regarde dans tes yeux.

thing [θiŋ], *s.* **1.** (*inanimate object*) chose *f*; *F:* truc *m*, machin *m*; (*a*) objet *m*, article *m*; **t. of beauty,** une belle chose; **expensive things,** articles coûteux, chers; **all the things on the mantelpiece are mine,** tous les objets sur la cheminée sont à moi; **the things of this world,** les choses de la terre, de ce monde; **to go the way of all things,** mourir; aller où va toute chose; **things to be washed,** du linge à laver; **we always send the big things to the laundry,** nous envoyons toujours le gros linge à la blanchisserie; **she likes chocolate, sweets, and things (like that), and (all) that sort of t.,** elle aime le chocolat, les bonbons, et autres choses sucrées, et ainsi de suite; (*b*) *F:* **what's that t.?** qu'est-ce que c'est que ce machin-là? *Pej:* **what's that blue veil t. you're wearing?** qu'est-ce que cette espèce de voile bleu que tu portes? (*c*) *usu. pl.* (*implements*) **the plumber hasn't brought his things,** le plombier n'a pas apporté ses outils; **tea things, dinner things,** service *m* à thé, à dîner; **to clear away the (dinner) things,** desservir; **to wash up the tea things, the dinner things,** laver la vaisselle; (*d*) *pl.* vêtements *m*, effets *m*; **to take off all one's things,** se déshabiller (complètement); **to put away one's winter things,** serrer, ranger, ses vêtements d'hiver; **bring along your swimming things,** apportez votre maillot de bain; (*e*) *pl.* affaires *f*, effets; **I forbid you to touch my things,** je vous défends de toucher à mes affaires; **they have sold all his things,** on a vendu tous ses effets; **to pack (up) one's things,** faire ses malles, ses valises; mettre ses affaires dans sa valise; (*f*) *Jur:* **things personal, real,** biens meubles, immeubles. **2.** *F:* (*pers.*) (*with adj. expressing pity, contempt, etc.*) être *m*, créature *f*; **poor t.!** le, la, pauvre! **you silly t.!** sot, sotte, que tu es! petit sot! petite sotte! **poor little things!** pauvres petits! **she's a dear old t.,** c'est une bonne vieille très sympathique; **the poor old thing's deaf and blind,** le pauvre vieux est sourd et aveugle; *O:* **hello, old t.!** salut mon vieux, ma vieille! **dumb things,** les animaux *m*; **he was like a mad t.,** il était fou de rage. **3.** (*a*) (*action, fact, etc.*) **that was a silly t. to do,** quelle bêtise! **how could you do such a t.?** comment avez-vous pu faire une chose pareille? **did you ever hear of such a t.?** on n'a pas idée d'une chose pareille! **of all the things to do!** comme si vous ne pouviez pas faire autre chose! **she was wearing a silk dress with, of all things, a top hat!** elle portait une robe de soie, et, tenez-vous bien, un chapeau haut de forme! **to expect great things of sth.,** attendre grand bien de qch.; **we expect great things of you,** nous pensons que vous allez vous acquitter brillamment; **you take things too seriously,** vous prenez les choses trop sérieusement, trop au sérieux; **he gets things done,** il fait marcher les choses; il ne perd pas son temps; **to think things over,** réfléchir; étudier la question; **it's just one of those things,** ce sont des choses qui arrivent; on ne peut rien y faire; *Lit:* **to be all things to all men,** être tout à tous; **he has a passion for things political,** la politique le passionne; il se passionne pour la politique; **to talk of one t. and another,** parler de choses et d'autres; parler de la pluie et du beau temps; **the t. agreed on,** le point arrêté; **that's the very t.,** c'est cela même; c'est juste ce qu'il faut; cela fait juste l'affaire, mon affaire; **I have the very t. for you,** j'ai votre affaire; **the t. is to find a substitute,** le difficile, c'est de trouver un remplaçant; **the t. is this,** voici ce dont il s'agit; **the t. is, I haven't got any money,** le problème c'est, le fait est, que je n'ai pas d'argent; **the only t. left is to . . .,** il ne reste plus qu'à . . .; **the important t. is that . . .,** l'important c'est que . . .; **that's quite another t.,** ça c'est tout autre chose; *F:* ça c'est une autre paire de manches; **neither one t. nor another,** ni l'un ni l'autre; *F:* entre le zist et le zest; **one t. or the other,** de deux choses l'une; **it's (just) one t. after another, if it's not one t. it's another,** ça n'arrête jamais, ça n'arrête pas; c'est ceci, c'est cela; **what with one t. and another. . .,** tant et si bien que . . .; **it's one t. to talk, another to write,** parler est une chose, écrire en est une autre; **for one t., I haven't got the time, for another . . .,** en premier lieu, d'abord, je n'ai pas le temps, ensuite . . .; **and another t.,** en plus; **it would be a good t. to make sure of it,** il serait intéressant, bon, de s'en assurer; **he makes a good t. out of it,** ça lui rapporte pas mal; il en tire bon parti; *F:* **to make a t. of sth.,** (i) considérer qch. comme essentiel; (ii) s'exciter sur qch.; *F:* **he's on to a good t.,** il a le filon, il est sur un bon filon; **I don't know a t. about algebra,** je ne comprends, n'entends, rien à l'algèbre; j'ignore le premier mot de l'algèbre; **it doesn't mean a t. to me,** (i) je n'y comprends (absolument) rien; (ii) je ne m'en souviens pas; (iii) ça ne me concerne pas; **do you know anything about cars?—not a t.,** savez-vous quelque chose sur les voitures?—absolument rien; **to know a t. or two,** (i) en savoir plus d'un(e); être malin; avoir plus d'un tour dans son sac; (ii) être bien renseigné; savoir de quoi il retourne; *F:* **he's got a t. about that, it's a t. with him,** c'est son idée fixe; il ne pense qu'à ça; **he's got a t. about X,** (i) X, c'est son dieu; (ii) il ne peut pas supporter X; *F:* **to do one's own t.,** faire ce qui vous intéresse personnellement; **do your (own) t.!** fais ce que tu veux, fais comme il te plaira! (*b*) **things are going badly,** les affaires vont mal; **that things should have come to this!** penser que les choses en sont là! **as thing are,** les choses étant comme elles sont; dans l'état actuel des choses; **since that's how things are,** puisqu'il en est ainsi; **we hope for better things,** nous espérons que les choses iront mieux; nous espérons mieux; *F:* **how are things? how's things?** (i) comment vont les affaires? ça marche, les affaires? (ii) comment ça va? et la santé, ça va? **4. a little t. of mine I'd like to read to you,** un petit exemple de mon ouvrage que j'aimerais vous lire; **the latest t. in shoes,** chaussure(s) dernier cri; **it's the (very) latest t.,** c'est tout ce qu'il y a de plus moderne; c'est la dernière mode; c'est tout à fait dernier cri. **5. the t. (to do),** l'usage *m*, l'etiquette *f*: **it's not the (done) t.,** cela ne se fait pas; c'est peu conforme aux règles; **it's quite the t.,** c'est tout à fait correct; c'est la mode; **he's not feeling quite the t. this morning,** il ne se sent pas dans son assiette ce matin; ça ne va qu'à moitié ce matin; *F:* il se sent tout chose ce matin.

thingummy, thingamy, thingumajig, thingumabob ['θiŋəmi, -dʒig, -bɔb], *s. F:* chose *m*, machin *m*; **Mr Thingamy, Thingummy,** M. Chose; M. Tartempion; **pass me the t.,** passez-moi le machin(-chouette), le truc(-chouette), le bidule.

Thinite ['θainait], *a. Archeol:* (monument, etc.) thinite.

think[1] [θiŋk], *s.* **to have a (quiet) t.,** réfléchir; *F:* **you've got another t. coming!** tu peux toujours courir! tu te mets le doigt dans l'œil! *F:* **t. tank,** (i) (réunion *f* d'un) comité consultatif; (ii) réservoir *m* d'idées.

think[2], *v.* (*p.t. & p.p.* **thought** [θɔːt])

I. *v.tr. & i.* **1.** penser, réfléchir; **to t. aloud,** penser tout haut; **he thinks for himself,** il pense par lui-même; **to t. hard,** réfléchir profondément; se creuser la tête; *F:* **to t. big,** être ambitieux; **to t. great thoughts,** avoir des pensées profondes; **to t. in philosophical terms,** penser philosophie; **we must t. European,** il faut penser européen; **he doesn't say much, but he thinks a lot,** il ne dit pas grand-chose mais il n'en pense pas moins; **he says all he thinks,** il dit tout ce qu'il pense; **what are you thinking?** à quoi pensez-vous? **I know what you're thinking,** je connais vos pensées; **the child didn't t. there was any harm (in) doing it,** l'enfant ne pensait pas à mal en le faisant, ne pensait pas que c'était mal; **I'm glad to t. that I have been of use to you,** je suis heureux à la pensée que j'ai pu vous être utile; **it was this that set me thinking,** c'est cela qui m'a intrigué, *F:* qui m'a mis la puce à l'oreille; **to act without thinking,** agir sans réflexion; **I did it without thinking,** je l'ai fait sans réfléchir, sans y penser; **t. first before accepting,** réfléchissez(-y) avant d'accepter; **t. before you speak,** pesez vos paroles; **just t. a minute!** réfléchissez un peu! *A:* **t. on it,** pensez-y; **he thought back to his childhood,** il s'est rappelé son enfance; **give me time to t. (and remember),** laissez-moi me reprendre; **his name was—let me t.—no, I've forgotten!** il s'appelait—voyons—non, je l'ai oublié! **to t. again,** se raviser; *F:* **t. again!** vous n'y êtes pas! réfléchissez donc! **(if that's what you're thinking) you can t. again,** tu peux toujours courir! **2.** songer, s'imaginer, se figurer; **I thought to myself that . . .,** je songeais en moi-même que . . .; **I (really) can't t. why, what, where . . .,** je me demande bien pourquoi, ce que, où . . .; **I can't t. what you mean,** je ne peux pas m'imaginer ce que vous voulez dire; **you can't t. what he looks like,** vous ne pouvez pas vous figurer de quoi il a l'air; **you can't t. how glad I am,** vous ne sauriez croire combien je suis content; **I no longer knew what to t.,** je ne savais plus que penser; **what will people t.?** qu'en dira-t-on? de quoi cela aura-t-il l'air? **when I heard the news, what do you t. I did?** quand j'ai appris la nouvelle, figurez-vous ce que j'ai fait! **he thinks he knows everything,** il s'imagine tout savoir; **one would have thought that . . .,** c'était à croire que . . .; **you might t. you were in Scotland,** on se dirait en Écosse; **anyone would t. he was asleep,** on dirait qu'il dort; **who'd have thought it!** qui l'aurait dit? a-t-on idée d'une chose pareille! **just t.!** songez donc! **to t. that he's only twenty!** et dire qu'il n'a que vingt ans! **3.** (*a*) (*conceive the notion of*) **I have been thinking that . . .,** l'idée m'est venue que . . .; **I thought I'd wait here,** j'ai pensé qu'il valait mieux attendre ici; **I only thought to help you,** ma seule pensée était de vous aider; (*b*) **did you t. to bring any money?** avez-vous pensé, songé, à apporter de l'argent? **4.** (*a*) **do you t. you could do it?—I t. I could,** pensez-vous que cela vous serait possible?—je pense que oui; **then you t. that . . .,** il vous semble donc que . . .; **it's better, don't you t., to get it over with?** il vaut mieux, n'est-ce pas, en finir? **one wouldn't have thought it,** on ne l'aurait pas cru; **I thought I ought to warn him,** j'ai cru devoir le prévenir; **what do you t. I ought to do?** que croyez-vous qu'il faudrait que je fasse? **the doctor thought it was scarlet fever,** le médecin a cru à une scarlatine; **I thought I heard him,** j'ai cru l'entendre; **I thought I heard a knock,** il m'a semblé entendre frapper; **I thought it was all over,** je me disais que tout était fini; **he thinks he may do anything,** il se croit tout permis; **everyone asked him what he thought,** chacun lui a demandé son avis; **I told him straight what I thought,** je lui ai dit carrément ce que j'en pensais, ce que je pensais, ma façon de penser; **I t. she's pretty,** je la trouve jolie; **everyone thought he was mad,** on le jugeait fou; on le tenait pour fou; **I t. he's looking unwell,** je lui trouve mauvaise mine; **I t. I'll go too,** ma foi! j'y vais aussi; **I (rather) t. people are leaving,** je crois qu'on part; **I rather t. it's going to rain,** j'ai dans l'idée qu'il va pleuvoir; **it is thought that . . .,** on suppose que +*ind.*; **I t. like you,** je pense comme vous; je suis de votre avis; **I t. so,** c'est ce qui me semble, je pense que oui; **I t. not, I don't t. so,** je pense que non; **so I thought, I thought so, I thought as much,** je le pensais bien; je m'y attendais; je m'en doutais (bien); **I (should) hardly t. so,** c'est peu probable; **I should t. so!** je crois bien! je vous crois! je vous en réponds! **I shouldn't t. so,** je ne crois pas: non, n'est-ce pas? *F:* **that's what you t.!** tu penses! *F:* **I don't t.!** jamais de la vie! quelle blague! sûrement pas! mon œil! (*b*) juger, considérer, croire, trouver, penser; **if you t. it necessary to . . .,** si vous jugez nécessaire de . . .; **I hardly t. it likely that . . .,** il n'est guère probable que +*sub.*; **you thought her (to be) a fool,** vous l'avez prise pour une sotte; **to t. oneself a hero,** se regarder comme, se prendre pour, un héros; **they were thought to be rich,** on les disait, supposait, riches; ils passaient pour (être) riches. **5.** s'attendre à (qch.); **I little thought I would see him again,** je ne m'attendais guère à le revoir; je ne comptais guère le revoir; *O:* **I had thought to make a fortune,** je m'étais imaginé, j'avais pensé, faire fortune.

II. (*compound verbs*) **1. think about, of,** *v.ind.tr.* (*a*) penser à (qn, qch.); songer à (qch.); **we're thinking of you,** nous pensons à vous; **I have thought about your proposal,** j'ai réfléchi à votre proposition; **she's always thinking about men,** elle a toujours un homme en tête; **one can't t. of everything, one never thinks of everything,** on ne saurait penser à tout; on ne songe pas à tout; on ne s'avise jamais de tout; **how could you t. of such a thing?** à quoi pensez-vous? **I have so much to t. about, of,** j'ai tant de choses auxquelles il me faut songer; **I never thought of it, about it,** je n'y ai pas pensé; je n'y ai jamais songé; **it's time we thought about going,** il est temps de songer au retour; **I can't t. of his name,** son nom ne me revient pas; **I can't t. of the right word,** le mot propre m'échappe; **the best thing I can t. of,** ce que je vois de mieux; **(when you) come to t. of it,** à la réflexion; **he can't sleep for thinking about it,** il perd le sommeil à force d'y penser; *F:* il n'en dort pas; **to give s.o. sth. else to t. about,** donner, procurer, des distractions à qn; **that's worth thinking about,** cela mérite réflexion; **it's a subject that doesn't bear thinking about,** c'est un sujet pénible qu'il faut éviter; **without her thinking about it,** sans qu'elle y pense; **what am I thinking about?** où ai-je la tête? **I never thought of warning you,** je n'ai pas pensé à vous avertir; (*b*) s'imaginer, se figurer, songer; **t. of a number,** pensez à un chiffre; **I thought of him as being tall,** je me le figurais grand; je le voyais grand; **t. of me having to do it!** (α) dire que je suis obligé de le faire! (β) me voyez-vous réduit à le faire! *F:* **(just) t. of that! to t. of**

it! ça, c'est pas banal! songez donc! qui l'aurait cru? **t. of it, he's in love with her!** il l'aime, figure-toi! **t. of the pleasure it gave me,** imaginez(-vous) le plaisir que cela m'a fait; **when I t. of what might have happened!** quand je pense à ce qui aurait pu arriver! (*c*) considérer (qn); avoir égard à (qn); songer à (qch.); **to t. of s.o.'s feelings,** avoir égard aux sentiments, aux susceptibilités, de qn; **to t. of the expense,** regarder à la dépense; **he never thinks of his mother,** il n'a aucune considération, il ne montre jamais de considération, pour sa mère; (*d*) **to t. of, about, doing sth.,** méditer, projeter, de faire qch.; penser à faire qch.; **I'm thinking of going tomorrow,** j'ai presque décidé de partir demain; **he thought of giving them a present,** il avait imaginé de leur offrir un cadeau; **I couldn't t. of it!** c'est impossible! il n'y a pas à y songer! **we could not t. of inviting them,** il ne saurait être question de les inviter; **I couldn't t. of allowing it,** je ne le tolérerais pas un instant; (*e*) (i) *v.tr.* penser (qch.) de (qch., qn); **what do you t. of it, about it?** qu'en pensez-vous? que vous en semble? **what do you t. of this picture?** que pensez-vous, que dites-vous, de ce tableau? **to t. a great deal of oneself, to t. too much of oneself,** avoir une haute idée de sa personne; **to t. too much of sth.,** attacher trop d'importance à qch.; **I told him what I thought of him,** je lui ai dit son fait; *F:* je lui ai donné, lâché, son paquet; (ii) **to t. well of s.o.,** estimer qn; avoir une bonne opinion de qn; penser du bien de qn; **to t. badly of s.o.,** avoir une mauvaise opinion de qn; penser du mal de qn; **I hope you won't t. badly of me because . . .,** j'espère que vous n'allez pas m'en vouloir de ce que . . .; **he is well thought of,** il est bien vu, bien considéré; **what will people t. of it?** de quoi cela aura-t-il l'air? qu'en dira-t-on?

2. think out, *v.tr.* (*a*) imaginer, méditer (qch.); **to t. out a plan,** combiner un plan; **well thought out plan,** projet bien médité, bien étudié; projet élaboré, mûri; **well thought out diet,** régime bien agencé; **carefully thought out answer,** réponse bien pesée; **that wants thinking out,** cela demande mûre réflexion; (*b*) arriver à la solution de (qch.); **he thinks things out for himself,** il juge des choses par lui-même; il se fait lui-même une opinion des choses; ses opinions lui sont personnelles.

3. think over, *v.tr.* réfléchir sur, aviser à (une question, etc.); délibérer de (qch.); **I'll t. it over,** j'y réfléchirai, j'y aviserai; **t. it over (carefully),** réfléchissez-y, songez-y, bien; **give me time to t. it over,** laissez-moi y réfléchir à tête reposée; **on thinking it over . . .,** après réflexion . . .; **this wants thinking over,** ceci demande qu'on y réfléchisse bien; cela mérite réflexion.

4. think up, *v.tr. F:* imaginer (un projet, une méthode); **carefully thought up plan,** projet bien médité; **to t. up a scheme to do sth.,** combiner de faire qch.; **what have you been thinking up?** qu'est-ce que tu as combiné?

thinkable ['θiŋkəbl], *a.* (projet, etc.) concevable, imaginable; **is it t. that . . .?** est-il admissible que +*sub.*; peut-on imaginer que +*sub.*

thinker ['θiŋkər], *s.* penseur, -euse.

thinking[1] ['θiŋkiŋ], *a.* pensant; qui pense; **I put this to the t. public,** je soumets cette question au public qui pense, à tous les hommes qui pensent.

thinking[2], *s.* **1.** pensée(s) *f(pl)*, méditation(s) *f(pl)*, réflexion(s) *f(pl)*; **deep t.,** pensées, méditations, profondes; **he did some hard t.,** il a réfléchi profondément; **to put on one's t. cap,** méditer une question; prendre le temps d'aviser, d'y réfléchir (sérieusement); *Med:* **compulsive t.,** pensée obsédante; *Th:* **t. part,** rôle muet; rôle de figurant. **2.** pensée, opinion *f*, avis *m*; **to my (way of) t.,** à mon avis, à mon sens; **that's my way of t.,** voilà ma façon de penser; **you are of my way of t.,** vous pensez comme moi; **I hope to bring you round to my way of t.,** j'espère vous amener à mon opinion, à mon point de vue.

thinly ['θinli], *adv.* **1.** à peine; **t. clad,** (i) vêtu légèrement; (ii) vêtu misérablement, insuffisamment; **t. veiled allusion,** allusion à peine voilée, transparente; **t. disguised hostility,** hostilité à peine déguisée. **2.** clair; d'une manière éparse; **to slice t.,** couper (qch.) en tranches minces; **to paint t.,** peindre mince; **to sow t.,** semer clair; **t. sown wheat,** blé clairsemé; **t. populated country,** pays de population peu dense, à population clairsemée; pays peu peuplé.

thinner ['θinər], *s.* (*also* **thinners**) diluant *m*, délayant *m*, (dis)solvant *m* (pour peinture, etc.).

thinness ['θinnis], *s.* **1.** (*a*) peu *m* d'épaisseur (de qch.); minceur *f* (d'une feuille de papier, etc.); ténuité *f*, finesse *f* (d'un fil, etc.); légèreté *f*, clarté *f* (d'un voile, etc.); (*b*) maigreur *f* (d'une personne). **2.** état clairsemé (du blé, etc.); rareté *f* (des cheveux, etc.). **3.** fluidité *f* (d'un liquide); manque *m* de corps (d'un vin); raréfaction *f*, légèreté (de l'air); caractère grêle, fluet (d'une voix). **4.** faiblesse *f* (d'une excuse, etc.); transparence *f* (d'un déguisement).

thinning ['θiniŋ], *s.* **1. t. (down),** amincissement *m*, amaigrissement *m*, démaigrissement *m*, affinage *m*, amenuisement *m* (de qch.); délardement *m* (d'une planche). **2.** délayage *m* (de la peinture); dilution *f*; *Ind:* **t. agent,** (dis)solvant *m*. **3. t. (out),** dépeuplement *m* (d'une forêt, d'un pays); éclaircie *f*, éclaircissage *m*, repiquage *m* (de jeunes plants); démariage *m* (des betteraves); effeuillage *m* (d'un arbre fruitier); épamprage *m* (d'une vigne); *For:* **light t.,** coupe *f* sombre, coupe d'ensemencement; **heavy t.,** coupe claire. **4.** *For: etc:* **thinnings,** bois *m* de déchet.

thinnish ['θiniʃ], *a.* **1.** (*a*) plutôt mince; (*b*) assez maigre; (*of pers.*) maigrichon, -onne, maigrelet, -ette, maigriot, -otte. **2.** (cheveux, etc.) assez rares. **3.** (vin) qui manque plutôt de corps; (voix) fluette, plutôt grêle.

Thinocoridae [θinou'kɔridi:], *s.pl. Orn:* thinocoridés *m*, thinocorythidés *m*.

Thinocorus [θi'nɔkərəs], *s. Orn:* thinocore *f*.

thio ['θaiou], *a. Ch:* **t. acid,** thioacide *m*; **salt of a t. acid,** sulfosel *m*.

thioacetic [θaiouə'si:tik], *a. Ch:* thioacétique.

thioalcohol [θaiou'ælkəhɔl], *s. Ch:* thioalcool *m*, thiol *m*, mercaptan *m*.

thioaldehyde [θaiou'ældihaid], *s. Ch:* thioaldéhyde *m*, thial *m*.

thioamide [θaiou'æmaid], *s. Ch:* thioamide *m*.

thioarsenic [θaiouɑ:'senik], *a. Ch:* sulfarsénique.

Thiobacteriales [θaioubæktiəri'eili:z], *s.pl. Bac:* thiobactériales *f*, sulfuraires *f*, sulfobactéries *f*.

thiocarbamide [θaiou'kɑ:bəmaid], *s. Ch:* thiocarbamide *m*, thio-urée *f*.

thiocarbanilide [θaioukɑ:bə'nilaid], *s. Ch:* thiocarbanilide *m*.

thiocarbonate [θaiou'kɑ:bəneit], *s. Ch:* thiocarbonate *m*, sulfocarbonate *m*.

thiocarbonic [θaioukɑ:'bɔnik], *a. Ch:* thiocarbonique.

thiocyanate [θaiou'saiəneit], *s. Ch:* thiocyanate *m*, sulfocyanate *m*, sulfocyanure *m*; **the sodium thiocyanates,** les thiocyanates alcalins.

thiocyanic [θaiousai'ænik], *a. Ch:* thiocyanique, sulfocyanique.

thiodiphenylamine [θaioudaife'niləmi(:)n], *s. Ch:* thiodiphénylamine *f*.

thioether [θaiou'i:θər], *s. Ch:* thioéther *m*.

thioflavin(e) [θaiou'fleivin], *s. Ch:* thioflavine *f*.

thioglycolic [θaiouglai'kɔlik], *a. Ch:* thioglycolique.

thioindamine [θaiou'indəmi(:)n], *s. Ch:* thio-indamine *f*, thiazine *f*.

thioindigo [θaiou'indigou], *s. Ch:* thio-indigo *m*.

thioketone [θaiou'ki:toun], *s. Ch:* thiocétone *f*.

Thiokol ['θaiəkɔl], *s. R.t.m:* Thiokol *m*.

thionaphthene [θaiou'næfθi:n], *s. Ch:* thionaphtène *m*.

thionate ['θaiəneit], *s. Ch:* thionate *m*.

thione ['θaioun], *s. Ch:* thione *f*, thiocétone *f*.

thionic [θai'ɔnik], *a. Ch:* thionique.

thionine ['θaiəni(:)n], *s. Ch:* thionine *f*.

thionyl ['θaiənil], *s. Ch:* thionyle *m*.

thiophene ['θaiəfi:n], *s. Ch:* thiofène *m*, thiophène *m*.

thiophenol [θaiou'fi:nɔl], *s. Ch:* thiophénol *m*, phénylmercaptan *m*.

thiophosgene [θaiou'fɔzdʒi:n], *s. Ch:* thiophosgène *m*.

thioplast ['θaiouplæst], *s. Ch:* thiogomme *f*.

thiosinamine [θaiousi'næmi(:)n], *s. Pharm:* thiosinamine *f*.

thiosulphate [θaiou'sʌlfeit], *s. Ch:* thiosulfate *m*, hyposulfite *m*; **sodium t.,** hyposulfite de soude.

thiosulphuric [θaiousʌl'fjuərik], *a. Ch:* thiosulfurique, hyposulfureux.

thiourea [θaiouju'ri:ə], *s. Ch:* thio-urée *f*.

thioxanthone [θaiou'zænθoun], *s. Ch:* thioxanthone *f*.

third [θə:d]. **1.** (*a*) *num.a.* troisième (jour, étage, etc.); tiers (état, etc.); **t. person,** (i) *Jur:* tierce personne, tiers *m*; (ii) *Gram:* troisième personne; **t. copy,** triplicata *m inv*; **to marry for the t. time,** se marier en troisièmes noces; *Sch:* **t. form, year,** *approx.* = classe *f* de quatrième, *F:* quatrième *f*; **Edward the T.,** Édouard Trois; **the T. World,** le tiers monde; **(on) the t. (of May),** le trois (mai); **on the t. floor,** (i) au troisième étage; (ii) *NAm:* au quatrième étage; **in (the) t. place,** en troisième lieu; troisièmement; **every t. day,** tous les trois jours; **the t. largest town,** la plus grande ville sauf deux; **he arrived t. or fourth,** il est arrivé trois ou quatrième; **t. rate,** de troisième qualité; **he's a very t. rate pianist,** c'est un joueur de piano de troisième ordre, très inférieur, au-dessous du médiocre; **information at t. hand,** renseignements de troisième main; **we got our car t. hand,** notre voiture est de troisième main; *Rail: A:* **to travel t. (class),** voyager en troisième (classe); **t. class carriage,** wagon de troisième classe; *Post: NAm:* **t. class matter,** imprimés *mpl* non périodiques; **t. man,** (i) *Cr:* troisième chasseur à droite du garde-guichet; (ii) (*lacrosse*) demi *m*; (*baseball, rounders*) **t. base,** (i) troisième base *f*; (ii) joueur, -euse, qui se tient à la troisième base; *El:* **t. brush generator,** générateur à balai auxiliaire; **t. rail,** rail *m* de contact (d'une voie ferrée électrifiée); (*b*) *s.* (*pers.*) tiers; **to make a t. in a game,** être en tiers dans un jeu. **2.** *s.* (*a*) *Astr: Mth:* soixantième *m* de seconde (de temps, de mesure angulaire); tierce *f*; (*b*) *Mus:* tierce; (*c*) *Fin:* **t. of exchange,** troisième *f* de change; (*d*) *Com:* **thirds,** articles *m* de troisième qualité, de qualité inférieure; (*e*) *Sch:* **to get a t. (class honours degree) in history,** obtenir la mention *passable* en histoire; être reçu tout juste; (*f*) *Aut:* **to go into t.,** passer en troisième *f*. **3.** *s.* (*fraction*) tiers; **to lose a t., two thirds, of one's money,** perdre le tiers, les deux tiers, de son argent; **a t., one t., of the inhabitants were killed,** un tiers des habitants a été tué, ont été tués.

thirdly ['θə:dli], *adv.* troisièmement; en troisième lieu.

thirst[1] [θə:st], *s.* **1.** (*a*) soif *f*; **great t.,** altération *f*; **to have a perpetual t.,** avoir toujours soif; **this work has given me a t.,** ce travail m'a donné soif, m'a altéré; **to satisfy one's t.,** étancher sa soif; **to die of t.,** mourir de soif; (*b*) *Rept:* **t. snake,** serpent *m* à grosse tête. **2.** *Lit:* **the t. for, after, knowledge,** la soif de connaître, de la science; **the t. to do sth.,** le désir immodéré de faire qch.; **to satisfy one's t. for adventure,** apaiser sa soif d'aventures.

thirst[2], *v.i.* **1.** *A: & Lit:* avoir soif; être altéré; être consumé par la soif. **2.** *Lit:* **to t. after sth., for sth.,** avoir soif de qch.; être avide, assoiffé, de qch.; **to t. for blood, for revenge,** être altéré de sang, de vengeance.

thirstily ['θə:stili], *adv.* **1. to drink t.,** boire à longs traits (pour étancher sa soif). **2.** *Lit:* avidement.

thirstiness ['θə:stinis], *s.* soif; soif habituelle; penchant *m* à boire.

thirsting[1] ['θə:stiŋ], *a. Lit:* assoiffé.

thirsting[2], *s. Lit:* soif *f* **(after, for,** de).

thirsty ['θə:sti], *a.* **1.** (*a*) altéré; assoiffé; **to be, feel, t.,** avoir soif; avoir la gorge sèche; *F:* avoir le gosier sec; **to become, get, t.,** s'altérer; **to make s.o. t.,** donner soif à qn; altérer qn; **fish makes me t.,** le poisson me donne soif, me fait boire; je trouve le poisson très altérant; *F:* **all this talking is t. work,** de tant parler, cela donne soif, cela vous altère, cela vous sèche le gosier; (*b*) *Lit:* **t. for blood, for riches,** assoiffé, altéré, avide, de sang, de richesses. **2.** (*of earth, etc.*) desséché, sec, *f.* sèche.

thirteen [θə:'ti:n, 'θə:ti:n], *num. a. & s.* treize (*m*); **t. houses,** treize maisons; **she's t. (years old),** elle a treize ans; **a girl of t.,** une jeune fille de treize ans; **I have t.,** j'en ai treize; **(the) number t.,** (le) numéro treize; **two thirteens are, twice t. is, twenty-six,** deux fois treize font vingt-six; **t. and a half,** treize et demi; **t. of my friends,** treize de, d'entre, mes amis; **there were t. of us,** nous étions treize; **at t. hundred (hours),** à treize heures; **at t. fifty (hours),** à treize heures cinquante.

thirteenth [θə:'ti:nθ]. **1.** *num.a. & s.* treizième (*mf*); **the t. house,** la treizième maison; **Louis the T.,** Louis Treize; **(on) the t. (of May),** le treize (mai); **Friday the t.,** vendredi treize; **he's, she's, (the) t. in his, her, class,** il est le, elle est la, treizième de sa classe. **2.** *s. Mus:* treizième *f*. **3.** *s.* (*fraction*) treizième *m*.

thirtieth ['θə:tiiθ], *num.a. & s.* trentième (*mf*); **(on) the t. (of June),** le trente (juin); **it's my t. birthday,** je fête mes trente ans.

thirty ['θə:ti], *num.a. & s.* trente (*m*); **t.-two, t.-three,** trente-deux, trente-trois; *Cards: etc:* **t.-one,** trente et un *m*; *Mus:* (*in organ*) **t.-two foot stop,** trente-deux-pieds *m inv*; **t.-first, t.-second,** trente et unième, trente-deuxième; **(on) the t.-first (of March),** le trente et un (mars); **about t. guests,** une trentaine d'invités; **to be t. (years old),** avoir trente ans; **she's not far off t.,** elle approche de la trentaine; **she's in her thirties,** elle a passé la trentaine; **she was in her early thirties,** elle n'avait guère plus de trente ans; **the thirties (of this century),** les années trente (de ce siècle); **the eighteen-thirties, the thirties of the last century,** les années trente du dernier siècle; les années entre 1830 et 1840, de 1830 à 1840; **the train leaves at two-t., at fourteen-t.,** le train part à deux heures trente, à quatorze heures trente; *Hist:* **the T. Years' War,** la guerre de Trente Ans; **t. years' lease,** concession *f* trentenaire.

thirtyish ['θə:tiiʃ], *a. F:* d'une trentaine d'années; **he's t.,** il a à peu près trente ans.

thirty-sixmo [θə:ti'siksmou], *a. & s. Typ:* in-trente-six (*m*); in-36 (*m*).

thirty-twomo [θə:ti'tu:mou], *a. & s. Typ:* in-trente-deux (*m*); in-32 (*m*).

this [ðis], *dem.pron., a. & adv.*

I. *dem.pron.pl.* **these** [ði:z]. **1.** ceci; ce; **what's t.? what**

are these? qu'est-ce que c'est (que ceci, *F:* que ça)? **what good is t.?** à quoi cela est-il bon? à quoi cela sert-il? **who's t.?** qui est-ce? *F:* qui ça? (dont vous parlez); **you'll be sorry for t.,** vous le regretterez; **at, upon, t.,** sur ce; ce disant; là-dessus; **I'd heard of it before t.,** j'en avais déjà entendu parler; **it ought to have come before t.,** cela devrait être déjà arrivé; **after t.,** après cela; ensuite; désormais; **t. is a free country,** nous sommes en pays libre; **t. is curious,** voilà qui est curieux; **t. is what he told me,** voici ce qu'il m'a dit; **t. is what it's all about,** voici ce dont il s'agit; **t. is why . . .,** voilà pourquoi . . .; voilà ce qui fait que . . .; **t. is true,** c'est bien vrai; voilà qui est vrai; **t. is Mr Thomas,** je vous présente M. Thomas; **these are my children,** voici mes enfants; **t. is where he lives,** c'est ici qu'il habite; **t. is my last will and testament,** ceci est mon testament; **these are things we cannot do without,** ce sont des choses dont on ne peut se passer; **listen to t.,** écoutez bien ceci; **what's t. (that) I hear?** qu'est-ce que j'entends? **it was like t.,** voici comment les choses se sont passées; **do it like t.,** fais comme ceci; fais-le ainsi; **the case is exceptional in t., that . . .,** le cas offre ceci de particulier que . . .; **in t. their first campaign,** dans cette campagne, qui était leur première; **all t. sort of thing is a reflexion on me,** tout ceci rejaillit sur moi; **what's all t. (noise)?** qu'est-ce qu'il y a? qu'est-ce qui se passe? **t. is not an hotel,** ce n'est pas ici un hôtel; **t. is the time to speak,** voici le moment de parler; **is t. the place to quarrel?** est-ce ici le lieu pour vous disputer? **t. is something like a meal,** voilà qui s'appelle un repas! **they are no ordinary houses, these,** ce ne sont pas là des maisons ordinaires; **t. I knew,** ceci, je le savais. **2.** (*opposed to* **that**) **will you have t. or that?** voulez-vous ceci ou cela? *F:* **they were talking about t. and that,** ils parlaient de choses et d'autres, de la pluie et du beau temps; **he told me t. and that, t., that and the other,** il m'a dit ceci et cela, *F:* ci et ça; **she told me all her worries and t., that and the other,** elle m'a raconté tous ses ennuis et patati et patata; **she's always asking "shall I do t., shall I do that?",** elle demande toujours "si je faisais (ce)ci, si je faisais cela, ça?" **it's always Charles t. and Charles that,** c'est Charles par-ci, Charles par-là. **3.** (*referring to sth. already mentioned*) celui-ci, *f.* celle-ci, *pl.* ceux-ci, *f.* celles-ci; **they're both very much alike, but t. (one) is new and that (one) is old,** les deux se ressemblent beaucoup, mais celui-ci est neuf et celui-là est ancien; **I prefer these to those,** je préfère ceux-ci à ceux-là; **perhaps these are the ones,** c'est peut-être ceux-ci.

II. *dem.a., pl.* **these** (*a*) ce, (*before vowel or h mute*) cet, *f.* cette, *pl.* ces; (*for emphasis and in opposition to* **that, those**) ce . . .-ci, cet . . .-ci, cette . . .-ci, ces . . .-ci; **t. book, these books,** ce livre(-ci), ces livres(-ci); **t. hat is Roger's, that one is Albert's,** ce chapeau-ci est à Roger; celui-là est à Albert; **t. morning, t. afternoon, t. week,** ce matin, cet après-midi, cette semaine; **where will you be going t. Easter?** où irez-vous à Pâques (prochain)? **what did you do t. Christmas?** qu'est-ce que vous avez fait à Noël (dernier)? **there's a nip in the air these mornings,** le matin, en cette saison, l'air est piquant; **one of these days,** un de ces jours; **(in) these days,** *esp. Journ:* **in t. day and age,** de nos jours; à notre époque; à cette époque(-ci); aujourd'hui; **t. day last year,** l'an dernier à pareil jour; **by t. time,** à l'heure qu'il est; **by t. time he must already be a qualified doctor,** il doit être déjà docteur; **you can't do that in t. country,** cela ne se fait pas dans ce pays(-ci), dans notre pays, chez nous; **to run t. way and that,** courir de-ci, de-là; **t. reader or that may disagree with the author,** un lecteur par-ci par-là se trouvera peut-être en désaccord avec l'auteur; **he will tell you that in t. or that case you should . . .,** il vous dira qu'en tel ou tel cas il faut. . .; **for t. reason,** voilà pourquoi; pour cette raison; *Jur:* **t. Convention,** la présente convention; **t. prime minister is an improvement on the last one,** le premier ministre actuel vaut mieux que l'ancien; **t. new pen of mine writes very well,** mon nouveau stylo, ce nouveau stylo, écrit très bien; *F:* (*in narrative*) **I was talking to t. man in the corridor when . . .,** je parlais à ce monsieur dans le couloir quand . . .; *P:* **t. here house,** cette maison(-ci); (*b*) *Pej:* **he's one of these artist chaps,** c'est un de ces artistes; (*c*) (**this** *with pl. noun;* **these** *with noun sg. coll.*) **I've been watching you these, t., ten minutes,** voilà dix minutes que je vous observe; **I've known him these three years,** je le connais depuis trois ans; **these vermin,** cette vermine; *O:* **t. many a day,** depuis bien des jours; depuis bien longtemps.

III. *dem.adv.* (*with adj. or adv. of quantity*) aussi . . . que ceci; **t. high, as high as t.,** aussi haut que ceci, que cela, *F:* que ça; **t. far,** jusqu'ici; jusque-là.

Thisbe ['θizbi], *Pr.n.f.* Thisbé.

thistle ['θisl], *s. Bot:* chardon *m*; **star t.,** chardon étoilé; chausse-trape *f, pl.* chausse-trapes; **cotton, Scotch, t.,** chardon aux ânes; pet-d'âne *m, pl.* pets-d'âne; chardonnette *f*; chardon d'Écosse; **woolly t.,** chardon laineux; **blue t.,** (i) vipérine *f,* herbe *f* aux vipères; (ii) *Austr:* argémone *f* du Mexique; **golden t.,** scolymus *m*; **saffron t.,** carthame *m*; **corn, creeping, cursed, t.,** *U.S:* **Canada t.,** chardon des champs; **blessed t.,** chardon bénit; **carline t.,** chardon doré; **edible t.,** cardon *m*; **t. seed oil,** huile *f* de chardon; **to clear the ground of thistles,** échardonner le terrain; **clearing the ground of thistles,** échardonnage *m.*

thistledown ['θisldaun], *s.* duvet *m* de chardon.

thistly ['θisli], *a.* **1.** (terrain) rempli de chardons. **2.** épineux, piquant.

thither ['ðiðər]. *A: & Lit:* **1.** *adv.* (*expressing motion*) là; y; **go ye t.,** rendez-vous dans cet endroit; allez-y; **to run hither and t.,** courir çà et là. **2.** *a.* plus lointain; plus éloigné; de l'autre côté; *Geog:* ultérieur; **they live on the t. side of the mountains,** ils habitent de l'autre côté des montagnes; **T. Calabria,** la Calabre Ultérieure.

thixotropic [θiksou'trɔpik], *a. Ch: etc:* thixotrope, thixotropique.

thixotropy [θiks'ɔtrəpi], *s. Ch: etc:* thixotropie *f.*

Thlaspi ['θlæspi], *s. Bot:* thlaspi *m.*

tho' [ðou], *conj. & adv. F:* = THOUGH.

thole[1] [θoul], *v.tr. A: & Scot:* **1.** endurer, souffrir (une douleur, un mal). **2.** tolérer, permettre (un abus, etc.).

thole[2], **tholepin** ['θoulpin], *s.* **1.** *Nau:* tolet *m,* dame *f,* toletière *f*; échaume *m,* échôme *m,* estrouif *m.* **2.** *Veh: A:* cheville *f* (de brancard).

tholos, *pl.* **-oi, tholus,** *pl.* **-i** ['θouləs, -ɔi, -ai], *s. Arch: Gr.Ant:* tholos *f, pl.* tholoï.

Thomas ['tɔməs], *Pr.n.m.* Thomas; **Saint T. Aquinas,** saint Thomas d'Aquin.

thomisid ['θoumisid], *s. Arach:* thomise *m,* thomisidé *m.*

Thomisidae [θou'misidi:], *s.pl. Arach:* thomisidés *m.*

Thomism ['toumizm], *s. Theol:* thomisme *m.*

Thomist ['toumist], *a. & s. Theol:* thomiste (*mf*).

Thomistic [tou'mistik], *a. Theol:* thomiste.

Thomomys ['θoumoumis], *s. Z:* thomomys *m.*

thomsenolite ['tɔmsənəlait], *s. Miner:* thomsenolite *f.*

thomsonite ['tɔmsənait], *s. Miner:* thomsonite *f.*

thong[1] [θɔŋ], *s.* (*a*) lanière *f* de cuir; courroie *f*; (*b*) lanière, longe *f* (de fouet); (*c*) *Algae:* **t. weed,** algue *f* en lanière.

thong[2], *v.tr.* **1.** attacher une lanière à (une cravache, etc.). **2.** assujettir (qch.) avec une courroie, avec des courroies. **3.** punir (qn) avec une courroie; sangler (qn).

thoracentesis [θɔ:rəsen'ti:sis], *s. Surg:* thora(co)centèse *f.*

thoracic [θɔ:'ræsik], *a.* (*a*) *Anat:* thoracique; **t. duct,** canal thoracique; (*b*) *Ich:* (nageoire pelvienne) thoracique.

Thoracica [θɔ:'ræsikə], *s.pl. Crust:* thoraciques *m.*

thoracopagus [θɔ:rə'kɔpəgəs], *s. Ter:* thoracopage *m.*

thoracoplasty ['θɔ:rəkouplæsti], *s. Surg:* thoracoplastie *f.*

thoracoscopy [θɔ:rə'kɔskəpi], *s. Med:* thoracoscopie *f.*

Thoracostraca [θɔ:rə'kɔstrəkə], *s.pl. Crust:* thoracostracés *m.*

thoracotomy [θɔ:rə'kɔtəmi], *s. Surg:* thoracotomie *f.*

thorax, *pl.* **thoraces** ['θɔ:ræks, θɔ:'reisi:z], *s.* **1.** *Anat: Ent: etc:* thorax *m.* **2.** *Gr.Ant:* corselet *m,* cuirasse *f.*

thoria ['θɔ:riə], *s. Ch:* thorine *f.*

thorianite ['θɔ:riənait], *s. Miner:* thorianite *f.*

thoric ['θɔrik, 'θɔ:-], *a. Ch:* thorique.

thorite ['θɔ:rait], *s. Miner:* thorite *f,* orangite *f.*

thorium ['θɔ:riəm], *s. Ch:* thorium *m*; **t. (di)oxide,** dioxyde *m* de thorium; thorine *f*; **t. series,** famille radioactive du thorium; *A:* **t. emanation,** émanation *f* du thorium; thoron *m.*

thorn [θɔ:n], *s.* **1.** (*a*) *Bot:* épine *f*; *Fig:* **a t. in one's flesh, in the flesh, in one's side,** une épine au pied; **to be a t. in s.o.'s flesh, side,** être un sujet continuel d'anxiété, d'irritation, à qn; **to be on thorns,** être, marcher, sur des épines, sur des charbons ardents; être dans une situation épineuse; (*b*) *Bot:* (arbrisseau) épineux *m*; épine; **Christ's, Egyptian, evergreen, fire, t.,** pyracanthe *f,* pyracantha *f*; buisson ardent; arbre *m* de Moïse; épine du Christ; **box t.,** lyciet *m*; **scorpion t.,** épine fleurie; **t. apple,** (i) pomme épineuse; stramoine *f*; (ii) *NAm:* (α) cenelle *f*; (β) aubépine *f*; **t. hedge,** haie *f* d'épines; *esp.* haie d'aubépine; (*c*) *Fish:* **t. hook,** épinette *f.* **2.** *Pal:* le caractère runique Þ.

thornback ['θɔ:nbæk], *s.* **1.** *Ich:* raie bouclée. **2.** *Crust:* grande araigne de mer; maïa *m,* maja *m.*

thornbird ['θɔ:nbɔ:d], *s. Orn:* annumbi *m.*

thornbush ['θɔ:nbuʃ], *s.* (arbrisseau) épineux *m*; épine *f.*

thornless ['θɔ:nlis], *a.* sans épines.

thorntail ['θɔ:nteil], *s. Orn: F:* gouldie *f.*

thorntree ['θɔ:ntri:], *s. Bot:* (*a*) (arbrisseau) épineux *m*; épine *f*; (*b*) aubépine *f*; (*c*) gleditschia *m*; févier *m* à trois épines; acacia *m* à trois épines; (*d*) (*S. Africa*) robinier *m,* faux acacia.

thorny ['θɔ:ni], *a.* épineux; *Bot:* spinifère, spinigère; *Rept:* **t. devil,** moloch *m*; *Fig:* **t. question,** question épineuse.

thorogummite [θɔ:rou'gʌmait], *s. Miner:* thorogummite *f.*

thoron ['θɔ:rɔn], *s. Ch: A:* thoron *m.*

thorough ['θʌrə], *prep., adv., a. & s.*

I. *prep. A:* = THROUGH I.

II. *adv. A:* **1.** = THROUGH II. **2.** = THOROUGHLY.

III. *a.* (*a*) (*of search, inspection, etc.*) minutieux; (*of knowledge, etc.*) profond; complet, -ète; parfait; (*of work, etc.*) consciencieux; **t. enquiry,** enquête approfondie; **t. distaste,** profond dégoût; **to give a room a t. cleaning,** nettoyer une pièce à fond; **t. knowledge of French,** connaissance approfondie du français; **he has a t. command of French,** il parle un français impeccable; **you must have a t. change,** il vous faut un changement complet; **you've got a t. chill,** vous avez pris un vrai refroidissement; **to be t. in one's work,** travailler consciencieusement, sérieusement; (*b*) **a t. Frenchman,** un vrai Français; **a t. musician,** un musicien consommé; **a t. republican,** un républicain convaincu; **a t. scoundrel,** un coquin fieffé, achevé; un scélérat consommé, accompli.

IV. *s. Eng.Hist:* politique intransigeante du système absolu; politique du "jusqu'au bout" (sous Charles Ier).

thoroughbass ['θʌrəbeis], *s. Mus: A:* **1.** basse continue; basse chiffrée; continuo *m.* **2.** composition *f* harmonique; l'harmonie *f* (en tant que science).

thoroughbrace ['θʌrəbreis], *s. Veh: U.S:* soupente *f* (de carrosse).

thoroughbred ['θʌrəbred]. **1.** *a.* (cheval) pur sang *inv*; racé; (chien, etc.) de race (pure), de sang; (*of pers.*) pur sang; racé; qui a de la race. **2.** *s.* (*a*) cheval *m* pur sang; pur-sang *m inv*; (*b*) animal, -aux *m,* de race; (*of pers.*) **she's a real t.,** elle est très racée.

thoroughfare ['θʌrəfeər], *s.* voie *f* de communication; **public t.,** voie publique; **one of the main thoroughfares of the town,** une des rues principales, une des artères, de la ville; **busy t.,** rue très passante; route à grande circulation, à circulation intense; *P.N:* **no t.,** (i) défense de passer; rue barrée; passage interdit (au public); entrée interdite; (ii) impasse; voie sans issue.

thoroughgoing ['θʌrəgouiŋ], *a.* (*a*) (*of search, inspection, etc.*) minutieux; approfondi; (*of knowledge, etc.*) profond; complet, -ète; parfait; (*of work, etc.*) consciencieux; (*b*) (travailleur, etc.) consciencieux; (moraliste, etc.) intransigeant; **a t. scoundrel,** un coquin fieffé, achevé; un scélérat consommé, accompli; **a t. democrat,** un démocrate enragé, effréné, à tous crins, à tout crin.

thoroughly ['θʌrəli], *adv.* (épuiser, etc.) tout à fait; (savoir une langue, etc.) parfaitement; (renouveler, etc.) complètement; entièrement; (nettoyer) à fond; **to go into a question t.,** examiner une question à fond, minutieusement; creuser, approfondir, une question; **to know sth. t.,** savoir qch. à fond, sur le bout du doigt; **the question was t. discussed,** la question a été l'objet d'un débat approfondi; **t. honest,** d'une honnêteté à toute épreuve; **t. reliable machine,** machine qui offre une sécurité à toute épreuve.

thoroughness ['θʌrənis], *s.* caractère approfondi (des recherches, d'un travail); perfection *f,* minutie *f* (du travail); **the t. with which this work has been done,** la conscience avec laquelle ce travail a été fait.

thoroughpin ['θʌrəpin], *s. Vet:* vessigon chevillé.

thoroughwax ['θʌrəwæks], *s. Bot:* buplèvre *m*; oreille-de-lièvre *f, pl.* oreilles-de-lièvre; perce-feuille *f, pl.* perce-feuilles.

thoroughwort ['θʌrəwɔ:t], *s. Bot:* eupatoire *f*; chanvre *m* d'eau.

thorp(e) [θɔ:p], *s. A:* village *m,* hameau *m.*

thortveitite [tɔ:t'vaitait], *s. Miner:* thortveitite *f.*

those. *See* THAT.

thou[1] [ðau], *pers.pron. A: & Poet:* (*except in prayers*) (*a*) (*unstressed*) tu; **t. seest,** tu vois; **there t. art,** te voilà! **hearest t.?** entends-tu? **t. rascal!** coquin que tu es! (*b*) (*stressed*) toi; **t. and I,** toi et moi; **it is t.,** c'est toi; **he is taller than t.,** il est plus grand que toi.

thou[2] [ðau], *v.tr. A:* tutoyer.

thou[3] [θau], *s. F:* **1.** (= *thousand pounds*) mille livres sterling. **2.** (= *thousandth of an inch*) millième *m* de pouce.

though [ðou], *conj. & adv.*

I. *conj.* **1.** (*also* **although**) quoique, bien que, encore que + *sub. or occ. ind.*; **t. he is poor he is generous,** quoiqu'il soit pauvre, quoique pauvre, il est généreux; **I'm sorry**

for him, t. he is nothing to me, je le plains, encore qu'il ne me soit rien; t. we are related, I've never seen him, quoique nous soyons parents, je ne l'ai jamais vu; I respect him t. I don't like him, je le respecte, bien qu'il ne me soit pas sympathique; you'll have to stay by her t. there'll be nothing for you to do, il faudra rester auprès d'elle, bien que vous n'aurez rien à faire; t. he had escaped from the pirates he was not yet safe, pour être échappé aux pirates il n'était pas encore en sûreté; t. I am a father, tout père que je suis; t. small he is none the less brave, pour être petit il n'en est pas moins courageux; t. (I am) unmarried, I am happy, je suis content, quoique célibataire; t. not beautiful, she was attractive, sans être belle elle plaisait; the bonds are strong even t. (they are) invisible, les liens sont forts encore qu'invisibles; t. aware of the crisis, I did nothing, bien qu'étant, tout en étant, conscient de la crise, je n'ai rien fait. 2. (a) *A: & Lit:* (*with sub.*) this statement, terrible t. it be, cette déclaration, pour terrible qu'elle soit; vice is infamous t. it be in a prince, le vice est infâme fût-ce chez un prince; t. your crimes be never so great, quelque grands que soient vos crimes; t. he slay me yet will I follow him, je le suivrai quand (même) il me tuerait, même s'il a l'intention de me tuer; (b) *A: & Lit:* (*with sub.*) what t. the way be long! qu'importe que le chemin soit long! (c) strange t. it may seem, si étrange que cela semble; even t. you'll laugh at me, quand vous devriez vous moquer de moi; even t. *he* can't come, *you* will, won't you? bien qu'il ne puisse pas venir, vous viendrez quand même, n'est-ce pas? he'll probably come, t. you never know, il est probable qu'il viendra, et pourtant, mais, on ne sait jamais. 3. as t., comme si; it's not as t. they would mind, ce n'est pas comme si cela leur faisait quelque chose; he sank into an armchair as t. (he were, he was) exhausted, il s'est affaissé dans un fauteuil comme s'il tombait d'épuisement; it looks as t. he's gone, il semble qu'il soit parti; as t. nothing had happened, comme si de rien n'était; he raised his hand as t. to take off his hat, il a levé la main comme pour enlever son chapeau.

II. *adv.* (a) cependant, pourtant; he had promised to go; he didn't t., il avait promis d'y aller; cependant, pourtant, il n'en a rien fait; he'll probably come; you never know t., il est probable qu'il viendra, et pourtant, mais, on ne sait jamais; (b) (*exclamatory*) did he t.! vraiment! il a dit, fait, cela?

thought [θɔ:t], *s.* 1. pensée *f*; t. is free, la pensée est libre; on est libre de penser; capable of t., capable de penser. 2. (a) pensée, idée *f*; he hasn't a t. in his head, il n'a pas une idée dans la tête; happy t., heureuse idée; the t. occurred to me that . . ., il m'est venu à l'esprit, l'idée m'est venue, j'ai réfléchi, que . . .; (b) dark, gloomy, thoughts, idées, pensées, sombres; papillons noirs; taken up with other thoughts, préoccupé; *F:* a penny for your thoughts, à quoi pensez-vous? tell me your thoughts on the matter, donnez-moi votre opinion à ce sujet; he keeps his thoughts to himself, il est peu communicatif; il ne se livre point; to follow the thread of one's thoughts, se laisser aller au fil de ses pensées; to let one's thoughts dwell on sth., penser à qch.; stray thoughts, pensées détachées; to read s.o.'s thoughts, lire dans la pensée de qn; to t.-read (s.o.), lire les pensées (de qn); t. reading, lecture *f* de la pensée, de l'âme; t. reader, liseur, -euse, de pensées; *Psychics:* t. transference, transmission *f* de pensée; télépathie *f*; t. wave, onde télépathique; (c) the mere t. of it makes my blood boil, rien que d'y penser, mon sang bout; at the mere t. of going there she . . ., à la seule pensée d'y aller elle . . .; have you ever given it a single t.? y avez-vous pensé un seul instant? y avez-vous jamais pensé? I didn't give a t. to the matter, je n'y ai pas accordé la moindre réflexion; I didn't give it another t., je n'y ai pas repensé; old age comes on without our having given it a t., la vieillesse arrive sans qu'on y pense; (d) *pl.* esprit *m*, pensée; to collect one's thoughts, rassembler ses idées, ses esprits; her thoughts were elsewhere, son esprit était ailleurs; you are in my thoughts, je pense à toi; to fix one's thoughts on a fact, arrêter sa pensée sur un fait; (e) contemporary, Greek, t., la pensée contemporaine, grecque. 3. (a) réflexion *f*, considération *f*; a few moments' t. made him change his mind, de brèves réflexions l'ont fait changer d'avis; after much t., après mûre réflexion; to give a great deal of t. to sth., réfléchir beaucoup à qch.; it required careful t., cela demandait mûre réflexion; he has no t. for his mother, il n'a pas de considération, pas d'égards, pour sa mère; il ne se soucie pas de sa mère; on second thoughts, (toute) réflexion faite; à la réflexion; après plus amples réflexions; tout bien considéré; *Lit:* to take no t. for the morrow, ne pas songer au lendemain; (b) pensées, rêverie *f*, méditation *f*, recueillement *m*; to fall into deep t., tomber dans une rêverie, une méditation, profonde; to be deep, lost, *Lit:* wrapt, in t., être perdu, absorbé, dans ses pensées; être plongé, abîmé, dans ses réflexions, dans la méditation; être songeur, -euse; to spend an hour in t., passer une heure à méditer. 4. (a) intention *f*, dessein *m*; to have a t., to have thoughts, of doing sth., avoir la pensée, l'intention, de faire qch.; songer à faire qch.; to have some t. of doing sth., avoir vaguement l'intention de faire qch.; I had no t. of offending you, je n'avais pas l'intention de vous offenser; you must give up all thought(s) of seeing him, il faut renoncer à le voir; il ne faut plus penser à le voir; his one t. is to get money, il ne pense qu'à l'argent; her one t. is to get married, elle ne songe, ne pense, qu'à se marier; with the t. of . . ., dans le dessein, dans l'intention, de . . .; I appreciate your t., j'apprécie votre bon mouvement, votre beau geste; (b) (*usu. neg.*) *O:* I had no t. of meeting you here, je ne m'attendais pas, je ne m'attendais guère, à vous rencontrer ici. 5. *adv.phr. F: O:* a t., un tout petit peu; un tantinet; a t. too sweet, un tout petit peu trop sucré; he's a t. better, il y a un léger mieux; the ribbon is a t. too blue, le ruban est d'un rien trop bleu.

thoughtful ['θɔ:tful], *a.* 1. (a) pensif, méditatif; rêveur, -euse; (b) réfléchi, prudent. 2. prévenant; attentionné; bien intentionné; plein d'égards; it's very t. of him to . . ., c'est une attention très délicate de sa part de . . .; c'est bien aimable à lui de . . .; il a eu la gentillesse de . . .; t. care, soins attentifs; he was t. enough to warn me, il a eu la prévenance, l'attention, de m'avertir. 3. (*of book, speech, writer, speaker*) profond.

thoughtfully ['θɔ:tfuli], *adv.* 1. (a) pensivement; d'une manière pensive; d'un air pensif, rêveur, méditatif; (b) d'une manière réfléchie, prudente. 2. avec prévenance; avec délicatesse.

thoughtfulness ['θɔ:tfulnis], *s.* 1. (a) méditation *f*, recueillement *m*; (b) réflexion *f*, prudence *f*. 2. prévenance *f*; délicatesse *f*; attentions *fpl*, égards *mpl* (pour, envers).

thoughtless ['θɔ:tlis], *a.* (*of pers., action, etc.*) 1. irréfléchi, mal avisé; inconséquent, étourdi; peu circonspect; t. action, étourderie *f*; acte inconsidéré. 2. t. of others, qui manque d'égards, de prévenance, de délicatesse, pour les autres.

thoughtlessly ['θɔ:tlisli], *adv.* 1. étourdiment; (agir) à l'étourdie, à la légère, sans réflexion. 2. to behave t. towards s.o., to treat s.o. t., manquer d'égards envers qn.

thoughtlessness ['θɔ:tlisnis], *s.* 1. irréflexion *f*; manque *m* de circonspection; étourderie *f*, inconséquence *f*. 2. manque d'égards, de prévenance, de délicatesse (pour, envers).

thousand ['θauz(ə)nd], *num.a. & s.* mille (*m*) *inv*; *s.* millier *m*; (*in dates A.D.* mil *is used instead of* mille, *except in* the year one t., the year two t., l'an mille, l'an deux mille); the year 4000 B.C., l'an quatre mille av. J.-C.; *Jur: Adm:* the year one t. nine hundred and thirty, l'an mil neuf cent trente; a t. years, mille ans; un millénaire; a t. men, mille hommes; a t. needles, un mille d'aiguilles; about a t. men, un millier d'hommes; quelque mille hommes; three hundred t. men, trois cent mille hommes; they died in hundreds of thousands, ils moururent par centaines de mille; they amounted to some thousands, ils s'élevaient à plusieurs mille; leur nombre s'élevait à plusieurs mille; I paid five t. (pounds) for it, je l'ai payé cinq mille livres; several t. inhabitants, plusieurs milliers d'habitants; thousands of people, des milliers de gens; they come in thousands, ils viennent par milliers; thousands upon thousands, des milliers (de milliers); he's a man, one, in a t., c'est un homme entre mille; c'est un homme comme il y en a peu, comme on en voit peu; a t. and one, mille un; *F:* I've got a t. and one things to ask you, j'ai mille et une choses à vous demander; I've told you a t. times, je vous l'ai dit mille fois; no, no, a t. times no! non, non, et cent fois non!

thousandfold ['θauz(ə)n(d)fould]. 1. *a.* multiplié par mille. 2. *adv.* mille fois autant.

thousandth ['θauz(ə)n(t)θ], *num.a. & s.* millième (*mf*).

Thrace [θreis], *Pr.n. A.Geog:* Thrace *f*.

Thracian ['θreiʃ(ə)n]. 1. *A.Geog:* (a) *a.* thrace; thracien; (b) *s.* Thrace *mf*. 2. *s. A. Ling:* thrace *m*.

thraldom ['θrɔ:ldəm], *s. Lit:* esclavage *m*, assujetissement *m*, asservissement *m*, servitude *f*, servage *m*; to keep s.o. in t., tenir qn dans l'assujetissement.

thrall [θrɔ:l], *s. Lit:* 1. esclave *mf*, serf *m*, serve *f* (of, to, de); to be a t. to one's passions, être l'esclave de ses passions. 2. kept in t., maintenu dans l'asservissement, en esclavage, en servitude.

thrash[1] [θræʃ], *s.* 1. battement *m* (de la pluie, des vagues, etc.). 2. *Mec.E:* vibration (d'un vilebrequin, etc.) due à la torsion; thrash *m*.

thrash[2], *v.tr. & i.*

I. *v.tr.* 1. (a) battre (qn, une bête); donner des coups de trique à, flanquer une (bonne) volée à (qn, une bête); rosser, *F:* cogner (qn); tanner le cuir à (qn); to t. s.o. soundly, donner une raclée, une (bonne) correction, à qn; (b) battre (un adversaire) à plate(s) couture(s); *F:* rosser (l'ennemi); they're going to get thrashed in the elections, ils vont prendre une belle raclée, recevoir une pile, aux élections; (c) to t. out a question, débattre, creuser, une question; discuter une question à fond. 2. (a) battre, défourrer (le blé); (b) to t. a walnut tree, gauler un noyer; the fish was thrashing the water with its tail, le poisson battait l'eau avec sa queue; *Swim:* to t. the water, battre l'eau (avec les jambes).

II. *v.i.* 1. (a) (*of water*) battre, clapoter (against, contre); (b) *Nau:* to t. to windward, marcher vent debout; (c) *Mec.E:* vibrer. 2. (*of pers.*) to t. about, se débattre des mains et des pieds.

thrasher[1] ['θræʃər], *s.* 1. (*pers.*) batteur, -euse, en grange. 2. *Paperm:* (a) tambour laveur de feutre; (b) blutoir *m*, batteuse, dépoussiéreur *m*. 3. *Ich:* t. (shark), renard (marin), renard de mer; *Z:* t. whale, orque *f*, épaulard *m*.

thrasher[2], *s. Orn:* moqueur *m*; brown t., moqueur roux; sage t., moqueur des armoises.

thrashing ['θræʃiŋ], *s.* 1. (a) volée *f* (de coups), correction *f*; *F:* raclée *f*, rossée *f*; to give s.o. a t., donner une raclée, flanquer une (bonne) volée, filer une trempe, à qn; a good t., une bonne raclée, une bonne correction; you're in for, you're going to get, a good t., tu vas recevoir une raclée, une bonne volée; (b) *Sp: etc:* défaite *f*; *F:* raclée; to give one's opponent a sound t., battre son adversaire à plate(s) couture(s). 2. (a) battage *m* (du blé); t. machine, batteuse *f*; (b) = THRASH[1].

Thrasybulus [θræ'sibju:ləs], *Pr.n.m. Gr.Hist:* Thrasybule.

Thraupidae ['θrɔ:pidi:], *s.pl. Orn:* tanagridés *m*.

thread[1] [θred], *s.* 1. (a) filament *m*, fil *m* (de soie, d'une plante, etc.); his life hung by a t., sa vie ne tenait qu'à un fil; *Paperm:* t. mark, filigrane *m* (des billets de banque); *Coel:* t. cell, nématocyste *m*, cnidocyste *m*; *Ent:* t.-waisted wasp, sphex *m*; (b) filon *m*, veine *f*, filet *m* (de minerai); (c) filet (d'eau, de fumée, de lumière, etc.). 2. (a) *Needlew:* fil (de coton, de nylon, etc.); linen t., fil de lin; gold t., fil d'or; button t., fil à boutons; gros fil; sewing t., fil à coudre; tacking, basting, t., coton *m*, fil, à bâtir; *Surg:* retaining, ligature, t., fil de contention, de ligature; *A:* t. gloves, gants de fil; (b) *Tex:* fil (de trame, de chaîne); t. counter, compte-fils *m inv*; quart-de-pouce *m*, *pl.* quarts-de-pouce; *Needlew:* t. drawing, ouvrage, travail, à jour(s); the t. of life, la trame de la vie; to lose the t. of one's argument, of the conversation, perdre le fil de son argument, de la conversation; I've lost the t., j'ai perdu le fil; je me suis embrouillé; to gather up the threads of a story, reprendre, rassembler, les fils d'une histoire; (c) (length of) t., brin *m*, bout *m* (de coton, de soie, etc.); aiguillée *f*; *Tchn:* filet *m*, filetage *m*, pas *m* (d'une vis, d'un boulon, etc.); right-hand t., filet à droite; left-hand(ed) t., filet à gauche; filet renversé; crossed t., filetage mâchuré; worn t., filetage usé, *F:* foiré; bastard t., filetage bâtard; full t. rod, tige filetée sur toute sa longueur; t. gauge, calibre pour filetage; t. cutter, machine *f* à fileter; taraudeuse *f*; t. milling machine, machine à fileter à la fraise; t. grinding machine, machine à fileter à la meule.

thread[2], *v.tr.* 1. (a) enfiler (une aiguille); *Tex:* to t. a heddle, rentrer une lisse; (b) enfiler (des perles) (on, sur); (c) enfiler (une ficelle dans un œillet, etc.); to t. elastic through sth., enfiler, passer, un élastique dans qch.; (d) to t. one's way between the cars, through the crowd, se faufiler, s'insinuer, entre les voitures, à travers la foule; se frayer un chemin à travers les voitures, la foule; the path threads its way between the hedges, le sentier file entre les haies. 2. *Tchn:* (a) fileter (une vis, etc.); tarauder (un tuyau, un écrou, etc.); threaded screw, vis filetée; threaded hole, trou taraudé; threaded rod, tige filetée, à vis; full threaded rod, tige filetée sur toute sa longueur; flat-threaded screw, vis à filet plat; (b) (*of screw, etc.*) to t. into sth., se visser dans qch.

threadbare ['θredbɛər], *a.* (a) (*of clothes, etc.*) râpé, élimé, usé (jusqu'à la corde), qui montre la corde; (b) (*of subject, argument, joke, etc.*) usé (jusqu'à la corde), rebattu; banal, -aux; t. story, vieille rengaine.

threader ['θredər], *s.* 1. (*pers.*) enfileur, -euse (d'aiguilles, etc.). 2. (a) enfile-aiguilles *m inv*; (b) (*bodkin*) passe-lacet *m*, *pl.* passe-lacets. 3. *Metalw:* machine *f* à fileter; taraudeuse *f*.

threadfin ['θredfin], *s. Ich:* capitaine *m*.

threading ['θrediŋ], *s.* 1. enfilement *m* (d'une aiguille, etc.). 2. *Tchn:* filetage *m* (d'une vis, etc.); taraudage *m* (d'un tuyau, etc.); **t. machine,** machine *f* à fileter; **t. lathe,** tour *m* à fileter.

threadlike ['θredlaik], *a.* filiforme.

threadworm ['θredwə:m], *s. Ann:* (*a*) nématode *m*; (*b*) *Med:* ascaride *m*, ascaris *m*, trichine *f*; **the threadworms,** les ascaridés *m*.

thready ['θredi], *a.* **1.** (*of substance, root, etc.*) fibreux, filamenteux; plein de fils. **2.** *Med:* (*of pulse*) filiforme, filant.

threat [θret], *s.* menace *f*; (*a*) **to utter a t.,** proférer une menace; **to carry out a t.,** mettre une menace à exécution; **to get sth. out of s.o. by threats,** arracher qch. à qn par des menaces; **idle t.,** vaine menace; menace en l'air; **threats and counterthreats,** menaces de part et d'autre; **the t. to Palestine,** la menace sur la Palestine; (*b*) **there is a t. of rain,** la pluie menace.

threaten ['θretn], *v.tr.* **1.** (*a*) menacer (qn); *Jur:* intimider (qn); **he was heard to t. them,** on l'a entendu leur adresser des menaces; **to t. s.o. with sth.,** menacer qn de qch.; **to t. s.o. with legal proceedings,** menacer qn de poursuites judiciaires; **he threatened him with dismissal,** il a menacé de le renvoyer; **(to be) threatened with sth.,** (être) menacé de qch.; **to be threatened with the law,** être sous le coup de plaintes au parquet; être sous le coup d'une plainte en justice; **race threatened with extinction,** race en voie de disparition; **the threatened strike didn't come off,** cette menace de grève n'a pas abouti; (*b*) **to t. to do sth.,** menacer de faire qch.; **to t. proceedings,** menacer de poursuivre; **this situation threatens to become dangerous,** cette situation menace de devenir dangereuse. **2.** *v.i.* **a storm is threatening,** l'orage menace, un orage s'annonce.

threatening ['θret(ə)niŋ], *a.* (ton, air) menaçant; **t. letter,** lettre de menaces; *Jur:* lettre comminatoire; **t. language,** menaces (verbales); *Jur:* intimidation *f*; **the weather looks t.,** le temps menace; le temps n'est pas sûr; **t. attitude,** attitude combative.

threateningly ['θret(ə)niŋli], *adv.* d'une manière menaçante; sur un ton menaçant.

three [θri:], *num.a. & s.* trois (*m*); (*a*) **t. weeks,** trois semaines; **every t. months, t. monthly,** tous les trois mois; trimestriellement; **I have t.,** j'en ai trois; **I live at number t.,** j'habite au (numéro) trois; **twenty-t.,** vingt-trois; **t. fours, four threes, are twelve,** trois fois quatre, quatre fois trois, font douze; **t. and a half,** trois et demi; **to be t. (years old),** avoir trois ans; **at t. (o'clock),** à trois heures, à quinze heures; **the train leaves at t. thirty, at half past t.,** le train part à trois heures trente, à trois heures et demie; le train part à quinze heures trente; *A:* **t. halfpence** [θri:'heipens], un penny et demi; **t. of them, t. of my friends,** trois d'entre eux; trois de mes amis; **to fold a sheet of paper in t.,** plier une feuille de papier en trois; **to come in t. by t., in threes, t. at a time,** entrer par trois; **attacked by forces t. times as great as ours,** attaqués par des forces triples des nôtres, trois fois supérieures aux nôtres; **one in t. of the inhabitants was killed,** un habitant sur trois a été tué; *Cards:* **t. of diamonds,** trois de carreau; (*at dominoes, etc.*) **double t.,** double-trois *m*, *pl.* doubles-trois; **to throw threes,** amener double-trois; (*telephone numbers*) **for numbers in France dial 33** [dʌbl'θri:], pour la France composez le trente-trois; **t. star hotel, brandy,** hôtel, cognac, trois-étoiles; *Th:* **t. act play,** pièce en trois actes; **t. lane road,** route à trois voies; *U.S: F:* **as phoney as a t. dollar bill,** faux comme un jeton; *Mus:* **t. four, t. eight (time),** trois-quatre *m*, trois-huit *m*; *Pol:* **the Big T.,** les Trois (Grands); *Pol: Dipl: etc:* **t. sided, t. party, conversations,** conversations tripartites, triparties; **t. power pact,** pacte tripartite, triparti; **t. per cent bonds, t. per cents,** le trois pour cent; *Ecc:* **the T. Hours' service,** *F:* **the T. Hours,** l'office du vendredi saint; *Theol:* **T. in One,** la Trinité; (*b*) **t.-stranded rope,** corde à trois cordons; **t.-bladed propeller,** hélice tripale; **t.-pointed,** à trois pointes; tricuspide; **t.-limb tube,** tube en T; *Aut: etc:* **t. seater,** triplace *m*; *Av:* **t.-engine(d) aircraft,** (avion) trimoteur *m*; *Metall:* **t.-high mill,** trio *m*; *El:* **t.-pole switch,** interrupteur tripolaire; **t.-phase generator,** alternateur triphasé; *El: etc:* **t.-cell capacitor,** condensateur triple; *W.Tel:* **t.-electrode valve, element,** lampe à trois électrodes; lampe triode; **t.-wire aerial,** antenne trifilaire; *Cmptr:* **t.-address instruction,** instruction à trois adresses; **t.-plus-one address,** à trois adresses d'opérande et une adresse de commande; **excess-t. code,** code plus trois.

three-ball ['θri:bɔ:l], *a. Golf:* **t.-b. match,** trois-balles *m inv*.

three-cable [θri:'keibl], *a.* tricâble.

three-card [θri:'kɑ:d], *a.* **t.-c. trick, set,** bonneteau *m*.

three-colour(ed) [θri:'kʌlər, -'kʌləd], *a. Phot: Phot.Engr:* trichrome; **t.-colour process,** trichromie *f*.

three-cornered [θri:'kɔ:nəd], *a.* (*of instrument, table, etc.*) triangulaire; **t.-c. hat,** (chapeau) tricorne *m*; *Tls:* **t.-c. file,** tiers-point *m*, *pl.* tiers-points; **t.-c. fight, discussion,** lutte, débat, à trois; *Pol:* **t.-c. election,** élection triangulaire.

three-course ['θri:kɔ:s], *a.* **1. t.-c. meal,** repas *m* à trois plats. **2.** *Agr:* **t.-c. system,** assolement triennal.

three-decker [θri:'dekər], *s.* **1.** *Nau: A:* trois-ponts *m inv*. **2.** *A:* roman *m* en trois volumes. **3.** *Ecc:* chaire *f* à trois étages. **4.** sandwich composé de trois tranches de pain.

three-dimensional [θri:d(a)i'menʃənəl], *a.* tridimensionnel; à trois dimensions.

three-field ['θri:'fi:ld], *a. Agr:* **t.-f. system,** assolement triennal.

threefold ['θri:fould]. **1.** *a.* triple. **2.** *adv.* trois fois autant; **to increase t.,** tripler.

three-handed [θri:'hændid], *a. Cards: etc:* **t.-h. game,** partie à trois.

three-legged [θri:'legid], *a.* (tabouret, etc.) à trois pieds; *Games:* **t.-l. race,** course à trois pieds.

three-masted [θri:'mɑ:stid], *a. Nau:* (vaisseau) à trois mâts.

three-master [θri:'mɑ:stər], *s. Nau:* trois-mâts *m inv*.

threepence ['θrəp(ə)ns], *s.* (la somme de) trois pence *m*.

threepenny ['θrep(ə)ni], *a.* (timbre, etc.) coûtant trois pence, à, de, trois pence; *A:* **t. (bit),** pièce *f* de trois pence.

three-piece ['θri:pi:s], *a.* en trois pièces; *Cost:* **t.-p. suit,** trois-pièces *m inv*; *Furn:* **t.-p. suite,** canapé et deux fauteuils assortis; *F:* salon *m*; **t.-p. fishing rod,** canne à pêche à trois brins.

three-ply ['θri:plai], *a.* **1. t.-p. wood,** contre-plaqué en trois, à trois épaisseurs; *Mec.E:* **t.-p. belt,** courroie en trois épaisseurs. **2.** (*of wool, etc.*) à trois fils, en trois brins; (*of rope*) en trois brins.

three-point ['θri:pɔint], *a. Mec.E:* **t.-p. support,** triangle *m* de sustentation; *Av:* **t.-p. landing,** atterrissage trois points; *Aut:* **to make a t.-p. turn,** faire demi-tour en trois mouvements.

three-quarter [θri:'kwɔ:tər]. **1.** *a.* **t.-q. inch nail,** clou de trois quarts de pouce; **t.-q. length coat,** trois-quarts *m inv*; **t.-q. face portrait,** portrait de trois quarts; **t.-q. violin,** trois-quarts; *Rugby Fb:* **t.-q. (back),** trois-quarts. **2.** *adv.* **the room was t.-quarters full,** la salle était pleine aux trois quarts, aux trois quarts pleine.

threescore ['θri:skɔ:r], *a. A: & Lit:* soixante; **t. (years) and ten,** soixante-dix ans.

threesome ['θri:səm], *s.* (*a*) groupe *m*, partie *f*, de trois personnes; (*b*) *Scot:* danse *f*, etc., à trois personnes; (*c*) *Golf:* partie *f* de trois; trois-balles *m inv*.

three-speed ['θri:spi:d], *a.* (bicyclette, etc.) à trois vitesses.

three-square ['θri:skwɛər], *a.* triangulaire; **t.-s. file,** tiers-point *m*, *pl.* tiers-points; lime triangulaire.

three-storey(ed), *NAm:* **-story, -storied** [θri:'stɔ:ri(d)], *a.* (maison) à trois étages.

three-way ['θri:wei], *a.* (robinet, etc.) à trois voies; *El:* (commutateur, etc.) à trois voies.

three-wheeled [θri:'(h)wi:ld], *a.* à trois roues; *Av:* **t.-w. undercarriage,** train d'atterrissage tricycle.

three-wheeler [θri:'(h)wi:lər], *s.* (*a*) *Aut:* (petite) voiture à trois roues; trois-roues *m inv*; tricyclecar *m*; (*b*) tricycle *m*.

threnody ['θrenədi], *s.* thrène *m*; chant *m* funèbre.

threose ['θri:ous], *s. Ch:* thréose *m*.

thresh [θreʃ], *v.tr.* **1.** battre, défourrer (le blé); **to t. corn by hand,** battre le blé en grange. **2.** (*of ship's screw, of whale's tail, etc.*) **to t. the water,** battre l'eau.

thresher ['θreʃər], *s.* **1.** (*a*) (*pers.*) batteur, -euse, en grange; (*b*) (*machine*) batteuse. **2.** *Ich:* **t. (shark),** renard (marin), renard de mer; *Z:* **t. whale,** orque *f*, épaulard *m*.

threshing ['θreʃiŋ], *s.* battage *m* (du blé); **t. floor,** aire *f*; **t. machine,** batteuse *f*.

threshold ['θreʃould], *s.* **1.** (*a*) seuil *m*, pas *m* (d'une porte, etc.); **on the t.,** sur le seuil; au seuil; **to cross the t.,** franchir le seuil; **to be on the t. of life,** être au seuil, au début, de la vie; **we were at the t. of a new era,** on entrait dans une ère nouvelle; (*b*) *Geol:* **glacial t.,** verrou *m* glaciaire. **2.** (*a*) *Physiol:* **t. of audibility, of hearing,** seuil d'audibilité; **stimulus t., t. of response,** seuil d'excitation (d'un muscle, etc.); seuil absolu; **t. of feeling,** seuil de sensibilité; **t. of pain,** seuil de douleur; **renal t.,** seuil d'élimination; *Psy:* **differential t.,** seuil différentiel; **t. of consciousness,** seuil de la conscience; **above the t.,** supraliminal, -aux; **below the t.,** subliminal, -aux; (*b*) *Ph: etc:* **fission t.,** seuil de fission; **photoelectric, photonuclear, t.,** seuil de sensibilité photoélectrique, photonucléaire; **t. of reaction, of response,** seuil de (la) réaction, de réponse, de sensibilité; **t. of (kinetic) energy,** seuil d'énergie (cinétique); *El: etc:* **t. indicator,** indicateur à seuil; **t. frequency,** seuil de fréquence, fréquence critique; **t. voltage,** tension de seuil; *W.Tel:* (*of valve*) **t. of oscillation,** limite *f* d'entretien; **t. wavelength,** seuil de longueur d'onde.

Threskiornithidae [θreskiɔ:'niθidi:], *s.pl. Orn:* threskiornithidés *m*.

thrice [θrais], *adv. A: & Lit:* **1.** trois fois; **t. as much,** trois fois autant; **t. as great,** trois fois aussi grand; trois fois plus grand. **2.** (*followed by adj. or p.p., e.g.*) **t.-told tale,** histoire rebattue; **t. blessed,** trois fois béni.

thridace ['θridəs], *s. Pharm:* thridace *f*.

thrift [θrift], *s.* **1.** économie *f*, épargne *f*; *Mil: etc:* **t. shop,** magasin spécialisé dans la vente des articles de seconde main. **2.** *Bot:* armérie, arméria, commune; **sea t.,** statice *m*; armérie, arméria, maritime; lavande *f* de mer; **(mountain) t.,** gazon *m* d'Olympe.

thriftily ['θriftili], *adv.* **1.** avec économie; avec épargne; **to live t.,** vivre frugalement. **2.** *NAm:* d'une façon florissante, prospère.

thriftiness ['θriftinis], *s.* (*a*) économie *f*, épargne *f*; (*b*) soins ménagers.

thriftless ['θriftlis], *a.* **1.** dépensier, prodigue. **2.** sans soin; imprévoyant; mou, *f.* molle.

thriftlessness ['θriftlisnis], *s.* **1.** prodigalité *f*; gaspillage *m*. **2.** manque *m* de soin; incurie *f*; imprévoyance *f*; mollesse *f* de caractère.

thrifty ['θrifti], *a.* **1.** économe, épargnant. **2.** *NAm:* prospère; florissant.

thrill[1] [θril], *s.* **1.** (*a*) frisson *m*, tressaillement *m*, frémissement *m*; **t. of joy,** tressaillement, frisson, de joie; **t. of pleasure,** frisson de plaisir; (*b*) (vive) émotion; **the crowd had the t. of their lives,** la foule était électrisée; **we've had the t. of a lifetime,** jamais nous ne revivrons une heure pareille; **it gave me quite a t.,** ça m'a fait quelque chose. **2.** *Med:* murmure *m* respiratoire; frémissement (à l'auscultation); thrill *m*.

thrill[2]. **1.** *v.tr.* (*a*) faire frissonner, faire frémir (qn); **to be thrilled with joy,** frissonner, tressaillir, de joie; *F:* **she's thrilled with her new car,** elle est ravie de sa nouvelle voiture; (*b*) faire vibrer le cœur de (qn); émouvoir, empoigner (qn); émotionner (qn); électriser (son auditoire); **scents that t. the senses,** parfums qui troublent les sens; **the news thrilled us,** la nouvelle nous a fait battre le cœur; **to be thrilled by a speech,** être électrisé par un discours; **to be thrilled at the sight of sth.,** ressentir une vive émotion, être profondément ému, à la vue de qch. **2.** *v.i. esp. Lit:* (*a*) tressaillir, frissonner, frémir; **to t. with fear,** frémir, tressaillir, de crainte; **we thrilled at the news,** la nouvelle nous a fait battre le cœur; (*b*) **joy thrilled through his heart,** la joie vibrait dans son cœur, le pénétrait jusqu'au cœur.

thriller ['θrilər], *s.* **1.** roman, film, policier; pièce *f*, film, à suspense. **2.** *F:* **this match is a t.,** ce match vous tient en haleine.

thrilling ['θriliŋ], *a.* (spectacle, discours, etc.) émouvant, qui vous empoigne, empoignant, saisissant, poignant, angoissant, émotionnant; (voyage, etc.) mouvementé; (roman, etc.) sensationnel, passionnant, à sensation, palpitant; *Rac:* **t. finish,** arrivée palpitante.

thrillingly ['θriliŋli], *adv.* d'une façon émouvante.

thrips [θrips], *s. Ent:* thrips *m*.

thrive [θraiv], *v.i.* (*p.t. & p.p.* **thrived** [θraivd]; *A: p.t.* **throve** [θrouv]; *p.p.* **thriven** ['θrivn]) (*a*) (*of child, plant*) se (bien) développer; *F:* profiter; (*of adult*) se bien porter; (*of plant, animal*) réussir, bien venir, prospérer; (*of business, etc.*) bien marcher, bien aller; **children who t. on milk,** enfants à qui le lait profite bien, à qui le lait réussit; **plant that thrives in all soils,** plante qui s'accommode de tous les sols, qui aime, qui se plaît à, tous les sols; **he thrives on it,** il s'en trouve bien; (*b*) (*of pers.*) prospérer (**on sth.,** de qch.); **to t. on other people's misfortunes,** s'engraisser de la misère d'autrui.

thriving[1] ['θraiviŋ], *a.* (*of pers., plant, etc.*) vigoureux; bien portant; (*of tree, herd, etc.*) qui réussit bien; bien venant; (*of pers., business*) prospère, florissant.

thriving[2], *s.* bien-être *m*, prospérité *f* (d'une personne); état vigoureux (d'une plante, etc.).

thro' [θru:], *prep. F:* = THROUGH.

throat [θrout], *s.* **1.** (*a*) *Anat:* gorge *f*; **to grip, pin, s.o. by the t.,** prendre, empoigner, qn par la gorge; serrer la gorge à qn; **he held me by the t.,** il me tenait par la gorge; il me serrait la gorge; **I've got him by the t.,** je le tiens à la gorge; **to cut s.o.'s t.,** couper la gorge à qn; égorger qn; **he's cutting his own t.,** il se perd lui-même; il travaille à sa propre ruine; **they were cutting each other's, one another's, throats,** ils se faisaient une concurrence désastreuse; **t. microphone,** laryngophone *m*; *A.Arms:* (*of helmet*) **t. piece,** gorgerin *m*; (*b*) (*gullet*) gorge, gosier *m*; **to have a fishbone in one's t.,** avoir une arête dans le gosier; **the back of the t.,** le fond de la gorge; l'arrière-gorge *f, pl.* arrière-gorges; **to have a sore t.,** avoir un mal de gorge; avoir mal à la gorge; **clergyman's (sore) t.,** pharyngite *f* chronique; **to clear one's t.,** s'éclaircir la voix, la gorge; se racler la gorge; tousser; *Med:* **t. sprayer,** insufflateur *m;* **t. wash,** gargarisme *m;* **fumes that catch your t.,** exhalaisons qui vous prennent à la gorge; *Lit:* **to give s.o. the lie in his t.,** donner à qn un démenti en plein visage, un démenti formel; *F:* **he's always ramming it down my t.,** il m'en rabat toujours les oreilles. **2.** *(a)* rétrécissement *m,* gorge (dans un cours d'eau, etc.); *(b) Nau:* (i) empointure *f* (de chute avant de voile goélette); (ii) mâchoire *f* (de corne); *(c)* **t. (piece),** cœur *m* (de raquette de tennis); *(d) Mec.E: etc:* portée *f* (d'une poinçonneuse); *(e) Metall:* gueulard *m* (de haut fourneau).

throatband ['θroutbænd], *s. Harn:* sous-gorge *f inv,* sougorge *f.*

throatily ['θroutili], *adv.* d'une voix gutturale.

throatiness ['θroutinis], *s.* qualité gutturale (de la voix).

throating ['θroutiŋ], *s.* rainure *f,* cannelure *f,* gorge *f.*

throatlash, throatlatch ['θroutlæʃ, -lætʃ], *s. Harn:* sous-gorge *f inv,* sougorge *f.*

throatwort ['θroutwəːt], *s. Bot:* (campanule) gantelée *f;* ganteline *f;* gant *m* de bergère, (de) Notre-Dame.

throaty ['θrouti], *a. (of voice)* d'arrière-gorge; guttural, -aux.

throb[1] [θrɔb], *s.* palpitation *f,* pulsation *f,* battement fort (du pouls, du cœur, etc.); vrombissement *m* (d'une machine, etc.); **his heart gave a t.,** il a eu un battement de cœur.

throb[2], *v.i.* **(throbbed)** *(a) (of pulse, heart, etc.)* battre fort, palpiter; *(of engine, etc.)* battre; vrombir; **his heart was throbbing violently,** son cœur battait à se rompre; **his heart throbbed with joy,** son cœur a tressailli de joie; **London is a city throbbing with activity,** Londres est une ville palpitante d'activité; *(b)* **my finger is throbbing,** mon doigt lancine; le doigt m'élance.

throbbing[1] ['θrɔbiŋ], *a. (of pulse, heart, etc.)* palpitant, qui bat fort; *(of engine)* vrombissant; **t. pain,** douleur lancinante, pulsative; lancinement *m,* élancement *m;* **t. sound of machines,** bruit ronflant de machines.

throbbing[2], *s. (a)* battement fort, palpitation *f,* pulsation *f* (du cœur, etc.); battement, vibration *f,* ronflement *m* (d'une machine, etc.); vrombissement *m* (d'une machine); *(b)* lancinement *m,* élancement *m,* lancées *fpl* (d'un panaris, etc.).

throes [θrouz], *s.pl.* douleurs *fpl,* angoisse *f,* agonie *f;* **the t. of childbirth,** les douleurs de l'accouchement; **the t. of death,** les affres *f* de la mort; l'agonie; **his death t. are beginning,** il entre en agonie; *Lit:* **in the t. of authorship,** en train d'enfanter une œuvre (littéraire); **England was in the t. of a general election,** l'Angleterre était au beau milieu d'une élection; **we're in the t. of moving house,** nous sommes en plein déménagement.

thrombasthenia [θrɔmbəs'θiːniə], *s. Med:* thrombasthénie *f.*

thrombin ['θrɔmbin], *s. Bio-Ch:* thrombine *f,* fibrinferment *m, pl.* fibrins-ferments, fibrine-ferment *m, pl.* fibrines-ferments.

thromboangiitis [θrɔmbouændʒi'aitis], *s. Med:* thrombo-angéite *f;* **t. obliterans,** thrombo-angéite oblitérante; thrombo-angiose *f;* maladie *f* de Buerger.

thrombocyte ['θrɔmbousait], *s. Physiol:* thrombocyte *m.*

thrombocytopenia [θrɔmbousaitou'piːniə], *s. Med:* thrombocytopénie *f.*

thrombocytopenic [θrɔmbousaitou'piːnik], *a. Med:* **t. purpura,** purpura thrombocytopénique.

thromboembolic [θrɔmbouem'bɔlik], *a. Med:* thrombo-embolique.

thrombokinase [θrɔmbou'kaineis], *s. Bio-Ch:* thrombokinase *f,* thromboplastine *f.*

thrombopenia [θrɔmbou'piːniə], *s. Med:* thrombopénie *f.*

thrombophlebitis [θrɔmboufli'baitis], *s. Med:* thrombophlébite *f.*

thromboplastic [θrɔmbou'plæstik], *a.* thromboplastique.

thromboplastin [θrɔmbou'plæstin], *s. Bio-Ch:* thromboplastine *f.*

thrombosed ['θrɔmbouzd], *a. Med:* thrombosé.

thrombosis [θrɔm'bousis], *s. Med:* thrombose *f;* **coronary t.,** infarctus *m* du myocarde.

thrombus, *pl.* **-bi** ['θrɔmbəs, -bai], *s. Med:* thrombus *m;* caillot sanguin.

throne[1] [θroun], *s.* **1.** *(a)* trône (royal, épiscopal); **to come to the t.; to ascend,** *Lit:* **mount, the t.,** monter sur le trône; **to instal, put, s.o. on the t.,** mettre, placer, qn sur le trône; **the heir to the t.,** l'héritier du trône; **the power behind the t.,** l'Éminence grise; *(b) F: (lavatory)* trône. **2.** *Theol: (order of Angles)* **the Thrones,** les Trônes.

throne[2]. *O:* **1.** *v.tr.* mettre (un roi, une reine) sur le trône; introniser (un évêque). **2.** *v.i. (a)* être sur le trône; *(b)* trôner.

throneroom ['θrounruːm], *s. (a)* salle *f* du trône; *(b) F:* les cabinets *mpl.*

throng[1] [θrɔŋ], *s.* **1.** *(a)* foule *f,* affluence *f,* multitude *f,* presse *f;* *(b)* cohue *f.* **2.** *A: & Dial:* **the t. of business,** la presse des affaires.

throng[2]. **1.** *v.i.* s'assembler en foule; affluer (à, dans, un endroit); **to t. round s.o.,** assiéger qn; se presser autour de qn; faire foule autour de qn; **they thronged into the square,** ils arrivèrent en foule sur la place. **2.** *v.tr.* encombrer, emplir, remplir (les rues, etc.); **the room was thronged with people,** la pièce était encombrée par la foule; la pièce était comble, bondée.

throng[3], *a. Scot: (a) (of pers.)* très occupé; *(b)* **the t. hours,** les heures de pointe; **the t. season,** la pleine saison.

thronging ['θrɔŋiŋ], *a. (of crowd, etc.)* serré, compact.

throstle ['θrɔsl], *s.* **1.** *Orn: Lit: & Dial:* grive musicienne. **2.** *Tex:* **t. (frame),** métier continu.

throttle[1] ['θrɔtl], *s.* **1.** gosier *m.* **2.** *Mec.E: (a) Mch:* régulateur *m;* modérateur *m;* prise *f* de vapeur; registre *m* de vapeur; **t. lever,** levier de régulateur; **t. rod, t. stem,** arbre *m* de commande, tringle *f* de manœuvre. du régulateur; **t. valve,** tiroir *m* de régulateur; glissière *f* du modérateur; étrangleur *m,* soupape *f* d'étranglement; **t. valve chamber,** tête de régulateur; *(b) I.C.E: etc:* étrangleur *m;* obturateur *m;* papillon *m;* **carburettor t.,** obturateur, papillon, de carburateur; **t. control, lever,** commande *f,* manette *f,* des gaz; **t. control unit,** bloc de commande des gaz; **t. chamber,** boisseau *m;* **t. clamp, lock,** blocage de la commande, de la manette, des gaz; **t. valve,** soupape de commande des gaz; papillon; **t. valve spindle,** axe du papillon; **t. valve screw,** vis de fixation des papillons; **t. quadrant,** secteur de commande des gaz; **t. idle stop,** butée *f* de ralenti; **to drive on full t., to give full t.,** aller, marcher, à pleins gaz; **to open the t.,** ouvrir, mettre, les gaz; **to close the t.,** couper, fermer, les gaz.

throttle[2], *v.tr.* **1.** *(a)* étrangler (qn); saisir, serrer (qn) à la gorge; *(b)* **to t. an offensive,** juguler une offensive. **2.** *Mch: I.C.E:* étrangler (la vapeur, le moteur); *v.i.* **to t. down,** mettre la machine, le moteur, au ralenti; *I.C.E:* couper, fermer, les gaz; **running throttled down,** marche au ralenti; *v.i. Av:* **to t. back,** couper, fermer, les gaz.

throttling ['θrɔtliŋ], *s.* **1.** étranglement *m, Jur:* strangulation *f* (de qn). **2.** *Mch: I.C.E:* étranglement; *Mch:* manœuvre *f* de registre; **t. down,** ralenti *m;* **t. valve,** soupape, vanne, d'étranglement, d'admission.

through [θruː], *prep., adv. & a.*

I. *prep.* **1.** *(a)* à travers; par; d'un côté à l'autre de (qch.); d'un bout à l'autre de (qch.); **t. a hedge,** au travers d'une haie; **there's a path t. the fields,** il y a un sentier qui passe à travers (les) champs; **the path goes, leads, t. the forest,** le sentier traverse, passe par, la forêt; **the sun is breaking t. the clouds,** le soleil perce les nuages; **I'm on my way t. Paris,** je suis de passage à Paris; **to pass t. the town,** passer par, traverser, la ville; **to pass t. the doorway,** passer par la porte; **the bill passed t. Parliament,** la loi a passé; **to look t. the window,** regarder par la fenêtre; **to look t. a telescope,** regarder dans un télescope; **he saw t. the trick,** il ne s'est pas laissé duper; *Mth:* **to draw a tangent t. an exterior point,** mener une tangente par un point extérieur; **to come, go, t. sth.,** traverser qch.; **to go out t. the kitchen,** sortir par la cuisine; **he came in t. the window,** il est entré par la fenêtre; **to go t. s.o.'s pockets,** fouiller qn; **to cycle, drive, ride, t. the countryside,** traverser la campagne à bicyclette, en voiture, à cheval; *Aut:* **to go t. a red light,** brûler un feu (rouge); **to go t. many dangers,** traverser beaucoup de dangers; **he's been t. it, t. a lot,** il en a vu de dures; il a mangé de la vache enragée; il en a vu de(s) vertes et de(s) pas mûres; il en a vu de toutes les couleurs; **to run right t. the town,** traverser la ville d'un bout à l'autre; **to speak t. one's nose,** parler du nez; **I can't hear a thing t. this noise,** il y a un tel bruit que je n'entends rien du tout; avec ce bruit je n'entends rien du tout; **to sleep t. a thunderstorm,** dormir à poings fermés pendant (toute la durée d')un orage; **he got t. his exam,** il a été reçu à son examen; *F:* **to put s.o. t. it,** faire subir à qn un interrogatoire très serré; **I'm half way t. this book,** j'ai lu la moitié de ce livre; **I've got t. this book,** j'ai fini ce livre; *NAm:* **when I'm t. my work,** quand j'aurai fini mon travail; *(b) (in expressions of time)* pendant, durant; **all t. his life,** sa vie durant; durant, pendant, toute sa vie; **I didn't sleep all t. the night, the whole night t.,** je n'ai pas dormi de la nuit; **to sleep all t. the winter, the whole winter t.,** dormir pendant tout l'hiver; **t. the ages,** à travers les âges; *esp. NAm:* **Monday t. Friday,** de lundi à vendredi; du lundi au vendredi. **2. t. s.o.,** par qn; par l'entremise, l'intermédiaire, de qn; en recourant à qn; **t. sth.,** par le moyen de qch.; **to receive sth. t. s.o.,** recevoir qch. par l'intermédiaire de qn; **to send sth. t. the post,** envoyer qch. par la poste; **I bought it t. my agent,** je l'ai acheté par l'entremise de mon homme d'affaires; **I heard of it t. a newspaper,** je l'ai appris par (l'intermédiaire d')un journal. **3.** *(a)* en conséquence de, par suite de, à cause de, par (qch.); **t. ignorance,** par ignorance; **absent t. illness,** absent par suite, pour cause, de maladie; **to act t. fear,** agir sous le coup de la peur; *(b)* par l'action de (qn, qch.); **it all happened t. him,** il est cause de tout; **it's (all) t. me that he missed his train,** c'est à cause de moi qu'il a manqué son train; c'est (entièrement) de ma faute s'il a manqué son train; **t. so much work you become exhausted,** à force de travailler on s'épuise.

II. *adv.* **1.** *(a)* à travers; **to drive a nail t.,** enfoncer un clou jusqu'à l'autre côté; **the water poured t.,** l'eau coulait à travers; **has it gone t.?** est-ce que ça a traversé? **to let s.o. t.,** laisser passer qn; **I got it t.,** je l'ai fait passer; **his trousers are t. at the knees,** son pantalon est percé aux genoux; *F:* **England are t. to the semi-final,** l'Angleterre jouera dans la demi-finale; *(b)* **t. (and t.),** de bout en bout; de part en part; **to run s.o. t. (with a sword, etc.),** transpercer qn; percer qn de part en part; **I know Paris t. and t.,** je connais Paris de bout en bout, comme (le fond de) ma poche; **I'm soaked t. (and t.),** la pluie m'a transpercé; *(c)* d'un bout à l'autre; jusqu'au bout; jusqu'à la fin; **to read a book (right) t.,** lire un livre jusqu'au bout, d'un bout à l'autre, en entier; **to hear s.o., a concert, t.,** écouter, entendre, qn, un concert, jusqu'au bout; **to see, carry, sth. t.,** mener qch. à bonne fin; **we must go t. with it,** il faut aller jusqu'au bout; **to be t. with sth.,** (i) avoir fini qch.; (ii) en avoir (eu) assez; **are you t. with your work?** avez-vous fini votre travail? **he'll change his tune when I'm t. with him,** il changera de ton quand je lui aurai réglé son compte; **I'm t. with you, we're t.,** j'en ai fini avec toi; je veux rompre avec toi; c'est fini entre nous; **to be t.,** (i) *esp. NAm:* avoir terminé, fini (de parler, etc.); (ii) *F:* être fichu. **2.** *(a)* directement; **the train runs t. to Paris,** le train va directement à Paris; **to book t. to Paris,** prendre son billet directement, prendre un billet direct, pour Paris; **to book the luggage t. to Rome,** enregistrer les bagages directement pour Rome; *(b)* **to get t. to s.o.,** (i) *Tp:* obtenir la communication avec qn; (ii) *F:* faire comprendre qch. à qn; *Tp:* **I'll put you t. to the secretary,** je vous passe le secrétaire; **you're t.,** vous êtes en communication; vous avez la communication; vous l'avez; *NAm:* **are you t.?** avez-vous terminé (la conversation)?

III. *a.* **1.** *Tchn: (a) (of shaft, etc.)* traversant; *(of mortise, etc.)* passant; **t. bolt,** boulon d'assemblage, boulon traversant; *Const:* **t. stone,** parpaing *m;* *(b)* **t. bridge,** pont à tablier inférieur, à tablier intermédiaire. **2.** *(of train, road, ticket, etc.)* direct; *Rail:* **t. wagon, coach,** wagon de groupage; **t. carriage for Paris,** voiture directe pour Paris; **t. connections,** relations directes; **t. passenger to Paris,** voyageur, -euse, direct(e) pour Paris; **t. traffic,** transit *m;* *P.N:* **no t. road,** voie sans issue; *NAm:* **t. street,** rue prioritaire; *Nau:* **t. bill of lading,** connaissement direct. **3.** *Min:* **t.(-and-t.) coal,** tout-venant *m.*

throughly ['θruːli], *adv. A:* = THOROUGHLY.

throughout [θruː'aut]. **1.** *prep. (a)* **t. the country,** d'un bout à l'autre du pays; dans tout le pays; partout dans le pays; **t. France,** partout en France; **t. the world,** à travers le monde; *(b) (time)* **t. the year,** pendant toute l'année; **t. his life,** toute sa vie durant; durant, pendant, toute sa vie. **2.** *adv. (a)* partout; **the wood was rotten t.,** le bois était complètement pourri; **the coat is lined with fur t.,** le manteau est entièrement doublé de fourrure; **to be wrong t.,** avoir tort sur tous les points, à tous égards; *(b) (time)* tout le temps; **he stuck to the same story t.,** il a persisté tout le temps dans la même histoire.

throughput ['θruːput], *s. (a)* capacité *f;* consommation *f;* débit *m;* **t. capacity,** capacité totale d'aspiration (d'une pompe centrifuge); *(b) Cmptr:* (i) débit, rendement *m;* (ii) capacité de traitement.

throughway ['θruːwei], *s. NAm:* (i) autoroute *f;* (ii) rue *f* prioritaire; **cross t.,** route transversale directe.

throw[1] [θrou], *s.* **1.** *(a)* jet *m,* lancement *m,* lancée *f,* lancer *m* (de qch.); **t. of dice,** coup *m* de dés; *(at dice)* **it's your t.,** à vous le dé; à vous de jouer; *A.Arms:* **t. stick = throwing stick;** *(b)* distance (à laquelle on lance un objet); **long t.,** jet de longue portée; *(c) Cr:* (i) lancement de la balle; (ii) balle lancée; (iii) balle nulle; *(d)*

Wr: lancer, mise *f* à terre (de l'adversaire); **head t.,** coup d'arpin. **2.** *Geol:* rejet *m*, cran *m*, accident *m* (dans une stratification, etc.). **3.** *Mec.E:* (*a*) **t. of the governor,** déviation *f*, écart *m*, du régulateur; **t. (of the eccentric),** (rayon *m* d')excentricité *f*; course *f* (de l'excentrique); course de la came; *Mch:* **t. (of the piston),** volée *f* (du piston); (*b*) *Aut: etc:* maneton *m* (de vilebrequin): *I.C.E:* **crank t.,** coude *m* de vilebrequin; **throws of the crankshaft,** bras *mpl* de manivelle du vilebrequin; **single-t. crankshaft,** arbre à un seul coude, à une seule manivelle; **two-t. crankshaft,** arbre à deux coudes, à deux manivelles; (*c*) **t. lathe,** tour à main. **4.** *NAm:* (*a*) couvre-lit *m*, *pl.* couvre-lits; (*b*) *Cost:* écharpe *f* (de femme).

throw[2], *v.tr.* (**threw** [θru:]; **thrown** [θroun])

I. 1. (*a*) jeter, lancer (une balle, etc.); **to t. the discus, the javelin,** lancer le disque, le javelot; **to t. bombs,** lancer des bombes; *v.i.* **he can t. a hundred metres,** il est capable de lancer à cent mètres; **to t. s.o. the ball, to t. the ball to s.o.,** lancer, jeter, la balle à qn; lancer le ballon à qn; **he threw the ball over the wall,** il a lancé la balle par-dessus le mur; *Cr:* **to t. (the ball),** (i) renvoyer la balle au guichet; (ii) lancer la balle en raidissant le coude (balle nulle); **to t. s.o. a kiss,** envoyer un baiser à qn; **to t. the dice,** jeter les dés; (*at dice*) **to t. a five, a six,** amener cinq, six; **to t. a (fishing) line,** jeter une ligne de pêche; **to t. a good line,** être habile à la pêche; être bon pêcheur; *Pol:* **to t. one's hat into the ring,** poser sa candidature; **to t. stones at s.o., at a dog,** lancer, jeter, des pierres sur, à, qn, à un chien; **to t. tomatoes at s.o.,** lancer des tomates à qn; recevoir qn à coups de tomates; **to t. sth. in s.o.'s face,** jeter qch. au nez, à la face, à la figure, de qn; **don't t. that in my face,** ne me faites pas de reproches à ce sujet; **to t. a glance at s.o.,** jeter un coup d'œil à, sur, qn; **to t. sth. out of the window,** jeter qch. par la fenêtre; **to t. one's arms in the air,** lever les bras en l'air; **to t. oneself in(to) the river,** se jeter dans la rivière; **to t. oneself forwards, backwards,** se jeter en avant; se rejeter en arrière; **to t. a bucket of water over s.o.,** jeter un seau d'eau sur qn; *F:* coiffer qn d'un seau d'eau; **to t. temptation in s.o.'s way,** exposer qn à la tentation; **to t. the blame, the responsibility, on s.o.,** rejeter la faute, la responsabilité, sur qn; (*b*) **to t. a bridge over, across, a river,** jeter, lancer, un pont sur une rivière; **to t. a sheet over sth.,** couvrir qch. d'un drap; **to t. a shawl over one's shoulders,** jeter un châle sur ses épaules; **to t. s.o. into prison,** jeter, mettre, qn en prison; **to t. a division against the enemy,** lancer une division sur, à, l'ennemi; *Lit:* **to t. oneself into the fray,** s'élancer à l'assaut, dans la mêlée; *Fig:* **to t. oneself at s.o.,** poursuivre qn dans le but (i) de l'épouser, (ii) de s'en faire un ami, une amie; **to t. oneself on, upon, s.o.,** s'attaquer, s'en prendre, à qn; *A:* **to be thrown upon the parish,** tomber à la charge de la commune, de l'assistance publique; **I was thrown by accident into their company,** je suis tombé par hasard dans leur société; **to t. s.o., an army, into confusion,** jeter qn dans l'embarras; jeter le désordre dans une armée; **to t. two rooms into one,** de deux pièces n'en faire qu'une; **to t. a switch,** basculer un interrupteur; **to t. open the door,** ouvrir la porte toute grande; ouvrir vivement la porte; **to t. open one's house to s.o.,** ouvrir sa maison à qn; **the competition was thrown open to people under 18,** le concours était ouvert aux personnes âgées de moins de 18 ans; **600 men were thrown idle,** 600 hommes ont été réduits au chômage, ont été privés de travail. **2.** (*a*) projeter (de l'eau, de l'huile, etc.); (*b*) **to t. a picture on the screen,** projeter une image sur l'écran; **to t. one's shadow, a beam of light, on the pavement,** projeter son ombre, un rayon de lumière, sur le trottoir; **to t. light on the matter,** jeter de la lumière sur la question; éclairer la question. **3. to t. a fit,** tomber en convulsions; piquer une attaque de nerfs; *F:* **to t. a party,** organiser une soirée. **4.** (*a*) *Wr:* **to t. an opponent,** terrasser, renverser, tomber, un adversaire; (*b*) (*of horse*) **to t. its rider,** désarçonner, démonter, son cavalier; (*of rider*) **to be thrown,** vider les arçons; être désarçonné; tomber (de cheval). **5.** (*of reptile*) **to t. its skin,** se dépouiller de sa peau; muer. **6.** (*of animals*) mettre bas (des petits). **7.** (*a*) tourner, façonner (un pot); (*b*) *Tex:* organiser, mouliner, tordre (la soie). **8.** *F:* étonner, déconcerter (qn); **his question threw me for a moment,** pendant un moment je ne savais que répondre à sa question. **9.** *esp. NAm: F:* **to t. a contest, a race,** perdre un match, une course, avec intention.

II. (*compound verbs*) **1. throw about,** *v.tr.* (*a*) jeter (des objets) çà et là, un peu partout; éparpiller, disséminer (des objets); **to t. one's money about,** dépenser largement, sans compter; gaspiller son argent; (*b*) (i) **to t. one's arms about,** faire de grands gestes; **to t. oneself about,** se démener; s'agiter; (ii) **to be thrown about,** être ballotté, cahoté, secoué.

2. throw aside, *v.tr.* (*a*) jeter (qch.) de côté; écarter (qch.); (*b*) se dépouiller de (toute haine, etc.).

3. throw away, *v.tr.* (*a*) (i) jeter (sa cigarette, etc.); rejeter (qch.); jeter, mettre (qch.) au rebut; abandonner (ses armes, etc.); **to be thrown away,** à jeter, jetable; (ii) *Cards:* **to t. away a card,** se défausser d'une carte; écarter, rejeter, une carte; (*b*) donner (qch.) inutilement; gaspiller; **a kind act is never thrown away,** une bonne action n'est jamais perdue; **to t. away a chance,** laisser passer une occasion; ne pas profiter d'une occasion; **to t. away one's life,** se sacrifier inutilement; (*of girl*) **to t. herself away,** se marier avec un homme indigne d'elle; (*c*) (*of actor*) **to t. away a line,** énoncer une phrase avec une indifférence calculée.

4. throw back. (*a*) *v.tr.* (i) jeter (un poisson dans l'eau, etc.); renvoyer, relancer (une balle, etc.); (*of mirror*) refléter, réfléchir, renvoyer (l'image, etc.); réverbérer (la lumière, la chaleur); (ii) repousser (les volets, etc.); **to t. one's head back,** rejeter la tête en arrière; **to t. back one's shoulders,** effacer les épaules; (iii) retarder (un travail, etc.); **this would t. me back,** cela me retarderait dans mon travail; (iv) **to be thrown back upon s.o., sth.,** être forcé de se rabattre sur qn, qch.; (*b*) *v.i. Biol:* (*of breed, specimen*) retourner à un type antérieur, à un type primitif.

5. throw down, *v.tr.* (*a*) (i) jeter (qch.) de haut en bas; **they threw down stones on the besiegers,** ils laissaient tomber, faisaient tomber, jetaient, des pierres sur les assiégeants; (ii) jeter (qch.) à terre, par terre; jeter bas (qch.); abattre (ses cartes, etc.); **to t. oneself down,** se jeter sur le sol; se jeter à plat ventre; (iii) **to t. down one's arms,** (α) abandonner ses armes; (β) se rendre; (iv) démolir, abattre (un mur, etc.); abattre (un arbre); (*b*) *Ch: etc:* déposer, précipiter (un sédiment); (*c*) *U.S: F:* rejeter, repousser (un projet, etc.); rejeter (qn).

6. throw in, *v.tr.* (*a*) jeter (qn, qch.) dedans; **when children are afraid to dive, they are thrown in,** quand les enfants hésitent à plonger, on les jette à l'eau; (*b*) (i) ajouter (qch.); donner (qch.) par-dessus le marché; **the butcher always throws in a bone for the dog,** le boucher ajoute toujours un os pour le chien; **you can have this piano for £60, with the stool thrown in,** je vous vends ce piano £60, avec le tabouret par-dessus le marché; (ii) intercaler, insérer, introduire (une observation, un mot); placer (un mot); (*c*) **to t. in one's lot with s.o.,** *v.i. U.S:* **to t. in with s.o.,** partager le sort, la fortune, de qn; unir sa destinée à celle de qn; s'attacher à la fortune de qn; (*d*) (i) **to t. in one's hand, one's cards,** abandonner, quitter, la partie; s'avouer vaincu; déclarer forfait; **to t. in the towel,** (α) *Box:* jeter l'éponge; (β) *Fig:* s'avouer vaincu; (ii) *Cr:* **to t. the ball in,** renvoyer la balle au guichet; (iii) *v.i. Fb:* **to t. in,** remettre en touche.

7. throw off, *v.tr.* (*a*) (*adv. use*) (i) jeter, rendre (de la vapeur, etc.); **the water is thrown off by centrifugal movement,** l'eau est projetée par le mouvement centrifuge; (ii) enlever, ôter, quitter (ses vêtements); se débarrasser, se défaire, de (qn, qch.); abandonner (un déguisement, etc.); lever (le masque); **to t. off a fever,** guérir de la fièvre; (iii) composer (un poème, etc.) au pied levé; (iv) (α) *Ven:* lancer (les chiens); (β) commencer, débuter; (*b*) (*prep. use*) (i) **to t. s.o. off his bicycle,** faire tomber qn de sa bicyclette; **to t. a train off the rails,** faire dérailler un train; (ii) **to t. the dogs off the scent,** mettre en défaut, dépister, les chiens.

8. throw on, *v.tr.* mettre, passer, (ses vêtements) à la hâte.

9. throw out, *v.tr.* (*a*) jeter (qn, qch.) dehors; expulser (qn); jeter (qn) à la porte; *Cr:* mettre (le batteur) hors jeu en lançant la balle sur le guichet; (*b*) (i) jeter, répandre, émettre (des rayons, de la chaleur, etc.); répandre (une odeur); (ii) **to t. out roots,** pousser des racines; (*c*) (i) rejeter, repousser (un projet de loi, etc.); écarter (un article défectueux, etc.); *Jur:* **to t. out a bill,** repousser une proposition de mise en accusation; rendre une ordonnance de non-lieu; (ii) *Aut: etc: O:* **to t. out the clutch,** débrayer; (*d*) (i) construire en saillie (l'aile d'une maison, une jetée, etc.); (ii) **to t. out one's chest,** bomber la poitrine; se cambrer; cambrer la taille; (iii) *Mil:* **to t. out skirmishers,** envoyer des tirailleurs en avant; (iv) faire ressortir (qch.); (*e*) lancer, laisser entendre (une remarque, etc.); **to t. out a challenge,** lancer un défi; **to t. out a suggestion,** émettre une proposition (sans insister); risquer un conseil; (*f*) (i) troubler, déconcerter, distraire (un orateur, etc.); **you've thrown him out,** vous lui avez fait perdre le fil de ses idées; (ii) **to t. s.o. out in his calculations,** tromper les calculs de qn.

10. throw over, *v.tr.* (*a*) abandonner (un ami, etc.); *F:* lâcher, plaquer (un amant, etc.); (*b*) renverser (un levier).

11. throw together, *v.tr.* (*a*) assembler (qch.) à la hâte; **his novels are thrown together,** ses romans sont écrits par-dessous la jambe, à la six-quatre-deux; (*b*) amener (des gens) à être ensemble, à se trouver en commun; **chance had thrown us together,** le hasard nous avait réunis.

12. throw up, *v.tr. & i.* (*a*) jeter (qch.) en l'air; (*b*) (i) *F:* vomir, rendre, *P:* dégueuler; (ii) **volcano that throws up lava,** volcan qui vomit de la lave; **wreckage thrown up by the sea,** débris de naufrage rejetés par la mer; (*c*) lever haut, mettre haut (les mains, etc.); **to t. up a window,** ouvrir (vivement) une fenêtre (à guillotine); **to t. up one's hands (in astonishment),** lever les bras au ciel; (*d*) construire (une maison. etc.) à la hâte; (*e*) faire ressortir (une couleur, etc.); (*f*) renoncer à, abandonner, lâcher (une affaire, etc.); **to t. up one's job,** se démettre de son poste; donner sa démission; **to t. up one's claims,** abandonner ses prétentions; **to feel like throwing everything up,** avoir envie de tout plaquer, de tout laisser tomber.

throwaway[1] ['θrouəwei], *a.* **1.** (couche, etc.) à jeter, jetable. **2.** *F:* **a t. line, remark,** un aparté.

throwaway[2], *s.* **1.** *Th: etc:* phrase énoncée avec une indifférence calculée; aparté *m.* **2.** *F:* prospectus *m.*

throwback ['θroubæk], *s.* **1.** recul *m* (dans le progrès); échec *m*, déconvenue *f.* **2.** retour *m* (en arrière); **this play is a t. to Shakespearian drama,** cette pièce tient du drame shakespearien. **3.** *Biol:* régression *f*; retour *m* atavique; atavisme *m.*

thrower ['θrouər], *s.* **1.** (*a*) jeteur, -euse; lanceur, -euse (de javelot, etc.); **discus t.,** discobole *m*; (*b*) joueur, -euse (aux dés); (*c*) *Gaming:* (*at boule*) **t.-in,** bouleur *m.* **2.** (*a*) *Cer:* potier *m*, tourneur *m*, tournas(s)eur *m*; (*b*) *Tex:* organsineur *m*, moulineur, -euse, moulinier, -ière, tordeur, -euse (de soie).

throw-in ['θrouin], *s. Fb:* (rentrée *f* en) touche *f*; remise *f* en jeu (du ballon).

throwing ['θrouiŋ], *s.* **1.** jet *m*, lancement *m*, lancer *m*, lancée *f* (d'une pierre, etc.); *A.Arms:* **t. stick,** (i) arme *f* de jet en forme de massue, de bâton recourbé; boumerang *m*; (ii) dispositif utilisé pour jeter une lance. **2.** projection *f* (d'une image, d'une ombre). **3.** renversement *m*, terrassement *m* (d'un adversaire); désarçonnement *m* (d'un cavalier). **4.** (*of reptile*) dépouillement *m* (de sa peau). **5.** *Z:* mise *f* bas (de petits). **6.** (*a*) tournage *m*, façonnage *m* (d'un pot); (*b*) *Tex:* organsinage *m*, moulinage *m*, tordage *m* (de la soie).

throw-off ['θrouɔf], *s.* **1.** (*a*) *Ven:* lancé *m* (des chiens); (*b*) commencement *m*; mise *f* en train. **2.** *Mec.E:* dispositif *m* de déclenchement, d'arrêt.

throw-out ['θrouaut], *s.* **1.** *Com:* **throw-outs,** rebuts *m*; articles défectueux, pièces *f* de rebut. **2.** *Mec.E:* débrayage *m* automatique.

throwster ['θroustər], *s. Tex:* organsineur *m*, moulineur, -euse, moulinier, -ière, tordeur, -euse (de soie).

throwstring ['θroustriŋ], *s. Tex:* organsinage *m*, moulinage *m*, tordage *m* (de la soie).

thru' [θru:], *prep. F:* = THROUGH.

thrum[1] [θrʌm], *s.* **1.** (*a*) *Tex:* (i) penne *f*; (ii) un des fils de la penne; (*b*) bout *m* de fil. **2.** *Nau:* lardage *m.*

thrum[2], *v.tr.* (**thrummed**) *Nau:* larder (un paillet).

thrum[3], *s.* son *m* monotone (d'une guitare, d'un piano).

thrum[4], *v.tr. & i.* **to t. (on) a guitar,** pincer de la guitare; s'escrimer sur une guitare; **to t. on the piano,** tapoter le piano; **to t. on the window pane,** tambouriner sur la vitre.

thrummy ['θrʌmi], *a.* (*of substance*) fibreux; poilu.

thrush[1] [θrʌʃ], *s. Orn:* (*a*) grive *f*; **song t.,** grive musicienne; **whistling t.,** grive sifflante; **laughing t.,** garrulax *m*; **black-throated t.,** grive à gorge noire; **red-throated t.,** grive à gorge rouge; **red-winged t.,** grive rouge, grive mauvis; roselle *f*; **grey-cheeked,** *NAm:* **gray-cheeked, t.,** grive à joues grises; **olive-backed t.,** grive petite; *Fr.C:* grive à dos olive; **green t.,** cochoa *m*; **dusky t.,** grive à ailes rousses, merle brun; **eyebrowed, dark, t.,** grive obscure; **jewel, painted, t.,** grive superbe, brève *f* (superbe); **varied t.,** merle à collier; **ant t.,** (i) fourmilier *m*; (ii) brève, grive superbe; **mistle(toe), missel, t.,** grive draine, grive de gui; **hermit t.,** grive ermite, *Fr.C:* grive solitaire; **ground t.,** (i) géocichle *m*, geocichla *m*; (ii) brève, grive superbe; **(Indian) orange-headed ground t.,** merle orange; **rock t.,** merle de roche; **blue rock t.,** merle bleu, monticole bleu; **wood t.,** grive des bois; **Siberian t.,** merle sibérien; **Louisiana water t.,** fauvette *f* hoche-queue; **northern, Grinnell's, water t.,** fauvette des ruisseaux; **Naumann's t.,** grive de Naumann; **Pallas's t.,** merle solitaire; **Swainsons's t.,** grive de Swainson; **Ticknell's t.,** grive micolore; **White's, golden mountain, t.,** grive dorée; **Wilson's t.,**

grive de Wilson; (*b*) **t. nightingale,** (rossignol) progné *m*.

thrush[2], *s*. **1.** *Med:* aphtes *mpl* (des nouveau-nés); muguet *m*, blanchet *m*. **2.** *Vet:* teigne *f*; échauffement *m* de la fourchette (du cheval).

thrust[1] [θrʌst], *s*. **1.** (*a*) poussée *f*; **with one t. he broke the door down,** d'une seule poussée il a enfoncé la porte; **t. hoe,** ratissoire *f* à pousser; (*b*) coup *m* de pointe; *Fenc:* coup d'estoc; passe *f*; *Fenc:* **t. and parry,** la botte et la parade; **lance t.,** coup de lance; **to make a t. at s.o.,** porter un coup de pointe, un coup de lance, *Fenc:* un coup d'estoc, à qn; porter, pousser, une botte à qn; *Fenc:* **to make a time t.,** tirer sur le temps; **a shrewd t.,** un trait, une critique, qui frappe juste; **that was a t. at you,** c'était un coup de boutoir, une attaque, à votre adresse; c'était une pierre dans votre jardin; (*c*) *Mil: etc:* poussée (d'une armée, etc.). **2.** (*a*) *Mec: Mec.E:* poussée, butée *f*; **axial t.,** poussée, butée, axiale; **cam t.,** poussée de la came; **connecting rod t.,** réaction *f* de la bielle; **dynamic t.,** poussée dynamique; **negative t.,** poussée négative; poussée réaction; **t. of an arch,** poussée d'une voûte; **t. of the ground,** poussée, butée, des terres; *Arch:* **lateral t.,** poussée latérale (d'une voûte); **t. passing outside material,** poussée au vide; **the thrusts meet,** les matériaux *m* se contrepoussent; **to take the t.,** (i) assurer la poussée; (ii) contre-buter, contre-bouter, la poussée; **to carry the t.,** travailler à la poussée; **t. line, line of t.,** axe *m* de poussée; **t. bearing, block,** (portée *f* de) palier *m* de butée; **t. collar,** collet *m* (du palier) de butée; rondelle *f* de butée; **t. rod,** bielle de poussée; **t. shaft,** arbre *m* de butée; **t. screw,** vis *f* à pression; **t. plate,** plaque *f* de choc, de butée (d'une emboutisseuse); (*b*) *Av: Nau:* poussée (d'une hélice); *Av:* **static t.,** poussée statique; **static jet t.,** poussée statique d'un réacteur, d'un moteur à réaction; **rated t.,** poussée nominale; (*of aero engine*) **to develop, produce, a 20,000 kilo t. at take-off,** développer une poussée de 20 000 kilos au décollage; **to take up the t.,** absorber la poussée; **t. coefficient,** coefficient de poussée; **t. load,** effort de poussée; **t. to weight ratio, t./weight ratio,** rapport de la poussée à la masse, rapport poussée/masse; **reverse t.,** contre-poussée *f*; poussée inverse; **t. reversal,** inversion de poussée; **t. reverser,** inverseur de poussée, de jet; **t. augmentation,** accroissement, augmentation, de la poussée; **t. augmenter,** augmentateur de poussée; **t. equalizer,** répartiteur de poussée; (*c*) *Geol:* chevauchement *m*, charriage *m* (des nappes de roche, des plissements); **t. plane,** plan de charriage.

thrust[2], *v*. (*p.t. & p.p.* **thrust**)

I. *v.tr. & i.* **1.** *v.tr.* (*a*) pousser (qn, qch.) (avec force); **to t. sth. into sth.,** enfoncer, fourrer, qch. dans qch.; **to t. one's hands into one's pockets,** fourrer, plonger, les mains dans ses poches; **to t. s.o. into a dungeon,** plonger, jeter, fourrer, qn dans un cachot; **to t. a dagger into s.o.'s back,** enfoncer, plonger, un poignard dans le dos de qn; **to t. sth. through sth.,** pousser qch. à travers qch.; **to t. sth. under s.o.'s nose,** fourrer qch. sous le nez de qn; (*b*) **to t. sth. on s.o.,** forcer qn à accepter qch.; imposer (son opinion) à qn; *F:* jeter qch. à la tête de qn; **to t. oneself (up)on s.o.,** s'imposer à qn, chez qn; imposer sa compagnie à qn; (*c*) **to t. oneself, one's way, through the crowd,** se frayer un chemin à travers la foule; **to t. past s.o.,** écarter qn pour passer. **2.** *v.i.* **to t. at s.o.,** (i) porter un coup de pointe à qn (avec sa canne, etc.); (ii) *Fenc:* porter un coup d'estoc à qn; frapper qn d'estoc; porter, pousser, une botte à qn; *Fenc:* **to t. in tierce, in quarte,** tirer en tierce, en quarte; *Fig:* **to t. and parry,** faire assaut d'esprit; riposter du tac au tac.

II. (*compound verbs*) **1. thrust aside, away,** *v.tr.* repousser, écarter (qn, qch., *Lit:* la tentation).

2. thrust back, *v.tr.* repousser violemment (la porte, etc.).

3. thrust forward, *v.tr.* (*a*) pousser (qn, qch.) en avant; avancer, tendre, brusquement (la main, etc.); (*b*) **to t. oneself forward,** (i) se faire valoir, se mettre en avant; (ii) s'ingérer dans une affaire.

4. thrust out, *v.tr.* (*a*) pousser (qn, qch.) dehors; **to t. out one's head,** passer la tête dehors; (*b*) **to t. out one's hand,** avancer brusquement, tendre vivement, la main; **to t. out one's chest,** bomber la poitrine; se cambrer.

thruster ['θrʌstər], *s*. **1.** *Fenc:* tireur, -euse (d'épée). **2.** (*a*) *Ven:* chasseur, -euse, à courre qui ne sait pas garder sa place, qui pousse de l'avant; (*b*) arriviste *mf*. **3.** *Mec.E: Av:* impulseur *m*; (*of spacecraft*) **apogee, perigee, t.,** impulseur d'apogée, de périgée; **re-entry t.,** impulseur de rentrée (dans l'atmosphère); **yaw t.,** impulseur de lacet.

thrusting ['θrʌstiŋ], *s*. **1.** poussée *f*; enfoncement *m* (de qch. dans qch.). **2.** *Fenc:* coup *m* d'estoc, de pointe; **t. weapon,** (i) (*sword*) arme *f* d'estoc; (ii) (*lance*) arme d'hast.

thrustor ['θrʌstər], *s*. *Mec.E: El:* servomoteur *m*.

thruway ['θru:wei], *s*. = THROUGHWAY.

Thryonomyidae [θraiɔnə'maiidi:], *s.pl. Z:* thryonomidés *m*.

Thryonomys [θrai'ɔnəmis], *s*. *Z:* thryonomys *m*.

thryothorus [θrai'ɔθərəs], *s*. *Orn:* thryothore *m*.

Thucydides [θ(j)u:'sididi:z], *Pr.n.m. Gr.Lit:* Thucydide.

thud[1] [θʌd], *s*. bruit sourd; bruit, son, mat; **to fall with a (dull) t.,** tomber avec un bruit sourd.

thud[2], *v.i.* (**thudded**) tomber, frapper, avec un bruit sourd; émettre un bruit, un son, mat; **his feet went thudding along the corridor,** ses pas résonnaient sourdement dans le couloir; **a bullet thudded into the wall,** une balle s'est enfoncée dans le mur avec un son mat.

thug [θʌg], *s*. **1.** *Hist:* thug *m*; étrangleur *m*. **2.** brute *f*, brutal, -aux *m*; **a political adventurer and his thugs,** un aventurier politique et ses hommes de main.

thuggee ['θʌgi:], *s*. *Hist:* thuggisme *m*.

thuggery ['θʌgəri], **thuggism** ['θʌgizm], *s*. **1.** *Hist:* thuggisme *m*. **2.** brutalité *f*, violence *f*.

thuja ['θu:jə], *s*. *Bot:* thuya *m*, thuia *m*, thuja *m*; **t. oil,** essence de thuya.

thujane ['θju:dʒein], *s*. *Ch:* thuyane *m*.

thujene ['θju:dʒi:n], *s*. *Ch:* thuyène *m*.

thujone ['θju:dʒoun], *s*. *Ch:* thuyone *f*.

Thujopsis [θju:'dʒɔpsis], *s*. *Bot:* thuiopsis *m*, thujopsis *m*, thuyopsis *m*.

thujyl ['θju:dʒil], *a*. *Ch:* **t. alcohol,** alcool *m* thuylique; thuyol *m*.

Thule ['θju:li(:)], *Pr.n. A.Geog:* Thulé *f*.

thulite ['θju:lait], *s*. *Miner:* thulite *f*.

thulium ['θju:liəm], *s*. *Ch:* thulium *m*.

thumb[1] [θʌm], *s*. **1.** (*a*) pouce *m*; **to hold sth. between finger and t.,** tenir qch. entre le pouce et l'index; *F:* **he's all thumbs, his fingers are all thumbs,** il est maladroit de ses mains; c'est un empoté, un brise-tout; il casse tout; **to be under s.o.'s t.,** être sous la domination, sous la coupe, de qn; être soumis à, dépendant de, qn; subir la loi de qn; **to keep s.o. (well) under one's t.,** mener qn en laisse, par le bout du nez; tenir qn en tutelle, comme un chien d'attache, comme un chien à l'attache; **she's got him right under her t.,** elle le mène à la baguette; elle le fait marcher comme elle veut; **to stick out like a sore t.,** sauter aux yeux, crever les yeux, choquer la vue; *F:* **thumbs up!** bravo! chic alors! *F:* **thumbs down on a proposition, a plan,** rejet *m* d'une proposition, d'un projet; *F:* **to give s.o. the thumbs down on his offer,** refuser tout net, rejeter, repousser, l'offre de qn; *A:* **to bite the t. at s.o.,** faire la figue à qn; narguer qn; **t. index,** (i) onglets *mpl* (d'un livre); (ii) répertoire *m* à onglets; **book bound with t. index,** livre relié avec encoches; **t.-indexed edition,** édition à onglets; **t. pot,** petit pot (à fleurs); godet *m*; **t. nut,** écrou à ailettes, à oreilles; papillon *m*; *Nau:* **t. cleat,** taquet *m* de hublot; (*b*) *F:* **to give a quick t. through a book,** feuilleter, parcourir, lire en diagonale, un livre. **2.** coquille *f* (de loquet); **t. latch, lock,** loquet *m* à poucier.

thumb[2], *v.tr. & i.* **1.** *O:* manier (qch.) maladroitement; **to t. the piano,** jouer du piano maladroitement; pianoter. **2. to t. (through) a book,** feuilleter, parcourir, lire en diagonale (les pages d')un livre; **well thumbed book,** livre bien feuilleté; livre qui porte la trace de nombreuses lectures. **3. to t. one's nose at s.o.,** faire un pied de nez à qn. **4. to t. a lift,** faire de l'auto-stop, du stop.

thumbling ['θʌmliŋ], *s*. *A: & Lit:* nain, *f*. naine; petit poucet.

thumbmark ['θʌmma:k], *s*. marque *f* de pouce.

thumbnail ['θʌmneil], *s*. ongle *m* du pouce; **t. sketch,** (i) *Art:* croquis *m* minuscule, hâtif; (ii) description concise.

thumbpiece ['θʌmpi:s], *s*. poucier *m*, bouton *m*, poussoir *m* (d'un loquet, etc.).

thumbprint ['θʌmprint], *s*. empreinte *f*, marque *f*, de pouce.

thumbscrew ['θʌmskru:], *s*. **1.** vis *f* à ailettes, à oreilles; papillon *m*. **2.** *Hist:* poucettes *fpl* (de torture).

thumbstall ['θʌmstɔ:l], *s*. **1.** poucier *m* (de cordonnier, etc.). **2.** *Med:* doigtier *m* pour pouce.

thumbtack ['θʌmtæk], *s*. *NAm:* punaise *f*.

thump[1] [θʌmp], *s*. **1.** coup sourd; battement *m*; cognement *m* (d'un mécanisme, etc.); **to fall with a t.,** tomber lourdement, avec un bruit sourd. **2.** coup de poing; bourrade *f*; **to give s.o. a friendly t. on the back,** donner à qn une bourrade amicale dans le dos.

thump[2], *v.tr. & i.* bourrer (qn) de coups; *F:* cogner (qn); frapper (qch.) à grands coups; marteler (qch.); **to t. (on) the table,** cogner sur la table, frapper la table du poing; **they began to t. one another,** ils ont commencé à se cogner, à se donner des coups de poing; **to t. the keys of a piano,** s'escrimer à jouer du piano; cogner sur le piano; **to t. out a tune,** taper un air (sur le piano); **we could hear feet thumping (about) overhead,** on entendait des pas qui résonnaient sourdement, lourdement, au-dessus de nous; **to t. (on) the big drum,** battre la grosse caisse; **my heart was thumping,** mon cœur battait fort, tumultueusement, à grands coups, à se rompre.

thumper ['θʌmpər], *s*. **1.** frappeur, -euse; **t. on the big drum,** batteur, -euse, de grosse caisse. **2.** *F: O:* (*a*) chose *f* énorme, ma(h)ousse; **isn't it a t.!** il, elle, est de taille! (*b*) **to tell thumpers,** débiter de gros mensonges; en conter de fortes; **that's a t.!** en voilà une forte!

thumping[1] ['θʌmpiŋ], *a*. **1.** qui cogne, qui frappe. **2.** *F: O:* énorme, colossal, -aux; mahous(s), mahousse, maousse; **what a t. (great) lie!** quel gros mensonge! ce mensonge est de taille!

thumping[2], *s*. **1.** coups sourds; battement *m*; cognement *m* (d'un mécanisme, etc.). **2.** coups de poings; bourrades *fpl*.

Thun [tu:n], *Pr.n. Geog:* Thoune; **the Lake of T., Lake T.,** le lac de Thoune.

thunder[1] ['θʌndər], *s*. **1.** (*a*) tonnerre *m*; **clap, peal, of t.,** coup *m* de tonnerre; **roll of t.,** roulement, grondement, de tonnerre; **there's t. in the air,** (i) le temps est à l'orage; (ii) l'atmosphère (de l'assemblée, etc.) est orageuse; (*b*) **the t. of the guns,** le tonnerre du canon; **t. of applause,** tonnerre d'applaudissements; **voice of, like, t.,** voix de tonnerre; voix tonnante, *F:* tonitruante. **2.** (*a*) *A: & Lit:* foudre *f*; (*b*) *Lit:* foudre *m*; **the thunders of Jupiter, of the Vatican,** les foudres *m* de Jupiter, les foudres romaines; **the t. bearer,** Jupiter tonnant; (*c*) **to steal s.o.'s t.,** anticiper qn; couper l'herbe sous le pied à qn. **3.** *F: O:* **why in the name of t. did you allow it?** pourquoi diable l'avez-vous permis?

thunder[2], *v.i. & tr.* **1.** tonner; **it's thundering,** il tonne; **the cannon was thundering,** le canon tonnait; **the avalanche thundered down,** l'avalanche roula dans un bruit de tonnerre; **the train thundered past,** le train a passé avec un bruit, un grondement, de tonnerre; **the sea thundered below us,** la mer grondait au-dessous de nous. **2.** *O:* **to t. (out) threats,** tonner, fulminer, des menaces; **to t. against sth.,** fulminer, tempêter, contre qch.; **to t. out an order,** donner un ordre d'une voix tonnante.

thunderbolt ['θʌndəboult], *s*. **1.** (coup *m* de) foudre *f*; (coup de) tonnerre *m*; **the news came upon me like a t.,** cette nouvelle a été un coup de foudre pour moi. **2.** nouvelle foudroyante. **3.** *A:* (*a*) météorite *f*; (*b*) bélemnite *f*, outil *m* en silex, etc. **4.** *Her:* foudre *m*.

thunderclap ['θʌndəklæp], *s*. **1.** coup *m* de tonnerre. **2.** *Fig:* coup de tonnerre, de foudre.

thundercloud ['θʌndəklaud], *s*. nuage orageux.

Thunderer ['θʌndərər], *s*. **the T.,** (i) *Myth:* Jupiter tonnant; (ii) *F: A:* (le journal) le *Times*.

thunderfish ['θʌndəfiʃ], *s*. *Ich:* **1.** loche *f* d'étang. **2.** (*of the Nile*) silure *m*, poisson-chat *m*, électrique; malaptérure *m*.

thunderflash ['θʌndəflæʃ], *s*. *Pyr:* grand pétard.

thunderhead ['θʌndəhed], *s*. *Meteor:* cumulus bourgeonnant (présageant l'orage).

thundering[1] ['θʌndəriŋ], *a*. **1.** tonnant; fulminant; **t. applause,** tonnerre *m* d'applaudissements; *Rom.Hist:* **the T. Legion,** la Légion fulminante. **2.** (*a*) **to be in a t. rage,** être dans une rage à tout casser; être transporté de fureur; (*b*) *F: O:* **what a t. nuisance!** ce que c'est embêtant! quelle scie! **what a t. (great) lie!** quel gros mensonge! ce mensonge est de taille; **a t. good licking,** une belle raclée; **he'll make a t. good sailor,** il fera un marin du tonnerre (de Dieu); **t. snakes!** tonnerre (de Dieu, de Brest)!

thundering[2], *s*. **1.** tonnerre *m*. **2.** bruit retentissant; bruit de tonnerre (de la mer, etc.).

thunderingly ['θʌndəriŋli], *adv*. **1.** avec un bruit de tonnerre. **2.** *F: O:* joliment, excessivement.

thunderous ['θʌnd(ə)rəs], *a*. **1.** *O:* (*of weather*) orageux; menaçant. **2.** (*of voice, etc.*) tonnant; **t. applause,** tonnerre *m* d'applaudissements.

thundershower ['θʌndəʃauər], *s*. pluie *f* d'orage; pluie, averse, accompagnée de tonnerre.

thunderstorm ['θʌndəstɔ:m], *s*. orage *m*; **local thunderstorms,** orages locaux.

thunderstroke ['θʌndəstrouk], *s*. *O:* coup *m* de tonnerre, de foudre.

thunderstruck ['θʌndəstrʌk], *a*. confondu, abasourdi, foudroyé, sidéré, ébahi; **to be t.,** tomber des nues; être atterré; **I was t. by the news,** cette nouvelle m'a foudroyé.

thundery ['θʌndəri], *a*. (temps, ciel) orageux; **t. weather, rain,** temps, pluie, d'orage; **the weather's t.,** le temps est à l'orage.

thurible ['θju:(ə)ribl], *s. Ecc:* encensoir *m.*
thurifer ['θju:(ə)rifər], *s. Ecc:* thuriféraire *m.*
thuriferous [θjuə'rifərəs], *a. Bot:* thurifère.
Thuringia [θə:'rindʒiə], *Pr.n. Geog:* Thuringe *f.*
Thuringian [θə:'rindʒiən]. *Geog:* (*a*) *a.* thuringien; (*b*) *s.* Thuringien, -ienne.
thuringite [θə:'rindʒait], *s. Miner:* thuringite *f.*
Thursday ['θə:zdi], *s.* (*a*) jeudi *m*; **Maundy T., the T. before Easter,** le jeudi saint; **Holy T.,** (i) (*in Anglican Church*) jour *m*, fête *f*, de l'Ascension; (ii) *R.C.Ch: & F:* le jeudi saint; **he's coming on T.,** il viendra jeudi; **he comes on a T., on Thursdays,** il vient le jeudi; **he comes every T.,** il vient tous les jeudis; *F:* **see you T.,** à jeudi; (*b*) *Geog:* **T. Island,** l'île *f* de Jeudi.
thus [ðʌs], *adv.* **1.** *Lit:* ainsi; de cette façon; de cette manière; comme ceci; **if you do it t.,** si vous le faites comme cela; **t. (spoke) Aeneas,** ainsi parla Énée; *U.S:* **she must have her coffee t. and t., t. and so,** il lui faut préparer son café de telle et telle manière. **2.** ainsi, donc; **t., when he arrived,** donc, lorsqu'il arriva; **t. we are no further forward,** de sorte que nous ne sommes pas plus avancés. **3. t. far,** jusqu'ici; jusque-là; **having gone t. far. . .,** en étant arrivé là. . .; **t. much,** autant que cela (et pas davantage).
thuya ['θu:jə], *s. Bot:* thuya *m*, thuia *m*, thuja *m.*
Thuyopsis [θju:'jɔpsis], *s. Bot:* thuiopsis *m*, thujopsis *m*, thuyopsis *m.*
thwack[1] [θwæk], *s.* (*a*) claquement *m*, clic-clac *m*, bruit sec (d'un marteau, etc.); (*b*) coup *m* (de bâton, etc.); claque *f*, taloche *f*; (*c*) *int.* vlan, v'lan; **to go t.,** faire clic-clac; claquer.
thwack[2], *v.tr. F:* battre (qn, qch.) (à coups retentissants); donner des coups à (qn, qch.).
thwart[1] [θwɔ:t, *Nau:* θɔ:t], *s.* banc *m* de nage, traversin *m* (d'une embarcation).
thwart[2]. *A:* **1.** *adv.* en travers; *Nau:* par le travers. **2.** *prep.* en travers de. **3.** *a.* transversal, -aux; transverse.
thwart[3], *v.tr.* contrarier (qn); barrer le chemin à (qn); déjouer (une intrigue); **to t. s.o.'s plans,** se mettre, se jeter, en travers des projets de qn; contrarier, contrecarrer, frustrer, déjouer, les projets de qn; **to be thwarted,** essuyer un échec; **hope thwarted by death,** espérance frustrée par la mort; **he's a thwarted actor,** c'est un acteur rentré.
thwartship ['θɔ:tʃip]. *Nau:* **1.** *adv.* transversalement; en travers. **2.** *a.* transversal, -aux.
thy [ðai], *poss.a.* (**thine,** *before a vowel*) *A: & Lit:* (*except in prayers*) ton, *f.* ta, *pl.* tes; (*in the fem. before a vowel sound*) ton; **t. service,** ton service; **t. glory,** ta gloire; **t. friendship,** ton amitié; **t. father and mother,** ton père et ta mère; tes père et mère; **thine own son,** ton propre fils.
Thyestes [θai'esti:z], *Pr.n.m. Gr.Lit:* Thyeste.
thyiad ['θaiiæd], *s. Gr.Ant:* thyade *f*, bacchante *f.*
thylacine ['θailəsi(:)n], *s. Z:* thylacine *m.*
Thylacoleo [θailə'kouliou], *s. Paleont:* thylacoleo *m.*
Thylogale [θai'lɔgəli:], *s. Z:* thylogale *m.*
thyme [taim], *s. Bot:* thym *m*; **wild t., shepherd's t.,** serpolet *m*; thym bâtard; **garden t.,** thym commun; **t. oil,** essence *f* de thym.
thymectomy [θai'mektəmi], *s. Surg:* thymectomie *f.*
Thymelaea [θaimə'liə], *s. Bot:* thymélée *f*, passerine *f.*
Thymelaeaceae [θaiməli'eisii:], *s.pl. Bot:* thyméléacées *f.*
thymele ['θiməli:], *s. A.Gr.Th:* thymélé *m.*
thymic[1] ['θaimik], *a. Anat: Med:* (asthme, etc.) thymique.
thymic[2] ['taimik, 'θai-], *a. Ch:* thymique; dérivé du thym; **t. acid,** acide thymique; thymol *m.*
thymol ['θaimɔl], *s. Pharm:* thymol *m.*
thymolphthalein [θaimɔl'θæliin], *s. Ch:* thymolphtaléine *f.*
thymoma, *pl.* **-as, -ata** [θai'moumə, -əz, -ətə], *s. Med:* thymome *m.*
thymonucleic [θaimounju:'kli:ik], *a. Bio-Ch:* (acide) thymonucléique.
thymus ['θaiməs], *s. Anat:* **t. (gland),** thymus *m.*
thyratron ['θaiərətrɔn], *s. El:* thyratron *m*; **t. inverter,** onduleur *m.*
thyreotropic [θairiou'trɔpik], *a. Physiol:* thyréotrope.
Thyrididae [θaiə'ridìdi:], *s.pl. Ent:* thyridides *m.*
thyristor [θai'ristər], *s. Elcs:* thyristor *m.*
thyro- ['θaiərou, θai(ə)'rɔ], *pref.* thyro-.
thyroarytenoid [θaiərouæri'ti:nɔid], *a. Anat:* thyro-aryténoïdien.
thyroepiglottic [θaiərouepi'glɔtik], *a. Anat:* thyro-épiglottique.
thyrogenic [θaiərou'dʒenik], **thyrogenous** [θaiə'rɔdʒənəs], *a. Physiol:* thyréogène.
thyroglobulin [θaiərou'glɔbjulin], *s. Bio-Ch:* thyroglobuline *f*, thyréoglobuline *f.*
thyrohyoid(ean) [θaiərou'haiɔid, -'ɔidiən], *a. Anat:* thyro-hyoïdien.
thyroid ['θaiərɔid], *a. Anat:* (cartilage, glande) thyroïde; **t. artery, vein,** thyroïdienne *f*; **t. hormone,** hormone thyroïdienne; *Pharm:* **t. (gland extract),** extrait *m* thyroïde.
thyroidal [θaiə'rɔidl], *a. Physiol: Med:* thyroïdien.
thyroid-deprived [θaiərɔiddi'praivd], *a. Med:* thyréoprivé.
thyroidectomize [θaiərɔi'dektəmaiz], *v.tr. Surg:* thyroïdectomiser.
thyroidectomy [θaiərɔi'dektəmi], *s. Surg:* thyroïdectomie *f.*
thyroidism ['θaiərɔidizm], *s. Med:* thyroïdisme *m.*
thyroiditis [θaiərɔi'daitis], *s. Med:* thyroïdite *f*; **ligneous t.,** maladie (ligneuse) de Riedel.
thyronine ['θai(ə)rəni(:)n], *s. Bio-Ch:* thyronine *f.*
thyropharyngeal [θaiəroufærin'dʒi:əl], *a. Anat:* thyropharyngien, -ienne.
thyroptera [θai(ə)'rɔptərə], *s. Z:* thyroptère *m.*
thyrotoxicosis [θaiəroutɔksi'kousis], *s. Med:* thyréotoxicose *f.*
thyrotrophic, -tropic [θaiərou'trɔfik, -'trɔpik], *a. Physiol:* thyréotrope; **t. hormone,** hormone *f* thyréotrope; thyréostimuline *f.*
thyrotrophin, -tropin [θaiərou'troufin, θai(ə)'rɔtrəfin, -pin], *s. Physiol:* hormone *f* thyréotrope; thyréostimuline *f.*
thyroxin(e) [θai'rɔksi(:)n], *s. Bio-Ch:* thyroxine *f.*
thyrse [θə:s], *s. Gr.Ant: Bot:* thyrse *m.*
Thyrsis ['θə:sis], *Pr.n.m. Lt.Lit:* Tircis, Thyrsis.
thyrsoid ['θə:sɔid], *a. Gr.Ant: Bot:* thyrsoïde.
thyrsus, *pl.* **-i** ['θə:səs, -ai], *s. Gr.Ant: & Bot:* thyrse *m.*
thysanopter(an)(on) [θaisə'nɔptər, -æn, -ɔn], *s. Ent:* thysanoptère *m*, thrips *m.*
Thysanoptera [θaisə'nɔptərə], *s.pl. Ent:* thysanoptères *m*, thrips *m.*
thysanopterous, -teran [θaisə'nɔptərəs, -tərən], *a. Ent:* des thysanoptères; des thrips.
Thysanura [θaisə'nju:rə], *s.pl. Ent:* thysanoures *m.*
thysanuran, -nurous [θaisə'nju:rən, -'nju:rəs]. *Ent:* **1.** *a.* appartenant aux thysanoures. **2.** *s.* thysanoure *m.*
thyself [ðai'self], *pers.pron. A: & Lit:* (*except in prayers, etc.*) toi(-même); (*a*) **thou hast loved her t.,** tu l'as aimée toi-même, toi aussi; (*b*) (*reflexive*) **know t.,** connais-toi toi-même; *B:* **physician, heal t.,** médecin, guéris-toi toi-même; **do t. no harm,** ne te fais point de mal.
tiara [ti'ɑ:rə], *s.* **1.** *Ecc:* tiare *f.* **2.** diadème *m.*
tiarella [tiə'relə], *s. Bot:* tiarella *m.*
tiaris [ti'ɑ:ris], *s. Orn:* tiaris *m.*
Tiber (the) [ðə'taibər], *Pr.n. Geog:* le Tibre.
Tiberian [tai'biəriən], *a.* **1.** tibérien; de Tibère. **2.** de Tibériade.
Tiberias [tai'biəriæs], *Pr.n. A. Geog:* Tibériade; **the Lake of T.,** le lac de Tibériade; la mer de Galilée.
Tiberius [tai'biəriəs], *Pr.n.m. Rom.Hist:* Tibère.
Tibet [ti'bet]. **1.** *Pr.n. Geog:* Tibet *m.* **2.** *s. Tex:* tibet *m*, thibet *m.*
Tibetan [ti'bet(ə)n]. **1.** *a. Geog:* tibétain; *Z:* **T. mastiff,** dogue *m* du Tibet; **T. terrier,** griffon *m* du Tibet. **2.** *s. Geog:* Tibétain, -aine.
tibia, *pl.* **-ae** ['tibiə, -i:], *s. Anat: etc:* tibia *m.*
tibial ['tibiəl], *a. Anat:* tibial, -aux.
tibiotarsal [tibiou'tɑ:s(ə)l], *a. Anat:* tibio-tarsien.
tibouchina [tibu'kainə], *s. Bot:* tibouchina *m.*
Tibullus [ti'buləs], *Pr.n.m. Lt.Lit:* Tibulle.
tic [tik], *s. Med:* tic *m*; **t. douloureux** [dulu'rø], tic douloureux.
tich [titʃ], *s. F:* (*of pers.*) atome *m.*
tichy ['titʃi], *a. F:* minuscule.
tichodroma [tikou'droumə], *s. Orn:* tichodrome *m.*
Ticino (the) [ðəti'tʃi:nou], *Pr.n. Geog:* **1.** le Tessin. **2. the river T.,** le Tessin.
tick[1] [tik], *s.* **1.** (*a*) **t. (tock),** tic-tac *m* (d'une pendule); *F:* **on the t.,** à l'heure sonnante, tapante; **you're on the t.,** vous êtes à la minute; **on the t. of seven,** à sept heures tapant; *Turf: F:* **t.-tack man,** aide *m* de bookmaker (qui fait des signaux à bras); (*b*) *F:* moment *m*, instant *m*; **I'd be recognized in a t.,** je serais reconnu en un instant; **just a t.! hang on a t.! half a t.!** un moment! un instant! **I'm coming in a t., in two ticks, in half a t.,** j'arrive dans un instant, en moins d'un instant, dans deux secondes, dans un quart de seconde; **he'll do it in two ticks,** il fera ça en moins de rien. **2.** marque *f*, pointage *m*, trait *m*, coche *f* (affirmant l'exactitude d'un compte, etc.); **to mark with a t.,** pointer, cocher; **to put a t. against a name,** faire une marque à un nom; pointer, cocher, un nom.
tick[2], *v.*
I. *v.tr. & i.* **1.** *v.i.* (*a*) (*of clock*) **to t.,** *F:* **to t.-tock,** faire tic-tac; tictaquer; battre; **the minutes are ticking by,** le temps passe; (*b*) *F:* **I'd like to know what makes him t.,** je voudrais bien savoir ce qui le pousse. **2.** *v.tr.* = TICK OFF (*a*).
II. (*compound verbs*) **1. tick off,** *v.tr.* (*a*) pointer (une liste, un article sur une liste, etc.); cocher (des noms sur une liste, etc.); **to t. off items in an account,** pointer les articles d'un compte; **to t. off a name,** faire une marque à un nom; pointer, cocher, un nom; (*b*) *F:* rembarrer (qn); remettre (qn) à sa place; **to get ticked off,** se faire rembarrer.
2. tick over, *v.i.* (*a*) *I.C.E:* (*of engine*) tourner au grand ralenti; (*b*) **my business is just ticking over,** mes affaires vont doucement, ne marchent plus; (*c*) (*of pers.*) suivre son petit bonhomme de chemin.
tick[3], *s.* **1.** *Arach:* tique *f* (du bétail, etc.); **dog t.,** tique, ricin *m*, des chiens. **2.** *Ent:* **t. (fly),** hippobosque *m*, mouche *f* araignée; **horse t.,** hippobosque des chevaux; **dog t. (fly),** mouche des chiens; *esp. U.S: F:* **as full as a t.,** plein comme un œuf. **3.** *P:* salaud *m*, saligaud *m.*
tick[4], *s. F:* crédit *m*; **to buy, get, sth. on t.,** acheter qch. à crédit.
tick[5], *s.* enveloppe *f*, toile *f* (à matelas).
ticker ['tikər], *s.* **1.** (*a*) échappement *m* (d'une montre); (*b*) *F:* montre *f*; pendule *f*, tocante *f*, toquante *f*, patraque *f*; (*c*) *F:* cœur *m*, palpitant *m.* **2.** *Tg:* (*a*) télégraphe imprimeur; **t. tape,** bande *f* (de téléimprimeur); ruban *m* (de téléscripteur); (*b*) (contact *m* à) trembleur *m*; ticker *m.*
ticket[1] ['tikit], *s.* **1.** (*a*) billet *m* (de chemin de fer, de théâtre, de loterie, etc.); ticket *m* (de métro, d'autobus, etc.); **book of tickets,** carnet *m* de cachets *m*, de tickets; **complimentary t.,** billet de faveur; billet donné à titre gracieux; *A:* **soup t.,** bon *m* de soupe; (*in library*) **reader's t.,** carte *f* de lecteur; *Rail:* **single t.,** billet simple; (billet d')aller *m*; **return t.,** billet d'aller et retour; **cheap t.,** billet à prix réduit; **through t.,** billet direct, pour tout le voyage; **left-luggage t., cloakroom t.,** bulletin *m*, ticket, de consigne; **platform t.,** ticket de quai; **season t.,** carte *f* d'abonnement; **t. holder,** voyageur, -euse, spectateur, -trice (muni(e) d'un billet); **season-t. holder,** abonné(e); **t. collector, t. inspector,** contrôleur, -euse (de billets); poinçonneur, -euse (de billets); *Austr: P:* **he's got tickets on himself,** il s'en fait accroire; (*b*) *Aut: F:* papillon *m*; **to get, collect, a t.,** se faire coller une contravention. **2.** (*a*) *Com:* **(price) t.,** étiquette *f*; (*b*) *St.Exch:* fiche *f*; **t. day,** jour *m* de la déclaration des noms; veille *f* de la liquidation. **3.** *Pol: U.S:* (*a*) liste *f* des candidats; **to vote a straight t.,** voter pour la liste entière; **to vote a split t., to split a t.,** faire du panachage; (*b*) *F:* **the democratic t.,** le programme du parti démocrate. **4.** (*a*) *Mil: etc:* ordre *m* de paiement (qui accompagne le congé définitif); **to get one's t.,** recevoir son congé définitif; être libéré (du service); *F: O:* **to work one's t.,** se faire réformer frauduleusement; (*b*) *Nau: F:* **to get one's (master's) t.,** passer capitaine; passer son brevet de capitaine; se faire breveter capitaine de vaisseau; (*c*) *Jur:* **t. of leave,** libération conditionnelle (d'un prisonnier). **5.** *P:* **that's the t.!** voilà qui fera l'affaire! à la bonne heure! c'est bien ça! c'est ça même!
ticket[2], *v.tr.* **(ticketed)** étiqueter, marquer (des marchandises, etc.).
ticketer ['tikitər], *s.* étiqueteur, -euse.
ticketing ['tikitiŋ], *s.* étiquetage *m.*
ticking[1] ['tikiŋ], *s.* **1.** tic-tac *m* (d'une pendule). **2. t. off,** (i) pointage *m*; (ii) *F:* réprimande *f*, savon *m.*
ticking[2], *s.* toile *f*, coutil *m*, à matelas; treillis *m* pour matelas.
tickle[1] ['tikl], *s.* chatouillement *m*; **to give s.o. a t.,** chatouiller qn; **to have a t. in one's throat,** avoir un chatouillement dans le gosier.
tickle[2]. **1.** *v.tr.* (*a*) chatouiller (qn); (*of food, wine*) **to t. the palate,** chatouiller le palais; **to t. s.o.'s fancy,** amuser qn; (*b*) *F:* amuser (qn); **I was tickled at the idea,** l'idée m'a beaucoup amusé; **to be tickled to death at, by, sth.,** (i) se tordre de rire à l'idée, à la vue, de qch.; (ii) être enchanté, ravi, de qch.; *O:* **I'd be tickled to death, tickled pink, to see you again,** je serais enchanté, ravi, de vous revoir; **I was tickled to death to hear it,** cette nouvelle m'a transporté de joie, m'a mis au comble de la joie; (*c*) *Aut: A:* **to t. the carburettor,** titiller le carburateur, agir sur le pointeau; (*d*) *Fish:* pêcher (la truite, etc.) à la main; (*e*) *F:* **to t. (s.o.) (up),** réveiller, stimuler, qn. **2.** *v.i.* **my hand tickles,** la main me démange.
tickler ['tiklər], *s.* **1.** *I.C.E:* titillateur *m*, poussoir *m* (du carburateur). **2.** (*a*) vrai problème; question embarrassante; (*b*) sujet délicat; affaire délicate. **3.** *F:* **memory t.,** aide-mémoire *m inv*; pense-bête *m*, *pl.* pense-bêtes.
tickling[1] ['tikliŋ], *a.* qui chatouille; **t. cough,** toux *f* d'irritation.

tickling², *s.* **1.** chatouillement *m*; **to feel a t. in one's throat,** éprouver un chatouillement dans la gorge. **2.** *Fish:* pêche *f* à la main (de la truite, etc.).

ticklish ['tikliʃ], *a.* **1.** chatouilleux, -euse; **to be t.,** craindre les chatouilles. **2.** (*a*) (*of pers.*) susceptible; (*b*) (*of task, etc.*) délicat, difficile; (*of undertaking*) scabreux; (*of question*) chatouilleux; **t. subject,** sujet délicat, brûlant; **to be in a t. situation,** se trouver dans une situation délicate, critique.

ticklishly ['tikliʃli], *adv.* **to be t. placed,** être dans une situation délicate.

ticklishness ['tikliʃnis], *s.* **1.** sensibilité *f* au chatouillement. **2.** (*a*) susceptibilité *f*; (*b*) difficulté *f*, délicatesse *f* (d'une tâche, etc.).

tick tack toe [tiktæk'tou], *s. U.S:* = morpion *m.*

tick-tick ['tiktik], *s.* (*child's word*) montre *f*, pendule *f.*

tidal ['taid(ə)l], *a.* **1. t. energy,** énergie marémotrice; **t. power station,** usine marémotrice; **t. wave,** (i) raz *m* de marée; (*on river*) barre *f* de flot; (ii) flot *m* de la marée; (iii) *F:* afflux *m* (de passion violente, etc.); (iv) vague *f* (d'enthousiasme, d'indignation populaire). **2.** (*a*) (*of river, etc.*) à marée; **t. harbour,** port *m* à, de, marée; **t. basin,** bassin *m* à flot; darse *f*; (*b*) **t. train,** train *m* de marée. **3.** *Physiol:* **t. air,** air *m* de respiration.

tidbit ['tidbit], *s.* = TITBIT.

tiddler ['tidlər], *s. F:* **1.** *Ich:* petit poisson, friture *f*, *esp.* épinoche *f.* **2.** petit enfant, môme *m.*

tiddl(e)y¹ ['tidli]. *F:* **1.** *a.* ivre, pompette, éméché. **2.** *s.* **a drop of t.,** une goutte de gnôle.

tiddl(e)y², *a. F:* minuscule.

tiddlywinks ['tidliwiŋks], *s. Games:* jeu *m* de (la) puce.

tide¹ [taid], *s.* **1.** *A:* temps *m*, époque *f*, saison *f*; *Ecc:* **Ascension t.,** temps, semaine *f*, de l'Ascension. **2.** marée *f*; **rising t., flood t.,** marée montante; flux *m*; (marée de) flot *m*; **ebb t.,** marée descendante, de jusant; **high t.,** marée haute; haute marée; **at high t.,** à la marée haute; au plein de la mer; **low t.,** marée basse; **lee t.,** marée qui porte comme le vent; **counter t.,** marée contraire; **neap t.,** marée de morte-eau; **spring t.,** grande marée; marée de vive eau; **t. race,** raz *m* de marée; mascaret *m*; **t. rip,** (i) revolin *m* de lame; clapotis *m* de marée; (ii) raz de marée; **t. gate,** porte *f* à flot; écluse *f* (de bassin); varaigne *f* (de marais salant); **t. gauge,** maré(o)mètre *m*, maré(o)graphe *m*; échelle *f* de marée; **the t. is coming in,** la marée arrive, gagne, monte; **rise, fall, of the t.,** montée *f*, baisse *f*, de l'eau; **there is a rise and fall of the t. of five metres,** la mer marne de cinq mètres; **against the t.,** à contre-marée; **against wind and t.,** contre vent et marée; *Fig:* **the rising t. of discontent,** le mécontentement qui croît de jour en jour; *Nau:* **to go out with the t.,** partir à la marée; **to go with the t.,** suivre le courant; **to go against the t.,** prendre le contresens de la marée; **to work double tides,** faire double marée; **the t. of battle,** la fortune de la bataille; **to turn the t. of battle,** changer l'issue de la bataille; *Prov:* **time and t. wait for no man,** la marée n'attend personne.

tide², *v.*

I. *v.tr. & i.* **1.** *v.tr.* (*of the tide*) porter, transporter; **driftwood tided up the river,** bois flottant porté en amont par la marée. **2.** (*a*) *v.i. Nau:* faire marée; (*b*) **to t. in, out,** entrer avec le flot, sortir avec le jusant; **to t. it into port,** entrer au port grâce à la marée; faire marée.

II. (*compound verb*) **tide over,** *v.tr.* aider (qn) à surmonter une difficulté; dépanner (qn); **this money will t. me over for another three months,** avec cet argent je vais encore pouvoir durer trois mois; **this sum will t. us over,** cette somme nous permettra de surmonter nos difficultés, de faire la soudure, va nous dépanner.

tideland ['taidlænd], *s. U.S:* terres inondées (i) aux grandes marées, (ii) à la haute marée.

tideless ['taidlis], *a.* sans marée.

tidemark ['taidmɑːk], *s.* **1.** (*a*) ligne *f* de marée haute, des hautes eaux; (*b*) laisse *f* de haute mer. **2.** échelle *f* de marée. **3.** *F:* ligne de crasse (dans une baignoire, sur la peau, etc.).

tidewaiter ['taidweitər], *s. A:* douanier *m* (de port).

tidewater ['taidwɑːtər], *s.* eau *f* de marée; *esp. U.S:* **t. land,** terre inondée à la marée haute; **t. glacier,** glacier *m* qui descend jusqu'à la mer.

tideway ['taidwei], *s.* lit *m* de la marée.

tidily ['taidili], *adv.* proprement; avec ordre; **everything was t. arranged,** tout était à sa place, en bon ordre; **t. dressed,** soigneusement habillé; habillé avec soin.

tidiness ['taidinis], *s.* bon ordre; (*in dress*) bonne tenue; (*of pers.*) le goût de l'ordre; **to have a mania for t.,** avoir la manie du rangement.

tidings ['taidiŋz], *s.pl. Lit:* nouvelle(s) *f(pl)*; **glad t.,** bonne nouvelle.

tidy¹ ['taidi], *a.* **1.** (*a*) (*of desk, room, etc.*) bien rangé, en bon ordre; **a clean and t. room,** une pièce propre et nette; **I must go and make myself t.,** je vais faire un brin de toilette; (*b*) (*of pers.*) ordonné, qui a de l'ordre; soigneux; **he's very t.,** il a beaucoup d'ordre. **2.** *F:* assez bon; passable; **at a t. pace,** à un bon petit train; **to cost a t. penny,** coûter chaud; **a t. fortune,** une fortune assez coquette; une jolie fortune; **a t. sum,** une somme rondelette.

tidy², *s.* **1.** *A:* vide-poche(s) *m inv.* **2.** *A:* voile *m*, voilette *f*, de chaise, de fauteuil. **3. sink t.,** coin *m* d'évier. **4.** *O:* **hair t.,** récipient *m* pour peignures.

tidy³, *v.tr.* ranger; mettre de l'ordre dans, arranger (une chambre, etc.); **to t. one's hair,** s'arranger les cheveux; **to t. oneself (up),** faire un bout, un brin, de toilette; s'apprêter; **to t. (things) up,** ranger; tout remettre à sa place; **to t. away the books,** ranger les livres; **to have a passion, a mania, for tidying things away,** avoir la manie du rangement; **to t. up a room,** mettre une pièce en ordre, (re)mettre de l'ordre dans une pièce; *Nau:* **to t. up the rigging,** alester le gréement.

tie¹ [tai], *s.* **1.** (*a*) lien *m*; attache *f*; **family ties,** liens de famille; **ties of friendship,** liens, nœuds *m*, de l'amitié; **our close ties with this district,** nos attaches dans cette région; **to break a t.,** rompre une attache; (*b*) assujettissement *m*; **her children are a t.,** ses enfants sont pour elle une entrave continuelle; **she was more of a t. than a companion,** elle était une gêne plutôt qu'une dame de compagnie. **2.** (*a*) lien (de corde, de paille, d'osier, etc.); centaine *f* (d'un écheveau); (*b*) *Nau:* itague *f*; (*c*) lacet *m*, cordon *m* (de soulier); (*d*) *Cost:* cravate *f*; **made-up t.,** cravate toute faite; *A:* **four-in-hand t.,** cravate-plastron *f*, *pl.* cravates-plastrons; **bow t.,** nœud *m* papillon; (*on invitation*) **black t.** = smoking *m*; **many of the men were in white ties,** beaucoup des hommes étaient en queue-de-morue; **the old school t.,** (i) la cravate portée par les anciens élèves d'une école; (ii) la franc-maçonnerie des anciens d'une école. **3.** *Const: etc:* chaîne *f*, crampon *m*, ancre *f*, ancrure *f*, moufle *f*, moise *f*, amoise *f*, entretoise *f*; tirant *m*; *Rail: NAm:* traverse *f* (portant les rails); *Av: A:* câble *m* d'haubannage; *Const:* **hooked t.,** harpon *m*, harpe *f*; ancre à fourchette; **t. iron,** chaîne de liaison; **t. irons,** chaînage *m*; **t. beam,** (i) *Const:* moufle *f*; longrine *f*, moise *f*; entrait *m*; blochet *m* (de toit); tirant (de charpente de fer, etc.); (ii) *Civ.E:* raineau *m* (de pilotis); **t. bar,** (i) *Const:* moufle (noyée dans la maçonnerie); (ii) *Mec.E: etc:* tirant; barre *f* d'entretoisement; *Rail:* entretoise (de rail); **t. rod,** tirant; barre d'accouplement; *Aut:* barre de connexion; *Const:* entrait (de toit); *Rail:* tringle *f* de connexion (des aiguilles); **boiler t. rod,** barre d'écartement de chaudière; *Mec.E: etc:* **t. bolt,** tirant; **t. plate,** (i) *Const:* ancre; plaque *f* d'assise; tôle *f* de jonction; (ii) *N.Arch:* virure *f* d'hiloire; (iii) *Rail:* selle *f* d'appui, d'arrêt (des rails). **4.** *Mus:* liaison *f* (rattachant deux notes liées). **5.** (*a*) *Sp:* match *m*, course *f*, à égalité, à points égaux, à égalité de points; **to play off a t.,** rejouer un match à égalité; **t. breaker,** match de barrage; **t. award,** prix *m* ex æquo; (*b*) **(cup) t.** = match de championnat; (*c*) **the election ended in a t.,** les candidats obtinrent un nombre égal de suffrages.

tie², *v.* **(tied; tying)**

I. *v.tr.* **1.** (*a*) attacher (un chien à sa niche, etc.); lier (qn à un poteau); **to t. two things together,** lier deux choses ensemble; *Fig:* **to t. s.o.'s hands,** enlever à qn toute liberté d'action; lier les mains à qn; **to be tied and bound, tied hand and foot,** (i) être ligoté; avoir pieds et poings liés; (ii) avoir les mains liées; **to be tied to one's bed,** être cloué au lit (par la maladie, etc.); **to be tied to the spot by urgent business,** être cloué sur place par des affaires pressantes; **to be tied to one's work,** être toujours à l'attache; **to be tied to one's mother's apron strings,** être pendu aux jupons de sa mère; (*b*) lier, nouer (un lacet, une ficelle, etc.); faire (un nœud, sa cravate); attacher, nouer (les brides de son capuchon); **I can't t. a tie,** je ne sais pas faire un nœud de cravate; *Fish:* **to t. a fly,** monter une mouche; *Surg:* **to t. an artery,** ligaturer une artère. **2.** *Const:* chaîner, moufler (les murs); *Mec.E:* renforcer (une chaudière, etc.) avec des tirants; entretoiser (un cadre, etc.). **3.** *Mus:* lier (deux notes).

II. *v.i. Sp: etc:* être, arriver, à égalité **(with,** avec); faire match nul; (*of candidates*) obtenir un nombre égal de suffrages; *Sch:* **to t. for first place,** être premier ex æquo **(with,** avec).

III. (*compound verbs*) **1. tie down,** *v.tr.* (*a*) immobiliser (qn) en l'attachant contre terre, sur son lit; assujettir (un objet qui pourrait se déplacer); (*b*) (i) assujettir (qn) à certaines conditions; (ii) **tied down to one's job,** assujetti à ses fonctions; **to t. s.o. down to facts,** obliger qn à ne pas s'écarter des faits.

2. tie in, *v.i. esp. NAm:* (*a*) se rattacher (à qch.); (*b*) avoir un rapport (avec qch.).

3. tie on, *v.tr.* attacher (une étiquette, etc.) avec une ficelle.

4. tie up. (*a*) *v.tr.* (i) attacher, ficeler (un paquet, etc.); se nouer (les cheveux); lier, ficeler (le haut d'un sac); bander, panser (un bras blessé, etc.); (ii) attacher (un animal); mettre (un animal) à l'attache; ligoter (qn); *v.tr. & i.* amarrer (un bateau); (iii) *Fin: etc:* arranger (un prêt, etc.); **to t. up a contract with s.o.,** passer un contrat avec qn; (iv) **to t. up one's capital,** immobiliser ses capitaux; **to t. up a succession,** rendre un legs, une succession, inaliénable; (v) *Bookb:* fouetter (un volume); (iv) *Hort:* accoler (un ceps, etc.); (vii) *F:* (*of priest, etc.*) marier (deux personnes); **to get tied up,** se marier; se mettre la corde au cou; (viii) *F:* **to be (all) tied up,** (α) être très occupé, avoir beaucoup à faire; (β) être géné, embarrassé, dans tous ses états; *NAm:* **the traffic was all tied up,** il y avait un embouteillage; (*b*) *v.i.* avoir des rapports (avec qch.); **our firm is tied up with theirs,** notre maison a des accords avec la leur; **that ties up with what I was just saying,** cela rejoint, correspond à, ce que je viens de dire.

tied [taid], *a.* **1.** assujetti (à son service, etc.). **2. t. cottage, house** = logement *m* de fonction; **t. house,** débit de boissons astreint par bail à vendre la bière d'une certaine brasserie; **t. garage,** garage astreint par contrat à vendre une certaine marque d'essence. **3.** *Mus:* **t. notes,** notes liées.

tie-in ['taiin], *s. NAm:* rapport *m*; association *f.*

tiemannite ['tiːmænait], *s. Miner:* tiemannite *f.*

tie-on ['taiɔn], *a.* **t.-on label,** étiquette *f* à œillets; fiche *f.*

tiepin ['taipin], *s.* épingle *f* de cravate.

tier¹ [tiər], *s.* **1.** (*a*) rangée *f* (de sièges, de barriques, etc.); étage *m*; *Nau:* plan *m* d'arrimage; **tiers of an amphitheatre,** gradins *m* d'un amphithéâtre; **hills rising t. upon t.,** collines disposées en gradins, en assises, en amphithéâtre; **two-t. postal service system,** courrier *m* à deux vitesses; **two-t., three-t., pricing,** fixation *f* des prix à deux, à trois, niveaux; **three-t. whatnot,** étagère *f* à trois tablettes; **to arrange in tiers,** disposer par étages; étager (des marchandises, etc.); **to rise, stand, in tiers,** s'étager; *Th: O:* **first-t. box,** première loge; (*b*) *Nau:* rangée, ligne *f*, de navires. **2.** *Nau:* **cable t.,** cale *f* à filin.

tier² ['taiər], *s.* **t. up,** ficeleur, -euse (de paquets, etc.).

tierce ['tiəs], *s.* **1.** *Cards: Fenc: etc:* tierce *f.* **2.** *Ecc:* tierce. **3.** *Com: A:* (*a*) tierçon *m* (de 42 *gallons*); (*b*) fût *m* de la contenance d'un tierçon. **4.** *Arch: etc:* **t. point,** tiers-point *m.*

tierced ['tiəst], *a. Her:* tiercé; **t. in fess, in bend, in bend-sinister, in pairle, in pairle reversed,** tiercé en fasce, en bande, en barre, en pairle, en pairle renversée.

tiercel ['tiəs(ə)l], *s.* = TERCEL.

tierceron ['tiəsərɔn], *s. Arch:* tierceron *m.*

tiered ['tiəd], *a.* (*a*) à gradins, à étages; (*b*) **three-t. cake,** pièce montée à trois étages; (*for flowers, etc.*) **three-t. stand, whatnot,** étagère *f* à trois tablettes.

Tierra del Fuego [ti'ɛərədel'fweigou], *Pr.n. Geog:* la Terre de Feu.

tie-up ['taiʌp], *s.* **1.** (*a*) amarrage *m* (pour un canot); (*b*) *U.S:* (i) étable *f* (à vaches); (ii) case *f* (d'étable); (*c*) *NAm:* (i) *Aut:* embouteillage *m*; (ii) suspension forcée (du travail). **2.** rapport *m* (entre deux choses); association *f* (d'idées, de maisons de commerce, etc.).

tie-wig ['taiwig], *s. A:* perruque *f* à nœuds, à marteaux.

tiff¹ [tif], *s.* petite querelle; fâcherie *f*; **they've had a t.,** ils se sont chamaillés; il y a entre eux de la fâcherie, de la pique; **to have a t. with s.o.,** avoir une légère difficulté avec qn; être en bisbille avec qn.

tiff², *v.i.* **1.** *O:* (*a*) être de mauvaise humeur; bouder; (*b*) se chamailler. **2.** *A:* boire un coup; *v.tr.* boire, lamper (qch.).

tiffany ['tifəni], *s. Tex:* gaze *f*; canevas *m* de soie, mousseline *f.*

tiffin ['tifin], *s.* (*Anglo-Indian*) déjeuner *m.*

tig¹ [tig], *s.* (jeu *m* de) chat *m*; **to play t.,** jouer à, au, chat; **cross t.,** chat coupé; **long t.,** chat perché.

tig², *v.tr.* **(tigged)** toucher (qn) (au jeu de chat).

tigella [ti'dʒelə], **tigelle** [ti'ʒel], *s. Bot:* tigelle *f.*

tigellate ['tidʒəleit], *a. Bot:* tigellé.

tiger ['taigər], *s.* **1.** (*a*) *Z:* tigre *m*; **Bengal t.,** tigre du Bengale; tigre royal; *Paleont:* **sabre-toothed t.,** félin *m* à dents de sabre; smilodon *m*; (*b*) *Z:* **American t.,** tigre d'Amérique; grande panthère des fourreurs; jaguar *m*; **red t.,** tigre rouge; lion *m* des Péruviens; couguar *m*; **t. cat,** chat-tigre *m*, *pl.* chats-tigres; serval, -als *m*; ocelot *m*; (*c*) *F:* homme (i) féroce, (ii) sanguinaire, (iii) âpre au gain; *Sp:* adversaire redoutable; (*d*) *F:* **paper t.,** tigre de papier (les États-Unis du point de vue chinois). **2.** (*a*) *Orn:* **t. bittern,** tigrisome *m*; (*b*) *Ich:* **t. fish,** poisson-tigre *m*, chien *m* d'eau; (*c*) *Rept:* **t. snake,** vipère(-)tigre *f*; (*d*) *Ent:* **t. beetle,** cicindèle *f* champêtre; **t. moth,** arctie *f*; (*e*) *Bot:* **t. flower,** tigridie *f*; **t. lily,** lis tigré; **t. nut,**

souchet *m* comestible; (*f*) *Lap:* **t. eye,** œil-de-chat *m*; œil-de tigre *m*, *pl.* œils-de-chat, -de-tigre. **3.** *A:* tigre, groom *m*, petit laquais. **4.** *NAm: F:* encore une acclamation, encore un hourra (en plus des trois acclamations réglementaires).

tigerish ['taigəriʃ], *a.* **1.** de tigre; (*of colour*) tigré. **2.** cruel (comme un tigre); sanguinaire; féroce.

tight [tait], *a. & adv.*

I. *a.* **1.** (*of partition, etc.*) imperméable (à l'eau, à l'air, etc.); à l'épreuve (du gaz, etc.); (*of ship, container*) étanche; (*of joint*) hermétique; **to make a ship t.,** mettre un navire à l'étanche. **2.** (*a*) (*of cord, etc.*) raide, tendu; **to draw a cord t.,** serrer un cordon; **cord that is too t.,** corde qui est trop tendue, qui bride trop, qui bande trop; *Nau:* **to haul a cable t.,** palanquer une amarre; *Fish:* **t. lines!** = lignes tendues! bonne pêche! *Equit:* **to keep a t. hand on the reins,** tenir la bride serrée; **to keep a t. hand, a t. hold, over s.o.,** tenir qn serré; tenir qn de court; mener, tenir, qn en laisse; **to keep t. hold of sth.,** se cramponner à qch.; **with t. lips,** les lèvres serrées; (*b*) (*of clothes*) **(skin) t.,** collant; **t. round the waist,** cintré; **too t.,** étriqué; trop juste; **my dress is (too) t. under the arms,** ma robe me gêne, me bride, aux entournures; **t. shoes,** chaussures trop petites, (trop) étroites, trop justes; *F:* **to be in a t. corner, a t. spot,** être en mauvaise passe; être dans une position critique, dans un mauvais pas, dans le pétrin; n'en pas mener large; (*c*) (*of furniture, mortise, etc.*) bien ajusté; (*of knot, screw*) serré; **the nut is t.,** l'écrou est serré à bloc, à refus; l'écrou est bloqué; **the mortise isn't t.,** la mortaise a du jeu; **the nut isn't t. (enough),** l'écrou n'est pas bloqué; **the cork was t. in the bottle,** le bouchon était solidement enfoncé dans la bouteille; (*d*) *Bookb:* **binding with a t. back,** reliure *f* à dos fixe, plein; (*e*) **t. schedule,** horaire minuté; **I work to a very t. schedule,** mon temps est très minuté. **3.** *A:* propret, gentil, coquet; **a t. little wench,** une gentille petite; **a t. little house,** une petite maison bien construite et commode. **4.** (*a*) (*of money, credit*) resserré, rare; *F:* **money's a bit t. with me,** je suis à court d'argent; (*b*) **t. bargain,** transaction *f* qui laisse très peu de marge; (*c*) *Sp:* (*of race, etc.*) serré, chaudement disputé. **5.** *F:* **to be t.,** être ivre, entamé, soûl, pompette; **to get t.,** prendre une cuite; **as t. as a fiddler, as a lord,** soûl comme une grive.

II. *adv.* **1.** hermétiquement; **to close t.,** (se) fermer hermétiquement; **shut t., t. shut,** (porte) hermétiquement close; (yeux) bien fermés; **window that doesn't shut t.,** fenêtre *f* qui joint mal. **2.** (*a*) fortement, fermement; **to hold sth. t.,** tenir qch. serré; serrer qch. dans ses bras, entre les mains; **to hold on t. to s.o., sth.,** se cramponner à qn, à qch.; **hold t.!** tenez bon! tenez ferme! **to screw a nut up t.,** visser, serrer, un écrou à bloc, à refus; *F: O:* **blow me t.!** par exemple! bigre! (*b*) étroitement; **to squeeze sth. t.,** serrer qch. étroitement; **to fit t.,** être bien ajusté.

tighten ['tait(ə)n]. **1.** *v.tr.* (*a*) serrer, resserrer (une vis, un nœud, etc.); bloquer (un écrou); revisser (une pièce de mécanisme); bander, tendre (un ressort); retendre (une courroie); tendre, raidir, *Nau:* embraquer (un cordage, etc.); *Nau:* rider (les haubans); **to t. a violin string,** remonter, tendre, une corde; *Aut:* **to t. up the steering,** rattraper le jeu de la direction; **to t. a screw hard,** serrer un écrou à bloc, à refus; bloquer un écrou; **to t. the bonds of friendship,** resserrer les liens de l'amitié; **to t. economic links,** resserrer les liens économiques; **to t. one's belt,** (i) serrer sa ceinture, son ceinturon; (ii) *F:* se serrer le ventre; se boucler la ceinture; **to t. one's purse strings,** serrer sa bourse; **with tightened lips,** les lèvres serrés; (*b*) **to t. (up) a blockade, restrictions,** renforcer un blocus, des restrictions. **2.** *v.i.* (*a*) se (res)serrer; **his lips tightened,** ses lèvres se sont serrées; il a pincé les lèvres; (*b*) (*of spring*) se bander; (*of cable, etc.*) devenir tendu; se tendre; raidir.

tightener ['tait(ə)nər], *s. Mec.E: etc:* (*device*) tendeur *m*, raidisseur *m*; **belt t.,** tendeur de courroie; *Tg: etc:* **stay t.,** tendeur de haubans.

tightening ['tait(ə)niŋ], *s.* **1.** serrage *m*, (res)serrement *m*; **t. nut,** écrou *m* de serrage, de tension; **t. end plate,** disque obturateur. **2.** raidissement *m* (d'un cordage); bandage *m* (d'un ressort). **3.** (*a*) renforcement *m* (d'un blocus, etc.); (*b*) *Fin:* resserrement (du crédit, etc.).

tightfisted [tait'fistid], *a. F:* **to be t.,** être très près de ses sous.

tightfistedness [tait'fistidnis], *s. F:* chicherie *f*, avarice *f*, pingrerie *f*.

tight-fitting [tait'fitiŋ], *a.* **1.** (vêtement) collant. **2.** (*of joint, etc.*) bien ajusté; (*of door*) qui ferme hermétiquement.

tightlaced [tait'leist], *a.* **1.** *O:* (*of figure*) étranglé par le corset; serré dans son corset. **2.** *F:* collet monté *inv*; guindé; prude.

tightly ['taitli], *adv.* **1. door that shuts t.,** porte *f* qui ferme hermétiquement; **eyes t. shut,** yeux bien fermés. **2.** (*a*) fortement, fermement; **a t. pulled knot,** un nœud fortement serré; **to hold sth. t.,** tenir qch. serré; serrer qch. dans ses bras, entre les mains; **to hold on t. to sth.,** se cramponner à qch.; (*b*) étroitement; **hands t. clasped,** mains étroitement serrées; **to fit t.,** être bien ajusté; **to fit too t.,** être (trop) serré, trop juste; **we were t. packed,** nous étions comme des sardines en boîte, comme des harengs en caque.

tightness ['taitnis], *s.* **1.** étanchéité *f*; imperméabilité *f* (d'un cloison, etc.); herméticité *f* (d'un masque à gaz, etc.). **2.** (*a*) tension *f*, raideur *f* (d'un cordage); (*b*) *Med:* **t. of the chest,** oppression *f* de la poitrine; difficulté *f* à respirer; **to feel a t. across the chest,** avoir la poitrine oppressée; **t. of the pulse,** tension du pouls; (*c*) étroitesse *f* (d'un lien, d'un nœud, etc.); force *f* (d'une étreinte); (*d*) étroitesse (d'un vêtement). **3.** *Fin:* resserrement *m*, rareté *f* (de l'argent).

tightrope ['taitroup], *s.* corde tendue; corde raide; **t. walker,** danseur, -euse, de corde; funambule *mf*; fildefériste *mf*; *F:* **t. walking,** acrobatie *f* politique.

tights [taits], *s.pl. Cost:* **1.** *A:* culotte collante; pantalon collant (se porte encore avec l'habit de cour). **2.** collant *m*; *Th: etc:* maillot *m*.

tightwad ['taitwɔd], *s F:* avare *m*; grippe-sou *m*, *pl.* grippe-sou(s); pingre *m*; **to be a t.,** être (très) près de ses sous.

tiglic ['tiglik], *a. Ch:* tiglique.

tigon ['taigɔn], *s. Z:* tigron *m*.

Tigranes [ti'greini:z], *Pr.n.m. A.Hist:* Tigrane.

tigress ['taigris], *s.f. Z:* tigresse.

tigrine ['taigrin], *a.* tigré.

Tigris (the) [ðə'taigris], *Pr.n. Geog:* le Tigre.

tike [taik], *s.* = TYKE.

til [til], *s. Bot:* till *m*, teel *m*; sésame *m* de l'Inde; **t. seed oil,** huile *f* de sésame.

tilapia [ti'leipiə], *s. Ich:* tilapie *m*.

tilasite ['tiləsait], *s. Miner:* tilasite *f*.

tilbury ['tilbəri], *s. A. Veh:* tilbury *m*.

tilde ['tildə], *s. Gram:* tilde *m*.

tile[1] [tail], *s.* **1.** (*a*) tuile *f* (de toiture, etc.); **flat t., plain t.,** tuile plate; **crest t., ridge t.,** tuile faîtière; **gutter t.,** tuile creuse; *F:* **to spend a night, one's nights, on the tiles,** traîner dehors toute la nuit; **to have a t. loose,** être toqué, timbré; (*b*) carreau *m*; **paving t.,** brique *f* à paver; carreau de carrelage; **floor(ing) t.,** carreau de pavage, de revêtement de sol; **Dutch t.,** carreau de céramique vernissée; carreau glacé; **wall t.,** carreau de revêtement; (*c*) **chimney (flue) t.,** boisseau *m*; (*d*) **t. clay,** argile téguline; **t. works,** tuilerie *f*; **t. kiln,** (i) tuilerie; (ii) four *m* à carreaux; **t. manufacturer, t. maker,** (i) tuilier *m*; (ii) carrelier *m*. **2.** *P: O:* chapeau *m*; *esp.* chapeau haut de forme; couvre-chef *m*, *pl.* couvre-chefs.

tile[2], *v.tr.* **1.** (*a*) couvrir (un comble) de tuiles, en tuiles; (*b*) carreler (un plancher, etc.). **2.** (*a*) (*freemasonry*) tuiler (la loge); garder l'entrée de (la loge); (*b*) *F: O:* faire jurer le secret à (qn).

tiled [taild], *a.* (*a*) (toit *m*) de, en, tuiles; (*b*) (pavage) carrelé, en carreaux; (paroi *f*, etc.) à carreaux vernissés, revêtue de carrelage, en céramique.

tilefish ['tailfiʃ], *s. Ich:* poisson-tuile *m*.

tiler ['tailər], *s.* **1.** (*a*) couvreur *m* (en tuiles); (*b*) tuilier *m*; (*c*) carreleur *m*. **2.** (*freemasonry*) (frère) couvreur; tuileur *m*.

tilery ['tailəri], *s.* (*a*) tuilerie *f*; (*b*) fabrique *f* de carreaux.

Tiliaceae [tili'eisii:], *s.pl. Bot:* tiliacées *f*.

tiliaceous [tili'eiʃəs], *a. Bot:* tiliacé.

tiling ['tailiŋ], *s.* **1.** (*a*) pose *f* des tuiles (sur une maison, etc.); (*b*) carrelage *m*; pose des carreaux. **2.** *coll.* (*a*) couverture *f*, toiture *f*, en tuiles; (*b*) carrelage, carreaux *mpl*.

till[1] [til], *v.tr.* labourer, cultiver (un champ, etc.).

till[2], *s. Com:* tiroir-caisse *m*, *pl.* tiroirs-caisses; casier *m* à monnaie; **t. money,** encaisse *f*; *F:* **to be caught with one's hand in the t.,** être surpris la main dans le sac, en flagrant délit; être pris sur le fait.

till[3]. **1.** *prep.* (*a*) jusqu'à; **t. tomorrow,** jusqu'à demain; **t. now, t. then,** jusqu'ici, jusque-là; **from morning t. night,** du matin au soir; **goodbye t. Thursday!** à jeudi! **he works t. late at night,** il travaille tard dans la nuit; **go and rest t. lunchtime,** allez vous reposer en attendant l'heure du déjeuner; **wait t. after the holidays,** attendez jusqu'après les vacances; **to wait t. later (on),** attendre à plus tard; (*b*) **not t. after ten o'clock,** pas avant dix heures passées; **he won't come t. after dinner,** il ne viendra qu'après le dîner; **it wasn't t. I met him that. . .,** ce ne fut qu'après notre rencontre que . . .; **I'd never heard of it t. now,** c'est la première fois que j'en entends parler; **I can't do anything t. Monday,** je ne peux rien faire avant lundi. **2.** *conj.* (*a*) jusqu'à ce que +*sub.*; **t. all the doors are shut,** jusqu'à ce que toutes les portes soient fermées; **he ran t. he fell exhausted,** il a couru jusqu'à tomber épuisé; **to laugh t. one cries,** rire aux larmes; (*b*) **he won't come t. you invite him, t. he's invited,** il ne viendra pas avant que vous (ne) l'invitiez, avant d'être invité; **I'm not going t. I get my money,** je ne sortirai d'ici que lorsque j'aurai mon argent; **I won't leave him t. the whole thing is settled,** je ne le quitterai pas que l'affaire ne soit terminée.

till[4], *s. Geol:* till *m*.

tillable ['tiləbl], *a.* labourable, cultivable, arable.

tillage ['tilidʒ], *s.* **1.** labour *m*, labourage *m*, agriculture *f*, culture *f*; **land in t.,** terre *f* en labour. **2.** terres en labour; labours.

tillandsia [ti'lændziə], *s. Bot:* tillandsie *m*.

tiller[1] ['tilər], *s.* **1.** *Nau:* barre franche (de direction); **to put the t. hard over,** donner un brusque coup de barre; **t. chain, t. rope,** drosse *f* du gouvernail; **sweep of t.,** tamisaille *f*. **2.** *Aut: A:* **t. steering,** direction *f* par levier à main.

tiller[2], *s.* laboureur *m*, cultivateur *m*.

tiller[3], *s.* **1.** *Agr:* talle *f* (du blé, etc.). **2.** *For:* baliveau *m*.

tiller[4], *v.i. Agr:* **the wheat has tillered well,** les blés ont bien tallé, bien gerbé.

tillering ['tiləriŋ], *s. Agr:* tallage *m*.

tilling ['tiliŋ], *s.* labour *m*, labourage *m*, culture *f*.

tillite ['tilait], *s. Geol:* tillite *f*.

tillodont ['tiloudɔnt], *s. Paleont:* tillodonte *m*.

Tillodontia [tilou'dɔnʃiə], *s.pl. Paleont:* tillodontes *m*.

Tilopteridales [tilɔptəri'deili:z], *s.pl. Algae:* tiloptéridales *f*.

tilt[1] [tilt], *s.* **1.** (*a*) inclinaison *f*, pente *f*; dévers *m*; dévoiement *m*; *Geol:* relèvement *m* (d'une couche, d'une faille); *Nau:* gîte *f*, bande *f*; *Veh:* carrossage *m* de l'essieu; **to be on the t.,** être penché, incliné, dévoyé; **to give a cask a t.,** faire pencher un tonneau; incliner un tonneau; *Tls:* **t. gauge,** règle *f* à dévers; *Nau:* **t. test,** essai *m* de gîte; essai de bande; (*b*) basculement *m*; *Av:* **t.-wing aircraft,** avion *m* à voilure basculante; **t. comparator,** comparateur *m* de basculement. **2.** *Cin:* panoramique vertical. **3.** (*a*) *A:* joute *f*, tournoi *m*; **t. yard,** carrousel *m*; lice *f*; champ clos; (*b*) *A:* coup *m* de lance; *Fig:* **to have a t. at s.o.,** jouter avec qn, donner un coup de patte à qn (dans un débat); (*c*) **(at) full t.,** à toute vitesse; à fond de train; au grand galop; **to run full t. into sth.,** donner en plein contre qch.; se jeter tête baissée, à corps perdu, contre qch.; **to ride (at) full t.,** aller à franc étrier, à bride abattue. **4.** (*a*) *Metall:* **t. (hammer),** martinet *m*; marteau *m* à soulèvement, à bascule; **t. hammerman,** martineur *m*; (*b*) *Leath:* **t. hammer,** triballe *f*.

tilt[2], *v.*

I. *v.i.* **1.** (*a*) **to t. (up),** s'incliner; pencher; *Geol:* (*of stratum*) se relever; **to t. backwards, forwards,** incliner vers l'arrière, vers l'avant; **to t. over,** (i) se pencher, s'incliner; (ii) (*of table, etc.*) se renverser; (*b*) (*of ship*) prendre de la bande, de la gîte; (*c*) (*of bench, etc.*) **to t. up,** basculer. **2.** *A:* (*a*) jouter (**with s.o.,** avec qn); (*b*) **to t. at s.o.,** (i) courir sur qn la lance en arrêt; courir une lance contre qn; fondre sur qn la lance en avant; (ii) *Fig:* donner un coup de patte à qn (dans un débat, etc.).

II. *v.tr.* **1.** (*a*) pencher, incliner (un tonneau, sa chaise, etc.); **to t. one's hat over one's eyes,** rabattre son chapeau sur ses yeux; **to t. one's chair back,** se balancer, se renverser, sur sa chaise; **to t. over a table,** renverser une table; (*b*) culbuter, (faire) basculer. **2.** *Metall:* martiner, marteler (le fer).

tilt[3], *s.* **1.** (*a*) *Veh:* bâche *f*, banne *f*; (*b*) *Nau:* tendelet *m*; (*c*) *Const:* **t. roof,** toit arrondi. **2.** (*in Labrador, Newfoundland, etc.*) cabane *f* (de bûcheron, de pêcheur).

tilt[4], *v.tr.* **1.** couvrir d'une bâche; bâcher, banner (une charrette, etc.). **2.** *Nau:* couvrir (une embarcation) d'un tendelet.

tilted[1] ['tiltid], *a.* incliné, penché.

tilted[2], *a.* bâché, banné.

tilter ['tiltər], *s.* **1.** *A:* jouteur *m*. **2.** (*a*) *Metall:* (*pers.*) martineur *m*; (*b*) dispositif *m* d'inclinaison; bascule *f*; culbuteur *m*.

tilth [tilθ], *s. Agr:* **1.** labour *m*, labourage *m*, culture *f*. **2.** (*a*) couche *f* arable; profondeur *f* de sol labourée; (*b*) cultures.

tilting[1] ['tiltiŋ], *a.* (i) incliné, penché; (ii) inclinable; (iii) basculant; (mouvement) basculaire; *Av:* **aircraft with t. rotors,** appareil *m* avec rotors basculants.

tilting[2], *s.* **1.** inclinaison *f*, pente *f*; dévoiement *m*; **t. device,** dispositif *m* d'inclinaison; bascule *f*; culbuteur *m*. **2.** *A:* joute *f*; **t. match,** carrousel *m*, joute; **t. lance, t. spear,** lance *f* de joute; lance courtoise; **t. at the ring,** jeu *m* de bagues. **3.** basculage *m*, culbutage *m*.

Tim [tim], *Pr.n.m.* (*dim.*) Timothée; *F: O:* **a tired T.,** un fainéant.

Timaeus [tai'mi:əs], *Pr.n.m. Gr.Phil:* Timée.

Timalidae [ti'mælidi:], *s.pl. Orn:* timalidés *m.*

timbale [tæm'bæl], *s.* **1.** *Ent:* timbale *f* (de la cigale). **2.** *Cu:* timbale.

timber[1] ['timbər], *s.* **1.** (*a*) bois *m* d'œuvre; bois à ouvrer; **building t.,** bois de construction, de service, de charpente; **rough(-hewn) t.,** bois en grume; bois dressé à la hache; **round t., t. in the round,** bois rond, non équarri; **squared t.,** bois équarri; **dimension t.,** bois débité; **cloven t.,** bois de fente; **to cut t.,** faire du bois; **the t. trade,** le commerce du bois; **t. merchant,** marchand *m* de bois; **t. yard,** chantier *m* (de bois de charpente); **t. bridge,** pont *m* en bois; (*b*) **standing t.,** bois sur pied; bois debout; arbres *mpl* de haute futaie; bois en état, en étant; **to fell t.,** abattre, couper, le bois; **to put an area under t.,** boiser une région; **t. shoot, chute,** lançoir *m*; **float, raft, of t.,** train *m* de bois. **2.** (*a*) **(piece of) t.,** poutre *f*, madrier *m*; (*b*) *N.Arch:* couple *m*, allonge *f*, membre *m*; **chief t.,** couple droit, couple de levée; **t. head,** jambette *f*, patin *m*; **stern timbers,** jambettes de voûte; quenouillettes *f*; (*c*) *F: O:* **t., t. toe,** jambe *f* de, en, bois; *F: A:* **shiver my timbers!** sapristi! nom d'un chien! mille tonnerres! tonnerre de Dieu! **shiver my timbers if . . .,** le diable m'emporte si . . .; (*d*) *Nau:* **t. hitch,** nœud *m* de bois, d'anguille; barbouquet *m.* **3.** *U.S: F:* qualité *f*, trempe *f* (de qn); **he's real ministerial t.,** il est du bois dont on fait les ministres.

timber[2]. **1.** *v.tr. O:* boiser, blinder, cuveler (un puits de mine, etc.). **2.** *v.i.* (*of lumberer*) faire du bois.

timber[3], *s. Her:* = TIMBRE[2].

timbered ['timbəd], *a.* (*a*) (maison *f*, etc.) en bois; **half t.,** à, en, colombage; en pans de bois; **t. excavation,** fouille blindée; (*b*) (*of land*) boisé.

timbering ['timb(ə)riŋ], *s.* **1.** boisage *m*, boisement *m* (d'une région). **2.** (*a*) boisage; (i) blindage *m*, cuvelage *m* (d'un puits de mine); (ii) armature *f* (de bois); *Arch:* forêt *f* de comble (d'une cathédrale, etc.); (*b*) **half t.,** colombage *m.*

timberline ['timbəlain], *s. For:* limite *f* des arbres.

timberman, *pl.* **-men** ['timbəmən], *s.m.* **1.** ouvrier en chantier. **2.** *Min: O:* boiseur.

timberwork ['timbəwə:k], *s.* **1.** construction *f* en bois. **2.** charpente *f.*

timbre[1] [tɛ̃:(m)br, 'tæmbər], *s.* timbre *m* (de la voix, d'un instrument de musique).

timbre[2] ['timbər], *s. Her:* timbre *m* (surmontant l'écu).

timbred ['timbəd], *a. Her:* timbré.

timbrel ['timbrəl], *s. Mus: B:* tambourin *m.*

Timbuktu [timbʌk'tu:], *Pr.n. Geog:* Tombouctou *m.*

time[1] [taim], *s.* **1.** temps *m*; **the ravages of t.,** les ravages *m* du temps; *Lit:* l'outrage *m* des ans; **work that takes t.,** ouvrage *m* de longue haleine; **(Father) T.,** le Temps; **t. will show,** qui vivra verra; *Prov:* **t. is money,** le temps c'est de l'argent; **t. is everything,** qui gagne du temps gagne tout; **lost in the mists of t.,** perdu dans la nuit des temps; **in (the course of) t., in process of t., as t. goes on,** dans le cours, dans la suite, du temps; avec le temps; à la longue; **it was a race against t.,** c'était une course contre la montre; il était de toute importance d'agir vite; **to do sth. against t.,** essayer de faire qch. contre la montre. **2.** (*a*) **in a short t.,** en peu de temps; sous peu; **in three weeks' t.,** en trois semaines; **in a month's t.,** dans un mois; **in no t.,** en un instant, en un clin d'œil, en un rien de temps, en moins de rien; **he was dressed, ready, in no t.,** il eut vite fait de s'habiller; il a été prêt en moins de rien; **they wear out in no t.,** ils s'usent en un rien de temps; **I'll have it done in next to, less than, no t.,** je vais vous faire ça en un rien de temps, en moins de rien; **in a very short space of t.,** au bout de très peu de temps; **within the required t.,** dans le délai prescrit; dans les délais voulus; **in the shortest possible t.,** dans le plus bref délai; le plus vite possible; le plus tôt possible; **to take a long t. over sth.,** mettre longtemps à faire qch.; **we shan't see him for a long t.,** on ne le verra pas d'ici longtemps; **we haven't seen him for a long t.,** nous ne l'avons pas vu de longtemps; voilà longtemps que nous ne l'avons vu; **for some t. past,** depuis quelque temps; **he'll be in bed for some t.,** il restera alité pendant quelque temps; **he stayed in London for a t.,** il est resté à Londres pendant quelque temps; **to stay for a short t.,** faire un bref séjour (à Londres, etc.); **a short t. after, after a short t.,** peu (de temps) après; **after a t.,** après quelque temps; au bout d'un certain temps; **after a long t.,** longtemps après; après un long intervalle; **it will take some t. to do it,** il faudra assez longtemps pour le faire; **what a (long) t. he's taking!** il n'en finit pas! il prend bien son temps! **all this t.,** pendant tout ce temps; **all the t. we were working,** pendant tout le temps que nous travaillions; **he does it all the t.,** il le fait toujours, continuellement; **he's been watching us all the t., the whole t.,** il n'a pas cessé de nous regarder, de nous observer; **I knew it, I've known it, all the t.,** je le sais depuis toujours; *Sp:* **official t.,** temps chronométré; **to keep the t.,** chronométrer; *Cin:* **running t.** (**of a film**), durée *f* de projection (d'un film); *Cmptr:* **t. sharing,** traitement *m* en temps partagé; *Gram:* **t. clause,** proposition temporelle; (*b*) *Fin:* **t. money,** prêts *mpl* à terme; **t. bill,** échéance *f* à terme; *St.Exch:* **dealings for t.,** négociations *f* à terme; **t. bargain,** marché *m* à terme, à livrer; vente *f* à découvert; *Nau:* **t. charter,** affrètement *m* à temps; *Ins:* **t. policy,** police *f* à terme, à forfait; *El:* **t. switch,** minuterie *f* (d'escalier, etc.); *Min: etc:* **t. fuse,** fusée fusante, à temps; **variable t. fuse,** fusée à influence; *Artil:* **t. fuse fire,** tir fusant; **t. bomb,** bombe *f* à retardement; *Phot:* **t. exposure,** pose *f*. **3.** (*a*) **my t. is my own,** je suis libre de mon temps; je ne suis pas soumis à l'heure; **my time's not, my t. isn't, my own,** mon temps n'est pas libre; **I'll write to him when I have t.,** je lui écrirai quand j'aurai le temps; **to have t. on one's hands,** avoir du temps de reste, à perdre; **to have no t. to do sth.,** ne pas avoir le temps de faire qch.; *F:* **I've no t. for him,** il m'embête; je ne peux pas le sentir; **we have no t. now,** nous n'avons pas le temps à présent; **to gain t.,** gagner du temps; **to play for t.,** chercher à gagner du temps; **you've plenty of t. to think it over,** vous avez tout le temps d'y réfléchir; **give me t. to think about it,** laissez-moi le temps d'y réfléchir; **you've plenty,** *F:* **heaps, oceans, of t.,** (i) vous avez tout le temps qu'il vous faut; (ii) ce n'est pas le temps qui vous manque; **there's no t. to be lost, to lose,** il n'y a pas de temps à perdre; **to make up for lost t.,** réparer, rattraper, le temps perdu; **to lose no t. doing sth.,** s'empresser, se hâter, à faire qch.; **to waste t.,** perdre du temps; **I didn't waste any (of my) t. reading that book,** je n'ai pas gaspillé mon temps à lire ce livre; **to make t. to do sth.,** trouver le temps de faire qch.; **it takes t.,** cela prend du temps; **to take one's t. over sth.,** mettre le temps à faire qch.; **take your t.,** prenez votre temps; ne vous pressez pas; **it will take you all your t. to . . .,** vous aurez fort à faire pour . . .; **it takes me all my t. to make both ends meet,** c'est à peine si je joins les deux bouts; **time's up!** l'heure a sonné! il est l'heure! c'est l'heure! *Box:* **t.!** allez! (*in public house*) **t., gentlemen, please!** on ferme! *Fb: etc:* **to play extra t.,** jouer les prolongations; *Fin:* **to ask for an extension of t.,** demander une prolongation d'échéance; (*b*) **soldier, convict, nearing the end of his t.,** soldat *m*, forçat *m*, qui a bientôt fait, fini, son temps; *F:* **to do t.,** faire de la prison, de la taule, tôle; **to serve one's t.** (**of apprenticeship**), faire son apprentissage; **the house will last our t.,** la maison durera autant que nous; **if I had my t. over again,** si j'avais à recommencer ma vie; *F:* **this hat has done, served, its t.,** ce chapeau a fait son temps. **4.** époque *f*; (*a*) **a sign of the times,** un signe de l'époque; **in Napoleonic times,** à l'époque, du temps, de Napoléon; **in times past, in former times,** autrefois, jadis; dans le temps (passé); **ancient times,** l'antiquité *f*; **the good old times,** le bon vieux temps; **those were happy times,** c'était le bon temps; **in happier times,** en un temps plus heureux; **it was the custom of those times, at that t.,** c'était l'usage alors; **t. out of mind, from t. immemorial,** de temps immémorial; **in times to come,** à l'avenir; dans l'avenir; dans les âges futurs; **in my t. it was different,** de mon temps c'était différent; **in our times, these times,** de nos jours; **the times we live in,** notre époque; notre siècle; (*b*) **to be ahead of, in advance of, one's t.,** avoir des idées avancées; **to move with the times, to be abreast of the times,** marcher, vivre, avec son temps; *F:* être à la page; **to be behind the times,** retarder, être en retard, sur son siècle; être arriéré, attardé; ne pas être de son temps; *F:* ne pas être à la page; **as times go,** par le temps qui court; **times are bad,** les temps sont difficiles, durs; (*c*) **t. capsule,** capsule-mémorial *f*, coffret-mémorial *m.* **5.** moment *m*; (*a*) **at the t. of delivery,** au moment de la livraison; **at the t. of his marriage,** lors de son mariage; **I wasn't there at the t.,** j'étais absent alors, à ce moment, à cette époque; **he was travelling at the t.,** il était alors en voyage; **at the t. I didn't notice it,** sur le moment je n'y ai pas fait attention; **I didn't know it at the t.,** je n'en savais rien (i) à ce moment-là, (ii) à cette époque; **at a t. when he was unknown,** alors qu'il était inconnu; **at that t.,** en ce temps-là; **at the present t.,** à l'heure qu'il est; actuellement; à présent; à l'heure actuelle; à l'époque actuelle; **at a given t.,** à un moment donné, déterminé; **at the t. fixed,** à l'heure convenue, dite; **at one t. . . ., at another t. . . .,** tantôt . . ., tantôt . . .; **at one t. it was different,** autrefois, dans le temps, il n'en était pas ainsi; **at one t. this book was very popular,** autrefois on lisait beaucoup ce livre; **at one t. priest of this parish,** ancien prêtre de cette paroisse; **at one t. I should have accepted,** à un moment donné j'aurais accepté; il y eut une heure où j'aurais accepté; *Lit:* **t. was when . . .,** il fut un temps où . . .; **at no t.,** (i) jamais; (ii) à aucun moment; **at times,** parfois, quelquefois; par moments; de temps à autre; **we've all said so at times,** nous avons tous parlé de même à certains moments; **at various times,** à diverses reprises; **at all times,** (i) en tout temps; toujours; à tous moments; (ii) à n'importe quel moment; **at all times and in all places,** en tout et partout; **between times,** entre temps; **(at) any t. (you like),** n'importe quand; quand vous voudrez, quand bon vous semblera; **repayable at any t.,** remboursable à toute date; **he may turn up at any t.,** il peut arriver d'un moment à l'autre; **if at any time . . .,** si à l'occasion . . .; **you will be welcome at any t.,** vous serez toujours le bienvenu; **at any other t.,** en toute autre occasion; **some t. or other,** un jour ou l'autre; tôt ou tard; **some time next month,** dans le courant du mois prochain; **this t. last year,** il y a un an à pareille époque, à pareil jour; **this t. next year,** l'an prochain à pareille époque, à la même date; **this t. tomorrow,** demain à la même heure; **by the t. that I got there,** (i) lorsque je suis arrivé; (ii) lorsque je serais arrivé; **by that t. we shall be old,** d'ici là nous aurons vieilli; **you ought to be ready by this t.,** vous devriez être prêt maintenant; **from t. to t.,** de temps en temps; de temps à autre; **from that t. (onwards),** dès lors; depuis lors; à partir de ce moment-là; **to do sth. when the t. comes, at the proper t.,** faire qch. en son temps, en temps utile; **we shall see when the t. comes,** nous verrons (cela) quand le moment sera venu; **to do things, everything, at the proper time,** faire chaque chose en son temps; **we'll speak of it at the proper t. and place,** nous en parlerons en son temps et lieu; **t. enough to attend to that tomorrow,** il sera bien temps de faire cela demain; **we must wait until such t. as business improves,** il faut attendre jusqu'au moment où les affaires iront mieux; il faut attendre que les affaires reprennent; **now is the t., our t., your t., to . . .,** voilà le moment pour . . ., c'est le bon moment pour . . .; **now is the t. for selling, to sell,** c'est le moment de vendre; **to appoint, fix, a t. for doing sth.,** fixer le moment, la date, le jour, l'heure, de faire qch.; **to choose one's t.,** prendre son temps; choisir son heure; **this is no t., this is not the t., to reproach me, for reproaching me,** ce n'est pas le moment, vous êtes mal venu, à me faire des reproches; (*b*) **in due t. and place,** en temps et lieu; **all in good t., in due t.,** tout viendra en son temps; chaque chose en son temps; il y a temps pour tout; **you'll hear from me in good t.,** je vous écrirai, vous préviendrai, en temps utile, le moment venu; **it will be done in due t.,** cela se fera à l'heure voulue; **in his own good t.,** à son heure; **in God's good t.,** à la grâce de Dieu. **6.** heure *f*; (*a*) **Greenwich mean t.,** l'heure de Greenwich; temps moyen de Greenwich; **New York t.,** heure de New York; **sidereal t.,** heure astronomique, temps sidéral; **astronomical t.,** temps astronomique; **solar t.,** temps solaire; **true t.,** temps vrai; **apparent t.,** temps apparent; **local mean t.,** temps moyen local; *Nau:* **ship's mean t.,** temps moyen du bord; **ship's t.,** heure du bord; **civil, official, t.,** heure légale; **standard t.,** heure du fuseau; **(standard) t. belt, t. zone,** fuseau *m* horaire; **summer t.,** *U.S:* **daylight saving t.,** heure d'été, *Fr.C:* heure avancée; (*b*) (*o'clock*) **what's the t.?** quelle heure est-il? **what t. do you make it?** quelle heure avez-vous? *W.Tel: etc:* **t. signal,** signal *m* horaire; *Nau:* **t. ball,** boule *f* horaire; balle *f*, ballon *m*, du signal horaire; **to look at the t.,** regarder (à) sa montre; regarder quelle heure il est; **watch that keeps (good) t.,** montre qui est exacte, qui va bien, qui est bien réglée; **clock that loses t.,** pendule qui retarde; **t. of day,** heure du jour; **at any t. of the day or night,** à n'importe quelle heure du jour ou de la nuit; **snacks at any t.,** casse-croûte à toute heure; **he turns up at any t.,** il n'a pas d'heure; *F:* **he turns up at the office at any old t.,** il arrive au bureau à n'importe quelle heure; **to pass the t. of day with s.o.,** échanger quelques mots, quelques paroles, avec qn; (*c*) **dinner t.,** l'heure du dîner; **to forget the t. of an appointment,** oublier l'heure d'un rendez-vous; **I must be there on t., at the right t.,** il faut que je sois à l'heure; **to be ahead of t.,** être en avance; être avant l'heure; **to be behind t.,** être en retard; **to arrive exactly on t.,** arriver à l'heure sonnante, tapante; **if the train is up to t., on t., here,** si le train arrive ici à l'heure; **the train wasn't up to t., was running behind t.,** le train avait du retard; **to be ten minutes behind t.,** avoir un retard de dix minutes, dix minutes de retard; être en retard de dix minutes; **I shall be back in t.,** je reviendrai à temps, en temps voulu; **I hope I'll arrive in t.,** pourvu que j'arrive à l'heure! **to arrive in t. for dinner,** arriver à temps pour dîner; **I was just in t. to see it,** je suis arrivé juste à temps pour le voir; **it was only just in t.,** il n'était que temps; **to start in good t.,** (i) s'y prendre (bien) à temps; (ii) se mettre en route de bonne heure; **to come in good t.,** arriver (grandement) à temps; **come in good t.!** ne soyez pas en retard! **it's t. she came down,** il est temps qu'elle descende; **it is t. we left,** il est temps à songer à partir; *F:* **it's high t.! and about t. too!** ce n'est pas, c'est pas, trop tôt! (*d*) **t. of the year,** époque de l'année; saison *f*; **at this t. of year,** en cette saison; **at my t. of life,** à mon âge; à l'âge que j'ai; **sowing t.,** la saison, le temps, de semailles; **it was holiday t.,** c'était l'époque des vacances; (*e*) **plant that is flowering before its t.,** plante qui fleurit prématurément; **to die before one's t.,** mourir avant l'âge; **his t. had not yet come,** son heure n'était pas encore venue; (*of pregnant woman*) **to be nearing her t.,** approcher de son terme. **7.** *Ind: etc:* (*a*) **to be paid by t.,** être payé à l'heure; **to put in t.,** faire des heures; **overtime counts t. and a half,** les heures supplémentaires sont payées à un taux de moitié plus élevé; **idle t.,** heures d'arrêt; durée *f* des arrêts; **to work, to be on, short t.,** être en chômage partiel; (*b*) **t. recorder, t. clock,** enregistreur *m* de temps; **t. sheet,** feuille *f* de présence; semainier *m*; **t. book,** (i) livret (individuel) des heures de travail; (ii) registre *m* de présence; **t. clerk,** chronométreur *m*, pointeur *m*, contrôleur *m* (de présence); (*c*) **t. and motion study,** étude *f* et ordonnancement des temps et mouvements; **t. and motion expert,** spécialiste *mf* des temps et méthodes; **t. and method engineering,** étude des temps et méthodes. **8.** *F:* **to have a good t. (of it),** (i) bien s'amuser; (ii) mener une vie agréable; **we had a good t.,** on s'est bien amusés; **to have a high old t., the t. of one's life,** faire la noce; bien rigoler; **I've had the t. of my life, I've had such a good t.,** jamais je ne me suis si bien amusé; **to have a bad t., a rough t., (of it),** (i) souffrir; manger de la vache enragée; en voir de dures; (ii) passer un mauvais quart d'heure; (*of woman*) **to have a bad t. of it with her baby,** subir des couches laborieuses, pénibles; **to give s.o. a rough t.,** en faire voir de dures à qn; **what a t. I had with him!** il m'a causé bien des ennuis! il m'en a fait voir! **9.** fois *f*; **five times,** cinq fois; **he has come three times, this is the third t. he's come,** voilà trois fois qu'il revient; c'est la troisième fois qu'il vient; **next t.,** la prochaine fois; **I'll forgive you this t.,** cette fois(-ci) je te pardonne; **another example, a more technical one this t.,** autre exemple, plus technique, celui-là; **another t.,** une autre fois; **at other times,** d'autres fois; **the first t. I saw him,** la première fois que je l'ai vu; **the one t. I got good cards there was a misdeal,** pour une fois que j'avais de bonnes cartes il y avait maldonne; **to do sth. several times over,** faire qch. à plusieurs reprises, plusieurs fois; **four times running,** quatre fois de suite, à quatre reprises; **times without number, t. and t. again, t. after t.,** à maintes reprises; maintes et maintes fois; mille et mille fois; vingt fois; cent fois; **t. and t. again he eluded the enemy,** il échappa vingt fois à l'ennemi; **I've told you so a hundred times,** je vous l'ai dit vingt fois, cent fois; **he succeeds every t.,** il réussit à chaque coup; **every t. that . . .,** chaque fois que . . ., toutes les fois que . . .; **to do two things at a t.,** faire deux choses à la fois; **don't try and do three things at a t.,** on ne peut pas faire trois choses à la fois; **to run upstairs four at a t.,** monter l'escalier quatre à quatre; **for weeks at a t.,** des semaines durant, d'affilée; pendant plusieurs semaines de suite; **it costs me £3 a t. to have my hair done,** ça me coûte trois livres chaque fois que je me fais coiffer; **pick any you like at 50p. a t.,** choisissez ceux que vous voudrez à cinquante pence chacun; **four times two is eight,** quatre fois deux font huit; **three times as big as the other,** trois fois plus grand que l'autre; **six times as much,** six fois autant; **three times as much jam, three times as many books,** trois fois plus de confiture, de livres; **there were five times fewer, less,** il n'y en avait que le cinquième. **10.** (*a*) **at the same t.,** en même temps; **don't all speak at the same t.,** ne parlez pas tous à la fois; *Prov:* **you can't be in two places at the same t.,** on ne peut pas se trouver dans deux endroits à la fois; on ne peut pas être au four et au moulin; **she was laughing and crying at the same t.,** elle pleurait et riait à la fois; elle pleurait d'un œil et riait de l'autre; (*b*) **at the same t., you mustn't forget that . . .,** d'autre part il ne faut pas oublier que . . .; **at the same t. I must say I don't envy her,** cependant, tout de même, néanmoins, j'avoue que je ne voudrais pas être à sa place. **11.** (*a*) *Mus:* **t. value,** valeur *f* (d'une note); (*b*) *Mus:* mesure *f*; **common t.,** (i) (*also* **quadruple t.**) mesure à quatre temps; (ii) (*also* **two-part t., duple t.**) mesure à deux temps; **two-four t.,** mesure à deux-quatre; **triple t., three-part t.,** mesure à trois temps, mesure ternaire; **t. signature,** fraction *f* indiquant la mesure; **to beat t.,** battre la mesure; **he was beating t. with his foot,** il marquait la mesure du pied; (*c*) **in strict t.,** en mesure; **to keep t., be in t.,** chanter, jouer, aller, danser, en mesure; suivre la mesure, la cadence; **to get out of t.,** perdre la mesure; *I.C.E:* **the ignition is in t., out of t.,** l'allumage est réglé; l'allumage est déréglé, décalé; (*d*) *Mus:* tempo *m*; **to quicken, to slow, the t.,** presser, ralentir, le tempo, le mouvement; *Gym: etc:* **to walk in quick t.,** marcher au pas accéléré; **to break into quick t.,** prendre le pas accéléré, le pas cadencé. **12.** *F:* **the big t.,** le haut de l'échelle; les couches supérieures (des affaires, du sport, etc. où l'on gagne gros); **to be in the big t., to have made the big t.,** être en haut de l'échelle; être parmi les huiles; **big-t. operator,** gros trafiquant; **a big-t. player,** un as (du jeu); **small-t. crook,** petit escroc.

time[2], *v.tr.* **1.** (*a*) fixer l'heure de (qch.); **to t. one's arrival to coincide with one's friend's,** s'arranger pour arriver en même temps que son ami; **the train was timed to leave at noon,** d'après l'horaire, le train devait partir à midi; **the arrival of the mayor was timed for three o'clock,** suivant le programme, le maire devait arriver à trois heures; l'arrivée du maire était fixée pour trois heures; (*b*) **to t. a blow, a remark,** choisir le moment de porter un coup, de placer un mot; mesurer un coup; (*c*) régler (une horloge); **to t. one's watch by the time signal,** régler sa montre sur le signal horaire; (*d*) *I.C.E:* régler, ajuster (l'allumage, les soupapes); caler (la magnéto, le distributeur); mettre (le moteur) au point; *Mch:* caler (une soupape); (*e*) régler (un obus); (*f*) *Row:* **to t. the stroke,** régler la nage. **2.** calculer la durée de (qch.); *Phot:* **to t. the exposure,** calculer le temps de pose. **3.** (*a*) **to t. how long it takes s.o. to do sth.,** mesurer le temps que qn met à faire qch.; (*b*) *Sp: etc:* chronométrer (qn, une course); prendre le temps (d'un coureur); **to t. s.o., a horse, over a mile,** chronométrer le temps employé pour parcourir un mille; **her last two laps were both timed at five seconds,** elle a fait l'avant-dernier et le dernier tour dans le même temps de cinq secondes; **timed race,** course contre la montre; (*c*) minuter; *Mil: etc:* **to t. an operation,** minuter une opération.

time-consuming ['taimkənsju:miŋ], *a.* (travail, etc.) qui prend beaucoup de temps.

timed [taimd], *a.* (*with adv. prefixed*) **1. well-t. remark,** observation opportune, à propos; **ill t. remarks,** propos inopportuns, intempestifs, hors de saison; **well t. stroke,** coup bien calculé, bien jugé; **well t. rowing,** nage cadencée, rythmée. **2. accurately-t. watch.** montre soigneusement réglée; **well t. engine,** moteur *m* au point.

time-expired ['taimikspaiəd], *a.* (soldat, etc.) qui a fait, servi, son temps.

time-fill[1], **time-filling** ['taimfil(iŋ)], *s. Cmptr:* temporisation *f*.

time-fill[2], *v.i. Cmptr:* temporiser.

time-honoured ['taimɔnəd], *a.* (*of custom, etc.*) consacré (par l'usage); vénérable, séculaire.

timekeeper ['taimki:pər], *s.* **1.** (*a*) *Ind:* chronométreur *m*, pointeur *m*, contrôleur *m* (de présence); (*b*) *Sp:* chronométreur. **2.** (*a*) **this watch is a good t.,** cette montre est toujours à l'heure; (*b*) **he's a good t.,** il est toujours à l'heure.

timekeeping ['taimki:piŋ], *s.* **1.** *Ind:* contrôle *m*, pointage *m*, de présence; comptabilité *f* du temps (du personnel). **2.** *Sp: etc:* chronométrage *m*; minutage *m*.

time-killing ['taimkiliŋ], *a.* (occupation *f*) pour tuer le temps.

timeless ['taimlis], *a.* (*a*) éternel; sans fin; (*b*) intemporel.

timelessness ['taimlisnis], *s.* intemporalité *f*.

Timeliidae [time'laiidi:], *s.pl. Orn:* timéliidés *m*, timaliidés *m*.

timeliness ['taimlinis], *s.* opportunité *f*; à-propos *m* (d'une intervention, etc.).

timely ['taimli], *a.* opportun, à propos; (mot) jeté à propos; **your arrival was t.,** vous êtes arrivé au bon moment, à point; **I made a t. escape,** je me suis échappé juste à temps.

timepiece ['taimpi:s], *s.* pendule *f*, chronomètre *m*; montre *f*.

timer ['taimər], *s.* **1.** (*pers.*) chronométreur *m*. **2.** (*device*) (*a*) *I.C.E: etc:* commutateur *m* d'allumage; rupteur *m*; (*b*) minuterie *f*; *Dom.Ec:* compte-minutes *m inv*; minuteur *m*; (*c*) *Cmptr:* **interval t.,** rythmeur *m*; (*d*) (*welding*) temporisateur *m*.

time(-)saver ['taimseivər], *s.* économiseur *m* de temps; **that's a t.,** voilà qui vous fait gagner du temps.

time(-)saving[1] ['taimseiviŋ], *a.* qui économise du temps; qui permet de gagner du temps; **t. device** = TIME(-) SAVER.

time(-)saving[2], *s.* économie *f* de temps.

timeserver ['taimsə:vər], *s.* complaisant, -ante (envers le pouvoir, etc.); opportuniste *mf*; **to be a t.,** faire de l'opportunisme.

timeserving[1] ['taimsə:viŋ], *a.* complaisant, opportuniste.

timeserving[2], *s.* basse complaisance (envers le pouvoir); louvoiement *m* (entre les partis); opportunisme *m*.

timetable ['taimteibl], *s.* **1.** horaire *m*; *Rail:* indicateur *m* (des chemins de fer); tableau *m* de marche (des trains); (*local*) livret *m* horaire; **to alter the t.,** modifier l'horaire; *Rail:* modifier la marche des trains. **2.** (*a*) *Sch:* emploi *m* du temps; (*b*) *Ind: Com:* plan *m* de mise en exécution.

timework ['taimwə:k], *s.* travail *m* à l'heure; *Typ:* travail en conscience; **to be on t.,** travailler à, être payé à, l'heure; *Typ:* être en conscience.

timeworker ['taimwə:kər], *s.* ouvrier, -ière, qui travaille à l'heure; *Typ:* ouvrier en conscience.

timeworn ['taimwɔ:n], *a. O:* **1.** usé par le temps. **2.** séculaire, vénérable.

timid ['timid], *a.* timide, timoré, peureux, appréhensif; craintif; (animal) fuyard.

timidity [ti'miditi], *s.* timidité *f*.

timidly ['timidli], *adv.* timidement, peureusement, craintivement; d'un air timoré.

timing ['taimiŋ], *s.* **1.** (*a*) *I.C.E:* réglage *m* (de l'allumage); *Mch:* calage *m* (d'une soupape); (*b*) *I.C.E:* distribution *f*; **t. gear,** (engrenage(s) *m(pl)* de) distribution; **t. (chain, gear) case,** carter de distribution; **t. control,** commande *f* de distribution; **t. disc,** plateau *m* de réglage (de la magnéto). **2.** *Phot:* calcul *m* (du temps de pose). **3.** (*a*) *Sp: etc:* chronométrage *m*; *Ind:* **t. apparatus,** garde-temps *m inv*; (*b*) *Mil: etc:* minutage *m* (d'une opération). **4.** (*a*) **error of t.,** mauvais calcul; erreur *f* de jugement; **good t., bad t., of a remark,** à-propos *m*, manque *m* d'à-propos, d'une observation; **poor t. of a move,** inopportunité *f* d'une démarche; (*b*) *Sp: etc:* rythme *m* (d'un mouvement).

timocracy [tai'mɔkrəsi], *s.* timocratie *f*.

timocratic [taimou'krætik], *a.* timocratique.

timorous ['timərəs], *a.* timoré, timide, peureux, craintif.

timorously ['timərəsli], *adv.* timidement, peureusement, craintivement; d'un air timoré.

timorousness ['timərəsnis], *s.* timidité *f*.

Timothy ['timəθi]. **1.** *Pr.n.m.* Timothée. **2.** *s. Bot:* **t. (grass),** fléole *f* des prés.

Timour ['ti:muər], *Pr.n.m. Hist:* Timour Lenk; *O:* Tamerlan.

timpani ['timpəni(:)], *s.pl. Mus:* timbales *f*.

timpanist ['timpənist], *s. Mus:* timbalier *m*.

tin[1] [tin], *s.* **1.** *Miner: Metall:* étain *m*; **sheet t.,** étain en feuilles; **bar t.,** étain en verges; **block t.,** étain en saumons, en blocs; **lode t.,** étain de roche; **wood, toad's eye, t.,** étain de bois; **t. deposit,** gîte *f* stannifère; **t. mine,** mine *f* d'étain; **t. pyrites,** étain pyriteux; stannine *f*; **t.-bearing,** stannifère; **t.-bearing ores,** cassitérides *m*; *Metalw:* **t. bath,** tain *m*; bain *m* d'étain (pour étamer le fer); **t. pot,** bain d'étain fondu (pour l'étamage); **t. cry,** cri *m* de l'étain; *Dy:* **t. liquor, spirit,** solution de sels d'étain (employée comme mordant); *Fin:* **t. shares,** valeurs *f* stannifères. **2.** (*a*) **t. (plate),** fer-blanc *m*; **t.-lined,** doublé de fer-blanc; **t. mug,** timbale *f*; **t. shop,** ferblanterie *f*; *Navy: F:* **t. fish,** torpille *f*; *Mil: etc: F:* **t. hat,** casque *m*; *F: O:* **that puts the t. hat, the t. lid, on it!** ça c'est le comble! il ne manquait plus que ça! c'est la fin des haricots! **t. pan,** plat *m* en fer-blanc; *F:* **T. Pan Alley,** (i) *U.S:* le quartier des éditeurs et des enregistreurs de musique populaire; (ii) (*also* **t. pan alley**) les compositeurs *m* et éditeurs *m*, le monde, de la musique populaire; (*b*) tôle *f*; **t. trunk,** malle *f* de tôle; *Mil:* cantine *f*; **t. roof,** toit *m* en tôle ondulée; (*c*) *Dom.Ec:* (*for cake*) moule *m*; (*for tart*) tourtière *f*; **baking t.,** plat à rôtir; *Bak:* **t. loaf,** pain cuit au moule; pain anglais; (*d*) boîte *f* (en fer-blanc); boîte à conserves; **t. of sardines,** boîte de sardines; **add a t. of tomato purée,** ajoutez le contenu d'une boîte de purée de tomates; **t. opener,** ouvre-boîtes *m inv*; **petrol t.,** bidon *m* à essence. **3.** *P: O:* galette *f*, braise *f*, pognon *m*, pèze *m*.

tin[2], *v.tr.* (**tinned**) **1.** *Metalw:* étamer. **2.** mettre (des sardines, etc.) en boîtes (de fer-blanc).

Tinamidae [ti'næmidi:], *s.pl. Orn:* tinamidés *m*.

Tinamiformes [tinæmi'fɔ:mi:z], *s.pl. Orn:* tinamiformes *m*.

tinamou ['tinəmu:], *s. Orn:* tinamou *m*.

tincal ['tiŋkəl], *s. Miner:* tincal *m*.

tincalconite [tin'kælkənait], *s. Miner:* tincalconite *f*.

tinctorial [tiŋk'tɔ:riəl], *a.* tinctorial, -aux.

tincture[1] ['tiŋ(k)tjər], *s.* **1.** *Pharm:* teinture *f* (d'iode, etc.). **2.** (*a*) *A:* teinte *f*, nuance *f*; coloration *f* (de la peau, etc.); (*b*) teinture (d'une science). **3.** *Her:* émail *m*, -aux; teinture; **shield of a single t.,** écu plein.

tincture[2], *v.tr.* teindre, colorer, teinter; *Fig:* **opinions**

tinctured with heresy, opinions teintées d'hérésie.

tinder ['tindər], *s.* mèche *f* de briquet; **(German) t.,** amadou *m*; **t. box,** (i) boîte *f* d'amadou; (ii) briquet *m* (à silex); (iii) *NAm:* chose *f* inflammable, qui prend feu aisément; *Fig:* situation explosive; *Fung:* **t. fungus, agaric,** amadouvier *m*.

tine [tain], *s.* **1.** dent *f*, fourchon *m* (de fourche); dent, pointe *f* (de herse, etc.). **2.** *Ven:* andouiller *m*, cor *m*, branche *f* (de bois de cerf); **brow t.,** andouiller de combat, de massacre; **bay t.,** surandouiller *m*.

tinea ['tiniə], *s. Ent: Med:* teigne *f*.

tined [taind], *a.* à dents, fourchons; **three-t., four-t.,** (i) (fourche) à trois, quatre, dents; (ii) (cerf) à trois, quatre, andouillers; **ten-t. stag,** cerf dix cors.

Tineidae [ti'ni:idi:], *s.pl. Ent:* tinéides *m*, tinéidés *m*.

tinfoil ['tin'fɔil], *s.* **1.** feuille *f* d'étain; étain battu en feuilles. **2.** papier *m* (d')étain, papier simili-étain; *F:* papier d'argent.

ting[1] [tiŋ], *s.* tintement *m* (d'une cloche).

ting[2], *v.i. & tr.* (faire) tinter.

ting-a-ling ['tiŋəliŋ], *s. & adv.* drelin drelin *(m)*; **to go t.-a-l.,** faire drelin drelin.

tinge[1] [tin(d)ʒ], *s.* teinte *f*, nuance *f*; **a t. of sadness,** une nuance, un soupçon, de tristesse; quelque chose de triste; **a t. of irony,** une teinte, une pointe, d'ironie; **in his smile there was just a t. of jealousy,** il y avait dans son sourire un rien de jalousie; **a t. of fennel improves the sauce,** un soupçon de fenouil améliore la sauce.

tinge[2], *v.tr.* teinter, colorer, nuancer; **sky tinged with pink,** ciel teinté de rose; **words tinged with malice,** paroles teintées de malice; **voice tinged with anger,** voix légèrement nuancée de colère; **songs tinged with melancholy,** chants qui ont une teinte de mélancolie; **memories tinged with sadness,** souvenirs empreints de tristesse.

Tingidae ['tindʒidi:], *s.pl. Ent:* tingidés *m*.

tingis ['tindʒis], *s. Ent:* tingis *m*; **pear t.,** tigre *m* du poirier.

tingle[1] ['tiŋgl], *s.* **1. t. in the ears,** tintement *m* d'oreilles. **2.** picotement *m*, fourmillement *m* (de la peau); *(in the finger tips)* onglée *f*; **to have a t. in one's legs,** avoir des fourmis dans les jambes.

tingle[2]. **1.** *v.i.* *(a)* *(of ears)* tinter; **my ears were tingling,** les oreilles me tintaient; *(b)* picoter; **my hand tingles,** j'ai des picotements à la main; la main me picote, me fourmille; **to t. with impatience,** vibrer d'impatience; **breeze that makes the blood t.,** brise qui fouette le sang; **her cheeks tingled,** les joues lui picotaient, lui cuisaient; **my eyes are tingling,** les yeux me cuisent; **my fingers are tingling with cold,** j'ai l'onglée aux doigts. **2.** *v.tr.* *(a)* faire tinter (les oreilles); *(b)* faire picoter (la peau).

tingling[1] ['tiŋgliŋ], *a.* **1.** (oreilles) qui tintent. **2.** fourmillant, picotant; **t. sensation,** picotement *m*; **t. conscience,** conscience inquiète.

tingling[2], *s.* = TINGLE[1].

tinhorn ['tinhɔ:n], *a. F:* *(of pers.)* prétentieux, insignifiant.

tininess ['taininis], *s.* petitesse *f* (extrême).

tinker[1] ['tiŋkər], *s.* **1.** *(a)* chaudronnier ambulant, au sifflet; étameur ambulant; *(b)* *Dial:* bohémien *m*; *(c)* *O:* *(to child)* **you little t.!** petit polisson! petit diable! *(d)* *F:* bousilleur *m*, savetier *m*; gâcheur *m* (d'ouvrage). **2. to have an hour's t. at sth.,** passer une heure à rafistoler, retaper, bricoler, qch. **3.** *U.S: Ich:* **t. (mackerel),** petit, jeune, maquereau. **4.** *Orn:* **t. bird,** barbu *m*, barbet *m*.

tinker[2]. **1.** *v.tr.* **to t. (sth.) up,** retaper, rafistoler, *F:* rabibocher, rabobiner (une machine, etc.); replâtrer (un contrat, etc.); **it has only been tinkered up,** ce n'est qu'un rhabillage. **2.** *v.i.* bricoler; **to t. (away) at the radio,** passer du temps à rafistoler le poste de radio; **to t. about the house,** bricoler dans la maison; **to t. with a literary work,** tripatouiller une œuvre littéraire; **don't t. with it,** ne vous mêlez pas (i) de le réparer, (ii) d'y apporter des retouches.

tinkering ['tiŋkəriŋ], *s.* **1.** (petite) chaudronnerie; rétamage *m*. **2.** bricolage *m*; (i) petites besognes de réparation, d'entretien; (ii) rafistolage *m*, raccommodage *m*, replâtrage *m*.

tinkle[1] ['tiŋkl], *s.* tintin *m*, tintement *m* (de clochettes, verres); son *m* grêle, *O:* drelin *m* (d'une clochette); *F:* **I'll give you a t.,** je vous donnerai un coup de téléphone, de fil.

tinkle[2]. **1.** *v.i.* tinter; **tinkling bells,** cloches argentines; **to t. on the piano,** tapoter sur le piano. **2.** *v.tr.* faire tinter (une sonnette, des grelots).

tinkler ['tiŋklər], *s. F:* clochette *f*.

tinkling ['tiŋkliŋ], *s.* = TINKLE[1].

tinman, *pl.* **-men** ['tinmən], *s.m.* = TINSMITH.

tinned [tind], *a.* **1.** *Metalw:* (fer, etc.) étamé. **2.** conservé (en boîtes métalliques); **t. foods,** conserves *f* alimentaires (en boîte, en boîtes métalliques); aliments conservés; **t. peas,** petits pois de conserve; *F:* **t. music,** musique enregistrée, *F:* de conserve. **3. t. loaf,** pain cuit au moule, pain anglais.

tinner ['tinər], *s.* **1.** *(a)* étameur *m*; *(b)* ferblantier *m*. **2.** *Min:* mineur *m* (de mine d'étain).

tinnery ['tinəri], *s.* **1.** exploitation *f* de l'étain. **2.** *(also pl.* **tinneries)** mine *f* d'étain; mine, exploitation, stannifère.

tinniness ['tininis], *s.* timbre grêle, métallique, fêlé.

tinning ['tiniŋ], *s.* **1.** *Metalw:* étamage *m*; **t. metal,** étamure *f*. **2.** mise *f* en boîte (de conserves alimentaires).

tinnitus [ti'naitəs], *s. Med:* tintement *m*.

tinny[1] ['tini], *a.* **1.** *(of earth, etc.)* stannifère. **2. t. smell,** odeur stanneuse; **food with a t. taste,** aliment qui a un goût d'étain, de boîte de conserve. **3. to sound t.,** sonner grêle; rendre un son métallique, fêlé. **4.** *P: A:* riche, cossu; *P:* au pèze.

tinny[2], *s. Austr: F:* boîte *f* de bière.

tinplate[1] ['tinpleit], *s.* fer-blanc *m*; **t. (ware),** ferblanterie *f*; **t. industry, trade,** ferblanterie.

tinplate[2], *v.tr. Metalw:* étamer (le fer).

tinpot ['tinpɔt], *a. F:* mesquin, misérable, méprisable; **a t. little shop,** un petit magasin de rien du tout; **a t. dictator,** un dictateur au petit pied.

tinsel ['tins(ə)l]. **1.** *s.* *(a)* clinquant *m*, oripeau *m*, paillettes *fpl*; *(Christmas decorations)* cheveux *mpl* d'ange; **to trim sth. with t.,** clinquanter qch.; *(b)* *Tex:* lamé *m*; **t. maker,** lamier *m*. **2.** *a.* *(a)* (fil, etc.) de clinquant; (tissu) lamé; *(b)* *Fig:* d'un faux brillant; éclatant, tapageur, clinquant.

tinselled ['tins(ə)ld], *a.* *(a)* orné, garni, de clinquant, d'oripeau; **t. finery,** oripeaux *mpl*; *(b)* *Tex:* *(of material)* lamé.

tinsmith ['tinsmiθ], *s.* étameur *m*; ferblantier *m*; potier *m* d'étain; **tinsmith's shop, works,** étamerie *f*, ferblanterie *f*.

tinsmithing ['tinsmiθiŋ], *s.* étamerie *f*, ferblanterie *f*.

tinstone ['tinstoun], *s. Miner:* cassitérite *f*, étain oxydé; mine *f* d'étain.

tint[1] [tint], *s.* **1.** teinte *f*, nuance *f*; **several tints of blue,** plusieurs nuances de bleu; **red with a blue t.,** teinte rouge bleuâtre; **warm tints,** tons chauds; *Art: etc:* **flat t.,** teinte plate; **t. drawing,** (i) (épure *f* au) lavis; (ii) camaïeu, -eux, *m*; **half t.,** demi-teinte *f*, *pl.* demi-teintes. **2.** *Engr:* *(in line engraving)* grisé *m*; **ruled t.,** grisé en hachures; **t. block,** cliché *m* du grisé. **3.** *Hairdr:* colorant *m*.

tint[2], *v.tr.* **1.** teinter, colorer; **tinted drawing,** (i) camaïeu, -eux, *m*; (ii) (épure *f* au) lavis; **tinted glasses,** verres teintés; **tinted (car) windows,** vitres teintées; *Hairdr:* **to have one's hair tinted,** se faire faire une coloration. **2.** *Engr:* ombrer, hachurer (une gravure). **3.** *Typ:* graisser par mouillage insuffisant.

tintack ['tintæk], *s.* broquette *f*; clou *m* de tapisserie; **tintacks,** semence *f*.

tinter ['tintər], *s.* colorieur *m* (de photographies, etc.).

tintinnabulate [tinti'næbjuleit], *v.i.* tintinnabuler.

tintinnabulation [tintinæbju'leiʃ(ə)n], *s.* tintinnabulement *m*.

tintinnabulum, *pl.* **-la** [tinti'næbjuləm, -lə], *s.* clochette *f*.

Tintoretto [tintə'retou], *Pr.n.m. Hist. of Art:* le Tintoret.

tintype ['tintaip], *s. Phot: A:* photographie *f* sur ferrotype.

tinware ['tinwɛər], *s.* articles *mpl* en fer-blanc; ferblanterie *f*.

tinwork ['tinwə:k], *s.* **1.** ferblanterie *f*. **2.** *pl.* *(usu. with sg. const.)* **tinworks,** ferblanterie.

tiny ['taini], *a.* minuscule; **a t. little house,** une toute petite maison; **a t. bit,** un tout petit peu; un tantinet; **t. figure,** forme menue.

tip[1] [tip], *s.* **1.** bout *m*, extrémité *f*, pointe *f*; sommité *f* (d'une plante, d'une branche); dard *m* (de flamme); *Sm.a:* sommet *m* (du guidon); **tips of a bow, of a crescent,** cornes *f* d'un arc, d'un croissant; **on the tips of the toes,** sur la pointe des pieds; **to have sth. on the t. of one's tongue,** avoir qch. sur le bout, le bord, de la langue; **from t. to toe,** de la tête aux pieds; **bird that measures four feet from t. to t. of its wings,** oiseau qui a une envergure de quatre pieds; *El:* **platinum t.,** grain *m* de platine; *Tls:* **drill t.,** pointe de mèche; *Cu:* **asparagus tips,** pointes d'asperge. **2.** *(a)* bout ferré, embout *m* (d'une canne, etc.); *Veh:* mouflette *f* (de brancard); *(b)* *Bill:* procédé *m* (de la queue); *(c)* *Fish:* (i) pointe *f* (de scion), (ii) scion *m* (de canne à pêche). **3.** palette *f* à dorer, de doreur. **4.** *Hatm:* calotte *f* (de chapeau melon).

tip[2], *v.tr.* **(tipped) 1.** mettre un bout à (un soulier); embouter, mettre un embout à (une canne, etc.); **to t. a stick with iron,** ferrer un bâton; **arrow tipped with poison,** flèche à bout empoisonné; **the sun tipped the hills with gold,** le soleil dorait les crêtes des montagnes. **2.** couper le bout à (qch.). **3.** *Bookb:* **to t. in plates,** coller les hors-texte.

tip[3], *s.* **1.** pente *f*, inclinaison *f*; **to give a cask a t.,** faire pencher un tonneau. **2.** coup léger; tape *f*; *Cr:* **t. and run,** jeu *m* de cricket où le batteur doit essayer de faire une course s'il a touché la balle; *Mil:* **t.-and-run raid,** raid *m* de surprise avec fuite précipitée. **3.** *(a)* pourboire *m*, gratification *f*; **tips included,** service compris; *(b)* don *m* d'argent de poche (à un neveu, etc.). **4.** *Turf: St. Exch: etc:* tuyau *m*; **if you take my t. you will have nothing to do with him,** si vous m'en croyez vous n'aurez aucun rapport avec lui; **to give s.o. a t.,** tuyauter, renseigner, qn; *Turf:* **straight t.,** tuyau increvable. **5.** *Civ.E: etc:* *(a)* (i) basculeur *m*, culbuteur *m*, verseur *m* (de wagons); (ii) élévateur *m* à bascule; *(b)* chantier *m* de versage; *Min:* terri(l) *m*; **rubbish t.,** dépotoir *m*; *(c)* tas *m*, monceau *m* (de déblais, d'ordures, etc.); *Metall:* crassier *m*; *(d)* **t. car, t. truck, t. wag(g)on,** wagon, wagonnet, basculant, à bascule, à renversement; **t. cart,** tombereau *m* (à bascule).

tip[4], *v.tr. & i.* **(tipped)**

I. *v.tr.* **1.** *(a)* **to t. (sth.) (over),** renverser (qch.); chavirer, verser (un canot, etc.); *(b)* **to t. (up),** soulever (un strapontin); faire basculer (une charrette); *Min:* verser (un wagon); **to t. (up) a barrel,** mettre un tonneau à cul; *(c)* **to t. (out),** déverser, décharger (le contenu d'une charrette, etc.); **t. the mixture into a watering can,** versez le mélange dans un arrosoir; **to t. s.o. into a ditch,** (ren)verser qn dans un fossé; **to t. rubbish,** verser, déposer, des immondices; *P:* **to t. a load of rubbish,** débiter des foutaises; *(d)* faire pencher, faire incliner; **to t. one's hat over one's eyes,** abaisser son chapeau sur ses yeux; *P: O:* **to t. one's lid, to t. one's hat, to s.o.,** tirer son chapeau à qn. **2.** *(a)* toucher légèrement, effleurer (qch.); *(b)* *P:* donner, passer, lancer (qch. à qn); *A:* **t. us your flipper,** donne ta pince que je la serre; *O:* **t. us a yarn,** raconte-nous quelque chose; *(c)* donner un pourboire, une gratification, à (qn); donner la pièce à (un domestique, etc.); **to t. the doorkeeper,** *F:* graisser le marteau; **to t. s.o. ten pence,** donner dix pence de pourboire à qn; **to t. a schoolboy,** donner de l'argent de poche à un collégien; **my uncle tipped me a pound,** mon oncle m'a donné une livre. **3.** *Turf: St. Exch: etc:* tuyauter (qn); donner un tuyau, des tuyaux, à (qn); **to t. a certain horse to win,** pronostiquer qu'un certain cheval sera le gagnant; *F:* **he's widely tipped for the job,** on lui donne toutes les chances pour le poste; **to t. s.o. (off),** (i) donner un tuyau à qn; (ii) avertir qn.

II. *v.i.* **1. to t. (over),** se renverser, basculer; *(of boat, etc.)* chavirer, verser. **2. to t. (up),** *(of plank, etc.)* se soulever; basculer. **3.** *Sp:* *(basketball)* **to t. off,** mettre le ballon en jeu (au commencement de la partie).

tipcat ['tipkæt], *s. Games:* bâtonnet *m*.

tip-off ['tipɔf], *s.* avertissement *m*, indication *f*, tuyau *m*; **to give s.o. a t.-o.,** tuyauter, renseigner, qn; mettre qn sur la piste.

tipped [tipt], *a.* **gold-t., silver-t.,** à bout doré, d'argent; **(filter-)t. cigarettes,** cigarettes à bout filtre.

tipper[1] ['tipər], *s.* **1. (waggon) t.,** (i) basculeur *m*, culbuteur *m*; verseur *m*; (ii) élévateur *m* à bascule. **2.** wagon, wagonnet, basculant, à bascule; camion-benne *m*, *pl.* camions-bennes. **3. to be a good t.,** donner des pourboires généreux.

tipper[2], *s.* ouvrier, -ière, qui met le(s) bout(s) à qch.; ferreur *m* (de cannes).

tippet ['tipit], *s.* **1.** *(a)* pèlerine *f*, palatine *f*; *(b)* pèlerine de fourrure (des juges). **2.** collet *m* de fourrure. **3.** *A:* **(hempen) t.,** cravate *f* de chanvre.

tipping[1] ['tipiŋ], *a.* basculant, culbutant, à bascule; **t. movement,** mouvement *m* basculaire, de bascule; **t. platform,** plate-forme *f*, *pl.* plates-formes, à bascule; **t. seat,** siège basculant, à bascule; strapontin *m*; **t. waggon,** wagon, wagonnet, basculant, à bascule.

tipping[2], *s.* **1.** *(a)* inclinaison *f*; *Nau:* cabanement *m* (d'un navire); *(b)* **t. (over),** renversement *m* (de qch.); chavirement *m* (d'un canot); *(c)* basculage *m*; **t. mechanism,** appareil *m* de basculage, à bascule, à renversement; **t. apparatus,** culbuteur *m* (pour wagons, etc.); *(d)* **t. (out),** versage *m*, déversement *m* (du contenu d'un wagon, etc.); *P.N:* **no t.,** décharge interdite; *(e)* *pl.* **tippings,** déblai *m* (d'une mine, etc.). **2.** (système *m* des) pourboires *m*; distribution *f* de pourboires. **3.** *Turf: etc:* tuyautage *m*.

tipple[1] ['tipl], *s. F:* boisson *f* alcoolique; **what's your t.?** qu'est-ce que vous allez prendre?

tipple[2], *v.i. F:* se livrer à la boisson; *P:* picoler, pinter.

tipple[3], *s. NAm: Min:* *(coal)* **1.** *(a)* basculeur *m* de wagons; *(b)* estrade *f*. **2.** installation *f* de criblage. **3.** chantier *m* de versage.

tippler ['tiplər], *s. F:* ivrogne *m*, buveur, -euse; *P:* poivrot, -ote, ivrognesse *f.*

tippling[1] ['tipliŋ], *a. F:* qui boit; buveur.

tippling[2], *s.* ivrognerie *f.*

tipsily ['tipsili], *adv.* d'une voix, avec une démarche, qui accuse l'ivresse.

tipsiness ['tipsinis], *s.* ivresse *f.*

tipstaff, *pl.* **-staffs, -staves** ['tipstɑːf, -stɑːfs, -steivz], *s. Jur:* huissier *m*; *A:* sergent *m* à verge.

tipster ['tipstər], *s. Turf: etc:* tuyauteur *m*; donneur *m* de tuyaux.

tipsy ['tipsi], *a.* **1.** (*a*) gris, ivre; *F:* pompette; **he's t.,** il a bu; *F:* il a son compte, son pompon; **slightly t.,** un peu éméché; **to get t.,** se griser, s'enivrer; (*b*) (titubation, rire, etc.) d'ivrogne; (*c*) *Cu:* **t. cake** = diplomate *m.* **2.** peu stable, peu solide; (*of table, etc.*) branlant. **3.** *Clockm:* **t. key,** clef *f* bréguet.

tip-tilted [tip'tiltid], *a.* à bout relevé; (nez) retroussé.

tiptoe[1] ['tiptou], *s. & adv.* **(on) t., on tiptoes,** sur la pointe des pieds; *Fig:* **to be on tiptoes with expectation,** être dans l'angoisse de l'attente; attendre fiévreusement (qch.); griller, bouillir, d'impatience.

tiptoe[2], *v.i.* (i) marcher, (ii) se dresser, sur la pointe des pieds; **to t. into, out of, the room,** entrer, sortir, sur la pointe des pieds.

tiptop ['tiptɔp]. *F: O:* **1.** *s.* sommet *m*, faîte *m*; le plus haut point. **2.** *a.* de premier ordre, de première force; excellent, extra; *P:* aux petits oignons; pépère; **t. dinner,** chic dîner; **t. hotel,** hôtel de premier ordre; **that's t.!** chouette! ça c'est tapé! c'est un (vrai) beurre! à la bonne heure! **he's a t. dancer,** il danse à la perfection; **I feel t.,** je me sens à merveille.

tipula, *pl* **-ae** ['tipjulə, -iː], *s. Ent:* tipule *f.*

Tipulidae [ti'pjuːlidiː], *s.pl. Ent:* tipulides *m.*

tip-up ['tipʌp], *a.* (charrette, cuvette, etc.) à bascule, à renversement, à rabattement; **t.-up seat,** strapontin *m.*

tirade[1] [tai'reid], *s.* **1.** tirade *f*; diatribe *f* **(against,** contre); **t. of invective,** tirade, bordée *f*, d'injures; **to break into a violent t. against s.o.,** prononcer une diatribe contre qn. **2.** *Mus:* tirade.

tirade[2], *v.i.* **to t. against s.o.,** débiter des tirades contre qn.

tire[1] ['taiər]. **1.** *v.tr.* fatiguer, lasser; **to t. oneself doing sth.,** se fatiguer, se lasser, à faire qch.; **to t. s.o. out, to death,** (i) épuiser, briser, rompre, qn de fatigue; (ii) excéder, assommer, qn; rompre le cerveau à qn; épuiser, lasser, la patience de qn. **2.** *v.i.* se fatiguer, se lasser; **I t. quickly coming up the hill,** je me fatigue vite à monter la côte; **to t. of s.o., sth., s.o.'s company,** se lasser, se fatiguer, de qn, de qch., de la compagnie de qn; **he never tires of telling me,** il ne se lasse, ne se fatigue, pas de me le dire.

tire[2], *s. A:* (*a*) atours *mpl*; (*b*) coiffure *f.*

tire[3], *v.tr. A:* parer (qn).

tire[4], *s.* **1.** *Veh:* bandage *m*, cercle *m*, de fer (d'une roue de charrette, etc.). **2.** *NAm: Aut: Cy:* = TYRE[1].

tire[5], *v.tr.* **1.** *Veh:* cercler (une roue de charrette, etc.) de fer. **2.** *NAm: Aut: Cy:* = TYRE[2].

tired ['taiəd], *a.* fatigué; (*a*) las, *f.* lasse; **to get t.,** devenir las; se fatiguer; **I'm too t. to stand,** je ne peux plus me tenir sur mes jambes; *F:* les jambes me rentrent dans le corps; **to be t. with standing,** être fatigué d'être resté debout; **t. out, t. to death,** épuisé; accablé, brisé, rompu, de fatigue; exténué, éreinté, fourbu; las à mourir; **she was t. out,** elle n'en pouvait plus de fatigue; elle n'avait plus de jambes; *F:* **to be born t.,** être né paresseux; **when you're t., go to bed,** quand vous serez fatigué, aurez sommeil, allez vous coucher; *F:* **you make me t.,** tu m'ennuies, m'embêtes; **to look t.,** avoir les traits tirés; **t. face,** visage fatigué, fané, fripé; *F:* **t. carpet,** tapis usé, défraîchi; (*b*) **to be t. of sth.,** être las de qch.; **t. of standing,** fatigué, las, de rester debout; **to grow, get, t. of doing sth.,** se lasser, s'impatienter, se fatiguer, s'ennuyer, de faire qch.; *F:* **I'm t. of you,** j'en ai assez de vous; **t. of arguing, he consented,** de guerre lasse, il a donné son consentement.

tiredness ['taiədnis], *s.* lassitude *f*, fatigue *f.*

tireless[1] ['taiəlis], *a.* inlassable, infatigable.

tireless[2], *a.* **1.** *Veh:* sans bandage(s). **2.** *NAm: Aut: Cy:* sans pneu(s).

tirelessly ['taiəlisli], *adv.* infatigablement, inlassablement.

tirelessness ['taiəlisnis], *s.* infatigabilité *f.*

tiresome ['taiəsəm], *a.* **1.** fatigant, lassant; (discours) fastidieux, ennuyeux, rebutant. **2.** exaspérant; (*of child*) fatigant, assommant; **how t.!** quel ennui! quel contretemps! c'est assommant! **how t. you are!** que vous êtes contrariant!

tiresomely ['taiəsəmli], *adv.* d'une façon ennuyeuse.

tirewoman, *pl.* **-women** ['taiəwumən, -wimin], *s.f. A:* femme de chambre, camériste.

tiring[1] ['taiəriŋ], *a.* **1.** lassant, fatigant; *Games;* **t. irons,** baguenaudier *m.* **2.** ennuyeux.

tiring[2], *s. A:* habillement *m*, toilette *f*; *NAm: Th:* **t. room,** loge *f* (d'acteur, d'actrice); **t. house,** loges des artistes.

Tiro[1] ['tairou], *Pr.n.m. Rom.Hist:* Tiron.

tiro[2], *pl.* **-o(e)s** ['tairou, -ouz], *s.* novice *mf*; commençant, -ante; néophyte *m*; apprenti, -ie; débutant, -ante; **t. in war,** novice à la guerre.

Tironian [tai'rouniən], *a. Rom.Hist:* de Tiron; **T. notes,** notes tironiennes.

tirralirra ['tirə'lirə], *s.* tire-lire *m* (de l'alouette, etc.).

Tiryns ['t(a)irinz], *Pr.n. A.Geog:* Tirynthe *m.*

'tis [tiz] = **it is.**

tissual ['tisjuəl], *a. Biol: Med:* tissulaire.

tissue ['tisjuː], *s.* **1.** tissu *m* (de soie, coton, etc.); étoffe *f*; *Fig:* **t. of lies, nonsense,** tissu de mensonges, d'absurdités. **2.** (*a*) *Biol:* tissu (nerveux, musculaire, etc.); **living t.,** tissu vivant; **t. system,** système *m* tissulaire; **t. culture,** culture *f* de tissus; *Med:* **granulation, cicatricial, t.,** bourgeon conjonctif; (*b*) *Arb:* **formative t.,** cambium *m.* **3.** (*a*) **t. (paper),** papier *m* de soie, papier mousseline; (*b*) **toilet t.,** papier hygiénique, papier toilette; **cleansing, face, t.,** (i) papier à démaquiller, papier démaquillant; (ii) serviette *f* à démaquiller; (*c*) (i) papier pelure (pour copies de lettres); (ii) *NAm: F:* copie *f* sur papier pelure; (*d*) *Bookb:* serpente *f* (pour protéger les gravures); (*e*) *Phot:* **carbon, autotype, t.,** papier (au) charbon.

tissued ['tisjuːd], *a.* tissé, tissu.

tit[1] [tit], *s.* **1.** *Orn:* mésange *f*; **azure t.,** mésange azurée; **bearded t.,** mésange à moustaches; **blue t.,** mésange bleue; **coal t.,** mésange noire; **crested t.,** mésange huppée; **great t.,** (mésange) charbonnière *f*; **long-tailed t.,** mésange à longue queue; **marsh t.,** nonnette (cendrée); **penduline t.,** mésange rémiz, (rémiz *m*) penduline (*f*); **Siberian t.,** mésange laponne, *Fr.C:* mésange à plastron; **sombre t.,** mésange lugubre; **sultan t.,** mésange sultane; *NAm:* **tufted t.,** mésange huppée; **willow t.,** mésange boréale; **wren t.,** fausse mésange de Californie. **2.** *A:* (*a*) cheval *m*, -aux, de petite taille; (*b*) bidet *m.* **3.** *P:* idiot, -ote, imbécile *mf,* crétin *m.*

tit[2], *s.* **t. for tat,** un prêté pour un rendu; donnant donnant; **to give s.o. t. for tat,** (i) rendre à qn la pareille, appliquer à qn la loi du talion; (ii) (*verbally*) riposter du tic au tac; renvoyer la balle à qn.

tit[3], *s. P:* **1.** (*a*) bout *m* de sein, tétin *m*; (*b*) sein *m*, néné *m.* **2.** bouton *m* (de démarreur, etc.).

Titan ['tait(ə)n]. **1.** *Pr.n.m. Myth: Astr:* Titan; **T. strength,** force *f* de titan. **2.** *s.m.* titan.

titanate ['taitəneit], *s. Ch:* titanate *m.*

Titanesque [taitə'nesk], *a.* titanesque; colossal, -aux; *O:* titanique.

Titaness ['taitənes], *s.f.* titan *m* femelle.

titanic[1] [tai'tænik], *a.* titanesque, de titan; géant, colossal; *O:* titanique.

titanic[2], *a. Ch:* titanique; *Miner:* **t. iron ore,** fer titané.

titaniferous [taitə'nifərəs], *a. Miner:* titanifère.

titanite ['taitənait], *s. Miner:* titanite *f*, titane *m* silicocalcaire.

titanium [tai'teiniəm], *s. Ch:* titane *m.*

Titanotheridae [taitənou'θeridiː], *s.pl. Paleont:* titanothéridés *m.*

titanous ['taitənəs], *a. Ch:* titaneux.

titanyl ['taitənil], *s. Ch:* titanyle *m.*

titbit ['titbit], *s.* **1.** morceau friand; friandise *f*; *F:* bonne bouche. **2.** passage piquant (d'un discours, etc.).

titch [titʃ], *s. F:* **a (little) t.,** *P:* un atome.

titchy ['titʃi], *a. F:* minuscule.

titfer ['titfər], *s. P:* chapeau *m*, galurin *m*, bitos *m*, bibi *m.*

tithable ['taiðəbl], *a.* dîmable, sujet à la dîme; décimable.

tithe[1] [taið], *s.* **1.** dîme *f*; *Hist:* **predial t.,** dîme réelle; **personal t.,** dîme personnelle; **to levy a t. on corn,** lever une dîme sur, dîmer (sur), le blé; *Fig:* **the plague took its t. of the people,** la peste décima le peuple; **t. barn,** grange *f* de la dîme, aux dîmes; **t. collector,** *A:* **proctor,** percepteur *m* de la dîme, dîmier *m*; **t. owner,** décimateur *m.* **2.** dixième *m*; **I don't believe a t. of what he says,** je ne crois pas le dixième, le quart, de ce qu'il dit.

tithe[2], *v.tr.* **1.** payer la dîme de, sur, (ses récoltes, etc.). **2.** (*a*) dîmer (sur) (le blé, etc.), soumettre (le blé, etc.) à la dîme; (*b*) faire payer la dîme à (qn), soumettre (qn) à la dîme.

tithing ['taiðiŋ], *s.* **1.** (*a*) paiement *m* de la dîme; (*b*) prélèvement *m* de la dîme. **2.** *Adm:* ancienne division administrative d'un comté; un dixième d'un *hundred.*

Tithonus [tai'θounəs], *Pr.n.m. Myth:* Tithon.

titi ['tiːtiː], *s. Z:* **t. (monkey),** (singe *m*) titi *m.*

Titian ['tiʃiən], *Pr.n.m. Hist. of Art:* le Titien.

Titianesque [tiʃiə'nesk], *a. Art:* titianesque.

titillate ['titileit], *v.tr.* titiller, chatouiller (le palais); émoustiller (les sens).

titillating ['titileitiŋ], *a.* titillant, chatouillant; émoustillant.

titillation [titi'leiʃ(ə)n], *s.* (*a*) titillation *f*, chatouillement *m* (de la plante du pied, etc.); (*b*) chatouillement *m*, émoustillement *m* (du palais, des sens, etc.).

titivate ['titiveit]. **1.** *v.tr.* faire (qn) beau; attifer, pomponner, bichonner (qn). **2.** *v.i.* se faire beau; s'apprêter, se pomponner, se bichonner.

titlark ['titlɑːk], *s. Orn:* pipit *m* (des prés).

title[1] ['taitl], *s.* titre *m.* **1.** (*a*) (*official*) **to have a t.,** avoir un titre, une qualification; **to give s.o. a t.,** donner un titre à, titrer, qn; **to have a t.,** avoir un titre, une qualification; **to deprive s.o. of his t.,** déqualifier qn; **to address s.o. by his correct t.,** qualifier qn de son titre, son grade; (*b*) **t. of honour, nobility,** titre d'honneur, de noblesse; **to have a t.,** avoir un titre de noblesse, être titré; **to have, bear, the t. of duke,** porter le titre de duc; **persons of t.,** les nobles *m*, la noblesse; (*c*) *Sp:* **to hold the t.,** (dé)tenir le titre (de champion); **t. holder,** tenant, -ante, du titre; *Box:* **t. fight, non t. fight,** combat *m* comptant, ne comptant pas, pour le titre; (*d*) *R.C.Ch:* **titles of the cardinals,** titres (= églises paroissiales) des cardinaux. **2.** (*a*) titre (d'un livre, d'un chapitre); intitulé *m* (d'un journal, acte); *Jur:* **full, short, t.,** intitulé complet, abrégé (d'un acte); *Cin:* **to insert the titles,** titrer le film; **insertion of the titles,** titrage; **the titles,** le titrage; *Publ:* **t. piece,** conte *m*, morceau *m*, qui donne le titre au recueil; *Th:* **t. rôle,** rôle *m* qui donne le titre à la pièce; **we went to see** *Hamlet* **with Olivier in the t. rôle,** nous sommes allés voir *Hamlet* joué par Olivier; *Typ:* **t. page,** (page *f* de) titre; (*with embellishments*) frontispice *m*; (*b*) **to publish fifty titles a year,** publier cinquante livres, ouvrages, par an. **3.** (*a*) **t. to property,** titre de propriété; **clear t.,** titre incontestable, incontesté; **to have a t. to sth.,** avoir un droit, des titres, à qch.; **by onerous t.,** à titre onéreux; **t. holder,** possesseur *m* du titre; *Fig:* **titles to fame,** titres de gloire; (*b*) **t. (deed),** titre (constitutif) de propriété; acte *m.* **4.** titre (de l'or): **to lower the t. of the coinage,** détitrer la monnaie.

title[2], *v.tr.* (*a*) intituler (un livre, etc.); (*b*) *A.Cin:* titrer, mettre les titres à (un film).

titled ['taitld], *a.* (*of pers.*) titré; **to be t.,** avoir un titre (de noblesse).

titler ['taitlər], *s. Cin:* **1.** *A:* (*pers.*) titulateur *m.* **2.** machine *f* à titrer; titreuse *f.*

titling ['taitliŋ], *s. Bookb:* impression *f* du titre (sur la reliure).

titmouse, *pl.* **-mice** ['titmaus, -mais], *s. Orn:* (*usu. called* **tit,** *q.v.*) mésange *f.*

Titoism ['tiːtouizm], *s. Pol:* titisme *m.*

Titoist ['tiːtouist], *s. Pol:* titiste *mf.*

titrant ['taitrənt], *s. Ch:* titré *m* (pour volumétrie).

titrate ['taitreit], *v.tr. Ch: Ind:* titrer, doser (une solution, etc.).

titrated ['taitreitid], *a.* (*of solution*) titré.

titration [tai'treiʃ(ə)n], *s. Ch: Ind:* (*a*) (*also* **titrating** [tai'treitiŋ]), titration *f*, titrage *m*, dosage *m*; (*b*) titrimétrie *f*, analyse *f* volumétrique.

titre ['taitər], *s. Ch: etc.* titre *m* (d'une solution, de l'or).

titrimeter [tai'trimitər], *s. Ch: etc:* titrimètre *m.*

titrimetry [tai'trimitri], *s. Ch: etc:* titrimétrie *f*, volumétrie *f.*

titter[1] ['titər], *s.* **1.** rire étouffé. **2.** petit rire nerveux; rire bébête.

titter[2], *v.i.* **1.** avoir un petit rire étouffé. **2.** rire nerveusement, bêtement.

tittering ['titəriŋ], *s.* petits rires.

tittivate ['titiveit], *v.tr. & i.* = TITIVATE.

tittle ['titl], *s.* **1.** *A:* point *m*; petit trait (de plume). **2.** la moindre partie; **not one t.,** pas un iota.

tittle-tattle[1] ['titltætl], *s.* commérages *mpl*; bavardage *m*, caquets *mpl* (de commères, etc.); **ill-natured t.-t.,** ragots *mpl*, cancans *mpl*, potins *mpl.*

tittle-tattle[2], *v.i.* bavarder; (*ill-naturedly*) potiner, cancaner.

tittle-tattler ['titltætlər], *s.* bavard, -arde, commère *f*; (*ill-natured*) potinier, -ière; cancanier, -ière.

tittup[1] ['titəp], *s.* **1.** (*of horse*) petit galop. **2.** (*of pers.*) air affecté, minauderie *f.*

tittup[2], *v.i.* **1.** (*of horse*) aller au petit galop. **2.** (*of pers.*) marcher à petits pas, d'un air affecté.

titty ['titi], *s. P:* = TIT[3]; **t. bottle,** biberon *m.*

titubation [titju'beiʃ(ə)n], *s. Med:* titubation *f.*

titular ['titjulər]. **1.** *a.* (*a*) (évêque, saint) titulaire; (*b*) (*of function, office, etc.*) nominal; (*c*) **t. possessions,** terres attachées à un titre; (*d*) **t. part in a play,** rôle *m* qui donne le titre à la pièce. **2.** *s.* (*a*) évêque *m*, saint *m*, titulaire; professeur *m*, etc., titulaire, en titre; (*b*) *Jur:* titulaire *mf* (d'un droit, etc.).

titularity [titu'læriti], *s.* titulariat *m.*
titularly ['titjuləli], *adv.* **1.** (que l'on possède) en vertu d'un titre. **2.** nominalement.
Titus ['taitəs], *Pr.n.m.* **1.** *Rom.Hist:* Titus. **2.** *Rel.H:* (saint) Tite.
tityra ['titirə], *s. Orn:* tityre *m.*
tizwas ['tizwɔz], **tizz** [tiz], **tizzy**[1] ['tizi], *s. F:* **to be in a t.,** être affolé, tout en émoi; ne (pas) savoir où donner de la tête.
tizzy[2], *s. P: A:* pièce *f* de six anciens pence.
tjaele ['tʃeili], *s. Geog:* tjaële *m*, tjäle *m.*
tmesis ['tmi:sis], *s. Gram:* tmèse *f.*
to [*stressed* tu; *unstressed before consonant* tə; *unstressed before vowel* tu.]
I. *prep.* à. **1.** (*a*) **to go to church, school,** aller à l'église, l'école; **what school do you go to?** à quelle école allez-vous? **the child ran to its mother,** l'enfant courut à sa mère; **I'm off to Paris,** je pars pour Paris; **he went to France, to Japan, to India,** il est allé en France, au Japon, aux Indes, dans les Indes; **we came to a village,** nous sommes arrivés à, dans, un village; **she returned home to her family,** elle est rentrée auprès de sa famille; **I am going to the grocer's,** je vais chez l'épicier; **to our house,** chez nous; **from town to town, from flower to flower,** de ville en ville, de fleur en fleur; **airlines to, from the Continent,** lignes aériennes à destination au, en provenance du, Continent; (*b*) **the road to London,** la route de Londres; **the road to ruin,** le chemin de la ruine; **journey to Paris,** voyage à Paris; **the way to the station,** le chemin de la gare; **the best, shortest, way to the station,** le meilleur, plus court, chemin pour aller à la gare; **it's twenty miles to London,** il y a vingt milles d'ici Londres; **to wear one's best clothes to church,** mettre ses plus beaux habits pour aller à l'église; **to bed!** (i) je vais me coucher; (ii) allez vous coucher! *A:* **to horse!** à cheval! **2.** (*a*) vers, à; **to the east,** vers l'est; **to hold up one's hands to heaven,** tendre les bras vers le ciel, lever les bras au ciel; *P.N:* **to the boat,** vers le bateau, **to the trains,** accès aux quais; **to the station,** direction de la gare; **to the right, left,** à droite, gauche; (*b*) **feet to the fire,** les pieds au feu; **the rooms to the back,** les chambres de derrière. **3. elbow to elbow,** coude à coude; **to fight man to man,** se battre homme à homme; **to put a revolver to s.o.'s head,** appliquer un revolver à la tête de qn; **I told him so to his face,** je le lui ai dit en face; **to clasp s.o. to one's heart,** serrer qn sur son cœur; **to fall to the ground,** tomber à, par, terre. **4.** (*of time*) (*a*) **from nine o'clock to twelve,** de neuf heures à midi; **from morning to night,** du matin au soir; **from day to day,** de jour en jour; d'un jour à l'autre; (*b*) **ten minutes to six,** six heures moins dix; **it's only 'ten 'to,** il est seulement moins dix; il n'est que moins dix. **5.** (*a*) jusqu'à; **stripped, naked, to the waist,** nu jusqu'à la ceinture; **shaken to the foundations,** ébranlé jusque dans les fondements; **to see s.o. to the end of the street,** accompagner qn jusqu'au bout de la rue; **to this day,** jusqu'à ce jour; **I shall remember it to my dying day,** je m'en souviendrai jusqu'à mon dernier jour; **to count up to ten,** compter jusqu'à dix; **from red to violet,** depuis le rouge jusqu'au violet; **moved to tears,** ému jusqu'aux larmes; **killed to a man,** tués jusqu'au dernier; **to defend one's country to the death,** défendre son pays jusqu'à la mort; (*b*) **to a high degree,** à un haut degré; **generous to a fault,** généreux à l'excès; **to the number of twenty,** au nombre de vingt; **accurate to a millimetre,** exact à un millimètre près; **to guess the weight of sth. to within a kilo,** deviner le poids de qch. à un kilo près; **a year to the day,** un an jour pour jour; (*c*) **to cut sth. down to a minimum,** réduire qch. au minimum; **evaporated to dryness,** évaporé jusqu'à siccité. **6.** (*a*) **to this end,** à cet effet, dans ce but; **with a view to my happiness,** dans le but d'assurer mon bonheur; **to come to s.o.'s aid,** venir à l'aide de qn; **to sit down to dinner,** se mettre à table (pour dîner); **to sentence s.o. to death,** condamner qn à mort; (*b*) **to my delight,** à mon grand désespoir; **to the general surprise,** à la surprise, à l'étonnement, de tous; **to the exclusion of all others,** à l'exclusion de tous les autres. **7.** (*a*) en; **to run to seed,** monter en graine; **to go to ruin,** tomber en ruine; **to put to flight,** mettre en fuite; **to pull to pieces,** mettre en pièces; (*b*) *O:* **to take s.o. to wife,** prendre qn pour femme; **called to witness,** pris à témoin. **8. to sing to the violin,** chanter avec accompagnement de violon, accompagné sur le violon; **what tune is it sung to?** sur quel air cela se chante-t-il? **9. Charles brother to John,** Charles frère de Jean; **heir to s.o., to an estate,** héritier de qn, d'une propriété; **purveyors to H.M. the Queen,** fournisseurs de Sa Majesté la Reine; **ambassador to the King of Sweden,** ambassadeur auprès du roi de Suède; **interpreter to U.N.O.,** interprète (au)près de l'O.N.U.; **secretary to the manager,** secrétaire du directeur; **apprentice to a joiner,** apprenti, en apprentissage, chez un menuisier; **there is no frame to this picture,** il n'y a pas de cadre à ce tableau; **the key to the door,** la clef de la porte. **10.** (*a*) (*effecting a comparison*) **superior to,** supérieur à; **to bear a similarity to sth.,** offrir une ressemblance avec qch.; **compared to this,** comparé à, en comparaison de, celui-ci; **that's nothing to what I have seen,** cela n'est rien auprès de, en comparaison de, à côté de, ce que j'ai vu; **to prefer walking to cycling,** préférer la marche à la bicyclette; (*b*) (*expressing a proportion*) **three is to six as six is to twelve,** trois est à six ce que six est à douze; **six votes to four,** six voix contre quatre; **three goals to nil,** trois buts à zéro; **three parts flour to one part butter,** trois parties de farine pour, contre, une partie de beurre; **one glass of wine to a pint, to each pint, of soup,** un verre de vin par demi-litre de bouillon; **to bet ten to one,** parier dix contre un; **it's a thousand to one (that) it won't happen,** il y a mille à parier contre un que cela n'arrivera pas; **one house to the square mile,** une maison par mille carré. **11. to all appearances,** selon les apparences; **not to my taste,** pas à mon goût; **to write to s.o.'s dictation,** écrire sous la dictée de qn; **to come to s.o.'s call,** venir à l'appel de qn; **to the best of my remembrance,** autant que je m'en souvienne, qu'il m'en souvienne. **12.** (*introducing object of honour, etc.*) **hail to thee!** salut à toi! **hymn to the sun,** hymne au soleil; **to build an altar to s.o.,** ériger un autel à qn; **to drink to s.o.,** boire à la santé de qn; **reply to s.o.,** réponse à qn. **13.** (*a*) (*concerning*) **what did he say to my suggestion?** qu'est-ce qu'il a dit de ma proposition? **to speak to a motion,** intervenir dans la discussion (d'une motion); **is there nothing more to civilization than a moral code?** est-ce que la civilisation consiste dans les lois de la moralité? **that's all there is to it,** c'est tout ce qu'il y a à dire; **is that all there is to it?** c'est tout? **there's nothing to it,** (i) ça ne vaut pas la peine; cela ne rapporte rien; (ii) c'est simple comme bonjour; (*b*) (*on bill*) **to repairing boiler . . .,** réparations à la chaudière . . .; **to taking out jets . . .,** pour avoir démonté les gicleurs . . .; *Com:* **to goods,** pour fourniture de marchandises. **14.** (*used to form the dative*) (*a*) **to give sth. to s.o.,** donner qch. à qn; **who did you give it to?** à qui l'avez-vous donné? **the man I gave it to,** l'homme à qui je l'ai donné; **to speak to s.o.,** parler à qn; **to whom?** à qui? **to whom, to which,** auquel, à laquelle, auxquels, auxquelles; **a courage (which) few men can lay claim to,** un courage auquel peu d'hommes sauraient prétendre; **the sum sent to him,** la somme à lui envoyée; **what's that to you?** qu'est-ce que cela vous fait? **what is life to me?** que m'importe la vie? **to have a compartment to oneself,** avoir un compartiment à soi (tout) seul; **to keep sth. to oneself,** garder qch. pour soi; **I said to myself that it wasn't possible,** je me suis dit (en moi-même) que ce n'était pas possible; (*s.a. all the personal pronouns*) **to allude to sth.,** faire allusion à qch.; *Th:* **to play to packed houses,** jouer devant des salles combles, à bureaux fermés; (*b*) envers, pour; **favourable to s.o.,** favorable à qn; **good to all,** bon pour tous, envers tous; **kind to me,** aimable à mon égard; aimable pour, envers, moi; **to be unjust to s.o.,** être injuste à l'égard de qn; **his duty to his country,** son devoir envers sa patrie; **he has been a father to me,** il a été comme un père pour moi; **his attitude to his work,** son attitude envers son travail; (*c*) **known to the ancients,** connu des anciens; **used to doing sth.,** accoutumé à faire qch.; **those who are born to a fortune,** ceux qui naissent héritiers d'une fortune.
II. (*with the infinitive*) **1.** (*inf. with adv. function*) (*a*) (*purpose, result*) pour; **he came to help me,** il est venu (pour) m'aider; **I gave him 5 francs to carry my bag,** je lui ai donné 5 francs pour qu'il porte ma valise; **we must eat (in order) to live,** il faut manger pour vivre; **they crowded together to give me more room,** ils se serrèrent dans le but de, afin de, me faire plus de place; **the chairs are painted to look the same,** les chaises sont peintes de manière à ce qu'elles aient l'air toutes pareilles; **so to speak,** pour ainsi dire; **born to rule,** né pour régner; **I have not done anything to rouse his anger,** je n'ai rien fait pour provoquer sa colère; **he has done much to provoke criticism,** il a fait bien des choses susceptibles de provoquer des critiques; (*b*) (*extension of adj. or adv.*) (i) de, à, pour; **happy to do it,** heureux de le faire; **ready to listen,** prêt à écouter; **old enough to go to school,** d'âge à aller à l'école; **too proud to fight,** trop fier pour se battre; **you are foolish to believe that,** vous êtes bien sot de croire cela; **you will do well to pay attention,** vous feriez bien de faire attention; **what a queer chap to be a mayor!** quel drôle d'homme pour un maire! (ii) (*inf. with pass. force*) à, pour; **good to eat,** bon à manger; **beautiful to look at,** beau à voir; **too hot to drink,** trop chaud pour qu'on puisse le boire; (*c*) (*parenthetic or absolute const.*) (i) **to look at her one would never imagine that she was a grandmother,** à la voir on ne s'imaginerait pas qu'elle est grand-mère; **to hear him talk you would imagine that he's somebody,** à l'entendre parler on s'imaginerait qu'il est un personnage important; (ii) (*expressing subsequent fact*) **he woke to find the lamp still burning,** en s'éveillant il a trouvé la lampe encore allumée; **he left the house never to return to it again,** il quitta la maison pour n'y plus revenir; **these times are gone never to return,** ces temps sont passés et ne reviendront plus. **2.** (*inf. with adjectival function*) (*a*) **to have a letter to write,** avoir une lettre à écrire; **to have a lot to do,** avoir beaucoup à faire; **knives to grind,** couteaux à repasser; **nothing to speak of,** rien qui vaille la peine qu'on en parle; **there is no one to see us,** il n'y a personne qui puisse nous voir; **there was not a sound to be heard,** on n'entendait pas le moindre bruit; **he is not a man to forget his friends,** il n'est pas homme à oublier ses amis; **he is not a man to be trusted,** ce n'est pas un homme à qui on peut, on puisse, se fier; **the first to complain,** le premier à se plaindre; **the third to arrive,** le troisième à venir; **trousers to fit 40 inch hips,** pantalon tour de hanches 102 cm.; **the conference to be held in Paris,** le congrès qui doit avoir lieu à Paris; (*b*) à, de; **tendency to do sth.,** tendance à faire qch.; **desire to do sth.,** désir de faire qch.; **this is the time to do it,** c'est le moment de le faire. **3.** (*inf. with substantival function*) **to go up was dangerous, to go down was impossible,** monter était périlleux, descendre était impossible; **to be or not to be,** être ou ne pas être; **to lie is shameful, it is shameful to lie,** il est honteux de mentir; **it was best to laugh,** le mieux était de rire; **it is better to do nothing,** il vaut mieux ne rien faire; **to learn to do sth.,** apprendre à faire qch.; **to refuse to do sth.,** refuser de faire qch. **4.** (*inf. in finite clause*) (*a*) **it seemed to grow,** il semblait croître; (*b*) **I wish him to do it,** je veux qu'il le fasse; **you would like it to be true,** vous voudriez bien que cela soit vrai. **5.** (*a*) (*interrogatively*) *A:* **what to do?** que faire! (*b*) (*expressing obligation*) (*in headline*) **a hundred employees to go,** cent employés vont recevoir leur congé. **6.** (*with ellipsis of verb*) **I didn't want to look, I** *had* to ['hætu:], je ne voulais pas regarder mais il le fallut bien, mais je n'ai pas pu m'en défendre; **take it; it would be absurd** *not* to, prenez-le; ce serait absurde de ne pas le faire, de manquer l'occasion; **he often says things one wouldn't expect him to,** il dit souvent des choses auxquelles on ne s'attendrait pas de sa part; **we shall have to,** il le faudra bien; **you ought to,** vous devriez le faire; **I want to,** je voudrais bien; j'ai envie de le faire.
III. *adv.* (*stressed*) **1.** (*a*) *NAm:* en avant; **to put on one's sweater wrong side to,** mettre son pull sens devant derrière; (*b*) **ship moored head to** (= *to the wind*), navire amarré vent debout; **keep her to!** tenez le vent! **to put the horses to** (= *to the carriage*), atteler les chevaux; **to turn to with a will,** se mettre résolument à l'ouvrage; **to come to** (= *to one's senses*), reprendre connaissance. *Note: for other examples see the verbs;* (*c*) **to pull the shutters to,** fermer les volets; **to leave the door to,** laisser la porte tout contre. **2. to go to and fro,** aller et venir; faire la navette; *Mec.E:* **movement to and fro, to-and-fro movement,** mouvement de va-et-vient.
toad [toud], *s.* **1.** (*a*) *Amph:* crapaud *m*; **clawed t.,** crapaud à griffes, (*African*) xenopus *m*; **European variable t., green t.,** crapaud vert; **fire-belly, -bellied, t.,** sonneur *m* (à ventre jaune); **midwife, obstetric, t.,** crapaud accoucheur; **running t.,** crapaud des roseaux; **spade-foot t.,** pélobate *m*, (*European*) pélobate brun; **Surinam t.,** crapaud de Surinam; pipa *m*; *Lit:* **to treat s.o. like a t. under the harrow,** fouler qn aux pieds, rabrouer qn; *A:* **to eat s.o.'s toads,** flagorner qn; **t. eater,** sycophante *m*, patelineur, -euse; lécheur *m* (de bottes); **t.(-)eating,** rampant, servile; *Med:* **t. test,** = test *m* de la lapine; *Ent:* **t. spit,** crachat *m* de coucou, écume printanière; (*b*) *P:* type répugnant, sale type; **he's, she's, a (filthy little) t.,** c'est une rosse. **2.** *Cu:* **t. in the hole,** morceau de viande, de saucisse, cuit au four dans de la pâte à crêpes.
toadfish ['toudfiʃ], *s. Ich:* poisson *m* crapaud; crapaud *m* de mer; baudroie *f.*
toadflax ['toudflæks], *s. Bot:* (*a*) linaire *f*, éperonnière *f*, muflier bâtard, lin *m* sauvage; *F:* velvote *f*; **ivy-leaved t.,** cymbalaire *f*; (*b*) **bastard t.,** thésium *m.*
toadstone ['toudstoun], *s. Miner:* crapaudine *f*; *F:* pierre *f* de crapaud, œil-de-serpent *m, pl.* œils-de-serpent.
toadstool ['toudstu:l], *s. Fung:* *F:* champignon, *esp.* champignon vénéneux.
toady[1] ['toudi], *s.* sycophante *m*, patelineur, -euse;

lécheur *m* (de bottes).

toady[2], *v.i.* **to t. to s.o.,** lécher les bottes à qn, flagorner qn; courber l'échine devant qn; *F:* faire du plat à qn, gratter qn où ça le démange, faire (de) la lèche à qn, *P:* lécher le cul à qn.

toadyism ['toudiizm], *s.* flagornerie *f.*

toast[1] [toust], *s.* **1.** pain grillé, toast *m;* **piece, round, of t.,** rôtie *f,* toast; **buttered t.,** rôtie au beurre, rôtie beurrée; **dry t.,** rôtie sans beurre; **anchovies on t.,** anchois sur canapé; *F:* **to have s.o. on t.,** (i) duper qn, mettre qn dedans; (ii) avoir qn à sa merci; mettre qn au pied du mur; tenir qn; **t. rack,** porte-rôties *m inv,* porte-toasts *m inv;* **t. water,** eau panée. **2.** *(a)* (i) personne à qui, chose à laquelle, on porte un toast; *esp.* (ii) *Hist:* beauté *f* célèbre, beauté à la mode; *(b)* toast; **to give, propose, a t.,** porter un toast; **to give s.o. a t.,** boire à la santé de qn; **to respond to s.o.'s t.,** répondre au toast de qn; **t. list,** liste *f* des toasts (à un banquet); **t. master,** préposé *m* aux toasts, annonceur *m* des toasts.

toast[2]. **1.** *v.tr.* *(a)* rôtir, griller (du pain); *F:* **to t. one's feet (in front of the fire),** se chauffer les pieds; *(b)* **to t. s.o.,** porter un toast à (la santé de) qn; boire à la santé de qn. **2.** *v.i.* rôtir, griller.

toaster ['toustər], *s.* grille-pain *m inv;* toaster *m,* toasteur *m.*

toasting ['toustiŋ], *s.* rôtissage *m,* grillage *m* (du pain); **t. fork,** (i) fourchette *f* à rôties; (ii) *P: O:* sabre *m,* épée *f,* lardoire *f.*

toat [tout], *s. Carp:* poignée *f* (de rabot).

tobacco, *pl.* **-os** [tə'bækou, -ouz], *s.* **1.** *Bot:* **t. (plant),** tabac *m;* **mountain t.,** arnica *f* des montagnes. **2. (smoking) t.,** tabac (à fumer); **leaf t.,** tabac en feuilles; **cut t.,** tabac haché; **fine-cut t.,** tabac haché fin; **coarse-cut t.,** tabac de grosse coupe; **chewing t.,** tabac à chiquer, mâcher; **t.-coloured,** tabac *inv;* **t. jar,** pot *m* à tabac; **t. juice,** (i) jus *m* de tabac; (ii) salive tachée de tabac; **t. shop,** débit *m* de tabac.

tobacconist [tə'bækənist], *s.* débitant, -ante (de tabac); **tobaconnist's (shop),** débit *m* de tabac.

Tobiah [tə'baiə], **Tobias** [tə'baiəs], *Pr.n.m.* Tobie.

Tobit ['toubit], *Pr.n.m. B:* **the Book of T.,** le livre de Tobie.

toboggan[1] [tə'bɔgən], *s.* **1.** toboggan *m; Fr.C:* traîne *f* sauvage; **(Swiss) t.,** luge *f; Sp:* **t. run, shoot, slide,** piste *f* de toboggan. **2.** *NAm:* dégringolade *f* (des cours en Bourse, etc.); **to be on the t.,** dégringoler.

toboggan[2], *v.i.* **1.** faire du toboggan; **to t. down a slope,** descendre une côte en toboggan. **2.** *NAm:* *(of share prices, etc.)* dégringoler.

tobogganer [tə'bɔgənər], *s.* tobogganiste *mf;* lugeur, -euse.

tobogganing [tə'bɔgəniŋ], *s. Sp:* (sport *m* du) toboggan; lugeage *m;* **to go in for t.,** faire du toboggan.

tobogganist [tə'bɔgənist], *s.* = TOBOGGANER.

Tobruk [tə'bruk], *Pr.n. Geog:* Tobrouk.

Toby ['toubi]. **1.** *Pr.n.m.* Tobie. **2.** *s.* **t. (jug),** pot *m* à bière (en forme de gros bonhomme à tricorne); = jacqueline *f.* **3.** chien (vivant) du guignol anglais; **t. collar,** collerette plissée, fraise *f.*

toc [tɔk], *s. Mil. Tg. & Tp: A:* la lettre T; **Toc H** [tɔk'eitʃ], (lettres initiales de Talbot House) association *f* pour l'étude des problèmes religieux et sociaux.

toccata [tə'kɑːtə], *s. Mus:* toccata *f.*

tocology [tə'kɔlədʒi], *s.* tocologie *f.*

tocopherol [tə'kɔferɔl], *s. Bio-Ch:* tocophérol *m,* tocoférol *m.*

tocsin ['tɔksin], *s.* tocsin *m.*

tod[1] [tɔd], *s. Scot:* **1.** renard *m.* **2.** *F:* vieux malin, fin renard.

tod[2], *s.* **1.** touffe *f,* masse *f* (de lierre, etc.). **2** poids *m* de vingt-huit livres (12,7 kg.) (de laine).

tod[3], *s. P:* **on my t., on his t.,** tout seul.

today [tə'dei], *adv. & s.* aujourd'hui *(m);* *(a)* **a week ago t.,** il y a aujourd'hui huit jours; **t. week,** (d')aujourd'hui en huit; **t. is the fifth, is Sunday,** c'est aujourd'hui le cinq, dimanche; **what is t.?** c'est quel jour aujourd'hui? **today's paper,** le journal d'aujourd'hui, du jour; **t. has been fine,** il a fait beau aujourd'hui; *F:* **he's here t. and gone tomorrow,** il est comme l'oiseau sur la branche; *Com:* **today's date, price,** la date, le prix, du jour; *(b)* **the young people of t.,** les jeunes gens d'aujourd'hui, de nos jours; **you can't find it t.,** on n'en trouve plus.

toddle[1] ['tɔdl], *s.* **1.** allure chancelante; pas chancelants (d'un jeune enfant). **2.** *F: O:* petite promenade; balade *f;* **let's go for a t.,** si on faisait un petit tour?

toddle[2], *v.i.* **1.** *(of young child)* marcher à petits pas chancelants. **2.** *F: O:* *(of adult)* marcher à petits pas; trottiner; **to t. along,** aller, faire, son petit bonhomme de chemin; **to t. round to the pub,** faire un saut jusqu'au café; **to t. off, away,** s'en aller; **I must be toddling,** il faut que je file.

toddler ['tɔdlər], *s.* enfant qui commence à marcher, à trottiner; **the toddlers,** les tout petits.

toddling ['tɔdliŋ], *a.* (enfant) trottinant, qui commence à marcher.

toddy ['tɔdi], *s.* **1.** toddy *m* (de palme). **2.** grog chaud; **a glass of t.,** un grog.

Todidae ['toudidiː], *s.pl. Orn:* todidés *m.*

to-do [tə'duː], *s. F:* bruit *m,* remue-ménage *m;* **to make a to-do,** (i) faire du tam-tam; (ii) faire des histoires, des chichis; **what a to-do!** quelle affaire! **there was a great to-do about it,** l'affaire a fait grand bruit.

todus ['toudəs], *s. Orn:* todier *m.*

tody ['toudi], *s. Orn:* todier *m;* **king t.,** roi *m* des gobe-mouches, moucherolle royale.

toe[1] [tou], *s.* **1.** orteil *m;* doigt *m* de pied; **great, big, t.,** gros orteil; **little t.,** petit orteil; *(of two pers.)* **to stand t. to t.,** se tenir face à face; **to come down on (the points of) one's toes,** retomber sur la pointe des pieds; **to turn one's toes in, out,** tourner les pieds en dedans, en dehors; *P:* **to turn up one's toes,** mourir; casser sa pipe; **to stand on the tips of one's toes,** se dresser sur la pointe des pieds; **stroke that brings the spectators up on their toes,** coup qui met l'assistance dans une attente fiévreuse; *Fig:* **to be on one's toes,** être alerte; *Danc:* **to dance on one's toes,** faire des pointes; *Aut: Av: etc:* **t. board,** plancher *m* oblique; **t. room,** dégagement *m; Geog:* **the t. of Italy,** le bout de la botte. **2.** *(a)* bout, pointe (de soulier, etc.); **to wear one's shoes out at the toes,** user ses chaussures du bout; **t. cap,** bout rapporté; pièce *f* de renfort; *(b) Farr:* (i) pince *f* (de sabot, de fer à cheval); **horse up on its toes,** cheval juché; *Vet:* **t. crack,** soie *f* (dans le sabot); (ii) griffe *f* (de fer à cheval); *(c) Golf:* pointe (de la crosse); *Sm.a:* bec *m* (de crosse de fusil); *(d) Mec.E:* pivot *m,* queue *f* (d'arbre vertical). **3.** *(a) Mec.E:* patin *m* (de serre-joint); *(b) Mec:* touche *f* (de distribution Corliss); *Mec.E:* ergot (actionné par une came, etc.); *(c) Metalw:* talon *m* de soudure. **4.** *Const:* empattement *m* (de mur); éperon *m,* saillie *f* (d'un arc-boutant); *Hyd.E:* **(downstream) t.,** base *f.*

toe[2], *v.tr.* **1. to t. a sock,** (i) tricoter, (ii) refaire, la pointe d'une chaussette; **to t. a shoe,** mettre, remettre, un bout à un soulier. **2. to t. the line, the mark,** s'aligner; *(at bowls)* piéter; *Fig:* **to t. the (party) line, the mark,** (i) s'aligner avec son parti; se conformer au mot d'ordre; (ii) obéir; s'exécuter; **to make s.o. t. the line,** faire aligner qn, faire rentrer qn dans les rangs; *Fig:* faire obéir qn. **3.** *F: O:* **to t. and heel it,** danser. **4.** *(a) v.i.* **to t. in, out,** tourner les pieds en dedans, en dehors, en marchant; *(b) Aut:* **to t. in,** (i) faire pincer (les roues avant); (ii) *v.i.* *(of front wheels)* être pincé (vers l'avant). **5.** *(a) Fb:* botter (le ballon) avec la pointe du pied; *(b) F:* flanquer un coup de pied à (qn), botter (qn). **6.** *Golf:* frapper (la balle) avec la pointe de la crosse. **7.** *Carp:* enfoncer (un clou) de biais.

toed [toud], *a.* **1.** *(with adj. or num. prefixed)* **two-t., three-t.,** à deux, trois, orteils; **square-t., pointed-t., shoes,** souliers à bouts carrés, pointus. **2.** (chaussettes) dont les doigts sont marqués. **3.** (soulier) à bout rapporté. **4.** *Carp:* *(a)* (clou) enfoncé de biais; *(b)* *(of rafter, etc.)* fixé par clous de biais.

toehold ['touhould], *s.* **1.** *Mount: etc:* prise *f* de pied. **2.** *Fig:* prise précaire.

toe-in ['touin], *s. Aut:* pincement *m* (des roues avant).

toenail[1] ['touneil], *s.* **1.** ongle *m* d'orteil. **2.** *Carp:* clou enfoncé de biais.

toenail[2], *v.tr. Carp:* fixer (une poutre) avec un clou, des clous, enfoncé(s) de biais.

toepiece ['toupiːs], *s. Bootm:* bout rapporté.

toeplate ['toupleit], *s.* fer *m* de bout de chaussure.

toff [tɔf], *s. F: O:* dandy *m,* aristo *m;* **the toffs,** la haute, le gratin, les rupins *m,* les gens huppés.

toffee, toffy ['tɔfi], *s.* *(a)* caramel *m* au beurre; **almond, walnut, t.,** caramel aux amandes, aux noix; **t. apple,** pomme enrobée de sucre et montée en sucette; *F:* **he can't sing for t.,** il ne sait pas chanter du tout; *F:* **t.-nosed,** pincé, dédaigneux; fiérot; *(b)* (bonbon *m* au) caramel.

toft [tɔft], *s. A: & Jur:* petite ferme; petite exploitation rurale.

toftman, *pl.* **-men** ['tɔftmən], *s.m. A:* exploitant d'une petite ferme; petit fermier.

tog [tɔg], *v.tr. & i.* **(togged)** *F:* **to t. a child up,** habiller un enfant (d'une manière ridicule), attifer un enfant; **to t. (oneself) up,** se faire beau; s'attifer; se mettre sur son trente et un; **to be (all) togged up,** être en grande toilette; être parée de ses plus beaux atours; être sur son tralala, en grand tralala.

toga ['tougə], *s. Rom.Ant:* toge *f.*

together [tə'geðər]. **1.** *adv.* ensemble; *(a)* **to tie two things t.,** lier deux choses ensemble, l'une à l'autre; **to go, belong, t.,** aller ensemble; **we stand or fall t.,** nous sommes tous solidaires; *Nau:* *(of ships)* **to sail t.,** naviguer de conserve; **the headmaster was present t. with his staff,** le proviseur y assistait avec le personnel enseignant; **the crew t. with the passengers were drowned,** l'équipage a été noyé ainsi que les passagers; **we arrived t. with our host,** nous sommes arrivés en même temps que notre hôte; *(b)* **to gather t., collect t.,** (i) réunir, rassembler; (ii) se réunir, se rassembler; **to add t., multiply t.,** additionner, multiplier, ensemble; **to strike two things t.,** frapper deux choses l'une contre l'autre; **to bring t.,** rassembler, réunir; *Bill:* **to bring the balls t.,** rappeler les billes; **lands lying t.,** terres tout d'un tenant; *(c)* **to act t.,** agir de concert; **all t.,** tout le monde ensemble; tous à la fois; *(in singing)* **the chorus all t.,** et tous ensemble pour le refrain; **now all t.!** tous en chœur! *(d)* **for months t.,** pendant des mois entiers, d'affilée, de suite; **to gossip for hours t.,** bavarder des heures durant; bavarder pendant des heures et des heures. **2.** *a. F:* **they are a very t. pair,** c'est un couple étroitement lié.

togetherness [tə'geðənis], *s. F:* **1.** unité *f,* harmonie *f,* ensemble parfait. **2.** solidarité *f.*

toggle[1] ['tɔgl], *s.* **1.** *(a) Nau:* **t. (pin),** cabillot *m,* chevillot *m* (d'amarrage); burin *m;* *(b) Cost:* olive *f* (de duffel-coat); *(c) Harn:* **halter rope t.,** billot *m* de longe de licou. **2.** *(a)* barrette *f* (de chaîne de montre): **small chain and t.,** chaînette *f* à T; *(b) Mec.E:* (i) *(at end of chain)* clef *f;* **brake t.,** clef de frein; (ii) levier articulé, genouillère *f;* **t. chuck,** mandrin *m* à genouillère; *El:* **t. switch,** interrupteur *m,* inverseur *m,* à bascule; basculeur *m;* *Metalw: etc:* **t. press,** presse *f* à genouillère; *Fish:* **t. iron,** harpon *m* à tête mobile.

toggle[2], *v.tr.* **1.** *(a) Nau:* fixer avec un cabillot, cabillotter (un cordage à un autre); *(b)* munir (un drapeau, etc.) d'un cabillot. **2.** *El:* basculer (un interrupteur).

Togo ['tougou], *Pr.n. Geog:* **the Republic of T.,** la République du Togo.

Togoland ['tougoulænd], *Pr.n. Hist:* le Togo.

Togolese [tougou'liːz], *Geog:* **1.** *a.* togolais. **2.** *s.* Togolais, -aise.

togs [tɔgz], *s.pl. F:* nippes *f,* fringues *f,* frusques *f,* hardes *f;* *Nau:* **harbour, long, t.,** frusques d'escale.

toil[1] [tɔil], *s.* travail dur, pénible; labeur *m,* peine *f;* **t. and trouble,** peine et ennuis; **after great t. he achieved his end,** à force de labeur il a gagné son but; **the toils of war,** les fatigues *f* de la guerre; **t.-worn,** usé par le travail; (visage) marqué par la fatigue.

toil[2], *v.i.* travailler, peiner; se donner du mal; **to t. and moil,** peiner, travailler dur; suer sang et eau; s'acharner; trimer; *F:* s'échiner; **to t. at sth., at doing sth.,** travailler ferme à qch.; s'épuiser à faire qch.; **to t. hard to maintain one's family,** travailler dur pour nourrir sa famille; **to t. up a hill,** gravir péniblement une colline; **to t. along the road,** avancer péniblement sur la route; **to t. on,** (i) continuer péniblement son travail; (ii) continuer péniblement sa route.

toile [twɑːl], *s.* *(a)* toile *f;* *(b) Dressm:* patron *m,* modèle *m* (en mousseline); *(c)* **t. de Jouy,** toile de Jouy.

toiler ['tɔilər], *s.* travailleur, -euse.

toilet ['tɔilit], *s.* **1.** *(a)* toilette *f;* **to make one's t.,** faire sa toilette; **t. bag, case,** nécessaire *m,* trousse *f,* de toilette; **t. glass, mirror,** glace *f,* miroir *m,* de toilette; **t. set,** garniture *f* de toilette; **t. soap,** savon *m* de toilette; **t. table,** *A:* **t.,** (table *f* de) toilette; coiffeuse *f;* **t. water,** eau *f* de toilette; *(b) Surg:* détersion *f,* mondification *f* (d'une plaie après l'opération). **2.** *(a)* *(lavatory) P.N:* **toilet(s),** toilettes; **t. paper,** papier *m* hygiénique; **t. paper holder,** porte-papier *m inv* (hygiénique); **t. roll,** rouleau *m* de papier hygiénique; *P:* **to go to the t.,** aller aux cabinets; *(b) U.S:* cabinet *m* de toilette.

toiletry ['tɔilitri], *s.* article *m* de toilette; **toiletries for men,** parfumerie *f* pour hommes.

toiling[1] ['tɔiliŋ], *a.* laborieux.

toiling[2], *s.* = TOIL[1].

toils [tɔilz], *s.pl. Ven:* filet *m,* lacs *m,* bricoles *fpl,* toiles *fpl;* **to be taken, get caught, in the t.,** se laisser prendre dans les lacs, les lacets, au filet; se laisser prendre au piège; se laisser engluer; s'engluer; être pris à la glu; **caught in the t.,** pris dans le(s) lacs; *Lit:* **to catch s.o. in one's t.,** prendre qn dans ses rets; **caught in his own t.,** pris dans ses propres lacets.

toilsome ['tɔilsəm], *a. Lit:* pénible, fatigant, laborieux.

toing ['tuːiŋ], *s.* **t. and froing,** va-et-vient *m.*

toison [twazɔ̃], *s. Her:* toison *f.*

tokay [tou'kei], *s. Rept:* tokeh *m;* **red-spotted t.,** tokeh à taches rouges.

token ['touk(ə)n], *s.* **1.** signe *m,* indication *f,* marque *f,* témoignage *m* (d'identité, de respect, etc.); **freemason's t.,** attouchement *m* maçonnique; **in t., as a t., of sincerity,** en signe, en témoignage, comme marque, de bonne foi; **to give s.o. sth. as a t. of one's esteem,** faire hommage de qch. à qn; **to give (some) t. of intelligence,** annoncer, indiquer, de l'intelligence; **by this, by the same, t.,** (i) donc, d'ailleurs; (ii) et la preuve c'est que; (iii) pareillement; **t. money,** monnaie *f* fiduciaire, circulation *f* fiduciaire; **t. payment,** paiement *m* symbolique (d'intérêts, etc., en reconnaissance d'une dette), paiement nominal; **t. strike,** grève *f* symbolique, d'avertissement; **t. withdrawal,** retrait *m* symbolique (de troupes, etc.). **2.** (*a*) *O:* signe; **to show a glove as a t.,** montrer un gant comme signe, comme preuve; **love t.,** gage *m* d'amour; (*b*) jeton *m* (de présence); *Ecc: A:* **communion t.,** méreau *m*; (*c*) jeton (pour distributeur automatique, etc.); (*d*) *A:* pièce *f* de monnaie fiduciaire; jeton; (*e*) **gift t.,** bon *m* d'achat; **book t.,** chèque-livre *m, pl.* chèques-livres; **flower t.,** chèque-fleurs *m, pl.* chèques-fleurs. **3.** *Typ:* dix mains *f* (de papier).

tokenism ['toukənizm], *s.* politique *f* de coopération symbolique.

tola ['toulə], *s. Bot:* tola *m.*

tolan(e) ['toulən, 'toulein], *s. Ch:* tolane *m.*

tolbooth ['tɔlbu:θ, -bu:ð], *s. Scot: A:* **1.** bureau *m* de péage. **2.** (*a*) hôtel *m* de ville; (*b*) prison *f.*

tol-de-rol ['tɔldirɔl]. (*song refrain*) = la faridondon, la faridondaine.

Toledan [tɔ'leid(ə)n]. *Geog:* **1.** *a.* tolédan. **2.** *s.* Tolédan, -ane.

Toledo [tɔ'leidou]. **1.** *Pr.n. Geog:* Tolède. **2.** [tɔ'li:dou] **T. blade,** *s. A:* **T.,** épée *f* de Tolède; lame *f* de Tolède.

tolerable ['tɔlərəbl]. **1.** *a.* (*a*) (*of pain, etc.*) tolérable, supportable; (*b*) **we were given a t. lunch,** on nous a servi un assez bon déjeuner, le déjeuner n'était pas mauvais; **they enjoy a t. amount of freedom,** ils jouissent d'une assez grande liberté; **we're in t. health,** *A:* **we are t.,** nous sommes en assez bonne santé, nous nous portons assez bien. **2.** *adv. A: & NAm:* assez; passablement.

tolerably ['tɔlərəbli], *adv.* tolérablement; **to draw t. (well),** dessiner passablement, tolérablement; **I'm t. well,** je suis en assez bonne santé, je me porte assez bien.

tolerance ['tɔlərəns], *s.* **1.** (*a*) **t. of a drug,** tolérance *f* d'une drogue; **increasing t. for a drug,** accoutumance *f* à une drogue; *Bot:* **t. of parasites,** tolérance des parasites; (*b*) *A:* **t. of heat, cold,** tolérance de la chaleur, du froid; endurcissement *m* à la chaleur, au froid. **2.** (*a*) tolérance (religieuse, etc.); (*b*) **to show great t.,** faire preuve de beaucoup de tolérance, d'une grande indulgence, de beaucoup de patience. **3.** (*a*) (*minting*) tolérance, faiblage *m*; (*b*) *Mec.E: etc:* tolérance, écart *m* admissible; **t. on fit,** tolérance d'ajustage; **factory t.,** tolérance de fabrication; **operational t.,** tolérance de fonctionnement; (*c*) *Cust:* tolérance (permise).

tolerant ['tɔlərənt], *a.* (*a*) *Med:* **patients t. of light, of a drug,** malades tolérants vis-à-vis des rayons lumineux, d'une drogue; *Bot:* **t. plant,** plante tolérante; (*b*) (*of parent, etc.*) tolérant, indulgent.

tolerantly ['tɔlərəntli], *adv.* avec tolérance.

tolerate ['tɔləreit], *v.tr.* (*a*) *Med:* tolérer (une drogue); **he can't t. iodine,** il ne supporte pas la teinture d'iode; (*b*) tolérer, supporter (la douleur, la contradiction, etc.); **I will not t. this behaviour,** cette conduite est insupportable; *F:* **I can't t. him,** je ne peux pas le souffrir, le sentir.

toleration [tɔlə'reiʃ(ə)n], *s.* **1.** tolérance *f.* **2.** (*minting*) tolérance, faiblage *m.*

tolite ['tɔlait], *s. Exp:* tolite *f.*

toll[1] [toul], *s.* **1.** (*a*) droit *m* de passage; péage *m*; **to pay t.,** payer un droit de passage; **to pay the t.,** acquitter le péage; *Jur:* **t. thorough,** droit de passage, péage, imposé par la ville; **t. traverse,** droit de passage (sur une propriété privée); **t. bar,** barrière *f* (de péage); **t. bridge,** pont *m* à péage, pont payant; **t. collector, keeper,** péager, -ère, (*on bridge*) pontonnier, -ière; **t. house,** (bureau *m* de) péage; **t. road,** route *f* à péage; (*b*) droit de place (au marché). **2.** (*a*) **miller's t.,** droit de mouture; mouture prélevée; (*b*) **rent takes a heavy t. of one's income,** le loyer retranche, mange, une grande partie de nos revenus; **accident that takes a heavy t. of human life,** accident qui occasionne beaucoup de morts; **the t. of the road,** les accidents, les hécatombes *f,* de la route. **3.** *Tp: O:* **t. call,** communication interurbaine entre villes peu éloignées; *NAm:* communication interurbaine.

toll[2], *s.* tintement *m*, son *m* (de cloche); (*for s.o.'s death*) glas *m.*

toll[3]. **1.** *v.tr.* (*a*) tinter, sonner (une cloche); *v.i.* **to t. for the dead,** sonner pour les morts; (*b*) (*of bell, clock*) sonner (l'heure); **to t. s.o.'s death,** sonner le glas pour la mort de qn; (*c*) **to t. the people to church,** appeler les fidèles à l'église (au son de la cloche); sonner l'office. **2.** *v.i.* (*of bell*) tinter, sonner; (*for death*) sonner le glas.

toll[4], *v.tr. Ven: NAm:* attirer (le gibier); *Fish:* amorcer (le poisson).

tollage ['toulidʒ], *s.* péage *m.*

tollbooth ['tɔlbu:θ, -bu:ð], *s.* **1.** *Scot:* = TOLBOOTH. **2.** *U.S:* guérite *f* (du péager).

tolling ['touliŋ], *s.* (*a*) tintement *m* (de cloche); (*b*) tintement funèbre, glas *m*; (*during funeral*) regret *m.*

tollway ['toulwei], *s. NAm:* autoroute *f* à péage.

Toltec ['tɔltek], *s. Ethn:* Toltèque *mf.*

Toltecan ['tɔltekən], *a. Ethn:* toltèque.

Tolu [tɔ'lju:], *Pr.n. Geog:* Tolu; *Pharm: etc:* **balsam of T., t. (balsam),** baume *m* de Tolu; tolu *m.*

toluate ['tɔljueit], *s. Ch:* toluate *m.*

toluene ['tɔljui:n], *s. Ch:* toluène *m.*

toluic [tɔ'lju:ik], *a. Ch:* toluique.

toluidine [tɔ'lju:idi:n], *s. Ch:* toluidine *f.*

toluifera [tɔlju'ifərə], *s. Bot:* toluifera *m.*

toluol ['tɔljuɔl], *s. Ch:* toluol *m.*

tolyl ['tɔlil], *s. Ch:* tolyle *m.*

Tom [tɔm], *Pr.n.m.* (*dim. of Thomas*) Thomas. **1.** *F:* **any T., Dick or Harry,** tout le monde, n'importe qui, le premier venu; **to be hail-fellow-well-met with T., Dick and Harry,** frayer avec Pierre, Paul et Jacques. **2.** (*a*) (nom donné à une) grande cloche; (*b*) *Navy: F: A:* **long T.,** grand canon, maître canon (monté au milieu du navire). **3.** *P: A:* **old T.,** gin *m*; *U.S:* **T. and Jerry,** grog chaud au rhum, épicé et qui contient des œufs. **4. t. (cat),** matou *m*; *NAm:* **t. (turkey),** dindon *m*; *he's a T.* **5. T. Thumb,** (*a*) le petit Poucet, Tom Pouce; **he's a T. Thumb,** c'est un courte-botte; (*b*) *attrib.* **T. Thumb nasturtium,** capucine naine; **T. Thumb umbrella,** parapluie court; tom-pouce *m, pl.* tom-pouces. **6. T. Tiddler's ground,** camp *m* du défenseur (dans un jeu d'enfants); **the Exhibition is a T. Tiddler's ground for pickpockets,** l'Exposition est l'endroit rêvé pour les pickpockets.

tomahawk[1] [tɔməhɔ:k], *s.* hache *f* de guerre (des Peaux-Rouges); tomahawk *m*; *Fig:* **to bury the t.,** enterrer la hache de guerre, faire la paix.

tomahawk[2], *v.tr.* (*a*) frapper (qn) avec un tomahawk; assommer (qn); (*b*) *Fig:* éreinter, tuer (un livre, etc.).

tomalley [tə'mæli], *s. Cu:* partie crémeuse du homard; **t. sauce,** sauce faite avec cette partie.

tomato, *pl.* **-oes** [tə'mɑ:tou, -ouz; *NAm:* tə'meitou], *s.* **1.** tomate *f*; **currant t.,** tomate groseille à grappes; *Cu:* **t. sauce,** sauce *f* tomate; **t. grower,** tomatier *m.* **2.** *Bot:* (*a*) **strawberry, husk, t.,** alkékenge *f,* coqueret officinal, coquerelle *f*; physalis *m*; (*b*) **tree t.,** tomate en arbre, cyphomandra *m.* **3.** *U.S: F:* jolie fille; gonzesse *f.*

tomb [tu:m], *s.* tombe *f*; (*with monument*) tombeau *m*; **table t.,** tombe couverte d'une pierre plate (dans les catacombes de Rome); **to rifle a t.,** violer une sépulture; **life beyond the t.,** la vie au delà de la tombe; *Lit:* **to go down into the t.,** descendre au tombeau, à la tombe.

tombac(k) ['tɔmbæk], *s. Metall:* tombac *m.*

tombola [tɔm'boulə], *s.* tombola *f.*

tombolo ['tɔmbəlou], *s. Geog:* tombolo *m,* flèche *f* isthme.

tomboy ['tɔmbɔi], *s.f.* fillette d'allures garçonnières; **she's a real t.,** c'est un vrai garçon, un garçon manqué; elle est très diable.

tombstone ['tu:mstoun], *s.* pierre tombale, tumulaire, funéraire; tombe *f.*

tome [toum], *s.* tome *m*; gros volume; **ponderous tomes in ancient bindings,** volumes massifs à reliure ancienne.

tomentose [tou'mentous], **tomentous** [tou'mentəs], *a. Bot: Biol:* tomenteux, laineux.

tomentum [tou'mentəm], *s. Bot: Biol:* laine *f,* duvet *m.*

tomfool [tɔm'fu:l]. *F:* **1.** *s.* idiot *m,* niais *m,* nigaud *m.* **2.** *a.* stupide, idiot; **t. scheme,** projet insensé.

tomfoolery [tɔm'fu:ləri], *s. F:* bêtise(s) *f(pl),* niaiserie(s) *f(pl),* nigauderie(s) *f(pl),* bouffonnerie(s).

Tommy ['tɔmi]. **1.** *Pr.n.m.* (*dim. of* **Thomas**) Thomas, Tom. **2.** (*a*) *Pr.n.m. O:* **T. Atkins,** sobriquet du soldat anglais; (*b*) *s.* **a t.,** un simple soldat; *F:* un troufion. **3.** *P: A:* (*a*) pain *m,* mangeaille *f,* bouffe *f*; *Nau:* **soft t.,** pain frais; (*b*) *Ind:* (i) provisions fournies par l'économat de l'usine; (ii) **t. (system),** paiement *m* en nature; **t. (shop),** cantine (dirigée par l'économat de l'usine). **4.** *s. Mec.E: Tls:* **t. (bar),** (i) broche *f* (à visser); (ii) pince *f*; **t. hole,** entaille *f,* encoche *f* (pour admettre la broche); **t. nut,** écrou *m* à trous (se vissant à la broche); **t. screw,** vis *f* à broche.

tommygun ['tɔmigʌn], *s. Mil:* mitraillette *f* Thompson; Thompson *f.*

tommyrot ['tɔmirɔt], *s. F:* bêtises *fpl,* inepties *fpl*; **that's all t.,** tout ça c'est idiot, de la blague, des sottises.

tomnoddy [tɔm'nɔdi], *s. F: A:* dadais *m,* nigaud *m.*

tomogram ['toumәgræm], *s. Med:* tomogramme *m,* tomographie *f.*

tomography [tɔ'mɔgrəfi], *s. Med:* tomographie *f.*

tomorrow [tə'mɔrou], *adv. & s.* demain (*m*); **t. morning,** demain matin; **t. week,** (de) demain en huit; **the day after t.,** après-demain; **tomorrow's paper,** le journal de demain; **t. is, will be, Sunday,** c'est demain dimanche; **the citizens of t.,** les citoyens de demain; *Prov:* **never put off till t. what you can do today,** ne remettez pas au lendemain ce que vous pouvez faire le jour même; **t. never comes,** demain veut dire jamais; **who knows what t. holds?** qui sait ce que demain nous réserve? **t. is another day,** demain il fera jour; à chaque jour suffit sa peine.

tompion ['tɔmpiən], *s.* = TAMPION.

tomtit ['tɔmtit], *s. Orn:* mésange bleue.

tomtom ['tɔmtɔm], *s.* tam-tam *m, pl.* tam-tams.

ton [tʌn], *s. Meas:* **1.** tonne *f*; **long t., gross t.,** tonne forte (= 1016.06 kg); **short t.,** tonne courte (= 907.185 kg); **metric t.,** tonne (métrique) (= 1000 kg); **t. mile,** tonne milliaire; **t. kilometre,** tonne kilométrique; **a t. of coal,** un mille de houille; **t. of refrigeration,** tonne de réfrigération; *F:* **there's tons of it,** il y en a des tas, des tonnes; **tons of money,** un argent fou; **this suitcase weighs a t.,** cette valise est rudement lourde. **2.** *Nau:* **gross, register, t.,** tonneau *m* de jauge; **freight t.,** tonneau d'affrètement, tonneau de mer; **measurement t.,** tonne d'arrimage, d'encombrement; **t. of displacement,** tonne de déplacement; **t. burden,** tonne de portée; **ship of 500 tons burden,** navire de 500 tonneaux. **3.** *F:* (*a*) 100 livres *fpl* sterling; (*b*) vitesse de 100 milles à l'heure; **t.-up boys,** motards bolides (qui font du 100 milles à l'heure).

tonal ['toun(ə)l], *a.* tonal, -aux.

tonality [tou'næliti], *s.* tonalité *f.*

tone[1] [toun], *s.* **1.** son *m*; sonorité *f*; **t. (colour),** timbre *m* (de la voix, d'une cloche, d'un instrument de musique); **the deep t. of the bell,** le son profond de la cloche; **this radio has a good t.,** ce poste a une bonne sonorité; **clean t.,** son pur; **high-pitched, low-pitched, t.,** son aigu, grave; **difference t.,** son différentiel; *Mus:* **stopped t.,** ton bouché (d'un cor, etc.); **t. quality,** timbre (d'un instrument, etc.); *Elcs: etc:* **t. control, correction,** correction de tonalité; **t. corrector device,** correcteur *m* de tonalité; *Rec:* **t. control,** touche *f* de tonalité; **t. arm,** bras *m* de lecture (d'un tourne-disque); *Tp:* **ringing t.,** tonalité d'appel. **2.** (*a*) ton, voix *f*; intonation *f*; **t. of voice,** accent *m*; **in an impatient t.,** d'un ton d'impatience; **in a low t.,** sur un ton bas; d'une voix basse; **in a gentle t.,** d'un ton doux; **to speak in a severe t.,** prendre, faire, la grosse voix; parler d'un ton sévère; **to raise the t. of one's voice,** hausser le ton; **to change one's t.,** changer de ton; (*b*) **to give a serious t. to a discussion,** donner un ton sérieux à une discussion; **the employees take their t. from the boss,** les employés prennent le ton du chef; *Fin: etc:* **the prevailing t.,** l'ambiance générale; **the t. of the market,** l'allure *f,* l'atmosphère *f,* du marché; (*c*) *Med:* tonicité *f,* tonus *m* (des muscles, etc.). **3.** *Mus: Ac:* ton; **whole t.,** ton entier; **quarter t.,** quart *m* de ton; *Mus:* **t. poem,** poème symphonique. **4.** ton, nuance *f* (d'une couleur); *Phot:* ton (d'une épreuve); **warm tones,** tons chauds; *Art:* **cut-out half t.,** simili détourée; **deepened half t.,** simili grand creux; **squared up half t.,** simili au carré. **5.** *Ling:* (*a*) ton; accent d'intensité, accent tonique; (*b*) accent de hauteur.

tone[2]. **1.** *v.tr.* (*a*) adoucir les tons, modifier la tonalité (d'un tableau); (*of voice, colour, etc.*) **low-toned, high-toned,** à ton bas, élevé; **full-toned note, voice,** note, voix, grave; **toned paper,** papier (i) teinté, (ii) crémé; (*b*) **to t. down a colour,** adoucir, atténuer, une couleur; (*on painting*) **to t. down sharp details,** estomper des détails trop crus; **the editor had to t. down the article,** le rédacteur a dû atténuer les termes de l'article; **to t. s.o. up,** tonifier, retremper, *F:* remonter, qn; (*c*) *Phot:* virer (une épreuve). **2.** *v.i.* (*a*) **to t. (in) with sth.,** s'harmoniser avec qch.; (*of voice, etc.*) **to t. down,** s'adoucir; (*of pers.*) **to t. up,** se tonifier; se remettre, *F:* se retaper (après une maladie); (*b*) *Phot:* (*of print*) virer.

tone deaf [toun'def], *a.* amusique, atteint d'amusie.

tone deafness [toun'defnis], *s.* amusie (sensorielle), surdité musicale.

toneless ['tounlis], *a.* **1.** (couleur) sans éclat. **2.** (voix) blanche, atone.

tonelessly ['tounlisli], *adv.* d'une voix blanche, atone.

tonelessness ['tounlisnis], *s.* absence *f* de ton, de tonalité.

toner ['tounər], *s. Toil:* (lotion *f*) tonique *m.*

tong [tɔŋ], *s.* (*in China*) société secrète.

tonga[1] ['tɔŋgə], *s.* (*in India*) charrette légère à deux roues.

Tonga[2]. **1.** *Geog:* (*a*) *Pr.n.* **the T. islands,** les îles Tonga;

les îles de l'Amitié, des Amis; (*b*) *s.* Tongan, -ane. **2.** *s. Ling:* tonga *m.*

Tongan ['tɔŋgən]. **1.** *a. Geog:* tongan. **2.** *s.* (*a*) *Geog:* Tongan, -ane; (*b*) *Ling:* tonga *m.*

Tongrian ['tɔŋgriən]. *Geol:* **1.** *a.* tongrien, -ienne. **2.** *s.* Tongrien *m.*

tongs [tɔŋz], *s.pl.* pince(s) *f(pl)*, tenailles *fpl*; *Glassm:* morailles *fpl*; **(pair of) t., (fire) t.,** pincettes *fpl*; **sealing t.,** pince à plomber; **soldering t.,** pince à souder; **riveting t.,** pince à river; **smith's t.,** (i) pinces de forgeron; tenailles de forge; (ii) (*wide-jawed*) goulues *fpl*; *Metall: Metalw:* **crucible t.,** happe *f*; pinces à creuset; **furnace t.,** pinces à four; **ingot t.,** pinces à lingot; *El:* **fuse t.,** pinces à fusibles; *Dom.Ec:* **sugar t., snail t.,** pince à sucre, à escargots.

tongue[1] [tʌŋ], *s.* **1.** langue *f*; (*a*) *Anat:* **t. bone,** (os *m*) hyoïde *m*; **bifid, cleft, t.,** langue bifide; *Med:* **coated t.,** langue pâteuse; **beefy, pellagrous, t.,** langue de bœuf, langue pellagre; *Med: Vet:* **black t.,** langue noire; *Vet:* **blue t.,** langue bleue; **to put out, stick out, one's t.,** tirer la langue **(at s.o.,** à qn); *Med:* **put out your t.,** montrez-moi votre langue; **t. depressor,** abaisse-langue *m inv*; *A.Med:* **t. traction,** tractions *fpl* de la langue (pour ranimer un asphyxié); (*of dog*) **to hang out its t.,** tirer la langue; *Fig:* **to have one's t. hanging out,** (i) tirer la langue; avoir soif; (ii) s'attendre à (qch.); **he could have bitten his t. off for having told his secret,** il se mordait, il s'en mordait, la langue d'avoir laissé échapper son secret; *Harn:* **t. bit,** mors *m* (pour cheval passant la langue); *Arach:* **t. worm,** linguatule *f*; (*b*) **to have a ready, a glib, t.,** avoir la langue déliée, bien pendue, bien affilée; n'avoir pas sa langue dans sa poche; **to keep a watch on one's t.,** gouverner sa langue; **to find one's t.,** retrouver la parole; (*of child*) retrouver sa langue; **to keep a civil t. in one's head,** rester courtois; **with one's t. in one's cheek,** en cachant ses sentiments véritables; avec une ironie masquée; **t. twister,** mot *m*, phrase *f*, difficile à prononcer; phrase à décrocher la mâchoire; *Prov:* **the t. is sharper than any sword,** un coup de langue est pire qu'un coup de lance; *Ven:* (*of hounds*) **to give t.,** donner de la voix; aboyer. **2.** langue, idiome *m* (d'un peuple); **the German t.,** la langue allemande; *esp. B:* **the gift of tongues,** le don des langues. **3.** (*a*) langue (de terre); langue, dard *m* (de feu); patte *f*, languette *f* (de chaussure); battant *m* (de cloche); ardillon *m* (de boucle); langue, languette, aiguille *f* (d'une balance); soie *f* (de couteau, etc.); *Mus:* languette, anche *f* (de hautbois); *Rail:* lame *f* d'aiguille (flexible); **t. rail,** aiguille; rail *m* mobile; **t. hounds,** fourchette *f* (d'un wagon); (*b*) *Carp:* languette de bois; **t. of a (frame) saw,** garrot *m* d'une scie; **loose, slipped, t.,** languette rapportée; **half-round t.,** noix *f.*

tongue[2]. **1.** *v.tr.* (*a*) *A:* réprimander, gronder (qn); (*b*) toucher (qch.) du bout de la langue; lécher (qch.); (*c*) *Carp:* langueter (le bord d'une planche); (*d*) *Mus:* (*on wind instrument*) **to t. a passage,** détacher les notes d'un passage. **2.** *v.i.* (*a*) *F: O:* **to t. (it),** jaser, bavarder; (*b*) *Ven:* (*of hounds*) donner de la voix; aboyer.

tongueless ['tʌŋlis], *a.* **1.** sans langue; élingué. **2.** muet.

tonguelet ['tʌŋlit], *s.* languette *f.*

tongue-tie ['tʌŋtai], *s. Med:* ankyloglosse *m*; soubrelangue *m.*

tongue-tied ['tʌŋtaid], *a.* **1.** qui souffre d'ankyloglosse. **2.** muet, -ette (d'étonnement, etc.); interdit; *F:* qui a le filet. **3.** tenu au silence.

tonguing ['tʌŋiŋ], *s.* **1.** *A:* remontrance *f*, réprimande *f*. **2.** *Carp:* bouvetage *m*; *Tls:* **t. plane,** bouvet *m* mâle, à languette. **3.** *Mus:* (*on wind instrument*) coup *m* de langue.

tonic ['tɔnik]. **1.** *a.* (*a*) *Med: etc:* tonique, remontant, reconstituant, réconfortant, fortifiant; (*b*) *Toil:* **t. (lotion),** (lotion *f*) tonique *m*; (*c*) (*drink*) **t. water,** eau tonique; **gin and t. (water),** gin-tonic *m*; (*d*) *Gram;* (accent) tonique; (*e*) *Mus:* (note) tonique *m;* **t. chord,** accord naturel; (*f*) *Med:* **t. spasm,** convulsion *f* tonique; tonisme *m*. **2.** *s.* (*a*) *Med:* tonique *m*, remontant *m*, incitant *m*, réconfortant *m*, reconstituant *m*, fortifiant *m*; **to take (sth. as) a t.,** prendre qch. pour se remonter; (*of news. etc.*) **to act as a t. on s.o.,** réconforter, remonter, qn; (*b*) *Mus:* tonique *f.*

tonicity [tou'nisiti], *s.* tonicité *f* (des muscles, etc.); tonus *m* (musculaire).

tonight [tə'nait], *adv. & s.* (*a*) ce soir; (*b*) cette nuit.

toning ['touniŋ], *s.* **1.** *Phot:* virage *m* (des épreuves); **blue t., iron t.,** virage bleu; **t. bath,** bain de virage, de chlorure; **t. and fixing bath,** (bain) viro-fixateur *m*. **2. t. down,** adoucissement *m*, atténuation *f*; (*of light*) assombrissement *m*; **a t. down of my criticisms,** un correctif à mes critiques.

tonk [tɔŋk], *v.tr.* (*a*) *Tchn:* frapper avec un marteau (le bandage d'une roue, etc.); (*b*) *F:* frapper, taper (qn).

tonka ['tɔŋkə], *s. Bot:* **t. bean (tree),** tonka *m*, tonca *m*; coumarou *m*; **t. (bean),** fève *f* tonka.

Tonkin ['tɔŋkin], **Tonking** ['tɔŋkiŋ], *Pr.n. Geog: Hist:* le Tonkin.

Tonkinese [tɔŋki'ni:z]. **1.** *a. Geog:* tonkinois. **2.** *s.* (*a*) *Geog:* Tonkinois, -oise; (*b*) *Ling:* tonkinois *m.*

tonlet ['tʌnlit], *s. Arm:* **t. suit,** armure *f* à tonne.

tonnage ['tʌnidʒ], *s.* **1.** *Nau:* tonnage *m*, jauge *f*; capacité *f* de chargement (d'un navire); **t. deck,** pont de tonnage; **register(ed) t.,** tonnage net; tonnage de jauge; jauge officielle, jauge de douane, de registre; **gross t.,** tonnage brut; jauge brute; **net t.,** jauge nette; **deadweight t.,** tonnage réel; **underdeck t.,** jauge sous le pont. **2.** tonnage (d'un port, d'un pays); **active t.,** tonnage actif, en service. **3.** *Hist:* (droit *m* de) tonnage.

tonne [tʌn], *s. Meas:* tonne *f* (métrique).

tonneau ['tɔnou], *s. Aut:* compartiment *m* arrière d'une voiture.

tonner ['tʌnər], *s.* (*with num. prefixed, e.g.*) *Nau:* **thousand-t., five-hundred-t.,** navire *m* de mille tonneaux, de cinq cents tonneaux.

tonofibril(la) [tɔnou'fibril(ə)], *s. Biol:* tonofibrille *f.*

tonometer [tou'nɔmitər], *s. Med: Ph:* tonomètre *m.*

tonometric [tɔnə'metrik], *a. Med: Ph:* tonométrique.

tonometry [tou'nɔmitri], *s. Med: Ph:* tonométrie *f.*

tonsil ['tɔnsl], *s. Anat:* amygdale *f*; *Med:* **enlarged tonsils,** amygdales hypertrophiées; hypertrophie *f*, tuméfaction *f*, des amygdales; *Surg:* **t. guillotine,** amygdalotome *m*, tonsillotome *m*, tonsillitome *m.*

tonsillectomy [tɔnsi'lektəmi], *s. Surg:* amygdalectomie *f*, tonsillectomie *f.*

tonsillitis [tɔnsi'laitis], *s. Med:* angine *f.*

tonsillotome [tɔn'silətoum], *s. Surg:* amygdalotome *m*, tonsillitome *m*, tonsillotome *m.*

tonsillotomy [tɔnsi'lɔtəmi], *s. Surg:* amygdalotomie *f*, tonsillotomie *f.*

tonsorial [tɔn'sɔ:riəl], *a. F:* capillaire; de barbier.

tonsure[1] ['tɔnʃər], *s.* tonsure *f*; **to submit to the t.,** recevoir, prendre, la tonsure.

tonsure[2], *v.tr.* tonsurer (un ecclésiastique).

tontine [tɔn'ti:n], *s. Ins:* tontine *f.*

tonus ['tounəs], *s. Med:* tonicité *f*, tonus *m* (musculaire).

Tony[1] ['touni], *Pr.n.m.* (*dim. of Antony*) Toine.

tony[2], *a. F: A:* dans le ton; chic, élégant; **a t. little hat,** un petit chapeau coquet.

too [tu:], *adv.* **1.** trop, par trop; **it's t. difficult,** c'est trop difficile; **t. difficult a job,** un travail (par) trop difficile; **it's not t. easy,** ce n'est pas si facile; **t. much money,** trop d'argent; **t. many people,** trop de gens; **t. far,** trop loin; **to work t. much, t. hard,** travailler trop, trop travailler; **50p t. much,** 50p de trop; **I have a card t. many,** j'ai une carte de trop; **I'm afraid I was one t. many,** je crains d'avoir été de trop; **this job's t. much for me,** ce travail est au-dessus de mes forces; **things are getting t. much for me,** je suis dépassé par les événements; **he was t. much, one t. many, for me,** il était trop fort pour moi; il était plus malin que moi; je n'étais pas de taille à lutter contre lui; **the hole was t. small for a rat (to come in by),** le trou était trop étroit pour laisser passer un rat; **you can't make the wall t. thick here,** (i) il n'est pas possible d'avoir un mur très épais ici; (ii) le mur ici doit être aussi épais que possible; **this dress is t. big, t. small, for me,** cette robe est trop large, trop étroite, pour moi; **he's t. talkative,** il parle trop; **I've listened to him t. long,** je l'ai trop écouté; **I'm t. tired to run,** je suis trop fatigué pour courir; **she loved him t. well,** elle l'a trop aimé; **I know him all t. well,** je ne le connais que trop; **you're t. kind,** vous êtes très, trop, gentil; **he's not t. well today,** il ne va pas très bien aujourd'hui; *F:* **it's t. t. charming!** c'est vraiment exquis! **2.** (*also*) aussi; également; **you're coming t.,** vous venez aussi; **he bought the picture and the frame t.,** il a acheté le tableau et le cadre aussi, et le cadre avec; **I need some t.,** il m'en faut également; moi aussi il m'en faut; il m'en faut à moi aussi; **I want, would like, some t.,** donnez-m'en aussi; **he t. is a painter,** (et) lui aussi est peintre. **3.** (*moreover*) d'ailleurs; de plus; en outre; **the prisoner, t., inspired little sympathy,** le prisonnier, d'ailleurs, inspirait peu de sympathie; **30°(C) in the shade and in September t.,** 30° à l'ombre et en septembre en plus.

toodle-oo ['tu:dl'u:], *int. F: O:* au revoir! salut!

tool[1] [tu:l], *s.* **1.** outil *m* (de menuisier, etc.); instrument *m*, ustensile *m*; **(set of) tools,** outillage *m*; **garden tools, gardening tools,** outils, matériel *m*, de jardin, de jardinage; **calibration tools,** outillage d'étalonnage; **small tools,** petit outillage; **hand t.,** outil à main; **power t.,** outil à moteur; **pneumatic, air, t.,** outil pneumatique; **diamond t.,** outil diamanté; **point t.,** outil à pointe; **gang t.,** outil multiple, sérié; **lathe t., turning t.,** outil de tour; **slide-rest t.,** outil à charioter, pour chariotage; **cutting t.,** outil coupant, tranchant; outil de coupe; burin *m*; **cutting-off t.,** outil à tronçonner, à saigner; **grinding t.,** outil abrasif; **boring t.,** (i) outil à percer, à aléser; (ii) *Min:* outil de forage, de sondage; **facing t., truing t.,** outil de forme, de reproduction; outil à profiler, à dresser; **roughing t.,** outil, ciseau *m*, à dégrossir; **stamping t.,** outil d'emboutissage; **planishing t.,** outil à planer; **neutralizing t.,** outil isolant; **finishing t.,** plane *f*; outil à finir; **(inside, outside) threading t.,** outil à fileter (intérieurement, extérieurement); *Const:* **cartridge-assisted fixing t.,** pistolet *m* de scellement; *Min:* **drilling t.,** outil de forage, de sondage; *Rail:* **platelayer's tools, track-laying tools,** outillage de la voie, de poseur de voie, de piqueur; *Atom.Ph: etc:* **remote handling t.,** outil de télémanipulation; télémanipulateur *m*; **t. angle,** angle de coupe, de taillant; *Min:* **t. joint,** manchon vissé; **t. post,** porte-outil *m*, *pl.* porte-outil(s); **t. holder,** (i) porte-outil; (ii) manche spécial pour divers outils; **revolving t. holder,** porte-outil revolver; **t. wrench,** clef à outils; **t. cabinet, chest,** casier *m*, boîte *f*, coffre *m*, à outils; **t. set,** jeu *m* d'outils; **t. rest,** support *m* d'outil; porte-outil; **t. rack,** râtelier à outils; **t. carriage,** chariot porte-outil; **t. crib,** petit magasin, *F:* cagibi *m*, à outils; **t. sharpener, grinder,** (i) (*device*) affûteuse *f*; (ii) (*pers.*) affûteur, -euse, aiguiseur *m*, rémouleur *m*, repasseur *m*; **t. sharpening, grinding,** affûtage *m*, aiguisage *m*, d'outils; **t. pusher,** surveillant, -ante, de forage; *Prov:* **a bad workman blames his tools,** mauvais ouvrier n'a jamais bons outils; à méchant ouvrier point de bon outil; les mauvais ouvriers ont toujours de mauvais outils. **2.** (*a*) instrument, créature *f*; **to make a t. of s.o.,** se servir de qn (dans un but intéressé); **man had become a t. in the hands of the dictator,** l'homme était un outil au service du dictateur; **he was a mere t. in their hands,** il était devenu leur créature; (*b*) **you have to learn the tools of your trade,** on ne peut pratiquer un métier sans apprentissage. **3.** *Bookb:* (*a*) ciselure *f*, dorure *f*; (*b*) fer *m* de relieur. **4.** *V:* pénis *m*, verge *f*, queue *f.*

tool[2], *v.tr. & i.* **1.** *v.tr.* (*a*) *Bookb:* ciseler, dorer (une tranche, une reliure); *Leath:* ciseler (le cuir); **tooled leather,** cuir repoussé; (*b*) *Stonew:* bretter, bretteler, layer (une pierre); (*c*) *Mec.E:* usiner, travailler (une pièce de fonte). **2.** *v.tr.* **t. (up),** outiller (une usine, etc.); *v.i.* s'équiper, s'outiller. **3.** *v.i. F: A:* **to t. along,** aller en voiture; rouler.

toolbag ['tu:lbæg], *s.* sac *m* à outils; (*of bicycle, etc.*) sacoche *f.*

toolbox ['tu:lbɔks], *s.* **1.** boîte *f*, coffre *m*, à outils. **2.** porte-outil *m*, *pl.* porte-outil(s).

tooler ['tu:lər], *s.* (*pers.*) *Leath:* ciseleur *m*; *Bookb:* doreur, -euse.

toolhouse ['tu:lhaus], *s.* resserre *f*, remise *f.*

tooling ['tu:liŋ], *s.* **1.** (*a*) *Leath:* ciselage *m*; (*b*) *Mec.E:* usinage *m*; **t. allowance,** surépaisseur *f* pour usinage; **t. hole,** trou *m* d'usinage, de fabrication; **t. lug,** patte *f* d'usinage; **t. reference,** gabarit *m* de réglage; (*c*) *Stonew:* bretture *f*. **2.** (*a*) *Bookb:* ciselure *f*, dorure *f* (du dos, etc.); **blind t.,** dorure à froid; **gold t.,** dorure à chaud; dentelles *fpl*; (*b*) *Stonew:* bretture. **3.** outillage *m*; **master t.,** outillage étalon.

toolkit ['tu:lkit], *s.* outillage *m*; jeu *m* d'outils; **this book is an essential part of the historian's t.,** ce livre est essentiel à tout historien qui se veut bien outillé.

toolmaker ['tu:lmeikər], *s.* fabricant *m* d'outils; outilleur *m*; taillandier *m.*

toolmaking ['tu:lmeikiŋ], *s.* fabrication *f* d'outils; taillanderie *f.*

toolroom ['tu:lru:m], *s.* atelier *m* d'outillage.

toolshed ['tu:lʃed], *s.* resserre *f*, remise *f.*

toolslide ['tu:lslaid], *s. Mch.Tls:* coulisseau *m* porte-outil.

toon [tu:n], *s. Bot:* toona *m*, cédrela *m.*

toot[1] [tu:t], *s.* **1.** son *m*, appel *m*, de clairon, etc. **2.** *Nau:* coup *m* de sirène; *Aut:* coup, appel, de klaxon, d'avertisseur.

toot[2]. **1.** *v.tr.* **to t. a horn, a trumpet,** sonner du cor, de la trompette; *Aut:* **to t. the horn,** klaxonner; donner un coup de klaxon, d'avertisseur. **2.** *v.i.* (*of pers.*) sonner du cor; (*of instrument*) sonner; *Aut:* klaxonner; avertir; **to t. on the trumpet,** sonner de la trompette.

tooth[1], *pl.* **teeth** [tu:θ, ti:θ], *s.* **1.** dent *f*; **(set of) teeth,** denture *f*, dentition *f*; **first, milk, teeth,** dents de lait; **deciduous, primary, t.,** dent temporaire, caduque; **natal t.,** dent présente à la naissance; **second, permanent, teeth,** dents permanentes; dentition définitive; **anterior, front, t.,** dent antérieure, du devant; **posterior, back, t.,** dent postérieure, dent du fond, grosse dent; **lower, mandibular, t.,** dent inférieure, dent du bas; **upper, maxillary, t.,** dent supérieure, dent du haut; **crowded, overlapping, teeth,** dents qui se chevauchent; chevauchement *m* des dents; **irregular t.,** surdent *f*; **unerupted, impacted, t.,** dent incluse; **hollow t.,** dent creuse; **loose t.,** dent branlante, qui se déchausse; dent mobile; **sensitive t.,** dent sensible; **buck t.,** dent qui avance; **buck teeth,** dents saillantes, proéminentes; **false, artificial, prosthetic, t.,** fausse dent; dent artificielle; **(set of) false teeth,** dentier *m*, appareil *m*; *F:* râtelier *m*; **pin t., pivot t.,** dent à crampon, à pivot; **abutment t.,** dent d'ancrage, dent pilier (d'une prothèse); **porcelain t.,** dent en porcelaine; **acrylic t.,** dent en acryl, en résine acrylique; *Orn: Rept:* **egg t.,** dent d'éclosion; *Orn:* **t. billed,** au bec dentelé; **t. glass,** verre à dents; **t. powder,** poudre *f* dentifrice; dentifrice *m*; *Med:* **t. rash,** strophulus *m*; *Moll:* **t. shell,** dentale *m*, dentalium *m*; **to have a fine set of teeth,** avoir de belles dents, une belle denture; *F:* avoir la bouche bien meublée; **horse with all its teeth,** cheval qui a tout mis, qui a la bouche faite; **to cut one's teeth,** faire, percer, ses dents; **to have a t. out,** se faire arracher une dent; **he knocked my t. out,** il m'a fait sauter une dent; *F:* **to knock s.o.'s teeth in,** battre qn, amocher le portrait à qn; **to kick s.o. in the teeth,** traiter qn avec mépris; **to cast, fling, sth. in s.o.'s teeth,** reprocher qch. à qn; **in the teeth of all opposition,** malgré, en dépit de, toute opposition; *Nau:* **to have the wind in one's teeth,** avoir le vent debout; **to show, bare, one's teeth,** (i) montrer, découvrir, ses dents; (ii) montrer les dents; menacer qn; **armed to the teeth,** armé jusqu'aux dents; **to fight t. and nail,** se battre avec acharnement; **to go for s.o. t. and nail,** attaquer qn du bec et des ongles; se jeter sur qn à bras raccourcis; **he went at it t. and nail,** il y est allé de toutes ses forces; *F:* il a travaillé d'achar; **to get one's teeth into sth.,** se mettre pour de bon à faire qch.; s'acharner à faire qch.; **it's sth. to get one's teeth into,** c'est qch. de substantiel, c'est qch. qui fait travailler; **to set one's teeth,** (i) serrer les dents; (ii) s'armer de résolution; **to say sth. between one's teeth,** grommeler qch. entre ses dents; *F:* **to be, get, long in the t.,** ne plus être jeune; vieillir; avoir, prendre, de la bouteille; **she's a bit long in the t.,** elle n'est plus dans sa première jeunesse. **2.** dent (de scie, de lime, de peigne); dent, alluchon *m* (de roue d'engrenage); (*of notching implements*) **teeth,** brettures *f*; **teeth of a wheel,** denture; **to break the teeth of a comb,** édenter un peigne; (*of cross-cut saw*) **champion t.,** dent double; **cross-cut teeth,** dents contournées, dents pour scie de travers; **fleam t.,** dent droite; **hook(ed) t.,** dent crochue, à crochet; **ripping teeth,** dents couchées; (*of milling cutter*) **cleared, relieved, teeth,** dents dégagées, denture dépouillée; **corrected t.,** dent à profil corrigé; **crown of t.,** sommet *m*, tête *f*, de la dent; **depth of t.,** creux *m* de la dent; **t. fillet,** rayon *m* de pied de denture; **t. pitch,** (i) module *m* de la dent; (ii) pas *m* des dents; *Mec.E:* **teeth of a rack,** dents d'une crémaillère; **gear teeth,** dents d'engrenage; **evolute teeth,** denture à développée; **involute teeth,** denture à développante; **guide t., marked t.,** dent de repère; **helical teeth,** denture hélicoïdale; **epicyclic teeth,** denture épicycloïdale; **herringbone teeth,** denture à chevrons, dents chevronnées; **ratchet t.,** dent d'arrêt; **skew teeth,** denture inclinée; **stub teeth,** denture tronquée; **spiral teeth,** denture spirale; **straight spur teeth,** denture droite; *El:* **armature t.,** dent d'induit; **t. induction,** induction dans les dents, dans la denture. **3.** *Const:* pierre *f* d'attente, d'arrachement; harpe *f*, amorce *f*. **4.** *Paperm:* (*grain*) grain *m* (du papier).

tooth². **1.** *v.tr.* (*a*) denter, endenter, créneler (une roue); (*b*) bretter, bretteler, layer (une pierre). **2.** *v.i.* (*of cogwheels*) s'engrener.

toothache ['tu:θeik], *s.* mal *m*, rage *f*, de dents; *Med:* odontalgie *f*; **to have t.,** avoir mal aux dents.

toothbrush ['tu:θbrʌʃ], *s.* brosse *f* à dents; **t. moustache,** moustache en brosse.

toothcomb ['tu:θkoum], *s.* peigne fin; **to go through (a document) with a fine t.,** passer (un document) au peigne fin, au crible; scruter (un document) à la loupe.

toothed [tu:θt], *a.* **1.** (*of animal*) denté; pourvu de dents; (*of leaf, etc.*) dentelé; **t. whale,** baleine denticèle. **2.** *Mec.E: etc:* denté, crénelé; **t. wheel,** roue dentée; roue à dents; roue d'engrenage; **t. gearing,** engrenage *m* à roues dentées; **t. plate,** peigne *m* (de rasoir, etc.); **t. rack,** crémaillère *f*; **t. jaw wrench,** clef *f* à mâchoires dentées; **t. quadrant, t. segment,** secteur denté; *El:* **t. armature,** induit denté.

toothful ['tu:θful], *s. O:* goutte *f*, soupçon *m* (de vin, etc.); *F:* de quoi remplir une dent creuse.

toothing ['tu:ðiŋ], *s.* **1.** (*a*) taille *f* des dents (d'une scie, d'une roue); (*b*) bretture *f* (de la pierre). **2.** (*a*) *Mec.E:* dents *fpl* (d'une roue); denture *f*, endentement *m*, crénelage *m*; (*b*) *Const:* (i) arrachement *m*, harpes *fpl*; (ii) appareil *m* en besace; **t. stone,** pierre d'attente, d'arrachement; harpe *f*, amorce *f*; (*c*) *Stonew:* bretture.

toothless ['tu:θlis], *a.* sans dents; édenté.

toothlessness ['tu:θlisnis], *s.* édentement *m*.

toothlike ['tu:θlaik], *a.* dentiforme.

toothpaste ['tu:θpeist], *s.* pâte *f* dentifrice; dentifrice *m*.

toothpick ['tu:θpik], *s.* **1.** cure-dent(s) *m*, *pl.* cure-dents. **2.** *Mil: F:* baïonnette *f*; Rosalie *f*.

toothsome ['tu:θsəm], *a. A:* **1.** savoureux; qui flatte le palais; agréable au goût; **t. morsel,** morceau friand, succulent; fin morceau. **2.** (*of pers.*) séduisant.

toothwort ['tu:θwə:t], *s. Bot:* dentaire *f*, lathræa *m*, lathrœa *f*; clandestine *f*.

toothy ['tu:θi], *a.* à dents saillantes; (*childish speech*) **t. pegs,** dents.

tooting ['tu:tiŋ], *s.* sonnerie *f* (de la trompette); cornement *m*.

tootle¹ ['tu:tl], *v.i.* corner, klaxonner (de façon continue); **to t. on the flute,** flûter.

tootle², *v.i. F: A:* **to t. along,** aller, suivre, son petit bonhomme de chemin.

tootsy(-wootsy) ['tu:tsi(wu:tsi)], *s. F:* (*childish speech*) pied *m*; peton *m*, paturon *m*, pâturon *m*.

top¹ [tɔp], *s. & a.*

I. *s.* **1.** haut *m*, sommet *m*, cime *f*, faîte *m* (d'un arbre); sommet, cime, faîte (d'une montagne); sommet, haut (d'une colline, d'une côte); sommet (d'une tour, de la tête); *Mch:* **t. of stroke,** haut de course (d'un piston); **we reached the t. of the hill,** nous sommes arrivés en haut de la colline; **at the t. of the stairs,** en haut de l'escalier; **at the t. of the tree,** (i) en haut de l'arbre; (ii) au premier rang de sa profession; **at the t. of the house,** sous les combles, sous le toit; **from t. to bottom,** de haut en bas; du haut en bas; de fond en comble; de la cave au grenier; **he slid from the t. to the bottom of the ladder,** il a glissé du haut en bas de l'échelle; **from t. to toe,** de la tête aux pieds; de pied en cap; *F:* **to blow one's t.,** s'emporter; sortir de ses gonds; **to put sth. on (the) t. of sth.,** mettre qch. sur qch., (tout) en haut de qch.; **we had to travel on t. of the luggage,** nous avons dû faire le trajet juchés sur les bagages; **she put the best apples on t.,** elle a mis les meilleures pommes (en, au) dessus; **he had a handkerchief round his head and his hat on t. (of it),** il avait un mouchoir autour de la tête et son chapeau par-dessus; **she had her hair taken up on t. (of her head),** elle avait les cheveux relevés en chignon; *Nau:* **cargo stowed on t.,** cargaison arrimée dans les hauts; **to be on t., to come out on t.,** avoir (pris) le dessus; avoir l'avantage; **it's just one thing on t. of another,** ça n'arrête jamais; c'est ceci, c'est cela; **on t. of it all he wanted to leave her,** et pour comble (de malheur), et en plus de tout cela, il voulait la quitter; **to be, to feel, on t. of the world,** être, se sentir, en pleine forme; être dans une forme éblouissante; *F:* **he just said it off the t. of his head,** il l'a dit sans y réfléchir; ce n'était qu'un mouvement d'instinct; c'était sa première réaction; **to go over the t.,** (i) *Mil:* monter à l'assaut; partir à l'attaque; (ii) *F:* exagérer; y aller fort; (iii) *F: O:* sauter le pas. **2.** (*a*) surface *f* (de l'eau, de la terre); dessus (d'une table, etc.); impériale *f* (d'un autobus); *A:* **to ride on t. (of a stage coach),** voyager sur la banquette; **oil always comes to the t.,** l'huile surnage toujours; **t. of the milk,** crème (séparée du lait); (*b*) *Mec.E:* **t. of a cam,** palier *m* de came. **3.** (*a*) dessus (d'une chaussure); revers *m* (d'une botte à revers, d'un bas); scion *m* (d'une canne à pêche); couvercle *m* (d'une boîte, d'une casserole, etc.); bouchon *m*, capsule *f* (d'une bouteille, etc.); capuchon *m* (d'un tube, etc.); ciel *m* (de fourneau); capote *f* (d'une voiture); *Aut:* **soft t.,** voiture *f* décapotable; (*of a circus*) **big t.,** chapiteau *m*; (*in kitchen, workroom*) **work(ing) t.,** table *f* de travail; *Cards:* **tops,** hautes cartes (du jeu); (*b*) *Cost:* (i) haut, corsage *m* (d'une robe); (ii) (*separate garment*) haut; **tank t.,** (i) *Cost:* débardeur *m*; (ii) *Nau:* plafond *m* de ballast; *Mch:* **t. of (shaft) tunnel,** plafond de tunnel (d'arbre). **4.** tête (de page, de carte, etc.); haut (d'un tableau, d'une page, etc.); *Bookb:* **gilt t.,** tête dorée. **5.** haut bout (de la table); **the t. of the street,** le haut de la rue; **at the t. of the street,** au bout de la rue; *Sch:* **to be (at) the t. of the form,** être à la tête de la classe; être le premier, la première, de la classe; (*of actor, etc.*) **to be (at) the t. of the bill,** faire tête d'affiche; *F:* **he's (at) the t. of the bill,** il fait tête d'affiche; *F:* **he's (the) tops!** c'est la crème de la crème, le dessus du panier! **6. to shout at the t. of one's voice,** crier à tue-tête, à pleine gorge; pousser des cris d'orfraie; **she was singing at the t. of her voice,** elle chantait à tue-tête, à pleine gorge, à gorge déployée; **to be on t. of one's form,** être, se sentir, en pleine forme; être au meilleur de sa forme, *Turf:* **to bring a horse to the t. of its form,** affûter un cheval; **this horse is at the t. of its form,** ce cheval est au mieux de sa forme, est bien en forme; **he ran at the t. of his speed,** il courait à toutes jambes; *F:* (*Irish phr.*) **(the) t. of the morning (to you),** bien le bonjour! *Aut: F:* **to climb a hill in t.,** monter une côte en prise (directe); *Nau:* **the t. of the flood, of the tide,** le haut de l'eau; les hautes eaux; le vif de la marée; l'étale *m* du flot. **7.** (*a*) *Bot: Hort:* **flowering, fruiting, t.,** sommité fleurie, fructifère; **turnip tops, carrot tops,** fanes *f* de navets, de carottes; (*b*) *Tex:* (i) laine peignée; peigné *m*; (ii) ruban *m*; **converted t.,** ruban converti; **combed t.,** ruban peigné. **8.** *Min:* toit *m* (d'une couche de houille). **9.** *Nau:* hune *f*; **main t.,** grand-hune *f*; **fore t.,** hune de misaine; *Navy:* **director t.,** hune de télépointage; **fire control t.,** hune de direction de tir. **10.** *Sp: esp. Ten: F:* **to put t. on a ball,** lifter; **he puts a lot of t. on,** il joue très lifté.

II. *a.* **1.** supérieur; du dessus, du haut, d'en haut; **the t. stones,** les pierres d'en haut; les pierres de faîte (d'un mur); **the t. floor, storey,** le plus haut étage; le dernier étage; l'étage du haut; **t. stair, t. step,** dernière marche (en montant); **the t. stair, the t. step (of the stairs),** la dernière marche de l'escalier; **the t. stair but one,** l'avant-dernière marche; **t. boots,** bottes à revers, à retroussis, à genouillères; **t. garment,** vêtement de dessus; **t. hat,** chapeau *m* haut de forme; haut-de-forme *m*, *pl.* hauts-de-forme; **t. hat insurance scheme** = retraite *f* des cadres; **the t. button of his coat,** le premier bouton de son manteau; **car with a t. speed of 150 km.p.h.,** voiture avec un plafond de 150 km/h; *Sp:* **to put t. spin on a ball,** lifter; (*at a sawpit*) **t. sawyer,** scieur *m* de long de dessus; **t. people,** personnalités *fpl*, gens éminents; *F:* **the t. brass,** (i) *Mil:* les officiers supérieurs; les galonnards *m*; les huiles *f*; (ii) les gros bonnets; les grosses légumes; *F:* **to be t. dog,** être le vainqueur, avoir le dessus; *Adm:* **t. secret,** très secret, ultra-secret; **to be, to feel, on t. form,** être, se sentir, en pleine forme; *Cu:* **t. ribs (of beef),** plat *m* de côtes; côtes plates; **t. gear,** (i) *Aut:* prise (directe); (ii) *Nau:* manœuvres hautes; **t. hamper,** superstructure *f* (d'un pont, etc.); *Nau:* **t. hamper (rigging),** fardage *m*; **t. chain,** suspente *f* de vergue; **t. crosstrees,** croisettes *f*; barres *f* (de perroquet); **t. lantern, light,** fanal *m*, lanterne *f*, de hune; **t. mark,** voyant *m* (de bouée); **t. tackle,** palan *m* de guinderesse; candelette *f*; *Metall:* **t. box, flask,** contrechâssis *m*, châssis *m* du dessus (de moulage); *Mec.E:* **t. brass,** contre-coussinet *m* (d'un palier); **t. cover,** (i) *Mch:* couvercle *m* de cylindre; (ii) *Mil.Av:* couverture aérienne (en altitude); *Tls:* **t. iron,** contre-fer *m* (d'un rabot); *Agr:* **t. dressing,** engrais *m* en couverture; fumure *f* en surface. **2.** premier; principal, -aux; **t. pupil,** premier, -ère, de la classe; **he got the t. mark,** *F:* **came t., in history,** il a eu la meilleure note en histoire; **he's one of the world's t. ten players,** c'est un des dix meilleurs joueurs du monde; **t. ten, twenty** = palmarès *m*; *F:* hit-parade *m*.

top², *v.tr.* **(topped** [tɔpt]**)** **1.** écimer (un arbre, une plante); étêter, élaguer (un arbre, un arbuste); *Hort:* pincer (l'extrémité d'une plante); *Petr:* étêter; **to t. and tail gooseberries,** éplucher des groseilles (à maquereau). **2.** (*a*) surmonter, couronner, coiffer **(with,** de); **a statue tops the column,** une statue surmonte la colonne; **the church is topped by a steeple,** l'église est coiffée d'un clocher; **to t. up a drink, a glass,** remplir un verre (à ras bords); *F:* **let me t. you up,** encore un peu? *Aut:* **to t. up,** *NAm:* **to t. off (the battery, the oil, the tank, etc.),** ajouter de l'eau, de l'huile, de l'essence; rétablir le niveau; faire un appoint; *F:* **t. her up,** faites le plein; **to t. out,** *NAm:* **to t. off (a tower block),** célébrer l'achèvement de la construction (d'un grand immeuble); (*b*) **he topped off the dinner with a liqueur,** il a couronné le dîner d'une liqueur; **and to t. it all,** et pour comble (de malheur), et en plus de tout cela. **3.** (*a*) excéder, dépasser, surpasser; **to t. sth. in height,** dépasser qch. en hauteur; **the takings have topped a thousand pounds,** les recettes dépassent mille livres; **she has never topped fifth place,** elle n'a jamais réussi à avoir une place plus haute que, au-dessus de, la cinquième; **to t. s.o. by a head,** dépasser qn de la tête; **to t. a given weight,** excéder un poids donné; (*b*) *Th:* **to t. one's part,** jouer son rôle à la perfection. **4. to t. a hill,** atteindre le sommet d'une colline; **the battalion topped the ridge,** le bataillon franchit l'arête; **the horse topped the fence,** le cheval a franchi la barrière; *Nau:* (*of ship*) **to t. the sea,** s'élever à la hauteur de la lame. **5. to t. a list, a class,** être à la tête d'une liste, de la classe. **6.** *Golf:* calotter (la balle). **7.** *Nau:* apiquer (une vergue).

top³, *s.* **(spinning, peg) t.,** toupie *f*; **to spin a t.,** faire aller une toupie; **t. shell,** (i) *Moll:* troche *f*, trochus *m*; maçon *m*; empereur *m*; (ii) *Conch:* coquille turbinée; **common t. shell,** troque *m*.

toparch ['tɔpa:k], *s. Ant:* toparque *m*.

toparchy ['tɔpa:ki], *s. Ant:* toparchie *f*.

topaz ['toupæz], *s. Lap:* topaze *f*; **oriental t.,** topaze orientale; **rose t., pink t.,** topaze brûlée; **smoky t.,** topaze enfumée; **burnt t.,** rubis *m* du Brésil; **quartz t., false t., Indian t.,** prime *f* de topaze; topaze occidentale; citrine *f*; **colourless t.,** goutte *f* d'eau du Brésil.

topazolite [tou'pæzəlait], *s. Miner:* topazolite *f.*

top-bracket ['tɔpbrækit], *a.* de première catégorie, de haute volée; d'élite, élitaire.

top(-)coat ['tɔpkout], *s.* **1.** *Cost:* pardessus *m*, manteau *m.* **2.** *Paint:* couche *f* de finition.

topcross(ing) ['tɔpkrɔs(iŋ)], *s. Breed:* croisement *m* d'un mâle d'une lignée consanguine avec des femelles quelconques non apparentées; topcrossing *m.*

top(-)dress ['tɔpdres], *v.tr. Agr:* fumer en surface (un terrain).

tope[1] [toup], *s. Ich:* milandre *m*; chien *m* de mer; hâ *m.*

tope[2], *s.* (*India*) bosquet *m*; verger *m* (de manguiers, etc.).

tope[3], *v.i. F: O:* boire (souvent et avec excès); pomper, biberonner, picoler; **he's always toping,** il a toujours un verre à la main.

topectomy [tɔ'pektəmi], *s. Surg:* topectomie *f.*

topee ['toupi], *s.* casque colonial.

toper ['toupər], *s. F: O:* ivrogne *m*, (gros) buveur, (grosse) buveuse; soiffard, -arde; sac *m* à vin.

topflight ['tɔpflait], *a.* de haute volée, de premier rang; d'élite; **a t. scientist,** un homme de science de première volée.

topgallant [tɔp'gælənt, tə'gælənt], *a. & s. Nau:* (voile *f*, mât *m*) de perroquet; **fore-t. sail,** petit perroquet; **main t. sail,** grand perroquet; **to put on the t. gear,** garnir les perroquets.

tophaceous [tɔ'feiʃəs], *a.* **1.** *Med:* tophacé. **2.** *Geol:* tufacé.

topheaviness [tɔp'hevinis], *s.* excès *m* de charge en hauteur; manque *m* de stabilité.

topheavy [tɔp'hevi], *a.* (*a*) trop lourd du haut; peu stable; (*b*) *Nau:* (*of ship*) trop chargé dans les hauts; volage.

tophole ['tɔphoul], *a. F: A:* épatant, formidable, excellent; **it's t.!** c'est bien tapé!

tophus, *pl.* **-i** ['toufəs, -ai], *s.* **1.** *Med:* tophus *m*; concrétions tophacées. **2.** *Geol:* tuf *m* calcaire.

topi[1] ['toupi], *s.* casque colonial.

topi[2] ['toupi:], *s. Z:* topi *m.*

topiary ['toupiəri], *a. & s. Hort:* **t. (work),** taille ornementale des arbres; art *m* topiaire.

topic ['tɔpik], *s.* **1.** matière *f* (d'un écrit, d'un discours, d'une discussion); sujet *m*, thème *m* (de conversation); **this is one of the main topics of the day,** c'est une des grandes questions d'actualité; **it's a favourite t. of his,** c'est un de ses sujets préférés. **2.** *Log: Rh:* lieu commun; topique *m.*

topical ['tɔpikl], *a.* **1.** (*a*) *O:* qui se rapporte au lieu; topique; local, -aux; (*b*) *Med:* (mal, remède) topique, local. **2. t. allusion,** allusion aux événements du jour; **t. question,** question d'actualité; question actuelle; **t. song,** chanson d'actualités (avec allusions aux événements du jour).

topicality [tɔpi'kæliti], *s.* actualité *f.*

topics ['tɔpiks], *s.pl.* (*usu. with sg. const.*) topique *f.*

topknot ['tɔpnɔt], *s.* **1.** *A.Cost:* fontange *f*; nœud *m* de rubans (sur la coiffure). **2.** (*a*) huppe *f* (d'un oiseau); (*b*) petit chignon. **3.** *Ich:* **(common) t.,** targeur *m*; cardine *f*, limande-salope *f.*

topless ['tɔplis], *a.* **1.** (*of tree*) étêté, écimé. **2.** *Lit:* d'une hauteur démesurée; qui se perd dans les nues. **3. t. dancer, waitress,** danseuse, serveuse, en monokini; **to go t.,** se mettre, aller, torse nu.

topman, *pl.* **-men** ['tɔpmən], *s.m.* **1.** *Nau:* gabier. **2.** (*in sawpit*) scieur de long de dessus.

topmast ['tɔpməst], *s. Nau:* mât *m* de hune; **main t.,** grand mât de hune.

topminnow ['tɔpminou], *s. Ich:* poeciliidé *m.*

topmost ['tɔpmoust], *a.* le plus haut; le plus élevé.

topnotch ['tɔpnɔtʃ], *a. F: O:* excellent, de premier ordre, de première classe.

topnotcher ['tɔpnɔtʃər], *s. F: O:* champion, -onne; crack *m*; **he's a t.,** c'est un caïd, un as.

topochemical [tɔpou'kemikl], *a.* topochimique.

topographer [tə'pɔgrəfər], *s.* topographe *m.*

topographic(al) [tɔpə'græfik(l)], *a.* topographique.

topographically [tɔpə'græfik(ə)li], *adv.* topographiquement.

topography [tə'pɔgrəfi], *s.* **1.** topographie *f.* **2.** anatomie *f* topographique.

topologic(al) [tɔpə'lɔdʒik(l)], *a.* topologique.

topology [tə'pɔlədʒi], *s.* topologie *f.*

toponym ['tɔpənim], *s.* toponyme *m.*

toponymic [tɔpə'nimik], *a.* toponymique.

toponymics [tɔpə'nimiks], *s.pl.* (*usu. with sg. const.*) toponymie *f.*

toponymy [tə'pɔnimi], *s.* toponymie *f.*

topophobia [tɔpou'foubiə], *s. Med:* topophobie *f.*

topotaxis [tɔpou'tæksis], *s. Biol:* tropisme *m.*

topped [tɔpt], *a. esp. Lit:* (*with noun prefixed, e.g.*) **cloud-t. peaks,** sommets couronnés de nuages; **gold-t. spire,** flèche à bout doré; **ivory-t. walking stick,** canne à pomme d'ivoire.

topper ['tɔpər], *s.* **1.** *F:* chapeau *m* haut de forme; haut-de-forme *m, pl.* hauts-de-forme. **2.** *F: O:* type épatant, chose épatante. **3.** *Agr:* **t. harvester,** arracheuse-décolleteuse *f.*

topping[1] ['tɔpiŋ], *a. F: O:* excellent, formidable, chouette.

topping[2], *s.* **1.** (*a*) écimage *m*, étêtement *m* (d'un arbre); pincement *m* (d'une plante); (*b*) *Petr:* étêtage *m*; **t. plant,** unité de fractionnement; (*c*) **t. out,** *NAm:* **t. off,** cérémonie *f* qui marque l'achèvement de la construction d'un grand immeuble. **2.** *Nau:* apiquage *m* (d'une vergue); **t. lift,** martinet *m*, balancine *f*, cartahu *m*. **3.** *Hort:* couverture *f* (de terreau, etc.). **4.** *Cu: F:* garniture *f* (pour un dessert, etc.).

topple ['tɔpl]. **1.** *v.i.* (*a*) **to t. (down, over),** tomber, s'écrouler, culbuter, dégringoler; **the whole lot toppled over,** tout a basculé; tout a chaviré; **to bring the government toppling,** faire tomber le gouvernement; renverser le gouvernement; (*b*) chanceler, vaciller, branler. **2.** *v.tr.* (*a*) **to t. sth. down, over,** faire tomber, faire dégringoler, qch.; jeter qch. à bas; (*b*) faire écrouler (un édifice, etc.); (*c*) renverser (un gouvernement, etc.).

top-rank(ing) ['tɔpræŋk(iŋ)], *a.* de haute volée, de première volée, de premier rang; **t.-r. civil servant,** haut fonctionnaire.

topsail ['tɔpsl], *s. Nau:* hunier *m*; (*of cutter*) flèche *f*; **main t.,** grand hunier; **t. schooner,** goélette carrée; goélette à huniers.

topside ['tɔpsaid], *s.* **1.** *Cu:* tende *f* de tranche (de bœuf). **2.** *Nau:* **topsides,** hauts *m*, œuvres mortes, accastillage *m* (d'un navire).

topsoil ['tɔpsɔil], *s.* terre végétale; couche *f* arable.

topsy-turvy [tɔpsi'tə:vi], *adv. & a.* sens (*m*) dessus dessous; **to turn sth. t.-t.,** mettre qch. sens dessus dessous; renverser, bouleverser, culbuter, qch.; *F:* chambouler qch.; **the whole world's t.-t., the whole world's turned t.-t.,** c'est le monde renversé; c'est le monde à l'envers; **everything's t.-t.,** tout est en désarroi.

top-up ['tɔpʌp], *s. F:* (*a*) *Aut:* (remplissage *m* d')appoint *m*; (*b*) (*when serving drinks*) **let me give you a t.-up,** encore un peu?

topweight ['tɔpweit], *s. Turf:* (*a*) poids attribué au cheval le plus chargé dans un handicap; top-weight *m*; (*b*) cheval le plus chargé (dans un handicap).

toque [touk], *s.* **1.** *Cost:* toque *f.* **2.** *Z:* **t. (monkey, macaque),** macaque *m.*

tor [tɔ:r], *s.* pic *m*, massif *m* de roche, tor *m* (dans le sud-ouest de l'Angleterre).

Torah ['tɔ:rə], *s. Jew.Rel:* Torah *f*, T(h)ora *f.*

torbanite ['tɔ:bənait], *s. Miner:* torbanite *f.*

torbernite ['tɔ:bə:nait], *s. Miner:* torbénite *f*, torbernite *f*, chalcolit(h)e *f.*

torc [tɔ:k], *s. A. Cost:* torque(s) *m*, torquis *m* (des Gaulois, etc.).

torcel ['tɔ:sel], *s. Ent:* (ver *m*) macaque *m.*

torch [tɔ:tʃ], *s.* **1.** torche *f*, flambeau *m*; **to hand on the t.,** passer, transmettre, le flambeau (à la génération suivante); **to carry a, the, t. for a cause,** prendre en main, embrasser, épouser, une cause; **t. fishing,** pêche *f* aux flambeaux; **t. race,** course *f* aux flambeaux; *Gr.Ant:* lampadophorie *f*, lampadodromie *f*; *Bot:* **t. thistle,** cierge épineux; **great t. thistle,** cierge du Pérou. **2. (electric) t.,** lampe *f* (électrique), torche (électrique) (de poche). **3.** (*a*) *Tchn: esp. NAm:* **oxyacetylene cutting t.,** chalumeau *m* (oxyacétylénique) de découpage; oxycoupeur *m*; (*b*) *Av:* allumeur *m*. **4.** *U.S: F:* pyromane *mf*, incendiaire *mf.*

torchbearer ['tɔ:tʃbɛərər], *s.* porte-flambeau *m inv.*

torchlight ['tɔ:tʃlait], *s.* lumière *f* de(s) torche(s), de(s) flambeau(x); **by t.,** à la clarté, à la lueur, des flambeaux; aux flambeaux; **t. procession, tattoo,** cortège, retraite, aux flambeaux; défilé aux flambeaux.

torchon ['tɔ:ʃ(ə)n], *s.* **t. (lace),** dentelle *f* torchon; **t. paper,** papier *m* torchon (pour peinture à l'aquarelle).

tore [tɔ:r], *s.* **1.** *Arch:* tore *m*, boudin *m*. **2.** *Mth:* tore.

toreador ['tɔriədɔ:r], *s.* toréador *m*, torero *m*; *Cost:* **t. pants,** pantalon corsaire.

toric ['tɔ:rik], *a. Mth: etc:* torique; *Opt:* **t. lens,** verre torique.

torment[1] ['tɔ:ment], *s.* **1.** *esp. Lit:* tourment *m*, torture *f*, supplice *m*; **the t. of Tantalus,** le supplice de Tantale; **the torments of jealousy,** les tourments de la jalousie; **he suffered torments,** il souffrait horriblement; il souffrait le martyre; **to be in t.,** être au supplice. **2.** (source *f* de) tourment; *F: O:* **that child is a positive t.,** cet enfant est assommant.

torment[2] [tɔ:'ment], *v.tr.* (*a*) *esp. Lit:* tourmenter, torturer (qn); **tormented with neuralgia,** en proie aux névralgies; **tormented with remorse,** tourmenté par les remords; rongé de remords; en proie aux remords; **he is not tormented by ambition,** l'ambition ne le travaille point; (*b*) faire enrager, embêter (qn); taquiner (qn, un chat, etc.); **the poor horse was being tormented by flies,** des taons harcelaient le pauvre cheval.

tormentil ['tɔ:məntil], *s. Bot:* tormentille *f.*

tormenting [tɔ:'mentiŋ], *a. esp. Lit:* (remords, etc.) torturant, brûlant.

tormentor [tɔ:'mentər], *s.* **1.** (*a*) *Hist:* tourmenteur *m*, bourreau *m*; (*b*) tourmenteur, -euse; harceleur, -euse; *F:* raseur, -euse. **2.** *Cin:* panneau insonorisé (de studio).

tormina ['tɔ:minə], *s.pl. Med:* tranchées *f*, coliques *f.*

torminal, torminous ['tɔ:minəl, -nəs], *a. Med:* torminal, -aux; tormineux.

tornado, *pl.* **-oes** [tɔ:'neidou, -ouz], *s.* tornade *f*; tornado *m*; **t. lantern, lamp,** lanterne de tempête; **t. of cheers,** acclamations effrénées.

toroid ['tɔ:rɔid], *s. Mth:* tore *m.*

toroidal [tɔ:'rɔidl], *a. Mth: etc:* toroïdal, -aux.

torose [tɔ'rous], **torous** ['tɔ:rəs], *a. Nat.Hist:* qui présente des protubérances; noueux.

Torpedinidae [tɔ:pi'dinidi:], *s.pl. Ich:* torpédinidés *m.*

torpedo[1], *pl.* **-oes** [tɔ:'pi:dou, -ouz], *s.* **1.** *Ich:* **t. (fish),** torpille *f.* **2.** *Navy: etc:* torpille; **aerial t.,** torpille aérienne; **t. bomber, carrier,** avion torpilleur; avion porte-torpilles; **homing t.,** torpille à tête chercheuse; **motor t. boat,** vedette lance-torpilles; vedette rapide; **t. recovery,** repêchage *m* de torpilles; **t. tube,** (tube *m*) lance-torpille(s) *m inv*; tube de lancement; **submerged t. tube,** tube lance-torpilles sous-marin; *O:* **t. net(ting),** filet pare-torpilles; filet de protection; **t. launching gear,** appareil, dispositif, lance-torpilles; **t. evasion,** manœuvre(s) d'autoprotection contre torpilles; **within t. range,** à portée de lancement (de torpilles); **t. officer,** officier torpilleur; **t. gunner,** maître principal torpilleur. **3.** (*a*) *Rail:* pétard *m*; (*b*) *Min:* torpille; **t. igniter,** inflammateur de torpille.

torpedo[2], *v.tr.* torpiller (un navire, un puits de pétrole); **to t. the negotiations,** faire échouer, torpiller, les pourparlers.

torpedoing [tɔ:'pi:douiŋ], *s.* torpillage *m* (d'un navire, d'un puits de pétrole, d'un projet, etc.).

torpedoman, *pl.* **-men** [tɔ:'pi:doumæn, -men], *s.m. Navy:* torpilleur.

torpid ['tɔ:pid]. **1.** *a.* engourdi, léthargique, inerte, torpide; **t. state of an animal,** engourdissement *m* d'un animal; *Med:* **t. liver,** foie paresseux. **2.** *s.pl.* (*at Oxford University*) **torpids,** courses *f* à l'aviron de début de saison.

torpidity [tɔ:'piditi], **torpidness** ['tɔ:pidnis], *s.* = TORPOR; *Nau:* **torpidity of the compass,** stagnation *f* du compas.

torpor ['tɔ:pər], *s.* torpeur *f*, engourdissement *m*, abattement *m*, léthargie *f*, inertie *f*; **summer t.,** estivation *f* (des serpents, etc.).

torps [tɔ:ps], *s. Navy: F:* officier *m* torpilleur.

torquate(d) ['tɔ:kweit, tɔ:'kweitid], *a. Nat.Hist:* (*of bird, etc.*) à collier.

torque[1] [tɔ:k], **torques** ['tɔ:kwi:z], *s. A.Cost:* torque(s) *m*, torquis *m* (des Gaulois, etc.).

torque[2], *s.* (*a*) *Mec: Ph: etc:* moment *m* de torsion, de rotation; couple *m* (de torsion); **(motor) t.,** couple (moteur); **starting t.,** couple de, au, démarrage; **opposing t.,** couple antagoniste; **resisting t.,** couple résistant; **restoring t.,** (i) couple de rappel; (ii) *Av:* couple redresseur; **locked rotor t.,** couple au frein; **pull-out t.,** couple maximum constant à vide, couple de décrochage; **pull-in t.,** couple maximum constant en charge, couple d'accrochage; **t. load,** couple de serrage; **t. (reaction),** couple de renversement; effort *m* de torsion; *Mch:* **t. tube,** arbre *m* de conjugaison; tube *m* de couple, de torsion, de réaction; **t. wrench,** clef *f*, bras *m*, dynamométrique; *Aut:* **t. arm,** jambe *f* de réaction, de force; *Av:* **propellor t.,** couple d'hélice; **stalling t.,** couple de décrochage; **t. limiter,** limiteur *m* de couple; **t. link,** ciseaux *mpl*; **t. pin,** support *m* de couple (frein); *El:* **armature t.,** couple d'induit; **t. motor,** moteur couple; (*b*) *Mec:* torseur *m.*

torqued [tɔ:kt], *a. Her:* tortillé.

torquemeter ['tɔ:kmi:tər], *s. Mec: Ph: etc:* torsiomètre *m.*

torrefaction [tɔri'fækʃ(ə)n], *s.* torréfaction *f.*

torrefy ['tɔrifai], *v.tr.* torréfier.

torrefying ['tɔrifaiiŋ], *a.* torréfiant.

torrent ['tɔrənt], *s.* torrent *m*; **mountain t.,** torrent de montagne; **it's raining in torrents,** il pleut à torrents, à verse; **t. of abuse, of tears,** torrent, déluge *m*, d'injures, de larmes.

torrential [tɔ'renʃ(ə)l], *a.* **1.** torrentiel; **we've had t. rain,** nous avons eu une pluie diluvienne, torrentielle. **2.** (*of stream*) torrentueux.

torrentially [tɔ'renʃəli], *adv.* torrentiellement; à torrents, à flots torrentiels.

Torricellian [tɔri'tʃeliən], *a. Ph:* (expérience, tube) de Torricelli; **T. vacuum,** vide *m* de Torricelli; chambre *f* barométrique.

torrid ['tɔrid], *a.* (chaleur, zone, terre) torride.

torridity [tɔ'riditi], **torridness** ['tɔridnis], *s.* chaleur *f*, caractère *m*, torride.

torsade [tɔ:'seid, -'sɑ:d], *s.* torsade *f.*

torse [tɔ:s], *s. Her:* torque *f* (de heaume).

torsel ['tɔ:sl], *s.* **1.** *Arch: etc:* ornement *m* en spirale; volute *f.* **2.** *Const:* tasseau *m.*

torsion ['tɔ:ʃ(ə)n], *s. Mec: etc:* torsion *f*; **t. test,** essai *m* de torsion; **t. balance,** balance *f* de torsion; **t. electrometer,** électromètre *m* de torsion; **t. meter,** torsiomètre *m*; *Mch: Aut:* **t. bar,** barre *f* de torsion.

torsional ['tɔ:ʃən(ə)l], *a. Mec: etc:* de torsion; **t. stress, strain,** effort *m* de torsion; **t. strength,** résistance *f* à la torsion; **t. stiffness,** rigidité *f*, raideur *f*, à la torsion; **t. deflection,** déformation due à la, par, torsion.

torsk [tɔ:sk], *s. Ich:* brosmius *m*, brosme *m*, torsk *m.*

torso, *pl.* **-os** ['tɔ:sou, -ouz], *s.* torse *m.*

tort [tɔ:t], *s. Jur:* acte *m* dommageable; préjudice *m*; délit civil.

torta ['tɔ:tə], *s. Metall:* tourte *f.*

torteau, *pl.* **-eaux** ['tɔ:tou, -ouz], *s. Her:* tourteau *m.*

torticollis [tɔ:ti'kɔlis], *s. Med:* torticolis *m.*

tortillé ['tɔ:tijei], *a. Her:* tortillé.

tortillon ['tɔ:tijɔn], *s. Art:* tortillon *m.*

tortilly [tɔ:'tili], *a. Her:* tortillé.

tortious ['tɔ:ʃəs], *a. Jur:* **1.** dommageable, préjudiciable. **2.** *A:* délictueux.

tortiously ['tɔ:ʃəsli], *adv. Jur:* d'une façon préjudiciable (à qn).

tortoise ['tɔ:təs], *s.* **1.** (*a*) *Rept:* tortue *f*; **freshwater, marsh, t.,** émyde *f*; **common, European, pond t., box t.,** cistude *f* (d'Europe), tortue boueuse, des marais; **Greek t.,** tortue grecque; **mud t.,** (tortue) bourbeuse *f*; **crevice t.,** tortue des fissures; **musk t.,** tortue musquée; **elephant t.,** tortue éléphantine; **giant elephant t., (of the Galapagos),** tortue éléphantine géante; **(African) leopard t.,** tortue léopard; **he moves like a t.,** il avance à pas de tortue, d'un pas de tortue; (*b*) *Ent:* **t. beetle,** scarabée *m* tortue; (*c*) *Bot:* **t. plant,** testudinaire *f*, pied *m* d'éléphant. **2.** *Rom.Ant:* tortue (de boucliers).

tortoiseshell ['tɔ:təʃel], *s.* (*a*) écaille *f* (de tortue, synthétique); **t. comb,** peigne en écaille; **spectacles with t. frames,** lunettes à monture d'écaille; (*b*) **t. cat,** chat écaille de tortue; (*c*) *Ent:* **t. (butterfly),** (vanesse *f*) tortue *f*; **large t.,** grande tortue; **small t.,** petite tortue; vanesse de l'ortie.

tortricid ['tɔ:trisid], *a.* & *s. Ent:* tortricide (*m*), tortricidé (*m*).

Tortricidae [tɔ:'trisidi:], *s.pl. Ent:* tortricides *m*, tortricidés *m.*

tortrix, *pl.* **trices** ['tɔ:triks, tɔ:'traisi:z], *s. Ent:* (*a*) **T.,** tortrix *m*; (*b*) tortricide *m*, tortricidé *m*, tordeuse *f.*

Tortuga [tɔ:'tu:gə], *Pr.n. Geog:* **La T.,** la Tortue.

tortuosity [tɔ:tju'ɔsiti], **tortuousness** ['tɔ:tjuəsnis], *s.* (*a*) courbures *fpl*, ondulations *fpl*, tortuosité *f* (d'un sentier, etc.); (*b*) détours *mpl*; tortuosité (de la pensée, etc.).

tortuous ['tɔ:tjuəs], *a.* **1.** (repli, moyen) tortueux; **t. descent,** descente sinueuse; **t. style,** style contourné; **to have a t. mind,** avoir l'esprit tortu. **2.** *Mth:* **t. curve,** courbe *f* gauche.

tortuously ['tɔ:tjuəsli], *adv.* tortueusement.

torture[1] ['tɔ:tʃər], *s.* **1.** torture *f*; **to put s.o. to (the) t.,** mettre qn à la torture; appliquer, infliger, la torture, le supplice, à qn; **instrument of t.,** instrument de torture; appareil tortionnaire; **t. chamber,** chambre de torture. **2.** torture, tourment *m*, supplice; **the day was one long t.,** cette journée fut un long calvaire.

torture[2], *v.tr.* torturer (qn); mettre (qn) à la torture, au supplice; appliquer, infliger, la torture, le supplice, à (qn); **tortured mind,** esprit à la torture; **tortured by remorse,** tenaillé par le remords; **he was tortured by jealousy,** la jalousie le torturait. **2.** torturer, dénaturer (un texte); forcer (le sens des mots).

torturer ['tɔ:tʃərər], *s.* (*a*) tortionnaire *m*; (*b*) *Hist:* bourreau *m.*

torturing[1] ['tɔ:tʃəriŋ], *a. Lit:* (remords) torturant.

torturing[2], *s.* (mise *f* à la) torture; (mise au) supplice.

torula, *pl.* **-ae** ['tɔr(j)ulə, -i:], *s.* **1.** *Fung:* torule *m.* **2.** *Med:* torulose *f*, cryptococcose *f*, blastomycose européenne.

torulose ['tɔr(j)ulous], **torulous** ['tɔr(j)uləs], *a. Nat.Hist:* toruleux.

torulosis [tɔr(j)u'lousis], *s. Med:* = TORULA 2.

torulus, *pl.* **-i** ['tɔr(j)uləs, -ai], *s. Ent:* torule *m* (d'antenne).

torus, *pl.* **-i** ['tɔ:rəs, -ai], *s.* **1.** *Arch:* tore *m*, boudin *m*; **lower t.,** toron *m*, tondin *m.* **2.** *Bot:* réceptacle (floral); thalamus *m.* **3.** *Mth:* tore.

Tory ['tɔ:ri], *a.* & *s. Pol:* tory (*m*).

Toryism ['tɔ:riizm], *s. Pol:* torysme *m.*

tosh [tɔʃ], *s. F: O:* bêtises *fpl*, blague(s) *f*(*pl*); bourrage *m* de crâne; **the papers are full of t.,** les journaux sont remplis d'idioties.

toss[1] [tɔs], *s.* **1.** (*a*) lancée *f*, lancement *m*, jet *m* (d'une balle, etc.); *Cr:* **full t.,** balle qui arrive sur le guichet sans avoir rebondi sur le sol; (*b*) coup *m* de pile ou face; **to win, lose, the t.,** gagner, perdre, à pile ou face; (*c*) *F:* **they didn't give a t. (about it),** ils s'en foutaient complètement. **2. t. of the head,** mouvement de tête impatient, dédaigneux; **she threw up her head with a scornful t.,** elle a eu un mouvement de tête dédaigneux. **3.** chute *f* (de cheval, etc.); **to take a t.,** tomber (de cheval, etc.); faire une chute (de cheval, etc.); *F:* ramasser une pelle, une gamelle.

toss[2], *v.* **(tossed** [tɔst])

I. *v.tr.* & *i.* **1.** *v.tr.* (*a*) lancer, jeter (une balle, etc.) en l'air; (*of bull*) lancer (qn) en l'air; (*of horse*) démonter, désarçonner (un cavalier); **to t. sth. to s.o.,** jeter qch. à qn; **to t. s.o. in a blanket,** faire sauter qn en l'air sur une couverture; **everything was tossed high into the air,** tout a été envoyé voltiger en l'air; **to t. the salad,** mélanger, *F:* fatiguer, touiller, la salade; *Nau:* **to t. (the) oars,** mâter les avirons; (*b*) **to t. a coin,** jouer à pile ou face; *v.i.* **to t. for sth.,** jouer qch. à pile ou face; **to t. who will begin,** jouer à pile ou face à qui commencera; **who's going to pay?—I'll t. you for it,** qui va payer?—décidons-le à pile ou face; **to t. for sides,** choisir les camps (à pile ou face); (*c*) **to t. one's head,** relever la tête d'un air dédaigneux, méprisant; faire un mouvement de tête; (*of horse*) **to t. its head,** hocher de la tête du nez; encenser; (*d*) agiter, secouer, ballotter; **to be tossed about,** être ballotté, cahoté, secoué; *Lit:* **tossed on the waves,** ballotté, tourmenté, par les flots; (*e*) *Min:* laver à la cuve (le minerai d'étain, etc.). **2.** *v.i.* (*a*) **to t. and turn, to t. (about), in bed,** se tourner et se retourner dans son lit; **to t. (and turn) in one's sleep,** s'agiter dans son sommeil; (*b*) **to t. on the waves,** être ballotté par les flots; ballotter sur les flots; (*of ship*) **to pitch and t.,** tanguer; **branches tossing in the wind,** branches secouées par le vent; (*c*) (*of waves*) s'agiter; clapoter.

II. (*compound verb*) **toss off,** *v.tr.* avaler d'un trait, lamper, *F:* siffler, s'enfiler (un verre de vin); expédier (une tâche); écrire (un article) au pied levé, de chic; trousser (une épigramme); laisser tomber, lâcher (une remarque).

tosser ['tɔsər], *s.* lanceur, -euse.

tossing ['tɔsiŋ], *s.* **1.** (*a*) lancement *m* en l'air (d'une balle, etc.); (*b*) **t. (up) of a coin,** jeu *m* à pile ou face. **2. t. of the head,** mouvement de tête impatient, dédaigneux. **3.** agitation *f*, secousses *fpl*, ballottement *m*; **we got a t. in the Channel,** nous avons été secoués dans la Manche; nous avons eu une mauvaise traversée. **4.** *Min:* lavage *m* à la cuve.

tosspot ['tɔspɔt], *s. A:* ivrogne *m.*

toss-up ['tɔsʌp], *s.* (*a*) (*of coin*) coup *m* de pile ou face; (*b*) affaire *f* à issue douteuse; **it's a complete t.-up,** les chances sont égales; **it's a t.-up which is the worse,** autant vaut être mordu d'un chien que d'une chienne.

tost [tɔst], *a. A:* & *Lit:* (= **tossed**) **tempest-t.,** ballotté par la tempête.

tot[1] [tɔt], *s.* **1. (tiny) t.,** tout(e) petit(e) enfant; **books for tiny tots,** livres pour les tout petits. **2.** *F:* goutte *f*, petit verre (de whisky, etc.); *Nau:* boujaron *m* (de rhum).

tot[2], *s.* colonne *f* de chiffres à additionner; addition *f.*

tot[3], *v.* **(totted) 1.** *v.tr.* **to t. up a column of figures,** additionner une colonne de chiffres; faire le total d'une colonne de chiffres; **to t. up expenses,** faire le compte des dépenses; additionner les dépenses; **he has totted up 2,500 hours flying time,** il totalise 2.500 heures de vol. **2.** *v.i.* (*of expenses, etc.*) **to t. up,** s'élever (**to,** à); **the bill tots up to £100,** la note se monte à £100.

total[1] ['toutl]. **1.** *a.* (*a*) total, -aux; entier; complet; global, -aux; **the t. number of inhabitants,** le nombre total des habitants; **the t. population,** la population totale; **the t. population is about 10,000,** la population totalise à peu près 10.000 personnes; **t. amount,** somme totale, globale; **t. capital,** capital global; **t. tonnage,** tonnage global; **t. war,** guerre totale; *Ph:* **t. (internal) reflection,** réflexion totale; (*b*) **the t. loss of his fortune,** la perte totale de sa fortune; **they were in t. ignorance of it,** ils l'ignoraient complètement; **t. failure,** échec complet; *F:* four noir; **t. eclipse,** éclipse totale. **2.** *s.* total *m*; montant *m*; tout *m*; **grand t.,** total global; **sum t.,** somme totale; **the t. amounts to £100,** la somme s'élève à £100; **to add up the t. of the amounts,** faire le total des sommes; *Cmptr:* **batch t.,** total par groupe.

total[2], *v.tr.* & *i.* **(totalled) 1.** additionner, totaliser (les dépenses). **2. to t., to t. up to, £100,** s'élever à, se monter à, totaliser, £100; **the armies totalled 300,000 men,** les armées s'élevaient à un total de 300.000 hommes.

totalitarian [toutæli'tɛəriən], *a. Pol:* totalitaire.

totalitarianism [toutæli'tɛəriənizm], *s. Pol:* totalitarisme *m.*

totality [tou'tæliti], *s.* **1.** totalité *f.* **2.** *Astr:* obscuration totale (d'un astre pendant une éclipse).

totalization [tout(ə)lai'zeiʃ(ə)n], *s.* totalisation *f.*

totalizator ['tout(ə)laizeitər], *s. Turf:* totalisateur *m*, totaliseur *m* (des paris).

totalize ['tout(ə)laiz], *v.tr.* additionner, totaliser (les dépenses, etc.).

totalizer ['tout(ə)laizər], *s. Turf:* = TOTALIZATOR.

totally ['tout(ə)li], *adv.* totalement, entièrement, complètement; **he's t. incapable of doing it,** il en est totalement incapable.

tote[1] [tout], *s. Turf: F:* = TOTALIZATOR.

tote[2], *v.tr. esp. NAm:* transporter (des marchandises, etc.); porter (un sac, un revolver, etc.); **t. bag,** grand sac (à provisions, etc.); *Ind:* **t. box,** caisse *f* de manutention.

totem ['toutəm], *s.* totem *m*; **t. pole,** mât *m* totémique; mât-totem *m.*

totemic [tou'temik], *a.* totémique.

totemism ['toutəmizm], *s.* totémisme *m.*

totemist ['toutəmist], *s.* totémiste *mf.*

totemistic [toutə'mistik], *a.* totémistique.

t'other, tother ['tʌðər], *a.* & *pron. Dial:* & *F:* (= **the other**) **where's t. cup?** où est l'autre tasse? **I can't tell one from t., t. from which,** je ne peux pas les distinguer l'un de l'autre.

Totipalmatae [toutipæl'meiti:], *s.pl. Orn:* totipalmes *m.*

totipalmate [touti'pælmeit], *a. Orn:* totipalme.

totter[1] ['tɔtər], *s.* chancellement *m*; **with a t.,** d'un pas chancelant; en chancelant.

totter[2], *v.i.* **1.** (*of pers.*) chanceler, tituber; vaciller sur ses jambes; **to t. to one's feet,** se relever en chancelant; **to t. in, out, away,** entrer, sortir, s'éloigner, en trébuchant, d'un pas mal assuré, d'un pas chancelant. **2.** (*of building, government*) menacer ruine; chanceler, branler.

totter[3], *s. F:* chiffonnier *m.*

tottering[1] ['tɔtəriŋ], *a.* chancelant, titubant, vacillant; **t. steps,** pas chancelants, mal assurés; **t. wall, empire,** mur, empire, qui menace ruine, qui croule.

tottering[2], *s.* chancellement *m*; démarche chancelante, titubante, vacillante.

tottery ['tɔtəri], *a.* chancelant, titubant; mal assuré; peu solide; (bâtiment) branlant, qui menace ruine.

totting ['tɔtiŋ], *s. F:* chiffonnerie *f.*

Touareg ['twɑ:reg], *s.* **1.** *Ethn:* Targui, *pl.* Touareg, *f.* Targuia, *pl.* Targuiat. **2.** *Ling:* tamachek *m.*

toucan ['tu:kæn], *s. Orn:* toucan *m*; **green-billed t.,** toucan à bec vert.

toucanet ['tu:kənet], *s. Orn:* toucanet *m*; **spot-billed t.,** toucanet à bec tacheté.

touch[1] [tʌtʃ], *s.* **1.** (*a*) toucher *m*, contact *m*; **to give s.o. a t.,** toucher qn; **I felt a t. on my arm,** j'ai senti qu'on me touchait le bras; **the engine starts at the first t. of the starter,** le moteur démarre du premier coup, au quart de tour; (*of firework, etc.*) **t. paper,** papier *m* d'amorce; (*b*) *Mil:* **elbow t.,** le coude à coude; **to keep t.,** garder le tact des coudes; (*c*) *Med:* **vaginal t.,** toucher vaginal; (*d*) *Games: A:* jeu *m* du chat. **2.** (le sens du) toucher; tact *m*; **hard, soft, to the t.,** dur, mou, au toucher; **to know sth. by the t.,** reconnaître qch. au toucher; **to have a delicate sense of t.,** avoir une grande finesse de tact. **3.** (*feel*) toucher; **the cold t. of marble,** le contact froid du marbre. **4.** (*a*) léger coup; **t. of, with, a stick,** léger coup de baguette; **to give one's horse a t. of the spurs,** toucher son cheval de l'éperon; (*b*) touche *f* (de pinceau); coup (de crayon); **to add a few touches to a picture,** faire quelques retouches *f*, ajouter quelques touches, à un tableau; **to put the finishing touch(es), to add the final t., to sth.,** mettre la dernière main, la dernière touche, à qch.; donner le coup de pouce, *F:* le coup de fion, à qch.; **as a final t.,** comme touche finale, comme dernière touche; (c) *Magn:* **magnetization by single, double, divided, t.,** aimantation *f* par touche simple, double, par touches séparées. **5.** (a) **sculptor with a bold, a light, t.,** sculpteur au ciseau hardi, délicat; **delicate t. (with, of, the brush),** coup de pinceau délicat; **this dress has an individual t. about it,** cette robe a un cachet spécial; **tennis player who has lost his t.,** joueur de tennis qui a perdu la main; **this room needs a woman's t.,** toute influence féminine fait défaut dans cette pièce; (b) *Mus:* toucher; **to have a light t. (on the piano),** avoir un toucher délicat. **6.** (a) pointe *f*, grain *m*, nuance *f*, soupçon *m*; **t. of salt, of garlic,** pointe de sel, d'ail; **t. of jealousy,** pointe, grain, de jalousie; **t. of malice, of irony,** teinte *f* de malice, d'ironie; **there's a t. of colour in her cheeks,** ses joues ont pris un peu de couleur; **handkerchief with just a t. of scent,** mouchoir discrètement parfumé; **the first touches of autumn,** les premières atteintes de l'automne; **there was a t. of bitterness in his reply,** il a répondu avec une nuance d'amertume; **he watched me with a t. of envy,** il m'a regardé avec un brin d'envie; **a t. of originality,** une note d'originalité; **t. of nature,** (i) trait naturel; (ii) action qui suscite la sympathie des autres; brin d'émotion; (b) **t. of fever, of flu, of malaria,** soupçon de fièvre; une petite grippe; légère attaque de paludisme. **7.** contact; **to be in t. with s.o.,** être, se tenir, en contact avec qn; avoir des relations, des rapports, avec qn; être en rapport avec qn; **to get in t. with s.o.,** joindre, contacter, qn; prendre, se mettre en, contact avec qn; *Mil:* prendre contact, établir la liaison, avec (une unité, etc.); **I'll be in t.,** je vous ferai signe; **to get in t. with the police,** se mettre en communication avec la police; **I can't get in t. with him,** je n'arrive pas à le joindre; **to put s.o. in t. with s.o.,** mettre qn en relations, en rapport, avec qn; **to put two people in t. with one another,** mettre deux personnes en contact; **to keep in t. with s.o.,** (i) rester en contact avec qn; (ii) être en sympathie avec qn; **to be in t. with the situation,** être au courant de la situation; **to keep s.o. in t. with sth.,** tenir qn au courant de qch.; **to be out of t. with foreign affairs,** ne plus être au courant des affaires étrangères; **to be out of t., to have lost t., with s.o.,** ne plus être en communication avec qn; perdre qn de vue. **8.** *Fb:* touche; **kick into t.,** envoi *m* de touche; **out of t.,** hors des touches; *Rugby Fb:* **t.-in-goal,** touche de but; **t. judge,** juge *m* de touche. **9.** (a) **it was t. and go whether we would catch the train,** nous courions grand risque de manquer le train; **it was t. and go with him,** il revient de loin; il a frôlé la mort; (b) **a t.-and-go affair,** une affaire très incertaine, très risquée; une affaire hasardeuse. **10.** *F:* **to make a t., to put the t. on s.o.,** emprunter de l'argent à qn, taper qn; **I'm broke, I'll have to try a t.,** je suis à sec, il me faut taper quelqu'un, trouver quelqu'un à taper; **easy, soft, t.,** personne à qui on emprunte de l'argent facilement. **11.** *A:* pierre *f* de touche; **to put sth. to the t.,** mettre qch. à l'épreuve.

touch[2], *v.tr. & i.*

I. *v.tr.* **1.** (a) toucher; **to t. sth. with one's finger, with a stick,** toucher qch. du doigt, avec un bâton; **to t. s.o. on the shoulder, on the arm,** toucher qn à l'épaule; toucher le bras à qn; **to t. s.o. lightly,** (i) toucher légèrement qn; (ii) effleurer qn; **to t. one's hat, one's forehead,** porter, mettre, la main à son chapeau, à son front; **he touched his hat to me,** il m'a salué; *Hist:* **to t. s.o. for the King's evil,** guérir les écrouelles par attouchement; **t. wood!** touche du bois! **don't t. those eggs, my papers,** ne touchez pas à ces œufs; ne tripotez pas, ne dérangez pas, mes papiers; **don't t.!** on ne touche pas! n'y touchez pas! *F:* pas touche! **I wouldn't t. it with a bargepole,** *U.S:* **a ten foot pole,** je ne voudrais pas y toucher avec des pincettes; je n'en veux à aucun prix; (*of ship*) **to t. a rock,** toucher un écueil; **to t. the bottom,** *v.i.* **to t.,** toucher le fond; toucher; **to t. land,** toucher terre; aborder, atterrir; *Nau:* **to t. the wind,** *v.i.* **to t.,** tâter le vent; (b) (*be in contact with*) toucher (à) (qch.); **his garden touches mine,** son jardin touche au mien, touche le mien; **point where the tangent touches the circle,** point où la tangente rencontre le cercle; point de contact de la tangente et du cercle; (c) toucher, effleurer (les cordes de la harpe); *Lit:* **to t. the harp,** toucher (de) la harpe; **to t. a spring,** faire jouer un ressort; **he touched the bell,** il a appuyé sur le bouton de la sonnette; *Equit:* **to t. one's horse with the spur,** piquer son cheval de l'éperon; (d) *v.ind.tr.* **to t. on a subject,** aborder, effleurer, un sujet; **I have already touched on these questions,** j'ai déjà abordé ces questions; (e) toucher, atteindre; *Fenc:* **to t. one's opponent,** toucher, boutonner, son adversaire; **the law can't t. him,** la loi ne peut rien contre lui; il est hors de l'atteinte de la loi; **I can just t. the ceiling,** je peux tout juste toucher le plafond; **the curtains t. the floor,** les rideaux descendent jusqu'au plancher; les rideaux touchent à terre; **no one can t. him in comedy,** il n'y a personne pour l'égaler, personne ne peut l'approcher, dans la comédie; (f) **I never t. wine,** (i) je ne bois jamais de vin; (ii) je ne supporte pas le vin. **2.** (a) produire de l'effet sur (qch.); **the file will not t. it,** la lime ne mord pas dessus; *F:* (*of remedy, etc.*) **to t. the spot,** aller à la racine du mal; **to t. s.o. on a raw spot, on a tender spot,** toucher qn à l'endroit sensible; toucher qn où cela le blesse. **3.** toucher, affecter, émouvoir, attendrir (qn); **to be touched by s.o.'s kindness,** être touché de, par, la bonté de qn; **it touched me to the heart,** cela m'a touché le cœur; **to t. s.o. to the quick,** toucher qn au vif. **4.** *O:* toucher, concerner, intéresser, regarder (qn); **the question touches you closely,** la question vous touche de près; c'est une question où vous êtes intéressé. **5. flowers touched by the frost,** fleurs atteintes par la gelée. **6.** *F:* **to t. s.o. for a fiver,** taper, faire casquer, qn de cinq livres.

II. *v.i.* **1.** (*of pers., thgs*) se toucher; (a) être en contact; (b) venir en contact; **the two ships touched,** les deux navires ont touché. **2.** *Nau:* **to t. at a port,** toucher, aborder à, un port; faire relâche, faire escale, à un port; mouiller.

III. (*compound verbs*) **1. touch down.** (a) *v.tr. & i. Rugby Fb:* toucher dans les buts; (b) *v.i. Av:* atterrir, faire escale; *Space: F:* alunir.

2. touch in, *v.tr. Art:* dessiner, ajouter (un trait, etc.).

3. touch off, *v.tr.* décharger (un canon, etc.); faire partir, faire exploser (une mine).

4. touch up, *v.tr.* (a) faire des retouches à (un tableau); (*of paintwork*) faire des raccords (de peinture); aviver, raviver, relever, rehausser, rafraîchir (les couleurs de qch.); enjoliver (un récit); retaper, retravailler, fignoler (un ouvrage); rafraîchir (le fil d'un outil, etc.); badigeonner (un vieux meuble, etc.); *P:* peloter (qn); **to t. up a manuscript (belonging to s.o. else),** blanchir un manuscrit; (b) toucher (un cheval) du fouet; *O:* **to t. up s.o.'s memory,** rafraîchir la mémoire de qn.

touchable ['tʌtʃəbl], *a.* tangible; palpable.

touchback ['tʌtʃbæk], *s. Fb: U.S:* touche *f* (dans son propre but).

touchdown ['tʌtʃdaun], *s.* **1.** *Rugby Fb:* touché-en-but *m.* **2.** *Av:* atterrissage *m*; *Space:* alunissage *m.*

touché ['tu:ʃei], *int.* touché!

touched ['tʌtʃt], *a.* **1.** *Nau:* **t. bill of health,** patente brute, suspecte. **2. t. (in the head),** toqué, timbré; qui a le cerveau un peu dérangé; **he's slightly t.,** il a un (petit) grain.

toucher ['tʌtʃər], *s.* (a) *Games:* (*at bowls*) boule *f* en contact avec le cochonnet; (b) *A:* **that was as near as a t.,** il était moins une.

touch(-)hole ['tʌtʃhoul], *s. Artil: A:* lumière *f* (d'un canon).

touchily ['tʌtʃili], *adv.* avec susceptibilité, avec humeur.

touchiness ['tʌtʃinis], *s.* susceptibilité *f*, irascibilité *f.*

touching[1] ['tʌtʃiŋ]. **1.** *a.* touchant, émouvant, attendrissant, pathétique. **2.** *prep. O: & Lit:* touchant, concernant; **as t. the defence of the town,** en ce qui concerne la défense de la ville.

touching[2], *s.* **1.** touche *f*; contact *m.* **2. t. up,** (i) retouches *fpl*; (ii) rehaussement *m*, avivage *m* (d'une couleur).

touchingly ['tʌtʃiŋli], *adv.* d'une manière touchante, émouvante.

touchline ['tʌtʃlain], *s. Fb: Rugby Fb:* ligne *f* de touche; *Rugby Fb:* **t. judge,** juge *m* de touche.

touch-me-not ['tʌtʃminɔt], *s. Bot:* balsamine *f*, impatiente *f.*

touchstone ['tʌtʃstoun], *s.* **1.** *Miner:* pierre *f* de touche; basanite *f*; jaspe noir. **2.** *Fig:* pierre de touche; critérium *m*; **time is the t. of merit,** le temps est la pierre de touche du mérite.

touch-type ['tʌtʃtaip], *v.i.* taper au toucher.

touch-typing ['tʌtʃtaipiŋ], *s.* dactylographie *f* (au toucher).

touch-up ['tʌtʃʌp], *s. Art: Dressm: etc:* retouche *f*; rehaut *m* (d'une couleur).

touchwood ['tʌtʃwud], *s.* amadou *m.*

touchy ['tʌtʃi], *a.* susceptible, irascible, ombrageux; **to be t.,** se piquer facilement, pour un rien; se froisser, s'offusquer, facilement; avoir l'épiderme chatouilleux, sensible; **he's very t.,** il prend feu comme de l'amadou; **he's very t. on that point,** il n'entend pas raillerie là-dessus; **to be t. on a point of honour,** être délicat, chatouilleux, sur le point d'honneur.

tough [tʌf], *a.* **1.** dur, tenace, résistant; *Bot:* cartilagineux; **t. meat,** viande coriace, dure; **t. wood, metal,** bois, métal, dur, résistant. **2.** (*of pers., etc.*) fort, solide; **t. constitution,** tempérament fort, solide, endurant; tempérament dur à la peine, à la tâche; **to become t. (through training),** s'endurcir. **3.** (*of pers.*) raide, inflexible, opiniâtre, obstiné; *F:* **a t. guy,** un dur, un coriace; **he's a t. customer,** il n'est pas commode; c'est un dur à cuire; **to be, get, t. with s.o.,** être, se montrer, dur envers qn. **4.** *F:* (a) (*of task, etc.*) rude, difficile; **it was a t. job,** ç'a été une dure, une rude, besogne; (b) **t. luck!** quelle malchance! quelle déveine! quelle guigne! pas de chance! **that's t.!** c'est dur pour vous! (c) **a t. cure,** un remède de cheval. **5.** *NAm: F:* (a) (homme) brutal, violent, criminel; (b) *s.* brute *f*, sale type *m.*

toughen ['tʌfn]. **1.** *v.tr.* (a) durcir; **toughened glass,** verre trempé; (b) endurcir (qn). **2.** *v.i.* (a) durcir; (b) (*of pers.*) s'endurcir.

toughie ['tʌfi], *s. F:* **1.** (a) homme brutal, violent; brute *f*; (b) un dur, un coriace. **2.** problème difficile à résoudre, casse-tête *m inv.*

toughly ['tʌfli], *adv.* **1.** durement; avec ténacité. **2.** vigoureusement. **3.** obstinément, avec opiniâtreté.

toughness ['tʌfnis], *s.* **1.** dureté *f*; ténacité *f*, résistance *f*; (*of meat*) coriacité *f*; **t. of a metal,** ténacité, résistance, d'un métal. **2.** (a) force *f*, solidité *f*; (b) résistance à la fatigue. **3.** (a) inflexibilité *f*, opiniâtreté *f*; (b) *F:* caractère *m* peu commode (de qn). **4.** difficulté *f* (d'un travail).

toupee, toupet ['tu:pei], *s. Hairdr:* **1.** *A:* toupet *m.* **2.** (faux) toupet; mèche *f* postiche.

tour[1] [tuər], *s.* **1.** voyage *m* (circulaire); voyage touristique; excursion *f*; **conducted t., guided t.,** (i) voyage touristique accompagné; voyage organisé; (ii) (*in museum, etc.*) visite dirigée, guidée; **inclusive t.,** *U.S:* **all-expense t.,** voyage à forfait, à prix forfaitaire; voyage organisé; **world t.,** voyage autour du monde; *Hist:* **the grand t.,** le grand tour (en Europe); **walking t.,** excursion, randonnée *f*, voyage, à pied; **we were on a t. through France,** nous faisions un voyage en France. **2.** tournée *f*; (a) **t. of inspection,** tournée d'inspection; **t. of duty,** (i) tour *m* d'équipe, de service; poste *m* de travail; (ii) journée *f* (de travail); durée quotidienne (de travail); (b) *Th:* **to take a company on t.,** emmener une troupe en tournée; **company, orchestra, on t.,** troupe, orchestre, en tournée.

tour[2]. **1.** *v.tr. & i.* (a) **to t. a country,** faire le tour d'un pays; voyager dans un pays; **they're touring in Canada,** ils font un grand voyage au Canada; (b) *Th:* **the play will t. the provinces in the spring,** la pièce passera en province au printemps, sera donnée en tournée au printemps. **2.** *v.tr. Th:* **the play has not been toured for some years,** la pièce n'a pas été au répertoire des tournées depuis quelques années.

touraco ['tuərəkou], *s. Orn:* touraco *m.*

tourbillion [tuə'biliən], *s. Pyr:* tourbillon *m.*

tourer ['tuərər], *s.* voiture *f* de tourisme; **open t.,** torpédo *f.*

touring[1] ['tuəriŋ], *a.* **t. cyclist,** cycliste en randonnée; **t. party,** groupe de touristes; **t. car,** voiture de tourisme; **open t. car,** torpédo *f*; *Th:* **t. company,** troupe en tournée.

touring[2], *s.* tourisme *m*; **t. information,** renseignements *m* touristiques.

tourism ['tuərizm], *s.* tourisme *m.*

tourist ['tuərist], *s.* touriste *mf*; *Hist:* **the English grand tourists in the 18th century,** les Anglais qui faisaient leur voyage en Europe au 18e siècle; **t. agency,** agence *f*, bureau *m*, de tourisme; **t. centre,** centre *m*, ville *f*, de tourisme, touristique; **t. ticket,** billet *m* circulaire; **t. information,** renseignements *m* touristiques; **the t. trade is a considerable source of income to this country,** le tourisme apporte à ce pays des revenus considérables; **this town has an important t. trade,** cette ville reçoit beaucoup de touristes; *F:* **t. trap,** attrape-touristes *m inv.*

touristic [tuə'ristik], *a.* touristique; de touriste(s).

touristy ['tuəristi], *a. F: Pej:* touristique; **this town is very t.,** cette ville est (toujours) inondée de touristes.

tourmalin(e) ['tuəməlin, -li:n], *s. Miner:* tourmaline *f*; **red t.,** rubellite *f*; apyrite *f*; **blue t.,** indicolite *f*; saphir *m* du Brésil; **green t.,** émeraude *f* du Brésil.

tournament ['tuənəmənt], *s.* **1.** *Hist:* (a) tournoi *m*; (b) carrousel *m.* **2.** *Games: Sp: etc:* tournoi (de tennis, etc.); concours *m* (d'échecs, etc.); **(challenge) t.,** challenge *m*; **ladder t.,** tournoi éliminatoire, pyramidal; **fencing t.,** poule *f* à l'épée; challenge d'escrime; **water t.,** joute *f* sur l'eau; joute lyonnaise, aquatique; *Cards:* **bridge t.,** tournoi de bridge; **pairs t.,** tournoi par paires.

tournette [tuə'net], *s. Cer:* tournette *f.*

tourney ['tə:ni], *s. Hist:* tournoi *m.*

tourniquet ['tuənikei], *s. Med:* tourniquet *m*, garrot *m.*

tousle ['tauzl], *v.tr.* **1.** *A:* houspiller, tirailler, maltraiter (qn). **2.** ébouriffer, écheveler (les cheveux de qn); mettre (les cheveux de qn) en désordre; **tousled hair,** cheveux ébouriffés, échevelés, en broussaille, embroussaillés, mal peignés.

tout[1] [taut], *s.* **1.** (*for hotels*) rabatteur, -euse; (*for insurance companies*) démarcheur, -euse; (*for shops, shows, etc.*) racoleur *m*; *F:* bonisseur *m*; **business t.,** rabatteur d'affaires; placier, -ière, démarcheur. **2.** *Turf:* **(racing) t.,** (i) individu qui suit secrètement l'entraînement des chevaux, à l'affût des tuyaux; espion, -onne; (ii) donneur, -euse, de tuyaux.

tout[2]. **1.** *v.tr.* (*a*) *A:* guetter (qn, qch.); espionner (qn); (*b*) *Turf:* suivre secrètement (les chevaux de course) à l'entraînement; *v.i.* **to t. round,** espionner dans les écuries. **2.** (*a*) *v.i.* **to t. for customers, for custom,** courir après la clientèle; racoler des clients; **to t. at the shop door,** faire la porte; (*b*) *v.tr.* **to t. s.o. for his custom,** solliciter les commandes de qn; importuner qn avec des offres de service; (*c*) **to t. a product (around),** faire l'article d'un produit.

touter ['tautər], *s. A:* = TOUT[1].

touting ['tautiŋ], *s.* **1.** racolage *m*, démarchage *m*. **2.** *Turf:* espionnage *m*.

touzle ['tauzl], *v.tr.* = TOUSLE.

tow[1] [tou], *s.* **1.** (câble *m*, corde *f*, de) remorque *f*. **2. to take a boat, a car, in t.,** prendre un bateau, une voiture, en, à la, remorque; donner la remorque à un bateau, à une voiture; touer un bateau; **to be taken in t.,** se mettre à la remorque; **one of the pressmen kindly took me in t.,** un des journalistes a bien voulu me servir de guide; **to be on, in, t.,** être à la remorque; **boat in t.,** embarcation à la traîne; **he always has his family in t.,** il remorque, trimbale, toujours toute sa famille avec lui; il traîne toujours avec lui toute sa smala; **we can give you a t.,** nous pourrons remorquer votre voiture; *Aut: etc:* **on t.,** en remorque; **t. hook,** croc de remorque; **t. bar,** (i) *Veh:* timon de remorque; (ii) *Av:* barre de remorquage (d'un planeur); *Aut: U.S:* **t. car, truck,** dépanneuse *f*. **3.** (*a*) (*vessel towed*) remorque; (*b*) **a t. of barges,** une rame de péniches.

tow[2], *v.tr.* remorquer (un navire, une voiture); prendre (un navire, une voiture) en, à la, remorque; touer (un chaland); donner la remorque à (un navire désemparé); (*from towpath*) haler (une péniche, un chaland); *Nau:* **to t. astern,** remorquer en arbalète, en flèche; **to t. a ship alongside,** remorquer un navire à couple; **to be towed out of harbour,** sortir du port à la remorque; **my car's been towed away by the police,** la police a saisi ma voiture.

tow[3], *s.* étoupe (blanche); filasse *f*; **to put, stuff, t. in a chink,** étouper une crevasse; *Nau:* **hank of t. (for caulking),** quenouillon *m*; (*of pers.*) **t.-headed,** aux cheveux (blond) filasse.

towage ['touidʒ], *s.* (*a*) remorquage *m*, touage *m*; (*on canal*) halage *m*; (*b*) **t. (dues),** (droit *m*, frais *mpl*, de) remorquage.

toward[1] ['touəd], *a. A:* **1.** (*also* **towards**) proche; tout près; **the feast is t.,** le festin est proche; le festin approche. **2.** (*of pers.*) (*a*) prometteur, -euse; (*b*) obligeant, affable.

toward[2] [tə'wɔ:d, twɔ:d], *prep. Lit:* = TOWARDS.

towardly[1] ['touədli], *adv. A:* **1.** d'une façon prometteuse. **2.** docilement, sagement.

towardly[2], *a. A:* **1.** (moment, etc.) propice, favorable. **2.** prometteur, -euse; **a t. child,** un enfant qui promet. **3.** (*a*) docile, obéissant; (*b*) obligeant, affable.

towards [tə'wɔ:dz, twɔ:dz], *prep.* **1.** (*a*) vers; du côté de; **t. the town,** vers la ville, du côté de la ville; **he came t. me,** il est venu vers moi; **scepticism is the first step t. truth,** le scepticisme est le premier pas vers la vérité; (*b*) (*with no idea of movement*) **t. the north,** vers le nord. **2.** envers, pour, à l'égard de (qn); **his attitude t. me,** son attitude envers moi; **his feelings t. me,** ses sentiments envers, pour, moi; ses sentiments vis-à-vis de moi, à mon égard; **the attitude of France t. foreign exchanges,** l'attitude de la France vis-à-vis des échanges internationaux; la France et les échanges internationaux. **3.** pour; **to save t. the children's education,** économiser pour, en vue de, l'éducation des enfants; **would you like to give something t. it?** voudriez-vous y contribuer quelque chose? **4.** (*of time*) vers, sur; **t. noon,** vers midi; **t. evening,** vers le soir; **t. the end of the journey,** vers la fin du voyage; **t. the end of the century,** vers la fin du siècle; **t. the middle, the end, of his life,** vers le milieu, sur la fin, de sa vie.

towboat ['toubout], *s.* remorqueur *m*, toueur *m*.

towel[1] ['tauəl], *s.* **1.** serviette *f* (de toilette); essuie-main(s) *m inv*; **roller t.,** essuie-main(s), serviette, sans fin (pour rouleau); essuie-main(s) à rouleau; **beach t.,** serviette de plage, pour la plage; **Turkish t.,** serviette éponge; **paper t.,** serviette en papier; *esp. NAm:* **dish t.,** torchon *m* (à vaisselle), essuie-verres *m inv*, *Fr.C:* linge *m* à vaisselle; **t. rail,** porte-serviettes *m inv* (en applique); séchoir *m* (à serviettes); **t. rack, horse,** chevalet *m* (pour serviettes); porte-serviettes *m inv* (mobile). **2. sanitary t.,** serviette hygiénique; serviette périodique.

towel[2], *v.tr.* **(towelled)** essuyer, frotter (qn) avec une serviette; **to t. oneself (dry),** s'essuyer (après le bain, etc.).

towelling ['tauəliŋ], *s.* **1.** friction *f* avec une serviette. **2.** tissu-éponge *m*; **t. robe,** peignoir en tissu-éponge; *F:* éponge *f*.

tower[1] ['tauər], *s.* **1.** (*a*) *Arch: Const:* tour *f*; **angle t.,** tour d'angle (d'un château); **t. of a windmill,** tour d'un moulin à vent; **the T. of Babel,** la tour de Babel; **the T. of London,** la Tour de Londres; **the Eiffel T.,** la Tour Eiffel: **the T. of silence,** la tour de silence; **church t.,** clocher *m*; **clock t.,** tour de l'horloge (de Westminster, etc.); **observation, conning, t.,** tour d'observation; baignoire *f*; **lookout, fire, t.,** tour de guet; **shot t.,** tour à fondre la dragée (de chasse); *Hyd.E:* **water t.,** château *m* d'eau; *Navy:* **armoured t.,** blockhaus *m*; **conning t.,** (i) (*in warship*) blockhaus; (ii) (*in submarine*) kiosque *m*, baignoire *f*; **t. block,** tour, immeuble-tour *m*, *pl.* immeubles-tours; *Moll:* **t. shell,** turritelle *f*; **he is a t. of strength,** c'est un puissant appui, un puissant secours; (*b*) *Av:* **control t.,** tour de contrôle; **beacon t.,** tour balise; **parachute t.,** tour d'instruction de parachutistes; *Ball:* **umbilical t.,** tour de remplissage (pour le ravitaillement de fusées); (*c*) *Ind: Ch:* **bubble, fractionating, t.,** tour de fractionnement; **stripping t.,** tour de rectification; *Ch:* **Gay-Lussac t.,** tour de Gay-Lussac; **Glover t.,** tour de Glover. **2.** (*a*) *Civ.E:* **(iron framework) t.,** pylône *m* (d'aérodrome, de réseau électrique, etc.); **t. crane,** grue à pylône; *W.Tel: etc:* **t. antenna,** antenne pylône; **radiating t.,** pylône d'émission; **television relay t.,** pylône relais de télévision; (*b*) *Rail: U.S:* **signal t.,** cabine *f* de signaux. **3.** *Ven:* montée *f* en chandelle (d'un oiseau blessé).

tower[2] ['tauər], *v.i.* **1. the castle towered above, over, the valley,** le château dominait la vallée; **he towered above the crowd,** sa haute taille dominait la foule; **he towers above his contemporaries,** il domine tous ses contemporains. **2.** (*of bird*) planer; monter très haut (en l'air); (*of wounded bird*) monter en chandelle; (*of hawk*) prendre son essor; monter.

tower[3] ['touər], *s.* haleur *m*, toueur *m* (d'une péniche, etc.).

towered ['tauəd], *a.* **1.** défendu par une tour, par des tours; surmonté d'une tour, de tours; flanqué de tours. **2.** *Lit:* (*with adj. prefixed, e.g.*) **high-t.,** aux tours élevées.

towering ['tauəriŋ], *a.* **1.** (*a*) très haut, très élevé; **a t. height,** une très grande hauteur; (*b*) *Lit:* **t. ambition,** ambition sans bornes, démesurée. **2.** (*of rage*) violent, extrême; **in a t. rage,** au paroxysme de la colère; dans une colère noire, furibonde; furieux.

towerman, *pl.* **-men** ['tauəmən], *s.m. Rail: U.S:* aiguilleur.

towhee [tə'(h)wi:, -'hi:, 'touhi:], *s. Orn:* **t. (bunting),** pinson *m* d'Amérique aux yeux rouges, *Fr.C:* tohi *m*; **eastern t.,** tohi commun; **green-tailed t.,** tohi à queue verte.

towing ['touiŋ], *s.* remorque *f*, remorquage *m*, touage *m*; (*from towpath*) halage *m*; *Aut:* **suspended t.,** remorquage suspendu; *Adm:* **t. zone,** zone de touage; **t. charge,** (droit *m*, frais *mpl*, de) remorquage; *Veh:* **t. pole,** timon de remorquage.

towline ['toulain], *s.* **1.** remorque *f*; câble *m*, corde *f*, de remorque; corde, grelin *m*, de halage; hale *f*; halin *m*; touline *f*; câbliau *m*, cordelle *f*; *Nau:* **to give, pass, a t.,** donner la remorque; **to haul the t. aboard,** prendre la remorque. **2.** *Fish:* ligne traînante.

town [taun], *s.* **1.** (*a*) ville *f*; **provincial, country, t.,** ville de province; **fortified t.,** place forte; place de guerre; **to go out on the t.,** faire la bombe, la noce; **t. life,** vie urbaine; **t. clothes,** toilette de ville (de femme); *Mil.Hist:* **t. major,** major de la garnison; commandant d'armes, de place; **t. adjutant,** adjudant de la garnison; **t. clerk** = secrétaire de marie; secrétaire de municipalité; **t. councillor,** conseiller municipal; **t. council,** conseil municipal; **t. hall,** hôtel *m* de ville; mairie *f*; maison commune; **t. house,** (i) maison de, en, ville; hôtel particulier; (ii) résidence urbaine; **town houses,** rangée *f* de maisons de style uniforme; **t. centre,** (i) centre *m* de la ville; (ii) *Aut: P.N:* centre ville; **t. gas,** gaz de ville; **t. water supply,** adduction *f* des eaux de ville; *Com:* **t. cheque,** chèque sur place; (*b*) *U.S:* (*in New England*) commune *f*; (*c*) (*inhabitants*) **the whole t. is talking about it,** toute la ville en parle; **half the t. was killed,** la moitié de la ville a été tuée. **2.** (*without article*) (*a*) Londres *m*; **to live in T.,** habiter Londres; **to do one's shopping in T.,** faire ses achats à Londres; (*b*) **to go into t., up to t.,** aller, se rendre, à la, en, ville; **to live in t.,** demeurer (i) dans la, en, ville, (ii) à la ville; **to be in t.,** être en ville; **he's in t.,** (i) (*of pers. living in the country*) il est à la ville; (ii) (*of pers. not at home*) il est en ville; **she's in t. shopping this morning,** elle fait ses courses en ville ce matin; **he's out of t.,** il est à la campagne, en voyage; **to leave t.,** quitter la ville; aller en province; **man, woman, about t.,** mondain, -aine; *F:* **they really went to t.,** ils s'y sont jetés à corps perdu; **she's really going to t. over the kitchen,** elle se lance dans de grosses dépenses pour la décoration de la cuisine; *Sch:* **t. and gown,** les habitants de la ville et les étudiants.

townee ['tauni(:)], *s. F: Pej:* habitant, -ante, de la ville.

townet ['tounet], *s. Fish:* filet traînant; drague *f*; senne *f*, seine *f*.

townsfolk ['taunzfouk], *s.pl.* habitants *m* de la ville; citadins *m*.

township ['taunʃip], *s.* **1.** commune *f*; bourg *m*. **2.** (*a*) *NAm:* municipalité *f*, *Fr. C:* canton *m*; (*in Canada*) **the Eastern Townships,** les cantons de l'est; (*b*) *U.S:* (*in New England*) commune; (*c*) *NAm: Surv:* lotissement *m* (de 36 milles carrés). **3.** *Austr:* site (aménagé en vue de la construction) d'une ville. **4.** (*in S. Africa*) banlieue noire.

townsite ['taunsait], *s. NAm:* site (aménagé en vue de la construction) d'une ville.

townsman, *pl.* **-men** ['taunzmən], *s.m.* habitant de la ville; citadin.

townspeople ['taunzpi:pl], *s.pl.* habitants *m* de la ville; citadins *m*.

townswoman, *pl.* **-women** ['taunzwumən, -wimin], *s.f.* habitante de la ville; citadine.

towpath ['toupɑ:θ], *s.* chemin, *m*, banquette *f*, de halage; halage *m*.

towrope ['touroup], *s.* remorque *f*; câble *m*, corde *f*, de remorque; corde, grelin *m*, de halage; hale *f*; halin *m*; touline *f*; câbliau *m*, cordelle *f*.

toxaemia [tɔk'si:miə], *s. Med:* toxémie *f*; **t. of pregnancy,** toxémie gravidique.

toxalbumins [tɔks'ælbju:minz], *s.pl. Bio-Ch:* toxalbumines *f*.

toxic ['tɔksik], *a. & s. Med:* toxique (*m*).

toxicant ['tɔksikənt], *a. & s.* toxique (*m*).

toxicity [tɔk'sisiti], *s.* toxicité *f*.

Toxicodendron [tɔksikou'dendrən], *s. Bot:* toxicodendron *m*; rhus *m*.

toxicoderma [tɔksikou'də:mə], *s. Med:* toxi(co)dermie *f*.

toxicogenic [tɔksikou'dʒenik], *a.* toxicogène.

toxicologic(al) [tɔksikə'lɔdʒik(l)], *a. Med:* toxicologique.

toxicologist [tɔksi'kɔlədʒist], *s.* toxicologue *mf*, toxicologiste *mf*.

toxicology [tɔksi'kɔlədʒi], *s. Med:* toxicologie *f*.

toxicomania [tɔksikou'meiniə], *s. Med:* toxicomanie *f*.

toxicophagous [tɔksi'kɔfəgəs], *a.* toxicophage.

toxicosis [tɔksi'kousis], *s. Med:* toxicose *f*.

toxigenic [tɔksi'dʒenik], *a. Bio-Ch:* toxigène.

toxi-infection [tɔksiin'fekʃ(ə)n], *s. Med:* toxi-infection *f*.

toxin ['tɔksin], *s. Bio-Ch:* toxine *f*.

toxinaemia [tɔksi'ni:miə], *s. Med:* toxinhémie *f*.

toxinfection [tɔksin'fekʃ(ə)n], *s. Med:* toxi-infection *f*.

toxinfectious [tɔksin'fekʃəs], *a. Med:* toxi-infectieux.

toxiphagus [tɔk'sifəgəs], *s.* toxicophage *mf*.

toxiphobia [tɔksi'foubiə], *s. Med:* toxicophobie *f*.

toxodont ['tɔksoudɔnt], *s. Paleont:* toxodonte *m*, toxodon *m*.

Toxodont(i)a [tɔksou'dɔnt(ʃi)ə], *s.pl. Paleont:* toxodontes *m*, toxodons *m*.

Toxoglossa [tɔksou'glɔsə], *s.pl. Moll:* toxoglosses *m*.

toxoglossate [tɔksou'glɔseit], *s. Moll:* toxoglosse *m*.

toxoid ['tɔksɔid], *s. Med:* toxoïde *m*, anatoxine *f*.

toxophilite [tɔk'sɔfilait], *s.* amateur *m* de tir à l'arc.

toxophily [tɔk'sɔfili], *s.* tir *m* à l'arc.

toxoplasm ['tɔksouplæzm], *s. Bac:* toxoplasme *m*.

toxoplasmosis [tɔksouplæz'mousis], *s. Med:* toxoplasmose *f*.

toy[1] [tɔi], *s.* **1.** (*a*) jouet *m*; amusette *f*; (*child's word*) joujou *m*, *pl.* joujoux; **t. shop,** magasin de jouets; **t. box,** boîte à jouets, à joujoux; **t. railway,** chemin de fer mécanique, électrique (d'enfant); **t. trumpet,** trompette d'enfant; **t. theatre,** théâtre de marionnettes; **t. soldier,** soldat de plastique, de plomb, etc.; *Mus:* **the T. Symphony,** la Foire des Enfants (de Haydn); (*b*) **t. dog,** (i) chien *m* de manchon; bichon *m*; (ii) chien en bois, en peluche, etc.; **t. spaniel, poodle,** épagneul, caniche, de petite taille; (*c*) *esp. Lit:* **a t. army, a t. Napoleon,** une petite armée pour rire; un Napoléon pour rire. **2.** *A: & Lit:* bagatelle *f*, brimborion *m*, colifichet *m*.

toy[2], *v.i.* **1. to t. with sth.,** jouer avec, manier, tripoter, qch.; **she was toying with her necklace,** elle jouait avec son collier; **to t. with one's food,** manger du bout des lèvres, des dents; grignoter, chipoter; **to t. with an idea,** caresser une idée; **he toyed with the idea of going to Australia,** il a envisagé la possibilité d'aller en

Australie. **2. to t. with s.o.,** badiner, flirter, avec qn; **to t. with s.o.'s affections,** jouer avec les affections de qn.
trabant ['træbənt], *s.* **1.** *A.Mil:* traban *m*, draban *m*. **2.** *Biol:* trabant *m*, satellite *m*.
trabea, *pl.* **-eae** ['treibiə, -ii:], *s. Rom.Ant:* trabée *f*.
trabeate(d) ['treibieit(id)], *a. Arch:* à entablement; **t. ceiling,** plafond *m* à poutres en saillie.
trabeation [treibi'eiʃ(ə)n], *s. Arch:* entablement *m*, trabéation *f*.
trabecula, *pl.* **-ae** [træ'bekjulə, -i:], *s. Anat: Nat.Hist:* trabécule *f*.
trabecular [træ'bekjulər], *a. Nat.Hist:* trabéculaire.
Trabzon ['træbzɔn], *Pr.n. Geog:* Trébizonde.
trace[1] [treis], *s.* **1.** *(a) usu.pl.* trace(s) *f(pl)* (de qn, d'un animal); empreinte *f* (d'un animal); **traces of wheels in the snow,** traces, empreinte, de roues dans la neige; *(b) U.S:* piste *f*; chemin *m*; **sheep t. (on a hill),** sentier fait par le passage de moutons (sur une pente). **2.** *(a)* trace, vestige *m*; **no t. was found of the explorers,** on n'a trouvé aucune trace des explorateurs; **they could find no t. of him,** on n'a pas pu retrouver sa trace; **there is no t. of the old castle,** il ne reste plus de trace, aucun vestige, du vieux château; **she has still some traces of beauty,** elle a des restes de beauté; **there's not a t. of it,** (i) il n'en reste pas de trace; (ii) cela ne se voit plus, n'y paraît plus; *(b)* trace, quantité *f* minime; soupçon *m*; **a t. of arsenic,** une trace, une quantité minime, d'arsénic; **a t. more salt,** encore un soupçon de sel; *(in tea, etc.)* **just a t. of milk,** un nuage, un soupçon, de lait; *Biol:* **t. element,** oligo-élément *m*, *pl.* oligo-éléments. **3.** *(a) Fort:* tracé *m*; *(b)* **radar t.,** signe *m*, image *f*, sur l'écran radar; **t. reader,** dispositif *m* de lecture de traces; *(c) (in cathode ray tube)* trace du spot. **4.** *St.Exch:* filière *f*.
trace[2], *v.*
I. *v.tr.* **1.** tracer (un plan); **to t. out a line of conduct (for oneself),** (se) tracer une ligne de conduite. **2.** *(a)* **to t. a plan, a diagram,** faire le tracé d'un plan, d'un diagramme; *(b)* calquer, contre-tirer (un dessin). **3.** suivre la trace, la piste (de qn, d'une bête); suivre (qn, une bête) à la trace, à la piste; **to t. lost goods,** recouvrer des objets perdus; **I can't t. it,** je n'en trouve pas la trace; **they traced him as far as Paris,** on a suivi sa piste jusqu'à Paris; **the crime was traced to him,** on a établi qu'il était l'auteur du crime; **to t. the evil to its source,** remonter à la source du mal. **4.** retrouver les vestiges, relever les traces (d'un ancien édifice, etc.); retracer, retrouver (une influence, etc.); **I can't t. any reference to it,** je n'en trouve trace d'aucune mention.
II. *(compound verb)* **trace back,** *v.tr.* **to t. sth. back to its source,** remonter jusqu'à l'origine de qch.; **to t. one's family back to the Conqueror,** faire remonter sa famille à Guillaume le Conquérant; **the rumour has been traced back to its originator,** on a découvert l'auteur de ce bruit.
trace[3], *s.* **1.** *Harn:* trait *m*; **in the traces,** attelé; **t. horse,** cheval *m* de renfort, en arbalète; côtier *m*; *Veh:* **t. block,** volée (de devant) (à laquelle sont attachés les traits); **the horse kicked over the traces,** le cheval s'est empêtré dans les traits; *F: (of pers.)* **to kick over the traces,** (i) s'insurger; ruer dans les brancards; (ii) s'émanciper; faire des frasques. **2.** *Fish:* bas *m* de ligne; armure *f*.
tracer ['treisər], *s.* **1.** *(a) (pers.)* traceur, -euse (d'un plan, etc.); calqueur, -euse; *(b) (device)* traçoir *m*; calquoir *m*. **2.** *Mil: etc:* **t. shell,** traçant *m*; **t. bullet,** (balle) traçante *f*. **3.** *(a) Ch:* **t. (substance),** substance révélatrice; *(b)* traceur (radioactif); corps marqué; indicateur *m*; élément marqueur.
traceried ['treisərid], *a.* (fenêtre) à réseau, à remplage.
tracery ['treisəri], *s.* **1.** *Arch:* réseau *m*, remplissage *m*, entrelacs *m* (d'une rosace, etc.); remplage *m*, tympan *m*, croisillons *mpl*, découpures *fpl* (d'une fenêtre gothique). **2.** réseau, filigrane *m*, nervures *fpl* (d'une feuille, d'une aile d'insecte, d'une dentelle, etc.).
trachea, *pl.* **-eae** [trə'ki:ə, -ii:], *s.* *(a) Anat:* trachée (-artère) *f*; *(b) Nat.Hist:* trachée (d'insecte, de plante).
tracheal [trə'ki:əl], *a. Anat: Ent:* trachéal, -aux; **t. gills,** trachéo-branchies *f*.
trachean [trə'ki:ən], *a. Nat.Hist:* trachéen.
tracheate [træ'ki:eit], *a. & s.* **t. (arthropod),** trachéate *m*.
tracheid [trə'ki:id], *s. Bot:* trachéide *f*.
tracheitis [træki'aitis], *s. Med:* trachéite *f*.
trachelobranchiate [trækəlou'bræŋkieit], *a.* trachélobranche.
trachelorrhaphy [trækəlɔ'ræfi], *s. Surg:* trachélorraphie *f*.
tracheloscapular [trækəlou'skæpjulər], *a. Anat:* trachéloscapulaire.
tracheobronchial [trækiou'brɔŋkiəl], *a. Anat:* trachéobronchique.
tracheobronchitis [trækioubrɔŋ'kaitis], *s. Med:* trachéo-bronchite *f*.
tracheocele [træ'ki:ousi:l], *s. Med:* trachéocèle *f*.
tracheole ['trækioul], *s. Ent:* trachéole *f*.
tracheophone ['trækioufoun], *s. Orn:* trachéophone *m*.
Tracheophonae [trækiou'founi:], *s.pl. Orn:* trachéophones *m*.
Tracheophyta [trækiou'faitə], *s.pl. Bot:* trachéophytes *m*.
tracheoscopy [træki'ɔskəpi], *s. Med:* trachéoscopie *f*.
tracheostenosis [trækiou'stenousis], *s. Med:* trachéosténose *f*.
tracheotomize [træki'ɔtəmaiz], *v.tr. Surg:* trachéotomiser.
tracheotomy [træki'ɔtəmi], *s. Surg:* trachéotomie *f*.
trachodont ['trækoudɔnt], *s. Paleont:* trachodon *m*.
trachoma [træ'koumə], *s. Med:* trachome *m*; conjonctivite granuleuse.
trachomatous [træ'koumətəs], *a. Med:* trachomateux.
Trachomedusae [trækioume'dju:si:], *s.pl. Coel:* trachyméduses *f*.
trachurus ['trækərəs], *s. Ich:* trachure *m*.
trachyandesite [træki'ændisait], *s. Miner:* trachyandésite *f*.
trachycarpus [træki'kɑ:pəs], *s. Bot:* trachycarpus *m*.
Trachylina, Trachylinae [træki'lainə, -i:], *s.pl. Coel:* trachylides *m*.
Trachymedusae [trækime'dju:si:], *s.pl. Coel:* trachyméduses *f*.
Trachypteridae [træki(p)'teridi:], *s.pl. Ich:* trachyptéridés *m*.
trachypteroid [træki(p)'terɔid], *s. Ich:* trachyptère *m*.
trachyte ['trækait], *s. Miner:* trachyte *m*.
trachytic [trə'kitik], *a. Miner:* trachytique.
tracing ['treisiŋ], *s.* **1.** *(a)* traçage *m*, tracement *m*, tracé *m*; calquage *m*; **t. paper,** papier *m* calque, à calquer; *Dressm: etc:* **t. wheel,** roulette *f* (à patron, à marquer); *(b) Carp: etc:* **t. iron,** rénette *f*; *(c) Bot:* **t. root,** racine traçante. **2.** *(a)* dessin calqué; calque *m*; **skeleton t.,** croquis-calque *m*, *pl.* croquis-calques; **to make, take, a t. of a plan,** contre-tirer un dessin; *(b) Magn: (of field in iron filings)* spectre *m* magnétique.
track[1] [træk], *s.* **1.** *(a) Ven:* voie *f*, foulées *fpl*, empreintes *fpl*, erre *f*, trace(s) *f(pl)*, piste *f* (d'un animal); **to follow the t.,** suivre la piste; *(in stag hunting)* chasser menée; *(b)* trace(s), piste (de qn); sillage *m*, houa(i)che *f* (d'un navire); trace, empreinte, sillon *m* (d'une roue); **to cross the t. of a ship,** couper, franchir, le sillage d'un navire; **tracks of a car in the snow,** traces d'une, piste tracée par une, voiture dans la neige; **to follow in s.o.'s tracks,** suivre la voie tracée par qn; **to be on s.o.'s t.,** suivre la piste de qn; **he's always on my tracks,** il est toujours sur mon dos; **that'll throw him off the t., cover up my tracks,** ça va le dépister; **to be on the right t.,** être dans la bonne voie, sur la voie; **to be on the wrong t., off the t.,** (i) avoir perdu la piste; être égaré; (ii) *F:* divaguer; **to keep t. of s.o., of sth.,** suivre les progrès de qn, d'une affaire; **I've lost t. of him,** je l'ai perdu de vue; **I've lost t. of his address,** je n'ai plus son adresse; *F:* **to make tracks,** partir, filer, décamper; **they made tracks for home,** ils ont filé vers la maison; **to stop in one's tracks,** s'arrêter net; **to fall, drop, dead in one's tracks,** tomber raide mort; *(c) Veh:* écartement *m* des roues, voie. **2.** *(a)* piste, chemin *m*, sentier *m*; **cart t.,** chemin de terre; **mule t.,** sentier muletier, piste muletière; **sheep t.,** sentier battu par les moutons; **cycle t.,** piste cyclable; *(b) Sp:* **(running, racing) t.,** piste; **cinder t.,** piste cendrée; **obstacle t.,** piste d'obstacles; **t. racing,** courses *fpl* de, sur, piste; **t. and field events,** épreuves *fpl* d'athlétisme; **t. shoes,** chaussures *f*, souliers *m*, de course à pointes; *Aut: etc:* **motor-racing, car-testing, t.,** autodrome *m*; **racing t.,** piste de vitesse; **test t.,** piste d'essai; **t. test,** essai *m* sur piste; *(of racehorse, car, F: of pers.)* **t. record,** carrière *f*, dossier *m*, antécédents *mpl*; **judging by his t. record,** s'il continue comme il a commencé; **to have a good t. record,** avoir remporté beaucoup de succès; avoir plusieurs réussites à son actif; *(c) Rail:* voie (ferrée); **main t.,** voie principale; **single t.,** voie simple, unique; **double t.,** voie double; **single-t., double-t., line,** ligne *f* à une voie, à deux voies; **t. signalled for two-way working,** voie banalisée; **t. clearer,** chasse-pierre(s) *m inv*; **t.-recording coach,** voiture *f* d'inspection; **on the open t.,** en pleine voie; **the train left the t.,** le train a déraillé; *U.S: F:* **across, on the other side of, the tracks,** dans les bas quartiers (de la ville); *(d) Mec.E: etc:* chemin de roulement, de glissement; *Rec: etc:* piste (de disque); voie, piste (de bande magnétique); **sound t.,** piste sonore; *Cmptr:* **card t.,** piste (d'entraînement) de cartes; **feed t.,** piste d'alimentation; **punching t.,** piste de perforation; **reading t.,** piste de lecture; **timing t.,** piste de synchronisation; **t. ball,** boule roulante; **t. pitch,** pas transversal; *(e) U.S: Sch:* **t. system** = TRACKING[1] 4. **3.** *(a)* route *f*, chemin; **t. of a comet,** route, cours *m*, d'une comète; *(b) Av: Nau:* route suivie; **t. angle,** angle *m* de route; **t. chart,** carte *f* de la route suivie; routier *m*; *(c) Av:* plan *m* de rotation (d'une hélice, d'un rotor); *(d) Atom.Ph:* trace (de particules); **nuclear t., ionization t.,** trace nucléaire, d'ionisation; **t. population,** nombre *m* de traces; **t. segment,** segment *m* de trace. **4.** *(a) Veh:* chenille *f*; **t., half-t., vehicle,** véhicule chenillé, semi-chenillé; **t. adjuster, stretcher,** tendeur *m* de chenilles; **t. shoe,** patin *m* de chenille; **t. guard,** garde-chenille *m*, *pl.* garde-chenilles; *(b) Ind:* **erecting t.,** chaîne *f* de montage; tapis roulant.
track[2], *v.*
I. *v.tr.* **1.** suivre (une bête, un voleur, etc.) à la trace, à la piste; pister (le gibier); traquer (un malfaiteur); suivre (un missile) à la trace; poursuivre (un objectif mobile, un satellite, etc.) (au moyen d'une lunette, d'un appareil électronique, etc.). **2.** tracer (un sentier, une voie). **3.** *N.Am:* **to t. the floor,** laisser des empreintes sur le plancher; **to t. mud into the house,** traîner de la boue dans la maison.
II. *v.i.* **1.** *(of gear wheels, etc.)* être en alignement, tourner dans le même plan. **2.** *Rec: (of stylus)* suivre la piste; **to t. at 2 grammes,** suivre la piste avec une force d'appui, d'application, de 2 grammes.
III. *(compound verb)* **track down,** *v.tr.* dépister (le gibier); dépister, acculer (un criminel); dépister (une maladie); rechercher (des erreurs); découvrir, retrouver, les traces de (qch., une influence, etc.).
track[3]. **1.** *v.tr.* haler (un chaland) (à la cordelle). **2.** *v.i. (of barge)* se faire haler, être halé (sur un canal).
trackage[1] ['trækidʒ], *s. N.Am:* réseau *m* ferroviaire.
trackage[2], *s.* **1.** halage *m* (sur les canaux). **2.** frais *mpl* de halage.
tracked [trækt], *a. Veh:* (tracteur, etc.) chenillé, à chenilles.
tracker[1] ['trækər], *s.* **1.** traqueur *m* (de gibier, de criminels); **t. dog,** chien policier. **2.** *(a) Artil:* appareil *m* de pointage continu; *(b) Elcs:* appareil, radar *m*, de poursuite; suiveur *m*; **sun t., star t.,** suiveur solaire, stellaire.
tracker[2], *s.* **1.** *(pers.)* haleur *m* (à la cordelle). **2.** *Mus:* abrégé *m*, demoiselle *f* (d'un orgue).
tracking[1] ['trækiŋ], *s.* **1.** poursuite *f* (d'un animal, de qn) à la piste; **t. (down),** dépistage *m* (du gibier, d'un criminel, d'un virus, d'une erreur, etc.); *Agr:* **t. powder,** poison *m* de piste. **2.** *(a) Elcs: Space:* poursuite; **t. systems,** systèmes *m* de repérage et de poursuite; **t. antenna,** antenne *f* de poursuite; **t. station,** station *f* de dépistage; **sun t., star t.,** poursuite du soleil, d'une étoile, aux instruments; *(b) Cin:* **t. shot,** travelling *m* en poursuite. **3.** *Av:* centrage *m* (d'une hélice, d'un rotor). **4.** *U.S: Sch:* répartition *f* (des élèves) en sections de force homogène.
tracking[2], *s.* halage *m*.
tracklayer ['trækleiər], *s. esp. U.S:* **1.** *Rail: (pers.)* poseur *m* de voie. **2.** véhicule *m* à chenilles.
tracklaying ['trækleiiŋ], *s.* **1.** *Rail:* pose *f* de voie. **2.** *esp. U.S:* **t. vehicle,** véhicule *m* à chenilles.
trackless ['træklis], *a.* **1.** qui ne laisse aucune trace, aucune piste. **2.** sans chemins, sans sentiers; **t. desert,** désert *m* vierge de tout chemin battu; **t. forest,** forêt *f* vierge. **3.** *N.Am:* **t. trolley,** trolleybus *m*.
trackman, *pl.* **-men** ['trækmən], *s.m. Rail:* *(a)* garde-ligne, *pl.* gardes-ligne(s); *(b) esp. U.S:* poseur de voie.
tracksuit ['træks(j)u:t], *s. Sp:* survêtement *m*.
trackway ['trækwei], *s. esp. U.S:* **1.** *(a) Rail:* voie *f*; *(b) (of roadway)* pavé *m*; chaussée *f*. **2.** *Archeol:* voie ancienne, préhistorique. **3.** *Ind:* pont roulant.
tract[1] [trækt], *s.* **1.** étendue *f* (de pays, de sable, d'eau); nappe *f* (d'eau); région (montagneuse, etc.); **vast tracts of desert,** vastes étendues désertiques. **2.** *(a) Anat:* **respiratory t.,** appareil *m* respiratoire; voies *f* respiratoires; **digestive t.,** appareil digestif; voies digestives; **optic tracts,** bandelettes *f* optiques; **sinus t.,** trajet fistuleux; *(b) Orn:* **feather t.,** ptérylie *f*. **3.** *A:* période *f*, espace *m* (de temps).
tract[2], *s.* petit traité; brochure *f*, opuscule *m*, tract *m*; **religious tracts,** petites brochures de piété; **to go round distributing tracts,** se faire colporteur, -euse, faire du colportage, de brochures de piété.
tractability [træktə'biliti], **tractableness** ['træktəbəlnis], *s.* humeur *f* traitable; docilité *f*, douceur *f*.
tractable ['træktəbl], *a.* **1.** *(of pers., character)* docile; traitable; doux, *f.* douce; menable; **t. disposition,** caractère *m* ductile. **2.** *(a) (of material)* facile à ouvrer; ouvrable; *(b) (of device, etc.)* maniable; d'usage facile.
Tractarian [træk'tɛəriən]. *Rel.H:* **1.** *s.* tractarien, -ienne; puseyiste *mf.* **2.** *a.* des tractariens; puseyiste.

Tractarianism [træk'tɛəriənizm], *s. Rel.H:* tractarianisme *m*; puseyisme *m*.
tractate ['trækteit], *s.* traité *m*.
traction ['trækʃ(ə)n], *s.* traction *f*, tirage *m*; (*a*) **steam t.,** traction à vapeur; **mechanical, motor, t.,** traction mécanique, par moteur; **electric t.,** traction électrique; **t. current,** courant *m* d'alimentation; **t. wheels,** roues motrices, roues tractives (d'une locomotive, etc.); **t. cable,** câble tracteur; **t. engine,** tracteur *m*; (*b*) *Med:* traction (d'une luxation); (*in artificial respiration*) **t. of the tongue,** tractions rythmées de la langue.
tractive ['træktiv], *a.* tractif, tirant; tractoire; **t. effort,** effort tractif, de traction.
tractor ['træktər], *s.* **1.** tracteur *m*, mototracteur *m*; *R.t.m:* **Caterpillar t.,** tracteur à chenilles; **wheel-type t.,** tracteur à roues; **breakdown t.,** tracteur à dépannage; **t. trailer unit,** semi-remorque *m*; *Civ.E:* **pusher t.,** pusher *m*; **t. driver,** tractoriste *mf*, conducteur *m* de tracteur; **t.-drawn,** tracté. **2.** *Av:* **t. propeller,** hélice tractive.
tractorist ['træktərist], *s. U.S:* conducteur *m* de tracteur; tractoriste *mf*.
tractory ['træktəri], *s. Mth:* tractoire *f*, tractrice *f*.
tractrix, *pl.* **-ices** ['træktriks, -isi:z], *s. Mth:* courbe *f* tractoire; tractoire *f*, tractrice *f*.
trad [træd]. *F:* (*a*) *a.* traditionnel; (*b*) *s.* jazz *m* Nouvelle Orléans (et ses dérivés).
trade[1] [treid], *s.* **1.** (*a*) métier *m*; commerce *m*; **to follow, carry on, a t.,** exercer un métier, un commerce; **to learn a t.,** apprendre un métier; **he's a plumber, a grocer, by t.,** il est plombier, épicier, de son métier; **he still doesn't know his t., hasn't learnt his t. yet,** il manque encore de métier; **everyone to his t.,** chacun son métier; (*b*) (corps *m* de) métier; **the building t.,** le bâtiment; **the publishing t.,** l'édition *f*; **the printing t.,** l'imprimerie *f*; **the tourist t.,** le tourisme; **to be in the t.,** être du métier; *F: A:* **the T.,** le commerce des boissons et spiritueux; **t. name,** (i) (*product*) appellation commerciale; (ii) (*firm*) nom commercial, raison commerciale; **t. secret,** secret *m* de fabrique; **t. journal, paper,** journal, organe, professionnel; **t. discount,** remise *f*, escompte *m*; **I'll let you have it at t. price,** vous pouvez l'avoir au prix de gros; (*c*) **t. association,** syndicat professionnel; **t., trades, union,** syndicat (ouvrier); (*of workers*) **to form a t. union,** se syndiquer; **t., trades, unionism,** syndicalisme (ouvrier); **t., trades, unionist,** syndicaliste *mf*; (ouvrier, -ière) syndiqué(e). **2.** (*a*) commerce; négoce *m*, affaires *fpl*; **to be in t.,** être dans le commerce; être négociant; être commerçant, -ante; **wholesale, retail, t.,** commerce de gros, de détail; **balance of t.,** balance commerciale; **foreign, external, t.,** commerce étranger, extérieur; **home, domestic, t.,** commerce intérieur; **coastal t.,** cabotage *m*; **t. route,** route commerciale; **the tea t., the cotton t.,** le commerce du thé, du coton; **the ivory t.,** la traite de l'ivoire; **t. is at a standstill,** le commerce est nul; **it's good for t.,** cela fait marcher le commerce; **he's doing a roaring t.,** il fait des affaires d'or; **t. cycle,** cycle *m* économique; **t. bills,** effets *m* de commerce; (*b*) *NAm:* (i) transaction (commerciale); (ii) clientèle *f* (d'une maison); (*c*) **t. winds, trades,** (vents) alizés *m*; (*d*) (**illicit**) **t.,** trafic *m* (des stupéfiants, etc.).
trade[2], *v.*
I. *v.i. & tr.* **1.** *v.i.* (*a*) faire le commerce, le négoce (**in sth.,** de, en, qch.; **with s.o.,** avec qn); faire des affaires, entretenir des relations commerciales (**with s.o.,** avec qn); (*b*) **to t. on, in, one's political influence,** trafiquer de, faire le trafic de, son influence politique; **to t. on s.o.'s ignorance,** exploiter, tirer profit de, l'ignorance de qn; (*c*) **what name does he t. under?** quelle est la raison sociale de sa maison? (*d*) *NAm:* **to t. with the local grocer,** se ravitailler chez l'épicier du quartier. **2.** *v.tr.* **to t. sth. for sth.,** échanger, troquer, qch. contre qch.
II. (*compound verbs*) **1. trade in,** *v.tr.* donner (une voiture, etc.) en reprise.
2. trade off. (*a*) *v.tr.* (i) échanger (qch. contre qch.) (pour arriver à un compromis); (ii) *U.S:* se servir (des outils, etc.) à tour de rôle (pour des besoins différents); (*b*) *v.i. U.S:* **they traded off with each other (year after year) for first place,** ou l'un ou l'autre était placé le premier (selon l'année).
trade-in ['treidin], *s.* objet donné en reprise.
trademark ['treidmɑ:k], *s.* marque *f* de fabrique, de commerce; estampille *f*; **registered t.,** marque déposée; *F:* **all her novels have her t.,** elle imprime sa marque sur tous ses romans.
trade-off ['treidɔf], *s. esp. U.S:* (*a*) échange *m*; compromis *m*; **they feel that they have been let down over the t.-o.,** ils se croient désavantagés par l'échange; **trade-offs between apparently unrelated topics are a feature of diplomacy,** en diplomatie on fait souvent des concessions qui ne semblent avoir aucun rapport l'une avec l'autre; **it was obvious that trade-offs had been made and decisions reached before the meeting,** il était évident qu'on avait déjà fait des concessions et que l'affaire était conclue avant la réunion; (*b*) **the education versus experience t.-o. which governs personnel practices,** l'importance relative du niveau d'enseignement et de la pratique du métier qui détermine le choix du personnel.
trader ['treidər], *s.* **1.** négociant, -ante; commerçant, -ante; marchand, -ande. **2.** *Nau:* navire marchand, de commerce.
tradescantia [trædes'kæntiə, -ʃə], *s. Bot:* tradescantia *m*, tradescantie *f*.
tradesman, *pl.* **-men** ['treidzmən], *s.m.* **1.** marchand, fournisseur; **tradesmen's entrance, tradesmen,** entrée *f* des fournisseurs. **2.** (*a*) artisan *m*; (*b*) *Mil: etc:* spécialiste *m*.
trading ['treidiŋ], *s.* **1.** (*a*) commerce *m*, négoce *m*; *Com: Book-k:* exercice *m*; **t. year,** année *f* d'exploitation; exercice; **t. company,** société commerciale; **t. stamp,** timbre-prime *m*, *pl.* timbres-prime(s); (*b*) (**illicit**) **t.,** trafic *m* (des stupéfiants, etc.); *A:* **slave t.,** traite *f* des noirs. **2. t. in,** vente *f* (de qch.) en reprise.
tradition [trə'diʃ(ə)n], *s.* **1.** tradition *f*; **t. has it that. . .,** selon la tradition . . .. **2.** *Jur:* tradition, transfert *m* (d'un bien).
traditional [trə'diʃənəl], *a.* traditionnel; de tradition.
traditionalism [trə'diʃənəlizm], *s.* traditionalisme *m*.
traditionalist [trə'diʃənəlist], *s.* traditionaliste *mf*.
traditionally [trə'diʃən(ə)li], *adv.* traditionnellement; selon la tradition.
traduce [trə'dju:s], *v.tr. O:* calomnier, diffamer (qn); médire de (qn).
traducement [trə'dju:smənt], *s. O:* calomnie *f*, diffamation *f*; médisance *f*.
traducer [trə'dju:sər], *s. O:* calomniateur, -trice; diffamateur, -trice.
traffic[1] ['træfik], *s.* **1.** (*a*) *A:* commerce *m*, négoce *m* (**in,** de); (*b*) *Pej:* trafic *m*; **the drug t.,** le trafic des stupéfiants; **t. in arms,** trafic des armes; **t. in women and children,** traite *f* des femmes et des enfants. **2.** (*a*) mouvement *m*, circulation *f*; **road t.,** circulation routière; **to block the t.,** arrêter la circulation; **t. jam,** embouteillage *m*; encombrement *m* (de circulation); *U.S:* **the backed-up t.,** les longues files de véhicules arrêtés; **line of moving t.,** colonne de véhicules en marche; **heavy t.,** circulation intense; **there's a great deal of t. on the roads,** les routes sont encombrées; **beware of t.!** attention aux voitures! **heavy t. crossing!** attention aux engins! **to open a road to t.,** livrer une route à la circulation; (**road**) **fit for t.,** (route) viable; **through t.,** circulation directe; **westbound t.,** circulation est-ouest; **restricted t.,** circulation réglementée; **t. regulations,** règlements *m* sur la circulation; **t. circle,** rond-point *m*; **t. island,** refuge *m*; *Aut:* **t. indicator,** indicateur *m* de direction; *Adm:* **t. lights, t. signals,** feux *m* de circulation, de signalisation routière; **turn right at the first t. lights,** tourner à droite au premier feu rouge; **t. control,** régulation de la circulation; **t. engineering,** technique *f* de la circulation (routière); **t. engineer,** technicien, -ienne, de la circulation (routière); *Mil:* **t. headquarters,** bureau *m* des mouvements et de la circulation; (*b*) **ocean t.,** navigation *f* au long cours; (*c*) **rail(way) t.,** trafic ferroviaire; **goods t.,** trafic marchandises; **passenger t.,** trafic voyageurs; **t. department,** (service *m* de) la traction; **t. manager, t. superintendent,** chef *m* du mouvement; (*d*) **telex t.,** trafic télex; **t. capacity,** capacité *f* d'écoulement de trafic.
traffic[2], *v.tr. & i.* (**trafficked** ['træfikt]) (*a*) *A:* faire le commerce (de); (*b*) *Pej:* trafiquer (en stupéfiants, etc.).
trafficator ['træfikeitər], *s. Aut: O:* indicateur *m*, flèche *f*, de direction.
trafficker ['træfikər], *s. Pej:* trafiquant, -ante, trafiqueur, -euse (**in,** de, en); **drug, dope, t.,** trafiquant, traffiqueur, de, en, dans les, stupéfiants.
tragacanth ['trægəkænθ], *s. Bot:* tragacanthe *f*; *Pharm: etc:* **gum t.,** gomme *f* adragante.
tragal ['treigəl], *a. Anat:* tragien.
tragedian [trə'dʒi:diən], *s.* (*a*) poète *m*, auteur *m*, tragique; (*b*) (*f.* **tragedienne** [trədʒi:di'en]) tragédien, -ienne.
tragedy ['trædʒidi], *s.* (*a*) *Th:* tragédie *f*; le tragique; (*b*) **to make a t. out of sth., to treat sth. as a t.,** prendre qch. au tragique; **the t. of his death,** sa mort tragique; **what a t.!** quel malheur! quelle tragédie!
tragelaph ['trædʒilæf], **tragelaphus** [trə'dʒeləfəs], *s. Z:* tragélaphe *m*.
Tragelaphinae [trædʒe'læfini:], *s.pl. Z:* tragélaphinés *m*.
tragic ['trædʒik], *a.* tragique; (*a*) **t. actor, actress,** tragédien, -ienne; **the great t. roles, parts,** les grands rôles tragiques; **the t. Muse,** la Muse tragique; la Muse de la tragédie; *F:* **to put on a t. act,** jouer la tragédie; (*b*) **t. event,** événement *m* tragique; **the t. side of the story is that . . .,** le tragique de l'histoire c'est que . . .; *F:* **don't be so t. about it!** ne le prenez pas si au tragique!
tragical ['trædʒikəl], *a. A:* = TRAGIC.
tragically ['trædʒik(ə)li], *adv.* tragiquement; **to take things t.,** prendre les choses au tragique.
tragicalness ['trædʒikəlnis], *s.* tragique *m*.
tragicomedy [trædʒi'kɔmidi], *s.* tragi-comédie *f*, *pl.* tragi-comédies.
tragicomic(al) [trædʒi'kɔmik(əl)], *a. Lit:* tragicomique.
tragopan ['trægoupæn], *s. Orn:* tragopan *m*.
tragule ['trægju:l], *s. Z:* tragule *m*.
tragulid [træ'gju:lid], *s. Z:* tragule *m*, tragulidé *m*.
Tragulidae [træ'gju:lidi:], *s.pl. Z:* tragulidés *m*.
tragus, *pl.* **-gi** ['treigəs, 'treidʒai], *s.* (*a*) *Anat:* tragus *m* (de l'oreille); (*b*) *Z:* oreillon *m* (d'une chauve-souris).
trail[1] [treil], *s.* **1.** (*a*) traînée *f* (de sang, de fumée, etc.); panache *m* (de fumée); queue *f* (d'un météore); **t. of light,** traînée lumineuse; sillon *m*, trace *f*, de lumière; (*of rocket, etc.*) **t. of fire,** sillon de feu; *Av:* **vapour t., condensation t.,** traînée (de condensation); (*b*) *Ball:* traînée réelle (d'une bombe); (*c*) *Artil:* flèche *f*, crosse *f* (d'affût); **double t.,** biflèche *f*; **t. box,** coffre *m* d'affût; **t. eye,** lunette *f* de crosse (pour raccord avec l'avant-train); **t. plate,** plaque *f* de crosse; bout *m* d'affût; talon *m* de flasque; **set of the t.,** angle *m* de recul; (*d*) *Aut:* chasse *f* (des roues directrices); (*e*) **t. bridge,** (bac *m* à) traille *f*; va-et-vient *m inv*; (*f*) *Fish:* **t. net,** (i) traîneau *m*, traîne *f*; (ii) chalut *m*. **2.** (*a*) piste *f*, trace (d'une bête, de qn); trace (d'un colimaçon); sillon (d'une roue); *Ven:* voie *f* (d'une bête); (*of hounds*) **to lose the t.,** perdre la piste, la trace, la voie; **to pick up the t.,** retrouver la trace; **false t.,** fausse piste; **to be on the t. of s.o.,** être sur la piste de qn; **to leave ruin in one's t.,** laisser la ruine sur son passage; *esp. NAm:* **in t.,** en file indienne; (*b*) sentier (battu); piste (dans une forêt, etc.); *Mount: Ski:* **to break t.,** faire la trace.
trail[2], *v.*
I. *v.tr.* **1.** (*a*) **to t. sth. (along),** traîner qch. après soi, à sa suite; (*of car, etc.*) remorquer (une caravane, etc.); **she was trailing five children after her,** elle traînait cinq enfants après elle; **to let one's dress t. in the dust,** traîner sa robe dans la poussière; **to t. one's coat,** (i) traîner son habit derrière soi en manière de défi; (ii) inviter les attaques; chercher noise à tout le monde; traîner son sabre; (*b*) *Mil:* **to t. arms,** porter l'arme à la main; **t. arms!** l'arme à la main! **2.** traquer, suivre à la piste (une bête, un criminel); (*of crook*) suivre, filer (une victime). **3.** *T.V: etc:* **to t. a programme, etc.,** faire de la publicité pour un programme, etc. (en donnant des extraits, etc.).
II. *v.i.* **1.** (*a*) traîner; **your skirt is trailing (on the ground),** votre jupe traîne (par terre); (*b*) **with a boat trailing behind,** avec un bateau à la traîne, à la remorque. **2.** (*of pers.*) **to t. along,** se traîner; avancer péniblement; **to t. behind,** traîner derrière (les autres); **wounded soldiers trailing past,** soldats blessés qui défilent péniblement, qui passent à la défilade; **to t. away, off,** s'en aller en traînant le pas; **her voice trailed away, off, in the distance,** sa voix se perdit dans le lointain. **3.** (*of plant*) grimper, ramper.
trailblazer ['treilbleizər], *s.* pionnier *m*.
trailer ['treilər], *s.* **1.** (*pers.*) traqueur *m*; (*b*) traînard *m*, retardataire *m*. **2.** plante grimpante, rampante. **3.** *Aut: etc:* (*a*) remorque *f*; **tent t.,** tente-remorque *f*; (*b*) *NAm:* caravane *f* (de camping). **4.** *Cin:* film *m* annonce, présentation *f*, bande-annonce *f*. **5.** *Turf:* (*horse*) partant *m* de seconde ligne. **6.** *Cmptr:* queue *f* de bande; **t. card,** carte *f* de fin de groupe; **t. block, record,** bloc *m* fin, article *m* fin.
trailing[1] ['treiliŋ], *a.* **1.** (*of skirt, etc.*) traînant. **2.** (*of plant*) grimpant, rampant. **3.** *Rail:* **t. axle,** essieu *m* arrière, axe *m* arrière (de locomotive); **t. wheel,** roue porteuse arrière (de locomotive); **t. points,** changement *m* de voie en talon; **t. edge,** (i) *Av:* bord *m* de sortie, de fuite; arêtier arrière; (ii) *Cmptr:* bord arrière (de carte, de document).
trailing[2], *s.* **1.** traîne *f*, traînement *m*. **2.** poursuite *f* (de qn) à la piste.
train[1] [trein], *s.* **1.** traîne *f*, queue *f* (d'une robe); queue (d'un paon, d'une comète); queue (d'un faucon); **two little pages carried her t.,** deux petits pages portaient sa traîne; **t. bearer,** porte-queue *m inv*; *Ecc:* caudataire *m* (d'un cardinal, etc.). **2.** (*a*) suite *f*, cortège *m*, équipage *m* (d'un prince, etc.); **to be in s.o.'s t.,** être à la suite de qn; (*b*) *Mil:* équipage, train *m*; **baggage t., wag(g)on t.,** train des équipages; **emergency supply t.,**

en-case *m* mobile; **bridging t., pontoon t.,** équipage de pont; *A:* **siege t.,** équipage de siège; **t. of artillery,** train d'artillerie; (*c*) **the evils that follow in the t. of war,** les maux que la guerre traîne à sa suite; **war brought famine in its t.,** la guerre a amené la disette; **who knows what this event will bring in its t.?** on ne sait quelles seront les conséquences, les suites, de cet événement; **the ruins that they left in their t.,** les ruines qu'ils ont semées sur leur passage. **3.** (*a*) train, convoi *m*, file *f* (de bêtes de somme, de wagons, de péniches); succession *f*, série *f*, enchaînement *m* (d'événements, de circonstances, de réflexions); **a long t. of tourists,** une longue file, une longue procession, de touristes; **t. of thought,** chaîne *f* d'idées; **to follow the t. of one's thoughts,** poursuivre le cours de ses idées; *Min:* **t. of tubs,** rame *f* de bennes; *W.Tel:* **t. of waves, wave t.,** train d'ondes; série d'ondes; *Elcs:* **pulse t.,** train d'impulsions; (*b*) *Min:* traînée *f* (de poudre); **to fire a t.,** allumer une traînée de poudre; (*c*) *O:* **to be in (good) t.,** être (bien) en train; **to set sth. in t.,** mettre qch. en train; **things are now in t.,** les choses sont maintenant bien en train. **4.** *Tchn:* système *m* d'engrenages; cadrature *f*, rouage(s) *m*(*pl*) (d'une montre, d'une horloge); **wheel t.,** train de roues; *Metall:* **t. of rolls,** train, jeu *m*, batterie *f*, de cylindres; **live roller t.,** transporteur *m* à rouleaux (de laminoir); *Civ.E:* (*of steel bridge*) **roller t.,** équipage de galets. **5.** (*a*) *Rail:* train; **passenger t., goods t.,** train de voyageurs, de marchandises; **main-line t.,** train de grande ligne; **local, branch-line t.,** train de petite ligne; **(fast) express t.,** (train) rapide *m*; **express t.,** train express; **slow, stopping, t.,** train omnibus, semi-direct; **high-speed t.,** train grande vitesse; **prestige t.,** *F:* **crack t.,** train-drapeau *m*, *pl.* trains-drapeaux; **relief t.,** train supplémentaire; **excursion t.,** train d'excursion, à prix réduit; **winter sports t.,** train de neige; **troop t.,** train militaire; **armoured t.,** train blindé; *Can:* **bullet t.,** ferrobus *m*; **to travel by t.,** voyager en train, par le train, par le chemin de fer; **t. journey,** voyage *m* en, par, chemin de fer; *F:* **t. jumper,** voyageur clandestin; **t. sickness,** mal *m* du rail; **to board the t.,** monter dans le train; **the train's in,** le train est en gare, à quai; **the t. home,** le train de retour; (*on suburban line*) **the last night t.,** le train-balai; *P.N:* **to the trains,** accès aux quais; (*b*) rame *f* (du métro); (*c*) **t. ferry,** ferry(-boat) *m*; **t. deck,** pont *m* des voies; (*d*) *Austr:* **road t.,** gros routier (à remorques); (*e*) *F:* **the gravy t.,** le bon filon; l'assiette *f* au beurre; **to ride the gravy t.,** taper dans l'assiette au beurre; se la couler douce.

train[2], *v.*

I. *v.tr.* **1.** (*a*) former, instruire (qn); faire l'éducation de (qn); former, styler (un domestique); former, exercer, faire faire l'exercice à, aguerrir (des conscrits); dresser (un animal); former (le caractère, l'esprit); exercer (l'oreille); **to t. a child,** élever un enfant; **this school trained many good officers,** cette école fut un séminaire de bons officiers; **he was trained at . . .,** il sort de (telle ou telle école); **engineers who have been trained at . . .,** les ingénieurs sortis de . . .; **to t. s.o. for sth., to do sth.,** exercer qn à qch., à faire qch.; **trained for public office,** préparé aux fonctions publiques; **to t. a youth for the navy,** préparer un jeune homme pour la marine; **to t. a dog to retrieve,** dresser un chien à rapporter; **to t. one's ear to distinguish various sounds,** exercer son oreille à distinguer des sons divers; **to t. s.o. in the use of a weapon,** instruire qn à se servir d'une arme; **he has been trained to cope with difficult business,** il est entraîné aux affaires difficiles; (*b*) *Sp:* entraîner (un coureur, un cheval de course, etc.); *Box: etc:* **he is being trained by X,** c'est le poulain de X; (*c*) *Hort:* diriger, conduire (une plante); faire grimper (une plante grimpante); palisser, mettre en espalier (un arbre fruitier, une vigne). **2.** pointer (un canon), braquer, diriger (une lunette, un projecteur, etc.) (**on, sur**); *Navy:* orienter (un canon); *Navy:* **to t. on the beam,** pointer par le travers.

II. *v.i.* **1.** (*a*) s'exercer; *Mil:* faire l'exercice; (*b*) *Sp:* s'entraîner; (*of athlete, jockey*) **to t. down,** réduire son poids; (*c*) **to t. for sth.,** s'exercer, se préparer, à qch.; préparer une carrière dans qch.; **to t. as a typist, a secretary,** suivre un cours de dactylographie. **2.** *F: O:* voyager par, en, chemin de fer; prendre le train.

trainband ['treinbænd], *s. Hist:* compagnie *f* de la milice bourgeoise (de Londres, etc.).

trained [treind], *a.* **1.** (*a*) (soldat, etc.) instruit; (chien, etc.) dressé; (domestique) stylé; (œil) exercé; **well t. child,** enfant bien élevé, bien appris; **badly t. servants,** domestiques mal stylés; **t. nurse,** infirmière diplômée; **t. army,** armée dressée, aguerrie; **t. soldier,** soldat *m* mobilisable; *Hist:* **t. band** = TRAINBAND; **t. horse,** cheval d'école; cheval fait; **well t. horse,** cheval bien dressé, qui a de l'école; **t. parrot,** perroquet savant; (*b*) *Sp:* entraîné. **2.** *Hort:* (rosier, pêcher) palissé, mis en espalier.

trainee [trei'ni:], *s.* stagiaire *mf*; élève *mf*; *Box: etc:* poulain *m*; *Cmptr:* **t. programmer,** élève-programmeur *m*.

trainer ['treinər], *s.* **1.** (*pers.*) (*a*) dresseur *m* (d'animaux); (*b*) *Sp: Turf:* entraîneur *m* (d'athlètes, de chevaux de course); **he's the Queen's t.,** c'est lui qui entraîne les chevaux de course de la Reine; (*c*) *Artil: U.S:* pointeur *m*. **2.** *Av:* avion-école *f*, *pl.* avions-écoles; appareil *m* d'école. **3.** (*for baby*) **t. pants,** culotte *f* de propreté.

trainful ['treinful], *s.* plein train (de marchandises, de voyageurs, etc.).

training ['treiniŋ], *s.* **1.** (*a*) éducation *f*, instruction *f*, formation *f*; **character t.,** formation du caractère; éducation morale; *NAm:* (*for baby*) **t. pants,** culotte *f* de propreté; **physical t.,** éducation physique; **vocational t.,** éducation professionnelle; **further t.,** perfectionnement *m*; **in-service t.,** cours *m* de perfectionnement (organisé par l'établissement où on travaille); **ear t.,** éducation de l'oreille; **I'm a historian by t.,** je suis historien de formation; **to have had a business t.,** être formé, rompu, aux affaires; **he had received a good t.,** il avait fait un bon apprentissage; **t. centre,** centre *m* de formation; (*b*) *Mil:* **military t.,** dressage *m* militaire; **preparatory t.,** instruction prémilitaire; **t. of troops,** aguerrissement *m* des troupes; **to keep troops in t.,** tenir des troupes en haleine; **battalion t.,** école *f* de bataillon; *Navy:* **t. squadron,** escadre *f* d'instruction; division *f* des écoles; **t. ship,** navire-école *m*; navire *m* d'application; *Av:* **t. aircraft,** appareil *m* d'école; avion-école *m*, *pl.* avions-écoles; **t. base,** base *f* école; (*c*) *Sp: Turf:* entraînement *m* (d'un athlète, d'un cheval de course, etc.); **to go into t.,** s'entraîner; **to be in t.,** (i) être à l'entraînement; (ii) être bien entraîné; être en forme; **to be out of t.,** ne plus être en forme; **team in good t.,** équipe entraînée à fond, en bon souffle; (*d*) dressage (d'un animal); *Equit:* **t. of horses,** manège *m*; **horse in t.,** cheval au dressage; **t. bit,** mors *m* d'Allemagne. **2.** (*a*) *Hort:* dressage, palissage *m* (d'une plante, d'un arbre fruitier); (*b*) *Hyd.E:* **t. works,** ouvrages directeurs; **t. wall,** digue directrice. **3.** *Artil:* pointage *m* en direction, braquage *m*, orientation *f* (d'une pièce); **arc of t.,** champ *m* de tir.

trainload ['treinloud], *s.* **t. of coal,** train chargé de houille; **t. of tourists,** plein train de touristes.

trainman, *pl.* **-men** ['treinmən], *s.m. NAm:* **1.** cheminot. **2.** serre-frein(s), *pl.* serre-freins; garde-frein(s), *pl.* gardes-frein(s).

train(-)oil ['treinɔil], *s.* (*a*) huile *f* de baleine; thran *m*; (*b*) *A:* huile de poisson.

traipse[1] [treips], *s.* **1.** *A:* (*pers.*) souillon *f*, guenipe *f*. **2.** (*a*) course longue et ennuyeuse; (*b*) longue promenade.

traipse[2]. **1.** *v.i.* traîner çà et là; se balader. **2.** *v.tr.* **to t. the fields, the streets,** traîner dans les champs, dans les rues.

trait [treit], *s.* (*a*) trait *m* (de caractère, etc.); (*b*) *A:* trait (du visage).

traitor ['treitər], *s.* traître *m*; (*applied to woman*) traîtresse *f*; **a t. to his country,** un traître à sa patrie; **to be a t. to (one's party, etc.),** trahir (son parti, etc.); **to turn t.,** passer à l'ennemi; se vendre.

traitoress ['treit(ə)ris], *s.f.* = TRAITRESS.

traitorous ['treit(ə)rəs], *a.* traître, *f.* traîtresse; perfide.

traitorously ['treit(ə)rəsli], *adv.* en traître; traîtreusement; perfidement.

traitorousness ['treit(ə)rəsnis], *s.* traîtrise *f*, perfidie *f*.

traitress ['treitris], *s.f.* traîtresse.

Trajan ['treidʒən], *Pr.n.m. Rom.Hist:* Trajan; **Trajan's Column,** la colonne Trajane.

traject[1] ['trædʒekt], *s.* trajet *m*.

traject[2] [trə'dʒekt], *v.tr.* transmettre (la lumière, etc.).

trajectory [trə'dʒektəri], *s.* trajectoire *f* (d'un projectile, d'une comète); *Mth:* ligne *f* trajectoire; *Ball:* **flat t., low t.,** trajectoire rasante, tendue; **curved t.,** trajectoire courbe; **sheaf of trajectories,** gerbe de trajectoires; *Artil:* **mean grazing t.,** trajectoire d'écrêtement.

tra la la [trɑ:lɑ:'lɑ:], *s.* (*in song*) tralala *m*.

tram[1] [træm], *s. Tex:* **t. (silk),** trame *f*.

tram[2], *s.* **1.** tramway *m*; **t. driver,** conducteur *m* de tramway; wattman *m*; **horse t.,** tramway *m* à cheval. **2.** **t. (rail),** rail *m* à ornière, à gorge; rail plat. **3.** = TRAMWAY 1. **4.** *Min:* benne *f*, berline *f*, herche *f*.

tram[3], *v.* (**trammed**) **1.** *v.i. F: A:* **to t. (it),** prendre le tramway. **2.** *v.tr. Min:* rouler, pousser, hercher (le minerai).

tramcar ['træmkɑ:r], *s. O:* tramway *m*.

tramline ['træmlain], *s.* **1.** ligne *f*, itinéraire *m*, de tramways. **2.** (*a*) **tramlines,** voie *f* de tramway; **the bicycle skidded on the tramlines,** la bicyclette a dérapé sur les rails du tramway; (*b*) *Ten:* **the tramlines,** le couloir.

trammel[1] ['træm(ə)l], *s.* **1.** *Fish:* **t. (net),** tramail *m*, trémail *m*, *pl.* -ails. **2.** (*a*) *A:* entrave *f* (de cheval en dressage); (*b*) *O:* **the trammels of superstition,** les langes *m* de la superstition; **the trammels of rhyme,** la contrainte de la rime. **3.** *Draw:* (*a*) compas *m* d'ellipse; compas elliptique; ellipsographe *m*; (*b*) **trammel(s),** compas à trusquin, à verge.

trammel[2], *v.tr.* (**trammelled**) entraver, embarrasser, empêtrer (**with,** de); **trammelled by prejudices,** entravé par les préjugés.

trammer ['træmər], *s. Min:* (*pers.*) rouleur *m*, hercheur *m*, moulineur *m*.

tramming ['træmiŋ], *s. Min:* roulage *m*, herchage *m* (du minerai).

tramontana [trɑ:mɔn'tɑ:nə], *s. Meteor:* tramontane *f*.

tramontane [træ'montein]. **1.** *a.* (pays, vent) ultramontain, d'outre-monts. **2.** *s. A:* = TRAMONTANA.

tramp[1] [træmp], *s.* **1.** bruit *m* de pas marqués; **I heard the (heavy) t. of the guard,** j'ai entendu le pas lourd de la garde; **to listen to the t. of the horses,** écouter le pas, le piétinement, des chevaux. **2.** (*a*) marche *f*; promenade *f* à pied; **to go for a long t. in the country,** faire (à pied) une grande excursion en campagne; (*b*) **to be on the t.,** (i) courir le pays; (ii) *F:* être chemineau, clochard. **3.** (*pers.*) (*a*) chemineau *m*, vagabond *m*, clochard *m*; (*b*) femme facile. **4.** *Nau:* **(ocean) t., t. steamer,** navire *m*, cargo *m*, sans ligne régulière; vapeur *m* en cueillette; tramp *m*. **5.** (*of boot*) semelle *f* de fer (pour appuyer sur la bêche, etc.).

tramp[2], *v.i.* & *tr.* **1.** marcher à pas marqués; marcher lourdement; **he tramped up and down the platform,** il arpentait le quai (à pas pesants). **2.** **to t. on sth.,** piétiner, écraser, qch. **3.** (*a*) marcher; se promener, voyager, à pied; **to t. the country,** parcourir le pays à pied; **to t. on in the rain,** cheminer sous la pluie; **to t. wearily along,** suivre péniblement son chemin; **I tramped ten kilometres,** j'ai fait dix kilomètres à pied; (*b*) vagabonder; courir le pays; être clochard; **to t. the streets (in search of work),** battre le pavé. **4.** *Nau:* (*of cargo vessel*) faire la cueillette, le tramping; naviguer à l'aventure.

tramper ['træmpər], *s. O:* chemineau *m*, vagabond *m*, clochard *m*.

tramping ['træmpiŋ], *s.* **1.** = TRAMP[1] 1. **2.** vagabondage *m*. **3.** *Nau:* navigation *f* à la cueillette; tramping *m*.

trample[1] ['træmpl], *s.* piétinement *m*; bruit *m* de pas.

trample[2]. **1.** *v.i.* **to t. on sth., s.o.,** piétiner, écraser, qch., qn; **to t. on s.o.'s feelings, reputation,** fouler aux pieds les susceptibilités, la réputation, de qn. **2.** *v.tr.* (*a*) **to t. s.o., sth., down, under foot,** fouler qn, qch., aux pieds; **to t. down the grass,** fouler l'herbe; **child trampled to death,** enfant écrasé (sous les pieds des chevaux, de la foule); (*b*) piétiner (le sol).

trampoline [træmpə'li:n], *s. Gym: etc:* tremplin *m*.

tramroad ['træmroud], *s.* tramway *m* de mine.

tramway ['træmwei], *s.* (voie *f* de) tramway *m*; **cable t.,** tramway à câbles; **overhead t.,** tramway aérien.

trance [trɑ:ns], *s.* (*a*) *Med:* (i) extase *f*; état *m* extatique; (ii) catalepsie *f*; **to fall into a t.,** tomber en extase; *F:* piquer une attaque d'hystérie; (*b*) **(hypnotic) t.,** transe *f*, hypnose *f*; **to send s.o. into a t.,** hypnotiser qn; (*c*) extase (religieuse).

tranche [trɑ:nʃ], *s. Fin:* tranche *f*.

tranquil ['træŋkwil], *a.* tranquille (et serein); calme, paisible.

tranquilite ['træŋkwilait], *s. Miner:* tranquilite *f*.

tranquillity [træŋ'kwiliti], *s.* tranquillité *f*, calme *m*, sérénité *f*.

tranquillization [træŋkwilai'zeiʃ(ə)n], *s.* tranquillisation *f*.

tranquillize ['træŋkwilaiz], *v.tr.* tranquilliser, calmer, apaiser, rendre tranquille (qn, l'esprit, etc.).

tranquillizer ['træŋkwilaizər], *s. Med: etc:* tranquillisant *m*, calmant *m*.

tranquillizing[1] ['træŋkwilaiziŋ], *a.* tranquillisant, calmant.

tranquillizing[2], *s.* apaisement *m*.

tranquilly ['træŋkwili], *adv.* tranquillement, paisiblement; avec calme; avec sérénité.

trans [træns, trænz], *a. Ch:* (isomère) trans.

trans- [trænz, træns], *pref.* trans-.

transact [træn'zækt], *v.tr.* **to t. business with s.o.,** faire des affaires avec qn; **the business was successfully transacted,** la transaction, l'affaire, a été conclue à notre satisfaction.

transaction [træn'zækʃ(ə)n], *s.* **1.** conduite *f* (d'une affaire); **business transactions,** les affaires; le commerce. **2.** (*a*) opération (commerciale); affaire (faite);

Stock Exchange transactions, opérations de Bourse; **cash t.,** opération, marché *m,* au comptant; *Fin: Bank:* **cash transactions,** mouvements *m* d'espèces; **transactions in securities,** mouvements des valeurs; (*b*) *Cmptr:* **t. data,** mouvements; **t. code, card,** code, carte, mouvement; **t. file,** fichier mouvements. **3. transactions (of a society),** travaux *m,* transactions (d'une société); mémoires *m,* actes *m,* procès-verbaux *m,* comptes rendus des séances (d'une société savante).

transactional [træn'zækʃən(ə)l], *a.* transactionnel.

transactor [træn'zæktər], *s.* négociateur, -trice (d'une affaire).

transafrican [trænz'æfrikən], *a.* transafricain.

transalpine [trænz'ælpain], *a.* transalpin.

transamerican [trænzə'merikən], *a.* transaméricain.

transaminase [træns'æmineis], *s. Bio-Ch:* transaminase *f.*

transandean [trænzæn'di:ən], *a. Geog:* transandin.

transatlantic [trænzət'læntik], *a.* transatlantique.

trans-Canada [træs'kænədə], *a.* transcanadien; **T.-C. Highway,** route transcanadienne.

Transcaucasia [trænzkɔ:'keisiə], *Pr.n. Geog:* Transcaucasie *f.*

transcaucasian [trænzkɔ:'keisiən], *a.* transcaucasien.

transceiver [træn'si:vər], *s. W.Tel:* émetteur-récepteur *m, pl.* émetteurs-récepteurs.

transcend [træn'send], *v.tr.* **1.** transcender; dépasser, outrepasser, les bornes de (la raison, etc.); aller au delà de (ce que l'on peut concevoir). **2.** surpasser (qn); l'emporter sur (qn).

transcendence, transcendency [træn'sendəns(i)], *s.* transcendance *f.*

transcendent [træn'sendənt], *a.* transcendant.

transcendental [trænsen'dentəl], *a.* **1.** *Phil:* (*a*) transcendental, -aux; (*b*) qui se conçoit a priori. **2.** *Mth:* transcendant; **t. function, geometry,** fonction, géométrie, transcendante.

transcendentalism [trænsen'dentəlizm], *s. Phil:* transcendantalisme *m.*

transcendentalist [trænsen'dentəlist], *s. Phil:* transcendantaliste *m.*

transcode [træns'koud], *v.tr. Cmptr:* transcoder.

transcoder [træns'koudər], *s. Cmptr:* transcodeur *m.*

transcontinental [trænzkɔnti'nent(ə)l], *a.* transcontinental, -aux.

transcribe [træns'kraib], *v.tr.* **1.** copier, transcrire (un manuscrit); traduire (des notes sténographiques). **2.** *Mus:* transcrire (un morceau pour un autre instrument).

transcriber [træns'kraibər], *s.* transcripteur *m;* copiste *mf.*

transcript ['trænskript], *s.* (*a*) transcription *f,* copie *f;* (*b*) traduction *f* (de notes sténographiques).

transcription [træns'kripʃ(ə)n], *s.* **1.** = TRANSCRIPT. **2.** *Mus:* transcription *f.*

transducer [trænz'dju:sər], *s. Ph: Elcs: etc:* transducteur *m;* **active t.,** transducteur actif.

transduction [trænz'dʌkʃ(ə)n], *s. Biol:* transduction *f.*

transect [træn'sekt], *v.tr.* couper, diviser (qch.) transversalement; *Anat:* disséquer (qch.) transversalement.

transection [træn'sekʃ(ə)n], *s.* coupe, division, transversale; *Anat:* dissection transversale.

transept ['trænsept], *s. Ecc.Arch:* transept *m;* **north, south, t.,** transept nord, sud; **arm of the t.,** croisillon *m.*

transesterification [trænzestərifi'keiʃ(ə)n], *s. Ch:* transestérification *f.*

transexual [træn'seksjuəl], *a & s. Psy:* transexuel, -elle.

transfer[1] ['trænsfə(:)r], *s.* **1.** (*a*) transfert *m;* transport *m* (de qch. à un autre endroit); déplacement *m* (d'un fonctionnaire, etc.); *Sch:* changement *m* (de section, de classe); **t. of population,** transfert de population; *Adm: etc:* **t. of personnel,** mutation *f* de personnel; **automatic t.,** mutation d'office; **I'm hoping to get a t. to the Dover branch,** j'espère être transféré à la succursale de Douvres; *Av:* **t. passengers,** voyageurs *m* en transit; *Rail:* **t. table,** transporteur *m* de wagons (à plate-forme roulante); *Jur:* **t. of a case to another court,** renvoi *m* d'une cause à un autre tribunal; *Cmptr:* **data t.,** transfert de données; **t. of control,** branchement *m;* **t. card,** carte *f* de branchement; **t. interpreter,** reporteuse *f;* **t. check,** contrôle *m* par répétition; *Fb: etc:* **t. fee,** prix *m* de transfert (d'un joueur); (*b*) *Jur:* transfert, transmission *f* (d'un droit, etc.); transmission, transport(-cession) *m* (de propriétés, de droits); translation *f,* mutation (de biens); **t. by death,** mutation par décès; **(capital) t. tax,** (i) droits de succession; (ii) droit de mutation (entre vifs); **t. of a debt,** cession *f,* revirement *m,* d'une créance; *St.Exch:* **t. of shares,** transfert, assignation *f,* d'actions; **t. form,** formule *f* de transfert; (*c*) *Book-k:* contre-passement *m,* contre-passation *f* (d'une écriture); transport, ristourne *f* (d'une somme d'un compte à un autre); **t. entry,** article *m* de contre-passement; **t. note,** filière *f;* **t. book, register,** journal *m,* livre *m,* registre *m,* des transferts; *Bank:* **t. of funds,** virement *m* de fonds. **2.** (*a*) *Jur:* **(deed of) t.,** acte *m* de cession, de transmission; acte translatif (de propriété); (*b*) *St.Exch:* (feuille *f* de) transfert. **3.** (*a*) *Lith:* report *m;* transport (sur la pierre); *Phot:* (*in carbon process, etc.*) **temporary t.,** transfert provisoire; **t. ink,** encre *f* lithographique, autographique; **t. paper,** (i) papier *m* à report, à transport, de transfert; (ii) papier à décalquer; (*b*) *Cer: Needlew: etc:* décalque *m; Needlew:* modèle *m* à décalquer; (*c*) **transfer (picture),** décalcomanie *f.*

transfer[2] [træns'fə:r], *v.tr.* **(transferred) 1.** (*a*) transférer (qch., qn, d'un endroit à un autre); déplacer (un fonctionnaire, etc.); muter (un militaire, un fonctionnaire); désaffecter (un soldat, pour raisons de santé); verser (des hommes à un régiment, etc.); **to t. a prisoner,** transférer un prisonnier d'une prison à une autre; **business transferred to new premises,** maison établie dans un nouveau local, dans de nouveaux bureaux; *Tp:* **transferred charge call,** communication *f* payable à l'arrivée, à la charge du destinataire; (*b*) *Jur:* transmettre, transporter, céder (une propriété, des droits, etc.); faire cession de, céder (un privilège, etc.); **to t. a right to s.o.,** passer un droit à qn; (*c*) *Book-k:* contre-passer, ristourner (une écriture); *Bank: etc:* virer (une somme). **2.** (*a*) *Lith: Phot:* reporter (un plan, etc.); (*b*) *Needlew: etc:* calquer, décalquer (un dessin, une image).

transferability [trænsfərə'biliti], *s.* transférabilité *f;* transmissibilité *f.*

transferable [træns'fə:rəbl], *a.* transmissible; *Jur:* (droit, bien) cessible; (droit) communicable, transférable; *Fin:* **t. securities,** valeurs négociables, cessibles, mobilières; **not t.,** (i) (*on ticket, etc.*) strictement personnel; (ii) invitation personnelle.

transferee [trænsfə:'ri:], *s. Jur: Fin:* cessionnaire *mf* (d'un bien, d'un effet de commerce, etc.).

transference ['trænsfərəns], *s. Psy:* transfert *m.*

transferential [trænsfə'renʃ(ə)l], *a. Psy:* transférentiel.

transferor [trænsfə(:)'rɔ:r], *s. Jur:* cédant, -ante; endosseur (cédant) (d'un effet de commerce).

transferrer [træns'fə:rər], *s.* **1.** *Lith:* reporteur *m,* transporteur *m.* **2.** = TRANSFEROR.

transferring [træns'fə:riŋ], *s.* **1.** transfert *m.* **2.** *Lith:* report *m;* **hand, machine, t.,** report à la main, à la machine; **(multi-)t. machine,** machine à reports.

transfiguration [trænsfigjə'reiʃ(ə)n], *s.* transfiguration *f;* **the T. (of Christ),** la Transfiguration (du Christ).

transfigure [træns'figər], *v.tr.* transfigurer; **to become transfigured,** se transfigurer.

transfix [træns'fiks], *v.tr.* **1.** transpercer (qn avec une lance, etc.). **2.** rendre (qn) immobile; pétrifier (qn); **transfixed with fear, with horror,** pétrifié, cloué au sol, par la peur, par l'horreur.

transfixion [træns'fikʃ(ə)n], *s.* **1.** transpercement *m.* **2.** *Surg:* transfixion *f* (dans certaines amputations).

transfluxor [træns'flʌksər], *s. Cmptr:* transfluxor *m.*

transform[1] [træns'fɔ:m], *v.tr.* **1.** (*a*) transformer; métamorphoser; **to t. the country,** renouveler, changer, la face du pays; (*b*) *Mth:* transformer (une équation). **2.** (*a*) *Ch: Mec: etc:* transformer, changer, convertir **(into,** en); **to t. heat into energy,** convertir la chaleur en énergie; (*b*) *El:* transformer (le courant).

transform[2], *s. Mth:* transformée *f.*

transformable [træns'fɔ:məbl], *a.* **1.** transformable. **2.** convertissable **(into,** en).

transformation [trænsfə'meiʃ(ə)n], *s.* **1.** (*a*) transformation *f;* métamorphose *f; Mth:* transformation (d'une équation); *Th:* **transformation scene,** (i) changement *m* à vue; (ii) apothéose *f* (d'une féerie, etc.); (*b*) *Ch: Mec: etc:* conversion *f* **(into,** en); **t. of heat into energy,** conversion de la chaleur en énergie; (*c*) *El:* transformation (du courant). **2.** *Hairdr: O:* faux toupet; transformation.

transformer [træns'fɔ:mər], *s.* (*a*) *El:* transformateur *m;* **static t.,** transformateur statique; **rotary t.,** transformateur rotatif; convertisseur rotatif; commutatrice *f;* **rotary-field t.,** transformateur à champ tournant; **balancing t.,** transformateur compensateur; **core t.,** transformateur à noyau; **air-gap t.,** transformateur à air; **oil t.,** transformateur à huile; **quadrature t.,** transformateur déphaseur; **step-up, step-down, t.,** transformateur élévateur, abaisseur; **t. ratio,** rapport *m* de transformation; **t. rectifier,** transformateur redresseur; **t. station,** station transformatrice; poste *m* de transformateurs; (*b*) *W.Tel:* **oscillation t.,** jigger *m.*

transforming [træns'fɔ:miŋ], *s.* transformation *f;* conversion *f* **(into,** en).

transformism [træns'fɔ:mizm], *s. Biol:* transformisme *m.*

transformist [træns'fɔ:mist]. *Biol:* **1.** *s.* transformiste *mf.* **2.** *a.* (théorie) transformiste.

transfuse [træns'fju:z], *v.tr.* **1.** transvaser; transfuser, verser (le contenu d'un récipient dans un autre). **2.** *Med:* (*a*) transfuser (du sang); (*b*) faire une transfusion de sang à (un malade).

transfusion [træns'fju:ʒ(ə)n], *s.* **1.** transvasement *m,* transfusion *f* (de liquides). **2.** *Med:* **blood t.,** transfusion de sang, transfusion sanguine; **exchange t.,** exsanguino-transfusion *f.* **3.** *Bot:* **t. tissue,** tissu *m* de transfusion.

transfusionist [træns'fju:zənist], *s. Med:* transfuseur *m.*

transgress [træns'gres], *v.tr. & i.* transgresser, violer, enfreindre (la loi); pécher; **to t. a rule,** violer une règle.

transgression [træns'greʃ(ə)n], *s.* **1.** (*a*) transgression *f,* violation *f* (d'une loi); infraction *f* (à la loi); (*b*) péché *m.* **2.** *Geol:* **marine t.,** transgression marine.

transgressive [træns'gresiv], *a.* **1.** coupable. **2.** *Geol:* (dépôt) transgressif; **t. stratification,** stratification transgressive.

transgressor [træns'gresər], *s.* transgresseur *m;* pécheur, *f.* pécheresse.

tranship [træn'ʃip]. **1.** *v.tr.* transborder (des voyageurs, des marchandises). **2.** *v.i.* (*of passengers*) faire un transbordement; changer de bateau.

transhipment [træn'ʃipmənt], *s.* transbordement *m.*

transhumance [træns(h)ju:'mæns], *s. Husb:* transhumance *f.*

transience, transiency ['trænziəns(i)], *s.* nature passagère, transitoire (d'un phénomène, etc.); courte durée (de la vie, d'une émotion).

transient ['trænziənt], *a.* (*a*) transitoire; (bonheur, etc.) passager, de passage; (beauté, etc.) éphémère, de courte durée; *NAm:* **t. visitor,** *s.* **transient,** client, -ente, de passage; **t. hotel,** hôtel qui reçoit essentiellement une clientèle de passage; (*b*) (coup d'œil, espoir) momentané; (coup d'œil) en passant; (*c*) *Mus:* (note) de passage, de transition; (*d*) *Phil:* (*of cause, etc.*) transitif.

transiently ['trænziəntli], *adv.* transitoirement; passagèrement; momentanément; en passant.

transillumination [trænzil(j)u:mi'neiʃ(ə)n], *s. Med:* transillumination *f.*

transire [træns'aiəri], *s. Cust:* passavant *m,* passe-debout *m inv,* laisser-passer *m inv;* acquit-à-caution (donné au capitaine d'un cabotier); **to have a permit for t.,** passer debout.

transistor [træn'zistər], *s. Elcs:* transistor *m;* **germanium t.,** transistor au germanium; **t. tester,** transistomètre *m;* **t. testing,** transistométrie *f;* **t. (set, radio),** poste *m* à transistors, *F:* transistor.

transistorization [trænzistərai'zeiʃ(ə)n], *s. Elcs:* transistorisation *f.*

transistorize [træn'zistəraiz], *v.tr. Elcs:* transistoriser.

transistorized [træn'zistəraizd], *a. Elcs:* transistorisé.

transit[1] ['trænsit], *s.* **1.** (*a*) passage *m,* voyage *m* (à travers un pays, etc.); **ships in t.,** navires transiteurs; (*b*) *Astr:* passage ((i) d'une planète sur le disque du soleil, (ii) d'un astre au méridien); **upper t., lower t.,** passage supérieur, inférieur, au méridien; **t. circle,** cercle méridien. **2.** transport *m* (de marchandises, etc.); **damage in t.,** avarie(s) *f(pl)* en cours de route; **goods lost in t.,** marchandises perdues pendant le transport, en cours de route, pendant parcours. **3.** *Cust:* transit *m;* **goods in t.,** marchandises en transit; (*warehoused*) **goods for t.,** marchandises de transit; **t. trade,** commerce *m* de transit; **t. permit,** document *m* de transit; **t. bill,** passavant *m;* **t. duty,** droit *m* de transit.

transit[2], *v.tr. Astr:* (*of planet, etc.*) passer sur (le méridien, le disque d'un corps céleste).

transition [træn'siʒ(ə)n], *s.* **1.** transition *f;* passage *m* (du jour à la nuit, de la crainte à l'espoir); **chapter that makes the t. between . . . and . . .,** chapitre qui fait transition entre . . . et . . .; **to pass from one state to another without t.,** passer d'un état à un autre sans aucune transition; **t. stage, period,** phase *f,* période *f,* de transition; période transitoire; *Ch:* **t. elements,** éléments *m* de transition; *Med:* **t. tumour,** tumeur bénigne qui tend à se transformer en tumeur maligne; *Cmptr:* **t. card,** carte *f* de branchement. **2.** *Mus:* modulation *f* (sans changement de mode).

transitional [træn'siʒən(ə)l], *a.* (*a*) transitionnel; de transition; *Arch: Art:* **t. style,** style *m* de transition; **Notre Dame is in t. style,** Notre-Dame de Paris est un édifice de la transition du roman au gothique; (*b*) *Geol:* **t. stratum,** couche transitive, de transition; (*c*) *Cmptr:* de transition; non-résident (en mémoire).

transitive ['trænzitiv], *a.* (verbe) transitif.

transitively ['trænzitivli], *adv.* transitivement.

transitorily ['trænsit(ə)rili], *adv.* transitoirement,

passagèrement.

transitoriness ['trænsit(ə)rinis], *s.* nature transitoire, passagère (**of,** de); courte durée (du bonheur, etc.).

transitory ['trænsit(ə)ri], *a.* transitoire, passager; (bonheur, etc.) fugitif, éphémère; (désir, etc.) momentané; (gloire, etc.) de courte durée.

transitron ['trænzitrɔn], *s. Elcs:* transitron *m.*

Transjordan, Transjordania [trænz'dʒɔːdən, -dʒɔː'deiniə], *Pr.n. Hist:* Transjordanie *f.*

Transjordanian [trænzdʒɔː'deiniən], *a. Hist:* transjordanien.

Transkei [træn'skai], *Pr.n. Geog:* Transkei *m.*

translatable [træns'leitəbl], *a.* traduisible.

translate [træns'leit], *v.tr.* **1.** traduire; **to t. a book,** traduire un livre; faire la traduction d'un livre; **to t. a sentence from French into English,** traduire une phrase du français en anglais; **book translated from (the) German,** livre traduit de l'allemand; **I translated his silence as a refusal,** j'ai pris son silence pour un refus; **to t. one's thoughts into words,** reproduire ses pensées en paroles; **to t. one's ideas into action,** convertir ses idées en actions. **2.** *(a)* transférer (un évêque) (**to,** à); *(b) B:* **Enoch was translated (to heaven),** Énoch fut enlevé au ciel; *(c) Mec: etc:* imprimer un mouvement de translation à (un corps). **3.** *A:* métamorphoser (qn) (**into,** en). **4.** *Tg:* répéter, retransmettre (une dépêche télégraphique, au moyen d'un répétiteur).

translation [træns'leiʃ(ə)n], *s.* **1.** *(a)* traduction *f* (d'un livre, etc.); **simultaneous t.,** traduction simultanée; *(b)* traduction; ouvrage traduit; *Sch:* version (latine, etc.); **to do, make, a t. of sth.,** faire une traduction de qch. **2.** *Com:* déchiffrement *m* (d'un câblogramme). **3.** *(a)* translation *f* (d'un évêque); *(b) Mec: etc:* **movement of t.,** mouvement *m* de translation; *(c) B:* enlèvement *m* (au ciel). **4.** *Tg:* translation (d'une dépêche).

translational [træns'leiʃən(ə)l], *a. Mec:* (mouvement) de translation.

translative [træns'leitiv], *a.* **1.** *Jur:* translatif. **2.** *Mec:* (mouvement) de translation.

translator [træns'leitər], *s.* **1.** *(a)* traducteur, -trice (d'un livre, etc.); *(b) A:* raccommodeur, -euse (de vêtements, de parapluies, etc.); ravaudeur, -euse (de vêtements). **2.** *Tg:* appareil *m* de translation; translateur *m,* répétiteur *m.* **3.** *Cmptr:* traducteur; **t. (routine),** programme *m* de traduction.

translatory [træns'leit(ə)ri], *a. Mec:* (mouvement) de translation.

transliterate [trænz'litəreit], *v.tr.* translit(t)érer; transcrire (en caractères différents, en caractères phonétiques).

transliteration [trænzlitə'reiʃ(ə)n], *s.* translit(t)ération *f*; transcription *f.*

translocation [trænzlou'keiʃ(ə)n], *s. (a) Biol:* translocation *f*; *(b)* déplacement *m* (d'une industrie, etc.); *(c)* **police t.,** relégation *f.*

translucence, translucency [trænz'luːsəns(i)], *s.* **1.** translucidité *f,* diaphanéité *f.* **2.** *A:* transparence *f.*

translucent, translucid [trænz'luːsənt, -sid], *a.* **1.** translucide, diaphane. **2.** *A:* transparent.

transmediterranean [trænzmeditə'reiniən], *a.* transméditerranéen.

transmethylation [trænzmeθi'leiʃ(ə)n], *s. Bio-Ch:* transméthylation *f.*

transmigrate [trænzmai'greit], *v.i.* (*of people, souls*) transmigrer.

transmigration [trænzmai'greiʃ(ə)n], *s.* transmigration *f* (d'un peuple, des âmes).

transmigrator [trænzmai'greitər], *s.* transmigré, -ée.

transmissibility [trænzmisi'biliti], *s.* transmissibilité *f.*

transmissible [trænz'misəbl], *a.* transmissible.

transmission [træns'miʃ(ə)n], *s.* **1.** *(a)* transmission *f* (d'un ordre, d'un message, d'un colis, etc.); *(b) Ph:* transmission (de la chaleur, du son, etc.); **neutron t.,** transmission de neutrons; **pulse t.,** transmission d'impulsions; **t. time,** durée *f,* temps *m,* de propagation (de la chaleur, etc.); *(c) Telecom: W.Tel: T.V: etc:* transmission; **radio t.,** transmission radio(électrique); **beam t.,** transmission aux ondes dirigées; **multiplex t.,** transmission multiplex; **multi-channel t.,** transmission à plusieurs voies; **multiway t.,** transmissions simultanées; **carrier t.,** transmission par courant porteur, par onde porteuse; **suppressed-carrier t.,** transmission à suppression d'onde porteuse; **parallel t.,** transmission en parallèle; **t. channel,** voie *f* de transmission; **t. band,** bande *f* de transmission; **t. band filter,** filtre *m* passe-bande; **t. level,** niveau *m* de transmission; **programme t.,** transmission de programmes (radiophoniques, etc.); *T.V:* **positive t.,** transmission positive; *Cmptr:* **t. control unit,** unité *f* de contrôle de transmission; contrôleur *m* de transmission; **synchronous t.,** transmission synchrone, isochrone; **start-stop t.,** transmission arythmique; *(d) El:* transport *m* (d'énergie); **high-voltage power t.,** transport de force; *(e) Mec.E: Aut:* **belt t.,** transmission par courroie; **gear t.,** transmission par engrenage; **selective t.,** engrenage sélectif; **automatic t.,** transmission automatique. **2.** *Aut:* **the t. (gear, system),** la transmission; les organes *m* de transmission. **3.** programme télévisé, radiodiffusé; **machine that records telegraphic transmissions,** machine qui enregistre des messages télégraphiés.

transmissive [træns'misiv], *a.* **1.** transmetteur. **2.** transmissible.

transmissivity [trænsmi'siviti], *s.* transmissibilité *f*; *Opt:* transmission *f.*

transmit [trænz'mit], *v.tr.* (**transmitted**) *(a)* transmettre (un colis, un ordre, une maladie, une nouvelle, etc.); *(b) Ph: etc:* transmettre (la lumière, etc.); *El:* transporter (la force); *Mec.E:* **to t. a motion to sth.,** imprimer, communiquer, un mouvement à qch.; *(c) W.Tel:* émettre, transmettre (un message, etc.).

transmittable [trænz'mitəbl], *a.* transmissible.

transmittal [trænz'mit(ə)l], *s.* transmission *f.*

transmittance [trænz'mitəns], *s. Ph:* transmittance *f*; **radiant t.,** transmittance radiante; **spectral t.,** transmittance spectrale.

transmittancy [trænz'mitənsi], *s. Ph:* coefficient *m* de transmittance.

transmitter [trænz'mitər], *s. (a) Tg: etc:* (i) (*sending apparatus*) transmetteur *m*; émetteur *m*; (ii) (*signalling key*) manipulateur *m*; **tape t.,** émetteur (télégraphique) à bande perforée; **t. distributor,** transmetteur-distributeur *m* (de téléimprimeur); *Tg: W.Tel:* **t. receiver,** émetteur-récepteur *m*; **lighthouse t. receiver,** émetteur-récepteur à tubes-phares, à mégatrons; *Cmptr:* **data t.,** transmetteur de données; *Elcs:* **t. distributor,** distributeur transmetteur; *(b) W.Tel: T.V:* (poste) émetteur; poste d'émission; **short, medium, long, wave t.,** émetteur (à) ondes courtes, moyennes, longues; **frequency-modulation t.,** émetteur à modulation de fréquence; **automatic t.,** émetteur automatique; **arc t.,** émetteur à arc; **(directional) beam t.,** émetteur dirigé, à radio-alignement; **spark t.,** émetteur à étincelles; **valve t., tube t.,** émetteur à lampe(s); **relay t.,** (i) émetteur de station relais; (ii) émetteur-relais; *T.V:* **image t.,** émetteur image; **film t.,** émetteur de télécinéma; **facsimile t.,** émetteur de fac-similés; **aural t.,** émetteur son; *(c) Nau:* émetteur de bord; **(turret) t.,** transmetteur d'ordres; *Av:* **onboard t.,** émetteur de bord; **glide-path t.,** émetteur de radioguidage.

transmitting [træns'mitiŋ], *attrib. (a) Mec.E:* **t. shaft,** arbre communicateur; **t. wire,** fil transmetteur; *(b) W.Tel: T.V:* **t. post,** poste émetteur; **t. station,** station émettrice; **t. tube, valve,** tube *m* d'émission; **t. antenna, aerial,** antenne *f* d'émission; **t. power,** pouvoir rayonnant (d'une antenne).

transmogrification [trænzmɔgrifi'keiʃ(ə)n], *s. Hum:* métamorphose *f.*

transmogrify [trænz'mɔgrifai], *v.tr. Hum:* changer, transformer, métamorphoser (qch. en qch.).

transmutability [trænzmjuːtə'biliti], *s.* transmutabilité *f.*

transmutable [trænz'mjuːtəbl], *a.* transmuable, transmutable.

transmutation [trænzmjuː'teiʃ(ə)n], *s.* **1.** *(a)* transmutation *f* (des métaux, des espèces biologiques, etc.) (**into,** en); *(b) A:* transformation *f* (d'une figure géométrique). **2.** *Jur:* **t. of possession,** mutation *f* (d'un bien).

transmute [trænz'mjuːt], *v.tr. (a)* transformer, changer, convertir (**into,** en); *(b) Alch:* transmuer (un métal).

transmuter [trænz'mjuːtər], *s. Alch: etc:* transmutateur *m.*

transoceanic [trænzousi'ænik], *a.* transocéanien.

transom ['trænsəm], *s.* **1.** *(a) Arch: Const:* traverse *f,* sommier *m,* linteau *m,* imposte *f* (de fenêtre, de porte); **t. (bar),** meneau horizontal (de croisée); *(b) Const:* épar(t) *m*; **scaffolding t.,** tendière *f* d'échafaudage; *(c) N.Arch:* (barre *f* d')arcasse *f*; (*in square-sterned vessel*) tableau *m* (d'arrière); **deck t., wing t.,** barre de pont, de hourdis; **t. floor,** varangue *f* d'arcasse; **t. board,** écusson *m*; **t. stern,** arrière *m* à tableau; *(d) A:* entretoise *f* (de fuselage d'avion, d'affût de canon); *(e) Veh:* épar(t), lisoir *m.* **2. t. (window),** (i) fenêtre *f* à meneau horizontal; (ii) *NAm:* vasistas *m,* imposte *f.*

transomed ['trænsəmd], *a.* (fenêtre) à meneaux.

transonic [træn'sɔnik], *a. Ph:* transsonique; *Av:* **t. range,** régimes *mpl,* vitesses *fpl,* transsoniques.

transpacific [trænzpə'sifik], *a.* transpacifique.

transparence [træns'pær(ə)ns, -'pɛər-], *s.* transparence *f*; clarté *f* (du verre, etc.).

transparency [træns'pærənsi, -'pɛər-], *s.* **1.** *(a)* transparence *f*; *Atom.Ph:* **t. matrix,** matrice *f* de transparence; **t. to neutrons,** transparence aux neutrons; *(b)* limpidité *f* (de l'eau, etc.). **2.** *(a)* (*picture*) transparent *m*; *(b) Phot:* diapositive *f*; **colour t.,** diapositive en couleurs.

transparent [træns'pær(ə)nt, -'pɛər-], *a.* **1.** (verre, etc.) transparent, diaphane; (eau, quartz, etc.) limpide; **t. effect,** effet *m* de transparence; **t. colours,** couleurs transparentes; **t.(-)winged,** à ailes diaphanes, *Ent:* vitripenne. **2.** évident, clair, qui saute aux yeux; à ne pas s'y méprendre; **of t. honesty,** d'une honnêteté évidente; **t. lies,** mensonges faciles à pénétrer.

transparently [træns'pærəntli, -'pɛər-], *adv.* **1.** d'une manière transparente. **2.** évidemment, clairement; **t. truthful,** d'une véracité incontestable.

transperitoneal [trænzperitə'niːəl], *a.* transpéritonéal, -aux.

transpierce [træns'piəs], *v.tr.* transpercer.

transpiration [trænspi'reiʃ(ə)n], *s. (a) Physiol:* transpiration *f*; perspiration *f*; exhalation *f*; *(b) Bot: Ph:* transpiration.

transpire [træns'paiər]. **1.** *v.tr.* (*of body, plant, etc.*) exsuder (un fluide); exhaler (une odeur). **2.** *v.i. (a) Physiol: Bot:* transpirer; *(b)* (*of news, secret*) transpirer, se répandre; **it transpired that . . .,** on a appris que . . .; *(c)* arriver, se passer, avoir lieu.

transplacental [trænzplæ'sentəl], *a. Anat:* transplacentaire.

transplant[1] ['trænsplɑːnt, 'trɑː-], *s.* **1.** *Hort:* plant repiqué. **2.** *Surg: (a)* transplantation *f,* greffe *f*; **t. surgery,** la chirurgie des greffes; **heart t.,** greffe du cœur; **heart t. patient,** greffé, -ée, du cœur; **inter-species t.,** greffe entre espèces différentes; *(b)* transplant *m,* greffon *m,* organe transplanté, greffé; **t. donor, recipient,** donneur, -euse, receveur, -euse, d'organe.

transplant[2] [træns'plɑːnt, trɑː-], *v.tr. (a) Hort:* transplanter, déplanter (des arbres, etc.); repiquer (des plants); *(b)* transplanter, transporter (une population, etc.); *(c) Surg:* transplanter, greffer (un organe); greffer (du tissu).

transplantable [træns'plɑːntəbl], *a.* transplantable.

transplantation [trænsplɑː'nteiʃ(ə)n], *s.* **1.** *Hort:* repiquage *m.* **2.** transplantation *f* (de populations, etc.). **3.** *Surg:* transplantation, greffe *f* (d'un organe); **heart t., kidney t.,** greffe, transplantation, du cœur, du rein.

transplanter [træns'plɑːntər], *s. Hort:* transplantoir *m.*

transplanting [træns'plɑːntiŋ], *s.* = TRANSPLANTATION.

transpleural [trænz'pləːrəl], *a.* transpleural, -aux; *Surg:* **t. incision,** incision transpleurale.

transpolar [trænz'poulər], *a.* transpolaire.

transponder [trænz'pɔndər], *s. Elcs:* transpondeur *m.*

transpontine [trænz'pɔntain], *a. (a)* transpontain; *(b) A:* de la rive droite (de la Tamise); **t. drama,** mélodrame *m* à gros effets.

transport[1] ['trænspɔːt], *s.* **1.** *(a)* transport *m* (de marchandises, de voyageurs, de troupes, etc.); **public t.,** les transports en commun; **road t.,** transport routier, par route; **rail t.,** transport ferroviaire, par chemin de fer; **air t.,** transport aérien, par air, par avion; **river t.,** transport fluvial; **inland water t.,** transport par voie(s) d'eau intérieure(s); **door-to-door t.,** transport à domicile; le porte à porte; **t. agent,** commissionnaire *m* de transport; transitaire *m*; **t. charges,** frais *m* de transport; *Mil: etc:* **military, army, t.,** les transports militaires; **concentration t.,** transports de concentration; **field t.,** transports de campagne; **first-line t.,** train *m* de combat; *Navy:* **attack t.,** transport d'assaut; *U.S:* **aircraft t.,** transport d'aviation; *(b) Cmptr:* transport, entraînement *m* (d'une bande magnétique, etc.); **t. mechanism,** mécanisme *m* d'entraînement; *(c) Atom.Ph:* transport (de particules); **t. of neutrons,** transport de neutrons; **t. cross section,** section *f* efficace de transport; **t. mean free path,** libre parcours moyen de transport. **2.** moyen *m* de transport; *Navy:* (bâtiment *m* de) transport; *Av:* **t. (aircraft, plane),** (avion *m* de) transport; avion cargo; *Adm: Mil: etc:* **your transport's waiting,** votre voiture est à la porte; *F:* **have you got t.?** est-ce que vous avez une, votre, voiture? **3.** *Jur: A:* déporté, -ée; transporté, -ée; forçat *m.* **4.** transport (de joie, de colère); élancement *m* (de l'esprit); **she was in transports of joy,** elle était transportée de joie.

transport[2] [træns'pɔːt], *v.tr.* **1.** *(a)* transporter (des voyageurs, des marchandises); **to t. goods by lorry, by truck,** camionner des marchandises; *(b) Cmptr:* acheminer (une carte); faire défiler (une bande). **2.** *Jur: A:* transporter, reléguer (un condamné). **3.** (*usu. passive*) **to be transported with joy, etc.,** être transporté de joie, etc.; délirer de joie, etc.; ne pas se connaître de joie, etc.

transportable [træns'pɔ:təbl], *a.* **1.** (*of goods, etc.*) transportable. **2.** *Jur: A:* (criminel, crime) punissable de transportation.

transportation [trænspɔ:'teiʃ(ə)n], *s.* **1.** (*a*) *esp. NAm:* (i) transport *m*; (ii) moyen *m* de transport (*see* TRANSPORT[1]); (*b*) *NAm: Rail: etc:* billet *m.* **2.** *Jur: A:* transportation *f*; relégation *f.*

transported [træns'pɔ:tid], *a. Jur: A:* (criminel) transporté, déporté.

transporter [træns'pɔ:tər], *s.* **1.** (*pers.*) entrepreneur *m* de transports. **2.** (*a*) transporteur *m*, transporteuse *f*; *Mil:* **tank t.,** porte-chars *m inv*; (*b*) **t. bridge,** (pont) transbordeur *m.*

transposable [træns'pouzəbl], *a.* transposable.

transpose [træns'pouz], *v.tr.* **1.** transposer (des mots, les termes d'une proposition, les termes d'une équation, etc.). **2.** *Mus:* transposer; **to t. a piece from C to D,** transposer un morceau d'ut en ré; **to t. a piece to a higher, lower, key,** élever, baisser, le ton d'un morceau.

transposer [træns'pouzər], *s. Mus:* transpositeur, -trice.

transposing[1] [træns'pouziŋ], *a. Mus:* **t. instrument,** transpositeur *m*; **t. piano,** piano transpositeur; **t. wind instruments,** instruments à vent transpositeurs.

transposing[2], *s. Mus:* transposition *f.*

transposition [trænspə'ziʃ(ə)n], *s.* (*a*) *Mus:* transposition *f*; (*b*) transposition, inversion *f* (de lettres, etc.); *Mth:* permutation *f* (de chiffres, de caractères); *Cmptr:* **t. error,** erreur *f* par inversion de deux chiffres; (*c*) *Tp:* croisement *m* (technique) des fils; **t. pole,** appui *m* de croisement; **t. section,** section *f* d'anti-induction; (*d*) *Anat:* **t. of the heart and liver,** transposition du cœur et du foie.

transpositional [trænspə'ziʃən(ə)l], **transpositive** [træns'pɔzitiv], *a.* transpositif.

transrectification [trænzrektifi'keiʃ(ə)n], *s. Elcs:* (*in vacuum tube*) redressement *m*; **t. characteristic,** diagramme *m* de redressement; **t. factor,** pourcentage *m* de redressement.

trans-Saharan [trænssə'hɑ:r(ə)n], *a.* transsaharien.

trans-ship, *v.tr.* **trans-shipment,** *s.* = TRANSHIP, TRANSHIPMENT.

trans-Siberian [træn(z)sai'biəriən], *a.* transsibérien.

trans(-)sonic [træn'sɔnik], *a. Ph:* transsonique.

transsubstantiate [trænsəb'stænʃieit], *v.tr. Theol:* transsubstantier.

transsubstantiation [trænsəbstænʃi'eiʃ(ə)n], *s. Theol:* transsubstantiation *f.*

transudate ['trænsju:deit], *s. Physiol:* transsudat *m.*

transudation [trænsju:'deiʃ(ə)n], *s. Physiol:* transsudation *f.*

transude [træn'sju:d], *v.tr. & i. Physiol:* transsuder.

transuranian, transuranic, transuranium [trænzju'reiniən, -ju'rænik, -ju'reiniəm], *a. Ch:* transuranien; **t. element,** élément transuranien.

Transvaal ['trɑ:nzvɑ:l]. **1.** *Pr.n.* **the T.,** le Transvaal. **2.** *a.* transvaalien.

Transvaaler [trɑ:nz'vɑ:lər], *s.* Transvaalien, -ienne.

transvaluate, transvalue [trænz'vælju(eit)], *v.tr. U.S:* réévaluer, réestimer.

transvaluation [trænzvælju'eiʃ(ə)n], *s.* (*a*) *Phil:* transvaluation *f*; (*b*) *U.S:* réévaluation *f.*

transverberate [trænz'və:bəreit], *v.tr.* transverbérer.

transverberation [trænzvə:bə'reiʃ(ə)n], *s.* transverbération *f.*

transversal [trænz'və:s(ə)l]. **1.** *a.* transversal, -aux. **2.** *s.* (*a*) *Mth:* transversale *f*; (*b*) *Anat:* transversal *m*; transverse *m.*

transversally [trænz'və:səli], *adv.* transversalement.

transverse ['trænzvə:s], *a.* (*occ. s.*) transversal, -aux; transverse; (*a*) *Anat:* **t. artery, vein,** artère *f*, veine *f*, transverse, transversaire; **t. colon,** côlon transversal, transverse; **t. fissure,** sillon transversal, transverse (du foie, du cerveau); **t. process,** apophyse *f* transverse; *a. & s.* **t. (muscle),** (muscle) transversal *m*; (muscle) transverse *m*; (*b*) *Mth: etc:* **t. line,** transversale *f*; **t. axis,** axe *m* transverse (d'une hyperbole); **t. section,** section transversale; coupe *f*, profil *m*, en travers; *Cmptr:* **t. parity,** parité transversale; **t. check,** contrôle *m* de parités transversales; (*c*) *Geol:* **t. valley,** vallée transversale; **t. fault,** décrochement (transversal); (*d*) *Const:* **t. beam,** traverse *f*; *N.Arch:* **t. construction,** construction transversale; **t. member,** liaison transversale; **t. metacentre,** métacentre latitudinal; *Av:* **t. frame,** couple *m*, cadre *m*; (*e*) *Mch.-Tls:* **t. feed,** avance transversale; **t. movement (of carriage),** course transversale (du chariot); *Rail:* **t. table,** transporteur *m* de wagons; plate-forme roulante; pont roulant; (chariot) transbordeur *m*; (*f*) *Ph: etc:* **t. field,** champ *m* transverse; **t. motion,** mouvement transversal; **t. diffusion,** diffusion transversale; **t. stability, vibration,** stabilité, vibration, transversale; **t. wave,** onde transversale.

transversely [trænz'və:sli], *adv.* transversalement; en travers.

transvestism [trænz'vestizm], *s. Psy:* travestisme *m*, transvestisme *m.*

transvestite [trænz'vestait], *s. Psy:* travesti, -ie.

Transylvania [trænsil'veiniə], *Pr.n. Geog:* Transylvanie *f.*

Transylvanian [trænsil'veiniən]. *Geog:* (*a*) *a.* transylvain, transylvanien; (*b*) *s.* Transylvain, -aine; Transylvanien, -ienne.

tranter ['træntər], *s. Dial:* (*a*) voiturier *m*; (*b*) colporteur *m.*

trap[1] [træp], *s.* **1.** (*a*) *Ven: etc:* piège *m*; (*for small game*) attrape *f*; (*for big game*) trappe *f*; (*for wolves, foxes, etc.*) chausse-trape *f, pl.* chausse-trapes; traquenard *m*, traquet *m*; (*for small birds*) trébuchet *m*, sauterelle *f*, cagette *f*, mésangette *f*; (*for hares, etc.*) panneau *m*; **spring t.,** piège à palette; **gin t., jaw t.,** piège à mâchoire; **to set a t. (for . . .),** dresser, tendre, un piège (à . . .); **to bait a t.,** amorcer un piège; **to catch an animal in a t.,** prendre une bête au piège; *Mil:* **tank t.,** chicane *f*; (*b*) *Fish:* **t. net,** filet *m* à cœur; paradière *f*; (*c*) *Atom.Ph:* piège (à particules); **ion t., neutron t.,** piège à ions, à neutrons; **magnetic t.,** piège magnétique; **vacuum t.,** piège à vide; (*d*) piège, ruse *f*, attrape; **police t.,** (i) souricière *f*; (ii) *Aut:* zone *f* de contrôle de vitesse; **to set, lay, a t. for s.o.,** dresser, tendre, un piège, une embûche, à qn; (*of police*) tendre une souricière à qn; **to be caught in the t.,** se laisser prendre au piège; **he's been caught in, he's fallen into, his own t.,** il est pris à son propre piège, dans son propre traquenard; **he fell into the t.,** il s'y laissa prendre; **to walk, fall, straight into the t.,** (i) donner, tomber, en plein dans le piège, dans le lacs, dans la nasse, dans le panneau; (ii) se jeter dans la souricière. **2.** (*a*) **t. (door),** (i) trappe *f*; abattant *m*; (*in hayloft*) abat-foin *m inv*; (ii) *Min:* porte *f* d'aérage; (*b*) *Th:* trappe; trappillon *m*; (*c*) trappe (de colombier); (*d*) *P:* bouche *f*, gueule *f*; **shut your t.!** ta gueule! la ferme! ferme ta boîte! **3.** *Sp:* (projecteur *m*) ball-trap *m, pl.* ball-traps (pour pigeons artificiels); boîte *f* de lancement (pour pigeons vivants). **4.** *Tchn:* collecteur *m* (d'eau, d'huile, etc.); *Mch:* **steam t.,** purgeur *m* de vapeur; **air t.,** (i) *Min:* ventilateur aspirant, porte *f* d'aérage; (ii) *Hyd.E:* poche *f* à air, collecteur à air; (iii) *Civ.E: Plumb:* siphon *m*, coupe-air *m inv* (d'un égout, d'un évier); **sink t.,** puisard *m.* **5.** *Cmptr:* interruption *f* (de programme); **t. handling routine,** sous-programme *m* de gestion d'interruption. **6.** *Veh:* charrette anglaise; cabriolet *m.* **7.** *esp. NAm: Mus:* **traps,** les instruments *m* à percussion.

trap[2] *v.tr.* **(trapped). 1.** *Ven: etc:* (*a*) prendre (une bête) au piège; piéger (une bête); **to t. s.o.,** prendre qn au piège; **trapped by the flames,** cerné par les flammes; (*b*) tendre des pièges dans (un bois, etc.); (*c*) *v.i. esp. Can:* trapper; (*d*) *Atom.Ph:* attraper, capturer (des particules). **2.** *Fb:* bloquer (le ballon) avec la plante du pied. **3.** *Tchn:* (*a*) **to t. a drain,** mettre, disposer, un siphon dans une conduite d'eaux ménagères; (*b*) arrêter (un gaz, des émanations) au moyen d'un siphon, d'un coupe-air, etc.; (*c*) *Mch:* purger (la vapeur). **4.** *Cmptr:* interrompre (le programme); **to t. to a location,** faire un branchement à une adresse.

trap[3], *s. Geog:* trapp *m*; roche trappéenne.

trap[4], *v.tr.* caparaçonner, harnacher (un cheval).

trapa ['træpə], *s. Bot:* trapa *m*, chataigne *f* d'eau, macre *f.*

trapes [treips], *s., v.i. & v.tr.* = TRAIPSE[1,2].

trapeze [trə'pi:z], *s. Gym: etc:* trapèze *m*; **flying t.,** trapèze volant; **to perform on the flying t.,** faire du trapèze volant, de la voltige; **t. artist,** trapéziste *mf*; voltigeur, -euse.

trapeziform [trə'pi:zifɔ:m], *a.* trapéziforme.

trapeziometacarpal [trəpi:zioumetə'kɑ:pl], *a. Anat:* trapézo-métacarpien.

trapezist [trə'pi:zist], *s. Gym: etc:* trapéziste *mf.*

trapezium [trə'pi:ziəm], *s.* **1.** *Mth:* trapèze *m.* **2.** *Anat:* **t. (bone),** os *m* trapèze; os trapézoïde.

trapezius [trə'pi:ziəs], *s. Anat:* **t. (muscle),** muscle *m* trapèze.

trapezohedron [træpi:zou'hi:dr(ə)n, -'hed-], *s. Mth: Cryst:* trapézoèdre *m.*

trapezoid ['træpizɔid], *s.* **1.** *Mth:* trapézoïde *m.* **2.** *Anat:* **t. (bone),** os *m* trapézoïde.

trapezoidal [træpi'zɔidl], *a.* trapézoïde; *Mth:* trapézoïdal, -aux; *Elcs:* **t. integration,** intégration trapézoïdale.

trapfall ['træpfɔ:l], trappe *f* (à bascule, au-dessus d'une fosse).

trapnest ['træpnest], *s.* nid-trappe *m, pl.* nids-trappes (de poulailler).

trappean [trə'pi(:)ən], *a. Geol:* trappéen.

trapped[1] [træpt], *a.* **1.** pris dans un piège; pris au piège; attrapé. **2.** *Tchn:* (*of drains, pipes*) muni d'un siphon, de pièces en chicane, d'un coupe-air; **light-t. cowl,** ventilateur *m* en chicane.

trapped[2], *a.* (cheval) harnaché, caparaçonné.

trapper ['træpər], *s.* **1.** *Ven:* piégeur *m*; *U.S: Can:* trappeur *m.* **2.** *Min:* ouvrier *m* à la manœuvre des portes d'aérage; portier *m*; fermeur *m* de portes.

trapping ['træpiŋ], *s.* **1.** (*a*) *Ven: etc:* piégeage *m*; chasse *f* au(x) piège(s); **t. and netting,** chasse au piège et au filet; (*b*) *Atom.Ph:* capture *f* (de particules); **t. of ions, of neutrons,** capture d'ions, de neutrons; (*c*) *Cmptr:* branchement *m* à une adresse (en cas d'incident); (*d*) *Physiol:* trappage *m* (de gaz inspirés). **2.** métier *m* de trappeur.

trappings ['træpiŋz], *s.pl.* **1.** harnachement *m*, caparaçon *m.* **2.** atours *mpl*; apparat *m*; **the t. of authority,** l'apparat de l'autorité.

Trappist ['træpist], *a. & s. Ecc:* trappiste (*m*).

Trappistine ['træpisti(:)n]. **1.** *Ecc: a. & s.* trappistine (*f*). **2.** *s.* (liqueur) trappistine *f.*

traprock ['træprɔk], *s. Geol:* = TRAP[3].

traps [træps], *s.pl. F:* effets (personnels); **to pack (up) one's t.,** faire ses valises; plier bagage.

trapshooter ['træpʃu:tər], *s. Sp:* tireur *m* au ball-trap, aux pigeons (artificiels ou vivants).

trapshooting ['træpʃu:tiŋ], *s. Sp:* ball-trap *m*; tir *m* aux pigeons; **live t.,** tir aux pigeons vivants.

trash [træʃ], *s.* **1.** (*a*) *Hort:* émondes *fpl*; (*b*) **(cane) t.,** bagasse *f* (de canne à sucre); (*c*) **t. ice,** glace flottante; débris *mpl* de banquise. **2.** (*a*) chose(s) *f*(*pl*) sans valeur; marchandises *fpl* de rebut, de pacotille; camelote *f*; *NAm:* détritus *mpl*, déchets *mpl*, ordures *fpl*; **t. can,** poubelle *f*; boîte *f* à ordures; **yard t.,** détritus du jardinage; (*b*) littérature *f* de camelote; (*c*) **to talk a lot of t.,** dire des sottises; parler pour ne rien dire; (*d*) *coll. Pej:* (*of pers.*) vauriens *mpl*, propres à rien *mpl*; *U.S:* **(poor) white t.,** les pauvres blancs, les petits blancs (des états méridionaux des États-Unis).

trashiness ['træʃinis], *s.* mauvaise qualité, peu *m* de valeur (d'une marchandise, etc.).

trashy ['træʃi], *a.* (marchandises, etc.) sans valeur, de mauvaise qualité, de rebut, de pacotille; (littérature *f*) de camelote.

Trasimene ['træzimi:n], **Trasimenus** [træzi'mi:nəs], *Pr.n. A.Geog:* **Lake Trasimene, Lake Trasimenus,** le lac Trasimène; *Geog:* **Lake Trasimene,** le lac de Pérouse.

trass [træs], *s. Miner:* trass *m*; pouzzolane *f* en pierre.

traulism ['trɔ:lizm], *s.* traulisme *m.*

trauma, *pl.* **-as, -ata** ['trɔ:mə, -əz, -ətə], *s. Med: Psy:* trauma *m.*

traumatic [trɔ:'mætik], *a. Med:* (fièvre, choc) traumatique.

traumatism ['trɔ:mətizm], *s. Med:* traumatisme *m.*

traumatize ['trɔ:mətaiz], *v.tr. Med:* traumatiser.

traumatology [trɔ:mə'tɔlədʒi], *s.* traumatologie *f.*

traumatopn(o)ea [trɔ:mətou'(p)ni:ə], *s. Med:* traumatopnée *f.*

travail[1] ['træveil], *s.* **1.** *A:* dur travail; labeur *m*, peine *f.* **2.** *A. & Lit:* douleurs *fpl* de l'enfantement; travail (d'enfant); mal *m* d'enfant; enfantement *m*; **woman in t.,** femme en travail.

travail[2], *v.i. A. & Lit:* (*of woman*) être en travail (d'enfantement).

travel[1] ['træv(ə)l], *s.* **1.** (*a*) voyages *mpl*; **to be fond of t.,** aimer voyager; aimer les voyages; **t. broadens the mind,** le voyage, voyager, ouvre l'esprit; **t. books,** récits *m* de voyages; **t. agency,** agence *f* de voyages; **t. agent,** agent *m* de voyages; **t. companion,** compagnon *m* de voyage; **t. bag,** sac *m* de voyage; **t. wear,** vêtements *mpl* de voyage; **t. goods,** articles *m* de voyage; (*b*) **I met him on, in the course of, my travels,** j'ai fait sa connaissance en voyage; **is he still on his travels?** est-il toujours en voyage? **2.** *Mec: Mch:* course *f*, avance *f* (du piston, du tiroir, du chariot); levée *f* (de piston, de soupape); déplacement *m* (d'une pièce mécanique); débattement *m* (de la caisse d'un véhicule); *Ball:* course, trajet *m* (d'un mobile, d'un projectile); **free t.,** course libre; **angular, axial, vertical, t.,** déplacement angulaire, axial, vertical; **upward, downward, t.,** course ascendante, descendante; **endwise t.,** déplacement longitudinal (d'une vis, etc.); **side t.,** translation latérale (d'un chariot de pont roulant); **t. follow-up,** détecteur *m* de déplacement; *Aut:* **clutch t.,** course de l'embrayage.

travel[2], *v.i.* **(travelled) 1.** (*a*) voyager; faire des voyages; **he has travelled a great deal, widely,** il a beaucoup voyagé; il a vu du pays, bien des pays; **to t. round the world,** faire le tour du monde; **to t. all over the world,**

courir le monde; **to t. through a country,** parcourir, traverser, un pays; **he travels up from Brighton (to London) every day,** il fait le trajet Brighton-Londres tous les jours; **I've travelled long distances on foot,** j'ai fait beaucoup de chemin à pied; **to t. a lonely road,** faire chemin seul; **to t. light,** voyager avec un minimum de bagages; **we travelled together,** nous avons fait le voyage ensemble; **to t. on business,** voyager pour affaires; **she let her thoughts t. over the past,** elle laissait errer ses pensées vers le passé; (*b*) aller, marcher; faire route; (*of news*) circuler, se répandre; **light travels faster than sound,** la lumière va, se propage, plus vite que le son; **the train was travelling at 150 km an hour,** le train marchait à 150 km à l'heure; *Aut:* **as we were travelling along the Dover road,** comme nous roulions sur la route de Douvres; **that day we travelled more than 800 km,** ce jour-là nous avons fait une étape de plus de 800 km; **this wine won't t.,** ce vin ne voyage pas. **2. to t. (for a firm),** voyager (pour une maison); représenter une maison; être représentant; **to t. in wine,** voyager pour les vins. **3.** *Mec.E:* (*of part*) se mouvoir, se déplacer; **to t. sideways,** se déplacer latéralement. **4.** *v.tr.* faire voyager (des troupeaux); *Equit: Turf:* **to t. a horse,** transporter, faire voyager, un cheval.

travelator ['trævəleitər], *s.* trottoir roulant.

travelled ['trævəld], *a.* (*of pers.*) **(much, well,) t.,** qui a beaucoup voyagé, qui connaît le monde, qui a vu bien des pays; **some of my t. friends tell me that . . .,** quelques-uns de mes amis, grands voyageurs, me disent, m'assurent, que . . ..

traveller ['træv(ə)lər], *s.* **1.** (*a*) voyageur, -euse; **he's been a great t.,** il a beaucoup voyagé; **fellow t.,** (i) *O:* compagnon *m* de voyage, de route; (ii) *Pej:* communisant, -ante; **traveller's cheque,** *U.S:* **check,** chèque *m* de voyage; (*b*) *Bot:* **traveller's joy,** clématite *f*; **traveller's tree,** arbre *m* du voyageur. **2.** *O:* **(commercial) t.,** voyageur de commerce; représentant *m*. **3.** (*a*) *Mec.E:* grue roulante; pont roulant; **shop t.,** pont roulant d'atelier; (*b*) (treuil *m*) chariot *m* (d'un pont roulant). **4.** (*a*) curseur *m* (de métier à filer, de règle à calcul, etc.); (*b*) *Nau:* **t. (ring),** bague *f* de conduite; guide *m* de drisse; rocambeau *m*; **backstay t.,** gouvernail *m* de drisse; (*c*) *U.S: Th:* **t. curtain,** rideau *m* à la grecque.

travelling[1] ['træv(ə)liŋ], *a.* **1.** (*a*) (cirque) ambulant; (prédicateur) itinérant; (*b*) *O:* (*now usu.* **mobile**) **t. library,** bibliobus *m*; *Rail:* **t. post office,** (bureau de poste) ambulant *m*; wagon-poste *m, pl.* wagons-poste; *Mil: etc:* **t. kitchen,** cuisine roulante, *F:* roulante *f*; **t. workshop,** camion-atelier *m, pl.* camions-ateliers. **2.** *Mec.E: etc:* (pont, treuil, portique, trottoir, etc.) roulant; (grille) mobile; **t. apron,** bande *f* souple de transport; toile transporteuse; **t. table,** (i) (*of lathe*) table *f* mobile; (ii) (*of rolling mill*) conducteur *m* de lingot. **3.** *Ph: etc:* **t. wave,** onde progressive; **t.-wave accelerator,** accélérateur *m* à ondes progressives, à propagation d'ondes.

travelling[2], *s.* (*a*) voyages *mpl*; **t. is expensive,** les voyages sont coûteux; **t. expenses,** frais *m* de voyage, de route; *Adm: Com: etc:* frais de déplacement; indemnité *f* de voyage; **t. scholarship,** bourse *f* de voyage; **t. companion,** compagnon *m* de voyage; **t. bag,** sac *m* de voyage; **t. clock,** réveil *m* de voyage; (*b*) *Artil:* **t. position,** position *f* de route (de l'ensemble tube-affût); *Mec.E:* **t. wheel,** galet *m* de roulement; roue *f* de translation; (*c*) *Cin:* **t. platform,** travelling *m*; **t. shot,** prise *f* de vues en travelling.

travelogue ['trævəlɔg], *s.* (*a*) documentaire *m* de voyage; (*b*) conférence *f* décrivant un voyage, une expédition.

travelstained ['trævəlsteind], *a.* sali par le voyage.

traversable [trə'vəːsəbl], *a.* **1.** (désert, etc.) traversable. **2.** *Jur:* (assertion) niable, contestable.

traverse[1] ['trævəs], *s.* **1.** (*a*) *O:* passage *m* à travers (une propriété, etc.); traversée *f* (d'une forêt, etc.); (*b*) *Mount:* (i) traverse *f* (sur la face d'un escarpement); vire *f*; (ii) traversée; **diagonal uphill t.,** montée diagonale; (*c*) *Mec.E:* (i) translation latérale (d'un chariot de tour, etc.); chariotage *m*; (ii) course verticale (de l'arbre porte-foret); **longitudinal t.,** chariotage longitudinal; **t. grinding,** rectification *f* par chariotage; *Mch.-Tls:* **t. feed,** avance *f* (de l'outil); (*d*) *Artil:* (i) pivotement (horizontal) (de la pièce); fauchage *m*; (ii) pointage *m* (de la pièce) en direction; **all-round t.,** pivotement tous azimuts; **t. circle,** circulaire *m* de tir; (*e*) *Th:* **t. curtain,** rideau *m* à la grecque. **2.** (*a*) *Mth:* (ligne) transversale *f*; (*b*) *Surv:* cheminement *m*; **t. survey,** levé *m* par cheminement; **closed t.,** cheminement fermé; **compass t., plane-table t., time t.,** cheminement à la boussole, à la planchette, à la montre; **leg of t.,** segment *m* de cheminement (entre deux stations successives); **taking of angles in t.,** cheminement d'angles; **to run a t.,** faire un cheminement; **t. map,** carte (topographique) établie par cheminements. **3.** *Nau:* route partielle; route en zigzag; **t. board,** renard *m* (de la timonerie); **t. table,** table *f* de point; **t. sailing,** point estimé avec de nombreuses routes; **to reduce, cast, work, solve, a t.,** réduire les routes. **4.** *Mec.E: Const: etc:* traverse, entretoise *f* (de châssis, de cadre, etc.). **5.** (*a*) *Fort:* traverse; (*b*) *Mil:* pare-éclats *m inv* (de tranchée). **6.** (*a*) *A:* traverse, revers *m*, obstacle *m*; (*b*) *Jur:* dénégation *f* (des faits allégués par l'adversaire). **7.** *Rail:* **t. (table)** = TRAVERSER.

traverse[2], *v.*

I. *v.tr.* **1.** *Lit:* (*a*) traverser, passer à travers (une région, le corps); franchir (une montagne); passer (un pont, un fleuve, la mer); (*b*) passer en revue (un sujet, une époque). **2.** (*a*) *Carp:* traverser (une planche) avec le rabot; (*b*) *Mec.E:* **to t. a piece on the lathe,** charioter, surfacer, une pièce. **3.** *Surv:* faire un cheminement (d'une région); faire le levé (d'une région) par cheminement. **4.** (*a*) *Artil: etc:* pointer (une pièce) en direction; (*b*) *Rail:* transborder (une locomotive). **5.** (*a*) *Lit:* contrarier, traverser (un dessein, une opinion); (*b*) *Jur:* dénier, renier (une accusation); opposer une fin de non-recevoir à (une réclamation).

II. *v.i.* **1.** *Mount:* prendre une traverse. **2.** (*of compass needle*) pivoter; **the compass does not t.,** le compas dort. **3.** (*of horse*) se traverser. **4.** (*of lathe cutting tool*) charioter.

traverser ['trævəsər], *s. Rail:* chariot *m* transbordeur; pont roulant; transporteur *m* de wagons.

traversing ['trævəsiŋ], *s.* **1.** (*a*) *Lit:* traversée *f* (d'une forêt, d'une mer); passage *m*, franchissement *m* (d'un fleuve, etc.); (*b*) *Lit:* passage en revue (d'une question, d'une époque); (*c*) *Mount:* prise *f* d'une traverse. **2.** (*a*) déplacement latéral (d'un pont roulant); (*b*) *Mec.E:* chariotage *m*; **t. tool,** outil chariotеur. **3.** *Surv:* (levé *m* par) cheminement *m*; **precise t.,** cheminement principal. **4.** (*a*) *Artil: etc:* (i) fauchage *m*; (ii) pointage *m* en direction; **t. fire,** tir *m* de fauchage; **t. and searching fire,** tir sur zone; **t. arc,** arc *m* de pointage en direction; **t. clamp handle,** levier *m* de blocage en direction; **t. gear, t. mechanism,** mécanisme *m* de pointage en direction; **t. handwheel, t. lever,** volant *m*, levier, de pointage en direction; **t. stop,** butée *f* de pointage en direction; (*b*) *Rail:* transbordement *m* (d'un wagon, etc.). **5.** *Jur:* dénégation *f* (d'une accusation).

travertine ['trævətain], *s. Geol:* travertin *m*, albâtre *m* (calcaire); silex *m* molaire.

travesty[1] ['trævəsti], *s.* travestissement *m* (d'une pièce de théâtre, etc.); parodie *f*; **a t. of the truth,** un travestissement de la vérité.

travesty[2], *v.tr. Lit:* parodier, travestir (une histoire, un personnage, etc.); **travestied play,** pièce travestie.

travis ['trævis], *s. Vet: etc:* travail *m, pl.* -ails.

travois, travoise, travoy[1] ['trævɔi(z), trə'vɔi(z)], *s. NAm: Veh:* travois *m*.

travoy[2], *v.tr. NAm:* transporter en travois.

trawl[1] [trɔːl], *s.* **1.** *Fish:* (*a*) **t. (net),** chalut *m*, chalon *m*; traille *f*; filet *m* à la trôle; (*b*) **t. (line),** palangre *f*, corde *f*; ligne flottante, dormante; **t. anchor,** petite ancre de palangre. **2.** *Navy:* (*for mines*) câble balayeur.

trawl[2]. *Fish:* **1.** *v.i.* pêcher à la traille, au chalut; chaluter. **2.** *v.tr.* (*a*) trainer (un chalut); (*b*) prendre (le poisson) à la traille, au chalut.

trawler ['trɔːlər], *s.* **1.** (*pers.*) pêcheur *m* au chalut; chalutier *m*. **2.** (*ship*) chalutier; **freezer t.,** chalutier frigorifique; **anti-submarine t.,** chalutier anti-sous-marin; **seaward-defence t.,** chalutier de défense vers le large.

trawling ['trɔːliŋ], *s. Fish:* pêche *f* au chalut; pêche chalutière; chalutage *m*; trôle *f*.

tray[1] [trei], *s.* **1.** (*a*) plateau *m, Fr.C:* cabaret *m*; **tea t.,** plateau à thé; **(hawker's flat) t.,** éventaire *m*; **(wicker) t.,** (i) (*for draining cheeses, etc.*) clayon *m*; (ii) (*for fruit, silkworms*) claie *f*; pantène *f*; **two-man t.,** bard *m*; *Surg: etc:* **instrument t.,** plateau à instruments; **sterilizing t.,** plateau pour stérilisation; (*b*) **a t. of sandwiches, etc.,** un plateau de sandwichs, etc.; (*c*) casier *m*, châssis *m* (d'une malle, etc.); compartiment *m* (d'une caisse, d'une malle); (*d*) (*in office, etc.*) corbeille *f* (à correspondance); **in t.,** corbeille à correspondance reçue; **out t.,** corbeille à courrier à expédier, à documents à classer; *Cmptr:* **card t.,** bac *m* à cartes; **loading t.,** rampe *f* à chargement; **t. truck,** chariot *m* à cartes. **2.** (*a*) cuvette *f*; (*b*) *Dent:* **impression t.,** porte-empreinte *m, pl.* porte-empreintes; **upper, lower, impression t.,** porte-empreinte du haut, du bas. **3.** (*a*) *Artil:* (*of gun*) **loading t.,** planchette *f* de chargement; (*b*) tambour *m* (de mitrailleuse Lewis).

tray[2], *s. Ven:* **t. (antler),** chevillure *f*.

traycloth ['treiklɔθ], *s.* dessus *m*, serviette *f*, napperon *m* (de plateau).

trayful ['treiful], *s.* plein plateau (de qch.).

treacherous ['tretʃərəs], *a.* (homme, caractère) traître, déloyal, -aux; (action) perfide; **t. blow,** coup déloyal; coup de Jarnac; **t. ice,** glace traîtresse; **t. weather,** temps traître; **t. memory,** mémoire infidèle, peu sûre.

treacherously ['tretʃərəsli], *adv.* (agir) en traître, perfidement, déloyalement, traîtreusement.

treacherousness ['tretʃərəsnis], *s.* (*a*) caractère dangereux (de la glace, etc.); (*b*) *occ.* = TREACHERY.

treachery ['tretʃəri], *s.* trahison *f*; perfidie *f*; **act of t.,** action *f* perfide; perfidie; **this is little short of t.,** c'est presque de la trahison.

treacle[1] [triːkl], *s.* **1.** mélasse *f*; **t. tart,** tarte *f* à la mélasse. **2.** *A.Pharm:* thériaque *f*.

treacle[2], *v.tr.* enduire (qch.) à la mélasse; engluer (des insectes).

treacly ['triːkli], *a.* (*a*) couvert de mélasse; gluant; **black t. oil,** huile noire et gluante; (*b*) (*of book, etc.*) d'une sentimentalité écœurante.

tread[1] [tred], *s.* **1.** (*a*) pas *m*; **heavy t.,** pas lourd; **measured, stately, t.,** pas mesuré, majestueux; démarche mesurée; **to walk with measured t.,** marcher à pas mesurés; s'avancer d'un train de sénateur; (*b*) bruit *m* de pas; (*c*) *A:* empreinte *f* de pas. **2.** (*a*) accouplement *m* (de l'oiseau mâle); (*b*) chalaze *f* (d'un œuf). **3.** (*a*) marche *f* (d'escalier); **t. (board),** giron *m*, ais *m* (de marche); **steps with a 15 cm t.,** marches avec 15 cm de giron; (*b*) semelle *f* (d'une chaussure, d'un étrier); plancher *m* (d'un étrier); (*c*) fourchon *m*, étrier (d'échasse); (*d*) échelon *m* (d'échelle, etc.); (*e*) *Rail:* surface *f*, table *f*, de roulement (d'un rail); *Civ.E:* table, semelle (de poutre); (*f*) *Aut:* (i) bande *f* de roulement, chape *f*, (ii) sculpture *f* (d'un pneu); portant *m* (d'une roue); **non-skid t.,** roulement antidérapant. **4.** *Cy:* longueur *f* des deux manivelles; distance *f* (entre pédales). **5.** *Veh:* empattement *m*; voie *f*.

tread[2], *v.* **(trod** [trɔd]; **trodden** ['trɔd(ə)n]) **1.** *v.i.* marcher; poser les pieds; **to t. on sth.,** marcher sur qch.; mettre le pied sur qch.; **somebody's been treading on the flower bed,** on a marché sur, on a piétiné, la plate-bande; **to t. on s.o.'s toes,** (i) marcher sur les pieds de qn; (ii) offenser, froisser, qn; **to t. on s.o.'s heels,** marcher sur les talons de qn; suivre qn de près; **we shall have to t. carefully, lightly, warily,** (i) il faut marcher légèrement, soigneusement; (ii) voilà un sujet délicat; nous marchons sur des œufs. **2.** *v.tr.* (*a*) marcher sur (le sol); **well trodden path,** (i) chemin battu; (ii) chemin (très) fréquenté; **to t. down the soil,** piétiner le sol; **to t. a plant in, into the ground,** enfoncer une plante dans le sol (en piétinant); **to t. sth. under foot,** écraser qch. du pied; fouler qch. aux pieds; **he was trodden to death by the elephants,** il a été écrasé sous les pieds des éléphants; (*b*) *O:* **to t. a path,** suivre un chemin; *A:* **to t. a measure,** faire un pas de danse; danser un menuet, une pavane, etc.; (*c*) **to t. grapes,** fouler la vendange; *Swim:* **to t. water,** nager debout; (*d*) (*of male bird*) couvrir, côcher (la femelle).

treadle[1] [tredl], *s.* pédale *f* (de meule à aiguiser, de machine à coudre, etc.); **to work the t.,** actionner la pédale; **t. machine,** machine *f* à pédale.

treadle[2], *v.i. & tr.* pédaler, actionner la pédale; actionner (une machine) avec la pédale.

treadmill ['tredmil], *s.* **1.** (*a*) (i) *A:* (*in prisons, etc.*) écureuil *m*; moulin *m* de discipline; (ii) besogne ingrate (quotidienne); collier *m* de misère; (*b*) = TREADWHEEL. **2.** (*for horses*) manège *m* à plan incliné; trépigneuse *f*.

treadwheel ['tred(h)wiːl], *s.* roue *f* à marches, à chevilles; treuil *m*; (roue à) tympan *m*.

treason ['triːz(ə)n], *s. Jur:* trahison *f*; **high t.,** haute trahison; lèse-majesté *f*; **t. felony,** infraction *f* à, complot *m* contre, la sûreté de l'État; **to talk t.,** tenir des propos séditieux.

treasonable ['triːzənəbl], *a.* séditieux; traître; (acte) de trahison.

treasure[1] ['treʒər], *s.* trésor *m*; **art treasures,** trésors, richesses *f*, artistiques; **t. hunt,** chasse *f* au(x) trésor(s); *Jur:* **t. trove,** trésor (découvert par le pur effet du hasard); *B:* **where your t. is there will your heart be also,** où est votre trésor là sera aussi votre cœur; **to lay up treasures in heaven,** amasser des trésors dans le ciel; *F:* **my help's a real t.,** ma femme de ménage est un trésor, une trouvaille; (*term of endearment*) **my t.!** mon bijou! mon trésor!

treasure[2], *v.tr.* **1.** priser, estimer, tenir beaucoup à, faire beaucoup de cas de (qch.). **2.** (*a*) **to t. sth. (up),** garder qch. soigneusement, comme une relique; conserver qch. précieusement; **to t. sth. in one's memory,** garder précieusement le souvenir de qch.; (*b*) *O:* **to t. up wealth,** accumuler, amasser, des richesses.

treasure(-)house ['treʒəhaus], *s. O:* trésor *m.*

treasurer ['treʒərər], *s.* trésorier, -ière; économe *mf* (d'une institution); **T. of the Household,** trésorier de la maison du souverain; *Hist:* **Lord High T.,** grand Trésorier.

treasury ['treʒəri], *s.* **1.** (*a*) trésor (public); trésorerie *f*; (*in Eng.*) **the T.** = le Ministère des finances; **First Lord of the T.** = Président *m* du Conseil (des ministres); *Fin:* **t. bonds, bills,** bons *m* du Trésor; *A:* **t. note,** coupure (de dix shillings ou d'une livre) émise par le Trésor; (*b*) trésor (d'une cathédrale, etc.). **2. t. (of verse),** anthologie *f* (de poésie).

treat[1] [tri:t], *s.* **1.** (*a*) régal, -als *m*; festin *m*; *O:* **Sunday-school t.,** fête offerte aux enfants de l'école du dimanche; (*b*) *P:* **to stand t.,** payer la tournée; **it's my t.,** c'est ma tournée; c'est moi qui paie. **2.** plaisir *m*; délice *m*; **it's a (great) t. to me,** cela me fait (infiniment de) plaisir; **it would be a great t. to go to the theatre,** ce serait une véritable fête d'aller au théâtre; **for us game is a t.,** pour nous le gibier est un régal; **to give oneself a t.,** faire un petit extra; **a t. in store,** un plaisir à venir; *Iron:* **you've got a t. in store!** je vous en souhaite! *Com:* **give yourself a t.! have a . . .!** succombez aux charmes de . . .! **3.** *P:* **that whisky went down a t.!** ce whisky m'a fait du bien; **he's getting on a (fair) t.!** (i) il fait des progrès épatants! (ii) ses affaires marchent à merveille!

treat[2], *v.i. & tr.* **1.** *v.i.* **to t. with s.o.,** traiter, négocier, avec qn; **to t. with the enemy,** pactiser avec l'ennemi; **to t. for peace,** traiter la paix. **2.** *v.tr.* traiter (qn, qch.); **to t. s.o. well,** traiter qn bien; se conduire bien avec qn; en bien user avec qn; **her aunt treats her badly,** sa tante la traite mal, la maltraite; **don't t. the poor cat so roughly,** il ne faut pas malmener, maltraiter, ce pauvre chat; **to t. s.o. like a friend,** traiter qn comme un ami, en ami; **my father still treats me like a child,** mon père me traite toujours en enfant, me considère toujours comme un enfant; **books should be treated carefully,** on devrait traiter les livres avec soin; **to t. sth. as a joke,** considérer qch. comme une plaisanterie; **he didn't t. my warning seriously,** il n'a pas pris mon avertissement au sérieux. **3.** *v.tr.* (*a*) **to t. s.o. to the theatre,** inviter qn au théâtre; **to t. oneself to oysters,** s'offrir des huîtres; *Iron:* **after that we were treated to the inevitable good advice,** après cela nous avons eu droit aux inévitables recommandations; (*b*) corrompre (des électeurs en leur offrant à boire ou à manger); *F:* arroser (des électeurs). **4.** *v.tr.* (*a*) *Med:* traiter (un malade, une maladie); **to t. s.o. for rheumatism,** soigner qn pour le rhumatisme; **he was treated in hospital,** il a reçu des soins à l'hôpital; (*b*) **to t. metal with an acid,** traiter un métal par un acide; **to t. wood with creosote,** imprégner le bois de créosote; injecter le bois à la créosote. **5.** *v.tr. Lit: Mus: etc:* traiter (un sujet, un thème).

treatable ['tri:təbl], *a.* traitable.

treating ['tri:tiŋ], *s. Jur:* corruption *f* (des électeurs, etc., en leur offrant à manger ou à boire).

treatise ['tri:tiz], *s.* traité *m* **(on,** de).

treatment ['tri:tmənt], *s.* **1.** (*a*) traitement *m* (de qn); (*of prisoners*) **special t.,** régime spécial; **he complained of the t. he had had,** il s'est plaint de la manière dont il avait été traité; **I didn't expect such t. from you,** je ne m'attendais pas à un traitement semblable de votre part, à ce que vous me traitiez ainsi; (*b*) traitement (d'une matière, d'un sujet). **2.** traitement (médical); **he's going into a nursing home for t.,** il va se faire soigner dans une clinique; **patients under t.,** les malades en traitement.

treaty ['tri:ti], *s.* **1.** traité *m* (de paix, de commerce); convention *f*; **arbitration t.,** traité d'arbitrage; **to enter into a t. with s.o.,** conclure un traité avec qn; **under this t.,** en vertu de ce traité; **t. obligations,** obligations conventionnelles; *Hist:* **t. port,** port ouvert (au commerce étranger). **2.** (*a*) accord *m*, contrat *m*; **to sell sth. by private t.,** vendre qch. de gré à gré, à l'amiable; (*b*) *O:* **to be in t. with s.o. for . . .,** être en traité, être en négociation, en pourparlers, avec qn pour . . ..

Treb(b)ia ['trebiə], *Pr.n. Geog:* **the (river) T.,** la Trébie.

Trebizond ['trebizɔnd], *Pr.n. Geog:* Trébizonde *f.*

treble[1] [trebl], *a., adv. & s.*

I. *a.* **1.** triple. **2.** *Mus:* de dessus; de soprano; **t. voice,** (voix *f* de) soprano *m*; **t. clef,** clef *f* de sol.

II. *adv.* trois fois autant.

III. *s.* **1.** triple *m.* **2.** (*a*) (*crochet*) **plain t.,** brides *f* simples; **alternating t.,** brides contrariées; (*b*) *Paperm:* étendoir *m*; **t. lines,** cordeaux *m* (de l'étendoir); guimées *f.* **3.** (*a*) *Mus:* dessus *m*; **to sing the t.,** chanter le dessus; (*b*) (*pers., voice*) soprano *m*; (*c*) *W.Tel: Elcs:* **t. control,** touche de tonalité aiguë. **4.** *Turf:* (pari) tiercé *m.*

treble[2]. **1.** *v.tr.* tripler (la valeur, le nombre). **2.** *v.i.* (se) tripler.

trebling ['trebliŋ], *s.* triplement *m.*

trebly ['trebli], *adv.* triplement; trois fois autant.

trebuchet ['trebuʃet], *s.* trébuchet *m* (de balance, *A:* de machine de guerre).

trecentist [tri'tʃentist], *s. Art: Lit.Hist:* trécentiste *m.*

trecento (the) [ðətri'tʃentou], *s. Art: Lit.Hist:* le XIVe siècle (italien).

trechmannite ['trekmənait], *s. Miner:* trechmannite *f.*

tree[1] ['tri:], *s.* **1.** (*a*) arbre *m*; **fruit t.,** arbre fruitier; **timber t.,** arbre de haute futaie; **clump of trees,** bouquet *m* d'arbres; *Geog:* **the t. line, limit,** la limite des arbres; **t. of liberty,** arbre de la liberté; **to climb a t.,** grimper sur, monter à, un arbre; **to be at the top of the t.,** être au premier rang de sa profession; être au sommet, au haut, de l'échelle; **to get to the top of the t.,** arriver; *F:* **to be up a (gum) t.,** être dans une impasse, dans le pétrin, dans de beaux draps; *F:* **they don't grow on trees,** on n'en trouve pas à la douzaine; *Prov:* **the t. is known by its fruit,** au fruit on connaît l'arbre; tel arbre tel fruit; (*b*) **the t. of life,** l'arbre de la vie; (*c*) *Bot:* **t. mallow,** lavatère arborée, grande mauve; **t. fern,** fougère arborescente; *F:* **crybaby t.,** (espèce d')érythrine *f*; **sausage t.,** arbre à saucisses, kigelia *m*; (*d*) *Z:* **t. hyrax, t. dassie, t. coney,** daman *m* arboricole, des arbres; dendrohyrax *m*; **t. porcupine,** porc-épic *m* arboricole; ourson *m* coquau; coendou *m*; éréthizontidé *m*; **t. kangaroo, t. wallaby,** dendrolague *m*, kangourou *m* arboricole; **t. shrew,** tupaïa *m*, tupaja *m*; *Amph:* **t. frog, t. toad,** rainette verte; grenouille *f* d'arbre; grasset *m*; *Crust:* **t. crab,** cancre *m* des cocotiers; (*e*) *Orn:* **t. creeper,** grimpereau *m* des bois; **short-toed t. creeper,** grimpereau des jardins; **t. duck,** dendrocygne *m*; **white-faced t. duck,** dendrocygne veuf: **fulvous t. duck,** dendrocygne fauve; **t. pipit,** pipit *m* des arbres; **t. runner,** sittelle *f*; (*f*) *Bookb:* **t. calf,** veau raciné. **2. genealogical, family, t.,** arbre généalogique. **3.** *A:* **gallows t.,** gibet *m*, potence *f*; *B:* **Jesus whom ye slew and hanged on a t.,** Jésus que vous avez fait mourir sur la croix. **4.** (*a*) *O: Const:* poutre *f*; *Min:* étai *m*, butte *f*; (*b*) *Leath:* chevalet *m* (de corroyeur); (*c*) **(shoe) t.,** tendeur *m* (pour chaussures).

tree[2], *v.tr.* (*p.t. & p.p.* **treed**; *pr.p.* **treeing**) (*a*) *Ven:* forcer (une bête) à se réfugier dans un arbre; (*b*) *F:* **he was treed by a bull,** un taureau l'a forcé à monter à, à se réfugier dans, un arbre.

treedozer ['tri:douzər], *s.* débroussailleuse *f*; *Civ.E: F:* treedozer *m.*

treehopper ['tri:hɔpər], *s. Ent:* membracide *m.*

treeless ['tri:lis], *a.* sans arbres.

treenail[1] ['tri:neil, 'tren(ə)l], *s.* cheville *f* de bois; fenton *m*; *Nau:* gournable *f*; *Rail:* trenail, -ails *m*; **t. wedge,** épite *f.*

treenail[2], *v.tr.* cheviller; *Nau:* gournabler.

treepie ['tri:pai], *s. Orn:* pie vagabonde; dendrocitte *f*, dendrocitta *f.*

treetop ['tri:tɔp], *s.* cime *f* d'un arbre; **just over the treetops,** juste au-dessus des arbres; **to skim the treetops,** voler en rase-mottes.

trefoil ['tri:fɔil, 'tref-], *s.* **1.** *Bot:* trèfle *m*; **bird's foot t.,** lotier *m*, *F:* corne *f* du diable; **hare's foot t.,** patte-de-lièvre *f*, *pl.* pattes-de-lièvre; **hop t.,** minette *f*; **bog t., marsh t., water t.,** ményanthe *m* à trois feuilles; trèfle d'eau. **2.** *Arch: Her:* trèfle; *Arch:* trilobe *m*; **t. arch,** arc trilobé.

trehalase ['tri:həleis], *s. Bio-Ch:* tréhalase *f.*

trehalose ['tri:həlous], *s. Ch:* tréhalose *f.*

trek[1] [trek], *s.* **1.** (*in S. Africa*) (*a*) voyage *m* en chariot (à bœufs); (*b*) étape *f* (d'un voyage); (*c*) *Hist:* migration *f.* **2. a long t.,** un trajet long et pénible (surtout à pied).

trek[2], *v.i.* **(trekked) 1.** (*in S. Africa*) voyager en chariot (à bœufs). **2.** faire un trajet long et pénible (surtout à pied).

trekboer ['trekbɔər], *s.* **1.** Boer *m* nomade. **2.** Boer qui émigra du Cap (1835–8).

trekker ['trekər], *s.* (*in S. Africa*) **1.** voyageur *m* (en chariot à bœufs). **2.** *Hist:* émigrant *m.*

trellis[1] ['trelis], *s.* **1.** (*a*) treillis *m*, treillage *m*; **t. window,** fenêtre treillissée; **t. mast,** (i) *N.Arch:* mât *m* en treillis; (ii) *Civ.E:* mât en treillis métallique; (*b*) *Hort:* rideau *m* de treillis; treille *f.* **2.** *Her:* treillis.

trellis[2], *v.tr.* **1.** treillisser, treillager (une fenêtre, etc.). **2.** échalasser (une vigne).

trellised ['trelist], *a.* garni de treillis, de treillage; treillissé; (grillage, etc.) entreillissé; **t. window,** fenêtre treillissée.

trellising ['trelisiŋ], *s.* **1.** échalassage *m*, échalassement *m* (des vignes). **2.** *coll.* = TRELLISWORK.

trelliswork ['treliswə:k], *s.* treillis *m*, treillage *m.*

Trematoda [tremə'toudə], *s.pl. Ann:* trématodes *m.*

trematode ['tremətoud], *a. & s.* **t. (worm),** (ver) trématode *m.*

Trematosaurus [tremətou'sɔ:rəs], *s. Paleont:* trématosaure *m*, trematosaurus *m.*

tremble[1] ['trembl], *s.* **1.** tremblement *m*, frisson *m*; (*in voice*) tremblotement *m*; **to be all of a t., all in a t.,** trembler comme une feuille; être tout tremblant; trembloter. **2.** *Vet:* **the trembles,** maladie tremblante. **3.** *U.S: Bot:* tremble *m.*

tremble[2], *v.i.* **1.** trembler, vibrer; **the bridge was trembling,** le pont tremblait. **2.** trembler, frissonner; frémir; **to t. like a leaf, like an aspen, to t. in every limb,** trembler comme une feuille; être tout tremblant; trembler de tout son corps, de tous ses membres; **to t. with fear,** trembler de peur; frémir de crainte; **I t. at the thought of, I t. to think of, meeting him,** je tremble de le rencontrer, à la pensée de le rencontrer.

trembler ['tremblər], *s.* **1.** (*pers.*) trembleur, -euse; peureux, -euse; poltron, -onne. **2.** *El:* trembleur; **t. coil,** bobine *f* à trembleur.

trembling[1] ['trembliŋ], *a.* tremblant, tremblotant; **to reassure the t. souls,** rassurer les trembleurs; *Bot:* **t. poplar,** (peuplier *m*) tremble *m*; **t. grass,** brize tremblante; amourette *f*; **t. bog,** tourbière flottante.

trembling[2], *s.* tremblement *m*; tremblotement *m* (d'une feuille, de la voix); **in fear and t.,** tout tremblant; *Med:* **t. fit,** accès *m* de tremblement nerveux (continu); tremblement de fièvre.

tremella [tri'melə], *s. Fung:* trémelle *f.*

Tremellaceae [tremi'leisii:], *s.pl. Fung:* trémellacées *f.*

Tremellales [tremi'leili:z], *s.pl. Fung:* trémellales *f.*

tremendous [tri'mendəs], *a.* **1.** terrible, épouvantable, effrayant; à faire trembler. **2.** *F:* immense, énorme; démesuré; formidable; **a t. lot of sth.,** une quantité énorme de qch.; un tas de qch.; **there was a t. crowd,** il y avait un monde fou; **t. success,** succès formidable, pyramidal; **a t. difference,** une énorme différence; **t. blow,** coup *m* d'assommoir; **at a t. speed,** à une vitesse vertigineuse; **he's a t. talker,** il est furieusement bavard; **he's a t. eater,** il mange comme un ogre.

tremendously [tri'mendəsli], *adv.* **1.** terriblement, épouvantablement; d'une manière effrayante; à faire trembler. **2.** *F:* énormément; démesurément; furieusement; **it was t. successful,** c'était un succès fou; **t. rich,** archiriche, qui roule sur l'or.

tremendousness [tri'mendəsnis], *s.* **1.** nature *f* terrible, caractère effrayant **(of,** de). **2.** énormité *f*; grandeur démesurée **(of,** de).

tremolite ['tremoulait], *s. Miner:* trémolite *f*, grammatite *f.*

tremolo ['treməlou], *s. Mus:* (*a*) tremolo *m*; **t. notes,** notes tremblées; (*b*) **t. (stop),** tremolo, tremblant *m* (d'un orgue).

tremor ['tremər], *s.* **1.** (*a*) tremblement *m*, frémissement *m*; tremblotement *m*; **t. of fear, of joy,** tremblement de peur, de joie; frisson *m* de peur; **a t. went through the audience,** un frémissement parcourut la salle; (*b*) *Med:* tremblement; trémulation *f*; (*c*) *Physiol:* **intention t.,** crispation *f* musculaire (sous le coup d'une volition). **2.** trépidation *f* (des vitres, d'une machine en marche, etc.); **earth t.,** tremblement de terre; secousse *f* sismique; baroséisme *m*; **preliminary t.,** choc avant-coureur (d'un séisme).

tremulous ['tremjuləs], *a.* tremblotant, frémissant; **t. smile,** sourire timide, craintif; **t. voice,** voix tremblante, chevrotante, mal assurée; **the t. ripple on the water,** les rides *f* qui font trembler, qui agitent, la surface de l'eau.

tremulously ['tremjuləsli], *adv.* en tremblant, en tremblotant; timidement, craintivement.

tremulousness ['tremjuləsnis], *s.* **1.** tremblotement *m* (de la voix, etc.). **2.** timidité *f.*

trench[1] [tren(t)ʃ], *s.* **1.** *Agr: Hort:* tranchée *f*, fossé *m*; (*for draining*) saignée *f*, rigole *f*; (*for young trees, etc.*) jauge *f*; **water t., irrigation t.,** fossé d'irrigation; **t. plough,** rigoleuse *f.* **2.** *Mil:* tranchée; **approach t.,** tranchée d'approche; **communication t.,** boyau, -aux *m*; **in t., out t.,** boyau d'adduction, d'évacuation; **dummy t.,** fausse tranchée; **first-line t.,** tranchée de première ligne; **jump-off t.,** tranchée de départ; **kneeling t., standing t.,** tranchée pour tireur à genou, debout; **slit t.,** tranchée individuelle, trou individuel; **switch t.,** bretelle *f*; **t.-crossing capacity,** puissance *f* de franchissement (d'un char); **to climb out of the t.,** escalader la tranchée; **to man a t.,** faire occuper une tranchée; **to go into the trenches,** monter aux tranchées; **to leave the trenches,** descendre des tranchées; **t. warfare,** guerre *f* de tranchées; **t. board,** caillebotis *m* de tranchée; **t. coat,** manteau *m* imperméable (d'officier); trench-coat *m*; *Med:* **t. fever,** fièvre récurrente, à rechutes; typhus récurrent; **t. foot, t. feet,** pieds gelés; gelure *f* des tranchées; **t. mouth,** angine *f*, stomatite *f*, de Vincent; stomatite ulcéro-membraneuse; *Artil:* **t. mortar,** mortier *m*, canon *m*, de tranchée; lance-bombes *m inv.* **3.** *Geol:* sillon *m.*

trench[2]. **1.** *v.tr.* (*a*) creuser un fossé, une tranchée, dans (le sol); (*for draining*) rigoler (un pré, etc.); *v.i.* creuser des fossés; (*b*) **to t. a piece of ground,** défoncer, effondrer, un terrain; (*c*) *Hort:* planter (le céleri) dans une rigole; (*d*) *Carp:* rainer (une planche). **2.** *v.i.* **to t. (up)on s.o.'s property, s.o.'s rights,** empiéter sur la propriété, sur les droits, de qn; **doctrine that trenches on heresy,** doctrine *f* qui frise l'hérésie.

trenchancy ['tren(t)ʃ(ə)nsi], *s.* mordacité *f,* causticité *f* (d'une réponse, d'une épigramme); énergie *f* (d'un discours).

trenchant ['tren(t)ʃ(ə)nt], *a.* **1.** *Lit:* (*of sword, etc.*) tranchant, coupant. **2.** (*a*) (style, ton) tranchant, net, incisif; (discours *m,* ton) énergique; (*b*) (*of reply, epigram*) mordant, cinglant, caustique.

trenchantly ['tren(t)ʃ(ə)ntli], *adv.* d'une manière tranchante, incisive; incisivement; caustiquement.

trencher[1] ['tren(t)ʃər], *s. A:* **1.** tranchoir *m,* tailloir *m;* **t. companion,** compagnon *m* de table. **2.** *Sch: F:* **t. (cap),** toque universitaire (anglaise); toque à plateau.

trencher[2], *s. Agr: Mil:* (*pers.*) creuseur *m* de fossés, de tranchées.

trencherman, *pl.* **-men** ['tren(t)ʃəmən], *s.* **(good, stout) t.,** (grand, gros, beau) mangeur; **to be nothing of a t.,** n'être qu'un petit mangeur; avoir un appétit d'oiseau.

trenching ['tren(t)ʃiŋ], *s.* creusement *m* d'une tranchée, de tranchées; défoncement *m,* effondrement *m* (d'un terrain); rigolage *m* (d'un pré, etc.); *Agr:* **t. plough,** charrue *f* à effondrer; (charrue) défonceuse *f.*

trenchworks ['tren(t)ʃwə:ks], *s.pl.* travaux *m* de tranchées.

trend[1] [trend], *s.* **1.** direction *f* (d'un cours d'eau, etc.); tendance *f,* marche *f* (de l'opinion publique, etc.); **current trends,** tendances actuelles; **the t. of business, of politics,** l'allure *f* des affaires; l'orientation *f* de la politique; **the t. of my thoughts,** le cours de mes pensées; **the t. of human thought,** la marche de la pensée humaine; **t. of prices,** tendance des prix; **t. of the birthrate,** mouvement *m* des naissances, de la natalité; *Mth:* **t. of a curve,** allure d'une courbe. **2.** *Nau:* bas *m* de la verge d'une ancre.

trend[2], *v.i.* se diriger, tendre, s'étendre, s'orienter (**to, towards,** vers); **prices are trending upwards,** les prix augmentent.

trendsetter ['trendsetər], *s.* lanceur, -euse, de modes.

trendy ['trendi], *a. F:* à la page; dans le vent; (évêque, etc.) qui suit la mode.

Trent [trent], *Pr.n. Geog:* **1. the (river) T.,** le Trent. **2.** Trente; *Ecc.Hist:* **the Council of T.,** le Concile de Trente.

trental ['trent(ə)l], *s. Ecc:* trentain *m.*

Trentine ['trentain], *a. Geog:* trentin.

Trentino (the) [ðətren'ti:nou], *Pr.n. Geog:* le Trentin.

trepan[1] [tri'pæn], *s. Surg: Min:* trépan *m.*

trepan[2], *v.tr.* **(trepanned)** *Surg: Min:* trépaner.

trepan[3], *v.tr.* **(trepanned)** *A:* (*a*) attraper, attirer (qn) (par des artifices); (*b*) escroquer (qn).

trepanation [trepə'neiʃ(ə)n], *s. Surg:* trépanation *f.*

trepang [tri'pæŋ], *s. Echin:* tripang *m,* trépang *m; F:* bêche-de-mer *f, pl.* bêches-de-mer.

trepanner [tri'pænər], *s. Surg:* trépanateur *m.*

trepanning [tri'pæniŋ], *s.* trépanation *f.*

trephine[1] [tri'fain], *s. Surg:* tréphine *f.*

trephine[2], *v.tr. Surg:* trépaner (qn, le crâne).

trephining [tri'fainiŋ], *s. Surg:* térébration *f;* trépanation *f.*

trephocyte ['trefousait], *s. Med:* tréphocyte *m.*

trephone ['trefoun], *s. Biol:* tréphone *f.*

trepidation [trepi'deiʃ(ə)n], *s.* **1.** trépidation *f;* agitation violente; émoi *m.* **2.** *Med: A:* trépidation; tremblement *m* des membres.

treponema [trepou'ni:mə], *s. Bac:* tréponème *m; Med:* **t. pallidum** ['pælidəm], tréponème pâle; spirochète *m* pâle.

treponematosis [trepouni:mə'tousis], *s. Med:* tréponématose *f,* tréponémose *f.*

treponemiasis [trepouni'maiəsis], *s. Med:* tréponémose *f.*

treponemicide [trepou'ni:misaid], *a. & s. Med:* tréponémicide (*m*).

trespass[1] ['trespəs], *s.* **1.** (*a*) contravention *f,* transgression *f,* de la loi; délit *m;* (*b*) *Theol:* offense *f,* péché *m;* **forgive us our trespasses,** pardonne-nous nos offenses. **2.** *Jur:* (*a*) violation *f* des droits de qn; trouble *m* de jouissance; (*b*) **t. to land,** violation *f* de propriété (sur un bien foncier); **t. of frontier,** violation de frontière.

trespass[2], *v.i.* **1.** *A: & Lit:* transgresser la loi; pécher **(against,** contre); **as we forgive them that t. against us,** comme nous pardonnons aussi à ceux qui nous ont offensés; **to t. against the law, against a principle,** violer, enfreindre, la loi, un principe. **2.** *Jur:* (*a*) **to t. (up)on s.o.'s rights,** violer, enfreindre, les droits de qn; empiéter sur les droits de qn; (*b*) **to t. ((up)on s.o.'s property),** empiéter, entrer, passer sans autorisation, sur la propriété de qn; (*c*) *O:* **to t. (up)on s.o.'s good nature,** abuser de la bonté de qn; **I don't wish to t. on your time,** je ne veux pas abuser de vos moments.

trespasser ['trespəsər], *s.* **1.** *Theol:* pécheur, *f.* pécheresse; transgresseur *m.* **2.** *Jur:* (*a*) violateur *m* des droits d'autrui; (*b*) auteur *m* d'une violation de propriété (foncière); intrus *m; P.N:* **trespassers will be prosecuted,** défense de passer, d'entrer, sous peine d'amende; propriété privée.

trespassing ['trespəsiŋ], *s.* = TRESPASS[1] 2.

tress [tres], *s.* (*a*) tresse *f,* boucle *f* (de cheveux); (*b*) *Lit:* **tresses,** chevelure *f,* cheveux *mpl* (d'une femme).

tressure ['treʃər, 'tresjər], *s. Her:* trêcheur *m,* trescheur *m;* **double t. flory-counterflory, t. of Scotland,** double trescheur fleuré-contrefleuré.

trestle ['tres(ə)l], *s.* tréteau *m,* chevalet *m;* **trestles, t. work, of a bridge,** chevalets de ponton, d'un pont; **t. bridge,** pont *m* de, sur, chevalets; ponton *m* à chevalets; **sawyer's t.,** chevalet de scieur; chèvre *f,* baudet *m;* **t. table,** table *f* à tréteaux; **t. bed,** lit *m* de sangle; *Nau:* **t. tree,** élongis *m* de chouque.

tret [tret], *s. Com: A:* réfaction *f.*

Treviso [tre'vi:zou], *Pr.n. Geog:* Trévise.

trews [tru:z], *s.pl. Cost:* pantalon *m* en tartan (que portent les soldats de certains régiments écossais).

trey [trei], *s.* (*at cards, dice*) (le) trois; (*dice*) **two treys,** terne *m.*

tri- [trai, tri], *pref.* tri-.

triacetin [trai'æsitin], *s. Ch:* triacétine *f.*

triacetonamin(e) [traiæsi'tɔnəm(a)in], *s. Ch:* triacétonamine *f.*

triacid [trai'æsid], *s. Ch:* triacide *m.*

triacontahedral [traiəkɔntæ'hedr(ə)l, -'hi:d-], *a. Cryst:* triacontaèdre.

triad ['traiæd], *s.* triade *f;* groupe *m* de trois; *Ch:* élément trivalent; *Mus:* accord *m* sans l'octave.

triadelphous [traiə'delfəs], *a. Bot:* triadelphe.

triadic [trai'ædik], *a.* triadique.

trial ['traiəl], *s.* **1.** *Jur:* (*a*) jugement *m* (d'un litige, d'un accusé); **to bring s.o. to t., to bring s.o. up for t.,** mettre, faire passer, qn en jugement; **to be brought to t., to stand one's t.,** passer en jugement; être jugé; comparaître devant le tribunal; **they were sent for t.,** ils furent renvoyés en jugement; **t. by jury,** jugement par jury; *Mil:* **t. by court martial,** renvoi *m* devant un conseil de guerre; (*b*) procès *m;* **civil t.,** action civile; **criminal t.,** procès criminel; **famous trials,** causes célèbres; **to grant s.o. a new t.,** accorder l'appel à qn; *U.S:* **t. judge** = juge *m* d'instance; **t. lawyer,** avocat plaidant; (*c*) *Hist:* **t. by combat,** combat *m* judiciaire; **to demand t. by battle,** demander le camp. **2.** (*a*) essai *m;* épreuve *f; Lit:* **his heart failed him in the hour of his t.,** le cœur lui manqua au moment de l'épreuve; **t. of strength,** épreuve de force; *Sp:* **t. (game),** match *m* de sélection; (*b*) **to give sth. a t.,** faire l'essai de qch.; **on t.,** à l'essai; **to take sth. on t.,** prendre qch. à l'essai; **by way of t.,** pour essayer; **as a t. measure,** à titre d'essai; **to proceed by t. and error,** procéder par tâtonnements, par approximations successives; **t. and error solution,** solution *f* empirique; *Com:* **t. lot,** envoi *m* à titre d'essai; **t. order,** commande *f* d'essai; *Book-k:* **t. balance,** balance *f* de vérification; **t.-balance book,** livre *m* de soldes; (*c*) essai (technique) (d'un appareil, d'un véhicule, etc.); **preliminary t., development t.,** essai préliminaire, de mise au point; **acceptance t.,** essai de recette, de réception; *Veh:* **speed t.,** essai de vitesse; **t. speed, speed on trials,** vitesse *f* aux essais; **t. run,** essai sur route; *Av:* **t. flight,** vol *m* d'essai; *Nau:* **dock trials, sea trials,** essais au point fixe, à la mer; *Artil:* **gun trials, firing trials,** essais de la pièce; essais de tir; *Min:* **t. boring,** forage *m* d'essai; sondage *m* d'exploration, de recherche; (*d*) *usu. pl.* concours *m;* **sheep dog trials, guard dog trials,** concours de chiens de berger, de chiens de défense. **3.** épreuve douloureuse; peine *f,* adversité *f;* **everyone has his trials,** tout le monde a ses tribulations; **he has had many trials,** il a été cruellement éprouvé; **the trials and troubles of life,** les peines et les épreuves de la vie; **that child is a great t. to his parents,** cet enfant fait le martyre de ses parents, met à l'épreuve l'indulgence de ses parents.

trialism ['traiəlizm], *s. Hist:* trialisme *m.*

trialist ['traiəlist], *s. Sp:* concurrent, -ente, aux épreuves de sélection (pour une équipe nationale, etc.).

triandria [trai'ændriə], *s. Bot:* triandrie *f.*

triandrous [trai'ændrəs], *a. Bot:* triandre.

triangle ['traiæŋgl], *s.* **1.** *Mth: etc:* triangle *m;* **congruent triangles,** triangles égaux; *Astr:* **the T.,** le Triangle (boréal, austral); *Mec:* **t. of forces,** triangle des forces; *Surv:* **t. of error,** chapeau *m; F:* **the eternal t.,** l'éternel triangle; le ménage à trois; la vie à trois. **2.** (*a*) *Draw: U.S:* équerre *f* (en triangle); triangle; (*b*) *Mus:* triangle.

triangular [trai'æŋgjulər], *a.* triangulaire; en triangle; *Nau:* **t. flag,** triangle *m; Const:* **t. tile,** tuile gironnée; *For:* **t. planting,** plantation *f* en triangle.

triangularis, *pl.* **-res** [traiæŋgju'leəris, -ri:z], *s. Anat:* **t. (muscle),** (muscle) triangulaire *m.*

triangularly [trai'æŋgjuləli], *adv.* en (forme de) triangle; triangulairement.

triangulate[1] [trai'æŋgjuleit], *v.tr. Surv:* **to t. an area,** trianguler une région; faire la triangulation d'une région.

triangulate[2], *a. Nat.Hist:* **1.** marqué de triangles; à triangles. **2.** triangulaire; en triangle.

triangulation [traiæŋgju'leiʃ(ə)n], *s. Surv:* triangulation *f;* **skeleton t.,** canevas *m;* **general t.,** canevas d'ensemble; **geodetic t.,** triangulation géodésique; **graphical t.,** triangulation graphique; **t. point,** point *m* géodésique; **t. station,** station *f* de triangulation.

triapsal, triapsidal [trai'æpsəl, -'æpsidl], *a. Arch:* à trois absides.

trias ['traiæs], *s. Geol:* trias *m.*

triassic [trai'æsik], *a. Geol:* triasique.

triatic [trai'ætik], *a. Nau:* **t. stay,** maroquin *m.*

triatoma [traiə'toumə], *s. Ent:* triatome *m.*

triatomic [traiə'tɔmik], *a. Ch:* triatomique; **t. oxygen,** ozone *m.*

triatomicity [traiætɔ'misiti], *s. Ch:* triatomicité *f.*

triatomid [trai'ætəmid], *s. Ent:* triatome *m.*

triaxial [trai'æksiəl], *a. Mth: etc:* à trois axes.

Triaxonia, Triaxonida [traiæk'souniə, -'sɔnidə], *s.pl. Spong:* triaxonides *m.*

triazine ['traiəzi:n], *s. Ch:* triazine *f.*

triazole ['traiəzoul], *s. Ch:* triazole *m.*

tribade ['tribəd], *s.f.* tribade, lesbienne.

tribadism ['tribədizm], *s.* tribadisme *m,* saphisme *m.*

tribal ['traib(ə)l], *a.* **1.** (*of race*) qui vit en tribus. **2.** qui appartient à la tribu; de tribu; tributif; **t. system,** système tribal; tribalisme *m.*

tribalism ['traibəlizm], *s.* tribalisme *m;* système tribal; organisation *f* par tribus.

tribally ['traibəli], *adv.* (vivre) en tribu; (être organisé) par tribus.

tribasic [trai'beisik], *a. Ch:* tribasique.

tribe [traib], *s.* **1.** tribu *f;* **the twelve tribes of Israel,** les douze tribus d'Israël; *F:* (*contemptuous*) **he and his t.,** lui et son clan, et sa caste; **a father with a whole t. of children,** un père avec toute une smala d'enfants. **2.** *Nat.Hist:* tribu.

tribesman, *pl.* **-men** ['traibzmən], *s.m.* membre (i) d'une tribu, (ii) de la tribu.

triblet ['triblit], *s. Metalw:* triboulet *m;* **t. tubes,** tubes coulissants.

triboelectricity [traibouelek'trisiti], *s.* tribo-électricité *f.*

tribology [trai'bɔlədʒi], *s. Tchn:* tribologie *f.*

triboluminescence [traiboulu:mi'nesəns], *s. Ph:* triboluminescence *f.*

tribometer [trai'bɔmitər], *s. Mec:* tribomètre *m.*

tribometry [trai'bɔmitri], *s. Ph:* tribométrie *f.*

Tribonian [trai'bouniən], *Pr.n.m. Hist:* Tribonien.

tribrach ['tribræk], *s. Pros:* tribraque *m.*

tribracteate [trai'bræktieit], *a. Bot:* tribractété.

tribracteolate [trai'bræktiouleit], *a. Bot:* tribractéolé.

tribromide [trai'broumaid], *s. Ch:* tribromure *m.*

tribromoethanol [traibroumou'eθənɔl], *s. Ch:* tribromoéthanol *m.*

tribromophenol [traibroumou'fi:nɔl], *s. Ch:* tribromophénol *m.*

tribulation [tribju'leiʃ(ə)n], *s.* tribulation *f,* affliction *f;* épreuves *fpl;* **his many tribulations,** ses nombreuses afflictions, tribulations; **his life was one long t.,** sa vie fut un long calvaire.

tribulus ['tribjuləs], *s. Bot:* tribulus *m;* croix *f* de Malte.

tribunal [tr(a)i'bju:nəl], *s.* tribunal *m,* -aux. **1.** (*a*) *Rom.Ant:* siège *m,* plate-forme *f* des magistrats; (*b*) siège, fauteuil *m,* du juge. **2.** cour *f* de justice; **to appear before a t.,** comparaître devant un tribunal.

tribunate ['tribjuneit], *s. Rom.Hist: etc:* tribunat *m.*

tribune[1] ['tribju:n], *s. Rom.Hist: etc:* tribun *m.*

tribune[2], *s.* **1.** (*a*) tribune *f* (d'orateur); (*b*) trône *m* (d'évêque). **2.** *Ecc.Arch: A:* tribunal *m* (de basilique).

tributary ['tribjutəri]. **1.** *a.* tributaire. **2.** *s.* (*a*) tributaire *m;* **the Jews were made tributaries of the Romans,** les Juifs furent faits tributaires des Romains; (*b*) *Geog:* affluent *m* (d'un fleuve).

tribute ['tribju:t], *s.* **1.** *Hist:* **t. (money),** tribut *m;* **to pay t.,** payer tribut (**to,** à); **to lay a nation under t.,** imposer un tribut à une nation. **2.** tribut, hommage *m;* **to pay a t. to s.o.,** faire, rendre, hommage à qn; **to pay a last t. to**

s.o., rendre à qn les derniers devoirs; **coffin covered with floral tributes,** cercueil caché sous un amas de gerbes et de couronnes; *Lit:* **to pay the t. of a tear,** rendre (à qn) l'hommage d'une larme. **3.** *Min:* **t. (system),** (i) rétribution proportionnelle, en nature ou en espèces, du propriétaire de la mine; (ii) abandon *m* à la main-d'œuvre d'une quote-part du minerai (en guise de salaires); **to work on t.,** (i) exploiter la mine à condition de payer une redevance proportionnelle; (ii) payer la main-d'œuvre en nature.

tributyrin [trai'bju:tirin], *s. Ch:* tributyrine *f.*

tricalcic, tricalcium [trai'kælsik, -'kælsiəm], *a. Ch:* tricalcique.

tricapsular [trai'kæpsjulər], *a. Bot:* tricapsulaire.

tricar ['traika:r], *s. Veh: O:* trois-roues *m inv*; (*commercial*) triporteur *m.*

tricarinated [trai'kærineitid], *a. Bot:* tricaréné.

tricarpous [trai'ka:pəs], *a. Bot:* à trois carpelles.

tricast ['traika:st], *s. Turf:* **(tote) t.** = tiercé *m.*

trice[1] [trais], *s.* **in a t.,** (faire qch.) en un clin d'œil, en moins de rien.

trice[2], *v.tr. Nau:* **to t. (up) a sail, the boom,** hisser une voile; relever, soulager, le gui.

tricenary [trai'si:nəri], *a.* tricénaire.

tricennial [trai'seniəl], *a. Jur:* (*of prescription*) tricennal, -aux.

tricentenary, *esp. U.S:* **tricentennial** [traisen'ti:nəri, -'teniəl], *a. & s.* tricentenaire (*m*).

tricephalic [traise'fælik], **tricephalous** [trai'sefələs], *a.* tricéphale.

tricephalus [trai'sefələs], *s. Ter:* tricéphale *m.*

triceps ['traiseps], *s. Anat:* **t. (muscle),** triceps *m.*

triceratops [trai'serətɔps], *s. Paleont:* tricératops *m.*

trichalcite [trai'kælsait], *s. Miner:* tricalcite *f*, trichalcite *f.*

Trichechidae [trai'kekidi:], *s.pl. Z:* trichécidés *m.*

trichiasis [tri'kaiəsis], *s. Med:* **1.** trichiasis *m* (des cils). **2.** trichosis *m*, trichiasis (de la vessie, etc.).

trichina, *pl.* **-ae** [tri'kainə, -i:], *s. Ann:* trichine *f.*

trichinal [tri'kainəl], *a. Vet: Med:* trichinal, -aux.

Trichinellidae [triki'nelidi:], *s.pl. Ann:* trichinidés *m.*

trichinoid [tri'kainɔid], *a.* trichinoïde.

trichinoscope [tri'kainouskoup], *s.* trichinoscope *m.*

trichinosed ['trikinouzd], *a. Med:* trichiné.

trichinosis [triki'nousis], *s. Med:* trichinose *f.*

trichinous ['trikinəs, tri'kainəs], *a.* (*of meat, etc.*) trichineux, trichiné.

trichion ['trikiɔn], *s. Anat:* trichion *m.*

trichite ['trikait], *s. Miner:* trichite *f.*

trichiura [triki'ju:rə], *s. Ent:* trichiure *m.*

Trichiuridae [triki'ju:ridi:], *s.pl. Ich:* trichiuridés *m.*

trichiurus [triki'ju:rəs], *s. Ich:* trichiure *m.*

trichloracetic [traiklɔ:rə'si:tik], *a. Ch:* trichloracétique.

trichlorethylene [traiklɔ:'reθili:n], *s. Ch:* trichloréthylène *m.*

trichloride [trai'klɔ:raid], *s. Ch:* trichlorure *m.*

trichloroacetic [traiklɔ:rouə'si:tik], *a. Ch:* trichloracétique.

trichloroethylene [traiklɔ:rou'eθili:n], *s. Ch:* trichloréthylène *m.*

tricho- [trikou, traikou], *comb.fm.* tricho-.

trichobezoar [trikou'bezoua:r], *s. Med:* trichobézoard *m.*

trichobothrium [trikou'bɔθriəm], *s. Z:* trichobothrie *f.*

trichocephaliasis [trikousefə'laiəsis], *s. Med:* trichocéphalose *f.*

trichocephalus [trikou'sefələs], *s. Med:* trichocéphale *m.*

trichoceras [tri'kɔsərəs], *s. Ent:* trichocère *f.*

Trichoceratidae [trikouse'rætidi:], *s.pl. Ent:* trichocéridés *m.*

trichoclasis [trikou'kleisis], *s. Med:* trichoclasie *f.*

trichocyst ['trikousist], *s.* trichocyste *m.*

trichodectes [trikou'dekti:z], *s. Ent:* trichodecte *m.*

trichogenic [trikou'dʒenik], **trichogenous** [tri'kɔdʒinəs], *a.* trichogénique.

trichoglossia [trikou'glɔsiə], *s. Med:* trichoglossie *f.*

Trichoglossidae [trikou'glɔsidi:], *s.pl. Orn:* trichoglossidés *m.*

Trichogrammidae [trikou'græmidi:], *s.pl. Ent:* trichogrammes *m.*

trichogyne ['trikoudʒain], *s. Algae:* trichogyne *f.*

trichology [tri'kɔlədʒi], *s.* trichologie *f.*

tricholoma [trikə'loumə], *s. Fung:* tricholome *m.*

trichoma [tri'koumə], *s. Med:* trichome *m*; trichoma *m*; plique (polonaise).

Trichomanes [trikou'meini:z], *s. Bot:* trichomanes *m.*

trichome ['traikoum], *s. Bot:* trichome *m.*

trichomonadal [trikou'mɔnədəl], *a. Med:* **t. vaginitis,** trichomonase *f* vaginale.

trichomoniasis [trikoumouni'eisis], *s. Med: Vet:* trichomonase *f*, trichomonose *f.*

trichomycosis [trikoumai'kousis], *s. Med:* trichomycose *f.*

Trichomycteridae [trikoumik'teridi:], *s.pl. Ich:* trichomyctères *m.*

trichophyte ['trikoufait], **trichophyton** [trikou'faitən], *s. Fung:* trichophyton *m.*

trichophytia [trikou'faitiə], **trichophytosis** [trikoufai'tousis], *s. Med:* trichophytie *f.*

Trichoptera [tri'kɔptərə], *s.pl. Ent:* trichoptères *m.*

Trichopterygidae [trikɔptə'ridʒidi:], *s.pl. Ent:* trichoptérygides *m.*

trichord ['traikɔ:d], *a. & s. Mus:* (instrument) tricorde (*m*).

trichorrhexis [trikɔ'reksis], *s. Med:* trichorhexis *f.*

trichosis [tri'kousis], *s. Med:* **1.** = TRICHIASIS 1. **2.** = TRICHOMA.

trichotillomania [trikoutilou'meiniə], *s. Med:* trichotillomanie *f.*

trichotomic, trichotomous [tri'kɔtəmik, -məs], *a.* trichotome, trichotomique.

trichotomy [tri'kɔtəmi], *s. Log: etc:* trichotomie *f.*

trichroic [trai'krouik], *a. Ph:* trichroïte.

trichroism ['traikrouizm], *s. Ph:* trichroïsme *m.*

trichromatic [traikrou'mætik], *a. Phot: etc:* trichrome.

trichuriasis [trikjuri'eisis], *s. Med:* trichocéphalose *f.*

tricing ['traisiŋ], *s. Nau:* **t. (up),** hissage *m*; **t. line, rope,** suspensoir *m*; lève-nez *m inv*, hale-breu *m inv.*

trick[1] [trik], *s.* **1.** (*a*) tour *m*, ruse *f*, finesse *f*; artifice *m*; supercherie *f*; **to get sth. by a t.,** obtenir qch. par ruse; **he would resort to any t. in order to . . .,** il userait de tous les artifices pour . . .; **there must be a t. in it,** cela ne me paraît pas honnête; il y a anguille sous roche; (*b*) farce *f*, tour; **tricks and jokes,** farces et attrapes; **to play a t. on s.o.,** faire une farce, une blague, à qn; **my memory's always playing me tricks,** je n'ai plus de mémoire; **my eyes must have been playing tricks on me, playing me tricks,** je n'ai pas pu voir ça; **that was a nasty, mean, dirty, t.!** ça c'était un vilain tour! **I know his little tricks,** je connais tous ses manèges; **you've been up to your tricks again,** vous avez encore fait des vôtres; (*c*) truc *m*; **the tricks of the trade,** les trucs, les tours, les astuces *f*, du métier; **he knows a t. or two, all the tricks of the trade,** il connaît le fort et le fin de son art; il en sait plus d'une; c'est un roublard; **that should do the t.,** ça fera l'affaire; **it's easy if you know the t.,** c'est facile si on sait comment le faire, si on a le truc; (*d*) tour d'adresse; **to teach a dog tricks,** apprendre des tours à un chien; **card t.,** tour de cartes; **conjuring t.,** tour de prestidigitation, de passe-passe; **the t. didn't come off,** le tour n'a pas réussi, a raté; *F:* **the whole bag of tricks,** tout le bataclan; tout le tremblement; **t. riding,** voltige *f*; **t. cyclist,** (i) cycliste acrobate; (ii) *P:* psychiatre *mf*; **I know a t. worth two of that,** je connais un truc encore meilleur que celui-là; **he doesn't miss a t.,** rien ne lui échappe; *F:* **how's tricks?** (i) comment vas-tu? (ii) quoi de neuf? **2.** manie *f*; habitude *f*; tic *m*; **it's a t. of his,** c'est une particularité chez lui; **he has a t. of repeating himself,** il se répète toujours. **3.** *Cards:* levée; **to take a t.,** faire une levée, un pli; **the odd t.,** la levée supplémentaire, le trick; **to take, lose, the odd t.,** faire, perdre, la carte; **to play for the odd t.,** jouer la belle. **4.** *Nau:* **t. at the wheel,** tour de barre; tour à la barre; **to take one's t. at the wheel,** prendre son tour de service à la barre.

trick[2], *v.tr.* **1.** attraper, duper (qn); mystifier (qn, *Sp:* un adversaire); **I've been tricked,** je me suis laissé duper; *F:* on m'a refait, on m'a eu; **to t. s.o. into doing sth.,** amener qn par ruse à faire qch.; **to t. s.o. into signing, into consenting,** surprendre la signature, le consentement, de qn; **to t. s.o. out of sth.,** (i) frustrer qn de qch.; (ii) escroquer qch. à qn; **he tricked me out of £1000,** il m'a refait de £1000. **2.** *Her:* blasonner (un écu). **3.** *F: O:* **to t. s.o. out,** parer, orner, attifer, qn.

trickery ['trikəri], *s.* tromperie *f*, tricherie *f*; duperie *f*; **piece of t.,** fraude *f*; supercherie *f*; **to get sth. by t.,** obtenir qch. par ruse.

trickiness ['trikinis], *s.* **1.** fourberie *f.* **2.** complication *f*, délicatesse *f* (d'un mécanisme, d'une situation, etc.).

tricking ['trikiŋ], *s.* **1.** duperie *f*, tromperie *f*, tricherie *f.* **2.** *Her:* blasonnement *m* (d'un écu).

trickle[1] [trikl], *s.* (*a*) filet *m*, filtrée *f* (d'eau, etc.); **there was only a t. of water in the river bed,** il n'y avait qu'un mince filet d'eau dans le lit de la rivière; **sales were down to a t.,** il n'y avait presque plus de ventes; (*b*) *El:* **t. charger,** chargeur *m* à régime lent.

trickle[2]. **1.** *v.i.* (*a*) couler (goutte à goutte); suinter; **water trickling through the rock,** eau (i) qui suinte; (ii) qui ruisselle, à travers la roche; **water that trickles from the rock,** eaux qui sourdent de la roche; **water was trickling down the wall,** l'eau dégoulinait le long du mur; **there was water trickling in under the door,** l'eau s'infiltrait sous la porte; **tears were trickling down her cheeks,** les larmes coulaient le long de ses joues; (*of liquid*) **to t. out,** découler, dégoutter; **news is beginning to t. through, out, from the devasted area,** on commence à recevoir peu à peu des nouvelles de la région sinistrée; (*b*) **there are still a few refugees trickling over the frontier,** il y a toujours un petit nombre de réfugiés qui passent la frontière; **the ball just trickled into the hole,** la balle a roulé tout doucement dans le trou. **2.** *v.tr.* (*a*) liasser dégoutter (un liquide); laisser tomber (un liquide) goutte à goutte; (*b*) *Golf: etc:* **to t. the ball into the hole,** faire rouler tout doucement la balle dans le trou.

trickler ['triklər], *s. Agr:* **t. irrigation,** irrigation *f* par goutte à goutte, par percolation.

trickling ['trikliŋ], *s.* dégouttement *m*; écoulement *m* goutte à goutte.

trickster ['trikstər], *s.* escroc *m*; **confidence t.,** voleur, -euse, à l'américaine.

tricky ['triki], *a.* **1.** rusé; astucieux; fin; **t. horse,** cheval qui a du vice; *F:* **he's a t. customer,** lui, c'est un rusé, un malin. **2.** (mécanisme, etc.) compliqué, (d'un maniement) délicat; **this door has a t. lock,** la serrure de cette porte n'est pas commode; **t. job,** tâche délicate, difficile, peu commode.

triclad ['traiklæd], *s. Ann:* triclade *m.*

Tricladida [trai'klædidə], *s.pl. Ann:* triclades *m.*

triclinic [trai'klinik], *a. Cryst:* triclinique; *Miner:* **t. feldspar,** plagioclase *f.*

triclinium [trai'kliniəm], *s. Rom.Ant:* triclinium *m.*

tricoccous [trai'kɔkəs], *a. Bot:* (fruit *m*) tricoque.

tricolo(u)r ['trikələr]. **1.** *a.* tricolore. **2.** *s.* (*a*) **the T.,** le drapeau tricolore (français); (*b*) cravate *f* (du drapeau).

tricoloured ['traikʌləd], *a.* tricolore.

Triconodon, triconodont [trai'kɔnədɔn(t)], *s. Paleont:* triconodon *m*, triconodonte *m.*

Triconodonta [traikɔnə'dɔntə], *s.pl. Paleont:* triconodontes *m.*

tricorn(e) ['traikɔ:n], *a. & s.* (chapeau) tricorne (*m*).

tricotyledonous [traikɔti'li:dənəs], *a. Bot:* à trois cotylédons.

Tricouni [trai'ku:ni:], *s. R.t.m: Mount:* Tricouni *m.*

tricuspid [trai'kʌspid], *a.* tricuspide; *Anat:* **t. valve,** valvule *f* tricuspide (du cœur).

tricycle[1] ['traisikl]. **1.** *s.* tricycle *m*; **motor t.,** tricycle à moteur: *O:* **carrier t., box t.,** triporteur *m.* **2.** *a. Av:* **t. undercarriage,** train *m* (d'atterrissage) tricycle.

tricycle[2], *v.i.* monter, aller, à tricycle; faire une promenade à tricycle.

tricyclic [trai'saiklik], *a. Ch:* tricyclique.

tricyclist ['traisiklist], *s.* tricycliste *mf.*

tridacna [trai'dæknə], *s. Moll:* tridacne *m.*

Tridacnidae [trai'dæknidi:], *s.pl. Moll:* tridacnes *m.*

tridactyl(ous) [trai'dæktil(əs)], *a. Z:* tridactyle.

trident ['traid(ə)nt], *s.* **1.** trident *m* (de Neptune, etc.). **2.** *Mth:* **t. (curve),** trident. **3.** *Med:* **t. hand,** main *f* en trident.

tridental, tridentate [trai'dent(ə)l, -eit], *a. Nat.Hist:* tridenté.

Tridentine [trai'dentain]. **1.** *a. Geog:* trentin; *Ecc.Hist:* tridentin, du Concile de Trente. **2.** *s. Rel: O:* catholique (romain).

tridermic [trai'də:mik], *a. Biol:* tridermique.

triduo ['tri:duou], **triduum** ['traidjuəm], *s. Ecc:* triduo *m*, triduum *m.*

tridymite ['traidimait], *s. Miner:* tridymite *f.*

tried [traid], *a.* éprouvé; **t. friend,** ami éprouvé, à toute épreuve; **well t. remedy,** remède éprouvé.

triennial [trai'eniəl], *a.* **1.** triennal, -aux; qui a lieu tous les trois ans. **2.** triennal; qui dure trois ans; **t. parliament,** parlement triennal; *Hort:* **t. (plant),** plante trisannuelle.

triennially [trai'eniəli], *adv.* tous les trois ans; **t. elected parliament,** parlement triennal.

triennium [trai'eniəm], *s.* triennat *m*; *Rel.H:* triennium *m.*

trientalis [traien'teilis], *s. Bot:* trientalis *m.*

trier ['traiər], *s.* **1.** *F:* **to be a t.,** ne pas se laisser décourager; fournir toujours son effort; **he's a t.,** il fait toujours de son mieux; il ne se décourage jamais; **he's not much of a t.,** il manque de persistance, de résolution. **2.** *Jur:* (*a*) juge *m*; **the t. of the case,** le magistrat qui a jugé la cause; (*b*) **triers,** arbitres (chargés d'apprécier la validité des récusations de jurés). **3.** *Tail: etc:* **t.-on,** essayeur, -euse.

trierarch ['traiəra:k], *s. Gr.Ant:* triérarque *m.*

trierarchy ['traiəra:ki], *s. Gr.Ant:* triérarchie *f.*

triester [trai'estər], *s. Ch:* triester *m.*

trieteric [traiə'terik]. *Gr.Hist:* **1.** *a.* triétérique. **2.** *s.* triétéride *f.*

triethyl- [trai'eθil], *comb.fm. Ch:* triéthyl-.

trifacial [trai'feiʃ(ə)l], *a. & s. Anat:* **t. (nerve),** (nerf) trijumeau (*m*); (nerf) trifacial (*m*).

trifid ['traifid], *a. Bot: etc:* trifide.

trifle[1] ['traifl], *s.* **1.** (*a*) chose *f* sans importance; bagatelle *f*, vétille *f*; **the merest t. puts him out,** il se fâche pour un rien, à propos de rien; (*of offence*) **it's a mere t.,** il n'y a pas de quoi fouetter un chat; **she would shed tears for a mere t.,** elle pleurait pour une bêtise; **to quarrel over a mere t.,** se quereller pour un oui, pour un non; se quereller sur un rien; **to be busy with trifles,** s'occuper à des futilités *f*; **to stick at trifles,** s'arrêter à des vétilles; vétiller; chercher la petite bête; **he doesn't stick at trifles,** il n'a pas (beaucoup) de scrupules; **he makes a fuss over trifles,** c'est un vétilleur; **it's not exactly a t.,** ce n'est pas une petite affaire; c'est toute une affaire; (*b*) petite somme d'argent; **£10, a mere t.!** £10, une misère, un rien! **it was sold for a mere t.,** on l'a vendu pour un rien; **I wouldn't call 1000 francs a t.,** pour moi, 1000 francs est une somme; (*c*) *adv.phr.* **a t.,** un tout petit peu, (un) tant soit peu; quelque peu; **he's a t. over forty,** il a un peu plus de quarante ans; **a t. too wide, too short,** trop large, trop court, d'un doigt; **he seemed a t. taken aback,** il parut légèrement surpris. **2.** (*a*) *Lit: O:* petit ouvrage d'esprit; (*b*) *Mus:* délassement *m*. **3.** *Cu:* = diplomate *m*. **4.** (*a*) étain *m* (pour vaisselle d'étain); (*b*) **trifles,** vaisselle *f* d'étain.

trifle[2]. **1.** *v.i.* (*a*) jouer, badiner (**with,** avec); **to t. with s.o.,** se jouer de qn; **he's not a man to be trifled with,** on ne joue pas, on ne plaisante pas, avec lui; on ne se moque pas de lui; **to t. with s.o.'s affections,** jouer avec les affections de qn; **feelings like that aren't to be trifled with,** on ne doit pas plaisanter avec ces sentiments-là; **to t. with one's health,** jouer avec sa santé; (*b*) **to t. with sth.,** manier nonchalamment (sa canne, etc.); jouer avec (son lorgnon, etc.); **to t. with one's food,** manger du bout des dents; chipoter ce qu'on a dans son assiette; (*c*) se montrer futile; vétiller; chipoter; s'amuser, s'occuper, à des futilités, à des riens; **he trifles a little with the arts,** il fait de l'art en dilettante. **2.** *v.tr.* **to t. away one's money, one's energy,** gaspiller, perdre à des riens, son argent, ses forces; **to t. one's time away,** gâcher, gaspiller, son temps.

trifler ['traiflər], *s.* (*a*) personne *f* frivole; (*b*) velléitaire *m*.

trifling[1], *a.* **1.** (*of pers.*) futile, léger. **2.** insignifiant, peu important, sans importance; négligeable; **t. incidents,** menus incidents; incidents futiles; **the most t. particulars,** les moindres détails *m*; **a few t. items,** quelques petites choses sans conséquences; **of t. value,** d'une valeur minime; **that's a t. matter,** c'est peu de chose; ce n'est qu'une bagatelle; **it's not just a t. business,** ce n'est pas une petite affaire; **our resources are not merely t.,** nos moyens ne sont pas négligeables; **in one evening he lost the t. sum of 10,000 francs,** il a perdu en une soirée la bagatelle de 10.000 francs.

trifling[2], *s.* (*a*) badinage *m*; (*b*) gaspillage *m* du temps (en futilités).

triflorous [trai'flɔːrəs], *a. Bot:* triflore; **ternately t.,** terniflore.

trifocal [trai'foukl], *a.* (*of lens*) trifocal, -aux.

trifoliate [trai'foulieit], *a. Bot:* trifolié; terné, ternifolié.

trifoliated [trai'foulieitid], *a. Arch:* (arc) tréflé.

trifoliolate [trai'fouliouleit], *a. Bot:* trifoliolé.

trifolium [trai'fouliəm], *s. Bot:* trifolium *m*, trèfle *m*.

trifoly ['trifəli], *s. Bot:* (*a*) *A:* trèfle *m*; (*b*) **sea t.,** glaux *m*.

triforium, *pl.* **-ia** [trai'fɔːriəm, -iə], *s. Arch:* triforium *m*.

triform ['traifɔːm], *a.* triforme.

trifurcate[1] [trai'fəːkeit], *a. Nat.Hist:* trifurqué.

trifurcate[2] ['traifəːkeit], *v.i.* se trifurquer.

trifurcation [traifəː'keiʃ(ə)n], *s.* trifurcation *f*.

trig[1] [trig], *s.* **1.** cale *f* (pour empêcher une roue, un tonneau, de rouler). **2.** sabot *m* d'enrayage; enrayure *f*.

trig[2], *v.tr.* **(trigged) 1.** caler (une roue, un tonneau). **2.** enrayer (une roue).

trig[3], *s. Mth: F:* trigo *f*.

trigamist ['trigəmist], *s. Jur:* trigame *mf*.

trigamous ['trigəməs], *a. Jur: Bot:* trigame.

trigamy ['trigəmi], *s. Jur:* trigamie *f*.

trigatron ['trigətrɔn], *s. Elcs:* trigatron *m*.

trigeminal [trai'dʒemin(ə)l], *a. & s. Anat:* **t. (nerve),** (nerf) trijumeau (*m*), (nerf) trifacial (*m*); nerf trigéminé; *Med:* **t. pulse,** pouls trigéminé; **t. neuralgia,** névralgie *f* du trijumeau, faciale.

trigeminous [trai'dʒeminəs], *a. Biol:* trigéminé.

trigeminus, *pl.* **-i** [trai'dʒeminəs, -ai], *s. Anat:* (nerf) trijumeau (*m*), (nerf) trifacial (*m*); nerf trigéminé *m*.

trigger[1] ['trigər], *s.* (*a*) *Mec.E: etc:* déclencheur *m*; poussoir *m* (à ressort); (*of pile driver, etc.*) déclic *m*; (*of latch*) poucier *m*; *Aut:* (*of hand brake*) manette *f*; **t. action,** déclenchement *m*; **t. mechanism,** mécanisme *m* de déclenchement; (*b*) *Sm.a:* détente *f*, *F:* gâchette *f*; **double t.,** double détente; **double-pull t.,** détente à double bossette; **light t.,** détente douce; **hard on the t.,** dur à la détente; **to pull, press, the t.,** agir, appuyer, sur la détente; **to release, let go, the t.,** lâcher la détente; **t. guard,** pontet *m*; sous(-)garde *f*; **t. finger,** index *m* (avec lequel on presse sur la détente); **to be quick on the t.,** *F:* **to be t. happy,** être prompt à la détente; ne pas hésiter à tirer; *F:* avoir la gâchette facile; *Fig:* **to be quick on the t.,** avoir la réaction, la réponse, facile; (*c*) **to use an A-bomb as t. for an H-bomb,** déclencher l'explosion d'une bombe H au moyen d'une bombe A; (*d*) *Nau:* **launching t.,** clef *f* de lancement (d'un navire); vérin *m* de retenue (d'un navire); (*e*) *Elcs:* **t. (circuit, pair),** bascule *f* (électronique); **t. relay,** relais *m* électronique; (*f*) *Physiol:* **t. area, zone,** zone *f* réflexogène; *Com:* **t. price,** prix indicatif.

trigger[2], *v.tr.* (*a*) déclencher (le départ du coup d'une arme à feu); (*b*) **to t. (off),** déclencher, provoquer (une réaction, une explosion, une révolution, etc.); **a neutron may t. off an extensive chain reaction,** un (simple) neutron peut déclencher une vaste réaction en chaîne; **this triggered off a series of strikes,** cela a provoqué une série de grèves.

triggerfish ['trigəfiʃ], *s. Ich:* baliste *m*.

triggering ['trigəriŋ], *s.* **t. (off),** déclenchement *m* (d'une explosion, d'une réaction, etc.); *Mec:* **t. pressure,** pression *f* de déclenchement; *El:* **t. voltage,** tension *f* de déclenchement.

trigla ['triglə], *s. Ich:* trigle *m*, grondin *m*.

triglid ['triglid]. *Ich:* (*a*) *a.* triglide; (*b*) *s.* triglide *m*, triglidé *m*.

Triglidae ['triglidiː], *s.pl. Ich:* triglidés *m*.

triglot ['traiglɔt], *a.* (dictionnaire, etc.) triglotte.

triglyph ['traiglif], *s. Arch:* triglyphe *m*.

trigon ['traigɔn], *s. Astrol:* trigone *m*.

trigona [trai'gounə], *s. Ent:* trigone *f*.

trigonal ['trigɔnəl], *a.* trigone.

trigone ['traigoun, tri'goun], *s. Anat:* trigone *m* (de la vessie).

trigonella [trigɔ'nelə], *s. Bot:* trigonelle *f*, trigonella *f*.

trigonocephaly [traigɔnou'sefəli], *s.* trigonocéphalie *f*.

trigonometric(al) [trigənə'metrik(l)], *a.* trigonométrique.

trigonometrically [trigənə'metrik(ə)li], *adv.* trigonométriquement.

trigonometry [trigə'nɔmitri], *s.* trigonométrie *f*; **plane t., spherical t.,** trigonométrie rectiligne, sphérique.

trigram ['traigræm], *s. Pal: etc:* trigramme *m*; sigle *m* de trois caractères réunis.

trigraph ['traigræf], *s. Gram: Typ:* trigramme *m*.

trigyn ['traidʒin], *s. Bot:* plante *f* trigyne.

Trigynia [trai'dʒiniə], *s.pl. Bot: O:* plantes *f* trigynes.

trigynous ['tridʒinəs], *a. Bot:* trigyne.

trihedral [trai'hiːdrəl, -'hedrəl], *a. & s. Mth:* (angle *m*) trièdre (*m*).

trihedron [trai'hiːdrən, -'hedrən], *s. Mth:* (angle *m*) trièdre *m*.

trihybrid [trai'haibrid], *s. Biol:* trihybride *m*.

trihydrol [trai'haidrɔl], *s. Ch:* trihydrol *m*.

triiodide [trai'aioudaid], *s. Ch:* triiodure *m*.

trijet ['traidʒet], *s. Av:* triréacteur *m*.

trilateral [trai'læt(ə)rəl], *a.* trilatéral, -aux.

trilby ['trilbi], *s.* **1. t. (hat),** chapeau mou. **2.** *pl. Austr: P:* jambes *f*.

trilinear [trai'liniər], *a.* trilinéaire.

trilingual [trai'liŋgw(ə)l], *a.* trilingue.

trilith, trilithon ['trailiθ(ɔn)], *s. Archeol:* trilithe *m*.

trilithic [trai'liθik], *a.* en forme de trilithe.

trill[1] [tril], *s.* **1.** *Mus:* (*a*) trille *m*; (*b*) cadence perlée. **2.** (*a*) chant perlé (des oiseaux); **trills of laughter,** des rires perlés; (*b*) chevrotement *m*. **3.** *Ling:* consonne roulée.

trill[2]. **1.** *v.i.* (*a*) *Mus:* faire des trilles (en chantant); (*b*) (*of bird*) perler son chant; **trilling laugh,** rire perlé; (*c*) chevroter. **2.** *v.tr.* (*a*) *Mus:* triller (une note, un passage); (*b*) *Ling:* rouler (les r); **trilled consonant,** consonne roulée.

triller ['trilər], *s. Orn:* échenilleur *m*.

trilling[1] ['triliŋ], *s.* (*a*) *Mus:* trilles *mpl*; (*b*) chant perlé (d'un oiseau).

trilling[2], *s.* (*a*) (*rare*) trijumeau, -elle (un de trois jumeaux); (*b*) *Cryst:* cristal *m* triple.

trillion ['triliən], *s.* **1.** trillion *m* (10^{18}). **2.** *U.S:* billion *m* (10^{12}).

Trillium ['triliəm], *s. Bot:* trillium *m*.

trilobate [trai'loubeit], *a. Bot: etc:* trilobé.

trilobite ['trailəbait], *s. Paleont;* trilobite *m*.

trilocular [trai'lɔkjulər], *a. Bot: etc:* triloculaire.

trilogy ['trilədʒi], *s.* trilogie *f*.

trilophodon [trai'lɔfədɔn], *s. Paleont:* tetrabelodon *m*.

trim[1] [trim], *s.* **1. in good t.,** (i) en bon ordre; (ii) (*of pers.*) en bonne santé; en (bonne) forme; **everything was in perfect t.,** tout était en parfait état, en ordre parfait; **in poor t.,** (i) en mauvais état; (ii) mal en train; **in fighting t.,** prêt pour le combat. **2.** (*a*) *Nau:* assiette *f*; *Av:* assiette; équilibrage *m*, centrage *m*; compensation *f*; **lateral t.,** compensation de gauchissement; **pitch t.,** (réglage *m* de l')assiette longitudinale; **t. angle,** angle *m* d'assiette, de calage; **t. tab,** volet correcteur; **t. actuator,** vérin *m* de volet correcteur; **in t., out of t.,** équilibré, non équilbré; (*b*) *Nau:* orientation *f* (des voiles); **sailing t.,** allure *f*; **in sailing t.,** bien orienté. **3.** (*a*) *O:* garniture *f*, ornements *mpl* (de vêtements, etc.); (*b*) *Aut:* équipement *m*; garnitures; (*c*) *NAm:* boiseries (ornementales) (d'une maison). **4.** *Hairdr:* coupe *f*; **just a t.,** simplement rafraîchir.

trim[2], *a.* (*a*) soigné; gentil, coquet; (*of pers.*) **to look t.,** avoir un air soigné; **to have a t. figure,** avoir une tournure élégante, une taille élégante; **a t. little garden,** un petit jardin coquet, bien tenu; (*b*) *Nau:* (navire) bien voilé; (voile) étarque.

trim[3], *v.tr.* **(trimmed) 1.** (*a*) arranger, mettre en ordre, mettre en état (qch.); (*b*) tailler, tondre, couper (une haie); émonder, ébourgeonner, esserter, ébrancher (un arbre); ravaler (des branches, etc.); ébarber, rogner, ajuster, parer (une pièce coulée); ébavurer, déborder (un moulage); dégrossir, corroyer (le bois); dégauchir, dresser (une pierre de taille); dégraisser, blanchir (une planche); égaliser, rafraîchir (les cheveux, la barbe, la queue d'un cheval); *Leath:* échantillonner (les peaux); *Phot:* calibrer (une épreuve); *Metall:* épiler (les blocs d'étain); *Hairdr:* couper, rafraîchir (les cheveux de qn); **to t. one's nails,** se faire les ongles; **to t. a lamp,** émécher une lampe; *Bookb:* **to t. the edges of a book,** ébarber, rogner, les tranches d'un livre; *Surg:* **to t. a wound,** (r)aviver une plaie; *Cu:* **to t. meat,** habiller, parer, la viande; enlever les tirants; **to t. off the fat,** enlever le gras; (*c*) (*of shoal of fish*) **to t. the shore,** longer la côte; (*d*) *Const:* enchevêtrer, enclaver (des solives); **trimmed joist,** poutre enchevêtrée; poutre secondaire. **2.** (*a*) équilibrer (un navire, un avion); donner de l'assiette à (un navire); balancer, redresser (un canot); mettre (un navire) en bon tirant d'eau; faire la pesée (d'un sous-marin); *Nau:* **trimmed even keel,** chargé à égal tirant d'eau; **trimmed by the head, by the stern,** chargé sur nez, sur cul; *Nau: Av:* **to t. the cargo,** arrimer le chargement; *Nau:* **to t. the tanks,** équilibrer les réservoirs; *Av:* **to t. the tabs,** régler les flettners; (*b*) *Nau:* orienter, appareiller, balancer (les voiles); **to t. (the sails) sharp,** brasser en pointe; (*c*) *v.i. Pol: etc:* tergiverser, louvoyer; faire de l'opportunisme; tendre les voiles du côté que vient le vent; ménager la chèvre et le chou; nager entre deux eaux. **3.** (*a*) *Dressm: etc:* orner, garnir, agrémenter (une robe, etc.) **(with,** de); garnir (un chapeau); **trimmed with lace,** garni, bordé, de dentelles; *esp. NAm:* **to t. the Christmas tree,** décorer l'arbre de Noël. **4.** *Carp: etc:* **to t. up,** dresser (une poutre, une meule, etc.); laver (du bois dégrossi); ragréer (un assemblage).

trimaran ['traimərӕn], *s. Nau:* trimaran *m*.

Trimera ['trimərə], *s.pl. Ent:* trimères *m*.

trimeran ['trimərən], *a. & s. Ent:* trimère (*m*).

trimerite ['trimərait], *s. Miner:* trimérite *f*.

trimerous ['trimərəs], *a. Ent: etc:* (coléoptère, etc.) trimère.

trimesic [trai'mesik], *a. Ch:* (acide) trimésique.

trimester [trai'mestər], *s.* trimestre *m*.

trimestrial [trai'mestriəl], *a.* trimestriel.

trimeter ['trimitər], *a. & s. Pros:* trimètre (*m*).

trimethylamine [traimeθil'æmain], *s. Ch:* triméthylamine *f*.

trimethylbenzene [traimeθil'benziːn], *s. Ch:* triméthylbenzène *m*.

trimethylcarbinol [traimeθil'kɑːbinɔl], *s. Ch:* triméthylcarbinol *m*.

trimethylene [trai'meθiliːn], *s. Ch:* triméthylène *m*.

trimetric [trai'metrik], *a.* **1.** *Pros:* trimètre. **2.** *Cryst:* trimétrique, orthorhombique.

trimmer ['trimər], *s.* **1.** (*pers.*) (*a*) *Ind:* appareilleur *m*; pareur, -euse; *Metall:* burineur *m* (de pièces venues de fonte, etc.); (*b*) *A:* **lamp t.,** lampiste *m*; (*c*) garnisseur, -euse (de chapeaux, de robes, etc.); (*d*) *Nau:* arrimeur *m*; *O:* **coal t.,** soutier *m*; (*e*) *Pol: etc:* opportuniste *m*; sauteur, -euse. **2.** (*a*) machine *f* à trancher, à dresser (le bois, etc.); (*b*) *Paperm: Bookb: etc:* massicot *m*; (*b*) *Const:* solive *f* d'enchevêtrure; chevêtre *m*; linçoir *m*, linsoir *m*; **to join joists by a t.,** enchevêtrer des solives; (*c*) *Av:* (dispositif) compensateur *m*; *Av: Nau:* équilibreur *m*; (*d*) *El:* **t. (capacitor),** condensateur *m* d'équilibrage; trimmer *m*; (*e*) *Fish:* (*for pike*) trimmer.

trimming ['trimiŋ], *s.* **1.** (*a*) arrangement *m*, mise *f* en ordre, mise en état (de qch.); (*b*) taille *f* (des haies, des arbres); ébranchage *m*, émondage *m* (des arbres); ravalement *m* (des branches); **t. axe,** émondoir *m*; (*c*) dégrossissage *m*, corroyage *m* (du bois); *Metall:* ébarbage *m* (des pièces coulées); débordage *m* (de fer en tôles, *Opt:* d'une lentille); *Leath:* échantillonnage *m* (des peaux); *Bookb:* ébarbage (des tranches); *Phot:* calibrage *m* (des épreuves); **t. machine,** (i) *Metall: etc:* ébarbeuse *f*; (ii) *Bookb:* rogneuse *f*; **trimmings,** rognures *f*, ébarbures *f* (de fer, de bois, de papier, etc.); *Phot:* **t. knife, t. nib,** lancette *f*; **t. board,** photo-cisaille *f, pl.* photo-cisailles; (*d*) *Carp:* enchevêtrement *m*, enclavement *m* (de solives); **t. joist,** chevêtrier *m*. **2.** (*a*) *Nau:* arrimage *m*, balancement *m* (de la cargaison); **t. tank,** caisse *f* d'assiette; (*b*) *Nau:* orientation *f*, balancement (des voiles); (*c*) *Av:* compensation *f*; équilibrage *m* (de l'avion); *Nau:* équilibrage (d'un navire); *Av:* **t. flap,** volet compensateur; **t. tab,** volet correcteur; (*d*) *F:* louvoyage *m* (politique, etc.). **3.** (*a*) garnissage *m* (de chapeaux, de linge, etc.); *Cu:* apprêt *m* (d'un mets); (*b*) garniture *f*, ornement *m* (de vêtements, de chapeaux, de rideaux, etc.); (*often pl.*) passementerie *f* (pour vêtements, ameublements, etc.); fournitures *fpl* (pour chapeaux, etc.); *Cu: F:* **the (usual) trimmings,** accompagnements *mpl*, garniture (d'un plat).

trimness ['trimnis], *s.* air soigné (de qn, de qch.); apparence bien tenue (d'un jardin, etc.); élégance *f* (de mise); **the t. of her figure,** sa taille élégante.

trimolecular [traimɔ'lekjulər], *a.* trimoléculaire.

trimorph ['traimɔ:f], *s. Cryst:* substance *f* trimorphe.

trimorphic [trai'mɔ:fik], *a. Cryst:* trimorphe.

trimorphism [trai'mɔ:fizm], *s. Cryst: Nat.Hist:* trimorphisme *m*.

trimorphous [trai'mɔ:fəs], *a.* trimorphe.

trinary ['trainəri], *a.* trinaire.

trine [train]. **1.** *a.* (*a*) triple; *Ecc:* **t. aspersion,** triple aspersion *f* (d'un baptême); (*b*) *Astrol:* trin; trine; **t. aspect,** trin(e) aspect *m*. **2.** *s. Astrol:* trin(e) aspect.

trinervate [trai'nə:veit], *a. Bot:* trinervé.

tringa ['triŋgə], *s. Orn:* tringa *m*.

tringle ['triŋgl], *s. Arch: Furn:* tringle *f*.

Trinidad ['trinidæd], *Pr.n. Geog:* (île de) Trinidad, (île de) la Trinité; **T. and Tobago,** (État de) Trinidad et Tobago.

trinitarian [trini'tɛəriən]. **1.** *a. & s. Theol:* trinitaire (*mf*). **2.** *s. Ecc:* **T. (monk, nun),** trinitaire *mf*.

trinitrate [trai'naitreit], *s. Ch:* trinitré *m*.

trinitrated [trainai'treitid], *a. Ch:* trinitré.

trinitrobenzene [trainaitrou'benzi:n], *s. Exp:* trinitrobenzène *m*.

trinitrocresol [trainaitrou'kresɔl], *s. Ch:* trinitrocrésol *m*.

trinitrophenol [trainaitrou'fenɔl], *s. Ch:* trinitrophénol *m*.

trinitrotoluene, trinitrotoluol [trainaitrou'tɔljui:n, -'tɔljuɔl], *s. Exp:* trinitrotoluène *m*, trinol *m*.

Trinity ['triniti], *s.* **1.** (*a*) *Theol:* **the (Holy) T.,** la (sainte) Trinité; **T. Sunday,** (fête *f* de) la Trinité; **T. term,** *Jur:* session *f* de la Trinité; session d'été; *Sch:* trimestre *m* d'été; (*b*) *F:* groupe *m* de trois; **this unholy t. of politicians,** ces trois salauds de politiciens. **2.** *Nau:* **T. House,** corporation chargée de l'entretien des phares, du balisage et du pilotage; **T. House boat** = (bateau) baliseur *m*, bateau pilote. **3.** *Bot:* **herb t.,** trinité.

trinket ['triŋkit], *s.* (*a*) petit objet de parure; petit bijou; colifichet *m*; breloque *f* (de chaîne de montre); (*b*) babiole *f*, bibelot *m*.

trinomial [trai'noumiəl], *a. & s. Mth:* trinôme (*m*).

Trinucleidae [trainju'kli:idi:], *s.pl. Paleont:* trinucléidés *m*.

trio, *pl.* **-os** ['tri:ou(z)], *s. Mus: etc:* trio *m*.

triode ['traioud], *s. Elcs:* triode *f*; **double t.,** double triode.

triodon ['traioudɔn], *s. Ich:* triodon *m*.

triol ['traiɔl], *s. Ch:* triol *m*, trialcool *m*.

triole ['tri:oul], *s. Mus:* triolet *m*.

triolein [trai'ouliin], *s. Ch:* trioléine *f*.

triolet ['tri:oulet], *s. Pros:* triolet *m*.

trional ['traiən(ə)l], *s. Pharm:* trional *m*.

Triones [trai'ouni:z], *Pr.n.pl. Astr:* Triones *m*.

Trionychidae [traiou'nikidi:], *s.pl. Rept:* trionychidés *m*.

trioxane [trai'ɔksein], *s. Ch:* trioxyméthylène *m*.

trioxide [trai'ɔksaid], *s. Ch:* trioxyde *m*; **sulphur t.,** anhydride *m* sulfurique.

trioxymethylene [traiɔksi'meθili:n], *s. Ch:* trioxyméthylène *m*.

trip[1] [trip], *s.* **1.** (*a*) excursion *f*; voyage *m* d'agrément; tour *m*; **holiday t.,** voyage de vacances; **honeymoon t.,** voyage de noces; **to go for, to make, a t.,** faire une excursion, un petit voyage; voyager; **to go for a short sea t., for a little t. on the sea,** faire une sortie en mer; **to go for a t. round the lake,** faire le tour du lac; **we always go for a t. somewhere on Sundays,** nous faisons toujours une sortie le dimanche; **the t. takes two hours,** on fait le trajet en deux heures; *Aut:* **t. recorder,** (totalisateur) journalier *m*; compteur *m* de trajet; *Nau:* **trial t.,** voyage d'essai; **maiden t.,** premier voyage; **round t.,** croisière *f*; voyage d'aller et retour; (*b*) **(drug) t.,** voyage; **to have a bad t.,** faire un mauvais voyage. **2.** pas léger; **I heard the t. of her feet in the corridor,** j'ai entendu ses pas légers dans le couloir. **3.** (*a*) faux pas; trébuchement *m*; bronchade *f* (d'un cheval); (*b*) faute *f*, erreur *f*; faux pas; (*c*) croc-en-jambe *m, pl.* crocs-en-jambe; croche-pied *m, pl.* croche-pieds; *Box:* enlaçage *m* de jambe; (*d*) **t. wire,** fil tendu (en guise de traquenard ou d'avertisseur). **4.** (*a*) *Mec.E:* **t. gear,** (i) déclic *m*, déclenche *f*, déclenchement *m* (de mouton, etc.); modificateur instantané; (ii) culbuteur *m* (de bennes, etc.); **t. lever,** levier *m* à déclic; **t. hammer,** marteau *m* à bascule, à soulèvement; *Metall: etc:* martinet *m*; (*b*) *El:* **t. coil,** bobine *f* de relais.

trip[2], *v.* **(tripped** [tript]**) 1.** *v.i.* (*a*) **to t. (along),** aller d'un pas léger; trotter, marcher, dru et menu; **to t. in, out, away,** entrer, sortir, s'en aller, d'un pas léger; **she tripped across the square,** elle a traversé la place à petits pas, de son pas menu, léger; **to t. up the stairs,** grimper lestement l'escalier; (*b*) trébucher; faire un faux pas; (*of horse*) broncher; **to t. over sth.,** trébucher sur, buter contre, qch.; (*c*) **to t. (up),** se tromper; **to catch s.o. tripping,** trouver, prendre, qn en défaut, en erreur; **to t. (up) over a word,** trébucher sur un mot; (*d*) *Mec.E:* (i) (*of catch, etc.*) se déclencher; (ii) (*of part of mechanism*) basculer, culbuter; (*e*) *Nau:* (*of anchor*) déraper; (*f*) *P:* (*drugs*) faire un voyage; être en voyage. **2.** *v.tr.* (*a*) **to t. s.o. (up),** (i) donner un croc-en-jambe à qn; renverser qn d'un croc-en-jambe; faire un croche-pied à qn; (*of obstacle*) faire trébucher, faire tomber, qn; (ii) prendre qn en défaut, en erreur; **to t. up a witness,** surprendre un témoin en contradiction; (*b*) *Mec.E:* déclencher, décliquer, débrayer (une pièce de machine); culbuter (un levier, etc.); **to t. a piece in,** embrayer une pièce; (*c*) *El:* déclencher; (*d*) *Nau:* **to t. the anchor,** déraper l'ancre.

tripack ['traipæk], *s. Phot:* jeu *m* de trois pellicules à écrans colorés (pour photographie trichrome).

tripalmitin [trai'pɑ:mitin], *s. Ch:* tripalmitine *f*.

tripartite [trai'pɑ:tait], *a.* **1.** tripartite; divisé en trois. **2.** triple; **t. alliance,** triple alliance; *Jur:* **t. indenture,** (i) contrat trilatéral, *pl.* contrats trilatéraux; (ii) contrat en trois exemplaires.

tripartition [traipɑ:'tiʃ(ə)n], *s.* tripartition *f*.

tripe [traip], *s.* **1.** (*a*) *Cu:* tripe(s) *f*(*pl*); gras-double *m*; **t. butcher,** tripier, -ière; **t. shop, t. butcher's,** triperie *f*; (*b*) *F:* fatras *m*, bêtises *fpl*; **to publish t.,** publier des ouvrages sans valeur, de la littérature de camelote; **sentimental t.,** sentimentalité *f* à l'eau de rose; **that's all t., that's a lot of t.,** tout ça c'est des sottises. **2.** *P: O:* **tripes,** (i) entrailles *f*, intestins *m*; (ii) panse *f*.

tripehound ['traiphaund], *s.* (*a*) journaliste *mf* (à la recherche des nouvelles sensationnelles); (*b*) *Austr:* chien *m*, *esp.* (i) berger australien, kelpie australien; (ii) chien de troupeaux australien.

tripeptide [trai'peptaid], *s. Bio-Ch:* tripeptide *m*.

tripery ['traipəri], *s.* triperie *f*.

tripetalous [trai'petələs], *a. Bot:* tripétale, tripétalé.

triphane ['traifein], *s. Miner:* triphane *m*.

triphase ['traifeiz], *a. El:* (courant) triphasé.

triphenol [trai'fenɔl], *s. Ch:* triphénol *m*.

triphenyl- [trai'fenil], *comb.fm. Ch:* triphényl-.

triphenylmethane [traifenil'meθein], *s.* triphénylméthane *m*.

triphthong ['trifθɔŋ], *s. Ling:* triphtongue *f*.

triphyline, triphylite ['traifili:n, -ait], *s. Miner:* triphyline *f*, triphylite *f*.

triphyllous [trai'filəs], *a. Bot:* triphylle.

tripinnate [trai'pineit], *a. Bot:* tripenné.

triplane ['traiplein], *a. & s. Av: A:* triplan (*m*).

triple[1] ['tripl], *a.* triple; *Mth:* **t. ratio,** raison *f* triple; *Mus:* **t. time,** mesure *f* ternaire, à trois temps; *Ch:* **t. salt,** sel *m* triple; *Astr:* **t. star,** étoile *f* triple; *Hist:* **the T. Alliance,** la Triplice, la triple Alliance; *Elcs:* **t. length working,** fonctionnement *m* en longueur triple; *F:* **t. chin,** triple menton *m*.

triple[2], **1.** *v.tr.* tripler **2.** *v.i.* (se) tripler.

triplegia [trai'pli:dʒiə], *s. Med:* triplégie *f*.

triple-huller [tripl'hʌlər], *s. Nau:* trimaran *m*.

triple-nerved [tripl'nə:vd], *a. Bot:* triplinervé.

triplet ['triplit], *s.* **1.** trio *m*; réunion *f* de trois personnes, de trois choses; (*a*) *Mus:* tercet *m*, triolet *m*; (*b*) *Pros:* tercet; (*c*) *Arch:* triplet *m* (de trois fenêtres); (*d*) *Opt:* **t. lens,** triplet. **2.** trijumeau, -elle; triplé(e); **to give birth to, to have, triplets,** mettre au monde des triplés; faire un accouchement trigémellaire.

triplex ['tripleks], *a.* (planche) en trois épaisseurs; (machine *f*) à trois cylindres; *NAm:* (*of building*) (i) à trois appartements; (ii) à trois étages; *Paperm:* **t. boards,** cartons *m* triplex.

triplicate[1] ['triplikət]. **1.** *a.* triplé; triple; *Mth:* **t. ratio,** raison triplée. **2.** *s.* triple *m*; triplicata *m*; **invoice, agreement, in t.,** facture, contrat, en triple, en triplicata, en triple exemplaire, en triple expédition.

triplicate[2] ['triplikeit], *v.tr.* **1.** tripler. **2.** rédiger (un document) en triple expédition.

triplication [tripli'keiʃ(ə)n], *s.* **1.** triplication *f*. **2.** tirage *m* à triple exemplaire.

triplicity [tri'plisiti], *s.* triplicité *f*.

triplinerved ['triplinə:vd], *a. Bot:* triplinervé.

tripling ['tripliŋ], *s.* **1.** triplement *m*. **2.** *Cryst:* groupe *m* de trois cristaux.

triplite ['triplait], *s. Miner:* triplite *f*.

triploid ['triplɔid], *a. Biol:* triploïde.

triply ['tripli], *adv.* triplement.

tripod ['traipɔd], *s.* (*a*) trépied *m*, trois-pieds *m inv*; pied *m* (à trois branches); **folding t.,** pied à brisures; pied pliant; **sliding t., adjustable t.,** trépied à coulisse; pied à branches coulissantes; **ladder t.,** trépied à échelle; pied praticable; **t. stand,** pied à trois branches; support à trois pieds; (*b*) *Nau:* **t. mast,** (mât) tripode *m*; **t. mounting,** affût trépied; (*c*) *Gr.Ant:* trépied.

tripodal ['tripədl], *a.* à trois pieds.

tripolar [trai'poulər], *a.* tripolaire.

Tripoli ['tripəli]. **1.** *Pr.n. Geog:* (*a*) Tripoli *m*; (*b*) (la province de) Tripoli; Tripolitaine *f*. **2.** *s. A:* **t. (powder),** tripoli *m*; terre pourrie (d'Angleterre).

Tripolitan [tri'pɔlitən]. *Geog:* (*a*) *a.* tripolitain; (*b*) *s.* Tripolitain, -aine.

Tripolitania [tripɔli'teiniə], *Pr.n. Geog:* Tripolitaine *f*.

tripos ['traipɔs], *s. Sch:* = licence ès lettres, ès sciences (à Cambridge).

tripper ['tripər], *s.* **1.** (*pers.*) excursionniste *mf*; **they're (just) day trippers,** ils sont venus pour passer la journée. **2.** *Mec.E:* culbuteur *m*.

trippery ['tripəri], *a. F: Pej:* (endroit) plein d'excursionnistes; (plage) populaire.

tripping[1] ['tripiŋ], *a.* **t. step,** pas léger.

tripping[2], *s.* **1.** = TRIP[1] 2, 3. **2.** (*a*) *Mec.E:* déclenchement *m* (d'un déclic); basculement *m* (d'une pièce de mécanisme); **t. gear,** (i) déclic *m*, déclenche *f*, déclenchement (de mouton, etc.); modificateur instantané; (ii) culbuteur *m* (de bennes, etc.); (*b*) *El:* disjonction *f*; **t. device,** disjoncteur *m*; **t. mechanism, t. system,** système *m* de disjonction. **3.** *Nau:* dérapage *m* (de l'ancre).

Triptolemus [trip'tɔliməs], *Pr.n.m. Gr.Myth:* Triptolème.

triptych ['triptik], *s. Art:* triptyque *m*.

triptyque ['triptik], *s. Aut: Adm:* triptyque *m*.

tripy ['traipi], *a. F:* sans valeur; de dernière catégorie; (littérature) de camelote; **t. stuff,** *esp.* littérature à l'eau de rose.

triquetrous [trai'kwetrəs], *a. Nat.Hist:* (tige, os, etc.) triquètre.

trireme ['trairi:m], *s. A.Nau:* trirème *f*, trière *f*.

trisect [trai'sekt], *v.tr. Mth: etc:* triséquer; diviser, couper, (une ligne, un angle, *F:* un gâteau) en trois.

trisecting[1] [trai'sektiŋ], *a.* trisecteur, -trice.

trisecting[2], **trisection** [trai'sekʃ(ə)n], *s.* trisection *f*.

trisector [trai'sektər], *s. Mth:* trisecteur *m*.

trisepalous [trai'sepələs], *a. Bot:* trisépale.

trishaw ['traiʃɔ:], *s. Veh:* vélo-pousse *m*.

triskele ['triski:l, 'trai-], **triskelion** [tris'keliən], *s. Num: etc:* triquètre *f*; triskèle *f*.

trismus ['trizməs], *s. Med:* trisme *m*, trismus *m*.

trisodium [trai'soudiəm], *a. Ch:* trisodique.

trisomic [trai'soumik]. **1.** *a.* trisomique. **2.** *s.* organisme *m* trisomique.

trisomy ['traisoumi], *s. Biol:* trisomie *f*.

trispermous [trai'spə:məs], *a. Bot:* trisperme.

tristearin [trai'sti:ərin], *s. Ch:* tristéarine *f*.

tristichous ['tristikəs], *a. Bot:* tristique.

Tristram ['tristrəm], *Pr.n.m. Lit:* Tristan.

trisubstituted [trai'sʌbstitjutid], *a. Ch:* trisubstitué.

trisulcate [trai'sʌlkeit], *a. Nat.Hist:* trisulce.

trisulphide [trai'sʌlfaid], *s. Ch:* trisulfure *m*.

trisyllabic [traisi'læbik], *a. Pros:* tris(s)yllabe, tris(s)yllabique.

trisyllable [trai'siləbl], *s. Pros:* tris(s)yllabe *m*.

trite [trait], *a.* banal, -als; rebattu; **t. subject,** sujet usé, rebattu; *Art: Lit:* poncif *m*; **t. remarks,** lieux communs; banalités *f*.

tritely ['traitli], *adv.* banalement.

triteness ['traitnis], *s.* banalité *f*.

triternate [trai'tə:neit], *a. Bot:* triterné.

tritheism ['traiθi:izm], *s. Theol:* trithéisme *m*.

tritheist ['traiθi:ist], *s. Theol:* trithéiste *m.*
trithionic [traiθai'ɔnik], *a. Ch:* trithionique.
trithrinax [trai'θrainæks], *s. Bot:* trithrinax *m.*
tritium ['tritiəm], *s. Ch:* tritium *m.*
tritomite ['traitoumait], *s. Miner:* tritomite *f.*
Triton[1] ['trait(ə)n]. **1.** *Pr.n.m. Myth:* Triton. **2.** *s.* (*a*) *Myth:* triton *m*; **to be a t. among the minnows,** éclipser tout son entourage; (*b*) *Amph:* triton; (*c*) *Moll:* **t. (shell),** triton, tritonie *f.*
triton[2], *s. Atom.Ph:* triton *m.*
tritone ['traitoun], *s. Mus:* triton *m.*
tritoness ['traitənes], *s.f. Myth:* tritonide, tritonne.
Tritondae [trai'tɔnidi:], *s.pl. Moll:* tritonidés *m.*
tritoxide [trai'tɔksaid], *s. Ch:* tritoxyde *m.*
tritubercular, trituberculate [traitju'bə:kjulər, -eit], *a. Nat.Hist:* trituberculé.
triturable ['tritjərəbl], *a.* triturable.
tritural ['tritjərəl], *a. Anat:* **t. surface (of a tooth),** face triturante (d'une dent).
triturate ['tritjəreit], *v.tr.* triturer; réduire (qch.) en poudre.
triturating ['tritjəreitiŋ], *s.* trituration *f*; **t. machine,** triturateur *m*; *Exp:* **t. ball,** gobille *f.*
trituration [tritjə'reiʃ(ə)n], *s.* trituration *f.*
triturator ['tritjəreitər], *s.* (*machine*) triturateur *m.*
trityl ['traitil], *s. Ch:* trityle *m.*
Tritylodon, tritylodont [trai'tiloudɔn(t)], *s. Paleont:* tritylodon *m.*
triumph[1] ['traiʌmf], *s.* **1.** *Rom.Ant:* triomphe *m.* **2.** (*a*) triomphe, succès *m*; **the t. of intelligence over brute force,** le triomphe de l'intelligence sur la force brutale; **to achieve great triumphs,** remporter de grands succès; *F:* **her dress is a t. of bad taste,** sa robe est un chef-d'œuvre de mauvais goût; (*b*) air *m* de triomphe; jubilation *f*; **there was a look of t. on his face,** un air de triomphe était répandu sur son visage; **he came home in t.,** il est rentré chez lui en triomphe.
triumph[2], *v.i.* **1.** *Rom.Ant:* triompher. **2.** triompher; remporter un succès éclatant; avoir l'avantage; **to t. over one's enemies,** triompher de ses ennemis; l'emporter sur ses ennemis; **to t. over opposition, difficulties,** avoir raison de l'opposition, des difficultés; **now it was my turn to t.,** c'était alors à moi de chanter, crier, victoire.
triumphal [trai'ʌmf(ə)l], *a.* triomphal, -aux; de triomphe; **t. arch,** arc *m* de triomphe.
triumphant [trai'ʌmfənt], *a.* triomphant; triomphateur, -trice; **the Church T.,** l'Église triomphante; **to have a t. expression,** avoir un air victorieux, un air de triomphe.
triumphantly [trai'ʌmfəntli], *adv.* en triomphe; triomphalement; d'un air, d'un ton, de triomphe; d'un air victorieux.
triumpher ['traiʌmfər], *s.* triomphateur, -trice; vainqueur *m.*
triumphing ['traiʌmfiŋ], *a.* triomphant; triomphateur, -trice.
triumvir, *pl.* **-virs, -viri** [trai'ʌmvə:r, -və:z, -viri:], *s. Rom.Hist: etc:* triumvir *m.*
triumviral [trai'ʌmvirəl], *a.* triumviral, -aux.
triumvirate [trai'ʌmvireit], *s.* (*a*) triumvirat *m*; (*b*) trio *m* (de personnes).
triune ['traiju:n], *a.* d'une unité triple; *Theol:* **t. godhead,** divinité *f* une en trois personnes; divinité trine.
triungulin [trai'ʌŋgjulin], *s. Ent:* triongulin *m.*
triunity [trai'ju:niti], *s.* trinité *f.*
trivalence [trai'veiləns], *s. Ch:* trivalence *f.*
trivalent [trai'veil(ə)nt]. **1.** *a. Ch:* trivalent. **2.** *a. & s. Biol:* trivalent (*m*).
trivalve ['traivælv], **trivalvular** [trai'vælvjulər], *a. Nat.Hist:* trivalve.
trivet[1] ['trivit], *s. Dom.Ec:* trépied *m*, chevrette *f* (pour bouilloire, etc.).
trivet[2], *s. Tex:* **t. (knife),** taillerol(l)e *f.*
trivia ['triviə], *s.pl.* des vétilles *f*, des riens *m*; **to get bogged down, immersed, in t.,** s'embarrasser de questions sans importance.
trivial ['triviəl], *a.* **1.** (*a*) insignifiant; sans importance; **t. loss,** perte légère, insignifiante; **t. offence,** peccadille *f*; (*b*) (*of pers.*) superficiel, léger, frivole, futile. **2.** banal, -aux; **the t. round,** le train-train de tous les jours. **3.** *Nat.Hist:* (nom *m*) (i) spécifique, (ii) populaire.
triviality [trivi'æliti], *s.* **1.** (*a*) insignifiance *f* (d'une perte, d'une offense, etc.); (*b*) banalité *f* (d'une observation, etc.). **2. to write trivialities,** écrire des banalités; **to talk polite trivialities,** dire des futilités; parler pour ne rien dire.
trivialize ['triviəlaiz], *v.tr.* banaliser; dire des inanités sur (un sujet d'importance).
trivially ['triviəli], *adv.* **1.** légèrement; d'une manière frivole. **2.** banalement.
trivoltine [trai'vɔltain], *a. Ent:* trivoltin.
triweekly [trai'wi:kli]. **1.** (*a*) *a.* de toutes les trois semaines; (*b*) *adv.* toutes les trois semaines; (*c*) *s.* périodique publié toutes les trois semaines. **2.** (*a*) *a.* trihebdomadaire; (*b*) *adv.* trois fois par semaine; (*c*) *s.* périodique trihebdomadaire.
Troad, Troas ['trouæd, -æs], *Pr.n. Geog:* La Troade.
troat[1] [trout], *s. Ven:* bramement *m* (de cerf).
troat[2], *v.i.* (*of stag*) bramer, réer, raire.
troating ['troutiŋ], *s. Ven:* bramement *m* (de cerf).
trocar ['troukər], *s. Surg:* trocart *m*; **exploring t.,** explorateur *m.*
trochaic [trou'keiik], *a. & s. Pros:* trochaïque (*m*).
trochal ['trouk(ə)l], *a. Nat.Hist:* rotiforme; en forme de roue; **t. disc,** disque rotateur (des rotifères).
trochanter [trɔ'kæntər], *s. Anat: Ent:* trochanter *m*; *Anat:* **the great t., t. major,** le grand trochanter; **the lesser t., t. minor,** le petit trochanter, le trochantin.
trochanteric [trɔkæn'terik], *a. Anat:* trochantérien.
trochantin(e) [trɔ'kænt(a)in], *s. Anat: Ent:* trochantin *m*; *Anat:* petit trochanter.
trochantinal [trɔ'kæntinəl], **trochantinian** [trɔkæn'tiniən], *a.* trochantinien.
troche [trouʃ], **trochee**[1] ['trouki:], *s. Pharm:* tablette *f*, pastille *f.*
trochee[2], *s. Pros:* trochée *m*, chorée *m.*
trochid ['troukid], *s. Moll:* trochidé *m.*
Trochidae ['troukidi:], *s.pl. Moll:* trochidés *m.*
Trochilidae [trou'kilidi:], *s.pl. Orn:* trochilidés *mpl.*
trochilus ['trɔkiləs], *s.* **1.** *Arch:* trochile *m.* **2.** *Orn:* (*a*) *Ant:* **(Egyptian) t.,** trochilus *m*; (*b*) **(American) t.,** trochile; colibri *m.*
trochite ['troukait], *s. Paleont:* entroque *m.*
trochlea, *pl.* **-eae** ['trɔkliə, -ii:], *s. Anat:* trochlée *f.*
trochlear ['trɔkliər], *a. Anat:* trochléen; trochléaire.
trochoid ['troukɔid]. **1.** *a.* (*a*) *Anat:* trochoïde; (*b*) *Mth:* cycloïdal, -aux. **2.** *s.* (*a*) *Anat:* articulation *f* trochoïde; trochoïde *f*; (*b*) *Mth:* (i) *A:* cycloïde *f*, roulette *f*; (courbe) trochoïde *f*; (ii) courbe cycloïdale; cycloïde allongée; cycloïde raccourcie; (*c*) *Moll:* trochoïde *m.*
trochoidal [trɔ'kɔidl], *a. Mth:* (*a*) *A:* trochoïde; (*b*) cycloïdal, -aux.
trochophore, trochosphere ['trɔkoufɔ(:)ər, -sfiər], *s. Nat.Hist:* trochophore *f*, trochosphère *f.*
trochus ['troukəs], *s. Moll:* troche *f*, trochus *m*, troque *m.*
troctolite ['trɔktoulait], *s. Miner:* troctolite *f.*
trod [trɔd], *s. Dial:* voie *f* (d'une bête); **sheep t.,** piste *f*, voie, d'un mouton, des moutons.
trodden ['trɔdn], *a.* (sentier, chemin) battu; **to follow, to stick to, the t. path,** suivre le chemin battu.
troegerite, trögerite ['trə:gərait], *s. Miner:* trœgérite *f.*
troglobiont [trɔglou'baiɔnt, trɔ'gloubiɔnt], *s. Biol:* troglobie *m.*
troglodyte ['trɔglədait], *s.* troglodyte *m.*
troglodytic [trɔglə'ditik], *a.* troglodytique.
Troglodytidae [trɔglə'ditidi:], *s.pl. Orn:* troglodytidés *m*, les troglodytes *m.*
trogon ['trougɔn], *s. Orn:* trogon *m*; courcourcou *m*; **masked t.,** trogon d'Amérique tropicale.
Trogonidae [trou'gɔnidi:], *s.pl. Orn:* trogonidés *m*, les trogons *m.*
Trogoniformes [trɔgɔni'fɔ:mi:z], *s.pl. Orn:* trogoniformes *m.*
troika ['trɔikə], *s. Veh:* troïka *f.*
troilite ['trɔilait], *s. Miner:* troïlite *f.*
Troilus ['trɔiləs], *Pr.n.m. Lit:* Troïlus.
Trojan ['troudʒən]. **1.** *a. A.Hist:* troyen; de Troie; **the T. War,** la guerre de Troie; **the T. Horse,** le cheval de Troie. **2.** *s.* (*a*) *A.Hist:* Troyen, -enne; (*b*) **he bore it like a T.,** il l'a supporté vaillamment, avec courage; **to work, fight, like a T.,** travailler sans relâche; se battre vaillamment; **he's a T.,** (i) c'est un courageux; (ii) c'est un chic type.
troll[1] [troul], *s.* **1.** *A:* chanson *f* à reprises; canon *m.* **2.** (*a*) *Fish:* cuiller *f*; (*b*) moulinet *m* (de canne à pêche).
troll[2]. **1.** *v.tr.* (*a*) *A:* chanter (un air) en canon; (*b*) chantonner (un air, une chanson); (*c*) *A:* passer (la bouteille) à la ronde. **2.** *v.i.* (*a*) *Fish:* **to t. for pike,** pêcher le brochet à la cuiller; (*b*) *A:* (*of bottle*) passer à la ronde.
troll[3], *s. Myth:* troll *m.*
troller ['troulər], *s. Fish:* pêcheur *m* à la cuiller.
trolley ['trɔli], *s.* **1.** (*a*) fardier *m*, binard *m*, binart *m*, chariot *m*; (*two wheeled*) diable *m*; *Min:* plate-forme *f* de roulage; *Rail:* **(luggage) t.,** chariot à bagages; (*two wheeled*) diable; **power t.,** locotracteur *m*; **platelayer's t.,** lorry *m*, wagonet *m*; *Aut:* **motor t.,** patin transbordeur (de voiture de dépannage, etc.); (*b*) **(shopping) t.,** (i) (*in supermarket, etc.*) chariot, *F:* caddie *m*; (ii) (*belonging to customer*) poussette *f*; **(dinner, tea) t.,** table roulante. **2.** *Ind:* **overhead t.,** chariot, baladeur *m*, transporteur aérien (de pont roulant, etc.). **3.** (*a*) moufle *m* or *f* (de transport sur câble aérien); *esp. U.S: F:* **to be off one's t.,** être fou, maboul; dérailler; (*b*) (poulie *f* de) trolley *m*; poulie de contact (d'un tramway, etc.); **t. pole,** perche *f* de trolley; archet *m*; **t. wire,** fil *m* de trolley; câble conducteur; *N.Am:* **t. (car),** tramway *m* à trolley.
trolleybus ['trɔlibʌs], *s.* trolleybus *m*, *F:* trolley *m.*
trolling ['trouliŋ], *s. Fish:* pêche *f* à la cuiller; **t. spoon,** cuiller *f*; **t. rod,** canne *f* (pour la pêche à la cuiller); **t. bait,** amorce *f* (pour la pêche à la cuiller).
trollop ['trɔləp], *s.f. A:* **1.** souillon, salope, guenipe. **2.** fille (de mauvaise vie).
trolly ['trɔli], *s.* = TROLLEY.
trombidiasis [trɔmbi'daiəsis], *s. Med: Vet:* trombidiose *f.*
trombidium [trɔm'bidiəm], *s. Ent:* trombidion *m.*
trombone [trɔm'boun], *s. Mus:* **1.** trombone *m*; **slide t.,** trombone à coulisse; **valve t.,** trombone à pistons; **alto, tenor, bass, t.,** trombone alto, ténor, basse. **2.** (*pers.*) trombone, tromboniste *mf.*
trombonist [trɔm'bounist], *s. Mus:* tromboniste *mf*, trombone *m*, joueur, -euse, de trombone.
trommel ['trɔm(ə)l], *s. Min: Civ.E:* trommel *m*, trieur *m.*
trompe l'œil ['trɔ̃plœ:j], *s. Art:* trompe-l'œil *m inv.*
trona ['trounə], *s. Miner:* trona *m.*
troop[1] [tru:p], *s.* **1.** troupe *f*, bande *f*, foule *f* (de personnes); **in troops,** par bandes. **2.** *Mil:* (*a*) **troops,** troupes *fpl*; **to raise troops,** lever des troupes; **troops told off for attack,** troupes d'attaque, unités chargées de l'attaque; **airborne troops,** troupes aéroportées; **picked troops,** troupes d'élite; **shock troops,** troupes de choc; **t. commander,** commandant *m* des troupes; **t. train,** train militaire; **t. carrier,** (i) véhicule blindé de transport de personnel; (ii) avion *m* de transport de troupes; (*b*) (*unit*) peloton *m* (de cavalerie, de l'arme blindée). **3.** *Th: A:* troupe (de comédiens, etc.). **4.** *Scout:* troupe.
troop[2]. **1.** *v.i.* **to come trooping up,** s'attrouper, s'assembler; **they all trooped off to the market,** ils se dirigeaient tous ensemble, en groupe, en bande, vers le marché; **hundreds of tourists were trooping into the castle after their guides,** des centaines de touristes suivaient leur guide en troupes, en foule, dans le château. **2.** *v.tr. Mil:* **to t. the colour(s),** faire la parade du drapeau, des drapeaux; présenter le drapeau.
trooper ['tru:pər], *s.* **1.** (*a*) *Mil:* cavalier *m*; soldat *m* de la cavalerie; *Pej:* **old t.,** (vieux) soudard; *F:* **to swear like a t.,** jurer comme un charretier, comme tous les diables; **to lie like a t.,** mentir comme un arracheur de dents; (*b*) cheval *m* de cavalerie; (*c*) *U.S: Austr:* membre *m* de la police montée; (*d*) *Th: A:* = TROUPER. **2.** = TROOPSHIP.
troopial ['tru:piəl], *s. Orn:* troupiale *m*; **red-winged t.,** commandeur *m.*
trooping ['tru:piŋ], *s. Mil:* **t. (of) the colour(s),** parade *f* du drapeau, des drapeaux; présentation *f* du drapeau; salut *m* au drapeau, aux couleurs.
troopship ['tru:pʃip], *s. Mil: etc:* transport *m* de troupes.
Tropaeolaceae [troupiou'leisii:], *s.pl. Bot:* tropéolées *f.*
tropaeolum [trou'pi:ələm], *s. Bot:* tropéolum *m.*
tropane ['trɔpein], *s. Ch:* tropane *m.*
trope [troup], *s. Rh:* trope *m.*
trophallaxis, *pl.* **-es** [trɔfə'læksis, -i:z], *s. Nat.Hist:* trophallaxie *f.*
trophic ['trɔfik], *a. Physiol:* (nerf, etc.) trophique.
trophism ['trɔfizm], *s.* trophie *f*, trophisme *m.*
tropho- ['trɔfou], *comb.fm.* tropho-.
trophobiont ['trɔfoubaiɔnt], *a. & s. Ent:* trophobionte (*m*).
trophobiotic [trɔfoubai'ɔtik], *a. Ent:* trophobionte.
trophoblast ['trɔfoublæst], *s. Biol:* trophoblaste *m.*
trophocyte ['trɔfousait], *s. Biol:* trophocyte *m.*
trophoedema [trɔ'fi:dimə], *s. Med:* trophœdème *m.*
trophology [trɔ'fɔlədʒi], *s.* trophologie *f.*
trophoneurosis, *pl.* **-es** [trɔfounjuə'rousis, -i:z], *s. Med:* trophonévrose *f.*
trophonucleus, *pl.* **-ii** [trɔfou'nju:kliəs, -kli:ai], *s. Biol:* trophonucléus *m.*
trophoplasm ['trɔfouplæzm], *s. Biol:* trophoplasma *m.*
trophosperm ['trɔfouspə:m], *s. Bot:* trophosperme *m.*
trophotaxis *pl.* **-es** [trɔfou'tæksis, -i:z], *s. Biol:* trophotaxie *f.*
trophotropism [trɔfou'troupizm], *s. Biol:* trophotropisme *m.*
trophy ['troufi], *s.* **1.** (*a*) *Gr. & Rom.Ant:* trophée *m*; (*b*) trophée (de guerre, de chasse, etc.). **2.** (*ornamental group of weapons*) trophée, panoplie *f.* **3.** *Sp:* trophée; coupe, etc., donnée en prix.
tropic ['trɔpik]. **1.** *s.* (*a*) *Astr: Geog:* tropique *m*; (*b*) **the tropics,** les tropiques. **2.** *attrib. Orn:* **t. bird,** phaéton *m*, *F: Fr.C:* paille-en-queue *m inv*; **red-billed t. bird,** paille-en-queue à bec rouge; **red-tailed t. bird,** paille-en-queue

à queue rouge; **white-tailed,** *NAm:* **yellow-billed, t. bird,** paille-en-queue à bec jaune.

tropical ['trɔpik(ə)l], *a.* **1.** *Astr:* (année*f*) tropique. **2.** (*a*) (climat, etc.) tropical, -aux, des tropiques; **t. heat,** chaleur tropicale; **t. diseases,** maladies *f* des tropiques. **3.** *Rh: A:* tropique; qui tient du trope; figuré; métaphorique.

tropicalization [trɔpikəlai'zeiʃ(ə)n], *s.* tropicalisation *f.*

tropicalize ['trɔpikəlaiz], *v.tr.* tropicaliser.

tropically ['trɔpik(ə)li], *adv.* **1.** comme sous les tropiques. **2.** *Rh: A:* sous forme de trope; figurativement; métaphoriquement; par métaphores.

tropicopolitan [trɔpikou'pɔlit(ə)n], *a. Nat.Hist:* tropical, -aux; qui se trouve partout sous les tropiques.

tropidine ['trɔpidi:n], *s. Ch:* tropidine *f.*

tropism ['trɔpizm], *s. Biol:* tropisme *m.*

tropological [trɔpou'lɔdʒik(ə)l], *a. Rh:* (sens) tropologique, figuré.

tropology [trɔ'pɔlədʒi], *s.* tropologie *f.*

tropometer [trɔ'pɔmitər], *s.* tropomètre *m.*

tropopause ['trɔpoupɔ:z], *s. Meteor:* tropopause *f.*

tropophilous [trɔ'pɔfiləs], *a. Bot:* tropophile.

tropophyte ['trɔpoufait], *s. Bot:* tropophyte *f.*

troposphere ['trɔpəsfiər], *s. Meteor:* troposphère *f.*

trot[1] [trɔt], *s.* **1.** *Equit: etc:* trot *m;* **close t., bumping t.,** trot assis; **rising t.,** *U.S:* **posting t.,** trot enlevé; **at a gentle, slow, controlled, t.,** au petit trot; **at a smart, brisk, t.,** au grand trot; **to set off at a t.,** partir au trot; **to break into a t.,** prendre le trot; **to put a horse to the t.,** trotter un cheval; **to go at a t.,** aller le trot, au trot; **he went off at a fast t.,** il est parti au grand trot; *Sp: F:* **they've had 22 wins on the t.,** ils ont gagné la partie vingt-deux fois à la file, de suite; *F:* **to keep s.o. on the t.,** faire trotter qn. **2.** *F:* (*a*) *O:* petit(e) enfant; mioche *mf* (qui commence à trottiner); (*b*) **old t.,** vieille commère. **3.** *P:* **to have the trot(s),** avoir la diarrhée, la courante.

trot[2], *v.* **(trotted)**

I. *v.i. & tr.* **1.** *v.i.* (*a*) *Equit:* trotter; aller le trot, au trot; **to t. away, off,** partir au trot; **to t. five kilometres,** faire cinq kilomètres au trot; **to t. close,** faire du trot assis; **to t. short,** trottiner; (*b*) (*of pers.*) trotter; (*of child, etc.*) trottiner; (*of athlete*) courir à une allure modérée, au pas gymnastique; *F:* **she's always trotting around,** elle est toujours à trotter; (*c*) *F: O:* **now I must be trotting,** maintenant il faut que je file, il faut que je me trotte. **2.** *v.tr.* (*a*) trotter (un cheval); (*b*) **to t. s.o. round,** faire voir la ville à qn; servir de guide à qn; **to t. s.o. off his legs,** éreinter qn (à force de la faire courir, de le faire marcher).

II. (*compound verb*) **trot out. 1.** *v.i.* allonger le pas; faire le grand trot. **2.** *v.tr.* (*a*) **to t. out a horse,** faire trotter, faire parader, un cheval (devant un client); (*b*) *F:* **he can always t. out excuses,** il est toujours prêt à débiter des excuses; **to t. out old grievances,** désenterrer de vieux griefs.

Trot[3], *a. & s. Pol: F:* trotskiste (*mf*), trotskyste (*mf*).

troth [trouθ], *s. A: & Lit:* **1.** foi *f;* **by my t.!** sur ma foi! **2.** vérité *f;* **in t.,** en vérité.

Trotskyist, Trotskyite ['trɔtskiist, -iait], *a. & s.* trotskiste (*mf*), trotskyste (*mf*).

trotter ['trɔtər], *s.* **1.** (*a*) cheval *m* de trot; trotteur, -euse; **this horse is a good t.,** ce cheval est bon trotteur; (*b*) (*pers.*) trotteur, -euse. **2.** (*a*) *Cu:* **sheep's trotters,** pieds *m* de mouton; **pigs' trotters,** pieds de porc, *Fr.C:* pattes *f* de cochon; (*b*) *F:* **trotters,** pieds, petons *m.*

trotting[1] ['trɔtiŋ], *a.* trotteur; (*of watch*) **t. seconds hand,** trotteuse *f.*

trotting[2], *s.* trot *m; Turf: etc:* **t. match, t. race,** course *f* de trot (monté, attelé); (*coll.*) **t. (races),** le trotting.

trotyl ['troutil], *s. Exp:* trinol *m.*

troubadour ['tru:bəduər], *s. Lit:* troubadour *m.*

trouble[1] [trʌbl], *s.* **1.** (*a*) peine *f;* chagrin *m;* affliction *f;* malheur *m;* **he has had a lot of t.,** il a eu de grands chagrins; il en a vu de toutes les couleurs; **he told me his troubles,** il m'a raconté ses malheurs; **his troubles are over,** (i) il est au bout de ses malheurs; les choses, ses affaires, vont mieux; (ii) il est mort; (*b*) ennui *m;* difficulté *f;* **family troubles,** ennuis de famille; **money troubles,** soucis *m* d'argent; **what's the t.?** qu'est-ce qu'il y a? *Prov:* **troubles never come singly,** un ennui ne vient jamais seul; **to meet t. halfway,** aller au-devant des ennuis; **we must get to the root of the t.,** il faut chercher les origines de la difficulté, la source du mal; **to know where the t. lies,** comprendre le problème; **the t. is that . . .,** l'ennui, la difficulté, c'est que . . .; **the t. with him is that . . .,** ce qu'on peut lui reprocher c'est que . . .; **you'll have t. with him,** il va vous causer des difficultés, des ennuis; il va vous donner du fil à retordre; (*c*) **to be in t.,** (i) avoir des ennuis, des difficultés; (ii) avoir du chagrin, des malheurs; (iii) *P: O:* être en prison; **to get into t.,** (i) s'attirer des ennuis, des désagréments; se trouver dans une situation difficile; (ii) *F:* (*of unmarried woman*) devenir enceinte; **to get into t. with the police,** avoir affaire à la police; **he's never been in t. (with the police),** son casier judiciaire est vierge; **to get s.o. into t., to make t. for s.o.,** créer, susciter, des ennuis à qn; attirer à qn des désagréments; *F:* **to get a girl into t.,** rendre une femme enceinte; engrosser une femme; **to get s.o. out of t.,** tirer qn d'affaire; **to keep out of t.,** éviter des ennuis; **to be looking, asking, for t.,** se préparer des ennuis; (*d*) **to make t.,** semer la discorde; **to make, cause, t. in the family,** mettre du trouble dans la famille; **to make t. for oneself,** s'attirer des ennuis; **he'll make t. if you don't agree,** si vous ne consentez pas il va se montrer désagréable; **there will be t.,** il y aura du vilain, *F:* de la casse; (*e*) **there was t. in the streets,** il y a eu des désordres *m* dans la rue; **t. spot,** point *m* névralgique; **labour troubles,** conflits ouvriers; **a strike might lead to further t.,** une grève pourrait amener des complications *f;* (*f*) *Med:* dérangement *m;* trouble(s); **eye t.,** (i) troubles de vision; (ii) affection *f* de l'œil; **stomach t.,** maux *m* d'estomac; troubles digestifs; **to have liver t.,** souffrir du foie; **to have heart t.,** être malade du cœur; avoir une maladie de cœur; **what's the t.?** de quoi souffrez-vous? de quoi vous plaignez-vous? où avez-vous mal? (*g*) *Mec.E: etc:* incident *m* (mécanique); panne *f;* **to locate, trace, the t.,** trouver la source de la panne; *U.S:* **t. man** = TROUBLESHOOTER 2; *Aut: etc:* **engine t.,** panne de moteur; **ignition t.,** ennuis d'allumage; **we're always having t. with our car,** notre voiture nous donne toujours des ennuis; **we had a t.-free journey,** nous avons eu un trajet sans incidents; *U.S: Tp:* **line in t.,** ligne *f* en dérangement; **signalling troubles,** dérangements d'appel. **2.** dérangement; peine; mal; **to take the t. to do sth., to go to the t. of doing sth.,** prendre, se donner, la peine de faire qch.; **I wanted to save you the t. (of doing it),** j'ai voulu vous épargner la peine (de le faire); **it's not worth the t.,** cela n'en vaut pas la peine; ce n'est pas la peine; **I don't want to give you, to put you to, any t.,** je ne veux pas vous déranger; **I went, put myself, to, took, a great deal of t. to do it, doing it,** je me suis donné beaucoup de mal, beaucoup de peine, à le faire; **you might take the t. to write legibly, go to the t. of writing legibly,** tu pourrais te donner la peine d'écrire de façon lisible; **to take, spare, no t. (in order to gain one's ends),** ne pas ménager sa peine (pour arriver à son but); **he thinks nothing too much t.,** rien ne lui coûte; **to have some, a great deal of, t. to do sth., doing sth.,** avoir de la peine, beaucoup de peine, du mal, beaucoup de mal, à faire qch.; **it's, that's, no t., won't be any t.,** cela ne donne pas de peine; cela se fait tout seul; cela ne me dérange pas; **to have had a lot of t., all one's t., for nothing,** en être pour sa peine; **that child must be a great deal of t. to her,** cet enfant doit lui donner bien du tracas, lui causer beaucoup de peine, d'ennuis; **it's the new customers who are the most t.,** c'est les nouveaux clients qui nous dérangement, tracassent, le plus, qui nous donnent le plus de mal.

trouble[2]. **1.** *v.tr.* (*a*) affliger, tourmenter, chagriner (qn); inquiéter, préoccuper, soucier (qn); **I'm troubled about my son,** mon fils m'inquiète, me donne des soucis; **I'm troubled about his future,** son avenir me préoccupe, m'inquiète; **that doesn't t. him much, hardly troubles him at all,** cela le, lui, soucie fort peu; cela ne le préoccupe guère; **don't let it t. you!** que cela ne vous inquiète pas! ne vous tourmentez pas à ce sujet! **don't t. your head about that!** ne vous inquiétez point de cela! (*b*) (*of disease, etc.*) affliger, faire souffrir (qn); **how long has this cough been troubling you?** depuis combien de temps souffrez-vous de cette toux? **my arm still troubles me,** mon bras me fait souffrir encore; (*c*) déranger, incommoder, gêner, ennuyer, embarrasser (qn); donner de la peine à (qn); **I'm so sorry to t. you,** excusez-moi de vous déranger; **I shan't t. you with the details,** je ne vous importunerai pas de tous les détails; *usu. Iron:* **may I t. you to shut the door?** cela vous dérangerait-il de fermer la porte? puis-je vous prier de (bien vouloir) fermer la porte? vous seriez bien aimable de fermer la porte; **may I t. you for the mustard?** voudriez-vous bien me passer la moutarde? (*d*) *A:* troubler (l'eau). **2.** *v.i.* (*a*) s'inquiéter, se tracasser **(about,** au sujet de, à propos de); **without troubling about the consequences,** sans s'inquiéter des conséquences; **don't t. about it,** ne vous inquiétez pas de cela; que cela ne vous inquiète pas; (*b*) se déranger; se mettre en peine; **don't t. to write,** ne vous donnez pas la peine d'écrire; **don't t. to answer it,** ne prenez pas la peine d'y répondre; **don't t. to change (your dress),** ce n'est pas la peine de changer (de robe); **don't t.! you needn't t.!** ne vous dérangez pas!

troubled ['trʌb(ə)ld], *a.* **1.** (*of liquid*) trouble; **to fish in t. waters,** pêcher en eau trouble. **2.** (*a*) inquiet; agité; **a t. expression,** un visage inquiet; **a t. soul,** une âme agitée, troublée, inquiète; **t. sleep,** sommeil agité; (*b*) **the t. period as the empire crumbled,** l'époque *f* de troubles pendant que l'empire croulait.

troublemaker ['trʌb(ə)lmeikər], *s.* fomentateur, -trice, de troubles; agitateur, -trice.

troubler ['trʌblər], *s.* perturbateur, -trice; agitateur, -trice.

troubleshoot ['trʌb(ə)lʃu:t], *v.i. & tr.* **1.** *Mec.E: etc:* rechercher, localiser, des pannes; dépanner. **2.** *Pol: Ind: etc:* servir de médiateur, de conciliateur.

troubleshooter ['trʌb(ə)lʃu:tər], *s.* **1.** *Mec.E: etc:* dépanneur *m;* déceleur *m,* détecteur *m,* de pannes. **2.** *Pol: Ind: etc:* médiateur, -trice; conciliateur, -trice.

troublesome ['trʌb(ə)lsəm], *a.* **1.** ennuyeux, gênant, incommode; **t. child,** enfant fatigant, ennuyant, énervant; **t. rival,** rival gênant; **a lot of t. luggage,** un tas de bagages embarrassants, incommodes; **the flies are t.,** les mouches sont agaçantes; **t. cough,** toux pénible, fatigante; **to take when the cough is t.,** à prendre dans les cas de quintes pénibles. **2.** *O:* (tâche, etc.) difficile, pénible.

troubling ['trʌbliŋ], *a.* (*of news, etc.*) inquiétant.

troublous ['trʌbləs], *a. A:* troublé, agité; **t. times,** époque *f* de troubles; temps *m* de confusion; **t. life,** vie orageuse.

trough [trɔf], *s.* **1.** (*a*) *Husb: etc:* **(feeding) t.,** auge *f;* mangeoire *f;* baquet *m;* (*small*) auget *m,* augette *f;* billot *m,* récipient *m,* à pâtée (pour la volaille); (*of bird cage*) **seed t.,** auget à grain; mangeoire; **drinking t.,** abreuvoir *m;* (*b*) *Tchn:* **grindstone t.,** auge de meule; *Ch: Ph:* **mercury t.,** cuvette *f* à mercure; **pneumatic t.,** cuve *f* à eau; *Metall:* **cementing t.,** caisse *f,* creuset *m,* de cémentation; **electrolytic t.,** cuve électrolytique; *Phot.Engr:* **water t.,** bassine *f* de mouillage (de machine offset); **etching t.,** bac *m* de morsure; *El:* **accumulator t.,** bac d'accumulateur; **t. accumulator,** accumulateur *m* à augets; (*c*) **book t.,** bac à livres; (*d*) = TROUGHFUL. **2.** (*a*) caniveau *m* (en bois, etc.); chéneau *m;* **t. gutter, eaves t.,** chéneau encaissé; *Civ.E:* **t. girder,** poutre *f* à ornière, en U; (*b*) *Min: etc:* **loading t., conveyor t.,** rigole *f* de chargement; **t. conveyor,** transporteur *m* à palettes; (*c*) *Anat:* **gingival t.,** sillon *m* gingivo-dentaire; **vestibular t.,** gouttière *f* vestibulaire. **3.** *Geol:* auge; fond *m* de bateau; **t. of a syncline,** charnière synclinale. **4.** (*a*) **t. of the sea,** creux *m* de la lame; entre-deux *m inv* des lames; **to be in the t. of the sea,** être en travers de la lame; (*b*) *Ph:* **t. of a wave,** creux, point bas, d'une onde; *Mth:* **t. of a graph,** creux d'un graphique; (*c*) *Meteor:* dépression *f* (barométrique); zone dépressionnaire.

troughful ['trɔfful], *s.* (*a*) augée *f;* (*b*) *Paperm:* pilée *f.*

trounce [trauns], *v.tr.* **1.** (*a*) *O:* rosser, étriller, houspiller (qn); rouer, bourrer (qn) de coups; (*b*) *Sp:* écraser (ses adversaires); battre (ses adversaires) à plates coutures. **2.** *O:* blâmer, réprimander, semoncer (qn).

trouncing ['traunsiŋ], *s.* (*a*) *O:* raclée *f;* étrillage *m;* (*b*) *Sp:* défaite écrasante.

troupe [tru:p], *s.* troupe *f* (de comédiens, etc.).

trouper ['tru:pər], *s. Th:* membre *m* d'une troupe.

troupial ['tru:piəl], *s. Orn:* troupiale *m.*

trouser ['trauzər], *s.* **(pair of) trousers,** pantalon *m;* **turn-up,** *NAm:* **cuff, trousers,** pantalon à bords relevés; **skiing trousers,** fuseaux *mpl; Com:* **this is a nice t., sir,** voilà un beau pantalon, monsieur; **t. suit,** tailleur-pantalon *m;* **t. strap,** sous(-)pied *m;* **t. press,** presse-pantalon *m;* **t. stretcher,** tendeur *m* pour pantalon; *F:* **she's the one who wears the trousers,** c'est elle qui porte la culotte; *F:* **to be caught with one's trousers down,** être pris au dépourvu, au pied levé.

trousering ['trauzəriŋ], *s.* drap *m,* tissu *m,* pour pantalon(s).

trousseau ['tru:sou], *s.* trousseau *m.*

trout [traut], *s.* **1.** *Ich:* (*inv. in pl.*) truite *f;* **brown t.,** truite de rivière; **rainbow t.,** truite arc-en-ciel; **steelhead t.,** truite à tête d'acier; **salmon t.,** truite saumonée; **speckled t.,** saumon *m* de fontaine; **t. stream,** ruisseau *m* à truites; **stream full of t.,** ruisseau plein de truites; **t. fishing,** pêche *f* à la truite; **t. fly,** (i) *Ent:* éphémère *m;* (ii) mouche *f* pour la pêche à la truite. **2.** *P:* (*woman*) **old t.,** vieille bique, vieille rombière.

troutlet, troutling ['trautlit, -liŋ], *s. Ich:* petite truite; truitelle *f,* truiton *m.*

trouvere [tru:'vɛər], *s. Lit:* trouvère *m.*

trove [trouv], *s.* **treasure t.,** trésor (découvert par le pur effet du hasard).

trover ['trouvər], *s. Jur:* **1.** appropriation *f* (d'une chose perdue). **2.** **(action for) t.,** action *f* en restitution (de biens illégalement détenus).

trow [trou], *v.tr. A:* croire, penser.

trowel[1] ['trauəl], *s.* **1.** *Const:* truelle *f*, gâche *f*; **notched t.,** truelle brettée; **brick t.,** truelle à mortier; **plastering t.,** plâtroir *m*, riflard *m*; **t. work,** truellage *m*. **2.** *Hort:* déplantoir *m*, transplantoir *m*, houlette *f*, manette *f*.

trowel[2], *v.tr.* (**trowelled**) *Const:* (*a*) étaler, lisser (le plâtre) avec une truelle; (*b*) appliquer le plâtre, le mortier, sur (une surface) avec une truelle.

trowelful ['trauəlful], *s.* clapée *f* (de mortier).

troy[1] [trɔi], *s. Meas:* **t. (weight),** poids *m* troy (pour la pesée de l'or et de l'argent); **t. ounce, ounce t.,** once *f* troy (31g, 1).

Troy[2], *Pr.n. A.Geog:* Troie *f*; **the siege of T.,** le siège de Troie.

truancy ['tru:ənsi], *s.* **1.** *A:* truanderie *f*. **2.** *Sch:* absentéisme *m* scolaire.

truant ['tru:ənt], *s.* **1.** *A:* truand *m*. **2.** *Sch:* élève absent (de l'école) sans permission; **to play t.,** faire l'école buissonnière.

truce [tru:s], *s.* trêve *f*; *Hist:* **the T. of God,** la trêve, la paix, de Dieu; **let's call it a t.!** c'en est assez! faisons la paix!

truceless ['tru:slis], *a.* (guerre) sans trêve.

Trucial ['tru:siəl], *Pr.n. Geog:* **T. Coast,** Côte *f* des Pirates, de la Trêve.

truck[1] [trʌk], *s.* **1.** troc *m*, échange *m*. **2.** *Hist:* marchandises données aux ouvriers en guise de paie; **t. (system),** paiement *m* des ouvriers en nature; **T. Act,** loi *f* interdisant le paiement des ouvriers en nature. **3.** *F: O:* rapports *mpl*, relations *fpl* (avec qn); **I've no t. with him,** (i) je n'ai pas affaire à lui; (ii) je n'ai rien à faire avec lui; je ne le fréquente pas. **4.** *F:* articles divers, de peu de valeur; de la camelote; articles de rebut. **5.** *NAm:* produits maraîchers; légumes *mpl*; **t. garden, farm,** jardin maraîcher; **t. gardener, farmer,** maraîcher *m*; **t. gardening, farming,** culture maraîchère; maraîchage *m*.

truck[2]. **1.** *v.i.* (*a*) troquer, faire un échange (avec qn); (*b*) *O:* faire le commerce (de qch.). **2.** *v.tr.* (*a*) troquer, échanger (qch. contre qch.); (*b*) *O:* troquer, échanger (des marchandises).

truck[3], *s.* **1.** (*a*) (*four-wheeled*) chariot *m*, fardier *m*, binard *m*, binart *m*; **fork-lift t.,** chariot élévateur à fourche; *Rail: etc:* **luggage t.,** (i) (*four-wheeled*) chariot à bagages; (ii) (*two-wheeled*) diable *m*; (*b*) *Min:* berline *f*, benne *f*, bac *m*; (*c*) *esp. NAm: Aut:* camion *m*; (*articulated*) semi-remorque *f*, *pl.* semi-remorques; **heavy t.,** gros routier; **flat t., platform t.,** camion plat, plateau *m*; *Civ.E:* **t. mixer,** camion-bétonnière *m*, *pl.* camions-bétonnières; bétonnière *f*; *Mil: etc:* **repair t.,** camion-atelier *m*, *pl.* camions-ateliers; *Av:* (*on aerodrome*) **refuelling t.,** camion-citerne *m*, *pl.* camions-citernes; *U.S:* **dump t.,** camion à benne basculante; *U.S:* **wrecking t.,** camion de dépannage, dépanneuse *f*; *Com:* **t. rental,** location *f* de camions. **2.** *Rail:* wagon *m* (à marchandises); **covered t., box t.,** wagon couvert, fermé; **open t.,** wagon découvert; tombereau *m*; **low-sided t.,** wagon à bords bas, à haussettes; **high-sided t.,** tombereau *m*; **flat t.,** wagon plat, (wagon) plate-forme *f*; **ballast t.,** wagon de terrassement; **tip t., tipping t.,** wagon à bascule, à benne; **cattle t.,** fourgon *m* à bestiaux. **3.** (*a*) *Rail:* (**bogie**) **t., radial t.,** bog(g)ie *m* (de locomotive, de wagon); **pilot t.,** bogie avant, bogie directeur; **trailing t.,** bogie arrière; **t. axle,** essieu porteur; **t. bolster,** traverse dansante (de bogie); (*b*) *Navy:* **trucks of a gun mounting,** roues *f* d'un affût; (*c*) *Civ.E:* chariot de dilatation (d'un pont en acier, etc.). **4.** *Nau:* (*a*) pomme *f* (de mât); (*b*) **bull's eye t.,** margouillet *m*; **seizing t., shroud t.,** pomme gougée.

truck[4], *v.tr.* camionner (des marchandises); transporter (des marchandises) par camion; *Min:* rouler (le minerai).

truckage ['trʌkidʒ], *s.* **1.** = TRUCKING. **2.** *coll.* chariots *mpl*; wagons *mpl*.

truckdriver ['trʌkdraivər], *s. esp. NAm:* **trucker** ['trʌkər], *s. NAm:* camionneur *m*; routier *m*.

truckful ['trʌkful], *s.* plein camion, plein wagon (de marchandises, etc.).

trucking ['trʌkiŋ], *s. esp. NAm:* camionnage *m*; transport *m* en camions; *Min:* roulage *m*.

truckle[1] ['trʌkl], *s.* **1.** poulie *f*. **2.** (*a*) *A:* roulette *f* (d'un meuble); (*b*) **t. bed,** lit bas à roulettes.

truckle[2], *v.i.* **to t. to s.o.,** ramper, s'abaisser, s'aplatir, devant qn.

truckler ['trʌklər], *s.* flagorneur *m*.

truckling ['trʌkliŋ], *s.* abaissement *m*, aplatissement *m* (devant qn).

truckload ['trʌkloud], *s.* = TRUCKFUL.

truckman, *pl.* **-men** ['trʌkmən], *s.m. esp. NAm:* camionneur; routier.

truculence, truculency ['trʌkjuləns(i)], *s.* agressivité *f*; caractère *m* agressif; férocité *f*; brutalité *f*.

truculent ['trʌkjulənt], *a.* agressif; féroce; brutal, -aux.

truculently ['trʌkjuləntli], *adv.* agressivement, d'une manière agressive; férocement; brutalement.

trudge[1] [trʌdʒ], *s.* marche *f* pénible; **a long t.,** un trajet long et pénible, long et fatigant.

trudge[2], *v.i.* marcher lourdement, péniblement; **to t. along,** cheminer, avancer, péniblement; suivre péniblement son chemin.

trudgen ['trʌdʒən], *s. Swim:* **t. (stroke),** trudgeon *m*; nage *f* à l'indienne.

true[1] [tru:], *a., adv. & s.*

I. *a.* **1.** vrai; conforme à la vérité; exact; **the story is t.,** l'histoire est vraie; c'est une vraie histoire; **t. adventures,** aventures réelles; **it's only too t.,** ce n'est que trop vrai; **it is t. that it would cost more,** il est vrai que cela coûterait plus cher; **is it t., can it be t. that, he refused?** est-il vrai, est-il possible, qu'il ait refusé? **if it were t. that . . .,** s'il était vrai que . . . + *sub.*; (**it is**) **t. I saw him only once,** il est vrai que je ne l'ai vu qu'une fois; (**that's**) **t.! t. enough!** vrai! vous avez raison! **to come t.,** se réaliser; **if my wishes come t.,** si mes désirs sont réalisés; **the rumour proved only too t.,** le bruit s'est malheureusement confirmé; **this also holds t. for . . .,** il en est de même pour . . .. **2.** véritable; vrai, réel, authentique; (*a*) **the t. God,** le vrai Dieu; **a t. poet,** un vrai, un véritable, poète; **a t. benefactor,** un véritable bienfaiteur; **t. repentance,** repentir *m* sincère, véritable; **his t. nature,** son véritable caractère; **the frog is not a t. reptile,** la grenouille n'est pas un véritable reptile; **to consider things in their t. light,** considérer les choses sous leur aspect véritable; bien prendre les choses; **to get a t. idea of the situation,** se faire une idée juste de la situation; (*b*) *Tchn:* **t. time,** temps vrai, heure vraie; **t. longitude,** longitude vraie; **t. pole,** pôle *m* géographique; **t. horizon,** horizon réel; **t. bearing,** azimut géographique, vrai; gisement vrai; *Av: Nau:* relèvement vrai; **t. altitude,** altitude vraie; hauteur vraie (d'un astre); *Av: Nau:* **t. position,** point vrai; **t. course,** route réelle, vraie; **t. heading,** cap vrai; **t. slip,** recul absolu, effectif (de l'hélice); *Ph: Mec:* **t. motion,** mouvement réel; *El:* **t. power, t. watt,** puissance *f*, watt *m*, efficace. **3.** (*a*) *Mec.E: Carp:* juste, droit, rectiligne; rectifié, ajusté; **to make a piece t.,** ajuster une pièce; **to file, grind, a piece t.,** ajuster, rectifier, une pièce à la lime, à la meule; **to centre a wheel dead t.,** assurer le parfait centrage d'une roue; (*b*) (terrain) égal, uni; **the table isn't t.,** la table n'est pas horizontale, n'est pas d'aplomb, n'est pas juste. **4.** (*a*) fidèle; loyal, -aux; **t. friend,** ami loyal; **to be t. to oneself,** ne pas se démentir; **to be t. to one's promise,** rester fidèle à une promesse; *O:* **he's a t. blue,** c'est un homme loyal, fidèle; (*b*) *A:* (*of pers.*) honnête, sincère; *Jur:* **a jury of twelve good men and t.,** un jury de douze citoyens de bonne renommée. **5.** (*of voice, instrument*) juste. **6.** *Biol:* **t. to type,** conforme au type ancestral.

II. *adv.* **1.** *F: O:* vraiment; (pour de) vrai. **2.** (*a*) (chanter) juste; (viser) juste; (*of wheel*) **to run t.,** tourner rond, sans balourd; **the wheel is not running t.,** la roue est désaxée, faussée; (*b*) **to breed t.,** se reproduire suivant un type invariable.

III. *s. Mec.E: etc:* **out of t.,** (i) (*of vertical post, member, etc.*) hors d'aplomb; (ii) (*of horizontal member, etc.*) dénivelé; (iii) (*of metal, plate, etc.*) gauchi, gondolé; (*of wheel rim, etc.*) voilé; (*of axle, etc.*) faussé, dévoyé; (*of timber*) déjeté, dévié, dévers; (*of overloaded beam, etc.*) fléchi; (iv) (*of cylinder, etc.*) ovalisé; (*of wheel, etc.*) décentré, excentré, désaxé; **to put (sth.) out of t.,** (i) mettre (qch.) hors d'aplomb; (ii) fausser, voiler, gauchir (une tôle, etc.); décentrer, désaxer, fausser, voiler (une roue); **to get out of t.,** (i) gauchir; (ii) (*of piston, etc.*) s'ovaliser; (iii) (*of wheel*) se décentrer, se fausser; se voiler; **to run out of t.,** (i) se décentrer; (ii) être décentré; tourner à faux; ne pas tourner rond.

true[2], *v.tr. Mec.E: etc:* **to t. (up),** ajuster (les pièces d'une machine); défausser, dégauchir (une tige, un essieu, etc.); rectifier, (re)dresser (une surface); dégauchir (une planche); mettre bien d'équerre (le bord d'une planche); *Mill:* ribler (une meule).

trueborn ['tru:bɔ:n], *a. O:* vrai, véritable; **a t. Englishman,** un vrai Anglais d'Angleterre.

truehearted [tru:'hɑ:tid], *a. O:* fidèle; loyal, -aux; sincère.

true(-)love ['tru:lʌv], *s.* **1.** bien-aimé(e); **t. knot** (*also* **true lover's knot**), lacs *m* d'amour (en 8 couché). **2.** *Bot: F:* parisette *f* à quatre feuilles; raisin *m* de renard.

trueness ['tru:nis], *s.* **1.** vérité *f* (**of,** de). **2.** fidélité *f*; sincérité *f*. **3.** justesse *f* (d'une note, de la voix). **4.** *Tchn:* équerrage *m*.

truffle ['trʌfl], *s.* (*a*) truffe *f*; **t. bed,** truffière *f*; **t. growing,** trufficulture *f*; **t. grower,** trufficulteur *m*; **t. dog, hound,** chien truffier; **t. eating,** tubérivore, tubérophage; **t. omelette,** omelette *f* aux truffes; (*b*) (*chocolate*) truffe.

truffled ['trʌfld], *a. Cu:* truffé; aux truffes.

trug [trʌg], *s. Hort:* corbeille *f* en bois éclaté.

truing ['tru:iŋ], *s. Tchn:* **t. (up),** dégauchissement *m*, dégauchissage *m* (d'une tige, d'une poutre, etc.); dressage *m* (d'un canon de fusil, etc.); rectification *f*, redressement *m* (d'une surface).

truism ['tru:izm], *s.* truisme *m*, axiome *m*; vérité *f* de La Palisse.

truly ['tru:li], *adv.* **1.** (*a*) vraiment, véritablement; sincèrement; **a t. difficult situation,** une situation vraiment difficile; **I am t. grateful to him,** je lui suis sincèrement reconnaissant; **I t. believe that. . .,** je crois vraiment, véritablement, sincèrement, que . . .; (*b*) *Corr:* **yours t.** = je vous prie d'agréer, de croire à, mes sentiments distingués; (*c*) *P:* **yours t.,** votre serviteur; moi-même. **2.** en vérité; à vrai dire; **t., it puzzles me,** à vrai dire cela me déconcerte; *F:* **really (and) t.?** vrai de vrai? **3.** (servir qn, etc.) fidèlement, loyalement. **4.** vraiment, exactement; justement; **it has been t. stated that . . .,** on a dit justement que . . .; **it may t. be called tragic,** on peut bien, vraiment, le qualifier de tragique.

trump[1] [trʌmp], *s. A: & Lit:* trompe *f*, trompette *f*; **the last t., the t. of doom,** la trompette du jugement dernier.

trump[2], *s.* **1.** *Cards:* **t. (card),** atout *m*; **what are trumps?** quel est l'atout? **spades are trumps,** c'est pique atout; **to play trumps,** jouer l'atout; **to call no trumps,** appeler, demander, sans-atout; **to hold the odd t., to be long in trumps,** avoir long-atout; *F:* **he always turns up trumps,** (i) *A:* la chance le favorise; il réussit toujours; (ii) il est toujours là pour donner un coup de main; *A:* **to be put to one's trumps,** être réduit aux abois. **2.** *F: O:* bon type; chic type; **you're a t.!** tu es un chic type!

trump[3], *v.tr. & i.* **1.** *Cards:* couper (une carte); jouer atout. **2. to t. up an excuse,** inventer, forger, une excuse; **to t. up a charge against s.o.,** déposer une fausse plainte contre qn; forger, fabriquer, une accusation contre qn; **trumped-up story,** histoire inventée à plaisir.

trumpery ['trʌmpəri]. **1.** *s.* (*a*) friperie *f*, camelote *f*; marchandise *f* de pacotille; (*b*) *A:* bêtises *fpl*, fadaises *fpl*. **2.** *a.* (*a*) (marchandises) sans valeur, de camelote, de pacotille; **to buy t. furniture,** se meubler avec de la camelote; (*b*) (argument, etc.) mesquin, ridicule, spécieux.

trumpet[1] ['trʌmpit], *s.* **1.** *Mus:* (*a*) trompette *f*; **keyed t.,** trompette à clefs; **valve t.,** trompette à pistons; trompette chromatique; **orchestral t.,** trompette d'harmonie; **to play the t.,** jouer de la trompette; **flourish of trumpets,** fanfare *f* de trompettes; **t. call,** coup *m* de trompette; sonnerie *f* de trompette; appel *m* de trompette; *Lit:* **to sound the t. call,** battre le rappel; **to publish sth. with a flourish of trumpets,** publier qch. à cor et à cri; *Lit:* **the t. sounds,** l'airain *m* retentit; *Jewish Rel:* **the Feast of Trumpets,** la fête des trompettes; (*b*) (*organ stop*) trompette. **2.** (*pers.*) (*a*) *Mil:* trompette *m*; **t. major,** trompette-major *m*, *pl.* trompettes-majors; (*b*) *Hist:* héraut *m*; (*c*) (*in orchestra*) trompette *f*. **3.** (*a*) (**ear**) **t.,** cornet *m* acoustique; (*b*) *O:* pavillon *m* (de phonographe, de cornet avertisseur, etc.). **4.** *Bot:* (*a*) trompette (du liseron, etc.); (*b*) **t. creeper, t. flower, t. vine,** jasmin *m* de Virginie; jasmin trompette; bignoniacée *f*; **t. leaf,** sarracénie *f*. **5.** (*a*) *Ich:* **t. fish,** poisson *m* trompette; centrisque *m*; *F:* bécasse *f* de mer; (*b*) *Moll:* **t. shell,** triton *m*. **6.** = TRUMPETING.

trumpet[2], *v.* (**trumpeted**) **1.** *v.i.* (*a*) trompeter; sonner de la trompette; (*b*) (*of elephant*) barrir. **2.** *v.tr.* publier (qch.) à son de trompe, à cor et à cri; crier (qch.) sur (tous) les toits; célébrer (un succès) à grand bruit; **the news was trumpeted abroad,** la nouvelle fut publiée à son de trompe.

trumpeter ['trʌmpitər], *s.* **1.** (*a*) *Mil: etc:* trompette *m*; sonneur *m* de trompette; (*b*) (*by profession*) trompettiste *m*; (*c*) (*in orchestra*) trompette *f*. **2.** *Orn:* **t. (bird),** agami *m*, *F:* oiseau-trompette *m*, *pl.* oiseaux-trompettes.

trumpeting ['trʌmpitiŋ], *s.* **1.** sonnerie *f* de trompette. **2.** (*of elephant*) barrit *m*, barrissement *m*.

trumpetweed ['trʌmpitwi:d], *s. Bot: NAm:* eupatoire pourprée.

trumpetwood ['trʌmpitwud], *s. Bot:* cécropie *f*; bois *m* trompette.

truncal ['trʌŋk(ə)l], *a. Anat:* du tronc.

truncate[1] [trʌŋ'keit], *v.tr.* tronquer, mutiler (un corps, un arbre, un texte, etc.); retrancher une partie essentielle (de qch.).

truncate[2] ['trʌŋkeit], *a.* tronqué.

truncated [trʌŋ'keitid], *a. Cryst: Arch: Nat.Hist: etc:* tronqué; *Mth:* **t. cone,** tronc *m* de cône; cône tronqué;

t. prism, prisme tronqué; **t. body, corpse,** corps tronqué, mutilé.

truncation [trʌŋ'keiʃ(ə)n], *s. Cryst: etc:* troncature *f*; *Ling:* troncation *f* (d'un mot).

truncheon ['trʌn(t)ʃ(ə)n], *s.* bâton *m* (d'agent de police); matraque *f*, casse-tête *m inv*; **rubber t.,** matraque en caoutchouc.

trundle[1] ['trʌndl], *s.* **1.** roulette *f* (de meuble); **t. bed,** (i) lit *m* gigogne; (ii) lit bas à roulettes. **2.** *Mec.E:* (*a*) **t. (wheel),** (roue *f* à) lanterne *f*; (*b*) (*stave*) fuseau *m* (de lanterne). **3.** binart *m*, fardier *m*. **4.** transport *m* sur fardier; roulage *m*; trajet *m* (en camion, etc.).

trundle[2]. **1.** *v.tr.* (*a*) faire rouler, faire courir (un cerceau, etc.); (*b*) pousser (une brouette, une voiture à bras); **they trundled him along in a wheelbarrow,** ils l'ont poussé dans une brouette. **2.** *v.i.* (*of hoop, etc.*) rouler; **to t. along a road,** rouler (doucement) sur une route.

trundlehead ['trʌndlhed], *s. Nau:* chapeau inférieur (de cabestan à double étage).

trunk[1] [trʌŋk], *s.* **1.** (*a*) tronc *m* (d'arbre); *For:* **fallen trunks,** bois mort gisant; (*b*) tronc (du corps); *Art:* torse *m*; (*c*) *Anat:* tronc (d'artère, etc.); **t. roads,** grandes routes; grands itinéraires; *Rail:* **t. line,** ligne principale; grande ligne; *Tp: O:* **t. line, t. circuit,** ligne interurbaine; circuit interurbain, entre centraux; **t. connections,** relations interurbaines; **t. call,** appel interurbain; *Hyd.E:* **t. main,** conduite, canalisation, principale; (*d*) *Arch:* fût *m* (d'une colonne). **2.** (*a*) malle *f*, coffre *m*; **wardrobe t.,** malle-armoire *f*, *pl.* malles-armoires; **to pack one's t.,** faire sa malle; (*b*) *NAm: Aut:* coffre; (*c*) *Min:* caisse *f* à débourber (le minerai); (*d*) *Mch:* fourreau *m*; **t. engine,** machine *f* à fourreau; **t. piston,** piston *m* à fourreau; (*e*) *Nau:* **rudder t.,** jaumière *f*. **3.** trompe *f* (d'éléphant). **4.** *Cost:* (*a*) *A:* **t. hose, trunks,** haut-de-chausse(s) *m*; (*b*) **trunks,** (i) caleçon court; short-slip *m*; (ii) short *m* (d'athlète); maillot *m* (de bain) (pour hommes).

trunk[2], *v.tr. Min:* débourber (le minerai).

trunkfish ['trʌŋkfiʃ], *s. Ich:* coffre *m*.

trunkful ['trʌŋkful], *s.* pleine malle (**of,** de).

trunking ['trʌŋkiŋ], *s. Min:* débourbage *m*.

trunnion ['trʌnjən], *s.* (*a*) *Artil:* tourillon *m*; **t. bed,** encastrement *m* des tourillons; **t. ring,** frette *f* à tourillons; (*b*) *Mch:* tourillon, goujon *m* (d'un cylindre oscillant); *Aut:* **t. block,** dé *m* du cardan.

truss[1] [trʌs], *s.* **1.** (*a*) botte *f* (de foin, de paille); (*b*) *Hort:* corymbe *m*; touffe *f* (de fleurs). **2.** (*a*) *Const:* (i) armature *f* (de poutre, etc.); (ii) ferme *f* (de comble, de pont); (iii) cintre *m* (de voûte); **hanging post t.,** arbalète *f*; **t. girder,** poutre armée; ferme *f*; **t. rod,** tirant *m* (d'armature); (*b*) *Civ.E:* treillis *m* (métallique); **t. member,** membrure *f* en treillis; **t. bridge,** pont *m* en treillis métallique; **hanging t. bridge,** pont suspendu à armatures; (*c*) *Arch:* console *f*; corbeau, -aux *m*; (*d*) *Mec.E: etc:* contre-fiche *f*, *pl.* contre-fiches; **t. actuating jack,** vérin *m* contre-fiche. **3.** *Nau:* drosse *f* (de vergue); **t. tackle,** palan *m* de drosse; **iron t.,** mulet *m*. **4.** *Med:* bandage *m* herniaire.

truss[2], *v.tr.* **1.** botteler (le foin); mettre (le foin) en bottes. **2.** *Const: Tchn:* armer, renforcer (une poutre, une pièce de mécanisme, etc.); *N.Arch:* latter (un navire). **3.** *Ven: A:* (*of hawk*) lier, saisir (sa proie). **4.** (*a*) *Cu:* trousser, brider (une volaille); *F:* **to t. s.o. up like a fowl,** ligoter qn; (*b*) *Nau:* **to t. a sail,** ramasser une voile. **5.** *A:* **to t. up a criminal,** pendre un malfaiteur haut et court.

trussed [trʌst], *a.* (*a*) armé, renforcé; *Veh:* **t. axle,** essieu renforcé; *Const: etc:* **t. beam, t. girder,** (i) poutre armée, renforcée; (ii) (*underbraced type*) poutre sous-bandée; (iii) poutre contre-fiche; **t. joist,** solive armée; (*b*) *Const:* **t. roof,** comble *m* sur fermes; (*c*) *Civ.E: etc:* en treillis (métallique); **t. arch,** arche *f* (de pont métallique) en treillis.

trussing[1] ['trʌsiŋ], *a. Her:* (*of hawk, etc.*) empiétant (sa proie).

trussing[2], *s.* **1.** bottelage *m* (du foin). **2.** *Const: etc:* (*a*) renforcement *m* (d'une poutre, d'une pièce de mécanisme); (*b*) armature *f*; ferme *f* en arbalète; *N.Arch:* **diagonal t.,** lattage *m*. **3.** *Cu:* (*a*) troussage *m*, bridage *m* (d'une volaille); (*b*) bridure *f*.

trust[1] [trʌst], *s.* **1.** confiance *f* (**in,** en); **to put one's t. in s.o., sth.,** avoir (de la) confiance en qn; mettre sa confiance en qn; se reposer sur qn, qch.; **to take sth. on t.,** (i) accepter qch. de confiance; (ii) croire qch., ajouter foi à qch., sans examen; **to buy sth. on t.,** acheter qch. de confiance. **2.** espérance *f*, espoir *m*; **it is my firm hope and t. that. . .,** j'espère avec confiance que. . .; j'ai le ferme espoir que. . .. **3.** *Com:* crédit *m*; **to supply goods on t.,** fournir des marchandises à crédit. **4.** (*a*) responsabilité *f*, charge *f*; **to be in a position of t.,** occuper un poste de confiance; **to fail in one's t.,** manquer à son devoir; (*b*) garde *f*; dépôt *m*; **he committed it to my t.,** il l'a confié à moi, à mes soins, à ma garde; **a sacred t.,** un dépôt sacré; **to hold sth. on t., in t.,** avoir qch. en dépôt; avoir la garde de qch. **5.** (*a*) *Jur:* fidéicommis *m*, fiducie *f*; **t. deed,** acte *m* fiduciaire, acte de fidéicommis; **to make, leave, a t.,** faire un fidéicommis; fidéicommisser; **to hold sth. in t.,** tenir qch. par fidéicommis; administrer (un bien, etc.) par fidéicommis; (*b*) **National T.,** société *f* pour la conservation des sites et monuments. **6.** (*a*) *Ind: etc:* trust *m*, syndicat *m*, cartel *m*; *Fin: U.S:* **t. company,** société financière; trust-company *f*; *St.Exch:* **investment t.,** trust de placement; coopérative *f* de placement; **unit t.,** société d'investissement à capital variable; (*b*) (*of a newspaper, etc.*) société fermière; (*c*) **t. funds,** fonds de dépôts (**of the F.A.O.,** de l'O.A.A.). **7.** *Pol:* **t. territories,** territoires *m* sous tutelle.

trust[2]. **1.** *v.tr.* (*a*) se fier à (qn, qch.); se confier à, en (qn, qch.); mettre sa confiance en (qn, qch.); **I've never trusted him,** je n'ai jamais eu confiance en lui; **he's not to be trusted,** on ne peut pas se fier à lui; il n'est pas digne de confiance; **this account is not to be trusted,** ce compte rendu est sujet à caution; **if we may t. his statement,** s'il faut en croire son affirmation; **I could scarcely t. my own eyes, my own ears,** c'était à n'en pas croire mes yeux, mes oreilles; **I can't t. my memory,** je ne peux pas compter sur ma mémoire, me fier à ma mémoire; **to t. s.o. with a job,** se fier à qn du soin de qch., du soin de faire qch.; **to t. s.o. with sth.,** confier qch. à qn; **he can't be trusted with a car,** il est trop novice, trop âgé, trop écervelé, etc. pour conduire; on ne peut pas se fier à lui pour conduire; **to t. s.o. to do sth., to get sth. done,** se fier à qn du soin de faire qch.; se fier à qn pour que qch. se fasse; (**you can**) **t. him!** laissez-le faire! *F:* **t. him to say that!** c'est bien de lui! on peut compter sur lui pour dire pareille chose; **you can t. him to be playing for his own hand,** il joue un jeu intéressé à coup sûr; **I t. you to make all the arrangements,** je vous laisse le soin de prendre toutes les dispositions; **he trusted her to make the best of the opportunity,** il avait toute confiance qu'elle tirerait tout le parti possible de cette occasion; **I couldn't t. myself to speak,** j'étais trop ému pour me risquer à rien dire; *F:* **she won't t. him out of her sight,** elle ne le perd jamais de vue; elle le surveille tout le temps; elle ne lui laisse aucune liberté; **in town you daren't t. the children out of doors,** en ville on n'ose pas laisser sortir les enfants seuls; (*b*) **to t. sth. to, with, s.o.,** confier qch. à qn, aux soins de qn, à la garde de qn; (*c*) *Com: F:* faire crédit à (un client); **the bank trusted him for a million dollars,** la banque lui a prêté un million de dollars; (*d*) *O:* espérer (que + *ind.*); exprimer le vœu (que + *sub.*); **I t. he is not ill,** j'espère bien, j'aime à croire, qu'il n'est pas malade; *Corr:* **I t. I shall hear from you soon,** j'espère bien avoir de vos nouvelles sous peu. **2.** *v.i.* (*a*) se confier (**in,** en); se fier (**in,** à); mettre sa confiance (**in,** en); **I want someone I can t. in,** il me faut un homme de confiance; (*b*) mettre ses espérances, son espoir (en qch.); **to t. to luck,** se confier au hasard; **to t. in God, in Providence,** s'abandonner à Dieu, à la Providence; **t. in your star(s)!** sois confiant dans ton étoile! **we must t. and not be afraid,** il faut avoir confiance et ne pas avoir peur.

trusted ['trʌstid], *a.* (personne) de confiance.

trustee [trʌs'tiː], *s.* **1.** *Jur:* (*a*) (*of testamentary estate*) fidéicommissaire *m*, fiduciaire *m*; curateur, -trice; **trustee's certificate,** certificat *m* fiduciaire; **the Public T.,** le curateur de l'État aux successions; (*b*) dépositaire *m*, consignataire *m*; (*c*) (*with powers of attorney*) mandataire *m*; **t. in bankruptcy,** administrateur *m*; syndic *m* de faillite. **2.** administrateur, curateur (d'un musée, etc.); membre *m* du conseil d'administration (d'une fondation); **board of trustees,** conseil *m* d'administration.

trusteeship [trʌs'tiːʃip], *s.* **1.** (*a*) fidéicommis *m*; (*b*) **t. in bankruptcy,** syndicat *m* de faillite. **2.** administration *f*, curatelle *f*. **3.** *Pol:* tutelle *f*.

trustful ['trʌstful], *a.* plein de confiance; confiant.

trustfully ['trʌstfəli], *adv.* avec confiance.

trustfulness ['trʌstfulnis], *s.* confiance *f*; nature confiante.

trustiness ['trʌstinis], *s.* fidélité *f*, loyauté *f*.

trusting ['trʌstiŋ], *a.* plein de confiance; confiant.

trustingly ['trʌstiŋli], *adv.* avec confiance.

trustless ['trʌstlis], *a.* **1.** infidèle; déloyal, -aux; décevant. **2.** méfiant, soupçonneux.

trustworthiness ['trʌstwəːðinis], *s.* **1.** (*of pers.*) loyauté *f*, honnêteté *f*; fidélité *f*. **2.** crédibilité *f*, véracité *f*, exactitude *f* (d'un témoignage, etc.).

trustworthy ['trʌstwəːði], *a.* **1.** (*of pers.*) digne de confiance, de foi; loyal, -aux; honnête, fidèle; **a t. person,** une personne de confiance; **t. witness,** témoin *m* irrécusable; **t. firm,** maison *f* de confiance. **2.** (renseignement *m*, etc.) digne de foi, croyable, exact; (témoignage) irrécusable; **we have it from a t. source that. . .,** nous savons de source certaine que. . .; **t. guarantee,** garantie *f* solide.

trusty ['trʌsti]. **1.** *a. A: & Lit:* sûr, fidèle; loyal, -aux; de confiance; **my t. blade,** ma fidèle épée; **t. friend,** ami *m* solide, à toute épreuve; **to our t. lieges,** à nos féaux sujets. **2.** *s.* forçat bien noté (à qui sont accordés certains privilèges).

truth [truːθ, *pl.* truːðz], *s.* **1.** (*a*) vérité *f*; véracité *f*; **to distinguish, tell, t. from falsehood,** distinguer le vrai du faux; **to speak, tell, the t.,** dire la vérité; *Jur:* **the t., the whole t., and nothing but the t.,** la vérité, toute la vérité, rien que la vérité; **the real, plain (unvarnished, unadulterated), honest, t.,** la pure vérité; la vérité vraie; la vérité pure et simple; **the t. (of the matter) is, if the t. must be told, to tell the t., I forgot it,** pour dire la vérité, à dire vrai, à ne point mentir, je l'ai oublié; la vérité est que je l'ai oublié; *A:* **t. to say, t. to tell, in t., of a t.,** en vérité, vraiment; à vrai dire; **to get at the t. of a matter,** tirer une affaire au clair; **that's the t. of it!** voilà la vérité! **here's the t. about what happened,** voici au vrai ce qui s'est passé; **you don't know how near you are to the t.,** vous ne croyez pas si bien dire; **there's some t. in what you say,** il y a du vrai dans ce que vous dites; vous êtes dans le vrai; **to keep well within the t.,** rester au-dessous de la vérité; **to fall short of the t.,** être en dessous de la vérité; **to overstep the t.,** outrepasser les bornes de la vérité; **to doubt the t. of a statement,** douter de la véracité, de l'exactitude *f*, d'une affirmation; *Prov:* **t. will out,** la vérité finit toujours par se découvrir; **t. is stranger than fiction,** la réalité dépasse la fiction; **nothing hurts like the t.,** il n'y a que la vérité qui blesse; (*b*) vérité; chose vraie; **scientific truths,** les vérités scientifiques; **home truths,** vérités bien senties; **I told him some, a few, home truths,** je lui ai dit son fait, ses quatre vérités; **half t.,** demi-vérité *f*, *pl.* demi-vérités. **2.** *Mec.E:* **out of t.** = **out of true,** *q.v. under* TRUE[1] **III.**

truthful ['truːθful], *a.* **1.** (*of pers.*) véridique; **he is t.,** il dit toujours la vérité; on peut le croire sur parole. **2.** (témoignage, etc.) vrai; (portrait *m*, etc.) fidèle.

truthfully ['truːθfuli], *adv.* **1.** véridiquement; sans mentir. **2.** fidèlement; *Lit:* **t. written novel,** roman écrit avec vérité.

truthfulness ['truːθfulnis], *s.* **1.** (*of pers.*) véracité *f*, véridicité *f*; bonne foi. **2.** vérité *f*; véracité (d'une assertion, etc.); fidélité *f* (d'un portrait, etc.); *Lit: Art:* **t. (to life),** vérité.

truxillic [trʌk'silik], *a. Ch:* truxillique.

try[1] [trai], *s.* **1.** essai *m*, tentative *f*; **to have a t. at (doing) sth.,** essayer de faire qch.; s'essayer à qch.; **to have another t.,** ressayer (qch.); **I shan't win the prize but I'll have a t.,** je ne vais pas gagner le prix mais je vais quand même essayer; **let's have a t.!** essayons toujours! **at the first t.,** au premier essai; du premier coup. **2.** *Rugby Fb:* **to score a t.,** marquer un essai; **to convert a t.,** transformer un essai (en but). **3.** *Carp:* **t. square,** équerre *f* à lame d'acier.

try[2], *v.* (*p.t. & p.p.* **tried** [traid])

I. *v.tr.* **1.** (*a*) éprouver (qn); mettre (qn, qch.) à l'épreuve; faire l'épreuve de (qch.); **to be tried and found wanting,** ne pas supporter l'épreuve; **to t. s.o.'s courage,** mettre à l'épreuve le courage de qn; (*b*) *Lit:* éprouver; affliger; **a people sorely tried,** une nation fort, durement, éprouvée; **sorely tried by fortune,** éprouvé par de grands revers; (*c*) **to t. one's eyes (reading),** se fatiguer les yeux (à lire). **2.** essayer, expérimenter (qch.); faire l'essai de (qch.); **to t. a dish,** goûter (à) un mets; goûter, tâter, d'un mets; **t. these chocolates,** goûtez ces chocolats; **t. this remedy,** essayez (de) ce remède; (*in fairs*) **t.-your-strength machine** = tête *f* de Turc; **to t. (out) a new process,** essayer, expérimenter, un nouveau procédé; **to t. (out) a medicine on an animal,** expérimenter un médicament, faire l'essai d'un médicament, sur une bête; **t. cleaning it with petrol,** essayez de l'essence, essayer voir si l'essence le nettoiera; **I'll have to t. it again,** il me faut le ressayer; *Mus:* **to t. over a piece,** essayer un morceau de musique. **3.** vérifier (un mécanisme); ajuster (des poids); essayer (un cordage, une voiture); **you'd better t. the brakes before starting,** vous feriez bien de vérifier le réglage des freins avant de vous mettre en route; *Nau:* **to t. the engines,** balancer la machine. **4.** (*a*) *Ind:* **to t. (out, down),** faire fondre (la graisse) pour la purifier; **to t. out (a metal),** épurer, affiner (un métal); (*b*) *Carp:* **to t. (up),** varloper (une planche). **5.** *Jur:* (*a*) juger (une cause, un accusé); mettre (un accusé) en jugement; **to be tried for theft,** passer en correctionnelle, être jugé, pour vol; **to be tried by one's peers,** être jugé par, passer en jugement devant, ses pairs; (*b*)

U.S: (*of advocate*) plaider (une cause). **6.** essayer, tenter; **to t. an experiment,** tenter une expérience; **t. your hand at it,** essayez par vous-même; voyez si vous pouvez le faire; **to t. one's strength against s.o.,** se mesurer avec qn; **to t. the door, the window,** essayer (douvrir) la porte, la fenêtre; **I can't find it; I'll t. another drawer,** je ne peux pas le trouver; je vais regarder dans un autre tiroir. **7. to t. to do,** *F:* **and do, sth.,** tâcher, essayer, de faire qch.; **t. to, and, write to him tonight,** tâchez de lui écrire ce soir; **t. to be ready in time,** tâchez d'être prêt à temps; **he tried to persuade me,** il a essayé de me persuader; **she tried to smile,** elle a essayé de sourire; **she was trying hard to keep back her tears,** elle faisait de grands efforts pour retenir ses larmes; **he tried his hardest to save them,** il a fait tout son possible pour les sauver; **it's worth trying,** cela vaut la peine d'essayer.

II. *v.i.* **1.** faire un effort, des efforts; **to t. again,** faire un nouvel effort; essayer de nouveau; **you must t. harder,** il faut faire de plus grands efforts; **the worst about him is that he never tries,** ce qu'on peut lui reprocher c'est qu'il ne veut jamais faire un effort; *F:* **you'd better not t.!** si tu y mets les pieds . . .! **2. to t. for sth.,** tâcher d'obtenir qch.; **to t. for a job,** poser sa candidature à un emploi. **3.** *Nau:* **to t. (under topsails),** être à la cape courante.

III. (*compound verbs*) **1. try back,** *v.i. Ven:* recommencer; revenir en arrière.

2. try on, *v.tr.* (*a*) essayer (un vêtement); **I'll t. the black dress on again,** je vais ressayer la robe noire; (*b*) *F:* **to t. it on (with s.o.),** bluffer; faire un ballon d'essai; chercher à mettre (qn) dedans, à donner le change (à qn); **he's trying it on; that's not worth £1,000,** c'est du bluff, il bluffe; ça ne vaut pas £1.000; **you're (just) trying it on!** ça ne marche pas, ne prend pas! pour qui me prends-tu? **just you t. it on!** ce n'est pas avec moi que ça marchera!

3. try out, *v.tr.* (*a*) faire l'essai de (qch.); *s.a.* TRY[2], 2; (*b*) *Sp:* **to be tried out for a team,** jouer dans un match à sélection.

trying[1] ['traiiŋ], *a.* **1.** difficile, pénible, rude, dur; **t. circumstances,** circonstances *f* difficiles; **t. situation,** situation difficile, fâcheuse, pénible; **t. winter,** hiver rigoureux, rude. **2.** vexant, contrariant; **that must have been very t. for you,** cela a dû vous contrarier beaucoup, a dû vous donner beaucoup de soucis; **he's very t.,** il est insupportable, *F:* embêtant. **3. t. light,** lumière fatigante (pour la vue).

trying[2], *s.* **1.** *Jur:* jugement *m* (d'une cause, d'un accusé). **2.** *Carp:* **t. (up),** varlopage *m*; **t. plane,** varlope *f*; rabot *m* à corroyer; jointout *m*. **3. t. on,** essayage *m* (de vêtements).

try-on ['traiɔn], *s. F:* (*a*) tentative *f* de déception; **I knew it was only a t.-on,** je savais bien que ce n'était que du bluff; (*b*) ballon *m* d'essai; **I asked £1,000 for it as a t.-on,** histoire de voir, à tout hasard, j'en ai demandé £1,000.

tryout ['traiaut], *s.* (*a*) premier essai, essai préliminaire (d'une machine, d'un procédé, etc.); (*b*) *F:* (i) *Sp:* joueur, -euse, dans un match à sélection; (ii) candidat pris à l'essai (pour un emploi, etc.).

trypanocidal [tripənou'said(ə)l], *a. Med:* trypanocide.

trypanocide [tri'pænousaid], *s. Med:* trypanocide *m*.

Trypanosomatidae [tripənousou'mætidi:], *s.pl. Prot:* trypanosomidés *m*.

trypanosome [tri'pænousoum], *s. Prot:* trypanosome *m*.

trypanosomiasis [tripənousou'maiəsis], *s. Med: Vet:* trypanosomiase *f*.

tryparsamide [tri'pɑ:səmaid], *s. Pharm:* tryparsamide *f*.

trypetid [tri'pi:tid], *s. Ent:* trypeta *f*; trypétidé *m*.

Trypetidae [tri'petidi:], *s.pl. Ent:* trypétidés *m*.

trypsin ['tripsin], *s. Ch:* trypsine *f*.

trypsinogen [trip'sinoudʒen], *s. Bio-Ch:* trypsinogène *f*.

tryptic ['triptik], *a. Ch:* trypsique.

tryptophan(e) ['triptoufæn, -fein], *s. Ch:* tryptophane *m*.

trysail ['traiseil, *Nau:* 'traisl], *s. Nau:* voile *f* goélette; senau *m*; **main t.,** grande voile goélette; benjamine *f*; **t. mast,** mât *m* de senau, baguette *f* de senau.

tryst [trist], *s. Lit:* rendez-vous *m*; **lover's t.,** assignation amoureuse; **to keep t., to break t.,** venir, manquer, à un rendez-vous.

trysting ['tristiŋ], *s. Lit:* **t. place,** (lieu *m* de) rendez-vous *m*.

tryworks ['traiwə:ks], *s.pl.* (*often with sg. const.*) fondoir *m* de graisse de baleine.

tsar [zɑ:r], *s.* tsar *m*, czar *m*.

tsarevitch ['zɑ:rəvitʃ], *s.* tsarévitch *m*, czarévitch *m*.

tsarina [zɑ:'ri:nə], *s.f.* tsarine, czarine.

tsarism ['zɑ:rizm], *s.* tsarisme *m*.

tsarist ['zɑ:rist]. (*a*) *a.* tsariste, tsarien; (*b*) *s.* tsariste *mf*.

tscheffkinite ['tʃefkinait], *s. Miner:* tscheffkinite *f*.

tsessebe, tsesseby ['(t)sesəbi], *s. Z:* (espèce *f* de) damalisque *m*.

tsetse ['t(s)etsi], *s. Ent:* **t. (fly),** (mouche *f*) tsé-tsé *f*, tsétsé *f*; glossine *f*.

tsunami [su:'nɑ:mi], *s. Oc:* tsunami *m*.

Tuareg ['twɑ:reg]. **1.** *a.* touareg. **2.** *s.* Targui, *pl.* Touareg, *f.* Targuia, *pl.* Targuiat.

tuatara [tu:ə'tɑ:rə], *s. Rept:* sphénodon *m*, hattérie *f*.

tub[1] [tʌb], *s.* **1.** (*a*) baquet *m*, bac *m*; *Hort:* bac, caisse *f* (à fleurs, à arbustes); *Nau:* baille *f*; *Vit:* bouge *m*; *Paperm:* bac, cuve *f*; **to plant, put, trees in tubs (again),** (r)encaisser des arbres; *Paperm:* **t. sizing,** collage *m* en bac, en cuve; *Leath:* **maceration t.,** confit *m*; **t. wheel,** (i) *Tan:* tonneau *m*; (ii) *Hyd.E:* roue *f* à cuve; (*b*) baquet, cuvier *m* (à lessive); (*in washing machine*) cuve; (*c*) *Com:* carton *m* (à glaces, à crème, etc.); (*d*) *Furn:* **t. chair,** crapaud *m*; (*e*) *F:* **t. thumper,** harangueur *m*; orateur *m* de carrefour; **t. thumping,** éloquence *f* de carrefour. **2.** (*a*) *F:* baignoire *f*; (*b*) **there's nothing like a hot t. to refresh you,** rien ne vous rafraîchit autant qu'un bain chaud. **3.** *Min:* (*a*) benne *f*, tonne *f*, tine *f*; cuf(f)at *m*; **tipping t.,** benne à renversement; (*b*) berline *f*, truck *m*, wagonnet *m*; bac, herche *f*. **4.** (*a*) *Nau: F:* **old t.,** vieux sabot; baille, barcasse *f*; rafiau *m*; rafiot *m*; (*b*) *Row:* canot *m* d'entraînement.

tub[2], *v.* (**tubbed**) **1.** *v.tr.* (*a*) encaisser (une plante); (*b*) *Min:* cuveler, boiser (un puits); (*c*) *Row:* entraîner (les rameurs) (dans un canot d'entraînement). **2.** *v.i.* (*a*) prendre un bain; (*b*) *Row:* s'exercer, faire de l'aviron, dans un canot d'entraînement.

tuba ['tju:bə], *s.* **1.** *Rom.Ant:* (*pl.* **tubae** ['tju:bi:]) tuba *f*. **2.** *Mus:* (*pl.* **tubas**) (*a*) (*organ*) trompette *f*; (*b*) (*in orchestra*) tuba *m*; **bass t.,** tuba basse; (*c*) **t. (player),** contrebassiste *m*; (*in brass band*) la contrebasse; le bombardon.

tubage ['tju:bidʒ], *s.* = TUBING 1.

tubal ['tju:b(ə)l], *a. Anat: Med:* tubaire; (i) des bronches; **t. respiration, breathing,** souffle *m* tubaire; (ii) de la trompe de Fallope; **t. pregnancy,** grossesse *f* tubaire.

tubbable ['tʌbəbl], *a. F:* (*of garment, fabric*) lavable.

tubbing ['tʌbiŋ], *s.* **1.** encaissage *m*, encaissement *m* (de plantes). **2.** bain *m*; **to give the child a good t.,** donner un bon bain à l'enfant; *F:* **to give the clothes a good t.,** bien laver le linge. **3.** *Min:* (*a*) cuvelage *m*, cuvellement *m*, boisage *m* (d'un puits); (*b*) (revêtement *m* de) boisage. **4.** *Row: F:* **to do a bit of t.,** s'exercer un peu dans un canot d'entraînement.

tubby ['tʌbi], *a. F:* rond comme un tonneau. **1.** (*of pers.*) boulot; gros et rond; pansu; **he's a t. little man,** c'est un (petit) pot à tabac. **2.** (*of boat*) aux formes ramassées, pansues; qui manque de galbe.

tube[1] [tju:b], *s.* **1.** (*a*) tube *m*; tuyau *m*; **angle t., bent t.,** tube coudé; **flared t., bell-mouthed t.,** tube épanoui, évasé; **drawn t.,** tube étiré; **to draw a t.,** étirer un tube, un tuyau; **t. drawing,** étirage *m* des tubes; **rolled t.,** tube laminé; **seamless t.,** tube sans soudure; **t. gauge,** calibreur *m* (pour tubes); **t. cutter,** coupe-tubes *m inv*; coupe-tuyaux *m inv*; **t. expander,** extendeur *m*, expanseur *m*; mandrin *m*, dudgeon *m*; **t. vice,** étau *m* à tuyaux; (*b*) tube (de couleur, de dentifrice); *Austr: F:* boîte *f* (de bière); (*c*) *Mch: etc:* **boiler t.,** tube de chaudière; **feeding t.,** tube alimentaire, d'alimentation; **t. brush,** brosse *f* à tubes (de chaudière); torche-tubes *m inv*; écouvillon *m*; *Mec.E:* **regulator t.,** tube régulateur; **torque t.,** tube de torsion; *I.C.E:* **choke t.,** buse *f*, diffuseur *m* (de carburateur); **flame t.,** tube à flamme (de moteur à réaction); *N.Arch:* **stern t.,** tube d'étambot, de sortie d'arbre; *Aut:* **rear axle flared t.,** trompette *f*; **inner t.,** chambre *f* à air (d'un pneu); *Artil:* **inner t., liner t.,** tube intérieur; **outer t.,** frette *f*, manchon *m*, de renfort; *Sm.a:* **Morris t.,** tube réducteur; *Navy:* **torpedo t.,** tube lance-torpille(s); (*d*) *Artil: A:* **firing t.,** étoupille *f*; **to extract the t.,** enlever l'étoupille; (*e*) *Ch: Ph: etc:* **capillary t.,** tube capillaire; **coiled t., spiral t.,** serpentin *m*; **funnel t.,** tube à entonnoir; **graduated glass t.,** tube de verre gradué; **siphon t.,** tube siphonal; **Torricellian t.,** tube de Torricelli; **filling t.,** tube d'affluence; **leading t.,** tube abducteur; *Av:* **Pitot t., static-pressure t.,** tube de Pitot; *Ind:* **fractional distillation t.,** tube pour distillation fractionnée; **soaker t.,** tube de maturation; (*f*) *Opt:* **(body) t.,** barillet *m* (d'un objectif); **eye t.,** tube porte-oculaire; **inner t.,** tube porte-réticule; **outer t.,** tube porte-objectif; **sight t.,** tube de visée; *Phot:* **extension t.,** (tube) allonge *f*; tube-rallonge *f*, *pl.* tubes-rallonges; (*g*) *Min:* tube (de pompage, d'exploitation); **core t.,** tube carottier; **drive t.,** tube perforateur; **guide t.,** tube-guide *m*, *pl.* tubes-guides; tube conducteur; (*h*) *Rail: F:* (*in London*) **the t.** = le métro; **to travel by t.** = voyager par le, en, métro; **t. station** = station *f* de métro; (*i*) *Med: etc:* (i) drain *m* (pour plaie profonde); tube (de drainage); (ii) tube, canule *f*, sonde *f* (pour tubage); **t. drainage,** drainage *m* par tube; **intratracheal t.,** sonde trachéale; **intubation t.,** tube pour intubation, pour tubage du larynx; **laryngotomy t.,** tube à laryngotomie; **tracheotomy t.,** tube, canule, pour trachéotomie; **stomach t.,** sonde pour tubage gastrique. **2.** (*a*) *Anat:* tube; canal, -aux *m*; trompe *f*; **Fallopian tubes,** trompes de Fallope; **bronchial tubes,** les bronches *f*; *P:* **it's my tubes!** c'est mes bronches (qui me font mal)! (*b*) *Ent:* **Malpighian tubes,** tubes de Malpighi; (*c*) *Moll:* **t. shell,** tubicole *f*; *Ann:* **t. worm,** tubicole. **3.** *El: Elcs: T.V: etc:* (*a*) tube (électronique, thermionique, à cathode chaude); lampe *f*; **cathode-ray t.,** tube cathodique, à rayons cathodiques; **Crookes t.,** tube de Crookes; **dark-trace t.,** tube cathodique à écran absorbant, tube à trace sombre; **derivation t.,** tube dérivateur; **discharge t.,** tube à décharge; **glow discharge t.,** tube à décharge luminescente; **grid glow t.,** tube à décharge à grille; **hard, soft, t.,** tube dur, mou; **image converter t.,** tube transformateur d'image; **memory t., storage t.,** tube de mémoire; **microwave t.,** tube hyperfréquences; **modulating t.,** tube modulateur; **modulator t.,** tube de modulation; **multi-electrode t.,** tube à grilles multiples, à plusieurs électrodes; **multigrid t.,** tube à plusieurs grilles; **multi-purpose t.,** tube universel; **neon t.,** tube au néon; **phase-inverter t.,** tube déphaseur; **picture t., television t.,** tube cathodique pour télévision; **power t.,** tube de puissance; **reactance t.,** tube de réactance; **receiving t.,** tube récepteur, lampe réceptrice; **rectification t.,** tube redresseur; **scanning t.,** tube de balayage; **screen-grid t.,** tube à grille écran; **(television) camera t.,** tube de prise de vues de télévision; **transmitting t.,** tube émetteur, lampe émettrice; **travelling-wave t.,** tube à propagation d'ondes; **t. wattmeter,** wattmètre *m* électronique; (*b*) *U.S: F:* **the t.,** la télé.

tube[2]. **1.** *v.tr.* (*a*) *Civ.E:* tuber, garnir de tubes (un sondage, un puits de mine, etc.); *Surg: Vet:* tuber (le larynx); drainer (une plaie profonde); (*b*) garnir de tubes (une chaudière, etc.). **2.** *v.tr. & i. F: A:* **to t. (it)** = voyager par le, en, métro.

tube-feed ['tju:bfi:d], *v.tr.* nourrir (un malade) à la sonde.

tubeflower ['tju:bflauər], *s. Bot:* clérodendron *m*.

tubeless ['tju:blis], *a. Aut:* (pneu) sans chambre (à air).

tubelike ['tju:blaik], *a. Anat: etc:* fistulaire.

tubemaker ['tju:bmeikər], *s. Nat.Hist:* annélide, etc., tubicole.

tubeman, *pl.* **-men** ['tju:bmən], *s.m.* employé du métro (londonien).

tuber ['tju:bər], *s.* **1.** (*a*) *Bot:* (i) racine tubéreuse; (ii) tubercule *m*; (*b*) *Fung:* tubéracée *f*, truffe *f*. **2.** (*a*) *Anat:* tubérosité *f*; (*b*) *Med:* tubercule.

Tuberaceae [tju:bə'reisii:], *s.pl. Fung:* tubéracées *f*.

tuberaceous [tju:bə'reiʃəs], *a. Fung:* tubéracé.

Tuberales [tju:bə'reili:z], *s.pl. Fung:* tubérales *f*.

tubercle ['tju:bə:kl], *s. Anat: Med:* tubercule *m*; **t. bacillus,** bacille *m* de Koch.

tubercled ['tju:bə:kld], *a.* tuberculé.

tubercular [tju:'bə:kjulər], *a.* **1.** *Bot:* tuberculeux; à tubercules; **t. root,** racine tuberculeuse. **2.** *Med:* tuberculeux.

Tuberculariaceae [tju:bə:kjulæri'eisii:], *s.pl. Fung:* tuberculariacées *f*.

tuberculate, tuberculated [tju:'bə:kjuleit(id)], *a. Nat.Hist: Med:* tuberculé.

tuberculation [tjubə:kju'leiʃ(ə)n], *s.* formation *f* de tubercules.

tuberculid(e) [tju'bə:kjulid, -laid], *s. Med:* tuberculide *f*.

tuberculiferous [tjubə:kju'lifərəs], *a. Nat.Hist:* tuberculifère.

tuberculiform [tju:'bə:kjulifɔ:m], *a.* tuberculiforme.

tuberculin [tju'bə:kjulin], *s. Med:* tuberculine *f*; lymphe *f* de Koch; **t. testing,** tuberculinisation *f*, tuberculination *f*; **t. test,** épreuve *f* de la tuberculinisation; tuberculino-diagnostic *m*; **t.-tested milk,** lait garanti exempt de tuberculose; lait de troupeaux tuberculinés; = lait cru certifié.

tuberculinic [tjubə:kju'linik], *a. Med:* tuberculinique.

tuberculinization [tjubə:kjulinai'zeiʃ(ə)n], *s. Med: Vet:* tuberculinisation *f*, tuberculination *f*.

tuberculinize [tju'bə:kjulinaiz], *v.tr. Med: Vet:* tuberculiner, tuberculiniser (un animal, etc.).

tuberculization [tjubə:kjulai'zeiʃ(ə)n], *s.* (*a*) *Med:* tuberculisation *f* (du poumon, etc.); (*b*) *Nat.Hist:* tuberculisation, formation *f* de tubercules.

tuberculize [tju'bə:kjulaiz]. *Med:* **1.** *v.tr.* tuberculiser. **2.**

v.i. (*of lung, etc.*) se tuberculiser.
tuberculoid [tju'bə:kjulɔid], *a.* tuberculoïde.
tuberculoma [tjubə:kju'loumə], *s. Med:* tuberculome *m.*
tuberculosed [tju'bə:kjuloust], *a. Med:* tuberculisé.
tuberculosis [tjubə:kju'lousis], *s.* **1.** *Med:* tuberculose *f,* bacillose *f;* **pulmonary t., t. of the lungs,** tuberculose pulmonaire; **t. of the hip joint,** coxotuberculose *f,* tuberculose ostéo-articulaire de la hanche; **t. dispensary,** dispensaire *m* antituberculeux. **2.** *Bot:* tuberculose (de l'olivier).
tuberculostat [tju'bə:kjuloustæt], *s. Med:* (médicament) tuberculostatique (*m*).
tuberculostatic [tjubə:kjulou'stætik], *a. Med:* tuberculostatique.
tuberculous [tju'bə:kjuləs], *a.* **1.** *Miner:* tuberculeux; *Nat.Hist:* tuberculeux; tuberculé; à tubercules. **2.** *Med:* tuberculeux; **t. meningitis,** méningite tuberculeuse; **t. lung,** poumon tuberculeux; **t. patient,** tuberculeux, -euse; *s. coll.* **the t.,** les tuberculeux.
tuberiform ['tju:bərifɔ:m], *a. Nat.Hist:* tubériforme.
tuberization [tju:bərai'zeiʃ(ə)n], *s. Bot:* tubérisation *f.*
tuberoid ['tju:bərɔid], *a. Nat.Hist:* tubéroïde.
tuberose[1] ['tju:bərous], *a. Bot:* tubéreux.
tuberose[2], *s. Bot:* tubéreuse *f.*
tuberosity [tju:bə'rɔsiti], *s.* tubérosité *f; Anat:* **great t. of the humerus,** trochéter *m;* **lesser t. of the humerus,** trochin *m.*
tuberous ['tju:bərəs], *a. Bot:* tubéreux, tubérisé; **t.-rooted,** à racines tubéreuses.
tubfast ['tʌbfɑ:st], *a. U.S:* (tissu) lavable.
tubful ['tʌbful], *s.* cuvée *f,* plein baquet (**of,** de).
tubicole ['tju:bikoul]. **1.** *a.* (annélide, etc.) tubicole. **2.** *s. Ann: Moll:* tubicole *m.*
tubicolous [tju'bikələs], *a. Nat.Hist:* tubicole.
tubicorn ['tju:bikɔ:n], *a. Z:* tubicorne.
tubiferous [tju'bifərəs], *a.* tubifère.
tubifex ['tju:bifeks], *s. Ann:* tubifex *m.*
tubiflorous [tju:bi'flɔ:rəs], *a. Bot:* tubiflore.
tubiform ['tju:bifɔ:m], *a.* tubiforme.
tubing ['tju:biŋ], *s.* **1.** (*a*) *Civ.E: Min: Surg: etc:* tubage *m* (d'un puits, du larynx, etc.); drainage *m* (d'une plaie); (*b*) pose *f* des tubes (d'une chaudière). **2.** *coll.* tubes *mpl;* tubulures *fpl;* tubage; tuyautage *m;* tuyauterie *f;* canalisation(s) *f*(*pl*); *Mec.E:* souplisseau(x) *m*(*pl*); *Min: Petr:* tubes de pompage, d'exploitation; *Petr:* colonne *f* de production; **flexible t.,** tuyautage souple; **rubber t.,** tuyau(x) *m*(*pl*) en caoutchouc.
tubiparous [tju'bipərəs], *a. Ann:* (ganglion *m*) tubipare.
Tubipora [tju'bipərə], **tubipore** ['tju:bipɔ:r], *s. Coel:* tubipora *m,* tubipore *m; F:* orgue *m* de mer.
tubiporid [tju:bi'pɔrid], *s. Coel:* tubiporide *m.*
Tubiporidae [tju:bi'pɔridi:], *s.pl. Coel:* tubiporides *m.*
Tubitelae [tju:bi'ti:li:], *s.pl. Arach:* tubitèles *m,* tubitélaires *m.*
tubo-ovarian [tjubouou'vɛəriən], *a. Anat:* tubo-ovarien.
tubular ['tju:bjulər], *a.* **1.** (*a*) tubulaire; **t. frame, chassis,** bâtis *m,* châssis *m,* tubulaire; **t. steel frame,** bâtis, châssis, en tubes d'acier; **t. framework,** carcasse *f* tubulaire, en tubes; **t. girder,** poutre *f* tubulaire; **t. pile,** pieux creux; **t. boiler,** chaudière *f* tubulaire, tubulée, à tubes; **t. shaft,** arbre *m* tubulaire; **t. spanner,** clef *f* à tube; **t. furniture,** meubles *m* tubulaires; *El:* **t. condenser,** condensateur *m* tubulaire; *Tex:* **t. fabric,** tissu *m* tubulaire; (*b*) *Nat.Hist:* tubulaire, tubiforme, tubulé, tubuleux; **t. flower,** fleur tubulée; **t. corolla,** corolle tubulée, tubuleuse; (*c*) *Mus:* **t. bells, t. chimes,** carillon *m* (d'orchestre). **2.** *Med:* **t. respiration, t. breathing,** souffle *m* tubaire.
Tubularia [tju:bju'lɛəriə], *s. Coel:* tubulaire *m.*
tubularian [tju:bju'lɛəriən], *a. & s. Coel:* tubulaire (*m*).
Tubulariidae [tju:bjulæ'raiidi:], *s.pl. Coel:* tubularidés *m.*
tubulate ['tju:bjuleit], *a. Nat.Hist:* tubulé.
tubulated ['tju:bjuleitid], *a. Ch: etc:* **t. retort,** cornue tubulée.
tubule ['tju:bju:l], *s. Nat.Hist:* tubule *m; Ent:* **Malpighian tubules,** tubes *m* de Malpighi.
Tubulidentata [tju:bjuliden'teitə], *s.pl. Z:* tubulidentés *m.*
tubulidentate [tju:bjuli'denteit], *a. & s. Z:* tubulidenté (*m*).
Tubulifera [tju:bju'lifərə], *s.pl. Ent:* tubulifères *m.*
tubuliflorous [tju:bjuli'flɔ:rəs], *a. Bot:* tubuliflore.
tubuliform [tju:'bju:lifɔ:m], *a.* tubuliforme.
Tubulipora [tju:bju'lipərə], **tubulipore** ['tju:bjulipɔ:r], *s. Biol:* tubulipore *m.*
tubulous ['tju:bjuləs], *a.* **1.** tubuleux. **2. t. boiler,** chaudière *f* tubulaire, tubulée, à tubes.
tubulure ['tju:bjuljuər], *s. Ch: Hyd.E:* tubulure *f.*
tuck[1] [tʌk], *s.* **1.** *Dressm:* (petit) pli; rempli *m,* plissé *m,* plissement *m,* relevé *m;* (*to shorten a garment*) troussis *m;* **to put, make, take up, a t. in a garment,** faire un rempli à, remplier, un vêtement; (*to shorten*) faire un troussis à un vêtement; **false t.,** biais *m.* **2.** *Nau:* cul *m,* fesses *fpl* (d'un navire). **3.** *Fish:* **t. net,** poche *f* (d'une seine). **4.** *Sch: F:* gâteaux *mpl,* friandises *fpl,* sucreries *fpl;* **t. box,** boîte *f* à provisions. **5.** *F:* **to be in tucks,** se tordre de rire.
tuck[2], *v.*
I. *v.tr.* **1.** *Dressm:* (*a*) faire des plis à, remplier (un vêtement); plisser, froncer (le tissu); (*b*) raccourcir (un vêtement). **2.** replier, rentrer, serrer, mettre; **to t. one's legs under one,** replier les jambes sous soi; **she tucked the flowers into her belt,** elle a mis les fleurs dans sa ceinture; **she tucked her arm in(to) mine,** elle a passé son bras sous le mien; **to t. a rug round s.o.,** envelopper qn d'une couverture; **the bird tucked its head under its wing,** l'oiseau a replié, a caché, sa tête sous son aile; **to t. sth. into, away in, a drawer,** serrer qch. dans un tiroir; **t. it (away) under the cushion,** fourrez-le sous le coussin; **village tucked away at the far end of the valley,** village blotti au fond de la vallée; (*with passive force*) **the flask will t. into the corner of your bag,** le flacon rentrera dans l'angle de votre valise.
II. (*compound verbs*) **1. tuck in.** (*a*) *v.tr.* serrer, rentrer (qch.); replier (le bord d'un vêtement, etc.); **t. in this flap,** replier, rentrer, cette extrémité; **in a tucked-in envelope,** sous enveloppe non cachetée; **to t. in the bedclothes,** border le lit; **to t. s.o. in,** border qn (dans son lit); (*b*) *v.i. F:* manger à belles dents; s'en mettre jusque-là; **t. in!** allez-y! mangez!
2. tuck into, *v.i. F:* **to t. into a meal,** attaquer un repas, manger un repas à belles dents; **t. into it!** allez-y! mangez!
3. tuck up, *v.tr.* (*a*) relever, retrousser (sa jupe, ses manches de chemise); **to t. up one's clothes (at the waist),** se trousser; (*b*) border (qn) (dans son lit); **to t. oneself up in bed,** se blottir dans son lit; (*c*) *Dressm:* rentrer (les fronces, etc.).
tuck[3], *s. A:* **1.** fanfare *f* (de trompettes). **2.** *Scot:* roulement *m* de tambour; **by t. of drum,** au son du tambour; à l'appel du tambour.
tuckamore ['tʌkəmɔ:ər], *s. Can:* bouquets d'arbres tordus par le vent.
tucker[1] ['tʌkər], *s.* **1.** *A.Cost:* fichu *m,* guimpe *f,* chemisette *f.* **2.** marqueur *m* de plis (d'une machine à coudre). **3.** *Austr: F:* nourriture *f,* mangeaille *f.*
tucker[2], *v.tr. F:* lasser, fatiguer (qn); **tuckered (out),** épuisé, éreinté, vanné.
tucket ['tʌkit], *s. A:* fanfare *f* (de trompettes).
tuck-in[1] ['tʌkin], *s. F:* (*a*) (*of bed*) **there isn't enough t.-in,** les couvertures ne sont pas assez larges; (*b*) repas copieux, gueuleton *m;* **to have a good t.-in,** s'envoyer un bon repas; s'en mettre jusqu'au menton.
tuck-in[2], *a. Cost:* **t.-in blouse,** corsage *m* qui rentre dans la jupe, dans le pantalon.
tuckshop ['tʌkʃɔp], *s. Sch: F:* annexe *f* de la cantine où se vendent les friandises.
tuco-tuco [tu:kou'tu:kou], **tucu-tucu** [tu:ku:'tu:ku:], *s. Z:* tuco(-)tuco *m;* tuto-tuco *m;* **burrowing t.-t.,** tucotuco fouisseur.
tucum ['tu:kəm], *s. Bot: Tex:* tucum *m.*
Tudor ['tju:dər], *Pr.n. Hist:* Tudor; **the Tudors,** la maison, la dynastie, des Tudors; *Arch:* **T. style,** style Tudor, élisabéthain; *Lit:* **the T. theatre,** le théâtre anglais de la période 1580–1640.
tue-iron ['tju:aiən], *s. Metall:* tuyère *f* (d'une forge).
Tuesday ['tju:zdi], *s.* mardi *m;* **he comes on Tuesdays,** il vient le mardi, *occ.* les mardis; **he comes every T.,** il vient tous les mardis.
tufa ['t(j)u:fə], *s. Geol:* = TUFF.
tufaceous [t(j)u(:)'feiʃəs], *a. Geol:* tufacé.
tuff [tʌf], *s. Geol:* tuf *m* (i) volcanique, (ii) calcaire; **ash t., vitric t.,** cinérite *f.*
tuffaceous [tʌ'feiʃəs], *a. Geol:* tufacé.
tuffet ['tʌfit], *s. Furn: O:* pouf *m.*
tuft[1], *s.* **1.** (*a*) touffe *f* (d'herbe); (*b*) touffe (de plumes, de cheveux); houppe *f* (de soie, de laine); mèche *f,* flocon *m* (de laine); freluche *f* (de soie); aigrette *f* (de plumes, etc.); huppe *f,* aigrette (d'un oiseau); (*in brush*) **t. of bristles,** loquet *m* de soies. **2.** *Anat:* glomérule *m* (de vaisseaux sanguins). **3.** (*a*) barbiche *f;* mouche *f;* (*b*) toupet *m* (de cheveux); **small t. of hair,** toupillon *m.* **4.** (*a*) gland *m,* houppe (d'une toque, d'un bonnet); pompon *m;* (*b*) **t. hunter,** adulateur, -trice, des grands; sycophante *m;* **t. hunting,** sycophantisme *m.*
tuft[2]. **1.** *v.tr.* (*a*) orner, garnir (qch.) d'une touffe, de touffes, d'une houppe, de houppes, de glands; (*b*) piquer, capitonner (un matelas). **2.** *v.tr. Ven:* (*a*) battre (un bois); (*b*) faire débucher (un cerf). **3.** *v.i.* (*of plant*) pousser en touffes; touffer.
tufted ['tʌftid], *a.* (*a*) orné d'une houppe, d'une touffe, de touffes; garni de houppes, de glands; (*b*) en touffe, en houppe; houppé; **t. clouds,** nuages *m* en paquet; (*c*) *Orn:* muni d'une aigrette; huppé; houppifère; **t. heron,** héron *m* à aigrette; aigrette; **t. duck,** morillon *m;* (*d*) *Bot:* cespiteux, aigretté.
tufter ['tʌftər], *s. Ven:* chien dressé à débucher le cerf; chien d'attaque.
tufty ['tʌfti], *a.* touffu.
tug[1] [tʌg], *s.* **1.** (*a*) traction (subite); saccade *f;* **to give a good t.,** tirer fort; (*of horse, etc.*) donner un bon coup de collier; **to give the rope a t.,** tirer sur la corde; **he gave a t. at the bell,** il a tiré (sur) la sonnette; **I felt a t. at my sleeve,** je me sentais tiré par la manche; **t. of war,** (i) *Sp:* lutte *f* de traction à la corde; lutte à la jarretière; (ii) lutte acharnée et prolongée; **t.-of-war rope,** corde *f* de traction; jarretière; (*b*) **to feel a t. at one's heartstrings,** avoir un serrement de cœur, un déchirement de cœur; être pris de pitié. **2.** (*a*) *Nau:* remorqueur *m,* toueur *m;* **harbour t.,** remorqueur de port; **ocean(-going) t.,** *Navy:* **fleet t.,** remorqueur de haute mer; **salvage t.,** *U.S:* **wrecking t.,** remorqueur de sauvetage; (*b*) **t. aircraft,** avion remorqueur. **3.** *Harn:* (*a*) trait *m* (d'attelage à deux chevaux); **t. hook,** crochet *m* d'attelage; **t. chain,** mancelle *f;* (*b*) porte-brancard *m, pl.* porte-brancards; boucleteau *m* (de sellette).
tug[2], *v.* (**tugged** [tʌgd]) **1.** *v.tr. & i.* tirer (qch.) avec effort; **to t. at the dog's lead,** tirer sur la laisse du chien; **to t. at sth.,** tirer (sur) qch.; **to t. at the oars,** tirer sur les rames; souquer (ferme); **the dog was tugging at the leash,** le chien tirait sur la laisse; **to t. (at) one's moustache,** tirer (sur), torturer, tourmenter, sa moustache. **2.** *v.tr. Nau:* remorquer (un navire).
tugboat ['tʌgbout], *s. Nau:* remorqueur *m;* toueur *m.*
tui ['tu:i], *s. Orn:* prosthemadère *m.*
tuille [twi:l], *s. Arm:* tuile *f* (de l'armure).
tuition [tju(:)'iʃ(ə)n], *s.* instruction *f,* enseignement *m;* **private t.,** leçons particulières; **to give t. on the violin,** donner des leçons de violon; **postal t.,** enseignement par correspondance.
tularemia [tu:læ'ri:miə], *s. Med: Vet:* tularémie *f.*
tule ['tu:li(:)], *s. Bot:* scirpe *m.*
tulip ['tju:lip], *s. Bot:* **1.** tulipe *f;* **t. grower,** tulipier *m,* tulipiste *m.* **2. t. tree,** tulipier *m;* **t. wood,** (i) (bois *m* de) tulipier; (ii) bois de rose.
tulipomania [tju:lipou'meiniə], *s. Hist:* tulipomanie *f.*
tulle [tju:l], *s. Tex:* tulle *m;* **t. embroidery,** broderie *f* sur tulle; **the t. industry,** l'industrie tullière.
tumble[1] ['tʌmbl], *s.* **1.** (*a*) culbute *f,* chute *f,* dégringolade *f;* **he had a nasty t.,** il a fait une rude chute, une mauvaise chute; (*b*) *P:* **to have a t. with a woman,** culbuter une femme; (*c*) *Dom.Ec:* **t. drier,** séchoir rotatif (à air chaud); *Fr.C:* sécheuse *f.* **2.** *Gym:* culbute (d'acrobate). **3.** désordre *m,* masse confuse; **everything was in a t.,** tout était en désordre; **a t. of rocks and trees,** (i) un désordre chaotique, (ii) un éboulis, de rochers et d'arbres. **4.** *N.Arch:* **t. home,** rentrée *f* (de la muraille); frégatage *m.*
tumble[2]. **1.** *v.i.* (*a*) **to t. (down, over),** tomber (par terre); faire une chute; culbuter, faire la culbute; **building that is tumbling down, tumbling to pieces,** édifice qui s'écroule, qui tombe en ruine; **her hair came tumbling down,** son chignon s'est défait tout d'un coup; **the river comes tumbling down,** la rivière dévale; (*b*) **to t. (about),** s'agiter; **to t. about in the water,** s'agiter dans l'eau; **to toss and t. (in bed),** s'agiter, se tourner et se retourner (dans son lit); (*c*) se jeter (précipitamment) (**into,** dans); **to t. into bed,** se jeter dans son lit; **to t. into one's clothes,** enfiler ses vêtements à la hâte; **to t. out of the window,** tomber par la fenêtre; **to t. out of bed,** (i) tomber de son lit; (ii) sauter (rapidement) du lit; **they were tumbling over one another,** ils se bousculaient; **he was tumbling over himself to please her,** il faisait tous ses efforts pour lui plaire; **to t. upstairs, downstairs,** trébucher en montant, en descendant, l'escalier; tomber du haut en bas de l'escalier; **to t. on sth.,** trouver qch. par hasard; (*d*) (*of acrobat, pigeon*) faire des culbutes; (*of acrobat*) faire ses tours; (*of projectile*) se renverser; (*e*) *F:* **to t. to an idea, to a fact,** comprendre, saisir, une idée; se rendre compte d'un fait; **d'you t. (to it)?** y êtes-vous? pigez-vous? **you've tumbled!** vous avez deviné! vous y êtes! (*f*) *N.Arch:* (*of ship*) **to t. home,** rentrer; avoir de la rentrée. **2.** *v.tr.* (*a*) **to t. sth., s.o., down, over,** culbuter, jeter à bas, renverser, faire tomber, faire rouler, qch., qn; **to t. everything into a box,** tout jeter pêle-mêle dans une boîte; (*b*) bouleverser, déranger; mettre en désordre; **to t. a bed,** mettre en désordre, défaire, un lit; *O:* **don't t. my hair,** ne m'ébouriffez pas; ne me décoiffez pas; **to t. s.o.'s dress,** chiffonner la robe de qn; (*c*) *P:* culbuter (une

femme); (*d*) *Metall:* dessabler (des pièces de fonte) au tonneau.

tumblebug ['tʌmb(ə)lbʌg], *s. Ent: NAm:* bousier *m*.

tumbled ['tʌmbld], *a. O:* **t. hair,** cheveux ébouriffés, en désordre; **t. dress,** robe chiffonnée, en désordre.

tumbledown ['tʌmb(ə)ldaun], *a.* croulant, délabré; qui menace ruine; **old t. house,** vieille maison décrépite, qui tombe en ruine(s); **t. wall,** mur à moitié écroulé.

tumbler ['tʌmblər], *s.* **1.** *A: (pers.)* jongleur *m*, acrobate *mf; A:* tombeur *m*. **2.** *Orn:* **t. (pigeon),** (pigeon) culbutant *m*. **3.** (*toy*) poussa(h) *m*, ramponneau *m*, bilboquet *m*, culbuteur *m*. **4.** verre *m* (à boire) sans pied; gobelet *m*. **5.** (*device*) (*a*) *El:* culbuteur *m* (d'interrupteur, etc.); (*b*) gorge *f* (mobile), arrêt *m* (de serrure); **t. lock,** serrure *f* à gorge(s); (*c*) **t. frame,** cœur *m* de renversement (d'un tour); (*d*) *Sm.a:* noix *f* (de platine); gâchette *f*; (*e*) *Nau:* mouilleur *m* (d'ancre); (*f*) *Hyd.E:* tambour *m* (d'une drague); (*g*) *Paperm:* (i) tambour *m* à décortication; (ii) cuve (tournante) de blanchiment; (iii) tambour culbuteur.

tumblerful ['tʌmbləful], *s.* plein verre (**of,** de).

tumbling[1] ['tʌmbliŋ], *a.* (*a*) croulant; (*b*) **t. stream,** ruisseau qui roule ses eaux, qui dévale en torrent; *Lit:* **t. billows,** flots agités.

tumbling[2], *s.* **1.** (*a*) culbute(s) *f(pl)*, chute(s) *f(pl)*; (*b*) *A:* tours *mpl* d'acrobate; acrobatie *f*. **2.** *Metall:* dessablage *m* au tonneau; **t. box, drum,** tonneau dessableur; tonneau à dessabler. **3.** *Paperm:* **t. machine,** tambour culbuteur. **4. t. shaft,** (i) *Mec.E:* arbre *m* à came(s); (ii) *Mch:* arbre de relevage, de changement de marche (de la distribution).

tumbrel ['tʌmbrəl], **tumbril** ['tʌmbril], *s. Hist:* charrette *f* (des condamnés).

tumefaction [tju:mi'fækʃ(ə)n], *s.* tuméfaction *f*.

tumefy ['tju:mifai]. **1.** *v.tr.* tuméfier. **2.** *v.i.* se tuméfier.

tumescence [tju:'mesəns], *s.* tumescence *f*, tuméfaction *f*.

tumescent [tju:'mesənt], *a.* tumescent.

tumid ['tju:mid], *a.* **1.** *Med:* enflé, gonflé. **2.** *Nat.Hist:* protubérant.

tumidity [tju:'miditi], *s.* **1.** *Med:* enflure *f*, gonflement *m*, turgescence *f*. **2.** *O:* enflure (de langage).

tummy ['tʌmi], *s. F:* (*a*) ventre *m*; **t. ache,** mal *m* de ventre; **to have t. ache,** avoir mal au ventre, à l'estomac; **to have t. trouble,** être sujet à des maux d'estomac; avoir des douleurs abdominales; avoir l'estomac dérangé; (*b*) bedaine *f*; **he's beginning to get a t.,** il commence à bâtir sur le devant, à prendre du ventre.

tumoral ['tju:mərəl], *a. Med:* tumoral, -aux.

tumorous ['tju:mərəs], *a. Med:* **1.** (excroissance) qui rentre dans la catégorie des tumeurs malignes; tumoral, -aux. **2.** affecté de tumeurs.

tumour ['tju:mər], *s. Med:* tumeur *f*; **indurated t.,** tumeur dure; **benign, malignant, t.,** tumeur bénigne, maligne; **false t.,** pseudo-tumeur *f*, *pl.* pseudo-tumeurs.

tumpline ['tʌmplain], *s. NAm:* sangle frontale.

tumular ['tju:mjulər], *a.* (*a*) en monticule, en tumulus; (*b*) (pierre *f*, etc.) tumulaire.

tumulary ['tju:mjuləri], *a.* tumulaire.

tumult ['tju:mʌlt], *s.* **1.** tumulte *m*; fracas *m*; **amid the t. of battle,** dans le fracas de la bataille. **2.** tumulte, agitation *f*, trouble *m*, émoi *m* (des passions).

tumultuous [tju'mʌltjuəs], *a.* tumultueux; **t. meeting,** réunion orageuse, assemblée houleuse; **t. crowds,** foules houleuses; **t. session,** séance mouvementée; *Ch:* **t. reaction,** réaction tumultueuse.

tumultuously [tju'mʌltjuəsli], *adv.* tumultueusement; en tumulte.

tumultuousness [tju'mʌltjuəsnis], *s.* nature tumultueuse (d'une réunion, etc.).

tumulus, *pl.* **-i** ['tju:mjuləs, -ai], *s.* tumulus *m*, *pl.* tumulus, tumuli.

tun[1] [tʌn], *s.* **1.** tonneau *m*, fût *m*; **the (great) t. of Heidelberg,** le foudre d'Heidelberg. **2.** *Brew:* cuve *f* (de fermentation).

tun[2], *v.tr.* **(tunned)** entonner, mettre en tonneaux (le vin, la bière).

tuna[1] ['t(j)u:nə], *s. Ich:* thon *m*; **bluefin t.,** thon rouge; **yellowfin t.,** albacore *m*; **blackfin t.,** patudo *m*.

tuna[2], *s. Bot:* tuna *m*, nopal *m*.

tundra ['tʌndrə], *s. Geog:* toundra *f*.

tune[1] [tju:n], *s.* **1.** air *m* (de musique); **to play a t.,** jouer un air; **to dance to a t.,** danser sur un air; **old song to a new t.,** vieille chanson sur un air nouveau; *F:* **give us a t.!** faites-nous un peu de musique! jouez-nous un air! **to call the t.,** donner la note; **to begin to sing (to) another t., to change one's t.,** changer de ton, de gamme, de langage; **to lower one's t.,** déchanter; *F: O:* **the t. the old cow died of,** (i) une vieille rengaine; (ii) des sons discordants; **to be fined to the t. of fifty pounds,** avoir une amende de cinquante livres; *F: O:* **we licked them to some t.!** nous les avons battus et comment! **2.** (*a*) *Mus:* accord *m*; **in t.,** (i) (*of note*) accordant; (ii) (*of instrument*) d'accord; **the piano is out of t.,** le piano est désaccordé, n'est pas d'accord; **to get out of t.,** (*of instrument*) se désaccorder, perdre l'accord; (*of band, choir, etc.*) se désaccorder, sortir du ton; (*of singer, player*) **to be out of t.,** détonner; (*of piano, etc.*) **to keep in t.,** tenir l'accord; **to sing in t., out of t.,** chanter juste, avec justesse; chanter faux; (*b*) *I.C.E:* **in perfect t.,** (moteur) au point. **3.** (*a*) accord, harmonie *f*; **to be in t. with s.o., with one's surroundings,** être en bon accord avec qn, avec son milieu; **to be out of t. with one's surroundings, with the times,** être en désaccord avec son environnement, avec son époque; (*b*) **to feel in t. for (doing) sth.,** se sentir en train, en bonne disposition, pour (faire) qch.; se sentir d'humeur à faire qch.

tune[2], *v.tr. & i.* **1.** *Mus:* accorder, mettre d'accord (un instrument); **to t. an instrument to concert pitch,** diapasonner un instrument; **to t. an instrument to a lower pitch,** baisser un instrument; (*of orchestra*) **to t. up,** s'accorder. **2.** *El: W.Tel: etc:* **to t. one circuit to another,** accorder, syntoniser, un circuit sur un autre; *W.Tel: etc:* **to t. in to Paris,** capter, prendre, Paris. **3.** *I.C.E: Mch: etc:* **to t. (up),** caler, régler, (re)mettre au point (un moteur); caler (une machine à vapeur, la magnéto); mettre au point (un yacht); *Tex:* appareiller (un métier à tisser); (*of engine*) **to be tuned (up),** être au point. **4.** *A:* jouer de (la lyre).

tuned [tju:nd], *a. El: etc:* **t. circuits,** circuits accordés, syntonisés; *Rec:* **t. amplifier,** amplificateur *m* à résonance.

tuneful ['tju:nful], *a.* mélodieux, harmonieux; **t. air, song,** mélodie, chanson, bien chantante.

tunefully ['tju:nfuli], *adv.* mélodieusement, harmonieusement.

tunefulness ['tju:nfulnis], *s.* qualité mélodieuse (d'un air, etc.).

tuneless ['tju:nlis], *a.* discordant; sans harmonie; (musique) sans mélodie.

tuner ['tju:nər], *s.* **1.** (*pers.*) (*a*) *Mus:* accordeur *m* (de pianos, etc.); (*b*) *Tex:* appareilleur *m* (de métiers à tisser); (*c*) *I.C.E: etc:* metteur *m* au point. **2.** (*device*) *W.Tel: etc:* syntonisateur *m*; tuner *m*; **t. amplifier,** *F:* **t. amp,** amplificateur-tuner *m*, ampli-tuner *m*.

tung [tʌŋ], *s. Bot:* **t. (tree),** abrasin *m*; **t. oil,** huile *f* d'abrasin, huile de Canton.

tungar ['tʌŋgər], *a. El:* **t. rectifier,** tungar *m*.

tungstate ['tʌŋsteit], *s. Ch:* tungstate *m*.

tungsten ['tʌŋstən], *s. Ch:* tungstène *m*, wolfram *m*; **t. lamp,** lampe *f* au tungstène; **t. steel,** acier *m* au tungstène.

tungstenite ['tʌŋstənait], *s. Miner:* tungsténite *f*.

tungstic ['tʌŋstik], *a. Ch:* tungstique; *Miner:* **t. ochre,** tungstite *f*.

tungstite ['tʌŋstait], *s. Miner:* tungstite *f*.

tungstosilicate [tʌŋstou'silikeit], *s. Ch:* tungstosilicate *m*.

tunic ['tju:nik], *s.* **1.** *Cost:* (*a*) tunique *f* (des peuples anciens, de soldat, etc.); (*b*) *Ecc:* = TUNICLE. **2.** *Nat.Hist:* tunique, enveloppe *f* (d'un organe); tunique (d'une ascidie).

tunica ['tju:nikə], *s. Anat:* tunique *f*.

Tunicata [tju:ni'keitə], *s.pl. Nat.Hist:* tuniciers *m*, uroc(h)ordés *m*.

tunicate[1] ['tju:nikeit], *s. Nat.Hist:* tunicier *m*.

tunicate[2], **tunicated** ['tju:nikeitid], *a. Nat.Hist:* tuniqué.

tunicle ['tju:nikl], *s. Ecc.Cost:* tunique *f*, tunicelle *f*; dalmatique *f*.

tuning ['tju:niŋ], *s.* **1.** *Mus:* accordage *m*, accordement *m*, accord *m* (d'un piano, d'un orgue, etc.); **fine t.,** accord précis; **t. fork,** diapason *m*; **t. hammer, t. key,** accordoir *m*; marteau *m*, clef *f*, d'accordage, d'accordeur; **t. peg, t. pin,** cheville *f* (d'un piano, d'un violon); **t. wire,** rasette *f* (de tuyau à anche d'un orgue). **2.** *I.C.E: Mch:* **t. (up),** calage *m*, réglage *m*; (re)mise *f* au point. **3.** *W.Tel: etc:* réglage de la tonalité, des tonalités; **t. in to a station,** accrochage *m* d'un poste; **t. dial,** cadran *m* d'accord.

Tunisia [tju:'niziə], *Pr.n. Geog:* Tunisie *f*.

Tunisian [tju:'niziən], (*a*) *a.* tunisien; (*b*) *s.* Tunisien, -ienne.

tunnel[1] ['tʌn(ə)l], *s.* **1.** (*a*) tunnel *m*; passage souterrain; *Min:* galerie *f* (d'accès) à flanc de coteau; **to drive a t. through a mountain,** percer un tunnel à travers, sous, une montagne; **the train stopped in the t.,** le train s'est arrêté sous le tunnel; *Mec: etc:* **wind t.,** tunnel aérodynamique; soufflerie *f*; *N.Arch:* **shaft t.,** tunnel de l'arbre; *El:* **cable t.,** galerie des câbles; (*b*) *Nat.Hist:* galerie (creusée par une taupe, etc.); (*c*) **t. vision,** rétrécissement *m* du champ visuel; *Pol: etc:* **it was a case of t. vision,** on regardait par le petit bout de la lorgnette. **2.** cuve *f*, vide *m* (de haut fourneau). **3. t. (net),** (i) *Ven: A:* tonnelle *f* (à prendre les perdrix, etc.); (ii) *Fish:* verveux *m*.

tunnel[2], *v.tr. & i.* **(tunnelled** ['tʌnld]) **1. to t. through, into, a hill,** percer un tunnel à travers, dans, sous, une colline; *F:* **we tunnelled our way through the snow,** nous nous sommes creusé un chemin à travers la neige, sous la neige; **rats had tunnelled under the foundations,** les rats avaient creusé des galeries sous les fondements, avaient miné les fondements; **moles can t. for a very long way,** les taupes peuvent creuser des galeries très longues. **2.** *Ven: A:* tonneler (des perdrix).

tunnelling ['tʌnəliŋ], *s.* **1.** (*a*) percement *m* d'un tunnel, de tunnels; (*b*) construction *f* d'une galerie de mine. **2.** *coll.* tunnels.

tunny ['tʌni], *s. Ich:* **t. (fish),** thon *m*; **bluefin t.,** thon rouge; **yellowfin t.,** albacore *m*; **blackfin t.,** patudo *m*; *Fish:* **t. boat,** thonier *m*; **t. net,** (i) madrague *f*; (ii) thonaire *f*.

tup[1] [tʌp], *s.* **1.** *Husb:* bélier *m*. **2.** *Tchn:* mouton *m*, pilon *m* (d'un marteau-pilon, d'une sonnette à battre les pieux).

tup[2], *v.* **(tupped) 1.** *v.tr.* (*of ram*) flécher (la brebis). **2.** *v.i.* (*a*) (*of ram, ewe*) béliner; (*b*) *P:* coïter (avec une femme).

Tupaiidae [t(j)u:'paiidi:], *s.pl. Z:* tupaiidés *m*.

tupelo ['t(j)u:pilou], *s. Bot:* nyssa *m*, tupélo *m*.

tuppence ['tʌp(ə)ns], *s. F: O:* = TWOPENCE; *A:* **t. coloured** = image *f* d'Épinal.

tuppenny ['tʌp(ə)ni], *a. F: O:* = TWOPENNY; **t. halfpenny** = TWOPENNY-HALFPENNY.

tuque [tju:k], *s. Cost:* tuque *f*.

turacin ['tju:rəsin], *s. Bio-Ch:* touracine *f*.

turaco ['t(j)u:rəkou], *s. Orn:* touraco *m*.

turban ['tə:bən], *s.* **1.** *Cost:* turban *m*. **2.** *Moll:* **t. (shell),** turbo *m*, turbinidé *m*; sabot *m*, turban. **3.** *Fung:* **t. top,** helvelle *f* (à turban). **4.** *Cu:* turban.

turbaned ['tə:bənd], *a.* turbané; à turban; coiffé d'un turban.

turbary ['tə:bəri], *s.* **1.** tourbière *f*. **2.** *Jur:* **(common of) t.,** droit *m* de prendre la tourbe; droit à la tourbe.

Turbellaria [tə:bi'lεəriə], *s.pl. Ann:* turbellariés *m*; planaires *f*.

turbellarian [tə:bi'lεəriən], *s. Ann:* turbellarié *m*.

turbid ['tə:bid], *a.* **1.** (liquide) trouble, bourbeux. **2.** (esprit) trouble, embrouillé, brouillon; **the t. depths of degradation,** l'abîme bourbeux de la dégradation.

turbidimeter [tə:bi'dimitər], *s.* turbidimètre *m*.

turbidimetric [tə:bidi'metrik], *a.* turbimétrique, turbidimétrique.

turbidimetry [tə:bi'dimitri], *s.* turbimétrie *f*, turbidimétrie *f*.

turbidity [tə:'biditi], **turbidness** ['tə:bidnis], *s.* état trouble, bourbeux; turbidité *f* (d'un liquide, d'esprit).

turbinal, turbinate(d) ['tə:binəl, -neit(id)]. **1.** *a. Nat.Hist:* turbiné. **2.** *a. & s. Anat:* **turbinal, turbinate (bone),** os turbiné; cornet *m* (du nez).

turbine ['tə:bain], *s.* **1.** turbine *f*; **compound t.,** turbine multi-rotors; **axial-flow t.,** turbine à débit, à écoulement, axial; **contra-flow t.,** turbine à débit, à écoulement, inverse; **inward-flow t.,** turbine centripète; **outward-flow t.,** turbine centrifuge; **radial-flow t.,** turbine à débit, à écoulement, radial: **tangential-flow t.,** turbine tangentielle; **cooling t.,** turbine de réfrigérateur; **reheat t.,** turbine à postcombustion; **ducted-fan t.,** turbine à ventilateur extérieur; **propeller t.,** turbine à hélice; **feathering-propeller t.,** turbine à pales mobiles; **geared t.,** turbine à engrenage; **impulse t.,** turbine à action, à impulsion; **reaction t.,** turbine à réaction; **gas t.,** turbine à gaz; **hydraulic, water, t.,** turbine hydraulique, à eau; **wind t.,** turbine éolienne; **steam t.,** turbine à vapeur; **ram-air t.,** turbine à air dynamique; **t. stage,** étage *m* de turbine; **velocity-stage t.,** turbine à étage de vitesse; **multistage t.,** turbine à étages; **two-stage, three-stage, t.,** turbine à deux, à trois, étages; **pressure-stage t.,** turbine à étage de pression; **t. engine,** moteur *m*, réacteur *m*, à turbine; turbomoteur *m*; **t. disc,** disque *m* de turbine; **t. rotor,** rotor *m* de turbine; **t. shaft,** arbre *m* de turbine; **t. wheel,** roue *f* de turbine; **t. nozzle,** tuyère *f* de turbine; **t. nozzle ring,** diffuseur *m* annulaire de turbine; **t. fuel,** turbocombustible *m*. **2.** *Sug.-R:* turbine, séparateur *m* centrifuge.

Turbinidae [tə:'binidi:], *s.pl. Moll:* turbinidés *m*.

turbiniform [tə:'binifɔ:m], *a. Nat.Hist:* turbiniforme, turbiné.

turbit ['tə:bit], *s. Orn:* pigeon cravaté, à cravate.

turbiteen ['tə:biti:n], *a. Orn:* (pigeon) turbitéen.

turbo, *pl.* **turbines** ['tə:bou, -bini:z], *s. Moll:* turbo *m*.

turbo- ['tə:bou], *pref.* turbo-.

turboalternator [tə:bou'ɔ:ltəneitər], *s. El:* turboalternateur *m*.

turboblower ['tə:boublouər], *s*. turbosoufflante *f*, turbosouffleuse *f*.

turbocharger ['tə:boutʃɑ:dʒər], *s*. *Av:* turbocompresseur *m* (sur gaz d'échappement).

turbocompressor [tə:boukəm'presər], *s*. *Mec.E: Av:* turbocompresseur *m*.

turbodrilling [tə:bou'driliŋ], *s*. *Min:* turboforage *m*.

turbodynamo [tə:bou'dainəmou], *s*. *El:* turbodynamo *f*.

turbo-electric [tə:boui'lektrik], *a*. (propulsion, etc.) turbo-électrique.

turbofan ['tə:boufæn], *s*. (*a*) *Av:* turboréacteur *m* à double flux; (*b*) *Mec.E:* turbine *f* à gaz à ventilateur auxiliaire.

turbofuel ['tə:boufjuəl], *s*. turbocombustible *m*.

turbogenerator [tə:bou'dʒenəreitər], *s*. *El:* turbogénérateur *m*, turbogénératrice *f*.

turbojet ['tə:boudʒet], *s*. *Av:* turboréacteur *m* (à simple flux); **two-spool t.**, turboréacteur à simple flux et à double corps.

turbo(-)mechanical [tə:boumi'kænikl], *a*. (propulsion) turbo-mécanique.

turbomotor ['tə:boumoutər], *s*. *Mch:* turbomoteur *m*.

turbonuclear [tə:bou'nju:kliər], *a*. (générateur) turbonucléaire.

turboprop ['tə:bouprɔp], *a*. & *s*. **t. (aircraft)**, avion *m* à turbopropulseur.

turbopropeller [tə:bouprə'pelər], *s*. *Av:* turbopropulseur *m*; **t. aircraft**, avion *m* à turbopropulseur.

turbopump ['tə:boupʌmp], *s*. *Mch:* turbopompe *f*; pompe *f* turbine; pompe centrifuge à diffuseur.

turboramjet [tə:bou'ræmdʒet], *s*. *Av:* turbostatoréacteur *m*.

turboreaction [tə:bouri'ækʃ(ə)n], *s*. turboréaction *f*.

turboshaft ['tə:bouʃɑ:ft], *s*. turbomachine *f*.

turbosupercharged [tə:bou'su:pətʃɑ:dʒd], *a*. (*of aircraft, etc.*) équipé d'un turbocompresseur sur gaz d'échappement.

turbosupercharger [tə:bou'su:pətʃɑ:dʒər], *s*. turbocompresseur *m* sur gaz d'échappement.

turbot ['tə:bət], *s*. *Ich:* turbot *m*; **spiny t.**, turbot épineux; **young t.**, turbotin *m*; **t. kettle**, turbotière *f*.

turbotrain ['tə:boutrein], *s*. *Rail:* turbotrain *m*.

turboventilator [tə:bou'ventileitər], *s*. turboventilateur *m*.

turbulence ['tə:bjuləns], *s*. **1.** (*a*) turbulence *f*, trouble *m*, tumulte *m*, agitation *f*; (*b*) indiscipline *f*. **2.** *I.C.E:* **(high) t. combustion chamber**, chambre *f* de combustion à (haute) turbulence; **high t. engine**, moteur *m* à haute turbulence. **3.** *Meteor: Av:* turbulence, remous *m* d'air.

turbulent ['tə:bjulənt], *a*. **1.** (*a*) turbulent, tumultueux; **t. sea**, mer tourmentée; (*b*) insubordonné. **2.** *I.C.E:* **t. cylinder head**, culasse *f* à turbulence. **3.** *Meteor: Av:* turbulent, agité, à turbulence; **t. air, atmosphere**, air agité, atmosphère agitée; *Av:* **t. boundary layer**, couche-limite *f* tourbillonnaire; **t. flow**, écoulement turbulent; **t. wake**, sillage turbulent.

turbulently ['tə:bjuləntli], *adv*. d'une manière turbulente; tumultueusement.

Turcoman, *pl*. **-mans** ['tə:koumæn, -mænz], *s*. = TURKMEN.

turcopole ['tə:koupoul], *s*. *Hist:* turcopole *m*.

turd [tə:d], *s*. *P:* (*not in polite use*) **1.** (*a*) étron *m*; merde *f*; (*b*) crotte *f* (de mouton, etc.). **2.** saligaud *m*; salaud *m*, salope *f*; couillon, -onne.

Turdidae ['tə:didi:], *s.pl*. *Orn:* turdidés *m*.

Turdinae ['tə:dini:], *s.pl*. *Orn:* turdinés *m*.

turdoid ['tə:dɔid], *a*. *Orn:* turdoïde.

tureen [tjuə'ri:n, tə'ri:n], *s*. **(soup) t.**, soupière *f*.

turf[1], *pl*. **turves, turfs** [tə:f, tə:vz, tə:fs], *s*. (*a*) (i) gazon *m*; (ii) motte *f* de gazon; **to cut t.**, lever des gazons, des mottes de gazon; **t. cutting**, dégazonnage *m*, dégazonnement *m*; **t. cutter**, dégazonneuse *f*, tranche-gazon *m inv*, coupe-gazon *m inv*; (*b*) (*in Ireland*) tourbe *f*; **a t. of peat**, une motte de tourbe; **t. moor**, (i) marais tourbeux; (ii) tourbière *f*; **t. cutting**, extraction *f* de la tourbe; (*c*) *Rac:* **the t.**, le turf, les courses *f* de chevaux; le monde des courses; **t. accountant**, bookmaker *m*; (*d*) *Tls:* **t. beetle**, batte *f* de terrassier.

turf[2], *v.tr*. **1.** gazonner (un terrain). **2.** *F:* **to t. s.o. out**, flanquer qn à la porte.

turfing ['tə:fiŋ], *s*. gazonnement *m*.

turfy ['tə:fi], *a*. (*a*) gazonné; couvert de gazon; (*b*) (*in Ireland*) tourbeux.

turgescence [tə:'dʒesəns], *s*. **1.** *Med: Bot:* turgescence *f*. **2.** emphase *f*.

turgescent [tə:'dʒesənt], *a*. **1.** turgescent; boursouflé, enflé. **2.** (*style*) emphatique, boursouflé, ampoulé.

turgid ['tə:dʒid], *a*. **1.** turgide, enflé, gonflé. **2.** (style, etc.) boursouflé, ampoulé.

turgidity [tə:'dʒiditi], *s*. **1.** enflure *f*, gonflement *m*; *Med:* turgescence *f*. **2.** boursouflure *f*, enflure, emphase *f* (de style, etc.).

turgidly ['tə:dʒidli], *adv*. avec emphase; emphatiquement.

turgor ['tə:gɔ:r], *s*. *Med: Bot:* turgescence *f*.

turion ['tju:riən], *s*. *Bot:* turion *m*; bourgeon *m* (d'asperge, etc.).

Turk [tə:k], *s*. (*a*) Turc, *f*. Turque; *Hist:* **the Grand T.**, le Grand Turc; (*b*) *F:* tyran *m*; **to turn T.**, faire le méchant; **he's a young T.**, c'est un petit démon, un enfant terrible; (*c*) *Bot:* **Turk's cap (lily)**, martagon *m*, *F:* turban *m*; **Turk's cap (cactus)**, mélocacte *m*; (*d*) *F:* **Turk's head**, (i) (*long broom*) tête-de-loup *f*, *pl*. têtes-de-loup; (ii) (*knot*) nœud *m* de bonnet turc; tête *f* de Maure, de Turc; (iii) *Mil: A:* tête de Turc, de Maure (pour exercices au sabre).

Turkestan [tə:kis'tɑ:n], *Pr.n*. *Geog:* Turkestan *m*.

Turkey[1] ['tə:ki], *Pr.n*. (*a*) *Geog:* Turquie *f*; **T. in Europe, in Asia**, la Turquie d'Europe, d'Asie; (*b*) **T. red**, rouge *m* d'Andrinople, rouge turc (*inv*); **T. carpet**, tapis *m* d'Orient, de Turquie, de Smyrne; **T. leather**, cuir chamoisé; **T. stone**, pierre *f* du Levant; novaculite *f*; coticule *f*; pierre à morfiler.

turkey[2], *s*. (*a*) *Orn:* **t. (cock)**, dindon *m*; **hen t.**, dinde *f*; **t. poult, young t.**, dindonneau *m*; **wild t.**, dindon sauvage; **ocellated t.**, dindon ocellé; (*b*) *Orn:* **water t.**, anhinga *m*, oiseau-serpent *m*; **brush t.**, mégapode *m* de Latham; **t. buzzard, t. vulture**, catharte *m* (aura), vautour *m* aura, *Fr.C:* vautour à tête rouge; (*c*) *Cu:* dinde, dindonneau; *F:* **to talk t.**, parler franchement, ne pas ménager ses mots; en venir aux faits; *P:* **cold t.**, (i) sevrage abrupt de drogues; (ii) *esp. U.S:* (*pers.*) pisse-froid *m*; (*d*) *Bot:* **t. grass**, gratteron *m*; gaillet accrochant.

Turkish ['tə:kiʃ]. **1.** *a*. turc, *f*. turque; de Turquie; *Hist:* **the T. Empire**, l'Empire *m* ottoman, du Croissant; *Com:* **T. cigarettes**, cigarettes *f* d'Orient; **T. delight**, rahat-lo(u)koum *m*; **T. carpet**, tapis *m* d'Orient, de Smyrne, de Turquie.

Turkmen ['tə:kmen]. **1.** *Ethn:* (*a*) *a*. turkmène, turcoman, turkoman; (*b*) *s*. Turkmène *mf*, Turcoman, -ane, Turkoman, -ane. **2.** *s*. *Ling:* turkmène *m*, turcoman *m*, turkoman *m*.

Turkmenian [tə:k'meniən], *a*. turkmène, turcoman, turkoman.

Turkmenistan [tə:kmeni'stɑ:n], *s*. *Geog:* Turkménistan *m*, Turkménie *f*.

Turkoman, *pl*. **-mans** ['tə:koumæn, -mænz], *s*. = TURKMEN.

turmeric ['tə:mərik], *s*. **1.** *Bot:* curcuma *m*. **2.** *Ch: Dy: etc:* curcuma; safran *m* des Indes; terre-mérite *f*; **t. paper**, papier *m* (de) curcuma.

turmoil ['tə:mɔil], *s*. (*a*) trouble *m*, tumulte *m*, désordre *m*, agitation *f*; **the whole town is in a t.**, toute la ville est agitée, est en ébullition; **the t. of politics**, la tourmente politique, le tumulte de la politique; (*b*) remous *m* (des eaux); tourbillon *m*.

turn[1] [tə:n], *s*. **1.** tour *m*, révolution *f* (d'une roue); *Nau: Av:* tour (d'hélice); **t. bench**, tour d'horloger; tour à archet; **a t. of Fortune's wheel**, un revirement du sort; **with a t. of the wrist**, avec un tour de poignet; **with a sharp t. of the handle**, en tournant brusquement la poignée; **to give another t. to the screw**, serrer la vis (à qn); **the meat is done to a t.**, la viande est cuite à point. **2.** (*a*) changement *m* de direction; virage *m*; *Nau:* giration *f*; **to finish a t.**, achever une giration; *Aut: Av:* **to take a short t.**, virer court; *Av:* **aileron t.**, tonneau *m* en descendant; **t. and bank indicator**, contrôleur *m* de virage; *Aut:* **sharp t.**, virage à la corde; **to make a t. to the right**, tourner à droite; **no right, left, t.**, défense de tourner à droite, à gauche; **U turn**, demi-tour *m*; **no U turns**, demi-tour interdit; **three-point t.**, demi-tour en trois mouvements; *Ski:* **kick t.**, virage en plaine; conversion *f*; **Christiania t.**, virage de Christiania; **snowplough t.**, virage en chasse-neige; **telemark t.**, virage de télémark; **at every t.**, à tout moment, à tout bout de champ, à tout propos; (*b*) tournure *f* (des affaires); **to take a tragic t.**, tourner au tragique; **to take a t. for the better**, prendre meilleure tournure, une meilleure allure; s'améliorer; **the patient has taken a t. for the better, for the worse**, l'état du malade s'est amélioré, a empiré; **the weather has taken a t. for the worse**, le temps se gâte; **the conversation took a new t.**, la discussion a pris une nouvelle tournure; (*c*) **t. of the tide**, étale *m*; changement, renverse *f*, renversement *m*, de la marée; virement *m* d'eau; **the tide is on the t.**, la marée change, est étale; **the milk is on the t.**, le lait est en train de tourner; **t. of the scale**, trait *m* de balance; **at the t. of the century**, au tournant du siècle; **at the t. of the month**, (i) à la fin du mois; (ii) avec le nouveau mois; (*d*) *Fin:* **t. of the market, jobbers' t.**, écart *m* entre le prix d'achat et celui de vente; (*e*) *F:* choc *m*, coup *m*; **it gave me quite a t.**, cela, ça, m'a donné un (vrai) coup, m'a bouleversé, m'a donné des émotions; **you gave me such a t.!** vous m'avez donné une belle peur! (*f*) *F:* **she had one of her turns**, elle a eu une de ses crises, de ses attaques. **3.** tour, petite promenade; **to take a t. in the garden**, faire un tour, vingt pas, dans le jardin; **he took a few turns up and down the deck**, il a fait les cent pas sur le pont. **4.** (*a*) tour (de rôle); **it's your t.**, c'est votre tour; c'est à vous (de jouer); **have a t.!** essayez donc! **each in his t., t. and t. about**, chacun (à) son tour; **it will be my t. some day**, (i) mon tour viendra, (ii) je prendrai ma revanche, un de ces jours; **in t.**, tour à tour; à tour de rôle; alternativement; **I'll serve you all in t.**, je vous servirai chacun à votre tour; **to drink in t.**, boire à la ronde; **laughing and crying in t.**, alternant les rires et les pleurs; **to speak out of one's t.**, parler avant son tour, mal à propos; **to take turns with s.o.**, relayer qn; **they take it in turns driving, to drive**, ils se relaient au volant; ils conduisent à tour de rôle; **to take one's t.**, prendre son tour; (*b*) *Th:* numéro *m* (de music-hall, etc.); **short t.**, flash *m*. **5.** (*a*) **to do s.o. a good t.**, rendre (un) service à qn; **to do s.o. a bad t.**, jouer un mauvais tour à qn; **to owe s.o. a good t.**, avoir des obligations envers qn; **t. for t.!** un service en vaut un autre; *Prov:* **one good t. deserves another**, à beau jeu beau retour; à charge de revanche; un service en vaut un autre; (*b*) intention *f*, but *m*; **it will serve my t.**, cela fera mon affaire (pour le moment). **6.** (*a*) disposition *f*; **humorous t. of mind**, esprit *m* humoristique; **to have a t. for sth.**, avoir un goût naturel pour qch.; être doué pour qch.; (*b*) forme *f*; **t. of phrase**, tournure de phrase; (*c*) **to have a good t. of speed**, (i) (*of car*) être rapide; rouler vite; (ii) (*of horse*) être capable de fournir un effort à grande allure. **7.** (*a*) tournant *m*, coude *m* (d'un chemin, etc.); **(sharp) t.**, virage; **twists and turns**, tours et détours; (*b*) tour (d'une corde); serpentement *m*; tour, spire *f* (d'une spirale); *Nau:* **take a t. round the cleat!** tournez au taquet! **round t. and two half hitches**, un tour et deux demi-clefs. **8.** *Mus:* gruppetto *m*, *pl*. gruppetti. **9.** *Typ:* caractère retourné; blocage *m*.

turn[2], *v*.

I. *v.tr*. **1.** (faire) tourner (une roue, une manivelle); (faire) tourner, faire jouer (une clef dans la serrure); **this key is hard to t.**, cette clef ne joue pas bien; **to t. the key in the lock**, donner un tour de clef à la porte; (*with passive force*) **the tap won't t.**, le robinet ne marche pas, ne tourne pas; **to t. the knife in the wound**, retourner le fer dans la plaie; **to t. the gas low**, mettre le gaz en veilleuse. **2.** tourner, retourner; **to t. (over) a page**, tourner une page; **freshly turned soil**, terre fraîchement retournée; **to t. the mattress**, retourner le matelas; **to t. a garment inside out**, retourner un vêtement; **my umbrella's turned inside out**, mon parapluie s'est retourné; **to t. everything upside down**, mettre tout sens dessus-dessous; **to t. the hay, an omelette**, retourner le foin, une omelette; **he turned the body over**, il a retourné le corps; **wood that turns the edge of the axe**, bois qui fait rebrousser la hache; *F:* **he didn't t. a hair**, il n'a pas bronché, sourcillé, tiqué; **onions t. me, t. my stomach**, les oignons m'écœurent, me donnent des nausées, me soulèvent le cœur. **3. there isn't room to t. the car**, il n'y a pas assez de place pour tourner la voiture; **to t. one's horse**, faire faire demi-tour à son cheval; **to t. one's horse to the right**, diriger son cheval à droite; **he turned his steps towards home**, il a dirigé ses pas vers la maison; **he never turned anyone from his door**, il n'a jamais renvoyé personne (de sa porte); **to t. a vessel from her course**, détourner un navire de sa route; **to t. (aside, away) a blow**, détourner, faire dévier, un coup; **to t. the conversation**, donner un autre tour à la conversation; orienter la conversation vers d'autres sujets; **to t. one's thoughts to God**, tourner ses pensées vers Dieu; se recueillir. **4.** tourner, retourner (la tête); tourner, diriger (les yeux) (vers qch.); **t. your face this way**, tournez-vous de ce côté; regardez de ce côté; **to t. a telescope on a star**, braquer une lunette sur une étoile. **5. they turned the laughter, his argument, against him**, ils ont retourné les rires, son argument, contre lui; **he turns everyone against him**, il se met tout le monde à dos. **6.** (*a*) **to t. the corner**, (i) tourner le coin; (ii) passer le moment critique; *Mil:* **to t. the enemy's flank, position**, tourner le flanc, la position, de l'ennemi; **to t. (aside) a difficulty**, tourner une difficulté; (*b*) **he's turned forty**, il a quarante ans passés; il a passé, franchi le cap de, la quarantaine; **Louise has just turned four**, Louise vient d'avoir quatre ans; **it's turned seven**, il est sept heures passées. **7.** (*a*) changer, convertir, transformer (**into**, en); **to t. the water into wine**, changer l'eau en vin; **his love turned to hate**, son amour s'est changé, s'est transformé, a tourné, en haine; **the drawing room was turned into a study,** on a transformé le salon en cabinet de travail; **to t. a theatre into a cinema,** convertir un théâtre en cinéma; **they turned her into a film star,** on l'a métamorphosée en vedette de cinéma; **our soldiers have been turned into a police force,** on a fait de nos soldats un corps de police; **to t. a partnership into a limited company,** transformer en société anonyme une société à nom collectif; **to t. one's land into money,** convertir ses terres en argent; *O:* **to t. a passage into French,** traduire un passage en français; (*b*) faire devenir; rendre; **the heat has turned the milk sour,** la chaleur a fait tourner le lait; **autumn turns the leaves yellow,** l'automne fait jaunir les feuilles; **the very thought (of it) made him t. pale,** cette seule pensée l'a fait pâlir; (*c*) **success has turned his head,** le succès lui a tourné la tête; **grief has turned his brain,** le chagrin lui a tourné la cervelle, l'a rendu fou. **8.** (*a*) tourner, façonner au tour (un pied de table, etc.); **turned in one piece with . . .,** venu de tour avec . . .; (*with passive force*) **metal that turns well,** métal qui se travaille bien au tour; **well turned leg,** jambe qui a du galbe; **well turned sentence,** phrase bien tournée; **to t. a compliment,** tourner un compliment; (*b*) *Knit:* **to t. a heel,** faire le talon.

II. *v.i.* **1.** (*a*) tourner; **the wheel turns,** la roue tourne; **to t. a complete circle,** virer un cercle complet; *Cr: etc:* **to make the ball t.,** donner de l'effet à la balle; **my head's turning,** la tête me tourne; **the door was turning on its hinges,** la porte tournait, roulait, pivotait, sur ses gonds; (*b*) **everything turns on your answer,** tout dépend de votre réponse; **our whole policy turned on this alliance,** cette alliance était le pivot de toute notre politique; **the conversation turned on a variety of subjects,** la conversation a roulé, a porté, sur une variété de sujets. **2.** (*a*) **to toss and t.,** se tourner et se retourner (dans son lit); *F:* **when father says t. we all t.,** il fait la pluie et le beau temps chez lui; (*b*) (*of edge of tool*) **to t. (up, over),** se rebrousser; (*c*) **to t. upside down,** se retourner. **3.** se tourner, se retourner; **to t. short,** se retourner tout à coup; **he turned towards me,** il s'est tourné de mon côté; **he turned to look at the landscape,** il s'est retourné pour regarder le paysage; *Th:* **he turns as if to go,** il va pour sortir; fausse sortie; *Mil:* **right t.! left t.!** à droite! à gauche! par le flanc droit, gauche! **4.** (*a*) tourner, se diriger; **the path turns to the left,** le chemin tourne à gauche; **he turned to the left,** il a tourné, a pris, à gauche; **he turned towards home,** il s'est dirigé vers la maison; **I turned down the avenue,** j'ai pris par l'avenue; *Nau:* **to t. to the east,** venir cap à l'est; **to t. sixteen points, to t. a half circle,** virer de bord cap pour cap; venir de seize quarts; décrire un demi-cercle; **the wind is turning,** le vent change; (*b*) se diriger (vers qch.); s'adresser (à qn); **my thoughts often t. to this subject,** mes réflexions se portent souvent sur ce sujet; je pense souvent à ce sujet; **to t. to another subject,** passer à une autre question; **to t. to the dictionary,** consulter le dictionnaire; **I don't know where, which way, to t.,** je ne sais pas de quel côté (me) tourner, où donner de la tête, à quel saint me vouer; **I didn't know to whom to t.,** je ne savais pas à qui m'adresser; **she turned to God in her suffering,** dans ses souffrances elle s'est tournée vers Dieu; **he turned to work (in order) to forget his worries,** il s'est mis à travailler pour oublier ses soucis. **5.** (*a*) **the tide is turning,** la marée change; **his luck has turned,** sa chance a tourné; (*b*) **to t. against s.o.,** se retourner contre qn. **6.** (*a*) se changer, se convertir, se transformer (**into,** en); **caterpillars t. into butterflies,** la chenille se transforme en papillon; **it is turning to rain,** le temps se met à la pluie; **the snow turned (in)to rain, into slush,** la neige s'est tournée en pluie, s'est convertie en boue; **everything he touches turns to gold,** tout ce qu'il touche se change en or; **it was turning to tragedy,** cela tournait au tragique; (*b*) **to t. acid,** tourner au vinaigre; (*of milk*) **to t. (sour),** tourner; **it's turning cold,** le temps tourne au froid, il commence à faire froid; **the leaves are beginning to t.,** les feuilles commencent à tourner, à jaunir; **the reds have turned to brown,** les rouges ont tourné au brun; **he turned red,** il a rougi; *Ch:* **to t. red, blue,** virer au rouge, au bleu; **ink that turns black in drying,** encre qui vire au noir en séchant; **to t. all colours of the rainbow,** passer par toutes les couleurs de l'arc-en-ciel; (*c*) **to t. sulky,** devenir maussade; **to t. socialist,** devenir socialiste; **to t. catholic,** embrasser le catholicisme; *O:* **to t. soldier,** se faire soldat.

III. (*compound verbs*) **1. turn around,** *v.tr. & i. esp. NAm:* = TURN ROUND.

2. turn away. (*a*) *v.tr.* (i) détourner (la tête, les yeux, etc.); (ii) détourner, écarter; *B:* **a soft answer turneth away wrath,** une réponse douce apaise la fureur; (iii) renvoyer (qn); *Th: etc:* **to t. people away,** refuser du monde; (*b*) *v.i.* (i) se détourner; **to t. away from s.o.,** (α) tourner le dos à qn; (β) délaisser, abandonner, qn; (ii) s'en aller; *Navy:* se dérober (**from,** à).

3. turn back. (*a*) *v.tr.* (i) faire rebrousser chemin à (qn); faire faire demi-tour à (qn); faire revenir (qn) sur ses pas; (ii) rabattre (son col, etc.); (iii) *Nau:* dévirer (le treuil, etc.); (*b*) *v.i.* rebrousser chemin; retourner sur ses pas; se retourner; faire demi-tour.

4. turn down, *v.tr.* (*a*) rabattre (un col); plier, corner (la page d'un livre); **to t. down the bed,** faire la couverture; ouvrir le lit; (*b*) *Cards:* renverser (une carte) (face à la table); (*c*) baisser (le gaz, la radio, etc.); (*d*) repousser (une offre); refuser (un candidat, etc.); écarter (une réclamation); *F:* **she turned me down flat,** elle m'a refusé catégoriquement.

5. turn in. (*a*) *v.tr.* (i) **to t. in one's toes,** tourner les pieds en dedans; (ii) *F:* rendre, rapporter (qch.); **to t. in an old car, (etc.),** échanger une vieille voiture contre une nouvelle; (iii) *F:* quitter, abandonner (son emploi); (iv) *F: esp. U.S:* livrer, vendre (qn) à la police; (v) *Sp: Th: etc:* **to t. in a good score, performance, etc.,** bien réussir; (*b*) *v.i.* (i) **his toes t. in,** il a les pieds tournés en dedans; (ii) **he turned in at the gate,** arrivé à la porte, il est entré; (iii) *F:* se coucher, se pieuter.

6. turn off. (*a*) *v.tr.* (i) fermer, couper (l'eau, le gaz); arrêter (l'eau); éteindre (le gaz, l'électricité); couper, arrêter (la vapeur); fermer (un robinet); **to t. off the radio,** fermer, arrêter, la radio; (ii) renvoyer, congédier (des ouvriers); (iii) *Tchn:* enlever (des inégalités, etc.) au tour; (iv) *P:* **he turns me off,** il me dégoûte; (*b*) *v.i.* (i) changer de route; tourner (à droite, à gauche); **I turned off to the left,** j'ai pris (la route) à gauche; j'ai tourné à gauche; **we t. off here for Dover,** c'est ici que nous prenons la route de Douvres; (ii) **we turned off the main road,** nous avons quitté la grande route; **a small street turning off the High Street,** une petite rue qui fait coin, fait angle, avec la Grande Rue.

7. turn on. (*a*) *v.tr.* donner (la vapeur, le courant); ouvrir, faire couler (l'eau); ouvrir (le robinet); allumer, ouvrir (le gaz); allumer (l'électricité); **shall I t. on the light?** voulez-vous que j'allume? **to t. on the fountains,** faire jouer les eaux; **I must t. on the bath for baby,** je vais préparer le bain du bébé; (*b*) *v.i.* **to t. on s.o.,** attaquer qn; se retourner contre qn; s'en prendre à qn; (*c*) *v.tr. & i.* **to t. s.o. on,** (i) *F:* éveiller l'intérêt, la curiosité, de qn; (ii) *P:* exciter qn (sexuellement); (iii) *P:* initier qn (par une première piqûre) à la drogue; *P:* **to t. on,** fumer de la marijuana; prendre une drogue; se droguer; *P:* **to be turned on,** être chargé (par les drogues, etc.).

8. turn out. (*a*) *v.tr.* (i) mettre, *F:* flanquer (qn) à la porte; déloger, évincer (un locataire); **to be turned out of one's job,** perdre son emploi; **t. him out!** à la porte! (ii) mettre (le bétail) au vert; (iii) *Nau:* réveiller (les hommes); *Mil:* alerter (les troupes); **to t. out the guard,** faire sortir la garde; mettre la garde sous les armes; **t. out the guard!** à la garde! (iv) **to t. out a room,** nettoyer une pièce à fond; **to t. out a drawer,** mettre de l'ordre dans un tiroir; **I was busy turning out papers from my desk,** j'étais occupé à trier les paperasses qui encombraient mon bureau; **to t. out one's pockets,** vider, retourner, ses poches; (v) *Cu:* démouler (une crème, etc.); (vi) couper, éteindre (le gaz, l'électricité); **don't forget to t. out the light!** n'oubliez pas d'éteindre (l'électricité)! (vii) produire, fabriquer (des marchandises); **turned out by the dozen,** confectionnés à la douzaine; (viii) (*of pers.*) **well turned out,** élégant, soigné; (ix) **to t. one's toes out,** tourner les pieds en dehors; (*b*) *v.i.* (i) sortir; **the whole town turned out to see it,** toute la ville est sortie pour le voir, le regarder; **the guard is turning out,** la garde sort; **guard t. out!** aux armes! (ii) *F:* se lever, sortir du lit; (iii) **his toes t. out,** il a les pieds tournés en dehors; (iv) **to t. out well,** bien tourner, réussir; **to t. out badly,** mal tourner, mal réussir; **it will t. out all right,** cela s'arrangera; **I don't know how it will t. out,** je ne sais pas comment cela finira, quelle en sera l'issue, à quoi cela aboutira; **as it turned out,** comme il est arrivé; en l'occurrence; **it turned out that . . .,** il est advenu que . . .; **she's turned out (to be) beautiful,** elle est devenue belle; **the weather turned out fine,** il a fait beau (temps); (v) **he turned out to be the son of an old friend of mine,** il s'est trouvé qu'il était le fils d'un de mes anciens amis; **he turned out to be a bore,** je l'ai trouvé, nous l'avons trouvé, assommant; **it turns out that . . .,** il apparaît, il se trouve, que . . .; **it turned out to be true,** cela est donc vrai.

9. turn over. (*a*) *v.tr.* (i) retourner (qch.); tourner (une page); **to t. over the pages of a book,** feuilleter un livre; **please t. over,** tournez s'il vous plaît; *Agr:* **to t. over the soil,** retourner le sol; **to t. over a field,** verser un champ; **to t. (sth.) over in one's mind,** ruminer (une idée); délibérer (une question); retourner (un projet) dans sa tête; (ii) **to t. sth. over to s.o.,** transférer, référer, qch. à qn; remettre qch. entre les mains de qn; **the thief was turned over to the police,** on a remis le voleur entre les mains de la police; (iii) *Typ:* faire sauter (un mot, une lettre); (*b*) *v.i.* se tourner, se retourner; **the dog turned over onto his back,** le chien s'est renversé sur le dos.

10. turn round. (*a*) *v.tr.* retourner (qch., qn); (*b*) *v.i.* (i) tourner; (*of crane, etc.*) virer, pivoter; (ii) tourner, se tourner, se retourner; faire volte-face; (*in one's opinions, etc.*) tourner casaque, (re)virer de bord; (*of horse*) **to t. round suddenly,** se replier; **to t. round to (face) s.o.,** se retourner vers qn; **t. round and let me see your face,** tournez-vous (un peu) que je voie votre visage; *F:* **I haven't time to t. round,** je n'ai pas le temps de me retourner; (iii) (*of ship in port*) se retourner; (iv) **to t. round on s.o.,** se retourner contre qn; s'en prendre à qn.

11. turn up. (*a*) *v.tr.* (i) relever (le col de son pardessus); retrousser (ses manches); *F:* **to t. up one's nose at sth.,** renifler sur qch.; faire le dédaigneux, le dégoûté; *P:* **to t. up one's toes,** mourir, casser sa pipe; (ii) retourner (le sol, une carte); déterrer (qch.); **I've just turned up a photograph of your mother,** je viens de découvrir une photo de votre mère; (iii) trouver, se reporter à (une citation, etc.); **to t. up a word in the dictionary,** chercher un mot dans le dictionnaire; (iv) *F:* **it (positively) turns me up!** ça m'écœure, me fait vomir! *P:* **t. it up!** arrête! ta gueule! j'en ai marre! (v) remonter (une mèche, une lampe); monter (le gaz); **to t. up the radio,** mettre la radio plus fort; (*b*) *v.i.* (i) se relever, se replier; (*of edge of tool*) se rebrousser; **his nose turns up,** il a le nez retroussé; (ii) **the ten of diamonds turned up,** le dix de carreau est sorti; (iii) arriver, se présenter (à l'improviste); **he turned up at my office this morning,** il s'est présenté à mon bureau ce matin; **he turned up ten minutes late,** il est arrivé, s'est amené, dix minutes en retard; **he'll t. up one of these days,** il reparaîtra un de ces jours; **something is sure to t. up,** il se présentera sûrement une occasion; **until something better turns up,** en attendant mieux.

turnabout ['tə:nəbaut], *s.* retournement *m*; revirement *m*; volte-face *f inv*.

turnaround ['tə:nəraund], *s. esp. NAm:* (*a*) retournement *m*; revirement *m*; changement *m* (en mieux); (*b*) *Trans:* rotation *f* (d'un navire, d'un avion, etc.); **t. period,** (i) durée *f* de rotation; (ii) *Ind: etc:* (période minimale de) repos quotidien, journalier.

turnaway ['tə:nəwei], *s. Navy:* dérobement *m* (de l'ennemi).

turnback ['tə:nbæk], *s.* retour *m* de drap (d'un lit).

turnbuckle ['tə:nbʌkl], *s.* **1.** *Mec.E:* lanterne *f* (de serrage); *Nau:* ridoir *m*; *Av:* tendeur *m*. **2.** tourniquet *m* (pour contrevent, etc.).

turncap ['tə:nkæp], *s.* capuchon *m* mobile (de cheminée).

turncoat ['tə:nkout], *s. Pol: etc:* renégat *m*; apostat, -ate; **to be a t.,** tourner casaque.

turncock ['tə:nkɔk], *s.* **1.** (*pers.*) fontainier *m*; employé *m* de la compagnie des eaux. **2.** robinet *m* d'arrêt, de fermeture.

turndown ['tə:ndaun]. **1.** *a.* (col, etc.) rabattu. **2.** *s.* = TURNBACK.

turned ['tə:nd], *a.* **1.** **(lathe, machine) t.,** façonné, fait, au tour; tourné; **t. work,** tournage *m*. **2.** (*a*) retourné; *Typ:* **t. letter,** caractère retourné; blocage *m*; (*b*) (*of collar, etc.*) **t. down,** rabattu; **t.-down piece,** rabat *m*; (*c*) **t. in,** rentré; (*d*) **t. up,** (col, etc.) relevé; (nez) retroussé.

turner ['tə:nər], *s. Ind:* tourneur *m*; **turner's wood,** bois *m* de tour, de tourneur.

turnery ['tə:nəri], *s.* **1.** art *m* du tourneur. **2.** (*a*) tournage *m*; travail *m* au tour; **wood t.,** tournage sur bois; (*b*) articles façonnés au tour. **3.** atelier *m* de tourneur; tournerie *f*.

Turnicidae [tə:'nisidi:], *s.pl. Orn:* turnicidés *m*.

turn-in ['tə:nin], *s.* (*a*) *Bookb:* rembord *m*; (*b*) *Dressm: F:* ourlet *m*.

turning ['tə:niŋ], *s.* **1.** (*a*) mouvement *m* giratoire, rotatoire; rotation *f*, giration *f*; *Aut: etc:* **t. circle,** rayon *m* de braquage; *Nau:* **t. basin,** bassin *m* d'évitage; (*b*) changement *m* de direction; virage *m*; **t. point,** (i) point décisif; moment *m* critique; (ii) *Surv:* point perdu; **the t. point in the negotiations,** le point pivot des négociations; le moment où les négociations ont pris une orientation nouvelle; **at the t. point of his career,** au tournant de sa carrière; (*c*) retournage *m* (de la terre, d'un vêtement etc.); *Typ:* blocage *m* (d'une lettre). **2.** (*a*) tournage *m*; travail *m* au tour; **bar t.,** décolletage *m*; **vertical t. machine, mill,** tour à plateau horizontal; (*b*) **turnings,** tournures *f*, copeaux *m* de tour; *Metalw:* bûchilles *f*. **3.** (*a*) tournant *m* (d'une route); coude *m*;

virage; *Adm:* **added t. lane,** surlargeur *f* avant un virage; **to take a t. too quickly,** prendre un virage trop vite; (*b*) **the first t. to the right,** la première route, rue, à droite.

turnip ['tə:nip], *s.* **1.** (*a*) *Hort:* navet *m*; **Swedish t.,** rutabaga *m,* chou-navet *m, pl.* choux-navets; **t. rape,** navette *f*; **t. cabbage,** chou-rave *m, pl.* choux-raves; turnep(s) *m*; (*b*) *Ent:* **t. moth,** agrotide *f* des moissons; **t. fly,** altise potagère; **t. sawfly,** tenthrède *f* de la rave; (*c*) *F:* **t. lantern,** griche-dents *f inv* (composée d'un navet évidé et garni d'une chandelle). **2.** *O:* **t. (watch),** grosse montre bombée, *F:* oignon *m.*

turnkey ['tə:nki(:)], *s.* **1.** guichetier *m* (d'une prison); porte-clefs *m inv.* **2.** (*a*) *O:* = TURNCOCK; (*b*) *U.S:* **t. job,** travail, ouvrage, livré clef en main.

turnoff ['tə:nɔf], *s.* sortie *f* (d'autoroute, etc.).

turnout ['tə:naut], *s.* **1.** concours *m,* assemblée *f* (de gens); **there was a large t. at his funeral,** il y avait foule à son enterrement. **2.** nettoyage *m* à fond (d'une pièce, etc.). **3.** *Ind: A:* grève *f.* **4.** *O:* (*a*) tenue *f,* uniforme *m* (d'un régiment, etc.); (*b*) attelage *m,* équipage *m.* **5.** *esp. NAm: Trans:* (voie *f* de) garage *m*; voie d'évitement.

turnover ['tə:nouvər], *s.* **1.** (*a*) *O:* renversement *m,* culbute *f*; (*b*) (*of tobacco*) **leaf t.,** inversion *f* des feuilles. **2.** *Com:* (*a*) chiffre *m* d'affaires; (*b*) **rapid t. of goods,** écoulement *m,* rotation *f,* rapide des marchandises; **t. of staff,** changement *m* de personnel. **3.** (*a*) retour *m* (de drap sur les courvertures du lit); (*b*) *Cost: O:* revers *m* (d'un chausson, etc.); (*c*) *Cu:* **apple t.,** chausson aux pommes.

turnpike ['tə:npaik], *s.* **1.** (*a*) *Hist:* barrière *f* de péage; **t. (road),** route *f* à péage; (*b*) *U.S:* autoroute *f* (à péage). **2.** *A:* tourniquet *m* (d'entrée). **3.** *Mil: A:* chevaux *mpl* de frise.

turnpin ['tə:npin], *s. Tls:* toupie *f* (de plombier).

turnround ['tə:nraund], *s.* (*a*) retournement *m*; changement *m* (en mieux); (*b*) *Trans:* rotation *f* (d'un navire, d'un avion, d'un camion).

turnscrew ['tə:nskru:], *s. A:* tournevis *m.*

turnsole ['tə:nsoul], *s. O:* **1.** *Bot:* tournesol *m* ((i) maurelle *f,* (ii) croton *m* des teinturiers, (iii) héliotrope *m*). **2.** *Dy:* tournesol.

turnspit ['tə:nspit], *s. A:* (*pers., dog*) tournebroche *m.*

turnstile ['tə:nstail], *s.* tourniquet(-compteur) *m* (pour entrées); moulinet *m.*

turnstone ['tə:nstoun], *s. Orn:* tourne-pierre *m*; **black t.,** tourne-pierre noir; *NAm:* **ruddy t.,** tourne-pierre interprête, à collier, *Fr.C:* tourne-pierre roux.

turntable ['tə:nteibl], *s.* **1.** (*a*) *Rail:* plaque tournante; (*b*) *Artil:* plate-forme tournante. **2.** (*a*) *Rec:* (plateau *m*) tourne-disques *m*; (*b*) selle *f,* sellette *f* (de modeleur).

turn(-)up ['tə:nʌp], *s.* (*a*) revers *m* (de pantalon); *A:* retroussis *m* (d'un chapeau); (*b*) *Cards:* retourne *f*; *F:* **what a t. (for the book)!** ça c'est une sacrée surprise! (*c*) *F: A:* (i) assaut *m* de boxe; (ii) rixe *f,* bagarre *f.*

turnwrest ['tə:nrest], *s. O:* **t. (plough),** (charrue *f*) tourne-oreille *m inv.*

Turonian [tju'rounian], *a. & s. Geol:* turonien (*m*).

turpentine ['tə:p(ə)ntain], *s.* (*a*) térébenthine *f*; **crude t.,** résine *f* vierge; (*b*) **(oil of) t.,** essence *f* de térébenthine; (*c*) **t. tree,** térébinthe *m.*

turpeth ['tə:piθ], *s. Pharm:* **1.** turbith *m.* **2. t. mineral,** turbith minéral; précipité *m* jaune.

turpitude ['tə:pitju:d], *s.* turpitude *f.*

turps [tə:ps], *s. F:* essence *f* de térébenthine.

turquoise ['tə:kwɔiz, -kwɑ:z], *s.* **1.** *Lap:* turquoise *f*; **true oriental t.,** turquoise de la vieille roche; **fossil t.,** turquoise osseuse, occidentale; **t. ring,** bague *f* de turquoises. **2.** *a. & s.* **t. (blue),** turquoise (*m*) *inv.*

turquoisine ['tə:kwɔizi:n], *s. Orn:* turquoisine *f,* perruche *f* d'Edwards.

turret ['tʌrit], *s.* **1.** *Arch:* tourelle *f*; **bell t.,** petit clocher. **2.** (*a*) *Mil: Navy:* **(gun) t.,** tourelle (de pièce d'artillerie, de mitrailleuse); *Navy:* **after t., forward t.,** tourelle de retraite, de chasse; *Fort: etc:* **disappearing t.,** tourelle à éclipse; **double-gun, triple-gun, quadruple-gun, t.,** tourelle double, triple, quadruple; **open t.,** tourelle à ciel ouvert; **offset t.,** tourelle excentrique; **revolving, rotating, t.,** tourelle pivotante; **t. turning gear,** vireur *m* de tourelle; **t. gun,** pièce *f* de tourelle; (*of tank*) **t. down,** à défilement de tourelle; (*b*) *Rail: U.S:* lanterneau *m* (de wagon). **3.** *Mec.E:* tourelle; (porte-outil(s) *m inv*) revolver *m*; barillet *m* porte-outils (de tour); **t. drill,** aléseuse *f* à revolver; **t. slide,** chariot *m* (de tour) à revolver.

turreted ['tʌritid], *a.* **1.** (*a*) *Arch:* (château, etc.) surmonté, garni, de tourelles, d'une tourelle; (*b*) *Her:* tourelé. **2.** *Conch:* turriculé.

turrethead ['tʌrithed], *s. Phot:* tourelle *f.*

turriculate, turriculated [tʌ'rikjuleit(id)], *a. Conch:* turriculé.

turrilite ['tʌrilait], *s. Paleont:* turrilite *m.*

turritella [tʌri'telə], *s. Moll:* turritelle *f,* térèbre *f.*

tursiops ['tə:siɔps], *s. Z:* tursiops *m,* souffleur *m.*

turtle[1] ['tə:tl], *s.* **1.** (*a*) (i) tortue *f* de mer; **t. shell,** carapace *f* de tortue; **t. soup,** consommé *m* à la tortue; *F:* **to turn t.,** *Nau:* chavirer; (*of small boat*) faire capot, capoter; (*of motor car, etc.*) capoter, se retourner; (ii) *Rept:* **alligator t.,** tortue vorace alligator; **(common) snapping t.,** tortue vorace; tortue alligator; **green t.,** chélonée franche; tortue verte; tortue marine; **leather t.,** tortue à cuir; tortue luth; **matamata t.,** tortue à gueule; **mud t.,** tortue bourbeuse; **musk t.,** tortue musquée; **(West Australian) snakeneck t.,** chélodine *f*; **soft-shelled t.,** trionix *m,* trionyx *m,* trionychidé *m*; **African, New Guinea, soft-shell t.,** tortue à carapace molle d'Afrique, de la Nouvelle-Guinée; **(American) box t.,** terrapène *m* des Carolines; **hawksbill t.,** tortue à écaille; (*b*) *Conch:* **t. cowrie,** porcelaine *f*; (*c*) *Cost:* **t. neck,** col roulé; vêtement *m* à col roulé; **t.-necked sweater,** chandail *m* à col roulé; (*d*) *Nau:* **t. back, t. (back) deck,** pont *m* en carapace de tortue; *Aer:* **t. back,** arête dorsale. **2.** (i) *Orn:* **t. dove,** tourterelle *f* des bois; **rufous t. dove, Eastern t. dove,** tourterelle orientale; **collared t. dove,** tourterelle turque; (ii) *F:* **a pair of t. doves, of turtles,** un couple d'amants, d'amoureux, de tourtereaux.

turtle[2], *v.i.* faire la pêche à la tortue.

turtler ['tə:tlər], *s.* **1.** pêcheur *m* de tortues. **2.** navire *m,* bateau *m,* pour la pêche à la tortue.

turtling ['tə:tliŋ], *s.* pêche *f* à la tortue.

turumtee [tə'rʌmti(:)], *s. Orn:* faucon *m* chiquera.

Tuscan ['tʌskən]. **1.** (*a*) *a. Geog: Arch:* toscan; *Hatm:* **t. straw,** paille *f* de Toscane; (*b*) *s. Geog:* Toscan, -ane. **2.** *s. Ling:* toscan *m.*

Tuscany ['tʌskəni], *Pr.n. Geog:* Toscane *f*; *Hist:* **Grand-Duke of T.,** grand-duc *m* de Toscane.

tush[1] [tʌʃ], *int. O:* bah! taratata! taisez-vous donc! chansons!

tush[2], *s.* canine *f,* écaillon *m* (du cheval); défense *f* (du sanglier).

tusk [tʌsk], *s.* **1.** (*a*) défense *f* (de sanglier, d'éléphant, de morse, etc.); dent *f* (d'éléphant); croc *m,* crochet *m* (de loup, etc.); (*b*) **boar's tusks,** broches *f,* dagues *f,* de sanglier; (*b*) *Moll:* **elephant's t. shell,** dentale *m.* **2.** *Ich:* torsk *m,* brosme *m.* **3.** (*a*) *Carp:* renfort *m,* mordâne *m* (de tenon); **t. tenon,** tenon *m* à renfort; (*b*) dent (d'une herse, etc.).

tusked [tʌskt], *s.* (*a*) (éléphant, sanglier) armé de défenses; (bête) à défenses; (*b*) *Her:* défendu.

tusker ['tʌskər], *s.* éléphant *m,* sanglier *m,* adulte, qui a ses défenses.

tussive ['tʌsiv], *a. Med:* de la toux; causé par la toux.

tussle[1] ['tʌsl], *s.* lutte *f,* mêlée *f,* corps-à-corps *m*; **sharp t.,** affaire chaude; **verbal t.,** passe *f* d'armes; prise *f* de bec; **to have a t. (with s.o.),** en venir aux mains (avec qn); **to have a t. for sth.,** disputer qch. (à qn).

tussle[2], *v.i.* **to t. with s.o.,** lutter avec qn; s'escrimer contre qn; **to t. over sth.,** se disputer qch.

tussock ['tʌsək], *s.* **1.** touffe *f* d'herbe. **2.** *Bot:* **t. (grass),** (i) tussack *m*; (ii) canche touffue, gazonnante. **3.** *Ent:* **t. (moth),** orgyie *f.*

tussore ['tʌsɔ:r], *s.* **1.** *Tex:* **t. (silk),** tussor(e) *m.* **2.** *Ent:* **t. worm,** ver *m* à soie sauvage.

tut [tʌt], *int.* (*a*) **t. (tut)!** allons donc! (*b*) (*of discouragement, impatience*) zut!

Tutankhamen, -un [tu:tæn'kɑ:mən, -kɑ:'mu:n], *Pr.n.m. A.Hist:* Toutânkhamon.

tutela [tju(:)'ti:lə], *s. Jur:* tutelle *f.*

tutelage ['tju:tilidʒ], *s.* (*a*) tutelle *f*; **child in t.,** enfant en tutelle; (*b*) (période *f* de) tutelle.

tutelar, tutelary ['tju:tilər, -ləri], *a.* tutélaire.

tutiorism ['tju:tiərizm], *s. Theol:* tutiorisme *m.*

tutor[1] ['tju:tər], *s.* **1.** *Sch:* (*a*) directeur, -trice, des études (d'un groupe d'étudiants); (*b*) **private t.,** précepteur *m*; répétiteur *m*; **army t.,** préparateur *m* aux écoles militaires. **2.** méthode *f* (de piano, etc.). **3.** *Jur: Scot:* tuteur, -trice (d'un mineur, d'un dément).

tutor[2], *v.tr.* instruire (qn); **to t. a boy in Latin,** enseigner le latin à un élève; donner à un élève des leçons particulières de latin.

tutorial [tju(:)'tɔ:riəl], *a.* **1.** (*a*) (cours, etc.) d'instructions; (*b*) (fonctions, etc.) de répétiteur, de préparateur. **2.** *Jur:* tutélaire. **3.** *s. Sch:* cours (individuel) fait par le directeur d'études.

tutoring ['tju:təriŋ], *s.* instruction *f,* enseignement *m*; leçons particulières; **to do t.,** donner des leçons particulières.

tutorship ['tju:təʃip], *s.* fonctions *fpl* de directeur, -trice, d'études; fonctions de répétiteur; **private t.,** préceptorat *m.*

tutory ['tju:təri], *s. Jur:* tutelle *f* (d'un mineur, d'un dément).

tutsan ['tʌts(ə)n], *s. Bot:* toute-saine *f,* androsème *m.*

tutty ['tʌti], *s. Metall: etc:* tut(h)ie *f,* cadmie *f.*

tutu ['tyty], *s. Cost:* tutu *m.*

tutwork ['tʌtwə:k], *s. Min:* travail *m* à la tâche (dans les mines d'étain, de plomb).

tu-whit, tu-whoo [tu'wittu'wu:]. **1.** *int.* hou hou! **2.** *s.* ululement *m* (du hibou).

tuxedo [tʌk'si:dou], *s. Cost: NAm:* smoking *m.*

tuyère ['twi:ɛər, 'twaiər], *s. Metall:* tuyère *f*; **t. arch,** embrasure *f*; **t. hole,** œil *m, pl.* yeux, de tuyère.

twaddle[1] ['twɔdl], *s. F:* fadaises *fpl*; futilités *fpl*; verbiage *m*; **to talk t.,** dire, débiter, des balivernes, des sottises; parler pour ne rien dire; parler en l'air.

twaddle[2], *v.i. F:* dire, conter, des sottises, des balivernes, des fadaises; radoter; parler pour ne rien dire; parler en l'air; débiter des platitudes.

twaddler ['twɔdlər], *s. F:* radoteur, -euse; débiteur *m* de fadaises, de futilités, de sottises.

twain [twein], *a. & s. Lit:* deux; **in t.,** en deux; **split in t.,** pourfendu; **never the t. shall meet,** les deux ne se rencontreront jamais.

twang[1] [twæŋ], *s.* **1.** bruit sec (de la corde d'un arc); son aigu (d'une guitare); **to hear the t. of harp strings,** entendre vibrer, résonner, les cordes de la harpe. **2. nasal t.,** ton nasillard; nasillement *m*; **to speak with a t.,** parler du nez, nasalement; parler d'une voix nasillarde; nasiller.

twang[2]. **1.** *v.tr.* (*a*) lâcher (la corde de l'arc tendu); (*b*) faire frémir, faire résonner (les cordes d'une harpe); **to t. a guitar,** *v.i.* **to t. on a guitar,** pincer de la guitare. **2.** *v.i.* (*a*) (*of string, harp, etc.*) vibrer, résonner, frémir; (*b*) (*of pers.*) nasiller.

twanging ['twæŋiŋ], *s.* (*a*) sons vibrants; vibration *f* (d'une corde); (*b*) nasillement *m.*

'twas [*stressed:* twʌz, *unstressed:* twəz] = **it was.**

twayblade ['tweibleid], *s. Bot:* listère *f.*

tweak[1] [twi:k], *s.* pinçon *m*; **he gave her nose a t.,** il lui a doucement tordu le nez.

tweak[2], *v.tr.* pincer; serrer entre les doigts (en tordant); **to t. a boy's ear,** tirer l'oreille à un gamin; **to t. s.o.'s nose,** tordre le nez à qn; moucher qn.

twee [twi:], *a. F: Pej:* gentillet, mignard.

tweed [twi:d], *s.* **1.** *Tex:* tissu *m* de laine à couleurs mélangées; tweed *m*; cheviote écossaise; **t. hat,** boléro *m* en tissu. **2. tweeds,** complet *m,* costume *m,* de cheviote.

tweedle ['twi:dl]. *A:* **1.** *v.i.* jouer sur un crincrin; seriner un air sur la flûte, etc. **2.** *v.tr.* **to t. s.o. into doing sth.,** enjôler qn.

tweedy ['twi:di], *a. F:* **1.** (tissu) qui tient du tweed. **2.** *Pej:* (*of pers.*) toujours vêtue de tweed; toujours vêtu comme si on était à la campagne; qui affecte la tenue d'un propriétaire rural.

'tween [twi:n], *adv. & prep.* **1.** *A: & Lit:* entre. **2.** *Nau:* **'t.-decks,** (i) *s.* le faux-pont, l'entrepont *m*; (ii) *adv.* dans l'entrepont.

tweeness ['twi:nis], *s. F: Pej:* mièvrerie *f,* mignardise *f.*

tweeny ['twi:ni], *s.f. F: A:* bonne qui aide la cuisinière et la femme de chambre.

tweet[1] [twi:t], *s.* pépiement *m,* gazouillement *m* (d'un oiseau).

tweet[2], *v.i.* (*of bird*) pépier, gazouiller.

tweeter ['twi:tər], *s. W.Tel: etc:* **t. (loudspeaker),** tweeter *m.*

tweezers ['twi:zəz], *s.pl.* petite pince; brucelles *fpl*; (*for pulling out hairs*) pince à épiler; épiloir *m.*

twelfth [twelfθ]. **1.** *num.a. & s.* douzième (*mf*); **to be the t. in one's class,** être le, la, douzième de sa classe; *F:* **the T.,** le douze août (ouverture de la chasse au lagopède d'Écosse); **Louis the T.,** Louis Douze; **T. Day (of Christmas),** le jour des Rois; **T. Night,** (i) la veille des Rois; (ii) la soirée du jour des Rois; **T.-night cake** = la galette des Rois. **2.** *s.* (*fractional*) douzième *m.*

twelfthly ['twelfθli], *adv.* douzièmement; en douzième lieu.

twelve [twelv], *num.a. & s.* douze (*m*); **t. o'clock,** (i) (*midday*) midi *m*; (ii) (*midnight*) minuit *m*; (*in 24-hour system*) **t. hours,** douze heures; **half past t., t. thirty,** midi, minuit, et demi; douze heures et demi, douze heures trente; *Tp:* **in twelves,** in-douze; *A.Artil:* **t. pounder,** pièce *f,* canon *m,* de douze; *B:* **the T.,** les Douze (apôtres *m*).

twelvemo ['twelvmou], *a. & s. Typ:* in-douze (*m*) *inv,* in-12 (*m*).

twelvemonth ['twelvmʌnθ], *s. O:* année *f*; **this day t.,** (i) d'aujourd'hui en un an; (ii) il y a un an aujourd'hui; **for a t.,** (i) depuis un an; (ii) pour un an.

twelve-note, twelve-tone ['twelvnout, -toun], *a. Mus:* dodécaphoniste, dodécaphonique; **t.-note, t.-tone, system,** dodécaphonie *f,* dodécaphonisme *m.*

twentieth ['twentiiθ]. **1.** *num.a. & s.* vingtième (*mf*); **(on) the t. of June,** le vingt juin; **it's my t. birthday,** je fête mes vingt ans; *A:* **one and t.,** vingt et unième. **2.** *s.* (*fractional*) vingtième *m.*

twenty ['twenti], *num.a. & s.* vingt (*m*); **t.-one,** *A: & Lit:* **one and t.,** vingt et un; **t.-two,** vingt-deux; **about t. people,** quelque vingt personnes; une vingtaine de personnes; **to be in the, one's, early twenties,** avoir vingt et quelques années; **to be in the, one's, late twenties,** approcher de la trentaine; **the twenties,** les années vingt (1920–1929); **the eighteen-twenties, the twenties of last century,** les années entre 1820 et 1829, de 1820 à 1829.

twenty-first [twenti'fə:st]. **1.** *num.a. & s.* vingt et unième (*mf*); **the t.-f. of May,** le vingt et un mai. **2.** *s. F:* (*a*) vingt et unième anniversaire *m*; (*b*) réunion *f* de vingt et unième anniversaire.

twenty-firster [twenti'fə:stər], *s. F:* = TWENTY-FIRST **2.**

twenty-five ['twentifaiv], *num.a. & s.* vingt-cinq (*m*); *Sp:* (*hockey*) **the t.-f.,** la ligne des vingt-deux mètres.

twentyfold ['twentifould]. **1.** *a.* vingtuple. **2.** *adv.* vingt fois autant; **to increase t.,** vingtupler.

twenty-four ['twentifɔ:ər]. **1.** *num.a. & s.* vingt-quatre (*m*). **2.** *s. Typ:* **twenty-fours,** in-vingt-quatre *m inv.*

twenty-fourmo [twenti'fɔ:mou], *a. & s. Typ:* in-vingt-quatre (*m*) *inv*, in-24 (*m*).

'twere [*stressed:* twə:r, *unstressed:* twər]. *Lit:* = **it were.**

twerp [twə:p], *s. P:* nouille *f*, andouille *f*; pauvre type *m*; crétin *m*; **nasty little t.,** salaud *m.*

twice [twais], *adv.* deux fois; **t. two is four,** deux fois deux font quatre; **t. as big as sth.,** deux fois plus grand que, deux fois grand comme, plus grand du double que, qch.; **I am t. as old as you (are), I am t. your age,** j'ai deux fois, le double de, votre âge; **t. as slow,** deux fois plus lent; **t. over,** à deux reprises; **to think t. before doing sth.,** y regarder à deux fois pour faire qch., avant de faire qch.; **he didn't have to think t. before accepting,** il a accepté sans hésiter; **he did not think t.,** il n'a fait ni une ni deux; **that made him think t.,** cela lui a donné à réfléchir; **he did not have to be asked t.,** il ne se fit pas prier; il ne se fit pas tirer l'oreille; **I shan't need to be told t.,** je ne me le ferai pas répéter; **t. told tale,** histoire répétée maintes fois; *P:* **to do sth. in, at, t.,** faire qch. (i) en deux coups, (ii) au deuxième coup.

twiddle[1] ['twidl], *s.* **1. to give sth. a t.,** tourner, faire tournoyer, qch. **2.** petite volute.

twiddle[2], *v.tr. & i.* **to t. (with) sth.,** jouer avec, tripoter, qch.; **to t. one's thumbs,** se tourner les pouces; **to t. one's moustache,** tortiller sa moustache.

twig[1] [twig], *s.* **1.** (*a*) brindille *f* (de branche); broutille *f*, ramille *f*; (*b*) *Anat:* petit vaisseau; (*c*) *El:* petit branchement. **2. (dowser's hazel) t.,** baguette *f* (divinatoire); baguette de coudrier; **to work the t.,** employer la baguette de sourcier, faire de l'hydroscopie, de la radiesthésie.

twig[2], *v.tr.* **(twigged)** *F: O:* **1.** apercevoir, observer (qn). **2.** comprendre, saisir; piger; **now I t. (it),** j'y suis maintenant; **I soon twigged his little game,** je me suis bientôt rendu compte de ses intentions; j'ai bien vu dans son jeu.

twiggy ['twigi], *a.* (arbre) qui a beaucoup de ramilles.

twilight ['twailait], *s.* **1.** crépuscule *m*, demi-jour *m*; **the morning t.,** l'aurore *f*, le petit jour; **in the (evening) t.,** au crépuscule, entre chien et loup, à la brune, à l'approche de la nuit; **in the t. of life,** dans le crépuscule de la vie; *Myth:* **the T. of the Gods,** le Crépuscule des Dieux. **2.** *attrib.* (*a*) crépusculaire; **the t. hour,** l'heure crépusculaire; *Astr:* **t. parallel,** cercle *m* crépusculaire; *Oc:* **t. zone,** zone crépusculaire; (*b*) **the t. zone between sleeping and waking,** l'état *m* intermédiaire entre le sommeil et la veille; **a t. zone of the city,** un quartier de la ville qui déchoit; *Obst:* **t. sleep,** demi-sommeil provoqué, chloroforme *m* à la reine.

twilit ['twailit], *a.* (ciel, paysage) crépusculaire, éclairé par le crépuscule.

twill[1] [twil], *s. Tex:* (*a*) (tissu) croisé (*m*); diagonale *f*, twill *m*; **cotton t.,** croisé en coton; **French t.,** florentine *f*; (*b*) **t. (weave),** croisé *m*, sergé *m.*

twill[2], *v.tr. Tex:* croiser (le drap).

'twill [twil] = **it will.**

twilled ['twild], *a. Tex:* croisé; **t. silk,** florentine *f.*

twilling ['twiliŋ], *s. Tex:* **1.** tissage *m* des étoffes croisées. **2.** tissus croisés; twills *mpl.*

twin[1] [twin], *a. & s.* **1.** jumeau, -elle; **t. brother, t. sister,** frère jumeau, sœur jumelle; **identical twins,** jumeaux univitellins, vrais jumeaux; **fraternal, non-identical, twins,** faux jumeaux; jumeaux dizygotes, bivitellins; *Astr:* **the Twins,** les Gémeaux *m.* **2.** *a.* (*a*) *Med: etc:* **t. pregnancy,** grossesse *f* gémellaire; **t. birth,** accouchement *m*, *Vet:* mise *f* bas, de jumeaux; (*b*) jumeau, jumelé, conjugué; **t. beds,** lits jumeaux; **t. tyres,** pneus jumelés; **t. columns,** colonnes géminées; **t. towns,** villes jumelées; *Rail:* **t. track,** ligne *f* à deux voies; *El:* **t. wire,** fil torsadé; *W.Tel:* **t. (wire) aerial,** antenne *f* bifilaire; *Nau:* **t. masts,** mâts jumelés; **t-screw steamer,** vapeur *m* à hélices jumelles, à deux hélices; **t. ships,** frères *m*; *Aut:* **t.-blade windscreen wiper,** essuie-glace *m inv* à double balai; **flat t. (cylinder) (engine),** moteur *m* à deux cylindres opposés; **V t. (cylinder) (engine),** moteur à deux cylindres en V; *Av:* **t.-boom aircraft,** avion *m* bipoutre; **t.-engine aircraft,** avion bimoteur; **t.-jet aircraft,** biréacteur *m*; *Cmptr:* **t. check,** double contrôle *m*; *Elcs:* **t. triode valve,** tube *m* triode double; (*c*) *Cost:* **t. set,** twin-set *m*; (*d*) *Bot:* **t. leaves,** feuilles géminées. **3.** *Cryst:* **t. (crystal),** macle *f*, cristal maclé; **contact t.,** macle par accolement; **t. crystallization,** hémitropie *f*; **t. axis,** axe *m* d'hémitropie; **t. plane,** plan *m* d'hémitropie; **t. aragonite,** aragonite confluente.

twin[2], *v.i.* **(twinned) 1.** accoucher de deux jumeaux; (*of animal*) mettre bas deux petits à la fois. **2.** (*a*) **to t. with s.o.,** être le frère jumeau, la sœur jumelle, de qn; (*b*) (*of thg*) **to t. with sth.,** s'apparier à qch.; (*c*) *v.tr.* jumeler (des villes). **3.** *Cryst:* (se) macler.

twine[1] [twain], *s.* **1.** ficelle *f*, fil retors; *Nau:* fil à voiles, lignerolle *f*; (*for netting*) lignette *f*; *Agr:* **binder t.,** ficelle lieuse, à lier; **t. cutter,** coupe-ficelle *m inv*; **t. holder,** porte-ficelle *m inv.* **2.** entrelacement *m*, enchevêtrement *m.*

twine[2]. **1.** *v.tr.* tordre, tortiller (des fils); entrelacer (une guirlande, les doigts, etc.); **to t. two cords together,** tordre deux fils ensemble, retordre deux fils; **to t. sth. about sth., round sth.,** (en)rouler qch. autour de qch.; entourer qch. de qch.; **she twined her arms round me,** elle m'a entouré de ses bras. **2.** (*a*) *v.i. & pr.* se tordre, se tortiller; **to t. round sth., about sth.,** s'enrouler, s'enlacer, s'entortiller, autour de qch.; **the ivy twines (itself) round the oak,** le lierre embrasse le chêne; (*b*) *v.i.* (*of road, etc.*) serpenter.

twiner ['twainər], *s.* **1.** *Bot:* plante *f* volubile. **2.** *Tex:* retordoir *m*, retorsoir *m.*

twinflower ['twinflauər], *s. Bot:* linnée *f.*

twinge[1] [twin(d)ʒ], *s.* (*a*) élancement *m* (de douleur); légère atteinte (de goutte, etc.); (*in stomach*) tiraillement *m*; (*b*) **t. of conscience,** remords *m* (de conscience); **he has some twinges of conscience,** il n'a pas la conscience tranquille; **this gave him a t. of conscience,** ceci lui a élancé la conscience.

twinge[2]. **1.** *v.i.* (*a*) élancer; **his finger was twinging,** son doigt lui élançait; (*b*) **his conscience twinges,** sa conscience le tourmente. **2.** *v.tr. A:* donner un élancement, causer des élancements, à qn.

twinging[1] ['twin(d)ʒiŋ], *a.* (*of pain*) lancinant, cuisant.

twinging[2], *s.* élancement *m.*

twining[1] ['twainiŋ], *a.* (*a*) *Bot:* (tige, plante) volubile; (*b*) (sentier, etc.) qui serpente, sinueux.

twining[2], *s.* (*a*) entortillement *m*, entrelacement *m*; **t. property of a plant,** volubilisme *m* d'une plante; (*b*) serpentement *m.*

twink[1] [twiŋk], *s.* = TWINKLE[1]; **in a t.,** en un clin d'œil, en un tour de main.

twink[2], *v.i.* = TWINKLE[2].

twinkle[1] ['twiŋkl], *s.* **1.** scintillement *m*, clignotement *m* (des étoiles, de feux lointains); **the t. of dancing feet,** le mouvement rapide des pieds des danseurs. **2.** (*a*) lueur fugitive; (*b*) clignement *m* (des paupières); pétillement *m* (du regard); **a mischievous t. in the eye,** un éclair de malice, une lueur de malice, dans les yeux; **in the t. of an eye, in a t.,** en un clin d'œil, en un tour de main; *F:* **you were just a t. in your father's eye,** tu étais encore en pointillés.

twinkle[2]. **1.** *v.i.* (*a*) (*of light, star*) scintiller, étinceler, papilloter, clignoter; (*of object in motion*) papillonner; (*b*) **his eyes twinkled (with amusement, mischief),** ses yeux pétillaient (d'envie de rire, de malice). **2.** *v.tr.* **to t. one's eyes,** clignoter des yeux; **glow worms twinkling their lights in the hedge,** vers luisants qui faisaient scintiller leurs lumières dans la haie.

twinkling[1] ['twiŋkliŋ], *a.* (*of star, etc.*) scintillant, étincelant, papillotant, clignotant; **t. eyes,** yeux pétillants d'esprit, de malice; **t. light,** feu scintillant.

twinkling[2], *s.* scintillement *m*, étincellement *m*, clignotement *m*; **in the t. of an eye,** en un clin d'œil, en un tour de main.

twinned ['twind], *a.* **1. t. towns,** villes jumelées. **2.** *Cryst:* maclé, hémitrope.

twinning ['twiniŋ], *s.* **1.** accouchement *m* de jumeaux, accouchement double; (*of animals*) mise *f* bas de deux petits. **2.** jumelage *m* (de deux villes, *Mil:* de deux armes). **3.** *Cryst:* hémitropie *f*; **repeated t.,** macle *f* polysynthétique; **t. axis,** axe *m* d'hémitropie; **t. plane,** plan *m* d'hémitropie. **4.** (*comb industry*) **t. machine, saw,** entrecoupeuse *f* double.

twinship ['twinʃip], *s.* (lien *m* de) parenté *f* entre jumeaux.

twirl[1] [twə:l], *s.* **1.** tournoiement *m*, révolution *f*; (*of dancer, etc.*) pirouette *f*; *Fenc:* moulinet *m.* **2.** volute *f* (de fumée, etc.); *Arch:* enroulement *m*, volute; *Conch:* spire *f*; (*in writing*) enjolivure *f* en spirale; fioriture *f.* **3.** *Ven:* (*for decoying larks*) miroir *m.*

twirl[2]. **1.** *v.tr.* (*a*) faire tournoyer, faire tourner; faire des moulinets avec (une canne, etc.); **to t. a mop,** faire tournoyer un guipon (pour l'égoutter); (*b*) **to t. one's thumbs,** se tourner les pouces; **to t. one's moustache,** tortiller, friser, sa moustache; **to t. up one's moustache,** retrousser sa moustache. **2.** *v.i.* tourner (comme une toupie), toupiller, tournoyer; (*of dancer*) pirouetter; **to t. on one's heels,** (i) pivoter; (ii) faire des pirouettes.

twirling ['twə:liŋ], *s.* tournoiement *m.*

twist[1] [twist], *s.* **1.** (*a*) fil retors; retors *m*, cordon *m*, cordonnet *m*; *Tex:* **machine t.,** câblé *m* de soie pour machines à coudre; **t. mill,** retorderie *f*; **t. yarn,** fil retors; (*b*) **t. of hair,** torsade *f*, tortillon *m*, de cheveux; **t. of wool,** écheveau *m* de laine; **t. of paper,** tortillon, cornet *m*, de papier; **sweet in a t. of paper,** bonbon dans une papillote; (*c*) **t. (tobacco),** tabac mis en corde; **to make t.,** filer, torquer, le tabac; **t. of tobacco,** rouleau *m*, andouille *f*, torquette *f*, boudin *m*, de tabac; (*d*) **t. of lemon (peel) in a cocktail,** zeste *m* de citron dans un cocktail; (*e*) *Glassm:* **enamel t. stem,** (verre à) pied rubané; (*f*) *Nau:* toron *m* (d'un cordage); (*g*) *F: A:* boisson mélangée; **gin t.,** grog *m* à base de gin. **2.** (*a*) (effort *m* de) torsion *f*; **to give sth. a t.,** exercer une torsion sur qch.; **to give one's ankle a t.,** se fouler la cheville, se donner une entorse; **to give oneself a t. in the back,** se donner un tour de reins; *Fig:* **to give the truth a t.,** donner une entorse à la vérité; *Mec.E: etc:* **t. joint,** torsade; *Mec.E:* **t. test,** essai *m* de torsion; (*b*) tors *m*, torsion (des brins d'un cordage); *Tex:* tordage *m* (de la soie, du chanvre); **there are twists in the wire,** le fil est tordu, est en tire-bouchon; **t.-fibred,** (bois) à fibres torses; *Artil: Sm.a:* **rifling with uniform, increasing, t.,** rayures à pas constant, à pas progressif; *F:* (*of thgs*) **to be in a t.,** être en confusion, en pagaille; *P:* **to get one's knickers in a t.,** se mettre dans tous ses états; (*c*) *Sp:* effet (donné à une balle); tour *m* de poignet; **he threw the ball with a quick t. of the wrist,** il a jeté la balle avec un tour de poignet; **it takes months to learn the t. of the wrist,** il faut des mois pour apprendre le tour de main; *Fenc:* **t. and thrust,** flanconade *f*; (*d*) contorsion *f* (des traits, du visage); **with a t. of the mouth,** en tordant la bouche, avec une grimace; (*e*) *Danc:* twist *m.* **3.** (*a*) spire *f*; **t. of rope round a post,** tour de corde autour d'un poteau; (*b*) tournant *m*, coude *m* (d'une rue, etc.); **road full of twists and turns,** chemin plein de tours et de détours, de tours et de retours; **final t. in a story,** tour inattendu à la fin d'un récit; **a queer t. of fate,** un coup étrange du destin; (*c*) *F:* **to be round the t.,** être fou, cinglé. **4.** (*a*) dévers *m*, gauchissement *m* (d'une pièce de bois); gondolage *m* (d'une tôle); déformation *f*; (*b*) perversion *f* (du sens d'un texte); **curious t. in the meaning of a word,** déformation curieuse du sens d'un mot; (*c*) (i) prédisposition *f*, propension *f* (à qch.); **criminal t.,** prédisposition au crime; (ii) **mental t.,** perversion, déformation, d'esprit; **to have a t. in one's character,** avoir l'esprit faussé; **his queer t. of mind,** sa singulière tournure d'esprit. **5.** *P: O:* escroquerie *f*, filouterie *f.* **6.** (*a*) *A:* enfourchure *f* (du corps); (*b*) entre-deux *m inv*, braie *f* (du bœuf, etc.). **7.** *F: O:* appétit *m*; **to have a t.,** avoir l'estomac creux; **the walk has given me a t.,** la promenade m'a creusé. **8.** *N.Am: P:* femme, gonzesse.

twist[2]. **1.** *v.tr.* (*a*) tordre, tortiller (ses cheveux, un cordage, etc.); *Tex: etc:* retordre (le fil); *Ropem:* commettre (un cordage); **to t. together,** torsader; câbler (des fils métalliques); **to t. (up) one's handkerchief,** tire-bouchonner son mouchoir; **to t. the linen (when wringing out),** bouchonner le linge; **to t. tobacco,** torquer le tabac; **to t. a garland,** tresser une guirlande; **to t. (up) sth. in a piece of paper,** entortiller qch. dans un morceau de papier; **to t. sth. round sth.,** rouler, entortiller, qch. autour de qch.; **the snake used to t. itself round my arm,** le serpent s'enroulait autour de mon bras; *F:* **you can t. him round your little finger,** c'est un homme facile à entortiller; il est du bois dont on fait les flûtes; **she can t. him round her little finger,** elle le mène par le bout du nez; elle lui fait faire ses quatre volontés; elle en fait ce qu'elle veut; elle le fait tourner comme un toton, à son gré; (*b*) se tordre (le bras, etc.); se déboîter (le genou); **to t. one's ankle,** se donner une entorse; se fouler la cheville; **he twisted his ankle,** il s'est tordu le pied; le pied lui a tourné; **to t. one's head round,** se tordre le cou (pour regarder en arrière); **to t. s.o.'s arm,** (i) tordre, retourner, le bras à qn; (ii) *Fig:* exercer une pression sur qn; *F:* (*on being offered sth.*) **well, if you t. my arm!** volontiers! je ne dis pas non! **to t. s.o.'s neck,** tordre le cou à qn; **to t. the head off a screw,** arracher la tête d'une vis; (*c*) **to t. one's mouth, one's face,** tordre la bouche; faire la grimace; **face twisted by pain,** visage tordu, contorsionné, par la douleur; (*d*) dénaturer, pervertir, altérer, fausser (le sens d'un texte); **to t. s.o.'s words into a confession,** essayer de donner aux paroles de qn le sens d'un aveu; **to t. the truth,** altérer la vérité; donner une entorse à la vérité; (*e*) donner de l'effet à (une balle). **2.** *v.i.* (*a*) (*of worm, etc.*) se tordre; se tortiller; **to t. about on one's chair,** se tortiller sur sa chaise; (*b*) se mettre en spirale; former une spirale, des spirales; (*of smoke*) former des volutes; (*of tendril*) vriller, vrillonner; (*c*) **to get (all) twisted (up),** s'entortiller; (*d*) (*of road, etc.*) tourner; faire des détours, des lacets; se replier; **to t. and turn,** serpenter; faire des tours et des détours; (*with cogn. acc.*) **to t. one's way through the crowd,** se faufiler à travers la foule; (*e*) **to t. round in one's seat,** se tourner sur son siège; (*f*) *Danc:* twister.

twisted ['twistid], *a.* **1.** tordu, tors; (fil, etc.) retors; **t. fringe,** torsade *f*; **t. hair,** cheveux en torsade; *Arch:* **t. pillar,** colonne torse; *Tex:* **t. cord fabric,** tissu corde retordue; *El:* **t. joint,** joint par torsade; *Glassm:* (*of wine-glass stem*) **enamel-t.,** rubané. **2.** (*distorted*) (*a*) tordu; (*of tree*) tortueux; (*of limb*) contourné; **face t. with pain,** traits contractés, tordus, par la douleur; (*b*) (*of piece of string, etc.*) vrillé; tire-bouchonnant. **3.** (*of meaning, etc.*) perverti, dénaturé, altéré; **t. mind,** esprit tordu, faussé. **4.** *P:* (*of drug addict*) chargé, défoncé. **5.** *Bot:* **t. stalk,** streptopus *m.*

twister ['twistər], *s.* **1.** (*pers.*) (*a*) tordeur, -euse (de chanvre, etc.); cordier *m*; (*b*) *Tex:* retordeur, -euse. **2.** (*a*) châssis *m* à cordeler; (*b*) *Tex:* tordoir *m*, retordoir *m*. **3.** *Equit:* plat *m* de la cuisse (du cavalier). **4.** *Cr: etc:* balle *f* qui a de l'effet, qui dévie. **5.** *A:* cabriolet *m* (d'agent de police). **6.** *F:* faux bonhomme; escroc *m*. **7.** *F: O:* argument déconcertant; question déconcertante, qui vous met à quia; **that's a t. for you!** voilà qui vous donnera du fil à retordre! **8.** *NAm: F:* cyclone *m*, tornade *f*. **9.** *P:* clef *f.*

twisting[1] ['twistiŋ], *a.* (sentier, etc.) tortueux, en lacets.

twisting[2], *s.* **1.** (*a*) *Tex:* retordage *m*; **t.-mill,** métier *m* à retordre; **silk-t. mill,** retorderie *f* de soie; (*b*) tressage *m* (d'une guirlande, etc.); (*c*) tortillement *m* (d'un ver, etc.); (*d*) **t. up,** entortillement *m*. **2.** (*a*) *Mec:* torsion *f*; **t. strain,** effort *m* de torsion; (*b*) contraction *f* (des traits); (*c*) perversion *f*, détournement *m*, altération *f* (du sens d'un mot, etc.); (*d*) *F:* escroquerie *f.*

twisty ['twisti], *a.* **1.** (chemin, etc.) tortueux. **2.** *F:* malhonnête, fripon.

twit[1] [twit], *s.* **1.** *P:* corniaud *m*, nouille *f*. **2.** *F:* = TWITTER[1] 2.

twit[2], *v.tr.* (**twitted**) narguer, taquiner (qn); railler (qn) d'une manière sarcastique; **to t. s.o. with sth.,** reprocher qch. à qn; railler qn de qch.

twitch[1] [twitʃ], *s.* **1.** saccade *f*; petit coup sec; **he felt a t. at his sleeve,** il s'est senti tiré par la manche. **2.** élancement *m* (de douleur); (*in the stomach*) tiraillement *m*; **t. of conscience,** remords *m* de conscience. **3.** (*a*) contraction soudaine (du visage); clignotement *m* (des paupières); crispation nerveuse (des mains); tic; mouvement convulsif (d'un membre); (*b*) **facial t.,** tic (convulsif); **he has a t.,** il a un tic. **4.** *Vet:* serre-nez *m inv*, tord-nez *m inv*, torche-nez *m inv.*

twitch[2]. **1.** *v.tr.* (*a*) tirer vivement, donner une saccade à (qch.); (*b*) contracter (ses traits); crisper (les mains, le visage); (*of cat*) **to t. its tail,** faire de petits mouvements de la queue. **2.** *v.i.* (*a*) (*of face*) se contracter nerveusement; (*of eyelids*) clignoter; (*of hands*) se crisper nerveusement; (*b*) **his face twitches,** il a un tic; il tique.

twitch[3], *s. Bot:* **t. (grass),** chiendent officinal, des boutiques.

twitching ['twitʃiŋ], *s.* (*a*) contraction nerveuse (du visage); clignotement *m* (des paupières); crispation nerveuse (des mains); **to have twitchings in one's legs,** avoir des tressaillements, *F:* des inquiétudes, dans les jambes; (*b*) tic *m* (du visage); (*c*) *Med:* convulsion *f* clonique (d'un membre); clonisme *m.*

twite [twait], *s. Orn:* **t. (finch),** linotte *f* à bec jaune, linotte montagnarde.

twitter[1] ['twitər], *s.* **1.** gazouillement *m*, gazouillis *m*. **2.** *F:* (*of pers.*) **to be in a t., all of a t.,** être tout agité, tout en émoi, dans tous ses états; **to have the twitters,** avoir la tremblote.

twitter[2], *v.i.* **1.** gazouiller; (*of swallow*) trisser. **2.** *F:* avoir la tremblote; être dans tous ses états.

twittering ['twitəriŋ], *s.* gazouillement *m*; babil *m* (des oiseaux).

'twixt [twikst], *prep. A: & Poet:* entre.

two [tu:], *num.a. & s.* deux (*m*); (*a*) **twenty-two,** vingt-deux; **one or t. books, a book or t.,** un ou deux livres, quelques livres; *F:* **he'd had one or t.,** il était entre deux vins; *Gym: etc:* **one t.! one t.!** une deux! une deux! *P:* une deusse! une deusse! **no t. men are alike,** il n'y a pas deux hommes qui se ressemblent; **to break, fold, sth. in t.,** casser, plier, qch. en deux; **to walk in twos, t. by t., t. and t.,** marcher deux à deux, (deux) par deux; **they came in in twos and threes,** ils entraient par groupes de deux ou trois; *Fig:* **to put t. and t. together,** tirer ses conclusions (après avoir rapproché les faits); **putting t. and t. together I came to this conclusion,** en rapprochant différents indices, je suis arrivé à cette conclusion; *F:* **in t. twos,** en un clin d'œil; **for your trip you must have t. of everything,** pour votre voyage il vous faudra avoir tout en double; **Martin's dog would have made t. of mine,** le chien de Martin était deux fois gros comme le mien; *F:* **that makes t. of us,** vous n'êtes, il n'est, pas le seul; c'est aussi mon cas; et moi aussi; **t. fours, four twos, are eight,** deux fois quatre, quatre fois deux, font huit; *Rail:* **to run a train in t. portions,** dédoubler un train; **at t. (o'clock),** à deux heures; **I live at number t.,** j'habite au (numéro) deux; *A:* **t. and six(pence),** deux shillings six pence; **a mother of t.,** la mère de deux enfants; *Cards:* **t. of spades,** deux de pique; (*at dominoes, etc.*) **double t.,** double-deux *m, pl.* doubles-deux; (*telephone number*) **for Geneva dial double t.,** pour Genève composez le vingt-deux; *Mus:* **t.-four time,** mesure *f* à deux quatre; deux-quatre *m*; (*b*) **t.-eyed,** (i) qui a deux yeux; (ii) (microscope, etc.) binoculaire; **t.-footed,** à deux pieds, pattes; bipède; **t. handled,** à deux poignées; (corbeille, etc.) à deux anses; **t.-monthly magazine,** revue bimestrielle; **t.-yearly,** (congrès, etc.) biennal; **t.-pointed,** (chapeau) bicorne; **t.-horse carriage,** voiture à deux chevaux; **t. oar,** embarcation *f* à deux avirons; *Mus:* **t. part song,** chanson *f* à deux voix; *Pol:* **t. chamber system,** système bicaméral; **t.-headed,** bicéphale; *Her:* (aigle) double, à deux têtes; *Bot:* **t.-lipped,** bilabié; **t.-stamened,** diandre, diandrique; *Ent:* **t.-winged,** diptère; **t.-wheeled vehicles,** véhicules *m* biroues, à deux roues; deux-roues *m*; *Aut:* **t.-door (car),** voiture *f* à deux portes; deux-portes *f*; *Aut: Av:* **t.-seater,** voiture, avion *m*, à deux places; biplace *m*; *Av:* **t.-bladed,** (hélice) bipale; **t.-engine(d),** bimoteur; **t.-engine(d) jet (plane),** biréacteur *m*; *I.C.E:* **t.-stroke engine,** moteur *m* à deux temps; *Mec.E: etc:* **t.-speed,** (machine, etc.) à deux vitesses; *El:* **t.-phase,** (courant) biphasé, diphasé; **t.-pin,** (contact) à deux fiches; **t.-pole,** (moteur) bipolaire, à deux pôles; **t.-wire,** (système, etc.) à deux fils, bifilaire; *Cmptr:* **t.-address instruction,** instruction *f* à deux adresses; **t.-plus-one address,** à deux adresses d'opérande et une adresse de commande; *Typ:* **t.-line capitals,** grandes majuscules.

two-bit ['tu:bit], *a. NAm: F:* (*a*) qui coûte 25 cents; (*b*) insignifiant, à la manque.

two-by-four ['tu:bai'fɔ:r]. **1.** *s. Carp:* pièce *f* de bois qui mesure deux pouces (5,08 cm) d'épaisseur sur quatre pouces (10,16 cm) de largeur (en grume). **2.** *a. esp. NAm: F:* tout petit, insignifiant.

two-cleft ['tu:kleft], *a. Bot:* bifide.

two-colour ['tu:kʌlər], *a.* de deux couleurs; *Typewr:* (ruban) bicolore; *Typ:* **t.-c. process,** bichromie *f.*

two-decker [tu:'dekər], *s. Nau:* navire *m* à deux ponts; deux-ponts *m.*

two-dimensional ['tu:di'menʃənəl, -dai-], *a.* (*a*) (espace, géométrie) à deux dimensions; (*b*) (roman, etc.) sans profondeur; (*c*) *Cmptr:* (tableau) à double entrée.

two-edged ['tu:edʒd], *a.* **1.** (épée, argument) à deux tranchants, à double tranchant; (compliment) ambigu. **2.** *Bot:* (*of stem, etc.*) ancipité.

two-faced ['tu:feist], *a.* **1.** *Tex:* (étoffe) sans envers, à double envers; *Sculp:* **t.-f. statue,** bifrons *m*. **2.** (*of pers.*) à double face, à deux visages, fourbe, faux, hypocrite.

twofer ['tu:fər], *s. esp. NAm: P:* **1.** cigare *m* de mauvaise qualité; *P:* crapulos *m*. **2.** *Th:* bon *m* pour l'achat de deux billets (à) demi-tarif.

two-fisted [tu:'fistid], *a. F:* **1.** maladroit, lourdaud. **2.** costaud.

twofold ['tu:fould]. **1.** *a.* double; (cordage) à deux brins. **2.** *adv.* doublement; **kindness returned t.,** bontés rendues au double.

two-handed [tu:'hændid], *a.* **1.** (*a*) **t.-h. sword,** épée *f* à deux mains, espadon *m*; (*b*) **t.-h. saw,** scie *f* passe-partout, arpon *m*. **2.** *Z: etc:* bimane. **3.** ambidextre. **4.** *Cards: etc:* (jeu) qui se joue à deux.

two-legged [tu:'legd, -'legid], *a.* à deux jambes, à deux pattes; bipède.

two-lipped [tu:'lipt], *a. Bot:* bilabié.

two-masted [tu:'mɑ:stid], *a.* (navire) à deux mâts.

two-master [tu:'mɑ:stər], *s. Nau:* deux-mâts *m inv.*

twopence ['tʌpəns], *s.* deux pence *m*; *F:* **one wouldn't have given t. for his chance of survival,** on n'aurait pas donné deux sous de sa vie; **it isn't worth t.,** ça ne vaut pas chipette; **t. coloured,** (article) criard, de mauvais goût.

twopenny ['tʌp(ə)ni]. **1.** *a.* (*a*) à, de, deux pence; (*b*) *Pej: O:* (article) de deux pence; (*b*) *Pej: O:* (article) de quatre sous. **2.** *s.* (*when talking to children*) *F:* tête *f*, *F:* caboche *f.*

twopenny-halfpenny ['tʌp(ə)ni'heipni], *a. O:* **1. a t.-h. stamp,** un timbre de deux pence et demi. **2.** *F:* insignifiant; sans importance; *F:* de quatre sous; **all that fuss over a t.-h. ring!** tout ça pour une méchante bague de quatre sous!

twopennyworth ['tu:peniwɔ:θ, *F:* -'penəθ], *s.* pour deux pence de (qch.); *F:* **if he had only t. of spunk,** s'il avait pour seulement quatre sous de courage.

two-piece ['tu:pi:s], *a. & s.* **t.-p. (suit, swimsuit),** complet, tailleur, maillot de bain, en deux pièces; deux-pièces *m.*

two-ply ['tu:plai], *a.* **1.** (cordage) à deux brins; **t.-p. wool,** laine *f* deux fils. **2.** (*of fabric, veneer, etc.*) à, en, deux épaisseurs.

two-sided [tu:'saidid], *a.* **1.** (*of paralysis, contract, etc.*) bilatéral. **2.** (*of question, argument, etc.*) qui comporte deux points de vue, qui a deux aspects.

twosome ['tu:səm], *s.* jeu *m*, partie *f*, à deux joueurs; danse *f* par couples; *Cards:* jeu à deux mains; paire *f*, couple *m* (d'amis, d'associés); *F: esp. Sp:* tandem *m.*

two-step ['tu:step], *s. Danc: Mus:* pas *m* de deux.

two-stroke ['tu:strouk]. **1.** *a.* (moteur, cycle) à deux temps. **2.** *s.* motocyclette *f* avec moteur à deux temps; **my motorcycle is a t.-s.,** ma moto est à deux temps, est un deux-temps; **t.-s. mixture,** (mélange *m*) deux-temps.

two-suiter ['tu:s(j)u:tər], *s. Cards:* jeu composé de deux couleurs.

two-time[1] ['tu:taim], *v.tr. NAm: F:* tromper (un amant, client, etc.).

two-time[2], *a. NAm: F:* **t.-t. loser,** récidiviste *mf* pour la deuxième fois.

two-timer ['tu:taimər], *s. NAm: F:* (*a*) mari, femme, amant(e), infidèle; (*b*) dupeur *m*, faux jeton.

two-tone ['tu:toun], *a.* **1. t.-t. paintwork, car,** peinture *f*, voiture *f*, deux tons. **2.** *Cmptr:* **t.-t. keying,** télégraphie *f* à deux fréquences porteuses.

'twould [twud] = **it would.**

two-up ['tu:ʌp], *s. Austr:* jeu *m* de hasard où l'on jette deux pièces pour avoir deux pile ou deux face.

two-way ['tu:wei], *a.* **1.** (*a*) (robinet) à deux voies, à deux eaux; (*b*) **t.-w. street,** rue *f* à double sens (de circulation); **t.-w. mirror,** miroir *m* sans tain. **2.** (*a*) **t.-w. communication,** *Telecom:* communication bilatérale; *Cmptr:* dialogue *m* (homme/machine); **t.-w. radio,** poste émetteur-récepteur; **t.-w. trade,** commerce *m* dans les deux sens; **t.-w. guarantee,** garantie *f* réciproque; (*b*) (outil, etc.) à deux modes d'emploi.

two-year-old ['tu:jərould], *a. & s.* **t.-y.-o. (child),** enfant (âgé) de deux ans; *Turf: etc:* **t.-y.-o. (colt, filly),** poulain *m*, pouliche *f*, de deux ans; deux-ans *m.*

twyer ['twiər], *s. Metall:* tuyère *f*; **t. sides,** costières *f*, côtières *f* (de haut fourneau).

tychism ['taikizm], *s. Phil:* tychisme *m.*

tycoon [tai'ku:n], *s.* **1.** *Jap.Hist:* taïcoun *m*. **2.** *F:* magnat *m*, brasseur *m* d'affaires; grand manitou.

Tydeus ['taidju:s], *Pr.n.m. Gr.Lit:* Tydée.

tye [tai], *s. Nau:* itague *f.*

tyg [tig], *s. Archeol:* coupe *f* à deux ou à plusieurs anses.

tying[1] ['taiiŋ], *a.* (poste, emploi) assujettissant.

tying[2], *s.* **1.** (*a*) nouage *m* (d'un nœud, etc.); (*b*) *Fish:* montage *m* (de l'hameçon, la mouche); (*c*) *Const:* chainage *m* (des murs); renforcement *m* (d'une chaudière, etc.) avec des tirants. **2. t. up,** (*a*) ficelage *m* (d'un paquet); bandage *m*, pansement *m* (d'un bras blessé); (*b*) mise *f* à l'attache (d'un cheval); ligotage *m* (de qn); (*c*) immobilisation *f* (de ses capitaux); (*d*) *Hort:* ligotage *m* (d'un cep).

tyke [taik], *s. F:* **1.** vilain chien, cabot *m*. **2.** rustre *m*. **3. (Yorkshire) t.,** homme du Yorkshire. **4.** *NAm:* enfant (*esp.* malicieux); petit coquin.

tyle [tail], *v.tr.* (*freemasonry*) tuiler, garder l'entrée de (la loge).

tyler ['tailər], *s.* (*freemasonry*) (frère) couvreur, tuilleur *m.*

Tylopoda [tai'lɔpədə], *s.pl. Z:* tylopodes *m.*

tylosis, *pl.* **-loses** [tai'lousis, -'lousi:z], *s.* **1.** (*a*) *Med:* blépharite *f* avec induration du rebord palpébral; (*b*) thyllose *f*. **2.** (*also* **tylose** ['tailous]) (*a*) *Med:* tylose *f*, cor *m* au pied; œil-de-perdrix *m, pl.* œils-de-perdrix; callosité *f*; (*b*) *Bot:* thylle *f.*

tymbal ['timbəl], *s. Ent:* timbale *f* (de cigale, etc.).

tymp [timp], *s. Metall:* tympe *f* (de haut fourneau); **t. arch,** encorbellement *m* de la tympe.

tympan ['timpən], *s. Arch: Typ: etc:* tympan *m*; *Typ:* **t. sheet,** marge *f*; **t. paper,** (papier *m* de, à) décharge (*f*), papier intercalaire.

tympanal ['timpənəl], *a. Anat: Z:* tympanal, -aux.

tympani ['timpəni], *s.pl. Mus:* timbales *f*.

tympanic [tim'pænik], *a. & s. Anat:* **t. membrane,** membrane *f* tympanique, du tympan (de l'oreille); **t. (bone),** (os) tympanal (*m*), -aux.

tympanist ['timpənist], *s. Mus:* timbalier *m*.

tympanites [timpə'naiti:z], *s. Med:* tympanisme *m*, tympanite *f*; gonflement *m* de l'abdomen.

tympanitic [timpə'nitik], *a. Med:* **t. resonance,** son *m* tympanique; tympanisme *m*.

tympanitis [timpə'naitis], *s. Med:* **1.** = TYMPANITES. **2.** tympanite *f*, otite moyenne.

tympanum, *pl.* **-a, -ums** ['timpənəm, -ə, -əmz], *s. Anat: Arch: Hyd.E:* tympan *m*; *NAm: Tp:* membrane (vibrante), plaque vibrante (d'un téléphone).

Tyndall ['tindəl], *Pr.n. Ph:* **T. effect,** effet *m* Tyndall.

tyndallization [tindəlai'zeiʃ(ə)n], *s.* tyndallisation *f*.

Tynwald ['tinwɔld], *s.* corps législatif de l'île de Man.

typal ['taip(ə)l], *a.* **1.** typique. **2.** typographique.

type[1] [taip], *s.* **1.** type *m*; (*a*) **the true French t.,** le vrai type français; **wine of the Sauterne t., Sauterne t. wine,** vin (de) genre sauternes; **people of this t.,** des personnes de ce genre, de cette catégorie; cette sorte de gens; **people of every t.,** des gens, de toutes sortes; *F:* **she's not my t.,** elle n'est pas mon genre; *NAm:* **he's not the t. of person we want,** il ne fera pas notre affaire du tout; **different types of goods,** différentes catégories de marchandises; *Ind: etc:* **equipment of the American t.,** équipement de type américain; **rifle of the French t.,** fusil (de) modèle français; **t. certificate, test,** certificat *m*, essai *m*, d'homologation; *Nat.Hist:* **t. genus,** genre type; **t. specimen,** échantillon *m* type; *Geol:* **t. locality,** région qui donne son nom à un minerai, etc.; **prehistoric t. site, station,** site *m*, station *f*, préhistorique (où fut pour la première fois définie une culture, etc.); (*b*) *F:* **what a t.!** quel type! **the t. with the red beard,** le type, l'individu, à barbe rousse; (*c*) *Num:* type (représenté sur une médaille). **2.** (*a*) *Typ:* (i) caractère *m*, type; (ii) *coll.* caractères; **old t.,** vieille matière; **to print in large t.,** imprimer en gros caractères; *Journ: etc:* **printed, displayed, in bold t.,** en vedette; **to set t.,** composer; **in t.,** composé; **packet of t.,** paquet *m* de composition; **to keep the t. standing,** conserver la forme; **to distribute the t.,** distribuer le plomb; **t. area,** justification *f*; **t. body,** corps *m* (de caractère); **t. face,** œil *m* (de caractère); **t. metal,** alliage *m* pour caractères d'imprimerie; **t. scale,** lignomètre *m*; *Typewr:* **t. wheel,** roulette *f* à caractères; *Cmptr:* roue *f* d'impression, à caractères; (iii) (*with pl.* **types**) sorte *f* de caractère; fonte *f* de caractères; (iv) *NAm:* imprimé *m*; (v) *NAm:* erreur *f* typographique; coquille *f*; (*b*) texte dactylographié.

type[2], *v.tr.* **1.** être le type de, typer (qn, qch.). **2.** *Med:* **to t. a blood sample,** déterminer le groupe d'un prélèvement de sang. **3.** *Th:* = TYPECAST.

type[3], *v.tr.* écrire, transcrire, à la machine; dactylographier; frapper, *F:* taper (une lettre, etc.) (à la machine); **everything she types is full of mistakes,** tout ce qu'elle tape est plein d'erreurs; **to t. in a correction,** écrire une correction à la machine; **to t. (out) a quotation,** copier une citation à la machine; *v.i.* **he types well,** il tape bien.

typebar ['taipbɑ:r], *s.* **1.** (*a*) *Typewr:* tige *f* à caractères; (*b*) *Cmptr:* barre *f* d'impression, à caractères, barre porte-caractères. **2.** *Typ:* ligne-bloc *f*, *pl.* lignes-blocs (de linotype).

typecast ['taipkɑ:st], *v.tr. Th: Cin:* (i) faire jouer à (un acteur) le rôle d'un personnage qui lui ressemble; (ii) donner toujours les mêmes rôles à (un acteur).

typecaster ['taipkɑ:stər], **typefounder** ['taipfaundər], *s.* fondeur *m* en caractères d'imprimerie; fondeur typographe.

typecutter ['taipkʌtər], *s. Typ:* graveur *m* de caractères.

typefoundry ['taipfaundri], *s. Typ:* fonderie *f* de caractères.

typescript ['taipskript], *s.* texte dactylographié.

typesetter ['taipsetər], *s. Typ:* **1.** (*pers.*) compositeur *m*. **2.** machine *f* à composer; compositeur, composeuse *f*.

typesetting ['taipsetiŋ], *s. Typ:* composition *f*; **t. machine** = TYPESETTER 2; *Cmptr:* **t. computer,** ordinateur *m* de composition automatique.

typewrite ['taiprait], *v.tr. O:* (*except in p.p.* **typewritten** *q.v.*) = TYPE[3].

typewriter ['taipraitər], *s.* **1.** machine *f* à écrire; **portable t.,** machine à écrire portative. **2.** *A:* = TYPIST.

typewriting ['taipraitiŋ], *s.* **1.** dactylographie *f*. **2.** écriture *f* à la machine.

typewritten ['taiprit(ə)n], *a.* (document, etc.) transcrit, écrit à la machine, dactylographié, *F:* tapé (à la machine).

typha ['taifə], *s. Bot:* typha *m*; *F:* massette *f*.

Typhaceae [tai'feisii:], *s.pl. Bot:* typhacées *f*.

typhlitis [ti'flaitis], *s. Med:* typhlite *f*.

typhlomegaly [tiflou'megəli], *s. Med:* typhlomégalie *f*.

typhlopexy ['tifloupeksi], *s. Surg:* typhlopexie *f*.

Typhlopidae [ti'flɔpidi:], *s.pl. Rept:* typhlopidés *m*.

typhoid ['taifɔid], *a. Med:* typhoïde; **t. bacillus,** bacille *m* typhoïdique; **t. fever,** *s.* **t.,** (fièvre *f*) typhoïde (*f*); *Vet:* **fowl t.,** typhose *f* aviaire.

typhoidal [tai'fɔidl], *a. Med:* typhoïque, typhoïdique.

typhomalaria [taifoumə'lɛəriə], *s. Med:* typhomalaria *f*.

typhomania [taifou'meiniə], *s. Med:* typhomanie *f*.

typhoon [tai'fu:n], *s. Meteor:* typhon *m*; ouragan *m*.

typhosis [tai'fousis], *s. Med:* typhose *f*.

typhotoxin [taifou'tɔksin], *s. Med:* typhotoxine *f*.

typhous ['taifəs], *a. Med:* typhique.

typhus ['taifəs], *s.* **1.** *Med:* (*a*) **t. (fever),** typhus *m*; **scrub t.,** typhus rural, fièvre fluviale du Japon; (*b*) *F: A:* fièvre typhoïde. **2.** *Vet:* **canine t.,** néphrite *f* des chiens; **equine t.,** purpura *m* des équidés.

typical ['tipikl], *a.* typique, typifié; **the t. Frenchman,** le vrai type français; le Français typique; **t. motor cycle,** motocyclette type; **three t. fashions of the year,** trois modes types de l'année; *F:* **isn't that t. (of him, her)!** c'est bien de lui, d'elle! **that action is t. of him,** cette action le peint bien, l'achève de peindre; **that is t. of France,** c'est un trait caractéristique de la France.

typically ['tipikəli], *adv.* d'une manière typique; typiquement; **he's t. French,** c'est le vrai type français, le vrai type du Français.

typify ['tipifai], *v.tr.* **1.** (*of symbol, etc.*) représenter (qch.); symboliser (qch.). **2.** (*of specimen, etc.*) être caractéristique de (sa classe, etc.); (*of pers.*) être le type de, personnifier (l'officier, etc.).

typing[1] ['taipiŋ], *s.* (*a*) identification *f*, détermination *f* des types (de bactéries, de virus); *Med:* **blood t. unit,** service *m* de détermination du groupage sanguin; (*b*) groupage *m* par types.

typing[2], *s.* dactylographie *f*, *F:* dactylo *f*; écriture *f* à la machine; **he's good at t.,** il tape bien à la machine; **t. error,** erreur *f*, faute *f*, de frappe; **t. exercises,** exercices *m* dactylographiques; **t. paper,** papier *m* (pour) machine (à écrire); **t. pool,** équipe *f* de dactylos.

typist ['taipist], *s.* **(copy) t.,** dactylographe *mf*, *F:* dactylo *mf*; **audio t.,** dactylo audio-magnéto; **t. invoice clerk,** dactylo-facturière *f*, *pl.* dactylos-facturières; **typist's error,** erreur *f*, faute *f*, de frappe.

typo ['taipou], *s. F:* **1.** typographe *m*, *F:* typo *m*. **2.** *NAm:* faute *f* typographique; *F:* coquille *f*.

typo- ['taipou, 'taipə, tai'pɔ], *comb.fm.* typo-.

typograph ['taipəgræf], *v.tr.* typographier.

typographer [tai'pɔgrəfər], *s.* **1.** typographe *m*, *F:* typo *m*. **2.** *Ent:* bostryche *m* typographe.

typographic(al) [taipə'græfik(l)], *a.* **1.** typographique. **2.** *Ent:* **typographic beetle,** bostryche *m* typographe.

typographically [taipə'græfikəli], *adv.* typographiquement.

typography [tai'pɔgrəfi], *s.* typographie *f*.

typolithography [taipouli'θɔgrəfi], *s.* typolithographie *f*.

typological [taipou'lɔdʒikl], *a.* typologique.

typology [tai'pɔlədʒi], *s.* typologie *f*.

typometer [tai'pɔmitər], *s. Typ:* typomètre *m*.

typotelegraph [taipou'teligræf], *s. Tg:* typotélégraphe *m*.

typotelegraphy [taipouti'legrəfi], *s. Tg:* typotélégraphie *f*.

tyramine ['tairəmi:n], *s. Bio-Ch:* tyramine *f*.

tyrannical [ti'rænikl], *a.* tyrannique.

tyrannically [ti'rænik(ə)li], *adv.* tyranniquement.

tyrannicidal [tiræni'saidəl], *a.* tyrannicide.

tyrannicide[1] [ti'rænisaid], *s.* tyrannicide *mf*.

tyrannicide[2], *s.* (crime *m* de) tyrannicide *m*.

Tyrannidae [ti'rænidi:], *s.pl. Orn:* tyrannidés *m*.

tyrannize ['tirənaiz], *v.i. & tr.* faire le tyran; **to t. (over) s.o.,** tyranniser qn; **he tyrannizes (over) his family,** il est le tyran de sa famille.

tyrannosaur(us) [ti'rænousɔ:r, -'sɔ:rəs], *s. Paleont:* tyrannosaure *m*.

tyrannous ['tirənəs], *a.* tyrannique.

tyrannously ['tirənəsli], *adv.* tyranniquement, en tyran.

tyranny ['tirəni], *s.* tyrannie *f*; **the t. of fashion,** la tyrannie, la servitude, de la mode.

tyrant ['tairənt], *s.* **1.** tyran *m*; **petty t.,** tyranneau *m*; **to play the t.,** faire le tyran; **woman who is a domestic t.,** femme qui tyrannise toute la famille. **2.** *Orn:* **t. (bird, flycatcher),** tyran.

tyre[1] ['taiər], *s.* (*a*) (*usu.* **tire**) bandage *m*, cerclage *m*, cercle *m* (de roue); **solid t.,** bandage plein; *Rail:* **flanged t.,** bandage à boudin; **blank t.,** bandage sans boudin; **t. press,** presse *f* à bandages; (*b*) *Aut: etc:* pneu *m*, *pl.* pneus; pneumatique *m*; **textile, metallic, cord t.,** pneu à carcasse textile, métallique; **cross ply, radial ply, t.,** pneu à carcasse croisée, radiale; **tubeless t.,** pneu sans chambre, pneu tubeless; *A:* **wired t., straight-sided t.,** pneu à tringles, à flancs droits; **aircraft t.,** pneu avion; **car t.,** *NAm:* **auto t.,** pneu tourisme; **giant, heavy lorry, t.,** *NAm:* **truck t.,** pneu poids lourd; **light giant t.,** *NAm:* **light truck t.,** pneu camionnette; **earth-mover t.,** pneu génie civil; **t. carrier,** porte-pneu *m inv*; **t. cover,** enveloppe *f* (pour pneu); **t. inflator, pump,** gonfleur *m*, pompe *f*, pour pneus; **t. lever,** démonte-pneu *m*, *pl.* démonte-pneus.

tyre[2], *v.tr.* **1.** (*usu.* **tire**) poser, monter, un bandage à (une roue); cercler (une roue); *Rail:* bander, embattre (une roue). **2.** *Aut: etc:* munir (une voiture, etc.) de pneus; chausser (une voiture).

Tyre[3], *Pr.n. Hist: Geog:* Tyr.

tyred ['taiəd], *a.* (*with adj. or noun prefixed*) **steel, solid, t.,** à bandage(s) d'acier, à bandage(s) plein(s); **rubber t. wheel,** roue caoutchoutée.

tyreless ['taiəlis], *a.* **1.** (*usu.* **tireless**) sans bandage(s). **2.** *Aut: etc:* sans pneu(s); (*of car*) non chaussé.

Tyrian ['tiriən], *a. & s. A. Geog:* tyrien, -ienne.

tyring ['taiəriŋ], *s.* **1.** pose *f* d'un bandage (à une roue); cerclage *m* (d'une roue); *Rail:* embat(t)age *m*. **2.** *Aut: etc:* mise *f* des pneus (à une voiture, etc.).

tyro ['tairou], *s.* novice *mf*; débutant, -ante.

Tyrol (the) [ðə'tirəl, ti'roul], *Pr.n. Geog:* le Tyrol.

Tyrolean [tirə'li:ən], *a. Geog:* tyrolien; *Cost:* **T. hat,** chapeau tyrolien.

Tyrolese [tirə'li:z]. *Geog:* **1.** *a.* tyrolien. **2.** *s.* Tyrolien, -ienne.

Tyrolienne [tirouli'en], *s. Mus:* tyrolienne *f*.

tyrolite ['tairəlait], *s. Miner:* tyrolite *f*.

tyrosinase [tai'rɔsineis], *s. Bio-Ch:* tyrosinase *f*.

tyrosin(e) ['tairəsi:n], *s. Bio-Ch:* tyrosine *f*.

tyrothricin [tairə'θrisin], *s. Pharm:* tyrothricine *f*.

Tyrrhenian [ti'ri:niən], **Tyrrhene** ['tiri:n]. *Hist: Geog:* **1.** *a.* tyrrhénien; **the Tyrrhenian Sea,** la Mer Tyrrhénienne. **2.** *s.* Tyrrhénien, -ienne.

Tyrtaeus [tə:'ti:əs], *Pr.n.m. Gr.Lit:* Tyrtée.

tysonite ['taisənait], *s. Miner:* tysonite *f*.

tzar [zɑ:r], *s.m.* czar, tsar.

tzarevitch ['zɑ:rəvitʃ], *s.m.* czarévitch, tsarévitch.

tzarina [zɑ:'ri:nə], *s.f.* czarine, tsarine.

tzigane [tsi'gɑ:n], *a. & s.* tzigane (*mf*).

U

U, u [ju:], *s.* (la lettre) U, u *m*; *Tp:* **U for uncle,** U comme Ursule; *Geog:* **U-shaped valley,** vallée (à profil) en U; *F:* **U and non U,** ce qui est bien, chic, comme il faut, et ce qui ne l'est pas; *Mec.E: etc:* **U-bolt,** étrier *m*; *Ch:* **U tube,** tube *m* coudé à deux branches; *Aut:* **U turn,** demi-tour *m, pl.* demi-tours; *P.N:* **no U turns,** demi-tour interdit; *Cin:* (= *universal*) **U film,** *F:* **U,** film *m* pour tout le monde; **U boat,** sous-marin allemand.

uakari [ju:ə'kɑ:ri], *s. Z:* ouakari *m*.

ubac ['ju:bæk], *s. Geog:* ubac *m*; (*in Alps*) ombrée *f.*

Ubangi [(j)u:'bæŋgi], *Pr.n. Geog:* Oubangui *m*; *Hist:* **U.-Chari** [-'ʃæri], Oubangui-Chari *m*.

uberous ['ju:bərəs], *a.* riche en lait; (vache) bonne laitière.

ubiquitarian [ju:bikwi'tɛəriən]. *Rel.H:* **1.** *a.* (doctrine) ubiquiste. **2.** *s.* ubiquitaire *mf*, ubiquiste *mf.*

ubiquitarianism [ju:bikwi'tɛəriənizm], **ubiquitism** [ju:'bikwitizm], *s. Rel.H:* ubiquisme *m*.

ubiquitous [ju:'bikwitəs], *a.* **1.** ubiquiste; doué d'ubiquité; qui se trouve, que l'on rencontre, partout; **I'm not u.,** je n'ai pas le don d'ubiquité. **2.** *Theol:* omniprésent.

ubiquity [ju:'bikwiti], *s.* **1.** ubiquité *f.* **2.** *Theol:* omniprésence *f.*

udder ['ʌdər], *s.* mamelle *f*, pis *m* (de vache, etc.).

udometer [ju:'dɔmitər], *s. Meteor:* udomètre *m*, pluviomètre *m*.

udometric [ju:dou'metrik], *a. Meteor:* udométrique, pluviométrique.

Ufa ['u:fɑ:], *Pr.n. Geog:* Oufa *m*.

ufoism ['ju:fouizm], *s.* ufologie *f.*

ufoist ['ju:fouist], *s.* ufologue *mf.*

ufologist [ju:'fɔlədʒist], *s.* ufologue *mf.*

Uganda [ju(:)'gændə], *Pr.n. Geog:* Ouganda *m*.

Ugandan [ju(:)'gændən]. *Geog:* **1.** *a.* ougandais. **2.** *s.* Ougandais, -aise.

ugh [ʌχ, u:], *int.* pouah! beuh!

ugli, *pl.* **ugli(e)s** ['ʌgli,-iz], *s. Hort:* tangelo *m*.

uglification [ʌglifi'keiʃ(ə)n], *s.* enlaidissement *m*.

uglify ['ʌglifai], *v.tr.* enlaidir.

ugliness ['ʌglinis], *s.* laideur *f.*

ugly ['ʌgli], *a.* (*a*) (*of pers.*) laid; disgracieux; **she's as u. as sin,** elle est laide comme les sept péchés capitaux, comme un pou, à faire peur; c'est un remède d'amour; **u. person,** laideron *m*; **to grow u.,** (s')enlaidir; **u. duckling,** vilain petit canard; *F:* **to turn, cut up, u.,** se fâcher, se mettre en colère, en rogne; (*b*) (*of thg*) vilain; **u. piece of furniture,** vilain meuble; **u. wound,** vilaine blessure; **u. rumour,** mauvais bruit; **u. incident,** incident regrettable.

Ugolino [ju:gou'li:nou], *Pr.n.m. Hist:* Ugolin.

Ugrian, Ugric ['ju:griən, -grik]. **1.** *a. Ethn:* ougrien. **2.** *s.* (*a*) *Ethn:* Ougrien, -ienne; (*b*) *Ling:* langue ougrienne.

uh [ə:], *int.* euh!

uhlan ['u:lɑ:n], *s. Mil.Hist:* uhlan *m*.

uinta(h)ite [ju:'intə(h)ait], *s. Miner:* uintahite *f*, gilsonite *f.*

Uintatherium [ju:intə'θi:əriəm], *s. Paleont:* uintatherium *m*, uintathérium *m*.

Uitlander ['eitləndər], *s. Hist:* (*in S. Africa*) uitlander *m*; étranger *m*.

ukase [ju:'keiz], *s.* (o)ukase *m*.

Ukraine [ju:'krein], *Pr.n. Geog:* Ukraine *f.*

Ukrainian [ju:'kreiniən]. **1.** *Geog:* (*a*) *a.* ukra(i)nien; (*b*) *s.* Ukra(i)nien, -ienne. **2.** *s. Ling:* ukra(i)nien *m*.

ukulele [ju:kə'leili], *s. Mus:* ukulele *m*; guitare hawaïenne.

ulama, ulema ['ju:ləmə, -im-], *s. Rel:* **1.** uléma *m*, ouléma *m*. **2.** membre *m* d'un uléma.

ulcer ['ʌlsər], *s.* ulcère *m*; (*produced by cauterizing*) cautère *m*; **stomach u.,** ulcère de, à, l'estomac; **peptic u.,** ulcère simple de l'estomac; **rodent, wasting, u.,** ulcère rongeant, rongeur; phagédène *f*; **endemic u.,** ulcère d'Orient; bouton *m* d'Orient, d'Alep.

ulcerate ['ʌlsəreit]. *Med:* **1.** *v.tr.* ulcérer; **ulcerated wound,** blessure ulcérée, ulcéreuse. **2.** *v.i.* s'ulcérer.

ulceration [ʌlsə'reiʃ(ə)n], *s.* ulcération *f.*

ulcerative ['ʌls(ə)rətiv], *a. Med:* ulcératif; *Vet:* **u. lymphangitis,** lymphangite ulcéreuse.

ulcered ['ʌlsəd], *a.* ulcéré, ulcéreux.

ulcerlike ['ʌlsəlaik], *a. Med:* ulcériforme, ulcéroïde.

ulcerogenic [ʌlsərou'dʒenik], *a. Med:* ulcérogène.

ulceromembranous [ʌlsərou'membrənəs], *a. Med:* ulcéro-membraneux.

ulcerous ['ʌlsərəs], *a. Med:* ulcéreux.

ulcus, *pl.* **ulcera** ['ʌlkəs, 'ʌlsərə], *s. Med:* ulcus *m*.

ulex ['ju:leks], *s. Bot:* ulex *m*; ajonc *m*.

ulexine [ju:'leksi(:)n], *s. Ch:* ulexine *f*, cytisine *f.*

ulexite ['ju:liksait], *s. Miner:* ulexite *f.*

uliginal, uliginous [ju:'lidʒin(ə)l, -dʒinəs], *a. Bot: etc:* uliginaire, uligineux.

ullage[1] ['ʌlidʒ], *s.* **1.** *Winem: etc:* (*a*) **(dry) u.,** vidange *f*; coulage *m*; *Cust:* manquant *m*; (*b*) **(wet) u.,** vin, etc. qui reste dans un tonneau; creux *m* du tonnoir; (*c*) *F: A:* lavasse *f.* **2.** *Engr:* copeaux (enlevés par le burin).

ullage[2], *v.tr. Winem: etc:* **1.** calculer, estimer, le manquant (d'un tonneau). **2.** tirer un peu de liquide (d'un tonneau). **3.** ouiller (un tonneau).

ullaged ['ʌlidʒd], *a. Winem: etc:* (tonneau) (i) en vidange, (ii) où il y a du vide.

ullaging ['ʌlədʒiŋ], *s. Winem: etc:* **1.** calcul *m*, estimation *f*, du manquant. **2.** ouillage *m*.

uller ['ʌlər], *s. Winem:* ouillette *f.*

ullmannite ['ʌlmənait], *s. Miner:* ullman(n)ite *f.*

Ulloa [u'ljouə], *Pr.n.m.* Ulloa; *Meteor: Opt:* **Ulloa's circle,** anthélie *f.*

ullucu [u:'ju:ku:], *s. Bot:* ullucu *m*, ulluco *m*, ulluque *m*.

Ulmaceae [ʌl'meisii:], *s.pl. Bot:* ulmacées *f.*

ulmaceous [ʌl'meiʃəs], *a. Bot:* ulmacé.

ulmaria [ʌl'mɛəriə], *s. Bot:* **(spiraea) u.,** ulmaire *f*; reine *f* des prés.

ulmic ['ʌlmik], *a. Ch:* (acide) ulmique.

ulmin ['ʌlmin], *s. Ch:* ulmine *f.*

ulmous ['ʌlməs], *a. Ch:* (acide) ulmique.

ulna ['ʌlnə], *s. Anat:* cubitus *m*.

ulnar ['ʌlnər], *a. Anat:* ulnaire; cubital, -aux.

Ulothrix ['ju:ləθriks], *s. Algae:* ulotrix *m*, ulotric *m*, ulotriche *m*.

Ulotrichales [ju:lɔtri'keili:z], *s.pl. Algae:* ulotricales *f.*

ulotrichan, ulotrichous [ju:'lɔtrikən, -əs], *a. Anthr:* ulotrique; ulotriche; aux cheveux crépus.

Ulster ['ʌlstər]. **1.** *Pr.n. Geog:* (i) Ulster *m*; (ii) Irlande *f* du Nord; Ulster; **U. Catholics,** catholiques de l'Irlande du Nord; *Pol:* **U. Unionist,** Ulstérien, -ienne. **2.** *s. Cost:* ulster *m*.

Ulsterian [ʌls'tiəriən], *a. & s. Geol:* ulstérien (*m*).

Ulsterman, *pl.* **-men** ['ʌlstəmən], *s.m. Geog:* Ulstérien.

Ulsterwoman, *pl.* **-women** ['ʌlstəwumən, -wimin], *s.f.* Ulstérienne.

ulterior [ʌl'tiəriər], *a.* **1.** ultérieur. **2.** secret; inavoué; **u. designs,** desseins secrets; **u. motive,** motif secret, caché; **without u. motive,** sans arrière-pensée.

ulteriorly [ʌl'tiəriəli], *adv.* ultérieurement; plus tard.

ultimate ['ʌltimət], *a.* (*a*) final, -als; **u. goal, end, purpose,** but final; **u. decision,** décision définitive; (*b*) *Ch:* **u. analysis,** analyse *f* ultime; *Mth:* **u. ratio,** extrême raison; (*c*) fondamental, -aux; **u. truth,** vérité fondamentale, élémentaire; **u. cause,** cause finale, profonde; *s.* **the quest for an u.,** la recherche de l'absolu; (*d*) *Ling:* (*of syllable, etc.*) ultime, dernier.

ultimately ['ʌltimətli], *adv.* (*a*) à la fin; en fin de compte; finalement; (*b*) fondamentalement.

ultimatum, *pl.* **-tums, -ta** [ʌlti'meitəm, -təmz, -tə], *s.* **1.** ultimatum *m*; **to deliver an u. to a country, to present a country with an u.,** signifier un ultimatum à un pays; **of the nature of an u.,** ultimatif. **2.** (*a*) principe fondamental; (*b*) but final.

ultimo ['ʌltimou], *adv. Com:* du mois dernier, du mois écoulé; **on the tenth u.,** le dix du mois dernier.

ultimogeniture [ʌltimou'dʒenitjər], *s.* ultimogéniture *f.*

Ultonian [ʌl'touniən]. *Geog:* **1.** *a.* ulstérien. **2.** *s.* Ulstérien, -ienne.

ultra ['ʌltrə]. **1.** *a.* extrême. **2.** *s. Pol:* ultra *mf.*

ultra- ['ʌltrə], *pref.* ultra-.

ultrabasic [ʌltrə'beisik], *a. Geol:* ultrabasique.

ultrabasite [ʌltrə'beisait], *s. Miner:* ultrabasite *f.*

ultracentrifugation [ʌltrəsentrifju'geiʃ(ə)n], *s.* ultracentrifugation *f.*

ultracentrifuge [ʌltrə'sentrifju:dʒ], *s.* ultracentrifugeur *m*, ultracentrifugeuse *f.*

ultrafashionable [ʌltrə'fæʃ(ə)nəbl], *a.* à la dernière mode; tout dernier cri.

ultrafilter[1] ['ʌltrəfiltər], *s. Ch:* ultrafiltre *m*.

ultrafilter[2], *v.tr. Ch:* ultrafiltrer.

ultrafiltration [ʌltrəfil'treiʃ(ə)n], *s. Ch:* ultrafiltration *f.*

ultraism ['ʌltrəizm], *s. Pol:* ultraïsme *m*, ultracisme *m*.

ultraist ['ʌltrəist], *s. Pol:* ultra *mf.*

ultraliberal [ʌltrə'lib(ə)rəl], *a. & s. Pol:* ultra-libéral, -aux.

ultramarine [ʌltrəmə'ri:n]. **1.** *a.* (*of colour, etc.*) ultra(-)marin; (*of country*) d'outre-mer; **u. (blue),** (blue d') outremer *m*. **2.** *s. Miner:* ultramarine *f.*

ultramicrometer [ʌltrəmai'krɔmitər], *s.* ultramicromètre *m*.

ultramicroscope [ʌltrə'maikrəskoup], *s.* ultramicroscope *m*.

ultramicroscopic [ʌltrəmaikrə'skɔpik], *a.* ultramicroscopique.

ultramicroscopy [ʌltrəmai'krɔskəpi], *s.* ultramicroscopie *f.*

ultramicrotome [ʌltrə'maikrətoum], *s.* ultramicrotome *m*.

ultramicrotomy [ʌltrəmai'krɔtəmi], *s.* ultramitrotomie *f.*

ultramodern [ʌltrə'mɔd(ə)n], *a.* ultramoderne.

ultramodernism [ʌltrə'mɔdənizm], *s.* ultramodernisme *m*.

ultramontane [ʌltrə'mɔntein]. **1.** *a.* (*a*) *Geog: Theol: Pol:* ultramontain. **2.** *s. Geog: Theol: Pol:* ultramontain, -aine.

ultramontanism [ʌltrə'mɔntənizm], *s. Theol: Pol:* ultramontanisme *m*.

ultramontanist [ʌltrə'mɔntənist], *s. Theol: Pol:* ultramontain, -aine.

ultramundane [ʌltrəmʌn'dein], *a.* ultramondain.

ultrared [ʌltrə'red], *a. Opt: A:* infra-rouge.

ultra(-)revolutionary [ʌltrərevə'lu:ʃ(ə)n(ə)ri], *a. & s.* ultra-révolutionnaire (*mf*), *pl.* ultra-révolutionnaires.

ultraroyalist [ʌltrə'rɔiəlist], *a. & s.* ultra-royaliste (*mf*), *pl.* ultra-royalistes.

ultrasensitive [ʌltrə'sensitiv], *a. Phot: etc:* ultrasensible.

ultrashort [ʌltrə'ʃɔ:t], *a. Ph:* **u. waves,** ondes ultracourtes.

ultrasonic [ʌltrə'sɔnik], *a. Ph:* ultra(-)sonore, ultra(-)sonique, supersonique; **u. waves,** ultra(-)sons *m*; **u. frequencies,** fréquences ultra(-)sonores; **ultrasonics,** science *f* des ultra(-)sons; *Metall:* **u. testing,** essai à ultra(-)son.

ultrasound ['ʌltrəsaund], *s. Ph:* ultra(-)son *m*; *Med:* **u. therapy,** ultrasonothérapie *f*.

ultrastructure ['ʌltrəstrʌktʃər], *s. Biol:* ultrastructure *f*.

ultraterrestrial [ʌltrəti'restriəl], *a.* ultraterrestre.

ultraviolet [ʌltrə'vaiələt]. *Ph:* **1.** *a.* ultra(-)violet; **u. rays,** rayons ultra(-)violets; **u. lamp,** lampe à rayons ultra(-)violets, à rayonnement ultra(-)violet; **u. spectrophotometry,** spectrophotométrie dans l'ultra(-)violet; *Med:* **u. therapy,** uviothérapie *f*. **2.** *s.* ultra(-)violet *m*.

ultra vires [ʌltrə'vaiəri:z, ultrə'vi:reiz]. *Lt.adj. & adv.phr. Jur:* au delà des pouvoirs; **action u. v.,** excès *m* de pouvoir; **to act u. v.,** commettre un excès de pouvoir.

ultravirus [ʌltrə'vaiərəs], *s. Bac:* virus filtrant, ultravirus *m*, ultragerme *m*.

ultrazodiacal [ʌltrəzou'daiək(ə)l], *a. Astr:* (*of planet*) ultra-zodiacal, -aux.

ululate ['ju:ljuleit], *v.i.* **1.** (*of owl, etc.*) ululer, huer. **2.** (*of jackal, etc.*) hurler, pousser des hurlements. **3.** (*of pers.*) se lamenter; pousser des lamentations.

ululation [ju:lju'leiʃ(ə)n], *s.* **1.** ululation *f*, ululement *m* (du hibou, etc.); hurlement *m* (du chacal, etc.). **2.** lamentation *f*.

ulva ['ʌlvə], *s. Algae:* ulve *f*; laitue *f* de mer.

Ulvaceae [ʌl'veisii:], *s.pl. Algae:* ulvacées *f*.

Ulysses ['ju:lisi:z, ju(:)'lisi:z], *Pr.n.m.* Ulysse.

umangite [(j)u:'mæŋgait], *s. Miner:* umangite *f*.

umbel ['ʌmbl], **umbella** [ʌm'belə], *s. Bot:* ombelle *f*.

umbellar [ʌm'belər], *a. Bot:* = UMBELLATE.

umbellate(d) ['ʌmbəleit(id)], *a. Bot:* ombellé, ombelliforme, en ombelle, en parasol.

umbellet ['ʌmbəlit], *s. Bot:* ombellule *f*.

umbellic [ʌm'belik], *a. Ch:* (acide) ombellique.

umbellifer [ʌm'belifər], *s. Bot:* ombellifère *f*.

Umbelliferae [ʌmbə'lifəri:], *s.pl. Bot:* ombellifères *f*.

umbelliferone [ʌmbə'lifəroun], *s. Ch:* ombelliférone *f*.

umbelliferous [ʌmbə'lifərəs], *a. Bot:* ombellifère.

Umbellula [ʌm'beljulə], *s. Coel:* ombellule *f*, ombellula *f*.

umbellule ['ʌmbəlju:l, ʌm'belju:l], *s. Bot:* ombellule *f*.

Umbellulidae [ʌmbə'lju:lidi:], *s.pl. Coel:* ombellulidés *m*.

umber[1] ['ʌmbər], *s.* **1.** *Ich:* ombre *m*. **2.** *Orn:* **u. (bird),** ombrette *f* (du Sénégal).

umber[2]. **1.** *s. Art:* terre *f* d'ombre, de Sienne; ombre *f*; **burnt u.,** terre d'ombre brûlée. **2.** *a.* couleur *inv* d'ombre.

umbilic [ʌm'bilik], *s. Mth:* ombilic *m*.

umbilical [ʌm'bilik(ə)l], *a.* **1.** (*a*) *Anat:* ombilical, -aux; **u. cord,** cordon ombilical; (*b*) *Ball:* **u. mast,** mât ombilical; **u. tower,** tour ombilicale, tour de remplissage (d'une fusée); **u. cord,** câble de liaison (d'un projectile filoguidé); **u. tether,** cordon ombilical (reliant l'astronaute à l'astronef); (*c*) (*of descent*) du côté maternel; utérin. **2.** *Mth:* **u. point,** ombilic *m*.

umbilicate(d) [ʌm'bilikət, -'bilikeitid], *a.* ombiliqué; déprimé en ombilic.

umbilication [ʌmbili'keiʃ(ə)n], *s.* ombilication *f*.

umbilicus [ʌm'bilikəs], *s.* (*a*) *Anat:* ombilic *m*, nombril *m*; (*b*) *Bot:* ombilic.

umbles ['ʌmblz], *s.pl. A:* entrailles *f*, abats *m* (de cerf, etc.).

umbo, *pl.* **-os, -ones** ['ʌmbou, -ouz, ʌm'bouni:z], *s.* **1.** *A.Arms:* ombon *m*, umbo *m* (de bouclier). **2.** *Nat.Hist:* protubérance *f*.

umbonate(d) ['ʌmbənət, -'neitid], *a. Nat.Hist:* omboné.

umbra[1], *pl.* **-ae** ['ʌmbrə, -i:], *s.* **1.** *Astr:* (*a*) cône *m* d'ombre, ombre *f* (dans une éclipse); (*b*) obscurité centrale (d'une tache solaire); (*c*) *Bot:* **u. tree,** phytolacca *m*. **2.** (*a*) *Ant:* ombre (d'un mort); (*b*) *Rom.Ant:* ombre (amenée par un invité).

umbra[2], *s. Ich:* umbrine *f*, ombrine *f*.

Umbraculidae [ʌmbrə'kju:lidi:], *s.pl. Moll:* umbraculidés *m*.

umbrage[1] ['ʌmbridʒ], *s.* **1.** *A: & Lit:* ombrage *m*. **2.** (*a*) *A:* ombrage, ressentiment *m*; (*b*) **to take u. at sth.,** prendre ombrage, se froisser, de qch.; **he didn't take u., he took no u.,** il ne s'offensait pas; *O:* **to give u. to s.o.,** porter ombrage, donner de l'ombrage, à qn.

umbrage[2], *v.tr. A: & Lit:* **1.** ombrager (un lieu). **2.** offenser, froisser (qn).

umbrageous [ʌm'breidʒəs], *a. A: & Lit:* **1.** (*a*) (arbre) ombreux; (*b*) (lieu) ombragé, ombreux. **2.** (*of pers.*) ombrageux.

umbrated ['ʌmbreitid], *a. Her:* ombragé.

umbre ['ʌmbər], *s. Orn:* ombrette *f* (du Sénégal).

umbrella [ʌm'brelə], *s.* **1.** (*a*) parapluie *m*; **to put up one's u.,** ouvrir son parapluie; **to put down, to take down, to fold (up), one's u.,** fermer, replier, son parapluie; **stumpy, dwarf, Tom Thumb, u.,** parapluie court; tom-pouce *m*, *pl.* tom-pouces; **telescopic, retractable, u.,** parapluie télescopique; **golf, fishing, u.,** grand parapluie de golf, de pêche; **beach u.,** parasol *m*; **u. frame,** monture *f*, carcasse *f*, de parapluie; **u. stand,** porte-parapluies *m inv*; **u.-shaped,** en forme de parasol; *W.Tel:* **u. aerial,** antenne *f* en parapluie; *Orn:* **u. bird,** céphaloptère *m*; *Moll:* **u. shell,** ombrelle *f*; *Bot:* **u. tree, magnolia,** magnolia *m*, magnolier *m*, (en) parasol; (*b*) *A:* ombrelle *f*; (*c*) parasol *m* (de chef de tribu, etc.); (*d*) **business u.,** consortium *m*, groupement *m* d'entreprises; **under the u. of the United Nations,** sous la protection (de l'Organisation) des Nations Unies; **under the u. of socialism,** sous la bannière, sous l'égide *f*, du socialisme; (*e*) *Mil.Av:* **air, aerial, u.,** parapluie aérien, ombrelle de protection aérienne; **fighter u.,** ombrelle de chasseurs; (*f*) *Civ.E:* bouclier *m* de creusement. **2.** *Coel: Moll:* ombrelle (de méduse, etc.).

umbrette [ʌm'bret], *s. Orn:* ombrette *f* (du Sénégal).

Umbria ['ʌmbriə], *Pr.n. Geog:* Ombrie *f*.

Umbrian ['ʌmbriən]. **1.** *Geog:* (*a*) *a.* ombrien; *Art:* **the U. School,** l'école d'Ombrie, l'école ombrienne; (*b*) *s.* Ombrien, -ienne. **2.** *s. Ling:* ombrien *m*.

umiak ['u:miæk], *s. Nau:* oumiac *m*, oumiak *m*.

umiri, umiry ['u:miri:], *s. Bot:* umiri *m*.

umlaut ['umlaut], *s. Ling:* (*a*) inflexion *f* vocalique, métaphonie *f*; umlaut *m*; (*b*) (*sign*) umlaut.

umph [hm], *int.* hum! hmm! (de doute ou de dégoût).

umpirage ['ʌmpaiəridʒ], *s.* arbitrage *m*.

umpire[1] ['ʌmpaiər], *s.* (*a*) arbitre *m*, juge *m*; (*b*) *Sp:* arbitre; **to be an u. at a match,** arbitrer un match; (*c*) *Jur:* surarbitre *m*, tiers-arbitre *m*, *pl.* tiers-arbitres.

umpire[2], *v.tr.* arbitrer (*Jur:* un différend, *Sp:* un match).

umpiring ['ʌmpaiəriŋ], *s.* arbitrage *m*.

umpteen ['ʌmp'ti:n], *s. F:* je ne sais combien; **she's got u. books on Africa,** elle a je ne sais combien, elle a des tas, de livres sur l'Afrique; **to have u. reasons for doing sth.,** avoir trente-six raisons de faire qch.

umpteenth [ʌmp'ti:nθ], *a. F:* **that's the u. time I've told you,** voilà Dieu sait combien de fois que je te le dis; c'est la n^{ième} fois que je te le dis.

'un [ən], *pron. P:* (= *one*) **a little 'un,** un petit, une petite; un petiot, une petiote; **he's a bad 'un,** c'est un sale type.

un-[1] [ʌn], *pref.* (*forming verbs expressing deprivation or reversal*) dé(s)-.

un-[2], *pref.* (*expressing negation*) **1.** in-. **2.** non. **3.** dé-. **4.** peu, mal. **5.** (ne) pas. **6.** a-. **7.** anti-. **8.** sans. **9.** manque *m* de, absence *f* de (qch.). **10.** indigne de (qn, qch.); dénué de (qch.); contraire à (qch.); exempt de (qch.).

unabashed [ʌnə'bæʃt], *a.* **1.** sans perdre contenance; sans se déconcerter, sans se décontenancer; **u. he replied,** il a répondu sans aucune confusion; *Pej:* il a répondu cyniquement. **2.** aucunement ébranlé.

unabated [ʌnə'beitid], *a.* qui n'a pas diminué; non diminué; **with u. speed,** toujours avec, à, la même vitesse; sans ralentir; **u. wind,** vent qui n'a rien perdu de sa violence; **for three days the storm continued u.,** pendant trois jours l'orage a continué sans répit.

unabating [ʌnə'beitiŋ], *a.* persistant, soutenu; **u. enthusiasm,** enthousiasme soutenu, constant.

unabbreviated [ʌnə'bri:vieitid], *a.* sans abréviation(s); non abrégé; en entier.

unabetted [ʌnə'betid], *a. Jur:* sans complice(s).

unable [ʌn'eibl], *a.* **1.** incapable; **to be u. to do sth.,** ne pas pouvoir faire qch., être impuissant à, hors d'état de, faire qch.; être dans l'impossibilité de faire qch.; **to be u. to escape,** se trouver dans l'impossibilité de s'échapper; **he seems u. to understand you,** il semble être incapable de vous comprendre; **we are u. to help you,** nous ne pouvons pas vous aider; nous ne sommes pas à même, en état, en mesure, de vous aider; **I was u. to persuade him,** je n'ai pas pu, je n'ai pas su, le persuader. **2.** *esp. Lit:* inhabile, incompétent; **in u. hands,** livré à des (gens) incapables.

unabridged [ʌnə'bridʒd], *a.* non abrégé; sans coupures; intégral, -aux; **u. edition,** édition complète, intégrale; **u. version,** texte intégral.

unabsolved [ʌnəb'sɔlvd], *a.* inabsous, *f.* inabsoute.

unaccented [ʌnək'sentid, ʌnæk-], *a.* sans accent(s); inaccentué; *Ling:* (*of syllable, etc.*) non accentué; atone; *Mus:* **u. beat,** temps faible.

unaccentuated [ʌnək'sentjueitid], *a.* inaccentué; non accentué.

unacceptable [ʌnək'septəbl], *a.* inacceptable; (théorie, défense, etc.) irrecevable; **his behaviour is quite u.,** sa conduite est complètement inadmissible; **conditions u. to us,** conditions que nous ne pouvons pas agréer; **a little help would not be u. to him,** un peu d'aide ne lui serait pas désagréable; **a glass of beer wouldn't be u.,** un verre de bière ne serait pas de refus.

unaccepted [ʌnək'septid], *a.* (don, etc.) inaccepté; *Com:* **u. bill,** effet non accepté.

unaccommodating [ʌnə'kɔmədeitiŋ], *a.* (*of pers.*) peu accommodant; (caractère) peu commode, désobligeant.

unaccompanied [ʌnə'kʌmp(ə)nid], *a.* **1.** inaccompagné, non accompagné, seul; **dog travelling u.,** chien qui voyage sans son maître (dans un avion, etc.). **2.** *Mus:* sans accompagnement; **passage for u. violin,** passage pour violon seul.

unaccomplished [ʌnə'kʌmpliʃt, -'kɔm-], *a.* **1.** (*a*) (projet) inaccompli, non réalisé; (*b*) (travail, etc.) inachevé. **2.** (*of pers.*) médiocre; qui ne se distingue guère.

unaccountable [ʌnə'kauntəbl], *a.* **1.** (*a*) (phénomène, etc.) inexplicable; (*b*) (conduite) bizarre, étrange, incompréhensible. **2.** (*of pers.*) qui n'est responsable envers personne (**for,** de).

unaccountably [ʌnə'kauntəbli], *adv.* inexplicablement; sans qu'on sache pourquoi.

unaccounted [ʌnə'kauntid], *a.* **1. u. mystery,** mystère inexpliqué; **the catastrophe is still u. for,** la catastrophe reste inexpliquée. **2. these £10 are u. for in the balance sheet,** ces £10 ne figurent pas au bilan; **five of the passengers are still u. for,** on reste sans nouvelles de cinq passagers; **two books are still u. for,** il manque toujours deux livres.

unaccredited [ʌnə'kreditid], *a.* (agent, etc.) non accrédité, sans pouvoirs.

unaccustomed [ʌnə'kʌstəmd], *a.* **1.** (événement, etc.) inaccoutumé, inhabituel. **2.** (*of pers.*) **u. to sth., to doing sth.,** inaccoutumé, peu habitué, inhabitué, à qch., à faire qch.; **I am u. to being kept waiting,** je n'ai pas l'habitude d'attendre; **u. as I am to public speaking, being u. to public speaking,** n'ayant pas l'habitude de faire des discours.

unachievable [ʌnə'tʃi:vəbl], *a.* (projet, etc.) irréalisable, inexécutable.

unacknowledged [ʌnək'nɔlidʒd], *a.* **1.** (*a*) *esp. Jur:* (enfant) non reconnu, non avoué; **u. agent,** agent non accrédité; (*b*) **u. quotation,** citation *f* sans nom d'auteur. **2.** (lettre) (restée, demeurée) sans réponse.

unacquainted [ʌnə'kweintid], *a.* **1. to be u. with s.o.,** ne pas connaître qn; **I am u. with him,** (i) il m'est étranger; (ii) je n'ai pas fait sa connaissance. **2. to be u. (with sth.),** ignorer (un fait, etc.); ne pas être au courant de (qch.).

unacquired [ʌnə'kwaiəd], *a.* (talent, etc.) non acquis, inné, naturel.

unacted [ʌn'æktid], *a. Th:* (pièce) qui n'a pas été jouée.

unadaptable [ʌnə'dæptəbl], *a.* (*of pers.*) qui ne s'adapte, ne s'accommode, pas aux circonstances; peu liant.

unadapted [ʌnə'dæptid], *a.* mal adapté, peu adapté (**to sth.,** à qch.).

unaddressed [ʌnə'drest], *a.* (colis, etc.) sans adresse, qui ne porte pas d'adresse.

unadjudged [ʌnə'dʒʌdʒd], *a.* **1.** *Jur:* (cas) pas encore décidé, en litige. **2.** (prix) non adjugé, non (encore) accordé, non (encore) attribué.

unadjusted [ʌnə'dʒʌstid], *a. Fin:* (différend) pas encore réglé.

unadmired [ʌnəd'maiəd], *a.* sans admirateurs; méconnu.

unadmitted [ʌnəd'mitid], *a. esp. Jur:* (tort, etc.) inavoué, non admis, non reconnu.

unadopted [ʌnə'dɔptid], *a.* **1.** non adopté; **u. measures,** mesures en souffrance; **to remain u.,** rester en souffrance. **2. u. road,** rue non entretenue, non prise en charge, par la municipalité.

unadorned [ʌnə'dɔ:nd], *a. Lit:* sans ornement, sans parure; naturel; **beauty u.,** la beauté sans parure, sans fard; **u. truth,** la vérité pure, sans fard, toute nue; la simple vérité.

unadulterated [ʌnə'dʌltəreitid], *a.* pur; sans mélange;

(vin) non falsifié, non frelaté; **u. joy,** joie *f* sans mélange; **the u. truth,** la vérité pure et simple, toute nue; **pure u. laziness,** paresse pure et simple.

unadventurous [ʌnəd'ventʃərəs], *a.* peu aventureux.

unadvertised [ʌn'ædvətaizd], *a.* (*of product, meeting, etc.*) sans publicité; (*of action, etc.*) discret, -ète.

unadvisable [ʌnəd'vaizəbl], *a.* (*a*) (*of pers.*) qui ne veut pas entendre raison; difficile à conseiller; opiniâtre; (*b*) (*of action*) peu sage, imprudent; (*c*) **alcohol is u. for people suffering from heart complaints,** l'alcool est à déconseiller aux cardiaques.

unadvised [ʌnəd'vaizd], *a. esp. Lit:* (*a*) (*of action*) imprudent, téméraire, irréfléchi; (*b*) (*of pers.*) irréfléchi, malavisé, imprudent.

unadvisedly [ʌnəd'vaizidli], *adv. esp. Lit:* imprudemment; sans réflexion; inconsidérément, précipitamment; à l'étourdie.

unaesthetic [ʌni:s'θetik], *a.* inesthétique.

unaffected [ʌnə'fektid], *a.* **1.** (*a*) sans affectation; véritable, sincère; **u. joy,** joie qui n'a rien de simulé; (*b*) naturel, simple; **u. style,** style sans recherche, sans apprêt; (*c*) (*of pers.*) sans affectation, sans pose; franc, *f.* franche; naïf, *f.* naïve; naturel; **u. modesty,** modestie simple. **2.** (*of pers.*) impassible, insensible (**by sth.,** à qch.); **to be u. by s.o.'s influence,** être réfractaire aux influences de qn. **3.** *Med:* (organe) qui n'est pas atteint; indemne. **4. u. by air or water,** inaltérable à l'air ou à l'eau; **metal u. by acids,** métal inattaquable aux acides; **organism u. by poison,** organisme réfractaire au poison.

unaffectedly [ʌnə'fektidli], *adv.* sans affectation; (*a*) sincèrement, vraiment; (*b*) naturellement, simplement; **to speak, write, u.,** parler, écrire, sans affectation, sans apprêt; (*c*) franchement, naturellement, naïvement; sans pose.

unaffectedness [ʌnə'fektidnis], *s.* absence *f* de toute affectation; sincérité *f*; simplicité *f*, naturel *m*; franchise *f*.

unaffiliated [ʌnə'filieitid], *a.* non affilié (**to,** à).

unafraid [ʌnə'freid], *a. esp. Lit:* sans crainte, sans peur.

unaggressive [ʌnə'gresiv], *a.* qui n'a rien d'agressif; pacifique.

unaided [ʌn'eidid], *a.* sans aide, sans secours; **he did it u.,** il l'a fait seul, à lui seul, sans assistance; **he can walk u. now,** il peut marcher tout seul maintenant.

unaired [ʌn'εəd], *a.* (*a*) (appartement, etc.) qui n'a pas été aéré; (*b*) (linge) qui n'a pas été aéré, éventé, complètement séché.

unalienated [ʌn'eiliəneitid], *a.* inaliéné.

unalike [ʌnə'laik], *a.* dissemblable, différent; **they are not u.,** ils se ressemblent un peu.

unallayed [ʌnə'leid], *a. A: & Lit:* **1.** (*of grief, etc.*) inapaisé; sans soulagement; (*of desire, etc.*) insatisfait. **2.** (*of joy, etc.*) sans mélange; pur, parfait; **u. with, by, . . .,** sans adjonction de . . ..

unalleviated [ʌnə'li:vieitid], *a.* sans soulagement; **u. despair,** désespoir que rien ne vient adoucir.

unallotted [ʌnə'lɔtid], *a.* **1.** (temps, etc.) disponible. **2.** *Fin:* **u. shares,** actions non réparties.

unallowable [ʌnə'lauəbl], *a. esp. Jur:* (prétention, etc.) inadmissible.

unalloyed [ʌnə'lɔid], *a.* (*a*) (métal) pur, sans alliage; (*b*) *esp. Lit:* **u. happiness,** bonheur pur, parfait, sans mélange, sans nuages.

unalterable [ʌn'ɔ:lt(ə)rəbl], *a.* immuable, invariable.

unalterably [ʌn'ɔ:lt(ə)rəbli], *adv.* immuablement, invariablement.

unaltered [ʌn'ɔ:ltəd], *a.* inchangé; toujours le même; sans changement; tel quel.

unambiguous [ʌnæm'bigjuəs], *a.* non équivoque; **u. answer,** réponse sans ambiguïté; réponse claire; **u. terms,** termes précis, clairs.

umambiguously [ʌnæm'bigjuəsli], *adv.* clairement; sans ambiguïté; (s'exprimer) avec précision, sans ambages; **to speak u. (to s.o.),** parler rondement (à qn), mettre les points sur les i (à qn).

unambitious [ʌnæm'biʃəs], *a.* **1.** (*of pers.*) sans ambition; peu ambitieux; **he's completely u.,** il manque entièrement d'ambition. **2.** (projet, etc.) modeste, sans prétention(s).

unambitiously [ʌnæm'biʃəsli], *adv.* **1.** sans ambition. **2.** modestement.

unamenable [ʌnə'mi:nəbl], *a.* **1. u. to discipline,** réfractaire, rebelle, à la discipline; indocile; **u. to reason,** qui ne veut pas entendre raison; **he is u. to persuasion,** il est impossible de le convaincre. **2.** *Jur:* non responsable, irresponsable (**to,** envers).

unamendable [ʌnə'mendəbl], *a. Jur: Parl:* (projet, etc.) qui ne peut pas être amendé, incapable d'amendement.

unamended [ʌnə'mendid], *a. Jur: Parl:* sans amendement.

un-American [ʌnə'merik(ə)n], *a.* peu américain, antiaméricain; contraire à l'esprit américain, aux usages, aux principes, des Américains.

unamiable [ʌn'eimiəbl], *a.* peu aimable, peu affable; **u. disposition,** caractère désagréable, rébarbatif, bourru.

unamiably [ʌn'eimiəbli], *adv.* d'une manière peu aimable; (répondre, etc.) d'un ton bourru.

unamusing [ʌnə'mju:ziŋ], *a.* peu amusant; **the story was not u.,** l'histoire ne manquait pas d'humour, n'était pas sans humour.

unaneled [ʌnə'ni:ld], *a. Ecc: A:* (mourir) sans avoir reçu l'extrême-onction, le viatique.

unanimism [ju(:)'nænimizm], *s. Lit.Hist:* unanimisme *m*.

unanimist [ju(:)'nænimist], *a. & s. Lit.Hist:* unanimiste (*mf*).

unanimity [ju:nə'nimiti], *s.* unanimité *f*, accord *m*; **with u.,** d'un commun accord; unanimement.

unanimous [ju(:)'næniməs], *a.* unanime; **they were u. in accusing him,** ils étaient unanimes à l'accuser; **we expressed the u. opinion that . . .,** nous avons été unanimes à, pour, reconnaître que . . .; **to reach a u. decision,** se prononcer à l'unanimité; **the vote was u.,** la décision a été votée à l'unanimité; **u. vote,** vote, résolution adoptée, à l'unanimité.

unanimously [ju(:)'nænimǝsli], *adv.* à l'unanimité; unanimement; **u. elected,** élu à l'unanimité.

unannealed [ʌnə'ni:ld], *a. Metall:* non recuit.

unannounced [ʌnə'naunst], *a.* (*a*) sans être annoncé; **he marched in u.,** il est entré sans se faire annoncer; (*b*) à l'improviste; **his arrival was completely u.,** on ne s'attendait pas du tout à le voir arriver; son arrivée était complètement imprévue, inattendue.

unanswerable [ʌn'ɑ:ns(ə)rəbl], *a.* (argument) incontestable, irréfragable, péremptoire, sans réponse; **u. question,** question (i) à laquelle on ne peut pas répondre, (ii) que l'on ne peut pas résoudre; *Jur:* **u. charge,** accusation irréfutable.

unanswerably [ʌn'ɑ:ns(ə)rəbli], *adv.* irréfutablement.

unanswered [ʌn'ɑ:nsəd], *a.* **1.** sans réponse; **u. letter,** lettre (i) sans réponse, (ii) à répondre; **our letter has remained u.,** notre lettre est restée sans réponse; nous restons sans réponse à notre lettre; **u. prayer,** prière inexaucée. **2.** (argument) irréfuté. **3.** *A: & Lit:* **u. love,** amour qui n'est pas payé de retour, non partagé.

unanticipated [ʌnæn'tisipeitid], *a.* imprévu, inattendu.

unappealable [ʌnə'pi:ləbl], *a. Jur:* (décision, jugement) sans appel.

unappeasable [ʌnə'pi:zəbl], *a.* **1.** (faim) inapaisable; (appétit, désir) insatiable, inassouvissable; (haine) implacable. **2.** (tumulte, etc.) que rien ne peut calmer.

unappeased [ʌnə'pi:zd], *a.* inapaisé; (*of hunger, passion*) inassouvi.

unappetizing [ʌn'æpitaiziŋ], *a.* peu appétissant.

unappreciated [ʌnə'pri:ʃieitid], *a.* peu apprécié, peu estimé; dont on ne fait pas grand cas; dont on ne se rend pas compte.

unappreciative [ʌnə'pri:ʃiətiv], *a.* (public) insensible; (compte rendu, etc.) peu favorable.

unapprehensive [ʌnæpri'hensiv], *a. esp. Lit:* sans appréhension (**of,** de); **to be u. of danger,** ne pas appréhender, ne pas redouter, le danger; être insouciant, sans crainte, du danger.

unapprised [ʌnə'praizd], *a. Lit:* non prévenu, non informé, ignorant (**of,** de).

unapproachable [ʌnə'proutʃəbl], *a.* **1.** (*a*) *A: & Lit:* (cime, etc.) inaccessible; (côte) inabordable; (*b*) (*of pers.*) inabordable, inaccessible; distant, froid; **an u. sort of person,** une personne d'un abord difficile, rebutant. **2.** incomparable, suréminent; sans pareil.

unappropriated [ʌnə'prouprieitid], *a.* **1.** (argent, etc.) inutilisé, disponible, sans destination spéciale; *Com:* **u. (profit) balance, u. profit,** solde bénéficiaire sans application déterminée. **2.** (siège, etc.) non réservé, non retenu; libre.

unapt [ʌn'æpt], *a.* **1.** *O:* qui ne convient pas; (mot) peu juste; (expression) impropre; (remarque) hors de propos; (remède) mal approprié. **2.** *A: & Lit:* peu disposé, peu enclin (**to do sth.,** à faire qch.).

unaptly [ʌn'æptli], *adv.* improprement; **not u. called . . .,** appelé assez justement . . ..

unarmed [ʌn'ɑ:md], *a.* (*a*) (*of pers.*) sans armes; **u. combat,** combat sans armes; corps-à-corps *m inv*; (*b*) *Nat. Hist:* (animal) sans défenses; (tige, ténia) inerme.

unarmoured [ʌn'ɑ:məd], *a.* **1.** (navire, etc.) non blindé, non cuirassé. **2.** (câble) sans armature.

unarrested [ʌnə'restid], *a.* **1.** (progrès, etc.) que rien n'arrête; continu. **2.** (voleur, etc.) pas encore arrêté, encore en liberté.

unascertainable [ʌnæsə'teinəbl], *a.* non vérifiable; indéterminable.

unashamed [ʌnə'ʃeimd], *a.* sans honte, sans vergogne; sans pudeur; éhonté; cynique; **to be u. about, of, doing sth.,** ne pas avoir honte de faire qch.

unashamedly [ʌnə'ʃeimidli], *adv.* sans honte, sans vergogne; sans pudeur; cyniquement.

unasked [ʌn'ɑ:skt], *a.* **1. to do sth. u.,** faire qch. spontanément; **she came to help quite u.,** elle est venue nous aider sans qu'on le lui demandât, sans y être invitée. **2. u. (for) gift,** cadeau qu'on n'a pas demandé; **his opinion was quite u. for,** on ne lui avait pas demandé son avis.

unaspirated [ʌn'æspireitid], *a. Ling:* non aspiré.

unaspiring [ʌnə'spaiəriŋ], *a.* (*of pers.*) sans ambition.

unassailable [ʌnə'seiləbl], *a.* (forteresse, droit) inattaquable; (conclusion) indiscutable, irréfutable; **his reputation is u.,** sa réputation est hors d'atteinte.

unassertive [ʌnə'sə:tiv], *a.* modeste, timide; effacé; qui ne sait pas se faire valoir; que ne sait pas imposer sa volonté.

unassessed [ʌnə'sest], *a.* **1.** (*of property, etc.*) non évalué. **2.** (*of price*) non imposé.

unassignable [ʌnə'sainəbl], *a. Jur:* (bien, droit) non transférable, intransférable, incessible, inaliénable.

unassigned [ʌnə'saind], *a.* **u. cause,** cause indéterminée; **u. revenue,** recettes non affectées (en garantie).

unassimilable [ʌnə'siməbl], *a.* inassimilable.

unassimilated [ʌnə'simileitid], *a.* (aliment) inassimilé; **u. knowledge,** connaissances mal assimilées; **u. (racial) minorities,** minorités (ethniques) qui ne se sont pas assimilées.

unassisted [ʌnə'sistid], *a.* sans aide, sans secours; **he did it u.,** il l'a fait tout seul, à lui seul, sans assistance.

unassuaged [ʌnə'sweidʒd], *a. Lit:* (souffrance, etc.) que rien ne vient calmer, ne vient adoucir; sans soulagement; inapaisé; (appétit) inassouvi.

unassuming [ʌnə'sju:miŋ], *a.* sans prétention(s); simple, modeste; effacé.

unassured [ʌnə'ʃuəd], *a.* **1.** (succès, etc.) douteux. **2.** (pas, air, etc.) mal assuré. **3.** *Ins:* non assuré.

unatonable [ʌnə'tounəbl], *a.* inexpiable.

unatoned [ʌnə'tound], *a.* **u. (for),** inexpié.

unattached [ʌnə'tætʃt], *a.* **1.** qui n'est pas attaché (**to,** à); indépendant (**to,** de). **2.** (journaliste, etc.) libre; (prêtre) sans fonctions régulières; *Mil:* (officier) disponible, en disponibilité; (*of pers.*) **to be u.,** être sans attaches; être libre (de toute attache); être célibataire.

unattackable [ʌnə'tækəbl], *a.* inattaquable.

unattainable [ʌnə'teinəbl], *a.* inaccessible (**by,** à); hors d'atteinte, hors de la portée (**by,** de); impossible.

unattempted [ʌnə'temptid], *a.* qu'on n'a pas encore essayé; **hitherto u. feat,** exploit que personne n'a tenté jusqu'ici, n'avait tenté jusqu'alors.

unattended [ʌnə'tendid], *a.* **1.** (*a*) (*of pers.*) seul; sans escorte; (*b*) **to leave a horse, one's car, u.,** laisser un cheval, sa voiture, sans surveillance; abandonner la garde d'un cheval; *P.N:* **do not leave your luggage u.,** surveillez toujours vos bagages; **it is a sport not u. by danger,** c'est un sport non dépourvu de danger. **2. u. to,** négligé; **to leave sth. u. (to),** négliger qch.

unattested [ʌnə'testid], *a.* (fait) inattesté, non attesté, non certifié; *Jur:* (certificat, etc.) non légalisé.

unattractive [ʌnə'træktiv], *a.* (projet, visage, etc.) peu attrayant, sans attrait, dépourvu d'attrait, peu séduisant; (caractère, personne) peu sympathique; **she is not u.,** elle ne manque pas de charme.

unau [ju:'nɔ:, 'ju:nɔ:, u:'nau], *s. Z:* unau *m*.

unaudited [ʌn'ɔ:ditid], *a. Com:* (bilan) non vérifié, non révisé.

unauthentic [ʌnɔ:'θentik], *a.* inauthentique, apocryphe.

unauthenticated [ʌnɔ:'θentikeitid], *a.* **1.** (*a*) dont l'authenticité n'est pas établie; (*b*) *Jur:* (*of document*) non légalisé. **2.** dont on ne connaît pas l'auteur.

unauthorized [ʌn'ɔ:θəraizd], *a.* **1.** non autorisé; sans autorisation, sans mandat; (commerce, etc.) illicite; *P. N:* **no entry to u. persons, u. persons prohibited, no u. access,** accès interdit à toute personne étrangère au service, aux travaux; **u. use,** usage abusif.

unavailability [ʌnəveilə'biliti], *s.* **1.** indisponibilité *f*. **2.** invalidité *f* (d'un billet).

unavailable [ʌnə'veiləbl], *a.* **1.** (*a*) indisponible; non disponible; (*b*) qu'on ne peut se procurer; (article) épuisé; (*c*) (*of pers.*) pas libre; non disponible. **2. ticket u. for certain trains,** billet inutilisable par, non valable pour, certains trains.

unavailing [ʌnə'veiliŋ], *a.* inutile; (*of tears, etc.*) vain, inefficace; (*of efforts, etc.*) infructueux.

unavailingly [ʌnə'veiliŋli], *adv.* inutilement; inefficacement; en vain.

unavenged [ʌnə'ven(d)ʒd], *a. esp. Lit:* invengé; sans être vengé.

unavoidable [ʌnə'vɔidəbl], *a.* (*a*) (conséquence, conclusion) inévitable; (sort) inéluctable, auquel on ne peut échapper; (*b*) (événement, etc.) qu'on ne peut prévenir; **my absence was u.,** mon absence a été due à un cas de force majeure.

unavoidably [ʌnə'vɔidəbli], *adv.* (*a*) inévitablement; inéluctablement; (*b*) **u. absent,** absent pour raison majeure.

unavowable [ʌnə'vauəbl], *a.* inavouable.

unavowed [ʌnə'vaud], *a.* inavoué.

unaware [ʌnə'wɛər], *a.* ignorant, non informé, pas au courant (**of sth.,** de qch.); **to be u. of sth.,** ignorer, ne pas se douter de, qch.; **I was u. that. . .,** j'ignorais que . . . + *ind. or sub.*; **I'm not u. that. . .,** je n'ignore pas que . . . + *ind.*; je ne suis pas sans savoir que . . . + *ind.*; **I was quite u. of his having written to you,** c'est complètement à mon insu qu'il vous a écrit.

unawares [ʌnə'wɛəz], *adv.* **1.** inconsciemment; par inadvertance, par mégarde, à son insu; **all u. I had agreed to do it,** j'y avais consenti sans m'en rendre compte, sans m'en douter. **2. to take, catch, s.o. u.,** prendre qn à l'improviste, au dépourvu, au pied levé.

unawed [ʌn'ɔ:d], *a. Lit:* aucunement intimidé.

unbacked [ʌn'bækt], *a.* **1.** *Turf:* (cheval) sur lequel on ne parie pas, sur lequel on n'a pas parié. **2.** (cheval) non dressé (à la selle). **3.** (mur, etc.) non renforcé.

unbag [ʌn'bæg], *v.tr.* (**unbagged**) *Ven:* lâcher (un renard).

unbait [ʌn'beit], *v.tr. Fish:* **to u. (a line),** déboëtter.

unbaked [ʌn'beikt], *a.* (*a*) (*of brick, etc.*) cru; (*b*) *Cu:* pas encore cuit.

unbalance[1] [ʌn'bæləns], *s.* **1.** *Mec.E:* déséquilibre *m*; balourd *m*. **2.** *Med: Psy:* déséquilibre.

unbalance[2], *v.tr.* **1.** déséquilibrer (un volant, etc.). **2.** déranger, déséquilibrer, désaxer (l'esprit de qn).

unbalanced [ʌn'bælənst], *a.* **1.** (*a*) *Ph:* en équilibre instable; *Mec.E:* (volant, etc.) mal équilibré, qui a du balourd; (*b*) (esprit) déséquilibré, dérangé, désaxé. **2.** (*a*) **u. forces,** forces non équilibrées; *El:* **u. phases,** phases inéquilibrées; (*b*) *Mec.E:* (*of crankshaft, etc.*) non compensé. **3.** *Book-k:* (*of account*) non soldé.

unballast [ʌn'bæləst], *v.tr.* délester (un navire).

unballasted [ʌn'bæləstid], *a.* **1.** *Nau:* délesté. **2.** *Civ.E: etc:* (*of track*) non ballasté.

unbandage [ʌn'bændidʒ], *v.tr.* débander (une plaie, etc.); retirer, enlever, le bandage (d'une plaie, etc.).

unbank [ʌn'bæŋk], *v.tr. Ind: Mch:* découvrir (le feu, les feux).

unbaptized [ʌnbæp'taizd], *a.* non baptisé; **to die u.,** mourir sans baptême.

unbar [ʌn'bɑ:*r*], *v.tr.* (**unbarred**) débarrer (une porte); *Nau:* dessaisir (un sabord).

unbarred [ʌn'bɑ:d], *a.* **1.** (*of door*) débarré. **2.** *Nau:* (*of harbour*) sans barre. **3.** *Mus:* qui n'est pas divisé en mesures.

unbearable [ʌn'bɛərəbl], *a.* insupportable, intolérable; **u. agony,** douleur atroce; **in this heat, the office is u.,** par cette chaleur le bureau n'est pas tenable.

unbearably [ʌn'bɛərəbli], *adv.* insupportablement, intolérablement; **it's u. hot,** il fait une chaleur étouffante.

unbeatable [ʌn'bi:təbl], *a.* imbattable, invincible; *Com:* **u. prices,** prix imbattables.

unbeaten [ʌn'bi:tn], *a.* **1.** non battu, non broyé. **2.** invaincu; **u. champion, record,** champion, record, qui n'a pas encore été battu; record encore debout.

unbecoming [ʌnbi'kʌmiŋ], *a.* **1.** peu convenable; malséant (**to,** à); déplacé, incongru; **u. of s.o.,** déplacé chez qn; **it's u. of him to act in this manner,** il lui sied mal d'agir de la sorte; **words u. in a child,** propos déplacés dans la bouche d'un enfant. **2.** (*of garment*) peu seyant.

unbegotten [ʌnbi'gɔt(ə)n], *a. Theol:* non engendré, inengendré.

unbeknown [ʌnbi'noun]. **1.** *a. Lit:* inconnu (**to,** de). **2.** *adv.* **to do sth. u. to anyone,** faire qch. à l'insu de tous.

unbelief [ʌnbi'li:f], *s.* incrédulité *f*; *Theol:* incroyance *f*, mécréance *f*.

unbelievable [ʌnbi'li:vəbl], *a.* incroyable; **it's u. that . . .,** il est incroyable que + *sub.*; *Com:* **u. reductions!** prix exceptionnels!

unbelievably [ʌnbi'li:vəbli], *adv.* incroyablement; **u. stupid,** d'une sottise sans pareille, bête comme ses pieds.

unbeliever [ʌnbi'li:vər], *s.* incrédule *mf*; *Theol:* incroyant, -ante; mécréant, -ante; infidèle *mf*; non-croyant, -ante.

unbelieving [ʌnbi'li:viŋ], *a.* incrédule; *Theol:* incroyant, infidèle.

unbeloved [ʌnbi'lʌvd], *a. A: & Lit:* peu aimé; **he lived and died u.,** il a vécu et il est mort sans avoir été aimé.

unbelt [ʌn'belt], *v.tr.* déboucler (son épée).

unbend [ʌn'bend], *v.* (*p.t. & p.p.* **unbent** [ʌn'bent])

I. *v.tr.* **1.** détendre, débander (un arc); détendre, relâcher (son esprit); *A:* **to u. one's brow,** se dérider. **2.** redresser (sa taille, une tige d'acier, etc.); détordre, dérouler (un ressort); déplier (la jambe). **3.** *Nau:* démarrer, défrapper (un câble); désenverguer, déverguer (une voile); détalinguer (la chaîne de l'ancre).

II. *v.i.* **1.** (*a*) s'abandonner, se laisser aller (un peu); se détendre; **he never unbends,** il ne se déride jamais; (*b*) *A:* (*of brow*) se dérider; (*of features*) se détendre. **2.** devenir droit; se redresser; (*of spring*) se détordre, se dérouler; (*of limb*) se déplier.

unbendable [ʌn'bendəbl], *a.* impliable, inflexible, infléchissable.

unbending[1] [ʌn'bendiŋ], *a.* inflexible, ferme; **u. character,** caractère inflexible, rigide, raide; **to maintain an u. attitude,** conserver une attitude intransigeante, inflexible.

unbending[2], *s.* **1.** détente *f* (d'un ressort, etc.); redressement *m*. **2.** affabilité *f*.

unbeneficed [ʌn'benifist], *a.* (prêtre) habitué; (prêtre) non pourvu d'un bénéfice.

unbeneficial [ʌnbeni'fiʃ(ə)l], *a.* peu avantageux; **he found the treatment to be u.,** il a trouvé le traitement inefficace, sans effet.

unbias(s)ed [ʌn'baiəst], *a.* **1.** (*of bowls, etc.*) qui n'a pas de fort. **2.** impartial, -aux; neutre; affranchi d'idées préconçues, de préjugés; sans parti pris; non prévenu (contre qn); (conseil) désintéressé; **u. praise,** critique *f* sans parti pris de louange; **u. observer,** observateur sans prévention.

unbiddable [ʌn'bidəbl], *a. O:* (enfant, etc.) désobéissant, indocile.

unbidden [ʌn'bid(ə)n], *a. O:* **1.** non invité; intrus. **2.** spontané; **to do sth. u.,** faire qch. spontanément, sans y avoir été invité.

unbigoted [ʌn'bigətid], *a.* (esprit, etc.) libre de préjugés, exempt de fanatisme.

unbind [ʌn'baind], *v.tr.* (*p.t. & p.p.* **unbound** [ʌn'baund]) (*a*) délier (un prisonnier, les mains); *Theol: A:* **to bind and u.,** lier et délier; (*b*) débander (une plaie); enlever le pansement (d'une plaie); (*c*) *Lit:* délier, défaire (un cordon, etc.).

unbitt [ʌn'bit], *v.tr. Nau:* débitter.

unblam(e)able [ʌn'bleiməbl], *a.* irréprochable, irrépréhensible; à l'abri de tout reproche.

unbleached [ʌn'bli:tʃt], *a.* non blanchi; écru; **u. linen,** toile bise, écrue; **u. calico,** toile jaune.

unblemished [ʌn'blemiʃt], *a.* sans défaut; sans tache, sans souillure; immaculé; (honneur) intact; **u. career,** carrière sans tache.

unblinking [ʌn'bliŋkiŋ], *a.* (*of pers.*) impassible, imperturbable; (regard) fixe; **with u. eyes,** sans ciller (des yeux).

unblock [ʌn'blɔk], *v.tr.* (*a*) dégager, désencombrer (un passage); déboucher (un tuyau, etc.); (*b*) *Cards:* **to u. a suit,** affranchir une couleur.

unblushing [ʌn'blʌʃiŋ], *a.* **1.** qui ne rougit pas; sans rougir. **2.** sans vergogne; impudent; éhonté, cynique.

unblushingly [ʌn'blʌʃiŋli], *adv.* **1.** sans rougir. **2.** sans vergogne, sans honte; (mentir) impudemment, cyniquement.

unboiled [ʌn'bɔild], *a.* (*a*) **u. water,** eau non bouillie; (*b*) *Tex: Paperm:* (*of silk, vegetable fibre, etc.*) non décreusé.

unbolt [ʌn'boult], *v.tr.* **1.** déverrouiller (une porte); tirer, ouvrir, le(s) verrou(s) (d'une porte). **2.** déboulonner, dévisser (un rail, etc.).

unbolted[1] [ʌn'boultid], *a.* **1.** (*a*) déverrouillé; (*b*) déboulonné. **2.** (*a*) non verrouillé; (*b*) non boulonné.

unbolted[2], *a. Mill:* (*of flour*) non bluté, non tamisé.

unbolting [ʌn'boultiŋ], *s. Mec.E:* déboulonnement *m*, déboulonnage *m*.

unborn ['ʌnbɔ:n], *a.* qui n'est pas (encore) né; **u. child,** enfant à naître; **generations yet u.** [ʌn'bɔ:n], générations à venir; générations futures.

unbosom [ʌn'buzəm], *v.tr. A: & Lit:* découvrir, révéler (ses sentiments, etc.); **to u. oneself,** épancher son cœur; s'épancher; se délester le cœur; **to u. oneself, one's sorrows, to s.o.,** ouvrir son cœur, son âme, à qn; s'épancher dans le sein de qn; se confier à qn.

unbound [ʌn'baund], *a.* **1.** (*a*) délié; **to come u.,** se délier; *Lit:* **Prometheus u.,** Prométhée délivré; (*b*) *Lit:* (*of hair*) dénoué, flottant. **2.** (*a*) libre (d'entraves); qui n'est pas lié (par un vœu, etc.); (*b*) (*of book*) non relié; broché.

unbounded [ʌn'baundid], *a.* sans bornes; illimité; (*of conceit, etc.*) démesuré; **u. ambition,** ambition sans mesure, démesurée.

unboundedly [ʌn'baundidli], *adv.* sans limites; démesurément.

unbreakable [ʌn'breikəbl], *a.* incassable, imbrisable.

unbreathable [ʌn'bri:ðəbl], *a.* irrespirable.

unbreech [ʌn'bri:tʃ], *v.tr. Artil: A:* déculasser (une pièce).

unbreeched [ʌn'bri:tʃt], *a. A:* **1.** *Artil:* déculassé. **2.** (petit garçon) qui n'a pas encore porté sa première culotte, qui porte encore le jupon.

unbribable [ʌn'braibəbl], *a.* incorruptible.

unbridle [ʌn'braidl], *v.tr.* (*a*) débrider (un cheval); ôter la bride à (un cheval); (*b*) lâcher la bride, donner libre cours, à (son indignation, ses sentiments, etc.).

unbridled [ʌn'braidld], *a.* **1.** (cheval) (i) débridé, (ii) sans bride. **2.** (*of passion, etc.*) débridé, effréné; sans frein; sans retenue, sans réserve.

unbridling [ʌn'braidliŋ], *s.* **1.** débridement *m* (d'un cheval). **2.** débridement, déchaînement *m*.

unbroached [ʌn'broutʃt], *a.* (tonneau) qui n'a pas été mis en perce; non entamé.

unbroken [ʌn'brouk(ə)n], *a.* **1.** (*a*) non brisé, non cassé; **u. coke,** coke non concassé; (*b*) intact; *Mil:* **u. front,** front inentamé; **u. spirit,** courage inentamé; fougue que rien ne peut abattre; (*c*) (*of rule, etc.*) toujours observé, respecté; qu'on n'enfreint pas; **the peace remained u. for ten years,** la paix n'a pas été troublée pendant dix ans; **u. vow,** serment inviolé; *Sp:* **record still u.,** record qui n'a pas été battu; record toujours imbattu; (*d*) (*of silence, etc.*) ininterrompu, continu; (*of ground*) non accidenté; **landscape u. by a single house,** paysage dont l'harmonie n'est rompue par aucune habitation; **u. sheet of ice,** nappe de glace continue. **2.** (*a*) (cheval) non rompu, non dressé; (*b*) **u. spirit,** esprit insoumis, indompté. **3.** *Agr:* **u. ground,** terre qui n'a pas encore été labourée; terre vierge.

unbrotherly [ʌn'brʌðəli], *a.* peu fraternel; indigne d'un frère.

unbruised [ʌn'bru:zd], *a.* **1.** sans meurtrissure; intact, indemne. **2.** *A:* non broyé, non concassé.

unbuckle [ʌn'bʌkl], *v.tr.* déboucler (une ceinture, etc.).

unbuilt [ʌn'bilt, 'ʌnbilt], *a.* (*a*) (bâtiment) non encore construit; (*b*) **u. plot, plot of u. (on) ground,** terrain vague, non construit.

unbung [ʌn'bʌŋ], *v.tr.* débonder (un tonneau).

unbuoyed [ʌn'bɔid], *a. Nau:* (*of channel, etc.*) non balisé.

unburden [ʌn'bə:d(ə)n], *v.tr.* **1.** (*a*) décharger, débarrasser; alléger (qn) d'un fardeau; (*b*) **to u. the mind,** soulager, alléger, l'esprit; **to u. oneself, one's heart,** s'épancher, se délester le cœur; épancher son cœur; **to u. oneself to s.o.,** se confier à qn; **to u. oneself of a secret,** se soulager du poids d'un secret. **2. to u. one's sorrows to s.o.,** épancher ses chagrins dans le sein de qn; raconter ses peines à qn.

unburied [ʌn'berid], *a.* sans sépulture; non enseveli, non enterré.

unburnable [ʌn'bə:nəbl], *a.* imbrûlable.

unburned, unburnt [ʌn'bə:nd, -'bə:nt], *a.* **1.** non brûlé, imbrûlé. **2.** (*of brick*) non cuit.

unbusinesslike [ʌn'biznislaik], *a.* **1.** (*of shop assistant, etc.*) peu commerçant; qui n'a pas le sens des affaires. **2. u. procedure,** procédé irrégulier, incorrect, contraire à toutes les règles du commerce; **to conduct one's affairs in an u. way,** mal conduire ses affaires; manquer de méthode, de sens pratique.

unbutton [ʌn'bʌtn], *v.tr.* défaire les boutons de (qch.); déboutonner (son manteau); **to u. (oneself),** se déboutonner.

unbuttoned [ʌn'bʌtnd], *a.* déboutonné, défait; (*of garment*) **to come u.,** se déboutonner; se défaire.

unbuttoning [ʌn'bʌtniŋ], *s.* déboutonnage *m*.

uncalled, *a.* **1.** ['ʌnkɔ:ld]. *Fin:* **u. capital,** capitaux non appelés. **2.** [ʌn'kɔ:ld], **u. for,** (i) (*of remark, etc.*) déplacé; (ii) (*of rebuke*) immérité, injustifié; **that remark was completely u. for,** cette observation était tout à fait déplacée.

uncancelled [ʌn'kæns(ə)ld], *a.* qui n'est pas (encore) annulé; (timbre) non oblitéré; (mot, chiffre) non effacé, non rayé.

uncannily [ʌn'kænili], *adv.* d'une manière étrange, surnaturelle; mystérieusement.

uncanny [ʌn'kæni], *a.* d'une étrangeté inquiétante; mystérieux; surnaturel; **u. noise,** bruit inquiétant, qui vous donne la chair de poule; **u. light,** lueur sinistre.

uncanonical [ʌnkə'nɔnik(ə)l], *a.* **1.** non canonique; contraire aux canons; (*of book*) apocryphe. **2.** (*a*) indigne d'un membre du clergé; (*b*) (*of dress*) laïque, séculier.

uncap [ʌn'kæp], *v.* (**uncapped**) **1.** *v.tr.* découvrir (qch.); **to u. a fuse,** décoiffer une fusée; *Ap:* **to u. a honeycomb,** désoperculer un rayon de miel. **2.** *v.i. A:* se découvrir; ôter son chapeau (**to s.o.,** à qn, devant qn).

uncapsizable [ʌnkæp'saizəbl], *a.* inchavirable, inversable.

uncared(-)for [ʌn'kɛədfɔ:r], *a.* dont on se soucie peu;

peu soigné; **to leave a garden u. for,** laisser un jardin à l'abandon.
Uncaria [ʌn'kɑːriə], *s. Bot:* uncaria *m.*
uncarpeted [ʌn'kɑːpitid], *a.* sans tapis, sans moquette.
uncastrated [ʌnkæs'treitid], *a. Husb:* (bœuf, etc.) non châtré, non castré; (cheval) entier.
uncatalogued [ʌn'kætəlɔgd], *a.* qui n'est pas catalogué; non catalogué; qui ne figure pas dans le catalogue.
unceasing [ʌn'siːsiŋ], *a.* (*a*) incessant, continu, continuel; (*b*) (travail) assidu; (effort) soutenu.
unceasingly [ʌn'siːsiŋli], *adv.* sans cesse; sans trêve; sans arrêt.
uncemented [ʌnsi'mentid], *a.* (*of stones, etc.*) non cimenté; **wall of u. stones,** mur en pierres meubles; *Opt: Phot:* **u. lens,** objectif à lentilles non collées.
uncensored [ʌn'sensəd], *a.* (article, etc.) qui n'a pas été soumis à la censure, au contrôle; (passage) non expurgé (par la censure).
uncensured [ʌn'sensjəd], *a.* qui n'est pas, n'a pas été, censuré; qui n'a été l'objet d'aucune critique; (*of pers.*) qui n'a été soumis à aucune réprobation; **to pass u.,** ne soulever aucune critique; passer sans protestation.
unceremonious [ʌnseri'mouniəs], *a.* **1.** sans cérémonie; peu cérémonieux; (*of pers.*) sans façons. **2.** (*of pers.*) sans façon, sans gêne.
unceremoniously [ʌnseri'mouniəsli], *adv.* **1.** sans cérémonie; **we dined u.,** nous avons dîné simplement, en famille. **2.** sans façon; sans gêne; brusquement.
uncertain [ʌn'səːt(ə)n], *a.* incertain. **1.** (*a*) (*of time, amount*) indéterminé; (*b*) (résultat) douteux, aléatoire; **it's u. who will win,** on ne sait pas au juste qui gagnera; *Fin:* **to quote u.,** donner l'incertain. **2.** (*a*) mal assuré; **u. steps,** pas mal assurés; pas chancelants, vacillants; **u. temper,** humeur inégale, changeante; **u. future,** avenir incertain, douteux; **he told him in no u. terms,** il lui a dit sans mâcher ses mots; il lui a dit tout cru; (*b*) **u. witness,** témoin vacillant; **his memory is u.,** sa mémoire vacille; **to be u. of the future,** être incertain de l'avenir, inquiet au sujet de l'avenir; **to be u. what to do,** être incertain de, indécis sur, ce qu'il faut faire; hésiter sur le parti à prendre; **he's u. whether to do it or not,** il ne sait pas au juste s'il doit le faire ou non.
uncertainly [ʌn'səːt(ə)nli], *adv.* d'une façon incertaine; (*a*) au hasard; (*b*) d'une manière mal assurée; (*c*) vaguement.
uncertainty [ʌn'səːt(ə)nti], *s.* incertitude *f.* **1. u. of the result,** incertitude du résultat; **there is some u. about . . .,** l'incertitude règne au sujet de . . .; **u. about, as to, the future,** incertitude quant à l'avenir; **to be in a state of u.,** être dans l'incertitude, dans le doute; **u. of tenure (of office),** amovibilité *f*; **to remove any u.,** pour dissiper toute équivoque; *Atom.Ph:* **(Heisenberg's) u. principle,** principe d'incertitude, d'indétermination (d'Heisenberg). **2. to prefer a certainty to an u.,** préférer le certain à l'incertain.
uncertificated [ʌnsə'tifikeitid], *a.* **1.** sans diplôme, non diplômé. **2.** *Jur:* **u. bankrupt,** failli qui n'a pas obtenu de concordat.
uncertified [ʌn'səːtifaid], *a.* non certifié.
unchain [ʌn'tʃein], *v.tr.* désenchaîner; **to u. a prisoner,** délivrer un prisonnier de ses chaînes; briser les chaînes d'un prisonnier; *Lit:* **to u. one's passions,** déchaîner ses passions, donner libre cours à ses passions.
unchallengeable [ʌn'tʃælindʒəbl], *a.* (affirmation) indiscutable; (argument) irréfutable; (droit) indisputable, incontestable; (témoignage, preuve) irrécusable, irréfragable.
unchallenged [ʌn'tʃælin(d)ʒd], *a.* **1.** (*a*) (interlocuteur) que personne ne vient contredire; **to continue u.,** continuer sans être contredit; (*b*) (droit) indisputé, incontesté; **to let (sth.) go, pass, u.,** ne pas relever, laisser passer sans protestation (une affirmation); ne pas disputer, ne pas contester (un droit); ne pas récuser (un témoignage, une preuve); **this principle stands u.,** ce principe n'a jamais été attaqué. **2.** *Mil: etc:* **to let s.o. pass u.,** laisser passer qn sans interpellation.
unchangeable [ʌn'tʃeindʒəbl], *a.* inchangeable; immuable; inaltérable.
unchangeableness [ʌn'tʃeindʒəbəlnis], *s.* immutabilité *f*, immuabilité *f*; inaltérabilité *f.*
unchanged [ʌn'tʃein(d)ʒd], *a.* inchangé; sans modification; inaltéré; intact; *Med:* **his condition remains u.,** son état est stationnaire.
unchanging [ʌn'tʃein(d)ʒiŋ], *a.* invariable, immuable; *Lit:* **the u. snows,** les neiges éternelles.
unchaperoned [ʌn'ʃæpəround], *a.* (*of young woman*) qui n'est pas chaperonnée; non accompagnée.
uncharged [ʌn'tʃɑːdʒd], *a.* **1.** *A:* (*of firearm*) qui n'est pas chargé; non chargé. **2.** non accusé. **3.** *Com:* (*a*) qui n'est soumis à aucune charge; (*b*) **u. for,** franco, gratuit.
uncharitable [ʌn'tʃæritəbl], *a.* peu charitable; (*a*) peu indulgent; *Lit:* **u. criticism,** critique sévère; (*b*) peu généreux.
uncharitableness [ʌn'tʃæritəblnis], *s.* manque *m* de charité.
uncharitably [ʌn'tʃæritəbli], *adv.* peu charitablement, sans charité.
uncharted [ʌn'tʃɑːtid], *a.* **1.** (*of island, etc.*) non porté sur la carte. **2.** (*of sea, etc.*) inexploré.
unchartered [ʌn'tʃɑːtəd], *a.* (société commerciale) sans charte.
unchaste [ʌn'tʃeist], *a. A: & Lit:* impudique; impur; incontinent.
unchastened [ʌn'tʃeis(ə)nd], *a.* (*of pers.*) aucunement ravalé; **he was u. by his experience,** son expérience n'a rien rabattu de ses prétentions, de son assurance.
unchastised [ʌntʃæs'taizd], *a.* inchâtié; impuni.
unchecked [ʌn'tʃekt], *a.* (*a*) auquel rien n'a été opposé; sans (la moindre) opposition; **the enemy advanced u.,** l'ennemi s'est avancé sans qu'on lui oppose de résistance, sans rencontrer d'obstacles; **u. advance,** libre marche en avant; **u. progress of a disease,** progrès *mpl* d'une maladie que rien ne parvient à enrayer; **u. anger, passion,** colère non contenue, qui a libre cours; passion non réprimée, sans frein; **to shed u. tears,** donner libre cours à ses larmes; (*b*) (compte rendu, bilan, etc.) non vérifié, non contrôlé; (document, etc.) non relu.
unchivalrous [ʌn'ʃiv(ə)lrəs], *a. Lit:* peu chevaleresque; peu galant; peu courtois; discourtois.
unchivalrously [ʌn'ʃiv(ə)lrəsli], *adv.* d'une manière peu chevaleresque, peu galante; peu courtoise; discourtoisement.
unchristened [ʌn'kris(ə)nd], *a.* **1.** non baptisé; sans baptême. **2.** *A: & Lit:* sans nom.
unchristian [ʌn'kristjən], *a.* **1.** infidèle, païen, non chrétien. **2.** (désir, etc.) peu chrétien. **3.** malséant, inconvenant; peu convenable; **at this u. hour,** à cette heure indue.
uncial ['ʌnsiəl]. **1.** *a.* (*of letters, MS*) oncial, -aux; **half u.,** demi-oncial, semi-oncial. **2.** *s.* (*a*) (écriture) onciale *f*; (*b*) lettre onciale; (*c*) majuscule *f.*
unciform ['ʌnsifɔːm]. **1.** *a. Nat.Hist:* unciforme, uncinulé, inciné; crochu. **2.** *s. Anat:* os *m* unciforme.
uncinaria [ʌnsi'nεəriə], *s. Ann:* uncinaire *f.*
uncinariasis [ʌnsinə'raiəsis], *s. Med:* uncinariose *f*, ankylostomiase *f.*
uncinate ['ʌnsineit], *a. Nat.Hist:* unciné, uncinulé, unciforme; crochu; **u. gyrus, convolution,** éminence unciforme; *Psy:* **u. fit, seizure,** crise uncinée.
Uncinula [ʌn'sinjulə], *s. Fung:* uncinula *m.*
uncinus, *pl.* **-cini** [ʌn'sainəs, -sainai], *s. Nat.Hist:* uncinule *f.*
uncircumcised [ʌn'səːkəmsaizd], *a.* incirconcis.
uncircumcision [ʌnsəːkəm'siʒ(ə)n], *s.* incirconcision *f.*
uncircumscribed [ʌn'səːkəmskraibd], *a.* incirconscrit; illimité.
uncivil [ʌn'siv(i)l], *a.* incivil, grossier, impoli; *Lit:* discourtois.
uncivilized [ʌn'sivilaizd], *a.* non civilisé, incivilisé, barbare.
uncivilly [ʌn'sivili], *adv.* incivilement, grossièrement, impoliment.
unclad [ʌn'klæd], *a. A: & Lit:* nu; sans vêtements; déshabillé.
unclaimed [ʌn'kleimd], *a.* non réclamé; **u. right,** droit non revendiqué; *Jur:* **u. animal,** animal errant; *Post:* **u. letter,** (lettre au) rebut.
unclamp [ʌn'klæmp], *v.tr.* (*a*) retirer (qch.) de la presse à serrer; ôter les crampons, les agrafes, de (qch.); (*b*) débrider (un tuyau, etc.); dévisser, débloquer (un instrument assujetti, etc.); (*c*) desserrer (un étau, etc.).
unclasp [ʌn'klɑːsp]. **1.** *v.tr.* (*a*) dégrafer, défaire, ouvrir (un bracelet); (*b*) desserrer (le poing, etc.). **2.** *v.i.* (*of hands*) se desserrer.
unclassable [ʌn'klɑːsəbl], *a.* inclassable.
unclassical [ʌn'klæsik(ə)l], *a.* contraire à la tradition classique.
unclassifiable [ʌn'klæsifaiəbl], *a.* inclassable.
unclassified [ʌn'klæsifaid], *a.* non classé.
uncle ['ʌŋkl], *s.* **1.** oncle *m*; *F:* (*of person other than true uncle*) parrain *m*; **u. on the mother's, the father's, side,** oncle paternel, maternel; *Fig:* **rich u.,** oncle d'Amérique, de comédie; *U.S: F:* **U. Tom,** noir *m* qui s'insinue dans les bonnes grâces des blancs. **2.** *F: O:* **my watch is at my uncle's,** ma montre est chez ma tante, au clou. **3.** *NAm: F:* **to say u.,** se soumettre, se rendre; céder.
unclean [ʌn'kliːn], *a.* **1.** (*a*) impur, obscène, immonde; *B:* **u. spirit,** esprit immonde; démon *m*; (*b*) *Rel:* (*of food, animal*) immonde, impur; (*c*) (*of fish*) hors de saison. **2.** *Lit:* malpropre, sale.
uncleanly [ʌn'klenli], *a. A: & Lit:* **1.** impur, immonde, obscène. **2.** malpropre, sale.
uncleanness [ʌn'kliːnnis], *s. A: & Lit:* **1.** impureté *f.* **2.** malpropreté *f*, saleté *f.*
uncleansed [ʌn'klenzd], *a. Lit:* **1.** non nettoyé; (*of pond*) non curé; sale, malpropre. **2.** non purifié.
unclear [ʌn'kliər], *a.* (*a*) peu transparent, peu clair; opaque; (*b*) (*of statement*) peu clair, obscur, confus, vague, nébuleux; (esprit) nuageux, fumeux.
uncleared [ʌn'kliəd], *a.* **1.** (sirop, etc.) non clarifié. **2.** non débarrassé **(of,** de); non dégagé; (*of pipe*) non dégorgé; (*of table*) non desservi; **u. ground,** terrain indéfriché. **3.** (accusé) non innocenté, non acquitté **(of a charge,** d'une accusation). **4.** (*a*) (*of debt*) non acquitté, non liquidé; (*b*) *Cust:* **u. goods,** marchandises non dédouanées; (*c*) (chèque) non compensé.
unclench [ʌn'klen(t)ʃ], *v.tr.* desserrer (le poing, les dents).
unclick [ʌn'klik], *v.tr. Mec.E:* décliqueter (une roue dentée, etc.).
unclicking [ʌn'klikiŋ], *s. Mec.E:* décliquetage *m* (d'une roue dentée, etc.).
unclimbable [ʌn'klaiməbl], *a.* (montagne) dont il est impossible de faire l'ascension, qu'on ne peut gravir.
unclipped [ʌn'klipt], *a.* (*of hedge*) non taillé; (*of sheep*) non tondu; (*of wing, coin*) non rogné.
uncloak [ʌn'klouk]. *Lit:* **1.** *v.tr.* (*a*) dépouiller, débarrasser (qn) de son manteau; (*b*) découvrir (des projets); démasquer, dévoiler (une imposture). **2.** *v.i.* se débarrasser de, ôter, son manteau.
unclog [ʌn'klɔg], *v.tr.* **(unclogged)** débloquer (une machine); déboucher, décrasser (une conduite).
uncloistered [ʌn'klɔistəd], *a.* **1.** décloîtré. **2.** non cloîtré.
unclosed [ʌn'klouzd], *a.* **1.** *A: & Lit:* (terrain) non enclos, non clôturé. **2.** non fermé; ouvert; (*of wound*) non refermé.
unclothed [ʌn'klouðd], *a.* **1.** déshabillé. **2.** nu; sans vêtements.
unclouded [ʌn'klaudid], *a.* **1.** (*of sky, future, etc.*) sans nuage(s), serein; (*of vision*) clair, lumineux. **2.** (*of liquid*) clair, limpide.
uncloudedness [ʌn'klaudidnis], *s.* clarté *f* (du ciel); sérénité *f* (du visage).
uncluttered [ʌn'klʌtəd], *a.* (style) concis, dépouillé; (esprit) clair, net.
unco ['ʌŋkou]. *Scot: A: & Lit:* **1.** *a.* (*a*) inconnu, insolite, inaccoutumé; (*b*) d'une étrangeté inquiétante; mystérieux; (*c*) grand, énorme; **I saw an u. shadow,** j'ai vu une ombre énorme; **he thinks an u. lot of you,** il vous tient en haute estime. **2.** *s.* (*a*) étranger, -ère; (*b*) **uncos,** nouvelles *f.* **3.** *adv.* remarquablement, très; **the u. guid,** les cagots *m*; les gens confits en dévotion.
uncoagulated [ʌnkou'ægjuleitid], *a.* (*of blood*) non coagulé.
uncock [ʌn'kɔk], *v.tr.* désarmer (un fusil); mettre (un fusil) à l'abattu.
uncocked [ʌn'kɔkt], *a.* (fusil) à l'abattu, désarmé.
uncog [ʌn'kɔg], *v.tr.* **(uncogged)** *Mec.E:* décliqueter (une roue dentée, etc.).
uncogging [ʌn'kɔgiŋ], *s. Mec.E:* décliquetage *m* (d'une roue dentée, etc.).
uncoil [ʌn'kɔil]. **1.** *v.tr.* dérouler; délover. **2.** *v.i. & pr.* **to u. (itself),** (*of snake, rope, etc.*) se dérouler; (*of snake*) se délover.
uncoiling [ʌn'kɔiliŋ], *s.* déroulement *m.*
uncoined [ʌn'kɔind], *a.* (or, etc.) non monnayé, non frappé.
uncollected [ʌnkə'lektid], *a.* non rassemblé; (*of luggage, etc.*) non réclamé; **u. taxes,** impôts non perçus.
uncoloured [ʌn'kʌləd], *a.* (*a*) non coloré; **u. account of sth.,** rapport fidèle, impartial, de qch.; (*b*) incolore; sans couleur.
uncombed [ʌn'koumd], *a.* (*of hair*) non peigné, mal peigné, ébouriffé; (*of wool*) non peigné.
uncombined [ʌnkəm'baind], *a. Ch: etc:* non combiné **(with,** avec).
un(-)come-at-able ['ʌnkʌm'ætəbl], *a. F:* **1.** inaccessible. **2.** difficile à obtenir, à se procurer.
uncomeliness [ʌn'kʌmlinis], *s.* **1.** manque *m* de grâce; laideur *f.* **2.** *A:* inconvenance *f*, malséance *f.*
uncomely [ʌn'kʌmli], *a.* **1.** peu joli; peu gracieux; disgracieux; laid. **2.** *A:* peu seyant; inconvenant; malséant.
uncomfortable [ʌn'kʌmf(ə)təbl], *a.* **1.** inconfortable; incommode; (fauteuil, etc.) peu confortable; (vêtement, etc.) gênant; **this is a very u. armchair,** on est très mal (assis) dans ce fauteuil. **2.** désagréable, inconfortable; fâcheux; **to make things u. for s.o.,** attirer, faire, créer, susciter, des ennuis à qn; causer du désagrément à qn. **3. to feel, be, u.,** (i) être mal à l'aise; (ii) *Fig:* ne pas être à son aise; être, se sentir, mal à l'aise; se sentir gêné; **to**

be, feel, u. about sth., être inquiet, ne pas avoir l'esprit tranquille, au sujet de qch.; **to make s.o. feel u.,** mettre qn mal à son aise; troubler qn.

uncomfortably [ʌn'kʌmf(ə)təbli], *adv.* **1.** peu confortablement; inconfortablement, incommodément. **2.** désagréablement, fâcheusement; **the enemy were u. near,** la proximité de l'ennemi était inquiétante.

uncommissioned [ʌnkə'miʃ(ə)nd], *a.* non commissionné, non délégué (**to do sth.,** pour faire qch.).

uncommitted [ʌnkə'mitid], *a.* **1.** (*a*) (*of pers.*) non engagé; libre; indépendant; **to be u. to any course of action,** n'être engagé à aucune ligne de conduite; (*b*) *Pol:* neutraliste, non aligné. **2.** *Parl:* (*of bill*) qui n'a pas été renvoyé à une commission.

uncommon [ʌn'kɔmən]. **1.** *a.* peu commun; (*a*) rare; **u. word,** mot rare, peu usité; (*b*) peu ordinaire; singulier, extraordinaire, particulier; (événement) qui sort de l'ordinaire. **2.** *adv. F: A:* singulièrement, remarquablement, particulièrement.

uncommonly [ʌn'kɔmənli], *adv.* **1. not u.,** assez souvent. **2.** singulièrement, remarquablement, particulièrement; **you're u. absentminded today,** vous êtes singulièrement distrait aujourd'hui; **u. good,** excellent.

uncommonness [ʌn'kɔmənnis], *s.* **1.** rareté *f.* **2.** *O: & Lit:* singularité *f.*

uncommunicative [ʌnkə'mju:nikətiv], *a.* peu communicatif; réservé, renfermé, taciturne.

uncompanionable [ʌnkəm'pæniənəbl], *a. Lit:* peu sociable; insociable.

uncompensated [ʌn'kɔmpənseitid], *a.* incompensé; (*a*) (*of pers.*) qui n'a pas été dédommagé (**for sth.,** de qch.); (*b*) *Mec.E:* (levier, etc.) non compensé.

uncomplaining [ʌnkəm'pleiniŋ], *a.* qui ne se plaint pas; patient, résigné; **u. submission,** soumission sans murmure, sans plainte.

uncomplainingly [ʌnkəm'pleiniŋli], *adv.* sans se plaindre, patiemment.

uncomplimentary [ʌnkɔmpli'ment(ə)ri], *a.* peu flatteur, -euse.

uncomplying [ʌnkəm'plaiiŋ], *a. Lit:* peu souple; intransigeant; (principe) rigide, inflexible.

uncompounded [ʌnkəm'paundid], *a.* simple, non composé.

uncomprehending [ʌnkɔmpri'hendiŋ], *a.* incompréhensif.

uncompromising [ʌn'kɔmprəmaiziŋ], *a.* intransigeant, inflexible; intraitable; **u. sincerity,** sincérité absolue, sans compromis; **to be too u. in business,** être trop rigide dans les affaires.

unconcealed [ʌnkən'si:ld], *a.* qui n'est pas caché; non dissimulé; fait à découvert; **u. dislike,** aversion que l'on ne cherche pas à dissimuler.

unconcern [ʌnkən'sə:n], *s.* insouciance *f*; indifférence *f*; **smile of u.,** sourire détaché; **to show u. in the face of danger,** se montrer indifférent en face du danger.

unconcerned [ʌnkən'sə:nd], *a.* **1.** (*a*) insouciant, indifférent; impassible; **u., he went on speaking,** sans se (laisser) troubler, il a continué de parler; **to be u. about s.o.'s unhappiness,** être indifférent au malheur de qn; ne pas se soucier du malheur de qn; (*b*) **he seems entirely u. about his results,** il ne semble pas du tout s'inquiéter au sujet de ses résultats. **2.** (*a*) neutre; impartial, -aux; (*b*) **to be u. in, with, a business,** être étranger à, ne pas être mêlé à, une affaire.

unconcernedly [ʌnkən'sə:nidli], *adv.* d'un air indifférent, dégagé; avec insouciance; sans se (laisser) troubler.

unconciliating, unconciliatory [ʌnkən'silieitiŋ, -'siliət(ə)ri], *a.* peu conciliant; intraitable; inflexible; rigide (en affaires, etc.).

uncondensable [ʌnkən'densəbl], *a.* (gaz) incondensable.

unconditional [ʌnkən'diʃən(ə)l], *a.* inconditionnel; absolu; **u. refusal,** refus net, catégorique, absolu; **u. surrender,** soumission inconditionnelle, sans condition; **u. acceptance,** acceptation inconditionnelle, sans réserve; *Fin:* **u. order,** ordre (de payer) pur et simple.

unconditionality [ʌnkəndiʃə'næliti], *s.* inconditionnalité *f.*

unconditionally [ʌnkən'diʃən(ə)li], *adv.* inconditionnellement; **to accept u.,** accepter sans réserve; **to surrender u.,** se rendre inconditionnellement, sans condition, à discrétion.

unconditioned [ʌnkən'diʃ(ə)nd], *a.* **1.** inconditionnel; absolu. **2.** inconditionné; qui ne dépend pas d'une condition antérieure.

unconfessed [ʌnkən'fest], *a.* **1.** (péché, etc.) inavoué, caché. **2. to die u.,** mourir sans confession.

unconfined [ʌnkən'faind], *a.* **1.** *Lit:* (*of joy, etc.*) illimité; sans bornes. **2.** *A: & Lit:* non enfermé; libre.

unconfirmed [ʌnkən'fə:md], *a.* non confirmé. **1.** (*of news, etc.*) qui n'est pas confirmé, qui n'a pas reçu de confirmation; non avéré; sujet à caution. **2.** *Ecc:* qui n'a pas reçu le sacrement de la confirmation.

unconformable [ʌnkən'fɔ:məbl], *a.* **1. u. to sth.,** qui n'est pas conforme à qch.; incompatible avec qch. **2.** indépendant, réfractaire. **3.** *Geol:* **u. stratum,** couche discordante.

unconformity [ʌnkən'fɔ:miti], *s.* **1.** incompatibilité *f,* désaccord *m* (**to,** avec). **2.** *Geol:* discordance *f* (d'une couche).

unconfuted [ʌnkən'fju:tid], *a. Lit:* irréfuté.

uncongealable [ʌnkən'dʒi:ləbl], *a.* incongelable.

uncongealed [ʌnkən'dʒi:ld], *a.* non congelé; (sang) non coagulé, non figé.

uncongenial [ʌnkən'dʒi:niəl], *a.* **1.** (*of pers.*) peu sympathique, antipathique. **2.** (*a*) (climat) peu favorable (**to,** à); (*b*) peu agréable (**to,** à); **u. atmosphere,** ambiance, atmosphère, hostile.

uncongeniality [ʌnkəndʒi:ni'æliti], *s.* **1.** caractère *m* peu sympathique (de qn). **2.** caractère (i) peu favorable (d'un climat), (ii) peu agréable (d'un travail, etc.).

unconnected [ʌnkə'nektid], *a.* (*a*) sans rapport, sans lien; qui n'a aucun rapport (**with,** avec); **the two events are totally u.,** les deux événements n'ont aucun rapport entre eux; (*b*) (style) décousu; **u. thoughts,** pensées sans suite; (*c*) *A: & Lit:* **u. with s.o.,** sans lien de parenté avec qn.

unconquerable [ʌn'kɔŋkərəbl], *a.* (ennemi) invincible; (cœur) qu'on ne peut conquérir; (courage) indomptable, invincible; (curiosité, etc.) irrésistible; (désir) irrépressible; (difficulté, aversion) insurmontable.

unconquerably [ʌn'kɔŋkərəbli], *adv.* invinciblement.

unconquered [ʌn'kɔŋkəd], *a.* (*a*) (peuple, etc.) invaincu, inasservi, non soumis; (passion) indomptée; (difficulté) insurmontable; (*b*) (peuple, pays) inconquis.

unconscientious [ʌnkɔnʃi'enʃəs], *a.* peu consciencieux; indélicat.

unconscionable [ʌn'kɔnʃənəbl], *a.* **1.** (*a*) *A: & Lit:* (*of pers.*) sans conscience; peu scrupuleux; indélicat; **u. rogue,** coquin fieffé; (*b*) *Jur:* **u. bargain,** marché léonin. **2.** énorme, déraisonnable, démesuré, excessif; (prix, etc.) exorbitant; **to take an u. time doing sth.,** mettre un temps invraisemblable à faire qch.

unconscionably [ʌn'kɔnʃənəbli], *adv.* **1.** *A: & Lit:* peu consciencieusement, peu scrupuleusement. **2.** énormément, déraisonnablement, démesurément, excessivement.

unconscious [ʌn'kɔnʃəs], *a.* **1.** inconscient; (*a*) **u. matter,** matière inanimée; (*b*) **to be u. of doing sth.,** ne pas avoir conscience de faire qch.; **to be u. of sth.,** (i) ne pas avoir conscience, ne pas s'apercevoir, de qch.; (ii) ignorer qch.; **he remained blissfully u. of it all,** il est resté parfaitement ignorant de tout; **he was u. of distinctions, of values,** il ne savait pas distinguer; il ne savait pas apprécier les choses à leur valeur; **he is not u. of her kindness,** il n'est pas insensible à, il n'est pas sans reconnaître, sa bonté. **2.** sans connaissance; inanimé; évanoui; **to become u.,** perdre connaissance; s'évanouir; **to knock s.o. u.,** assommer qn raide; **to be knocked u.,** être assommé (par le coup); *F:* être (complètement) k.-o. **3.** *s. Psy:* **the u.,** l'inconscient *m.*

unconsciously [ʌn'kɔnʃəsli], *adv.* inconsciemment; (i) à son insu; sans le savoir; (ii) sans s'en rendre compte.

unconsciousness [ʌn'kɔnʃəsnis], *s.* **1.** inconscience *f* (**of,** de). **2.** évanouissement *m,* insensibilité *f.*

unconsecrated [ʌn'kɔnsikreitid], *a.* (église, terre) non consacrée; (évêque) non sacré; (eau) non bénite.

unconsenting [ʌnkən'sentiŋ], *a.* non consentant.

unconsidered [ʌnkən'sidəd], *a.* **1.** (*of remark, opinion*) inconsidéré, irréfléchi, indiscret. **2.** *A: & Lit:* (objet, fait, événement) auquel on n'attache aucune importance.

unconsolable [ʌnkən'souləbl], *a.* inconsolable.

unconsoled [ʌnkən'sould], *a.* inconsolé; sans consolation.

unconsolidated [ʌnkən'sɔlideitid], *a.* non consolidé.

unconstitutional [ʌnkɔnsti'tju:ʃən(ə)l], *a.* inconstitutionnel, anticonstitutionnel.

unconstitutionality [ʌnkɔnstitju:ʃə'næliti], *s.* inconstitutionnalité *f.*

unconstitutionally [ʌnkɔnsti'tju:ʃən(ə)li], *adv.* inconstitutionnellement, anticonstitutionnellement.

unconstrained [ʌnkən'streind], *a.* non contraint; sans contrainte; libre; (acte) spontané; **u. laughter,** hilarité franche, débordante; **u. freedom,** liberté complète; **u. manner,** allure aisée, désinvolte, décontractée.

unconstrainedly [ʌnkən'streinidli], *adv.* sans contrainte, sans aucune gêne; librement; spontanément.

unconstraint [ʌnkən'streint], *s. esp. Lit:* absence *f* de contrainte; liberté *f*; aisance *f,* désinvolture *f,* décontraction *f*; franchise *f* (de langage).

unconstricted [ʌnkən'striktid], *a.* (*of pers.*) à l'aise; **u. movement,** mouvement libre, qui n'est pas gêné.

unconsumed [ʌnkən'sju:md], *a.* qui n'est pas consumé (par le feu).

unconsummated [ʌn'kɔnsəmeitid], *a.* inconsommé; *esp.* **u. marriage,** mariage inconsommé; mariage blanc.

uncontainable [ʌnkən'teinəbl], *a.* (*of laughter, etc.*) qu'on ne peut réprimer.

uncontaminated [ʌnkən'tæmineitid], *a.* incontaminé, non corrompu (**by,** par).

uncontested [ʌnkən'testid], *a.* (droit, etc.) incontesté; *Jur:* **u. owner,** possesseur paisible, pacifique; *Pol: etc:* **u. seat,** siège (à la Chambre, etc.) qui n'est pas disputé, pour lequel il n'y a qu'un candidat.

uncontracted [ʌnkən'træktid], *a.* (*of word*) non contracté; entier.

uncontradictable [ʌnkɔntrə'diktəbl], *a.* irréfutable, irréfragable, irrécusable.

uncontradicted [ʌnkɔntrə'diktid], *a.* non contredit; irréfuté; incontroversé.

uncontrite [ʌn'kɔntrait], *a.* impénitent.

uncontrollability [ʌnkəntroulə'biliti], *s.* caractère *m* ingouvernable; indocilité *f,* insoumission *f* (d'un enfant, etc.).

uncontrollable [ʌnkən'trouləbl], *a.* **1.** *A:* (pouvoir, droit) absolu. **2.** (enfant, peuple) ingouvernable; (mouvement) irréprimable; (désir) irrésistible, irrépressible, indomptable; **u. laughter,** fou rire; rire irrépressible, convulsif, inextinguible; **fits of u. temper,** violents accès de colère; emportements *m*; **u. causes,** causes qui ne dépendent pas de la volonté humaine.

uncontrollably [ʌnkən'trouləbli], *adv.* irrésistiblement.

uncontrolled [ʌnkən'trould], *a.* **1.** indépendant; (monarque, etc.) irresponsable. **2.** sans frein; effréné; **u. passions,** passions effrénées, indomptées. **3.** *Med:* **u. diabetes,** diabète *m* instable.

uncontroversial [ʌnkɔntrə'və:ʃ(ə)l], *a.* (sujet) qui ne soulève pas, qui ne provoque pas, de controverses.

uncontrovertible [ʌnkɔntrə'və:tibl], *a.* incontroversable, incontestable, indiscutable; **u. proof,** preuve qui ne saurait être mise en doute; preuve irréfutable.

uncontrovertibly [ʌnkɔntrə'və:tibli], *adv.* indisputablement, incontestablement.

unconventional [ʌnkən'venʃən(ə)l], *a.* qui va à l'encontre des conventions sociales, littéraires, artistiques, etc.; peu conventionnel; non-conformiste, individualiste; original, -aux; **u. dress,** robe originale; **he leads an u. life,** il mène une vie irrégulière; **u. war,** (i) guerre avec des armes non classiques, non conventionnelles; (ii) guerre de subversion, de partisans; guerre non conventionnelle; **u. weapon,** arme non classique, non conventionnelle.

unconventionality [ʌnkənvenʃə'næliti], *s.* indépendance *f* à l'égard des conventions sociales, littéraires, artistiques, etc.; non-conformisme *m,* individualisme *m*; originalité *f.*

unconventionally [ʌnkən'venʃən(ə)li], *adv.* de manière peu conventionnelle; **to act u.,** aller à l'encontre de l'usage.

unconversant [ʌnkən'və:s(ə)nt], *a.* **u. with sth.,** peu versé dans (une science, etc.); peu familier avec (un sujet); **to be u. with a question,** ne pas être au courant d'une question.

unconverted [ʌnkən'və:tid], *a.* **1.** inconverti, non converti (**into,** en). **2.** *Rel:* inconverti.

unconvertible [ʌnkən'və:tibl], *a.* **1.** inconvertible, inconvertissable (**into,** en). **2.** *Log:* (proposition) inconversible.

unconvicted [ʌnkən'viktid], *a.* (*a*) non condamné; (*b*) dont la culpabilité n'a pas été établie.

unconvinced [ʌnkən'vinst], *a.* sceptique (**of,** à l'égard de, au sujet de); incrédule; **I am still u.,** je ne suis toujours pas convaincu.

unconvincing [ʌnkən'vinsiŋ], *a.* (témoignage, etc.) peu convaincant, peu probant; (excuse, etc.) peu vraisemblable.

uncooked [ʌn'kukt], *a.* (aliment) non cuit, inapprêté, cru.

uncooperative [ʌnkou'ɔprətiv], *a.* peu coopératif, -ive.

uncoordinated [ʌnkou'ɔ:dineitid], *a.* non coordonné; **u. manœuvre,** manœuvre désunie, qui manque de coordination.

uncork [ʌn'kɔ:k], *v.tr.* déboucher (une bouteille, etc.).

uncorrected [ʌnkə'rektid], *a.* **1.** (*of exercise, proof*) non corrigé. **2.** (*of error*) non rectifié; *Ph: etc:* **result u. for temperature, for pressure,** résultat brut. **3.** *A: & Lit:* (*of child*) impuni. **4. u. time,** temps réel.

uncorroborated [ʌnkə'rɔbəreitid], *a.* non corroboré, non confirmé.

uncorroded [ʌnkə'roudid], non corrodé; non rongé.

uncorrupted [ʌnkə'rʌptid], *a.* incorrompu; intègre.

uncounted [ʌn'kauntid], *a.* **1.** non compté; non énuméré. **2.** *Lit:* incalculable, innombrable.

uncouple [ʌn'kʌpl], *v.tr.* **1.** découpler, désaccoupler, détacher, lâcher (des chiens); *Ven:* **to u. the hounds,** laisser courre. **2.** *Mec.E: etc:* débrayer (une machine); déboîter (des tuyaux); dételer, découpler, désaccoupler, détacher (des wagons, une locomotive); *v.i.* *Mus:* (*in organ playing*) découpler.

uncoupled [ʌn'kʌp(ə)ld], *a.* non accouplé.

uncoupling [ʌn'kʌpliŋ], *s.* **1.** *Ven:* découple *m*, découpler *m* (des chiens). **2.** *Mec.E:* débrayage *m* (d'une machine); déboîtage *m* (des tuyaux); dételage *m*, désaccouplement *m* (des wagons).

uncouth [ʌn'ku:θ], *a.* **1.** (usage, etc.) grossier, barbare; (pays) sauvage. **2.** (*of pers.*) malappris, impoli, grossier; lourd, balourd, rustaud; **u. manner,** manières gauches, frustes, agrestes; **he's still rather u.,** il est encore un peu rustre. **3.** *A:* singulier, étrange, bizarre.

uncouthly [ʌn'ku:θli], *adv.* **1.** grossièrement. **2.** impoliment, grossièrement; gauchement. **3.** *A:* singulièrement, étrangement, bizarrement.

uncouthness [ʌn'ku:θnis], *s.* **1.** grossièreté *f*, barbarie *f*, rudesse *f*. **2.** (*of pers.*) grossièreté *f*, impolitesse *f*; gaucherie *f*, lourdeur *f*, balourdise *f*. **3.** *A:* étrangeté *f*, bizarrerie *f*.

uncovenanted [ʌn'kʌvənəntid], *a.* **1.** non stipulé par contrat. **2.** (*a*) *Theol:* **the u. mercy of God,** la miséricorde inconditionnelle de Dieu; (*b*) *B.Hist:* en dehors de l'alliance. **3.** *Hist:* qui n'a pas signé de pacte.

uncover [ʌn'kʌvər]. **1.** *v.tr.* (*a*) découvrir (son visage, etc.); dévoiler, révéler, découvrir (un complot, etc.); débâcher (un wagon); **to u. one's head,** *Lit: v.i.* **to u.,** se découvrir; ôter son chapeau; *Mch:* **to u. a port,** démasquer une lumière; (*b*) *Chess:* **to u. a piece,** découvrir, dégarnir, une pièce; *Fenc:* (*when parrying*) **to u. oneself,** aller à l'épée. **2.** *v.i.* (*of reef*) découvrir.

uncovered [ʌn'kʌvəd], *a.* **1.** mis à nu, à découvert; découvert; sans couverture; (*of pers.*) **to remain u.,** rester la tête découverte; garder son chapeau à la main. **2.** *Ten:* **the player left part of the court u.,** le joueur a laissé une région découverte, un trou dans son court. **3.** *Bank: etc:* (achat, vente) à découvert; (chèque) sans provision; **u. balance,** découvert *m*.

uncoveted [ʌn'kʌvitid], *a.* *Lit:* non désiré.

uncrate [ʌn'kreit], *v.tr.* sortir (qch.) de sa caisse; déballer (des marchandises, etc.).

uncreasable [ʌn'kri:səbl], *a.* (tissu, etc.) infroissable.

uncredited [ʌn'kreditid], *a.* (*of rumour, etc.*) auquel on ne peut se fier.

uncritical [ʌn'kritik(ə)l], *a.* **1.** non critique; dépourvu de sens critique; sans discernement; **u. audience,** auditoire peu exigeant. **2.** contraire aux règles de la critique.

uncross [ʌn'krɔs], *v.tr.* décroiser (les jambes, etc.).

uncrossable [ʌn'krɔsəbl], *a.* (abîme, etc.) infranchissable; (route) qu'on ne peut traverser.

uncrossed [ʌn'krɔst], *a.* **1.** non croisé. **2.** *Bank:* **u. cheque,** chèque non barré, ouvert.

uncrowned [ʌn'kraund], *a.* **1.** sans couronne. **2.** non couronné.

uncrushable [ʌn'krʌʃəbl], *a.* (tissu) infroissable.

uncrystallizable [ʌn'kristəlaizəbl], *a.* incristallisable.

uncrystallized [ʌn'kristəlaizd], *a.* non cristallisé; amorphe.

unction ['ʌŋkʃ(ə)n], *s.* **1.** (*a*) onction *f*; *Ecc:* **extreme u.,** extrême-onction *f*; (*b*) *A: & Lit:* **to speak, preach, with u.,** parler, prêcher, avec onction; **to relate a scandal with u.,** raconter un scandale avec saveur, avec plaisir. **2.** *A: & Lit:* (*a*) onguent *m*; (*b*) baume *m* (pour l'âme).

unctuous ['ʌŋktjuəs], *a.* *A: & Lit:* **1.** onctueux, graisseux; (sol) gras. **2.** (*a*) (prédicateur, sermon, etc.) onctueux; (*b*) *Pej:* onctueux, patelin, mielleux.

unctuously ['ʌŋktjuəsli], *adv.* *A: & Lit:* **1.** onctueusement. **2.** *Pej:* d'un air, d'un ton, onctueux, mielleux; d'un ton patelin.

unctuousness ['ʌŋktjuəsnis], *s.* *A: & Lit:* onctuosité *f*.

uncultivable [ʌn'kʌltivəbl], *a.* (terre) incultivable, inexploitable.

uncultivated [ʌn'kʌltiveitid], *a.* (*a*) (terrain) inculte, incultivé; (terre) en friche; (personne) inculte, sans culture; (esprit) inculte; (*b*) (plante) à l'état sauvage.

uncultured [ʌn'kʌltjəd], *a.* (esprit) inculte; (*of pers.*) peu lettré; sans culture, inculte.

uncurbed [ʌn'kə:bd], *a.* **1.** (cheval) sans gourmette. **2.** (*a*) libre; (autorité, etc.) sans restriction; (*b*) (*of passion, etc.*) débridé, déchaîné, effréné; sans frein.

uncured [ʌn'kjuəd], *a.* **1.** non guéri. **2.** (hareng) frais.

uncurl [ʌn'kə:l]. **1.** *v.tr.* défriser, déboucler (les cheveux, etc.). **2.** *v.i. & pr.* (*of hair*) se défriser, se déboucler; (*of cat*) s'étirer.

uncurtained [ʌn'kə:tənd], *a.* (fenêtre) sans rideaux.

uncustomary [ʌn'kʌstəm(ə)ri], *a.* inaccoutumé, inhabituel.

uncustomed [ʌn'kʌstəmd], *a.* **u. goods,** marchandises introduites en contrebande, en fraude; (marchandises de) contrebande *f*.

uncut, *a.* **1.** [ʌn'kʌt]. (*a*) sans coupure, sans entaille; (*b*) *Jur:* **u. fruit,** fruits pendants par les racines. **2.** ['ʌnkʌt]. (*a*) (*of hedge, etc.*) non coupé, non taillé; **u. diamond,** diamant brut, non taillé; *Const:* **u. stone,** pierre brute, velue, non dégrossie; **u. book,** livre (i) non coupé, (ii) *Bookb:* non rogné; *Tex:* **u. pile,** poil non coupé; (*b*) *Th:* (représentation) en entier, sans coupures, intégrale.

undamaged [ʌn'dæmidʒd], *a.* non endommagé, sans être endommagé; non avarié, sans avarie; indemne; en bon état; **u. reputation,** réputation intacte.

undamped [ʌn'dæmpt], *a.* **1.** non mouillé; sec, *f.* sèche. **2.** (son) non étouffé, non assourdi. **3.** *Ph: etc:* (*of oscillation*) non amorti, non éteint; *W.Tel:* **u. waves,** ondes entretenues. **4.** (*a*) (courage, etc.) non affaibli; persistant, soutenu; (*b*) **u. by this failure,** nullement découragé de cet échec.

undated [ʌn'deitid], *a.* non daté; sans date; *St.Exch:* **u. (government) stocks,** fonds (d'État) sans date d'échéance; **u. debenture,** obligation perpétuelle.

undaunted [ʌn'dɔ:ntid], *a.* (*a*) intrépide; *Lit:* impavide; sans peur; (*b*) aucunement intimidé; aucunement ébranlé (**by,** de, par).

undauntedly [ʌn'dɔ:ntidli], *adv.* intrépidement; sans peur.

unde ['ʌndei], *a.* *Her:* ondé.

undebased [ʌndi'beist], *a.* non avili; non dégradé; (argent) non altéré, de bon aloi; (style) de bon aloi.

undebatable [ʌndi'beitəbl], *a.* indiscutable.

undebated [ʌndi'beitid], *a.* indiscuté; qui n'a pas (encore) été l'objet de débats; **to accept a motion u.,** accepter une motion sans débat.

undecagon [ʌn'dekəgɔn], *s.* *Mth:* undécagone *m*, hendécagone *m*.

undecanoic [ʌndekə'nouik], *a.* *Ch:* **u. acid,** undécanoïque *m*.

undecayed [ʌndi'keid], *a.* **1.** *Lit:* (édifice, etc.) intact, en bon état. **2.** (bois, etc.) non pourri.

undecaying [ʌndi'keiiŋ], *a.* *Lit:* impérissable; **u. beauty,** beauté toujours jeune.

undeceive [ʌndi'si:v], *v.tr.* *esp. Lit:* désabuser (**of,** de); détromper, désillusionner, désenchanter (qn); tirer (qn) d'erreur; dessiller les yeux de, à (qn); **to u. oneself,** se détromper, se désabuser; se dépouiller de ses illusions.

undecided [ʌndi'saidid], *a.* (*a*) (problème, etc.) indécis, non résolu, irrésolu; (match) sans résultat; (procès, etc.) pendant; **the match was left u.,** c'était match nul; (*b*) (*of pers.*) indécis, irrésolu, hésitant, vacillant; (caractère) flottant; (*c*) **to be u. how to act,** être indécis quant au parti à prendre; rester indécis entre plusieurs partis; ne pas savoir quel parti prendre; **he was u. whether he would go or not,** il se demandait, il ne savait pas, s'il irait ou non.

undecipherable [ʌndi'saif(ə)rəbl], *a.* indéchiffrable.

undeciphered [ʌndi'saifəd], *a.* indéchiffré.

undecked [ʌn'dekt], *a.* **1.** *Lit:* (*a*) sans parure, sans ornement; (*b*) déparé; dépouillé de ses beaux atours. **2.** *Nau:* (navire) non ponté.

undeclared [ʌndi'klɛəd], *a.* (*of war, etc.*) non déclaré; *Cust:* **u. goods,** marchandises non déclarées.

undecomposable [ʌndi:kəm'pouzəbl], *a.* (élément, etc.) indécomposable.

undecomposed [ʌndi:kəm'pouzd], *a.* *esp. Ch:* indécomposé.

undecylenic [ʌndesi'lenik], *a.* *Ch:* **u. acid,** acide *m* undécylénique.

undee ['ʌndei], *a.* *Her:* ondé.

undefaced [ʌndi'feist], *a.* **1.** (*a*) (monument, etc.) non mutilé, non défiguré, non dégradé; intact; (*b*) **landscape u. by posters,** paysage non enlaidi par l'abus des affiches. **2.** (timbre, etc.) non oblitéré.

undefeated [ʌndi'fi:tid], *a.* invaincu; non battu; **to withdraw u.,** se replier sans avoir subi l'échec.

undefended [ʌndi'fendid], *a.* **1.** sans défense, sans protection; sans protecteur, sans défenseur. **2.** *Jur:* (*a*) (accusé) sans défenseur, qui n'est pas représenté par un avocat; (*b*) **u. case, trial,** débats non contentieux; **u. suit,** cause où le défendeur s'abstient de plaider.

undefiled [ʌndi'faild], *a.* sans souillure, sans tache; immaculé; pur.

undefinable [ʌndi'fainəbl], *a.* indéfinissable, indéterminable.

undefined [ʌndi'faind], *a.* **1.** non défini. **2.** indéterminé; vague.

undelivered [ʌndi'livəd], *a.* **1.** (*a*) *esp. Lit:* non délivré, non libéré, non débarrassé (**from,** de); (*b*) *A:* (femme) pas encore accouchée. **2. u. goods,** marchandises non livrées; **u. message,** commission dont on ne s'est pas acquitté; *Post:* **u. parcel,** colis en souffrance; **u. letter,** lettre pas encore remise au destinataire; **u. letters,** (lettres au) rebut; **if u. please return to sender,** en cas de non-livraison prière de retourner à l'expéditeur.

undemanding [ʌndi'mɑ:ndiŋ], *a.* peu exigeant; qui n'exige rien.

undemocratic [ʌndemə'krætik], *a.* antidémocratique.

undemonstrable [ʌndi'mɔnstrəbl, 'ʌn'demən-], *a.* indémontrable.

undemonstrated [ʌn'demənstreitid], *a.* non démontré; sans démonstration.

undemonstrative [ʌndi'mɔnstrətiv], *a.* (*of pers.*) peu expansif, peu démonstratif; réservé.

undeniable [ʌndi'naiəbl], *a.* indéniable, incontestable, indiscutable; qu'on ne peut nier; (témoignage, etc.) irrécusable, irréfragable, irréfutable; **of u. worth,** dont la valeur s'impose.

undeniably [ʌndi'naiəbli], *adv.* incontestablement, indiscutablement, irréfutablement; indéniablement.

undenominational [ʌndinɔmi'neiʃən(ə)l], *a.* non confessionnel.

undependable [ʌndi'pendəbl], *a.* sur lequel on ne peut pas compter; auquel on ne peut se fier; (renseignement, etc.) peu sûr, peu digne de foi.

undepreciated [ʌndi'pri:ʃieitid], *a.* non déprécié.

under ['ʌndər], *prep. & adv.*

I. *prep.* **1.** sous; au-dessous de; (*a*) **the dog is u. the table,** le chien est sous la table; **he sat down u. a tree,** il s'est assis sous un arbre; **u. water,** sous l'eau; **he went u. the table,** (i) il s'est mis sous la table; (ii) il a passé par-dessous la table; **I crept u. it,** (i) je me suis glissé (là-)dessous; (ii) j'ai passé par-dessous; **here's a table, get u. it,** voici une table, mettez-vous dessous; **put it u. that,** mettez-le là-dessous; **to wear a waistcoat u. one's jacket,** porter un gilet sous son veston; **he pulled a stool out from u. the table,** il a tiré un tabouret de sous la table; **her curls peeped out from u. her hat,** ses boucles ressortaient de dessous son chapeau; **the village u. the castle,** le village au-dessous du château; **to grow sth. u. a wall,** cultiver qch. à l'abri d'un mur; **to look up a word u. (the letter) S,** chercher un mot sous la lettre S; **to look for, to file, sth. u.** *miscellaneous*, chercher, classer, qch. sous la rubrique *divers*; **computers come u. (the heading of) data processing,** les ordinateurs sont classés sous (la rubrique de l')informatique; (*b*) (*less than*) **sold (at) u. its value,** vendu au-dessous de sa valeur; **all their books were u. £5,** tous leurs livres coûtaient moins de £5; **salaries u. £3000,** salaires inférieurs à, au-dessous de, £3000; **a temperature (of) u. 30°,** une température au-dessous de 30°; **he's u. thirty,** il a moins de trente ans; **people u. thirty, the u. thirties,** les moins de trente ans; **children u. ten,** les enfants au-dessous de dix ans; **in u. ten minutes,** en moins de dix minutes; **to speak u. one's breath,** parler à mi-voix; **nobody u. the rank of captain,** personne au-dessous du grade de capitaine; **alcohol that is u. proof,** alcool au-dessous de preuve. **2.** (*a*) **u. lock and key,** sous clef; **visible u. the microscope,** visible au microscope; **u. pain of death,** sous peine de mort; **to be u. sentence of death,** être condamné à mort; **to be u. orders to do sth.,** avoir reçu l'ordre de faire qch.; **to be u. a deportation order,** être sous le coup d'un arrêté d'expulsion; **u. these conditions,** dans ces conditions; **u. the circumstances,** dans les circonstances; **u. the rules of the club,** selon les règles du club; **u. the terms of the agreement,** aux termes, en vertu, de la convention; selon, suivant, les termes de la convention; **u. article twelve,** conformément à, d'après, aux termes de, l'article douze; **u. his father's will,** d'après le testament de son père; **he had returned u. an amnesty,** il était rentré en vertu d'une amnistie; **to be u. a promise to do sth.,** être engagé (par sa promesse) à faire qch.; **she wrote it u. a pseudonym,** elle l'a écrit sous un pseudonyme; (*b*) **he had a hundred men u. him,** il avait cent hommes sous ses ordres; **to be u. s.o.,** être au service, sous les ordres, de qn; **to be, to come, u. the authority of the Home Office,** relever du Ministère de l'Intérieur; **u. government control,** soumis, assujetti, au contrôle de l'État; **country u. French influence,** pays soumis à l'influence française; **to be u. the influence of alcohol,** *F:* **to be u. the influence,** être sous l'empire de la boisson; être dans les vignes (du Seigneur); **u. Louis XIV,** sous Louis XIV; *Hist:* **mandate u. the League of Nations,** mandat sous l'égide de la Société des Nations; *F:* **to be u. the doctor,** être sous les ordres du médecin; (*c*) **to sink u. the burden,** plier sous les faix; **the people were u. a crushing yoke,** le peuple subissait un joug écrasant. **3.** en; (*a*) **u. repair,** en (voie de) réparation; **u. construction,** en construction; **patients u. treatment,** malades qui suivent un traitement; **patient u. observation,** malade en observation; **the question is u. examination,**

la question a été prise en considération; (*b*) **field u. wheat, u. grass,** champ mis en blé, en herbe.
II. *adv.* **1.** (au-)dessous; **to stay u. for two minutes,** rester deux minutes sous l'eau; *F:* **to get out from u.,** se tirer d'affaire; *Com: etc:* **as u.,** comme ci-dessous; **children seven years old and u.,** des enfants (âgés) de sept ans et au-dessous. **2.** en soumission; **to keep s.o. u.,** opprimer, écraser, dominer, qn; tenir qn dans la soumission; **to keep a fire, an epidemic, a rebellion, u.,** maîtriser un incendie; enrayer une épidémie; mater une rébellion; **he was u. sedation,** on lui avait donné des tranquillisants; **he was kept u. by means of morphine (injections),** des injections de morphine le maintenaient dans un état d'insensibilité.

underact [ʌndə'rækt], *v.tr. & i. Th: etc:* **to u. (a part),** ne pas faire assez, trop, ressortir un rôle.

underarm. 1. *adv.* [ʌndə'rɑːm, 'ʌndərɑːm], *Cr: Ten: etc:* **to bowl, to serve, u.,** lancer, servir, la balle par en dessous. **2.** *a.* ['ʌndərɑːm]. (*a*) *Cr: Ten: etc:* (lancement, coup, etc.) par en dessous; **u. service,** (i) *Ten:* service par en dessous, coupé en dessous; (ii) (*volleyball*) service bas; (*b*) **u. deodorant,** déodorant *m*, désodorisant *m*, pour les aisselles; déodorant corporel.

underbelly ['ʌndəbeli], *s.* (*a*) bas-ventre *m, pl.* bas-ventres (d'un animal, etc.); ventre *m* (d'un avion, etc.); surface inférieure, dessous *m* (d'un nuage, etc.); poitrine *f* (de porc); (*b*) point *m*, côté *m*, vulnérable; endroit *m* faible (d'un pays, d'un projet, etc.).

underbid [ʌndə'bid], *v.tr. & i.* (**underbid; underbid(den)** [-'bidn]) **1.** *Ind: etc:* faire des soumissions, offrir des conditions, plus avantageuses que celles de (qn); demander moins cher que (qn). **2.** *Cards:* **to u. (one's hand),** demander au-dessous de son jeu.

underblanket ['ʌndəblæŋkit], *s.* protège-matelas *m inv.*

underbody ['ʌndəbɔdi], *s.* face ventrale (d'un animal); dessous *m* (d'un animal, d'une voiture, etc.); ventre *m* (d'un avion); carène *f* (d'un navire).

underbrush ['ʌndəbrʌʃ], *s.* broussailles *fpl*, sous-bois *m.*

undercall [ʌndə'kɔːl], *v.tr. & i. Cards:* **to u. (one's hand),** demander au-dessous de son jeu.

undercapitalization [ʌndəkæpitəlai'zeiʃ(ə)n], *s. Pol.Ec:* sous-capitalisation *f.*

undercarriage ['ʌndəkæridʒ], *s.* **1.** *Veh: O:* (*a*) train *m* de roulement (d'un véhicule); châssis *m* (d'un wagon de chemin de fer, etc.); (*b*) *Aut:* dessous *m* (d'une voiture). **2.** *Av:* train d'atterrissage, atterrisseur *m* (d'un avion); **main u.,** atterrisseur principal; **nose, tail, u.,** atterrisseur avant, arrière; **fixed, retractable, droppable, u.,** train (d'atterrissage) fixe, escamotable, largable; **tricycle u.,** train tricycle; **ski u.,** train à skis; **split u.,** train d'atterrissage sans essieu; **tread-type u.,** atterrisseur chenillé; **u. well,** logement *m* du train (escamotable); **u. circuit,** circuit *m* (hydraulique) de l'atterrisseur; **to let down, extend, the u.,** sortir, descendre, le train d'atterrissage; **to retract the u.,** rentrer, escamoter, le train d'atterrissage.

undercharge[1] ['ʌndətʃɑːdʒ], *s.* **1.** *Artil:* charge (d'explosif) insuffisante. **2.** *Com: Fin:* liquidation trop basse.

undercharge[2] [ʌndə'tʃɑːdʒ]. **1.** *v.tr. Artil: El:* ne pas assez charger (un fusil, un accumulateur). **2.** (*a*) *v.tr.* **they undercharged him,** on ne lui a pas, on ne l'a pas, fait assez payer; on lui a, on l'a, fait trop peu payer; **they undercharged her, she was undercharged, by 50p,** on aurait dû lui, la, faire payer 50 pence de plus; (*b*) *v.i.* demander trop peu (**for sth.,** pour qch.).

undercharged [ʌndə'tʃɑːdʒd], *a. Min:* (*of mine*) sous-chargé.

underclad [ʌndə'klæd], *a. O: & Lit:* insuffisamment vêtu (pour la saison); mal protégé contre le froid.

underclay ['ʌndəklei], *s. Min:* schiste argileux (au mur d'une couche de charbon).

underclothes ['ʌndəklouðz], *s.pl.* **underclothing** ['ʌndəklouðiŋ], *s.* (*for men and women*) sous-vêtements *mpl*; vêtements *mpl* de dessous, linge *m* (de corps); (*for women*) lingerie *f*, dessous *mpl*; (*matching set*) parure *f.*

undercoat ['ʌndəkout], *s.* **1.** duvet *m* (d'un chien, etc.). **2.** (*a*) *Paint:* couche *f* de fond, première couche; (*b*) *NAm: Aut:* couche, revêtement *m*, antirouille (pour dessous de caisse, châssis).

undercoating ['ʌndəkoutiŋ], *s.* = UNDERCOAT 2.

undercook[1] [ʌndə'kuk], *v.tr.* ne pas assez cuire (du porc, etc.).

under(-)cook[2] ['ʌndəkuk], *s.* aide-cuisinier *m, pl.* aides-cuisiniers; aide *mf* de cuisine.

undercooled ['ʌndəkuːld], *a. Ph:* surfondu.

undercooling ['ʌndəkuːliŋ], *s. Ph:* surfusion *f.*

undercover [ʌndə'kʌvər], *a.* secret, -ète, clandestin; **u. agent,** agent secret.

undercoveralls [ʌndə'kʌvərɔːlz], *s.pl.* sous-vêtement *m*, combinaison *f* (de pilote, d'astronaute).

undercroft ['ʌndəkrɔft], *s. Arch:* crypte *f.*

undercurrent ['ʌndəkʌrənt], *s.* **1.** courant *m* de fond; (*in sea*) courant sous-marin; (*in atmosphere, etc.*) courant inférieur. **2.** courant, mouvement *m* (de l'opinion, etc.); **u. of discontent,** vague *f* de fond, courant profond, de mécontentement; **the u. of his emotions, his thoughts,** ses émotions, ses pensées, sous-jacentes.

undercut[1] ['ʌndəkʌt], *s.* **1.** *Cu:* filet *m* (de bœuf). **2.** *Metalw:* contre-dépouille *f* (d'une boîte à noyau). **3.** *Ten: etc:* coup tranchant (coupé en dessous); *Ten:* **u. spin,** rotation inverse. **4.** *NAm: For:* entaille creusée du côté où l'arbre doit tomber.

undercut[2], *v.tr.* (*p.t. & p.p.* **undercut**; *pr.p.* **undercutting**) **1.** (*a*) (*of the sea*) miner, affouiller, saper (une falaise, etc.); (*b*) *Min:* haver (du charbon); sous-caver, souchever (de la pierre); (*c*) *Sculp: etc:* fouiller (un bas-relief, etc.). **2.** *Ten: etc:* couper, lifter (la balle). **3.** *NAm: For:* entailler (un arbre) (du côté où il doit tomber). **4.** *Com: Ind:* (*a*) faire des soumissions plus avantageuses que celles de (qn); (*b*) vendre moins cher, à meilleur marché, que (qn); (*c*) travailler pour un salaire plus bas que (qn).

undercut[3], *a.* **1.** (*of cliff, etc.*) affouillé, miné, sapé. **2.** *Sculp: etc:* (bas-relief, etc.) fouillé.

undercutter ['ʌndəkʌtər], *s.* **1.** *Min:* (*a*) (*pers.*) haveur *m*, soucheveur *m*; (*b*) (*machine*) haveuse *f*. **2.** *NAm: For:* bûcheron *m* (qui entaille des arbres).

undercutting ['ʌndəkʌtiŋ], *s.* **1.** (*a*) affouillement *m* (d'une falaise, etc.); (*b*) *Min:* havage *m* (du charbon, etc.); sous-cavage *m*, souchevage *m* (de la pierre); (*c*) *Sculp: etc:* (r)enfoncement *m*, fouillement *m* (d'un bas-relief, etc.). **2.** *Com: Ind:* vente *f* à des prix qui défient la concurrence.

underdamping ['ʌndədæmpiŋ], *s. Mec.E: El:* amortissement *m* faible.

underdeveloped [ʌndədi'veləpt], *a.* **1.** *Phot:* (cliché) insuffisamment développé. **2.** (enfant) retardé; (muscle, etc.) pas complètement, pas assez, développé, formé. **3.** *Pol.Ec:* **u. countries,** pays sous-développés, en voie de développement; **u. area,** région sous-exploitée.

underdevelopment [ʌndədi'veləpmənt], *s.* **1.** *Phot:* développement insuffisant (d'un cliché). **2.** sous-développement *m*, sous-exploitation *f* (d'une région, d'une industrie, etc.).

underdog ['ʌndədɔg], *s.* (*a*) perdant, -ante (au jeu, dans un match, une lutte); (*b*) opprimé, -ée, défavorisé, -ée (d'une société); **to plead for, to side with, the underdog(s),** plaider la cause des opprimés.

underdone [ʌndə'dʌn], *a. Cu:* (*a*) pas assez cuit; (*b*) pas trop cuit; (bœuf, etc.) saignant; (bifteck) bleu.

underdrain[1] ['ʌndədrein], *s.* conduit souterrain; drain *m.*

underdrain[2] [ʌndə'drein], *v.tr.* drainer (un terrain) (au moyen de conduits souterrains).

underdrawers ['ʌndədrɔːəz], *s.pl. U.S: Cost:* caleçon *m* (d'homme).

underdressed [ʌndə'drest], *a.* **to be u.,** ne pas être vêtu avec l'élégance qu'il faut; **to feel u. at a smart party,** ne pas se sentir habillé dans une réunion élégante.

underdriven [ʌndə'drivn], *a. Mec.E:* à commande par le bas.

under-eaves ['ʌndəriːvz], *a. Const:* **u.-e. tile,** tuile *f* d'égout.

underemployed [ʌndərem'plɔid], *a.* sous-employé; (*of resources, etc.*) sous-exploité; **the staff are seriously u.,** les employés n'ont presque rien à faire.

underemployment [ʌndərem'plɔimənt], *s.* sous-emploi *m* (d'une personne, etc.); sous-exploitation *f* (de ressources, etc.).

under-equipped [ʌndəri'kwipt], *a.* (pays, etc.) sous-équipé.

underestimate[1], **underestimation** [ʌndə'restimeit, -esti'meiʃ(ə)n], *s.* sous-estimation *f*, sous-évaluation *f.*

underestimate[2], *v.tr.* sous-estimer, sous-évaluer (les dépenses, un adversaire, etc.); méconnaître, mésestimer, méjuger (les difficultés, un concurrent, etc.); **he underestimated the importance of what she said,** il n'a pas attaché assez d'importance à, il a fait trop peu de cas de, ses paroles; *Artil:* **to u. the range,** apprécier court.

underexpose [ʌndəreks'pouz], *v.tr. Phot:* sous-exposer (un film, etc.).

underexposure [ʌndəreks'pouʒər], *s. Phot:* sous-exposition *f* (d'un film, etc.).

underfed [ʌndə'fed], *a.* sous-alimenté; insuffisamment nourri; mal nourri.

underfeed[1] ['ʌndəfiːd], *a. Mec.E:* **u. stoker,** foyer *m* à alimentation sous grille.

underfeed[2] [ʌndə'fiːd], *v.tr.* (*p.t. & p.p.* **underfed** [-'fed]) sous-alimenter; nourrir insuffisamment; mal nourrir.

underfeeding [ʌndə'fiːdiŋ], *s.* sous-alimentation *f.*

underfelt ['ʌndəfelt], *s.* thibaude *f* (pour moquette); assise *f* de feutre (pour matelas, etc.).

underfired [ʌndə'faiəd], *a. Cer:* pas assez cuit; *Brickm:* demi-cuit.

underfiring [ʌndə'faiəriŋ], *s. Cer:* cuisson insuffisante; *Brickm:* demi-cuisson *f.*

underfloor ['ʌndəflɔːr], *a.* **u. heating,** chauffage *m* par le sol.

underflow ['ʌndəflou], *s.* **1.** courant *m* de fond. **2.** *Cmptr:* dépassement *m* de capacité négatif.

underfoot [ʌndə'fut], *adv.* sous les pieds; **it's wet u.,** il fait mouillé à marcher; le sol est humide; **the snow crunched u.,** la neige craquait sous les pieds; **to trample, tread, sth. u.,** fouler qch. aux pieds.

underframe ['ʌndəfreim], *s.* **1.** infrastructure *f* (d'un pont). **2.** *Rail:* châssis *m* (de wagon, etc.); *Aut:* soubassement *m* (de châssis).

underfur ['ʌndəfəːr], *s.* (*furriery*) bourre *f* (d'une peau).

under(-)gardener ['ʌndəgɑːdnər], *s.* aide-jardinier *m, pl.* aides-jardiniers.

undergarment ['ʌndəgɑːmənt], *s.* sous-vêtement *m*; vêtement *m* de dessous.

underglaze ['ʌndəgleiz], *a. Cer:* **u. painting,** peinture *f* sous la couverte.

undergo [ʌndə'gou], *v.tr.* (**underwent** [-'went]; **undergone** [-'gɔn]) **1.** (*a*) passer par, subir (un changement, etc.); **his feelings underwent a change,** une révolution, un revirement, s'est opéré(e) dans son esprit; **to u. a complete change,** subir une métamorphose complète; **undergoing repairs,** en (voie de) réparation; (*b*) subir (une épreuve, un examen); **to u. a test successfully,** sortir vainqueur d'une épreuve; **they are undergoing a great trial,** ils sont sous le coup d'une grande épreuve; **to u. a punishment,** subir un châtiment; **he is at present undergoing a prison sentence,** il purge actuellement une peine de prison; **to u. an operation,** subir une opération, une intervention chirurgicale; se faire opérer; *Med:* **to u. treatment,** suivre un traitement. **2.** supporter, souffrir, essuyer, endurer, passer par (des souffrances); **to u. a disappointment,** éprouver une déception; **she has undergone much suffering,** elle a essuyé, subi, passé par, de dures épreuves.

undergrad [ʌndə'græd], *s. F:* = UNDERGRADUATE.

undergraduate [ʌndə'grædjuət], *s.* étudiant, -ante (qui prépare la licence); **in my u. days,** lorsque j'étais étudiant; **u. life,** la vie d'étudiant; la vie étudiante, estudiantine; **u. organizations,** organisations étudiantes, estudiantines; **u. accommodation,** logement *m* des étudiants.

underground. 1. *adv.* [ʌndə'graund]. (*a*) sous (la) terre; (*of miner, etc.*) **to work u.,** travailler sous (la) terre; **to rise from u.,** surgir de dessous, de sous, la terre; (*b*) clandestinement, secrètement; **to go u.,** passer dans la clandestinité; prendre le maquis. **2.** *a.* ['ʌndəgraund]. (*a*) (travail, etc.) sous (la) terre; (tuyau, etc.) sous le sol; (lac, abri, câble, etc.) souterrain; **u. atomic explosion,** explosion atomique souterraine; **u. water level,** nappe *f* phréatique; **u. railway,** chemin de fer souterrain; **u. gallery, passage,** souterrain *m*; **u. workings,** chantier souterrain, travaux souterrains; *Min:* **u. worker,** mineur de fond; travailleur au fond; **u. fire,** incendie de mine; (*b*) (*of organization, press, etc.*) clandestin, secret, -ète; (*of film, music, etc.*) d'avant-garde; **u. movement,** mouvement clandestin; (*in occupied country, etc.*) résistance *f*; **u. forces,** armée clandestine; (*c*) *Geol: Bot:* (cours d'une rivière, cotylédon) hypogé; *Bot:* (rhizome) souterrain. **3.** *s.* ['ʌndəgraund]. (*a*) sous-sol *m* (du terrain); (*b*) chemin de fer souterrain; **the u.** = le métro; (*c*) (*in occupied country, etc.*) **the u.,** la résistance.

undergrown [ʌndə'groun], *a.* **1.** (*of pers., plant*) mal venu; (*of child*) retardé; (*of plant*) rabougri; pas complètement, pas assez, développé, formé. **2.** (*of forestland, etc.*) plein de broussailles.

undergrowth ['ʌndəgrouθ], *s.* **1.** broussailles *fpl*; sous-bois *m*; **new u.,** jeune(s) vente(s) *f*; **to clear a forest, a field, of u.,** soutrager une forêt, débroussailler un champ; **u. remover,** débroussailleuse *f*. **2.** croissance insuffisante (d'un enfant, etc.); rabougrissement *m* (d'une plante).

underhand ['ʌndəhænd]. **1.** *adv.* (*a*) *Cr: Ten: etc: O:* (lancer, servir, la balle) par en dessous; (*b*) *A: & Lit:* (agir) (en) sous main, en cachette, en secret, sournoisement. **2.** *a.* (*a*) *Cr: Ten: etc: O:* (lancement, coup, etc.) par en dessous; (*b*) ['ʌndəhænd] secret, -ète; clandestin; (*of pers.*) sournois; **to behave in an u. way, to play an u. game,** agir en cachette, en tapinois, (en) sous main, en secret; agir sournoisement, sourdement; **u. dealings, methods,** agissements clandestins; menées clandestines; manœuvres tortueuses; **there's something u. going on,** il se trouve quelque manigance, il y a quelque chose, là-dessous; il se trame quelque chose; il y a anguille sous roche; **I'm not doing anything u.,** je ne fais de sournois.

underhanded [ʌndə'hændid]. **1.** *adv. esp. U.S:* = UNDERHAND 1. *(a)*. **2.** *a.* = UNDERHAND 2. *(b)*. **3.** *a. esp. U.S:* à court de personnel, de main-d'œuvre, d'ouvriers; **to be u.,** manquer de personnel.

underhandedly [ʌndə'hændidli], *adv.* sournoisement; (en) sous main, en secret, en cachette, en tapinois.

underhung [ʌndə'hʌŋ], *a.* **1.** *(a)* (chien, etc.) dont la mâchoire inférieure fait saillie; (personne) prognathe, *F:* à menton en galoche; *(b)* **u. jaw,** menton prognathe, *F:* en galoche; **man with an u. jaw,** homme prognathe. **2.** (porte, etc.) à coulisse inférieure.

underinsurance [ʌndərin'sju:rəns], *s.* sous-assurance *f.*

underinsured [ʌndərin'sjud], *a.* sous-assuré.

underjaw ['ʌndədʒɔ:], *s.* mâchoire inférieure; *(of horse)* (i) ganache *f,* (ii) *Farr:* sous-barbe *f.*

underkeeper ['ʌndəki:pər], *s.* *(a)* gardien, -ienne, auxiliaire; *(b)* garde-chasse *m* auxiliaire, *pl.* gardes-chasse(s).

underlay[1] ['ʌndəlei], *s.* **1.** *Typ:* mise *f* de hauteur sous cliché; hausse *f.* **2.** *Min:* pendage *m,* inclinaison *f* (d'un filon, etc.); **u. lode, shaft,** filon, puits, incliné. **3.** *(a)* thibaude *f* (pour moquette); assise *f* de feutre, de carton, de bois (pour matelas, carrelage, etc.); *(b) Const:* feutre, papier, carton, bitumé.

underlay[2] [ʌndə'lei], *v.tr.* *(p.t. & p.p.* **underlaid** [-'leid]) **1. to u. sth. with sth.,** mettre qch. sous qch.; **carpet underlaid with felt,** moquette sur thibaude. **2.** *Typ:* mettre des hausses à, rehausser (la composition).

underlayment [ʌndə'leimənt], *s. Const:* revêtement *m* de mortier (sur plancher de béton).

underlease[1] ['ʌndəli:s], *s. O:* sous-bail *m, pl.* sous-baux; (contrat *m* de) sous-location *f.*

underlease[2] [ʌndə'li:s], *v.tr. O:* sous-louer (un appartement) (avec bail); donner (un appartement) en sous-location; sous-(af)fermer (une terre).

underlessee [ʌndəle'si:], *s. O:* sous-locataire *mf;* sous-preneur *m.*

underlessor ['ʌndəlesɔ:r], *s. O:* sous-bailleur, -eresse.

underlet [ʌndə'let], *v.tr.* *(p.t. & p.p.* **underlet;** *pr.p.* **underletting) 1.** *O:* sous-louer (un appartement). **2.** louer à trop bas prix, à perte.

underletting [ʌndə'letiŋ], *s.* **1.** *O:* sous-location *f.* **2.** location *f* à trop bas prix, à perte.

underlie[1] [ʌndə'lai], *v.tr.* *(p.t.* **underlay** [-'lei]; *p.p.* **underlain** [-'lein]; *pr.p.* **underlying** [-laiiŋ]) *(a)* être sous (qch.), en dessous, au-dessous, de (qch.); **the strata underlying the coal,** les couches sur lesquelles repose la houille; *(b)* être à la base, à l'origine, de (qch.); servir de base à (qch.); **the principles that u. automobile construction,** les principes fondamentaux de la construction automobile; **the truths underlying a satire,** les vérités cachées sous une satire.

underlie[2] ['ʌndəlai], *s. Min:* pendage *m,* inclinaison *f* (d'un filon, etc.).

underline[1] ['ʌndəlain], *s.* **1.** trait *m* qui souligne. **2. underlines,** transparent *m* (pour guider l'écriture). **3.** légende *f* (d'une illustration). **4.** (contour *m* de la) face ventrale (d'un animal).

underline[2] [ʌndə'lain], *v.tr.* **1.** souligner (un mot, etc.). **2.** souligner, appuyer sur, insister sur (un mot, un fait, etc.).

underlinen ['ʌndəlinin], *s. A:* linge *m* de corps, de dessous.

underling ['ʌndəliŋ], *s. Pej:* subalterne *mf,* subordonné, -ée; sous-ordre *m;* inférieur, -e; *F:* sous-fifre *mf;* **I'm only an u.,** je ne suis qu'un tout petit employé.

underlining [ʌndə'lainiŋ], *s.* soulignement *m,* soulignage *m.*

underlip ['ʌndəlip], *s.* lèvre inférieure.

underlying ['ʌndəlaiiŋ], *a.* **1.** au-dessous; *(of rock, etc.)* sous-jacent, subjacent. **2.** (principe) fondamental, -aux; (qui sert) de base; caché, secret, -ète; **there is an u. bitterness in his writings,** il y a dans ses écrits un fond d'amertume; **u. causes, meaning, of an event,** raisons profondes, signification profonde, d'un événement; **u. hatred, sadness,** haine, tristesse, latente.

undermanager ['ʌndəmænidʒər], *s.* sous-directeur *m,* sous-chef *m.*

undermanned [ʌndə'mænd], *a.* *(a)* à court de personnel, de main-d'œuvre, d'ouvriers; **to be u.,** manquer de personnel; *(b) Nau: etc:* à court d'équipage; à équipage insuffisant; (navire) mal armé.

undermentioned ['ʌndəmenʃ(ə)nd], *a.* (cité, mentionné) ci-dessous; **in the u. rules,** dans les règles ci-après; **the u. persons,** les personnes dont les noms suivent.

undermine [ʌndə'main], *v.tr.* *(a)* miner, saper (la côte, une muraille, etc.); *(of sea, river, etc.)* affouiller (les falaises, les berges); **foundations undermined by water,** fondements minés par l'eau; **to u. the ground,** fouiller sous le terrain; *(b)* **to u. morals, s.o.'s authority,** saper les fondements de la morale, l'autorité de qn; **to u. a principle,** saper un principe (à sa base); **to u. the foundations of society,** miner, saper, ébranler, les fondements de la société; attaquer les bases de la société; **to u. one's health,** s'abîmer lentement la santé; **the work has undermined his health,** le travail a miné, ébranlé, usé, sa santé; le travail l'a miné; **to u. s.o.'s confidence,** ébranler la confiance de qn.

undermining [ʌndə'mainiŋ], *s.* affouillement *m* (de la côte, etc.); ébranlement *m* (d'un régime, de la confiance, etc.).

undermost ['ʌndəmoust], *a.* *(a)* le, la, plus en dessous; le plus bas, *f.* la plus basse; inférieur; *(b)* **to be u.,** avoir le dessous (dans une lutte, etc.).

underneath [ʌndə'ni:θ]. **1.** *prep.* au-dessous de; sous; **the rabbit is u. the hedge,** le lapin est sous la haie; **he pushed the letter u. the door,** il a glissé la lettre sous la porte; **he went u. the table,** (i) il s'est mis sous la table; (ii) il a passé par-dessous la table; **the cat slipped u. it,** (i) le chat s'est glissé (là-)dessous; (ii) le chat a passé par-dessous; **put it u. that,** mettez-le là-dessous; **he pulled it (out) from u. the blanket,** il l'a tiré de dessous, de sous, la couverture. **2.** *adv.* au-dessous; dessous; par-dessous; **it's rotten u.,** c'est pourri en dessous, par-dessous; **he picked up the book and found the ticket u.,** il a soulevé le livre et a trouvé le billet en dessous; **he bent down and went u.,** il s'est baissé et a passé par-dessous; **he was standing u.,** il était dessous; **she was wearing a dressing gown with nothing u.,** sous sa robe de chambre elle ne portait rien. **3.** *s.* dessous *m;* **the u. of the box is black,** la boîte est noire en dessous, par-dessous. **4.** *a.* de dessous, d'en dessous; inférieur.

undernourished [ʌndə'nʌriʃt], *a.* sous-alimenté; insuffisamment nourri; mal nourri.

undernourishment [ʌndə'nʌriʃmənt], *s.* sous-alimentation *f.*

underpaid [ʌndə'peid], *a.* (travail, ouvrier, etc.) sous-payé, sous-rémunéré; insuffisamment rétribué; *Post:* (colis, etc.) insuffisamment affranchi.

underpaint [ʌndə'peint], *v.tr. Art:* préparer le dessous (d'un tableau); ébaucher (un tableau).

underpainting [ʌndə'peintiŋ], *s. Art:* (i) préparation *f* du dessous, ébauchage *m,* (ii) dessous, ébauche *f* (d'un tableau).

underpan ['ʌndəpæn], *s. Aut: etc:* carter inférieur (d'un moteur, etc.).

underpants ['ʌndəpænts], *s.pl.* *(for men)* slip *m;* *(with legs)* caleçon *m;* *(occ. for women)* culotte *f,* slip.

underpart ['ʌndəpɑ:t], *s.* **1.** *(a)* dessous *m;* partie inférieure; *(b)* face ventrale (d'un animal). **2.** *Th: etc:* petit rôle; rôle secondaire.

underpass ['ʌndəpɑ:s], *s.* *(a)* passage *m* en dessous, inférieur; *(b)* (passage) souterrain *m.*

underpay [ʌndə'pei], *v.tr.* *(p.t. & p.p.* **underpaid** [-'peid]) sous-payer, sous-rémunérer, insuffisamment rétribuer (un ouvrier, etc.).

underpayment [ʌndə'peimənt], *s.* rémunération, rétribution, insuffisante (d'un ouvrier, d'un travail, etc.); *Post:* affranchissement insuffisant (d'un colis, etc.).

underpin [ʌndə'pin], *v.tr.* **(underpinned) 1.** *(a)* étayer; étançonner, (en)chevaler (un mur, etc.); *(b)* étayer (une société, etc.); soutenir (une thèse, une opinion, etc.); renforcer (un argument, etc.). **2.** *Civ.E: Const:* reprendre en sous-œuvre, battre, mettre, des pieux en dessous (des fondations, etc.); rechausser (un mur, etc.).

underpinning ['ʌndəpiniŋ], *s.* **1.** *(a)* étayage *m,* étayement *m,* étaiement *m,* étançonnement *m* (d'un mur, etc.); *(b)* reprise *f* en sous-œuvre (des fondations, etc.); **excavation for u.,** fouille en sous-œuvre; travaux *mpl* de soutènement. **2.** *(a)* (en)chevalement *m,* étais *mpl,* chevalet(s) *m(pl)* (d'un puits de mine, etc.); *(b)* étançons *mpl,* maçonnerie *f* en sous-œuvre; soutènement *m* (d'un mur, etc.); *(c)* soutien *m,* appui *m* (d'un argument, etc.); base *f,* fondement *m* (d'une société, etc.).

underplant [ʌndə'plɑ:nt], *v.tr. For:* créer un sous-étage dans (une futaie).

underplay [ʌndə'plei]. **1.** *v.tr. Cards:* **he underplayed his ace,** il a joué une carte au-dessous de son as; *Fig:* **to u. one's hand,** cacher son jeu; dissimuler ses intentions, ses projets. **2.** *(a) v.tr. & i. Th: etc:* minimiser, réduire (la comédie d'une pièce, etc.); **to u. (a part),** ne pas faire assez, trop, ressortir un rôle; *(b) v.tr.* minimiser (l'importance de qch.).

underplot ['ʌndəplɔt], *s.* **1.** intrigue *f* secondaire (d'une pièce de théâtre, d'un roman, etc.). **2.** *A:* basse intrigue; complot *m.*

underpopulated [ʌndə'pɔpjuleitid], *a.* (pays) sous-peuplé.

underpowered [ʌndə'pauəd], *a.* (voiture, etc.) à moteur trop faible.

underprice [ʌndə'prais], *v.tr. Com: Ind:* **1.** mettre un prix trop bas à (un article); minorer (des marchandises). **2.** *(a)* faire des soumissions plus avantageuses que celles de (qn); *(b)* vendre moins cher, à meilleur marché, que (qn).

underprint [ʌndə'print], *v.tr.* imprimer trop légèrement.

underprivileged [ʌndə'privilidʒd], *a.* déshérité, défavorisé; économiquement faible; *s.* **the u.,** les défavorisés (sociaux), les moins favorisés; les économiquement faibles.

underproduction [ʌndəprə'dʌkʃ(ə)n], *s. Ind: etc:* sous-production *f.*

underproductive [ʌndəprə'dʌktiv], *a. Ind: etc:* sous-productif.

underproof [ʌndə'pru:f], *a.* (alcool) au-dessous de preuve.

underprop [ʌndə'prɔp], *v.tr.* **(underpropped)** étayer, étançonner (un mur, etc.); reprendre en sous-œuvre (des fondations, etc.).

underpunch ['ʌndəpʌntʃ], *s. Cmptr:* perforation *f* 1 à 9 (dans carte 80 colonnes).

underquote [ʌndə'kwout], *v.tr. Com: Ind:* faire une soumission plus avantageuse que celle de (qn).

underrate [ʌndə'reit], *v.tr.* sous-estimer, sous-évaluer (un adversaire, les difficultés, l'importance de qch., etc.); méconnaître, mésestimer (qn, qch., les qualités de qch., etc.); faire trop peu de cas de (qch.).

underream [ʌndə'ri:m], *v.tr. Petr:* élargir (un trou de sonde).

underreamer ['ʌndəri:mər], *s. Petr:* élargisseur *m.*

underreaming [ʌndə'ri:miŋ], *s. Petr: Civ.E:* élargissement *m* (du fond d'un trou).

underripe [ʌndə'raip], *a.* pas assez mûr; vert.

underrun[1] ['ʌndərʌn], *s.* **1.** *Ind: Com: etc:* production, livraison, inférieure, tirage inférieur, à la quantité commandée, estimée. **2.** *Rail:* frotteur *m* (du rail conducteur).

underrun[2] [ʌndə'rʌn], *v.tr.* *(p.t.* **underran** [-'ræn]; *p.p.* **underrun,** *pr.p.* **underrunning)** *Nau: etc:* paumoyer (un cordage).

underscore [ʌndə'skɔ:r], *v.tr.* souligner.

underscoring [ʌndə'skɔ:riŋ], *s.* soulignement *m,* soulignage *m.*

undersea. 1. ['ʌndəsi:], *a.* sous-marin. **2.** *adv.* [ʌndə'si:], *(also* **underseas)** sous la mer.

underseal[1] ['ʌndəsi:l], *s. Aut:* couche *f,* revêtement *m,* antirouille (pour dessous de caisse, châssis).

underseal[2], *v.tr.* **to u. (the chassis of) a car,** traiter contre la rouille le châssis d'une voiture.

undersecretary [ʌndə'sekrit(ə)ri], *s.* sous-secrétaire *mf;* **u. of state,** sous-secrétaire d'État; **permanent u.,** directeur général (d'un ministère).

undersecretaryship [ʌndə'sekrit(ə)riʃip], *s.* sous-secrétariat *m.*

undersell [ʌndə'sel], *v.tr.* *(p.t. & p.p.* **undersold** [-'sould]) **1.** vendre à meilleur marché, moins cher, que (qn); **we are never knowingly undersold,** à notre connaissance personne ne vend meilleur marché. **2.** vendre (qch.) à bas prix, à vil prix, au-dessous de sa valeur; **he has a tendency to u. himself,** il a tendance à se sous-estimer, à se méjuger, à se mésestimer.

underset[1] ['ʌndəset], *s.* **1.** courant *m* de fond; *(in sea)* courant sous-marin. **2.** *Min:* couche profonde (de minerai, etc.).

underset[2] [ʌndə'set], *v.tr.* *(p.t. & p.p.* **underset;** *pr.p.* **undersetting) 1.** *(a)* étayer, étançonner (un mur, etc.); reprendre en sous-œuvre (des fondations, etc.); *(b) A: & Lit:* soutenir (une opinion, etc.); renforcer (un argument, etc.). **2.** *A:* sous-louer (une terre).

undersexed [ʌndə'sekst], *a.* de, à, faible libido.

undersheriff ['ʌndəʃerif], *s.* *(a)* sous-shérif *m;* *(b) U.S:* sous-chef *m* de la police (d'un comté).

undershirt ['ʌndəʃə:t], *s. NAm:* *(for men)* maillot *m,* tricot *m,* de corps; tricot de peau; gilet *m* de dessous, de peau; *(for women)* chemise américaine, *Fr.C:* camisole *f.*

undershoot[1] ['ʌndəʃu:t], *s. Av:* présentation trop courte, atterrissage trop court.

undershoot[2] [ʌndə'ʃu:t], *v.tr. & i.* *(p.t. & p.p.* **undershot** [-'ʃɔt]) *Av:* **to u. (the runway),** se présenter, atterrir, trop court (sur la piste); atterrir avant d'atteindre la piste.

undershore [ʌndə'ʃɔ:r], *v.tr.* *(a)* étayer, étançonner (un mur, etc.); reprendre en sous-œuvre (des fondations, etc.); *N.Arch:* épontiller; *(b)* soutenir (une opinion, etc.); renforcer (un argument, etc.).

undershoring [ʌndə'ʃɔ:riŋ], *s.* (*a*) étayage *m*, étaiement *m*, étayement *m*, étançonnement *m* (d'un mur, etc.); reprise *f* en sous-œuvre (des fondations, etc.); *N.Arch:* épontillage *m*; (*b*) soutien *m*, appui *m* (d'un argument, etc.).

undershot ['ʌndəʃɔt], *a.* **1.** *Hyd.E: etc:* **u. wheel,** *s.* **u.,** roue *f* à aubes, à palettes. **2.** (chien, etc.) dont la mâchoire inférieure fait saillie; (personne) prognathe, *F:* à menton en galoche.

underside ['ʌndəsaid], *s.* dessous *m*; surface inférieure.

undersign [ʌndə'sain], *v.tr. esp. Jur:* soussigner (un document).

undersigned [ʌndə'saind], *a.* & *s.* soussigné, -ée; **I, the u.,** je soussigné; **the u. declare that. . .,** les soussignés déclarent que . . ..

undersize ['ʌndəsaiz], *s. Min:* refus *m* de crible.

undersize(d) [ʌndə'saiz(d)], *a.* (*a*) de (trop) petite taille, trop petit; (*of pers.*) rabougri; d'une taille au-dessous de la moyenne; (*b*) *Ind: etc:* inférieur à la cote; (projectile, etc.) sous-calibré.

underskirt, underslip ['ʌndəskə:t, -slip], *s.* fond *m* de robe; jupon *m*.

underslung [ʌndə'slʌŋ], *a.* (*a*) (ressort) sous l'essieu, en dessous; *Aut:* **u. frame,** châssis surbaissé, suspendu; **u. car,** voiture à châssis surbaissé, à carrosserie surbaissée; (*b*) *Nau: etc:* **u. load,** charge à l'élingue.

undersoil ['ʌndəsɔil], *s. Geol: etc:* sous-sol *m*.

understaffed [ʌndə'stɑ:ft], *a.* à court de personnel; **the office is u.,** le bureau manque de personnel.

understand [ʌndə'stænd], *v.* (*p.t.* & *p.p.* **understood** [-'stud])

I. *v.tr.* & *i.* **1.** (*a*) comprendre, entendre; **I don't u. French,** je ne comprends pas le français; **he can't make himself understood in German,** il ne peut pas, il n'arrive pas à, se faire comprendre en allemand; **I can't u. modern poetry,** je ne comprends pas, je n'entends pas, la poésie moderne; je ne comprends, je n'entends, rien à la poésie moderne; **to u. this passage fully,** pour bien comprendre ce passage; **he understands business matters,** il s'y connaît, il s'entend, en affaires; **to u. horses,** s'y connaître en chevaux; **he doesn't u. the difficulties,** il ne comprend pas les difficultés; il ne se rend pas compte des difficultés; **this sentence can be understood in several ways,** cette phrase peut se comprendre, s'entendre, s'interpréter, de plusieurs façons; **I don't u. your brother,** je ne comprends pas votre frère; **he doesn't u. children,** il ne comprend rien aux enfants; **no one understands me,** (i) personne ne me comprend; (ii) je suis un incompris, une incomprise; **to u. each other, one another,** se comprendre, s'entendre; **I quite u. that he must be tired,** je comprends très bien qu'il soit fatigué; **I know he understands how I feel,** je sais qu'il comprend mes sentiments, mon état d'esprit; **do you u. how he did it?** comprenez-vous comment il l'a fait? **I don't u. why he did it,** je ne comprends pas, je ne m'explique pas, je ne conçois pas, pourquoi il l'a fait; **I u. what you mean,** je comprends bien, j'entends bien, ce que vous voulez dire; **do you u. what he's talking about?** comprenez-vous quelque chose à ce qu'il raconte? **now I u. what it's all about,** maintenant je comprends de quoi il s'agit; **in order to u. what follows,** pour comprendre, pour se rendre compte de, pour l'intelligence de, ce qui va suivre; **what I can't u. is that . . .,** ce que je ne peux pas comprendre, ce que je ne comprends pas, c'est que + *sub.*; **I can u. your being angry,** je comprends que vous soyez fâché; **I can't u. his daring to apply to them,** je n'arrive pas à comprendre, à concevoir, je ne peux pas m'expliquer, qu'il ait osé s'adresser à eux; **I can't u. it,** je ne (le) comprends pas; **I'm at a loss to u. it, I can't u. a word of it, I don't u. the first thing about it,** je n'y comprends (absolument) rien; **I can u. it all the better because . . .,** je le conçois d'autant mieux que . . .; **(is that) understood?** (vous avez, c'est bien) compris? (c'est) entendu? **that's easily understood, I can u. that,** cela se comprend, se conçoit, facilement; (cela) s'entend; c'est facile à comprendre; *children* **is understood to mean those under 14,** quand on dit *enfants* on veut dire, il s'agit de, ceux au-dessous de 14 ans; (*b*) **I understood that I should be, that I was to be, paid for my work,** j'ai cru comprendre que je devais être payé pour mon travail, que mon travail serait rémunéré; **I u. (that) you're coming to work here,** il paraît que, j'ai appris que, d'après ce qu'on m'a dit, si je comprends bien, si j'ai bien compris, si je ne me trompe pas, vous venez travailler ici; vous venez travailler ici, semble-t-il; **am I to u. that . . .?** ai-je bien compris que . . .? dois-je comprendre que . . .? **I understand him to mean, to say, next Saturday,** j'ai compris qu'il voulait dire, qu'il a dit, samedi prochain; **he is understood to be, it is understood that he is, abroad,** il paraît, on croit, on pense, qu'il est à l'étranger; **it must be understood, you must u., that . . .,** il doit être (bien) entendu, il faut (bien) comprendre, que . . .; **it being understood that . . .,** étant entendu que . . .; **it was understood that, it was the understood thing that, they would send for him,** il a été convenu qu'ils le feraient venir; **to give s.o. to u. that . . .,** donner à entendre, laisser (à) entendre, faire comprendre, faire entendre, à qn que . . .; **I have made it understood, I have let it be understood, that . . .,** j'ai donné à entendre, j'ai laissé entendre, que . . .. **2.** *Gram: etc:* sous-entendre (un mot); présumer, supposer (une condition, etc.); **in this sentence the verb is understood,** dans cette phrase le verbe est sous-entendu; **that's understood,** cela va sans dire; cela va de soi.

II. *v.i.* comprendre; **now I u.!** je comprends, j'y suis, j'y vois clair, maintenant! **you don't u.,** vous ne comprenez pas; vous n'y êtes pas; **do you u.?** vous comprenez? vous saisissez? c'est bien compris? (c'est) entendu? **he left yesterday, I u.,** il est parti hier, si j'ai bien compris, si je ne me trompe (pas); **to u. about sth.,** comprendre qch.; savoir ce qu'il faut faire au sujet de, à propos de, qch.

understandable [ʌndə'stændəbl], *a.* compréhensible; intelligible; **that's u.,** cela se comprend (facilement); c'est bien normal; c'est (tout) naturel; **it's quite u. that he should want to go,** il est normal, on peut comprendre, qu'il ait envie d'y aller.

understandably [ʌndə'stændəbli], *adv.* naturellement; comme on peut le comprendre.

understanding[1] [ʌndə'stændiŋ], *a.* compréhensif, bienveillant (**about sth.,** au sujet de qch.); **he's bound to forgive you, he's very u.,** il vous excusera sûrement, il est très compréhensif; **u. parents,** parents compréhensifs, indulgents, qui comprennent; **u. smile,** sourire (i) d'intelligence, compatissant, (ii) entendu; **he behaved in a very u. way,** il a agi avec beaucoup de discernement.

understanding[2], *s.* **1.** compréhension *f*, entendement *m*, intelligence *f*; *esp. Phil:* appréhension *f*, intellection *f*; **the age of u.,** l'âge de discernement *m*; **he is a man of good u., he has a good u.,** c'est un homme intelligent; il comprend très vite; **lacking in u.,** incompréhensif, inintelligent; dépourvu d'intelligence; **it's beyond u.,** on n'y comprend rien; cela dépasse l'entendement; **according to my u. of it,** si je l'ai bien compris. **2.** (*a*) entente *f*, accord *m*; **to come to a perfect u.,** arriver, parvenir, à une entente parfaite; **our good u. with France,** nos bons rapports avec la France; **spirit of u.,** esprit d'entente; (*b*) accord, arrangement *m*; **to have an u. with s.o.,** avoir un arrangement, être d'intelligence, avec qn; **there was an u. between them,** ils étaient d'intelligence; **to come to, to reach, an u. with s.o.,** s'entendre, s'accorder, s'arranger, avec qn; (*c*) condition *f*; **on the u. that he gives it me back,** à (la) condition de me le rendre; à (la) condition qu'il me le rende, qu'il me le rend; **on the firm, distinct, u. that . . .,** à la condition expresse que . . .; **on this u. I accept,** à cette condition, à ces conditions, j'accepte. **3.** *F: A:* **understandings,** (i) jambes *f*; (ii) pieds *m*; (iii) chaussures *f*.

understandingly [ʌndə'stændiŋli], *adv.* avec compréhension, avec bienveillance, avec compassion; **to look u. at s.o.,** regarder qn d'un air (i) compatissant, (ii) entendu; **he smiled u.,** il a eu un sourire (i) d'intelligence, compatissant, (ii) entendu.

understate [ʌndə'steit], *v.tr.* minimiser, amoindrir (les faits); rester au-dessous de la vérité en racontant (les faits).

understatement [ʌndə'steitmənt], *s.* **1.** amoindrissement *m* (des faits); *Ling:* litote *f*. **2.** affirmation *f*, exposé *m*, au-dessous de la vérité; **to say it's expensive is an u.,** dire que c'est cher est bien au-dessous de la vérité; **that would be an u.,** dire cela serait demeurer au-dessous de la réalité; *F:* **that's the u. of the year!** si tu crois que c'est assez dire! et comment! tu parles!

understeer [ʌndə'stiər], *v.i.* (*of car*) sous-virer.

understeering [ʌndə'stiəriŋ], *s.* sous-virage *m* (d'une voiture).

understock ['ʌndəstɔk], *s. Hort:* porte-greffe *m inv.*

understrapper ['ʌndəstræpər], *s. F: O:* subalterne *mf*; sous-ordre *m*; sous-fifre *m*.

understratum, *pl.* **-a** ['ʌndəstrɑ:təm, -ə], *s.* couche inférieure; sous-couche *f*; *Geol:* substrat *m*.

understructure ['ʌndəstrʌktʃər], *s. Civ.E: Const:* infrastructure *f*.

understudy[1] ['ʌndəstʌdi], *s. Th: etc:* doublure *f*.

understudy[2], *v.tr.* & *i. Th: etc:* **to u. (a part, an actor),** doubler un rôle, un acteur; étudier un rôle en double.

undersubscribed [ʌndəsʌb'skraibd], *a. Fin:* (emprunt) non couvert.

undersurface ['ʌndəsə:fis], *s.* surface inférieure; dessous *m*; *Av:* intrados *m* (de l'aile).

undertake [ʌndə'teik], *v.tr.* (*p.t.* **undertook** [-'tuk]; *p.p.* **undertaken** [-'teik(ə)n]) **1.** entreprendre (un voyage, etc.). **2.** (*a*) se charger de, entreprendre, s'imposer (une tâche); assumer (une responsabilité); contracter (des obligations); **to u. a guarantee,** s'engager à donner une garantie; (*b*) **to u. to do sth.,** se charger de, entreprendre de, promettre de, s'engager à, s'obliger à, faire qch.; prendre à tâche de, se faire fort de, faire qch.; (*c*) *O:* **to u. that . . .,** garantir, assurer, répondre, que . . .. **3.** *A:* prendre (qn) à partie; s'attaquer à (qn); entreprendre (qn).

undertaker [ʌndə'teikər], *s.* **1.** celui, celle, qui entreprend, qui a entrepris (une tâche, etc.). **2.** *A:* entrepreneur *m* (de bâtiments, etc.). **3.** ['ʌndəteikər] entrepreneur, ordonnateur *m*, des pompes funèbres; **she phoned the undertaker's,** elle a téléphoné au service des pompes funèbres, aux pompes *f* funèbres.

undertaking [ʌndə'teikiŋ], *s.* **1.** (*a*) action *f* d'entreprendre (qch.); entreprise *f* (de qch.); (*b*) ['ʌndəteikiŋ] métier *m* d'entrepreneur de pompes funèbres. **2.** entreprise (commerciale, industrielle, etc.); **it's quite an u.,** c'est toute une affaire; c'est une grande entreprise. **3.** engagement *m*, promesse *f*; *Jur:* soumission *f*; **he gave an u. to do it, that he would do it,** il s'est engagé à, il a promis de, le faire; **on the u. that . . .,** sous promesse, à (la) condition, que . . ..

undertenancy ['ʌndətenənsi], *s. O:* sous-location *f*.

undertenant ['ʌndətenənt], *s. O:* sous-locataire *mf*.

underthrust ['ʌndəθrʌst], *s. Geol:* sous-charriage *m*.

undertone ['ʌndətoun], *s.* **1. to speak in an u.,** parler à mi-voix, à voix basse; parler bas. **2.** (*a*) **u. of discontent,** courant sourd de mécontentement; **u. of hostility,** hostilité sourde; **u. of sadness,** fond *m* de tristesse; tristesse sous-jacente; (*b*) **grey with an u. of blue, with blue undertones,** gris nuancé de bleu.

undertow ['ʌndətou], *s.* contre-marée *f*; courant sous-marin, courant de fond (opposé à celui de la surface); ressac *m*.

undertrick ['ʌndətrik], *s. Cards:* levée manquante.

undertrump [ʌndə'trʌmp], *v.tr. Cards:* couper trop faible, trop bas.

underutilization [ʌndəju:tilai'zeiʃ(ə)n], *s.* sous-utilisation *f*.

undervaluation [ʌndəvælju'eiʃ(ə)n], *s.* **1.** sous-estimation *f*, sous-évaluation *f*. **2.** mésestimation *f*, dépréciation *f* (du mérite de qn, etc.).

undervalue [ʌndə'vælju:], *v.tr.* **1.** sous-estimer, sous-évaluer, minorer, déprécier (des marchandises, etc.). **2.** méconnaître, mésestimer, méjuger, faire trop peu de cas de, déprécier (qn, qch.).

undervest ['ʌndəvest], *s. esp. NAm:* (*for men*) maillot *m*, tricot *m*, de corps; tricot de peau; gilet *m* de dessous, de peau; (*for women*) chemise américaine, *Fr.C:* camisole *f*.

undervoltage ['ʌndəvoultidʒ], *s. El:* sous-tension *f*, sous-voltage *m*.

underwater. 1. ['ʌndəwɔ:tər], *a.* sous l'eau; sous-marin; immergé; submergé; **u. camera,** caméra sous-marine; **u. fishing,** pêche sous-marine, subaquatique; **u. diving,** plongée subaquatique; **u. crossing,** tronçon, passage, immergé (d'une canalisation, d'un pipeline, etc.); **u. river crossing,** traversée sous-fluviale (pour câbles). **2.** (*occ.* **underwaters** [ʌndə'wɔ:tər, -əz]), *adv.* sous l'eau; sous la mer.

underway ['ʌndəwei], *a. U.S:* **u. refueling,** ravitaillement en chemin.

underwear ['ʌndəwɛər], *s.* (*for men and women*) sous-vêtements *mpl*; vêtements *mpl* de dessous, linge *m* (de corps); (*for women*) lingerie *f*, dessous *mpl*; **(woman's) matching (set of) u.,** parure *f*.

underweight[1] ['ʌndəweit], *s.* poids insuffisant, trop faible.

underweight[2] [ʌndə'weit], *a.* (article) d'un poids insuffisant, trop léger; (*of pers.*) **to be u.,** ne pas peser assez; être trop léger, maigre.

underwing ['ʌndəwiŋ], *s. Ent:* **1.** aile postérieure (d'un insecte). **2. the u. moths,** les catocalas *f*.

underwood ['ʌndəwud], *s.* sous-bois *m*, broussailles *fpl*, (bois *m*) taillis *m*.

underwork [ʌndə'wə:k]. **1.** *v.tr.* ne pas faire travailler suffisamment (qn, un animal). **2.** *v.i. O:* ne pas assez travailler.

underworld ['ʌndəwə:ld], *s.* **1.** *A:* (*a*) monde *m* sublunaire; (*b*) antipodes *mpl*. **2.** *esp. Myth:* enfers *mpl*. **3.** pègre *f*, milieu *m*; bas-fonds *mpl* (de la société, d'une ville); **u. vendetta,** vendetta du milieu.

underwrite ['ʌndərait], *v.tr.* (*p.t.* **underwrote** [-rout]; *p.p.* **underwritten** [-ritn]) **1.** *A:* souscrire (son nom). **2.** (*a*) *Fin:* garantir, souscrire (une émission);

soumissionner (un emprunt, une nouvelle émission); **the number of shares underwritten by him,** le nombre de titres garantis par lui; (*b*) *Ins:* souscrire (une police, un risque); **the company underwrites a part of the risk,** la compagnie souscrit une partie du risque; **the sum underwritten by each insurer,** la somme souscrite par chaque assureur; **policy underwritten at Lloyd's, in London,** police souscrite chez Lloyd, à Londres.

underwriter ['ʌndəraitər], *s.* **1.** *Fin:* syndicataire *m*; soumissionnaire *mf* (d'un emprunt, etc.); **the underwriters,** le syndicat de garantie. **2.** *Ins:* assureur *m*; **marine u.,** assureur maritime; **fire u.,** assureur contre l'incendie; **Lloyd's underwriters,** assureurs du Lloyd; *M.Ins:* **leading u.,** apériteur *m*; **underwriters' committee,** comité d'assureurs; **the amount subscribed by each u.,** la somme souscrite par chaque assureur.

underwriting ['ʌndəraitiŋ], *s.* **1.** *Fin:* garantie *f* (d'émission); souscription *f* (d'un risque); **firm u.,** garantie de prise ferme; **u. syndicate,** syndicat *m* de garantie; **u. share,** part syndicale; part syndicataire; **u. commission,** commission de garantie, syndicale; **u. contract, letter,** acte syndical; convention syndicale; contrat de garantie. **2.** (*a*) souscription (d'une police, d'un risque); **u. account,** note d'assurance; (*b*) assurance *f* maritime.

undescended [ʌndi'sendid], *a. Med:* **u. testes,** ectopie inguinale des testicules, ectopie testiculaire.

undescribed [ʌndis'kraibd], *a.* non décrit.

undeserved [ʌndi'zə:vd], *a.* (*of praise, reproach*) immérité; (*of reproach*) injuste.

undeservedly [ʌndi'zə:vidli], *adv.* **1.** à tort; injustement. **2.** (être décoré, etc.) sans le mériter, sans l'avoir mérité.

undeserving [ʌndi'zə:viŋ], *a.* (*of pers.*) peu méritant; sans mérite; (*of thg*) peu méritoire; **u. of attention,** qui ne mérite pas l'attention; indigne d'attention.

undeservingly [ʌndi'zə:viŋli], *adv.* de manière peu méritoire.

undesignated [ʌn'dezigneitid], *a.* non désigné; non indiqué.

undesigned [ʌndi'zaind], *a.* (*of action, etc.*) (*a*) involontaire, non prémédité, accidentel; (*b*) (résultat) inattendu, imprévu, non envisagé.

undesignedly [ʌndi'zainidli], *adv.* involontairement, sans intention; sans préméditation.

undesigning [ʌndi'zainiŋ], *a.* candide; sans artifice, sans malice.

undesirable [ʌndi'zaiərəbl], *a.* & *s.* indésirable (*mf*); peu désirable; peu souhaitable; **he's an u. character,** c'est un personnage peu désirable; *For:* **u. tree, shrub,** mort-bois *m, pl.* morts-bois.

undesired [ʌndi'zaiəd], *a.* peu désiré; inopportun.

undesirous [ʌndi'zaiərəs], *a. Lit:* peu désireux (**of,** de); **to be u. of doing sth.,** n'avoir aucun désir de faire qch.

undespairing [ʌndis'peəriŋ], *a.* qui ne désespère pas; à l'espoir tenace.

undestroyed [ʌndis'trɔid], *a.* non détruit; intact.

undetachable [ʌndi'tætʃəbl], *a.* non détachable; indétachable; (partie d'une machine, etc.) non amovible.

undetected [ʌndi'tektid], *a.* non détecté, non décelé; (crime) insoupçonné; (*of mistake, etc.*) **to go u.,** passer inaperçu.

undetermined [ʌndi'tə:mind], *a.* **1.** (*of quantity, date, etc.*) indéterminé, incertain; *Ch: etc:* non dosé. **2.** (*of question*) indécis; *esp. Lit:* (*of pers.*) irrésolu, indécis; **he was u. whether he would go or not,** il se demandait s'il irait ou non.

undeterred [ʌndi'tə:d], *a.* non découragé, sans se laisser décourager, aucunement ébranlé (**by,** par); **to carry on u.,** continuer comme si de rien n'était; **u. by the weather, he went out for a walk,** en dépit du mauvais temps, il est sorti se promener.

undeveloped [ʌndi'veləpt], *a.* non développé; (*a*) **u. plant, animal,** avorton *m*; (*b*) (*of land, resources*) inexploité, non exploité; (*of mind, intelligence*) non développé, non formé; (*c*) *Phot:* (*of film*) non développé.

undeviating [ʌn'di:vieitiŋ], *a.* **1.** (cours, chemin) droit, direct, qui ne dévie pas. **2.** constant; (honnêteté) rigide; (fidélité, loyauté) qui ne se dément pas.

undeviatingly [ʌn'di:vieitiŋli], *adv.* **1.** sans dévier; directement. **2.** constamment; rigidement; sans jamais se démentir.

undies ['ʌndiz], *s.pl. F:* (*esp. for women*) lingerie *f*; sous-vêtements *m*, dessous *mpl.*

undifferenced [ʌn'difərənst], *a. Her:* **u. arms,** armes pleines.

undifferentiated [ʌndifə'renʃieitid], *a.* indifférencié; *Mth:* **u. expression,** expression non différenciée, non différentiée.

undiffused [ʌndi'fju:zd], *a.* (*of light*) non diffus; cru.

undigested [ʌnd(a)i'dʒestid], *a.* (*of food*) non digéré, mal digéré; *esp. Lit:* (*of facts, knowledge*) indigeste, confus.

undignified [ʌn'dignifaid], *a.* peu digne; qui manque de dignité, de tenue; **a show of emotion would be u.,** ce serait s'abaisser, manquer à sa dignité, que de montrer de l'émotion.

undiluted [ʌndai'lju:tid], *a.* non dilué, non délayé; (vin) pur, non étendu; (acide) concentré; *F:* **to talk u. nonsense,** divaguer.

undiminished [ʌndi'miniʃt], *a.* non diminué; sans diminution; **my respect for him remains u.,** mon respect pour lui reste le même, n'a point diminué.

undimmed [ʌn'dimd], *a. Lit:* brillant; (*of light*) qui n'est pas atténué (**by,** par); (*of eyes*) non ternis (**by,** par); (*of vision*) clair, inobscurci.

undine[1] ['ʌndi:n], *s.f. Myth:* ondine.

undine[2] ['ʌndain], *s. Med:* œillère *f.*

undiplomatic [ʌndiplə'mætik], *a.* peu diplomatique; peu adroit, peu prudent; (*of pers.*) peu diplomate.

undipped [ʌn'dipt], *a. Aut:* **to drive with u. headlights,** conduire avec les phares allumés, ne pas se mettre en code.

undirected [ʌndi'rektid], *a.* **1.** (lettre) sans adresse. **2.** (faire qch.) sans ordres, sans instructions.

undiscerned [ʌndi'sə:nd], *a.* inaperçu.

undiscernible [ʌndi'sə:nəbl], *a.* indiscernable.

undiscerning [ʌndi'sə:niŋ], *a.* (esprit) sans discernement, peu pénétrant.

undischarged [ʌndis'tʃɑ:dʒd], *a.* **1.** (*of ship, firearm, accumulator, etc.*) non déchargé. **2.** (*a*) (débiteur) non libéré, non déchargé (d'une obligation); (*b*) *Jur:* **u. bankrupt,** failli non réhabilité; **u. debt,** dette non acquittée, non liquidée, non soldée. **3.** (devoir) inaccompli, inexécuté.

undisciplined [ʌn'disiplind], *a.* indiscipliné; sans discipline.

undisclosed [ʌndis'klouzd], *a.* non révélé; non divulgué; caché.

undiscountable [ʌndis'kauntəbl], *a. Fin:* (billet) inescomptable.

undiscouraged [ʌndis'kʌridʒd], *a.* (*a*) non découragé; aucunement abattu; (*b*) *Lit:* (soupirant) non rebuté.

undiscovered [ʌndis'kʌvəd], *a.* non découvert, caché; **the murderer remains u.,** l'assassin reste introuvable; **u. country,** terre inconnue.

undiscriminating [ʌndis'krimineitiŋ], *a.* (*of pers.*) sans discernement, qui manque de discernement; **u. praise,** éloges prodigués sans discernement.

undiscriminatingly [ʌndis'krimineitiŋli], *adv.* **to praise u.,** prodiguer des éloges sans discernement.

undiscussed [ʌndis'kʌst], *a.* indiscuté; non débattu; **this plan remains u.,** ce projet n'a encore jamais été discuté.

undisguised [ʌndis'gaizd], *a.* (*of voice, etc.*) non déguisé; (*of feelings*) non dissimulé; franc *f.* franche; sincère; **to show u. satisfaction,** manifester une satisfaction sincère; témoigner franchement sa satisfaction.

undisguisedly [ʌndis'gaizidli], *adv.* ouvertement; franchement; sincèrement.

undismayed [ʌndis'meid], *a.* non consterné, non découragé; impavide; **he was quite u. by the incident,** l'incident ne l'a nullement consterné.

undispatched [ʌndis'pætʃt], *a. esp. Lit:* **1.** (*of letter*) non expédié; (*of object*) non envoyé; (*of messenger*) non dépêché. **2.** (*of business*) non expédié.

undispelled [ʌndi'speld], *a. Lit:* non dissipé.

undispersed [ʌndis'pə:st], *a. esp. Lit:* (*of army, etc.*) non dispersé; (*of art collection*) intact.

undisposed [ʌndis'pouzd], *a.* **1.** (*a*) **stock u. of,** marchandises non écoulées, non vendues; (*b*) **house, car, u. of,** maison, voiture, dont on n'a pas encore disposé. **2.** *A:* peu enclin, peu disposé (**to do sth.,** à faire qch.).

undisputed [ʌndis'pju:tid], *a.* incontesté, indisputé, incontroversé.

undissolved [ʌndi'zɔlvd], *a.* **1.** non dissous, -oute. **2.** (*of obligation, contract, etc.*) qui reste entier, dont on n'est pas délié; (*of marriage*) non dissous.

undistilled [ʌndis'tild], *a.* non distillé.

undistinguished [ʌndis'tiŋgwiʃt], *a.* **1.** (*a*) non distingué (**from,** de); (*b*) que l'on n'avait pas distingué, reconnu, remarqué. **2.** (*a*) médiocre; banal, -als; quelconque; (*b*) (*of appearance*) peu distingué.

undistorted [ʌndis'tɔ:tid], *a.* (*of image, sound*) non déformé; (*of truth*) non altéré.

undistressed [ʌndis'trest], *a. Lit:* aucunement affligé.

undistributed [ʌndis'tribjutid], *a.* non distribué; non réparti; non partagé; *Log:* **u. middle,** dénombrement imparfait.

undisturbed [ʌndis'tə:bd], *a.* **1.** (*a*) *esp. Lit:* (*of pers.*) tranquille; (*b*) (*of sleep, etc.*) paisible, calme. **2.** (*of peace*) que rien ne vient troubler; (*of the ground, etc.*) qui n'a pas été remué; (*of papers, etc.*) non dérangé, non déplacé. **3.** *Cmptr:* **u. one, zero, output signal,** signal de sortie un, zéro, sans perturbation; **u. output signal, u. response voltage,** signal de sortie sans perturbation.

undiversified [ʌndai'və:sifaid], *a.* non diversifié; monotone.

undivided [ʌndi'vaidid], *a.* **1.** indivisé; non divisé; entier. **2.** non partagé, impartagé; **u. profits,** bénéfices non répartis; **u. property,** biens indivis; **he gave her his u. attention,** il lui a donné toute son attention. **3.** (*a*) non séparé (**from,** de); (*b*) **u. opinion,** opinion unanime.

undivulged [ʌndi'vʌl(d)ʒd], *a.* non divulgué.

undo [ʌn'du:], *v.tr.* (*p.t.* undid [-'did]; *p.p.* undone [-'dʌn]) **1.** détruire, annuler (une œuvre, etc.); réparer (une faute, etc.); **you can't u. the past,** ce qui est fait est fait; à chose faite point de remède. **2.** (*a*) défaire, dénouer (un nœud, ses cheveux); défaire (un tricot); (*b*) défaire (un bouton); décrocher (une agrafe); ouvrir (un fermoir); desserrer (une vis); *Mec.E:* décliqueter (un échappement); (*c*) défaire, ouvrir, déficeler (un paquet); délier (une botte de foin); délacer (ses chaussures); dégrafer, déboutonner, défaire (sa robe, etc.). **3.** *A: & Lit:* perdre, ruiner (qn); causer la ruine de (qn).

undock [ʌn'dɔk]. **1.** *v.tr.* faire sortir (un navire) du bassin. **2.** *v.i.* (*of ship*) (i) sortir du bassin; (ii) sortir de cale sèche.

undocking [ʌn'dɔkiŋ], *s. Nau:* sortie *f* du bassin.

undocumented [ʌn'dɔkjumentid], *a.* non documenté.

undoer [ʌn'du(:)ər], *s. A: & Lit:* auteur *m* de la ruine (de qn); séducteur *m* (d'une femme).

undoing [ʌn'du(:)iŋ], *s.* **1.** action *f* de défaire (un travail, ses cheveux, un nœud, une robe, etc.). **2.** *esp. Lit:* ruine *f,* perte *f*; **drink was his u.,** l'alcool a causé sa perte, l'a perdu; **such an action would be your u.,** vous vous perdriez par cette démarche.

undomesticated [ʌndə'mestikeitid], *a. F:* **he's completely u.,** il ne sait rien faire dans la maison.

undone [ʌn'dʌn], *a.* **1.** (*a*) défait; **to come u.,** (*of knot, button, etc.*) se défaire; (*of hair*) se dénouer; (*of screw*) se desserrer; (*of shoe, etc.*) se délacer; (*of dress*) se dégrafer; (*of seam, etc.*) se découdre, se défaire; (*of parcel*) se déficeler; (*b*) *A: & Lit:* ruiné; perdu; *Hum: A:* **I am u.!** je suis perdu! c'en est fait de moi! **2.** inaccompli, non accompli; inachevé; **we have left u. those things which we ought to have done,** nous n'avons pas fait les choses que nous aurions dû faire.

undoubted [ʌn'dautid], *a.* (fait, etc.) indiscutable, incontestable, indubitable.

undoubtedly [ʌn'dautidli], *adv.* indubitablement, incontestablement, indiscutablement, assurément.

undoubting [ʌn'dautiŋ], *a.* certain, convaincu.

undrainable [ʌn'dreinəbl], *a.* **1.** (terrain) qu'on ne peut pas drainer, qu'il est impossible d'assécher. **2.** (source, mine) inépuisable.

undrained [ʌn'dreind], *a.* (terrain) non drainé, non asséché.

undramatic [ʌndrə'mætik], *a.* (ouvrage, style) peu dramatique, qui manque de sens dramatique.

undrawable [ʌn'drɔ:əbl], *a.* (métal) inétirable.

undrawn [ʌn'drɔ:n], *a.* **the curtains were still u.,** les rideaux n'étaient toujours pas tirés.

undreamt [ʌn'dremt], **undreamed** [ʌn'dremt, *occ.* ʌn'dri:md], *a.* **u. of,** (i) dont on ne s'aviserait jamais; insoupçonné; inattendu; (ii) qui dépasse l'imagination; inimaginable.

undress[1] [ʌn'dres], *v.* (**undressed** [ʌn'drest]) **1.** *v.i. & pr.* se déshabiller, se dévêtir. **2.** *v.tr.* (*a*) déshabiller, dévêtir; (*b*) **to u. a wound,** ôter les pansements d'une plaie.

undress[2], *s.* (i) *Mil: etc:* petite tenue; (ii) *A: & Lit:* (*for women*) déshabillé *m*, négligé *m*; **in u.,** (i) en petite tenue; (ii) *A: & Lit:* en déshabillé, en négligé; *Mil: etc:* **u.** ['ʌndres] **uniform,** petite tenue; tenue de service.

undressed [ʌn'drest], *a.* **1.** (*a*) déshabillé, dévêtu; (*b*) en déshabillé, en négligé. **2.** (*a*) non préparé; inapprêté; brut; non dégrossi; **u. stone,** pierre brute, non taillée; **u. timber,** bois en grume; **u. leather, cloth,** cuir d'œuvre; tissu inapprêté; **u. skin,** peau verte, crue; (*b*) *Agr:* (champ) non façonné; (*c*) *Cu:* (*of meat*) non habillé; non accommodé; (*of lobster, etc.*) nature *inv*; (*of salad*) non garni, non assaisoné; (*d*) *O:* non paré, non arrangé; peu soigné; (*e*) **u. wound,** blessure non pansée.

undried [ʌn'draid], *a.* non séché.

undrilled [ʌn'drild], *a.* **1.** (*of troops*) inexercé. **2.** (*of iron plate, etc.*) non perforé, non percé.

undrinkable [ʌn'driŋkəbl], *a.* imbuvable; non potable.

undrunk [ʌn'drʌŋk], *a.* **1.** (vin, etc.) non bu. **2.** *A: & Lit:* (toast) non porté.

undue [ʌn'dju:], *a.* **1.** (paiement) inexigible, indu; *Fin:* (billet) non échu. **2.** (*a*) (*of exaction, etc.*) injuste, inique, injustifiable; *Jur:* illégitime; (*of reward*) immérité; **to cast u. suspicions on s.o.,** soupçonner qn à tort; *Jur:* **use of u. authority,** abus *m* d'autorité; excès *m* de pouvoir; **u. influence,** abus d'influence; intimidation *f*; manœuvres *f* captatoires; (*b*) (*of haste, etc.*) exagéré, indu; **u. optimism,** optimisme excessif, peu justifié.

undulant ['ʌndjulənt], *a. Med:* **u. fever,** brucellose *f*; fièvre ondulante.

undulate[1] ['ʌndjuleit], *a. Nat.Hist:* ondulé.

undulate[2] ['ʌndjuleit]. 1. *v.tr.* onduler. 2. *v.i.* onduler, ondoyer.

undulated ['ʌndjuleitid], *a.* (*of surface*) ondulé, onduleux.

undulating ['ʌndjuleitiŋ], *a.* ondulé, onduleux; (blé) ondoyant; **u. country,** pays ondulé, mouvementé, accidenté, vallonné.

undulation [ʌndju'leiʃ(ə)n], *s.* 1. ondulation *f*; *Lit:* houle *f* (d'un champ de blé, etc.). 2. pli *m*, accident *m* (de terrain); mouvement *m* (de terrain).

undulator ['ʌndjuleitər], *s. Telecom:* ondulateur *m*.

undulatory [ʌndju'leitəri], *a.* 1. (*a*) ondulatoire; (*b*) *Ph:* **u. theory,** théorie des ondulations. 2. *Lit:* ondulé, onduleux.

undulous ['ʌndjuləs], *a. Lit:* onduleux.

unduly [ʌn'dju:li], *adv.* 1. (*a*) (réclamer, payer) indûment. 2. (*a*) injustement, iniquement; *Jur:* illégitimement; (*b*) à l'excès, outre mesure, trop; exagérément; **to sell sth. at an u. high price,** vendre qch. excessivement cher; **to be u. optimistic,** faire preuve d'un optimisme excessif, peu justifié; **he worries u., he's u. worried, about his health,** sa santé le préoccupe (i) sans raison, (ii) trop.

undutiful [ʌn'dju:tif(u)l], *a.* (personne) qui ne remplit pas ses devoirs; (enfant) insoumis.

undutifully [ʌn'dju:tif(u)li], *adv.* (agir, etc.) en manquant à ses devoirs, avec insoumission.

undyed [ʌn'daid], *a.* non teint; sans teinture; **u. cloth,** tissu en beige.

undying [ʌn'daiiŋ], *a.* immortel, impérissable; **u. love,** amour éternel.

unearned [ʌn'ə:nd], *a.* 1. (*of reward, punishment*) immérité. 2. (*of money*) non gagné (par le travail); **u. income,** rentes *fpl*.

unearth [ʌn'ə:θ], *v.tr.* 1. (*a*) déterrer, exhumer; (*b*) découvrir, dénicher (qch.); **to u. an old manuscript,** déterrer, dénicher, un vieux manuscrit; **wherever did you u. that?** où diable as-tu déniché ça? 2. faire sortir (un animal) de son trou; **to u. a fox,** faire sortir un renard de son terrier; faire bouquer un renard.

unearthing [ʌn'ə:θiŋ], *s.* déterrage *m*, déterrement *m*, exhumation *f*, dénichement *m*; *Husb:* déchaussement *m* (des arbres, etc.).

unearthly [ʌn'ə:θli], *a.* 1. céleste, sublime. 2. (*a*) surnaturel; mystérieux; (*b*) *Lit:* **u. pallor,** pâleur mortelle; **u. light,** lueur sinistre, lugubre, blafarde; (*c*) *F:* **he woke her up at an u. hour,** il l'a réveillée à une heure indue, impossible; **u. din,** bruit, vacarme, de tous les diables.

unease [ʌn'i:z], *s. esp. Lit:* malaise *m*; gêne *f*.

uneasily [ʌn'i:zili], *adv.* 1. (*a*) d'un air gêné; avec gêne; (*b*) avec inquiétude; **to sleep u.,** dormir d'un sommeil agité; *esp. Lit:* **to listen u.,** écouter anxieusement. 2. *A:* avec difficulté; difficilement.

uneasiness [ʌn'i:zinis], *s.* 1. gêne *f*, embarras *m*. 2. inquiétude *f*. 3. *A:* difficulté *f* (d'un travail, etc.).

uneasy [ʌn'i:zi], *a.* 1. (*a*) mal à l'aise; gêné; (*b*) tourmenté; inquiet, -ète; **he has an u. conscience,** il n'a pas la conscience tranquille; **there was an u. silence,** il y a eu un silence gêné; **to be u.,** ressentir de l'inquiétude; être inquiet, anxieux (**about,** au sujet de); **to be u. in one's mind about sth.,** avoir l'esprit inquiet, ne pas avoir l'esprit tranquille, au sujet de qch.; **I have an u. feeling that she won't come,** je ne peux pas m'empêcher de penser qu'elle ne viendra pas; j'ai l'impression déconcertante qu'elle ne viendra pas; **my baby has a cough and it makes me u.,** mon bébé tousse et cela m'inquiète; **don't be u. on that score,** ne vous tracassez pas de ce côté-là; tranquillisez-vous là-dessus; **u. sleep,** sommeil agité; (*c*) (*of situation*) incommode, gênant. 2. *A:* (travail, voyage) difficile, ardu.

uneatable [ʌn'i:təbl], *a.* immangeable; pas mangeable.

uneaten [ʌn'i:tn], *a.* non mangé; **u. food,** restes *mpl*.

uneclipsed [ʌni'klipst], *a. Astr:* non éclipsé; *Lit:* (*of fame, etc.*) non éclipsé, non surpassé.

uneconomic [ʌni:kə'nɔmik], *a.* 1. non économique; contraire aux lois de l'économie. 2. (travail, etc.) non rentable, non rémunérateur.

uneconomical [ʌni:kə'nɔmik(ə)l], *a.* (*of method, car, etc.*) peu économique; inéconomique.

unedifying [ʌn'edifaiiŋ], *a.* peu édifiant.

unedited [ʌn'editid], *a.* (texte) non édité; (film) non monté.

uneducated [ʌn'edjukeitid], *a.* 1. (*of pers.*) (*a*) sans instruction, sans éducation; (*b*) *O:* illettré, analphabète. 2. (*of speech, accent*) populaire.

uneffaced [ʌni'feist], *a. Lit:* ineffacé; intact.

uneffected [ʌni'fektid], *a.* ineffectué, inaccompli; (*of purpose*) irréalisé.

unelected [ʌni'lektid], *a.* (candidat) non élu.

uneliminated [ʌni'limineitid], *a.* non éliminé.

unelucidated [ʌni'lju:sideitid], *a.* non élucidé; inéclairci.

unemancipated [ʌni'mænsipeitid], *a.* (mineur, etc.) non émancipé; (esclave) non affranchi(e).

unembarrassed [ʌnim'bærəst], *a.* peu embarrassé, peu gêné; désinvolte, dégagé.

unembellished [ʌnim'beliʃt], *a.* non orné, non embelli, sans ornement; (*of story*) non enjolivé; sans enjolivures, sans enjolivements.

unembittered [ʌnim'bitəd], *a. esp. Lit:* (*of pers.*) nullement aigri; nullement rancunier; (*of tone*) sans amertume.

unemotional [ʌni'mouʃən(ə)l], *a.* 1. (*of pers.*) peu émotif; peu émotionnable; (*of reaction*) peu émotionnel; (*of style*) neutre, dépourvu de passion. 2. (*of pers.*) peu impressionnable, impassible; qui ne montre, ne trahit, aucune émotion.

unemotionally [ʌni'mouʃən(ə)li], *adv.* sans émotion; avec impassibilité, avec sang-froid.

unemphatic [ʌnim'fætik], *a.* 1. (*of manner, tone*) peu énergique. 2. (*of syllable, word*) non accentué.

unemployability [ʌnemplɔiə'biliti], *s.* non qualification *f* pour un emploi.

unemployable [ʌnim'plɔiəbl], *a.* (*of pers.*) inapte à travailler.

unemployed [ʌnim'plɔid], *a.* 1. (*of pers.*) (*a*) désœuvré, inoccupé; (*b*) *Ind: etc:* en chômage; sans travail; sans emploi, sans occupation; (fonctionnaire) en inactivité, en non-activité; *Mil:* (officier) en non-activité; *s.* **the u.,** les chômeurs *m*, les sans-travail *m*; **the number of u. has risen since last year,** le chômage a augmenté depuis l'année dernière. 2. (*of time, etc.*) inemployé; inutilisé; **u. capital,** fonds inactifs, dormants, inemployés.

unemployment [ʌnim'plɔimənt], *s. Ind:* chômage *m*; manque *m* de travail; **u. benefit, relief,** *NAm:* **u. compensation,** allocation *f*, indemnité *f*, secours *m*, de chômage; **u. figures,** statistiques du chômage; **u. has risen to over a million,** il y a maintenant plus d'un million de chômeurs.

unemptied [ʌn'em(p)tid], *a.* non vidé; non déchargé; encore plein.

unenclosed [ʌnin'klouzd], *a.* 1. (champ) sans clôture. 2. *Ecc:* (religieux) non cloîtré.

unencumbered [ʌnin'kʌmbəd], *a.* 1. non encombré (**by, with,** de). 2. non embarrassé (**by, with,** par); libre (**by,** de); *Jur:* **u. estate,** propriété franche d'hypothèques, non grevée, libre d'inscription; **u. widow,** veuve sans enfants.

unending [ʌn'endiŋ], *a.* 1. interminable, qui n'en finit plus; sans fin; sempiternel. 2. éternel.

unendorsed [ʌnin'dɔ:st], *a.* 1. sans inscription (au dos); (chèque) non endossé; (passeport) sans visa. 2. non appuyé; non sanctionné; **proposal u. by the government,** proposition à laquelle le gouvernement ne donne pas son adhésion, ne souscrit pas.

unendowed [ʌnin'daud], *a. Lit:* 1. non doué, peu doué (**with,** de). 2. *A:* (jeune fille) sans dot.

unendurable [ʌnin'djuərəbl], *a.* insupportable, intolérable.

unenforceable [ʌnin'fɔ:səbl], *a.* (contrat, jugement, etc.) non exécutoire.

unenforced [ʌnin'fɔ:st], *a.* 1. (*a*) (*of law, regulation*) non appliqué, qui n'est pas en vigueur; (*b*) (argument) qu'on ne fait pas valoir; **u. claim,** demande non appuyée. 2. (*of rule, obedience, etc.*) non imposé.

unenfranchised [ʌnin'fræn(t)ʃaizd], *a.* 1. (esclave) non affranchi(e). 2. *Pol:* (*a*) (personne) qui n'a pas le droit de vote; (*b*) (ville) sans droits municipaux.

unengaged [ʌnin'geidʒd], *a.* 1. qui n'est lié par aucun serment; libre. 2. libre de son temps. 3. (domestique) non engagé.

unengaging [ʌnin'geidʒiŋ], *a.* (*of manner*) peu engageant, peu attrayant; (*of pers.*) sans charme; peu sympathique.

un-English [ʌn'iŋgliʃ], *a.* peu anglais; (i) (conduite, etc.) indigne d'un Anglais; (ii) contraire à l'esprit anglais; (iii) (*of phrase, idiom*) qui n'est pas anglais.

unenjoyable [ʌnin'dʒɔiəbl], *a.* peu agréable; **I spent a rather u. afternoon at the dentist,** j'ai passé une après-midi assez désagréable chez le dentiste.

unenlightened [ʌnin'laitnd], *a.* (peuple, siècle) peu éclairé, rétrograde, ignorant.

unenlightening [ʌnin'laitniŋ], *a.* (remarque) qui jette peu de lumière (sur une question); (commentaire) qui ne dit rien, qui ne nous apprend rien.

unenriched [ʌnin'ritʃt], *a. Atom.Ph:* (*of uranium, etc.*) non enrichi.

unentered [ʌn'entəd], *a.* non inscrit, non enregistré.

unenterprising [ʌn'entəpraiziŋ], *a.* (*of pers.*) peu entreprenant, peu actif, qui manque d'initiative; (*of plan, etc.*) qui manque d'audace.

unentertaining [ʌnentə'teiniŋ], *a.* peu divertissant; ennuyeux.

unenthusiastic [ʌninθju:zi'æstik], *a.* (esprit, etc.) peu enthousiaste, froid; **he seems rather u. about it,** ça n'a pas l'air de l'enthousiasmer.

unenthusiastically [ʌninθju:zi'æstikli], *adv.* sans enthousiasme; froidement.

unentitled [ʌnin'taitld], *a. esp. Lit:* **to be u. to sth.,** n'avoir aucun droit à qch.; **u. to do sth.,** non autorisé à faire qch.

unenviable [ʌn'enviəbl], *a.* peu enviable.

unequable [ʌn'ekwəbl, -'i:k-], *a. A: & Lit:* (*of movement*) irrégulier; (*of temper, etc.*) inégal, -aux; changeant.

unequal [ʌn'i:kwəl], *a.* 1. (*a*) (*of size, amount, etc.*) inégal, -aux; (*b*) **he was, felt, u. to the job,** il était, il se sentait, au-dessous de la tâche; il n'était pas, ne se sentait pas, à la hauteur de la tâche; **to be u. to doing sth.,** ne pas être de force, de taille, à faire qch. 2. *O:* inégal, irrégulier; *Med:* **u. pulse,** pouls inégal, variable, irrégulier; *Aut:* **u. braking action,** freinage irrégulier.

unequalled [ʌn'i:kwəld], *a.* inégalé, sans égal, sans pareil.

unequally [ʌn'i:kwəli], *adv.* inégalement.

unequipped [ʌni'kwipt], *a.* non équipé; (navire) non armé; (laboratoire) mal installé; **he was u. for bad weather,** il était mal équipé pour le mauvais temps.

unequivocal [ʌni'kwivək(ə)l], *a.* (*of language, proof*) clair, net, univoque; sans équivoque; **u. position,** situation franche; **to give an u. answer,** répondre sans ambiguïté; **he gave an u. refusal,** il a refusé catégoriquement.

unequivocally [ʌni'kwivək(ə)li], *adv.* sans équivoque; clairement, nettement.

uneradicated [ʌni'rædikeitid], *a.* (préjugé, etc.) indéraciné, non extirpé.

unerased [ʌni'reizd], *a. Cmptr: Rec: etc:* non effacé.

unerring [ʌn'ə:riŋ], *a.* (jugement, etc.) infaillible, sûr; **to strike an u. blow,** frapper un coup sûr, frapper à coup sûr; frapper sûrement; **with u. aim, he hit the target,** visant avec précision, il a touché la cible.

unerringly [ʌn'ə:riŋli], *adv.* infailliblement, sûrement; avec précision.

unerupted [ʌni'rʌptid], *a.* (*of tooth*) n'ayant pas fait son éruption; enclavé.

Unesco [ju:'neskou], *s.* l'Unesco *f*.

unescorted [ʌni'skɔ:tid], *a.* sans escorte; **u. group (of tourists, etc.),** groupe (de touristes, etc.) non accompagné.

unessayed [ʌni'seid], *a. Lit:* non essayé.

unessential [ʌni'senʃ(ə)l], *a. esp. Lit:* non essentiel; peu important; accessoire; *s.* **the unessential(s),** l'accessoire *m*.

unestablished [ʌni'stæbliʃt], *a.* 1. (*of power, reputation, etc.*) mal établi. 2. (*of fact, etc.*) non établi, non avéré. 3. (*of church*) non établi; séparé de l'État. 4. (personnel, etc.) auxiliaire.

unethical [ʌn'eθik(ə)l], *a.* (*a*) non conformiste; (*b*) **u. conduct,** conduite qui manque de probité.

uneven [ʌn'i:v(ə)n], *a.* 1. inégal, -aux; (*a*) (papier, etc.) rugueux; (chemin) raboteux; (*b*) (terrain) accidenté, dénivelé, anfractueux; **to make a surface u.,** déniveler une surface; **the floorboards are u.,** les planches ne sont pas de niveau; (*c*) irrégulier; **u. breathing,** respiration inégale, irrégulière; **u. temper,** humeur inégale; **his style is very u.,** son style est très inégal. 2. (nombre) impair.

unevenly [ʌn'i:v(ə)nli], *adv.* 1. inégalement; **the opponents were u. matched,** les adversaires étaient de force inégale; **u. distributed load,** charge répartie inégalement. 2. irrégulièrement.

unevenness [ʌn'i:v(ə)nnis], *s.* inégalité *f*; (*a*) aspérités *fpl* (d'un chemin, etc.); rugosité *f* (du papier, etc.); (*b*) dénivellement *m*, dénivellation *f* (d'une surface, etc.); anfractuosité *f*, montuosité *f* (d'un terrain); (*c*) désaffleurement *m* (d'un plancher); (*d*) irrégularité *f* (de la respiration, etc.); **u. of temper,** inégalité d'humeur.

uneventful [ʌni'ventful], *a.* (voyage, etc.) sans incidents; **u. life,** vie calme, tranquille, peu mouvementée.

unexamined [ʌnig'zæmind], *a.* 1. non examiné, non inspecté; (compte) non vérifié; (passeport) non contrôlé; *Cust:* (bagages) non visités. 2. *Jur:* (témoin, etc.) non (encore) interrogé, qui n'a pas (encore) subi d'interrogatoire.

unexampled [ʌnig'zɑ:mpld], *a. esp. Lit:* sans exemple, sans égal, sans pareil; unique.
unexcavated [ʌn'ekskəveitid], *a.* (terrain, etc.) qui n'a pas (encore) été fouillé, où l'on n'a pas (encore) fait de fouilles.
unexcelled [ʌnik'seld], *a.* **1.** qui n'a jamais été surpassé. **2.** sans pareil; insurpassable.
unexceptionable [ʌnik'sepʃənəbl], *a.* irréprochable; (conduite) inattaquable; (témoignage) irrécusable, irréfragable; **u. person,** personne tout à fait convenable, personne inattaquable.
unexceptionableness [ʌnik'sepʃənəbəlnis], *s.* caractère *m* irréprochable (de la conduite de qn, etc.).
unexceptionably [ʌnik'sepʃənəbli], *adv.* (se conduire) irréprochablement, d'une manière irréprochable.
unexceptional [ʌnik'sepʃən(ə)l], *a.* **1.** *A: & Lit:* = UNEXCEPTIONABLE. **2.** *(a)* (règle, etc.) sans exception, qui ne souffre pas d'exception; *(b)* (ordre) formel, auquel on ne peut se soustraire. **3.** ordinaire; banal, -als; (incident, etc.) qui n'a rien d'exceptionnel, qui ne sort pas de l'ordinaire.
unexchangeability [ʌnikstʃeindʒə'biliti], *s. Fin:* impermutabilité *f* (de titres, d'actions, etc.).
unexchangeable [ʌniks'tʃeindʒəbl], *a.* inéchangeable; *Fin:* **u. security,** valeur impermutable.
unexcised[1] [ʌn'eksaizd], *a.* exempt de droits de régie.
unexcised[2] [ʌnek'saizd], *a.* **1.** *Surg: (of organ, tumour, etc.)* non excisé, non coupé. **2.** *(of passage in book, etc.)* non coupé, non retranché.
unexcitable [ʌnik'saitəbl], *a.* **1.** *(of pers.)* peu émotionnable; imperturbable; qui ne s'émeut pas facilement. **2.** *Physiol: etc:* inexcitable.
unexcited [ʌnik'saitid], *a.* **1.** *(of pers., crowd)* calme, tranquille; **to be u. about sth.,** ne pas s'échauffer au sujet de qch.; rester indifférent à (une nouvelle, etc.). **2.** *Atom.Ph:* non excité.
unexciting [ʌnik'saitiŋ], *a.* plat; (conte, etc.) insipide, peu passionnant, peu intéressant; (spectacle) peu sensationnel; (roman, etc.) peu palpitant; **u. life,** vie monotone, dépourvue d'intérêt; **u. day,** journée calme; **this restaurant serves very u. food,** on sert des repas très ordinaires dans ce restaurant.
unexecuted [ʌn'eksikju:tid], *a.* **1.** (projet, etc.) inexécuté, non réalisé; (travail) inaccompli; (devoir) inacquitté; *Jur:* **u. deed,** acte non souscrit, non validé. **2.** (condamné) pas encore exécuté.
unexercised [ʌn'eksəsaizd], *a.* **1.** (droit, influence) qu'on n'exerce pas, dont on ne fait pas usage. **2.** (corps) inexercé, non exercé; (esprit) non exercé; **u. horses,** chevaux qu'on n'a pas promenés. **3.** inexercé, inexpérimenté.
unexpansive [ʌniks'pænsiv], *a.* (corps, fluide, etc.) non expansif, non dilatable.
unexpectant [ʌniks'pektənt], *a.* qui n'attend rien; qui ne s'attend à rien.
unexpected [ʌniks'pektid]. *(a) a.* (visiteur, résultat, etc.) inattendu; (événement) imprévu; (départ) inopiné; (secours, bonheur) inespéré; **u. meeting,** rencontre inopinée; **it was all so u.,** on ne s'y attendait pas du tout; *(b) s.* **you must allow for the u.,** il faut parer à l'imprévu; **the u. is always round the corner,** l'aventure est au coin de la rue.
unexpectedly [ʌniks'pektidli], *adv.* de manière inattendue, imprévue; inopinément; inespérément; **he arrived u. early,** il est arrivé plus tôt que prévu, plus tôt qu'on ne s'y attendait; **to arrive u.,** arriver à l'improviste, inopinément.
unexpectedness [ʌniks'pektidnis], *s.* soudaineté *f* (d'un événement, etc.); l'inattendu *m,* l'imprévu *m.*
unexpended [ʌniks'pendid], *a.* **1.** (argent) non dépensé; *Fin:* **u. balance,** reliquat *m.* **2.** *Mil: (of food)* inconsommé.
unexpiated [ʌn'ekspieitid], *a.* inexpié.
unexpired [ʌniks'paiəd], *a.* (bail, etc.) non expiré; (passeport, billet, etc.) non périmé, encore valable.
unexplainable [ʌniks'pleinəbl], *a.* inexplicable.
unexplained [ʌniks'pleind], *a.* inexpliqué; (mystère) inéclairci.
unexplicit [ʌniks'plisit], *a.* peu explicite, peu clair; confus.
unexploded [ʌniks'ploudid], *a.* **1.** (obus) non explosé, non éclaté. **2. u. theory,** théorie toujours accréditée.
unexploited [ʌniks'plɔitid], *a.* inexploité.
unexplored [ʌniks'plɔ:d], *a.* (pays, etc.) inexploré, encore inconnu; *Mil:* (terrain) non reconnu.
unexposed [ʌniks'pouzd], *a.* **1.** *(a)* **u. to sth.,** à l'abri de qch.; *(b) Phot:* (film) vierge. **2.** non découvert; **u. crime, thief,** crime caché; voleur non démasqué.
unexpressed [ʌniks'prest], *a.* **1.** (sentiment, souhait, etc.) inexprimé. **2.** (mot, etc.) sous-entendu.
unexpurgated [ʌn'ekspəgeitid], *a.* (livre, texte) non expurgé; (auteur) non épuré; **u. edition,** édition intégrale.
unextinguishable [ʌniks'tiŋgwiʃəbl], *a.* inextinguible.
unextinguished [ʌniks'tiŋgwiʃt], *a.* non éteint; qui brûle (encore); **u. passion,** passion toujours ardente.
unfaded [ʌn'feidid], *a.* non fané, non flétri; encore frais, *f.* fraîche; non effacé.
unfading [ʌn'feidiŋ], *a.* qui ne se fane pas, ne se flétrit pas; **u. flowers,** fleurs toujours fraîches; **u. memories,** souvenirs ineffaçables, impérissables; **u. glory,** gloire immortelle, impérissable.
unfailing [ʌn'feiliŋ], *a.* **1.** qui ne se dément pas; qui ne se dément jamais; (moyen, remède) infaillible, certain, sûr; (courage, etc.) inlassable; (zèle, etc.) infatigable, inépuisable, intarissable; (mémoire) sans défaillance, qui n'est jamais en défaut; **to listen with u. interest,** écouter avec un intérêt soutenu; **u. good humour,** bonne humeur inaltérable; **u. hope, optimism,** espoir, optimisme, inébranlable; **to be u. in one's duty,** ne jamais faillir à son devoir. **2.** (source) intarissable, inépuisable.
unfailingly [ʌn'feiliŋli], *adv.* **1.** infailliblement, immanquablement; sûrement; inlassablement, infatigablement; **he was u. kind, polite,** il était d'une bonté, d'une politesse, inaltérable, qui ne se démentait jamais. **2.** intarissablement, inépuisablement.
unfair [ʌn'fɛər], *a.* **1.** injuste (**to s.o.,** envers qn); peu équitable; partial, -aux; **to be u. to s.o.,** défavoriser qn; **it's u.!** ce n'est pas juste! **it's very u. to ask him,** il est injuste, il n'est pas juste, de le lui demander; **it's so u. of him to behave like that,** il est si injuste de sa part d'agir ainsi; **to have an u. advantage over everybody else,** être avantagé, favorisé (injustement) au détriment, au préjudice, de tous les autres; **he has been put at an u. disadvantage,** on l'a défavorisé, désavantagé; il a été défavorisé, désavantagé. **2.** *(a)* inéquitable; **u. price,** prix déraisonnable, exorbitant, excessif; *(b)* déloyal, -aux; **u. play,** jeu déloyal; **u. competition,** concurrence déloyale.
unfairly [ʌn'fɛəli], *adv.* **1.** injustement; peu équitablement; **he has been u. treated,** il est (la) victime d'une injustice. **2.** (jouer, etc.) déloyalement; **to act u.,** commettre une déloyauté; agir avec mauvaise foi.
unfairness [ʌn'fɛənis], *s.* **1.** injustice *f*; partialité *f.* **2.** déloyauté *f*; mauvaise foi; **with great u.,** au mépris de toute loyauté.
unfaithful [ʌn'feiθful]. **1.** *a. (a)* **to be u. to one's wife, to one's husband,** tromper sa femme, son mari; être infidèle à sa femme, à son mari; **her husband is u. to her,** son mari la trompe, la trahit; *(b)* (compte rendu, etc.) inexact, infidèle; *(c) O:* infidèle; déloyal, -aux; **he has been u. to his master,** il a été infidèle à, déloyal envers, son maître; il a trahi son maître. **2.** *s.pl. Ecc:* **the u.,** les infidèles *m.*
unfaithfully [ʌn'feiθfuli], *adv.* **1.** *(a)* infidèlement; *(b) O:* infidèlement, déloyalement. **2.** (raconter, citer) inexactement.
unfaithfulness [ʌn'feiθfulnis], *s.* **1.** *(a)* infidélité *f* (d'un mari, etc.); *(b)* inexactitude *f,* infidélité (d'un portrait, d'un traducteur, etc.); *(c) O:* infidélité, déloyauté *f* (à un maître, etc.).
unfaltering [ʌn'fɔ:ltəriŋ], *a.* **u. voice,** voix ferme, résolue, décidée; **u. steps,** pas assurés, fermes; **u. courage,** courage sans défaillance, soutenu.
unfalteringly [ʌn'fɔ:ltəriŋli], *adv.* (parler) d'une voix ferme, sans hésiter, sans défaillance; (marcher) d'un pas bien assuré, soutenu.
unfamiliar [ʌnfə'miliər], *a.* **1.** peu familier, peu connu, mal connu; étranger; **u. face,** visage étranger, inconnu, nouveau; **u. word,** mot nouveau; **u. phrase,** expression peu habituelle. **2.** *(of pers.)* **to be u. with sth.,** ne pas connaître, mal connaître, qch.; ne pas être au fait, au courant, de qch.; **I'm totally u. with this town,** je ne connais pas du tout cette ville; **he is quite u. with this subject,** il ne sait absolument rien de, il est tout à fait étranger à, ce sujet; ce sujet lui est tout à fait étranger.
unfamiliarity [ʌnfəmili'æriti], *s.* **1.** caractère étranger, aspect inconnu, nouveauté *f* (d'un lieu, etc.). **2.** ignorance *f* (**with,** de); **u. with legal procedure,** inexpérience *f* de la procédure.
unfashionable [ʌn'fæʃ(ə)nəbl], *a.* (vêtement, etc.) démodé, passé de mode; qui n'est pas, qui n'est plus, à la mode; **it's u. to wear miniskirts,** les mini-jupes ne se portent plus, ne se font plus; **it's u. to read Dickens at the moment,** ce n'est plus à la mode de lire du Dickens.
unfashionably [ʌn'fæʃ(ə)nəbli], *adv.* sans se préoccuper de la mode; à l'ancienne mode; **he was u. dressed,** ses vêtements étaient démodés, passés de mode.
unfashioned [ʌn'fæʃ(ə)nd], *a.* (marbre, etc.) brut, qui n'est pas façonné; (bois, métal) non ouvré.
unfasten [ʌn'fɑ:sn], *v.tr.* **1. to u. sth. from sth.,** détacher, délier, qch. de qch.; dégager qch. **2.** défaire, dégrafer, détacher, déboutonner (des vêtements); desserrer (une ceinture); défaire (une cravate, un nœud, une corde, etc.); dénouer, délier (de la ficelle, etc.); délacer (des chaussures); ouvrir, déverrouiller (une porte).
unfastened [ʌn'fɑ:snd], *a.* (vêtement, etc.) défait, dégrafé, détaché, déboutonné; (cordon, etc.) dénoué, délié; *(of door)* déverrouillé; **to come u.,** *(of garment)* se dégrafer, se déboutonner; *(of knot, hair, etc.)* se défaire, se dénouer; *(of belt)* se desserrer.
unfatherly [ʌn'fɑ:ðəli], *a.* peu paternel; indigne d'un père.
unfathomable [ʌn'fæðəməbl], *a.* (abîme, mystère) insondable; (abîme) sans fond; (mystère) impénétrable; (visage) impénétrable, inscrutable; **u. distance,** distance infinie, incommensurable.
unfathomed [ʌn'fæðəmd], *a.* (gouffre, etc.) insondé; **u. seas,** mers insondées; **u. depths,** profondeurs inexplorées; **u. mystery,** mystère insondé, impénétré.
unfavourable [ʌn'feiv(ə)rəbl], *a. (of circumstances, conditions, etc.)* défavorable, peu favorable, désavantageux (**to,** à); (moment, etc.) peu propice, inopportun; (vent) contraire; **u. weather, report,** temps, compte rendu, défavorable; **u. criticism,** critique adverse; **to appear in an u. light,** se montrer sous un jour désavantageux.
unfavourably [ʌn'feiv(ə)rəbli], *adv.* défavorablement, désavantageusement; **to treat s.o. u.,** désavantager qn; **to be u. disposed towards sth., s.o.,** être hostile, opposé, à qch., à qn; **his work compares u. with his brother's,** ses œuvres supportent mal la comparaison avec celles de son frère.
unfeasible [ʌn'fi:zibl], *a.* (projet, etc.) peu faisable, irréalisable, impraticable.
unfeeling [ʌn'fi:liŋ], *a.* **1.** sans sensation; insensible. **2.** *(of pers.)* insensible, impitoyable; sans pitié, sans cœur; dur; inflêchissable; **u. heart,** cœur sec, froid, indifférent, aride.
unfeelingly [ʌn'fi:liŋli], *adv.* (agir, etc.) sans émotion, sans pitié; impitoyablement; (répondre, etc.) froidement, sèchement, durement.
unfeigned [ʌn'feind], *a.* non simulé; sincère, vrai, réel.
unfeignedly [ʌn'feinidli], *adv.* sincèrement; réellement, vraiment.
unfelt [ʌn'felt], *a.* **1.** (coup) auquel on est insensible. **2.** (force, influence) qui ne se fait pas sentir, dont on ne se rend pas compte.
unfeminine [ʌn'feminin], *a.* peu féminin.
unfenced [ʌn'fenst], *a.* (terrain, etc.) sans clôture, sans barrière.
unfermentable [ʌnfə'mentəbl], *a.* infermentescible.
unfermented [ʌnfə'mentid], *a.* non fermenté; **u. grape juice,** moût *m.*
unfertilized [ʌn'fə:tilaizd], *a.* **1.** (œuf) non fécondé. **2.** *Agr:* (sol) non amendé, non fumé, non fertilisé; qui n'a pas reçu d'engrais.
unfetter [ʌn'fetər], *v.tr. (a) A: & Lit:* désenchaîner, déferrer (un prisonnier); délier (les mains d'un prisonnier); briser les fers (d'un prisonnier); débarrasser (un cheval) de ses entraves; *(b) Lit:* libérer, affranchir (l'art, etc.).
unfettered [ʌn'fetəd], *a.* libre de tous liens; *(a) A: & Lit:* (prisonnier) désenchaîné, déferré; (cheval, etc.) sans entrave(s); *(b) Lit:* **to leave s.o. u. to act u.,** laisser agir librement qn; donner toute latitude à qn pour agir; **u. by conventions,** libre de toute convention.
unfettering [ʌn'fetəriŋ], *s. A: & Lit:* déferrage *m,* déferrement *m,* déferrure *f* (d'un prisonnier, d'un cheval); libération *f*; affranchissement *m* (d'un prisonnier, de l'esprit, etc.).
unfilial [ʌn'filiəl], *a.* peu filial, -aux; indigne d'un fils, d'une fille.
unfiltered [ʌn'filtəd], *a.* non filtré.
unfinished [ʌn'finiʃt], *a.* **1.** inachevé, incomplet, -ète; (ouvrage) imparfait; **u. game,** partie interrompue; **to have some u. business,** avoir (i) quelques affaires pendantes, (ii) une affaire à régler; **I've only got one left u.,** il ne m'en reste qu'un à finir. **2.** *(a) Ind:* brut; non façonné; non usiné; *(b)* qui manque de fini, mal fini; **it looks u.,** la finition semble insuffisante.
unfired [ʌn'faiəd], *a.* **1.** *(of brick, etc.)* non cuit; cru. **2.** (canon) non déchargé; (coup) qui n'est pas parti.
unfit[1] [ʌn'fit], *a.* **1.** *(a)* impropre, peu propre, qui ne convient pas (**for,** à); **u. for (human) consumption, for food, u. to eat,** impropre à la consommation, non comestible, incomestible, inconsommable; immangeable; **u. to drink,** impropre à boire; imbuvable; non potable; **it's u. for publication,** on ne saurait le publier; c'est impubliable; **this house is u. for habitation,** cette maison est inhabitable; **road u. for heavy traffic,** chemin impraticable aux poids lourds; *(b) (of pers.)* inapte, peu

apte (**for,** à); **u. for military service,** inapte, impropre au service militaire; **u. for business,** inapte aux affaires; **to be u. for one's job,** ne pas convenir à son poste; **u. for a position of trust,** incapable d'occuper un poste de confiance; **u. to rule,** indigne de régner. **2.** (*physically unfit*) (*a*) **to be u.,** être en mauvaise santé; ne pas être en forme; être peu dispos; **he's u. to travel, for travelling,** il n'est pas en état, il est incapable, de voyager; il ne devrait pas voyager; **the patient is temporarily u. for the operation,** pour le moment le malade ne va pas, ne se porte pas, assez bien pour subir l'opération; **u. for duty,** incapable de faire son service; (*b*) faible de constitution; *Mil: etc:* **to turn a man down as u.,** réformer un homme; **to be discharged as u.,** être réformé; **to be declared u.,** être déclaré inapte.

unfit[2], *v.tr.* (**unfitted**) rendre (qn) inapte (**for sth.,** à qch.); rendre (qch.) impropre (**for a use,** à un usage); **his wound unfits him for work,** sa blessure le rend incapable de travailler, le met hors d'état de travailler, le met dans l'impossibilité de travailler.

unfitness [ʌn'fitnis], *s.* **1.** *A: & Lit:* disconvenance *f* (du climat, etc.); manque *m* d'à-propos (d'une observation, etc.). **2. u. for sth., to do sth.,** inaptitude *f* à qch., à faire qch.; incapacité *f* de faire qch.; incompétence *f.* **3.** (**physical**) **u.,** (i) mauvaise santé; (ii) constitution *f* faible; incapacité.

unfitted [ʌn'fitid], *a.* **to be u. for sth., to do sth.,** (i) (*of equipment, etc.*) être impropre à qch., à faire qch.; (ii) (*of pers.*) ne pas convenir à, ne pas être fait pour (un poste, etc.); être inapte à, incapable de, faire qch.; (iii) être indigne de faire qch.

unfitting [ʌn'fitiŋ], *a.* peu convenable; peu séant; (*of remark, etc.*) mal à propos, déplacé, inopportun.

unfix [ʌn'fiks], *v.tr.* détacher, défaire; *Mil:* **to u. bayonets,** remettre la baïonnette.

unfixed [ʌn'fikst], *a.* **1.** détaché, mobile; libre; **to come u.,** se détacher, se défaire. **2.** *A: & Lit:* (*a*) (*of spelling, ideas, etc.*) indéterminé, variable, flottant; (*b*) (*of pers.*) irrésolu, incertain; instable, changeant.

unflagging [ʌn'flægiŋ], *a.* (intérêt) soutenu, qui ne se dément pas; (courage, vigueur, etc.) inlassable, infatigable, inépuisable, intarissable; (optimisme, espoir) inébranlable.

unflaggingly [ʌn'flægiŋli], *adv.* inlassablement, infatigablement.

unflappable [ʌn'flæpəbl], *a. F:* imperturbable, calme; **his secretary is completely u.,** sa secrétaire affiche toujours un calme imperturbable, garde toujours son calme, son sang-froid, son flegme, ne s'affole, ne s'emballe, jamais.

unflattering [ʌn'flætəriŋ], *a.* peu flatteur, -euse (**to,** pour); **her hat was most u.,** son chapeau ne la flattait point, ne la mettait point en valeur, ne l'avantageait point.

unflatteringly [ʌn'flætəriŋli], *adv.* sans flatterie; d'une manière peu flatteuse.

unfledged [ʌn'fledʒd], *a.* **1.** (oiseau) sans plumes; (poussin) frais éclos; *Ven:* (faucon) saure; (perdreaux) en traîne. **2.** *Lit:* (*of pers.*) sans expérience (de la vie); jeune; novice; **u. youth,** la prime jeunesse.

unfleshed [ʌn'fleʃt], *a.* **1.** *Ven:* (chien) non acharné. **2.** *Lit:* sans expérience (de la vie); novice; nouveau (**in sth.,** à qch.).

unflinching [ʌn'flinʃiŋ], *a.* qui ne bronche pas; ferme, résolu; stoïque, impassible; **u. policy,** politique sans défaillance; **with u. eyes,** d'un regard franc.

unflinchingly [ʌn'flinʃiŋli], *adv.* sans broncher; sans sourciller; de pied ferme, résolument; stoïquement; sans défaillance.

unfold[1] [ʌn'fould]. **1.** *v.tr.* (*a*) déplier, ouvrir (un journal, une serviette, etc.); déployer (une carte, etc.); **to u. one's arms,** décroiser les bras; (*of bird*) **to u. its wings,** déployer ses ailes; (*b*) révéler; expliquer, exposer (ses intentions, etc.); développer, exposer (un projet); dévoiler, découvrir (ses plans, un secret); raconter tout au long (une histoire). **2.** *v.i. & pr.* (*a*) se déployer, se dérouler, s'étaler; (*of flower*) s'ouvrir, s'épanouir; **a superb landscape unfolded (itself) before us,** un paysage magnifique se déroulait, s'étendait, se développait, devant nous; **the story, the action, slowly unfolded,** le récit, l'action, se déroulait lentement; (*b*) (*of secret, etc.*) se dévoiler, se développer.

unfold[2], *v.tr. A:* déparquer (des moutons).

unforced [ʌn'fɔːst], *a.* **1.** qui n'est pas forcé; libre; **u. obedience,** obéissance librement consentie; obéissance volontaire. **2.** naturel, spontané; **u. laugh,** rire franc. **3.** (*of plant, fruit*) qui n'a pas été forcé.

unfordable [ʌn'fɔːdəbl], *a.* (ruisseau, etc.) non guéable, que l'on ne peut pas passer à gué.

unforeseeable [ʌnfɔː'siːəbl], *a.* (événement, etc.) imprévisible.

unforeseeing [ʌnfɔː'siːiŋ], *a. esp. Lit:* imprévoyant; aux vues courtes.

unforeseen [ʌnfɔː'siːn], *a.* imprévu, inattendu; inopiné; **u. developments,** événements imprévus, non envisagés, fortuits; **u. event, contingency,** imprévu *m*; **unless something u. happens,** sauf imprévu; à moins d'imprévu; **if something u. happens, write to me,** en cas d'imprévu, écrivez-moi; **u. circumstances,** (i) circonstances imprévues; (ii) *Jur:* force majeure.

unforgettable [ʌnfə'getəbl], *a.* inoubliable.

unforgivable [ʌnfə'givəbl], *a.* impardonnable; inexcusable; irrémissible.

unforgivably [ʌnfə'givəbli], *adv.* inexcusablement; irrémissiblement; **he was u. rude,** on ne pouvait pas lui pardonner son impolitesse.

unforgiven [ʌnfə'givn], *a.* impardonné; sans pardon.

unforgiving [ʌnfə'giviŋ], *a.* implacable, impitoyable; sans merci.

unforgotten [ʌnfə'gɔtn], *a.* inoublié; **he remains u.,** son souvenir est toujours présent, toujours vivace.

unformatted [ʌn'fɔːmætid], *a. Cmptr:* non mis en forme, non édité; brut.

unformed [ʌn'fɔːmd], *a.* **1.** (os, etc.) qui n'est pas (encore) formé. **2.** (masse, etc.) informe. **3.** (esprit, etc.) inculte.

unformulated [ʌn'fɔːmjuleitid], *a.* (*of thoughts, etc.*) informulé.

unforthcoming [ʌnfɔːθ'kʌmiŋ], *a.* réservé; **to be u. about sth.,** être, se montrer, réticent au sujet de qch.

unfortified [ʌn'fɔːtifaid], *a.* non fortifié; sans défenses; sans fortifications; **u. town,** ville ouverte.

unfortunate [ʌn'fɔːtʃənət]. **1.** *a.* (*a*) malheureux, malchanceux; infortuné; **he's been most u.,** il a eu beaucoup de malchance; il n'a pas eu beaucoup de chance; il a eu bien du malheur; **you were u. in missing him,** (c'est) dommage que vous l'ayez manqué; (*b*) (accident, événement, etc.) malheureux, malencontreux, fâcheux; (erreur, etc.) regrettable; **u. business venture,** entreprise malheureuse, fâcheuse; **u. state of affairs,** situation regrettable, fâcheuse; **u. consequences,** suites malheureuses; **u. remark,** observation malheureuse, malencontreuse, regrettable; **u. choice of words,** choix de mots peu heureux, déplorable; mauvais choix de mots; **in u. circumstances,** dans de tristes circonstances; **it's my u. duty to tell you,** c'est mon triste devoir de vous faire part (que); **it's u. that she has to leave today,** il est malheureux, regrettable, triste, il est dommage, qu'elle soit obligée de partir aujourd'hui; **how (very) u.!** quel malheur! quelle malchance! quel dommage! que c'est (bien) malheureux! **2.** *s.* malheureux, -euse; *coll. Lit:* **the u.,** les déshérités *m*; les disgraciés *m* de la fortune; les infortunés *m.*

unfortunately [ʌn'fɔːtʃənətli], *adv.* malheureusement; malencontreusement; par malheur; **an u. phrased, worded, statement,** déclaration formulée, rédigée, d'une façon regrettable, malencontreuse; déclaration dont les termes sont mal choisis; **u. he decided to post the letter,** pour son malheur, il s'est décidé à mettre la lettre à la poste; **u. for him,** malheureusement pour lui; pour son malheur.

unfounded [ʌn'faundid], *a.* (*of accusation, etc.*) sans fondement, sans base, non fondé, infondé; **u. rumour,** bruit dénué de tout fondement, sans consistance, qui ne repose sur rien, de pure imagination; **u. supposition,** supposition infondée, gratuite; **u. suspicions,** soupçons sans fondement, injustifiés; faux soupçons; **u. criticism,** critique injustifiée, qui manque de fondement.

unframed [ʌn'freimd], *a.* (tableau, etc.) non encadré; sans cadre.

unfreezable [ʌn'friːzəbl], *a.* incongelable.

unfreeze [ʌn'friːz], *v.* (*p.t.* **unfroze** [ʌn'frouz]; *p.p.* **unfrozen** [ʌn'frouzn]) **1.** *v.tr.* (faire) dégeler; décongeler; *Fin:* **to u. funds,** dégeler, débloquer, des crédits. **2.** *v.i.* (se) dégeler.

unfreezing [ʌn'friːziŋ], *s.* décongélation *f* (d'un terrain, de la viande, etc.); *Fin:* déblocage *m* (de crédits).

un-French [ʌn'fren(t)ʃ], *a.* peu français; pas français.

unfrequented [ʌnfri'kwentid], *a.* peu fréquenté, infréquenté; (chemin) impratiqué; **u. spot,** endroit écarté, peu fréquenté, solitaire.

unfriendliness [ʌn'frendlinis], *s.* manque *m* d'amitié (**towards,** pour); froideur *f,* disposition *f* défavorable (**towards,** envers, à l'égard de); hostilité *f* (**towards,** envers, contre).

unfriendly [ʌn'frendli], *a.* **1.** (ton, sentiment, etc.) peu amical, -aux; inamical, -aux; peu bienveillant; **u. action,** action inamicale, hostile; acte d'hostilité; **to be u. to(wards) s.o.,** être mal disposé pour, envers, qn; traiter qn avec froideur; être hostile à qn; **he's been very u. towards me,** il n'a pas été très gentil avec moi. **2.** (*of circumstances, atmosphere, etc.*) défavorable; peu propice; **u. reception,** accueil froid, hostile; *Lit:* **u. wind,** vent contraire.

unfrock [ʌn'frɔk], *v.tr.* défroquer (un prêtre, etc.); **an unfrocked priest,** un (prêtre) défroqué.

unfrozen [ʌn'frouzn], *a.* (*a*) (terrain, etc.) (i) dégelé, (ii) non gelé; (produit alimentaire) (i) décongelé, (ii) non congelé; (*b*) *Fin:* (crédit) dégelé, débloqué.

unfruitful [ʌn'fruːtful], *a.* (arbre, terrain, esprit, etc.) stérile, infécond, infertile, improductif; **u. research,** recherche infructueuse, improductive, peu profitable.

unfruitfully [ʌn'fruːtfuli], *adv.* sans profit, sans succès; en vain.

unfruitfulness [ʌn'fruːtfulnis], *s.* (*a*) stérilité *f,* infécondité *f* (d'un arbre, du sol, etc.); infertilité *f* (du sol, etc.); (*b*) caractère *m* peu profitable, improductivité *f* (d'une recherche, etc.).

unfulfilled [ʌnful'fild], *a.* (*a*) **u. prophecy,** prophétie inaccomplie; (*b*) (désir) non satisfait, inassouvi; (*of pers.*) **to feel u.,** éprouver un sentiment d'insatisfaction; se sentir insatisfait, frustré; (*c*) **u. prayer, wish,** prière inexaucée, vœu inexaucé; (*d*) (devoir) inaccompli; (dessein) inexécuté; **u. condition,** condition non remplie; **u. task,** tâche inachevée; **u. promise,** promesse non tenue.

unfulfilment [ʌnful'filmənt], *s. Psy:* incomplétude *f.*

unfunded [ʌn'fʌndid], *a. Fin:* **u. debt,** dette flottante, non consolidée.

unfurl [ʌn'fəːl]. **1.** *v.tr.* (*a*) *Nau:* déferler, larguer, ouvrir (une voile); déployer, déferler (un drapeau, *Nau:* un pavillon); (*b*) dérouler (un parapluie); déplier, défaire (une tente, etc.). **2.** *v.i.* se déferler, s'ouvrir; se déplier.

unfurling [ʌn'fəːliŋ], *s.* déferlage *m* (d'une voile); déploiement *m* (d'un pavillon, etc.).

unfurnished [ʌn'fəːniʃt], *a.* (appartement, etc.) non meublé; **u. room to let, room to let u.,** chambre non meublée à louer.

ungainliness [ʌn'geinlinis], *s.* gaucherie *f*; air *m* gauche; lourdeur *f.*

ungainly [ʌn'geinli], *a.* gauche, lourd, disgracieux; dégingandé.

ungallant [ʌn'gælənt, *A:* ʌngə'lænt], *a. O:* peu galant; discourtois.

ungarbled [ʌn'gɑːbld], *a.* (texte) non mutilé, intégral, -aux; (rapport) vrai, exact; **I want an u. version of the story,** je veux qu'on me raconte l'histoire exactement comme elle s'est passée.

ungarnered [ʌn'gɑːnəd], *a. Lit:* non moissonné; (récolte) non rentrée.

ungarnished [ʌn'gɑːniʃt], *a.* dépourvu d'ornements, de garniture; simple; *Cu:* sans garniture(s); sans accommodement(s).

ungarrisoned [ʌn'gæris(ə)nd], *a.* (ville) sans garnison.

ungeared [ʌn'giːəd], *a. Mec.E:* **1.** (*of machine part*) débrayé. **2.** sans engrenage.

ungemachite ['ʌngəmɑːkait], *s. Miner:* ungémachite *f.*

ungenerous [ʌn'dʒen(ə)rəs], *a.* peu généreux; (*a*) peu magnanime; mesquin, bas, *f.* basse; (*b*) avare, parcimonieux; cupide; (*c*) *Lit:* (sol) ingrat, stérile.

ungenerously [ʌn'dʒen(ə)rəsli], *adv.* (*a*) mesquinement, bassement; (*b*) avec avarice; parcimonieusement, cupidement.

ungentlemanly [ʌn'dʒentlmənli], *a.* peu galant, discourtois; (homme) mal élevé, qui n'a pas de savoir-vivre; **u. behaviour,** (i) procédés indélicats; (ii) impolitesse *f*; manque *m* de tenue, de savoir-vivre.

ungetatable [ʌnget'ætəbl], *a. F:* inaccessible.

ungird [ʌn'gəːd], *v.tr.* (**ungirded, ungirt**) *Lit:* **1.** détacher, ôter, la ceinture de (qn); **to u. oneself,** ôter sa ceinture. **2.** *A:* déceindre (son épée); ôter, déboucler (son armure).

ungirded, ungirt [ʌn'gəːdid, ʌn'gəːt], *a. Lit:* **1.** sans ceinture. **2.** *A:* (*of sword, armour*) débouclé.

ungirth [ʌn'gəːθ], *v.tr.* dessangler (un cheval).

unglazed [ʌn'gleizd], *a.* **1.** (*of window, etc.*) non vitré; sans vitres. **2.** (*a*) (papier, etc.) non glacé, non lustré; *Phot:* **u. print,** épreuve mate, non émaillée; (*b*) *Cer:* non verni, non vernissé, non émaillé; poreux; (*of brick*) non vitrifié; **u. porcelain,** biscuit *m*; (*c*) (gâteau) non glacé.

ungloved [ʌn'glʌvd], *a.* déganté; sans gant(s); **u. hand,** main nue, dégantée.

unglue [ʌn'gluː], *v.tr.* (**unglued; ungluing**) décoller; **it came, got, unglued, it unglued itself,** il s'est décollé.

ungodliness [ʌn'gɔdlinis], *s.* impiété *f.*

ungodly [ʌn'gɔdli], *a.* (*a*) impie, irréligieux; (*b*) *F:* **an u. row,** un bruit de tous les diables; **he got up at an u. hour,** il s'est levé à une heure impossible, indue.

ungovernable [ʌn'gʌv(ə)nəbl], *a.* **1.** (peuple, pays) ingouvernable; (enfant) indisciplinable, indocile. **2.** (désir, passion) irrésistible, irrépressible; **he has fits of u. temper,** il a des emportements *m* de colère, il n'est pas toujours maître de lui-même.

ungoverned [ʌn'gʌv(ə)nd], *a.* **1.** (peuple, pays) libre de tout gouvernement. **2.** (*of passion, etc.*) indompté, effréné; sans frein.

ungraceful [ʌn'greisful], *a.* disgracieux; sans grâce; gauche.

ungracefully [ʌn'greisfuli], *adv.* sans grâce; gauchement.

ungracious [ʌn'greiʃəs], *a.* **1.** *O:* (devoir, etc.) désagréable, déplaisant, ingrat. **2.** (*of pers., manner, etc.*) peu gracieux; incivil; peu aimable; **it would be u. of me to refuse,** j'aurais mauvaise grâce de refuser; **it would be u. of me to blame you,** je serais mal venu de, j'aurais mauvaise grâce à, vous faire des reproches.

ungraciously [ʌn'greiʃəsli], *adv.* de, avec, mauvaise grâce; **not u.,** de bonne grâce.

ungraciousness [ʌn'greiʃəsnis], *s.* mauvaise grâce.

ungraded [ʌn'greidid], *a. NAm:* **1.** *Civ.E:* (*of ground*) non nivelé. **2. u. school,** école primaire où les élèves ne sont pas divisés par classes.

ungraduated [ʌn'grædjueitid], *a.* **1.** non gradué, sans gradation. **2.** *esp. Ch:* (*of beaker, etc.*) sans graduations, non gradué.

ungrafted [ʌn'grɑ:ftid], *a.* (arbre) franc de pied.

ungrammatical [ʌngrə'mætikl], *a.* non grammatical, -aux; incorrect; agrammatical, -aux.

ungrammatically [ʌngrə'mætik(ə)li], *adv.* incorrectement.

ungrateful [ʌn'greitful], *a.* ingrat; (*a*) peu reconnaissant; **to be u. to s.o. (for sth.),** être peu reconnaissant envers qn de qch.; se montrer ingrat envers qn; payer qn d'ingratitude; (*b*) *Lit:* **u. soil,** sol ingrat; **u. task,** tâche ingrate.

ungratefully [ʌn'greitfuli], *adv.* avec ingratitude; sans reconnaissance.

ungratefulness [ʌn'greitfulnis], *s.* ingratitude *f*; manque *m* de reconnaissance.

ungratifiable [ʌngræti'faiəbl], *a.* (désir) incontentable, inassouvissable.

ungratified [ʌn'grætifaid], *a.* **1.** (*of pers.*) peu satisfait; mécontent. **2.** (désir) incontenté, inassouvi, non satisfait; (vœu) inexaucé.

ungreased [ʌn'gri:st], *a.* non graissé; non lubrifié.

ungrudging [ʌn'grʌdʒiŋ], *a.* **1.** (*of gift, etc.*) donné de bon cœur, de bonne grâce, sans rechigner; (*of admiration*) (très) sincère. **2.** (*of pers.*) généreux; large.

ungrudgingly [ʌn'grʌdʒiŋli], *adv.* de bonne grâce; de bon cœur; sans rechigner; généreusement; **to praise (s.o.) u.,** se prodiguer en éloges, ne pas ménager ses louanges à qn.

ungual ['ʌŋgwəl], *a. Anat:* unguéal, -aux; unguinal, -aux.

unguarded [ʌn'gɑ:did], *a.* **1.** (*a*) non gardé; sans garde; sans surveillance; (ville, etc.) sans défense; *Ten:* **to leave part of one's court u.,** laisser un trou dans son court; *Fb: etc:* **to leave the goal u.,** dégarnir le but; (*b*) *Cards:* (roi) sec; *Chess:* (pièce) non gardée. **2.** (*of pers.*) qui n'est pas sur ses gardes; qui agit par inadvertance; (*of remark, etc.*) indiscret, -ète, imprudent, inconsidéré, irréfléchi; **in an u. moment,** dans un moment d'inattention, d'inadvertance, d'irréflexion. **3.** (précipice, etc.) sans garde-fou; (mécanisme) sans dispositif protecteur; (engrenage) sans carter.

unguardedly [ʌn'gɑ:didli], *adv.* **1.** inconsidérément; sans réflexion. **2.** par inadvertance, par mégarde.

unguardedness [ʌn'gɑ:didnis], *s.* inadvertance *f*, inattention *f*; imprudence *f*.

unguent ['ʌŋgwənt], *s.* onguent *m*.

unguessable [ʌn'gesəbl], *a.* indevinable.

Unguiculata [ʌngwikju'leitə], *s.pl. Z:* onguiculés *m*.

unguiculate(d) [ʌŋ'gwikjuleit(id)], *a. Nat.Hist:* onguiculé.

unguided [ʌn'gaidid], *a.* **1.** *Mount: etc:* sans guide. **2.** *Ball:* **u. missile,** missile non guidé.

unguiferate, unguiferous [ʌŋ'gwifərət, -'gwifərəs], *a. Nat.Hist:* unguifère.

unguiform ['ʌŋgwifɔ:m], *a. Nat.Hist:* onguiforme.

unguinal ['ʌŋgwinəl], *a. Anat:* unguinal, -aux; unguéal, -aux.

unguis, *pl.* **ungues** ['ʌŋgwis, -i:z], *s.* **1.** *Anat:* unguis *m*; os lacrymal. **2.** *Bot:* onglet *m* (d'un pétale). **3.** *Z:* ongle *m*; sabot *m*.

ungula, *pl.* **-ae** ['ʌŋgjulə, -i:], *s.* **1.** *Mth:* onglet *m* (sphérique, etc.). **2.** *Bot:* onglet (d'un pétale). **3.** *Z:* ongle *m*; sabot *m*.

Ungulata [ʌŋgju'leitə], *s.pl. Z:* ongulés *m*.

ungulate ['ʌŋgjuleit], *a. & s. Z:* ongulé (*m*).

unguled ['ʌŋgju:ld], *a. Her:* onglé.

unguligrade ['ʌŋgjuligreid], *a. Z:* onguligrade.

ungum [ʌn'gʌm], *v.tr.* (**ungummed**) dégommer; décoller (un timbre, etc.).

unhaft [ʌn'hɑ:ft], *v.tr.* démancher (un poignard, un outil).

unhair [ʌn'hɛər], *v.tr. Tan:* dépiler, débourrer, ébourrer, peler (une peau).

unhairing [ʌn'hɛəriŋ], *s. Tan:* dépilage *m*, débourrage *m*, ébourrage *m*, pelage *m* (d'une peau).

unhallowed [ʌn'hæloud], *a.* (*a*) non béni, non consacré; (*b*) profane.

unhampered [ʌn'hæmpəd], *a.* non entravé (**by,** par); libre (de ses mouvements); **u. by rules,** sans être gêné, qui n'est pas gêné, par des règles.

unhand [ʌn'hænd], *v.tr. A: & Lit:* lâcher, laisser aller (qn); **u. me, sir!** lâchez-moi, monsieur!

unhandled[1] [ʌn'hændəld], *a.* (cheval) non rompu, non dressé.

unhandled[2], *a.* (outil, etc.) (i) démanché, (ii) sans manche.

unhandsome [ʌn'hænsəm], *a.* **1.** qui manque de beauté; **he's not u.,** il n'est pas laid, vilain. **2.** *A: & Lit:* (*of conduct, etc.*) indélicat, malséant. **3.** *A: & Lit:* peu généreux; peu libéral, -aux; mesquin.

unhandy [ʌn'hændi], *a.* **1.** *esp. Lit:* (*of pers.*) maladroit, malhabile, gauche. **2.** (outil, etc.) peu maniable, mal commode.

unhang [ʌn'hæŋ], *v.tr.* (**unhung** [ʌn'hʌŋ]) *Nau:* démonter (le gouvernail).

unhanged [ʌn'hæŋd], *a.* qui n'est pas (encore) pendu; non pendu; **one of the greatest rogues u.,** un des plus grands coquins qui aient échappé à la potence; un vrai gibier de potence.

unhappily [ʌn'hæpili], *adv.* **1.** (*a*) malheureusement; par malheur, par malchance; *O:* **u. he fell ill the following day,** malheureusement il est tombé malade le lendemain; (*b*) tristement; **he looked at her u.,** il l'a regardée d'un air triste, malheureux. **2. thought u. expressed,** pensée mal exprimée, exprimée de manière peu heureuse.

unhappiness [ʌn'hæpinis], *s.* **1.** chagrin *m*, tristesse *f*; peine *f*. **2.** *esp. Lit:* inopportunité *f* (d'une expression, etc.).

unhappy [ʌn'hæpi], *a.* **1.** (*a*) malheureux, triste; **to look u.,** avoir l'air triste; **to make s.o. u.,** causer du chagrin à qn; rendre qn malheureux; **to be u. at leaving s.o.,** avoir du chagrin de quitter qn; **it made me u. to see how changed he was,** j'avais du chagrin de le voir si changé; **he's u. in his new flat,** il ne se plaît pas dans son nouvel appartement; **to be u. with s.o., sth.,** être mécontent de qn, qch.; (*b*) inquiet; **I'm u. about leaving the house empty,** je n'aime pas laisser la maison vide, ça m'inquiète de laisser la maison vide. **2.** (*of remark, etc.*) mal inspiré; malheureux; (*of choice*) malencontreux, malheureux; **the author was u. in his choice of words,** l'auteur a mal choisi ses mots; **this is an u. state of affairs,** c'est une situation regrettable, fâcheuse.

unharbour [ʌn'hɑ:bər], *v.tr. Ven:* débusquer, débucher (la bête).

unhardened [ʌn'hɑ:dənd], *a.* (*of substance*) non durci, non endurci; (*of steel, glass*) non trempé.

unharmed [ʌn'hɑ:md], *a.* (*of pers.*) sans mal; sain et sauf; indemne; (*of thg*) intact; non endommagé.

unharmonious [ʌnhɑ:'mouniəs], *a.* peu harmonieux; discordant.

unharness [ʌn'hɑ:nis], *v.tr.* **1.** (*a*) déharnacher (un cheval); (*b*) dételer (un cheval). **2.** *A:* débarrasser (un chevalier) de son armure; désarmer (un chevalier).

unharnessing [ʌn'hɑ:nisiŋ], *s.* (*a*) déharnachement *m* (d'un cheval); (*b*) dételage *m* (d'un cheval).

unharvested [ʌn'hɑ:vistid], *a.* (blé, etc.) non moissonné, non récolté, non rentré.

unhasp [ʌn'hɑ:sp], *v.tr. A: & Lit:* ouvrir le loquet (d'une porte); décadenasser (une porte, etc.).

unhealed [ʌn'hi:ld], *a.* **1.** non guéri. **2.** (*of wound*) non cicatrisé.

unhealthiness [ʌn'helθinis], *s.* **1.** insalubrité *f* (de l'air, d'un endroit); caractère dangereux, malsain (d'un travail). **2.** (*a*) mauvaise santé; état maladif; manque *m* de santé; (*b*) **u. of mind,** esprit malsain; morbidité *f* d'esprit.

unhealthy [ʌn'helθi], *a.* **1.** (air, endroit) malsain, insalubre; (travail) dangereux, malsain; *F:* **the engine sounds a bit u.,** le moteur fait un drôle de bruit. **2.** (*a*) (*of pers.*) maladif; **u. complexion,** visage terreux; (*b*) **u. state of mind,** état d'esprit malsain; **u. curiosity,** curiosité morbide.

unheard [ʌn'hə:d], *a.* **1.** non entendu; **to condemn s.o. u.,** condamner qn sans l'entendre, sans l'avoir entendu. **2. u. of,** (i) inouï; (ii) (auteur, etc.) inconnu, ignoré; (iii) sans précédent; **that's u. of!** c'est vraiment inouï, incroyable!

unheated [ʌn'hi:tid], *a.* non chauffé.

unheeded [ʌn'hi:did], *a.* à qui, auquel, on ne fait pas, on ne prête pas, attention; inaperçu; (*of warning, etc.*) négligé, ignoré, dédaigné; **his warning went u.,** on n'a pas tenu compte de, on a ignoré, son avertissement.

unheeding [ʌn'hi:diŋ], *a.* inattentif (**of,** à); insouciant (**of,** de); distrait, absent; **he walked on u. through the rain,** il a continué à marcher sans se soucier de la pluie.

unhelped [ʌn'helpt], *a.* sans aide, sans secours; **to do sth. u.,** faire qch. tout seul.

unhelpful [ʌn'helpful], *a.* (*a*) (critique, etc.) peu utile, d'aucune utilité; (conseil) vain, futile; (*b*) (*of pers.*) peu secourable, peu serviable, peu obligeant; **don't be so u.!** tâche donc un peu de nous aider!

unhelpfully [ʌn'helpfuli], *adv.* inutilement; **to stand by u.,** rester là sans aider (qn).

unheralded [ʌn'herəldid], *a. esp. Lit:* **1.** qui n'est pas annoncé, proclamé. **2.** imprévu, inattendu.

unheroic [ʌnhi'rouik], *a.* peu héroïque; lâche; pusillanime.

unhesitating [ʌn'heziteitiŋ], *a.* qui n'hésite pas; ferme, résolu; **u. reply,** réponse faite sans hésitation; réponse prompte, immédiate.

unhesitatingly [ʌn'heziteitiŋli], *adv.* sans hésiter; sans hésitation; **he answered u.,** il a répondu sans hésiter, d'un ton ferme.

unhewn [ʌn'hju:n], *a.* (*of stone, etc.*) non taillé, non dégrossi, brut.

unhindered [ʌn'hindəd], *a.* sans encombre, sans obstacle, sans entrave, sans empêchement; librement; sans être dérangé (**by,** par).

unhinge [ʌn'hindʒ], *v.tr.* **1.** dégonder, démonter (une porte); enlever (une porte) de ses gonds. **2.** déranger, détraquer (l'esprit).

unhinged [ʌn'hindʒd], *a.* **1.** (porte) hors de ses gonds. **2.** (esprit) dérangé, déséquilibré, détraqué; **his mind is u.,** il a le cerveau détraqué; il a perdu l'esprit; il n'a plus sa raison.

unhistorical [ʌnhis'tɔrik(ə)l], *a.* peu historique. **1.** contraire à l'histoire. **2.** (fait) dépourvu de tout caractère historique, non historique; (fait) légendaire.

unhitch [ʌn'hitʃ], *v.tr.* **1.** détacher, décrocher (qch.). **2.** dételer (un cheval).

unhobble [ʌn'hɔbl], *v.tr.* désentraver (un cheval, etc.).

unholiness [ʌn'houlinis], *s.* **1.** impiété *f*. **2.** caractère *m* profane (**of,** de).

unholy [ʌn'houli], *a.* **1.** (*of pers.*) impie; (*of thg*) profane. **2.** *F:* **u. muddle,** désordre invraisemblable, affreux; **there was an u. row,** il y a eu un charivari de tous les diables.

unhonoured [ʌn'ɔnəd], *a.* sans être honoré; qui n'est pas honoré; dédaigné.

unhood [ʌn'hud], *v.tr. Ven:* déchaperonner (le faucon).

unhook [ʌn'huk]. **1.** *v.tr.* (*a*) décrocher (un tableau, etc.); (*b*) dégrafer (un vêtement); **to u. one's dress,** se dégrafer; (*of dress, etc.*) **to come unhooked,** se dégrafer. **2.** *v.i.* (*a*) se décrocher; (*b*) se dégrafer.

unhoped [ʌn'houpt], *a.* **u. for,** inespéré; inattendu.

unhorse [ʌn'hɔ:s], *v.tr. esp. Lit:* **1.** désarçonner, démonter (un cavalier); **to be unhorsed,** vider les arçons; perdre, quitter, vider, les étriers. **2.** dételer (une voiture).

unhoused [ʌn'hauzd], *a.* **1.** (*of animal*) sans abri. **2.** (*of pers.*) (*a*) délogé; (*b*) sans logement.

unhung [ʌn'hʌŋ], *a.* **1.** (tableau) non exposé. **2. one of the biggest rogues u.,** un des plus grands coquins qui aient échappé à la potence, un vrai gibier de potence.

unhurt [ʌn'hə:t], *a.* (*of pers.*) sans mal, sans blessure; indemne; sain et sauf; **to escape u.,** sortir indemne, s'en tirer sans aucun mal, sain et sauf; **I escaped u.,** je n'ai pas eu une égratignure.

unhusk [ʌn'hʌsk], *v.tr.* dépouiller (un fruit, etc.) de son tégument, de son écorce; décortiquer.

unhygienic [ʌnhai'dʒi:nik], *a.* non hygiénique, contraire à l'hygiène.

uni- ['ju:ni], *pref.* **1.** uni-. **2.** mono-.

uniangulate [ju:ni'æŋgjuleit], *a. Bot:* uniangulaire.

uniarticulate [ju:niɑ:'tikjulət], *a. Ent: etc:* uniarticulé.

Uniat, Uniate ['ju:niæt, 'ju:nieit], *s. & a. Rel.H:* uniate (*m*).

uniaxial [ju:ni'æksiəl], *a.* **1.** *Cryst:* uniaxe. **2.** *Bot:* unicaule.

unicameral [ju:ni'kæmərəl], *a. Pol:* qui n'a qu'une assemblée législative.

unicameralism [ju:ni'kæmərəlizm], *s. Pol:* monocamér(al)isme *m*.

unicapsular [ju:ni'kæpsjulər], *a. Bot:* unicapsulaire.

unicellular [ju:ni'seljulər], *a. Biol:* unicellulaire; **u. organism,** protiste *m*.

unicity [ju:'nisiti], *s. Phil:* unicité *f*.

unicolour(ed), unicolorous ['ju:nikʌlər, -kʌləd, -'kʌlərəs], *a.* unicolore.

unicorn ['ju:nikɔ:n]. **1.** *a.* unicorne, unicornis; à une seule corne. **2.** *s.* (*a*) *Myth: Her:* licorne *f*, unicorne *m*;

Astr: **the U.,** la Licorne; (*b*) *Z:* **sea u., u. fish, u. whale,** licorne de mer; narval *m*, -als; (*c*) *A:* **u. (team),** attelage *m* en arbalète; **to drive u.,** conduire un attelage en arbalète.

unicornous [ju:ni'kɔ:nəs], *a.* unicorne, unicornis.

unicursal [ju:ni'kə:s(ə)l], *a. Mth:* **u. curve,** (courbe) unicursale *f*.

unicuspid [ju:ni'kʌspid], *a. Nat.Hist:* unicuspidé.

unicycle ['ju:nisaikl], *s. Cy:* monocycle *m*.

unidentified [ʌnai'dentifaid], *a.* non identifié; **u. flying object,** objet volant non identifié; soucoupe volante.

unidimensional [ju:nidai'menʃən(ə)l], *a.* unidimensionnel.

unidiomatic [ʌnidiə'mætik], *a.* peu idiomatique.

unidirectional [ju:nid(a)i'rekʃən(ə)l], *a. Ph: etc:* unidirectionnel.

unifacial [ju:ni'feiʃ(ə)l], *a.* uniface.

unification [ju:nifi'keiʃ(ə)n], *s.* unification *f*.

unified ['ju:nifaid], *a.* unifié.

unifier ['ju:nifaiər], *s.* unificateur, -trice.

unifilar, [ju:ni'failər], *a. El: etc:* (circuit) unifilaire.

unifloral, uniflorous [ju:ni'flɔ:rəl, -'flɔ:rəs], *a. Bot:* uniflore.

unifoliate [ju:ni'foulieit], *a. Bot:* unifolié, monophylle.

uniform ['ju:nifɔ:m]. **1.** *a.* (*of colour, style, etc.*) uniforme; **u. life,** vie uniforme; **u. temperature,** température constante; **u. acceleration,** accélération uniforme; **u. velocity, pace,** vitesse, allure, uniforme; *Equit:* **u. step,** pas écouté; **u. houses,** maisons uniformes; **these boxes are all of u. size,** ces boîtes sont toutes de la même grandeur; **to make u.,** uniformiser. **2.** *s.* (*a*) *Mil: Sch: etc:* uniforme *m*; **in u.,** en tenue, en uniforme; **out of u.,** en civil, *F:* en pékin; **(in) full (dress) u.,** (en) grande tenue, (en) grand uniforme; **field service u.,** tenue de campagne; **drill u.,** tenue d'exercice; **regulation, service, u.,** tenue, uniforme réglementaire; **u. trousers,** pantalon d'uniforme; *Mil:* **u. case, chest,** cantine *f* (à bagages); (*b*) costume *m* (d'infirmière, etc.).

uniformed ['ju:nifɔ:md], *a.* en uniforme, en tenue.

uniformitarian [ju:nifɔ:mi'teəriən], *a. & s. Geol:* uniformitariste (*mf*).

uniformitarianism [ju:nifɔ:mi'teəriənizm], *s. Geol:* uniformitarisme *m*.

uniformity [ju:ni'fɔ:miti], *s.* **1.** (*a*) uniformité *f*, unité *f* (de style, etc.); (*b*) régularité *f* (de fonctionnement); constance *f* (d'un courant, etc.). **2.** *Anglican Ch:* **Act of U.,** acte d'uniformité.

uniformly ['ju:nifɔ:mli], *adv.* uniformément.

unify ['ju:nifai]. **1.** *v.tr.* unifier (des idées, un parti politique, etc.); **to u. the whole population,** donner de l'unité à toute la population. **2.** *v.i.* s'unifier.

unifying ['ju:nifaiiŋ], *a.* unificateur, -trice.

unijugate [ju:ni'dʒu:geit], *a. Bot:* unijugué.

unilabiate [ju:ni'leibieit], *a. Bot:* unilabié.

unilateral [ju:ni'læt(ə)rəl], *a.* unilatéral, -aux; *Jur:* **u. contract,** contrat unilatéral.

unilaterally [ju:ni'læt(ə)rəli], *adv.* unilatéralement.

unilinear [ju:ni'liniər], *a.* unilinéaire.

unilingual [ju:ni'liŋgwəl], *a.* (dictionnaire, etc.) unilingue.

unilluminated [ʌni'lju:mineitid], *a.* non illuminé; (i) obscur, non éclairé; (ii) peu inspiré.

unilluminating [ʌni'lju:mineitiŋ], *a.* **1.** (*of explanation, etc.*) peu clair, peu lumineux. **2.** (*of book, etc.*) vide d'idées, peu intéressant.

unillustrated [ʌn'iləstreitid], *a.* **1.** non illustré; sans images. **2.** (grammaire, etc.) sans exemples.

unilobate [ju:ni'loubeit], *a. Nat.Hist:* unilobé.

unilocular [ju:ni'lɔkjulər], *a. Bot:* (ovaire) uniloculaire.

unilocularity [ju:nilɔkju'læriti], *s. Bot:* unilocularité *f*.

unimaginable [ʌni'mædʒinəbl], *a.* inimaginable, inconcevable.

unimaginative [ʌni'mædʒinətiv], *a.* dénué, qui manque, d'imagination; peu imaginatif.

unimaginatively [ʌni'mædʒinətivli], *adv.* sans imagination; d'une manière peu imaginative.

unimaginativeness [ʌni'mædʒinətivinis], *s.* manque *m* d'imagination.

unimagined [ʌni'mædʒind], *a.* inimaginé.

unimodal [ju:ni'moud(ə)l], *a. Stat:* unimodal, -aux.

unimpaired [ʌnim'pɛəd], *a.* (*of health, hearing, etc.*) non altéré; intact; **u. strength, quality,** force, qualité, non diminuée; force, qualité, intacte; **her sight is u.,** sa vue ne s'est pas détériorée, n'a pas faibli; **his mind is u.,** il conserve toute sa vigueur d'esprit; il a encore toute sa tête.

unimpassioned [ʌnim'pæʃ(ə)nd], *a.* sans passion; tranquille, froid, calme; **u. speech,** discours mesuré.

unimpeachable [ʌnim'pi:tʃəbl], *a.* (*a*) inattaquable; (droit) incontestable; **I have it from an u. source,** je le tiens de source sûre, d'une source incontestable; (*b*) (témoignage, témoin) inattaquable, irrécusable, irréfragable; (conduite) irréprochable, impeccable.

unimpeached [ʌnim'pi:tʃt], *a.* **1.** (témoignage) qui n'a pas été mis en doute; incontesté. **2.** non accusé.

unimpeded [ʌnim'pi:did], *a.* libre (d'entraves); non entravé; sans obstacle; sans empêchement.

unimportance [ʌnim'pɔ:t(ə)ns], *s.* manque *m*, peu *m*, d'importance; insignifiance *f*.

unimportant [ʌnim'pɔ:t(ə)nt], *a.* sans importance; de peu d'importance; peu important; insignifiant, négligeable; **it's quite u.,** c'est sans conséquence; cela n'a pas d'importance, pas la moindre importance.

unimposing [ʌnim'pouziŋ], *a.* (air, aspect) peu imposant, peu impressionnant.

unimpregnated [ʌn'impregneitid], *a.* **1.** *Biol:* non fécondé; *Breed:* **u. mare,** jument vide. **2.** (*of cloth, etc.*) non imprégné.

unimpressed [ʌnim'prest], *a.* **1.** qui n'est pas impressionné, peu impressionné (**by,** par); **I was u. by his speech,** son discours ne m'a fait aucune impression, m'a laissé froid, ne m'a pas convaincu. **2.** (*of medal, etc.*) sans impression; non (encore) frappé.

unimpressionable [ʌnim'preʃ(ə)nəbl], *a.* peu impressionnable; (juge) froid, impassible.

unimpressive [ʌnim'presiv], *a.* peu impressionnant; peu émouvant; (discours) terne, peu convaincant; (paysage, etc.) peu frappant.

unimproved [ʌnim'pru:vd], *a.* (*a*) non amélioré, non perfectionné; sans amélioration; inchangé; *Agr:* (sol) non amendé; (*b*) *O:* (*of opportunity*) inutilisé.

unimpugnable [ʌnim'pju:nəbl], *a.* (*of statement, etc.*) incontestable, inattaquable.

unimpugned [ʌnim'pju:nd], *a.* (*of statement, etc.*) incontesté.

unimpulsive [ʌnim'pʌlsiv], *a. esp. Lit:* peu impulsif; calme.

unindexed [ʌn'indekst], *a.* (livre, etc.) sans index.

uninervate, uninerved [ju:ni'nə:veit, 'ju:ninə:vd], *a. Bot:* (*of leaf*) uninervé, uninervié.

uninfected [ʌnin'fektid], *a.* **1.** (air, etc.) non infecté, non vicié (**with, by,** par). **2.** *Med:* (*of pers.*) non contaminé, non contagionné; qui a échappé à la contagion; (*of wound*) non infecté.

uninflammable [ʌnin'flæməbl], *a.* ininflammable, incombustible.

uninflated [ʌnin'fleitid], *a.* (*of tyre, etc.*) non gonflé.

uninflected [ʌnin'flektid], *a.* (voix, langue) sans inflexions; (mot) sans inflexion, sans flexion.

uninfluenced [ʌn'influənst], *a.* **1.** (opinion, etc.) libre de toute prévention. **2. to remain u. by s.o.,** ne pas se laisser influencer par qn.

uninfluential [ʌninflu'enʃ(ə)l], *a.* sans influence; qui n'a pas d'influence; peu influent.

uninformed [ʌnin'fɔ:md], *a.* **1. to be u. on a subject,** ne pas connaître un sujet; **to be u. about sth.,** être mal informé, mal renseigné, sur qch.; ne pas être au courant de qch. **2.** (*of pers.*) ignorant, inaverti; (*of mind*) inculte.

uninhabitable [ʌnin'hæbitəbl], *a.* inhabitable.

uninhabited [ʌnin'hæbitid], *a.* inhabité, désert; sans habitants.

uninhibited [ʌnin'hibitid], *a.* sans inhibitions, qui n'a pas d'inhibitions; non refréné.

uninitiated [ʌni'niʃieitid], *a.* non initié (**in,** à); *s.* **the u.,** les profanes *m*, les non-initiés *m*; **this book is too complicated for the u.,** ce livre est trop compliqué pour les profanes.

uninjured [ʌn'indʒəd], *a.* **1.** (*of pers.*) (*a*) sans blessure, sans mal; sain et sauf; indemne; **he escaped u.,** il s'en est tiré sans aucun mal; (*b*) *Jur:* non lésé. **2.** (*of thg*) intact; sans dommage; non endommagé.

uninominal [ju:ni'nɔmin(ə)l], *a.* uninominal, -aux; **u. voting,** scrutin, vote, uninominal, individuel; votation uninominale.

uninquisitive [ʌnin'kwizitiv], *a.* peu curieux, qui n'est pas curieux; discret, -ète.

uninspired [ʌnin'spaiəd], *a.* qui manque d'inspiration, qui n'est pas inspiré; (*of style, etc.*) banal, -als.

uninspiring [ʌnin'spaiəriŋ], *a.* peu inspirant, qui n'est pas inspirant; (film, repas, etc.) (plutôt) médiocre.

uninstructed [ʌnin'strʌktid], *a.* **1.** sans instruction; ignorant. **2.** sans instructions.

uninstructive [ʌnin'strʌktiv], *a.* non instructif; ininstructif.

uninsulated [ʌn'insjuleitid], *a. Ph: etc:* non isolé.

uninsurable [ʌnin'ʃuərəbl], *a.* non assurable.

uninsured [ʌnin'ʃuəd], *a.* non assuré (**against,** contre).

unintellectual [ʌninti'lektjuəl], *a.* peu intellectuel.

unintelligent [ʌnin'telidʒənt], *a.* inintelligent.

unintelligently [ʌnin'telidʒəntli], *adv.* inintelligemment; d'une manière inintelligente; sans intelligence.

unintelligibility [ʌnintelidʒi'biliti], *s.* inintelligibilité *f*.

unintelligible [ʌnin'telidʒibl], *a.* inintelligible.

unintelligibleness [ʌnin'telidʒib(ə)lnis], *s.* inintelligibilité *f*.

unintelligibly [ʌnin'telidʒibili], *adv.* d'une manière peu intelligible; inintelligiblement.

unintended [ʌnin'tendid], *a.* (*a*) (résultat) non prémédité, non voulu; (*b*) involontaire, fait sans intention, non intentionnel.

unintentional [ʌnin'tenʃən(ə)l], *a.* involontaire; non intentionnel; fait sans intention; **it was quite u.,** ce n'était pas fait exprès.

unintentionally [ʌnin'tenʃənəli], *adv.* involontairement; sans intention; **to offend s.o. u.,** froisser qn sans le vouloir; **he did it quite u.,** il ne l'a pas fait exprès.

uninterested [ʌn'int(ə)restid], *a.* non intéressé (**in,** par); indifférent (**in,** à); **to be u. in sth.,** prendre peu d'intérêt à qch.

uninteresting [ʌn'int(ə)restiŋ], *a.* inintéressant; non intéressant; sans intérêt; (*of pers.*) ennuyeux.

uninterestingly [ʌn'int(ə)restiŋli], *adv.* d'une manière peu intéressante.

uninterpretable [ʌnin'tə:pritəbl], *a.* ininterprétable.

uninterpreted [ʌnin'tə:pritid], *a.* ininterprété.

uninterred [ʌnin'tə:d], *a.* non enterré; sans sépulture.

uninterrupted [ʌnintə'rʌptid], *a.* **1.** ininterrompu; sans interruption. **2.** continu; **u. correspondence,** correspondance suivie.

uninterruptedly [ʌnintə'rʌptidli], *adv.* **1.** sans interruption. **2.** d'une façon continue; continuellement.

uninuclear, uninucleate [ju:ni'nju:kliər, -'nju:klieit], *a. Biol:* (cellule) mononucléaire.

uninured [ʌni'njuəd], *a.* non accoutumé, peu habitué, non endurci, non aguerri (**to,** à).

uninvaded [ʌnin'veidid], *a.* non envahi; (domaine, etc.) qui n'a pas subi d'invasion, d'incursion.

uninventive [ʌnin'ventiv], *a.* peu inventif.

uninvested [ʌnin'vestid], *a.* **1.** *esp. Lit:* non revêtu (**with,** de). **2.** (argent) non placé.

uninvited [ʌnin'vaitid], *a.* sans être invité; sans invitation; **u. guest,** (i) visiteur, -euse, inattendu(e), (ii) intrus, -use; **to come u.,** venir sans invitation; **to do sth. u.,** faire qch. sans y avoir été invité.

uninviting [ʌnin'vaitiŋ], *a.* (*of pers., appearance, etc.*) peu attirant, peu attrayant; (*of appearance*) peu engageant; (*of food*) peu appétissant.

unio, *pl.* **-os, -onides** ['ju:niou, -ouz, -'ounidi:z], *s. Moll:* unio *m*, mulette *f*.

uniocular [ju:ni'ɔkjulər], *a. Z: etc:* unioculé.

union ['ju:niən], *s.* **1.** union *f*; (*a*) **u. of a province with France,** réunion *f* d'une province à la France; *Hist:* **the U.,** l'union (i) des couronnes de l'Angleterre et de l'Écosse (1603), (ii) des parlements (1707), (iii) de la Grande Bretagne avec l'Irlande (1801); (*b*) union, mariage *m*; (*c*) concorde *f*, harmonie *f*, entente *f*; **they lived together in perfect u.,** ils ont vécu ensemble en parfaite harmonie. **2.** (*a*) **the (American) U.,** les États-Unis, l'Union (américaine); *Hist:* **the South African U.,** l'Union sud-africaine; *Hist:* **the French U.,** l'Union française; **Western European U.,** union de l'Europe occidentale; **customs u.,** union douanière, des douanes; **Universal Postal U.,** Union postale universelle; (*b*) syndicat (ouvrier); **to form, join, a u.,** se syndiquer; **u. member,** syndiqué(e); membre *m* du, d'un, syndicat; **u. regulations,** règles syndicales; **u. hours,** heures conformes aux règles syndicales; **non-u. workers,** ouvriers, -ières, non syndiqué(e)s; **u. recognition,** reconnaissance syndicale; *Fr.C:* agrément syndical; *NAm:* **u. shop,** atelier *m* d'ouvriers syndiqués; (*c*) *Hist:* union de plusieurs communes pour l'administration de l'Assistance publique; **u. (workhouse),** asile *m* des pauvres à l'usage de plusieurs communes. **3.** (*a*) soudure *f* (des os, etc.); raccordement *m* (de fils, de tuyaux, etc.); (*b*) *Mec.E: etc:* **u. (joint),** raccord *m*; **joint u.,** raccord manchon; **pipe u.,** raccord de tuyaux; **elbow u.,** raccord coudé; **T u.,** raccord en T; té *m*; **u. nut,** raccord fileté; **u. nut joint,** raccord à vis; **movable u.,** raccord movible. **4. U. Flag, Jack,** pavillon *m* britannique, du Royaume-Uni. **5.** *Tex:* **u. (cloth),** tissu mélangé; tissu mi-laine. **6.** *Cost: U.S:* **u. suit,** combinaison *f* (une pièce).

Unionidae [ju:ni'ɔnidi:], *s.pl. Moll:* unionidés *m*.

unionism ['ju:niənizm], *s.* **1.** *Ind:* syndicalisme (ouvrier). **2.** *Pol:* unionisme *m*.

unionist ['ju:niənist], *s.* **1.** *Ind:* syndicaliste *mf*, (ouvrier, -ière) syndiqué(e). **2.** *Pol:* unioniste *mf*; *Hist:* **the u. party,** le parti unioniste ((i) les adversaires du *Home Rule* (pour l'Irlande); (ii) *U.S:* le parti qui s'opposait à la Sécession).

unionize ['ju:niənaiz], *v.tr. Ind:* syndiquer (des ouvriers, etc.).

unionized[1] ['ju:niənaizd], *a. Ind:* syndiqué.

unionized[2] [ʌn'aiənaizd], *a.* non ionisé.

uniovular, uniovulate [ju:ni'ouvjulər, -'ouvjuleit], *a. Nat.Hist:* uniovulé.

uniparous [ju:'nipərəs], *a. Biol:* unipare.

unipersonal [ju:ni'pə:s(ə)n(ə)l], *a.* **1.** *Gram:* (verbe) unipersonnel, impersonnel. **2.** (Dieu) en une personne.

unipetalous [ju:ni'petələs], *a. Bot:* unipétale, monopétale.

uniphase ['ju:nifeiz], *a. El:* monophasé.

uniplanar [ju:ni'pleinər], *a.* sur un seul plan; *Mth:* **u. figure,** figure plane.

unipolar [ju:ni'poulər], *a. El:* unipolaire; *Biol:* **u. cell,** cellule unipolaire; *Pol:* **u. coalition,** coalition unipolaire.

unipolarity [ju:nipou'læriti], *s. El:* unipolarité *f.*

uniprocessing [ju:ni'prousesiŋ], *s. Cmptr:* traitement *m* (des données) avec une seule unité centrale.

uniprocessor [ju:ni'prousesər], *s. Cmptr:* unité centrale unique.

uniprogramming [ju:ni'prougræmiŋ], *s. Cmptr:* monoprogrammation *f.*

unipunch ['ju:nipʌntʃ], *s. Cmptr:* poinçonneuse manuelle, trou par trou; perforateur manuel.

unique [ju:'ni:k]. **1.** *a.* unique; seul en son genre; **a u. opportunity,** une occasion unique, exceptionnelle; **a u. talent,** un talent unique, d'exception, exceptionnel, extraordinaire; **his position is u.,** son cas est tout à fait particulier. **2.** *s.* (*a*) chose *f* unique; *Num: etc:* médaille *f*, pièce *f*, amphore *f*, verre *m*, etc., unique; (*b*) *Lit:* **the u.,** l'unique *m.*

uniquely [ju:'ni:kli], *adv.* d'une manière unique; exceptionnellement, extraordinairement; **u. beautiful,** d'une beauté unique.

uniqueness [ju:'ni:knis], *s.* caractère *m* unique, exceptionnel; nature *f* unique, extraordinaire; unicité *f.*

uniradical [ju:ni'rædik(ə)l], *a. Bot: Anat:* uniradiculaire.

uniserial, uniseriate [ju:ni'siəriəl, -'siərieit], *a. Nat.Hist:* (filament, etc.) unisérié.

unisex ['ju:niseks], *a.* (pantalon, boutique, etc.) unisexe.

unisexual [ju:ni'seksjuəl], *a. Nat.Hist:* unisexué, unisexuel.

unisexuality [ju:niseksju'æliti], *s. Nat.Hist:* unisexualité *f.*

unison ['ju:nis(ə)n, -z(ə)n], *s.* **1.** *Mus: etc:* unisson *m*; **in u.,** à l'unisson (**with,** de); **u. (string),** corde qui résonne à l'unisson; **they both replied in u.,** tous les deux ont répondu en même temps, simultanément, ensemble. **2.** unisson, accord *m*; **to be in u. with s.o.,** être à l'unisson de, en accord avec, qn; agir de concert avec qn; (*of parts*) **to rotate in u.,** tourner à la même vitesse.

unisonal, unisonant, unisonous [ju:'nisən(ə)l, -nənt, -nəs], *a. Mus: etc:* à l'unisson (**with,** de); unissonnant.

unissued [ʌn'isju:d], *a. Fin:* **u. stocks, shares,** titres non encore émis; actions non encore émises; titres, actions, à la souche.

unit ['ju:nit], *s.* **1.** unité *f*; *Mth:* **units and tens,** unités et dizaines; **units column,** colonne des unités; *Com: Ind:* **each box contains a hundred units,** chaque boîte contient cent unités; **u. cost (price),** prix de revient unitaire; **u. price,** prix unitaire, de l'unité; *Pharm:* **(biological) u.,** unité (biologique); **a 500,000 u. antibiotic,** un antibiotique à 500 000 unités; *Biol:* **u. character,** caractère *m* unité; *Cryst:* **u. cell,** maille *f*, motif *m* (du réseau). **2.** (*a*) unité (de longueur, de poids, etc.); **u. of capacity, of volume, of time,** unité de capacité, de volume, de temps; **u. of area, u. area, u. of surface,** unité de surface; **u. of angle,** unité d'angle; *Mth:* **arbitrary u.,** unité arbitraire; **derived u.,** unité dérivée; **practical u.,** unité pratique; **standard u.,** module *m*; **u. vector,** vecteur unitaire; *Ph:* **physical u.,** unité physique; **SI units,** unités SI; **CGS units,** unités CGS; **u. of mass,** unité de masse; **u. of heat, thermal u.,** unité de chaleur, unité thermique; *Atom.Ph:* **atomic u.,** unité atomique; **radiation u.,** unité de rayonnement; **irradiation u.,** unité d'irradiation; *El:* **electrical u.,** unité électrique; **u. of current,** unité de courant; **u. of resistance,** unité de résistance; **u. of illumination,** unité d'éclairement; **u. of light,** unité d'intensité lumineuse; **u. of luminous flux, of magnetic flux,** unité de flux lumineux, de flux magnétique; **u. step function,** pas *m* unité; *Mec:* **mechanical u.,** unité mécanique; **u. of energy, of work,** unité d'énergie, de travail; **u. of force, of power,** unité de force, de puissance; **u. of stress,** unité de charge; **u. of acceleration,** unité d'accélération; **u. of velocity,** unité de vitesse; *Av:* **u. thrust,** poussée *f* unitaire (d'un réacteur); *Tp:* **u. call,** unité de conversation, de communication; **u. charge,** taxe *f* unitaire; *Tg:* **u. interval,** pas, intervalle *m* (au collecteur); *Fin:* **u. of account,** unité de compte; **monetary u.,** unité monétaire; **u. trust,** société de placement(s), d'investissement à capital variable; *Pol.Ec:* **u. of consumption, of production,** unité de consommation, de production; **man work u., labour u.,** unité de travail; *Mil:* **u. of supply,** unité d'approvisionnement; *Artil:* **u. of fire,** unité de feu; (*b*) **the species is the u. of the genus,** l'espèce est l'unité du genre; **in England the county is the largest administrative u. for local government,** en Angleterre le comté est la plus grande division administrative; **information u.,** service *m* d'informations; *Med:* **intensive care, intensive therapy, u.** = service, centre *m*, de réanimation; **X-ray u.,** service de radiologie; *Petr:* **cracking u.,** unité de craquage, de cracking; **topping and cracking u.,** unité, installation *f*, de fractionnement et de craquage; **dewaxing u.,** unité de déparaffinage; *Mil:* **administrative u.,** unité administrative; **leading u.,** unité de premier échelon; **major, minor, u.,** grande, petite, unité; **basic u.,** unité élémentaire; **basic tactical u.,** unité tactique élémentaire; **tactical u.,** unité tactique; **adjacent units,** unités encadrantes; **auxiliary units,** formations *f* auxiliaires; **component u.,** unité constitutive; **self-contained u.,** unité autonome, organique, formant corps; **support u.,** unité de soutien, d'appui, de deuxième échelon; **follow-up u.,** unité de deuxième échelon; **subordinate u.,** unité subordonnée; **skeleton u.,** unité cadre; **reserved units,** unités réservées, en réserve; **fighting u.,** *U.S:* **combat u.,** unité combattante; **attacking u., u. told off for (the) attack,** unité d'attaque; **shock u.,** unité de choc; **naval u.,** unité navale; **air force u.,** unité, groupe *m*, de l'aéronautique, de l'armée de l'air; **air, aviation, u.,** unité aérienne, d'aviation; **u. reserves,** réserves d'unité; **u. equipment,** matériels organiques d'unité; **to activate, form, a u.,** constituer, mettre sur pied, une unité; **to disband, inactivate, a u.,** dissoudre une unité; (*c*) *Mec.E: etc:* unité, élément *m*, organe *m*; ensemble *m*, bloc *m*, groupe; **control u.,** élément de contrôle, de régulation, de réglage; **safety u.,** élément de sécurité; **generating u.,** élément générateur; **heating u.,** élément chauffant; **construction u.,** élément de construction; **standardized units,** éléments normalisés; **self-contained u.,** ensemble autonome; *Aut:* **motor u.,** bloc-moteur *m*; **motor cycle u.,** groupe moto; **hydraulic u.,** groupe hydraulique; **connecting u.,** bloc de raccordement; **the engine forms a u. with the transmission,** le moteur fait bloc avec la transmission; *Veh:* **haulage u.,** engin *m* de transport, véhicule moteur; *Min: Petr:* **rotary u.,** trépan rotatif; rotary *m*; *El:* **power supply u.,** groupe d'alimentation; *Av:* **ground power u.,** groupe de démarrage au sol; *Cmptr:* **arithmetic, calculating, computer, u.,** organe, unité, élément, de calcul(ateur), de calculatrice, électronique; calculateur *m*; calculatrice *f*; **processing u.,** unité de traitement; **central processing u.,** unité centrale; **terminal u.,** (poste) terminal *m*; appareil terminal; **input u.,** organe, appareil, unité, d'entrée; **output u.,** appareil périphérique, élément, de sortie; **input/output u.,** élément, dispositif *m*, équipement *m* (d')entrée-sortie; **gating u.,** élément porté; **(magnetic) tape u.,** dérouleur *m*, unité, de bande (magnétique); **disc storage u.,** unité de disques; **audio response u.,** unité de réponse vocale; **(visual) display u.,** dispositif, unité, d'affichage; (terminal à) écran *m* de visualisation; **u. distance code,** code à signaux à espacement unitaire; **u. record,** support *m* de mémoire, *esp.* carte perforée; **u. string,** chaîne unitaire; *Cin:* **sound(-reproducing) u.,** lecteur *m* de son; *Const:* **u. construction,** préfabrication *f*; **u. furniture,** meubles par éléments, formés d'éléments; **kitchen u.,** élément de cuisine; **hob u.,** table *f* de cuisson; **u. heater,** aérotherme *m.*

Unitarian [ju:ni'tɛəriən]. **1.** *a. & s. Rel:* unitarien, -ienne; unitaire (*mf*). **2.** *a. Pol: etc:* (système, etc.) unitaire.

Unitarianism [ju:ni'tɛəriənizm], *s. Rel: Pol: etc:* unitarisme *m.*

unitary ['ju:nit(ə)ri], *a.* (système, gouvernement, etc.) unitaire.

unite [ju:'nait]. **1.** *v.tr.* (*a*) unir, amalgamer (une chose à une autre, deux choses ensemble); relier, raccorder (deux voies, etc.); **to u. one country to, with, another,** réunir un pays à un autre; **when Brittany was united to, with, France,** lorsque la Bretagne fut unie à la France; **to u. two armies,** joindre, combiner, deux armées; **to u. idealism with practical common sense,** allier l'idéalisme au bon sens pratique; (*b*) mettre (les gens) d'accord; unifier (un parti, etc.); **common interests that u. two countries,** intérêts communs qui allient, associent, deux pays; (*c*) unir (en mariage). **2.** *v.i.* (*a*) s'unir, se joindre, s'unifier (**with,** à); (*b*) (*of two or more pers. or thgs*) s'unir; se réunir; (*of party, etc.*) s'unifier; (*of states*) se confédérer; (*of styles, movements, etc.*) s'amalgamer, confluer; (*of colours*) s'allier, s'accorder; (*of water*) se conglomérer; *Ch:* (*of atoms*) s'unir, se combiner; **to u. against s.o., sth.,** s'unir contre qn, qch.; **to u. in doing sth.,** se mettre d'accord pour faire qch.; *Pol:* **to u. against a party,** faire bloc contre un parti.

united [ju(:)'naitid], *a.* uni, réuni; unifié; **u. efforts,** efforts conjugués, réunis; **u. we stand, divided we fall,** l'union fait la force; **to present a u. front,** présenter un front uni; *Geog:* **the U. Kingdom (of Great Britain and Northern Ireland),** le Royaume-Uni (de Grande-Bretagne et de l'Irlande du Nord); **the U. States (of America),** les États-Unis (d'Amérique); **the U. States of Mexico,** les États-Unis mexicains; **the U. States of Brazil,** la République des États du Brésil; **the U. Arab Republic,** la République Arabe Unie, **the U. Arab Emirates,** les Émirats arabes unis; *Hist:* **the U. Provinces,** les Provinces-Unies (des Pays-Bas).

unitedly [ju(:)'naitidli], *adv.* (*a*) conjointement, ensemble; (*b*) de concert, d'accord.

uniterm ['ju:nitə:m], *s. Cmptr:* descripteur *m*; **u. system,** système de recherche documentaire à descripteurs.

uniterming ['ju:nitə:miŋ], *s. Cmptr:* choix descripteur.

uniting[1] [ju(:)'naitiŋ], *a.* qui unit, qui joint; unitif; unificateur, -trice.

uniting[2], *s.* union *f*, réunion *f.*

unitive ['ju:nitiv], *a.* unitif.

unity ['ju:niti], *s.* unité *f.* **1.** *Mth:* **to reduce a coefficient to u.,** réduire un coefficient à l'unité; **the family considered as a u.,** la famille considérée comme une unité. **2.** concorde *f*, accord *m*, harmonie *f*; **national, political, u.,** unité nationale, politique; **to live together in u.,** vivre en bonne intelligence, en parfait accord, en parfaite harmonie; *Prov:* **u. is strength,** l'union fait la force. **3.** (*a*) **the U. of God,** l'unité de Dieu; (*b*) **there is no u. in his work,** ses œuvres manquent d'unité, d'harmonie; *Lit:* **the three (dramatic) unities,** les trois unités (dramatiques); **u. of time, of place, of action,** unité de temps, de lieu, d'action; (*c*) *Jur:* **u. of interest, of title, of time,** communauté *f* de droit, de titre, de durée; **u. of possession,** (i) communauté de possession; (ii) consolidation *f* de la possession; extinction *f* de servitude (par fusion).

univalent [ju:ni'veilənt], *a. Ch:* univalent, monovalent.

univalve ['ju:nivælv], *a. & s. Moll:* univalve (*m*).

univalved ['ju:nivælvd], *a. Nat.Hist:* univalve.

universal [ju:ni'və:s(ə)l]. **1.** *a.* (*a*) (remède, langage, etc.) universel; **u. suffrage,** suffrage universel; **he's a u. favourite,** tout le monde l'aime; **this practice is becoming u.,** cet usage devient universel, commence à s'universaliser; cet usage commence à se répandre, à se généraliser, dans le monde entier; *Log:* **u. proposition,** proposition universelle; *Jur:* **u. legatee,** légataire universel; *Com: Jur:* **u. agent,** mandataire général; (*b*) *Mec.E: etc:* **u. calliper,** compas universel; **u. chuck,** mandrin universel; **u. wrench,** clef universelle; *El:* **u. motor,** moteur universel, moteur tous courants; *W.Tel:* **u. receiver,** récepteur *m* toutes ondes, tous courants; *Atom.Ph:* **u. manipulator,** manipulateur universel. **2.** *s.* (*a*) *Log:* **(abstract) u.,** proposition universelle; (*b*) *Phil: A:* universel *m*, *pl.* -aux.

universalism [ju:ni'və:səlizm], *s. Theol: Phil:* universalisme *m.*

universalist [ju:ni'və:səlist], *s. Theol: Phil:* universaliste *mf.*

universality, universalness [ju:nivə:'sæliti, -'və:s(ə)lnis], *s.* universalité *f* (d'une église, d'une langue, etc.).

universalization [ju:nivə:səlai'zeiʃ(ə)n], *s.* universalisation *f.*

universalize [ju:ni'və:səlaiz], *v.tr.* universaliser, généraliser, répandre (un usage, etc.).

universally [ju:ni'və:səli], *adv.* universellement; **it is u. agreed that he is a most intelligent man,** tout le monde s'accorde à reconnaître l'intelligence de cet homme; **his genius is u. acknowledged,** on lui reconnaît du génie dans le monde entier.

universe ['ju:nivə:s], *s.* univers *m*; **the wonders of the u.,** les merveilles de la création.

university [ju:ni'və:siti], *s.* (*a*) université *f*; **he's been to u., he's had a u. education,** il a étudié à l'université, il a fait des études supérieures; **he was at, he went to, London U.,** il a fait ses études à l'université de Londres; **when I was at u.,** quand j'étais à l'université, à la faculté, *F:* à la fac; quand j'étais étudiant; **u. education,** études universitaires; enseignement supérieur; éducation universitaire; **u. lecture,** conférence de faculté; **u. professor,** professeur de faculté; (professeur) universitaire *mf*; **u. student,** étudiant, -ante, à l'université; **u. library,** bibliothèque de l'université; bibliothèque universitaire; **u. town,** ville universitaire; **the redbrick universities,** certaines universités anglaises de fondation moderne; **the Open U.,** *A:* **the U. of the Air** = le centre de Télé-enseignement universitaire; (*b*) **the whole u. is**

against it, toute l'université s'y oppose.
univibrator [ju:nivai'breitər], *s. Telecomm:* multivibrateur *m* monostable.
univocal [ju:'nivək(ə)l], *a.* univoque.
univoltine [ju:ni'voulti:n], *a. Ent:* univoltin, monovoltin.
unjoined [ʌn'dʒɔind], *a.* **1.** disjoint, séparé. **2.** qui n'a pas été joint, uni.
unjudged [ʌn'dʒʌdʒd], *a.* **1.** qui n'est pas (encore) jugé; à être jugé. **2.** (être condamné) sans procès, sans jugement.
unjudicial [ʌndʒu:'diʃ(ə)l], *a.* (conduite, etc.) peu judiciaire.
unjust [ʌn'dʒʌst], *a.* **1.** (*a*) injuste (**to,** envers, avec); **my suspicions were u.,** mes soupçons étaient mal fondés; (*b*) **u. weight,** faux poids. **2.** *A:* infidèle; déloyal, -aux.
unjustifiable [ʌndʒʌsti'faiəbl], *a.* injustifiable, inexcusable.
unjustifiably [ʌndʒʌsti'faiəbli], *adv.* d'une manière injustifiable, inexcusable; sans justification.
unjustified [ʌn'dʒʌstifaid], *a.* (*a*) injustifié; non justifié; (*of action, etc.*) non motivé; **he was absolutely u. in doing this,** il était absolument dans son tort en faisant cela; *Jur:* **u. enrichment,** enrichissement sans cause; (*b*) *Typ: Cmptr:* (*of line*) non justifié, mal justifié.
unjustly [ʌn'dʒʌstli], *adv.* injustement.
unkempt [ʌn'kem(p)t], *a.* **1.** (*of hair, etc.*) mal peigné, ébouriffé; (*of appearance*) négligé, débraillé; (*of pers.*) hirsute, dépeigné; débraillé. **2.** (*of garden, etc.*) peu soigné; mal tenu; négligé; en désordre.
unkennel [ʌn'kenl], *v.tr.* (**unkennelled**) **1.** *Lit:* faire sortir (les chiens) du chenil. **2.** *Ven:* lancer (un renard).
unkey [ʌn'ki:], *v.tr. Mec.E: etc:* décaler (un piston, etc.); déclaveter (une poulie, etc.).
unkind [ʌn'kaind], *a.* (i) dur; cruel; sévère; (ii) peu aimable; pas gentil; *esp. Lit:* (*of weather*) peu favorable; (*of climate*) rude; **u. fate,** sort impitoyable, cruel; **that's very u. of him,** c'est très mal à lui; ce n'est pas gentil de sa part; **to say u. things to s.o., about s.o.,** dire des méchancetés *f* à qn, sur le compte de qn; **to be u. to s.o.,** être méchant avec qn; se montrer dur envers qn; **her aunt is u. to her,** sa tante la traite mal; **he was u. enough to say it to me,** il a eu la méchanceté de me le dire.
unkindliness [ʌn'kaindlinis], *s.* manque *m* d'amabilité, de gentillesse (**to,** envers, pour).
unkindly[1] [ʌn'kaindli], *adv.* **1.** (i) méchamment, durement; sévèrement; (ii) sans gentillesse; peu aimablement; **to look u. at, on, s.o.,** regarder qn d'un œil malveillant; **don't take it u. if I say it frankly,** ne soyez pas offensé, ne le prenez pas en mauvaise part, si je vous le dis franchement; **he took u. to that remark,** il a mal accepté cette réflexion.
unkindly[2], *a.* **1.** peu aimable, peu gentil; (*of remark*) méchant. **2.** *Lit:* (temps) peu favorable; (climat) rude.
unkindness [ʌn'kaindnis], *s.* manque *m* de gentillesse; méchanceté *f*, sévérité *f*; rigueur *f* (du climat); cruauté *f* (du sort).
unkingly [ʌn'kiŋli], *a.* indigne d'un roi; peu royal, -aux.
unknightly [ʌn'naitli], *a. A: & Lit:* indigne d'un chevalier; déloyal, -aux.
unknot [ʌn'nɔt], *v.tr.* (**unknotted**) dénouer; défaire les nœuds (d'une ficelle, etc.).
unknowable [ʌn'nouəbl], *a. & s.* inconnaissable (*m*).
unknowing [ʌn'nouiŋ], *a.* ignorant; inconscient (**of,** de).
unknowingly [ʌn'nouiŋli], *adv.* inconsciemment; sans le savoir; (pécher) par ignorance; (offenser qn) en toute ignorance.
unknown [ʌn'noun]. **1.** *a.* (*a*) inconnu (**to,** à, de); ignoré (**to,** de); **u. land,** terre inconnue; **u. person,** inconnu, -ue; **u. writer,** écrivain obscur, sans renom, inconnu; **the U. Soldier,** le Soldat inconnu; *Jur:* **verdict against person or persons u.,** verdict contre inconnu; **this is a process u. to us, this process is u. to us,** c'est un procédé qui nous est inconnu; nous ignorons ce procédé; nous ne savons rien de ce procédé; *adv.* **he did it u. to me,** il l'a fait à mon insu, sans que je le sache; (*b*) *Mth: etc:* **u. quantity,** (quantité) inconnue *f*; **he's an u. quantity,** il a des réactions imprévisibles; on ne sait pas comment il va réagir. **2.** *s.* (*a*) (*pers.*) inconnu; (*b*) *Mth:* inconnue; (*c*) **the u.,** l'inconnu.
unlabelled [ʌn'leib(ə)ld], *a.* (*of bottle, etc.*) non étiqueté, sans étiquette; (*of document, etc.*) sans référence, sans indication; *Cmptr:* (*of magnetic tape, etc.*) sans labels.
unlaboured [ʌn'leibəd], *a.* (style) non travaillé, non élaboré, facile, naturel, coulant.
unlace [ʌn'leis], *v.tr.* délacer, défaire (ses chaussures, etc.); délacer (un corset, qn).
unlade [ʌn'leid], *v.tr.* (*p.t.* **unladed;** *p.p.* **unladen**) décharger (un bateau, une cargaison); débateler (des marchandises); *v.i.* **we will u. tomorrow,** nous effectuerons le déchargement demain.
unladen [ʌn'leidn], *a. Nau:* sans charge; à vide; *Av: Veh:* **u. weight,** poids à vide.
unlading [ʌn'leidiŋ], *s.* déchargement *m*, débatelage *m*.
unladylike [ʌn'leidilaik], *a.* indigne d'une femme bien élevée; mal élevée; (*of manners*) peu distingué; **it's u. to yawn in public,** une jeune fille bien élevée ne bâille pas en public.
unlaid [ʌn'leid], *a.* **1.** (cordage) décommis, détordu. **2.** (*a*) non posé; **the carpets were still u.,** les tapis n'étaient pas encore posés; **supper was ready and the table was still u.,** le dîner était prêt et la table n'était pas encore mise; (*b*) **u. ghost,** esprit, revenant, non exorcisé; (*c*) (papier) non vergé, sans vergeures.
unlamented [ʌnlə'mentid], *a.* non regretté, non pleuré; **he died u.,** il est mort sans être regretté.
unlash [ʌn'læʃ], *v.tr.* démarrer, détacher (un bateau); déguinder, débréler (une charge); défrapper (un palan).
unlatch [ʌn'lætʃ], *v.tr.* déloqueter, ouvrir (une porte); lever le loquet (d'une porte).
unlawful [ʌn'lɔ:ful], *a.* (*a*) illégal, -aux; contraire à la loi; (*b*) (moyen, etc.) illicite; (acte, etc.) irrégulier, illégitime; (*c*) (enfant) illégitime.
unlawfully [ʌn'lɔ:fuli], *adv.* (*a*) illégalement; contrairement à la loi; (*b*) illicitement; irrégulièrement, illégitimement.
unlawfulness [ʌn'lɔ:fulnis], *s.* (*a*) illégalité *f*; (*b*) illégitimité *f*, irrégularité *f* (d'un acte, etc.).
unlay [ʌn'lei], *v.tr.* (**unlaid** [-'leid]) décommettre, détordre, décorder (des cordages).
unlead [ʌn'led], *v.tr. Typ:* désinterligner (la composition); enlever les interlignes (de la composition).
unleaded [ʌn'ledid], *a. Typ:* désinterligné; sans interlignes.
unlearn [ʌn'lə:n], *v.tr.* (*p.t. & p.p.* **unlearnt** [-'lə:nt], *occ.* **unlearned** ['lə:nd]) désapprendre, oublier (qch.); **to u. a habit,** se défaire d'une habitude.
unlearned, *a.* **1.** [ʌn'lə:nid], ignorant; sans instruction; inculte. **2.** [ʌn'lə:nd] (*a*) peu versé (**in,** dans); **he was not u. in philosophy,** il connaissait bien la philosophie; (*b*) (*also* **unlearnt** [ʌn'lə:nt]) non appris; **to leave a lesson u.,** ne pas apprendre une leçon.
unleash [ʌn'li:ʃ], *v.tr.* (*a*) détacher, lâcher, découpler (des chiens); (*b*) déchaîner (les passions, etc.); **to u. a nuclear war,** déclencher, provoquer, une guerre nucléaire.
unleavened [ʌn'lev(ə)nd], *a.* **1.** (pain) sans levain, azyme; *Jew.Rel:* **the feast of u. bread,** la fête des azymes. **2.** *Lit:* **her dislike of him is not u. with jealousy,** son aversion pour lui n'est pas sans un levain de jalousie.
unless [ʌn'les]. **1.** *conj.* à moins que + *sub*; **u. it's you,** à moins que ce ne soit vous; **he will do nothing u. you ask him to,** il ne fera rien à moins que vous ne le lui demandiez; **you'll be too late u. you leave at once,** vous arriverez trop tard à moins de partir immédiatement, si vous ne partez pas immédiatement; **they never go out u. they have to,** ils ne sortent jamais à moins d'y être contraints; **u. I'm mistaken,** à moins que je (ne) me trompe, si je ne me trompe (pas); **u. otherwise stated,** sauf indication contraire; **u. I hear to the contrary,** sauf avis contraire; sauf contrordre; **u. and until I receive a full apology,** à moins d'amende honorable. **2.** *prep. A:* sauf, excepté; **no other mineral, u. iron,** aucun autre minéral, sauf peut-être le fer.
unlettable [ʌn'letəbl], *a.* (maison, etc.) qu'on ne peut louer.
unlettered [ʌn'letəd], *a.* peu lettré; inculte; ignorant.
unlicensed [ʌn'lais(ə)nst], *a.* (*a*) non autorisé; illicite; (*b*) non patenté; non breveté; **u. premises,** établissement où la vente des boissons alcooliques n'est pas autorisée; **u. taxi, broker,** taxi, courtier, marron; (*c*) (*of car, etc.*) = sans vignette.
unlighted [ʌn'laitid], *a. Lit:* **1.** (feu) non allumé. **2.** (couloir, etc.) non éclairé, sans lumière.
unlike [ʌn'laik], *a. & prep.* (*a*) différent, dissemblable; **u. s.o., sth.,** différent de qn, qch.; dissemblable de qn, qch.; **the portrait is utterly u. him,** le portrait n'est absolument pas ressemblant, ne lui ressemble absolument pas; **they're completely u. (each other),** ils ne se ressemblent pas du tout; **he's not u. his sister,** il ressemble assez à sa sœur; **his house is not so very much u. ours,** sa maison ressemble assez à la nôtre, ne diffère pas beaucoup de la nôtre; **he, u. his father,** lui, à la différence de, contrairement à, son père; (*b*) **it's u. him to do such a thing,** cela ne lui ressemble pas, ce n'est pas dans ses habitudes, de faire une chose pareille; **that was very u. him!** on ne le reconnaît pas là! on ne s'attendait pas à ça de sa part!
unlikeable [ʌn'laikəbl], *a.* (*of pers.*) antipathique; peu sympathique; (*of thg*) peu agréable.
unlikelihood, unlikeliness [ʌn'laiklihud, -'laiklinis], *s.* improbabilité *f*.
unlikely [ʌn'laikli], *a.* **1.** (*a*) improbable, peu probable; (*of explanation*) peu plausible, invraisemblable; **that's most, very, u.,** c'est fort improbable, très peu probable; **it's not (at all) u.,** c'est très probable, bien possible; cela se pourrait bien; il y a des chances; **it's not at all u. that he'll come,** il se pourrait bien, il n'est pas impossible, qu'il vienne; **it's u. to happen,** cela ne risque pas d'arriver; (*b*) **he's u. to do it,** il est peu probable qu'il le fasse; il y a peu de chances pour qu'il le fasse. **2. he's an u. man for the job,** il ne semble pas être destiné à ce travail; **he married the most u. girl,** on ne s'attendait pas à ce qu'il épouse une femme comme elle; **we found the ring in a most u. place,** nous avons retrouvé la bague dans un endroit auquel nous n'aurions jamais pensé; *F:* **she wears the most u. clothes,** elle s'habille d'une façon invraisemblable.
unlikeness [ʌn'laiknis], *s.* dissemblance *f* (**to,** de); différence *f*.
unlimber [ʌn'limbər], *v.tr. & i. Artil:* décrocher l'avant-train (d'une pièce).
unlimited [ʌn'limitid], *a.* (*of time, resources, etc.*) illimité; sans limites; (*of patience, etc.*) sans borne(s); (*of hired car*) **u. mileage** = kilométrage illimité; *Fin:* **u. liability,** responsabilité illimitée; **there were u. supplies of beer,** la bière était à discrétion.
unlined[1] [ʌn'laind], *a.* (manteau, etc.) sans doublure.
unlined[2], *a.* (visage) sans rides; (papier) uni, non réglé.
unlink [ʌn'liŋk], *v.tr.* **1.** défaire les anneaux (d'une chaîne). **2.** détacher (deux choses liées ensemble); décrocher, détacher (une remorque, etc.).
unliquidated [ʌn'likwideitid], *a.* (*of debt*) non liquidé, non amorti; (*of company*) non liquidé.
unlisted [ʌn'listid], *a.* non inscrit, qui ne figure pas, sur une liste; *St.Exch:* non inscrit à la cote (officielle).
unlit [ʌn'lit], *a.* **1.** (couloir, etc.) non éclairé, sans lumière. **2.** (feu) non allumé.
unlivable [ʌn'livəbl], *a.* **1.** (vie) impossible, insupportable, intenable; (existence) invivable. **2. u. (in),** (chambre, pays) inhabitable.
unload [ʌn'loud], *v.tr. & i.* **1.** (*a*) décharger (un bateau, une voiture, des marchandises); décharger, débarquer (une cargaison); faire le déchargement; (*of ship's master*) débarquer la cargaison; (*b*) *Fig:* se débarrasser, se défaire, de (qch.); *Com: F:* mettre (des marchandises) sur le marché à bas prix (pour les vendre plus rapidement); *St.Exch:* **to u. stock on the market,** se décharger d'un paquet d'actions. **2.** décharger, désarmer (un fusil); *Phot:* décharger (un appareil).
unloaded [ʌn'loudid], *a.* **1.** (*a*) déchargé; (*b*) (fusil) déchargé, désarmé. **2.** (*a*) non chargé; sans chargement; (*b*) (fusil) non armé, non chargé.
unloader [ʌn'loudər], *s.* (*pers.*) débardeur, -euse; docker *m*; (*device*) déchargeur *m*.
unloading [ʌn'loudiŋ], *s.* déchargement *m*; débarquement *m*.
unlock [ʌn'lɔk], *v.tr.* **1.** ouvrir, déverrouiller (une porte, etc.); faire jouer la serrure (d'une porte, etc.); **I heard him u. the door,** je l'ai entendu tourner la clef dans la serrure. **2.** révéler, découvrir (un secret, etc.). **3.** (*a*) débloquer (une roue, un écrou); *Typ:* desserrer (la forme); (*b*) *Rail:* déclencher (un signal); **to u. the switch,** déverrouiller l'aiguille de raccordement; *Aut:* **to u. the steering gear,** déverrouiller le mécanisme de direction; (*c*) déverrouiller (une arme); (*d*) (*with passive force*) se débloquer, se desserrer, se déclencher, se déverrouiller.
unlocked [ʌn'lɔkt], *a.* (*of door, etc.*) qui n'est pas fermé à clef.
unlocking [ʌn'lɔkiŋ], *s.* **1.** ouverture *f*, déverrouillage *m* (d'une porte, etc.). **2.** (*a*) *Mec.E:* déblocage *m*; déverrouillage; (*b*) déverrouillage (d'une arme).
unlooked [ʌn'lukt], *a.* **1. u. at,** négligé, oublié; qu'on ne regarde pas; qu'on n'a pas examiné. **2. u. for,** (événement) inattendu, imprévu.
unloose(n) [ʌn'lu:s(n)], *v.tr.* délier, détacher; **to unloosen one's grip,** lâcher prise; **to u. s.o.'s tongue,** délier la langue à qn.
unlovable [ʌn'lʌvəbl], *a.* peu attachant.
unloved [ʌn'lʌvd], *a.* qui n'est pas aimé.
unlovely [ʌn'lʌvli], *a.* (*of pers.*) sans charme, disgracieux; (*of thg*) laid, déplaisant; peu attrayant.
unloving [ʌn'lʌviŋ], *a.* peu affectueux, peu aimant; froid.
unluckily [ʌn'lʌkili], *adv.* malheureusement, par malheur, malencontreusement.
unluckiness [ʌn'lʌkinis], *s.* malchance *f*, malheur *m*; *F:* déveine *f*.
unlucky [ʌn'lʌki], *a.* **1.** (*a*) (*of pers.*) malheureux, malchanceux, infortuné; **to be u.,** ne pas avoir de chance; avoir de la malchance; jouer de malheur, de

malchance; *F:* ne pas avoir de veine; avoir de la déveine, avoir la guigne; **it was u. for him that she arrived just at that moment,** malheureusement pour lui, elle est arrivée à cet instant précis; (*b*) (*of thg*) malheureux, malencontreux; **u. day,** jour de malheur, jour néfaste; **that's u.,** ce n'est pas de chance. **2.** qui porte malheur; **u. star,** étoile maléfique; **don't walk under a ladder, it's u.,** ne passez pas sous une échelle, ça porte malheur.

unlute [ʌn'lu:t], *v.tr. Cer:* déluter.

unluting [ʌn'lu:tiŋ], *s. Cer:* délutage *m.*

unmade [ʌn'meid], *a.* qui n'est pas (encore) fait; **u. bed,** lit non encore fait, lit défait; **u. road,** chemin non goudronné.

unmade-up [ʌnmeid'ʌp], *a.* (*of pers., face*) non maquillé, sans maquillage.

unmaidenly [ʌn'meidənli], *a. A: & Lit:* indigne d'une jeune fille; qui ne sied pas à une jeune fille; immodeste.

unmaintainable [ʌnmein'teinəbl], *a.* **1.** (position) intenable. **2.** (opinion) insoutenable; *Jur:* (défense) inadmissible.

unmake [ʌn'meik], *v.tr.* (*p.t. & p.p.* **unmade** [-'meid]) défaire; détruire, démolir.

unmalleable [ʌn'mæliəbl], *a.* **1.** (métal) peu malléable. **2.** (personne, caractère, etc.) peu malléable; indocile.

unmalted [ʌn'mɔ:ltid], *a. Brew: etc:* non malté.

unman [ʌn'mæn], *v.tr.* (**unmanned**) **1.** *A: & Lit:* (*a*) amollir, émasculer (une nation, etc.); (*b*) émouvoir, toucher, (qn) jusqu'aux larmes; attendrir (qn); (*c*) abattre, décourager, démoraliser (qn); **this news unmanned us,** cette nouvelle nous ôta, nous fit perdre, tout courage. **2.** dégarnir d'hommes; désarmer (un bateau).

unmanageable [ʌn'mænidʒəbl], *a.* **1.** (*of pers.*) intraitable; difficile à diriger; (*of child, horse*) indocile, ingouvernable; (*of vehicle, ship, etc.*) difficile à manœuvrer, à gouverner. **2.**(*of business, etc.*) difficile à diriger. **3.** (*of large book, etc.*) difficile à manier, peu mainable; **u. hair,** cheveux difficiles à coiffer.

unmanliness [ʌn'mænlinis], *s.* (*a*) manque *m* de virilité; (*b*) lâcheté *f.*

unmanly [ʌn'mænli], *a.* (*a*) indigne d'un homme; peu viril; efféminé; (*b*) lâche.

unmanned [ʌn'mænd], *a.* (*of vehicle, etc.*) non habité, sans équipage; *Space:* **u. flight,** vol inhabité, non habité; *Rail:* **u. halt,** halte non gérée; **to leave sth. u.,** laisser qch. sans surveillance; **the reception desk must never be left u.,** il doit toujours y avoir quelqu'un au bureau de réception.

unmannered [ʌn'mænəd], *a. esp. Lit:* = UNMANNERLY.

unmannerliness [ʌn'mænəlinis], *s. Lit:* manque *m* de savoir-vivre; mauvaises manières; impolitesse *f.*

unmannerly [ʌn'mænəli], *a. Lit:* qui a de mauvaises manières, qui manque de savoir-vivre; discourtois, impoli; mal élevé; **u. behaviour,** conduite de rustre, de goujat; **an u. lout,** un ours mal léché.

unmanufactured [ʌnmænju'fæktʃəd], *a. Ind:* (à l'état) brut; non manufacturé.

unmapped [ʌn'mæpt], *a.* (pays, etc.) dont on n'a pas dressé la carte.

unmarked [ʌn'mɑ:kt], *a.* **1.** (*a*) (visage, surface, etc.) sans marque(s), sans tache(s); qui n'a pas (encore) été marqué; non marqué; **u. (police) car,** voiture (de police) banalisée; *St.Exch:* **u. shares,** actions non estampillées; (*b*) *Games:* **u. player,** joueur démarqué; (*c*) **my essay was still u.,** ma dissertation n'était toujours pas corrigée. **2.** (*of remark, etc.*) **to pass u.,** passer inaperçu, inobservé.

unmarketable [ʌn'mɑ:kitəbl], *a.* (*of goods*) invendable; non marchand; de débit difficile; *Com:* **u. assets,** actif non liquide.

unmarred [ʌn'mɑ:d], *a.* **1.** (plaisir, etc.) que rien ne vient troubler, ne vient gâter; (bonheur) sans mélange. **2.** (beauté, etc.) que rien ne vient déparer.

unmarriageable [ʌn'mæridʒəbl], *a.* **1.** immariable; que l'on ne peut pas marier. **2.** qui n'est pas (encore) d'âge à se marier.

unmarried [ʌn'mærid], *a.* (*a*) célibataire; qui n'est pas marié; non marié; **he, she, is u.,** il est garçon, elle est demoiselle; il, elle, ne s'est pas (encore) marié(e); **he remained u.,** il est resté célibataire, garçon; **she remained u.,** elle est restée célibataire, demoiselle; **an u. man, woman,** un, une, célibataire; **u. mother,** mère célibataire; **u. state,** célibat *m*; (*b*) *Cin:* **u. print,** copie pas encore synchronisée.

unmask [ʌn'mɑ:sk]. **1.** *v.tr.* (*a*) démasquer (qn); ôter, arracher, le masque à (qn); (*b*) *Mil: A:* **to u. a battery,** démasquer une batterie; (*c*) *Lit:* dévoiler (un complot, etc.). **2.** *v.i. & pr.* (*a*) se démasquer; enlever son masque; (*b*) lever le masque; ôter son masque; se montrer tel qu'on est.

unmasked [ʌn'mɑ:skt], *a.* (*a*) démasqué; (*b*) sans masque.

unmast [ʌn'mɑ:st], *v.tr. Nau:* démâter.

unmastered [ʌn'mɑ:stəd], *a.* (*of passion, etc.*) non maîtrisé; indompté; rebelle; (*of difficulty*) qu'on n'a pas (encore) surmonté; (*of subject*) qu'on ne possède pas (encore) bien.

unmasting [ʌn'mɑ:stiŋ], *s. Nau:* démâtage *m.*

unmatchable [ʌn'mætʃəbl], *a.* **1.** (laine, etc.) impossible à assortir; (objet) impossible à appareiller. **2.** qui n'a pas de pendant.

unmatched [ʌn'mætʃt], *a.* **1.** sans égal, *pl.* sans égaux; inégalé; sans pareil; incomparable (**for courage,** pour son courage; **as a boxer,** comme boxeur). **2.** désassorti, dépareillé; (*of one of a pair*) déparié. **3.** *Cmptr:* (article) sans correspondant.

unmeasured [ʌn'meʒəd], *a. esp. Lit:* infini, illimité; sans mesure, sans bornes; démesuré.

unmeet [ʌn'mi:t], *a. A: & Lit:* (*a*) peu convenable; inconvenable; (*b*) **u. to do sth., for sth.,** (i) inapte, impropre, à faire qch.; (ii) indigne de faire qch.

unmelodious [ʌnmə'loudiəs], *a.* peu mélodieux; discordant, inharmonieux.

unmelted [ʌn'meltid], *a.* (*of ice, etc.*) pas encore fondu.

unmemorable [ʌn'mem(ə)rəbl], *a.* (événement, discours, etc.) peu mémorable, peu remarquable, banal, -als.

unmendable [ʌn'mendəbl], *a.* (vêtement, etc.) impossible à raccommoder, irraccommodable; (outil, etc.) impossible à réparer.

unmentionable [ʌn'menʃ(ə)nəbl]. **1.** *a.* (mot, etc.) qu'il ne faut pas prononcer; (événement, chose, etc.) dont il ne faut pas faire mention, dont il ne faut pas parler; *Lit:* (péché) inavouable, innomable. **2.** *s.pl. F: A:* **unmentionables,** (i) sous-vêtements *m*; (ii) pantalon *m.*

unmentioned [ʌn'menʃənd], *a.* dont on ne fait pas mention, dont il n'a pas été fait mention; **to leave s.o., sth., u.,** ne pas faire mention, ne pas parler, de qn, de qch.; passer qn, qch., sous silence.

unmercenary [ʌn'mə:sən(ə)ri], *a.* non mercenaire; désintéressé; sans but intéressé.

unmerchantable [ʌn'mə:tʃ(ə)ntəbl], *a. Com:* invendable; non marchand; de débit difficile.

unmerciful [ʌn'mə:sif(u)l], *a.* impitoyable; sans pitié; sans indulgence; sans miséricorde.

unmercifully [ʌn'mə:sif(u)li], *adv.* impitoyablement; sans pitié; sans indulgence; sans miséricorde; **to tease s.o. u.,** faire des misères continuelles à qn.

unmerited [ʌn'meritid], *a.* (reproche, etc.) immérité.

unmet [ʌn'met], *a. U.S:* (*a*) (besoin, etc.) non envisagé, nouveau; (*b*) (problème, etc.) non résolu, sans réponse.

unmetalled [ʌn'metld], *a.* (chemin) non empierré, non ferré.

unmethodical [ʌnmi'θɔdik(ə)l], *a.* **1.** (organisation, etc.) peu méthodique; (travail) décousu. **2.** (*of pers.*) qui manque de méthode, d'ordre; sans méthode; brouillon, -onne.

unmilled [ʌn'mild], *a.* **1.** (*a*) (blé, etc.) non moulu; (*b*) *Mec.E:* (écrou) non moleté, non godronné; (*c*) *Num:* non crénelé; sans crénelage, sans grènetis, sans cordon. **2.** *Tex:* (drap) non foulé.

unmindful [ʌn'maindful], *a.* **1.** *esp. Lit:* **to be u. of sth.,** être oublieux, peu soucieux, de qch.; être indifférent, inattentif, à qch.; **u. of one's own interests,** sans penser à ses propres intérêts; **to be u. of one's own interests,** (i) méconnaître, ignorer, ses propres intérêts; (ii) faire peu de cas de ses propres intérêts; **he was never u. of his responsibilities,** il ne négligeait, il n'oubliait, jamais ses responsabilités. **2.** *A: & Lit:* (*of pers.*) négligent.

unmined [ʌn'maind], *a.* **1.** *Navy:* (chenal, etc.) non semé de mines, libre. **2.** (gisement, minerai, domaine, etc.) inexploité.

unmingled [ʌn'miŋg(ə)ld], *a. Lit:* pur, sans mélange; **joy u. with regret,** joie exempte de regret.

uninted [ʌn'mintid], *a.* (or) non monnayé, en lingots.

unmistakable [ʌnmis'teikəbl], *a.* (*a*) (preuve, etc.) indubitable; qui ne laisse aucune place au doute; (sentiment, etc.) clair, net, *f.* nette; évident; **u. change,** changement marqué; **u. difference,** différence marquée, manifeste; (*b*) facilement reconnaissable.

unmistakably [ʌnmis'teikəbli], *adv.* sans aucun doute, indubitablement; clairement, nettement; manifestement.

unmitigated [ʌn'mitigeitid], *a.* **1.** (mal, etc.) non mitigé, que rien ne vient adoucir. **2.** (*intensive*) véritable; **u. idiot,** parfait imbécile; âne bâté; **he's an u. liar,** c'est un sacré menteur; **u. lie,** pur mensonge.

unmixed [ʌn'mikst], *a.* sans mélange; pur; **u. joy,** joie pure, franche, parfaite.

unmodified [ʌn'mɔdifaid], *a. Tchn:* non modifié; *Cmptr:* **u. instruction,** instruction sous forme initiale.

unmodulated [ʌn'mɔdjuleitid], *a. W.Tel: etc:* **u. waves,** ondes non modulées; **u. keyed continuous waves,** ondes A1 non modulées; ondes entretenues manipulées; **u. groove,** sillon non modulé, non enregistré; sillon blanc, vierge; *Cin:* (*of sound track*) **u. track,** bande sonore sans enregistrement, non modulée.

unmolested [ʌnmə'lestid], *a.* sans être molesté; (vivre) en paix, tranquillement, sans être inquiété; (voyager) sans obstacle, sans encombre.

unmonitored [ʌn'mɔnitəd], *a. Elcs:* **u. control system,** système de commande à boucle ouverte.

unmoor [ʌn'mɔ:r], *v.tr. Nau:* (*a*) démarrer, désamarrer (un navire); (*b*) lever une des ancres d'affourche; désaffourcher (un navire).

unmooring [ʌn'mɔ:riŋ], *s. Nau:* (*a*) démarrage *m*, désamarrage *m*; (*b*) désaffourchage *m.*

unmoral [ʌn'mɔrəl], *a.* amoral, -aux.

unmortgaged [ʌn'mɔ:gidʒd], *a.* libre d'hypothèques; franc, *f.* franche, d'hypothèques; non hypothéqué.

unmotherly [ʌn'mʌðəli], *a.* peu digne d'une mère; peu maternel.

unmotivated [ʌn'moutiveitid], *a.* (*a*) (*of pers., behaviour, etc.*) sans motif(s), non motivé; (*of behaviour, action*) immotivé; (*b*) (*of pers.*) dépourvu d'ambition.

unmounted [ʌn'mauntid], *a.* **1.** non monté; (*a*) (*of gem*) non serti; (*b*) (*of photograph, etc.*) non encadré; non collé; sans support. **2.** (soldat) à pied.

unmourned [ʌn'mɔ:nd], *a.* non pleuré; *Lit:* impleuré; **he died u.,** on n'a pas pleuré sa mort; il est mort sans être pleuré, sans laisser de regrets.

unmoved [ʌn'mu:vd], *a.* **1.** impassible; **u. by sth.,** aucunement ému, aucunement touché, de, par, qch.; **he was u. by her entreaties,** ses prières ne l'ont pas touché, ne l'ont pas ému; **he remained u. by all our arguments,** il restait insensible, inflexible, à tous nos arguments; tous nos arguments le laissaient indifférent; **to hear, see, sth. u.,** entendre, voir, qch. sans émotion. **2.** (*a*) (objet) toujours à la même place; (*b*) *Cmptr:* (article) non mouvementé.

unmown [ʌn'moun], *a.* (foin) non coupé; (gazon) non tondu.

unmuffle [ʌn'mʌfl], *v.tr.* enlever le voile (d'un tambour, etc.).

unmusical [ʌn'mju:zik(ə)l], *a.* **1.** (*of voice, etc.*) peu musical, -aux; peu mélodieux, peu harmonieux; discordant. **2.** (*a*) (*of pers., ear, etc.*) peu musicien, -ienne; (*b*) qui n'aime pas la musique.

unmuzzle [ʌn'mʌzl], *v.tr.* démuseler (un chien, etc.).

unnail [ʌn'neil], *v.tr.* déclouer.

unnameable [ʌn'neiməbl], *a.* innommable.

unnamed [ʌn'neimd], *a.* (*of pers.*) au nom inconnu; anonyme; (*of thg*) innom(m)é, sans nom; **u. benefactor,** bienfaiteur anonyme.

unnatural [ʌn'nætjərəl], *a.* non naturel, qui n'est pas naturel; (*a*) anormal, -aux; **the u. lustre of his eyes,** l'éclat anormal de ses yeux; (*b*) (*of habit, vice, etc.*) contre nature, pervers; dénaturé, cruel; **u. friendship,** amitié particulière; **u. parents,** parents cruels; (*c*) (*of style, etc.*) peu naturel; factice, artificiel; forcé, affecté; **u. laugh,** rire forcé.

unnaturalized [ʌn'nætjərəlaizd], *a.* (*of alien*) non naturalisé.

unnaturally [ʌn'nætjərəli], *adv.* **1.** (i) de manière peu naturelle; (ii) de manière anormale; **he hoped not u. that she would come,** naturellement, bien entendu, il espérait qu'elle viendrait. **2.** avec une cruauté dénaturée; perversement. **3.** facticement, artificiellement.

unnaturalness [ʌn'nætjərəlnis], *s.* **1.** caractère anormal, anormalité *f* (**of,** de). **2.** perversité *f*, cruauté *f.* **3.** manque *m* de naturel (du style); affectation *f.*

unnavigable [ʌn'nævigəbl], *a.* (rivière, etc.) innavigable.

unnecessarily [ʌnnesi'serəli], *adv.* **1.** sans nécessité, inutilement, pour rien. **2.** plus que de raison; **to travel with u. bulky luggage,** voyager avec trop de bagages.

unnecessary [ʌn'nesis(ə)ri], *a.* peu nécessaire; inutile, superflu, oiseux; **it is u. to say that . . .,** (il est) inutile de dire que . . .; **to do without u. things,** se passer de superfluités *f*; **she's always making an u. fuss,** elle fait beaucoup d'histoires pour rien.

unneeded [ʌn'ni:did], *a.* inutile; dont on n'a pas besoin.

unneighbourliness [ʌn'neibəlinis], *s.* **1.** mauvais rapports (entre voisins). **2.** humeur peu obligeante (envers un voisin).

unneighbourly [ʌn'neibəli], *a.* peu obligeant; (conduite) de mauvais voisin; peu sociable; **to behave in an u. manner,** se conduire en mauvais voisin.

unnerve [ʌn'nə:v], *v.tr.* **1.** *A: & Lit:* énerver, affaiblir. **2.** faire perdre son courage, son sang-froid, son assurance, à (qn); effrayer, démonter, dérouter (qn); **it**

unnerved him, cela l'a déconcerté.
unnerving [ʌn'nəːviŋ], *a.* déconcertant, déroutant, effrayant.
unnoted [ʌn'noutid], *a.* (phénomène, etc.) inobservé, inaperçu.
unnoticeable [ʌn'noutisəbl], *a.* qui échappe à l'attention; qui passe inaperçu; imperceptible.
unnoticed [ʌn'noutist], *a.* **1.** inaperçu, inobservé; qui échappe, qui a échappé, à l'attention; **to pass u.,** passer inaperçu; **the film did not pass u.,** le film a eu un grand retentissement. **2. to let an interruption, an insult, pass u.,** ne pas relever une interruption, une injure; faire comme si on n'avait pas entendu.
unnotified [ʌn'noutifaid], *a.* sans avertissement, qui n'a pas reçu d'avertissement, préalable; non avisé, non averti (**of,** de).
unnumbered [ʌn'nʌmbəd], *a.* **1.** *esp. Lit:* que l'on ne saurait compter; sans nombre; innombrable. **2.** (*of page, etc.*) non numéroté; sans numéro.
unobjectionable [ʌnəb'dʒekʃnəbl], *a.* (personne) à qui on ne peut rien reprocher; (chose) à laquelle on ne peut trouver à redire; acceptable, passable.
unobliging [ʌnə'blaidʒiŋ], *a.* peu obligeant, désobligeant; peu complaisant; inserviable.
unobliterated [ʌnə'blitəreitid], *a.* **1.** (*of traces, stain, etc.*) ineffacé. **2.** (*of stamp*) non oblitéré.
unobscured [ʌnəb'skjuəd], *a.* non caché; visible; **u. view,** vue dégagée, libre.
unobservant [ʌnəb'zəːv(ə)nt], *a.* peu perspicace; peu observateur, -trice; inattentif.
unobserved [ʌnəb'zəːvd], *a.* inaperçu, inobservé; **he went out u.,** il est sorti sans être vu, sans éveiller l'attention.
unobstructed [ʌnəb'strʌktid], *a.* (tuyau, canal, sentier, etc.) non bouché, non obstrué; **u. road,** chemin non encombré, dégagé, libre; **u. view,** vue dégagée, libre. **2.** sans rencontrer d'obstacle(s); (agir) sans encombre, sans obstacle.
unobtainable [ʌnəb'teinəbl], *a.* (consentement, etc.) impossible à obtenir; (article) impossible à se procurer, introuvable; *Tp:* **the number is u.,** il est impossible d'obtenir, d'avoir, le numéro; **number u. tone,** tonalité (entendue quand on a composé un numéro hors service).
unobtrusive [ʌnəb'truːsiv], *a.* (*of remark, colour, etc.*) discret, -ète; **a very u. woman,** une femme très effacée, très discrète; **he always tried to remain u.,** il cherchait toujours à s'effacer, à se faire remarquer le moins possible; **u. part,** rôle effacé, modeste.
unobtrusively [ʌnəb'truːsivli], *adv.* discrètement, modestement; d'une manière effacée.
unoccupied [ʌn'ɔkjupaid], *a.* **1.** (*of pers.*) inoccupé, désœuvré; sans occupation, sans travail. **2.** (*a*) (*of house, land, etc.*) inoccupé, inhabité; (*b*) *Mil:* **u. zone,** zone libre; **the town was still u.,** la ville n'était toujours pas occupée. **3.** (*of table, seat, etc.*) libre, disponible; vide; **u. post,** poste vacant.
unoffending [ʌnə'fendiŋ], *a.* inoffensif, innocent; **he kicked an u. dog,** il a donné un coup de pied à un chien qui n'avait rien fait, qui n'y était pour rien.
unofficial [ʌnə'fiʃ(ə)l], *a.* (*of meeting, etc.*) non officiel, officieux; **u. visit,** visite privée; *Ind: etc:* **u. strike,** grève sauvage; **in an u. capacity,** à titre non officiel; à titre officieux, privé, personnel; **u. report,** renseignements officieux, non confirmés; **from an u. source,** de source officieuse; **it's still u.,** on ne l'a pas encore confirmé.
unofficially [ʌnə'fiʃəli], *adv.* non officiellement, officieusement; à titre officieux.
unopened [ʌn'oup(ə)nd], *a.* non ouvert, qui n'a pas été ouvert; (*of letter*) non décacheté; **the box was u.,** la boîte n'avait pas été ouverte; **the door remained u.,** la porte restait fermée.
unopposed [ʌnə'pouzd], *a.* sans opposition; non contrarié; **they continued u.,** ils ont continué sans rencontrer d'opposition, de résistance; *Pol:* **u. candidate,** candidat unique; **to be returned u.,** être élu sans opposition; *Parl:* **the bill was given an u. second reading,** le projet de loi a été accepté sans opposition à la deuxième lecture.
unordained [ʌnɔː'deind], *a. Ecc:* qui n'a pas (encore) reçu les ordres.
unordered [ʌn'ɔːdəd], *a.* **1.** *Cmptr: etc:* (*of data, documents, etc.*) non ordonné, non trié, non classé. **2.** *Com: etc:* (article) pas encore commandé, non commandé.
unorganizable [ʌnɔːgə'naizəbl], *a.* inorganisable.
unorganized [ʌn'ɔːgənaizd], *a.* **1.** (*a*) non organisé; mal organisé; (*b*) *Pol:* **u. labour,** main-d'œuvre inorganisée. **2.** *Biol:* (corps, état, etc.) inorganisé.
unoriginal [ʌnə'ridʒinl], *a.* (*of pers., life, work, etc.*) sans originalité; peu original, -aux, qui manque d'originalité; (*of style, idea, etc.*) banal, -als.
unornamented [ʌn'ɔːnəmentid], *a.* sans ornements, simple.
unorthodox [ʌn'ɔːθədɔks], *a.* peu orthodoxe; hétérodoxe.
unostentatious [ʌnɔsten'teiʃəs], *a.* (*of pers., decoration, style, etc.*) peu fastueux, sans ostentation; simple, modeste, discret, -ète; sobre; (*of behaviour, etc.*) peu ostentatoire; (*of ceremony, etc.*) sans faste.
unostentatiously [ʌnɔsten'teiʃəsli], *adv.* (agir) sans ostentation, sans faste; (vêtu) simplement, modestement, discrètement, sobrement.
unostentatiousness [ʌnɔsten'teiʃəsnis], *s.* manque *m* d'ostentation, de faste, de simplicité; sobriété *f* (de qn, du décor, etc.); modestie *f,* discrétion *f* (de qn).
unowned [ʌn'ound], *a.* **1.** (terre) sans propriétaire; (chien) sans maître. **2.** *A: & Lit:* (enfant, etc.) non reconnu.
unoxidizable [ʌn'ɔksidaizəbl], *a.* inoxydable.
unoxidized [ʌn'ɔksidaizd], *a.* inoxydé.
unpacified [ʌn'pæsifaid], *a.* non pacifié.
unpack [ʌn'pæk], *v.tr.* **1.** déballer, dépaqueter, décaisser (des objets); déplier (son attirail, etc.). **2.** défaire (une valise, etc.); *v.i.* défaire sa valise, etc. **3.** *Cmptr:* éclater (des données).
unpacked [ʌn'pækt], *a.* **1.** (*a*) déballé, dépaqueté; (*b*) (*of suitcase, etc.*) défait. **2.** (*a*) pas encore empaqueté, emballé; (*b*) **my suitcase is still u.,** je n'ai pas encore défait ma valise.
unpacker [ʌn'pækər], *s.* déballeur *m.*
unpacking [ʌn'pækiŋ], *s.* **1.** déballage *m,* décaissement *m.* **2. the u. didn't take long,** nous n'avons pas été longtemps à défaire nos bagages. **3.** *Cmptr:* éclatement *m* (des données).
unpaged [ʌn'peidʒd], *a.* (livre) non folioté, non paginé.
unpaid [ʌn'peid], *a.* non payé. **1.** (*a*) (*of pers.*) qui ne reçoit pas de salaire; non salarié, non rétribué, non appointé; (*of post, etc.*) non rétribué, non rémunéré; qui ne comporte pas d'appointements; **u. agent,** mandataire *mf* bénévole; **u. services,** services à titre gracieux, non rétribués; (*b*) qui n'a pas touché son salaire, ses appointements; (troupes) sans solde. **2.** (*a*) (*of bill*) impayé; (*of debt*) non acquitté; (*of letter*) non affranchi; **the bill is still u.,** la facture n'a pas encore été réglée, payée; **to leave an account u.,** laisser arrérager un compte; **to return a bill u.,** retourner une traite faute de paiement; **the meal is u. for,** le repas n'a pas été payé; (*b*) (*of money*) non versé.
unpaintable [ʌn'peintəbl], *a.* (sujet) impossible à peindre.
unpainted [ʌn'peintid], *a.* non peint; **u. china,** porcelaine blanche.
unpaired [ʌn'peəd], *a.* **1.** non apparié, non appareillé, non assorti; dépareillé. **2.** *Anat: A:* **u. organ,** organe impair. **3.** *Parl:* (membre) qui ne s'est pas pairé avec qn (en vue d'un vote).
unpalatable [ʌn'pælətəbl], *a.* (*a*) d'un goût désagréable; désagréable au goût; (*b*) (*of truth, etc.*) désagréable; dur, difficile, à avaler.
unparalleled [ʌn'pærəleld], *a.* (*of beauty, etc.*) incomparable, sans pareil, sans égal; hors (de) pair; (*of cruelty, rudeness, etc.*) inouï; (*of action, event*) sans précédent.
unpardonable [ʌn'pɑːdənəbl], *a.* **1.** impardonnable; **u. weakness,** faiblesse inexcusable. **2.** *Ecc:* (péché) irrémissible.
unpardoned [ʌn'pɑːdnd], *a.* sans pardon, impardonné; *Ecc:* (*of pers.*) non absous, -oute.
unparliamentary [ʌnpɑːlə'ment(ə)ri], *a.* (langage, action) antiparlementaire, peu parlementaire.
unpatented [ʌn'peit(ə)ntid, -'pæ-], *a.* non breveté.
unpatriotic [ʌnpeitri'ɔtik, -pæ-], *a.* (*of pers.*) peu patriote; (*of action*) peu patriotique; antipatriotique; **to be u.,** être mauvais patriote.
unpatriotically [ʌnpeitri'ɔtikli, -pæ-], *adv.* de manière peu patriotique, antipatriotique; (agir) en mauvais patriote.
unpatronized [ʌn'pætrənaizd], *a.* **1.** sans protecteur, sans mécène. **2.** (magasin, cinéma, etc.) sans clientèle, sans clients.
unpaved [ʌn'peivd], *a.* (trottoir, etc.) non pavé, sans pavés.
unpayable [ʌn'peiəbl], *a.* **u. debt,** dette inacquittable.
unpeeled [ʌn'piːld], *a.* (fruit, légume) non épluché, avec sa peau.
unpeg [ʌn'peg], *v.tr.* (**unpegged**) arracher, ôter, la cheville, les chevilles, de (qch.); décheviller; enlever, arracher, les piquets (d'une tente, etc.).
unpen [ʌn'pen], *v.tr.* (**unpenned**) déparquer (du bétail).
unpenetrated [ʌn'penitreitid], *a.* impénétré.
unpensioned [ʌn'penʃ(ə)nd], *a.* non pensionné; sans pension, sans retraite.
unperceived [ʌnpə'siːvd], *a.* **1.** non perçu. **2.** inaperçu.
unperforated [ʌn'pəːfəreitid], *a.* non perforé, sans perforations.
unperformed [ʌnpə'fɔːmd], *a.* **1.** *esp. Lit:* (*of work*) inexécuté, inaccompli. **2.** (*of play*) non joué, non représenté; (*of symphony, etc.*) non joué, non exécuté.
unpersevering [ʌnpəːsi'viəriŋ], *a.* non persévérant, non assidu.
unpersuadable [ʌnpə'sweidəbl], *a.* non persuasible.
unpersuaded [ʌnpə'sweidid], *a.* non convaincu; non persuadé; **she shook her head u.,** elle hocha la tête pour montrer qu'on ne l'avait pas convaincue.
unpersuasive [ʌnpə'sweiziv, -siv], *a.* (argument, etc.) peu convaincant.
unperturbed [ʌnpə'təːbd], *a.* **1.** impassible. **2.** non déconcerté, non découragé; **u. by this event,** aucunement inquiété par cet événement.
unphilosophical [ʌnfilə'sɔfik(ə)l], *a.* peu philosophique.
unpick [ʌn'pik], *v.tr.* défaire (une couture); découdre (une robe).
unpicked [ʌn'pikt], *a.* **1.** non choisi; non trié. **2.** (fruit) non cueilli; **the fruit was still u.,** les fruits étaient encore sur l'arbre.
unpigmented [ʌnpig'mentid], *a.* (*of animal, skin*) non pigmenté.
unpiloted [ʌn'pailətid], *a.* (navire) sans pilote.
unpin [ʌn'pin], *v.tr.* (**unpinned**) **1.** *Mec.E: etc:* décheviller, dégoupiller (qch.). **2.** désépingler, dépingler, défaire (qch.); ôter les épingles de (qch.); *F:* **can you please u. me?** pouvez-vous m'enlever toutes ces épingles?
unpitied [ʌn'pitid], *a.* qui n'est pas plaint; sans être plaint.
unpitying [ʌn'pitiiŋ], *a.* sans pitié; sans compassion; impitoyable.
unplaced [ʌn'pleist], *a.* (cheval, etc.) non placé; (candidat) non classé.
unplait [ʌn'plæt], *v.tr.* dénatter (ses cheveux, etc.).
unplaned [ʌn'pleind], *a.* (bois) non raboté, non dégauchi; (bois, métal) non aplani, non plané.
unplanned [ʌn'plænd], *a.* (événement, etc.) imprévu; (enfant) non prévu.
unplanted [ʌn'plɑːntid], *a.* **u. (flower) bed,** parterre sans fleurs; **she leaves her garden u.,** elle ne plante rien dans son jardin.
unplastered [ʌn'plɑːstəd], *a.* (mur, etc.) non crépi, non plâtré.
unplayable [ʌn'pleiəbl], *a.* (musique) injouable, inexécutable; *Golf: etc:* **u. ball,** balle injouable.
unpleasant [ʌn'plez(ə)nt], *a.* désagréable, déplaisant; **u. weather,** mauvais temps; **he lives in a rather u. part of the town,** il habite dans un quartier peu attrayant de la ville; **he made some u. remarks,** il a dit des choses désobligeantes; **she was very u. with me,** elle a été très désagréable avec moi.
unpleasantly [ʌn'plez(ə)ntli], *adv.* désagréablement; **the room was u. cold,** il faisait désagréablement froid dans la pièce; la pièce était désagréablement froide.
unpleasantness [ʌn'plez(ə)ntnis], *s.* **1.** caractère *m* désagréable (de qch.); aspect, caractère, déplaisant (d'un endroit, etc.); **you can imagine the u. of my position,** vous pouvez vous figurer ce que ma situation offrait de désagréable. **2.** désagrément *m,* ennui *m;* **to cause s.o. u.,** attirer du désagrément, des désagréments, à qn; **there was some u.,** il y a eu une dispute; **don't let that u. spoil our friendship,** il ne faut pas que ce désaccord gâche notre amitié.
unpleasing [ʌn'pliːziŋ], *a.* peu agréable; peu attrayant; qui manque de grâce; déplaisant.
unpleated [ʌn'pliːtid], *a.* **u. skirt,** jupe sans plis, non plissée.
unpledged [ʌn'pledʒd], *a.* non engagé; libre.
unpliable, unpliant [ʌn'plaiəbl, -'plaiənt], *a.* (*of pers.*) peu souple; peu complaisant; buté; inflexible.
unploughed [ʌn'plaud], *a.* **1.** (*of field*) non labouré. **2.** *Bookb:* (*of edge*) non rogné.
unplucked [ʌn'plʌkt], *a.* **1.** *A: & Lit:* (*of flowers, etc.*) non cueilli. **2.** (poulet, etc.) non plumé.
unplug [ʌn'plʌg], *v.tr.* (**unplugged**) **1.** déboucher (une ouverture, un tuyau); détaper (un canon). **2.** débrancher (une télévision, etc.).
unplumbed [ʌn'plʌmd], *a. Lit:* **u. depths,** profondeurs insondées.
unpoetic(al) [ʌnpou'etik(əl)], *a.* peu poétique; antipoétique; terre(-)à(-)terre *inv.*
unpointed [ʌn'pɔintid], *a.* **1.** *Gram:* (*a*) (phrase) sans ponctuation; (*b*) (hébreu, etc.) sans points-voyelles. **2.** sans pointe; émoussé; obtus. **3.** *Const:* **u. brickwork,** briquetage à joints bruts de truelle.

unpoised [ʌn'pɔizd], *a.* **she's very u.,** elle n'a pas de prestance.
unpolarized [ʌn'poulǝraizd], *a.* (*of light*) non polarisé; naturel.
unpolished [ʌn'pɔliʃt], *a.* **1.** (*a*) non poli; mat; (*of stone*) brut; (*b*) (*of floor, furniture*) non ciré, non astiqué; (*of shoes*) non ciré. **2.** (*a*) (*of pers.*) fruste, rude, mal dégrossi; (*b*) **u. style,** style fruste, non poli.
unpolluted [ʌnpǝ'lu:tid], *a.* impollué, non pollué; pur.
unpopular [ʌn'pɔpjulǝr], *a.* impopulaire; **he makes himself u. with everybody, he's generally u.,** il se fait mal voir de tout le monde, il est mal vu de tous; **he's u. with his employees,** ses employés ne l'aiment pas (beaucoup); **this decision was very u.,** cette décision a été très mal accueillie.
unpopularity [ʌnpɔpju'læriti], *s.* impopularité *f.*
unpopulated [ʌn'pɔpjuleitid], *a.* (*of area, region*) impeuplé; non peuplé; sans population.
unportrayable [ʌnpɔ:'treiǝbl], *a. Lit:* (scène, etc.) impossible à dépeindre, indescriptible.
unpot [ʌn'pɔt], *v.tr.* (**unpotted**) dépoter (une plante).
unpotting [ʌn'pɔtiŋ], *s.* dépotage *m*, dépotement *m* (d'une plante).
unpractical [ʌn'præktikl], *a.* **1.** (*of pers.*) peu pratique. **2.** (*of plan, etc.*) impraticable, irréalisable.
unpractised [ʌn'præktist], *a.* inexercé, inexpérimenté; inhabile; inexpert; novice; **u. in business,** sans expérience des affaires.
unprecedented [ʌn'presidentid], *a.* sans précédent; inouï; inédit.
unpredictability [ʌnpridiktǝ'biliti], *s.* imprévisibilité *f.*
unpredictable [ʌnpri'diktǝbl], *a.* imprévisible; **the weather's u.,** le temps est incertain; **she's u.,** on ne sait jamais ce qu'elle va faire.
unprejudiced [ʌn'predʒudist], *a.* impartial, -aux; sans parti pris; sans préjugés, sans prévention(s); non prévenu; désintéressé.
unpremeditated [ʌnpri'mediteitid], *a.* (départ, etc.) inopiné, imprévu; (discours, etc.) spontané, improvisé, impromptu; *Jur:* (délit) non prémédité.
unprepared [ʌnpri'pɛǝd], *a.* **1.** (*a*) (*of food, etc.*) inapprêté, non préparé; **u. speech,** discours improvisé, impromptu; *Sch:* **u. translation,** traduction à livre ouvert; (*b*) **to find everything u.,** trouver que rien n'a été préparé, que rien n'est prêt. **2.** **to be u. for sth.,** ne pas être prêt à qch.; ne pas s'attendre à qch.; **he was u. for what was to come,** il ne s'attendait pas à ce qui allait arriver. **3.** sans préparation, sans préparatifs; sans avoir pris les dispositions nécessaires; **to go u. into an undertaking,** se lancer à tête perdue dans une entreprise; **I took the exam quite u.,** j'ai passé l'examen sans l'avoir suffisamment préparé.
unpreparedness [ʌnpri'pɛǝdnis, -'pɛǝridnis], *s.* impréparation *f* (**for,** à).
unprepossessing [ʌnpri:pǝ'zesiŋ], *a.* (*of pers.*) peu engageant; peu séduisant; peu avenant; rébarbatif; **he's a man of u. appearance,** c'est un homme qui fait mauvaise impression, *F:* qui marque mal.
unpresentable [ʌnpri'zentǝbl], *a.* peu présentable, qui n'est pas présentable.
unpressed [ʌn'prest], *a.* (pantalon, etc.) non repassé.
unpresuming [ʌnpri'zju:miŋ], *a.* modeste; peu présomptueux; sans présomption.
unpretending, unpretentious [ʌnpri'tendiŋ, -'tenʃǝs], *a.* sans prétention(s); modeste, simple.
unpretentiously [ʌnpri'tenʃǝsli], *adv.* modestement; **u. dressed,** vêtu simplement.
unpretentiousness [ʌnpri'tenʃǝsnis], *s.* absence *f* de prétention; modestie *f*; simplicité *f* (de mise, etc.).
unpreventable [ʌnpri'ventǝbl], *a.* (malheur, etc.) qu'on ne peut empêcher, qu'on ne peut prévenir.
unpriced [ʌn'praist], *a.* (article) sans indication de prix, dont le prix n'est pas marqué.
unprime [ʌn'praim], *v.tr. Exp: etc:* désamorcer (un fusible, etc.).
unprimed [ʌn'praimd], *a. Exp: etc:* (fusible, etc.) désamorcé.
unprincipled [ʌn'prinsipld], *a.* (*of pers.*) sans principes; improbe; **u. conduct,** conduite peu scrupuleuse, sans scrupules; **he's completely u.,** il ne s'embarrasse d'aucun scrupule.
unprintable [ʌn'printǝbl], *a.* (livre) inimprimable, inéditable; **at that time these words were literally u.,** à cette époque on ne pouvait imprimer ces mots sous peine d'amende.
unprinted [ʌn'printid], *a.* non imprimé; inimprimé.
unprivileged [ʌn'privilidʒd], *a.* sans privilège(s), défavorisé.
unprized [ʌn'praizd], *a. Lit:* peu estimé; mésestimé.
unprobed [ʌn'proubd], *a.* (secret, mystère) insondé.
unprocessable [ʌnprou'sesǝbl], *a. Cmptr: etc:* (*of data, information*) inexploitable, ne pouvant être traité.
unprocessed [ʌn'prousest], *a. Cmptr: etc:* non traité; **u. data,** données brutes.
unprocurable [ʌnprǝ'kju:rǝbl], *a.* impossible à obtenir; que l'on ne peut se procurer; introuvable.
unproducible [ʌnprǝ'dju:sibl], *a.* improductible.
unproductive [ʌnprǝ'dʌktiv], *a.* improductif; (travail, etc.) stérile; (capital) improductif, qui dort; **u. land,** terre ingrate, stérile, qui ne rend rien; terre en non-valeur; **u. consumption,** consommation irreproductive.
unproductively [ʌnprǝ'dʌktivli], *adv.* de façon improductive; improductivement; stérilement.
unproductiveness [ʌnprǝ'dʌktivnis], *s.* improductivité *f*; stérilité *f.*
unprofessional [ʌnprǝ'feʃn(ǝ)l], *a.* (*a*) **u. conduct,** conduite contraire au code professionnel, aux usages du métier; manquement *m* à l'étiquette professionnelle, aux devoirs de la profession; (*b*) **for an architect he's very u.,** comme architecte il est plutôt amateur.
unprofessionally [ʌnprǝ'feʃǝn(ǝ)li], *adv.* (*a*) contrairement au code professionnel, aux usages du métier; (*b*) en amateur, d'une façon gauche.
unprofitable [ʌn'prɔfitǝbl], *a.* peu profitable, peu avantageux; peu lucratif; sans profit; (travail, etc.) inutile; (sol, etc.) ingrat.
unprofitability, unprofitableness [ʌnprɔfitǝ'biliti, -'prɔfitǝblnis], *s.* nature peu profitable, peu avantageuse.
unprofitably [ʌn'prɔfitǝbli], *adv.* sans profit; inutilement, vainement; infructueusement, stérilement.
unprogrammable [ʌnprou'græmǝbl], *a. Cmptr:* non programmable.
unprogrammed [ʌn'prougræmd], *a. Cmptr:* non programmé.
unprogressive [ʌnprǝ'gresiv], *a.* non progressif, rétrograde.
unprohibited [ʌnprǝ'hibitid], *a.* non prohibé, non interdit; licite.
unprolific [ʌnprǝ'lifik], *a.* peu fécond, peu fertile.
unpromising [ʌn'prɔmisiŋ], *a.* peu prometteur, -euse; **the weather looks u.,** le temps s'annonce mal.
unprompted [ʌn'prɔmptid], *a.* (*of answer, etc.*) spontané; **to do sth. u.,** faire qch. spontanément, sans y être incité.
unpromulgated [ʌn'prɔmǝlgeitid], *a.* impromulgué.
unpronounceable [ʌnprǝ'naunsǝbl], *a.* imprononçable, inarticulable.
unpronounced [ʌnprǝ'naunst], *a.* non prononcé.
unpropitious [ʌnprǝ'piʃǝs], *a.* défavorable, peu favorable (**to,** à); impropice.
unprosperous [ʌn'prɔspǝrǝs], *a.* peu prospère; peu florissant.
unprotected [ʌnprǝ'tektid], *a.* **1.** (*a*) sans protection, sans défense; inabrité; **u. balcony,** balcon (i) mal abrité, (ii) sans garde-fou; (*b*) (*of pers.*) sans patronage, sans protection, sans appui. **2.** *Tchn:* (*of moving part, etc.*) exposé; nu; sans garde-fou; sans carter, sans garde.
unprotested [ʌnprǝ'testid], *a. Com:* (effet) non protesté.
unprovable [ʌn'pru:vǝbl], *a.* qu'on ne peut prouver; improuvable; indémontrable.
unproved, unproven [ʌn'pru:vd; -'pru:v(ǝ)n, -'prou-], *a.* (*of accusation, etc.*) improuvé; non prouvé; sans preuve.
unprovided [ʌnprǝ'vaidid], *a.* **1.** (*a*) **u. with sth.,** (i) sans qch.; (ii) dépourvu, démuni, dénué, de qch.; (*b*) *A: & Lit:* **to be u. against an attack,** être sans moyens pour, ne pas être prêt à, résister à une attaque; (*c*) **to be left u. for,** être laissé sans ressources. **2.** imprévu; **case u. for by the rules,** cas non prévu dans les règlements. **3.** non fourni (par qn); *A:* **u. school,** école (primaire) libre.
unprovoked [ʌnprǝ'voukt], *a.* non provoqué; fait sans provocation; **u. abuse,** insultes imméritées, injustes.
unpruned [ʌn'pru:nd], *a.* (arbre, etc.) non taillé.
unpublicized [ʌn'pʌblisaizd], *a.* (fait, etc.) non publié; (produit) pour lequel on ne fait pas de publicité.
unpublishable [ʌn'pʌbliʃǝbl], *a.* (livre) impubliable, qu'on ne peut publier, éditer.
unpublished [ʌn'pʌbliʃt], *a.* inédit, non publié; **the u. facts,** les faits qui n'ont pas été livrés, révélés, au public; les faits que l'on a tenus secrets.
unpunctual [ʌn'pʌŋktjuǝl], *a.* inexact; peu ponctuel; qui n'est pas, jamais, à l'heure.
unpunctuality [ʌnpʌŋktju'æliti], *s.* inexactitude *f*; manque *m* de ponctualité.
unpunctually [ʌn'pʌŋktjuǝli], *adv.* inexactement; peu ponctuellement.
unpunctuated [ʌn'pʌŋktjueitid], *a.* (texte, etc.) non ponctué, sans ponctuation.
unpunishable [ʌn'pʌniʃǝbl], *a.* impunissable.
unpunished [ʌn'pʌniʃt], *a.* impuni, *Lit:* inchâtié; **to go u.,** rester impuni, sans punition.
unpurified [ʌn'pju:rifaid], *a.* inépuré, non épuré.
unqualifiable [ʌn'kwɔlifaiǝbl], *a.* (conduite, etc.) inqualifiable.
unqualified [ʌn'kwɔlifaid], *a.* **1.** (*a*) incompétent; non qualifié; **to be u. for sth.,** ne pas avoir les qualités requises, ne pas satisfaire aux conditions requises pour qch.; **to be u. to do sth.,** être incompétent, impropre, inapte, à faire qch.; **this court is u. to hear the case,** ce tribunal est incompétent à juger la cause; (*b*) (médecin, professeur, etc.) sans diplôme(s), qui n'a pas (encore) reçu ses diplômes; non diplômé, non qualifié; **he's completely u.,** il n'a aucun diplôme; il n'a pas (reçu) de formation professionnelle; **she's u. for the job,** elle n'est pas qualifiée, elle n'a pas les diplômes requis, pour occuper le poste; **I'm quite u. to talk about it,** je ne suis nullement qualifié pour en parler. **2.** (*a*) (*of accusation, etc.*) sans réserve; sans restriction; sans conditions; **u. denial,** dénégation absolue, catégorique; **u. praise,** éloges sans réserve; **with my u. consent,** avec tout mon consentement; **it was an u. success,** c'était un succès formidable; (*b*) *Gram:* (adjectif) non modifié.
unquantified [ʌn'kwɔntifaid], *a.* **1.** (*a*) *Log:* (prédicat) non quantifié; (*b*) *Ling:* (expression) sans quantifieur, sans quantificateur, sans quantitatif. **2.** dont on n'a pas évalué la quantité.
unquenchable [ʌn'kwenʃǝbl], *a.* (soif, feu) inextinguible; (soif, curiosité, etc.) insatiable; (cupidité, etc.) inassouvissable.
unquenched [ʌn'kwenʃt], *a.* (feu) non éteint; (désir, etc.) inassouvi; **u. thirst,** soif non étanchée.
unquestionable [ʌn'kwestjǝnǝbl], *a.* (habileté, preuve, etc.) indiscutable, indubitable; (droit, etc.) incontestable; (jugement, etc.) inattaquable, indisputable; **u. fact,** fait hors de doute, indiscutable.
unquestionably [ʌn'kwestjǝnǝbli], *adv.* indubitablement, incontestablement; sans contestation, sans conteste; sans aucun doute; **he is u. the best,** il est sans contredit le meilleur; **she is u. guilty,** elle est indiscutablement coupable.
unquestioned [ʌn'kwestj(ǝ)nd], *a.* **1.** (droit, etc.) indiscuté, incontesté. **2.** (*a*) **to let s.o. in u.,** laisser entrer qn sans interpellation, sans l'interroger, sans le questionner; (*b*) **to let a statement pass u.,** laisser passer une affirmation sans la relever, sans la mettre en doute.
unquestioning [ʌn'kwestjǝniŋ], *a.* (obéissance, etc.) aveugle, sans hésitation ni murmure; **u. trust,** confiance absolue, totale.
unquestioningly [ʌn'kwestjǝniŋli], *adv.* aveuglément; sans question; sans poser de question; **to believe s.o. u.,** croire qn sur parole.
unquiet [ʌn'kwaiǝt], *a. A: & Lit:* **1.** inquiet, -ète; agité; **u. soul,** âme inquiète, tourmentée; **u. times,** époque troublée, mouvementée, de troubles, d'agitation. **2.** (peuple, etc.) bruyant, turbulent.
unquote ['ʌnkwout], *v.i.* (*used only in imp.*) (*in dictation*) fermez les guillemets; **he said there would be no price rise quote "before the middle of February" u.,** il a dit que les prix ne s'élèveraient pas, début de citation, "avant la mi-février", fin *f* de citation.
unquoted [ʌn'kwoutid], *a.* **1.** non cité. **2.** *St.Exch:* **u. securities,** valeurs non cotées, incotées.
unransomed [ʌn'rænsǝmd], *a.* **1.** *Lit:* (péché, etc.) non racheté. **2.** (prisonnier) non rançonné; **he was allowed to go u.,** on l'a laissé aller sans rançon.
unratified [ʌn'rætifaid], *a.* (traité, etc.) sans ratification; qui n'est pas encore ratifié; qui n'a pas été ratifié.
unrationed [ʌn'ræʃ(ǝ)nd], *a. War Adm:* en vente libre.
unravel [ʌn'ræv(ǝ)l], *v.* (**unravelled**) **1.** *v.tr.* (*a*) effiler, effilocher, érailler (un tissu, etc.); défaire (du tricot); défaire, détordre (une corde, etc.); (*b*) débrouiller, démêler, détortiller (des fils, de la ficelle, etc.); **to u. a plot,** dénouer, démêler, une intrigue; **he loves unravelling mysteries,** il adore débrouiller les mystères; **to u. the situation,** éclaircir, élucider, la situation; **to u. the truth,** démêler la vérité. **2.** *v.i. & pr.* (*a*) **to u. (itself), to come unravelled,** (*of cloth, etc.*) s'effiler, s'effilocher, se défaire, s'érailler; (*of knitting*) se défaire; (*of rope, etc.*) se détordre; (*b*) (*of facts*) s'éclaircir.
unravelling [ʌn'ræv(ǝ)liŋ], *s.* (*a*) effilage *m*, effilement *m*, effilochage *m* (d'un tissu, etc.); (*b*) débrouillement *m*, démêlage *m*, démêlement *m* (d'un écheveau, d'une intrigue); dénouement *m* (d'une intrigue); éclaircissement *m*, élucidation *f* (d'un mystère, etc.).
unread [ʌn'red], *a.* **1.** (roman, etc.) (i) qui n'a pas été lu, (ii) sans lecteurs, que personne ne lit; **to leave sth. u.,** ne pas lire qch.; **he left the magazine on the table u.,** il a laissé la revue sur la table sans la lire. **2.** (*of pers.*) sans instruction; illettré, ignorant, ignare; inculte; **he's completely u. in political economy,** il ne connaît rien à

l'économie politique.

unreadable [ʌn'ri:dəbl], *a.* **1.** (livre) illisible, indigeste, difficile à lire; **this is u. rubbish,** cela ne vaut absolument rien. **2.** (écriture) illisible.

unreadiness [ʌn'redinis], *s.* **1.** (*a*) manque *m* de préparation; impréparation *f*; (*b*) manque de préparatifs. **2.** *Lit:* manque de promptitude.

unready[1] [ʌn'redi], *a.* **1. to be u. for sth.,** ne pas être prêt à qch.; ne pas être préparé, être mal préparé, pour qch.; **to be u. to do sth.,** (i) ne pas être prêt, (ii) ne pas être disposé, à faire qch. **2.** *Lit:* (*a*) (esprit, etc.) peu prompt; (*b*) *A:* qui manque de résolution; irrésolu.

unready[2], *a. A:* peu avisé; malavisé; *Hist:* **Ethelred the U.,** Ethelred le Malavisé.

unreal [ʌn'riəl], *a.* irréel; sans réalité; imaginaire, chimérique, mensonger; **everything seemed u. to him,** il avait l'impression de rêver.

unrealism [ʌn'riəlizm], *s.* irréalisme *m.*

unrealist [ʌn'riəlist], *s.* irréaliste *mf.*

unrealistic [ʌnriə'listik], *a.* irréaliste.

unreality [ʌnri'æliti], *s.* **1.** irréalité *f*; absence *f* de réalité; caractère *m* imaginaire, chimérique. **2.** chimère *f*; vaine imagination.

unrealizable [ʌn'riəlaizəbl], *a.* **1.** *Lit:* (qualité, etc.) incompréhensible, inintelligible, dont on ne peut pas se rendre compte. **2.** (projet, etc.) irréalisable, inexécutable.

unrealized [ʌn'riəlaizd], *a.* **1.** *esp. Lit:* (courage, etc.) dont on ne s'est pas rendu compte; inapprécié. **2.** (*a*) (espoir, désir, etc.) irréalisé; (*b*) *Fin:* (capital) non réalisé; **u. profits,** profits fictifs.

unreaped [ʌn'ri:pt], *a.* (champ, blé, etc.) pas encore moissonné; **the crops are still u.,** les récoltes sont toujours sur pied; **u. benefits,** avantages dont on n'a pas profité.

unreason [ʌn'ri:zn], *s. A: & Lit:* déraison *f*; **the Abbot of U.,** le pape, le prince, des fous.

unreasonable [ʌn'ri:z(ə)nəbl], *a.* **1.** (*of pers.*) déraisonnable; **don't be u.,** soyez raisonnable; **you are being most u.,** vous n'êtes pas raisonnable; vous êtes trop exigeant; vous exigez trop, vous exagérez. **2.** (*a*) **u. assumption,** supposition déraisonnable; **u. demands,** demandes immodérées, démesurées, extravagantes; **u. price,** prix excessif, exorbitant; (*b*) **at this u. hour,** à cette heure indue.

unreasonableness [ʌn'ri:z(ə)nəblnis], *s.* exorbitance *f* (d'une revendication, etc.); absurdité *f* (de la conduite, etc.).

unreasonably [ʌn'ri:z(ə)nəbli], *adv.* déraisonnablement; d'une manière extravagante, excessive, exorbitante, peu raisonnable.

unreasoned [ʌn'ri:z(ə)nd], *a.* irraisonné.

unreasoning [ʌn'ri:z(ə)niŋ], *a.* (*of pers.*) qui ne raisonne pas; **u. hatred,** haine irraisonnée, aveugle.

unrebuked [ʌnri'bju:kt], *a.* non réprimandé, sans réprimande; **they let him go u.,** ils l'ont laissé aller sans le réprimander, sans le reprendre.

unreceipted [ʌnri'si:tid], *a. Com:* non acquitté.

unreceptive [ʌnri'septiv], *a.* (*a*) (*of pers.*) aucunement, peu, réceptif (**to sth.,** à qch.); incompréhensif, indifférent, froid; (*b*) (*of mind, etc.*) obtus.

unreclaimed [ʌnri'kleimd], *a.* **1.** *Lit:* (pécheur, etc.) non corrigé, qui ne s'est pas corrigé. **2.** (*a*) (terrain) (resté) en friche, indéfriché, inculte; (*b*) (marais, etc.) que l'on n'a pas encore asséché.

unrecognizable [ʌn'rekəgnaizəbl, -'naizəbl], *a.* méconnaissable; impossible, difficile, à reconnaître.

unrecognizably [ʌn'rekəgnaizəbli, -'naizəbli], *adv.* **they are u. alike,** il est impossible de les distinguer l'un de l'autre; **the fog had u. blurred the outlines,** le brouillard en avait estompé les contours et les avait rendus méconnaissables.

unrecognized [ʌn'rekəgnaizd], *a.* **1.** (*of genius, etc.*) méconnu. **2.** (*of ruler, government, etc.*) non reconnu.

unreconciled [ʌn'rekənsaild], *a.* irréconcilié.

unreconstructed [ʌnri:kən'strʌktid], *a. NAm:* (homme, etc.) attaché à des principes dépassés; de (la) vieille roche, de l'ancienne roche.

unrecorded [ʌnri'kɔ:did], *a.* **1.** (*of fact, comment, etc.*) non enregistré, non mentionné, non relevé; dont on n'a aucun rapport; dont on ne trouve aucune mention. **2.** (*of music, tape, etc.*) non enregistré; *Cmptr: etc:* (*of tape*) vierge.

unrecoverable [ʌnri'kʌv(ə)rəbl], *a.* irrécouvrable.

unrectified [ʌn'rektifaid], *a.* **1.** *Ph: etc:* (résultat) brut. **2.** (alcool) inépuré, brut. **3.** *El:* (courant) non redressé.

unredeemable [ʌnri'di:məbl], *a.* **1.** (*a*) (crime, faute, etc.) irrachetable; (défaut, désastre, etc.) irrémédiable; (*b*) (criminel, etc.) incorrigible, irrachetable. **2.** *Fin:* (fonds, etc.) irremboursable, irréalisable; (papier) non convertible.

unredeemed [ʌnri'di:md], *a.* **1.** (péché, etc.) non racheté; **he has a bad character u. by any good points,** il a une mauvaise nature que ne rachète aucune qualité réelle; il n'a aucune qualité réelle pour compenser sa mauvaise nature; **it is a town of u. ugliness,** c'est une ville uniformément laide. **2.** (*a*) **u. promise,** promesse non remplie, non tenue; (*b*) (gage) non retiré (des mains du prêteur sur gages); **his watch is still u. (from pawn),** il n'a pas encore dégagé sa montre (du crédit municipal); (*c*) *Fin:* (emprunt) non amorti, non remboursé; **u. bill,** traite non honorée; **u. mortgage,** hypothèque non purgée.

unredeemedly [ʌnri'di:midli], *adv.* **u. ugly town,** ville uniformément laide.

unredressed [ʌnri'drest], *a. Lit:* (mal, etc.) non redressé, qui n'a pas été réparé.

unreduced [ʌnri'dju:st], *a.* **1.** qui n'a subi aucune diminution, aucune réduction; **u. speed,** vitesse aucunement ralentie; vitesse soutenue. **2.** *Med:* (*of fracture*) irréduit.

unreel [ʌn'ri:l]. **1.** *v.tr.* dérouler (un film, un câble, etc.). **2.** *v.i. & pr.* se dérouler.

unreeve [ʌn'ri:v], *v.tr.* (*p.t.* **unrove** [ʌn'rouv], **unreeved;** *p.p.* **unreeved, unrove,** *A:* **unroven** [ʌn'rouvn]) *Nau:* dépasser (un cordage).

unrefined [ʌnri'faind], *a.* **1.** brut; (métal, sucre, pétrole) non raffiné; (pétrole) inépuré. **2.** (homme, goût) peu raffiné, grossier, vulgaire; (langage) inapprêté; **u. manners,** manières frustes; manque *m* de raffinement.

unreflecting [ʌnri'flektiŋ], *a. Lit:* irréfléchi.

unreformed [ʌnri'fɔ:md], *a.* **1.** (*of pers.*) qui ne s'est pas corrigé; (*of institution, etc.*) non réformé; (*of law*) non amendé. **2.** (*of church, etc.*) qui n'a pas subi l'influence de la Réforme.

unrefracted [ʌnri'fræktid], *a. Ph:* (rayon) non réfracté.

unrefreshed [ʌnri'freʃt], *a.* **1.** non rafraîchi. **2. to wake up u.,** se réveiller peu reposé, encore fatigué.

unrefreshing [ʌnri'freʃiŋ], *a.* **1.** peu rafraîchissant. **2. u. sleep,** sommeil peu réparateur.

unrefuted [ʌnri'fju:tid], *a.* irréfuté.

unregarded [ʌnri'gɑ:did], *a.* négligé; à qui, à quoi, on ne fait pas attention; **her joke passed totally u.,** personne n'a tenu compte de sa plaisanterie; on a fait peu de cas de sa plaisanterie.

unregardful [ʌnri'gɑ:dful], *a. A:* peu soigneux (**of,** de); inattentif, indifférent (**of,** à); négligent (**of,** de).

unregenerate [ʌnri'dʒenərət], *a.* **1.** non régénéré; impénitent. **2.** (*a*) (*of pers.*) qui ne s'est pas corrigé; attaché à des principes dépassés; (*b*) (*of pers., beliefs, etc.*) obstiné, entêté; (*of opposition, etc.*) opiniâtre.

unregimented [ʌn'redʒimentid], *a.* (bataillon, système, etc.) non réglementé, non discipliné; sans réglementation, sans discipline.

unregistered [ʌn'redʒistəd], *a.* (*of pers.*) non inscrit, non immatriculé, non enrôlé; (*of luggage, etc.*) non enregistré; **u. car,** voiture non immatriculée; **u. trademark,** marque non déposée; **u. birth,** naissance non déclarée. **2.** *Post:* (*of letter, parcel*) (i) non recommandé; (ii) non chargé.

unregretted [ʌnri'gretid], *a.* (*of act, statement, etc.*) que l'on ne regrette pas; **she died u.,** elle est morte sans laisser de regrets; personne n'a pleuré sa mort.

unregulated [ʌn'regjuleitid], *a.* (*a*) (*of machine, etc.*) non réglé, non régularisé; *El:* **u. voltage,** voltage non stabilisé; **u. frequency,** fréquence non asservie; (*b*) (*of pers., business, etc.*) non réglé, non réglementé.

unrehearsed [ʌnri'hə:st], *a.* (*of play, etc.*) (joué) sans répétition(s); (*of speech, etc.*) improvisé, spontané; **u. effect, incident,** effet, incident, non préparé, imprévu, inattendu.

unrelatable [ʌnri'leitəbl], *a.* irracontable.

unrelated [ʌnri'leitid], *a.* **1.** (*a*) (*of events, etc.*) sans rapport (**to each other,** l'un avec l'autre); **these facts are totally u.,** il n'y a aucun rapport entre ces faits; (*b*) (*of pers.*) **they are entirely u.,** il n'y a aucun lien de parenté entre eux; ils ne sont pas parents entre eux; (*c*) *Gram:* (participe) isolé, indépendant, sans soutien. **2. to leave a fact u.,** ne pas raconter un fait; passer un fait sous silence.

unrelaxing [ʌnri'læksiŋ], *a. esp. Lit:* **1.** (assiduité, etc.) sans relâche; (effort, etc.) assidu, soutenu. **2. u. grip,** prise de fer.

unrelenting [ʌnri'lentiŋ], *a.* (*a*) (*of pers.*) implacable, impitoyable, inexorable (**towards,** à, pour, à l'égard de); **he was u.,** il restait inflexible; (*b*) (*of persecution, struggle, etc.*) acharné; sans rémission, sans relâche; **an u. series of disasters,** une série continue de désastres.

unrelentingly [ʌnri'lentiŋli], *adv.* (*a*) inexorablement, impitoyablement, implacablement; (*b*) sans rémission, sans relâche, sans répit; continuellement.

unreliability [ʌnrilaiə'biliti], *s.* **1.** instabilité *f*, inconstance *f*, manque *m* de sérieux (d'une entreprise, de qn). **2** (*a*) incertitude *f*, inexactitude *f* (d'un résultat, d'un calcul, etc.); (*b*) manque de fiabilité, de sécurité (d'une machine, etc.).

unreliable [ʌnri'laiəbl], *a.* **1.** (homme, etc.) auquel, à qui, on ne peut pas se fier, sur lequel, sur qui, on ne peut pas compter; (caractère) inconstant, instable; **I think he's u.,** je ne peux pas avoir confiance en lui. **2.** (*a*) (renseignement, etc.) inexact, sujet à caution; (résultat) incertain, douteux; **to have sth. from an u. source,** tenir quelque chose d'une source douteuse, incertaine, peu sûre; (*b*) (appareil, machine, etc.) non fiable, au fonctionnement incertain, irrégulier; (entreprise, etc.) qui manque de sérieux; **u. clock,** horloge déréglée, à laquelle on ne peut se fier; **u. map,** carte peu fidèle, peu fiable; **u. road,** route à viabilité douteuse; *Turf:* **u. runner,** tocard *m.*

unreliably [ʌnri'laiəbli], *adv.* **I am u. informed that. . .,** selon une source douteuse, incertaine, peu sûre. . . .

unrelieved [ʌnri'li:vd], *a.* **1.** (*a*) *A:* (*of pers.*) qui reste sans secours; laissé sans secours; (*b*) (*of pain*) non soulagé; sans soulagement. **2.** qui manque de relief, de variété; monotone; **the u. monotony of the concrete walls,** la monotonie absolue, l'uniformité lassante, des murs de béton; **u. mediocrity,** médiocrité absolue, totale; **news of u. gloom,** nouvelles uniformément désolantes; **u. poverty,** misère noire; **u. boredom,** ennui mortel.

unremarkable [ʌnri'mɑ:kəbl], *a.* (*of pers., style, dress, etc.*) médiocre, (qui ne sort pas de l')ordinaire; peu remarquable; **it's a very u. case,** c'est un cas très banal.

unremarked [ʌnri'mɑ:kt], *a.* inobservé, inaperçu; **it went u.,** cela a passé sous silence, sans commentaires.

unremedied [ʌn'remidid], *a.* (*of situation, etc.*) auquel, à laquelle, auxquels, auxquelles, on n'a pu remédier.

unremembered [ʌnri'membəd], *a. Lit:* oublié, immémoré.

unremittable [ʌnri'mitəbl], *a.* irrémissible.

unremitted [ʌnri'mitid], *a.* (péché) non remis, non pardonné; **u. debt,** dette non remise.

unremitting [ʌnri'mitiŋ], *a.* **1.** (travail, etc.) ininterrompu; sans relâche; (appui, etc.) inlassable, infatigable; **u. efforts,** efforts soutenus, assidus, constants; **u. opposition to a project,** opposition opiniâtre à un projet; **u. rain,** pluie incessante, ininterrompue, sans cesse. **2.** (*of pers.*) **he was u. in his attentions,** son assiduité ne s'est pas démentie un instant.

unremittingly [ʌnri'mitiŋli], *adv.* sans cesse, sans relâche; sans interruption; (travailler, etc.) assidûment, inlassablement, infatigablement; **he was u. opposed to it,** il s'y opposait de la façon la plus opiniâtre.

unremorseful [ʌnri'mɔ:sful], *a.* sans remords.

unremunerated [ʌnri'mju:nəreitid], *a.* (ouvrier, travail) non rémunéré; irrémunéré; non payé, impayé.

unremunerative [ʌnri'mju:nərətiv], *a.* peu rémunérateur, -trice; peu lucratif; mal payé; **u. research,** recherches peu fructueuses, peu rentables, improductives.

unrenewed [ʌnri'nju:d], *a.* non renouvelé.

unrepaid [ʌnri'peid], *a.* **1.** (emprunt, argent, etc.) non remboursé, non rendu; (service) non payé de retour; (tort) non vengé. **2.** (*of pers.*) (i) non remboursé; (ii) non récompensé; **u. for his kindness,** sans récompense de sa bonté.

unrepealable [ʌnri'pi:ləbl], *a.* inabrogeable, irrévocable.

unrepealed [ʌnri'pi:ld], *a.* (*of law, etc.*) non abrogé, inabrogé; non révoqué.

unrepeatable [ʌnri'pi:təbl], *a.* (remarque, etc.) qu'on ne peut répéter; (histoire) irracontable; **he said sth. u.,** je n'ose pas répéter ce qu'il a dit; **u. prices, offer,** prix exceptionnels, offre unique.

unrepentant, unrepenting [ʌnri'pentənt, -'pentiŋ], *a.* impénitent; **to die unrepentant,** mourir dans le péché; **she was unrepentant about what she had done,** elle ne s'est pas repentie de ce qu'elle avait fait.

unrepented [ʌnri'pentid], *a.* (péché) non regretté, dont on ne se repent pas.

unrepining [ʌnri'painiŋ], *a. Lit:* qui ne se plaint pas.

unrepiningly [ʌnri'painiŋli], *adv. Lit:* sans se plaindre; sans murmurer.

unreplenished [ʌnri'pleniʃt], *a.* non réapprovisionné.

unreported [ʌnri'pɔ:tid], *a.* (*of meeting, etc.*) non rapporté; dont on n'a pas donné le compte rendu; (*of accident, etc.*) non signalé.

unrepresentative [ʌnrepri'zentətiv], *a.* peu représentatif; peu typique; **u. legislature,** législature peu représentative.

unrepresented [ʌnrepri'zentid], *a.* non représenté; **u. nation,** nation sans représentant, sans délégué.

unrepressed [ʌnri'prest], *a.* irréprimé, non réprimé.

unreproducible [ʌnriːprəˈdjuːsibl], *a.* que l'on ne peut reproduire.
unreproved [ʌnriˈpruːvd], *a.* non réprimandé, non censuré; sans réprimande, sans blâme.
unrequested [ʌnriˈkwestid], *a.* spontané; qui n'a pas été demandé; **he did it u.,** il l'a fait spontanément, sans qu'on le lui ait demandé.
unrequired [ʌnriˈkwaiəd], *a.* qui n'est pas nécessaire; dont on n'a pas, plus, besoin.
unrequitable [ʌnriˈkwaitəbl], *a.* qu'on ne peut récompenser; irrécompensable.
unrequited [ʌnriˈkwaitid], *a.* **1.** (*of service, etc.*) non récompensé. **2. u. love,** amour non payé de retour, non partagé; amour malheureux.
unrescinded [ʌnriˈsindid], *a.* (*of law, etc.*) inabrogé, non abrogé, toujours en vigueur.
unresented [ʌnriˈzentid], *a.* dont on ne s'offense pas, dont on ne se froisse pas; **u. criticism,** critique prise en bonne part.
unresentful, unresenting [ʌnriˈzentful, -ˈzentiŋ], *a.* sans ressentiment, non rancunier.
unreserved [ʌnriˈzəːvd], *a.* **1.** sans réserve; non réservé; (*a*) franc, *f.* franche; ouvert, expansif; **he spoke to me with u. confidence,** il m'a parlé avec abandon; (*b*) (*of approval, etc.*) entier; complet, -ète; **u. praise,** éloges sans réserve. **2. u. seats,** places non réservées, non retenues.
unreservedly [ʌnriˈzəːvidli], *adv.* sans réserve; (*a*) franchement; à cœur ouvert; (*b*) entièrement, complètement; sans restriction; **to trust s.o. u.,** avoir pleine confiance en qn.
unreservedness [ʌnriˈzəːvidnis], *s.* manque *m* de réserve.
unresisted [ʌnriˈzistid], *a.* **1.** (*of temptation, etc.*) auquel on ne résiste pas; auquel on n'a pu résister. **2. to do sth. u.,** faire qch. sans rencontrer d'opposition.
unresisting [ʌnriˈzistiŋ], *a.* qui ne résiste pas; soumis, docile.
unresolved [ʌnriˈzɔlvd], *a.* **1.** (*of pers.*) irrésolu, hésitant, indécis; **he was u. whether he would go or not,** il se demandait s'il irait ou non. **2.** (problème, etc.) non résolu, irrésolu. **2.** *Mus:* (*of discord*) non résolu.
unrespectable [ʌnriˈspektəbl], *a.* peu respectable, peu honorable.
unrespected [ʌnriˈspektid], *a.* (personne) que l'on ne respecte pas.
unresponsive [ʌnriˈspɔnsiv], *a.* difficile à émouvoir; insensible (**to,** à); **she was totally u. when he told her the news,** elle n'a pas réagi du tout quand il lui a appris la nouvelle.
unrest [ʌnˈrest], *s.* **1.** inquiétude *f.* **2.** troubles *mpl,* agitation *f;* **social u.,** malaise social; **labour u.,** agitation ouvrière; **there was u. among the workers,** les ouvriers s'agitaient.
unrestored [ʌnriˈstɔːd], *a.* **1.** (*of stolen goods, etc.*) non rendu, non restitué. **2.** (*of monument, picture*) non restauré; (*of picture*) non réparé; (*of furniture*) non rénové. **3.** (*a*) (*of object*) non remis (en place); (*b*) (*of pers.*) non rétabli (dans ses fonctions, ses droits).
unrestrainable [ʌnriˈstreinəbl], *a.* irréprimable, incontrôlable.
unrestrained [ʌnriˈstreind], *a.* **1.** non restreint; non contenu; non réprimé, irréprimé; libre, effréné; **u. laughter,** rires immodérés. **2.** *Lit:* **u. by our presence, he continued to talk,** aucunement gêné par notre présence, il a continué de parler.
unrestrainedly [ʌnriˈstreinidli], *adv.* librement; sans contrainte; immodérément.
unrestricted [ʌnriˈstriktid], *a.* sans restriction; illimité; (pouvoir) absolu; (accès) libre; *Adm: Aut:* **u. road,** voie sans limitation de vitesse.
unretentive [ʌnriˈtentiv], *a.* **u. memory,** mémoire courte; mauvaise mémoire.
unretracted [ʌnriˈtræktid], *a.* non rétracté, non désavoué.
unrevealable [ʌnriˈviːləbl], *a.* que l'on ne peut révéler, dévoiler, divulguer.
unrevealed [ʌnriˈviːld], *a.* non révélé, non dévoilé, non divulgué.
unrevenged [ʌnriˈvendʒd], *a.* invengé. **1.** sans être vengé. **2.** sans s'être vengé.
unrevised [ʌnriˈvaizd], *a.* (*of text*) non revu, non relu, non révisé; (*of proof*) non corrigé, non révisé.
unrevoked [ʌnriˈvoukt], *a.* non révoqué; (décret) non abrogé.
unrewarded [ʌnriˈwɔːdid], *a.* non récompensé; sans récompense.
unrewarding [ʌnriˈwɔːdiŋ], *a.* (*a*) peu rémunérateur, -trice; (*b*) **it's a very u. book,** ce livre ne vaut pas la peine d'être lu.
unrhymed [ʌnˈraimd], *a.* **u. verse,** vers blancs.
unrhythmical [ʌnˈriðmikl], *a.* non rythmique; non rythmé; non cadencé.
unrhythmically [ʌnˈriðmik(ə)li], *adv.* sans (aucun) rythme.
unridable [ʌnˈraidəbl], *a.* (cheval) immontable.
unridden [ʌnˈridn], *a.* (cheval) qui n'a jamais été monté.
unriddle [ʌnˈridl], *v.tr. A: & Lit:* résoudre (un mystère, etc.).
unrifled[1] [ʌnˈraifld], *a.* non pillé, non violé, intact.
unrifled[2], *a. Sm.a:* (canon) lisse.
unrig [ʌnˈrig], *v.tr.* (**unrigged**) *Nau:* dégréer, dégarnir, déséquiper (un navire); dégréer, décapeler (un mât); dégarnir (le cabestan); **to u. a crane,** désappareiller une grue.
unrigging [ʌnˈrigiŋ], *s. Nau:* décapelage *m,* dégarnissement *m,* désappareillement *m.*
unrighteous [ʌnˈraitʃəs], *a.* (*of pers., action*) **1.** mauvais, malveillant, méchant; funeste. **2.** inique, injuste.
unrighteously [ʌnˈraitʃəsli], *adv.* **1.** méchamment, funestement. **2.** iniquement, injustement.
unrighteousness [ʌnˈraitʃəsnis], *s.* **1.** mal *m,* malveillance *f,* méchanceté *f.* **2.** iniquité *f,* injustice *f,* improbité *f.*
unripe, unripened [ʌnˈraip, -ˈraip(ə)nd], *a.* (*of fruit, wine, etc.*) vert; qui n'est pas mûr; (*of wheat*) en herbe; vert; (*of plan, etc.*) insuffisamment médité, pas encore mûr; **the fruit must be picked u.,** il faut cueillir les fruits avant qu'ils soient mûrs.
unripeness [ʌnˈraipnis], *s.* verdeur *f,* immaturité *f* (d'un fruit, du vin, etc.); immaturité *f* (d'âge, d'un projet).
unrippled [ʌnˈripld], *a.* (*of surface of sea, etc.*) calme, plat; sans une ride.
unrivalled [ʌnˈraiv(ə)ld], *a.* sans rival; sans pareil; incomparable; hors de pair, hors ligne; **our goods are u.,** nos articles sont sans concurrence.
unrivet [ʌnˈrivit], *v.tr.* (**unrivet(t)ed**) dériver, dériveter (un clou, etc.).
unroadworthy [ʌnˈroudwəːði], *a.* (*of vehicle*) qui n'est pas en état de rouler; qui n'est pas en état de marche.
unroasted [ʌnˈroustid], *a.* non rôti; (*of coffee*) non torréfié, non grillé.
unroll [ʌnˈroul]. **1.** *v.tr.* dérouler (une carte, du tissu); **to u. a banner,** déferler une bannière. **2.** *v.i. & pr.* se dérouler.
unromantic [ʌnrəˈmæntik], *a.* peu romanesque; peu romantique; terre(-)à(-)terre *inv.*
unroof [ʌnˈruːf], *v.tr.* **to u. a house,** enlever le toit d'une maison.
unrope [ʌnˈroup], *v.i. Mount:* se décorder.
unruffled [ʌnˈrʌfld], *a.* **1.** (*of pers., temper, etc.*) calme, serein, imperturbable, placide; **u., he continued to speak,** sans se troubler, il a continué de parler. **2.** (*of sea, etc.*) calme, uni, sans rides; (*of hair, feathers*) lisse.
unruled [ʌnˈruːld], *a.* **1.** (*of a people*) non gouverné; (*of passion*) déchaîné, effréné. **2.** (*of paper*) uni; sans lignes; non réglé.
unruliness [ʌnˈruːlinis], *s.* indiscipline *f,* insoumission *f,* insubordination *f,* turbulence *f* (d'un enfant, etc.); caractère fougueux (d'un cheval).
unruly [ʌnˈruːli], *a.* (enfant, etc.) indiscipliné, insoumis, rebelle, turbulent; (cheval) fougueux.
unsaddle [ʌnˈsædl], *v.tr.* **1.** desseller (un cheval); débâter (un âne). **2.** (*of horse*) désarçonner, démonter (un cavalier).
unsafe [ʌnˈseif], *a.* (*of place, etc.*) dangereux; (*of position, Ins: of life*) peu sûr; (*of undertaking*) hasardeux; (*of chair, etc.*) peu solide; (*of rope, etc.*) mal assujetti, mal attaché; *Nau:* **u. anchorage,** mauvais mouillage.
unsaid [ʌnˈsed], *a.* (*of word, etc.*) non prononcé; **to leave sth. u.,** passer qch. sous silence; **it's better left u.,** mieux vaut se taire, ne rien dire; **consider that u.,** mettez que je n'ai rien dit.
unsalaried [ʌnˈsælərid], *a.* non rétribué; non rémunéré; non salarié.
unsaleable [ʌnˈseiləbl], *a.* (*of goods*) invendable, peu vendable; hors de vente; de mauvaise vente.
unsaleableness [ʌnˈseiləb(ə)lnis], *s.* difficulté *f* d'écoulement (d'une marchandise).
unsalted [ʌnˈsɔːltid], *a.* (*of meat, fish, etc.*) non salé; (*of dish*) sans sel; **u. butter,** beurre frais.
unsanctified [ʌnˈsæŋ(k)tifaid], *a.* non consacré; profane.
unsanctioned [ʌnˈsæŋ(k)ʃ(ə)nd], *a.* **1.** (*of action, etc.*) non autorisé, non approuvé. **2.** (*of law, decree*) non sanctionné, non ratifié.
unsated, unsatiated [ʌnˈseitid, -ˈseiʃieitid], *a. Lit:* (*of appetite, desire, etc.*) inassouvi, non rassasié.
unsatisfactorily [ʌnsætisˈfækt(ə)rili], *adv.* d'une manière peu satisfaisante; d'une manière qui laisse à désirer; mal.
unsatisfactoriness [ʌnsætisˈfækt(ə)rinis], *s.* caractère peu satisfaisant.
unsatisfactory [ʌnsætisˈfækt(ə)ri], *a.* peu satisfaisant; qui laisse à désirer; décevant; (*of explanation, etc.*) peu convaincant; (*of method, system*) défectueux; (*of result, etc.*) au-dessous de la moyenne; médiocre; **it's most u.,** cela laisse beaucoup à désirer.
unsatisfiable [ʌnsætisˈfaiəbl], *a.* (désir, etc.) inassouvissable.
unsatisfied [ʌnˈsætisfaid], *a.* **1.** mécontent, peu satisfait (**with,** de); **I'm u. with it,** je n'en suis pas satisfait; **he was u. with (mere) guesswork,** il ne se satisfaisait pas de conjectures. **2. to be u. about sth.,** avoir des doutes sur qch.; **I'm still u. about it,** je n'en suis pas encore convaincu. **3.** (*of appetite, etc.*) inassouvi, non rassasié; *Psy:* **u. instincts,** inassouvissements *m.* **4.** (*of debt*) insatisfait; non réglé.
unsatisfying [ʌnˈsætisfaiiŋ], *a.* **1.** peu satisfaisant, peu convaincant; peu rassurant. **2.** (*of meal, etc.*) insuffisant; **I found the meal u.,** (i) après le repas j'avais encore faim; (ii) le repas était plutôt décevant.
unsaturable [ʌnˈsætjərəbl], *a. Ch: etc:* insaturable.
unsaturated [ʌnˈsætjəreitid], *a. Ch: etc:* insaturé; non saturé.
unsave [ʌnˈseiv], *v.tr. Cmptr:* détruire (une information devenue inutile).
unsavouriness [ʌnˈseiv(ə)rinis], *s.* **1.** (*a*) goût *m* désagréable (d'un mets, etc.); (*b*) odeur désagréable, nauséabonde (d'un endroit). **2.** caractère répugnant (d'un scandale, d'un roman, etc.).
unsavoury [ʌnˈseiv(ə)ri], *a.* **1.** (*a*) (goût) désagréable; (plat) d'un goût désagréable, répugnant; (*b*) **u. smell,** mauvaise odeur; odeur déplaisante, désagréable, nauséabonde. **2.** (scandale, etc.) répugnant; **u. business,** affaire louche; **u. reputation,** réputation équivoque; *F:* **he's really u.,** ce qu'il est répugnant, ce qu'il me dégoûte.
unsawn [ʌnˈsɔːn], *a.* (bois) non scié, non débité.
unscalable [ʌnˈskeiləbl], *a.* (*of cliff, wall*) qu'il est impossible d'escalader.
unscaled [ʌnˈskeild], *a.* (*of cliff, etc.*) qui n'a jamais été escaladé.
unscarred [ʌnˈskɑːd], *a.* sans cicatrice; indemne; **he came out of it u.,** il en est sorti indemne, sain et sauf.
unscathed [ʌnˈskeiðd], *a.* indemne; sain et sauf.
unscented [ʌnˈsentid], *a.* (savon, etc.) sans parfum.
unscheduled [ʌnˈʃedjuːld, -ˈskedjuːld], *a.* (*a*) (départ, etc.) imprévu; *Rail: etc:* **u. stop,** arrêt qui n'est pas indiqué dans l'horaire; (*b*) *Cmptr:* non planifié; **u. maintenance,** entretien curatif.
unscholarly [ʌnˈskɔləli], *a.* peu savant; indigne d'un savant; (auteur, etc.) qui manque d'érudition.
unschooled [ʌnˈskuːld], *a.* **1.** (*a*) *O:* (*of pers.*) sans instruction; illettré, ignorant; (*b*) **u. horse,** cheval non dressé. **2.** *A: & Lit:* (*a*) indiscipliné; (*b*) (sentiment, etc.) spontané, naturel.
unscientific [ʌnsaiənˈtifik], *a.* non scientifique; peu scientifique; **u. name,** nom courant (d'une plante, etc.).
unscientifically [ʌnsaiənˈtifik(ə)li], *adv.* peu scientifiquement.
unscramble [ʌnˈskræmbl], *v.tr.* déchiffrer (un code).
unscraped [ʌnˈskreipt], *a.* non gratté; *Leath:* **u. sheepskin,** parchemin en cosse.
unscratched [ʌnˈskrætʃt], *a.* sans (une) égratignure.
unscreened [ʌnˈskriːnd], *a.* **1.** (*a*) (*of place*) exposé, non abrité; (*b*) sans écran; *El:* (condensateur, etc.) non blindé. **2.** (*of coal*) non criblé. **3.** non examiné (par les services de contre-espionnage). **4.** (*of film*) pas encore mis à l'écran.
unscrew [ʌnˈskruː]. **1.** *v.tr.* (*a*) dévisser (un boulon, etc.); déboulonner (une machine); (*b*) *Med: etc:* desserrer (un tourniquet, etc.). **2.** *v.i. & pr.* se dévisser; se desserrer; (*of capstan*) dévirer.
unscrewed [ʌnˈskruːd], *a.* **1.** dévissé; déboulonné. **2.** (*of bolt, etc.*) sans filet; non taraudé; uni.
unscrewing [ʌnˈskruːiŋ], *s.* **1.** dévissage *m,* déboulonnage *m.* **2.** dévirage *m* (du cabestan).
unscripted [ʌnˈskriptid], *a. W.Tel: T.V:* (*of interview, etc.*) spontané.
unscrupulous [ʌnˈskruːpjuləs], *a.* peu scrupuleux; indélicat; sans scrupules; sans conscience.
unscrupulously [ʌnˈskruːpjuləsli], *adv.* peu scrupuleusement; indélicatement; sans scrupule(s).
unscrupulousness [ʌnˈskruːpjuləsnis], *s.* indélicatesse *f;* manque *m* de conscience, de scrupule.
unseal [ʌnˈsiːl], *v.tr.* **1.** desceller (un acte, etc.); décacheter (une lettre, etc.). **2.** *Lit:* **to u. s.o.'s lips,** rendre à qn sa liberté de parole.
unsealed [ʌnˈsiːld], *a.* **1.** descellé; (*of letter*) décacheté. **2.** sans sceau; (document) non scellé.
unseamanlike [ʌnˈsiːmənlaik], *a.* peu digne d'un marin.
unsearched [ʌnˈsəːtʃt], *a.* (*of ship, luggage, etc.*) qui n'a

pas été visité; **to let a suspect go u.,** laisser partir un suspect sans le fouiller.

unseasonable [ʌn'si:z(ə)nəbl], *a.* **1.** (*of fish, fruit, etc.*) hors de saison; **this weather's very u.,** ce temps n'est pas normal pour la saison. **2.** (*of time, etc.*) inopportun; mal venu; déplacé; mal à propos; *Lit:* **u. request,** demande inopportune, importune.

unseasonableness [ʌn'si:z(ə)nəblnis], *s.* **1. the u. of the weather,** l'état anormal du temps. **2.** *Lit:* inopportunité *f* (d'une demande, etc.).

unseasonably [ʌn'si:z(ə)nəbli], *adv.* **1.** hors de saison. **2.** mal à propos; inopportunément; à contretemps.

unseasoned [ʌn'si:z(ə)nd], *a.* **1.** (*of food*) non assaisonné. **2.** (*a*) **u. timber,** bois vert, vif; (*b*) *O:* (*of pers.*) (i) inexpérimenté; (ii) inacclimaté; (*of troops*) inaguerri; (*of sailor*) non amariné.

unseat [ʌn'si:t], *v.tr.* **1.** (*a*) désarçonner, démonter (un cavalier); (*b*) renverser, faire tomber (qn). **2.** *Parl:* (*a*) faire perdre son siège à (un député); (*b*) annuler l'élection de (qn); invalider (un membre élu).

unseaworthiness [ʌn'si:wə:ðinis], *s.* *Jur:* (état *m* d')innavigabilité *f*; vice *m* propre (d'un navire).

unseaworthy [ʌn'si:wə:ði], *s.* (navire) hors d'état de prendre la mer; incapable de tenir la mer; en mauvais état de navigabilité; *Jur:* innavigable.

unseconded [ʌn'sekəndid], *a.* (*a*) (*of pers.*) non secondé; non soutenu; non appuyé; (*b*) (*of motion in debate, etc.*) non appuyé.

unsecured [ʌnsi'kjuəd], *a.* **1.** (*of door, etc.*) mal fermé; (*of plank, etc.*) mal assujetti; non assujetti; (*of boat, etc.*) non amarré. **2.** (*of loan, etc.*) non garanti, à découvert, en blanc; (*of debt, creditor*) sans garantie; chirographaire.

unseeded [ʌn'si:did], *a.* *Ten: etc:* (*of player*) non classé.

unseeing [ʌn'si:iŋ], *a.* qui ne voit pas; aveugle; **to look at s.o., sth., with u. eyes,** regarder qn, qch., sans (le) voir; **to look at nature with u. eyes,** regarder la nature en aveugle.

unseemliness [ʌn'si:mlinis], *s.* *O:* inconvenance *f*, incongruité *f*, messéance *f* (de conduite, d'une remarque).

unseemly [ʌn'si:mli], *a.* *O:* (*of behaviour, remark, etc.*) inconvenant, incongru; peu convenable, messéant.

unseen [ʌn'si:n]. **1.** *a.* (*a*) inaperçu, invisible; **to do sth. u.,** faire qch. à la dérobée, sans être vu; **to buy sth. u.,** acheter qch. sans l'avoir vu; (*b*) *Sch:* **u. translation,** *s.* **u.,** version *f*. **2.** *s.* **the u.,** (i) l'autre monde *m*; l'au-delà *m*; (ii) le surnaturel.

unsegmented [ʌnseg'mentid], *a.* non segmenté.

unsegregated [ʌn'segrigeitid], *a.* sans ségrégation.

unselfconscious [ʌnself'kɔnʃəs], *a.* (*of pers., manner*) naturel; sans contrainte; désinvolte.

unselfconsciousness [ʌnself'kɔnʃəsnis], *s.* absence *f* de contrainte; naturel *m*; désinvolture *f*.

unselfish [ʌn'selfiʃ], *a.* (*of pers., life, etc.*) généreux; dévoué; sans égoïsme; **u. life,** vie d'abnégation; **u. motive,** motif désintéressé.

unselfishly [ʌn'selfiʃli], *adv.* généreusement; sans égoïsme; avec dévouement; pour des motifs de bonté.

unselfishness [ʌn'selfiʃnis], *s.* désintéressement *m*; générosité *f*; dévouement *m*.

unsensitized [ʌn'sensitaizd], *a.* *Phot:* (papier) non sensibilisé.

unsent [ʌn'sent], *a.* (*of letter*) non expédié.

unsentenced [ʌn'sentənst], *a.* (détenu, etc.) non condamné, dont le jugement n'a pas (encore) été prononcé.

unsentimental [ʌnsenti'ment(ə)l], *a.* (*a*) peu sentimental, -aux; (*b*) (*of pers.*) positif, prosaïque; terre à terre.

unserve [ʌn'sə:v], *v.tr.* *Nau:* défourrer (un cordage).

unserved [ʌn'sə:vd], *a.* (*of customer, food*) non servi.

unserviceable [ʌn'sə:visəbl], *a.* (*a*) inutilisable; d'aucune utilité; (*b*) (vêtement, etc.) peu pratique, qui s'use trop vite; (*c*) (*of machine, etc.*) hors d'usage; *Mil:* (*of arms, stores, etc.*) hors service; **it has become u.,** il est maintenant hors d'état de servir.

unset [ʌn'set], *a.* **1.** (*of diamond, etc.*) non serti; hors d'œuvre. **2.** *Med:* (fracture) qui n'a pas été remise. **3.** (ciment, béton) qui n'a pas encore pris.

unsettle [ʌn'setl], *v.tr.* ébranler (les idées de qn, etc.); déranger (un projet, etc.); troubler le repos de (qn); **the storm has unsettled the weather,** l'orage a dérangé le temps.

unsettled [ʌn'setld], *a.* **1.** (pays, gouvernement) troublé, instable; (temps) variable, changeant, incertain; (esprit) (i) inquiet, troublé, agité, (ii) dérangé, détraqué; **the u. state of the weather, the market,** l'incertitude *f* du temps, du marché; les fluctuations *f* du marché. **2.** (*of pers.*) sans domicile fixe; pas encore établi. **3.** (esprit, caractère) indécis, irrésolu; **I'm still u. in my mind about it,** je ne suis pas encore décidé là-dessus. **4.** (*a*) (*of question, dispute*) indécis, douteux, pas encore réglé; (*b*) (*of bill, etc.*) impayé, non réglé; (*c*) *Jur:* (*of estate of deceased*) non constitué. **5.** (pays) sans habitants; (territoire) non habité.

unsettling [ʌn'setliŋ], *a.* (*of news, etc.*) inquiétant, troublant.

unsewn [ʌn'soun], *a.* **to come u.,** se découdre.

unsex [ʌn'seks], *v.tr.* priver (qn) de son sexe; émasculer (un mâle); déféminiser (une femelle).

unsexed [ʌn'sekst], *a.* (*of chickens, etc.*) dont on n'a pas encore déterminé le sexe.

unshackle [ʌn'ʃækl], *v.tr.* **1.** désentraver (un cheval, etc.); ôter les fers à (un prisonnier). **2.** *Nau: etc:* démaniller, démailler (une chaîne); détalinguer (une ancre). **3.** *Tg:* enlever l'isolateur d'arrêt (d'un fil).

unshackled [ʌn'ʃækld], *a.* **1.** sans fers, sans entraves. **2.** libre, sans entraves, sans contrainte.

unshackling [ʌn'ʃækliŋ], *s.* *Nau:* démanillage *m*.

unshakeable [ʌn'ʃeikəbl], *a.* (volonté) inébranlable, ferme; (amitié) à toute épreuve; **u. devotion,** attachement *m* irréductible.

unshaken [ʌn'ʃeik(ə)n], *a.* inébranlé, ferme; (*of perseverance, etc.*) constant; **with u. constancy,** avec une constance inébranlable.

unshapely [ʌn'ʃeipli], *a.* mal fait; difforme, disgracieux.

unshattered [ʌn'ʃætəd], *a.* (*a*) (*of nerves, spirit, etc.*) inébranlé; (*b*) **there was only one (window)pane u.,** une seule vitre est restée intacte.

unshaved, unshaven [ʌn'ʃeivd, -'ʃeiv(ə)n], *a.* non rasé.

unsheathe [ʌn'ʃi:ð], *v.tr.* **1.** dégainer (une épée, etc.); *Lit:* **to u. the sword,** commencer les hostilités; tirer le glaive. **2.** *N.Arch:* (*also* **unsheath** [ʌn'ʃi:θ]) dédoubler (un navire); enlever la doublure (d'un navire).

unsheathed [ʌn'ʃi:ðd], *a.* **1.** (*a*) (*of sword*) dégainé; (*b*) (*of ship*) dédoublé. **2.** sans gaine.

unsheathing [ʌn'ʃi:ðiŋ], *s.* **1.** dégainement *m* (d'une épée). **2.** *N.Arch:* dédoublage *m*.

unsheltered [ʌn'ʃeltəd], *a.* sans abri, non abrité, sans protection (**from,** contre); **u. on any, every, side,** exposé à tous les vents.

unshielded [ʌn'ʃi:ldid], *a.* **u. from sth.,** non protégé contre qch.; exposé à qch.

unshifted [ʌn'ʃiftid], *a.* *Cmptr:* non décalé.

unship [ʌn'ʃip], *v.tr.* (**unshipped**) *Nau:* **1.** décharger, débarquer, désembarquer (les marchandises); débarquer (les passagers, etc.). **2.** (*a*) enlever (un mât); démonter (le gouvernail, une hélice, etc.); (*b*) déborder, désarmer, rentrer (les avirons); **u. oars!** rentrez!

unshod [ʌn'ʃɔd], *a.* **1.** (*a*) (*of pers.*) déchaussé; (*b*) (*of horse*) déferré; (*c*) (*of wheel*) désembattu; (*of stake, etc.*) désarmé. **2.** (*a*) (*of pers.*) nu-pieds *inv*; les pieds nus; sans chaussures; (*b*) (*of horse*) sans fers; (*c*) (*of wheel*) sans bande; (*of stake, etc.*) sans sabot; sans fer.

unshoe [ʌn'ʃu:], *v.tr.* (*p.t.* & *p.p.* **unshod, unshoed** [-'ʃɔd, -'ʃu:d]) **1.** déferrer (un cheval). **2.** (*a*) *A:* **to u. a wheel,** désembattre une roue; ôter la bande d'une roue; (*b*) **to u. a stake, pile,** désarmer un pieu; ôter le sabot d'un pieu.

unshorn [ʌn'ʃɔ:n], *a.* (*a*) (*of sheep, cloth*) non tondu; intondu; (*b*) *Lit:* (*of head*) non rasé; (*of hair*) non coupé.

unshrinkable [ʌn'ʃriŋkəbl], *a.* *Tex:* irrétrécissable.

unshrinking [ʌn'ʃriŋkiŋ], *a.* crâne, hardi, ferme; qui ne recule pas, ne bronche pas.

unshrinkingly [ʌn'ʃriŋkiŋli], *adv.* hardiment, crânement, sans broncher.

unshriven [ʌn'ʃriv(ə)n], *a.* *A:* & *Lit:* **to die u.,** mourir sans confession; mourir inabsous, -oute; mourir dans son péché.

unshrunk [ʌn'ʃrʌŋk], *a.* *Tex:* non rétréci; qui n'a pas été soumis au rétrécissement.

unshut [ʌn'ʃʌt], *a.* (*of door, eyes*) non fermé; ouvert.

unshutter [ʌn'ʃʌtər], *v.tr.* enlever, ouvrir, les volets (d'une fenêtre).

unshuttered [ʌn'ʃʌtəd], *a.* (fenêtre) (i) dont les volets ne sont pas fermés, (ii) sans volets.

unsifted [ʌn'siftid], *a.* (*a*) (*of sand, cinders, etc.*) non criblé; (*of sugar*) non passé au tamis; (*of flour*) non sassé; (*b*) (*of information, etc.*) non examiné (à fond); non passé au tamis.

unsighted [ʌn'saitid], *a.* **1.** (*a*) inaperçu, invisible; (*b*) **the ship is still u.,** le navire n'a pas encore été aperçu; on est encore sans nouvelle du navire. **2.** (*of gun*) sans hausse. **3.** *Games:* **to be u.,** avoir la vue bouchée pour un instant; perdre le ballon, etc., de vue. **4.** *s.* **the u.,** les aveugles.

unsightliness [ʌn'saitlinis], *s.* laideur *f*.

unsightly [ʌn'saitli], *a.* laid; peu agréable à la vue; désagréable à voir; **landscape marred by u. advertisements,** paysage déparé par des panneaux qui offusquent la vue.

unsigned [ʌn'saind], *a.* (document) non signé, sans signature; *Cmptr:* sans signe, non signé.

unsilt [ʌn'silt], *v.tr.* écurer (un puits); dévaser (un port); décolmater (une canalisation).

unsingable [ʌn'siŋəbl], *a.* inchantable; **the thing's u.!** impossible à chanter cela!

unsinkable [ʌn'siŋkəbl], *a.* (*of boat, etc.*) insubmersible.

unsisterly [ʌn'sistəli], *a.* (*of pers.*) peu comme une sœur; (conduite) indigne d'une sœur.

unsizeable [ʌn'saizəbl], *s.* *Fish:* (poisson) au-dessous des dimensions requises pour la pêche.

unsized[1] [ʌn'saizd], *a.* (*of paper, etc.*) sans colle, sans apprêt.

unsized[2], *a.* sans classification de taille.

unskilful [ʌn'skilful], *a.* malhabile, inhabile, inexpert, maladroit (**in, at,** à).

unskilfully [ʌn'skilfuli], *adv.* inhabilement, malhabilement, maladroitement; peu expertement.

unskilled [ʌn'skild], *a.* (*of pers.*) inexpérimenté (**in,** à); inexpert (**in,** dans, en); inexercé (**in,** à); **u. in, at, doing sth.,** inexpérimenté à faire qch.; *Ind:* **u. worker,** ouvrier non qualifié; manœuvre *m*; **u. labour,** main-d'œuvre non qualifiée, non spécialisée.

unslaked [ʌn'sleikt], *a.* **1. u. lime,** chaux vive, non éteinte, anhydre. **2.** (*of thirst*) non étanché, non apaisé.

unsleeping [ʌn'sli:piŋ], *a.* *Lit:* toujours en éveil; vigilant.

unslept [ʌn'slept], *a.* **u. in,** (lit, chambre) où l'on n'a pas couché; (lit) non défait.

unsling [ʌn'sliŋ], *v.tr.* (*p.t.* & *p.p.* **unslung** [-'slʌŋ]) **1. to u. a hammock,** dégréer, décrocher, un hamac. **2.** *Nau: etc:* enlever les élingues (d'un ballot).

unslung [ʌn'slʌŋ], *a.* (hamac) non gréé.

unsmiling [ʌn'smailiŋ], *a.* sérieux; qui ne sourit pas.

unsmirched [ʌn'smə:tʃt], *a.* (*of reputation, etc.*) sans tache, sans souillure; **to come out u.,** sortir indemne (d'une affaire délicate).

unsmokable [ʌn'smoukəbl], *a.* (cigare, etc.) infumable.

unsmoked [ʌn'smoukt], *a.* ((i) *of bacon, etc.*, (ii) *of cigar, etc.*) non fumé.

unsociability [ʌnsouʃə'biliti], **unsociableness** [ʌn'souʃəblnis], *s.* insociabilité *f*.

unsociable [ʌn'souʃəbl], *a.* insociable; sauvage, farouche; peu sociable.

unsocial [ʌn'souʃ(ə)l], *a.* **1.** insocial, -aux; **to work u. hours,** travailler à des heures indues, quand la plupart des gens sont libres. **2.** = UNSOCIABLE.

unsoiled [ʌn'sɔild], *a.* propre; (réputation) sans tache, sans souillure.

unsold [ʌn'sould], *a.* invendu.

unsolder [ʌn'souldər], *v.tr.* *Metalw:* dessouder.

unsoldered [ʌn'souldəd], *a.* **1.** dessoudé; **u. seam,** dessoudure *f*. **2.** non soudé.

unsoldierlike, unsoldierly [ʌn'souldʒəlaik, -li], *a.* peu militaire.

unsolicited [ʌnsə'lisitid], *a.* non sollicité; (*of action*) volontaire, spontané; **u. testimonial,** lettre d'attestation spontanée; **to do sth. u.,** faire qch. volontairement, spontanément.

unsolidified [ʌnsə'lidifaid], *a.* non solidifié; liquide.

unsolvable [ʌn'sɔlvəbl], *a.* (problème, etc.) insoluble.

unsolved [ʌn'sɔlvd], *a.* (problème) non résolu; (mystère) impénétré.

unsophisticated [ʌnsə'fistikeitid], *a.* **1.** pur; non adultéré; non frelaté; non sophistiqué; (vin) naturel. **2.** (*a*) (*of pers.*) ingénu, naïf, simple, candide; (*b*) *Tchn:* peu évolué, peu élaboré; primitif.

unsorted [ʌn'sɔ:tid], *a.* non assorti, non trié, non classé; **u. coal,** (houille *f*) tout-venant *m*.

unsought [ʌn'sɔ:t], *a.* **1. u. (for),** que l'on n'a pas cherché, recherché, demandé. **2.** *Lit:* **to do sth. u.,** faire qch. spontanément, volontairement, de soi-même.

unsound [ʌn'saund], *a.* **1.** (*a*) (*of pers.*) malsain, maladif; (*of health*) précaire, chancelant; **to be of u. mind,** ne pas avoir toute sa raison; ne pas jouir de toutes ses facultés; être fou, folle; **to commit suicide while of u. mind,** se suicider en état de démence temporaire; **u. horse,** cheval taré; (*b*) (*of timber*) avarié; vermoulu; (*of fruit, etc.*) gâté; en mauvais état; (*c*) (*of ice, foundations, bridge, etc.*) peu solide; en mauvais état; dangereux; (*of position*) mal affermi; (*of business, etc.*) périclitant; (*d*) (*of theory, argument*) mal fondé; qui pèche par la base; (*of doctrine, opinion*) faux; discutable; (*of decision, judgement*) peu judicieux; discutable; (*of investment*) peu sûr, hasardeux; (*of politician, etc.*) incompétent; **some passages in this book are u.,** ce livre contient des passages discutables; **it is u. financially,** c'est de la mauvaise finance; *Ins:* **u. risk, life,** mauvais risque; mauvais sujet d'assurance. **2.** *A:* (*of pers., character*) corrompu, dépravé, vicieux.

unsoundable [ʌn'saundəbl], *a.* (abîme, etc.) insondable.

unsounded[1] [ʌn'saundid], *a.* (syllabe) non prononcée; (lettre) muette, nulle.

unsounded[2], *a.* (*of depth*) insondé.

unsoundly [ʌn'saundli], *adv.* (raisonner, etc.) à faux, d'une manière discutable, peu judicieuse.

unsoundness [ʌn'saundnis], *s.* **1.** (*a*) **u. of mind,** faiblesse *f* d'esprit; (*b*) (*of timber, etc.*) mauvais état; (*c*) fausseté *f* (d'une doctrine, d'un raisonnement); manque *m* de jugement (d'une décision, etc.); incompétence *f* (d'un homme politique, etc.); caractère hasardeux (d'un placement). **2.** *A:* caractère dépravé (de qn).

unsowed, unsown [ʌn'soud, -'soun], *a.* **1.** (*of seed*) non semé. **2.** (*of field, etc.*) non ensemencé.

unspan ['ʌnspæn], *v.tr.* (**unspanned**) (*in S. Africa*) dételer (les bœufs).

unsparing [ʌn'spɛəriŋ], *a.* prodigue; libéral, -aux; **to be u. in one's efforts,** être infatigable, ne pas ménager ses efforts.

unsparingly [ʌn'spɛəriŋli], *adv.* libéralement; infatigablement, sans ménager ses efforts.

unspeakable [ʌn'spi:kəbl], *a.* **1.** (douleur) indicible, inexprimable; (joie) ineffable. **2.** *F:* détestable, infect, ignoble, répugnant, exécrable, indescriptible, inqualifiable; **it's u.!** c'est exécrable! ça n'a pas de nom! **he's really u.!** il est au-dessous de tout!

unspeakably [ʌn'spi:kəbli], *adv.* **1.** ineffablement, indiciblement, d'une façon inexprimable. **2.** *F:* **u. bad,** exécrable; au-dessous de tout.

unspecified [ʌn'spesifaid], *a.* non spécifié; **certain u. persons,** certaines personnes, dont on taira les noms.

unspectacular [ʌnspek'tækjulər], *a.* peu frappant; peu spectaculaire; qui fait peu d'impression; **he left in a completely u. manner,** il est parti tout simplement, sans se faire remarquer.

unspent [ʌn'spent], *a.* **1.** (*of money*) non dépensé. **2.** (*of cartridge, etc.*) qui n'a pas servi.

unspoiled [ʌn'spɔild], *a.* **1.** *A: & Lit:* (*of town, etc.*) non pillé; non mis à sac. **2.** *occ.* = UNSPOILT.

unspoilt [ʌn'spɔilt], *a.* (*a*) bien conservé; intact; (*b*) **the child has remained u. in spite of . . .,** en dépit de . . . l'enfant est toujours bien élevé; (*c*) (paysage) qui n'a pas été défiguré, qui n'a pas été touché pas l'industrialisation.

unspoken [ʌn'spouk(ə)n], *a.* non prononcé; (accord) tacite; **the power of the u. word,** la force du sous-entendu.

unsporting [ʌn'spɔ:tiŋ], **unsportsmanlike** [ʌn'spɔ:tsmənlaik], *a.* peu loyal, -aux; indigne d'un (vrai) sportif.

unspotted [ʌn'spɔtid], *a.* (*a*) sans tache(s); (*b*) *Lit:* immaculé; (*of pers., mind*) pur; non corrompu; (*of reputation*) sans tache; **to keep oneself u. from the world,** se préserver de la souillure du monde.

unsprocketed [ʌn'sprɔkitid], *a. Tchn:* (bande de contrôle, etc.) sans perforations marginales.

unsprung [ʌn'sprʌŋ], *a.* **1.** (*of vehicle, etc.*) sans ressorts. **2.** (*of weight*) non suspendu; **u. weight on the axle,** poids porté à cru sur l'essieu.

unstable [ʌn'steibl], *a.* **1.** instable; (climat) instable, changeant; (atome, élément, etc.) instable; (économie) fragile, instable; **prices are u.,** les prix, les cours, sont instables, fluctuants; *Mec: etc:* **u. equilibrium,** équilibre instable; *Ch:* **u. compound,** composé instable. **2.** (*of pers., character*) instable, inconstant, vacillant.

unstack [ʌn'stæk], *v.tr.* désempiler (du bois).

unstageable [ʌn'steidʒəbl], *a. Th:* (*of play*) irreprésentable.

unstained [ʌn'steind], *a.* **1.** propre, sans tache. **2.** (*of wood, etc.*) non teint. **3.** *Lit:* (*of reputation, etc.*) sans tache; sans souillure; immaculé.

unstamped [ʌn'stæmpt], *a.* **1.** (*of coin, etc.*) non frappé; (*of silver, gold*) non poinçonné; (*of leather, etc.*) non estampé. **2.** (*a*) (*of letter*) sans timbre, non timbré, non affranchi; (*b*) *Adm: Jur:* (*of weights, document*) non estampillé.

unstarched [ʌn'stɑ:tʃt], *a.* (linge) non empesé, non amidonné.

unstated [ʌn'steitid], *a.* non mentionné; passé sous silence.

unstatesmanlike [ʌn'steitsmənlaik], *a.* peu digne d'un homme d'État; peu diplomatique.

unsteadily [ʌn'stedili], *adv.* (marcher) d'un pas chancelant, (*of drunkard*) en titubant; (tenir qch.) d'une main tremblante; (écrire) d'une main tremblante, mal assurée; **the table stood u. on the uneven floor,** placée sur un plancher inégal, la table manquait d'aplomb.

unsteadiness [ʌn'stedinis], *s.* **1.** (*a*) instabilité *f*; manque *m* d'aplomb (d'une table, etc.); manque de sûreté (de la main, etc.); (*b*) démarche chancelante (d'un ivrogne, etc.); (*c*) affolement *m* (du compas). **2.** (*a*) irrésolution *f*, indécision *f*, vacillation *f* (de la volonté, etc.); (*b*) manque de stabilité (d'un jeune homme, etc.). **3.** variabilité *f* (des prix); agitation *f* (du marché).

unsteady [ʌn'stedi], *a.* **1.** (*a*) (*of table, etc.*) instable, peu stable, peu solide; mal affermi, vacillant; boiteux, branlant; (*of legs, footsteps*) chancelant; incertain; (*of hand, voice*) mal assuré, tremblant; (*of position, foothold*) mal assuré; incertain; (*of ship*) rouleux; **to be u. on one's legs, feet,** avoir une démarche chancelante; marcher d'un pas chancelant, incertain; vaciller (sur ses jambes); (*of drunkard*) tituber; (*b*) (*of flame*) tremblant, vacillant; (*of compass*) affolé, volage; *Ph:* **u. balance,** balance folle. **2.** (*a*) (*of purpose, etc.*) vacillant, irrésolu; indécis; inconstant; (*b*) (*of pers.*) instable, qui manque de stabilité; peu rangé. **3.** irrégulier; (*of barometer*) variable; **prices are u.,** les prix sont instables; **the market is u.,** le marché est agité; **output is u.,** la production varie, est irrégulière.

unstep [ʌn'step], *v.tr.* (**unstepped**) *Nau:* **to u. the mast,** ôter le mât de son emplanture.

unsterilized [ʌn'sterilaizd], *a.* non stérilisé.

unstick [ʌn'stik], *v.tr.* (*p.t. & p.p.* **unstuck** [-'stʌk]) décoller, dégommer (qch.); **to come unstuck,** (i) se décoller, se dégommer; (ii) *F:* (*of plan*) s'effondrer, tomber à l'eau; (iii) *F:* (*of pers.*) tomber sur un bec.

unstinted [ʌn'stintid], *a.* (*a*) (*of supplies, etc.*) abondant, copieux; à volonté, à discrétion; sans restriction; (*b*) illimité; sans réserve; **u. admiration,** admiration sans bornes; **u. efforts,** efforts illimités; **to give u. praise,** ne pas ménager ses louanges.

unstinting [ʌn'stintiŋ], *a.* (*a*) généreux, prodigue; libéral, -aux; (*b*) = UNSTINTED (*b*).

unstintingly [ʌn'stintiŋli], *adv.* (*a*) abondamment, copieusement; (*b*) généreusement, libéralement; (louer qn) sans réserve.

unstitch [ʌn'stitʃ], *v.tr.* dépiquer, découdre (une couture); débrocher (un livre); **to come unstitched,** se découdre, se dépiquer.

unstock [ʌn'stɔk], *v.tr.* (*a*) *Sm.a:* enlever le fût (d'un fusil); (*b*) *Nau:* déjaler (une ancre).

unstocked [ʌn'stɔkt], *a.* (*a*) (*of gun*) sans fût; (*b*) (*of anchor*) sans jas.

unstockinged [ʌn'stɔkiŋd], *a.* **in one's u. feet,** nu-pieds.

unstop [ʌn'stɔp], *v.tr.* (**unstopped**) **1.** (*a*) déboucher, désobstruer (un tuyau, etc.); (*b*) *B:* **the ears of the deaf shall be unstopped,** les oreilles des sourds s'ouvriront. **2.** *Mus:* (*organ*) tirer (un registre, un jeu).

unstoppable [ʌn'stɔpəbl], *a. Fb: etc:* (*of shot*) imparable.

unstow [ʌn'stou], *v.tr. Nau:* désarrimer (la cargaison).

unstrained [ʌn'streind], *a.* **1.** (*of cable, etc.*) non tendu. **2.** (*of laughter, etc.*) spontané; non forcé. **3.** (*of liquid*) non filtré; (*of vegetables, etc.*) non égoutté.

unstressed [ʌn'strest], *a.* (*of syllable*) sans accent; inaccentué; à accentuation faible; atone.

unstretchable [ʌn'stretʃəbl], *a. Tex:* (tissu) indéformable.

unstring [ʌn'striŋ], *v.tr.* (*p.t. & p.p.* **unstrung** [-'strʌŋ]) **1.** (*a*) enlever les cordes, les ficelles, de (qch.); (*b*) débander (un arc); **to u. a violin,** (i) ôter les cordes, (ii) détendre, relâcher, les cordes, d'un violon. **2.** défiler, désenfiler (des perles, etc.). **3.** (*of pers.*) **to be unstrung,** avoir les nerfs détraqués, à fleur de peau.

unstriped [ʌn'straipt], *a. Anat:* (muscle) lisse.

unstripped [ʌn'stript], *a.* non dépouillé; (*of tree*) (i) non écorcé; (ii) non dénudé, non effeuillé; (*of tobacco leaf*) non écôté.

unstudied [ʌn'stʌdid], *a.* spontané; (style, etc.) inapprêté, facile; (langage, etc.) naturel.

unsubdued [ʌnsəb'dju:d], *a.* indompté; (*of passion, etc.*) non maîtrisé.

unsubmissive [ʌnsəb'misiv], *a.* insoumis, indocile, rebelle.

unsubscribed [ʌnsəb'skraibd], *a.* **1.** (document) non souscrit, non signé. **2.** *Fin:* (capital) non souscrit.

unsubsidized [ʌn'sʌbsidaizd], *a.* non subventionné; sans subvention.

unsubstantial [ʌnsəb'stænʃ(ə)l], *a.* insubstantiel; sans substance; (repas) léger, peu satisfaisant, peu nourrissant.

unsubstantiated [ʌnsəb'stænʃieitid], *a.* (*of accusation*) non prouvé; (*of rumour*) non confirmé, non corroboré, sans confirmation; (*of claim*) dont on ne peut pas établir le bien-fondé.

unsubtle [ʌn'sʌtl], *a.* peu subtil; qui manque de finesse, de pénétration; sans nuances.

unsuccessful [ʌnsək'sesful], *a.* **1.** (*of effort, etc.*) vain, infructueux; (*of application, etc.*) refusé; **u. attempt,** tentative qui n'a abouti à rien; coup manqué; **after several u. attempts,** après avoir essayé plusieurs fois sans succès; après avoir échoué plusieurs fois; **u. outcome,** insuccès *m*; **u. marriage,** mariage malheureux; **our visit was u.,** notre visite a été infructueuse; **it was completely u.,** cela a été un échec complet. **2.** (*of pers.*) **to be u.,** ne pas réussir; échouer; **I tried to do it but I was u.,** j'ai essayé de le faire mais en vain, sans succès; **u. candidate,** candidat refusé, malheureux, ajourné, (*at election*) non élu; *Jur:* **the u. party,** le perdant; *s.* **the u.,** ceux qui ne réussissent pas dans la vie, *F:* les ratés.

unsuccessfully [ʌnsək'sesfuli], *adv.* sans succès; vainement, en vain.

unsuitability [ʌns(j)u:tə'biliti], **unsuitableness** [ʌn's(j)u:təb(ə)lnis], *s.* **1.** inaptitude *f* (de qn à qch.). **2.** caractère *m* impropre (de qch. à qch.); disconvenance *f* (du climat, etc); **he insisted on the u. of taking such a step,** il a insisté sur le fait qu'une telle démarche ne conviendrait pas du tout.

unsuitable [ʌn's(j)u:təbl], *a.* **1.** (*pers.*) peu fait (pour qch.); inapte (à qch.); **he's quite u. for the job,** ce n'est pas l'homme qu'il faut pour cet emploi. **2.** (*of thg*) impropre, mal adapté (à qch.); (*of time, etc.*) inopportun; (*of marriage, etc.*) mal assorti; **u. for, to, the occasion,** peu approprié, qui ne convient pas, à la circonstance; **her clothes were quite u. for a funeral,** sa toilette était peu appropriée à, peu convenable pour, un enterrement; **she always wears the most u. clothes,** elle n'a aucun goût pour s'habiller; **you have chosen a most u. time to . . .,** vous avez mal choisi le moment de . . .; vous arrivez mal à propos pour . . .; **film u. for children,** film à déconseiller aux enfants; **the climate is u. for wheat,** le climat ne convient pas au blé; le blé ne pousse pas dans ce climat.

unsuitably [ʌn's(j)u:təbli], *adv.* **u. dressed,** habillé d'une façon qui ne convient pas à l'occasion; habillé sans goût.

unsuited [ʌn's(j)u:tid], *a.* **1.** (*of pers.*) inapte (à qch.); (*of thg*) mal adapté, mal approprié (à qch.); **u. to a man in his position,** tout à fait déplacé chez un homme de son rang. **2.** *O:* (*a*) *Com:* (*of customer*) pas satisfait; qui n'a pas trouvé son affaire; (*b*) (*of domestic servant*) sans situation; qui n'a pas trouvé une place; (*of employer*) qui n'a pas trouvé quelqu'un qui lui convient.

unsullied [ʌn'sʌlid], *a. Lit:* sans souillure; sans tache; immaculé; **u. honour,** honneur immaculé; **u. reputation,** réputation intacte, sans tache, sans souillure.

unsung [ʌn'sʌŋ], *a.* **1.** non chanté. **2.** *Lit:* (*of deed, victory, etc.*) non célébré, non commémoré.

unsupervised [ʌn'su:pəvaizd], *a.* non surveillé.

unsupported [ʌnsə'pɔ:tid], *a.* **1.** (*a*) (*of statement, etc.*) non confirmé; sans preuves; (*b*) (*of pers.*) non appuyé; non soutenu; (agir) seul, sans encouragement; (*c*) *Parl: etc:* **u. amendment,** amendement qui n'a pas été appuyé. **2.** *Civ.E: etc:* sans support, sans appui; non étayé; en porte-à-faux. **3.** *Mil:* **u. battalion,** bataillon découvert; **to be u.,** être découvert, être en l'air.

unsure [ʌn'ʃuər], *a.* **1.** (*of position, etc.*) peu sûr; précaire. **2.** (*of pers.*) peu sûr, incertain (**about,** de); **I'm u. of the date,** je ne suis pas sûr de la date; **to be u. of oneself,** manquer de confiance en soi-même.

unsurmountable [ʌnsə(:)'mauntəbl], *a.* insurmontable; **our difficulties are not u.,** il nous sera possible de surmonter nos difficultés.

unsurpassable [ʌnsə(:)'pɑ:səbl], *a.* insurpassable.

unsurpassed [ʌnsə(:)'pɑ:st], *a.* qui n'a jamais été surpassé, égalé; sans égal, -aux; sans pareil.

unsuspected [ʌnsəs'pektid], *a.* insoupçonné (**by,** de); dont on ne soupçonnait pas l'existence; **u. by anyone,** à l'insu de tout le monde.

unsuspecting [ʌnsəs'pektiŋ], *a.* qui ne se doute de rien; qui ne soupçonne rien; confiant; sans soupçons; sans défiance; **u. by nature,** peu soupçonneux.

unsuspicious [ʌnsəs'piʃəs], *a.* peu soupçonneux.

unsustained [ʌnsəs'teind], *a.* (*of effort, etc.*) non soutenu.

unswayed [ʌn'sweid], *a.* non influencé, non gouverné (**by,** par); sans se laisser influencer (par).

unsweetened [ʌn'swi:tnd], *a.* (*of tea, etc.*) non sucré.

unswept [ʌn'swept], *a.* (*of room, etc.*) non balayé.

unswerving [ʌn'swə:viŋ], *a.* **1.** (*of loyalty, purpose, etc.*) inébranlable, constant, ferme. **2. to pursue an u. course,** ne pas s'écarter de son chemin, du but.

unsworn [ʌn'swɔ:n], *a.* **1.** (*of pers.*) qui n'a pas prêté serment. **2.** (témoignage) qui n'a pas été rendu sous serment.

unsymmetrical [ʌnsi'metrik(ə)l], *a.* asymétrique, dissymétrique; sans symétrie.

unsymmetrically [ʌnsi'metrik(ə)li], *adv.* sans symétrie.

unsympathetic [ʌnsimpə'θetik], *a.* (*a*) peu compatissant; froid; indifférent; **he's so u. if she doesn't feel well,** ses malaises le laissent indifférent; **she's so u.,** elle est si froide; (*b*) **I find the characters of this novel u.,** les personnages de ce roman me sont peu sympathiques, me répugnent.

unsympathetically [ʌnsimpə'θetik(ə)li], *adv.* froidement; d'un ton, d'un air, indifférent.

unsystematic [ʌnsistə'mætik], *a.* non systématique; sans méthode.

unsystematically [ʌnsistə'mætik(ə)li], *adv.* sans méthode.

untack [ʌn'tæk], *v.tr.* détacher. **2.** *Needlew:* défaufiler, débâtir (un vêtement, etc.). **2.** retirer les pointes (d'un tapis, etc.).

untainted [ʌn'teintid], *a.* non corrompu; non infecté; pur; (*of food*) frais, *f.* fraîche, non gâté, non altéré; (*of reputation*) sans tache, sans souillure.

untalented [ʌn'tæləntid], *a.* sans talent(s), peu doué.

untalked-of [ʌn'tɔ:ktɔv], *a.* (sujet, etc.) que l'on ne mentionne pas, duquel on ne parle pas.

untam(e)able [ʌn'teiməbl], *a.* (*of animal, etc.*) inapprivoisable, indomptable; (*of spirit, etc.*) indomptable.

untamed [ʌn'teimd], *a.* (*of animal, etc.*) inapprivoisé, indompté; sauvage; (*of spirit, etc.*) indompté.

untangle [ʌn'tæŋgl], *v.tr.* démêler (de la laine, ses cheveux, etc.); détortiller, désentortiller (une ficelle, etc.); éclaircir (un mystère); dénouer (une intrigue).

untanned [ʌn'tænd], *a.* (cuir) non tanné, cru.

untapped [ʌn'tæpt], *a.* **1.** (*a*) (*of barrel*) qui n'a pas été mis en perce; (*b*) *For:* (*of pine*) non gemmé; (*c*) **u. resources,** ressources inexploitées. **2.** *Tchn:* (*of rod, nut, etc.*) non taraudé.

untarnishable [ʌn'tɑ:niʃəbl], *a.* (*of steel, etc.*) qui ne ternit pas; qui garde son brillant, son éclat.

untarnished [ʌn'tɑ:niʃt], *a.* **1.** (métal) non terni, toujours brillant; (cadre) non dédoré, toujours neuf. **2.** (honneur, etc.) non terni, sans tache, sans souillure.

untarred [ʌn'tɑ:d], *a.* (*of road*) non goudronné; **u. rope,** franc filin, filin blanc.

untasted [ʌn'teistid], *a.* non goûté; auquel on n'a pas goûté; **to send a dish away u.,** renvoyer un plat sans y goûter, sans y toucher.

untaught [ʌn'tɔ:t], *a.* (*a*) (*of pers.*) sans instruction; ignorant, ignare; inculte; (*b*) (*of skill, etc.*) naturel, spontané.

untaxable [ʌn'tæksəbl], *a.* non imposable, non taxable; *Jur:* non taxatif.

untaxed [ʌn'tækst], *a.* exempt, exempté, d'impôts, de taxes; (produit) non imposé; (revenu) non imposable; *Jur:* (frais) non taxés.

unteachable [ʌn'ti:tʃəbl], *a.* **1.** (*of pers.*) à qui l'on ne peut rien apprendre; incapable d'apprendre. **2.** (*of subject, art*) non enseignable, impossible à enseigner.

untempered [ʌn'tempəd], *a.* **1.** (*a*) (*of cement*) non gâché, non délayé; (*b*) (*of steel*) non trempé. **2.** (*of feeling*) non tempéré, non atténué, non adouci.

untempted [ʌn'tem(p)tid], *a.* non tenté. **1.** peu séduit (**by,** par). **2.** qui n'a pas subi de tentation.

untenability, untenableness [ʌntenə'biliti, -'tenəblnis], *s.* caractère *m* intenable (d'une position, d'une forteresse, etc.); nature *f* insoutenable (d'une théorie, etc.).

untenable [ʌn'tenəbl], *a.* (position, forteresse, etc.) intenable; (théorie, etc.) insoutenable; peu soutenable; **an opinion u. by those who know the facts,** une opinion que ne saurait soutenir ceux qui ont connaissance des faits.

untenantable [ʌn'tenəntəbl], *a.* (*of house, etc.*) inhabitable; qui ne peut pas être loué.

untenanted [ʌn'tenəntid], *a.* (*of house, etc.*) sans locataire(s); inoccupé; vide; inhabité.

untended [ʌn'tendid], *a.* (malade, etc.) non soigné, sans soins; (enfant, etc.) non surveillé; (jardin) non entretenu.

untested [ʌn'testid], *a.* (*of pers., theory, etc.*) inéprouvé; qui n'a pas (encore) été mis à l'épreuve; (*of invention, etc.*) non essayé, qui n'a pas (encore) été essayé; (*of result*) non vérifié, invérifié; (*of water, etc.*) non analysé.

untether [ʌn'teðər], *v.tr.* détacher (un cheval, etc.).

untethered [ʌn'teðəd], *a.* (*of horse, etc.*) **1.** détaché. **2.** non attaché; en liberté.

unthankful [ʌn'θæŋkful], *a.* peu reconnaissant; ingrat.

unthankfully [ʌn'θæŋkfuli], *adv.* sans reconnaissance, ingratement.

unthinkable [ʌn'θiŋkəbl], *a.* inconcevable, impensable; inimaginable; **it's u. that he should want to do such a thing,** c'est incroyable qu'il veuille faire une chose pareille.

unthinking [ʌn'θiŋkiŋ], *a.* (*of pers.*) irréfléchi, sans discernement, étourdi; **in an u. moment,** dans un moment d'inattention.

unthinkingly [ʌn'θiŋkiŋli], *adv.* (faire qch.) sans réfléchir, sans discernement, sans réflexion, avec inattention, étourdiment.

unthought [ʌn'θɔ:t], *a.* (*of circumstance, etc.*) **u. of,** inattendu, imprévu; à quoi on n'avait pas pensé.

unthoughtful [ʌn'θɔ:tful], *a.* (*of pers., action, etc.*) irréfléchi; inconséquent, étourdi.

unthread [ʌn'θred], *v.tr.* désenfiler, défiler (une aiguille, etc.).

untidily [ʌn'taidili], *adv.* sans ordre, sans soin; **she's always u. dressed,** elle a toujours l'air débraillé; **his clothes lay u. around the room,** ses vêtements jonchaient la pièce.

untidiness [ʌn'taidinis], *s.* désordre *m*; manque *m* d'ordre, de soin.

untidy [ʌn'taidi], *a.* (*a*) (*of room, etc.*) en désordre, mal tenu; mal rangé; (*of hair*) ébouriffé; mal peigné; (*of writing*) brouillon; **u. appearance,** tenue négligée, débraillée; **to make s.o.'s hair u.,** dépeigner qn; *Mus:* **his playing is u.,** son jeu manque de netteté; (*b*) (*of pers.*) désordonné; qui manque d'ordre; sans soin; peu soigneux; **he looks u.,** il ne s'habille pas avec soin, il a l'air débraillé.

untie [ʌn'tai]. (**untied; untying**) **1.** *v.tr.* dénouer (sa ceinture, etc.); défaire, délier (un nœud, un paquet); déficeler, ouvrir (un paquet); démarrer (un cordage); délier, détacher (un chien, etc.). **2.** *v.i. & pr.* (*of knot*) **to u. (itself), to come untied,** se défaire, se dénouer.

untighten [ʌn'tait(ə)n], *v.tr.* desserrer (sa ceinture, etc.).

until [ʌn'til]. **1.** *prep.* (*a*) jusqu'à; **u. tomorrow,** jusqu'à demain; **u. now,** jusqu'ici, jusque-là; **you can rest u. lunchtime,** vous pouvez vous reposer en attendant l'heure du déjeuner; **she didn't arrive u. yesterday,** elle n'est arrivée qu'hier; (*b*) **not u. (after) eight o'clock,** pas avant huit heures (passées); **it wasn't u. I met her that . . .,** ce n'est qu'après notre rencontre que . . .; **I've never seen it u. now,** c'est la première fois que je le vois. **2.** *conj.* (*a*) jusqu'à ce que + *sub.*; **u. all the windows are open,** jusqu'à ce que toutes les fenêtres soient ouvertes; (*b*) **he won't come u. he's invited,** il ne viendra pas avant d'être invité, pas avant que vous ne l'invitiez; **I won't leave him u. he's completely recovered,** je ne le quitterai pas tant qu'il n'est pas tout à fait guéri.

untile [ʌn'tail], *v.tr.* **to u. a house, a roof,** ôter les tuiles d'une maison, d'un toit.

untiled [ʌn'taild], *a.* (toit) sans tuiles; (plancher) sans carreaux, non carrelé.

untillable [ʌn'tiləbl], *a.* (*of land*) non labourable, non arable, incultivable; infertile, aride.

untilled [ʌn'tild], *a.* (*of land*) inculte, incultivé, non cultivé, non labouré; en friche.

untimeliness [ʌn'taimlinis], *s.* **1.** (*a*) prématurité *f* (d'une naissance); caractère prématuré (d'une mort); (*b*) précocité *f* (d'un fruit, etc.); (*c*) précocité (de la saison, des pluies). **2.** inopportunité *f* (d'une question, etc.).

untimely[1] [ʌn'taimli], *a.* **1.** (*a*) (*of death, birth, etc.*) prématuré; **to come to an u. end,** mourir prématurément, avant son temps, avant l'âge; (*b*) (*of fruit, etc.*) précoce. **2.** (*of snow, etc.*) hors de saison. **3.** (*of question, action, etc.*) inopportun, mal venu, intempestif, mal à propos.

untimely[2], *adv.* **1.** prématurément; avant l'heure. **2.** inopportunément, intempestivement; mal à propos.

untinged [ʌn'tin(d)ʒd], *a. Lit:* sans teinte (**with,** de); **joy not u. with sadness,** joie mêlée de tristesse, qui ne va pas sans tristesse.

untirable [ʌn'taiərəbl], *a.* infatigable, inlassable.

untiring [ʌn'taiəriŋ], *a.* infatigable, inlassable.

untiringly [ʌn'taiəriŋli], *adv.* infatigablement, inlassablement.

untitled [ʌn'taitld], *a.* (*of book, etc.*) non titré; (*of pers.*) sans titre.

unto ['ʌntu(:), -ʌntə], *prep. A: & Lit:* (= **to** *in certain uses*) **1. to liken s.o., sth., u. s.o., sth.,** comparer qn, qch. à, avec, qn, qch.; **to hearken u. sth.,** écouter qch.; **known u. few,** connu de peu de gens; (*with ellipsis of verb*) **let us u. our ships,** allons à nos vaisseaux; *B:* **suffer little children to come u. me,** laissez venir à moi les petits enfants; **u. us a child is born,** un enfant nous est né; **and I say u. you . . .,** et je vous dis . . .; **render u. Caesar the things that are Caesar's,** rendez à César ce qui est à César. **2.** vers; to **turn u. s.o.,** se tourner vers qn; **to come, be, nigh u. sth.,** s'approcher, être près, de qch. **3.** jusqu'à; **u. this day,** jusqu'à ce jour.

untoggle [ʌn'tɔgl], *v.tr. Nau:* décabillotter (des cordages).

untold [ʌn'tould], *a.* **1.** (richesse, etc.) immense, énorme; **u. quantities,** quantités démesurées, énormes, incalculables; **during u. centuries,** pendant des siècles innombrables; **u. suffering,** souffrances inouïes; **u. joy,** joie indicible, ineffable. **2.** (*of tale, etc.*) non raconté; (*of secret*) non dévoilé, non divulgué; **his exploits remain u.,** nul n'a encore fait le récit de ses exploits.

untorn [ʌn'tɔ:n], *a.* non déchiré; intact.

untouchable [ʌn'tʌtʃəbl]. **1.** *a.* intouchable; intangible. **2.** *s.* (*in India*) intouchable *mf,* paria *m.*

untouched [ʌn'tʌtʃt], *a.* **1.** (*a*) non touché; non manié; **the piano has stood u. for weeks,** le piano n'a pas été joué depuis des semaines; **food product u. by (human) hand,** produit alimentaire non manié; (*b*) **he'd left the meal u.,** il n'avait pas touché à son repas; il n'avait rien mangé. **2.** (*of pers.*) indemne, sain et sauf; (*of thg*) intact; (*of reputation*) sans tache; sans souillure. **3.** (*of fact, subject*) **u. (upon),** non mentionné; non discuté. **4.** (*of pers.*) non ému; indifférent; insensible (**by,** à). **5.** (*of quality, etc.*) sans rival, -aux; sans égal, -aux.

untoward [ʌntə'wɔ:d; *NAm:* ʌn'tɔ:d], *a.* **1.** *A:* (*of pers.*) insoumis, indocile; rétif; rebelle; indiscipliné; (*of thg*) incommode; peu commode; difficile (à façonner, à travailler). **2.** (événement, etc.) fâcheux, malencontreux, malheureux; **I hope nothing u. has happened,** j'espère qu'il n'est pas arrivé un malheur. **3.** (*of conditions, etc.*) peu favorable, défavorable. **4.** (*of thoughts, behaviour, etc.*) malséant, inconvenant.

untowardly [ʌntə'wɔ:dli], *adv.* **1.** malencontreusement; fâcheusement. **2.** d'une manière peu séante.

untraceable [ʌn'treisəbl], *a.* introuvable, indécouvrable; *Jur:* **u. beneficiary,** bénéficiaire introuvable.

untracked [ʌn'trækt], *a.* **1.** (*of land, snow, etc.*) sans sentier frayé; sans voie. **2.** (criminel, etc.) (i) non suivi; (ii) non dépisté.

untrained [ʌn'treind], *a.* (ouvrier, professeur, etc.) qui n'a pas reçu de formation professionnelle; (danseur, coiffeur, etc.) qui n'a pas reçu d'instruction; inexpérimenté, inexpert, inexercé; **u. staff,** personnel non spécialisé, non formé; **u. horse,** cheval non dressé.

untrammelled [ʌn'træm(ə)ld], *a.* sans entraves, sans contrainte; non entravé (**by,** par); non empêtré (**by,** de); libre (**by,** de).

untransferable [ʌntræns'fə:rəbl], *a.* non transmissible; non transférable; intransférable; *Jur:* (droit, propriété) incessible, inaliénable; (billet, etc.) strictement personnel.

untranslatable [ʌntræns'leitəbl], *a.* (mot, auteur, etc.) intraduisible.

untranslated [ʌntræns'leitid], *a.* (livre, etc.) qui n'a pas (encore) été traduit; intraduit.

untransportable [ʌntræns'pɔ:təbl], *a.* intransportable.

untravelled [ʌn'trævəld], *a.* **1.** (*of pers.*) qui n'a pas, qui n'a jamais, voyagé. **2.** (pays) inexploré, peu fréquenté, peu connu.

untraversable [ʌntrə'və:səbl], *a.* (torrent, etc.) intraversable.

untraversed [ʌn'trævəst], *a.* (desert, etc.) que l'on n'a jamais traversé; (pays) inexploré, peu fréquenté.

untried [ʌn'traid], *a.* **1.** (article, produit, etc.) qui n'a pas été essayé; non essayé; **they left no remedy u.,** il n'y a pas de remède qu'ils n'aient essayé. **2.** (moteur, système, etc.) qui n'a pas été mis à l'épreuve; **u. troops,** troupes qui n'ont pas encore vu le feu. **3.** (détenu, cas) qui n'a pas encore été jugé.

untrimmed [ʌn'trimd], *a.* **1.** (*a*) *A:* non arrangé; non mis en ordre; (*b*) (*of hedge, etc.*) non taillé, non coupé; (*of hair, beard, etc.*) non rafraîchi, non égalisé; *Carp:* (*of wood*) non dégrossi, non corroyé; **u. floor,** plancher qui repose seulement sur des lambourdes; **u. book edges,** tranches non ébarbées, non rognées; **u. casting,** pièce non ébarbée, non parée, brute de fonte; **u. lamp,** lampe non mouchée; *Cu:* **u. meat,** viande non parée. **2.** (chapeau, etc.) non garni, sans garniture(s).

untrodden [ʌn'trɔdn], *a. Lit:* (chemin) impratiqué, peu fréquenté, non frayé; (terrain) inexploré, que le pied de l'homme n'a jamais foulé; (forêt) vierge; **u. snow,** neige immaculée, vierge.

untroubled [ʌn'trʌb(ə)ld], *a.* **1.** (*of pers., features, etc.*) calme, tranquille, paisible; **he seemed u. by the news,** la nouvelle ne semblait nullement le troubler, l'inquiéter, l'émouvoir; il restait impassible en apprenant la nouvelle. **2.** *Lit:* (*of water, etc.*) non troublé, non brouillé.

untrue [ʌn'tru:], *a. & adv.*

I. *a.* **1.** (*of statement, etc.*) faux, *f.* fausse; inexact, erroné; mensonger, contraire à la vérité; **the story he told was u.,** l'histoire qu'il a racontée était fausse, n'était pas vraie; **it's absolutely u.,** c'est complètement faux. **2.** *Mec.E: etc:* inexact, faux; qui n'est pas juste. **3.** (*of pers.*) infidèle (**to,** à); déloyal, -aux (**to,** envers).

II. *adv.* **1.** *Mec.E: etc:* **the shaft is running u.,** l'arbre tourne à faux, a du balourd. **2.** *A:* **to speak u.,** ne pas dire la vérité; mentir.

untruly [ʌn'tru:li], *adv.* **1.** faussement; inexactement, erronément; mensongèrement, contrairement à la vérité. **2.** *Mec.E: etc:* inexactement.

untrustworthiness [ʌn'trʌstwə:ðinis], *s.* **1.** (*of pers.*) manque *m* d'honnêteté, de probité; fausseté *f,* déloyauté *f.* **2.** caractère douteux, peu sûr (d'un renseignement, etc.); inexactitude *f* (d'un témoignage, etc.).

untrustworthy [ʌn'trʌstwəːði], *a.* **1.** (*of pers.*) indigne de confiance; à qui on ne peut pas se fier; déloyal, -aux; faux, *f.* fausse; infidèle; (témoin) récusable; **u. memory,** mémoire infidèle, peu sûre, labile. **2.** (renseignement, etc.) douteux, peu sûr, sujet à caution; (livre, etc.) auquel on ne peut pas se fier; (témoignage) récusable.

untruth [ʌn'truːθ, 'ʌntruːθ], *s.* **1.** *A: & Lit:* = UNTRUTHFULNESS. **2.** (*pl.* **untruths** [ʌn'truːðz, 'ʌntruːðz], mensonge *m*; contre(-)vérité *f*; **to tell an u.,** dire, faire, commettre, un mensonge.

untruthful [ʌn'truːθful], *a.* **1.** (*of pers.*) menteur; peu véridique; **he's an u. boy,** c'est un garçon qui ne dit jamais la vérité. **2.** (*of story, etc.*) mensonger; faux, *f.* fausse; inexact; peu véridique, dénué de vérité.

untruthfully [ʌn'truːθfuli], *adv.* mensongèrement; inexactement; peu véridiquement; **he replied u.,** il a répondu en mentant.

untruthfulness [ʌn'truːθfulnis], *s.* **1.** (*of pers.*) caractère menteur, mensonger; fausseté *f.* **2.** fausseté, inexactitude *f,* caractère mensonger, caractère peu véridique (d'une histoire, d'un témoignage, etc.).

untuck [ʌn'tʌk], *v.tr.* **1.** défaire des (rem)plis (d'un vêtement); déplisser, défroncer (du tissu, etc.). **2.** déborder (un lit); **the bed's come untucked,** le lit s'est débordé; **his shirt had come untucked,** il était en pans (de chemise). **3. he untucked his legs (from under him),** il a déplié ses jambes de dessous lui.

untunable [ʌn'tjuːnəbl], *a. Mus:* (instrument) que l'on ne peut pas accorder, mettre d'accord, qui ne tient pas l'accord.

untuned [ʌn'tjuːnd], *a. Mus:* (instrument) mal accordé, discordant; *Aut: etc:* (moteur) qui n'est pas au point.

untuneful [ʌn'tjuːnful], *a.* peu harmonieux, peu mélodieux; **u. melody,** mélodie peu chantante.

unturf [ʌn'təːf], *v.tr. Agr:* dégazonner (du terrain).

unturned [ʌn'təːnd], *a.* **1.** (*of card, etc.*) non (re)tourné. **2.** *Carp:* (*of post, table leg, etc.*) non tourné; non façonné au tour.

untutored [ʌn'tjuːtəd], *a. esp. Lit:* **1.** (*of pers.*) sans instruction; peu instruit; simple, naïf, *f.* naïve; (esprit, goût) non formé. **2.** (talent, etc.) naturel.

untwine [ʌn'twain], *v.tr.* **1.** détordre, détortiller, dérouler, défaire (des fils, etc.). **2. she untwined her arms from round his neck,** elle a cessé de l'étreindre.

untwist [ʌn'twist]. **1.** *v.tr.* détordre, détortiller (des fils, etc.); décorder (un cordage, etc.); **untwisted thread,** fil détors. **2.** *v.i. & pr.* **to u. (itself), to come untwisted,** se détordre, se détortiller.

untypical [ʌn'tipikl], *a.* peu caractéristique; **it was not u.,** ce n'était pas anormal.

unusable [ʌn'juːzəbl], *a.* inutilisable.

unused, *a.* **1.** [ʌn'juːzd] (*a*) dont on ne se sert pas; inutilisé; non employé; **u. building,** bâtiment désaffecté; (*b*) qui n'a pas encore servi; dont on ne s'est pas encore servi; neuf; (*c*) (mot) inusité; (*d*) *Cmptr:* **u. time,** temps d'inutilisation. **2.** [ʌn'juːst] (*of pers.*) peu habitué, inhabitué (à qch.).

unusual [ʌn'juːʒ(ə)l], *a.* (*a*) peu commun; peu ordinaire; exceptionnel, extraordinaire; inhabituel, insolite; **it's u.,** (i) cela se fait peu; ce n'est pas l'usage; (ii) cela se voit, se produit, rarement; **it's u. to see him at the theatre,** il est rare qu'on le voie au théâtre; **nothing u.,** rien d'anormal; **of u. interest,** d'un intérêt exceptionnel; (*b*) (mot) peu usité.

unusually [ʌn'juːʒu(ə)li], *adv.* exceptionnellement; d'une manière insolite; rarement; **u. tall,** d'une taille exceptionnelle; **he was u. attentive,** il s'est montré plus attentif que d'habitude, que d'ordinaire.

unutilized [ʌn'juːtilaizd], *a.* (*of resources, etc.*) inutilisé.

unutterable [ʌn'ʌt(ə)rəbl], *a.* (*of astonishment, etc.*) inexprimable, indicible, inénarrable; **that's u. nonsense,** ça c'est d'une absurdité sans nom.

unutterably [ʌn'ʌt(ə)rəbli], *adv.* d'une façon inexprimable; **u. lazy,** d'une paresse invraisemblable, inimaginable.

unvaccinated [ʌn'væksineitid], *a.* non vacciné.

unvanquished [ʌn'væŋkwiʃt], *a. Lit:* invaincu.

unvaried [ʌn'vɛərid], *a.* invariable; uniforme, constant; non varié; **u. diet,** repas qui manquent de variété.

unvarnished [ʌn'vɑːniʃt], *a.* **1.** (*of surface*) non verni; (*of pottery*) non vernissé; **plain u. wood,** bois cru. **2.** (*of statement, etc.*) simple; **the plain u. truth,** la vérité pure et simple.

unvarying [ʌn'vɛəriiŋ], *a.* invariable; uniforme, constant.

unveil [ʌn'veil]. **1.** *v.tr.* dévoiler (qn, un secret, etc.); **to u. a statue,** inaugurer une statue. **2.** *v.i.* se dévoiler.

unveiled [ʌn'veild], *a.* (visage, etc.) dévoilé, sans voile.

unveiling [ʌn'veiliŋ], *s.* dévoilement *m*; inauguration *f* (d'une statue).

unverifiable [ʌnveri'faiəbl], *a.* invérifiable; incontrôlable.

unventilated [ʌn'ventileitid], *a.* non ventilé, non aéré; sans ventilation, sans aérage.

unverified [ʌn'verifaid], *a.* invérifié, incontrôlé; non contrôlé, non vérifié.

unversed [ʌn'vəːst], *a. Lit:* peu versé (**in,** dans).

unviable [ʌn'vaiəbl], *a.* inviable, non viable.

unviolated [ʌn'vaiəleitid], *a.* inviolé.

unvisited [ʌn'vizitid], *a.* non visité.

unvitiated [ʌn'viʃieitid], *a.* non vicié.

unvitrified [ʌn'vitrifaid], *a. Cer: etc:* invitré.

unvoiced [ʌn'vɔist], *a.* **1.** *Ling:* (*of vowel, consonant*) sourd, muet; (*of consonant*) dévoisé; (*of vowel*) nonvoisé. **2.** (*of opinion, etc.*) non exprimé. **3.** (tuyau, jeu d'orgue) qui n'a pas encore été harmonisé.

unvouched [ʌn'vautʃt], *a.* **u. for,** non garanti; non confirmé.

unwanted [ʌn'wɔntid], *a.* **1.** (*a*) non désiré, non voulu; qu'on ne désire plus; dont on n'a plus envie; (*b*) qu'on n'a pas désiré; dont on n'a pas eu envie. **2.** superflu; **to give away all one's u. books,** se débarrasser de tous les livres dont on n'a pas besoin.

unwarily [ʌn'wɛərili], *adv.* imprudemment; sans précaution; étourdiment; en étourdi.

unwariness [ʌn'wɛərinis], *s.* imprudence *f,* imprévoyance *f*; manque *m* de précaution; irréflexion *f,* étourderie *f.*

unwarmed [ʌn'wɑːmd], *a.* (*of plate, etc.*) non réchauffé.

unwarrantable [ʌn'wɔrəntəbl], *a.* (action) injustifiable, inexcusable; (assertion) insoutenable; **u. conduct,** conduite peu qualifiable.

unwarrantably [ʌn'wɔrəntəbli], *adv.* inexcusablement; d'une manière injustifiable.

unwarranted [ʌn'wɔrəntid], *a.* **1.** sans garantie. **2.** (*of action, etc.*) injustifié; peu justifié; injustifiable; **u. insult,** injure gratuite; **u. display of force,** emploi abusif de la force; **u. remark,** observation déplacée; **u. familiarity,** familiarité indue.

unwary [ʌn'wɛəri], *a.* imprudent, imprévoyant; irréfléchi, étourdi.

unwashed [ʌn'wɔʃt], *a.* (*a*) (*of pers.*) non lavé; malpropre, sale; *s. F: O:* **the great u.,** les prolétaires, les prolos, les pouilleux, les crasseux; (*b*) *Ind:* (charbon, etc.) non lavé.

unwatched [ʌn'wɔtʃt], *a.* non surveillé; sans surveillance.

unwater [ʌn'wɔːtər], *v.tr. Min:* assécher, dénoyer (une mine).

unwatered [ʌn'wɔːtəd], *a.* **1.** (*a*) (*of garden, etc.*) non arrosé; (*b*) *Fin:* **u. capital,** capital non dilué. **2.** (*a*) (*of region*) (i) sans eau, (ii) non irrigué, sans irrigation; (*b*) (*of horse, etc.*) non abreuvé.

unwavering [ʌn'weivəriŋ], *a.* constant, ferme, résolu; inébranlable; qui ne vacille pas; **u. fortitude,** fermeté qui ne se dément jamais; **u. policy,** politique ferme et suivie; **u. stare,** regard fixe.

unwaveringly [ʌn'weivəriŋli], *adv.* résolument; sans hésiter; (regarder qn) fixement.

unwaxed [ʌn'wækst], *a.* (*of floor, etc.*) non ciré.

unweaned [ʌn'wiːnd], *a.* (enfant, chaton) non sevré.

unwearable [ʌn'wɛərəbl], *a.* (vêtement) immettable, qui n'est pas mettable, qu'on ne peut pas porter.

unwearying [ʌn'wiəriiŋ], *a.* inlassable, infatigable.

unweeded [ʌn'wiːdid], *a.* (jardin) non sarclé, envahi par les mauvaises herbes.

unweighed [ʌn'weid], *a.* non pesé.

unweighted [ʌn'weitid], *a. Pol.Ec:* (*of index*) non pondéré; **u. figures,** chiffres bruts.

unwelcome [ʌn'welkəm], *a.* (*a*) (visiteur, etc.) mal venu, importun; **u. visits,** visites importunes; **a not u. visit,** une visite opportune; (*b*) **u. news,** nouvelle fâcheuse, ennuyeuse, désagréable; **it's not u.,** cela fait tout de même plaisir.

unwelded [ʌn'weldid], *a. Tchn:* non soudé.

unwell [ʌn'wel], *a.* indisposé; souffrant; *occ.* (*of woman*) **to be u.,** avoir ses règles, être indisposée.

unwholesome [ʌn'houlsəm], *a.* (aliment) malsain; (atmosphère) insalubre; (air) vicié.

unwholesomeness [ʌn'houlsəmnis], *s.* insalubrité *f*; caractère malsain (d'un aliment, etc.).

unwieldiness [ʌn'wiːldinis], *s.* manque *m* de maniabilité (d'un colis, etc.).

unwieldy [ʌn'wiːldi], *a.* **1.** (*of pers.*) lourd et gauche; à la démarche lourde. **2.** (outil, colis, etc.) peu maniable; difficile, incommode, à porter, à manier; (colis) encombrant.

unwifely [ʌn'waifli], *a.* (conduite) indigne d'une épouse.

unwilling [ʌn'wiliŋ], *a.* **1.** peu serviable; rétif. **2. to be u. to do sth.,** être peu, mal, disposé à faire qch.; ne pas vouloir faire qch.; **he appeared u. to accept,** il paraissait peu disposé à accepter; **u. acquiescence,** assentiment donné à contrecœur; **he excited our u. admiration,** nous étions bien forcés de l'admirer; **I was u. that my wife should know, for my wife to know,** je ne voulais pas que ma femme le sache.

unwillingly [ʌn'wiliŋli], *adv.* à contrecœur; de mauvais 'cœur, de mauvaise grâce, de mauvaise volonté; à regret.

unwillingness [ʌn'wiliŋnis], *s.* **1.** mauvaise volonté; mauvaise grâce. **2.** hésitation *f,* manque *m* d'enthousiasme (à faire qch.).

unwind [ʌn'waind], *v.* (*p.t. & p.p.* **unwound** [ʌn'waund]) **1.** *v.tr.* dérouler (la corde d'un treuil, etc.); développer (un câble); dépelotonner (une pelote de laine); *Tex:* dévider (un cocon, etc.); *El:* débobiner (une bobine); *Nau:* dériver (le cabestan). **2.** *v.i.* (*a*) se dérouler; se dévider; (*of ball of wool*) se dépelotonner; (*of capstan*) dévirer; (*b*) *F:* se détendre, se relaxer.

unwinding [ʌn'waindiŋ], *s.* déroulement *m*; dévidage *m*; *El:* débobinage *m*; *Nau:* dévirage *m* (du cabestan).

unwise [ʌn'waiz], *a.* **1.** (*of pers.*) imprudent; peu prudent, peu sage; malavisé, indiscret. **2.** (*of action*) contraire au bon sens; déraisonnable, peu judicieux; malavisé; **that was very u. of you,** c'était très imprudent, malavisé, de votre part.

unwisely [ʌn'waizli], *adv.* imprudemment; peu sagement.

unwitnessed [ʌn'witnist], *a.* **1.** sans témoin; qui n'a pas été vu, entendu. **2. u. signature,** signature non certifiée; **u. document,** document qui n'a pas été signé par des témoins.

unwitting [ʌn'witiŋ], *a.* **1.** inconscient (**of,** de); qui n'a pas conscience (**of,** de; **that,** que). **2.** (*of action*) fait sans dessein; accidentel, non intentionnel.

unwittingly [ʌn'witiŋli], *adv.* sans le savoir; sans intention; sans le vouloir; sans y penser; inconsciemment; accidentellement.

unwomanly [ʌn'wumənli], *a.* peu féminin; peu digne d'une femme.

unwonted [ʌn'wountid], *a. Lit:* peu coutumier; inaccoutumé, inhabituel; (événement) peu commun, rare, extraordinaire, insolite; **to show u. generosity,** faire preuve d'une générosité inaccoutumée.

unworkable [ʌn'wəːkəbl], *a.* **1.** (projet, etc.) inexécutable, impraticable; (organisation, etc.) difficile à gouverner. **2.** *Min: etc:* (gisement, etc.) inexploitable.

unworked [ʌn'wəːkt], *a.* **1.** (métal, etc.) non ouvré, non travaillé, non façonné. **2.** *Min: etc:* (gisement) inexploité.

unworkmanlike [ʌn'wəːkmənlaik], *a.* indigne d'un bon ouvrier; (travail) mal fait.

unworldliness [ʌn'wəːldlinis], *s.* **1.** détachement *m* de ce monde. **2.** simplicité *f,* candeur *f.*

unworldly [ʌn'wəːldli], *a.* **1.** (*a*) peu mondain; détaché de ce monde; (*b*) simple, candide. **2.** céleste; qui n'est pas de ce monde.

unworn [ʌn'wɔːn], *a.* (vêtement, etc.) tout neuf, qu'on n'a pas encore porté, qu'on n'a jamais porté.

unworthiness [ʌn'wəːðinis], *s.* indignité *f* (d'une action, etc.); **he was obsessed by his own u.,** c'était une obsession chez lui de se croire indigne.

unworthy [ʌn'wəːði], *a.* **1.** indigne (de qch.); **u. of notice,** qui ne mérite pas qu'on y fasse attention; **her last novel is u. of her,** son dernier roman est indigne d'elle. **2.** *O:* (personne, conduite) méprisable.

unwounded [ʌn'wuːndid], *a.* non blessé; sans blessure; indemne; sain et sauf; *Mil: etc:* **there were only ten men u.,** il ne restait que dix hommes valides.

unwrap [ʌn'ræp], *v.tr.* (**unwrapped**) défaire, désenvelopper (un paquet, etc.); détortiller (un bonbon); désengainer (une momie); **to come unwrapped,** (*of parcel*) se défaire, (*of contents*) sortir du papier, de l'enveloppe.

unwrinkled [ʌn'riŋkld], *a.* sans rides; lisse; **u. face,** visage sans rides.

unwritten [ʌn'rit(ə)n], *a.* non écrit; (*of tradition, etc.*) oral, -aux; (*of agreement, etc.*) verbal, -aux; **u. letters,** lettres à écrire, qu'on doit écrire; **an u. law,** une convention toujours respectée; une loi morale; **according to the u. law,** selon la tradition (établie); **this is an u. law of the game,** c'est une des conventions du jeu qui a force de règle.

unyielding [ʌn'jiːldiŋ], *a.* qui ne cède pas; (*of substance, support, etc.*) raide, ferme; (*of pers., determination*) inébranlable, ferme; opiniâtre; inflexible; **u. grip,** prise indesserrable, de fer; **of u. principles,** inflexible dans ses principes.

unyoke [ʌn'jouk], *v.tr.* (*a*) dételer, découpler (des bœufs); ôter le joug (des bœufs); (*b*) dételer (la charrue).

unzip [ʌnzip], *v.* (**unzipped**) **1.** *v.tr.* dégrafer (une robe, etc.); (*of dress*) **to come unzipped,** se dégrafer. **2.** *v.i. F:*

(*of garment*) **it unzips at the side,** ça s'ouvre sur le côté.

up[1] [ʌp], *adv., prep., a. & s.*

I. *adv.* **1.** (*a*) en montant; vers le haut; **all the way, the whole way, up, right up (to the top),** jusqu'au haut (de la colline); jusqu'en haut (de l'escalier); **half way up,** jusqu'à mi-hauteur; **a hundred metres up,** à cent mètres d'altitude; **to live three flights up,** habiter au troisième, *NAm:* au quatrième (étage); **two floors up from me,** deux étages au-dessus de moi; *F: often Pej:* **a two up two down,** une maison à quatre pièces à deux étages (sans salle de bains); **to throw sth. up in the air,** jeter qch. en l'air; **up went his stick,** il a levé sa canne (d'un geste menaçant); **to put one's hand up,** lever la main; **hands up!** haut les mains! (*to dog, etc.*) **up (, now)!** allons, hop! lève-toi! **to put up the results,** afficher les résultats; (*b*) **to go up on one side of the street and down on the other,** monter la rue d'un côté et redescendre de l'autre; **to walk up and down,** se promener de long en large; **to go up north,** aller dans le nord; **to go up to London, to town, for the day,** aller passer la journée à Londres; **he's going up to Oxford,** il va faire ses études à l'université d'Oxford; **when do you go up?** quand est-ce que le trimestre commence? **to go up for an examination,** se présenter à un examen; **to come up before the bench,** être cité devant les magistrats; (*c*) *Nau:* **up to windward,** au vent; **hard up with the helm!** la barre au vent toute! (*d*) **from £10 up,** à partir de £10; **from my youth up,** dès ma jeunesse. **2.** (*a*) haut, en haut; **what are you doing up there?** qu'est-ce que vous faites là-haut? *Nau:* **up top!** ohé de la hune! ohé là-haut! **up above,** en haut; dans le ciel; **up above sth.,** au-dessus de qch.; **the moon is up,** la lune est levée; **before the sun was up,** avant le lever du soleil; **have you never been up in a plane?** vous n'avez jamais volé, jamais pris l'avion? *Games:* **I'll play you a hundred up,** je vous fais cent points; **game of a hundred up,** partie *f* en cent; **the new building is up,** le nouveau bâtiment est terminé; **at last we've got the curtains up,** nous avons enfin posé les rideaux; **are the blinds up?** est-ce qu'on a relevé les stores? **the shutters are up,** on a mis les volets; (*in car*) **would you like the window up a bit?** voulez-vous que je remonte un peu la glace? *Nau:* **the anchor is up,** l'ancre est haute; **the anchor is up and down,** l'ancre est à pic; *Turf:* (*of jockey*) **to be up,** être en selle; **Comet with Thomas up,** Comet monté par Thomas; **the cat's back was up,** le chat faisait le gros dos; **with his tail up,** avec la queue en cierge; **the tide's up,** la marée est haute; **the river's up,** la rivière est haute, en crue; **this road's always up,** cette route est toujours en réparation; (*b*) en dessus; (*on packing case*) **this side up, this end up,** haut; dessus; **put it the other side, the other way, up,** retournez-le; (*c*) **up in London,** à Londres; **up in Yorkshire,** au nord dans le Yorkshire; **up at Oxford,** à l'université d'Oxford; **relations up from the country,** parents de province en visite à la ville. **3.** (*a*) **prices have gone up 10% since last year, are 10% up on last year's,** les prix ont augmenté de dix pour cent depuis l'année dernière; **bread is up again,** le pain a encore augmenté; **the temperature is going up,** la température est en hausse; **business is looking up,** les affaires sont à la hausse; *F:* **he's something quite high up in the civil service,** il est haut placé dans l'administration; *Sp:* **to be one game up, one goal up,** *Golf:* **one hole up,** être en avance d'une partie; mener par un but; avoir un trou d'avance; **to be one up on s.o.,** (i) avoir un point d'avance sur un adversaire; (ii) *F:* faire la barbe à qn; (*b*) *Mch:* **steam is up,** nous sommes sous pression; **his blood was up,** il était monté; le sang lui bouillait; (*c*) **to be well up in a subject,** connaître un sujet à fond; **well up in Latin,** fort, *F:* calé, en latin; (*d*) **speak up!** parlez plus fort, plus haut, plus distinctement! *F:* (**up** *redundant*) **to praise s.o. up,** vanter, prôner, qn. **4.** (*close proximity*) (*a*) **put it up near, against, the other,** mettez-le tout près de l'autre; **lean it up against the wall,** appuyez-le contre le mur; **they were standing close up to each other,** ils se tenaient tout près l'un de l'autre; (*b*) **to be up against difficulties,** se heurter à des difficultés; **you're up against a strong man,** vous avez affaire à forte partie; **to be up against it,** avoir de la malchance; être dans le pétrin; **to be up against the law,** avoir des démêlés avec la justice. **5.** (*a*) debout; levé; **to be up late,** veiller tard; **to be up all night,** ne pas se coucher de la nuit; **I was up late this morning,** je me suis levé tard ce matin; **I was up late last night,** je me suis couché tard hier soir; **he's always up and about, up and doing, by seven,** à sept heures il est toujours levé et au travail; (*after illness*) **to be up and about again,** être de nouveau sur pied; **we shall have to be up and doing,** il faut nous remettre au travail; (*of pers.*) **to be up and doing,** être actif et entreprenant; **to be up and coming,** (i) (*of pers.*) être plein d'avenir; promettre bien; (ii) (*of town, etc.*) être progressif; (*b*) **Parliament is up,** le parlement est en vacances; (*c*) **up guards!** debout, les gardes! **up with X!** vive X! **6.** (*a*) **to be up in arms,** être en révolte; (*b*) *F:* **what's up?** qu'est-ce qui se passe? qu'y a-t-il? **what's up with you?** qu'avez-vous! qu'est-ce qui vous prend? **I wonder what's up,** je me demande ce qui se passe, se mijote; **something's up,** il y a quelque chose (i) qui ne va pas, (ii) qui se mijote. **7. time is up,** il est l'heure (de fermer, de finir, etc.); **he completed it two days before the time was up,** il l'a terminé deux jours avant l'expiration du délai; **his leave is up,** sa permission est expirée; (*of prisoner*) **his term is up,** son temps est fini; *F:* **the game's up, it's all up,** tout est perdu; c'est fichu, flambé; **I thought it was all up with me,** j'ai pensé mourir; j'ai cru que ma dernière heure était venue; **it's all up with him,** (i) c'en est fait de lui; il n'en réchappera pas; il a son affaire, son compte; (ii) il est fichu; c'est le bout du rouleau pour lui. **8.** (*a*) **to go up to s.o.,** s'approcher de, s'avancer vers, qn; **he went straight up to the door,** il est allé droit à la porte; **covered in mud up to the ears,** couvert de boue, crotté, jusqu'aux oreilles; **where, what page, are you up to?** où en êtes-vous (du livre que vous lisez)? (*b*) **up to now, up to here,** jusqu'ici; **up to this day,** jusqu'à ce jour; **up to then,** jusqu'alors, jusque-là; **to be up to date,** être moderne, à la mode, *F:* à la page; **an up-to-date house,** une maison moderne; **up to £100 a week,** jusqu'à £100 par semaine; (*of investment, etc.*) **up to £5000,** jusqu'à concurrence, jusqu'à concours, de £5000; **to live up to one's income,** dépenser tout ce qu'on gagne, tout son revenu; **up to what age did you live in France?** jusqu'à quel âge avez-vous vécu en France? (*c*) **to be up to one's job,** être à la hauteur de sa tâche; **he's not up to it,** il n'est pas capable de le faire; **he's not up to the journey,** il n'est pas à même de faire le voyage; **I don't feel up to it,** (i) je ne m'en sens pas la capacité, le courage, la force; (ii) (*also* **I don't feel up to much**), je ne me sens pas bien; je ne suis pas dans mon assiette; **it's not up to much,** ça ne vaut pas grand-chose; **I'm not up to him, to his tricks,** je ne suis pas de force à lutter avec lui; (*d*) **he's up to something,** il a quelque chose en tête; il mijote quelque chose; **what are the children up to?** qu'est-ce que font les enfants? **she'd be up to anything,** elle est capable de tout; elle n'a pas froid aux yeux; (*e*) **it's up to him to do it,** c'est à lui de le faire; **it's up to you to accept,** il ne tient qu'à vous d'accepter; (*f*) (*in some schools*) **I'm up to Mr Martin for Latin,** je suis dans la classe de latin de M. Martin.

II. *prep.* **1.** au haut de; dans le haut de; **to go up the stairs,** monter l'escalier; **the cat is up a tree,** le chat est en haut, dans le haut, d'un arbre. **2. up the river,** en amont; vers la source de la rivière; **it's u. river from here,** c'est en amont d'ici; **to go up the street,** remonter la rue; **further up the street,** plus loin dans la rue; **to walk up and down the platform, the room,** arpenter le quai, la pièce; **he's somewhere up the garden,** il est quelque part dans le jardin.

III. *a.* ascendant, montant; *Rail:* **up line, up road,** voie paire, de gauche; voie en direction de Londres (ou d'un terminus important); **up train,** train montant.

IV. *s.* (*a*) **ups and downs,** (i) ondulations *f* (du terrain); (ii) les hauts et les bas, vicissitudes *f*, péripéties *f* (de la vie); (iii) avatars *m* (de la politique); (iv) *Com: etc:* oscillations *f* (du marché); **life is full of ups and downs,** la vie est faite de hauts et de bas; *F:* **to give s.o. the up and down,** mesurer qn des yeux; *attrib.* **up-and-down movement,** (i) mouvement *m* de montée et de descente, de monte et baisse; (ii) jeu vertical (d'une pièce); (*b*) *F:* **to be on the up and up,** être en bonne voie; être en train de monter, de faire son chemin; prospérer; (ii) être honnête, correct.

NOTE. *When* **up** *is an integral part of a verb, e.g.* **come up, go up, get up, take up,** *etc., etc., the user should consult the verb in question.*

up[2], *v.* (**upped**) **1.** *v.tr.* (*a*) **to up the swans,** recenser les cygnes; (*b*) *F: esp. U.S:* hausser (les prix); (*c*) *F:* lever (son bâton, son fusil, etc.); **to up sticks,** déménager. **2.** *v.i. P:* (*a*) se lever d'un bond; **they upped and went,** sans plus attendre ils sont partis, ils ont fichu le camp; **I upped and told him what I thought of him,** et moi de lui dire ses quatre vérités; (*b*) **he upped with his stick and hit the dog,** levant son bâton il a frappé le chien; **then he ups with a stone,** puis il ramasse une pierre.

Upanishads (the) [ðiu:'pɑ:niʃædz], *s.pl. Rel:* les Oupanichads *f*.

upas ['ju:pəs], *s. Bot:* (*a*) **u. (tree),** upas *m*; (*b*) **u. (juice),** upas.

upbeat ['ʌpbi:t], *s.* (*a*) *Mus:* levé *m*; temps *m* faible; (*b*) *Mus: Pros:* anacrouse *f*.

upbraid [ʌp'breid], *v.tr.* reprocher, faire des reproches à (qn); réprimander (qn).

upbraiding [ʌp'breidiŋ], *s.* reproches *mpl*; **to give s.o. an u.,** reprocher, faire des reproches à, qn.

upbringing ['ʌpbriŋiŋ], *s.* éducation *f* (d'un enfant); **what sort of (an) u. has she had?** comment a-t-elle été élevée?

upcast[1] ['ʌpkɑ:st], *s.* **1.** *Geol:* rejet *m* en haut; relèvement *m* (d'un filon). **2.** *Min:* (*a*) **u. (air current),** courant d'air ascendant; (*b*) **u. (shaft),** puits *m* de retour, de sortie (d'air).

upcast[2], *a.* **1.** (*of eyes, look*) tourné vers le ciel. **2.** (*a*) jeté en l'air; (*b*) *Geol:* **u. dyke,** rejet *m* en haut.

upcountry [ʌp'kʌntri]. *esp. NAm: Austr:* (*a*) *s.* l'intérieur *m* (du pays); (*b*) *a.* de l'intérieur (du pays); (*c*) *adv.* **to go u.,** aller vers l'intérieur.

update [ʌp'deit], *v.tr.* (*a*) mettre (qch.) à jour; (*b*) moderniser (qch.).

upend [ʌp'end], *v.* **1.** *v.tr.* (*a*) dresser (qch.) debout; mettre (un tonneau) à cul; (*b*) *Nau:* (*of wave*) mâter (un canot). **2.** *v.i.* (*of duck*) plonger (et lever le croupion).

uperization [ju(:)pərai'zeiʃ(ə)n], *s. Tchn:* upérisation *f*.

uperize ['ju:pəraiz], *v.tr. Tchn:* upériser.

upgrade[1] ['ʌpgreid], *s.* pente ascendante; rampe *f*, montée *f* (d'une route, d'une ligne de chemin de fer); **to be on the u.,** (i) (*of prices, etc.*) monter; tendre à la hausse; (ii) (*of business, etc.*) reprendre, se relever, se ranimer; (iii) (*of invalid*) être en bonne voie de guérison.

upgrade[2], *v.tr.* **1.** améliorer (un produit, *Breed:* une race). **2.** monter en grade (un fonctionnaire, etc.); nommer (qn), élever (qch.), à un niveau supérieur.

upgrading [ʌp'greidiŋ], *s.* **1.** amélioration *f* (d'une race, d'un produit). **2.** (*a*) *Adm: etc:* montée *f* en grade; avancement *m*; (*b*) élévation *f* du niveau (de la production, des bénéfices, etc.).

upheaval [ʌp'hi:v(ə)l], *s.* (*a*) *Geol: etc:* soulèvement *m*; commotion *f*, bouleversement *m*; (*b*) bouleversement, agitation *f* (de la société, etc.); **political u.,** convulsion *f*, commotion, politique.

uphill ['ʌphil]. **1.** *a.* (*a*) (*of road*) montant; (*b*) (*of task, etc.*) ardu, pénible, difficile, rude, fatigant, rebutant. **2.** *adv.* **to go u.,** monter; aller en montant.

uphold [ʌp'hould], *v.tr.* (*p.t. & p.p.* **upheld** [-'held]) supporter, soutenir, maintenir (une opinion, etc.); **to u. the law,** faire observer la loi; **to u. s.o.,** soutenir, encourager, qn; prêter son appui à qn; **to u. a decision,** confirmer une décision; **contract that can be upheld,** contrat *m* valide.

upholder [ʌp'houldər], *s.* **1.** partisan *m* (d'un usage, etc.); défenseur *m* (d'une opinion, d'une cause). **2.** *A:* (*a*) tapissier *m*; (*b*) entrepreneur *m* de pompes funèbres.

upholster [ʌp'houlstər], *v.tr.* (i) capitonner, garnir, rembourrer, (ii) tendre, tapisser, couvrir (un canapé, etc.) (**with, in,** de).

upholstered [ʌp'houlstə(:)d], *a.* (canapé, etc.) (i) capitonné, garni, rembourré, (ii) tapissé, couvert; **u. in, with, velvet,** garni de velours; **leather u. seat,** siège garni, tapissé, de cuir; *F:* **she's well u.,** elle est bien rembourrée.

upholsterer [ʌp'houlstərər], *s.* **1.** tapissier *m* (garnisseur, décorateur); tapissier en ameublement. **2.** *Ent:* **u. bee,** abeille coupeuse de feuilles.

upholstering [ʌp'houlstəriŋ], *s.* = UPHOLSTERY 1.

upholstery [ʌp'houlstəri], *s.* **1.** capitonnage *m*, rembourrage *m* (d'un fauteuil, etc.). **2.** (i) capiton *m*; tapisserie *f* d'ameublement; capitonnage; (ii) garniture intérieure, d'intérieur (d'une voiture); **leather u.,** garniture en cuir. **3.** (*trade*) tapisserie.

upholstress [ʌp'houlstris], *s.f.* tapissière.

upkeep ['ʌpki:p], *s.* (frais *mpl* d')entretien *m* (d'un établissement, d'un jardin, etc.); *Jur:* **u. and improvements,** impenses *fpl* et améliorations *f*.

upland ['ʌplənd]. **1.** *s. usu. pl.* région montagneuse; **the uplands,** le haut pays; les hautes terres; les collines *f*. **2.** *a.* (*a*) (village, etc.) des montagnes, dans les montagnes; (*b*) *Tex:* **u. cotton,** coton *m* à fibres courtes.

uplander ['ʌpləndər], *s.* montagnard, -arde; habitant, -ante, des hautes terres.

uplift[1] ['ʌplift], *s.* **1.** (*a*) élévation *f* (du terrain, etc.); haussement *m* (des sourcils, etc.); *Geol:* soulèvement *m*; *Civ.E:* (*of dam*) sous-pression *f*, *pl.* sous-pressions; (*b*) **u. bra, brassière,** soutien-gorge pigeonnant, au maintien parfait. **2. moral u.,** élévation morale; inspiration (morale).

uplift[2] [ʌp'lift], *v.tr.* **1.** soulever, élever (qch.). **2.** élever (l'âme, le cœur, la voix, etc.).

uplifted [ʌp'liftid], *a.* (*a*) (*of hand, etc.*) levé; (*of head, etc.*) haut; (*b*) (*of mind, etc.*) (i) élevé; (ii) exalté, inspiré.

up(-)link ['ʌpliŋk], *s. Telecom:* liaison montante.

up-market ['ʌpmɑ:kit], *a. F:* de qualité supérieure; (journal, etc.) sérieux.

upmost ['ʌpmoust], *a.* = UPPERMOST 1.

upon [ə'pɔn], *prep.* (= ON) sur; **on** *and* **upon** *are interchangeable in meaning, and the difference between them is one of style; in modern English* **upon** *is used mainly where greater formality or emphasis is required, sometimes to introduce variety of style into a sentence, e.g.* **he was relying on the votes of his constituents, not upon the vote of the assembly,** il comptait sur les voix de ses électeurs, pas sur la décision de l'assemblée; *in certain phrases and contexts, however,* **upon** *is preferable:* **upon my word!** ma foi! mon Dieu! **the enemy was upon us,** l'ennemi nous attaquait; **I came upon it by accident,** je l'ai trouvé par hasard; **you brought it upon yourself,** ne t'en prends qu'à toi-même!

upper ['ʌpər], *a. & s.*

I. *a.* 1. (*a*) supérieur; (plus) haut; (plus) élevé; de dessus; d'au-dessus; **the u. air,** les couches supérieures de l'atmosphère; *Geol:* **u. strata,** couches supérieures; **u. jaw, lip,** mâchoire, lèvre, supérieure; **the u. branches,** les hautes branches; **the u. rooms,** les pièces d'en haut; **u. storey,** étage supérieur; *F:* **to be weak, wrong, to have sth. missing, in the u. storey,** avoir une araignée au plafond; *Bootm:* **u. leather,** empeigne *f*; *Nau:* **u. mast,** mât supérieur; **u. sails,** hautes voiles; **u. topsail,** (hunier) volant *m*; **u. deck,** pont supérieur; *Th:* **u. circle,** deuxième balcon *m*; **temperature in the u. twenties,** température qui dépasse 25°; (*b*) **u. reaches, u. waters, of a river,** amont *m* d'une rivière; **the u. Rhine,** le haut Rhin; **U. Canada,** le haut Canada; **U. Egypt,** la Haute-Égypte; **U. Silesia,** la Haute-Silésie. 2. supérieur (en rang, etc.); **u. servants,** principaux domestiques; **u. end of the table,** haut bout de la table; *Parl:* **the u. House,** la Chambre haute; **the u. classes,** la haute société; **u.-class milieu,** milieu aristocratique; **the u. middle classes,** la haute bourgeoisie; *Sch:* **the u. school, the u. forms,** les grandes classes; les classes supérieures; **to get the u. hand,** prendre le dessus; prévaloir; **to get the u. hand of s.o., of a horse,** avoir raison de qn; subjuguer un cheval; **to let s.o. get the u. hand,** se laisser tyranniser, subjuguer, par qn; **we must keep the u. hand,** il faut garder l'avantage. 3. *Mus:* (*a*) (clavier) du côté droit; (*b*) (registre) aigu; **to pass from the u. to the lower register,** passer de l'aigu au grave.

II. *s.* (*a*) *Bootm:* (i) empeigne *f*; (ii) tige *f* (de botte); (*b*) *F:* **to be down on one's uppers,** être très pauvre; être dans la dèche, dans la purée.

uppercut[1] ['ʌpəkʌt], *s. Box:* coup porté de bas en haut; uppercut *m.*

uppercut[2], *v.tr.* (*p.t. & p.p.* **-cut;** *pr.p.* **-cutting**) *Box:* porter à (qn) un coup de bas en haut.

uppermost ['ʌpəmoust]. 1. *a.* (*a*) le plus haut; le plus élevé; (*b*) premier; de la plus grande importance; **to be u.,** prédominer; tenir le premier rang; **the problem (which is) u. in our minds,** le problème qui nous préoccupe le plus; notre principale préoccupation. 2. *adv.* (le plus) en dessus; **face u.,** face en dessus; **wheels, u.,** les roues en l'air.

uppish, uppity ['ʌpiʃ, -iti], *a. F:* présomptueux, arrogant, suffisant; qui se donne des airs; **don't be so u. about it!** ne le prenez pas de si haut, sur ce ton! **he's getting very u.,** il se croit quelqu'un.

uppishly ['ʌpiʃli], *adv. F:* d'un air, d'un ton, suffisant.

uppishness ['ʌpiʃnis], *s. F:* arrogance *f*; suffisance *f.*

upraised ['ʌpreizd], *a.* levé; **with u. hand,** en levant la main.

upright[1] ['ʌprait], *a., adv. & s.*

I. *a.* 1. (*of line, etc.*) vertical, -aux; perpendiculaire; (*of wall, writing, etc.*) droit; **u. boiler,** chaudière verticale; (*of scaffolding*) **u. pole,** écoperche *f*; **u. joint,** joint montant; **u. piano,** piano droit; **u. freezer,** congélateur vertical, droit. 2. (*of pers., dealings, etc.*) droit, juste, honnête; équitable; intègre; **u. judge,** magistrat juste, intègre.

II. *adv.* debout; (*of pers.*) **to stand u.,** se tenir droit; **sitting u. on his chair,** assis raide sur sa chaise; **to put, stand, sth. u.,** mettre qch. debout, d'aplomb; **to be kept u.,** tenir debout.

III. *s.* 1. **out of u.,** hors d'aplomb. 2. *Carp: etc:* montant *m*; pied-droit *m, pl.* pieds-droits; chandelle *f*, jambage *m*; *Rail:* ranchet *m* (de wagon plat); **uprights of a ladder,** montants, bras *m*, d'une échelle; **uprights of a mine,** bois *mpl* de mine; *Fb: etc:* **the uprights,** les montants de but. 3. piano droit.

upright[2], *v.tr. esp. U.S: F:* **to u. sth.,** (re)mettre qch. debout.

uprightly ['ʌpraitli], *adv.* avec droiture; justement, avec justesse; équitablement; intègrement; honnêtement.

uprightness ['ʌpraitnis], *s.* 1. verticalité *f*, perpendicularité *f*, aplomb *m.* 2. (*of pers., etc.*) droiture *f*, intégrité *f*, rectitude *f*, honnêteté *f*, probité *f*, équité *f.*

uprising [ʌp'raiziŋ], *s.* soulèvement *m* (du peuple); insurrection *f.*

uproar ['ʌprɔ:r], *s.* 1. tumulte *m*, vacarme *m*, tapage *m*, brouhaha *m*, chahut *m*; **it was a deafening u.,** c'était un vacarme assourdissant, un bruit de tous les diables. 2. **the town was in an u.,** la ville était en effervescence.

uproarious [ʌp'rɔ:riəs], *a.* tumultueux; tapageur, -euse; **u. crowd,** foule tumultueuse; **the class was getting u.,** la classe commençait à faire du tapage; **u. laughter,** grands éclats de rire; **the new farce is really u.,** la nouvelle farce est désopilante.

uproariously [ʌp'rɔ:riəsli], *adv.* tumultueusement; tapageusement; (rire) à grands éclats, à gorge déployée; **u. funny,** désopilant.

uproot [ʌp'ru:t], *v.tr.* déraciner, extirper, arracher (une plante, un mal, etc.); **to u. s.o. from his home,** arracher qn de son foyer; **to feel uprooted,** se sentir déraciné.

uprooting [ʌp'ru:tiŋ], *s.* déracinement *m*, extirpation *f.*

uprush ['ʌprʌʃ], *s.* montée soudaine (d'eau, etc.); jaillissement *m* (de pétrole, etc.); bouffée (montante) (de gaz, d'air).

upsadaisy ['ʌpsədeizi, ʌpsə'deizi], *int. F:* houp là!

upsaddle [ʌp'sædl], *v.i.* (*esp. in S. Africa, N Am.*) seller son cheval.

Upsala [ʌp'sɑ:lə], *Pr.n. Geog:* Upsal.

upset[1] ['ʌpset], *s.* 1. renversement *m*; chavirage *m*, chavirement *m* (d'un bateau). 2. (*a*) désorganisation *f*; bouleversement *m*; désordre *m*; remue-ménage *m inv*; **we're moving, and you can imagine the u.,** nous déménageons; vous pouvez vous figurer le bouleversement, le désordre; (*b*) ennui *m*; **that's going to cause a bit of an u.,** cela va causer des difficultés, des ennuis; (*c*) bouleversement (d'esprit); **it was a terrible u. to, for, me,** cela m'a bouleversé, m'a donné un coup; (*d*) indisposition *f*; dérangement *m* (d'estomac).

upset[2] [ʌp'set], *v.* (*p.t. & p.p.* **upset;** *pr.p.* **upsetting**) 1. *v.tr.* (*a*) renverser (un vase, son contenu, etc.); (faire) chavirer (un bateau); (*b*) désorganiser, bouleverser, déranger (les projets de qn); tromper (les calculs de qn); *Mil: etc:* **to u. a manœuvre,** déjouer une manœuvre; **to u. everything,** mettre tout en confusion; tout bouleverser, détraquer, chambarder; (*c*) troubler, émouvoir, bouleverser (qn); **the accident u. me very much,** cet accident m'a vraiment bouleversé; **the least thing upsets him,** la moindre chose le bouleverse; il s'impressionne pour un rien; **don't get u., don't u. yourself, don't be upset,** ne vous impressionnez pas; ne vous frappez pas; ne le prenez pas au tragique; il ne faut pas vous en rendre malade; (*d*) indisposer (qn); déranger (l'estomac); troubler (la digestion); **beer upsets me,** la bière me rend malade, m'est contraire, ne me réussit pas, ne me vaut rien. 2. *v.tr. Metalw: etc:* refouler (la tête d'un boulon, etc.); (*of projectile*) **to become u.,** se refouler. 3. *v.i.* (*of cup, contents, etc.*) se renverser; (*of boat*) chavirer.

upset[3]. [*before noun* 'ʌpset, *otherwise* ʌp'set], *a.* 1. (*a*) renversé; (*of boat*) chaviré; (*b*) (*of pers.*) bouleversé; ému; (*c*) (estomac) dérangé; (*of pers.*) **to feel u.,** être indisposé; avoir l'estomac dérangé. 2. (*at auctions, etc.*) **u. price,** mise *f* à prix; prix de départ; prix demandé; **knocked down for £100 from an u. price of £60,** adjugé à £100 sur demande de £60.

upsetting[1] [ʌp'setiŋ], *a.* (*of news, etc.*) bouleversant, inquiétant.

upsetting[2], *s.* 1. (*a*) renversement *m*; chavirage *m*, chavirement *m*; (*b*) bouleversement *m*; désorganisation *f*; dérangement *m* (de projets); **u. of the equilibrium,** rupture *f* de l'équilibre. 2. *Metalw:* refoulement *m*; **u. press,** presse *f* à refouler.

upshot ['ʌpʃɔt], *s.* résultat *m*, issue *f*, dénouement *m*, conclusion *f* (d'une affaire); **what will be the u. of it?** quelle en sera l'issue? cela finira comment? **the u. of it all was that he resigned,** pour conclure l'affaire il a donné sa démission.

up(-)side ['ʌpsaid]. 1. *s.* (*a*) *F:* dessus *m* (de qch.); (*b*) *Tg:* amont *m.* 2. *adv.phr:* **upside down:** (*a*) sens dessus dessous; la tête en bas; cul par-dessus tête; **to hold sth. u. down,** tenir qch. renversé, à l'envers, sens dessus dessous; **book bound u. down,** livre relié à l'envers; (*b*) bouleversé; en désordre; **to turn everything u. down,** tout bouleverser; tout mettre en désordre, sens dessus dessous. 3. *a. F:* **upside-down,** renversé; mis sens dessus dessous; **u.-down ideas,** idées biscornues; **to have an u.-down way of looking at things,** voir les choses à l'envers. 4. *adv. F: O:* **to get upsides with s.o.,** rendre la pareille à qn; prendre sa revanche.

upsilon [jup'sailən, 'ʌpsilən], *s. Gr.Alph:* upsilon *m.*

upslope ['ʌpsloup], *s.* pente ascendante.

upstage[1] [ʌp'steidʒ]. 1. *s. Th:* arrière-scène *f.* 2. *a.* (*a*) *Th:* de l'arrière-scène; (*b*) *F:* arrogant, hautain, dédaigneux; **to behave in an u. manner,** se donner des airs. 3. *adv.* à l'arrière-scène.

upstage[2], *v.tr.* prendre la vedette à (qn); reléguer (qn) au second plan.

upstairs. 1. *adv.* [ʌp'stɛəz] (*a*) en haut (de l'escalier); à l'étage; aux étages supérieurs; **to go u.,** monter (l'escalier); **to call s.o. u.,** faire monter qn; *F:* **to kick, boot, s.o. u.,** donner de l'avancement à qn (pour s'en débarrasser); limoger qn en lui conférant une dignité; (*b*) *O:* (*as opposed to the servants' quarters*) chez les maîtres; (*c*) *F:* **he hasn't got much u.,** il n'est pas très intelligent, il n'a pas beaucoup de cervelle; **he's got plenty u.,** il y a quelque chose là-dedans. 2. (*a*) *a.* (*also* **upstair**) ['ʌpstɛəz, 'ʌpstɛər] (*of room, etc.*) d'en haut, du haut; (situé) à l'étage (supérieur); **we have an u. sitting room,** nous avons un salon au premier; (*b*) *s. F:* (**the**) **u.** [ʌp'stɛəz], l'étage; les pièces d'en haut; **the house has no u.,** la maison n'a pas d'étage; **I'm going to clean the u. this morning,** ce matin je vais faire le ménage en haut.

upstanding [ʌp'stændiŋ], *a.* (*of pers.*) (*a*) droit, qui se tient bien; (*b*) honnête, droit, intègre.

upstart ['ʌpstɑ:t], *s.* 1. parvenu, -ue; nouveau riche; **u. official,** petit bureaucrate arrogant (qui se croit important). 2. *Bot:* colchique *m* d'automne.

upstream ['ʌpstri:m], *a.* (*a*) (bief, etc.) d'amont; **u. cutwater,** avant-bec *m* (d'une pile de pont); (*b*) (vent) d'aval.

upstroke ['ʌpstrouk], *s.* 1. (*in writing*) délié *m.* 2. (*of violin bow*) poussé *m.* 3. *I.C.E: Mch:* course montante, course ascendante, (re)montée *f*, levée *f*, ascension *f*, mouvement ascensionnel (du piston).

upsurge ['ʌpsə:dʒ], *s.* poussée *f*; vague *f* (d'enthousiasme, etc.); regain *m* (d'activité, etc.).

upswept ['ʌpswept], *a. Aut: Av:* surélevé; profilé; **u. hair(style),** coiffure relevée.

upswing ['ʌpswiŋ], *s.* 1. mouvement ascendant. 2. amélioration *f* sensible; **business is on the u.,** les affaires sont en progression constante.

uptake ['ʌpteik], *s.* 1. *F:* entendement *m*, intelligence *f*; **to be quick in, on, the u.,** être intelligent; avoir la compréhension facile; avoir l'esprit vif, éveillé; **he's a bit slow in, on, the u.,** il est lent à comprendre, à saisir; il n'est pas dégourdi pour deux sous. 2. (*a*) colonne *f* d'air montant (d'un système d'aérage, etc.); **u. pipe,** tuyau ascendant, montant; tuyau de montée; *Min:* **u. (shaft),** puits *m* de retour d'air; (*b*) *Mch:* culotte *f*, rampant *m* (de cheminée); (*c*) captage *m.*

uptight ['ʌplait], *a. F:* tendu; ému; agité; crispé.

uptown. 1. *adv.* [ʌp'taun] *esp. U.S:* dans, vers, les quartiers résidentiels de la ville. 2. *s.* ['ʌptaun] (*a*) la partie la plus élevée de la ville; (*b*) *esp. U.S:* les quartiers résidentiels; **u. society,** les milieux bourgeois.

upturn[1] ['ʌptə:n], *s.* amélioration *f*; progression *f* (dans les affaires, etc.); avancement *m*; **there has been an u. in oils,** les actions pétrolières ont remonté; **there is an u. in prices,** les prix sont à la hausse.

upturn[2] [ʌp'tə:n], *v.tr.* retourner; mettre à l'envers; renverser.

upturned ['ʌptə:nd], *a.* (*a*) retourné; renversé; (*b*) (bord) relevé; (nez) retroussé; (yeux) tournés vers le ciel; **u. faces,** visages tournés en l'air.

Upupidae [ju:'pju:pidi:], *s.pl. Orn:* upupidés *m*, les huppes *f.*

upward ['ʌpwəd]. 1. *a.* (*of road, etc.*) montant, ascendant; **u. movement,** (i) mouvement ascensionnel, d'ascension; (ii) mouvement de reprise; phase ascendante; **u. slope, gradient,** pente ascendante; rampe *f*; *Av:* (*following dive*) **u. motion,** remontée *f*; **eyebrows with a somewhat satanic u. curve,** sourcils à la remontée un peu satanique; *Com: etc:* **u. tendency, movement,** tendance *f* à la hausse, mouvement de hausse; **prices show an u. tendency,** les prix sont à la hausse, en hausse. 2. *adv.* = UPWARDS.

upwards ['ʌpwədz], *adv.* 1. de bas en haut; vers le haut; en montant; **concave u.,** concave vers le haut; **the road runs u.,** la route monte; **to look u.,** regarder en haut. 2. en dessus; **to put sth. face u. on the table,** mettre qch. à l'endroit sur la table; (*of pers.*) **lying face u.,** couché sur le dos; (*of cat, etc.*) **paws u.,** les pattes en l'air; **the knife fell with the edge u.,** le couteau est tombé le tranchant en dessus. 3. au-dessus; **£100 and u.,** £100 et au-dessus, et au-delà; **u. of 500 pupils,** plus de 500 élèves; **children from ten (years) u.,** des enfants à partir de dix ans.

upwash ['ʌpwɔʃ], *s. Av: etc:* déflexion *f* des filets d'air vers le haut.

urachus ['ju:rəkəs], *s. Anat:* ouraque *m.*

uracil ['ju:rəsil], *s. Ch:* uracile *m.*

uraemia [ju'ri:miə], *s. Med:* urémie *f.*

uraemic [ju'ri:mik], *a. Med:* urémique.

uraeus [ju'ri:əs], *s. Ant:* uræus *m.*

Ural ['ju:rəl], *Pr.n. Geog:* **the U. (river),** l'Oural *m*; **the U. mountains,** *s.* **the Urals,** les monts Ourals, l'Oural.

Ural-Altaic [ju:rəlæl'teiik], *a.* & *s. Ling:* ouralo-altaïque (*m*).
Uralian [ju'reiliən], *a. Geog:* ouralien.
uralite ['ju:rəlait], *s. Miner:* ouralite *f.*
uralitization [jurælitai'zeiʃ(ə)n], *s. Miner:* ouralitisation *f*, ouralisation *f.*
uramil ['ju:rəmil], *s. Ch:* uramile *m.*
uranate ['ju:rəneit], *s. Ch:* uranate *m.*
Urania [ju'reiniə]. **1.** *Pr.n.f. Myth: Astr:* Uranie. **2.** *s. Bot: Ent:* uranie *f.*
uranic [ju'rænik], *a. Ch:* uranique.
uraniferous [jurə'nifərəs], *a.* uranifère.
uraniid [ju'reiniid], *s. Ent:* uranie *f*, uraniidé *m.*
Uraniidae [jurei'ni:idi:], *s.pl. Ent:* uraniidés *m.*
uraninite [ju'reininait], *s. Miner:* uraninite *f.*
uranism [ju'reinizm], *s. Med:* uranisme *m.*
uranist [ju'reinist], *a.* & *s. Med:* uraniste (*m*).
uranite ['ju:rənait], *s. Miner:* uranite *f.*
uranium [ju'reiniəm], *s. Ch:* uranium *m*; **u. oxide,** urane *m*; **u. glass,** verre *m* d'urane; **enriched u.,** uranium enrichi.
uranocircite [jureinou'sə:sait], *s. Miner:* uranocircite *f.*
uranography [ju(:)rə'nɔgrəfi], *s. Astr:* uranographie *f.*
uranometry [ju(:)rə'nɔmitri], *s. Astr:* uranométrie *f.*
uranophane [ju'rænoufein], *s. Miner:* uranophane *f.*
uranopilite [ju(:)rənou'pailait], *s. Miner:* uranopilite *f.*
uranoscopid [jurə'nɔskəpid], *s. Ich:* uranoscope *m.*
uranosph(a)erite [ju(:)rənou'sferait], *s. Miner:* uranosphérite *f.*
uranospinite [jurə'nɔspinait], *s. Miner:* uranospinite *f.*
uranothallite [ju(:)rənou'θælait], *s. Miner:* uranothallite *f.*
uranothorite [ju(:)rənou'θɔ:rait], *s. Miner:* uranothorite *f.*
uranotil(e) [ju'rænout(a)il], *s. Miner:* uranotile *f.*
uranous ['ju:rənəs], *a. Ch:* uraneux.
Uranus [ju'reinəs], *Pr.n.m. Myth: Astr:* Uranus.
uranyl ['ju:rənil], *s. Ch:* uranyle *m.*
urazole ['ju:rəzoul], *s. Ch:* urazole *m.*
urban[1] ['ə:bən], *a.* urbain; **u. life,** la vie urbaine; **over-populated u. areas,** agglomérations urbaines surpeuplées.
Urban[2], *Pr.n.m.* Urbain.
urbane [ə:'bein], *a.* courtois; d'une politesse raffinée.
urbanely [ə:'beinli], *adv.* courtoisement; d'une politesse raffinée; avec urbanité.
urbanification [ə:bænifi'keiʃ(ə)n], *s.* urbanification *f.*
urbanism ['ə:bənizm], *s.* urbanisme *m.*
urbanist[1] ['ə:bənist], *s.* **1.** *Rel.H:* urbaniste *m* (partisan d'Urbain VI). **2.** *Ecc:* **u. (nun),** urbaniste *f.*
urbanist[2], *s. Town P:* urbaniste *mf.*
urbanity [ə:'bæniti], *s.* urbanité *f*; courtoisie *f.*
urbanization [ə:bənai'zeiʃ(ə)n], *s.* urbanisation *f.*
urbanize ['ə:bənaiz], *v.tr.* urbaniser.
Urbino [ə:'bi:nou], *Pr.n. Hist:* **Duchy of U.,** duché *m* d'Urbin.
urceolate ['ə:siəleit], *a. Nat.Hist:* urcéolé.
urceolus [ə:'si:ələs], *s. Nat.Hist:* urcéole *m.*
urchin ['ə:tʃin], *s.* **1.** *F:* (*a*) **(street) u.,** galopin *m*; gamin, -ine (des rues); (*b*) gosse *mf*; marmot *m*; bambin, -ine. **2.** (*a*) *A:* hérisson *m*; (*b*) *Echin:* **(sea) u.,** oursin *m*; **heart u.,** spatangue *m*; **edible sea u.,** oursin violet; (*c*) *Her:* hérisson; (*d*) *Tex:* hérisson (de machine à carder).
Urdu ['uədu:], *s. Ling:* ourdou *m.*
urea [ju'ri:ə], *s. Ch:* urée *f.*
ureal [ju'ri:əl], *a. Ch:* uréique.
ureameter [ju:ri'æmitər], *s. Med:* uréomètre *m.*
ureametry [ju:ri'æmitri], *s. Med:* uréométrie *f.*
urease ['ju:rieis], *s. Bio-Ch:* uréase *f.*
Uredinales [juridi'neili:z], *s.pl. Fung:* urédinales *f.*
uredo [ju'ri:dou], *s. Fung:* urédo *m.*
uredospore [ju'ri:douspɔ:r], *s. Fung:* urédospore *f.*
ureic [ju'ri:ik], *a. Ch:* uréique.
uremia, uremic [ju'ri:miə, -mik] = URAEMIA, URAEMIC.
urena [ju'ri:nə], *s. Bot:* urena *m.*
ureometer [ju:ri'ɔmitər], *s. Med:* uréomètre *m.*
ureometry [ju:ri'ɔmitri], *s. Med:* uréométrie *f.*
ureter [ju'ri:tər], *s. Anat:* uretère *m.*
ureteral [ju'ri:tər(ə)l], *a. Anat:* urétéral, -aux.
ureterectomy [juri:tə'rektəmi], *s. Surg:* urétérectomie *f.*
ureteric [juri'terik], *a. Anat:* urétérique.
ureteritis [juri:tə'raitis], *s. Med:* urétérite *f.*
ureterolithiasis [juri:tərouli'θi'eisis], *s. Med:* urétérolithiase *f.*
ureterolithotomy [juri:tərouli'θɔtəmi], *s. Surg:* urétérolithotomie *f.*
ureterorrhaphy [juri:tərou'ræfi], *s. Surg:* urétérorraphie *f.*
ureterostomy [juri:tə'rɔstəmi], *s. Surg:* urétérostomie *f.*
ureterotomy [juri:tə'rɔtəmi], *s. Surg:* urétérotomie *f.*
urethan(e) ['ju:riθein], *s. Ch:* uréthane *m.*
urethra [ju'ri:θrə], *s. Anat:* urètre *m.*
urethral [ju'ri:θrəl], *a. Anat:* urétral, -aux.
urethrectomy [juri'θrektəmi], *s. Surg:* urétrectomie *f.*
urethritis [juri'θraitis], *s. Med:* urétrite *f.*
urethrobulbar [juri:θrou'bʌlbər], *a. Anat:* urétrobulbaire.
urethrocele [ju'ri:θrousi:l], *s. Med:* urétrocèle *f.*
urethroplasty [juri:θrou'plæsti], *s. Surg:* urétroplastie *f.*
urethrorectal [juri:θrou'rekt(ə)l], *a. Anat:* urétro-rectal, -aux.
urethrorrhagia [juri:θrou'reidʒiə], *s. Med:* urétrorragie *f.*
urethroscope [ju'ri:θrəskoup], *s. Med:* urétroscope *m.*
urethroscopy [ju(:)ri:θ'rɔskəpi], *s. Med:* urétroscopie *f.*
urethrostomy [ju(:)ri:θ'rɔstəmi], *s. Surg:* urétrostomie *f.*
urethrotomy [ju(:)ri:θ'rɔtəmi], *s. Surg:* urétrotomie *f*; **external, perineal, u.,** urétrotomie externe.
urethrovesical [juri:θrou'vesikl], *a. Anat:* urétro-vésical, -aux.
urge[1] [ə:dʒ], *s.* incitation *f*, impulsion *f*; poussée *f*; mobile *m*; **to feel an u. to do sth.,** se sentir poussé à, se sentir le besoin de, faire qch.; **u. to write,** démangeaison *f* d'écrire.
urge[2], *v.tr.* **1.** (*a*) **to u. s.o. (on),** encourager, exhorter, exciter, qn; **to u. a horse forward, on,** pousser, presser, animer, talonner, lancer, forcer, enlever, un cheval; hocher le mors à, serrer les côtes à, un cheval; chasser en avant; *Ven:* **to u. on the hounds,** baudir les chiens; **to u. s.o. to do sth.,** pousser, exhorter, qn à faire qch.; presser qn de faire qch.; prier instamment qn de faire qch.; **to u. s.o. to action,** exhorter qn à l'action; **to u. s.o. to revolt,** inciter, exciter, qn à la révolte, à se révolter; (*b*) hâter, pousser (qch.); **to u. on, forward, a piece of work,** hâter, activer, un travail. **2.** mettre en avant, avancer, alléguer, objecter (une raison, etc.); faire valoir (une raison, une excuse, etc.); insister sur (un point); **I urged that. . .,** j'ai fait valoir que . . .; **to u. sth. against s.o.,** objecter qch. contre qn; faire un démérite à qn de qch. **3.** conseiller fortement, recommander (une démarche, etc.); **"let's make haste," he urged,** "dépêchons-nous," répétait-il; **to u. the necessity of doing sth.,** insister sur la nécessité de faire qch.
urgency ['ə:dʒənsi], *s.* **1.** urgence *f* (d'une question, etc.); extrémité *f* (d'un besoin); *Parl:* **to call for a vote of u.,** demander l'urgence; **it's a matter of u.,** il y a urgence; c'est urgent. **2.** besoin pressant; nécessité urgente.
urgent ['ə:dʒ(ə)nt], *a.* **1.** urgent, pressant; immédiat; **u. need,** besoin pressant; **u. case,** cas urgent, pressant; **the matter is u.,** l'affaire presse; il y a urgence; c'est urgent; **to deal with the most u. thing first,** s'occuper d'abord du plus pressé; courir au plus pressé; **the doctor had an u. call,** on a appelé le médecin d'urgence; *Parl:* **the business is reported as u.,** l'urgence est déclarée; **u. entreaty,** prière instante; **at their u. request,** sur leurs instances pressantes; *Post:* **u.,** urgent. **2.** *A:* (*of pers.*) qui insiste; pressant, insistant; **they were u. for him to start at once,** ils ont beaucoup insisté pour qu'il parte aussitôt; **they were very u. with him,** ils ont beaucoup insisté auprès de lui; **do not be too u.,** n'allez pas jusqu'à l'importunité.
urgently ['ə:dʒəntli], *adv.* d'urgence; avec instance; **a doctor is u. required,** on demande d'urgence un médecin; **his return is most u. required,** il y a grande urgence à ce qu'il revienne; **to press u. for sth.,** réclamer qch. de façon urgente.
urginea [ə:'dʒiniə], *s. Bot:* urginea *m.*
Uriah [ju'raiə], *Pr.n.m. B.Hist:* Urie.
urial ['u:riəl], *s. Z:* urial *m.*
uric ['ju:rik], *a.* (acide, etc.) urique.
uric(a)emia [juri'si:miə], *s. Med:* uricémie *f.*
uricase ['ju:rikeis], *s. Bio-Ch:* uricase *f.*
uricosuric [ju(:)rikou's(j)u:rik], *a.* & *s. Med:* uricosurique (*m*); urico-éliminateur, -trice.
urinal ['ju:rin(ə)l, ju:'rain(ə)l], *s.* **1. (bed) u.,** urinal *m*, -aux (de lit). **2.** *Hyg:* urinoir *m*; *F:* pissotière *f.*
urinalysis [juri'nælisis], *s.* analyse *f* d'urine.
urinarium [juri'neəriəm], *s. Husb:* fosse *f* à purin.
urinary ['ju:rinəri]. **1.** *a. Anat:* urinaire; **the u. system,** les voies *f* urinaires; **u. calculus,** urolithe *m.* **2.** *s.* (*a*) = URINAL 2; (*b*) *Husb:* fosse *f* à purin.
urinate ['ju:rineit], *v.i.* uriner.
urination [ju(:)ri'neiʃ(ə)n], *s.* urination *f*; miction *f.*
urine ['ju:rin], *s.* urine *f.*
urinometer [ju:ri'nɔmitər], *s. Med:* urinomètre *m*; pèse-urine *m.*
urinous ['ju:rinəs], *a.* urineux.
urite ['ju:rait], *s. Ent:* urite *m*; uromère *m.*
urn [ə:n], *s.* **1.** (*a*) *Cer: etc:* urne *f*; (*b*) **cinerary u.,** urne cinéraire, sépulcrale; (*c*) *Rom.Ant:* urne électorale. **2.** *Dom.Ec:* **(tea) u.,** fontaine *f* (à thé).
urobilin [ju:rou'bailin], *s. Physiol:* urobiline *f.*
urobilinuria [ju:roubaili'nju:riə], *s. Med:* urobilinurie *f.*
Urochorda(ta) [ju:rou'kɔ:də(tə)], *s.pl. Nat.Hist:* uroc(h)ordés *m.*
urochrome ['ju:roukroum], *s. Physiol:* urochrome *m.*
urocoptid [ju:rou'kɔptid], *s. Moll:* urocoptidé *m.*
Urocoptidae [ju:rou'kɔptidi:], *s.pl. Moll:* urocoptidés *m.*
urocyon [ju'rɔsiən], *s. Z:* urocyon *m.*
urocystis [ju:rou'sistis], *s. Fung:* urocystis *m.*
urodele ['ju:roudi:l], *s. Amph:* urodèle *m.*
urodynia [ju(:)rou'dainiə], *s. Med:* urodynie *f.*
urogaster ['ju:rougæstər], *s. Crust:* urogastre *m.*
urogenital [ju(:)rou'dʒenit(ə)l], *a. Anat:* urogénital, -aux.
urography [ju'rɔgrəfi], *s. Med:* urographie *f.*
urolagnia [jurou'lægniə], *s. Med:* urolagnie *f.*
urolith ['ju:rouliθ], *s. Med:* urolithe *m.*
urologic [jurou'lɔdʒik], *a. Med:* urologique.
urologist [ju'rɔlədʒist], *s.* urologiste *mf*, urologue *mf.*
urology [ju'rɔlədʒi], *s. Med:* urologie *f.*
uromere ['ju:roumiər], *s. Ent:* uromère *m*; urite *m.*
uromyces [jurou'maisi:z], *s. Fung:* uromyces *m.*
uromys ['ju:roumis], *s. Z:* uromys *m.*
Uropeltidae [jurou'peltidi:], *s.pl. Rept:* uropeltidés *m.*
uropod ['ju:roupɔd], *s. Crust:* uropode *m.*
uropoietic [ju(:)roupɔi'etik], *a. Physiol:* (fonction) uropoïétique.
uropteran [ju'rɔptərən], *s. Crust:* uroptère *m.*
uropygial [ju(:)rou'pidʒiəl], *a. Orn:* uropygial, -aux; **u. gland,** glande uropygienne, uropygiale.
uropygium [ju(:)rou'pidʒiəm], *s. Orn:* uropyge *m*, uropygium *m.*
uroscopy [ju'rɔskəpi], *s. Med:* uroscopie *f.*
urostyle ['ju:roustail], *s. Amph:* urostyle *m.*
urotoxic [ju(:)rou'tɔksik], *a. Med:* urotoxique.
urotoxicity [juroutɔk'sisiti], *s. Med:* urotoxie *f.*
uroxanic [jurɔk'sænik], *a. Ch:* uroxanique.
Ursa ['ə:sə], *s. Astr:* **U. Major, U. Minor,** la Grande, la Petite, Ourse.
Ursidae ['ə:sidi:], *Z:* ursidés *m*; les ours *m.*
ursigram ['ə:sigræm], *s. Telecom:* ursigramme *m.*
ursine ['ə:sain], *a. Z:* ursin, oursin; **u. seal,** phoque oursin; ours marin.
Ursula ['ə:sjulə], *Pr.n.f.* Ursule.
Ursuline ['ə:sjul(a)in, -li:n], *a.* & *s.* **U. (nun),** ursuline *f*; **U. convent,** (un) couvent d'ursulines; (le) couvent des ursulines, *F:* (*school*) les ursulines.
urtica ['ə:tikə], *s. Bot:* ortie *f.*
Urticaceae [ə:ti'keisii:], *s.pl. Bot:* urticacées *f.*
Urticales [ə:ti'keili:z], *s.pl. Bot:* urticales *f.*
urticaria [ə:ti'keəriə], *s. Med:* urticaire *f.*
urtication [ə:ti'keiʃ(ə)n], *s.* urtication *f.*
urubu [u:ru'bu:], *s. Orn:* urubu *m.*
Uruguay ['urugwai], *Pr.n. Geog:* Uruguay *m.*
Uruguayan [uru'gwaiən]. *Geog:* (*a*) *a.* uruguayen; (*b*) *s.* Uruguayen, -enne.
urunday [u:run'dai], *s. Bot:* urunday *m.*
urus, *pl.* **uri, uruses** ['ju:rəs, 'ju:rai, 'ju:rəsiz], *s. Z:* urus *m*, aurochs *m.*
urutu [u:'ru:tu:], *s. Rept:* urutu *m.*
urva ['ə:və], *s. Z:* urva *m.*
us, *pers. pron., objective case.* **1.** (*unstressed*) [əs] (*a*) nous; **he sees us,** il nous voit; **in front of us,** devant nous; **he gave it to us,** il nous l'a donné; **tell us,** dites-nous; **he wrote us a long letter,** il nous a écrit une longue lettre; **he stayed with us a month,** il est resté un mois chez nous; **there are three of us,** nous sommes trois; **we'll take the boxes with us,** nous prendrons les boîtes avec nous; (*b*) *A:* & *Lit:* **we sat us down,** nous nous sommes assis. **2.** (*stressed*) [ʌs] (*a*) nous; **that concerns** ***us*** **alone,** cela nous regarde, nous seuls; cela ne regarde que nous; **between them and us,** entre eux et nous; **will you be one of us?** voulez-vous être des nôtres? **as for us Englishmen,** quant à nous autres Anglais; (*b*) (*after the verb* **to be**) **he couldn't believe that it was us,** il ne pouvait pas croire que c'était nous. **3.** (= **me**) (*a*) (*plural of majesty, etc.*) nous; **it appears to us that. . .,** nous sommes persuadé que . . .; (*b*) *F:* **let's have a look,** laissez-moi regarder; **give us a bit of it,** donnez-m'en un peu.
usable ['ju:zəbl], *a.* utilisable, employable; exploitable.
usage ['ju:sidʒ], *s.* **1.** traitement *m*; **this book has had rough u.,** ce livre a été maltraité. **2.** (*a*) usage *m*, coutume *f*; pratique consacrée; **an old u.,** une vieille coutume; **sanctified by u.,** consacré par l'usage; **modern English u.,** l'usage de l'anglais d'aujourd'hui; (*b*) *Jur:* droit *m* de passage. **3.** (*a*) emploi *m*, usage (d'un mot, etc.); (*b*) utilisation *f*, destination *f* (d'un appareil, etc.); **u. time,** disponibilité *f*, *Cmptr:* temps utile.

usance ['ju:z(ə)ns], *s. Com:* usance *f*; **local u.,** l'usance de la place; **bill at double u.,** effet *m* à double usance.

use[1] [ju:s], *s.* **1.** (*a*) emploi *m*, usage *m*; **a new u. for a product,** une nouvelle utilisation d'un produit; **the u. of steel in modern building,** l'emploi de l'acier dans la construction moderne; **to make (good) u. of sth.,** se servir de qch.; utiliser qch.; employer qch.; tirer parti, profit, de qch.; mettre qch. à contribution; **to make the best possible u. of sth.,** tirer le meilleur parti possible de qch.; utiliser qch. aussi avantageusement que possible; **he makes good u. of his time,** il emploie bien son temps; **he hasn't made very good u. of it,** il n'en a pas profité; **can't you make u. of me?** je ne puis donc pas vous aider, vous rendre service? **everything has a, its, u.,** il y a un emploi pour tout; **I'll find a u. for it,** je trouverai un moyen de m'en servir; **it's for u., not for ornament,** ce n'est pas un objet d'art; il faut s'en servir; **word in everyday u.,** mot d'usage courant; mot très usité; **not in u.,** (i) hors d'usage; dont on ne se sert plus; (ii) (machine) qui n'est pas en marche; **this machine has been in u. for ten years,** cette machine sert depuis dix ans; **is this machine in u. (at the moment)?** est-ce que cette machine est disponible? (*at reference library*) **book in u.,** livre en lecture; **out of u.,** hors d'usage; (mot) désuet, tombé en désuétude; *P.N:* (*on door of lift, etc.*) hors de service; **for u. in case of fire,** à employer en cas d'incendie; **for u. in schools,** à l'usage des écoles; **directions, instructions, for u.,** mode d'emploi; indications du mode d'emploi; *Pharm:* **for external u.,** pour usage externe; *Cust:* **home u. entry,** sortie *f* de l'entrepôt pour consommation; (*b*) usage; **to improve with u.,** s'améliorer à l'usage. **2.** jouissance *f*, usage; (*a*) **to have full u. of one's faculties,** jouir de toutes ses facultés; **to lose the u. of a leg,** perdre l'usage d'une jambe; être impotent d'une jambe; **to recover the u. of one's limbs,** recouvrer l'usage, le maniement, de ses membres; (*b*) **to have one room and the u. of the bathroom,** avoir une chambre et l'usage, le droit de se servir, de la salle de bains; **you can have the u. of my car while I'm in London,** tu peux te servir de ma voiture pendant que je suis à Londres; (*c*) *Jur:* détention *f* précaire; usufruit *m*; **full right and u. (of sth.),** plein usufruit, pleine jouissance (de qch.). **3.** utilité *f*; **to be of u. (for sth.),** être utile (à qch.); **can I be of any u. (to you)?** puis-je vous être utile à quelque chose? puis-je vous aider? **this is no longer of any u.,** cela n'est plus bon à rien; on ne peut plus se servir de ça; **it's of no u.,** cela ne sert à rien; **it's not much u.,** cela ne sert pas à grand-chose, n'est pas très utile; **for all the u. it is to me,** pour ce que j'en fais; *F:* **a fat lot of u. that'll be to you!** si tu crois que ça va t'avancer! *F: Iron: you're* **a lot of u.!** je vous retiens! **I'm no u. here,** je suis inutile ici; *F:* **he's no u.,** il est incapable; il ne vaut rien; **to have no u. for sth.,** n'avoir que faire, ne savoir que faire, de qch.; **I've no further u. for it,** je n'en ai plus besoin; *F:* **I haven't much u. for him,** il ne me dit rien; il m'est antipathique; je ne peux pas le voir; **it was no u.,** c'était inutile; **it's no u. discussing the question,** rien ne sert de discuter la question; inutile de discuter la question; **it's no u. crying,** ce n'est pas la peine de pleurer; **it's no u. my talking,** je perds ma peine à parler; ce sont paroles perdues; **it's no u.(, I can't do it)!** c'est peine perdue(; je ne peux pas le faire); **is it any u. writing to him?** est-ce que ça servirait de lui écrire? **what's the u. of doing it, of going there?** à quoi bon le faire, y aller? **4.** *A:* (*a*) usage, coutume *f*, accoutumance *f*, habitude *f*; **according to u. and wont,** suivant l'usage; selon l'usage; (*b*) *Ecc:* liturgie *f*, rite *m* (particuliers à une église).

use[2] [ju:z], *v.tr.* **1.** (*a*) employer, se servir de (qch.); **are you using this knife?** est-ce que vous vous servez de ce couteau? **to know how to u. one's hands,** savoir se servir de ses mains; **u. your intelligence!** ne sois pas si bête! débrouille-toi! **u. your eyes!** ouvrez les yeux! (*of thg*) **to be used for sth.,** servir à qch.; être employé à qch.; **it's there to be used,** c'est là pour s'en servir; *F:* ce n'est pas fait pour les chiens; **I used the money to rebuild my garage,** j'ai utilisé l'argent à reconstruire mon garage; **this word is no longer used,** ce mot est désuet; **this expression is not used any more,** cette expression ne s'emploie plus; **word used figuratively,** mot employé au (sens) figuré; **the roots are used for food,** on en mange les racines; **I u. a lot of thyme in cooking,** je me sers beaucoup de thym dans la cuisine; (*b*) avoir recours à (qch.); user de (qch.); **to u. force,** user de force; employer la force; avoir recours à la force; **to u. discretion,** agir avec discrétion; **to u. one's influence,** user de son influence; **to u. every means (at one's disposal),** employer tous les moyens (à sa disposition); (*c*) *esp. U.S: F:* **I could u. some coffee,** je prendrais volontiers du café; une tasse de café ne serait pas de refus. **2.** traiter (qn); (bien, mal) agir envers qn; **I've been very badly, roughly, used,** j'ai été maltraité, rudoyé; **this tool has been roughly, hardly, used,** cet outil a été maltraité; **it will last a long time if you u. it carefully,** cela vous servira longtemps si vous le traitez avec soin; *F:* **how's the world been using you lately?** comment ça va ces temps-ci? **3.** (*a*) **to u. sth. (up),** user, épuiser, consommer, qch.; **we've used (up) all the milk,** il ne reste plus de lait; **to u. up all one's provisions,** consommer toutes ses provisions; **don't u. it all,** il ne faut pas tout employer; (*b*) **to u. up scraps, remains, leftovers,** utiliser, *Cu:* accommoder, les restes; tirer parti des restes; (*c*) *O:* **to be used up,** être épuisé, surmené, éreinté. **4.** (*as aux., p.t.*) **when we were children we used** [ju:st] **to play together,** quand nous étions enfants nous jouions ensemble; **my father used to tell me that . . .,** mon père m'a souvent raconté que . . .; **it used to be a pleasant town to live in,** c'était autrefois une ville agréable à habiter; **things aren't what they used to be,** ce n'est plus comme autrefois; **you used to love me!—used to?** tu m'aimais autrefois!—autrefois? **she used not, usen't, to like oysters,** autrefois elle n'aimait pas les huîtres; **I used not to like him,** *F:* **didn't use to** ['ju:stə] **like him,** autrefois je ne l'aimais pas.

used, *a.* **1.** [ju:zd] (vêtement, etc) usé, usagé; (timbre-poste) oblitéré; (nappe, etc.) sale, qui a déjà servi; **u. car,** voiture d'occasion; **hardly u.,** presque neuf; à l'état de neuf; *Ind: etc:* **u. material,** déchets *mpl*; *Atom.Ph:* **u. (nuclear, reactor,) fuel,** combustible (nucléaire) usé. **2.** [ju:st] **u. to (doing) sth.,** habitué, accoutumé, à (faire) qch.

useful ['ju:sful], *a.* **1.** utile; (vêtement, etc.) pratique; **this book was very u. to me,** ce livre m'a été très utile, d'une grande utilité, m'a rendu grand service; **it's u. to know,** c'est utile à savoir; **it will come in very u.,** cela sera d'une grande utilité, rendra bien service; **a u. man to know,** un homme utile à connaître; **to make oneself u.,** se rendre utile; **let me make myself u.,** je vais vous donner un coup de main; *Av:* **u. weight,** poids *m* utile; **u. lift,** force ascensionnelle disponible; **this machine has a u. life of ten years,** cette machine donnera dix ans de service; **he's a u. player,** c'est un joueur compétent; **he played a u. game,** il s'est acquitté honorablement, il s'est très bien acquitté; **he's quite, pretty, u. with his fists,** il sait se servir de ses poings; **to be u. with a gun,** savoir manier un fusil; *Iron:* **that's u.!** nous voilà bien avancés!

usefully ['ju:sfuli], *adv.* utilement; **one might u. write a book on . . .,** on pourrait utilement écrire un livre sur . . .; **dictionary that can be u. consulted,** dictionnaire utile à consulter.

usefulness ['ju:sfulnis], *s.* utilité *f*; **institution that has outlived its u.,** institution qui a perdu sa raison d'être; **this has outlived its u.,** cela ne sert plus à rien, n'a plus d'utilité.

useless ['ju:slis], *a.* inutile; bon à rien; (effort, etc.) vain, infructueux; **this gadget is u.,** ce machin ne sert à rien; **these goods are u.,** ces marchandises ne sont bonnes à rien; **a map without a key is u.,** une carte sans légende est inutilisable; **it would be u. to make further requests,** d'autres demandes seraient inutiles; **u. regrets,** regrets superflus; **u. remedy,** remède inefficace; **a u. person,** un(e) incompétent(e); une non-valeur; un bon à rien; **I feel completely u.,** je me sens bon à rien, complètement inutile; *F:* **to be worse than u.,** être au-dessous de tout.

uselessly ['ju:slisli], *adv.* inutilement; en pure perte; en vain.

uselessness ['ju:slisnis], *s.* inutilité *f*; (*of pers.*) incompétence *f*.

user[1] ['ju:zər], *s.* **1.** usager, -ère (de la route, d'un moyen de transport, etc.); utilisateur, -trice (d'un appareil, d'un véhicule, etc.); abonné, -ée (du téléphone, etc.); *Cmptr:* **u. coded,** (programme) écrit par l'utilisateur; **u. core,** zone utilisateur en mémoire. **2.** *Jur:* détenteur *m* précaire; usufruitier *m*.

user[2], *s. Jur:* droit *m* d'usage continu; **to reserve the u. of sth.,** se réserver l'usage de qch.; **full right of u. of sth.,** plein usufruit de qch.; **land subject to a right of u.,** propriété grevée d'une servitude.

Ushant ['ʌʃənt], *Pr.n. Geog:* Ouessant *m*.

usher[1] ['ʌʃər], *s.* **1.** (*a*) **(gentleman) u.,** huissier *m*; introducteur *m* (auprès des grands, à une réception); *Jur:* **court u.,** (huissier) audiencier *m*; (*b*) **theatre u.,** ouvreuse *f*; (*c*) (*at wedding*) **the ushers,** les garçons *m* d'honneur. **2.** *Sch: A: or Iron:* (*a*) maître *m* d'étude; surveillant *m* d'études; *F:* pion *m*; (*b*) maître, professeur *m*.

usher[2], *v.tr.* **1.** précéder (un roi, etc.) comme huissier. **2. to u. s.o. in (to the room),** introduire, faire entrer, qn (dans le salon); annoncer qn; **to u. s.o. into the presence of s.o.,** introduire qn en présence de qn, auprès de qn; **to u. in a new epoch,** inaugurer une époque; *Cmptr:* **to u. in, out,** introduire (un programme) en mémoire; sortir, extraire (un programme) de la mémoire. **3.** *v.i. F:* (*at wedding*) servir de garçon(s) d'honneur; *Th: Cin:* servir d'ouvreuse.

usherette [ʌʃə'ret], *s.f. Th: Cin:* ouvreuse.

usnea ['ʌsniə], *s. Moss:* usnée *f*.

usquebaugh ['ʌskwibɔ:], *s. A: & Dial:* whisky *m*; usquebac *m*.

ustilago [ʌsti'leigou], *s. Fung:* ustilago *m*.

usual ['ju:ʒu(ə)l], *a.* usuel, habituel, ordinaire; **at the u. time,** à l'heure habituelle; **the u. terms,** les conditions d'usage; **his u. clothes,** ses vêtements d'habitude, de tous les jours; **our u. waiter didn't serve us,** ce n'est pas notre garçon habituel qui nous a servis; **it's u. to pay in advance,** c'est la coutume, il est d'usage, de coutume, de payer d'avance; **it's the u. practice,** c'est la pratique courante; cela se fait couramment; **earlier, later, than u.,** plus tôt, plus tard, que de coutume, que d'habitude, que d'ordinaire; **more than u.,** plus que d'habitude; **as u.,** comme à l'ordinaire; comme d'ordinaire, d'habitude, d'usage, de coutume; comme à l'accoutumée; **business as u.,** les affaires continuent, la vente continue (à l'intérieur) (pendant les réparations, etc.); *s. F:* (*in bar, etc.*) **(are you having) your u.?** votre demi, votre whisky, etc., comme d'habitude?

usually ['ju:ʒu(ə)li], *adv.* ordinairement, usuellement, habituellement; d'ordinaire, d'habitude, de coutume; à l'ordinaire, à l'accoutumée; **I u. get up at seven,** j'ai l'habitude, j'ai coutume, de me lever à sept heures; je me lève d'habitude à sept heures; **he was more than u. polite,** il s'est montré (i) d'une politesse qui ne lui est pas habituelle, (ii) encore plus poli que d'habitude.

usucapion, usucaption [ju:zju'keipiən, -'kæpʃ(ə)n], *s. Jur:* usucapion *f*.

usucapt ['ju:zjukæpt], *v.tr. Jur:* usucaper.

usufruct ['ju:zjufrʌkt], *s. Jur:* usufruit *m* **(of,** de); **quasi u., imperfect u.,** quasi-usufruit *m*; **ownership without u.,** nue propriété.

usufructuary [ju:zju'frʌktjəri], *a. & s. Jur:* usufruitier, -ière; **u. right,** droit *m* usufructuaire.

usurer ['ju:ʒərər], *s.* usurier, -ière.

usurious [ju:'zju:riəs], *a.* **1.** (intérêt *m*, etc.) usuraire. **2.** (*of pers.*) usurier.

usurp [ju:'zə:p, -'sə:p]. **1.** *v.tr.* usurper (un trône, un titre, etc.) **(from,** sur); voler (un titre) **(from,** à). **2.** *v.i.* **to u. (up)on s.o.'s rights, upon one's neighbours,** empiéter, usurper, sur les droits de qn, sur ses voisins.

usurpation [ju:zə'peiʃ(ə)n, -sə:-], *s.* usurpation *f*.

usurpatory [ju:'zə:pət(ə)ri, -'sə:-], *a.* usurpatoire.

usurper [ju'zə:pər, -'sə:-], usurpateur, -trice.

usurping [ju:'zə:piŋ, -'sə:-], *a.* usurpateur, -trice.

usury ['ju:ʒuri], *s.* usure *f*; **to practise u.,** pratiquer l'usure.

usward ['ʌswə:d], *adv. A: & B:* **to usward(s),** vers nous, de notre côté.

uta ['u:tə], *s. Med:* uta *m*.

utahlite ['ju:təlait], *s. Miner:* variscite *f*.

utensil [ju(:)'tensəl], *s.* ustensile *m*; **household utensils,** ustensiles de ménage; **(set of) kitchen utensils,** batterie *f* de cuisine.

uterine ['ju:tərain], *a.* **1.** *Med:* utérin. **2.** *Jur:* **u. brother, u. sister,** frère utérin, sœur utérine; frère, sœur, de mère.

uterogestation [ju:təroudʒes'teiʃ(ə)n], *s. Physiol:* gestation utérine.

utero-ovarian [ju:tərouou'vɛəriən], *a. Anat:* utéro-ovarien.

uteroplacental [ju:tərouplæ'sentəl], *a. Obst:* utéro-placentaire.

uterosacral [ju:tərou'sækrəl], *a. Anat:* utéro-sacré.

uterovaginal [ju:tərouvə'dʒainəl], *a. Anat:* utéro-vaginal, -aux.

uterus, *pl.* **-ruses, -ri** ['ju:tərəs, -rəsiz, -rai], *s. Anat:* utérus *m*, matrice *f*.

Utica ['ju:tikə], *Pr.n.* (*a*) *A.Geog:* Utique *f*; (*b*) (*in U.S:*) Utica.

utilitarian [ju:tili'tɛəriən], *a. & s.* utilitaire (*mf*).

utilitarianism [ju:tili'tɛəriənizm], *s. Phil:* utilitarisme *m*.

utility [ju'tiliti], *s.* **1.** (*a*) utilité *f*; **to be of great u.,** être d'une grande utilité; *Pol.Ec:* **marginal u.,** utilité marginale; **u. vehicle, car,** véhicule, voiture, utilitaire, tous usages; *Mil.Av:* **u. aircraft,** avion du service général; *Com:* **u. goods,** articles *m* utilitaires, de consommation courante; (*World War II*) articles d'utilité sociale; **u. footwear,** la chaussure nationale; **u. room,** débarras *m*; *Cmptr:* **u. program(me), u. routine,** programme *m* de service; **u. tape,** bande *f* de manœuvre; (*b*) **public utilities, public u. services,** *NAm:* **utilities,** services publics; (*c*) *NAm:* entreprise *f* de service public. **2.** *Phil:* utilitarisme *m*. **3.** personne *f*, chose *f*, utile; *Th:* **to be a u. (man), to play utilities,** jouer les utilités; **u. actor, actress,** *Th:* utilité, doublure *f*; *Cin:* acteur, actrice, de complément; doublure.

utilizable [ju:ti'laizəbl], *a.* utilisable.

utilization [ju:tilai'zeiʃ(ə)n], *s.* utilisation *f*; mise *f* en valeur; *Bank:* réalisation *f*; **u. of a patent,** exploitation *f* d'une invention; **better u. of resources,** mobilisation *f* des ressources; **u. factor,** *El: etc:* facteur *m* d'utilisation (d'une génératrice, etc.); *Ind:* taux *m* du rendement.

utilize ['ju:tilaiz], *v.tr.* utiliser, se servir de (qn, qch.); tirer parti de, tirer profit de, mettre en valeur (qch.).

utmost ['ʌtmoust]. **1.** *a.* extrême; dernier; **the u. ends of the earth,** les (derniers) confins, les extrémités *f*, de la terre; **the room was in the u. confusion,** la pièce était dans la plus grande confusion; **to make the u. efforts to do sth.,** faire tout son possible pour faire qch.; **the u. poverty,** la misère la plus profonde, le dernier degré de la misère; **treated with the u. contempt,** traité avec le dernier mépris; **it is of the u. importance that he should be present,** il est de toute importance, de la dernière importance, qu'il soit présent; **with the u. ease,** avec la plus grande facilité. **2.** *s.* extrême *m*; dernière limite; dernier degré; **to the u.,** le plus possible; à l'extrême; au suprême degré; **I'll help you to the u. of my ability,** je vous aiderai autant qu'il est en mon pouvoir, de tout mon pouvoir; **to do one's u. to achieve sth.,** faire tout son possible, faire l'impossible, faire des pieds et des mains, se mettre en quatre, pour arriver à un but; s'ingénier à accomplir qch.; **that is the u. one can do,** c'est tout ce qu'on peut faire; c'est le plus qu'on puisse faire.

utopia [ju:'toupiə], *s.* utopie *f*.

utopian [ju:'toupiən]. **1.** *a.* utopique; d'utopie. **2.** *s.* utopiste *mf*.

utopianism [ju:'toupiənizm], *s.* utopisme *m*.

utricle ['ju:trikl], *s. Nat.Hist: Anat:* utricule *m*.

utricular [ju'trikjulər], *a. Nat.Hist: Anat:* utriculaire; *Bot:* utriculé, utriculeux.

utricularia [jutrikju'lɛəriə], *s. Bot:* utriculaire *f*.

Utriculariaceae [jutrikjulɛəri'eisii:], *s.pl. Bot:* utriculariacées *f*.

utriform ['ju:trifɔ:m], *a.* utriforme.

utter[1] ['ʌtər], *a.* **1.** *A:* extérieur; **the u.** (= *outer*) **darkness,** les ténèbres extérieures. **2.** complet, -ète; absolu; **he's an u. stranger to me,** il m'est complètement étranger; je ne le connais ni d'Ève ni d'Adam; **we were in u. darkness,** il faisait noir comme dans un four; **u. rubbish,** (i) de la pure camelote; (ii) des absurdités; **u. scoundrel,** coquin fieffé, de la plus belle eau; **he's an u. fool,** il est complètement idiot; **u. poverty,** la misère la plus profonde; **to my u. horror,** à ma grande horreur.

utter[2]. **1.** *v.tr.* (*a*) jeter, pousser, faire entendre (un cri, un gémissement, etc.); dire, prononcer, articuler, proférer (un mot, etc.); lancer (un juron); **you must never u. his name in her presence,** il ne faut jamais prononcer son nom devant elle; **I didn't u. a word,** je n'ai pas desserré les dents, soufflé mot; (*b*) dire; exprimer (ses sentiments); débiter (des mensonges). **2.** *v.tr.* émettre, faire circuler, mettre en circulation, passer (de la fausse monnaie, un faux chèque); **to u. a forged document,** faire usage d'un faux document. **3.** *v.i. F:* **he didn't u.,** il n'a pas desserré les dents; **he looked at me without uttering,** il m'a regardé sans mot dire.

utterance ['ʌtər(ə)ns], *s.* **1.** expression *f* (des sentiments, etc.); prononciation *f* (d'un discours); émission *f* (d'un son); **to give u. to one's feelings,** exprimer ses sentiments. **2.** articulation *f*, prononciation. **3. utterances,** propos *m*, mots *m* (de qn).

utterer ['ʌtərər], *s.* émetteur, -trice (de fausse monnaie).

uttering ['ʌtəriŋ], *s.* émission *f* (de fausse monnaie).

utterly ['ʌtəli], *adv.* complètement, absolument, entièrement, parfaitement, tout à fait; **u. stupid,** d'une bêtise extrême.

uttermost ['ʌtəmoust], *a. & s.* = UTMOST; **the u. parts of the earth,** les derniers confins, les extrémités *f*, de la terre.

utters ['ʌtəz], *s.pl. Mec.E:* (*on lathe work, etc.*) broutages *m*, broutements *m* (causés par les saccades de l'outil).

uva, *pl.* **-ae** ['ju:və, -i:], *s.* **1.** *Bot:* uva *m*, raisin *m*. **2.** *Bot: Pharm:* **u. ursi,** uva-ursi *m*.

uvala ['u:vələ], *s. Geog:* ouvala *m*.

uvarovite [(j)u:'vɑ:rouvait], *s. Miner:* ouvarovite *f*, ouwarowite *f*.

uvea ['ju:viə], *s. Anat:* uvée *f*.

uveal ['ju:viəl], *a. Anat:* uvéal, -aux.

uveitis [ju:vi'aitis], *s. Med:* uvéite *f*.

uveoparotid [ju:vioupæ'rɔtid], *a. Med:* **u. fever,** uvéoparotidite *f*.

uveoparotitis [ju:vioupærou'taitis], *s. Med:* uvéoparotidite *f*.

uvitic [ju:'vitik], *a. Ch:* uvitique.

uvula, *pl.* **-as, -ae** ['ju:vjulə, -əs, -i:], *s. Anat:* uvule *f*; luette *f*.

uvular ['ju:vjulər], *a. Anat:* uvulaire; *Ling:* **u. r,** r uvulaire, vélaire, grasseyé.

uvularia [ju:vju'lɛəriə], *s. Bot:* uvulaire *f*.

uvulitis [ju:vju'laitis], *s. Med:* uvulite *f*, staphylite *f*.

uvulotomy [ju:vju'lɔtəmi], *s. Surg:* uvulotomie *f*.

uxoricide [ʌk'sɔ(:)risaid], *s.* uxoricide *m*.

uxorious [ʌk'sɔ:riəs], *a.* (mari) (i) qui fait preuve d'un attachement exagéré pour sa femme, (ii) dominé par sa femme.

uxoriousness [ʌk'sɔ:riəsnis], *s.* attachement exagéré (d'un mari) pour sa femme.

Uzbek ['ʌzbek], *s. Geog:* Uzbek *m*, Ouzbek *m*; **U. Soviet Socialist Republic,** République socialiste soviétique d'Uzbékistan, d'Ouzbékistan.

Uzbekistan [ʌzbeki'stɑ:n], *Pr.n. Geog:* Uzbékistan *m*, Ouzbékistan *m*.

V

V, v [vi:], *s.* (la lettre) V, v *m.* **1.** *Tp:* **V for Victor,** V comme Victor; **V-shaped,** en (forme de) V; *Geog:* **V-shaped valley,** vallée (à profil) en V; **V-necked dress,** robe à encolure, (*low*) à décolleté, en pointe, en V; **V. sign,** (i) *Hist:* (1939–45) le V de la victoire; (ii) geste *m* obscène, de dérision; **V Day,** le jour de la victoire; *I.C.E:* **V. (type) engine,** moteur *m* à cylindres en V; *Mec.E:* **V block,** support *m* en V (pour traçage), V de traçage, de mécanicien; *Rail:* **V crossing,** croisement de changement, croisement aigu; *Mec.E:* **V gear,** engrenage à chevrons, engrenage hélicoïdal double; **V pulley,** poulie *f* à corde; **V thread,** filet *m*, pas *m*, triangulaire (de vis); *Sm.a:* **backsight V,** cran *m* de mire. **2.** *Cmptr:* **V format,** format en longueur variable. **3.** *Mil:* (1939–45) **V 1, V 2 (bomb),** V 1 *m*, V 2 *m*.

vaalite ['vɑ:lait], *s. Miner:* vaalite *f*.

vac [væk], *s. Sch: F:* vacances *fpl*.

vacancy ['veikənsi], *s.* **1.** vide *m*, vacuité *f*; **to stare, gaze, into v.,** fixer les yeux dans l'espace, le vide, le vague. **2.** vide (de l'esprit), nullité *f* d'esprit; absence *f* d'idées. **3.** vide; espace *m* vide, lacune *f*; *Cryst:* défaut *m* de Schottky. **4.** (*a*) place vacante, poste vacant; (*for dignitary, professional, etc.*) vacance *f*; **to fill a v.,** pourvoir un poste vacant, un vide; *P.N:* **v. for a bricklayer,** on demande maçon; (*b*) (*at hotel, etc.*) chambre *f* libre; (*at camp site, etc.*) place libre; *P.N:* **no vacancies,** complet.

vacant ['veikənt], *a.* **1.** vacant, vide, libre; **v. space,** place vide; **v. site,** *NAm:* **v. lot,** terrain *m* vague; **v. room, seat,** chambre, place, libre, inoccupée; **v. throne,** trône vacant; (*of official post, etc.*) **to be v.,** vaquer; **every time the throne was v. a civil war followed,** chaque vacance du trône était suivie d'une guerre civile; *Jur:* **v. succession,** succession vacante. **2.** (esprit) inoccupé; (regard) distrait, vague, atone, sans expression; **v. eyes,** yeux vides d'expression; **v. expression,** air hébété; **with a v. stare,** le regard perdu.

vacantly ['veikəntli], *adv.* d'un air distrait; d'un regard perdu; **to stare v. at sth.,** regarder qch. (i) d'un air vague, d'un œil atone, sans voir, (ii) d'un air hébété.

vacate [və'keit], *v.tr.* **1.** (*a*) quitter (un emploi, une situation, etc.); **to v. office,** donner sa démission, démissionner, se démettre; (*b*) quitter, laisser libre (un siège, etc.); évacuer (un appartement); quitter (une chambre d'hôtel); déménager (d'une maison); *Jur:* **to v. the premises,** vider les lieux. **2.** *Jur:* annuler (un contrat, etc.).

vacating [və'keitiŋ], *s.* **1.** (*a*) **v. of office,** démission *f*; (*b*) évacuation *f* (d'une maison, etc.). **2.** *Jur:* annulation *f* (d'un contrat).

vacation[1] [və'keiʃ(ə)n], *s.* **1.** (*a*) **the v.,** les vacances *fpl*; **the long v.,** *Jur:* les vacances judiciaires, les vacations *fpl*; *Sch:* (*at university*) les grandes vacances; (*b*) *esp. NAm:* **to take a v.,** prendre des vacances; **two weeks' v. with pay,** un congé payé de deux semaines. **2.** = VACATING.

vacation[2], *v.i. NAm:* prendre des vacances; **to v. in the mountains,** passer ses vacances, faire une villégiature, à la montagne.

vacationist, vacationer [və'keiʃ(ə)nist, -ər], *s. NAm:* villégiaturiste *mf*, vacancier, -ière; (*in summer*) estivant, -ante.

vacationland [və'keiʃ(ə)nlænd], *s. NAm:* centre de tourisme, de villégiature, très fréquenté.

vaccinate ['væksineit], *Med:* **1.** *v.tr.* vacciner (*esp.* contre la variole); **to get vaccinated,** se faire vacciner. **2.** *v.i.* faire une vaccination, des vaccinations.

vaccination [væksi'neiʃ(ə)n], *s. Med:* vaccination *f* (*esp.* contre la variole); **first, primary, v.,** primovaccination *f*; **v. mark,** vaccin *m*.

vaccinationist [væksi'neiʃ(ə)nist], *s. Med.Hist:* partisan, -ane, de la vaccination.

vaccinator ['væksineitər], *s.* **1.** (*pers.*) vaccinateur *m*. **2.** lancette *f* à vacciner; vaccinostyle *m*.

vaccine ['væksi:n]. **1.** *a.* (*a*) de vache, relatif aux vaches; (*b*) *Vet:* vaccinal, de la vaccine; **v. pustule,** pustule vaccinale; **v. virus,** virus *m* de la vaccine; **v. lymph,** lymphe vaccine. **2.** *s. Med:* vaccin *m*; **(smallpox) v.,** vaccin antivariolique; **yellow fever v.,** vaccin antiamaril; **tetravalent v.,** vaccin tétravalent; **v. reactions,** réactions vaccinales; **v. inoculation,** vaccination *f*, (i) inoculation *f* de la vaccine, (ii) inoculation de vaccin; **v. point,** plume *f* pour vaccination, vaccinostyle *m*; **v. tube,** tube *m* à vaccin; **v.(-)producing,** vaccinogène; **v. therapy,** vaccinothérapie *f*.

vaccinia [væk'siniə], *s.* **1.** *Vet:* variole *f* des vaches; vaccine *f*; **pustules of v.,** pustules vaccinales. **2.** *Med:* vaccinelle *f*, vaccinoïde *f*.

vaccinid(e) ['væksin(a)id], *s. Med:* vaccinide *f*.

vacciniferous [væksi'nifərəs], *a. Med: Vet:* vaccinifère.

vacciniform [væk'sinifɔ:m], *a.* vaccinoïde.

vacciniola [væk'sinioulə], *s. Med:* vaccinelle *f*, vaccinoïde *f*.

vaccinium [væk'siniəm], *s. Bot:* vaccinier *m*.

vaccinoid ['væksinɔid], *a. Med:* vaccinoïde.

vaccinogenic [væksinou'dzenik], *a.* vaccinogène.

vaccinostyle ['væksinoustail], *s. Med:* vaccinostyle *m*.

vaccinotherapy [væksinou'θerəpi], *s. Med:* vaccinothérapie *f*.

vacillate ['væsileit], *v.i.* vaciller; (i) chanceler (en marchant); (ii) hésiter (entre deux opinions, etc.).

vacillating[1] ['væsileitiŋ], *a.* vacillant, inconstant, irrésolu.

vacillating[2], *s.* vacillation *f*.

vacillation [væsi'leiʃ(ə)n], *s.* vacillation *f*; hésitation *f*.

vacillatory ['væsilət(ə)ri], *a.* vacillatoire; irrésolu, hésitant.

vacoa [və'kouə], *s. Bot:* vaquois *m*.

vacuist ['vækjuist], *s. A.Phil:* vacuiste *mf*.

vacuolar ['vækjuələr], *a. Biol:* (membrane, etc.) vacuolaire.

vacuolate[1] ['vækjuəleit], **vacuolated** ['vækjuəleitid], *a. Biol:* vacuolaire, qui renferme des vacuoles.

vacuolate[2], *v.i. Biol:* vacuoliser.

vacuole ['vækjuoul], *s. Biol:* vacuole *f*.

vacuol(iz)ation [vækjuou'leiʃ(ə)n, -lai'zeiʃ(ə)n], *s. Biol:* vacuolisation *f*.

vacuome ['vækjuoum], *s. Biol:* vacuome *m*.

vacuometer [vækju'ɔmitər], *s. Ph:* vacuomètre *m*.

vacuous ['vækjuəs], *a.* (*a*) (espace, etc.) vide; (*b*) vide de pensée, d'expression; **v. remark,** observation bête, dénuée de bon sens; **v. laugh,** rire niais, bête; **he's completely v.,** c'est un parfait idiot; **v. look,** air hébété, regard *m* vide d'expression.

vacuously ['vækjuəsli], *adv.* (regarder) avec des yeux vides d'expression; (rire) bêtement.

vacuousness ['vækjuəsnis], *s.* vacuité *f*, vide *m*.

vacuum, *pl.* **-ua, -uums** ['vækjuəm, -juə, -juəmz], *s.* **1.** *Ph:* (*a*) vide *m*, vacuum *m*; **absolute v.,** vide absolu, parfait; **high, hard, v.,** vide élevé, poussé; **very high, ultra-high, v.,** vide très poussé, ultra-poussé; ultravide *m*; **low, partial, v.,** vide imparfait, partiel; **to produce, create, a v. in a vessel,** faire le vide dans un récipient; **v. bottle, flask, jug,** bouteille, cruche, isolante; *El:* **v. lamp,** lampe *f* à vide; **v. arc lamp,** lampe à arc dans le vide; **v. switch,** interrupteur *m* dans le vide; *Rad.A:* **v. (photo-emittent) cell,** cellule *f* à vide; *Elcs:* **v. tube,** tube *m* (à vide), électronique; **v. tube rectifier,** redresseur *m* à lampe; **v. valve,** lampe à vide; *I.C.E:* **v. (feed) tank,** exhausteur *m*, réservoir *m* à élévateur; *Ph:* **v. filter,** filtre *m* à vide; *Sug.-R:* **v. pan,** autoclave *m*, chaudière *f*, à vide; chaudière de concentration par le vide; **v. distillation, distilling,** distillation *f* sous vide; *Petr:* **v. rerun,** redistillation *f* sous vide; **v. filtration,** filtration *f* par le vide; *Ind:* **v. packing,** emballage *m* sous vide; (*b*) (*partial*) dépression *f*; *Mec.E:* **v. system,** circuit *m* de dépression; **v. leak,** fuite *f* dans un circuit de dépression; **v. test,** essai *m* de dépression. **2.** *Dom.Ec: etc:* **v. cleaner,** aspirateur *m*; **to run the v. (cleaner) over a room,** passer une pièce à l'aspirateur; **v. cleaning,** nettoyage *m* par le vide, dépoussiérage *m* par aspirateur.

vacuum(-clean) ['vækjuəm(kli:n)], *v.tr.* passer (une pièce, etc.) à l'aspirateur.

vacuum-controlled, -operated ['vækjuəmkən'trould, -'ɔpəreitid], *a. Mec.E:* commandé par dépression.

vacuum-distilled [vækjuəmdi'stild], *a.* distillé sous le vide.

vacuum-packed [vækjuəm'pækt], *a.* emballé, serti, sous vide.

vade-mecum [veidi'mi:kəm, vɑ:di'meikəm], *s.* vade-mecum *m inv*, aide-mémoire *m inv*.

vadose ['veidous], *a. Geol:* **v. water,** eaux *fpl* d'infiltration.

vagabond ['vægəbɔnd]. **1.** *a.* vagabond, errant; *Arach:* **v. spiders,** araignées vagabondes. **2.** *s.* (*a*) vagabond, -onde; chemineau *m*; (*b*) vaurien *m*, homme sans aveu.

vagal ['veig(ə)l], *a. Anat:* vagal, -aux.

vagary ['veigəri, və'gɛəri], *s.* caprice *m* (de qn, du temps, etc.); **I'm tired of his vagaries,** j'en ai assez de ses fantaisies *f*, lubies *f*, lunes *f*, boutades *f*; **the vagaries of the human mind,** les écarts *m* de l'esprit humain; **the vagaries of fashion,** les caprices de la mode.

vagina, *pl.* **-ae, -as** [və'dʒainə, -i:, -əz], *s.* **1.** *Anat:* vagin *m*. **2.** *Nat.Hist:* gaine *f*, enveloppe *f*.

vaginal ['vædʒinəl, və'dʒainəl], *a.* **1.** (*of membrane, etc.*) vaginal, -aux; engainant; vaginant. **2.** *Anat:* vaginal; *Med:* **v. douche,** douche vaginale.

vaginant ['vædʒinənt], *a.* vaginant, engainant.

vaginate ['vædʒineit], *a. Nat.Hist:* (*a*) vaginé, engainé; (*b*) vaginiforme.

vaginicola [vædʒi'nikələ], *s. Prot:* vaginicole *f*.

vaginiform [væ'dʒinifɔ:m], *a. Nat.Hist:* vaginiforme.

vaginismus [vædʒi'nizməs], *s. Med:* vaginisme *m*, vaginodynie *f*.

vaginitis [vædʒi'naitis], *s. Med:* vaginite *f*.

vaginoscopy [væ'dʒainouskɔpi, vædʒi'nɔskəpi], *s. Med:* vaginoscopie *f*.

vagino-vesical [vædʒ(a)inou'vesikl], *a. Med:* vaginovésical, -aux.

vaginula, *pl.* **-ae** [væ'dʒainjulə, -i:], **vaginule** ['vædʒinju:l], *s. Nat.Hist:* vaginule *f*, petite gaine.

vagitus [və'dʒaitəs], *s.* vagissement *m* (du nouveau-né).

vagolytic ['veigoulitik], *a. Med:* vagolytique.

vagosympathetic [veigousimpə'θetik], *a. & s. Anat:* (nerf *m*) vago-sympathique.

vagotomy [vei'gɔtəmi], *s. Surg:* vagotomie *f*.

vagotonia [veigou'touniə], **vagotony** [vei'gɔtəni], *s. Med:* vagotonie *f*.

vagotonic [veigou'tɔnik], *a. Med: Psy:* vagotonique.

vagrancy ['veigrənsi], *s.* **1.** (*a*) *Jur:* vagabondage *m*, mendicité *f*; (*b*) vie *f* de vagabond, vie errante. **2.** *NAm:* caprice *m*, fantaisie *f*, lubie *f*.

vagrant ['veigrənt]. **1.** *a.* vagabond, errant; **v. knife grinder,** remouleur ambulant. **2.** *s.* (*a*) *Jur:* vagabond, -onde; (*b*) homme sans aveu; mendiant, -ante; chemineau *m*.

vague [veig], *a.* (*of pers., look, etc.*) vague; (*of impression, memory*) imprécis; (*of colour, etc.*) indéterminé, indécis; (*of shape, outline*) estompé, flou, **v. answers,** réponses vagues; **I haven't the vaguest idea,** je n'en ai pas la moindre idée; **I had a v. idea that he was dead,** j'avais vaguement l'idée qu'il était mort; **you must not be so v. in your statements,** il faut préciser vos affirmations; **to leave sth. v.,** laisser un point dans l'imprécision.

vaguely ['veigli], *adv.* vaguement; **he was v. American,** il était vaguement Américain.

vagueness ['veignis], *s.* vague *m*, imprécision *f*.

vagus, *pl.* **-gi** ['veigəs, -dʒai], *s. Anat:* **v. (nerve),** (nerf) pneumogastrique (*m*).

vail [veil]. *A:* **1.** *v.tr.* **to v. one's bonnet, cap,** se découvrir; **to v. one's pride,** rabattre son orgueil. **2.** *v.i.* s'incliner **(to s.o.,** devant qn); céder **(to s.o.,** à qn).

vain [vein], *a.* **1.** (*of pleasure, hope, etc.*) vain, mensonger, creux; **v. promises,** vaines promesses; promesses vaines; **under a v. pretext,** sous un prétexte frivole. **2.** (*unavailing*) vain, inutile, infructueux, stérile, superflu; **v. efforts,** efforts vains, futiles, stériles. **3.** (*conceited*) vaniteux, glorieux, orgueilleux, fier, vain; **she was v. about her beauty,** elle était fière, *O:* vaine, de sa beauté; **as v. as a peacock,** glorieux comme un paon; fier comme Artaban. **4.** *adv.phr.* **in v.,** en vain; (*a*) vainement; **in v. I tried to help him,** en vain ai-je tâché de l'aider; **we protested in v., it was in v. that we protested,** nous avons eu beau protester; **to labour in v.,** travailler inutilement; perdre sa peine; **it was all in v.,** rien n'y faisait; c'était peine perdue; c'étaient des efforts en pure perte; (*b*) **to take God's name in v.,** prendre le nom de Dieu en vain; *F:* **who's taking my name in v.?** qui est-ce qui parle de moi?

vainglorious [vein'glɔ:riəs], *a.* vaniteux, glorieux, orgueilleux.

vaingloriously [vein'glɔ:riəsli], *adv.* vaniteusement, avec vanité, orgueilleusement.

vaingloriousness [vein'glɔ:riəsnis], *s.* vanité *f*, orgueil *m*; *A: & Lit:* superbe *f*.

vainglory [vein'glɔ:ri], *s.* (*a*) vaine gloire; gloriole *f*; (*b*) = VAINGLORIOUSNESS.

vainly ['veinli], *adv.* **1.** vainement, en vain, inutilement. **2.** vaniteusement, avec vanité; orgueilleusement.

vainness ['veinnis], *s.* **1.** vanité *f* (du monde, des plaisirs). **2.** futilité *f*, inutilité *f* (des efforts de qn, etc.). **3.** vanité, fierté *f*, orgueil *m*.

vair [vɛər], *s. Her:* vair *m*; **v. ancient, in pale,** vair antique, en pal.

vairy ['vɛəri], *a. Her:* vairé.

Vaishnavism [vai'ʃnɑ:vizm], *s. Rel:* vichnouisme *m*, vishnuisme *m*.

Vaisya ['vaisjə], *s.m. Ethn:* vaiçya, hindou de la troisième caste.

valance ['væləns], *s.* **1.** *Furn:* (*a*) frange *f* de lit, draperie *f* de bas de lit; soubassement *m*; tour *m* de lit; jupon *m* de lit; (*b*) cantonnière *f*, lambrequin *m*, pente *f* (d'un ciel de lit, d'une fenêtre). **2.** *Aut: A:* bavolet *m*; **inside v.,** bajoue *f*.

vale[1] [veil], *s. A: & Lit:* vallon *m*; vallée *f*; val *m*, *pl.* vals, vaux; **this v. of tears, of woe,** cette vallée de larmes, de misère; ce triste vallon de pleurs; **the v. of years,** la vieillesse; *Geog:* **the V. of Evesham,** la vallée d'Evesham; *Myth:* **the Sacred V.,** le sacré vallon.

vale[2] ['veili, 'vɑ:li], *s. & int.* adieu (*m*).

valediction [væli'dikʃ(ə)n], *s.* **1.** adieu(x) *m*(*pl*). **2.** *NAm:* = VALEDICTORY 2.

valedictorian [vælidik'tɔ:riən], *s. NAm: Sch:* membre *m* d'une promotion qui prononce le discours d'adieu.

valedictory [væli'diktəri]. **1.** *a.* (allocution, dîner) d'adieu. **2.** *s. NAm: Sch:* discours *m* d'adieu (à la sortie d'une promotion, etc.).

valence[1] ['veiləns], *s. Ch: Atom.Ph:* valence *f*; **v. link, bond,** liaison *f* de valence; **v. electron,** électron valentiel, de valence; **v. shell,** couche *f* de valence.

valence[2] ['væləns], *s.* = VALANCE.

Valencia [və'lensiə]. **1.** *Pr.n. Geog:* (*in Spain*) Valence; (*in Venezuela*) Valencia. **2.** (*a*) **V. orange,** valence *f*; *O:* **valencias,** (i) raisins secs, (ii) amandes *f*, d'Espagne; (*b*) *Tex:* **v.,** valencia *m*.

Valencian [və'lensiən], *Geog:* **1.** *a.* valencien, de Valence. **2.** *s.* Valencien, -ienne.

Valenciennes [valɑ̃'sjɛn]. **1.** *Pr.n. Geog:* Valenciennes. **2.** *s.* **V. (lace),** dentelle *f* de Valenciennes; valenciennes *f*.

valency ['veilənsi], *s.* = VALENCE[1].

Valentine ['væləntain]. **1.** *Pr.n.* Valentin *m*, Valentine *f*; **Saint Valentine's Day,** la Saint-Valentin (le 14 février). **2.** *s.* (*a*) carte envoyée le jour de la Saint-Valentin; (*b*) celui, celle, qui reçoit cette carte; **Robert is my v.,** c'est Robert que j'aime.

Valentinian[1] [vælən'tiniən], *Pr.n.m. Rel.H:* Valentinien.

Valentinian[2], *a. & s. Rel.H:* valentinien, -ienne.

valentinite ['væləntinait], *s. Miner:* valentinite *f*.

Valentinus [vælən'tainəs], *Pr.n.m.* Valentin.

valerate ['væləreit], *s. Ch:* valérate *m*.

Valeria [və'liəriə], *Pr.n.f.* Valérie.

Valerian[1] [və'liəriən], *Pr.n.m. Rom.Hist:* Valérien.

valerian[2], *s.* **1.** *Bot:* (*a*) valériane *f*; **red v., spur v.,** valériane rouge, centranthe *m* rouge, barbe-de-Jupiter *f*; (*b*) **Greek v.,** valériane grecque, polémonie bleue, échelle *f* de Jacob; (*c*) **African v.,** fédie *f*. **2.** *Pharm:* valériane.

Valerianaceae [vəliəriə'neisii:], *s.pl. Bot:* valérianacées *f*.

valeric [və'lerik], *a. Ch:* (acide) valérique.

Valerie ['væləri], *Pr.n.f.* Valérie.

Valerius [və'liəriəs], *Pr.n.m.* Valère; *Lt.Lit:* **V. Maximus,** Valère Maxime.

valet[1] ['vælei, 'vælit], *s.* **1.** (*a*) valet *m* de chambre; (*b*) (*in hotel, etc.*) employé qui s'occupe de l'entretien des vêtements des clients; **v. service,** service *m* de buanderie et de nettoyage; buanderie *f* et nettoyage *m*. **2.** *Furn:* valet.

valet[2], *v.tr.* **(valeted** ['vælitid]) **1.** servir (qn) comme valet de chambre. **2.** remettre en état (un vêtement d'homme).

valeting ['vælitiŋ], *s.* **1.** service *m* de valet de chambre. **2.** **v. company,** maison *f* pour la remise en état des vêtements d'hommes.

Valetta [və'letə], *Pr.n. Geog:* la Valette.

valetudinarian [vælitju:di'nɛəriən]. **1.** *a.* valétudinaire. **2.** *s.* (*a*) valétudinaire *mf*; (*b*) malade *mf* imaginaire.

valetudinarianism [vælitju:di'nɛəriənizm], *s.* **1.** valétudinarisme *m*. **2.** hypocondrie *f*.

valetudinary [væli'tju:dinəri], *a. & s.* = VALETUDINARIAN.

valgus ['vælgəs], *a. & s. Med:* valgus (*m*) *inv*, valgum (*m*) *inv*.

Valhalla [væl'hælə], *s. Myth:* le Walhalla.

valiancy ['væliənsi], *s. A:* vaillance *f*.

valiant ['væliənt], *a.* vaillant, valeureux, brave.

valiantly ['væliəntli], *adv.* vaillamment, valeureusement, bravement.

valid ['vælid], *a.* (contrat, etc.) valide, valable; (passeport) en règle; **v. argument,** argument valable, solide; **ticket v. for three months, no longer v.,** billet bon pour trois mois, périmé; **to make v.,** valider, rendre valable (un contrat, etc.).

validate ['vælideit], *v.tr.* valider, rendre valable (un acte, etc.); *U.S:* **to v. an election, s.o.,** valider une élection, qn.

validation [væli'deiʃ(ə)n], *s.* validation *f* (d'une élection, d'un mariage, etc.).

validity [və'liditi], *s.* (*a*) validité *f* (d'un contrat, d'une élection, d'un passeport, etc.); *Jur:* **to dispute the v. of a document,** s'inscrire en faux contre un document; **v. of an argument, a conclusion,** justesse *f* d'un argument, d'une conclusion; force *f*, validité, d'un argument; *Elcs:* **v. check,** contrôle *m* de validité; (*b*) durée *f* (de validité), période *f* de validité.

validly ['vælidli], *adv.* validement, valablement.

valine ['veili:n], *s. Bio-Ch:* valine *f*.

valise [və'li:s, -i:z], *s.* **1.** *NAm:* valise *f*; sac *m* de voyage. **2.** *Mil:* sac de voyage (d'officier); **sleeping v.,** rouleau *m* (de matériel) de couchage.

Valkyrie [væl'kai(ə)ri], *s.f. Myth:* Walkyrie, Valkyrie.

vallecula, *pl.* **-ae** [væ'lekjulə, -i:], *s.* **1.** *Anat:* (*a*) fosse *f*; (*b*) scissure médiane du cervelet. **2.** *Bot:* vallécule *f*.

valleculate [væ'lekjuleit], *a.* **1.** *Anat:* muni de fosses, de scissures. **2.** *Bot:* valléculé.

valley ['væli], *s.* **1.** vallée *f*; (*small, narrow*) vallon *m*; **the Rhone V.,** la vallée du Rhône; **up, down, v.,** en montant, en descendant, la vallée; en amont, en aval; *B:* **the v. of the shadow of death,** la vallée de l'ombre de la mort; *Archeol:* **the V. of the Kings,** la Vallée des Rois; *Geog:* **transverse v.,** cluse *f*, percée *f*; **glacial v.,** vallée glaciaire; auge *f*; **drowned v.,** vallée noyée, enfoncée; **hanging v.,** vallée suspendue; **v. bottom,** fond *m* de vallée. **2.** (*a*) *Const:* noue (cornière), cornière *f* (de toit, de comble); **v. gutter,** noulet *m*; **v. piece, rafter,** arêtier *m* de noue; **v. tile,** tuile cornière; (*b*) creux *m*, point bas (d'une courbe, etc.). **3.** *Anat:* scissure médiane du cervelet.

vallisneria [vælis'niəriə], *s. Bot:* vallisnérie *f*.

vallum ['væləm], *s. Rom.Ant:* vallum *m*.

val(l)onia [və'louniə], *s.* **1.** *Com: Tan: etc:* vélanède *f*, avelanède *f*, vallonnée *f*. **2.** *Bot:* **v. oak,** chêne *m* vélani; vélanède.

valorization [vælərai'zeiʃ(ə)n], *s. Com: Fin:* valorisation *f*.

valorize ['væləraiz], *v.tr. Com: Fin:* valoriser.

valorous ['vælərəs], *a. Lit:* valeureux, vaillant.

valorously ['vælərəsli], *adv. Lit:* valeureusement, vaillamment.

valour ['vælər], *s. Lit:* valeur *f*, vaillance *f*, bravoure *f*.

Valsalva [væl'sælvə], *Pr.n. Med:* **V. manœuvre,** manœuvre *f* de Valsalva.

Valtellina [vælte'li:nə], *Pr.n. Geog:* la Valteline.

valuable ['væljuəbl]. **1.** *a.* (*a*) précieux; de valeur, de prix; **v. discovery,** découverte précieuse; **v. gift,** cadeau de valeur; **as rubber becomes more v.,** depuis la (re)valorisation du caoutchouc; *Jur:* **for v. consideration,** à titre onéreux; **v. collaborator,** collaborateur précieux; (*b*) évaluable; **service not v. in terms of money,** service auquel on ne peut pas donner une valeur d'argent, que l'on ne saurait estimer en termes d'argent. **2.** *s.pl.* **valuables,** objets *m* de valeur, de prix.

valuation [vælju'eiʃ(ə)n], *s.* **1.** (*a*) évaluation *f*, estimation *f*, appréciation *f*; *Jur:* prisée *f* et estimation; expertise *f*; **at a v. the ring is worth £1,000,** à dire d'expert la bague vaut £1,000; **to get a v. of sth.,** faire expertiser qch.; **to make a v. of the goods,** faire l'expertise, l'appréciation, des marchandises; **to draw up the v. of the furniture,** dresser l'état appréciatif du mobilier; (*b*) inventaire *m* (d'une succession, du portefeuille d'une coopérative de placement, etc.). **2.** valeur estimée; (*a*) **to set too high, too low, a v. on goods, on a building,** surestimer, sous-estimer, des marchandises; surimposer, sous-imposer, un immeuble; **to put 5% on to the v. of a building,** frapper un immeuble d'une majoration de 5%; (*b*) **to take, accept, s.o. at his own v.,** estimer, coter, qn selon l'opinion qu'il a de lui-même.

valuator ['væljueitər], *s.* estimateur *m*, appréciateur *m*, commissaire-priseur *m*, *pl.* commissaires-priseurs; expert *m*.

value[1] ['vælju(:)], *s.* **1.** valeur *f*, prix *m*; **to be of v.,** avoir de la valeur; **of great v.,** de grande, de haute, valeur; **of little v.,** de peu de valeur; **to be of great v.,** avoir une haute valeur; **to be of little v.,** valoir peu de chose; **of no v.,** sans valeur; **it is nothing of any v.,** ce n'est rien qui vaille; **to lose v., to fall in v.,** s'avilir; *Fin:* se dévaloriser; **loss of v., fall in v.,** dévalorisation *f*; **to have a certain v.,** valoir son prix; **he doesn't seem to know the v. of time,** il semble ignorer le prix du temps; **to set v. upon sth., to attach value to sth.,** attacher de la valeur à qch.; **to set a low v. on sth.,** attacher peu de prix à qch.; faire peu de cas de qch.; **to set a low v. on the stock,** estimer à un bas prix la valeur des marchandises en magasin; évaluer les marchandises à un bas prix; **to set a high v. on sth.,** faire grand cas de qch., attacher un grand prix à qch., tenir beaucoup à qch.; **to set a v. upon sth.,** (i) priser qch.; (ii) évaluer qch.; *Com:* attribuer une cote de valeur à qch.; **to set too high a v. on sth.,** attacher trop de valeur, trop de prix, à qch.; surestimer qch.; **v. judgment,** jugement *m* de valeur; **commercial v., market v.,** valeur vénale, valeur marchande, valeur négociable; cours *m*; *St.Exch:* **market values of equities,** valeurs boursières des actions; **exchange v.,** valeur d'échange; **capital v.,** valeur en capital; **v. in gold currency,** valeur-or *f*, *pl.* valeurs-or; **customs v.,** valeur en douane; *Com:* **decrease in v.,** moins-value *f*, *pl.* moins-values; **loss in v. owing to damage or waste,** tare *f*; **increase in v.,** plus-value *f*, *pl.* plus-values; *Adm:* **v. added tax,** taxe *f* à la valeur ajoutée; *Ins:* **v. of a policy,** aliment *m*, risque *m*, intérêt *m*, valeur, d'un police; **replacement v.,** valeur de remplacement; *Min:* **commercial v. of an ore,** qualité industrielle d'un minerai; **the values contained in an ore,** les richesses contenues dans un minerai. **2.** (*a*) **to pay s.o. the v. of a lost article,** rembourser à qn le prix d'un article perdu; *Com:* **for v. received,** valeur reçue; **v. received in cash,** valeur reçue comptant; **to get (good) v. for one's money,** en avoir pour son argent; s'assurer d'un bon rendement-coût; **he gives you v. for**

money, il vous en donne pour votre argent; **this book is quite good v. at £5,** ce livre n'est pas cher à cinq livres; **it's v. for money,** cela vaut son prix, n'est pas cher; **it's very good v.,** c'est (à un prix) avantageux, d'un bon marché exceptionnel; *F:* **he's good v.,** il est bien amusant; c'est un bon compagnon; (*b*) **calorific, heating, v.,** pouvoir *m*, puissance *f*, calorifique; **thermal v.,** équivalent *m* thermique; **insulating v.,** pouvoir isolant. **3.** (*a*) *Mth:* **to give** *x* **a v.,** attribuer une valeur à *x*; **positive, negative, v.,** valeur positive, négative; **limiting v.,** condition *f* limite; (*b*) *Av:* **slip v.,** coefficient *m* de recul; (*c*) *Mus:* **time v.,** valeur (d'une note); *Th:* **to give full v. to each word,** détailler les mots, la phrase; (*d*) **sense of values,** sentiment *m* des valeurs; *Art:* **colour out of v.,** couleur qui manque de valeur; **foreground out of v.,** premier plan qui n'est pas en valeur; (*e*) *Ch:* **iodine v.,** indice *m* d'iode; (*f*) *Elcs:* **threshold v.,** valeur-seuil *f*, *pl.* valeurs-seuil.

value[2], *v.tr.* **1.** (*a*) *Com:* **to v. goods,** évaluer, estimer, apprécier, priser, inventorier, des marchandises; **to v. each object,** attribuer une cote de valeur à chaque objet; **to v. a set of furniture,** faire l'expertise, dresser l'état appréciatif, d'un mobilier; **to get sth. valued,** faire expertiser qch.; **to v. work done,** faire l'expertise d'un travail; (*b*) *Bank:* **to v. cheques on London,** valoriser des chèques sur Londres. **2.** estimer, tenir à, faire grand cas de (qn, qch.); *Lit:* **to v. sth. above rubies,** priser qch. plus que des rubis; **to v. one's life,** tenir à la vie; **if you v. your life,** si vous tenez à la vie; **he doesn't v. his skin,** il fait bon marché de sa peau. **3.** *v.i. Com:* **to v. upon s.o.,** disposer, faire traite, sur qn.

valued ['vælju(:)d], *a.* estimé, précieux; **my v. friend Mr Martin,** M. Martin dont l'amitié m'est si précieuse.

valueless ['vælju(:)lis], *a.* sans valeur; *Fin:* **v. securities, stock,** non-valeurs *f*.

valuer ['vælju(:)ər], *s.* estimateur *m*, appréciateur *m*; **official v.,** commissaire-priseur *m*, *pl.* commissaires-priseurs; expert *m*.

valuing ['vælju(:)iŋ], *s.* **1.** évaluation *f*, estimation *f*, appréciation *f*. **2.** *Bank:* valorisation *f* (de chèques) (**on Paris,** sur Paris).

valvar ['vælvər], **valvate** ['vælveit], *a. Bot: etc:* valvé, valvaire; **valvate dehiscence,** déhiscence valvaire.

Valvata [vælveitə], *s.pl. Moll:* valvates *f*, valvées *f*.

valve[1] [vælv], *s.* **1.** (*a*) soupape *f*; **(clack, flap) v.,** (soupape à) clapet *m*; valve *f*; **needle, pin, v.,** soupape à pointeau; **plunger v.,** clapet à piston plongeur; **valves of a bellows,** soupapes, âmes *f*, venteaux *m*, d'un soufflet; **(pressure) reducing, (pressure) relief, v.,** soupape, clapet, de décharge; détendeur *m*; **vacuum relief v.,** clapet, soupape, de décompression; **pump v.,** clapet de pompe; **suction v.,** soupape, clapet, d'aspiration; **exhaust v.,** clapet de refoulement (d'une pompe); **back-pressure, feed-check, v.,** soupape de retenue; **forcing v.,** soupape de refoulement; **shut-off v.,** clapet, soupape, de retenue; soupape d'arrêt; clapet de fermeture; obturateur *m*; **drain v.,** soupape, clapet, de vidange; *Av:* **flow regulating v.,** valve régulatrice de débit; **air v.,** soupape à air, soupape atmosphérique; reniflard *m*; *Mch:* (*on furnace door*) ventouse *f*; *Navy:* **air valves of a submarine,** purges *f* d'un sous-marin; *I.C.E: etc:* **throttle v.,** soupape d'étranglement, de réglage; *Mch:* **sentinel v.,** soupape d'avertissement; (*b*) *I.C.E:* **mushroom v., poppet v.,** soupape à champignon, à déclic; **automatically operated v.,** soupape à levée automatique; **mechanically operated v.,** soupape commandée (mécaniquement); **inlet, induction, v.,** soupape d'admission, d'arrivée; **exhaust, outlet, v.,** soupape d'échappement, de décharge; **side valves,** soupapes latérales, en chapelle; **v. chamber,** chapelle *f*; **v. cover,** cache-soupape(s) *m inv*; **v. guide,** guide *m* de soupape; **v. lever,** levier *m* de distribution; **v. lifter,** (i) (*tappet*) poussoir *m* de soupape; (ii) *Motor Cy:* décompresseur *m*; (iii) *Tls:* démonte-soupapes *m inv*, lève-soupape(s) *m inv*; **v. rocking lever, v. rocker,** culbuteur *m*; **v. rod,** tige *f* (de commande) de soupape; **v. stem,** tige, queue *f*, de soupape; **v. spring,** ressort *m* de soupape; **v. spring lifter,** démonte-soupapes, lève-soupape(s); **v. seat, seating,** siège *m*, portée *f*, de soupape; **v. gear, motion,** (organes *mpl*, engrenages *mpl* de) distribution *f*; **v. diagram,** diagramme *m*, épure *f*, de distribution; **v. grinding,** rodage *m* des soupapes; **v. grinding tool,** rodeur *m*; (*c*) *Mch:* **(slide) v.,** tiroir *m* (de distribution), distributeur *m*; **brake v.,** distributeur de freinage; (*of Corliss engine, etc.*) **segment v.,** tiroir cylindrique tournant; **sequence v.,** distributeur d'ordonnancement; **v. box, casing, chest,** boîte *f* à vapeur, boîte de distribution (de vapeur); chapelle du tiroir; chambre *f* de distribution; **v. eccentric,** excentrique *m* (de commande) du tiroir; **v. face, seat, seating,** table *f*, barrette *f*, glace *f*, du tiroir; **v. gear, motion,** appareil *m*, mécanisme *m*, de distribution (de la vapeur); (*link motion*) (distribution par) coulisse *f*; (*expansion*) (distribution à) détente *f*; **v. rod,** bielle *f* du tiroir; (*d*) (*tap, cock*) robinet *m*; **valves and fittings,** robinetterie *f*; **hose v.,** robinet de branchement (pour manche à incendie); **three, four, way v.,** robinet à trois, quatre, voies; **cross-feed v.,** robinet d'intercommunication; **change v.,** robinet (d'ascenseur hydraulique); **drain v.,** robinet de vidange; **king, master, v.,** robinet chef; *Mch:* **steam v.,** robinet de prise de vapeur; **brake v.,** robinet de frein; (*e*) *Aut: Cy:* valve (de chambre à air); **needle, pin, v.,** valve à pointeau; **self-sealing v.,** valve auto-obturatrice; **v. cap,** capuchon *m*, chapeau *m*; **v. inside,** garniture intérieure de valve; (*f*) vanne *f*; **gas, water, v.,** vanne à gaz, d'eau; **gate v.,** vanne à guillotine, à obturateur; *Hyd.E:* **(sluice) v.,** vanne de communication; vannelle *f*; robinet-vanne *m*, *pl.* robinets-vannes; **paddle v.,** vantelle *f*; *Nau:* **Kingston v.,** vanne pour le remplissage des ballasts; (*g*) *Mus:* (i) **rotary valves,** cylindres *m* (d'un instrument en cuivre); (ii) **v. board,** ais *m* à valve (de piano mécanique). **2.** *Anat:* valvule *f* (du cœur, etc.); **aortic, mitral, tricuspid, semilunar, v.,** valvule aortique, mitrale, tricuspide, semi-lunaire; **coronary v.,** valvule de Thébésius. **3.** *Elcs: W.Tel:* lampe *f* (de radio); lampe, tube *m* (à vide); valve; **amplifying v.,** lampe amplificatrice, tube amplificateur; **rectifying v.,** lampe, valve, redresseuse; tube redresseur; **transmitting v.,** lampe émettrice, tube émetteur; **reactance v.,** tube à réactance; **light v. recording of sound,** enregistrement *m* du son par valve de lumière; **five v. set,** poste *m*, appareil *m*, à cinq lampes; **v. holder,** support *m* de lampe; **v. noise,** souffle dû au tube; **electron, thermionic, vacuum, v.,** tube électronique; lampe, tube, à vide; **beam power v.,** tube de puissance à faisceau électronique; *Elcs:* **band lighter v.,** valve lumineuse à amorçage par couche conductrice extérieure. **4.** *Bot: Moll:* valve; **v.-shaped,** valviforme. **5.** battant *m* (de porte à battants).

valve[2], *v.tr.* **1.** munir (qch.) d'une soupape, d'un clapet, d'un robinet. **2.** (*a*) régler (le cours d'un liquide, etc.) avec une soupape, un robinet; (*b*) *Aer:* laisser échapper (le gaz du ballon).

valved [vælvd], *a.* à valve(s), à soupape(s); *Moll:* **two-v. shell,** coquille *f* à deux valves, bivalve; *Bot:* **three-v. fruit,** fruit *m* à trois valves, trivalve.

valveless ['vælvlis], *a.* sans soupape(s), valve(s).

valviform ['vælvifɔ:m], *a.* valviforme.

valvula, *pl.* **-ae** ['vælvjulə, -i:], *s. Anat: etc:* valvule *f*.

valvular ['vælvjulər], *a.* **1.** *Med: etc:* valvulaire; **v. disease (of the heart),** valvulite *f*; insuffisance *f* valvulaire. **2.** *Nat.Hist:* valvulaire, valvulé.

valvulate ['vælvjulət], *a. Nat.Hist:* valvulé, valvulaire.

valvule ['vælvju:l], *s. Anat: Nat.Hist:* valvule *f*.

valvulitis [vælvju'laitis], *s. Med:* valvulite *f*.

valvuloplasty ['vælvjuləplæsti], *s. Surg:* valvuloplastie *f*.

vambrace ['væmbreis], *s. Arm:* (canon *m* d')avant-bras *m inv*.

vamoose [və'mu:s], **vamose** [və'mous], *v.i. F:* décamper, filer.

vamp[1] [væmp], *s.* **1.** *Bootm:* empeigne *f*, claque *f*. **2.** *F: esp. Lit:* (*a*) assemblage *m* de pièces et de morceaux; assemblage disparate; (*b*) morceau rajouté. **3.** *Mus: F:* accompagnement tapoté, improvisé.

vamp[2], *v.tr.* **1.** *Bootm:* remonter (un soulier); mettre une empeigne à (un soulier); **vamped boot,** chaussure claquée. **2.** *Mus: F:* (*a*) tapoter au piano (un accompagnement ad hoc); (*b*) *v.i.* tapoter, improviser, l'accompagnement. **3. to v. up,** (*a*) rapiécer, rafistoler (qch.); (*b*) composer, bâtir (un article de journal, etc.) de pièces et de morceaux; fagoter (un article).

vamp[3], *s.f. F: O:* (*abbr. of* **vampire**) (*a*) aventurière, femme fatale; ensorceleuse, enjôleuse, sirène; *F:* vamp; (*b*) allumeuse, flirteuse.

vamp[4]. *F: O:* (*a*) *v.tr.* (*of woman*) ensorceler, envoûter, vamper (un homme); dominer, exploiter (un homme); enjôler (un homme); (*b*) *v.i.* flirter.

vamper ['væmpər], *s.* **1.** *Mus:* improvisateur, -trice (d'un accompagnement en accords simples); accompagnateur, -trice qui improvise. **2.** rafistoleur, -euse.

vamping ['væmpiŋ], *s.* **1.** (*a*) remontage *m* (de chaussures); (*b*) rapiècement *m*, rafistolage *m*. **2.** *Mus:* accompagnement improvisé.

vampire ['væmpaiər], *s.* **1.** (*a*) *Myth:* vampire *m*; strige *f*; (*b*) *F:* (i) vampire; extorqueur, -euse; *F:* sangsue *f*; (ii) = VAMP[3]. **2.** *Z:* **v. (bat),** vampire; **true v.,** desmode *m*; **false, great, v.,** vampire spectre. **3.** *Th:* **v. (trap),** trappe *f*.

vampiric [væm'pirik], *a.* vampirique.

vampirism ['væmpaiərizm], *s.* vampirisme *m*.

vamplate ['væmpleit], *s. Arm:* rondelle *f* (de lance de joute).

van[1] [væn], *s. Mil: etc:* (i) avant-garde *f*; (ii) front *m* (de bataille); *Fig:* **to be in the v.,** être à l'avant-garde.

van[2], *s. Min:* (*a*) vannage *m* (du minerai); (*b*) pelle *f* à vanner; van *m*.

van[3], *v.tr.* (**vanned**) *Min:* vanner (le minerai).

van[4], *s. Veh:* **1.** (*a*) fourgon *m*; **furniture v., removal v.,** voiture *f* de déménagement; **delivery v.,** camion *m*, camionnette *f*, de livraison; **v. horse,** cheval *m* de trait léger; camionneur *m*; **v. horse parade,** défilé *m* de voitures de livraison; *Cin:* **recording v.,** camion d'enregistrement; *W.Tel:* **outside broadcasting v.,** car *m* de radio-reportage; **police (loudspeaker) v.,** camionnette de police; (*b*) **gipsy v.,** roulotte *f*. **2.** *Rail:* wagon *m*, fourgon; **goods v.,** fourgon à marchandises; **luggage v.,** fourgon à bagages; **guard's v.,** fourgon du chef de train; fourgon de queue.

van[5], *s. Ten:* avantage *m*; **v. in,** avantage au servant, dedans; **v. out,** avantage au relanceur, dehors.

vanadate ['vænədeit], *s. Ch:* vanadate *m*.

vanadic [və'nædik], *a. Ch:* (acide) vanadique.

vanadiferous [vænə'difərəs], *a. Ch: Miner:* vanadifère.

vanadinite [və'nædinait], *s. Miner:* vanadinite *f*.

vanadious [və'neidiəs], *a. Metall:* (alliage) vanadié, vanadeux.

vanadium [və'neidiəm], *s. Ch:* vanadium *m*; *Metall:* **v. steel,** acier *m* au vanadium.

vanadyl ['vænədil], *s. Ch:* vanadyle *m*.

Van Allen [væn'ælən], *Pr.n. Meteor:* **V.A. radiation belts,** ceintures *f*, zones *f*, de Van Allen.

vanda ['vændə], *s. Bot:* vanda *m*.

Vandal ['vænd(ə)l], *s.* **1.** *Hist:* Vandale *mf*. **2. vandal,** vandale.

vandalic [væn'dælik], *a. Hist:* (invasion, etc.) vandalique.

vandalism ['vændəlizm], *s.* vandalisme *m*; **piece of v.,** acte *m* de vandalisme; **it's positive v. to touch up these pictures,** c'est un meurtre de retoucher ces tableaux.

vandalistic [vændə'listik], *a.* (acte, etc.) de vandalisme, vandalique.

vandalize ['vændəlaiz], *v.tr.* **several pictures have been vandalized,** plusieurs tableaux ont été mutilés par des vandales, ont subi des actes de vandalisme.

Van de Graaff ['vændə'græf], *Pr.n. Atom.Ph:* **V. de G. generator,** générateur *m* Van de Graaff.

Van der Waals ['vændə'wɑ:lz], *Pr.n. Ph:* **V. d. W. forces,** forces *f* Van der Waals; **V. d. W. equation of state,** équation *f* de l'état de Van der Waals.

Vandyke[1] [væn'daik, 'væn-]. **1.** *Pr.n.m. Art:* Van Dyck; **V. beard,** *s.* **v.,** barbe *f* à la Van Dyck; **V. brown,** brun foncé; *A.Cost:* **V. collar, cape,** *s.* **v.,** col *m* à la Van Dyck. **2.** *s. A.Cost:* **vandykes,** pointes *f*, crêtes *f* (d'un col à la Van Dyck, etc.).

vandyke[2], *v.tr. A:* crêter, denteler, échancrer (un col, etc.).

vane [vein], *s.* **1.** (*a*) **(wind, weather) v.,** girouette *f*; (*b*) moulinet *m* (d'un anémomètre, etc.); turbine *f* (d'un compteur à eau); **v. anemometer,** anémomètre à moulinet; *Ph:* **electric v.,** tourniquet *m* électrique. **2.** (*a*) bras *m* (de moulin à vent); (*b*) pale *f* (d'hélice); ailette *f*, pale (de ventilateur, etc.); aube *f*, ailette, palette *f* (de turbine, turboréacteur, compresseur); aube (de tunnel aérodynamique); **moving, runner, v.,** aube mobile; **stationary v.,** aube fixe; **swirl v.,** aube de turbulence; déflecteur *m*; **the vanes,** l'aubage *m* (d'une turbine, d'un tunnel aérodynamique); **anti-vortex vanes,** aubage redresseur de l'écoulement; **twist vanes,** aubage hélicoïdal; *Hyd.E:* **v. pump,** pompe rotative à ailettes; *Av:* **v. supercharger,** compresseur *m* à palette; (*c*) *Ball:* ailette *f* (d'une bombe, torpille); **the vanes,** l'empennage *m*; (*d*) *W.Tel:* lamette *f* (de condensateur variable). **3.** *Surv:* **(sight) v.,** pinnule *f* (d'une alidade, etc.); viseur *m* (de compas); **slide v.,** voyant *m* (d'une mire de nivellement). **4.** *Orn:* lame *f* (d'une plume).

vanessa [və'nesə], *s. Ent:* vanesse *f*.

vang [væŋ], *s. Nau:* palan *m* de garde; garde *f* (de la corne); **v. fall,** garant *m* de garde.

vanguard ['væŋgɑ:d], *s. Mil:* tête *f* d'avant-garde; *Fig:* **to be in the v. of a movement,** être un des pionniers d'un mouvement; **to be in the v.,** être d'avant-garde.

vanilla [və'nilə], *s.* **1.** *Bot:* **v. (plant),** vanille *f*, vanillier *m*; **v. plantation,** vanillerie *f*; (*b*) **v. (bean, pod),** gousse *f* de vanille. **2.** *Cu:* **v. (flavouring),** vanille; **flavoured with v.,** vanillé, parfumé à la vanille; **v. custard,** crème vanillée; **v. ice,** glace à la vanille; **v. sugar,** sucre vanillé.

vanillin [və'nilin], *s. Ch:* vanilline *f*.

vanillism [və'nilizm], *s. Med:* vanillisme *m*.

vanillon [və'ni:jən], *s. Com:* vanillon *m*.

vanish[1] ['væniʃ], *s. Ling:* son *m* transitoire; détente *f*.

vanish[2]. **1.** *v.i.* disparaître; (*of visions, suspicions, etc.*) se dissiper, s'évanouir; (*of difficulties, etc.*) s'aplanir;

Mth: (*of quantity*) (i) tendre vers zéro; (ii) s'évanouir; **the ghost vanished (before our eyes),** le fantôme disparut à nos yeux; **he vanished from sight,** il a disparu; **he vanished in the crowd,** il s'est perdu dans la foule; **at the moment of danger he vanished,** au moment du danger il s'est éclipsé; **vanished friends,** amis disparus; **she saw her last hope v.,** elle a vu s'évanouir, s'anéantir, son dernier espoir; **vanished hopes,** espérances évanouies. **2.** *v.tr.* (*of conjuror*) faire disparaître (qch.).

vanishing[1] ['væniʃiŋ], *a.* qui disparaît; *Toil: O:* **v. cream,** crème *f* de jour, crème support de poudre.

vanishing[2], *s.* disparition *f*; (*a*) *Art:* **v. line,** ligne *f* d'horizon; **v. point,** point *m* de fuite, de concours; (*b*) **profits have dwindled to v. point,** les bénéfices se sont réduits à néant.

vanity ['væniti], *s.* **1.** (*a*) vanité *f*, vide *m* (des grandeurs humaines, etc.); futilité *f* (d'une tentative, etc.); **all is v.,** tout est vanité; tout n'est que vanité, que mensonge, que fumée; **all is v. and vexation of spirit,** tout passe, tout casse, tout lasse; **V. Fair,** la foire aux vanités; (*b*) **to forsake the vanities of this world,** dire adieu aux vanités de ce monde. **2.** vanité; orgueil *m*; **to do sth. out of v.,** faire qch. par vanité, pour la gloriole; **to feed s.o.'s v.,** chatouiller l'orgueil de qn. **3.** (*a*) **v. bag,** (petit) sac de dame (pour soirée, etc.); **v. case,** (i) nécessaire *m* de maquillage; (ii) mallette *f*, trousse *f*, de toilette; (iii) *A:* poudrier *m*; (*b*) *NAm: Furn:* coiffeuse *f*.

vanman, *pl.* **-men** ['vænmən], *s.m.* livreur.

vanner[1] ['vænər], *s. Min:* (*pers., machine*) vanneur *m*.

vanner[2], *s.* cheval *m* de trait léger; camionneur *m*.

vanning ['væniŋ], *s. Min:* vannage *m*; **v. shovel,** pelle *f* à vanner; van *m*; **v. machine,** vanneur *m*.

vanquish ['væŋkwiʃ]. *Lit:* **1.** *v.tr.* vaincre; triompher de (qn, ses passions, etc.). **2.** *v.i.* être vainqueur; vaincre.

vanquishable ['væŋkwiʃəbl], *a.* qui peut être vaincu; (passion, etc.) que l'on peut subjuguer, dont on peut triompher.

vanquisher ['væŋkwiʃər], *s.* vainqueur *m*.

vanquishing[1] ['væŋkwiʃiŋ], *a.* vainqueur (*m*).

vanquishing[2], *s.* conquête *f*; subjugation *f* (d'un peuple).

vantage ['vɑ:ntidʒ], *s.* **1. (coign, place, point, of) v., v. ground,** terrain avantageux, position avantageuse; avantage *m* du terrain. **2.** *Ten:* avantage; **v. in,** avantage au servant, dedans; **v. out,** avantage au relanceur, dehors.

vanthoffite [vænt'hɔfait], *s. Miner:* vanthoffite *f*.

vapid ['væpid], *a.* (*of beverage*) plat, insipide, éventé; (*of conversation*) fade, insipide, plat; **v. style,** style fade, sans saveur.

vapidity [və'piditi], **vapidness** ['væpidnis], *s.* évent *m* (d'une boisson); fadeur *f*, insipidité *f* (de la conversation, etc.).

vapidly ['væpidli], *adv.* **to talk v.,** débiter des fadaises, des fadeurs.

vaporimeter [veipə'rimitər], *s.* vaporimètre *m*.

vaporizable ['veipəraizəbl], *a.* vaporisable.

vaporization [veipərai'zeiʃ(ə)n], *s.* **1.** vaporisation *f*. **2.** pulvérisation *f* (d'un liquide); *I.C.E:* carburation *f* (du combustible).

vaporize ['veipəraiz]. **1.** *v.tr.* (*a*) vaporiser, gazéifier; (*b*) pulvériser, vaporiser (un liquide); *I.C.E:* carburiser (le combustible). **2.** *v.i.* (*a*) se vaporiser, se gazéifier; (*b*) (*of liquid*) se pulvériser.

vaporizer ['veipəraizər], *s.* (*a*) (*evaporator*) vaporisateur *m*; *I.C.E: etc:* réchauffeur *m*; (*b*) (*producing fine spray*) pulvérisateur *m*, atomiseur *m*, vaporisateur.

vaporizing ['veipəraiziŋ], *s.* = VAPORIZATION; *I.C.E:* **v. chamber,** chambre *f* de mélange, de vaporisation.

vaporous ['veipərəs], *a. Lit:* (ciel, etc.) vaporeux; (style) vaporeux, nuageux, vague.

vaporously ['veipərəsli], *adv. Lit:* vaporeusement.

vapour[1] ['veipər], *s.* **1.** (*a*) vapeur *f*; buée *f* (sur les vitres, etc.); **v. laden,** (atmosphère) humide; (*b*) *Ph: etc:* **water, aqueous, v.,** vapeur d'eau; **v. bath,** (i) *Med:* bain *m* de vapeur; (ii) étuve *f* humide (de hammam); **ether, alcoholic, v.,** vapeur d'éther, d'alcool. **2.** *pl. Med: A:* **vapours,** vapeurs; **to have the vapours,** avoir des vapeurs.

vapour[2], *v.i.* **1.** (*of liquid*) s'évaporer; se vaporiser; jeter de la vapeur. **2.** *F:* (*of pers.*) (*a*) se vanter; faire le fanfaron, faire le rodomont; (*b*) débiter des fadaises, des sottises, des platitudes; parler pour ne rien dire.

vapourer ['veipərər], *s.* **1.** *F: A:* (*a*) vantard, -arde; (*b*) radoteur, -euse. **2.** *Ent:* **v. moth,** orgyie *f*.

vapourish ['veipəriʃ], *a.* **1.** = VAPOROUS. **2.** *A.Med:* (malade) qui a des vapeurs, vaporeux; hypocondriaque.

var [vɑ:r], *s. El: etc:* var *m*.

varactor [və'ræktər], *s. Elcs:* varactor *m*.

varan ['værən], *s. Rept:* varan *m*.

Varangian [və'rændʒiən]. *Hist:* **1.** *s.m.* Varègue, Variague. **2.** *a.* des Variagues, des Varègues; **the V. guard,** la garde palatine des Varanges.

varanian [və'reiniən]. *Rept:* **1.** *s.* varan *m*. **2.** *a.* des varans.

Varanidae [və'rænidi:], *s.pl. Rept:* varanidés *m*.

varec(h) ['værek], *s. Com: Ind:* soude *f* de varech; *F:* varech *m*.

varia ['vεəriə], *s.pl. Lit:* varia *m*.

variability [vεəriə'biliti], *s.* variabilité *f* (du temps, etc.); *Nat.Hist:* inconstance *f* (de type).

variable ['vεəriəbl]. **1.** *a.* (*a*) variable, changeant, inconstant; **v. weather,** temps variable; *Astr:* **v. star,** étoile variable; *Mec:* **v. motion,** mouvement varié; *Mth:* **v. quantity,** quantité variable; (*b*) *Cmptr:* **v. address,** adresse indexée; **v. multiplier,** multiplicateur analogique; (*c*) *Mec.E: etc:* **v. (at will),** réglable; **v. transmission,** variateur *m*; *Av:* **v. geometry nose,** nez articulé (du Concorde). **2.** *s.* (*a*) *Mth: etc:* variable *f*; **basic v.,** variable de base, principale; **dependent, independent, v.,** variable dépendante, indépendante; *Cmptr:* **binary, two-state, two-valued, v.,** variable binaire; *Pol.Ec:* **random v.,** variable aléatoire; **shadow v.,** variable fictive; *Atom.Ph:* **process variables,** paramètre *m* du procédé; (*b*) *Nau:* vent *m* variable; **the variables,** la zone des vents variables.

variableness ['vεəriəblnis], *s.* = VARIABILITY.

variably ['vεəriəbli], *adv.* variablement, avec inconstance.

variance ['vεəriəns], *s.* **1.** (*a*) désaccord *m*; discorde *f*; **to be at v. with s.o.,** être en désaccord, en contestation, en contradiction, en mésintelligence, en querelle, avec qn; être brouillé avec qn; avoir un différend avec qn; **to set two people at v.,** mettre deux personnes en désaccord; mettre la discorde entre deux personnes; brouiller deux personnes; **family at v.,** famille désunie; **states at v.,** états en désaccord; **historians are at v. on this point,** les historiens diffèrent entre eux, varient, sur ce point; **the witnesses are at v.,** les témoins ne sont pas d'accord; **theory at v. with the facts,** théorie incompatible, en désaccord, en contradiction, avec les faits; (*b*) *Jur:* écart *m*, divergence *f*, entre la preuve testimoniale et les conclusions échangées avant les débats. **2.** (*a*) variation *f* (de température, volume, etc.); (*b*) *Stat: Ch:* variance *f*; **error v.,** variance de l'erreur; **sampling v.,** variance de l'échantillon; **v. analysis,** analyse *f* de variance; **v. component,** composante *f* de la variante; **v. ratio,** rapport *m* des variances.

variant ['vεəriənt]. **1.** *a.* (*a*) *A:* variant, qui change souvent; (*b*) différent **(from,** de); qui diffère (de); *Lit:* **v. reading,** variante *f*; (*c*) *Biol:* qui s'écarte, a dévié, du type. **2.** *s.* (*a*) *Lit:* variante; (*b*) *Biol:* variant *m*.

variate ['vεəriət], *s. Stat:* variable *f* aléatoire.

variation [vεəri'eiʃ(ə)n], *s.* **1.** variation *f*, changement *m*; **variations in public opinion,** oscillations *f* de l'opinion publique; *Nat.Hist:* **v. of species,** variation des espèces; *Mec.E:* **v. of load,** fluctuation *f* de charge; **torque v.,** irrégularité *f* du couple moteur; *El:* **current v.,** variation de courant; *Magn:* **v. of terrestrial magnetism,** variation du magnétisme terrestriel; **magnetic v.,** *Nau: etc:* **v. of the compass,** déclinaison magnétique (locale); **easterly v.,** variation nord-est; **v. chart,** carte de déclinaison; **v. compass,** compas de variation; boussole de déclinaison; *Astr:* **periodic v., secular v.,** variation périodique, séculaire. **2.** différence *f*; écart *m*; **v. between two readings,** écart entre deux lectures (d'un appareil scientifique); *Mth:* **calculus of variations,** calcul *m* des variations. **3.** *Mus:* variation **(on, sur); air with variations,** air avec variations; **to write variations on an air,** varier un air.

variational [vεəri'eiʃən(ə)l], *a.* sujet à des variations, variationnel.

variator ['vεərieitər], *s. Mec.E:* **speed v.,** variateur *m* de vitesse.

varicated ['værikeitid], *a.* variqueux; **v. shell,** coquille variqueuse.

varicella [væri'selə], *s. Med:* varicelle *f*; petite vérole volante.

varicellous [væri'seləs], *a. Med:* **1.** affecté de la varicelle. **2.** (éruption, etc.) de la varicelle.

varicocele ['værikəsi:l], *s. Med:* varicocèle *m or f*.

varicoloured ['vεərikʌləd], *a.* aux couleurs variées; versicolore.

varicose ['værikous], *a. Med:* **1.** variqueux; **v. vein,** varice *f*. **2. v. stocking,** bas *m* à varices.

varicosed ['værikoust], *a.* (*of vein, etc.*) variqueux; *Moll:* **v. shell,** coquille variqueuse.

varicosity [væri'kɔsiti], *s. Med:* **1.** état variqueux (d'une veine, etc.). **2.** varice *f*.

varied ['vεərid], *a.* **1.** varié, divers; **very v. opinions,** opinions très diverses; **v. style,** style accidenté, varié. **2.** *Nat.Hist:* multicolore, diversicolore.

variegate ['vεərigeit], *v.tr.* **1.** varier, diversifier (les couleurs). **2.** bigarrer, barioler; diaprer.

variegated ['vεərigeitid], *a.* **1.** varié, divers. **2.** bigarré, bariolé; diapré; versicolore; *Nat.Hist:* panaché, diversicolore; *Miner:* panaché; (*of flower, leaf, etc.*) **to become v.,** se panacher; **the v. colours of the meadows,** *Lit:* l'émail *m* des prés; *Z:* **v. monkey,** douc *m*.

variegation [vεəri'geiʃ(ə)n], *s.* diversité *f* de couleurs; bigarrure *f*; *Bot:* panachure *f*, diaprure *f*.

varietal [və'raiətəl], *a. Nat.Hist:* variétal; **v. name,** nom *m* de variété.

variety [və'raiəti], *s.* **1.** (*a*) variété *f*, diversité *f*; **v. of opinions,** diversité d'opinions; **to lend v. to the menu, the programme,** donner de la variété au menu, au programme; **hillocks that give v. to the landscape,** petites collines qui accidentent le paysage; *Prov:* **v. is the spice of life,** le changement donne du piquant à la vie; (*b*) **a v. of patterns,** un assortiment d'échantillons; **I did it for a v. of reasons,** je l'ai fait pour des raisons diverses; **in a v. of ways,** de diverses manières, diversement; **to deal in a v. of goods,** faire le commerce de toutes sortes d'articles; *NAm:* **v. store,** petit magasin qui vend toutes sortes d'articles. **2.** *Nat.Hist:* variété *f* (de fleur, etc.). **3.** *Th:* **v. show,** spectacle *m* de variétés; **v. theatre,** théâtre *m* de variétés; théâtre des boulevards; **v. turns,** numéros *m* de music-hall. **4.** *NAm:* **v. meat,** abats *mpl*.

variform ['vεərifɔ:m], *a.* dont la forme est variable; diversiforme.

variocoupler ['vεəriouk ʌplər], *s. W.Tel:* variocoupleur *m*.

variola [və'raiələ], *s. Med:* variole *f*; petite vérole.

variolar [və'raiələr], *a. Med:* variolaire.

variolation [vεəriə'leiʃ(ə)n], *s. Med:* variolisation *f*.

variole ['vεərioul], *s.* **1.** petite cavité, petit trou. **2.** *Miner:* sphérolithe *m* (dans la variolite).

variolite ['vεəriəlait], *s. Miner:* variolite *f*.

variolitic [vεəriə'litik], *a. Miner:* qui ressemble à la variolite.

variolization [vεəriəlai'zeiʃ(ə)n], *s.* = VARIOLATION.

varioloid ['vεəriəlɔid], *a. Med:* **1.** varioliforme. **2.** varioloïde.

variolous [və'raiələs], *a. Med:* (*of eruption, etc.*) varioleux, variolique; (*of patient*) varioleux.

variometer [vεəri'ɔmitər], *s. El: Av:* variomètre *m*; **disk coil v.,** variomètre à bobines plates.

varioplex ['vεəriəpleks], *s. Elcs:* varioplex *m*.

variorum [vεəri'ɔ:rəm], *a. & s. Lit:* **v. (edition),** (édition *f*) variorum (*m*).

various ['vεəriəs], *a.* **1.** varié, divers; **of v. kinds,** de diverses sortes; **v. types,** types variés, divers; **to talk about v. things,** parler d'une chose et d'une autre, de chose(s) et d'autre(s). **2.** (*a*) différent, dissemblable; divers; **known under v. names,** connu sous des noms divers; *Lit:* **v. reading,** variante *f*; (*b*) plusieurs; plus d'un; **for v. reasons,** pour plusieurs raisons; **at v. times,** à différentes reprises; en diverses occasions; **in v. ways,** de diverses, plusieurs, manières; diversement.

variously ['vεəriəsli], *adv.* diversement; de diverses, plusieurs, manières.

variscite ['værisait], *s. Miner:* variscite *f*.

varistor [və'ristər], *s. Elcs:* varistance *f*, varistor *m*.

varix, *pl.* **-ices** ['vεəriks, 'værisi:z], *s. Med: Conch:* varice *f*.

varlet ['vɑ:lit], *s.m.* **1.** (*a*) *Hist:* varlet, page; (*b*) *A:* palefrenier, valet. **2.** *A:* coquin, vaurien, drôle; *A:* maraud.

varletry ['vɑ:litri], *s. A:* valetaille *f*.

varmint ['vɑ:mint], *s. Dial:* (= VERMIN) **1.** (*a*) vermine *f*; (*b*) *Ven:* renard *m*. **2.** *F: A:* **young v.,** petit polisson.

varnish[1] ['vɑ:niʃ], *s.* **1.** vernis *m*; **spirit v.,** vernis à l'alcool, à l'esprit de vin; vernis spiritueux; **turpentine v.,** vernis à l'essence; **oil v.,** vernis gras; **transparent, clear, v.,** vernis blanc; *Toil:* **nail v.,** vernis à ongles; **v. remover,** (i) *Ind: etc:* décapant *m* pour vernis; (ii) *Toil:* dissolvant *m*. **2. (coat of) v.,** (enduit *m* de) vernis; vernissage *m*, vernissure *f*; *Fig:* **to take the v. off sth.,** enlever l'attrait de qch., révéler qch. dans toute sa misère. **3.** *NAm:* mauvais alcool, casse-pattes *m*, tord-boyaux *m*. **4.** *Bot:* **v. tree,** (i) sumac *m* vernis; vernis du Japon; (ii) courbaril *m*; (iii) **black v. tree,** mélanorrhœa *m*.

varnish[2], *v.tr.* **1.** vernir (du bois, un tableau); vernir, vernisser (de la poterie). **2.** *Fig: O:* **to v. (over),** farder (les faits), glisser sur, vernir (les défauts de qn); jeter un voile complaisant sur (une infamie).

varnisher ['vɑ:niʃər], *s.* vernisseur *m*.

varnishing ['vɑ:niʃiŋ], *s.* vernissage *m*, vernissure *f*; peinture *f* au vernis; **v. day,** vernissage *m* (au Salon de peinture).

Varro ['værou], *Pr.n.m. Lt.Lit:* Varron.

varsity ['vɑ:siti], *s. F:* **1.** *A:* université *f*; *Can:* **Varsity,** l'Université de Toronto. **2.** *U.S:* équipe *f* universitaire.
Varsovian [vɑ:'souviən]. *Geol:* **1.** *a.* varsovien, de Varsovie. **2.** *s.* Varsovien, -ienne.
varsoviana [vɑ:souvi'ɑ:nə], **varsovienne** [vɑ:souvi'en], *s. Danc: Mus:* varsovienne *f*, varsoviana *f*.
varus[1] ['vɛərəs], *s. Med:* pied bot; varus *m*.
varus[2], *s. Med:* **1.** goutte *f* rose. **2.** papule *f* (de la petite vérole).
varve [vɑ:v], *s. Geol:* varve *f*.
varved [vɑ:vd], *a. Geol:* (argile) à varve.
varvel ['vɑ:vel], *s. Ven: A:* vervelle *f*.
vary ['vɛəri]. **1.** *v.tr.* varier, diversifier; faire varier; accidenter (son style); **to v. the menu, the programme,** donner de la variété au menu, au programme; **to v. one's methods,** varier de méthode. **2.** *v.i.* (*a*) varier, changer; être variable; **this type has never varied,** ce type ne s'est jamais modifié, n'a jamais varié; **to v. in quality,** varier en qualité; *Mth: y* **varies as** *x*, *y* varie dans le même sens que et proportionnellement à *x*; *y* **varies directly as** *x*, *y* varie en raison directe de *x*, est directement proportionnel à *x*; *y* **varies inversely as** *x*, *y* varie en raison inverse de *x*, est inversement proportionnel à *x*; *y* **varies inversely as the square of** *x*, *y* varie comme l'inverse du carré de *x*; (*b*) **to v. from sth.,** dévier, s'écarter, de, différer de, qch.; **this edition varies very little from its predecessor,** cette édition s'écarte très peu de la précédente; (*c*) *Biol:* s'écarter du type; présenter une variation; (*d*) **as to date, authors v.,** quant à la date, les auteurs ne sont pas d'accord, varient là-dessus.
varying[1] ['vɛəriiŋ], *a.* qui varie; variable, changeant; varié, divers; **with v. results,** avec des résultats divers.
varying[2], *s.* variation *f*, changement *m*.
vas, *pl.* **vasa** [væs,'veisə], *s. Anat: Bot:* vaisseau *m*; *Anat:* vas *m*, *pl.* vasa; **v. deferens,** canal déférent; **v. aberrans,** vas aberrans.
vasal ['veisəl], *a.* appartenant à un canal; dans un canal.
Vascones [væs'kouni:z], *Pr.n. pl. A.Hist:* Vascons *m*.
vascular ['væskjulər], *a. Nat.Hist: etc:* (tissu, cryptogame, plante, système, etc.) vasculaire; *Bot:* **v. bundle,** faisceau *m* fibro-vasculaire.
vascularity [væskju'læriti], *s. Physiol:* vascularité *f*.
vascularization [væskjulərai'zeiʃ(ə)n], *s. Physiol:* vascularisation *f*.
vascularize ['væskjuləraiz], *v.tr. Med:* vasculariser.
vasculature ['væskjulətjər], *s. Nat.Hist: etc:* vascularisation *f*.
vasculose ['væskjulous], *s. Bot: Ch:* vasculose *f*.
vasculum, *pl.* **-a, -ums** ['væskjuləm, -ə, -əmz], *s.* **1.** *Bot:* ascidie *f*. **2.** boîte *f* en fer blanc (d'herborisateur, de botaniste); coquette *f*, jeannette *f*.
vase [vɑ:z], *s.* **1.** vase *m*; **flower v.,** vase à fleurs; **Chinese v., China v., Japanese v.,** potiche *f*; *Art:* **v. painting,** peinture *f* sur vase; **v. shaped,** en forme de vase, vasiforme. **2.** *Arch:* vase (de chapiteau corinthien).
vasectomize [və'sektəmaiz], *v.tr. Surg:* faire une vasectomie à (qn).
vasectomy [və'sektəmi], *s. Surg:* vasectomie *f*, vasotomie *f*.
Vaseline[1] ['væsəli:n], *s. R.t.m.* Vaseline *f*; **white V.,** Vaseline officinale; **to smear, coat, sth. with V.,** enduire qch. de Vaseline; graisser qch. à la Vaseline; vaseliner qch.
Vaseline[2], *v.tr.* frotter, graisser, avec de la Vaseline, enduire de Vaseline; vaseliner.
Vashti ['væʃti], *Pr.n.f. B.Hist:* Vasthi.
vasiform ['veizifɔ:m], *a.* en forme de vase; vasiforme.
vaso- ['veizou], *comb.fm. Physiol: Med:* vaso-.
vasoconstriction [veizoukən'strikʃ(ə)n], *s. Med:* vasoconstriction *f*.
vasoconstrictive [veizoukən'striktiv], *a. Anat:* vasoconstricteur, -trice.
vasoconstrictor [veizoukən'striktər], *a.* & *s. Anat:* vaso-constricteur (*m*), -trice, *pl.* vaso-constricteurs, -trices; vaso-presseur *m*, *pl.* vaso-presseurs.
vasodilation [veizoudai'leiʃ(ə)n], *s. Med:* vaso-dilation *f*.
vasodilator [veizoudai'leitər], *a.* & *s. Anat:* vasodilateur (*m*), -trice, *pl.* vaso-dilateurs, -trices.
vasoformative [veizou'fɔ:mətiv], *a. Physiol:* vasoformatif.
vasoligation, vasoligature [veizouli'geiʃ(ə)n, -'ligətjər], *s. Surg:* ligature *f* du canal déférent.
vasomotor ['veizoumoutər], *a.* & *s. Anat:* vaso-moteur (*m*), -trice, *pl.* vaso-moteurs, -trices.
vasopressin [veizou'presin], *s. Physiol:* vasopressine *f*.
vasopressor [veizou'presər], *s. Med:* vaso-presseur *m*, *pl.* vaso-presseurs.
vasospasm ['veizouspæzm], *s.* spasme *m* d'un vaisseau, d'un canal.
vasotocin [veizou'tousin], *s. Physiol:* vasotocine *f*.
vassal ['væs(ə)l], *a.* & *s.* **1.** *Hist:* vassal (*m*), -aux; feudataire (*m*) (to, de); **the great vassals,** les grands vassaux; **the rear vassals,** les arrière-vassaux. **2.** subordonné, vassal.
vassalage ['væsəlidʒ], *s.* **1.** *Hist:* vassalité *f*, vasselage *m*; **to hold land in v.,** tenir une terre en fief; **to reduce s.o. to v.,** vassaliser qn, réduire qn à l'état de vassal. **2.** *Fig:* sujétion *f*.
vassalize ['væsəlaiz], *v.tr.* vassaliser (qn), réduire (qn) à l'état de vassal.
vast[1] [vɑ:st], *a.* vaste, immense; **a v. number of people,** un nombre immense de gens; **his v. reading,** l'étendue *f* de ses lectures; son savoir immense; sa vaste érudition; **a v. horizon,** un vaste horizon; **to spend a v. amount, v. sums (of money),** dépenser énormément d'argent, dépenser des sommes folles; **there's a v. difference between them,** il y a une différence énorme entre eux.
vast[2], *int. Nau:* tiens bon! tenez bon! baste! **v. heaving!** tiens bon virer!
vastitude ['vɑ:stitju:d], *s. Lit:* = VASTNESS.
vastly ['vɑ:stli], *adv.* vastement, immensément; **you're v. mistaken,** vous vous trompez énormément, du tout au tout; **they're not v. different,** il y a peu de différence entre eux.
vastness ['vɑ:stnis], *s.* immensité *f*, *Lit:* vastitude *f*; vaste étendue *f*; amplitude *f* (de l'espace, etc.).
vastus ['vɑ:stəs], *s. Anat:* **the v. externus, internus,** le (muscle) vaste externe, interne.
vasty ['vɑ:sti], *a. Poet:* vaste, immense.
vat[1] [væt], *s.* (*a*) cuve *f*; (*small*) cuveau *m*; bac *m*, bain *m*; **v. house,** salle *f* des cuves; *Dy:* **v. dyes,** colorants *m* de cuve; *Paperm:* **v. paper,** papier *m* à la cuve; **v. mill,** papeterie *f* à la cuve; *Leath:* **tan v.,** fosse *f* de tannage; rodoir *m*; **maceration v.,** confit *m*; *Metalw:* **quenching v.,** bain de trempage; *Ind:* **lye v.,** chaudière *f* à lessive; *Vit:* **v. for carrying grapes,** bouge *m*; (*b*) (*contents*) cuvée *f*.
vat[2], *v.tr.* (**vatted**) mettre (le raisin) en cuve; encuver, mettre en fosse (des peaux à tanner, etc.).
vatful ['vætful], *s.* cuvée *f*.
Vatican ['vætikən], *s.* **the V.,** le Vatican; **the V. library,** la bibliothèque vaticane, la Vaticane; **a V. spokesman,** un porte-parole du Vatican; **the V. City,** la cité du Vatican; *Hist:* **the V. State,** les États pontificaux; **the V. Council,** le concile du Vatican; Vatican I; **the second V. Council,** le deuxième concile du Vatican; Vatican II.
Vaticanism ['vætikənizm], *s. Theol: Pol:* ultramontanisme *m*.
Vaticanist ['vætikənist], *s. Theol: Pol:* ultramontain, -aine.
vaticinal [væ'tisin(ə)l], *a.* prophétique; *Pej:* vaticinateur, -trice.
vaticinate [væ'tisineit], *v.tr.* prophétiser; *Pej:* vaticiner.
vaticination [vætisi'neiʃ(ə)n], *s.* prophétie *f*; *Pej:* vaticination *f*.
vaticinator [væ'tisineitər], *s.* prophète *m*; *Pej:* vaticinateur, -trice.
vatman, *pl.* **-men** ['vætmən], *s.m. Paperm:* plongeur, puiseur.
vatting ['vætiŋ], *s.* mise *f* en cuve; *Tan:* encuvage *m*, mise en fosse.
vaudeville ['voudəvil, 'vɔ:-], *s. Th:* **1.** vaudeville *m*. **2.** spectacle varié; spectacle de music-hall.
vaudevillist ['voud(ə)vilist, 'vɔ:-], *s.* **1.** vaudevilliste *m*. **2.** auteur *m* de spectacles du genre revue.
Vaudism ['voudizm], *s. Rel.H:* valdisme *m*.
Vaudois[1] ['voudwɑ:]. *Geog:* **1.** *a.* vaudois. **2.** *s.* Vaudois, -oise.
vaudois[2], *a.* & *s. Rel.H:* vaudois (*m*).
vault[1] [vɔ:lt, vɔlt], *s.* **1.** (*a*) *Arch:* voûte *f*; **barrel, cradle, tunnel, v.,** voûte en berceau, cylindrique; **basket-handle v.,** voûte en anse de panier; **cross, groin, v.,** voûte d'arêtes; **domical v.,** voûte en arc-de-cloître; **fan v.,** voûte en éventail; **ribbed v.,** voûte d'ogives, à nervures; **semicircular v.,** voûte à plein cintre; *Lit:* **the v. of heaven,** le dôme des cieux; *Poet:* les célestes lambris *m*; (*b*) *Const:* chapelle *f* (de four de boulangerie); voûte (d'un fourneau); (*c*) *Anat:* voûte (du crâne, etc.). **2.** (*a*) souterrain *m*; (*of bank, etc.*) **safety v.,** chambre forte; (*b*) (i) (**wine**) **v.,** cave *f*, cellier *m*; (ii) *pl.* **vaults,** débit *m* de boissons; (*c*) (**sepulchral**) **v.,** caveau *m*; **family v.,** caveau, tombeau *m*, de famille.
vault[2]. **1.** *v.tr.* **to v. (over) a cellar,** voûter une cave, couvrir une cave d'une voûte. **2.** *v.i.* (*of roof, etc.*) se voûter.
vault[3], *s. Gym: etc:* saut *m* (de barrière, etc., en s'aidant de la main, d'une perche); saut au cheval d'arçons; saut latéral.
vault[4]. **1.** *v.i.* (*a*) **to v. over a gate,** sauter une barrière, franchir une barrière d'un saut (en s'aidant de la main, des mains); **to v. over a stream,** sauter un ruisseau à la perche; *Gym:* **to v. over the horse,** sauter le cheval d'arçons, pratiquer le saut latéral avec appui, faire des exercices de volte; (*b*) **to v. into the saddle,** sauter à cheval, sauter en selle. **2.** *v.tr.* sauter (une barrière, etc.), franchir (une barrière, etc.) d'un saut (en s'aidant de la main, des mains).
vaultage ['vɔ:ltidʒ, 'vɔl-], *s. Arch:* voûtes *fpl*.
vaulted ['vɔ:ltid, 'vɔl-], *a.* **1.** voûté, couvert d'une voûte. **2.** en (forme de) voûte, voussé.
vaulter ['vɔ:ltər, 'vɔl-], *s.* sauteur, -euse; (*acrobatic*) voltigeur, -euse; acrobate *mf*.
vaulting[1] ['vɔ:ltiŋ, 'vɔl-], *s.* **1.** construction *f* de voûtes. **2.** *coll.* voûte(s) *f(pl)*; **barrel v.,** voûte en berceau; **the cathedral v.,** la voûte de la cathédrale.
vaulting[2], *a. Lit:* **v. ambition,** ambition démesurée, qui vise (trop) haut.
vaulting[3], *s. Gym:* exercice *m* du saut; voltige *f* (sur le cheval d'arçons); **side v.,** saut latéral avec appui des mains.
vaunt [vɔ:nt]. *Lit:* **1.** *v.i. A:* se vanter; fanfaronner; faire de la gloriole. **2.** *v.tr.* (*a*) vanter (qch.); **our much vaunted justice,** notre justice tant vantée, si célèbre; (*b*) se vanter de (qch.), se faire gloire de (qch.).
vaunting[1] ['vɔ:ntiŋ], *a.* vantard.
vaunting[2], *s.* vanterie *f*, jactance *f*.
vauntingly ['vɔ:ntiŋli], *adv.* avec jactance, en se vantant.
vauquelinite ['vouk(ə)linait], *s. Miner:* vauquelinite *f*.
vavasory ['vævəsəri], *s. Hist:* vavassorie *f*.
vavasour ['vævəsuər], *s. Hist:* vavasseur *m*, vavassal *m*, -aux.
veal [vi:l], *s.* **1.** *Cu:* veau *m*; **v. cutlet,** côtelette *f* de veau; **fillet of v.,** rouelle *f* de veau; **v. olive,** alouette *f* sans tête. **2.** *Med:* **v. skin,** vitiligo *m*.
vealer ['vi:lər], *s.* veau *m* de boucherie.
vectocardiogram [vektə'kɑ:diəgræm], *s. Med:* vectocardiogramme *m*, vectogramme *m*.
vectocardiographic [vektəkɑ:diə'græfik], *a. Med:* vectocardiographique.
vectocardiography [vektəkɑ:di'ɔgrəfi], *s. Med:* vectocardiographie *f*.
vectograph ['vektəgræf], *s. Med:* vectographie *f*.
vector[1] ['vektər], *s.* **1.** *Mth: Ph:* vecteur *m*; *attrib.* **v. calculus,** calcul vectoriel; **v. function,** fonction vectorielle; **v. (cross) product,** produit vectoriel; **v. quantity,** quantité, grandeur, vectorielle; *El:* **v. resistance,** résistance vectorielle. **2.** *Med:* (agent) vecteur (d'une maladie).
vector[2], *v.tr. Av:* diriger (un avion) par radio.
vectorial [vek'tɔ:riəl], *a. Mth:* vectoriel; *El:* **v. power,** puissance vectorielle.
Veda ['veidə, 'vi:-], *s. Rel:* **the Veda(s),** les Védas *m*.
Vedanta [vi'dæntə, vei'dɑ:n-], *s. Rel:* védânta *m*.
Vedantic [vi'dæntik, vei'dɑ:n-], *a. Rel:* védantin, védantiste.
Vedantist [vi'dæntist, vei'dɑ:n-], *s.* védantiste *mf*, védantin, -ine.
Veddas ['vedəz], *s.pl. Ethn:* Veddas *m*, Védas *m*.
vedette [vi'det], *s. Mil:* vedette *f*; **to be on v. duty,** être en vedette; *Navy:* **v. boat,** vedette.
Vedic ['veidik, 'vi:-]. *Rel:* **1.** *a.* védique. **2.** *s.* sanscrit *m* védique.
Vedism ['veidizm, 'vi:-], *s. Rel:* védisme *m*.
vee [vi:], *s.* V (dans certains termes techniques).
veep [vi:p], *s.m. U.S: F:* vice-président.
veer[1] ['viər], *s.* **1.** changement *m* de direction, saute *f* (de vent, *esp.* à droite). **2.** (*of ship*) virage *m* vent arrière. **3.** changement, revirement *m* (d'opinion).
veer[2]. **1.** *v.i.* (*a*) (*of wind*) tourner, sauter (*esp.* à droite); **to v. aft, abaft,** adonner; **to v. ahead,** venir debout; **to v. forward,** refuser; **to v. to the west,** haler l'ouest; ouestir; **to v. round to the north,** anordir, ranger le nord, se ranger au nord; (*b*) (*of ship*) virer (vent arrière); changer de bord; **to v. at anchor,** rôder sur son ancre; (*of rocket, etc.*) **to v. off course,** virer en s'éloignant de la direction prévue; (*c*) *Fig:* **the conversation veered to politics,** la conversation a tourné à la politique; (*d*) (*of pers.*) **to v. round,** changer d'opinion; **to v. round to an opinion,** se ranger à une opinion. **2.** *v.tr.* (faire) virer (un navire) vent arrière.
veer[3], *v.tr. Nau:* **to v. away, out, the cable,** filer du câble; **to v. the capstan,** dévirer le cabestan; *v.i.* **to v. and haul,** (i) filer et haler (un cordage) alternativement; (ii) *Fig:* manœuvrer avec adresse.
veering ['viəriŋ], *s.* = VEER[1].
veery ['viːri], *s. Orn:* grive *f* fauve.
veg [vedʒ], *s. F:* légume(s) *m*.
Vega ['vi:gə], *Pr.n. Astr:* Véga *m*.

vegan ['viːgən], *s.* végétalien, -ienne.

vegetable ['vedʒ(i)təbl]. **1.** *a.* (*a*) végétal, -aux; **the v. kingdom,** le règne végétal; **v. life,** la vie végétale, la végétalité; **v. soil,** terre végétale; **v. oils,** huiles végétales; **v. oil materials,** matières végétales oléagineuses; oléagineux *m* d'origine végétale; (*b*) *Fig:* **to lead a v. existence,** mener une existence végétative. **2.** *s.* (*a*) *Bot:* végétal *m*; (*b*) *Hort: Cu:* légume *m*; **dried vegetables,** légumes secs; **green vegetables,** légumes verts; **early vegetables,** primeurs *f*; **v. diet,** régime végétal, de légumes; **v. dish,** légumier *m*; **v. garden,** (jardin) potager (*m*); jardin légumier; **v. cutter, slicer,** taille-racines *m inv*, taille-légumes *m inv*, coupe-légumes *m inv*; (*c*) *Fig:* être végétatif, vieux routinier.

vegetal ['vedʒitl], *a. & s. Bot:* végétal (*m*), -aux; *Biol:* **v. pole,** pôle végétatif.

vegetarian [vedʒi'tɛriən], *a. & s.* végétarien, -ienne.

vegetarianism [vedʒi'tɛəriənizm], *s.* végétar(ian)isme *m*.

vegetate ['vedʒiteit], *v.i.* **1.** (*a*) (*of plant*) végéter; (*b*) **to v. in an office,** végéter, moisir, dans un bureau. **2.** *Metall:* (*of silver, etc.*) rocher.

vegetating ['vedʒiteitiŋ], *a.* végétant.

vegetation [vedʒi'teiʃ(ə)n], *s.* **1.** (*a*) végétation *f*; *Fig:* **a life of v.,** une vie végétative; (*b*) *Metall:* rochage *m*. **2.** *coll.* végétation (d'une région). **3.** *Med:* **vegetations,** végétations.

vegetative ['vedʒitətiv, -'teitiv], *a.* végétatif; (*a*) *Bot:* **v. reproduction,** reproduction végétative; (*b*) *Fig:* **v. existence,** existence végétative.

vegetatively [vedʒi'teitivli], *adv.* végétativement.

Vegetius [ve'dʒiːʃiəs], *Pr.n.m. Lit.Hist:* Végèce.

vegetive ['vedʒitiv], *a.* **1.** végétal, -aux. **2.** végétatif.

vegeto-animal [vedʒitou'æniməl], *a.* végéto-animal, -aux.

vegeto-mineral [vedʒitou'minərəl], *a.* végéto-minéral, -aux.

vegeto-sulphuric [vedʒitousʌl'fjuːrik], *a.* végéto-sulfurique, *pl.* végéto-sulfuriques.

vehemence ['viːəməns], *s.* véhémence *f* (du vent, d'un orateur); impétuosité *f*, ardeur *f* (de la jeunesse, etc.).

vehement ['viːəmənt], *a.* (vent, orateur, etc.) véhément; (vent) impétueux; (amour) passionné; (effort) violent.

vehemently ['viːəməntli], *adv.* véhémentement; avec véhémence; impétueusement, passionnément, avec violence.

vehicle[1] ['viːikl], *s.* **1.** (*a*) véhicule *m*, voiture *f*; *Adm:* **commercial v.,** véhicule industriel; (véhicule) utilitaire (*m*); **(extra) long v.,** convoi *m* grande longueur; convoi exceptionnel; (*at ferry, etc.*) **v. check-in,** contrôle *m* des véhicules; (*b*) *Space:* **space v.,** véhicule spatial; **launching v.,** véhicule de lancement, laceur *m*, vecteur *m*. **2.** véhicule; moyen *m* de transmission, de propagation; (*a*) **air is the v. of sound,** l'air est le véhicule du son; **speech is the v. of thought,** le langage est le véhicule de la pensée; **the newspaper as a v. for advertising,** le journal comme moyen de publicité; **he used the press as a v. for the propagation of his ideas,** il se servait de la presse comme véhicule pour la propagation de ses idées; (*b*) *Med:* **v. of a disease,** agent vecteur, véhicule, d'une maladie; **direct contagion without v.,** contage immédiat sans agent vecteur. **3.** *Paint: Pharm:* véhicule; *Pharm:* excipient *m*. **2.** *Rel:* (*Buddhism*) **the Great, Little, V.,** le grand, petit, véhicule.

vehicle[2], *v.tr.* véhiculer, voiturer.

vehicular [vi'hikjulər], *a.* des voitures; véhiculaire; **v. traffic,** circulation *f* des voitures; **v. ferry,** bac *m* à voitures.

Vehmgericht ['feimgəriχt], *Pr.n. Hist:* (la) Sainte Vehme.

Vehmic ['feimik], *a. Hist:* (tribunal, etc.) vehmique.

Veii ['viːjai], *Pr.n. A.Geog:* Véies.

veil[1] [veil], *s.* **1.** *Cost:* (*a*) voile *m* (de religieuse, de deuil); **bridal v.,** voile de mariée; *Ecc:* (*of woman*) **to take the v.,** prendre le voile; **taking of the v.,** prise *f* de voile; (*b*) **hat v., eye v.,** voilette *f*; *A.Aut:* **dust v.,** pare-poussière *m inv*, voilette anti-poussière *inv*. **2.** (*a*) *A:* voile, rideau *m*; *Jew.Ant:* **the v. of the temple,** le voile du temple; (*b*) *Lit:* **beyond the v.,** au delà de la tombe. **3.** *F:* voile, rideau, gaze *f*, déguisement *m*; **under the v. of anonymity,** sous le voile de l'anonyme; **to draw, throw, a v. over sth.,** jeter un voile sur qch.; tirer le voile sur qch.; gazer (les faits). **4.** *Nat.Hist:* voile; *Fung:* **universal v.,** voile général.

veil[2], *v.tr.* **1.** voiler (son visage, un tableau); **to v. oneself,** se voiler; **to v. one's face,** se voiler la face. **2.** *O:* voiler, cacher, dissimuler (ses sentiments, desseins).

veiled [veild], *a.* **1.** voilé, couvert d'un voile. **2.** voilé, caché, dissimulé; **in thinly v. terms,** en termes peu voilés; **v. hostility,** hostilité sourde; **scarcely v. hostility,** hostilité à peine déguisée. **3.** *Mus:* **v. voice,** voix sombrée, voilée.

veiling ['veiliŋ], *s.* **1.** action *f*, fait *m*, de voiler (la face), de dissimuler (la vérité, etc.). **2.** *coll.* voile(s) *m(pl)*; *Tex:* **nun's v.,** flanelle *f* mousseline. **3.** *Phot:* voile.

veiltail ['veilteil], *s. Ich:* cyprin *m* à queue de voile.

vein[1] [vein], *s.* **1.** *Anat:* veine *f*; **companion veins,** veines satellites; **he has foreign blood in his veins,** du sang étranger coule dans ses veines. **2.** *Bot: Ent:* nervure *f* (de feuille, d'aile); veine (de feuille). **3.** (*a*) *Geol: Min:* veine, filon *m*, rameau *m*, gîte filonien; **horizontal v.,** plateure *f*; *Min:* **rake, gash, v.,** filon à pendage fort, vertical; **soft v. in quarry stone,** moye *f* dans la pierre de taille; **v. gold,** or filonien; **v. stone,** roche *f* de filon, roche filonienne; (*b*) *O:* **he has a v. of meanness in his character,** il y a dans son caractère une légère dose de mesquinerie. **4.** (*in wood, marble*) veine. **5.** veine, disposition *f*, humeur *f*; **the poetic v.,** la veine poétique; **other remarks in the same v.,** d'autres observations faites dans le même esprit; **to be in the v. for doing sth.,** être en veine, en humeur, de faire qch.

vein[2], *v.tr. Paint:* veiner, marbrer (une porte, etc.).

veined [veind], *a.* **1.** veiné, veineux, à veines; **v. wood,** bois veiné, madré. **2.** *Bot: Ent:* nervuré.

veining ['veiniŋ], *s.* **1.** *Paint:* (*action*) veinage *m*; **v. brush,** veinette *f*. **2.** *coll.* (*a*) veinure *f*, marbrure *f*; (*b*) veines *fpl*; *Bot: Ent:* nervures *fpl*.

veinlet ['veinlit], *s.* veinule *f*, filet *m*.

veinous ['veinəs], *a.* **1. v. blood, system,** sang, système, veineux. **2.** (*of hands, etc.*) veineux, couvert de veines, où les veines ressortent.

veinstuff ['veinstʌf], *s. Min:* gangue *f*.

veiny ['veini], *a.* (*of leaf, wood*) veineux.

Velabrum (the) [ðəvi'læbrəm], *Pr.n. Rom.Ant:* le Vélabre.

velamen, *pl.* **-lamina** [vi'leimən, -'leiminə], *s. Bot:* enveloppe extérieure, tégument *m*, voile *m* (d'une racine d'orchidée).

velamentous [velə'mentəs], *a.* vélamenteux.

velar ['viːlər], *a. & s. Ling:* vélaire (*f*); **v. consonant,** (consonne) vélaire, consonne vélarisée.

velarium, *pl.* **-ia** [vi'lɛəriəm, -iə], *s. Rom.Ant:* vélarium *m*.

velarization [viːlərai'zeiʃ(ə)n], *s. Ling:* vélarisation *f*.

velarize ['viːləraiz], *v.tr. Ling:* vélariser.

veld(t) [velt], *s.* veld(t) *m*.

velella [və'lelə], *s. Cœl:* vellèle *f*, vélelle *f*.

veleta [və'liːtə], *s. Danc:* sorte *f* de valse d'origine anglaise.

veliform ['viːlifɔːm], *a. Nat.Hist:* véliforme.

veliger ['viːlidʒər], *s. Moll:* véligère *f*.

veligerous [vi'lidʒərəs], *a. Nat.Hist:* véligère.

velite ['viːlait], *s. Rom.Ant:* vélite *m*; *Fr.Hist:* **velites,** vélites.

vell [vel], *s.* feuillet *m* (d'estomac de veau).

velleity [ve'liːiti], *s.* velléité *f*.

vellum ['veləm], *s.* vélin *m*; **rough v.,** parchemin *m* en cosse; **Japanese v.,** papier *m* du Japon; **v. paper,** papier vélin.

velocimeter [velə'simitər], *s. Ball: etc:* vélocimètre *m*.

velocipede [vi'lɔsipiːd], *s.* **1.** *A:* vélocipède *m*. **2.** *NAm:* tricycle *m* d'enfant.

velocipedist [vilɔsi'piːdist], *s.A:* vélocipédiste *mf*.

velocity [vi'lɔsiti], *s.* vitesse *f*, *occ.* vélocité *f*; **uniformly accelerated, retarded, v.,** vitesse uniformément accélérée, retardée; **comparative, relative v.,** vitesse relative; *Ac:* **particle v.,** vitesse corpusculaire; *Astr: Space:* **escape v.,** vitesse d'évasion, de libération; *Hyd.E:* **v. of approach,** vitesse d'arrivée; *Atom.Ph:* **v. band,** bande *f* de vitesse; *Mec:* **v. range,** gamme *f*, éventail *m*, des vitesses; *Mec.E:* **v. ratio,** rapport *m* de démultiplication; *Tp: etc:* **v. microphone,** microphone *m* à vitesse; *T.V:* **v. modulation,** modulation *f* de vitesse; **v. modulated tube,** tube *m* acoustique à modulation de vitesse; *Fin:* **v. of circulation of money,** vitesse de circulation de la monnaie.

velour(s) [və'luər], *s. Com:* **1.** *Tex:* velouté *m*; velours *m* de laine. **2.** feutre taupé; **v. (hat),** chapeau (en feutre) taupé. **3.** bichon *m* (pour chapeaux de soie).

velum, *pl.* **vela** ['viːləm, -ə], *s.* (*a*) *Anat:* voile *m* du palais; (*b*) *Anat: Nat.Hist:* voile.

velutinous [vi'ljuːtinəs], *a. Nat.Hist:* velouteux.

velvet ['velvit], *s.* **1.** *Tex:* velours *m*; **plain v.,** velours plain, uni; **raised, stamped, v.,** velours frappé; **brocaded v.,** velours broché; **figured v.,** velours façonné; **printed v.,** velours imprimé; **shot v.,** velours glacé; **cut v.,** velours ciselé; **uncut v., terry v.,** velours bouclé, frisé, épinglé; **ribbed v., corduroy v.,** velours à côtes, côtelé; velours de chasse; **cotton v.,** velours de coton; **worsted v.,** velours de laine; **mock v.,** tripe *f* de velours; **v. manufacturer,** veloutier *m*; **soft as v.,** velouté; *F:* **to be on v.,** (i) (*also* **to play**) jouer sur le velours; (ii) mener une vie de château, être comme un coq en pâte. **2.** *Nat.Hist:* velouté *m*; **v. of a stag's horns,** peau velue du bois de cerf. **3.** *P:* **black v.,** mélange *m* de champagne et de stout. **4.** *NAm: P:* bénéfice *m*, gains *mpl*. **5.** *attrib.* (*a*) de velours, velouté; **v. coat,** habit de velours; **v. braid,** velouté; **v. pile,** moquette *f*; *Phot:* **v. paper,** papier velouté; *Fig:* **with v. tread,** à pas feutrés; (*b*) *Bot:* **v. grass,** houlque laineuse; **v. leaf,** lavatère *f*, mauve *f*, en arbre; abutilon *m*; (*c*) *Ent:* **v. ant,** mutille *f*.

velveted ['velvitid], *a.* **1.** *Nat.Hist:* velouté. **2.** vêtu de velours.

velveteen [velvi'tiːn], *s.* **1.** *Tex:* velours *m* de coton; tripe *f* de velours; velours de chasse; velvantine *f*, velventine *f*; **ribbed v., corduroy v.,** velours (de coton) côtelé, à côtes. **2.** *pl. A:* **velveteens,** (i) *Cost:* pantalon *m* en velours de chasse; (ii) *F:* (*with sg. const.*) le garde-chasse.

velvet-eyed ['velvit'aid], *a. Lit:* au regard velouté; aux yeux doux.

velvetiness ['velvitinis], *s.* velouté *m*.

velvetings ['velvitiŋz], *s.pl. Com:* velours *mpl*; étoffes *f* de velours.

velvety ['velviti], *a.* velouté, velouteux; doux comme du velours; *Bot:* pruiné, pruineux; **v. wine,** vin velouté, moelleux, qui a du velouté.

vena cava, *pl.* **venae cavae** [viːnə'keivə, 'viːni 'keiviː], *s. Anat:* veine *f* cave.

venal ['viːnl], *a.* (*of pers., conduct, etc.*) vénal, aux; (*of pers.*) mercenaire; **v. justice,** justice vénale, *F:* justice à l'encan.

venality [vi'næliti], *s.* vénalité *f*.

venally ['viːnəli], *adv.* vénalement.

venation [vi'neiʃ(ə)n], *s. Bot: Ent:* nervation *f*, nervulation *f*.

venational [vi'neiʃən(ə)l], *a.* de la nervation.

vend [vend], *v.tr.* **1.** (*a*) *Jur:* vendre; (*b*) faire le commerce de (choses de peu de valeur); vendre (des journaux). **2.** *O:* annoncer, proclamer hautement (une théorie, etc.).

vendace ['vendeis], *s. Ich:* vendace *m*.

vendaval ['vendəvæl], *s. Meteor:* vent *m* du sud-ouest (du détroit de Gibraltar).

Vendean [ven'di(ː)ən], *Hist: Geog:* **1.** *a.* vendéen. **2.** *s.* Vendéen, -éenne.

vendee [ven'diː], *s. Jur:* acheteur, -euse, acquéreur, -euse.

vender ['vendər], *s.* **1.** vendeur, -euse; **street v.,** (i) marchand, -ande des quatre saisons; (ii) camelot *m*; **illicit street v.,** marchand à la sauvette. **2.** (*machine*) distributeur *m* automatique.

vendetta [ven'detə], *s.* **1.** vendetta *f*. **2.** *Fig:* guerre *f*, hostilités *fpl* (entre des groupes sociaux, etc.).

vending ['vendiŋ], *s.* vente *f*; **automatic v.,** vente par distributeur(s) automatique(s); **v. machine,** distributeur *m* automatique.

vendor ['vendɔːr], *s.* **1.** (*a*) *Com:* vendeur, -euse; *Fin:* **vendor's shares,** actions *f* d'apport, de fondation; **v. company,** compagnie apporteuse; (*b*) *Jur:* vendeur, -eresse; **vendor's lien,** privilège *m* du vendeur. **2.** *also* ['vendər] = VENDER.

vendue ['vendjuː], *s. NAm:* vente *f* aux enchères.

veneer[1] [və'niər], *s.* **1.** (*a*) placage *m*, revêtement *m* (de bois mince); (*b*) bois *m* de placage, bois à plaquer; **leaf, sheet, of v.,** feuille *f*, feuillet *m*, copeau *m*, de placage; plaque *f* (d'ébéniste); **v. cutter,** (i) machine *f* à trancher le bois; (ii) (*pers.*) scieur *m*, trancheur *m*, fendeur *m*, de bois de placage; (*c*) *Const:* revêtement, enduit *m* (de béton, etc.). **2.** *Fig:* masque *m*, apparence extérieure, vernis *m* (de connaissances, etc.); **a v. of politeness,** un vernis de politesse; une politesse toute en surface. **3.** *Ent:* **v. (moth),** crambe *m*.

veneer[2], *v.tr.* plaquer (le bois).

veneerer [və'niərər], *s.* plaqueur, -euse.

veneering [və'niəriŋ], *s.* **1.** (*process*) placage *m*; **v. hammer,** marteau *m* à plaquer; **v. press,** presse *f* à plaquer; **v. wood,** bois *m* de placage. **2.** (*a*) (*layer of wood*) placage, revêtement *m*; (*b*) bois de placage.

venenific [venə'nifik], *a. Nat.Hist:* (glande, etc.) vénénifique, vénénipare.

venepuncture ['venipʌŋktjər], *s. Surg:* ponction *f* d'une veine.

venerability [ven(ə)rə'biliti], **venerableness** ['ven(ə)rəbəlnis], *s.* vénérabilité *f*.

venerable ['ven(ə)rəbl], *a.* **1.** (vieillard, etc.) vénérable; **v. beard,** barbe de vieillard vénérable; **v. oaks,** chênes séculaires. **2.** (*a*) titre honorifique accordé aux archidiacres de l'Église anglicane; (*b*) *R.C.Ch:* vénérable. **3.** *s.* vénérable *m* (d'une loge de francs-maçons).

venerably ['ven(ə)rəbli], *adv.* vénérablement; d'une

manière vénérable.

venerate ['venəreit], *v.tr.* vénérer; avoir de la vénération pour (qn).

veneration [venə'reiʃ(ə)n], *s.* vénération *f* (**for,** pour); **to hold s.o. in v.,** avoir de la vénération pour qn.

venerator ['venəreitər], *s.* vénérateur, -trice.

venereal [vi'niəriəl], *a. Med:* vénérien.

venereologist [viniəri'ɔlədʒist], *s. Med:* vénéréologue *mf.*

venereology [viniəri'ɔlədʒi], *s. Med:* vénéréologie *f.*

venery[1] ['venəri], *s. A:* vénérie *f*; la chasse; **hounds of v.,** chiens courants.

venery[2], *s. A:* plaisirs sexuels.

venesection [veni'sekʃ(ə)n], *s. Surg:* saignée *f*; phlébotomie *f.*

Veneti ['venitai], *s.pl. Hist:* Vénètes *m*, Vénèdes *m.*

Venetia [vi'ni:ʃə], *Pr.n. A.Geog:* la Vénétie.

Venetian [vi'ni:ʃən]. *Geog:* **1.** *a.* vénitien; (i) de Venise, (ii) de Vénétie; **V. chalk,** talc *m* de Venise; **V. glass,** verre *m* de Venise; *Needlew:* **V. lace,** point *m* de Venise; *Furn:* **V. blinds,** *s.* **venetians,** jalousies *f* (à lames mobiles); *Paint:* **V. white,** blanc vénitien. **2.** *s.* Vénitien, -ienne.

Venetic [vi'netik], *a. Ethn:* des Vénètes.

Venezuela [vene'zweilə], *Pr.n.* le Vénézuéla.

Venezuelan [vene'zweilən]. *Geog:* **1.** *a.* vénézuélien. **2.** *s.* Vénézuélien, -ienne.

vengeance ['ven(d)ʒ(ə)ns], *s.* vengeance *f*; **to take v. on s.o.,** tirer, prendre, vengeance de qn, se venger de qn; **to wreak one's v. on s.o.,** se venger, exercer sa vengeance, sur qn; **to take v. for sth.,** tirer vengeance de qch.; venger qch.; **to take v. for an insult,** se venger d'une injure; **to swear v. against s.o.,** jurer de se venger; **crime that cries for v.,** crime qui crie vengeance; **the v. of God,** la vengeance de Dieu; *B:* **v. is mine; I will repay, saith the Lord,** c'est moi qui ferai justice, moi qui rétribuerai, dit le Seigneur; *F:* **with a v.,** furieusement; à outrance; pour de bon; **to punish s.o. with a v.,** corriger qn d'importance, de la bonne façon; **he's making up for lost time with a v.,** il rattrape le temps perdu, pas d'erreur! **it is raining with a v.,** maintenant qu'il pleut, c'est pour de bon; voilà qui s'appelle pleuvoir; **it was raining with a v.,** il pleuvait que c'était une bénédiction! **he's a gambler with a v.,** c'est un joueur s'il en fut jamais; **that was a game with a v.,** ç'a été un beau match ou je ne m'y connais pas.

vengeful ['ven(d)ʒful], *a.* **1.** (*of pers.*) vindicatif. **2.** *Lit:* (*of arm, sword, etc.*) vengeur, -eresse.

vengefully ['ven(d)ʒfuli], *adv.* vindicativement, par vengeance.

vengefulness ['ven(d)ʒfulnis], *s.* caractère vindicatif, esprit *m* de vengeance.

venial ['vi:niəl], *a.* (*a*) *Theol:* (péché) véniel; (*b*) (*of fault, etc.*) léger, pardonnable, excusable, véniel.

veniality [vi:ni'æliti], *s.* (*a*) *Theol:* caractère véniel (d'un péché); (*b*) caractère léger, véniel (d'une faute).

venially ['vi:niəli], *adv.* (*a*) *Theol:* véniellement; (*b*) d'une manière pardonnable, excusable; véniellement.

Venice ['venis], *Pr.n. Geog:* Venise *f*; **V. glass,** verre *m* de Venise.

venipuncture ['venipʌŋktjər], *s. Surg:* = VENEPUNCTURE.

venire [və'niəri], *s. Jur:* (*a*) **v. facias** ['fæʃiəs], *U.S:* **v.,** injonction *f* d'assigner un jury; (*b*) *U.S:* tableau *m*, liste *f*, des jurés assignés.

venireman, *pl.* **-men** [və'niərimən], *s. U.S:* personne nommée sur la liste des jurés assignés.

venisection [veni'sekʃ(ə)n], *s. Surg:* = VENESECTION.

venison ['ven(i)z(ə)n], *s. Cu:* venaison *f*; **haunch of v.,** quartier *m* de chevreuil.

Venite [ve'ni:tei, ve'naiti], *s. Ecc:* Venite exultemus *m inv.*

Venn [ven], *Pr.n. Log:* **V. diagram,** diagramme *m* de Venn.

vennel ['ven(ə)l], *s. Scot:* ruelle *f*, venelle *f.*

venom ['venəm], *s.* (*a*) venin *m*; (*b*) **tongue full of v.,** langue pleine de venin, mauvaise langue, langue de vipère.

venomed ['venəmd], *a.* envenimé, plein de venin.

venomous ['venəməs], *a.* **1.** (*of animal*) venimeux; (*of plant*) vénéneux. **2.** (*of criticism, etc.*) venimeux, plein de venin, envenimé; **v. tongue,** langue de vipère; **she has a v. tongue,** c'est une mauvaise langue.

venomously ['venəməsli], *adv.* d'une manière venimeuse, avec venin, méchamment.

venomousness ['venəməsnis], *s.* **1.** nature venimeuse (d'un animal); nature vénéneuse (d'une plante); venimosité *f* (d'une piqûre, etc.). **2.** méchanceté *f* (de langue, d'un potin); venimosité (d'une critique).

venosclerosis [venouskla'rousis], *s. Med:* phlébosclérose *f.*

venose ['vi:nous], *a. Bot: Ent:* nervé.

venosity [vi'nɔsiti], *s. Anat: Med:* vénosité *f.*

venostasis ['vi:nəsteisis], *s. Med:* stase *f* dans une veine.

venous ['vi:nəs], *a.* **1.** *Physiol:* (système, sang) veineux. **2.** *Ent:* nervé.

vent[1] [vent], *s.* **1.** (*a*) trou *m*, orifice *m* (pour laisser entrer l'air, sortir un gaz, etc.); **v. of a cask,** trou de fausset d'un tonneau; **the gas found v. through a crack in the pipe,** le gaz s'est échappé par une fissure du tuyau; **to give v. to a cask,** donner vent, de l'évent, à un tonneau; **v. to air, atmosphere,** mise *f* à l'air libre; **air v.,** bouche *f* d'aération, évent *m*; **v. (hole),** évent, trou d'évent, d'aération; prise *f* d'air (d'un réservoir à essence, etc.); aspirail *m*, -aux (d'un fourneau); soupirail *m*, -aux (d'un puits d'aérage, d'une meule de carbonisation, etc.); *Metall:* trou d'air, d'évent (d'un moule); *El:* trou d'aération (d'un élément de pile); **v. (line),** canalisation *f* de mise à l'air libre; *Nau:* collecteur *m*, tuyau, de dégazage (d'un pétrolier); **v. opening,** ouverture *f* d'aérage, de ventilation; **v. pipe,** tube *m* de mise à l'air; **v. stack,** (i) *Ind: Cin:* aspirateur *m* de fumée; (ii) *Plumb:* prolongation *f* hors toiture de la canalisation sanitaire; **v. valve,** soupape *f* de respiration (d'un réservoir); **v. peg, plug,** fausset *m* (de barrique, etc.); (*b*) (i) *A:* lumière *f* (d'une arme à feu); *Artil:* lumière (d'une culasse, fusée d'obus); **v. plug,** tampon *m* de lumière, étoupillon *m*; (ii) *Ball:* évent (d'une fusée spatiale); (*c*) *Mus:* **vents of a flute,** trous d'une flûte; (*d*) tuyau de cheminée; *Geol:* cheminée *f* (de volcan); *Aer:* cheminée (de parachute); (*e*) *Nat.Hist:* orifice anal (d'un oiseau, poisson, etc.). **2.** cours *m*, libre cours; **to give v. to one's grief, to one's anger,** donner libre cours à sa douleur, à sa colère; donner vent à sa colère; laisser échapper son chagrin; **to give v. to one's indignation,** manifester, faire éclater, son indignation; *Lit:* **to give v. to one's spleen, one's resentment,** décharger, évaporer, sa bile; exhaler son ressentiment; **he gave v. to his anger by smashing the crockery,** il soulageait sa colère en brisant la vaisselle. **3.** (*of otter*) retour *m* à la surface, remontée *f* (pour respirer).

vent[2]. **1.** *v.tr.* (*a*) décharger, vider (une canalisation, etc.) des gaz (qu'elle contient); (*b*) évacuer (les gaz d'une canalisation, la vapeur d'une chaudière, etc.); (*c*) munir (un réservoir, etc.) d'un évent, d'une prise d'air, d'un trou d'aération; *A:* pratiquer une lumière dans (une arme à feu); (*d*) mettre (un réservoir, un réacteur d'avion, etc.) à l'air libre; *A:* donner vent, de l'évent, à (une pièce de vin); (*e*) décharger, laisser éclater, exhaler, jeter (sa colère); **to v. one's ill humour, anger, on s.o.,** décharger sa bile, épancher, passer, sa colère, sur qn. **2.** *v.i.* (*a*) (*of piping, tank, boiler, etc.*) se décharger, se vider; (*b*) *Ven:* (*of otter*) remonter à la surface (pour respirer).

vent[3], *s. Cost:* fente *f* (dans la basque d'un veston).

ventage ['ventidʒ], *s.* **1.** *Mus:* trou *m* (d'un instrument à vent sans clefs). **2.** = VENT HOLE *q.v. under* VENT[1].

ventail ['venteil], *s. Arm: Her:* ventail *m*, -aux, ventaille *f* (du heaume).

vented ['ventid], *a.* pourvu d'évents.

venter ['ventər], *s.* **1.** *A:* ventre *m*, abdomen *m*; *Jur:* **his two sons by another v.,** ses deux fils d'un autre lit. **2.** *Anat: etc:* (i) protubérance *f*, (ii) dépression *f* (d'un os, etc.); *Bot:* ventre (de l'archégone); *Moll:* ventre (d'une coquille bivalve).

ventiduct ['ventidʌkt], *s. Arch: Const:* conduit *m* d'air; ventouse *f.*

ventifact ['ventifækt], *s. Geol:* caillou éolisé.

ventilate ['ventileit], *v.tr.* **1.** (*a*) aérer (une chambre, etc.); ventiler (un tunnel); éventer (une houillère); *Aut:* **ventilated bonnet,** capot ajouré; (*b*) *Physiol: A:* oxygéner (le sang). **2.** agiter (une question) (au grand jour, devant l'opinion publique); mettre (une question) en discussion; faire connaître (publiquement) (ses opinions, griefs); **the whole question needs to be ventilated,** toute la question demande à être ventilée.

ventilating[1] ['ventileitiŋ], *a.* aérant, aérateur, -trice.

ventilating[2], *s.* ventilation *f*, aération *f*, aérage *m*; **v. engine,** machine *f* à ventiler; **v. fan,** ventilateur *m*; **v. pipe,** manche *f* à vent, à air; *Bot:* **v. tissue,** parenchyme *m* aérifère.

ventilation [venti'leiʃ(ə)n], *s.* **1.** (*a*) ventilation *f*, aération *f*, aérage *m*; **to stop the v.,** empêcher l'air de circuler; **exhaust v.,** ventilation par succion; **vacuum v.,** ventilation par aspiration, aérage négatif; **v. aperture,** prise *f* d'air; bouche *f* d'aération (d'un tunnel, etc.); **v. plant,** installation *f* d'aérage; *Min: etc:* **v. shaft,** puits *m* de ventilation, d'aération, d'aérage; *Nau:* **v. port,** sabord *m* d'aération; (*b*) *Physiol: A:* oxygénation *f* (du sang). **2.** mise *f* en discussion publique (d'une question); **the matter requires v.,** c'est une question qu'il faudra soumettre à l'opinion, qui demande à être ventilée.

ventilator ['ventileitər], *s.* **1.** (i) ventilateur *m*, aérateur *m*; (ii) ventouse *f*, éolipile *m* (d'une cheminée); (iii) soupirail *m*, -aux (d'une cave); *Nau:* manche *f* à air, à vent; **vacuum v.,** ventilateur aspirant, négatif; *Nau:* **exhaust v.,** manche d'évacuation; **v. cowl,** capuchon *m* de ventilation, pavillon *m* de manche à air; **v. shaft,** colonne *f* d'aération. **2.** (*in window, over door*) vasistas *m*. **3.** *Aut:* volet *m* d'aération; persienne *f* (de capot); (*window*) déflecteur *m*. **4.** *Med:* appareil *m* à respiration artificielle; poumon artificiel.

Ventimiglia [venti'mi:ljə], *Pr.n. Geog:* Vintimille.

venting ['ventiŋ], *s. Metall:* perçage *m* d'un trou, des trous, d'évent (dans un moule).

ventral ['ventr(ə)l], *a.* **1.** *Anat: Nat.Hist:* ventral, -aux; *Ich:* **v. fins,** *s.* **ventrals,** (nageoires) ventrales; *Med:* **v. rupture,** hernie ventrale; *Av:* **v. tank,** réservoir ventral. **2.** *Ph:* **v. segment,** ventre *m* (d'une onde).

ventrally ['ventrəli], *adv.* ventralement.

ventricle ['ventrikl], *s. Anat:* ventricule *m* (du cœur, du cerveau).

ventricose ['ventrikous], *a.* **1.** *Nat.Hist:* ventru, bombé, renflé. **2.** (*of pers.*) ventru.

ventricular [ven'trikjulər], *a. Anat:* ventriculaire.

Ventriculitidae [ventrikju'laitidi:], *s.pl. Paleont:* ventriculitidés *m.*

ventriculo-bulbous [ventrikjulou'bʌlbəs], *a. Anat:* ventriculo-aortique, *pl.* ventriculo-aortiques.

ventriculogram [ven'trikjuləgræm], *s. Med:* ventriculogramme *m.*

ventriculography [ventrikju'lɔgrəfi], *s. Med:* ventriculographie *f.*

ventriloquial [ventri'loukwiəl], *a.* ventriloque, de ventriloque, de la ventriloquie; *Th:* **v. turn,** numéro *m* de ventriloquie, de ventriloque.

ventriloquism [ven'triləkwizm], *s.* ventriloquie *f.*

ventriloquist [ven'triləkwist], *s.* ventriloque *mf.*

ventriloquistic [ventrilə'kwistik], *a.* (art, etc.) de la ventriloquie, du ventriloque.

ventriloquous [ven'triləkwəs], *a.* ventriloque.

ventriloquy [ven'triləkwi], *s.* ventriloquie *f.*

ventripotent [ven'tripətənt], *a. Lit:* (*a*) ventripotent, pansu; (*b*) glouton, goulu.

venture[1] ['ventjər], *s.* **1.** risque *m*; entreprise hasardeuse, risquée; **he declined the v.,** il n'a pas voulu prendre le risque; **ready for any v.,** prêt aux entreprises les plus hasardeuses; **desperate v.,** tentative désespérée; *Scout:* **v. scout,** routier *m*. **2.** (*a*) *Com:* entreprise, spéculation *f*, opération *f*, affaire *f*, aventure *f*; **to have a share in a v.,** avoir part à une aventure; **joint v.,** entreprise à risques partagés; *O:* **we wish success to this new and interesting v.,** nous souhaitons le succès à cette initiative intéressante; (*b*) *A:* chose hasardée, aventurée; enjeu *m*. **3.** (*a*) *A:* hasard *m*; (*b*) **at a v.,** à l'aventure, au hasard; **to answer at a v.,** répondre au petit bonheur; **to fire at a v.,** tirer au jugé; *Fig:* **to draw a bow at a v.,** lancer une flèche au hasard; plaider le faux pour savoir le vrai.

venture[2]. **1.** *v.tr.* (*a*) **to v. to do sth.,** oser faire qch.; s'enhardir, se risquer, à faire qch.; se permettre de faire qch.; **I v. to affirm he knew nothing about it,** j'ose affirmer qu'il n'en savait rien; **I ventured to go in,** je me hasardai à entrer; **I wouldn't v. to appear in public,** je n'oserais pas affronter les regards du public; (*b*) **to v. an opinion,** se hasarder, se risquer, à donner une opinion; **to v. a guess,** hasarder une conjecture; (*c*) hasarder, aventurer, risquer (sa vie, son argent); **to v. one's fortune in an enterprise,** aventurer sa fortune dans une entreprise; **I'll v. a small bet,** je risquerai bien un petit enjeu; **nothing ventured nothing gained,** qui n'ose rien ne gagne rien. **2.** *v.i.* (*a*) se risquer (à faire qch.); prendre le risque (de faire qch.); **it's worth venturing on,** c'est un risque à courir; (*b*) **to v. into unknown country, on to a shaky bridge,** s'aventurer en pays inconnu, sur un pont tremblant; **to v. out (of doors),** se risquer à sortir; **I wouldn't v. out in such weather,** je ne me risquerais pas dehors par un temps pareil; **to v. too far,** être trop osé; aller trop loin.

venturer ['ventjurər], *s.* (*a*) aventurier *m*; **venturers into unknown lands,** ceux qui s'aventurent en pays inconnus; (*b*) *A:* marchand aventurier.

venturesome ['ventjəsəm], *a.* **1.** (*of pers.*) aventureux, entreprenant, osé. **2.** (*of action, opinion, etc.*) aventuré, risqué, hasardeux.

venturesomeness ['ventjəsəmnis], *s.* nature aventureuse; esprit aventureux.

venturi [ven'tju:ri], *s.* **v. (tube),** venturi *m.*

venue ['venju:], *s.* **1.** *Jur:* lieu *m* du jugement; juridiction *f*; **to lay the v.,** désigner la cour qui sera saisie de l'affaire; **to change the v. of a trial,** renvoyer une affaire devant une autre cour (pour assurer l'ordre public, etc.). **2.** lieu de réunion; rendez-vous *m*; **v. of the meet,**

rendez-vous de chasse.
venule ['venju:l], *s. Anat: Bot: Ent:* veinule *f.*
Venus ['vi:nəs], *Pr.n.f. Rom.Myth: Astr:* Vénus; *F:* **she's no V. but she's a good sort,** ce n'est pas une Vénus mais elle est aimable (et secourable); *Astr:* **transit of V.,** passage *m* de Vénus; *Anat:* **mount of V.,** mont *m* de Vénus; *Bot:* **Venus's basin, bath,** cardère *f* sauvage, chardon *m* à foulon, cabaret *m* des oiseaux, bain *m* de Vénus; **Venus's comb,** scandix *m*, peigne *m* de Vénus, aiguillette *f*, aiguille *f* de berger; **Venus's flytrap,** dionée *f* gobe-mouches; (Vénus) attrape-mouche(s) (*m*); **Venus's hair fern,** cheveu *m* de Vénus; **Venus's slipper,** cypripède *m*, sabot *m* de Vénus, de la Vierge; *Cœl:* **Venus's girdle,** ceste *m*; *Miner:* **Venus's hair stone(s),** flèches *f* d'amour, cheveux de Vénus; *Moll:* **V. (shell),** Vénus, praire *f*; *Spong:* **Venus's flower basket,** euplectelle *f.*
venushair ['vi:nəshεər], *s. Bot:* cheveu *m* de Vénus.
venusian [vi'nju:ziən], *a. Astr:* vénusien.
veracious [və'reiʃəs], *a.* (*of pers., account, etc.*) véridique.
veraciously [və'reiʃəsli], *adv.* véridiquement, avec véracité.
veracity [və'ræsiti], **veraciousness** [və'reiʃəsnis], *s.* véracité *f*, véridicité *f* (de qn, d'un rapport); **authors of the greatest v.,** auteurs des plus véridiques.
veranda(h) [və'rændə], *s. Arch:* véranda *f*, galerie *f* à jour.
veranda(h)ed [və'rændəd], *a.* à véranda.
veratric [və'rætrik], *a. Ch:* vératrique.
veratrine ['verətri:n], *s. Ch: etc:* vératrine *f.*
veratrol ['verətrɔl], *s. Ch: Pharm:* vératrol(e) *m.*
veratrum [və'reitrəm], *s. Bot: Pharm:* vératre *m.*
verb [və:b], *s. Gram:* verbe *m.*
verbal ['və:bəl], *a.* **1.** (*a*) verbal, -aux, oral, -aux; **v. agreement,** convention verbale; **v. offer,** offre verbale; *Dipl:* **v. note,** note verbale; (*b*) de mots, verbal; **v. dispute,** dispute de mots; **v. criticism,** critique qui ne s'attache qu'aux mots; **v. distinction,** distinction verbale; *F:* **v. diarrhoea,** verbomanie *f*; (*c*) (*of translation, etc.*) mot à mot, mot pour mot; littéral, -aux. **2.** *Gram:* **v. noun, adjective,** nom, adjectif, verbal. **3.** *s.* (*a*) *Gram:* nom, adjectif, verbal; (*b*) déclaration verbale.
verbalism ['və:bəlizm], *s.* **1.** (*a*) *A:* expression *f*, locution *f*; (*b*) expression verbeuse, qui signifie peu. **2.** *Phil: etc:* verbalisme *m.*
verbalist ['və:bəlist], *s.* (*a*) critique, etc., qui ne s'attache qu'aux mots; (*b*) personne qui sait bien employer les mots.
verbalization [və:bəlai'zeiʃ(ə)n], *s.* **1.** emploi *m* (d'un nom) comme verbe. **2.** rendement *m* (d'une idée) par des mots; *Psy:* verbalisation *f.*
verbalize ['və:bəlaiz]. **1.** *v.i.* verbiager, être verbeux. **2.** *v.tr.* (*a*) *Gram:* employer (un nom) comme verbe, transformer (un mot) en verbe; (*b*) rendre (une idée) par des mots; *Psy:* verbaliser (une expérience).
verbally ['və:bəli], *adv.* **1.** verbalement, oralement; de vive voix; **v. or in writing,** verbalement ou par écrit. **2.** littéralement; (traduire, etc.) mot à mot, mot pour mot.
verbascum [və:'bæskəm], *s. Bot:* verbascum *m*, molène *f*, cierge *m.*
verbatim [və:'beitim]. **1.** *adv.* mot à mot; textuellement. **2.** *a.* (*of reprint, etc.*) reproduit exactement, exact, mot à mot; **v. report of the proceedings,** (i) compte rendu sténographique, sténogramme *m*, des débats; (ii) les débats enregistrés sur bande.
verbena [və(:)'bi:nə], *s. Bot:* verveine *f*; **lemon(-scented) v.,** citronnelle *f.*
Verbenaceae [və:bi'neisii:], *s.pl. Bot:* verbénacées *f.*
verbenaceous [və:bi'neiʃəs], *a. Bot:* verbénacé.
verbiage ['və:biidʒ], *s.* verbiage *m*; **to lose oneself in v.,** délayer sa pensée.
verbicide[1] ['və:bisaid], *s. F:* personne qui estropie, massacre, les mots.
verbicide[2], *s.* massacre *m* de mots.
verbigeration [və:bidʒə'reiʃ(ə)n], *s. Med:* verbigération *f.*
verbomania [və:bə'meiniə], *s. Psy:* verbomanie *f.*
verbose [və:'bous], *a.* (écrivain, style, etc.) verbeux, diffus.
verbosely [və:bousli], *adv.* avec verbosité, prolixement, avec prolixité, verbeusement.
verboseness [və:'bousnis], **verbosity** [və:'bɔsiti], *s.* verbosité *f*, prolixité *f.*
verb. sap. ['və:b'sæp]. *Lt. phr.* (= *verbum sapienti sat est*) à bon entendeur demi-mot suffit; à bon entendeur salut.
Vercelli [və:'tʃeli], *Pr.n. Geog:* Verceil.
verdancy ['və:d(ə)nsi], *s.* **1.** *Lit:* verdure *f* (d'un pré, du feuillage, etc.). **2.** *A:* inexpérience *f*, naïveté *f*, candeur *f.*
verdant ['və:d(ə)nt], *a.* **1.** *Lit:* vert, verdoyant. **2.** *A:* (*of pers.*) inexpérimenté, naïf, candide.
verd antique ['və:dæn'ti:k], *s.* **1.** *Miner:* (*a*) vert *m* antique, vert de Florence; (*b*) (*of the ancients*) vert d'Égypte; **Oriental v. a.,** porphyre vert. **2.** (*on bronze*) patine verte.
Verde [və:d], *Pr.n. Geog:* **Cape V.,** le cap Vert.
verdea [və:'di(:)ə], *s. Vit:* verdée *f* (raisin blanc et vin de Toscane).
verderer ['və:dərər], *s. Hist:* verdier *m* (du domaine royal).
verdict ['və:dikt], *s.* **1.** *Jur:* (*a*) verdict *m*; réponse *f* du jury (portant sur les questions posées par le juge); **to bring in a v. of guilty, of not guilty,** rendre un verdict positif, de culpabilité, négatif, d'acquittement; déclarer l'accusé coupable, non coupable; **to return a v.,** prononcer, rendre, un verdict; **the jury retire to find their v.,** le jury se retire pour délibérer, pour formuler ses conclusions; **to reach a v.,** conclure, décider; (*b*) (*in coroner's court*) **the jury returned a v. of suicide,** le jury a conclu au suicide; **open v.,** jugement *m* (i) qui ne formule aucune conclusion sur les circonstances dans lesquelles la mort a eu lieu; (ii) qui conclut au crime sans désigner le coupable; **special v.,** déclaration *f* des faits établis qui n'en tire aucune conclusion. **2.** jugement, décision *f*, avis *m*, opinion *f*; **to stick to one's v.,** maintenir le bien-fondé de son jugement; **the doctor has not yet given his v.,** le médecin ne s'est pas encore prononcé; **I read the doctor's v. in his face,** j'ai lu l'arrêt du médecin sur son visage.
verdigris ['və:digris], *s.* (*a*) vert-de-gris *m*; (*of bronze*) **to become covered with v.,** se vert-de-griser; verdir; (*b*) *Dy:* vert-de-gris, verdet *m.*
verdigrised ['və:digrist], *a.* vert-de-grisé, verdi.
verditer ['və:ditər], *s. Art: etc:* vert *m* de terre; **blue v.,** cendre bleue, bleu *m* de montagne; **green v.,** cendre verte, vert de montagne.
verdure ['və:dʒər], *s.* **1.** (*a*) verdure *f*; (i) couleur verte; (ii) herbage *m*, feuillage *m*; (*b*) *Lit:* verdeur *f*, jeunesse *f*, vigueur *f*. **2.** *A:* (tapisserie *f* de) verdure.
verdurous ['və:dʒərəs], *a. Lit:* verdoyant.
veretillum [verə'tiləm], *s. Cœl:* vérétille *m or f.*
Verey ['veri, 'viəri], *Pr.n.* = VERY[2].
verge[1] [və:dʒ], *s.* **1.** (*a*) bord *m* (d'un fleuve); extrémité *f*, limite *f* (d'un pays); orée *f* (d'une forêt); *Civ.E:* accotement *m* (d'une route); **sitting on the grass v. of the road,** assis sur l'herbe du bord de la route; *P.N:* **soft v.,** accotement non stabilisé; *Cmptr:* **v. perforated card,** carte à bords perforés, à perforations marginales; (*b*) bordure *f* (d'une plate-bande); (*c*) **to be on the v. of forty,** friser la quarantaine; **on the v. of manhood,** au seuil de l'âge viril; **he is on the v. of ruin,** il est sur le penchant de la ruine; il est proche de la ruine, à deux doigts de la ruine; sa ruine est imminente; **on the v. of war,** à la veille de la guerre; **on the v. of (bursting into) tears,** au bord des larmes, sur le point d'éclater en larmes; **to carry daring to the v. of rashness,** pousser la hardiesse jusqu'à la témérité. **2.** *Jur:* **v. of a court,** ressort *m* d'une juridiction; *Hist:* **within the v.,** dans un rayon de douze milles autour de la Cour du Roi. **3.** *Const:* saillie *f* de la couverture au-dessous du pignon; **v. board,** bordure de pignon. **4.** *Ecc:* verge (portée devant l'évêque). **5.** *Z:* verge (d'un invertébré). **6.** (*a*) *Mec.E: NAm:* tringle *f*, tige *f*; (*b*) *Clockm:* axe *m* (du balancier).
verge[2], *v.i.* (*a*) **to v. on sth.,** toucher à, être contigu, -uë, à, être voisin de, côtoyer, qch.; **the path verges on the edge of the precipice,** le sentier côtoie le bord du précipice; (*b*) **that verges on disingenuousness,** cela frise la mauvaise foi; **courage verging on foolhardiness,** courage qui confine à la témérité; **colour verging on red,** couleur qui tire sur le rouge; **he was verging on sixty,** il frisait la soixantaine.
verge[3], *v.i.* **1.** (*a*) (*of the sun, etc.*) baisser; **to v. towards the horizon,** descendre vers l'horizon; (*b*) approcher (**towards,** de); **he was verging towards sixty,** il approchait de la soixantaine. **2.** passer (**into,** à l'état de).
vergency ['və:dʒ(ə)nsi], *s. Opt:* vergence *f.*
verger ['və:dʒər], *s.* (*a*) *Ecc:* bedeau *m*; (*b*) huissier *m* à verge.
Vergil ['və:dʒil], *Pr.n.m. Lt.Lit:* Virgile.
Vergilian [və:'dʒiliən], *a.* virgilien.
veridical [və'ridikl], *a. Psy: etc:* véridique.
verifiability [verifaiə'biliti], **verifiableness** [veri'faiəbəlnis], *s.* vérifiabilité *f.*
verifiable [veri'faiəbl], *a.* vérifiable, facile à vérifier; constatable.
verification [verifi'keiʃ(ə)n], *s.* vérification *f*, contrôle *m.*
verificatory [verifi'keitəri], *a.* (*of experiment, etc.*) vérificatif; de contrôle.
verifier ['verifaiər], *s.* **1.** (*pers.*) vérificateur, -trice; contrôleur, -euse. **2.** *Cmptr:* (*machine*) vérificatrice, vérifieuse *f*; **v. operator,** vérificateur, -trice, vérifieur, -euse.
verify ['verifai], *v.tr.* **1.** (*a*) *Jur:* prouver (son dire); (*b*) (*of evidence, etc.*) confirmer (une affirmation, un fait); **this verifies my suspicions, my fears,** cela confirme, donne raison à, mes soupçons, mes craintes. **2.** vérifier, contrôler (des renseignements, des comptes); *Cmptr:* **(key) verified card,** carte vérifiée.
verily ['verili], *adv. A:* en vérité, vraiment, véritablement; *B:* **for v. I say unto you,** car je vous dis en vérité.
verisimilar [veri'similər], *a.* vraisemblable.
verisimilitude [verisi'militju:d], *s.* vraisemblance *f*; **beyond the bounds of v.,** au-delà du vraisemblable; **to give a spice of v. to a story,** donner un peu de vraisemblance, une apparence de vérité, au récit.
verism ['viərizm], *s. Art: etc:* vérisme *m.*
verist ['viərist], *a. & s. Art: etc:* vériste (*mf*).
veristic [viə'ristik], *a. Art: etc:* vériste.
veritable ['veritəbl], *a.* véritable; **we had a v. deluge,** ce fut un véritable, vrai, déluge.
veritably ['veritəbli], *adv.* véritablement.
verity ['veriti], *s. Lit:* vérité *f.* **1. to challenge the v. of sth.,** mettre en doute la vérité de qch. **2. the eternal verities,** les vérités éternelles. **3.** fait réel; **these things are verities,** ces choses sont vraies; ce sont là des faits; **unquestionable verities,** faits, vérités, indiscutables; *A:* **of a v.,** en vérité.
verjuice ['və:dʒu:s], *s.* verjus *m*; **v. grape,** verjus; *Fig:* **she looked vinegar and v.,** elle avait un air, elle eut un regard, aigre comme verjus.
verjuiced ['və:dʒu:st], *a.* (*a*) verjuté; (*b*) *Fig:* aigre comme verjus.
vermeil ['və:meil, -mil], *s.* **1.** (*a*) (*silver gilt*) vermeil *m*; (*b*) **v. varnish,** (vernis) vermeil. **2.** *Lap: Com:* grenat *m* (tirant sur l'orange). **3.** *a. Poet:* (*of lips, etc.*) vermeil, -eille.
vermetid ['və:mitid], *s. Moll:* vermet *m.*
vermi- ['və:mi], *comb.fm.* vermi-.
vermian ['və:miən], *a.* **1.** *Anat:* vermien. **2.** vermiforme, vermiculaire.
vermicelli [və:mi'tʃeli], *s. Cu:* vermicelle *m.*
vermicidal ['və:misaidl], *a. Pharm:* (*of drug*) vermicide.
vermicide ['və:misaid], *s. Pharm:* vermicide *m.*
vermicular [və:'mikjulər], *a.* **1.** vermiculaire, vermiforme; **v. markings,** vermiculures *f*, vermiculations *f*; *Anat:* **v. appendix,** appendice *m* vermiculaire. **2.** *Physiol:* **v. action,** mouvement *m* péristaltique, vermiculaire (des intestins). **3.** *occ.* vermoulu. **4.** *Arch:* vermiculé.
vermiculate [və:'mikjulət], *a. Arch: Nat.Hist: etc.* vermiculé.
vermiculated [və:'mikjuleitid], *a.* **1.** vermoulu, piqué des vers. **2.** *Arch: Nat.Hist:* vermiculé.
vermiculation [və:mikju'leiʃ(ə)n], *s.* **1.** *Arch: etc:* (*a*) vermiculure *f*; (*b*) vermiculation(s) *f*, vermiculure *f.* **2.** vermoulure *f.*
vermicule ['və:mikju:l], *s.* vermisseau *m*, petit ver, asticot *m*, larve *f.*
vermiculite [və:'mikjulait], *s. Miner:* vermiculite *f.*
vermiform ['və:mifɔ:m], *a.* vermiforme, helminthoïde; *Anat:* **v. processes of the brain,** éminences *f* vermiformes du cervelet; **v. appendix,** appendice *m* vermiculaire, vermiforme, iléo-cæcal, -aux.
vermifugal [və:mi'fju:g(ə)], *a Med: Pharm:* vermifuge, helminthagogue.
vermifuge [və:mi'fju:g(ə)l], *a. & s. Med: Pharm:* ver(*m*). anthelminthique (*m*); helminthagogue (*m*).
vermigrade ['və:migreid], *a.* vermigrade.
Vermilinguia [və:mi'liŋgwiə], **Vermilingues** [və:mi'liŋgwi:z], *s.pl. Rept:* vermilingues *m.*
vermilinguial [və:mi'liŋgwiəl], *a. Rept:* vermilingue.
vermilion[1] [və'miljən]. **1.** *s.* vermillon *m*, cinabre *m.* **2.** (*a*) *s.* (*colour*) vermillon; (*b*) *a.* (de) vermillon *inv*, vermeil.
vermilion[2], *v.tr.* vermillonner; (i) enduire de vermillon; (ii) rendre rouge comme du vermillon.
vermilioning [və'miljəniŋ], *s.* vermillonnement *m.*
vermin ['və:min], *s.* **1.** (*a*) (*body parasites*) vermine *f*; (*b*) *Z:* les nuisibles *m*; (*weasels, etc.*) bêtes puantes; (*rats and mice*) *occ.* vermine. **2.** *Pej:* (*people*) vermine.
verminate ['və:mineit], *v.i.* **1.** grouiller de vermine. **2.** engendrer de la vermine.
vermination [və:mi'neiʃ(ə)n], *s. Med:* vermination *f.*
verminous ['və:minəs], *a.* **1.** couvert de vermine; *F:* grouillant de vermine. **2.** *Med:* (*a*) **v. disease,** maladie vermineuse, due aux vers (intestinaux); (*b*) (*of pers.*) qui souffre de vers intestinaux.
vermis ['və:mis], *s. Anat:* vermis *m.*
vermivorous [və:'mivərəs], *a. Nat.Hist:* vermivore.
Vermonter [və:'mɔntər], *s. U.S:* originaire *mf* du

Vermont.

Vermontese [vəː'mɔntiːz], *a. & s.* (originaire *mf*, habitant, -ante) du Vermont.

verm(o)uth ['vəːməθ], *s.* vermout(h) *m.*

vernacular [və'nækjulər], *s.* **1.** *a.* (*a*) *Ling:* vernaculaire; du pays; indigène; (idiome) national; **v. Arabic,** l'arabe *m* vulgaire; (*b*) **v. building, architecture,** construction (d'habitations, etc.) dans le style indigène, propre au pays. **2.** *s.* (*a*) vernaculaire *m*; langue *f* du pays; idiome national; **our own v.,** notre propre langue; notre langue maternelle; (*b*) la langue vulgaire; (*c*) langage *m* (d'un métier, d'une profession); (*d*) *P:* gros mots, jurons *mpl.*

vernacularism [və'nækjulərizm], *s.* mot *m* du pays; locution *f* propre au pays, idiotisme *m.*

vernacularize [və'nækjuləraiz], *v.tr.* **1.** traduire (qch.) dans le langage du pays, métier, etc. **2.** acclimater (un mot, une locution).

vernal ['vəːn(ə)l], *a.* printanier; du printemps; *Astr: Bot:* vernal, -aux; *Astr:* **the v. signs,** les signes vernaux; *Bot:* **(sweet) v. grass,** flouve odorante.

vernalization [vəːnəlai'zeiʃ(ə)n], *s. Agr: Hort:* vernalisation *f*, printanisation *f*, jarovisation *f* (du blé, etc.).

vernalize ['vəːnəlaiz], *v.tr.* soumettre (des graines) à la vernalisation.

vernation [vəː'neiʃ(ə)n], *s. Bot:* vernation *f*, préfoliaison *f*, préfoliation *f*, feuillaison *f*.

vernicle ['vəːnikl], *s. Ecc:* véronique *f*, suaire *m.*

vernier ['vəːniər], *s. Astr: Mth: Surv:* vernier *m*; **v. calliper,** jauge *f* micrométrique; **v. setting,** repère *m* pour mise au point précise; *Ball:* **v. engine, motor,** moteur *m* vernier; *W.Tel: etc:* **v. dial,** cadran *m* à démultiplicateur.

Verona [və'rounə], *Pr.n. Geog:* Vérone.

veronal ['verən(ə)l], *s. Pharm:* véronal *m.*

Veronese[1] [verə'niːz]. *Geog:* **1.** *a.* véronais, de Vérone. **2.** *s.* Véronais, -aise.

Veronese[2] [verou'neizi], *Pr.n.m. Hist: of Art:* Véronèse.

Veronica [və'rɔnikə]. **1.** *Pr.n.f.* Véronique. **2.** *s.* (*a*) *Bot:* véronique *f*; (*b*) *Ecc:* véronique, suaire *m*; (*c*) (*bull fighting*) véronique.

Verrine ['verain], *a. Lt.Lit:* **the V. Orations,** les Verrines *f* (de Cicéron).

verruca, *pl.* **-ae** [ve'ruːkə, -siː], *s.* verrue *f*.

verrucaria [veru'kɛəriə], *s. Moss:* verrucaire *f*, herbe *f* aux verrues.

verrucose [ve'ruːkous, 'verukous], **verrucous** [ve'ruːkəs], *a.* verruqueux.

verrucosity [veru'kɔsiti], *s. Med:* verrucosité *f*.

verruga [ve'ruːgə], *s. Med:* **v. peruana, peruviana,** verruga *f* du Pérou.

versal ['vəːsl], *s.* lettrine *f* (dans un manuscrit enluminé).

versant ['vəːs(ə)nt], *s.* **1.** *Geog:* versant *m* (d'une montagne). **2.** pente *f* (de terrain, etc.).

versatile ['vəːsətail], *a.* **1.** (*a*) (*of pers.*) (i) aux talents variés; *F:* qui a plus d'une corde à son arc; **v. genius,** génie universel; **he's a v. writer,** il écrit dans tous les genres; (ii) capable d'entreprendre n'importe quoi, qui se plie à tout; **v. mind,** esprit souple; (*b*) (*of tool, machine, etc.*) polyvalent, plurivalent, d'une grande souplesse d'emploi; universel. **2.** (*a*) pivotant, capable de tourner; (*b*) *Nat.Hist:* versatile; *Bot:* **v. anther,** anthère oscillante, versatile. **3.** *A:* (*of pers.*) versatile, inconstant.

versatility [vəːsə'tiliti], *s.* **1.** (*a*) souplesse *f*, universalité *f* (d'esprit, etc.), (faculté *f* d')adaptation *f*; (*b*) polyvalence *f*, grande souplesse d'emploi (d'un outil, d'une machine, etc.). **2.** *Nat.Hist:* versatilité *f* (d'un organe, membre, etc.). **3.** *A:* (*of pers.*) versatilité, inconstance *f*.

verse[1] [vəːs], *s.* **1.** vers *m*; **a hexameter v.,** un vers hexamètre. **2.** (*of song*) couplet *m*; (*of poem, hymn*) strophe *f*, stance *f*; **a three v. poem,** un poème en trois strophes. **3.** *coll.* vers *mpl*; **to write in v. and in prose,** écrire en vers et en prose; **free v.,** vers libres; **light v.,** poésie légère. **4.** (*a*) *Ecc:* verset *m* (de la Bible); (*b*) *Mus:* solo *m* (d'un motet).

verse[2]. **1.** *v.i. A:* versifier; faire des vers. **2.** *v.tr.* (*a*) rendre, mettre (qch.) en vers; (*b*) dire, exprimer (qch.) en vers.

versed[1] [vəːst], *a.* versé (**in,** en, dans); **v. in the arts,** versé dans les arts; **to be well v. in mathematics,** avoir de profondes connaissances en mathématiques, être fort instruit dans les mathématiques.

versed[2], *a. Mth:* **v. sine,** sinus *m* verse.

verselet ['vəːslit], *s.* petit vers; poème court.

versicle ['vəːsikl], *s.* **1.** *Ecc: Typ:* verset *m.* **2.** petit vers, versicule *f*, versiculet *m.*

versicolour(ed) ['vəːsikʌlər, -kʌləd], *a.* versicolore.

versification [vəːsifi'keiʃ(ə)n], *s.* **1.** versification *f*. **2.** facture *f* (du vers); métrique *f* (d'un auteur). **3.** rédaction versifiée (d'une fable, etc.).

versifier ['vəːsifaiər], *s.* versificateur, -trice.

versify ['vəːsifai], *v.tr. & i.* versifier; mettre (un récit, etc.) en vers.

versifying ['vəːsifaiiŋ], *s.* versification *f*, mise *f* en vers.

versin ['vəːsin], **versine** ['vəːsain], *s. Mth:* sinus *m* verse.

version ['vəːʃ(ə)n], *s.* **1.** (*a*) version *f*, traduction *f*; **the English v. of the Bible,** la version anglaise de la Bible; **the Alexandrian v.,** la version des Septante; la Septante; **the English v. of a French film,** la version anglaise d'un film français; **the T.V. version of a novel, the concert v. of an opera,** l'adaptation *f* d'un roman à la télévision, d'un opéra à la salle de concert; (*b*) *Sch: Scot:* thème latin. **2.** version (des faits); interprétation *f* (d'un fait); **he gave us a very different v. of the affair,** il nous a donné de cette affaire un récit très différent; son interprétation de l'affaire est tout autre; **according to his v. he had no chance of avoiding an accident,** selon son dire, d'après lui, il a été dans l'impossibilité d'éviter un accident; **that's a very different v.,** *F:* voilà un tout autre son de cloche. **3. the military v. of this aircraft,** la version militaire de cet avion. **4.** *Obst:* version (du fœtus).

vers libres ['vɛə'liːbr], *s.pl.* vers *m* libres.

vers librist [vɛə'liːbrist], *s.* vers-libriste *m.*

verso ['vəːsou], *s.* **1.** verso *m* (d'une page); *Typ:* **printing of the v.,** retiration *f*. **2.** *Num:* revers *m* (d'une médaille).

verst [vəːst], *s. Russ.Meas:* verste *f*.

versus ['vəːsəs]. *Lt.prep. esp. Jur: Sp:* contre; **Martin v. Thomas,** Martin contre Thomas.

vert [vəːt], *s.* **1.** *Hist: Jur:* (*a*) tout ce qui, dans une forêt, croît et porte des feuilles; arbres verts; bois vert; (*b*) droit *m* de couper, d'abattre, du bois vert. **2.** *Her:* sinople *m*, vert *m.*

vertebra, *pl.* **-ae, -as** ['vəːtibrə, -iː, -əz], *s. Anat:* vertèbre *f*.

vertebral ['vəːtibrəl], *a. Anat:* vertébral, -aux; **the v. column,** la colonne vertébrale.

Vertebrata [vəːti'breitə], *s.pl. Z:* vertébrés *m.*

vertebrate ['vəːtibreit]. **1.** *a.* (*a*) (animal) vertébré; (*b*) des vertébrés. **2.** *s.* vertébré *m.*

vertebro-iliac [vəːtibrou'iliæk], *a. Anat:* vertébro-iliaque, *pl.* vertébro-iliaques.

vertex, *pl.* **-ices** ['vəːteks, -tisiːz], *s.* **1.** sommet *m* (d'un angle, cône, d'une pyramide, courbe, etc.); **v. angle,** angle *m* de rencontre; *Cmptr:* **v. matrix,** matrice associée à un graphe. **2.** *Anat:* vertex *m*; sommet *m* de la tête. **3.** *Astr:* zénith *m*, vertex.

vertical ['vəːtikl]. **1.** *a.* (*a*) vertical, -aux; **v. plane,** plan vertical; **v. line,** (ligne) verticale (*f*); **v. elevation,** altitude *f*; **v. circle,** (i) cercle vertical (d'un théodolite, etc.); (ii) *Astr:* grand cercle, vertical *m* (de la sphère céleste); **v. scale,** échelle verticale, des hauteurs; **v. exaggeration,** exagération de l'échelle verticale; *Ph:* **v. polarization,** polarisation verticale; *Const:* **v. joint,** joint montant; *T.V:* **v. scanning, sweep,** balayage vertical; *Cmptr:* **v. format,** mise en page verticale; **v. format unit tape,** bande *f* pilote; (*b*) *Artil: Ball:* **v. deflection,** correction *f* en hauteur; **v. error,** écart *m* en hauteur; *Artil:* (*anti-aircraft*) **v. lead,** correction-but *f* en site; (*c*) **v. cliff,** falaise à pic, à la verticale; *Av:* **v. bank,** virage vertical; **v. take-off, landing,** décollage, atterrissage, vertical; **v. climb,** montée *f* en chandelle; (*d*) *Pol.Ec:* **v. combination,** intégration, concentration, verticale; (*e*) *Astr:* du zénith, situé au zénith; zénithal, -aux; **v. shade,** ombre zénithale; (*f*) *Anat:* du sommet de la tête; *NAm:* **v. index,** indice *m* céphalique; (*g*) *Mth:* **v. angles,** angles opposés par le sommet. **2.** *s.* (*a*) *Mth:* verticale *f*; (*b*) *Astr:* (cercle) vertical (*m*); **prime v.,** premier vertical.

verticality [vəːti'kæliti], *s.* verticalité *f*.

vertically ['vəːtik(ə)li], *adv.* verticalement, à la verticale; (i) à plomb, d'aplomb; (ii) de haut en bas, de bas en haut; **v. to the horizon,** à la verticale, à l'aplomb, de l'horizon; **Chinese is written v.,** le chinois s'écrit de haut en bas; **to take off, land, v.,** décoller, atterrir, à la verticale; **to climb v.,** monter en chandelle; *Ph:* **v. polarized wave,** onde polarisée verticalement.

verticil ['vəːtisil], *s. Bot:* verticille *m.*

verticillate [vəː'tisileit], *a. Bot:* verticillé.

verticity [vəː'tisiti], *s. Magn:* verticité *f*.

vertiginous [vəː'tidʒinəs], *a.* **1.** (*of height, speed, etc.*) vertigineux. **2.** *A:* **to grow, get, v.,** avoir le vertige. **3.** *NAm:* inconstant, volage. **4.** (*of motion, etc.*) rotatif, rotatoire, de rotation.

vertigo ['vəːtigou], *s.* **1.** *Med:* vertige (ténébreux, apoplectique); scotodinie *f*; *F:* tournement *m* de tête; **epileptic v.,** absence *f*. **2.** *Moll:* vertigo *m.*

vertu [vəː'tjuː], *s.* goût *m* des arts, des objets d'art; **articles of v.,** objets *m* d'art; antiquités *f*, curiosités *f*.

verumontanum [veruːmɔn'teinəm], *s. Anat:* vérumontanum *m.*

verve [vəːv, vɛəv], *s.* verve *f*; **to play, act, with v.,** jouer avec verve.

vervein ['vəːvein], *s. Bot:* verveine *f*; herbe sacrée; **common v.,** verveine officinale.

vervel ['vəːvel], *s. Ven: A:* vervelle *f*.

vervet ['vəːvit], *s. Z:* **v. (monkey),** vervet *m.*

very[1] ['veri], *a. & adv.*

I. *a.* **1.** *Lit:* (*real, true*) vrai, véritable, complet, -ète, parfait; **the v. truth,** la vérité vraie; **v. God of v. God,** vrai Dieu de vrai Dieu; **the veriest fool knows that,** le plus parfait idiot sait cela; **I could not do so for v. shame,** j'aurais honte de le faire. **2.** (*emphatic use*) (*a*) (*identical*) même; **he lives in this v. place, in this v. house,** il habite ici même; **sitting in this v. room,** assis dans cette salle même; **to stop in the v. middle of the square,** s'arrêter en plein milieu, au beau milieu, de la place; **you are the v. man I wanted to see,** vous êtes justement l'homme que je voulais voir; **the v. man we want,** l'homme de la circonstance; **we shall appoint X, he is the v. man,** nous nommerons X, il est tout indiqué; **here's the v. letter I was waiting for,** voilà justement la lettre que j'attendais; **at the v. moment,** à cet instant même; **come here this v. minute!** venez ici à l'instant! **from this v. day,** à partir d'aujourd'hui même; dès aujourd'hui; **it was a year ago to the v. day,** c'était il y a un an jour pour jour; **he died a year ago this v. night,** il y a juste un an ce soir qu'il est mort; **I shall do it this v. evening,** je le ferai pas plus tard que ce soir; **these are his v. words,** ce sont là ses propres paroles; **I repeat his v. words,** je répète ce qu'il a dit mot pour mot; (*b*) **he lives at the v. end of the town,** il demeure à l'extrême limite de la ville; **at the v. beginning,** tout au commencement; **it grieves me to the v. heart,** cela me touche au plus profond du cœur; **he drank it to the v. dregs,** il le but jusqu'à la lie; **they took the v. shirt off his back,** on lui prit jusqu'à sa chemise; **he knows our v. thoughts,** il connaît jusqu'à nos pensées; **the v. children knew of it,** les enfants mêmes le savaient; (*c*) **the v. thought frightens me,** la seule pensée m'effraie; **I shudder at the v. thought of it,** je frémis rien que d'y penser.

II. *adv.* **1.** très; (*in affective uses*) fort, bien; **these herbs are v. poisonous,** ces herbes sont très toxiques; **v. good,** (i) très bon, fort bon; (ii) très bien, fort bien; **he is v. well known in Paris,** il est très connu à Paris; **you are not v. polite,** vous êtes peu poli; **not v. rich,** pas très riche; **not v. well pleased,** médiocrement satisfait; **that's v. kind of you,** c'est bien gentil de votre part; **he's v. pleasant,** il est très agréable; **if you want to be v. kind,** si vous voulez être tout à fait gentil(le); **you are v. kind,** vous êtes bien bon; **I'm not so v. sure,** je n'en suis pas plus sûr que ça; **not so v. small,** déjà pas si petit; **so v. little,** si peu; **I took only a v. little,** j'en ai pris très peu; j'en ai pris un tout petit peu (seulement); **it isn't so v. difficult,** ce n'est pas tellement difficile; ce n'est pas si difficile que ça; **I find v. few instances of it,** je trouve très peu, un très petit nombre, d'exemples; **v. v. few,** très très peu; **are you hungry?—yes, v.,** avez-vous faim?—oui, très; **a v. trying time,** une période très difficile; **a v. dazzling effect,** un effet absolument éblouissant; **he wore a v. pleased expression,** il avait l'air tout à fait satisfait; (*with past part*) **I was v. much surprised,** *F:* **v. surprised,** j'en ai été très surpris; **so v. much astonished,** tellement étonné; (*with comparatives*) **I feel v. much better,** je me sens beaucoup mieux; **it is v. much warmer,** il fait beaucoup plus chaud; **it is v. much better to wait,** il vaut bien mieux attendre. **2.** (*emphatic use*) **the v. first,** le tout premier; **we were the v. first to arrive,** nous sommes arrivés les tout premiers, tout les premiers; **the v. last,** le tout dernier; **the v. best,** le meilleur de tous; tout ce qu'il y a de mieux, de meilleur; **I did the v. best I could,** j'ai fait tout mon possible; **it was the v. last thing I expected,** c'était (absolument) la dernière chose à laquelle je m'attendais; **the v. next day,** dès le lendemain; **at the v. most, at the v. least,** tout au plus; tout au moins; **at the v. latest,** au plus tard; **the v. same,** absolument le même; précisément le même; **it's my v. own,** c'est à moi tout seul.

Very[2] ['veri, 'viəri], *Pr.n. Mil: etc:* **V. light,** fusée éclairante; **V. (light) pistol,** pistolet *m* lance-fusée(s), pistolet Very.

Vesalius [ve'seiliəs], *Pr.n.m. Med.Hist:* Vésale.

vesania [vi'seiniə], *s. Med:* vésanie *f*, aliénation mentale.

vesica, *pl.* **-ae** [ve'saikə, -iː], *s.* **1.** (*a*) *Anat: Z:* vessie *f*; *Ich:* **v. natatoria,** vessie natatoire, vésicule aérienne; (*b*) *Bot:* vésicule. **2.** *Art:* **v. piscis,** amande *f* mystique; auréole *f* elliptique.

vesical ['vesikl], *a. Anat: Med:* vésical, -aux.

vesicant ['vesikənt], *a. & s. Med: Pharm:* vésicant (*m*); *Mil:* **v. (gas),** gaz vésicant.

vesicate ['vesikeit]. **1.** *v.tr.* produire des vésicules, des ampoules, sur (la peau). **2.** *v.i.* (*a*) (*of vesicant*) produire des ampoules, des vésicules; (*b*) (*of skin, etc.*) s'ampouler.

vesication [vesi'keiʃ(ə)n], *s.* vésication *f.*

vesicatory [vesi'keitəri, ve'sikətəri], *a. & s. Med: Pharm:* vésicatoire (*m*), vésicant (*m*); vésicateur *m.*

vesicle ['vesikl], *s.* **1.** *Anat: Nat.Hist: Med:* vésicule *f*; *Med:* phlyctène *f*, ampoule *f.* **2.** *Geol:* vacuole *f.*

vesico- ['vesikou], *comb.fm.* vésico-.

vesico-intestinal [vesikouintes'tain(ə)l, -'testin(ə)l], *a. Anat:* vésico-intestinal, -aux.

vesicorectal [vesikou'rekt(ə)l], *a. Anat:* vésico-rectal, -aux.

vesico-uterine [vesikou'juːtər(a)in], *a. Anat:* vésico-utérin, -ins.

vesicovaginal [vesikouvə'dʒain(ə)l], *a. Anat:* vésico-vaginal, -aux.

vesicular [ve'sikjulər], *a.* **1.** (*a*) *Anat: Med: Nat.Hist:* vésiculaire; **v. pustule,** vésico-pustule *f, pl.* vésico-pustules; (*b*) *Med:* **normal v. murmur of the respiration,** murmure *m* vésiculaire de la respiration. **2.** *Geol:* vacuolaire.

vesiculate [ve'sikjulət], *a.* vésiculeux.

vesiculation [vesikju'leiʃ(ə)n], *s.* **1.** *Med:* vésiculation *f.* **2.** *Geol:* disposition *f* des vacuoles.

vesiculectomy [vesikju'lektəmi], *s. Surg:* vésiculectomie *f.*

vesiculitis [vesikju'laitis], *s. Med:* vésiculite *f.*

vesiculous [ve'sikjuləs], *a.* vésiculeux.

Vespasian [ves'peiʒiən], *Pr.n.m. Rom.Hist:* Vespasien.

Vesper ['vespər]. **1.** *Pr.n. Astr:* Vesper *m*; l'étoile *f* du soir. **2.** *s. Poet:* le soir; **v. breeze,** brise du soir, vespérale. **3.** *Ecc:* (*a*) *s.pl.* **vespers,** vêpres *f*, office *m* du soir; **to sing vespers,** chanter les vêpres; *Hist:* **the Sicilian Vespers,** les Vêpres Siciliennes; (*b*) **the v. (bell),** la cloche des vêpres, du soir.

vesperal ['vespərəl], *s. Ecc:* vespéral *m*, -aux.

vespertilio [vespə'tiliou], *s. Z:* vespertilion *m.*

Vespertilionidae [vespətili'ɔnidiː], *s.pl. Z:* vespertilionidés *m.*

vespertine ['vespətain], *a. Astr: Nat.Hist:* vespéral, -aux; du soir.

vesperus ['vespərəs], *s. Ent:* vespère *m.*

vespiary ['vespiəri], *s.* guêpier *m*, nid *m* de guêpes.

vespid ['vespid], *a. & s. Ent:* vespidé (*m*).

Vespidae ['vespidiː], *s.pl. Ent:* vespidés *m*, guêpes *f.*

vespiform ['vespifɔːm], *a.* vespiforme.

vespine ['vespain], *a. Ent:* des vespidés, des guêpes.

Vespucci [ves'pjuːtʃi], *Pr.n. Hist:* **Amerigo V.,** Améric Vespuce.

vessel ['ves(ə)l], *s.* **1.** (*receptacle*) récipient *m*, vase *m*; *Ph:* **communicating vessels,** vases communicants; **graduated v.,** vase gradué; *Atom.Ph:* **reactor v.,** récipient de réacteur. **2.** *Nau:* navire *m*; bateau *m*; bâtiment *m*; **sailing v.,** voilier *m*; bateau, navire, à voiles; **steam v.,** vapeur *m*; **ocean-going v.,** navire au long cours; long-courrier *m, pl.* longs-courriers; **merchant v.,** navire marchand, de commerce; **passenger v.,** navire à passagers, à voyageurs; paquebot *m*; **fishing v.,** navire de pêche; pêcheur *m*; **light v.,** bateau feu; phare flottant; *Navy:* **escort v.,** aviso *m*; escorteur *m*; **patrol v.,** vedette *f* (de la marine); **boom defence v.,** bateau gardien de barrage; **torpedo recovery v.,** ramasseur *m* de torpilles; **fishery protection v.,** garde-pêche *m inv.* **3.** *Anat: Bot:* vaisseau *m*; *Bot:* trachée *f.* **4.** *Lit:* vaisseau, vase, instrument *m*; *B:* **chosen v.,** vaisseau, vase, d'élection; **weaker v.,** (le) sexe faible; **vessels of wrath, of mercy,** vases, vaisseaux, de colère, de miséricorde.

vest[1] [vest], *s.* **1.** *Tail: NAm:* (*waistcoat*) gilet *m*; **sleeved v.,** gilet à manches, de travail; **v. pocket,** poche *f* du gilet. **2.** (*a*) (*for men*) maillot *m* de corps; *Com:* gilet (de dessous, hygiénique); (*knitted*) tricot *m* de corps; **string v.,** gilet en point noué, en filet maille (aérée); **long-sleeved v.,** gilet à manches longues; **short-sleeved v.,** gilet à manches courtes; **sleeveless v.,** gilet athlétique; *Sp:* **(running, boxing, rowing) v.,** maillot; (*b*) (*for women*) (i) chemise américaine; *Fr.C:* camisole *f*; (ii) *O:* **modesty v.,** modestie *f*; (*c*) (*for baby*) brassière *f.*

vest[2]. **1.** *v.tr.* (*a*) **to v. s.o. with authority,** investir, revêtir, qn de l'autorité; **to v. s.o. with a function,** investir qn d'une fonction; **vested with absolute authority, with the power of life and death,** investi d'une autorité absolue, du droit de vie ou de mort; *Jur:* **to v. s.o. with an inheritance,** saisir qn d'un héritage; (*b*) **to v. property in s.o.,** assigner des biens à qn; mettre qn en possession d'un bien; *Jur:* **the estate is vested in the heir the very moment the owner dies,** le mort saisit le vif, le vif chasse le mort; **vesting order,** envoi *m* en possession; **right vested in the Crown,** droit dévolu à la Couronne; **this right is vested in the Crown,** ce droit est assigné à, appartient à, la Couronne; **authority vested in the people,** autorité exercée par le peuple; (*c*) *Lit: Ecc:* vêtir, revêtir (un dignitaire, le prêtre, etc.); **to v. the altar,** parer l'autel. **2.** *v.i.* (*a*) (*of priest*) revêtir ses vêtements sacerdotaux; se revêtir; (*b*) (*of property, etc.*) **to v. in s.o.,** être dévolu à qn.

Vesta ['vestə]. **1.** *Pr.n.f. Rom.Myth: Astr:* Vesta. **2.** *s.* **(wax) v.,** allumette-bougie *f, pl.* allumettes-bougies.

vestal ['vest(ə)l]. *Rom.Ant:* **1.** *a.* (i) de Vesta; (ii) de vestale, des vestales; **v. virgin,** vestale *f.* **2.** *s.f.* vestale.

vested ['vestid], *a.* **1.** (*of priest*) dans ses vêtements sacerdotaux. **2.** *Jur:* **v. interests, rights,** droits acquis; **to have a v. interest in a firm,** avoir des capitaux, être intéressé, dans une entreprise; **to have a v. interest in maintaining, retaining, sth.,** avoir un intérêt matériel à conserver qch.; **to come up against v. interests,** se heurter contre (les gens ayant) des intérêts de longue date.

vestee [ves'tiː], *s. Cost: O:* **1.** (*for men*) faux plastron. **2.** (*for women*) modestie *f.*

vestiary ['vestiəri], *s. A:* vestiaire *m.*

vestibular [ve'stibjulər], *a. Anat: Med:* (face de l'incisive, syndrome, etc.) vestibulaire.

vestibule ['vestibjuːl], *s.* **1.** (*a*) vestibule *m*, antichambre *f*; (*b*) (*of public building*) salle *f* des pas perdus; (*c*) *NAm: Rail:* soufflet *m*; **v. car, coach,** wagon à soufflets; **v. train,** train à soufflets. **2.** *Anat:* vestibule (de l'oreille); (*of mouth*) avant-bouche *f, pl.* avant-bouches.

vestige ['vestidʒ], *s.* (*a*) vestige *m*, trace *f* (de civilisation, etc.); **not a v. of common sense, of evidence, of clothing,** pas la moindre trace, un grain, de bon sens; pas la moindre preuve; complètement nu; (*b*) *Biol:* organe *m* qui persiste à l'état rudimentaire.

vestigial [ves'tidʒiəl], *a.* (*a*) résiduel; *Elcs:* **v. side band transmission,** transmission avec bande résiduelle; (*b*) *Biol:* (organe) qui persiste à l'état rudimentaire, qui s'est atrophié au cours des âges.

vestimentary [vesti'mentəri], *a.* vestimentaire.

vesting ['vestiŋ], *s.* **1.** mise *f* des vêtements sacerdotaux (à un prêtre, par un prêtre). **2.** *Com:* étoffe *f* pour gilets.

vestiture ['vestitʃər], *s. Nat.Hist:* revêtement *m* (de poils, d'aiguillons, etc.); vestiture *f.*

vestment ['vestmənt], *s.* **1.** vêtement *m* (de cérémonie, d'apparat); *Ecc: esp.* chasuble *f*; **(church) vestments,** vêtements sacerdotaux; ornements sacerdotaux; *Ecc:* **v. maker,** chasublier *m.* **2.** *Ecc:* nappe *f* d'autel. **3.** *A:* revêtement *m* (de la terre).

vestry ['vestri], *s. Ecc:* **1.** (*a*) sacristie *f*; (*b*) salle *f* de patronage (d'un temple protestant). **2. common v.,** l'ensemble *m* des membres imposables de la paroisse (responsables de l'entretien de la fabrique); **select v.,** conseil paroissial. **3. v. (meeting),** réunion *f* du conseil paroissial. **4.** *attrib.* **v. book,** registre *m* de l'état civil de la paroisse; **v. clerk,** secrétaire *m* du conseil paroissial; **v. room,** (i) sacristie; (ii) salle *f* de réunion du conseil paroissial.

vestryman, *pl.* **-men** ['vestrimən], *s.m. Ecc:* membre du conseil paroissial.

vesture[1] ['vestjər], *s.* **1.** *Lit:* vêtement(s) *m*(*pl*). **2.** *Jur:* produits *mpl* de la terre (à l'exception des arbres).

vesture[2], *v.tr.* revêtir (un prêtre, la terre).

vesturer ['vestjərər], *s. Ecc:* **1.** sacristain *m.* **2.** sous-trésorier *m, pl.* sous-trésoriers.

Vesuvian [vi'suːviən]. **1.** *a.* vésuvien; volcanique. **2.** *s.* (*a*) *Miner:* vésuvienne *f*, vésuvianite *f*, idocrase *f*; (*b*) allumette-tison *f, pl.* allumettes-tisons; *F:* tison *m.*

vesuvianite [vi'suːviənait], *s. Miner:* vésuvianite *f*, vésuvienne *f*, idocrase *f.*

Vesuvius [vi'suːviəs], *Pr.n. Geog:* le Vésuve.

veszelyite ['vesiljait], *s. Miner:* veszélyite *f.*

vet[1] [vet], *s. F:* vétérinaire *mf*; *F:* véto *m.*

vet[2], *v.tr.* **(vetted)** *F:* **1.** (*a*) examiner, traiter (un animal); **to have a horse vetted,** soumettre un cheval au traitement, à l'examen, d'un vétérinaire; (*b*) examiner (qn) médicalement; **to get vetted by a doctor,** se faire examiner par un médecin. **2.** (*a*) revoir, corriger, mettre au point (l'œuvre littéraire de qn); (*b*) *Cmptr:* valider (un programme); (*c*) *Adm: etc:* effectuer un contrôle de sécurité sur (un candidat, etc.).

vet[3], *a. & s. NAm:* = VETERAN.

vetch [vetʃ], *s. Bot:* (*a*) vesce *f*; **common v.,** vesce commune; (*b*) **bitter v.,** orobe *m or f.*

vetchling ['vetʃliŋ], *s. Bot:* **(yellow) v.,** gesse *f* des prés; **hairy v.,** gesse velue.

veteran ['vet(ə)r(ə)n]. **1.** *s.* (*a*) (*pers.*) vétéran *m*; *F:* vieux *m* de la vieille; **the veterans of 1870,** les anciens *m* de 1870; **(war) v.,** ancien combattant; (*b*) *For:* (*tree*) ancien de première classe. **2.** *a.* (*a*) de vétéran, des vétérans; vieux, *f.* vieille, ancien, aguerri, expérimenté; **v. soldier,** vieux soldat, soldat aguerri; **v. army,** armée *f* de vétérans; **v. golfer,** vétéran du golf; (*b*) *Aut:* **v. car,** (i) (*in Eng.*) ancêtre *m* (vieille voiture d'avant 1905), (ii) (*international categories*) vétéran *m* (1905–1918).

veterinarian [vet(ə)ri'nɛəriən], *s.* vétérinaire *mf.*

veterinary ['vet(ə)rin(ə)ri], *a.* vétérinaire; **v. (surgeon),** vétérinaire *mf.*

vetiver ['vetivər], *s. Bot:* vétiver *m.*

veto[1], *pl.* **-oes** ['viːtou, -ouz], *s.* veto *m*; **to put, place, set, a v., one's v., on sth.,** mettre le veto, son veto, à qch.; **right of v.,** droit *m* de veto; **to have the right, power, of v.,** avoir voix négative, avoir le veto; **absolute v.,** veto absolu; **suspensive v.,** veto suspensif; **local v.,** interdiction du débit des boissons alcooliques votée par les habitants d'une localité.

veto[2], *v.tr.* mettre son veto à (qch.); interdire (qch.).

vetting ['vetiŋ], *s.* (*a*) *F:* examen (médical, etc.); contrôle *m* de sécurité (sur un candidat, etc.); (*b*) *Cmptr:* passage *m* de validation, de contrôle préalable.

vex [veks], *v.tr.* **1.** vexer, fâcher, ennuyer, contrarier, chagriner (qn). **2.** *A:* faire de la peine à (qn); affliger (qn). **3.** *Lit:* troubler, tourmenter, agiter (la mer, etc.).

vexation [vek'seiʃ(ə)n], *s.* **1.** (*a*) action *f* de vexer; *O:* vexation *f*; **v. on the part of the landlord,** tracasserie *f*, harassement *m*, de la part du propriétaire; (*b*) action de se tourmenter; **v. of spirit,** tourment *m.* **2.** (*a*) contrariété *f*, ennui *m*, désagrément *m*; **the little vexations of life,** les petites contrariétés, petits déboires, de la vie; (*b*) chagrin *m*, dépit *m*; **imagine my v.!** pensez si j'étais contrarié, humilié, si cela m'a chagriné!

vexatious [vek'seiʃəs], *a.* **1.** (*of pers., thg*) fâcheux, irritant, ennuyeux, contrariant; tracassier; (*of pers.*) vexateur, -trice; **it's most v. to miss one's train,** c'est vexant, ennuyeux, de manquer son train. **2.** *Jur:* (*of measure, suit, tax*) vexatoire.

vexatiously [vek'seiʃəsli], *adv.* d'une manière contrariante, vexante. **2.** à seule fin de contrarier.

vexatiousness [vek'seiʃəsnis], *s.* **1.** caractère fâcheux, contrariant (de qn, qch.). **2.** nature *f* vexatoire (d'une loi, etc.).

vexed [vekst], *a.* **1.** vexé, contrarié, mortifié, dépité. **2. v. question,** question controversée, souvent débattue, très débattue, non résolue.

vexil ['veksil], *s. Bot:* étendard *m.*

vexillar ['veksilər], *a. Bot: Orn:* vexillaire.

vexillary ['veksiləri]. *Rom.Ant:* (*a*) *s.* vexillaire *m*; (*b*) *a.* (soldat) vexillaire.

vexillate ['veksilət], *a. Bot:* vexillé.

vexillum, *pl.* **-a** [vek'siləm, -ə], *s.* **1.** (*a*) *Rom.Ant:* (i) vexille *m*, enseigne *f*; (ii) troupe *f* vexillaire; (*b*) *Ecc:* écharpe *f* (de crosse d'évêque). **2.** *Bot:* étendard *m.* **3.** *Orn:* vexille (de plume).

vexing ['veksiŋ], *a.* vexant, contrariant, ennuyeux, chagrinant; *P:* bisquant.

via ['vaiə], *prep.* via, par la voie de; par (une route); **we came home v. Ostend,** nous sommes revenus par, via, Ostende; **to learn sth. v. the press,** apprendre qch. par la voie de la presse.

viability[1] [vaiə'biliti], *s.* (*a*) *Biol: Obst:* viabilité *f*, aptitude *f* à vivre; (*b*) viabilité (d'un projet).

viability[2], *s. A:* viabilité *f*, bon état (d'une route).

viable[1] ['vaiəbl], *a.* (*a*) *Biol: Obst:* viable, apte à vivre; (*b*) (gouvernement, etc.) viable; (projet, etc.) viable, praticable.

viable[2], *a. A:* (route) viable, en bon état.

viaduct ['vaiədʌkt], *s.* viaduc *m.*

viagraph ['vaiəgræf], *s. Civ.E:* viagraphe *m.*

vial ['vaiəl], *s.* fiole *f*; *Lit:* **to pour out the vials of one's wrath,** lâcher la bonde à sa colère.

viameter [vai'æmitər], *s. Surv:* odomètre *m.*

viand ['vaiənd], *s. A: & Lit:* mets *m*; *usu.pl.* **viands,** aliments *m*; **choice viands,** mets délicats.

viaticum [vai'ætikəm], *s.* **1.** *Ecc:* viatique *m.* **2.** (*a*) *O:* provisions *fpl* (en vue d'un voyage), viatique; (*b*) (*travel allowance*) viatique.

vibes [vaibz], *s.pl. F:* **1.** *Mus:* vibraphone *m.* **2.** vibrations *f*; **my v. are good,** ça marche, ça gaze.

vibex, *pl.* **-ices** ['vaibeks, -isiːz], *s. Med:* vergeture *f*; *pl.* vibices *f.*

vibist ['vaibist], *s. Mus: F:* vibraphoniste *mf.*

vibracularium, *pl.* **-ia** [vaibrækju'lɛəriəm, -iə], **vibraculum,** *pl.* **-a** [vai'brækjuləm, -ə], *s. Z:* vibraculaire *m.*

vibrancy ['vaibrənsi], *s.* vibrance *f*, qualité vibrante.

vibrant ['vaibrənt], *a.* (*of string, sound, pulse, etc.*) vibrant; **city v. with commercial activity,** ville palpitante d'activité commerciale; **v. personality,** nature vibrante, émotive.

vibraphone ['vaibrəfoun], *s. Mus:* vibraphone *m.*

vibrate [vai'breit]. **1.** *v.i.* (*a*) vibrer; (i) trépider; (ii) retentir **(in, on, the ear,** à l'oreille); **voice vibrating with emotion,** voix vibrante d'émotion; (*b*) *Ph:* vibrer, osciller. **2.**

v.tr. (*a*) faire vibrer; agiter; (i) faire trépider; (ii) faire osciller; *Const:* **vibrated concrete,** béton (per)vibré, désaéré; (*b*) **pendulum that vibrates seconds,** pendule qui a une durée d'oscillation d'une seconde.

vibratile ['vaibrətail], *a. Biol:* (*of cilium*) vibratile.

vibrating[1] [vai'breitiŋ], *a.* vibrant; (mouvement) vibratoire, oscillant; **v. sieve, screen,** tamis oscillant; *Aut:* **v. plate of the horn,** disque *m* de résonance de l'avertisseur; *Opt:* **v. mirror,** miroir oscillant; *Civ.E:* **v. roller,** rouleau vibrateur; *El:* **v. capacitor, rectifier, relay,** condensateur, redresseur, relais, vibrant; **v. current,** courant vibré; **v. contactor,** vibreur *m.*

vibrating[2], *s. Tchn:* vibrage *m*; *Const:* **v. of concrete,** vibrage du béton; *Paperm:* **v. frame,** appareil *m* de branlement (de la toile).

vibration [vai'breiʃ(ə)n], *s.* **1.** vibration *f*; *Ph: etc:* oscillation *f*, pulsation *f*; **atomic v.,** vibration des atomes; **erratic v.,** vibration irrégulière; *Opt:* **linear v.,** vibration rectiligne; *Veh: Mch: etc:* **v. of the car windows,** trépidation *f* des vitres d'une voiture; *Const:* **insulating of the foundations of buildings against v.,** isolement *m* antivibratile des fondations des bâtiments; *Mec.E: etc:* **anti-v. mounting,** montage *m* anti-vibrations; **v. damper,** amortisseur *m* de vibrations; **v. meter,** vibromètre *m*; **v.(-)free,** exempt de vibration(s); **v. proof,** résistant aux vibrations. **2.** *Const:* (per)vibration *f*, vibrage *m* (du béton).

vibrational [vai'breiʃ(ə)nl], *a.* de (la) vibration, des vibrations; d'oscillation, des oscillations; vibratoire; **v. energy,** énergie de vibration, d'oscillation; **v. spectrum,** spectre de vibration; **v. period of the magnetic compass,** période vibratoire du compas magnétique.

vibrato [vi'brɑ:tou], *s. Mus:* vibrato *m.*

vibrator [vai'breitər], *s.* **1.** (*a*) *El:* vibrateur *m*, vibreur *m*; trembleur *m* (de bobine); **quartz v.,** vibrateur à quartz; **synchronous v.,** vibreur synchrone; **v. coil,** bobine *f* à trembleur; (*b*) *Mus:* anche *f* (d'harmonium, etc.); (*c*) *Typ:* distributeur *m* (d'encre). **2.** (*a*) *Const:* pervibr(at)eur *m* (pour béton); (*b*) *Med:* (*for massage*) **(electric) v.,** vibromasseur *m*; (*c*) *Agr:* **v. digger, tiller,** vibroculteur *m.*

vibratory [vai'breitəri], *a. Ph: etc:* vibratoire.

vibrio, *pl.* **-oes** ['vaibriou, -ouz], **vibrion,** *pl.* **-ones** ['vaibriən, -'ouni:z], *s. Bac:* vibrion *m.*

vibrionic [vaibri'ɔnik], *a. Bac: Med:* vibrionien; *Vet:* **v. abortion,** vibriose *f.*

vibriosis, *pl.* **-oses** [vaibri'ousis, -'ousi:z], *s. Vet:* vibriose *f.*

vibrissae [vai'brisi:], *s.pl. Anat: Z:* vibrisses *f.*

vibrograph ['vaibrougræf], *s. Ph:* vibrographe *m.*

vibro machine ['vaibroumәʃi:n], *s. Med:* vibromasseur *m.*

vibromassage [vaibrou'mæsɑ:ʒ], *s. Med:* massage *m* vibratoire, vibro(-)massage *m*, sismothérapie *f.*

vibrometer [vai'brɔmitər], *s. Ph:* vibromètre *m.*

vibroscope ['vaibrəskoup], *s. Ph:* vibroscope *m.*

viburnum [vai'bə:nəm], *s. Bot:* viorne *f.*

vicar ['vikər], *s.* **1.** *Ch. of Eng:* ecclésiastique préposé à l'administration d'une paroisse et titulaire du bénéfice, mais non de la dîme; = curé *m*; *Can:* vicaire de paroisse. **2.** *Ch. of Eng:* **clerk v., lay v., secular v., v. choral,** chantre *m.* **3.** *R.C.Ch:* **Cardinal v.,** cardinal-vicaire *m*, *pl.* cardinaux-vicaires; **v. apostolic,** vicaire apostolique. **4. the V. of (Jesus) Christ,** le vicaire de Jésus-Christ, le Pape.

vicarage ['vikəridʒ], *s. Ch. of Eng:* **1.** (*benefice*) cure *f* (d'un *vicar*). **2.** (*residence*) presbytère *m* (d'un *vicar*); cure.

vicar-general ['vikə'dʒen(ə)r(ə)l], *s. Ch. of Eng: R.C.Ch:* vicaire général, grand vicaire.

vicariate [vai'kɛərieit], *s.* **1.** *Ch. of Eng: R.C.Ch:* vicariat *m.* **2.** *Ch. of Eng:* office *m*, autorité *f*, de *vicar.*

vicarious [vai'kɛəriəs], *a.* **1.** (*of power, authority*) délégué. **2.** (*a*) (travail) fait (i) par un autre, (ii) pour un autre; (châtiment) souffert (i) par un autre, (ii) pour un autre; **v. pleasure,** plaisir donné par le plaisir d'un autre; *Theol:* **v. satisfaction,** satisfaction vicaire; (*b*) (méthode) de substitution. **3.** *Physiol:* (organe, etc.) vicariant.

vicariously [vai'kɛəriəsli], *adv.* (*a*) par délégation, par délégué; par substitution, par procuration; (*b*) à la place d'un autre; (*c*) **to live v.,** vivre par l'imagination.

vicariousness [vai'kɛəriəsnis], *s. Physiol:* vicariance *f.*

vice[1] [vais], *s.* **1.** vice *m*; (*a*) **to live in v.,** vivre dans le vice; **to sink into v.,** tomber dans le vice, la débauche; (*b*) **avarice is a v.,** l'avarice est un vice; **his many vices,** ses nombreux vices. **2.** défaut *m*, défectuosité *f*, imperfection *f*; *Jur:* (*in deed, etc.*) **v. of form,** vice de forme. **3.** (i) vice, (ii) nature vicieuse (d'un cheval); **stable v.,** tic *m.* **4.** *A.Th:* **the V.,** (i) le Vice, (ii) le bouffon.

vice[2], *s. Tls:* étau *m*; **standing v., leg v., staple v.,** étau à pied, à table; **bench v.,** étau, servante *f*, d'établi; âne *m*; **instantaneous-grip v.,** étau à serrage instantané; **hand v.,** étau à main, à vis; tenaille *f* à vis; détret *m*; **blacksmith's v.,** étau à chaud; **v. with detachable jaws,** étau à mâchoires rapportées; **machine v.,** étau mécanique; **shaping v.,** étau-limeur *m*, *pl.* étaux-limeurs; **twisting v.,** mâchoire *f* à tordre; **v. bench,** étau roulant, établi roulant pour étaux; banc *m* d'âne; **v. cap, clamp, jaw,** (*of metal*) mordache *f*; (*of wood*) mordache, entibois *m*; **bevelled v. clamp,** tenaille à chanfrein(er); **v. plate,** étau-plateau *m*, *pl.* étaux-plateaux; plateau-étau *m*, *pl.* plateaux-étaux; **v. press,** presse *f* à vis.

vice[3], *v.tr.* serrer (qch.) dans un étau; coincer (qch.).

vice[4], *s. F:* = VICE-CHAIRMAN, -PRESIDENT; *Sch:* = VICE-CHANCELLOR.

vice[5] ['vaisi], *prep.* en remplacement de (qn); **Treasurer: Mr Martin v. Mr Thomas (resigned),** Trésorier: M. Martin qui succède à M. Thomas démissionnaire.

vice- [vais], *pref.* vice-.

vice-admiral [vais'ædmərəl], *s.* vice-amiral *m*, -aux; **the vice-admiral's flagship,** *F:* le vice-amiral.

vice-admiralship, -admiralty [vais'ædmərəlʃip, -'ædmərəlti], *s.* vice-amirauté *f*, *pl.* vice-amirautés.

vice-chairman, *pl.* **-men** [vais'tʃɛəmən], *s.* vice-président, -ente, *pl.* vice-président(e)s.

vice-chairmanship [vais'tʃɛəmənʃip], *s.* vice-présidence *f*, *pl.* vice-présidences.

vice-chamberlain [vais'tʃeimbəlin], *s.* vice-chambellan *m*, *pl.* vice-chambellans.

vice-chancellor [vais'tʃɑ:nsələr], *s.* **1.** vice-chancelier *m*, *pl.* vice-chanceliers; *Ecc:* cardinal vice-chancelier (de la Chancellerie de Rome). **2.** *Sch:* recteur *m* (d'une université).

vice-chancellorship [vais'tʃɑ:nsələʃip], *s.* **1.** fonction *f*, dignité *f*, de vice-chancelier. **2.** *Sch:* rectorat *m* (d'université).

vice-consul [vais'kɔns(ə)l], *s.* vice-consul *m*, *pl.* vice-consuls.

vice-consular [vais'kɔnsjulər], *a.* de, du, vice-consul; des vice-consuls.

vice-consulate [vais'kɔnsjulat], *s.* (*post or premises*) vice-consulat *m*, *pl.* vice-consulats.

vice-consulship [vais'kɔns(ə)lʃip], *s.* vice-consulat *m.*

vicegerent [vais'dʒer(ə)nt], *s.* représentant *m*, délégué *m*; *Ecc: A:* vice-gérent *m*, *pl.* vice-gérents.

vice-governor [vais'gʌvənər], *s.* sous-gouverneur *m*, *pl.* sous-gouverneurs.

vice-legate [vais'legət], *s.* vice-légat *m*, *pl.* vice-légats.

vice-legateship [vais'legətʃip], *s.* vice-légation *f.*

vicelike ['vaislaik], *a.* **squeezed in a v. grip,** serré dans une poigne de fer.

vice-marshal [vais'mɑ:ʃ(ə)l], *s. Mil.Av:* **air v.-m.,** général *m*, -aux, de division aérienne.

vicenary ['visənəri], *a. Mth:* (*of notation*) vicésimal, -aux.

vicennial [vi'seniəl], *a.* vicennal, -aux.

Vicenza [vi'tʃentsə], *Pr.n. Geog:* Vicence.

vice-presidency, vice-presidentship [vais'prezidənsi, -dəntʃip], *s.* vice-présidence *f.*

vice-president [vais'prezid(ə)nt], *s.* (*a*) vice-président *m*, *pl.* vice-présidents; (*b*) sous-délégué, -ée, *pl.* sous-délégués, -ées (d'une société de bienfaisance).

vice-presidential [vaisprezi'denʃ(ə)l], *a.* de, du, vice-président; des vice-présidents.

vice-principal [vais'prinsip(ə)l], *s. Sch:* sous-directeur, -trice, *pl.* -teurs, -trices; sous-principal *m*, -aux; préfet *m* des études.

vice-rector [vais'rektər], *s.* vice-recteur *m*, *pl.* vice-recteurs.

vice-rectorship [vais'rektəʃip], *s.* vice-rectorat *m.*

viceregal [vais'ri:gl], *a.* vice-royal, -aux.

vice-regent [vais'ri:dʒənt], *s.* **1.** suppléant, -e, du régent, de la régente. **2.** *Ecc: A:* vice-gérent *m*, *pl.* vice-gérents.

vice-reine [vais'rein], *s.f.* vice-reine, *pl.* vice-reines.

viceroy ['vaisrɔi], *s.m.* **1.** vice-roi, *pl.* vice-rois. **2.** *Ent:* **v. (butterfly),** (papillon *m*) vice-roi.

viceroyalty [vais'rɔiəlti], *s.* **1.** (*status*) vice-royauté *f.* **2.** (*domain*) vice-royaume *m*, *pl.* vice-royaumes; *Hist:* **the Spanish v. of Mexico,** le vice-royaume espagnol de Mexico.

vicesimal [vai'sesim(ə)l], *a. Mth:* vigésimal, -aux.

vice versa [vais(i)'və:sə]. *Lt. adv.phr.* vice versa; réciproquement.

Vichy ['vi:ʃi:], *Pr.n. Geog:* Vichy; *Hist:* **the V. government,** le gouvernement de Vichy; *Med:* **V. (water),** eau *f* de Vichy; **V. tablet,** pastille *f* de Vichy.

Vichyism ['vi:ʃiizm], *s. Hist:* vichysme *m.*

Vichyist ['vi:ʃiist], *a. & s.* vichyste (*mf*), (homme) de Vichy; vichyssois, -oise.

vicinage ['visinidʒ], *s. A:* **1.** = VICINITY. **2.** *coll.* **the v.,** les voisins *m.*

vicinal ['visin(ə)l], *a.* **1.** *A:* (chemin) vicinal, -aux. **2.** *Ch:* vicinal.

vicinity [vi'siniti], *s.* **1.** voisinage *m*, proximité *f* (**to, with,** de). **2.** abords *mpl*, alentours *mpl*, environs *mpl*; **the church and its v.,** l'église et ses abords; **in the v. of Dover,** (i) à proximité de, du côté de, dans les environs de, Douvres; (ii) *Nau:* dans les parages de Douvres; **in the immediate v. of the factory,** aux abords de l'usine.

vicious ['viʃəs], *a.* **1.** (*of habits, practice, pers.*) vicieux, corrompu, dépravé. **2.** (*of horse*) vicieux, méchant, hargneux, rétif. **3.** (*of language, reasoning*) vicieux, défectueux, incorrect. **4.** (*a*) méchant, haineux; **v. criticism,** critique méchante, pleine d'acrimonie; **v. gossip,** commérages méchants; **she has a v. tongue,** c'est une mauvaise langue; (*b*) rageur; **to give a v. tug at the bell,** tirer rageusement la sonnette; **v. fight,** combat acharné.

viciously ['viʃəsli], *adv.* **1.** vicieusement. **2.** incorrectement. **3.** (*a*) méchamment, haineusement; (*b*) rageusement; **he banged the door v.,** il a claqué rageusement la porte.

viciousness ['viʃəsnis], *s.* **1.** nature vicieuse (d'un cheval, des mœurs de qn). **2.** méchanceté *f* (d'une critique, etc.).

vicissitude [vi'sisitju:d], *s.* vicissitude *f*; péripétie *f*; **the vicissitudes of life,** les vicissitudes de la vie; **the vicissitudes of fortune,** les changements *m*, retours *m*, de la fortune.

vicissitudinous [visisi'tju:dinəs], *a.* sujet à, marqué par, des vicissitudes.

victim ['viktim], *s.* **1.** victime (offerte en sacrifice). **2. to be the v. of s.o.,** être la victime de qn; **v. of s.o.'s trickery,** victime, dupe *f*, de la fourberie de qn; **a v. to his devotion,** victime de son dévouement; **v. of an accident,** accidenté, -ée; (*of fire*) incendié, -ée; (*of flood*) inondé, -ée; (*of fire, flood, shipwreck, etc.*) sinistré, -ée; **to die a v. to smallpox,** mourir victime de la petite vérole; **to fall a v. to a press campaign, to one's duty,** périr, être, (la) victime d'une campagne de presse, de son devoir; **to fall a v. to s.o.'s charm,** succomber au charme de qn; **to offer oneself as a ready v.,** tendre le cou; **to make a v. of oneself,** se poser en victime.

victimization [viktimai'zeiʃ(ə)n], *s.* **1.** prise *f* (de qn) comme victime; (*b*) (*in strike settlement*) **there is to be no v.,** on n'exercera pas de représailles contre des individus. **2. a case of v.,** une duperie.

victimize ['viktimaiz], *v.tr.* **1.** (*a*) prendre (qn) comme victime; (*b*) exercer des représailles contre (les meneurs d'une grève, etc.); **he felt that he was being victimized,** il se croyait brimé. **2.** tromper, duper, escroquer (qn).

victor[1] ['viktər], *s.* vainqueur *m*, triomphateur, -trice; **the victors of the ladies' doubles,** les vainqueurs du double dames.

Victor[2], *Pr.n.m.* Victor.

Victoria [vik'tɔ:riə]. **1.** *Pr.n.f.* Victoire, Victoria; *Hist:* **Queen V.,** la reine Victoria; *Mil: etc:* **V. Cross,** Croix *f* de Victoria; *Can:* **V. Day,** fête nationale célébrée le lundi qui précède le 24 mai. **2.** *s.* (*a*) *Bot:* **v. regia,** victoria *f* regia, maïs *m* d'eau; (*b*) *Hort:* **v. (plum),** (variété *f* de) grosse prune rouge; (*c*) *Orn:* (variété de) pigeon *m* domestique; (*d*) *A.Veh:* victoria *f.*

Victorian [vik'tɔ:riən]. **1.** (*a*) *a.* victorien, du règne de la reine Victoria; (*b*) *s.* Victorien, -ienne. **2.** *a. & s. Geog:* (originaire *mf*, habitant, -ante) du Victoria (en Australie).

Victoriana [viktɔ:ri'ɑ:nə], *s.* bric-à-brac *m*, antiquités *f*, de l'ère victorienne.

Victorianism [vik'tɔ:riənizm], *s.* goûts *mpl*, esprit *m*, de l'ère victorienne.

Victorine ['viktəri:n], *a. & s. Ecc.Hist:* **V. (canon),** victorin *m.*

victorious [vik'tɔ:riəs], *a.* **1.** victorieux, vainqueur *m*; **to be v. over s.o.,** être victorieux de qn; vaincre, battre, qn; *Sp:* **Alice Martin who was v. in the ladies' singles,** Alice Martin, vainqueur du simple dames. **2.** (journée, etc.) de victoire.

victoriously [vik'tɔ:riəsli], *adv.* victorieusement, en vainqueur.

victory ['viktəri], *s.* **1.** victoire *f*; **to gain a, the, v.,** remporter la victoire (**over,** sur); être victorieux; remporter la palme (dans un concours, etc.). **2.** *Art:* **(statue of) v.,** victoire; **the Winged V. of Samothrace,** la Victoire ailée de Samothrace.

victual[1] ['vitl], *s.* **1.** *O:* aliment *m.* **2. victuals,** (i) vivres *m*, provisions *f*; (ii) victuailles *f*; **he doesn't quarrel with his victuals,** il ne boude pas sur la nourriture.

victual[2], *v.* **(victualled** ['vitld]**) 1.** *v.tr.* approvisionner; fournir de vivres, ravitailler (un navire, une garnison). **2.** *v.i.* (*a*) s'approvisionner, se ravitailler; (*b*) *F:O:* manger, bâfrer.

victualler ['vitlər], *s.* **1.** (*a*) approvisionneur *m*; pourvoyeur *m*; fournisseur *m* de vivres; (*b*) **licensed v.,** débitant *m* de boissons, de spiritueux; **the licensed victuallers,** le commerce des boissons et spiritueux. **2.** navire *m* de ravitaillement.

victualling ['vitliŋ], *s.* approvisionnement *m*, ravitaillement *m*; *Mil: etc:* **v. book,** cahier *m*, rôle *m*, de rations; *Navy:* **v. office,** bureau *m* des subsistances.

vicuña [vi'ku:njə], **vicuna, vicugna** [vi'ku:njə, vi'kju:nə], *s. Z: Tex:* vigogne *f*.

vidame ['vi:dæm], *s. Fr. Hist:* vidame *m*.

vidameship ['vi:dæmʃip], *s. Fr. Hist:* vidamé *m*.

vide ['videi, 'vaidi]. *Lt. imp.* voir.

videlicet [vi'di:lisit, vi'deiliket], *adv.* à savoir; c'est-à-dire.

video ['vidiou]. **1.** *s. T.V:* vidéo *m*; vision *f*; (voie *f*) image *f*. **2.** *a. Elcs: T.V:* vidéo *inv*; **v. amplifier,** amplificateur *m* vidéo; **v. characteristics,** caractéristiques *f* de la voie image; **v. circuit,** circuit *m* vidéo; **v. frequency,** vidéofréquence *f*, fréquence *f* image; **v. signal,** signal *m* de vision; **v. tape,** bande *f* vidéo; **v. tape recorder,** magnétoscope *m*; **v. tape recording,** enregistrement *m* magnétoscope; magnétoscopie *f*; **v. cassette,** vidéocassette *f*; *Cmptr:* **v. printer,** imprimante *f* vidéo.

videophone ['vidioufoun], *s.* vidéophone *m*; **v. system,** visiotéléphonie *f*.

vidian ['vidiən], *a. Anat:* (*of artery, canal, nerve*) vidien.

Vidicon ['vidikɔn], *s. R.t.m. T.V:* Vidicon *m*.

vidimus ['vaidiməs], *s. Jur:* vidimus *m*.

viduage ['vidjuidʒ], *s. A:* **1.** veuvage *m*, viduité *f*. **2.** *coll.* veuves *fpl*.

vidual ['vidjuəl], *a. A:* vidual, -aux; de veuve.

viduity [vi'dju:iti], *s. A:* viduité *f*, veuvage *m*.

vie [vai], *v.* (**vied** [vaid], **vying** ['vaiiŋ]) **1.** *v.i.* le disputer (**with s.o.,** à qn); rivaliser, entrer en rivalité, lutter (**with s.o.,** avec qn); **to v. with s.o. in beauty,** le disputer en beauté à qn, avec qn; rivaliser de beauté avec qn; **to v. with s.o. in politeness, in wit,** faire assaut de politesse, d'esprit, avec qn; **to v. with each other in doing sth.,** (*of two pers.*) faire qch. à l'envi l'un de l'autre, rivaliser d'efforts l'un avec l'autre; (*of more than two pers.*) faire qch. à l'envi les uns des autres, faire qch. à qui mieux mieux; **they v. with one another as to who shall speak,** c'est à qui parlera; **they vied with one another in generosity,** il y eut entre eux un combat de générosité. **2.** *v.tr. U.S:* mettre (de l'argent) en jeu; jouer (une somme).

vielle [vi'el], *s. A.Mus:* vielle *f*.

Vienna [vi'enə], *Pr.n. Geog:* Vienne *f*.

Viennese [viə'ni:z, vie-]. *Geog:* **1.** *a.* viennois; *Bak:* **V. bread,** viennoiserie *f*. **2.** *s.* Viennois, -oise.

Vietnam [viet'nɑ:m, -'næm], *Pr.n. Geog:* le Vietnam.

Vietnamese [vietnə'mi:z]. *Geog:* **1.** *a.* vietnamien. **2.** *s.* Vietnamien, -ienne.

view[1] [vju:], *s.* vue *f*. **1.** (*a*) regard *m*, coup *m* d'œil, inspection *f*, examen *m*; **I should like to get a nearer v. of it,** je voudrais l'examiner de plus près; **the collection is on v. (to the public),** la collection est ouverte au public; **private v.,** entrée *f* sur invitation personnelle; avant-première *f*, *pl.* avant-premières (d'une exposition, etc.); vernissage *m* (d'une exposition de peinture); **v. day,** avant-première; (*b*) *Jur:* descente *f* sur les lieux. **2.** (*a*) **exposed to v.,** exposé aux regards *m*; à la vue de tous; **hidden from v.,** caché aux regards; **in v.,** en vue; **in full v. of the crowd,** sous les regards de (toute) la foule; **at last a hotel came into v.,** enfin nous avons aperçu un hôtel; **we were in v. of land, of Dieppe,** nous étions en vue de la terre, en vue de Dieppe; **land in v.!** terre! (*b*) (*of telescope*) **field of v.,** champ *m*; *Opt: Phot:* **angle of v.,** angle *m* de champ. **3.** (*scene, prospect*) (*a*) vue, perspective *f*; champ visuel; **front v.,** vue de face; **front v. of the hotel,** l'hôtel vu de face; **what a splendid v.!** quel coup d'œil magnifique; **here you have a good v. of the castle,** d'ici on a une très belle vue du château; **one gets a beautiful v. from the hill,** de la colline se découvre un magnifique tableau; **you will get a better v. from here,** vous verrez mieux d'ici; **it was worth while coming up for the v.,** le panorama valait le déplacement; (*on hill, etc.*) **v. indicator,** guide *m* panoramique; **views of Paris,** vues de Paris; *Opt:* **dissolving views,** vues fondantes; (*b*) *Arch: Draw: etc.:* **front, back, v.,** élévation *f* du devant, du derrière; **sectional v.,** vue en coupe; profil *m*; écorché *m*; **exploded v.,** (vue) éclatée (*f*); **to keep sth. in v.,** ne pas perdre qch. de vue. **4.** (*mental survey*) aperçu *m*, exposé *m*; **to offer a general v. of the subject,** donner un aperçu général de la question. **5.** manière *f* de voir; opinion *f*, idée *f*, avis *m*, conception *f*; **to express a v.,** exprimer une opinion, un avis; **to have sound views on a question,** avoir des vues saines, des opinions saines, sur une question; **to take a right v. of things,** voir juste; **he always takes a wrong v. of things,** il voit toujours faux; **to hold extreme views,** avoir des idées extrémistes; **to have very decided views on sth.,** avoir des idées arrêtées au sujet de qch.; **to take a shortsighted v. of sth.,** voir qch. en myope; **what are your views on the matter?** comment envisagez-vous la question? **in my v.,** à mon avis; **my v. is that we should accept the offer,** mon opinion c'est que nous devrions accepter l'offre; **to share s.o.'s views,** partager les sentiments de qn. **6. in v. of what has happened,** en considération de, eu égard à, par suite de, en raison de, ce qui est arrivé; **in v. of these facts,** en présence de ces faits; prenant en considération tous ces faits; **in v. of the state of things,** devant cet état de choses; **in v. of this answer,** considérant cette réponse; **in v. of the distance, of the great heat,** vu l'éloignement, la grande chaleur; **in v. of existing divergencies,** étant donné les divergences qui existent. **7.** (*intention*) vue, intention *f*, but *m*, dessein *m*; **to fall in with, meet, s.o.'s views,** entrer dans les vues de qn; se mettre d'accord avec qn; **will this meet your views?** cela vous conviendra-t-il? **to have sth. in v.,** avoir qch. en vue; méditer (un voyage, etc.); **to have nothing but one's own interests in v.,** rapporter tout à soi, à ses intérêts; **this law has two objects, two aims, in v.,** cette loi vise un double but; **to attain the end that we have in v.,** pour aboutir aux fins que nous poursuivons; **what is the object in v.?** à quoi vise tout cela? **with a special object in v.,** avec, dans, un but précis; **with this in v.,** dans cet objet, à cette fin; **I have nothing in v. for this evening,** je n'ai rien en vue pour ce soir; **whom have you in v.?** qui avez-vous en vue? à qui pensez-vous? vous avez un candidat (à proposer)? **with a v. to, a v. of, doing sth.,** en vue de, dans le but de, dans l'intention de, faire qch.; avec l'idée de, dans l'idée de, dans le dessein de, faire qch.; **with a v. to carrying out this plan,** en vue de réaliser ce projet; **with a v. to learning the truth,** dans le but, dans l'intention, d'apprendre la vérité; **negotiations with a v. to an alliance,** négociations visant une alliance.

view[2], *v.tr.* **1.** (*a*) regarder, porter sa vue sur (qn, qch.); **to v. (photographic) slides,** visionner des diapositives; *T.V:* **to v. a programme,** regarder une émission; (*b*) inspecter, examiner (qch.); visiter (une maison à vendre). **2.** envisager, regarder (qch.); **the subject may be viewed in different ways,** on peut envisager la question à des points de vue différents; **I don't v. it in that light,** je ne l'envisage pas ainsi; **the proposal was viewed unfavourably by the authorities,** la proposition était regardée d'un œil peu favorable par les autorités; **to v. everything from a personal angle,** rapporter tout à soi. **3.** voir, apercevoir (qn, qch.); *Ven:* **to v. the fox away,** voir débucher le renard. **4.** *v.i. T.V:* regarder la télévision.

viewer ['vju:ər], *s.* **1.** (*pers.*) (*a*) spectateur, -trice; *T.V:* téléspectateur, -trice; (*b*) inspecteur, -trice; expert *m*; **colliery v.,** gérant *m* de mine. **2.** (*device*) visionneuse *f*, passe-vues *m inv*.

viewfinder ['vju:faindər], *s.* **1.** *Phot:* viseur *m*; **brilliant v.,** viseur clair. **2.** *T.V:* viseur électronique.

view-halloo [vju:hə'lu:], *s. Ven:* (*fox hunting*) vue *f*.

viewing ['vju:iŋ], *s.* **1.** examen *m*, inspection *f*. **2.** *Opt: Elcs:* vision *f*, visualisation *f*, observation *f*; *Phot: etc:* visée *f*; **v. angle,** angle *m* de vision, d'observation; **v. point,** point *m* de visée (d'un sujet, d'une scène); *Rad:* cornet *m* d'observation (d'écran radar); *Cin: etc:* **v. room,** salle *f* de projection, de vision; salle de cinéma; (*for slides*) salle de visionnement; **v. screen,** *Cin: T.V:* écran *m* (de visualisation); *X Rays:* négatoscope *m*; **v. system,** système *m* de contrôle optique; **v. unit,** appareil *m*, équipement *m*, de visualisation; **v. window,** fenêtre *f*, orifice *m*, trou *m*, d'observation; *Cmptr:* viseur *m* (de machine à calculer); *T.V:* **v. time,** temps *m* d'antenne.

viewless ['vju:lis], *a.* **1.** *Lit:* invisible. **2.** (*a*) (maison, etc.) qui n'a pas de vue; (*b*) (personne) sans opinions, sans vues.

viewpoint ['vju:pɔint], *s.* (*a*) (*place*) point *m* de vue; (*at beauty spot, etc.*) belvédère *m*; (*b*) **from the international v.,** du point de vue international.

vigesimal [vai'dʒesim(ə)l], *a.* vicésimal, -aux.

vigil ['vidʒil], *s.* **1.** veille *f*. **to keep v.,** veiller; **worn out by his long vigils,** usé par les veilles; *A:* **the v. of arms,** la veille, la veillée, des armes. **2.** *Ecc:* (*a*) vigile *f*; (*b*) **vigils of the dead,** vigiles des morts; (*c*) **v. candle, light,** cierge brûlé devant une image sainte.

vigilance ['vidʒiləns], *s.* **1.** vigilance *f*; *U.S:* **v. committee,** comité *m* de surveillance; **v. man,** membre *m* du comité de surveillance. **2.** *Med: O:* insomnie *f*.

vigilant ['vidʒilənt], *a.* vigilant, éveillé, alerte.

vigilante [vidʒi'lænti], *s.* membre *m* d'un comité de surveillance.

vigilantly ['vidʒiləntli], *adv.* vigilamment, avec vigilance.

Vigilius [vi'dʒiliəs], *Pr.n.m. Ecc. Hist:* Vigile.

vignette[1] [vi'njet], *s.* **1.** *Art: Engr:* vignette *f*; **to ornament a book with vignettes,** vignetter un livre; **ornamentation with vignettes,** vignetage *m*; **v. engraver,** vignettiste *m*. **2.** (*a*) *Art:* buste peint sur un fond dégradé; (*b*) *Phot:* (i) photographie *f* en dégradé; buste sous cache dégradé; (ii) cache dégradé. **3.** (*a*) *Lit:* petit portrait (en prose); (*b*) *Th:* saynète *f*.

vignette[2], *v.tr.* **1.** (*a*) peindre (qn) en buste sur un fond dégradé; (*b*) *Phot:* dégrader (un portrait). **2.** *Lit:* faire un petit portrait (en prose) de (qn).

vignetter [vi'njetər], *s.* **1.** *Art:* vignettiste *m*. **2.** *Phot:* dégradateur *m*; cache dégradé; *Cin:* **iris v.,** iris extérieur (pour fondus).

vignetting [vi'njetiŋ], *s. Phot:* tirage *m* (de photographies) en dégradé; **iris v. mask,** dégradateur *m* iris.

vignettist [vi'njetist], *s. Art:* vignettiste *m*.

vigogne [vi'gouŋ], *s. Z: Tex:* vigogne *f*.

Vigornian [vi'gɔ:niən], *a.* & *s. Geog:* (originaire *mf*, habitant, -ante) de Worcester.

vigorous ['vigərəs], *a.* **1.** vigoureux, robuste; **v. in body and mind,** robuste de corps et d'esprit; **to grow more v.,** se renforcer; **v. blow,** coup de poing solide; *Hort:* **v. plant,** plante vigoureuse. **2.** (*a*) (*of style, opposition, etc.*) vigoureux; (*b*) (*of colour*) corsé.

vigorously ['vigərəsli], *adv.* vigoureusement; **to shake s.o. v.,** secouer qn d'un bras vigoureux; **to express oneself v.,** s'exprimer avec vigueur; **he maintained v. that he knew nothing about it,** il affirmait énergiquement qu'il n'en savait rien; *F:* **to go at it v.,** y aller avec vigueur, d'attaque.

vigour ['vigər], *s.* **1.** vigueur *f*, énergie *f*; vitalité *f*; **to die in the full v. of manhood,** mourir dans la force de l'âge; **the v. of youth,** la sève de la jeunesse; **man of v.,** homme énergique. **2.** (*a*) **v. of colouring, of style,** vigueur de coloris, de style; **wanting in v.,** qui manque de vigueur, de force; (coloris) terne; (style) mou, lâche, languissant; (couleurs) effacées; (*b*) *Mus:* brio *m*. **3.** *NAm:* **laws in v.,** lois en vigueur.

Viking ['vaikiŋ]. *Hist:* **1.** *s.* (*a*) Viking *m*; (*b*) *F:* écumeur *m* de mer. **2.** *a.* viking *inv. in f*; des Vikings; **V. ship,** drakkar *m*.

vile [vail], *a.* **1.** *A:* & *Lit:* vil; (*a*) sans valeur; **they dreamt of changing v. metals into gold,** ils rêvaient de changer en or les métaux vils; (*b*) abject; **reduced to the v. position of a lackey,** réduit au vil emploi de laquais; **to render v.,** avilir. **2.** vil; bas, basse, infâme, ignoble; **a v. calumny,** une vile calomnie; une calomnie infâme; **a v. song,** une chanson ignoble; **the vilest of men,** le dernier des hommes; le plus vil des hommes. **3.** *F:* abominable, exécrable, mauvais; sale; **he lived in a v. hovel,** il vivait dans un réduit ignoble, dans un taudis infect; **v. weather,** un sale temps; **what a v. pencil!** quel sale crayon! **v. handwriting,** écriture désespérante, exécrable; **he's in a v. temper,** il est d'une humeur exécrable; **v. whisky,** whisky abominable, exécrable, infect.

vilely ['vailli], *adv.* **1.** *A:* & *Lit:* abjectement. **2.** vilement, bassement. **3.** d'une manière abominable, exécrable.

vileness ['vailnis], *s.* **1.** *A:* & *Lit:* (*a*) vileté *f* (d'un métal, etc.); (*b*) nature abjecte (d'un emploi, etc.). **2.** bassesse *f*, caractère *m* ignoble (de qn, d'un sentiment), vileté (de caractère, de langage). **3.** *F:* **the v. of the weather, of the food,** le temps, la nourriture, abominable.

vilification [vilifi'keiʃ(ə)n], *s.* **1.** avilissement *m* (d'une denrée, etc.). **2.** dénigrement *m* (de qn).

vilifier ['vilifaiər], *s.* détracteur, -trice.

vilify ['vilifai], *v.tr.* **1.** *A:* avilir; ravilir, dégrader. **2.** vilipender, diffamer, dénigrer, noircir (qn); dire des infamies, des noirceurs, de (qn); médire de (qn); décrier la conduite de (qn); déchirer (qn) à belles dents; **to v. s.o. in the papers,** éreinter qn dans les journaux.

vilipend ['vilipend], *v.tr. Lit:* vilipender.

villa ['vilə], *s.* **1.** (*a*) villa *f*; maison *f* de campagne; (*b*) **Roman v.,** villa romaine. **2.** petite maison, villa, de banlieue.

Villafranchian [vilə'frænkiən], *a.* & *s. Prehist: Geol:* villafranchien (*m*).

village ['vilidʒ], *s.* **1.** village *m*; bourgade *f*; bourg *m*; **she's from our v.,** *F:* elle vient de notre patelin; c'est une payse; **the whole v. was talking about it,** tout le village en parlait; **v. custom,** coutume villageoise; **the v. grocer,** l'épicier du village; **v. inn,** auberge *f* de campagne. **2.** *U.S:* petite municipalité.

villager ['vilidʒər], *s.* villageois, -oise.

villain ['vilən], *s.* **1.** (*a*) scélérat *m*; bandit *m*, gredin *m*, misérable *m*; *F:* **you little v.!** petit garnement! petite coquine! petit polisson! oh, le vilain, la vilaine! *F:* **the horse was a v. to drive,** le cheval était une rosse entre les brancards; (*b*) *Th:* **the v. (of the piece),** le traître; *F:* **so you are the v. of the piece!** alors c'est vous qui êtes responsable de tout ça! **2.** = VILLEIN.

villainous ['vilənəs], *a.* **1.** vil, infâme, scélérat, de scélérat; **v. deed,** action scélérate; **v. face,** vilain visage; *F:* sale mine; *P:* gueule d'empeigne. **2.** *F:* abominable, exécrable, mauvais; **v. weather,** un sale temps; **v. handwriting,** écriture désespérante, exécrable.

villainously ['vilənəsli], *adv.* **1.** d'une manière infâme; en scélérat. **2.** *F:* (écrire, etc.) abominablement, exécrablement.

villainy ['viləni], *s.* **1.** infamie *f, A: & Lit:* scélératesse *f,* (d'une action, etc.). **2.** action scélérate, infâme; infamie *f,* vilenie *f; F:* sale coup *m.*

villanella [vilə'nelə], *s. Mus: Danc:* villanelle *f.*

villanelle [vilə'nel], *s. Lit:* villanelle *f.*

Villanovan [vilə'nouvən], *a. & s. Prehist:* villanovien (*m*).

villein ['vilin], *s. Hist:* vilain *m;* serf *m;* **land in v. tenure,** terre serve.

villeinage ['vilinidʒ], *s. Hist:* **1.** (*a*) vilainage *m;* (*b*) servage *m.* **2. (tenure in) v.,** tenure *f* de roture.

villiaumite ['viːjoumait], *s. Miner:* villiaumite *f.*

villiform ['vilifɔːm], *a. Nat.Hist:* villiforme.

villose ['vilous], **villous** ['viləs], *a. Nat.Hist:* villeux.

villosity [vi'lɔsiti], *s. Anat: etc:* villosité *f;* velu *m* (d'une plante, etc.).

villus, *pl.* **-i** ['viləs, -ai], *s.* **1.** *Bot:* poil *m.* **2.** *Anat: Z:* villus *m;* villosité *f* (de l'intestin grêle, du chorion).

vim [vim], *s. F:* vigueur *f,* énergie *f;* **full of v.,** plein de sève, d'énergie; **put a bit of v. into it!** activez! mets-y du nerf, du jus! mets-y-en! **to put plenty of v. into it,** ne pas y aller de main morte.

vinaceous [vai'neiʃəs], *a.* vineux; couleur *inv* de vin, de lie de vin.

vinage ['vainidʒ], *s. A.Jur:* vinage *m.*

vinaigrette [vin(e)i'gret], *s.* **1.** *A:* flacon *m* de sels. **2.** *A.Veh:* vinaigrette *f.* **3.** *Cu:* **v. (sauce),** vinaigrette.

vinasse [vi'næs], *s. Sug.-R:* vinasse *f* (de betterave).

Vincent ['vins(ə)nt], *Pr.n.m.* Vincent; *Med:* **Vincent's angina, bacillus,** angine *f,* bacille *m,* de Vincent.

Vincentian [vin'senʃ(ə)n]. **1.** *a.* de saint Vincent (de Paul, de Lérins). **2.** *s.* prêtre *m* de la Mission; lazariste *m.*

vincetoxicum [vinsi'tɔksikəm], *s. Bot:* dompte-venin *m.*

vincible ['vinsibl], *a.* qui peut être dompté; pas invincible.

vinculum, *pl.* **-la** ['viŋkjuləm, -lə], *s.* **1.** lien *m.* **2.** *Anat:* frein *m,* filet *m* (de la langue, etc.). **3.** *Typ:* (*a*) accolade *f;* (*b*) *Mth:* barre tirée au-dessus d'un groupe de symboles.

vindicable ['vindikəbl], *a.* justifiable, défendable, soutenable.

vindicate ['vindikeit], *v.tr.* **1.** défendre, soutenir (qn, sa foi, etc.); justifier, faire l'apologie de (qn, sa conduite, etc.); prouver, maintenir (son dire); **to v. one's character,** se justifier; **to v. one's veracity,** justifier de sa bonne foi. **2. to v. one's rights,** revendiquer ses droits; faire valoir son bon droit.

vindication [vindi'keiʃ(ə)n], *s.* **1.** défense *f,* apologie *f;* justification *f;* **in v. of his conduct,** pour justifier, en justification de, sa conduite. **2.** revendication *f* (d'un droit, etc.).

vindicative ['vindikətiv, -kei-], *a.* **1.** justificatif; *Theol:* apologétique. **2.** *A:* = VINDICTIVE.

vindicator ['vindikeitər], *s.* défenseur *m.*

vindicatory [vindi'keitəri], *a.* **1.** justificatif; *Theol:* apologétique. **2.** vindicatif; vengeur, -eresse; **v. justice,** justice vindicative.

vindictive [vin'diktiv], *a.* **1.** vindicatif; vengeur, -eresse; (acte, etc.) de vengeance; *Jur:* **v. justice,** justice vindicative; **v. damages,** dommages-intérêts infligés à titre de pénalité. **2.** (*of pers., character*) vindicatif, rancunier.

vindictively [vin'diktivli], *adv.* par rancune, par esprit de vengeance, avec une méchanceté rancunière.

vindictiveness [vin'diktivnis], *s.* caractère vindicatif; esprit *m* de vengeance; esprit rancunier.

vine[1] [vain], *s.* **1.** vigne *f* (vinifère); **wild v.,** vigne sauvage; *Dial:* lambruche *f,* lambrusque *f;* **v. shoot,** sarment *m;* **v. growing,** viticulture *f;* **v. grower,** viticulteur *m;* vigneron, -onne; **v.-growing country, region,** pays *m* vinicole; **v. harvest,** vendange *f;* **v. arbour,** treille *f;* **v. prop,** échalas *m; Ent:* **v. beetle,** altise *f* de la vigne; pucerotte *f;* **v. fretter, v. louse,** phylloxéra *m;* **v. grub,** (i) eumolpe *m* de la vigne; (ii) ver-coquin *m, pl.* vers-coquins; **v. moth,** eudémis *m* de la vigne; **v. weevil,** charançon *m* de la vigne. **2.** (*a*) *NAm:* plante grimpante, rampante; (*b*) *Bot:* **balloon v.,** cardiosperme *m;* **Madeira v.,** boussingaultia *f.* **3.** sarment *m,* tige *f* (de houblon, melon, etc.).

vine[2], *v.i. U.S:* (*of plant*) pousser des sarments.

vinegar ['vinigər], *s.* **1.** vinaigre *m;* (*a*) **wine v.,** vinaigre de vin; **wood v.,** vinaigre de bois; acide pyroligneux; **tarragon v.,** vinaigre à l'estragon; *Cu:* **oil and v. dressing,** vinaigrette *f;* **v. cruet,** burette *f* à vinaigre; vinaigrier *m; Ann:* **v. eel,** anguille *f,* anguillule *f,* du vinaigre; *Bot:* **v. tree,** sumac *m* de Virginie; (*b*) *Fig:* acidité *f,* âpreté *f* (du caractère de qn, etc.); **v. countenance,** visage revêche; **v.-faced,** au visage revêche; (*c*) **toilet, aromatic, v.,** vinaigre parfumé, de toilette; **rose v.,** vinaigre rosat; *A:* **Marseilles v.,** vinaigre des quatre voleurs. **2.** *NAm: F:* vigueur *f,* allant *m.*

vinegarish ['vinigəriʃ], *s. F:* = VINEGARY 2.

vinegary ['vinigəri], *a.* **1.** (goût, etc.) de vinaigre. **2.** *F:* (visage) revêche; (ton) acerbe, aigre.

vineland ['vainlænd], *s.* vignoble *m.*

vineleaf ['vainliːf], *s.* feuille *f* de vigne.

vinery ['vainəri], *s.* serre *f* à vignes; forcerie *f* de raisins; grapperie *f.*

vinestock ['vainstɔk], *s.* cep *m* de vigne.

vineyard ['vinjəd], *s.* clos *m,* champ *m,* de vigne; vigne *f;* vignoble *m;* **the best vineyards,** les meilleurs crus; *Lit:* **to work in the Lord's v.,** travailler à la vigne du Seigneur; *Vit:* **v. plough,** charrue vigneronne; déchausseuse *f.*

vineyardist ['vinjədist], *s.* vigneron, -onne.

vinhatico [viː'njætikou], *s. Bot:* **v. (wood),** vinhaticou *m.*

vinic ['vinik], *a. Ch:* (alcool, éther, etc.) vinique.

vinicultural [vini'kʌltjərəl], *a.* (région, etc.) vinicole.

viniculture ['vinikʌltjər], *s.* viniculture *f,* viticulture *f.*

viniculturist [vini'kʌltjərist], *s.* viticulteur *m.*

viniferous [vi'nifərəs], *a.* (sol, etc.) vinifère.

vinification [vinifi'keiʃ(ə)n], *s.* vinification *f* (du moût).

vinificator ['vinifikeitər], *s. Vit:* (*apparatus*) vinificateur *m.*

vino ['viːnou], *s. F:* vin *m;* gros rouge, pinard *m.*

vinology [vi'nɔlədʒi], *s.* vinologie *f,* œnologie *f.*

vinometer [vi'nɔmitər], *s.* vinomètre *m.*

vinosity [vi'nɔsiti], *s.* vinosité *f.*

vinous ['vainəs], *a.* **1.** (*a*) (goût, etc.) vineux; (*b*) couleur *inv* de vin; vineux. **2.** (*of pers.*) (*a*) aviné; (*b*) ivrogne.

vint [vint], *v.tr.* faire (le vin).

vintage[1] ['vintidʒ], *s.* **1.** (*a*) récolte *f* du raisin; vendanges *fpl;* (*b*) (*crop*) vendange, vinée *f;* **a good v.,** une bonne vinée; **the 1964 v.,** le cru de 1964; (*c*) temps *m* de vendange, les vendanges. **2.** (*a*) année *f* (de belle récolte); **of the 1964 v.,** de l'année 1964, au millésime de 1964; **v. year,** année de bon vin, bonne année, grande année; *F:* **a v. year for fashionable weddings,** une bonne année pour les mariages dans le beau monde; **v. wine,** vin de marque, vin cacheté, grand vin; **v. champagne,** champagne *m* d'origine; **v. burgundies,** (i) bourgognes *m* d'appellation; (ii) bourgognes de la bonne année; **guaranteed v.,** appellation contrôlée; *Fig:* **this is v. Shaw,** c'est du Shaw et du meilleur; **an old v. joke,** plaisanterie qui a de la bouteille; **bicycle of the 1890 v.,** bicyclette du modèle de 1890; (*b*) *Aut:* **v. car,** vintage *m,* voiture construite entre 1916 et 1930.

vintage[2], *v.tr.* **1.** cueillir (le raisin). **2.** faire (le vin).

vintager ['vintidʒər], *s.* vendangeur, -euse.

vintaging ['vintidʒiŋ], *s.* cueillette *f* (du raisin).

vintner ['vintnər], *s.* négociant *m* en vins.

vintnery ['vintnəri], *s.* commerce *m* des vins.

vinyl ['vainil], *s. Ch:* vinyle *m;* **v. acetate, chloride,** acétate *m,* chlorure *m,* de vinyle; **v. alcohol,** alcool *m* vinylique; **v. resins,** résines *f* vinyliques.

vinylacetylene [vainilə'setiliːn], *s. Ch:* vinylacétylène *m.*

vinylbenzene [vainil'benziːn], *s. Ch:* vinylbenzène *m.*

vinylog ['vainilɔg], *s. Ch:* vinylogue *m.*

vinylogous [vai'niləgəs], *a. Ch:* vinylogue.

vinylpyridine [vainil'pairidiːn], *s. Ch:* vinylpyridine *f.*

viol ['vaiəl], *s. Mus:* **1.** = VIOLA[1] 2. **2. bass v.,** contrebasse *f.*

viola[1] [vi'oulə], *s. Mus:* **1.** alto *m* (à cordes); quinte *f;* **v. player,** altiste *mf.* **2.** viole *f;* **v. da gamba, bass v.,** viole de gambe, basse *f* de viole; **v. d'amore,** viole d'amour.

viola[2] [vi'oulə, 'vaiələ], *s.* **1.** *Bot:* violacée *f,* violariée *f.* **2.** *Hort:* pensée *f* (unicolore); violette *f* (de jardin).

violable ['vaiələbl], *a.* violable.

Violaceae [vaiə'leisiiː], *s.pl. Bot:* violariées *f,* violacées *f.*

violaceous [vaiə'leiʃəs], *a.* **1.** *Bot:* violacé, de la famille des violacées. **2.** (*colour*) violacé.

violan(e) ['vaiələn, -ein], *s. Miner:* violane *f.*

violanthrone [vaiou'lænθroun], *s. Ch: Dy:* violanthrone *f.*

violate ['vaiəleit], *v.tr.* **1.** violer (un serment, traité, secret, sanctuaire, la neutralité d'un pays); profaner (un sanctuaire); manquer à (une règle); **to v. a clause,** enfreindre les dispositions d'un article; **to v. the law,** violer, enfreindre, blesser, la loi; **to v. s.o.'s privacy,** troubler la solitude de qn, faire intrusion auprès de qn. **2.** violer, outrager (une femme).

violation [vaiə'leiʃ(ə)n], *s.* **1.** violation *f* (d'un serment, d'une loi, de frontière, etc.); viol *m,* profanation *f* (d'un sanctuaire); **v. of a rule,** manquement *m,* infraction *f,* à une règle; **v. of an order,** infraction à un ordre; **v. of professional secrecy,** violation, viol, du secret professionnel; **v. of the laws governing the press,** délit *m* de presse; **v. of all justice,** injure *f* à toute justice; **to act in v. of a treaty,** agir en violation d'un traité; **v. of s.o.'s privacy,** intrusion *f* auprès de qn. **2.** viol (d'une femme).

violator ['vaiəleitər], *s.* **1.** violateur, -trice (des lois, etc.); contrevenant, -ante (d'un règlement). **2.** violateur, violeur *m* (d'une femme).

violence ['vaiələns], *s.* **1.** (*a*) violence *f,* intensité *f* (du feu, du vent, d'une passion); (*b*) **to die by v.,** mourir de mort violente; **to use v.,** user de violence; **to do v. to a text, one's principles, a woman,** faire violence à un texte, ses principes, une femme; **to do v. to one's conscience,** violenter sa conscience; aller à l'encontre de sa conscience; **to do v. to one's feelings,** se faire violence; **to do v. to the law,** faire violence à la loi; *F:* donner une entorse au Code. **2.** *Jur:* **to commit acts of v., to resort to v.,** se livrer, se porter, à des voies de fait; **robbery with v.,** vol avec violence(s), avec agression.

violent ['vaiələnt], *a.* **1.** violent; **v. storm,** orage violent; tempête *f;* **(very) v. wind,** vent corsé, à écorner les bœufs; *Aut:* **v. braking,** freinage brutal; **to die a v. death,** mourir de mort violente; **to lay v. hands on s.o.,** attaquer brutalement qn; *Jur:* se porter à des voies de fait contre qn; **to lay v. hands on oneself,** attenter à ses jours; **to lay v. hands on sth.,** s'emparer de qch. par la violence, s'emparer de force de qch.; **v. abuse,** injures violentes; **to be in a v. temper,** être furieux, monté; (*of pers.*) **to become v.,** se livrer à des actes de violence; s'emporter, être en fureur; **he became positively v. on hearing the decision,** il est entré dans une colère à tout casser en apprenant cette décision. **2.** (*a*) violent, vif, aigu, -uë, fort; **v. poison,** poison violent; **v. pain,** douleur aiguë, violente; **v. dislike,** vive aversion; **in a v. hurry,** extrêmement pressé; **a v. cold,** un gros rhume, un rhume carabiné; **v. fever,** fièvre carabinée, violente; *Jur:* **v. presumption,** forte présomption; (*b*) **v. colours,** couleurs criardes, crues; **hair of a v. red,** cheveux d'un roux éclatant.

violently ['vaiələntli], *adv.* **1.** violemment, avec violence; **to push s.o. v. away,** repousser violemment qn; **his heart was throbbing v.,** son cœur battait à se rompre. **2.** vivement; extrêmement; **after supper I became v. ill,** après le souper j'ai été pris d'un violent malaise, j'ai été terriblement malade; **to fall v. in love with s.o.,** tomber follement amoureux de qn.

violet ['vaiələt]. **1.** *s.* (*a*) *Bot:* (i) violette *f;* **sweet (scented) v.,** violette odorante; **Parma v.,** violette de Parme; **v. scented,** parfumé à la violette; *F: O:* **to play the shrinking v.,** faire sa violette; (ii) **corn v.,** violette des blés, miroir *m* de Vénus; (iii) **water v.,** hottonie *f* des marais; *F:* giroflée *f* d'eau; mille-feuille *f* aquatique; plumeau *m;* (*b*) *Algae:* **rock v.,** trentepohlia *m* jolithus. **2.** (*colour*) (*a*) *s.* violet *m;* (*b*) *a.* **v. (coloured),** violet, de couleur violette; **v. (coloured) eyes,** yeux de violette; **v. purple,** améthystin; *Ph:* **v. rays,** rayons violets; *Moll:* **v. snail, shell,** violet *m; Com:* **v. wood,** palissandre *m,* bois violet, bois de violette, bois royal.

violin [vaiə'lin], *s. Mus:* violon *m;* **first v.,** premier violon, violon principal; **second v.,** second violon; **v. case,** boîte *f* à violon.

violine ['vaiəliːn], *a.* violine.

violinist ['vaiəlinist], *s. Mus:* violoniste *mf.*

violist[1] ['vaiəlist], *s. Mus:* joueur, -euse, de viole; violiste *mf.*

violist[2] [vi'oulist], *s. Mus:* joueur, -euse, d'alto; altiste *mf.*

violoncellist [vaiələn'tʃelist], *s. Mus:* violoncelliste *mf.*

violoncello [vaiələn'tʃelou], *s. Mus:* violoncelle *m.*

violone ['vaiəloun], *s. Mus:* violone *f.*

violuric [vaiou'ljuːrik], *a. Ch:* violurique.

viomycin [vaiou'maisin], *s. Bio-Ch:* viomycine *f.*

viper ['vaipər], *s.* **1.** (*a*) *Rept:* vipère *f;* **young v.,** vipereau *m;* **common (European) v., rat-tailed v.,** (vipère) fer-de-lance (*m*), *pl.* fers-de-lance; vipère péliade; **horned v.,** vipère à cornes; céraste *m;* **South-West African dwarf v.,** vipère du sud-ouest de l'Afrique; **African tree v.,** vipère arboricole d'Afrique; **pit v.,** trigonocéphale *m;* **Gaboon v.,** vipère du Gabon; **(European) sand v.,** ammodyte *m; Bot: Cu:* **viper's grass,** scorsonère *f;* salsifis noir, d'Espagne; (*b*) (*pers.*) vipère; **to cherish a v. in**

one's bosom, réchauffer un serpent dans son sein. **2.** *Her:* guivre *f.*
Viperidae [vai'peridi:], *s.pl. Rept:* vipéridés *m.*
viperine ['vaipərain], *a.* vipérin; **v. snake,** vipérine *f.*
viperish ['vaipəriʃ], **viperous** ['vaipərəs], *a.* vipérin, de vipère; *Fig:* **viperish tongue,** langue venimeuse, de vipère, vipérine.
vipio ['vaipiou], *s. Ent:* vipion *m.*
viraemia [vai'ri:miə], *s. Med:* virémie *f.*
virago [vi'reigou, -'rɑ:-], *s.f.* **1.** *A:* amazone; virago; (*b*) grande bringue de femme, vrai gendarme, vrai dragon; virago. **2.** mégère.
viral ['vairəl], *a. Med:* viral, virien.
virazone ['virəzən], *s. Meteor:* virazon *m.*
vire ['viər], *s. A:* (*archery*) vireton *m.*
virelay ['virəlei], *s. A:* virelai *m.*
viremia [vai'ri:miə], *s. Med:* virémie *f.*
vireo ['viriou], *s. Orn:* viréo *m*; **blue-headed, solitary, v.,** viréo à tête bleue; **Hutton's v.,** viréo de Hutton; **Philadelphia v.,** viréo de Philadelphie; **red-eyed v.,** viréo à œil rouge; *Fr.C:* aux yeux rouges; **warbling v.,** viréo mélodieux; **white-eyed v.,** viréo aux yeux blancs; **yellow-green v.,** viréo jaune verdâtre; **yellow-throated v.,** viréo à gorge jaune.
Vireonidae [viri'ɔnidi:], *s.pl. Orn:* viréonidés *m.*
virescence [vi'resəns], *s.* **1.** *Bot:* virescence *f.* **2.** *Lit:* couleur verte; verdure *f* (du printemps, etc.).
virescent [vi'resənt], *a. Lit:* **1.** qui commence à verdoyer. **2.** verdoyant.
virga ['və:gə], *s. Meteor: A.Mus:* virga *f.*
virgate[1] ['və:geit], *a. Nat.Hist:* en verge; élancé.
virgate[2], *s. Hist:* mesure *f* agraire le plus souvent de 12 hectares.
virgation [və:'geiʃ(ə)n], *s. Geol:* virgation *f.*
Virgil ['və:dʒil], *Pr.n.m. Lt.Lit:* Virgile.
Virgilian [və:'dʒiliən], *a.* virgilien.
virgin ['və:dʒin]. **1.** *s.* (*a*) vierge *f*; **the (Blessed) V.,** la Sainte Vierge; **the foolish virgins,** les vierges folles; *Ap:* **v. queen,** reine non fécondée; *Hist:* **the V. Queen,** la Reine Vierge (Élizabeth I); *Geog:* **the V. Islands,** les îles *f* Vierges; *Bot:* **virgin's bower,** clématite *f,* berceau *m* de la Vierge; (*b*) *Astr:* **the V.,** la Vierge. **2.** *a.* (*a*) de vierge; virginal, -aux; **v. modesty,** modestie virginale; **v. birth,** naissance virginale; *Theol:* (la) maternité divine; *Biol:* parthénogénèse *f*; (*b*) **v. forest,** forêt *f* vierge; **v. snow,** neige virginale; **v. (vegetable) oil,** huile vierge, naturelle; **v. wax,** cire *f* vierge; *Cer:* **v. clay,** argile crue, non cuite; *Cmptr:* **v. tape,** bande *f* vierge.
virginal ['və:dʒin(ə)l]. **1.** *a.* virginal, -aux; de vierge; *Biol:* **v. generation,** parthénogénèse *f.* **2.** *s. A.Mus:* **virginal(s), pair of virginals,** virginale *f,* virginal *m.*
Virginia [və(:)'dʒiniə]. **1.** *Pr.n.* (*a*) *Geog:* la Virginie; **West V.,** la Virginie de l'Ouest, la Virginie-Occidentale; *Bot:* **V. creeper,** vigne *f* vierge; **V. willow,** itea *m*; (*b*) (*girl's name*) Virginie. **2.** *s.* **V. (tobacco),** tabac *m* de Virginie; virginie *f.*
Virginian [və(:)'dʒiniən]. *Geog:* **1.** *a.* virginien; *Bot:* **V. willow,** itea *m.* **2.** *s.* Virginien, -ienne.
virginity [və(:)'dʒiniti], *s.* virginité *f.*
virginoparous [və:dʒin'ɔpərəs], *a. Ent:* (insecte) virginipare.
Virglorian [və:'glɔriən], *s. Geol:* Virglorien *m.*
Virgo ['və:gou], *Pr.n. Astr:* la Vierge.
virgula ['və:gjulə], *s. Paleont:* virgula *f.*
virgularia [və:gju'lɛəriə], *s. Coel:* virgulaire *f.*
Virgulariidae [və:gjulə'raiidi:], *s.pl. Coel:* virgulariidés *m.*
virgule ['və:gju:l], *s. Typ:* barre transversale, oblique.
Virgulian [və(:)'gju:liən], *a. & s. Geol:* virgulien (*m*).
virial ['viriəl], *s. Ph:* viriel *m.*
viricidal [vairi'saidl], *a. Med:* virulicide.
viricide ['vairisaid], *s. Med:* agent *m* virulicide.
viridescent [viri'des(ə)nt], *a.* **1.** = VIRESCENT. **2.** verdâtre.
viridian [vi'ridiən], *s. Art:* vert *m* Guignet.
viridine ['viridi:n], *s. Ch: Dy:* viridine *f.*
viridite ['viridait], *s. Miner:* viridite *f.*
viridity [vi'riditi], *s.* **1.** viridité *f,* verdeur *f.* **2.** *Fig:* naïveté *f,* ingénuité *f.*
virile ['virail], *a.* viril, mâle; (*a*) *Anat:* **the v. member,** le membre viril, la verge, le pénis; (*b*) **v. mind,** esprit viril; **a v. old age,** une mâle vieillesse; **v. eloquence,** mâle éloquence; **v. style,** style mâle; *Art:* **v. touch,** touche mâle.
virilia [vi'riliə], *s.pl. Anat:* virilités *f*; parties viriles.
virilism ['virilizm], *s. Med:* virilisme *m.*
virility [vi'riliti], *s.* virilité *f.*
virilizing ['virilaiziŋ], *a. Med:* (traitement, etc.) virilisant.
virilocal ['viriloukl], *a. Ethn:* virilocal, -aux.
virion ['vairiən], *s. Bac:* virion *m.*
virole [vi'roul], *s. Her:* virole *f* (autour d'un cor, etc.).
viroled [vi'rould], *a. Her:* (cor, etc.) virolé.
virological [vairə'lɔdʒikl], *a.* virologique.
virology [vai'rɔlədʒi], *s.* virologie *f.*
virose ['vairous], *a.* (*of plant*) vireux, vénéneux; (*of smell*) vireux, fétide.
virosis [vai'rousis], *s. Med:* virose *f.*
virtu [və:'tu:], *s.* goût *m* des arts, des objets d'art; **articles of v.,** objets *m* d'art; antiquités *f,* curiosités *f.*
virtual ['və:tjuəl], *a.* **1.** de fait, en fait; **he's the v. head of the business,** c'est lui le vrai chef de la maison; de fait c'est lui qui mène tout; **a v. promise,** une quasi-promesse, ce qui équivaut à une promesse; **this was a v. admission of guilt,** de fait c'était un aveu. **2.** (*Theol: of intention; Mec: of displacement, velocity; Opt: of image, focus; Cmptr: of memory, etc.*) virtuel. **3.** *El:* **v. value of electromotive force,** force électromotrice efficace; *Mth:* **v. value of a variable quantity,** valeur *f* efficace d'une quantité variable.
virtuality [və:tju'æliti], *s.* virtualité *f.*
virtually ['və:tjuəli], *adv.* virtuellement; de fait; par le fait; en pratique; **I'm v. certain of it,** j'en ai la quasi-certitude; **there's v. nobody who doesn't know all about it,** il n'y a pour ainsi dire personne qui n'en sache pas tout.
virtue ['və:tju:], *s.* **1.** (*a*) vertu *f*; **Christian virtues,** vertus chrétiennes; **the three theological, the Christian, the supernatural, virtues,** les trois vertus théologales; **the four cardinal virtues,** les trois vertus cardinales; **he's a personification of all the virtues,** il personnifie toutes les vertus; on lui donnerait le bon Dieu sans confession; **a woman of v.,** une femme vertueuse, chaste; *O:* **woman of easy v.,** femme de petite vertu, de mœurs faciles; **to make a v. of necessity,** faire de nécessité vertu; *Prov:* **v. is its own reward,** la vertu trouve sa récompense en elle-même; (*b*) *Theol:* (*angelic order*) **the Virtues,** les Vertus. **2.** qualité *f*; avantage *m*; **it has the v. of being unbreakable,** cela a l'avantage d'être incassable; **the hotel has the v. of being cheap,** l'hôtel se recommande par son bon marché; **he has the v. of not being touchy,** il a cette qualité qu'il ne se froisse pas facilement. **3.** efficacité *f* (de certaines drogues, de certaines eaux); **plants that have healing virtues,** plantes qui ont la vertu de guérir, qui ont des propriétés curatives; **there is no v. in this drug,** ce médicament n'a aucune efficacité. **4.** *prep.phr.* **by v. of, in v. of,** en vertu de; en raison de; à titre de; **he had a vote in v. of his ownership of a house,** il était électeur à titre de propriétaire; **by v. of one's office,** à titre d'office; **by v. of his father's millions,** de par les millions de son père.
virtuosa, *pl.* **-ose** [və:tju'ouzə,-'ouzei], *s.f. A:* virtuose
virtuosity [və:tju'ɔsiti], *s.* **1.** goût *m* des arts. **2.** *Mus: etc:* virtuosité *f.*
virtuoso, *pl.* **-sos, -si** [və:tju'ouzou, -zouz, zi:; -'ousou, -'ousouz, -'ousi:], *s.* **1.** connaisseur *m*; (i) amateur *m* des arts; (ii) amateur d'antiquités, de curiosités. **2.** *Mus: etc:* virtuose *mf*; **he gave a v. performance,** il a fait montre d'une grande virtuosité.
virtuous ['və:tjuəs], *a.* vertueux.
virtuously ['və:tjuəsli], *adv.* vertueusement.
virtuousness ['və:tjuəsnis], *s.* vertu *f.*
virucidal [vairə'saidl], *a. Med:* virulicide.
virucide ['vairəsaid], *s. Med:* agent *m* virulicide.
virulence ['vir(j)uləns], **virulency** ['vir(j)ulənsi], *s.* virulence *f* (d'une maladie, d'un poison, d'un microbe, d'une critique, etc.).
virulent ['vir(j)ulənt], *a.* virulent; **v. disease,** maladie virulente; **v. satire, speech,** satire venimeuse, discours virulent.
virulently ['vir(j)uləntli], *adv.* avec virulence.
virus, *pl.* **-uses** ['vairəs, -əsiz], *s.* **1.** *Med:* virus *m*; **v. disease,** maladie virale, à virus; virose *f.* **2.** *Fig:* venin *m*; poison (moral); influence mauvaise.
vis, *pl.* **vires** [vis, 'vairi:z], *s.* force *f*; *Jur:* **v. major,** force majeure; *Mec:* **v. inertiae** [in'ə:ʃii], force d'inertie; **v. viva** ['vaivə], force vive; *Physiol:* **v. a tergo,** vis *m* a tergo.
visa[1] ['vi:zə], *s.* (*on passport, document*) visa *m*; **transit v.,** visa de transit.
visa[2], *v.tr.* (**visaed, -a'd**) viser, apposer un visa à (un passeport).
visage ['vizidʒ], *s.* **1.** *Lit:* visage *m,* figure *f.* **2.** *NAm:* aspect *m,* visage (de qch.).
visagiste [vi:zɑ:'ʒi:st], *s. Th: etc:* visagiste *mf.*
vis-à-vis ['vi:zɑ:vi:]. **1.** *s.* (*a*) (i) *Danc: etc:* vis-à-vis *m*; (ii) *U.S:* ami(e) que l'on accompagne (dans une réunion, etc.); (*b*) (i) *Furn:* vis-à-vis; (ii) *A. Veh:* vis-à-vis. **2.** *adv.* vis-à-vis (**to, with, s.o.,** de qn). **3.** *prep.* **to sit vis-à-vis s.o.,** être assis vis-à-vis de qn; **v.-à-v. the economic situation,** par rapport à, vis-à-vis de, la situation économique.
visbreaking ['visbreikiŋ], *s. Petr:* visbreaking *m.*
viscaria [vis'kɛəriə], *s. Bot:* viscaire *f,* viscaria *m.*
viscera ['visərə], *s.pl. Anat:* viscères *m.*
visceral ['visər(ə)l], *a.* **1.** *Anat:* viscéral, -aux. **2.** (*of feelings, etc.*) viscéral.
visceralgia [visə'rældʒiə], *s. Med:* viscéralgie *f.*
visceroptosis [visərɔp'tousis], *s. Med:* viscéroptôse *f,* entéroptôse *f,* splanchnoptôse *f.*
viscerotonic [viserou'tɔnik], *a. Psy:* (caractère) du type pycnique.
viscid ['visid], *a.* visqueux, mucilagineux, gluant.
viscidity [vi'siditi], *s.* viscosité *f.*
viscin ['visin], *s. Ch:* viscine *f.*
viscometer [vis'kɔmitər], *s. Ph: Ind:* viscomètre *m.*
viscometric [viskə'metrik], *a. Ph:* viscométrique.
viscometry [vis'kɔmitri], *s. Ph:* viscométrie *f.*
viscose ['viskous], *s. Ch: Ind:* viscose *f.*
viscosimeter [viskə'simitər], *s. Ph:* viscosimètre *m.*
viscosimetric [viskousi'metrik], *a. Ph:* viscosimétrique.
viscosimetry [viskou'simitri], *s. Ph:* viscosimétrie *f.*
viscosity [vis'kɔsiti], *s.* viscosité *f*; *Ph:* **coefficient of v.,** coefficient *m* de viscosité; **v. index,** indexe *m* de viscosité; *Petr:* **v. breaking,** visbreaking *m.*
viscount ['vaikaunt], *s.m.* vicomte.
viscountcy ['vaikauntsi], **viscountship** ['vaikauntʃip], *s.* vicomté *f.*
viscountess ['vaikauntis], *s.f.* vicomtesse.
viscounty ['vaikaunti], *s.* vicomté *f.*
viscous ['viskəs], *a.* visqueux.
viscousness ['viskəsnis], *s.* viscidité *f.*
viscus, *pl.* **viscera** ['viskəs, 'visərə], *s. Anat:* viscère *m.*
vise [vais], *s. NAm: Tls:* = VICE[2].
visé[1] ['vi:zei], *s.* = VISA[1].
visé[2], *v.tr.* (**viséd, visé'd**) = VISA[2].
Vishnu ['viʃnu:], *Pr.n.m. Rel:* Vichnou.
Vishnuism ['viʃnu:izm], *s. Rel:* vichnouisme *m.*
visibility [vizi'biliti], *s.* **1.** visibilité *f*; **v. range,** distance *f* de visibilité; *Surv:* **v. diagram,** croquis *m* des parties vues et cachées. **2.** (*a*) **good, bad, v.,** bonne, mauvaise, visibilité; **v. scale,** échelle *f* de visibilité; **v. was down to a few yards,** la visibilité était réduite à quelques mètres; (*b*) *Aut: Av:* vue *f*; champ visuel, de visibilité; **good v.,** bonne visibilité, vue dégagée; **car with good front and rear v.,** voiture avec une bonne visibilité avant et arrière; **bad, poor, v.,** visibilité défectueuse, insuffisamment dégagée; (*in aircraft*) **downward, forward, v.,** (champ de) visibilité vers le bas, vers l'avant; (*c*) *Ph:* **v. curve,** courbe *f* de visibilité (des ondes lumineuses).
visible ['vizibl], *a.* visible; (*a*) **to become v.,** apparaître; **the hand of man is everywhere v.,** la main de l'homme se montre partout; **the Church v.,** l'Église visible; **with v. satisfaction,** avec une satisfaction évidente; **v. horizon,** horizon visuel, visible, apparent; **v. signal,** signal *m* optique; **v. speech,** (i) système *m* de caractères phonétiques associés aux positions articulatoires; (ii) paroles reproduites par la spectrographie acoustique; *Cmptr:* **v. record computer,** ordinateur à support visible; (*b*) *F:* **I'm not v.!** je ne puis voir personne! je ne suis pas habillé(e)! *O:* **she's not v. before lunch,** elle ne reçoit pas, n'est pas visible, avant le déjeuner.
visibly ['vizibli], *adv.* visiblement, manifestement; (grandir, etc.) à vue d'œil.
Visigoth ['vizigɔθ], *s. Hist:* Wisigoth, -e.
Visigothic [vizi'gɔθik], *a. Hist:* wisigothique, wisigoth.
visiogenic [viziou'dʒenik], *a.* (sujet) bon à téléviser, qui réussit bien à la télévision.
vision[1] ['viʒ(ə)n], *s.* **1.** (*a*) vision *f,* vue *f*; **the theory of v.,** la théorie de la vision; **within the range of v.,** à portée de vue; **beyond our v.,** au delà de notre vue; **the accident had impaired his v.,** cet accident avait affaibli sa vue; *Med:* **double v.,** double vision, diplopie *f*; **field, angle, of v.,** champ, angle, visuel; **forward v.,** visibilité *f* vers l'avant; **horizontal v.,** visibilité latérale; (*b*) **man of v.,** homme d'une grande pénétration, d'une grande perspicacité, qui voit loin dans l'avenir; **prophetic v.,** vision prophétique; (*c*) clairvoyance *f.* **2.** (*a*) imagination *f,* vision; **a poet's visions,** les visions, imaginations, d'un poète; **visions of wealth, success,** visions de richesses, de succès; *F:* **I had visions of being had up for speeding,** je me voyais déjà recevoir une contravention pour excès de vitesse; (*b*) vision, apparition *f*; **the beatific v.,** la vision béatifique; **he has visions,** il a des visions; *F:* **what a v. she was!** ce qu'elle était ravissante à voir! **3.** *T.V:* image *f.*
vision[2], *v.tr.* **1.** voir (qch.) comme dans une vision. **2.** montrer (qch.) comme dans une vision; donner une vision de (qch.).
visional ['viʒ(ə)n(ə)l], *a.* **1.** fondé sur des visions; de vision. **2.** imaginaire, chimérique.
visionary ['viʒ(ə)nəri]. **1.** *a.* (*a*) (*of pers.*) visionnaire, rêveur; (*b*) (projet, etc.) chimérique, fantastique; (*c*)

(mal, danger, etc.) imaginaire; (*d*) qui paraît, a paru, dans une vision. **2.** *s.* (*a*) visionnaire *mf*; idéologue *m*; (*b*) *A:* visionnaire; illuminé, -ée.

visionist [ˈviʒ(ə)nist], *s.* visionnaire *mf.*

visionless [ˈviʒ(ə)nlis], *a.* **1. v. eyes,** yeux sans regard, éteints. **2.** (*of pers.*) dépourvu d'imagination, d'inspiration; à l'esprit fermé.

visit[1] [ˈvizit], *s.* **1.** (*a*) **(social) v.,** visite *f*; **courtesy, duty, v.,** visite de politesse; **to pay s.o. a v.,** faire (une) visite à qn, rendre visite à qn; **to pay a formal v. to s.o.,** (i) aller présenter ses devoirs, ses compliments, à qn; (ii) (*of official*) faire une visite de cérémonie à qn; **to go on a v.,** sortir faire une visite; **to return s.o.'s v.,** rendre sa visite à qn; *F:* **to pay a v.,** aller faire pipi, aller faire une petite commission; (*b*) **doctor's round of visits,** tournée *f* de visites d'un médecin; *Com:* **representative's v.,** passage *m*, visite, d'un représentant; (*c*) *NAm: F:* causerie *f*, causette *f* (**with s.o.,** avec qn). **2.** visite, séjour *m*; **to be on a v. to friends,** être en visite chez des amis; **we decided to prolong our v. to Rome,** nous avons décidé de prolonger notre séjour à Rome; **the President is on an official v. to Italy,** le Président s'est rendu en visite officielle en Italie; **to make a return v. to Moscow,** faire un second voyage, refaire un voyage, à Moscou. **3.** tournée d'inspection, visite d'inspection; *Jur:* **v. to the scene of a crime,** descente *f* sur les lieux; **domiciliary v.,** visite domiciliaire; *Nau:* **right of v. (and search),** droit *m* de visite (en mer).

visit[2], *v.tr.* **1.** (*a*) rendre visite, faire (une) visite, à (qn); aller voir (qn); **to v. a friend's house,** visiter la maison d'un ami; (*b*) **to v. the sick,** visiter les malades; (*c*) (*of doctor*) visiter (un malade); *Com:* (*of representative*) passer chez (un client); (*d*) visiter, aller voir (un endroit); **we visited the museums,** nous avons visité les musées; **a spot which few people v.,** un endroit peu fréquenté; (*e*) *v.i. NAm: F:* causer, bavarder (**with s.o.,** avec qn). **2.** (*of official*) visiter, inspecter; *Jur:* **to v. a place,** faire une perquisition dans un lieu; perquisitionner un lieu; **to v. the scene of a crime,** faire une descente sur les lieux. **3.** *O:* (*of disease, calamity*) visiter (qn), s'abattre sur (qn); **visited with, by, a disease,** affligé, atteint, d'une maladie. **4.** (*a*) *B:* punir, châtier (qn); punir (un péché); **to v. the sins of the fathers upon the children,** punir les enfants pour les péchés des pères; faire retomber sur les enfants, faire expirer aux enfants, les péchés des pères; *Lit:* **to v. one's wrath on s.o.,** répandre sa colère sur qn; (*b*) *A:* **to v. s.o. with salvation, a blessing,** accorder le salut, une bénédiction, à qn.

Visitandine [viziˈtændain], *a. & s. Ecc:* **V. (nun),** Visitandine *f*, religieuse *f* de l'ordre de la Visitation.

visitant [ˈvizitənt]. **1.** *a. A: & Poet:* en visite. **2.** *s.* (*a*) *Poet:* visiteur, -euse; (*b*) *Orn:* oiseau *m* de passage; (*c*) *R.C.Ch:* Visitandine *f*; (*d*) être surnaturel qui se manifeste à un mortel; apparition *f.*

visitation [viziˈteiʃ(ə)n], *s.* **1.** (*a*) visite *f* (d'inspection); (*of bishop*) visite pastorale; *Nau:* **right of v.,** droit *m* de visite; (*b*) tournée *f* (d'inspection); (*c*) *F:* visite fâcheuse, trop prolongée; visite d'un fâcheux. **2.** (*a*) *Ecc:* (i) **v. of the sick,** visites aux malades; (ii) **(Feast of) the V.,** (fête *f* de) la Visitation; **the Order of the V.,** l'Ordre de la Visitation; (*b*) *Z:* migration insolite, anormale. **3.** (*a*) **v. (of God),** épreuve *f*, affliction *f*, châtiment *m*; (ii) récompense *f*, faveur *f*; **to die by v. of God,** mourir subitement; (*b*) calamité *f*; **that year the country suffered a v. of the plague,** en cette année le pays fut ravagé par la peste. **4.** apparition (surnaturelle).

visitator [ˈviziteitər], *s. Ecc:* visitatrice *f.*

visitatorial [vizitəˈtɔːriəl], *a.* = VISITORIAL.

visiting[1] [ˈvizitiŋ], *a.* **1.** en visite; *Sp:* **the v. team,** les visiteurs; (*freemasonry*) **v. brother,** (frère) visiteur; *U.S: F:* **v. fireman,** visiteur de marque. **2.** *Sch:* **v. teacher,** maître externe; (*at pupils' homes*) maître à domicile; **v. lecturer,** conférencier, -ière, de l'extérieur; **v. professor,** professeur (de faculté) invité.

visiting[2], *s.* (*a*) visites *fpl*; **to go v.,** aller en visites; **they are not on v. terms,** ils ne se voient pas chez eux; **v. card,** carte *f* de visite; *A:* **v. book,** carnet *m* de visites; **v. hours,** heures *f* de visite (dans un hôpital, etc.); (*b*) (*of museum, etc.*) **worth v.,** qui vaut la visite; *F:* visitable.

visitor [ˈvizitər], *s.* **1.** (*a*) visiteur, -euse; **she has visitors,** (i) elle a du monde, reçoit de la visite, des visites; (ii) *F: A:* elle a ses règles, *F:* ses affaires; **we're expecting visitors,** nous attendons des invités; **visitors' bell,** sonnette *f* des visiteurs; (*b*) visiteur (d'un musée); client, -ente (d'un hôtel); **visitors' book,** livre des voyageurs (à un hôtel); registre *m* des visiteurs (à un musée); (*for distinguished visitors*) livre d'or (d'un hôtel de ville, etc.); **to enter one's name in the visitors' book,** s'inscrire dans le livre; **visitors' tax,** taxe *f* de séjour; **summer, winter, visitors at a seaside resort,** estivants *m*, hivernants *m*, d'une station balnéaire; **bird that is a winter v.,** oiseau qui est de passage en hiver; **a v. from Mars,** un voyageur venu de Mars; (*freemasonry*) **brother v.,** frère visiteur. **2.** *Jur: Adm:* visiteur; inspecteur *m*.

visitorial [viziˈtɔːriəl], *a.* (droit, devoir, etc.) de visite, d'inspection; (fonctions, etc.) d'inspecteur.

vismia [ˈvismiə], *s. Bot:* vismie *f.*

visne [ˈviːni], *s. Jur:* **1.** voisinage *m*. **2.** jury constitué dans le voisinage (d'un crime, etc.).

vison [ˈvais(ə)n], *s. Z:* vison *m*.

visor [ˈvaizər], *s.* **1.** (*a*) *Arm:* visière *f* (de casque); (*b*) *A:* masque *m*; (*c*) *esp. NAm:* visière (de casquette). **2.** *Aut:* (*a*) pare-soleil *m inv*; (*over windscreen*) parasol *m*; (*b*) visière (de phare).

vista [ˈvistə], *s.* **1.** échappée *f* de vue; (*in forest*) percée *f*, éclaircie *f*, trouée *f*. **2.** perspective *f*; **a long v. of beeches,** une longue perspective de hêtres; *Cin:* **v. shot,** plan *m* d'ensemble; *Rail:* **v. dome,** vistadôme *m*; *Fig:* **to open up new vistas,** ouvrir de nouvelles perspectives, de nouveaux horizons.

vistaed [ˈvistəd], *a.* (parc, etc.) qui présente de belles perspectives, de belles échappées; (rue, etc.) qui offre une belle perspective, une belle percée.

Vistula (the) [(ðə)ˈvistjulə], *Pr.n. Geog:* (la) Vistule.

visual [ˈvizjuəl, ˈviʒ-], *a.* **1.** (*of perception, art, memory, etc.*) visuel; *Opt:* **v. angle,** angle visuel, optique; **v. field,** champ visuel, de vision, de vue; *Mil: Nau: etc:* **v. signal, signalling, telegraphy,** signal *m*, signalisation *f*, télégraphie *f*, optique; *Av:* **v. flight,** vol *m* à vue; **v. distance,** distance *f* de visibilité; **v. range,** portée *f* optique; **to keep within v. range,** se tenir à portée de vue; *Nau:* garder le contact visuel; *Sch:* **v. methods (of teaching),** enseignement *m* par l'image; *Elcs:* **v. display,** appareil *m*, écran *m*, de visualisation. **2.** perceptible à l'œil; *Astr:* **v. binary,** binaire visuelle. **3.** *Anat:* **v. nerve,** nerf *m* optique; **v. purple,** pourpre rétinien.

visualization [vizjuəlaiˈzeiʃ(ə)n, viʒ-], *s.* visualisation *f.*

visualize [ˈvizjuəlaiz, ˈviʒ-], *v.tr.* visualiser; (*a*) rendre (qch.) visible; (*b*) se représenter (qch.); évoquer l'image de (qch.); se faire une image de (qch.); **I know his name but I can't v. him,** je connais son nom mais je ne me souviens pas de sa physionomie, *F:* mais je ne le revois pas.

visually [ˈvizjuəli, ˈviʒ-], *adv.* visuellement.

Vitaceae [vaiˈteisiiː], *s.pl. Bot:* ampélidacées *f*, vit(ac)ées *f.*

vital [ˈvaitl], *a. & s.*

I. *a.* **1.** vital, -aux; essentiel à la vie; **v. organ,** partie vitale; **v. force,** force vitale; **v. capacity,** volume des poumons (mesuré après une inspiration maximum); *Biol:* **v. staining of cells,** coloration *f* des cellules vivantes. **2.** essentiel; capital, -aux; vital; **v. question,** question vitale; **question of v. importance,** question d'une importance vitale, de toute première importance, d'importance capitale; **secrecy is v. to the success of the scheme,** le secret est la condition fondamentale du succès de l'affaire; le secret dans cette affaire est une condition essentielle; **our v. interests,** le plus vif de nos intérêts. **3.** mortel; fatal, -als; **v. wound,** blessure mortelle; **v. error,** erreur fatale, irrémédiable. **4.** (*of pers.*) vif, animé, plein d'entrain.

II. *s.pl.* **vitals. 1.** *Anat: etc:* organes vitaux. **2.** parties essentielles, vitales (de qch.); *Nau:* œuvres vives.

vitalism [ˈvaitəlizm], *s. Biol:* vitalisme *m*.

vitalist [ˈvaitəlist], *s. Biol:* vitaliste *mf.*

vitalistic [vaitəˈlistik], *a. Biol:* (théorie, etc.) vitaliste.

vitality [vaiˈtæliti], *s.* **1.** vitalité *f* (d'un organisme); vitalité, vigueur *f* (d'une race, d'une institution, etc.). **2.** vie *f*, animation *f*, vigueur (de qn, de style, etc.); **style devoid of v.,** style inanimé, sans vigueur; **I wish I had her v.,** j'aimerais bien avoir sa vitalité, son énergie *f.*

vitalization [vaitəlaiˈzeiʃ(ə)n], *s.* vitalisation *f.*

vitalize [ˈvaitəlaiz], *v.tr.* vitaliser, vivifier, animer.

vitalizing [ˈvaitəlaiziŋ], *s.* (*of power, influence, etc.*) animateur, -trice, vivifiant.

vitally [ˈvaitəli], *adv.* d'une manière vitale; **this affects us v.,** cela tranche dans le plus vif de nos intérêts, touche nos plus graves intérêts; cela nous intéresse au premier chef.

vitamin [ˈv(a)itəmin], *s. Bio-Ch:* vitamine *f*; *Med:* **v. deficiency,** avitaminose *f*, carence *f* vitaminique; **v. therapy,** vitaminothérapie *f.*

vitaminization, vitaminizing [v(a)itəminaiˈzeiʃ(ə)n, -ˈaiziŋ], *s.* vitaminisation *f.*

vitaminized [ˈv(a)itəminaizd], *a.* vitaminé.

vitaminology [v(a)itəmiˈnɔlədʒi], *s. Med:* vitaminologie *f.*

vitellarium, *pl.* **-ia** [viteˈlɛəriəm, -iə], *s. Biol:* glande *f* vitellogène.

vitellary [ˈvitelәri], *a. Biol:* vitellin.

vitelliferous [viteˈlifərəs], *a.* vitellifère.

vitelligenous [viteˈlidʒinəs], *a. Biol:* **v. cell,** cellule vitelline.

vitellin [viˈtelin], *s. Ch:* vitelline *f.*

vitelline [viˈtelin, -ain], *a. Biol:* vitellin; **v. membrane,** membrane vitelline (de l'œuf); **v. gland,** glande *f* vitellogène.

vitellogen, vitellogene [viˈtelədʒen, -dʒiːn], *s. Biol:* glande *f* vitellogène.

vitellogenesis [viteləˈdʒenisis], *s. Biol:* vitellogénèse *f.*

vitellus, *pl.* **-i** [viˈteləs, -ai], *s. Biol:* vitellus *m*, lécithe *m*.

Viterbo [viˈtɔːbou], *Pr.n. Geog:* Viterbe.

vitex [ˈvaiteks], *s. Bot:* vitex *m*.

vitiable [ˈviʃiəbl], *a.* viciable.

vitiate [ˈviʃieit], *v.tr.* **1.** vicier, corrompre (le sang, etc.); méphitiser, vicier (l'air); gâter, vicier (les goûts de qn); fausser (le résultat d'un essai, etc.). **2.** *Jur:* vicier (un contrat, etc.); **to v. a transaction,** rendre une opération nulle; **act vitiated by a fundamental flaw,** acte entaché d'un vice radical.

vitiated [ˈviʃieitid], *a.* (air, goût, etc.) vicié.

vitiating [ˈviʃieitiŋ], *a.* viciateur, -trice.

vitiation [viʃiˈeiʃ(ə)n], *s.* viciation *f.*

viticultural [vitiˈkʌltjər(ə)l], *a.* viticole.

viticulture [ˈvitikʌltjər], *s.* viticulture *f.*

viticulturist [vitiˈkʌltjərist], *s.* viticulteur *m*.

vitiligo [vitiˈlaigou], *s. Med:* vitiligo *m*.

vitrage [viˈtrɑːʒ], *s.* **v. (curtain, net),** vitrage *m*.

vitrain [ˈvitrein], *s. Miner: O:* vitrain *m*, houille brillante.

vitreous [ˈvitriəs], *a.* **1.** *Ch: Geol: etc:* vitreux; hyalin; *Med:* **v. degeneration,** dégénérescence vitreuse. **2.** *Anat:* **v. body, humour,** corps, vitré, humeur vitrée (de l'œil). **3.** *A:* **v. electricity,** électricité vitrée.

vitreousness [ˈvitriəsnis], *s.* vitrosité *f.*

vitrescence [viˈtresəns], *s.* vitrosité *f.*

vitrescent [viˈtresənt], *a.* vitrescible, vitreux.

vitrescibility [vitresiˈbiliti], *s.* vitrescibilité *f*, vitrifiabilité *f.*

vitrescible [viˈtresibl], *a.* vitrescible, vitrifiable.

vitrifiability [vitrifaiəˈbiliti], *s.* vitrifiabilité *f*, vitrescibilité *f.*

vitrifiable [vitriˈfaiəbl], *a.* vitrifiable, vitrescible.

vitrification [vitrifiˈkeiʃ(ə)n], *s.* vitrification *f.*

vitrified [ˈvitrifaid], *a.* vitrifié; **v. drain tile,** tuile *f* en grès verni.

vitriform [ˈvitrifɔːm], *a.* vitreux, qui a l'apparence du verre.

vitrify [ˈvitrifai]. **1.** *v.tr.* vitrifier. **2.** *v.i.* se vitrifier.

vitrifying [ˈvitrifaiiŋ], *a.* vitrificateur, -trice; vitrificatif.

vitrinite [ˈvitrinait], *s. Miner:* vitrain *m*, houille brillante.

vitriol [ˈvitriəl], *s.* **1.** (*a*) *Ch: A:* vitriol *m*, sulfate *m*; (*b*) *Miner:* **blue, copper, v.,** vitriol bleu, couperose bleue, sulfate *m* de cuivre; **green v.,** vitriol vert, couperose verte, sulfate de fer, sulfate ferreux; **white v.,** vitriol blanc, couperose blanche, sulfate de zinc; **red v.,** biebérite *f*, rhodalose *f*. **2. (oil of) v.,** (huile *f* de) vitriol; acide *m* sulfurique; **to throw v. at s.o.,** lancer du vitriol sur qn, vitrioler qn; **v. throwing,** vitriolage *m*; **v. thrower,** vitrioleur, -euse; *Fig:* **pen dipped in v.,** plume trempée dans le vitriol.

vitriolated [ˈvitriəleitid], *a.* vitriolé.

vitriolation [vitriəˈleiʃ(ə)n], *s.* vitriolisation *f.*

vitriolic [vitriˈɔlik], *a.* **1.** (acide) vitriolique. **2.** *Fig:* **v. criticism,** critique *f* au vitriol.

vitriolization [vitriəlaiˈzeiʃ(ə)n], *s. Ch: Ind:* vitriolisation *f.*

vitriolize [ˈvitriəlaiz], *v.tr.* **1.** *Ch: Ind:* vitrioler (un sulfure, etc.). **2.** lancer du vitriol sur, vitrioler (qn).

vitroclastic [vitrəˈklæstik], *a. Geol:* à cassure vitreuse.

vitrodentine [vitrouˈdentiːn], *s. Anat:* émail *m* (des dents).

vitrophyre [ˈvitroufaiər], *s. Geol:* vitrophyre *m*.

Vitruvian [viˈtruːviən], *a. Arch:* de Vitruve; **V. scroll,** postes *fpl.*

Vitruvius [viˈtruːviəs], *Pr.n.m. Rom.Hist:* Vitruve.

vitta, *pl.* **-ae** [ˈvitə, -iː], *s.* **1.** (*a*) *Rom.Ant:* vitta *f*; (*b*) *pl. Ecc.Cost:* **vittae,** fanons *m* (de mitre d'évêque). **2.** (*a*) *Nat.Hist:* bande *f* (de couleur), raie *f*; (*b*) *Bot:* canal *m*, -aux, résinifère, bandelette *f* (du fruit des ombellifères).

vittate [ˈviteit], *a. Nat.Hist:* vittigère.

vitular [ˈvitjulər], *a. Vet:* vitulaire.

vituperate [viˈtjuːpəreit]. **1.** *v.tr.* injurier, *Lit:* vitupérer (qn); dire des injures à, insulter, outrager, vilipender (qn). **2.** *v.i.* déblatérer, vitupérer (**against s.o., sth.,** contre qn, qch.).

vituperation [vitjuːpəˈreiʃ(ə)n], *s.* injures *fpl*, insultes *fpl*, invectives *fpl*; vitupération *f*; **when he turns to v.,** lorsqu'il se met à déblatérer.

vituperative [viˈtjuːpərətiv], *a.* injurieux, hargneux, vitupérateur, -trice.

vituperator [vi'tju:pəreitər], *s.* vitupérateur, -trice.
Vitus ['vaitəs], *Pr.n.m. Ecc:* (Saint) Guy; *Med:* **Saint Vitus's dance,** chorée *f*; danse *f* de Saint-Guy.
viva[1] ['vi:və], *int. & s.* vivat (*m*).
viva[2] ['vaivə], *s. Sch: F:* = VIVA VOCE 3.
vivace [viv'ɑ:tʃei], *adv. & a. Mus:* vivace *inv.*
vivacious [vi'veiʃəs], *a.* **1.** (*of pers.*) vif, animé, enjoué, éveillé; **to be v.,** (i) avoir de la vivacité; (ii) se montrer plein d'entrain, de verve. **2.** (*a*) *A:* (*of pers.*) robuste; *A:* vivace; (*b*) *Bot:* (plante) vivace.
vivaciously [vi'veiʃəsli], *adv.* avec enjouement, avec verve, avec entrain, d'un air enjoué.
vivaciousness [vi'veiʃəsnis], **vivacity** [vi'væsiti], *s.* vivacité *f*, verve *f*, vie *f*; animation *f*, enjouement *m*, entrain *m*.
vivarium, *pl.* **-iums, -ia** [vai'vɛəriəm, -iəmz, -iə], *s.* **1.** (*for animals, plants*) vivarium *m.* **2.** *Pisc: A:* (*fishpond*) vivier *m.*
vivat ['vaivæt], *int. & s.* vivat (*m*).
viva voce ['vaivə'vousi, -'voutʃi]. **1.** *adv.* de vive voix, oralement. **2.** *a.* oral, -aux. **3.** *s. Sch:* (*often shortened to* **viva**) examen oral, épreuves orales; *F:* (l')oral *m.*
vivax ['vaivæks], *s. Med:* plasmodium *m* vivax.
viverricula [vive'rikjulə], *s. Z:* viverricula, *f*, viverricule *f.*
Viverridae [vi'veridi:], *s.pl. Z:* viverridés *m.*
viverrine [vi'verain], *a. Z:* viverrin; **v. cat,** chat viverrin; **v. otter,** cynogale *f.*
vivers ['vaivəz], *s.pl. Scot:* (*a*) vivres *m*, provisions *f*; (*b*) victuailles *f*; *F:* mangeaille *f.*
vives [vaivz], *s.pl. Vet:* avives *f*; parotidite *f.*
Vivian ['viviən]. **1.** *Pr.n.m.* Vivien. **2.** *Pr.n.f.* (*also* **Vivien(ne)**, Vivienne; *Lit:* **Merlin and V.** Merlin et Viviane.
vivianite ['viviənait], *s. Miner:* vivianite *f.*
vivid ['vivid], *a.* **1.** (*of light, colour*) vif, éclatant, brillant, tranchant; **meadow of v. green,** pré d'un vert éclatant, cru; **v. flash of lightning,** éclair aveuglant. **2.** (*a*) (*of pers.*) vif, vigoureux; (*b*) **v. imagination, interest,** imagination vive; vif intérêt; **I have a v. recollection of the scene,** j'ai un souvenir très vif, très net, de la scène; **v. description, picture, of sth.,** description, image, vivante de qch.; **v. expression,** expression qui fait image.
vividly ['vividli], *adv.* **1.** vivement, avec éclat; **to burn v.,** brûler avec éclat; **v. coloured,** (i) aux couleurs tranchantes; (ii) haut en couleur. **2. to describe sth. v.,** décrire qch. d'une manière vivante, sous de vives couleurs.
vividness ['vividnis], *s.* **1.** vivacité *f*, éclat *m* (de la lumière, des couleurs). **2. the v. of his style,** la vigueur, le pittoresque, de son style; **the v. of his images,** ses images frappantes; *Psy:* **v. of images,** vividité *f* des images.
vivific [vi'vifik], *a.* vivifiant.
vivification [vivifi'keiʃ(ə)n], *s.* vivification *f*, vivifiement *m.*
vivifier ['vivifaiər], *s.* vivificateur, -trice.
vivify ['vivifai]. **1.** *v.tr.* vivifier, (r)animer; rendre la vie à, ranimer (une institution, etc.). **2.** *v.i.* prendre de la vie; s'animer.
vivifying ['vivifaiiŋ], *a.* vivifiant.
Viviparidae [vivi'pæridi:], *s.pl. Moll:* viviparidés *m.*
viviparity [vivi'pæriti], *s. Biol:* viviparité *f.*
viviparous [vi'vipərəs], *a. Bot: Z:* vivipare.
viviparously [vi'vipərəsli], *adv.* viviparement, à la façon des vivipares.
viviparousness [vi'vipərəsnis], *s. Biol:* viviparité *f.*
viviparus [vi'vipərəs], *s. Moll:* paludine *f*, viviparus *m.*
vivisect [vivi'sekt, 'vivisekt]. **1.** *v.tr.* pratiquer des vivisections sur (des animaux). **2.** *v.i.* faire de la vivisection.
vivisection [vivi'sekʃ(ə)n], *s.* **1.** vivisection *f.* **2.** *Fig:* critique minutieuse (et brutale).
vivisectionist [vivi'sekʃənist], *s.* **1.** celui qui pratique (habituellement) la vivisection; vivisecteur *m.* **2.** partisan *m* de la vivisection.
vivisector [vivi'sektər], *s.* vivisecteur *m.*
vixen ['viksn], *s.f.* **1.** *Z:* renarde. **2.** *F:* mégère, femme acariâtre; *F:* teigne.
vixenish ['viksəniʃ], *a.* (femme) acariâtre, méchante; (caractère, etc.) de mégère.
vixenishly ['viksəniʃli], *adv.* méchamment.
viz [viz] (*when reading aloud usu.* **namely** ['neimli]), *adv.* (*abbr. for* VIDELICET) à savoir; c'est-à-dire.
viza ['vi:zə], *s. Ich:* **v. (sturgeon),** (esturgeon *m*) viza (*m*).
vizcacha [vis'kætʃə], *s. Z:* (i) (*also* **vizcachon** [viskæ'tʃɔn]) **(plains, pampas) v.,** viscache *f*, lièvre *m* des pampas; lagostomus *m*; (ii) **mountain v.,** lagidium *m*, lagotis *m.*
vizcachera [viskæ'tʃɛərə], *s. Z:* viscachère *f.*
vizier [vi'ziər], *s. Hist:* vizir *m*; **grand v.,** grand vizir.
vizierate [vi'ziəreit], **viziership** [vi'ziəʃip], *s. Hist:* vizir(i)at *m.*
vizierial [vi'ziəriəl], *a.* vizirial, -aux.
vizor ['vaizər], *s.* = VISOR.
Vlach [vlæk], *a. & s. Ethn: Geog:* Valaque (*mf*).
vlei [flei], *s.* (*in S. Africa*) marécage *m.*
vocab [və'kæb, 'voukæb], *s. Sch: F:* vocabulaire *m.*
vocable ['voukəbl], *s.* vocable *m.*
vocabulary [və'kæbjuləri], *s.* **1.** (*a*) vocabulaire *m*, lexique *m* (accompagnant un texte); **book published with an English–French v.,** livre édité avec un vocabulaire anglais–français; (*b*) vocabulaire, glossaire *m* (faisant fonction de dictionnaire restreint). **2.** vocabulaire (d'une langue, d'un métier, auteur); lexique (d'une langue); **to enlarge one's v.,** enrichir son vocabulaire; **Balzac has a large v.,** le vocabulaire de Balzac est très riche.
vocal ['voukl]. **1.** *a.* (*a*) (*of sound, music*) vocal, -aux; **v. score,** partition *f* de chant; **v. impairment,** altération *f* de la voix; *Anat:* **v. cords,** cordes, bandes, vocales; *Ecc:* **v. prayer,** prière vocale; (*b*) *Ling:* (*of vowel*) voisé; (*of consonant*) sonore; (*of sound*) vocal, vocalique; (*c*) doué de voix; capable de produire des sons; **the v. statue of Memnon,** la statue de Memnon qui faisait entendre des sons harmonieux; *F:* **the most v. member of the audience,** le membre de l'auditoire qui s'est fait le plus entendre, qui s'est montré le plus bruyant, qui a eu le plus à dire; **it's the most v. who carry the day,** ce sont ceux qui crient le plus fort qui l'emportent; (*of animal, bird*) **to be more v. than usual,** miauler, etc., chanter, plus que d'habitude; (*d*) *Lit: Poet:* bruyant, sonore; **the woods are v. with the song of birds,** les bois retentissent du chant des oiseaux. **2.** *s.* (*a*) *Ling:* son vocal; (*b*) **vocals,** (i) *Mus:* musique vocale, vocaux *m*, chant *m*; (ii) *R.C.Ch:* vocaux, vocales; *NAm: P:* **to give with (the) vocals,** chanter, *P:* goualer.
vocalic [və'kælik], *a.* **1.** (langue) qui a beaucoup de voyelles. **2.** (son) vocalique; *Ling:* **v. change,** changement *m* vocalique. **3.** *s. Ling:* voyelle *f.*
vocalise ['voukəli:z], *s. Mus:* chant *m* sans paroles.
vocalism ['voukəlizm], *s. Ling: Mus:* vocalisme *m.*
vocalist ['voukəlist], *s.* chanteur *m*, cantatrice *f.*
vocalization [voukəlai'zeiʃ(ə)n], *s.* **1.** prononciation *f*, articulation *f* (d'un mot). **2.** *Mus:* vocalisation *f.* **3.** *Ling:* vocalisation; (*a*) changement *m* (d'une consonne sourde) en consonne sonore; (*b*) changement en voyelle.
vocalize ['voukəlaiz]. **1.** *v.tr.* (*a*) prononcer, articuler (un mot); chanter (un air); (*b*) *Ling:* (i) vocaliser (une consonne); changer (une consonne) en voyelle; (ii) sonoriser, voiser (une consonne); (iii) ajouter les points-voyelles à (un texte hébreu); (*c*) *Mus:* vocaliser (un air). **2.** *v.i.* (*a*) *Mus:* faire des vocalises, vocaliser; (*b*) *F:* chanter, chantonner; (*c*) *F:* se faire entendre; crier; vocaliser.
vocally ['voukəli], *adv.* **1.** (*a*) vocalement, oralement; (*b*) **to protest v.,** protester à haute voix. **2.** par des chants, à l'aide du chant.
vocation [və'keiʃ(ə)n], *s.* **1.** (*a*) vocation *f*; **v. to the ministry,** vocation sacerdotale; (*b*) **the V. of the Gentiles,** la vocation des gentils; (*c*) **a v. for literature,** la vocation littéraire. **2.** vocation, profession *f*, métier *m*, état *m*, emploi *m*; **to mistake, miss, one's v.,** manquer sa vocation; **all vocations are open to the youth of today,** tous les métiers sont ouverts à la jeunesse d'aujourd'hui.
vocational [və'keiʃ(ə)n(ə)l], *a.* (enseignement, cours) professionnel; **v. bias,** déformation professionnelle; **v. guidance,** orientation professionnelle; **v. adviser,** *NAm:* **v. guidance counselor,** orienteur professionnel, conseiller, -ère, d'orientation scolaire et professionnelle.
vocationalism [və'keiʃ(ə)nəlizm], *s. Sch:* enseignement professionnel.
vocationally [və'keiʃ(ə)nəli], *adv.* du point de vue professionnel.
vocative ['vɔkətiv], *a. & s. Gram:* **v. (case),** (cas) vocatif *m*; **in the v.,** au vocatif.
vociferance [və'sifərəns], *s.* **1.** vociférations *fpl*, clameur(s) *f*(*pl*). **2.** ton criard.
vociferant [və'sifərənt], *a.* qui vocifère; vociférant, bruyant, criard.
vociferate [və'sifəreit], *v.i. & tr.* (*a*) vociférer, crier (**against,** contre); (*b*) crier à pleins poumons; s'égosiller.
vociferation [vəsifə'reiʃ(ə)n], *s.* **1.** cri *m*, clameur *f.* **2.** vociférations *fpl*, cris, clameurs.
vociferator [və'sifəreitər], *s.* vociférateur, -trice, braillard, -arde.
vociferous [və'sifərəs], *a.* vociférant, bruyant, criard, braillard.
vociferously [və'sifərəsli], *adv.* en vociférant, avec des vociférations; bruyamment; **they were crying their wares v.,** ils s'égosillaient à crier leur marchandise.
vodka ['vɔdkə], *s.* vodka *f.*
voe [vou], *s. Geog:* (*in Orkney and Shetland Islands*) crique *f.*
voglite ['vouglait], *s. Miner:* voglite *f.*
vogue [voug], *s.* vogue *f*, mode *f*; **the v. of short skirts,** la vogue des jupes courtes; **when short skirts were the v.,** quand les jupes courtes étaient à la mode; **they have had a great v.,** ils ont eu une grande vogue; **to be in v.,** être en vogue, à la mode, de mode; avoir de la vogue, une vogue; **it's all the v.,** c'est la mode; **to bring sth. into v.,** mettre qch. en vogue, en faveur, à la mode; **to come into v.,** entrer en vogue; **v. word,** mot à la mode.
voice[1] [vɔis], *s.* **1.** voix *f*; (*a*) **to raise, lower, one's v.,** hausser, baisser, la voix; **in a gentle v.,** d'une voix douce, d'un ton doux; **in a low v.,** à voix basse, à mi-voix, à demi-voix; **to speak in a loud v.,** parler à haute voix, à voix haute, d'une voix retentissante; **to raise one's v. against sth.,** élever la voix contre qch.; **he likes to hear his own v.,** il aime à s'entendre parler; (*of singer*) **she's not in (good) v.,** elle n'est pas en voix; **cracked v.,** voix fêlée; **to lose one's v.,** attraper une extinction de voix; **loss of v.,** extinction de voix; *Mus:* **a soprano v.,** une voix de soprano; **v. test,** audition *f*; **v. box,** larynx *m*; **v. production,** (i) élocution *f*, diction *f*; (ii) *Mus:* mise *f* de voix; *Mil:* **v. drill,** école *f* d'intonation; **v. tube, pipe,** porte-voix *m inv*; *Av:* aviophone *m*; *NAm:* **v. vote,** vote par acclamation; *T.V:* **v. in,** voix dans le champ; **v. off, over,** voix hors champ; *Elcs: W.Tel:* **v. circuit,** circuit *m* de phonie; **v. communication, transmission,** phonie *f*, radiotéléphonie *f*; **v. dialling,** sélection *f* à distance par fréquence vocale; **v. frequency,** fréquence vocale; **v. operated,** à commande par fréquence vocale; **v. grade channel,** voie *f* à fréquence vocale; *Cmptr:* **v. response unit,** unité *f* de réponse vocale; **v. test,** essai *m* téléphonique, téléphonométrique; (*b*) *Fig:* **the v. of the storm,** la voix de la tempête; **the v. of conscience,** la voix de la conscience. **2.** (*a*) voix, suffrage *m*; **I count on your v.,** je compte sur votre voix; (*b*) **to give v. to one's indignation,** exprimer son indignation; **we have no v. in the matter,** nous n'avons pas voix au chapitre; **they refused with one v.,** ils refusèrent tout d'une voix, à l'unanimité. **3.** *Gram:* voix (du verbe); **in the active, passive, v.,** à la voix active, passive; à l'actif, au passif. **4.** *Ling:* phonème sonant; son voisé.
voice[2], *v.tr.* **1.** exprimer, énoncer (une opinion); **he was chosen to v. their grievances,** il fut choisi pour exprimer, pour exposer, leurs griefs; **to v. the general feeling,** exprimer, interpréter, le sentiment général, l'opinion générale. **2.** *Mus:* (*a*) ajouter le chant à (un morceau de musique); (*b*) harmoniser (un orgue, un tuyau d'orgue). **3.** *Ling:* voiser, sonoriser, démuétiser (une consonne).
voiced [vɔist], *a.* **1.** *with adj. prefixed, e.g.* **sweet(-)v., low(-)v., loud(-)v.,** à la voix douce, basse, forte. **2.** *Ling:* (voyelle) voisée, (consonne) sonore, voisée, (son) vocalique; *f* **became v.,** *f* s'est sonorisé.
voiceful ['vɔisful], *a. Lit:* sonore, retentissant.
voiceless ['vɔislis], *a.* **1.** sans voix; muet; *Med:* aphone; **the v. minorities,** les minorités silencieuses, qui ne savent pas se faire entendre. **2.** *Ling:* sourd, non voisé; (son) soufflé.
voicelessly ['vɔislisli], *adv.* silencieusement, en silence.
voicelessness ['vɔislisnis], *s.* **1.** mutisme *m*, silence *f.* **2.** *Ling:* caractère sourd (d'une consonne).
voicer ['vɔisər], *s. Mus:* harmoniste *m* (d'orgues).
voicing ['vɔisiŋ], *s.* **1.** *Mus:* harmonisation *f* (d'un tuyau d'orgue). **2.** *Ling:* voisement *m* (d'une voyelle, consonne), sonorisation *f* (d'une consonne).
void[1] [vɔid], *a. & s.*
I. *a.* **1.** (*a*) *Lit:* vide; **v. space,** espace vide; (*b*) *Cards:* **v. suit,** couleur *f* dont on n'a pas de cartes dans son jeu. **2.** (*of office, etc.*) vacant, inoccupé; **to fall v.,** devenir inoccupé, vaquer. **3.** *Jur:* (*of deed, contract, etc.*) nul, *f.* nulle; **absolutely v.,** radicalement nul; **to make a clause v.,** annuler une clause, frapper une clause de nullité; **under pain of being declared v.,** sous peine de nullité; **v. (voting) paper,** bulletin nul; **v. money order,** mandat-poste prescrit, nul; *Cmptr:* **v. date,** date de péremption. **4.** *Poet:* vain, inutile, sans valeur. **5.** dépourvu, dénué, exempt, libre (**of,** de); **proposal v. of reason,** proposition dénuée, dépourvue, de raison, proposition déraisonnable; **style v. of all affectation,** style libre, exempt, de toute affectation.
II. *s.* **1.** vide *m*; **to fill the v.,** combler le vide; **he disappeared into the v.,** il a disparu dans le vide; **the aching v. in his heart,** la perte douloureuse qui lui tenait

au cœur; *F:* **to have an aching v.,** avoir l'estomac dans les talons, avoir des tiraillements *m*, crampes *f*, d'estomac; avoir l'estomac tenaillé (par la faim); *Cards:* **hand with a v. in hearts,** jeu *m* sans cœur. **2.** *Cmptr:* défaut *m* d'encrage.

void[2], *v.tr.* **1.** *Jur:* résoudre, résilier, annuler (un contrat, etc.). **2.** évacuer (des matières fécales, etc.).

voidable ['vɔidəbl], *a. Jur:* (contrat, etc.) résoluble, annulable.

voidableness ['vɔidəbəlnis], *s. Jur:* annulabilité *f.*

voidance ['vɔid(ə)ns], *s.* **1.** *Ecc:* expulsion *f* (de qn) d'un bénéfice. **2.** *Ecc:* vacance *f* (d'un bénéfice). **3.** *Jur:* annulation *f* (d'un contrat, etc.); résiliation *f.* **4.** évacuation *f* (des selles).

voided ['vɔidid], *a. Her:* vidé.

voiding ['vɔidiŋ], *s.* = VOIDANCE 3, 4.

voidness ['vɔidnis], *s.* **1.** vide *m*, vacuité *f.* **2.** *Jur:* nullité *f.*

voile [vɔil], *s. Tex:* voile *m.*

voivode ['vɔivoud], *s. Hist:* voïvode *m*, vayvode *m.*

volant ['voulənt], *a.* **1.** *Nat.Hist:* volant. **2.** *Her:* volant, essorant; **eagle v.,** aigle volant.

Volapük, -puk ['vɔləpjuk, -puk], *s. Ling: A:* volapük *m.*

volar ['voulər], *a. Anat:* (i) palmaire; (ii) plantaire.

volatile ['vɔlətail], *a.* **1.** *O:* (*of insect*) qui vole, peut voler; *O:* volatile. **2.** *Ch: etc:* volatil, gazéfiable; *s.* substance *f* volatile; **v. oil,** huile volatile; huile essentielle; *A:* **v. alkali,** alcali volatil. **3.** (*a*) gai, vif, folâtre; (*b*) volage, inconstant, étourdi; (*c*) versatile.

volatileness ['vɔlətailnis], *s.* caractère *m* volage; inconstance *f*, étourderie *f.*

volatility [vɔlə'tiliti], *s.* **1.** *Ch:* volatilité *f*; *I.C.E:* **fuel of low v.,** combustible peu volatil. **2.** = VOLATILENESS.

volatilizable ['vɔlətilaizəbl], *a. Ch:* volatilisable.

volatilization [vəlætilai'zeiʃ(ə)n], *s. Ch:* volatilisation *f*, subtilisation *f.*

volatilize [və'lætilaiz], *v. Ch:* **1.** *v.tr.* volatiliser (un liquide). **2.** *v.i.* se volatiliser.

Volcae ['vɔlsiː], *s.pl. A.Hist:* Volces *m.*

volcanic [vɔl'kænik], *a.* **1.** volcanique; **by v. action,** volcaniquement; *Miner:* **v. glass,** verre *m* volcanique, obsidiane *f*, obsidienne *f*; pierre *f* des volcans. **2. v. temperament,** tempérament *m* volcanique.

volcanically [vɔl'kænikəli], *adv.* volcaniquement, de façon volcanique.

volcanicity [vɔlkə'nisiti], *s.* vulcanicité *f*, volcanisme *m.*

volcanism ['vɔlkənizm], *s. Geol:* volcanisme *m*, vulcanisme *m.*

volcanist ['vɔlkənist], *s.* **1.** volcaniste *m*, vulcanologue *mf.* **2.** partisan *m* de la théorie du vulcanisme; vulcaniste *m.*

volcano, *pl.* **-oes** [vɔl'keinou, -ouz], *s.* volcan *m*; **active, dormant, extinct, v.,** volcan actif, dormant, éteint; **shield v.,** volcan bouclier, hawaïen; **plug v.,** volcan péléen; **mud v.,** source boueuse; salse *f*, soufflard *m*; *Fig:* **to be on the edge of a v.,** être sur un volcan.

volcanologic(al) [vɔlkənə'lɔdʒik(l)], *a.* vulcanologique.

volcanologist [vɔlkə'nɔlədʒist], *s.* vulcaniste *m*, vulcanologue *mf*, volcanologue *mf.*

vole[1] [voul], *s. Cards:* vole *f.*

vole[2], *v.i. Cards:* faire la vole.

vole[3], *s. Z:* campagnol *m*; **(field) v.,** campagnol commun, des champs; **bank v.,** campagnol roussâtre; **short-tailed field v.,** campagnol agreste; **pine v.,** campagnol souterrain; **Mediterranean pine v.,** campagnol à douze côtes; **snow v.,** campagnol de Crespan, des neiges; **water v.,** campagnol rat d'eau.

volet ['vɔlei], *s. Art:* volet *m* (d'un triptyque).

volitant ['vɔlitənt], *a.* (*of insect, etc.*) voltigeant, qui se déplace sans cesse.

volition [və'liʃ(ə)n], *s.* volition *f*, volonté *f*; **to do sth. of, by, one's own v.,** faire qch. de son propre gré, de plein gré, spontanément.

volitional [və'liʃən(ə)l], **volitionary** [və'liʃ(ə)nəri], *a.* volitif, volitionnel, de la volonté.

volitive ['vɔlitiv], *a.* volitif.

volley[1] ['vɔli], *s.* **1.** volée *f*, salve *f* (d'armes à feu, de canon); volée, grêle *f* (de coups de bâton); grêle (de pierres); **to fire, discharge, a v.,** tirer une volée, une salve; tirer un feu de peloton, un feu de salve; **v. firing,** (i) feu *m* de salve, de peloton; (ii) *Min:* tir *m*, tirage *m*, en volée. **2.** volée, bordée *f* (d'injures, d'invectives); salve (d'applaudissements); **a v. of oaths,** une bordée de jurons. **3.** *Ten: etc:* (balle prise de) volée; **low v.,** volée basse.

volley[2]. **1.** *v.tr.* (*a*) lancer une volée de (missiles); **to v. stones at s.o.,** lancer une grêle de pierres à, contre, qn; (*b*) *Mil: etc:* tirer une volée, une salve, de (projectiles); **to v. (forth, out) abuse,** lâcher une bordée d'injures; (*c*) *Ten: etc:* **to v. the ball, a return,** *v.i.* **to v.,** reprendre la balle de volée; relancer la balle à la volée; **to half v. (the ball),** prendre la balle entre bond et volée. **2.** *v.i.* (*a*) (*of guns*) partir ensemble; tirer simultanément; (*b*) tonner, faire un bruit retentissant.

volleyball ['vɔlibɔːl], *s. Sp:* volley-ball *m*; **v. player,** volleyeur, -euse.

volleyer ['vɔliər], *s. Ten:* volleyeur, -euse.

volplane[1] ['vɔlplein], *s. Av:* vol plané.

volplane[2], *v.i. Av:* **1.** faire du vol plané; planer. **2.** descendre en vol plané; **to v. to the ground,** atterrir en vol plané.

Volscian ['vɔlʃiən]. **1.** *A.Hist:* (*a*) *a.* volsque; (*b*) *s.* Volsque *mf.* **2.** *s. Ling:* le volsque.

volt[1] [voult], *s. Equit: Fenc:* volte *f*; *Fenc:* **to make a v.,** volter; *Equit:* **to cut a v.,** couper le rond.

volt[2], *s. El.Meas:* volt *m*; **hundred v. dynamo,** dynamo pour cent volts; **no-v. release,** déclenchement de tension nulle; **v. rise,** surtension *f*; **v. ampere,** voltampère *m*; **v. ampere meter,** voltampèremètre *m*; **v. ampere hour,** voltampère-heure *m*, *pl.* voltampères-heures; **v. box,** boîte *f* de résistances.

Volta ['vɔltə], *Pr.n. Geog:* **the (River) V.,** la Volta; **Upper V.,** (la République de) la Haute-Volta.

voltage ['voultidʒ], *s. El:* tension *f*; **at a v. of 120 volts,** à une tension de 120 volts; **to apply the v. to a circuit,** mettre un circuit sous tension; **application of the v. to a circuit,** mise *f* d'un circuit sous tension; **applied v.,** tension appliquée; **excessive v.,** surtension *f*; **high, low, v.,** haute, basse, tension; **high v. test,** essai *m* de claquage; **zero v.,** tension nulle; **v. drop,** chute *f* de tension; **rated v., v. rating,** tension nominale; **terminal v., pole v.,** tension aux bornes; *W.Tel:* **negative grid v.,** polarisation négative de grille; **v. driver,** diviseur *m* de tension; **v. recorder,** voltmètre enregistreur; **v. transformer,** transformateur *m* de tension.

voltaic[1] [vɔl'teiik], *a. El:* (pile, courant, arc) voltaïque.

Voltaic[2], *a. Geog:* voltaïque, de la Haute-Volta.

Voltairean, Voltairian [vɔl'tɛəriən], *a. & s.* voltairien, -ienne.

Voltair(ian)ism [vɔl'tɛər(iən)izm], *s.* voltairianisme *m.*

voltaism ['vɔltəizm], *s. El:* voltaïsme *m.*

voltaite ['vɔltəait], *s. Miner:* voltaïte *f.*

voltameter [vɔl'tæmitər], *s. El:* voltamètre *m.*

voltammeter [vɔlt'æmitər], *s. El:* voltampèremètre *m.*

volte [voult], *s.* = VOLT[1].

volte-face[1] ['vɔltfɑːs], *s.* volte-face *f inv.*

volte-face[2], *v.i.* faire volte-face.

voltinism ['vɔltinizm], *s. Ent:* voltinisme *m.*

voltmeter ['voultmiːtər], *s. El:* voltmètre *m*; **dead-beat v.,** voltmètre apériodique.

voltzine ['vɔltsin], **voltzite** ['vɔltsait], *s. Miner:* voltzine *f*, voltzite *f.*

volubility [vɔlju'biliti], *s.* volubilité *f.*

voluble ['vɔljubl], *a.* **1.** (*of speech*) facile, aisé, coulant; (*of pers.*) volubile; (*of tongue*) délié, bien, pendu; **to be a v. talker,** parler avec beaucoup de volubilité, être grand parleur, avoir la langue bien pendue. **2.** *A:* roulant, tournant, pivotant. **3.** *Bot:* volubile.

volubly ['vɔljubli], *adv.* avec volubilité.

volucella [vɔlju'selə], *s. Ent:* volucelle *f.*

volume ['vɔlju(ː)m], *s.* **1.** volume *m*, livre *m*; **large v.,** tome *m*; **work in six volumes, six-v. work,** ouvrage en six volumes; **v. one,** volume premier, premier volume, tome premier; **it would take volumes to relate all the details,** il faudrait des volumes pour raconter tous les détails; **her look spoke volumes,** sa mine en disait long; **it speaks volumes for him,** cela en dit long en sa faveur. **2.** *Archeol:* volume; parchemin enroulé autour d'un bâton, parchemin en rouleau. **3. volumes of smoke,** nuages *m*, tourbillons *m*, de fumée; **volumes of water,** flots *m*, torrents *m*, d'eau. **4.** (*a*) *Ch: Ph:* volume; **densities for equal volumes,** densités à volume égal; **atomic, molecular, nuclear, v.,** volume atomique, moléculaire, nucléaire; *Atom.Ph:* **sensitivity v.,** volume efficace; **v. absorption,** absorption *f* volumétrique; **v. concentration,** concentration *f* en volume; **v. recombination,** recombinaison *f* volumétrique; (*b*) volume, cubage *m*; **v. of a cone, cylinder, sphere,** volume d'un cône, cylindre, d'une sphère; **the v. of the case must not exceed one cubic metre,** le volume du colis ne doit pas dépasser un mètre cube, le colis ne doit pas cuber plus d'un mètre; **the v. of a reservoir,** le cubage d'un réservoir; *Anat:* **v. of the brain,** volume du cerveau; *I.C.E:* **v. of charge,** cylindrée *f*; **v. efficiency,** rendement *m* volumétrique; **swept v.,** rapport *m* volumétrique. **5. v. of business, exports,** volume des affaires, des exportations; **v. index of imports,** indice *m* du volume des importations. **6.** volume, intensité *f*; (*a*) *Mus: W.Tel:* volume (de la voix, du son); *Mus:* **to give v. to the tone,** nourrir le son; *W.Tel:* **to turn the v. up, down,** augmenter, diminuer, le volume; **v. control,** réglage *m* de volume, de puissance (sonore); **automatic, manual, v. control,** réglage automatique, manuel, du volume; **v. indicator, meter,** indicateur *m* de puissance (sonore); décibelmètre *m*; **v. unit,** unité d'intensité, de puissance, sonore; décibel *m*; **v. range,** gamme *f* de puissance (sonore); (*b*) *Mil:* **v. of fire,** volume, intensité, du feu; *Ball:* **damage v.,** zone *f* d'efficacité (d'une arme atomique).

volumenometer [vɔlju(ː)mi'nɔmitər], *s. Ph:* voluménomètre *m.*

volumeter [vɔ'ljuːmitər], *s. Ph:* volumètre *m.*

volumetric(al) [vɔlju'metrik(l)], *a. Ch: Ph:* volumétrique; **v. analysis,** analyse *f* volumétrique.

volumetrically [vɔlju'metrik(ə)li], *adv.* volumétriquement.

voluminal [və'ljuːmin(ə)l], *a. Ph:* (*of mass*) volumique.

voluminosity [vɔlju(ː)mi'nɔsiti], *s.* = VOLUMINOUSNESS.

voluminous [və'ljuːminəs], *a.* **1.** *A:* (ouvrage) volumineux, en un grand nombre de volumes. **2.** (auteur) volumineux, abondant, fertile, prolifique. **3.** (paquet, etc.) volumineux; **v. curtains,** amples rideaux; **wrapped in a v. cloak,** enveloppé d'un grand manteau.

voluminously [və'ljuːminəsli], *adv.* en grande quantité; abondamment, énormément; **to write v.,** écrire abondamment.

voluminousness [və'ljuːminəsnis], *s.* grand nombre (d'ouvrages); immense quantité *f* (de documents); **the v. of her correspondence,** son énorme correspondance.

Volumnia [və'lʌmniə], *Pr.n.f. Rom.Hist:* Volumnie, Volumnia.

voluntariate [vɔlən'tɛəriət], *s. Mil: A:* volontariat *m.*

voluntarily ['vɔləntərili], *adv.* volontairement, de son propre mouvement, de (son) plein gré.

voluntariness ['vɔləntərinis], *s.* nature *f* volontaire (d'un acte); spontanéité *f.*

voluntarism ['vɔləntərizm], *s.* **1.** *Phil:* volontarisme *m.* **2.** *Ecc: A:* = VOLUNTARYISM.

voluntarist ['vɔləntərist]. *Phil:* **1.** *a. also* **voluntaristic** [vɔlənt'ristik], volontariste. **2.** *s.* volontariste *mf.*

voluntary ['vɔlənt(ə)ri]. **1.** *a.* (*a*) volontaire, spontané; **v. offer,** offre spontanée; **v. service,** service volontaire; **v. confession of guilt,** confession volontaire; aveu spontané; **v. homicide,** homicide volontaire; **v. discipline,** discipline librement consentie; **he was a v. agent in the matter,** il agissait librement dans l'affaire; (*b*) (i) *Adm: Pol.Ec:* non-gouvernemental, -aux; (ii) **v. school, hospital,** école soutenue, hôpital soutenu, par des contributions volontaires; **v. organization,** organisation bénévole; (*c*) *Physiol:* **v. nerve, muscle,** nerf, muscle, volontaire; (*d*) *Jur:* **v. conveyance, disposition,** cession *f* à titre gratuit; cession volontaire; **v. oath,** serment extrajudiciaire. **2.** *s.* (*a*) *Ecc.Mus:* morceau d'orgue (joué avant, pendant, ou après le service); **concluding, outgoing, v.,** sortie *f*; (*b*) *A:* (*pers.*) partisan *m* de la séparation de l'Église et de l'État et du soutien de l'Église par contributions volontaires.

voluntaryism ['vɔlənt(ə)riizm], *s. Ecc: A:* principe *m* de la séparation de l'Église et de l'État et du soutien de l'Église par contributions volontaires.

volunteer[1] [vɔlən'tiər]. **1.** (*a*) *Mil:* volontaire *m*; **as a v.,** en volontaire; **v. service,** service volontaire; **v. army,** armée de volontaires; *Hist:* **the Volunteers,** armée de simples particuliers embrigadés pour la défense du pays; les Volontaires; (*b*) **to call for volunteers,** demander des hommes de bonne volonté, des volontaires (pour une œuvre de bienfaisance, etc.). **2.** *Jur:* bénéficiaire *mf* d'une cession à titre gratuit. **3.** *Bot: Hort:* **v. plants,** plantes spontanées.

volunteer[2]. **1.** *v.tr.* offrir volontairement, spontanément (ses services); **to v. information,** donner spontanément des renseignements; **to v. to do sth.,** se proposer (volontairement) pour faire qch.; s'offrir à faire qch.; faire qch. de bonne volonté. **2.** *v.i.* (*a*) s'offrir (pour une tâche); (*b*) *Mil:* s'engager comme volontaire; **to v. for a campaign,** s'engager pour une campagne.

voluptuary [və'lʌptjuəri]. **1.** *a.* voluptueux, sybarite, sybaritique. **2.** *s.* voluptueux, -euse, sybarite *mf*, épicurien *m.*

voluptuous [və'lʌptjuəs], *a.* voluptueux, sensuel.

voluptuously [və'lʌptjuəsli], *adv.* voluptueusement.

voluptuousness [və'lʌptjuəsnis], *s.* sensualité *f.*

voluta [və'ljuːtə], *s. Moll:* volute *f.*

volute[1] [və'ljuːt], *s.* **1.** *Arch:* volute *f*, corne *f* (de chapiteau ionique). **2.** (*a*) *Conch:* volute; (*b*) *Moll:* volute. **3.** *Mec.E: I.C.E:* volute, diffuseur *m*; **inlet v.,** volute d'aspiration; *Mec.E:* **delivery v.,** volute de refoulement (de pompe centrifuge); **v. drain,** (dispositif *m* de) vidange *f* de volute.

volute[2], *a.* en volute; voluté; **v. spring,** ressort *m* en volute; **v. chamber,** (i) canal collecteur (de pompe cen-

trifuge); (ii) *I.C.E:* conque *f,* diffuseur *m* (du compresseur).
voluted [və'lju:tid], *a.* voluté; (i) à volutes; (ii) enroulé en spirale.
Volutidae [və'lju:tidi:], *s.pl. Moll:* volutidés *m.*
volutin ['vɔljutin], *s. Ch:* volutine *f.*
volution [və'lju:ʃ(ə)n], *s.* **1.** tour *m* (de spire, spirale). **2.** spire *f* (de coquille). **3.** *Anat:* circonvolution *f.*
volva ['vɔlvə], *s. Fung:* volve *f,* volva *f.*
volvate ['vɔlveit], *a. Fung:* volvé.
Volvocaceae [vɔlvə'keisii:], *s.pl. Algae:* volvocacées *f.*
Volvocales [vɔlvə'keili:z], *s.pl. Algae:* volvocales *f.*
Volvocidae [vɔl'vɔsidi:], *s.pl. Prot:* volvocidés *m.*
volvox ['vɔlvɔks], *s. Prot:* volvox *m,* volvoce *m.*
volvulus ['vɔlvjuləs], *s. Med:* volvulus *m,* iléus *m.*
Vombatidae [vɔm'bætidi:], *s.pl. Z:* vombatidés *m.*
vomer ['voumər], *s. Anat:* vomer *m.*
vomerine ['voumərain], *a. Anat:* vomérien.
vomica, *pl.* **-cas, -cae** ['vɔmikə, -kəz, -si:], *s. Med:* **1.** caverne *f* pulmonaire. **2.** vomique *f*; expectoration *f* de sérosités, de pus, de sang.
vomicine ['vɔmisi:n], *s. Ch:* vomicine *f.*
vomit[1] ['vɔmit], *s.* **1.** matières vomies, vomissure *f,* vomi *m,* vomissement *m*; *Med:* **black v.,** vomito *m* negro, fièvre *f* jaune; *B:* **as the dog returneth to his v.,** comme le chien retourne à son vomissement. **2.** *Med:* vomitif *m.* **3.** *Bot: Pharm:* **v. nut,** noix *f* vomique.
vomit[2], *v.tr. & i.* (*a*) vomir, rendre; **to v. blood,** vomir du sang; **he vomits up everything he eats,** il rejette, il rend, tout ce qu'il mange; **he began to v.,** il fut pris de vomissements; (*b*) (*of chimney, etc.*) **to v. smoke,** vomir de la fumée.
vomiter ['vɔmitər], *s.* vomisseur, -euse.
vomiting ['vɔmitiŋ], *s.* **1.** vomissement *m.* **2.** *Paperm:* **v. boiler,** lessiveur *m* à vomissement, avec tubes de circulation (pour la cuisson de l'alfa).
vomition [və'miʃ(ə)n], *s.* vomissement *m.*
vomitive ['vɔmitiv], *a. & s.* vomitif (*m*).
vomito ['vɔmitou], *s. Med:* vomito *m* (negro), fièvre *f* jaune.
vomitory ['vɔmitəri]. **1.** *a. & s. Med:* vomitif (*m*). **2.** *s. Rom.Ant: ect:* (*also* **vomitorium** [vomi'tɔ:riəm]) vomitoire *m.*
vomiturition [vɔmitju'riʃ(ə)n], *s. Med:* vomiturition *f.*
voodoo[1] ['vu:du:], *s. Anthr:* **1.** vaudou *m.* **2.** **v. (doctor, priest),** vaudou, *pl.* -ous, -oux; sorcier *m* (nègre).
voodoo[2], *v.tr.* (*of voodoo doctor*) ensorceler.
voodooism, voodouism ['vu:duizm], *s.* vaudou *m.*
voracious [və'reiʃəs, vɔr-], *a.* vorace, dévorant; **v. appetite,** appétit dévorant, de loup; **v. reader,** lecteur vorace, grand dévoreur de livres.
voraciously [və'reiʃəsli], *adv.* voracement, avec voracité; **to eat v.,** manger avec avidité, goulûment, de toutes ses dents.
voraciousness [və'reiʃəsnis], **voracity** [və'ræsiti], *s.* voracité *f.*
vorant ['vɔ:rənt], *a. Her:* **serpent v. a child,** guivre *f,* vivre *f,* vouivre *f.*
vortex, *pl.* **-ices, -exes** ['vɔ:teks, -isi:z, -eksiz], *s.* **1.** (*a*) *Ph:* tourbillon *m*; **v. line, filament,** ligne *f,* filet *m,* de tourbillon; **v. motion,** mouvement *m* tourbillonnaire; **v. ring,** vortex *m*; *A.Phil:* **the v. theory,** la théorie des tourbillons; (*b*) *Aedcs: Meteor:* tourbillon, remous *m* (d'air); **v. generator,** générateur *m* de turbulence; **v. sheet,** nappe *f* tourbillonnaire; **v. street,** ligne des tourbillons; (*c*) tourbillon (de fumée, poussière, etc.); (*d*) (*whirlpool*) tourbillon; gouffre *m*; *Fig:* **the v. of pleasure, politics,** le tourbillon des plaisirs, de la politique. **2.** *Anat:* vortex (des fibres du cœur, etc.). **3.** *Ann:* vortex.
vortical ['vɔ:tikl], *a. & s.* **1.** tourbillonnaire, en tourbillon; *Ph:* **v. (motion),** mouvement *m* tourbillonnaire. **2.** tourbillonnant.
vorticel ['vɔ:tisel], **vorticella,** *pl.* **-ae** [vɔ:ti'selə, -i:], **vorticellid** [vɔ:ti'selid], *s. Prot:* vorticelle *f.*
Vorticellidae [vɔ:ti'selidi:], *s.pl. Ann:* vorticellidés *m.*
vorticism ['vɔ:tisizm], *s. Art:* vorticisme *m.*
vorticist ['vɔ:tisist], *s.* **1.** *Art:* vorticiste *m.* **2.** *Ph: Phil:* tourbillonniste *m.*
vorticular [vɔ:'tikjulər], *a.* tourbillonnaire.
vortiginous [vɔ:'tidʒinəs], *a. A:* **1.** tourbillonnaire. **2.** tourbillonnant.
votaress ['voutəris], *s.f.* fervente, adoratrice, sectatrice (**of,** de).
votary ['voutəri], *s.* fervent, -ente (**of,** de). dévot, -ote (**of,** à), adorateur, -trice (**of,** de), sectateur, -trice (**of,** de); *F:* suppôt *m* (**of,** de); **to be a v. of a saint,** être dévot à un saint; **v. of the arts,** partisan zélé des arts, amateur, des arts; **they were all votaries of poetry,** ils étaient tous adonnés à la poésie.
vote[1] [vout], *s.* **1.** (*a*) vote *m,* scrutin *m*; (*by white or black balls*) ballottage *m*; **secret v.,** scrutin secret; **open v.,** scrutin découvert; **popular v.,** consultation *f* populaire; **v. of an assembly,** délibération *f* d'une assemblée; **to put a question to the v., to take a v. on a question,** mettre une question aux voix; aller aux avis; **to take the v.,** procéder au scrutin; **to take a v. by calling over the names of the members,** voter par appel nominatif; (*b*) **(individual) v.,** voix *f,* suffrage *m*; **postal v.,** vote postal; **proxy vote,** vote par personne interposée; **ten thousand votes,** dix mille suffrages; **to give one's v. to, for, s.o.,** donner son vote, sa voix, à qn; **to count, tell, the votes,** énumérer les voix; dépouiller le scrutin; compter les bulletins; **number of votes recorded,** nombre de suffrages exprimés; **to have a v.,** avoir le droit de vote; **to record one's v.,** voter; **votes for women!** la femme doit voter! le droit de vote aux femmes! *coll.* **to lose the trade union v.,** perdre les suffrages des syndicalistes; **the floating v.,** les suffrages des indécis; (*c*) droit *m* de voter; **to have the v.,** avoir le droit de voter. **2.** (*a*) motion *f,* résolution *f*; **v. of censure,** (motion de) censure (*f*); **the v. of censure was defeated,** la motion de censure a été repoussée; **to carry a v.,** adopter une résolution; (*b*) *Parl: Fin:* crédit *m*; **the Army v.,** le crédit militaire.
vote[2]. **1.** *v.i.* voter, se lever (**for, against,** pour, contre); donner sa voix, son vote (**for sth.,** pour qch.); prendre part au vote; **to v. by (a) show of hands,** voter à mains levées; **to be entitled to speak and v.,** avoir voix délibérative; **to v. in the affirmative, negative,** donner un vote affirmatif, négatif; **to v. Communist,** voter communiste; **v. for Thomas!** votez Thomas! **2.** *v.tr.* (*a*) **to v. a sum,** voter une somme, *Parl:* un crédit; **to v. £50,000 for the victims of the disaster,** voter 50,000 livres pour les sinistrés; (*b*) *F:* **she was voted charming,** on déclara à l'unanimité qu'elle était charmante; **I v. (that) we go,** je propose que nous y allions. **3.** (*compound verbs*) (*a*) **to v. down a motion,** repousser une motion; (*b*) **to v. s.o. in,** élire qn.
voter ['voutər], *s.* (*a*) votant, -ante; (*b*) électeur, -trice; **registered v.,** inscrit *m.*
voting[1] ['voutiŋ], *a.* (*of assembly, member*) votant; (*of elector*) voteur, -euse; **v. and tax paying citizen,** citoyen actif.
voting[2], *s.* (participation *f* au) vote; votation *f,* scrutin *m*; (*by white or black balls*) ballottage *m*; **manner of v.,** mode de votation; **result of the v.,** vote; **v. paper,** bulletin *m,* billet *m,* de vote; **to return a blank v. paper,** voter blanc; *Fin:* **v. stock, shares,** actions qui donnent le droit de vote (aux assemblées des actionnaires).
votive ['voutiv], *a.* votif; **v. offering,** offrande votive; ex-voto *m inv*; **v. mass,** messe votive.
vouch [vautʃ]. **1.** *v.tr.* (*a*) affirmer, maintenir, garantir (qch.); **I can v. that he was not there,** je peux garantir qu'il n'y était pas; (*b*) *Jur:* **to v. s.o. to warrant, to warranty,** appeler qn en garantie; (*c*) (i) prouver, confirmer (une affirmation); (ii) appuyer (des dépenses, etc.) de pièces justificatives. **2.** *v.i.* (*a*) **to v. for the truth of sth.,** témoigner de, répondre de, attester, affirmer, la vérité de qch.; **to publish news without vouching for its accuracy,** publier une nouvelle sous toutes réserves; **I can v. for it,** je m'en porte garant; je vous en assure; (*b*) **to v. for s.o.,** répondre de qn; se rendre garant de qn; **I can v. for his good conduct, for his honesty,** je peux attester sa bonne conduite; je le garantis honnête.
vouchee [vau'tʃi:], *s.* caution *f*; répondant, -ante.
voucher ['vautʃər], *s.* **1.** (*pers.*) garant, -ante. **2.** (*a*) justification produite à l'appui de dépenses; pièce justificative, pièce à l'appui, pièce certificative; *Book-k:* pièce comptable; (*b*) *Com: etc:* fiche *f,* bon *m*; **v. for receipt,** recépissé *m,* quittance *f,* pièce *f* de recette; **v. for goods received,** reçu *m* de marchandises; *Mil: etc:* **issue v.,** bon de distribution, de sortie; **return to store v.,** bon de réintégration; (*c*) **cash v.,** bon de caisse; **gift v.,** (i) bon d'achat; (ii) coupon-prime *m, pl.* coupons-prime; **luncheon, meal, v.,** ticket-restaurant *m, pl.* tickets-restaurant; ticket-repas *m, pl.* tickets-repas; chèque-repas *m, pl.* chèques-repas; *Mil: etc:* **travel v.,** feuille *f* de route; (*d*) *Navy:* **sick v.,** certificat *m* de maladie; billet *m* d'hôpital; (*e*) *Publ:* **v. copy,** (exemplaire) justificatif (*m*).
vouchsafe [vautʃ'seif], *v.tr. Lit:* (*a*) **to v. s.o. sth.,** accorder, octroyer, qch. à qn; (*b*) **to v. to do sth.,** daigner faire qch.; **he vouchsafed no reply,** il ne daigna pas répondre.
voussoir ['vu:swa:r], *s. Arch:* voussoir *m,* vousseau *m,* claveau *m*; **centre v.,** clef *f* (de voûte).
vow[1] [vau], *s.* vœu *m,* serment *m*; **the three, monastic, vows,** les trois vœux, les vœux monastiques; **to take the vows,** prononcer, faire, ses vœux, entrer en religion; **baptismal vows,** vœux de baptême; **lovers' vows,** serments d'amoureux; **to make a v.,** faire un vœu; **to make, take, a v. to do sth.,** faire vœu de faire qch.; **to take a v. of poverty,** faire vœu de pauvreté; **to be under a v. to do sth.,** avoir fait le vœu de faire qch.; **to fulfil a v.,** accomplir un vœu; **to keep a v.,** rester fidèle à un vœu; **to break a v.,** violer un vœu.
vow[2], *v.tr.* vouer, jurer; **to v. a temple to Jupiter,** vouer un temple à Jupiter; **to v. obedience,** jurer obéissance; **to v. vengeance against s.o.,** faire vœu, jurer, de se venger sur qn; **to v. an implacable hatred to s.o.,** vouer à qn une haine implacable; *v.i.* **to v. and protest,** jurer ses grands dieux; **to v. a vow,** faire, prononcer, un vœu.
vow[3], *v.tr. A:* (*avow*) affirmer, déclarer (**that,** que); **she vowed that she was delighted,** elle déclara qu'elle était ravie, elle se déclara enchantée.
vowel ['vauəl], *s. Ling:* voyelle *f*; **open, closed, v.,** voyelle ouverte, fermée; **v. sound,** son vocalique; **v. change,** changement vocalique; *Hebrew Gram:* **v. point,** point-voyelle *m, pl.* points-voyelles.
vowelize ['vauəlaiz], *v.tr.* **1.** vocaliser (une consonne). **2.** *Hebrew Gram:* mettre les points-voyelles à (un texte).
vox, *pl.* **voces** [vɔks, 'vousi:z]. *Lt. s.* voix *f*; **v. populi** ['pɔpjul(a)i], la voix du peuple; *Mus:* (*organ*) **v. angelica,** voix céleste; **v. humana** [hju'ma:nə], voix humaine.
voyage[1] ['vɔiidʒ], *s.* (**sea**) **v.,** voyage *m* sur mer, au long cours; (grande) traversée; **v. by air,** voyage aérien; **v. in space,** voyage spatial; **on the v. out, home,** à l'aller, au retour; **to go on a v.,** faire un voyage (**to,** à); (*on luggage*) **not wanted on v.,** bagages *mpl* de cale; **wanted on v.,** malle *f* de cabine.
voyage[2]. **1.** *v.i.* voyager (autrement que par terre, *esp.*) sur, par, mer; naviguer. **2.** *v.tr.* traverser (la mer, l'espace, l'air); parcourir (les mers).
voyager ['vɔiədʒər], *s.* voyageur, -euse, par mer, par avion, dans l'espace; passager, -ère; navigateur *m.*
voyageur [vɔiə'ʒə:r], *s. Hist:* (*in Canada*) batelier *m* qui assurait la liaison entre les comptoirs.
voyaging ['vɔiədʒiŋ], *s.* voyage(s) *m(pl)* sur mer, par avion, dans l'espace.
voyeur [vwa:'jə:r], *s.* voyeur, -euse.
voyeurism [vwa:'jə:rizm], *s.* voyeurisme *m.*
vraic [vreik], *s.* (*in Channel Islands*) varech *m.*
vrbaite ['və:bəait], *s. Miner:* vrbaïte *f.*
Vulcan ['vʌlkən], *Pr.n.m. Myth: Astr:* Vulcain.
Vulcanian [vʌl'keiniən], *a. Myth:* vulcanien, vulcanal; *Geol:* vulcanien, plutonien; **the V. theory,** le vulcanisme.
vulcanicity [vʌlkə'nisiti], **vulcanism** ['vʌlkənizm], *Geol:* vulcanicité *f,* volcanisme *m.*
vulcanist ['vʌlkənist], *s. Geol:* vulcaniste *m.*
vulcanite ['vʌlkənait], *s.* vulcanite *f,* ébonite *f.*
vulcanization [vʌlkənai'zeiʃ(ə)n], *s. Ind:* vulcanisation *f* (du caoutchouc, etc.).
vulcanize ['vʌlkənaiz]. **1.** *v.tr.* vulcaniser, cuire (le caoutchouc, etc.). **2.** *v.i.* se vulcaniser; cuire.
vulcanizer ['vʌlkənaizər], *s.* (*device*) vulcanisateur *m.*
vulcanizing ['vʌlkənaiziŋ], *s.* vulcanisation *f*; **hot, cold, v.,** vulcanisation à chaud, à froid.
vulcanological [vʌlkənə'lɔdʒikl], *a. Geol:* vulcanologique.
vulcanologist [vʌlkə'nɔlədʒist], *s. Geol:* vulcanologue *mf,* vulcanologiste *mf.*
vulcanology [vʌlkə'nɔlədʒi], *s. Geol:* vulcanologie *f.*
vulgar ['vʌlgər], *a.* **1.** vulgaire, commun; de mauvais goût; trivial, -aux; du peuple; **v. mind,** esprit vulgaire; **v. manners,** manières communes; **v. display of wealth,** gros luxe de mauvais goût; **v. expressions,** expressions vulgaires, triviales; **to make v. remarks,** dire des vulgarités *f*; **to be v. in one's speech,** s'exprimer vulgairement; **to grow v.,** se vulgariser; *A:* **the v. herd,** *s.* **the v.,** le vulgaire; le commun des hommes; le populaire; **there was something v. about her,** elle avait un je ne sais quoi de peuple; **v. doggerel,** vers de mirliton. **2.** (*a*) vulgaire; communément reçu; du commun des hommes; commun; **v. errors,** erreurs très répandues, vulgaires; (*b*) **the v. tongue,** la langue commune; la langue vulgaire; **v. Latin,** le latin vulgaire; (*c*) *Mth:* **v. fraction,** fraction *f* ordinaire.
vulgarian [vʌl'gɛəriən], *s.* (*a*) personne vulgaire, commune; (*b*) parvenu(e) mal décrassé(e).
vulgarism ['vʌlgərizm], *s.* **1.** expression *f* vulgaire. **2.** vulgarité *f,* trivialité *f.*
vulgarity [vʌl'gæriti], *s.* vulgarité *f,* trivialité *f*; **to lapse into v.,** donner dans le vulgaire, tomber dans le trivial.
vulgarization [vʌlgərai'zeiʃ(ə)n], *s.* vulgarisation *f.*
vulgarize ['vʌlgəraiz], *v.tr.* **1.** vulgariser (une science, etc.). **2.** vulgariser, trivialiser (son style, etc.).
vulgarly ['vʌlgəli], *adv.* **1.** vulgairement, trivialement, grossièrement. **2.** *A:* vulgairement, communément.
vulgate ['vʌlgit, -eit], *s.* **1.** **the V.,** la Vulgate. **2.** leçon reçue (d'un texte classique, d'un passage).

vulgus ['vʌlgəs], *s. Sch: O:* composition *f* en vers latins (sur un sujet donné).

vulnerability [vʌln(ə)rə'biliti], **vulnerableness** ['vʌln(ə)rəbəlnis], *s.* vulnérabilité *f.*

vulnerable ['vʌln(ə)rəbl], *a.* (*a*) vulnérable; **v. to temptation,** sans défense contre la tentation; **v. to criticism,** sensible à la critique; **to find s.o.'s v. spot,** trouver le défaut dans la cuirasse de qn; **that's his v. spot,** c'est son point faible, son talon d'Achille; (*b*) *Cards:* (*at bridge*) vulnérable.

vulnerary ['vʌlnərəri], *a. & s. Pharm:* vulnéraire (*m*).

vulpine ['vʌlpain], *a.* **1.** qui a rapport au renard. **2.** qui tient du renard; rusé, astucieux.

vulpinite ['vʌlpinait], *s. Miner:* vulpinite *f.*

vulture ['vʌltjər], *s.* **1.** *Orn:* vautour *m, F:* charognard *m*; **bearded v.,** gypaète barbu; **black v.,** (i) vautour moine; (ii) *NAm:* vautour noir; **cinereous v.,** vautour moine; **Egyptian v.,** percnoptère *m* d'Égypte, néophron *m*; **(African) hooded v.,** petit vautour; **palm nut v.,** vautour pêcheur, des palmes; **sociable v.,** vautour oricou; **white-backed v.,** vautour à dos blanc; *NAm:* **turkey v.,** vautour aura, catharte *m* aura, *Fr. C:* vautour à tête rouge. **2.** *Fig:* homme *m* rapace, âpre à la curée; affameur *m*, vautour.

Vulturidae [vʌl'tju:ridi:], *s.pl. Orn:* vulturidés *m.*

vulturine ['vʌltʃərain], *a.* **1.** de vautour, des vautours. **2.** *Orn:* vulturin; **v. fish eagle,** vautour-pêcheur *m, pl.* vautours-pêcheurs.

vulturish ['vʌltʃəriʃ], *a.* de vautour; rapace.

vulva ['vʌlvə], *s. Anat:* vulve *f.*

vulval ['vʌlv(ə)l], **vulvar** ['vʌlvər], *a. Anat:* vulvaire.

vulvectomy [vʌl'vektəmi], *s. Surg:* vulvectomie *f.*

vulvismus [vʌl'vismǝs], *s. Med:* vaginisme *m*, vaginodynie *f.*

vulvitis [vʌl'vaitis], *s. Med:* vulvite *f.*

vulvo-vaginal [vʌlvouvə'dʒainl], *a. Anat: Med:* vulvo-vaginal, -aux.

vulvo-vaginitis [vʌlvouvædʒi'naitis], *s. Med:* vulvo-vaginite *f.*

vying ['vaiiŋ], *s.* rivalité *f,* lutte *f.*

W, w ['dʌblju:], *s.* (la lettre) W, w *m*; *Tp:* **W for William,** W comme William; *Biol:* **W chromosome,** chromosome *m* W; *Av:* **W engine,** moteur *m* en W.

Waac [wæk], *s.f. Hist:* (1914–1918) membre *m* du W.A.A.C. (Women's Army Auxiliary Corps).

Waaf [wæf], *s.f. Hist:* membre *m* du W.A.A.F. (Women's Auxiliary Air Force).

wabble[1,2] ['wɔbl], *s.* & *v.i.* & *tr.* = WOBBLE[1,2].

wack [wæk], *s. F:* (*esp. in Liverpool*) copain, -ine, pote *m*; **how're you doing, w.?** alors mon vieux, comment ça va?

wacke ['wækə], *s. Geol:* wacke *f.*

wackily ['wækili], *adv. esp. NAm: F:* **to behave w.,** faire des loufoqueries.

wackiness ['wækinis], *s. esp. NAm: F:* loufoquerie *f.*

wacky ['wæki], *a. esp. NAm: F:* cinglé; loufoque; farfelu; **they're a w. bunch,** c'est une coterie de cinglés.

wad[1] [wɔd], *s.* **1.** (*a*) tampon *m*, bouchon *m*, bourrelet *m*, pelote *f* (de linge, d'ouate, etc.); (*b*) liasse *f* (de billets de banque). **2.** *Sm.a:* rondelle *f*, bourre *f* (de cartouche); *Artil:* bourre (de charge); **w. hook,** tire-bourre *m inv*; dégorgeoir *m*. **3.** *Cer:* cerceau *m* de ciment.

wad[2], *v.tr.* (**wadded**) **1.** bourrer (une arme à feu). **2.** *Dressm: Needlew:* ouater, capitonner, cotonner (un vêtement, une couverture, etc.). **3.** rouler en liasse (des billets de banque, etc.).

wad[3], *s. Miner:* wad *m.*

wadding ['wɔdiŋ], *s.* **1.** ouatage *m*, capitonnage *m*; rembourrage *m*. **2.** (*a*) ouate *f* (pour vêtements, etc.); bourre *f* (pour armes à feu); **some w.,** de l'ouate, de la ouate; (*b*) *coll.* tampons *mpl* d'ouate.

waddle[1] ['wɔdl], *s.* dandinement *m*; tortillement *m* des hanches; démarche *f* de canard.

waddle[2], *v.i.* (*a*) (*of duck, etc.*) marcher cahin-caha; (*b*) (*of pers.*) se dandiner (comme un canard); marcher en canard; **to w. along,** avancer en se dandinant; **the stout lady waddled off,** la grosse dame s'est éloignée avec un dandinement de canard.

waddling[1] ['wɔdliŋ], *a.* dandinant; qui se dandine; (allure, démarche) de canard.

waddling[2], *s.* = WADDLE[1].

waddy ['wɔdi], *s.* **1.** *Austr:* assommoir *m* (des aborigènes). **2.** *U.S:* (*a*) cowboy *m*; (*b*) voleur *m* de bétail.

wade [weid]. **1.** *v.i.* marcher (avec effort) dans l'eau, dans la vase; (*of child*) **to w. in the sea,** patauger dans la mer; **to w. across a stream,** passer à gué un cours d'eau; **to w. through a book, a mass of figures,** venir péniblement à bout d'un livre; se diriger péniblement dans un océan de chiffres; **to w. in,** (i) entrer dans l'eau; (ii) *F:* intervenir; prendre part (à qch.); (iii) *F:* s'attaquer à son adversaire; (iv) *F:* s'y mettre; *F:* **to w. into s.o.,** s'attaquer à qn. **2.** *v.tr.* (*a*) passer à gué (un cours d'eau); (*b*) **to w. a horse across a stream,** faire passer à gué un cours d'eau à un cheval.

wader ['weidər], *s.* **1.** *Orn:* échassier *m*. **2.** **he was watching the waders in the stream,** il regardait les gens qui marchaient, qui pataugeaient, dans le ruisseau. **3.** **waders,** bottes cuissardes imperméables; waders *mpl*; **sewerman's waders,** bottes d'égoutier.

wadi ['wɔdi], *s. Geog:* oued *m.*

wading[1] ['weidiŋ], *a. Orn:* **w. bird** = WADER **1.**

wading[2], *s.* pataugeage *m* dans l'eau; *U.S:* **w. pool,** grenouillère *f* (pour les enfants); **to cross a stream by w.,** passer à gué un cours d'eau; **w. boots** = *waders, q.v. under* WADER **3.**

Wadjak ['wɑ:dʒɑ:k, -djɑ:k], *Pr.n. Prehist:* **W. man,** l'homme de Wadjak.

Wafdist ['wɔftist], *a.* & *s. Hist:* wafdiste (*mf*).

wafer[1] ['weifər], *s.* **1.** *Cu:* gaufrette *f.* **2.** *Ecc:* hostie *f*; **unconsecrated w.,** pain *m* à chanter; **w. cloth,** tavaïol(l)e *f.* **3.** (*a*) *A:* pain à cacheter; (*b*) *Jur:* disque *m* de papier rouge (collé sur un document en guise de cachet). **4.** *Pharm:* cachet *m* (de quinine, etc.).

wafer[2], *v.tr.* **1.** *A:* mettre un pain à cacheter à (une lettre); fermer (une lettre) avec un pain à cacheter; cacheter (une lettre). **2.** apposer un cachet en papier rouge à (un document).

waffle[1] [wɔfl], *s. Cu:* gaufre (américaine); **w. iron,** gaufrier *m*; moule *m* à gaufre(s).

waffle[2], *s. F:* verbosité *f*; verbiage *m*; (*in writing*) remplissage *m*; **it's just w.,** ce n'est que du laïus; c'est parler pour ne rien dire.

waffle[3], *v.i. F:* laïusser; débiter des niaiseries; parler dans le vague; parler pour ne rien dire; (*in writing*) faire du remplissage; **he just waffles on,** (il n'a rien à dire mais) il ne sait pas s'arrêter.

waffler ['wɔflər], *s. F:* laïusseur *m*; type verbeux.

waft[1] [wɑ:ft], *s.* **1.** *Lit:* bouffée *f*, souffle *m* (de vent, d'air); bouffée (de musique, de parfum). **2.** coup *m* d'aile (d'un oiseau). **3.** *Nau: A:* pavillon couplé; flamme couplée; **flag with a w.,** pavillon en berne.

waft[2], *v.tr. Lit:* (*of wind*) **to w. a sound, a scent, through the air,** porter, transporter, un son, un parfum, dans les airs; **music wafted on the breeze,** musique *f* qui flotte, qui arrive, sur la brise; musique apportée par la brise; **scent wafted from the flowers,** parfum qui vient, qui s'exhale, des fleurs; (*of wind*) **to w. the ship along,** faire avancer le navire.

wag[1] [wæg], *s.* **1.** *O:* farceur, -euse; blagueur *m*, plaisant *m*, plaisantin *m*. **2.** *Sch: F: A:* **to play, hop, the w.,** faire l'école buissonnière.

wag[2], *s.* agitation *f*, mouvement *m* (d'un membre, de la queue); hochement *m* (de la tête); (*of dog*) **with a w. of his tail,** en remuant la queue.

wag[3], *v.* (**wagged**) **1.** *v.tr.* agiter, remuer (le bras, etc.); **to w. its tail,** (*of dog*) remuer, agiter, la queue; frétiller de la queue; (*of bird*) hocher la queue; **to w. one's tongue,** (i) jaser; jacasser; (ii) avoir la langue bien pendue; **to w. one's finger at s.o.,** menacer qn du doigt; **to w. one's head,** hocher la tête. **2.** *v.i.* s'agiter, se remuer; (*of pendulum*) osciller; (*of dog*) **his tail was wagging,** sa queue frétillait; **his tongue was beginning to w.,** sa langue se déliait; **her tongue's always wagging,** elle a la langue déliée, bien pendue; **to set (people's) tongues wagging,** faire aller les langues; faire jaser les gens.

wage[1] [weidʒ], *s.* (*a*) salaire *m*; paie *f*; gages *mpl* (de domestique); **basic w.,** salaire de base; **index-linked w.,** salaire indexé; **living w.,** minimum vital; **guaranteed minimum w.** = salaire minimum interprofessionnel de croissance (S.M.I.C.); **to get one's weekly w.,** recevoir son salaire de la semaine; *F:* toucher sa semaine; **to earn good wages,** être bien payé; gagner gros; avoir un bon salaire; **w. earner,** (i) salarié, -iée; (ii) soutien *m* de famille; **wages sheet,** feuille *f* des salaires; (*b*) *Lit:* prix *m*, salaire, récompense *f*; **the wages of sin is death,** la mort est le salaire du péché.

wage[2], *v.tr.* **1.** **to w. war,** faire la guerre (**with, on, against,** à). **2.** *A:* = WAGER[2].

wager[1] ['weidʒər], *s.* **1.** pari *m*; gageure *f*; **to lay, make, a w.,** faire un pari, une gageure; parier, gager; **to take up a w.,** accepter, soutenir, une gageure; *Ins:* **w. policy,** police gageuse. **2.** *Hist:* **w. of battle,** combat *m* judiciaire, duel *m* judiciaire; *Jur: A:* **w. of law,** témoignage justificateur (porté par les amis de l'accusé).

wager[2], *v.tr.* parier, gager (cent livres, etc.); **to w. that . . .,** parier que . . ..

wagerer ['weidʒərər], *s.* parieur, -euse; gageur, -euse.

wagering ['weidʒəriŋ], *s.* paris *mpl*, gageures *fpl.*

waggery ['wægəri], *s. A:* **1.** plaisanterie(s) *f*(*pl*); moquerie *f*; espièglerie *f*; facétie(s) *f*(*pl*). **2.** (**piece of**) **w.,** plaisanterie, facétie.

wagging ['wægiŋ], *s.* agitation *f*, remuement *m* (de la queue, etc.); branlement *m*, hochement *m* (de la tête); *F:* **there was a lot of tongue w. going on,** on jasait, bavardait, beaucoup.

waggish ['wægiʃ], *a. O:* plaisant, badin; moqueur, -euse, blagueur, -euse; facétieux.

waggishly ['wægiʃli], *adv. O:* plaisamment, facétieusement; en plaisantant.

waggishness ['wægiʃnis], *s. O:* caractère blagueur; disposition *f* à la plaisanterie.

waggle ['wægl]. **1.** *v.tr.* & *i. F:* = WAG[3]. **2.** *v.tr. Golf:* agiter (sa crosse) avant de viser la balle.

waggon ['wægən], *s. see* WAG(G)ON.

Wagnerian [vɑ:g'niəriən], **Wagnerite**[1] ['vɑ:gnərait], *a.* & *s. Mus:* wagnérien, -ienne; wagnériste (*mf*).

wagnerite[2] ['wægnərait, 'vɑ:g-], *s. Miner:* wagnérite *f.*

wag(g)on ['wægən], *s.* (*the spelling* **waggon** *is now rare except for* **1.** (*a*)) **1.** (*a*) (*usu. horse drawn*) charrette *f* (à quatre roues), chariot *m*, char *m*; voiture *f* de roulage, de roulier; **covered w.,** chariot bâché; **hay w.,** charrette à foins; (*b*) *F:* **to be on the (water) w.,** s'abstenir de boissons alcooliques; (*c*) = WAG(G)ONLOAD. **2.** (*a*) **station w.,** canadienne *f*; *NAm:* **patrol w.,** *F:* **paddy w.,** voiture *f* cellulaire, *F:* panier *m* à salade; *P:* **meat w.,** (i) ambulance *f*; (ii) corbillard *m*, roulotte *f* à refroidis; (*b*) *Mil: esp. U.S:* voiture *f*, fourgon *m*; **ammunition w.,** camionnette *f* à munitions; **baggage w.,** voiture d'allègement; **combat w.,** voiture du train de combat; **first-line wag(g)ons,** train *m* de combat; **general service w.,** fourgon, véhicule *m*, voiture, du service général; **quartermaster battalion w.,** voiture à vivres et à bagages de bataillon. **3.** (*a*) *Rail:* wagon (découvert) (pour le transport des matériaux, des marchandises); **goods w.,** wagon à marchandises; **covered goods w.,** fourgon; **high-sided w.,** tombereau *m*; **hopper w.,** trémie *f*; **permanent-way w.,** wagon de service de la voie; (*b*) *Rail: Min:* wagonnet *m*; *Min:* berline *f*; **drop-bottom w.,** wagonnet à fond mobile; **tip w., tipping w.,** wagonnet basculant, à bascule; **box-tipping w.,** wagonnet à caisse basculante; **end-tipping w.,** wagonnet basculant longitudinalement; **side-tipping w.,** wagonnet basculant latéralement; *Min:* **w. way,** galerie *f*, voie *f*, de roulage. **4.** *Furn:* **dinner w.,** servante *f.*

wag(g)oner ['wægənər], *s.* **1.** roulier *m*, voiturier *m*, charretier *m*. **2.** *Astr:* **the W.,** le Cocher; Auriga *m*,

Aurige *m.*
wag(g)onette [wægə'net], *s. Veh:* wagonnette *f,* break *m.*
wag(g)onload ['wægənloud], *s.* charretée *f,* enlevée *f* (de foin, etc.); *Rail:* (charge *f* de) wagon *m.*
wagtail ['wægteil], *s. Orn:* (*a*) bergeronnette *f,* hochequeue *m,* lavandière *f;* **grey w.,** bergeronnette des ruisseaux; **pied w.,** bergeronnette de Yarrell; **white w.,** bergeronnette grise; **yellow-headed w.,** bergeronnette citrine; **blue-headed w.,** bergeronnette printanière; **ashy-headed w.,** bergeronnette printanière à tête cendrée; **black-headed w.,** bergeronnette printanière à tête noire; **grey-headed w.,** bergeronnette printanière nordique; **Spanish w.,** bergeronnette printanière d'Espagne; **yellow w.,** bergeronnette printanière flavéole; (*b*) **crested w.,** seisure *m;* gobemouches *m* turbulent; **willy w.,** rhipidure *f* à sourcils blancs.
Wah(h)abi, Wah(h)abite [wə'hɑ:bi, -bait], *s. Rel.H:* wahhabite *m.*
wahine [wæ'hi:nei], *s. N.Z: F:* femme *f.*
waif [weif], *s.* (*a*) *Jur:* épave *f;* (*b*) enfant abandonné; **waifs and strays,** (enfants) abandonnés.
wail[1] [weil], *s.* (*a*) cri plaintif, (cri de) lamentation *f;* plainte *f,* gémissement *m;* (*b*) vagissement *m* (de nouveau-né).
wail[2], *v.i.* (*a*) gémir; (*of new-born child*) vagir; (*of siren*) mugir; (*b*) **to w. over sth.,** se lamenter, pleurer, sur qch.
wailing[1] ['weiliŋ], *a.* (cri, chant) plaintif; (*of pers.*) qui gémit; gémissant; **w. infant,** enfant vagissant.
wailing[2], *s.* = WAIL[1]; (*at Jerusalem*) **the W. Wall,** le mur des Lamentations.
wailingly ['weiliŋli], *adv.* plaintivement; en gémissant; d'un ton larmoyant.
wain [wein], *s.* **1.** *A:* charrette *f;* **hay w.,** charrette à foins. **2.** *Astr:* **the W., Charles's W.,** le Grand Chariot, la Grande Ourse.
wainscot[1] ['weinskɔt], *s.* lambris *m;* boiseries *fpl* (d'une pièce).
wainscot[2], *v.tr.* (**wainscot(t)ed**) lambrisser, boiser (une pièce).
wainscot(t)ing ['weinskɔtiŋ], *s.* **1.** lambrissage *m,* boisage *m.* **2.** lambris *m,* boiseries *fpl.*
wainwright ['weinrait], *s. A:* charron *m.*
waist [weist], *s.* (*a*) (*of pers.*) taille *f,* ceinture *f;* mi-corps *m;* **down to the w., up to the w.,** jusqu'à la ceinture; jusqu'à mi-corps; **to have a small w.,** avoir un petit tour de taille; avoir la taille fine; **w. measurement,** tour de taille; *Dressm:* **dress with a long, a short, w.,** robe *f* à taille longue, à taille courte; *F:* **to have no waist,** être corpulent; **to put one's arm round s.o.'s w.,** prendre qn par la taille; **to seize, grip, one's adversary round, by, the w.,** saisir son adversaire à bras le corps; *Wr:* ceinturer, porter une ceinture à, son adversaire; *Wr:* **hold round the w., w. lock,** ceinture; (*b*) étranglement *m* (d'un sablier, d'un violon, etc.); rétrécissement *m* (d'un tuyau); (*c*) *Nau:* embelle *f,* passavant *m* (d'un navire).
waistband ['weistbænd], *s.* ceinture *f* (de jupe, de pantalon).
waistbelt ['weistbelt], *s. Cost: O:* ceinture *f; Mil:* ceinturon *m.*
waistcoat ['weskət], *s.* **1.** *Tail:* gilet *m;* **single-breasted, double-breasted, w.,** gilet droit, gilet croisé; **sleeved w.,** gilet à manches; **w. hand, w. maker,** giletier, -ière. **2.** **strait w.,** camisole *f* de force.
waisted ['weistid], *a.* **1. long w., short w.,** long, court, de taille; qui a la taille longue, courte. **2.** *Mec.E:* (*of wheel*) **w. teeth,** denture entaillée à la racine.
waistline ['weistlain], *s. Dressm:* taille *f;* **natural w.,** taille normale; **to watch one's w.,** soigner sa ligne; **to keep one's w.,** garder la ligne.
wait[1] [weit], *s.* **1.** (*a*) attente *f;* **we had a long w. at the station,** nous avons dû attendre longtemps à la gare; *Rail:* **ten minute(s') w. at the next station,** arrêt *m* de dix minutes à la prochaine gare; **twenty minute(s') w. between the two trains,** battement *m* de vingt minutes entre les deux trains; (*b*) **to lie in w.,** se tenir en embuscade; être à l'affût, être aux aguets; **to lie in w. for s.o.,** tendre un guet-apens à qn; guetter le passage de qn; attendre qn au passage; *Jur:* **lying in w.,** guet-apens *m;* (*of animal*) **to lie in w. for its prey,** guetter sa proie. **2. waits,** chanteurs *m* de noëls (qui vont de porte en porte aux approches de Noël).
wait[2]. **1.** *v.i.* (*a*) attendre; **w. a moment, a minute, a bit,** attendez un moment, un instant, un peu; *P.N:* **w.!** (piétons) attendez! **to keep s.o. waiting,** faire attendre qn; **to w. about,** *esp. NAm:* **to w. around,** attendre (longtemps); faire le pied de grue; faire planton; **to wait for s.o., sth.,** attendre qn, qch.; **what are you waiting for?** qu'attendez-vous? **to w. for another opportunity,** se réserver pour une autre occasion; **I'll be late, so don't w. up for me,** comme je rentrerai tard tu n'as qu'à te coucher; **mother always waits up for me,** maman veille toujours jusqu'à ce que je rentre; **you always have to w. for him,** il se fait toujours attendre; **I'll w. for you to give me the signal,** j'attendrai que vous me donniez le signal; **we're waiting to be served,** nous attendons qu'on nous serve; **the enemy fled without waiting to be attacked,** l'ennemi s'enfuyait sans attendre l'attaque; **he didn't w. to be told twice,** il ne se l'a pas fait dire deux fois; **w. until tomorrow,** attendez jusqu'à demain; **I shall w. until he's ready,** j'attendrai qu'il soit prêt; **w. until you see the result,** attendez le résultat; **these orders will have to w. until next week,** ces commandes devront attendre jusqu'à la semaine prochaine; *Com:* **repairs while you w.,** réparations *f* à la minute; *Prov:* **everything comes to him who waits,** tout vient à point, tout vient en son temps, qui sait attendre; **to w. and see,** attendre voir ce qui arrive; (**we must**) **w. and see,** il faudra voir; **I shall w. and see,** je me réserve; **w.-and-see policy,** politique *f* attentiste; attentisme *m;* (*b*) **to w. at,** *NAm:* **on, table,** servir (à table); faire le service; *v.ind.tr.* **to w. on s.o.,** (i) servir qn; (ii) *A:* se présenter chez qn; présenter ses respects à qn; **our representative will w. on you,** notre représentant passera chez vous; **to w. on s.o. hand and foot,** être aux petits soins auprès de qn; être l'esclave de qn; *A:* **to w. on, upon, sth.,** être la conséquence de qch.; suivre qch. **2.** *v.tr.* (*a*) attendre, guetter (une occasion, un signal, etc.); (*b*) **to w. a meal for s.o.,** différer un repas jusqu'à l'arrivée de qn; **don't w. dinner for me,** ne m'attendez pas pour vous mettre à table; (*c*) *Typ:* **to w. copy,** manquer de copie.
wait-a-bit ['weitəbit], *s. Bot:* jujubier *m* (de l'Afrique du Sud).
waiter ['weitər], *s.* **1.** garçon *m* (de restaurant); **head w.,** maître *m* d'hôtel (de salle de restaurant, etc.); **wine w.,** sommelier *m;* **w.!** garçon! **2. dumb w.,** serveuse *f,* servante *f;* monte-plats *m inv.*
waiting ['weitiŋ], *s.* **1.** attente *f; P.N: Aut:* **no w.,** stationnement interdit; **after a good hour's w.,** après une bonne heure d'attente; **w. room,** salle *f* d'attente, salle des pas perdus (de gare, etc.); antichambre *f* (chez un médecin); **to be on the w. list,** être sur la liste d'attente; **to play a w. game,** jouer un jeu d'attente; *Turf:* **to ride a w. race,** faire une course d'attente. **2.** service *m;* **in w.,** de service; **gentleman-in-w.,** gentilhomme servant, de service (to, auprès de); **lady-in-w.,** dame *f* d'honneur.
waitress[1] ['weitris], *s.f.* serveuse (dans un restaurant, etc.); **w.!** mademoiselle!
waitress[2], *v.i. F:* (*of woman*) servir à table; **she waitresses in a transport café,** elle est serveuse dans un restaurant routier.
waive [weiv], *v.tr.* renoncer à, abandonner, se désister de, se départir de (ses prétentions, ses droits); écarter, mettre à l'écart (ses intérêts privés); déroger à (un principe); ne pas insister sur (une condition); **to w. the age limit for s.o.,** dispenser qn de la limite d'âge.
waiver ['weivər], *s. Jur:* **w. of a right,** abandon *m* d'un droit, renonciation *f* à un droit; **w. of a claim,** désistement *m* (de revendication); **w. clause,** clause *f* d'abandon, de désistement.
waiving ['weiviŋ], *s.* abandonnement *m,* désistement *m* (d'un droit); mise *f* à l'écart (de ses intérêts); dérogation *f* (à un principe); **w. of the age limit,** dispense *f* d'âge.
wake[1] [weik], *s.* (*a*) *Nau:* sillage *m;* houache *f* (d'un navire); **to be in the w. of a ship,** être dans les eaux d'un navire; **propeller w.,** (i) *Nau:* brassage *m,* remous *m,* (ii) *Av:* remous, souffle *m,* de l'hélice; *Av:* **the wing is in the propeller w.,** la voilure est baignée par le souffle de l'hélice; **aircraft with wing in the propeller w.,** avion *m* à aile, à voilure, soufflée; (*b*) **in the w. of the storm,** à la suite de la tempête; **to follow in s.o.'s w.,** suivre la trace de qn; marcher à la suite de, dans le sillage de, sur les traces de, qn; se mettre, être, à la remorque de qn.
wake[2], *s.* **1.** (*in Ireland*) veillée *f* de corps; veillée mortuaire. **2.** (*a*) *Hist:* fête *f* de la dédicace (d'une église); (*b*) (*N. of Eng.*) **wakes week,** semaine *f* de congé annuel.
wake[3], *v.* (*p.t.* **woke** [wouk], **waked** [weikt]; *p.p.* **woke, waked, woken** ['wouk(ə)n]) **1.** *v.i.* (*a*) veiller; être éveillé; rester éveillé; **waking or sleeping that thought never left her,** éveillée ou endormie, cette pensée ne la quittait jamais; *Lit:* **can it be that I w.?** serait-ce vrai que je ne dors pas? (*b*) **to w. (up),** (i) (*from sleep*) s'éveiller, se réveiller; (ii) (*from inaction*) s'animer; sortir de sa torpeur; se réveiller; **come on, w. up!** allons, (i) réveillez-vous! (ii) activez-vous! remuez-vous! secouez-vous! **to sleep without waking,** dormir tout d'un somme; ne faire qu'un somme; **to w. (up) with a start,** se réveiller en sursaut; **he had always woken up when she came to bed,** il s'était toujours réveillé lorsqu'elle se couchait; **I woke up to find it was ten o'clock,** en me réveillant j'ai vu qu'il était dix heures; quand je me suis réveillé il était dix heures; **to w. up to find oneself famous,** se réveiller célèbre; **he is waking up to the truth,** la vérité se fait jour dans son esprit; **all nature is waking again,** toute la nature se réveille, s'anime; **his jealousy woke again,** sa jalousie se réveilla. **2.** *v.tr.* (*a*) **to w. s.o. (up),** (*from sleep*) réveiller qn; (*from inaction*) tirer qn de sa torpeur; secouer (les puces à) qn; **to be hard to w.,** avoir le sommeil dur; **w. me at six,** réveillez-moi à six heures; **he wants something to w. him up,** il lui faut quelque chose qui l'émoustille, le secoue; **he's going to w. up the whole country,** il va donner le branle à, va secouer, tout le pays; *Equit:* **to w. up a horse,** avertir un cheval; (*b*) **to w. the dead,** réveiller, ranimer, les morts; rappeler les morts à la vie; (*c*) éveiller, exciter (une émotion, un souvenir, etc.); (*d*) troubler (le silence); **to w. echoes in the valleys,** faire retentir les vallées; (*e*) (*in Ireland*) veiller (un mort).
wakeful ['weikful], *a.* **1.** (*a*) éveillé; peu disposé à dormir; (*b*) sans sommeil; **w. night,** nuit blanche; nuit d'insomnie. **2.** vigilant; sur ses gardes.
wakefully ['weikfuli], *adv.* **1.** sans dormir. **2.** vigilamment; avec vigilance.
wakefulness ['weikfulnis], *s.* **1.** (*a*) insomnie *f;* (*b*) état *m* de veille. **2.** vigilance *f.*
waken ['weik(ə)n]. **1.** *v.tr.* (*a*) éveiller, réveiller (qn); ranimer (un mort); **noise fit to w. the dead,** bruit *m* à réveiller les morts; (*b*) éveiller, exciter (une émotion, un souvenir, etc.). **2.** *v.i.* se réveiller, s'éveiller.
wakener ['weikənər], *s.* **1.** *Ind: etc: A:* réveilleur, -euse; éveilleur *m.* **2.** *F: A:* gros coup, taloche. *f.* **3.** *F: A:* surprise *f;* coup inattendu.
wakening ['weik(ə)niŋ], *s.* réveil *m.*
waker ['weikər], *s.* **to be an early w.,** se réveiller (habituellement) de bonne heure.
wakerobin ['weikrɔbin], *s. Bot:* arum maculé; pied-de-veau *m, pl.* pieds-de-veau.
wakey ['weiki], *int. F:* **w. (w.)!** debout! réveillez-vous! réveille-toi! secouez-vous!
waking[1] ['weikiŋ], *a.* éveillé; de veille; **w. hours,** heures *f* de veille.
waking[2], *s.* **1.** veille *f;* **between sleeping and w.,** entre la veille et le sommeil; *Med:* **suggestion in the w. state,** suggestion *f* à l'état de veille. **2.** réveil *m;* **the sleep with no w.,** le sommeil qui n'a pas de réveil. **3.** (*in Ireland*) veillée *f* (d'un mort).
Walchia ['wɔ:lkiə], *s. Paleont:* walchia *m.*
Waldenses [wɔl'densi:z], *s.pl. Rel.H:* vaudois *m.*
Waldensian [wɔl'densiən], *a. & s. Rel.H:* vaudois, -oise.
wale[1] [weil], *s.* **1.** marque *f,* trace *f* (d'un coup de fouet); vergeture *f.* **2.** *Tex:* côte *f* (de drap). **3.** *Civ.E:* **w. (piece),** moise *f* (de palplanches). **4.** *Nau: A:* (*a*) platbord *m, pl.* plats-bords; (*b*) **the wales,** les préceintes *f.*
wale[2], *v.tr.* **1.** marquer (d'un coup de fouet); zébrer (de coups de fouet). **2.** *Civ.E:* moiser (des pieux). **3.** *Mil:* clayonner (un gabion).
Wales [weilz], *Pr.n. Geog:* le pays de Galles; **North W., South W.,** la Galles du Nord, du Sud; **New South W.,** la Nouvelle Galles du Sud; **the Prince of W.,** le Prince de Galles; **the Prince of Wales's feathers,** l'emblème *m* du Prince de Galles; *Tex:* **Prince of Wales check,** Prince de Galles.
waling ['weiliŋ], *s.* **1.** *Hyd.E:* (*a*) moisage *m* (des pieux); (*b*) moise *f.* **2.** *Mil:* (*a*) clayonnage *m* (des gabions); (*b*) clayonnage; claies *fpl.* **3.** *Nau:* bordage épais (autour d'un navire).
walk[1] [wɔ:k], *s.* **1.** marche *f;* **it's half an hour's w. from here,** c'est à une demi-heure de marche à pied d'ici; **it's a long w. from here to the station,** c'est un long trajet à pied d'ici jusqu'à la gare; **it's only a short w. (from here),** ce n'est qu'une petite promenade. **2.** promenade (à pied); tour *m;* **to go for a w.,** (aller) se promener; faire un tour, une promenade; **charity w., sponsored w.,** promenade en groupe entreprise au profit d'une œuvre de bienfaisance; **space w.,** promenade dans l'espace; **to take s.o. for a w.,** emmener qn en promenade; faire faire une promenade à qn; mener promener qn; **to take the dog for a w.,** sortir, promener, le chien; **that will make a little w. for you,** cela vous promènera un peu. **3.** (*a*) manière *f* de marcher; démarche *f;* marcher *m,* marche, allure *f;* **graceful w.,** marcher gracieux; marche gracieuse; **I know him by his w.,** je le reconnais à sa marche, à sa démarche; (*b*) **to go, move, at a w.,** aller, avancer, marcher, au pas; (*of horse*) **to drop into a w.,** se mettre au pas. **4.** (*a*) allée *f* (de jardin, etc.); avenue *f,* promenade; (*b*) trottoir *m;* (*c*) **covered w.,** allée couverte; promenoir *m; Arch:* péristyle *m,* ambulatoire *m;* (*d*) *Nau:* **stern w.,** galerie *f*

de poupe; (*e*) *A:* parquet *m* d'élevage (de coqs de combat); *Ven:* établissement *m* pour l'éducation, le dressage, des jeunes chiens; (*f*) *O:* **sheep w.,** pâturage *m*; (*g*) *Fort:* **parapet, rampart, wall, w.,** chemin *m* de ronde; (*h*) *Can:* **cross w.,** passage *m* pour piétons. **5. w. of life,** (i) milieu *m*; position sociale; (ii) métier *m*, carrière *f*.

walk², *v.*

I. *v.i.* **1.** marcher; cheminer; **to w. on, in, the road,** marcher sur la chaussée; **to w. on to the road,** s'engager sur la chaussée; **to w. two paces forward,** faire deux pas en avant; avancer de deux pas; **to w. on all fours,** marcher à quatre pattes; (*of dog*) **to w. on three legs,** marcher à trois pattes; **to w. on one's hands,** faire l'arbre fourchu; **to w. in one's sleep,** être somnambule, noctambule; **I'll w. a little way with you,** je vais vous accompagner un bout de chemin; **to walk quickly towards s.o.,** marcher sur qn; **to w. lame, to w. with a limp,** boiter (en marchant); clocher; traîner la jambe; *NAm: P.N:* **w.! don't w.!** (piétons) passez, attendez. **2.** (*a*) (*as opposed to ride, drive, etc.*) aller à pied; **to w. home, to w. back,** rentrer, retourner, à pied; **I always w. to the office,** je me rends toujours à pied à mon bureau; **I had to w.,** j'ai dû faire le trajet à pied; **to w. ten kilometres,** faire dix kilomètres à pied; **you can w. there, w. it, in ten minutes,** vous en avez pour dix minutes à pied; (*b*) **to w. up, down, the street, the stairs,** monter, descendre, la rue, l'escalier; **he walked up to the fifth floor,** il est monté (à pied) jusqu'au cinquième (étage); **to w. up and down,** (i) monter et descendre à pied; (ii) se promener de long en large; faire les cent pas; **to w. up to s.o.,** s'avancer vers qn; s'approcher de qn; (*at fair, etc.*) **w. up!** approchez, entrez, messieurs-dames! **to w. across, over, to speak to s.o.,** traverser (la rue, etc.) pour parler à qn; **to w. into a room,** entrer dans une pièce; **to w. out of a room,** sortir d'une pièce; **please w. in,** entrez sans frapper; **to w. into s.o., sth.,** se heurter à, contre, qn, qch.; se trouver nez à nez avec qn; *F: O:* **to w. into one's food,** se jeter sur sa nourriture; **to w. through the town, the crowd,** traverser la ville, la foule (à pied); **he walked through the open door,** il a passé par la porte ouverte; (*c*) (*for exercise, pleasure*) se promener (à pied); **I like walking by, along, the river,** j'aime bien me promener au bord de la rivière; **he was walking (about) in the shade of the trees,** il se promenait à l'ombre des arbres. **3.** (*of horse, rider, vehicle*) aller au pas. **4.** (*of ghost*) revenir. **5.** *A:* marcher, se conduire; *B:* **to w. in His laws,** marcher dans ses statuts; **to w. uprightly,** cheminer droit; bien vivre.

II. *v.tr.* **1. to w. the streets,** (i) courir les rues; battre le pavé; (ii) (*of prostitute*) faire le trottoir; (*of sentry*) **to w. one's beat, one's round,** faire sa faction; *Th:* **to w. the boards,** être sur les planches; être acteur, actrice. **2.** (*a*) faire marcher, faire promener (un stupéfié, etc.); (*b*) **to w. s.o. off his feet,** exténuer, éreinter, qn à force de le faire marcher; **he has walked himself lame,** il a tant marché qu'il traîne la patte; (*c*) **to w. a horse,** (i) conduire, promener, un cheval (au pas); (ii) mettre un cheval au pas, lui faire prendre le pas; (*d*) **to w. the dog,** faire faire sa promenade au chien. **3.** *Ven:* prendre (un jeune chien) en pension pour l'éduquer, le dresser. **4.** *Ven:* **to w. up game,** lever le gibier.

III. (*compound verbs*) **1. walk away,** *v.i.* s'en aller; partir; *Sp:* **to w. away from a competitor,** distancer facilement, semer, un concurrent; *F:* **to w. away with sth.,** (i) emporter, (ii) voler, faucher, qch.

2. walk off. (*a*) *v.i.* s'en aller; partir; *F:* **to w. off with sth.,** (i) emporter, (ii) voler, faucher, qch.; **he's walked off with my dictionary!** il a emporté mon dictionnaire! (*b*) *v.tr.* **to w. off one's lunch,** faire une promenade de digestion.

3. walk on, *v.i. Th:* figurer (sur la scène); faire, remplir, un rôle de figurant(e).

4. walk out, *v.i.* (*a*) sortir (en colère); *Ind:* débrayer, se mettre en grève; (*b*) *F:* **to w. out on s.o.,** (i) abandonner, lâcher, plaquer, qn; (ii) quitter qn en colère; (*c*) *F: O:* **to w. out with a young man,** sortir avec un jeune homme (en vue de fiançailles).

5. walk over. (*a*) *v.i. Sp:* **to w. over the course;** inspecter le terrain (avant l'épreuve); (*b*) *v.tr.* **to w. one's shoes over (to, on, one side),** tourner ses chaussures.

6. walk round, *v.i.* faire le tour.

walkabout ['wɔːkəbaut], *s.* (*a*) *Austr:* (*of aborigines*) **to go w.,** courir le pays; (*b*) promenade au milieu de la foule (faite par un souverain, un président, etc.).

walkaway ['wɔːkəwei], *s. Sp:* victoire *f* facile.

walker ['wɔːkər], *s.* **1.** marcheur, -euse; promeneur, -euse; piéton *m*; **he's a fast w., a slow w.,** il marche vite, lentement; **to be a good w.,** être bon marcheur; avoir de bonnes jambes; **I'm not the w. I used to be,** je n'ai plus mes jambes de vingt ans. **2.** (*a*) *Orn:* oiseau marcheur; (*b*) *Ent:* insecte marcheur; phasmidoptère *m*. **3.** *Th:* **w. on,** figurant, -ante; (*in ballet*) marcheuse *f*.

walkie-talkie [wɔːki'tɔːki], *s. W.Tel:* émetteur-récepteur (portatif), *pl.* émetteurs-récepteurs; *F:* walkie-talkie *m*, *pl.* walkies-talkies; talkie-walkie *m*, *pl.* talkies-walkies.

walking¹ ['wɔːkiŋ], *a.* **1.** (voyageur, spectre) ambulant; *Mil: Med:* **w. cases, w. wounded,** blessés *m* qui marchent, qui peuvent marcher; **he's a w. dictionary,** c'est un dictionnaire ambulant. **2.** *Th: A:* **w. gentleman, w. lady,** figurant, -ante. **3.** (*a*) *Ich:* **w. catfish,** clarias *m*; (*b*) *Bot:* **w. fern,** (i) camptosore *m*; (ii) lycopode *m* en massue; **w. leaf,** (i) *Ent:* phyllie *f*; (ii) *Bot:* camptosore.

walking², *s.* marche *f*; promenades *fpl* à pied; **w. is the best exercise,** la marche est le meilleur des exercices; **two hours' w.,** deux heures de marche, de promenade; **six kilometres an hour is fair w.,** six kilomètres à l'heure, ce n'est pas mal marcher, c'est une bonne allure; **it's within ten minutes' w. distance,** vous en avez pour dix minutes à pied; c'est à moins de dix minutes de marche; **it's within w. distance,** on peut aisément s'y rendre à pied; *Th:* **w. on part,** rôle *m* de figurant(e); **at a w. pace,** au pas; **to go, drive, at a w. pace,** aller, avancer, au pas; *Sp:* **w. race,** concours *m* de marche; épreuve *f* de marche; **w. shoes,** chaussures *f* de marche; **w. stick,** (i) canne *f*; (ii) *Ent:* phasmidé *m*; *esp. NAm: F:* **to give s.o. his w. orders, his w. papers,** congédier qn; donner son congé à qn.

walk-on ['wɔːkɔn], *s. Th:* rôle *m* de figurant(e).

walkout ['wɔːkaut], *s.* (*a*) (*at meeting, etc.*) **to cause a w.,** provoquer le départ d'un groupe, d'une faction; (*b*) *Ind: etc:* débrayage *m*, mise *f* en grève.

walkover ['wɔːkouvər], *s.* (*a*) victoire *f* facile; **it would have been a w. for them,** ils auraient gagné dans un fauteuil; (*b*) *Turf:* walk-over *m*.

walk-round ['wɔːkraund], *a. & s.* **w.-r. (store),** (magasin *m* à) entrée *f* libre.

walk-up ['wɔːkʌp], *a. & s. NAm:* (immeuble *m*) sans ascenseur.

walkway ['wɔːkwei], *s.* allée (couverte); passage (couvert); *NAm:* sentier (forestier); **moving w.,** tapis roulant.

wall¹ [wɔːl], *s.* (*a*) (*of building*) mur *m*; **main walls,** gros murs; gros ouvrages; **supporting w., breast w.,** mur de soutènement; **partition w.,** paroi *f*; **cross w., internal (partition) w.,** mur de refend; **party w.,** mur mitoyen; (*of bridge*) **abutment w.,** mur de culée; **blind w., blank w.,** mur nu, orbe; renard *m*; **battened w.,** cloison *f* en lattes; **cavity w.,** mur double; **bearing w.,** mur d'appui, de support; mur portant, porteur; **face w.,** mur de revêtement; **w. tie,** ancrage *m*; **w. string,** faux limon (d'un escalier); **w. plate,** (i) sablière *f* (de comble); (ii) plaque *f* d'assise (de poutre); lambourde *f*, ligneul *m* (pour les solives du plancher); (iii) *Mec.E:* plaque murale; contre-plaque *f* (de chaise); **w. rib,** formeret *m* (d'une voûte); **w. arcade,** arcade aveugle, feinte; *Ecc.Arch:* **w. belfry,** clocher-mur *m*, *pl.* clochers-murs; **to leave only the four walls, the bare walls, standing,** ne laisser que les quatre murs; **between these four walls,** entre ces quatre murs; entre nous; *O:* **to give s.o. the w., the w. side of the pavement,** donner à qn le haut du pavé; **to take the w.,** prendre le haut du pavé; **w. bracket,** (i) console murale; (ii) *Mec.E:* (*for shaft*) chaise-console *f*, chaise-applique *f*; palier mural; **w. fitting,** applique *f*; **w. lamp,** (lampe *f* d')applique; **w. paintings,** peintures murales; **the paintings, pictures, hanging on the w.,** les peintures, les tableaux, qui pendent au mur; **w. clock,** pendule murale; **w. mirror,** miroir mural; **w. map,** carte murale; **w. chart,** tableau mural; **w. press,** placard *m*; **w. to w. carpet,** moquette *f*; *esp. U.S: F:* **w. to w. grin,** sourire énorme; **w. box,** boîte aux lettres (encastrée dans un mur); *N.Arch:* **w.-sided,** (navire) à murailles droites; (*b*) (*boundary, barrier*) **surrounding w.,** mur d'enceinte; **enclosing w.,** mur de clôture; **dry(stone) w.,** mur de pierres sèches; muraillon *m*; perré *m*; **sea w.,** digue *f*, endiguement *m*; **the town walls,** les murs, les murailles *f*, de la ville; **inside, within, the walls,** dans la ville; intra muros; **outside,** *A:* **without, the walls,** extra muros; **Hadrian's W.,** le mur d'Adrien; **the Great W. of China,** la grande muraille de Chine; **the Wailing W.,** le mur des Lamentations; **the Berlin W.,** le mur de Berlin; **w. of death,** mur, ravin *m*, de la mort; **W. Street,** la Bourse, le centre financier, de New-York; *Sp:* (*at Eton*) **the w. game,** jeu spécial de football joué contre un mur; *Pol.Ec:* **high tariff walls,** hautes barrières douanières; (*c*) muraille, paroi (de rochers); *Geol:* paroi, éponte *f* (d'un filon); lèvre *f* (d'une faille); **outer w. of a volcano,** rempart *m* d'un volcan; **ledger w.,** chevet *m* (d'un filon); *Min:* **hanging w.,** toit *m*; **w. face,** paroi (d'une galerie de mine); face *f* (d'un puits); **village surrounded by a w. of mountains,** village enfermé dans une enceinte de montagnes; (*d*) paroi (d'une chaudière, de la poitrine, d'une cellule, etc.); flanc *m* (d'un pneu); **white w. tyre,** pneu à flancs blancs; *Metall:* **lining w.,** contre-mur *m* (d'un haut fourneau); *Biol:* **w. pressure,** pression *f* membranaire; *Ph:* **cosmic w.,** mur cosmique; (*e*) *Orn:* **w. creeper,** tichodrome *m* échelette; grimpereau *m* de muraille; *Rept:* **w. lizard,** lézard *m* des murailles; *Ent:* **w. bee,** chalicodome *f* (des hangars); *Bot:* **w. cress,** arabette *f*; **w. lettuce,** laitue *f* des murs; **w. fern,** polypode *m* vulgaire, du chêne; **w. pepper,** orpin *m* âcre; poivre *m* de muraille; **w. rue,** rue *f* (des murailles); doradille *f*; sauve-vie *f*; (*f*) *Fig:* **to come up against a blank w.,** se heurter à un mur; **to have one's back to the w.,** en être réduit à la dernière extrémité; **to go to the w.,** (i) être mis à l'écart; être laissé de côté; (ii) être ruiné, acculé; perdre la partie; faire faillite; **the weakest always goes to the w.,** le plus faible est toujours écrasé; les battus paient l'amende; **to run, beat, one's head against a (brick) w.,** donner de la tête, se heurter, se cogner, se battre, la tête, contre un mur; se buter à l'impossible; *F:* **you might as well talk to a brick w.,** autant vaut parler à un sourd; *F:* **he can see as far through a brick w. as most people,** plus fin que lui n'est pas bête; *F:* **you're sending, driving, me up the w.,** vous allez me rendre fou.

wall², *v.tr.* **1. to w. (in) a town, a garden,** murer, entourer de murs, une ville, un jardin; *A:* **to w. in, up, a prisoner,** murer, emmurer, un prisonnier; **to w. up a window, a door,** murer, maçonner, une fenêtre, une porte; **to w. off (a room),** séparer (une pièce) par un mur, par une paroi.

wallaba ['wɔləbə], *s. Bot:* walaba *m*.

wallaby ['wɔləbi], *s.* **1.** *Z:* wallaby *m*; **scrub w.,** thylogale *m*; **rock w.,** pétrogale *m*; *Austr: F:* **to be on the w. (track),** être sur le trimard; trimarder. **2.** *F:* Australien, -ienne.

Wallace ['wɔləs], *Pr.n. Geog: Nat.Hist:* **W. line, Wallace's line,** ligne *f* de Wallace.

Wallach ['wɔlək], *s. Geog:* Valaque *mf*.

Wallachia [wɔ'leiʃiə], *Pr.n. Geog:* Valachie *f*.

Wallachian [wɔ'leiʃiən]. **1.** *Geog:* (*a*) *a.* valaque; (*b*) *s.* Valaque *mf*. **2.** *s. Ling:* valaque *m*.

wallah ['wɔlə], *s. O:* (*in India*) employé *m*, garçon *m*; **punkah-w.,** tireur *m* de panka.

wallaroo [wɔlə'ruː], *s. Z:* kangourou géant.

wallboard ['wɔːlbɔːd], *s. Const:* panneau *m* de revêtement.

wallcovering ['wɔːlkʌvəriŋ], *s. Com:* tapisserie *f*; tenture *f*.

walled [wɔːld], *a.* **1.** (*a*) (*of garden, town, etc.*) muré; clos de murs, d'une enceinte; (*b*) (talus, puits) muraillé. **2.** (*with adj. or noun prefixed*) **double-w.,** à double paroi; **brick-w. house,** maison *f* en brique.

Wallerian [wɔ'leəriən], *a. Physiol:* **W. degeneration,** dégénérescence wallérienne.

wallerite ['wɔlərait], *s. Miner:* wallérite *f*.

wallet ['wɔlit], *s.* **1.** *A:* (*a*) havresac *m*; (*b*) bissac *m*; besace *f* (de mendiant). **2.** *A:* sacoche *f* (de bicyclette, d'arçon, etc.); giberne *f* (de musicien); *Sch:* **(pen and) pencil w.,** trousse *f* d'écolier. **3.** portefeuille *m*.

walleye ['wɔːlai], *s. Med: Vet:* **1.** œil vairon. **2.** œil à strabisme divergent.

walleyed ['wɔːlaid], *a.* **1.** (*of horse, pers.*) vairon; qui a un œil vairon. **2.** (*of pers.*) à strabisme divergent.

wallflower ['wɔːlflauər], *s.* **1.** *Bot:* (*a*) giroflée *f* jaune, des murailles; ravenelle *f*; violier *m* jaune; (*b*) érysimon *m*, erysimum *m*; *NAm:* **western w.,** (i) (espèce d')érysimon; (ii) (espèce d')apocynum *m*. **2.** *F:* (*of girl at a dance*) **to be a w.,** faire tapisserie.

walling ['wɔːliŋ], *s.* **1. w. (in),** murage *m* (d'une ville, d'un jardin, etc.); **w. (round),** muraillement *m* (d'un puits); **w. up,** (i) *A:* emmurement *m* (de qn); (ii) murage *m*, maçonnage *m* (d'une fenêtre, etc.). **2.** murs *mpl*, maçonnerie *f*; **rough w.,** limo(u)sinage *m*.

Wallis ['wɔlis], *Pr.n. Geog:* **W. and Futuna** [fuː'tuːnə], les îles *f* Wallis et Futuna.

Wallonia [wɔ'louniə], *Pr.n. Geog:* Wallonie *f*.

Walloon [wɔ'luːn]. **1.** *Geog:* (*a*) *a.* wallon; (*b*) *s.* Wallon, -onne. **2.** *s. Ling:* wallon *m*.

wallop¹ ['wɔləp], *s. F:* **1.** gros coup; fessée *f*; torgn(i)ole *f*. **2. to fall with a w., to go (down) w.,** tomber lourdement, avec fracas; **and then he went (down with a) w., and down he went with a w.!** et patatras, le voilà qui tombe, le voilà par terre! **3.** *F.* bière (brune).

wallop², *v.tr. F:* rosser (qn); tanner le cuir à (qn); flanquer une tournée à (qn); *Sp:* battre (qn) à plate(s) couture(s).

walloping¹ ['wɔləpiŋ], *a. F: O:* énorme; épatant; de première force; **a w. great lie,** un mensonge énorme.

walloping[2], *s. F:* volée *f* (de coups); rossée *f*, tannée *f*; *Sp:* **to give s.o. a w.,** battre qn à plate(s) couture(s).

wallow[1] ['wɔlou], *s.* **1.** fange *f*, bourbe *f*, boue *f* (où se vautre une bête). **2.** trou bourbeux (où se roulent les buffles, les rhinocéros, etc.); souille *f*, bauge *f* (de sanglier); *Ven:* (*of boar*) **to return to his w.,** prendre souille.

wallow[2], *v.i.* (*of animals*) se vautrer; se rouler dans la boue; **wallowing place,** trou bourbeux; souille *f*, bauge *f* (de sanglier); (*of pers.*) **to w. in blood,** se baigner, se plonger, dans le sang; **to w. in vice,** croupir, se plonger, dans le vice; crapuler; **to be wallowing in luxury,** être à la paille jusqu'au ventre; *F:* **he's wallowing in money,** c'est un richard; il roule sur l'or.

wallower ['wɔlouər], *s. Mec.E:* **w. (wheel),** (roue *f* à) lanterne *f*.

wallpaper ['wɔːlpeipər], *s.* papier peint, papier à tapisser, (papier) tenture *f*.

walnut ['wɔːlnʌt], *s.* **1.** noix *f*; **green w.,** cerneau *m*; **pickled walnuts,** cerneaux confits au vinaigre; **w. oil,** huile *f* de noix; *Tex:* **w. dye,** racinage *m*; **w. juice, stain,** brou *m* de noix; **to stain one's skin with w.,** se frotter la peau avec du brou de noix; **w. shell,** coquille *f* de noix; *F: O:* **to sit over the walnuts and wine,** parler entre la poire et le fromage. **2.** *Bot:* **w. (tree),** noyer *m*; **American w., black w.,** noyer américain, noir; **African w.,** lovoa *m* klaineana; noyer du Gabon; **w. plantation,** noiseraie *f*. **3.** (bois *m* de) noyer; **figure(d) w.,** ronce *f* de noyer; **w. furniture,** mobilier *m* en noyer; **w. (colour), w. brown,** couleur *m* de noyer.

Walpurgis [væl'pəːdʒis], *Pr.n.f.* **Saint W.,** Sainte Walpurgis, Sainte Walburge; **W. Night,** nuit *f* de Walpurgis (nuit du 30 avril au 1er mai).

walpurgite [wɔl'pəːdʒait], *s. Miner:* walpurgine *f*.

walrus ['wɔːlrəs], *s. Z:* morse *m*; **the w. family,** les odobénidés *mpl*; *Orn:* **w. bird,** bécasseau tacheté; *F:* **w. moustache,** moustache tombante, à la gauloise.

Walter ['wɔːltər], *Pr.n.m.* Gauthier.

waltherite ['væltərait], *s. Miner:* walthérite *f*.

waltz[1] [wɔːls], *s.* **1.** valse *f*; **Viennese w.,** valse viennoise; **slow w.,** valse lente; **he asked me for a w.,** il m'a fait valser. **2.** *Mus:* air *m* de valse; **one of Johann Strauss's waltzes,** une valse de Johann Strauss.

waltz[2], *v.i. & tr.* **1.** valser; **to w. round the room,** faire un tour de valse; **I waltzed with Louise a bit, I waltzed Louise round a bit,** j'ai fait valser Louise un peu. **2.** *F:* danser (de joie, etc.); **they joined hands and waltzed round the statue,** se donnant la main ils se sont mis à danser autour de la statue; **to w. off,** partir, s'en aller; **to w. off with a prize,** remporter un prix. **3.** *Austr: F:* (*of bushman*) **to w. Matilda,** courir le pays avec son baluchon.

waltzer ['wɔːlsər], *s.* valseur, -euse.

waltzing ['wɔːlsiŋ], *s.* valse *f*.

wampum ['wɔmpəm], *s.* (*a*) wampoum *m*; (*b*) *NAm: F:* argent *m*, fric *m*.

wan [wɔn], *a.* pâlot, -otte; blême; blafard; **w. child,** enfant pâlot; **to grow w.,** pâlir, blêmir; **w. light,** lumière blafarde, pâle, faible; **w. smile,** pâle sourire; sourire faible, triste, défaillant.

wananish ['wɔnəniʃ], *s. Ich:* saumon *m* d'eau douce, *Fr.C:* ouananiche *f*.

wand [wɔnd], *s.* **1.** baguette *f* (de fée, de magicien); **(dowser's) hazel w.,** baguette de coudrier; baguette divinatoire. **2.** bâton *m* (de commandement, etc.); verge *f* (d'huissier); **Mercury's w.,** caducée *m*.

wander[1] ['wɔndər], *s.* **1.** course errante, vagabonde; **to go for a w. in the woods,** aller se promener dans les bois. **2.** *El:* **w. plug,** fiche *f* de prise de courant (sur une batterie sèche de haute tension à éléments multiples).

wander[2]. **1.** *v.i.* (*a*) errer (sans but); se promener au hasard; **to w. in the woods, about the streets,** errer dans les bois, par les rues; **to w. about,** aller à l'aventure; aller le nez au vent; vaguer; se balader; **to w. (about) aimlessly, forlornly,** errer à l'abandon; errer à l'aventure; **to w. about the world,** rouler sa bosse (un peu partout); **his eyes wandered over the scene,** ses regards se promenaient sur cette scène; il promenait ses yeux sur cette scène; **to let one's thoughts w.,** laisser vaguer ses pensées; **his thoughts wandered back to the past,** sa pensée vagabonde est revenue sur le passé; (*b*) **to w. from the right way,** s'écarter, sortir, du droit chemin; s'égarer; **to w. from the point, from the subject,** s'écarter, sortir, du sujet, de la question; digresser; faire une digression; se lancer, se perdre, dans une digression; **my thoughts were wandering,** je n'étais pas à la conversation; **his mind wanders at times, is apt to w.,** il est sujet à des absences; il a des absences; (*c*) **to w. (in one's mind),** divaguer; avoir le délire; battre la campagne. **2.** *v.tr. A: & Lit:* parcourir (au hasard); **to w. the world,** errer de, par, le monde; **to w. the whole world through,** parcourir le monde entier.

wanderer ['wɔndərər], *s.* **1.** vagabond, -onde; *F:* baladeur, -euse; **to be a w.,** errer par voies et par chemins; *B:* **they shall be wanderers among the nations,** ils seront errants parmi les nations; **our w. has returned,** notre voyageur nous est revenu; (*of pet*) notre chien, chat, nous est revenu. **2. a w. from the fold,** *Ecc:* une brebis égarée; *Pol: etc:* un membre dévoyé (du parti).

wandering[1] ['wɔnd(ə)riŋ], *a.* **1.** (*a*) errant, vagabond; (*of tribe*) nomade; **w. tribes,** nomades *m*; **w. life,** vie errante, vagabonde; **w. minstrels,** chanteurs, ménestrels, ambulants; (*b*) (esprit) distrait; **w. eyes,** yeux distraits; **w. attention,** attention vagabonde; (*c*) *Med:* (maladie *f*, douleur *f*) mobile; **w. kidney,** rein flottant, mobile; (*d*) **w. sheep,** (i) *Ecc:* brebis égarée; (ii) *Pol:* membre dévoyé du parti. **2.** (*a*) *Med:* qui a le délire; qui délire; qui divague; (*b*) (discours, récit) incohérent.

wandering[2], *s.* **1.** (*a*) vagabondage *m*; errance *f*; **my w. days are over,** j'en ai fini avec mes voyages; je n'ai plus l'âge de voyager; **wanderings,** pérégrinations *f*; (*b*) *El:* **w. of the arc,** migration *f* de l'arc. **2.** (*a*) rêverie *f*; inattention *f*; (*b*) *Med:* égarement *m* (de l'esprit); délire *m*; **in his wanderings,** dans ses divagations. **3. to indulge in a good many wanderings from the point, the subject,** digresser beaucoup, faire beaucoup de digressions.

wanderingly ['wɔnd(ə)riŋli], *adv.* **to talk w.,** parler d'une façon incohérente; divaguer.

wanderlust ['wɔndəlʌst], *s.* manie *f*, passion *f*, des voyages.

wanderoo [wɔndə'ruː], *s. Z:* singe *m* lion; ouanderou *m*.

wane[1] [wein], *s.* décroît *m*, déclin *m*, décours *m* (de la lune, d'une puissance); **moon on the w.,** lune à son décours; **beauty on the w.,** beauté *f* sur le déclin; **to be on the w.,** (*of moon*) décroître; (*of pers., civilization*) être à, sur, son déclin; (*of beauty*) être sur le retour; (*of fame, etc.*) être à son couchant; (*of illness*) être dans le décours; **his star is on the w.,** son étoile pâlit.

wane[2], *v.i.* (*of the moon, of power, popularity, etc.*) décroître, décliner; (*of beauty*) être sur le retour; (*of enthusiasm, etc.*) s'affaiblir, s'attiédir; **his star, his glory, is waning,** son étoile pâlit; sa gloire diminue.

wane[3], *s. Carp:* flache *f* (d'une planche).

waney ['weini], *a.* (*of plank*) flacheux, flache.

wangle[1] ['wæŋgl], *s. F:* moyen détourné; truc *m*; **his appointment was a w., he got the appointment by a w.,** il a été nommé par intrigue, à la suite de manigances.

wangle[2], *v.tr. & i.* **1.** obtenir (qch.) par subterfuge, par intrigue; carotter, fricoter (qch.); resquiller; pratiquer le système D; **to w. leave,** se faire accorder un congé, *Mil:* carotter une permission; **to w. a decoration,** décrocher la croix, un ordre, etc. **2.** cuisiner (des comptes, un procès-verbal, etc.).

wangler ['wæŋglər], *s. F:* resquilleur, -euse; fricoteur, -euse.

wangling ['wæŋgliŋ], *s. F:* resquillage *m*, resquille *f*; carottage *m*, fricotage *m*.

waning[1] ['weiniŋ], *a.* décroissant, déclinant; **w. moon,** lune décroissante; lune à son déclin, à son décours; **w. light,** lumière défaillante, faiblissante; **w. power,** pouvoir déclinant; **w. empire,** empire *m* en décadence.

waning[2], *s.* décroissance *f*, décroissement *m*, décours *m* (de la lune); déclin *m* (de la beauté, etc.); décadence *f* (d'un empire); attiédissement *m* (de l'enthousiasme, etc.).

wanion ['wɔnjən], *s. A:* décroît *m* (de la lune); **with a w. to him!** et que le diable l'emporte!

wanly ['wɔnli], *adv.* **to smile w.,** sourire d'un air triste; **the moon was shining w.,** la lune donnait une lumière faible.

wanness ['wɔnnis], *s.* pâleur *f*.

want[1] [wɔnt], *s.* **1.** (*a*) *O:* (*now usu.* **lack**) manque *m*, défaut *m*; **w. of judgment,** défaut de jugement; **w. of imagination,** manque d'imagination; **my w. of memory,** mon peu de mémoire; **w. of respect,** manque de respect; **to suffer from the w. of friends,** se sentir seul(e); **I was out of tobacco but didn't feel the w. of it,** je n'avais plus de tabac mais ce n'était pas une privation; **for w. of sth.,** faute de qch.; à défaut de qch.; par manque de (prévoyance, etc.); **the thing fell through for w. of money,** faute d'argent l'affaire a échoué; *Bank:* **for w. of funds,** faute de provision; **for w. of something better to do,** faute de mieux; **for w. of something to do,** par désœuvrement; *Prov:* **for w. of a nail the shoe was lost, for w. of a shoe the horse was lost,** faute d'un point Martin perdit son âne; **for w. of saying a word, of speaking, in time,** faute d'avoir parlé à temps; **there is no w. of talent or money,** ce n'est ni le talent, ni l'argent, qui manque; **to make up for the w. of sth.,** suppléer à l'absence de qch.; (*b*) *Mec.E:* **w. of balance,** balourd *m*; (*c*) *O:* (*now usu.* **need**) **to be in w. of sth.,** avoir besoin de qch.; **to be in w. of money,** être à court d'argent; **to be badly in w. of money,** être à sec, sans le sou; être presque dans la misère; **I am in w. of . . .,** il me manque, il me faut, . . .; **I'm badly in w. of a hundred pounds,** j'ai grand besoin de cent livres; il me faut cent livres d'urgence; *esp. NAm: F:* **is there a w. ad for a typist?** y a-t-il une offre d'emploi pour une dactylo? y a-t-il quelqu'un qui recherche une dactylo? **2.** indigence *f*, misère *f*, besoin *m*; **to be in w.,** être dans le besoin, dans la peine, dans la gêne; **to be living in w.,** vivre dans la misère, dans le besoin, dans la privation; vivre de privations; **to be in great w.,** être dans le dénuement; *F:* être sur la paille; **war on w.,** lutte *f* contre la misère. **3.** besoin *m*; **to minister, to attend, to s.o.'s wants,** servir qn dans ses besoins; pourvoir aux besoins de qn; **a long-felt w.,** une lacune à combler; **this book meets a long-felt w.,** ce livre, ce volume, comble un vide. **4.** *Scot:* **to have a w.,** être faible d'esprit.

want[2]. **1.** *v.i.* (*a*) manquer (de); être dépourvu (de); *O:* **to w. for bread,** manquer de pain; **to w. for nothing,** ne manquer de rien; (*b*) **her family will see to it that she doesn't w.,** sa famille veillera à ce qu'elle ne se trouve pas dans la nécessité, dans le besoin; (*c*) *esp. U.S: F:* **if you w. in there's nothing stopping you,** si tu le veux rien ne t'empêche d'entrer, d'y prendre part; **stay if you like but I w. out,** reste si tu veux mais moi je me sauve. **2.** *v.tr.* (*a*) *O:* (*be without*) manquer de, ne pas avoir (qch.); ne pas être pourvu de (qch.); être dépourvu de (qch.); **statue that wants a head,** statue qui n'a pas de tête, qui est sans tête, à laquelle il manque la tête; **to w. patience, intelligence,** manquer de patience, d'intelligence; **I w. one card,** il me manque une carte; *impers. NAm:* **it wants six minutes to ten (o'clock),** il est dix heures moins six; **it still wanted an hour to dinnertime,** il y avait encore une heure à passer avant le dîner; *Lit:* **it wanted only a few days to Christmas,** c'était juste quelques jours avant Noël; (*b*) (*need*) (*of pers.*) avoir besoin de (qch.); (*of thg*) exiger, réclamer, demander (qch.); **to w. rest,** avoir besoin de repos; **he wants a new hat,** il lui faut un nouveau chapeau; *F:* **it wants a lot of patience to do this work,** ce travail exige, demande, beaucoup de patience; *F:* **situation that wants tactful handling,** situation qui demande à être maniée avec tact; **I shall w. you,** j'aurai besoin de vous; **if nobody wants me, my help, here, I'm going home,** si personne n'a plus besoin de moi, je rentre; **if you don't w. this book may I borrow it?** si vous n'avez pas besoin de ce livre, voulez-vous me le prêter? **have you everything you w.?** avez-vous tout ce qu'il vous faut, tout ce que vous désirez? **he doesn't w. all this,** il n'a que faire de tout cela; **we've more than we w.,** nous en avons plus qu'il n'en faut; **you shall have as much as you w.,** vous en aurez autant que vous voudrez; vous en aurez à plaisir; **I've had all I want(ed),** j'en ai assez; **the goods can be supplied as (and when) they are wanted,** on peut fournir les articles au fur et à mesure des besoins; **these are not wanted,** ceux-ci sont de trop; **that's the very thing I w., that's just what I w.,** c'est juste, voilà tout juste, ce qu'il me faut; cela fait tout juste mon affaire; c'est juste mon affaire; **I have the very thing you w.,** j'ai juste votre affaire; **the very man we w.,** l'homme de la circonstance; **to w. a job,** être en quête d'un emploi; **wanted, a good cook,** on demande, on recherche, une bonne cuisinière; **he's wanted by the police,** il a la police à ses trousses; la police le recherche; il est recherché par la police; (*c*) **you w. to eat more than you do,** vous devriez manger plus que vous ne faites; **you w. to be on your guard,** il faut vous méfier; **your hair wants cutting,** vous avez besoin de vous faire couper les cheveux; **it wants some doing,** ce n'est pas (si) facile à faire; (*d*) (*desire*) désirer, vouloir; **he knows what he wants,** il sait ce qu'il veut; *Prov:* **the more you get the more you w.,** l'appétit vient en mangeant; **do you w. any?** en voulez-vous? **is that all you w.?** est-ce tout ce que vous voulez? **take all you w.,** prenez tant que vous voudrez; **what more do you w.?** que voudriez-vous de plus? **those who wanted war,** ceux qui voulaient la guerre; **I do not w. a throne,** je ne veux point d'un trône; **what, how much, do you w. for this armchair?—I w. fifty pounds,** combien vendez-vous ce fauteuil?—J'en demande cinquante livres; **how much, what price, do you w. for your house?** quel prix voulez-vous de votre maison? *Iron:* **you don't w. much!** tu n'es pas dégoûté! **she makes him do everything she wants,** elle lui fait faire ses quatre volontés; **to w. s.o. for king,** vouloir qn pour roi; **you're wanted, somebody wants (to see) you,** on vous demande; **we're not wanted here,** nous sommes de trop ici; **we don't w. you,** nous n'avons que faire de vous;

they don't w. to have me, ils ne veulent pas de moi; **I see you don't w. me here,** je vois que ma présence vous déplaît; **if nobody wants me I'm going home,** si personne ne désire ma compagnie, je rentre; **what does he w. with me?** que me veut-il? que veut-il de moi? **to w. sth. of s.o., from s.o.,** désirer, vouloir, qch. de qn; **what do you w. of him?** que lui voulez-vous? **I w. to tell you that . . .,** je voudrais vous dire que . . .; **he wants to taste it,** il a envie d'y goûter; **to w. to see s.o., to speak to s.o.,** demander qn; avoir à parler à qn; **he could have done it if he had wanted to,** il l'aurait bien fait s'il avait voulu; **I'm asked to take the chair and I don't w. to,** on m'a prié de présider, et j'aimerais mieux n'en rien faire; **don't come unless you w. to, if you don't w. to,** ne venez pas à moins que le cœur ne vous en dise; **I w. him to come,** je désire qu'il vienne; **he wanted a tree cut down,** il voulait faire abattre un arbre; **I don't w. it known,** je ne veux pas que cela se sache; **he wants it finished by tomorrow,** il désire que ce soit fini demain au plus tard; **what do you w. done?** que désirez-vous qu'on fasse? **I w. you to be cheerful,** je vous veux gai; **I don't w. you turning everything upside down,** je ne veux pas que vous mettiez tout sens dessus dessous; **I wanted her to live,** je désirais tant qu'elle vécût.

wantage ['wɔntidʒ], *s. U.S: Com:* manque *m*, déficit *m*.

wanted ['wɔntid], *a.* **1.** désiré, voulu, demandé; *Fin:* **stocks w.,** valeurs demandées. **2.** (criminel) recherché par la police.

wanting ['wɔntiŋ]. **1.** *a.* (*a*) manquant, qui manque; **to be w., faire défaut; in this animal the teeth are w.,** chez cet animal les dents sont absentes; **courage is not w. in him,** le courage ne lui fait pas défaut; **one sheet is w., there is one sheet w.,** il manque une feuille; **there is something w.,** le compte n'y est pas; *Gram:* **verb of which the past participle is w.,** verbe *m* dont le participe passé manque; (*b*) (*of pers.*) **w. in intelligence,** dépourvu d'intelligence; **he is not w. in courage,** il ne manque pas de courage; ce n'est pas le courage qui lui manque, qui lui fait défaut; **to be w. in patience, in courtesy,** manquer de patience, de politesse; *Lit:* **to be found w.,** se trouver en défaut; **he was tried and found w.,** il n'a pas supporté l'épreuve; (*c*) *F:* (*of pers.*) faible d'esprit; **he's slightly w.,** il lui manque un petit quelque chose. **2.** *prep.* sans; sauf; **w. energy all work becomes tedious,** sans l'énergie tout travail devient monotone; **w. beauty she was nevertheless attractive,** sans être belle elle plaisait; **he arrived w. both money and luggage,** il est arrivé sans argent ni bagages; *A:* **six thousand w. only ten,** six mille sauf seulement dix, à dix près.

wanton[1] ['wɔntən]. **1.** *a.* (*a*) *O:* (*of woman*) licencieuse, lascive, lubrique, impudique; folle de son corps; **w. thoughts,** pensées *f* impudiques; (*b*) *O:* folâtre; d'une gaieté étourdie, qui suit ses caprices; *Lit:* **w. winds,** vents *m* folâtres; **w. tresses,** boucles ondoyantes; **w. love,** folles amours; (*c*) *Lit:* (*of vegetation*) surabondant, luxuriant; (*d*) gratuit; sans motif; **w. cruelty, w. insult,** cruauté, insulte, gratuite; **w. destruction,** destruction *f* pour le simple plaisir de détruire; **they committed the w. crime of destroying the village,** ils ont commis gratuitement le crime de détruire le village. **2.** *s.f. O:* femme impudique; voluptueuse; paillarde; *A:* **to play the w.,** être folle de son corps.

wanton[2], *v.i. A:* folâtrer; s'ébattre.

wantonly ['wɔntənli], *adv.* **1.** *O:* lascivement; en libertin, en libertine; impudiquement. **2.** (*a*) *O:* en folâtrant; de gaieté de cœur; (*b*) **to spread false news w.,** répandre comme à plaisir des nouvelles fausses; (*c*) *Lit:* (*of vegetation*) (pousser) surabondamment, profusément. **3.** (blesser, insulter) gratuitement, sans motif.

wantonness ['wɔntənnis], *s.* **1.** *O:* libertinage *m*. **2.** *O:* gaieté *f* de cœur; irréflexion *f*, étourderie *f*; **to do sth. in sheer w.,** faire qch. de gaieté de cœur, par étourderie. **3.** gratuité *f* (d'une insulte, etc.); **to act from sheer w.,** agir gratuitement.

wapentake ['wɔpənteik], *s. Hist:* division *f* de certains comtés.

wapiti ['wɔpiti], *s. Z:* wapiti *m*.

waps, *pl.* **wapses** [wɔps, -siz], *s. Hum:* = WASP.

war[1] [wɔːr], *s.* guerre *f*; (*a*) **atomic, nuclear, w.,** guerre atomique, nucléaire; **contained w., local w.,** guerre localisée; **defensive, offensive, w.,** guerre défensive, offensive; **global w.,** guerre planétaire, universelle; **holy w.,** guerre sainte; **cold w.,** guerre froide; **hot w., shooting w.,** guerre chaude; **latent w.,** guerre larvée; **lightning w.,** guerre éclair; **limited w.,** (i) guerre à objectif(s) limité(s); (ii) guerre localisée; **minor w.,** petite guerre, guerre de harcèlement; **preventive w.,** guerre préventive; **civil w.,** guerre civile; **revolutionary w.,** guerre révolutionnaire; **subversive w.,** guerre subversive; **total w.,** guerre totale; **w. of attrition,** guerre d'usure; **w. of extermination,** guerre d'extermination; guerre à mort, à outrance; **w. of manoeuvre,** guerre de manœuvre; **w. of nerves,** guerre des nerfs; **state of w.,** état *m* de guerre; **in time of w.,** en temps de guerre; **in the midst of w.,** en pleine guerre; **w. establishment, w. footing, w. strength,** effectif(s) *m(pl)* de guerre; **to bring a unit to w. strength,** porter une unité à effectif de guerre; **to set a unit on a w. footing,** mettre une unité sur pied de guerre; **w. preparations, preparations for w.,** préparatifs *m* de guerre; **w. talk,** (i) rumeurs *fpl* de guerre; (ii) chauvinisme agressif; **w. zone,** zone *f* de guerre; **to inure troops to w.,** aguerrir des troupes; *Lit:* **to let loose the dogs of w.,** déchaîner les fureurs de la guerre; **to start a w.,** déclencher une guerre; **to unleash an atomic w.,** déclencher une guerre atomique; **outbreak of w.,** début *m*, déclenchement *m*, de la guerre; **to be at w. with a country,** être en guerre avec, contre, un pays; être en état de guerre avec un pays; **to make, wage,** *A:* **levy, w. on, against, a country,** faire la guerre à, contre, un pays; guerroyer contre un pays; **to go to the war(s),** partir, s'en aller, en guerre; partir à la guerre; *F:* **he's always in the wars,** il ne rêve que plaies et bosses; **you look as if you'd been in the wars,** vous avez l'air de vous être battu, de revenir de la guerre; **w. fever,** psychose *f* de guerre; **w. cloud,** menace *f* de guerre; **the w. clouds are gathering,** l'horizon *m* s'assombrit; **w. game,** kriegspiel *m*; exercice *m* sur la carte; **W. Department** = Ministère *m* de la Guerre; **W. Council,** Conseil supérieur de la Guerre; **w. loan,** emprunt *m* de guerre; **w. debts,** dettes *f* de guerre; **w. correspondent,** correspondant, -ante, de guerre; **w. work,** travail de guerre, fait pendant la guerre; **I did my w. work in a hospital,** pendant la guerre j'ai travaillé dans un hôpital; **to be w. weary,** être fatigué, las, de la guerre; **w. baby,** (i) enfant né pendant la guerre; (ii) enfant illégitime né à cause de la guerre; **w. widow,** veuve *f* de guerre; **w. grave,** sépulture *f* militaire; **w. cemetery,** cimetière *m* militaire; **w. memorial,** monument *m* aux morts; **w. damage,** dommages *mpl* de guerre; **w. crimes,** crimes *m* de guerre; **w. criminal,** criminel, -elle, de guerre; *A:* **w. axe,** hache *f* d'armes; **w. hammer,** maillotin *m*; **w. god, goddess,** dieu, déesse, de la guerre; **w. chant, song,** chant *m* de guerre; **w. dance,** danse guerrière; (*b*) *Hist:* **the Trojan W.,** la guerre de Troie; **the Punic Wars,** les guerres puniques; **the Wars of the Roses,** la guerre des Deux Roses; **the American Civil W.,** *U.S:* **the w. between the States,** la guerre de Sécession; **the Great W.** (1914–1918), la Grande Guerre; **the first, second, World W., World W. I, II,** la première, deuxième, guerre mondiale; **the Korean W.,** la Guerre de Corée; **the phoney w.** (1939–1940), la drôle de guerre; **the w. to end all wars,** la dernière guerre que verra l'Humanité, *F:* la der des der; (*c*) guerre, lutte *f*, conflit *m*; **private w., family w.,** guerre entre deux familles; *Pol.Ec:* **price w., tariff w.,** guerre des prix, des tarifs; **w. of words,** dispute *f*, altercation *f*; **w. of the elements,** conflit des éléments; **the elements at w.,** les éléments *m* en guerre; **to be at w. with s.o., sth.,** être en guerre avec, contre, qn; être en guerre, en lutte, contre qch.; être en conflit avec qn, qch.; **to be openly at w. with s.o.,** être en guerre ouverte contre qn; **to make, wage, w. on, against, s.o., sth.,** faire la guerre à, contre, qn; faire la guerre à qch.; lutter, militer, contre qch.; **to go to w. against s.o., sth.,** partir en guerre, entrer en lutte, contre qn, qch.; entrer en conflit avec qn, qch.

war[2], *v.i.* **(warred) to w. against s.o., sth.,** mener une campagne contre qn, qch.; guerroyer, lutter, contre qn, qch.; **to w. against abuses,** faire la guerre aux abus; **one of these feelings, instincts, warred with, against, the other,** ces deux émotions étaient en conflit.

warble[1] ['wɔːbl], *s.* gazouillement *m*, gazouillis *m*, ramage *m* (des oiseaux); doux murmure.

warble[2]. **1.** *v.i.* (*a*) gazouiller; (*of lark*) grisoller; (*b*) *F:* (*of pers.*) (i) chanter; (ii) parler d'une voix roucoulante, affectée; (*c*) *O:* (*of stream*) couler en murmurant. **2.** *v.tr.* chanter (qch.) en gazouillant; *F:* (*of pers.*) **to w. a song,** roucouler une chanson.

warble[3], *s.* **1.** *Vet: usu. pl.* **warbles,** (i) cors *m* (sur le dos du cheval); indurations (dues à la selle); (ii) (*of cattle, etc.*) var(r)ons *m*. **2.** *Ent:* (*maggot*) var(r)on *m*; **w. (fly),** œstre *m*; hypoderme *m* du bœuf; **w. fly infestation,** hypodermose *f*.

warbled ['wɔːbld], *a. Vet: Leath:* var(r)onné.

warbler ['wɔːblər], *s.* **1.** (*a*) (oiseau) chanteur *m*; (*b*) *usu. Pej:* chanteur, -euse; **nightclub w.,** chanteuse de boîte. **2.** *Orn:* (*a*) fauvette *f*, pouillot *m*, rousserolle *f*; **barred w.,** fauvette épervière; **Dartford w.,** fauvette pitchou; **garden w.,** fauvette des jardins; **Marmora's w.,** fauvette sarde; **Orphean w.,** fauvette orphée; **Sardinian w.,** fauvette mélanocéphale; **spectacled w.,** fauvette à lunettes; **subalpine w.,** fauvette passerine, subalpine; **desert w.,** fauvette naine; **Rüppell's w.,** fauvette de Rüppell; **wren w.,** fauvette-roitelet *f*; **Arctic w., Eversmann's w.,** pouillot boréal; **Bonelli's w.,** pouillot de Bonelli; **greenish w.,** pouillot verdâtre; **willow w.,** pouillot fitis; **wood w.,** pouillot siffleur; **yellow-browed w.,** pouillot à grands sourcils; **dusky w.,** pouillot brun; **Pallas's w.,** pouillot de Pallas; **Radde's bush w.,** pouillot de Schwarz; **hedge w.,** rousserolle des buissons; **marsh w.,** rousserolle verderolle; **reed w.,** rousserolle effarvatte; **great reed w.,** rousserolle turdoïde; **Blyth's reed w.,** rousserolle des buissons; **paddyfield w.,** rousserolle isabelle; **Cetti's w.,** bouscarle *f* de Cetti; **grasshopper w.,** locustelle tachetée; **river w.,** locustelle fluviatile; **Savi's w.,** locustelle luscinoïde; **Gray's grasshopper w.,** locustelle fasciée; **Pallas's grasshopper w.,** locustelle de Pallas; **Temminck's grasshopper w., lanceolated w.,** locustelle lancéolée; **moustached w.,** lusciniole *f* à moustaches; **aquatic w.,** phragmite *m* aquatique; **sedge w.,** phragmite des joncs; **icterine w.,** hypolaïs *f* ictérine; **melodious w.,** hypolaïs polyglotte; **olivaceous w.,** hypolaïs pâle; **olive-tree w.,** hypolaïs des oliviers; **booted w.,** hypolaïs russe; **rufous, brown-backed, w.,** agrobate roux; **fantailed w.,** cisticole *f* des joncs; **Australian fantail w.,** cisticole couturière d'Australie; **(Australian) rock w.,** fauvette des rochers; **flycatcher w.,** fauvette gobe-mouches; (*b*) *NAm:* **Audubon's w.,** fauvette d'Audubon; **bay-breasted w.,** fauvette à poitrine baie; **black and white w.,** fauvette noire et blanche; **Blackburnian w.,** fauvette à gorge orangée; **blackpoll w.,** fauvette rayée; **blackthroated blue w.,** fauvette bleue à gorge noire; **blackthroated gray w.,** fauvette grise à gorge noire; **blackthroated green w.,** fauvette à poitrine, à gorge, noire, *Fr.C:* fauvette verte à gorge noire; **bluewinged w.,** fauvette à ailes bleues; **Canada w.,** fauvette du Canada; **Cap May w.,** fauvette tigrée; **cerulean w.,** fauvette azurée; **chestnut-sided w.,** fauvette à flancs marron; **Connecticut w.,** fauvette à gorge grise; **golden-winged w.,** fauvette à ailes dorées; **hooded w.,** fauvette à capuchon; **Kentucky w.,** fauvette du Kentucky; **Kirtland's w.,** fauvette de Kirtland; **Macgillivray's w.,** fauvette des buissons; **magnolia w.,** fauvette à tête cendrée; **mourning w.,** fauvette triste; **myrtle w.,** fauvette à croupion jaune; **Nashville w., Calaveras w.,** fauvette à joues grises; **orange-crowned w.,** fauvette verdâtre; **palm w.,** fauvette à couronne rousse; **parula w.,** fauvette parula; **pine w.,** fauvette des pins; **prairie w.,** fauvette des prés; **prothonotary w.,** fauvette orangée; **Tennessee w.,** fauvette obscure; **Townsend's w.,** fauvette de Townsend; **Wilson's w., pileolated w.,** fauvette à calotte noire; **worm-eating w.,** fauvette vermivore; **yellow w.,** fauvette jaune.

warbling[1] ['wɔːbliŋ], *a.* (oiseau) gazouillant; (son, murmure) doux, mélodieux.

warbling[2], *s.* = WARBLE[1].

warcry ['wɔːkrai], *s.* cri *m* de guerre (d'une tribu, *F:* d'un parti politique).

ward[1] [wɔːd], *s.* **1.** (*a*) guet *m*; **to keep watch and w.,** faire le guet; faire bonne garde; (*b*) *A:* tutelle *f*; **to put a child in w.,** mettre un enfant en tutelle; **to be in w. to s.o.,** être sous la tutelle de qn; (*c*) (*pers.*) pupille *mf*; *Jur:* **w. in Chancery, w. of court,** pupille sous tutelle judiciaire. **2.** *Fenc: A:* garde *f*, défense *f*, parade *f*. **3.** (*a*) **hospital w.,** salle *f* d'hôpital; **w. maid,** fille *f* de salle; (*of medical student*) **to walk the wards,** assister aux leçons cliniques; faire les hôpitaux; suivre la clinique d'un hôpital; (*b*) quartier *m* (d'une prison). **4.** *Adm:* arrondissement *m*, quartier (d'une ville); **electoral w.,** circonscription électorale. **5. wards of a lock,** gardes *f*, bouterolles *f*, garnitures *f*, râteau *m*, d'une serrure; **wards of a key,** dents *f*, bouterolles (du panneton) d'une clef.

ward[2], *v.tr.* **1.** (*a*) *A:* & *Lit:* garder **(from,** de); défendre, protéger **(from,** contre); (*b*) **to w. off a blow,** parer, écarter, un coup; **to w. off a danger, an illness,** détourner, écarter, un danger; prévenir une maladie. **2.** façonner les bouterolles (d'une clef).

warded ['wɔːdid], *a.* (serrure) à garnitures; (clef) à bouterolles.

warden[1] ['wɔːd(ə)n], *s.* **1.** (*a*) directeur *m* (d'une institution, d'une prison); *Ecc:* (père) gardien, supérieur, -eure (d'un monastère, d'un couvent); **w. of a hostel,** (i) directeur, -trice, d'un foyer; (ii) (*of youth hostel*) père *m* aubergiste, mère *f* aubergiste; (*b*) (*freemasonry*) surveillant *m*; **senior w.,** premier surveillant; (*c*) gardien *m*; gouverneur *m*; conservateur *m* (d'un parc national); (*d*) gouverneur (d'une ville); **Lord W. of the Cinque Ports,** gouverneur des Cinq Ports. **2.** (*a*) *Mil:* portier-consigne *m*, *pl.* portiers-consigne (d'un arsenal); (*b*) **air-raid w.,** chef *m* d'îlot; **traffic w.,** contractuel, -elle; *NAm:* **game w.,** garde-chasse *m*, *pl.* gardes-chasse; (*c*)

Adm: **W. of the Standards,** Gardien des poids et mesures; (*d*) *Ecc:* marguillier *m.*

warden[2], *s. Hort:* **w. (pear),** catillac *m,* catillard *m.*

warder [ˈwɔːdər], *s.* **1.** gardien, -ienne, de prison; **chief w.,** gardien-chef *m.* **2.** *Hist:* bâton *m* de commandement.

wardership [ˈwɔːdəʃip], *s.* charge *f,* fonctions *fpl,* de gardien de prison; gardiennage *m.*

warding [ˈwɔːdiŋ], *s.* **1.** garde *f.* **2.** *Pol:* découpage électoral. **3.** façonnage *m* des bouterolles (d'une clef).

wardite [ˈwɔːdait], *s. Miner:* wardite *f.*

wardmote [ˈwɔːdmout], *s. Adm:* conseil *m* d'arrondissement (de la Cité de Londres).

wardress [ˈwɔːdris], *s.f.* gardienne de prison.

wardrobe [ˈwɔːdroub], *s.* **1.** *Furn:* armoire *f,* garde-robe *f, pl.* garde-robes; **hanging w.,** penderie *f.* **2.** (ensemble *m* de) vêtements *mpl*; garde-robe; **to have a large w.,** avoir beaucoup de vêtements; **to sell one's w.,** vendre sa garde-robe; **w. dealer,** fripier, -ière; **w. keeper,** (i) *Th:* costumier, -ière; (ii) (*in school, etc.*) lingère *f.*

wardroom [ˈwɔːdruːm], *s. Navy:* carré *m* des officiers; **w. officers,** officiers *m* du carré; **w. mess,** table *f* des officiers; **warrant-officers' w.,** poste *m* des maîtres; **w. servant,** matelot *m* d'office; **w. cutter,** canot-major *m.*

wardship [ˈwɔːdʃip], *s.* tutelle *f*; **to have the w. of a minor,** avoir un mineur sous sa tutelle.

ware[1] [wɛər], *s.* **1.** *coll.* (*a*) articles fabriqués; **aluminium w.,** ustensiles *m* en aluminium; **Japan w.,** articles de laque; **cast-iron w.,** poterie *f* en fonte; **toilet w.,** ustensiles, garniture *f,* de toilette; (*b*) *Cer:* faïence *f*; **china w.,** porcelaine *f*; **Delft w.,** faïence de Delft. **2. wares,** marchandise(s) *f*; *O:* **to puff one's wares,** vanter, faire valoir, sa marchandise.

ware[2], *v.tr.* (*used only in the imp.*) (*a*) *Ven:* **w. wire!** gare le fil de fer! **w. wheat!** attention au blé! (*b*) méfiez-vous! attention!

warehouse[1] [ˈwɛəhaus], *s.* **1.** entrepôt *m*; dépôt *m* de marchandises; magasin *m*; *Cust:* **bonded w.,** entrepôt réel, entrepôt de la douane; **unbonded w.,** entrepôt fictif; **w. certificate,** certificat *m* de dépôt de marchandises; *Com:* **ex w.,** à prendre en entrepôt; *Navy:* **w. of the arsenal,** magasin de l'arsenal. **2.** *A:* magasin; maison *f* de commerce; **Italian w.,** magasin de comestibles; épicerie *f.* **2.** (*for depositing furniture*) garde-meuble *m, pl.* garde-meubles.

warehouse[2] [ˈwɛəhauz], *v.tr.* **1.** (*a*) (em)magasiner, mettre en magasin; (*b*) *Cust:* entreposer (des marchandises); (*c*) *P:* mettre en gage, mettre au clou (sa montre, etc.). **2. to w. one's furniture,** mettre son mobilier au garde-meuble.

warehouseman, *pl.* **-men** [ˈwɛəhausmən], *s.m.* **1.** (*a*) emmagasineur, entrepositaire, *Cust:* entreposeur; (*b*) garde-magasin, *pl.* gardes-magasin; magasinier. **2.** *A:* **Italian w.,** marchand de comestibles; épicier.

warehousing [ˈwɛəhauziŋ], *s.* (*a*) (em)magasinage *m,* mise *f* en magasin; (*b*) *Cust:* entreposage *m* (de marchandises).

warfare [ˈwɔːfɛər], *s.* la guerre; **total w.,** guerre totale; **conventional w.,** guerre classique, conventionnelle; **unconventional w.,** guerre non classique, non conventionnelle; guerre de partisans; **guerilla w., partisan w.,** guérilla *f*; guerre de partisans; **static w., position w.,** guerre de positions; **stabilized w.,** guerre stabilisée; **mobile w.,** guerre de mouvement; **trench w.,** guerre de tranchées; **land w.,** guerre sur terre; **field w., open w.,** guerre en rase campagne; **bush w., jungle w.,** guerre dans la brousse, dans la jungle; **desert w.,** guerre dans le désert, dans les régions désertiques; **mountain w.,** guerre en montagne; **naval w.,** guerre navale, guerre sur mer; **submarine w.,** guerre sous-marine; **anti-submarine w.,** guerre anti-sous-marine; **aerial w., air w.,** guerre aérienne, dans les airs; **atomic, nuclear, w.,** guerre atomique, nucléaire; **bacteriological w., germ w.,** guerre bactériologique; **biological w.,** guerre biologique; **chemical w.,** guerre chimique; **electronic w.,** guerre électronique; **radiological w.,** guerre radiologique; **psychological w.,** guerre psychologique; **class w.,** lutte *f* des classes.

warfarin [ˈwɔːfərin], *s. Ch:* warfarine *f.*

warfaring [ˈwɔːfɛəriŋ], *a.* militant; qui combat; **w. nation,** nation militante, guerrière.

warhead [ˈwɔːhed], *s.* (*a*) cône *m* de charge (d'une torpille); (*b*) *Artil: Ball:* ogive *f*; tête *f* (de fusée); **atomic, nuclear, w.,** ogive atomique, nucléaire; tête nucléaire; **conventional w.,** ogive classique.

warhorse [ˈwɔːhɔːs], *s.* **1.** *A:* destrier *m*; cheval *m* de bataille. **2.** *F:* **an old w.,** (i) un vieux soldat; (ii) un vétéran de la politique.

warily [ˈwɛərili], *adv.* avec circonspection; prudemment; précautionneusement; **to proceed w.,** agir avec circonspection.

wariness [ˈwɛərinis], *s.* circonspection *f*; prudence *f*; défiance *f.*

warlike [ˈwɔːlaik], *a.* (exploit, maintien) guerrier; (peuple) belliqueux; (air) martial.

warlock [ˈwɔːlɔk], *s.m. A:* sorcier, magicien.

warlord [ˈwɔːlɔːd], *s.* (*esp. in China*) seigneur *m* de la guerre.

warm[1] [wɔːm], *a. & s.*

I. *a.* **1.** (*a*) (relativement) chaud; **w. water,** eau chaude (mais pas très chaude); **the water's only just w.,** l'eau n'est que tiède; **to have w. hands and feet,** avoir les pieds et les mains chauds; **the body was still w.,** le cadavre était encore chaud; **I'm not very w., not w. enough,** je n'ai pas assez chaud; **to get w.,** se réchauffer; *Aut: etc:* **to get the engine w.,** chauffer le moteur; **to keep w.,** se tenir chaud; **to keep a dish w.,** garder un plat au chaud; *Com:* **to be kept in a w. place,** tenir au chaud; *F:* **to keep a place w. for s.o.,** garder un emploi pour qn; **wash in w. water,** à laver à l'eau tiède, pas trop chaude; (*b*) (vêtement) chaud; **w. blanket,** couverture chaude; (*c*) *Paperm:* **w. bleach,** blanchiment *m* à chaud; (*d*) *Meteor:* **w. front,** front chaud; (*of weather*) **it's w.,** il fait (assez) chaud; **it's getting warmer,** il commence à faire plus chaud; *Games:* **you're getting warmer,** tu brûles; *F:* **it's nice and w. here,** il fait bien chaud ici. **2.** (*a*) (accueil, remerciements, etc.) chaleureux; **to meet with a w. reception,** (i) être accueilli chaleureusement, avoir un accueil chaleureux; (ii) *Iron:* être accueilli par des huées; (*b*) **w. heart,** cœur généreux, chaud; **w. smile,** sourire accueillant; (*c*) **w. temper,** caractère emporté, vif, violent; **it was w. work,** c'était une rude besogne; *O:* **w. argument,** discussion animée; *A:* **w. with wine,** échauffé par le vin; *F:* **to make things, it, w. for s.o.,** rendre la vie intenable pour qn; en faire voir de dures à qn; (*d*) (*of colour*) chaud; **w. tints,** tons chauds; tons tirant sur le rouge; **w. red,** rouge chaud, à tons chauds; **w. yellow,** jaune orangé. **3.** *esp. N. of Eng: F:* (*of pers.*) riche, cossu, qui a de quoi.

II. *s.* **1. to have a w.,** se réchauffer; **to give sth. a w.,** chauffer qch. **2.** *Cost:* **British w.,** pardessus *m* trois-quarts beige de coupe militaire.

warm[2]. **1.** *v.tr.* (*a*) **to w. sth. (up),** (faire) chauffer qch.; **to w. up the soup,** (faire) réchauffer le potage; **to w. a bed,** bassiner un lit; **to w. a bottle of wine,** chambrer une bouteille de vin; **to w. oneself by the fire, in the sun,** se chauffer près du feu, au soleil; **to w. oneself up walking,** se réchauffer en marchant; *Aut:* **to w. up the engine,** chauffer le moteur; (*b*) **wine, news, that warms the heart,** vin, nouvelle, qui réchauffe le cœur; **that will w. the cockles of your heart,** voilà qui vous réchauffera; (*c*) *F: O:* **to w. s.o.'s ears,** échauffer, frotter, les oreilles à qn; *A:* **to w. s.o.'s jacket,** flanquer une tripotée à qn; secouer les puces à qn. **2.** *v.i.* (*a*) (se) chauffer; s'échauffer, se réchauffer; **to w. to s.o.,** concevoir de la sympathie pour qn; se sentir attiré vers qn; (*b*) **to w. (up),** (i) s'animer; (ii) devenir plus cordial, plus animé; *F:* se dégeler; (iii) *Sp:* se mettre en train; **the lecturer was warming up (to his subject),** le conférencier s'animait (peu à peu).

warm-blooded [wɔːmˈblʌdid], *a.* **1.** (animal) à sang chaud. **2.** (*of pers.*) (*a*) prompt à s'emporter; (*b*) passionné, au sang chaud.

warmer [ˈwɔːmər], *s.* **dish w.,** chauffe-plats *m inv*; **foot w.,** chaufferette *f.*

warmhearted [wɔːmˈhɑːtid], *a.* au cœur chaud, généreux; **w. welcome,** accueil chaleureux.

warmheartedly [wɔːmˈhɑːtidli], *adv.* chaleureusement, avec chaleur.

warming[1] [ˈwɔːmiŋ], *a.* chauffant; qui réchauffe.

warming[2], *s.* **1.** (*a*) chauffage *m*; **w. pan,** bassinoire *f*; *Artil: A:* **to fire a w. shot,** flamber le canon; (*b*) **w. up,** réchauffement *m,* réchauffage *m.* **2.** *F: A:* rossée *f,* raclée *f,* tripotée *f.*

warmly [ˈwɔːmli], *adv.* **1.** (vêtu) chaudement. **2.** (*a*) (applaudir, etc.) chaudement, avec ardeur; (accueillir qn, remercier qn, etc.) chaleureusement; (défendre qn, etc.) vivement, chaudement; *O:* **I'm w. attached to them,** je les aime beaucoup; (*b*) (répondre, etc.) avec chaleur, avec vivacité.

warmonger [ˈwɔːmʌŋgər], *s.* belliciste *mf*; fauteur, -trice, de guerre.

warmongering [ˈwɔːmʌŋg(ə)riŋ], *s.* bellicisme *m*; propagande *f* de guerre.

warmth [wɔːmθ], *s.* **1.** chaleur *f* (du soleil, du feu, etc.). **2.** (*a*) ardeur *f*; chaleur; (*of style, etc.*) **to lack w.,** manquer de chaleur; être froid; (*b*) cordialité *f,* chaleur (d'un accueil); (*c*) emportement *m,* vivacité *f.* **3.** *Art:* chaleur (du coloris).

warm-up [ˈwɔːmʌp], *s.* réchauffement *m,* réchauffage *m*; **come and have a w.-up by the fire,** viens te réchauffer auprès du feu; *Aut:* **to give the engine a w.-up,** chauffer le moteur; (*b*) *Sp:* mise *f* en train; **w.-up match,** match *m* préparatoire, d'entraînement; *esp. U.S:* **w.-up suit,** survêtement *m*; tenue *f* d'entraînement.

warn [wɔːn], *v.tr.* **1.** (*a*) avertir; prévenir; **to w. s.o. of a danger,** avertir qn d'un danger; **to w. s.o. against sth.,** mettre qn en garde, sur ses gardes, contre qch.; **he warned her against going, he warned her not to go,** il lui a conseillé (fortement) de ne pas y aller; **I had been warned that the police were after me,** on m'avait prévenu que la police était à mes trousses; **I w. you that he's dangerous,** je vous préviens que c'est un homme dangereux; **I had warned him of it, against it,** je l'en avais averti; **you have been warned!** vous voilà prévenu! **be warned by me,** que mon exemple vous serve d'avertissement, de leçon; (*b*) **the magistrate warned him not to do it again,** le juge lui a dit de ne pas recommencer; **I shan't w. you again,** tenez-vous-le pour dit. **2.** informer, donner l'éveil à (qn); **to w. the police,** alerter la police. **3.** *Turf:* **to w. s.o. off (the course),** exclure qn des champs de course; exécuter (un jockey, etc.).

warning [ˈwɔːniŋ], *s.* (*a*) avertissement *m*; avis *m,* préavis *m*; **to sound a note of w.,** (i) donner l'alarme; (ii) recommander la prudence; **gale w.,** avis, signal *m,* de tempête; **air-raid w.,** alerte *f*; **strike w.,** préavis de grève; **w. strike,** grève *f* d'avertissement; **without w.,** sans préavis; sans déclaration préalable; **without a moment's w.,** à l'improviste; *attrib.* **w. signal,** signal avertisseur, signal d'alarme, d'alerte; **w. device,** (appareil, dispositif) avertisseur; **w. bell,** sonnette *f,* sonnerie *f,* avertisseuse; sonnette, sonnerie, d'alarme, d'alerte; **w. lamp,** lampe *f* témoin; **w. light,** (i) avertisseur lumineux; voyant (lumineux); alarme lumineuse; lampe témoin; (ii) *Nau:* feu *m* d'avertissement; *Aut:* **hazard w. lights system,** signalisation *f* détresse; *Av:* **stall w. indicator, terrain clearance w. indicator,** avertisseur de décrochage, de marge d'altitude; *Tchn:* **w. plate,** plaquette *f* d'alarme; *Navy:* **w. shot,** coup *m* de semonce; **w. sign,** (i) signe avertisseur, signe précurseur, signe avant-coureur; (ii) pancarte *f,* plaque *f,* d'avertissement; **w. system,** système *m,* dispositif *m,* d'avertissement, d'alarme, d'alerte; avertisseur; **audio w. system,** avertisseur sonore; **fire w. system,** avertisseur d'incendie; *Mch:* *etc:* **overheat w. system,** avertisseur de surchauffe; *Mil:* **early w. system,** système de détection lointaine, de surveillance avancée; **early w. radar,** radar d'alerte avancée, de détection lointaine; (*b*) **he was let off with a w.,** il en a été quitte pour une réprimande; **I'm giving you fair w.,** vous voilà averti! (*c*) **let this be a w. to you,** que cela vous serve de leçon, d'exemple, d'avertissement; (*d*) *A:* (*of employer, landlord, etc.*) **to give s.o. w.,** donner son congé à qn; (*of maid, etc.*) **to give a week's w.,** donner ses huit jours au patron; (*e*) *Turf:* **w. off,** exécution *f* (d'un jockey).

warp[1] [wɔːp], *s.* **1.** (*a*) *Tex:* chaîne *f*; (*for tapestry*) lisse *f,* lice *f*; **with cotton w.,** à chaîne de coton; **backing w.,** chaîne de l'envers; **pile w.,** chaîne à poil; **w. beam,** ensouple dérouleuse; **w. end,** fil *m* de chaîne; **w. frame,** ourdissoir *m*; **w. protector,** casse-chaîne *m inv*; **high-w., low-w., tapestry,** tapisserie *f* de haute lice, de basse lice, de haute lisse, de basse lisse; (*b*) *Paperm:* chaîne; **triple w.,** toile *f* triple chaîne. **2.** *Nau:* amarre *f*; aussière *f* de halage; touée *f,* grelin *m*; chableau *m,* chablot *m*; **to make fast with four warps,** s'amarrer avec quatre grelins. **3.** voilure *f,* courbure *f* (d'une planche, d'une tôle, etc.); gauchissement *m.* **4.** *Agr:* colmate *f.*

warp[2], *v.*

I. *v.tr.* **1.** (*a*) déjeter, (faire) voiler, fausser, gauchir, déverser (le bois, une tôle, etc.); voiler (une roue); faire travailler (le bois); (*b*) fausser, pervertir (l'esprit, le caractère); (*c*) *Av:* gauchir (les ailes). **2.** (*a*) ourdir (un tissu, une corde); (*b*) *Tex:* empeigner (le métier). **3.** *Nau:* haler, touer (un navire); **to w. out, off, a ship,** déhaler un navire. **4.** *Agr:* colmater (un champ).

II. *v.i.* **1.** se déformer; (*of timber, etc.*) se déjeter, gauchir; se dévier, (se) déverser; se voiler, travailler; (*of sheet metal*) se fausser, se voiler, (se) gondoler; (*in tempering*) s'envoiler; (*of wheel*) se voiler; **the wood is warping,** le bois joue, travaille; **the beam is beginning to w.,** la poutre commence à se cambrer. **2.** *Nau:* **to w. out of port,** sortir du port à la touée; déhaler.

warpage [ˈwɔːpidʒ], *s. Nau:* (*a*) touage *m,* halage *m*; (*b*) **w. (dues),** (droits *mpl* de) touage.

warpaint [ˈwɔːpeint], *s.* **1.** peinture *f* de guerre (des Amérindiens). **2.** *F:* grande tenue; habits *mpl* de gala, de cérémonie; **decked out in all one's w.,** en grande toilette, en grand tralala; sur son trente et un. **3.** *F:* maquillage *m*; **to put on one's w.,** se maquiller.

warpath [ˈwɔːpɑːθ], *s.* sentier suivi par les guerriers amérindiens; **like an Indian on the w.,** comme un Mohican sur le sentier de la guerre; **to be on the w.,** (i) être parti en campagne; (ii) *F:* en vouloir à tout le monde; chercher noise à tout le monde; **country on the w.,** pays qui ne demande qu'à faire la guerre; **the boss is on the w.,** le patron est d'une humeur massacrante; **you're on the w. tonight,** tu cherches querelle, tu es agressif, ce soir.

warped [wɔ:pt], *a.* **1.** (*a*) (bois) déjeté, dévers, gauchi, gondolé, retrait; (essieu, etc.) faussé, fléchi; **w. wheel,** roue voilée; (*b*) (esprit) perverti, faussé; **w. nature,** caractère mal fait. **2.** *Tex:* (métier) empeigné.

warper ['wɔ:pər], *s. Tex:* ourdisseur, -euse.

warping ['wɔ:piŋ], *s.* **1.** (*a*) déjettement *m*, déversement *m*, gauchissement *m* (d'une planche, etc.); gondolement *m*, gondolage *m* (d'une tôle, etc.); voilure *f*, voile *m* (d'une roue); déformation *f*, flexion *f* (d'une pièce coulée); (*in tempering*) envoilure *f* (du métal); (*b*) perversion *f* (de l'esprit, du caractère); (*c*) *Av:* gauchissement *m* (des ailes); **w. control,** commande *f* de gauchissement; **w. wires,** câbles *m* à gauchissement. **2.** *Tex:* ourdissage *m*; **w. frame,** métier *m* à ourdir; ourdissoir *m*. **3.** *Nau:* touage *m*, halage *m*; **w. rope, w. cable,** touée *f*; **w. out, off,** déhalage *m* (avec amarres). **4.** *Agr:* (*a*) colmatage *m* (d'un champ); (*b*) colmate *f*.

warrandice ['wɔrəndis], *s. Jur: Scot:* garantie *f*.

warrant[1] ['wɔrənt], *s.* **1.** (*a*) garantie *f*; **a w. for s.o.'s good behaviour,** une garantie pour la bonne conduite de qn; **his interest is a w. for his discretion,** son intérêt est le garant de sa discrétion; (*b*) garant *m*; **I maintain, and I quote the Scriptures as my w., that . . .,** j'affirme, et je cite pour garant les Écritures Saintes, que . . .. **2.** autorisation *f*; justification *f*; **they had no w. for doing that,** ils n'étaient pas justifiés à faire cela. **3.** (*a*) mandat *m*, ordre *m*; *Jur:* **w. of arrest,** mandat d'arrêt, d'arrestation; mandat d'amener, de prise de corps; **there's a w. out against him,** il est sous le coup d'un mandat d'amener; **search w.,** mandat de perquisition; (*b*) autorisation écrite; autorité *f*; pouvoir *m*; **w. of attorney,** procuration *f*, mandat, pouvoir; (*c*) certificat *m*; **warehouse w., dock w.,** certificat d'entrepôt; bulletin *m* de dépôt; warrant *m*; **to issue a warehouse w. for goods,** warranter des marchandises; **goods covered by a warehouse w.,** marchandises warrantées; **produce w.,** warrant en marchandises; **w. bank,** banque *f* assignataire; (*d*) *Adm: etc:* mandat; chèque *m*; **my pension is paid by quarterly w.,** je reçois ma retraite trimestriellement par chèque; **w. for payment,** ordonnance *f* de paiement; **travel w.,** feuille *f* de route; *Mil: etc:* **detached service w.,** lettre *f* de mission; **royal w.,** brevet *m* de fournisseur du souverain; *St. Exch:* **dividend w.,** chèque-dividende *m*; **interest w.,** mandat d'intérêts. **4. w. officer,** (i) *Mil:* adjudant *m*; (ii) *Navy: A:* = maître principal; **w. officer class I,** *U.S:* **chief w. officer,** adjudant chef; **w. officer class II,** *U.S:* **w. officer junior grade,** adjudant.

warrant[2], *v.tr.* **1.** garantir, attester, certifier (qch.); répondre de (qch.); *O:* **I w. that the sum shall be paid,** je garantis le paiement de la somme; **it won't happen again, I w. you!** cela n'arrivera pas deux fois, je vous en réponds! **2.** *A: & Lit:* **to w. s.o. to do sth.,** autoriser qn à faire qch. **3.** justifier; **nothing can w. such conduct,** rien ne justifie une pareille conduite; rien ne peut excuser une telle conduite; **sufficient to w. a conviction,** suffisant pour motiver une condamnation; **that warrants a celebration,** cela mérite d'être fêté; il faut arroser cela.

warrantable ['wɔrəntəbl], *a.* **1.** (*a*) justifiable; légitime, permis; (*b*) que l'on peut garantir. **2.** *Ven:* **w. stag,** cerf *m* courable.

warrantably ['wɔrəntəbli], *adv.* justifiablement.

warranted ['wɔrəntid], *a.* **1.** *Com:* garanti; **colours w. fast,** couleurs garanties bon teint; **w. free from adulteration,** garanti pur de toute falsification. **2.** *Jur:* autorisé; légitime.

warrantee [wɔrən'ti:], *s.* **1.** receveur, -euse, d'une garantie. **2.** personne *f* sous le coup d'un mandat d'amener.

warranter ['wɔrəntər], *s.* garant, -ante.

warrantor ['wɔrəntɔ:r], *s. Jur:* répondant, -ante; garant, -ante.

warranty ['wɔrənti], *s.* **1.** autorisation *f*; justification *f* (**for doing sth.,** pour faire qch., pour avoir fait qch.); **have you any w. for such a charge?** êtes-vous fondé à porter une telle accusation? **2.** *Com: etc:* garantie *f*; *Jur:* **w. of title,** attestation *f* du titre; **breach of w.,** rupture *f* de garantie.

warren[1] ['wɔrən], *s.* (**rabbit**) **w.,** garenne *f*, lapinière *f*.

Warren[2], *Pr.n. Civ.E:* **W. girder, truss,** poutre *f* Warren; poutre en V symétrique.

warrener ['wɔrinər], *s.* garennier *m*.

warring ['wɔ:riŋ], *a.* **w. nations,** nations *f* hostiles, antagoniques; nations en lutte, en guerre; **w. interests,** intérêts *m* contraires; **w. creeds,** croyances *f* contraires, en conflit.

warrior ['wɔriər], *s.* guerrier *m*, soldat *m*; **the Unknown W.,** le Soldat inconnu; **w. tribes,** tribus guerrières; *Ent:* **w. ant,** (fourmi *f*) amazone *f*.

Warsaw ['wɔ:sɔ:], *Pr.n. Geog:* Varsovie *f*.

warship ['wɔ:ʃip], *s.* navire *m*, vaisseau *m*, de guerre.

wart [wɔ:t], *s.* (*a*) verrue *f*; **plantar w.,** verrue plantaire; *F:* **to paint s.o. warts and all,** peindre un portrait très exact de qn (sans le flatter); (*b*) *Vet:* poireau *m*; fic *m*; (*c*) *Bot:* excroissance *f*; loupe *f*; (*d*) *Bot:* **w. cress,** coronope *m*; **w. spurge,** (euphorbe *f*) réveille-matin *m inv*.

warted ['wɔ:tid], *a. Bot: Z:* verruqueux.

warthog ['wɔ:thɔg], *s. Z:* phacochère *m*; sanglier *m* d'Afrique.

wartime ['wɔ:taim], *s.* temps *m* de guerre; **in w.,** en temps de guerre; **w. regulations,** règlements *m* du temps de guerre.

wartweed ['wɔ:twi:d], *s. Bot:* (i) grande éclaire, herbe *f* aux verrues; (ii) (euphorbe *f*) réveille-matin *m inv*; (iii) herbe aux mamelles.

wartwort ['wɔ:twɔ:t], *s.* **1.** *Bot:* = WARTWEED. **2.** *Moss:* verrucaire *f*; herbe *f* aux verrues.

warty ['wɔ:ti], *a.* verruqueux.

warwickite ['wɔrikait], *s. Miner:* warwickite *f*.

wary ['wɛəri], *a.* (*a*) avisé, prudent, circonspect; défiant; cauteleux, précautionneux; **to be too w. to do sth.,** être trop avisé pour faire qch.; **we shall need to be w.,** (i) il faudra s'observer; (ii) il faudra être sur nos gardes; **to keep a w. eye on s.o.,** guetter qn; surveiller qn attentivement; (*b*) **to be w. of sth.,** se méfier de qch.; être sur ses gardes; **be w. of strangers,** méfiez-vous des étrangers.

wash[1] [wɔʃ], *s.* **1.** (*a*) lavage *m*; savonnage *m*; **to give sth. a w.,** laver qch.; **this table needs a w.,** cette table a besoin d'être lavée; (*b*) (*of pers.*) **to have a w.,** se laver; **to have a w. and brush up,** faire un brin, un bout, de toilette; (*c*) lessive *f*, blanchissage *m*; **to send clothes to the w.,** envoyer du linge au blanchissage; donner du linge à blanchir; **all my sheets are at the w.,** tous mes draps sont à la blanchisserie; *F:* **it will all come out in the w.,** (i) les faits se révéleront un jour ou l'autre; (ii) ça se tassera; *Aut:* **car w.,** installation *f*, aire *f*, de lavage; *F:* **we'll take her along to the car w.,** on l'amènera au lavage rapide; (*d*) *St. Exch: U.S:* **w. sale,** vente fictive. **2.** (*a*) *Med: Vet:* lotion *f* (pour plaies, etc.); **hair w.,** lotion capillaire; (*b*) *Hort: etc:* lessive (insecticide, etc.); *Vit:* (*against mildew, etc.*) bouillie *f*. **3.** (*a*) (*for walls, etc.*) **colour w.,** badigeon *m*; (*b*) couche légère, badigeonnage *m* (de couleur sur une surface); (*c*) *Art:* lavis *m* (d'aquarelle, d'encre de Chine); **w. drawing,** dessin *m*, épure *f*, au lavis; lavis; (*d*) dorure *f*, argenture *f*, au trempé; (*e*) **w. primer,** wash-primer *m inv*. **4.** (*a*) *Dist:* vinasse *f*; (*b*) *F:* (**hog, pig**) **w.,** lavasse *f*. **5.** (*a*) remous *m* (des vagues); **the w. of the waves,** le bruit des flots qui passent; (*b*) *Nau:* houache *f*, remous (d'un navire); *Av:* souffle *m* (de l'hélice); (*c*) *Nau:* **w. strakes,** fargues *f* (de canot). **6.** *Min:* (**gold**) **w.,** alluvions *f* (aurifères); **w. trough,** battée *f* (pour le lavage des sables aurifères). **7.** pelle *f*, pale *f* plat *m* (d'un aviron).

wash[2], *v.*

I. *v.tr.* **1.** (*a*) laver; **to w. sth. in cold w.,** laver qch. à l'eau froide; **to w. sth. clean,** nettoyer qch. à grande eau; bien laver qch.; **to w. one's face,** se laver le visage; **to w. one's hands,** (i) se laver les mains; (ii) *Ecc:* s'ablutionner; (iii) *F:* se frotter les mains (comme si on se les lavait); *F:* **would you like to w. your hands?** les toilettes sont par ici; *F:* **to w. one's hands of sth., s.o.,** se laver les mains de qch., de qn; **I've washed my hands of the affair,** je ne suis plus pour rien dans l'affaire; *Ecc:* **to w. the chalice,** ablutionner le calice; **to be washed of one's sins,** expier, se laver de, ses péchés; *Bookb: etc:* **to w. the parchment,** abluer le parchemin; (*b*) *v.pr. & i.* **to w.** (**oneself**), se laver; (*c*) *Med:* lotionner, déterger (une plaie). **2.** (*a*) blanchir, lessiver, laver (le linge); **to w. a few things,** faire une petite lessive; **w. in cool, hot, water,** à laver à l'eau tiède, chaude; **hand w. only,** ne laver qu'à la main (pas à la machine); *v.i.* **to w. for s.o.,** blanchir le linge de qn; (*b*) (*with passive force*) (*of fabric*) supporter le lavage; **material that washes well,** tissu qui lave bien; *F:* **that won't w.!** ça ne prend pas, ne passe pas! **3.** *Ind:* débourber (le minerai, le charbon); clairer (le minerai); épurer (le gaz d'éclairage). **4.** (*a*) **to w. the walls,** badigeonner les murs (**with,** de); (*b*) **to w. a metal, a coin, with gold,** dorer un métal, une pièce, au trempé, par immersion; (*c*) *Art:* laver (un dessin). **5.** (*a*) (*of sea*) baigner (une côte); **the sea washes the foot of the cliff,** la mer baigne le pied de la falaise; (*b*) (*of current*) dégrader, affouiller (les berges d'une rivière). **6.** (*of sea*) **to w. s.o., sth., ashore,** rejeter qn, qch., sur le rivage; **some debris that has been washed ashore,** des débris qui ont échoué sur la côte; **sailor washed overboard,** matelot enlevé par une lame. **7.** *St. Exch: U.S:* **to w. sales of stock,** faire des ventes fictives d'une valeur.

II. *v.i.* **the waves washed over the deck,** les vagues *f* balayaient le pont; **waves washing against the cliff,** vagues qui baignent la falaise.

III. (*compound verbs*) **1. wash away,** *v.tr.* (*a*) enlever (une tache, etc.) par le lavage; *Ch: etc:* éliminer (un sel) à l'eau courante; **to w. one's sins away,** se laver de ses péchés; (*b*) (i) (*of running water*) **to w. away the gravel from a river bed,** enlever le gravier du lit d'une rivière; dégravoyer le lit d'une rivière; **the flood washed away part of the river bank,** l'inondation a dégradé la berge, a enlevé une partie de la berge; (ii) emporter, entraîner; **washed away by the tide,** emporté, enlevé, par la mer.

2. wash down, *v.tr.* (*a*) laver (les murs) à grande eau; (*b*) (*of the rain*) emporter, entraîner (le sol, le gravier); *F:* **to w. down one's dinner with a glass of beer,** arroser son dîner d'un verre de bière; faire descendre son dîner avec un verre de bière.

3. wash off, *v.tr.* enlever, effacer, éliminer (qch.) par le lavage; (*with passive force*) **it will w. off,** (i) cela s'effacera à l'eau; (ii) cela s'en ira à la lessive.

4. wash out, *v.tr.* (*a*) (i) enlever (une tache); passer l'éponge sur (une tache); *Lit:* **to w. out an insult in blood,** laver un affront dans le sang; *F:* **better w. the whole thing out,** le mieux sera d'oublier toute cette affaire; mieux vaut passer l'éponge là-dessus; **you can w. that right out,** il ne faut pas compter là-dessus; (ii) **to w. out a few clothes, things,** faire une petite lessive; *F:* **to be, look, completely washed out,** être, avoir l'air, complètement lessivé; **I'm completely washed out,** je suis complètement vanné, à plat; (iii) laver, rincer, nettoyer (une tasse, une bouteille); *Paperm:* élaver (les chiffons); (iv) *Art:* dégrader (une couleur); (v) *Min:* **to w. out the gold,** extraire l'or (en lavant le sable, etc.); (vi) *Sp:* (*of match*) **to be washed out,** être décommandé à cause de la pluie; (*b*) (*with passive force*) (*of stain, colour*) partir au lavage; **it will w. out,** cela s'en ira à la lessive.

5. wash up. (*a*) *v.tr. & i.* (i) **to w. up** (**the dishes**), laver, faire, la vaisselle; (ii) (*of sea*) rejeter (qn, qch.) sur le rivage; **wreckage washed up by the sea,** débris rejetés par la mer; (iii) *U.S:* **we've washed up that subject,** on a épuisé, *F:* liquidé, ce sujet; **he's all washed up,** c'est un homme fini, liquidé; (*b*) *v.i.* (i) **the water washed up on to the bank,** l'eau refluait sur la berge; (ii) *U.S:* se laver (les mains et la figure).

washability [wɔʃə'biliti], *s.* lavabilité *f*.

washable ['wɔʃəbl], *a.* lavable; (*of wallpaper, etc.*) lessivable; **w. ink,** encre *f* délébile.

wash-and-wear [wɔʃənd'wɛər], *a. NAm:* lavé-repassé *inv*.

washbasin ['wɔʃbeis(ə)n], *s.* (cuvette *f* de) lavabo *m*.

washboard ['wɔʃbɔ:d], *s.* **1.** (*a*) planche *f* à laver; selle *f*, planche, de blanchisseuse; (*b*) *U.S:* **w. track,** chemin plein d'ornières, à la surface ravinée. **2.** *Nau:* **washboards,** (i) fargues volantes (d'un canot); (ii) *A:* fargues de sabord; **to fit a boat with washboards,** farguer un bateau.

washboiler ['wɔʃbɔilər], *s. Laund:* cuve *f* à lessive; lessiveuse *f*.

washbowl ['wɔʃboul], *s.* cuvette *f*; (*large*) bassine *f*.

washcloth ['wɔʃklɔθ], *s. U.S:* = gant *m* de toilette.

washday ['wɔʃdei], *s.* jour *m* de la lessive.

washdown ['wɔʃdaun], *s.* (*a*) toilette complète; **I'll give the car a w.,** je vais laver (rapidement) la voiture; (*b*) *Av:* aire *f* de lavage.

washed [wɔʃt], *a.* **1.** (*a*) (enfant, linge) lavé; (*b*) *Ind:* (gaz) épuré; (minerai) débourbé, clairé; (*c*) **w. out,** (i) (*of colour, material*) délavé, déteint, décoloré; (ii) *F:* (*of pers.*) à plat, vanné; (iii) *Sp:* (match) décommandé (à cause de la pluie). **2.** *Art:* **w. drawing,** dessin lavé, au lavis. **3.** *St. Exch: U.S:* **w. sale,** vente fictive.

washer[1] ['wɔʃər], *s.* **1.** (*pers.*) laveur, -euse; (*b*) **w. up,** *F:* **w. upper,** laveur, -euse, de vaisselle; (*in restaurant, etc.*) plongeur, -euse. **2.** (*device*) (*a*) *F:* (i) machine *f* à laver; (ii) lave-vaisselle *m inv*; *Paperm:* cylindre *m* à laver; pile défileuse; pile laveuse; *Min:* patouillet *m* (pour le lavage des minerais); (*b*) *Gasm:* laveur *m*, scrubber *m*; (*c*) *Phot:* **plate w., print w.,** cuve *f* de lavage; (*d*) *Aut:* **windscreen w.,** lave-glace *m, pl.* lave-glaces.

washer[2], *s. Mec.E: Hyd.E: etc:* rondelle *f*; bague *f* (d'appui); **cork, felt, leather, metal, rubber, w.,** rondelle de liège, de feutre, de cuir, de métal, de caoutchouc; **adjusting w.,** rondelle de réglage; **balance w.,** rondelle d'équilibrage; **base w.,** rondelle embase; **bland w., blank w.,** rondelle obturatrice; **countersunk w.,**

rondelle fraisée; **cupped w.,** rondelle de Belleville; **cup w.,** rondelle chambrée, rondelle cuvette, rondelle hémisphérique; **dished w.,** rondelle de raccordement; **domed w.,** rondelle bombée; **friction w.,** rondelle de frottement; **lock w.,** rondelle frein; **machine-made w., punched w.,** rondelle décolletée; **packing w.,** rondelle de garniture; bague, grain *m*, de presse-étoupe; **rivet w.,** rondelle de contre-rivure; **sealing w.,** rondelle d'étanchéité; **setting w.,** rondelle de calage; **shearing w.,** rondelle de cisaillement; **spacing w.,** rondelle d'écartement, d'épaisseur; rondelle entretoise; **split w.,** rondelle fendue, ouverte; **spring w.,** rondelle à ressort; rondelle élastique, rondelle Grower; **stop w.,** rondelle d'arrêt, de butée; rondelle à crans; **tab w.,** rondelle à ergot, à flancs rabattus; **tap w.,** rondelle de robinet; **thick, heavy, w.,** rondelle épaisse; **thin w.,** rondelle mince; **thrust w.,** rondelle d'appui, de poussée; **w. seat,** portée *f* de rondelle; *Rail:* **spring w.,** étoile *f.*

washerman, *pl.* **-men** ['wɔʃəmən], *s.m.* (*a*) blanchisseur; (*b*) *Min:* laveur, débourbeur (de minerai).

washerwoman, *pl.* **-women** ['wɔʃəwumən, -wimin], *s.f.* blanchisseuse.

washery ['wɔʃəri], *s. Ind:* laverie *f.*

wash(-)hand ['wɔʃhænd], *a.* **w. basin,** (cuvette *f* de) lavabo *m.*

wash-house ['wɔʃhaus], *s.* (*a*) buanderie *f*, lavanderie *f*; (*with copper*) fournil *m*; (*b*) laverie *f*; lavoir (public); (*c*) *U.S:* blanchisserie *f.*

washin ['wɔʃin], *s. Av:* augmentation *f* de l'incidence à l'extrémité de l'aile.

washiness ['wɔʃinis], *s. F:* fadeur *f*, insipidité *f.*

washing ['wɔʃiŋ], *s.* **1.** (*a*) lavage *m*; ablutions *fpl*; (*b*) *Ecc:* lavement *m* (des pieds, des mains); ablution *f* (du calice). **2.** (*a*) blanchissage *m*, lessive *f* (du linge); **to do the w.,** faire la lessive; **to do a bit of w.,** faire une petite lessive; **w. day,** jour *m* de lessive, de blanchissage; **it's our w. day,** on blanchit aujourd'hui chez nous; **w. machine,** machine *f* à laver; **to do one's own w.,** se blanchir soi-même; faire la lessive à la maison; (*b*) linge (i) à laver, (ii) lavé; le blanchissage; la lessive; **my w. hasn't come back yet,** on ne m'a pas encore rapporté mon blanchissage; *O:* **she takes in w.,** elle fait le blanchissage; *F:* **to take in one another's w.,** se rendre mutuellement service; *F:* **you're showing next week's w.,** votre jupon dépasse; vous cherchez belle-mère; (*c*) **to do the w. up,** faire la vaisselle, (*in restaurant*) la plonge; **w.-up bowl,** cuvette *f*, bassine *f*; **w.-up water.,** eau *f* de vaisselle; **w.-up machine,** machine à laver la vaisselle, lave-vaisselle *m inv*; *Fr.C:* laveuse *f* à vaisselle; (*d*) *Aut:* **w. bay,** installation *f*, aire *f*, de lavage. **3.** *Ind:* (*a*) débourbage *m* (du charbon, du minerai); clairage *m* (du minerai); épurage *m* (du gaz); *Min:* **w. cylinder,** patouillet *m* (pour le minerai); *Ind:* **w. tower,** tour *f* de lavage; *Ch:* **w. bottle,** flacon laveur; barboteur *m* pour lavage; (*b*) lavée *f* (du minerai, de la laine, etc.); (*c*) **washings,** produits *m* de lavage; (*d*) *Min:* **washings,** chantier *m* de lavage (du quartz aurifère, etc.). **4.** (*a*) badigeonnage *m* (d'une surface); (*b*) *Art:* lavis *m* (d'un dessin). **5.** *St.Exch: U.S:* vente fictive.

washingtonia [wɔʃiŋ'touniə], *s. Bot:* washingtonia *m.*

washleather ['wɔʃleðər], *s.* **1.** peau *f* de chamois; chamois *m* lavable; cuir chamoisé; **w. gloves,** gants *m* chamois. **2.** peau de chamois (pour nettoyage de vitres).

washout ['wɔʃaut], *s.* **1.** lavage *m*, rinçage *m*; *Mch: etc:* **w. hole,** regard *m* de lavage; trou *m* de sel (d'une chaudière). **2.** *Min: Geol:* affouillement *m* de terrain; poche *f* (de dissolution); *Rail:* effondrement *m* de la voie (causé par les pluies). **3.** (*a*) fiasco *m*; **the whole thing's a w.,** c'est une perte sèche! (*b*) (*pers.*) raté *m*; propre *m* à rien. **4.** *Av:* diminution *f* de l'incidence à l'extrémité de l'aile.

washpot ['wɔʃpɔt], *s. Metalw:* bain *m* d'étain fondu (pour étamage).

washrag ['wɔʃræg], *s. U.S:* = gant *m* de toilette.

washroom ['wɔʃru:m], *s.* (*a*) *esp. NAm:* (*in hotel, etc.*) toilette *f*; (*b*) salle *f* d'eau; cabinet *m* de toilette.

washstand ['wɔʃstænd], *s.* **1.** *Furn:* (*a*) table *f* de toilette; (*b*) *NAm:* lavabo *m.* **2.** *U.S: Aut:* installation *f*, aire *f*, de lavage.

washtrading ['wɔʃtreidiŋ], *s. St.Exch: NAm:* ventes fictives de valeurs.

washtub ['wɔʃtʌb], *s. Dom.Ec:* cuvier *m*; baquet *m* (à lessive).

washup ['wɔʃʌp], *s.* (*a*) lavage *m* (de vaisselle); (*b*) *Surg: F:* stérilisation *f* des mains, etc. (avant de procéder à une opération); (*c*) *NAm:* **to have a w.,** se laver (les mains et la figure).

washy ['wɔʃi], *a. F:* (*a*) fade, fadasse; insipide; (*b*) **w. tea, coffee,** lavasse *f*; (*c*) (*of colour*) délavé, fade.

wasp [wɔsp], *s. Ent:* guêpe *f*; **solitary w.,** guêpe solitaire; **social wasps,** guêpes sociales; **mason w.,** guêpe maçonne; **hunting w.,** pompile *m*; **wood w.,** tremex *m*; **w. bee,** nomade *f*; **w. moth,** sésie *f*; **w. beetle,** clyte *m*; **w. fan beetle,** rhipiphore *m*; **w. fly,** (i) *Ent:* mouche-guêpe *f*, *pl.* mouches-guêpes; asile *m* frelon; (ii) *Fish:* mouche (artificielle) (à saumon); **wasp's nest,** guêpier *m*; (*of pers.*) **w. waist,** taille *f* de guêpe; *Cost: O:* **w. waisted corset, w. waister,** guêpière *f.*

waspish ['wɔspiʃ], *a. F: O:* méchant; acerbe; (ton) aigre.

waspishly ['wɔspiʃli], *adv. F: O:* d'une manière acerbe; méchamment; d'un ton aigre, acerbe.

waspishness ['wɔspiʃnis], *s. F: O:* méchanceté *f*, aigreur *f* (d'une réponse, etc.).

wasplike ['wɔsplaik], *a.* vespiforme.

wassail[1] ['wɔseil, wɔ'seil, 'wɔsəl]. **1.** *A:* (*a*) santé portée (à qn); (*b*) *int.* à votre santé! **2.** *Hist:* (*a*) bière épicée, sucrée, additionnée de pommes (bue à Noël et à la Fête des Rois); **w. bowl,** coupe *f* de *wassail,* (*b*) soirée passée à boire. **3. w. (song),** chanson *f* à boire; noël *m.*

wassail[2], *v.i. A:* (*a*) passer la soirée à boire; (*b*) aller de maison en maison en chantant des noëls.

wassailer ['wɔseilər], *s. A:* (*a*) convive *mf* à une réunion où on boit le *wassail;* (*b*) chanteur, -euse, de noëls (qui va de maison en maison).

Wassermann ['væsəmæn], *Pr.n. Med:* **Wassermann('s) reaction, test,** réaction *f* de (Bordet-) Wassermann.

wastage ['weistidʒ], *s.* **1.** (*a*) déperdition *f*, perte *f* (de chaleur etc.); coulage *m*; (*b*) gaspillage *m.* **2.** *coll.* déchets *mpl*, rebuts *mpl.*

waste[1] [weist], *a.* **1.** (*a*) **w. land, ground,** (i) terre *f* inculte, en friche; (ii) terre indéfrichable; (iii) (*in town*) terrains *m* vagues; *Jur:* terres vaines et vagues; (*of ground*) **to lie w.,** rester en friche; (*b*) **to lay w.,** dévaster, ravager, piller (un pays, etc.). **2.** (*a*) **w. products, material, etc.,** déchets *mpl*; matière *f* de rebut; **w. paper,** papier *m* de rebut; **waste-paper basket,** corbeille *f* à papier(s); *Typ:* **w. sheets,** (i) passe *f*, maculatures *f*; (ii) défets *m*; **w. print,** déchets d'imprimés; **w. water,** (i) eaux ménagères; (ii) *Ind:* eaux résiduaires, vannes, usées; (iii) *Mch:* eau de condensation; (*b*) *Ind:* (produit) non utilisé, perdu; *Mch:* **w. steam,** vapeur perdue; **w.-steam pipe,** tuyau *m* d'échappement (de la vapeur); **w. gas,** gaz perdus; *Metall:* gaz de gueulard; *Metall:* **w. gas main,** gargouille *f.*

waste[2], *s.* **1.** région *f* inculte; désert *m*; lande *f*; friche *f*; **a w. of water(s),** une étendue désolée d'eaux. **2.** gaspillage *m* (d'argent, d'efforts, etc.); **house where there is a lot of w.,** maison où on gaspille beaucoup; **w. of time,** perte *f* de temps; **it was a sheer w. of effort,** c'était une pure perte d'effort; **to run, go, to w.,** (i) (*of liquid, etc.*) se perdre, se gaspiller, se dissiper; (ii) (*of land, garden, etc.*) s'affricher; être envahi par de mauvaises herbes; **all that potential going to w.!** toutes ces possibilités qui se perdent! **to cut cloth to w.,** gaspiller le drap; *Prov:* **wilful w. makes woeful want,** après le gaspillage la misère. **3.** (*a*) déperdition *f* (de force, d'énergie); (*b*) détérioration *f*, dépérissement *m*, déperdition (de tissus, etc.); (*c*) *Ind: etc:* freinte *f.* **4.** (*a*) déchets *mpl*; débris *mpl*; résidu(s) *m(pl)*; rebut *m*; *Min:* déblais *mpl*; *Tex:* bouts *m* veules; bouts tors; **cotton w.,** déchets, bourre *f*, de coton; chiffons *mpl*; étoupe *f*, chiffons, de nettoyage; *Metalw:* **stamping w.,** déchets d'estampage; *Typ:* **printing w.,** (i) (*superfluous sheets*) défets *mpl*; (ii) (*spoilt*) maculatures *fpl*; la passe; **w. of a beam,** gras *m* d'une poutre; *Atom.Ph: etc:* **atomic, nuclear, radioactive, w.,** déchets, résidus, atomiques, nucléaires, radioactifs; **hot, cool, w.,** déchets à haute, à faible, activité; **cold w.,** déchets inactifs; **w. recovery,** récupération *f* des déchets; **w. disposal,** élimination *f*, destruction *f*, des déchets, des résidus; *Dom.Ec:* **w. disposal unit,** broyeur *m* à ordures; **the w. was buried in the ground, disposed of at sea,** on a enfoui, immergé, les déchets; (*b*) *Hyd.E:* trop-plein *m*; **w. gate,** écluse *f* de fuite, de dégagement; **w. weir,** déversoir *m*; trop-plein; livon *m*; *Hyd.E: etc:* **w. (pipe),** tuyau *m* d'écoulement (du trop-plein); tuyau de décharge, de dégagement, de vidange; épanchoir *m*; écoulement *m* (d'une baignoire); *Mch: etc:* **w. cock,** robinet purgeur, de purge. **5.** *Jur:* dégradations *fpl* (qui surviennent pendant une location); **voluntary w.,** dégradations commises sur le fonds par l'usufruitier; **permissive w.,** détérioration *f* du fonds faute d'entretien.

waste[3], *v.*

I. *v.tr.* **1.** *A:* dévaster, ravager, désoler (un pays, etc.). **2.** consumer, user, épuiser, faire dépérir (qn, le corps, la force, etc.); **patient wasted by a disease,** malade amaigri, miné, par une maladie. **3.** (*a*) gaspiller (les provisions, son argent, etc.); brouiller, gâcher (du papier); dissiper, dilapider (une fortune); perdre, gaspiller (du temps); *Lit:* **to w. one's substance,** gaspiller son bien; **nothing is wasted,** rien ne se perd; **one shouldn't w. anything,** il ne faut rien laisser perdre; **I haven't any time to w. on, over, that, doing that,** je n'ai pas de temps à perdre à faire cela, ça; **I haven't any time to w. on him,** je n'ai pas de temps à perdre pour lui; **that would be wasted on me,** ce serait trop beau pour moi; moi, je n'en aurais que faire; **to w. one's youth,** gaspiller sa jeunesse; **to w. one's life,** gâcher sa vie; **he's wasted in that job,** cet emploi est bien au-dessous de ses capacités; **to w. one's eloquence,** dépenser inutilement son éloquence; **to w. one's words,** (i) parler en pure perte; (ii) prêcher dans le désert; **why w. words?** à quoi bon tant de mots? **you're wasting your energy,** vous vous dépensez inutilement, en pure perte; **the allusion, the joke, was wasted on him,** il n'a pas saisi l'allusion, n'a pas compris la plaisanterie; (*b*) **to w. an opportunity,** perdre une occasion. **4.** *Jur:* (i) dégrader, (ii) laisser détériorer (le fonds d'un usufruit).

II. *v.i.* **1.** (*a*) se perdre; s'user, se consumer; s'épuiser; (*b*) *Prov:* **w. not, want not,** qui ne gaspille pas trouve toujours; qui épargne gagne. **2.** (*of living being*) **to w. (away),** dépérir; se miner, se décharner; s'affaiblir, maigrir; **he is visibly wasting away,** il maigrit, diminue, s'affaiblit, à vue d'œil; **to w. away for lack of food,** dépérir faute de nourriture; **his leg is wasting away,** sa jambe s'atrophie; **to be wasting away with anxiety,** se consumer d'inquiétude.

wastebasket ['weistbɑ:skit], *s. NAm:* corbeille *f* à papier(s).

wasted ['weistid], *a.* **1.** (pays, etc.) dévasté, ravagé, ruiné. **2.** (*a*) (malade, corps) affaibli, amaigri, décharné, atténué; (membre) atrophié; **w. hands,** mains flétries; **he's terribly w.,** il n'a plus que la peau et les os; (*b*) (*of thg*) usé, détérioré; épuisé. **3.** (argent, etc.) gaspillé; **w. life,** vie manquée; **w. time,** (i) temps perdu; (ii) (*in mechanical movement*) temps mort; *Tchn:* **w. energy,** dépense *f* à vide.

wasteful ['weistful], *a.* gaspilleur, -euse; prodigue; (habitudes) de gaspillage; (dépense) en pure perte; **don't be so w. with the hot water!** ne gaspillez pas l'eau chaude!

wastefully ['weistfuli], *adv.* prodigalement; avec prodigalité; en gaspillant; (dépenser) en pure perte.

wastefulness ['weistfulnis], *s.* prodigalité *f*; gaspillage *m.*

wasteheap ['weisthi:p], *s.* tas *m* de déchets; *Min:* halde *f* de déblais.

waster ['weistər], *s.* **1.** (*pers.*) (*a*) gaspilleur, -euse; **time w.,** (i) personne qui perd son temps; (ii) travail, chose, qui vous fait perdre votre temps; (*b*) raté *m*; propre *m* à rien. **2.** *Ind: Metall:* pièce *f* de rebut, pièce manquée; loup *m* (de fonderie); rebut *m.*

wasteway ['weistwei], *s. Hyd.E:* déversoir *m.*

wasting ['weistiŋ], *s.* **1.** gaspillage *m* (de ses ressources, de son temps, etc.); dissipation *f*, dilapidation *f* (de sa fortune). **2. w. (away),** dépérissement *m*, amaigrissement *m*, atténuation *f* (du corps); atrophie *f* (d'un membre).

wastrel ['weistrəl], *s.* **1.** *Ind: etc:* = WASTER 2. **2.** (*pers.*) (*a*) gaspilleur *m*; (*b*) rebut *m* de la société; vaurien *m*; propre *m* à rien; mauvais sujet.

watch[1] [wɔtʃ], *s.* **1.** *A:* veille *f*; (*still so used in*) **in the watches of the night, in the night watches,** pendant les veilles de la nuit; pendant les heures de veille; *Lit:* **it passed as a w. in the night,** ce fut bientôt oublié. **2.** garde *f*; surveillance *f*; **to be on the w.,** (i) être en observation; être, se tenir, aux aguets, au guet, à l'affût; avoir l'œil au guet; être aux écoutes; (ii) être sur ses gardes; **to be on the w. for s.o.,** épier, guetter, qn; être à l'affût de qn; **he was on the w. to keep anyone from going in,** il était attentif à ce que personne n'entre, n'entrât; **to keep w.,** monter la garde; **to keep (a) good, close, w.,** faire bonne garde; **to keep a close w. on one's interests,** être très près de ses intérêts, suivre ses intérêts de très près; **to keep a close w. on, over, s.o.,** surveiller qn de près; garder qn à vue; **to keep a discreet w. on s.o.,** exercer une surveillance discrète sur qn; **to keep a w. on one's tongue,** (i) surveiller son langage; (ii) savoir se taire; **he kept close w. on what was happening,** il surveillait de près ce qui se passait; **to set a w. on s.o.,** faire surveiller qn; **w. house,** (i) guérite *f* (d'homme de veille); (ii) *A:* corps *m* de garde; (iii) *U.S:* poste *m* de police; *Mil:* **w. post,** (i) poste *m* de garde; (ii) corps *m* de garde; **w. radar,** radar *m* de veille; **w. tower,** (i) tour *f* d'observation, de guet; (*in prison camp*) mirador *m*; (ii) *A.Fort:* échauguette *f*; **w. fire,** feu *m* de bivouac; *Ind: etc:* **w. clock,** contrôleur *m* de ronde. **3.** (*a*) *A:* (*pers.*) garde *m*, veilleur *m*; (*b*) *coll. Hist:* **the w.,** la garde, le guet; **the constables of the w.,** le guet; la ronde de nuit; les archers *m*; (*c*) *Adm:* **w. committee,** comité *m* qui veille au maintien de l'ordre de la commune. **4.** *Nau:* (*a*) quart *m*; **the morning w.,** le quart du jour; **the night w.,** le quart de nuit; **first w.,** quart de huit heures à minuit; **middle w.,** quart de minuit à quatre heures; **in two, three, watches,** service *m* par bordée, par tiers; **to set the w.,** régler les quarts; **to come on w.,** prendre le quart; **to be on w.,** être de quart; **to keep w.,** faire le quart; **the officer of the w.,** l'officier *m* du quart; **the w. on deck,** le quart en haut; **to have w. and w.,** faire le quart par bordées; **the w. bell,** la cloche; **radio w.,** quart radio; **w. bill,** rôle *m* de(s) quart(s); **w. and quarter bill,** rôle de quart et de manœuvre; **w. keeper,** (i) homme *m* de quart; (ii) chef *m* de quart; **engineroom w. keeper,** mécanicien *m* de quart; (*b*) (*men*) bordée *f*; **the port w.,** la bordée de bâbord; les bâbordais *m*; **the starboard w.,** la bordée de tribord; les tribordais *m*; **the w. on deck,** la bordée de quart; **the w. below,** la bordée libre de quart. **5.** (*a*) montre *f*; **self-winding w.,** montre à remontage automatique; **electronic w.,** montre électronique; **quartz w.,** montre à quartz; **dress w.,** montre-bijou *f*; **to wind one's w.,** remonter sa montre; **to put one's w. right,** mettre sa montre à l'heure; **it's six o'clock by my w.,** il est six heures à ma montre; **w. case,** (i) boîte *f*, boîtier *m*, (ii) étui *m*, de montre; **w. chain,** chaîne *f* de montre, de gilet; **w. glass,** verre *m* de montre; **w. guard,** chaîne *f* de gilet; giletière *f* (en cuir, etc.); **w. pocket,** gousset *m* (de montre); **w. stand,** porte-montre *m inv*; **w. spring,** ressort *m* de montre; **w. train,** mouvement *m* (d'une montre); (*b*) *Nau:* **the deck w., the hack w.,** le compteur.

watch[2]. **1.** *v.i.* (*a*) veiller; **I watched all night,** j'ai veillé jusqu'au jour; *Ecc:* **w. and pray,** veillez et priez; (*b*) **to w. by a sick person,** veiller un malade; veiller auprès d'un malade; **to w. over a child, a flock,** veiller sur, surveiller, garder, un enfant, un troupeau, *Ecc:* ses ouailles *f*; **to w. over the safety of the state,** veiller au salut de l'état; (*c*) **to w. (out),** être aux aguets; être au guet, à l'affût; avoir l'œil au guet; être sur ses gardes; prendre garde; **w. out!** attention! prenez garde! **w. out for X!** gare à X! (*d*) **to w. (out) for s.o.,** attendre qn; épier, guetter, qn; **he was watching for an opportunity,** il attendait que l'occasion se présentât; il guettait l'occasion; **to w. (for wildfowl, etc.),** être au guet, *Fr.C:* faire la guette (du gibier, etc.); *P.N: NAm:* **w. for deer,** attention grands animaux; **w. for slow-moving vehicles,** attention aux véhicules lents; (*e*) *O:* **to w. after s.o.,** suivre qn du regard, des yeux. **2.** *v.tr.* (*a*) veiller (un mort); garder, veiller sur (qn, qch.); (*b*) observer; regarder attentivement; *Prov:* **a watched pot never boils,** plus on désire une chose, plus elle se fait attendre; **to w. s.o. closely,** surveiller qn de près; épier qn; garder qn à vue; ne pas quitter qn des yeux; **to w. s.o. like a cat watching a mouse,** guetter qn comme le chat fait de la souris; **to have s.o. watched,** faire surveiller, faire épier, qn; faire pister qn; **we are being watched,** on nous observe; **to w. birds, wildlife,** observer les oiseaux, les bêtes, la nature; (*c*) avoir l'œil sur (qch.); **we shall have to w. the expenses,** il nous faudra avoir l'œil sur la dépense; **w. the step!** attention à la marche! **w. your step!** (i) prenez garde de tomber; (ii) allez-y discrètement; **I had to w. my step all through the discussion,** pendant toute la discussion il m'a fallu éviter tout faux pas; *F:* **w. it!** attention! (*d*) regarder; voir; **I watched him go down the path,** je l'ai regardé descendre le sentier; **I watched her working,** je la regardais travailler; **I watched his face fall,** j'ai vu son visage s'allonger petit à petit; **I watched him do it,** je le regardais faire; **to w. a football match,** assister à un match de football; **she's gone to w. her brother playing for the University,** elle est allée voir le match où son frère joue pour l'université; **I was watching the procession,** je regardais passer le cortège; **to w. the course of events, to w. s.o.'s career,** suivre le cours des événements, la carrière de qn; *Jur:* **to w. a case,** veiller (en justice) aux intérêts de qn; (*e*) **to w. one's opportunity, one's time,** guetter l'occasion, le moment propice.

watchband ['wɔtʃbænd], *s.* bracelet *m* de montre.

watchcock ['wɔtʃkɔk], *s. Clockm:* pont *m* de rouage.

watchdog ['wɔtʃdɔg], *s.* **1.** chien *m* de garde; chien de défense; chien d'attache; **good w.,** chien de bonne garde, de bon guet; *F:* **w. committee,** comité *m* qui veille à la dépense d'un projet, etc. **2.** *Cmptr:* contrôleur *m* de séquence.

watcher ['wɔtʃər], *s.* **1.** veilleur, -euse (d'un mort, d'un malade). **2.** *A:* **night w.,** veilleur de nuit; gardien *m* de nuit. **3.** (*a*) observateur, -trice; guetteur *m*; **bird w.,** observateur des mœurs des oiseaux; **bird watchers' societies,** sociétés *f* d'études ornithologiques, pour l'étude des oiseaux, d'ornithologie; (*b*) **to be a weight w.,** surveiller son poids.

watchful ['wɔtʃful], *a.* vigilant; alerte; attentif; **to be w.,** être sur ses gardes; être aux aguets; **to keep a w. eye on, over, s.o.,** surveiller qn de près; **to be w. of s.o.,** observer, épier, qn d'un œil méfiant, d'un œil jaloux.

watchfully ['wɔtʃfuli], *adv.* avec vigilance; d'un œil attentif.

watchfulness ['wɔtʃfulnis], *s.* vigilance *f*.

watching ['wɔtʃiŋ], *s.* **1.** veille *f*; veillée *f*. **2.** observation *f*; **bird w.,** observation des oiseaux; étude *f* des oiseaux; études ornithologiques.

watchmaker ['wɔtʃmeikər], *s.* horloger *m*.

watchmaking ['wɔtʃmeikiŋ], *s.* horlogerie *f*.

watchman, *pl.* **-men** ['wɔtʃmən], *s.m.* gardien, garde; guetteur; *Nau:* homme de garde (au mouillage); factionnaire; *Hist:* veilleur (de nuit); *Ind: etc:* **night w.,** gardien de nuit; *Rail:* **track w.,** garde-ligne, *pl.* gardes-ligne(s); *Com:* **market w.,** hallier.

watchnight ['wɔtʃnait], *s. Ecc:* **w. service,** office *m* de minuit (à la veille du jour de l'an).

watchstrap ['wɔtʃstræp], *s.* bracelet *m* de montre (en cuir).

watchword ['wɔtʃwɔ:d], *s.* (*a*) *Mil: A:* mot *m* d'ordre; (*b*) *Pol: etc:* mot d'ordre (du parti, etc.).

water[1] ['wɔ:tər], *s.* eau *f*. **1.** (*a*) **spring w.,** eau de source; **hard w., soft w.,** eau calcaire, douce; **sea w., salt w.,** eau de mer, eau salée; **fresh w.,** (i) (*newly drawn*) eau fraîche; (ii) (*not salt*) eau douce; **drinking w.,** eau potable; **w. cooler,** gargoulette *f*; alcarazas *m*; **w. carrier,** (i) porteur, -euse, d'eau; (ii) *Astr: F:* (*also* **w. bearer**) le Verseau; **hot w.,** eau chaude; *F:* **to get into hot w.,** se mettre dans le pétrin, dans de mauvais draps; **cold w.,** eau froide, fraîche; **to drink a glass of cold w.,** boire un verre d'eau fraîche; **to pour cold w. on a scheme,** dénigrer, décourager, jeter une douche froide sur, un projet; **to put w. in one's wine,** couper son vin d'eau; mouiller son vin; *F:* **w. bewitched (and tea begrudged),** thé faiblard; lavasse *f*; **to take the horses to w.,** conduire, mener, les chevaux à l'abreuvoir; *Prov:* **you can, may, lead, take, a horse to (the) w. but you cannot make him drink,** on ne saurait faire boire un âne qui n'a pas soif; **to let in w.,** prendre eau; **my shoes let in w.,** mes chaussures prennent l'eau; **to take in w.,** (i) (*of ship*) embarquer son eau; faire de l'eau; (ii) (*of steam locomotive*) faire de l'eau; (*of ship*) **to make w.,** avoir une voie d'eau; faire eau; **w. repellent, resisting,** hydrofuge; imperméable; *Ch:* **w. soluble,** hydrosoluble; *Myth:* **w. sprite,** ondin, -ine; (*of graceful swimmer*) **she's a real w. sprite,** c'est une véritable ondine; (*b*) *Dom.Ec: etc:* **w. supply,** (i) arrivée *f* d'eau; (ii) service *m* des eaux; **w. pipe,** tuyau *m* d'eau; **w. main,** conduite *f* d'eau; **main(s) w.** = eau de la ville; **running w.,** eau courante; **to have w. laid on,** (i) faire mettre, (ii) avoir, l'eau courante; **w. cock,** robinet *m* (d'arrivée d'eau); **to turn on the w.,** ouvrir l'eau; **to cut off, turn off, the w.,** couper, fermer, arrêter, l'eau; **w. softener,** adoucisseur *m* d'eau; **w. heater,** chauffe-eau *minv*; **w. closet,** water-closet *m*; toilette *f*; *Adm:* **w. rate,** taux *m* d'abonnement à l'eau; **w. cart,** arroseuse *f* (des rues); voiture *f* d'arrosage; **w. jug,** pot *m*, cruche *f*, broc *m* à eau; **w. bottle,** gourde *f*, bidon *m* (à eau); **hot w. bottle,** bouillotte *f*; *Cu:* **w. ice,** sorbet *m*; **w. biscuit,** *NAm:* **cracker,** galette salée; *Hyd.E:* **w. tower,** château *m* d'eau; (*c*) *Paperm: Tex: etc:* **w. of condition,** eau hygroscopique; (degré *m* d')humidité *f*; **w. stain,** (i) goutte *f*; (ii) teinture *f* (du bois, etc.) à l'eau; *Paperm:* **white w.,** eau collée, blanche; **w. finish,** calandrage *m* humide; (*d*) *Ind: etc:* **w. mill,** moulin *m* à eau; **w. engine,** (i) machine *f* hydraulique; (ii) (*also* **w. elevator**) élévateur *m* d'eau; machine élévatrice d'eau; *A:* **w. clock,** clepsydre *f*; *Mch:* **w. feed,** alimentation *f* en eau; **w. drum,** collecteur inférieur (d'une chaudière); **w. space,** cloison *f* d'eau, chambre *f* d'eau, lame *f* d'eau, réservoir *m* d'eau, bouilleur *m* (d'une chaudière); **w. tube,** tube *m* d'eau, bouilleur; **w. tube boiler,** chaudière à tubes d'eau; chaudière aquatubulaire; **w. bearing,** palier glissant; **w. seal,** fermeture *f*, clôture *f*, à eau (de récipient de gaz, etc.); *I.C.E: etc:* **w. jacket,** chemise *f* d'eau; chambre, culotte *f*, d'eau, de circulation; enveloppe *f* de circulation d'eau; **w.-cooled engine,** moteur à refroidissement d'eau, refroidi par l'eau; **w. gauge,** (i) *Mch:* (indicateur *m* de) niveau *m* d'eau; (ii) *Hyd.E:* indicateur de niveau d'eau; hydromètre *m*; (*in river*) échelle *f* d'étiage; *Hyd.E:* **w. gate,** (i) porte *f* d'écluse; vanne *f*, vannelle *f*, vantelle *f* (d'écluse); retenue *f* d'eau; (ii) robinet-vanne *m*, *pl.* robinets-vannes; vanne (de communication); vannelle; (iii) grille *f* d'accès (donnant sur un fleuve); **w. hammer,** (i) *Ph:* marteau *m* d'eau; (ii) *Hyd.E:* coup *m* de bélier (dans une conduite d'eau ou de vapeur); *Min: etc:* **w. shaft,** puits *m* d'épuisement; **w. level,** galerie *f* d'écoulement; **w. blast,** trompe *f*; (*e*) *Art:* **w. colours,** couleurs *f* à l'eau, pour l'aquarelle; **to paint in w. colours,** faire de l'aquarelle; (*a painting*) **a w. colour,** une aquarelle; **w. colourist,** aquarelliste *mf*; (*f*) *Sp:* **w. polo,** polo *m* nautique; water-polo *m*; **w. skiing,** ski *m* nautique; **to w. ski,** faire du ski nautique; *Rac:* **w. jump,** douve *f*, brook *m*. **2.** (*a*) *Geol:* **ground w.,** nappe *f* d'eau souterraine; **w. level,** niveau piézométrique; **w. table,** (i) surface *f* piézométrique; niveau hydrostatique; nappe aquifère, phréatique; (ii) *Arch:* chanfrein *m* du socle; **w.-bearing stratum,** couche *f* aquifère; (*b*) (*mineral springs*) **iron waters,** eaux ferrugineuses; **to take, drink, the waters,** prendre les eaux; faire une cure; (*c*) eaux (d'une rivière, d'un océan, etc.); **the waters of the Danube,** les eaux du Danube; **shark-infested waters,** eaux infestées par les requins; *Lit:* **to cast one's bread upon the waters,** jeter son pain sur la face des eaux; *Myth:* **to drink the waters of Lethe, of forgetfulness,** boire les eaux du Léthé, du fleuve d'oubli; **on land and w.,** sur terre et sur mer; sur la terre et sur l'océan; **to cross the w.,** traverser la mer, l'océan; **on the other side of the w.,** de l'autre côté de l'Atlantique; **by water,** par eau; en bateau; **to transport goods by w.,** transporter des marchandises par voie d'eau; **w. bus** = bateau-mouche *m*, *pl.* bateaux-mouche; galiote fluviale; (*of animal, etc.*) **to take to the w.,** se jeter à l'eau; se mettre à la nage; **under w.,** (i) (*of land, roots, etc.*) submergé; inondé; (ii) (*of submarine*) en plongée; **to swim under w.,** nager entre deux eaux; **above w.,** à flot; surnageant; **to keep (oneself), to keep one's head, above w.,** (i) se maintenir à la surface, sur l'eau; (ii) arriver à se subvenir; faire face à ses engagements; **deep w.,** eau profonde; **in deep w.,** par de grands fonds; **to swim in deep w.,** nager en pleine eau; (*of pers.*) **to be in deep water(s),** faire de mauvaises affaires; être dans la gêne; *Nau:* **shallow w., white w.,** petits fonds, hauts fonds, fond diminuant; (*d*) **high w.,** marée haute; haute mer, hautes eaux; **high w. mark,** (i) ligne *f* de la marée haute, des hautes eaux; (ii) apogée *m* (de la carrière de qn); **low w.,** marée basse; bas *m* de l'eau; eaux basses; (*of pers.*) **to be in low w.,** (i) être dans la gêne; être sans fonds; (ii) être déprimé, malade; être bien bas; être dans le marasme; (iii) être tombé dans la déconsidération; être peu estimé; (*e*) *Bot:* **w. chestnut,** châtaigne *f* d'eau, marron *m* d'eau; truffe *f* d'eau; mache *f*, macre *f*, trapa *m*; **w. fern,** osmonde royale; **w. germander,** germandrée *f* aquatique; **w. gladiole,** butome *m* à ombelles; **w. hemlock,** ciguë vireuse; cicutaire *f* aquatique; **w. horehound,** lycope *m*; marrube *m* aquatique; patte-de-loup *f*, pied-de-loup *m*; **w. hyacinth,** eichornia *m*, lis *m* d'eau; **w. hyssop,** herbe *f* au pauvre homme; **w. lentil,** lentille *f* d'eau; **w. lemon,** pomme-liane *f*; **w. lily,** nénuphar *m*; lis *m* d'eau, des étangs; **white w. lily, w. nymph, w. rose,** nymphée *f*; nénuphar blanc; blanc *m* d'eau; lune *f* d'eau; **yellow w. lily,** nuphar *m*; lis jaune; jaune *m*, jaunet *m*, d'eau; **royal, Amazon, giant w. lily, w. platter,** victoria *m* regia; **w. lotus,** rose *f* d'Inde; lotus sacré; **w. milfoil,** (i) volant *m* d'eau; (ii) mille-feuille *f* aquatique; **w. mint,** menthe *f* aquatique; **w. parsnip,** berle *f*; ache *f* (d'eau); **w. parsley,** ache; **w. pepper,** poivre *m* d'eau; persicaire *f* âcre; curage *m*; **w. rice,** riz *m* du Canada; zizanie *f*; **w. soldier,** stratiote *f* (faux aloès); **w. spike,** potamot *m*; épi *m* d'eau; **w. tree,** tetracère *f*; **red w. tree,** mancône *m*; *Arb:* **w. sprout,** branche gourmande; (*f*) *Orn:* **w. crake,** râle *m* à crête; **w. hen,** poule *f* d'eau; **w. ouzel,** merle *m* d'eau; cincle plongeur; hydrobate *m*; **Louisiana w. thrush,** fauvette *f* hoche-queue; **northern, Grinnell's, w. thrush,** fauvette des ruisseaux; *Z:* **w. antelope,** kob *m* singsing; **w. buffalo,** kérabau *m*; **w. deer,** hydropote *m*; **(African) w. deer,** chevrotain *m* aquatique; **w. hog, w. pig, w. cavy,** cabiai *m*; *Austr:* **w. mole,** ornithor(h)ynque *m*; **w. rat,** rat *m* d'eau; campagnol nageur; **w. shrew,** musaraigne *f* d'eau; **European w. shrew,** crossope *f*; **Szechwan w. shrew of Tibet,** crocidure *m or f* aquatique du Tibet; **w. spaniel,** épagneul *m* d'eau; chien *m* canard; **w. vole,** campagnol, rat d'eau; *Rept:* **w. dragon,** dragon *m* aquatique, d'eau; physignathe *m* de Lesneur; **w. lizard,** varan *m*; *Ent:* **w. boatman,** notonecte *m or f*; **w. bug,** nèpe *f*; **w. devil,** hydrophile brun; **w. fly,** (i) perle *f*; (ii) gyrin *m*, tourniquet *m*; **w. scorpion,** scorpion *m* aquatique, d'eau; nèpe; **w. spider,** (i) *Ent:* (*also* **w. tick**) hydromètre *f*; araignée *f* d'eau; (ii) *Arach:* argyronète *f*; *Ent:* **w. strider,** gerris *m*; **w. tiger,** dytique *m*; *Arach:* **w. bear,** tardigrade *m*; **w. mite,** hydrachne *f*; *Crust:* **w. flea,** daphnie *f*; puce *f* d'eau; **w. slater,** aselle *m* aquatique; **w. snail,** (i) *Moll:* hélice *f* aquatique; (ii) *Hyd.E:* pompe spirale; *Ann:* **w. worm,** naïs *f*, naïde *f*. **3.** (*liquid resembling or containing water*) (*a*) **lavender w.,** eau de lavande; *A:* **strong waters,** eau-de-vie *f*; (*b*) *Med:* **w. on the brain,** hydrocéphalie *f*; **w. on the knee,** hydarthrose *f* du genou; épanchement *m* de synovie; **w. brash,** pyrosis *m*, pituite *f*, aigreurs *fpl* (d'estomac);

Obst: **breaking of the waters,** perte *f* des eaux; (*c*) (*saliva*) **it brings (the) w. to one's mouth,** cela fait venir l'eau à la bouche; (*d*) **to pass, make, w.,** uriner; *Vet:* **red w.,** eaux rousses; (*e*) *Ch: etc:* **w. of crystallization,** eau de cristallisation; **constitution w.,** eau de constitution. **5.** transparence *f*, eau (d'un diamant); **diamond of the first w.,** diamant de première eau; *F: O:* **a swindler of the first w.,** un escroc de la plus belle eau, de premier ordre. **6.** *Fin: F:* actions émises pour diluer le capital.

water[2], *v.*

I. *v.i. & tr.* **1.** *v.tr.* (*a*) arroser (une plante, une route, une région); **country watered by many rivers,** pays arrosé, baigné, par de nombreux cours d'eau; **Egypt is watered by the Nile,** l'Égypte est arrosée par le Nil; **I have to w. the garden every evening,** chaque soir il me faut arroser le jardin; *Lit:* **to w. sth. with one's tears,** arroser qch. de ses larmes; (*b*) diluer, mouiller, délayer (un liquide); **to w. the milk,** mouiller le lait; **to w. one's wine,** mouiller, couper, *F:* baptiser, son vin; **to w. an acid,** étendre d'eau un acide; *Fin:* **to w. the capital,** diluer le capital; (*c*) faire boire, donner à boire à, abreuver (des bêtes); alimenter en eau (une machine); **to w. the horses,** conduire, mener, les chevaux à l'abreuvoir; donner à boire aux chevaux; (*d*) *Tex:* moirer, tabiser (la soie). **2.** *v.i.* (*a*) (*of eyes*) pleurer, larmoyer; **it makes one's mouth w.,** cela fait venir l'eau à la bouche; (*b*) (*of ship*) faire de l'eau; faire provision d'eau; aller à l'aiguade; (*c*) (*of animals*) aller à l'abreuvoir; s'abreuver; aller boire.

II. (*compound verb*) **water down,** *v.tr.* diluer, délayer (un liquide); atténuer (une expression, une affirmation); **to w. down one's claims,** en rabattre.

waterage ['wɔːtəridʒ], *s.* **1.** batelage *m*; transport *m* par eau. **2.** (droit(s) *m(pl)* de) batelage; prix *m* de transport par eau.

waterborne ['wɔːtəbɔːn], *a.* (*a*) (*of vessel*) à flot, flottant; (*b*) (*of goods*) transporté par voie d'eau; (*c*) (*of disease*) d'origine hydrique.

waterbuck ['wɔːtəbʌk], *s. Z:* (*a*) kob *m*, kobus *m*; cob onctueux; (*b*) adénote *m*; (*c*) redunca *m*; antilope *f* des roseaux.

waterbutt ['wɔːtəbʌt], *s.* tonneau *m* pour recueillir l'eau de pluie.

watercourse ['wɔːtəkɔːs], *s.* **1.** cours *m* d'eau. **2.** conduit *m*.

watercress ['wɔːtəkres], *s. Bot:* cresson *m* de fontaine.

watercup ['wɔːtəkʌp], *s. Bot:* hydrocotyle *f*; écuelle *f* d'eau.

watered ['wɔːtəd], *a.* **1.** arrosé; **well w. country,** pays bien arrosé. **2.** (vin, etc.) coupé, mouillé; (lait) mouillé. **3. w. silk,** soie moirée; tabi(s); **w. ribbon,** ruban moiré, ridé.

waterer ['wɔːtərər], *s.* arroseur, -euse.

waterfall ['wɔːtəfɔːl], *s.* chute *f* d'eau; cascade *f*; saut *m*.

waterflood ['wɔːtəflʌd], *s.* **1.** inondation violente. **2.** *Petr:* injection *f* d'eau (dans un puits).

waterfowl ['wɔːtəfaul], *s.* (*a*) oiseau *m* aquatique; (*b*) *coll.* gibier *m* d'eau; sauvagine *f*.

waterfowler ['wɔːtəfaulər], *s.* chasseur *m* de sauvagine.

waterfowling ['wɔːtəfauliŋ], *s.* chasse *f* à la sauvagine, au gibier d'eau.

waterfront ['wɔːtəfrʌnt], *s.* bord *m* de mer; bord de l'eau; les quais *m*; *U.S: F:* **on the w.,** chez les dockers.

waterglass ['wɔːtəglɑːs], *s. Com:* silicate *m* (i) de potasse, (ii) de soude; *F:* verre *m* soluble.

water-harden ['wɔːtəhɑːd(ə)n], *v.tr. Metalw:* tremper (l'acier) à l'eau.

waterhole ['wɔːtəhoul], *s.* mare *f* (dans un cours d'eau à sec).

wateriness ['wɔːt(ə)rinis], *s.* **1.** insipidité *f*, fadeur *f* (d'un potage, de qch. cuit à l'eau). **2.** (*a*) aquosité *f*; (*b*) *Med:* sérosité *f*.

watering ['wɔːt(ə)riŋ], *s.* **1.** (*a*) arrosage *m* (d'une plante, etc.); **w. can, pot,** arrosoir *m*; (*long spouted*) chantepleure *f*; *Moll:* **w. pot shell,** aspergillum *m*, bréchite *m*, *F:* arrosoir; (*b*) irrigation *f* (des champs). **2.** mouillage *m*, dilution *f* (d'un liquide); *Fin:* dilution (de capital). **3.** abreuvage *m* (des bêtes); alimentation *f* en eau (d'une machine); approvisionnement *m* d'eau (d'un navire); **w. place,** (i) (*for cattle*) abreuvoir *m*; (ii) (*for ships*) aiguade *f*; (iii) ville *f* d'eau, station thermale; (iv) station balnéaire, plage *f*. **4.** *Tex:* moirage *m* (de la soie). **5.** (*of eyes*) larmoiement *m*.

waterleaf ['wɔːtəliːf], *s.* **1.** (*a*) *Bot:* hydrophylle *f*; (*b*) *Algae:* rhodyménie palmée. **2.** *Paperm:* papier *m* brouillard, sans colle, sans apprêt.

waterless ['wɔːtəlis], *a.* sans eau; aride.

waterline ['wɔːtəlain], *s.* **1.** *Nau:* (*a*) (ligne *f* de) flottaison *f*; **load w., deep w.,** ligne de flottaison en charge; **light w.,** ligne de flottaison lège; **laden to the w.,** chargé au ras de l'eau; **repairs above the w.,** réparations *f* dans les œuvres mortes; *Artil:* **to aim at the w.,** viser à la flottaison. **2.** = WATERMARK[1] 2.

waterlogged ['wɔːtəlɔgd], *a.* **1.** (*a*) (navire) plein d'eau, entre deux eaux, qui a engagé; (*b*) (bois) alourdi par absorption d'eau. **2.** (terrain) détrempé, envahi par les eaux, imbibé d'eau; (sous-sol) aqueux; *Geol:* **w. bed,** gîte *m* d'eau.

Waterloo [wɔːtə'luː], *Pr.n.* **the Battle of W.,** la bataille de Waterloo; **a W.,** un combat décisif; **to meet one's W.,** arriver au désastre; être décisivement battu; voir la ruine, l'effondrement, de tous ses projets.

waterman, *pl.* **-men** ['wɔːtəmən], *s.m.* (*a*) batelier, marinier; (*b*) **good w.,** canotier expérimenté.

watermark[1] ['wɔːtəmɑːk], *s.* **1.** *Nau:* laisse *f* (de haute, de basse, mer, marée). **2.** *Paperm:* filigrane *m*; **countersunk w.,** filigrane enfoncé.

watermark[2], *v.tr. Paperm:* filigraner.

watermarked ['wɔːtəmɑːkt], *a.* (papier) à filigrane.

waterpot ['wɔːtəpɔt], *s.* **1.** pot *m*, broc *m*, à eau; cruche *f*; *Tex: etc:* (*for moistening fingers*) mouilloir *m*. **2.** *Moll:* aspergillum *m*, bréchite *m*, *F:* arrosoir *m*.

waterpower ['wɔːtəpauər], *s.* énergie *f* hydraulique, hydroélectrique.

waterproof[1] ['wɔːtəpruːf]. **1.** *a.* (toile, tissu, etc.) imperméable, caoutchouté; (enduit) hydrofuge; **w. varnish,** vernis *m* hydrofuge. **2.** *s. Cost:* imperméable *m*; caoutchouc *m*.

waterproof[2], *v.tr.* imperméabiliser (une toile, un tissu, un bâtiment); hydrofuger (un enduit); imperméabiliser, caoutchouter (un vêtement).

waterproofing ['wɔːtəpruːfiŋ], *s.* (*a*) imperméabilisation *f*; (*b*) hydrofugation *f*, hydrofugeage *m*; **w. compound,** enduit *m* hydrofuge.

watershed ['wɔːtəʃed], *s. Geog:* **1.** ligne *f* de partage des eaux. **2.** *NAm:* bassin *m* hydrographique.

watershoot ['wɔːtəʃuːt], *s.* (*a*) gargouille *f*, gouttière *f*; (*b*) = WATERSPOUT 3.

waterside ['wɔːtəsaid], *s.* bord *m* de l'eau; les quais *m*; **on the w.,** au bord de l'eau; sur le rivage, la rive; **w. flowers,** fleurs du bord de l'eau; *U.S:* **w. workers,** dockers *m*.

waterskin ['wɔːtəskin], *s.* outre *f*.

waterspout ['wɔːtəspaut], *s.* **1.** tuyau *m*, descente *f* (d'eau). **2.** gouttière *f*, gargouille *f*. **3.** *Meteor:* trombe *f* (d'eau), trombe marine; siphon *m*; colonne *f* d'eau.

watertight ['wɔːtətait], *a.* étanche (à l'eau); imperméable (à l'eau); (*of vessel*) **to be w.,** retenir l'eau; **w. barrel,** baril qui tient l'eau; **to keep the roof w.,** entretenir la toiture à étanche d'eau; *Nau:* **w. bulkhead,** cloison étanche; **w. regulations,** règlement qui a prévu tous les cas, qui ne permet pas d'échappatoire.

watertightness ['wɔːtətaitnis], *s.* étanchéité *f* (à l'eau).

waterway ['wɔːtəwei], *s.* **1.** voie *f* d'eau; voie navigable; voie fluviale. **2.** *Civ.E: etc:* (*a*) cunette *f*; (*b*) *N.Arch:* gouttière *f* (de pont); (*c*) débouché *m*, ouverture *f* (d'un pont); (*d*) (*in cock or valve*) passage *m*, voie, d'eau.

waterweed ['wɔːtəwiːd], *s. Bot:* plante *f* aquatique.

waterwheel ['wɔːtə(h)wiːl], *s.* roue *f* hydraulique; turbine *f* hydraulique; roue à aubes; *Pyr:* soleil *m* d'eau.

waterworks ['wɔːtəwəːks], *s.pl.* **1.** usine *f* de distribution d'eau; usine hydraulique; usine élévatoire; (*b*) *F:* (*of pers.*) voies *f* urinaires. **2.** (*a*) *A:* jeux *mpl* d'eaux; (*b*) *F:* **to turn on the w.,** (i) se mettre à pleurer, à chialer; ouvrir la fontaine; (ii) faire pipi.

waterwort ['wɔːtəwəːt], *s. Bot:* élatine *f*.

watery ['wɔːtəri], *a.* (*a*) (terrain) humide, aquatique, aquifère; (*b*) aqueux; qui contient de l'eau; **w. clouds,** nuages chargés de pluie; (*c*) noyé d'eau; **w. eyes,** (i) yeux larmoyants, qui pleurent; (ii) yeux mouillés de larmes; **w. potatoes,** pommes de terre aqueuses; **this cabbage is w.!** ce chou est insipide et nage dans l'eau! **w. fish,** poisson insipide, fade, noyé d'eau; **w. soup,** potage trop clair, peu consistant; (*d*) (*of colour*) pâle, déteint; délavé; (*e*) (temps, etc.) pluvieux; **w. moon,** lune voilée, embrumée, entourée d'un halo; **w. sun,** soleil *m* d'eau, qui annonce la pluie; **w. sky,** ciel chargé de pluie; (*f*) *Lit:* **to find a w. grave,** être enseveli par les eaux.

watsonia [wɔt'souniə], *s. Bot:* watsonia *m*.

watt [wɔt], *s. El.Meas:* watt *m*; voltampère *m*; **w. current,** courant watté, courant énergétique; **watts per candle,** watts par bougie; **w. hour,** watt-heure *m*, *pl.* watt-heures; **w.-hour meter,** watt-heuremètre *m*; wattmètre *m*.

wattage ['wɔtidʒ], *s. El:* puissance *f*, consommation *f*, en watts; wattage *m*.

wattful ['wɔtful], *a. El:* watté, actif; **w. component,** composante wattée, active.

wattle[1] ['wɔt(ə)l], *s.* **1.** (*a*) **w. (work),** clayonnage *m*; **w. fence,** enclos *m* en clayonnage; **w.-and-daub wall,** mur en clayonnage revêtu de boue, d'argile; *Mil:* **w. hut,** baraque-gourbi *f*; (*b*) (i) (*hurdle*) claie *f*; (ii) (*tray, stand*) claie, clayon *m*; (*for picking wool, etc.*) volette *f*. **2.** *Bot:* (*a*) *Austr:* acacia *m*; **silver w.,** acacia dealbata, acacia blanc; (*b*) mimosa *m*.

wattle[2], *v.tr.* **1.** clayonner; garnir de claies (un talus, etc.). **2.** tresser, entrelacer (l'osier, etc.).

wattle[3], *s.* caroncule *f* (d'une poule, d'un dindon); fanon *m* (d'un porc, d'un dindon); barbillon *m*, barbe *f* (d'un poisson, d'un coq).

wattled[1] ['wɔt(ə)ld], *a.* **1.** clayonné; garni de claies; **w. wall,** mur *m* en clayonnage. **2.** (*of branches, reeds, etc.*) entrelacé; tressé.

wattled[2], *a.* **1.** *Orn:* caronculé. **2.** *Her:* (*of cock, cockatrice*) **w. gules,** barbé de gueules.

wattless ['wɔtlis], *a. El:* (courant) déwatté, réactif; **w. component,** composante déwattée, réactive; **w. power,** puissance réactive.

wattling ['wɔtliŋ], *s.* clayonnage *m*.

wattmeter ['wɔtmiːtər], *s. El:* wattmètre *m*; voltampèremètre *m*.

wave[1] [weiv], *s.* **1.** (*a*) *Nau:* vague *f*, lame *f*; **crest, hollow, of a w.,** crête *f*, creux *m*, d'une vague; **bow w.,** lame d'étrave; moustache *f*; **stern waves,** lames de l'arrière; **synchronous w.,** houle synchrone; **transverse waves,** lames, vagues, transversales; **w. amplitude,** amplitude *f* de l'onde; (*b*) *Lit: etc:* **new w.,** nouvelle vague; (*c*) *Com: Fin:* **w. of depression,** vague de baisse; **w. of enthusiasm,** vague d'enthousiasme; **w. of anger,** bouffée *f* de colère; **a w. of bitterness, of repulsion, swept over him,** un flot d'amertume l'envahit; il eut un mouvement de répulsion; **a great w. of public opinion,** un déchaînement de l'opinion publique. **2.** (*a*) *Ph:* onde *f* (électrique, magnétique, etc.); **w. mechanics,** mécanique *f* ondulatoire; **heat w.,** onde calorifique; **light w.,** onde lumineuse; **w. theory of light,** théorie *f* ondulatoire de la lumière; **longitudinal, transverse, w.,** onde longitudinale, transversale; **plane w.,** onde plane; **reflected w.,** onde réfléchie; **sine w.,** onde sinusoïdale; **plane sine w.,** onde sinusoïdale plane; **standing, stationary, w.,** onde stationnaire; **steep-front w.,** onde à front raide; **travelling w.,** onde progressive; **waves out of phase,** ondes décalées; *Artil:* **blast w., detonation w., explosive w.,** onde explosive; **muzzle blast w.,** onde de bouche; *Geol:* **seismic w.,** onde s(é)ismique; *Av:* **shock w.,** onde de choc; **w. amplitude,** amplitude, élongation *f*, de l'onde; **w. equation,** équation *f* d'onde; **w. form, w. shape,** forme *f* d'onde; **w. front,** front *m* d'onde; **w. path,** parcours *m* de l'onde; **w. surface,** surface *f* d'onde; **w. train,** train *m* d'ondes; **w. velocity,** vitesse *f* (de propagation) de l'onde; (*b*) *W.Tel: Elcs:* **audio-frequency w., low-frequency w., kilometric w.,** onde kilométrique, onde basse fréquence; **carrier w.,** onde porteuse; **continuous, undamped, sustained, waves,** ondes entretenues; **damped waves,** ondes amorties; **directed waves,** ondes dirigées; **extremely-high-frequency w.,** onde millimétrique; **ground w.,** onde de sol, de surface; **hertzian w.,** onde hertzienne; **high-frequency w., decametric w.,** onde décamétrique, onde haute fréquence; **super-high-frequency w.,** onde centimétrique; **ultra-high-frequency w., decimetric w.,** onde décimétrique; **ultra-short waves,** ondes ultra-courtes; **very-high-frequency w., metric w.,** onde métrique; **very-low-frequency w., myriametric w.,** onde myriamétrique; **ionospheric w., sky w.,** onde ionosphérique; **long waves,** grandes ondes; **long-w. station,** émettrice *f* sur grandes ondes; **medium-frequency w., hectometric w.,** onde hectométrique, onde moyenne fréquence; **medium waves,** ondes moyennes; **modulated waves,** ondes modulées; **radio w.,** onde radioélectrique; *W.Tel:* **sending, transmitting, working, w.,** onde d'émission, de transmission, de travail; **short waves,** ondes courtes; **signal w., traffic w.,** onde de trafic; **speech w.,** onde acoustique; **w. band, w. range,** gamme *f* d'ondes, plage *f* (d'ondes); **w. collector,** collecteur *m* d'ondes; **w. detector,** détecteur *m* d'ondes; **w. generator,** générateur *m* d'ondes; **w. guide,** guide *m* d'ondes. **3.** (*a*) ondulation *f* (des cheveux); **to have a natural w. (in one's hair),** avoir les cheveux ondulés naturellement; (*b*) *Hairdr:* ondulation; **blow w.,** brushing *m*. **4.** (*a*) balancement *m*, ondoiement *m*, ondulation; (*b*) geste *m*, signe *m* (de la main, du chapeau, etc.); **with a w. of his hand,** d'un geste, d'un signe, de la main. **5.** *Ent:* **w. (moth),** cabère *f*.

wave[2], *v.*

I. *v.i.* **1.** s'agiter; (*of flag*) flotter (au vent); (*of corn, grass, plume*) ondoyer, onduler; **hair waving in the breeze,** cheveux agités par la brise. **2. to w. to s.o.,** (i) faire signe à qn (en agitant le bras, un mouchoir); essayer d'attirer l'attention de qn; (ii) saluer qn de la main; adresser de la main un salut à qn; **he was waving to me with his hat, with his stick,** il me faisait signe avec son chapeau, avec sa canne; il agitait son chapeau; il brandissait sa canne; **I waved to him to stop,** je lui ai fait signe d'arrêter. **3.** (*of the hair*) être ondé; onduler; former des ondulations; **my hair waves naturally,** mes cheveux ondulent naturellement.

II. *v.tr.* **1.** agiter (le bras, un mouchoir, son chapeau, un fanion); brandir (un parapluie, une canne); **to w. one's hand,** faire signe de la main; agiter le bras; **to w. one's arms about,** agiter les bras. **2.** (*a*) **to w. a welcome, to w. goodbye, to s.o.,** agiter la main, son mouchoir, son chapeau, en signe de bienvenue, en signe d'adieu; faire adieu à qn (d'un signe de main); **he waved us goodbye,** il nous a fait un signe d'adieu; (*b*) **to w. s.o. aside, away,** écarter qn d'un geste; faire signe à qn de s'écarter; **he waved us on,** de la main il nous a fait signe de continuer; **he waved me back,** de la main il m'a fait signe de (i) revenir, (ii) reculer; **to w. sth. away,** (i) refuser qch. d'un geste; (ii) faire signe d'écarter qch.; **to w. aside an objection,** écarter une objection; **to w. s.o. off,** faire signe de la main à qn de s'en aller; **I waved him, his car, down,** je lui ai fait signe d'arrêter. **3.** *Hairdr:* onduler (les cheveux); **to have one's hair waved,** se faire faire une mise en plis.

waved [weivd], *a.* **1.** ondé, ondulé, en ondes; **w. hair,** cheveux ondulés. **2.** *Mec.E:* **w. wheel,** came *f* à montagne russe. **3.** *Typ:* **w. rule,** tremblé *m.*

wavelength ['weivleŋθ], *s. Ph:* longueur *f* d'onde; **distinctive w.,** caractéristique *f* (d'une radiation, etc.); *F:* **we weren't on the same w.,** nous n'étions pas sur la même longueur d'onde.

wavelet ['weivlit], *s.* vaguelette *f*, petite vague.

wavelike ['weivlaik], *a.* (*a*) ondoyant; (*b*) *Ph:* sinusoïdal, -aux.

wavellite ['weivəlait], *s. Miner:* wavellite *f.*

wavemeter ['weivmi:tər], *s. W.Tel:* ondemètre *m*, cymomètre *m.*

waver ['weivər], *v.i.* vaciller. **1.** (*of flame*) trembloter. **2.** (*a*) hésiter, balancer, être indécis, flotter, osciller (entre deux opinions, etc.); (*of the voice, etc.*) se troubler; (*of courage*) défaillir; (*of virtue*) chanceler; **to w. in one's resolution,** chanceler dans sa résolution; (*b*) *Mil:* (*of troops*) fléchir; être près de lâcher pied; **the line wavered and broke,** le front de bataille fléchit et se disloqua.

waverer ['weivərər], *s.* indécis, -ise; irrésolu, -ue.

wavering[1] ['weivəriŋ], *a.* **1.** (*of flame*) vacillant, tremblotant. **2.** (homme, esprit) irrésolu, hésitant, indécis, vacillant; (voix) défaillante, qui se trouble; (courage) défaillant.

wavering[2], *s.* **1.** tremblement *m*, vacillement *m* (d'une flamme). **2.** (*a*) vacillation *f*, irrésolution *f*, hésitation *f*, flottements *mpl* (de l'esprit); trouble *m* (de la voix); défaillance *f* (du courage); (*b*) flottement (d'une ligne de troupes).

waveringly ['weivəriŋli], *adv.* avec indécision; en hésitant; irrésolument.

waviness ['weivinis], *s.* caractère onduleux, ondulé (d'une surface, des cheveux); ondulations naturelles (des cheveux).

waving[1] ['weiviŋ], *a.* **1.** (blé) ondoyant, ondulant; (drapeau) flottant (au vent). **2.** (main, canne) qui s'agite.

waving[2], *s.* **1.** (*a*) agitation *f* (d'un mouchoir, etc.); **w. of the hand,** geste *m*, mouvement *m*, de la main; (*b*) ondoiement *m*, ondulation *f* (du blé, etc.). **2.** *Hairdr:* ondulation (des cheveux).

wavy ['weivi], *a.* onduleux; **w. surface,** surface onduleuse, ondulée; **w. line,** ligne tremblée; **w. hair,** chevelure ondoyante; *Her:* **barry w.,** fascé ondé; *Nau: F:* **the W. Navy** = les officiers de réserve de la marine.

wax[1] [wæks], *s.* **1.** (*a*) cire *f*; **bleached w., unbleached w.,** cire blanche, jaune; **virgin w.,** cire vierge; **w. modelling,** céroplastique *f*; **to mould s.o. like w.,** façonner, former, (le caractère de) qn comme de la cire; *Ent:* **w. gland,** glande cirière; *Art:* **lost w. process,** *Metall:* **waste w. casting,** moulage *m*, fonte *f*, à cire perdue; *Engr:* **wall w.,** cire à border; *Rec:A:* **w. record,** plateau *m* de cire; **w. chandler,** cirier *m*; marchand *m*, fabricant *m*, de bougies, de cierges; **w. taper,** (i) rat *m* de cave; (*small*) queue-de-rat *f*, *pl.* queues-de-rat; (ii) *Ecc:* cierge *m*; **w. doll,** poupée *f* (i) de cire, (ii) à tête en cire; (*b*) *Petr:* cire (minérale), paraffine *f*; **amorphous w.,** paraffine amorphe; **sea w.,** cire marine; **slack w.,** paraffine brute; **paraffin w.,** paraffine; **w. tailings,** résidus paraffineux; **w. paper,** papier paraffiné. **2.** (*sth. resembling wax*) (*a*) *Physiol:* cérumen *m* (des oreilles); (*b*) **Chinese w.,** cire de Chine; **fossil w., mineral w.,** cire fossile, minérale; ozokérite *f*, ozocérite *f*; *Miner:* **w. opal,** résinite *m*; (*c*) *Bot:* **w. palm,** (i) céroxyle *m*, ceroxylon *m*; arbre *m* à cire; (ii) carnauba *m*; palmier *m* à cire; **w. myrtle,** = WAXBERRY 1; **w. tree,** (i) = WAXBERRY 1; (ii) troène *m* de la Chine; (iii) vismie *f* (de l'Amérique du Sud); **Japanese w. tree,** sumac *m* cirier; **w. pink,** pourpier *m*; **w. bearing,** cérifère; **carnauba w., palm w.,** carnauba; **vegetable w.,** cire végétale; (*d*) *Ski:* fart *m.*

wax[2], *v.tr.* **1.** (*a*) cirer, enduire de cire, encaustiquer (un plancher, un meuble); astiquer (un meuble, etc.); *Ski:* farter; (*b*) *Bootm:* empoisser (le fil). **2.** *Dressm: O:* bougier (un tissu). **3.** *Leath:* mettre (le cuir) en cire.

wax[3], *v.i.* **1.** (*of the moon*) croître; **to w. and wane,** croître et décroître; **the moon is waxing,** la lune est dans son croissant. **2.** *esp. Lit:* devenir, se faire; **to w. eloquent in support of sth.,** déployer toute son éloquence en faveur de qch.; **he waxed more and more eloquent,** il devenait, il se faisait, de plus en plus éloquent; **he waxed indignant,** il s'indigna.

wax[4], *s. F: O:* rage *f*, colère *f*; **to be in a w.,** rager; être en colère, en rogne; **to get into a w.,** se mettre en colère; **to put s.o. in a w.,** mettre qn en colère; faire enrager qn.

waxberry ['wæksberi], *s. Bot:* **1.** myrica *m*; cirier *m*; arbre *m* à cire. **2.** symphorine *f* boule-de-neige.

waxbill ['wæksbil], *s. Orn:* astrild *m*, sénégali *m*, bengali *m*, *F:* oiseau *m* des Iles; **blue-breasted w.,** astrild bleu; **golden-breasted w.,** astrild à ventre orange; **orange-cheeked w.,** astrild à joues orange; **St. Helena w., common w.,** astrild ondulé; **Sydney w.,** astrild de Sydney, bec-de-cire *m*, *pl.* becs-de-cire.

waxed [wækst], *a.* **1.** ciré; enduit de cire; **w. floor,** parquet frotté à la cire; parquet ciré; **w. moustache,** moustache cosmétiquée; **w. leather,** cuir ciré, en cire. **2. w. thread,** fil poissé.

waxen ['wæks(ə)n], *a.* (*a*) de cire, en cire; (*b*) cireux; **w. pallor, paleness,** pâleur cireuse; **w. complexion,** teint *m* de cire; (*c*) *O:* (caractère, cœur, etc.) mou comme la cire.

waxing[1] ['wæksiŋ], *s.* **1.** cirage *m*; encaustiquage *m.* **2.** empoissage *m.* **3.** *Ski:* fartage *m.*

waxing[2], *a.* (*of moon, anxiety, force, etc.*) croissant; grandissant.

waxing[3], *s.* croissance *f*, croissant *m* (de la lune); grandissement *m* (d'une lumière).

waxwing ['wækswiŋ], *s. Orn:* jaseur *m*; **w.,** *NAm:* **Bohemian w.,** jaseur de Bohême, jaseur boréal; **cedar w.,** jaseur des cèdres.

waxwork ['wækswə:k], *s.* **1.** modelage *m* en cire. **2.** (*a*) figure *f* de cire; (*b*) **waxworks,** (musée *m* de) figures de cire. **3.** *Bot: U.S:* célastre grimpant; *F:* bourreau *m* des arbres.

waxy[1] ['wæksi], *a.* **1.** cireux; (*a*) **w. complexion,** teint cireux, de cire; **w. potatoes,** pommes de terre cireuses; (*b*) *Med:* **w. degeneration,** dégénérescence cireuse; **w. (degeneration of the) liver,** amylose *f* du foie. **2.** *O:* (*of pers., mind*) mou comme la cire; plastique.

waxy[2], *a. F: O:* en colère; en rogne; **to be, get, w.,** être, se mettre, en colère.

way[1] [wei], *s.* **1.** chemin *m*, route *f*, voie *f*; **the public w.,** la voie publique; **on either side of the w.,** de chaque côté de la route; **over the w., across the w.,** de l'autre côté de la route, du chemin, de la rue; **the house, the people, over the w., across the w.,** la maison, les gens *m*, d'en face; **covered w.,** *Arch:* ambulatoire *m*; *Fort:* chemin couvert; *Nau:* cale couverte; *Ven:* **hollow w.,** cavée *f*; *Rel:* **the narrow w., the w. of salvation,** la voie étroite, du salut; le chemin du paradis; *Rail:* **permanent w.,** voie ferrée; **six-foot w.,** entre-voie *f*; *U.S:* **w. train,** (train *m*) omnibus *m*; **w. station,** halte *f*. **2.** (*a*) (*route*) **the w. to the station,** le chemin qui mène, qui conduit, à la gare; le chemin de la gare; **I forget the w. to your house,** j'oublie le chemin de votre maison; **to show s.o. the w.,** montrer la route à qn; **to ask one's w.,** demander son chemin; **to lose one's w.,** s'égarer, se perdre; **that's the w. to ruin,** c'est là le chemin de la ruine; **the right w.,** le bon chemin; la bonne voie; la bonne route; **to go the wrong w., to mistake the, one's, w.,** se tromper de chemin; faire fausse route; **to go the nearest, the shortest, w.,** prendre par le plus court; **to know one's w. about (a house),** connaître les aîtres; *F:* **he knows his w. about, around,** il sait se débrouiller; il est débrouillard; **to prepare the w.,** préparer les voies; **to light the w. for s.o.,** éclairer qn; **to set s.o. on his w.,** (i) remettre qn dans son chemin; (ii) *A:* faire un bout de chemin avec qn; faire un bout de conduite à qn; **to start on one's w.,** se mettre en route; **on the w.,** chemin faisant; en chemin; en cours de route; **to stop on the w.,** s'arrêter en chemin; **to be on one's, the, w. to Paris,** être en route pour, sur la route de, Paris; **on my, the, w. home,** en revenant chez moi; en rentrant; **on the, my, w. here, back from church,** en venant ici, en revenant de l'église; **on the w. to the restaurant,** sur le trajet du restaurant; **he's well on the w. to doing it,** il est en bonne voie de le faire; *F:* **there's a baby on the w.,** elle attend un bébé; **she was about three months on the w.,** elle était enceinte de trois mois, à peu près; **to go the w. of all things, of all flesh,** aller où va toute chose; mourir; **to go one's w.,** passer son chemin; **to go one's own w.,** (i) faire à sa guise; suivre son idée; (ii) se désolidariser d'avec ses collègues; faire bande à part; (iii) suivre son petit bonhomme de chemin; **her husband goes his own w.,** son mari vit à sa guise; **let him go his own w.!** qu'il s'arrange comme il voudra; qu'il s'accommode! **he always goes his own w.,** il ne fait jamais qu'à sa guise; **to go out of one's w.,** s'écarter de son chemin; dévier de sa route; faire un détour; **it wasn't worth going out of our w. for,** cela ne valait pas le détour; **to go out of one's w. to oblige s.o.,** se déranger, se donner de la peine, se mettre en quatre, pour être agréable à qn; **I wouldn't go out of my w. to hear him,** je ne me dérangerais pas pour l'écouter; **he seems to go out of his w. to find difficulties,** il semble prendre à tâche de découvrir, il a l'air de rechercher, la difficulté; **he goes out of his w. to offend the locals,** il recherche toutes les occasions d'offenser les gens du pays; **she's always out of the w. when she's wanted,** elle n'est pas jamais là quand on a besoin d'elle; **the village is rather out of the w.,** le village est un peu écarté; **his talent is nothing out of the w.,** son talent n'est pas hors ligne; **that's nothing out of the w.,** rien d'extraordinaire à cela; *Ecc:* **the W. of the Cross,** le chemin de la Croix; le calvaire; (*b*) **w. in,** entrée *f*; **w. out,** sortie *f*; **w. through,** passage *m*; **w. up,** montée *f*; **w. down,** descente *f*; **to find a w. out, in,** trouver moyen de sortir, d'entrer; **to find a w. out of a deadlock,** trouver une issue à une impasse; **to leave s.o. a w. out,** laisser à qn le moyen de s'échapper, de sortir (d'une difficulté, etc.); **easy w. out,** solution *f* de facilité; (*c*) **to find one's w. to a place,** parvenir à un endroit; **can you find your w. out?** vous savez le chemin pour sortir? vous savez où est la sortie, par où on sort? **he found his w. back,** il a trouvé moyen de revenir; **it's time we began to find our w. back,** il est temps de songer au retour; **to find one's w. into a place,** s'introduire dans un endroit; **however did it find its w. into print?** comment en est-on venu à l'imprimer? **to make one's w. towards a place, towards s.o.,** se diriger vers, se rendre dans, un endroit; s'avancer vers qn; **I made my w. to York,** j'ai réussi à aller jusqu'à York; **to make, work, push, one's w., to make a w. for oneself, through the crowd,** se frayer un chemin, s'ouvrir un chemin, se faire jour, à travers la foule; traverser, percer, la foule; fendre la foule; **he made his w. into the house,** il a pénétré dans la maison; **to make one's w. out of the house,** sortir de la maison; **to make one's w. back,** retourner, revenir; *Mil:* **the scouts made their w. back to their unit,** les éclaireurs rallièrent leur unité; **to make a w. for oneself,** se faire jour; **how to make one's w. (in the world),** le moyen de parvenir; **he's anxious to make his w.,** il est impatient de percer; **to work one's w. westward,** se diriger vers l'ouest; **to work one's w. up,** (i) s'élever; (ii) s'élever à force de travail; **to pay one's w.,** se suffire; **he can't pay his w.,** il ne peut pas suffire à ses besoins; **firm that pays its w.,** entreprise qui fait, qui couvre, ses frais; **to see one's w. to doing sth.,** se croire à même de faire qch.; (entre)voir la possibilité de, juger possible de, faire qch.; trouver moyen de, voir jour à, faire qch.; **I can't see my w. to doing it now,** je ne vois pas pour le moment comment le faire; **couldn't you see your w. to doing it?** ne trouveriez-vous pas moyen de le faire? **I hope you'll see your w. to doing it,** j'espère qu'il vous sera possible de le faire; **as soon as I see my w. to something better,** dès que je trouverai mieux, le moyen de faire mieux; (*d*) **to stand in s.o.'s w.,** être dans le chemin de qn; barrer le passage à qn; faire obstacle à qn; **he (came and) stood in my w.,** il m'a barré le passage; **I don't wish to stand in the w. of your happiness,** je ne voudrais pas faire obstacle à votre bonheur; **to stand in the w. of a scheme, of a marriage,** s'opposer à un projet, à un mariage; **the obstacles that stand in our w.,** les obstacles qui se dressent sur notre chemin; **there's only one obstacle in my w.,** un seul obstacle m'arrête; **to put difficulties in s.o.'s w., in the w. of sth.,** opposer, créer, des difficultés à qn; susciter des tracas à qn; apporter des difficultés à qch.; **to get in one another's w.,** se gêner (les uns les autres); **he gets in my w.,** il se met dans mes jambes; **to be in s.o.'s w.,** gêner, embarrasser, qn; **am I in the, your, w.?** est-ce que je vous gêne? **this table is in the w.,** cette table nous gêne, est encombrante; **is my chair in your w.?** est-ce que ma chaise vous incommode? **that child is in the w.,** cet enfant est embarrassant; **a man is terribly in the w. in a house,** un homme, c'est tellement encombrant dans la maison! **to get out of s.o.'s w.,** faire place à qn; céder le pas à qn; **to get out of the w.,** se ranger, s'effacer;

s'ôter du chemin; se garer; s'écarter (pour laisser passer qn); *Nau:* s'écarter de sa route; **get out of the w.!** rangez-vous! ôtez-vous de là, de mon chemin! **to get s.o., sth., out of the w.,** se débarrasser de qn; écarter, éloigner, qn, qch.; **to keep out of the w.,** se tenir à l'écart; **to keep out of s.o.'s w.,** se cacher de qn; éviter qn; **to make w. for s.o.,** s'écarter, s'effacer, pour laisser passer qn; faire place à qn; **they made w. for him to pass,** on s'est rangé pour le laisser passer; **the crowd made w. for him,** la foule s'est écartée pour lui faire passage; (*e*) *Jur:* servitude *f* de passage. **3.** (*distance*) **to go part of the w., a little w., a bit of the w., with s.o.,** accompagner qn un bout de chemin; faire un bout de chemin avec qn; **all the w.,** tout le long du chemin; jusqu'au bout; **I don't go all the w. with him,** je n'accepte pas absolument ses théories, etc.; **to walk all the, the whole, w., all the, the whole, w. back,** faire, refaire, toute la route à pied; **I flew most of the w.,** j'ai fait la plupart du voyage en avion; **we've done a good w.,** nous avons fait un bon bout de chemin; **I've come a long w.,** j'ai fait une longue traite; *F:* **he's come a long w.,** il a bien réussi (dans la vie); **it's a long w. to London, London's a long w. from here,** Londres est bien loin; Londres, c'est loin d'ici; c'est loin d'ici à Londres; **it's a long w. from Paris to Rome,** il y a loin de Paris à Rome; **to have a long w. to go,** avoir beaucoup de chemin à faire; **a little, a short, w. off,** à peu de distance; pas trop loin; **it's a long w. off,** c'est loin, il y a loin; c'est à une grande distance; **it's quite a short w. (off),** le trajet n'est pas long; c'est assez proche; **I saw him a long w. off,** je l'ai aperçu d'assez loin; *Fig:* **he'll go a long w.,** il ira loin; il fera son chemin; **first impressions go a long w.,** presque tout dépend de la première impression; **a little sympathy goes a long w.,** un peu de sympathie fait grand bien; **a little kindness will go a long w. with him,** avec un peu de bonté vous ferez de lui tout ce que vous voudrez; **a little of it goes a long w.,** on en use très peu, il en faut très peu; *F:* **a little of him, of his company, goes a long w.,** on se lasse bien vite de sa compagnie; **to make one's money,** *A:* **a penny, go a long w.,** savoir ménager ses sous; **by a long w.,** de beaucoup; **he's heavier than I am by a long w.,** il est de beaucoup plus lourd que moi; **she's more intelligent than he is by a long w.,** elle est de loin plus intelligente que lui; **the best known by a long w.,** de loin le plus célèbre (des monuments historiques, etc.); **not by a long w.,** pas à beaucoup près; il s'en faut de beaucoup; **you're a long w. out, out by a long w.,** vous êtes loin de compte; vous vous trompez de beaucoup. **4.** (*direction*) (*a*) côté *m*, direction *f*; **which w. is the wind blowing?** d'où vient, d'où souffle, le vent? *F:* **so that's the w. the wind blows!** ça se passe donc comme ça! **this w., that w.,** de ce côté-ci, par ici; de ce côté-là, par là; **(step) this w.!** (venez, passez) par ici! **this w. out,** par ici la sortie; **is this the way?** c'est par ici? **which w. did you come?** par où êtes-vous venu? quel chemin avez-vous pris? **which w. did he go?** par où est-il passé? **which w. do we go?** de quel côté, par où, allons-nous? **you're going this w.?** vous passez par ici? **this w. and that,** de-ci de-là; **she was turning her head this w. and that,** elle tournait la tête de tous (les) côtés; **you're not looking the right w.,** vous ne regardez pas du bon côté; **he didn't know which w. to look,** il a perdu contenance; il était tout décontenancé; **to look the other w.,** détourner les yeux; **I've nothing to say one w. or the other,** je n'ai rien à dire pour ou contre; **the tendency is all the other w.,** la tendance est tout à fait contraire; **to be too much (inclined) the other w.,** pécher par l'excès contraire; **ships going the same w.,** navires faisant la même route; **they set off, each going his own w.,** ils sont partis chacun de son côté; **I'm going your w.,** je vais de votre côté; **the next time you're that w.,** la prochaine fois que vous passerez par là; *F:* **down our w.,** chez nous; **he lives Hampstead w.,** il habite du côté de Hampstead; **have you never been our w.?** vous n'êtes jamais venu de nos côtés? **people like that don't often come my w.,** je n'ai pas souvent eu affaire à des gens pareils; **these things often come my w.,** j'ai souvent l'occasion d'acheter des objets de ce genre, de traiter des affaires de ce genre; **I take on anything that comes my w.,** j'entreprends n'importe quoi; **if the chance comes your w.,** si vous en trouvez l'occasion; si l'occasion se rencontre; (*b*) sens *m*; **both ways,** dans les deux sens; **(in) the wrong w.,** à contre-sens; **to brush sth. the wrong w.,** brosser qch. à rebours, à contre-poil, à rebrousse-poil; **the wrong w. up,** sens dessus dessous; à l'envers; **to hold sth. (the) right w. up,** tenir qch. dans le bon sens; **the same w. as the current,** dans le sens du courant; (*c*) voie (d'un robinet, etc.); **two-w. cock,** robinet à deux voies; *El:* **two-w. wiring system,** va-et-vient *m*; (*d*) **to split a sum of money three ways, five ways,** partager une somme entre trois, entre cinq, personnes. **5.** (*means*) moyen *m*; **the only w. to earn money,** le seul moyen de gagner de l'argent; **to find a w. of doing sth.,** trouver (le) moyen de faire qch.; *Adm:* **ways and means,** voies et moyens; *Parl:* **Committee of Ways and Means** = Commission *f* du Budget. **6.** (*a*) façon *f*, manière *f*; **in this w.,** de cette façon; **it can be done in many ways,** cela peut se faire de bien des façons; **in a friendly w.,** en ami; amicalement; **speaking in a general w.,** (parlant) d'une manière générale; **in such a w. as to . . .,** de façon à . . .; **in no w.,** en aucune façon; en rien; nullement; tant s'en faut; *F: esp. U.S:* **no w.!** jamais de la vie! aucunement! des clous! **he is in no sort of w. an extremist,** il n'est d'aucune façon extrémiste; **without in any w. wishing to criticize,** sans aucunement vouloir critiquer; **that's the w. he treated me, spoke to me,** voilà de quelle façon il m'a traité; voilà en quels termes il m'a parlé; **that's the w. the money goes!** voilà comme l'argent file! **that's the w.!** ça y est! voilà! à la bonne heure! **to go to work another w.,** (i) s'y prendre autrement; (ii) prendre un biais; **in such and such a way,** de telle et telle façon; **whichever w. he sets about it,** de quelque façon qu'il s'y prenne; **to go, set, about it (in) the right w.,** s'y prendre de la bonne manière, comme il faut; **you're going the right w. to make him angry,** ça c'est la meilleure manière de le mettre en colère; **that's not the right w.,** il ne faut pas le faire comme ça; **the best w. is to say nothing,** le mieux est de ne rien dire; **in one w. or another,** de façon ou d'autre; d'une façon ou d'une autre; **in what w. should I take that remark?** comment dois-je entendre, dans quel sens faut-il prendre, cette observation? **there are no two ways about it,** il n'y a pas à discuter; **to go on in the same old w.,** aller toujours son train; **I don't like the w. things are going,** c'est inquiétant, l'allure *f* des affaires; **they'll never finish it the w. things are going,** ils n'en finiront jamais, du train que vont, que prennent, les choses; **well, it's this w.,** voici ce que c'est; **w. of doing sth.,** manière, façon, de faire qch.; **I do it in the same w. as you, (in) the w. (that) you do it,** je le fais de la même façon que vous; **w. of speaking, writing,** façon de parler, d'écrire; **our w. of living,** notre train *m*, genre *m*, de vie; **his w. of looking at things,** sa manière de voir; **I don't like his w. of going on,** je n'aime pas sa conduite, sa manière d'agir; **it isn't what he says, it's the w. he says it,** ce n'est pas ce qu'il dit mais le ton dont il le dit; **to my w. of thinking,** selon moi; à mon sens; **that's not my w. (of doing things),** ce n'est pas ma manière de faire; **that's his w.,** c'est sa manière de faire; il est comme cela; voilà comme il est; **that's always the w. with him,** il est toujours comme ça; il n'en fait jamais d'autres; je le reconnais bien là; **to do things in one's own w.,** faire les choses à sa guise, à sa façon, à sa manière; **to have a w. of one's own, one's own w., of doing sth.,** avoir une façon à soi de faire qch.; avoir sa méthode; **he's happy in his own w.,** il est heureux à sa manière; **he's a genius in his w.,** c'est un génie dans son genre; **in its w. it's very beautiful,** c'est très beau dans son genre; **he does what he can for them in his small w.,** il les aide dans la mesure de ses moyens; **the ways of God,** les voies de Dieu; **you'll soon get into our ways,** vous vous ferez bientôt à nos habitudes; **to get, fall, into the w. of doing sth.,** (i) prendre l'habitude de faire qch.; s'habituer à faire qch.; (ii) apprendre à faire qch.; **you'll get into the w. of it,** vous vous y ferez; **when you get into the w. of things,** quand vous serez au courant; **I've got out of the w. of smoking,** j'ai perdu l'habitude de fumer; **to put s.o. in the w. of doing sth.,** (i) montrer à qn comment faire qch.; (ii) offrir à qn l'occasion de faire qch.; **if that's the w. you feel about it!** si c'est ça l'effet que ça te fait; **that's one w. of looking at it!** c'est une manière de voir; (*b*) **engaging ways, pretty ways,** petites façons engageantes; gentillesses *f*; **he disliked her free and easy ways,** il n'aimait pas sa liberté d'allure; **I don't like his ways,** je n'aime pas sa façon d'agir; **I know his little ways,** je connais ses petites manies; **he has a w. with him,** il est insinuant; **he has a w. with children,** il sait se faire bien voir des enfants; il sait prendre les enfants; (*c*) **ways and customs,** us *m* et coutumes *f*; **the good old ways,** les usages *m* du bon vieux temps; *Lit:* (*of pers.*) **to stand, walk, in the ancient ways,** être très vieux jeu; vivre dans le passé; s'en tenir au passé; en tenir pour le passé; (*d*) **to have one's (own) w.,** agir à sa guise; faire à sa tête; **to get one's (own) w.,** suivre sa volonté; faire valoir sa volonté; (en) faire à sa volonté; arriver à ses fins; **he wants his own w.,** il veut n'en faire qu'à sa tête; **in the end he always gets his (own) w.,** il finit toujours par faire ce qu'il veut, par n'en faire qu'à sa tête; **if I had my w.,** si j'étais le maître; si on me laissait faire; **if the law had its w.,** si la loi suivait son cours; **have it your own w.,** (i) faites comme vous l'entendez, à votre guise; faites ce que vous voulez; (ii) soit; **he had it all his own w.,** il n'a pas rencontré de résistance; cela n'a fait aucune difficulté; tout lui a souri; il a réussi d'emblée; **you can't expect to have it all your own w.,** (i) vous vous heurterez sûrement à des obstacles; (ii) il faut de temps en temps laisser faire les autres; **they're allowed to have it all their own w.,** (i) on les laisse faire; (ii) on ne leur fait pas de concurrence; **you can't have it both ways,** on ne peut pas être et avoir été. **7.** (*respect*) **in many ways,** à bien des égards; **it's a good thing in many ways that . . .,** il est heureux sous bien des rapports que . . .; **in some ways,** à certains points de vue, par certains côtés; **in every w.,** sous tous les rapports, en tous points; **he was a gentleman in every w.,** c'était un parfait gentleman, sous tous rapports un gentleman; **in one w.,** d'un certain point de vue; **you're right in a w.,** en un certain sens vous avez raison; **she's certainly clever in a w.,** elle ne manque pas d'une certaine adresse. **8.** cours *m*, course *f*; **the moon keeps on her w.,** la lune poursuit sa course; **I met him in the ordinary w. of business,** je l'ai rencontré dans le courant de mes affaires; **it wouldn't happen in the ordinary w. of business,** cela ne se fait pas dans le cours normal des affaires; **in the ordinary w. (of things) I'm home by five,** de coutume, en général, je suis rentré à cinq heures. **9.** (*a*) **the flood is making w.,** l'inondation fait des progrès; **to make no great w.,** ne pas faire de grands progrès; (*b*) *Nau:* erre *f*; **to have w. on,** avoir de l'erre; **to check the w.,** briser, casser, étaler, l'erre; **to lose w.,** perdre l'erre, son erre; **give w. (ahead)!** donnez de l'erre! **steerage w.,** erre pour gouverner; **ship under w.,** navire en marche, en route, faisant route; **to get under w.,** (i) *Nau:* appareiller; (ii) *Nau: etc:* se mettre en route; (*in rowing*) **give w.!** avant partout! **give w. (starboard)!** avant (tribord)! souquez (tribord)! **w. enough!** laisse courir! **when I arrived the meeting was already under w.,** lorsque je suis arrivé la réunion avait déjà commencé; **an important experiment is under w.,** une expérience importante est en cours. **10.** (*state, condition*) (*a*) (*of mind, body, estate*) **to be in a good w., a bad w.,** être bien, mal, en point; **the crops are in a bad w.,** (i) la récolte souffre; (ii) la récolte s'annonce mal; **things seem in a bad w.,** les choses ont l'air d'aller mal; **his business is in a bad w.,** ses affaires vont mal, périclitent; ses affaires sont engagées dans une mauvaise voie; **the country is in a bad w.,** le pays court à, vers, la ruine; **his health is in a bad w.,** sa santé est chancelante, délabrée; **he's in a worse w. than you,** il est plus malade que vous; **to be in a good w. of business,** faire de bonnes affaires; (*b*) *F: O:* **he's in a fine w. about it,** (i) il ne décolère pas; il est dans tous ses états; (ii) il a pris la chose très à cœur; (*c*) **to be in a fair w. to . . .,** être en voie de, en (bonne) passe de (faire fortune, etc.); **he's in a fair w. to becoming a millionaire,** il est en passe de devenir millionnaire; **to put s.o. in the w. of earning a few pounds,** mettre qn à même de gagner quelques livres. **11. w. of business,** genre *m* d'affaires; métier *m*, emploi *m*; **to be in a small w. of business,** avoir un petit commerce; **to be in a large way of business,** faire de grandes affaires; faire les affaires en grand; faire des affaires importantes, un commerce important; être à la tête d'une grosse maison; **he lives in a small w.,** il vit petitement, modestement; il a un train de maison très modeste; **he makes furniture in a small w.,** il a un petit commerce d'ébénisterie; **to be doing quite well in a small w.,** aller (toujours) son chemin. **12.** (*a*) **by the way:** (i) chemin faisant; en route; **he stopped by the w.,** il s'arrêta en route; (ii) incidemment; en passant; **(let it be said) by the w.,** soit dit en passant, (soit dit) par parenthèse; **all this is by the w.,** tout ceci est par parenthèse; (iii) à (ce) propos; **by the w., did you see him yesterday?** à propos, l'avez-vous vu hier? **by the w.!** ah, j'y pense! (*b*) **by w. of,** (i) (*via*) par la voie de, par (un endroit); (ii) en guise de, à titre de; **by w. of introduction, of warning,** à titre d'introduction, d'avertissement; (iii) **what have you by w. of, in the w. of, fruit?** qu'est-ce que vous avez en fait de fruits, comme fruits? **would you like something in the w. of ties?** désirez-vous quelque chose comme cravates? (iv) (*followed by gerund*) **he's by w. of being a socialist,** il se dit, il fait profession d'être, socialiste; il passe pour être, il est vaguement, socialiste; **he's by w. of being an artist,** c'est un artiste; (v) **he asked after her dog by w. of changing the conversation,** il a demandé des nouvelles de son chien, histoire de changer de sujet. **13.** (*a*) *N.Arch:* **ways,** couettes *f*; **ground ways, standing ways,** couettes mortes; (*b*) *Mec.E:* glissière *f* (d'une machine); **circular w.,** rail *m* circulaire (d'une machine); **ways of a lathe,** guidages *m*, guides *m*, d'un tour.

way[2], *adv. F:* **it was w. back in the twenties,** cela remonte aux années vingt; **I knew him w. back in 1930,** je l'ai connu dès 1930; *esp NAm:* **w. back when I was a child,** il y a des années quand j'étais enfant; **w. down south,** là-bas dans le sud; **w. up north,** dans le nord; **w. out west,** dans l'ouest; **to be w. out,** (i) être original, excentrique, anti-conformiste; (ii) faire une grosse erreur; se tromper sérieusement.

waybill ['weibil], *s.* **1.** *Com:* (*a*) lettre *f* de voiture, de mouvement; feuille *f* de route; bulletin *m*, bordereau *m*, d'expédition; (*b*) *A:* liste *f* des voyageurs (par diligence, etc.). **2.** *Adm: A:* bon *m* de secours (délivré à un chemineau).

wayfarer ['weifɛərər], *s.* voyageur, -euse (à pied); passant *m*.

wayfaring ['weifɛəriŋ], *s.* **1.** voyages *mpl* (à pied); **w. man,** voyageur *m* (à pied). **2.** *Bot:* **w. tree,** viorne cotonneuse, flexible; *F:* mantiane *f*, mancienne *f*.

Wayland ['weilənd], *Pr.n.m. Lit:* Galant.

waylay [wei'lei], *v.tr.* (*p.t. & p.p.* **waylaid** [wei'leid]). **1.** attirer (qn) dans une embuscade; dresser, tendre, un guet-apens, une embûche, à (qn); **to be waylaid,** tomber dans un guet-apens. **2.** arrêter (qn) au passage; guetter le passage de (qn); accrocher (qn) au passage (pour lui parler).

wayleave ['weili:v], *s.* **1.** *Min: Telecom: etc:* droit *m*, jouissance *f*, de passage. **2.** *Av:* droit de survol (**over a place,** d'un endroit).

ways-end ['weizend], *s. N.Arch:* avant-cale *f*, *pl.* avant-cales.

wayshaft ['weiʃɑ:ft], *s.* = WEIGHSHAFT.

wayside ['weisaid], *s.* bord *m* de la route; **to fall by the w.,** rester en chemin; **w. chapel, inn,** chapelle *f*, auberge *f*, au bord de la route, en bordure de route; **w. flowers,** fleurs *f* qui croissent en bordure de route.

wayward ['weiwəd], *a.* (*of pers.*) (*a*) volontaire, rebelle, indocile, difficile, entêté, pervers; (*b*) capricieux, fantasque; **to be w.,** avoir des caprices; **w. imagination,** imagination libertine, vagabonde, fantasque.

waywardly ['weiwədli], *adv.* (*a*) volontairement; avec entêtement; (*b*) capricieusement.

waywardness ['weiwədnis], *s.* (*a*) entêtement *m*, obstination *f*, caractère *m* difficile, volontaire; (*b*) caractère fantasque, capricieux.

wayzgoose ['weizgu:s], *s.* fête annuelle d'une imprimerie.

we [wi(:)], *pers. pron. nom. pl.* **1.** (*a*) (*unstressed*) nous; **we were playing,** nous jouions; **here we are!** nous voilà! **where shall we go?** où irons-nous? **we both thank you,** nous vous remercions tous (les) deux; **we all four went out,** nous sommes sortis tous les quatre; *F:* **we're sure to catch it!** on est sûrs de se faire attraper! (*b*) (*stressed*) nous; **we are English, they are French,** nous, nous sommes anglais, eux, ils sont français; **they are not as happy as we are,** eux, ils sont moins heureux que nous; **you don't think that we did it!** vous ne pensez pas que c'est nous qui l'avons fait? **we doctors, we English,** nous autres médecins, nous autres Anglais; (*c*) (*indefinite*) on; nous; **as we say in England,** comme on dit en Angleterre; **we are living in difficult times,** nous vivons dans une période difficile; **we are lazy by nature,** l'homme est paresseux de nature; **we all make mistakes sometimes,** tout le monde se trompe parfois. **2.** (*plural of majesty, editorial* **we,** *etc.*) nous; **we are convinced that . . .,** nous sommes convaincu que . . . .

weak [wi:k], *a.* **1.** (*a*) faible; (*of health*) débile; (*of body*) infirme, chétif; **w. in body,** faible de corps; **to have a w. heart,** être cardiaque; **to have a w. stomach,** avoir l'estomac délicat; **horse w. in the back,** cheval faible des reins; **to have w. (eye)sight,** avoir la vue faible; **my eyes are w.,** mes yeux se fatiguent facilement; j'ai souvent mal aux yeux; **w. legs,** jambes faibles; *F:* **I feel all w. at the knees,** j'ai les jambes en coton; **to grow w.,** s'affaiblir; **w. with hunger,** affaibli par la faim; **to feel as w. as a cat, as a kitten, as water,** se sentir mou, molle, comme une chiffe; *F:* **to be w. in the head, to be w. headed,** être faible d'esprit; **to have a w. head,** supporter mal l'alcool; **the weaker sex,** le sexe faible; (*b*) (mémoire) faible. **2.** (*a*) (style) sans vigueur, sans énergie, sans caractère; (décision) qui dénote de la faiblesse, un manque d'énergie; **in a w. moment,** dans un moment de faiblesse; (*b*) (*of pers.*) faible, amorphe; inefficace; peu capable; qui manque d'énergie; *esp. NAm:* **w. sister,** personne inefficace, qui a besoin d'aide; (*of members of a group*) **our weaker brethren,** les moins capables; **her discipline is very w., she is w. on discipline,** elle manque de discipline, d'autorité, de fermeté; **his w. side, spot,** son côté, son point, faible; **the w. point in the plan,** le point faible du projet; **w. argument,** argument faible, peu solide, peu tenable; *St.Exch:* **the market is w.,** les actions sont en baisse; (*c*) **the weaker pupils,** les élèves moins doués; **to be w. in French,** être faible en français; **my weakest subject is chemistry,** c'est en chimie que je suis le plus faible; (*d*) *Cards:* **to have a w. hand,** avoir mauvais jeu; (*e*) *Mus:* **w. beat,** temps *m* faible; temps secondaire. **3.** (*a*) (*of solution*) dilué, étendu; **w. tea,** thé (i) trop faible, (ii) léger; **a w. whisky,** un whisky bien arrosé, avec beaucoup d'eau; (*b*) *I.C.E:* **w. mixture,** mélange *m* pauvre; (*c*) *Phot:* **w. negative,** cliché *m* faible. **4.** (*a*) *Gram:* **w. conjugation, verb,** conjugaison *f* faible; (*b*) *Gr.Gram:* **w. aorist,** aoriste sigmatique; premier aoriste; (*c*) **w. syllable,** syllabe non accentuée.

weaken ['wi:k(ə)n]. **1.** *v.tr.* affaiblir (le corps, l'esprit, un ressort, une teinte, etc.); amollir (l'esprit, le courage); appauvrir (la constitution de qn); **her illness has weakened her,** sa maladie l'a affaiblie, l'a amoindrie; **voice weakened by illness,** voix affaiblie par la maladie; **the floods have weakened the foundations of the house,** les inondations ont miné les fondations de la maison; *I.C.E:* **to w. the mixture,** appauvrir le mélange. **2.** *v.i.* s'affaiblir, faiblir, s'amollir; (*of sound, current, etc.*) fléchir; *I.C.E:* (*of mixture*) s'appauvrir; **his courage weakened,** son courage a fléchi, a faibli; **his will is weakening,** il perd sa volonté; **the market weakened,** le marché a fléchi, s'est tassé; **the dollar has weakened,** le dollar a baissé; **the ship is weakening,** le navire se délie.

weakening[1] ['wik(ə)niŋ], *a.* affaiblissant; faiblissant; **such an illness is very w.,** une telle maladie vous affaiblit beaucoup.

weakening[2], *s.* affaiblissement *m*, amollissement *m*; fléchissement *m* (de son, de courant, etc.); défaillance *f* (du courant, *Fin:* du marché, du dollar, etc.); *I.C.E:* appauvrissement *m* (du mélange); *Med:* déperdition *f* (de volonté).

weakfish ['wi:kfiʃ], *s. NAm: Ich: F:* (*a*) truite *f* de mer; (*b*) maigre *m*.

weakhearted [wi:k'hɑ:tid], *a.* sans courage; pusillanime; mou, *f.* molle.

weak-kneed [wi:k'ni:d], *a.* (*a*) faible des genoux; (*b*) sans caractère; irrésolu.

weakliness ['wi:klinis], *s.* débilité *f*; manque *m* de santé.

weakling ['wi:kliŋ], *s.* (*a*) être *m* faible, débile; enfant chétif; (*b*) **he's a w.,** c'est un faible, un irrésolu; il manque de résolution.

weakly[1] ['wi:kli], *a.* (*of pers.*) débile, faible (de santé), peu robuste, chétif.

weakly[2], *adv.* (*a*) faiblement; sans force; (*b*) sans résolution; sans force de caractère; sans énergie; **they yielded w.,** ils n'ont pas eu l'énergie de résister; **he w. allowed them to have their own way,** il a eu la faiblesse de leur permettre de faire ce qu'ils voulaient.

weakminded [wi:k'maindid], *a.* (*a*) faible d'esprit; (*b*) irrésolu, indécis, qui manque de résolution; (*c*) **it was a w. decision,** c'était la décision d'un faible.

weakmindedness [wi:k'maindidnis], *s.* (*a*) faiblesse *f* d'esprit; (*b*) irrésolution *f*, manque *m* de résolution.

weakness ['wi:knis], *s.* (*a*) faiblesse *f* (de corps, de caractère, d'un lien); débilité *f* (de corps); **the weakness of human nature,** les faiblesses de la nature humaine; **the w. of his argument,** la faiblesse, le peu de solidité, de son argument; *I.C.E:* **w. of the mixture,** pauvreté *f* du mélange; *Mec.E:* **torsional w.,** manque *m* de résistance à la torsion; (*b*) faible *m*; **to have a w. for sth., s.o.,** avoir un faible pour qch., qn.

weal[1] [wi:l], *s. A: & Lit:* bien *m*, bien-être *m*, bonheur *m*; **w. and woe,** bonheur et malheur; **for w. or (for) woe, whate'er betide of w. or woe,** quoi qu'il arrive; bonheur ou malheur; quoi qu'il advienne; advienne que pourra; vaille que vaille; **the general w., the public w.,** le bien commun; le bien public.

weal[2], *s.* marque *f*, trace *f* (d'un coup de fouet); vergeture *f*.

weal[3], *v.tr.* marquer (d'un coup de fouet); zébrer (de coups de fouet).

Wealden ['wi:ldən], *a. & s. Geol:* wealdien (*m*).

wealth [welθ], *s.* **1.** richesse(s) *f*(*pl*); opulence *f*; **he was a man of great w.,** il était très riche. **2.** abondance *f* (de détails, d'illustrations, de cheveux, etc.); profusion *f* (de détails, etc.). **3.** *A:* bien-être *m*; prospérité *f*.

wealthy ['welθi]. (*a*) *a.* riche; opulent; **w. heiress,** grosse héritière; **a w. merchant,** un riche négociant; (*b*) *s.* **the w.,** les riches *m*.

wean[1] [wi:n], *s. Scot:* enfant *mf*.

wean[2], *v.tr.* (*a*) sevrer (un nourrisson, un agneau, etc.); (*b*) **to w. s.o. (away) from a bad habit,** détacher, détourner, qn d'une mauvaise habitude.

weaner ['wi:nər], *s.* **1.** *Husb:* muselière *f* (pour empêcher le jeune animal de téter). **2.** jeune animal qui vient d'être sevré.

weaning ['wi:niŋ], *s.* sevrage *m*; ablactation *f*; *Husb:* **w. lamb,** agneau *m* en sevrage; **w. muzzle** = WEANER 1.

weanling ['wi:nliŋ], *s.* nourrisson *m*, jeune animal (i) en sevrage, (ii) qui vient d'être sevré.

weapon ['wepən], *s.* arme *f*; **conventional w.,** arme classique, traditionnelle, conventionnelle; **unconventional, non conventional w.,** arme non classique, non conventionnelle; **atomic, nuclear, weapons,** armes atomiques, nucléaires; **chemical w.,** arme chimique; **bacteriological w.,** arme bactériologique; **biological w.,** arme biologique; **military weapons,** armes de guerre; **defensive weapons,** armes défensives; **improvised w.,** arme improvisée, de fortune; **missile weapons,** armes de jet; **weapons of percussion,** armes de choc; **shafted w., thrusting w.,** arme d'hast; **cutting and thrusting weapons,** armes blanches; **hand weapons,** armes de main; **stand-off w.,** arme tirée à distance; **political w.,** arme politique; **to beat s.o. with his own weapons,** battre qn avec ses propres armes; **nobody yet knows the radius or the effectiveness of the new w.,** personne ne sait encore ni le rayon d'action ni l'efficacité de la nouvelle arme; **the carrying of weapons is illegal,** le port d'armes est prohibé; **a flick knife is an illegal w.,** le couteau à cran d'arrêt est une arme prohibée.

weaponless ['wepənlis], *a.* sans armes; désarmé.

weaponry ['wepənri], *s. esp. NAm: coll.* armes *fpl*; armements *mpl.*

wear[1] [wɛər], *s.* **1.** (*a*) **men's, women's** (*Com:* **ladies'**), **children's, w.,** vêtements *mpl* pour hommes, pour femmes, pour enfants; (*in department store*) **men's w. department,** rayon *m* hommes; **evening w.,** toilettes *fpl* de soirée; **suits for spring w.,** tailleurs *mpl* pour le printemps; **for country w.,** pour la campagne; (*of garment*) **in w.,** en usage; qu'on porte; (*b*) (*of material*) **to stand hard w.,** être d'un bon usage; **these shoes still have some w. in them,** ces chaussures sont toujours portables. **2.** (*a*) usure *f*; détérioration *f* (par usure); fatigue *f* (d'une machine); dégradation *f* (d'une route, etc.); attrition *f* (d'une meule, etc.); **one-sided w.,** usure unilatérale; *Mec.E:* **w. plate,** plaque *f* de friction, de frottement; **it hasn't shown any signs of w.,** cela paraît inusable; **the seams are showing signs of w.,** les coutures présentent des traces de fatigue, commencent à s'user; **w. and tear,** usure; dépréciation *f*, détérioration; dégradation (d'un immeuble); **the cost of w. and tear,** les frais *mpl* d'entretien; **to stand w. and tear,** résister à l'usure; *Jur:* **fair w. and tear,** usure naturelle, normale (du mobilier loué, etc.); **to be the worse for w.,** (i) (*of garment, etc.*) être usé, défraîchi; ne plus être présentable; (ii) (*of pers.*) avoir l'air débauché; (iii) *F:* (*of pers.*) avoir la gueule de bois; **to be little the worse for w.,** être peu usé, presque à l'état neuf; **he came out of the wrecked car little the worse for w.,** il est sorti presque indemne de la voiture accidentée; (*b*) frai *m* (d'une pièce d'argent).

wear[2], *v.* (**wore** [wɔ:r]; **worn** [wɔ:n])

I. *v.tr. & i.* **1.** *v.tr.* porter (un vêtement, une épée, la pourpre, une couronne); **he wears the same suit every day,** il porte tous les jours le même complet; **to w. good clothes,** s'habiller bien; être toujours bien habillé; **she was wearing a blue dress,** elle portait une robe bleue; **blue is being worn,** le bleu se porte (beaucoup) actuellement; **to wear black,** porter du noir; **he was wearing a black hat,** il portait un chapeau noir; il était coiffé d'un chapeau noir; **which coat do you think I should w. with this dress?** quel manteau devrais-je mettre avec cette robe? **I've nothing (fit) to w.,** je n'ai rien à me mettre sur le dos, rien de mettable; **she wears short skirts,** elle porte des jupes courtes; **he was wearing his slippers,** il était en pantoufles, était chaussé de pantoufles; **he was wearing all his medals,** il avait mis, arboré, toutes ses médailles; **to w. one's hair long,** porter les cheveux longs; **to w. a beard,** porter la barbe; **to w. a set smile,** arborer un sourire; **to w. one's arm in a sling,** porter, avoir, le bras en écharpe; **she wears her age well,** elle porte bien son âge; elle ne paraît pas avoir son âge; *F:* **I can w. it!** je le supporterai! **if you think I'm going to w. that!** si tu penses que je vais tolérer, supporter, ça! ça, c'est trop fort! **I won't w. it,** je ne marche pas. **2.** *v.tr.* user; **to w. one's coat threadbare,** user son manteau jusqu'à la corde; **to w. a dress to rags,** porter une robe jusqu'à ce qu'elle tombe en loques; **to w. holes in sth., to w. sth. into holes,** faire des trous à qch. (à force d'usage); trouer qch.; **to w. oneself out, to death,** se tuer, s'éreinter (à force de travail); **worn with anxiety,** usé par les soucis; **to w. a surface flat,** araser une surface. **3.** (*with passive force*) (*a*) (*of gun*) se chambrer; (*at the muzzle*) s'égueuler; **the edges will w. in time,** les bords s'useront avec le temps; (*of garment*) **to w. into holes,** se trouer; (*of stone, etc.*) **to w. smooth,** se lisser par le frottement; (*of pers.*) **to be worn to a shadow,** ne plus être que l'ombre de soi-même; (*b*) **to w. well,** (i) (*of material*) être de bon usage; faire bon usage; résister à l'usure; (ii) (*of pers.*) bien porter son âge; être bien conservé; **this coat has worn well,** ce manteau m'a bien servi; **guaranteed to w. well,** garanti à l'usage; **it will w. for ever,** c'est inusable; **it will w. for years,** cela durera des années. **4.** *v.i. Lit:* **the year was wearing to its close,** l'année tirait à sa fin.

II. (*compound verbs*) **1. wear away.** (*a*) *v.tr.* user, ronger; effacer, détruire; **the inscription has been worn away by the passage of time,** le temps a effacé l'inscription; (*b*) *v.i.* (i) s'user; s'effacer; disparaître (peu à peu); (ii) **she was wearing away,** elle se consumait (de chagrin, d'inquiétude, etc.).

2. wear down. (*a*) *v.tr.* user; **to w. down the edge of a tool,** user le tranchant d'un outil; **to w. one's heels down,** user ses talons; **to w. down the enemy's resistance,** user à la longue, épuiser peu à peu, la résistance de l'ennemi; **to w. s.o. down,** briser la résistance à qn; **you're wearing me down,** tu m'épuises; (*b*) *v.i.* s'user; **the heels (of my shoes) have worn down,** mes talons sont usés.

3. wear off, *v.i.* s'effacer; disparaître; (*of pain*) se calmer; **it will w. off,** cela disparaîtra (à la longue); **the novelty soon wore off,** la nouveauté a vite passé; **his shyness is wearing off,** sa timidité disparaît peu à peu.

4. wear on, *v.i.* (*of time*) s'écouler (lentement); s'avancer; **as the evening wore on,** à mesure que la soirée s'avançait.

5. wear out. (*a*) *v.tr.* (i) user (ses vêtements, etc.); **to w. oneself out,** s'user; s'épuiser; se consumer; **to w. oneself out with work,** se tuer au travail, à travailler; (ii) *Lit:* **to w. out one's days in captivity,** passer le reste de ses jours dans la captivité; (*b*) *v.i.* s'user; **this material will never w. out,** ce tissu ne s'use pas, paraît inusable; **my shoes have worn out,** mes chaussures sont usées; **the elastic has worn out,** l'élastique est étiré.

6. wear through. (*a*) *v.tr.* **I've worn my jacket through at the elbows,** j'ai fait des trous dans les coudes de mon veston; (*b*) *v.i.* (*of material, etc.*) se trouer (à force d'usage).

wear[3], *v.* (*p.t. & p.p.* **wore**) *Nau:* **1.** *v.i.* (*of ship*) virer lof pour lof; virer vent arrière. **2.** *v.tr.* faire virer (un navire) lof pour lof; virer (un navire) vent arrière.

wearable ['wɛərəbl], *a.* (*of garment, etc.*) portable, mettable.

wearer ['wɛərər], *s.* **clothes too heavy for the w.,** vêtements trop lourds pour celui, celle, qui les porte; **the crown and its w.,** la couronne et le souverain.

wearied ['wiərid], *a.* lassé; fatigué; épuisé; **my w. brain,** mon cerveau fatigué.

wearily ['wiərili], *adv.* **1.** (répondre, regarder qn) d'un ton, d'un air, las, fatigué; **he went w. back to his work,** (i) visiblement fatigué, (ii) avec un air de dégoût, il a repris son travail. **2.** (marcher) péniblement, d'un pas fatigué.

weariness ['wiərinis], *s.* **1.** lassitude *f,* fatigue *f.* **2.** dégoût *m,* lassitude, ennui *m.*

wearing[1] ['wɛəriŋ], *a.* fatigant, lassant; épuisant; **I've had a very w. day,** j'ai eu une journée très fatigante.

wearing[2], *s.* **1. w. apparel,** vêtements *mpl,* habits *mpl.* **2.** usure *f;* **w. parts of a machine,** parties frottantes, organes sujets à l'usure, d'une machine; **w. surface,** surface frottante, de frottement, d'usure; **one-sided w.,** usure unilatérale; *Mec.E:* **w. piece,** pièce *f* de frottement; **w. quality,** résistance *f* à l'usure; durabilité *f.*

wearing[3], *s. Nau:* virement *m* de bord lof pour lof.

wearisome ['wiəris(ə)m], *a.* fatigant, ennuyeux, fastidieux.

wearisomeness ['wiərisəmnis], *s.* ennui *m,* caractère fastidieux (de qch.).

weary[1] ['wiəri], *a.* fatigué; las, *f.* lasse; **it's too much for my w. brain,** j'ai le cerveau trop fatigué pour le faire; *Lit:* **not to be w. in well doing,** persévérer à faire le bien; *F:* **a w. Willie,** un fainéant, un traîne-la-patte. **2.** las, dégoûté (of, de); **to be w. of life,** être dégoûté de la vie; **to grow w. of waiting,** se lasser d'attendre; **I am w. of his complaints,** ses plaintes m'excèdent, me dégoûtent. **3.** fatigant, fastidieux, ennuyeux; **a w. day,** une journée fatigante; **it is w. waiting,** le temps est, semble, long à qui attend; **a w. wait,** une attente fatigante, pénible; **it was a w. climb,** la montée était pénible; *F:* **you make me w.!** tu me fatigues! tu me tapes sur les nerfs.

weary[2], *v.* (**wearied**) **1.** *v.i.* (*a*) se lasser, se fatiguer; **the horses were wearying,** les chevaux donnaient des signes de fatigue; *esp. Lit:* **to w. of (doing) sth.,** se lasser de (faire) qch.; **to w. of s.o.,** se fatiguer de la compagnie de qn; (*b*) trouver le temps long; (*c*) *Lit:* **to w. for sth.,** désirer ardemment qch.; soupirer, languir, après qch. **2.** *v.tr.* (*a*) lasser, fatiguer (qn); (*b*) **he wearies me with all his complaints,** je suis las de ses plaintes éternelles; **he wearies us to death with his stories,** ses histoires nous font mourir d'ennui.

wearying ['wiəriiŋ], *a.* fatigant, ennuyeux, fastidieux; **I find it very w.,** cela me fatigue, m'ennuie, excessivement.

weasand ['wi:zənd], *s. A: & Dial:* **1.** trachée-artère *f.* **2.** gorge *f,* gosier *m.*

weasel[1] ['wi:z(ə)l], *s.* **1.** (*a*) *Z:* belette *f;* **least w.,** belette pygmée; **white-naped, striped, w.,** pœcilogale *m;* (*b*) *F:* fouine *f;* homme furtif, rusé; (*c*) *U.S: F:* habitant, -ante, de la Caroline du Sud; (*d*) *U.S: F:* **w. word,** mot ambigu; (mot qui constitue une) échappatoire. **2.** *Veh:* crabe *m.*

weasel[2], *v.i. F:* (*a*) *esp. NAm:* ruser; agir d'une manière évasive; (*b*) **to w. out,** se rétracter.

weasel-faced ['wi:zəlfeist], *a.* (*of pers.*) à figure de fouine.

weather[1] ['weðər], *s.* (*a*) temps *m* (qu'il fait); **in all weathers,** par tous les temps; **fine w.,** beau temps; **the w. is settled, we're in for a spell of fine w.,** le temps est au beau; **seasonable w.,** un temps de saison; **overcast w.,** temps couvert; **what's the w. like? what sort of w. is it?** quel temps fait-il? **the weather's awful, appalling,** il fait un temps de chien; **in spite of bad w.,** en dépit du mauvais temps, des intempéries; **it depends on the w.,** cela dépend du temps qu'il fait; **in this, in such, w.,** par un temps pareil; **(wind and) w. permitting,** si le temps le permet, s'y prête; **if there is a break in the w.,** si le temps (i) se gâte, (ii) se met au beau; (*b*) *Nau:* **heavy w.,** gros temps; (*of ship*) **to make heavy w.,** bourlinguer; (*of scheme, etc.*) **to run into heavy w.,** rencontrer des obstacles; (*of pers.*) **to make heavy w. (of sth.),** faire un tas d'histoires (pour faire qch.); avoir toutes les peines du monde (à faire qch.); (*c*) *Av:* **to fly over the w.,** voler au-dessus des nuages; *F:* (*of pers.*) **to be under the w.,** être (i) malade, indisposé, souffrant, (ii) déprimé, (iii) étamé, un peu ivre; (*d*) **w. (situation), state of the w.,** état *m* du temps; *F:* **did you listen to the w. this morning?** as-tu écouté la météo ce matin (à la radio)? **w. bulletin, forecast,** bulletin *m* météorologique; prévisions *fpl* météorologiques; **today's w.,** le temps (qu'il fera) aujourd'hui; **w. map, w. chart,** carte *f* météorologique (synoptique); **w. station,** station *f* météorologique; **w. ship,** navire *m,* frégate *f,* météorologique; navire-météo *m;* *Av: Nau:* **w. log,** journal *m* météorologique; *Nau:* **w. signal,** signal *m* atmosphérique, d'indication du temps; (*e*) **w. side,** (i) côté (d'une maison, etc.) exposé au vent; (ii) *Nau:* bord *m* du vent; *Nau:* **w. quarter,** hanche *f* du vent; **w. shore,** côte *f* du vent; (*of ship*) **w. rode,** évité au vent; **w. bow,** l'avant *m* du côté vent; **w. deck,** pont supérieur; partie du pont exposée au vent et à la mer; **w. helm,** barre *f* au vent; (*of ship*) **to carry a w. helm,** être ardent; **w. sheet,** écoute *f* du vent; **w. leech,** chute *f* du vent (d'une voile); lof *m;* *Fig:* **to keep one's w. eye open,** veiller au grain; (*f*) *Arch:* **w. moulding,** larmier *m;* jet *m* d'eau; (*g*) (*of windmill sails*) **angle of w.,** airage *m.*

weather[2], *v.tr. & i.*

I. *v.tr.* **1.** (*usu. passive*) *Geol:* désagréger, altérer (des roches); **weathered rocks,** roches désagrégées; *Furn:* **weathered oak,** chêne patiné. **2.** *Nau:* (*a*) **to w. a headland,** doubler un cap (à la voile); gagner le vent d'un cap; **to w. a ship,** passer au vent d'un navire; **to w. the shore,** s'élever au vent de la côte; (*b*) **to w. (out) a gale,** étaler un coup de vent; **to w. (out) a storm,** étaler, remonter, une tempête; survivre, résister, à une tempête; *Fig:* **to w. the, a, storm,** se tirer d'affaire; *Pol: etc:* se maintenir contre des attaques. **3.** donner l'airage (aux ailes d'un moulin). **4.** *Const:* tailler en rejéteau (une pierre de corniche, etc.).

II. *v.i.* **1.** (*of rock*) se désagréger, s'altérer. **2.** (*of copper, bronze, building*) prendre la patine; se patiner.

weatherbeaten ['weðəbi:tən], *a.* **1.** battu des vents; battu par la tempête. **2.** (*a*) (*of pers., face*) bronzé, hâlé, basané; (*b*) (*of thg*) usé, fatigué; (*of wall*) dégradé par le temps.

weatherboard[1] ['weðəbɔ:d], *s.* **1.** *Const:* (*a*) (*for roof, wall*) planche *f* à recouvrement; (*b*) (*for window*) jet *m* d'eau; reverseau *m;* auvent *m;* (*c*) *Row:* hiloire *f.* **2.** *Nau:* (*a*) côté *m* du vent; (*b*) (*screen*) cagnard *m;* (*c*) auvent (de sabord).

weatherboard[2], *v.tr.* garnir (une maison, etc.) de planches à recouvrement; **weatherboarded upper storey,** étage *m* en planches à recouvrement.

weatherboarding ['weðəbɔ:diŋ], *s. Const:* planches *fpl* à recouvrement.

weatherbound ['weðəbaund], *a.* retenu, arrêté, par le mauvais temps.

weathercock ['weðəkɔk], *s.* (*a*) girouette *f;* (*b*) *F:* (*pers.*) girouette; **to be a w.,** tourner, virer, à tout vent, à tous les vents.

weatherfish ['weðəfiʃ], *s. Ich:* loche *f* d'étang.

weatherglass ['weðəglɑ:s], *s.* **1.** baromètre *m* (à cadran). **2.** *Bot: F:* **poor man's, shepherd's, w.,** mouron *m* rouge.

weathering ['weðəriŋ], *s.* **1.** (*a*) désagrégation *f,* altération *f* (des roches); **w. agent,** agent *m* de désagrégation. **2.** *Const:* (*a*) glacis *m;* (*b*) rejéteau *m.*

weatherly ['weðəli], *a. Nau:* **w. ship,** voilier fin, ardent, qui tient bien le plus près; boulinier *m.*

weatherman, *pl.* **-men** ['weðəmæn, -men], *s. F:* météo *m.*

weathermost ['weðəmoust], *a. Nau:* (navire, îlot) le plus au vent.

weatherproof[1] ['weðəpru:f], *a.* (*a*) à l'épreuve du gros temps; étanche; (*b*) qui résiste aux intempéries.

weatherproof[2], *v.tr.* protéger contre les intempéries.

weatherstrip[1] ['weðəstrip], *s.* **1.** (*for door, window*) bourrelet *m* étanche; garniture *f* d'encadrement; calfeutrage *m;* coupe-froid *m inv.* **2.** *Veh: etc:* gouttière *f* d'étanchéité.

weatherstrip[2], *v.tr.* calfeutrer (une porte, etc.).

weatherwise ['weðəwaiz], *a.* (*a*) qui sait prévoir le temps; (*b*) sensible aux changements politiques, etc.

weave[1] [wi:v], *s. Tex:* **1.** armure *f;* **ground w.,** armure fondamentale; **plain w.,** armure toile. **2.** tissage *m;* texture *f.*

weave[2], *v.* (**wove** [wouv]; **woven** ['wouv(ə)n]) **1.** *v.tr.* (*a*) *Tex:* tisser; (*b*) *Lit:* **skilfully woven plot,** intrigue bien imaginée; **to w. a spell,** composer un charme; (*c*) tresser (une guirlande, un panier); entrelacer (des fils, des fleurs, des rameaux). **2.** *v.i.* (*a*) *Tex:* être tisserand, -ande (de métier); (*b*) **to w. through the traffic,** se frayer un chemin parmi les voitures; **the road weaves through the valley,** la route suit la vallée en serpentant; *Av:* **the fighters were weaving around the formation,** les chasseurs allaient et venaient autour de la formation; (*c*) *F:* **to get weaving,** s'y mettre; **get weaving!** vas-y!

weaver ['wi:vər], *s.* **1.** *Tex:* tisserand, -ande; tisseur, -euse. **2.** *Arach:* araignée fileuse. **3.** *Orn:* **w. (bird),** tisserin *m, F:* tisserand *m;* **black-headed w.,** tisserin à tête noire; **dark-backed w.,** tisserin bicolore; **rufous-necked w.,** tisserin Cap-Moor; **village w.,** tisserin à capuchon; **buffalo w.,** alecto *m;* **Napoleon w.,** worabée *m;* **orange w.,** ignicolore *m;* **sociable w.,** républicain *m;* **(South African) w. (bird),** tisserin républicain (d'Afrique du Sud); **red-faced w. finch,** beau-marquet *m.* **4.** *Ent:* psyché *f.*

weaving ['wi:viŋ], *s.* **1.** *Tex:* tissage *m;* **figure w.,** brochage *m;* **w. (trade),** tisseranderie *f.* **2.** entrelacement *m* (de rameaux, etc.).

weazen(ed) ['wi:zən(d)], *a.* = WIZENED.

web [web], *s.* **1.** (*a*) *Tex:* tissu *m;* **w. of lies,** tissu de mensonges; *Lit:* **the w. of life,** la trame de nos jours; (*b*) *Mil:* **w. equipment,** équipement *m* en toile. **2.** (*a*) **spider's w.,** toile *f* d'araignée; (*b*) *Av:* **lift w.,** corde *f* de suspension (d'un parachute). **3.** *Nat.Hist:* palmure *f,* membrane *f* (d'un palmipède); **w.-fingered,** syndactyle; **w.-footed, w.-toed,** palmipède; aux pieds palmés; syndactyle. **4.** *Vet:* cul *m* de verre (de l'œil du cheval). **5.** *Orn:* lame *f* (d'une plume). **6.** *Tchn:* bras *m,* joue *f,* flasque *m* (de manivelle); âme *f* (d'un rail); corps *m,* estomac *m* (d'enclume); panneton *m* (de clef); lame *f* (de scie, de coutre); *Civ.E:* **w. (plate),** âme (d'une poutre); *N.Arch:* **w. frame,** porque *f.* **7.** (*a*) *Tex:* pièce *f,* rouleau *m* (de tissu); **w. beam,** ensouple enrouleuse (de métier); (*b*) **w. of newsprint,** rouleau de papier pour presse rotative; **w. press,** presse rotative; **w. paper,** papier continu; (*c*) *Cmptr:* rouleau de bande magnétique; bande *f* de papier en continu.

webbed [webd], *a.* **1.** palmé, membrané; **w. foot,** pied palmé, patte palmée. **2.** (*of beam, etc.*) évidé.

webbing ['webiŋ], *s.* **1.** sangles *fpl* (de chaise, de lit, etc.). **2.** toile *f* à sangles; ruban *m* à sangles.

weber ['veibər], *s. El.Meas:* weber *m.*

websterite ['webstərait], *s. Miner:* webstérite *f.*

webworm ['webwə:m], *s. Ent:* tisseuse *f;* **Hawaiian beet w.,** tisseuse de la betterave hawaïenne.

wed [wed], *v.* (*p.t. & p.p.* **wedded,** *occ.* **wed;** *pr.p.* **wedding**) **1.** *v.tr.* (*a*) épouser (qn); se marier avec (qn); (*b*) (*of priest*) marier (un couple); (*of parent*) marier (sa fille); (*c*) unir (des qualités, etc.); **to be wedded to an idea,** être obstinément attaché à une idée. **2.** *v.i.* se marier.

wedded ['wedid], *a.* marié; **my (lawful) w. wife, husband,** mon épouse, époux, légitime; **the newly w. pair,** les nouveaux mariés; **w. life,** vie conjugale.

wedding ['wediŋ], *s.* mariage *m;* noce(s) *f(pl);* **church w.,** mariage religieux, à l'église; **to have a quiet w.,** se marier dans l'intimité; **w. day,** (i) jour *m* du mariage, des noces; (ii) anniversaire *m* du mariage; **silver, golden, diamond, w.,** noces d'argent, d'or, de diamants; **w. ring,** alliance *f;* **w. dress,** robe *f* de mariée;

the **w. guests,** les invités (au mariage); **w. breakfast,** repas *m* de noces; lunch *m* de noces; **w. cake,** gâteau *m* de noces (en pièce montée); *Pej:* **it's sheer w. cake architecture,** c'est de la vraie pâtisserie; **w. present,** cadeau *m* de mariage, de noces; **w. list,** liste *f* de mariage; **w. card** = faire-part *m inv* de mariage; **w. night,** nuit *f* de noces; **w. trip,** voyage *m* de noces.

wedeln ['vedəln], *s. Ski:* godille *f.*

wedge[1] [wedʒ], *s.* **1.** *Tchn:* coin *m*; (*a*) **fixing w.,** coin de serrage; cale *f* de fixation; *Min:* (*in timbering*) picot *m*; *Mec.E:* clavette *f*, clef *f*; **flat w.,** clavette plate, méplate; **taper w.,** clavette conique; *Carp:* **plane w.,** coin de rabot; *Const:* **indented w.,** coin à échelons; **w. of the lewis,** louveteau *m*; *Mec.E:* **coupling w.,** cône *m* de pression pour accouplement; *Artil:* **recoil w.,** coin de recul; **w. key,** clef de serrage; *Bootm:* **w. heeled shoes,** *F:* **wedges,** chaussures *f* à semelles compensées; (*b*) **splitting w.,** coin à fendre; **hafted w.,** contre *m*; **quarry w.,** cale de carrière d'abattage; quille *f*; *Stonew:* **spalling w.,** coin à tranche; *Metalw:* (**blacksmith's**) **steel(-cutting) w.,** casse-fer *m inv*; **to drive in a w.,** enfoncer un coin; **thin end of the w.,** tranchant *m* du coin; *Fig:* **it's the thin end of the w.,** c'est un premier empiétement; c'est un pied de pris; c'est un premier avantage de pris. **2.** (*a*) *Ten:* cœur *m* (d'une raquette); *Orn:* **w. of geese,** bande *f*, vol *m*, d'oies (sauvages); **w. of cake, of cheese,** morceau *m* (triangulaire) de gâteau, de fromage; **to take a w. out of a tart,** échancrer une tarte; (*b*) *Opt:* **photometric w.,** coin optique; **w. constant,** coefficient *m* du coin.

wedge[2], *v.tr.* **1.** *Tchn:* coincer, assujettir; caler (des rails); claveter (une roue sur son axe, etc.); picoter (un puits de mine). **2. to w. (up) a piece of furniture,** caler un meuble; **to w. a door open,** maintenir une porte ouverte avec une cale. **3. to w. sth. in sth.,** enclaver, insérer, implanter, enfoncer, serrer, qch. dans qch.; **two bottles wedged tightly into a basket,** deux bouteilles étroitement serrées dans un panier; **with his pipe firmly wedged in the corner of his mouth,** la pipe bien calée au coin de la bouche; **I was wedged in between two large women,** je me suis trouvé coincé entre deux grosses femmes. **4. to w. sth. apart, open,** fendre, forcer, qch. avec un coin.

wedge-shaped ['wedʒʃeipt], *a.* en (forme de) coin; cunéaire; *Bot: etc:* cunéiforme; **with w.-s. leaves,** cunéifolié.

wedge-tailed ['wedʒteild], *a. Orn:* à queue cunéiforme.

wedgewise ['wedʒwaiz], *adv.* (disposé) en triangle.

wedging ['wedʒiŋ], *s.* (*a*) coinçage *m*; coincement *m*; *Mec.E:* calage *m*, clavetage *m*; *Min:* picotage *m*; (*b*) calage (d'un meuble, etc.).

Wedgwood ['wedʒwud], *s. Cer:* porcelaine, faïence, anglaise (inventée par Josiah Wedgwood).

wedlock ['wedlɔk], *s.* (*a*) *Jur:* mariage *m*; **to be born in, out of, w.,** être légitime, illégitime; (*b*) *esp. Lit:* la vie conjugale.

Wednesday ['wenzdi], *s.* mercredi *m*; **he opens on Wednesdays,** il ouvre le mercredi; **he comes every Wednesday,** il vient tous les mercredis; **Ash W.,** le mercredi des Cendres.

wee[1] [wi:], *a. F:* **1.** petit; tout petit; minuscule; **a w. bit,** un tout petit peu; **she's a w. bit, the weest** ['wi:ist] **bit, jealous,** elle est tant soit peu jalouse; **a w. drop of whisky,** un doigt, une larme, de whisky. **2.** *Rel.H:* **the W. Frees,** petite minorité dans l'Église réformée d'Écosse qui a refusé de faire partie de l'Union presbytérienne.

wee[2], *s. & v.i. F:* = WEE(-)WEE[1,2].

weed[1] [wi:d], *s.* **1.** *Bot:* mauvaise herbe; herbe folle; **garden running to weeds, overgrown with weeds,** jardin envahi par les mauvaises herbes; jardin à l'abandon; **to get up a few weeds,** désherber un peu, faire un peu de désherbage; *Prov:* **ill weeds grow apace,** mauvaise herbe croît toujours. **2.** *F:* (*a*) *O:* **the w.,** le tabac; (*b*) *O:* cigare *m*; (*c*) *O:* cigarette *f*; (*d*) marijuana *f*, herbe *f*. **3.** *F:* (*a*) personne étique, chétive; gringalet *m*; (*b*) cheval efflanqué, étique.

weed[2]. **1.** *v.tr.* (*a*) désherber (un jardin, etc.); arracher, extirper, enlever, les mauvaises herbes de (l'allée, etc.); sarcler, éplucher (un champ, une allée, un jardin); (*b*) **to w. out,** éliminer (les candidats faibles, etc.); **to w. out the bad (from the good),** éliminer, rejeter, ce qui est de mauvaise qualité. **2.** *v.i.* désherber; arracher, enlever, les mauvaises herbes.

weeder ['wi:dər], *s.* **1.** (*pers.*) sarcleur, -euse. **2.** *Tls:* *Hort:* sarcloir *m*; sarclette *f*; sarcleuse *f*; *Agr:* extirpateur *m.*

weediness ['wi:dinis], *s.* (*a*) **look at the w. of those fields,** regardez-moi ces champs, comme ils sont couverts de mauvaises herbes! (*b*) *F:* maigreur *f*; apparence *f* malingre, peu robuste.

weeding ['wi:diŋ], *s.* sarclage *m*; désherbage *m.*

weedkiller ['wi:dkilər], *s.* herbicide *m*; désherbant *m.*

weeds [wi:dz], *s.pl. O:* (**widow's**) **weeds,** vêtements *m* de deuil (d'une veuve); deuil *m* de veuve.

weedy ['wi:di], *a.* **1.** (sentier, champ) couvert de mauvaises herbes. **2.** *F:* (*a*) (*of pers.*) maigre, poussé en asperge, à l'air malingre; (*b*) (cheval, etc.) efflanqué, étique.

week [wi:k], *s.* **1.** (*a*) semaine *f*; **the days of the w.,** les jours de la semaine; **what day of the w. is it?** quel jour de la semaine sommes-nous? **he comes twice a w.,** il vient deux fois par semaine; **next w., last w.,** la semaine prochaine, dernière; *F:* **to knock s.o. into the middle of next w.,** (i) donner à qn un coup décisif, un fameux coup; (ii) bouleverser qn; **w. in w. out,** toutes les semaines que Dieu nous envoie; sans trêve; **I haven't seen him for,** *esp. NAm:* **in, weeks,** je ne l'ai pas vu depuis des semaines; voilà des semaines que je ne l'ai vu; *Mil: etc:* **officer on duty for the w.,** officier *m* de semaine; *Ecc:* **Holy W.,** la semaine sainte; *Jewish Rel:* **the Feast of Weeks,** la fête des semaines; (*b*) semaine, huit jours; **about a w.,** une huitaine; **once a w.,** une fois par semaine; tous les huit jours; **every w.,** tous les huit jours; **within the w., in the course of the w.,** dans la semaine; dans la huitaine; **within a w.,** sous huitaine; **a w. from now, this day w., today w., in a week's time,** (d')aujourd'hui en huit; dans une huitaine; **tomorrow w., Tuesday w.,** demain, mardi, en huit; **yesterday w.,** il y a eu hier huit jours; **last Saturday w.,** il y a eu huit jours samedi dernier; **in a w. or so,** dans une huitaine; **in six weeks' time,** dans six semaines; **a w. ago today,** il y a (aujourd'hui) huit jours; *Jur:* **to adjourn a case for a w.,** remettre une cause à huitaine; **I'm taking a week's holiday, a w. off,** je vais prendre huit jours de congé; **the week's rent,** le loyer de la semaine; *Ind: etc:* **forty hour w.,** semaine de quarante heures; **a week's wages,** le salaire hebdomadaire, de la semaine; **to be paid by the w.,** être payé à la semaine. **2.** (*opposed to Sunday*) la semaine; **what I can't get done in the w. I do on Sundays,** ce que je n'arrive pas à faire en semaine je le fais le dimanche.

weekday ['wi:kdei], *s.* jour *m* ouvrable; jour de semaine; **on weekdays,** en semaine; **weekdays only,** (i) la semaine seulement; (ii) sauf samedi et dimanche; **w. service,** (i) *Ecc:* office *m* de (jour de) semaine; (ii) *Rail:* service *m* de semaine; **his w. suit,** son complet de tous les jours, de semaine.

weekend[1] [wi:k'end], *s.* fin *f* de semaine; week-end *m*; **to have one's weekends free,** être libre le week-end; faire la semaine anglaise; **I stayed with them for the w.,** j'ai passé le week-end chez eux; **long w.,** week-end prolongé; **as Tuesday's a holiday we'll make a long w. of it,** comme c'est jour férié mardi on fera le pont; **w. cottage,** résidence *f* secondaire (où on passe le week-end); **w. driver,** chauffeur *m* du dimanche; *Rail:* **w. return,** aller (et) retour *m* valable du vendredi soir jusqu'au lundi.

weekend[2], *v.i.* passer le week-end, la fin de semaine (à un endroit).

weekender [wi:k'endər], *s.* **they're weekenders,** ils viennent, vont, y passer le week-end, la fin de semaine; **most of the houses belong to weekenders,** la plupart des maisons sont des résidences secondaires.

weekly ['wi:kli]. **1.** *a.* (*a*) (salaire *m*) de la semaine; (revue *f*, visite *f*, paiement *m*, etc.) hebdomadaire; **w. rest-day Act,** loi *f* sur le repos hebdomadaire; *Ind:* **w. wage earner,** salarié(e) payé(e) à la semaine; (*b*) (locataire, etc.) à la semaine; *Sch:* **w. boarder** = demi-pensionnaire *mf.* **2.** *s.* journal *m*, revue *f*, hebdomadaire; hebdomadaire *m.* **3.** *adv.* par semaine; hebdomadairement; tous les huit jours; **twice w.,** deux fois par semaine; **to be paid w.,** être payé à la semaine.

week-old ['wi:kould], *a.* âgé d'une semaine; **w.-o. kitten,** chaton né il y a huit jours; **w.-o. chicks,** poussins *m* de huit jours; **w.-o. paper,** journal vieux d'une semaine.

ween [wi:n], *v.tr. A: & Lit:* **I w.,** j'imagine; je crois; voire; **weenst thou that . . .?** croyez-vous, crois-tu, que . . .?

weeny ['wi:ni], *a. F:* minuscule; tout petit; **give me just the weeniest morsel, drop,** donnez-moi un rien, une larme.

weep[1] [wi:p], *s.* pleurs *mpl*; **to have a good w.,** pleurer à chaudes larmes; pleurer tout son content, tout son soûl; **to have a little w.,** verser quelques larmes.

weep[2], *v.* (**wept** [wept]; **wept**) **1.** *v.i.* (*a*) pleurer; répandre, verser, des larmes; **to w. bitterly,** pleurer amèrement; pleurer à chaudes larmes; pleurer comme une Madeleine; **to w. for joy,** pleurer de joie; **to w. with annoyance, from vexation,** pleurer de dépit; **to w. for s.o.,** (i) pleurer (la mort de) qn; (ii) pleurer sur l'absence de qn; (iii) pleurer sur les malheurs de qn; **to w. for one's lost youth,** pleurer sa jeunesse perdue; **to w. over the heroine (of a novel),** pleurer sur le sort de l'héroïne; **to w. for, over, one's sins,** pleurer, regretter vivement, gémir de, ses péchés; **that's nothing to w. about, over,** (i) ce n'est pas une raison de pleurer; il n'y a pas de quoi pleurer; (ii) tant mieux! **it's enough to make you w.,** c'est à faire pleurer; **I could have wept to see it,** je gémissais de le voir; (*with cogn. acc.*) **to w. tears,** répandre, verser, des larmes; **to w. tears of blood,** verser des larmes de sang; **to w. tears of joy,** pleurer de joie; (*b*) (*of wall, rock, etc.*) suinter, suer; (*of tree*) pleurer; (*of sore*) couler, exsuder, baver; **the smoke was making my eyes w.,** la fumée m'a fait venir les larmes aux yeux. **2.** *v.tr.* **she has wept herself blind,** elle s'est brûlé les yeux à force de pleurer; **to w. one's heart, one's eyes, out,** pleurer à chaudes larmes; se consumer dans les larmes.

weeper ['wi:pər], *s.* **1.** (*a*) pleureur, -euse; (*b*) *Art:* pleurant, deuillant. **2.** *Z:* (singe) pleureur *m*; saï *m*; capucin *m.* **3.** *A:* **weepers,** (i) pleureuses *f*; manchettes *f* de deuil; (ii) crêpe de deuil à bouts pendants; (iii) voile *m* de deuil (d'une veuve); (iv) favoris très longs. **4.** = WEEPHOLE.

weephole ['wi:phoul], *s. Const:* chantepleure *f* (dans un mur); barbacane *f* (dans un mur de soutènement).

weeping[1] ['wi:piŋ], *a.* **1.** (enfant, etc.) pleurant, qui pleure. **2.** (*of rock, etc.*) suintant, humide; *Med:* **w. wound,** plaie baveuse; **w. eczema,** eczéma *m* humide. **3.** *Bot:* **w. willow,** saule pleureur; **w. ash,** frêne pleureur.

weeping[2], *s.* **1.** pleurs *mpl*, larmes *fpl*; **a fit of w.,** une crise de larmes. **2.** suintement *m* (d'un mur, etc.); exsudation *f.*

weepingly ['wi:piŋli], *adv.* en pleurant; d'un ton larmoyant.

weepy ['wi:pi], *a. F:* (*a*) (ton, air) larmoyant; **w. eyes,** yeux larmoyants, mouillés de larmes; (*b*) **to feel w.,** se sentir une envie de pleurer.

weever ['wi:vər], *s. Ich:* vive *f*; **lesser w.,** vive vipère, petite vive; **greater w.,** grande vive.

weevil ['wi:v(i)l], *s. Ent:* charançon *m*; **corn w., grain w.,** calandre *f*; charançon du blé; **nut w.,** charançon des noisettes; balanin *m*; **seed w., gorse w.,** apion *m.*

weevil(l)ed ['wi:vəld], **weevil(l)y** ['wi:vili], *a.* (blé, etc.) charançonné.

wee(-)wee[1] ['wi:wi:], *s. F:* (*child's word*) pipi *m.*

wee(-)wee[2], *v.i. F:* faire pipi; faire une petite commission.

weft [weft], *s. Tex:* (*a*) trame *f*; **w. fork,** (fourchette *f*) casse-trame *m inv*; **w. winding,** trametage *m*; (*pers.*) **w. winder,** trameur, -euse; (*b*) **w. (yarn),** fil *m* de trame.

wehrlite ['wεəlait], *s. Miner:* wehrlite *f.*

weigh[1] [wei], *s.* (*of ship*) **under w.,** appareillé, en marche.

weigh[2], *v.*

I. *v.tr. & i.* **1.** *v.tr.* (*a*) peser (un paquet, etc.); faire la pesée de (qch.); **to w. sth. in one's hand,** soupeser qch.; **to w. oneself,** se peser; **to get weighed,** se faire peser; (*b*) **to w. one's words,** peser, mesurer, ménager, ses paroles; **to w. sth. in one's mind,** considérer qch.; méditer (sur) qch.; **to w. the consequences (of sth.),** calculer les conséquences (de qch.); **to w. the pros and the cons,** peser le pour et le contre; **to w. one thing against another,** mettre deux choses en balance; (*c*) *Nau:* **to w. anchor,** lever, virer, déraper, l'ancre; appareiller. **2.** *v.i.* (*a*) peser, avoir du poids; **to w. heavy, light,** peser lourd; peser peu, être léger; **how much does it w.?** combien pèse-t-il? **it weighs two kilos,** il pèse deux kilos; **I don't w. much,** je ne pèse pas lourd; (*b*) **it's weighing on my mind,** cela me trouble, me tracasse; **the silence was beginning to w. on us,** le silence commençait à nous peser; (*c*) **that doesn't w. with me,** cela ne compte pas pour moi; je ne fais pas grand cas de cela.

II. (*compound verbs*) **1. weigh down,** *v.tr.* (*a*) faire pencher (la balance); (*b*) surcharger; appesantir; **branch weighed down with fruit,** branche surchargée de fruits; **weighed down with sorrow,** accablé de chagrin, par le chagrin; affaissé sous le poids des chagrins; **weighed down by heavy responsibilities,** accablé de grosses responsabilités; **they were weighed down with sleep,** le sommeil pesait sur eux; ils étaient alourdis par le sommeil.

2. weigh in, *v.i.* (*a*) (*of jockey*) se faire peser après la course; (*of boxer*) se faire peser avant l'assaut; (*b*) *F:* (*of pers.*) arriver, s'amener; **to w. in (with an argument),** intervenir avec un argument; se joindre à la discussion; **to w. in with a fiver,** verser cinq livres.

3. weigh out. (*a*) *v.tr.* peser (du sucre, etc.) en petites quantités; **to w. out the required amounts,** peser les quantités requises; (*b*) *v.i.* (*of jockey*) se faire peser avant la course.

4. weigh up, *v.tr.* **to w. up the situation,** peser la situation; **to w. s.o. up,** estimer (i) la valeur, (ii) les intentions, de qn.

weighbeam ['weibi:m], *s.* **1.** fléau *m*, verge *f* (d'une balance romaine). **2.** balance romaine.

weighbridge ['weibridʒ], *s.* pont-bascule *m*, *pl.* ponts-bascules; poids public.

weigher ['weiər], *s.* peseur, -euse.

weigh-house ['weihaus], *s.* bureau (public) de pesage.

weigh-in ['weiin], *s. Box: Turf:* pesée *f.*

weighing ['weiiŋ], *s.* **1.** (*a*) pesée *f* (de denrées, etc.); *Ph:* **(method of) double w.,** double-pesée *f*; **w. machine,** machine *f* à peser; **w. hopper,** trémie peseuse; (*b*) **w. in,** pesage *m* (d'un jockey, d'un boxeur); **w.-in room, w. enclosure,** le pesage. **2.** *Nau:* levage *m* (de l'ancre); appareillage *m*.

weigh-out ['weiaut], *s.* pesage *m* (d'un jockey) avant la course.

weight¹ [weit], *s.* **1.** (*a*) poids *m*; **to try, feel, the w. of sth.,** soupeser qch.; **net w., gross w.,** poids net, brut; **to sell by w.,** vendre au poids; **to give good w., short w.,** faire bon poids, faux poids; **excess w.,** excédent *m* de poids; **it's ten pounds in w.,** cela pèse dix livres; **ten pounds' w., ten pounds in w., of sugar,** dix livres *f* de sucre; **it's worth its w. in gold,** cela vaut son pesant d'or; **coin of standard w.,** monnaie *f* de poids; **I can't cope with the w. of this case,** cette valise est trop lourde pour moi; **what a w.!** que ça pèse lourd! que c'est lourd! (*of pers.*) **to lose w.,** perdre du poids; **to gain, put on, w.,** prendre du poids; **to put on w. again,** reprendre du poids; **he's twice your w.,** il pèse deux fois autant que vous; **to practise w. control,** surveiller son poids; *F:* **I've got a w. problem,** je n'arrive pas à maigrir; **to pull one's w.,** (i) *Row:* fournir un effort (en rapport avec son poids); (ii) *Fig:* fournir un effort (en rapport avec ses capacités); y mettre du sien; (*of horse*) **to put its full w. into the collar,** tirer à plein collier; *Turf:* **to give w. (to another horse),** rendre le poids (à un autre cheval); **to carry w.,** être handicapé; (*b*) *Tchn:* poids; pesanteur *f*; *Ph: Ch:* **atomic, molecular, w.,** poids atomique, moléculaire; **statistical w.,** poids statistique; *Mec.E: Veh: etc:* **distribution of w.,** répartition *f* du poids; **w. breakdown,** devis *m* de poids; **design w.,** poids de calcul; **w. factor,** indice *m* de poids; **all-up w.,** poids total; **balance, balancing, w.,** poids compensateur; contrepoids *m*; masse *f* d'équilibrage; **power-to-w. ratio, w. efficiency,** puissance *f* massique; **maximum permissible w.,** poids maximum admissible; **dead w., live w.,** poids utile (d'un véhicule); **w. when empty,** poids à vide; **laden, loaded, w.,** poids en charge; charge *f* utile; **hauled w.,** poids remorqué, tracté; **static w.,** poids statique; *Av:* **static w. on nose gear,** poids statique sur l'atterrisseur avant; **flying w., w. in flying order,** poids en ordre de vol; **w. per pound thrust,** poids par livre de poussée; *Nau:* **launching w.,** poids au lancement; *Petr:* **w. indicator,** peson *m* (de forage); (*c*) *Cmptr:* poids (binaire, etc.); (*d*) *Stat:* coefficient *m* de pondération. **2.** (*a*) poids (en cuivre, etc.); **set of weights,** série *f* de poids; **I can't find the 50 gramme w.,** j'ai perdu le poids de 50 grammes; **sliding w.,** poids mobile, curseur; **weights and measures,** poids et mesures; (*b*) (*corps lourd*) poids (d'une horloge, etc.); olive *f* (de plomb); *Gym: etc:* gueuse *f* (d'athlétisme); **weights and dumb bells,** poids et haltères; **w. lifting,** haltérophilie *f*; **w. lifter,** haltérophile *mf*; **weights of a fishing net,** lest *m* d'un filet. **3.** charge; **this pillar bears the w. of the whole building,** cette colonne soutient tout le bâtiment; **to put the w. on, to take the w. off, a beam,** charger, décharger, une poutre; **to give way under the w. of sth.,** fléchir sous le poids de qch.; **to lean on sth. with all one's w.,** appuyer de tout son poids sur qch.; **he feels the w. of his responsibilities,** sa responsabilité lui pèse; **that takes a w. off my mind,** cela me soulage; *F:* **I'm going to take the w. off my feet for a bit,** je vais m'asseoir, me reposer, un peu; *Lit:* **the w. of years,** le fardeau, le faix, le poids, des ans, des années. **4.** force *f* (d'un coup); **blow with no w. behind it,** coup sans force; **to put all one's w. into a blow,** asséner un coup avec toute sa force. **5.** importance *f*; **to give w. to an argument,** donner du poids à un argument; **what he says carries w.,** sa parole a du poids, de l'autorité; **he doesn't carry much w. with the committee,** il n'a pas beaucoup d'influence auprès du comité; **the w. of the evidence was against him,** les témoignages pesaient contre lui; *F:* **to throw one's w. about,** faire l'important.

weight², *v.tr.* **1.** (*a*) attacher un poids à (qch.); charger (qch.) d'un poids; lester, plomber (un filet, une corde, etc.); plomber (une canne); (*b*) **to w. the left ski,** appuyer sur le ski de gauche; (*c*) *Stat:* pondérer; (*d*) *Turf:* handicaper (un cheval). **2.** (*a*) *Tex:* charger, engaller (des fils de soie); (*b*) *Paperm:* charger (la pâte, le papier).

weighted ['weitid], *a.* **1.** (*a*) chargé d'un poids; lesté; alourdi; (*of walking stick*) plombé; **w. safety valve,** soupape *f* de sûreté à contrepoids; (*b*) *Stat:* (*of average, index*) pondéré. **2.** (*a*) *Tex:* (fil de soie) chargé, engallé; (*b*) *Paperm:* (papier) chargé.

weightily ['weitili], *adv.* **1.** pesamment. **2.** (raisonner) puissamment, avec force.

weightiness ['weitinis], *s.* **1.** pesanteur *f*, lourdeur *f* (d'un paquet, etc.). **2.** importance *f*, puissance *f*, force *f* (d'un raisonnement, etc.).

weighting ['weitiŋ], *s.* **1.** (*a*) lestage *m*, plombage *m* (d'un filet, etc.); plombage (d'une canne); (*b*) *Stat:* pondération *f*. **2.** *Tex:* engallage *m* (des fils de soie).

weightless ['weitlis], *a.* (*a*) qui pèse presque rien; très léger; (*b*) *Space:* **w. conditions,** état *m* d'apesanteur.

weightlessness ['weitlisnis], *s.* (*a*) absence *f* de poids; (extrême) légèreté *f*; (*b*) *Space:* apesanteur *f.*

weighty ['weiti], *a.* **1.** (fardeau, etc.) pesant, (très) lourd. **2.** (*a*) (motif, etc.) grave, important, sérieux; (affirmation, etc.) d'une grande portée; (raisonnement, etc.) puissant, d'un grand poids; (*b*) (*occ. of pers.*) qui exerce une grande influence.

weinschenkite ['vi:nʃeŋkait], *s. Miner:* weinschenkite *f.*

weir [wiər], *s.* **1.** barrage *m* (dans un cours d'eau); reversoir *m*; **cylindrical w.,** barrage à tambour; **sluice w.,** barrage à vannes; **needle w.,** barrage à aiguilles; **w. keeper,** barragiste *m*. **2.** déversoir *m*, égrilloir *m* (d'un étang, etc.).

weird¹ ['wiəd], *s. Scot:* sort *m*; destin *m*; destinée *f.*

weird², *a.* **1.** **the w. sisters,** (i) *Myth:* les Parques *f*; (ii) les sorcières *f* (dans *Macbeth*). **2.** (*a*) surnaturel; mystérieux; d'une étrangeté inquiétante; **w. light,** lueur mystérieuse; **I heard a w. noise,** j'ai entendu un bruit mystérieux, étrange, qui m'a donné la chair de poule; (*b*) étrange, singulier, curieux; bizarre; *F:* (*of pers.*) **talk about w.!** quel drôle d'oiseau!

weirdie ['wiədi], *s. F:* excentrique *mf*; olibrius *m*; drôle d'oiseau; phénomène *m*.

weirdly ['wiədli], *adv.* (*a*) mystérieusement, d'une façon mystérieuse, étrangement inquiétante; (*b*) étrangement; bizarrement.

weirdness ['wiədnis], *s.* (*a*) étrangeté inquiétante, surnaturelle, mystérieuse (d'un spectacle, etc.); (*b*) caractère singulier, étrange, bizarre (de qn, des vêtements, d'une idée, etc.).

weirdo, weirdy ['wiədou, -di], *s. F:* = WEIRDIE.

Weismannism ['vaismænizm], *s. Biol:* théorie *f* de Weismann.

weka ['wekə], *s. Orn:* ocydrome *m*.

Welch, welch, *see* WELSH[1,2].

welcome¹ ['welkəm], *a.* **1.** (*a*) bienvenu; **to make s.o. w.,** faire bon accueil à qn; **a w. guest,** un invité qu'on reçoit avec plaisir; **you're always w.,** vous êtes toujours le bienvenu; **your letters are, a letter from you is, always w.,** vos lettres sont toujours les bienvenues; **to be as w. as the flowers in May,** arriver comme marée en carême; (*b*) *as int.* **w.!** soyez le bienvenu, la bienvenue, (chez nous)! **w. to England!** soyez le bienvenu en Angleterre! **to bid s.o. w.,** souhaiter la bienvenue à qn. **2.** (*of thg*) **his gift was very w.,** son cadeau m'a fait grand plaisir; **this is w. news,** nous nous réjouissons de cette nouvelle; **a w. change,** un changement bienvenu, agréable; **this cheque is most w.,** ce chèque est très acceptable, tombe à merveille. **3.** **you're w. to borrow any of my books,** ma bibliothèque est à votre disposition; **you're w. to it,** (i) c'est à votre service, à votre disposition; c'est de bon cœur que je vous l'offre; usez-en à votre aise; (ii) *Iron:* je ne vous l'envie pas; grand bien vous fasse! **he's w. to do as he likes,** il est libre de faire ce qui lui plaît; **you're w. to try,** libre à vous d'essayer; **have it and w.,** je vous le donne et volontiers; *esp. NAm:* (*on being thanked*) **you're w.!** je vous en prie! c'est un plaisir!

welcome², *s.* (*a*) bienvenue *f*; **to outstay, overstay, one's w.,** lasser l'amabilité de ses hôtes; s'incruster; (*b*) accueil *m*; **to give s.o. a hearty w.,** faire bon accueil, faire un accueil cordial, chaleureux, à qn; **he gave us a very poor, cold, w.,** il nous a reçus froidement; il ne nous a pas fait bon accueil; **to give s.o. an enthusiastic w.,** faire à qn un accueil enthousiaste; faire une ovation à qn; **w. mat,** essuie-pieds marqué du mot *welcome*; *F:* **to put out the w. mat,** accueillir qn à bras ouverts.

welcome³, *v.tr.* **1.** (*a*) souhaiter la bienvenue à (qn); faire bon accueil, faire fête, à (qn); bien accueillir (qn); **they welcomed us home,** ils nous ont accueillis cordialement à notre retour; **dinner to w. the new member,** dîner pour fêter le nouveau membre; (*b*) accueillir, recevoir, avec plaisir; **to welcome an opportunity to do sth.,** se réjouir de l'occasion, saluer l'occasion, de faire qch.; **to w. a piece of news,** se réjouir d'une nouvelle; (*at the end of a speech*) **to w. discussion,** encourager la discussion; **he doesn't w. discussion of his beliefs,** il n'aime pas que ses croyances soient mises en question; **his efforts weren't welcomed,** ses efforts ont reçu peu d'encouragement. **2.** accueillir; **to w. s.o. warmly,** faire un accueil chaleureux à qn.

welcoming ['welkəmiŋ], *a.* (sourire, etc.) accueillant.

weld¹ [weld], *s. Bot:* réséda *m* des teinturiers; gaude *f*; herbe *f* aux juifs; fleur *f* du soleil.

weld², *s. Metalw:* soudure *f*; joint *m*, ligne *f*, de soudure. *s.a.* WELDING 2.

weld³, *v. Metalw:* **1.** *v.tr.* (*a*) souder (deux pièces) (au blanc soudant); unir (deux pièces) à chaud; joindre à chaud (un tube, etc.); **to arc w.,** souder à l'arc (électrique); **to spot w.,** souder par points; **to flash w.,** souder par étincelage; **butt welded, lap welded,** soudé à, par, rapprochement, à, par, recouvrement; **cold welded,** soudé (par pression) à froid; (*b*) corroyer (l'acier); (*c*) *Fig:* unir, joindre, étroitement. **2.** *v.i.* (*of metals*) (i) se souder; (ii) se corroyer.

weldability [weldə'biliti], *s. Metalw:* soudabilité *f.*

weldable ['weldəbl], *a.* (acier, etc.) soudable; **w. to glass,** soudable au verre; **not w.,** insoudable.

welded ['weldid], *a.* (tube, etc.) soudé; (acier) corroyé; **w. joint,** soudure *f*; joint *m*, ligne *f*, de soudure.

welder ['weldər], *s.* **1.** (*pers.*) soudeur *m*; **spot w.,** soudeur par points; **lamp, torch, w.,** soudeur au chalumeau. **2.** soudeuse *f*; machine *f* à souder; **spot w.,** soudeuse par points; **w. generator,** poste *m* de soudure (autogène).

welding ['weldiŋ], *s. Metalw:* **1.** (*process*) soudure *f*, soudage *m* (autogène); corroyage *m* (de l'acier); (NOTE: *in the processes listed below, only* soudure *is given as a translation for* **welding,** *though either* soudure *or* soudage *may be used*); **oxyacetylene w.,** soudure oxyacétylénique, autogène; **pressure w.,** soudure par pression; **cold w.,** soudure (par pression) à froid; **forge, blacksmith, hammer, w.,** soudure par forgeage, à la forge; **electric w.,** soudure électrique; **gas w.,** soudure au gaz; **electron-beam w.,** soudure par bombardement, par faisceau, électronique; **arc w.,** soudure à l'arc; **carbon-arc w.,** soudure à l'arc (à électrode) en charbon; **argon-arc w.,** soudure à l'arc à l'argon; **submerged-arc w.,** soudure à l'arc immergé, à l'arc sous flux; **inert-gas, reducing-gas, w.,** soudure à l'arc en atmosphère inerte, réductrice; **tig w.,** soudure à l'arc au tungstène; **pulsation w.,** soudure par courant pulsé; **projection w.,** soudure par projection; **flash w.,** soudure par étincelage, par étincelles; **fusion w.,** soudure par fusion; **spot w., stitch w.,** soudure par points; **aluminothermic, thermit, w.,** soudure aluminothermique, par aluminothermie; **cascade w.,** soudure en cascade; **underwater w.,** soudage sous l'eau; **w. machine,** machine à souder; soudeuse *f*; **w. heat,** blanc soudant; **w. flux,** flux *m* de soudure; **w. rod,** baguette *f* de soudure, d'apport pour soudage; **w. torch,** chalumeau soudeur; **w. steel,** acier soudant; acier soudable, corroyable; **w. test,** essai *m*, épreuve *f*, de soudabilité. **2.** soudure; **joint** *m*, ligne *f*, de soudure; (*in the following, either* **weld** *or* **welding** *may be used*) **butt w.,** soudure bord à bord, en bout, bout à bout, à franc bord, à, par, rapprochement; **lap w.,** soudure à, par, recouvrement, à clin, en écharpe, par amorces; **flat w.,** soudure à plat; **flush w.,** soudure affleurée, arasée; **backhand, forehand, w.,** soudure à droite, à gauche; **bead w.,** soudure en cordon longitudinal; **w. bead,** cordon de soudure; **continuous w., seam w.,** soudure continue, à la molette; **intermittent w.,** soudure discontinue; **chain intermittent w.,** soudure en chaîne; **girth-seam w.,** soudure circulaire; **overhead w.,** soudure au plafond; **seamless w.,** soudure sans joints; **spot w., stitch w.,** soudure par points; **tack w.,** soudure d'agrafage, d'assemblage; **staggered w.,** soudure alternée; **vertical w.,** soudure montante; **fillet w.,** soudure d'angle; **plug w.,** soudure en bouchon.

weldless ['weldlis], *a.* (tube, etc.) sans soudure, sans couture.

welfare ['welfeər], *s.* bien-être *m*; bonheur *m*; **to have s.o.'s w. at heart,** avoir à cœur le bonheur, le bien-être, de qn; **public w.,** bien-être et santé publics; **social w.,** sécurité sociale; **child w., infant w.,** protection *f* de l'enfance; puériculture sociale; **w. work,** = assistance sociale; **w. centre** = centre d'assistance sociale; **infant w. centre,** consultations *fpl* de nourrissons; **w. worker** = assistant(e) social(e); **the W. State,** l'État *m* providence.

welfarism ['welfeərizm], *s. esp. U.S:* le culte de l'État providence.

welfarist ['welfeərist], *s. esp. U.S:* partisan, -ane, de l'État providence.

welkin (the) [ðə'welkin], *s. Lit:* le firmament, la voûte céleste; **to make the w. ring,** (i) (*of sound*) retentir; (ii) faire retentir l'air, la voûte céleste.

well[1] [wel], *s.* **1.** (*a*) *A: & Lit:* source *f*, fontaine *f*; (*b*) **hot w.,** source chaude (d'eau minérale). **2.** puits *m*; **artesian w.,** puits artésien; **driven w., tube w., Abyssinian w.,** puits abyssinien, puits instantané; **open, uncovered, w.,** puits à ciel ouvert; **pump w.,** puits à bras; **draw w.,** puits à poulie; **dead w.,** puits absorbant, puits perdu; *Petr:* **(oil) w.,** puits (de pétrole); **clear w.,** puits de décantation; **wild w.,** puits fou, sauvage; **directional w.,** puits directeur; **beam w.,** sondage *m* à balancier; **staggered wells,** sondages disposés en quinconces; **driven w.,** puits à production forcée; **exploratory w.,** puits d'exploration; **pulling w.,** puits en nettoyage; **w. logging,** diagraphie *f*; **to drive, sink, a w.,** forer, creuser, un puits; **w. sinking, boring,** (i) sondage, forage *m*, (ii) fonçage *m*, de puits; **w. sinker, borer,** (i) foreur *m* de puits; sondeur *m*; (ii) puisatier *m*; *Agr: etc:* **w. drain,** puits d'écoulement; **w. water,** eau *f* de puits. **2.** (*a*) (*shaft*) puits, cage *f* (d'un ascenseur); cage, jour *m* (d'un escalier); (*b*) partie encaissée, creux *m* (de qch.); *Mec.E: etc:* fond *m* de carter, etc. (formant réservoir d'huile); *Metall:* (i) ouvrage *m*, (ii) creuset *m* (d'un haut fourneau); *Aut:* baignoire *f* (de roue de secours); *Nau:* puisard *m*, archipompe *f*, sentine *f* (d'un navire); plat-fond *m* (d'un canot); cockpit *m* (d'un yacht); vivier *m*, réservoir *m* (d'un bateau de pêche); **w. deck,** coffre *m*; **w. decker,** navire à coffre; *Av:* **landing gear w.,** compartiment *m* de logement de train; *Const:* **w. fire,** foyer *m* à âtre surbaissé; *Cu:* **make a w. in the flour,** faire une fontaine dans la farine; mettre la farine en fontaine. **3.** *Atom.Ph:* **potential w.,** puits de potentiel.

well[2], *v.i.* (*of water, spring*) **to w. up, out,** jaillir; *Lit:* sourdre; **tears were welling from her eyes,** des larmes jaillissaient de ses yeux.

well[3], *adv., a. & s.*

I. *adv.* (*comp.* **better,** *sup.* **best,** *q.v.*) **1.** (*a*) **to work w.,** bien travailler; **to do as w. as one can,** faire de son mieux; **it's remarkably w. done,** c'est fait à merveille, à miracle; **this boy will do w.,** ce garçon ira loin, réussira bien, fera son chemin; **w. done!** bravo! très bien! **w. played!** bien joué! *F:* **to do oneself w.,** bien se soigner; bien manger (et bien boire); s'enfiler un bon repas; **we did ourselves w. last night,** on s'est offert un bon dîner hier soir; **it looks w. up there,** cela fait bien là-haut; **it wouldn't look w. if we refused,** si on refusait cela ferait mauvaise impression; **she looked after them (very) w.,** elle les a bien soignés; **you would do w. to be quiet (about it),** vous feriez bien, le mieux serait, de vous taire; **to know a subject w.,** connaître un sujet à fond; **I know him w.,** je le connais bien; **I know only too w. what patience it needs,** je ne sais que trop quelle patience cela exige; **I can't very w. tell you,** je ne saurais trop vous dire; **I can't very w. do it,** il ne m'est guère possible de le faire; **he accepted, as w. he might,** il a accepté et rien d'étonnant; **one might as w. say that black is white,** autant dire que le blanc est le noir; **you might (just) as w. stay,** (i) autant vaut rester; (ii) vous n'êtes pas de trop; **you could just as w. have stayed until tomorrow,** vous auriez tout aussi bien pu rester jusqu'à demain; **we might (just) as w. have stayed at home!** cela ne valait pas la peine de venir! **now you're here you might as w. help me,** puisque tu es là, tu peux bien m'aider, me donner un coup de main; **very w.!** (très) bien! entendu! (*b*) **to entertain s.o. w.,** faire bon accueil à qn; **everyone speaks w. of him,** tout le monde parle bien, dit du bien, de lui; **it speaks w. for his courage,** cela fait honneur à son courage; **to do w. by s.o.,** se montrer généreux envers qn; **she deserves w. of you,** elle mérite bien votre reconnaissance; **he won't take this decision (very) w.,** il aura (bien) du mal à accepter cette décision; **he meant it w.,** il l'a fait, l'a dit, à bonne intention; (*c*) **you're w. out of it,** soyez heureux d'en être quitte; **I came out of it (very) w., I came off (very) w.,** j'ai eu de la chance; j'ai bien réussi; tout s'est bien passé; **the fête went off (very) w.,** la fête s'est bien passée, a été une réussite; *O:* **w. met!** heureuse rencontre! vous arrivez bien à propos! **2.** (*intensive*) **it's w. worth trying,** cela vaut bien la peine d'essayer, *F:* ça vaut le coup; **it's w. after six,** il est six heures bien sonnées; **w. on into the small hours,** bien avant, fort avant, dans la nuit; **he's w. over fifty,** *F:* **w. up the fifties,** il a largement dépassé la cinquantaine; il a cinquante ans bien sonnés; **to be w. on in years,** être âgé, avancé en âge; ne plus être jeune; **to be w. up in a subject,** connaître un sujet à fond; bien posséder un sujet; **he's w. up in history,** il est ferré, *F:* calé, en histoire. **3. pretty w. all,** presque tout; **it's pretty w. finished,** c'est presque, pratiquement, terminé; **it comes to pretty w. the same thing,** c'est à peu près la même chose; *F:* **it serves him damn w., jolly w., right!** il l'a bien cherché! **4.** (*a*) **as w.,** aussi; **keep these as w.,** gardez aussi ceux-ci; **take me as w.,** emmenez-moi aussi; **I'd like some as w.,** j'en ai envie, moi aussi; **I need some as w.,** il m'en faut également; (*b*) **as w. as,** de même que; comme; ainsi que; non moins que; **his enemies as w. as his friends respected him,** ses ennemis ainsi que ses amis le respectaient; **I'm taking an umbrella as w. as a raincoat,** je vais prendre un parapluie et aussi un imperméable; **by day as w. as by night,** de jour comme de nuit; le jour comme la nuit. **5.** (*a*) (*introducing remark*) **w., as I was telling you,** eh bien, donc, comme je vous disais; **w., who was it?** eh bien, qui était-ce? **w., what of it?** eh bien, et après? **w., here we are (at last)!** enfin nous voilà! **you told him—w., I'm afraid I didn't,** vous le lui avez dit?—eh bien, non! c'est-à-dire que non! (*b*) (*exlamatory*) ça alors! pas possible! **(oh) w.! (ah) w.!** (i) eh bien! (ii) (*expressing resignation*) tant pis! **w., w.!** (i) (eh bien,) que voulez-vous! (ii) (*expressing incredulity*) vrai de vrai? **w., it can't be helped!** tant pis! on n'y peut rien! **w., that's life!** enfin, quoi! c'est la vie! (*c*) **w. then,** eh bien, alors; **w. then, why worry about it?** eh bien alors, pourquoi se faire du mauvais sang? **w. then, are you coming?** alors, vous venez? **6.** (*used as comb.fm. with participles to give a virtual adj.; a hyphen is incorrect if the adj. is predicative and permissible but not obligatory if it precedes the noun*) **w. advised,** sage, prudent, judicieux; **he would be w. advised to do it,** ce serait sage, prudent, de sa part de le faire; **w. balanced,** bien équilibré; (*of pers.*) posé; **w. behaved,** (i) (*of child*) bien élevé, sage; (ii) (*of animal*) bien dressé; **w. built,** bien construit; bien bâti; solide; **w. chosen,** bien choisi; **w. disposed,** (i) (*of pers.*) bien disposé (envers); (ii) (*of thgs*) bien arrangé, bien disposé; **w. earned,** (bien) mérité; **w. educated,** instruit; cultivé; **w. fed,** bien nourri; **w. grown,** (i) (*of child, animal*) grand, bien venu; (ii) (*of tree, etc.*) d'une belle venue; **w. informed,** bien renseigné; instruit; bien documenté; (*of pers., mind*) averti; **to be w. informed on a subject,** bien connaître un sujet; connaître un sujet à fond; **to keep w. informed,** se tenir au courant; **w. intentioned,** bien intentionné; **w. kept,** (*of garden, etc.*) bien (entre)tenu; soigné; (*of hands, etc.*) soigné; (*of secret*) bien gardé; **w. known,** (bien) connu; célèbre; (*of expert, etc.*) réputé; **it is w. known that . . .,** tout le monde sait que . . .; **w. made,** bien fait, bien fini; de fabrication soignée; (*of garment*) de coupe soignée; **w. mannered,** poli, bien élevé; qui a du savoir-vivre; **w. matched,** bien assorti; (*of teams*) de force égale; **they are w. matched,** ils sont bien assortis; ils vont bien ensemble; **w. meaning,** bien intentionné; **he's very w. meaning,** il a bon esprit; il a les meilleures intentions du monde; **w. meant,** fait avec une bonne intention, avec les meilleures intentions; **w. off,** *F:* **w. lined,** *esp. NAm: F:* **w. fixed, w. heeled,** *Austr: F:* **w. in,** riche; prospère; **to be (very) w. off,** avoir de la fortune, *F:* avoir de quoi; **you don't know when you're well off,** vous ne connaissez pas votre bonheur; **w. oiled,** (i) (*of machinery*) bien graissé; (ii) *F:* (*of pers.*) ivre, rétamé; **w. paid,** bien payé, bien rétribué; **w. preserved,** bien conservé; **w. read,** (i) (*pers.*) instruit, cultivé, qui a de la culture; (ii) (*of book*) qui porte les traces de nombreuses lectures; **w. spent,** (*of money, time*) bien utilisé; bien employé; (*of money*) dépensé avantageusement; **w. spoken,** (i) qui parle bien, qui a un accent cultivé; (ii) qui parle courtoisement; **w. stocked,** bien approvisionné; bien achalandé; **w. timed,** opportun, bien calculé; **w. worn,** (i) (*of garment, etc.*) usé, vieux; fortement usagé; (*of book, etc.*) qui a beaucoup servi; (*of argument, etc.*) rebattu; usé jusqu'à la corde.

II. *a.* **(better; best) 1.** (*in good health*) **to be w.,** être bien portant, en bonne santé; se porter, aller, bien; **w. and strong,** robuste; **how are you?—very w.,** comment allez-vous?—très bien, merci; **people who are w. don't understand invalids,** les gens bien portants ne comprennent pas les malades; **I don't feel w.,** je ne me sens pas bien; **he's not very w.,** il est indisposé, souffrant; **he's not so w.,** il va moins bien; **to get w.,** guérir; se rétablir; se remettre; **I'm quite w. again now,** me voilà remis; *esp. U.S:* **he's not a w. man,** il ne se porte pas bien; il n'a pas de santé; *F:* (*in a hospital*) **the w. patients,** ceux qui sont déjà bien portants. **2.** (*a*) (*advisable*) **it is w. to . . .,** il est opportun de . . .; **it would be w. to . . .,** il serait bon, utile, recommandable, de . . .; il serait à propos de . . .; il y a lieu de . . .; **it would be w. to start early,** nous ferions bien de partir de bonne heure; **it would be just as w. if you were present,** il y aurait avantage à ce que vous soyez présent; **it would be just as w. for you to stay a little longer,** il serait prudent que vous restiez encore un peu; **it might be as w. to . . .,** peut-être conviendrait-il de . . .; il serait peut-être bon de . . .; (*b*) (*lucky*) **it was w. for you that you were there,** vous avez eu de la chance de vous trouver là; **it was w. for him that nobody saw him,** heureusement pour lui personne ne l'a vu; (*c*) (*satisfactory*) **all's w. that ends w.,** tout est bien qui finit bien; **all's w.!** *Mil:* tout va bien! *Nau:* bon quart! (*d*) **that's all very w., but. . .,** tout cela est bel et bon, c'est bon à dire, mais. . .; **that's all very w.!** cela vous plaît à dire! **a written contract is all very w., but . . .,** un contrat par écrit c'est parfait, c'est très bien, mais. . .; **it is all very w. for you to say that . . .,** libre à vous, permis à vous, de dire que . . .; **it's all very w. to say it's none of your business,** vous avez beau dire que cela ne vous regarde pas; **he's all very w. in his way, but. . .,** il n'y a rien à dire contre lui, mais . . .; **w. and good!** (i) soit! bon! (ii) passe encore pour cela! **if he returns tomorrow, well and good,** qu'il revienne demain, et cela ira bien; **that's all very w. and good, but. . .,** tout ça c'est très bien, mais . . .

III. *s.* **1.** *pl.* **the w. and the sick,** les bien portants et les malades. **2. to wish s.o. w.,** vouloir du bien à qn; être bien disposé envers qn.

welladay ['weladei], *int. A:* hélas!

wellbeing ['welbiiŋ], *s.* bien-être *m*; **physical and moral w.,** santé physique et morale; **public w.,** le salut public; **to have a sense of (general) w.,** se trouver en bonne forme; se sentir bien disposé envers tout le monde.

wellborn ['welbɔ:n], *a.* bien né; de bonne famille.

wellbred [wel'bred], *a.* (*of pers.*) bien élevé; courtois; distingué; de bonne famille.

welldigger ['weldigər], *s.* puisatier *m.*

welldoing [wel'du:iŋ], *s. Lit:* **to find pleasure, not to weary, in w.,** trouver son plaisir à faire le bien.

welling ['weliŋ], *s.* (*of liquid*) **w. (up),** jaillissement *m.*

wellington ['weliŋtən], *s.* **wellingtons, w. boots,** bottes *f* en caoutchouc.

Wellingtonia [weliŋ'tounia], *s. Bot:* wellingtonia *m*; sequoia *m.*

wellnigh ['welnai], *adv. Lit:* presque; **he was w. drowned,** il a failli se noyer.

wellsite ['welzait], *s. Miner:* wellsite *f.*

wellspring ['welspriŋ], *s. Lit:* source *f*; **the w. of life,** la source de la vie.

well-to-do [weltə'du:], *a.* aisé, riche; prospère; cossu; *s.pl.* **the w.-to-do,** les riches, les fortunés.

wellwisher ['welwiʃər], *s.* partisan, -ane (d'une cause, etc.); **surrounded by wellwishers,** entouré d'admirateurs; (*in anonymous letter*) **a w.,** quelqu'un qui vous veut du bien.

Welsh[1] [welʃ]. **1.** (*a*) *a.* (*in regimental names* **Welch**) gallois; du pays de Galles; *Pol:* **W. nationalist,** nationaliste *mf* gallois; **W. nationalism,** nationalisme gallois; *Furn:* **W. dresser,** vaisselier *m*; (*b*) *s.pl.* **the W.,** les Gallois *m.* **2.** *s. Ling:* gallois *m.*

welsh[2], *v.tr. & i.* (*occ.* **welch**) partir, filer, décamper, sans payer; lever le pied; escroquer (qn); **to w. on s.o.,** manquer à une obligation à qn.

welsher ['welʃər], *s.* (*occ.* **welcher**) escroc *m* (qui part sans payer); tire-au-flanc *m*; *Turf:* bookmaker marron.

welshing ['welʃiŋ], *s.* (*occ.* **welching**) fuite *f* (d'un bookmaker marron, etc.).

Welshman, -woman, *pl.* **-men, -women** ['welʃmən, -wumən, -mən, -wimin], *s.* Gallois, -oise.

welt[1] [welt], *s.* **1.** (*a*) *Bootm:* trépointe *f* (de semelle); (*b*) bordure *f* (de gant); haut *m* (d'un bas); passepoil *m* (de coussin, etc.); *Knit:* bordure à côtes; (*c*) *Mec.E:* couvre-joint *m, pl.* couvre-joints; fourrure *f*, bande *f* de recouvrement (d'une rivure); (*d*) *Plumb:* **w. (joint),** agrafe *f* (de feuilles de plomb). **2.** marque *f*, trace *f* (d'un coup de fouet, etc.); vergeture *f*; zébrure *f.*

welt[2], *v.tr.* **1.** (*a*) *Bootm:* mettre des trépointes à (des chaussures); (*b*) border (un gant, une chaussette); (*c*) *Plumb:* **to w. (joint) lead sheets,** agrafer des feuilles de plomb. **2.** *F: O:* rosser, battre (qn).

welted ['weltid], *a.* (*a*) *Bootm:* (chaussure, semelle) à trépointes; (*b*) **w. pocket,** poche passepoilée; poche à patte de gilet; (*c*) *Mec.E:* (assemblage) à couvre-joints; (*d*) *Plumb:* **w. joint,** agrafe *f.*

welter[1] ['weltər], *s.* (*a*) confusion *f*, désordre *m*; (*b*) masse confuse, fouillis *m* (de choses disparates).

welter[2], *v.i. esp. Lit:* se vautrer, se rouler (dans la boue, etc.); **to be weltering in one's (own) blood,** nager, baigner, dans son sang.

welterweight ['weltəweit], *s.* **1.** *Rac: O:* (*a*) (*pers.*) cavalier lourd; poids lourd; (*b*) poids supplémentaire; surcharge *f*. **2.** *Box:* (*pers.*) poids mi-moyen; welter *m.*

welting ['weltiŋ], *s.* **1.** (*a*) *Bootm:* mise *f* des trépointes; (*b*) bordurage *m* (d'un gant, d'une chaussette); (*c*) *Plumb:* agrafage *m* (de feuilles de plomb). **2.** = WELT[1] 1 (*a*), (*b*). **3.** *F: O:* rossée *f*, raclée *f*; **to give s.o. a w.,**

rosser, battre, qn.

wen [wen], *s. Med:* **1.** kyste sébacé; *F:* loupe *f.* **2.** *F: A:* goitre *m.*

wench[1] [wen(t)ʃ], *s.f.* (*a*) *F: & Hum:* (jeune) fille, jeunesse, jeune femme; **strapping great w.,** grande gaillarde; (*b*) *A:* jeune fille du peuple; servante; serveuse (dans une auberge); **kitchen w.,** fille de cuisine; (*c*) *A:* fille des rues; coureuse.

wench[2], *v.i. F:* **to go wenching,** courir la gueuse, les filles, le jupon.

wencher [ˈwen(t)ʃər], *s.* coureur *m* de jupon.

wend[1] [wend], *v.tr. Lit:* **to w. one's way,** porter, diriger, ses pas (**to,** vers); se diriger, s'acheminer (**to,** vers); **to w. one's way homeward,** s'acheminer vers sa maison.

Wend[2], *s. Ethn:* Wende *mf.*

Wendish [ˈwendiʃ]. **1.** *a.* wende. **2.** *s. Ling:* wende *m.*

went [went], *s. A: & Dial:* chemin *m*, sentier *m*; **three-w. way,** carrefour *m* à trois voies; échaudé *m.*

wentletrap [ˈwentltræp], *s. Moll:* (**common**) **w.,** scalaire *f.*

werewolf, *pl.* **-wolves** [ˈwiəwulf, -wulvz; ˈwəː-], *s. Myth:* loup-garou *m, pl.* loups-garous.

wernerite [ˈwəːnərait], *s. Miner:* wernérite *f.*

werwolf [ˈwəːwulf], *s.* = WEREWOLF.

Wesleyan [ˈweslіən], *a. & s. Rel.H:* wesleyen, -enne; **W. Methodism,** méthodisme wesleyen.

Wesleyanism [ˈwesliənizm], *s. Rel.H:* méthodisme wesleyen.

west[1] [west]. **1.** *s.* (*a*) ouest *m*, occident *m*, couchant *m*; **the wind is blowing from the w.,** le vent vient, souffle, de l'ouest; **house facing (the) w.,** maison exposée à l'ouest; **look towards the w.,** regardez vers l'ouest; **on the w., to the w.,** à l'ouest, au couchant (**of,** de); (*b*) **the W.,** l'Occident; (*c*) **to live in the w. of England,** demeurer dans l'ouest de l'Angleterre; *U.S:* **the W.,** les États occidentaux (des États-Unis); **the Far W.,** les États des Montagnes Rocheuses et du littoral du Pacifique; le Far-West; **the Mid(dle) W.,** les États de la Prairie. **2.** *adv.* (*a*) à l'ouest, à l'occident; **to travel w.,** voyager vers l'ouest; **Ireland lies w. of England,** l'Irlande est située à l'ouest de l'Angleterre; **to sail due w.,** faire route droit vers l'ouest; avoir le cap à l'ouest; faire de l'ouest; **w. by south,** ouest-quart-sud-ouest; **w. by north,** ouest-quart-nord-ouest; (*b*) **to go w.,** (i) partir pour l'ouest; se diriger vers l'ouest; (ii) *F:* mourir; casser sa pipe; *Mil:* passer l'arme à gauche; **there's ten pounds gone w.!** voilà (un billet de) £10 de claqué! **there's another plate gone w.!** encore une assiette de cassée! **3.** *a.* (*a*) ouest *inv.*; (vent) d'ouest; (mur, etc.) qui fait face, qui est exposé, à l'ouest; **the W. coast,** (i) la côte ouest; (ii) les plages *f* de l'ouest; **the W. Country,** le sud-ouest de l'Angleterre; **the W. End,** le quartier (chic) du centre-ouest de Londres; **W.-end tailor,** tailleur chic (du centre-ouest de Londres); *U.S:* **the W. Side,** les quartiers ouest de New York; **W. Sider,** habitant, -ante, des quartiers ouest de New York; *Geog: Pol:* **the W. Bank,** la rive occidentale du Jourdain; Cisjordanie *f*; (*b*) (*in Pr.n. Geog:*) **W. Africa,** l'Afrique occidentale; **W. Berlin,** Berlin Ouest; **W. Germany,** l'Allemagne de l'Ouest; la République fédérale allemande; **W. German,** *a. & s. F:* ouest-allemand, -ande; **the W. Indies,** les Antilles *f*; **W. Indian,** (i) *a.* des Antilles; antillais; (ii) *s.* Antillais, -aise; *Hist:* **W. Indiaman,** navire *m* faisant le commerce des Antilles; *U.S:* **W. Virginia,** Virginie-Occidentale.

west[2], *v.i.* (*of sun, ship*) passer à l'ouest.

westbound [ˈwes(t)baund], *a.* allant vers l'ouest.

wester [ˈwestər], *v.i.* **1.** (*of sun, moon, stars*) passer à l'ouest. **2.** (*of wind*) sauter à l'ouest.

westering [ˈwest(ə)riŋ], *a.* qui passe à l'ouest; (*of wind*) qui saute à l'ouest; **the w. sun,** le soleil couchant.

westerly [ˈwestəli]. **1.** *a.* **w. wind,** vent *m* d'ouest, qui vient de l'ouest; **w. current,** courant *m* qui se dirige vers l'ouest; **w. point,** point situé à, vers, l'ouest. **2.** *adv.* vers l'ouest. **3.** *s.* **westerlies,** vents d'ouest; westerlies *m.*

western [ˈwestən]. **1.** *a.* (*a*) ouest, de l'ouest; occidental, -aux; **the W. Empire,** l'Empire d'Occident; **W. Europe,** l'Europe occidentale; **the W. Church,** l'Église d'Occident; l'Église latine; *Pol:* **the W. powers,** les puissances occidentales; l'Occident; (*b*) **the W. States,** les États occidentaux (des États-Unis); **W. Australia,** l'Australie occidentale. **2.** *s.* (*a*) occidental (*pl.* -aux), -ale; (*b*) (i) *Cin:* western *m*; (ii) *Lit:* roman *m* de cowboys.

westerner [ˈwestənər], *s.* (*a*) occidental (*pl.* -aux), -ale; (*b*) *U.S:* habitant, -ante, des États de l'ouest, occidentaux.

westernization [westənaiˈzeiʃ(ə)n], *s.* occidentalisation *f.*

westernize [ˈwestənaiz], *v.tr.* occidentaliser (un peuple); **country that has westernized itself,** pays qui s'est occidentalisé.

westing [ˈwestiŋ], *s. Nau:* marche *f*, route *f*, vers l'ouest; chemin *m* ouest.

west-north-west [westnɔːθˈwest, *Nau:* -nɔːˈwest]. **1.** *s.* ouest-nord-ouest *m.* **2.** *adv.* à l'ouest-nord-ouest. **3.** *a.* (vent) qui vient de l'ouest-nord-ouest; (courant) qui se dirige vers l'ouest-nord-ouest.

west-north-westerly [westnɔːθˈwestəli, *Nau:* -nɔːˈwestəli], *a.* (vent) qui vient de l'ouest-nord-ouest.

Westphalia [westˈfeiliə], *Pr.n. Geog:* Westphalie *f.*

Westphalian [westˈfeiliən]. *Geog:* (*a*) *a.* westphalien; (*b*) *s.* Westphalien, -ienne.

Westralian [wesˈtreiliən], *a. & s. F: Geog:* ouest-australien, -ienne; de l'Australie occidentale; *St.Exch: O:* **Westralians,** valeurs minières de l'Australie occidentale.

west-south-west [westsauθˈwest, *Nau:* -sauˈwest]. **1.** *s.* ouest-sud-ouest *m.* **2.** *adv.* à l'ouest-sud-ouest. **3.** *a.* = WEST-SOUTH-WESTERLY.

west-south-westerly [westsauθˈwestəli, *Nau:* -sauˈwestəli], *a.* (vent) qui vient de l'ouest-sud-ouest; (courant) qui se dirige vers l'ouest-sud-ouest.

westward [ˈwestwəd]. **1.** *s.* direction *f* de l'ouest; **to w.,** vers l'ouest. **2.** *a.* à l'ouest; de l'ouest. **3.** *adv.* = WESTWARDS.

westwards [ˈwestwədz], *adv.* vers l'ouest; à l'ouest.

wet[1] [wet], *a.* (**wetter; wettest**) **1.** (*a*) mouillé, humide; imbibé d'eau; **to get w.,** (i) se mouiller; (ii) *Austr: P:* se fâcher; **to get one's feet w.,** se mouiller les pieds; **he's afraid of getting his feet w.,** c'est un douillet, une poule mouillée; **to be w. through, w. to the skin, dripping w.,** être trempé, mouillé, jusqu'aux os; **as w. as a drowned rat,** trempé comme un canard, comme une soupe; **wringing w., sopping w., soaking w.,** (*of clothes, etc.*) mouillé à tordre; (*of pers.*) trempé comme une soupe, jusqu'aux os; **cheeks w. with tears,** joues baignées de larmes; **ink still w.,** encre encore fraîche; *F:* (*pers.*) **w. blanket,** rabat-joie *m inv*; trouble-fête *m inv*; (*b*) **w. weather,** temps humide, pluvieux; temps de pluie; **it's going to be w.,** il va pleuvoir; **three w. days,** trois jours de pluie; **when it's w.,** quand il pleut, les jours où il pleut; **the w. season,** la saison des pluies; (*c*) *Ch:* **w. assay,** essai *m* par voie humide; **w. treatment,** traitement *m* à l'eau; *El:* **w. cell,** pile *f* à élément humide; **w. bulb thermometer,** thermomètre mouillé, à boule mouillée; (*d*) *Paperm:* **w. pulp,** pâte grasse; **w.-beaten pulp,** pâte engraissée; (*e*) **w. nurse,** nourrice *f*; (*f*) *F:* **he's, she's, w., so w. it's not true,** c'est une nouille; **w. joke,** astuce vaseuse; **he's w. behind the ears,** on lui pincerait le nez qu'il en sortira encore du lait; (*g*) **w. dream,** pollution *f* nocturne, rêve *m* érotique (d'un homme). **2.** *F:* (*of country, state*) qui permet la vente des boissons alcooliques.

wet[2], *s.* **1.** humidité *f.* **2.** pluie *f*; *esp. Austr:* saison *f* des pluies; **to go out in the w.,** sortir sous la pluie; **come in out of the w.,** ne restez pas là sous la pluie; **he hasn't enough sense to come in out of the w.,** il est bête comme ses pieds. **3.** *F: O:* **to have a w.,** boire un coup, prendre un pot. **4.** *F:* (*pers.*) nouille *f.*

wet[3], *v.tr.* (**wetted**) **1.** (*a*) mouiller, humecter; imbiber (une éponge); arroser (de la pâte, etc.); (*of child, etc.*) **to w. the bed,** mouiller le lit; **to w. one's pants,** *F:* **oneself,** mouiller sa culotte; *F:* (*of dog, etc.*) **to w.,** *v.i.* **to w. on, the carpet,** pisser, faire pipi, sur le tapis; *F: O:* **to w. the tea,** infuser le thé; *Nau:* **to w. a sail,** empeser une voile; (*b*) *Pharm:* madéfier (un emplâtre, etc.). **2.** *F: O:* **to w. a bargain, a deal,** arroser une affaire; boire le vin du marché.

wet-grind [wetˈgraind], *v.tr.* meuler (un outil) à l'eau.

wether [ˈweðər], *s. Husb:* bélier châtré; mouton; **w. hog,** mouton d'un an (pas encore tondu); **w. lamb,** agneau *m.*

wetlands [ˈwetlændz], *s.pl.* (*a*) marécages *mpl*; (*b*) marais salants.

wet-lease [ˈwetliːs], *v.tr. Av:* louer (un avion) avec personnel navigant et non-navigant.

wetly [ˈwetli], *adv.* (*a*) **his clothes clung w. to him,** ses vêtements détrempés lui collaient à la peau; (*b*) *F:* (parler, etc.) bêtement.

wetness [ˈwetnis], *s.* (*a*) humidité *f*; (*b*) *F:* bêtise *f.*

wetting [ˈwetiŋ], *s.* mouillage *m*, mouillement *m*; arrosage *m* (de la pâte); humectage *m*; *F: O:* infusion *f* (du thé); **to get a w.,** se faire tremper; **to have a thorough w.,** être trempé jusqu'aux os; **bed w.,** incontinence *f* nocturne; *Tchn:* **w. agent,** mouillant *m*; *Typ:* **w. board,** ais *m* à tremper.

whack[1] [(h)wæk]. *F:* **1.** *s.* (*a*) coup (de bâton, etc.) retentissant, bien appliqué; claque *f*, taloche *f*; **we gave the carpet a good w.,** nous avons bien battu le tapis; (*b*) **to have a w. at sth.,** essayer de faire qch.; tenter le coup; **to have first w. at sth.,** attaquer qch., y aller, le premier; (*c*) part *f*, portion *f*, (grand) morceau; **a good w. of cake,** un gros morceau de gâteau; **he didn't get his w.,** il n'a pas eu sa part; **he didn't do his w.,** il n'y a pas mis du sien; **he did, paid, more than his w.,** il a fait, a payé, plus que sa part; (*d*) *U.S:* (*of mechanism, etc.*) **out of w.,** dérangé, détraqué. **2.** *int.* v'lan!

whack[2], *v.tr. F:* (*a*) battre (qn) (à coups retentissants); bourrer (qn) de coups; rosser (qn); fesser (un enfant); (*b*) *Sp: etc:* battre (ses adversaires) à plates coutures; défaire, rouler (une équipe, etc.).

whacked [(h)wækt], *a. F:* épuisé, éreinté, vanné; **completely w., w. to the wide,** complètement abruti.

whacker [ˈ(h)wækər], *s. F:* **1.** quelque chose de colossal, de pépère; mastodonte *m*; **what a w.! isn't it a w.!** il est pépère, celui-là! **2.** *O:* gros mensonge; mensonge de taille; **what a w.!** en voilà une forte!

whacking[1] [ˈ(h)wækiŋ], *a. & adv. F:* énorme; colossal, -aux; **a w. great cabbage,** un maître chou, un fameux chou; **a w. great lie,** un mensonge de taille.

whacking[2], *s. F:* **1.** rossée *f*, raclée *f*; fessée *f.* **2.** *Sp: etc:* **we gave them a w.,** on les a bien battus.

whacko [(h)wæˈkou], *int. esp. Austr: P:* magnifique! épatant!

whacky [ˈ(h)wæki], *a.* = WACKY.

whale[1] [(h)weil], *s.* (*a*) *Z:* baleine *f*; cétacé *m*; **right w., Greenland w., northern w., arctic w., great polar w.,** baleine franche; **pigmy right w.,** baleine franche naine; **Basque w., black w., North Atlantic right w., scrag w., southern right w.,** baleine de Biscaye; **blue w.,** baleine bleue; **Californian grey w.,** baleine grise de Californie; **sperm w.,** cachalot *m*; **pygmy sperm w.,** cachalot pygmée, kogia *m*; **fin(-back) w., finny w., furrow-throated w.,** rorqual, -als *m*, baleinoptère *m*; **sei w.,** rorqual du nord; **bottle-nosed w., beaked w.,** hyperoodon *m*; **hump(backed) w.,** mégaptère *f*, jubarte *f*; **white w.,** bél(o)uga *m*; **toothed w.,** odontocète *m*; **whalebone w.,** mysticète *m*; **bull w.,** baleine mâle; **cow w.,** baleine femelle; **w. calf,** baleineau *m*; **w. oil,** huile *f* de baleine; **w. hunter** = WHALER; **w. chaser** = WHALER 2; (*b*) *Ich:* **w. shark,** requin-baleine *m*, *pl.* requins-baleines; (*c*) *Crust:* **w. barnacle,** coronule *f*; **w. louse,** (i) cyame *m*, cyamus *m*; (ii) coronule; (*d*) *F:* **a w. of a crop,** une récolte fantastique; **a w. of a cold,** un rhume carabiné; **we had a w. of a time,** on s'est drôlement bien amusés; **to be a w. (at sth.),** être un as (à qch.); **he's a w. for work,** il abat du travail.

whale[2], *v.i.* faire la pêche à la baleine; pêcher la baleine.

whale[3], *v.tr. NAm: F:* (*a*) battre, rosser (qn); (*b*) *Sp: etc:* battre (qn) à plates coutures.

whaleback [ˈ(h)weilbæk], *a. & s.* **w. (boat),** (navire *m*) à dos de baleine.

whalebird [ˈ(h)weilbəːd], *s. Orn:* prion *m.*

whaleboat [ˈ(h)weilbout], *s.* baleinière *f*; bateau-chasseur *m*, *pl.* bateaux-chasseurs.

whalebone [ˈ(h)weilboun], *s.* (*a*) (fanon *m* de) baleine *f*; (*b*) busc *m*, baleine (d'un corset).

whalehead [ˈ(h)weilhed], *s. Orn:* balaeniceps *m*, baléniceps *m*; *F:* bec-en-sabot *m*, *pl.* becs-en-sabot.

whaler [ˈ(h)weilər], *s.* **1.** (*pers.*) baleinier *m*; pêcheur *m* de baleines. **2.** (*vessel*) baleinier; baleinière *f*; bateau-chasseur *m*, *pl.* bateaux-chasseurs. **3.** *Ich:* **w. (shark),** carcharhinus *m.*

whalery [ˈ(h)weiləri], *s.* industrie baleinière.

whaling[1] [ˈ(h)weiliŋ], *s.* pêche *f*, chasse *f*, à la baleine; **w. ship, boat,** baleinier *m*; baleinière *f*; bateau-chasseur *m*, *pl.* bateaux-chasseurs; **w. ground,** parages fréquentés par les baleines; **w. gun,** canon *m*, fusil *m*, à harpon; **w. spade,** louchet *m.*

whaling[2], *s. NAm: F:* rossée *f*, raclée *f.*

wham[1] [ˈ(h)wæm]. *F:* **1.** *s.* coup retentissant; **to fall with a w.,** tomber v'lan. **2.** *int.* vlan!

wham[2], *v.tr. & i. F:* **to w. (into) s.o., sth.,** battre (qn, qch.) (de coups retentissants); botter (qn); flanquer une raclée à (qn).

whammy [ˈ(h)wæmi], *s. NAm: F:* **to put the w. (on s.o.),** mettre les bâtons dans les roues.

whang[1] [(h)wæŋ], *v.tr. F:* cogner, battre (qn, qch.) (d'un coup retentissant).

whang[2], *s. F:* coup retentissant; détonation *f*; **I fell (with a) w. on the pavement,** je suis tombé vlan sur le trottoir.

whare [ˈ(h)wɔːri], *s. N.Z:* case, habitation (maorie).

wharf[1], *pl.* **-s, wharves** [(h)wɔːf, -s, (h)wɔːvz], *s.* **1.** (*a*) appontement *m*, débarcadère *m*, embarcadère *m*; entrepôt maritime; wharf *m*, quai *m*; **oil w.,** quai des pétroles; *Com:* **ex w.,** à prendre sur quai; (*b*) **w. rat,** (i) *Z:* surmulot *m*; (ii) *P: O:* rôdeur *m*, chapardeur *m* (qui fréquente les quais); *Crust:* **w. monkey,** ligie *f.* **2.** (*coke-making*) glacis *m* (d'un four à coke).

wharf[2], *v.tr.* **1.** (*a*) déposer (des marchandises) sur le quai; (*b*) débarquer (les marchandises). **2.** (*a*) amarrer (un navire) à quai; (*b*) *v.i.* (*of ship*) venir à quai;

amarrer à quai.

wharfage [ˈ(h)wɔːfidʒ], *s.* **1.** débarquement *m*, embarquement *m*; mise *f* en entrepôt (de marchandises). **2.** quayage *m*; droits *mpl* de quai, de bassin. **3.** quais *mpl* et appontements *mpl*.

wharfie [ˈwɔːfi], *s.m. Austr: F:* débardeur, déchargeur.

wharfing [ˈ(h)wɔːfiŋ], *s.* = WHARFAGE 1, 3.

wharfinger [ˈ(h)wɔːfin(d)ʒər], *s.* (*a*) (i) propriétaire *m*, (ii) gardien *m*, d'un quai; maître *m* de quai; (*b*) mesureur juré.

wharfman, *pl.* **-men** [ˈ(h)wɔːfmən], *s.m.* débardeur, déchargeur.

wharfmaster [ˈ(h)wɔːfmɑːstər], *s.m.* maître de quai; (*on river*) garde-port, *pl.* gardes-port(s).

what [(h)wɔt], *a. & pron.*

I. *a.* **1.** (*relative*) (ce, la chose, etc.) que, qui; **lend me w. money you can,** prêtez-moi l'argent dont vous pouvez disposer; **he took w. little I had left,** il m'a pris le peu qui me restait; **w. little he did say was always well said,** le peu qu'il disait, il le disait toujours bien; **w. few friends he had,** le peu d'amis qu'il avait; **he traded with w. capital he had,** il faisait le commerce avec ce qu'il possédait de capital. **2.** (*interrogative, direct or indirect*) quel, *f.* quelle, *pl.* quels, quelles; **w. time is it?** quelle heure est-il? **tell me w. time it is,** dites-moi l'heure qu'il est; **w. paper do you read?** quel journal lisez-vous? **w. job does he do?** quel est son métier? qu'est-ce qu'il fait? **tell me w. books you want,** dites-moi quels livres vous désirez; **tell me w. man it was you saw,** dites-moi quel était l'homme que vous avez vu; **w. right has he to give orders?** de quel droit donne-t-il des ordres? **w. good, w. use, is this?** à quoi cela sert-il? **w. part of speech are these words?** à quelle partie du discours appartiennent ces mots? **w. news is there?** quoi de nouveau? quelles nouvelles? **w. price do you reckon for this horse?** à combien évaluez-vous ce cheval? **what's the date (today)?** quelle est la date (aujourd'hui)? **w. sort of (a) book is it?** quelle sorte, quelle espèce, de livre est-ce? **w. colour, w. size, is it?** c'est de quelle couleur, de quelle taille? **3.** (*exclamatory*) **w. an idea!** quelle idée! **w. a fine hotel!** quel bel hôtel! **w. a fool he is!** qu'il est bête! comme il est bête! **w. a fuss about nothing!** voilà bien de bruit pour rien! **w. a question!** quelle question! **w. a man!** quel homme! **w. a pity!** quel dommage! **w. a (long) time you are getting dressed!** comme vous êtes longtemps à vous habiller! **w. a lot of people!** que de gens! que de monde!

II. *pron.* **1.** (*rel.*) ce qui, ce que; **w. is done cannot be undone,** ce qui est fait est fait; **I don't know w. has happened,** je ne sais pas ce qui est arrivé; **w. I like is a detective story,** ce que j'aime c'est un roman policier; **w. I object to is . . .,** ce à quoi je m'oppose, ce contre quoi je proteste, c'est . . .; **w. is most remarkable is that . . .,** ce qu'il y a de plus remarquable c'est que . . .; **he had a key and w. is more he still has it,** il avait une clef et qui plus est il l'a encore; **this is w. it's all about,** voici ce dont il s'agit; *F:* **that's w. football's all about!** mais c'est ça le football! **that's just w. I was driving at,** c'est là où je voulais en venir; **but that's not w. I said,** mais je n'ai pas dit cela; **w. I expected has happened,** ce à quoi je m'attendais est arrivé; **come w. may,** advienne que pourra; **say w. he will, w. he likes,** quoi qu'il dise; il a beau dire; **he never speaks of w. he has gone through,** il ne parle jamais de ce qu'il a enduré; **I took w. was given me,** j'ai pris ce qu'on m'a donné; **w. with one thing and another the scheme miscarried,** pour une raison ou pour une autre le projet a échoué; **w. with golf and w. with tennis I have no time to write,** entre le golf et le tennis il ne me reste pas une minute pour écrire; *Dial:* **not a day but w. it rains,** il ne passe un jour qu'il ne pleuve; **not but w. she still loves him,** néanmoins elle l'aime toujours; *P:* **to give s.o. w. for,** laver la tête à qn; flanquer une bonne raclée à qn. **2.** (*interrogative*) (*a*) (*direct*) qu'est-ce qui? qu'est-ce que? que? quoi? **w. has happened?** qu'est-ce qui est arrivé? **what's happening?** que se passe-t-il? **what's burning?** qu'est-ce qui brûle? **w. on earth are you doing here?** qu'est-ce que vous pouvez bien faire ici? qu'est-ce que vous venez faire ici? pourquoi êtes-vous venu ici? **w. is it?** (i) qu'est-ce? qu'est-ce que c'est? (ii) qu'est-ce qu'il y a? **what's that?** qu'est-ce que cela? qu'est-ce que c'est que ça? **what's that you're telling me?** qu'est-ce que vous me dites? **w. will become of him?** que deviendra-t-il? **what's the matter?** qu'y a-t-il? qu'est-ce qu'il y a? de quoi s'agit-il? **what's her address?** quelle est son adresse? **what's his name?** quel est son nom? comment s'appelle-t-il? **w. is half of twenty-eight? w. does half twenty-eight come to?** quelle est la moitié de vingt-huit? **w. is a powder?** qu'est-ce (que c'est) qu'une poudre? **what's that to you?** qu'est-ce que cela vous fait? est-ce que ça vous regarde? **w. is there to see in this town?** qu'y a-t-il à voir dans cette ville? **what's the good, the use?** à quoi bon? **w. do you want?** qu'est-ce que vous désirez? qu'est-ce que vous voulez? **what's to be done?** que faire? *F:* **what's taken him I ask you?** je vous demande un peu qu'est-ce qui lui prend! **w. did I tell you?** quand je vous le disais! je vous l'avais bien dit! **what's the news today?** quoi de neuf aujourd'hui? **w. will people say?** que dira-t-on? qu'en dira-t-on? **what's the French for** *dog*? comment dit-on *dog* en français? **w. gave you that idea?** qu'est-ce qui vous a donné cette idée? **what's that gun meant for shooting?** ce fusil c'est pour chasser quoi? **w. else could bring me here?** quoi d'autre pourrait m'amener ici? **w. better is there?** qu'y a-t-il de meilleur, de mieux? **w. could be more beautiful?** quoi de plus beau? **w. would be more natural than to ask that?** quoi de plus naturel que de demander cela? **w. do seven and eight make?** combien font sept et huit? **w. are potatoes today?** à combien (sont) les pommes de terre aujourd'hui? **w. is the rent?** de combien est le loyer? **w. do I owe you?** combien vous dois-je? (*in shop*) c'est combien? ça fait combien? **w. is he like?** comment est-il? quelle espèce d'homme est-il, est-ce? **w. do you take me for?** pour qui me prenez-vous? **what's it made of?** en quoi est-ce? c'est en quoi? **w. are you thinking of?** à quoi pensez-vous? **w. are you talking about?** de quoi parlez-vous? **what's it all about, (all) in aid of?** de quoi s'agit-il? **w. about the £10 I lent you?** et les dix livres que je vous ai prêtées? **w. about a game of bridge?** si on faisait une partie de bridge? **w. about you?** et vous donc? **w. about that coffee?** et ce café? **and w. about our guests?** et nos invités, avec tout ça? **and your cousins?—w. about my cousins?** et vos cousins?—quoi, mes cousins? **w. about Martin?—well, w. about him?** et Martin?—eh bien quoi, Martin? **well, w. about it?** (i) eh bien, quoi? eh bien, et puis après? (ii) la belle histoire! le grand malheur! (iii) eh bien, qu'en dites-vous? **what's that for?** à quoi sert cela? à quoi ça sert? **w. did he do that for?** pourquoi a-t-il fait cela? **w. (on earth) for?** mais pourquoi donc? pourquoi faire? **w. ever for?** mais pourquoi, enfin? **and w. if she hears about, of, it?** et si elle l'apprend? **w. now?** qu'y a-t-il à présent? quoi encore? **w. then?** et après? **and w. then?** et alors? alors quoi? *F:* **so w.?** et (puis) après? alors? **w. do we do, shall we do, now, next?** qu'est-ce que nous allons faire maintenant? *F:* **d'you think I'm mad or w.?** dis, tu me crois donc fou? **w. if we** ***are*** **poor?** qu'importe que nous soyons pauvres? **paper, pens, pencils, and w. not, and w. have you,** du papier, des stylos, des crayons et d'autres choses encore, et que sais-je encore; **theatres and dances and w. not, and w. have you,** le théâtre, les bals, et tout ce qui s'ensuit; **w. did you say?** vous disiez? pardon? **w. of that?** qu'est-ce que cela fait? eh bien, et puis après? la belle affaire! **to w. do I owe the pleasure of your visit?** qu'est-ce qui me vaut le plaisir de votre visite? *F:* **what's yours? gin or whisky?** qu'est-ce que tu prends? gin ou whisky? (*b*) (*indirect*) ce qui, ce que; **tell me what's happened,** dites-moi ce qui s'est passé; **I don't know w. you want,** je ne sais pas ce que vous désirez; **he didn't know w. to say,** il ne savait que dire; **I don't know w. to do,** je ne sais que faire, quel parti prendre; **I don't know w. to do to get rid of him,** je ne sais (pas) comment faire pour me débarrasser de lui; **there were books and I don't know w.,** il y avait des livres et que sais-je encore; **tell me w. you're crying for,** dites-moi pourquoi vous pleurez; **see w. courage can do!** ce que c'est que le courage! **do you know w. he was asking for it?** savez-vous combien il en demandait? **I'll tell you w.,** je vais vous dire; écoutez; *F:* **to know what's w.,** savoir son monde; savoir de quoi il retourne; avoir de la jugeotte; **he knows what's w.,** il en sait long; il la connaît (dans tous les coins); il s'y connaît; c'est un malin; il a le fil; **I'll show you what's w.!** on verra de quel bois je me chauffe! **he told me w. was w.,** il m'a mis au courant. **3.** (*exclamatory*) (*a*) **w. he has suffered!** ce qu'il a souffert! **w. next!** par exemple! (*b*) **w.! you can't come!** comment! vous ne pouvez pas venir! *F:* **w.! no eggs!** quoi! pas d'œufs! *O:* **nice girl, w.!** joli brin de fille, hein! **you know my wife, w.?** vous connaissez ma femme, n'est-ce pas?

what-d'ye-call-'em, -her, -him, -it [ˈ(h)wɔtjəkɔːləm, -ər, -im, -it], *s. F:* machin *m*, truc *m*; (*of pers.*) chose *mf*; **pass me the what-d'ye-call-'em,** passez-moi le machin; **Miss What-d'ye-call-her,** mademoiselle Chose; **old What-d'ye-call-him,** le père Machin.

whate'er [(h)wɔtˈɛər], *pron. Poet:* = WHATEVER.

whatever [(h)wɔtˈevər]. **1.** *pron.* (*a*) (*relative*) tout ce qui, tout ce que; **w. you like,** tout ce qui vous plaira; tout ce que vous voudrez; n'importe quoi; **w. is interesting,** n'importe quoi d'intéressant; ce qu'il y a d'intéressant; (*b*) (*introducing a dependent clause with sub. or indic.*) quoi qui, quoi que + *sub.*; **w. it is, may be,** quoi que ce soit; **w. happens, keep calm,** quoi qui survienne, restez calme; **w. you hear, say nothing,** quoi que vous entendiez, ne dites rien; **he shall have w. he wants,** quoi qu'il désire, il l'aura; **w. we may think of his wisdom there is no doubting his courage,** quoi que nous pensions de sa sagesse on ne saurait douter de son courage; **w. you say I shan't go, I'm not going,** vous avez beau dire, je n'irai pas; **w. she says, may say,** en dépit de ce qu'elle dit; (*c*) *F:* **pens, pencils, paper and w.,** des stylos, des crayons, du papier et tout ce qui s'ensuit, et tout ce que vous voulez; . . . **or w.,** (i) ou quelque chose de ce genre; (ii) ou tout ce que vous voulez, tout ce qui vous passe par la tête; ou n'importe quoi. **2.** *a.* (*a*) **w. price they are asking,** quel que soit le prix qu'on demande; **at w. time,** quelle que soit l'heure; à n'importe quelle heure; **w. mistakes I (may) have made,** quelles que soient les erreurs que j'ai faites; **w. sort it is, may be,** de quelque genre qu'il soit, que ce soit; de n'importe quel genre; (*b*) (*emphatic*) **under any pretext w.,** sous quelque prétexte que ce soit; **no hope w.,** pas le moindre espoir; **is there any hope w.?** y a-t-il un espoir quelconque? **if there is any hope w.,** s'il y a une lueur d'espoir; **no books w.,** pas un seul livre; **none w.,** pas un seul; **nothing w.,** absolument rien; **he won't say anything w., he just says nothing w.,** il refuse de dire quoi que ce soit; **I don't mean that I have any intention w. of resigning,** je ne veux pas dire que j'aie la moindre intention de démissionner.

whatho [(h)wɔtˈ(h)ou], *int. F:* (*a*) *O:* eh bien! et alors? (*b*) bonjour! salut!

whatnot [ˈ(h)wɔtnɔt], *s.* **1.** *Furn:* étagère *f.* **2.** *F:* machin *m*, truc *m*.

what's her, his, its, name, *s.* [ˈ(h)wɔtsə, -iz, -its, neim], *s. F:* = WHAT-D'YE-CALL-HER, *etc.*

whatsit, what's it [ˈ(h)wɔtsit], *s. F:* machin *m*, truc *m*.

whatsoever [(h)wɔtsouˈevər]. **1.** *pron. Lit:* **w. it may be,** quoi que ce soit. **2.** *a.* (*emphatic*) = WHATEVER **2** (*b*).

whaup [hwɔːp], *s. Orn: Scot:* courlieu *m*, courlis *m*.

wheal [(h)wiːl], *s. Med:* papule *f*; élevure rosée (de l'urticaire, etc.).

wheat [(h)wiːt], *s.* (*a*) blé *m*, froment *m*; **hard w.,** *U.S:* **durum w.,** blé dur; blé vitreux; **soft w.,** blé tendre, blé farineux; **bearded w.,** blé barbu; **winter w.,** blé d'hiver; **spring w.,** blé de mars; **grain of w.,** grain *m* de blé; **to plant, crop, land with w.,** mettre une terre en blé; **w. country, w.-growing land,** terre à blé; **the w. crop has yielded well,** le blé a bien donné; **to divide the w. from the chaff,** séparer le bon grain de l'ivraie; (*b*) **w. grass,** agropyre *m*; **(creeping) w. grass,** chiendent (officinal, des boutiques); (*c*) *Ann:* **w. worm,** anguillule *f*; anguillule *f* du blé.

wheatear[1] [ˈ(h)wiːtiər], *s.* épi *m* de blé.

wheatear[2], *s. Orn:* traquet(-)motteux; **black w.,** traquet rieur; traquet noir; **white-rumped black w.,** traquet à tête blanche; **black-eared w.,** traquet oreillard, traquet stapazin; **desert w.,** traquet du désert; **isabelline w.,** traquet isabelle; **pied w.,** traquet leucomèle.

wheaten [ˈ(h)wiːt(ə)n], *a.* (pain, etc.) de froment, de blé; **fine w. bread,** pain de gruau; **pure w. flour,** fleur *f* de farine.

wheatmeal [ˈ(h)wiːtmiːl], *s.* farine grossière, grosse farine, de froment, de blé; **w. loaf** = pain complet.

wheatsheaf [ˈ(h)wiːtʃiːf], *s.* gerbe *f* de blé; *Her:* gerbe.

wheatstalk [ˈ(h)wiːtstɔːk], *s.* tige *f* de blé.

Wheatstone [ˈ(h)wiːtstən], *Pr.n. El:* **W. bridge,** pont *m* de Wheatstone.

wheedle [ˈ(h)wiːdl], *v.tr.* enjôler, cajoler, câliner, amadouer, entortiller, embobiner, embobeliner (qn); **to w. s.o. into doing sth.,** amener qn à faire qch. en le cajolant, à force de cajoleries; **to w. money from, out of, s.o.,** soutirer de l'argent à qn; se faire donner de l'argent par qn.

wheedler [ˈ(h)wiːdlər], *s.* enjôleur, -euse; cajoleur, -euse; amadoueur, -euse; patelin, -ine; patelineur, -euse; **the little w.!** (la) petite câline!

wheedling[1] [ˈ(h)wiːdliŋ], *a.* (*of manner, etc.*) enjôleur, cajoleur, amadoueur, câlin; **w. voice,** voix pateline; **w. ways,** câlineries *f*, chatteries *f*.

wheedling[2], *s.* enjôlement *m*, cajolerie *f*, câlinerie *f*, amadouement *m*.

wheedlingly [ˈ(h)wiːdliŋli], *adv.* d'une manière enjôleuse, cajoleuse; d'un ton câlin.

wheel[1] [(h)wiːl], *s.* **1.** roue *f*; (*small*) roulette *f*; (*a*) *Veh: etc:* **wheels,** roues; (*of plough*) avant-train *m*; *Artil:* **truck wheels (of gun carriage),** roulettes (d'affût); *For:* **bar wheels,** fardier *m* (pour le transport des troncs d'arbres); **on wheels,** sur roues, sur roulettes; **to run on wheels,** marcher sur des roues, sur des roulettes; *F:* **meals on wheels,** repas livrés à domicile (aux personnes âgées, etc.); **back w., rear w.,** (i) *Aut: etc:* roue arrière; (ii) *Cy:* roue motrice; **front w.,** (i) *Aut: etc:* roue avant; (ii) *Cy:* roue directrice; **spare w.,** roue de secours; **dual wheels,** roues jumelées; **solid w., spokeless w.,** roue pleine; **spoked w.,** roue à rayons, à raies; **wire w.,** roue à fils, à rayons, métalliques; roue à fils d'acier; **w. disc,** enjoliveur *m*; **w. alignment,** (i) parallélisme *m* des roues; (ii) réglage *m* du train avant; **four-w. independent suspension,** suspension *f* à quatre roues indépendantes; **to put one's shoulder to the w.,** pousser à la roue; se mettre à l'œuvre; **the fifth w.,** la cinquième roue du carrosse; personne inutile, superflue, qui regarde travailler les autres; *Rail:* **coupled wheels,** roues couplées (de locomotive); **carrying w.,** roue porteuse; **leading w.,** roue (porteuse) avant; **trailing w.,** roue (porteuse) arrière; **flange w.,** roue à boudin, à bourrelet; *Av:* **landing wheels,** roues (du train) d'atterrissage; **nose w.,** roue (d'atterrisseur) avant; **tail w.,** roue, roulette, de queue, de béquille; **retractable wheels,** roues escamotables; train escamotable, rentrant; **wheels up, down,** roues rentrées, sorties; train rentré, sorti; (*b*) *Hyd.E:* **hydraulic w.,** roue hydraulique; **bucket w.,** roue (hydraulique) à augets, à godets; **(water) raising w.,** roue élévatoire; **reaction (water) w.,** roue à réaction, à tuyaux; (*c*) *Mec.E:* roue (de transmission, d'engrenage, de turbine, etc.); **adhesion w.,** roue à adhérence; **blower w.,** roue soufflante; **cam w.,** roue à cames; **driven w.,** roue menée; **driving w.,** roue menante; **eccentric w.,** roue excentrique; **fast w., fixed w.,** roue calée, roue fixe; **friction w.,** roue à friction; **grooved w.,** roue à gorge; **loose w.,** roue folle, roue indépendante; **master w.,** roue maîtresse; **split w.,** roue, poulie *f*, démontable; **sprocket w.,** roue dentée, roue à cames; **straight-tooth w.,** roue à dents droites, à denture droite; **toothed w., cog w., rack w.,** roue dentée, roue à dents, roue d'engrenage; **worm w.,** roue (d'engrenage) à vis; roue dentée de vis sans fin; **(rail) w.,** galet *m* (à boudin, à joue); **travelling, running, w.,** galet de roulement (de pont roulant, etc.); **idle(r) w.,** galet de guidage, galet guide; **bogie w.,** galet de roulement (de chenille); **the wheels (of a mechanism, of a watch),** les rouages *m* (d'un mécanisme, d'une montre); (*to child*) **come and watch the wheels go round,** viens regarder comment ma montre marche; **the wheels of government,** les rouages de l'administration; **there are wheels within wheels,** c'est une affaire très compliquée, dont il faut connaître les dessous; il y a toutes sortes de forces en jeu; c'est plus compliqué que cela n'en a l'air; (*d*) **(hand) w.,** volant *m* (de manœuvre, de commande); *Mch: Mec.E:* **balance w.,** volant régulateur; **brake w.,** volant de frein (à main); **capstan w., pilot w.,** volant à poignée radiale; **control w.,** volant de commande; **w. control,** commande *f* par volant; *Mch.Tls:* **feed w.,** volant d'avance; **operating w.,** volant de manœuvre; **reversing w.,** volant de changement de marche; *Artil: etc:* **adjusting w.,** volant de réglage; **training w.,** volant de pointage; **elevating w.,** volant de pointage en hauteur; **traversing w.,** volant de pointage en direction; **(steering) w.,** (i) *Aut:* volant (de direction); (ii) *Nau:* roue du gouvernail; la barre; *Av:* **control w.,** volant (de commande); **to be at the w.,** (i) *Aut:* être au volant; (ii) *Nau:* tenir la barre, le gouvernail; (iii) *Fig:* tenir la barre, être à la tête de l'entreprise, des affaires; *Aut:* **to be killed at the w.,** être tué au volant; **the man at the w.,** (i) *Aut:* le conducteur; l'homme au volant; (ii) *Nau:* l'homme de barre, le timonier; (iii) *Fig:* l'homme à la tête des affaires, *F:* le grand patron; **don't speak to the man at the w.,** défense de parler, ne parlez pas, au conducteur, au pilote; (*e*) **(grinding) w., abrasive w.,** meule *f*; **cup w.,** meule assiette, en cuvette; **carborundum w.,** meule au carborundum; **diamond w.,** meule diamantée; **roughing w.,** meule à dégrossir; **sharpening w.,** meule à aiguiser, à affûter; **trimming w.,** meule à ébarber; **tru(e)ing w.,** meule à rectifier; (*e*) **potter's w.,** tour *m* de potier; **(spinning) w.,** rouet *m*; (*f*) **cutting w.,** molette *f* (à couper le verre, etc.); **(flint) w.,** molette (d'un briquet); **pastry w.,** roulette (à couper la pâte); *Needlew: etc:* **tracing w., pricking w.,** roulette (à piquer, à pointiller); *Surv:* **measuring w.,** rouet d'arpenteur; (*g*) (i) *F: O:* bicyclette *f*, vélo *m*; (ii) *F:* **my wheels,** ma bagnole; (*h*) *Hist:* **to condemn a criminal to the w.,** condamner un criminel à la roue; **to break s.o. on the w.,** rouer qn; *Fig:* **it's like breaking a butterfly on the w.,** c'est un pavé pour écraser une mouche; (*i*) **w. of life,** (i) *Toys:* zootrope *m*; (ii) *Rel:* (*Buddhism*) la ronde de la transmigration; **big w.,** (i) (*at fair*) grande roue; (ii) *NAm: F:* personnage important, gros bonnet, grosse légume; **the w. of fortune,** la roue de la fortune. **2.** (*a*) révolution *f*; mouvement *m* de rotation; (*b*) *Mil: etc:* (mouvement de) conversion *f*; **left w., right w.,** conversion à gauche, à droite; **w. through 90°,** quart *m* de conversion.

wheel². **1.** *v.tr.* (*a*) tourner; faire pivoter; **to w. one's chair round,** faire pivoter sa chaise; *Mil:* **to w. a line of men,** faire faire une conversion à une ligne d'hommes; *Rugby Fb:* **to w. the scrum,** tourner la mêlée; (*b*) rouler (une brouette, etc.); pousser, conduire (une bicyclette) à la main; **to w. sth. in a barrow,** transporter qch. en brouette; brouetter qch.; **to w. (a child in) a pram,** promener un enfant dans sa voiture; *Mil:* **to w. a gun into line,** amener une pièce en ligne; (*c*) *Needlew: Leath:* marquer (le cuir, etc.) avec une roulette, avec une molette. **2.** *v.i.* (*a*) tourner en rond, en cercle; tournoyer; **the gulls were wheeling round the headland,** les mouettes tournoyaient autour du cap; (*b*) *Mil:* (i) opérer, effectuer, une conversion; **to w. about,** faire la roue; (ii) **left w.!** par file à gauche, gauche! **right w.!** par file à droite, droite! (iii) **w. him in!** qu'il entre! (*c*) (*of pers.*) **to w. about, round,** faire demi-tour; se retourner (brusquement); faire volte-face; (*of horse, etc.*) pirouetter; (*d*) *NAm: F:* aller à bicyclette, à bécane; (*e*) *F:* **to w. and deal,** brasser des affaires (plus ou moins louches).

wheelbarrow ['(h)wi:lbærou], *s.* brouette *f.*

wheelbase ['(h)wi:lbeis], *s. Veh: Rail:* empattement *m*; distance *f* entre les deux essieux.

wheelchair ['(h)wi:ltʃɛər], *s.* fauteuil roulant; voiture *f* de malade.

wheeled [(h)wi:ld], *a.* **1.** roulant; à roues; muni de roues; sur roues. **2.** (*with adj. prefixed*) **two-w., three-w.,** à deux, à trois, roues.

wheeler ['(h)wi:lər], *s.* **1.** (*pers.*) (*a*) *A:* = WHEELWRIGHT; (*b*) *Min: etc:* rouleur *m*, brouetteur *m*; (*c*) *F:* (i) *A:* cycliste *mf*; (ii) *esp. U.S:* moto *f* à side-car; (*d*) *F:* **w. dealer,** brasseur *m* d'affaires (plus ou moins louches). **2.** cheval *m* de derrière; timonier *m*; **the wheelers,** l'attelage *m* (de derrière); **off w.,** sous-verge *m inv* de derrière; **near w.,** porteur *m* de derrière. **3.** *Veh:* (*with num. a. prefixed*) **two-w., three-w.,** voiture *f* à deux, à trois, roues. **4.** *Av: F:* atterrissage *f* à deux roues.

wheelhorse ['(h)wi:lhɔ:s], *s.* = WHEELER 2.

wheelhouse ['(h)wi:lhaus], *s. Nau:* abri *m* de navigation; kiosque *m*, chambre *f*, de barre; la timonerie.

wheeling¹ ['(h)wi:liŋ], *a.* tournoyant; *Mil:* (ligne d'hommes) qui fait une conversion; **w. gulls,** mouettes tournoyantes, qui tournoient.

wheeling², *s.* **1.** tournoiement *m* (des oiseaux, etc.). **2.** *Mil:* conversion *f.* **3.** *U.S: F: A:* promenades *fpl* à bicyclette, à bécane. **4.** *F:* **w. and dealing,** brassage *m* d'affaires (plus ou moins louches).

wheelless ['(h)wi:llis], *a.* sans roues.

wheelman, *pl.* **-men** ['(h)wi:lmən], *s.m. U.S: F:* (*a*) *Nau:* timonier; (*b*) *Aut:* conducteur; (*c*) cycliste.

wheelspin ['(h)wi:lspin], *s. Aut: etc:* patinage *m* de la roue, des roues.

wheelwork ['(h)wi:lwə:k], *s. Mec.E:* rouage(s) *m(pl).*

wheelwright ['(h)wi:lrait], *s.* charron *m*; **wheelwright's work,** charronnage *m.*

wheeze¹ [(h)wi:z], *s.* **1.** respiration bruyante, pénible, asthmatique, sifflante. **2.** *F:* (*a*) *esp. Th:* (vieille) plaisanterie; (*b*) ruse *f*, truc *m*; **a good w.,** une bonne astuce.

wheeze². **1.** *v.i.* (*a*) respirer péniblement, en asthmatique; faire entendre un sifflement en respirant; (*b*) (*of horse*) corner. **2.** *v.tr.* **to w. out sth.,** dire qch. d'une voix rauque, asthmatique; **a barrel organ was wheezing out a tune,** un orgue de Barbarie asthmatique serinait un air.

wheezer ['(h)wi:zər], *s.* cheval cornard, corneur, poussif.

wheezily ['(h)wi:zili], *adv.* (respirer) avec peine, en asthmatique; (dire qch.) d'une voix rauque, asthmatique.

wheezing¹ ['(h)wi:ziŋ], *s.* = WHEEZY.

wheezing², *s.* (*a*) respiration *f* asthmatique; sifflement gras (d'asthmatique); (*b*) (*of horse*) cornage *m.*

wheezy ['(h)wi:zi], *a.* (*a*) (*of pers.*) asthmatique; *F:* poussif; (*b*) (*of horse*) cornard; poussif; gros d'haleine; (*c*) **a w. old barrel organ,** un vieil orgue de Barbarie asthmatique.

whelk¹ [(h)welk], *s. Moll:* buccin *m*; **dog w.,** pourpre *m*; **netted dog w.,** nasse *f.*

whelk², *s. Med: A:* papule *f.*

whelm [(h)welm], *v.tr. A: & Lit:* (*a*) engouffrer, engloutir, ensevelir (qch.); (*b*) écraser, accabler (qn).

whelp¹ [(h)welp], *s.* **1.** (*a*) jeune chien *m*, chiot *m*; (*b*) petit *m* (d'un fauve); **lion's w.,** lionceau *m*; **wolf's w.,** louveteau *m*; (*c*) *F:* mauvais garnement; drôle *m*; (*d*) *F:* petit morveux. **2.** *Nau:* flasque *m*, taquet *m* (de guindeau, de cabestan).

whelp², *v.i. & tr.* (*of bear, lion, etc., P: Pej: of pers.*) mettre bas (des petits).

when [(h)wen], *adv., conj., pron. & s.*

I. *adv.* **1.** (*interr.*) quand? **w. will you come?** quand viendrez-vous? **I wonder w. he will come,** je me demande quand il viendra; **w. will the wedding be?** à quand le mariage? **w. is the meeting?** pour quand est la réunion? **w.** *ever*, **w. on earth, will be come?** quand donc, quand diable, viendra-t-il? *F:* (*when pouring drinks*) **say w.!** arrêtez-moi! comme ça? **2. the day w. I first met her,** le jour où je l'ai rencontrée pour la première fois; **one day w. I was on duty,** un jour que j'étais de service; **at the very time w. . . .,** au moment même où . . .; alors même que . . .; **I was waiting for the moment w. he would be free,** je guettais le moment où il serait libre; **now is w. I need him most,** c'est maintenant que j'ai le plus besoin de lui.

II. *conj.* **1.** quand, lorsque; **w. I came into the room I saw it,** lorsque je suis entré dans la pièce je l'ai vu; **it was only a couple of seconds later w. I heard a shot,** ce n'était que deux secondes plus tard que j'ai entendu un coup de feu; **w. I was young I lived in Paris,** quand, au temps que, j'étais jeune j'habitais à Paris; **w. he was married he left London,** lors de son mariage il a quitté Londres; **we'll try again w. you have rested,** on essaiera de nouveau quand, lorsque, vous vous serez reposé; **he will speak when I have finished,** il parlera après que j'aurai fini; (*exclamatory*) **w. you have** *quite* **finished!** quand vous aurez fini! **w. I think of what he must have suffered!** quand je pense à ce qu'il a dû souffrir! (*elliptical*) **w. writing I get very tired,** en écrivant je me fatigue beaucoup; *Cu:* **w. cool, turn out on to a dish,** après refroidissement, démouler sur un plat. **2. the prince will arrive on the 10th., w. he will open the new university,** le prince arrivera le dix et inaugurera la nouvelle université; **he was a major until 1970, w. he left the army,** il était commandant jusqu'en 1970, année où il a quitté l'armée. **3. he walked there w. he could have taken the car,** il y est allé à pied, alors qu'il aurait pu faire le trajet en voiture; **what's the good of telling you w. you won't listen to me?** à quoi bon vous le dire du moment que vous ne voulez pas m'écouter?

III. *pron.* **1.** (*interr.*) **until w. can you stay?** jusqu'à quand pouvez-vous rester? **since w. have you been living in Paris?** depuis quand habitez-vous Paris? **since w. have children of your age been allowed to do that?** depuis quand des enfants de ton âge ont-ils le droit de faire ça? **2.** (*rel.*) **since w. I have always bought a car of that make,** depuis quand j'achète toujours cette marque de voiture; **until w. I shall stay here,** jusqu'à quand je resterai ici.

IV. *s.* **the w. and the how of it,** le pourquoi et le comment de l'affaire; quand et comment cela est arrivé.

whence [(h)wens], *adv. A: & Lit:* **1.** (*now* **from where** *or* **where . . . from**) d'où; **w. came they?** d'où sont-ils venus? **no one knows w. he comes,** personne ne sait d'où il vient; **the source w. these evils spring,** la source d'où découlent ces maux. **2.** (*now* **from which**) **w. I conclude that . . .,** d'où je conclus que . . .; de là je conclus que . . ..

whencesoever, *Poet:* **whencesoe'er** [(h)wenssou'evər, -'ɛər], *adv. A: & Lit:* (i) d'où, de quelque endroit que ce soit; (ii) quelle qu'en soit la source; **w. these evils spring,** d'où que découlent ces maux.

whenever, *Poet:* **whene'er** [(h)wen'evər, -'ɛər], *conj. & adv.* (*a*) toutes les fois, chaque fois, que; **w. I see it I think of you,** chaque fois que je le vois je pense à vous; **I go w. I can,** j'y vais aussi souvent que possible, chaque fois que je suis libre; (*b*) à n'importe quel moment (que); **come w. you like,** venez quand vous voudrez, à n'importe quel moment; *F:* **. . . or w.,** . . . ou n'importe quand; . . . ou à peu près à ce moment-là; **Sunday, Monday, or w.,** dimanche, lundi, ou n'importe quel jour; *s.a.* WHEN I, 1.

whensoever, whensoe'er [(h)wensou'evər, -'ɛər], *conj. & adv. A: & Lit:* = WHENEVER.

where [(h)weər], *adv., conj., pron. & s.*

I. *interr. adv.* (*a*) **w. am I?** où suis-je? **tell me w. he is,** dites-moi où il est; **w. on earth, w. ever, were you?** où diable étiez-vous (donc)? **I wonder w. it is,** je me demande où cela peut bien se trouver; **w. did you put it?** où l'avez-vous mis? (*in work*) **w. have you reached? w. are you?** où en êtes-vous? **w. should I be if I had followed your advice?** qu'est-ce que je serais devenu si j'avais suivi vos conseils? (*b*) par où; **w. is the exit?** par où sort-on? **I have no idea w. to begin,** je n'ai aucune idée où commencer; (*c*) **w. is the use, the good, of it?** à quoi bon (faire) cela? **w. can be the harm in doing it?** qu'y a-t-il de mal à faire cela?

II. *rel. conj. & adv.* (*a*) (là) où; **I'll stay w. I am,** je resterai (là) où je suis; **you'll find it w. I left it,** vous le trouverez là où je l'ai laissé; **go w. you like,** allez où vous voudrez; (*b*) **that's w. we've got to,** voilà où nous

en sommes; **that is w. you are mistaken,** voilà, c'est là, que vous vous trompez; **I'll show you w. you went wrong,** je vous montrerai où vous vous êtes trompé; (*c*) **he came to (the place) w. I was fishing,** il est venu à l'endroit où je pêchais; **I can see it from w. we are,** je le vois d'où nous sommes; **I'll take you to w. we can get a better view,** je vais vous mener à un endroit où nous aurons une meilleure vue; **that's w. they found the body,** c'est là où l'on, qu'on, a trouvé le cadavre; **delete w. inapplicable,** rayer les mentions inutiles; (*d*) où, dans lequel; **the house w. I was born,** la maison où, dans laquelle, je suis né; ma maison natale; **countries w. it never snows,** les pays où il ne neige jamais; **they went to Paris w. they stayed a week,** ils sont allés à Paris et y sont restés huit jours.
III. *pron.* **w. are you going to?** où allez-vous? **w. does he come from?** (i) d'où vient-il? (ii) de quel pays est-il? IV. *s.* **the w. and the when,** le lieu et la date; le lieu et l'heure; **I don't grasp the w. and the how of it,** je ne comprends ni où ni comment cela est arrivé.

whereabouts ['(h)wɛərəbauts]. **1.** *adv. & conj.* où; de quel côté; **w. are you?** où donc êtes-vous? **do you know w. the town hall is?** savez-vous de quel côté se trouve l'hôtel de ville? **he's in Canada, but I don't know exactly w.,** il est au Canada, mais je ne sais pas au juste dans quel endroit. **2.** *s.* lieu *m* où se trouve qn, qch.; **nobody knows his w.,** personne ne sait où il est, où il habite.

whereafter [(h)wɛə'rɑːftər], *rel. adv. A: & Lit:* après quoi; à la suite de quoi.

whereas [(h)wɛə'ræz], *conj.* **1.** *Jur: etc:* (*introducing preamble*) attendu que, vu que, puisque, considérant que + *ind.* **2.** alors que, tandis que + *ind.*; **I like living in the country w. Louise prefers the town,** moi, j'aime habiter à la campagne tandis que Louise préfère la ville.

whereat [(h)wɛə'ræt], *adv. & conj. A: & Lit:* à quoi, sur quoi, de quoi, etc.; **w. he replied that . . .,** à quoi il répondit que . . ..

whereby [(h)wɛə'bai], *adv.* **1.** *A: & Lit:* (*interr.*) par quoi? par quel moyen? **2.** *Lit: Jur: etc:* (*rel.*) par lequel, au moyen duquel; **decision w. . . .,** décision par laquelle . . ..

wherefore ['(h)wɛəfɔːr]. **1.** *adv. A: & Lit:* (*a*) (*interr.*) pourquoi? pour quelle raison? *B:* **w. didst thou doubt?** pourquoi as-tu douté? (*b*) (*rel.*) donc; pour cette raison. **2.** *s.* **the whys and the wherefores,** les pourquoi et les comment.

wherein [(h)wɛə'rin], *adv. & conj. A: & Lit:* **1.** (*interr.*) en quoi? **w. have we offended you?** en quoi vous avons-nous offensé? **2.** (*rel.*) dans lequel; (là) où; **w. the difficulty lies,** là où se trouve la difficulté.

whereof [(h)wɛə'rɔv], *adv. & conj. A: & Lit:* **1.** (*interr.*) en quoi? de quoi? **2.** (*rel.*) (*a*) de quoi, dont; (*b*) duquel, dont.

whereon [(h)wɛə'rɔn], *adv. & conj. Lit:* **1.** *A:* (*interr.*) sur quoi? **2.** (*rel.*) (*a*) *A:* sur quoi, sur lequel; **the day w. . . .,** le jour où . . ., que . . .; (*b*) sur quoi; après quoi; là-dessus; sur ce(la); **w. he left us,** sur quoi il nous quitta.

wheresoever, *Poet:* **wheresoe'er** [(h)wɛəsou'evər, -'ɛər], *adv. & conj. esp. Lit:* = WHEREVER.

whereupon [(h)wɛərə'pɔn], *adv. & conj. Lit:* **1.** (*interr.*) *A:* sur quoi? **2.** (*rel.*) (*a*) *A:* sur quoi, sur lequel; (*b*) sur quoi; après quoi; là-dessus; sur ce(la); **w. he left us,** sur quoi il nous quitta.

wherever [(h)wɛə'revər], *conj. & adv.* **1.** partout où; n'importe où; **I shall remember it w. I go,** où que j'aille, je m'en souviendrai; j'en porterai partout le souvenir; **w. I go I see them,** partout où je vais je les vois; **I'll go w. you want (me to),** j'irai où vous voudrez (que j'aille); **w. I see them,** n'importe où je les rencontre; **w. possible,** n'importe où où il y a de la place; partout où cela est possible; *F:* **at home, in the office, or w.,** chez moi, au bureau ou n'importe où. **2. w. they come from,** d'où qu'ils viennent; **he comes from Glossop, w. that may be,** il est originaire d'un endroit, il habite un endroit, qui s'appellerait Glossop; *s.a.* WHERE I, (*a*).

wherewith [(h)wɛə'wið], *adv. & conj. A: & Lit:* **1.** (*interr.*) avec quoi? *B:* **if the salt have lost his savour, w. shall it be salted?** si le sel perd sa saveur, avec quoi va-t-on le saler? **2.** (*rel.*) (*a*) avec lequel; avec quoi; par lequel; au moyen duquel; (*b*) = WHEREUPON 2 (*b*).

wherewithal ['(h)wɛərwiðɔːl], *s. F:* **the w.,** l'argent *m*, les fonds *m*, le nécessaire, les moyens *m*; **I haven't the w. to buy it,** je n'ai pas de quoi l'acheter; je n'ai pas les moyens de l'acheter.

wherry ['(h)weri], *s.* **1.** esquif *m*. **2.** bachot *m* (de rivière).

wherryman, *pl.* **-men** ['(h)werimən], *s.m.* bachoteur.

whet[1] [(h)wet], *s.* **1.** = WHETTING. **2.** stimulant *m*, aiguillon *m*, excitement *m*; **w. to the appetite,** stimulant de l'appétit.

whet[2], *v.tr.* (**whetted**) **1.** aiguiser, affûter, affiler, repasser (un outil, un couteau, etc.). **2.** stimuler, aiguiser, exciter, aiguillonner (l'appétit, les désirs, etc.).

whether ['(h)weðər], *conj.* **1.** (*indirect question*) si; **I don't know w. it's true,** je ne sais pas si c'est vrai; **it's doubtful, uncertain, w. . . .,** il est douteux, peu certain, si . . ., **the question arose w. . . .,** la question a été soulevée de savoir si . . .; **I want to know w. . . . or w. . . .,** je voudrais savoir si . . . ou si . . .; **I don't know w. it's true or not,** je ne sais pas si c'est vrai ou non; **it depends on w. you're in a hurry or not,** cela dépend (de) si vous êtes pressé ou non; **it's all one, the same, to me w. you agree or w. you don't,** que vous soyez d'accord ou non, cela ne m'intéresse pas; **the question was w. or not to take David with him,** la question était de savoir si, oui ou non, il devait emmener David. **2.** (*conditional*) **w. it rains or (w. it) snows, he always goes out,** soit qu'il pleuve, soit qu'il neige, il sort toujours; pluie ou neige, il sort toujours; **w. he comes or not, or no, we shall leave,** qu'il vienne ou non, qu'il vienne ou qu'il ne vienne pas, nous allons partir; **w. or not . . .,** qu'il en soit ainsi ou non . . .; **w. expensive or not, this is a luxury,** que ce soit cher ou bon marché, cela est un luxe.

whetstone ['(h)wetstoun], *s.* pierre *f* à aiguiser, à repasser; aiguisoir *m*, affiloir *m*, affiloire *f*.

whetting ['(h)wetiŋ], *s.* **1.** affûtage *m*, affilage *m*, aiguisage *m*, repassage *m* (d'un outil, etc.); **to give sth. a w.,** affûter, affiler, aiguiser, repasser (un outil, etc.). **2.** stimulation *f*, excitation *f*, aiguillonnement *m* (des sens, de l'appétit).

whew [hjuː], *int.* **1.** (*of relief, fatigue*) ouf! **2.** (*astonishment*) mon Dieu!

whewellite ['hjuːəlait], *s. Miner:* whewellite *f*.

whey [(h)wei], *s.* petit lait; lait clair; lactosérum *m*; **w.-faced,** à figure de papier mâché.

which [(h)witʃ], *a. & pron.*
I. *a.* **1.** (*interr.*) quel, *f.* quelle; *pl.* quels, *f.* quelles? **w. colour do you like best?** quelle couleur aimez-vous le mieux? **w. way do we go?** par où allons-nous? **w. way is the wind blowing?** d'où vient le vent? **I don't know w. side to back,** je ne sais pas de quel côté parier; **w. one?** lequel? laquelle? **w. ones?** lesquels? lesquelles? **I know w. one you want,** je sais celui que vous désirez; **I'm going with the girls—w. girls?** j'y vais avec les filles—lesquelles? **w. twin did he marry?** laquelle des jumelles a-t-il épousée? **2.** (*rel.*) lequel, *f.* laquelle; *pl.* lesquels, *f.* lesquelles; **he was told to apply to a police station, w. advice he followed,** on lui a dit de s'adresser à un commissariat, conseil qu'il a suivi; **he stayed here two weeks during w. time he never left the house,** il est resté ici deux semaines, pendant lesquelles, au cours desquelles, il n'a pas quitté la maison; **he came at noon, at w. time I'm usually in the garden,** il est venu à midi, heure à laquelle je suis ordinairement au jardin; **look w. way you will,** de quelque côté que vous regardiez.
II. *pron.* **1.** (*interr.*) lequel, *f.* laquelle; *pl.* lesquels, *f.* lesquelles? **w. have you chosen?** lequel, laquelle, avez-vous choisi(e)? **w. of you can answer?** lequel d'entre vous peut, lesquels d'entre vous peuvent, répondre? **w. of you (girls) did that?** laquelle d'entre vous a fait cela? **w. of the two (girls) is the prettier?** laquelle des deux est la plus jolie? **he told me w. of the paintings were valuable,** il m'a dit lesquelles des peintures étaient de valeur; **w. would you rather have?** lequel préférez-vous? **of w. is he speaking? w. is he speaking of, about?** duquel parle-t-il? **w. will you take, milk or cream?** que prendrez-vous, du lait ou de la crème? **tell me w. is w.,** dites-moi comment les distinguer; dites-moi lequel est le bon, le vrai; **they're so alike I can never tell w. is which,** ils se ressemblent tellement que je ne sais jamais les distinguer; **I don't know w. to choose,** je ne sais (pas) lequel choisir; **do say w. you will have!** choisissez donc! **I don't mind w.,** n'importe (lequel); cela m'est égal; **w. is the best shop for fish?** quelle est la meilleure poissonnerie? **2.** (*rel.*) (*a*) qui; que; lequel; **the house w. is for sale,** la maison qui est à vendre; **the book w. I bought yesterday,** le livre que j'ai acheté hier; **the one w. you like best,** celui que vous préférez; **the penalty w. he has escaped,** la peine à laquelle il est échappé; *B:* **Our Father w. art in Heaven,** Notre Père qui es aux cieux; (*b*) ce qui, ce que; **he looked like a retired colonel, which in fact he was,** il avait l'air d'un colonel en retraite, ce qu'il était en effet; **he detailed a great many incidents, which were all perfectly true,** il énuméra de nombreux incidents qui étaient tous exacts, dont chacun était exact; **if this happens, w. God forbid,** si cela arrive, ce qu'à Dieu ne plaise; **he told me to shut the door, w. I had already done,** il m'a dit de fermer la porte, ce que j'avais déjà fait; **when overworked, w. he often was,** lorsqu'il était surmené, comme il l'était souvent, ce qui lui arrivait souvent; **he was back in London, w. I didn't know,** il était de retour à Londres, fait que j'ignorais. **3.** (*a*) **to w., at w.,** auquel, *f.* à laquelle; *pl.* auxquels, *f.* auxquelles; **of w., from w.,** duquel, *f.* de laquelle; *pl.* desquels, *f.* desquelles; dont; **the house of w. I am speaking,** la maison dont je parle; **the drawer of w. I have lost the key,** le tiroir dont j'ai perdu la clef; **the countries to w. we are going, w. we're going to,** les pays où nous irons; **the hotels at w. we stayed,** les hôtels où nous sommes descendus; **the pen w. I'm writing with,** la plume avec laquelle j'écris; **the town in w. we live,** la ville où nous demeurons, que nous habitons; **in the times in w. we live,** par le temps qui court, les temps qui courent; **we want a house with a room in w. we can dance,** il nous faut une maison avec une salle où l'on puisse danser; (*b*) **he insists that actors should have talent, in w. he is right,** il exige que les acteurs aient du talent, (ce) en quoi il a raison; **there are no trains on Sunday, w. I hadn't thought of,** il n'y a pas de trains le dimanche, ce à quoi je n'avais pas pensé; **after w. he went out,** après quoi il est sorti; **he gave me some books, all of w. are new,** il m'a donné des livres qui sont tous nouveaux.

whichever [(h)witʃ'evər], *pron. & a.* **1.** *pron.* (*a*) celui qui; celui que; n'importe lequel, laquelle; **take w. you like best,** prenez celui que vous préférez; prenez n'importe lequel; **w. of you comes in first had better switch on the fire,** celui (d'entre vous) qui arrive le premier doit allumer le radiateur; (*b*) n'importe lequel; **w. you choose, you will have a good bargain,** n'importe lequel vous choisirez, vous aurez fait une bonne affaire. **2.** *a.* (*a*) le . . . que; n'importe quel; **take w. book you prefer,** prenez le livre que vous préférez, n'importe quel livre; (*b*) n'importe quel; quelque . . . que; **w. way he turned he saw nothing but sand,** de quelque côté qu'il se soit tourné, de n'importe quel côté il se tournait, il ne voyait (rien) que du sable; **the foreign policy remains the same w. party is in power,** la politique étrangère reste la même, quel que soit le parti politique au pouvoir, quelque parti politique qui détienne le pouvoir.

whichsoever [(h)witʃsou'evər], *pron. & a. A:* = WHICHEVER.

whidah ['(h)widə], *s. Orn:* = WHYDAH.

whiff[1] [(h)wif], *s. Ich:* cardine *f*; mère *f* des soles.

whiff[2], *s.* **1.** (*a*) bouffée *f* (de vent, de fumée, d'air, etc.); odeur *f* (de vin, etc.); **there wasn't a w. of wind,** il n'y avait pas un souffle de vent; **to go out for a w. of fresh air,** sortir pour respirer un peu, pour prendre l'air; **to get a w. from the sewers,** attraper un relent des égouts; (*b*) *F:* **what a w.!** que ça pue! (*c*) **w. of grapeshot,** décharge *f* de mitraille. **2.** petit cigare; ninas *m inv*; cigarillo *m*. **3.** *Row:* skiff *m*.

whiff[3]. **1.** *v.i.* (*a*) émettre des bouffées; (*b*) souffler par bouffées; (*c*) *F:* puer; **it whiffs of garlic,** ça pue l'ail; **his feet w.,** il sent des pieds. **2.** *v.tr.* (*a*) **to w. smoke,** émettre des bouffées de fumée; (*b*) *F:* **I can w. rosemary and garlic in it,** j'y sens le romarin et l'ail.

whiffet ['(h)wifit], *s. U.S:* personne nulle; zéro *m*.

whiffle[1] ['(h)wifl], *s.* souffle *m*, bouffée *f*.

whiffle[2], *v.tr. & i.* souffler légèrement, par bouffées.

whiffy ['(h)wifi], *a. F:* puant, qui pue.

Whig [(h)wig], *s. Pol. Hist:* whig *m*; libéral *m*, -aux (de vieille roche); *attrib.* (historien, etc.) partisan des whigs, du parti whig.

whiggamore ['(h)wigəmɔːr], *s. Hist:* insurgé écossais (de 1648).

whiggery ['(h)wigəri], *s. Pol. Hist: Pej:* = WHIGGISM.

whiggish ['(h)wigiʃ], *a. Pol. Hist: Pej:* des whigs.

whiggism ['(h)wigizm], *s. Pol. Hist:* whiggisme *m*, libéralisme *m*.

while[1] [(h)wail], *s.* **1.** (*a*) (espace *m* de) temps *m*; **after a w.,** au bout de quelque temps; quelque temps après; **after a little w., a little w. later,** peu de temps après; bientôt après; **for a (short) w.,** pendant quelque temps, quelques instants; pendant un moment; **in the shortest w. possible,** aussitôt que possible; **in a short, little, w.,** bientôt; dans un instant; sous peu; avant peu; **a short, little, w. ago,** il n'y a pas bien longtemps; il y a peu de temps; **a long w.,** longtemps; **a long w. ago,** il y a longtemps; **I've been here (for) a long w.,** je suis ici depuis longtemps; **not for a long w.,** (i) (*future*) pas avant longtemps; (ii) (*past*) pas depuis longtemps; **a good w.,** pas mal de temps; **it's a good w. since she died,** il y a beau jour, pas mal de temps, longtemps, qu'elle est morte; **I haven't seen him for a good w.,** il y a longtemps que je ne l'ai vu; **it will be a good w. before you see him again,** vous ne le reverrez pas de si tôt; **that will do for a w., just for the w.,** cela suffira pour le moment; **I shall be away for some w.,** je vais m'absenter pour, pendant, un certain temps; **it will take me quite a w.,** cela me prendra un certain temps, pas mal de temps; **stay a little w. longer,** restez encore un peu; **what a long w. you are!** quel temps vous y mettez! vous en mettez du temps! **all the w.,** tout le temps; **once in a w.,** de temps en temps; de temps à autre; (*b*) *adv.phr. A:* **the w.,** en attendant; pendant ce temps; **take a book to read the w.,** prenez un livre à lire en attendant. **2. to be worth (one's) w.,** valoir la peine; *F:* valoir le coup; **it's not worth our w. waiting,** nous ne gagnerons rien à attendre; cela ne vaut pas la peine, ce n'est pas la peine, d'attendre; **it's not, you won't find it, worth your w. to do it,** cela ne vaut pas la peine que vous le fassiez; **you'll find it worth your w. visiting the castle,** vous trouverez que c'est un château qui vaut la visite; **it wasn't worth your w. going (there), it wasn't worth w. your going,** vous auriez aussi bien fait de ne pas y aller; **it is perhaps worth w. pointing out that . . .,** il vaut peut-être la peine de faire remarquer que . . .; **I'll make it worth your w.,** je vous récompenserai, rémunérerai, de votre dérangement; vous serez bien payé de votre peine.

while², *v.tr.* **to w. away,** faire passer, tromper (le temps); tuer (une heure, le temps); **I played patience to w. away the time,** j'ai fait des réussites pour me désennuyer.

while³, *A:* **whiles** [(h)wailz], *conj.* **1.** (*a*) (*during the time that*) pendant que, tandis que; *A: & Lit:* cependant que; **w. (he was) here,** pendant qu'il était ici; **let's be happy w. we are young,** soyons heureux pendant que nous sommes jeunes; **w. in Paris he attended a few classes,** pendant son séjour à Paris il a suivi quelques cours; **he died w. eating his dinner,** il est mort en dînant; **your meals w. travelling will be paid for,** on vous paiera les repas pris en cours de route; **w. reading I fell asleep,** tout en lisant, je me suis endormi; **w. this was going on,** sur ces entrefaites; **she reads the paper before breakfast and he reads it w. he is having his,** elle lit le journal avant le petit déjeuner et lui, il le lit en le mangeant; (*b*) (*as long as*) tant que; **w. I live there's nothing you shan't have,** tant que je vivrai vous ne manquerez de rien; **w. there's life there's hope,** tant qu'il y a de la vie il y a de l'espoir. **2.** (*concessive*) quoique, bien que; **w. I admit, w. admitting, it's difficult, I don't think it's impossible,** quoique j'admette, tout en reconnaissant, que c'est difficile, je ne le crois pas impossible, je n'admets pas que ce soit impossible; **he's generous to his wife w. denying himself necessities,** il est généreux pour sa femme en même temps qu'il se refuse, tout en se refusant, le nécessaire. **3.** (*whereas*) tandis que; **one of the sisters was (dressed) in white w. the other was all in black,** une des sœurs était vêtue de blanc, tandis que l'autre était tout en noir.

whilom ['(h)wailəm]. *A:* **1.** *a.* ancien; d'autrefois, d'antan. **2.** *adv.* jadis, autrefois.

whilst [(h)wailst], *conj.* = WHILE³.

whim [(h)wim], *s.* **1.** caprice *m*; fantaisie *f*, lubie *f*; **a mere w.,** une simple fantaisie; **passing w.,** toquade *f*; lubie fugace; **a sudden w. of his,** un caprice qui lui a pris; **that's another of his whims,** c'est encore une de ses lubies; **he expects one to fall in with all his whims,** il faut faire ses quatre volontés. **2.** *Min: etc: A:* **(horse) w., w. (gin),** cabestan *m* à cheval; treuil *m* d'extraction à manège; manège *m*; baritel; **w. engine,** cabestan à vapeur. **3.** *Veh: Austr:* trique-balle *m*.

whimbrel ['(h)wimbrəl], *s. Orn:* courlieu *m*.

whimper¹ ['(h)wimpər], *s.* **1.** (i) pleurnicherie *f*, pleurnichement *m*; (ii) geignement *m*, plainte *f*. **2.** (*of dog*) petit cri plaintif; plainte.

whimper². **1.** *v.i.* (*a*) pleurnicher, geindre; (*b*) (*of dog*) pousser de petits cris plaintifs. **2.** *v.tr.* dire (qch.) en pleurnichant.

whimpering¹ ['(h)wimp(ə)riŋ], *a.* qui pleurniche; pleurnicheur; geignard; (chien) qui pousse de petits cris plaintifs.

whimpering², *s.* (*a*) pleurnichement *m*, pleurnicheries *fpl*; (*b*) plaintes *fpl*; (*c*) petits cris plaintifs (d'un chien).

whimsical ['(h)wimzik(ə)l], *a.* **1.** (*of pers., mind*) capricieux, fantasque. **2.** (*of thg*) bizarre, baroque.

whimsicality [(h)wimzi'kæliti], *s.* **1.** caractère capricieux, fantasque. **2.** bizarrerie *f* (de caractère).

whimsically ['(h)wimzikəli], *adv.* capricieusement; bizarrement, baroquement.

whimsy ['(h)wimzi], *s.* (*occ.* **whimsey**) (*a*) fantaisie *f*, lubie *f*; **as my w. takes me,** selon ma fantaisie; (*b*) **her novels are all sentimental whimsies,** ses romans sont tous de la sentimentalité à l'eau de rose.

whin¹ [(h)win], *s. Bot:* ajonc *m*; genêt épineux; ulex *m*; *F:* jonc marin, sainfoin *m* d'hiver.

whin², *s. Geol:* trapp *m*.

whinberry ['(h)winb(ə)ri], *s. Bot:* airelle *f*, myrtille *f*.

whinchat ['(h)wintʃæt], *s. Orn:* traquet *m* tarier.

whine¹ [(h)wain], *s.* **1.** plainte *f*; cri dolent (d'une personne); pleurnicherie *f*, geignement *m* (d'un enfant); gémissement *m*, plainte, geignement (d'un chien). **2.** jérémiade *f*.

whine², *v.i. & tr.* (*of pers.*) se plaindre; gémir; (*of child*) pleurnicher, piauler; (*of dog*) gémir, geindre; **you've nothing to w. about,** il n'y a pas de quoi vous plaindre, vous n'avez pas à vous plaindre; *Pej:* **they are whining for another increase in wages,** ils demandent sans raison encore une augmentation de salaire; **stop whining!** assez de jérémiades!

whiner ['(h)wainər], *s.* (*pers.*) geigneur, -euse; plaignard, -arde; (*child*) pleurnicheur, -euse; piauleur, -euse; **they are habitual whiners,** ce sont des gens qui ont toujours à se plaindre.

whinge [(h)win(d)ʒ], *v.i. Dial: F:* pleurnicher, geindre; grognonner; *Austr:* **a whing(e)ing Pom,** un Anglais qui se plaint de tout.

whining¹ ['(h)wainiŋ], *a.* (*a*) gémissant, geignant; (enfant) pleurnicheur; (ton) plaintif, pleurard; **w. voice,** voix dolente; (*b*) geignard.

whining², *s.* (*a*) gémissement *m*, geignement *m*; **the w. of the shells,** le piaulement des obus; (*b*) jérémiades *fpl*; plaintes *fpl*; **that's enough of your w.! stop your w.!** assez de jérémiades!

whinny¹ ['(h)wini], *s.* hennissement *m* (de cheval).

whinny², *v.i.* (*of horse*) hennir.

whinny³, *a. Dial:* (terrain) couvert d'ajoncs.

whinnying ['(h)winiiŋ], *s.* hennissement(s) *m(pl)* (de cheval).

whinstone ['(h)winstoun], *s. Geol:* trapp *m*.

whip¹ [(h)wip], *s.* **1.** (*a*) fouet *m*; **long w., lunging w.,** chambrière *f*; (*b*) *F:* **to get a fair crack of the w.,** avoir sa (bonne) part; en tirer un bon parti. **2.** (*a*) *A:* cocher *m*, conducteur *m* (d'un mail-coach, etc.); **to be a good, a bad, w.,** bien, mal, conduire; **he's a fine w.,** c'est une fine guide; (*b*) *Ven:* piqueur *m*. **3.** *Parl:* (*a*) (membre désigné par un parti comme) chef *m* de file; whip *m*; **the government has taken off the whips,** le gouvernement laisse ses adhérents libres de voter comme bon leur semblera; (*b*) appel *m* aux membres d'un groupe; **three-line w.,** appel urgent. **4.** fouettement *m*, coup *m* de fouet (d'un câble, etc.). **5.** aile *f*, bras *m* (d'un moulin à vent). **6.** *Nau:* cartahu *m*, palan *m*; **single w.,** cartahu simple. **7.** *Needlew:* **w. stitch,** (i) point *m* de surjet; (ii) point roulé. **8.** *Cu:* **strawberry w.** = mousse *f* aux fraises. **9.** *Arach:* **w. scorpion,** pédipalpe *m*.

whip², *v.* (**whipped** [(h)wipt])

I. *v.tr.* **1.** (*a*) fouetter (un cheval, un enfant, etc.); donner des coups de fouet à (un cheval); donner le fouet à (un enfant, etc.); corriger (un enfant); **to w. a top,** fouetter, faire aller, un sabot; **the rain was whipping the window panes,** la pluie fouettait, cinglait, les vitres; (*b*) *Cu:* battre (des œufs); fouetter, faire mousser (de la crème); **whipped cream,** crème fouettée; **to w. in the cream, to w. the cream into sth.,** incorporer la crème (à une sauce, etc.) (avec un fouet); (*c*) *Fish:* fouetter (un cours d'eau); (*d*) *F:* vaincre (qn); battre (qn) (à plate(s) couture(s)). **2.** (*a*) *Nau:* surlier, garnir (un cordage); (*b*) ligaturer (un brancard, une canne à pêche, etc.); (*c*) *Needlew:* **to w. a seam,** surjeter une couture; faire un surjet. **3.** (*a*) *A:* **to w. out one's sword,** dégainer; (*b*) **he whipped a revolver out of his pocket, whipped out a revolver,** il a sorti vivement, brusquement, un revolver (de sa poche); **he whipped it away, out of sight,** il l'a caché d'un mouvement rapide; **to w. on, off, a garment,** enfiler, ôter, rapidement un vêtement; **I'll w. you up something to eat,** je vais te préparer rapidement quelque chose à manger. **4.** *Nau:* hisser (une vergue, etc.) avec un cartahu. **5.** *F:* voler, faucher.

II. *v.i.* **1.** fouetter; **the rain was whipping against the panes,** la pluie fouettait, cinglait (contre) les vitres. **2. to w. behind sth.,** se jeter, s'élancer, derrière qch.; **to w. in, out, off,** entrer, sortir, partir, brusquement; **to w. down the stairs,** dévaler, dégringoler, l'escalier; **to w. round,** se retourner vivement; faire (un) tête-à-queue; **to w. round the corner,** tourner vivement le coin; **I'll just w. over, across, round, to the grocer's,** je vais faire un saut jusqu'à l'épicerie. **3.** *Mec.E: etc:* (*of shaft, etc.*) fouetter; (*of cable, etc.*) **to w. back,** fouetter.

III. (*compound verbs*) **1. whip round,** *v.i.* **to w. round (for subscriptions),** faire la quête.

2. whip up, *v.tr.* (*a*) activer, stimuler (un cheval); toucher (un cheval) (du fouet); (*b*) *Parl:* faire passer un appel urgent à (des membres d'un parti); **to w. up one's friends,** rallier ses amis.

whipbird ['(h)wipbə:d], *s. Orn:* psophode *m*.

whipcord ['(h)wipkɔ:d], *s.* **1.** (*a*) mèche *f* de fouet; (*b*) corde *f* à fouet; ficelle *f* à fouet; forcet *m*; (*c*) *Algae:* **sea w.,** lacet *m* de mer. **2.** *Tex:* whipcord *m*; fil *m* de fouet.

whipfish ['(h)wipfiʃ], *s. Ich:* hénioque *m*; *F:* cocher *m*.

whip-graft ['(h)wipgrɑ:ft], *v.tr. Hort:* greffer (un arbre) en fente anglaise.

whiphand ['(h)wiphænd], *s.* main *f* du fouet; main droite du cocher; *Fig:* **to have, hold, the w.,** avoir l'avantage; avoir le dessus; tenir le haut bout; **to have the w. over, of, s.o.,** avoir barres, une barre, sur qn; avoir la haute main sur qn.

whiplash ['(h)wiplæʃ], *s.* mèche *f* de fouet; *Aut: etc:* **w. (injury),** coup *m* de fouet; *F:* **tongue like a w.,** langue *f* qui cingle.

whipper ['(h)wipər], *s.* fouetteur, -euse; *Ven:* **w. in,** piqueur *m*.

whippersnapper ['(h)wipəsnæpər], *s. F:* petit jeune homme suffisant, qui fait l'important; *P:* petit merdeux.

whippet ['(h)wipit], *s.* **1.** (*dog*) whippet *m*. **2.** *Mil: F: A:* char d'assaut léger, de petit modèle.

whipping ['(h)wipiŋ], *s.* **1.** (*a*) fouettage *m* (d'un cheval, d'un sabot, de la crème, etc.); *Com:* **w. cream,** crème à fouetter; (*b*) fouettée *f*; *Jur:* (châtiment *m* du) fouet; peine *f* du fouet, de la flagellation; **to give (s.o.) a w.,** donner le fouet à (qn); donner une fouettée à (un enfant); **to get a w.,** (i) recevoir le fouet; être fouetté; (ii) *Sp: etc:* être battu à plate(s) couture(s); **w. boy,** (i) *Hist:* jeune garçon élevé avec un prince et qui reçoit le fouet au lieu de celui-ci; (ii) *F:* bouc *m* émissaire; *A:* **w. post,** poteau *m* des condamnés au fouet. **2.** (*a*) fouettement *m* (de la pluie, etc.); (*b*) *Mec.E:* fouettement, battement *m* (d'un arbre, *Aut:* du vilebrequin, etc.). **3.** (*a*) *Nau:* surliure *f* (d'un cordage); (*b*) ligature(s) *f(pl)* (d'une canne à pêche, etc.); (*c*) *Needlew:* (i) surjet *m* (d'une couture); (ii) **w. (stitch),** point roulé.

whippletree ['(h)wipəltri:], *s. Veh:* palonnier *m*.

whip-poor-will ['(h)wippuəwil], *s. Orn:* engoulevant *m* de la Virginie; *Fr.C:* engoulevent bois-pourri.

whippy ['(h)wipi], *a.* (crosse de golf, etc.) flexible, souple.

whipround ['(h)wipraund], *s. F:* quête *f*; **to have a w. for s.o.,** organiser une souscription en faveur de qn.

whipsaw¹ ['(h)wipsɔ:], *s. Tls:* (*a*) scie *f* à chantourner; (*b*) scie de long.

whipsaw², *v.tr. & i.* (*a*) chantourner; (*b*) scier en long.

whipstock ['(h)wipstɔk], *s.* **1.** manche *m* de fouet. **2.** *Petr:* sifflet *m* de déviation; sifflet déviateur amovible.

whiptailed ['(h)wipteild], *a. Nat.Hist:* à queue en fouet; *Ich:* **w. sting ray,** pastenague *f*.

whip-up ['(h)wipʌp], *s. Parl: etc:* appel urgent (à faire acte de présence).

whir¹,² [(h)wə:r], *s. & v.i.* = WHIRR¹,².

whirl¹ [(h)wə:l], *s.* **1.** (*a*) mouvement *m* giratoire, giration *f* (d'une roue, etc.); (*b*) tourbillon *m*, tourbillonnement *m*, tournoiement *m*; **a w. of dead leaves, of dust,** un tourbillon de feuilles mortes, de poussière; **a w. of pleasure,** un tourbillon de plaisirs; **my head's in a w.,** la tête me tourne; j'ai la tête à l'envers; *Ph:* **sound w.,** tourbillon acoustique. **2.** *Ropem:* molette *f*. **3.** *Ph:* **electric w.,** tourniquet *m* électrique.

whirl². **1.** *v.i.* (*a*) **to w. (round),** tourbillonner, tournoyer; (*of dancer*) pirouetter; (*of rocket*) vriller; **whirling dervish,** derviche tourneur; **my head's whirling,** la tête me tourne; j'ai le vertige; (*b*) **to w. along,** filer à toute vitesse, à toute allure; aller comme le vent; se précipiter; **the leaves came whirling down,** les feuilles descendaient en tournoyant; **to w. past sth.,** passer qch. à toute vitesse, en trombe; **to w. into the room,** entrer précipitamment dans la pièce; **the thoughts that were whirling through my head,** les pensées qui tourbillonnaient dans mon cerveau. **2.** *v.tr.* (*a*) faire tournoyer, faire tourbillonner (les feuilles mortes, etc.); **the wind was whirling the leaves about,** le vent faisait voler, danser, les feuilles; (*b*) entraîner (à toute vitesse, à fond de train); **the train whirled us along,** le train nous emportait à toute vitesse.

whirligig ['(h)wə:ligig], *s.* **1.** (*a*) *Toys:* tourniquet *m*; (*b*) manège *m* de chevaux de bois. **2.** mouvement *m* rapide de giration; tournoiement *m*. **3.** *Ent:* **w. (beetle),** gyrin *m*; *F:* tourniquet aquatique.

whirling¹ ['(h)wə:liŋ], *a.* tourbillonnant; tournoyant; giratoire, rotatoire.

whirling², *s.* (*a*) tourbillonnement *m*; tournoiement *m*; giration *f*; (*b*) course précipitée.

whirlpool ['(h)wə:lpu:l], *s.* tourbillon *m* (d'eau); remous *m* d'eau; gouffre *m*, maelström *m*.

whirlwind ['(h)wə:lwind], *s.* tourbillon *m* (de vent); trombe *f* (de vent); **to come in like a w.,** entrer en trombe, en coup de vent.

whirlybird ['(h)wə:libə:d], *s. F:* hélicoptère *m*, moulin *m*, batteur *m* (à œufs), banane *f*.

whirr¹ [(h)wə:r], *s.* bruissement *m* (d'ailes); bruit ronflant, ronflement *m*, ronron *m*, ronronnement *m* (de machines); sifflement *m* (d'obus); vrombissement *m* (d'une hélice d'avion, d'une turbine).

whirr[2], *v.i.* (*of machinery, etc.*) tourner à toute vitesse; ronfler, ronronner; (*of propeller*) vrombir; (*of shell*) siffler; **the birds were whirring past,** les oiseaux passaient avec un bruissement d'ailes.

whirring[1] ['(h)wəːriŋ], *a.* (*of wheel, etc.*) qui tourne à toute vitesse; qui ronfle; ronflant; (*of wings*) bruissant.

whirring[2], *s.* = WHIRR[1].

whirtle ['(h)wəːtl], *s. Tchn:* **w. (plate),** filière *f.*

whisht [hwiʃt], *Scot:* (*a*) *int.* chut! (*b*) *s.* **hold your w.!** taisez-vous! tais-toi!

whisk[1] [(h)wisk], *s.* **1.** (*light, rapid movement*) **a w. of the tail, of a duster,** un coup de queue, de torchon. **2.** verge *f*, vergette *f* (de brindilles, de plumes, etc.); *Dom.Ec:* (*for dusting, etc.*) époussette *f*; plumeau *m*; balayette *f*; (*for beating eggs, etc.*) fouet *m*, batteur *m*.

whisk[2]. **1.** *v.i.* **to w. away, off,** partir comme un trait, comme une flèche; partir, disparaître, à toute allure; **to w. past,** passer comme un trait, comme le vent. **2.** *v.tr.* (*a*) agiter (qch.) d'un mouvement vif; (*of cow, etc.*) **to w. its tail,** agiter sa queue; se battre les flancs avec sa queue; (*b*) **to w. sth. away, off,** enlever qch. d'un geste rapide; **to w. away a fly, a tear,** chasser une mouche, une larme (d'un revers de main); **to w. s.o. away,** entraîner, emporter, qn à toute vitesse; **I was whisked up, down, in the lift,** l'ascenseur m'a emporté rapidement; (*c*) *Cu:* battre (des œufs); fouetter (de la crème).

whisker ['(h)wiskər], *s.* **1.** (*a*) **whiskers,** (i) favoris *m*, (ii) barbe *f* (d'homme); moustache(s) *f* (de chat, de souris, etc.); *F:* **he thinks he's the cat's whiskers,** il se croit quelqu'un; il croit qu'il est sorti de la cuisse de Jupiter; (*b*) *Cryst:* **whiskers,** moustache, trichite *f*; (*c*) *Sp: F:* **to win by a w.,** gagner dans un mouchoir. **2.** *N.Arch:* arc-boutant *m*, *pl.* arcs-boutants (de beaupré).

whiskered ['(h)wiskəd], *a.* (homme) à favoris, à barbe.

whiskery ['(h)wiskəri], *a.* (visage) barbu; (fromage) moisi.

whiskeyjack ['(h)wiskidʒæk], *s. Can: Orn:* mésangeai *m* du Canada, *Fr.C:* geai gris.

whisky[1] ['(h)wiski], *s.* (*Irish or U.S:* **whiskey**) whisky *m*; **a w. and soda,** un whisky soda; **w. on the rocks,** whisky frappé; **w. sour,** cocktail de whisky et de jus de citron sucré.

whisky[2], *s. A.Veh:* wiski *m*.

whisper[1] ['(h)wispər], *s.* **1.** (*a*) chuchotement *m*; **to speak in a w., in whispers,** parler bas; **to say sth. in a w.,** chuchoter qch.; dire qch. tout bas; (*b*) *Lit:* bruissement *m* (des feuilles); murmure *m* (de l'eau). **2.** *O:* rumeur *f*, bruit *m* (que l'on se transmet à voix basse).

whisper[2]. **1.** *v.i.* chuchoter; parler bas; *Lit:* (*of leaves*) susurrer; (*of water*) murmurer; **to w. to s.o.,** chuchoter à l'oreille de qn; dire, souffler, qch. à l'oreille de qn; **stop whispering!** (i) c'en est assez de chuchotements! (ii) parlez un peu plus distinctement! **2.** *v.tr.* (*a*) **to w. sth. to s.o.,** dire, chuchoter, glisser, couler, un mot à l'oreille de qn; **he whispered (to me) the word I had forgotten,** il m'a soufflé (à l'oreille) le mot que j'avais oublié; **whispered conversation,** conversation à voix basse; (*b*) *O:* faire circuler secrètement (une nouvelle).

whisperer ['(h)wispərər], *s.* chuchoteur, -euse.

whispering ['(h)wisp(ə)riŋ], *s.* **1.** (*a*) chuchotement *m*; (*b*) *Pej:* chuchoterie(s) *f*(*pl*); **w. campaign,** campagne sournoise, de chuchoteries, de bouche à l'oreille; (*c*) *Arch:* **w. gallery,** voûte *f* acoustique; galerie *f* à écho. **2.** *Lit:* bruissement *m* (de feuilles); murmure *m* (d'eaux).

whist[1] [(h)wist], *s. Cards:* whist *m*; **dummy w.,** whist à trois (avec un mort); **short, long, w.,** petit, grand, whist; **w. player,** joueur, -euse, de whist; **w. drive,** tournoi *m* de whist.

whist[2], *int.* = WHISHT.

whistle[1] ['(h)wisl], *s.* **1.** (*a*) sifflement *m*; coup *m* de sifflet; *Sp:* **final w.,** coup de sifflet final; **blackbird's w.,** le sifflement du merle; (*b*) **the w. of the wind in the trees,** le sifflement du vent dans les arbres. **2.** (*a*) sifflet *m*; *Mil: etc:* **w. signal,** commandement *m* au sifflet; **to blow a w.,** donner un coup de sifflet; *F:* **to blow the w.,** vendre la mèche; *Sp:* **to blow the w. for a foul, for half time,** siffler une faute, la mi-temps; (*b*) **tin w.,** *A:* **penny w.,** flageolet *m*. **3.** *P:* **to wet, whet, one's w.,** s'arroser la gorge; se rincer la dalle; boire un coup.

whistle[2]. **1.** *v.i.* (*a*) (*of pers., bird, wind, etc.*) siffler; **to w. for one's dog, for a taxi,** siffler son chien, un taxi; *F:* **he can w. for his money,** il peut courir après son argent; **you can w. for it!** tu peux toujours courir, te fouiller! *Nau:* **to w. for a wind,** être accalminé; siffler pour avoir du vent; **the bullet whistled past his ear,** la balle a passé en sifflant tout près de son oreille; **cars were whistling past,** des voitures passaient à toute allure; (*b*) donner un coup de sifflet; *Rail:* **to w. for the road,** demander la voie; siffler au disque; (*c*) *P: A:* vendre la mèche; vendre ses complices. **2.** *v.tr.* (*a*) siffler, siffloter (un air); (*b*) *F:* **to w. s.o., sth., down the wind,** laisser aller qn, qch.; ne plus se soucier de qn, de qch.; (*c*) *F:* **I'll w. up a few friends to help us,** je vais trouver quelques amis pour nous aider; **can you w. up some more sandwiches?** peux-tu préparer encore quelques sandwichs?

whistler ['(h)wislər], *s.* **1.** (*a*) siffleur, -euse; (*b*) cheval cornard. **2.** *Orn:* **w. (bird),** pachycéphale *m*, oiseau siffleur. **3.** *Z:* siffleur, marmotte canadienne, *Fr.C:* siffleux *m*.

whistle-stop[1] ['(h)wis(ə)lstɔp], *s. esp. U.S:* (*a*) *Rail:* halte *f* (à arrêt facultatif); **w.-s. tour,** (i) tournée électorale rapide (faite par train spécial); (ii) tour rapide; (*b*) *F:* patelin *m*, bled *m*.

whistle-stop[2], *v.i. U.S:* faire une tournée électorale par train spécial.

whistling[1] ['(h)wisliŋ], *a.* (oiseau, etc.) siffleur; **w. sound,** sifflement *m*; **w. note,** note sifflante; *Nau:* **w. buoy,** bouée *f* à sifflet.

whistling[2], *s.* sifflement *m*; sifflerie *f*.

whit[1] [(h)wit], *s.* (*usu. in neg.*) brin *m*, iota *m*; petit morceau; **he's not a w. the better for it,** il ne s'en porte aucunement, nullement, mieux; **without a w. of regret,** sans un brin de regret; **he's every w. as good as you,** il vous vaut bien.

Whit[2], *a. & s.* **W. Sunday,** (le dimanche de) la Pentecôte; **W. Monday,** le lundi de la Pentecôte; **at W.,** à la Pentecôte.

white[1] [(h)wait], *a. & s.*

I. *a.* **1.** (*a*) blanc, *f.* blanche; **as w. as snow,** blanc comme la neige; **we had a w. Christmas,** il a neigé à Noël; **w. beard,** barbe blanche; **w. hair,** cheveux blancs; **he's going w.,** il commence à blanchir; **w.(-)headed,** (i) *Z:* à tête blanche; (ii) (*of pers.*) (*also* **w.(-)haired**) aux cheveux blancs; *O:* **the w.-headed boy of the family,** le chouchou de la famille; **w.(-)faced,** (i) *Z:* à face blanche; (ii) (*of pers.*) au visage pâle, blême; **w.-faced horse,** cheval *m* belle-face; **w.(-)nosed,** à nez blanc; **w.-nosed monkey,** blanc-nez *m*, *pl.* blancs-nez; hocheur *m*; *F:* (*of pers.*) **w.(-)livered,** poltron, pusillanime; *Anat:* **w. tissues,** tissus albuginés; **w. line,** ligne blanche; trait blanc; *Typ:* ligne de blanc; **w. collar,** col blanc; **w.-collar worker,** employé *m* de bureau; col-blanc *m*, *pl.* cols-blancs; *Fr.C:* collet-blanc *m*, *pl.* collets-blancs; *Cu:* **w. sauce,** sauce blanche; **w. meat,** chair blanche, blanc *m* (de poulet, etc.); *Com:* **w. goods,** articles *m* de blanc; *Navy:* **w. uniform,** tenue *f* en blanc; les blancs; **the W. House,** (i) la Maison Blanche (à Washington); (ii) le gouvernement américain, la Maison Blanche; **w. paper,** (i) *Parl:* livre blanc; (ii) *Fin:* papier *m* de haut commerce; *Geog:* **the W. Sea,** la Mer Blanche; **W. Russia,** Russie Blanche; *Hist:* **W. Russian,** Russe blanc, blanche; (*b*) **the w. races,** les races blanches; **a w. man,** (i) un blanc; (ii) *esp. U.S:* un homme loyal; (*c*) **w. with fear,** blanc de peur; **w.(-)lipped,** (i) aux lèvres blanches, pâles; (ii) blême, livide (de peur); **to turn, go, w.,** devenir blanc, pâle, blême; blanchir, blêmir; **as w. as a ghost, as a sheet,** pâle comme la mort, comme un linge; **in a w. rage,** dans une colère blanche; blanc, blême, de colère; (*d*) **w. wine,** vin blanc; **w. bread,** pain blanc; **w. coffee,** café *m* au lait; (*e*) *Bot:* **w. hellebore,** vératre *m*, ellébore blanc; **w. vine,** (i) vigne blanche; couleuvrée *f*; (ii) clématite *f* des haies, berceau *m* de la Vierge; (*f*) **w. metal, w. alloy,** (i) métal blanc; (ii) antifriction *f*, régule *m*; **w. iron,** (i) fer blanc; (ii) fonte blanche; *Petr:* **water w. oil,** huile extra-blanche; *F:* **w. electricals,** appareils ménagers (réfrigérateurs, machines à laver, etc.). **2.** *Lit:* (*of pers., etc.*) pur, innocent; (*of reputation, etc.*) sans tache.

II. *s.* **1.** (*a*) blanc *m*; **dead w.,** blanc mat; **a line of w.,** une ligne de blanc; un trait blanc; (*b*) *Metall:* **w. hot,** chauffé, porté, à blanc. **2. Chinese w.,** blanc de Chine; **zinc w.,** blanc de zinc, de neige. **3. dressed in w.,** habillé en blanc, de blanc; **w. wedding,** mariage *m* en blanc; **whites,** (i) *Com:* linge blanc; (ii) *Sp:* pantalon blanc; *Com:* **w. sale,** vente *f* de blanc; **wash your whites with X,** lavez votre linge avec X. **4.** (*pers.*) blanc, *f.* blanche; *Pej:* **poor w.,** petit blanc. **5.** (*a*) **w. (of egg),** blanc (d'œuf); **the w. of an egg,** un blanc d'œuf; (*b*) **the w. of the eyes,** le blanc des yeux; *F:* **to turn up the whites of one's eyes,** (i) faire des yeux de carpe pâmée; (ii) tourner de l'œil; (*c*) *Mill:* **whites,** fleur *f* de farine. **6.** *Typ:* ligne *f* de blanc. **7.** *Med: F:* **whites,** leucorrhée *f*, pertes blanches, fleurs blanches.

white[2], *v.tr.* **1.** *A:* blanchir; *Lit:* **whited sepulchre,** sépulcre blanchi. **2.** *Typ:* blanchir (la composition).

whitebait ['(h)waitbeit], *s. Cu:* blanchaille *f*; **a dish of w.** = une friture.

whitebeam ['(h)waitbiːm], *s. Bot:* alisier blanc; (alisier) allouchier *m*.

white-eye ['(h)waitai], *s. Orn:* zostérops *m*, oiseau *m* à lunettes.

whitefish ['(h)waitfiʃ], *s. Ich:* (*a*) corégone *m*; (*b*) menhaden *m*; (*c*) huso *m*.

Whitehall ['(h)waithɔːl], *s.* l'Administration *f* (britannique) (du nom de la rue à Londres où se trouvent beaucoup de ministères).

whiteheart ['(h)waithaːt], *a. & s.* **w. (cherry),** bigarreau *m*.

whiteleg ['(h)waitleg], *s. Med: F:* leucophlegmasie *f*, œdème blanc douloureux.

whiten ['(h)wait(ə)n]. **1.** *v.tr.* (*a*) blanchir (les cheveux, la peau, le linge, etc.); (*b*) blanchir à la chaux, badigeonner en blanc; (*c*) *Leath:* écharner, blanchir (les peaux); (*d*) *Metalw:* étamer (un métal). **2.** *v.i.* (*a*) blanchir; (*b*) (*of pers.*) pâlir, blêmir.

whitener ['(h)wait(ə)nər], *s.* (*a*) *Leath:* blanchisseur *m* (de peaux); (*b*) *Metalw:* étameur, blanchisseur (d'épingles, etc.).

whiteness ['(h)waitnis], *s.* (*a*) blancheur *f* (de la neige, de la peau, etc.); (*b*) pâleur *f* (du visage, etc.); (*c*) *A: & Lit:* innocence *f*, pureté *f*.

whitening ['(h)wait(ə)niŋ], *s.* **1.** (*a*) blanchiment *m* (d'un mur, etc.); (*b*) *Leath:* écharnage *m*, blanchiment (des peaux); **w. machine,** écharneuse *f*; **w. knife,** doloir *m*; (*c*) *Metalw:* étamage *m*. **2.** blanchissement *m* (des cheveux, etc.). **3.** *O:* = WHITING[1].

white-out ['(h)waitaut], *s.* brouillard blanc aveuglant (particulier aux régions polaires).

whiteprint ['(h)waitprint], *s.* photocopie *f* sur blanc.

whitesmith ['(h)waitsmiθ], *s.* **1.** ferblantier *m*. **2.** serrurier *m*; ouvrier *m* en métaux.

whitethorn ['(h)waitθɔːn], *s. Bot:* épine blanche; aubépine *f*.

whitethroat ['(h)waitθrout], *s. Orn:* fauvette grisette; **lesser w.,** fauvette babillarde.

whitewash[1] ['(h)waitwɔʃ], *s.* **1.** blanc *m*, lait *m*, de chaux; badigeon *m* à la chaux; échaudage *m*; **to give a wall a coat of w.,** badigeonner un mur (en blanc). **2.** *Sp: F:* défaite *f* à zéro.

whitewash[2], *v.tr.* **1.** (*a*) peindre, blanchir, à la chaux; badigeonner en blanc; chauler, échauder (un mur); (*b*) blanchir, disculper (qn). **2.** *Sp: F:* battre (ses adversaires) sans qu'ils aient marqué un point.

whitewasher ['(h)waitwɔʃər], *s.* **1.** badigeonneur *m*. **2.** apologiste *mf*.

whitewashing ['(h)waitwɔʃiŋ], *s.* **1.** peinture *f* à la chaux; badigeonnage *m*; chaulage *m*, échaudage *m*. **2.** blanchiment *m* (d'une réputation, etc.).

whitewood ['(h)waitwud], *s. Com:* bois blanc.

whither ['(h)wiðər], *adv. & conj. A: & Lit:* **1.** (*interr.*) où? vers quel lieu? **w. Japan?** où va le Japon? **2.** (*rel.*) (là) où; **I shall go w. fate leads me,** j'irai là où me mènera le destin.

whithersoever [(h)wiðəsou'evər], *adv. & conj. A: & Lit:* n'importe où; vers n'importe quel endroit; où que + *sub.*

whiting[1] ['(h)waitiŋ], *s. Com: O:* blanc *m* d'Espagne, de Meudon.

whiting[2], *s. Ich:* merlan *m*.

whitish ['(h)waitiʃ], *a.* blanchâtre.

whitleather ['(h)witleðər], *s. Leath:* cuir mégis.

whitlow ['(h)witlou], *s.* **1.** *Med:* panaris *m*; (*round a nail*) tourniole *f*. **2.** *Bot:* **w. grass,** drave printanière; **w. wort,** paronychia *m*, paronyque *f*.

whitneyite ['(h)witniait], *s. Miner:* whitneyite *f*.

Whitsun(tide) ['(h)witsən(taid)], *s.* (fête *f*, saison *f*, de) la Pentecôte; **at Whitsun,** à la Pentecôte.

whittle ['(h)wit(ə)l], *v.tr.* **to w. (down),** amenuiser, parer (un bâton, une cheville, etc.); **to w. down, away, one's capital,** rogner, dilapider peu à peu, son capital.

whiz(z) [(h)wiz], *s. F:* **w. kid,** jeune prodige *m*; jeune coq *m*.

whizz[1] [(h)wiz]. **1.** *int.* pan! **2.** *s.* (*a*) sifflement *m* (d'une balle, etc.); *F:* **w.-bang,** (i) *Mil: A:* obus *m* (à haute vitesse, de petit calibre); (ii) *Pyr:* pétard *m*; (*b*) *esp. U.S: F:* as *m*, crack *m* (**at,** en).

whizz[2], *v.i.* (*of bullet, etc.*) siffler; **the bullet whizzed past his head,** la balle a passé tout près de sa tête en sifflant; **cars were whizzing down, along, the road, were whizzing past, by,** des voitures passaient (sur la route) à toute vitesse.

who [huː], *pers. pron. nom.* **1.** (*interr.*) qui? qui est-ce qui? *occ.* lequel, etc., quel, etc.; **w. is it?** qui est-ce? **w. is that woman?** qui, quelle, est cette femme? **nobody knows w.,** personne ne sait qui; **w. on earth told you that?** qui diable vous a dit cela? **w. on earth is it?** qui cela peut-il bien être? **who's speaking?** qui est-ce qui parle? *Tp:* c'est de la part de qui? **ask him w. found it,** demandez-lui qui l'a trouvé; **he's arrived—w.?** il est arrivé—qui donc? **w. did you say?** qui ça? **Mr w. did you say?** vous disiez M. qui? **w. did you say you expected?** qui disiez-vous que vous attendiez? **he**

knows who's w., il connaît les gens; **tell me who's w.,** dites-moi qui sont tous ces gens-là; **w. am I to deserve this?** qui suis-je pour recevoir un tel honneur? **w. does he think he is?** pour qui se prend-il? **w. are in the running (for the job)?** quels sont les candidats ayant des chances? **w. of us can still remember it?** qui, lesquels, d'entre nous se le rappelle(nt) encore? (*b*) *F:* (*grammatically incorrect, in formal speech always* **whom**) **w. do you want?** qui voulez-vous? **w. were you talking to?** à qui parliez-vous? **2.** (*a*) (*rel.*) qui; **the friends w. came yesterday,** les amis qui sont venus hier; **the man w. gave it to me,** l'homme qui me l'a donné; (*b*) (*to avoid ambiguity*) lequel; **Louise's father, w. is very rich,** le père de Louise, lequel est très riche; (*c*) (*independent rel.*) (celui) qui; **deny it w. may,** le nie qui voudra; **as w. should say,** comme qui dirait.

whoa [wou], *int.* (*a*) (*to stop horse*) **w. (back)!** ho! holà! (*b*) *F:* (*to pers.*) doucement! attendez!

whodun(n)it [hu:'dʌnit], *s. F:* roman policier.

whoever (*Poet:* **whoe'er**) [hu(:)'evər, -'ɛər], *pers. pron. nom.* **1.** celui qui, etc.; quiconque; **w. finds it may keep it,** celui qui, quiconque, le trouvera pourra le garder; **we shall welcome w. comes,** quiconque viendra sera le bienvenu. **2.** qui que + *sub.*; **w. you are, speak!** qui que vous soyez, parlez! **w. wrote that letter,** qui que ce soit qui ait écrit cette lettre; *F:* . . . **or w.,** ou qui que ce soit. **3.** *F:* (*replaces* **whomsoever** *in ordinary conversation*) **w. she marries,** celui qu'elle épousera; **w. you like,** qui vous voudrez.

whole [houl], *a. & s.*

I. *a.* **1.** (*a*) *A:* sain; en bonne santé; *B:* **his hand was made w.,** sa main fut guérie; **they that are w. need not a physician,** ceux qui se portent bien n'ont pas besoin de médecin; (*b*) (*of pers.*) sain et sauf; (*of thg*) intact; en bon état; **to come back w.,** revenir sain et sauf. **2.** (*a*) (*entire*) intégral, -aux; entier; complet, -ète; total, -aux; **ox roasted w.,** bœuf rôti entier; **he swallowed it w.,** (i) il l'a avalé sans le mâcher; (ii) *F:* il a pris ça pour de l'argent comptant; **a w. loaf,** un pain entier; *Mth:* **w. number,** nombre entier; **w. length,** longueur totale; **w. outfit,** trousseau complet; **w. holiday,** jour entier de congé; **w. life insurance,** assurance *f* en cas de décès, pour la vie entière; **w. pulley,** poulie *f* en une seule pièce; **w. coffee,** café *m* en grains; **to cut out of w. cloth,** tailler en plein drap; (*b*) (*emphatic*) tout, entier, tout entier; **to tell the w. truth,** dire toute la vérité; **the w. world,** le monde entier; **to last a w. week,** durer toute une semaine; **I waited for you a w. hour,** je vous ai attendu une bonne heure; **I never saw him the w. evening,** je ne l'ai pas vu de la soirée; **the w. work must be done again,** l'œuvre est tout entière à recommencer; **sobs shook her w. frame,** des sanglots la secouaient tout entière; **to eat a w. goose,** manger une oie tout entière; **w. families died of it,** des familles entières en sont mortes; **to do sth. with one's w. heart,** faire qch. de tout son cœur; *F:* **the w. lot of you,** vous tous.

II. *s.* tout *m*, totalité *f*, intégralité *f*, ensemble *m*; **the w. of the school,** l'école entière; toute l'école; **to pay the w. of one's rent,** payer l'intégralité de son loyer; **to bequeath to s.o. the w. of one's estate,** léguer à qn l'universalité *f* de ses biens; **nearly the w. of our resources,** la presque totalité de nos ressources; **he spent the w. of that year in London,** il a passé toute cette année-là à Londres; **the w. amounts to . . .,** le total se monte à . . .; **the various parts blend into a harmonious w.,** les différentes parties se fondent en un ensemble harmonieux; **as a w.,** dans son ensemble; en totalité; **taken as a w.,** pris dans sa totalité; **on the w.,** à tout prendre; tout bien considéré; absolument parlant; en somme; dans l'ensemble; au total; somme toute; **on the w. I am satisfied,** somme toute je suis satisfait; **the work on the w. is good,** l'ensemble du travail est bon; dans l'ensemble le travail est bon; **prices are steady on the w.,** les prix sont plutôt soutenus; (*in charades*) **my w.,** mon tout; mon entier.

whole-coloured ['houlkʌləd], *a.* (tissu, etc.) unicolore, de teinte uniforme; (cheval, chien) zain.

wholehearted [houl'hɑ:tid], *a.* (qui vient) du cœur; sincère; (rire) épanoui.

wholeheartedly [houl'hɑ:tidli], *adv.* de tout (son) cœur; de bon, de grand, cœur; sincèrement; avec élan.

wholehogger [houl'hɔgər], *s. F:* jusqu'auboutiste *mf.*

wholehoggism [houl'hɔgizm], *s. F:* jusqu'auboutisme *m.*

wholemeal ['houlmi:l], *s. Mill:* bisaille *f*; **w. bread,** pain complet.

wholeness ['houlnis], *s.* état complet; intégralité *f*; intégrité *f.*

wholesale[1] ['houlseil]. **1.** *s. & a.* (*a*) *s.* (vente *f* en) gros *m*; **w. and retail,** gros et détail; (*b*) **w. trade,** commerce *m* de gros, en gros; **w. goods,** marchandises *f* en gros; **w. warehouse,** maison *f* de gros, de fournitures en gros; **w. dealer, merchant,** grossiste *mf*; commerçant, -ante, en gros; **w. price,** prix *m* de, en, gros; (*c*) *a.* **by w. borrowing,** en empruntant de tous côtés; **a w. slaughter,** un massacre, une tuerie en masse. **2.** *adv.* **to sell, buy, w.,** vendre, acheter, en gros.

wholesale[2], *v.tr.* vendre (des marchandises) en gros.

wholesaler ['houlseilər], *s.* grossiste *mf*; commerçant, -ante, en gros.

wholesaling ['houlseiliŋ], *s.* vente *f* en gros.

wholesome ['houlsəm], *a.* (aliment) sain; (air, climat) salubre; (remède) salutaire; **good, w. food,** bonne nourriture (simple).

wholesomely ['houlsəmli], *adv.* sainement; salutairement; salubrement.

wholesomeness ['houlsəmnis], *s.* nature saine (de la nourriture, etc.); salubrité *f* (de l'air, etc.).

wholly ['houlli], *adv.* **1.** tout à fait; complètement, entièrement. **2.** intégralement, en totalité.

whom [hu:m], *pers. pron.* (*objective case*) **1.** (*interr.*) qui? qui est-ce que? **w. did you see?** qui avez-vous vu? qui est-ce que vous avez vu? **to w. are you speaking?** à qui parlez-vous? **of w. are you speaking?** de qui parlez-vous? **on w. can we count for certain?** sur qui pouvons-nous compter sûrement? **I don't know to w. to turn,** je ne sais à qui m'adresser; **go and fetch you know w.,** allez chercher qui vous savez; **w. else?** qui d'autre? **2.** (*rel.*) (*a*) (*direct object*) que; lequel, *f.* laquelle; *pl.* lesquels, *f.* lesquelles; **the man w. you saw,** l'homme que vous avez vu; **he is a man w. no one respects,** c'est un homme que ne respecte personne; (*b*) (*indirect object and after prep.*) qui; **he wanted to find somebody to w. he might talk,** il voulait trouver quelqu'un à qui parler; **the two officers between w. she was sitting,** les deux officiers entre lesquels elle était assise; **the friend of w. I speak,** l'ami dont je parle; **these two men, both of w. were quite young,** ces deux hommes, qui tous deux étaient tout jeunes; **a man about w. much good is spoken,** un homme dont on dit beaucoup de bien; (*c*) (*after* **than**) **Hannibal, no greater soldier than w. ever existed,** Annibal, le plus grand soldat qui ait jamais existé; **here is Mr Long, than w. nobody could advise you better,** voilà M. Long qui est plus autorisé que personne à vous donner des conseils. **3.** (*independent rel.*) celui que, etc.; qui; **w. the gods love die young,** qui est aimé des dieux meurt jeune; **talk with w. I will,** n'importe à qui je parle.

whomsoever, *Poet:* **whomsoe'er** [hu:msou'evər, -'ɛər], *pers. pron esp. Lit:* **1.** celui (quel qu'il soit) que; **w. they choose,** celui qu'ils choisiront. **2.** n'importe qui que; qui que ce soit que.

whoop[1] [hu:p]. **1.** *int.* houp! **2.** *s.* (*a*) *Ven:* huée *f*; (*b*) *Med:* quinte *f* (de la coqueluche), *F:* chant *m* de coq; (*c*) cri *m* (de rage, de joie); (*d*) *NAm:* (h)ululement *m* (d'un hibou).

whoop[2], *v.i.* (*a*) *Ven:* huer; (*b*) *Med:* faire entendre la toux convulsive de la coqueluche; **whooping cough,** coqueluche; (*c*) crier, pousser des cris (de rage, de joie); (*d*) *NAm:* (*of owl*) (h)ululer; (*e*) *NAm:* *F:* **to w.** [wu:p] **it up,** faire un bruit de tous les diables.

whoopee [wu:'pi:], *s. F: O:* **to make w.,** (i) fêter bruyamment; faire la noce, la bombe; (ii) bien s'amuser.

whooper ['hu:pər], *s.* **w. swan,** cygne chanteur, sauvage.

whoops [(h)wu:ps], *int.* houp-là!

whop[1] [(h)wɔp], *s. F:* coup (retentissant, lourd, ou mat); **to fall with a w.,** tomber comme une masse, comme un sac.

whop[2], *v.tr.* (**whopped**) *F:* (*a*) battre, rosser (qn); (*b*) battre, rouler (une équipe, etc.).

whopper ['(h)wɔpər], *s. F:* (*a*) quelque chose de colossal; mastodonte *m*; (*b*) mensonge *m* de taille.

whopping[1] ['(h)wɔpiŋ], *a. F:* énorme; **w. great lie,** mensonge *m* de taille.

whopping[2], *s. F:* rossée *f*, raclée *f.*

whore[1] [hɔ:r], *s.f.* prostituée; putain; *P:* **w. house,** bordel *m.*

whore[2], *v.i.* (*a*) (*of man*) **to w., to go whoring,** fréquenter les prostituées; courir les filles; courir la gueuse; (*b*) (*of woman*) se prostituer; se livrer à la débauche.

whoremonger ['hɔ:mʌŋgər], *s.m.* débauché; coureur de filles; coureur de la gueuse.

whoreson ['hɔ:sən], *s. A:* bâtard *m.*

whoring ['hɔ:riŋ], *s.* (*a*) prostitution *f*; (*b*) débauche *f.*

whorl [(h)wɔ:l, (h)wə:l], *s.* **1.** *Bot:* verticille *m.* **2.** tour *m* d'une spirale; spire *f*, circonvolution *f*, volute *f*; vortex *m* (d'une coquille). **3.** *Tex:* (*a*) volant *m* (d'un fuseau); (*b*) *Archeol:* **(spindle) w.,** fusaïole *f.*

whorled [(h)wɔ:ld, (h)wə:ld], *a.* (*of flowers, leaves, etc.*) verticillé; (*of shell, etc.*) convoluté, turbiné; *Arch: etc:* voluté.

whortleberry ['(h)wə:t(ə)lberi], *s. Bot:* airelle *f* (myrtille); myrtille *f*; **red w.,** airelle rouge; airelle canche; **bog w.,** airelle uligineuse, des marais.

whose [hu:z], *poss.pron.* **1.** de qui? (*denoting ownership*) à qui? **w. is this?** à qui ceci appartient-il? **w. are these gloves?** à qui sont ces gants? **w. umbrella is this?** à qui est ce parapluie? **w. daughter are you?** de qui êtes-vous la fille? **w. fault is it?** à qui la faute? **w. book did you take?** c'est le livre de qui que vous avez pris? **2.** (*rel.*) (*a*) dont; **the pupil w. work I showed you,** l'élève dont je vous ai montré le travail; **the house w. windows are broken,** la maison dont les fenêtres sont cassées; **a mother w. children give her more trouble than joy,** une mère à qui ses enfants donnent plus d'ennuis que de joie; (*b*) (*after prep.*) de qui; duquel, *f.* de laquelle; *pl.* desquels, *f.* desquelles; **the man to w. wife I gave the money,** l'homme à la femme de qui, duquel, j'ai donné l'argent; **the person for w. sake he did it,** la personne par égard pour qui il l'a fait.

whoso ['hu:sou], *pron. A:* = WHOEVER, 1, 2.

whosoever, *Poet:* **whosoe'er** [hu:sou'evər, -'ɛər], *pron. esp. Lit:* (*emphatic*) = WHOEVER.

why [(h)wai]. **1.** *adv. & conj.* (*a*) pourquoi? pour quelle raison? **w. did you do that?** pourquoi avez-vous fait cela? **w. didn't you say so?** que ne le disiez-vous? il fallait le dire! **w. do you say that?** pour quelle raison, à cause de quoi, dites-vous cela? **w. not?** pourquoi pas? **w. not let him do as he pleases?** que ne le laisse-t-on faire! **w. so?** pourquoi cela? **w. on earth does he meddle?** de quoi diable se mêle-t-il? (*b*) (*rel.*) pourquoi; **that is (the reason) w. . . .,** voilà pourquoi . . .; c'est ce qui fait que . . .; **w. he should always be late I do not understand,** qu'il soit toujours en retard, je ne me l'explique pas; **I'll tell you w.,** *F:* **for w.,** je vous dirai pourquoi. **2.** *s.* (*pl.* **whys**) pourquoi *m*, raison *f*, cause *f*, motif *m*; **I like to know the whys and wherefores of a thing,** j'aime à savoir le pourquoi et le comment d'une chose. **3.** *int.* (*a*) (*expressing surprise*) **w., it's David!** tiens, mais c'est David! **w., that's true!** tiens, c'est vrai! c'est bien vrai! (*b*) (*expressing protest*) **w., you're not afraid, are you?** voyons, vous n'avez pas peur? **w., what's the harm?** voyons, quel mal y a-t-il à cela? mais quel mal y a-t-il? (*c*) (*expressing hesitation*) **w. I really don't know,** vraiment, franchement, je ne sais pas; (*d*) (*introducing apodosis*) **if this doesn't do, w. we must try something else!** si ceci ne réussit pas, alors, eh bien, il faudra essayer autre chose!

whydah ['(h)widə], *s. Orn:* **w. (bird),** veuve *f*; **long-tailed w.,** veuve géante; **paradise w.,** veuve à collier d'or; **pin-tailed w.,** veuve dominicaine; **red-collared w.,** veuve en feu; **shaft-tailed w.,** veuve royale.

wick[1] [wik], *s.* **1.** mèche *f* (d'une lampe, d'une bougie); **w. trimmer,** mouchettes *fpl.* **2.** *Mch: etc:* **(oil) w.,** mèche de graisseur, de graissage; **w. yarn,** coton *m* pour mèches. **3.** *P:* **he gets on my w.,** il me tape sur les nerfs.

wick[2], *s. A:* (*found in place names*) village *m*, hameau *m.*

wicked ['wikid], *a.* **1.** (*evil*) mauvais, méchant; pervers; **a truly w. man,** un homme essentiellement mauvais; **a w. crime,** un crime atroce, affreux; **a w. lie,** un mensonge (i) inique, (ii) mal intentionné; **it's a w. lie,** c'est faux et archifaux; *s.pl.* **the w.,** les méchants. **2.** (*attenuated meanings*) (*a*) (*unpleasant, severe*) (*of weather*) affreux, atroce; (*of pain, etc.*) cruel, atroce; **the cold was w.,** il faisait un froid terrible, atroce; **he's got a w. temper,** il a très mauvais caractère; (*b*) **it's w. to waste so much food,** c'est un crime de gaspiller tant de nourriture; *F:* **a w. price,** un prix scandaleux; **it's a w. shame that . . .,** il est scandaleux que + *sub.*; (*c*) (*mischievous*) malicieux, espiègle, fripon; **w. smile,** sourire malicieux; *F:* (*to child*) **you w. little thing!** petit vilain! petite vilaine! **3.** *F:* excellent; réussi; **a w. shot,** un coup de tonnerre.

wickedly ['wikidli], *adv.* **1.** méchamment; d'une manière perverse. **2.** (*a*) terriblement, affreusement; cruellement; abominablement; **it was w. cold,** il faisait terriblement, abominablement, froid; **w. expensive,** hors de prix; (*b*) malicieusement; d'une manière espiègle; **she was smiling w.,** elle avait un sourire malicieux.

wickedness ['wikidnis], *s.* **1.** méchanceté *f*; perversité *f*; **we were horrified by the sheer w. of the crime,** l'atrocité *f* de ce crime nous a profondément choqués. **2. this horse has no w.,** ce cheval n'a pas de vice.

wicker ['wikər], *s.* (*a*) osier *m*; *attrib.* **w. chair,** chaise *f* en osier (tressé), en vannerie; (*b*) = WICKERWORK.

wickerwork ['wikəwə:k], *s.* (*a*) vannerie *f*; osier (tressé); *Aut:* **w. body,** carrosserie cannée; (*b*) *Fort: etc:* clayonnage *m.*

wicket ['wikit], *s.* **1.** guichet (d'une porte, d'une porte d'écluse, pratiqué dans un mur, etc.). **2.** (*a*) **w. (door),** porte à piétons; (*b*) **w. (gate),** petite porte à claire-voie;

barrière *f*; portillon *m* (de passage à niveau, etc.). 3. *NAm:* (*in bank, etc.*) guichet. 4. *Cr:* (*a*) guichet; **wickets pitched at 12 o'clock,** la partie commence à midi; **the w. is down,** le guichet est renversé; **w. keeper,** garde-guichet *m, pl.* gardes-guichet; gardien *m* de guichet; (*b*) le terrain entre les guichets; **soft w.,** terrain mou; *Fig:* **to be on a good, a sticky, w.,** être dans une position avantageuse, difficile. 5. *NAm:* (*at croquet*) arceau *m.*

widdershins ['widəʃinz], *adv.* = WITHERSHINS.

wide [waid], *a., adv. & s.*

I. *a.* 1. large; **a w. road,** une route large; **the road gets wider after the village,** au-delà du village la route s'élargit; **to be five metres w.,** avoir cinq mètres de large, de largeur; avoir une largeur de cinq mètres; **how w. is the room?** quelle est la largeur de la pièce? de quelle largeur est la pièce? **to give a w. yawn,** bâiller en ouvrant largement la bouche; *Cin:* **w. screen,** grand écran; *Aut:* (*on vehicle*) **w. load** = convoi exceptionnel. 2. (*of range, experience, knowledge, etc.*) étendu, vaste, ample; (*of influence, etc.*) répandu; **the w. world,** le vaste monde; **w. plain,** plaine *f* d'une grande étendue; **to vary within w. limits,** varier avec des écarts importants; **there is a w. difference between . . .,** il y a une grande différence entre . . .; **business with w. ramifications,** entreprise *f* aux ramifications très étendues; **in a wider sense,** par extension; *Ph:* **w. range of frequencies,** grande gamme de fréquences; *Phot:* **w. angle of view,** grand angle de champ; *St.Exch:* **w. quotation,** cours *m* avec un grand écart entre le prix d'achat et celui de vente. 3. (*a*) (vêtement) ample, large; (*b*) (vues, opinions) larges, libérales, sans étroitesse; **w. definition,** définition très large; **in the widest sense of the word,** dans l'acception la plus large du mot. 4. (*a*) éloigné, loin; **to be w. of the mark,** être loin de compte; (*b*) *Cr:* **w. ball,** balle écartée, qui passe hors de la portée du batteur. 5. *F:* malin, retors; **a w. boy,** un malin, un débrouillard, un filou; un chevalier d'industrie.

II. *adv.* 1. (*a*) loin; **far and w.,** de tous côtés; partout; **to fall w. of the mark,** tomber loin du but; (*b*) **w. apart,** espacé; **with one's legs w. apart,** les jambes très écartées. 2. (ouvrir, etc.) largement, grandement; **to fling the door open w., w. open,** ouvrir la porte toute grande; **w.-open door,** porte toute grande ouverte; **to open all the windows w.,** ouvrir toutes les fenêtres en grand; **to open one's eyes w.,** ouvrir les yeux tout grands; **to be w. awake,** être complètement, bien, éveillé; *Box:* **to leave oneself w. open,** se découvrir; *Aut: etc:* **to take a bend w.,** prendre un virage large.

III. *s.* 1. *Cr:* balle écartée, qui passe hors de la portée du batteur. 2. *F:* **broke to the w.,** fauché, sans le sou.

wide-angle ['waidæŋgl], *a. Phot:* **w.-a. lens,** (objectif) grand angulaire *m.*

wideawake ['waidəweik]. 1. *a. & s.* **w. (hat),** chapeau *m* en feutre à larges bords; chapeau ecclésiastique. 2. *s. Orn:* sterne fuligineuse.

wide-eyed ['waidaid], *a.* les yeux grands ouverts, les yeux écarquillés, en écarquillant les yeux; **he looked at me in w.-e. amazement,** il m'a regardé les yeux comme des portes cochères.

widely ['waidli], *adv.* 1. largement; d'une manière étendue; **w. distributed material,** matière très répandue; **w. read newspaper,** journal répandu, très lu, à grande circulation; **the most w. read papers,** les journaux les plus lus; **to be w. read,** (i) (*of author, etc.*) avoir un public très étendu; (ii) (*of pers.*) avoir beaucoup lu; avoir de la lecture; **he has travelled w.,** il a beaucoup voyagé. 2. (planter, etc.) à de grands intervalles, en espaçant les plants. 3. extrêmement, excessivement, très; **w. different versions of what happened,** versions très différentes de ce qui est arrivé; versions de l'événement qui diffèrent du tout au tout.

widen ['waid(ə)n]. 1. *v.tr.* (*a*) élargir (une route, etc.); agrandir (qch.) en large; donner plus d'ampleur à (un vêtement); (*b*) évaser (un trou, etc.); (*c*) étendre (l'influence, les limites, de qch.); **to w. the terms of a law,** étendre les termes d'une loi; donner plus d'extension aux termes d'une loi. 2. *v.i.* (*a*) **to w. (out),** s'élargir; s'agrandir (en large); s'évaser; (*b*) **the breach is widening,** la rupture s'accentue; (*c*) (*of influence, etc.*) s'étendre.

wideness ['waidnis], *s.* 1. largeur *f* (considérable) (d'un escalier, etc.). 2. vaste étendue *f* (d'une plaine, d'une influence, etc.).

widening ['waid(ə)niŋ], *s.* 1. élargissement *m*; agrandissement *m* (en large). 2. extension *f* (d'une influence, etc.).

widespread ['waidspred]. 1. (*of plain, wings, etc.*) étendu. 2. répandu; universel; général, -aux; **the shortage is w.,** la disette est générale; **w. opinion,** opinion largement répandue; **w. sense of insecurity,** sentiment universel d'insécurité; **w. damage,** de grands dégâts.

widgeon ['widʒən], *s. Orn: NAm:* (*a*) **European w.,** canard siffleur, *Fr.C:* canard siffleur d'Europe; **American w.,** canard siffleur d'Amérique; (*b*) *Ven: F:* vingeon *m.*

widow[1] ['widou], *s.* 1. veuve *f*; **she was left a w. at (the age of) thirty,** elle a été laissée veuve à l'âge de trente ans; **she remained a w.,** elle est restée veuve. 2. *Orn:* **w. bird,** veuve.

widow[2], *v.tr.* **to be widowed,** devenir veuf, veuve; perdre son mari, sa femme.

widowed ['widoud], *a.* (homme) veuf; (femme) veuve; **his w. mother,** sa mère qui est veuve; **w. life,** veuvage *m.*

widower ['widouər], *s.m.* veuf.

widowhood ['widouhud], *s.* veuvage *m.*

width [widθ], *s.* 1. largeur *f* (d'une route, de la poitrine, etc.); ampleur *f* (d'un vêtement); ouverture *f* (d'une voûte, etc.); grosseur *f* (d'un pneu); **w. of wings,** envergure *f* (d'un oiseau, d'un avion); **to be three metres in w.,** avoir trois mètres de large; **w. between the columns,** écartement *m* des colonnes; *Const:* **w. of stair,** longueur *f* d'emmarchement; *N.Arch:* **extreme w.,** largeur au fort (d'un navire); *Rail:* **w. of vehicle and load,** gabarit *m* du véhicule. 2. largeur (de vues, d'idées). 3. *Tex:* lé *m,* laize *f,* largeur (d'un tissu); **double w.,** grande largeur; **single w.,** petite largeur; **you need three widths for the skirt,** il vous en faut trois lés pour la jupe.

widthwise ['widθwaiz], *adv.* dans la largeur.

wield [wi:ld], *v.tr. esp. Lit:* manier (l'épée, la plume); tenir (le sceptre, etc.); **brush wielded by a skilful hand,** pinceau conduit par une main exercée; **to w. power,** exercer le pouvoir; avoir l'autorité, la haute main.

wife, *pl.* **wives** [waif, waivz], *s.f.* 1. femme (mariée); *esp. Adm: & Lit:* épouse; **Mr Martin and his w.,** M. Martin et sa femme; **she was his second w.,** il l'avait épousée en secondes noces; **she will make a good w.,** elle fera une bonne épouse; **the baker's, butcher's, grocer's, w.,** la boulangère, la bouchère, l'épicière; *O:* **to take a w.,** se marier, prendre femme; **to take s.o. to w.,** épouser qn; prendre qn pour femme; **lawful, wedded, w.,** épouse légitime; **she's his common law w.,** ils cohabitent, vivent comme mari et femme; *F:* ils se sont mariés derrière l'église; **battered wives,** femmes battues; *P:* **the w.,** la ménagère, la bourgeoise. 2. (*a*) *A:* femme; commère; (*b*) **old wives' remedy,** remède *m* de bonne femme; **old wives' tale,** conte de vieille femme, de bonne femme; conte bleu.

wifely ['waifli], *a.* conjugal, -aux, de bonne épouse.

wifie ['waifi], *s. P:* la ménagère, la bourgeoise.

wig [wig], *s.* 1. (*a*) perruque *f*; **bob w.,** perruque à marteaux; **bobtail w.,** perruque ronde; **theatrical w.,** perruque de théâtre; **w. block, stand,** tête *f* à perruque; champignon *m*; *Lit:* **the w., the scalpel and the cloth,** le droit, la médecine et l'église; les trois professions libérales; *A:* **there were wigs on the green,** il y a eu une bagarre; *P:* **to blow one's w.,** fulminer, sortir de ses gonds; (*b*) postiche *m.* 2. *F: O:* chevelure *f*; tignasse *f*; **what a w.!** quelle perruque!

wigeon ['widʒən], *s. Orn:* canard siffleur, *Fr.C:* canard siffleur d'Europe; **American w.,** canard siffleur d'Amérique.

wigged [wigd], *a.* (juge, etc.) à perruque.

wigging ['wigiŋ], *s. F: O:* verte semonce; grondée *f*; savon *m*; **to give s.o. a good w.,** tancer vertement qn; **to get a good w.,** se faire bien gronder; se faire laver la tête; recevoir un savon.

wiggle[1] ['wig(ə)l], *v. F:* (*a*) *v.tr.* agiter, remuer (qch.) (d'un mouvement de va-et-vient); **to w. one's hips,** se tortiller les hanches; (*b*) *v.i.* se remuer, se tortiller; (*of fish*) frétiller; (*c*) *v.i. & tr.* **to w. (one's way) out of a difficulty,** se tirer, s'extraire, d'une position difficile; **to try to w. out of it,** chercher une échappatoire; **to w. one's way in,** se faufiler, s'insinuer.

wiggle[2], *s.* (*a*) *F:* **w. (waggle),** tortillement *m* (du corps, etc.); **to give sth. a w.,** agiter, remuer, qch.; **the worm gave a w.,** le ver s'est tortillé; (*b*) *P:* **to get a w. on,** se dépêcher, se grouiller.

wiggly ['wigli], *a. F:* qui se remue, se tortille; **w. line,** trait ondulé.

wight [wait], *s. A:* être *m,* personne *f*; **a poor, sorry, w.,** un pauvre hère.

wigmaker ['wigmeikər], *s.* perruquier, -ière; posticheur, -euse.

wigwam ['wigwæm], *s.* wigwam *m.*

wilco ['wilkou], *int. esp. U.S: W.Tel:* (= **will comply**) j'exécute.

wild [waild], *a., adv. & s.*

I. *a.* 1. (*of animal, plant, etc.*) sauvage; **w. flowers,** fleurs *f* des champs, fleurs sauvages; **w. boar,** sanglier *m*; **w. rabbit,** lapin *m* de garenne; **w. country,** pays inculte, sauvage, désert. 2. (*a*) (vent) furieux, violent; (torrent) impétueux; **w. sea,** mer agitée; **a w. (and stormy) night,** une nuit de tempête; (*b*) (animal) farouche, inapprivoisé; *Hist:* **to be drawn by w. horses,** être écarté à quatre chevaux; *F:* **w. horses wouldn't drag it out of me,** rien au monde ne me le ferait dire; (*c*) (*of pers.*) dissipé, dissolu, désordonné; (*of adolescent*) fougueux et indiscipliné; (*of behaviour*) déréglé; **to lead a w. life,** mener une vie déréglée, *F:* de bâton de chaise; (*d*) **in w. disorder,** dans un désordre indescriptible; (*e*) *Paperm:* **w. look-through,** épair nuageux, irrégulier; (*f*) *Cards:* (carte) libre. 3. (*a*) **w. applause,** applaudissements *m* frénétiques; **w. enthusiasm,** enthousiasme délirant, débordant; **w. eyes,** yeux égarés; **w. with joy,** fou, éperdu, de joie; **w. with rage, anger,** fou de rage, de colère; en fureur, furieux; **it makes me w. to think that . . .,** j'enrage, cela me met en rage, quand je pense que . . .; **to drive s.o. w.,** mettre qn en fureur; **it's enough to drive you w.,** c'est à vous rendre fou; *F:* **to be w. with s.o.,** être furieux contre qn; **to be w. about s.o.,** être emballé pour qn; **to be w. about sth.,** (i) être furieux au sujet de qch.; (ii) être passionné par qch.; trouver qch. passionnant; **I'm really w. about it,** ça me met en rage, en boule; **I'm not w. about it,** ça ne m'emballe pas; (*b*) (idée) fantasque; (projet) insensé, extravagant; **w. talk,** propos *mpl* en l'air; **w. rumour,** bruit absurde, extravagant, sans fondation; **w. promises,** promesses extravagantes; **w. exaggeration,** exagération insensée; **to make a w. guess (at the answer),** répondre à tout hasard, à l'aveuglette; **w. delusions,** illusions folles; **w. gallop,** galop furieux; **w. dance,** danse échevelée; **to make a w. rush at sth.,** se ruer sur qch.

II. *adv.* (*a*) (*of plant*) **to grow w.,** retourner, pousser, à l'état sauvage; (*b*) **to run w.,** (i) (*of children*) mener une vie sans discipline; courir les rues; (ii) (*of hooligans*) se livrer à des actes de violence; (iii) (*of escaped bull, etc.*) s'emballer; **she lets her children run w.,** elle ne surveille aucunement ses enfants; elle a lâché la bride à ses enfants; (*c*) (*of oil well*) **to blow w.,** jaillir violemment; être difficile à capter.

III. *s.* (*of animal*) **in the w.,** à l'état sauvage; **the call of the w.,** l'appel de la jungle; **in the wilds,** dans une région sauvage, déserte, inculte; dans la brousse; **to go out into the wilds,** pénétrer dans une région inexplorée, dans la brousse; **he disappeared into the wild(s),** il a disparu dans la nature; **he lives in the wilds of Afghanistan,** il habite au fin fond de l'Afghanistan.

wildcat[1] ['waildkæt], *s.* (*a*) *Z:* chat sauvage; (*b*) *F:* homme, femme, colérique, qui s'emporte facilement; (*c*) *Petr:* sondage *m* d'exploration, forage *m* de reconnaissance; (*d*) *attrib.* **w. scheme,** projet insensé, extravagant; spéculation risquée; **w. strike,** grève surprise, sauvage; *NAm: Rail:* **w. engine,** machine *f* haut-le-pied; **w. train,** train *m* qui ne figure pas dans l'horaire.

wildcat[2], *v.i. Petr:* faire des sondages d'exploration, des forages de reconnaissance.

wildcatter ['waildkætər], *s. Petr:* foreur *m* d'exploration.

wildebeest ['wildibi:st, 'vil-], *s. Z:* gnou *m*; **black w.,** gnou à queue blanche; **blue w.,** gnou gorgon, taurin, rayé, bleu.

wilderness ['wildənis], *s.* 1. (*a*) désert *m*; lieu *m* sauvage; pays *m* inculte; **a voice in the w.,** *B:* **the voice of one crying in the w.,** une voix qui prêche dans le désert; *F:* (*of politician, party*) **to be in the w.,** ne plus être au pouvoir; (*b*) partie inculte, laissée à l'état sauvage (d'un jardin, etc.). 2. *Lit:* solitude *f*; lieu éloigné.

wildfire ['waildfaiər], *s.* 1. (*a*) *A:* feu grégeois; (*b*) (*of report, etc.*) **to spread like w.,** se répandre comme une traînée de poudre; se propager avec la rapidité de l'éclair. 2. *Med: A:* érysipèle *m.*

wildfowl ['waildfaul], *s. coll.* (*a*) gibier *m* à plume; (*b*) gibier d'eau; sauvagine *f.*

wildfowler ['waildfaulər], *s.* chasseur *m* au, de, gibier d'eau, à la sauvagine; huttier *m.*

wildfowling ['waildfauliŋ], *s.* chasse *f* au gibier d'eau, à la sauvagine, au marais.

wilding ['waildiŋ], *s. Bot:* 1. plante sauvage; *Arb:* sauvageon *m.* 2. (*a*) pommier *m* sauvage; (*b*) pomme *f* sauvage.

wildlife ['waildlaif], *s.* faune *f* (et flore *f*).

wildly ['waildli], *adv.* 1. (écrire, parler) d'une manière extravagante; **to talk w.,** dire des folies; parler en l'air; **to rush about w.,** courir çà et là comme un fou; **to look at s.o. w.,** regarder qn éperdument, avec des yeux hagards; **to clap w.,** applaudir frénétiquement; **her heart was beating w.,** son cœur battait à se rompre; **w. happy,** follement heureux; **to be w. excited,** être dans les nues; *F:* **I'm not w. enthusiastic about it,** ça ne m'emballe pas. **2.** (vivre, se comporter) d'une manière dissolue. **3.** (répondre) au hasard, au petit bonheur, sans réflexion, à l'aveuglette; **to hit out w.,** lancer des coups au hasard.

wildness ['waildnis], *s.* **1.** état *m* sauvage (d'un pays, d'un animal, d'une plante); état inculte (d'une région). **2.** (*a*) fureur *f*, impétuosité *f* (du vent, des vagues); déchaînement *m* (de la tempête); (*b*) nature *f* farouche (du gibier, etc.); sauvagerie *f*; (*c*) dérèglement *m* (de mœurs); égarements *mpl* (de conduite). **3.** frénésie *f*, délire *m* (d'applaudissements); extravagance *f* (d'idées, de sentiments, de paroles).

wile[1] [wail], *s. usu. pl.* ruse *f*, artifice *m*, finasserie *f*; **to fall a victim to s.o.'s wiles,** succomber aux séductions de qn.

wile[2], *v.tr.* **1.** tromper, séduire, charmer (qn). **2.** = WHILE[2].

wilful ['wilfəl], *a.* **1.** (*of pers.*) obstiné, entêté, opiniâtre, volontaire. **2.** (*of action*) fait avec intention; fait exprès, de propos délibéré, à dessein; commis de parti pris; *Jur:* **w. murder,** homicide volontaire, prémédité; assassinat *m*; **w. damage,** bris *m*; dommage délibéré.

wilfully ['wilfəli], *adv.* **1.** obstinément; avec entêtement; opiniâtrement, volontairement. **2.** exprès, à dessein, avec intention, avec préméditation, de parti pris.

wilfulness ['wilfəlnis], *s.* **1.** obstination *f*, entêtement *m*, opiniâtreté *f*. **2.** préméditation *f*, intention *f*.

Wilhelmina [wilhel'mi:nə], *Pr.n.f.* Wilhelmine.

wiliness ['wailinis], *s.* astuce *f*; caractère rusé (de qn).

will[1] [wil], *s.* **1.** (*a*) volonté *f*; **to have a strong, weak, w.,** avoir la volonté forte, faible, **w. of iron, iron w.,** volonté de fer; **he has a w. of his own,** ce qu'il veut il le veut bien; il sait ce qu'il veut; il est volontaire; **he has no w. of his own,** il n'a pas, il manque, de volonté; **strength of w.,** force *f* de volonté; détermination *f*; **the w. to live,** la volonté de vivre; **to take the w. for the deed,** accepter l'intention *f* pour le fait; tenir compte de l'intention; **where there's a w. there's a way,** vouloir c'est pouvoir; **with the best w. in the world,** avec la meilleure volonté du monde; **to do sth. of one's own free w. (and accord),** faire qch. de sa propre, de bonne, volonté; *Phil:* **free w.,** libre arbitre *m*; (*b*) **to work with a w.,** travailler de bonne volonté; **to go at it with a w.,** y aller de bon cœur, de toutes ses forces. **2.** (*a*) décision *f*; volonté; **the w. of God,** la volonté de Dieu; ce que Dieu veut; **the Lord's w. be done!** que la volonté du Seigneur s'accomplisse, soit faite! **Thy w. be done on earth as it is in heaven,** que ta volonté soit faite sur la terre comme au ciel; **to impose one's w. on s.o.,** imposer sa volonté à qn; (*b*) bon plaisir; gré *m*; *Lit:* **such is our w. and pleasure,** tel est notre bon plaisir; **at one's w. and pleasure, at w.,** selon son bon plaisir; à volonté; à discrétion; **to have one's w.,** (i) obtenir ce qu'on veut; avoir ce qu'on désire; (ii) faire à sa tête, à sa guise; *A:* **to have one's w. of a woman,** posséder une femme; **to change one's face at w.,** changer de visage à volonté; **one can't shed tears at w.,** les larmes ne se commandent pas; **at the w. of the wind,** au caprice des vents; **to do sth. of one's own free w.,** faire qch. de son plein gré; *O:* **she comes and goes at her own sweet w.,** elle va et vient à son (bon) gré, à son bon plaisir, à sa guise; *Mil:* **fire at w.,** feu *m* à volonté; **to do sth. against one's w.,** faire qch. contre son gré, malgré soi, à contrecœur; **to get married against one's father's w.,** se marier contre le gré, la volonté, de son père. **3. good w., ill w.,** bonne, mauvaise, volonté. **4.** *Jur:* testament *m*; acte *m* de dernière volonté; **the last w. and testament of. . .,** les dernières volontés de . . .; **this is my last w. and testament,** ceci est mon testament; **to make one's w.,** faire son testament; **to mention s.o. in one's w.,** mettre, coucher, qn sur son testament; **to dispute a w.,** attaquer un testament; **executor, -trix, of a w.,** exécuteur, -trice, testamentaire; **w. form,** formule *f* de testament; *Jur:* **nuncupative w.,** testament noncupatif.

will[2], *v.tr.* (*p.t. & p.p.* **willed** [wild]) **1.** (*a*) *A: & Lit:* **God so willed (it),** Dieu l'a voulu ainsi; **the king wills it (so),** telle est la volonté du roi; **Fate willed (it) that he should die,** le sort voulut qu'il mourût; **those who willed the revolution,** ceux qui ont voulu la révolution; **as we w. the end we must w. the means,** qui veut la fin veut les moyens; (*b*) **to w. s.o. to do, into doing, sth.,** faire faire qch. à qn par un acte de volonté, en lui imposant sa volonté; (*by hypnotism*) suggestionner qn. **2.** léguer (qch.); disposer de (qch.) par testament; **to w. one's money to a charity,** léguer son argent à une société de bienfaisance; **to w. one's property away from s.o.,** déshériter qn.

will[3], *modal aux. v. def.* (*I* **will,** *A: thou* **wilt** [wilt], *he, we, etc.,* **will;** *p.t. & condit.* **would** [wud], *A: thou* **wouldst** [wudst] *or* **wouldest** ['wudist]. *I will, he will, etc. are often contracted into* **I'll** [ail], **he'll** [hi:l], *etc.; I would, they would, etc., to* **I'd** [aid], **they'd** [ðeid], *etc. A: thou wilt to* **thou'lt** [ðault]; *will not and would not to* **won't** [wount], **wouldn't** ['wud(ə)nt])

I. vouloir. **1.** vouloir, désirer; (*a*) *A:* **what wilt thou?** que désires-tu? **what would they?** que désirent-ils? (*b*) *esp. Lit:* **do as you w.,** faites comme vous voudrez, comme vous l'entendrez; **let him do it when he w.,** qu'il le fasse quand il voudra, quand bon lui semblera; **the place where I would be,** l'endroit où je voudrais être; **I would have stayed there for ever,** j'aurais voulu y rester toujours; **what would you have me do?** que voulez-vous que je fasse? **I would advise you to read this book,** je vous conseille de lire ce livre; **say what you w., you won't be believed,** quoi que vous disiez, vous aurez beau dire, malgré vos protestations, on ne vous croira pas; **look which way you w.,** de quelque côté que vous regardiez; **look at it as I would I couldn't excuse him,** de n'importe quel point de vue je ne pouvais l'excuser; (*c*) *esp. Lit:* (*optative*) **would (that) I were a bird!** je voudrais être un oiseau! **would it were not so!** je voudrais qu'il n'en fût pas ainsi! plût à Dieu qu'il n'en fût pas ainsi! **would to God, to heaven, it were not, wasn't, true!** plût à Dieu, au ciel, que cela ne fût pas vrai! **2.** (*consent*) **the great** *I will,* le grand oui; **I w. not do it,** je refuse de le faire; je ne le ferai pas; **I w. not have that said of me,** je ne veux pas qu'on dise cela de moi; **I wouldn't do it for anything,** je ne le ferais pour rien au monde; **he could if he would,** il le pourrait s'il le voulait; **I'm looking for a chauffeur who would look after the garden as well,** je cherche un chauffeur qui s'occuperait aussi du jardin; *F:* **will do!** (n'ayez pas peur) je le ferai! **the wound wouldn't heal,** la blessure ne voulait pas se cicatriser; **the engine won't start,** le moteur ne veut pas démarrer; **just wait a moment, w. you?** voulez-vous bien attendre un instant? **would you pass the mustard please?** voudriez-vous bien me passer la moutarde? **he will, would, go no further,** il ne veut pas, ne voulait pas, n'a pas voulu, aller plus loin; **he would have nothing to do with it,** il a refusé de s'y mêler; **he w., would, have none of it,** (i) il n'en veut, n'en voulait, à aucun prix; (ii) il refuse, refusait, d'en entendre parler; **I won't have it sold,** je n'entends pas qu'on le vende; **I w.** *not* **have it!** je ne le veux pas! **so he won't come, won't he?** il refuse donc de venir? **won't you sit down?** asseyez-vous, je vous en prie; *will* **you be quiet!** voulez-vous bien vous taire? *Prov:* **he that w. not when he may, when he w. he shall have nay,** qui refuse muse. **3.** (*emphatic*) **accidents** *will* **happen,** on ne peut pas éviter les accidents; **he** *will* **have it that I was wrong,** il veut absolument que je me sois trompé; **he** *will* **have it that it was a ghost,** il affirme que c'était un revenant; **he** *will* **go out in spite of his cold,** il persiste à sortir malgré son rhume; **oh, he** *will,* **w. he?** ah, vraiment! c'est comme ça? **he** *will* **get in my way,** il est toujours dans mon chemin, dans mes jambes; **he** *will, would,* **make me stay in bed,** il veut, voulait, a voulu, à toute force me faire garder le lit; il insiste, a insisté, pour que je garde le lit; **the doctor** *will* **have his little joke,** il aime (à) plaisanter, le docteur; **I quite forgot!—you would!** j'ai oublié!—c'est bien de vous! **you** *would* **go and tell him about that!** vous aviez besoin d'aller lui parler de ça! **I met him in a bar yesterday—that's where you** *would* **meet him,** je l'ai rencontré dans un bar hier—c'est bien là qu'on le rencontre en effet; **he** *will* **talk out of turn,** il faut toujours qu'il parle quand on ne lui demande rien; *F:* **I wouldn't know!** je ne saurais dire. **4.** (*habit*) **this hen w. lay up to six eggs a week,** cette poule pond jusqu'à six œufs par semaine; **she would often return home exhausted,** elle rentrait souvent très fatiguée. **5.** (*of conjecture*) **this w. be the Strand I suppose,** c'est bien le Strand, n'est-ce pas? **that would be your cousin?** ça c'est sans doute votre cousin? **you'll be tired,** vous devez être fatigué; **he's very late, he'll have missed the train,** il est terriblement en retard, il a dû manquer le train; **I was quite young at the time; it would be before the war,** j'étais assez jeune alors; c'était, me semble-t-il, avant la guerre.

II. (*used as aux. v. forming future tenses*) **1.** (*used in the 1st pers.; for the 2nd and 3rd pers. see* SHALL) **we would have come if you had, had you, invited us earlier,** nous serions venus si vous nous aviez invités plus tôt; **I won't be caught again,** on ne m'y reprendra plus. **2.** (*simple futurity; used in the 2nd and 3rd pers.; for the 1st pers. see* SHALL) (*a*) **I shall tell you everything and you w. give me your opinion,** je vous dirai tout et vous me donnerez votre opinion; **w. he be there?—he w.,** y sera-t-il?—oui (, il y sera); **no, he w. not, he won't,** non (, il n'y sera pas); **but I shall starve!—no, you won't,** mais je mourrai de faim!—pas du tout; **you won't forget, w. you?** vous n'oublierez pas, hein? **you'll write to me, won't you?** vous m'écrirez, n'est-ce pas? **he told me he would be there,** il m'a dit qu'il serait là; **he had finished his work and would be home in an hour's time,** son travail était fini et dans une heure il serait de retour chez lui; (*b*) (*immediate future*) **Mr. Long w. explain the situation to you,** M. Long va vous expliquer la situation; (*verb of motion omitted*) *A:* **I'll to the kitchen,** je vais me rendre à la cuisine; (*c*) (*in injunctions*) **you'll be careful to . . .,** vous aurez soin de . . .; **you'll be here at three,** soyez ici à trois heures; (*d*) (*in Scot. & N. of Engl.* **I will = I shall**) **I will be happy to see you again,** je serai heureux de vous revoir; **we will be there,** nous serons là. **3.** (*in conditional sentences*) **if he comes she w. speak to him,** s'il vient elle lui parlera; **he would come if you invited him,** il viendrait si vous l'invitiez; **had he, if he had, let go he would have fallen,** s'il avait lâché prise il serait tombé; *Austr: P:* **wouldn't it!** que c'est dégueulasse!

Will[4], *Pr.n.m.* (*dim. of William*) Guillaume.

willed[1] [wild], *a.* **1.** (acte, etc.) voulu, volontaire. **2.** (argent, etc.) légué.

willed[2], *a.* **1.** *A:* disposé (à faire qch.). **2.** (*with adj. prefixed*) **strong-w., weak-w.,** de forte volonté, sans volonté.

willet ['wilit], *s. Orn:* symphémie semi-palmée, *Fr.C:* chevalier semi-palmé.

willey[1,2] [wili], *s. & v.tr.* = WILLOW[2,3].

William ['wiljəm]. **1.** *Pr.n.m.* Guillaume; *Hist:* **W. the Conqueror,** Guillaume le Conquérant; **W. Rufus,** Guillaume le Roux; **W. the Silent,** Guillaume le Taciturne; **W. of Orange,** Guillaume d'Orange. **2.** *Hort:* **W. pear,** poire *f* Williams; *Bot:* **sweet w.,** œillet *m* du poète; jalousie *f*.

williamsite ['wiljəmzait], *s. Miner:* williamsite *f*.

willies ['wiliz], *s.pl. F:* **to have the w.,** avoir le trac, la frousse; **it gives me the w.,** cela me met les nerfs en pelote, en boule.

willing ['wiliŋ], *a.* **1.** (*a*) de bonne volonté; bien disposé; serviable; **w. men,** hommes de bonne volonté; **w. hands,** mains empressées; **we found plenty of w. hands,** il y avait beaucoup de gens prêts à nous donner un coup de main; **w. horse,** (i) cheval franc du collier; (ii) homme de bonne volonté (qui se laisse imposer); *Prov:* **do not spur the w. horse,** bon cheval n'a pas besoin d'éperon; **w. sacrifice,** sacrifice fait de bonne volonté; (*b*) consentant. **2. to be w. to do sth.,** vouloir bien faire qch.; être disposé à faire qch.; **w. to help,** prêt à rendre service; complaisant; **to be w. to listen to an argument,** être accessible à un raisonnement; **I am more than w. to come with you,** je ne demande pas mieux que de vous accompagner; **I am w. for you to come,** je veux bien que vous veniez; **to be able and w.,** avoir à la fois le pouvoir et la volonté; **I am able and w. to help them,** je peux les aider et je le ferai très volontiers; **w. or not,** bon gré mal gré; **God w.,** s'il plaît à Dieu; *F:* **to show w.,** faire preuve de bonne volonté.

willingly ['wiliŋli], *adv.* **1.** volontairement; spontanément; de plein gré. **2.** (*a*) de bonne volonté; de bon cœur; (*b*) volontiers; avec plaisir; de grand cœur.

willingness ['wiliŋnis], *s.* **1.** bonne volonté; empressement *m*; **with the utmost w.,** de très bon cœur. **2.** consentement *m*; complaisance *f*; **to express one's w. to do sth.,** accepter de faire qch.; consentir à faire qch.

williwaw ['wiliwɔ:], *s. Meteor:* williwans *m*, rafale violente (du détroit de Magellan).

will-less ['willis], *a.* sans volonté; sans caractère.

will-o'-the-wisp [wiləðə'wisp], *s.* feu follet; flammerole *f*.

willow[1] ['wilou], *s.* **1.** *Bot:* (*a*) **w. (tree),** saule *m*; **weeping w.,** saule pleureur; **crack w.,** saule fragile; **goat w., sallow w.,** (saule) marceau *m*; **grey w.,** saule cendré; **white w., swallowtail w., bat w.,** saule blanc; **water w.,** osier *m*; **almond w.,** osier brun; **almond-leaved w.,** osier à trois étamines; **golden w.,** osier jaune; **w. plantation,** saulaie *f*; (*b*) **false w.,** baccharis *m*; **bush w.,** combretum *m*; **primrose w.,** jussiée *f*; **Virginia(n) w.,** itea *m*; (*c*) *Cer:* **w. pattern plate,** assiette *f* à décoration à la chinoise en teinte bleue, à motif de saule pleureur. **2.** *Cr: F:* **the w.,** la batte. **3.** *Orn:* **w. grouse,** *NAm:* **w. ptarmigan,** lagopède *m* des saules; lagopède blanc, subalpin; **w. warbler, w. wren,** pouillot *m* fitis; pouillot chantre. **4.** *a. & s.* **w. green,** céladon (*m*) *inv.*

willow[2], *s. Tex: Paperm:* effilocheuse *f*; batteuse *f*, ouvreuse *f*; willow *m*; loup *m*, diable *m*.

willow[3], *v.tr. Tex: Paperm:* louveter, effilocher, battre, ouvrir (les chiffons, etc.).

willower ['wilouər], *s. Tex:* **1.** (*pers.*) louveteur *m*. **2.** = WILLOW[2].

willowherb ['wilouhə:b], *s. Bot:* épilobe *m*; *F:* osier fleuri; laurier *m* (de) Saint-Antoine; **rosebay w.,** épilobe à épi(s); **milk w.,** salicaire *f.*

willowing ['wilouiŋ], *s. Tex:* louvetage *m.*

willowy ['wiloui], *a.* (*of figure, form*) souple, svelte, élancé, flexible.

willpower ['wilpauər], *s.* volonté *f*; **lack of w.,** manque *m* de volonté.

willy[1,2] ['wili], *s. & v.tr.* = WILLOW[2,3].

willy-nilly ['wili'nili], *adv.* bon gré mal gré; de gré ou de force; qu'on le veuille ou non.

willy-willy ['wiliwili], *s. Meteor:* (*in Austr.*) (*a*) cyclone *m*; (*b*) tourbillon *m.*

wilt [wilt]. **1.** *v.i.* (*a*) (*of plant*) se flétrir, se faner; (*b*) (*of pers.*) dépérir, languir; perdre son énergie; (*c*) *F:* perdre contenance (devant des reproches); se dégonfler. **2.** *v.tr.* (*of the heat, etc.*) flétrir (les fleurs).

Wilton ['wiltən], *a. Prehist:* wiltonien.

wily ['waili], *a.* rusé, astucieux; fin, finaud; malin, -igne; roublard; *F:* ficelle; **he's a w. old bird,** c'est un vieux roublard.

wimble ['wimb(ə)l], *s. Tls:* **1.** *A:* vrille *f.* **2.** (*a*) tarière *f*; *Min:* tarière à glaise; (*b*) vilebrequin *m.*

wimple[1] ['wimp(ə)l], *s.* **1.** (*a*) guimpe *f* (de religieuse); (*b*) voile *m.* **2.** *A: & Lit:* (*of stream*) méandre *m.*

wimple[2]. **1.** *v.tr.* (*a*) envelopper (la tête) d'une guimpe; (*b*) voiler (qch.). **2.** *v.i. Scot: Lit:* (*of stream*) (*a*) se rider; (*b*) serpenter; faire des méandres; (*c*) couler en murmurant; gazouiller.

win[1] [win], *s. Sp:* victoire *f*; **to have three wins in succession,** gagner trois fois de suite; **to back a horse for a w.,** jouer un cheval gagnant.

win[2], *v.tr. & i.* (*p.t. & p.p.* **won** [wʌn]; *pr.p.* **winning**) **1.** gagner (une bataille, une course, un pari); remporter, gagner (un prix); remporter la victoire; **to w. one's spurs,** gagner ses éperons; (*at cards, etc.*) **to w. money from s.o.,** gagner de l'argent à qn; **to w. one's money back,** regagner son argent; **to w. back a province from the enemy,** reconquérir une province sur l'ennemi; **to w. the toss,** gagner (à pile ou face); **heads you w. tails I lose,** vous gagnez de toute façon; *Golf:* **to w. by four up and three to play,** gagner par quatre et trois à jouer; *Rac:* **to w. by a length,** gagner d'une longueur; **to w. by a short head,** coiffer d'une courte tête; **to back a horse to w.,** jouer un cheval gagnant; **who's winning?** qui est-ce qui gagne? *F:* **you (just) can't w.,** j'aurai, on aura, toujours tort; **you can't w. them all,** on ne peut pas plaire à tout le monde; **go in and w.!** vas-y! tu réussiras! **2.** acquérir (de la popularité, la bienveillance de qn); captiver (l'attention de qn); gagner (la confiance de qn); **his bravery won him a decoration,** son action courageuse lui a valu une médaille; **to w. s.o.'s love,** se faire aimer de qn. **3. to w. all hearts,** gagner, conquérir, tous les cœurs; **to w. the admiration of one's audience,** gagner l'admiration de ses auditeurs; **to w. s.o. away from sth.,** détourner, détacher, qn de qch.; **see whether you can w. him over,** essayez de le persuader de se mettre avec nous, d'accepter notre point de vue; **I won him round to my point of view,** j'ai réussi à lui faire accepter mon point de vue. **4. to w. one's way to . . .,** parvenir à . . .; **he won his way to the top of his profession,** il a réussi (par ses propres efforts) à atteindre le sommet de sa profession; **to w. through,** y arriver, parvenir, réussir; venir à bout; gagner droit de cité; **to w. home,** (i) regagner sa maison (en dépit des obstacles); (ii) parvenir à son but; *O:* **to w. the shore,** gagner le rivage; **to w. free,** arriver à se dégager. **5.** (*a*) *A: & Lit:* **to w. one's living, one's daily bread,** gagner sa vie, son pain quotidien; (*b*) *O:* extraire (le charbon, le minerai); **to w. metal from ore,** extraire, récupérer, le métal du minerai; (*c*) *A:* **to w. the crops,** récolter la moisson; (*d*) *P:* voler; **I won it,** je l'ai chauffé.

wince[1] [wins], *s.* crispation (nerveuse, de douleur); tressaillement *m*; **without a w.,** sans sourciller; sans tiquer; sans broncher.

wince[2], *v.i.* faire une grimace de douleur, tressaillir de douleur; **he didn't w. in spite of the pain,** en dépit de la douleur il n'a pas sourcillé, son visage est resté calme; **the remark made him w.,** à cette observation il s'est crispé, a tressailli.

winceyette [winsi'et], *s. Tex:* flanelle *f* de coton.

winch[1] [win(t)ʃ], *s.* **1.** *Mec.E:* manivelle *f.* **2.** *Mec.E:* treuil *m* (de hissage); *F:* bourriquet *m*, singe *m* (d'une chèvre); **hand w., crank w.,** treuil à manivelle, treuil à bras; **geared w.,** treuil composé, à engrenages; **worm w.,** treuil à vis tangente, à vis sans fin; *Rail:* **shunting w.,** treuil de manœuvre; *Av:* **w. launch(ing),** lancement (d'un planeur) au treuil; **w. handle,** manivelle de treuil. **3.** *Fish:* moulinet *m.* **4.** *Nau:* (*a*) treuil, guindeau *m*; (*b*) *Y:* winch *m.*

winch[2], *v.tr. Mec.E: etc:* **to w. sth. (in, up),** tirer, soulever, qch. à l'aide d'un treuil; *Av:* **to w.-launch a glider,** lancer un planeur au treuil.

Winchester ['win(t)ʃistər], *Pr.n. Sm.a:* **W. (rifle),** winchester *f.*

wind[1] [wind], *s.* **1.** vent *m*; (*a*) **north w., south w.,** vent du nord, du sud; **east w., west w.,** vent d'est, d'ouest; **mountain w.,** vent de montagne; **there was a terrible w.,** il faisait un vent à écorner les bœufs; **house exposed to all the winds, to the four winds of heaven, to every w. that blows,** maison exposée à tous les vents, aux quatre vents du ciel; **where's the w. coming, blowing, from?** d'où vient le vent? *Fig:* **to see, to find out, which way the w. blows,** regarder de quel côté vient le vent; **with her hair streaming in the w.,** la chevelure au vent; **sound carried by, that comes on, the w.,** son qui est porté par le vent; *F:* **there's something in the w.,** il se prépare, se mijote, quelque chose; il y a anguille sous roche; il y a quelque chose en train; **to have the w. in one's face,** aller contre le vent, avoir vent debout; *Ven:* (*of bird*) **to fly down, before, the w.,** aller à vau-vent; **to hunt, shoot, down (the) w.,** chasser à vau-vent; *F:* **to go like the w.,** aller comme le vent, plus vite que le vent; **one might as well talk to the w.,** c'est prêcher dans le désert; c'est comme si on chantait; **to throw one's cares to the w.,** chasser les soucis; **to sow the w. and reap the whirlwind,** semer le vent et récolter la tempête; **to raise the w.,** (i) faire souffler le vent; (ii) *F:* se procurer de l'argent; obtenir du crédit; battre monnaie; *F:* **to have, get, the w. up,** avoir le trac, la frousse; avoir une peur bleue; **to put the w. up s.o.,** donner, flanquer, le trac à qn; faire une peur bleue à qn; (*b*) **cross w.,** vent de travers; *Nau: etc:* **fair w.,** bon vent; vent favorable, propice; **foul w.,** vent contraire; **w. and weather permitting,** si le temps le permet; **head w.,** vent debout; **to have a head w.,** avoir vent debout; **to sail against the w.,** avoir le vent droit debout; **rear w., stern w., following w.,** vent arrière; *Nau:* vent de poupe; **to sail, run, before the w.,** courir vent arrière, courir le vent en poupe; **to sail with w. and tide,** avoir vent et marée; **against w. and tide,** contre vent et marée; **in the teeth of the w.,** contre le vent; **to sail into the w.,** venir, aller, au lof; **to sail off the w.,** naviguer vent largue; avoir du largue; **to sail on a w., close to the w., near the w.,** pincer, serrer, le vent; courir près du vent; tenir le vent; aller, courir, naviguer, au plus près; *F:* **to sail close to, near, the w.,** friser (i) l'indécence, (ii) la malhonnêteté; faire des affaires douteuses; **it's a bit near the w.,** il y a du louche là-dedans; **to set a sail to the w.,** aventer une voile; **sails all in the w.,** voiles en ralingue; **to take the w. out of a ship's sails,** déventer un navire; *F:* **to take the w. out of s.o.'s sails,** déjouer les projets de qn; devancer qn; couper l'herbe sous le pied de qn; **that took all the w. out of my sails,** ça m'a coupé, cassé, bras et jambes; ça m'a paralysé; **to keep the better w.,** serrer le vent de plus près (qu'un autre navire); **between w. and water,** à fleur d'eau, à la flottaison; (*c*) *Av:* **surface w.,** vent de sol; **upper w.,** vent en altitude; **up w., down w., cross w., landing,** atterrissage *m* dans le vent, vent arrière, vent de travers, de côté; **w. indicator,** indicateur *m* de direction du vent; **w. sock, sleeve, stocking,** manche *f* à air; *F:* biroute *f*; *Nau:* **w. scoop,** (i) manche à air, à vent; (ii) bonnette *f* de hublot. **2.** *Ven: etc:* vent; **to have the w. of the game,** avoir le vent de son gibier; *F:* **to get w. of sth.,** avoir vent de qch.; éventer (un secret, etc.). **3.** *Med: F:* vent(s); flatuosité *f*; **to break w.,** lâcher un vent, avoir des gaz; **to have w.,** (i) roter; (ii) péter. **4.** souffle *m*, respiration *f*, haleine *f*; **to have plenty of w.,** avoir du souffle; **to get one's second w.,** reprendre haleine; **let me get my w.,** laissez-moi souffler; *O:* **to hit, catch, s.o. in the w.,** couper la respiration à qn. **5.** (*a*) *Ind: etc:* vent; air, vent, de soufflerie; *Mus:* **w. supply (of an organ),** soufflerie *f*; *Aedcs:* **w. tunnel,** soufflerie; tunnel *m* aérodynamique; **Eiffel-type w. tunnel, open-circuit w. tunnel,** soufflerie Eiffel, soufflerie en circuit ouvert; **closed-jet, open-jet, w. tunnel,** soufflerie à veine fermée, à veine ouverte; **return-flow w. tunnel,** soufflerie à écoulement de retour; **small-scale w. tunnel,** soufflerie pour essais de maquettes; **supersonic w. tunnel,** soufflerie supersonique; **w. tunnel cascade,** aubage directeur de soufflerie; **w. tunnel nozzle,** diffuseur *m* de soufflerie; (*b*) *Aedcs:* **w. resistance,** résistance *f* de l'air. **6.** *Mus:* **w. instrument,** instrument *m* à vent; (*in orchestra*) **the w.,** les instruments à vent.

wind[2], *v.tr.* **1.** [waind] (*p.t. & p.p.* **winded** ['waindid] *or* **wound** [waund]) **to w. a, the, horn,** sonner du cor; sonner une fanfare. **2.** [wind] (**winded**) (*a*) *Ven:* (*of hounds*) éventer, flairer (le gibier); avoir vent (du gibier); (*b*) faire perdre le souffle à (qn); couper la respiration, le souffle, à (qn); essouffler (qn, un cheval); **the stiff climb winded him,** la rude montée l'a essoufflé; (*c*) laisser reprendre haleine à, laisser souffler (un cheval).

wind[3] [waind], *s.* **1.** *Tchn:* déformation *f* (du bois, etc.); **out of w.,** non gauchi, non faussé. **2.** = WINDING[3] 1, 6.

wind[4] [waind], *v.* (*p.t. & p.p.* **wound** [waund])

I. *v.i.* **1.** tourner; faire des détours; serpenter; aller en spirale; (*of path, river*) serpenter, se replier; (*of staircase*) monter en colimaçon; **the path winds round the lawn,** le sentier contourne la pelouse, tourne autour de la pelouse; **river that winds across the plain,** rivière *f* qui serpente à travers la plaine; **the road winds up, down, the hill,** le chemin monte, descend, en serpentant. **2.** (*of thread, etc.*) **to w. round sth.,** s'enrouler autour de qch. **3.** (*of board*) (se) gauchir.

II. *v.tr.* **1.** enrouler; *Tex:* dévider, envider (le fil); *Ser:* dévider (la soie); **to w. wool into a ball,** enrouler de la laine en peloton; **to w. string round sth.,** enrouler de la corde autour de qch.; **to w. cotton on a reel,** bobiner du coton; *Fish:* **to w. in the line,** ramener la ligne; **she wound her arms round the child,** elle a entouré l'enfant de ses bras; **the serpent was winding itself round its prey,** le serpent s'enroulait autour de sa proie. **2. to w. a bobbin,** enrouler le fil sur une bobine; *El:* **to w. a dynamo,** armer une dynamo. **3.** remonter (l'horloge). **4.** *Min:* extraire, hisser, remonter (le minerai, etc.). **5.** *Nau:* **to w. the ship,** éviter, virer, cap pour cap.

III. (*compound verb*) **wind up.** (*a*) *v.tr.* (i) enrouler (de la laine, un cordage, etc.); (ii) bander, remonter (un ressort); remonter (sa montre); *F:* (*of pers.*) **to be all wound up,** être remonté; (iii) *Turf: F:* affûter (un cheval); (iv) finir, terminer (qch.); *Com:* liquider (une société); régler, clôturer (un compte); **to w. up the debate,** terminer les débats; **he wound up his speech by announcing that . . .,** il a terminé son discours en faisant savoir que . . .; (*b*) *v.i. F:* finir; terminer; **how does the novel w. up?** comment le roman s'achève-t-il, se dénoue-t-il? quel est le dénouement?

windage ['windidʒ], *s.* **1.** *Ball:* (*a*) dérivation *f*, dérive *f* (due au vent); (*b*) vent *m* (entre le projectile et l'âme). **2.** *Mec.E:* jeu *m*; espace *m* libre.

windbag ['windbæg], *s.* **1.** réservoir *m* à air. **2.** outre *f* (d'une cornemuse). **3.** *F:* orateur verbeux; moulin *m* à paroles; **what a w.!** quel bavard!

windblown ['windbloun], *a.* **1.** emporté par le vent. **2. w. hair,** cheveux ébouriffés par le vent.

windborne ['windbɔːn], *a.* porté par le vent.

windbound ['windbaund], *a. Nau:* retenu par des vents contraires; retardé par le vent.

windbox ['windbɔks], *s.* **1.** boîte *f* à vent, caisse *f* à vent, chambre *f* à air (d'un cubilot, d'un haut fourneau). **2.** *Mus:* (*also* **wind chest**) laie *f*, sommier *m* (d'un orgue).

windbreak ['windbreik], *s. Hort: etc:* abrivent *m*; brise-vent *m inv*; abat-vent *m inv.* **2.** *For:* (*broken treetop*) volis *m.*

windburn ['windbəːn], *s. Agr:* ventaison *f.*

windcheater ['windtʃiːtər], *s. Cost:* blouson *m*; *Fr.C:* coupe-vent *m inv.*

windcutter ['windkʌtər], *s.* **1.** *Rail:* coupe-vent *m inv* (d'une locomotive). **2.** *Mus:* lèvre supérieure (de la bouche d'un tuyau d'orgue).

winded ['windid], *a.* hors d'haleine; essoufflé; à bout de souffle.

winder ['waindər], *s.* **1.** (*pers.*) (*a*) *Tex: etc:* bobineur, -euse; dévideur, -euse; **ball w.,** peloteur, -euse; pelotonneur, -euse; **weft w.,** trameur, -euse; *El:* **coil w.,** bobinier *m*; (*b*) remonteur, -euse (d'horloges); (*c*) *Min:* mécanicien *m* d'extraction. **2.** (*device*) (*a*) *Tex:* bobinoir *m*, dévidoir *m*; **pirn, weft, cop, w.,** can(n)etière *f*; (*b*) *Cin:* embobineur *m*, embobineuse *f*, bobinoir (du film); (*c*) *Paperm:* bobineuse *f*; (*d*) *Fish:* plioir *m*; (*e*) remontoir *m* (d'une horloge, d'une montre); (*f*) *Min:* machine *f*, moteur *m*, d'extraction, de hissage; (*g*) *Aut: etc:* lève-glace(s) *m inv* (de portière). **3.** *Const:* **winders,** marches tournantes, dansantes, gironnées (d'un escalier).

windfall ['windfɔːl], *s.* **1.** (*a*) bois gisant; chablis *m*, chable *m*, ventis *m*; (*b*) fruit abattu par le vent; fruit tombé. **2.** (*a*) aubaine *f*; bonne fortune; (*b*) héritage inattendu; *Jur:* acquêt *m.*

windfallen ['windfɔːlən], *a.* (fruit) abattu par le vent, tombé.

windflower ['windflauər], *s. Bot:* anémone *f* des bois; sylvie *f*; gentiane *f* des marais; **narcissus-flowered w.,** anémone à fleurs de narcisse.

windgall ['windgɔːl], *s. Vet:* molette *f*, vessigon *m.*

windhover ['windhɔvər], *s. Orn:* (faucon *m*) crécerelle *f.*

winding[1] ['waindiŋ], *s.* sonnerie *f* (du cor).

winding[2], *a.* (chemin, cours d'eau) sinueux, plein de détours, qui serpente; (chemin) anfractueux; (route) en lacets; **w. streets,** rues tortueuses; **w. stairs,** marches gironnées, en limaçon.

winding[3], *s.* **1.** mouvement sinueux; cours sinueux; serpentement *m*; replis *mpl.* **2.** (*a*) *Tex: etc:* bobinage *m*, embobinage *m*; **w. frame,** dévideuse *f*; *El:* enroulage *m*, enroulement *m*, bobinage; **barrel w.,** enroulement en manteau; **closed w., re-entrant w.,** enroulement fermé; (*b*) *Tex:* **w. back,** déroulement; (*c*) **w. of sth. in sth.,** enroulement de qch. dans qch.; *A:* **w. sheet,** linceul *m*, suaire *m*. **3.** *Carp:* gauchissement *m*. **4.** *Min:* extraction *f*, remonte *f*, remontée *f*; **w. shaft,** puits *m* d'extraction; **w. engine,** machine *f*, moteur *m*, d'extraction, de hissage; **w. gear,** (i) *Min:* appareils *mpl*, machine, d'extraction; (ii) treuil *m* (d'un ascenseur); **w. drum,** (i) *Min: Mec.E:* tambour *m*, poulie *f*, d'enroulage; (ii) cylindre enrouleur. **5.** (*a*) **w. (up),** remontage *m* (d'une horloge, d'une montre); (*b*) **w. (up),** bandage *m* (d'un ressort). **6.** (*a*) méandre *m*, repli *m*; (*b*) spire *f* (d'un bobinage, etc.). **7.** (*a*) **windings,** sinuosités *f*, replis, méandres (d'une rivière); lacets *m* (d'un chemin); détours *m* (d'une route); contournements *m* (d'une côte); tortuosités *f* (d'un labyrinthe); (*b*) spires, enroulement (d'une bobine, etc.); *El:* **armature w.,** enroulement d'enduit; **closed w., re-entrant w.,** enroulement fermé; **field w.,** enroulement inducteur; **lap w.,** enroulement imbriqué; **pie w.,** bobine *f* à galettes. **8. w. up,** (*a*) fin *f*, conclusion *f* (de qch.); *F:* dénouement *m* (d'un roman, etc.); (*b*) *Com:* liquidation *f*, dissolution *f* (d'une société); clôture *f* (d'un compte).

windjammer ['win(d)dʒæmər], *s.* **1.** *Nau:* grand voilier. **2.** *Cost:* blouson *m*.

windlass[1] ['windləs], *s.* treuil *m*, vindas *m*; *F:* singe *m*; (*on dray, etc.*) pouliot *m*; (*small*) vireveau(t) *m*, vireveau *m*; *Nau:* guindeau *m*; cabestan horizontal; **differential w., Chinese w.,** treuil différentiel, treuil de la Chine; **Spanish w.,** (é)trésillon *m*; **w. end,** poupée *f* de guindeau.

windlass[2], *v.tr.* élever, hisser (qch.) au treuil, au guindeau; guinder (qch.).

windlestraw ['wind(ə)lstrɔ:], *s. Bot:* tige desséchée (de certaines graminées).

windmill[1] ['windmil], *s.* **1.** moulin *m* à vent; (*for pumping*) aéromoteur *m*, aermotor *m* (pour puits); épuise-volante *f*, *pl.* épuises-volantes; éolienne *f*; *F:* **to tilt at windmills,** se battre contre des moulins à vent (comme Don Quichotte). **2.** *Toys:* moulinet *m*. **3.** *Com: F:* traite *f* en l'air; cerf-volant *m*, *pl.* cerfs-volants.

windmill[2], *v.i. Av:* (*of propeller*) tourner en moulinet; (*of engine*) tourner en autorotation.

windmilling ['windmiliŋ], *s. Av:* autorotation *f*.

window ['windou], *s.* (*a*) fenêtre *f*; **casement w.,** fenêtre croisée, à battants; **sash w.,** fenêtre à coulisse, à guillotine; *Fr.C:* fenêtre anglaise; **bay w., bow w.,** fenêtre en saillie; **sliding w.,** fenêtre à glissière; **balance w.,** fenêtre oscillante, à bascule, à charnière; **attic w.,** fenêtre en mansarde; **double windows,** contre-châssis *m*; **blank, blind, false, w.,** fausse fenêtre; fenêtre feinte, aveugle; *Jur:* **to block up the windows,** condamner les vues; *Ecc.Arch:* **stained-glass w.,** vitrail, -aux *m*; **rose w.,** rosace *f*; **w. frame,** dormant *m* de fenêtre; bâti dormant, de croisée; châssis dormant, de fenêtre; chambranle *m*; **w. seat,** banquette *f* (dans l'embrasure d'une fenêtre); coussiège *m*; **w. cleaner,** laveur *m* de vitres, de carreaux; *Adm: A:* **w. tax, duty,** impôt *m* sur les fenêtres; **to look in at, out of, the w.,** regarder par, à la, fenêtre; **to break a w.,** casser une vitre, un carreau; *Lit:* **the windows of heaven opened,** les cataractes du ciel s'ouvrirent; *F:* **you make a better door than a w.,** tu n'es pas transparent; ton père n'était pas vitrier; (*b*) **French w.,** porte-fenêtre *f*, *pl.* portes-fenêtres; (*c*) (*of ticket office*) guichet *m*; (*d*) **(shop) w.,** vitrine *f*, devanture *f*; **w. display,** étalage *m*; **to put sth. in the w.,** mettre qch. à l'étalage, à la devanture; **premises with extensive w. space,** local *m* aux vitrines spacieuses; **w. dressing,** (i) (l'art de) l'étalage; (ii) *F:* façade *f*, décor *m* de théâtre, camouflage *m*; **w. dresser,** étalagiste *mf*; *F:* **he puts all his goods in the w.,** il est tout façade; *F:* **w. shopping,** lèche-vitrines *m*; **to go w. shopping,** faire du lèche-vitrines; (*e*) *Aut: Rail:* vitre *f*; glace *f*; *Aut:* **rear w.,** lunette *f* arrière; **wrap-round rear w.,** lunette arrière panoramique, enveloppante; **tinted windows,** vitres teintées; **car with electrically operated windows,** voiture à lève-glaces électriques; (*f*) fenêtre (d'une enveloppe); panneau transparent; (*g*) *Anat:* fenêtre (du tympan); (*h*) **firing, launching, w.,** fenêtre de lancement (d'un spationef d'exploration); (*i*) *Elcs:* **windows,** bandes *f* métalliques (de brouillage de radar).

windowledge ['windouledʒ], *s.* rebord *m*, appui *m*, banquette *f*, de fenêtre.

windowless ['windoulis], *s.* **1.** sans fenêtres. **2.** *Cmptr:* (bobine de bande) sans évidement.

windowpane ['windoupein], *s.* vitre *f*, carreau *m*.

windowsill ['windousil], *s.* appui *m*, rebord *m*, tablette *f*, de fenêtre.

windpipe ['windpaip], *s. Anat: F:* trachée-artère *f*, *pl.* trachées-artères.

windpower ['windpauər], *s.* énergie éolienne.

windproof ['windpru:f], *a.* à l'épreuve du vent.

wind-rode ['windroud], *a. Nau:* évité au vent.

windrow ['windrou], *s. Agr:* andain *m*.

windrower ['windrouər], *s. Agr:* andaineur *m*.

windsail ['windseil], *s. Nau:* manche *f* à vent, à air (en toile).

windscreen ['windskri:n], *s.* **1.** abrivent *m*; abat-vent *m inv*; brise-vent *m inv*; pare-vent *m inv*. **2.** *Aut:* pare-brise *m inv*; **laminated w.,** pare-brise feuilleté; **w. wiper,** essuie-glace *m*, *pl.* essuie-glaces; **self-parking w. wiper,** essuie-glace à retour automatique; **w. washer,** lave-glace *m*, *pl.* lave-glaces.

windshield ['windʃi:ld], *s.* **1.** = WINDSCREEN 1. **2.** *N.Am:* = WINDSCREEN 2.

windstorm ['windstɔ:m], *s.* tempête *f* de vent; tourbillon *m*.

windsucker ['windsʌkər], *s.* cheval cornard, tiqueur; tiqueur, -euse.

windsurfer ['windsə:fər], *s. Sp:* planche *f* à voile.

windsurfing ['windsə:fiŋ], *s.* **to go w.,** faire de la planche à voile.

windswept ['windswept], *a.* **1.** (*of place*) balayé par le vent, venteux. **2. w. hairstyle,** coiffure *f* en coup de vent; **w. hair,** cheveux ébouriffés, balayés, par le vent.

wind-up ['waindʌp], *s. F:* fin *f*, conclusion *f* (de qch.).

windward ['windwəd]. **1.** *a.* au vent; *Geog:* **the W. Islands,** les îles du Vent; **the W. and Leeward Islands,** les îles Caraïbes. **2.** *s.* côté *m* au vent; *Nau:* **to work, ply, to w.,** louvoyer; **to fetch to w.,** gagner le vent; gagner dans le vent, au vent; **lying to (the) w. of . . .,** situé au vent de . . ..

windy ['windi], *a.* **1.** venteux; **w. weather,** temps venteux; **w. day,** journée de grand vent; **it's very w.,** il fait beaucoup de vent. **2.** (*of place, etc.*) balayé par le vent; battu du vent; exposé au vent, aux quatre vents. **3.** *A:* (côté) du vent; *F:* **to keep on the w. side of the law,** se tenir hors de l'atteinte de la loi. **4.** (*a*) *Med: F:* venteux, flatueux; (*b*) *F:* **to be w.,** avoir le trac, la frousse. **5.** *F: O:* (*a*) (*of plan, etc.*) vain, vide, qui n'est que du vent; (*b*) (*of speech, etc.*) ampoulé, enflé, verbeux.

wine[1] [wain], *s.* (*a*) vin *m*; **white, red, rosé, w.,** vin blanc, rouge, rosé; **dry, sweet, w.,** vin sec, doux; **sparkling w.,** vin mousseux; **this wine's a bit thin,** ce vin c'est de la piquette; **the w. trade,** le commerce des vins; **w. merchant,** négociant *m* en vins; marchand *m* de vins; **w. taster,** (i) (*pers.*) dégustateur, -trice; piqueur *m* de vins; (ii) (*thg*) tasse *f* à déguster; sonde *f* à vin, tâte-vin *m inv*; **w. cellar, w. vault(s),** cave *f*, caveau *m* (à vin); **w. bottle,** bouteille *f* à vin; **w. basket,** panier verseur à vin; **w. bin,** porte-bouteilles *m inv*; **w. cooler,** rafraîchissoir *m*, rafraîchisseur *m* (à vin); seau *m* à glace, à rafraîchir; (*in restaurant*) **wine list,** carte *f* des vins; **w. waiter,** sommelier, -ière; **(cheese and) w. party,** réunion *f* où l'on boit du vin (servi avec du fromage); **w. producing district,** pays *m* vignoble, de vignobles; **w. vinegar,** vinaigre *m* de vin; *Lit: Pej:* **w. bibber,** buveur, -euse (de vin); **w. bibbing,** la boisson; l'ivrognerie *f*; (*b*) **rhubarb w., ginger w.,** vin de rhubarbe, de gingembre.

wine[2], *v.tr.* **to w. and dine s.o.,** fêter qn; offrir à qn un bon dîner arrosé de bons vins.

wine-coloured ['wainkʌləd], *a.* couleur de vin; lie de vin *inv*.

wineglass ['wainglɑ:s], *s.* verre *m* à vin.

wineglassful ['wainglɑ:sful], *s.* plein verre à vin.

winepress ['wainpres], *s.* pressoir *m*.

winery ['wainəri], *s.* établissement vinicole; chai *m*; **bottled at the w.** = mis en bouteilles au château.

wineskin ['wainskin], *s.* outre *f* à vin.

wing[1] [wiŋ], *s.* **1.** (*a*) aile *f* (d'oiseau, d'insecte, d'ange); **w. span, spread,** envergure *f*; **w. beat,** coup *m* d'aile; *Orn:* **w. quill,** rémige *f*; *Ent:* **w. case, sheath,** élytre *m*; *Moll:* **w. shell,** avicule *f*; strombe *m*; *Danc:* **pigeon w.,** aile de pigeon; **to take s.o. under one's w.,** prendre qn sous son aile, sous sa protection, sous son égide; *Lit:* **to come on the wings of the wind,** venir sur les ailes du vent; **fear lent him wings,** la peur lui donnait des ailes; *Nau:* **w. and w.,** avec bonnettes des deux bords; les voiles en paire de ciseaux; (*b*) course *f*, vol *m*, essor *m*; **to shoot a bird on the w.,** tirer un oiseau au vol, à la volée; **w. shooting,** tir *m* au vol, à la volée; (*of bird*) **to be on the w.,** voler; **to take w.,** s'envoler; prendre son vol, son essor; (*c*) *Mil. Av:* **wings,** insigne *m* de pilote. **2.** *Av:* aile (d'un avion); **wings, w. unit,** voilure *f*; **cambered w.,** aile cambrée, aile courbe; **cantilever w.,** aile en porte-à-faux, aile cantilever; **delta w.,** aile (en) delta; **fixed w.,** aile, voilure, fixe; **retractable w.,** aile rentrante; **flying w., all w. aircraft,** aile volante; **folding w.,** aile, voilure, repliable; **high w.,** aile, voilure, haute; **low w.,** aile, voilure, basse, surbaissée; **lower, upper, w.,** plan inférieur, supérieur; **receding w.,** aile fuyante; **rotary w.,** voilure tournante; **slotted w.,** aile à fente; **stub w.,** (i) amorce *f* d'aile; (ii) nageoire *f* (d'hydravion); **swept-back w.,** aile en flèche; **swing-w. aircraft,** avion à flèche, à voilure, variable; **tapered w.,** aile effilée; **tilting w.,** voilure basculante; **tilt-w. aircraft,** avion à voilure basculante; **variable-w. aircraft,** avion à voilure, à géométrie, variable; **w. area,** surface *f* alaire; **w. span, spread,** envergure *f*; **w. curve,** cambrure *f*, courbure *f*, de l'aile; **w. flap,** volet *m* d'aile, d'atterrissage, de courbure; **w. support,** attache *f* d'aile; **w. drag,** traînée *f* de l'aile; **w. loading,** charge *f* alaire; **w. panel,** élément *m* d'aile; **w. section,** (i) profil *m* d'aile; (ii) élément d'aile; **w. socket,** emplanture *f* d'aile; **w. sweepback,** flèche *f* d'aile; **w. tip,** extrémité *f*, saumon *m*, d'aile; **w. undersurface,** intrados *m*; **w. upper-surface,** extrados *m*. **3.** (*a*) battant *m* (d'une porte); (*b*) aile (d'un bâtiment); pavillon *m* (d'un hôpital, etc.); *Hyd.E:* **w. wall,** jouière *f*, musoir *m* (d'une écluse); *Th:* **the wings,** la coulisse, les coulisses; **in the wings,** (i) dans la coulisse; (ii) à la cantonnade; (*c*) *Mil:* aile, flanc *m* (d'une armée); *Fb: etc:* (i) aile; (ii) (*pers.*) ailier *m*; **the w. halves,** les demis *m* aile; *Pol:* **the left w. (of the party),** l'aile gauche (du parti); (*d*) aile (d'un moulin à vent, d'une selle); aile, ailette *f* (d'un ventilateur); oreille *f*, ailette (d'une vis); **w. bolt, screw,** boulon *m*, vis, à oreilles; *Furn:* **w. chair,** fauteuil *m* à oreillettes; (*e*) quart *m* de cercle (d'un compas à dessiner); **w. compass,** compas quart de cercle; (*f*) *Cin:* secteur *m* d'obscuration, secteur opaque (de l'obturateur). **4.** (*a*) *N.Arch:* flanc (d'un navire); **bridge w.,** aileron *m* de passerelle; **w. turret,** tourelle latérale; (*of cargo*) **in the wings,** en abord dans la cale; **w. feeder,** réservoir latéral; **w. furnace,** foyer *m* de côté; (*b*) (*of paddle steamer*) jardin *m* de tambour; (*c*) *Aut:* aile (d'une voiture); **w. mirror,** rétroviseur *m* de côté. **5.** (*a*) *Mil:* **headquarters w.,** compagnie *f* des services; (*b*) *Mil.Av:* escadre aérienne; *U.S:* brigade aérienne; **w. headquarters,** poste *m* de commandement d'escadre; **w. commander,** lieutenant-colonel *m*.

wing[2], *v.tr. & i.* **1.** (*a*) empenner (une flèche); (*b*) *Lit:* **fear winged his steps, his flight,** la peur lui donnait, lui prêtait, des ailes; (*c*) **to w. an arrow at s.o.,** lancer, décocher, une flèche à qn; (*d*) (*of bird, etc.*) **to w. the air, to w. its flight, its way,** voler; **birds winging towards the south,** oiseaux volant vers le sud. **2.** frapper, blesser (un oiseau) à l'aile; **I've winged him,** je lui ai mis du plomb dans l'aile.

winged [wiŋd, *Lit: often* 'wiŋid], *a.* (*a*) ailé; **w. words,** paroles ailées; *Ven:* **w. game,** gibier *m* à plumes, gibier ailé; *Bot:* **w. seed,** graine ailée; (*of ash, sycamore, etc.*) samare *f*; **the w. gods,** les dieux aligères; *Mil:* **w. bomb,** bombe empennée; *Gr.Ant:* **the W. Victory of Samothrace,** la Victoire de Samothrace; (*b*) (*with adj. prefixed, e.g.*) **white(-)w.,** aux ailes blanches.

winger ['wiŋər], *s. Fb: etc:* ailier *m*.

wingless ['wiŋlis], *a.* sans ailes; aptère; *Gr.Ant:* **the W. Victory,** la Nikê, la Victoire, aptère.

winglet ['wiŋlit], *s.* ailette *f*, cuilleron *m* (de diptère).

wing(-)shaped ['wiŋʃeipt], *a.* aliforme.

wink[1] [wiŋk], *s.* clignement *m* d'œil; clignotement *m*; clin *m* d'œil; **with a w.,** en clignant de l'œil, avec un clin d'œil; **in a w.,** en un clin d'œil; en un rien de temps; *F:* **to tip s.o. the w.,** prévenir, avertir, qn; faire signe à qn que le moment est venu d'agir; **to have forty winks,** faire un petit somme, une petite sieste; **I didn't sleep a w., didn't get a w. of sleep all night,** je n'ai pas dormi, fermé l'œil, de toute la nuit; *Prov:* **a nod is as good as a w. to a blind horse,** c'est comme si vous parliez à un sourd; **a nod's as good as a w. to him,** il entend à demi-mot.

wink[2]. **1.** *v.i.* (*a*) cligner de l'œil; cligner les yeux; **to w. at s.o.,** cligner de l'œil, lancer un clignement d'œil, à qn; (*b*) **to w. at an abuse,** fermer les yeux sur un abus; (*c*) (*of star, light*) vaciller, trembler, clignoter. **2.** *v.tr.* **she winked an eye,** elle a cligné de l'œil, a fait un clin d'œil; **she winked away a tear,** elle a clignoté des yeux pour chasser une larme.

winker ['wiŋkər], *s. Aut: F:* clignotant *m*.

winking[1] ['wiŋkiŋ], *a.* clignotant; (*of light, etc.*) vacillant, tremblant.

winking[2], *s.* **1.** clignement *m* de l'œil; clignotement *m*; *Anat:* **w. muscle,** orbiculaire *m* des paupières; **as easy as w.,** simple comme bonjour; *F:* **like w.,** en un clin d'œil; en un rien de temps. **2.** vacillation *f*, tremblement *m*, clignotement (d'une lumière).

winkle[1] [wiŋkl], *s.* **1.** *Moll:* bigorneau *m*; **sting w.,** cormaillot *m*, rocher épineux. **2.** *F:* **w. pickers,** chaussures *f* à bout pointu.

winkle[2], *v.tr. F:* **see if you can w. it out,** pourquoi ne pas essayer de l'extraire; **I couldn't manage to w. him out**

of his office, je n'ai pas réussi à le persuader de quitter son bureau, de le déloger de son bureau; **to w. out the enemy,** déloger l'ennemi.

winner ['winər], *s.* (*a*) vainqueur *m*; gagnant, -ante; gagneur, -euse; *Turf:* (cheval) gagnant; (*in major race*) lauréat, -ate; **the w. of the contest,** le vainqueur de l'épreuve; *Ten:* **the w. of the women's singles,** le vainqueur du simple dames; (*in lottery, etc.*) **the w. of the big prize,** le gagnant du gros lot; *Turf:* **Thomas rode three winners at Chantilly yesterday,** hier à Chantilly Thomas a gagné trois fois, a trois fois remporté le prix; **to back a w.,** (i) *Turf:* jouer un cheval gagnant; (ii) *F:* jouer gagnant, bien miser; **to be a sure w.,** partir gagnant; *Turf:* **all the winners!** résultat des courses! (*at fair, etc.*) **every time a w.!** à tous les coups l'on gagne! (*b*) *F:* roman, pièce, etc., à grand succès; **this book, this car, will be a w.,** ce livre, cette voiture, a un succès assuré, sera certainement une réussite; **I think you've a w. with your new assistant,** je crois que votre nouveau collaborateur ira loin.

winning[1] ['winiŋ], *a.* **1.** gagnant; **w. number,** numéro gagnant; (*in a lottery*) numéro sortant; **w. stroke,** coup décisif; **the w. game,** la partie décisive; la belle; **the w. side,** les vainqueurs *m*; **the w. horse,** le cheval gagnant; *Sp:* **w. streak, sequence,** suite *f* de victoires; **to have, hold, the w. hand,** détenir les cartes maîtresses. **2.** attrayant, séduisant, engageant, insinuant, attachant, attirant; **w. smile,** sourire engageant.

winning[2], *s.* **1.** (*a*) victoire *f*; conquête *f*, acquisition *f* (de qch.); **the w. of a battle,** le gain d'une bataille; **the w. of the battle doesn't mean the w. of the war,** gagner la bataille ne veut pas dire qu'on a gagné la guerre; (*b*) *Min:* extraction *f* (du charbon, etc.). **2. winnings,** (i) gains (aux courses, etc.); (ii) *Min:* (*gold*) récolte *f*.

winnow[1] ['winou], *s.* = WINNOWER 2.

winnow[2], *v.tr.* **1.** (*a*) *Agr:* vanner, sasser, tararer (le grain); **to w. (away, out) the chaff from the grain,** séparer l'ivraie d'avec le grain; (*b*) éplucher, sasser, examiner minutieusement (des preuves, etc.); **to w. the evidence,** passer les témoignages au crible. **2.** *Lit:* (*of bird, etc.*) battre (l'air); (*of wind*) agiter (les cheveux de qn).

winnower ['winouər], *s.* **1.** (*pers.*) vanneur, -euse. **2.** (*machine*) vanneuse *f*; cribleur *m*; sasseur *m* mécanique; van *m* mécanique; tarare *m*.

winnowing ['winouiŋ], *s.* **1.** (*a*) vannage *m*, ventage *m*; **w. basket,** van *m*; **w. machine** = WINNOWER 2; (*b*) examen minutieux; triage *m*. **2. winnowings,** vannure *f*.

winsome ['winsəm], *a.* (*of child, young woman*) captivant, séduisant, attrayant; **w. smile,** sourire séduisant.

winsomely ['winsəmli], *adv.* d'une manière captivante, attrayante.

winsomeness ['winsəmnis], *s.* charme *m*, attrait *m* (d'une jeune fille).

winter[1] ['wintər], *s.* (*a*) hiver *m*; **in w.,** en hiver; **on a fine winter('s) day,** par un beau jour d'hiver; *Lit:* **he has seen sixty winters,** il compte soixante hivers; **winter clothing,** vêtements *mpl* d'hiver; **the w. season,** la saison d'hiver; la saison hivernale; *Agr:* **w. ploughing,** entre-hivernage *m*; **w. resort,** station hivernale; **w. visitors,** hivernants *m*; **w. sports,** sports *m* d'hiver; **the W. Olympics,** les jeux olympiques d'hiver; *Mil: A:* **w. quarters,** quartiers *m* d'hiver; hivernage *m*; **to go into w. quarters,** prendre ses quartiers d'hiver; hiverner; *Nat.Hist:* **w. sleep,** sommeil hibernal; (*b*) *Bot:* **w. berry,** apalachine *f*; **w. cherry,** (i) alkékenge *f*; coquerelle *f*, coqueret *m*; herbe *f* à cloques; cerise *f* de suif, de juif, d'hiver, en chemise; (ii) cerisette *f*; morelle *f* faux piment; (iii) (*tree*) cerisier *m* d'amour; petit cerisier d'hiver; **w. cress,** barbarée *f*; roquette *f* des jardins; **w. lodge,** hibernacle *m*; (*c*) *Ent:* **w. moth,** phalène *f* d'hiver; chéimatobie *f*, *F:* nonne *f*.

winter[2]. **1.** *v.i.* hiverner, passer l'hiver (**at,** à). **2.** *v.tr.* hiverner (le bétail); conserver (des plantes) pendant l'hiver.

winter-flowering [wintə'flauəriŋ], *a.* (*of plant*) hibernal, -aux; hiémal, -aux.

wintergreen ['wintəgri:n], *s. Bot:* **1.** pyrole *f*. **2.** gaulthérie *f* du Canada; *F:* palommier *m*; thé *m* du Canada; thé rouge; *Pharm:* **oil of w.,** essence *f* de wintergreen.

wintering ['wintəriŋ], *s.* hivernage *m*.

winterization [wintərai'zeiʃ(ə)n], *s.* **1.** *Ch:* démargarination *f*, wintérisation *f*. **2.** *esp. NAm:* mise *f* en condition pour l'hiver (d'une voiture, d'une maison, etc.); *Fr.C:* hivérisation *f*.

winterize ['wintəraiz], *v.tr.* **1.** démargariner (les huiles). **2.** *esp. NAm:* mettre (une voiture, une maison, etc.) en condition pour passer l'hiver; *Fr.C:* hivériser.

winter-plough [wintə'plau], *v.tr. Agr:* entre-hiverner.

wintertime, *Lit:* **wintertide** ['wintətaim, -taid], *s.* l'hiver *m*.

winterweight ['wintəweit], *a.* (sous-vêtement etc.) d'hiver.

wint(e)ry ['wintri], *a.* d'hiver; hivernal, -aux; hiémal, -aux; **w. weather,** temps *m* d'hiver; temps rigoureux; **w. smile,** sourire (i) décourageant, (ii) de découragement; **w. reception,** accueil glacial.

winy ['waini], *a.* vineux; (odeur, etc.) du vin, de vin.

winze [winz], *s. Min:* descenderie *f*, descente *f*; beurtia(t) *m*.

wipe[1] [waip], *s.* **1.** (*a*) coup *m* de torchon, de mouchoir, d'éponge; **to give sth. a w. (over),** essuyer qch.; donner un coup de torchon à qch.; (*b*) *Cin:* (fermeture *f* en) fondu *m*; *T.V:* volet *m*. **2.** *F: A:* tape *f*, taloche *f*. **3.** *P:* (**nose**) **w.,** mouchoir *m*, tire-jus *m inv*.

wipe[2], *v.*

I. *v.tr. & i.* **1.** *v.tr.* essuyer (une table, une assiette, un tableau noir, etc.); **w. it clean, dry,** nettoyez-le, essuyez-le, bien; **to w. one's face, one's hands,** s'essuyer la figure, les mains; **to w. one's nose,** se moucher; **to w. a child's nose,** moucher un enfant; **to w. one's eyes,** s'essuyer les yeux; *F: O:* **to w. s.o.'s eye,** devancer qn; couper l'herbe sous le pied à qn. **2.** *v.tr. Plumb:* ébarber (un joint). **3.** *v.i.* (*a*) **the windscreen wiper isn't wiping,** l'essuie-glace ne marche pas; **I'll wash if you'll w.,** je vais laver si tu veux bien essuyer (la vaisselle); (*b*) *P: A:* **to w. at s.o.,** allonger un coup à qn.

II. (*compound verbs*) **1. wipe away,** *v.tr.* essuyer (ses larmes); enlever, ôter (une tache); **the rain wiped the footprints away,** la pluie a enlevé la trace des pas.

2. wipe off, *v.tr.* (*a*) enlever, essuyer (une éclaboussure, etc.); régler, liquider (une dette); (*b*) *F:* **that'll w. the smile off his face,** ça va lui enlever, supprimer, le sourire; **to w. a town off the map,** rayer une ville de la carte.

3. wipe out, *v.tr.* (*a*) essuyer (une baignoire, etc.); (*b*) liquider, amortir (une dette); effacer (une injure, etc.); passer l'éponge sur (qch.); (*c*) exterminer (une armée, etc.); *P:* tuer, lessiver (qn); **the fire wiped out the whole district,** l'incendie a rasé tout le quartier.

4. wipe up, *v.tr. & i.* nettoyer, enlever (une saleté); essuyer (la vaisselle).

wiper ['waipər], *s.* **1.** (*pers.*) essuyeur, -euse. **2.** (*a*) racleur *m*; **felt w.,** racleur en feutre; *Aut:* **windscreen w.,** essuie-glace(s) *m*; (*b*) *P:* (**nose**) **w.,** mouchoir *m*, tire-jus *m inv*. **3.** *Mec.E:* came *f*, mentonnet *m*; frotteur *m*; *I.C.E:* **ignition w.,** came d'allumage; **oil w.,** racleur d'huile; **w. lubrication,** graissage *m* par frotteur; **w. shaft,** arbre *m* à cames, des cames; **w. wheel,** roue *f* à cames.

wiping ['waipiŋ], *s.* **1.** essuyage *m*, nettoiement *m*; **w. out,** liquidation *f*, amortissement *m* (d'une dette); effacement *m* (d'une injure). **2.** *Mec.E:* **w. action,** mouvement glissant (d'une came, etc.); *El:* **w. contact,** contact frottant, à frottement.

wire[1] ['waiər], *s.* **1.** fil *m* métallique, fil de fer; (*a*) **iron w.,** fil de fer; **steel w.,** fil d'acier; **brass w.,** fil de laiton, d'archal; **silver w., copper w.,** fil d'argent, de laiton; **gold w.,** fil d'or; (*for lace, etc.*) or trait; trait *m*; **stranded w., twin w.,** fil torsadé; **galvanized w.,** fil (de fer) galvanisé; **fine w.,** fil ténu; **drawn w.,** fil étiré, tréfilé; **hard-drawn w.,** fil étiré à froid; **w. drawing,** tréfilerie *f*, tréfilage *m*, étirage *m*; **w.-drawing machine,** machine *f* à tréfiler; **w. drawer,** tréfileur *m*, étireur *m*; **w. stretcher, strainer,** tendeur *m* pour fil de fer; raidisseur *m*; cric-tenseur *m*, *pl.* crics-tenseurs; **w. netting,** treillis *m*, treillage *m*, métallique, en fil de fer; grillage *m*; *Mil:* **w. entanglement,** réseau(x) *m* (*pl*) de fil de fer (barbelé); **w. cloth,** toile *f* métallique; *Paperm:* toile de fabrication; (*for hand-made paper*) toile véline; *Paperm:* **w.-wove paper,** papier vélin; **w. mark,** vergeure *f*; *Bookb:* **w. stitcher,** brocheuse *f*; **continuous w. stitcher,** encarteuse-piqueuse *f*, *pl.* encarteuses-piqueuses; **w. edge,** morfil *m*, bavure *f* (d'un outil); **w. brush,** brosse *f* en fil de fer; carde *f* métallique (pour nettoyer les limes, etc.); *Engr:* boësse *f*; **w. mat,** décrottoir *m*, essuie-pieds *m*, métallique; **w. sieve,** tamis *m* métallique, de fil de fer; **w. mattress,** sommier *m* métallique; **w. glass,** verre armé; cristal armé; verre à fil de fer noyé; *Aut:* **w. wheels,** roues *f* fil; **w. stay,** hauban *m* en fil métallique; **w. bracing,** haubannage *m* en fil métallique; **w. cage,** cage *f* en fil de fer; *Vet:* **w. heel,** seime *f*; *Bot:* **w. grass,** pâturin comprimé; (*b*) *El: Telecom:* **telegraph, telephone, w.,** fil télégraphique, téléphonique; **w. tapping,** captage *m* de messages télégraphiques, téléphoniques; branchement *m* pour écoute clandestine; **w. tapper,** capteur *m* de messages télégraphiques, téléphoniques; *F:* **to get one's wires crossed,** se tromper, s'embrouiller; *U.S: Tp:* **party w.,** ligne partagée; *El:* **high-tension w.,** fil (à) haute tension; **connecting w.,** fil de connexion; **earth w.,** *NAm:* **ground w.,** fil de masse; **return w.,** fil de retour; **line w.,** fil de section; **feed w.,** fil d'aller, d'amenée; **live w.,** (i) fil sous tension, fil électrisé; (ii) *F:* homme, femme, dynamique; *Ball:* **w. guidance,** guidage *m* par fil; **w.-guided missile,** missile filoguidé; *Mec.E:* **bracing, staying, w.,** fil tendeur; *Av:* **drag w.,** fil de traînée; **locking w.,** fil à freiner; **retaining w., safety w.,** fil d'arrêt; **span w.,** fil aérien, fil tendeur; *Surg:* **ligature w., retaining w.,** fil de ligature, de contention; *Dent:* **arch w.,** fil d'arc; *Com:* **cheese w.,** fil à couper le beurre; (*in circus*) **the high w.,** la corde raide; *Th: etc:* **puppet wires,** ficelles *f* de marionnettes; *F:* **to pull the wires,** tirer les ficelles, faire jouer le piston; **w. pulling,** intrigues *fpl*; **w. puller,** intrigant, -ante; (*c*) *Cmptr:* **w. printing,** impression *f* par points; **w. printer,** imprimante *f* par points. **2.** télégramme *m*, dépêche *f*.

wire[2], *v.*

I. *v.tr. & int.* **1.** *v.tr.* (*a*) munir (qch.) d'un fil métallique; armer (un bouchon de bouteille) de fil de fer; rattacher (qch.) avec du fil de fer; monter (des fleurs) sur fil de fer; enfiler (des perles) sur un fil de fer; grillager (une ouverture); fermer (une ouverture) avec un réseau de fils de fer; (*b*) *El:* faire l'installation électrique (d'une maison); **to w. a hall for sound,** sonoriser une salle; *Tg:* **to w. a station on to a circuit,** relier un poste; (*c*) *Metalw:* **to w. the edge of a plate,** enrouler le bord d'une tôle. **2.** *v.i. & tr.* télégraphier (à qn); **they wired for his son,** on a télégraphié pour faire venir son fils; on a appelé son fils par télégramme; **he wired that he would arrive at twelve,** il a télégraphié qu'il arriverait vers midi.

II. (*compound verbs*) **1. wire in.** (*a*) *v.tr.* grillager (un terrain, etc.); (*b*) *v.i. F:* **to w. in (to a meal),** s'attaquer (à un repas).

2. wire off, *v.tr.* isoler (un terrain) au moyen d'un grillage, de fils métalliques.

wirecutter ['waiəkʌtər], *s. Tls:* (*a*) coupe-fil *m inv*; (*b*) (**pair of**) **wirecutters,** pince(s) coupante(s); coupe-net *m inv*, coupe-fil.

wired ['waiəd], *a.* (*a*) monté sur fil de fer; armé de fil de fer; **w. glass,** verre armé; (*b*) (*of enclosure, etc.*) grillagé.

wire(-)draw ['waiədrɔ:], *v.tr. Metalw:* tréfiler; tirer, fileter (le métal); travailler, passer (un métal) à la filière; affiler, tirer à l'argue (l'or, l'argent).

wirehaired ['waiəhɛəd], *a.* (chien terrier) à poil dur.

wireless[1] ['waiəlis]. **1.** *a.* sans fil. **2.** *s. O:* télégraphie *f*, téléphonie *f*, sans fil; radio *f*; **w. (set),** poste *m* de T.S.F., radio.

wireless[2], *v.tr. O:* envoyer (un message) par la radio; radiotélégraphier (un message).

wire(-)stitch ['waiəstitʃ], *v.tr.* brocher (un livret).

wirework ['waiəwə:k], *s.* **1.** (*a*) tréfilerie *f*, tréfilage *m*, étirage *m*; (*b*) (*factory*) **wireworks,** tréfilerie. **2.** grillage *m* métallique.

wireworm ['waiəwə:m], *s.* **1.** *Ent:* larve *f* de taupin. **2.** *Myr:* iule *m*.

wiriness ['waiərinis], *s.* (*a*) vigueur (alliée à un corps sec, nerveux); (*b*) raideur *f* (des cheveux); (*c*) *Med:* caractère *m* filiforme (du pouls).

wiring ['waiəriŋ], *s.* **1.** (*a*) montage *m* (de fleurs, etc.) sur fil de fer; (*b*) *El:* câblage *m*; canalisation *f* (électrique); pose *f* (de fils électriques); **w. plan,** schéma *m* de câblage, de montage; (*c*) *Mil:* pose des barbelés; (*d*) *Med:* cerclage *m* (d'un os fracturé). **2.** *Metalw:* repliage *m* du bord (d'une tôle). **3.** transmission *f* (d'un message) par télégraphe; envoi *m* d'une dépêche. **4.** (*a*) fils *m* métalliques; (*b*) grillage *m* métallique; (*c*) bordage *m* en cordon (d'une tôle, etc.); (*d*) installation *f* électrique (d'une maison, etc.).

wiry ['waiəri], *a.* **1.** *A:* de, en, fil métallique. **2.** (*a*) (*of hair*) raide, rude; (*b*) (*of pers.*) (sec et) nerveux; (*c*) *Med:* (*of pulse*) filiforme.

wisdom ['wizdəm], *s.* sagesse *f*; **to have the w. of the serpent,** avoir la prudence du serpent; **I doubt the w. of trusting him,** je me demande si on serait bien avisé de se fier à lui; *B:* **the Book of W., the W. of Solomon,** (le livre de) la Sagesse; **w. tooth,** dent *f* de sagesse.

wise[1] [waiz], *a.* **1.** sage; prudent; sagace; **the seven w. men of Greece,** les sept sages de la Grèce; **the W. Men (of the East), the Three W. Men,** les (Rois) Mages *m*; **it would be a w. man that could tell,** bien avisé qui saurait le dire; **to get, grow, wise(r),** (i) s'assagir; (ii) acquérir de l'expérience; **it wouldn't be w. to do it,** il ne serait pas sage, prudent, de le faire; **w. after the event,** sage après coup; *Prov:* **a w. man can learn from a fool,** un fou avise un sage. **2.** (*a*) **to look w.,** prendre un (petit) air entendu; **with a w. shake of the head,** en secouant la tête d'un air entendu; (*b*) **I'm no wiser than you,** je n'en sais pas plus long que vous; **he's none, not any, the wiser (for it),** il n'en sait pas plus long pour cela; il n'en est pas plus avancé (pour cela); il n'est pas plus avancé qu'auparavant; **without anyone being the wiser,** (faire qch.) à l'insu de tout le monde; **hold your tongue and nobody will be any the wiser,** si tu te tais, ni vu ni connu; **we came in by the back door and he was none the wiser,** nous sommes entrés par la petite porte et il n'en a rien su; (*c*) *F:* **to get w. to a fact,** saisir un fait; se rendre compte d'un fait; **to put s.o. w. (to sth.),** avertir qn (de qch.); donner le mot à qn (sur qch.); mettre qn à la page; **put me w. about it,** expliquez-moi ça; **when you've got w. to things,** quand vous serez au courant. **3.** *A:* **w. man,** devin *m*; sorcier *m*; **w. woman,** (i) devineresse *f*; sorcière *f*; (ii) sage-femme *f*, *pl.* sages-femmes.

wise[2], *s. Lit:* manière *f*, façon *f*; guise *f*; **in no w.,** en aucune manière, d'aucune manière; en aucune façon, d'aucune façon; nullement, aucunement; **in some w.,** en quelque façon; de quelque manière, de quelque façon; **in any w.,** en, de, quelque manière que ce soit; **the letter ran in this w.,** la lettre était ainsi conçue; *B:* **and God spake on this w.,** et Dieu parla ainsi; *A:* **in solemn w.,** solennellement; *F:* **salary w.,** en ce qui concerne la paie.

wise[3], *v. F:* **to w. s.o. up,** mettre qn à la page; **w. me up about it,** explique-moi ça; mets-moi au courant.

wiseacre ['waizeikər], *s.* prétendu sage; pédant *m*; benêt sentencieux et suffisant.

wisecrack[1] ['waizkræk], *s.* bon mot; saillie *f* (d'esprit); facétie *f*.

wisecrack[2], *v.i.* dire des bons mots; faire de l'esprit; dire des facéties.

wisely ['waizli], *adv.* (*a*) sagement, prudemment; avec sagesse; (*b*) **to shake one's head w.,** secouer la tête d'un air entendu.

wisent ['vi:zənt], *s. Z:* aurochs *m*.

wish[1] [wiʃ], *s.* (*a*) désir *m*, vœu *m*; **to express a w.,** (i) émettre un vœu; (ii) exprimer un désir; **he has a great w. to go,** il éprouve un grand désir d'y aller; **I have no w. to go, to see it,** je n'ai pas envie, je suis peu désireux, peu curieux, d'y aller, de le voir; **the w. to please,** le désir de plaire; **by my father's w.,** sur le désir de mon père; **it was done against, contrary to, my wishes,** cela s'est fait à l'encontre de mon désir; **everything succeeds according to his wishes,** tout lui réussit à souhait; **to frame one's policy according to the wishes of the electorate,** orienter sa politique au gré des électeurs, selon les vœux des électeurs; **I cannot grant your w.,** je ne peux pas vous accorder ce que vous désirez; **you shall have your w.,** votre désir sera exaucé; **to go against s.o.'s wishes,** agir contre les désirs de qn; *Prov:* **the w. is father to the thought,** on croit aisément ce qu'on désire; c'est le désir qui fait naître, qui engendre, la pensée; (*b*) **quick! make a w.!** vite! fais un vœu! **your w. will come true,** ton vœu se réalisera; (*c*) souhait *m*, vœu; **to send all good wishes to s.o.,** adresser tous ses vœux de bonheur à qn; présenter ses souhaits à qn; **New Year's wishes,** souhaits (et félicitations) à l'occasion du nouvel an; souhaits de bonne année.

wish[2]. **1.** *v.ind.tr.* **to w. for sth.,** désirer, vouloir, souhaiter, qch.; **what do you w. (for)?** que désirez-vous? **to w. for happiness, for peace,** désirer, souhaiter, le bonheur, la paix; **to have everything one can, could, w. for,** avoir tout à souhait; **he has nothing left to w. for,** il n'a plus rien à désirer; **the weather is all one could w. for,** le temps est à souhait; **I couldn't w. for anything better,** je ne pourrais désirer mieux; c'est à souhait; **what more can you, do you, w. for?** que voudriez-vous de plus? **2.** *v.tr.* vouloir; (*a*) **to w. to do sth.,** désirer, vouloir, faire qch.; **I w. you to do it,** je voudrais que vous le fassiez; c'est mon désir que vous le fassiez; **I w. it to be done,** je désire, je veux bien, que cela se fasse; **I w. it to be done this way, like this,** je le veux ainsi; **I don't w. anything to be said about it,** je ne veux pas qu'on en dise rien; *U.S:* **do you w. advice?** est-ce que vous me demandez conseil? **have a cup of coffee, or do you w. tea?** prenez du café, ou voulez-vous du thé? (*b*) (*optative*) **I w. I were a bird!** je voudrais être un oiseau! si je pouvais être un oiseau! **I w. it were, was, already done,** je voudrais que cela soit déjà fait; **I w. I were in your place,** je voudrais bien être à votre place; **I w. you were in my place,** je voudrais bien vous voir à ma place; **I w. you were more attentive,** je voudrais vous voir plus attentif; **I w. I had never seen her,** je voudrais ne l'avoir jamais vue; **I w. I had seen it!** j'aurais bien voulu voir cela! **I w. I hadn't left so early,** je regrette d'être parti si tôt; **I w. I had the money I spent on all that,** je regrette l'argent que j'ai dépensé à tout cela; **I w. he would come!** que ne vient-il! **I w. you'd come and help us,** vous seriez bien gentil de venir nous aider; **how I w. I could (do it)!** si seulement je pouvais (le faire)! **I wished myself a hundred miles away,** j'aurais voulu être à cent milles de là; **I wished myself dead, wished I were dead,** j'aurais voulu être mort; (*c*) **it's to be wished that. . .,** il est à souhaiter que . . .; **do you w. you'll, you could, live to see it?** souhaitez-vous (de) vivre assez longtemps pour le voir? *F: Iron:* **I w., don't you w., you may get it!** je vous en souhaite! tu peux te brosser! **I w. we may see our money back (from them)!** ils nous rembourseront la semaine des quatre jeudis; (*d*) **he wishes me well,** il est bien disposé envers moi; **he wishes everybody well,** il veut du bien à tout le monde; **he wishes nobody ill,** il ne veut du mal à personne; **to w. s.o. happiness,** *O:* **to w. s.o. happy,** souhaiter que qn soit heureux; **to w. s.o. a pleasant journey,** souhaiter à qn bon voyage; **to w. s.o. goodnight,** souhaiter bonne nuit à qn; dire bonsoir à qn; **that's a fate I wouldn't w. my worst enemy,** je ne souhaiterais pas un tel sort à mon pire ennemi; (*e*) **it was wished on me,** c'est une chose que je n'ai pas pu refuser; j'ai été obligé de l'accepter; **he wished himself on us,** il nous a infligé sa présence. **3.** *v.i.* **go on! w.!** vite! fais un vœu! **to w. on a shooting star,** faire un vœu lorsqu'on aperçoit une étoile filante.

wishbone ['wiʃboun], *s.* lunette *f*, fourchette *f* (d'une volaille).

wishful ['wiʃfəl], *a.* (*a*) **w. to do sth., of doing sth.,** désireux de faire qch.; (*b*) *F:* **w. thinking,** pensée née du désir (que telle ou telle chose soit); **that's a bit of w. thinking** = c'est prendre ses désirs pour des réalités; **to indulge in w. thinking,** détourner les choses dans le sens de son désir.

wishwash ['wiʃwɔʃ], *s. F:* lavasse *f*.

wishywashy ['wiʃiwɔʃi], *a. F:* fade, insipide; faible; **w. stew,** ragoût délavé, nageant dans la sauce; **w. speech,** discours fade, terne; (*of tea, soup, etc.*) **w. stuff,** lavasse *f*.

wisp[1] [wisp], *s.* **1.** (*a*) bouchon *m*, poignée *f* (de paille, de foin, d'herbe); (*b*) tortillon *m*, toron *m* (de paille); (*for tying up plants*) accolure *f*; **w. of smoke,** ruban *m*, traînée *f*, de fumée; **w. of hair,** mèche folle; **little w. of a man,** tout petit bout d'homme; (*c*) bourrelet *m* (en paille). **2.** *Ven:* troupe *f*, vol *m* (de bécassines).

wisp[2], *v.tr.* **to w. down, w. over, a horse,** bouchonner un cheval.

wispy ['wispi], *a.* (*of wool, etc.*) mécheux.

wist [wist], *v.tr. A:* savoir.

wistaria [wis'tiəriə], *s. Bot:* glycine *f*.

wistful ['wistfəl], *a.* plein d'un vague désir, d'un vague regret; (regard, air) désenchanté; **w. smile,** (i) sourire désenchanté; sourire de regret; (ii) sourire pensif.

wistfully ['wistfəli], *adv.* avec un regard, d'un air, plein d'un vague désir, d'un vague regret; d'un air songeur et triste; (regarder qn, qch.) avec un peu d'envie.

wistiti ['wistiti], *s. Z:* ouistiti *m*.

wit[1] [wit], *s.* **1.** (*often pl.*) esprit *m*, entendement *m*; intelligence *f*; **he hasn't the w., the wits, hasn't w. enough, to see it,** il n'est pas assez intelligent pour s'en apercevoir; **to have quick wits,** avoir l'esprit vif; **to be out of one's wits, to have lost one's wits,** avoir perdu l'esprit, la raison, la tête; **are you out of your wits?** vous avez perdu le sens commun! **to send, drive, s.o. out of his wits,** faire perdre la tête à qn; **to collect one's wits,** se ressaisir; **to sharpen s.o.'s wits,** aiguiser l'intelligence de qn; déniaiser, délurer, qn; **to have, keep, one's wits about one,** avoir, conserver, toute sa présence d'esprit; avoir l'œil ouvert; ne pas perdre la carte; **he has all his wits about him,** c'est un malin; **to be at one's wit's end,** ne plus savoir que faire; ne plus savoir de quel côté se tourner, à quel saint se vouer; être à bout d'expédients; être au bout de son rouleau, de ses écus, à bout de course; être aux abois; être aux cent coups; **to have, to engage in, a battle of wits,** jouer au plus fin; **to live by one's wits,** vivre d'expédients; vivre d'invention, d'industrie; **he lives by his wits,** c'est un aventurier; **to set one's wits to work to please s.o.,** s'ingénier pour faire plaisir à qn; **to put one's wits to work on, exercise one's wits on, a problem,** s'attaquer à un problème; **she was trying to set her wits against his,** elle a voulu faire assaut d'esprit avec lui, se mesurer avec lui. **2.** vivacité *f* d'esprit; **he has both w. and humour,** il est doué à la fois d'esprit et d'humour; **flash of w.,** trait *m* d'esprit; **sparkling with w.,** étincelant d'esprit.

wit[2], *s.* (*pers.*) bel esprit; homme, femme, d'esprit.

wit[3], *v.tr. A:* (*the only parts used are: pr.ind.* **I wot, thou wottest, he wot;** *p.t.* **wist;** *pr.p.* **witting**) savoir; **God wot that. . .,** Dieu sait que . . .; **God wot,** en vérité; *B:* **wist ye not that I must be about my Father's business?** ne saviez-vous pas qu'il me faut être occupé aux affaires de mon Père? **little witting that her child was dead,** ne sachant pas que son enfant était mort; *Jur:* **to w.,** à savoir; c'est-à-dire.

witch[1] [witʃ], *s.* (*a*) sorcière *f*, *occ.* sorcier *m*; **the W. of Endor,** la pythonisse d'Endor; **witch's hat,** chapeau pointu; **w. hunt,** (i) chasse *f* aux sorcières; (ii) persécution *f* des ennemis politiques; (*b*) *F:* **old w.,** vieille bonne femme (déplaisante); vieille sorcière; (*c*) *F: O:* jeune charmeuse; ensorceleuse; (*d*) *Anthr:* **w. doctor,** sorcier guérisseur; (*e*) *Ent:* **witches' horse,** phasme *m*, phasmidé *m*; **w. moth, black w. (moth),** érèbe *m*; sorcière noire; (*f*) *Bot:* **w. hazel,** (i) (*also* **w. elm**) orme blanc, de montagne, des montagnes; (ii) hamamélis *m*; *Pharm:* teinture *f* d'hamamélis; **w. broom, witches' broom,** balai *m* de sorcière; *Algae:* **witches' butter,** nostoc *m*, nodulaire *f*.

witch[2], *v.tr. A:* ensorceler, fasciner, envoûter (qn).

witchcraft ['witʃkra:ft], *s.* **1.** sorcellerie *f*; magie noire; **white w.,** magie blanche. **2.** *F:* magie; **as if by w., like w.,** comme par magie, par enchantement.

witchery ['witʃəri], *s.* (*a*) ensorcellement *m*, enchantement *m*; (*b*) fascination *f*; magie *f*; charme *m* magique.

witchetty ['witʃəti], *s. Ent: Austr:* **w. (grub),** larve *f* (comestible) du cossus.

witching ['witʃiŋ], *a.* **1.** enchanteur, -eresse; charmant, séduisant. **2.** magique; **w. hour,** heure *f* propice à la sorcellerie; heure des sorciers; minuit *m*.

wite [wit], *s. A.Jur:* prix *m* du sang.

with[1] [wið], *prep.* avec. **1.** (*expressing accompaniment*) (*a*) **to travel w., work w., s.o.,** voyager, travailler, avec qn; **he is staying w. friends,** il est chez des amis; **he lives w. his parents,** il vit auprès de, avec, ses parents; **they aren't married but she lives w. him,** ils ne sont pas mariés mais elle habite avec lui; **to mingle w. the crowd,** se mêler à la foule; **I don't mix w. them,** je ne fraye pas avec eux; **the king (together) w. his courtiers,** le roi accompagné de ses courtisans; **are you alone or is there someone w. you?** êtes-vous seul ou accompagné? **he always has a nurse w. him,** il a toujours une garde-malade auprès de lui; **he was there w. his wife,** il y était avec sa femme; **to be w. the colours, w. one's regiment, etc.,** être sous les drapeaux; **I have nobody to go out w.,** je n'ai personne avec qui sortir; **there I am w. nobody to talk to,** je suis là, me voilà, sans personne à qui parler; **I'll be w. you in a moment,** je serai à vous dans un moment; **you will lose your money and your honour w. it,** vous perdrez votre argent et votre honneur avec; **some cheese to eat w. it,** du fromage pour manger avec; *F:* **you'll get yourself killed and me w. you,** tu te feras tuer et moi avec; **question that is always w. us,** question *f* qui est toujours d'actualité; (*b*) (*having*) **knife w. a silver handle,** couteau *m* à manche d'argent; **girl w. blue eyes,** jeune fille aux yeux bleus; **child w. a cold, w. measles,** enfant enrhumé, atteint de rougeole; **old ladies w. camp stools,** vieilles dames à pliant; **house w. green shutters,** maison *f* à volets verts; **house w. walls freshly whitewashed,** maison avec ses murs nouvellement blanchis; **w. his hat on,** le chapeau sur la tête; **w. his (over)coat on,** en pardessus; **w. a bundle under his arm,** un paquet sous le bras; **w. your intelligence you'll easily guess what followed,** intelligent comme vous l'êtes vous devinerez facilement la suite; (*c*) **w. child,** enceinte; (*of animal*) **w. young,** pleine; (*d*) **he came in w. a suitcase,** il est entré avec une valise; **bring it w. you when you come,** apportez-le (avec vous) quand vous viendrez; **have you a pencil w. you?** avez-vous un crayon sur vous? **to leave a child w. s.o.,** laisser un enfant à la garde de qn, aux soins de qn; **the decision rests, lies, w. you,** c'est à vous de décider; **he rests w. God,** il repose en Dieu; **he took refuge w. his uncle,** il s'est réfugié auprès de son oncle; (*e*) (*in spite of*) **w. all his faults I love him,** malgré tous ses défauts je l'aime; **I couldn't, w. all my efforts, make way against the tide,** je ne pouvais, en dépit de tous mes efforts, avancer contre la marée; **w. all his knowledge he cannot teach,** en dépit de tout son savoir il est incapable d'enseigner; (*f*) **what will happen to her w. both her parents dead?** que va-t-elle devenir maintenant que son père et sa mère sont morts, avec ses parents morts? **2.** (*expressing association*) (*a*) **to trade w. France,** faire du commerce avec la France; **to correspond w. s.o.,** correspondre avec qn; **to have to do w. s.o.,** avoir affaire avec qn; **to have nothing to do w. s.o.,** n'avoir rien à faire avec qn; **the next move is w. him,** c'est à lui d'agir maintenant; **I can do nothing w. him,** je ne peux rien en faire; **you never can tell w. women how they'll take things,** on ne peut jamais prédire d'une femme comment elle va prendre une chose; **w. God all things are possible,** à Dieu rien n'est impossible; **w. him all men are equal,** tous les hommes sont égaux à ses yeux; **to be patient w. s.o.,** être patient avec qn; **he has cordial relations w. his neighbours,** ses rapports avec ses voisins sont cordiaux; **to be honest w. oneself,** être sincère envers soi-même; **it's a habit w. me,** c'est une habitude chez moi; **that often happens w. business men,** cela arrive souvent chez les hommes d'affaires; **he was in favour w. the queen,** il était en faveur auprès de la reine; **he pleaded his cause w. the king,** il a plaidé sa cause auprès du roi; **to use one's influence w. s.o.,** agir auprès de qn; **there's nothing wrong w. you?** *A:* **is it well w. you?** est-ce que vous vous portez bien? **the difficulty w. poetry is to read it well,** le plus difficile en ce qui concerne la poésie c'est de bien la lire; (*b*) **I sympathize w. you,** je vous plains; **I think w. you,** je pense comme vous; **I don't agree w. you,** je ne suis pas de votre avis; **I'm w. you there!** j'en conviens! **the whole country is w. him,** tout le pays est avec lui; **to vote w. a party,** voter avec un parti; *F:* **to be w. it,** être à la page, dans le vent, dans la course; **w.-it colour,** coloris *m* vedette; (*c*) **to rise w. the lark,** se lever avec l'alouette; **his health will improve w. the spring,** sa santé s'améliorera avec le printemps; **our hopes died w. him,** nos espérances sont mortes en même temps que lui; **prejudices will die w. time,** les préjugés disparaîtront avec le temps; **the countryside changes w. the seasons,** le paysage change avec les saisons; **w. these words he dismissed me,** là-dessus, ce disant, il m'a congédié; **he said this w. a smile,** il a accompagné ces mots d'un sourire; **I accept, she said, w. a happy smile,** j'accepte, dit-elle dans un sourire de joie; **w. a cry,** en poussant un cri; **she disappeared w. a soft rustling of silk,** elle a disparu dans un doux bruissement de soie; (*d*) (*against*) **to compete w. s.o.,** concourir avec qn; **to fight w. s.o.,** se battre contre qn. **3.** (*dissociation*) **to part w. sth.,** se dessaisir, se défaire, de qch. **4.** (*expressing instrument*) (*a*) **to cut sth. w. a knife,** couper qch. avec un couteau, au couteau; **to write w. a pen,** écrire avec une plume; **to walk w. (the aid of) a stick,** marcher avec une canne; **to fight w. swords,** se battre à l'épée; **killed w. a bayonet,** tué d'un coup, à coups, de baïonnette; **to take sth. w. both hands,** prendre qch. à deux mains; **to look at sth. w. the naked eye,** regarder qch. à l'œil nu; **to write w. one's left hand,** écrire de la main gauche; **to strike w. all one's might,** frapper de toutes ses forces; **w. God's help, w. the help of time,** Dieu, le temps, aidant; (*b*) **to tremble w. rage,** trembler de rage; **to be stiff w. cold, red w. shame,** être engourdi par le froid, rouge de honte; **to be ill w. measles,** être malade de la rougeole, atteint de rougeole; (*c*) **to fill a vase w. water,** remplir un vase d'eau; **eyes flooded w. tears,** yeux inondés de larmes; **lorry loaded w. timber,** camion chargé de bois; **endowed w. beauty,** doué de beauté; **it's pouring w. rain,** il pleut à verse. **5.** (*forming adv. phrs.*) **to work w. a will,** travailler avec courage; **to fight w. great courage,** se battre avec un grand courage; **to advance w. great strides,** (s')avancer à grands pas; **to write w. ease,** écrire avec facilité; **to receive s.o. w. open arms,** recevoir qn à bras ouverts; **his return was greeted w. cheers,** son retour a été salué par des acclamations; **w. all due respect,** avec tout le respect que je vous dois; **w. respect,** ne vous en déplaise; **w. your permission,** si vous voulez bien me le permettre; **w. this object,** dans ce but; **w. intent to defraud,** dans le but de frauder; **I say it w. regret,** je le dis à regret; **w. a few exceptions,** à part quelques exceptions; à peu d'exceptions près (*the uses of* **with** *as a general link between vb. or adj. and its complement are shown under the respective words that take this construction, e.g.* **to dispense with, pleased with**). **6.** (*elliptical*) **away w. care!** bannissons les soucis! *F:* **down w. the police!** à bas les flics! **to blazes, to hell, w. him!** qu'il aille au diable!

with² [wiθ], *s. Const:* languette *f* (entre conduites de fumée).

withal [wi'ðɔ:l]. **1.** *adv. A: & Lit:* aussi; en même temps; d'ailleurs, en outre, de plus; **she is young and fair, and rich w.,** elle est jeune et belle et riche aussi. **2.** *prep. A:* **he hath nothing to fill his belly w.,** il n'a rien pour remplir son ventre.

withamite ['wiðəmait], *s. Miner:* withamite *f.*

withdraw [wið'drɔ:], *v.* (*p.t.* **withdrew** [-'dru:]; *p.p.* **withdrawn** [-'drɔ:n]) **1.** *v.tr.* (*a*) retirer (sa main); retirer, enlever (un étai); (*b*) ramener (des troupes) en arrière; faire replier (des troupes); lever (une sentinelle); *O:* **to w. a child from school,** retirer un enfant de l'école; (*c*) **to w. coins from circulation,** retirer des pièces de la circulation; démonétiser des pièces; **to w. a sum of money,** retirer une somme d'argent (de la caisse d'épargne, etc.); **you can w. £50 without notice,** on peut retirer £50 sans préavis; **sum withdrawn from the bank,** prélèvement *m* sur les fonds déposés en banque; (*d*) retirer (une offre, une promesse, sa parole, sa candidature); reprendre (sa parole); revenir sur (une promesse); renoncer à (une réclamation); **to w. a charge,** se rétracter; **I w. that remark,** mettez que je n'ai rien dit; *O:* **to w. one's friendship, one's favour, from s.o.,** retirer son amitié, sa faveur, à qn; **to w. an order,** (i) *Com:* annuler une commande; (ii) *Adm:* rapporter un décret; **to w. one's claims,** se désister, *Jur:* se déporter, de ses prétentions; **to w. an action,** abandonner un procès; retirer sa plainte. **2.** *v.i.* (*a*) se retirer (**from,** de); s'éloigner; *Mil:* (*of outposts*) se replier; **to w. from an undertaking,** se retirer, se dégager, d'une affaire; **to w. from a treaty,** cesser d'être partie à un traité; dénoncer un traité; (*of candidate*) **to w. in favour of s.o.,** se désister pour qn; (*b*) *A:* **after dinner the ladies w.,** après le dîner les dames se retirent, les dames passent au salon; (*c*) **to w. into oneself, into silence,** se renfermer en soi-même, dans le silence.

withdrawal [wið'drɔ:əl], *s.* **1.** (*a*) retrait *m*; **w. of troops,** retrait des troupes; évacuation *f* de troupes; **w. of a sum of money,** retrait, décaissement *m*, d'une somme d'argent; **w. of money (from circulation),** retrait des monnaies; **w. of capital,** retrait de fonds; *Bank: etc:* **w. notice,** avis *m* de retrait de fonds; *Med:* **w. symptoms,** (i) (*from alcohol*) symptômes d'abstinence; symptômes de sevrage; (ii) (*from drugs*) (état *m*, crise *f* de) manque *m*; **w. during sexual intercourse,** retrait pendant l'acte sexuel; (*b*) rappel *m* (d'un décret, d'un ordre); rétractation *f* (d'une promesse, d'une accusation); retrait (d'une plainte); *Jur:* (*to a marriage, etc.*) **w. of opposition,** mainlevée *f* d'opposition. **2.** (*a*) retraite *f*; *Mil:* repli *m*, repliement *m* (des troupes); mouvement *m* de repli, mouvement rétrograde; (*b*) **w. of a candidate,** désistement *m* d'un candidat.

withdrawing [wið'drɔ:iŋ], *s.* **1.** retrait *m*, enlèvement *m* (de qch.). **2.** retraite *f.*

withdrawn [wið'drɔ:n], *a.* (*of pers.*) réservé.

withe [wiθ], *s.* brin *m*, lien *m*, d'osier; hart *f*, pleyon *m*, accolure *f.*

wither ['wiðər]. **1.** *v.i.* (*of plant, etc.*) **to w. (up, away),** se dessécher, se flétrir, se faner; dépérir; sécher sur pied; (*of flowers, beauty*) passer; (*of pers.*) dépérir; **his arm had withered,** son bras s'était séché. **2.** *v.tr.* (*a*) (*of wind, heat*) dessécher, flétrir, faner, dépérir (une plante, etc.); (*of illness*) dessécher (qn); **time will w. her beauty,** sa beauté passera avec le temps; (*b*) **to w. s.o. with a look,** foudroyer qn du regard, d'un regard.

withered ['wiðəd], *a.* desséché, flétri, fané; **w. arm,** bras desséché, atrophié.

withering¹ ['wið(ə)riŋ], *a.* **1.** qui se dessèche, qui se flétrit, qui se fane, qui dépérit. **2.** (*a*) qui dessèche, qui flétrit; (vent) desséchant; (*b*) (regard) foudroyant, écrasant; (ton) de souverain mépris; **to give s.o. a w. look,** foudroyer qn du regard; (*c*) **to keep up a w. fire against the enemy,** maintenir un feu meurtrier contre l'ennemi.

withering², *s.* dessèchement *m*; **w. away,** dépérissement *m*; amenuisement *m* (d'un parti politique, etc.).

witheringly ['wiðəriŋli], *adv.* d'un regard foudroyant, d'un ton de mépris.

witherite ['wiðərait], *s. Miner:* withérite *f.*

withers ['wiðəz], *s.pl.* garrot *m* (du cheval, du bœuf); *Lit:* **our withers are unwrung,** cela ne nous touche pas.

withershins ['wiðəʃinz], *adv. esp. Scot:* à contre-sens; dans le sens inverse des aiguilles d'une montre; de droite à gauche.

witherwrung ['wiðərʌŋ], *a. Vet:* garrotté; blessé au garrot.

withhold [wið'hould], *v.tr.* (*p.t. & p.p.* **withheld** [-'held]) **1.** (*a*) refuser (son consentement, son aide); (*b*) **to w. the truth from s.o.,** cacher la vérité à qn; **to w. an important fact,** taire, supprimer, un fait important; (*c*) *O:* **to w. so much out of s.o.'s pay,** retenir tant sur la paie de qn; (*d*) *Jur:* **to w. property,** détenir des biens; **to w. release of the property,** s'abstenir de libérer un bien; **to w. a document,** refuser de communiquer une pièce. **2.** *A:* **to w. s.o. from doing sth.,** retenir, empêcher, qn de faire qch.; **to w. one's hand,** arrêter sa main; s'abstenir (au moment de frapper, etc.).

withholder [wið'houldər], *s. Jur:* détenteur, -trice (**of,** de).

withholding [wið'houldiŋ], *s.* refus *m* (de consentement, etc.); *Jur:* détention *f*, rétention *f*; **w. of the truth,** dissimulation *f* de la vérité; *U.S: Adm:* **w. tax,** impôt retenu à la source.

within [wið'in]. **1.** *adv.* (*a*) *A: & Lit:* à l'intérieur, au dedans; à la maison, chez soi; **w. and without,** à l'intérieur et à l'extérieur; *prep.* **w. and without the realm,** dedans et dehors le royaume; **to go w.,** entrer dans la maison, dans la chambre; **a voice w. shouted to me to enter,** une voix à l'intérieur m'a crié d'entrer; **make me pure w.,** purifiez mon âme, mon cœur; **Bishopsgate w.,** Bishopsgate ès murs; (*b*) *Th:* à la cantonade; (*c*) *adv.phr.* **from w.,** de l'intérieur; **seen from w.,** vu de l'intérieur, du dedans; *Pol: etc:* **to act from w. (a party),** agir du dedans. **2.** *prep.* (*a*) *O: & Lit:* à l'intérieur de, en dedans de; **w. the house,** dans la maison; en dedans de la maison; **safe w. the walls,** en sûreté à l'intérieur des murs; **w. four walls,** entre quatre murs; **w. the frontier,** en deçà des frontières; **the enemy is w. our frontiers, w. our walls,** l'ennemi est dans nos frontières, dans nos murs; **notwithstanding her smile she trembled w. her at the thought,** tout en souriant elle tremblait intérieurement à cette pensée; **he thought w. himself that she loved him all the same,** il pensait dans son for intérieur que néanmoins elle l'aimait; **a voice w. me told me to set out at once,** une voix intérieure me disait de partir tout de suite; **w. the committee,** au sein de la commission; **dissensions w. (the bosom of) the Church,** dissensions *f* dans le sein de l'église; (*b*) (*not beyond*) **w. reason,** dans des limites raisonnables; **to keep w. the law,** rester dans (les bornes de) la légalité; **strictly w. the law,** dans les limites strictes de la légalité; **to come w. the provisions of the law,** tomber sous le coup de la loi; **w. the meaning of the Act,** selon les prévisions de l'acte; **to keep, live, w. one's income,** ne pas dépenser plus que son revenu; ne pas dépasser son revenu; vivre selon ses moyens; **task well w. his powers,** tâche *f* qui ne dépasse pas ses capacités; **to be well w. the truth,** être en deça, au-dessous, de la vérité; **he'll tell you your weight w. a pound,** il vous dira combien vous pesez à une livre près; (*c*) **w. sight,** en vue; **w. call,** à (la) portée de la voix; **born w. the sound of Bow Bells,** né à la portée du son des cloches de Bow (c.-à-d. dans la Cité de Londres); **w. two miles of the town,** à moins de deux milles de la ville; **w. a radius of ten kilometres,** dans un rayon de dix kilomètres; à dix kilomètres à la ronde; **w. a couple of paces of me,** à deux pas de moi; **we were w. an inch of death,** nous étions à deux doigts de la mort; **w. a short distance of the enemy,** tout près de l'ennemi; (*d*) (*in expressions of time*) **w. an hour,** avant une heure; en moins d'une heure; **w. the week,** avant la fin de la semaine; **he died w. a week,** il est mort dans la semaine; **w. a year of his death,** (i) moins d'un an après sa mort; dans l'année qui a suivi sa mort; (ii) moins d'un an avant sa mort; dans l'année qui a précédé sa mort; **I've spoken to him w. the last week,** je lui ai parlé il n'y a pas huit jours; **w. the next week,** dans le courant de la semaine prochaine, la semaine suivante; **w. the next five years (from now),** d'ici cinq ans; avant cinq ans d'ici; **w. the required time,** dans le délai prescrit, dans les délais voulus; **ordered to vacate the premises w. twenty-four hours,** sommé de vider les lieux dans les vingt-quatre heures; **delivery w. a month,** délai de livraison: un mois; **w. a short time,** (i) à court délai; (ii) à court intervalle (**of each other,** l'un de l'autre); (iii) peu de temps après; **there were two fires w. a short space of time, w. a short time of each other,** deux incendies se sont déclarés à court intervalle, coup sur coup; **they're the same age w. a few months,** ils sont du même âge à quelques mois près; **w. the memory of man,** de mémoire d'homme.

without [wið'aut]. **1.** *adv. A: & Lit:* (*a*) à l'extérieur, au dehors; **within and w.,** à l'intérieur et à l'extérieur; (*b*) *adv.phr.* **from w.,** de l'extérieur; **seen from w.,** vu de l'extérieur, du dehors. **2.** *prep.* (*a*) *A: & Lit:* en dehors de; **w. the walls,** en dehors des murailles; hors des murs; **things w. oneself,** les choses extérieures; (*b*) sans; **to be w. friends,** être sans amis; **to be w. food,** manquer de nourriture; être privé de nourriture; **w. fear,** sans peur; **he came back w. the money,** il est revenu sans l'argent; **he came back w. any money,** il est revenu sans argent; **w. any difficulty,** sans aucune difficulté; **rumour w. foundation,** bruit dénué de fondement, mal fondé; **rule not w. exceptions,** règle *f* qui comporte des exceptions; **not w. difficulty,** non sans difficulté; **w. end,** sans fin; *Ecc:* **world w. end,** pour les siècles des siècles; **he passed by w. seeing me, w. being seen,** il est passé sans me voir, sans être vu; **w. hesitating any further,** sans plus hésiter; **I won't do it w. being paid,** je ne le ferai pas à moins d'être payé; **it goes w. saying that . . .,** il va sans dire, va de soi, que . . .; **that goes w. saying,** cela va sans dire; **can you do it w. his knowing about it?** pouvez-vous le faire sans qu'il le sache? **it was done w. France being able to intervene,** cela s'est fait sans que la France ait pu intervenir; **a year never passes w. his writing to us,** il ne se passe jamais une année sans qu'il nous écrive; **readers w. any knowledge of French,** lecteurs qui ignorent le français; **to do w., go w., sth.,** se passer de qch.

withstand [wið'stænd], *v.tr.* (*p.t. & p.p.* **withstood** [-'stud]) résister à, s'opposer à (qn); résister à (la douleur, la tentation, etc.); **to w. pressure, wear, the heat,** supporter, résister à, la pression; résister à l'usage; supporter la chaleur; *Mil: etc:* **to w. an attack,** soutenir une attaque; **to w. the blow,** supporter, *F:*

tenir, le coup.

withy ['wiði], *s.* **1.** osier *m.* **2.** = WITHE.

witless ['witlis], *a.* **1.** (*a*) sans intelligence; sot, *f.* sotte; (*b*) imbécile; faible d'esprit; (*c*) (*of action*) stupide. **2.** *A:* **w. of what was happening,** ignorant de ce qui se passait.

witloof ['witlouf], *s. Bot:* chicorée *f* des jardins; endive *f*, witloof *m.*

witness[1] ['witnis], *s.* **1.** témoignage *m*; **to bear w. to, of, sth.,** rendre, porter, témoignage de qch.; témoigner de qch.; attester qch.; **to bear w. to the success of the scheme,** rendre témoignage au succès du projet; **to bear w. to having done sth.,** attester avoir fait qch.; **in w. whereof,** en témoin, en témoignage, en foi, de quoi; **to call, to take, s.o. to w.,** prendre, appeler, qn à témoin; invoquer le témoignage de qn; **I call you to w.,** j'en appelle à votre témoignage; **I call Heaven to w.!** j'en atteste les cieux! **2.** (*pers.*) (*a*) témoin *m* (d'un incident, d'un mariage, etc.); (*b*) *Jur:* **w. to a document, to a deed,** témoin instrumentaire; témoin à un acte; (*c*) *Jur:* témoin judiciaire; déposant *m*; **to call s.o. as w.,** citer qn comme témoin; assigner qn; **w. for the defence, for the prosecution,** témoin à décharge, à charge; **the first w. was the wife of the accused,** le premier témoin a été la femme de l'accusé; **w. asserted that . . .,** le témoin affirma que . . .; **w. box,** *U.S:* **w. stand,** banc *m* des témoins; (*d*) **prehistoric bridge that is a w. to the ingenuity of primitive man,** pont préhistorique qui fait preuve de l'habileté technique des hommes primitifs; **they're not all stay-at-homes; w. the three brothers who went to America,** ils ne sont pas tous casaniers; témoin les trois frères qui sont allés en Amérique.

witness[2]. **1.** *v.tr.* (*a*) *A:* (*of pers.*) témoigner, être témoin, de (qch.); déposer (**that . . .,** que . . .); **to call s.o. to w. sth.,** prendre qn à garant de qch.; (*b*) *A:* (*of thg*) témoigner de; **his pale face witnessed his distress,** son visage pâle témoignait de sa détresse; (*c*) être spectateur, témoin (d'une scène); assister à (une entrevue, etc.); **to have witnessed many a battle,** avoir vu bien des batailles; (*d*) attester, certifier véritable, signer à (un acte); certifier (une signature); **to have a document witnessed,** faire légaliser un document. **2.** *v.i.* (*a*) **to w. to sth.,** témoigner de qch.; **to w. against, for, s.o.,** témoigner contre qn, en faveur de qn; (*b*) *A:* **w. Heaven!** que le ciel me soit témoin!

witnessing ['witnisiŋ], *s.* **1.** témoignage *m.* **2.** attestation *f*; certification *f*, légalisation *f*, (d'une signature).

wittichenite [wi'tiʃinait], *s. Miner:* wittichénite *f*, wittichite *f.*

witticism ['witisizm], *s.* trait *m* d'esprit; jeu *m* d'esprit; bon mot; saillie *f*, pointe *f.*

wittily ['witili], *adv.* spirituellement; avec esprit.

wittiness ['witinis], *s.* esprit *m*; sel *m* (d'une observation, etc.).

wittingly ['witiŋli], *adv.* sciemment, à dessein.

wittol ['wit(ə)l], *s. A:* mari cocu et complaisant; mari commode.

witty ['witi], *a.* (*of pers.*) spirituel; (*of remark, etc.*) spirituel; piquant; plein d'esprit, de sel.

wivern ['waivəːn], *s. Her:* dragon ailé à deux pattes.

wizard[1] ['wizəd], *s.* sorcier *m*, magicien *m*; **I'm not a w., no w.,** je ne suis pas devin; je ne puis pas faire des miracles.

wizard[2], *a. F: O:* épatant, excellent, chic; au poil.

wizardry ['wizədri], *s.* sorcellerie *f*, magie *f*; **there's no w. in, about, that,** ce n'est pas bien sorcier; *Art:* **the w. of his brush, his w. with the brush,** son pinceau magicien.

wizened ['wiz(ə)nd], *a.* desséché, ratatiné; (*of cheeks, etc.*) parcheminé; (*of face*) vieillot; **to become w.,** se ratatiner; se parcheminer; **a w. old man,** un vieux sec et ridé; **little w. old woman,** petite vieille ratatinée.

wo(a) [wou], *int.* (*to horse*) ho!

woad [woud], *s.* (*a*) *Bot:* **(dyer's) w.,** pastel *m* des teinturiers; guède *f*; (*b*) guède, vouède *f*, teinture bleue (dont se peignaient les anciens Bretons); (*c*) *Bot:* **w. waxen,** genêt *m* des teinturiers, *F:* cornéole *f.*

wobble[1] ['wɔbl], *s.* (*a*) vacillation *f*; branlement *m*, oscillation *f*, flottement *m*; tremblement *m*; dandinement *m* (d'une roue); *Aut:* **front-wheel w.,** shimmy *m*; **tail w.,** queue *f* de poisson; **w. plate,** plateau oscillant (de moteur, etc.); (*b*) chevrotement *m* (de la voix).

wobble[2], *v.i.* **1.** (*a*) vaciller, ballotter; osciller; (*of table, etc.*) branler; (*of pers.*) chanceler; (*of wheel*) tourner à faux; ne pas tourner rond; avoir du jeu; *Aut:* **the front wheels are wobbling,** les roues avant font le shimmy; (*b*) (*of voice, etc.*) chevroter. **2.** *F: O:* (*of pers.*) hésiter, vaciller; tergiverser.

wobbler ['wɔblər], *s.* (*a*) *Metalw:* branleur *m*; trèfle *m*; **w. action,** mouvement *m* excentrique à secousses; **w. shaft,** arbre *m* à cames; (*b*) *Elcs:* vobulateur *m*, wobbulateur *m.*

wobbling[1] ['wɔbliŋ], *s.* = WOBBLY.

wobbling[2], *s.* = WOBBLE[1].

wobbly ['wɔbli], *a.* (*a*) branlant, vacillant; hors d'aplomb; **w. chair,** chaise boiteuse, branlante; **my legs feel w.,** j'ai les jambes en coton; (*b*) (*of voice, etc.*) tremblant, chevrotant.

wobbulation [wɔbju'leiʃ(ə)n], *s. Elcs:* vobulation *f*, wobbulation *f*; exploration *f* en fréquence.

wobbulator ['wɔbjuleitər], *s. Elcs:* vobulateur *m*, wobbulateur *m.*

wodge [wɔdʒ], *s.* gros morceau (de pain, etc.).

woe [wou], *s. esp. Lit:* malheur *m*, affliction *f*, chagrin *m*, peine *f*; **to tread the path of w.,** gravir son calvaire; **a tale of woes,** une odyssée de malheurs; **to tell a tale of w.,** faire le récit de ses peines, de ses malheurs, de ses infortunes; **w. is me!** pauvre de moi! malheureux que je suis! **w. to the vanquished!** malheur aux vaincus!

woebegone ['woubigɔn], *a.* (air, visage, etc.) désolé, abattu; (*of pers.*) **to look w.,** avoir l'air désolé, abattu, inconsolable, navré; faire une figure d'enterrement.

wo(e)ful ['wouful], *a. esp. Lit:* (air) affligé, malheureux, désolé; (cri) d'affliction; (nouvelle) attristante, déplorable.

wo(e)fully ['woufuli], *adv. esp. Lit:* tristement, d'un air affligé, désolé.

wog [wɔg], *s. P: Pej:* **1.** Arabe *m*, Levantin *m*, Égyptien *m*, bicot *m*, moricaud *m*, bougnoule *m.* **2.** étranger, -ère.

woggle ['wɔgl], *s. Scout:* nœud *m* de foulard.

wohlfahrtia [voul'fɑːtiə], *s. Z:* wohlfahrtia *f.*

wold [would], *s. Geog:* (*used mainly in Pr.n.*) (petite) chaîne de collines crayeuses (ou calcaires).

wolf[1], *pl.* **wolves** [wulf, wulvz], *s.* **1.** (*a*) *Z:* loup *m*; **she w.,** louve *f*; **maned w.,** loup à crinière; **timber w.,** loup gris (de l'Amérique du Nord); **Tasmanian w.,** thylacine *m*; **prairie w.,** coyote *m*; *Ven:* **w. cub,** louveteau *m* (moins de 6 mois); **young w.,** louvart *m* (6 mois à un an); **old w.,** grand vieux loup (4 ans et plus); (*in children's rhyme*) **the big, bad w.,** le grand méchant loup; **w. hunt,** chasse *f* au loup; louveterie *f*; **to be as hungry as a w.,** avoir une faim de loup; **to cry w.,** crier loup; **to have, hold, the w. by the ears,** tenir le loup par les oreilles; **that will keep the w. from the door,** (i) voilà quelque chose pour écarter la faim; (ii) cela vous, nous, mettra à l'abri du besoin; **a w. in sheep's clothing,** un loup déguisé en brebis; (*b*) *Z:* **w. dog,** chien-loup *m*, *pl.* chiens-loups; *Ven:* chien *m* de loup; **w. tooth,** surdent *f*, dent *f* de loup (d'un cheval, etc.); *Ich:* **w. fish,** loup marin; poisson-loup *m*, *pl.* poissons-loups; crapaudine *f*; *Arach:* **w. spider,** lycose *f*; araignée-loup *f*, *pl.* araignées-loups; (*c*) *Bot:* **wolf's milk,** euphorbe *f* réveille-matin; herbe *f* aux verrues; (*d*) (i) *O:* homme rapace; (ii) *F:* coureur *m* de jupons; (iii) *P:* homosexuel, pédé *m*; *F:* **w. whistle,** sifflement admiratif (au passage d'une jolie fille); *F:* **lone w.,** (i) cavalier seul; (ii) célibataire endurci, vieux bouc. **2.** *Mus:* note *f* qui sonne le tambour (sur le violoncelle, etc.).

wolf[2], *v.tr.* **to w. (down) one's food,** ingurgiter, engloutir, dévorer, sa nourriture; avaler sa nourriture à grosses bouchées.

wolfachite ['vɔlfəkait], *s. Miner:* wolfachite *f.*

wolffia ['wulfiə], *s. Bot:* wolffia *f or m.*

wolfhound ['wulfhaund], *s.* chien *m* de loup; **Irish w.,** lévier *m* d'Irlande.

wolfish ['wulfiʃ], *a.* (*a*) de loup; rapace, vorace; cruel; (*b*) **w. appetite,** appétit énorme.

wolfling [wulfliŋ], *s.* louveteau *m.*

wolfram ['wulfrəm], *s. Miner:* wolfram *m.*

wolframine ['wulfrəmain], *s. Miner:* wolframine *f.*

wolframite ['wulfrəmait], *s. Miner:* wolframite *f.*

wolfsbane ['wulfsbein], *s. Bot:* aconit *m*; tue-loup *m inv*; mort *f* aux loups; coqueluchon *m*, napel *m.*

wolfsbergite ['wulfsbəːdʒait], *s. Miner:* wolfsbergite *f*, chalcostibite *f.*

wolf-whistle ['wulf(h)wisl], *v.i. F:* siffler une fille.

wollastonite ['wuləstounait], *s. Miner:* wollastonite *f.*

wolverene, -ine ['wulvəriːn], *s. Z:* glouton *m.*

woman, *pl.* **women** ['wumən, 'wimin], *s.f.* **1.** femme; **single w.,** femme célibataire; **a young w.,** une jeune femme; **an old w.,** une vieille femme; **a little old w.,** une petite vieille; *F: O:* **the little w.,** ma femme; **he's an old w.,** il est comme une vieille fille; **the old w. who lived in a shoe** = la mère Gigogne; **the w. in her,** ses instincts féminins; (*of man*) **to run after women,** courir le jupon; **woman's man,** galant *m*; **there's a w. in it, at the bottom of it** = cherchez la femme; **a woman's work is never done,** on n'a jamais fini de faire le ménage; **women's rights,** les droits *m* de la femme; **w. must have her way** = ce que femme veut, Dieu le veut; **Women's Liberation Movement,** *F:* **Women's Lib.,** le Mouvement pour la Libération de la Femme (M.L.F.); **Women's liberationist,** *F:* **Women's libber,** (i) membre *m*, (ii) partisan, -ane, du M.L.F.; *Journ:* **women's page,** page *f* des lectrices; **women's magazines,** revues féminines; *F:* **it's just women's magazine stuff,** c'est de la littérature à l'eau de rose; **w. doctor,** femme médecin, *F:* doctoresse; **w. artist,** femme peintre; **w. friend,** amie; **a career woman,** une femme professionnelle; **it was a w. driver,** c'était une femme qui conduisait, il y avait une femme au volant; *F:* **we have a w., our w. comes in, three times a week,** nous avons une femme de ménage trois fois par semaine. **2.** *A:* femme, suivante (d'une princesse, etc.).

womanhater ['wumənheitər], *s.* misogyne *m.*

womanhood ['wumənhud], *s.* **1.** (*a*) **to come, grow, to w.,** devenir femme; devenir adulte; (*b*) *A:* féminité *f.* **2.** *coll. O:* les femmes.

womanish ['wumәniʃ], *a.* (*a*) *A:* féminin; (*b*) (*of man*) efféminé.

womanize ['wumənaiz], *v.i. F:* courir les femmes, courir le jupon.

womanizer ['wumənaizər], *s.* coureur *m* de femmes.

womankind ['wumənkaind], *s.* les femmes.

womanlike ['wumənlaik], *a.* de femme; en femme.

womanliness ['wumənlinis], *s.* féminité *f.*

womanly ['wumənli], *a.* féminin; de femme; digne d'une femme; **she has a very w. nature,** elle est très femme.

womb [wuːm], *s. Anat:* matrice *f*; **the child she bore in her w.,** l'enfant qu'elle portait dans son ventre; *B:* **the fruit of thy w.,** le fruit de vos entrailles; **in the w. of the earth,** dans le sein, dans les entrailles, de la terre.

wombat ['wɔmbæt], *s. Z:* wombat *m*, vombat *m*; phascolome *m.*

womenfolk ['wiminfouk], *s.f.pl.* (*a*) *coll.* les femmes; (*b*) *F:* **his w.,** les femmes de sa famille.

womenkind ['wiminkaind], *s. coll.* les femmes.

womp [wɔmp], *s. T.V: Cin: U.S: F:* superintensité lumineuse brusque.

wonder[1] ['wʌndər], *s.* **1.** merveille *f*, miracle *m*, prodige *m*; **to work, do, wonders,** faire, accomplir, opérer, des merveilles; faire des prodiges; faire merveille; **w. worker,** faiseur *m* de prodiges; **to promise wonders,** promettre monts et merveilles; **the seven wonders of the world,** les sept merveilles du monde; **a nine-days' w.,** la merveille d'un jour; **a w. of architecture,** un miracle d'architecture; **it's a w. (that) he hasn't lost it,** c'est merveille, il est étonnant, c'est miracle, qu'il ne l'ait pas perdu; **the w. is that he found it,** ce qu'il y a d'étonnant, ce qui m'étonne, c'est qu'il l'ait (re)trouvé; **no w., little w., small w., that the scheme failed,** il n'est guère étonnant que le projet n'ait pas réussi, ait échoué; **no w. she felt uneasy,** rien d'étonnant si elle se sentait inquiète; **for a w. he was in time,** chose étonnante, surprenante, remarquable, par miracle, par extraordinaire, il est arrivé à l'heure; **the only w. to me is that . . .,** la seule chose dont je m'étonne c'est que . . .; **he's ill and no w., and little w.,** il est malade et ce n'est pas étonnant, et rien d'étonnant, et il n'y a pas à s'en étonner; **that's no w.,** rien d'étonnant à cela. **2.** (*a*) étonnement *m*, surprise *f*; *F:* ébahissement *m*; **to fill s.o. with w.,** étonner qn; remplir qn d'étonnement; **to look at s.o. with, in, w.,** regarder qn dans l'étonnement, d'un air étonné; (*b*) émerveillement *m*, admiration *f*; **to fill s.o. with w.,** émerveiller qn; **to be lost in w.,** être, tomber, en admiration; être saisi d'admiration; **I stared at it in w.,** je le regardais émerveillé. **3.** *a. F:* **w. product,** produit miracle *a. inv.*

wonder[2]. **1.** *v.i.* s'étonner, s'émerveiller, être étonné, surpris (**at,** de); **I don't w. at it,** cela ne m'étonne pas; cela ne me surprend pas; **I w. at that!** voilà qui m'étonne! **I w. at your doing that,** je n'aurais pas cru cela de vous; **can you w. that he refused?** comment s'étonner qu'il ait refusé? **that isn't to be wondered at,** ce n'est pas étonnant; il n'y a pas de quoi s'ébahir, à s'en étonner; rien d'étonnant à cela; **it's not to be wondered at that he left,** il n'est pas étonnant, rien d'étonnant, qu'il soit parti; **I shouldn't w.,** cela ne m'étonnerait pas, ne me surprendrait pas; **I shouldn't w. if he were late arriving,** il pourrait bien arriver en retard; **I shouldn't w. if it rained soon,** rien de surprenant s'il va bientôt pleuvoir; **that set me wondering,** cela m'a intrigué. **2.** *v.tr.* (*a*) **to w. that . . .,** s'étonner que . . .; **I w. he didn't kill you,** je m'étonne qu'il ne vous ait pas tué; (*b*) se demander, vouloir savoir; **one wonders!** sait-on jamais? **I w. what the time is,** je me demande quelle heure il est; **I w. why he doesn't come,** je me demande pourquoi il ne vient pas; **I w. whether he'll come,** je me demande, je voudrais savoir, s'il viendra; **I do w. how he manages to do it,** je voudrais bien savoir comment il arrive à le faire; **one wonders whether he hasn't done it, didn't do it, on purpose,** c'est à se demander s'il ne l'a pas fait exprès; **I w. who invented that,** je suis curieux de savoir qui a inventé cela; **I w. why!** je voudrais bien savoir pourquoi! **a lot of people w. why,** plusieurs s'en demandent la raison; **their son will help them—I w.!** leur fils leur viendra en aide—est-ce bien sûr? vous croyez? **are you going to London tonight?—why?—oh, I just wondered,** allez-vous à Londres ce soir?—pourquoi?—oh, pour rien!

wonderful ['wʌndəfəl], *a.* étonnant, merveilleux, prodigieux, admirable; **you've got a w. memory,** vous avez une mémoire merveilleuse; **she's a w. mother,** c'est une mère merveilleuse; **w. to relate,** chose étonnante, remarquable; **he did a w. job of it,** il s'en est acquitté à merveille; **it was w.!** c'était merveilleux, magnifique! **we had a w. time,** nous nous sommes très bien amusés.

wonderfully ['wʌndəfəli], *adv.* étonnamment, merveilleusement, prodigieusement, extraordinairement; **w. well,** merveilleusement bien; à merveille; **she looks w. well,** elle a très bonne mine; **we enjoyed ourselves w., had a w. good time,** nous nous sommes très bien amusés; **it was w. hot all the time we were at Nice,** pendant tout notre séjour à Nice la chaleur a été magnifique; **he came out of it w. in spite of all the difficulties,** en dépit de toutes les difficultés il s'en est tiré à merveille.

wondering ['wʌnd(ə)riŋ], *a.* étonné, surpris, émerveillé.

wonderingly ['wʌnd(ə)riŋli], *adv.* d'un air étonné, surpris; avec étonnement.

wonderland ['wʌndəlænd], *s.* pays *m* des merveilles, pays enchanté.

wonderment ['wʌndəmənt], *s. esp. Lit:* étonnement *m*; émerveillement *m*; **it is a matter of w. that she is still alive,** il est bien étonnant qu'elle soit encore vivante.

wondrous ['wʌndrəs]. **1.** *a. A: & Lit:* étonnant, surprenant; incroyable, inimaginable; prodigieux; **w. dexterity,** dextérité prestigieuse; **a w. vision,** une apparition merveilleuse. **2.** *adv. A:* **w. strange,** incroyablement étrange; **w. fair,** d'une beauté incomparable.

wondrously ['wʌndrəsli], *adv.* étonnamment; merveilleusement; **w. well,** à merveille.

wonky ['wɔŋki], *a. F: O:* patraque; disloqué; chancelant, branlant; (*of chair, table*) boiteux; **to feel w.,** se sentir patraque.

wont[1] [wount], *a. Lit:* **to be w. to do sth.,** avoir coutume, avoir l'habitude, de faire qch.; **as it was w.,** de même que dans le temps; tout comme auparavant.

wont[2], *s. Lit:* coutume *f*, habitude *f*; **use and w.,** l'usage *m*; les us *m* et coutumes; **it is my w. to . . .,** c'est mon habitude de . . .; **he spoke more often of it than was his w.,** il en parlait plus souvent que d'habitude, que de coutume, qu'il n'en avait l'habitude; **according to his w., as is, was, his w.,** selon sa coutume; à, selon, suivant, son habitude.

wonted ['wountid], *a. Lit:* habituel, accoutumé.

woo [wu:], *v.tr. A: & Lit:* **1.** faire la cour à, courtiser (une femme); rechercher (une femme) en mariage. **2.** rechercher, courtiser (la fortune, la célébrité). **3. to w. s.o. to do sth.,** solliciter qn de faire qch.

wood [wud], *s.* **1.** (*a*) (*collection of trees*) bois *m*; *For:* peuplement *m*; **dense w.,** peuplement serré; **pine w.,** bois de pins; **you can't see the w. for the trees,** les arbres empêchent de voir la forêt; l'ensemble disparaît dans les détails; on se perd dans les détails; **we're not yet out of the w.,** nous ne sommes pas encore quittes de toutes les difficultés, hors de danger, tirés d'affaire, au bout; **to take to the woods,** (i) (*of animal, etc.*) s'enfuir, se sauver; gagner le taillis; (ii) *U.S: F:* (*of pers.*) se dérober à ses responsabilités; se défiler; (*b*) *attrib.* des bois; (fleur) sylvestre, sylvatique; (oiseau, bête) sylvicole; *Bot:* **w. anemone,** anémone *f* des bois; sylvie *f*; **w. rush,** luzule *f*; *Ent:* **w. ant,** fourmi *f* fauve; *Z:* **w. rat,** néotome *m*; *Orn:* **w. pigeon,** pigeon *m* ramier; palombe *f*; **w. rail,** aramide *m*, grand râle de Cayenne; **w. sandpiper,** chevalier *m* sylvain; **w. swallow,** langrayen *m*; **masked w. swallow,** langrayen à face noire; **w. warbler, w. wren,** pouillot *m* siffleur; *Myth:* **w. nymph,** nymphe *f* des bois; dryade *f*, hamadryade *f*. **2.** (*a*) (*material*) bois; **box made of w.,** boîte faite de bois; boîte en bois; **hard w.,** bois dur; bois d'ouvrage, d'œuvre; **soft w.,** bois doux, tendre; bois blanc; bois conifère; **seasoned w.,** bois séché, desséché; bois sec; **close-grained w.,** bois serré; **to chop w. (for lighting fires),** faire du petit bois; *F:* **touch w.!** *U.S:* **knock on w.!** touchez du bois! *F:* **he's w. from the neck up,** il est bouché à l'émeri; *U.S: F:* **to saw w.,** s'occuper de son affaire; rester coi; (*b*) *For:* (*in coppice*) **young w.,** cépée *f*, revenue *f*; (*of tree*) **to run to w.,** s'emporter; (*c*) **w. ash, ashes,** cendre *f* de bois; **w. floor,** plancher *m* de bois; **w. mosaic floor,** parquet *m* mosaïque; **w. pavement,** pavage *m* en bois; pavé *m* de bois; **w. block,** *Civ.E:* pavé de bois; *Engr:* planche *f*, bois; **w. engraver,** graveur *m* sur bois; xylographe *m*; **w. engraving,** (i) (*process*) gravure *f* sur bois de bout; xylographie *f*; (ii) (*print*) gravure, planche, sur bois; **w. carving,** sculpture *f* sur bois; **w. carver,** sculpteur *m* sur bois; **w. alcohol, w. spirit,** esprit *m* de bois; esprit pyroxylique; alcool *m* méthylique; *Paperm:* **w. pulp,** pâte *f* de bois; pâte à papier; *Ent:* **w. borer, w. fretter,** perce-bois *m inv*; artison *m*; vrillette *f*; **w. eater,** limebois *m inv*; **w. wasp,** siricidé *m*; *Miner:* **w. opal,** opale *f* xyloïde. **3.** *Wine-m:* **the w.,** le tonneau, la pièce, le fût; **wine in the w.,** vin logé; vin en fût, en pièce, en cercles; **wine three years in the w.,** vin qui a trois ans de barrique; **beer (drawn) from the w.,** bière tirée au fût. **4.** *Bowls:* boule *f*. **5.** *Mus:* = WOODWIND.

woodbine ['wudbain], *s. Bot:* (*a*) chèvrefeuille *m* des bois; (*b*) *U.S:* vigne *f* vierge.

woodburning ['wudbə:niŋ], *s. U.S:* pyrogravure *f*.

woodchat ['wudtʃæt], *s. Orn:* **w. (shrike),** pie-grièche rousse, *pl.* pies-grièches.

woodchuck ['wudtʃʌk], *s. Z:* marmotte *f* d'Amérique.

woodcock ['wudkɔk], *s.* (*usu. inv. in pl.*) **1.** *Orn:* bécasse *f* (des bois); *Ven: F:* videcoq *m*; **(American) w.,** bécasse américaine; **w. are very plentiful this year,** les bécasses sont nombreuses cette année. **2.** *Cu:* **Scotch w.,** œufs *mpl* aux anchois.

woodcraft ['wudkrɑ:ft], *s.* **1.** connaissance *f* (i) de la forêt, (ii) de la chasse à courre. **2.** pratique *f* du travail sur bois.

woodcraftsman, *pl.* **-men** ['wudkrɑ:ftsmən], *s.m.* trappeur; veneur.

woodcut ['wudkʌt], *s.* gravure *f* sur bois; *F:* bois *m*; estampe *f*; xylographie *f*; (*as page ornament*) vignette *f*.

woodcutter ['wudkʌtər], *s.* **1.** bûcheron *m*; **woodcutter's saw,** scie *f* à bûches. **2.** graveur *m* sur bois.

woodcutting ['wudkʌtiŋ], *s.* **1.** coupe *f* des bois. **2.** gravure *f* sur bois de fil.

wooded ['wudid], *a.* boisé; **w. hill,** colline couverte de bois; **w. country,** pays boisé, couvert.

wooden ['wud(ə)n], *a.* **1.** de bois, en bois; **w. shoes,** sabots *m*; *A:* **the w. walls of England,** (les navires de) la marine anglaise; *Vet:* **w. tongue,** actinomycose *f*. **2.** (*a*) (*of movement, manner, etc.*) raide, gauche; inexpressif; sans animation; **w. face,** visage fermé; visage de bois; (*b*) *F* **w.(-headed),** stupide, sans intelligence; à l'esprit obtus; **w. headedness,** stupidité *f*; manque *m* d'intelligence.

woodenness ['wudənnis], *s.* **1.** maintien compassé; raideur *f*. **2.** manque *m* d'intelligence; stupidité *f*.

woodhen ['wudhen], *s. Orn:* ocydrome *m*.

woodhewer ['wudhju(:)ər], *s. Orn:* picucule *m*.

woodhouse ['wudhaus], *s.* bûcher *m*.

woodland ['wudlənd], *s.* pays boisé; bois *m*; **w. nymph,** nymphe *f* des bois; dryade *f*; **w. scenery,** paysage boisé; **w. tree,** arbre *m* sylvestre; *Geog:* **w. steppe,** steppe *f* sylvatique.

woodlander ['wudləndər], *s.* habitant, -ante, des bois; forestier *m*.

woodlark ['wudlɑ:k], *s. Orn:* alouette *f* lulu; alouette des bois.

woodlouse, *pl.* **-lice** ['wudlaus, -lais], *s. Crust:* cloporte *m*, *F:* porcelet *m*; **armadillo w.,** armadille *f*.

woodman, *pl.* **-men** ['wudmən], *s.m.* **1.** bûcheron. **2.** *A:* trappeur; homme des bois. **3.** garde forestier.

woodmite ['wudmait], *s. Ent:* oribate *m*; oribatidé *m*.

woodnotes ['wudnouts], *s.pl. Lit:* le chant des bois, des oiseaux.

woodpecker ['wudpekər], *s. Orn:* pic *m*; **green w.,** pic vert, pivert *m*; **great(er) spotted w.,** pic épeiche; **lesser spotted w.,** pic épeichette; **middle spotted w.,** pic mar; **black w.,** pic noir; **grey-headed w.,** pic cendré; **Asiatic rufous w.,** pic brun d'Asie; **Syrian w.,** pic syriaque; **three-toed w.,** pic tridactyle; **American three-toed w., northern three-toed w.,** pic à dos rayé; **black-backed three-toed w., arctic three-toed w.,** pic à dos noir; **downy w.,** pic minule, *Fr.C:* pic mineur; **hairy w.,** pic chevelu; **ivory-billed w.,** pic à bec d'ivoire; **Lewis's w.,** pic de Lewis; **pileated w.,** grand pic; **red-bellied w.,** pic à ventre roux; **redheaded w.,** pic à tête rouge; **slaty w.,** pic meunier; **white-backed w.,** pic à dos blanc; **whiteheaded w.,** pic à tête blanche; **Williamson's w.,** pic de Williamson.

woodpile ['wudpail], *s.* tas *m*, monceau *m*, de bois.

woodruff ['wudrʌf], *s. Bot:* aspérule odorante; hépatique *f* des bois; petit muguet; reine *f* des bois.

woodshed ['wudʃed], *s.* bûcher *m*; *F:* **there's something nasty in the w.,** il se passe du vilain; il y a un cadavre dans la grange.

woodsman, *pl.* **-men** ['wudzmən], *s.m. esp. U.S:* chasseur (en forêt); trappeur; homme des bois.

woodstack ['wudstæk], *s.* = WOODPILE.

woodstone ['wudstoun], *s.* bois pétrifié.

woodwardia [wud'wɑ:diə], *s. Bot:* woodwardia *m*.

woodwaxen ['wudwæks(ə)n], *s. Bot:* genêt *m* des teinturiers, *F:* cornéole *f*.

woodwind ['wudwind], *s. Mus:* **the w.,** les bois *m* (flûtes, clarinettes, hautbois et bassons).

woodwork ['wudwə:k], *s.* **1.** travail *m* du bois; (*a*) construction *f* en bois; charpenterie *f*; (*b*) menuiserie *f*, ébénisterie *f*. **2.** bois travaillé; (*a*) boiserie *f*, charpente *f*; (*b*) menuiserie, ébénisterie; *Veh:* carrosserie *f*.

woodworker ['wudwə:kər], *s.* ouvrier *m* du bois; charpentier *m*, menuisier *m*, ébéniste *m*.

woodworking ['wudwə:kiŋ], *s.* = WOODWORK 1.

woodworm ['wudwə:m], *s. Ent:* artison *m*; ver *m* du bois; **this table's got w.,** cette table est vermoulue, est rongée des vers.

woody ['wudi], *a.* **1.** (*a*) boisé; **w. tract,** région couverte de bois, plantée d'arbres; (*b*) (*of path, etc.*) sylvestre, sylvatique. **2.** (*a*) *Bot: etc:* ligneux; **w. tissue,** tissu ligneux; **w. stem of a plant,** tige ligneuse d'une plante; (*of young shoot*) **to get w.,** (s')aoûter; (*b*) **w. sound,** son mat, comme si l'on cognait sur du bois. **3.** (*in plant names, etc.*) des bois; **w. nightshade,** morelle *f* douce-amère; vigne *f* de Judée, de Judas.

woodyard ['wudjɑ:d], *s.* chantier *m* (de bois).

wooer ['wu:ər], *s. A: & Lit:* amoureux *m*; prétendant *m*; soupirant *m*.

woof[1] [wu:f], *s. Tex:* trame *f*.

woof[2] [wuf], *s.* (*of dog*) aboi *m*, aboiement *m*.

woof[3] [wuf], *v.i.* (*of dog*) aboyer.

woofer ['wufər], *s. Ac:* boomer *m*; haut-parleur *m* électrodynamique pour reproduire les sons graves.

wooing ['wu:iŋ], *s. A: & Lit:* cour *f*; recherche *f* en mariage; *Fig:* recherche (de la fortune, la célébrité).

wool [wul], *s.* **1.** laine *f*; (*a*) **w. growing,** élevage *m* de moutons; **w. grower,** éleveur, -euse, de moutons; **raw w.,** laine brute, crue; (laine) surge *f*; **short (staple) w.,** laine courte, basse, à fibres courtes, à court brin; **long (staple) w.,** laine longue, haute, à long brin; **greasy w., w. in the yolk, in the grease,** laine en suint, laine grasse; **back w.,** laine mère; **breech w., livery w.,** laine cuisse; loquet *m*; **pelt w.,** pelade *f*; **wether w.,** laine bâtarde; **picklock w.,** laine prime; **dead w.,** moraine *f*, morine *f*; **sliped w.,** laine morte; **washed w.,** laine lavée; **fleece-washed w.,** laine lavée à dos; **scoured w.,** laine lavée à chaud; **waste w.,** ploc *m*; **dyed in the w., w. dyed,** teint en laine; **a dyed in the w. reactionary, etc.,** un conservateur, etc. à tous crins; *Lit:* **to go for w. and come home shorn,** aller chercher de la laine et revenir tondu; *F:* **keep your w. on! don't lose your w.!** ne te fâche pas! (*b*) **the w. industry,** l'industrie lainière; **the w. trade,** le commerce des laines; **w. mill,** fabrique *f* de lainages; **combed w.,** laine peignée; **w. comber,** (i) (*pers.*) peigneur, -euse, de laine; (ii) (*machine*) peigneuse; **w. breaker,** loup *m*; **carded w.,** laine cardée; **reworked, reclaimed w.,** laine renaissance; **recovered w. fibre,** effiloché *m*; **w. waste,** bourre *f* de laine; **w. cloth,** tissu *m*, étoffe *f*, de laine; **pure w. suit,** complet pure laine; **w. mattress,** matelas *m* de laine; **w. stapler,** négociant, -ante, en laine, marchand, -ande, de laine; **w. hall,** (i) marché *m* aux laines; (ii) bourse *f* des laines; (*c*) **knitting w., darning w.,** laine à tricoter, à repriser; **embroidery w.,** laine à broder, laine de tapisserie; **a ball of w.,** une pelote de laine. **2.** (*a*) pelage *m* (d'animal); (*b*) *Bot: etc:* laine, duvet *m*; (*c*) *F:* cheveux crépus, laine. **3. mineral w.,** coton minéral, laine minérale; laine de scorie(s); **steel w.,** paille *f* de fer.

woolball ['wulbɔ:l], *s. Vet:* égagropile *m*; gob(b)e *f*.

woold [wu:ld], *v.tr. Nau:* rouster, velter (une vergue, etc.).

woolding ['wu:ldiŋ], *s. Nau:* rousture *f*, velture *f*.

woolfell ['wulfel], *s.* peau couverte de sa laine; peau de mouton.

woolgathering ['wulgæð(ə)riŋ]. *F:* (*a*) *s.* rêvasserie *f*; (*b*) (*used verbally*) **to be w.,** rêvasser; **you're w., your mind's gone w.,** vous êtes distrait; vous rêvassez; **he's always w.,** il a toujours l'esprit ailleurs.

woolled [wuld], *a.* couvert de laine; **long(-)w.,** à longue laine.

woollen ['wulən], *a. & s.* **w. materials, woollens,** (i) *Tchn:* tissus *m* de laine cardée; (ii) (*in general parlance*) laines *f*, lainages *m*; **w. dress,** robe *f* de laine; **woollens,** vêtements *m* de laine; **winter woollens,** (sous-)vêtements chauds d'hiver; **w. merchant,** négociant, -ante, en lainages.

woolliness ['wulinis], *s.* **1.** nature laineuse (**of,** de). **2.** *F:* imprécision *f* (de raisonnement, du style, etc.); nébulosité *f* (d'idées, etc.); manque *m* de netteté; flou *m* (d'un dessin, des contours).

woolly ['wuli]. **1.** *a.* (*a*) laineux; de laine; **a little w. puppy,** un petit chien qui est une vraie boule de laine; **(soft) w. toys,** animaux *m* en peluche; **w. clouds,** nuages ouatés; **(child's) w. suit,** esquimau *m*; **w. hair,** cheveux crépus; *F:* (*of pers.*) **wild and w.,** rude, mal léché; hirsute; (*b*) *Bot: etc:* laineux; lanigère, lanifère; *Ent:* **w. bear (caterpillar),** hérissonne *f*; *Z:* **w. monkey,** singe laineux, lagothrix *m*; *Paleont:* **w. mammoth,** mammouth *m* à toison; **w. rhinoceros,** rhinocéros laineux; (*c*) (*of fruit*) cotonneux; pâteux; (*d*) *F:* peu net; imprécis; nébuleux; vaseux; (*of painting, etc.*) flou; **w. ideas,** idées vagues, vaseuses, nébuleuses, fumeuses; **w. minded,** aux idées imprécises, vagues; **w. style,** style vague, qui manque de précision; **w. outlines,** contours flous; profils ouatés. **2.** *s. F:* tricot *m*, laine *f*; **put on your w.,** mets ton tricot; **winter woollies,** (sous-) vêtements chauds d'hiver.

woolpack ['wulpæk], *s.* (*a*) *O:* sac *m*, ballot *m*, de laine; (*b*) **w. (clouds),** balle(s) *f(pl)* de coton.

woolsack ['wulsæk], *s.* (*a*) *O:* sac *m* de laine; (*b*) *Parl:* **the W.,** le siège du *Lord Chancellor* (à la Chambre des Lords).

woolskin ['wulskin], *s.* = WOOLFELL.

woolsorter ['wulsɔːtər], *s.* tireur, -euse, assortisseur, -euse, de laine; **woolsorter's disease,** pustule charbonneuse (chez l'homme).

woolwork ['wulwəːk], *s.* tapisserie *f*, broderie *f* en laine.

woomera ['wuːmərə], *s.* arme *f* de jet (des indigènes australiens).

woorali [wu'rɑːli], *s.* **1.** *Bot:* strychnos *m*. **2.** *A:* curare *m*.

wop [wɔp], *s. P: Pej:* Italien *m*, macaroni *m*.

word[1] [wəːd], *s.* **1.** (*a*) mot *m*; vocable *m*; **to repeat sth. w. for w.,** répéter qch. mot pour mot; **to translate sth. w. for w.,** traduire qch. mot à mot, textuellement, à la lettre; **a play on words,** un jeu de mots, sur les mots; **to a w.,** à la lettre; littéralement; **in a w., in one w.,** en un mot; bref; pour tout dire; en définitive; **he's rude and spiteful, in a w., a thoroughly bad child,** il est mal élevé et vindicatif, enfin un mauvais enfant; **in a few words,** en quelques mots; en termes brefs; en raccourci; **in other words,** en d'autres mots, en d'autres termes; **I told him in so many words that . . .,** je lui ai dit en termes propres, en termes exprès, que . . .; **in the full sense of the w.,** dans toute la force du terme; dans toute l'acception du terme; **he doesn't know a w. of Latin,** il ne sait pas un mot de latin; **I don't know the first w. about chemistry,** je ne sais pas un traître mot de chimie; **the French have a w. for it,** les Français ont un mot pour dire cela; **bad isn't the w. for it,** mauvais n'est pas assez dire; (*b*) **w. group,** groupe *m* de mots; locution *f*, membre *m* de phrase; **w. stress,** accent *m* tonique (d'un mot); **w. picture, painting,** description imagée, pittoresque; portrait *m* en prose (de qn); *Med:* **w. blindness,** alexie *f*, cécité verbale; (*of actor*) **to be w. perfect,** savoir son rôle sur le bout des doigts; (*c*) *Cmptr:* mot machine; **w.-organized store, memory,** mémoire organisée par mots; **key w.,** mot-clef *m*; **control w.,** mot de commande; **status w.,** mot qualificatif, d'état; (*d*) **spoken words,** paroles *f*; **these are the actual words he used,** ce sont ses propres paroles; **he didn't say it in so many words,** ce n'est pas exactement ça qu'il a dit (mais quelque chose d'approchant); **in the words of Voltaire,** selon (l'expression de) Voltaire; comme Voltaire a dit; **I can't put it into words,** je n'arrive pas à l'exprimer par des mots; **if that is the right w.,** si on peut s'exprimer ainsi; **song without words,** romance *f* sans paroles; **I said a few words to them,** (i) j'ai échangé quelques mots avec eux; (ii) je leur ai fait un petit discours; **to ask s.o. to say a few words,** demander à qn de prendre la parole, de dire quelques mots; **I told him in a few words that . . .,** je lui ai dit carrément que . . .; **he's a man of few words,** c'est un homme qui parle peu, qui ne parle pas beaucoup; **I can't get a w. out of him,** je ne peux pas le faire parler; **I've never spoken a w. to him,** je ne lui ai jamais dit un mot; **I tried to get a w. in (edgeways),** j'ai essayé de dire, de placer, un mot; **I managed to put my w. in,** j'ai réussi à placer mon mot; **he didn't say a w.,** il n'a rien dit; il n'a pas soufflé mot; **not a w.!** pas un mot! bouche close! **without a w.,** sans mot dire; **with these words, he went,** ce disant, à, sur, ces mots, là-dessus, il est parti; **you're putting words into my mouth,** vous me prêtez des paroles (que je n'avais aucune intention de dire); **to take the words out of s.o.'s mouth,** anticiper les paroles de qn; **you've taken the words out of my mouth,** c'est exactement ce que j'allais dire; **no words can describe it,** il n'y a pas de mots pour le décrire; **words fail me to express my feelings (about it),** les paroles me manquent, me font défaut, pour exprimer mes sentiments là-dessus; **words fail me!** j'en perds la parole! **too stupid for words, stupid beyond words,** d'une bêtise sans nom; **too beautiful for words,** d'une beauté ineffable; **hard words,** paroles dures; **fine words,** belles paroles; **fine words won't take me in,** je ne me paie pas de phrases; *Prov:* **fine, fair, soft, words butter no parsnips,** la belle cage ne nourrit pas l'oiseau; les belles paroles ne mettent pas de beurre dans les épinards; je vis de bonne soupe et non de beau langage; (*e*) **may I have a w. with you, I'd like a w. with you,** puis-je vous parler un instant? **I'll have a w. with him about it,** je lui en toucherai deux mots; **a truer w. was never spoken,** on n'a jamais dit si vrai; **to put in a good w. for s.o.,** dire, glisser, un mot en faveur de qn, pour qn; **he has always a good, a kind, w. for everybody,** il a du bien à dire de tout le monde; **he never has a good w. for anyone,** il ne peut pas s'empêcher de dire du mal de son prochain; **nobody has a good w. for him,** personne ne dit un mot en sa faveur; **a w. in season, out of season,** un conseil opportun, inopportun; *Prov:* **a. w. to the wise (is sufficient),** à bon entendeur demi-mot suffit; à bon entendeur salut; (*f*) **to have words with s.o.,** se disputer, se quereller, avec qn; **to come to words,** en venir aux injures; **words were running high,** la querelle s'échauffait. **2.** (*speech*) parole; **in w. or in thought,** par la parole ou par la pensée; **by w. of mouth,** de vive voix; de bouche à oreille; verbalement; **battle of words,** guerre oratoire. **3.** (*message*) avis *m*; nouvelle *f*; **I'll send you w. as soon as he arrives,** je vous en ferai part dès son arrivée; **we received w. that. . .,** on nous a apporté la nouvelle que . . .; **I'll leave w. at your house,** je vous préviendrai chez vous. **4. to give s.o. one's w.,** donner sa parole à qn; **to keep one's w.,** tenir (sa) parole; **to break one's w.,** manquer à sa parole; se dédire d'une promesse; **I give you my w., take my w. for it,** je vous en donne ma parole; croyez-m'en; je vous en réponds; vous pouvez me croire sur parole; **I'll take your w. for it,** je vous crois sur parole; je m'en rapporte à vous; **he's a man of his w., he's as good as his w.,** c'est un homme de parole; **his w. is as good as his bond,** sa parole vaut sa signature; il n'a qu'une parole; **my w.!** tiens! mon Dieu! **5.** (*a*) **w. of command,** ordre *m*; **to give the w. to do sth.,** donner (i) l'ordre, (ii) le signal, de faire qch.; *F: O:* **sharp's the w.!** dépêchez-vous! (*b*) mot de passe. **6.** *Theol:* (*a*) **the w. of God, God's w.,** la parole de Dieu; (*b*) **the W. (of God, of the Father), the Eternal W.,** le Verbe; **the W. was made flesh,** le Verbe s'est fait chair.

word[2], *v.tr.* **1.** *A:* exprimer (une idée, etc.). **2.** formuler, rédiger (un document, etc.); **well worded,** bien exprimé, bien rédigé; **I don't know how to w. this letter,** je ne sais pas en quels termes je dois écrire cette lettre; **it might have been differently worded,** on aurait pu l'exprimer autrement, en d'autres termes.

wordbook ['wəːdbuk], *s.* vocabulaire *m*, lexique *m*.

wordiness ['wəːdinis], *s.* verbosité *f*; diffusion *f*, prolixité *f*.

wording ['wəːdiŋ], *s.* **1.** (*a*) *A:* expression *f* (d'une idée); (*b*) rédaction *f* (d'un document); libellé *m* (d'une traite, d'une lettre de change); énoncé *m* (d'un acte, d'un problème). **2.** (*a*) mots *mpl*; langage *m*; (choix *m* de) termes *mpl* (d'un article, d'un acte, etc.); **form of w.,** modèle *m*, formule *f* (de chèque, de lettre de change); (*b*) phraséologie *f*; **the meaning is clear, but I'm not happy about the w.,** le sens est clair mais la phraséologie laisse à désirer.

wordless ['wəːdlis], *a.* sans paroles.

wordy ['wəːdi], *a.* (orateur, discours, etc.) verbeux, prolixe, diffus.

work[1] [wəːk], *s.* **1.** travail, -aux *m*; **to be at w.,** travailler; être au travail; **the forces at w.,** les forces en jeu; **there is some hidden influence at w.,** il y a une influence secrète qui agit (en notre faveur, contre nous); **to be hard at w.,** être en plein travail; **he was hard at w. ploughing, gardening,** il était en plein labour, en plein jardinage; **this invention takes much of the hard w. out of gardening,** cette invention facilite beaucoup le jardinage; **after a great deal of hard w.,** après beaucoup d'effort, bien des efforts; *Prov:* **all w. and no play makes Jack a dull boy,** on ne peut pas toujours travailler sans se délasser; **to start w., to set to w.,** se mettre au travail; **I'll set them to w.,** je les mettrai au travail; **I don't (quite) know how to set, to go, to w. about it,** je ne sais pas comment m'y prendre; **to stop, knock off, w.,** cesser le travail; suspendre le travail (pour la journée); **I've stopped w. for today,** je ne travaillerai plus aujourd'hui; **the w. is suspended, is in abeyance,** on a suspendu les travaux; **what happened was no w. of mine,** ce qui est arrivé n'est pas mon ouvrage; *Iron:* **that looks like some of his w.!** voilà un chef-d'œuvre de sa façon! **2.** (*a*) travail, ouvrage, besogne *f*, tâche *f*; **I've w. to do,** j'ai (du travail) à faire; **to have plenty of w. to do,** avoir du pain sur la planche; **to have too much w. to do,** avoir trop à faire; **to get through a lot of w.,** abattre de la besogne; **to make w. for s.o.,** tailler de la besogne à qn; **to give s.o. a piece, a job, of w. to do,** donner une tâche à qn; **he gives me all the dirty w. to do,** il me donne toujours les tâches ingrates, les sales besognes; **let's get down to w.!** au travail! *F:* **nice w. if you can get it!** une bonne planque si on a de la veine! **a fine piece of w.,** un beau travail; *Iron:* **that's a nice, a fine, piece of w.!** ça c'est un joli travail! **the brandy had done its w.,** l'eau-de-vie avait fait son effet; **I'll have my w. cut out to finish in time,** j'aurai de quoi faire, fort à faire, pour finir à l'heure (voulue); **you'll have your w. cut out with him,** il vous donnera du fil à retordre; **a w. that needs, will take, time,** un ouvrage de longue haleine; **day's w.,** (travail d'une) journée; **a full day's w.,** une journée bien remplie; **it's all in a, the, day's w.,** c'est l'ordinaire de mon existence; c'est comme ça tous les jours; **you did a good day's w. when you bought that house,** vous avez été bien inspiré d'acheter cette maison; (*b*) (*needlework, etc.*) ouvrage; **bring your w. with you,** apportez votre ouvrage; (*c*) **it was thirsty w., dry w.,** c'était un travail qui donnait soif. **3.** (*a*) **the works of God,** les œuvres *f* de Dieu; **to renounce the devil and all his works,** renoncer au démon, à ses pompes et à ses œuvres; **good works,** bonnes œuvres; (*b*) ouvrage, œuvre; **a(n) historical w.,** un ouvrage historique; **the works of Shakespeare,** les œuvres *f* de Shakespeare; l'œuvre *m* de Shakespeare; **Shakespeare's last w.,** le dernier ouvrage de Shakespeare; **a w. of art, of genius,** une œuvre d'art, de génie. **4.** (*a*) travail, emploi *m*; **office w., factory w.,** travail de bureau, d'usine; **to be in regular w.,** avoir un travail régulier; **to be off w.,** ne pas travailler (parce qu'on est malade); **to be out of w.,** être sans travail; être en chômage; chômer; (*b*) (lieu *m* de) travail; bureau *m*, usine *f*, etc.; **he's not at w. today,** il ne travaille pas, il n'est pas à son bureau, etc., aujourd'hui. **5.** *Mil:* **works,** ouvrages, travaux; **advanced, detached, defensive, works,** ouvrages avancés, détachés, défensifs; **field works,** travaux de campagne. **6.** *Civ.E: etc:* **works,** travaux; **public works,** travaux publics; *P.N:* **road works ahead!** *U.S:* **w. zone!** travaux! chantier! *U.S:* **w. zone ends,** fin de chantier. **7. works,** rouages *m*, mécanisme *m*, mouvement *m* (d'une montre, etc.); **there's something wrong with the works,** ça ne marche pas; *F:* **the whole works,** tout le bataclan, tout le tralala; *P:* **to give s.o. the works,** (i) passer qn à tabac; tabasser qn; (ii) tuer, descendre, qn; (iii) recevoir qn avec la croix et la bannière; *esp. U.S:* **to shoot the works,** tenter le coup; aller jusqu'au bout. **8. works,** usine *f*; atelier *m*; **chemical works,** usine de produits chimiques; **engineering works,** atelier de constructions mécaniques; **works council,** comité *m* d'entreprise. **9. chased w., hammered w.,** ouvrage ciselé, martelé; **stucco w.,** ouvrage de stuc; **bright w.,** parties polies (d'une machine, etc.); *Publ:* **art w.,** illustration *f* (d'un ouvrage). **10.** *Nau:* **upper works,** accastillage *m*, œuvres mortes; **inboard, outboard, works,** œuvres intérieures, extérieures.

work[2], *v.* (*p.t. & p.p.* **worked** [wəːkt]; *A: and in a few expressions* **wrought** [rɔːt])

I. *v.i.* **1.** (*a*) travailler; **to w. hard,** travailler dur, ferme; **to w. away, to w. steadily, at sth.,** travailler assidûment à qch.; **to w. like a navvy, like a slave, like a (cart)horse,** *U.S:* **to w. like a beaver,** travailler comme un bœuf, comme un cheval, comme un forçat, comme une brute, comme quatre; peiner comme un cheval; travailler d'arrache-pied **(at sth.,** à qch.); **to w. five days a week, a 40-hour week,** travailler cinq jours par semaine; faire une semaine de 40 heures; **to w. unsocial hours,** travailler à des heures indues, quand la plupart des gens sont libres; **to w. day and night to finish sth.,** travailler vingt-quatre heures sur vingt-quatre pour finir qch.; *Ind: etc:* **to w. to rule,** faire la grève du zèle; **to w. easily, slowly,** avoir le travail facile, lent; **to w. in leather, in brass,** travailler dans le cuir, dans le cuivre; **he's hard to w. with,** il est difficile de travailler avec lui; **to w. on a newspaper,** collaborer à un journal; **he's working on an edition of** ***Hamlet,*** il travaille, prépare, une édition de *Hamlet;* (*b*) **to w. for a good cause,** travailler pour une bonne cause; **to w. for an end,** travailler pour atteindre un but; **to w. for s.o.,** (i) être employé par qn; travailler sous les ordres de qn; (ii) prêter son secours à qn; **to w. against s.o.,** intriguer, travailler, contre qn; **they have worked together to achieve their object,** ils se sont concertés pour atteindre leur but; **all these things have worked together for good,** toutes ces choses ont contribué au bien; **working from the principle that . . .,** partant du principe que . . .. **2.** (*a*) (*of machine, etc.*) fonctionner, aller, marcher, jouer; **system that works well,** système qui fonctionne bien; **everything is working smoothly,** tout fonctionne normalement; **such a process couldn't be**

made to w., on ne saurait mettre en pratique un tel procédé; **I have forgotten how it works,** j'en ai oublié le fonctionnement; **machine that works well,** appareil *m* facile à manœuvrer, qui marche bien; **the pump isn't working,** la pompe ne marche pas; **the lift isn't working,** l'ascenseur est hors de service, est en panne; **the brake is not working,** le frein ne fonctionne pas; **the manometer is not working,** le manomètre dort; **strap that works on a wheel,** courroie qui passe sur une roue; **wheel that works on a fixed axle,** roue qui tourne sur un axe fixe; **all these tools w. by compressed air,** tous ces outils sont actionnés par l'air comprimé; (*b*) **drug that works,** médicament *m* qui produit son effet, qui agit; **his plan didn't w.,** son projet a échoué, n'a pas réussi; *F:* **that won't w. with me,** ça ne prend pas avec moi. **3.** fermenter; **the beer is working,** la bière guille; **the yeast is beginning to w.,** la levure commence à fermenter. **4.** (*a*) *O:* **his face was, his features were, working horribly,** ses traits *m* se contractaient horriblement; **his mouth was working,** il tordait la bouche; sa bouche se crispait; (*b*) *Nau:* **the ship works,** le navire fatigue; (*c*) (*of sailing ship*) **to w. southwards,** remonter vers le sud (contre le vent); **to w. to windward,** chasser dans le vent; louvoyer; (*d*) (*of angler*) **to w. upstream,** remonter le courant; (*e*) **the smaller particles w. to the bottom,** les petites particules descendent lentement au fond. **5. to w. loose,** se desserrer, se détacher; prendre du jeu.

II. *v.tr.* **1.** faire travailler (qn, un cheval, etc.); **he works his staff too hard,** il exige trop de travail de son personnel; il surmène ses employés; **to w. oneself ill, to death,** se rendre malade, se tuer, à force de travailler; se tuer à la tâche; **to w. one's fingers to the bone,** se tuer à travailler, au travail. **2.** faire travailler, faire fonctionner, faire marcher (une machine, etc.); *Nau: etc:* manœuvrer (un navire, les voiles, une pompe); **it's worked by steam, by electricity,** cela marche à la vapeur, à l'électricité. **3.** faire, opérer (un miracle); opérer (une guérison); exercer (une influence); amener (un changement); produire (un effet); **to w. mischief,** semer la discorde; **the great change wrought in him,** le grand changement qui s'est opéré en lui; **the destruction wrought by the fire,** la dévastation causée par l'incendie; **I'll w. it, things, so that. . .,** je ferai de sorte que + *sub.*; **I'll w. it if I can,** je vais tâcher de le faire, de le mener à bien; *F: O:* **I worked the ex-serviceman on him,** je la lui ai faite à l'ancien combattant. **4.** broder (un dessin, des initiales); **the flowers are worked in silk,** les fleurs sont brodées à la soie; **worked with silver, with gold,** lamé d'argent, d'or; **with silver threads worked into the woof,** avec des fils d'argent tissés dans la trame. **5.** (*a*) **to w. an incident into a book,** introduire un incident dans un livre; **to w. a staircase into the thickness of the wall,** pratiquer, ménager, un escalier dans l'épaisseur du mur; **to w. a pin into a hole,** faire entrer peu à peu une goupille dans un trou; **his keys had worked a hole in his pocket,** ses clefs avaient fini par faire un trou dans sa poche; (*b*) **to w. one's hands free,** parvenir à dégager ses mains; (*c*) **to w. one's way down, up,** descendre, monter, petit à petit, peu à peu, avec précaution; **to work oneself along on one's elbows,** ramper à l'aide des coudes; avancer sur ses coudes; **he worked his way along the ledge,** il s'est avancé péniblement sur la corniche; **they worked their way through the crowd,** ils se sont frayé un chemin à travers la foule. **6.** (*a*) travailler, façonner (le bois, le fer); ouvrer (les métaux précieux); pétrir (l'argile); brasser (la fonte); malaxer, délaiter (le beurre); travailler (la pâte); cuver, faire fermenter (le moût); **to w. a constituency,** chauffer les électeurs; (*b*) **to w. the iron into a horseshoe,** façonner, forger, le fer en fer à cheval; **to w. the clay into a statuette,** façonner une statuette avec l'argile; (*c*) **to w. oneself (up) into a rage,** laisser monter sa colère. **7.** (*a*) exploiter (une mine, une carrière); (*b*) *Com:* (*of representative*) **to w. the south-east,** faire, couvrir, le sud-est. **8.** *Nau:* **to w. one's passage,** payer son passage par son travail; (*of student*) **to w. one's way through university,** travailler pour payer ses études.

III. (*compound verbs*) **1. work in,** *v.tr.* incorporer, mélanger (qch. à qch.); introduire (un incident dans un roman, etc.); *Cu:* **w. in the butter,** incorporer le beurre.

2. work off. (*a*) *v.tr.*(i) se débarrasser de (qch.); cuver (sa colère); **to w. off one's bad temper on s.o.,** passer sa mauvaise humeur sur qn; **I'm doing some gardening to try to w. off a bit of fat,** je fais du jardinage pour essayer de perdre du poids; (ii) *Typ:* tirer (les feuilles); (*b*) *v.i.* (*of nut, etc.*) se détacher.

3. work on, *v.i.* (*a*) **he worked on after the others had left,** il a continué à travailler après le départ des autres; (*b*) **have you any data to w. on?** avez-vous des données sur lesquelles vous baser? (*c*) influencer (qn); agir sur (l'esprit de) (qn); travailler (qn); **you'll have to w. on him if you want him to do it,** il faudra le travailler si vous voulez qu'il le fasse.

4. work out. (*a*) *v.tr.* (i) exécuter (un projet); mener à bien (une entreprise); développer (une idée); **the plan was well worked out,** le projet a été bien étudié; **to w. out one's own salvation,** faire son salut; **to w. out one's (own) destiny,** être l'artisan de sa propre destinée; (ii) faire (un calcul); établir, calculer (un prix); résoudre (un problème); calculer (un azimut); *Artil: etc:* **to w. out the range,** calculer la portée; (iii) (*of mine, seam, etc.*) **to be worked out,** être épuisé; (*b*) *v.i.* (i) sortir peu à peu; **the needle gradually worked out,** l'aiguille a fini par ressortir; (ii) **I wonder how it will all w. out,** je me demande comment cela finira, va finir; **it worked out very well for me,** je m'en suis bien trouvé; (iii) **how much does it all w. out at?** le total s'élève à combien? c'est combien en tout? **it works out at £10 a head,** cela fait £10 par personne; **the problem won't w. out,** je n'arrive pas à résoudre ce problème; (iv) *Sp:* s'entraîner.

5. work round, *v.tr. & i.* (i) **the wind has worked round,** le vent a tourné; (ii) **what are you working round to?** à quoi voulez-vous en venir? **I'll try to w. him round,** je vais essayer de le convaincre.

6. work up. (*a*) *v.i.* (i) (*of skirt, etc.*) remonter; (ii) avancer par degrés; **we worked up to 150 km an hour,** notre vitesse a monté à 150 km par heure; **it's working up for a storm,** un orage se prépare; **what are you working up to?** à quoi voulez-vous en venir? (*b*) *v.tr.* (i) préparer (un discours, etc.); élaborer (un article, etc.); *Com:* **to w. up a connection,** se faire une clientèle; (ii) **to get worked up,** s'échauffer, s'emballer.

workability [wəːkə'biliti], *s.* maniabilité *f*; ouvrabilité *f*.

workable ['wəːkəbl], *a.* (*a*) *Tchn:* (*of material*) ouvrable, maniable; (*b*) (mine, etc.) exploitable; (*c*) (projet, etc.) réalisable, exécutable, pratique.

workaday ['wəːkədei], *a.* de tous les jours; **w. clothes,** habits *m* de tous les jours; vêtements *m* de travail.

workbag ['wəːkbæg], *s. Needlew: etc:* sac *m* à ouvrage; travailleuse *f*.

workbasket ['wəːkbɑːskit], *s. Needlew: etc:* corbeille *f*, panier *m*, nécessaire *m*, à ouvrage.

workbench ['wəːkben(t)ʃ], *s.* établi *m*.

workbox ['wəːkbɔks], *s. Needlew: etc:* boîte *f* à ouvrage; coffret *m* de travail.

workday ['wəːkdei], *s.* jour *m* ouvrable.

worker ['wəːkər], *s.* (*a*) travailleur, -euse; **heavy w.,** travailleur de force; **hard w.,** travailleur assidu; abatteur *m* de besogne; **to be a hard w.,** travailler dur; **horse that is a good w.,** cheval franc de collier; (*b*) *Ind:* ouvrier, -ière; (*as opposed to management*) **the workers,** le personnel; **w. priest,** prêtre-ouvrier *m*, *pl.* prêtres-ouvriers; (*c*) *Ent:* (*bee, ant*) ouvrière; (*d*) **w. of miracles,** faiseur, -euse, de miracles.

workforce ['wəːkfɔːs], *s.* main-d'œuvre *f*; personnel *m*.

workhouse ['wəːkhaus], *s.* **1.** *A:* asile *m* des pauvres; hospice *m*; **to end one's days in the w.,** finir ses jours à l'hospice; **w. child,** enfant assisté. **2.** *U.S:* maison *f* de correction.

working[1] ['wəːkiŋ], *a.* **1.** (*a*) qui travaille; ouvrier; **w. man, woman,** ouvrier, -ière; **w. farmer,** agriculteur exploitant; **the w. classes,** la classe ouvrière; les classes populaires; **w.-class family,** famille ouvrière; **w.-class district,** quartier populaire; (*b*) **he's very hard w.,** c'est un grand travailleur; (*c*) **w. party,** (i) *Pol: Ind:* groupe *m* de travail; (ii) *Mil:* atelier *m*, équipe *f*. **2.** (*a*) qui fonctionne; **w. parts of a machine,** mécanisme *m* d'une machine; parties démontables; œuvres vives, organes *m* mobiles; (*b*) **w. agreement,** modus vivendi *m*; accord *m*, entente *f*, convention *f* (entre deux entreprises, etc.); **w. majority,** majorité suffisante; **w. procedure,** méthode *f* de travail; mode opératoire; **w. theory,** théorie *f* admissible, qui donne des résultats.

working[2], *s.* **1.** travail *m*; **w. clothes,** vêtements *m* de travail; **w. hours,** heures *f* de travail; **w. day,** (i) jour ouvrable; (ii) journée *f* (de travail). **2.** (*a*) manœuvre *f* (d'une machine, etc.); **w. gear,** organes *mpl* de manœuvre; (*b*) mise *f* en œuvre (d'un procédé); exploitation *f* (d'une mine, d'une forêt, etc.); *Min:* abattage *m* (de la roche); *Min:* **w. face,** face *f*, front *m*, de travail, de taille, d'abattage; **w. expenses,** frais généraux; frais d'exploitation; **w. capital,** capital *m* d'exploitation; fonds *m* de roulement; **w. capital fund,** compte *m* d'avances; **w. plant,** matériel *m* d'exploitation; **w. drawing,** épure *f*; (*c*) fonctionnement *m* (d'une loi); fonctionnement, pratique *f* (d'un système); application *f* (d'une convention, d'une règle). **3.** marche *f*, fonctionnement, jeu *m* (d'un mécanisme); allure *f*, marche (d'un fourneau); **to alter the w. of the trains,** modifier la marche des trains; *Tg:* **multiple(x) w.,** communication *f* multiplex; *Mec.E: etc:* **w. load,** charge *f* de travail; charge pratique; **w. speed,** vitesse *f* de régime; vitesse normale; *El:* **w. voltage,** tension *f* de régime; **in w. order,** en état de marche, de service; en exploitation normale; **are the brakes in w. order,** est-ce que les freins fonctionnent? **to put a machine in w. order,** mettre une machine en état de fonctionnement; **to be in good w. order,** bien fonctionner; **everything is in w. order,** tout est au point; tout est en bon état; tout va bien. **4. w. of the digestion,** travail de la digestion; **the workings of the mind, of the conscience,** le travail de l'esprit, de la conscience; **principles that guide the workings of human thought,** principes *m* qui guident la marche de la pensée humaine. **5.** *Mth:* **w. out,** calcul *m*; résolution *f* (d'un problème). **6.** fermentation *f* (du vin, de la bière). **7.** (*a*) *Nau:* fatigue *f* (du navire); (*b*) contraction *f*, crispation *f* (des traits, de la bouche, du front). **8.** délaitement *m* (du beurre). **9.** *pl. Min:* **workings,** chantiers *m* d'exploitation; siège *m* d'exploitation, d'extraction; **first workings,** (travaux de) traçage *m*; **old workings,** vieux travaux.

workless ['wəːklis], *a.* sans travail; *s.pl.* **the w.,** les chômeurs *m*.

workman, *pl.* **-men** ['wəːkmən], *s.m.* ouvrier; artisan; **Workmen's Compensation Act,** la loi sur les accidents du travail; *Prov:* **a (good) w. is known by his work, by his chips,** à l'œuvre on connaît l'ouvrier, l'artisan; **a poor, bad, w. blames his tools,** à méchant ouvrier point de bon outil.

workmanlike ['wəːkmənlaik], *a.* (*a*) bien fait, bien travaillé; **to do sth. in a w. manner,** faire qch. en professionnel; (*b*) *A:* (*of pers.*) habile, capable, compétent.

workmanship ['wəːkmənʃip], *s. Ind: etc:* exécution *f*; travail *m*, façon *f*; **sound w.,** fabrication, exécution, soignée; **fine (piece of) w.,** beau travail.

work(-)out ['wəːkaut], *s. Sp:* séance *f* d'entraînement.

workpeople ['wəːkpiːpl], *s.pl.* ouvriers *m*; personnel *m*.

workroom ['wəːkruːm], *s.* (*a*) atelier *m*; salle *f* de travail; (*b*) ouvroir *m* (d'une communauté, d'une œuvre de bienfaisance).

workshop ['wəːkʃɔp], *s.* atelier *m*; **mobile w.,** camion-atelier *m*, *pl.* camions-ateliers; *Mil:* **field w.,** atelier de campagne; **ordnance w.,** atelier du matériel.

workshy ['wəːkʃai], *a.* fainéant; **to be w.,** bouder, renâcler, à la besogne; **he isn't w.,** le travail ne lui fait pas peur.

workstand ['wəːkstænd], *s. Tchn:* plate-forme *f* d'accès.

worktable ['wəːkteibl], *s.* table *f* de travail; *Needlew: etc:* table à ouvrage; travailleuse *f*.

work-to-rule [wəːktə'ruːl], *s. Ind: etc:* grève *f* du zèle.

world [wəːld], *s.* monde *m*. **1.** (*a*) **in this w.,** en ce monde; ici-bas; **the other w., the next w., the w. to come,** l'autre monde; **he's too good for this w.,** il est trop bon pour le siècle; **he's not long for this w.,** il n'en a pas pour longtemps à vivre; il ne fera pas de vieux os; **justice is not of this w.,** la justice n'est pas de ce monde; **to bring a child into the w.,** mettre un enfant au monde; **to make the best of both worlds,** concilier le salut de son âme avec les plaisirs d'ici-bas, de ce monde; combiner deux façons de vie très différentes; **he wants the best of both worlds,** il veut tout avoir; **the end of the w.,** la fin du monde; **w. without end,** jusqu'à la fin des siècles; éternellement; *Ecc:* pour les siècles des siècles; (*b*) **the whole w.,** le monde entier; tout l'univers; **are there any other inhabited worlds?** y a-t-il d'autres mondes habités? **to be alone in the w.,** être seul au monde; **the happiest man in the w.,** l'homme le plus heureux du monde; **he doesn't have a care in the w.,** il n'a aucun souci; **he lives in a w. of his own,** il vit dans un monde à part; **I don't know what in the w. to do with it,** je ne sais absolument pas qu'en faire; **what in the w. is the matter with you?** que diable avez-vous? **I wouldn't do it for (all) the w., for anything in the w., nothing in the w. will make me do it,** je ne le ferais pour rien au monde; **he's for all the w. like my father,** il a exactement l'air de mon père; il ressemble tout à fait à mon père; **she's all the w. to me,** elle est tout pour moi, elle est toute ma vie; **I would give the w. to know what it is,** je donnerais n'importe quoi pour savoir ce que c'est; **he carries the w. before him,** il passe de succès en succès; il ne connaît que le succès. **2.** (*earth*) **to go round the w.,** faire le tour du monde; **round-the-w. trip, tour,** voyage autour du monde; **he has seen the w.,** il a vu du pays; il a connu le monde; il a beaucoup voyagé; **map of the w.,** carte universelle; (*in two hemispheres*) mappemonde *f*; **(all) the w. over, all over the w.,** dans le monde entier; par tout l'univers; **to the end of the w., to the world's end,** jusqu'au bout du monde; **it's a small w.!** (que) le monde est petit! le monde est bien petit! **the Old W.,** l'ancien monde; **the New W.,** le nouveau monde; *Z:* **the New-W. monkeys,** les platy(r)rhiniens *m*; **the New-W. porcupines,** les éréthizontidés *m*; **the roof of the w.,** le toit du monde; le Tibet; **the English-speaking w.,** le monde anglophone; **w. power,** (i) le pouvoir séculier; (ii) *Pol:* puissance mondiale; **w. politics,** politique mondiale; **w. revolution,** révolution mondiale; **w. war,** guerre mondiale; **w. congress,** congrès mondial; **w. record,** record mondial; **w.-beater,** champion, -onne (du monde); **this car's a w.-beater,** cette voiture bat tous les records; *Fb:* **the W. Cup,** la coupe du monde; *U.S:* (*baseball*) **the W. Series,** le championnat du monde; **w. language,** langage universel; langue répandue dans le monde entier; **w. history,** histoire universelle. **3.** (*a*) (*human affairs*) **it's the way of the w.,** ainsi va le monde; **we must take the w. as we find it,** il faut prendre le monde comme il est; **as the w. goes. . .,** de la façon dont va le monde. . .; par le temps qui court. . .; **what is the w. coming to?** où allons-nous? **to see the w.,** voir le monde; **man of the w.,** homme qui connaît la vie, qui a l'expérience du monde; **w.-wise,** qui a l'expérience de la vie, qui connaît la vie; **w.-weary,** las, *f.* lasse, de ce monde; las de vivre; **w.-weariness,** dégoût *m* de la vie; **to live out of the w.,** vivre loin du monde; *F:* **it's out of this w.,** c'est (qch. d') extraordinaire, (d')épatant; c'est mirifique; **he's gone up in the w.,** il a eu beaucoup de succès (dans sa carrière, etc.); il a fait du chemin; **he's gone down in the w.,** il a connu des jours meilleurs; **to have the w. before one,** avoir toute sa carrière devant soi; **this company leads the w. in canned foods,** cette entreprise est à la pointe de l'industrie des conserves; **all the w. knows,** c'est bien connu; **w. famous, w. known,** de renommée mondiale; célèbre, connu, dans le monde entier; **all the w. and his wife,** tout le monde sans exception; **what will the w. say?** qu'en dira-t-on? (*b*) *Ecc:* siècle *m*; **to live apart from the w.,** vivre en dehors du siècle; se séparer du siècle. **4.** (*a*) **the w. of literature, of letters, the literary w.,** le monde littéraire; **the theatrical w.,** le milieu du théâtre; **the sporting w.,** le monde du sport; **the dog w.,** le monde cynophile, d'éleveurs de chiens; les sociétés canines; **the financial w.,** le monde de la finance; le monde financier; **the w. of high finance,** la bancocratie; la haute finance; **the w. of dreams,** le monde des rêves; (*b*) **the animal, vegetable, mineral, w.,** le monde animal, végétal, minéral; **the w. of birds,** le monde des oiseaux. **5.** *F:* **that will do you a w. of good,** cela vous fera un bien infini; **there's a w. of difference between margarine and butter,** il y a une différence énorme entre la margarine et le beurre; **their opinions are worlds apart,** leurs opinions sont totalement différentes; **she thinks the w. of him,** elle l'admire énormément; elle l'estime hautement.

worldliness ['wə:ldlinis], *s.* mondanité *f*; attachement *m* aux biens de ce monde.

worldling ['wə:ldliŋ], *s.* mondain, -aine.

worldly ['wə:ldli], *a.* (*a*) du monde, de ce monde, d'ici-bas; terrestre; **he's a child in w. matters,** il n'a aucune expérience du monde; **all his w. goods,** toute sa fortune, *F:* tout son saint-frusquin; **w. wisdom,** la sagesse du monde, du siècle; **w. interests,** soucis matériels; (*b*) mondain; **w.(-)minded,** attaché aux choses matérielles, aux biens de ce monde; mondain; **w. mindedness,** attachement *m* aux biens de ce monde; mondanité *f.*

worldwide ['wə:ldwaid]. (*a*) *a.* universel; mondial, -aux; partout dans le monde; **w. financial crisis,** crise financière mondiale; **w. reputation,** réputation universelle, mondiale, universellement reconnue; **the w. problem of under-development,** le problème planétaire du sous-développement; (*b*) *adv.* **the programme was heard w.,** le programme a été entendu dans le monde entier.

worm[1] [wə:m], *s.* ver *m.* **1.** (*a*) *Prov:* **even a w. will turn,** la patience a des limites; il n'y a si petit chat qui n'égratigne; **the w. has turned,** il en a assez de se laisser mener par le bout du nez; **he's a w.,** c'est un minable, un miteux; **worm's-eye view,** perspective vue (i) d'en bas, (ii) d'une humble position; *F:* **it's going to worms,** tout va de travers; *U.S: F:* **that's opening another can of worms,** (i) ça va être très compliqué; (ii) ça va nous mettre dans de beaux draps; nous allons nous fourrer dans un véritable guêpier; **that's a can of worms we don't have to open,** il n'y a pas besoin de, nous n'avons pas à, nous occuper de cela; cela ne nous regarde pas; laissons cela! (*b*) *Fish:* **worms,** *coll.* **w.,** arénicole *f*; ver (de sable, des pêcheurs); **to fish with worms,** pêcher au ver; **w. fishing,** pêche au ver; (*c*) *Ent:* larve *f*; asticot *m*; ver blanc; **apple w.,** ver des fruits; (**yellow**) **meal w.,** ver de farine; larve du ténébrion meunier; (*d*) *Med: Vet:* (*of pers., dog*) **to have worms,** avoir des vers; *Ann:* **palisade w.,** strongle, strongyle, géant; sclérostome *m* du cheval; **red w. disease,** strongylose *f* du cheval; *Pharm:* **w. powder,** poudre *f* à vers; poudre vermifuge, anthelminthique; (*e*) *Bot:* **w. grass,** spigélie *f.* **2.** (*a*) filet *m* (de vis); (*b*) **w. (screw),** vis *f* sans fin; **w. and segment,** vis (sans fin) et secteur; **conveyor w.,** hélice, spirale, transporteuse; *Mec.E:* **w. gear,** engrenage *m* à vis sans fin; **w. gear (reduction),** réducteur *m* à vis sans fin, à vis tangente; **w. pinion,** pignon *m* à vis sans fin; **w. wheel,** roue *f* (d'engrenage) à vis; *Aut: etc:* **w. drive,** commande *f,* transmission *f,* par vis sans fin; **overhead w. drive,** transmission par vis en dessus; (*c*) *Sm.a: A:* tire-bourre *m inv*; (*d*) serpentin *m* (d'alambic). **3.** le nerf sous la langue d'un chien.

worm[2]. **1.** *v.tr.* (*a*) **he wormed himself, his way, along the tunnel,** il a avancé dans le tunnel en rampant, en se tortillant; **to w. one's way out of, into, sth.,** se faufiler hors de, dans, qch.; **to w. oneself into s.o.'s favour, into s.o.'s confidence, into society,** s'insinuer, s'ingérer, dans les bonnes grâces de qn, dans la confiance de qn, dans le monde; **how did he w. his way into our group?** comment s'est-il immiscé, insinué, dans notre groupe? (*b*) **to w. a secret out of s.o.,** tirer un secret de, arracher un secret à, qn; **I'll w. it out of him,** je saurai lui tirer les vers du nez; (*c*) (i) **to w. a dog,** débarrasser un chien de ses vers; (ii) **to w. a dog's tongue,** couper le nerf sous la langue d'un chien; (*d*) fileter (un boulon); (*e*) *Nau:* congréer (un cordage). **2.** *v.i.* (*of boars, etc.*) vermiller.

wormcast ['wə:mkɑ:st], *s.* déjection *f* de ver de terre.

wormeaten ['wə:mi:t(ə)n], *a.* (*a*) piqué des vers; mangé aux vers; rongé par les vers; (*of wood*) vermoulu; (*of fruit*) véreux; (*of tree*) cussonné; (*b*) (*of method, etc.*) suranné, désuet.

wormed [wə:md], *a.* **1.** = WORMEATEN (*a*). **2.** (boulon) fileté.

wormhole ['wə:mhoul], *s.* (*in wood, in the ground*) trou *m* de ver; (*in cloth, wood*) piqûre *f* (de ver).

worming ['wə:miŋ], *s. Nau:* (*a*) congréage *m*; (*b*) filin *m* à congréer.

wormlike ['wə:mlaik]. **1.** *a.* vermiforme, vermiculaire. **2.** *adv.* comme un ver (de terre).

wormseed ['wə:msi:d], *s. Bot:* ambroisie *f,* santonine *f*; *Pharm:* (**Levant**) **w.,** semen-contra *m*; armoise *f* d'Alep; santonine.

wormwood ['wə:mwud], *s. Bot:* armoise (amère); (armoise) absinthe *f*; **spicate w.,** armoise en épi; *Lit:* **life to him was gall and w.,** la vie pour lui n'était qu'amertume et dégoût, que fiel et absinthe.

wormy ['wə:mi], *a.* **1.** infesté, plein, de vers; véreux; piqué des vers. **2.** vermiforme, vermiculaire.

worn [wɔ:n], *a.* **1.** (*a*) **w. (out),** (vêtement) usé, fatigué, râpé; **these shoes are w. out,** ces chaussures sont tout usées; (*b*) (cordage) mâché; (rocher) rongé par les intempéries; **w. cable,** câble fatigué; (*c*) usé, fatigué; (visage) fripé, marqué par les soucis; **travel-w.,** fatigué par le voyage; **w. features,** traits usés (par le chagrin, par l'âge, etc.); **I'm absolutely w. out!** je suis épuisé, exténué, éreinté! je n'en peux plus! (*d*) *Farr:* **w. hoof,** pied dérobé. **2. w. out,** (*of idea, etc.*) rebattu, usé.

worried ['wʌrid], *a.* tourmenté, tracassé, soucieux; ennuyé; **I'm w. about this,** cela m'inquiète, me tracasse; **he's w. about the car,** il est inquiet au sujet de la voiture; **he looks w.,** il a l'air préoccupé, soucieux.

worriedly ['wʌridli], *adv.* anxieusement, soucieusement; avec inquiétude.

worrier ['wʌriər], *s.* **1.** chien *m,* loup *m,* qui attaque les moutons, qui les prend à la gorge. **2.** (*of pers.*) harceleur, -euse; tourmenteur, -euse; persécuteur, -trice. **3.** (*a*) personne qui tracasse les autres; tracassier, -ière; (*b*) personne qui se tracasse, qui se fait de la bile; **he's such a w.,** il s'inquiète tout le temps; il se fait trop de soucis; il se met toujours martel en tête.

worriment ['wʌrimənt], *s. A: & Lit:* souci *m,* tracas *m.*

worrisome ['wʌrisəm], *a.* tracassant, inquiétant; ennuyeux.

worrit[1,2] ['wʌrit], *s., v.tr. & i. Dial:* = WORRY[1,2].

worry[1] ['wʌri], *s.* **1.** (*a*) *Ven:* (*of hounds*) action *f* de fouler la bête; (*b*) **bun w.,** goûter copieux (pour des élèves, des membres d'une association, etc.) où il y a cohue. **2.** ennui *m,* souci *m,* tracasserie *f,* tracas *m*; **little domestic worries,** petites misères domestiques; chagrins *m* domestiques; **he is a constant w. to me,** il m'est un perpétuel souci; **it's causing me a lot of w.,** cela m'inquiète beaucoup; **that's the least of my worries,** c'est le moindre, le dernier, le cadet, de mes soucis; *F:* **what's your w.?** qu'est-ce qui ne va pas?

worry[2]. **1.** *v.tr.* (*a*) (*of dog, wolf*) prendre (les moutons) à la gorge; attaquer, harceler (les moutons); déchirer (une bête); (*b*) *Ven:* (*of hounds*) fouler (la bête); (*c*) *O:* **to w. out a problem,** s'évertuer, s'escrimer, à résoudre un problème; (*d*) tourmenter, tracasser, ennuyer, harceler, importuner (qn); *F:* asticoter (qn); **to w. one's horse,** tourmenter son cheval; **don't w. him,** laissez-le tranquille; **something is worrying him,** il y a quelque chose qui le préoccupe, qui le travaille; **the noise of the traffic worries me,** le bruit de la circulation m'importune; **my baby has a cough and it rather worries me,** mon bébé tousse et cela m'inquiète; **to w. oneself,** se tourmenter, se tracasser; se faire du souci; se faire du mauvais sang, de la bile; **she'll w. herself to death,** elle se tourmentera à s'en rendre malade; elle sera folle d'inquiétude; **don't w. your head about him!** ne vous inquiétez pas de lui; ne vous en faites pas sur son compte. **2.** *v.i.* se tourmenter, se tracasser, s'inquiéter; se travailler l'esprit; se faire du souci, de la bile, du mauvais sang; se ronger les sangs; **to w. about sth.,** être, se mettre, en peine de qch.; **he keeps worrying about that business,** cette affaire lui travaille l'esprit; **you have no cause to w.,** vous pouvez dormir sur les deux oreilles; **they had never worried whether people were polite or not,** ils ne s'étaient jamais souciés que les gens fussent polis ou non; **don't (you) w.!** *F:* **not to w.!** ne vous tracassez pas, ne vous inquiétez pas! soyez tranquille! ne vous en faites pas! **don't (you) w. about me, over me,** ne vous tracassez pas sur mon compte, ne vous faites pas de soucis à mon sujet; ne vous inquiétez pas pour moi; **don't w. about looking for it now!** vous n'allez pas le chercher maintenant! **he worries about nothing,** (i) il se tracasse pour (un) rien; (ii) rien ne le tracasse; **it's nothing to w. about,** ce n'est rien d'inquiétant; *F:* ce n'est pas le diable; **what's the use of worrying?** à quoi bon se tourmenter? *F:* **I should w.!** ce n'est pas mon affaire! ça m'est égal!

worryguts ['wʌrigʌts], *s. P:* personne qui se fait de la bile, qui se tracasse; bileux, -euse.

worrying[1] ['wʌriiŋ], *a.* **1. w. dog,** chien traître, qui attaque le troupeau. **2.** tracassant, inquiétant.

worrying[2], *s.* tracasserie *f,* tracas *m,* tourment *m*; inquiétude *f.*

worse [wə:s]. **1.** *a. & s.* pire, plus mauvais; **I'm a w. player than he (is),** je joue plus mal que lui; **he makes himself out (to be) w. than he is,** il se noircit à plaisir; **in w. condition,** dans un plus mauvais état; **this is w. and w.,** c'est, ça va, de mal en pis, de pis en pis; **you're only making things w.,** vous ne faites qu'empirer les choses; **to make matters w. . . .,** par, pour, surcroît de malheur. . .; **that only makes matters w.,** cela n'a pas arrangé les choses; cela n'a fait qu'aggraver le mal; **it might have been w.,** il n'y a que demi-mal; **he escaped with nothing w. than a fright,** il en fut quitte pour la peur; **what is w. . . .,** qui pis est. . .; **to go from bad to w.,** aller de mal en pis; **he's getting w.,** (i) (*in behaviour*) il se tient de plus en plus mal; (ii) (*in health*) il va plus mal; il va de plus en plus mal; il va de mal en pis; **his illness is getting w.,** sa maladie s'aggrave, empire; **my eyesight is growing w. every day,** ma vue baisse de jour en jour; **the w. his arguments are the more he believes in them,** plus ses arguments sont mauvais plus il y croit; **so much the w. for him,** tant pis pour lui; **he escaped none the w.,** il s'en est tiré sans aucun mal; **I am none the w. for it,** je ne m'en trouve pas plus mal; je ne m'en ressens pas; je ne m'en porte pas plus mal; **he is none the w. for his accident,** son accident n'a pas eu de suites; il ne se ressent pas, il se ressent à peine, de son accident; **I think none the w. of him because he accepted,** je n'ai pas moins bonne opinion de lui parce qu'il a accepté. **2.** *s.* (*a*) **I have w. to tell,** j'ai quelque chose de pire à dire; je n'ai pas encore dit le pire; **but w. followed, there was w. to follow, to come,** mais il y a eu plus grave; ce qui a suivi était encore pire; **I have seen w., been through w., than that,** j'en ai vu bien d'autres; (*b*) **to change for the w.,** s'altérer; **change for the w.,** changement *m* en mal; altération *f*; **he has taken a sudden turn for the w.,** son état s'est subitement aggravé. **3.** *adv.* (*a*) plus mal; *Lit:* pis; **he is behaving w. than ever,** il se conduit plus mal que jamais; il recommence de plus belle; **he has been taken w.,** il va plus mal; son état a empiré; **w. still, he didn't leave his address,** ce qui est pire, il n'a pas laissé son adresse; **you might do w. than to accept,** accepter n'est pas ce que vous pourriez faire de pire; vous pourriez faire pire que d'accepter; **to think w. of s.o.,** avoir plus mauvaise opinion de qn; **to think w. of s.o. for doing sth.,** estimer qn moins pour avoir fait qch.; **he is w. off than before,** sa situation a empiré; **your remedy is w. than useless,** votre remède est non seulement inefficace, mais dangereux; (*b*) **I hate him w. than before,** je le déteste plus qu'auparavant; **the noise went on w. than ever,** le vacarme a recommencé de plus belle.

worsen ['wə:s(ə)n]. **1.** *v.tr.* empirer, aggraver (un mal); rendre pire. **2.** *v.i.* empirer, devenir pire; (*of health, etc.*) s'aggraver; **the situation has since worsened,** la situation a empiré depuis.

worsening ['wə:s(ə)niŋ], *s.* aggravation *f.*

worship[1] ['wə:ʃip], *s.* **1.** culte *m,* adoration *f*; **w. of im-**

ages, iconolâtrie *f*; culte, adoration, des images; **divine w.,** le culte divin; **private w.,** culte privé; **public w.,** (i) culte public; (ii) *Adm:* les Cultes; **freedom of w.,** liberté *f* du culte; **forms of w.,** formes *f* de culte; formes cultuelles; **hours of w.,** heures *f* des offices; **place of w.,** lieu consacré au culte; édifice cultuel; église *f*, temple *m*; **to be an object of w.,** être un objet d'adoration; **gazing at her with w. in his eyes,** la regardant avec des yeux adorateurs. **2.** (*a*) *A:* honneur *m*, considération *f*, dignité *f*; (*b*) **His W. the Mayor,** monsieur le maire; **yes, your W.,** oui, monsieur le maire, monsieur le juge.

worship² (**worshipped**) **1.** *v.tr.* (*a*) rendre un culte à, adorer (un dieu, une idole); vouer un culte à, vénérer (un saint); vénérer (une relique); **to w. the golden calf,** adorer le veau d'or; (*b*) adorer (qn); aimer (qn) à l'adoration, jusqu'à l'idolâtrie; avoir un véritable culte pour (qn); **to w. money,** faire son idole de l'argent; **he worships the ground she treads on,** il vénère jusqu'au sol qu'elle foule; **to w. one's body,** idolâtrer son corps. **2.** *v.i.* **the parish church where his family had worshipped for years,** l'église paroissiale où sa famille a prié, a fait ses dévotions, pendant des années; **where does he w.?** à quelle église, à quel temple, va-t-il?

worshipful ['wəːʃipful], *a.* (*a*) honorable (titre des membres des Corporations de Londres, des juges de paix, des *aldermen*, etc.); (*b*) (*Freemasonry*) **w. master,** vénérable *m*.

worshipper ['wəːʃipər], *s.* adorateur, -trice; (*in church*) **the worshippers,** les fidèles *m*.

worshipping ['wəːʃipiŋ], *s.* culte *m*, adoration *f*.

worst¹ [wəːst]. **1.** *a.* (le) pire, (le) plus mauvais; **the w. of all evils,** le pire de tous les maux; **that was his w. mistake,** c'était sa plus grave erreur; **his w. enemy,** son pire ennemi; **it was the w. winter for 40 years,** c'était l'hiver le plus rude depuis 40 ans. **2.** *s.* **the w. that could happen,** le pire, la pire chose, qui puisse arriver; **the w. of the storm is over,** le plus fort de l'orage est passé; **the w. of it is that. . .,** le pire c'est que, l'ennui c'est que, le malheur c'est que + *ind.*; **that's the w. of cheap shoes,** c'est l'inconvénient des chaussures bon marché; voilà ce que c'est que d'acheter des chaussures bon marché; **you saw him at his w.,** vous l'avez vu dans un de ses plus mauvais jours, dans un de ses plus mauvais moments; **when things are at their w., at the w.,** quand les choses vont au plus mal; **I'll only be 10 minutes late at the w.,** en tout cas, en mettant les choses au pire, je n'aurais que 10 minutes de retard; (*in a fight, etc.*) **to get the w. of it,** avoir les dessous; essuyer un échec; être battu; avoir le désavantage; être le perdant; **I fear the w.,** je crains le pire; **he's prepared for the w.,** il s'attend au pire; **they are the w. off,** ils sont les plus démunis; **if it comes to the w., if the w. comes to the w.,** *U.S:* **if the worse comes to the w.,** en mettant les choses au pire; au pis aller; **the w. is yet to come,** on n'a pas encore vu le pire; le pire n'est pas encore arrivé; **do you w.!** allez -y! essayez toujours! **let him do his w.,** il peut bien faire tout ce qu'il voudra! **the w. is over,** le plus mauvais moment est passé; **the w. has happened!** c'est la catastrophe! c'en est fait! **and that's not the w. of it!** et ce n'est pas le pire! et il y a pire encore! **3.** *adv.* (le) plus mal; *Lit:* (le) pis; **that frightened me w. of all,** c'est cela qui m'a effrayé le plus.

worst², *v.tr.* battre, vaincre, défaire (qn); **to be worsted,** succomber; avoir le dessous.

worsted ['wustid], *s. Tex:* laine peignée; peigné *m*; **w. fabrics,** tissus *m* de laine peignée.

wort [wəːt], *s.* **1.** (*rare except in compounds*) plante *f*, herbe *f*. **2.** moût *m* (de bière); *Brew:* **to run off the w.,** donner un avoi.

worth [wəːθ]. **1.** *a.* valant; (*a*) **to be w. so much, little, nothing,** valoir tant; valoir peu; ne rien valoir; **what is the franc w.?** combien vaut le franc? **two houses w. £30,000 each,** deux maisons valant £30,000 chacune; **that's w. something,** cela a de la valeur; **this old piano is surely w. something,** ce vieux piano a bien son prix; **it's not w. much,** cela ne vaut pas grand-chose; **whatever it may be w.,** vaille que vaille; **I'll buy it whether it's w. the money or not,** je l'achète, vaille que vaille; **I tell you this for what it is w.,** je vous passe ce renseignement sans y attribuer grande valeur; **it would be as much as my life is w.,** ce serait risquer ma vie; **society is w. more than the individual,** la société l'emporte en valeur sur l'individu; (*b*) **it's not w. the trouble,** cela ne, n'en, vaut pas la peine; **is it w. while? is it w. it?** cela (en) vaut-il la peine? **it isn't w. it,** ça ne vaut pas le coup; **it's not w. anything,** cela ne vaut pas quatre sous; **this novel is not w. reading,** ce roman ne vaut pas la peine d'être lu, qu'on le lise, ne mérite pas d'être lu; **she's not w. bothering about,** elle ne vaut pas qu'on s'occupe d'elle; ce n'est pas la peine de s'occuper d'elle; **something w. having,** une chose précieuse; **it's not w. having,** ce n'est rien qui vaille; **it's not w. mentioning,** cela ne vaut pas la peine qu'on en parle; **life wouldn't be w. living,** la vie serait intolérable; **it's w. thinking about,** cela mérite réflexion; **it's w. seeing, hearing, remembering,** cela mérite d'être vu, entendu; **it's w. knowing, remembering,** c'est bon à savoir, à se rappeler; **it's w. a special visit,** cela vaut le détour; (*c*) **he's w. millions,** il est énormément riche, riche à millions; **to be w. £40,000 a year,** avoir, posséder, £40,000 de rente; **to die w. a million,** mourir en laissant un million; **that is all I am w.,** voilà toute ma fortune; **he was running, pulling, for all he was w.,** il courait, tirait, tant qu'il pouvait, tant et plus, de toutes ses forces. **2.** *s.* valeur *f*, mérite *m*; **of great, little, no, w.,** de grande valeur; de peu de valeur; d'aucune valeur; **people of (sterling) w.,** personnes de valeur, de mérite, de bon aloi, du meilleur aloi; **give me £4 w. of petrol,** donnez-moi pour £4 d'essence; **a hundred pounds' w. of goods,** des marchandises pour une valeur de cent livres; **to have, to want, one's money's w.,** en avoir, en vouloir, pour son argent; **he gives you your money's w.,** il vous en donne pour votre argent.

worthily ['wəːðili], *adv.* **1.** dignement. **2.** à juste titre.

worthiness ['wəːðinis], *s.* mérite *m*.

worthless ['wəːθlis], *a.* sans valeur, sans mérite; qui ne vaut rien; indigne; **he's completely w.,** c'est un vaurien; **w. excuses,** excuses qui ne valent rien; *Com:* **w. bill,** titre *m* sans valeur; non-valeur *f*.

worthlessness ['wəːθlisnis], *s.* peu *m* de valeur; indignité *f*; nature *f* méprisable (de qn).

worthwhile [wəːθ'(h)wail], *a.* qui en vaut la peine, *F:* le coup; **at last I've found a w. job,** j'ai enfin trouvé un poste qui me donne satisfaction.

worthy ['wəːði]. **1.** *a.* digne; (*a*) **a w. man,** un digne homme; un homme honorable, estimable; un homme de mérite; **a w. life,** une vie honorable, vertueuse; (*b*) **to be w. of s.o., of sth.,** être digne de qn, de qch., mériter qch.; **to be w. to do sth.,** être digne de faire qch.; **to be w. of death,** mériter la mort; **w. of respect,** digne de respect; **he is w. of punishment, of being punished,** il mérite d'être puni; **it is w. of note that. . .,** il est à noter que. . .; (*c*) **the town has no museum w. of the name,** la ville n'a aucun musée digne du nom; **speech w. of the occasion,** discours digne de l'occasion. **2.** *s.* (*a*) *A:* personnage éminent, illustre, célèbre par son courage, sa grandeur d'âme; **the nine Worthies,** les neuf Preux *m*; (*b*) *F:* personnage (de l'endroit); **the village worthies,** (i) les notables du village; (ii) les anciens *m* du village.

wot [wɔt], *v.i. A:* **to w. of. . .,** savoir. . .; **him you w. of,** celui que vous savez; **dangers that none w. of,** dangers insoupçonnés.

wotcher ['wɔtʃər], *int. P:* **w. mate!** comment ça gaze mon vieux?

would-be ['wudbiː], *a.* prétendu, soi-disant, voulu; **w.-be assassin,** prétendu assassin; **a w.-be note of cynicism,** un ton de scepticisme voulu, affecté; **a w.-be candidate,** un aspirant à la candidature.

wound¹ [wuːnd], *s.* (*a*) blessure *f*; **w. in the arm,** blessure au bras; **slight w. in the arm,** atteinte *f* au bras; **bullet w.,** blessure par balle; **lacerated w.,** déchirure *f*; **operation w.,** incision chirurgicale; *Mil:* **w. stripe,** chevron *m* de blessé; (*b*) plaie *f*; **the w. is festering,** la plaie s'envenime; **to reopen a w.,** rouvrir une plaie; **the five wounds of Christ,** les cinq plaies de Notre-Seigneur; *Fig:* **to rub salt in the w.,** retourner le fer dans la plaie; (*c*) *Lit:* **to inflict a w. upon s.o.'s honour,** porter atteinte à l'honneur de qn; **it was a w. to my pride,** ce fut une blessure pour mon amour-propre.

wound² [wuːnd], *v.tr.* blesser; faire une blessure à (qn); (*in duel*) toucher (son adversaire); **wounded in the shoulder,** blessé, atteint, à l'épaule; **to w. s.o.'s pride,** blesser qn dans son orgueil, dans son amour-propre; **to w. s.o.'s feelings,** blesser les susceptibilités de qn; froisser qn.

wound³ [waund], *a.* enroulé, entortillé; **w. rotor,** rotor bobiné.

wounded ['wuːndid], *a.* blessé; **the w. man,** le blessé; **seriously w.,** grièvement blessé; *s.pl.* **the w.,** les blessés; *Mil:* **the seriously w.,** les grands blessés; **w. pride,** orgueil froissé, blessé; **w. heart,** cœur ulcéré.

wounding ['wuːndiŋ], *a.* blessant; **he found it w. to his pride,** cela a blessé son amour-propre.

woundwort ['wuːndwəːt], *s. Bot:* **1.** stachys *m*, épiaire *m*, bétoine *f*. **2.** anthyllide *f*, anthyllis *f*, vulnéaire; vulnéaire *f*. **3.** consoude *f*.

wow¹ [wau]. *F:* **1.** *int.* oh là là! **2.** *s.* succès fou.

wow², *s. Ac:* pleurage *m*.

wowser ['wauzər], *s. Austr:* puritain, -aine, à outrance; rabat-joie *mf inv*.

wrack¹ [ræk], *s.* **1.** varec(h) *m*, goémon *m*; **(sea, knotted) w.,** goémons épaves; **brown w.,** goémon jaune; **denticulated w.,** goémon jaune denticulé; **holy, channelled, w.,** pelvetia *f*, goémon noir; **flat w.,** fucus noir. **2.** laisse (déposée sur le rivage).

wrack², *s.* **(cloud) w.,** légers nuages chassés par le vent; diablotins *mpl*.

wrack³, *s.* **to go to w. and ruin,** aller à la ruine, tomber en ruine, (s'en) aller à vau-l'eau; (*of house, etc.*) se délabrer.

Wraf [ræf], *s.f. F:* membre *m* de la *Women's Royal Air Force*.

wraith [reiθ], *s.* **1.** apparition *f*; (i) esprit revenu de l'autre monde (peu après la mort de la personne); (ii) double spectral d'une personne (présage de la mort). **2.** *F:* personne maigre (comme un clou); fantôme *m*. **3.** filet *m* de fumée, de vapeur.

wrangle¹ ['ræŋgl], *s.* dispute *f*, querelle *f*, altercation *f*, chamaillerie *f*.

wrangle². **1.** *v.i.* se disputer, se quereller, se chamailler; **to w. over trifles,** *F:* chipoter, chicoter; **they're always wrangling,** ils sont toujours à se disputer, ce sont entre eux des chamailleries continuelles; **he paid without wrangling,** il a payé sans chicaner. **2.** *v.tr. NAm:* garder, soigner (les chevaux) sur les pâturages non clôturés.

wrangler ['ræŋglər], *s.* **1.** querelleur, -euse; *F:* chamaillard *m*; **a terrible w.,** un insupportable argumentateur. **2.** *Sch:* (*at Cambridge University*) candidat sorti dans la première classe à l'examen du tripos de mathématiques; *A:* **senior w.,** candidat sorti le premier (à cet examen). **3.** *NAm:* cowboy *m*.

wrangling¹ ['ræŋgliŋ], *a.* querelleur, disputeur.

wrangling², *s.* disputes *fpl*, querelles *fpl*, chamailleries *fpl*.

wrap¹ [ræp], *s.* (*a*) *usu. pl.* **wraps,** (i) couvertures *f* (de voyage, etc.); (ii) pardessus *m*, châle *m*, cache-nez *m inv* (dont on s'enveloppe pour se garantir du froid); (*b*) pèlerine *f*, manteau *m* (de voyage); (*c*) **evening w.,** manteau du soir, sortie *f* de bal, de théâtre; (*d*) *Tchn:* enveloppe *f*, couverture *f* (d'un fil, etc.); **w. thickness,** épaisseur *f* d'enroulement; (*e*) *esp. U.S: F:* **to keep sth. under wraps,** tenir, garder, qch. secret; **to take the wraps off a secret,** dévoiler un secret.

wrap², *v.tr. & i.* (**wrapped** [ræpt], *A:* **wrapt**) **1.** *v.tr.* (*a*) envelopper; **to w. sth. (up) in paper,** envelopper, empaqueter, qch. dans du papier; **to w. up a book,** envelopper un livre; **to w. up a parcel,** faire un paquet; envelopper un paquet; **to w. (up) sweets in a screw of paper,** entortiller des bonbons dans un morceau de papier; *P:* **w. up!** la ferme! (*b*) **to w. oneself up,** *v.i.* **to w. up,** s'envelopper; se couvrir de vêtements chauds; s'emmitoufler; **do w. up!** couvrez-vous bien! **to w. oneself up in a blanket,** s'envelopper, s'entortiller, dans une couverture; **to w. a baby (up) in a shawl,** emmitoufler un enfant dans un châle; **fog wrapped the streets in darkness,** le brouillard plongeait les rues dans les ténèbres; **mountain wrapped in mist,** montagne enveloppée de brouillard; *Fig:* **to w. sth. up,** déguiser, cacher, qch.; **wrapped in mystery,** enveloppé, entouré, de mystère. **2.** *v.tr.* **to w. sth. round sth.,** enrouler, entortiller, qch. autour de qch.; **the cable wrapped (itself) round the capstan,** le câble s'enroula sur le cabestan; **he wrapped a cloak round her,** il l'a enveloppée d'un manteau; **he wrapped the blanket close round him,** il s'est bien enveloppé dans sa couverture; *F:* **he wrapped his car round a tree,** il a encadré un arbre. **3.** *v.tr. F:* **to w. up a deal,** boucler une affaire; **it's all wrapped up,** tout est arrangé; c'est une affaire bouclée; **the government has the crisis wrapped up,** le gouvernement a la crise en main; *Sp:* **they had the match wrapped up from the start,** dès le début du match leur victoire était assurée. **4.** *v.i.* (*of garment*) **to w. over,** croiser. **5.** *v.tr.* **to w. a tyre,** bandeler un pneu; **to w. a spring with cord,** ficeler un ressort; *El:* **to w. a cable (in cotton),** guiper un câble (de coton).

wraparound ['ræpəraund], *s. Cost: esp. NAm:* **w. (skirt),** jupe *f* portefeuille; *Mec.E: etc:* **w. ring,** bague *f* de serrage.

wrapover ['ræpouvər], *s. Cost:* **w. (skirt),** jupe *f* portefeuille.

wrappage ['ræpidʒ], *s.* (*a*) enveloppe *f*, couverture *f*; (*b*) papier *m*, toile *f*, d'emballage.

wrapped [ræpt], *a.* **1.** (*a*) **w. bread,** pain préemballé; **w. sweets,** bonbons en papillotes *f*; *El:* **metal-w. cable,** câble avec revêtement de métal; (*b*) (*of pers.*) **w. up,** bien enveloppé; emmitouflé. **2.** (*a*) **w. in meditation, in thought,** plongé, enfermé, perdu, dans ses pensées; absorbé dans ses réflexions; songeur, -euse; **w. in slumber,** plongé dans un profond sommeil; (*b*) **to be w. up in s.o.,** vivre entièrement pour qn; être épris, engoué, de qn; **she was w. up in her son,** elle ne vivait que pour son fils; elle ne songeait qu'à son fils; **to be w. up in sth.,** être uniquement préoccupé de qch.; **he is w.**

up in his work, il est entièrement absorbé par son travail; **to be w. up in oneself,** être replié sur soi-même, concentré en soi-même.

wrapper ['ræpər], *s.* **1.** (*pers.*) emballeur, -euse; empaqueteur, -euse. **2.** toile *f* d'emballage; feuille *f* de papier d'emballage. **3.** (*a*) chemise *f* (d'un dossier, de documents); (*b*) **book w.,** (i) couverture *f* (d'un livre); couvre-livre *m, pl.* couvre-livres; (ii) liseuse *f.* **4.** bande *f* (de journal); **to do a newspaper up in a w.,** mettre un journal sous bande. **5.** (*a*) robe *f,* cape *f* (de cigare); (*b*) *U.S: F:* cigare *m.* **6.** *Tchn:* couvre-joint *m, pl.* couvre-joints; fourrure *f;* bande de recouvrement. **7.** robe de chambre (de dame); saut-de-lit *m, pl.* sauts-de-lit.

wrapping ['ræpiŋ], *s.* **1.** enveloppement *m;* mise *f* en paquet; entortillage *m;* enroulement *m;* ficelage *m;* (*of newspapers*) mise *f* sous bande; **w. paper,** papier *m* d'emballage; *NAm:* **paper w.,** guipage *m* (d'un câble) au papier; **paper w. machine,** guipeuse *f* à papier. **2.** (*a*) enveloppe *f,* couverture *f;* (*b*) (i) papier *m,* (ii) toile *f,* d'emballage; (*c*) **wrappings,** bandelettes *f* (de momies).

wrap-rascal ['ræprɑːskl], *s. A:* pardessus *m.*

wrap(-)round ['ræpraund], *a. Aut:* **w.(-)r. rear window,** lunette arrière panoramique, enveloppante; *Cost:* **w.(-)r. skirt,** jupe *f* portefeuille.

wrap-up ['ræpʌp], *s. NAm: F:* **1.** résumé *m; F:* topo *m.* **2.** tâche *f* facile; *Sp:* certitude *f;* **it was a w.-up,** c'était donné. **3.** commande *f* par poste; achat *m* sur catalogue.

wrasse [ræs], *s. Ich:* labre *m, F:* vieille *f,* rouillé *m,* rouquier *m;* **Ballan w.,** labre commun; **corkwing w.,** crénilabre *m;* **rainbow, goldfinny, goldsinny, w.,** girelle *f.*

wrath [rɔθ, rɔːθ], *s. Lit:* courroux *m; B:* **vessels, children, of w.,** vases *m,* enfants *m,* de colère; **slow to w.,** lent à la colère; **to bottle up one's w.,** rentrer sa colère.

wrathful ['rɔ(ː)θful], *a. Lit:* courroucé, en colère, irrité.

wrathfully ['rɔ(ː)θfuli], *adv. Lit:* avec colère, avec courroux.

wrathfulness ['rɔ(ː)θfulnis], *s. Lit:* colère *f,* courroux *m.*

wrathy ['ræθi, 'rɔθi], *a. NAm:* = WRATHFUL.

wreak [riːk], *v.tr.* assouvir (sa colère, haine); **to w. one's rage on, upon, s.o.,** décharger, passer, sa colère sur qn; **to w. (one's) vengeance upon s.o.,** exercer, assouvir, sa vengeance sur qn; se venger de qn.

wreath [riːθ, *pl.* riːðz, riːθs], *s.* **1.** (*a*) couronne *f,* guirlande *f* (de fleurs); **bridal w.,** (i) couronne de mariée; (ii) *Bot:* (*also* **Saint Peter's w.**) (espèce *f* de) spirée *f;* **funeral w.,** couronne mortuaire; **artificial (funeral) w.,** couronne de perles; (*b*) *Her:* **crest w.,** torque *f,* tortil *m* (de casque); (*c*) *Astr:* **the W.,** la couronne boréale, australe. **2.** volute *f,* panache *m,* tourbillon *m,* filet *m* (de fumée); spirale *f* (de fumée). **3.** *Scot:* amoncellement *m* de neige.

wreathe [riːð]. **1.** *v.tr.* (*a*) enguirlander; couronner, ceindre (la tête, le front, de qn); **statue wreathed with flowers,** statue enguirlandée de fleurs; **mountain wreathed with mist,** montagne entourée de brouillard; **face wreathed in smiles,** visage rayonnant; (*b*) entrelacer, tresser (des fleurs, etc.); tresser (une guirlande); (*c*) **to w. sth. round sth.,** enrouler, entortiller, qch. autour de qch.; **to w. one's arms round s.o.,** enlacer qn dans ses bras. **2.** *v.i.* (*a*) (*of smoke*) tourbillonner; s'élever en volutes; (*b*) (*of foliage, etc.*) s'enrouler, se tordre **(round,** autour de).

wreathed [riːðd], *a.* **1.** entrelacé, enguirlandé. **2.** *Arch:* **w. column,** colonne torse. **3.** *Her:* tortillé.

wreathing ['riːðiŋ], *s.* entrelacement *m,* tressage *m.* **2.** tourbillonnement *m.*

wreck[1] [rek], *s.* **1.** (*a*) *Jur:* **w. of the sea,** épaves *fpl* de mer; agan *m;* (*b*) navire naufragé, épave; **the w. is visible at low tide,** l'épave est visible à la marée basse; **to break up a w.,** détruire une épave; *Ins:* **total w.,** navire entièrement perdu; *Jur:* **receivers of wrecks,** fonctionnaires chargés de surveiller les bris et naufrages; **w. master,** receveur *m* des épaves; (*c*) **the building, car, is a mere w.,** le bâtiment n'est qu'une ruine; la voiture est en morceaux; **my car's a total w.,** ma voiture est bonne pour la casse; **an old w. (of a car),** une voiture délabrée, disloquée; *Rail: NAm:* **w. train,** convoi *m* de secours; **human wrecks,** épaves humaines; **he's a perfect w.,** sa santé est ruinée, fortement atteinte; **he's a physical, mental, w.,** son physique, sa mentalité, est abîmé(e); **to be a nervous w.,** avoir les nerfs détraqués, avoir les nerfs en piteux état; **war wrecks,** les grands invalides de guerre; **she's the w. of her former self,** elle n'est plus que l'ombre d'elle-même. **2.** naufrage *m* (d'un navire); **to suffer w.,** faire naufrage; **to save a ship from w.,** sauver un navire du naufrage; **to be saved from the w.,** échapper au naufrage; **this was the w. of his fortune, of his hopes, of his life,** ce fut le naufrage de sa fortune, ses espérances, sa vie; *Cmptr:* **card w.,** bourrage *m* de cartes.

wreck[2]. **1.** *v.tr.* (*a*) faire faire naufrage à (un navire), causer le naufrage (d'un navire); (*of pers., ship*) **to be wrecked,** faire naufrage; (*b*) faire dérailler (un train); démolir (une voiture, etc.); démolir, détruire, ruiner (un édifice, etc.); **the car wrecked the telegraph pole,** la voiture a fauché le poteau télégraphique; **to w. one's health,** ruiner sa santé; **to w. one's digestion,** se détraquer l'estomac; **to w. s.o.'s nerves, nervous system,** ébranler les nerfs de qn; (*c*) faire échouer, saboter (une entreprise); détruire, ruiner, briser (les espérances de qn); **to w. s.o.'s plans,** faire échouer les projets de qn; **he's wrecking our cause,** il est en train de ruiner notre cause; *Parl:* **wrecking amendment,** amendement proposé dans le but de faire échouer un projet de loi. **2.** *v.i.* (*a*) faire naufrage; (*b*) *NAm:* faire le commerce des voitures disloquées, délabrées.

wreckage ['rekidʒ], *s.* **1.** naufrage *m* (d'un navire, de la fortune de qn). **2.** *coll.* épaves éparses; débris *mpl;* ce qui reste (d'un sinistre); **piece of w.,** épave.

wrecked [rekt], *a.* (*a*) (navire) naufragé, qui a fait naufrage; (marin) naufragé; (*b*) (édifice, etc.) ruiné, écroulé; (village) dévasté; (train) déraillé; **w. life,** existence brisée; **w. health,** santé ruinée.

wrecker ['rekər], *s.* **1.** naufrageur *m,* pilleur *m* d'épaves. **2.** destructeur, -trice (d'une ville, civilisation, etc.); *Rail:* dérailleur *m* (de trains); *Const:* démolisseur *m* (de bâtiments). **3.** *NAm:* (*a*) *Nau:* (i) navire *m* qui va au secours d'un navire naufragé; sauveteur *m* d'épaves; (ii) acheteur *m,* exploiteur *m,* d'épaves; (*b*) *Aut:* (i) membre *m* d'une équipe de secours; **w. (car),** camion *m* de dépannage; dépanneuse *f;* camion-grue *m, pl.* camions-grues; (ii) acheteur, marchand *m,* de voitures délabrées; (*c*) *Rail:* convoi *m* de secours. **4.** *Fish: F:* pêcheur *m* (qui pêche) aux environs d'une épave.

wreckfish ['rekfiʃ], *s. Ich:* cernier *m.*

wrecking ['rekiŋ], *s.* **1.** (*a*) action *f* de détruire; destruction *f* (d'un navire en l'attirant à la côte); *Rail:* déraillement *m* (d'un train par malveillance); *Const:* démolition *f* (d'un bâtiment); *Const:* **w. bar,** pince *f* (pied-de-biche) à clous; (*b*) ruine *f* (d'une fortune, des espérances de qn); *Pol:* **w. policy,** politique *f* de sabotage. **2.** *NAm:* (*a*) *Nau:* sauvetage *m* (d'un navire); (*b*) *Aut:* dépannage *m;* **w. crew,** corvée *f,* équipe *f,* de secours; **w. car,** camion *m* de dépannage; dépanneuse *f;* camion-grue *m, pl.* camions-grues; (*c*) *Rail:* **w. train,** convoi *m* de secours. **3.** *Fish: F:* pêche *f* aux environs d'une épave.

wren[1] [ren], *s. Orn:* **(common) w.,** *F:* **Jenny Wren,** *NAm:* **winter w.,** troglodyte (mignon), *F:* roitelet *m; Fr.C:* troglodyte des forêts; **gold(en)-crested w.,** roitelet huppé; **fire-crested w.,** roitelet à triple bandeau; **w. warbler,** fauvette *f* roitelet; *NAm:* **Carolina w.,** thryothore *m,* troglodyte de la Caroline; **house w.,** troglodyte familier; **long-billed marsh w.,** troglodyte des marais; **short-billed marsh w.,** troglodyte à bec court; **w. tit,** fausse mésange de Californie; *Austr:* **emu w.,** stipiture *m;* **New Zealand w.,** xenicus *m.*

Wren, wren[2], *s.f.* membre *m* du **Women's Royal Naval Service (W.R.N.S.).**

wrench[1] [ren(t)ʃ], *s.* **1.** (*a*) mouvement violent de torsion, effort violent; *Ph:* torsion *f;* **to give sth. a w.,** tordre qch. violemment; **with a w. he pulled off the knocker,** d'un effort violent il a arraché le marteau; **to force the lid with a single w.,** forcer le couvercle d'une seule pesée; **he gave his ankle a w.,** il s'est donné une entorse; il s'est foulé la cheville; **I felt a w.,** j'ai ressenti une violente douleur; (*b*) **the separation was a terrible w.,** la séparation fut un déchirement (de cœur) affreux, un terrible crève-cœur; **it will be a w. to leave them,** il m'en coûtera de les quitter; ce sera un arrachement de les quitter. **2.** *Med: Surg:* arrachement. **3.** *Tls:* (*a*) clef *f,* tourne-à-gauche *m inv;* **open-end w.,** clef plate ordinaire; **adjustable w.,** clef à ouverture variable, clef universelle; **hexagonal w.,** clef (à) six pans; **Allen w.,** clef (à) six pans (mâle); **twelve point w.,** clef (à) douze pans; **fork w.,** clef à fourche; **double-headed w.,** clef double (à fourches); **tube w.,** clef à pipes, à, pour, tubes, pour tuyaux; **chain w.,** clef à chaîne; (*b*) pince *f;* **claw w.,** pince à panne fendue, arrache-clou *m, pl.* arrache-clous.

wrench[2], *v.tr.* **1.** (*a*) tordre; tourner violemment; **to w. a key,** fausser une clef; **to w. the lid open,** forcer le couvercle; **to w. off, out, away,** arracher, enlever (avec un violent effort de torsion); (*b*) **to w. sth. from s.o.,** arracher qch. à qn; **to w. oneself from s.o.'s clutches,** s'arracher de force à l'étreinte de qn; **she wrenched herself free,** d'une secousse elle se dégagea; (*c*) **to w. one's ankle,** se fouler la cheville; se donner une entorse; **to w. one's shoulder,** se fouler, se forcer, l'épaule. **2.** forcer, fausser (le sens d'un mot, etc.); torturer (le sens d'un passage); faire une entorse à (la vérité).

wrenched [ren(t)ʃt], *a.* **1.** tordu, déchiré, forcé. **2.** (pied, etc.) foulé.

wrenching ['ren(t)ʃiŋ], *s.* torsion *f;* (*away, from sth.*) arrachement *m.*

wrest[1] [rest], *s.* **1.** *A:* torsion violente. **2.** *Mus:* clef *f* d'accordeur; **w. block, plank,** sommier *m,* table *f* (d'un piano); **w. pin,** cheville *f* (d'accordage) (d'un piano).

wrest[2], *v.tr.* **1.** arracher **(from,** à); **to w. a confession from s.o.,** arracher un aveu à qn. **2.** forcer, fausser, tordre (le sens d'un passage); *F:* donner une entorse à (la vérité, un passage, etc.).

wrestle[1] [resl], *s.* (*a*) lutte *f* (corps à corps); assaut *m* de lutte (à main plate, etc.); **to have a w. with s.o.,** lutter avec, contre, qn; (*b*) **w. with temptation,** lutte contre la tentation.

wrestle[2]. **1.** *v.i.* (*a*) **to w. with s.o.,** lutter avec, contre, qn; colleter qn; **to w. (together),** lutter, se prendre corps à corps, combattre à la lutte; (*with cogn. acc.*) **to w. a fall with s.o.,** faire un assaut de lutte avec qn; **to w. for a prize,** disputer un prix à la lutte; (*b*) **to w. with one's umbrella, lawn mower,** lutter avec son parapluie, sa tondeuse à gazon; **to w. with difficulties,** lutter contre les difficultés; **to w. with temptation,** résister à la tentation; **to w. with one's passions,** lutter, réagir, contre ses passions; **to w. with adversity,** lutter contre, être aux prises avec, l'adversité; **to w. with death,** se débattre contre la mort; **to w. with a problem,** s'attaquer à un problème; s'acharner à résoudre un problème; **to w. in prayer, to w. with God,** prier avec ferveur. **2.** *v.tr.* (*a*) lutter avec, contre (qn); **he offered to w. me for £10,** il offrit de se mesurer avec moi à la lutte pour un enjeu de £10; **to w. down one's opponent,** faire toucher la terre à, terrasser, son adversaire (à la lutte); (*b*) *U.S:* atterrer, renverser (un bouvillon, pour le marquer au fer chaud).

wrestler ['reslər], *s.* lutteur *m.*

wrestling ['resliŋ], *s.* **1.** sport *m* de la lutte; lutte corps à corps; **Graeco-Roman w.,** lutte gréco-romaine; **freestyle w.,** lutte libre; **tag w.,** catch *m* à quatre. **2. w. with difficulties, temptation,** lutte contre les difficultés, la tentation.

wretch [retʃ], *s.* **1.** malheureux, -euse; infortuné, -ée; **poor w.,** pauvre diable *m,* pauvre hère *m;* **poor little wretches,** pauvres petits. **2.** (*a*) misérable *mf,* scélérat, -ate; **you w.!** misérable! (*b*) **you little w.!** petit fripon, petite friponne!

wretched ['retʃid], *a.* **1.** (*of pers.*) misérable, malheureux, infortuné; **to feel w.,** être mal en train, broyer du noir, avoir le cafard; **to look w.,** avoir l'air misérable, malheureux; faire peine à voir; faire triste mine; **to be in w. poverty,** être dans une misère affreuse. **2.** (*a*) pitoyable, tout à fait mauvais, lamentable; **this coffee is w.,** ce café est une abomination; **w. meal,** triste, pauvre, maigre, repas; **what w. weather!** quel temps abominable! quel temps de chien! quel chien de temps! **he has w. health,** il a une santé pitoyable; (*b*) **w. hovel,** taudis *m;* **w. lodgings,** appartement minable; **w. little shop,** petite boutique de rien du tout; (*c*) (*vague intensive*) **I can't find that w. umbrella, key,** je ne retrouve pas ce diable de parapluie, cette diable de clef; **what's that w. boy doing?** qu'est-ce qu'il fait, ce sacré garçon?

wretchedly ['retʃidli], *adv.* **1.** (vivre, etc.) misérablement. **2.** (s'acquitter, etc.) de façon pitoyable, lamentable. **3. to be w. poor,** être dans une misère affreuse; **to be w. ill,** être malade à faire pitié; **I was w. ill between Calais and Dover,** entre Calais et Douvres j'ai été malade comme un chien.

wretchedness ['retʃidnis], *s.* **1.** (*a*) misère *f,* malheur *m,* infortune *f;* (*b*) tristesse *f,* idées noires. **2.** caractère *m* méprisable; mauvaise qualité, mauvais état.

wrick[1] [rik], *s.* **to give oneself a w.,** se donner, attraper, un effort; **to have a w. in the neck,** avoir le torticolis.

wrick[2], *v.tr.* **to w. oneself, a muscle,** se donner, attraper, un effort; **to w. one's back,** se donner un effort dans le dos; **to w. one's ankle,** se fouler la cheville; se donner, *F:* se flanquer, une entorse.

wriggle[1] ['rigl], *s.* **1.** tortillement *m* du corps. **2.** détour *m,* sinuosité *f.*

wriggle[2]. **1.** *v.i.* (*a*) (*of worm*) se contorsionner, se tortiller; (*of fish*) frétiller; (*of pers.*) se tortiller, s'agiter, se remuer; **to w. through a hedge,** se faufiler à travers une haie (en se tortillant); **to w. out of one's vest,** se dévêtir de son maillot en se tortillant; **the fish wriggled out of my hands,** le poisson s'est échappé d'entre mes doigts; (*b*) **to w. out of a difficulty, of an undertaking,** se tirer, s'extraire, d'une position difficile par des moyens évasifs; se retirer adroitement d'une entreprise; **to try to w. out of it,** chercher une échappatoire; (*c*) *Fig:* tortiller; tergiverser; chercher des échappatoires, des faux-fuyants. **2.** *v.tr.* (*a*) tortiller; **to w. one's body,**

one's legs, remuer, tortiller, le corps; agiter les jambes; se tortiller; se contorsionner; (*b*) **to w. one's way, oneself, into a crowded hall,** se faufiler, s'insinuer, dans une salle comble.

wriggler ['riglər], *s.* **1.** (*a*) ver *m*, crustacé *m*, etc., qui se tortille; *esp.* larve *f* de moustique; (*b*) enfant qui ne sait pas se tenir tranquille sur sa chaise. **2.** personne *f* qui s'insinue partout. **3.** tergiversateur, -trice.

wriggling[1] ['rigliŋ], *F:* **wriggly** ['rigli], *a.* qui se tortille, se remue; frétillant.

wriggling[2], *s.* **1.** tortillement *m*, grouillement *m* (des vers). **2.** *Fig:* tergiversation *f*.

wright [rait], *s. A:* (*now found only in compounds, shipwright, wheelwright, etc.*) ouvrier *m*, artisan *m*, fabricant *m*.

wring[1] [riŋ], *s.* **1.** (mouvement *m* de) torsion *f*, action *f* de tordre; **to give the clothes a w.,** tordre le linge, passer le linge à l'essoreuse. **2. he gave my hand a w.,** il m'a donné une vigoureuse poignée de main.

wring[2], *v.tr.* (*p.t. & p.p.* **wrung** [rʌŋ]) **1.** (*a*) tordre; **to w. (out) the linen,** tordre, essorer, le linge; **to w. s.o.'s hand,** serrer à briser, étreindre, la main de qn; **to w. one's hands in despair,** se tordre les mains, les bras, de désespoir; **to w. a bird's neck,** tordre le cou à une volaille; *F:* **I'd like to w. your neck,** tu m'exaspères, à la fin! **it wrings my heart to go,** cela me déchire le cœur de partir; (*b*) *Leath:* biller (une peau). **2. to w. sth. out of, from, sth., s.o.,** exprimer, faire sortir (l'eau d'un vêtement mouillé); arracher (un secret à qn); arracher, extorquer (de l'argent à qn); **to w. tears from s.o.,** faire pleurer qn; arracher des larmes à qn; **he managed to w. out a tear,** *F:* il y est allé de sa larme. **3.** (*a*) forcer, déformer (une plaque métallique, etc.); bistourner (une lame d'épée); (*b*) *A:* & *Lit:* **to w. the truth,** faire, donner, une entorse à la vérité.

wringer ['riŋər], *s.* **1.** *Laund:* essoreuse *f* (à rouleaux); *P:* **to put s.o. through the w.,** (i) faire subir à qn de dures épreuves, passer qn à tabac; (ii) cuisiner, griller, qn. **2.** *Ind:* tordoir *m*. **3.** *Exp:* **acid w.,** turbine *f*.

wringing[1] ['riŋiŋ], *a.* (*a*) (*of pain*) déchirant; (*b*) **w. (wet),** (*of clothes*) mouillé à tordre; (*of pers.*) trempé comme une soupe, trempé jusqu'aux os.

wringing[2], *s.* tordage *m*, essorage *m*.

wrinkle[1] ['riŋkl], *s.* **1.** (*a*) (*on face*) ride *f*; (*b*) rugosité *f*; (*of ground*) plissement *m*, sillon *m*; (*on water*) ondulation *f*, ride; (*c*) (*in garment, etc.*) faux pli; **her left stocking was in wrinkles,** son bas gauche était tire(-)bouchonné; **dress that fits without a w.,** robe qui ne fait pas un pli. **2.** *F:* renseignement *m* utile, tuyau *m*, recette *f* de métier, chose bonne à savoir; (*b*) **that's a new w.,** ça c'est une nouvelle idée, une idée originale.

wrinkle[2]. **1.** *v.tr.* rider, plisser; (*a*) **old age wrinkles the forehead,** l'âge ride, plisse, le front; **to w. one's forehead,** froncer le(s) sourcil(s); **a smile wrinkled his face,** un sourire plissait sa figure; (*b*) **to w. a dress,** plisser, froisser, chiffonner, une robe; **her stockings were wrinkled,** ses bas faisaient des plis, étaient tire(-)bouchonnés. **2.** *v.i.* **to w. (up),** se rider; se plisser; faire des plis; **the skin of these apples wrinkles,** la peau de ces pommes se fronce, se ratatine.

wrinkled ['riŋk(ə)ld], *a.* (*of forehead, etc.*) ridé, plissé; (*of dress, etc.*) froncé, chiffonné; (*of skin*) ratatiné.

wrinkling ['riŋkliŋ], *s.* **1.** ridement *m*, plissement *m*; **w. of the forehead,** froncement *m* du sourcil, des sourcils. **2.** rides *fpl*, plis *mpl*.

wrinkly ['riŋkli], *a.* **1.** (*of forehead, etc.*) ridé, plein de rides, couvert de rides. **2.** (*of dress, etc.*) qui a des faux plis; chiffonné; (*of stocking*) tire(-)bouchonné.

wrist [rist], *s.* **1.** (*a*) poignet *m*; attache *f* de la main; *Sp:* **w. stroke,** coup exécuté avec le poignet; tour *m* de poignet; *Med:* **dropped w.** = WRISTDROP; (*b*) *Anat:* = WRISTBONE; (*c*) *Cost:* poignet *m* (d'une manche). **2.** *Mec.E:* **w. plate,** plateau conducteur; plateau oscillant; **w. (pin),** (i) *Mch:* tourillon *m* de crosse; tourillon de la tête de piston; (ii) *Mec.E:* bouton *m* de manivelle, de bielle, tourillon de manivelle; maneton *m*.

wristband ['ristbænd], *s.* **1.** poignet *m*, manchette *f* (de chemise, etc.). **2.** *Gym: etc:* bracelet *m* de force (en cuir).

wristbone ['ristboun], *s. Anat:* os *m* du carpe; carpe.

wristdrop ['ristdrɔp], *s. Med:* paralysie *f* des extenseurs de la main; fléchissement *m* du poignet.

wristlet ['ristlit], *s.* **1.** (*a*) bracelet *m*; **w. watch,** montre-bracelet *f*, *pl.* montres-bracelets; (*b*) **woollen w.,** miton *m*. **2.** *F:* **wristlets,** menottes *f*.

wristwatch ['ristwɔtʃ], *s.* montre-bracelet *f*, *pl.* montres-bracelets; montre *f* de poignet.

wristy ['risti], *a. Sp:* (coup, etc.) de poignet.

writ [rit], *s.* **1. Holy, Sacred, W.,** les saintes Écritures, l'Écriture sainte. **2.** *Jur:* (*a*) acte *m* judiciaire, mandat *m*, ordonnance *f*, assignation *f*; **w. of summons,** (i) citation *f* (à comparaître); assignation *f*, sommation *f*; (ii) mandat de comparution, ajournement *m*; **w. of attachment,** ordre *m* de saisie; **w. of possession,** envoi *m* en possession; **w. of prohibition,** défense de statuer (adressée par une cour supérieure à une cour inférieure); **to draw up a w.,** dresser un exploit; **to serve a w. on s.o., issue a w. against s.o., have a w. issued against s.o.,** assigner qn (en justice); signifier, faire donner, une assignation à qn; signifier un exploit à qn; **to serve a w. on the other party,** signifier un à-venir à la partie adverse; **w. server,** porteur *m* de contraintes; **a w. is out for his arrest,** il est décrété de prise de corps, il est sous le coup d'un mandat d'arrêt; (*b*) **the King's, Queen's, w. does not run in these parts,** ces régions sont en dehors de la loi britannique; (*c*) (i) ordonnance au *sheriff* de procéder à l'élection d'un membre du Parlement; (ii) lettre *f* de convocation (d'un Lord).

write[1] [rait], *s. Cmptr:* écriture *f*, enregistrement *m*; **gather w.,** écriture avec regroupement; **w. head,** tête *f* d'écriture, d'enregistrement; **w. lock-out,** verrouillage *m*, interdiction *f*, d'écriture; **w. pulse,** impulsion *f* d'écriture, d'enregistrement; **w. time,** durée *f* d'enregistrement, d'écriture; **to be w. inhibited,** être en interdiction d'écriture.

write[2], *v.tr. & i.* (*p.t.* **wrote** [rout], *p.p.* **written** ['rit(ə)n], *A:* **writ** [rit])

I. *v.tr.* écrire. **1.** (*a*) **to w. one's name,** écrire son nom; **to w. sth. in one's own hand,** écrire qch. de sa main, autographier qch.; **that was not written by me,** cela n'est pas écrit de ma main; **to w. sth. again,** écrire qch. de nouveau, récrire qch.; **how is it written?** comment cela s'écrit-il? **this word is written with a g,** ce mot s'écrit avec, par, un g; **to w. 1,000 words a day,** écrire 1,000 mots par jour; **the paper is written all over,** le papier est couvert d'écriture; **his guilt was written on his face,** on lisait sur son visage qu'il était coupable; **innocence is written on his brow,** l'innocence se peint sur son front; **there's policeman written all over him,** il sent son policier d'une lieue; **writ large,** (i) écrit en gros, en grosses lettres; (ii) écrit sous une forme exagérée; *Lit:* **their name is writ in water,** leur renommée n'est qu'éphémère; (*b*) *Cmptr:* **to w. data into storage,** introduire des données en mémoire; (*c*) *Ins:* souscrire (une police, un risque); **to w. business,** souscrire un risque, des risques. **2.** écrire (un roman, une lettre); rédiger (un article, etc.); **carefully written report,** rapport rédigé avec soin, bien étudié; **to w. (out) a cheque,** faire, établir, remplir, libeller, un chèque; **I'll w. you (out) a cheque,** je vous fais un chèque; (*in S. Africa*) **to w. an exam,** passer un examen.

II. *v.i.* écrire. **1. to learn to read and w.,** apprendre à lire et à écrire; **to w. legibly,** écrire lisiblement; **to w. small, large,** écrire fin, gros; *with cogn. acc.* **he writes a good hand,** il a une belle écriture, une belle main; **this pen won't w.,** ce stylo ne marche, ne va, pas. **2.** (*a*) **he writes,** il fait profession d'écrire, il est écrivain; **to w. for the papers,** faire du journalisme; **to w. for a paper,** écrire dans, collaborer à, un journal; **he writes on, about, gardening,** il écrit des articles sur l'horticulture, des livres d'horticulture; (*b*) **he writes home every Sunday,** il écrit chez lui tous les dimanches; *F:* **that's nothing to w. home about,** il n'y a là rien d'étonnant, il n'y a pas là de quoi s'émerveiller; ce n'est pas bien extraordinaire; il n'y a pas de quoi se vanter; *F:* ça ne casse rien; **the cooking was nothing to w. home about,** la cuisine était plutôt moche; **he wrote to me,** *F:* **he wrote me, yesterday,** il m'a écrit hier; **what did he w. to you about?** à quel sujet vous a-t-il écrit? **I have written to (ask) him to come,** je lui ai écrit de venir; **he wrote to her (saying) that he was sorry about it,** il lui a écrit qu'il le regrettait; **w. (in) for our catalogue,** demandez notre catalogue; **I'll w. (off) for it at once,** je vais le commander, le faire venir, tout de suite.

III. (*compound verbs*) **1. write back,** (*a*) *v.i.* répondre (à une lettre); (*b*) *v.tr. Book-k:* contre-passer, ristourner (un article).

2. write down. (*a*) *v.i.* **to w. down to one's readers,** se mettre à la portée de ses lecteurs (avec condescendance); (*b*) *v.tr.* (i) coucher, consigner (qch.) par écrit; inscrire (son nom); marquer, noter (ses dépenses, etc.); **to w. down the facts,** coucher les faits sur le papier; **to w. sth. down from dictation,** écrire qch. sous la dictée de quelqu'un; (ii) décrier, vilipender (qn), *F:* éreinter (qn, une pièce, un roman); (iii) *Fin:* réduire (le capital).

3. write in, *v.tr.* (*a*) (i) insérer (une correction, un mot, etc.); (ii) *U.S: Pol:* voter pour (un candidat qui n'est pas nommé) par l'insertion de son nom sur le bulletin de vote; (*b*) *see* **II.2.** *above*; *NAm:* **to w. in a complaint,** envoyer une plainte à la direction.

4. write off, *v.tr.* (*a*) écrire (un article, etc.) d'un trait, au courant de la plume; *s.a.* **II. 2.** *above*; (*b*) (i) *Fin:* **to w. off capital,** réduire le capital; **to w. so much off for wear and tear,** déduire tant pour l'usure; (ii) *Com:* **to w. off a bad debt,** défalquer une mauvaise créance, passer une créance par profits et pertes; (iii) *F:* **my car can be written off,** ma voiture a été complètement démolie, est bonne pour la casse; **three planes were written off,** il y a eu trois appareils de détruits.

5. write out, *v.tr.* (*a*) transcrire (qch.); mettre (une copie, etc.) au net; (*b*) **to w. sth. out in full,** écrire qch. en toutes lettres; (*c*) *see* **I.2.** *above*; *Med:* **to w. out a prescription,** formuler, rédiger, une ordonnance; (*d*) **to w. oneself out,** épuiser ses idées (comme écrivain), *F:* vider son sac, se vider; **author who wrote himself out in his first novel,** auteur qui a jeté son feu dans son premier roman.

6. write up, *v.tr.* (*a*) (i) *Journ:* écrire, rédiger (un fait-divers, un compte rendu); (ii) faire l'éloge de (qn, qch.); *F:* prôner, faire mousser (qn, qch.); (*b*) (i) mettre (son agenda, sa comptabilité, etc.) au courant, à jour; (ii) *Sch:* **w. up your notes,** recopiez vos notes; (*c*) *Fin:* augmenter (la valeur des stocks).

write(-)down ['rait'daun], *s. Fin: etc:* dépréciation *f*.

write-in ['raitin], *s. NAm: Pol:* voix *f* pour un candidat pas nommé sur le bulletin de vote dont le nom est ajouté par le votant.

write-off ['raitɔf], *s.* **1.** *Book-k:* annulation *f* par écrit. **2.** *F:* **my car was a complete w.-o.,** ma voiture a été complètement démolie, n'était plus qu'un tas de ferraille, était bonne pour la casse.

writer ['raitər], *s.* **1.** (*a*) scripteur *m* (d'un document, manuscrit); **public w.,** écrivain public; (*b*) **to be a good, bad, w.,** avoir une belle, mauvaise, écriture; **writer's cramp,** crampe *f* des écrivains, mogigraphie *f*; (*c*) **the present w., the w. (of this letter),** celui qui écrit, l'auteur de cette lettre; **it's the writer's belief that it's a mistake,** moi qui vous écris je crois que c'est une erreur; (*d*) auteur *m* (d'un roman, d'une chanson, *Cin:* du scénario); (*e*) écrivain; **woman w.,** femme auteur, femme écrivain; **to be a good, bad, w.,** être bon, mauvais, écrivain; écrire bien, mal; **to be a ready w.,** avoir la plume facile; (*f*) commis *m* (aux écritures); expéditionnaire *m*, *Navy:* fourrier *m*; (*g*) *Scot: Jur:* notaire *m*; **w. to the signet,** avoué *m*. **2.** *O:* **letter w.,** recueil *m* de modèles de lettres. **3.** *Tg:* **ink w.,** récepteur-imprimeur *m*, *pl.* récepteurs-imprimeurs; appareil *m* à molette.

write-up ['raitʌp], *s.* **1.** (*a*) *Journ:* article *m*; **pre-performance w.-up,** avant-première *f*, *pl.* avant-premières; **a (good) w.-up,** un article élogieux; (*b*) éloge exagéré (de qn); réclame tapageuse (de qch.). **2.** *Cmptr:* **programme w.-up,** description *f* de programme. **3.** *Book-k:* augmentation *f* de la valeur comptable (du stock).

writhe[1] [raið], *s.* contorsion *f* (d'une personne, d'un animal, qui souffre).

writhe[2], *v.i.* (*a*) se tordre (de douleur); se tortiller; se crisper; se contorsionner; **to w. in agony,** se tordre dans des souffrances atroces; (*b*) **to w. under s.o.'s sarcasm,** sentir ses nerfs se crisper sous les remarques ironiques de qn; **he writhed at, under, the insult,** il ressentit vivement cette injure; cette injure l'a mis au supplice; **to make s.o. w.,** donner des crispations à qn; crisper les nerfs à qn.

writhing ['raiðiŋ], *s.* contorsions *fpl*.

writing ['raitiŋ], *s.* **1.** écriture *f*; (*a*) **the art of w.,** l'art d'écrire; **to be fond of w.,** aimer à écrire; **I'm very bad about w.,** je suis très mauvais correspondant; **at the time of w.,** au moment où j'écris; **w. case,** nécessaire *m* (contenant ce qu'il faut pour écrire); **w. desk, table,** pupitre *m*, bureau *m*, secrétaire *m*; **w. materials,** tout ce qu'il faut pour écrire; **w. pad,** (i) sous-main *m*, *pl.* sous-mains; buvard *m*, cartable *m*; (ii) bloc-correspondance *m*, *pl.* blocs-correspondance; **w. paper,** (i) papier *m* écolier; (ii) papier à lettres; (*b*) **his (hand)w. is bad,** il a une mauvaise écriture; **I do not recognize the w.,** je ne reconnais pas l'écriture; **cuneiform w.,** écriture cunéiforme; **the w. on the wall,** (i) *B:* Mané, Thécel, Pharès (inscrits sur les murs au festin de Balthazar); (ii) un avertissement (d'une catastrophe imminente, etc.); **to set sth. down in w., to put sth. in w.,** coucher qch. par écrit; **to answer in w.,** répondre par écrit; **agreement in w.,** convention *f* par écrit; **to commit the facts to w.,** consigner les faits par écrit; *Jur:* **evidence in w.,** preuve littérale. **2.** (*a*) *Lit:* l'art d'écrire; **the w. profession,** le métier d'écrivain; **a fine piece of w.,** (i) un beau morceau; (ii) une œuvre bien écrite; (*b*) ouvrage *m* littéraire; **the writings of an author,** les ouvrages littéraires, l'œuvre *m*, le bagage, d'un auteur. **3.** (*a*) *Book-k:* **w. back,** contre-passation *f* (d'un article); (*b*) **w. down,** inscription *f* (de son nom, etc.); (*c*) **w. in,** insertion *f* (d'un mot, etc.); (*d*) **w. off,** (i) *Book-k:* annulation *f* par écrit; (ii) *Fin: Com:* déduction *f* (pour l'usure); défalcation *f* (d'une mauvaise créance); amortissement *m* (du capital); (*e*) **w. out,** mise *f* (d'une copie, etc.) au net; transcription *f* (de ses notes, etc.); (*f*) **w. up,** (i) *Journ:* rédaction *f* (d'un fait-divers); (ii) mise au courant, à jour (de son agenda, etc.).

written ['rit(ə)n], *a.* écrit; par écrit; **the w. word,** le mot écrit; **w. consent,** consentement *m* par écrit; **to submit a w. statement of a case,** exposer un cas par écrit; **w. law,** loi écrite.

wrong[1] [rɔŋ], *a., s. & adv.*

I. *a.* **1.** (*morally bad*) mauvais; mal *inv*; **you know what is right and w.,** vous savez ce qui est bien et ce qui est mal; **it is wrong to steal, stealing is w.,** c'est mal de voler; **that was very w. of you!** c'était très mal de votre part! **it is very w. of you to say so,** c'est bien mal à vous de dire cela; *P:* **a w. 'un,** (i) un mauvais sujet; un vaurien; (ii) *Cr:* balle *f* qui a de l'effet à droite du batteur. **2.** (*a*) incorrect, inexact; erroné; faux, *f.* fausse; **my watch is w.,** ma montre va mal, n'est pas à l'heure; **my watch is two minutes w.,** ma montre avance, retarde, de deux minutes; **the answer is obviously w.,** la réponse (au problème, etc.) est manifestement erronée; **you've got the answer w.,** votre solution est incorrecte, n'est pas juste; **a w. calculation,** un calcul faux; **he gave a w. age in order to join the club,** il s'est rajeuni, vieilli, afin de devenir membre du club; **w. use of a word,** emploi abusif, vicieux, d'un mot; **a w. expression,** une expression impropre; **a w. meaning,** un sens inexact; **w. ideas,** idées fausses; **his ideas are all w.,** il a des idées toutes de travers; (*b*) (*of pers.*) **to be w.,** avoir tort; se tromper; être dans l'erreur; **you are not far w.,** vous ne vous trompez pas de beaucoup; **that's just where you are w.,** c'est justement ce qui vous trompe; **you were w. to contradict him,** vous avez eu tort de le contredire. **3.** (*a*) **to be in the w. place,** être mal placé; ne pas être à sa place; **picture in the w. light,** tableau dans un faux jour; **to drive on the w. side of the road,** circuler à contre-voie, conduire du mauvais côté de la route; **to enter a (one-way) street at the w. end,** prendre une rue (à sens unique) à rebours; **to get out on the w. side of the train,** descendre du train à contre-voie; *F:* **to get out of bed on the w. side,** se lever du pied gauche; **the w. side of the material,** l'envers *m,* le revers, de l'étoffe; **your sock is w. side out,** votre chaussette est à l'envers, n'est pas à l'endroit; **to wear a coat (the) w. side out,** porter un manteau retourné, à l'envers; **to be w. side up,** être sens dessus dessous; **to be w. side foremost,** être sens devant derrière; **to be on the w. side of forty,** avoir (dé)passé la quarantaine; **to brush cloth the w. way,** brosser l'étoffe à contre-poil, à rebrousse-poil; **to stroke a cat the w. way,** caresser un chat à rebrousse-poil; **to hold sth. by the w. end,** tenir qch. par le mauvais bout; **you are setting about it in the w. way,** vous vous y prenez mal, de travers; **to take a word in the w. sense,** prendre un mot à contre-sens; prendre le contre-sens d'un mot; **to put a w. construction on s.o.'s words, to take s.o. the w. way,** prendre le contre-sens des paroles de qn; prendre une observation à contre-pied; comprendre qn à rebours; **to swallow sth. the w. way,** avaler qch. de travers; (*of food*) **it went down the w. way,** je l'ai avalé de travers; *Mec.E: etc:* (*of pin*) **to go the w. way,** refouler; *Nau:* **to cast in the w. way,** abattre du mauvais bord; abattre à contre; *Sp:* **to take the ball on the w. foot,** prendre la balle à contre-pied; (*b*) (*mistaken*) **I went to the w. house,** je me suis trompé de maison, de porte; **to take the w. train,** se tromper de train; **that is the w. book,** ce n'est pas là le livre qu'il faut; **the police have arrested the w. man,** la police a arrêté l'homme qu'il ne fallait pas; la police a commis une erreur; il y a eu erreur d'identité; **to back the w. horse,** miser sur le mauvais cheval; **to take the w. road,** se tromper de chemin, de direction; faire fausse route; prendre le mauvais chemin; **to put s.o. on the w. road,** mal diriger qn; **I was sent the w. way,** on m'a mal dirigé; **to put s.o. on the w. track,** mettre qn sur une fausse piste; **to be on the w. scent, track,** suivre une mauvaise piste; faire fausse piste; se fourvoyer; **to laugh in the w. place,** rire au mauvais endroit; **to come at the w. time,** venir dans un mauvais moment, mal à propos; **to do, say, the w. thing,** commettre un impair; faire une gaffe; gaffer; mettre les pieds dans le plat; *Tp:* **w. number,** erreur *f* de numéro; numéro erroné; communication erronée; **to dial the w. number,** composer un mauvais numéro; **you have been given the w. number, the w. connection,** on vous a mal branché; on vous a donné un mauvais numéro, un faux numéro; *NAm: F:* **a w. number,** (i) une idée fausse; (ii) un mauvais sujet, un vaurien, une vaurienne; (iii) un fou, une folle, un(e) aliéné(e); *Mus:* **w. note,** fausse note; *Typ:* **w. fount,** lettre *f* d'un autre œil, d'un œil étranger. **4.** (*amiss*) **what's w. with you?** de quoi souffrez-vous? qu'avez-vous? qu'est-ce qu'il y a qui ne va pas? **there's something w. with me,** j'ai quelque chose, il y a quelque chose, qui ne va pas; **there's something w. with his throat,** il a quelque chose à la gorge; **something w. with the machinery,** un défaut de fonctionnement dans le mécanisme; **something is w.,** il y a quelque chose de détraqué; **there was something w. with our car,** nous avons eu des ennuis avec la voiture; **there's something w. somewhere,** il y a quelque chose qui cloche; **I hope there's nothing w.,** j'espère qu'il n'est rien arrivé (de malheureux); **things are all w., everything is w.,** tout est à l'envers, tout va mal, de travers; **what do you find w. with this book?** qu'est-ce que vous reprochez à ce livre? *F:* **what's w. with that?** qu'avez-vous à redire à cela? **things are going the w. way,** les affaires se gâtent.

II. *s.* **1.** **(moral w.)** mal *m*; **the difference between right and w.,** la différence entre le bien et le mal; **to know right from w.,** distinguer le bien et le mal; distinguer le bien du mal; **to make w. right,** changer le mal en bien; **two wrongs do not make a right,** deux noirs ne font pas un blanc; **the king can do no w.,** le roi ne peut pas mal faire; le roi n'est pas responsable. **2.** (*a*) (*unjust action*) tort *m,* injustice *f,* injure *f*; **to acknowledge one's wrongs,** avouer ses torts; **right and w.,** le juste et l'injuste; **to do s.o. w., to do w. to s.o.,** faire tort à qn; (i) être injuste envers qn; (ii) faire injure à qn, léser qn; *P: O:* **he did her w.,** il l'a séduite; **to labour under a sense of w.,** nourrir un sentiment d'injustice; **she complains of her wrongs,** elle se plaint des torts qu'on lui a faits; **the wrongs that I have suffered,** les injustices, le mal, dont j'ai été l'objet, que j'ai eu à subir; (*b*) *Jur:* (*tort*) dommage *m,* préjudice *m.* **3.** **to be in the w.,** être dans son tort; avoir tort; **to admit one is in the w., to acknowledge oneself to be in the w.,** avouer son tort; se rendre à l'évidence; **to put s.o. in the w.,** mettre qn dans son tort; **to put oneself in the w.,** se mettre dans son tort.

III. *adv.* mal. **1.** (*a*) inexactement, incorrectement; **to guess w.,** mal deviner; **to do a sum w.,** faire un calcul incorrectement; **you have spelt, written, my name w.,** vous avez mal orthographié mon nom; (*b*) à tort; à faux; **you did w.,** vous avez mal agi; **you would do w. to punish him,** vous feriez mal, vous auriez tort, de le punir; **to lead s.o. w.,** tromper, égarer, qn; fourvoyer qn; **you told me w.,** (i) vous m'avez trompé; (ii) vous m'avez mal renseigné; vous m'avez mis sur une mauvaise voie; *F:* **you've got me w.,** vous m'avez mal compris; *Dial: & NAm:* **to get in w. with s.o.,** se faire mal voir de qn; **to get s.o. in w. with s.o.,** mettre qn en défaveur auprès de qn. **2.** **to go w.:** (*a*) (*of pers.*) (i) se tromper de chemin, de direction; se fourvoyer; faire fausse route; (ii) se tromper; commettre une erreur; (iii) *F:* tomber dans le vice, dans l'inconduite; se dévoyer; mal tourner; **girl who has gone w.,** fille qui a failli, qui a fauté; (*b*) (*of mechanism, etc.*) se déranger, se dérégler, se détraquer; (*of business, etc.*) aller mal; aller de travers; **something went w. with the electric light,** nous avons eu une panne d'électricité; **my digestion has gone w.,** ma digestion est détraquée; j'ai l'estomac détraqué; **all our plans went w.,** tous nos projets ont avorté; **things are going w.,** tout va mal; **things have gone w.,** les choses ont mal tourné; **do what I tell you, otherwise everything will go w.,** faites ce que je vous dis, autrement tout ira de travers.

wrong[2], *v.tr.* (*a*) faire (du) tort à (qn); faire injure à (qn), léser (qn); **the woman he had so grievously wronged,** la femme qu'il avait traitée si cruellement; (*b*) être injuste pour, envers (qn); **I thought he had stolen it but I wronged him,** j'ai cru que c'était lui qui l'avait volé, mais je lui faisais tort.

wrongdoer ['rɔŋdu(:)ər], *s.* (*a*) auteur *m* d'une injustice, d'un dommage; injuste *m*; *B:* méchant *m*; (*b*) *Jur:* celui qui fait une infraction à la loi; délinquant, -ante.

wrongdoing ['rɔŋdu(:)iŋ], *s.* (*a*) mal *m*; injustice *f*; (*b*) **wrongdoings,** méfaits *m,* écarts *m* de conduite; (*c*) infraction *f* à la loi.

wrong-foot ['rɔŋ'fut], *v.tr. Sp:* prendre (son adversaire) à contre-pied; *Fig:* prendre (qn) à l'improviste, au dépourvu, au pied levé.

wrongful ['rɔŋful], *a.* **1.** (*a*) injuste; *Jur:* **w. dismissal,** renvoi injustifié (d'un employé); (*b*) *Jur:* illégal, -aux; préjudiciable; dommageable. **2.** faux (héritier, roi, etc.).

wrongfully ['rɔŋfuli], *adv.* injustement, à tort.

wrongheaded [rɔŋ'hedid], *a.* qui a mauvaise tête; qui a l'esprit pervers, de travers; **wilfully w.,** opiniâtre.

wrongheadedly [rɔŋ'hedidli], *adv.* avec une obstination que rien ne justifie; à tort.

wrongheadedness [rɔŋ'hedidnis], *s.* mauvaise tête, perversité *f* de jugement; obstination *f* que rien ne justifie, opiniâtreté *f.*

wrongly ['rɔŋli], *adv.* **1.** à tort, à faux; **I've been w. accused,** on m'a accusé injustement, à tort, à faux; **rightly or w.,** à tort ou à raison. **2.** mal; **to choose w.,** mal choisir; **w. put together,** mal assemblé.

wrongness ['rɔŋnis], *s.* **1.** erreur *f,* inexactitude *f.* **2.** injustice *f* (d'une accusation, etc.).

wroth [rəθ], *a. Lit:* courroucé, en courroux, en colère (**at,** contre); **to wax w.,** se courroucer, entrer en courroux, se mettre en colère.

wrought [rɔ:t], *a.* (*a*) travaillé, ouvré, ouvragé, façonné; (*b*) (*of metals*) ouvré, forgé, battu; **w. iron,** (i) fer forgé, battu, martelé, soudé, corroyé; (ii) fer ouvré; **w. iron pipe,** tuyau *m* en fer forgé; **w. iron worker,** ferronnier *m*; **w. steel,** acier soudé, soudant; **w. copper,** cuivre battu.

wrought up [rɔ:t'ʌp], *a.* excité, agité, ému.

wrung [rʌŋ], *a.* **1.** (cœur) déchiré. **2.** (*of beam, plate*) faussé, gondolé.

wry [rai], *a.* (**wrier, wryer**) tordu, tors; de travers; **w. neck,** cou tors; **to pull a w. face,** faire la grimace; faire une vilaine moue; *O:* **to make a w. mouth,** tordre la bouche; **a w. smile,** un sourire forcé, pincé; un petit sourire moitié figue moitié raisin, mi-figue mi-raisin; **he gave a w. smile,** il a grimacé un sourire.

wry-faced ['raifeist], *a.* aux traits tirés, de travers.

wryly ['raili], *adv.* avec un sourire forcé; en grimaçant.

wry-mouthed ['raimauθt], *a.* qui a la bouche de travers.

wryneck ['rainek], *s.* **1.** *Med:* torticolis *m.* **2.** *Orn:* torcol (fourmilier).

wrynecked ['rainekt], *a.* qui a le cou tordu, de travers.

wryness ['rainis], *s.* **1.** manque *m* de régularité, de symétrie (des traits). **2.** acidité *f* (d'une remarque); caractère forcé, contraint (d'un sourire).

wulfenite ['wulfənait], *s. Miner:* wulfénite *f,* plomb *m* jaune.

wurley ['wə:li], *s. Austr:* **1.** hutte *f* (d'aborigène). **2.** nid *m* (de rat, etc.).

Würmian ['wə:miən], *a. & s. Geol:* würmien (*m*).

Würtemberger ['və:təmbɛəgər], *s. Geog:* Wurtembergeois, -oise.

wurtzite ['wə:tsait], *s. Miner:* wurtzite *f.*

wuzzy ['wʌzi], *a. NAm: F:* **I feel w.,** la tête me tourne.

wyandotte ['waiəndɔt], *s. Husb:* (poule) wyandotte *f.*

wych-elm ['witʃelm], *s. Bot:* orme blanc, de(s) montagne(s).

Wyclif(f)ite ['wiklifait], *a. & s. Rel.H:* wicléfiste (*mf*).

wye [wai], *s.* **1.** (la lettre) y *m.* **2.** *Plumb:* branche *f* culotte.

Wykehamist ['wikəmist], *a. & s.* (élève, ancien élève) du collège de Winchester.

wynd [waind], *s. Scot:* ruelle *f,* allée *f.*

wyvern ['waivə(:)n], *s. Her:* dragon ailé à deux pattes.

X

X, x [eks], *s.* (la lettre) X, x *m*; *Tp:* **X for Xmas,** X comme Xavier; *Mth:* **the x-axis,** l'axe *m* des abscisses; *Cmptr:* **X punch,** perforation *f* X; *W.Tel: O:* **X's,** bruits *m* parasites; *Biol:* **X chromosome,** chromosome *m* X; *Ph:* **X rays,** rayons *m* X; **deep X rays,** rayons X pénétrants; *Cin:* **X film,** film interdit aux moins de 18 ans.
xancus ['zæŋkəs], *s. Moll:* xancus *f.*
xanthate ['zænθeit], *s. Ch:* xanthate *m.*
xanthein ['zænθiin], *s. Ch:* xanthéine *f.*
xanthelasma [zænθi'læzmə], *s. Med:* xanthélasma *m.*
xanthene ['zænθi:n], *s. Ch:* xanthène *m.*
xanthic ['zænθik], *a. Ch: Bot:* xanthique.
xanthin(e) ['zænθ(a)in], *s. Ch:* xanthine *f.*
Xanthippe [zæn'θipi], *Pr.n.f. Gr.Hist:* Xanthippe.
Xanthippus [zæn'θipəs], *Pr.n.m. Gr.Hist:* Xanthippe.
xanthium ['zænθiəm], *s. Bot:* xanthium *m*, lampourde *f.*
xanth(o)- ['zænθ(ou)], *comb.fm. Ch: etc.:* xanth(o)-.
xantho ['zænθou], *s. Crust: (genus)* xanthe *m.*
xanthoarsenite [zænθou'ɑ:sinait], *s.* xantharsénite *m.*
xanthocarpous [zænθou'kɑ:pəs], *a.* xanthocarpe.
xanthochromia [zænθou'kroumiə], *s. Med:* xanthochromie *f.*
xanthoconite [zænθou'kounait], *s. Miner:* xanthoconite *f.*
xanthoderm ['zænθoudə:m], *a. Anthr:* xanthoderme.
xanthogenate [zæn'θɔdʒəneit], *s. Ch:* xanthogénate *m.*
xanthogenic [zænθou'dʒenik], *a. Ch:* xanthogénique.
xanthoma, *pl.* **-as, -ata** [zæn'θoumə, -əs, ətə], *s. Med:* xanthoma *m*, xanthome *m.*
xanthomatosis [zænθoumə'tousis], *s. Med:* xanthomatose *f.*
xanthone ['zænθoun], *s. Ch:* xanthone *f.*
Xanthophyceae [zænθou'faisii:], *s.pl. Algae:* xanthophycées *m.*
xanthophyll ['zænθoufil], *s. Ch: Bot:* xanthophylle *f.*
xanthophyllite [zænθou'filait], *s. Miner:* xanthophyllite *f.*
xanthoproteic [zænθouprou'teiik], *a. Ch:* xanthoprotéique.
xanthopsia [zæn'θɔpsiə], *s. Med:* xanthopsie *f.*
xanthorrhiza [zænθou'raizə], *s. Bot:* xanthorrhize *f.*
xanthorrhœa [zænθou'ri:ə], *s. Bot:* xanthorrhée *f.*
xanthosoma [zænθou'soumə], *s. Bot:* xanthosoma *m.*
xanthoura [zæn'θu:rə], *s. Orn:* xanthoura *m.*
xanthous ['zænθəs], *a.* jaune.
xanthoxylin [zæn'θɔksilin], *s. Ch:* xanthoxyline *f.*
xanthoxylum [zæn'θɔksiləm], *s. Bot:* xanthoxylum *m.*
Xanthus ['zænθəs], *Pr.n. A.Geog:* Xanthe *m* (ville et fleuve).
xanthydrol ['zænθidrɔl], *s. Ch:* xanthydrol *m.*
Xantusiidae [zænt(j)u'si:idi:], *s.pl. Rept:* xantusiidés *m.*
Xavier ['zeiviər], *Pr.n.m.* Xavier.
xebec ['zi:bek], *s. Nau:* chébec *m.*
Xenarthra [ze'nɑ:θrə], *s.pl. Z:* xénarthres *m.*
xenia ['zi:niə], *s. Bot:* xénie *f.*
xen(o)- ['zen(ou)], *comb.fm.* xén(o)-.
Xenocrates [ze'nɔkrəti:z], *Pr.n.m. Gr.Phil:* Xénocrate.
xenodiagnosis [zenoudaiəg'nousis], *s. Med:* xénodiagnostic *m.*
xenogamous [ze'nɔgəməs], *a. Bot:* xénogame.
xenogamy [ze'nɔgəmi], *s. Bot:* xénogamie *f.*
xenogenesis [zenou'dʒenəsis], *s. Biol:* xénogénèse *f.*
xenoglossy ['zenouglɔsi], *s. Psychics:* xénoglossie *f.*
xenolite ['zenoulait], *s. Miner:* xénolite *f.*
xenolith ['zenouliθ], *s. Geol:* enclave *f.*
xenomorphic [zenou'mɔ:fik], *a. Geol:* xénomorphe.
xenon ['zenɔn], *s. Ch:* xénon *m.*
xenoparasitism [zenou'pærəsitizm], *s. Biol:* xénoparasitisme *m.*
Xenopeltidae [zenou'peltidi:], *s.pl. Rept:* xénopeltidés *m.*
Xenophanes [ze'nɔfəni:z], *Pr.n.m. Gr.Phil:* Xénophane.
xenophile ['zenoufail], *s.* xénophile *mf.*
xenophilism [ze'nɔfilizm], *s.* xénophilie *f.*
xenophilous [ze'nɔfiləs], *a.* xénophile.
xenophobe ['zenoufoub], *a. & s.* xénophobe *(mf).*
xenophobia [zenou'foubiə], *s.* xénophobie *f.*
xenophobic [zenou'foubik], *a.* xénophobe.
Xenophon ['zenəfɔn], *Pr.n.m. Gr.Lit:* Xénophon.
xenophoran [zə'nɔfərən], *s. Moll:* xénophore *m.*
Xenophoridae [zenou'fɔridi:], *s.pl. Moll:* xénophoridés *m.*
xenoplastic [zenou'plæstik], *a. Biol:* xénoplastique.
Xenopsylla [ze'nɔpsilə], *s. Ent:* xénopsylla *f.*
Xenopus ['zenəpəs], *s. Amph:* xénopus *m.*
xenos ['zenɔs], *s. Ent:* xénos *m.*
Xenosauridae [zenou'sɔ:ridi:], *s.pl. Rept:* xénosauridés *m.*
xenotime ['zenoutaim], *s. Miner:* xénotime *m.*
xeranthemum [ziə'rænθiməm], *s. Bot:* xéranthème *m.*
xerasia [ziə'reiziə], *s. Med:* xérasie *f.*
xer(o)- ['ziər(ou)], *comb.fm.* xér(o)-.
xerocopy ['ziəroukɔpi], *s.* copie *f* xérographique.
xeroderm(i)a [ziərou'də:m(i)ə], *s. Med:* xérodermie *f.*
xerographic [ziərou'græfik], *a.* xérographique.
xerography [ziə'rɔgrəfi], *s.* xérographie *f.*
xerophagy [ziə'rɔfədʒi], *s. Rel.H:* xérophagie *f.*
xerophilous [ziə'rɔfiləs], *a.* xérophile.
xerophthalmia [ziərɔf'θælmiə], *s. Med:* xérophtalmie *f.*
xerophyte ['ziəroufait], *s. Bot:* xérophyte *m.*
xerophytic [ziərou'fitik], *a. Bot:* xérophyt(iqu)e.
xerosis [ziə'rousis], *s. Med:* xérose *f*; *(ophthalmology)* xérosis *f.*
xerostomia [ziərou'stoumiə], *s. Physiol: Med:* xérostomie *f.*
xerothermic [ziərou'θə:mik], *a. Nat.Hist:* xérothermique.
Xerox ['ziərɔks], *s. R.t.m.* machine *f* Xerox.
Xerus ['ziərəs], *s. Z:* xérus *m.*
Xerxes ['zə:ksi:z], *Pr.n.m. A.Hist:* Xerxès.
Xhosa [kousə, kɔ:-]. *Ethn:* **1.** *a.* xhosa. **2.** *s.* Xhosa *mf*; **the X.,** les Xhosa(s).
xi [ksai, (g)zai], *s. Gr.Alph:* xi *m.*
ximenia [zi'mi:niə], *s. Bot:* ximénie *f.*
xiphias ['zifiəs]. **1.** *s. Ich:* xiphias *m*, espadon *m*; épée *f* de mer. **2.** *Pr.n. Astr:* la Dorade.
xiphisternal [zifi'stə:n(ə)l], *a. Anat:* xiphoïdien.
xiphisternum [zifi'stə:nəm], *s. Anat:* appendice *m* xiphoïde.
xiph(o)- ['zif(ou)], *comb.fm.* xiph(o)-.
xiphodon ['zifoundɔn], *s. Paleont:* xiphodon *m.*
xiphoid ['zifɔid], *a. & s. Anat:* **x. (appendage, cartilage, process),** (appendice *m*) xiphoïde.
xiphoidian [zi'fɔidiən], *a. Anat:* xiphoïdien.
xiphopagus [zi'fɔpəgəs], *s. Ter:* xiphopage *m.*
xiphophorus [zi'fɔfərəs], *s. Ich:* xiphophore *m.*
Xiphosura [zifou's(j)u:rə], *s.pl. Ent:* xiphosures *m.*
Xmas ['krisməs, *F:* 'eksməs], *s. F:* (= *Christmas*) Noël *m.*
xoanon ['zouənɔn], *s. A.Sculp:* xoanon *m.*
xonotlite ['zounətlait], *s. Miner:* xonotlite *f.*
X(-)ray[1] ['eksrei], *s.* **1. X rays,** rayons *m* X; *attrib.* **X-r. examination,** examen *m* radiographique, radioscopique, radiologique; radioscopie *f*; **X-r. diagnosis,** radiodiagnostic *m*; **X-r. photograph,** radio(graphie) *f*; **X-r. photography,** radio(graphie); **X-r. spectrograph,** radiospectrographe *m*; **X-r. cinematography,** radiocinématographie *f*; **X-r. treatment,** radiothérapie *f*; **X-r. crystallography,** radiocrystallographie *f*; **X-r. tube,** ampoule *f* radiogène; **X.-r. dermatitis,** radiodermite *f*; **X-r. lesion,** radiolésion *f.* **2.** radiographie, radioscopie *f*; **full-throat X-r.,** radiographie complète de la gorge.
X-ray[2], *v.tr. Med:* radiographier (qn); **to be X-rayed,** se faire radiographier, *F:* passer à la radio.
xylan ['zailæn], *s. Bot:* xylane *m.*
xylem ['zailem], *s. Bot:* xylème *m.*
xylene ['zaili:n], *s. Ch:* xylène *m.*
xylenol ['zailənɔl], *s. Ch:* xylénol *m*; acide *m* crésylique.
xylic ['z(a)ilik], *a.* xylique.
xylidine ['z(a)ilidi:n], *s. Ch:* xylidine *m.*
xylitol ['z(a)ilitɔl], *s. Ch:* xylite *f*, xylitol *m.*
xyl(o)- ['zail(ou), zai'lɔ, zil], *comb.fm.* xyl(o)-.
xylocarpous [zailou'kɑ:pəs], *a.* xylocarpe.
xylocopa [zailou'koupə], *s. Ent:* xylocope *m.*
xyloglyphy [zai'lɔglifi], *s.* xyloglyphie *f*, xyloglyptique *f.*
xylograph ['zailougræf], *s.* xylographie *f*; gravure *f* sur bois; estampe *f.*
xylographer [zai'lɔgrəfər], *s.* xylographe *m*; graveur *m* sur bois.
xylographic [zailou'græfik], *a.* xylographique.
xylography [zai'lɔgrəfi], *s.* xylographie *f*; (l'art *m* de la) gravure sur bois.
xylol ['zailɔl], *s. Ind: Ch:* xylol *m.*
xylology [zai'lɔlədʒi], *s.* xylologie *f.*
xylophagan [zai'lɔfəgən], **xylophage** ['zailoufeidʒ], *s. Ent:* xylophage *m.*
xylophagous [zai'lɔfəgəs], *a. Ent:* xylophage.
xylophilous [zai'lɔfiləs], *a.* lignicole.
xylophone ['zailəfoun], *s. Mus:* xylophone *m.*
xylophonist [zai'lɔfənist], *s. Mus:* joueur, -euse, de xylophone.
xylopia [zai'loupiə], *s. Bot:* xylopia *m.*
xylose ['zailous], *s. Ch:* xylose *m.*
xylotomous [zai'lɔtəməs], *a. Ent:* xylotome.
Xyridaceae [ziri'deisii:], *s.pl. Bot:* xyridacées *f.*
xyst [zist], *s. Gr.Ant:* xyste *m.*
xystus, *pl.* **-i** ['zistəs, -ai], *s. Gr.Ant:* xyste *m.*

Y

Y, y, *pl.* **y's, ys** [wai, waiz], *s.* (la lettre) Y, y *m*; i grec; y-grec *m*; *Tp:* **Y for yellow,** Y comme Yvonne; *Mth:* **the y axis,** l'axe *m* des ordonnées; *Biol:* **Y chromosome,** chromosome *m* Y; **Y-shaped,** fourchu; à fourche; en Y; *Ent:* **Y moth,** plusie *f*; *Tchn:* **Y joint,** raccord *m* en Y; *Hyd.E: etc:* **Y pipe, Y branch,** culotte *f*; *El:* **Y connection,** couplage *m*, montage *m*, en étoile, montage en Y; **Y junction box,** boîte *f* de jonction à bifurcation; *Surv:* **Y level,** niveau *m* à lunette; *U.S: Mil:* **Y gun,** canon anti-sous-marin à deux tubes, en fourche; *Cmptr:* **Y punch,** perforation *f* Y.

yacht[1] [jɔt], *s.* yacht *m*; **sailing y.,** yacht à voiles; **motor y.,** yacht à moteur; autoyacht *m*; **steam y.,** yacht à vapeur; **racing y.,** yacht de course; **sand y.,** aéroplage *f*; **ice y.,** yacht à glace; **y. club,** yacht-club *m, pl.* yacht-clubs.

yacht[2], *v.i.* faire du yachting; **we went yachting,** nous avons fait (i) une promenade, (ii) une croisière, en yacht.

yachting ['jɔtiŋ], *s.* yachting *m*; navigation *f* de plaisance; **to go y.,** faire du yachting; **y. cruise,** croisière *f* en yacht; **y. cap,** casquette *f* de yachtman.

yachtsman, *pl.* **-men** ['jɔtsmən], *s.m.* yachtman, *pl.* yachtmen; plaisancier.

yack(ety-yack)[2], *v.i. P:* jacasser.

yack(ety-yach)[2], *v.i. P:* jacasser.

yaffle ['jæfl], *s. Orn: Dial:* pic vert; pivert *m*.

yah [jɑ:], *int.* **1.** (*disgust*) pouah! **2.** (*derision*) oh, là là!

yahoo [jə'hu:, 'jɑ:hu:], *s. F:* homme bestial; brute *f*.

Yahveh ['jɑ:vei], **Yahweh** ['jɑ:wei, -vei], *Pr.n. B.Lit:* Jahvé *m*, Yahvé *m*, Jéhovah *m*.

Yahwist ['jɑ:wist], *a. & s. Rel:* yahviste (*mf*).

Yahwistic [jɑ:'wistik], *a. Rel:* yahviste.

yak[1] [jæk], *s. Z:* ya(c)k *m*; vache *f* de Tartarie.

yak[2], *s. P:* jacasserie *f*.

yak[3], *v.i. P:* jacasser.

yakety-yak[1,2] ['jækəti'jæk], *s. & v.i.* = YAK[2,3].

Yakut [jæ'kut]. **1.** *a.* iakoute, yakoute. **2.** *s.* Iakoute *mf*, Yakoute *mf*.

Yakutsk [jæ'kutsk], *Pr.n. Geog:* Iakoutski *m*, Yakoutsk *m*.

Yalu (the) [ðəjæ'lu:], *Pr.n. Geog:* le (fleuve) Yalou.

yam [jæm], *s. Bot:* igname *f*.

yammer ['jæmər], *v.i.* **1.** *F:* gémir, geindre; pousser des cris. **2.** *F:* jacasser. **3.** (*of machine*) ronfler, bourdonner, vrombir.

yang [jæŋ], *s. Phil:* yang *m*.

Yangtze Kiang (the) [ðə'jæŋtsiki'æŋ], *Pr.n. Geog:* le Yang-tsé-Kiang.

yank[1] [jæŋk], *s.* (*a*) *F:* secousse *f*, saccade *f*; (*b*) *Scot:* coup sec.

yank[2], *v.tr. F:* tirer (d'un coup sec); **to y. on the brake,** tirer vivement sur le levier du frein; freiner vivement; **to y. out a tooth,** arracher une dent d'un seul coup; **to y. s.o. off,** emmener qn de force.

Yank[3], **Yankee (Doodle)** ['jæŋki('du:dl)], *s. F:* (*a*) Américain, -aine (des États-Unis); Yankee *mf*; (*b*) (*in U.S.A.*) *usu. Pej:* habitant, -ante, des États du Nord.

Yankeefied ['jæŋkifaid], *a. P:* américanisé; à l'allure américaine; à l'accent américain.

Yankeeism ['jæŋkiizm], *s.* mot américain; locution américaine; américanisme *m*.

yap[1] [jæp], *s.* jappement *m* (d'un chien).

yap[2], *v.i.* **(yapped)** (*a*) (*of dog*) japper; (*b*) *F:* (*of pers.*) criailler; en dégoiser; jacasser.

yapo(c)k ['jæpɔk], *s. Z: U.S:* crabier *m*.

yapp [jæp], *s. Bookb:* reliure *f* en cuir souple débordant amplement la page.

yapping[1] ['jæpiŋ], *a.* jappeur; glapissant.

yapping[2], *s.* = YAP[1].

yappy ['jæpi], *a. F:* jappeur.

yarborough ['jɑ:b(ə)rə], *s. Cards:* main *f* qui ne contient aucune carte au-dessus du neuf.

yard[1] [jɑ:d], *s.* **1.** *Meas:* yard *m* (0,914 m); (*in Canada*) verge *f*; **square y.,** yard carré (0,765 m^2); **a y. of sand, gravel** = un mètre cube de sable, de gravier; **how many yards do you want?** quel métrage désirez-vous? *F:* **I can't see a y. in front of me,** je ne vois pas à un mètre; **face a y. long,** figure longue d'une aune; **yards of statistics, statistics by the y.,** des statistiques à n'en plus finir. **2.** *Nau:* vergue *f*; **main y.,** grande vergue; grand-vergue; **topsail y.,** vergue de hunier; **topgallant y.,** vergue de perroquet; **lower yards,** basses vergues; **signal yards,** vergues de, à, signaux; **y. and stay,** (manœuvre *f* en) colis volant.

yard[2], *s.* **1.** (*a*) (i) cour *f* (de maison, de ferme, d'écurie, etc.); *Sch:* cour, préau *m*; **y. dog,** chien *m* de garde; (ii) *U.S:* jardin *m* (autour d'une maison); (iii) *Austr: pl. usu. with sg. const.* parc *m* à bétail, à bestiaux; (iv) (*in Can.*) *Ven:* ravage *m*; (*b*) **New Scotland Y.,** *F:* **the Y.** = la Sûreté. **2.** (*a*) chantier *m*; **timber, lumber, y.,** chantier de bois; **builder's y.,** chantier (de construction); *N.Arch:* **repair y.,** chantier de radoub; **shipbuilding y.,** chantier de construction(s) navale(s); **shipbreaker's y.,** chantier de démolition; **naval (dock)y.,** *U.S:* **navy y.,** chantier de l'État; arsenal *m* maritime; (*b*) dépôt *m*; **coal y., fuel y.,** dépôt de charbon; parc *m* aux combustibles; **contractor's y.,** gare *f* dépôt de matériaux; *Rail:* **goods y.,** cour, dépôt, de marchandises; **switching y., railway y.,** gare de triage; centre *m* de triage; **y. master,** chef *m* de dépôt.

yardage[1] ['jɑ:didʒ], *s.* métrage *m*.

yardage[2], *s.* **1.** parcage (attaché à un atelier, etc.). **2.** frais *mpl* de dépôt. **3.** *Rail:* manœuvres *fpl*.

yardang ['jɑ:dæŋ], *s. Geog:* jardang *m*, yardang *m*.

yardarm ['jɑ:dɑ:m], *s. Nau:* fusée *f* de vergue; bout *m* de vergue; **y. and y.,** vergue à vergue.

yardbird ['yɑ:dbə:d], *s. F:* **1.** *Mil:* homme *m* de corvée. **2.** prisonnier *m*, forçat *m*.

yard(s)man, *pl.* **-men** ['jɑ:d(z)mən], *s.m.* **1.** manœuvre, homme, de cour, de chantier. **2.** *Rail:* gareur, classeur, de trains. **3.** (*in stables*) palefrenier; garçon d'écurie.

yardstick ['jɑ:dstik], *s.* (i) yard *m* (en bois, en métal); (ii) *Fig:* (*as standard of comparison*) aune *f*, étalon *m*, jauge *f*; modèle *m*, exemple *m*; **to measure others by one's own y.,** mesurer les autres à son aune.

yarmulka ['jɑ:məlkə], *s.* calotte juive.

yarn[1] [jɑ:n], *s.* **1.** (*a*) *Tex:* fil *m*; filé *m* (de coton); **woollen y.,** laine filée; fil de laine, filé de laine; **jute y.,** fil de jute; **glazed y.,** fil glacé; **y. beam, y. roll,** ensouple dérouleuse; (*b*) *Nau:* **(rope)y.,** fil de caret; **spun y.,** bitord *m*; **three-y. spun y.,** bitord en trois; **spun-y. winch,** moulinet *m* à bitord. **2.** *F:* (i) histoire *f* de matelot; (ii) histoire merveilleuse; longue histoire; **to spin a y.,** raconter, débiter, une histoire; **what y. is he spinning now?** qu'est-ce qu'il dévide?

yarn[2], *v.i. F:* débiter des histoires, bavarder.

yarn-dye ['jɑ:ndai], *v.tr. Tex:* teindre avant tissage.

yarrow ['jærou], *s. Bot:* achillée *f*, mille-feuille *f*, herbe *f* aux charpentiers.

yashmak ['jæʃmæk], *s. Cost:* yachmak *m*.

yataghan ['jætəgən], *s.* yatagan *m*.

yatter ['jætər], *v.i. F:* bavarder.

yaw[1] [jɔ:], *s.* (*a*) *Nau:* embardée *f*; (*b*) *Av: etc:* (mouvement *m* de) lacet *m*; **angle of y.,** angle *m* de lacet; **y. axis,** axe *m* de lacet; **y.-axis accelerometer,** accéléromètre latéral; **(automatic) y. damper,** amortisseur *m*, correcteur *m* (automatique) de lacet; **y. damping,** amortissement *m* du lacet; **y. rate,** amplitude *f* de lacet.

yaw[2], *v.i.* (*a*) *Nau:* embarder; faire des embardées; **don't let her y.!** défiez l'embardée! (*b*) *Av: etc:* faire un mouvement de lacet.

yawing ['jɔ:iŋ], *s.* (*a*) *Nau:* embardées *fpl*; (*b*) *Av: etc:* lacet *m*; **y. moment, plane,** moment *m*, plan *m*, de lacet.

yawl [jɔ:l], *s. Nau:* **1.** yole *f* (à rames). **2.** sloop *m*, cotre *m*, à tape-cul; yawl *m*.

yawn[1] [jɔ:n], *s.* **1.** bâillement *m*; **to give a y.,** bâiller; **to stifle a y.,** étouffer un bâillement; **with a sleepy y.,** avec un bâillement de sommeil. **2.** *Lit:* crevasse béante; abîme *m*.

yawn[2]. **1.** *v.i.* (*a*) bâiller (de sommeil, etc.); (*b*) (*of chasm, etc.*) être béant; bâiller; **the gulf yawned at his feet,** le gouffre s'ouvrait, s'entrouvrait, à ses pieds. **2.** *v.tr.* **to y. one's life away,** bâiller sa vie; languir d'ennui; *F:* **to y. one's head off,** bâiller à se décrocher la mâchoire; bâiller comme une carpe.

yawner ['jɔ:nər], *s.* bâilleur, -euse.

yawning[1] ['jɔ:niŋ], *a.* **1.** qui bâille d'ennui. **2.** (gouffre) béant, ouvert, entrouvert.

yawning[2], *s.* bâillement *m*; **y. is catching,** le bâillement est communicatif.

yawningly ['jɔ:niŋli], *adv.* en bâillant.

yawny ['jɔ:ni], *a. F:* (*a*) qui fait bâiller; **it's a y. day,** il fait un temps lourd, soporifique; *U.S:* **y. tale,** histoire à dormir debout; (*b*) qui bâille; **to feel y.,** avoir sommeil.

yawp[1] [jɔ:p], *s. U.S: F:* cri *m* rauque.

yawp[2] [jɔ:p], *v.i. U.S: F:* criailler.

yaws [jɔ:z], *s.pl. Med:* pian *m*.

yclept [i'klept], *a. A:* appelé; dit, nommé.

ye[1] [ji:]. *A:* (*& pseudo archaic*) le, la, les; **Ye Olde Shoppe,** la Vieille Boutique.

ye[2], *pers.pron.* **1.** *nom. or voc.* (*a*) *pl. A: & Lit:* vous; **where were ye?** où étiez-vous? **be ye merciful,** soyez miséricordieux; **seek and ye shall find,** cherchez et vous trouverez; (*b*) *sg. F: & Dial:* tu, vous; **how d'ye do?** comment vas-tu? comment allez-vous? **2.** *acc.* (*a*) *A:* vous; **I do beseech ye,** je vous en prie; (*b*) *F: & Dial:* **Heaven be with ye!** Dieu te, vous, garde!

yea [jei]. **1.** *adv. B: & Lit:* (*a*) oui; **I answered him y.,** je lui répondis oui; (*b*) en vérité; voire; *B:* **y. though I walk through the valley of the shadow of death,** même quand je marcherais dans la vallée de l'ombre de la mort; **the remedy is useless, y. harmful,** ce remède est inutile, voire (même) pernicieux. **2.** *s.* oui *m*; (*a*) **to fall out over a y. or nay,** se quereller pour un oui, pour un non; (*b*) *U.S:* (*in voting*) **yeas and nays,** voix *f* pour et contre.

yeah [jɛə], *adv. P:* oui; *Iron:* **oh y.?** vraiment? vous m'en direz tant!

yean [ji:n]. *A:* **1.** *v.i.* (*of ewe*) agneler; (*of goat*) chevreter. **2.** *v.tr.* (*of ewe, goat*) mettre bas (un petit).

yeanling ['ji:nliŋ], *s. A:* (*a*) agnelet *m*; (*b*) chevreau *m*.

year [jiər], *s.* an *m*, année *f*; (*a*) *usu.* an; **in the y. (of our Lord, of grace) 1850,** en l'an, en l'année (du Seigneur, de grâce) 1850; **I have known him for ten years,** je le connais depuis dix ans; **the Thirty Years' War,** la Guerre de Trente Ans; **sentenced to ten years' imprisonment,** condamné à dix ans de prison; **a y. last, next, September,** il y a eu, il y aura, un an en septembre; **last y.,** l'an dernier; l'année dernière; **next y.,** l'an prochain; l'année prochaine; **this day next y.,** dans un an jour pour jour; dans un an à pareil jour; *Jur:* **a y. and a day,** an et jour; **every y.,** tous les ans; chaque année; annuellement; **twice a y.,** deux fois par an; deux fois l'an, l'année; **(i) to earn, (ii) to have, £10,000 a y.,** (i) gagner £10.000 par an, (ii) avoir £10.000 de rente; **a y.-old child, a one-y.-old (child),** un enfant (âgé) d'un an; **to be ten years old,** avoir dix ans; **a hundred y. old tree,** (i) un arbre de cent ans; (ii) un arbre séculaire; **new y.,** nouvel an; **New Y.'s Day,** le jour de l'an; **Happy New Y.!** bonne année! **to wish s.o. a happy new y.,** souhaiter la bonne année, *F:* la souhaiter bonne et heureuse, à qn; **to see the old y. out, the new y. in,** faire la veillée, le réveillon, de la Saint-Sylvestre; réveillonner; *Ecc:* **y.'s mind,** (service *m* du) bout de l'an; (*b*) *usu.* année; **leap y.,** année bissextile; **solar y.,** année solaire; **calendar, civil, y.,** année civile; **Gregorian y.,** année grégorienne; **financial, fiscal, tax, y.,** année budgétaire; exercice (financier); **company's financial y.,** exercice social, comptable; **crop y.,** campagne agricole; **school y.,** année scolaire; *Ind:* **man y.,** année-homme, *pl.* années-hommes; **third y. student,** étudiant de troisième année; **he was in my y.,** il est de ma promotion; **to be the first in one's y.,** être le premier de sa promotion; **rainy y.,** année pluvieuse; **to rent, hire, sth. by the y.,** louer qch. à l'année; **document valid for one y.,** document valable pour un an; **for many long years,** pendant de longues années; **for several years on end,** pendant plusieurs années de suite; **all the y. round,** (pendant) toute l'année; **y.-round service,** service permanent; **from year's end to year's end,** d'un bout de l'année à l'autre, tout le long de l'année; **from y. to y.,** d'une année à l'autre; **y. in (and) y. out,** une année après l'autre; **y. by y.,** d'année en année; **taking one y. with another,** bon an, mal an; **years ago,** il y a bien des années; *F:* **it's years since I saw him, I haven't seen him for, in, years,** il y a des éternités que je ne l'ai vu; **in later years,** dans la suite; **the best years of our life,** les plus belles années de notre vie; **to be in one's twentieth y.,** être dans sa vingtième année; **from his earliest years,** dès son plus jeune âge; **a boy in years, a man in intelligence,** un enfant quant au nombre des années, un homme quant à l'intelligence; **old for his years,** plus vieux que son âge; (enfant) précoce; **disparity in years,** différence *f* d'âge; **to be getting on in years, to advance in years,** prendre de l'âge; avancer en âge; tirer sur l'âge; **advanced in years,** âgé; *Lit:* **stricken in years,** chargé d'années; **to die full of years,** mourir plein de jours; *Com: Ind:* **y. of manufacture,** année de construction, millésime *m* (d'une machine, etc.); (*c*) *Vit:* millésime; **a good y. for claret,** une bonne année pour le bordeaux rouge.

yearbook ['jiəbuk], *s.* annuaire *m*, almanach *m*; recueil annuel (de jurisprudence etc.).

yearling ['jiəliŋ], *a. & s.* (*a*) (animal *m*) d'un an; (*of roe-deer*) brocard *m*; *esp. y.* **(colt),** poulain *m* d'un an; laiteron *m*, yearling *m*; (*b*) (plante *f*) d'un an; (*c*) *Fin:* **y. (bond),** bon *m* à un an.

yearlong ['jiəlɔŋ], *a.* **1.** qui dure (tout) un an, toute l'année. **2.** qui dure pendant des années; (coutume, etc.) séculaire.

yearly ['jiəli]. **1.** *a.* annuel; (*a*) qui se fait, qui revient, chaque année; **debt redeemable by y. payments,** dette *f* annuitaire; *Ecc:* **y. festival,** annuel *m*; (*b*) qui dure un an; **y. letting,** location annale. **2.** *adv.* annuellement; (i) une fois par an; (ii) tous les ans.

yearn [jə:n], *v.i.* **1. to y. for, after, sth.,** languir pour, après, qch.; soupirer pour, après, à, vers, qch.; attendre qch. avec impatience; **to y. for the sight of one's native land,** brûler de revoir son pays natal; **to y. for, after, home,** avoir la nostalgie du pays; **to y. to do sth.,** avoir bien envie de faire qch.; brûler de faire qch.. **2.** *A:* s'affliger, s'attrister; s'émouvoir; **to y. to, towards, s.o.,** être plein de compassion pour qn.

yearning[1] ['jə:niŋ], *a.* (désir) vif, ardent; (regard) (i) plein d'envie, de désir, (ii) plein de tendresse.

yearning[2], *s.* désir ardent; envie *f* **(for,** de); aspiration *f* **(for,** à).

yearningly ['jə:niŋli], *adv.* avec envie; avec un vif désir; **to look at sth. y.,** couver qch. des yeux.

yeast [ji:st], *s.* levure *f*; **brewer's y.,** levure de bière; **y. fungus,** saccharomyces *m*; **y. powder,** poudre *f* de levure.

yegg [jeg], *s.m. NAm: P:* cambrioleur.

yeld [jeld], *a. Scot:* (vache, etc.) stérile.

yell[1] [jel], *s.* **1.** (*a*) hurlement *m*; cri aigu; vocifération *f*; **to give a y.,** pousser un cri, un hurlement; (*b*) *NAm:* cri de guerre, de bataille (des étudiants, etc.). **2.** *F: O:* personne *f*, chose *f*, affaire *f*, extrêmement drôle; **it was a y.,** c'était (tout ce qu'il y a de plus) cocasse; c'était d'un rigolo!

yell[2]. **1.** *v.i.* hurler; crier à tue-tête; crier comme un sourd; **to y. with pain,** hurler de douleur; *O:* **to y. with laughter,** *F:* **to y.,** se tordre de rire; rire aux éclats; s'esclaffer (de rire). **2.** *v.tr.* **to y. (out) a song,** hurler, beugler, une chanson; **to y. out an order,** hurler, *F:* gueuler, un ordre; **to y. out abuse,** vociférer, hurler, des injures.

yelling[1] ['jeliŋ], *a.* (*of crowd, etc.*) hurlant.

yelling[2], *s.* hurlements *mpl*; grands cris; vociférations *fpl.*

yellow[1] ['jelou]. **1.** *a.* (*a*) jaune; **y. as a lemon, a guinea,** jaune comme un citron, comme un coing; **to turn, go, y.,** jaunir; **y. gloves,** des gants *m* jaune paille; **y. hair,** cheveux blonds; cheveux d'or; **y. metal,** cuivre *m* jaune; laiton *m*; **y. Jack,** (i) fièvre *f* jaune; (ii) pavillon *m* de quarantaine; **y. soap** = savon *m* de Marseille; *NAm:* **y. jacket,** (i) petite guêpe; (ii) *P:* barbiturique *m*; **y.-tail,** (i) *Ich:* sériole *f*; (ii) *Ent:* cul-doré *m*, *pl.* culs-dorés; *F: A:* **y.(-)back,** (i) roman (anglais) cartonné en jaune (bibliothèque des chemins de fer, etc.); (ii) livre broché (français); *F: A:* **y.-boy,** pièce *f* d'or; jaunet *m*; **the y. races,** les races *f* jaunes; **the y. peril,** le péril jaune; *U.S:* **y. negro,** nègre *m* au teint clair; *U.S:* **y. dog,** (i) chien bâtard; (ii) sale type *m*; *Ind:* **y.-dog contract,** convention *f* qui n'est pas conforme aux règlements syndicaux; **the y. pages,** les pages jaunes (de l'annuaire téléphonique); *Anat:* **y. spot,** tache jaune (de la rétine); **y. body,** corps jaune, corps progestatif; *Med:* **y. gum,** ictère *m* des enfants; *Agr:* **y. berry,** mitadinage *m*; blé mitadin; *Miner:* **y. ore,** pyrite cuivreuse; pyrite de cuivre; chalcopyrite *f*; *Geog:* **the Y. Sea,** la mer Jaune; *Bot:* **y. waterlily,** nuphar *m*; **y. oxeye,** (i) (*also* **y. bottle)** marguerite dorée; (ii) (*also* **y. daisy)** rudbeckia *f*, rudbeckie *f*; **y. root,** xanthorrhize *f* (à feuilles de persil); **y. vetchling,** gesse *f* des prés; *U.S:* **y. poplar,** tulipier *m*; *NAm:* **y. devil,** épervière *f*; *F:* trouillard, froussard, lâche; **to turn y.,** caner, caponner. **2.** *s. & a.* (*in Fr. a.inv.*) **golden y.,** jaune (*m*) d'or; aurore; **pale y., faint y.,** jaune pâle; **lemon y.,** jaune citron. **3.** *s.* (*a*) jaune *m*; **chrome y.,** jaune de chrome; **Naples y., Neapolitan y.,** jaune de Naples; (*b*) *Med: F: A:* **the yellows,** la jaunisse; (*c*) *Miner: Dy:* **king's y.,** orpiment *m*. **4.** *a. Paperm:* **y. wove** (= azure wove), vélin azuré.

yellow[2]. **1.** *v.tr.* jaunir (qch.); teindre (qch.) en jaune; **papers yellowed with age,** papiers jaunis par le temps. **2.** *v.i.* jaunir; (*of corn*) javeler.

yellowbelly ['jeloubeli], *s. P:* froussard *m*; trouillard *m*.

yellowcake ['jeloukeik], *s. Miner:* oxyde *m* d'uranium.

yellowfin ['jeloufin], *a. & s. Ich:* **y. (tunny),** albacore *m*.

yellowhammer ['jelouhæmər], *s. Orn:* (*a*) bruant *m* jaune; (*b*) *NAm:* colapte doré.

yellowing[1] ['jelouiŋ], *a.* jaunissant.

yellowing[2], *s.* jaunissement *m*.

yellowish ['jelouiʃ], *a.* jaunâtre; jaunet; **y. red,** rouge jaune *inv.*

yellowlegs ['jeloulegz], *s. Orn:* **greater, lesser, y.,** grand, petit, chevalier à pattes jaunes.

yellowness ['jelounis], *s.* ton *m* jaune, teinte *f* jaune (de qch.); teint *m* jaune (de qn).

yellowthroat ['jelouθrout], *s. Orn:* cou-jaune *m*, *pl.* cous-jaunes; gorge-jaune *f*, *pl.* gorges-jaunes.

yellowweed ['jelouwi:d], *s. Bot:* (*a*) réséda *m* des teinturiers; gaude *f*; fleur *f* du soleil; (*b*) helenium *m*; (*c*) solidage *f*, solidago *m*; (*d*) colza *m*.

yellow(-)wood ['jelouwud], *s. Bot:* **1.** santal citrin (de Cochinchine). **2.** podocarpe *m* Thunbergii. **3.** cladrastis *m* tinctoria.

yelp[1] [jelp], *s.* jappement *m*, glapissement *m*.

yelp[2], *v.i.* japper, glapir.

yelper ['jelpər], *s.* jappeur, -euse.

yelping[1] ['jelpiŋ], *a.* jappant, glapissant.

yelping[2], *s.* jappement *m*, glapissement *m*; *Ven:* clabaudage *m* (des chiens).

Yemen (the) [ðə'jemən], *Pr.n. Geog:* le Yémen; **South Y.,** Sud-Yémen, Yémen du Sud.

Yemeni(te) ['jeməni, -ait]. **1.** *a.* yéménique, yéménite. **2.** *s.* Yéménite *mf.*

yen[1] [jen], *s. Num:* yen *m*.

yen[2], *s. F:* envie *f.*

yen[3], *v.i. F:* = YEARN.

yeoman, *pl.* **-men** ['joumən], *s.m.* **1.** *O:* petit propriétaire; franc-tenancier, *pl.* francs-tenanciers; gros fermier; **to do y. service,** fournir un effort précieux; rendre des services inestimables. **2.** (*a*) soldat du *yeomanry, q.v.*; (*b*) **Y. of the Guard,** hallebardier (i) de la garde du corps, (ii) de service, à la Tour de Londres. **3.** *Navy:* (*a*) gardien; magasinier; garde-magasin, *pl.* gardes-magasin; (*b*) *U.S:* sous-officier, commis, aux écritures; sous-officier chargé de l'administration.

yeomanry ['joumənri], *s. coll.* **1.** petits propriétaires; francs-tenanciers. **2.** *Hist:* corps de cavalerie composé surtout de petits propriétaires fonciers qui fournissaient leurs montures; = garde nationale à cheval, montée.

yep [jep], *adv. U.S: P:* oui.

yerba maté [jə:bə'mɑ:tei], *s.* maté *m*, thé *m* du Paraguay, des Jésuites.

yes [jes]. **1.** *adv.* (*a*) oui; parfaitement; (*contradicting negation*) si; **to answer y. or no,** répondre par oui ou non; **to say y.,** dire oui; dire que oui; **y., certainly, oh y.!** mais oui! **are you hungry?**—**y. (, I am),** avez-vous faim?—oui; **do you love him?**—**y. (, I do),** l'aimez-vous?—oui (, bien sûr)! **yes, rather! good heavens, y.!** bien sûr que oui! mais parfaitement! **you didn't hear me?**—**y., I did,** vous ne m'avez pas entendu?—(mais) si; **you said so; oh y., you did,** vous l'avez dit; si, si, vous l'avez dit; (*b*) (*interrogatively*) **y.?** (i) vraiment? (ii) et puis après? (*in answer to summons*) **waiter!**—**y. sir,** garçon!—voilà, monsieur; (*c*) (*introducing emphatic statement*) **I will do it, y. and enjoy doing it,** je le ferai, oui certes, et même très volontiers; **I could do it, y. and well too,** je pourrais le faire, et même bien. **2.** *s.* (*pl.* **yeses** ['jesiz]) oui *m inv.*; **an emphatic y.,** un oui énergique.

yes-man, *pl.* **-men** ['jesmæn, -men], *s. F:* béni-oui-oui *m.inv.*

yesterday ['jestədei], *adv. & s.* hier (*m*); **I only arrived y.,** je ne suis arrivé qu'hier, *A:* que d'hier; **only y. I heard that . . .,** pas plus tard qu'hier j'ai appris que . . .; **the day before y.,** avant-hier (*m*); **y. week,** il y a eu hier huit jours; **a week (from) y.,** d'hier en huit; **y. was the sixteenth,** c'était hier le seize; **y. was a good day,** la journée d'hier a été bonne; **you had all y. to make up your mind,** vous aviez toute la journée d'hier pour vous décider; **yesterday's paper,** le journal d'hier; **y. morning, evening,** hier (au) matin, (au) soir; *pl. Lit:* **yesterdays,** jours *m* d'autrefois, d'antan.

yestereve(n) [jestər'i:v(n)], *adv. & s. A: & Poet:* hier (au) soir.

yestermorn(ing) [jestə'mɔ:n(iŋ), *adv. & s. Lit:* hier (au) matin.

yesternight [jestə'nait], *adv. & s. Lit: & Poet:* la nuit passée, la nuit dernière; hier (au) soir.

yesteryear [jestə'jiər]. **1.** *adv. Lit:* l'an dernier. **2.** *s. Poet:* **the snows of y.,** les neiges *f* d'antan.

yestreen [je'stri:n], *adv. & s. A: Scot:* hier (au) soir.

yet [jet], *adv. & conj.*

I. *adv.* **1.** *esp. Lit:* (*a*) encore; **I can see him y.,** je le vois encore; **we have ten minutes yet,** nous avons encore dix minutes; **jobs y. to be done,** tâches encore à faire; tâches qui restent à faire; **y. untrodden regions,** des régions encore inexplorées; **he has y. to learn. . .,** il lui reste à savoir . . .; (*b*) **y. more,** encore plus; **y. more difficult,** encore plus difficile; **y. again, y. once more,** encore une fois; **y. one more,** encore un autre; **there's another loaf y.,** il nous reste encore un pain. **2.** déjà; jusqu'à présent; jusqu'ici; **need you go y.?** faut-il que vous partiez déjà? **not y.,** pas encore; **do not go y.,** ne partez pas encore; **lilac not y. in bloom,** des lilas pas encore en fleur(s); **it will not happen just y.,** cela n'arrivera pas tout de suite; nous n'en sommes pas encore là; **I have never found a fault in him y.,** j'en suis encore à lui trouver un défaut; **the biggest found y.,** le plus grand qu'on ait jamais trouvé, qu'on ait trouvé jusqu'à maintenant; **as y. nothing has been done,** jusqu'à maintenant, jusqu'à présent, jusqu'ici, on n'a rien fait; *Poet:* **ere y. the dawn breaks,** avant qu'il fasse jour encore. **3.** malgré tout; **he will win y.,** malgré tout, cependant, il gagnera; **I shall catch him y.!** je finirai bien par l'attraper! **I'll do it y.!** j'y arriverai! **4. not finished nor y. started,** pas achevé, pas même commencé, ni même commencé; **not me nor y. you,** ni moi ni vous non plus.

II. *conj.* néanmoins, cependant; tout de même; **he seems honest, (but) y. I don't trust him,** il a l'air d'un honnête homme, néanmoins, mais tout de même, je ne me fie pas à lui; **not very good, y. not bad,** pas très bon, mais tout de même pas mauvais; **and y. I like him,** et cependant, et malgré tout, néanmoins, il me plaît.

yeti ['jeti], *s.* yeti *m*.

yew [juː], *s.* **1.** *Bot:* **y. (tree),** if *m.* **2.** *(a)* (*wood*) (bois *m* d'if); *(b) A: & Poet:* **the y.,** l'arc *m* (en bois d'if).

Yid [jid], *s. P: Pej:* Juif, Juive; youpin, -ine.

Yiddish ['jidiʃ], *a. & s. Ling:* judéo-allemand (*m*); yiddis(c)h (*m*).

yield[1] [jiːld], *s.* **1.** production *f*, produit *m*, débit *m* (d'une mine); rapport *m* (d'un arbre fruitier, d'une mise de fonds, etc.); rendement *m*, récolte *f* (d'un champ); rendement (d'une forêt, d'une machine, d'un impôt); *Atom.Ph:* rendement de matière; énergie libérée; (*of bomb*) puissance *f*; **if there is a good y. of wheat this year,** si les blés donnent cette année; **the y. on these shares is large,** ces actions *f* rapportent beaucoup, rendent beaucoup; **net y.,** revenu net; (*of industry, tree, etc.*) **in full y.,** en plein rapport, en plein rendement; **y. capacity,** productivité *f* (d'une forêt, etc.); *Atom.Ph:* **neutron y.,** rendement en neutrons; **ion y.,** rendement ionique; **chain-fission y.,** rendement de fission en chaîne; **energy y.,** rendement énergétique; **thermal-energy y.,** rendement thermique; **y. of radiation,** rendement en radiations, en rayonnement. **2.** affaissement *m* (des fondements, etc.); fléchissement *m* (d'une poutre, etc.); **y. point, y. limit,** limite *f* de la résistance (élastique), limite d'élasticité; **y. stress,** résistance *f* élastique.

yield[2]. **1.** *v.tr.* *(a)* rendre, donner; offrir, présenter (une vue); émettre, exhaler (une odeur); *(b)* rapporter, produire, donner; **tree that yields fruit,** arbre qui donne des fruits; **ground that yields well,** terre qui donne un bon rendement; terre qui rend bien; terre de bon rapport; **spring that yields a thousand litres an hour,** fontaine qui débite mille litres par heure; **money that yields interest,** argent qui produit un intérêt; argent qui rapporte; **shares that y. high interest,** actions *f* à gros rendement; **to y. a 10% dividend,** produire, rapporter, rendre, un dividende de 10%; *(c)* céder (une forteresse à l'ennemi, un droit, etc.); **to y. ground,** céder le terrain; **to y. one's rights,** céder ses droits; renoncer à ses droits; **to y. a point to s.o.,** céder à qn sur un point; admettre un point; concéder un point; *Lit:* **to y. (up) the ghost, one's soul,** rendre l'âme; **to y. consent to sth.,** donner son consentement à qch. **2.** *v.i.* *(a)* se rendre, se soumettre; faire sa soumission; céder (**to,** à); capituler (**to,** devant); **they yielded (to us) eventually,** ils ont fini par mettre pavillon bas (devant nous); **to y. to circumstances,** céder aux circonstances; **to y. to force, to reason,** céder devant la force; obéir à la force; se rendre à la raison; **to y. to temptation,** succomber à la tentation; se laisser tenter; **to y. to s.o.'s persistence,** céder devant l'insistance de qn; **to y. to s.o.'s prayers, to s.o.'s entreaties,** se laisser fléchir (par les prières de qn); **to y. to s.o.'s arguments,** céder, s'incliner, devant les arguments de qn; **the disease was yielding to treatment,** la maladie cédait aux remèdes; **the frost is yielding,** la gelée s'adoucit; **to y. to pleasure,** se prêter au plaisir; **to y. to enthusiasm,** se laisser aller à l'enthousiasme; **to y. to s.o.'s wishes,** condescendre aux désirs de qn; *Nau:* (*of ship*) **to y. to the helm,** obéir à la barre; *(b)* (*of rope, etc.*) céder; (*of beam, etc.*) s'affaisser, fléchir, plier; **to y. under pressure,** céder à la pression; **the plank yielded under our weight,** la planche a manqué, a cédé, sous nos pieds.

yielding[1] ['jiːldiŋ], *a.* **1.** (*of pers.*) facile, complaisant, accommodant; **in a y. moment,** dans un moment de faiblesse. **2.** *(a)* mou, *f.* molle; **y. ground,** sol mou, peu résistant; **y. snow,** neige souple *f*; *(b)* souple, élastique, flexible; **steel is more y. than iron,** l'acier obéit plus que le fer. **3.** (*of tree, soil*) en plein rapport.

yielding[2], *s.* **1.** rendement *m.* **2.** *(a)* soumission *f*; *(b)* reddition *f* (d'une forteresse); abandon *m* (d'un argument); cession *f* (d'un droit). **3.** affaissement *m* (de fondements, etc.); fléchissement *m* (d'une poutre, etc.).

yieldingly ['jiːldiŋli], *adv.* avec soumission; avec complaisance.

yieldingness ['jiːldiŋnis], *s.* **1.** (*of pers.*) complaisance *f.* **2.** mollesse *f* (du sol, etc.); élasticité *f*, flexibilité *f* (d'un métal, etc.).

yin [jin], *s. Phil:* yin *m.*

yip[1] [jip], *s. U.S: P:* rouspétance *f*; protestation violente.

yip[2], *v.i. U.S: P:* rouspéter; protester violemment.

yippee [ji'piː], *int. F:* hourra! bravo!

ylang-ylang ['iːlæŋ'iːlæŋ], *s. Bot: Toil:* ilang-ilang *m*, ylang-ylang *m.*

ylem ['ailəm], *s. Biol: Miner:* ylem *m.*

yob [jɔb], **yobbo** ['jɔbou], *s.m. P:* *(a)* voyou, loubar(d); *(b)* type.

yod [jɔd], *s. Ling:* yod *m.*

yodel[1] ['joud(ə)l], *s. Mus:* (chant *m* à la) tyrolienne.

yodel[2], *v.i.* **(yodel(l)ing),** *Mus:* jodler, yodler; chanter à la tyrolienne; faire des tyroliennes.

yod(el)ler ['joud(ə)lər], *s.* jodleur, -euse, yodleur, -euse.

yoga ['jougə], *s.* yoga *m.*

yog(h)urt ['jɔgət], *s. Comest:* yaourt *m*; **y. making machine,** yaourtière *f.*

yogi ['jougi], *s.* yogi *m.*

yogic ['jougik], *a.* (exercice, etc.) de yoga.

yo-heave-ho ['jouhiːv'hou], *int. Nau:* o, hisse!

yohimbe, yohimbi [jou'himbi], *s. Bot:* yohimbehe *m.*

yohimbine [jou'himbiːn], *s. Pharm:* yohimbine *f.*

yoho [jou'hou], *int. Nau:* o, hisse!

yoicks [jɔiks], *int. Ven:* = taïaut!

yoke[1] [jouk], *s.* **1.** joug *m*; *(a)* **y. oxen,** bœufs *m* d'attelage; **y. of oxen,** paire *f*, couple *f*, attelage *m* (de bœufs); **two, three, y. of oxen,** deux, trois, couples de bœufs; *Bot:* **y.-elm,** charme *m*; *(b) Hist:* **to send, pass, an army under the y.,** faire passer une armée sous le joug; *(c)* **the y. of convention, of marriage,** le joug des conventions, du mariage; **to throw off, cast off, the y.,** secouer le joug; s'affranchir du joug; **impatient of, under, the y.,** impatient du joug; *(d) Hist:* mesure agraire équivalente à l'aire qu'on pouvait labourer dans une journée avec une paire de bœufs (20 hectares). **2.** *(a)* (*for carrying two pails*) palanche *f*; *(b) Husb:* carcan *m*, tribart *m* (pour porcs, etc.). **3.** *(a) Anat:* **y. bone,** os *m* malaire; *(b) Dressm:* empiècement *m.* **4.** *(a) Const: etc:* moufle *f*, longrine *f*, moise *f* (d'une charpente); *(b)* mouton *m* (d'une cloche); *(c) Veh:* **pole y.,** support *m* de timon; *(d) El:* culasse *f* (d'aimant, de transformateur); carcasse *f*, bâti *m* (de dynamo); **magnetic y.,** culasse magnétique; **y. stray field,** champ *m* de dispersion de culasse; *(e) Mch:* (*cross head*) joug; *(f) Mec.E:* chape *f* (pour tuyaux); étrier *m* (de fixation); attache *f*; **tie-rod y.,** chape de barre d'accouplement; **driving y.,** chape d'entraînement; **y. pin,** axe *m* de chape; broche *f* d'étrier; *Nau:* **tiller y.,** barre *f* à tire-v(i)eilles; **y. lines,** tire-v(i)eilles *f*; *Av:* **connecting twin y.,** jumelle *f* de liaison; *(g) Cmptr:* **print y.,** bloc *m* d'impression; bloc-tambour *m*, *pl.* blocs-tambours.

yoke[2], *v.tr.* **1.** accoupler (des bœufs); mettre (des bœufs) au joug; atteler (des bœufs) **(to the plough,** à la charrue); unir (deux personnes en mariage); (*with passive force*) **oxen that do not y. well together,** bœufs *m* qui ne vont pas bien ensemble dans un attelage. **2.** mettre un carcan à (un porc, etc.). **3.** suspendre (une cloche) avec un mouton. **4.** accoupler (les pièces d'un appareil).

yoked [joukt], *a.* **1.** sous le joug. **2. well y., ill y.,** (*of oxen*) bien appariés, bien appareillés; mal appariés, mal appareillés; *A:* (*of persons*) bien, mal, assortis.

yokefellow ['joukfelou], **yokemate** ['joukmeit], *s.* **1.** compagnon, *f.* compagne, de travail. **2.** époux, -ouse.

yokel ['jouk(ə)l], *s.* rustre *m*; campagnard *m.*

yoking ['joukiŋ], *s.* *(a)* mise *f* sous le joug; attelage *m*, attellement *m*; *(b)* accouplement *m.*

Yokohama [joukə'hɑːmə], *Pr.n. Geog:* Yokohama; *Husb:* **Y. cock,** phénix *m.*

yoldia ['jɔldiə], *s. Moll:* yoldia *f.*

yolk[1] [jouk], *s.* *(a)* jaune *m* (d'un œuf); *Cu:* **take the y. of an egg, one egg y.,** prenez un jaune d'œuf; *(b) Biol:* vitellus *m*; **formative y.,** vitellus formatif; **nutritive, food, y.,** vitellus nutritif; **y. bag, sac,** membrane vitelline.

yolk[2], *s.* suint *m*; **wool in the y.,** laines *fpl* en suint.

yolkless ['jouklis], *a.* (œuf) nain.

Yom Kippur [jɔmki'puər], *s. Jew.Rel:* Yom-Kippour *m.*

yon [jɔn], *a. & adv. A: & Dial:* = YONDER.

yonder ['jɔndər]. *Lit:* **1.** *adv.* **down y., over y.,** là-bas; **up y.,** là-haut. **2.** *a.* ce . . . -là, *f.* cette . . . -là, *pl.* ces . . . -là; **y. elms,** ces ormes *m* là-bas; ces ormes-là; **look at y. cloud!** regardez ce nuage là-bas!

yoohoo ['juːhuː], *int.* ohé!

yore [jɔːr], *s. A: & Lit:* **of y.,** (d')autrefois; **in days of y.,** au temps jadis; autrefois, anciennement; du temps que Berthe filait; **as of y.,** comme autrefois, comme jadis.

yorker ['jɔːkər], *s. Cr: F:* balle lancée de manière à ce qu'elle rebondisse sur la ligne de camp du batteur.

Yorkist ['jɔːkist], *s. Hist:* partisan, -ane, de la maison d'York.

Yorkshire ['jɔːkʃiər], *Pr.n. Geog:* le comté d'York; *Const:* **Y. stone,** grès *m* du Yorkshire; *Cu:* **Y. pudding,** pâte cuite au-dessous du rôti, dont elle absorbe le jus et la graisse qui s'écoulent; *F: A:* **to put Y. on s.o.,** tromper, duper, qn.

Yorkshireman, *pl.* **-men** ['jɔːkʃiəmən], *s.m.* originaire du comté d'York.

you [ju(ː)], *pers. pron.* (i) *sg. & pl.* vous; (ii) *sg.* (*when addressing relatives, intimate friends, children, animals, deities, often*) tu, te, toi. **1.** (*unstressed*) *(a)* (*nom.*) vous; tu; **y. are very kind,** vous êtes bien aimable(s); tu es bien aimable; **how are y.?** comment allez-vous? comment vas-tu? **there y. are,** vous voilà, te voilà; *Tp:* **are y. there?** allô! **when did y. leave?** quand êtes-vous parti(s)? quand es-tu parti? **y. are all guilty,** vous êtes tous coupables; **y. are all four responsible,** vous êtes responsables tous les quatre; *(b)* (*as object of verb*) vous; te; **I hope to see y. tomorrow,** j'espère vous voir, te voir, demain; **I'll give y. some,** je vous en donnerai; je t'en donnerai; **who saw y.?** qui vous a vu(s)? qui t'a vu? **I told y. so!** je vous, te, l'avais bien dit! *(c)* (*as object of preposition*) vous, toi; **between y. and me,** (i) entre vous et moi, entre toi et moi; (ii) entre nous soit dit; **there's a fine apple for y.!** regardez-moi ça si ce n'est pas une belle pomme! **away with y.!** allez-vous-en! va-t'en! **all of y.,** vous tous; **all four of y. were there,** vous étiez là tous les quatre. **2.** (*stressed*) *(a)* vous; toi; **y. and I will go by train,** vous et moi, nous irons par le train; **I am older than y.,** je suis plus âgé que vous, que toi; **it's y.,** c'est vous, toi; *F:* **it's just not y.,** ce n'est pas ton genre; **it's y. I'm speaking to,** c'est à vous que je parle; **if I were y.,** (si j'étais) à votre place, à ta place; **y. are the master,** c'est vous le maître; **all y. who went in first,** vous tous qui êtes entrés les premiers; **hi! y. there!** eh! dites donc, là-bas! *(b)* (*in the imperative*) **now y. make a speech,** à votre tour de parler; **don't y. be afraid!** n'ayez pas peur! **y. sit down and eat your lunch!** toi, assieds-toi et prends ton déjeuner! **don't y. talk so much!** n'en dis pas tant, toi! **never y. mind!** (i) ça, c'est mon affaire! (ii) ne t'en fais pas; *(c)* (*in apposition*) **y. lawyers, y. Englishmen,** vous autres avocats, vous autres Anglais; **y. English are not like us,** vous autres Anglais, vous ne nous ressemblez pas; **y. idiot (, y.)!** idiot que vous êtes, que tu es! imbécile, va! espèce d'idiot! **y. darling!** chéri(e)! **3.** (*refl.*) *A:* **sit y. down,** asseyez-vous; assieds-toi; **get y. gone,** allez-vous-en. **4.** (*indefinite*) on; **y. never can tell,** on ne sait jamais; **y. cannot predict your fate,** on ne peut prédire son sort; **he is a great orator, but his speeches leave y. cold,** c'est un grand orateur, mais ses discours vous laissent froid; **the joy y. feel when y. meet a friend,** la joie qui vous saisit quand on rencontre un ami; **when y. ask a girl to be your wife,** quand on demande à une jeune fille d'être votre, sa, femme.

you-all ['juːɔːl, jɔːl], *pers.pron.pl. U.S: Dial:* vous (autres).

You-Know-Who [juːnou'huː], (*in lieu of*) *Pr.n.* qui-vous-savez *mf.*

young [jʌŋ]. **1.** *a.* *(a)* jeune; (*of animal*) petit; **younger,** plus jeune; **younger son, younger daughter,** fils cadet, fille cadette; **my younger brother,** mon jeune frère; mon frère cadet; **youngest,** le, la, plus jeune; le cadet, la cadette; **little Louise was our youngest child,** la petite Louise était notre dernière; **he is younger than I,** il est plus jeune, moins âgé, que moi; il est mon cadet; **she is two years younger than I,** elle est plus jeune que moi, elle est ma cadette, de deux ans; **when I was twenty years younger,** quand j'avais vingt ans de moins; **we are only y. once,** jeunesse n'a qu'un temps; **I am not so y. as I was,** je n'ai plus mes jambes de vingt ans; **a not-so-y. woman,** une femme plus très jeune; **man still y.,** homme encore jeune; **y. man,** jeune homme; **y. men,** jeunes gens *m*; **y. lady,** demoiselle *f*; **y. person,** jeune personne *f*; **y. woman,** jeune femme; **when you have a y. family, when your family is y.,** quand on a des petits enfants, des gosses; quand vos enfants sont jeunes; **his y. woman,** sa petite amie; sa fiancée; **y. folk, y. people,** jeunes gens; les jeunes; **y. Mr Smith,** (i) M. Smith fils; (ii) le jeune M. Smith; **Pliny the Younger,** Pline le Jeune; **the younger generation,** la jeune génération; *F:* **you y. monkey,** petit(e) espiègle; *O:* **well, y. 'un,** (i) eh bien, jeune homme; (ii) eh bien, mon petit; **in his younger days,** dans son jeune temps; dans sa jeunesse; **y. nation,** nation jeune; **y. grass,** herbe nouvelle; **y. tree,** arbre adolescent; **lake like a y. sea,** lac grand comme une petite mer, comme une mer en miniature; *(b)* **y. for his years,** jeune pour son âge; qui paraît plus jeune que son âge; qui porte bien son âge; **y. in mind,** jeune d'esprit; **to grow, get, y. again, to grow younger,** rajeunir; **you are looking younger!** comme vous avez rajeuni! *(c) Cards:* **younger hand,** deuxième *m* à jouer (dans les jeux qui se jouent à deux); *(d)* **y. wine,** vin vert; **the night is still y.,** la nuit n'est que peu avancée; **y. moon,** nouvelle lune; *(e)* **y. England,** l'Angleterre *f* d'aujourd'hui; la jeunesse anglaise; *(f)* **information from a younger source,** renseignement fourni par une source plus récente. **2.** *s.pl. inv.* *(a)* les jeunes gens; la jeunesse; **books for the y.,** livres pour la jeunesse; **old and y.,** les grands et les petits; **y. and old,** tout le monde; **the y. and the not so y.,** les jeunes et les moins jeunes; *(b)* **animal and its y.,** animal et ses petits; **mare with y.,** jument pleine; **to bring forth y.,** faire des petits.

youngish ['jʌŋiʃ], *a.* assez jeune; *F:* jeunet, -ette.

youngling ['jʌŋliŋ], *s. A:* jeune homme *m*; jeune fille *f*;

jeune femme *f*; (*animal*) petit, -ite.

youngster ['jʌŋstər], *s.* (*a*) jeune personne *f*, *esp.* jeune homme *m*, garçon *m*; (*b*) petit, -ite; *F:* gosse *mf*; gamin, -ine; môme *mf*; **are the youngsters all right?** est-ce que les petits, les jeunes, vont bien?

younker ['jʌŋkər], *s. A:* **1.** *F:* (*a*) jeune monsieur *m*; (*b*) = YOUNGSTER. **2.** junker *m*.

your [jɔ:r], *poss.a.* **1.** (i) *sg. & pl.* votre, *pl.* vos; (ii) *sg.* (*when addressing relatives, intimate friends, children, deities, often*) ton, *f.* ta, *pl.* tes; **y. house,** votre maison, ta maison; **he lives in y. road,** il habite la même rue que vous; **y. friends,** vos ami(e)s, tes ami(e)s; **y. help,** votre aide *f*, ton aide; **y. father and mother,** votre père et votre mère; (*in official style*) vos père et mère; (*in formal correspondence, etc.*) **y. father, y. mother, y. sister,** monsieur votre père, madame votre mère, mademoiselle votre sœur; **he is y. best friend,** c'est votre meilleur ami; **is it the most recent of y. books, y. most recent book?** c'est votre livre le plus récent? **have you hurt y. hand?** vous vous êtes fait mal à la main? **turn y. head(s),** tournez la tête: *Games: etc:* **y. turn! y. ball!** à vous! **Y. Majesty,** votre Majesté; **Y. Worship,** monsieur le juge, monsieur le maire. **2.** (*indefinite; cf.* YOU 4) son, *f.* sa, *pl.* ses; **you cannot alter y. nature,** on ne peut pas changer son caractère; **on y. right,** à (votre) droite. **3.** (*ethic*) **he isn't one of y. narrow-minded Christians,** ce n'est pas un de vos chrétiens à l'esprit étroit; **y. true reformer cannot discriminate,** le vrai réformateur ne sait pas distinguer.

yours [jɔ:z], *poss.pron.* (i) *sg. & pl.* le vôtre, la vôtre, les vôtres; (ii) *s.* (*when addressing relatives, intimate friends, children, often*) le tien, la tienne; les tiens, les tiennes; (*a*) **here is our place and there is y.,** voici notre place et voilà la vôtre, la tienne; **this is y.,** ceci est à vous, à toi; ceci vous appartient, t'appartient; *F:* **the bathroom's all y.,** la salle de bains est libre maintenant; **it's all y.!** c'est à vous, à toi! *F:* **what's y.?** qu'est-ce que tu veux boire? qu'est-ce que tu prends? **I am entirely y.,** je vous suis tout acquis; *Corr:* **y. (sincerely),** bien amicalement à vous; **the idea is y.,** l'idée *f* est de vous; **y. is a nation of travellers,** vous êtes une nation de voyageurs; **I should like to read something of y.,** je voudrais bien lire quelque chose de vous; **he is a friend of y.,** c'est un de vos amis; c'est un ami à vous; il est de vos amis; **that's no business of y.,** cela ne vous regarde pas; ce n'est pas votre affaire; **that dog of y.,** votre chien; **that pride of y.,** votre orgueil *m*; cet orgueil dont vous ne pouvez vous défaire; *Com:* **y. of the 16th inst.,** votre estimée, votre honorée, du seize de ce mois; (*b*) (*your kindred*) **you and y.,** vous et les vôtres; toi et les tiens.

yourself [jɔ:'self], *pl.* **yourselves** [jɔ:'selvz], *pers.pron.* (*a*) (*emphatic*) (i) *sg. & pl.* vous, vous-même(s); (ii) (*when addressing relatives, intimate friends, children, deities, often*) toi(-même); **you could do it y.,** vous pourriez le faire vous-même, tu pourrais le faire toi-même; *F:* **you don't look quite y.,** vous avez, tu as, l'air mal en train; (*b*) *refl.* (i) vous; (ii) te; **are you enjoying y., yourselves?** vous amusez-vous? **have you hurt y.?** vous êtes-vous fait mal? **you ought to get y. a car,** tu devrais t'acheter une voiture; *F:* **have y. a good time,** amuse-toi bien; (*c*) (*after preposition*) **see for y., yourselves,** voyez vous-même(s); **speak for y.,** cela vous plaît à dire; **we're all going then?—speak for y.!** nous y allons donc, tous?—parle pour toi! vas-y si tu veux! **keep it for y.,** garde-le pour toi(-même), gardez-le pour vous(-même); **here's sth. for y.,** voilà pour vous; **what do you do with y. all day?** à quoi vous occupez-vous toute la journée? **do you live by y.?** vous vivez (tout) seul? (*reciprocal*) **among yourselves,** entre vous; (*d*) (*used impersonally*) soi(-même); (*refl.*) se; **you have to do it y.,** il faut le faire soi-même; **you can't take y. too seriously,** il ne faut pas se prendre trop au sérieux.

yourt ['ju:ət], *s.* iourte *f*, yourte *f*.

yous(e) [ju:z], *pers. pron. pl. U.S: & Dial: P:* vous; **he'll settle y., y. guys,** il vous fera votre affaire, à vous autres.

youth [ju:θ, *pl.* ju:ðz], *s.* **1.** jeunesse *f*, adolescence *f*, jeune âge *m*; **the days of y.,** le bel âge; **in his early y.,** dans sa première jeunesse; **she is not in the first blush of y., she is past her first y.,** elle n'est pas de la première jeunesse; elle n'est pas si jeune; **from y. upwards he showed talent,** dès sa jeunesse, il a fait preuve de talent; **mind which has kept its y.,** esprit qui est resté jeune; *Myth:* **the fountain of Y.,** la Fontaine de Jouvence; *Prov:* **y. will have its way, will have its fling,** il faut que jeunesse se passe. **2.** jeune homme, adolescent *m*. **3.** *coll.* jeunes gens *m*; jeunesse (du village, etc.).

youthful ['ju:θful], *a.* **1.** (*of pers., face, etc.*) jeune; **y. hat,** chapeau coiffant jeune; chapeau rajeunissant; **to look y.,** avoir l'air jeune; avoir un air de jeunesse. **2.** (erreur, enthousiasme) de jeunesse. **3.** *Geol:* **y. stage,** jeunesse *f* (d'un cycle d'érosion).

youthfully ['ju:θfuli], *adv.* en jeune homme, en jeune fille; comme un jeune homme, comme une jeune fille.

youthfulness ['ju:θfulnis], *s.* jeunesse *f*; juvénilité *f*; air *m* de jeunesse; air jeune, juvénile.

yowl¹ [jaul], *s.* hurlement *m* (de chien); miaulement *m* (de chat).

yowl², *v.i.* (*of dog*) hurler; (*of cat*) miauler.

yo-yo ['joujou], *s. Toys: R.t.m.* yo-yo *m*; **to play with a yo-yo,** yoyoter.

yperite ['i:pərait], *s. Ch: Mil:* ypérite *f*.

Yponomeutidae [ipɔnou'mju:tidi:], *s.pl. Ent:* yponomeutidés *m*.

ytterbium [i'tə:biəm], *s. Ch:* ytterbium *m*; **y. oxide,** ytterbine *f*.

yttria ['itriə], *s. Ch: Miner:* yttria *m*.

yttrialite ['itriəlait], *s. Miner:* yttrialite *f*.

yttric ['itrik], *a. Ch:* yttrique.

yttriferous [i'trifərəs], *a. Miner:* yttrifère.

yttrium ['itriəm], *s. Ch:* yttrium *m*; **the y. group,** le groupe yttrique.

yttrocerite [i'trɔsərait], *s. Ch:* yttrocérite *f*; yttrocalcite *f*.

yttrocolumbite [itrou'kələmbait], *s. Miner:* yttrocolumbite *f*.

yttrocrasite [itrou'kreisait], *s. Miner:* yttrocrasite *f*.

yttrofluorite [itrou'flu:ərait], *s. Miner:* yttrofluorite *f*.

Yucatec ['jʌkətek]. *Geog:* (*a*) *a.* yucatèque; (*b*) *s.* Yucatèque *mf*.

Yucatecan [jʌkə'tekən], *a. Geog:* yucatèque.

yucca ['jʌkə], *s. Bot:* yucca *m*; *Ent:* **y. moth,** papillon *m* du yucca.

yuck [jʌk], *int. F:* pouah!

yucky ['jʌki], *a. F:* dégueulasse.

Yugoslav ['ju:gousla:v]. *Geog:* **1.** *a.* yougoslave. **2.** *s.* Yougoslave *mf*.

Yugoslavia [ju:gou'sla:viə], *Pr.n. Geog:* Yougoslavie *f*.

Yugoslavian [ju:gou'sla:viən], *a.* yougoslave.

Yukon ['ju:kɔn], *Pr.n. Geog:* le Youkon.

yule [ju:l], *s.* (*a*) *A:* Noël *m*; (*b*) **y. log,** bûche *f* de Noël.

yuletide ['ju:ltaid], *s. A:* l'époque *f* de Noël; les fêtes *f* de Noël.

yummy ['jʌmi], *a. F:* délicieux.

yum-yum [jʌm'jʌm], *int. F:* miam-miam!

yup [jup], *adv. U.S: P:* oui.

yurt ['ju:ət], *s.* iourte *f*, yourte *f*.

Ywain [i'wein], *Pr.n.m. Lit:* Gauvain.

Z

Z, z, *pl.* **zs, z's** [zed, *U.S:* ziː, *pl.* zedz, ziːz], *s.* (la lettre) Z, z *m*; *Tp:* **Z for zebra,** Z comme Zoé; *Mec.E:* **Z bar,** barre *f*, fer *m*, en Z.

zabaglione [zæbæl'jouni], *s. Cu:* sabayon *m.*

zabrus ['zæbrəs], *s. Ent:* zabre *m.*

Zacchaeus [zæ'kiːəs], *Pr.n.m. B.Hist:* Zachée.

Zachariah [zækə'raiə], *Pr.n.m. B.Hist:* ((i) le prophète, (ii) le prêtre) Zacharie.

Zacharias [zækə'raiəs], *Pr.n.m.* Zacharie.

Zachary ['zækəri], *Pr.n.m. Ecc.Hist:* (le pape) Zacharie.

zaffer, zaffre ['zæfər], *s. Ch: Cer:* safre *m*; oxyde bleu de cobalt.

Zaire [zɑː'iər], *Pr.n. Geog:* Zaïre *m.*

Zairean [zɑː'iəriən]. **1.** *a.* zaïrois. **2.** Zaïrois, -oise.

Zalophus [zə'loufəs], *s. Z:* zalophe *m.*

Zambezi (the) [ðəzæm'biːzi], *Pr.n. Geog:* le Zambèze.

Zambia ['zæmbiə], *Pr.n. Geog:* Zambie *f.*

zambo ['zæmbou], *s. Ethn:* zambo *m*; métis, -isse.

zamenis ['zæminis], *s. Rept:* zamenis *m.*

zamia ['zeimiə], *s. Bot:* zamia *m*; **z. tree,** zamier *m.*

zamindar [zæ'mindɑːr], *s. Hist:* (*India*) zémindar *m.*

zanclus ['zæŋkləs], *s. Ich:* zancle *m*; tranchoir *m.*

zanily ['zeinili], *adv. F:* d'une manière loufoque.

zaniness ['zeininis], *s. F:* loufoquerie *f.*

zannichellia [zæni'keliə], *s. Bot:* zannichellia *m*, zannichellie *f.*

zantedeschia [zænti'deskiə], *s. Bot:* zantedeschia *m.*

zany ['zeini]. **1.** *s. A.Th:* zan(n)i *m*, bouffon *m.* **2.** *s. F:* sot, *f.* sotte; niais, -aise; nigaud, -aude. **3.** *a. F:* loufoque.

zap [zæp], *v.tr.* **(zapped)** *P:* descendre, flinguer (qn).

zapatero [zæpə'tɛərou], *s. Bot:* zapatero *m.*

zaphrentid [zæ'frentid], *s. Paleont:* zaphrentis *m.*

Zaphrentis [zæ'frentis], *s. Paleont:* zaphrentis *m.*

Zapodidae [zæ'pɔdidiː], *s.pl. Z:* zapodidés *m.*

Zapotec ['zæpoutek]. *Geog:* **1.** *a.* zapotèque. **2.** *s.* Zapotèque *mf.*

zapus ['zæpəs], *s. Z:* zapode *m*, zapus *m.*

Zarathustrian [zærə'θustriən], *a. & s.* zoroastrien, -ienne.

zaratite ['zærətait], *s. Miner:* zaratite *f.*

zareba, zariba [zə'riːbə], *s.* (*in N.Africa*) clôture (fortifiée de ronces); camp *m* de fortune.

zax [zæks], *s.* hache *f* d'ouvrage (de couvreur).

zeal [ziːl], *s.* zèle *m*, ardeur *f*; **misguided z.,** faux zèle; **religious z.,** zèle, ferveur *f*; **to make a show of z.,** faire du zèle; **full of z. for sth.,** plein de zèle, plein d'ardeur, pour qch.

Zealand ['ziːlənd], *Pr.n. Geog:* **1.** Zélande *f.* **2.** (l'île *f* de) Seeland.

Zealander ['ziːləndər], *s. Geog:* Zélandais, -aise.

zealot ['zelət], *s.* **1.** *B. Hist:* zélateur, -trice; zélote *m.* **2.** fanatique *mf*, zélateur (**for,** de).

zealotism ['zelətizm], **zealotry** ['zelətri], *s.* **1.** *Hist:* zélotisme *m.* **2.** fanatisme *m*, ferveur *f.*

zealous ['zeləs], *a.* zélé; zélateur, -trice; ardent, enthousiaste; empressé; **to be z. in doing sth.,** montrer du zèle à faire qch.; **z. for sth.,** plein de zèle pour qch.

zealously ['zeləsli], *adv.* avec zèle; ardemment; avec ferveur.

Zebedee ['zebədiː], *Pr.n.m. B.Hist:* Zébédée.

zebra ['ziːbrə, 'zebrə], *s.* **1.** *Z:* zèbre *m*; **Burchell's z.,** da(u)w *m*; **z. wolf,** thylacine zébré; **striped like a z.,** zébré; **z. markings,** zébrure *f.* **2.** *U.S:* (*a*) **z. suit,** costume *m* de forçat; (*b*) forçat *m.* **3. z. crossing,** passage *m* pour piétons.

zebrawood ['ziːbrəwud, 'zeb-], *s.* (arbre *m* au) bois zébré, *esp.* zingana *m.*

zebroid ['ziːbrɔid, 'zeb-], **zebrula** ['ziːbruːlə, 'zeb-], **zebrule** ['ziːbruːl, 'zeb-], *s. Z:* zébrule *m.*

zebu ['ziːb(j)uː], *s.* zébu *m*; bœuf *m* à bosse; taureau *m* des Indes.

Zebulon, Zebulun ['zeibjulən], *Pr.n.m. B.Hist:* Zabulon.

Zechariah [zekə'raiə], *Pr.n. B.Hist:* ((i) le prophète, (ii) le prêtre) Zacharie.

zed [zed], *s.* (la lettre) z *m.*

Zedekiah [zedi'kaiə], *Pr.n.m. B.Hist:* Sédécias.

zedoary ['zedouəri], *s. Bot: A.Pharm:* zédoaire *f*; **long z., round z.,** zédoaire longue, ronde.

zee [ziː], *s. U.S:* (la lettre) z *m.*

Zeeland ['ziːlənd], *Pr.n. Geog:* Zélande *f.*

Zeidae ['ziːidiː], *s.pl. Ich:* zéidés *m.*

zein ['ziːin], *s. Ch:* zéine *f.*

zemindar [ze'miːndɑːr], *s.* (*India*) zémindar *m.*

zemmi ['zemi], *s. Z:* zemmi *m.*

Zen [zen], *s. Rel:* **Z. (Buddhism),** (bouddhisme) zen *m.*

zenaida [ze'neidə, ze'naidə], *s. Orn:* zénaïde *f.*

zenana [ze'nɑːnə], *s.* (*India*) zénana *m*, harem *m*; *Tex:* **z. cloth,** zénana.

Zend [zend], *a. & s. Ling:* zend (*m*); **the Z. Avesta,** le Zend-Avesta.

zenith ['zeniθ], *s. Astr:* zénith *m*; **z. distance,** distance zénithale; **at the z. of his fame,** à l'apogée, au sommet, au zénith, de sa gloire; **at his z.,** à son zénith; **the z. of his influence, of his power,** le plus haut période de son influence, le point culminant de sa puissance.

zenithal ['zeniθ(ə)l], *a.* zénithal, -aux.

Zeno ['siːnou], *Pr.n.m. Gr.Phil:* Zénon.

Zenobia [ze'noubiə], *Pr.n.f. A.Hist:* Zénobie.

Zenonian [ze'nouniən], **Zenonic** [ze'nɔnik]. *Gr.Phil:* **1.** *a.* (doctrine, etc.) zénonique. **2.** *s.* zénoniste *m.*

Zenonism ['zenənizm], *s.* zénonisme *m.*

zeolite ['ziːoulait], *s. Miner:* zéolit(h)e *f.*

zeolitic [ziːou'litik], *a. Miner:* zéolit(h)ique.

zeolitization [zioulitai'zeiʃ(ə)n], *s. Geol:* zéolitisation *f.*

zeoscope ['ziːəskoup], *s. Ph:* zéoscope *m.*

Zephaniah [zefə'naiə], *Pr.n.m. B.Lit:* Sophonie.

zephyr ['zefər], *s.* **1.** *Lit:* zéphyr *m*; ((i) vent *m* de l'ouest, (ii) vent doux). **2.** (*a*) *a. & s.* tissu zéphyr (*a. inv*); le zéphyr. (*b*) *Sp:* maillot *m* (de canotage, etc.).

zephyranthes [zefi'rænθiːz], *s. Bot:* zephyrantes *m.*

Zephyrus ['zefirəs], *s. Myth:* Zéphire *m*, Zéphyre *m.*

zeppelin ['zepəlin], *s. Aer:* zeppelin *m.*

zeriba [zə'riːbə], *s.* = ZAREBA.

zero[1] ['ziərou], *s.* **1.** *Mth:* zéro *m*; **z. point two (0.2),** zéro virgule deux (0,2); **power z.,** puissance *f* zéro; **the terms in** *x* **reduce to z.,** les termes en *x* s'annulent; **z. hour,** l'heure H; *Cmptr:* **z. fill,** remplissage *m* avec des zéros; **z. suppression,** suppression *f* des zéros; *F:* (*pers.*) **a z.,** un zéro (en chiffre). **2.** (*a*) **z. (point),** (point *m*) origine *f*, zéro (d'une échelle graduée, etc.); **determination of the z. point,** zérotage *m*; **z. adjustment,** réglage *m* du zéro; **z. drift,** déplacement *m*, glissement *m*, du zéro (d'un instrument); **z. resetting,** remise *f* à zéro; *Mth:* **z. on the time co-ordinate (of a graph),** origine du temps; **the thermometer is at z., below z.,** le thermomètre est à zéro, au-dessous de zéro; *Adm:* **z. rating,** imposition nulle; **books are z. rated** = la TVA sur les livres est de 0%; **his courage fell to z.,** son courage est tombé à zéro; **exports are down to z.,** les exportations sont tombées à zéro, à néant; (*b*) *Surv:* **z. altitude,** altitude zéro, nulle; niveau *m* de la mer; *Ph:* **z. energy,** énergie nulle; *El:* **z. bias,** polarisation nulle; **z.-loss circuit,** circuit *m* sans pertes; *Mec:* **z. allowance,** tolérance nulle; **z. line,** axe *m* neutre (des tensions); **z. tension,** tension nulle; *Av:* **z. lift,** portance nulle; *Meteor:* **z.-z. fog,** brouillard *m* avec plafond et visibilité nuls.

zero[2]. **1.** *v.tr.* (*a*) déterminer le zéro (d'un instrument, etc.); (*b*) (re)mettre (un instrument, etc.) à zéro. **2. zero in,** *v.tr.* (*a*) *Artil: U.S:* régler la hausse (d'une pièce); (*b*) *Artil: U.S:* régler le tir (d'une pièce) **(on a target,** sur un objectif); (*c*) *Mec.E:* synchroniser. **3. zero in,** *v.i.* (*a*) *Artil:* **to z. in on sth.,** régler le tir sur qch.; (*b*) *Av:* amener l'avion dans la position voulue pour lui faire effectuer une manœuvre; (*c*) *Fig:* se diriger (**on sth.,** vers qch.).

zeroize [ziərouaiz], *v.i. Cmptr:* mettre des zéros, mettre à zéro.

zerovalent [ziərou'veilənt], *a. Ch:* nullivalent.

Zerubbabel [zə'rʌbəb(ə)l], *Pr.n.m. B.Hist:* Zorobabel.

Zervanite ['zəːvənait], *s. Rel:* zervanite *mf.*

zest [zest], *s.* **1.** (*a*) enthousiasme *m*, entrain *m*; délectation *f*, plaisir *m*; verve *f*; **to fight with z.,** combattre avec élan, avec entrain; **to eat with z.,** manger avec appétit, de bon appétit; **without z.,** sans entrain; avec tiédeur; (*b*) saveur *f*, goût *m*; **story that lacks z.,** conte *m* qui manque de saveur; **to add z. to the adventure,** donner du piquant à l'aventure. **2.** zeste *m* (d'orange, de citron).

zestful ['zestful], *a.* plein d'enthousiasme, de verve.

zeta ['ziːtə], *s. Gr.Alph:* (d)zéta *m.*

zetetic [ze'tetik]. *Phil:* **1.** *a. & s.* zététique (*mf*). **2.** *s.pl.* *usu. with sg. const.* **zetetics,** zététique *f.*

zeuglodon(t) ['zjuːgloudɔn(t)], *s. Paleont:* zeuglodon *m.*

Zeuglodontia [zjuːglou'dɔntiə], *s.pl. Paleont:* zeuglodontidés *m.*

zeugma ['zjuːgmə], *s. Gram: Rh:* zeugme *m*, zeugma *m.*

zeugmatic [zjuːg'mætik], *a. Gram: Rh:* (phrase etc.) qui contient un zeugma.

zeunerite ['zjuːnərait], *s. Miner:* zeunérite *f.*

Zeus [zjuːs]. **1.** *Pr.n.m. Myth:* Zeus. **2.** *s. Ich:* zée *m*; zeus *m.*

zeuzera [zuː'zerə], *s. Ent:* zeuzère *f.*

zibel(l)ine ['zibəliːn, -ain], *s.* zibeline *f.*

zibet(h) ['zibit], *s. Z:* civette *f*, zibeth *m* (d'Asie ou des Indes).

ziff [zif], *s. P: Austr:* barbe *f.*

ziggurat ['zigəræt], *s. Archeol:* ziggourat *f.*

zigotene ['zigoutiːn], *s. Biol:* stade *m* zigotène.

zigzag[1] ['zigzæg]. **1.** *s.* zigzag *m*; **in zigzags,** en zigzag; **to move in zigzags,** faire des zigzags; **z. road, path,** chemin, sentier, en lacets, en zigzag; *Nau:* **to steer a z. course,** faire route en zigzag, en zigzagant; faire des zigzags; *Arch:* **z. moulding(s),** bâtons rompus; *Metalw:* **z. riveting,** rivetage *m* en quinconce; *Mil:* **z. trenches,** tranchées *f* en zigzag. **2.** *adv.* **the road runs z.,** le chemin fait des zigzags.

zigzag[2], v. (**zigzagged**) 1. v.i. zigzaguer; faire des zigzags; avancer en zigzagant; Nau: zigzaguer; faire route en zigzag, en zigzagant; faire des zigzags. 2. v.tr. (a) disposer (des obstacles, etc.) en zigzag; disposer (des rivets) en quinconce; (b) traverser (une plaine, etc.) en zigzag.

zigzagging ['zigzægiŋ], s. zigzags mpl; marche serpentine; lacets mpl; tournées f et virées f.

zilch [ziltʃ], s. esp. NAm: F: zéro m; rien de rien.

zillion ['ziliən], s. U.S: F: des millions m (et des millions).

Zimbabwe [zim'bɑ:bwi], Pr.n. Geog: **Z.-Rhodesia,** Zimbabwe-Rhodésie m.

zinc[1] [ziŋk], s. 1. zinc m; **z.(-)bearing,** zincifère; Miner: **red z. ore, red oxide of z.,** zincite f; **crude z.,** zinc brut; **z. alkyl,** zinc-alcoyle m; **z. diethyl,** zinc-éthyle m; **z. dimethyl,** zinc-méthyle m; **z. sulphide,** sulphure m de zinc; **z. oxide,** Paint: **z. white,** oxyde m de zinc, blanc m de zinc; **z. powder,** poussière f de zinc; Metall: **z. dust,** fleurs fpl de zinc; **sublimated oxide of z.,** cadmie f des fourneaux; Pharm: **z. ointment,** pommade f à l'oxyde de zinc; **z. works, trade,** zinguerie f; **z. plate,** zinc en feuilles; **z. coating,** zingage m. 2. Phot: Engr: **z. engraving, etching,** zincogravure f.

zinc[2], v.tr. (**zin(c)ked**) zinguer; (i) couvrir (un toit, etc.) de zinc; (ii) galvaniser (le fer, etc.).

zincaluminite [ziŋkə'lju:minait], s. Miner: zincaluminite f.

zincate ['ziŋkeit], s. Ch: zincate m.

zincblende ['ziŋkblend], s. Miner: blende f, sphalérite f.

zincic ['ziŋkik], a. Ch: zincique.

zinciferous, zin(c)kiferous [ziŋ'kifərəs], a. zincifère.

zincite ['ziŋkait], s. Miner: zincite f.

zinckenite ['ziŋkənait], s. Miner: zinckénite f.

zinc(k)ing ['ziŋkiŋ], s. zingage m, zincage m; étamage m au zinc.

zincograph[1] ['ziŋkougræf], s. Phot.Engr: zincogravure f; gravure f sur zinc.

zincograph[2], v.tr. zincographier.

zincographer [ziŋ'kɔgrəfər], s. zincographe m, zincograveur m.

zincography [ziŋ'kɔgrəfi], s. Phot.Engr: zincographie f, zincogravure f, photogravure f sur zinc; **to reproduce by z.,** zincographier (un dessin, etc.).

zincosite ['ziŋkousait], s. Miner: zincosite f.

zincotype ['ziŋkoutaip], s. Phot.Engr: zincogravure f.

zincware ['ziŋkwɛər], s. Com: zinguerie f.

zing [ziŋ], s. F: vitalité f, entrain m.

zingana [ziŋ'gɑ:nə], s. Bot: zingana m.

Zingiberaceae [zindʒibə'reisii:], s.pl. Bot: zingibéracées f.

zingiberene [zin'dʒibəri:n], s. Ch: zingibérène m.

zinjanthropus [zin'dʒænθrəpəs], s. Prehist: zinjanthrope m.

zinking ['ziŋkiŋ], s. = ZINCING.

zinnia ['ziniə], s. Bot: zinnia m.

zinnwaldite ['zinwɔ:ldait], s. Miner: zinnwaldite f.

Zion ['zaiən]. 1. Pr.n.m. Sion ((i) la colline; (ii) Jérusalem; (iii) l'Église). 2. s. O: (often Pej:) chapelle f, temple m (non-conformiste).

Zionism ['zaiənizm], s. Pol: sionisme m.

Zionist ['zaiənist], a. & s. Pol: sioniste (mf).

zip[1] [zip], s. 1. (a) sifflement m (d'une balle); (b) bruit m de déchirure; crissement m. 2. F: énergie f, vitesse f; **put some z. into it!** mets-y du nerf! 3. **z. (fastener, fastening),** fermeture f éclair inv (R.t.m.), fermeture à glissière, à curseur, à crémaillère; Belg: tirette f.

zip[2] (**zipped**) 1. v.i. siffler (comme une balle); (of car, etc.) **to z. past,** passer comme un éclair. 2. v.i. crisser. 3. v.tr. **to z. in a lining,** attacher une doublure par moyen d'une fermeture à glissière; F: **z. me up,** agrafe ma robe.

zip[3], s. U.S: **z. code,** code postal.

Ziphiinae [zi'fi:ini:], s.pl. Z: ziphiinés m.

zippeite ['zipiait], s. Miner: zippéite f.

zipper ['zipər], s. F: = **zip (fastener); z. bag,** (sac m) fourre-tout m inv à fermeture éclair.

zippy ['zipi], a. F: plein d'énergie; plein d'entrain, d'allant; **look z.!** grouille-toi!

zircon ['zə:kɔn], s. Miner: zircon m.

zirconate ['zə:kəneit], s. Ch: zirconate m.

zirconia [zə:'kouniə], s. Ch: Ind: zircone f.

zirconic [zə:'kɔnik], a. Ch: zirconique.

zirconifluoride [zə:kɔni'flju:əraid], s. Ch: zirconifluorure m.

zirconite ['zə:kənait], s. Miner: zirconite f.

zirconium [zə:'kouniəm], s. Ch: zirconium m.

zirconyl ['zə:kounil], s. Ch: zirconyle m.

zither ['ziðər], A: **zithern** ['ziðən], s. Mus: cithare f.

zitherist ['ziðərist], s. cithariste mf.

zithum ['zaiθəm], s. Ant: zython m, zythum m.

zizania [zi'zeiniə], s. Bot: zizanie f; riz m du Canada.

ziziphus ['zizifəs], s. Bot: ziziphus m.

zloty ['zlɔti], s. Num: zloty m (de Pologne).

Zoantharia [zouæn'θεəriə], s.pl. Coel: zoanthaires m.

zoantharian [zouæ'θεəriən], a. & s. Coel: zoanthaire (m).

Zoanthidae [zou'ænθidi:], s.pl. Coel: zoanthides m.

zoanthodeme [zou'ænθoudi:m], s. Coel: zoanthodème m.

zoanthropy [zou'ænθrəpi], s. zoanthropie f.

Zoarces [zou'ɑ:si:z], s. Ich: zoarcès m.

zodiac ['zoudiæk], s. Astr: zodiaque m; **the signs of the z.,** les signes m du zodiaque.

zodiacal [zou'daiək(ə)l], a. zodiacal, -aux; **z. light,** lumière zodiacale.

Zoe ['zoui], Pr.n.f. Zoé.

zoea [zou'i:ə], s. Crust: zoé f.

zoetrope ['zouitroup], s. Toys: A: zootrope m.

zoic ['zouik], a. zoïque.

Zoilus ['zouiləs], Pr.n.m. Gr.Lit: Zoïle.

zoisite ['zɔisait], s. Miner: zoïsite f.

zokor ['zɔkɔ:r], s. Z: myospalax m.

zombi(e) ['zɔmbi], s. 1. Rel: (a) dieu m python; (b) zombi m; (c) esprit m qui ranime un zombi. 2. F: crétin, -ine; imbécile mf.

zona ['zounə], s. Med: zona m.

zonal ['zoun(ə)l], a. zonal, -aux; Cryst: zonaire; Meteor: **z. climate,** climat zonal.

zonality [zou'næliti], s. Geog: zonalité f.

zonaria [zou'nεəriə], s. Algae: zonaire f.

zonate ['zouneit], a. Bot: Z. Miner: zoné.

zonation [zou'neiʃ(ə)n], s. zonage m; distribution f, formation f, par zones.

zone[1] [zoun], s. 1. A: & Poet: ceinture f. 2. zone f; (a) Mth: **spherical z.,** zone sphérique; (b) Miner: **zones of crystal, of onyx,** zones du cristal, de l'onyx; **z. axis,** axe zonal; Bot: **annual z. (of tree),** anneau annuel; (c) Geog: **tropical z.,** zone tropicale; **time z.,** fuseau m horaire; **z. time,** l'heure f du fuseau; (coastal waters) **splash z.,** zone subterrestre, niveau m des balanes blanches; **Fuchs z.,** niveau des goémons jaunes; **thongweed z., low-tide z.,** niveau des algues en lanières; (d) Adm: **no parking z.,** zone d'interdiction de stationner; **parking meter z.,** A: **pink z.** = zone bleue; U.S: **slow-drive z.,** zone à vitesse limitée; **postal delivery z.,** zone de livraison postale; **monetary z.,** zone monétaire; **frontier z.,** zone frontière; (e) Mil: **battle z., z. of the front,** zone de l'avant; **z. fire,** tir m sur zone; **z. of fire,** zone à battre, à tenir sous le feu; **z. of the interior,** zone de l'intérieur; **z. of operations,** zone des armées; **the non-operational z.,** l'arrière f, les arrières; **danger z.,** zone dangereuse; (f) Ac: **z. of silence,** zone de silence; W.Tel: **skip z.,** zone de silence radio; (g) Atom.Ph: **radiation z.,** zone d'irradiation; **radiation danger z.,** zone de rayonnement dangereux; (h) Cmptr: (i) groupe m de caractères; (ii) partie f hors texte (d'une carte perforée); **z. punch,** perforation f hors texte; **z. punching,** perforation en hors texte.

zone[2], v.tr. répartir (une ville, etc.) en zones.

zoned [zound], a. 1. Town P: réparti, découpé, en zones. 2. Bot: Z: Miner: zoné; (albâtre, etc.) zonaire; Arb: **broad-z., fine-z., tree,** arbre à couches épaisses, minces.

zoning ['zouniŋ], s. répartition f en zones; Town P: zonage m, zoning m.

Zonitidae [zou'nitidi:], s.pl. Moll: zonitidés m.

zonula ['zounjulə], **zonule** ['zounju:l], s. Anat: **z. of Zinn,** zonule f.

zonular ['zounjulər], a. Anat: zonulaire.

zonure ['zounjuər], s. Rept: zonure m.

Zonuridae [zoun'juəridi:], s.pl. Rept: zonuridés m.

zoo [zu:], s. jardin m zoologique, F: zoo m; **open-air z.,** parc m zoologique; F: **this house is a perfect z.,** c'est une vraie ménagerie que cette maison.

zoo- ['zouə, zou'ɔ], comb.fm. zoo-.

zoobiological [zouəbaiə'lɔdʒik(ə)l], a. zoobiologique.

zoobiology [zouəbai'ɔlədʒi], s. zoobiologie f.

zoocecidium, pl. **-ia** [zouəsi'sidiəm, -iə], s. Bot: zoocécidie f.

zoochemical [zouə'kemik(ə)l], a. zoochimique.

zoochemistry [zouə'kemistri], s. zoochimie f.

zoochlorella, pl. **-ae** [zouəklə'relə, -i:], s. Algae: zoochlorelle f.

zoochore ['zouəkɔ:r], s. Bot: zoochore f.

zooerasty [zouə'eræsti], s. Psy: zoophilie f érotique.

zooflagellate [zouə'flædʒəleit], s. Nat.Hist: zooflagellé m.

zoogenic [zouə'dʒenik], a. Paleont: Geol: zoogénique, zoogène.

zoogeny [zou'ɔdʒəni], s. zoogénie f.

zoogeographer [zouədʒi'ɔgrəfər], s. zoogéographe mf.

zoogeography [zouədʒi'ɔgrəfi], s. zoogéographie f.

zoogloea [zouə'gli:ə], s. Biol: zooglée f.

zoographer [zou'ɔgrəfər], s. zoographe mf.

zoographic(al) [zouə'græfik(l)], a. zoographique.

zoography [zou'ɔgrəfi], s. zoographie f.

zooid ['zouɔid], a. & s. zooïde (m).

zooidal [zou'ɔid(ə)l], a. zooïde.

zoolator [zou'ɔlətər], s. zoolâtre mf.

zoolatrous [zou'ɔlətrəs], a. zoolâtre.

zoolatry [zou'ɔlətri], s. zoolâtrie f.

zoolite ['zouəlait], s. Paleont: zoolit(h)e m.

zoological [zouə'lɔdʒik(ə)l, zu:ə'lɔdʒik(ə)l], a. zoologique; **z. garden(s),** jardin m zoologique.

zoologically [zouə'lɔdʒik(ə)li, zu:ə-], adv. zoologiquement.

zoologist [zou'ɔlədʒist, zu:-], s. zoologiste m.

zoology [zou'ɔlədʒi, zu:-], s. zoologie f; **descriptive z.,** zoographie f.

zoom[1] [zu:m], s. 1. bourdonnement m; vrombissement m. 2. Av: (montée f en) chandelle f. 3. Cin: changement m rapide de plan, F: zoom m, zoum m; **z. lens,** objectif m à (distance) focale variable, à foyer variable; zoom.

zoom[2], v.i. 1. bourdonner; vrombir; **the cars are zooming along the road,** les voitures vrombissent sur la route; F: **to z. up,** arriver en trombe. 2. Av: F: monter en chandelle. 3. Cin: **to z. in, on,** changer de plan.

zoomagnetism [zouə'mægnətizm], s. zoomagnétisme m.

zoomancy ['zouəmænsi], s. zoomancie f.

zoometric [zouə'metrik], a. zoométrique.

zoometry [zou'ɔmətri], s. zoométrie f.

zoomorphic [zouə'mɔ:fik], a. Biol: zoomorph(iqu)e.

zoomorphism [zouə'mɔ:fizm], s. Biol: zoomorphisme m.

zoomorphy ['zouəmɔ:fi], s. Biol: zoomorphie f.

zoonomy [zou'ɔnəmi], s. Biol: zoonomie f.

zoonosis [zouə'nousis], s. Biol: zoonose f.

zooparasite [zouə'pærəsait], s. zooparasite m.

zoopathology [zouəpə'θɔlədʒi], s. zoopathologie f.

Zoophaga [zou'ɔfəgə], s.pl. Biol: zoophages m.

zoophagan [zou'ɔfəgən], a. & s. Biol: zoophage (m).

zoophagous [zou'ɔfəgəs], a. zoophage.

zoophilia [zouə'filiə], s. zoophilie f.

zoophilous [zou'ɔfiləs], a. zoophile.

zoophobia [zouə'foubiə], s. Psy: zoophobie f.

zoophorus [zou'ɔfərəs], s. Gr.Ant: zoophore m.

Zoophyta [zouə'faitə], s.pl. Biol: les zoophytes m.

zoophytal [zouə'fait(ə)l], **zoophytic(al)** [zouə'fitik(ə)l], a. zoophytique.

zoophyte ['zouəfait], s. Biol: zoophyte m.

zoophytology [zouəfit'ɔlədʒi], s. zoophytologie f.

zooplankton [zouə'plæŋktən], s. Biol: zooplancton m.

zoopsia [zou'ɔpsiə], s. Med: zoopsie f.

zoosperm ['zouəspə:m], s. Physiol: zoosperme m, spermatozoïde m.

zoosporange ['zouəspɔ:rændʒ], **zooporangium** [zouəspɔ:'rændʒiəm], s. Bot: zoosporange m.

zoospore ['zouəspɔ:r], s. Biol: zoospore f.

zoosporic [zouə'spɔrik], **zoosporous** [zouə'spɔ:'rəs], a. Biol: zoosporé.

zootaxy ['zouətæksi], s. zootaxie f.

zootechnic(al) [zouə'teknik(l)], a. zootechnique.

zootechnician [zouətek'niʃ(ə)n], s. zootechnicien, -ienne.

zootechny [zouə'tekni], s. zootechnie f.

zootherapy [zouə'θerəpi], s. zoothérapie f.

zootomic(al) [zouə'tɔmik(l)], a. zootomique.

zootomist [zou'ɔtəmist], s. zootomiste mf.

zootomy [zou'ɔtəmi], s. zootomie f.

zootrope ['zouətroup], s. Toys: zootrope m.

zoot suit ['zu:tsu:t], s. U.S: F: costume m zazou.

zoot-suiter ['zu:tsu:tər], s. U.S: F: = zazou m.

Zooxanthellae [zouək'sænθeli:], s.pl. Algae: zooxanthelles f.

Zoraptera [zɔ'ræptərə], s.pl. Ent: zoraptères m.

zoril ['zɔril], **zorillo** [zɔ'ri:jou], s. Z: zorilla f, zorille f; **z. fur,** zorrino m.

Zoroaster [zɔrou'æstər], Pr.n.m. Rel.H: Zoroastre.

Zoroastrian [zɔrou'æstriən], a. & s. zoroastrien, -ienne.

Zoroastrianism [zɔrou'æstriənizm], s. zoroastrisme m.

zostera ['zɔstərə], s. Bot: zostère f.

Zosteropidae [zɔstə'rɔpidi:], s.pl. Orn: zostéropidés m.

zosterops ['zɔstərɔps], s. Orn: zostérops m, oiseau m à lunettes.

zouave [zwɑ:v], s. zouave m.

zounds [zaundz], int. A: morbleu! ventrebleu! sacrebleu!

zucchetto [tsu'ketou], s. Ecc: calotte f (de prêtre).

zucchini [zu'ki:ni], s. inv. courgette f.

Zulu ['zu:lu:]. 1. a. Ethn: zoulou inv. in f, pl. zoulous. 2. s. Ethn: Zoulou mf. 3. s. Ling: zoulou m. 4. s. Fish: mouche f fantaisie.

Zululand ['zu:lu:lænd], Pr.n. Geog: le Zoulouland.

Zungaria [zʌŋ'geəriə], *Pr.n. Geog: A:* la Dzougarie.
zunyite ['zju:niait], *s. Miner:* zunyite *f.*
Zweibrücken ['tsvaibrykən], *Pr.n. Geog:* Deux-Ponts.
zwieback ['tsvi:bæk], *s. Cu:* = biscotte *f.*
Zwingli ['zwiŋgli], *Pr.n.m. Rel.H:* Zwingle.
Zwinglian ['zwiŋgliən], *a. & s. Rel.H:* zwinglien, -enne.
Zwinglianism ['zwiŋgliənizm], *s. Rel.H:* zwinglianisme *m.*
zygaenid [zi'dʒi:nid], *s. Ent:* zygène *f.*
Zygaenidae [zi'dʒi:nidi:], *s.pl. Ent:* zygénides *m*, zygaénides *m*, zygénidés *m.*
zygapophysis, -es [zaigə'pɔfisis, -i:z], *s. Anat:* apophyse *f* articulaire.
zygnema [zig'ni:mə], *s. Algae:* zygnéma *m.*
Zygnemales [zigni'meiliz], **Zygnematales** [zignimə'teiliz], *s.pl. Algae:* zygnémales *f.*
zygo- ['zaigou, 'zigou], *comb.fm.* zygo-.
zygobranchiate [zaigou'bræŋkieit], *a.* zygobranche.
zygodactyl(e) [zaigou'dæktil], *a. & s. Orn:* zygodactyle (*m*).
zygodactylous [zaigou'dæktiləs], *a. Orn:* zygodactyle.
zygodont ['zaigoudɔnt], *a.* zygodonté.
zygoma, *pl.* **-ata** [zai'goumə, -ətə], *s. Anat:* zygoma *m*; os *m* malaire.
zygomatic [zaigou'mætik], *a. Anat:* zygomatique; **the z. arch,** larcade *f* zygomatique.
zygomorphic [zaigou'mɔ:fik], **zygomorphous** [zaigou'mɔ:fəs], *a. Bot:* zygomorphe.
zygomorphism [zaigou'mɔ:fizm], **zygomorphy** [zaigou'mɔ:fi], *s. Bot:* zygomorphie *f.*
Zygomycetes [zaigoumai'si:ti:z], **Zygomycetidae** [zaigoumai'setidi:], *s.pl. Fung:* zygomycètes *m.*
zygoneurous [zaigou'nju:rəs], *a.* zygonèvre.
Zygophyllaceae [zaigoufi'leisii:], *s.pl. Bot:* zygophyllacées *f.*
zygophyllaceous [zaigoufi'leiʃəs], *a. Bot:* zygophyllacé.
zygophyllum [zaigou'filəm], *s. Bot:* zygophylle *f.*
Zygoptera [zai'gɔptərə], *s.pl. Ent:* zygoptères *m.*
zygosis [zai'gousis], *s. Biol:* zygose *f*, conjugaison *f.*
zygospore ['zaigouspɔ:r], *s. Bot:* zygospore *m.*
zygote ['zaigout], *s. Biol:* zygote *m.*
zymase ['zaimeis], *s. Ch:* zymase *f.*
zym(o)- ['zaim(ou)], *comb.fm.* zym(o)-.
zymogen ['zaimoudʒen], *s. Bio-Ch:* zymogène *m*, prodiastase *f*, proenzyme *f*, proferment *m*, prozymase *f.*
zymohydrolysis [zaimouhai'drɔlisis], *s.* zymohydrolyse *f.*
zymology [zai'mɔlədʒi], *s. Ch:* zymologie *f.*
zymometer [zai'mɔmitər], **zymosimeter** [zaimou'simitər], *s. Brew: etc:* zymosimètre *m.*
zymosis [zai'mousis], *s.* fermentation *f.*
zymotechnics [zaimou'tekniks], *s.pl.* (*usu. with sg. const.*) zymotechnie *f.*
zymotic [zai'mɔtik], *a. Med:* (maladie) zymotique.
zythum ['zaiθəm], *s. Ant:* zython *m*, zythum *m.*

Common Abbreviations

French translations and their abbreviations have been given except where there is no real equivalent in French or where the same phrase has several meanings.

Abréviations courantes

La traduction et les abréviations françaises sont données sauf quand il n'y a pas d'équivalent véritable en français ou quand il y a plusieurs acceptions d'une même expression.

A., **1.** *Mus: alto*, alto. **2.** *Ph: angström*, angström. **3.** *atomic*, atomique. **4.** *answer*, réponse.
a., **1.** *accepted*, accepté. **2.** *acre*, acre. **3.** *acceleration*, accélération, a. **4.** *annus*, an. **5.** *ante*, avant.
A.A., **1.** *anti-aircraft* = défense contre avions, D.C.A. **2.** *Automobile Association.* **3.** *Alcoholics Anonymous*, Alcooliques Anonymes, AA.
aa, *Pharm: ana*, aa.
A.A.A., **1.** *Amateur Athletics Association.* **2.** *anti-aircraft artillery*, artillerie pour la défense contre avions. **3.** *American Automobile Association.*
A.A.A.A., **1.** *Amateur Athletic Association of America.* **2.** *American Association of Advertising Agencies.*
A.A.A.S., *American Association for the Advancement of Science.*
A.A.M., **1.** *Association of Assistant Mistresses.* **2.** *air-to-air missile*, engin air-air.
a.a.r., *Ins: against all risks*, tous risques.
A.A.S., *Academiae Americanae Socius, Fellow of the American Academy.*
A.A.U., **1.** *Association of American Universities.* **2.** *U.S: Amateur Athletic Union.*
A.A.U.P., *American Association of University Professors.*
A.A.U.W., *American Association of University Women.*
A. B., **1.** *Nau: able(-bodied) seaman*, matelot de deuxième classe. **2.** *U.S: Artium Baccalaureus, Bachelor of Arts.*
A.B.A., **1.** *Amateur Boxing Association.* **2.** *American Bar Association.*
Abb., (*a*) *Abbess*, abbesse; (*b*) *Abbot*, abbé; (*c*) *Abbey*, abbaye.
abbr., (*a*) *abbreviation*, abréviation; (*b*) *abbreviated*, abrégé.
A.B.C., **1.** *American Broadcasting Company.* **2.** *Australian Broadcasting Corporation.*
abd., *abdicated*, abdiqué.
ab init., *ab initio*, dès le commencement.
abl., *ablative*, ablatif.
A.B.M., *antiballistic missile*, engin antimissile.
Abp., *Archbishop*, archevêque.
abr., *abridged*, réduit.
A.B.S., *American Bible Society.*
abs., **absol.**, *absolute(ly)*, absolu(ment).
abs., *abstract*, abstrait.
abs. re., *absente reo*, the accused being absent.
abt., *about*, environ.
A.B.T.A. ['æbtə], *Association of British Travel Agents.*
abv., *above*, au-dessus, ci-dessus.
A.C., **1.** *Aero Club*, Aéro Club. **2.** *Alpine Club*, Club alpin. **3.** *El: alternating current*, courant alternatif, c.a.
A/C, **a/c.**, *Com: account*, compte, c.
acad., (*a*) *academic*, académique; (*b*) *academy*, académie.
acc., **1.** *Com: Fin:* (*a*) *acceptance*, acceptation, acc.; (*b*) *account*, compte, c.; (*c*) *accountant*, comptable. **2.** *Gram: accusative*, accusatif. **3.** *accompanied*, accompagné. **4.** *according to*, d'après, selon.
accrd. int., *accrued interest*, intérêts accumulés.
acct., (*a*) *account*, compte, c(pte).; (*b*) *accountant*, comptable.
accus., *accusative*, accusatif.
AC/DC, **1.** *El: alternating current or direct current*, courant alternatif ou courant continu. **2.** *F: bisexual*, bisexuel.
A.C.G.B., *Arts Council of Great Britain.*
A.C.G.I., *Associate of the City and Guilds of London Institute* = ingénieur diplômé.
ack., (*a*) *acknowledge*, accuser réception (de); (*b*) *acknowledgement*, quittance.
A.C.L. *allowable cargo load*, chargement permis.
A.C.L.U., *American Civil Liberties Union.*
A.-Com.-in-C., *Air-Commodore-in-Chief.*
acpt., *acceptance*, acceptation.
A.C.R.A., *Associate of the Corporation of Registered Accountants.*
A.C.S., **1.** *American Cancer Society.* **2.** *American Chemical Society.*
a/cs pay., *accounts payable*, dettes passives.
a/cs rec., *accounts receivable*, dettes actives.
A.C.T., *Air Cargo Transport.*
act., *Gram: active*, actif.
actg., *acting*, suppléant, intérimaire.
A.C.T.H., *Biol: adrenocorticotrophic hormone*, adréno-cortico-trophic-hormone, A.C.T.H.
A.C.T.U., *Australian Council of Trade Unions.*
act. wt., *actual weight*, poids effectif.
A.C.W., **1.** *W.Tel: alternating continuous waves.* **2.** *aircraftwoman*, femme soldat de la W.R.A.F.
A.D., **1.** *anno Domini*, A.D., après Jésus-Christ, ap(r). J.-C. **2.** *Air Defence*, défense de l'air. **3.** *Air Division*, Division de l'Air.
a.d., **1.** *Com: after date.* **2.** *active duty*, service actif. **3.** *ante diem*, before the day.
ad., **1.** *advertisement*, annonce; affiche. **2.** *adapted*, adapté.
A.D.A., **1.** *American Dairy Association.* **2.** *American Dental Association.* **3.** *Atomic Development Authority.*
A.D.C., **1.** *aide-de-camp*, officier d'ordonnance. **2.** *Tp: advise duration and charge*, indication de durée, I.D.
add., **1.** *Pharm: addatur*, ajouter. **2.** *addition*, addition. **2.** *addenda*, addenda, supplément.
ad fin., *ad finem*, à, vers, la fin.
A.D.G., *Assistant Director General.*
ad inf., *ad infinitum*, à l'infini.
ad init., *ad initium*, au commencement.
ad int., *ad interim*, par l'intérim.
adj., **1.** *adjective, adjectival*, adjectif. **2.** *adjacent*, contigu. **3.** *adjourned*, ajourné, différé. **4.** *adjustment*, ajustement.
Adjt, *adjutant*, adjudant; **Adjt-Gen.**, *Adjutant-General*, adjudant général.
ad lib., *ad libitum*, à volonté.
ad loc., *ad locum*, au lieu.
adm., *admission*, accès.
Adm., **1.** *Admiral*, amiral. **2.** *Admiralty*, amirauté.
A.D.M., *atomic demolition mine*, charge nucléaire de destruction.
Adm. Co., *Admiralty Court*, Tribunal maritime.
admin., *administration*, administration.
A.D.P., *Cmptr: automatic data processing*, traitement automatique de l'information.
A.D.S., *Mil: advanced dressing station.*
adv., **1.** *Com: ad valorem*, selon la valeur. **2.** *adverb*, adverbe. **3.** *advocate*, avocat. **4.** *advance*, avance. **5.** *advisory*, consultatif.
ad val., *Com: ad valorem*, selon la valeur.
advt, *advertisement*, annonce; affiche.
A.E.A., **1.** *American Economic Association.* **2.** *Atomic Energy Authority.* **3.** *Actors' Equity Association.*
A.E.C., *U.S: Atomic Energy Commission* = Commissariat à l'énergie atomique, C.E.A.
A.E.F., **1.** *Amalgamated Union of Engineering and Foundry Workers.* **2.** *American Expeditionary Forces.*
aet., **aetat.**, *aetatis*, âgé.
A.E.U., *Amalgamated Engineering Union.*
a.f., *Elcs: audiofrequency*, audiofréquence, A.F.
A.F.A., **1.** *Academy of Fine Arts*, Académie des Beaux-Arts. **2.** *American Forestry Association.* **3.** *Amateur Football Association.*
A.F.B.F., *American Farm Bureau Federation.*
A.F.B.S., *American and Foreign Bible Society.*
A.F.C., **1.** *Air Force Cross.* **2.** *Association Football Club.*
a.f.c., **1.** *automatic frequency control*, correcteur automatique de fréquence. **2.** *automatic flight control*, commande automatique de vol.
A.F.F., *Army Field Forces.*
afft, *Jur: affidavit*, déclaration sous serment.
AFL-CIO, *American Federation of Labour and Congress of Industrial Organizations.*
A.F.M., *Air Force Medal.*
A.F.N., *American Forces Network.*
A.F.S., **1.** *Auxiliary Fire Service.* **2.** *American Field Service.*
A.F.T., *American Federation of Teachers.*
aft., *afternoon*, après-midi.
A.G., **1.** *Adm: Accountant General*, chef de la comptabilité. **2.** *Jur: Attorney-General.* **3.** *Mil: Adjutant-General*, adjudant général. **4.** *Agent General*, agent général.
agcy, *agency*, agence.
agitprop, *agitation and propaganda*, agitation et propagande.
A.G.M., **1.** *Annual General Meeting*, assemblée générale annuelle. **2.** *air-to-ground missile*, engin air-sol.
A.G.R., *advanced gas-cooled reactor.*
agri(c)., *agriculture*, agriculture, agr.

A.G.S., 1. *American Geographical Society*. 2. *Army General Staff.*
Agt, *agent*, commissionnaire, caire.
A.H., *anno Hegirae*, de l'ère des Mahométans.
a.h., *El: ampere-hour(s)*, ampère(s)-heure, Ah.
A.H.Q., *Army, Air, Headquarters.*
A.I., 1. *Amnesty International*. 2. *artificial insemination*, insémination artificielle.
A.I.A., 1. *American Institute of Accountants*. 2. *Archeological Institute of America*. 3. *Associate of the Institute of Actuaries.*
A.I.D., 1. *Army Intelligence Department*. 2. *U.S: Agency for International Development*. 3. *artificial insemination by donor*, insémination artificielle par donneur.
A.I.F., 1. *Australian Imperial Forces*. 2. *Allied Invasion Forces.*
A.I.G., *Assistant Inspector General*, sous-inspecteur général.
A.I.H., *artificial insemination by husband*, insémination artificielle par époux.
A.I.M.M., *Associate of the Institution of Mining and Metallurgy.*
A.I.S.A., *Associate of Incorporated Secretaries' Association.*
A.I.W.M., *American Institute of Weights and Measures.*
A.J.C., *Australian Jockey Club.*
A.J.R.C., *American Junior Red Cross.*
A.L., *American Legion.*
Ala., *Geog: Alabama.*
A.L.A., 1. *American Library Association*. 2. *Authors' League of America.*
Alas., *Geog: Alaska.*
A.L.C., *American Lutheran Church.*
Ald(m)., *alderman*, conseiller municipal.
alg., *algebra*, algèbre.
alt., 1. *altitude*, altitude. 2. *alternate*, alternatif, alterné. 3. *Mus: alto*, alto.
Alta, *Geog: Alberta.*
A.M., 1. *U.S: Artium Magister*, Master of Arts. 2. *Albert Medal*. 3. *Air Marshall*, général de corps d'armée aérienne. 4. *W.Tel: amplitude-modulation*, modulation d'amplitude. 5. *anno mundi, in the year of the world.*
a.m., *ante meridiem, before noon*, avant midi, a.m.
a.-m., *El: ampere-minute*, ampère-minute, a.-m.
A.M.A., 1. *American Medical Association*. 2. *Australian Medical Association*. 3. *Assistant Masters' Association.*
amal(g)., *amalgamate(d)*, fusionné, fusionner.
Amb., 1. *ambassador*, ambassadeur. 2. *ambulance*, ambulance.
A.M.C., *Army Medical Centre*, centre médical de l'armée.
A.M.D.G., *ad majorem Dei gloriam*, pour la plus grande gloire de Dieu.
amdt, *amendment*, amendement.
Am(er)., *America, American*, Amérique, Américain.
A.M.G., *Allied Military Government.*
amp., 1. *ampere*, ampère, amp. 2. *Elcs: amplitude*, amplitude.
A.M.P.A.S., *Academy of Motion Picture Arts and Sciences.*
Amph., *U.S: Mil: amphibious*, amphibie.
amt, *amount*, somme; quantité; montant.
A.M.W.A., *American Medical Women's Association.*
A.N.A., *Australian National Airways.*
anal., 1. *analogy, analogous*, analogie, analogue. 2. *analysis*, analyse.
analyt., *analytical*, analytique.
anat., *anatomy, anatomical*, anatomie, anatomique.
A.N.C., *U.S: Army Nurse Corps*, Corps d'infirmières militaires.
anc., *ancient*, ancien, anc.
and., *Mus: andante.*
Angl., 1. *Anglican*. 2. *Anglice.*
ann., 1. *annual*. 2. *annuity*, annuité, rente.
anniv., *anniversary*, anniversaire.
annot., *annotated*, avec commentaire.
anon., *anonymous*, anonyme.
A.N.P.A., *American Newspaper Publishers Association.*
A.N.R.C., *American National Red Cross.*
ans., *answer*, réponse.
ant., *Gram: antonym*, antonyme.
anthol., *anthology*, anthologie.
anthrop., *anthropological*, anthropologique.
A.O., 1. *Accounting Officer*, officier comptable. 2. *Administration Officer*, officier, fonctionnaire, administratif.
a/o, *to the account of*, au compte de.
A.O.B., *Com: Any Other Business.*
A.O.C.(-in-C.), *Air Officer Commanding(-in-Chief).*
A.O.D., *Army Ordnance Department.*
A.O.F., *Ancient Order of Foresters.*
A. of F., *Admiral of the Fleet* = amiral commandant en chef.
a.p., 1. *accounts payable*, dettes passives. 2. *atmospheric pressure*, pression atmosphérique. 3. *atomic power*, énergie nucléaire.
Ap., *apostle*, apôtre.
Ap., Apr., *April*, avril.
ap., 1. *apothecary*, apothicaire. 2. *apud*, selon.
A.P., 1. *M.Ins: additional premium*, surprime. 2. *Mth: arithmetical progression*, progression arithmétique. 3. *Navy: Assistant Paymaster*, sous-commissaire. 4. *Associated Press.*
A.P.C., *Mil: armoured personnel carrier*, véhicule blindé de transport de troupe, de personnel.
A.P.M., *Assistant Provost-Marshal.*
A.P.O., *U.S: Army Post Office.*
apo., *apogee*, apogée.
Apocr., *Apocrypha*, Apocryphes.
app., 1. *appendix*, appendice. 2. *apparently*, apparemment. 3. *appointed*, désigné. 4. *apprentice*, apprenti. 5. *apparatus*, appareil, dispositif.
appd, *approved*, approuvé, agréé.
appro (on) [ɔn'æprou], *on approval*, à condition, à l'essai.
approx., *approximately*, à peu près.
A.P.S., 1. *American Philosophical Society*. 2. *American Physical Society*. 3. *Army Postal Service.*
apt., *U.S: apartment*, appartement.
A.P.T., *Rail: advanced passenger train.*
aq., *aqua*, eau.
A.Q.M.G., *Mil: Assistant Quartermaster General*, sous-intendant.
A.R., *annual return*, revenu annuel.
a.r., 1. *accounts receivable*, dettes actives. 2. *anno regni*, en l'an du règne.
a/r, *Ins: all risks*, tous risques.
A.R.A., 1. *Amateur Rowing Association*. 2. *Associate of the Royal Academy of Arts*, membre associé de l'Académie royale des Beaux-Arts.
A.R.A.M., *Associate of the Royal Academy of Music.*
ARAMCO [æ'ræmkou], *Arabian-American Oil Company.*
A.R.C., *American Red Cross.*
A.R.C.A., *Associate of the Royal College of Art.*
A.R.Cam.A., *Associate of the Royal Cambrian Academy.*
arch., 1. *archaic, archaism*, archaïque, archaïsme. 2. *archipelago*, archipel. 3. *archive(s)*, archives.
archaeol., *archaeology*, archéologie.
Archbp, *archbishop*, archevêque.
Archd., 1. *archdeacon*, archidiacre. 2. *archduke*, archiduc.
archit., *architecture*, architecture.
archt, *architect*, architecte.
A.R.C.M., *Associate of the Royal College of Music.*
A.R.C.O., *Associate of the Royal College of Organists.*
A.R.C.S., 1. *Associate of the Royal College of Science*. 2. *Associate of the Royal College of Surgeons.*
A.R.H.A., *Associate of the Royal Hibernian Academy.*
A.R.I.B.A., *Associate of the Royal Institute of British Architects.*
A.R.I.C., *Associate of the Royal Institute of Chemists.*
A.R.I.C.S., *Associate of the Royal Institute of Chartered Surveyors.*
arith., *arithmetic(al)*, arithmétique.
Ariz., *Geog: Arizona.*
Ark., *Geog: Arkansas.*
A.R.P., *Air Raid Precautions*, défense passive (anti-aérienne).
arr., 1. (*a*) *arrives*, arrive; (*b*) *arrival*, arrivée. 2. *arranged*, arrangé.
arrgt, *arrangement.*
A.R.S.A., 1. *Associate of the Royal Scottish Academy*. 2. *Associate of the Royal Society of Arts.*
A.R.S.L., *Associate of the Royal Society of Literature.*
A.R.S.M., *Associate of the Royal School of Mines.*
art., 1. *article*, article, art. 2. *artificial*, artificiel. 3. *artillery*, artillerie, art. 4. *artist*, artiste.
arty, *artillery*, artillerie, art.
A.R.U., *American Railway Union.*
A.S., 1. *Academy of Science*, Académie des Sciences, A.d.S. 2. *Assistant Secretary.*
A.S., A/S, *Com: account sales*, compte de vente.
A.-S., *Anglo-Saxon*, Anglo-Saxon.
a/s, *Com: at sight*, (payable) à vue.
A.S.A., 1. *Advertising Standards Authority*. 2. *American Standards Association*. 3. *Amateur Swimming Association.*
A.S.C., 1. *Mil: Army Service Corps*. 2. *Allied Supreme Council*, conseil supérieur interallié.
A.S.C.A.P., *American Society of Composers, Authors and Publishers.*
A.S.C.E., *American Society of Civil Engineers.*
Asdic ['æzdik], *Anti-Submarine Detection Investigation Committee*, asdic.
A.S.E., *Amalgamated Society of Engineers.*
ASH [æʃ], *Action on Smoking and Health* = Ligue contre la Fumée du Tabac en Public, L.C.F.T.P.
ASLEF ['æzlef], *Associated Society of Locomotive Engineers and Firemen.*
A.S.M., *air to surface missile*, engin air-sol.
A.S.M.E., *American Society of Mechanical Engineers.*
A.S.P.C.A., *American Society for the Prevention of Cruelty to Animals.*
Ass(n)., *association*, association, A.
ass(t)., 1. *assistant*, adjoint, aide, auxiliaire. 2. *assorted*, variés, assortis.
A.S.T., *U.S: Atlantic Standard Time.*
A.S.T.M.S., *Association of Scientific, Technical and Managerial Staffs.*
astrol., *astrology*, astrologie.
astr(on)., *astronomy*, astronomie.
A.S.U., *American Students' Union.*
A.T., *anti-tank*, anti-chars, anti-tank.
at., 1. *atmosphere*, atmosphère, atm. 2. *atomic*, atomique. 3. *attorney.*
A.T.A., 1. *American Teachers' Association*. 2. *U.S: Air Transport Association*. 3. *American Trucking Association.*
A.T.C., 1. *Air Training Corps* = préparation militaire supérieure (pour l'aviation), P.M.S. 2. *Air Traffic Control*, réglementation du trafic aérien. 3. *automatic train control*, arrêt automatique des trains.
atm., *atmosphere*, atmosphère, atm.; **atm. pr.**, *atmospheric pressure*, pression atmosphérique.
A.T.P.L., *Air transport Pilot's Licence*, brevet de pilote de ligne.
A.T.S., 1. *A: Mil: Auxiliary Territorial Service* (*now W.R.A.C.*). 2. *American Television Service*. 3. *Army Transport Service.*
ats., *Jur: at the suit of*, à la diligence de.
Atty, *Jur: Attorney*: **Atty Gen.**, *Attorney General.*
A.T.V., *Associated Television.*
at. wt, *atomic weight*, poids atomique, p.at.
A.U., *Ph: Angström unit*, unité d'Angström.
A.U.C., *ab urbe condita. anno urbis conditae*, après la fondation de Rome.
aud., *auditor*, commissaire aux comptes.
A.U.E.W., *Amalgamated Union of Engineering Workers.*
Aug., 1. *August*, août. 2. *Augustan*, (le siècle) d'Auguste.

A.U.S., *Army of the United States.*
A.U.T., *Association of University Teachers.*
aut(o)., *automatic*, automatique.
auth., **1.** *author*, auteur. **2.** *authorized*, autorisé, sanctionné.
aux(il)., *auxiliary*, auxiliaire.
A.V., *Authorized Version*, la traduction anglaise de la Bible de 1611.
av., **1.** *Meas: avoirdupois*, avoirdupois, avdp. **2.** *average*, (i) avaries, (ii) moyen(ne).
a/v, *ad valorem*, selon la valeur.
Av(e)., *Avenue*, avenue, av.
A.V.C., **1.** *W.Tel: automatic volume control*, dispositif antifading. **2.** *American Veterans' Committee.*
avdp., *Meas: avoirdupois*, avoirdupois, avdp.
avg., *average*, (i) avaries, (ii) moyen(ne).
avn, *aviation*, aviation.
avoir., *Meas: avoirdupois*, avoirdupois, avdp.
a.w., **1.** *atomic weight*, poids atomique, p.at. **2.** *actual weight*, poids effectif.
A.W.G., *American wire gauge*, jauge américaine.
A.W.L., *absent with leave*, absent en permission.
A.W.O.L., *Mil: absent without leave*, en absence illégale.
A.W.V.S., *American Women's Voluntary Service.*
ax., *axiom*, axiome.
A.Y.H.A., *American Youth Hostels Association.*

B., **1.** *baron*, baron, B. **2.** *Mus: bass*, basse. **3.** *black (pencil lead).*
b., **1.** *born*, né. **2.** *Cr: bowled.*
B.A., **1.** *Baccalaureus Artium, Bachelor of Arts* = licencié ès lettres. **2.** *British Association (for the Advancement of Science).* **3.** *F: Geog: Buenos Aires.* **4.** *British Airways.*
B.A.A., *British Airports Authority.*
B.A.A.S., *British Association for the Advancement of Science.*
B.A.C., *British Aircraft Corporation.*
back., *St.Exch: backwardation*, déport, D.
bact., *bacteriology*, bactériologie.
B.A.F.T.A. ['bæftə], *British Academy of Film and Television Arts.*
B.A.I., *Baccalaureus in Arte Ingeniaria.*
bal., *Book-k: balance*, solde.
B.A.L.P.A. ['bælpə], *British Airline Pilots' Association.*
b. & b., *bed and breakfast*, chambre et petit déjeuner.
B. & S., *Mec.E: Brown & Sharpe (wire gauge)*, (jauge) Brown et Sharpe.
B.A.O.R., *British Army of the Rhine.*
bap., *baptized*, baptisé.
Bap(t)., *Ecc: baptist*, baptiste.
B.App.Arts, *Bachelor of Applied Arts.*
bar., **1.** *Com: barrel*, tonneau, t., baril, b. **2.** *barometer*, baromètre. **3.** *barrister*, avocat.
barit., *baritone*, baryton.
Bart, *baronet*, baronnet.
Bart's [bɑːts], *St Bartholomew's Hospital (London).*
bat(t)., *Mil: (a) battalion*, bataillon, bat., bon, btn; *(b) battery*, batterie, batt., bie.
B.B., **1.** *Boys' Brigade.* **2.** *U.S: Bureau of the Budget.* **3.** *Jur: bail bond*, engagement signé par la caution. **4.** *double black (pencil).*
B.B.B., *U.S: Better Business Bureau.*
B.B.C., *British Broadcasting Corporation*, la Corporation britannique de radiodiffusion.
bbl., *barrels*, barils.
BC., **1.** *before Christ*, avant Jésus-Christ, av. J.-C. **2.** *(also B. Ch:) Baccalaureus Chirurgiae*, Bachelier en Chirurgie. **3.** *British Columbia.* **4.** *British Council.*
b/c, *bill for collection*, effet à encaisser.
B.C.D., *Cmptr: binary coded decimal*, décimal codé binaire.
B.C.E., *esp. U.S: before the Christian Era, before the Common Era*, avant Jésus-Christ, av. J.-C.
B.C.G., *Med: bacillus Calmette-Guérin*, bacille Calmette-Guérin.
B.C.M.A., *British Country Music Association.*
B.Com(m)., *Bachelor of Commerce.*
B.D., *Baccalaureus Divinitatis, Bachelor of Divinity*, Bachelier en Théologie.
bd, **1.** *bundle*, paquet, ballot. **2.** *Publ: bound*, relié.
Bd, *Boulevard*, boulevard.
B/D, **1.** *bank draft*, traite, tr. **2.** *bills discounted*, effets escomptés.
B.D.A., *British Dental Association.*
Bde, *Brigade*, brigade, bde.
bdl., *bundle*, paquet, ballot.
B.D.S., *Bachelor of Dental Surgery.*
B.E., **1.** *Bachelor of Education.* **2.** *Bachelor of Engineering.*
B/E, b/e, *bill of exchange*, lettre de change.
Bé, *Ph: Baumé.*
B.E.A., **1.** *A: British European Airways (now British Airways).* **2.** *British Electricity Authority.* **3.** *British Epilepsy Association.*
B.Econ., *Bachelor of Economics.*
B.Ed., *Bachelor of Education.*
Beds, *Geog: Bedfordshire.*
B.E.F., *British Expeditionary Force.*
bef., *before*, avant.
beg., *begin(ning)*, commencer, commencement.
B.E.M., **1.** *British Empire Medal.* **2.** *F: bug-eyed monster*, monstre aux yeux menaçants.
Berks., *Geog: Berkshire.*
bet(w)., *between*, entre.
B.E.V., *Elcs: billion electron volts.*
B.F., *P: bloody fool.*
B/F, b/f, *Book-k: brought forward*, à reporter; report.
bf, *Jur: brief*, dossier (d'une procédure).
b.f., *Typ: boldface*, caractères gras.
B.F.A., *Bachelor of Fine Arts.*
B.F.B.S., *British and Foreign Bible Society.*
BFI, *British Film Institute*, la Cinémathèque britannique.
B.F.N., *British Forces Network.*
B.F.O., *Elcs: beat frequency oscillator*, oscillateur à battements.
B.F.P.O., *British Forces Post Office.*
B.G., *Tchn: Birmingham gauge*, jauge de Birmingham.
B.Gen., *brigadier-general.*
B'ham, *Geog: Birmingham.*
b.h.p., *brake horse-power*, puissance au frein.
Bib., *Bible, biblical*, Bible, biblique.
bibl(iog)., *bibliography*, bibliographie.
bicarb., *bicarbonate (of soda)*, bicarbonate (de soude).
B.I.F., *British Industries Fair.*
B.I.M., *British Institute of Management.*
biog., *biographical, biography, biographer*, biographique, biographie, biographe.
biol., *biological, biology*, biologique, biologie.
B.I.S., *Bank for International Settlements.*
B.I.S.F., *British Iron and Steel Federation.*
bk, **1.** *book*, livre. **2.** *bank*, banque, banq., bque.
bkcy, *Jur: bankruptcy*, faillite.
bkg, *banking*, banque.
Bkge, *Fin: brokerage*, courtage, cage.
bklr, *Typ: black letter*, caractères gothiques.
bkpr, *bookkeeper*, teneur de livres.
bks, *barracks*, caserne.
B. L., *Bachelor of Law*, licencié en droit.
bl., **1.** *Com: bale*, balle, B.; ballot, bot. **2.** *black*, noir. **3.** *blue*, bleu. **4.** *block*, bloc.
B/L, b/l, *Com: bill of lading*, connaissement, connt.
b.l., *Artil: Sm.a: breech-loading*, se chargeant par la culasse.
B.L.A., *British Liberation Army.*
bldg, *building*, construction.
B.Litt., *Baccalaureus Litterarum*, Bachelier ès Lettres, B. ès L.
blk, **1.** *black*, noir. **2.** *block*, bloc. **3.** *bulk*, gros.
blvd, *boulevard*, boulevard, boul., bd.
B.M., **1.** *British Museum.* **2.** *Mec: bending moment*, moment de flexion. **3.** *Bachelor of Medicine.*
B.M.A., *British Medical Association.*
B.M.E.W.S., *ballistic missile early warning system*, système de couverture radar pour l'approche d'engins téléguidés.
B.M.I., *U.S: Broadcast Music, Incorporated.*
B.M.J., *British Medical Journal.*
B.Mus., *Baccalaureus Musicae*, licencié en musique.
Bn, *Baron*, baron, Bon.
bn, *Mil: battalion*, bataillon, bat., bon, btn.
B.N.C., *Brasenose College, Oxford.*
Bnss, *Baroness*, baronne, Bonne.
B.O., *body odour*, odeur corporelle.
B/O, *branch office*, agence, bureau de quartier.
b.o., *St. Exch: buyer's option*, prime acheteur.
B.O.A.C., *A: British Overseas Airways Corporation (now British Airways).*
B.O.D., *biochemical oxygen demand.*
B. of E., **1.** *Bank of England.* **2.** *A: Board of Education.*
Bomb., *Mil: bombardier* (i) brigadier, (ii) *U.S:* bombardier.
Bor., Boro', *borough.*
bot., *botanical, botany*, botanique.
B.O.T., *A: Board of Trade.*
Boul., *Boulevard*, boulevard, bd, bld, boul.
BOW, *Elcs: backward wave oscillator*, oscillateur à ondes inverses.
B.P., **1.** *British Pharmacopoeia.* **2.** *boiling point*, point d'ébullition. **3.** *Dist: below proof*, moins de la teneur exigée. **4.** *British Petroleum.* **5.** *blood pressure*, tension artérielle.
Bp, *bishop*, évêque; **Bp Suff.**, *Bishop Suffragan.*
b.p., *Com: bill payable*, billet, effet, à payer, b. à p., e. à p.
b.pl., *birthplace*, lieu de naissance.
Br, *Ecc: brother*, frère, F(r).
br., **1.** *branch*, succursale, succle. **2.** *(a) bronze*, bronze; *(b) brass*, laiton, cuivre jaune. **3.** *brown*, brun, marron. **4.** *Nau: brig*, brick. **5.** *Jur: brief.*
B.R., *British Rail.*
B/R, *Fin: bill receivable*, effet à recevoir, e. à r.
B.R.C.S., *British Red Cross Society.*
brev., **1.** *Mil: brevet*, (brevet d')honorariat. **2.** *Typ: brevier*, gaillarde.
Brig., *Mil: (a) brigade*, brigade, bde, brig.; *(b) brigadier.*
Brig. Gen., *Brigadier General.*
Brit., *Britain, British*, Grande-Bretagne, britannique.
bro(s), *brother(s)*, frère(s).
B.R.S., *British Road Services.*
B.S., **1.** *Bachelor of Surgery.* **2.** *Blessed Sacrament*, Saint Sacrement, S.S. **3.** *Civ. E: British Standard.*
B/S, b.s., **1.** *Com: balance sheet*, bilan. **2.** *bill of sale*, acte de vente.
B.Sc., *Baccalaureus Scientiae*, licencié ès sciences; **B. Sc. Econ.**, *Bachelor of Science in the Faculty of Economics.*
B.S.C., *British Steel Corporation.*
B.S.C.P., *British Standard Code of Practice.*
B.S.G., *British Standard Gauge*, norme britannique.
bsh., *Meas: bushel.*
B.S.I., *British Standards Institution*, institut britannique de normalisation.
B.S.M., *British School of Motoring.*
B.S.S., *British Standard Specification*, norme britannique.
B.S.T., *(a) British summer time*, heure d'été britannique; *(b) British Standard Time*, heure légale britannique.

B/St, *Cust: bill of sight,* déclaration provisoire.
B.S.W.G., *British Standard Wire Gauge,* jauge britannique (pour fils métalliques).
Bt, *Baronet,* baronnet.
bt, **1.** *bought,* acheté. **2.** *boat,* bateau.
B.T.A.F., *British Tactical Air Force.*
B.T.C., *British Transport Commission.*
bt fwd, *Book-k: brought forward,* report.
B.Th.U., *Meas: British thermal unit (252 cal.).*
btl., *bottle,* bouteille.
btn, *Mil: battalion,* bataillon, bat., bon, btn.
btry, *Mil: battery,* batterie, batt.
B.T.U., *British thermal unit (252 cal.).*
Bucks., *Geog: Buckinghamshire.*
bull., *bulletin,* bulletin.
B.U.P., *British United Press.*
BUPA ['bu:pə], *British United Provident Association.*
bur., *bureau,* bureau.
bus, *business,* affaire(s).
b.v., *Com: book value,* valeur comptable.
B.V.A., *British Veterinary Association.*
B.V.M., *Blessed Virgin Mary,* la Sainte Vierge.
B.W.D., *Vet: bacillary white diarrhoea,* diarrhée blanche des poussins, pullorose.
B.W.G., *Tchn: Birmingham wire gauge,* jauge de Birmingham.
bx, *box,* boîte; caisse.
Bz., (*a*) *benzene nucleus,* noyau benzénique; (*b*) *benzoyl radical,* radical benzoyle.

C., **1.** *centum,* cent, c. **2.** *Ph:* (*a*) *centigrade,* centigrade, c.; (*b*) *Celsius,* Celsius, C.; (*c*) *curie,* curie, Ci. **3.** *El: coulomb,* coulomb, C., coul. **4.** *Geog: Cape,* cap, promontoire. **5.** *central,* central. **6.** *Conservative,* conservateur.
c., **1.** *circa, circiter,* environ, env. **2.** *Num:* (*a*) *cent,* cent, c.; (*b*) *centime,* centime, c. **3.** *St.Exch: coupon,* coupon, c. **4.** *cube, cubic,* cube, cubique, cub. **5.** *century,* siècle. **6.** *Ph:* (*a*) *candle,* bougie, b.; (*b*) *capacitance,* capacitance; (*c*) *cathode,* cathode; (*d*) *condenser,* condensateur; (*e*) *current,* courant. **7.** *concentration,* concentration. **8.** *Com: case,* caisse, csse. **9.** *Cr: caught.*
c/-, *Austr: Post: care of,* aux bons soins de, a.b.s.
c-, (*a*) *cyclo-,* cyclo-; (*b*) *cis-,* cis-.
C.A., **1.** (*a*) *chartered accountant,* expert comptable; (*b*) *chief accountant,* chef comptable. **2.** *Fin: current account,* compte courant, C.C., c/c. **3.** *County Alderman.* **4.** *Church Army.* **5.** *Consumers' Association.* **6.** *Court of Appeal,* cour d'appel.
c/a., **1.** *Fin:* (*a*) *capital account,* compte capital; (*b*) *credit account,* compte créditeur; (*c*) *commercial agent,* agent de commerce. **2.** *Com:* = **1.** (*c*).
ca., **1.** *El: cathode,* cathode. **2.** *Meas: centiare,* centiare, ca. **3.** *circa,* environ, env. **4.** *case,* (i) cas, (ii) caisse.
C.A.A., *Civil Aviation Authority.*
C.A.B., **1.** *Citizens' Advice Bureau.* **2.** *U.S: Civil Aeronautics Board.*
Caer., *Geog: Hist: Caernarvonshire.*
C.A.F., c.a.f., *Com: cost, assurance and freight,* coût, assurance, fret, C.A.F.
C.A.I., *computer-assisted instruction,* enseignement à l'aide d'un ordinateur.
Cal., **1.** *Ph: kilogramme calorie, large, great, calorie,* grande calorie, C(al). **2.** *Geog: California,* Californie.
cal., **1.** *Ph: gramme calorie, lesser, small, calorie,* petite calorie, c(al). **2.** *calibre,* calibre.
Calif., *Geog: California,* Californie.
CALTEX, *California-Texas Oil Corporation.*
Cam., Camb., *Geog: Cambridge.*
Cambs., *Geog: Cambridgeshire.*
Can., **1.** *Geog: Canada.* **2.** *Ecc: canon,* chanoine; **Can. Res.,** *canon residentiary,* chanoine résidant.
can., *canto,* chant, ch.
can(c)., *cancel,* annuler; supprimer.
c. & f., *Com: cost and freight,* coût et fret, C.F.
C. & W., *Mus: country and western.*
Cant., **1.** *Ecc: canticle,* cantique. **2.** *Geog: Canterbury,* Cantorbéry.
Cantab., *Cantabrigiensis,* de l'Université de Cambridge.
C.A.P., *Common Agricultural Policy.*
cap., **1.** *capitulum,* chapitre, ch(ap). **2.** *Typ: capital,* majuscule. **3.** *Geog: capital,* capitale, cap. **4.** *Fin: capital,* capital, cap.
caps, **1.** *Typ: capitals,* majuscules. **2.** *Med: capsules,* capsules.
Capt., *captain,* capitaine, Cap., commandant, comm.
C.A.R., *Geog: Central African Republic,* République centrafricaine.
car., *Meas: carat,* carat.
CARIFTA [kæ'riftə], *Caribbean Free Trade Area.*
Carm., *Geog: Hist: Carmarthenshire.*
carp., *carpentry,* grosse menuiserie.
carr., *carriage,* port.
carr. pd, *carriage paid,* port payé, p.p.
C.A.S., *Chief of the Air Staff.*
C.A.T., **1.** *College of Advanced Technology.* **2.** *clear air turbulence.*
cat., **1.** *catalogue,* catalogue. **2.** *catechism,* catéchisme.
Cath., *Catholic,* catholique.
cath., *cathedral,* cathédrale.
Cav., *cavalry,* cavalerie, cav.
C.B., **1.** *Companion of the Order of the Bath.* **2.** *Com: cash book,* livre de caisse. **3.** *Adm: County Borough.* **4.** *Mil: confinement to barracks,* consigne au quartier. **5.** *W.Tel: U.S: citizens' band.*
C.B.C., *Canadian Broadcasting Corporation.*
C.B.E., (i) *Commander,* (ii) *Companion, of the Order of the British Empire.*
C.B.I., *Confederation of British Industries.*
C.B.S., *Columbia Broadcasting System.*
C.B.W., *chemical and biological* (i) *warfare,* (ii) *weapons.*
C.C., **1.** (*a*) *county court;* (*b*) *county council;* (*c*) *county councillor.* **2.** *Mil: company commander,* commandant de compagnie. **3.** *cricket club.* **4.** *Chamber of Commerce,* chambre de commerce. **5.** *cycling club.*
c.c., **1.** *Meas: cubic centimetre(s),* centimètre(s) cube(s), cm^3, cc. **2.** *El: continuous current,* courant continu. **3.** *chapters,* chapitres. **4.** *carbon copy,* copie au papier carbone. **5.** *Com: cash credit,* crédit par caisse.
cc, *copies,* copies.
C.C.C., **1.** *Central Criminal Court.* **2.** *Corpus Christi College.*
C.C.F., *Combined Cadet Force* = préparation militaire (élémentaire), P.M. (E.)
C.C.P., *Jur: Court of Common Pleas,* Cour des Plaids communs.
C.C.R., *Commission on Civil Rights.*
C.C.S., *Mil: casualty clearing station,* centre d'évacuation.
Cd., *Ph: candela,* (*new*) *candle,* nouvelle bougie, cd.
C.D., **1.** *civil defence* = défense passive, D.P. **2.** *Corps Diplomatique.* **3.** *Pol: Christian Democrat(ic) (Party).*
c.d., **1.** *St.Exch: cum dividend,* coupon attaché, c. at(t)., exercice attaché, ex.att. **2.** *cash discount,* escompte au comptant.
C/D, c/d., *Book-k: carried down,* à reporter.
cd fwd., *Book-k: carried forward,* à reporter; report.
Cdr, *Mil: commander,* commandant.
Cdre, *Navy: Av: etc: commodore.*
Cdt, *Mil: commandant,* commandant, Cdt, Comm., Comt.
C.D.T., *U.S: Central Daylight Time.*
C.E., **1.** *civil engineer,* ingénieur des travaux publics. **2.** *esp. U.S: Christian Era.*
C.E.A., *county education authority.*
C.E.D., *Committee for Economic Development.*
C.E.G.B., *Central Electricity Generating Board.*
C.E.M.A., *Council for the Encouragement of Music and the Arts.*
c.e.m.f., *El: counter-electromotive force,* force contre-électromotive, f.c.é.m.
cen., **1.** *central,* central. **2.** *century,* siècle.
C.Eng., *chartered engineer.*
Cent., *Ph: centigrade,* centigrade, c.
cent., **1.** *century,* siècle. **2.** *central,* central. **3.** *centum,* cent. **4.** *Num: centime,* centime, cent. **5.** *Meas:* (*a*) *centimetre(s),* centimètre(s), cm.; (*b*) *cental(s),* quintal, -aux; (*c*) *centiare,* centiare, cent.
CENTO ['sentou], *Central Treaty Organization,* Cento.
cert., *certificate,* certificat.
C.E.T., *Central European Time,* heure de l'Europe centrale.
cf., **1.** *Lt: confer,* comparez; voir. **2.** *Bookb: calf,* veau.
C.F., *Chaplain to the Forces,* aumônier militaire.
C/F, c/f, *Book-k: carried forward,* à reporter, report.
c.f.i., C.F.I., *Com: cost, freight, insurance,* coût, fret et assurance, c.f.a.
cg., *Meas: centigramme,* centigramme, cg.
C.G., *coastguard,* garde-côte.
c.g., *Ph: centre of gravity,* centre de gravité.
C.-G., **1.** *Mil: commissary-general,* intendant général d'armée. **2.** *consul-general,* consul général, C.G.
C.G.M., *Navy: Conspicuous Gallantry Medal.*
cgm., *Meas: centigramme,* centigramme, cg.
C.G.S., *Mil: Chief of the General Staff,* chef de l'état-major.
c.g.s., *Ph: Meas: centimetre-gramme-second,* centimètre-gramme-seconde, C.G.S.
C.H., **1.** *Companion of Honour.* **2.** *Sch: Christ's Hospital.* **3.** *Fin: clearing house,* chambre de compensation, clearing. **4.** *customs house,* (bureau de) douane. **5.** *central heating,* chauffage central.
ch., **1.** *chapter,* chapitre, ch(ap). **2.** *church,* église. **3.** *child,* enfant. **4.** *cheque,* chèque.
Ch., **1.** *Chancery,* chancellerie. **2.** *Charles.* **3.** *chief,* chef.
Chamb., *chamberlain,* chambellan.
Chan(c)., **1.** *chancellor,* chancelier. **2.** *Chancery,* chancellerie.
chap., **1.** *chaplain,* aumônier. **2.** *chapter,* chapitre, ch(ap).
Chas, *Charles.*
Ch.B., *Chirurgiae Baccalaureus, Bachelor of Surgery,* licencié en chirurgie.
Ch.E., *chief engineer.*
chem., *chemistry,* chimie; *chemical,* chimique; *chemist,* chimiste.
Ches., *Geog:* Cheshire.
chg., **1.** *change.* **2.** *charge.*
Ch.J., *Chief Justice.*
chm., **1.** *chairman,* président. **2.** *checkmate,* échec et mat.
choc., *chocolate,* chocolat.
chq., *cheque,* chèque.
Chr., (*a*) *Christ,* Christ; (*b*) *Christian,* chrétien.
Chron., *B: Chronicles,* Chroniques, Chron.
C.I., **1.** *Geog: Channel Islands,* îles Anglo-normandes. **2.** (*Order of the*) *Crown of India.*
c/i, *Com: certificate of insurance,* certificat d'assurance.
C.I.A., *U.S: Central Intelligence Agency,* service de renseignements.
C.I.C., *U.S:* **1.** *Combat Information Centre.* **2.** *Counterintelligence Corps.*
C.I.D., *Criminal Investigation Department* = police judiciaire, P.J.
C.I.E., **1.** *Companion of the Order of the Indian Empire.* **2.** *Irish: Coras Iompair Eireann,* Irish Transport Commission.
C.I.F., c.i.f., *Com: cost, insurance and freight,* coût, assurance, fret, C.A.F.
c.i.f.c., *Com: cost, insurance, freight and commission,* coût, assurance, fret et commission.
C.I.G.S., *Mil: Chief of the Imperial General Staff.*
C.-in-C., *Mil: commander-in-chief,* commandant en chef.
C.I.O., *U.S: Congress of Industrial Organizations.*
C.I.P., *F: Commercially Important Person.*
circ., **1.** *circa,* environ, env. **2.** *circuit,* circuit. **3.** *circulation,* circulation. **4.** *circumference,* circonférence.
cit., **1.** *citation,* citation. **2.** *citizen,* citoyen, -enne.
civ., (*a*) *civilian,* civil; (*b*) *civil,* civil.
C.J., *Chief Justice.*
ckw., *clockwise,* dans le sens des aiguilles d'une montre.
cl., **1.** *Meas: centilitre,* centilitre, cl. **2.** *clause,* clause. **3.** *Bookb: cloth,* toile. **4.** *class,*

classe. **5.** *clerk*, employé, commis.
C.Lit., *Companion of Literature.*
Cllr, *councillor.*
C.M., **1.** *Corresponding Member*, membre correspondant. **2.** *Nau: Certified Master.* **3.** *Common Market*, Marché commun. **4.** *common metre.*
cm., *Meas: centimetre(s)*, centimètre(s), cm.; **cm²**, **cm³**, *square, cubic, centimetre(s)*, centimètre(s) carré(s), cube(s), cm², cm³.
C.M.A., *U.S: Country Music Association.*
C.M.B., *A: Navy: coastal motor boat*, vedette torpilleur, V.T.
Cmdr., **1.** *commodore.* **2.** *commander.*
C.M.F., *Central Mediterranean Force.*
C.M.G., *Companion of the Order of St Michael and St George.*
C.M.S., *Church Missionary Society.*
C/N, *Com: credit note*, note de crédit.
C.N.A.A., *Council for National Academic Awards.*
C.N.D., *Campaign for Nuclear Disarmament.*
C.N.O., *Chief of Naval Operations.*
cnr, *corner*, coin.
Co., **1.** *Com: company*, compagnie, société, Cie, Co., Sté. **2.** *Adm: county.*
C.O., **1.** (*a*) *A: Colonial Office*; (*b*) *Crown office.* **2.** *Mil: commanding officer*, officier commandant. **2.** *conscientious objector*, objecteur de conscience.
C/O, *certificate of origin*, certificat d'origine.
c/o, **1.** *Post: care of*, aux bons soins (de), a.b.s. **2.** *Book-k: carried over*, reporté.
coch(l)., *Pharm: cochleare*, cuillerée, cochl.
C.O.D., **1.** *Com: cash on delivery, U.S: collect on delivery*, (livraison) contre remboursement. **2.** *Concise Oxford Dictionary.*
C. of E., *Church of England*, l'Église anglicane.
C. of S., **1.** *Mil: Chief of Staff*, chef d'état-major. **2.** *Church of Scotland.*
cog., *cognate.*
C.O.I., *Central Office of Information.*
Col., **1.** *Mil: colonel*, colonel, Col. **2.** *Geog:* (*a*) *Colombia*; (*b*) *Colorado.* **3.** *B: Colossians*, (Épître aux) Colossiens, Col.
col., **1.** *colony*, colonie; *colonial*, colonial. **2.** *column*, colonne. **3.** *colour*, couleur.
colat., *Pharm: colature*, colature, colat.
Coll., *college*, collège.
coll., **1.** *colloquial*, familier. **2.** *collection*, collection; *collector*, collectionneur. **3.** *college*, collège. **4.** *colleague*, confrère, collègue.
collat., *collateral(ly).*
colloq., *colloquial*, familier.
Colo., *Geog: Colorado*, Colorado.
Coloss., *B: Colossians*, Colossiens.
Com., **1.** *commander*, (i) commandant, Cdt, Comt; Comm.; (ii) commandeur, Comm. **2.** *Com: commission*, commission, cion, com., con. **3.** *commissioner*, commissaire. **4.** *committee*, comité. **5.** *communist*, communiste. **6.** *Navy: commodore.* **7.** *Commonwealth*, Commonwealth.
com., **1.** *comedy*, comédie. **2.** *commerce*, commerce. **3.** *commission*, commission, com., con, cion. **4.** *common*, commun.
comb., *combined*; *combining.*
comdg, *commanding*, commandant.
Comdr, *commander*, (i) commandant, Cdt, Comm., Comt; (ii) commandeur, Comm.
Comdt, *Mil: commandant*, commandant, Cdt, Comm.
COMECON ['kɔmikɔn], *Council for Mutual Economic Aid*, Conseil pour l'aide économique mutuelle, COMECON.
Com.H., *Parl: Committee of the House*, la Chambre constituée en comité.
Cominform ['kɔminfɔ:m], *Communist Information Bureau*, Kominform.
Comintern ['kɔmintə:n], *Communist International*, Komintern.
comm., **1.** *commentary*, commentaire. **2.** *commander*, commandant, Cdt, Comt, Comm.; commandeur, Comm. **3.** *commerce*, commerce. **4.** *commission*, commission, cion, com., con. **5.** *committee*, comité. **6.** *commonwealth*, commonwealth.
Commissr, *commissioner*, commissaire.
commn, *commission*, commission, cion, com., con.
Commy, *commissary*, commissaire.
comp., **1.** (*a*) *comparative*, comparatif, compar.; (*b*) *compare*, comparer, compar. **2.** *compiled*, compilé, rédigé, composé. **3.** *composed*, composé. **4.** *compound*, composé, compound. **5.** *compositor*, compositeur, typographe. **6.** *comprising*, comprenant.
compar., (*a*) *comparative*, comparatif, compar.; (*b*) *comparison*, comparaison.
comps, *compliments*, compliments.
Con. **1.** *consul*, consul. **2.** *Pol: Conservative*, conservateur.
con., **1.** *contra*, contre. **2.** *conclusion*, conclusion. **3.** *consolidated*, consolidé. **4.** *conju(n)x*, époux, épouse.
conc., **1.** (*a*) *concentrated*, concentré; (*b*) *concentration*, concentration. **2.** *conclusion*, conclusion. **3.** *concerning*, concernant.
conch., *conchology*, conchyliologie.
cond., **1.** *condenser*, condensateur; condenseur. **2.** *conditional*, conditionnel, condit. **3.** *conductor*, conducteur.
conf., *conference*, conférence.
cong., **1.** *congress*, réunion, congrès. **2.** *congregation*, assistance; assemblée.
Cong., *Congregational(ist)*, Congrégationaliste.
conj., *conjunction*, conjonction.
Conn., *Geog: Connecticut.*
conn., **1.** *connection.* **2.** *connotation*, connotation; signification.
Cons., *Pol: conservative*, conservateur.
cons., **1.** *Fin: consols*, consolidés. **2.** *consonant*, consonne.
consec., *consecutive*, consécutif.
con. sec., *Mth: conic section*, la conique.
const., **1.** *constant*, constant. **2.** *constitution*, constitution.
const(r)., *construction*, construction.
cont., **1.** *contents*, contenu. **2.** *continued*, suite. **3.** *continent(al)*, continent(al).
contd, *continued*, suite.
contr., (*a*) *contracted*, contracté; (*b*) *contraction*, contraction.
contrib., (*a*) *contribution*, contribution; (*b*) *contributor*, collaborateur.
conv., *conventional*, conventionnel.
convd, *Fin: converted*, converti, conv.
co-op., *cooperative society*, société coopérative.
Cor., **1.** *B: Corinthians*, (Épître aux) Corinthiens, Cor. **2.** *coroner*, coroner.
cor, **1.** *correction*, correction. **2.** *U.S: corner*, coin.
C.O.R.E., *U.S: Congress of Racial Equality.*
Cor. Mem., *corresponding member*, membre correspondant.
Corn., *Geog: Cornwall.*
coroll., *Geom: corollary*, corollaire, cor.
corp., **Corp.**, **1.** *corporation*, compagnie, Cie. **2.** *Mil: corporal*, caporal.
corr., **1.** (*a*) *corresponding*, correspondant; **Corr. Mem.**, *corresponding member*, membre correspondant (d'une société savante); (*b*) *correspondence*, correspondance. **2.** *correction*, correction. **3.** *corrupt(ed)*, altéré.
cort., *Pharm: cortex*, cortex, cort.
cos., *Mth: cosine*, cosinus, cos.
cosec., *Mth: cosecant*, cosécante, coséc.
C.O.S.I.R.A. [kou'sairə], *Council for Small Industries in Rural Areas.*
COSPAR ['kouspɑ:r], *Committee on Space Research.*
cot., *Mth: cotangent*, cotangente, cot(g)., ctg.
Coy, *esp. Mil: company*, compagnie.
cp., **1.** *compare*, comparer. **2.** *St.Exch: coupon*, coupon, coup.
C.P., **1.** *Com: carriage paid*, port payé, p.p., franco, fco, fro. **2.** *Jur:* (*a*) *Clerk of the Peace*, greffier de la session des juges de paix; (*b*) (*Court of*) *Common Pleas*, Cour des Plaids communs. **3.** *Pol:* (*a*) *Communist Party*, parti communiste, P.C.; (*b*) *Austr: Country Party.*
C/P, *Com: charter party*, charte-partie.
c.p., *Ph: candle power*, bougie, b.
C.P.A., *U.S: Certified Public Accountant.*
cpd, *compound*, composé; compound.
C.P.I., *Consumer Price Index.*
Cpl, *corporal*, caporal.
C.P.M., *Cmptr: critical path method*, méthode de chemin critique.
C.P.O., *Navy: Chief Petty Officer.*
C.P.R., *Canadian Pacific Railway.*
C.P.R.E., *Council for the Protection of Rural England.*
C.P.S., *Custos Privati Sigilli*, Keeper of the Privy Seal.
c.p.s., *El.E: cycles per second*, périodes par seconde, p.p.s., hertz, hz.
C.P.S.U., *Communist Party of the Soviet Union.*
C.Q.M.S., *Mil: Company Quartermaster Sergeant*, sergent chef.
cr., **1.** *Book-k:* (*a*) *credit*, crédit, cr, avoir, Av.; (*b*) *creditor*, créancier. **2.** *Paperm: crown*, format couronne. **3.** *concillor*, conseiller.
C.R.C.C., *Canadian Red Cross Committee.*
Cres., *Crescent*, (nom de) rue.
cresc., *Mus: crescendo*, crescendo.
crim. con., *Jur: A: criminal conversation*, adultère.
crit., *criticism, critical*, critique.
C.R.M.P., *Corps of Royal Military Police.*
C.R.O., *Criminal Records Office* = l'Identité judiciaire.
C.R.T., *W.Tel: cathode ray tube*, tube à rayons cathodiques.
cryst., (*a*) *crystalline*, cristallin; (*b*) *crystallography*, cristallographie.
cs, *case(s)*, cas.
C.S., **1.** *Civil Service*, Administration civile. **2.** (*a*) *Clerk of Sessions*, greffier; (*b*) *clerk to the Signet*, avoué; (*c*) *Custos Sigilli*, garde des sceaux. **3.** *Scot: Court of Session*, Cour Suprême. **4.** *Christian Science*, Science chrétienne. **5.** *Chartered Surveyor.*
C.S.C., *Civil Service Commission.*
C.S.E., *Sch: Certificate of Secondary Education*, certificat de fin d'études secondaires.
C.S.I., *Companion of the Order of the Star of India.*
C.S.M., *Mil: company sergeant-major*, adjudant de compagnie, (*W.R.A.C.*) deuxième catégorie.
C.S.O., *U.S: Chief Signal Officer*, directeur du service des transmissions.
C.S.T., *U.S: Central Standard Time.*
ct, **1.** *Num: cent*, cent. **2.** *Meas:* (*a*) *carat*, carat; (*b*) *cental*, quintal.
Ct, **1.** *count*, comte, Cte. **2.** *Geog: Connecticut.* **3.** *court*, cour, tribunal.
C.T., *U.S: Central Time.*
c.t.l., *M.Ins: constructive total loss*, perte censée totale.
C.U., *Cambridge University*, Université de Cambridge.
cu(b), *cube, cubic*, cube, cubique, cub.
cu.ft., *cubic foot, feet*, pied(s) cube(s).
cum., *St.Exch: cumulative*, cumulatif, cum.
Cumb., *Geog: Hist: Cumberland.*
cum div., *St.Exch: cum dividend*, coupon attaché.
C.U.P., *Cambridge University Press.*
cur(t)., *current*, (mois) courant.
cusec., *cubic feet per second*, pieds cubes par seconde.
C.V.O., *Commander of the Royal Victorian Order.*
C.W., *W.Tel: continuous waves*, ondes entretenues.
c.w.o., *Com: cash with order*, payable à la commande.
C.W.O., *Mil: chief warrant officer.*
C.W.S., *Co-operative Wholesale Society*, société coopérative de consommation.
cwt(s), *Meas: hundredweight(s).*
cy., **1.** *capacity*, capacité. **2.** *cycle*, cycle.
cyl., *cylinder*, cylindre.
C.Z., *Geog: Canal Zone*, Zone du Canal.

D., **1.** *dimension(al)*, dimension(nel); **3D film**, film à réfraction. **2.** *Pol: U.S: democrat*, démocrate.
d., **1.** *diameter*, diamètre. **2.** *Astr: declination*, déclinaison, d(éclin). **3.** *died, deceased*, mort, m. **4.** *Num: Lt: denarius, -ii*, penny, pence. **5.** *Com: debit*, doit, débit, D. **6.** *daughter*, fille. **7.** *Ph: density*, densité, d. **8.** *Pharm: dose*, dose, d. **9.** *day*, jour, jr. **10.** *date*, date. **11.** *departs*, part. **12.** *Typ: delete, dele*, à supprimer.

D.A., **1.** *U.S: District Attorney* = procureur de la République. **2.** *F: Hairdr: duck's arse*, (coiffure en) queue de canard.
D/A, *Bank: deposit account*, compte de dépôts.
dag., *Meas: decagramme*, décagramme, dag.
Dak., *Geog: Dakota.*
dal., *Meas: decalitre*, décalitre, dal.
dam., *Meas: decametre*, décamètre, dam.
D. & C., *Med: dilation and curettage*, dilatation et curettage.
D.A.P., *Com: documents against payment*, documents contre paiement, D.P.
D.A.R., *Daughters of the American Revolution.*
D.A.S., *Com: delivered alongside ship*, livré sous palan.
dat., *Gram: dative*, datif.
d.b., *Book-k: day-book*, journal, jl.
dB, db., *decibel*, décibel, dB.
D.B.E., *Dame Commander of the Order of the British Empire.*
dbk, *Cust, drawback.*
dbl., *double*, double.
D.C., **1.** (*a*) *District Commissioner*, commissaire régional; (*b*) *Deputy Consul*, consul suppléant. **2.** *El: direct current*, courant continu, c.c. **3.** *Geog: District of Columbia.* **4.** *Mus: da capo*, D.C. **5.** *U.S: District Court*, tribunal d'instance.
D.C.B., *Dame Commander of the Order of the Bath.*
D.C.L., *Doctor of Civil Law*, docteur en droit civil.
D.C.M., *Distinguished Conduct Medal.*
D.C.M.G., *Dame Commander of the Order of St Michael & St George.*
D.C.V.O., *Dame Commander of the Royal Victorian Order.*
D.D., *Doctor of Divinity*, docteur en théologie.
d.d., **D/D**, *Com:* (*a*) *days after date*, jours de date, j/d.; (*b*) *demand draft*, traite à vue.
dd, *delivered*, livré.
d/d, *dated*, daté.
D.D.D., *Tp: NAm: direct distance dialling* = téléphone automatique, *F:* l'automatique.
D.D.T., *dichloro-diphenyl-trichloroethane*, D.D.T.
deb., **1.** *Fin: debenture*, obligation. **2.** *Book-k: debit*, débit, déb. **3.** *debutante*, débutante.
Dec., *December*, décembre.
dec., **1.** *Astr: declination*, déclinaison, d(éclin). **2.** *declaration*, déclaration. **3.** *Gram: declension*, déclinaison. **4.** *decrease*, diminution. **5.** *deceased*, décédé, déc.
decl., *Gram: declension*, déclinaison.
decoct., *Pharm: decoction*, decoctio, dec.
def., **1.** *Fin: deferred*, différé, dif. **2.** *Jur: defendant*, défendeur, -eresse. **3.** *definite; defined; definition*, défini(tion).
deg., *degree(s)*, degré(s).
Del., *Geog: Delaware.*
del. 1. *Engr: delineavit*, del(t). **2.** *St.Exch: delegation*, délégation, délég. **3.** *delegate*, délégué. **4.** *delete*, effacer; à supprimer.
delt, *Engr: delineavit*, del(t).
dely, *Com: delivery*, livraison, liv(r).
dem., **1.** *Paperm: demy*, format carré. **2.** *Com: demand*, demande, d. **3.** *Pol: U.S: democrat*, démocrate. **4.** *Gram: demonstrative*, démonstratif.
Denb., *Geog: Hist: Denbighshire.*
denom., *Fin: denomination*, coupure, coup.
dent., *dental, dentistry*, (art) dentaire.
dep., **1.** *department*, service. **2.** (*a*) *Rail: departs*, part; (*b*) *Nau: departure*, chemin est et ouest. **3.** *deposit*, dépôt. **4.** *Gram: deponent*, déponent. **5.** *deposed*, déposé. **6.** *deputy*, suppléant.
dept, *department*, service; rayon.
der(iv)., *derived, derivative, derivation*, dérivé, dérivation.
D.E.S., *Department of Education and Science.*
det., **1.** (*a*) *Mil: detachment*, détachement, détt.; (*b*) *detached*, séparé, détaché. **2.** *detail*, détail.
Deut., *B: Deuteronomy*, Deutéronome, Deut.
D.E.W., *Distant Early Warning.*
D.F., *W.Tel: Nau: direction finder, finding*, radiogoniomètre, -métrie.
D.F.C., *Distinguished Flying Cross.*
D.F.M., *Distinguished Flying Medal.*
dft., **1.** *Com: draft*, traite, T/, tr. **2.** *Jur: defendant*, défendeur, -eresse.
D.G., **1.** *Dei gratia*, par la grâce de Dieu, D.G. **2.** *Director-General.*
dg., *Meas: decigramme*, décigramme, dg.
D.H.S.S., *Department of Health and Social Security.*
dia., *diameter*, diamètre.
diag., *diagram*, diagramme.
dial., **1.** *dialect*, dialecte. **2.** *dialectical*, dialectique.
diam., *diameter*, diamètre.
dict., **1.** *dictionary*, dictionnaire. **2.** *dictation*, dictée.
dif(f)., *different, difference*, différent, différence.
dig., *Pharm: digest*, faites digérer, dig.
dil., *Pharm: dilute*, faites diluer, dil.
dim., **1.** *Gram: diminutive*, diminutif. **2.** *dimension*, dimension.
dioc., *diocese*, diocèse.
dip., *diploma*, diplôme.
Dip.A.D., *Diploma in Art and Design.*
Dip.Ed., *Diploma in Education* = Certificat d'aptitude au professorat de l'enseignement secondaire, C.A.P.E.S.
Dir., *director*, administrateur, directeur; *Cin:* réalisateur.
disc., *discoverer*, découvreur.
dis(c), **disct**, *Com: discount*, escompte, esc(te).
diss., *dissertation*, dissertation.
dist., **1.** *Adm: district*, arrondissement, arr., quartier, qer. **2.** *distance*, distance. **3.** *distinguish*, distinguer.
distr., *distribution, distributor*, distribution, répartition; distributeur.
div., **1.** *Fin: dividend*, dividende, div. **2.** *Mil: division*, division, div.
D.I.Y., *do-it-yourself*, bricolage.
D.J., **1.** *dinner jacket*, smoking. **2.** *disc jockey*, présentateur de disques.
dkg., *Meas: decagram(me)(s)*, décagramme(s).
dkl., *Meas: decalitre*, décalitre.
dkm., *Meas: decametre(s)*, décamètre(s).
dl., *Meas: decilitre*, décilitre, d(éci)l.
D.L., *deputy lieutenant.*
D.Lit(t)., *Doctor Litterarum, Litteraturae, Doctor of Letters*, docteur ès lettres.
D.L.O., *Post: dead letter office*, bureau des rebuts.
dlr, *dealer*, marchand.
D.M., Deutsche Mark.
dm., *Meas: decimetre(s)*, décimètre(s), dm.; **dm²**, *square decimetre(s)*, décimètre(s) carré(s), dm²; **dm³**, *cubic decimetre(s)*, décimètre(s) cube(s), dm³.
D.Mus., *Doctor of Music*, docteur en musique.
D.M.Z., *demilitarized zone*, zone démilitarisée.
D.N.A., *desoxyribonucleic acid*, acide désoxyribonucléique, A.D.N.
D.N.B., *Dictionary of National Biography.*
do, *ditto*, dito, do.
D/O, d.o., *Com: delivery order*, bon de livraison.
D.O.A., *dead on arrival.*
doc., *document*, document.
D.O.E., *Department of the Environment.*
dol., **1.** *Mus: dolce*, dol. **2.** *dollar*, dollar, dol(l).
Dom., *Dominion*, dominion.
dom., *domestic*, domestique.
Dom. Rep., *Geog: Dominican Republic.*
D.O.R.A. ['dɔːrə], *Hist: Defence of the Realm Act.*
doz., *dozen*, douzaine, d(ou)z.
D.P., *displaced person*, personne déplacée, D.P.
D/P, *Com: documents against payment*, documents contre paiement.
D/PA, *Director of Personnel and Administration.*
D.Phil., *Doctor of Philosophy*, docteur en philosophie.
D.P.P., *Director of Public Prosecutions* = Procureur de la République.
D.P.R., *director of public relations*, chef du service des relations avec le public.
dpt, *department*, service; rayon.
Dr, **1.** *doctor*, docteur, Dr. **2.** *Com: debtor*, débiteur. **3.** *Drive*, avenue, av.
dr, **1.** *Book-k: debit*, débit, d. **2.** (*a*) *Meas: dra(ch)m*, drachme; (*b*) *Num: drachma*, drachme. **3.** *Com: drawer*, souscripteur, tireur.
D.R., *Nau: dead reckoning*, estime.
ds., *Meas: decistere*, décistère.
D.S., *Defence Secretary.*
d.s., **d/s**, *Com: days after sight*, jours de vue, j/v.
D.S.C., *Navy: Distinguished Service Cross.*
D.Sc., *Doctor of Science*, docteur ès sciences.
D.S.L., *Oc: deep scattering layer*, couche diffusante profonde.
D.S.M., *Navy: Distinguished Service Medal.*
D.S.O., *Distinguished Service Order.*
D.S.T., *U.S: Daylight Saving Time*, heure d'été.
D.T.(s) ['diː'tiː(z)], *Med: F: delirium tremens.*
D.T.I., *Department of Trade and Industry.*
D.U.K.W. [dʌk], *Veh: Detroit United Kaiser Works*, véhicule amphibie.
dup., *duplicate.*
D.V., *Deo volente*, si Dieu le veut.
d.w., *dead weight*, poids mort, p.m.
dwt., *A. Meas: pennyweight.*
D.X., *U.S: W.Tel: distance*, distance.
dyn., *dynamics*, dynamique.
D.Z., *Mil: Av: dropping zone*, D.Z.
dz., *dozen*, douzaine, d(ou)z.

E., *east*, est, E.
ea., *each*, chacun.
E. & F.C., *examined and found correct*, lu et approuvé.
E. & O.E., *Com: errors and omissions excepted*, sauf erreur ou omission, s.e. & o., s.e. ou o.; erreur ou omission exceptée, e.o.o.e.
E.B.U., *European Broadcasting Union.*
E.C., *East Central.*
E.C.A., *U.S: Economic Cooperation Administration.*
Eccl(es)., *B: Ecclesiastes*, Ecclésiaste, Eccl.
eccl(es)., *ecclesiastic*, ecclésiastique.
E.C.E., *Economic Commission for Europe*, Commission économique (des Nations Unies) pour l'Europe, C.E.E.
E.C.G., *electrocardiogram*, électrocardiogramme.
E.C.L.A., (*United Nations*) *Economic Commission for Latin America.*
ecol., *ecological, ecology*, écologique, écologie.
econ., *economic(s)*, économique.
E.C.S.C., *European Coal and Steel Community*, Communauté européenne du charbon et de l'acier, C.E.C.A.
E.C.T., *Med: electroconvulsive therapy*, électrochoc.
E.C.U., *English Church Union.*
ed., **1.** (*a*) *edition*, édition, éd(it).; (*b*) *editor;* (*c*) *edited.* **2.** *educated.*
E.D.C., *European Defence Community*, Communauté européenne de défense, C.E.D.
Ed(in)., *Geog: Edinburgh*, Édimbourg.
edit., (*a*) *edited;* (*b*) *edition*, édition, éd(it).
E.D.P., *electronic data processing*, informatique.
E.D.T., *U.S: Eastern Daylight Time.*
educ., *education(al), educated.*
E.E., *errors excepted*, sauf erreur, s.e.
E.E. & M.P., *Envoy Extraordinary and Minister Plenipotentiary*, envoyé extraordinaire et ministre plénipotentiaire, E.e. & M.pl.
E.E.C., *European Economic Community*, Communauté économique européenne,

C.E.E.
E.E.G., *Med: electroencephalogram,* électroencéphalogramme, E.E.G.
E.F.T.A. ['eftə], *European Free Trade Association,* Association européenne de libre-échange, A.E.L.E.
e.g., *exempli gratia,* par exemple, p.ex.
E.G.M., *Empire Gallantry Medal.*
E.G.O., *Eccentric Orbiting Geophysical Observatory.*
E.H.F., *extremely high frequency.*
E.H.P., *(a) effective horsepower; (b) electric horsepower.*
E.I.B., *European Investments Bank,* Banque européenne d'investissement, B.E.I.
E.I.S., *Educational Institute of Scotland.*
el., *U.S: elevated railroad,* chemin de fer, *F:* métro, aérien.
E.L(ong)., *east longitude,* longitude est.
E.L.D.O. ['eldou], *European Launcher Development Organization* = Comité Européen pour la Construction de Lanceurs d'Engins Spatiaux, CECLES.
elec(t)., *electric(al), electricity,* électrique, électricité.
elem., **1.** *element,* élément. **2.** *elementary,* élémentaire.
E.L.F., *extremely low frequency.*
Eliz., *Elizabethan,* élisabéthain.
E.L.R., *Meteor: environment lapse rate.*
E.M.A., *European Monetary Agreement,* Accord monétaire européen.
e.m.f., *El: electromotive force,* force électromotrice, f.é.m.; **back e.m.f.,** force contre-électromotrice, f.c.é.m.
E.M.S., *European Monetary System,* Systéme Monétaire Européen, SME.
e.m.u., *electromagnetic unit.*
enc(l)., *enclosure(s),* document(s) ci-inclus.
Ency(c)., *encylopaedia,* encyclopédie.
E.N.E., *east-north-east,* est-nord-est, E.-N.-E.
Eng(l)., *(a) England,* Angleterre; *(b) English,* anglais.
eng., **1.** *(a) engineer,* ingénieur, ing(én).; *(b) engineering,* génie. **2.** *engraving,* gravure. **3.** *engaged.*
E.N.I.A.C., *Electronic Numerical Integrator and Computer.*
enl., **1.** *enlarge,* agrandir. **2.** *enlisted.*
ens., *ensign.*
E.N.S.A. ['ensə], *Entertainments National Service Association.*
E.N.T., *Med: ear, nose and throat,* oto-rhino-laryngologie, O.R.L.
ent(om)., *entomology,* entomologie.
e.o.d., *every other day,* tous les deux jours.
Ep., *B: Epistle,* Épître.
E.P., **1.** *Rec: extended play,* super 45 tours. **2.** *electroplated,* plaqué; argenté.
Eph., *B: Ephesians,* (Épître aux) Éphésiens, Éph.
E.P.N.S., *electroplated nickel silver.*
E.P.T., *Excess Profits Tax.*
E.P.U., *European Payments Union,* Union européenne des paiements, U.E.P.
eq., **1.** *equal,* égal. **2.** *equivalent,* équivalent. **3.** *equation,* équation.
equiv., *equivalent,* équivalent.
E.R., *(a) Edwardus Rex,* le Roi Edward; *(b) Elizabeth Regina,* la reine Elizabeth.
E.R.A., *Emergency Relief Administration.*
ERNIE ['ə:ni], *Cmptr: Electronic Random Number Indicator Equipment.*
E.R.P., *European Recovery Programme.*
E.R.S., *Earth resources satellite; environmental research satellite.*
E.S.E., *east-south-east,* est-sud-est, E.-S.-E.
E.S.N., *educationally subnormal,* arriéré.
esp., *especially,* surtout.
E.S.P., *extrasensory perception,* perception extra-sensorielle.
Esq., *Esquire.*
E.S.R.O., *European Space Research Organization,* organisation européenne de recherches spatiales, O.E.R.S.
E.S.S.A., *U.S: Environmental Science Services Administration.*
est., **1.** *(a) established; (b) establishment.* **2.** *estimated,* estimatif. **3.** *estate,* bien. **4.** *estuary,* estuaire.
E.S.T., **1.** *U.S: (a) Eastern Standard Time; (b) Eastern Summer Time.* **2.** *Med: electro-shock treatment,* électrochoc.
e.s.u., *electrostatic unit.*
&, et, et commercial.
E.T.A., *estimated time of arrival.*
et al., *et alia, et alii,* et tout le monde.
etc., *etcetera,* et cætera, etc.
E.T.O., *European Transport Organization.*
et seq., *et sequentia,* et la suite.
E.T.U., *Electrical Trades Union.*
Eur., *(a) Europe,* Europe; *(b) European,* européen.
Euratom [ju:'rætɔm], *European Atomic Energy Community,* Communauté européenne de l'énergie atomique, C.E.E.A., Euratom.
eV, *electron-volt,* électron-volt, eV.
E.V.A., *Space: extravehicular activity.*
eve., evg, *evening,* soir.
Ex(od)., *B: Exodus,* Exode.
ex., *example,* exemple, ex.
Exc., *Excellency,* Excellence, Exc.
exc., *except,* excepté.
Exch., **1.** *Exchequer,* Échiquier. **2.** *exchange,* échange.
excl., *exclusive, excluding,* exclusif, à l'exclusion de.
excl(am)., *exclamation, exclamatory,* exclamation, exclamatif.
ex cp., *Fin: ex coupon,* coupon détaché, ex-c(oup).
ex div., *Fin: ex dividend,* ex-dividende, ex-d., x.-d.
exec., **1.** *Jur: executor,* exécuteur testamentaire. **2.** *executive.*
ex int., *Com: without interest,* sans intérêt.
exix, *Jur: executrix,* exécutrice testamentaire.
ex lib., *ex libris.*
ex off., *ex officio.*
exor, *Jur: executor,* exécuteur testamentaire.
exp., **1.** *export,* exportation. **2.** *expenses,* frais. **3.** *expired,* périmé.
exr, exrx, *executor, executrix,* exécuteur, exécutrice, testamentaire.
exsec., *Mth: exsecant.*
ext., **1.** *Tp: etc: extension.* **2.** *external,* externe.

F., **1.** *Ph: Fahrenheit,* Fahrenheit, F. **2.** *Mth: function,* fonction. **3.** *Ecc: Father,* Père, P. **4.** *fine (pencil lead).*
f., **1.** *Meas: (a) foot, feet,* pied(s), p.; *(b) fathom,* brasse; *(c) furlong.* **2.** *Num: (a) farthing(s),* quart(s) d'un ancien penny; *(b) franc(s),* franc(s), fr., f. **3.** *El: farad,* farad, F. **4.** *Phot: focal length,* distance focale, F. **5.** *Ph: (a) force,* force, F.; *(b) frequency,* fréquence, f.
F.A., **1.** *Football Association.* **2.** *Mil: field artillery,* artillerie de campagne. **3.** *P: Fanny Adams,* rien du tout.
F.A.A., **1.** *Navy: Fleet Air Arm.* **2.** *U.S: Federal Aviation Administration.*
f.a.a., *M.Ins: free of all average,* franc de toutes avaries.
F.A.A.A.S., **1.** *Fellow of the American Academy of Arts and Sciences.* **2.** *Fellow of the American Association for the Advancement of Science.*
fac., **1.** *facsimile,* fac-similé. **2.** *factor,* facteur.
F.A.G.S., *Fellow of the American Geographical Society.*
Fahr., *Fahrenheit,* Fahrenheit, F.
F.A.I., *Fellow of the Auctioneers' Institute.*
F.A.I.A., *Fellow of the American Institute of Architects.*
fam., **1.** *family,* famille. **2.** *familiar,* familier, fam.
F.A.N.Y., *First Aid Nursing Yeomanry.*
F.A.O., *Food and Agriculture Organization,* Organisation pour l'alimentation et l'agriculture, O.A.A.
f.a.q., *Com: free alongside quay,* franco quai.
f.a.s., *Com: free alongside ship,* franco sous palan.
F.A.S., **1.** *Fellow of the Society of Arts.* **2.** *Fellow of the Antiquarian Society.* **3.** *Foreign Agricultural Service.*
fath., *Meas: fathom,* brasse.
F.B.A., *Fellow of the British Academy.*
F.B.A.A., *Fellow of the British Association of Accountants and Auditors.*
F.B.I., *U.S: Federal Bureau of Investigation.*
F.C., **1.** *Football Club.* **2.** *Free Church,* Église libre (d'Écosse). **3.** *Ph: foot-candle.*
fc(s), *Num:* **franc(s),** franc(s), fr.
F.C.A., *Fellow of the Institute of Chartered Accountants* = expert comptable.
fcap, *foolscap,* papier ministre.
F.C.C., *U.S: Federal Communications Commission.*
F.C.I.S., *Fellow of the Chartered Institute of Secretaries.*
fco, *Com: franco,* franco, fco.
F.C.O., **1.** *Fire Control Officer.* **2.** *Foreign and Commonwealth Office.*
F.C.P., *Fellow of the College of Preceptors.*
fcp, *foolscap,* papier ministre.
F.C.S., *Fellow of the Chemical Society.*
fd, **1.** *field.* **2.** *fund.*
F.D., *Fidei Defensor,* défenseur de la foi.
F.D.A., *U.S: Food and Drug Administration.*
Feb., *February,* février, fév.
fec., *fecit.*
Fed., *Federal,* fédéral.
F.E.I.S., *Fellow of the Educational Institute of Scotland.*
fem., *feminine,* féminin, f.
F.E.R.A., *Federal Emergency Relief Administration.*
F.E.T., **1.** *W.Tel: Field Effect Transistor,* transistor à effet de champ, T.E.C. **2.** *Federal Excise Tax.*
ff., **1.** *following pages,* pages suivantes. **2.** *folios,* folios.
F.F.F., *Hist: (1939–45) Free French Forces,* Forces françaises libres, F.F.L.
F.F.I., **1.** *Hist: (1939–45) French Forces of the Interior,* Forces françaises de l'intérieur. **2.** *Mil:* free from infection.
F.F.V., *U.S: First Families of Virginia.*
f.g.a., *M.Ins: free of general average,* franc d'avarie commune, f.a.c.
F.G.S., *Fellow of the Geological Society.*
F.H., *fire hydrant,* bouche d'incendie.
f'hold, *freehold,* tenu en propriété perpétuelle et libre.
F.I., *Falkland Islands.*
F.I.A., *Fellow of the Institute of Actuaries,* actuaire diplômé.
F.I.C., *Fellow of the Institute of Chemists.*
f.i.c., *Com: freight, insurance, carriage.*
F.I.C.E., *Fellow of the Institution of Civil Engineers.*
fict., *fiction,* fiction.
Fid. Def., *Fidei Defensor,* défenseur de la foi.
F.I.D.O. ['faidou], *Fog Investigation Dispersal Operation,* F.I.D.O.
fi. fa., *Jur: fieri facias,* ordonnance de saisie-exécution.
F.I.F.A. ['fi:fə], Fédération internationale de football association.
fig., **1.** *figure,* figure, fig. **2.** *figurative,* figuré, fig.
F.I.J., *Fellow of the Institute of Journalists.*
filt., *Pharm: filter,* filtrez, filt.
F.I.Mech.E., *Fellow of the Institution of Mechanical Engineers.*
fl., **1.** *A.Num: florin,* florin, fl. **2.** *Pharm: flowers,* fleurs, fl. **3.** *floruit,* florissait.
F.L., **1.** *Mil: flight lieutenant,* capitaine d'aviation. **2.** *Ph: focal length,* longueur focale. **3.** *P: French letter,* capote anglaise.
F.L.A., **1.** *First Lord of the Admiralty.* **2.** *Fellow of the Library Association.*
Fla., *Geog: Florida,* Floride.
F.L.C.M., *Fellow of the London College of Music.*
flor., *floruit,* florissait.
fl.oz., *Meas: fluid ounce(s).*
F.L.Q., Front de libération du Québec.
F.L.S., *Fellow of the Linnaean Society.*
F/Lt, Flt Lt, *flight lieutenant,* capitaine d'aviation.

fm, *fathom*, brasse.
F.M., **1.** *El: field magnet*, inducteur. **2.** *Mil: field marshal*, maréchal. **3.** *Field Manual*, manuel de service en campagne. **4.** *W.Tel: Frequency Modulation*, modulation de fréquence, F.M.
F.M.B., *Federal Maritime Board.*
fo., *folio*, folio, f°; in-folio, inf(o), in-fo.
F.O., **1.** *Foreign Office*, ministère des affaires étrangères. **2.** *Mil: field officer*, officier supérieur. **3.** *Flying Officer*, lieutenant (aviateur). **4.** *Mus: full organ*, orgue à plein jeu, plein. **5.** *fallout*, retombées (radioactives).
f.o.b., *Com: free on board*, franco à bord, f. à b.
F.O.B.S., *Fractional Orbit Bombardment System.*
F.O.C. *(of Union) Father of Chapel.*
f.o.c., *Com: free of charge*, franco, fco, fro.
fol., *folio*, folio, f°, in-folio, in-f(o), in-fol.
foll., *following*, suivant, suiv.
F.O.O., *Mil: Forward Observation Officer.*
f.o.q., *Com: free on quay*, franco à quai.
f.o.r., *Com: free on rail*, franco sur wagon.
for., **1.** *foreign*, étranger. **2.** *forestry*, sylviculture.
f.o.s., *Com: (a) free on shipboard*, franco à bord, f.à b.; *(b) free on station*, franco gare.
f.o.w., *Com: (a) free on wharf*, franco quai; *(b) free on wagon*, franco sur wagon.
f.oz., *Meas: fluid ounce(s).*
F.P., **1.** *fire plug*, prise d'eau, bouche d'incendie. **2.** *freezing point*, point de congélation. **3.** *esp. Scot: former pupil*, ancien élève.
f.p., **1.** *Fin: fully paid*, libéré, lib. **2.** *Mec.Meas: foot-pound(s)*, pied(s)-livre(s). **3.** *fixed price*, prix fixe.
f.p.a., *M.Ins: free of particular average*, franc d'avaries particulières, f.a.p.
F.P.A., **1.** *Family Planning Association.* **2.** *Foreign Press Association.* **3.** *Film Producers' Association.*
F.P.C., *U.S: Federal Power Commission.*
F.P.H.A., *U.S: Federal Public Housing Authority.*
F.P.S., **1.** *Fellow of the Philological Society.* **2.** *Mec.Meas: foot-pound-second*, pied-livre-seconde.
Fr., **1.** *Geog: (a) France*, France, Fr.; *(b) French*, français. **2.** *Ecc: Father*, Père, P. **3.** *Ecc: friar*, frère, Fr. **4.** *Frau*, madame.
fr., **1.** *Num: franc(s)*, franc(s), fr. **2.** *(a) frequent*, fréquent; *(b) Gram: frequentative*, fréquentatif, itératif. **3.** *fragment*, fragment. **4.** *from*, de.
F.R.A.M., *Fellow of the Royal Academy of Music.*
F.R.A.S., **1.** *Fellow of the Royal Astronomical Society.* **2.** *Fellow of the Royal Asiatic Society.*
F.R.B., *U.S:* **1.** *Federal Reserve Bank.* **2.** *Federal Reserve Board.*
F.R.B.S., *Fellow of the Royal Botanical Society.*
F.R.C., *U.S:* **1.** *Federal Radio Commission.* **2.** *Flight Research Center.*
F.R.C.M., *Fellow of the Royal College of Music.*
F.R.C.O., *Fellow of the Royal College of Organists.*
F.R.C.P., *Fellow of the Royal College of Physicians.*
F.R.C.S., *Fellow of the Royal College of Surgeons.*
F.R.C.V.S., *Fellow of the Royal College of Veterinary Surgeons.*
F.R.Econ.S., *Fellow of the Royal Economic Society.*
freq., *(a) frequent*, fréquent; *(b) Gram: frequentative*, fréquentatif, itératif.
F.R.G.S., *Fellow of the Royal Geographical Society.*
F.R.H.S., *Fellow of the Royal Horticultural Society.*
F.R.H(ist).S., *Fellow of the Royal Historical Society.*
Fri., *Friday*, vendredi, vend.
F.R.I.B.A., *Fellow of the Royal Institute of British Architects.*
F.R.I.C., *Fellow of the Royal Institute of Chemistry.*
F.R.I.C.S., *Fellow of the Royal Institution of Chartered Surveyors.*
Frl., *Fräulein*, mademoiselle, mlle.
F.R.Met.S., *Fellow of the Royal Meteorological Society.*
F.R.P.S., *Fellow of the Royal Photographic Society.*
F.R.S., **1.** *Fellow of the Royal Society.* **2.** *Federal Reserve System.*
F.R.S.A., *Fellow of the Royal Society of Arts.*
F.R.S.E., *Fellow of the Royal Society, Edinburgh.*
F.R.S.G.S., *Fellow of the Royal Scottish Geographical Society.*
F.R.S.L., *Fellow of the Royal Society of Literature.*
F.R.S.S., *Fellow of the Royal Statistical Society.*
frt, *freight*, fret.
F.S., **1.** *Mil: field service*, service en campagne. **2.** *feasibility study*, étude de faisabilité. **3.** *Fabian Society*, Association fabienne.
f.-s., *Mec: foot-second(s)*, pied(s) par seconde.
F/S, *financial statement*, situation de trésorerie.
F.S.A., *Fellow of the Society of Antiquaries.*
F.S.H., *follicle-stimulating hormone*, folliculino-stimuline hypophysaire.
F.S.R., *Mil: Field Service Regulation*, règlement du service en campagne.
Ft, *Fort*, fort.
ft, *Meas: foot, feet*, pied(s), p., pd; *Mec:* **ft-lb.,** *foot-pound*, pied-livre.
F.T.C., *U.S: Federal Trade Commission.*
fth(m), *Meas: fathom*, brasse.
ft/s, *feet per second*, pieds par seconde.
fur., *Meas: furlong.*
fur(l)., *Mil: furlough*, congé, permission.
furn., *furnished*, meublé.
fut., *future*, futur; avenir.
fwd, *forward.*
f.y., *fiscal year*, année fiscale.
F.Z.S., *Fellow of the Zoological Society.*

g., **1.** *Meas: gramme*, gramme, gr. **2.** *Num: A: guinea*, guinée. **3.** *Com: goods*, marchandise, mise. **4.** *gauge*, jauge. **5.** *Gram: (a) gender*, genre; *(b) genitive*, génitif. **6.** *gravitational acceleration*, accélération de la pesanteur; *gravity*, gravité, g.
g.a., g/a, *M.Ins: general average*, avaries communes.
Ga, *Geog: Georgia, Géorgie.*
G.A., **1.** *Ecc: General Assembly.* **2.** *Com: general agent.*
Gael., *Gaelic*, gaélique.
Gal., *B: Galatians*, Galates, Gal.
gal(l)., *Meas: gallon(s).*
G.A.O., *General Accounting Office.*
G.A.T.T., *General Agreement on Tariffs and Trade*, arrangement général pour les tarifs et le commerce.
G.A.W., *U.S: guaranteed annual wage.*
G.B., *Geog: Great Britain*, Grande-Bretagne, G.B.
G.B.E., *Grand Cross of the Order of the British Empire.*
G Branch, **1.** *Mil: General Staff Branch*, Troisième Bureau. **2.** *Navy: U.S:* **G1, G2, G3, G4 Branch,** *General Staff Division 1, 2, 3, 4*, Premier, Deuxième, Troisième, Quatrième, Bureau.
G.B.S., **1.** *George Bernard Shaw.* **2.** *U.S: Government Bureau of Standards.*
G.C., **1.** *George Cross.* **2.** *Grand Cross (of the Legion of Honour)*, Grand'croix, G(r).C.
G.C.A., *Av: (a) ground controlled approach*, système international d'approche et d'atterrissage contrôlés; *(b) ground control apparatus.*
g.cal., *Ph: gramme-calorie(s)*, petite(s) calorie(s), c.
G.C.B., *Grand Cross of the Order of the Bath.*
G.C.D., *Mth: greatest common divisor*, plus grand commun diviseur, p.g.c.d.
G.C.E., *General Certificate of Education.*
G.C.I., *Mil: ground controlled interception*, interception commandée de la terre.
G.C.I.E., *Hist: Knight Grand Commander of the Order of the Indian Empire.*
G.C.L.H., *Grand Cross of the Legion of Honour*, grand'croix de la Légion d'Honneur, G(r).C.
G.C.M., *U.S: General court martial*, Tribunal militaire général.
G.C.M.G., *Grand Cross of the Order of St Michael and St George.*
G.C.R., *ground controlled radar.*
G.C.S.I., *Grand Commander of the Order of the Star of India.*
G.C.V.O., *Grand Cross of the Royal Victorian Order.*
gd, *good*, bon.
g.d., *gravimetric density*, densité gravimétrique.
Gdns, *Gardens*, rue.
G.D.R., *German Democratic Republic*, République démocratique allemande, R.D.A.
Gen., **1.** *Mil: General*, général, gal. **2.** *B: Genesis*, Genèse, Gen.
gen., *Gram: (a) gender*, genre; *(b) genitive*, génitif.
gen.av., *Com: general average*, avaries communes, a.c.
genit., *Gram: genitive*, génitif.
gent., *gentleman*, monsieur.
Geo., **1.** *George.* **2.** *Geog: Georgia, Géorgie.*
geog., *geographical, geography*, géographique, géographie.
geol., *geological, geology*, géologique, géologie.
geom., *geometric(al), geometry*, géométrique, géométrie.
ger., *Gram: (a) gerund*, gérondif; *(b) gerundive*, gérondif.
GeV., *El: gigaelectron volt*, gigaélectron-volt, GeV.
G.F.R., *Geog: German Federal Republic*, République fédérale allemande, R.F.A.
G.F.T.U., *U.S: General Federation of Trade Unions.*
G.G., **1.** *Governor General.* **2.** *Girl Guides.*
g.gr., *Com: great gross*, douze grosses.
G.H.A., *Nav: Greenwich hour angle.*
G.H.Q., *Mil: General Headquarters*, grand quartier général, G.Q.G.
G.I., *U.S: Mil: (a) Government issue, general issue*, matériel réglementaire de l'armée; *(b) F:* soldat (américain).
Gib., *Geog: Gibraltar.*
Glam., *Geog: Glamorganshire.*
G.L.C., *Adm: Greater London Council.*
Glos., *Geog: Gloucestershire.*
gm., *Meas: gramme(s)*, gramme(s), g.
G.M. **1.** *George Medal.* **2.** *Freemasonry: Grand Master*, Grand-Maître, G.-M. **3.** *guided missile*, engin téléguidé.
G-man, *(Government man)*, agent de la police fédérale.
G.M.C., *General Medical Council.*
G.M.T., *Hor: Greenwich mean time*, temps moyen de Greenwich, temps universel, T.U.
G.M.W.U., *General and Municipal Workers' Union.*
gn., *Num: A: guinea*, guinée.
G.N., *U.S: graduate nurse.*
G.N.P., *gross national product*, produit national brut, P.N.B.
gnr., *Mil: gunner.*
G.O., **1.** *Grand Officer (of the Legion of Honour)*, Grand Officier, G(r).O. **2.** *Mil: general orders*, ordres généraux, consigne générale.
G.O.C., *Mil: general officer commanding*, officier général commandant.
G.O.M., *Grand Old Man.*
G.O.P., *U.S: Grand Old Party*, le Parti républicain.
Goth., *Gothic*, gothique.
Gov., *(a) government*, gouvernement; *(b) governor*, gouverneur.
Gov.-Gen., *Governor-General*, Gouverneur général.
Govt, *government*, gouvernement.
G.P., *Med:* **1.** *General Practitioner*, médecin de médecine générale, M.G. **2.** *general paralysis*, paralysie générale, p.g.
Gp Capt., *Mil.Av: colonel.*
G.P.I., **1.** *Rad: ground position indicator*, indicateur de position au sol. **2.** *Med: general paralysis of the insane.*
G.P.O., **1.** *A: General Post Office* = Postes et Télécommunications, P.E.T. **2.** *U.S: Government Printing Office.*
G.Q., *Navy: general quarters*, postes de combat.
gr., **1.** *Com: gross*, (i) grosse(s), (ii) brut. **2.** *Meas: (a) gramme(s)*, gramme(s), g.; *(b) grain(s)*, grain(s). **3.** *Ph: gravity*, gravité, g. **4.** *great*, grand. **5.** *grammar*, grammaire. **6.** *grade*, rang.

G.R., *Georgius Rex*, le roi George.
grad., **1.** *graduate*, diplômé. **2.** *gradient*.
gram., *grammar*, grammaire.
grm., *Meas: gramme(s)*, gramme(s), g(r).
gro., *Com: gross*, (i) grosse, (ii) brut.
G.R.T., *Com: gross registered tonnage*, jauge brute.
gr.wt., *gross weight*, poids brut.
G.S., **1.** *gold standard*, étalon (d')or. **2.** *Mil: General Staff*, état-major général. **3.** *Mil: general service*.
gs, *A. Num: guineas*, guinées.
G.S.A., *Girl Scouts of America*.
G.S.C., *General Staff Corps*, corps d'officiers brevetés d'état-major.
G.S.O., *Mil: general staff officer*, officier d'état-major.
G.S.T., *Hor: Greenwich sidereal time*, temps sidéral de Greenwich.
G.T., **1.** *Meas: gross ton*, tonne forte. **2.** *Aut: gran turismo*.
gt, *great*, grand.
gtd, *guaranteed*, avec garantie.
gu(in)., *Num: A: guinea*, guinée.
guar., *guaranteed*, avec garantie.
G.W.R., *Hist: Great Western Railway*.
gym., (*a*) *gymnastics*, gymnastique; (*b*) *gymnasium*, gymnase.

H., **1.** *Ph: henry*, henry, H. **2.** *hydrant*, bouche d'eau. **3.** (*a*) (*of pencil lead*) *hard*, dur: (*b*) *hardness*, dureté.
h., **1.** *hour(s)*, heure(s), h. **2.** *hecto-*, hecto-. **3.** *horse*, cheval. **4.** *hot*, chaud. **5.** *husband*, mari.
ha., *Meas: hectare*, hectare, ha.
H.A., (*a*) *Horse Artillery*, artillerie montée; (*b*) *Heavy Artillery*, artillerie lourde, A.L.
H.A.C., *Honourable Artillery Company*.
h. & c., *hot and cold* (*water*), eau courante chaude et froide.
Hants., *Geog: Hampshire*.
HB, (*of pencil lead*) *hard black*.
H.B.M., *Her, His, Britannic Majesty*, Sa Majesté Britannique, S.M.B.
H.C., **1.** *House of Commons*, Chambre des Communes. **2.** *Ecc: Holy Communion*, sainte communion.
h.c., *honoris causa*.
hcap., *Sp: handicap*, handicap.
H.C.F., **1.** *Mth: highest common factor*, plus grand commun diviseur, p.g.c.d. **2.** *Honorary Chaplain to the Forces*.
H.C.M., *His, Her, Catholic Majesty*, Sa Majesté Catholique, S.M.C.
hcp, *Sp: handicap*, handicap.
hd, *Meas:* **1.** *hogshead*. **2.** *hand*, paume. **3.** *head*, tête.
hdbk, *handbook*, manuel.
H.E., **1.** (*a*) *His Eminence*, son Éminence, S.E(m).; (*b*) *His, Her, Excellency*, son Excellence, S.E(xc). **2.** *high explosive*, haut explosif.
Heb., (*a*) *Hebrew*, hébreu; (*b*) *B: Hebrews*, Hébreux, Hébr.
hect., *Meas: hectolitre*, hectolitre, hl.
hectog., *Meas: hectogramme*, hectogramme, hg.
her., (*a*) *heraldic*, héraldique; (*b*) *heraldry*, science héraldique.
Herts., *Geog: Hertfordshire*.
HEW, *U.S: Department of Health, Education and Welfare*.
hf., *half*, moitié.
HF., **1.** *Ecc: Holy Father*, Saint-Père, S.-P. **2.** *El: high frequency*, haute fréquence.
hfc, *El: high-frequency current*, courant à haute fréquence.
hg., *Meas: hectogramme*, hectogramme, hg.
H.G., **1.** *His, Her, Grace*, Sa Grâce, S.G. **2.** *Hist: Home Guard*. **3.** *Horse Guards*, Garde du corps (à cheval).
H.G.V., *heavy goods vehicle*, poids lourd; **H.G.V. licence**, permis (de conduire un) poids lourd.
H.H., **1.** *His, Her, Highness*, Son Altesse, S.A. **2.** *His Holiness*, Sa Sainteté, S.S.
hhd., *Meas: hogshead*.
H.I., *Geog: Hawaiian Islands*.
H.I.H., *His, Her, Imperial Highness*, son Altesse Impériale, S.A.I.
H.I.M., *His, Her, Imperial Majesty*, sa Majesté Impériale, S.M.I.
hist., (*a*) *historical*, historique; (*b*) *history*, histoire.
H.K., **1.** *House of Keys*, le parlement de l'île de Man. **2.** *Geog: Hong Kong*.
H.L., *House of Lords*, Chambre des Lords.
hl., *Meas: hectolitre*, hectolitre, hl.
hm., *Meas: hectometre*, hectomètre, hectom., hm.
H.M., **1.** *His, Her, Majesty*, sa Majesté, S.M. **2.** *Sch: Headmaster, Headmistress*, directeur, -trice.
H.M.A.S., *His, Her, Majesty's Australian Ship*.
H.M.C.S., *His, Her, Majesty's Canadian Ship*.
H.M.I., *His, Her, Majesty's Inspector* (*of schools*) = Inspecteur d'Académie.
H.M.N.Z.S., *His, Her, Majesty's New Zealand Ship*.
H.M.S., *His, Her, Majesty's Ship*.
H.M.S.O., *His, Her, Majesty's Stationery Office*, service des fournitures et des publications de l'Administration.
H.M.V., *Rec: His Master's Voice*.
ho., *house*, maison.
H.O., **1.** *Home Office*, Ministère de l'Intérieur. **2.** *head office*, bureau central.
Hon., **1.** *Honourable*. **2.** *Honorary*, honoraire; **Hon. Sec.**, *Honorary Secretary*.
Hons, *Sch: Honours*.
hor., *horizon*, horizon.
hort., *horticulture*, horticulture.
hosp., *hospital*, hôpital.
H.P., **1.** *hire purchase*. **2.** *House Physician* = interne (en médecine).
h.p., **1.** *high pressure*, haute pression, h.p. **2.** *Mec: horsepower*, cheval-vapeur, c.v., ch.v(ap).; chevaux, chx.
H.Q., *headquarters*, (i) poste de commandement, P.C.; (ii) quartier général, Q.G.; (iii) état-major, E.M.
hr, *hour*, heure, h.
H.R., *Pol:* **1.** *Hist: Home Rule*, autonomie. **2.** *U.S: House of Representatives*, Chambre des Représentants.
h.r., *El: high resistance*, haute résistance.
H.R.H., *His, Her, Royal Highness*, son Altesse Royale, S.A.R.
hrs., *hours*, heures.
H.S.H., *His, Her, Serene Highness*, son Altesse Sérénissime, S.A.S.
H.S.T., *Rail: high speed train* = train grande vitesse, T.G.V.
ht., **1.** *heat*, chaleur. **2.** *height*, hauteur.
H.T., *El: high tension*, haute tension, H.T.
hund., *hundred*, cent.
Hung., *Geog:* (*a*) *Hungarian*, hongrois; (*b*) *Hungary*, Hongrie.
H.V., *El: high voltage*, haute tension, H.T.
h.w., *Cr: hit wicket*.
H.W.M., *Nau: high water mark*, niveau de haute mer.
Hy, *Henry*, Henri.
hyd., **1.** *hydraulics*, hydraulique. **2.** *hydrostatics*, hydrostatique.
hyp., (*a*) *hypothesis*, hypothèse; (*b*) *hypothetical*, hypothétique.
Hz., *El: hertz*, hertz, hz.

I., *Island, Isle*, île.
Ia, *Geog: Iowa*.
IAAF, *International Amateur Athletic Federation*.
IAEA, *International Atomic Energy Agency*.
I.A.F., *International Automobile Federation*, Fédération internationale de l'automobile, F.I.A.
IATA, *International Air Transport Association*, Association internationale des transports aériens, A.I.T.A.
I.B.A., *Independent Broadcasting Authority*.
ibid., *ibidem*, ibid.
I.B.M., *Cmptr: International Business Machines*.
IBRD, *International Bank for Reconstruction and Development*.
I.C., **1.** *Jesus Christ*, Jésus-Christ, I.C. **2.** *Intelligence Corps*.
i/c, **1.** *in charge* (*of*). **2.** *internal combustion*, combustion interne.
I.C.A., **1.** *Institute of Contemporary Arts*. **2.** *Institute of Chartered Accountants*.
I.C.A.O., *International Civil Aviation Organization*, Organisation de l'aviation civile internationale, O.A.C.I.
ICBM, *intercontinental ballistic missile*, missile balistique intercontinental.
Ice., *Geog: Iceland*, Islande.
I.C.E., *Institute of Civil Engineers*.
I.C.I., *Imperial Chemical Industries*.
icon., *iconography*, iconographie.
ID, *identification*, identification; *U.S:* **ID card**, carte d'identité.
id., *idem*, id.
I.D., *Mil: etc: Intelligence Department*.
Ida., *Geog: Idaho*.
I.D.A., *International Development Association*.
I.D.T.A., *International Dance Teachers' Association*.
i.e., *id est, that is*, c'est-à-dire, c.-à-d.
I.E.C., *International Electrotechnical Commission*, Commission électrotechnique internationale, C.E.I.
I.F., *W.Tel: intermediate frequency*, fréquence moyenne.
IFC, *International Finance Corporation*.
I.F.R., *Av: instrument flight rules*, règles de vol aux instruments.
I.F.T.U., *International Federation of Trade Unions*, Fédération syndicale internationale, F.S.I.
ign., *ignition*, allumage.
i.h.p., *indicated horsepower*, chevaux indiqués.
I.H.S., *Jesus*, Jésus (from Greek ΙΗΣΟΥΣ).
I.L., *Institute of Linguists*.
I.L.E.A., *Inner London Education Authority*.
Ill., *Geog: Illinois*.
ill(us)., (*a*) *illustrated*, illustré; (*b*) *illustration*, illustration.
I.L.O., *International Labour Organization*, Organisation internationale du travail, O.I.T.
I.L.P., *Pol: Independent Labour Party*, Parti travailliste indépendant.
I.L.S., *Av: instrument landing system*, dispositif d'atterrissage aux instruments.
I.M., *intramuscular*, intramusculaire.
IMCO, *Intergovernmental Maritime Consultative Organization*, Organisation consultative maritime intergouvernementale, OCMI.
I.M.F., *International Monetary Fund*, Fonds monétaire international, F.M.I.
I.M.M., *Institution of Mining and Metallurgy*.
Imp., *Imperator, -trix*, empereur, impératrice.
imp., **1.** *Typ: imprimatur*. **2.** *Paperm: imperial*, format grand jésus. **3.** (*a*) *imported*, importé; (*b*) *importer*, importateur.
imper., *Gram: imperative*, impératif.
imperf., *Gram: imperfect*, imparfait.
in., *Meas: inch*, pouce, p(o).
Inc., *Incorporated*.
inc., **1.** *increase*, augmentation. **2.** *income*, revenu.
incl., (*a*) *inclusive*, inclusivement; (*b*) *including*, y compris.
Ind., **1.** *Independent*, indépendant. **2.** *Geog: India*, Inde. **3.** *Geog: Indiana*.
ind., **1.** *industry*, industrie, ind. **2.** *Gram: indicative*, indicatif. **3.** *independence*, indépendance.
inf., **1.** *infantry*, infanterie, inf. **2.** *infra, below*, infra, au-dessous. **3.** *Gram: infinitive*, infinitif.
inj., *Pharm: injection*, injection, inj.
I.N.R.I., *Ecc: Iesus Nazarenus Rex Iudaeorum*, Jésus de Nazareth, Roi des Juifs.
ins., **1.** *insurance*, assurance, asse. **2.** *Meas: inches*, pouces, ppo.
Insp., *Inspector*, inspecteur.
Inst., (*a*) *Institute*, institut; (*b*) *Institution*, institution.

inst., *Corr: instant*, courant, c., cour., ct.
instr., **1.** *instructor*, moniteur; enseignant. **2.** *instrument*, instrument.
int., **1.** *Fin: interest*, intérêt, in(er). **2.** *interior*, intérieur. **3.** *internal*, intérieur.
inter., **1.** *intermediate*, intermédiaire. **2.** *Gram: interrogative*, interrogatif.
intr., **1.** *Gram: intransitive*, intransitif. **2.** *introduction*, introduction.
inv., **1.** *Com: invoice*, facture, fre. **2.** *invenit*, (*he*) *designed* (*it*), inv. **3.** *inventor*, inventeur. **4.** *inventory*, inventaire. **5.** *invariable*, invariable, inv.
I.O.M., *Geog: Isle of Man.*
I.O.W., *Geog: Isle of Wight.*
IPA, **1.** (*a*) *International Phonetic Association*; (*b*) *International Phonetic Alphabet.* **2.** *R.t.m.* (*beer*) *India Pale Ale.*
i.p.s., *Rec: inches per second* = centimètres par seconde, cm/s.
I.Q., *intelligence quotient*, quotient intellectuel, Q.I.
Ir., *Geog:* (*a*) *Ireland*, Irlande; (*b*) *Irish*, irlandais.
I.R., **1.** *Inland Revenue*, le fisc. **2.** *infrared*, infra(-)rouge.
I.R.A., *Irish Republican Army.*
IRBM, *intermediate range ballistic missile*, missile balistique à portée moyenne.
I.R.C. (C.), *International Red Cross* (*Committee*), Comité international de la Croix-Rouge, C.I.C.R.
IRO, **1.** *Inland Revenue Office*, bureau du fisc. **2.** *International Refugee Organization.*
I.R.S., *U.S: Internal Revenue Service.*
Is., *Isle, Island*, île.
Is(a)., *B: Isaiah*, Ésaïe.
I.S.B.N., *Publ: international standard book number*, I.S.B.N.
I.S.C., (*motor racing*) *International Sporting Commission* = Code sportif international, C.S.I.
ISIS ['aisis], *International Student Insurance Service.*
I.S.O., **1.** *Imperial Service Order.* **2.** *International Standards Organization.*
It., *Geog: Italy*, Italie.
I.T.A., *Independent Television Authority.*
Ital., *Italian*, italien.
ital., *Typ: italics*, italique.
ITN, *Independent Television News.*
ITO, *International Trade Organization.*
I.T.U., **1.** *International Telecommunications Union*, Union internationale des télécommunications, U.I.T. **2.** (*in hospital*) *Intensive Therapy Unit.*
ITV, *Independent Television.*
I.U.D., (*for birth control*) *intra-uterine device*, stérilet.
I.U.S., *International Union of Students.*
I.V., *intravenous*, intraveineux.
I.W.W., *Industrial Workers of the World.*

J., **1.** *El: joule*, joule, J., j. **2.** *Cards: jack*, valet. **3.** *Judge*, juge. **4.** *Justice*, justice.
J.A., *Judge Advocate*, rapporteur.
J/A, *Bank: joint account*, compte conjoint.
J.A.G., *Judge advocate general*, Président du tribunal militaire de cassation.
Jam., **1.** *Geog: Jamaica*, la Jamaïque. **2.** *B: James*, Jacques.
Jan., *January*, janvier, janv.
Jap., *Geog:* (*a*) *Japan*, Japon; (*b*) *Japanese*, japonais.
Jas., (i) *James*; (ii) *B: James*, Jacques.
J.C., **1.** *Jesus Christ*, Jésus-Christ, J.-C. **2.** *Jur: Juris Consultus*, jurisconsulte. **3.** *Justice Clerk*, assesseur du président du tribunal.
J.C.R., *Sch:* **1.** *Junior Common Room.* **2.** *Junior Combination Room.*
jct(n)., *junction*, jonction.
Jer., **1.** *B: Jeremiah*, Jérémie, Jér. **2.** *Geog: Jersey.*
J.F.K., *John Fitzgerald Kennedy* (*Airport*).
jn, *junction*, jonction.
Jno, *John*, Jean.
Jnr, *Junior*, jeune, Je, Jne.
Josh., *B: Joshua*, Josué.
jour., *journal*, journal, jl.
journ., *journalism*, journalisme.
J.P., *Justice of the Peace* = juge de paix.
Jr, *Junior*, jeune, Je, Jne.
jt, *joint*, jointure.
Jud., *B: Judith.*
jud., *judicial*, judiciaire.
Judg., *B: Judges*, Juges.
Jul., *July*, juillet, juil.
Jun., **1.** *June*, juin. **2.** *Junior*, jeune, Je, Jne.

K., **1.** *Ph: Kelvin* (*scale*), (échelle de) Kelvin, K. **2.** *King('s)*, (du) roi. **3.** *Knight*, Chevalier, Ch(ev). **4.** *Mus: Köchel.*
k, *kilo*, kilo, k.
kA., *El: kiloampere*, kiloampère, kA.
Kan(s)., *Geog: Kansas.*
KANU ['kɑ:nu:], *Kenya African National Union.*
K.B., **1.** *Knight Bachelor.* **2.** *Jur: King's Bench.*
K.B.E., *Knight Commander* (*of the Order*) *of the British Empire*, Chevalier de l'Ordre de l'Empire britannique.
kc., *El: kilocycle*, kilocycle, kc; kilohertz, kHz.
K.C., **1.** *Jur: King's Counsel.* **2.** *King's College.*
kc(a)l., *Ph: kilocalorie*, kilocalorie, kcal.
K.C.B., *Knight Commander* (*of the Order*) *of the Bath*, Chevalier Commandeur de l'Ordre du Bain.
K.C.I.E., *Knight Commander* (*of the Order*) *of the Indian Empire*, Chevalier Commandeur de l'Ordre de l'Empire des Indes.
K.C.M.G., *Knight Commander* (*of the Order*) *of St Michael and St George*, Chevalier Commandeur de l'Ordre de Saint-Michel et Saint-Georges.
K.C.S.I., *Knight Commander* (*of the Order*) *of the Star of India*, Chevalier Commandeur de l'Ordre de l'Étoile des Indes.
K.C.V.O., *Knight Commander of the Royal Victorian Order*, Chevalier Commandeur de l'Ordre royal de Victoria.
K.E., *kinetic energy*, énergie cinétique.
Ken., *Geog: Kentucky.*
keV, *El: kilo-electron-volt*, kilo-électron-volt.
kg., **1.** *Meas: kilogramme*, kilogramme, kg. **2.** *Com: keg.*
K.G., *Knight* (*of the Order*) *of the Garter*, Chevalier de l'Ordre de la Jarretière.
K.G.B., *secret police in the Soviet Union*, police secrète en Union soviétique, K.G.B. (from Russian Komitet Gosudarstvennoï Bezopasnosti).
kgm., *Mec: kilogrammeter*, kilogrammètre, kgm.
kg/m³, *Ph: kilogramme per cubic metre*, kilogramme par mètre cube, kg/m³.
Kgs, *B: Kings*, Rois.
kHz, *El: kilohertz*, kilohertz, kHz.
kJ, *El: kilojoule*, kilojoule, kJ.
K.K.K., *U.S: Ku Klux Klan.*
kl, *Meas: kilolitre*, kilolitre, kl.
km., *Meas: kilometre(s)*, kilomètre(s), km; **km²**, *square kilometre(s)*, kilomètre(s) carré(s), km²; **km³**, *cubic kilometre(s)*, kilomètre(s) cubes, km³.
km.p.h., *kilometres per hour*, kilomètres (à l')heure, km/h.
kn., *Nau: knot(s)*, nœud(s).
Knt., *Knight*, Chevalier, Ch(ev).
K.O., *Box: knockout*, knock-out, k.o.; **he was K.O.'d**, il a été mis k.o.
K.P., *Knight* (*of the Order*) *of St Patrick*, Chevalier de l'Ordre de Saint-Patrice.
k.p.h., *Meas: kilometres per hour*, kilomètres (à l')heure, km/h.
K.S., *Sch: King's scholar.*
K.St.J., *Knight* (*of the Order*) *of St John*, Chevalier de l'Ordre de Saint-Jean.
Kt., *Knight*, Chevalier, Ch(ev).
K.T., **1.** *Knight* (*of the Order*) *of the Thistle*, Chevalier de l'Ordre du Chardon. **2.** *Knight Templar.*
kV, kv, *El: kilovolt*, kilovolt, kV.
kva., *El: kilovoltampere*, kilovoltampère, kVA.
kvar, *Elcs: kilovar*, kilovar, kvar.
kvarh, *Elcs: kilovar-hour*, kilovarheure, kvarh.
kW, kw, *El: kilowatt*, kilowatt, kW.
kWhr, kwhr, *El: kilowatt-hour(s)*, kilowatt(s)-heure, kWh.
Ky, *Geog: Kentucky.*

L., **1.** *Lake*, lac. **2.** *Aut: learner* (*driver*), apprenti conducteur; **L plate**, plaque d'apprenti conducteur. **3.** *Pol: Liberal*, libéral. **4.** *Licentiate*, diplômé. **5.** *Latin*, latin, lat.
£, *Num: libra, librae, pound sterling*, livre(s) sterling, l(iv). s(t); **£E.**, *Egyptian pound(s)*, livre(s) égyptienne(s); **£T.**, *Turkish pound(s)*, livre(s) turque(s).
l., **1.** *Num: lira*, lire. **2.** *Meas:* (*a*) *litre*, litre, l.; (*b*) *league*, lieue, l. **3.** *length*, longueur, long. **4.** *line*, ligne. **5.** *left*, gauche, g. **6.** *El: lumen*, lumen, lm, lu.
La., *Geog: Louisiana.*
L.A., **1.** *Library Association.* **2.** *Geog: Los Angeles.*
l.a., *Pharm: lege artis, as directed*, l.a.
Lab., **1.** *Pol: Labour*, travailliste. **2.** *Geog: Labrador.*
L.A.C., *Leading Aircraftman*, caporal.
L.A.C.W., *Leading Aircraftwoman*, femme caporal de la W.R.A.F.
Lam., *B: Lamentations*, Lamentations, Lam.
Lancs., *Geog: Lancashire.*
lang., *language*, langue.
Lat., *Latin*, latin, lat.
lat., *Geog: latitude*, latitude, lat.
lb., **1.** *Meas: libra, pound*, livre, lb. **2.** *Cr: leg bye.*
l.b.w., *Cr: leg before wicket.*
L.C., **1.** *Lord Chamberlain*, Chambellan. **2.** *Lord Chancellor*, Grand Chancelier.
l.c., **1.** *Typ: lower case*, bas de casse. **2.** *Th: left centre*, à gauche au second plan. **3.** *loco citato, in the passage already quoted*, l(oc). c(it). **4.** *Bank: letter of credit*, lettre de crédit, l/cr.
L.C.C., *A: London County Council.*
L.C.D., *Mth: least, lowest, common denominator*, plus petit commun dénominateur, p.p.c.d.
L.C.J., *Lord Chief Justice*, président du Tribunal du banc de la Reine, du Roi.
L.C.M., *Mth: lowest common multiple*, plus petit commun multiple, p.p.c.m.
L/Cpl, *Mil: Lance Corporal*, soldat de première classe.
Ld, *Lord.*
Ldg, *Leading.*
Ldn, *Geog: London*, Londres.
Ldp, (*a*) *Lordship*; (*b*) *Ladyship.*
L.D.S., *Licentiate in Dental Surgery* = chirurgien-dentiste diplômé.
L.E.A., *Adm: Local Education Authority.*
led., *Book-k: ledger*, grand livre, g.l.
leg., **1.** *legal*, légal. **2.** *legislative*, législatif.
Leics., *Geog: Leicestershire.*
L.E.M., *lunar excursion module*, module lunaire d'excursion.
Lev., *B: Leviticus*, Lévitique, Lévit.
lex., (*a*) *lexical*, lexicologique; (*b*) *lexicon*, lexique.
L.F., *El: low frequency*, basse fréquence.
lg., **1.** *large*, grand. **2.** *long*, long.
lgth., *length*, longueur, long.
l.h., *Mus: etc: left hand*, main gauche.
L.I., **1.** *Light Infantry*, infanterie légère. **2.** *Geog: Long Island.*
Lib., **1.** *Pol: Liberal*, libéral. **2.** *F: Liberation*, libération.
lib., *library*, bibliothèque, Bib.
Lieut., *Mil: Lieutenant*, lieutenant, Lieut, Lt.
Lieut.-Col., *Mil: Lieutenant-Colonel*, lieutenant-colonel, Lieut-Col.
lin., **1.** *Pharm: liniment*, liniment, lin. **2.** *lineal*, linéal. **3.** *linear*, linéaire.
Lincs., *Geog: Lincolnshire.*
ling., *linguistics*, linguistique.
lit., **1.** *literary*, littéraire. **2.** *literature*, littérature.

Lith., *Geog:* (*a*) *Lithuania*, Lithuanie; (*b*) *Lithuanian*, lithuanien.
lith., (*a*) *lithograph*, lithographie; (*b*) *lithography*, lithographie.
Litt. D., *Litterarum Doctor, Doctor of Letters*, Docteur ès lettres.
L.J., *Lord Justice*, juge de la cour de cassation.
ll., *lines*, lignes.
L.L., *Lord Lieutenant.*
l.l., *loco laudato, at the place indicated*, l.l.
LL.B., *Legum Baccalaureus, Bachelor of Laws*, Bachelier en Droit.
LL.D., *Legum Doctor, Doctor of Laws*, Docteur en Droit.
LL.M., *Legum Magister, Master of Laws.*
L.M., *lunar module*, module lunaire.
L.M.H., *Sch:* (*at Oxford*) *Lady Margaret Hall.*
L.O., *Liaison Officer*, officier de liaison.
loc. cit., *loco citato, in the passage already quoted*, l(oc). c(it).
log., *Mth: logarithm*, logarithme, log.
Lond., *London*, Londres.
long., *Geog: longitude*, longitude, long.
L.P., **1.** *Lord Provost.* **2.** *Ph: low pressure*, basse pression. **3.** *long-playing* (*record*), (disque) de longue durée, 33 tours.
L.P.G., *liquefied petroleum gas.*
L'pool., *Geog: Liverpool.*
L.R.A.M., *Licentiate of the Royal Academy of Music.*
LRBM, *long-range ballistic missile*, missile balistique de longue portée.
L.R.C.M., *Licentiate of the Royal College of Music.*
L.R.C.P., *Licentiate of the Royal College of Physicians* = médecin diplômé.
L.R.C.S., *Licentiate of the Royal College of Surgeons* = chirurgien diplômé.
LSD, *Pharm: lysergic acid diethylamide*, acide lysergique diéthylamide, LSD.
£.s.d., *A: librae, solidi, denarii, pounds, shillings, and pence.*
L.S.E., *London School of Economics.*
L.S.O., *London Symphony Orchestra.*
Lt., *Mil: Lieutenant*, lieutenant, Lieut., Lt.
L.T., **1.** *London Transport.* **2.** *El: low tension*, basse tension, B.T.
l.t., **1.** *Meas: long ton*(*s*). **2.** *local time*, heure légale.
L.T.A., *Lawn Tennis Association.*
Lt.-Col., *Mil: Lieutenant-Colonel*, lieutenant-colonel, Lieut-Col.
Ltd, *Com: Limited* (*company*), à responsabilité limitée, *Fr.C:* Ltée; = Société Anonyme, S.A.
L.V., *luncheon voucher*, chèque-repas, ticket-repas.
l.v., *El: low voltage*, basse tension, B.T.
L.W., *W.Tel: long waves*, grandes ondes, G.O.
L.W.M., *Nau: low water mark*, niveau de basse mer.
lx, *Ph: Meas: lux*, lux, lx.

M., **1.** *Majesty*, Majesté, M. **2.** *Master*, Maître. **3.** Monsieur, M. **4.** *member*, membre. **5.** *motorway*, autoroute; **M1**, autoroute No 1. **6.** *mega-*, mega-, M.
m., **1.** *metre*(*s*), mètres, *m*; **m²**, *square metres*, mètres carrés, m²; **m³**, *cubic metres*, mètres cubes, m³. **2.** *mile*(*s*), mille(*s*). **3.** (*a*) *male*, mâle; (*b*) *masculine*, masculin, m. **4.** *married*, marié. **5.** *mare*, jument. **6.** *milli-*, milli. **7.** *million*(*s*), million(s). **8.** *minute*(*s*), minute(s), mn. **9.** *Num: mark*, mark. **10.** *month*, mois, m. **11.** *midday*, midi, M. **12.** *Pharm: mix*, misce, m. **13.** *Cr: maiden* (*over*).
ma., *El: milliampere*(*s*), milliampère(s); mA.
M.A., **1.** *Sch: Magister Artium, Master of Arts* = (i) maîtrise, (ii) maître (ès lettres). **2.** *Hist: Middle Ages*, moyen âge, M.A. **3.** *Military Academy*, École militaire.
m/a., *Com: my account*, mon compte, m/c.
MAA, *Master-at-arms.*
mag., **1.** *F: magazine*, revue. **2.** (*a*) *magnet*, aimant; (*b*) *magnetic*, magnétique; (*c*) *magnetism*, magnétisme. **3.** *magneto*, magnéto. **4.** *magnitude*, grandeur.
Maj., *Mil: Major*, commandant, Cdt, Comm., Comt; Major, Maj.; **Maj.-Gen.**, *Major-General*, général de division.
m.amp., *milliampere*, milliampère, mA.
Man(it)., *Geog: Manitoba.*
manuf., (*a*) *manufactory*, fabrique; (*b*) *manufacturer*, fabricant; (*c*) *manufacture*, fabrication, fab.
Mar., *March*, mars, M.
mar., **1.** *marine*, marin. **2.** *maritime*, maritime. **3.** *married*, marié.
March., *Marchioness*, marquise.
Marq., *Marquess, Marquis*, marquis.
masc., *masculine*, masculin, m.
Mass., *Geog: Massachusetts.*
math., (*a*) *mathematics*, mathématiques; (*b*) *mathematical*, mathématique; (*c*) *mathematician*, mathématicien, -ienne.
Matt., *Matthew*, Mat(t)hieu, Mat(t).
Max., *Ph: Maxwell*, Maxwell, M.
max., *maximum*, maximum, max.
mb., *Meteor: millibar*, millibar, mb.
M.B., *Medicinæ Baccalaureus, Bachelor of Medicine* = (i) licence, (ii) licencié, en médecine.
M.B.E., *Member of the Order of the British Empire*, membre de l'Ordre de l'Empire britannique.
Mc., *W.Tel: megacycle*, mégacycle, Mc.
mc., *Ph.Meas:* **1.** *millicycle.* **2.** *millicurie*, millicurie.
m/c., *Com: my account*, mon compte, m/c.
M.C., **1.** *Master of Ceremonies*, maître des cérémonies. **2.** *U.S: Member of Congress*, député. **3.** *Military Cross* = Croix de guerre. **4.** *Mil: Medical Corps*, personnel médical du service de santé.
M.Ch(ir)., *Magister Chirurgiae, Master of Surgery.*
mcht., *merchant*, marchand, -ande, md(e).
Md., *Geog: Maryland.*
M.D., **1.** *Medicinæ Doctor, Doctor of Medicine*, Docteur en médecine. **2.** *Managing Director* = Président directeur général, P.D.G. **3.** *mentally deficient*, débile.
m.d., **M/D**, *Com: month's date*, mois de date, m/d.

Mddx., *Geog: Post: Middlesex.*
MDS, M.D.S., *Master of Dental Surgery.*
Me., *Geog: Maine.*
M.E., **1.** *Middle English.* **2.** *Mining Engineer*, ingénieur des mines. **3.** *Mechanical Engineer*, ingénieur mécanicien.
meas., *measure*, mesure.
mech., (*a*) *mechanical*, mécanique; (*b*) *mechanics*, mécanique.
Med., *Geog: F: Mediterranean* (*Sea*), (mer) Méditerranée.
med., **1.** *medieval*, médiéval. **2.** (*a*) *medical*, médical; (*b*) *medicine*, médecine. **3.** *medium*, moyen. **4.** *medius, middle*, milieu.
M.E.F., *Middle East Forces.*
mem., **1.** *member*, membre. **2.** (*a*) *memorandum*, mémorandum; mém; (*b*) *memoir*, mémoire. **3.** *memento*, mémento.
memo., *memorandum*, mémorandum, mém.
meq., *Ch: milliequivalent*, milliéquivalent, mEq.
mer., **1.** *meridian*, méridien. **2.** *meridional*, méridional.
merc., **1.** *mercantile*, mercantile. **2.** (*a*) *Pharm: mercurial*, mercuriel; (*b*) *Ch: mercury*, mercure.
Messrs. ['mesəz], Messieurs, MM.
Met., *Metropolitan*, métropolitain.
metal(l)., *metallurgy*, métallurgie.
met(aph)., **1.** (*a*) *metaphor*, métaphore; (*b*) *metaphorical*, métaphorique. **2.** *metaphysics*, métaphysique.
met(eor)., (*a*) *meteorological*, météorologique; (*b*) *meteorology*, météorologie.
Meth., *Methodist*, méthodiste.
mev, MeV, *mega-electron-volt*(*s*), *million electron volts*, méga-électron-volt(s), meV.
Mex., *Geog:* (*a*) *Mexican*, mexicain; (*b*) *Mexico*, Mexique.
mf, *Mus: mezzo forte*, mezz.f.
M.F., *W.Tel: medium frequency*, fréquence moyenne, intermédiaire.
mfd, **1.** *Com: manufactured*, fabriqué. **2.** *El.Meas: microfarad*, microfarad.
M.F.H., *Ven: Master of Foxhounds*, maître d'équipage de la chasse au renard.
mfr(s), *Com: manufacturer*(*s*), fabricant(s).
mg., *Meas: milligram*(*me*), milligramme; mg.
M.G., *machine-gun*, mitrailleuse.
mGal, *Ph: milligal*, milligal, mgal.
M.G.B., *motor gunboat*, aviso-torpilleur.
Mgr, **1.** *manager*, directeur. **2.** *Ecc: Monsignor*, Monseigneur; Mgr.
mgt, *management*, direction.
M.H., *Medal of Honour*, médaille d'honneur.
M.H.R., *Member of the House of Representatives.*
M.I., **MI**, **1.** *Military Intelligence*; **MI5**, *security service*, la sécurité; **MI6**, *espionage department*, espionnage. **2.** *Mounted Infantry.*
M.I.C.E., *Member of the Institution of Civil Engineers.*
Mich., **1.** *Geog: Michigan.* **2.** *Michaelmas*, la Saint-Michel.
M.I.Chem.E., *Member of the Institution of Chemical Engineers.*
MIDAS, M.I.D.A.S. ['maidəs], *missile defence alarm system*, système d'alarme pour la défense contre les missiles.
Middx, *Geog: Middlesex.*
M.I.E.E., *Member of the Institute of Electrical Engineers.*
mil., **1.** *military*, militaire. **2.** *militia*, milice.
M.I.Mech.E., *Member of the Institution of Mechanical Engineers.*
M.I.Min.E., *Member of the Institution of Mining Engineers.*
Min., (*a*) *Minister*, Ministre, Min.; (*b*) *Ministry*, Ministère.
min., **1.** *minimum*, minimum, min. **2.** *minute*(*s*), minute(s), mn. **3.** *Mus: minim*, blanche. **4.** *mineralogy*, minéralogie.
Minn., *Geog: Minnesota.*
M.I.Prod.E., *Member of the Institution of Production Engineers.*
MIRV, (*of missile*) *multiple independently targeted re-entry vehicle.*
misc., **1.** *miscellaneous*, divers. **2.** *miscellany*, mélange.
Miss., *Geog: Mississippi.*
miss., **1.** *mission*, mission. **2.** *missionary*, missionnaire.
M.I.T., *Massachusetts Institute of Technology.*
Mk, *mark*, marque.
M.K.S.A., *Ph.Meas: metre-kilogram*(*me*)*-second-ampere*, mètre-kilogramme-seconde-ampère, M.K.S.A.
mkt., *market*, marché.
ml., **1.** *mile*(*s*), mille(s). **2.** *millitre*, millilitre, ml.
M.L.A., *Austr: Member of the Legislative Assembly.*
MLF, *multilateral* (*nuclear*) *force*, force (nucléaire) multilatérale.
M.Litt., *Magister Litterarum, Master of Letters* = (i) maîtrise, (ii) maître (ès lettres).
M.L.R., *Fin: Minimum Lending Rate*, taux (officiel) d'escompte.
mm., *millimetre*(*s*), millimètre(s), mm; **mm²**, *square millimetres*, millimètres carrés, mm²; **mm³**, *cubic millimetres*, millimetres, cubes, mm³.
MM., *Military Medal* = Croix de guerre.
m.m.f., *Ph: magnetomotive force.*
M.Mus., *Master of Music.*
M.N., *Merchant Navy*, Marine Marchande, M.M.
Mo., *Geog: Missouri.*
M.O., **1.** *Medical Officer*, (i) (*in hospital*) chef de service; (ii) médecin militaire. **2.** *Post: money order*, mandat-poste.
m/o., *Fin: my order*, mon ordre, m/o.
mod., **1.** *modern*, moderne. **2.** *moderate*, modéré.
M.O.D., *Ministry of Defence*, Ministère de la Défense.
mod. cons., *F: modern conveniences*, confort moderne.
M.O.H., *Medical Officer of Health*, médecin de l'état civil.
mol., *Ch:* (*a*) *molecular*, moléculaire; (*b*) *molecule*, mol.; (*c*) **mol.wt.**, *molecular weight*, poids moléculaire, p.mol.
Mon., *Monday*, lundi.
mon., **1.** *monastery*, monastère. **2.** *monetary*, monétaire.
Mont., *Geog: Montana.*
Mor., *Geog: Morocco*, Maroc.

morn., *morning*, matin.
mortg., *mortgage*, hypothèque, h., hyp(oth).
M.O.T., *Ministry of Transport*; *F:* **M.O.T. test**, examen annuel obligatoire des véhicules âgés de trois ans ou plus.
mp, *Mus: mezzo piano*, mezz.p.
M.P., **1.** (*a*) *Metropolitan Police*, police métropolitaine; (*b*) *Military Police*, police militaire. **2.** *Member of Parliament*, membre de la Chambre des Communes.
m.p., *melting point*, point de fusion.
m.per sec.², *metre(s) per second per second*, mètre(s) par seconde par seconde, m/s^2.
m.p.g., *miles per gallon* = litres au cent (kilomètres).
m.p.h., *miles per hour*, milles à l'heure.
M.Phil., *Master of Philosophy*.
m.p.s., *metre(s) per second*, mètre(s) par seconde, m/s.
M.P.S., **1.** *Member of the Pharmaceutical Society*. **2.** *Member of the Philological Society*. **3.** *Member of the Physical Society*.
Mr ['mistər], *Mister*, Monsieur, M.
M.R., *Jur: Master of the Rolls* = vice-président de la Cour de Cassation.
M.R.A., *Moral Rearmament*, réarmement moral.
M.R.B.M., *medium range ballistic missile*, missile balistique de moyenne portée.
M.R.C., *Medical Research Council*.
M.R.C.A., *multi-role combat aircraft*, avion de combat polyvalent.
Mrs. ['misiz], *Mistress*, Madame, Mme.
MS, *manuscript*, manuscrit; **MSS**, *manuscripts*, manuscrits.
Ms [miz], madame ou mademoiselle.
M.S., **1.** *Master of Surgery*. **2.** *Master of Science*. **3.** *Med: multiple sclerosis*, sclérose en plaques.
M.S., M/S, *Com: months (after) sight*, mois de vue, m/v.
m/s, *metre(s) per second*, mètre(s) par seconde, m/s.
M.Sc., *Master of Science*.
m.s.l., *mean sea level*, niveau moyen de la mer.
Mt., *Mount*, mont, montagne.
M.T., **1.** *mechanical transport*, transport mécanique. **2.** *Meas: metric ton*, tonne (métrique). **3.** *mean time*, temps moyen.
M.T.B., *motor torpedo boat*, vedette lance-torpilles.
M.Tech., *Master of Technology*.
mtge., *mortgage*, hypothèque, h., hyp(oth).
mth., *month(s)*, mois, m.
M.Th., *Master of Theology*.
M.T.I., *Rad: moving target indicator*, indicateur d'objectifs mobiles.
Mtl, *Geog: Montreal*, Montréal.
mtn., *mountain*, montagne.
M.U., *mobile unit*.
M/U., *St.Exch: making-up price*, cours de compensation, c.c.
mun., (*a*) *municipal*, municipal; (*b*) *municipality*, municipalité.
mus., **1.** (*a*) *music*, musique; (*b*) *musical*, musical; (*c*) *musician*, musicien, -ienne. **2.** *museum*, musée.
Mus.B(ac)., *Musicae Baccalaureus, Bachelor of Music*.
Mus.D(oc)., *Musicae Doctor, Doctor of Music*.
M.V., **1.** *motor vessel*, bateau à moteur. **2.** *muzzle velocity*, vitesse initiale.
M.V.O., *Member of the Royal Victorian Order*, membre de l'Ordre royal de Victoria.
MW, *El.Meas: megawatt(s)*, mégawatt(s).
M.W., *W.Tel: medium wave*, onde moyenne.
Mx, *Ph: Maxwell(s)*, Maxwell, M.
M.Y., *motor yacht*, yacht à moteur.
myg., *Meas: myriagramme*, myriagramme, myg.
mym., *Meas: myriametre*, myriamètre, myriam.
myth., (*a*) *mythology*, mythologie; (*b*) *mythological*, mythologique.

N., **1.** (*a*) *North*, nord, N; (*b*) *northern*, boréal, B. **2.** *New*, nouveau. **3.** *Ph: Newton*, Newton, N. **4.** (*chess*) *knight*, cavalier.
n., **1.** *noon*, midi, M. **2.** *name*, nom, N. **3.** *neuter*, neutre, n. **4.** *noun*, substantif. **5.** *Fin: nominal*, nominal, N. **6.** *Meas: nano-*, nano-, n.
N/A, *Adm: not applicable*, sans objet, S.O.
N.A.A.C.P., *U.S: National Association for the Advancement of Colored People*.
N.A.A.F.I. ['næfi], *Navy, Army, and Air Force Institutes* = coopérative militaire.
N.A.L.G.O. ['nælgou], *National and Local Government Officers' Association*.
NAS, **1.** *National Association of Schoolmasters*. **2.** *Noise Abatement Society*.
NASA ['næsə], *U.S: National Aeronautics and Space Administration*, administration des questions aéronautiques et de l'espace.
nat., **1.** (*a*) *national*, national; (*b*) *nationalist*, nationaliste. **2.** (*a*) *natural*, naturel; (*b*) *naturalist*, naturaliste. **3.** *native*, natif.
N.A.T.O. ['neitou], *North Atlantic Treaty Organization*, Organisation du Traité de l'Atlantique Nord, OTAN.
NATSOPA [næt'soupə], *National Society of Operative Printers and Assistants*.
NATTKE ['nætki], *National Association of Theatrical, Television and Kine Employees*.
naut., *nautical*, nautique.
nav., **1.** *naval*, naval. **2.** *navigation*, navigation.
N.B., **1.** *nota bene*, N.B. **2.** *Geog: New Brunswick*, Nouveau-Brunswick.
NBC, *U.S: National Broadcasting Company*.
n.b.g., *P: no bloody good*, ça ne vaut rien.
N.C., *Geog: North Carolina*.
N.C.B., *National Coal Board*.
N.C.O., *Mil: non-commissioned officer*, sous-officier, gradé.
n.d., *no date, not dated*, sans date.
N.D(ak)., *Geog: North Dakota*.
NE, N.E., **1.** *north-east*, nord-est, N-E. **2.** *Geog: New England*, Nouvelle-Angleterre.
N.E.B., *New English Bible*.
Neb(r)., *Geog: Nebraska*.
NEDC (*also* **Neddy**), *National Economic Development Council*.
neg., *negative*, négatif.
nem. con., nem. diss., *nemine contradicente, nemine dissentiente, no-one contradicting, dissenting; unanimously*.
NEP, *New Economic Policy*.
Neth., *Geog: Netherlands*, Pays-Bas, P.-B.
neut., *neuter*, neutre, n.
Nev., *Geog: Nevada*.
N.F., **1.** (*also* **Nfld.**) *Geog: Newfoundland*, Terre-Neuve. **2.** *Bank:* (*also* **N/F**) *no funds*, défaut de provision. **3.** *Pol: National Front*.
N.F.T., *National Film Theatre*.
NFU, *National Farmers' Union*.
N.G.A., *National Graphical Association*.
N.H., *Geog: New Hampshire*.
n.h.p., *nominal horsepower*, cheval nominal.
N.H.S., *National Health Service* = Sécurité Sociale, S.S.
N.I., **1.** *National Insurance*. **2.** *Geog: Northern Ireland*, Irlande du Nord.
N.J., *Geog: New Jersey*.
N.L., **1.** *north latitude*, latitude nord. **2.** *non licet*, non permis.
N.L.I., *National Lifeboat Institution*.
NLRB, N.L.R.B., *U.S: National Labor Relations Board*.
N.M., *Geog: New Mexico*, Nouveau Mexique.
NNE, N.N.E., *north-north-east*, nord-nord-est, N.-N.-E.
NNW, N.N.W., *north-north-west*, nord-nord-ouest, N.-N.-O.
No., no., *number*, numéro, No, N°, n°.
N.O., *Geog: New Orleans*, Nouvelle-Orléans.
nom., **1.** *Gram: nominative*, nominatif. **2.** *nominal*, nominal.
non seq., *non sequitur*, illogicité.
nor., *north*, nord, N.
Northants., *Geog: Northamptonshire*.
Northumb., *Geog: Northumberland*.
Nor(w)., *Geog:* (*a*) *Norway*, Norvège; (*b*) *Norwegian*, norvégien.
Notts., *Geog: Nottinghamshire*.
Nov., *November*, novembre, nov.
Np., *Ph: neper*, néper, Np.
N.P., *Jur: notary public*, notaire.
n.p., **1.** *new paragraph*, à la ligne. **2.** *no place of publication*.
NPA, *Newspaper Publishers' Association*.
nr, *near*, près.
N.R., *Geog: North Riding* (*of Yorkshire*).
N.S., **1.** *Chr: New Style*, nouveau style, N.S. **2.** *Geog: Nova Scotia*, Nouvelle-Écosse. **3.** *nuclear ship*, bateau nucléaire.
N.S.B., *National Savings Bank* = Caisse Nationale d'Épargne, C.N.E.
NSC, *U.S: National Security Council*.
N.S.F., *Bank: not sufficient funds*, insuffisance de provision.
N.S.P.C.C., *National Society for the Prevention of Cruelty to Children*.
N.S.W., *Geog: New South Wales*.
N.T., **1.** *B: New Testament*, Nouveau Testament, N.T. **2.** *Geog: Austr: Northern Territory*, Territoire du Nord. **3.** *National Theatre*.
Nth., *North*, nord, N.
NUJ, *National Union of Journalists*.
NUM, *National Union of Mineworkers*.
Num., *B: Numbers*, Nombres, Nomb.
num., **1.** *number*, nombre. **2.** *numeral*, nombre.
NUPE ['nju:pi], *National Union of Public Employees*.
NUR, *National Union of Railwaymen*.
NUS, *National Union of Students* = Union Nationale des Étudiants de France, UNEF.
NUT, *National Union of Teachers* = Fédération de l'éducation nationale, F.E.N.
NW, N.W., *north-west*, nord-ouest, N.-O.; *Nau:* N.-W.
N.Y., *Geog: New York*.
N.Y.C., *Geog: New York City*.
N.Z., *Geog: New Zealand*, Nouvelle-Zélande.

O., **1.** *Old*, vieux. **2.** *Geog: Ohio*. **3.** *El: ohm*, ohm. **4.** *Sch:* **O level**, *Ordinary level examination*.
o., *Ch: ortho*, ortho, o.
o/a., *Com: on account*, pour compte, p/c.
O. & M., *Organization and Methods* = Organisation scientifique du travail, O.S.T.
O.A.P., (*a*) *Old Age Pension*, retraite de vieillesse; (*b*) *Old Age Pensioner*, retraité(e).
O.A.S., **1.** *on active service* (i) *Mil:* en service actif; (ii) *Post:* franchise militaire, F.M. **2.** *Organization of American States*, Organisation des États américains, O.E.A.
O.A.U., *Organization of African Unity*, Organisation de l'unité africaine, O.U.A.
ob., *obiit*, décédé.
O.B., **1.** *Old Boy*. **2.** *outside broadcast*, production extérieure.
obdt, *obedient*, obéissant.
O.B.E., (*Officer of the*) *Order of the British Empire*.
obj., **1.** *object*, objet. **2.** *objective*, objectif. **3.** *objection*, objection.
obs., **1.** *obsolete*, désuet. **2.** *observation*, observation. **3.** *observatory*, observatoire.
O.C., *Mil: Officer Commanding*, chef de corps.
oc., *ocean*, océan.
o/c, *Com: overcharge*, surcharge, trop-perçu.
Oct., *October*, octobre, oct.
oct., *Paperm: octavo*, in-octavo.
O.C.T.U., *Mil: Officer Cadet Training Unit*.
OD, *Mil: Officer of the Day*, officier de jour.
O/D, o/d, **1.** *Bank: overdraft*, (annonce à) découvert. **2.** *Com: on demand*, sur demande, à vue.
ODM, *Overseas Development*, Ministère du Développement Outre-mer.
OE, *Old English*.
o.e., *omissions excepted*.
O.E.C.D., *Organization for Economic Co-operation and Development*, Organisation de coopération et de développement économiques, O.C.D.E.

O.E.D., *Oxford English Dictionary.*
OF, *Old French.*
off., **1.** *official*, officiel, O. **2.** *office*, bureau. **3.** *officer*, officier, O. **4.** *offered*, offert, off.
O.F.M., *Ecc: Order of Friars Minor*, Ordre de Saint-François d'Assise, les Frères mineurs.
O.G., *Mil: Officer of the Guard*, officier de garde.
O.H.M.S., *On His, Her, Majesty's Service*, au service de Sa Majesté.
Okla., *Geog: Oklahoma.*
O.M., *(Member of the) Order of Merit.*
o.n.o., *or near(est) offer.*
Ont., *Geog: Ontario.*
op., **1.** *Mus: opus*, op. **2.** *opposite*, en face. **3.** *operation*, opération. **4.** *opera*, opéra.
O.P., **1.** *Ecc: Order of Preachers*, les Frères prêcheurs. **2.** *Th: opposite prompt (side)*, côté de la scène à la droite, *U.S:* à la gauche, des acteurs; côté cour. **3.** *Mil: observation post*, poste d'observation.
o/p, *Publ: out of print*, tirage épuisé.
op. cit., *opere citato, in the work already quoted*, op. cit.
O.P.E.C. ['oupek], *Organization of Petroleum Exporting Countries*, Organisation des pays exportateurs de pétrole, O.P.E.P.
opp., **1.** *opposed*, opposé. **2.** *opposite*, en face.
opt., **1.** (*a*) *optical*, optique; (*b*) *optician*, opticien, -ienne; (*c*) *optics*, optique. **2.** *Gram: optative*, optatif.
O.R., *operational research*, recherche opérationnelle.
orch., (*a*) *orchestra*, orchestre; (*b*) *orchestral*, orchestral.
ord., **1.** *ordinary*, ordinaire, ord. **2.** *order*, ordre. **3.** *ordinal*, ordinal. **4.** *ordained*, ordonné. **5.** *ordnance*. **6.** *ordinance*, ordonnance.
Ore(g)., *Geog: Oregon.*
org., **1.** *organic*, organique. **2.** *organized*, organisé.
orig., **1.** *origin*, origine. **2.** (*a*) *original*, original; (*b*) *originally*, originairement.
O.S., **1.** *Chr: Old Style*, vieux style. **2.** *Nau: ordinary seaman*, matelot de pont. **3.** *Com:* (*a*) *out of stock*, manque en magasin; (*b*) *outsize*, dimension hors série. **4.** *Ordnance Survey* = Institut Géographique National, I.G.N.
o/s, *Com: outstanding*, à percevoir.
O.S.A., *Ecc: Order of St Augustine.*
O.S.B., *Ecc: Order of St Benedict.*
O.S.F., *Ecc: Order of St Francis.*
O.St.J., *Officer of the Order of Saint John of Jerusalem.*
O.T., *B: Old Testament*, Ancien Testament, A.T.
O.T.C., *Mil: Officers' Training Corps.*
O.U., *Sch: Oxford University.*
OUP, *Oxford University Press.*
Oxf., *Geog: Oxford.*
OXFAM ['ɔksfæm], *Oxford Committee for Famine Relief.*
Oxon., **1.** *Geog: Oxfordshire.* **2.** *Oxoniensis, of Oxford*, d'Oxford.
oz., *Meas: ounce(s)*, once(s).

P., *(chess) pawn*, pion.
p., **1.** *page*, page, p. **2.** *per*, par, pour, p. **3.** *Mus: piano*, piano, p. **4.** *Fin: premium*, prime, p. **5.** *penny, pence.* **6.** *Gram: past*, passé.
Pa., *Geog: Pennsylvania.*
P.A., **1.** *Com: particular average*, avaries particulières, a.p. **2.** *personal assistant.* **3.** *Publishers' Association.* **4.** *Press Association.* **5.** *public address (system)*, sonorisation extérieure.
p.a., **1.** *per annum*, par an, p. an. **2.** *Jur: power of attorney*, procuration; mandat, mat. **3.** *Com: private account*, compte particulier.
PABA, *Bio-Ch: para-aminobenzoic acid*, acide para-amino-benzoïque, P.A.B.
P.A.B.X., *private automatic branch (telephone) exchange.*
pam., *pamphlet*, brochure.
Pan., *Geog: Panama.*
Pan Am, *Pan American Airways.*
p. & p., *postage and packing*, port et emballage.
par., **1.** *parallel*, parallèle. **2.** *paragraph*, paragraphe. **3.** *parenthesis*, parenthèse. **4.** *parish*, paroisse.
para., *paragraph*, paragraphe.
Parag., *Geog: Paraguay.*
Parl., *Parliament(ary)*, parlement(aire).
part., **1.** *Gram: participle*, participe. **2.** *particular*, particulier.
P.A.S., *para-aminosalicylic acid*, acide para-amino-salicylique, P.A.S.
pass., **1.** *passenger*, voyageur. **2.** *passim*, pass. **3.** *passive*, passif.
pat., **1.** *patent*, brevet. **2.** *pattern*, modèle, mle.
path(ol)., (*a*) *pathological*, pathologique; (*b*) *pathology*, pathologie.
P.A.X., *private automatic (telephone) exchange.*
P.A.Y.E., **1.** *pay-as-you-earn* = impôt retenu à la source, à la base. **2.** *(on buses) pay-as-you-enter.*
P.B.X., *W.Tel: private branch exchange.*
pc., *piece*, morceau.
P.C., **1.** *Police Constable.* **2.** (*a*) *Privy Council*, Conseil privé du Roi, de la Reine; (*b*) *Privy Councillor*, conseiller privé.
p.c., **1.** *postcard*, carte postale. **2.** *percent*, pour cent, p.c. **3.** *Com: petty cash*, petite caisse.
p/c, *Com: price(s) current*, prix courant(s).
P.C.M., *W.Tel: pulse code modulation*, modulation par impulsions codées, M.I.C.
pd, *paid*, payé.
P.D., *Nau: Police Department.*
p.d., **1.** *El: potential difference*, différence de potentiel, D.D.P. **2.** *per diem, per day*, par jour.
P.D.S.A., *People's Dispensary for Sick Animals.*
P.E., **1.** *physical education*, éducation physique. **2.** *Typ: printer's error*, faute d'impression.
p/e, *price/earnings (ratio).*
P.E.I., *Geog: Prince Edward Island.*
pen., *peninsula*, péninsule.
P.E.N., (*also* **PEN Club**) *International Association of Poets, Playwrights, Editors, Essayists and Novelists.*
Penn(a)., *Geog: Pennsylvania.*
perf., **1.** *Gram: perfect*, parfait. **2.** *perforated*, perforé. **3.** (*a*) *performed*, représenté; (*b*) *performance*, représentation; (*c*) *performer*, acteur; artiste.
per pro., *per procurationem, by proxy*, par procuration, p.p., p. pon.
Pers., *Geog:* (*a*) *Persia*, Perse; (*b*) *Persian*, persan.
pers., (*a*) *person*, personne; (*b*) *personal*, personnel; (*c*) *personally*, personnellement.
persp., *perspective*, perspective.
pert., *pertaining*, appartenant.
pf., **1.** *Fin: preferred*, (actions) de préférence. **2.** *perfect*, parfait.
p.f., *El: power factor*, facteur de puissance.
Pfc., *Mil: U.S: private first class*, soldat de première classe.
P.G., *paying guest*, pensionnaire.
P.G.A., *Professional Golfers' Association.*
ph, *Ph: phot*, ph.
phar(m)., (*a*) *pharmaceutical*, pharmaceutique; (*b*) *pharmacopoeia*, pharmacopée; (*c*) *pharmacy*, pharmacie.
Ph.D., *Philosophiae Doctor, Doctor of Philosophy*, Docteur en Philosophie.
Phil., *Geog: Philadelphia.*
phil., **1.** (*a*) *philosopher*, philosophe; (*b*) *philosophical*, philosophique; (*c*) *philosophy*, philosophie. **2.** *philharmonic*, philharmonique.
phr., *phrase*, locution.
P.I.B., *Prices and Incomes Board.*
pk, **1.** *pack*, paquet. **2.** *park*, parc. **3.** *peak*, pic.
pkg., (*a*) *package*, paquet; (*b*) *packing*, emballage.
pkt., **1.** *packet*, paquet. **2.** *pocket*, poche.
Pl., *Place*, rue.
pl., **1.** *plural*, pluriel. **2.** *Mil: platoon*, section, sec(t).
P/L, P. & L., *profit and loss*, profits et pertes, P. et P.
P.L.A., **1.** *Port of London Authority.* **2.** *Rail: Passenger Luggage in Advance.*
plat., **1.** *plateau*, plateau. **2.** *platform*, plate-forme. **3.** *platoon*, section, sec(t).
P.L.O., *Palestinian Liberation Organization*, Organisation pour la Libération de la Palestine, O.L.P.
P.L.P., *Parliamentary Labour Party.*
P.L.R., *Public Lending Right.*
pm., *Fin: premium*, prime, pr.
P.M., **1.** *Prime Minister*, premier ministre. **2.** *Postmaster*, directeur des Postes. **3.** *Paymaster*, trésorier. **4.** *Mil: Provost Marshal*, grand prévôt.
p.m., **1.** *post meridiem, after noon*, après midi, p.m., P.M. **2.** *post-mortem*, autopsie.
P.M.G., **1.** *Postmaster General*, directeur général des Postes. **2.** *Paymaster General*, trésorier.
pmk., *postmark*, cachet de la poste.
P.M.T., *Physiol: premenstrual tension*, syndrome prémenstruel.
P.N., p.n., P/N, *Com: promissory note*, billet à ordre.
P.O., **1.** *Post Office* = Postes et Télécommunications, P.E.T.; **P.O. Box,** *post office box*. Boîte Postale, B.P. **2.** *postal order*, mandat-poste, M.-P. **3.** *Navy: Petty Officer*, officer marinier; *F:* chef. **4.** *Av: Pilot Officer*, sous-lieutenant (aviateur).
P.O.D., *pay on delivery*, paiement à la livraison.
pop., **1.** *population*, population. **2.** *popular*, populaire.
P.O.P., **1.** *(of size of envelopes, etc.) Post Office Preferred.* **2.** *printing(-out) paper*, (*a*) *Phot:* papier aristotypique; (*b*) *Ind:* papier héliographique.
Port., *Geog:* (*a*) *Portugal*, Portugal; (*b*) *Portuguese*, portugais.
pos., **1.** *position*, position. **2.** *positive*, positive, positif. **3.** *possession*, possession.
P.O.S.B., *Post Office Savings Bank* = Caisse Nationale d'Épargne, C.N.E.
poss., **1.** (*a*) *possible*, possible; (*b*) *possibly*, c'est possible. **2.** *possession*, possession.
pot., *potential*, potentiel.
P.O.W., *Prisoner of War*, prisonnier de guerre, P.G.; **ex-P.O.W.,** *ex-Prisoner-of-War*, ancien prisonnier de guerre, A.P.G.
pp., *pages*, pages, pp.
p.p., **1.** *per procurationem*, par procuration, p.p., p. pon. **2.** *Gram: past participle*, participe passé. **3.** *post paid*, port payé, p.p.
PPE, *Sch: philosophy, politics and economics*, philosophie, politique et économie.
P.P.L., *private pilot's licence*, brevet de pilote (d'avion de tourisme).
p.p.m., *parts per million.*
P.P.S., **1.** *Adm: Parliamentary Private Secretary.* **2.** *post postscriptum, additional postscript.*
P.Q., *Geog: Province of Quebec*, Province de Québec.
Pr., **1.** *Prince*, Prince, Pr. **2.** *Priest*, prêtre.
pr., **1.** *pair*, paire. **2.** *price*, prix. **3.** *present*, présent. **4.** *Ph: power*, puissance, p. **5.** *pronoun*, pronom.
P.R., **1.** *proportional representation*, représentation proportionnelle, R.P. **2.** *public relations (office)*, service des relations publiques; **P.R. man,** chef du service des relations publiques. **3.** *Geog: Puerto Rico.*
P.R.A., *President of the Royal Academy.*
Preb., *Ecc: Prebendary*, prébendier.
prec., *preceding*, précédent, préc.
pred., *Gram:* (*a*) *predicate*, attribut; (*b*) *predicative*, prédicatif.
pref., **1.** *Fin: preference*, préférence, préf. **2.** *preface*, préface. **3.** *prefix*, préfixe.
prelim., *preliminary*, préliminaire.
prep., **1.** (*a*) *preparation*, préparation; (*b*) *preparatory*, préparatoire. **2.** *Gram: preposition*, préposition.
Pres., *President*, président.
pres., **1.** *present*, présent. **2.** *presidency*, présidence.
pret., *Gram: preterite*, prétérit.
prim., **1.** *primary*, primaire. **2.** *primitive*, primitif.
prin., **1.** *principal(ly)*, principal(ement). **2.** *principle*, principe.
prm., *Fin: premium*, prime, pr.

P.R.O., 1. *public relations officer*, chef du service des relations publiques. 2. *Public Record Office*, bureau des archives nationales.
prob., 1. (*a*) *probable*, probable; (*b*) *probably*, probablement. 2. *problem*, problème.
proc., 1. *proceedings*, procédé. 2. *process*, processus. 3. *proclamation*, proclamation. 4. *proctor*.
prod., 1. (*a*) *produce*, produit; (*b*) *produced*, produit; (*c*) *producer*, producteur. 2. *product*, produit.
Prof., *Professor*, professeur.
prog., 1. (*a*) *progress*, progrès; (*b*) *progressive*, progressif. 2. *programme*, programme.
pron., 1. *Gram:* (*a*) *pronoun*, pronom; (*b*) *pronominal*, pronominal. 2. (*a*) *pronounced*, prononcé; (*b*) *pronunciation*, prononciation.
prop., 1. *proprietor*, propriétaire. 2. *property*, propriété. 3. *properly*, correctement. 4. *proposition*, proposition.
pros., *prosody*, prosodie.
Prot., 1. *Protestant*, protestant. 2. *Protectorate*, protectorat.
Prov., *B: Proverbs*, Proverbes, Prov.
prov., 1. (*a*) *province*, province, prov; (*b*) *provincial*, provincial. 2. *provisional*, provisoire. 3. *provost*, prévôt, principal.
prox., *Com: proximo*, *of next month*, du mois prochain, prox.
prox. acc., *proxime accessit*, *runner-up*, (bon) second.
P.R.S., *President of the Royal Society*.
ps., *pseudonym*, pseudonyme.
P.S., 1. (*also* **PS**) *postscript*, post-scriptum, P.S. 2. (*a*) *Permanent Secretary*, secrétaire permanent; (*b*) *Private Secretary*, secrétaire privé. 3. *Police Sergeant*. 4. *Privy Seal*, Garde du petit Sceau. 5. *Th: prompt side*, côté de la scène à la gauche, *U.S:* à la droite, des acteurs; côté jardin.
Pss, *B: Psalms*, Psaumes, Ps.
pseud., *pseudonym*, pseudonyme.
P.S.V., *public service vehicle*.
psych., (*a*) *psychological*, psychologique; (*b*) *psychology*, psychologie; (*c*) *psychic(al)*, psychique.
pt., 1. *part*, partie. 2. *payment*, paiement. 3. *pint*, pinte. 4. *point*, point. 5. *port*, port.
P.T., *physical training*, éducation physique.
P.T.A., *Parent-Teacher Association* = Association des Parents d'Élèves, A.P.E.
pta, *Num: peseta*, peseta.
Pte, *Mil: Private*, simple soldat.
ptg., *printing*, imprimerie.
P.T.O., *please turn over*, tournez s'il vous plaît, T.S.V.P.
pub(l)., 1. *public*, public. 2. (*a*) *published*, publié; (*b*) *publication*, publication; (*c*) *publisher*, éditeur.
PVC, *polyvinyl chloride*, chlorure de polyvinyle.
Pvt., *Mil: Private*, simple soldat.
P.W., *policewoman*, femme-agent.
PX, *Mil: U.S: post exchange* = coopérative militaire.

Q., 1. *Queen('s)*, (de la) reine. 2. *Geog: Quebec*, Québec. 3. *Quartermaster*, (i) *Nau:* maître de timonerie; (ii) *Mil:* officier chargé des vivres et des fournitures; *Mil:* **Q Department**, *Quartermaster's Department* = Quatrième Bureau.
q., 1. (*a*) *query*, question; (*b*) *question*, question. 2. *Meas:* (*a*) *quart*; (*b*) *quarter*, quart; (*c*) *quintal*, quintal, q(t).
Q.A.N.T.A.S. ['kwɔntæs], *Av: Queensland & Northern Territory Aerial Services* (*Australian international airline*).
Q.A.R.A.N.C., *Queen Alexandra's Royal Army Nursing Corps.*
Q.A.R.N.N.S., *Queen Alexandra's Royal Naval Nursing Service.*
Q.B., *Jur: Queen's Bench.*
Q.C., *Jur: Queen's Counsel.*
q.e., *quod est*, *which is*, ce qui est.
Q.E.D., *quod erat demonstrandum, which was to be proved*, ce qu'il fallait démontrer, C.Q.F.D., Q.E.D.
Q.E.F., *quod erat faciendum, which was to be done*, ce qu'il fallait faire.
Q.E.I., *quod erat inveniendum, which was to be found out*, ce qu'il fallait découvrir.
Q.E.2., *F: Queen Elizabeth II*, (le paquebot) la reine Elizabeth II.
Q.F., *quick-firing*, à tir rapide.
ql., *Meas: quintal*, quintal, q(t).
Qld, *Geog: Queensland.*
qlty., *quality*, qualité.
Q.M., *Mil: Quartermaster*, (i) *Nau:* maître de timonerie; (ii) *Mil:* officier chargé des vivres et des fournitures; **Q.M.G.**, *Quartermaster general* = Directeur de l'Intendance (militaire); **Q.M.S.**, *Quartermaster sergeant*, fourrier; **Q.M.C.**, *Quartermaster Corps* = Service de l'Intendance.
qnty, *quantity*, quantité.
q.p., *Pharm: etc: quantum placet, as much as desired*, à volonté, q.p.
Q.P.M., *Queen's Police Medal.*
qq., 1. *questions*, questions. 2. *Paperm: quartos*, in-quarto.
qr., 1. *Meas: quarter*, quart. 2. *quire* = (*approx.*) main de papier.
Q.S., *Jur: quarter sessions*, assises trimestrielles.
q.s., *Pharm: etc: quantum sufficit, sufficient quantity*, quantité suffisante, Q.S.
qt, 1. *Meas: quart(s)*. 2. *quantity*, quantité, q.
qto, *Paperm: quarto*, in-quarto.
qtr, 1. *quarter*, quart. 2. *quarterly*, trimestriel.
qu., (*a*) *question*, question; (*b*) *query*, question.
quad., *quadrant*, quadrant.
quar., 1. *Meas: quarter*, quart. 2. *quarterly*, trimestriel.
Que., *Geog: Quebec*, Québec.
ques., *question*, question.
quot., *St.Exch: quotation*, cours, cs.
q.v., 1. *quod vide, which see*, voyez, voir, v., q.v. 2. *Pharm: etc: quantum vis, as much as desired*, à volonté, q.v.
qy., *query*, question.

R., 1. (*a*) *Rex*, *king*, roi; (*b*) *Regina*, *queen*, reine. 2. *Royal*, royal. 3. *Railway*, chemin de fer, c(h), de f. 4. *River*, rivière. 5. *Ph: Réaumur*, Réaumur, R. 6. *Ecc: Response*, répons, R. 7. (*chess*) *rook*, tour. 8. *NAm: Republican*, républicain. 9. *registered*, déposé, (ii) *Post:* recommandé.
r., 1. *Meas: rod*, perche. 2. *Num: rupee*, roupie. 3. *right*, droit, d. 4. *recto*, recto, R°, Ro, ro. 5. *Ph: röntgen*, röntgen, R. 6. *run(s)*.
R.A., 1. (*a*) *Royal Academy* = Académie des Beaux-Arts; (*b*) *Royal Academician* = membre de l'Académie des Beaux-Arts. 2. *Astr: right ascension*, ascension droite, *ascensio recta*, a.r. 3. *Mil: Royal Artillery*. 4. *Mil: Rear Admiral*, contre-amiral.
R.A.A.F., *Royal Australian Air Force.*
R.A.C., 1. *Royal Automobile Club* = Touring Club de France, T.C.F. 2. *Royal Armoured Corps.*
Rad., 1. *Mth: radian(s)*, radian(s), radiant(s). 2. *Radical*, radical.
R.A.D., *Royal Academy of Dancing.*
R.A.D.A. ['rɑːdə], *Royal Academy of Dramatic Art.*
R.A.D.C., *Royal Army Dental Corps.*
R.Ae.S., *Royal Aeronautical Society.*
R.A.F., *Royal Air Force*, armée de l'air.
R.A.F.V.R., *Royal Air Force Volunteer Reserve.*
R.A.M., *Royal Academy of Music.*
R.A.M.C., *Royal Army Medical Corps.*
R.A.N., *Royal Australian Navy.*
R. and A., *Royal and Ancient* (*Golf Club, St Andrews*).
R. & B., *Mus: rhythm and blues.*
R. & D., *research and development*, recherche et développement.
R.A.O.C., *Mil: Royal Army Ordnance Corps.*
R.A.P.C., *Royal Army Pay Corps.*
R.A.S., *Royal Astronomical Society.*
R.A.S.C., *Hist: Mil: Royal Army Service Corps* = (*approx.*) train des équipages militaires, T.E.M.
R.B.A., *Royal Society of British Artists.*
R.C., 1. *Roman Catholic*, catholique. 2. *Red Cross*, Croix rouge. 3. *reinforced concrete*, béton armé. 4. *El:* **R.-C. coupling**, couplage par résistance capacité.
r.c., *Th: right centre*, à droite au second plan.
R.C.A., 1. *Royal College of Art*. 2. *Radio Corporation of America.*
R.C.A.F., *Royal Canadian Air Force.*
rcd., *received*, reçu, r.
R.C.M., *Royal College of Music.*
R.C.M.P., *Royal Canadian Mounted Police.*
R.C.N., 1. *Royal College of Nursing*. 2. *Royal Canadian Navy.*
R.C.O., *Royal College of Organists.*
R.C.P., *Royal College of Physicians.*
rcpt., *receipt*, (i) recette; (ii) reçu.
R.C.S., 1. *Royal College of Surgeons*. 2. *Royal College of Science*. 3. *Royal Corps of Signals.*
rct, 1. *receipt*, (i) recette; (i) reçu. 2. *Mil: recruit*, recrue.
R.C.T., *Mil: Royal Corps of Transport.*
rcvr, *receiver*, receveur.
R.C.V.S., *Royal College of Veterinary Surgeons.*
Rd, *road*, rue, r.
rd, *round*, rond.
R.D., 1. *Bank: refer(red) to drawer*, voir le tireur. 2. *Royal Naval Reserve Decoration.*
R.E., 1. *Mil: Royal Engineers*. 2. *Royal Exchange*, Bourse du Commerce.
rec., 1. *receipt*, (i) recette; (ii) reçu. 2. *recipe*, recette. 3. *recorded*, enregistré.
recd, *received*, reçu, r.
rect., *Ecc:* (*a*) *rector* = curé; (*b*) *rectory* = cure.
red., (*a*) *reduced*, réduit; (*b*) *reduction*, réduction.
ref., 1. *Corr: reference*, référence, Réf. 2. *referred*, rapporté. 3. *referee*, arbitre. 4. *reformed*, réformé. 5. *refund(ing)*, remboursement.
refl., 1. *Gram: reflexive*, réfléchi. 2. *reflection*, réflexion.
Reg., *Regina*, *queen*, reine.
reg., 1. *regular*, régulier. 2. *Post: registered*, recommandé, r. 3. *regulation*, règlement. 4. (*on electric oven*) *regulo.*
regd, *Post: registered*, recommandé, r.
Reg. Prof., *Regius Professor.*
Regt., *Regiment*, régiment, rég.
rel., 1. *relating*, relatif. 2. *relative*, relatif. 3. *religious*, religieux.
R.E.M., *Physiol: rapid eye movement*, mouvement oculaire rapide.
R.E.M.E., *Mil: Royal Electrical and Mechanical Engineers.*
Rep., 1. (*a*) *Republic*, république; (*b*) *Republican*, républicain. 2. *U.S: Representative.*
rep., *Fin: report*, report, R.
repr., 1. *Publ: reprint(ed)*, nouveau tirage. 2. *represented*, représenté.
req., 1. *required*, exigé. 2. *requisition*, demande.
res., 1. *research*, recherche. 2. *reserve*, réserve. 3. (*a*) *residence*, résidence; (*b*) *resident*, riverain, habitant.
resp., 1. (*a*) *respective*, respectif; (*b*) *respectively*, respectivement. 2. *respondent*, répondant. 3. *respiration*, respiration, r.
ret., 1. *retired*, retraité. 2. *returned*, renvoyé.
retd, 1. *retired*, retraité. 2. *returned*, renvoyé. 3. *retained*, retenu.
Rev., 1. *B: Revelation(s)*, Apocalypse, Révélation. 2. *Ecc: Reverend*, révérend, Rd, Revd.
rev., 1. *revolution*, tour, t(r). 2. *revenue*, revenu. 3. *review*, revue. 4. *revised*, révisé. 5. *reverse*, inverse.
r.f., 1. *radio frequency*, fréquence radio(électrique). 2. *range finder*, télémètre. 3. *rapid fire*, tir rapide.
R.F.C., *Rugby Football Club.*
R.F.D., *Post: U.S: rural free delivery.*
R.G.S., *Royal Geographical Society.*
Rgt, *regiment*, régiment, rég.
Rh., *Med: rhesus*, rhésus, Rh.
r.h., *Mus: etc: right hand*, main droite.

R.H.A., *Royal Horse Artillery.*
R.H.G., *Royal Horse Guards.*
R.H.S., **1.** *Royal Horticultural Society.* **2.** *Royal Humane Society.* **3.** *Royal Historical Society.*
R.I., **1.** *Geog: Rhode Island.* **2.** *Rex et Imperator, Regina et Imperatrix,* roi et empereur, reine et impératrice. **3.** *Royal Institute, Institution.*
R.I.B.A., *Royal Institute of British Architects.*
R.I.C.S., *Royal Institution of Chartered Surveyors.*
R.I.P., *requiescat in pace, may he, she, rest in peace,* qu'il, qu'elle, repose en paix, R.I.P.
R.L., *Rugby League.*
rly, *railway,* chemin de fer, c(h). de f.
rm, **1.** *ream,* rame. **2.** *room,* pièce, chambre.
R.M., **1.** *Post: Royal Mail.* **2.** *resident magistrate,* juge résident. **3.** *Navy: Royal Marines,* fusiliers marins.
R.M.A., *Royal Military Academy.*
R.M.P., (*Corps of*) *Royal Military Police.*
R.M.S., *Nau: Royal Mail Steamer.*
R.N., **1.** *Royal Navy.* **2.** *NAm: Registered Nurse,* infirmière diplômée.
R.N.A., *ribonucleic acid,* acide ribonucléique, A.R.N.
R.N.A.S., *Hist: Royal Naval Air Service, Station.*
RNIB, *Royal National Institute for the Blind.*
RNID, *Royal National Institute for the Deaf.*
RNLI, *Royal National Lifeboat Institution.*
R.N.(V.)R., *Royal Naval* (*Volunteer*) *Reserve.*
R.N.Z.A.F., *Royal New Zealand Air Force.*
R.N.Z.N., *Royal New Zealand Navy.*
ro., **1.** *recto,* recto, R°, Ro, ro. **2.** *Bookb: roan,* rouan.
R.O., **1.** *Receiving Office,* bureau des messageries. **2.** *Recruiting Officer.* **3.** *Regimental Order,* ordre régimentaire. **4.** *Royal Observatory.*
Rom., **1.** *B: Romans,* Romains, Rom. **2.** *Roman,* romain. **3.** *Romance,* roman. **4.** *Romanic,* roman, romain.
rom., *Typ: roman type,* romain.
rot., (*a*) *rotating,* rotatif; (*b*) *rotation,* rotation.
R.O.T.C., *Mil: U.S: Reserve Officers' Training Corps,* système de cours préparatoires d'officiers de réserve.
R.P., **1.** *Regius Professor.* **2.** *reply paid,* réponse payée, r.p.
R.P.C., *Royal Pioneer Corps.*
rpm, r.p.m., **1.** *resale price maintenance.* **2.** *revolutions per minute,* tours (par) minute, t.m., t/mn.
R.P.S., *Royal Photographic Society.*
r.p.s., *revolutions per second,* tours par seconde.
rpt., **1.** *report,* rapport. **2.** *repeat,* reprise.
R.R., **1.** *Right Reverend,* très révérend. **2.** *NAm: Railroad,* chemin de fer, c(h). de f.
R.S., **1.** *Royal Society.* **2.** *Royal Scots.*
r.s., *right side,* côté droit.
R.S.A., **1.** (*a*) *Royal Scottish Academy;* (*b*) *Royal Scottish Academician.* **2.** *Royal Society of Arts.*
R.S.F.S.R., *Russian Soviet Federal Socialist Republic,* république soviétique fédérative socialiste de Russie, R.S.F.S.R.
R.S.M., *Mil: Regimental Sergeant-major* = adjudant chef.
R.S.P.B., *Royal Society for the Protection of Birds.*
R.S.P.C.A., *Royal Society for the Prevention of Cruelty to Animals,* Société protectrice des animaux, S.P.A.
R.S.V., (*of Bible*) *Revised Standard Version.*
R.S.V.P., *please answer,* répondez s'il vous plaît, R.S.V.P.
R.T., (*a*) *radiotelegraphy,* radiotélégraphie; (*b*) *radiotelephony,* radiotéléphonie, R.T.
Rt Hon., *Right Honourable,* très honorable.
Rt Rev., *Right Reverend,* très révérend.
Ru., *Geog:* **1.** (*a*) *Rumania,* Roumanie; (*b*) *Rumanian,* roumain. **2.** (*a*) *Russia,* Russie; (*b*) *Russian,* russe.
R.U., *Rugby Union.*
R.U.C., *Royal Ulster Constabulary.*
R.V., (*of Bible*) *Revised Version.*
R/W, *right of way,* droit de passage.
Ry, *Railway,* chemin de fer, c(h). de f.
R.Y.S., *Royal Yacht Squadron.*
R.Z.S., *Royal Zoological Society.*

S., **1.** *Saint,* Saint, S(t)., Ste. **2.** (*a*) *South,* sud, S; (*b*) *southern,* austral, A. **3.** *Society,* société. **4.** *Sabbath,* sabbat.
s., **1.** *Meas:* (*a*) *second(s),* second(s), s(ec).; (*b*) *stere(s),* stère(s), s(t). **2.** *A.Num: shilling(s).* **3.** *Gram:* (*a*) *singular,* singulier; (*b*) *substantive,* substantif. **4.** *son,* fils. **5.** *steamer,* vapeur, vap. **6.** *small,* petit.
S.A., **1.** *Salvation Army,* Armée du Salut. **2.** *Geog:* (*a*) *South Africa,* Afrique du Sud; (*b*) *South Australia,* Australie méridionale; (*c*) *South America,* Amérique du Sud; (*d*) *Saudi Arabia,* Arabie Saoudite. **3.** *small arms,* armes portatives. **4.** *Hist: Sturmabteilung, Storm troops,* section d'assaut, S.A.
s.a., **1.** *Pharm: secundum artem,* s.a. **2.** *sine anno, without year, date,* sans date. **3.** *semiannual,* semi-annuel, semestriel. **4.** *see also,* voir.
Sab., *Sabbath,* sabbat.
S.A.C., **1.** *Strategic Air Command.* **2.** *Senior Aircraftman.*
S.A.C.W., *Senior Aircraftwoman.*
s.a.e., *stamped addressed envelope,* enveloppe timbrée et sur laquelle on a écrit l'adresse.
SALT [sɔlt], *Strategic Arms Limitation Talks.*
Sam., *B: Samuel,* Samuel, Sam.
S.A.M., *surface-to-air missile,* missile sol-air.
SAS, *Scandinavian Airlines System.*
Sat., *Saturday,* samedi.
S.A.Y.E., *save-as-you-earn,* économie à la source.
sb., *Gram: substantive,* substantif.
sc., **1.** *sculpsit,* (*he*) *carved* (*it*), (il l'a) sculpté, sc. **2.** *scilicet, that is,* c'est-à-dire. **3.** *scene,* scène, sc. **4.** *science,* science.
S.C., **1.** *Geog: South Carolina,* Caroline du Sud. **2.** *Mil: Signal Corps,* service des transmissions. **3.** *Special Constable.*
s.c(aps)., *Typ: small capitals,* petites capitales.
Sc.D., *Scientiae Doctor, Doctor of Science,* Docteur ès Sciences.
S.C.E., *Scottish Certificate of Education.*
sch., **1.** *school,* école. **2.** *scholar,* boursier. **3.** *schooner,* schooner.
S.C.M., **1.** *Student Christian Movement.* **2.** *State Certified Midwife.*
Scot., *Geog:* (*a*) *Scotland,* Écosse; (*b*) *Scottish,* écossais.
S.C.R., *Sch:* **1.** *Senior Common Room.* **2.** *Senior Combination Room.*
s.d., **1.** *sine die,* indéfiniment. **2.** *Stat: standard deviation,* écart type.
S/D, *Com: sight draft,* traite à vue.
S.D(ak)., *Geog: South Dakota.*
S.D.R., *special drawing right* (*from International Monetary Fund*).
SE, S.E., *South-East(ern),* (du) sud-est. S.-E.
S.E.A.C., *South-East Asia Command.*
S.E.A.T.O. ['si:tou], *South-East Asia Treaty Organization,* Organisation du Traité de l'Asie du Sud-Est, O.T.A.S.E.
SEC, S.E.C., *U.S: Securities and Exchange Commission.*
sec., **1.** *secretary,* secrétaire. **2.** *Mth: secant,* sécante, séc. **3.** *second(s),* seconde(s), s(ec). **4.** *secondary,* secondaire. **5.** *sector,* secteur.
sec(t)., *section,* section, sec(t).
sel., (*a*) *selected,* choisi; (*b*) *selection,* choix.
Sem., **1.** *Semitic,* sémitique. **2.** *seminary,* séminaire.
Sen., **1.** (*a*) *Senate,* Sénat; (*b*) *Senator,* sénateur. **2.** *senior,* aîné; père.
S.E.N., *State Enrolled Nurse* = infirmière diplômée.
senr., *senior,* aîné; père.
Sept., **1.** *September,* septembre, sept. **2.** *B: Septuagint,* Septante.
seq., *sequens, following,* suivant, suiv., svt.
ser., **1.** *series,* série. **2.** *sermon,* sermon.
Sergt., *Mil: Sergeant,* sergent, sgt.
S.E.T., *Selective Employment Tax.*
S.F., *science fiction,* science-fiction.
S.F.A., *Scottish Football Association.*
sf(z)., *Mus: sforzando,* sf.
S.G., *Solicitor General,* conseiller juridique de la Couronne.
s.g., **1.** *Ph: specific gravity,* gravité spécifique. **2.** *Elcs: screen grid,* grille-écran.
sgd., *signed,* signé, s.
Sgt., *Sergeant,* sergent, sgt.; **Sgt. Maj.,** *Sergeant Major* = sergent major.
sh., **1.** *A.Num: shilling(s).* **2.** *sheet,* feuille (de papier).
S.H.A.E.F. [ʃeif], *Hist: Supreme Headquarters of the Allied Expeditionary Force.*
SHAPE [ʃeip], *Supreme Headquarters Allied Powers Europe,* quartier général suprême des forces alliées en Europe.
shpt., *shipment,* chargement.
shr., *Fin: share,* action, act.
shtg., *shortage,* insuffisance, manque.
S.I., **1.** (*Order of the*) *Star of India.* **2.** *International System of Units,* Système d'unités international, SI.
Sig., *Signor.*
sig., *signature,* signature.
sim., **1.** *similar,* semblable. **2.** *simile,* comparaison.
sin., *Mth: sine,* sinus, sin.
sing., *singular,* singulier.
S.J., *Societas Jesu, Society of Jesus,* Société de Jésus.
S.L.B.M., *submarine launched ballistic missile.*
sld., **1.** *sailed,* (qui a) navigué. **2.** *sealed,* scellé; fermé.
S.M., *Mil: Sergeant Major* = sergent major.
S.M.O., *Senior Medical Officer.*
S.N.P., *Pol: Scottish National Party.*
So., *NAm:* (*a*) *south,* sud, S.; (*b*) *southern,* austral, A.
S.O., **1.** *Stationery Office,* service des fournitures et des publications de l'Administration. **2.** *Mil: Staff Officer,* officier d'état-major. **3.** *Mil: Signal Officer,* officier des transmissions. **4.** *special order,* ordre spécial. **5.** *standing order,* ordre permanent.
s.o., *St.Exch: seller's option,* prime vendeur.
S.O.B., *P: NAm: son of a bitch,* fils de pute.
Soc., **1.** *Society,* société, association. **2.** *Socialist,* socialiste.
SOGAT ['sougæt], *Society of Graphical and Allied Trades.*
sol., **1.** *solution,* solution. **2.** *soluble,* soluble.
solv., *Pharm: dissolve,* dissolvez, solv.
Som., *Geog: Somerset.*
S.O.S., *W.Tg:* signal de détresse, appel de détresse international, S.O.S.; **to send out an S.O.S.,** lancer un S.O.S.
sov., **1.** *sovereign,* souverain. **2.** *soviet,* soviet.
Sp., *Geog:* (*a*) *Spain,* Espagne; (*b*) *Spanish,* espagnol.
sp., **1.** *speed,* vitesse, v. **2.** *species,* espèce. **3.** *special,* spécial. **4.** *specific,* spécifique.
s.p., **1.** *sine prole,* sans enfants. **2.** *Turf: starting price,* dernière cote avant le départ. **3.** *Fin: supra protest,* sous protêt.
S.P.C.K., *Society for the Promotion of Christian Knowledge.*
spec., **1.** *special,* spécial. **2.** *specimen,* spécimen. **3.** *specification,* spécification.
sp. gr., *Ph: specific gravity,* gravité spécifique.
sp. ht., *Ph: specific heat,* chaleur spécifique.
Spr., *Sapper,* sapeur.
Sq., *Square,* place, square.
sq., **1.** *sequens, sequentia, the following,* le suivant, sq. **2.** *Meas: square,* carré. **3.** *Mil: etc: squadron,* escadron, esc. **4.** *sequence,* séquence.
sqd., *Mil: squad,* escouade.
sq. ft., *Meas: square foot,* pied carré.
Sqn. Ldr, *Av: Squadron Leader.*
sqq., *sequentia,* suivant, ssq.

Sr., 1. *senior*, aîné; père. 2. *Señor*.
S.R.B.M., *short range ballistic missile*, missile balistique de courte portée.
S.R.C., *Science Research Council*.
S.R.N., *State Registered Nurse*.
SS., *Saints*, Saints, SS.
S.S., 1. *Sunday School*, école du dimanche. 2. *steamship*, steamer, ss. 3. *German Hist: Schutzstaffel, Nazi special police force*, S.S.
S.S.A.F.A., *Soldiers', Sailors' and Airmen's Families Association*.
S.S.C., *Jur: Scot: Solicitor to the Supreme Court*.
SSE, S.S.E., *South-south-east*, sud-sud-est, S.-S.-E.
S.S.R.C., *Social Science Research Council*.
SSW, S.S.W., *South-south-west*, sud-sud-ouest, S.-S.-O.
St, 1. *Street*, rue. 2. *Saint*, Saint, S(t), Ste. 3. *Strait*, détroit.
st., 1. *Cr: stumped (by)*. 2. *Meas: stone*. 3. *stanza*, stance. 4. *statute*, statut.
Sta., *Station*, gare.
Staffs., *Geog: Staffordshire*.
stat., 1. *statistics*, statistique. 2. *statute*, statut. 3. *statue*, statue.
std., *standard*, ordinaire, standard.
STD, *Tp: subscriber trunk dialling*, (téléphone) automatique; **are you on STD?** avez-vous l'automatique?
stg, *sterling*.
stge., *storage*, emmagasinage.
Sth., *South*, sud, S.
stk., *Fin: stock*, titre, t.; valeur, v/., val.
S.T.O.L. [stɔl], *Av: short takeoff and landing*, décollage et atterrissage courts.
str., 1. *strait*, détroit. 2. *Row: stroke*, chef de nage.
sub., 1. *suburb*, faubourg, faub. 2. *subscription*, souscription. 3. *subway*, passage souterrain.
subj., 1. *subject*, sujet. 2. *Gram: subjunctive*, subjonctif.
subst., 1. *Gram: substantive*, substantif. 2. *substitute*, suppléant.
succ., *successor*, successeur, succ.
suff., 1. *suffix*, suffixe. 2. *sufficient*, suffisant.
Sun., *Sunday*, dimanche, dm.
sup., 1. *Gram: superlative*, superlatif. 2. *superior*, supérieur.
supp(l)., *supplement*, supplément.
Supt, *Superintendent*.
surg., (*a*) *surgeon*, chirurgien; (*b*) *surgical*, chirurgical; (*c*) *surgery*, chirurgie.
surv., *surveyor*.
s.v., *sub voce, sub verbo, under the word*, (voir) à ce mot.
S.W., 1. *South-west*, sud-ouest, S.-O. 2. *Geog: South Wales*. 3. *W.Tel: short wave*, ondes courtes, O.C.
S.W.A.(L.)K. [swæk, swɔlk], *F: (on back of envelope) sealed with a (loving) kiss*.
S.W.A.P.O. ['swɑːpou], *South West African People's Organization*.
Sw(ed)., *Geog:* (*a*) *Sweden*, Suède; (*b*) *Swedish*, suédois.
S.W.G., *standard wire gauge*.
Switz., *Geog: Switzerland*, Suisse.
Sx., *Geog: Sussex*.
syl(l)., *syllable*, syllabe.
sym., 1. *symbol*, symbole. 2. *symmetrical*, symétrique. 3. *symphony*, symphonie.
syn., (*a*) *synonym*, synonyme; (*b*) *synonymous*, synonyme.
syr., *Pharm: syrup*, sirop, sir., syr.

T., *Meas:* 1. *tesla*, tesla, T. 2. *tera-*, téra-, T.
t., 1. *Meas: ton(s), tonne(s)*, tonne(s), t. 2. *Turf: taken*, accepté. 3. *Pharm: take*, recipe, r. 4. *Com: tare*, tare, T. 5. *Gram: tense*, temps, t. 6. *time*, temps, t.
T.A., 1. *Mil: Territorial Army*. 2. *telegraphic address*, adresse télégraphique, adr. tél.
tab., *table*, table.
T.A.B., *typhoid-paratyphoid A and B vaccine*, vaccin antityphoparatyphoïdique A et B, T.A.B.
tan., *Mth: tangent*, tangente, tang., tg.
T. & A.V.R., *Territorial and Army Volunteer Reserve*.
TASS [tæs], *Telegraphic news agency of the Soviet Union*, agence de presse de l'Union soviétique, TASS.
T.B., 1. *Med:* (*a*) *tubercle bacillus*, bacille de Koch; (*b*) *F: tuberculosis*, tuberculose. 2. *Fin: trial balance*, balance de vérification. 3. *torpedo boat*, torpilleur.
tbs(p)., *tablespoon(ful)*, cuiller à soupe.
TC, 1. *Technical College* = lycée technique. 2. *Touring Club*. 3. *Town Councillor*, conseiller municipal. 4. *Training Centre*, centre de formation.
T.C.P., *Ch: trichlorophenoxyacetic acid*.
tech(n)., 1. *technical*, technique. 2. *technology*, technologie.
tel., 1. *telephone*, téléphone, tel. 2. (*a*) *telegraph*, télégraphe; (*b*) *telegraphic*, télégraphique, tel.
temp., 1. *temperature*, température, t. 2. *temporary*, temporaire. 3. *tempore, in the time of*, du temps de.
Tenn., *Geog: Tennessee*.
ter., 1. *terrace*, terrasse. 2. *territory*, territoire.
term., 1. *terminal*, terminal. 2. *termination*, terminaison. 3. *terminology*, terminologie.
T.E.S., *Times Educational Supplement*.
Test., *B: Testament*, Testament.
Teut., *Teutonic*, teutonique.
Tex., *Geog: Texas*.
tfr., *Fin: transfer*, virement, virt.
TGWU, *Transport and General Workers Union*.
Th.D., *Doctor of Theology*, docteur en théologie.
theor., *Mth: theorem*, théorème, th.
therm., *thermometer*, thermomètre.
Thess., *B: Thessalonians*, Thessaloniciens, Thess.
Thos., *Thomas*.
Thur(s)., *Thursday*, jeudi.
Tim., *B: Timothy*, Timothée, Tim.
tinct., *Pharm: tincture*, tincture, tinct.; *tinctura*, tra.
Tit., *B: Titus*, (Épître à) Tite.
tit., *title*, titre.
t.l.o., *Ins: total loss only*, perte totale seulement.
T.L.S., 1. *Times Literary Supplement*. 2. *typed letter signed*, lettre tapée à la machine et signée.
T.M., *Their Majesties*, leurs Majestés.
TMO, *telegraph money order*, mandat télégraphique.
tn., 1. *Meas: ton(s)*, tonne(s), t. 2. *town*, ville. 3. *train*, train.
tng., *training*, formation.
T.N.T., *Exp: trinitrotoluene*, trinitrotoluène, T.N.T.
T.O., 1. *Telegraph Office*, bureau télégraphique. 2. *Transport Officer*.
tom., *tomus, tome*, tome, t.
tp., 1. *township*, commune. 2. *troop*, troupe.
t.p., *Typ: title page*, (page de) titre.
Tpr., *Mil: Trooper*, soldat de la cavalerie.
tr., 1. *treasurer*, trésorier. 2. *trustee*, curateur. 3. *transaction*, opération (d'une affaire). 4. *Typ: transpose*, transposer. 5. *transferred*, transféré. 6. *Com: tare*, tare, T.
trans., 1. *Gram: transitive*, transitif. 2. (*a*) *translated*, traduit; (*b*) *translation*, traduction. 3. *transaction*, opération (d'une affaire).
treas., (*a*) *treasurer*, trésorier; (*b*) *treasury*, trésor.
T.R.H., *Their Royal Highnesses*, leurs Altesses Royales, LL.AA.RR.
trib., *Geog: tributary*, confluent, confl.
T.S.H., 1. *Their Serene Highnesses* = leurs Altesses Sérinissimes. 2. *Med: thyroid stimulating hormone*.
tsp., (*a*) *teaspoon*, cuiller à thé; (*b*) *teaspoonful*, cuiller à café.
TT., 1. *teetotal(ler)*, abstinent. 2. *St.Exch: telegraphic transfer*, transfert télégraphique, t.t. 3. *tuberculin tested*, garanti exempt de tuberculose. 4. (*also* **T.T. race**) *Tourist Trophy*.
T.U., 1. *Ph: transmission unit*, décibel. 2. *Trade Union*, syndicat.
TUC, *Trades Union Congress*.
Tue(s)., *Tuesday*, mardi, M.
T.V., *television*, télévision, T.V.; **T.V. game**, jeu vidéo; *NAm:* **T.V. dinner**, repas préparé spécialement pour pouvoir le manger devant la télévision.
T.W.A. (*also* [twɑː]), *Transworld Airlines*.
typ., (*a*) *typographer*, typographe; (*b*) *typographic*, typographique; (*c*) *typography*, typographie.

U., 1. *Unionist*. 2. *Cin: universal*, pour tout le monde. 3. *university*, université.
u., *upper*, supérieur.
U.A.E., *United Arab Emirates*, Émirats arabes unis. E.A.U.
U.A.R., *United Arab Republic*, République arabe unie, R.A.U.
U.C., 1. *under construction*, en construction. 2. *University College*.
u.c., *Typ: upper case*, haut de casse.
U.C.C.A. ['ʌkə], *Universities Central Council on Admissions*.
U.D.C., 1. *Hist: Urban District Council*. 2. *Universal Decimal Classification*.
UDI, *Unilateral Declaration of Independence*.
U.D.R., *Ulster Defence Regiment*.
UEFA, *Union of European Football Associations*.
U.F.C., *Ecc: United Free Church (of Scotland)*.
U.F.O. (*occ.* ['juːfou]), *unidentified flying object*, objet volant non identifié, O.V.N.I.
U.G.C., *University Grants Committee*.
UHF, *W.Tel: ultra-high frequency*, fréquence ultra-haute.
UK., *Geog: United Kingdom*, Royaume-Uni.
UKAEA, *United Kingdom Atomic Energy Authority*.
ult., 1. *Corr: ultimo*, dernier, der(r). 2. (*a*) *ultimate*, final; (*b*) *ultimately*, en fin de compte.
U.N., *United Nations*, Nations Unies.
UNA, *United Nations Association*.
unbd., *Bookb: unbound*, non relié.
UNCTAD, *United Nations Commission for Trade & Development*.
UNDRO, *United Nations Disaster Relief Organization*.
UNEF, *United Nations Emergency Force*.
UNESCO [ju'neskou], *United Nations Educational, Scientific and Cultural Organization*, Organisation des Nations Unies pour l'éducation, la science et la culture, UNESCO.
ung(t)., *Pharm: unguentum, ointment*, ung.
UNICEF ['juːnisef], *United Nations (International) Children's (Emergency) Fund*, Fonds international de secours à l'enfance, FISE.
UNIDO [ju'niːdou], *United Nations Industrial Development Organization*.
univ., 1. *universal*, universel. 2. *university*, université.
UNO, U.N.O. ['juːnou], *United Nations Organization*, Organisation des Nations Unies, O.N.U.; **UNO expert**, expert onusien.
unpub., *unpublished*, inédit, inéd.
UNRRA['ʌnrɑː], *United Nations Relief and Rehabilitation Administration*, Organisation des Nations Unies pour l'assistance et la reconstruction.
UNRWA., *United Nations Relief and Works Agency*.
U.N.S.C., *United Nations Security Council*.
U.P., 1. *Geog: Uttar Pradesh*. 2. *Dist: underproof*, au-dessous de preuve. 3. *Journ: United Press*. 5. *F: O:* **it's all U.P. with him**, il est foutu.
up., *upper*, supérieur.
UPI, *United Press International*.
U.P.U., *Universal Postal Union*, Union postale universelle, U.P.U.
U.R.I., *Med: upper respiratory infection*.
Uru., *Geog: Uruguay*.
U.S., 1. *Geog: United States*, États-Unis, É.-U. 2. *Mil: etc: unserviceable*, hors service, H.S.
u.s., *ut supra*, comme ci-dessus.
U.S.A., 1. *Geog: United States of America*, États-Unis d'Amérique. 2. *United States Army*.
USAEC, *Hist: United States Atomic Energy Commission*.
U.S.A.F., *United States Air Force*.

U.S.C.G., *United States Coast Guard.*
U.S.D.A., *United States Department of Agriculture.*
USDAW, *Union of Shop, Distributive and Allied Workers.*
U.S.I.A., **U.S.I.S.**, *United States Information Agency, Service.*
USM, *underwater-to-surface missile*, missile mer-sol.
U.S.M., **1.** *United States Mail.* **2.** *Mil: United States Marines.* **3.** *Fin: United States Mint.*
U.S.N., *United States Navy.*
U.S.N.G., *United States National Guard.*
U.S.N.R., *United States Naval Reserve.*
U.S.S., **1.** *United States Senate.* **2.** *United States Ship.* **3.** *United States Service.* **4.** *Universities Superannuation Scheme.*
U.S.S.R., *Union of Soviet Socialist Republics*, Union des républiques socialistes soviétiques, U.R.S.S.
usu., (*a*) *usual*, usuel, ordinaire; (*b*) *usually*, ordinairement.
U.S.W., *Ph: ultra-short waves*, ondes ultra-courtes.
Ut., *Geog: Utah.*
u.i., *ut infra*, comme ci-dessous.
U.V., *ultra-violet*, ultraviolet, U.V.
U/W, **u/w**, *Fin: underwriter*, syndicataire, assureur.
UXB, *unexploded bomb*, obus non explosé.

V, *El: volt*, volt, v.
v., **1.** *vide, see*, voir, voyez, v. **2.** *Jur: etc: versus*, contre, c. **3.** *verse*, (i) *B:* verset, v.; (ii) *Lit:* strophe. **4.** *velocity*, vitesse, v. **5.** *valve*, soupape. **6.** *very*, très.
Va, *Geog: Virginia*, Virginie.
va., *El. Meas: volt-ampere*, volt-ampère, VA.
V.A., **1.** *Order of Victoria and Albert.* **2.** *Vicar Apostolic*, vicaire apostolique. **3.** *Vice-Admiral*, vice-amiral. **4.** *U.S: Veterans' Administration.*
V. & A., *Victoria & Albert Museum.*
V.A.D., (*Member of*) *Voluntary Aid Detachment*, (membre de la) société de secours aux blessés.
val., (*a*) *value*, valeur; (*b*) *valuation*, évaluation.
VAR, *Av: visual aural (radio) range*, radiophare d'alignement audio-visuel.
var., **1.** *variety*, variété. **2.** *variant*, variante.
var. lect., *varia lectio, variant reading*, variante.
V.A.T., (*also* [væt]), *value added tax*, taxe sur, à, la valeur ajoutée, T.V.A.
V.C., **1.** *Victoria Cross.* **2.** (*a*) *Vice-chairman*, vice-président; (*b*) *Vice-chancellor*, vice-chancelier; (*c*) *Vice-consul*, vice-consul, V.-C.
VCR, *Rec: video cassette recorder*, magnétoscope.
VD, *Geog:* Vaud.
V.D., **1.** *Med: Venereal Disease*, maladie vénérienne. **2.** *Volunteer (Officers') Decoration.*
v.d., *various dates.*
V.D.U., *visual display unit*, dispositif d'affichage.
V.E., *Victory in Europe*, victoire en Europe; **V.E. day**, jour de la victoire en Europe.
Ven., *Ecc: Venerable*, vénérable.
Venez., *Geog:* (*a*) *Venezuela*; (*b*) *Venezuelan*, vénézuélien.
ver., **1.** *verse*, (i) *B:* verset, v.; (ii) *Lit:* strophe. **2.** *version*, version.
vers., *Mth: versed sine*, sinus verse.
vert., **1.** *Anat:* (*a*) *vertebra*, vertèbre; (*b*) *vertebrate*, vertébré. **2.** *vertical*, vertical.
Vet(er)., *Veterinary*, vétérinaire.
Vet. Surg., *veterinary surgeon*, vétérinaire.
VF, **1.** *video frequency*, vidéofréquence. **2.** *voice frequency*, fréquence vocale.
V.F.R., *Av: visual flight rules*, règles de vol à vue.
V.F.W., *U.S: Veterans of Foreign Wars.*
VG., **1.** *Vicar-General*, vicaire général. **2.** *very good*, très bien. **3.** *verbi gratia, for example*, par exemple.
VHF, *W.Tel: very high frequency*, très haute fréquence, THF.
V.I., *Geog:* **1.** *Vancouver Island.* **2.** *Virgin Islands*, îles Vierges.
Vic., *Victoria.*
vic., *Ch. of Eng:* (*a*) *vicar* = curé; (*b*) *vicarage*, cure.
vid., **1.** *vide, see*, voir, voyez, v. **2.** *Elcs: T.V: video*, vidéo.
vil., *village*, village.
V.I.P., *very important person*, personnage de marque; **to give s.o. V.I.P. treatment**, recevoir qn avec la croix et la bannière.
Vis(c)., *Viscount*, vicomte, Vcte; *Viscountess*, Vicomtesse, Vctesse.
viz., *videlicet, namely*, c'est-à-dire, à savoir.
VJ, *Victory over Japan*, victoire sur le Japon; **VJ day**, jour de la victoire sur le Japon.
v.l., *varia lectio, variant reading*, variante.
V.L.C.C., (*of oil tankers*) *Very Large Crude Carriers.*
VLF., *Elcs: very low frequency*, très basse fréquence, TBF.
V.M.H., *Victoria Medal of Honour* (*of the Royal Horticultural Society*).
vo., *verso*, verso, vo.
V.O., *Royal Victoria Order.*
VOA, *W.Tel: Voice of America.*
voc., **1.** *Gram: vocative*, vocatif. **2.** *vocational*, professionnel.
vol., **1.** *Ph: volume*, volume, vol. **2.** *volume*, tome, t(om). **3.** *volunteer*, volontaire. **4.** (*a*) *volcano*, volcan; (*b*) *volcanic*, volcanique.
VOR, *Av: visual omnirange*, radiophare omni-directionnel.
VP., *Vice-President*, vice-président.
V.R., *Victoria Regina, Queen Victoria*, la Reine Victoria.
V.R.D., *Voluntary Reserve Decoration.*
V.R.I., *Victoria Regina et Imperatrix, Victoria, Queen and Empress*, Victoria, Reine et Impératrice.
vs., **1.** *Jur: etc: versus*, contre, c. **2.** *verse*, (i) *B:* verset, v.; (ii) *Lit:* strophe.
V.S., **1.** *Veterinary Surgeon*, vétérinaire. **2.** *volti subito*, tournez vite.
V.S.O., *Voluntary Service Overseas.*
V.S.O.P., (*of brandy*) *Very Special Old Pale.*
Vt., *Geog: Vermont.*
VTOL, *Av: vertical take-off and landing* (*aircraft*), avion à décollage et atterrissage verticaux, ADAV.
VTR, *Rec: video tape recorder*, magnétoscope.
Vul(g)., *B.Lit: Vulgate*, Vulgate.
vul(g)., *vulgar*, vulgaire.
vv., *verses*, (i) *B:* versets; (ii) *Lit:* strophes.
vv. ll., *variae lectiones, various readings*, variantes.
v.y., *various years.*

W., **1.** *El: watt(s)*, watt(s), w. **2.** (*a*) *west*, ouest, O.; *Nau:* W.; (*b*) *western*, occidental. **3.** *Welsh*, Gallois. **4.** *Com: women's (size).*
w., **1.** *Cr: wicket.* **2.** (*a*) *wide*, large; (*b*) *width*, largeur, larg. **3.** *with*, avec. **4.** *wife*, épouse.
W.A., *Geog:* **1.** *West Africa.* **2.** *Western Australia.*
W.A.A.C., *Hist:* (1914–18) *Women's Army Auxiliary Corps.*
W.A.A.F., *Hist:* (1939–45) *Women's Auxiliary Air Force.*
W.A.C., *U.S: Women's Army Corps.*
W.A.F., *U.S: Women in the Air Force.*
w.a.f., *Com: with all faults.*
Wall., *Walloon*, Wallon.
War., *Geog: Warwickshire.*
warr., *warranty.*
Wash., *Geog: Washington.*
W.A.S.P. [wɔsp], *Pej: White Anglo-Saxon Protestant.*
WAVES, *U.S: Navy: Women's Appointed Volunteer Emergency Service.*
wb., *Ph: weber*, weber, wb.
w.b., **1.** *water board.* **2.** *westbound*, vers l'ouest. **3.** *waybill*, feuille de route.
W.C., **1.** *water closet*, water-closet, W.C. **2.** *West Central.* **3.** *without charge.*
W.C.C., *World Council of Churches.*
W/Cdr, *Av: Wing Commander*, lieutenant-colonel.
W.D., **1.** *War Department*, Ministère de la guerre. **2.** *Works Department.*
w/e., *week ending*, semaine se terminant . . .
W.E.A., *Workers' Educational Association.*
Wed., *Wednesday*, mercredi, M(e).
W.E.U., *Western European Union*, Union de l'Europe occidentale, U.E.O.
w.f., *Typ: wrong fount*, œil étranger.
W.F.T.U., *World Federation of Trade Unions*, Fédération syndicale mondiale, F.S.M.
Wg.Cdr., *Av: Wing Commander*, lieutenant-colonel.
wh., *El: watt-hour(s)*, watt(s)-heure, wh.
W.H.O., *World Health Organization*, Organisation mondiale de la santé, O.M.S.
W.I., **1.** *Geog: West Indies*, Indes occidentales. **2.** *Women's Institute.*
Wilts., *Geog: Wiltshire.*
Wis., *Geog: Wisconsin.*
Wisd., *B: Wisdom of Solomon.*
wk., **1.** *weak*, faible. **2.** *week*, semaine. **3.** *work*, travail.
WL, *W.Tel: wavelength*, longueur d'onde.
Wm., *William*, Guillaume.
W.M.O., *World Meteorological Organization.*
WNW, **W.N.W.**, *west-north-west*, ouest-nord-ouest, O.-N.-O.
W.O., **1.** *Hist: War Office*, Ministère de la guerre. **2.** *Warrant Officer.*
w.o., *Sp: walkover.*
Worcs., *Geog: Worcestershire.*
W.P., *weather permitting*, si le temps le permet.
W.P.B., *waste paper basket*, corbeille à papier(s).
W.P.C., *woman police constable*, femme-agent.
w.p.m., *words per minute*, mots par minute.
W.R., **1.** *Geog: West Riding* (*of Yorkshire*). **2.** *Jur: with rights*, avec droit, av. dt.
w.r., *war risk*, risque de guerre.
W.R.A.C., *Women's Royal Army Corps* = Auxiliaire féminine de l'armée de terre, A.F.A.T.
W.R.A.F., *Women's Royal Air Force.*
W.R.N.S., *Women's Royal Naval Service*, Services féminins de la Flotte, S.F.F.
W.R.V.S., *Women's Royal Voluntary Service.*
W.S., *Jur: Scot: Writer to the Signet.*
WSW, **W.S.W.**, *west-south-west*, ouest-sud-ouest, O.-S.-O.
wt, *weight*, poids, p.
W.T., *wireless telegraphy, telephony*, télégraphie, téléphonie, sans fil, T.S.F.
W.Va., *Geog: West Virginia.*
WW, *World War*, Guerre mondiale.
W.W.F., *World Wildlife Fund.*
W.X., *Com: women's extra large (size).*
Wyo., *Geog: Wyoming.*

X., *cross*, croix.
x.c., *St.Exch: ex coupon*, ex-coupon, x.c(oup).
x.d(iv)., *Fin: ex dividend*, ex-dividende, ex-d., x.d.
x.i., *St.Exch: ex interest*, sans intérêt.
XL, *Cost: extra large (size).*
Xn, *Christian*, chrétien.
Xnty, *Christianity*, Christianisme.
x.r., *St.Exch: ex rights*, ex-droits, x.dr.
Xt(ian), *Christian*, chrétien.
Xty, *Christianity*, Christianisme.

Y., **1.** *Num: yen*, yen. **2.** *Yeomanry.* **3.** *U.S: F:* = Y.M.C.A., Y.W.C.A.
y., **1.** *year*, an. **2.** *Meas: yard.*
yd(s), *Meas: yard(s).*
Yeo(m)., *Yeomanry.*
Y.H.A., *Youth Hostels Association.*
Y.M.C.A., *Young Men's Christian Association.*
Yorks., *Geog: Yorkshire.*
yr., **1.** *Corr: your*, votre, v. **2.** *year*, an. **3.** *younger*, plus jeune, cadet.

yrs, 1. *Corr: yours*, votre, v. **2.** *years*, ans.
Y.T., *Geog: Yukon Territory.*
Y.W.C.A., *Young Women's Christian Association.*

Z., 1. *zero*, zéro. **2.** *zinc*, zinc. **3.** *zone*, zone. **4.** *Num: zloty*, zloty.

Z.A.N.U. ['zɑ:nu:], *Zimbabwe African National Union.*
Z.A.P.U. ['zɑ:pu:], *Zimbabwe African People's Union.*
Zech., *B: Zechariah*, Zacharie, Zach.
Zool., (*a*) *zoological*, zoologique; (*b*) *zoology*, zoologie; (*c*) *zoologist*, zoologiste.
Z.P.G., *zero population growth.*